D1690121

Schlechtriem / Schwenzer
CISG-Kommentar

Schlechtriem/Schwenzer

Kommentar zum Einheitlichen UN-Kaufrecht

Das Übereinkommen der Vereinten Nationen
über Verträge über den internationalen Warenkauf
– CISG –

Bearbeitet
von

Klaus Bacher, Franco Ferrari, Christiana Fountoulakis, Pascal Hachem,
Florian Mohs, Markus Müller-Chen, Martin Schmidt-Kessel,
Ulrich G. Schroeter, Ingeborg Schwenzer, Corinne Widmer Lüchinger

Herausgegeben von
Ingeborg Schwenzer

6., völlig neu bearbeitete Auflage

Verlag C. H. Beck München 2013
Helbing Lichtenhahn Verlag Basel 2013

Hinweis zur Rechtschreibung:

Die im vorliegenden Kommentar verwendete Orthografie folgt teils den in Deutschland, Österreich und deutschsprachigen Regionen weiterer Länder geltenden Regeln, teils der in der Schweiz gebräuchlichen Schreibweise, die auf den Buchstaben "ß" verzichtet. Die resultierenden Abweichungen sind auf Wunsch der Herausgeberin nicht harmonisiert worden.

www.beck.de
www.helbing.ch

ISBN 978 3 406 64423 8 (C. H. Beck)
ISBN 978 3 7190 3335 4 (Helbing Lichtenhahn)

© 2013 Verlag C. H. Beck oHG
Wilhelmstraße 9, 80801 München
Satz, Druck und Bindung: Druckerei C. H. Beck
(Adresse wie Verlag)

Gedruckt auf säurefreiem, alterungsbeständigem Papier
(hergestellt aus chlorfrei gebleichtem Zellstoff)

Vorwort zur 6. Auflage

Mit der jetzt vorliegenden 6. Auflage haben sich wiederum bezüglich des Kreises der Autoren eine Reihe von Änderungen ergeben. Mit seiner Pensionierung ist Günter Hager, der die Artt. 53–70 kommentierte und darin in der 5. Auflage von Felix Maultzsch unterstützt wurde, aus dem Kreis der Autoren ausgeschieden. Die von ihm betreuten Bestimmungen werden in der 6. Auflage von Florian Mohs (Artt. 53–65) und Pascal Hachem (Artt. 66–70) übernommen. Den ausgeschiedenen Autoren gilt unser aufrichtiger Dank; sie haben am Ansehen dieses Kommentars entscheidenden Anteil. Im Übrigen konnte die Kommentierung durch die bewährten Autoren konsolidiert werden.

Der bereits im Vorwort zu den Vorauflagen festzustellende Erfolg des CISG ist ungebrochen. Heute gilt das Übereinkommen in 78 Vertragsstaaten (s. Anhang I). Nicht nur die wissenschaftliche Aufarbeitung in Kommentaren, Lehrbüchern, Monographien, Beiträgen in Fachzeitschriften etc. hat weiter zugenommen. Vor allem liegt inzwischen eine – in den Kernbereichen des Übereinkommens – kaum mehr überschaubare Zahl von Entscheidungen staatlicher und vor allem auch nichtstaatlicher Gerichte aus fast allen Vertragsstaaten vor. Es ist gerade die Aufgabe eines Kommentars, die verschiedenen Entwicklungslinien nachzuzeichnen und zusammenzuführen, damit der durch das Übereinkommen an Rechtseinheit und Rechtssicherheit erreichte Gewinn nicht durch divergierende Auslegung in den einzelnen Vertragsstaaten wieder verloren geht. Der vorliegende Kommentar macht es sich deshalb besonders zur Aufgabe, Literatur und vor allem auch Rechtsprechung ausserhalb des deutschen Rechtskreises auf- und einzuarbeiten. Wesentlich erleichtert wird der internationale Diskurs durch die Erfassung der Rechtsprechung, aber auch der Literatur in über das Internet zugänglichen Datenbanken, die in verschiedenen Ländern existieren und untereinander verlinkt sind.[1]

Die Neuauflage reflektiert die inzwischen eingetretenen Entwicklungen. Der zunehmenden Bedeutung auch ausländischer Rechtsprechung für die Auslegung des CISG wird durch eine noch stärker rechtsvergleichende Kommentierung Rechnung getragen. Dabei muss auch eine sich überwiegend an deutschrechtlichen Begriffen anlehnende Auslegung des CISG, wie sie von Literatur und Rechtsprechung im deutschen Rechtskreis oftmals erfolgt, hinterfragt werden. Entsprechend der zentralen Bedeutung, die der in- und ausländischen Judikatur in der Praxis zukommt, wird in den einzelnen Kommentierungen besonderes Gewicht auf die Entscheidungen und die Auseinandersetzung mit ihnen gelegt. Um die Zugänglichkeit namentlich auch ausländischer Rechtsprechung zu erleichtern, wird für sämtliche Entscheidungen ein Web-Zitat der frei zugänglichen Datenbank CISG-online angegeben, das ein sofortiges Auffinden der Entscheidung im Volltext ermöglicht. Wiederum erleichtert das Entscheidungsregister die Möglichkeit, von einer der Leserin oder dem Leser bereits bekannten Entscheidung direkt zu den entsprechenden Anmerkungen im Kommentar zu gelangen.

Die Aufgabe der Herausgabe eines Grosskommentars, wie er hier in 6. Auflage vorgelegt wird, ist ohne die engagierte, ja aufopferungsvolle Hilfe von Mitarbeitern nicht zu leisten. Dank gebührt deshalb zuvörderst Herrn David Tebel für die Koordinierung des Projektes sowie den studentischen Hilfskräften Herrn Christoph Burckhardt, Frau Antonia Füller, Frau Sophie Holdt, Frau Florence Jäger, Herrn Sandro Jaisli, Herrn Lukas Meyer, Herrn Christian Schlumpf, und Frau Nicole Schmidt für die Betreuung der Manuskripte der Autoren, des Apparats und für ihre Mithilfe bei der Fahnenkorrektur. Weiterer Dank gilt Herrn Daniel Roggenkemper, der im Rahmen eines Kurzpraktikums an der Erstellung der

---

[1] Vgl. nur CISG-online, abrufbar unter http://www.globalsaleslaw.org (Stand: 12.2.2013).

Vorwort

Verzeichnisse sowie der Fahnenkorrektur mitwirkte. Die Verantwortung für alle Unvollkommenheiten bleibt eine solche der Herausgeberin.

Für grosszügige finanzielle Unterstützung dankt die Herausgeberin dem Schweizerischen Nationalfonds sowie der Stiftung zur Förderung der rechtlichen und wirtschaftlichen Forschung an der Universität Basel.

Basel, Sommer 2012   Die Herausgeberin

Verzeichnis der Bearbeiter

Dr. iur. Klaus Bacher .... Artt. 78, 85–88
Richter am Bundesgerichtshof

Dott. Franco Ferrari, LL. M. (Universität Augsburg) .... Präambel, Artt. 1–7, 10, 89–101,
ordentlicher Professor an der New York University   Unterzeichnungsklausel

Dr. iur. Christiana Fountoulakis .... Artt. 26, 71–73, 81–84
ordentliche Professorin an der Universität Freiburg i. Ue.

Dr. iur. Pascal Hachem .... Artt. 66–70
ACIArb, Lehrbeauftragter an der Universität Basel

Dr. iur. Florian Mohs, LL. M. (Vict. U. Wellington) .... Artt. 53–65
Rechtsanwalt (Zürich), Lehrbeauftragter an der Universität Basel

Dr. iur. Markus Müller-Chen .... Artt. 28, 45–52, VerjÜbk
Rechtsanwalt, ordentlicher Professor an der Universität St. Gallen

Dr. iur. Martin Schmidt-Kessel .... Artt. 8, 9, 11–13
ordentlicher Professor an der Universität Bayreuth

Dr. iur. Ulrich G. Schroeter .... Artt. 14–25, 27, 29, VertragsG
Professor an der Universität Mannheim

Dr. iur. Ingeborg Schwenzer, LL. M. (U. C. Berkeley) .... Einleitung, Artt. 35–44, 74–77,
ordentliche Professorin an der Universität Basel   79, 80, Gesamtredaktion

Dr. iur. Corinne Widmer Lüchinger .... Artt. 30–34
Rechtsanwältin, ordentliche Professorin an der Universität Basel

Inhaltsübersicht

Vorwort V
Verzeichnis der Bearbeiter VII

Inhaltsverzeichnis XI
Abkürzungen XVII
Einleitung *(Schwenzer)* 1

Übereinkommen der Vereinten Nationen über Verträge über den internationalen Warenkauf 13

Präambel *(Ferrari)* 13

Teil I. Anwendungsbereich und allgemeine Bestimmungen 19
   Kapitel I. Anwendungsbereich *(Ferrari)* 19
   Kapitel II. Allgemeine Bestimmungen *(Ferrari/Schmidt-Kessel)* ... 156

Teil II. Abschluss des Vertrages *(Schroeter)* 265

Teil III. Warenkauf 427
   Kapitel I. Allgemeine Bestimmungen *(Schroeter/Fountoulakis/Müller-Chen)* 427
   Kapitel II. Pflichten des Verkäufers *(Widmer Lüchinger/Schwenzer/Müller-Chen)* . 509
   Kapitel III. Pflichten des Käufers *(Mohs)* 783
   Kapitel IV. Übergang der Gefahr *(Hachem)* 910
   Kapitel V. Gemeinsame Bestimmungen über die Pflichten des Verkäufers und des Käufers *(Fountoulakis/Schwenzer/Bacher)* 957

Teil IV. Schlußbestimmungen *(Ferrari)* 1177

Gesetz zu dem Übereinkommen der Vereinten Nationenvom 11. April 1980 über Verträge über den internationalen Warenkauf sowie zur Änderung des Gesetzes zu dem Übereinkommen vom 19. Mai 1956 über den Beförderungsvertrag im internationalen Straßengüterverkehr (CMR) [VertragsG] *(Schroeter)* 1211

Übereinkommen über die Verjährung beim internationalen Warenkauf *(Müller-Chen)* 1221

Anhang *(Schwenzer)* 1271
Sachregister *(Schwenzer)* 1413

Inhaltsverzeichnis

Vorwort V
Verzeichnis der Bearbeiter VII

Inhaltsübersicht IX
Abkürzungen XVII
Einleitung *(Schwenzer)* 1

Übereinkommen der Vereinten Nationen über Verträge über den internationalen Warenkauf

Präambel *(Ferrari)* 13

Teil I. Anwendungsbereich und allgemeine Bestimmungen

Kapitel I. Anwendungsbereich
(Ferrari)

Vorbemerkungen zu Artt. 1–6 19
Art. 1 [Anwendungsbereich] 35
Art. 2 [Anwendungsausschlüsse] 73
Art. 3 [Verträge über herzustellende Waren oder Dienstleistungen] 91
Art. 4 [Sachlicher Geltungsbereich] 101
Art. 5 [Ausschluß der Haftung für Tod oder Körperverletzung] 129
Art. 6 [Ausschluß, Abweichung oder Änderung durch Parteiabrede] 135

Kapitel II. Allgemeine Bestimmungen

Art. 7 [Auslegung des Übereinkommens] *(Ferrari)* 156
Art. 8 [Auslegung von Erklärungen und Verhalten] *(Schmidt-Kessel)* 194
Art. 9 [Handelsbräuche und Gepflogenheiten] *(Schmidt-Kessel)* 228
Art. 10 [Mehrere Niederlassungen; gewöhnlicher Aufenthalt] *(Ferrari)* . 242
Art. 11 [Formfreiheit] *(Schmidt-Kessel)* 247
Art. 12 [Wirkungen eines Vorbehaltes hinsichtlich der Formfreiheit]
  (Schmidt-Kessel) 258
Art. 13 [Schriftlichkeit] *(Schmidt-Kessel)* 261

Teil II. Abschluss des Vertrages
(Schroeter)

Vorbemerkungen zu Artt. 14–24 265
Art. 14 [Begriff des Angebots] 299
Art. 15 [Wirksamwerden des Angebots; Rücknahme] 337
Art. 16 [Widerruf des Angebots] 342
Art. 17 [Erlöschen des Angebots] 351
Art. 18 [Begriff der Annahme] 353
Art. 19 [Ergänzungen, Einschränkungen und sonstige Änderungen zum Angebot] 370
Art. 20 [Annahmefrist] 389
Art. 21 [Verspätete Annahme] 393

Inhalt

Art. 22 [Rücknahme der Annahme] 403
Art. 23 [Zeitpunkt des Vertragsschlusses] 406
Art. 24 [Begriff des Zugangs] 409

Teil III. Warenkauf

Kapitel I. Allgemeine Bestimmungen

Art. 25 [Wesentliche Vertragsverletzung] *(Schroeter)* 427
Art. 26 [Aufhebungserklärung] *(Fountoulakis)* 463
Art. 27 [Absendetheorie] *(Schroeter)* 472
Art. 28 [Erfüllungsanspruch] *(Müller-Chen)* 482
Art. 29 [Vertragsänderung oder -aufhebung] *(Schroeter)* 493

Kapitel II. Pflichten des Verkäufers

Art. 30 [Pflichten des Verkäufers] *(Widmer Lüchinger)* 509

Abschnitt I. Lieferung der Ware und Übergabe der Dokumente
(Widmer Lüchinger)

Art. 31 [Inhalt der Lieferpflicht und Ort der Lieferung] 513
Art. 32 [Verpflichtungen hinsichtlich der Beförderung der Ware] 548
Art. 33 [Zeit der Lieferung] 559
Art. 34 [Übergabe von Dokumenten] 569

Abschnitt II. Vertragsmäßigkeit der Ware sowie Rechte oder Ansprüche Dritter
(Schwenzer)

Art. 35 [Vertragsmäßigkeit der Ware] 576
Art. 36 [Maßgeblicher Zeitpunkt für die Vertragsmäßigkeit] 603
Art. 37 [Nacherfüllung bei vorzeitiger Lieferung] 609
Art. 38 [Untersuchung der Ware] 615
Art. 39 [Mängelrüge] 629
Art. 40 [Bösgläubigkeit des Verkäufers] 648
Art. 41 [Rechtsmängel] 653
Art. 42 [Belastung mit Schutzrechten Dritter] 664
Art. 43 [Rügepflicht] 678
Art. 44 [Entschuldigung für unterlassene Anzeige] 683

Abschnitt III. Rechtsbehelfe des Käufers wegen Vertragsverletzung durch den Verkäufer
(Müller-Chen)

Art. 45 [Rechtsbehelfe des Käufers; keine zusätzliche Frist] 691
Art. 46 [Recht des Käufers auf Erfüllung oder Nacherfüllung] 706
Art. 47 [Nachfrist] 723
Art. 48 [Recht des Verkäufers zur Nacherfüllung] 731
Art. 49 [Vertragsaufhebung] 742
Art. 50 [Minderung] 763
Art. 51 [Teilweise Nichterfüllung] 772
Art. 52 [Vorzeitige Lieferung und Zuviellieferung] 777

Kapitel III. Pflichten des Käufers
(Mohs)

Art. 53 [Zahlung des Kaufpreises; Abnahme der Ware] 783

Abschnitt I. Zahlung des Kaufpreises

Art. 54 [Kaufpreiszahlung]	802
Art. 55 [Bestimmung des Preises]	806
Art. 56 [Kaufpreis nach Gewicht]	815
Art. 57 [Zahlungsort]	817
Art. 58 [Zahlungszeit; Zahlung als Bedingung der Übergabe; Untersuchung vor Zahlung]	832
Art. 59 [Zahlung ohne Aufforderung]	848

Abschnitt II. Abnahme

Art. 60 [Begriff der Abnahme]	851

Abschnitt III. Rechtsbehelfe des Verkäufers wegen Vertragsverletzung durch den Käufer

Art. 61 [Rechtsbehelfe des Verkäufers; keine zusätzliche Frist]	858
Art. 62 [Zahlung des Kaufpreises; Abnahme der Ware]	866
Art. 63 [Nachfrist]	875
Art. 64 [Vertragsaufhebung]	883
Art. 65 [Spezifizierung durch den Verkäufer]	901

Kapitel IV. Übergang der Gefahr
(Hachem)

Vorbemerkungen zu Artt. 66–70 CISG	910
Art. 66 [Wirkung des Gefahrübergangs]	917
Art. 67 [Gefahrübergang bei Beförderung der Ware]	926
Art. 68 [Gefahrübergang bei Verkauf der Ware, die sich auf dem Transport befindet]	936
Art. 69 [Gefahrübergang in anderen Fällen]	944
Art. 70 [Wesentliche Vertragsverletzung und Gefahrübergang]	952

Kapitel V. Gemeinsame Bestimmungen über die Pflichten des Verkäufers und des Käufers

Abschnitt I. Vorweggenommene Vertragsverletzung und Verträge über aufeinander folgende Lieferungen
(Fountoulakis)

Art. 71 [Verschlechterungseinrede]	957
Art. 72 [Antizipierter Vertragsbruch]	978
Art. 73 [Sukzessivlieferungsvertrag; Aufhebung]	993

Abschnitt II. Schadenersatz
(Schwenzer)

Art. 74 [Umfang des Schadenersatzes]	1008
Art. 75 [Schadensberechnung bei Vertragsaufhebung und Deckungsgeschäft]	1035
Art. 76 [Schadensberechnung bei Vertragsaufhebung ohne Deckungsgeschäft]	1043
Art. 77 [Schadensminderungspflicht des Ersatzberechtigten]	1050

Abschnitt III. Zinsen
(Bacher)

Art. 78 [Zinsen]	1057

Inhalt

Abschnitt IV. Befreiungen
(Schwenzer)

Art. 79 [Hinderungsgrund außerhalb des Einflußbereiches des Schuldners] 1072
Art. 80 [Verursachung der Nichterfüllung durch die andere Partei] 1097

Abschnitt V. Wirkungen der Aufhebung
(Fountoulakis)

Vorbemerkungen zu Artt. 81–84 1104
Art. 81 [Erlöschen der Leistungspflichten; Rückgabe des Geleisteten] 1108
Art. 82 [Verlust der Rechte auf Vertragsaufhebung oder Ersatzlieferung wegen Unmöglichkeit der Rückgabe im ursprünglichen Zustand] 1122
Art. 83 [Fortbestand anderer Rechte des Käufers] 1135
Art. 84 [Ausgleich von Vorteilen im Falle der Rückabwicklung] 1138

Abschnitt VI. Erhaltung der Ware
(Bacher)

Vorbemerkungen zu Artt. 85–88 1153
Art. 85 [Pflicht des Verkäufers zur Erhaltung der Ware] 1155
Art. 86 [Pflicht des Käufers zur Inbesitznahme und Erhaltung der Ware] 1161
Art. 87 [Einlagerung bei Dritten] 1167
Art. 88 [Selbsthilfeverkauf] 1170

Teil IV. Schlußbestimmungen
(Ferrari)

Vorbemerkungen zu Artt. 89–101 1177
Art. 89 [Depositar] 1180
Art. 90 [Konventionskonflikte] 1181
Art. 91 [Unterzeichnung, Ratifikation, Annahme, Genehmigung, Beitritt] 1185
Art. 92 [Teilweise Ratifikation, Annahme, Genehmigung oder Beitritt] 1187
Art. 93 [Föderative Staaten] 1190
Art. 94 [Erklärung über Nichtanwendung des Übereinkommens] 1193
Art. 95 [Erklärung zum Ausschluss der Anwendung des Art. 1 Abs. 1 lit. b)] 1196
Art. 96 [Erklärung über Schriftform] 1198
Art. 97 [Wirksamkeitsvoraussetzungen einer Vorbehaltserklärung] 1202
Art. 98 [Zulässigkeit von Vorbehalten] 1203
Art. 99 [Zeitpunkt des Inkrafttretens] 1204
Art. 100 [Zeitlicher Anwendungsbereich] 1207
Art. 101 [Kündigung des Übereinkommens] 1209
[Unterzeichnungsklausel] 1210

Gesetz zu dem Übereinkommen der Vereinten Nationen vom 11. April 1980 über Verträge über den internationalen Warenkauf sowie zur Änderung des Gesetzes zu dem Übereinkommen vom 19. Mai 1956 über den Beförderungsvertrag im internationalen Straßengüterverkehr (CMR) [VertragsG]
(Schroeter)

Erster Teil. Zustimmung zu dem Übereinkommen über Verträge

Art. 1 [Zustimmung] 1211
Art. 2 [Anwendung aufgrund IPR-Verweisung] 1211

Art. 3 [Verjährung von Ansprüchen wegen vertragswidriger Beschaffenheit] 1214

Zweiter Teil. Änderung des Gesetzes zu dem Übereinkommen vom 19. Mai 1956 über den Beförderungsvertrag im internationalenStraßengüterverkehr (CMR)

Art. 4 (hier nicht abgedruckt) 1219

Dritter Teil. Schlussbestimmungen

Art. 5 [Aufhebung von EAG und EKG] 1219
Art. 6 (gegenstandslos) 1219
Art. 7 [Inkrafttreten des Gesetzes] 1219

Übereinkommen über die Verjährung beim internationalen Warenkauf
(Müller-Chen)

Einleitung 1221
Teil I. Allgemeine Bestimmungen 1223
Teil II. Anwendungsbestimmungen 1261
Teil III. Erklärungen und Vorbehalte 1262
Teil IV. Schlußbestimmungen 1265

Anhang
(Schwenzer)

I. Vertragsstaaten des Übereinkommens der Vereinten Nationen über Verträge über den internationalen Warenkauf – CISG – 1271
II. Vertragsstaaten des Übereinkommens über die Verjährung beim internationalen Warenkauf – VerjÜbk – 1277
III. Materialien zu CISG und VerjÜbk 1279
IV. Incoterms® 2010 1283
V. UNIDROIT Principles of International Commercial Contracts 2010 1331
VI. Entscheidungsregister 1362

Sachregister 1413

Abkürzungsverzeichnis

A. 2d	Atlantic Reporter, Second Series (USA)
AAA	American Arbitration Association
a. A.	anderer Ansicht
A.-A. Leg. Cons. Comm. R.	Asian-African Legal Consultative Committee Report
aaO	am angegebenen Ort
A. B. A.	American Bar Association
A. B. A. J.	American Bar Association Journal (USA)
ABGB	Allgemeines Bürgerliches Gesetzbuch vom 1.6.1811 (Österreich)
abgedr.	abgedruckt
abl.	ablehnend
AblEG Nr. L	Amtsblatt der Europäischen Gemeinschaften, Ausgabe L (Rechtsvorschriften)
AblEG Nr. C	Amtsblatt der Europäischen Gemeinschaften, Ausgabe C (Mitteilungen und Bekanntmachungen)
Abs.	Absatz, Absätze
AbzG	Gesetz betreffend die Abzahlungsgeschäfte
A. C.	Appeal Cases (Großbritannien)
AcP	Archiv für die civilistische Praxis
Act. Jur. Hung.	Acta Juridica Academiae Scientiarum Hungaricae (Ungarn)
Actes	Conférence diplomatique sur l'Unification du droit en matière de la vente internationale, Den Haag, 2.–25. April 1964, Actes et Documents de la Conférence, Bd. I: Actes, Ministère de la Justice des Pays-Bas (Hrsg.), Den Haag: Imprimerie Nationale (1966)
ADB 1963	Allgemeine Deutsche Binnen-Transportversicherungs-Bedingungen von 1963
ADC	Anuario de Derecho Civil (Spanien)
ADHGB	Allgemeines Deutsches Handelsgesetzbuch von 1861
ADS Güterversicherung	Allgemeine Deutsche Seeversicherungsbedingungen von 1919. Besondere Bestimmungen für die Güterversicherung von 1973 i. d. F. von 1984
ADSp	Allgemeine Deutsche Spediteurbedingungen i. d. F. vom 1.1.2003, veröffentlicht unter http://www.spediteure.de
Adv.	The Advocate (Kanada)
Advoc. Q.	The Advocate's Quarterly
a. E.	am Ende
a. F.	alte Fassung
Afr. J. Int'l L.	African Journal of International Law (Großbritannien)
AG	Amtsgericht
AGB	Allgemeine Geschäftsbedingungen
AGBG	Gesetz zur Regelung des Rechts der Allgemeinen Geschäftsbedingungen vom 9.12.1976, BGBl. I, S. 3317 (außer Kraft)
ähnl.	ähnlich
AJP	Aktuelle Juristische Praxis (Schweiz)
ALB/RGW	Allgemeine Bedingungen für die Warenlieferungen zwischen den Organisationen der Mitgliedsländer des Rates für gegenseitige Wirtschaftshilfe i. d. F. von 1979, GBl. II, S. 81 (DDR)
A. L. I.	American Law Institute (USA)
ALI-ABA	American Law Institute-American Bar Association (USA)
All E. R.	All England Law Reports (Großbritannien)
Alt.	Alternative, Alternativen
a. M.	am Main
Am. Bus. L. J.	American Business Law Journal (USA)
Am. For. L. Assn. Newsletter	American Foreign Law Association Newsletter (USA)
Am. J. Comp. L.	American Journal of Comparative Law (USA)

XVII

Abkürzungen

Abkürzungsverzeichnis

Am. J. Int'l L.	American Journal of International Law (USA)
ÄndProt	Protocol Amending the Convention on the Limitation Period in the International Sale of Goods vom 11.4.1980 (Änderungsprotokoll) (A/CONF. 97/18, annex II), YB XI (1980), 162–164
Anh.	Anhang
An. Jur.	Anuario jurídico (Mexiko)
Annals Fac. L. Belgrade	Annals of the Faculty of Law in Belgrade (also known as Anali Pravnog fakulteta)
Anm.	Anmerkung
Ann. dr. mar. & aero-spat	Annuaire de droit maritime et aero-spatiale (Frankreich)
Ann. Genova	Annuario Genova (Italien)
AnwBl	Anwaltsblatt
A. Pac. L. Rev.	Asia Pacific Law Review
App.	Corte d'Appello (italienisches Berufungsgericht)
AppGer	Appellationsgericht
AppHof	Appellationshof
Arb.	Arbitration
Arb.Ct. Bulgarian CCI	Arbitration Tribunal of Bulgarian Chamber of Commerce & Industry
Arb. Int'l	Arbitration International (Großbritannien)
Arb. J.	The Arbitration Journal (USA)
Arch. iur. Cracov.	Archivum iuridicum Cracoviense (Polen)
Ariz. J. Int'l L.	Arizona Journal of International Law (USA)
Ariz. J. Int'l & Comp. L.	Arizona Journal of International and Comparative Law (USA)
Art(t).	Artikel (pl.)
Asper Rev. Int'l Bus. & Trade L.	Asper Review of International Business and Trade Law
Ass'n	Association
Ass. plén.	Cour de Cassation, Assemblée plénière
Ateneo L. J.	Ateneo Law Journal (Philippinen)
AUDCG	L'Acte Uniforme sur le Droit Commercial Général
Aufl.	Auflage
ausf.	ausführlich
Ausg.	Ausgabe
Aust. Bus. L. Rev.	Australian Business Law Review (Australien)
Aust. L. J.	The Australian Law Journal (Australien)
AW	DDR-Außenwirtschaft. Informationen, Dokumente, hrsg. v. Zentrum für Information & Dokumentation für Außenwirtschaft, Beilage 1: Recht im Außenhandel (DDR)
AWD	Außenwirtschaftsdienst des Betriebs-Beraters, s. RIW
AW-Prax	Außenwirtschaftliche Praxis, Zeitschrift für Aussenwirtschaft in Recht und Praxis
A. y D.	Actualidad y Derecho (Spanien)
BAnz.	Bundesanzeiger
Bankr. D. Or.	Bankruptcy District Court for the District of Oregon
Bankr. M. D. Fla.	Bankruptcy District Court for the Middle District of Florida
BB	Betriebs-Berater
B. B. J.	Boston Bar Journal (USA)
Bbl.	Bundesblatt (Schweiz)
Bd(e).	Band (Bände)
bearb.	bearbeitet
Begr./begr.	Begründung/begründet
Beil.	Beilage
Bek. v.	Bekanntmachung vom
Belgr. L. Rev.	Belgrade Law Review
Bem.	Bemerkung(en)
Ber.	Bericht
bes.	besondere(r, s)

Abkürzungen

betr.	betrifft (betreffend)
BezG	Bezirksgericht (Österreich/Schweiz)
bezgl.	bezüglich
BGer	Bundesgericht (Schweiz)
BGB	Bürgerliches Gesetzbuch
BGB-InfoV	Verordnung über Informations- und Nachweispflichten nach bürgerlichem Recht v. 2.1.2002 (BGBl. I S. 342)
BGBl.	Bundesgesetzblatt
BGE	Entscheidungen des Schweizerischen Bundesgerichts (amtliche Sammlung)
BGer	Bundesgericht (Schweiz)
BGH	Bundesgerichtshof
BGHZ	Entscheidungen des Bundesgerichtshofes in Zivilsachen (amtliche Sammlung)
BJM	Basler Juristische Mitteilungen (Schweiz)
BlgNR	Beilagen zu den Stenographischen Protokollen des Nationalrats (Österreich)
BMJ	Bundesministerium der Justiz
Bol. Mex. Der. Comp.	Boletín Méxicano de Derecho Comparado (Mexiko)
BR	Bundesrepublik
BR/DC	Baurecht/Droit de la construction; Mitteilungen zum privaten und öffentlichen Baurecht, Seminar für Schweizerisches Baurecht, Universität Freiburg (Schweiz)
BR-Drs.	Bundesrats-Drucksache
Brooklyn J. Int'l L.	Brooklyn Journal of International Law (USA)
Bsp.	Beispiel
BT	Bundestag
BT-Drs.	Bundestags-Drucksache
BTTA	Bulgarska turgosko-promishlena palata (Bulgarische Industrie- und Handelskammer)
Btx	Bildschirmtext
Buff. L. Rev	Buffalo Law Review (USA)
Bull. Civ.	Bulletin des arrêts de la Cour de Cassation, Chambres civiles (Frankreich)
Bull. Transp. Int. Ferrov.	Bulletin des Transports Internationaux Ferroviaires/Zeitschrift für den internationalen Eisenbahnverkehr (Schweiz)
Bus. Law.	The Business Lawyer (USA)
BVerfG	Bundesverfassungsgericht
BW	Burgerlijk Wetboek i. d. F. vom 1.1.1992 (Bürgerliches Gesetzbuch der Niederlande)
B. Y. U. L. Rev.	Brigham Young University Law Review (USA)
bzgl.	bezüglich
bzw.	beziehungsweise
C. A.	Court of Appeal(s)
CA	Cour d'appel (Frankreich)/Corte d'appello (Italien)
CAEM	Conseil d'assistance économique mutuelle (Rat für gegenseitige Wirtschaftshilfe, s. a. RGW)
Cah. de Dr.	Les Cahiers de Droit (Kanada)
Cah. jur. fisc. exp.	Cahiers juridiques et fiscaux de l'exportation (Frankreich)
Calif. West. Int'l L. J.	California Western International Law Journal (USA)
Cambridge Lect.	The Cambridge Lectures (Kanada)
Cambridge L. J.	Cambridge Law Journal (Großbritannien)
Can. Bus. L. J.	Canadian Business Law Journal (Kanada)
Can. Counc. Int'l L.	Canadian Council on International Law (Kanada)
Can. Int'l L.	Canadian International Lawyer (Kanada)
Can.- U. S. L. J.	Canada – United States Law Journal
Cardozo J. Int'l & Comp. L.	Cardozo Journal of International and Comparative Law
Cass.	La Suprema Corte di Cassazione (Italienischer Kassationshof)
Cass. Civ.	La Suprema Corte di Cassazione (Italienischer Kassationshof; Zivilkammer)

Abkürzungen

Abkürzungsverzeichnis

Cc/CC	Code civil (Frankreich)/Codice civile (Italien)/Código civil (u. a. Spanien)
CCI	Chambre de Commerce Internationale, Paris (s. a. IntHK, ICC)
CCI Ct. Arb.	Arbitration Court (attached to the Hungarian) Chamber of Commerce and Industry
Ccom	Code de Commerce (Frankreich)/Código de Comercio (u. a. Spanien)
CCP	Civil code of procedure
C. D. C.	Cuadernos de Derecho y Comercio (Spanien)
C. D. Cal.	U. S. District Court, Central District of California
C. D. Ill.	U. S. District Court, Central District of Illinois
CESL	China-EU School of Law
CFR	cost and freight (Kosten und Fracht, Incoterm)
ch., chap.	chapter
Ch. D.	Law Reports, Chancery Division (Großbritannien)
China Bus. Rev.	China Business Review (USA)
China L. R.	China Law Reporter (USA)
Chron.	Chronique
cic	culpa in contrahendo
CIETAC	China International Economic and Trade Arbitration Commission
C&F	cost and freight (Kosten und Fracht) (Incoterm)
CIF, cif	cost, insurance, freight (Kosten, Versicherung, Fracht) (Incoterm)
CIM	Convention internationale concernant le transport des marchandises par chemins de fer/Einheitliche Rechtsvorschriften für den Vertrag über die internationale Eisenbahnbeförderung von Gütern, COTIF, Anhang B
Cir.	Circuit
CISG	United Nations Convention on Contracts for the International Sale of Goods/Übereinkommen der Vereinten Nationen über Verträge über den internationalen Warenkauf vom 11.4.1980 (A/CONF. 97/18, annex I), O. R., S. 178 ff., YB XI (1980), S. 151 ff. (s. a. VertragsG)
CISG-AC	Advisory Council of the Vienna Convention on Contracts for the International Sale of Goods (http://www.cisg.law.pace.edu)
CISG Austria	Internet-Datenbank österreichischer Entscheidungen zum CISG (s. Literaturverzeichnis)
CISG Belgium	Internet-Datenbank belgischer Entscheidungen zum CISG, Universität Leuven (s. Literaturverzeichnis)
CISG France	CISG France, Internet-Datenbank französischer Entscheidungen zum CISG, Universität Saarbrücken (s. Literaturverzeichnis)
CISG-online	Internet-Datenbank, Universität Basel (s. Literaturverzeichnis)
CISG Pace	CISG W3 Database, Internet-Datenbank, Pace University School of Law (s. Literaturverzeichnis)
CISG Spain	CISG Spain and Latin America, Internet-Datenbank, Universität Carlos III Madrid (s. Literaturverzeichnis)
Civ.	Cour de Cassation, Chambre civile (Zivilkammer des französischen Kassationshofs)
CLOUT	Case Law on UNCITRAL Texts (s. Literaturverzeichnis)
C. L. R.	Commonwealth Law Reports (Australien)
CMEA	Council of Mutual Economic Assistance (Rat für gegenseitige Wirtschaftshilfe, s. a. RGW)
CMR	Convention relative au Contrat de transport international de marchandises par route/Übereinkommen über den Beförderungsvertrag im internationalen Straßengüterverkehr vom 19. Mai 1956, BGBl. 1961 II, S. 1120
c. o. d.	cash on delivery (Lieferung gegen Nachnahme)
COFREUROP	Geschäftsbedingungen für frische, essbare Gartenbauerzeugnisse im nationalen und internationalen Verkehr, Stand: Oktober 1999 (s. http://www.dfhv.de/)
Colo. Law.	The Colorado Lawyer (USA)
Colum. J. Transnat'l L.	Columbia Journal of Transnational Law (USA)
Colum. L. Rev.	Columbia Law Review (USA)
Com.	Cour de Cassation, Chambre civile, Section Commerciale (Kammer für Handelssachen des französischen Kassationshofs)
Com. L. J.	Commercial Law Journal (USA)

Abkürzungen

Comp. L. J.	Comparative Law Journal
Comp. L. Y. B.	Comparative Law Yearbook (USA)
Comp. & Int'l L. J. S. Afr.	Comparative and International Law Journal of Southern Africa (Südafrika)
Com. int. Ban.	Comercio internacional Banamex (Mexiko)
Computer Law.	The Computer Lawyer (USA)
Computer L. J.	Computer Law Journal (USA)
Conf.	Conference
Conn. B. J.	Connecticut Bar Journal (USA)
Cons. Fin. L. Q. R.	Consumer Finance Law Quarterly Report (USA)
Contemp. Trends	Contemporary Trends (Großbritannien)
Contr. Imp.	Contratto e Impresa (Italien)
Contr. Imp. E.	Contratto e Impresa, Europa (Italien)
Cornell Int'l L. J.	Cornell International Law Journal (USA)
Cornell L. Rev.	Cornell Law Review (USA)
Corp.	Corporation
Corr. giur.	Corriere giuridico (Italien)
COTIF	Convention relative aux transports internationaux ferroviaires/Übereinkommen über den internationalen Eisenbahnverkehr vom 9.5.1980, BGBl. 1985 II, S. 130
CPC	Codice di Procedura Civile (Italien)/Code de Procedure Civile (vgl. NCPC)
C. P. N.	Cours de perfectionnement du notariat (Frankreich)
CR	Computer und Recht
Ct.	Court
Ct. App.	Court of Appeals (USA)
Ct. Int'l Trade	United States Court of International Trade
CTO	Combined Transport Operator (Beförderer im kombinierten Transport)
Cu. der. int.	Curso de Derecho Internacional (Jahrbuch der OAS, USA)
Cum. L. Rev.	Cumberland Law Review (USA)
CVIM	Convention de Vienne sur la vente internationale de marchandises
D.	Receuil Dalloz Sirey (Frankreich)
D. Alaska	U. S. District Court, District of Alaska
D. Ariz.	U. S. District Court, District of Arizona
Das Recht	Das Recht, Beilage zum Zentralblatt für Handelsrecht
DB	Der Betrieb
DCFR	Draft Common Frame of Reference
D. Chron.	Receuil Dalloz Sirey, Chronique (Frankreich)
D. Col.	U. S. District Court, District of Colorado
D. Conn.	U. S. District Court, District of Connecticut
D. D. C.	U. S. District Court, District of Columbia
DDR	Deutsche Demokratische Republik
DDR-AW/RiA	DDR-Außenwirtschaft, Beilage „Recht im Außenhandel"
Defensor Legis	Defensor Legis (Finnland)
D. Del.	U. S. District Court, District of Delaware
Del. Law.	Delaware Lawyer (USA)
Denkschrift	Denkschrift der deutschen Bundesregierung zum Entwurf eines Gesetzes zu dem Übereinkommen der Vereinten Nationen vom 11. April 1980 über Verträge über den internationalen Warenkauf (s. Literaturverzeichnis)
Denkschrift zum EKG	Denkschrift der deutschen Bundesregierung zu den internationalen Kaufrechtsübereinkommen (s. Literaturverzeichnis)
dens.	denselben
Der. com. int.	Derecho del comercio internacional (Kolumbien)
Der. comp.	Derecho comparado (Argentinien)
Der. neg.	Derecho de los negocios (Mexico)
ders.	derselbe
dgl.	dergleichen
D. Guam.	U. S. District Court, District of Guam
d. h.	das heißt
D. H.	Dalloz, Recueil hebdomadaire de jurisprudence (1924–1940) (Frankreich)

Abkürzungen

D. Haw.	U. S. District Court, District of Hawaii
Dick. J. Int'l L.	Dickinson Journal of International Law (USA)
Dick. L. Rev.	Dickinson Law Review
D. Idaho.	U. S. District Court, District of Idaho
dies.	dieselbe(n)
Dig. Com. L.	Digest of Commercial Laws of the World (USA)
DIHK	Deutscher Industrie- und Handelskammertag
D. IR.	Receuil Dalloz Sirey, Informations Rapides (Frankreich)
Dir. com. int.	Diritto del Commercio Internazionale (Italien)
Dir. comun. sc. int.	Diritto Comunitario e degli scambi Internazionale (Italien)
Diss.	Dissertation
Dist.	District (USA)
D. Kan.	U. S. District Court, District of Kansas
D. Mass.	U. S. District Court, District of Massachusetts
D. Md.	U. S. District Court, District of Maryland
D. Me.	U. S. District Court, District of Maine
D. M. F.	Le Droit maritime français (Frankreich)
D. Minn.	U. S. District Court, District of Minnesota
D. Mont.	U. S. District Court, District of Montana
D. N. D.	U. S. District Court, District of North Dakota
D. Neb.	U. S. District Court, District of Nebraska
D. Nev.	U. S. District Court, District of Nevada
D. N. H.	U. S. District Court, District of New Hampshire
D. N. J.	U. S. District Court, District of New Jersey
D. N. M..	U. S. District Court, District of New Mexico
D. N. Mar. I.	U. S. District Court, District of the Northern Mariana Islands
DNotZ	Deutsche Notar-Zeitschrift
Doc.	Conférence diplomatique sur l'Unification du droit en matière de la vente internationale, Den Haag, 2.–25. April 1964, Actes et Documents de la Conférence, Bd. II: Documents, Ministère de la Justice des Pays-Bas (Hrsg.), Den Haag: Imprimerie Nationale (1966)
Doc. dir. comp.	Documentacão e Direito Comparado (Portugal)
D. Or.	U. S. District Court, District of Oregon
DÖV	Die Öffentliche Verwaltung
D. P.	Dalloz, Recueil périodique et critique mensuel (vor 1941) (Frankreich)
D. P. R.	U. S. District Court, District of Puerto Rico
DR	Deutsches Recht (1931–1945)
Drake L. Rev.	Drake Law Review (USA)
D. R. I.	U. S. District Court, District of Rhode Island
Dr. prat. com. int.	Droit et pratique du commerce international/International Trade Law and Practice (Paris, New York)
D. S. C.	U. S. District Court, District of South Carolina
D. S. D.	U. S. District Court, District of South Dakota
D. Somm.	Receuil Dalloz Sirey, Sommaires Commentés (Frankreich)
dt.	deutsch(en)
DTI	Department of Trade and Industry
dto.	dito
DtZ	Deutsch-Deutsche Rechts-Zeitschrift
DtZ-Inf.	Informationsbeilage zur Deutsch-Deutschen Rechts-Zeitschrift
Duq. L. Rev.	Duquesne Law Review (USA)
D. Utah	U. S. District Court, District of Utah
D. Vt.	U. S. District Court, District of Vermont
D. V. I.	U. S. District Court, District of the Virgin Islands
D. Wyo.	U. S. District Court, District of Wyoming
DZWir	Deutsche Zeitschrift für Wirtschaftsrecht

E	Entwurf
E 1958	Entwurf zum EAG 1958
E 1976	s. Genfer E 1976

Abkürzungen

E 1977	s. New Yorker E 1977
E 1978	s. New Yorker E 1978
EAG	Einheitliches Gesetz über den Abschluß von internationalen Kaufverträgen über bewegliche Sachen vom 17.7.1973, BGBl. I, S. 868
ebd.	ebenda
E. C. E.	Economic Commission for Europe/Europäische Wirtschaftskommission der Vereinten Nationen
ecolex	ecolex (Österreich)
E-Commerce-RL	RL 2000/31/EG des Europäischen Parlaments und des Rates vom 8. Juni 2000 über bestimmte rechtliche Aspekte der Dienste der Informationsgesellschaft, insbesondere des elektronischen Geschäftsverkehrs, im Binnenmarkt
E. D.	Eastern District
E. D. Ark.	U. S. District Court, Eastern District of Arkansas
E. D. Cal.	U. S. District Court, Eastern District of California
EDI	Electronic Data Interchange
EDI L. Rev.	EDI Law Review
E. D. Ky.	U. S. District Court, Eastern District of Kentucky
E. D. La.	U. S. District Court, Eastern District of Louisiana
E. D. Mich.	U. S. District Court, Eastern District of Michigan
E. D. Mo.	U. S. District Court, Eastern District of Missouri
E. D. N. C.	U. S. District Court, Eastern District of North Carolina
E. D. N. Y.	U. S. District Court, Eastern District of New York
E. D. Ok.	U. S. District Court, Eastern District of Oklahoma
E. D. Pa.	U. S. District Court, Eastern District of Pennsylvania
E. D. Tenn.	U. S. District Court, Eastern District of Tennessee
E. D. Tex.	U. S. District Court, Eastern District of Texas
E. D. Va.	U. S. District Court, Eastern District of Virginia
E. D. Wash.	U. S. District Court, Eastern District of Washington
E. D. Wis.	U. S. District Court, Eastern District of Wisconsin
ed(s).	editor(s) (Hrsg.)/edition (Aufl.)
EG	Europäische Gemeinschaft
EGBGB	Einführungsgesetz zum Bürgerlichen Gesetzbuch
EG-RL	Richtlinie der Europäischen Gemeinschaften
EG-VO	Verordnung der Europäischen Gemeinschaften
Einf.	Einführung
EJLR	European Journal of Law Reform
EKG	Einheitliches Gesetz über den internationalen Kauf beweglicher Sachen vom 17.7.1973, BGBl. I, S. 856
El Derecho	El Derecho (Argentinien)
Electr. J. Comp. L.	Electronic Journal of Comparative Law
el. ERA	Anhang zu den Einheitlichen Richtlinien und Gebräuche für Dokumenten-Akkreditive für die Vorlage elektronischer Dokumente, Fassung 2002
El Foro	El Foro (Mexiko)
Emory Int'l L. Rev.	Emory International Law Review (USA)
Emory J. Int'l Disp. Resol.	Emory Journal of International Dispute Resolution (USA)
Enc. D.	Enciclopedia del diritto (Italien)
Enc. Pub. Int'l L.	Encyclopedia of Public International Law
Energy L. J.	Energy Law Journal (USA)
engl.	englisch(e, es, er)
EPÜ	Europäisches Patentübereinkommen von 1973, BGBl. 1976 II, S. 826
ERA 600	Einheitliche Richtlinien und Gebräuche für Dokumenten-Akkreditive (Revision 2007; s. auch UCP 500)
ERI 522	Einheitliche Richtlinien für Inkasso (Revision 1996; s. auch URC 522)
erl.	Erläutert
ERPL	European Review of Private Law (NL)
Esq.	Esquire
etc.	et cetera
EuGH	Gerichtshof der Europäischen Gemeinschaften

Abkürzungen

EuGHE .... Gerichtshof der Europäischen Gemeinschaften (bis 1958: Gerichtshof der Europäischen Gemeinschaften für Kohle und Stahl). Sammlung der Rechtsprechung des Gerichtshofes
EuGVO .... EG-VO Nr. 44/2001 vom 22.12.2000 über die gerichtliche Zuständigkeit und die Anerkennung und Vollstreckung von Entscheidungen in Zivil- und Handelssachen
EuGVÜ .... Europäisches Übereinkommen über die gerichtliche Zuständigkeit und die Vollstreckung gerichtlicher Entscheidungen in Zivil- und Handelssachen vom 27.9.1968, BGBl. 1972 II, S. 773
EuGVVO .... Verordnung über die gerichtliche Zuständigkeit und die Anerkennung und Vollstreckung von Entscheidungen in Zivil- und Handelssachen (Brüssel I Verordnung)
EuLF .... The European Legal Forum
EuIPRÜ .... Europäisches Übereinkommen über das auf vertragliche Schuldverhältnisse anzuwendende Recht vom 19.6.1980 (Rom-Übereinkommen), BGBl. 1986 II, S. 810
European L. Rev. . European Law Review (Großbritanien)
Eur. Transp. L. .... European Transport Law (Belgien)
EuZW .... Europäische Zeitschrift für Wirtschaftsrecht
EvBl .... Evidenzblatt der Rechtsmittelentscheidungen, in: Österreichische Juristen-Zeitung (seit 1946); vorher selbstständig (1934–1938); dann: Beilage zu „Deutsches Recht" Teil C (DREvBl)
EVHGB .... Verordnung zur Einführung handelsrechtlicher Vorschriften im Lande Österreich
evtl. .... eventuell
EWG .... Europäische Wirtschaftsgemeinschaft
EWiR .... Entscheidungen zum Wirtschaftsrecht
EWS .... Europäisches Wirtschafts- und Steuerrecht
Ex. .... Court of Exchequer
ex ship .... ab Schiff

F. .... Federal Reporter (USA)
f(f). .... folgend(e)
F. 2 d. .... Federal Reporter, Second Series 1988–1993 West's Federal Reporter, Second Series (USA)
F. 3rd. .... West's Federal Reporter, Third Series (USA)
FAS .... free alongside ship (Frei Längsseite Seeschiff, Incoterm)
F. B. I. .... Federal Bureau of Investigation
FCA .... Federal Court of Australia
F. C. R. (Aus) ...... Federal Court Reports (Australia)
FD&C .... Food, Drug and Cosmetic Act
Fed. Reg. .... Federal Register (USA)
FF .... Französischer Franc
FGPrax .... Praxis der Freiwilligen Gerichtsbarkeit (vormals OLGZ)
FIATA .... Fédération Internationale des Associations de Transitaires et Assimilés (Internationale Föderation der Spediteurorganisationen)
Fla. B. J. .... Florida Bar Jounal (USA)
Fla. Int'l L. J. ...... Florida International Law Journal (USA)
Fn. .... Fußnote
FOB, fob .... free on board (Frei an Bord, Incoterm)
Fordham Int'l L. J. Fordham International Law Journal (USA)
Fordham L. Rev. .. Fordham Law Review (USA)
Foro it. .... Foro italiano (Italien)
Foro Pad. .... Foro Padano (Italien)
fortgef. .... fortgeführt
frz. .... französisch
FS .... Festschrift
F. Supp. .... Federal Supplement (USA)

Ga. J. Int'l & Comp. L. .... Georgia Journal of International and Comparative Law (USA)
Ga. L. Rev. ...... Georgia Law Review (USA)

Abkürzungen

Gaz. Pal.	La Gazette du Palais (Frankreich)
GBl.	Gesetzblatt
GebrMG	Gebrauchsmustergesetz i. d. Bek. vom 28.8.1990, BGBl. I, S. 1455 (Deutschland)
G. com.	Giurisprudenza commerciale (Italien)
gem.	gemäß
GemO	Gemeindeordnung
Genfer E 1976	Entwurf der Arbeitsgruppe der UNCITRAL, 7. Sitzung (Genf 5.–16. Januar 1976), YB VII (1976), 89–96
Genfer E 1977	Entwurf eines Kaufvertragsabschlußgesetzes der Arbeitsgruppe der UNCITRAL, 9. Sitzung (Genf 19.–30. September 1977), YB IX (1978), 83–85, 107–121
Geo. Mason J. Int'l Comm. L.	George Mason Journal of International Commercial Law (USA)
Geo. Wash. J. Int'l L. & Econ.	The George Washington Journal of International Law and Economics (USA)
Ges.	Gesellschaft
Ges. Aufs.	Gesammelte Aufsätze
GG	Grundgesetz für die Bundesrepublik Deutschland vom 23.5.1949, BGBl. I, S. 1
ggf.	gegebenenfalls
G. it.	Giurisprudenza italiana (Italien)
Giust. civ.	Giustizia civile (Italien)
GIW	Gesetz über internationale Wirtschaftsverträge vom 5.2.1976, GBl. I, S. 61 (DDR)
GL	Gefährliche Ladung (Deutschland)
GP	Gesetzgebungsperiode
GPÜ	Übereinkommen über das Europäische Patent für den Gemeinsamen Markt, BGBl. 1979 II, S. 834 (nicht in Kraft getreten)
GPR	Zeitschrift für Gemeinschaftsprivatrecht
GrS	Großer Senat
grunds.	grundsätzlich
GS	Gesammelte Schriften
GVBl.	Gesetz- und Verordnungsblatt
GWB	Gesetz gegen Wettbewerbsbeschränkungen (Kartellgesetz)
h. A.	herrschende Ansicht
Halbbd.	Halbband
Harv. Int'l L. J.	Harvard International Law Journal (USA)
Harv. L. Rev.	Harvard Law Review (USA)
Hastings Int'l & Comp. L. Rev.	Hastings International and Comparative Law Review (USA)
HGB	Handelsgesetzbuch
HGer	Handelsgericht (Schweiz/Österreich)
High Ct. Sing.	High Court Singapore
HIPRÜ	Haager Übereinkommen betreffend das auf internationale Kaufverträge über bewegliche Sachen anzuwendende Recht vom 15. Juni 1955
H. K.	Hikakohu Kenkyu (Japan)
H. L.	House of Lords
h. L.	herrschende Lehre
h. M.	herrschende Meinung
Hofstra L. Rev.	Hofstra Law Review (USA)
Hong Kong L. J.	Hong Kong Law Journal
Houst. J. Int'l L.	Houston Journal of International Law (USA)
HR	Hooge Raad (Niederlande)
HRR	Höchstrichterliche Rechtsprechung (1928–1942)
Hrsg./hrsg.	Herausgeber/herausgegeben
HS.	Halbsatz
HSG	Handelsrechtliche Schiedsgerichtspraxis, fortgeführt unter dem Titel Rechtsprechung kaufmännischer Schiedsgerichte (s. Literaturverzeichnis, Allgemeine Literatur: Straatmann/Ulmer)
HWiG	Gesetz über den Widerruf von Haustürgeschäften und ähnlichen Geschäften vom 16.1.1986, BGBl. I, S. 122 (außer Kraft)

Abkürzungen

I. A. L. S.	International Association of Legal Science
i. c.	in casu
I. C. A. B.	The ICC International Court of Arbitration Bulletin
ICC	International Chamber of Commerce (s. a. IntHK., CCI)/Court of Arbitration of the International Chamber of Commerce (Paris, Frankreich)
ICC Ct. Bull.	ICC International Court of Arbitration Bulletin (Frankreich)
iContr.	I Contratti (Italien)
Idaho L. Rev.	Idaho Law Review (USA)
i. d. F.	in der Fassung
i. d. R.	in der Regel
i. E.	im Einzelnen; im Ergebnis
i. e. S.	im engeren Sinne
IHR	Internationales Handelsrecht, Zeitschrift für das Recht des internationalen Warenkaufs und -vertriebs (seit 2001, Nachfolge von TranspR-IHR)
ILM	International Legal Materials (USA)
Inc.	Incorporated
Incoterms	International Commercial Terms der IntHK. von 1936, ergänzt und neu ausgelegt 1953, 1974, 1976, 1980, 1990 und 2000, IntHK.-Publikation Nr. 460
Indian J. Int'l L.	Indian Journal of International Law (Indien)
Indiana Int'l & Comp. L. Rev.	Indiana International and Comparative Law Review (USA)
Inf. Bull. Eur. Ass. Chin. L.	Information Bulletin for the Members of the European Association for Chinese Law (Belgien)
insbes.	insbesondere
InsO	Insolvenzordnung vom 5.10.1994, BGBl. I, S. 2866
int.	international
Int. Contract	The International Contract. Law and Finance Review (Schweiz)
Int. Ct. Hungarian CCI	Tribunal of International Commercial Arbitration of the Hungarian Chamber of Commerce and Industry
Int. Ct. Russian CCI	Internationales Schiedsgericht der Industrie- und Handelskammer der Russischen Föderation
Int. Ct. Ukrainian CCI	Tribunal of International Commercial Arbitration at the Ukrainian Chamber of Commerce and Industry
Int. Enc. Comp. L.	International Encyclopedia of Comparative Law
IntHK	Internationale Handelskammer Paris (s. a. CCI, ICC)
In-house c. int.	In-house counsel international (Großbritannien)
Int. Leg. Mat.	International Legal Materials (Hrsg. American Association of International Law, Washington D. C.)
Int'l	International
Int'l Arb. J.	International Arbitration Journal (USA)
Int'l Arb. Rep.	International Arbitration Report (USA)
Int'l Bus. Law.	International Business Lawyer (Großbritannien)
Int'l Bus. L. J.	International Business Law Journal/Revue de Droit des Affaires Internationales (Frankreich)
Int'l Contr. Adviser	International Contract Adviser (USA)
Int'l Fin. L. Rev.	International Financial Law Review (Großbritannien)
Int'l J. Leg. Inf.	International Journal of Legal Information (USA)
Int'l Law.	The International Lawyer (USA)
Int'l law pract. (NYSBA)	International law practicum, New York State Bar Association (USA)
Int'l Pro. Com. Rep.	International Procurement Committee Report
Int'l Rev. L. & E.	International Review of Law and Economics
Int'l Tax J.	The International Tax Journal (USA)
Int'l Tax & Bus. Law.	The International Tax & Business Lawyer (USA)
Int'l Trade & Bus. L. Ann	International Trade and Business Law Annunal (Australien)
Int'l Trade Forum	International Trade Forum/Forum du Commerce International (Schweiz)

Abkürzungen

Int'l & Comp. L. Q.	The International and Comparative Law Quarterly (Großbritannien)
Iowa L. Rev.	Iowa Law Review (USA)
IPR	Internationales Privatrecht
IPRax	Praxis des Internationalen Privat- und Verfahrensrechts
IPRG	Bundesgesetz über das Internationale Privatrecht vom 18.12.1987 (SR 291) (Schweiz)
i. S.	im Sinne
i. S. d.	im Sinne der (des)
Israel L. Rev.	Israel Law Review (Israel)
IStR	Internationales Steuerrecht
i. S. v.	im Sinne von
ital.	italienisch
Ital. Y. B. Int'l L.	Italian Yearbook of International Law (Italien)
i. Ü.	im Übrigen
i. V. m.	in Verbindung mit
i. w. S.	im weiteren Sinne
J.	Justice
JA	Juristische Ausbildung
J. Air L. & Com.	Journal of Air Law and Commerce (USA)
Jb. It. R.	Jahrbuch für Italienisches Recht
J. Bus. L.	The Journal of Business Law (Großbritannien)
J. C. Civ.	Juris Classeur Civil (Frankreich)
J. C. P. éd. E	Juris Classeur Périodique. La Semaine Juridique. Cahiers de Droit de l'Entreprise (Frankreich), (1966–1983 éd. commerce et industrie; 1984–1997 éd. entreprise; ab 1998 entreprise et affaires)
J. C. P. éd. G	Juris Classeur Périodique. La Semaine Juridique. Édition Générale (Frankreich)
J. Com. Arb.	Journal of Commercial Arbitration (Süd Korea)
J. Cont. L.	Journal of Contract Law (Australien)
J. der. marítimo	Jornadas de Derecho Marítimo, Universidad de la Rabida (Spanien/Argentinien)
J. D. I.	Journal du Droit International (Frankreich)
JF	Jura Falconis (Belgien)
JFT	Tidskrift, utgiven av juridiska föreningen i Finland (Finnland)
J. Int'l Arb.	Journal of International Arbitration (Schweiz)
J. Int'l Bus. L.	Journal of International Business Law (USA)
J. Közlöny	Jogtudományi Közlöny (Türkei)
J. L. & Com.	The Journal of Law and Commerce (USA)
J. Leg. Stud.	The Journal of Legal Studies (USA)
J. Leg. Educ.	Journal of Legal Education (USA)
J. Mar. L. & Com.	Journal of Maritime Law and Commerce (USA)
JN	Jurisdiktionsnorm (Österreich)
Journal des Tribunaux	Journal des Tribunaux (Belgien)
JR	Juristische Rundschau
J. Small & Emerg. Bus. L.	Journal of Small & Emerging Business Law (USA)
JT	Juridisk Tidskrift (Schweden)
J. Transnat'l L. & Pol'y	Journal of Transnational Law & Policy (USA)
Jur.	Jurisprudence
Jura	Juristische Ausbildung
Jur. gén.	Jurisprudence générale, Répertoire méthodique et alphabéthique de législation, de doctrine et de jurisprudence, Dalloz (Frankreich)
Juridica Int.	Juridica International
Juris Data	Internet-Datenbank für französische Entscheidungen
JuS	Juristische Schulung
JW	Juristische Wochenschrift
J. World Trade L.	Journal of World Trade Law (USA)
JZ	Juristenzeitung

Abkürzungen

Kaigai S. H.	Kaigai Shoji Homu (Japan)
Kan.	Kansas Supreme Court (USA)
K. B.	Law Reports, King's Bench Division (Großbritannien)
KassGer	Kassationsgericht
Kap.	Kapitel
KauflPRÜ 1985	Convention on the Law Applicable to the International Sale of Goods/Convention sur la loi applicable aux contrats de vente internationale de marchandises (Übereinkommen über das auf Verträge über den internationalen Warenkauf anzuwendende Recht), Den Haag, 30.10.1985, abgedruckt in RabelsZ 51 (1987), 196–213
KG	Kammergericht (Deutschland)/Kantonsgericht (Schweiz); Kommanditgesellschaft (Deutschland)
KKG	Konsumkreditgesetz (Schweiz)
KO	Konkursordnung i. d. F. vom 20.5.1898, RGBl., S. 612 (außer Kraft; s. jetzt InsO)
Kokusai S. H.	Kokusai Shoji Homu (Japan)
KOM	Dokument der Kommission bestimmt für die Öffentlichkeit
Köpl	Köplagen (schwedisches Kaufgesetz)
KreisG	Kreisgericht
krit.	kritisch
KSchG	Konsumentenschutzgesetz (Österreich)
KW	Kalenderwoche
L. & Pol'y Int'l Bus.	Law and Policy in International Business
La Ley	La Ley (Spanien)
Lakimies	Lakimies (Finnland)
Law Inst. J.	Law Institute Journal (Australien)
Law YB China	Law Yearbook of China (Volksrepublik China)
Leg. Stud.	Legal Studies
Lesotho L. J.	Lesotho Law Journal
Lex Mundi W. R.	Lex Mundi World Reports
LEXIS	Datenbank von LEXIS-NEXIS
LG	Landgericht
lit.	littera
Lit.	Literatur
Liverpool L. Rev.	Liverpool Law Review (Großbritannien)
L. J.	Lord Justice
L. J. Ex.	Law Journal Reports, Exchequer, New Series, 1831–1875 (Großbritannien)
Ll. L. R.	Lloyd's List Law Reports
Lloyd's Mar. & Com. L. Q.	Lloyd's Maritime and Commercial Law Quarterly (Großbritannien)
Lloyd's Rep.	Lloyd's List Law Reports (Großbritannien)
LM	Entscheidungen des Bundesgerichtshofs, Nachschlagewerk mit Leitsätzen und Entscheidungen, hrsg. von Lindenmaier und Möhring
La. L. Rev.	Louisiana Law Review (USA)
Loy. L. Rev.	Loyola Law Review (USA)
Loy. L. A. Int'l & Comp. L. J.	Loyola of Los Angeles International and Comparative Law Journal (USA)
Loy. L. A. L. Rev.	Loyola University of Los Angeles Law Review (USA)
L. Q. R.	The Law Quarterly Review (Großbritannien)
L. Soc. J.	Law Society Journal (USA)
L. T.	Law Times Reports (Großbritannien)
Ltd.	Limited
LuganoÜ	Lugano-Übereinkommen über die gerichtliche Zuständigkeit und die Vollstreckung gerichtlicher Entscheidungen in Zivil- und Handelssachen vom 16. September 1988
LZ	Leipziger Zeitschrift für das deutsche Recht

Abkürzungen

MarkenG	Markengesetz vom 25.10.1994, BGBl. I, S. 3082
m. a. W.	mit anderen Worten
McGill L. J.	McGill Law Journal (Kanada)
M. D. Ala.	U. S. District Court, Middle District of Alabama (USA)
M. D. Fla.	U. S. District Court, Middle District of Florida
M. D. Ga.	U. S. District Court, Middle District of Georgia
Md. J. Int'l L. & Trade	Maryland Journal of International Law and Trade (USA)
M. D. La.	U. S. District Court, Middle District of Louisiana
M. D. N. C.	U. S. District Court, Middle District of North Carolina
M. D. Pa.	U. S. District Court, Middle District of Pennsylvania
MDR	Monatsschrift für deutsches Recht
M. D. Tenn.	U. S. District Court, Middle District of Tennessee
m. E.	meines Erachtens
Mealey's Int'l Arb. Rep.	Mealey's International Arbitration Report
Meredith Lect.	Meredith Memorial Lectures (Kanada)
Mich. B. J.	Michigan Bar Journal (USA)
Mich. J. Int'l L.	Michigan Journal of International Law (USA)
Minn.	Minnesota (USA)
Minn. J. Global Trade	Minnesota Journal of Global Trade (USA)
MMA	Madrider Abkommen über die internationale Registrierung von Fabrik- oder Handelsmarken von 1891 i. d. F. von Nizza 1957, BGBl. 1962 II, S. 125
MMR	Multimedia und Recht (Zeitschrift)
Mod. L. Rev.	The Modern Law Review (Großbritannien)
Molengrafica	Molengrafica (Niederlande)
MünchKomm (BGB)	Münchener Kommentar zum Bürgerlichen Gesetzbuch (s. Literaturverzeichnis)
MünchKommHGB	Münchener Kommentar zum Handelsgesetzbuch (s. Literaturverzeichnis)
m. w. N.	mit weiteren Nachweisen
Nachw.	Nachweise
N. b.	nota bene
NBW	Nieuw Burgerlijk Wetboek, s. BW
N. C. J. Int'l L. & Com Reg.	North Carolina Journal of International Law and Commercial Regulation (USA)
NCPC	Nouveau code de procédure civile (Frankreich, s. CPC)
N. D. Ala.	U. S. District Court, Northern District of Alabama
N. D. Cal.	U. S. District Court, Northern District of California
N. D. Fla.	U. S. District Court, Northern District of Florida
N. D. Ga.	U. S. District Court, Northern District of Georgia
N. D. Ill.	U. S. District Court, Northern District of Illinois
N. D. Ind.	U. S. District Court, Northern District of Indiana
N. D. Iowa.	U. S. District Court, Northern District of Iowa
N. D. Miss.	U. S. District Court, Norhtern District of Mississippi
N. D. N. Y.	U. S. District Court, Northern District of New York
N. D. Ohio.	U. S. District Court, Norhtern District of Ohio
N. D. Ok.	U. S. District Court, Norhtern District of Oklahoma
N. D. Tex.	U. S. District Court, Norhtern District of Texas
N. D. W. Va.	U. S. District Court, Norhtern District of West Virginia
NE Int'l Bus.	Northeast International Business (USA)
Neth. Int'l L. Rev.	Netherlands International Law Review (Niederlande)
New Yorker E 1977	Entwurf eines Kaufvertragsabschlussgesetzes der Arbeitsgruppe der UNCITRAL, 8. Sitzung (New York 4.–14. Januar 1977), YB VIII (1977), 88–90
New Yorker E 1978	Entwurf der UNCITRAL, 11. Plenarsitzung (New York 30. Mai – 16. Juni 1978), YB IX (1978), 14–21

Abkürzungen

n. F.	neue Fassung
NIPR	Nederlands Internationaal Privaatrecht (Niederlande)
NJ	Nederlandse Jurisprudentie
NJB	Nederlands Juristenblad (Niederlande)
N. J. Law.	New Jersey Lawyer (USA)
N. J. L. J.	New Jersey Law Journal (USA)
NJOZ	Neue Juristische Online-Zeitschrift
N. J. Super. Ct.	New Jersey Superior Court (USA)
NJW	Neue Juristische Wochenschrift
NJW-RR	Neue Juristische Wochenschrift – Rechtsprechungsreport Zivilrecht
NL	Niederlande
N. L. Civ. Comm.	Le Nuove Leggi Civili Commentate (Italien)
N. L. J.	New Law Journal (Großbritannien)
no.	number (Nummer)
Nordic J. Com. L.	Nordic Journal of Commercial Law
Nordic J. Int'l L.	Nordic Journal of International Law (Dänemark)
Nr.	Nummer(n)
NWB	Neue Wirtschaftsbriefe (Deutschland)
Nw. J. Int'l L. & Bus.	Northwestern Journal of International Law and Business (USA)
N. Y.	New York
N. Y. – CPLR	New York Civil Practice Law and Rules (USA)
N. Y. Ct. Cl.	New York Court of Constitutional Legislation (USA)
N. Y. Int'l L. Rev.	New York International Law Review (USA)
N. Y. L. Sch. J. Int'l & Comp. L.	New York Law School Journal of International and Comparative Law (USA)
N. Y. L. J.	New York Law Journal (USA)
N. Y. St. B. J.	New York State Bar Journal (USA)
N. Y. U. J. Int'l Law & Pol.	New York University Journal of International Law and Politics (USA)
NYSBA	New York State Bar Association
NZG	Neue Zeitschrift für Gesellschaftsrecht
N. Z. L. J.	New Zealand Law Journal
o. ä.	oder ähnliches
obs.	observation
OG	Oberster Gerichtshof (Israel)
OGer	Obergericht (Schweiz)
OGH	Oberster Gerichtshof (Österreich)
OHADA	Organisation pour l'Harmonisation en Afrique du Droit des Affaires
Ohio St. L. J.	Ohio State Law Journal (USA)
ÖJZ	Österreichische Juristenzeitung
OLG	Oberlandesgericht (Deutschland/Österreich)
OLG-Rp.	OLG-Report (getrennt für jedes OLG)
OLGRspr.	Die Rechtsprechung der Oberlandesgerichte auf dem Gebiete des Zivilrechts (1900–1928)
OLGZ	Entscheidungen der Oberlandesgerichte in Zivilsachen einschließlich der freiwilligen Gerichtsbarkeit (seit 1994: FGPrax)
Op.	Opinion
Or.	Supreme Court of Oregon
Or. Ct. App.	Court of Appeals of Oregon
OR	Schweizerisches Obligationenrecht vom 30.3.1911
O. R.	Official Records (s. Literaturverzeichnis bei United Nations)
O. R. VerjÜbk	Official Records zum Verjährungsübereinkommen (s. Literaturverzeichnis bei United Nations)
ÖRiZ	Österreichische Richter-Zeitung
östJBl	Österreichische Juristische Blätter
östZRVgl	Österreichische Zeitschrift für Rechtsvergleichung (siehe auch ZRVgl)
Oxford J. Legal Stud.	Oxford Journal of Legal Studies (Großbritannien)

Abkürzungen

P. 2d	Pacific Reporter, Second Series (USA)
Pace Int'l L. Rev.	Pace International Law Review (USA)
par.	Paragraph
PatG	Patentgesetz i. d. Bek. vom 16.12.1980, BGBl. I 1981, S. 1
PECL	Principles of European Contract Law (Fassung 1995, hrsg. v. *Lando/Beale* [s. Literaturverzeichnis] zitiert als a. F.; Fassung 1997 zitiert als n. F.)
Petites aff.	Les petites affiches (Les journaux judiciaires associés) (Frankreich)
Philippine L. J.	Philippine Law Journal (Philippinen)
PICC	UNIDROIT-Principles of International Commercial Contracts (s. Literaturverzeichnis)
plädoyer	plädoyer. Das Magazin für Recht und Politik (Schweiz)
Preadviezen	Preadviezen uitgebracht voor de Vereniging voor Burgerlijk Recht (Niederlande)
ProdHaftG	Gesetz über die Haftung für fehlerhafte Produkte (Produkthaftungsgesetz) vom 15.12.1989, BGBl. I, S. 2198
PrPG	Gesetz zur Stärkung des Schutzes des geistigen Eigentums und zur Bekämpfung der Produktpiraterie vom 3.7.1990, BGBl. I, S. 422
PVÜ	Pariser Verbandsübereinkunft zum Schutz des gewerblichen Eigentums von 1983 i. d. F. von Stockholm 1967, BGBl. 1979 II, S. 391
Q. B.	Law Reports, Queen's Bench Division (Großbritannien)
Q. C.	Queen's Counsel
Queensl. L. S. J.	Queensland Law Society Journal (Australien)
RabelsZ	Rabels Zeitschrift für ausländisches und internationales Privatrecht
RAG	Gesetz über die Anwendung des Rechts auf internationale zivil-, familien- und arbeitsrechtliche Beziehungen sowie auf internationale Wirtschaftsverträge – Rechtsanwendungsgesetz – vom 5.12.1975, GBl. I, S. 748 (DDR)
RB	Arrondissementsrechtbank (niederländisches Landgericht)/Rechtbank van Koophandel (belgisches Landgericht)
RCEA	Revista de la Corte Española de Arbitraje (Spanien)
R. D. A. I.	Revue de Droit des Affaires Internationales/International Business Law Journal (Frankreich)
R. D. I. D. C.	Revue de Droit International et de Droit Comparé (Belgien)
RdL	Recht der Landwirtschaft (Zeitschrift)
RdW	Österreichisches Recht der Wirtschaft
Rec. des Cours	Recueil des Cours, Collected Courses of the Hague Academy of International Law
recht	recht, Zeitschrift für juristische Ausbildung und Praxis (Schweiz)
Record of N. Y. C. B. A.	Record of the Association of the Bar of the City of New York (USA)
Req.	Cour de Cassation, Chambre des requêtes (Frankreich)
Rev. CISG	Cornell Review of the Convention on Contracts for the International Sale of Goods (USA)
Rev. crit. dr. int. privé	Revue critique de droit international privé (Frankreich)
Rev. de la Fac. de Cien Jur. y Pol.	Revista de la Facultad de Ciencias Jurídicas y Políticas (Venezuela)
Rev. der. com. oblig.	Revista del Derecho comercial y de las Obligaciones (Argentinien)
Rev. der. priv.	Revista de derecho privado (Mexiko)
Rev. Der. Com. Oblig.	Revista del Derecho Comercial y de las Obligaciones (Argentinien)
Rev. Der. Mercantil	Revista de Derecho Mercantil (Venezuela)
Rev. Dir. Econ.	Revista de Direito e Economia
Rev. dir. merc. ind.	Revista de direito mercantil, industrial, econômico e financeiro (Brasilien)
Rev. dr. aff. int.	Revue de droit des affaires internationals
Rev. dr. com. belge	Revue de droit commercial belge (Belgien)
Rev. dr. int.	Revue de droit international et de droit comparé (Belgien)

Abkürzungen

Rev. dr. unif. ...... Revue de droit uniforme/Uniform Law Review (Hrsg. UNIDROIT, Rom) (s. a. Uniform L. Rev.)
Rev. fac. der. México .... Revista de la facultad de derecho de México
Rev. fac. der. Univ. Cat. Andrés .... Revista de la facultad de derecho de la Universidad Bello Católica Andrés Bello (Venezuela)
Rev. fac. der. Univ. Complutense .... Revista de la facultad de derecho de la Universidad Complutense (Curso) (Spanien)
Rev. Fac. Dir. UFRGS .... Revista da Faculdade de Direito da UFRGS (Brasilien)
Rev. for. .... Revista forense (Brasilien)
Rev. gen. der. ..... Revista general de derecho (Spanien)
Rev. gén. dr. .... Revue générale de droit (Kanada)
Rev. Ghana L. .... Review of Ghana Law
Rev. Inf. Leg. ..... Revista de Informação Legislativa (Brasilien)
Rev. Inst. belge ... Revue de droit international et de droit comparé (Belgien)
Rev. int. dr. comp. Revue internationale de droit comparé (Frankreich)
Rev. Int'l Bus. L. . Review of International Business Law (Kanada)
Rev. inv. jur. ...... Revista de investigaciones jurídicas (Mexiko)
Rev. jur. Cat. ...... Revista jurídica de Catalunya (Spanien)
Rev. jur. com. ..... Revue de jurisprudence commerciale (Frankreich)
Rev. Jur. Thémis .. La Revue Juridique Thémis (Kanada)
Rev. jur. Univ. Puerto Rico .... Revista jurídica de la Universidad de Puerto Rico (USA)
Rev. Sup. Trib. Just. Dur. .... Revista del Suprema Tribunal de Justicia de Durango (Mexiko)
Rev. trav. de l'Acad. S. M. P. et C. R. S. .... Revue des travaux de l'Académie des Sciences Morales Politiques et Comptes Rendus de ses Séances (Frankreich)
Rev. trim. dr. civ. . Revue Trimestrielle de Droit Civil (Frankreich)
Rev. Univ. Panamericana .... Revista del Instituto de Documentacin e Investigacin Jurdicas de la Facultad de la Universidad Panamericana (Mexiko)
Rev. Ur. Der. Int. - Priv. .... Revista uruguaya de derecho internacional privado
RG .... Reichsgericht
RGBl. .... Reichsgesetzblatt
RGRK .... Reichsgerichtsrätekommentar (s. Literaturverzeichnis)
RGW .... Rat für gegenseitige Wirtschaftshilfe
RGZ .... Entscheidungen des Reichsgerichts in Zivilsachen
RheinZ .... Rheinische Zeitschrift für Zivil- und Prozeßrecht (1909–1926)
RiA .... Recht in Afrika
Riv. arb. .... Rivista dell' arbitrato (Italien)
Riv. di diritto privato .... Rivista di diritto privato (Italien)
RiVeVo .... Richtlinien für die Fassung von Vertragsgesetzen und vertragsbezogenen Verordnungen
Riv. dir. civ. .... Rivista di Diritto civile (Italien)
Riv. dir. com. ..... Rivista del diritto commerciale e del diritto generale delle obligazioni (Italien)
Riv. dir. int. priv. proc. .... Rivista di diritto internazionale privato e processuale (Italien)
Riv. trim. dir. proced. civ. .... Rivista trimestrale di diritto e procedura civile (Italien)
Riv. vr. giur. ec. impr. .... Rivista veronese di giurisprudenza ed economia dell'impresa (Italien)
RIW .... Recht der Internationalen Wirtschaft, Außenwirtschaftsdienst des Betriebs-Beraters
RL .... Richtlinie
R. M. Themis ..... Rechtsgeleerd magazijn Themis

Rn.	Randnummer(n)
ROHGE	Entscheidungen des Reichsoberhandelsgerichts (amtliche Sammlung, 1872–1880)
ROW	Recht in Ost und West
Rs.	Rechtssache
R. S. C.	Rules of Supreme Court (Order)
Rspr.	Rechtsprechung
RTDciv	Revue trimestrielle de droit civil
RTD com.	Revue trimestrielle de droit commercial et économique (Frankreich)
Rutgers Computer & Tech. L. J.	Rutgers Computer and Technology Law Journal (USA)
RvV	Richtlinien für die Behandlung völkerrechtlicher Verträge
R. W.	Rechtspraak van de Week
s.	siehe
S.	Seite/Satz
SA	South Australia
SAcLJ	Singapore Academy of Law Journal
s. a.	siehe auch
SachenR	Sachenrecht
S. Afr. L. J.	The South African Law Journal (Südafrika)
sämtl.	sämtliche
San Diego L. Rev.	San Diego Law Review (USA)
Scand. Stud. L.	Scandinavian Studies in Law (Schweden)
SchiedsVZ	Zeitschrift für Schiedsverfahren
SchR	Schuldrecht
SchuldModG	Gesetz zur Modernisierung des Schuldrechts v. 26.11.2001, BGBl. I 3138
schweiz. IPRG	Bundesgesetz über das Internationale Privatrecht vom 18.12.1987 (Schweiz)
schweiz.	schweizerisch(e, s)
SCC	Stockholm Chamber of Commerce
S. D.	Southern District (USA)
S. D. Ala.	U. S. District Court, Southern District of Alabama
S. D. Cal.	U. S. District Court, Southern District of California
S. D. Fla.	U. S. District Court, Southern District of Florida
S. D. Ga.	U. S. District Court, Southern District of Georgia
S. D. Ill.	U. S. District Court, Southern District of Illinois
S. D. Ind.	U. S. District Court, Southern District of Indiana
S. D. Iowa.	U. S. District Court, Southern District of Iowa
S. D. Miss.	U. S. District Court, Southern District of Mississippi
S. D. N.	Société des Nations
S. D. N. Y.	U. S. District Court, Southern District of New York
S. D. Ohio	U. S. District Court, Southern District of Ohio
S. D. Tex.	U. S. District Court, Southern District of Texas
S. D. W. Va.	U. S. District Court, Southern District of West Virginia
sec.	section(s)
Sekretariatskommentar	Commentary on the Draft Convention on Contracts for the International Sale of Goods (s. Literaturverzeichnis: Commentary)
Sem. jud.	La Semaine Judiciaire (Schweiz)
Sess. Cas.	Session Cases, Court of Sessions (Schottland)
SeuffArch.	Seufferts Archiv für Entscheidungen der obersten Gerichte in den deutschen Staaten (1847–1944)
SF	Schweizer Franken
SGA	Sale of Goods Act 1979, zuletzt geändert durch den Sale and Supply of Goods Act 1994 und den Sale of Goods (Amendment) Act 1995 (Großbritannien)
SSGA 1994	Sale and Supply of Goods Act 1994 (Großbritannien)
SGAA 1995	Sale of Goods (Amendment) Act 1995 (Großbritannien)
SigG	Gesetz zur digitalen Signatur vom 22.7.1997, BGBl. 1997, I, 1870
Singapore YB. Int'l L.	Singapore Yearbook of International Law

Abkürzungen

SJZ	Schweizerische Juristen-Zeitung
skand.	skandinavisch
Slg.	Sammlung der Rechtsprechung des EuGH
SLR	Singapore Law Review
s. o.	siehe oben
Soc. Pravo	Socialisticesko Pravo (Bulgarien)
Software L. J.	Software Law Journal (USA)
sog.	sogenannt(e, en)
Somm.	Sommaires
SortSchG	Sortenschutzgesetz vom 20.5.1968, BGBl. I, S. 429
South. Cal. L. Rev.	Southern California Law Review (USA)
Stan. J. Int'l L.	Stanford Journal of International Law (USA)
STEG	Gesetz über die Sicherheit technischer Einrichtungen und Geräte (Schweiz)
St. John's L. Rev.	St. John's Law Review (USA)
str.	streitig
st. Rspr.	ständige Rechtsprechung
Stud. L. & Econ.	Studies of Law and Economics (Japan)
Stud. Transnat'l Econ. L.	Studies in Transnational Economic Law (USA)
Stu. mez. práva	Studie z mezinárodního práva (Tschechoslowakei)
StuR	Staat und Recht
s. u.	siehe unten
Sub.	Subchapter
Sup. Ct. BC	Supreme Court of British Columbia
Sup. Ct. Ontario	Superior Court Ontario (Kanada)
Sup. Ct. QLD	Supreme Court of Queensland (Australien)
Svensk Jurist.	Svensk Juristtidning (Schweden)
Syracuse J. Int'l L. & Com.	Syracuse Journal of International Law and Commerce (USA)
SZ	Entscheidungen des österreichischen Obersten Gerichtshofs in Zivilsachen
SZIER	Schweizerische Zeitschrift für Internationales und Europäisches Recht (Schweiz)
SZW/RSDA	Schweizerische Zeitschrift für Wirtschaftsrecht/Revue suisse de droit des affaires (Schweiz)
T. civ.	Tribunale civile (Zivilgericht, Italien)
Temp. Int'l & Comp. L. J.	Temple International and Comparative Law Journal (USA)
Tex. Int'l L. J.	Texas International Law Journal (USA)
TfR	Tidsskrift for Rettsvitenskap (Norwegen)
TGI	Tribunal de grande instance (Frankreich)
Transnat'l Law.	The Transnational Lawyer (USA)
TranspR	Transport- und Speditionsrecht
TranspR-IHR	Internationales Handelsrecht, Mitteilungen für die Wirtschaftsrechtliche Praxis, Beilage zu der Zeitschrift Transportrecht (1998–2000)
Trav. dr. comp.	Travaux de droit comparé (Tschechoslowakei)
Trib.	Tribunal (Schweiz)/Tribunale (Italien)
Trib. com.	Tribunal de Commerce (Belgien/Frankreich)
TRIPS	Agreement on Trade-Related Aspects of Intellectual Property Rights [der WTO] (http://www.wto.org/english/docs_e/legal_e/27-trips.pdf)
Tul. Civ. L. F.	Tulane Civil Law Forum (USA)
Tul. Eur. & Civ. L. Forum	Tulane European & Civil Law Forum (USA)
Tul. L. Rev.	Tulane Law Review (USA)
TvP	Tijdschrift voor privaatrecht (Belgien)
u.	und
u. a.	unter anderem/und andere
u. ä.	und ähnliche(s)
UAGCL	Uniform Act Relating to General Commercial Law
U. B. C. L. Rev.	University of British Columbia Law Review (Kanada)

U. B. L. R.	University of Baltimore Law Review (USA)
UCC	Uniform Commercial Code (USA)
UCC L. J.	Uniform Commercial Code Law Journal (USA)
UCC Rep. Serv.	Uniform Commercial Code Reporting Service (Callaghan, USA)
U. Chic. L. Rev.	University of Chicago Law Review (USA)
U. Cin. L. Rev.	University of Cincinnati Law Review (USA)
UCLA L. Rev.	University of California Los Angeles Law Review
UCP 600	ICC Uniform Customs and Practice for Documentary Credits (Einheitliche Richtlinien und Gebräuche für Dokumenten-Akkreditive), von der ICC veröffentlicht 1935, revidiert 1951, 1962, 1974, 1983, 1993 und 2007 (s. auch el. ERA, ERA)
U. Detr. L. Rev.	University of Detroit Law Review (USA)
u. dgl.	und dergleichen
U. D. P.	Institut International pour l'Unification du Droit privé/International Institut for the Unification of Private Law (s. a. UNIDROIT)
UdSSR	(ehem.) Union der Sozialistischen Sowjetrepubliken
UfR	Ugeskrift for Retsvaesen (Dänemark)
ULIS	Uniform Law on the International Sale of Goods (s. a. EKG)
U. Miami Inter-Am. L. Rev.	University of Miami Inter-American Law Review (USA)
U. Miami Y. B. Int'l L.	University of Miami Yearbook of International Law (USA)
UN	United Nations (Vereinte Nationen)
UNCITRAL	United Nations Commission on International Trade Law
UNCITRAL-E	UNCITRAL-Entwurf
UN-Dok.	UN-Dokumente
UNECIC	United Nations Convention on the Use of Electronic Communications in International Contracts (2005)
UNIDROIT	Institut International pour l'Unification du Droit Privé/International Institute for the Unification of Private Law
Unif. L. Conf.	Uniform Law Conference of Canada, Proceedings of the Annual Meeting (Kanada)
Uniform L. Rev.	Uniform Law Review/Revue de droit uniforme (Hrsg. UNIDROIT, Rom)
UNILEX	International Case Law, UNIDROIT (s. Literaturverzeichnis)
UNO	United Nations Organization
unstr.	unstreitig
Unterabs.	Unterabschnitt, Unterabsatz
UnterzKl	Unterzeichnungsklausel
U. Pa. L. Rev.	University of Pennsylvania Law Review (USA)
U. Pitt. L. Rev.	University of Pittsburgh Law Review (USA)
URC 522	ICC Uniform Rules for Collections (Einheitliche Richtlinien für Inkassi), von der ICC veröffentlicht 1956, revidiert 1967, 1979 und 1996 (s. auch ERI)
UrhG	Urheberrechtsgesetz vom 9.9.1965, BGBl. I, S. 1273
Urt.	Urteil
US/U. S.	United States
USA	United States of America
U. S. C. S.	United States Code Service
U. S. Dep. Agric.	United States Department of Agriculture
U. S. Dist. LEXIS	LEXIS Datenbank der Entscheidungen der US-District Courts
U. So. Fla. L. Rev.	University of Southern Florida Law Review (USA)
U. S. F. L. Rev.	University of San Francisco Law Review (USA)
usw.	und so weiter
u. U.	unter Umständen
U. W. Ont. L. Rev.	University of Western Ontario Law Review (Kanada)
UWG	Gesetz gegen den unlauteren Wettbewerb vom 7.6.1909, RGBl. S. 499
u. z.	und zwar
v.	von (vom)/versus
Va. J. Int'l L.	Virginia Journal of International Law (USA)
Vand. J. Transnat'l L.	Vanderbilt Journal of Transnational Law (USA)

Abkürzungen

VE .... Vorentwurf
VerbrKrG .... Verbraucherkreditgesetz vom 17.12.1990, BGBl. I, S. 2840 (außer Kraft)
VerjÜbk .... Convention on the Limitation Period in the International Sale of Goods (Übereinkommen über die Verjährung beim internationalen Warenkauf) vom 14.6.1974 (A/CONF. 63/15), YB V (1974), 210–215 in der Fassung des Protocol Amending the Convention on the Limitation Period in the International Sale of Goods vom 11.4.1980 (A/CONF. 97/18, annex II), YB XI (1980), 162–164
VerjÜbk 74 .... Convention on the Limitation Period in the International Sale of Goods (Übereinkommen über die Verjährung beim internationalen Warenkauf) vom 14.6.1974 (A/CONF. 63/15), YB V (1974), 210–215
Ver. Sen. .... Vereinigte Senate
VersR .... Versicherungsrecht
VertragsG .... Gesetz zu dem Übereinkommen der Vereinten Nationen vom 11. April 1980 über Verträge über den internationalen Warenkauf sowie zur Änderung des Gesetzes zu dem Übereinkommen vom 19. Mai 1956 über den Beförderungsvertrag im internationalen Straßengüterverkehr (CMR) vom 5.7.1989, BGBl. II, S. 586
vgl. .... vergleiche
Vict.
U. Well. L. Rev. ... Victoria University of Wellington Law Review (Neuseeland)
VJ .... Vindobona Journal of Commercial Law and Arbitration (Österreich)
VLK .... Vestre Landsret (Western High Court, Dänemark)
VN .... Vereinte Nationen
VO .... Verordnung
VOB/A .... Verdingungsordnung für Bauleistungen, Teil A
vol. .... volume (Band)
Vor Artt. .... Vorbemerkungen zu den Artikeln
Vorbem. .... Vorbemerkungen
VP .... Die Versicherungs-Praxis
VVG .... Gesetz über den Versicherungsvertrag idF. vom 23.11.2007, BGBl. I, S. 2833

WarnR .... Rechtsprechung des Reichsgerichts, soweit sie nicht in der amtlichen Sammlung der Entscheidungen des Reichsgerichts abgedruckt ist, begr. v. Warneyer (1908–1943); ab 1961: Rechtsprechung des Bundesgerichtshofs in Zivilsachen
Wash. L. Rev. ..... Washington Law Review (USA)
Wash. U. L. Q. .... Washington University Law Quarterly (USA)
WBl. .... Wirtschaftsrechtliche Blätter, Beilage zu Österreichische Juristische Blätter (Österreich)
W. D. Ark. .... U. S. District Court, Western District of Arkansas
W. D. Ky. .... U. S. District Court, Western District of Kentucky
W. D. La. .... U. S. District Court, Western District of Louisiana
W. D. Mich. ...... U. S. District Court, Western District of Michigan
W. D. Mo. .... U. S. District Court, Western District of Missouri
W. D. N. C. .... U. S. District Court, Western District of North Carolina
W. D. N. Y. .... U. S. District Court, Western District of New York
W. D. Ok. .... U. S. District Court, Western District of Oklahoma
W. D. Pa. .... U. S. District Court, Western District of Pennsylvania
W. D. Tenn. ...... U. S. District Court, Western District of Tennessee
W. D. Tex. .... U. S. District Court, Western District of Texas
W. D. Va. .... U. S. District Court, Western District of Virginia
W. D. Wash. ...... U. S. District Court, Western District of Washington
W. D. Wis. .... U. S. District Court, Western District of Wisconsin
West Int'l L. Bull. . West's International Law Bulletin (USA)
wg. .... wegen
W. G. .... Working Group
WiB .... Wirtschaftsrechtliche Beratung (seit 1998 NZG)
Wi. Bl. .... Wirtschaftliche Blätter
Wiener E 1977 ... Entwurf der UNCITRAL, 10. Plenarsitzung (Wien 23. Mai–17. Juni 1977), YB VIII (1977), S. 15–21

Wiener Vertrags-rechtskonvention	Wiener Konvention über das Recht der Verträge vom 23. Mai 1969 (in Kraft seit 27. Januar 1980)
Willamette L. Rev.	Willamette Law Review (USA)
WiR	Wirtschaftsrecht
WiRO	Wirtschaftsrecht in Osteuropa
Wis. B. Bull.	Wisconsin Bar Bulletin (USA)
WL	West Law, Datenbank
W. L. R.	The Weekly Law Reports (Großbritannien)
WM	Wertpapier-Mitteilungen
WPNR	Weekblad voor privaatrecht, notariaat en registratie (Niederlande)
W. R.	Weekly Reporter (Großbritannien)
WTO	World Trade Organization, Sitz: Genf, Schweiz (http://www.wto.org)
WZG	Warenzeichengesetz vom 5.5.1936, RGBl. II, S. 134 (außer Kraft)
Yale L. J.	The Yale Law Journal (USA)
Yale J. Int'l L.	The Yale Journal of International Law (USA)
YB	UNCITRAL-Yearbook, New York: United Nations Publication (1971 ff.)
YB. Comm. Arb.	Yearbook Commercial Arbitration (USA)
zahlr.	zahlreich
Zahlungsverzugs-RL	RL 2000/35/EG des Europäischen Parlaments und des Rates v. 29.6.2000 zur Bekämpfung von Zahlungsverzug im Geschäftsverkehr
ZaiP	Zeitschrift für ausländisches und internationales Privatrecht
z. B.	zum Beispiel
ZBJV	Zeitschrift des Bernischen Juristenvereins
ZEuP	Zeitschrift für Europäisches Privatrecht
ZfBR	Zeitschrift für deutsches und internationales Baurecht
ZfRVgl	Zeitschrift für Rechtsvergleichung, intern. Privatrecht und Europarecht (Österreich, seit 1991, davor: Zeitschrift für Rechtsvergleichung, s. a. östZRVgl)
ZG	Zeitschrift für Gesetzgebung
ZGB	Schweizerisches Zivilgesetzbuch vom 10.12.1907
ZGer	Zivilgericht (Schweiz, s. a. ZivG)
ZHR	Zeitschrift für das gesamte Handelsrecht und Wirtschaftsrecht
Ziff.	Ziffer, Ziffern
ZIP	Zeitschrift für Wirtschaftsrecht
ZivG	Zivilgericht (Schweiz, s. a. ZGer)
ZNotP	Zeitschrift für die NotarPraxis
ZRP	Zeitschrift für Rechtspolitik
ZSR	Zeitschrift für Schweizerisches Recht (Schweiz)
z. T.	zum Teil
zust.	zustimmend
ZVerglRWiss	Zeitschrift für vergleichende Rechtswissenschaft
z. Zt.	zur Zeit

Literaturverzeichnis[1]

Achilles, Wilhelm-Albrecht Kommentar zum UN-Kaufrechtsübereinkommen (CISG), Neuwied: Luchterhand (2000)
Achilles, Wilhelm-Albrecht: Zur Rechtsmängelhaftung des Verkäufers bei Schutzrechtsverwarnungen und Berechtigungsanfragen, in: *Bühler/Müller-Chen* (Hrsg.), Festschrift für Ingeborg Schwenzer zum 60. Geburtstag, Bern: Stämpfli (2011), S. 1–20 (Kurztitel: FS Schwenzer)
Adame Goddard, Jorge: El contrato de compraventa internacional, Mexiko: McGraw-Hill (1994) (Kurztitel: Compraventa internacional)
Adame Goddard, Jorge: Reglas de interpretación de la Convención sobre Compraventa Internacional de Mercaderías, Dir. com. int. 1990, 103–125
Adami, Francesco: Les contrats „open price" dans la Convention des Nations Unies sur les contrats de vente international de marchandises, R. D. A. I. 1989, 103–120 = Int'l Bus. L. J. 1989, 103–120
Aicher, Josef/Koppensteiner, Hans-Georg (Hrsg.): Beiträge zum Zivil- und Handelsrecht, in: Festschrift für Rolf Ostheim zum 65. Geburtstag, Vienna: Orac (1990), S. 211 ff. (Kurztitel: FS Ortheim)
Aicher, Josef: Leistungsstörungen aus der Verkäufersphäre, in: *Hoyer/Posch* (Hrsg.), Das Einheitliche Wiener Kaufrecht, Wien: Orac (1992), S. 111–142
Allmendinger, K.-H.: Gestaltung von Liefer-(Kauf-)Verträgen im Auslandsgeschäft, Köln: Bundesstelle für Aussenhandelsinformation (1984)
Almén, Tore: Das skandinavische Kaufrecht, Bde. I–III, Deutsche Ausgabe von Neubecker, Heidelberg: Winter (1922)
Alpa, Guido/Bessone, Mario: Inadempimento, rimedi contrattuali, effetti della risoluzione nella vendita internazionale di cose mobili, (Convenzione di Vienna, marzo 1980), in: *Tedeschi/Alpa* (Hrsg.), Il contratto nel diritto nord-americano, Mailand: Giuffrè (1980), S. 279–310
Alpa, Guido/Bessone, Mario: Inadempimento, rimedi, effetti della risoluzione nella vendita internazionale di cose mobili (Convenzione di Vienna, marzo 1980), in: La Vendita Internazionale, Mailand: Giuffrè (1981), 165–212 = Foro it. 1980, 233–254
van Alstine, Michael P.: Consensus, Dissensus, and Contractual Obligation Through the Prism of Uniform International Sales Law, 37 Va. J. Int'l L. (1996), 1–105
van Alstine, Michael P.: Dynamic Treaty interpretation, 146 U. Pa. L. Rev. (1998), 687–793
van Alstine, Michael P.: Fehlender Konsens beim Vertragsabschluß nach dem einheitlichen UN-Kaufrecht: eine rechtsvergleichende Untersuchung auf der Grundlage des deutschen sowie des US-amerikanischen Rechts (Diss. Bonn 1994), Baden-Baden: Nomos (1995)
van Alstine, Michael P.: The UNCITRAL Digest, the Right to Interest, and the Interest Rate Controversy, in: *Flechtner/Brand/Walter* (Hrsg.), Drafting Contracts under the CISG, Oxford: Oxford University Press (2008), S. 505–528 (Kurztitel: Drafting Contracts)
Amato, Paul: Recent Developments: CISG. U. N. Convention on Contracts for the International Sale of Goods – The Open Price Term and Uniform Application: an Early Interpretation by the Hungarian Courts, 13 J. L. & Com. (1993), 1–29
Amstutz, Marc/Breitschmid, Peter/Furrer, Andreas/Girsberger, Daniel/Huguenin, Claire/Müller-Chen, Markus/Roberto, Vito/Rumo-Jungo, Alexandra/Schnyder, Anton K. (Hrsg.): Kommentar zum Schweizer Privatrecht, Zürich: Schulthess (2007)
Ancel, Bertrand/Muir Watt, Horatia: Note [commenting on Cass. Civ. 16.7.1998], Rev. crit. dr. int. privé 1999, 123–132
Andersen, Camilla Baasch: Comparative analysis between the provisions of the CISG regarding notice requirements (Arts. 39 & 26) and the counterpart provisions of the UNIDROIT Principles and the PECL, in: Felemegas, John (Hrsg.): An International Approach to the Interpretation of the United Nations Convention on Contracts for the International Sale of Goods (1980) as Uniform Sales Law, Cambridge, New York u. a.: Cambridge University Press (2007), 133–138 (Kurztitel: Comparative analysis)
Andersen, Camilla Baasch: Noblesse Oblige…? Revisiting the «Noble Month» and the Expectations and Accomplishments it has prompted, in: *Bühler/Müller-Chen* (Hrsg.), Festschrift für Ingeborg Schwenzer zum 60. Geburtstag, Bern: Stämpfli (2011), S. 33–50 (Kurztitel: FS Schwenzer)

---

[1] Dieses Literaturverzeichnis enthält grds. nur die im Kommentar zitierten Arbeiten. Ein umfassendes und ständig aktualisiertes Verzeichnis der Literatur zum CISG findet sich in der Datenbank CISG-online (http://www.globalsaleslaw.org/index.cfm?pageID=638)

Literatur

Andersen, Camilla Baasch: Reasonable Time in Article 39(1) of the CISG – Is Article 39(1) Truly a Uniform Provision?, CISG Pace (Kurztitel: Reasonable Time)

Andersen, Camilla Baasch: Uniform Application of the International Sales Law: Understanding Uniformity, the Global Jurisconsultorium and Examination and Notification Provisions of the CISG, Alphen am Rhein: Kluwer Law International (2007) (Kurztitel: Uniform Application)

Andreason, Rod N.: MCC-Marble Ceramic Center: the Parol Evidence Rule and Other Domestic Law Under the Convention on Contracts for the International Sale of Goods, 1999 B. Y. U. L. Rev., 351–379

Annibale, Silverio: Riforma del sistema del italiano di diritto internazionale privato, Padua: Cedam (1997)

Anson, William R./Beatson, Jack: Anson's Law of contract, 28. Aufl., Oxford: Oxford University Press (2002) (Kurztitel: Ansons/Beatson)

Antweiler, Clemens: Beweislastverteilung im UN-Kaufrecht. Insbesondere bei Vertragsverletzungen des Verkäufers (Diss. Mainz 1994), Frankfurt a. M.: Lang (1995)

AnwaltKommentar BGB, Band 1: Allgemeiner Teil und EGBGB, hrsgg. v. *Noack, Mansel* u. *Hüßtege,* Bonn: Deutscher Anwaltverlag (2005) (Kurztitel: AnwK/*Bearbeiter*)

Armbrüster, Christian: Standard Contract Terms and Information Rules, in: *Collins, Hugh* (Hrsg.), Standard Contract Terms in Europe: A Basis for and a Challenge to European Contract Law, Alphen an den Rijn: Kluwer (2009), 163–175 (Kurztitel: Standard Contract Terms)

Asam, Herbert: Aktuelle Fragen zur Anwendung des Kaufrechtsübereinkommens der UN vom 11.4.1980 im deutsch-italienischen Rechtsverkehr seit 1.1.1988, Jb. It. R. 3 (1990), 3–47

Asam, Herbert: Die Verjährung kaufvertraglicher Ansprüche im italienischen Recht, RIW 1992, 798–802

Asam, Herbert: Instrumente des Inflationsausgleichs im italienischen und deutschen Privatrecht. Eine rechtsvergleichende Untersuchung (Diss. München 1983), München: Florentz (1984)

Asam, Herbert: Rechtsfragen der Verjährung kaufvertraglicher Ansprüche im deutsch-italienischen Rechtsverkehr, Jb. It. R. 5 (1992), 59–90

Asam, Herbert: UN-Kaufrechtsübereinkommen im deutsch-italienischen Rechtsverkehr, RIW 1989, 942–946

Asam, Herbert/Kindler, Peter: Ersatz des Zins- und Geldentwertungsschadens nach dem Wiener Kaufrechtsübereinkommen vom 11.4.1980 bei deutsch-italienischen Kaufverträgen, RIW 1989, 841–849

Atamer, Yeşim Müride: Availability of Remedies other than Damages in Case of Exemption According to Art. 79 CISG, in: *Büchler/Müller-Chen* (Hrsg.), Private Law, national – global – comparative, Festschrift für Ingeborg Schwenzer zum 60. Geburtstag, Bern: Stämpfli (2011), S. 83–98 (Kurztitel: FS Schwenzer)

Atamer, Yeşim Müride: Grenzen des Erfüllungsanspruchs im System des Leistungsstörungsrechts der PICC, PECL und des DCFR im Vergleich zum CISG – Probleme und Änderungsvorschläge, in: *Grundmann/ Haar/Merkt u. a.* (Hrsg.), Festschrift für Klaus J. Hopt zum 70. Geburtstag am 24. August 2010: Unternehmen, Markt und Verantwortung, Berlin: De Gruyter (2010), 3–26 (Kurztitel: FS Hopt)

Atiyah, Patrick Selim: An Introduction to the Law of Contracts, 5. Aufl., Oxford: Oxford Press (1995)

Atiyah Patrick Selim/Adams, John N./Macqueen, Hector: The Sale of Goods, 10. Aufl., London: Pitman (2001)

Atiyah, Patrick Selim/Smith, Stephan A.: Atiyah's Introduction to the Law of Contract, 6. Aufl., Oxford: Clarendon Press (2005)

Aubrey, Michael: The Formation of International Contracts, with Reference to the Uniform Law on Formation, 14 Int'l & Comp. L. Q. (1965), 1011–1022

Audit, Bernard: Anmerkung zu CA Paris, 14.1.1998, D. 1998. Somm. 288–299

Audit, Bernard: La vente internationale de marchandises, Paris: L. G. D. J. (1990) (Kurztitel: Vente internationale)

Audit, Bernard: The Vienna Sales Convention and the Lex Mercatoria, in: *Carbonneau* (Hrsg.), Lex Mercatoria and Arbitration: a Discussion of the New Law Merchant, Dobbs Ferry, New York: Transnational Juris Publications (1990), 139–160 (Kurztitel: Lex Mercatoria)

Aue, Joachim: Mängelgewährleistung im UN-Kaufrecht unter besonderer Berücksichtigung stillschweigender Zusicherungen (Diss. Heidelberg), Frankfurt a. M.: Lang (1989) (Kurztitel: Mängelgewährleistung im UN-Kaufrecht)

Augner, Jörn: Vertragsschluß ohne Zugang der Annahmeerklärung. § 151 in rechtshistorischer und rechtsvergleichender Sicht (Diss. Hamburg 1985)

Azeredo da Silveira, Mercédeh: Anticipatory Breach Under the United Nations Convention on Contracts for the International Sale of Goods, 2 Nordic J. Com. L. (2005), http://www.njcl.utu.fi/2_2005/article1.pdf

Literatur

Babiak, Andrew: Defining „Fundamental Breach" under the United Nations Convention on Contracts for the International Sale of Goods, 6 Temp. Int'l & Comp. L. J. (1992), 113–143

Babusiaux, Ulrike: Conditions d'application des usages du commerce international sous la Convention de Vienne, D. 2002, Jur. 320–322

Bach, Ivo: Neuere Rechtsprechung zum UN-Kaufrecht, IPRax (2009), 299–306

Bacher, Klaus: Landesspezifische Auslegung von Einheitsrecht?, in: *Schwenzer/Hager* (Hrsg.), Festschrift für Peter Schlechtriem zum 70. Geburtstag, Tübingen: Mohr (2003), S. 155–163 (Kurztitel: FS Schlechtriem)

Bacher, Klaus: Rechte und Ansprüche aus Patenten als Rechtsmangel im Sinne von Art. 42 CISG, in: *Bühler/Müller-Chen* (Hrsg.), Festschrift für Ingeborg Schwenzer zum 60. Geburtstag, Bern, Stämpfli (2011), S. 115–128 (Kurztitel: FS Schwenzer)

Bailey, James E.: Facing the Truth: Seeing the Convention on Contracts for the International Sale of Goods as an Obstacle to a Uniform Law of International Sales, 32 Cornell Int'l L. J. (1999), 273–317

Bainbridge, Stephen: Trade Usages in International Sales of Goods: An Analysis of the 1964 and 1980 Sales Convention, 24 Va. J. Int'l L. (1984), 619–665

Baldus, Christian: Beweislastverteilung im UN-Kaufrecht, Frankfurt a. M.: Lang (1995)

Bamberger, Heinz Georg/Roth, Herbert (Hrsg.): Beck'scher Online-Kommentar zum BGB, Stand: 1.2.2013 Edition: 26, München: Beck (2013) (Kurztitel: *Bamberger/Roth/Autor*)

Bamberger, Heinz Georg/Roth, Herbert (Hrsg.): Kommentar zum Bürgerlichen Gesetzbuch, Band 1, §§ 1–610, CISG, 2. Aufl., München: Beck (2007) (Kurztitel: *Bamberger/Roth/Saenger*)

Bamberger, Heinz Georg/Roth, Herbert (Hrsg.): Kommentar zum Bürgerlichen Gesetzbuch, Band 3, §§ 1297–2385, EGBGB, CISG, München: Beck (2007) (Kurztitel: *Bamberger/Roth/Saenger*)

Bammarny, Bawar: Treu und Glauben und UN-Kaufrecht (CISG): Eine rechtsvergleichende Untersuchung mit Schwerpunkt auf dem islamischen Rechtskreis (Diss. Heidelberg, 2010), Frankfurt a. M. u. a.: Lang (2011) (Kurztitel: Treu und Glauben)

Bankrecht und Bankpraxis, hrsg. von *Hellner/Steuer,* Loseblatt, Köln: bank-verlag (Stand: Juni 2007) (Kurztitel: BuB/*Bearbeiter*)

von Bar, Christian/Mankowski, Peter: Internationales Privatrecht, Bd. 2, Besonderer Teil, 2. Aufl., München: Beck (2003) (Kurztitel: IPR Bd. 2)

von Bar, Christian/Zimmermann, Reinhard: Grundregeln des Europäischen Vertragsrechts, Teile I und II, München: Sellier. European Law Publishers (2002)

Barbic, Jaksa: Uniform Law on the International Sale of Goods, Uniform Law on the Formation of Contracts for the International Sale of Goods (1964) and United Nations Convention on Contracts for the International Sale of Goods (Vienna 1980), in: *Voskuil/Wade* (Hrsg.), Hague-Zagreb Essays 4, Den Haag: Asser Instituut/Martinus Nijhoff (1983), S. 3–21 (Kurztitel: Uniform Law)

Bardo, Ulrike: Die „abstrakte" Berechnung des Schadensersatzes wegen Nichterfüllung beim Kaufvertrag (Diss. Köln), Berlin: Duncker & Humblot (1989)

Barfuss, Werner: Das Einheitliche Kaufgesetz im Spiegel der Rechtsprechung deutscher Gerichte, in: *Barfuss u. a.* (Hrsg.), Festschrift für Karl H. Neumayer zum 65. Geburtstag, Baden-Baden: Nomos (1985), S. 59–77 (Kurztitel: FS Neumayer)

Bariatti, Stefania: L'interpretazione delle convenzioni internazionali di diritto uniforme, Padua: Cedam (1986)

Barrière Brousse, Isabelle: La création normative des États. Point de vue privatiste, in: *Loquin/Kessedjian* (Hrsg.), La mondialisation du droit, Dijon: Litec (2000), S. 133–148

Bartels, Hans-Joachim/Motomura, Hiroshi: Haftungsprinzip, Haftungsbefreiung und Vertragsbeendigung beim internationalen Kauf, RabelsZ 43 (1979), 649–707

Basedow, Jürgen: Depositivierungstendenzen in der Rechtsprechung zum Internationalen Einheitsrecht, in: *Canaris u. a.* (Hrsg.), 50 Jahre Bundesgerichtshof, München: Beck (2000), S. 779–798 (Kurztitel: 50 Jahre BGH)

Basedow, Jürgen: Germany, in: *Bonell* (Hrsg.), A New Approach to International Commercial Contracts – The UNIDROIT Priniciples of International Commercial Contracts, Deventer: Kluwer (1999), S. 125–150 (Kurztitel: Germany)

Basedow, Jürgen: Uniform Law Conventions and the UNIDROIT Principles of International Commercial Contracts, Uniform L. Rev. 2000, 129–139

Basler Kommentar: Kommentar zum Schweizerischen Privatrecht, Obligationenrecht I, Art. 1–529 OR, hrsg. von *Honsell/Vogt/Wiegand,* 4. Aufl., Basel, Genf, München: Helbing & Lichtenhahn (2007) (Kurztitel: BaslerKomm/*Bearbeiter*)

Batiffol, Henri/Lagarde, Xavier: Droit international privé, 8. Aufl., Paris: Pichon (1993)

Bauer, Jobst-Hubertus/Diller, Martin: Kündigung durch Einwurf-Einschreiben – ein Kunstfehler!, NJW 1998, 2795–2796

Literatur

Baumann, Antje: Regeln der Auslegung internationaler Handelsgeschäfte: eine vergleichende Untersuchung der UNIDROIT Principles, der Principles of European Contract Law, des Uniform Commercial Code und des deutschen Rechts (Diss. Osnabrück 2003), Göttingen: V & R Unipress (2004) (Kurztitel: Auslegung)

Baumbach, Adolf/Hefermehl, Wolfgang: Wettbewerbsrecht, 22. Aufl., München: Beck (2001)

Baumbach, Adolf/Hopt, Klaus J.: Handelsgesetzbuch mit GmbH & Co., Handelsklauseln, Bank- und Börsenrecht, Transportrecht (ohne Seerecht), bearb. v. *Hopt* und *Merkt,* 33. Aufl., München: Beck (2008) (Kurztitel: Baumbach/Hopt)

Baumgärtel, Gottfried: Handbuch der Beweislast im Privatrecht, Bd. 2, BGB Sachen-, Familien- und Erbrecht, Recht der EG, UN-Kaufrecht, hrsg. v. *Laumen,* Artt. 1–101 CISG erläutert v. *Hepting,* 2. Aufl., Köln: Heymann (1999) (Kurztitel: Baumgärtel/Laumen/Hepting)

Bayer, Wilhelm F.: Auslegung und Ergänzung international vereinheitlichter Normen durch staatliche Gerichte, RabelsZ 20 (1955), 603–642

Bazinas, Spiros V.: Case Law on UNCITRAL Texts, in: *Majoros* (Hrsg.), Emptio – venditio inter nationes, Basel: Recht und Gesellschaft (1997), S. 195–210 (Kurztitel: FS Neumayer)

Bazinas Spiros V.: Uniformity in the Interpretation and Application of the CISG: The Role of Clout and the Digest, in: Singapore International Arbitration Centre (Hrsg.), Celebrating Success: 25 Years United Nations Convention o Contracts for the International Sale of Goods, Singapur (2006), S. 18–27 (Kurztitel: Uniformity)

Beale, Hugh G. (Hrsg.): Chitty On Contracts, Vol. I & II, 31. Aufl., London: Sweet & Maxwell (2012) (Kurztitel: Chitty On Contracts)

Bednarikova, Jarmila: Les réformes législatives en Tchécoslovaquie: la réception est une chose, l'application une autre, in: Schweizerisches Institut für Rechtsvergleichung (Hrsg.), Osmose zwischen Rechtsordnungen, Berichte des Kolloquiums anläßlich des zehnjährigen Bestehens des Schweizerischen Instituts für Rechtsvergleichung, Zürich: Schulthess (1992), S. 61–68

Behling, Thorsten B.: Der Zugang elektronischer Willenserklärungen in modernen Kommunikationssystemen (Diss. Bochum 2006), Baden-Baden: Nomos (2007)

Behn, Michael: Das Wirksamwerden von schriftlichen Willenserklärungen mittels Einschreiben: Zur Bedeutung der Zurücklassung des Benachrichtigungszettels, AcP 178 (1978), 505–532

Behr, Volker: Commentary to Journal of Law and Commerce Case I: OLG Frankfurt a. M. 17. Sept. 1991, 12 J. L. & Com. (1993), 271–276

Behr, Volker: The Sales Convention in Europe: From problems in drafting to problems in Practice, 17 J. L. & Com. (1998), 263–299

Beinert, Dieter: Wesentliche Vertragsverletzung und Rücktritt (Diss. Bonn 1977), Bielefeld: Gieseking (1979) (Kurztitel: Wesentliche Vertragsverletzung)

Bejcek, Josef/Fritzsche, Jörg: Die Vertragsstrafe im Geschäftsverkehr mit der CR, WiRO 1994, 111–115 (Kurztitel: Vertragsstrafe)

Bell, Gary F.: How the Fact of Accepting Good Faith as a General Principle of the CISG will Bring More Uniformity, Rev. CISG (2005/2006), 3–22

Bell, Gary F.: Taking the Languages of the CISG Seriously, in: *Bühler/Müller-Chen* (Hrsg.), Festschrift für Ingeborg Schwenzer zum 60. Geburtstag, Bern: Stämpfli (2011), S. 143–158 (Kurztitel: FS Schwenzer)

Bell, Gary F.: Why Singapore Should Withdraw Its Reservation to the United Nations Convention on Contracts for the International Sale of Goods (CISG), 9 Singapore Y B. Int'l L. (2005), 55–73

Bell, Kevin: The Sphere of Application of the Vienna Convention on Contracts for the International Sale of Goods, 8 Pace Int'l L. Rev. (1996), 237–258

Ben Abderrahmane, Dahmane: La conformité des marchandises dans la convention de Vienne du 11 avril 1980 sur les contrats de vente internationale de marchandises, Dr. prat. com. int. 1989, 551–563

Benedick, Gilles: Die Informationspflichten im UN-Kaufrecht (CISG) und ihre Verletzung. Unter Berücksichtigung des Zusammenspiels mit dem nationalen schweizerischen Recht (Diss. Luzern), München: Sellier. European Law Publisher (2008) (Kurztitel: Informationspflichten)

Benicke, Christoph: Rügeobliegenheit und Beweislast für Vertragswidrigkeit im UN-Kaufrecht, in: *Gropp Walter/Lipp, Martin/Steiger, Heinhard* (Hrsg.): Rechtswissenschaft im Wandel – Festschrift des Fachbereichs Rechtswissenschaft zum 400jährigen Gründungsjubiläum der Justus-Liebig-Universität Gießen, Tübingen: Mohr Siebeck (2007), S. 373–394 (Kurztitel: FS Fachbereich Rechtswissenschaft)

Benicke, Christoph: Zur Vertragsaufhebung nach UN-Kaufrecht bei Lieferung mangelhafter Ware, IPRax 1997, 326–331

Benjamin, Judah Philip: Benjamin's Sale of Goods, hrsg. v. *Guest,* 7. Aufl., London: Sweet & Maxwell (2006)

Literatur

Bérando, Jean-Paul: Convention de Vienne du 11 avril 1980 sur la vente internationale de marchandises: l'interprétation du contrat, Der. comp. 1993 Nr. 9, 33–43

Bérando, Jean-Paul: Droit uniforme et règles de conflit de lois dans les conventions internationales récentes, J. C. P. 1992, éd. G, I, 3626 (507–510)

Bérando, Jean-Paul: Le Règlement (CE) du Conseil du 22 décembre 2000 concernant la compétence judiciaire, la reconnaissance et l'exécution des décisions en matière civile et commerciale, J. D. I. 2001, 1033–1106

Bérando, Jean-Paul: The United Nations Convention on Contracts for the international Sale of Goods and Arbitration, 5 I. C. A. B. (1994), 60–64

Bérando, Jean-Paul/Kahn, Philippe: Le nouveau droit de la vente internationale de marchandises: Convention de Vienne – 11 avril 1980, Paris: Chambre de commerce et d'industrie de Paris (1989) (Kurztitel: Vente Internationale)

Berg, Daniel Friedrich: Die Rückabwicklung gescheiterter Verträge im spanischen und deutschen Recht – Eine rechtsvergleichende Untersuchung unter besonderer Berücksichtigung des Einheitsrechts (Diss. Freiburg 2002), Köln: Lang (2002)

Berger, Klaus Peter: Die Einbeziehung von AGB in internationale Kaufverträge, in: *Berger/Borges/Herrmann/Schlüter/Wackerbarth* (Hrsg.), Zivil- und Wirtschaftsrecht im Europäischen und Globalen Kontext. Festschrift für Norbert Horn zum 70. Geburtstag, Berlin: De Gruyter Recht (2006), S. 3–20 (Kurztitel: FS Horn)

Berger, Klaus Peter: Formalisierte oder „schleichende" Kodifizierung des transnationalen Wirtschaftsrechts: zu den methodischen und praktischen Grundlagen der lex mercatoria, Berlin: de Gruyter (1996) (Kurztitel: Kodifizierung des transnationalen Wirtschaftsrechts)

Berger, Klaus Peter: Vertragsstrafen und Schadenspauschalierungen im Internationalen Wirtschaftsvertragsrecht, RIW 1999, 401–411

Berger, Klaus Peter/Scholl, Bernd: Das Konkurrenzverhältnis der Rechte des Käufers wegen Vertragsverletzung durch den Verkäufer im UN-Kaufrecht, in: *Büchler/Müller-Chen* (Hrsg.), Private Law, national – global – comparative, Festschrift für Ingeborg Schwenzer zum 60. Geburtstag, Bern: Stämpfli (2011), S. 159–174 (Kurztitel: FS Schwenzer)

Bergsten, Eric E.: Basic Concepts of the UN Convention on the International Sale of Goods, in: *Doralt* (Hrsg.), Das UNCITRAL-Kaufrecht im Vergleich zum österreichischen Recht, Wien: Manz (1985), 15–27 (Kurztitel: Basic Concepts)

Bergsten, Eric E.: Methodological Problems in the Drafting of the CISG, in: *Janssen/Meyer* (Hrsg.), CISG Methodology, München: Sellier European Law Publishers (2009), S. 5–32 (Kurztitel: CISG Methodology)

Bergsten, Eric E./Miller, Anthony J.: The Remedy of Reduction of Price, 27 Am. J. Comp. L. (1979), 255–277

Berman, Harold J.: Excuse for Nonperformance in the Light of Contract Practices in International Trade, 63 Colum. L. Rev. (1963), 1413–1439

Berman, Harold J.: The Law of International Commercial Transactions (Lex Mercatoria), (1988) 2 Emory J. Int'l Disp. Resol. 235–310

Berman, Harold J.: The Law of International Commercial Transactions (Lex Mercatoria), in: *Surrey/Wallace jr.* (Hrsg.), A Lawyer's Guide to International Business Transactions, 2. Aufl., Philadelphia, Pa.: A. L. I./A. B. A. (1979), 42–49 (Part III, Folio 3) (Kurztitel: Lex Mercatoria)

Berman, Harold J./Ladd, Monica: Risk of Loss or Damage in Documentary Transactions Under The Convention on the International Sale of Goods, 21 Cornell Int'l L. J. (1988), 423–437

Berman, Harold J.: The Law of International Commercial Transactions (Lex Mercatoria), 2 Emory J. Int'l Disp. Resol. (1988), 235–310

Bernardini, Piero: Hardship e force majeure, in: *Bonell/Bonelli* (Hrsg.), Contratti commerciali internazionali e principi UNIDROIT, Mailand: Giuffrè (1997), S. 193–214 (Kurztitel: Hardship e Force majeure)

Bernardini, Piero: La compravendita internazionale, in: *Mirabelli,* Rapporti contrattuali nel diritto internazionale, Mailand: Giuffrè (1991), 77–94 (Kurztitel: Compravendita internazionale)

Bernasconi, Christophe: The Personal and Territorial Scope of the Vienna Convention on Contracts for the International Sale of Goods (Article 1), 46 Neth. Int'l L. Rev. 1999, 137–170

Berner Kommentar: Kommentar zum schweizerischen Privatrecht, 2. Abt., Die einzelnen Vertragsverhältnisse, 1. Teilbd. Kauf und Tausch – Die Schenkung, 1. Abschnitt: Allgemeine Bestimmungen – Der Fahrniskauf, Art. 184–215 OR, erläutert v. *Hans Giger,* Bern: Stämpfli (1979) (Kurztitel: Berner Komm/Giger)

Bernstein, Herbert/Lookofsky, Joseph M.: Understanding the CISG in Europe, 2. Aufl., Den Haag/London/New York: Kluwer Law International (2002)

Literatur

Graf von Bernstorff, Christoph: Ausgewählte Rechtsprobleme im Electronic Commerce, RIW 2000, 14–20
Graf von Bernstorff, Christoph: Der Abschluss elektronischer Verträge, RIW 2002, 179–182
Graf von Bernstorff, Christoph: Gesetzliche Regelung der lex rei sitae, AW-Prax 1999, 368–370
Graf von Bernstorff, Christoph: Incoterms 2010 der Internationalen Handelskammer (ICC), Köln: Bundesanzeiger Verlag (2010) (Kurztitel: Incoterms 2010)
Bertrams, Roeland I. V. F./Kruisinga, Sonja A.: Overeenkomsten in het internationaal privaatrecht en het Weens Koopverdrag, 3. Ausg., Deventer: Kluwer (2007)
Bertrams, Roeland I. V. F./van der Velden, Frans J. A.: Overeenkomsten in het internationaal privaatrecht en het Weense Koopverdrag, Zwolle: Tjeenk Willink (1994)
Bess, Jürgen: Die Haftung des Verkäufers für Sachmängel und Falschlieferungen im Einheitlichen Kaufgesetz im Vergleich mit dem englischen und deutschen Recht, (Diss. Heidelberg 1969), Heidelberg: Winter (1971) (Kurztitel: Die Haftung des Verkäufers)
Bess, Jürgen: Grundprinzipien des Haager Einheitlichen Kaufgesetzes, RIW 1975, 14–18
Bianca, Cesare Massimo: Convenzione di Vienna sui contratti di vendita internazionale die beni mobili, Estrato da „Le Nuove Leggi Civile Commentate", Fasc. 1–2/1989, Mailand: CEDAM (1992) (Kurztitel: *Bianca/Bearbeiter*)
Bianca, Cesare Massimo: Wesentliche Vertragsverletzung im italienischen und internationalen Kaufrecht. Vorträge, Reden und Berichte aus dem Europa-Institut Nr. 176, Saarbrücken: Europa-Institut (1989) (Kurztitel: Wesentliche Vertragsverletzung)
Bianca, Cesare Massimo/Bonell, Michael Joachim: Commentary on the International Sales Law, Mailand: Giuffrè (1987) (Kurztitel: *Bianca/Bonell/Bearbeiter*)
Bijl, Maartje: Fundamental Breach of Contract in Documentary Sales Contracts: The Doctrine of Strict Compliance and the Underlying Sales Contract, EJCCL 2009, 19–28
Bisazza Giovanni: Auslegung des Wiener UN-Kaufrechts unter Berücksichtigung ausländischer Rechtsprechung: ein amerikanisches Beispiel, EuLF 2004, 380–384
Bitter, Jan Willem/Drion, Coen/Groenewegen, Pieter Sippens: Kaufvertragsrecht in den Niederlanden, in: *Graf von Westphalen* (Hrsg.), Handbuch des Kaufvertragsrechts in den EG-Staaten, Köln: O. Schmidt (1992), S. 683–763 (Kurztitel: Handbuch des Kaufvertragsrechts)
Bitter, Walter/Bitter, Georg: Wandelungsmöglichkeit des professionellen Käufers und Nachlieferungsrecht des Verkäufers bei aliud-Lieferung. Eine Untersuchung zum deutschen und UN-Kaufrecht, BB 1993, 2315–2326
Blaurock, Uwe: Übernationales Recht des internationalen Handels, ZEuP 1993, 247–267
Blodgett, Paul C.: The UN Convention on the Sale of Goods and the „Battle of the Forms", 18 Colo. Law. (1989), 423–430
Blomeyer, Arwed: Allgemeines Schuldrecht, 4. Aufl., Berlin: Vahlen (1969)
Bock, Anne-Florence: Gewinnherausgabeansprüche gemäss CISG, in: *Büchler/Müller-Chen* (Hrsg.), Private Law, national – global – comparative, Festschrift für Ingeborg Schwenzer zum 60. Geburtstag, Bern: Stämpfli (2011), S. 175–189 (Kurztitel: FS Schwenzer)
Bock, Anne-Florence: Gewinnherausgabe als Folge einer Vertragsverletzung: eine rechtsvergleichende Untersuchung der vertraglichen Vorteilsherausgabe unter Berücksichtigung des schweizerischen, deutschen und englischen Rechts (Diss. Basel), Basel: Helbing Lichtenhahn (2010) (Kurztitel: Gewinnherausgabe)
Böckstiegel, Karl-Heinz: Beurteilung von Exportverboten nach den Vertrags-Schiedsgerichtsregeln der Refinded Sugar Association, London, in: *Glossner* (Hrsg.), Festschrift für Martin Luther zum 70. Geburtstag am 13. Juli 1976, München: Beck (1976), S. 21–29 (Kurztitel: Beurteilung von Exportverboten)
Böckstiegel, Karl-Heinz: Vertragsklauseln über nicht zu vertretende Risiken im internationalen Wirtschaftsverkehr, RIW 1984, 1–7
Boele-Woelki, Katharina: De verjarung van vorderingen uit internationale koopovereenkomsten, Molengrafica 1996, 99–146
Boele-Woelki, Katharina: Die Anwendung der UNIDROIT-Principles auf internationale Handelsverträge, IPRax 1997, 161–171
Boggiano, Antonio: La Convención de las Naciones Unidas sobre los contratos de compraventa internacional de mercaderías: En el ámbito del derecho internacional privado argentino, 13 Rev. der. com. oblig. (1980), 355–364 (Anexo I: 365–391) = *Boggiano* (Hrsg.), Derecho internacional privado, T., Buenos Aires: Depalma (1988), 175–197
Boghossian, Nayiri: A Comparative Study of Specific Performance Provisions in the United Nations Convention on Contracts for the International Sale of Goods, Rev. CISG 1999–2000, 3–78
Bollée, Sylvain: The Theory of Risks in the 1980 Vienna Sale of Goods Convention, Pace Review of the Convention on Contracts for the International Sale of Goods, Kluwer (1999–2000), 245–290

Literatur

Bonell, Michael Joachim (Hrsg.): UNILEX. International Case Law & Bibliography on the U. N. Convention on Contracts for the International Sale of Goods, Unilex-Website, Irvington-on-Hudson, N. Y.: Transnational Publishers (1995 ff.)
Bonell, Michael Joachim: A Proposal for the Establishment of a „Permanent Editorial Board" for the Vienna Sales Convention, in: UNIDROIT (Hrsg.), International Uniform Law in Practice, New York: Oceana/Rom: Unidroit (1988), 241–244 (Kurztitel: Proposal)
Bonell, Michael Joachim: An International Restatement of Contract Law, 2. Aufl., The UNIDROIT Principles of International Commercial Contracts, Irvington-on-Hudson, N. Y.: Transnational Publishers (1997) (Kurztitel: International Restatement)
Bonell, Michael Joachim: Die allgemeinen Geschäftsbedingungen nach italienischem Recht, ZVerglRW 1979, 1–20
Bonell, Michael Joachim: Die Bedeutung der Handelsbräuche im Wiener Kaufrechtsübereinkommen von 1980, östJBl 1985, 385–395
Bonell, Michael Joachim: I Principi UNIDROIT – Un approccio moderno al diritto dei contratti, Riv. dir. civ. 1997–I, 231–247
Bonell, Michael Joachim: La convenzione di Vienna sulla vendita internazionale: origini, scelte e principi fondamentali, Riv. trim. dir. proced. civ. 1990, 715–732
Bonell, Michael Joachim: La formazione del contratto di compravendita, in: La Vendita Internazionale, Mailand: Giuffrè (1981), 113–136
Bonell, Michael Joachim: La nouvelle Convention des Nations-Unies sur les contrats de vente internationale de marchandises, Dr. prat. com. int. 1981, 7–35
Bonell, Michael Joachim: La prima decisione italiana in tema di Convenzione di Vienna sulla vendita internazionale (nota a sent. Tribunale Monza 14 gennaio 1993), G. it. (1994), I, 145–150
Bonell, Michael Joachim: La revisione del diritto uniforme della vendita internazionale, G. com. 1980, 116–145
Bonell, Michael Joachim: L'entrata in vigore della Convenzione di Vienna sulla vendita el le sue conseguenze nella prassi delle contrattazioni commerciali internazionali, Dir. com. int. 1987, 415–427
Bonell, Michael Joachim: L'interpretazione del diritto uniforme alla luce dell' Art. 7 della Convenzione di Vienna sulla vendita internazionale, Riv. dir. civ. 1986, II, 221–224
Bonell, Michael Joachim: The CISG and the Unidroit Principles of International Commercial Contracts: Two Complementary Instruments, 10 Wuhan U. Int'l L. Rev. (2008/09), 100–117
Bonell, Michael Joachim: The CISG, European Contract Law and the Development of a World Contract Law, 56 Am. J. Comp. L. (2008), 1–28
Bonell, Michael Joachim: The UNIDROIT Principles and CISG – Sources of Inspiration for English Courts?, Uniform L. Rev. 2006, 305–318
Bonell, Michael Joachim: The UNIDROIT Principles in Practice: The Experience of the First Two Years, Uniform L. Rev. 1997, 34–45
Bonell, Michael Joachim: The UNIDROIT Principles of International Commercial Contracts and the CISG – Alternatives or Complementary Instruments?, 26 Uniform L. Rev. (1996), 26–39
Bonell, Michael Joachim: Un „codice" internazionale del diritto dei contratti: i principi UNIDROIT dei contratti commerciali internazionali, Milano: Giuffrè (1995) (Kurztitel: Codice internazionale)
Bonell, Michael Joachim: Una nuova disciplina in materia di rappresentanza: la convenzione di Ginevra del 1983 sulla rappresentanza nella compravendita internazionale de merci, Riv. dir. com. 1983, 273–315
Bonell, Michael Joachim: UNILEX. International Case Law & Bibliography on the UN Convention on Contracts for the International Sale of Goods, Unilex-Website, Irvington-on-Hudson, New York: Transnational Publishers (1995 ff.)
Bonell, Michael Joachim: UN-Kaufrecht und das Kaufrecht des Uniform Commercial Code im Vergleich, RabelsZ 58 (1994), 20–39
Bonell, Michael Joachim: Vertragsverhandlungen und culpa in contrahendo nach dem Wiener Kaufrechtsübereinkommen, RIW 1990, 693–702
Bonell, Michael Joachim: Zum Verhältnis des Wiener Kaufrechtsübereinkommens zum Haager Kauf-IPR-Übereinkommen von 1955 aus italienischer Sicht, Jb. It. R. 3 (1990), 117–119
Bonsau/Feuerriegel: Die Probleme der Bestimmung von Fälligkeitszinsen im UN-Kaufrecht, IPRax 2003, 421–425
Bopp, Thomas: Vertragsstrukturen internationaler Kompensationsgeschäfte, Stuttgart: Schäffer-Poeschel (1992)
Borges, Georg: Verträge im elektronischen Geschäftsverkehr (Habil. Köln 2002), München: Beck (2003) (Kurztitel: Elektronischer Geschäftsverkehr)
Borisova, Bojidara: Freedom of contract: Remarks on the manner in which the UNIDROIT Principles may be used to interpret or supplement Article 6 of the CISG, in: *Felemegas* (Hrsg.), An International

Literatur

Approach to the Interpretation of the United Nations Convention on Contracts for the International Sale of Goods (1980) as Uniform Sales Law, Cambridge: Cambridge University Press (2007), S. 39–44 (Kurztitel: Art. 6 CISG-UP)

Bortolotti, Fabio: Remedies Available to the Seller and Seller's Right to Require Specific Performance (Articles 61, 62 and 28), 25 J. L. & Com. (2005–06), 335–338

Borysewicz, Michel: Conventions et projets de convention sur la vente internationale de marchandises, in: Les Ventes Internationales de Marchandises, Paris: Economica (1981), 16–61

Boschiero, Nerina: Il coordinamento delle norme in materia di vendita internazionale, Padova: CEDAM (1990) (Kurztitel: Coordinamento delle norme)

Boschiero, Nerina: Le convenzioni internazionali in tema di vendita, in: *Rescigno* (Hrsg.), Trattato di Diritto Privato, Bd. 21, Turin: UTET (1987), 233–279 (Kurztitel: Le convenzioni)

Botzenhardt, Bertrand: Die Auslegung des Begriffs der wesentlichen Vertragsverletzung im UN-Kaufrecht (Diss. Augsburg 1997), Frankfurt a. M.: Lang (1998)

Boulanger, David: Erreur, non-conformité, vice caché: la fin d'une confusion, J. C. P. 1996, I, 1585–1590

Boving, Dagmar: Internationale Vertragsgestaltung, Bonn: DIHT (2001)

Brand, Ronald A.: Nonconvention Issues in the Preparation of Transnational Sales Contracts, 8 J. L. & Com. (1988), 145–186

Brand, Ronald A./Flechtner, Harry M.: Arbitration and Contract Formation in International Trade: First Interpretations of the U. N. Sales Convention, 12 J. L. & Com. (1993), 239–260 = 6 Int'l Q. (1994), 1–25

Brandi-Dohrn, Matthias: Das UN-Kaufrecht – Entstehungsgeschichte und Grundstruktur, CR 1991, 705–708

Brandner, Hans-Erich/Ulmer, Peter: EG-Richtlinie über mißbräuchliche Klauseln in Verbraucherverträgen, BB 1991, 701–709

Braun, Edwin: Produktpiraterie: Rechtsschutz durch Zivil-, Straf- und Verwaltungsrecht sowie ausgewählte Probleme der Rechtsdurchsetzung, Köln: Heymanns (1993)

Bredow, Jens/Seiffert, Bodo: Incoterms 2000, Kommentar und deutsch/englischer Text der ICC-Incoterms, Bonn: Economica (2000)

Breitling, Siegfried: Bedeutung und Wirkung von Schriftformklauseln, Pfaffenweiler: Centaurus (1994)

Bridge, Michael G.: A Commentary on Articles 1–13 and 78, in: *Ferrari u. a.* (Hrsg.), The Draft UNCITRAL Digest and Beyond: Cases, Analysis and Unresolved Issues in the U. N. Sales Convention, München/London: Sellier. European Law Publishers/Sweet&Maxwell (2004), S. 235–258 (Kurztitel: Draft Digest)

Bridge, Michael G.: A Comment on „Towards A Universal Doctrine of Breach–The Impact of the CISG" by Jürgen Basedow, 25 Int'l Rev. L. & Econ. (2005), 501–511

Bridge, Michael G.: Avoidance for Fundamental Breach of Contract Under the UN Convention on the International Sale of Goods, 59 Int'l & Comp. L. Q. (2010), 911–940

Bridge, Michael G. (Hrsg.): Benjamin's Sale of Goods, 8. Aufl., London: Sweet & Maxwell (2010) (Kurztitel: Benjamin's Sale of Goods)

Bridge, Michael G.: Curing a Seller's Defective Tender or Delivery of Goods in Commercial Sales, in: *Büchler/Müller-Chen* (Hrsg.), Private Law, national – global – comparative, Festschrift für Ingeborg Schwenzer zum 60. Geburtstag, Bern: Stämpfli (2011), S. 221–235 (Kurztitel: FS Schwenzer)

Bridge, Michael G.: Issues Arising Under Articles 64, 72 and 73 of the United Nations Convention on Contracts for the International Sale of Goods, 25 J. L. & Com. (2005), 405–421

Bridge, Michael G.: The International Sale of Goods: Law and Practice, 2. Aufl., Oxford/New York: Oxford University (2007) (Kurztitel: Int'l Sale of Goods)

Bridge, Michael G.: The Sale of Goods, Oxford: Clarendon Press (1997) (Kurztitel: Sale of Goods)

Bridge, Michael G.: The Transfer of Risk under the UN Sales Convention 1980 (CISG), in: *Andersen/Schroeter* (Hrsg.), Sharing International Commercial Law Across National Boundaries: Festschrift in Honour of Albert H. Kritzer on the Occasion of his 80th Birthday, London: Wildly, Simmons & Hill (2008), S. 77–105 (Kurztitel: FS Kritzer)

Brölsch, Martin: Schadensersatz und CISG, (Diss. Hamburg 2006), Frankfurt a. M.: Peter Lang (2007) (Kurztitel: Schadensersatz)

Brüggemeier, Gert/Hart, Dieter: Soziales Schuldrecht, Bremen: Universität Bremen (1987)

Brunner, Christoph: Force Majeure and Hardship under General Contract Principles (Habil. Bern 2008), Austin: Wolters Kluwer Law and Business (2009) (Kurztitel: Force Majeure)

Brunner, Christoph: UN-Kaufrecht – CISG, Kommentar zum Übereinkommen der Vereinten Nationen über Verträge über den internationalen Warenkauf von 1980, Bern: Stämpfli (2004)

Brussel, Gabrielle S.: The 1980 United Nations Convention on Contracts for the International Sale of Goods: A Legislative Study of the North-South Debates, 6 N. Y. Int'l L. Rev. (1993), 53–74

Literatur

Bucher, Eugen (Hrsg.): Wiener Kaufrecht – Der schweizerische Aussenhandel unter dem UN-Übereinkommen über den internationalen Warenkauf, Bern: Stämpfli (1991) (Kurztitel: Wiener Kaufrecht)

Bucher, Eugen: Gefahrenübergang, in: Schweizerisches Institut für Rechtsvergleichung (Hrsg.), Lausanner Kolloquium 1984, Zürich: Schulthess (1985), S. 207–218 (Kurztitel: Gefahrenübergang)

Bucher, Eugen: Preisvereinbarung als Voraussetzung der Vertragsgültigkeit beim Kauf. Zum angeblichen Widerspruch zwischen Art. 14 und Art. 55 des „Wiener Kaufrechts", in: *Bucher* (Hrsg.), Wiener Kaufrecht, Bern: Stämpfli (1991), S. 53–82 (Kurztitel: Preisvereinbarung)

Bucher, Eugen: Preisvereinbarung als Voraussetzung der Vertragsgültigkeit beim Kauf. Zum angeblichen Widerspruch zwischen Art. 14 und Art. 55 des „Wiener Kaufrechts", in: *Sturm* (Hrsg.), Mélanges Paul Piotet: Recueil de travaux offerts à M. P. Piotet, Bern: Staempfli (1990), S. 371–408 (Kurztitel: FS Piotet)

Bucher, Eugen: Überblick über die Neuerungen des Wiener Kaufrechts, dessen Verhältnis zur Kaufrechtstradition und zum nationalen Recht, in: *Bucher* (Hrsg.), Wiener Kaufrecht, Bern: Stämpfli (1991), S. 13–52 (Kurztitel: Neuerungen)

Bülow, Peter/Artz, Markus: Heidelberger Kommentar zum Verbraucherkreditrecht, 6. Aufl., Heidelberg: C. F. Müller (2006)

Bultmann, Fritz A./Rahn, Gerd-Jürgen: Rechtliche Fragen des Teleshopping, NJW 1988, 2432–2438

Bund, Jennifer M.: Force Majeure Clauses: Drafting advice for the CISG Practitioner, 17 J. L. & Com. (1998), 381–413

Bundesamt für Justiz (Schweiz): Rechtsprechung zum Wiener Kaufrecht, 3 SZIER (1993), 653–668

Bundesamt für Justiz (Schweiz): Rechtsprechung zum Wiener Kaufrecht in der Schweiz, 1–2 SZIER 2008, 173–207

Bundesstelle für Außenhandelsinformation (Hrsg.): Wiener UNCITRAL-Übereinkommen über internationale Warenkaufverträge vom 11 April 1980, 3. Aufl., Köln: Bundesstelle für Außenhandelsinformation (1988)

Bundesstelle für Außenhandelsinformation (Hrsg.): Zur Vertragsgestaltung im Auslandsgeschäft nach UNCITRAL-Kaufrecht, Berichte und Dokumente zum ausländischen Wirtschafs- und Steuerrecht Nr. 179, Köln: Bundesstelle für Außenhandelsinformation (1984) (Kurztitel: Bundesstelle für Außenhandelsinformation, Berichte und Dokumente)

Bunte, Hermann-Josef: Die Aufhebung des Schriftformerfordernisses nach § 34 GWB, BB 1998, 1600–1601

Bunte, Hermann-Josef: Gedanken zur Rechtsharmonisierung in der EG auf dem Gebiet der mißbräuchlichen Klauseln in Verbraucherverträgen, in: *Löffelmann* (Hrsg.), Festschrift für Horst Locher zum 65. Geburtstag, Düsseldorf: Werner (1990), S. 325–336 (Kurztitel: FS Locher)

Burghard, Ulrich: Das Wirksamwerden empfangsbedürftiger Willenserklärungen im Zeitalter moderner Telekommunikation, AcP 195 (1995), 74–136

Burgstaller, Alfred: Internationales Zivilverfahrensrecht, Wien: Orac (2000) (Kurztitel: *Burgstaller/Bearbeiter*)

Burkart, Fabian: Interpretatives Zusammenwirken von CISG und UNIDROIT Principles, Baden-Baden: Nomos (2000)

Burr, Wolfgang: Fragen des kontinental-europäischen internationalen Verjährungsrechts (Diss. Bonn 1968)

Burrows, Andrew: Remedies for Torts and Breach of Contract, 3. Aufl., Oxford 2003. (Kurztitel: Remedies)

Butler, Allison E.: A Practical Guide to the CISG: Negotiations through Litigation, New York: Aspen Publishers (2007) (Kurztitel: Guide to the CISG)

Butler, Allison E.: Cause of Action by Buyer to Avoid a Contract Pursuant to Article 49(1) of the United Nations Convention for the International Sale of Goods (CISG) When the Seller has Fundamentally Breached an express Contractual Term, in: 27 Causes of Action 2d (2006), 597

Butler, Allison E.: Caveat Emptor: Remedy-Oriented Approach Restricts Bayer's Right to Avoidance under Article 49(1)(a) of the United Nations Convention on Contracts for the International Sale of Goods, IHR 2003, 208–212

Butler, Allison E.: Interpretation of „place of business": Comparison between provisions of the CISG (Article 10) and counterpart provisions of the Principles of European Contract Law, VJ (2002), 275–280

Butler, Allison E.: „Place of Business": Comparison between the of CISG Article 10 and the counterpart provisions of UNIDROIT Principles Article 1.10, in: *Felemegas, John* (Hrsg.): And International Approach to the Interpretation of the United Nations Convention on Contracts for the International Sale of Goods (1980) as Uniform Sales Law, Cambridge, New York u. a.: Cambridge University Press (2007), 59–62 (Kurztitel: Art. 10 CISG-UP)

Literatur

Butler, Allison E.: The International Contract: Knowing when, why and how to „opt out" of the United Nations Convention on Contracts for the International Sale of Goods, 76 Fla. B. J. (2002), 24–33

Butler, Petra: The Doctrines of Parol Evidence Rule and Consideration – A Deterrence to the Common Law Lawyer?, in: Singapore International Arbitration Centre (Hrsg.), Celebrating Success: 25 Years United Nations Convention on Contracts for the International Sale of Goods, Singapore (2006), S. 54–66 (Kurztitel: Parol Evidence Rule and Consideration)

Butler, Petra: The Use of the CISG in Domestic Law, Annals Fac. L. Belgrade 2011, 7-27

Bydlinski, Franz: Das allgemeine Vertragsrecht, in: *Doralt* (Hrsg.), Das UNCITRAL-Kaufrecht im Vergleich zum österreichischen Recht, Wien: Manz (1985), 57–90 (Kurztitel: Allgemeines Vertragsrecht)

Bydlinski, Franz: Der Vertragsschluß nach der Wiener UN-Kaufrechtskonvention in komparativer Betrachtung, Arch. iur. Cracov. 1985, 143–156 (Kurztitel: Vertragsschluß)

Bydlinski, Franz: Erklärungsbewußtsein und Rechtsgeschäft, JZ 1975, 1–6

Bydlinski, P.: Probleme des Vertragsschlusses ohne Annahmeerklärung, JuS 1988, 36–38

Byok, Jan/Jaeger, Wolfgang: Kommentar zum Vergaberecht, 2. Aufl., Heidelberg: Verlag Recht und Wirtschaft (2003) (Kurztitel: *Byok/Jaeger/Bearbeiter*)

Calais-Auloy, Jean: Ventes Maritimes Nr. 190, in: Encyclopédie Dalloz Commercial, Paris: Dalloz (Stand 1974)

Calamari, John D./Perillo, Joseph M.: The Law of Contracts, St. Paul (Minn.): West (1970)

Calleo, Peter J.: The Inapplicability of the Parol Evidence Rule to the United Nations Convention on Contracts for the International Sale of Goods, 28 Hofstra L. Rev. (2000), 799–833

Canaris, Claus-Wilhelm: Die Reform des Rechts der Leistungsstörungen, JZ 2001, 499–530

Canaris, Claus-Wilhelm: Handelsrecht, 24. Aufl., München: C.H. Beck (2006)

Cañellas, Anselmo Martinez: The Scope of Article 44 CISG, 25 J. L. & Com. (2005), 261–271

Capuccio, Jacopo: La deroga implicita nella convenzione di Vienna del 1980, Dir. com. int. 1994, 861–873

Carbone, Sergio M.: L'ambito di applicazione ed i criteri interpretativi della Convenzione di Vienna sulla vendita internazionale, in: La Vendita Internazionale, Mailand: Giuffrè (1981), 61–88 = Riv. dir. int. priv. proc. 1980, 513–534

Carbone, Sergio M.: Principi dei contratti internazionali e norme di origine internazionale (con particolare riguardo al diritto uniforme), in: *Bonell/Bonelli* (Hrsg.), Contratti commerciali internazionali e principi unidroit, Mailand: Giuffrè (1997), 23–38 (Kurztitel: Principi)

Carbone, Sergio M./Luzzatto, Riccardo: I contratti del commercio internazionale, in: *Rescigno* (Hrsg.), Trattato di diritto privato, Bd. 11, Turin: UTET (1984)

Carter, J. W.: Suspending Contract Performance for Breach, in: *Beatson, Jack/Friedmann, Daniel* (Hrsg.), Good Faith and Fault in Contract Law, Oxford: Clarendon Press (1995), 485–522 (Kurztitel: Carter, Suspending Contract Performance)

Carter, J. W./Phang, A./Phang, S. Y.: Performance Following Repudiation: Legal and Economic Interests, 15 J. Cont. L. (1999), 100–123

Carver, Jeremy: Uniform Law and Its Impact on Business Circles: The Experience of the Legal Profession, in: UNIDROIT (Hrsg.), International Uniform Law in Practice, New York: Oceana/Rom: UNIDROT (1988), 411–430

Case Law on UNCITRAL Texts (CLOUT) (http://www.uncitral.org/english/clout/index.htm)

Cassoni, Giuseppe: La compravendita nelle Convenzioni e nel diritto internazionale privato italiano, in: Studi in memorio di Gian Carlo Venturini, Mailand: Giuffrè (1984), 113–167 = Riv. dir. int. priv. proc. 1982, 429–483

Castellanos Ruiz, Esperanza: Autonomia de la voluntad y derecho uniforme en la compraventa internacional, Granada: Comares (1998)

Catalano, John M.: More Fiction than Fact: The Perceived Differences in the Application of Specific Performance under the United Nations Convention on Contracts for the International Sale of Goods, 71 Tul. L. Rev., (1997) 1807–1834

Caytas, Ivo G.: Der unerfüllbare Vertrag, anfängliche und nachträgliche Leistungshindernisse und Entlastungsgründe im Recht der Schweiz, Deutschlands, Österreichs, Frankreichs, Italiens, Englands, der Vereinigten Staaten, im Völkerrecht und im internationalen Handelsrecht (Diss. St.Gallen), Wilmington: Morgan/Zürich: Schulthess (1984) (Kurztitel: Der unerfüllbare Vertrag)

Cerutti, Romeo: Das U. S. amerikanische Warenkaufrecht. Mit rechtsvergleichenden Hinweisen auf das schweizerische und das deutsche Recht, das CISG sowie die UNIDROIT Principles, Baden-Baden: Nomos, 1998

Cetiner, Bilgehan: Die Sachmängelhaftung des Verkäufers im UN-Kaufrecht und im neuen deutschen Schuldrecht: Eine rechtsvergleichende Studie, Frankfurt a. M.: Peter Lang Verlag (2006) (Kurztitel: Sachmängelhaftung)

Literatur

Charters, Andrea L.: Specifications and the Contractual Relationship: Art. 65 of the CISG in Light of PECL Art. 7:105, in: *Felemegas* (Hrsg.), An International Approach to the Interpretation of the United Nations Convention on Contracts for the International Sale of Goods (1980) as Uniform Sales Law, Cambridge: Cambridge University Press (2007), 456–461 (Kurztitel: Specifications and the Contractual Relationship)

Chaudet, Francois: La garantie des défauts de la chose vendue en droit suisse et dans la Convention de Vienne sur les contrats de vente internationale de marchandises, in: *Dessemontet* (Hrsg.), Contrats de vente internationale, Lausanne: CEDIDAC (1991), 83–130

Chen, Laura Carlson: Guide to the U. N. Convention on the Limitation Period in the International Sale of Goods, 7 International Quarterly (1995), 400–449

Chen-Wishart, Mindy: Contract law, Oxford: Oxford University Press (2005)

Cheshire, Geoffrey C./Fifoot, Cecil H./Furmston, Michael P.: Cheshire, Fifoot and Furmston's Law of Contract, 15. Aufl., London: Butterworths (2007)

Chiomenti, Cristina: Does the choice of a national rules entail an implicit exclusion of the CISG?, EuLF 2005, 141–148

Chitty, Joseph: Chitty On Contracts, hrsg. v. *Beale*, 31. Aufl., London: Sweet & Maxwell (2012) (Kurztitel: Chitty On Contracts)

Chong, Kah Wie/Chao, Joyce: United Nations Convention on the Use of Electronic Communications in International Contracts – A New Global Standard, 18 SAcLJ (2006), 116–202

Christandl, Gregor: The 'dying' offer Rule in European Contract Law, ERCL 2011, 463–489

Chrocziel, Peter: Einführung in den gewerblichen Rechtsschutz und das Urheberrecht, 2. Aufl., München: Beck (2002)

CISG Austria, Internet-Datenbank österreichischer Entscheidungen zum CISG (http://www.cisg.at)

CISG Belgium, Internet-Datenbank belgischer Entscheidungen zum CISG (http://www.rechtspraak.nl)

CISG France, Internet-Datenbank französischer Entscheidungen zum CISG, Universität Saarbrücken (http://www.jura.uni-sb.de/FB/LS/Witz/cisg.htm)

CISG Pace, Internet-Datenbank, Pace University School of Law (http://www.cisg.law.pace.edu)

CISG Spain and Latin America, Internet-Datenbank, Universität Carlos III Madrid (http://www.cisgspanish.com)

CISG-AC (Hrsg.): CISG-AC Opinion No. 1, Electronic Communications under CISG, 15.8.2003, *Ramberg, Christina* (Rapporteur), http://www.cisgac.com/default.php?ipkCat=128&ifkCat=143&sid=143 (Kurztitel: CISG-AC, Op. 1 *(Ramberg)*)

CISG-AC (Hrsg.): CISG-AC Opinion No. 2, Examination of the Goods and Notice of Non-Conformity – Articles 38 and 39, 7.6.2004, *Bergsten, Eric* (Rapporteur), http://www.cisgac.com/default.php?ipkCat=128&ifkCat=144&sid=144 (Kurztitel: CISG-AC, Op. 2 *(Bergsten)*)

CISG-AC (Hrsg.): CISG-AC Opinion No. 3, Parol Evidence Rule, 23.10.2004, *Hyland, Richard* (Rapporteur), http://www.cisgac.com/default.php?ipkCat=128&ifkCat=145&sid=145 (Kurztitel: CISG-AC, Op. 3 *(Hyland)*)

CISG-AC (Hrsg.): CISG-AC Opinion No. 4, Contracts for the Sale of Goods to Be Manufactured or Produced and Mixed Contracts – Article 3 CISG, 24.10.2004, *Perales Viscasillas, Maria del Pilar* (Rapporteur), http://www.cisgac.com/default.php?ipkCat=128&ifkCat=146&sid=146 (Kurztitel: CISG-AC, Op. 4 *(Perales Viscasillas)*)

CISG-AC (Hrsg.): CISG-AC Opinion No. 5, The buyer's right to avoid the contract in case of non-conforming goods or documents, 7.5.2005, *Schwenzer, Ingeborg* (Rapporteur), http://www.cisgac.com/default.php?ipkCat=128&ifkCat=147&sid=147 (Kurztitel: CISG-AC, Op. 5 *(Schwenzer)*)

CISG-AC (Hrsg.): CISG-AC Opinion No. 6, Calculation of Damages under CISG Article 74, Frühjahr 2006, *Gotanda, John Y.* (Rapporteur), http://www.cisgac.com/default.php?ipkCat=128&ifkCat=148&sid=148 (Kurztitel: CISG-AC, Op. 6 *(Gotanda)*)

CISG-AC (Hrsg.): CISG-AC Opinion No. 7 Exemption of Liability for Damges under Article 79 of the CISG, 12.10.2007, *Garro, Alejandro M.* (Rapporteur), http://www.cisgac.com/default.php?ipkCat=128&ifkCat=148& sid=169 (Kurztitel: CISG-AC, Op. 7 *(Garro)*)

CISG-AC (Hrsg.): CISG-AC Opinion No. 8, Calculation of Damages under CISG Articles 75 and 76, 15.11.2008, *Gotanda, John y.* (Rapporteur), http://www.cisgac.com/default.php?ipkCat=128&ifkCat=148&sid=184 (Kurztitel: CISG-AC, Op. 8 *(Gotanda)*)

CISG-AC (Hrsg.): CISG-AC Opinion No. 9, Consequences of Avoidance of the Contract, 15.11.2008 *Bridge, Michael* (Rapporteur), http://www.cisgac.com/default.php?ipkCat=128&ifkCat=148&sid=185 (Kurztitel: CISG-AC, Op. 9 *(Bridge)*)

CISG-AC (Hrsg.): CISG-AC Opinion No. 10, Agreed Sums Payable upon Breach of an Obligation in CISG Contracts, 3.8.2012 *Hachem, Pascal* (Rapporteur), http://www.cisgac.com/default.php?ipkCat= 128&ifkCat=218&sid=218 (Kurztitel: CISG-AC, Op. 10 *(Hachem)*)

Literatur

CISG-online, Internet-Datenbank, Universität Basel (http://www.cisg-online.ch = http://www.globalsaleslaw.org/index.cfm?pageID=28)
Clausson, Olof: Avoidance in Nonpayment Situations and Fundamental Breach Under the 1980 U. N. Convention on Contracts for the International Sale of Goods, 6 N. Y. L. Sch. J. Int'l & Comp. L. (1984), 93–117
CLOUT (Case Law on UNCITRAL Texts), UN Doc. A/CN.9/SER.C/ABSTRACTS/1–12, edited and published by the UNCITRAL Secretariat, Vienna International Centre, www.uncitral.org/uncitral/en/case_law.html
Coen, Christoph: Teilbeendigung von Verträgen wegen Leistungsstörungen im Einheitsrecht, in: *Schwenzer/Hager* (Hrsg.), Festschrift für Peter Schlechtriem zum 70. Geburtstag, Tübingen: Mohr (2003), S. 189–206 (Kurztitel: FS Schlechtriem)
Coen, Christoph: Vertragsscheitern und Rückabwicklung – Eine rechtsvergleichende Untersuchung zum englischen und deutschen Recht, zum UN-Kaufrecht sowie zu den Unidroit Principles und den Principles of European Contract Law (Diss. Freiburg 2002), Berlin: Duncker & Humblot (2003)
Coester-Waltjen, Dagmar: Die Bedeutung des § 279 BGB für Leistungsverzögerungen, AcP 183 (1983), 279–294
Coetzee, Juana: Securing the Future of Electronic Sales in the Context of International Sales, 11 VJ (2007), 11–24
Coetzee, Juana/de Gama, Mustaqeem: Harmonisation of Sales Law: An International and Regional Perspective, 10 VJ (2006), 15–26
Cohn, Ernst J.: The Defence of Uncertainty: A Study in the Interpretation of the Uniform Law on International Sales Act 1967, 23 Int'l & Comp. L. Q. (1974), 520–538
Colligan, Arthur B. Jr.: Applying the General Principles of the United Nations Convention on Contracts for the International Sale of Goods to Fill the Article 78 Interest Rate Gap in Zapata Hermanos, S. A. v. Hearthside Baking Co. Inc., VJ (2002), 40–56
Commentary on the Draft Convention on Contracts for the International Sale of Goods. Prepared by the Secretariat (A/CONF. 97/5), O. R., 14–66 (Kurztitel: Sekretariatskommentar)
Comoglio, Luigi Paolo: Libertà di forma e libertà di prova nella compravendita internazionale di merci, Riv. trim. dir. proced. civ. 1990, 785–810
Conetti, Giorgio: Disciplina uniforme della compravendita internazionale, Riv. trim. dir. proced. civ. 1983, 272–282
Conetti, Giorgio: Internationalprivatrechtliche Probleme, die sich aus dem Beitritt Italiens zur Wiener Konvention über Verträge über den Internationalen Kauf ergeben, ZfRVgl 1987, 83–86
Conetti, Giorgio: Problemi di diritto internazionale privato derivanti dalla partecipazione dell'Italia alla convenzione di Vienna del 1980, Riv. dir. int. priv. proc. 1987, 41–46
Conetti, Giorgio: Uniform Substantive and Conflict Rules on the International Sale of Goods and their Interaction, in: *Šarčević/Volken* (Hrsg.), Dubrovnik Lectures, New York: Oceana (1986), 385–399 (Kurztitel: Uniform Substantive and Conflicts Rules)
Conrad, Peter: Die Lieferung mangelhafter Ware als Grund für eine Vertragsaufhebung im einheitlichen UN-Kaufrecht (CISG): unter Berücksichtigung des öffentlich-rechtlich bedingten Sachmangels, Zürich: Schulthess (1999)
Cook, V. Susanne: The Need for Uniform Interpretation of the 1980 United Nations Convention on Contracts for the International Sale of Goods, 50 U. Pitt. L. Rev. (1988), 197–226
Cook, V. Susanne: The Sales Convention in the United States, Presentation at seminar „Ten Years of the United Nations Sales Convention", University of Pittsburgh School of Law (16./17. Oktober 1997)
Cook, V. Susanne: The U. N. Convention on Contracts for the International Sale of Goods: A Mandate to Abandon Legal Ethnocentricity, 16 J. L. & Com. (1997), 257–264
Coote, Brian: Contract Damages, Ruxley, and the Performance Interest, 56 CLJ (1997), 537–570
Corbin, Arthur Linton: Corbin On Contracts. A Comprehensive Treatise on the Rules of Contract Law IV, St. Paul (Minn.): West (1951)
Corbisier, Isabelle: La détermination du prix dans les contrats commerciaux portant vente de marchandises. Réflexions comparatives, Rev. int. dr. comp. (1988), 767–831
Cortérier, André: A New Approach to Solving the Interest Rate Problem of Art. 78 CISG, 5 Int'l Trade & Bus. L. Ann. (2000), 33 ff.
Cortérier, André: Cortérier's Commentary on the United Nations Convention on Contracts for the International Sale of Goods, http://ccisg.org/ (Kurztitel: ccisg.org)
Cortérier, André: Interest in Uniform Application – How to Solve the UN Sales Law's Interest Rate Problem Under CISG Article 78 and CISG Article 84, 16 Pace Int'l L. Rev. (2004), 1–18
Corvaglia, Stefano: Das einheitliche UN-Kaufrecht – CISG, Bern: Stämpfli (1998)

Literatur

Cosnard, Henri: La compétence teritoriale en matière contractuelle, Mélanges offerts à Pierre Hébraud, Toulouse (1981), 207–218

von Caemmerer, Ernst: Die Haager Konferenz über die internationale Vereinheitlichung des Kaufrechts vom 2. bis 25. April 1964, RabelsZ 29 (1965), 101–145

von Caemmerer, Ernst: Die wesentliche Vertragsverletzung im international Einheitlichen Kaufrecht, in: *Horn* (Hrsg.), Aspekte europäischer Rechtsgeschichte, Festgabe für Helmut Coing zum 70. Geburtstag, Bd. 2, München: Beck (1982), S. 33–52 = GS Bd. 3, Tübingen: Mohr (1983), 67–86 (Kurztitel: Wesentliche Vertragsverletzung)

von Caemmerer, Ernst: Internationale Vereinheitlichung des Kaufrechts, SJZ 1981, 257–267 = GS Bd. 3, Tübingen: Mohr (1983), 87–107

von Caemmerer, Ernst: Mortuus redhibetur, in: *Paulus* (Hrsg.), Festschrift für Karl Larenz zum 70. Geburtstag, München: Beck (1973), S. 621–642 = GS Bd. 3, Tübingen (1983), 167–188 (Kurztitel: FS Larenz)

von Caemmerer, Ernst: Probleme des Haager Einheitlichen Kaufrechts, AcP 178 (1978), 121–149 = GS Bd. 3, Tübingen: Mohr (1983), 23–51

von Caemmerer, Ernst: Vertragspflichten und Vertragsgültigkeit im internationalen Einheitlichen Kaufrecht, in: *Sandrock* (Hrsg.), Festschrift für Günther Beitzke zum 70. Geburtstag, Berlin/New York: de Gruyter (1979), S. 35–42 = GS Bd. 3, Tübingen: Mohr (1983), 59–66 (Kurztitel: Vertragspflichten und Vertragsgültigkeit)

von Caemmerer, Ernst: Zahlungsort, in: *ders.,* GS Bd. 3, 1968–1982, Tübingen: Mohr (1983), S. 108–124 (Kurztitel: GS Bd. 3)

von Caemmerer, Ernst/Schlechtriem, Peter (Hrsg.): Kommentar zum Enheitlichen UN-Kaufrecht: Das Übereinkommen der Vereinten Nationen über Verträge über den internationalen Warenkauf – (CISG-Kommentar), 1. Aufl., München: Beck (1990)

von Caemmerer, Ernst/Schlechtriem, Peter (Hrsg.): Kommentar zum Enheitlichen UN-Kaufrecht: Das Übereinkommen der Vereinten Nationen über Verträge über den internationalen Warenkauf – (CISG-Kommentar), 2. Aufl., München: Beck (1995)

Crawford, B. Blair: Drafting Considerations Under the 1980 United Nations Convention on Contracts for the International Sale of Goods, 8 J. L. & Com. (1988), 187–205

Crawford, B. Blair/Rich, Janet L.: A. L. I. – A. B. A. Course of Study, Going International: International Trade for the Nonspecialist, New Rules for Contracting in the Global Market Place: the United Nations Convention on Contracts for the International Sale of Goods („CISG"), Chicago (1989), 13–37 (Kurztitel: ALI-ABA Course of Study)

Cumming, Newell E.: United Nations Commission on International Trade Law: Will a Uniform Law in International Sales Finally Emerge?, 9 Calif. West. Int'l L. J. (1979), 157–184

Cuniberti, Giles: Is the CISG Benefiting Anybody?, 39 Vand. J. Transnat'l L. (2006), 1511–1550

Cunnington, Ralph: Should punitive damages be part of the judicial arsenal in contract cases?, 26 Legal Studies (2006), 369–393

Cvetkovic, Predag: Remarks on the manner in which the PECL may be used to interpret or supplement Article 14 CISG, publiziert unter http://www.cisg.law.pace.edu/cisg/text/peclcomp14.html

Czerwenka, Beate: Rechtsanwendungsprobleme im internationalen Kaufrecht, Berlin: Duncker & Humblot (1988) (Kurztitel: Rechtsanwendungsprobleme)

Czerwenka, Beate/Drobnig, Ulrich: Diskussionsbeiträge in: *Schlechtriem* (Hrsg.), Einheitliches Kaufrecht und nationales Obligationenrecht, Baden-Baden, 1987, S. 170 f., 175 f.

Dageförde, Carsten: Internationales Finanzierungsleasing, München: Beck (1992)

Dannemann, Gerhard: Formation of Contracts on the Internet, in: *Birks/Pretto* (Hrsg.), Themes in Comparative Law – In Honour of Bernard Rudden, Oxford: Oxford University Press (2002), S. 179–197 (Kurztitel: FS Rudden)

Dannemann, Gerhard: The „Battle of the Forms" and the Conflict of Laws, in: *Rose* (Hrsg.), Lex Mercatoria, Essays on International Commercial Law in Honour of Francis Reynolds, London: LLP (2000), S. 199–218 (Kurztitel: FS Reynolds)

Darkey, Joanne M.: A U. S. Court's Interpretation of Damage Provisions Under the U. N. Convention on Contracts for the International Sale of Goods: A Preliminary Step Towards an International Jurisprudence of CISG or a Missed Opportunity?, 15 J. L. & Com. (1995), 139–152

Date-Bah, Samuel K.: Problems of the Unification of International Sales Law from the Standpoint of Developing Countries, in: Problems of Unification, New York: Oceana (1980), 39–52 = 7 Dig. Com. L. (1980), 39–52 (Kurztitel: Problems of Unification)

Date-Bah, Samuel K.: The Convention on the International Sale of Goods from the Perspective of the Developing Countries, La Vendita Internazionale, Mailand: Giuffrè (1981), 23–38 (Kurztitel: Perspective of Developing Countries)

Literatur

Date-Bah, Samuel K.: The United Nations Convention on Contracts for the International Sale of Goods, 1980: Overview and Selective Commentary, 11 Rev. Ghana L. (1979), 50–67
Daun, Johannes: Grundzüge des UN-Kaufrechts, JuS 1997, 811–816
Daun, Johannes: Öffentlichrechtliche „Vorgaben" im Käuferland und Vertragsmäßigkeit der Ware nach UN-Kaufrecht, NJW 1996, 29–30
De Cristofaro, Marco: Critical remarks on the Vienna Sales Convention's impact on jurisdiction, Uniform L. Rev. 2000, 43–68
De Ly, Filip: Obligations of the Buyer and Remedies for the Buyer's Breach of Contract (Articles 53–65), in: *Ferrari/Flechtner* (Hrsg.), The Draft UNCITRAL Digest and Beyond. Cases, Analysis and Unresolved Issues in the UN Sales Convention, München: Sellier/London: Sweet & Maxwell (2003), 468–481 (Kurztitel: Draft Digest)
De Ly, Filip: Opting-Out: Some Observations on the Occasion of the CISG's 25th Anniversary, in: *Ferrari* (Hrsg.), Quo Vadis CISG? Celebrating the 25th anniversary of the United Nations Convention on Contracts for the International Sale of Goods, München: Sellier (2005), S. 25–42 (Kurztitel: Opting-Out)
De Ly, Filip: Sources of International Sales Law: An Eclectic Model, 25 J. L. & Com. (2005), 1–12
De Ly, Fillip: Uniform Interpretation: What is Being Done? Official Efforts, in: *Ferrari* (Hrsg.), The 1980 Uniform Sales Law. Old Issues Revisited in the Light of Recent Experiences, Mailand/München: Giuffrè/Sellier European Law Publishers (2003) S. 335–360 (Kurztitel: Uniform Interpretation)
De Nova, Giorgio: L'àmbito di applicazione „ratione materiae" della convenzione di Vienna, Riv. trim. dir. proced. civ. 1990, 749–753
Del Duca, Louis F.: Implementation of Contract Formation Statute of Frauds, Parol Evidence, and Battle of Forms CISG Provisions in Civil and Common Law Countries, 25 J. L. & Com. (2005–06), 133–146
Del Duca, Louis F./Del Duca, Patrick: Practice Under the Convention of International Sale of Goods (CISG): A Primer for Attorneys and International Traders (Part I), 27 UCC L. J. (1995), 331–370
Del Duca, Louis F./Del Duca, Patrick: Practice Under the Convention on International Sale of Goods (CISG): A Primer for Attorneys and International Traders (Part II), 29 UCC L. J. (1996), 99–167
Dejaco, Stefan: Das UN-Kaufrecht – Untersuchung der Anwendung und Auslegung in der deutschen, italienischen und österreichischen Rechtsprechungspraxis (Dipl.-Arb. Innsbruck, 2007), Saarbrücken: VDM Verlag Dr. Müller (2010)
De Lukowicz, Daniela: Divergenzen in der Rechtsprechung zum CISG – Auf dem Weg zu einer einheitlichen Auslegung und Anwendung?, Frankfurt a. M.: Lang (2001)
Demogue, René: Traité des obligations en général, Bd. 2, Paris: Rousseau (1923)
Denkschrift der deutschen Bundesregierung zum Übereinkommen der Vereinten Nationen vom 11. April 1980 über Verträge über den Internationalen Warenkauf, BT-Drs. 11/3076, 38–63 (Kurztitel: Denkschrift)
Derains, Yves: La jurisprudence arbitrale de la CCI en matière de vente internationale: expérience et perspectives, in: La Vendita Internazionale, Mailand: Giuffrè (1981), 341–356 (Kurztitel: Jurisprudence arbitrale de la CCI)
Derains, Yves/Ghestin, Jacques (Hrsg.): La Convention de Vienne sur la vente internationale et les incoterms. Actes du Colloque des 1er et 2 décembre 1989, Paris: L. G. D. J. (1990) (Kurztitel: Convention de Vienne et les incoterms)
Dessemontet, Francois (Hrsg.): Les contrats de vente internationale de marchandises, Lausanne: CEDIDAC (1991) (Kurztitel: Contrats de vente internationale)
Dessemontet, Francois: La convention des Nations Unies du 11 avril 1980 sur les contrats de vente internationale de marchandises, in: *Dessemontet* (Hrsg.), Contrats de vente internationale, Lausanne: CEDIDAC (1991), 47–82 (Kurztitel: Convention)
Dessemontet, François: The legal protection of know-how in the United States of America, 2. Aufl., Genf: Droz/South Hackensack N. J.: Rothmann & Co. (1976)
Detzer, Klaus/Thamm, Manfred: Überblick über das neue UN-Kaufrecht, BB 1992, 2369–2381
Diederichsen, Eva: Commentary to Journal of Law and Commerce: Case I; Oberlandesgericht, Frankfurt am Main, 14 J. L. & Com (1995), 177–181
Diedrich, Frank: Anwendbarkeit des Wiener Kaufrechts auf Softwareüberlassungsverträge, RIW 1993, 441–452
Diedrich, Frank: Autonome Auslegung von Internationalem Einheitsrecht. Computersoftware im Wiener Kaufrecht (Diss. Hannover), Baden-Baden: Nomos (1994) (Kurztitel: Autonome Auslegung)
Diedrich, Frank: Lückenfüllung im Internationalen Einheitsrecht – Möglichkeiten und Grenzen richterlicher Rechtsfortbildung im Wiener Kaufrecht, RIW 1995, 353–364

Literatur

Diedrich, Frank: Maintaining Uniformity in International Uniform Law via Autonomous Interpretation: Software Contracts and the CISG, 8 Pace Int'l L. Rev. (1996), 303–338

Diedrich, Frank: The CISG and Computer Software Revisited, 6 VJ (Supplement) (2002), 55–75

Diedrich, Frank: Voraussetzungen einer Vertragsaufhebung wegen Sachmängeln nach dem Wiener Kaufrecht, RIW 1995, 11–16

Diesse, François: La bonne foi, la cooperation et le raisonnable dans la Convention des Nations Unies relative à la vente internationale de merchandises (CVIM), J. D. I. 2002, 55–112

Dietze, Jan/Schnichels, Dominik: Die aktuelle Rechtsprechung des EuGH zum EuGVÜ, EuZW 1997, 459–462 und 1998, 485–490

Díez-Picazo, Luis (Hrsg.): La compraventa internacional de mercaderías: comentario de la Convencion de Viena, Madrid: Civitas (1998) (Kurztitel: *Díez-Picazo/Bearbeiter*)

Digenopoulos, Vassilios: Die Abwandlung der CIF- und FOB-Geschäfte im modernen Überseekauf (Diss. Hamburg 1977), Frankfurt a. M.: Metzner (1978)

Dilger, Konrad: Das Zustandekommen von Kaufverträgen im Aussenhandel nach internationalem Einheitsrecht und nationalem Sonderrecht, RabelsZ 45 (1981), 169–195

DiMatteo, Larry A.: An International Contract Law Formula: The Informality of International Business Transactions Plus the Internationalization of Contract Law Equals Unexpected Contractual Liability, 23 Syracuse J. Int'l L. & Com. (1997), 67–111

DiMatteo, Larry A.: Case Law Precedent and Legal Writing, in: *Janssen/Meyer* (Hrsg.), CISG Methodology, München: Sellier European Law Publishers (2009), S. 113–132 (Kurztitel: CISG Methodology)

DiMatteo, Larry A.: The CISG and the Presumption of Enforceability: Unintended contractual Liability in International Business Dealings, 22 Yale J. Int'l L. (1997), 111–170

DiMatteo, Larry A./Dhooge, Lucien/Greene, Stephanie/Maurer, Virginia/Pagnattaro, Marisa: International Sales Law: A Critical Analysis of CISG Jurisprudence, Cambridge u. a.: Cambridge University Press (2005) (Kurztitel: International Sales Law)

DiMatteo, Larry A./Dhooge, Lucien/Greene, Stephanie/Maurer, Virginia/Pagnattaro, Marisa: The Interpretive Turn in International Sales Law: An Analysis of Fifteen Years of CISG Jurisprudence, 34 Nw. J. Int'l L. & Bus. (2004), 299–440

Dimsey, Mariel: Consequences of Avoidance Under the CISG, in: *Kröll/Mistelis/Perales Viscasillas/Rogers* (Hrsg.), International Arbitration and International Commercial Law: Synergy, Convergence and Evolution, Liber Amicorum Eric Bergsten, London: Wolters Kluwer (2011), 525–550 (Kurztitel: Consequences of Avoidance)

DiPalma, Maryellen: Nachfrist under National Law, the CISG, and the UNIDROIT and European Principles, Int'l Contr. Adviser 1999, 28–38

Dixon, David B.: Que Lastima Zapata! Bad CISG Ruling on Attorneys, Fees Still haunts U. S. Courts, 38 U. Miami Inter-Am. L. Rev., 405–429

Djordjevic, Milena: Declaration of Price Reduction under the CISG: Much Ado About Nothing?, in: *Kröll/Mistelis/Perales Viscasillas/Rogers* (Hrsg.), International Arbitration and International Commercial Law: synergy, convergence, and evolution: liber amicorum Eric Bergsten, Alphen aan den Rijn, Kluwer Law International (2011), S. 551–569 (Kurztitel: FS Bergsten)

Dobbs, Dan B.: Law of Remedies. Damages – Equity – Restitution, 2. Aufl., St. Paul (Minn.): West Publishing (1993)

Dodge, William S.: Teaching the CISG in Contracts, 50 J. Leg. Educ. (2000), 72–94

Dokter, Daan: Interpretation of exclusion-clauses of the Vienna Sales Convention, RabelsZ 68 (2004), 430–443

Dokter, Daan/Kruisinga, Sonja A.: The application of the CISG in the Netherlands: a Dutch treat for the CISG?, IHR 2003, 105–115

Dölle, Hans (Hrsg.): Kommentar zum Einheitlichen Kaufrecht, München: Beck (1976) (Kurztitel: *Dölle/Bearbeiter*)

Dölle, Hans: Bedeutung und Funktion der „Bräuche" im Einheitsgesetz über den internationalen Kauf beweglicher Sachen, in: *von Caemmerer u. a.* (Hrsg.), Ius privatum gentium: Festschrift für Max Rheinstein zum 70. Geburtstag am 5. Juli 1969, Tübingen: Mohr (1969), S. 447 ff. (Kurztitel: FS Rheinstein)

Dölle, Hans: Bemerkungen zu Art. 17 des Einheitsgesetzes über den internationalen Kauf dinglicher körperlicher Gegenstände, in: *Ferid u. a.* (Hrsg.), Festschrift für Hans G. Ficker, Frankfurt a. M.: Metzner (1967), S. 138 ff. (Kurztitel: Bemerkungen zu Art. 17 EKG)

Dölle, Hans: Einheitliches Kaufgesetz und Internationales Privatrecht, RabelsZ 32 (1968), 438–449

Doralt, Peter (Hrsg.): Das UNCITRAL-Kaufrecht im Vergleich zum österreichischen Recht. Referate und Diskussionen des Symposiums in Baden bei Wien, 17.–19. April 1983, Wien: Manz (1985) (Kurztitel: Das UNCITRAL-Kaufrecht im Vergleich zum österreichischen Recht)

Literatur

Dore, Isaak I.: Choice of Law Under the International Sales Convention: A U. S. Perspective, 77 Am. J. Int'l L. (1983), 521–540

Dore, Isaak I./DeFranco, James E.: A Comparison of the Non-Substantive Provisions of the UNCITRAL Convention on the International Sale of Goods and the Uniform Commercial Code, 23 Harv. Int'l L. J. (1982), 49–67 = Hancock (Hrsg.), Guide to the International Sale of Goods Convention, Chesterland, Ohio: Business Laws (1988), 104.01–104.17

Draetta, Ugo: La „battle of forms" nella prassi del commercio internazionale, Riv. dir. int. priv. proc. 1986, 319–326

Draetta, Ugo: Les clauses de force majeure et de hardship dans les contrats internationaux, R. D. A. I. 2002, 347–358

Drasch, Wolfgang: Einbeziehungs- und Inhaltskontrolle vorformulierter Geschäftsbedingungen im Anwendungsbereich des UN-Kaufrechts, Zürich: Schulthess (1999)

Drobnig, Ulrich: Allgemeine Geschäftsbedingungen im internationalen Handelsverkehr, in: *Flume* (Hrsg.), Internationales Recht und Wirtschaftsordnung, Festschrift für F. A. Mann zum 70. Geburtstag, München: Beck (1977), S. 591–615 (Kurztitel: FS Mann)

Drobnig, Ulrich: Anwendungsnormen in Übereinkommen zur Vereinheitlichung des Privatrechts, in: *Stoffel/Volken* (Hrsg.) Kollision und Vereinheitlichung, Festschrift für Alfred E. Overbeck zum 65. Geburtstag, Fribourg: Editions Universitaires (1990), S. 15–30 (Kurztitel: FS Overbeck)

Drobnig, Ulrich: Regionale Vereinheitlichung des Rechts der Mobiliarsicherheiten außerhalb Europas, in: *Schwenzer/Hager* (Hrsg.), Festschrift für Peter Schlechtriem zum 70. Geburtstag, Tübingen: Mohr (2003), S. 855–867 (Kurztitel: FS Schlechtriem)

Drobnig, Ulrich: Standard Forms and General Conditions in International Trade: Dutch, German and Uniform Law, in: *Voskuil/Wade* (Hrsg.), Hague-Zagreb Essays 4, Den Haag: Asser Instituut/Martinus Nijhoff (1983), S. 117–134 (Kurztitel: Standard Forms)

Drobnig, Ulrich: The UNIDROIT Principles in the Conflict of Laws, Uniform L. Rev. 1998, 385–395

Drobnig, Ulrich: The Use of the Unidroit Principles by National and Supranational Courts, Use of the Unidroit Principles, in: Institute of International Business Law and Practice (Hrsg.), Unidroit Principles for International Commercial Contracts: A New Lex Mercatoria, Paris: ICC-Publication Nr. 490/1 (1995), S. 223–232 (Kurztitel: Unidroit Principles)

Drobnig, Ulrich: Transfer of Property, in: *Hartkamp/Hondius/Hesselink/Du Perron/Vranken* (Hrsg.), Towards a European Civil Code, 2. Aufl., Dordrecht/Boston/London: Martinus Nijhoff (1998), S. 495–542 (Kurztitel: Transfer of Property)

Drobnig, Ulrich: Vereinheitlichung von Zivilrecht durch soft law: neuere Erfahrungen und Einsichten, in: *Basedow u. a.* (Hrsg.), Aufbruch nach Europa, 75 Jahre Max-Planck-Institut für Privatrecht, Tübingen: Mohr (2001), S. 745–755 (Kurztitel: Vereinheitlichung durch soft law)

Droste, Monica: Der Liefervertrag mit Montageverpflichtung (Diss. Köln 1989/90), Heidelberg: Recht und Wirtschaft (1991)

Dübbers, Robert: Das neue „Einwurf-Einschreiben" der Deutschen Post AG und seine juristische Einordnung, NJW 1997, 2503–2504

Duintjer Tebbens, Harry: Internationale Kaufverträge und EuGVÜ: Gerichtsstandsklausel in AGB und Erfüllungsort nach EKG, IPRax 1985, 262–265

Duncan, John C., Jr.: Nachfrist Was Ist? Thinking Globally and Acting Locally: Considering Time Extension Principles of the U. N. Convention on Contracts for the International Sale of Goods in Revising the Uniform Commercial Code, Brigham Young U. L. Rev. (2000), 1363–1411

Ebenroth, Carsten Thomas: Das kaufmännische Bestätigungsschreiben im internationalen Handelsverkehr, ZfRVgl 1978, 161–206

Ebenroth, Carsten Thomas: Internationale Vertragsgestaltung im Spannungsverhältnis zwischen AGBG, IPR-Gesetz und UN-Kaufrecht, östJBl 1986, 681–695

Ebers, Martin/Janssen, André/Meyer, Olaf: Comparative Report, in: *Ebers/Janssen/Meyer* (Hrsg.), European Perspectives on Producers' Liability, München: Sellier (2009), 3–73

Ebke, Werner F.: Artikel VIII Abschnitt 2(b) des Übereinkommens über den Internationalen Währungsfonds und die Schweiz: „2(b) or Not 2(b)", in: *Gehrig/Schwander* (Hrsg.), Banken und Bankrecht im Wandel, Festschrift für Beat Kleiner, Zürich: Schulthess (1993), S. 303–323

Ebnet, Peter: Rechtsprobleme bei der Verwendung von Telefax, NJW 1992, 2985–2991

Eckardt, Udo: Die „Vergleichsfalle" als Problem der Auslegung adressatenloser Annahmeerklärungen nach § 151 S. 1 BGB, BB 1996, 1945–1953

Eckhardt, Udo: Die Entlastung des Verkäufers nach Art. 74 EKG: eine rechtstatsächliche und rechtsvergleichende Untersuchung unter besonderer Berücksichtigung der Entlastungswirkung arbeitskampfbedingter Leistungshindernisse (Diss. Konstanz 1982), Frankfurt a. M.: Lang (1983) (Kurztitel: Entlastung des Verkäufers nach Art. 74 EKG)

Eckert, Hans-Werner/Maifeld, Jan/Matthiessen, Michael: Handbuch des Kaufrechts. Der Kaufvertrag nach bürgerlichem Recht, München: Beck (2007)

Ehrenberg, Victor: Handbuch des gesamten Handelsrechts mit Einschluß des Wechsel-, Scheck-, See- und Binnenschiffahrtsrechts, des Versicherungsrechts sowie des Post- und Telegraphenrechts, Bd. 8, 1. Abteilung: Versicherungsrecht, bearb. v. *Hagen,* Leipzig: Reisland (1922) (Kurztitel: *Ehrenberg/ Hagen*)

Ehrenzweig, Armin: System des österreichischen allgemeinen Privatrechts, 2. Buch: Das Recht der Schuldverhältnisse, 1. Abteilung: Allgemeine Lehren, bearb. v. *Mayrhofer,* 3. Aufl., Wien: Manz (1986) (Kurztitel: *Ehrenzweig/Mayrhofer*)

Eiselen, Sieg: Anticipatory breach: Remarks on the manner in which the Principles of European Contract Law may be used to interpret or supplement Articles 71 and 72 of the CISG, in: *Felemegas* (Hrsg.), An International Approach to the Interpretation of the United Nations Convention on Contracts for the International Sale of Goods (1980) as Uniform Sales Law, Cambridge/New York u. a.: Cambridge University Press (2007), S. 461–465 (Kurztitel: Anticipatory breach)

Eiselen, Sieg: Anticipatory breach: Remarks on the manner in which the UNIDROIT Principles of International Commercial Contracts may be used to interpret or supplement Articles 71 and 72 of the CISG, in: *Felemegas* (Hrsg.), An International Approach to the Interpretation of the United Nations Convention on Contracts for the International Sale of Goods (1980) as Uniform Sales Law, Cambridge, New York u. a.: Cambridge University Press (2007), S. 207–211 (Kurztitel: Anticipatory breach)

Eiselen, Sieg: E-Commerce and the CISG: Formation, Formalities and Validity, 6 VJ (2002), 305–318

Eiselen, Sieg: Electronic commerce and the United Nations Convention on Contracts for the International Sale of Goods (CISG) 1980, 6 EDI L. Rev. (1999), 21–46

Eiselen, Sieg: Literal Interpretation: The Meaning of the Words, in: *Janssen/Meyer* (Hrsg.), CISG Methodology, München: Sellier European Law Publishers (2009), S. 61–90 (Kurztitel: CISG Methodology)

Eiselen, Sieg: Modification or termination of contract and formalities: Remarks on the manner in which the UNIDROIT Principles of International Commercial Contracts may be used to interpret or supplement Article 29 of the CISG, in: *Felemegas* (Hrsg.): An International Approach to the Interpretation of the United Nations Convention on Contracts for the International Sale of Goods (1980) as Uniform Sales Law, Cambridge: Cambridge University Press (2007), S. 163–166 (Kurztitel: Modification)

Eiselen, Sieg: Remarks on the Manner in which the UNIDROIT Principles of International Commercial Contracts May Be Used to Interpret or Supplement Article 78 of the CISG, www.cisg.law.pace.edu/cisg/biblio/eiselen3.html (Kurztitel: PICC – Art. 78 CISG)

Eiselen, Sieg: The CISG and Electronic Issues, 10 Wuhan University International Law Review (2008–2009), 138–155

Eiselen, Sieg: The Interaction between the Electronic Communications Convention and the United Nations Convention on the International Sale of Goods, in: *Boss/Kilian* (Hrsg.), The United Nations Convention on the Use of Electronic Communications in International Contracts: An In-Depth Guide and Sourcebook, Austin, Boston, Chicago, New York, The Netherlands: Wolters Kluwer (2008), 333–352 (Kurztitel: Interaction)

Eisemann, Frédéric: La practique des incoterms: usages de la vente internationale, 3. Aufl., Paris: Jupiter (1988) (Kurztitel: Incoterms)

Eisemann, Frédéric: Usages de la vente commerciale internationale, Paris: Jupiter (1980)

Eisemann, Frédéric/Schütze, Rolf A.: Das Dokumentenakkreditiv im internationalen Handelsverkehr, 5. Aufl., Heidelberg: Recht und Wirtschaft (1999)

Elsing, Siegfried H./van Alstine, Michael P.: US-amerikanisches Handels- und Wirtschaftsrecht, 2. Aufl., Heidelberg: Recht und Wirtschaft (1999)

Elzer, Oliver/Jakobi, Florian: Durch Fax übermittelte Willenserklärungen und Prozeßhandlungen, ZIP 1997, 1821–1830

Emmerich, Volker: Das Recht der Leistungsstörungen, 6. Aufl., München: Beck (2005)

Enderlein, Fritz: Das UN-Verjährungsübereinkommen und seine Geltung in Deutschland, in: *Jayme/ Furtak* (Hrsg.), Der Weg zur deutschen Rechtseinheit: internationale und interne Auswirkungen im Privatrecht, Heidelberg: C. F. Müller (1991), S. 65–81 (Kurztitel: UN-Verjährungsabkommen)

Enderlein, Fritz: Das Wiener UN-Kaufrechtsübereinkommen 1980 und die ALB/RGW, ZfRVgl 1988, 10–24

Enderlein, Fritz: Die Interpretation internationalen Einheitsrechts, DDR-AW 1987/RiA Nr. 98, I–VII

Literatur

Enderlein, Fritz: Die Verpflichtung des Verkäufers zur Einhaltung des Lieferzeitraums und die Rechte des Käufers bei dessen Nichteinhaltung nach dem UN-Übereinkommen über Verträge über den internationalen Warenkauf, IPRax 1991, 313–316

Enderlein, Fritz: Rights and Obligations of the Seller under the UN Convention on Contracts for the International Sale of Goods, in: Šarčević/Volken (Hrsg.), Dubrovnik Lectures, New York: Oceana (1986), S. 133–201 (Kurztitel: Rights and Obligations of the Seller)

Enderlein, Fritz/Graefrath, Bernhard: Nochmals: Deutsche Einheit und internationales Kaufrecht, BB 1991, Beil. Nr. 6, 8–13

Enderlein, Fritz/Maskow, Dietrich: International Sales Law, New York: Oceana (1992)

Enderlein, Fritz/Maskow, Dietrich/Stargardt, Monika: Kaufrechtskonvention der UNO (mit Verjährungskonvention) – Kommentar, Berlin: Staatsverlag DDR (1985) (Kurztitel: *Enderlein/Maskow/Stargardt*)

Enderlein, Fritz/Maskow, Dietrich/Strohbach, Heinz: Internationales Kaufrecht, Berlin: Haufe (1991) (Kurztitel: *Enderlein/Maskow/Strohbach*)

Endler, Maximilian/Daub, Jan: Internationale Softwareüberlassung und UN-Kaufrecht, CR 1993, 601–606

Enneccerus, Ludwig/Lehmann, Heinrich: Lehrbuch des bürgerlichen Rechts, begr. v. *Ludwig Enneccerus, Theodor Kipp* u. *Martin Wolff,* Bd. 2: Recht der Schuldverhältnisse, 15. Bearb., Tübingen: Mohr (1958)

Ensthaler, Jürgen (Hrsg.): Gemeinschaftskommentar zum Handelsgesetzbuch mit UN-Kaufrecht, 7. Aufl., Neuwied: Luchterhand (2007) (Kurztitel: *Ensthaler/Bearbeiter,* GK-HGB)

Ensthaler, Jürgen: Haftungsrechtliche Bedeutung von Qualitätssicherungsvereinbarungen, NJW 1994, 817–823

Eörsi, Gyula: A Propos for the 1980 Vienna Convention on Contracts for the International Sale of Goods, 31 Am. J. Comp. L. (1983), 333–356

Eörsi, Guyla: Problems of Unifying Law on the Formation of Contracts for the International Sale of Goods, 27 Am. J. Comp. L. (1979), 311–323

Eörsi, Gyula: General Provisions, in: Galston/Smit (Hrsg.), International Sales, New York: Matthew Bender (1984), Kap. 2, S. 1–36 (Kurztitel: General Provisions)

Eörsi, Guyla: The Validity of Clauses Excluding or Limiting Liability, 23 Am. J. Comp. L. (1975), 215–237

Erauw, Johan: The Delivery Terms and the Passing of Risk – Drafting Clauses Related to Articles 66–70 CISG, in: Fletchner/Brand/Walter (Hrsg.), Drafting Contracts under the CISG, Oxford: Oxford University Press (2007), S. 383–410 (Kurztitel: Delivery and Passing of Risk)

Erauw, Johan/Flechtner, Harry: Remedies under the CISG and Limits to their Uniform Character, in: Šarčević/Volken (Hrsg.), The International Sale of Goods Revisited, The Hague/London/New York: Kluwer (2001), S. 35–76 (Kurztitel: Remedies under the CISG)

Erdem, Ercüment H.: La livraison des marchandises selon la Convention de Vienne, La convention des Nations Unies sur le contrat de vente internationale de marchandises du 11 avril 1980 (Diss. Fribourg), Fribourg: Editions Universitaires (1990)

Erman, Walter: Handkommentar zum Bürgerlichen Gesetzbuch. Mit EinfGes., AGBG, etc., früher hrsg. v. *Erman,* hrsg. v. *H. P. Westermann,* 12. Aufl., Münster: Aschendorff (2008) (Kurztitel: *Erman/Bearbeiter*)

Ernst, Birgit: Das Wiener Übereinkommen von 1980 über Verträge über den internationalen Warenkauf (UN-Kaufrecht) im Recht der Produkthaftung: Abgrenzungsprobleme gegenüber dem „ansonsten anwendbaren" Recht, Aachen: Shaker (2002) (Kurztitel: Produkthaftung)

Escher, Alfred: UN-Kaufrecht: Stillschweigender Verzicht auf Einwand einer verspäteten Mängelrüge? Zugleich Anmerkung zu BGH, RIW 1999, 385 f., RIW 1999, 495–502

Espinassous, Valentine: L'uniformisation du droit substantiel et le conflit de lois (Diss. Paris, 2008) (Kurztitel: L'uniformisation du droit substantial)

Esser, Michael J.: Die letzte Glocke zum Geleit? – Kaufmännische Bestätigungsschreiben im Internationalen Handel: Deutsches, Französisches, Österreichisches und Schweizerisches Recht und Einheitliches Recht unter der Kaufrechtskonvention von 1980, östZRVgl 1988, 167–193

Esslinger, Anita C.: Contracting in the Global Marketplace: The UN Conventions on Contracts for the International Sale of Goods and The Limitation Period in the International Sale of Goods, ALI-ABA (1999), 69–88

Fadlallah, Ibrahim: Le projet de convention sur la vente de marchandises, J. D. I. 1979, 755–769

Fagan, David: The Remedial Provisions of the Vienna Convention on the International Sale of Goods 1980: A Small Business Perspective, J. Small & Emerg. Bus. L. (1998), 317–354

Fairlie, David: A Commentary on Issues Arising under Articles 1 to 6 of the CISG (with Special Reference to the Position in Australia), in: Singapore International Arbitration Centre (Hrsg.),

Celebrating Success: 25 Years United Nations Convention on Contracts for the International Sale of Goods, Singapur (2006), S. 18–27

Fakes, Arthur: The Application of the United Nations Convention on Contracts for the International Sale of Goods to Computer Software and Database Transactions, 3 Software L. J. (1990), 559–588

Fallon/Philippe: La Convention de Vienne sur les contrats de vente internationale de marchandises, Journal des Tribunaux 1998, 17–37

Faria, José Angelo Estrella: Online contracting: Legal certainty for global business – The new U. N. Convention on the Use of Electronic Communications in International Contracts, 39 UCC L. J. (2006), 25–73

Faria, José Angelo Estrella: The United Nations Convention on the Use of Electronic Communications in International Contracts – An Introductory Note, 55 Int'l & Comp. L. Q. (2006), 689–694

Farnsworth, E. Allan: Contracts, 2. Aufl., Boston: Little, Brown (1982) (Kurztitel: Contracts)

Farnsworth, E. Allan: Damages and Specific Relief, 27 Am. J. Comp. L. (1979), 247–253

Farnsworth, E Allan: Farnsworth on Contracts, 32. Aufl., New York: Aspen Publishers (2004) (Kurztitel: Farnsworth on Contracts)

Farnsworth, E. Allan: Formation of Contract, in: *Galston/Smit* (Hrsg.), International Sales, New York: Matthew Bender (1984), Kap. 3, S. 1–18 (Kurztitel: Formation of Contract)

Farnsworth, E. Allan: Formation of International Sales Contracts: Three Attempts at Unification, 110 U. Pa. L. Rev. (1961/1962), 305–329

Farnsworth, E. Allan: Legal Remedies for Breach of Contract, 70 Colum. L. Rev. (1970), 1145–1216

Farnsworth, E. Allan: Negotiation of Contracts and Precontractual Liability: General Report, in: *Stoffel/Volken* (Hrsg.), Kollision und Vereinheitlichung, Festschrift für Alfred E. von Overbeck zum 65. Geburtstag, Fribourg (Schweiz): Editions Universitaires (1990), S. 657–680 (Kurztitel: FS von Overbeck)

Farnsworth, E. Allan: Precontractual Liability and Preliminary Agreements: Fair Dealing and Failed Negotiations, 87 Colum. L. Rev. (1987), 217–294

Farnsworth, E. Allan: Problems of the Unification of Sales Law from the Standpoint of the Common Law Countries, in: Problems of Unification, New York: Oceana (1980), 3–25 = 7 Dig. Com. L. (1980), 3–25

Farnsworth, E. Allan: Review of Standard Forms or Terms Under the Vienna Convention, 21 Cornell Int'l L. J. (1988), 439–447

Farnsworth, E. Allan: Rights and Obligations of the Seller, in: Schweizerisches Institut für Rechtsvergleichung (Hrsg.), Lausanner Kolloquium 1984, Zürich: Schulthess (1985), S. 83–90 (Kurztitel: Rights and Obligations)

Farnsworth, E. Allan: The Convention on the International Sale of Goods from the Perspective of the Common Law Countries, in: La Vendita Internazionale, Mailand: Giuffrè (1981), S. 3–21 (Kurztitel: Convention)

Farnsworth, E. Allan: UNCITRAL – Why? What? How? When?, 20 Am. J. Comp. L. (1972), 314–322

Farnsworth, E. Allan: Unification of Sales Law: Usage and Course of Dealing, in: Unification and Comparative Law in Theory and Practice: Liber amicorum Jean Georges Sauveplanne, Deventer: Kluwer Law and Taxation (1984), S. 81–89 (Kurztitel: Usage and Course of Dealing)

Fastrich, Lorenz: Richterliche Inhaltskontrolle im Privatrecht (Habil. München 1989), München: Beck (1992)

Faust, Florian: Die Vorhersehbarkeit des Schadens gemäß Art. 74 Satz 2 UN-Kaufrecht (CISG), Tübingen: Mohr (1996)

Faust, Florian: Argentinische Hasen, belgische Schweine und österreichische Wein – Der Verdacht als Mangel, in: *Wilhelm/Richardi/Lobinger* (Hrsg.), Festschrift für Eduard Picker zum 70. Geburtstag: am 3. November 2010, Tübingen: Mohr Siebeck (2010), S. 185–200 (Kurztitel: FS Picker)

Faust, Florian: Zinsen bei Zahlungsverzug, RabelsZ 68 (2004), 511–527

Feil, Erich: Produkthaftung, Produktsicherheit und Verbraucherschutz beim Fernabsatz, Wien: Linde (2001)

Felemegas, John: Introduction, in: *Felemegas* (Hrsg.): An International Approach to the Interpretation of the United Nations Convention on Contracts for the International Sale of Goods (1980) as Uniform Sales Law, Cambridge/New York u. a.: Cambridge University Press (2007), S. 1–38 (Kurztitel: Introduction)

Felemegas, John: The United Nations Convention on Contracts for the International Sale of Goods: Article 7 and Uniform Interpretation, Rev. CISG (2000/2001), 115–265

Feltham, J. D.: C. I. F. and F. O. B. Contracts and the Vienna Convention on Contracts for the International Sale of Goods, 34 J. Bus. L. (1991), 413–425

Literatur

Feltham, J. D.: The United Nations Convention on Contracts for the International Sale of Goods, 24 J. Bus. L. (1981), 346–361

Ferid, Murad: Das französische Zivilrecht, Bd. 1, Allgemeine Lehren, Recht der Schuldverhältnisse, Frankfurt a. M.: Metzner (1971)

Ferid, Murad: Internationales Privatrecht, 3. Aufl., Frankfurt a. M.: Metzner (1986)

Ferrari, Franco (Hrsg.): The 1980 Uniform Sales Law – Old Issues Revisited in the Light of Recent Experiences, Berlin: Sellier. European Law Publishers (2003)

Ferrari, Franco: Applying the CISG in a Truly Uniform Manner: *Tribunale di Vigevano* (Italy), 12 July 2000, Uniform L. Rev. 2001, 203–215

Ferrari, Franco: Assumption of Debts as a Subject Matter Excluded from the UN Sales Convention (Commentary to OGH [Austria] 24 April 1997), Forum International 1997, 90–93

Ferrari, Franco: Auslegung von Parteierklärungen und -verhalten nach UN-Kaufrecht, IHR 2003, 10–15

Ferrari, Franco: Ausschluß des UN-Kaufrechts, Rügefrist und Beweislast in einem italienischen Urteil zum deutsch-italienischen Rechtsverkehr, IPRax 2001, 354–358

Ferrari, Franco: Brevi considerazioni critiche in materia di interpretazione autonoma ed applicazione uniforma della convenzione di vienna, Riv. dir. civ. 1998, 81–98

Ferrari, Franco: Brief Remarks on Electronic Contracting and the United Nations Convention on Contracts for the International Sale of Goods (CISG), 6 VJ (2002), 289–304

Ferrari, Franco: Burden of Proof under the CISG, Rev. CISG (2000/2001), 1–8

Ferrari, Franco: CISG and Private International Law, in: *Ferrari* (Hrsg.), The 1980 Uniform Sales Law – Old Issues Revisited in the Light of Recent Experiences, Berlin: Sellier European Law Publishers (2003), S. 19–55 (Kurztitel: CISG and PIL)

Ferrari, Franco: Choice of Forum and CISG: Remarks on the Latter's Impact on the Former, in: *Flechtner/Walter* (Hrsg.), Drafting Contracts Under the CISG, Oxford: University Press (2008), S. 103–148 (Kurztitel: *Ferrari,* Choice of Forum)

Ferrari, Franco: CISG Article 1 (1) (b) and Related Matters: Brief Remarks on Occasion of a Recent Dutch Court Decision, NIPR 13 (1995), 317–328

Ferrari, Franco: CISG case law on the rate of interest on sums in arrears, Int'l Bus. L. J. 1999, 86–93

Ferrari, Franco: CISG Case Law: A New Challenge for Interpreters?, 17 J. L. & Com. (1998), 245–261

Ferrari, Franco: Commentary: Uniform Law of International Sales: Issues of Applicability and Private International Law, J. L. & Com. (1995), 159–174

Ferrari, Franco: Comparative Ruminations on the Foreseeability of Damages in Contract Law, 53 Lou. L. Rev. (1993), 1257–1269

Ferrari, Franco: Contrat de vente internationale. Applicabilité et applications de la Convention de Vienne sur les contrats de vente internationale de marchandises, 2. Aufl., Brüssel/Basel/Paris: Bruylant/Helbing & Lichtenhahn/FEC (2005) (Kurztitel: Contrat de vente)

Ferrari, Franco: Contrattazione via mezzi informatici e la Convenzione delle Nazioni Unite sui contratti di vendita internazionale di beni mobili, Dir. commun. sc. int. 2004, 1–22

Ferrari, Franco: Contratti di distribuzione, ambito di applicazione ratione materiae della Convenzione di Vienna del 1980: gli insegnamenti che si possono trarre dalla giurisprudenza straniera, Giust. civ. 2000, 2334–2342

Ferrari, Franco: Das Verhältnis zwischen den Unidroit-Grundsätzen und den allgemeinen Grundsätzen internationaler Einheitsprivatrechtskonventionen, Zugleich ein Beitrag zur Lückenfüllung durch staatliche Gerichte, JZ 1998, 9–17

Ferrari, Franco: Der Begriff des „internationalen Privatrechts" nach Art. 1 Abs. 1 lit. b) des UN-Kaufrechts, ZEuP 1998, 162–172

Ferrari, Franco: Der internationale Anwendungsbereich des Ottawa-Übereinkommens von 1998 über Internationales Factoring, RIW 1996, 181–188

Ferrari, Franco: Der Vertriebsvertrag als vom UN-Kaufrechtsübereinkommen (nicht) erfasster Vertragstyp oder wie der italienische Kassationshof einen groben Fehler hätte vermeiden können, EuLF 2000, 7–12

Ferrari, Franco: Die Schuldübernahme als vom UN-Kaufrecht nicht geregelte Rechtsmaterie (Anmerkung zu OGH [Österreich] 24.4.1997), Forum International 1997, 89–92

Ferrari, Franco: Diritto uniforme della Vendita Internazionale: Questioni di applicabilità e diritto internazionale privato, Riv. dir. civ. 1995, II, 669–685

Ferrari, Franco: Divergences in the application of the CISG's rules on non-conformity of goods, RabelsZ 68 (2004), 473–494

Ferrari, Franco: Do Courts Interpret the CISG Uniformly?, in: *Ferrari* (Hrsg.), Quo Vadis CISG? Celebrating the 25th anniversary of the United Nations Convention on Contracts for the International Sale of Goods, München: Sellier (2005), S. 3–23 (Kurztitel: Uniform Interpretation)

Literatur

Ferrari, Franco: Einheitsrecht, in: *Basedow/Hopt/Zimmermann* (Hrsg.), Handwörterbuch des Europäischen Privatrechts, Bd. 1, Tübingen: Mohr Siebeck (2009), S. 376 ff.

Ferrari, Franco: Einige kurze Anmerkungen zur Awendbarkeit des UN-Kaufrechts beim Vertragsschluss über das Internet, EuLF 2001, 301–307

Ferrari, Franco: Estudios comparativos en materia de conclusion del contrato en los paises de America del Sur con referencias a la Convencion de Viena sobre la venta internacional, Rev. Der. Com. Oblig. 1992, 51–84

Ferrari, Franco: Exclusion et inclusion de la Convention de Vienne sur les contrats de vente international de merchandises de 1980, Rev. gén. dr. 2002, 335–357

Ferrari, Franco: Exclusion et inclusion de la CVIM, Int'l Bus. L. J. 2001, 401–414

Ferrari, Franco: Gap-filling and Interpretation of the CISG: Overview of International Case Law, Int'l Bus. L. J. 2003, 221–239

Ferrari, Franco: General Principles and International Uniform Commercial Law Conventions: A Study of the 1980 Vienna Sales Convention and the 1988 UNIDROIT Conventions, Uniform L. Rev. 1997, 451–473

Ferrari, Franco: Hadley v Baxendale v Foreseeability under Article 74 CISG, in: *Saidov/Cunnington* (Hrsg.), Contract Damages: Domestic and International Perspectives, Oxford: Hart (2008), S. 305–327 (Kurztitel: Foreseeability)

Ferrari, Franco: Homeward Trend and Lex Forism Despite Uniform Sales Law, 13 VJ (2009), 15–42

Ferrari, Franco: Homeward Trend: What, Why and Why Not, IHR 2009, 8–24

Ferrari, Franco: I rapporti tra le convenzioni di diritto materiale uniforme in materia contrattuale e la necessita di un'interpretazione interconvenzionale, Riv. dir. int. priv. proc. 2000, 669–688

Ferrari, Franco: International Sales Law and the Inevitability of Forum Shopping, 23 J. L. & Com. (2004), 169–192

Ferrari, Franco: Internationales Kaufrecht einheitlich ausgelegt – Anmerkungen anläßlich eines italienischen Urteils, IHR 2001, 56–60

Ferrari, Franco: Interpretation of the Convention and gap-filling: Article 7, in: *Ferrari u. a.* (Hrsg.), The Draft UNCITRAL Digest and Beyond: Cases, Analysis and Unresolved Issues in the U. N. Sales Convention, München/London: Sellier. European Law Publishers/Sweet&Maxwell (2004), S. 138–171 (Kurztitel: Interpretation and gap-filling)

Ferrari, Franco: Interprétation uniforme de la Convention de Vienne de 1980 sur la vente internationale, Rev. int. dr. comp. 1996, 813–852

Ferrari, Franco: Italienische CISG-Rechtsprechung – Eine Übersicht, IHR 2001, 179–186

Ferrari, Franco: La Convention de Vienne sur la vente internationale et le droit international privé, J. D. I. 2006, 27–61

Ferrari, Franco: La determinazione del foro competente in materia di compravendita internazionale: breve guida agli errori da evitare, Corr. giur. 2002, 372–376

Ferrari, Franco: La jurisprudence sur la CVIM: un nouveau défi pour les interprètes?, Int'l Bus. L. J. 1998, 495–508

Ferrari, Franco: La place de la régionalisation dans l'unification d droit de la vente, Int'l Bus. L. J. 2004, 445–460

Ferrari, Franco: La vendita internazionale. Applicabilità ed applicazione della convenzione delle Nazioni Unite sui contratti di vendita internazionale di beni mobili, in: *Galgano* (Hrsg.), Trattato di diritto commerciale e di diritto pubblico dell'economia, Bd. 21, Padua: Cedam (2006) (Kurztitel: Applicabilità ed applicazioni)

Ferrari, Franco: La vendita internazionale: Applicabilità ed applicazioni della Convenzione di Vienna del 1980, in: *Galgano* (Hrsg.), Trattato di diritto commerciale e di diritto pubblico dell'economia, Bd. 21, Padua: CEDAM (1997) (Kurztitel: Applicabilità ed applicazioni)

Ferrari, Franco: L'ambito di applicazione della convenzione di Vienna sulla vendita internazionale, Riv. trim. dir. proced. civ. 1994, 893–934

Ferrari, Franco: Nuove e vecchie questioni in materia di vendita internazionale tra interpretazione autonoma e ricorso alla giurisprudenza straniera, Giur. it. 2004, 1405–1419

Ferrari, Franco: Overview of case law on the CISG's international sphere of application and its applicability requirements (Articles 1(1)(a) and (b)), Int'l Bus. L. J. 2002, 961–975

Ferrari, Franco: PIL and CISG: Friends or Foes?, IHR 2012, 89–113

Ferrari, Franco: Problematiche tipiche della Convenzione di Vienna sui contratti di vendita internazionale di beni mobili risolte in una prospettiva uniforme, Giur. it. 2002, 281–290

Ferrari, Franco: Quelles sources de droit pour les contrats de vente internationale de merchandises? Des raisons pour lesquelles il faut aller au-delà de la CVIM, Int'l Bus. L. J. 2006, 403–429

Literatur

Ferrari, Franco: Rapporto tra diritto materiale uniforme di origine convenzionale e diritto internazionale privato, Corr. giur. 2000, 933–939

Ferrari, Franco: Recent Italian court decisions on the CISG, Int'l Bus. L. J. 2001, 224–230

Ferrari, Franco: Remarks on the Autonomy and the Uniform Application of the CISG on the Occasion of its Tenth Anniversary, Int'l Contr. Adviser 1998, 33–46

Ferrari, Franco: Scope of Application: Articles 4–5, in: *Ferrari u. a.* (Hrsg.), The Draft UNCITRAL Digest and Beyond: Cases, Analysis and Unresolved Issues in the U. N. Sales Convention, München/London: Sellier. European Law Publishers/Sweet&Maxwell (2004), S. 96–113 (Kurztitel: Scope of Application)

Ferrari, Franco: Specific Topics of the CISG in Light of Judicial Application and Scholarly Writing, 15 J. L. & Com. (1995), 1–126

Ferrari, Franco: Specific Topics of the CISG in Light of Judicial Application and Scholarly Writing, 10 Preadviezen uitgebracht voor de Vereniging voor Burgerlijk Recht (1995), 81–176

Ferrari, Franco: The CISG and Domestic Remedies, RabelsZ 71 (2007), 52–80

Ferrari, Franco: The CISG and Its Impact on National Legal Systems – General Report, in: *ders.* (Hrsg.), The CISG and Its Impact on National Legal Systems, München: Sellier. European Law Publishers (2008), S. 413–480 (Kurztitel: CISG and Its Impact)

Ferrari, Franco: The CISG's Sphere of Application: Articles 1–3 and 10, in: *Ferrari u. a.* (Hrsg.), The Draft UNCITRAL Digest and Beyond: Cases, Analysis and Unresolved Issues in the U. N. Sales Convention, München/London: Sellier. European Law Publishers/Sweet&Maxwell (2004), S. 21–95 (Kurztitel: The CISG's Sphere of Application)

Ferrari, Franco: The CISG's Uniform Interpretation by courts – An Update, 9 VJ (2005), 233–252

Ferrari, Franco: The Formal Validity of Contracts for the International Sale of Goods Governed by the CISG, Int'l Bus. L. J. 2004, 85–90

Ferrari, Franco: The Interaction between the United Nations Convention on Contracts for the International Sale of Goods and Domestic Remedies (Rescission for Mistake and Remedies in Tort), RabelsZ 71 (2007), 52–80

Ferrari, Franco: The relationship between international uniform contract law conventions, Uniform L. Rev. 2000, 69–84

Ferrari, Franco: The relationship between the UCC and the CISG and the construction of uniform law, 29 Loy. L. A. L. Rev. (1996), 1021–1033

Ferrari, Franco: The Sphere of Application of the Vienna Sales Convention, Deventer: Kluwer Law and Taxation (1995) (Kurztitel: Sphere of Application)

Ferrari, Franco: Tribunale di Vigevano: Specific Aspects of the CISG Uniformly Dealt With, 21 J. L. & Com. (2001), 225–239

Ferrari, Franco: Uniform application and interest rates under the 1980 Vienna Sales Convention, 24 Ga. J. Int'l & Comp. L. (1995), 467–483 = 1 Rev. CISG (1995), 3–19

Ferrari, Franco: Uniform Interpretation of the 1980 Uniform Sales Law, 24 Ga. J. Int'l & Comp. L. (1994), 183–228

Ferrari, Franco: Universal and Regional Sales Law: Can They coexist?, Uniform L. Rev. 2003, 177–189

Ferrari, Franco: Vendita internazionale di beni mobili, in: *Scialoja/Branca* (Hrsg.), Commentario del Codice Civile, 4. Buch, III. Titel, Kap. I, Della vendita, Supplemento, Legge 11 dicembre 1985 n. 765, Bd. 1 (Art. 1–13), Bologna: Zanichelli (1994) (Kurztitel: Vendita internazionale)

Ferrari, Franco: Vendita internazionale di beni mobili, in: *Galgano* (Hrsg.), Commentario del Codice civile Scialoja-Branca, 4. Buch, III. Titel, Kap. I, Della vendita, Supplemento, Legge 11 dicembre 1985 n. 765, Bd. 2, Art. 14–24, Bologna: Zanichelli (2006) (Kurztitel: Vendita internazionale)

Ferrari, Franco: Verzugszinsen nach Art. 78 UN-Kaufrecht, IHR 2003, 153–160

Ferrari, Franco: Vom Abstraktionsprinzip und Konsensualprinzip zum Traditionsprinzip, ZEuP 1993, 52–78

Ferrari, Franco: Wesentliche Vertragsverletzung nach UN-Kaufrecht, IHR 2005, 1–8

Ferrari, Franco: What sources of law for contracts for the international sale of goods? Why one has to look beyond the CISG, IHR 2006, 1–20

Ferrari, Franco: Writing requirements: Articles 11–13, in: *Ferrari u. a.* (Hrsg.), The Draft UNCITRAL Digest and Beyond: Cases, Analysis and Unresolved Issues in the U. N. Sales Convention, München/London: Sellier. European Law Publishers/Sweet&Maxwell (2004), S. 206–215 (Kurztitel: Writing Requirements)

Ferrari, Franco: Zum vertraglichen Ausschluss des UN-Kaufrechts, ZEuP 2002, 737–746

Ferrari, Franco: Zur Bedeutung von Handelsbräuchen und Gepflogenheiten nach UN-Kaufrecht, EuLF 2002, 272–277

Ferrari, Franco/Flechtner, Harry/Brand, Ronald A. (Hrsg.): The Draft UNCITRAL Digest and Beyond: Cases, Analysis and Unresolved Issues in the U. N. Sales Convention. München/London: Sellier. European Law Publishers (2004) (Kurztitel: Draft Digest)

Ferrari, Franco/Kieninger, Eva-Maria/Mankowski, Peter/Otte, Karsten/Saenger, Ingo/Schulze, Götz Joachim/ Staudinger, Ansgar: Internationales Vertragsrecht, Rom I-VO, CISG, CMR, FactÜ, 2. Aufl., München: C. H. Beck (2012) (Kurztitel: *Ferrari u. a./Autor*, Internationales Vertragsrecht)

Ficker, Hans Claudius: Die Gefahrtragung im Haager Einheitlichen Kaufgesetz, in: *Leser/Marschall von Bieberstein* (Hrsg.), Das Haager Einheitliche Kaufgesetz und das Deutsche Schuldrecht, Kolloquium zum 65. Geburtstag von Ernst von Caemmerer, Karlsruhe: C. F. Müller (1973), S. 131–140 (Kurztitel: Das Haager Einheitliche Kaufgesetz)

Finke, Karin: Die Bedeutung der Internationalen Handelsklauseln für den Gefahrübergang nach deutschem und US-amerikanischem Recht, Eine rechtsvergleichende Studie unter Berücksichtigung des Haager Einheitlichen Kaufrechts und des UNCITRAL-Kaufrechts am Beispiel der Klauseln cif, fob und der Klauseln des Ankunftsvertrags (Diss. Augsburg 1983), Frankfurt a. M.: Lang (1984)

Fisanich, Frank N.: Application of the U. N. Sales Convention in Chinese International Commercial Arbitration: Implications for International Uniformity, 10 Am. Rev. Int'l Arb. (1999), 101–122

Fischer, Detlev: Vertragsstrafe und vertragliche Schadenspauschalierung in der neueren deutschen und französischen Rechtsentwicklung (Diss. Freiburg 1980), Frankfurt a. M.: Metzner (1981) (Kurztitel: Vertragsstrafe)

Fischer, Jörg: Die Unsicherheitseinrede. Eine rechtsvergleichende Untersuchung über die Rechte eines Vertragspartners bei Vermögensverschlechterung der anderen Partei zum deutschen und US-amerikanischen Recht sowie zu den einheitlichen Kaufrechten (Diss. Freiburg 1987), Frankfurt a. M.: Lang (1988) (Kurztitel: Die Unsicherheitseinrede)

Fischer, Nicole: Die Unmöglichkeit der Leistung im internationalen Kauf- und Vertragsrecht, Berlin: Duncker & Humblot (2001) (Kurztitel: Unmöglichkeit)

Fischer, R. Reinhard: Vor- und Nachteile des Ausschlusses des UN-Kaufrechts aus Sicht des deutschen Exporteurs (Diss. Köln), Hamburg: Verlag Dr Kova (2008) (Kurztitel: Vor- und Nachteile)

Fitzgerald, John: CISG, Specific Performance, and the Civil Law of Louisiana and Quebec, 16 J. L. & Com. (1997), 291–313

Fitzgerald, Peter L.: International Contracting Practices Survey Project: An Empirical Study of the Value and Utility of the United Nations Convention on the International Sale of Goods (CISG) and the Unidroit Principles of International Commercial Contracts to Practitioners, Jurists, and Legal Academics in the United States, 27 J. L. & Com. (2008), 1–112

Flambouras, Dionysios P.: The Doctrines of Impossibility of Performance and Clausula rebus sic stantibus in the 1980 Convention on Contracts for the International Sale of Goods and the Principles of European Contract Law – A Comparative Analysis, 13 Pace Int'l L. Rev. (2001), 261–293

Flambouras, Dionysios P.: When Bullets Penetrate Bullet-Proof Vests: Conformity of the Bullet-Proof Material to the Contract of Sale and Concurrent Remedies (a Note on the Judgment of the Multi-Member Court of First Instance of Athens 4505/2009), 29 J. L. & Com. (2011), 171–232

Flechtner, Harry M.: Another CISG Case in the U. S. Courts: Pitfalls for the Practitioner and the Potential for Regionalized Interpretations, 15 J. L. & Com. (1995), 127–138

Flechtner, Harry M.: Buyer's Obligation to give notice of lack of conformity (Articles 38, 39, 40 and 44), in: *Ferrari/Flechtner/Brand* (Hrsg.): The Draft UNCITRAL Digest and Beyond: Cases, Analysis and Unresolved Issues in the U. N. Sales Convention. München/London: Sellier. European Law Publishers (2004), S. 377–391 (Kurztitel: Draft Digest)

Flechtner, Harry M.: Conformity of Goods, Third Party Claims, And Buyer's Notice of Breach under the United Nations Convention („CISG"), with Comments on the „Mussels Case", the „Stolen Automobile Case", and the „Ugandan Used Shoes Case", University of Pittsburgh School of Law Working Paper Series (2007), Paper 64

Flechtner, Harry M.: Excluding CISG Article 35(2) Quality Obligations: The 'Default Rule' – View vs the 'Cumulation' View, in: *Kröll/Mistelis/Perales Viscasillas/Rogers* (Hrsg.), International Arbitration and International Commercial Law: synergy, convergence, and evolution: liber amicorum Eric Bergsten, Alphen aan den Rijn, Kluwer Law International (2011), S. 571–584 (Kurztitel: FS Bergsten)

Flechtner, Harry M.: Funky Mussels, a Stolen Car, and Decrepit Used Shoes: Non-Conforming Goods and Notice Thereof under the United Nations Sales Convention („CISG"), 26 B. U. Int'l L. J. (2008), 1–28

Flechtner, Harry M.: Recent Developments: CISG, 14 J. L. & Com. (1995), 153–176

Flechtner, Harry M.: Recovering Attorneys' Fees as Damages under the U. N. Sales Convention, 22 Nw. J. Int'l. L. & Bus. (2002), 121

Literatur

Flechtner, Harry M.: Remedies Under the New International Sales Convention: The Perspective from Article 2 of the U. C. C., 8 J. L. & Com. (1988), 53–108

Flechtner, Harry M.: Selected Issues Relating to the CISG's Scope of Application, 13 VJ (2009), 91–108

Flechtner, Harry M.: Substantial Revisions to U. S. Domestic Sales Law (Article 2 of the Uniform Commercial Code), IHR 2004, 225–236

Flechtner, Harry M.: The CISG in U. S. Courts: The Evolution (and Devolution) of the Methodology of Interpretation, in: *Ferrari* (Hrsg.), Quo Vadis CISG? Celebrating the 25th anniversary of the United Nations Convention on Contracts for the International Sale of Goods, München: Sellier (2005), S. 91–111 (Kurztitel: The CISG in U. S. Courts)

Flechtner, Harry M.: The CISG's Impact on International Unification Efforts: the UNIDROIT Principles of International Commercial Contracts and the Principles of European Contract Law, in: *Ferrari* (Hrsg.), 1980 Uniform Sales Law. Old issues revisited in the light of recent experiences, Mailand/München: Giuffrè/Sellier (2003), S. 169–197 (Kurztitel: The CISG's Impact)

Flechtner, Harry M.: The Future of the Sales Convention: In Defense of Diversity (Some Non-Uniformity) in Interpreting the CISG, in: *Büchler/Müller-Chen* (Hrsg.), Private Law, national – global – comparative, Festschrift für Ingeborg Schwenzer zum 60. Geburtstag, Bern: Stämpfli (2011), S. 493–514 (Kurztitel: FS Schwenzer)

Flechtner, Harry M.: The Several Texts of the CISG in a Decentralized System: Observations on Translation, Reservations and Other Challenges to the Uniformity Priciple in Article 7 (1), 17 J. L. & Com. (1998), 187–217

Flechtner, Harry M.: The U. N. Sales Convention (CISG) and MCC-Marble Ceramic Center, Inc. v. Ceramica Nuova dAgostino, S. p. A.: The Eleventh Circuit Weights in on Interpretation, Subjective Intent, Procedural Limits to the Conventions Scope, and Parol Evidence Rule, 18 J. L. & Com (1999), 259–287

Flechtner, Harry M.: Transcript of a Workshop on the Sales Convention: Leading CISG scholars discuss Contract Formation, Validity, Excuse for Hardship, Avoidance, Nachfrist, Contract Interpretation, Parol Evidence, Analogical Application, and much more, 18 J. L. & Com. (1999), 191–258

Flechtner, Harry M./Brand, Ronald A./Walter, Mark S. (Hrsg.), Drafting Contracts Under the CISG, Oxford: Oxford University Press (2008)

Flechtner, Harry M./Lookofsky, Joseph: Viva Zapata! American Procedure and CISG in a U. S. Circuit Court of Appeals, 7 VJ (2003), 93–104

Flesch, Karin: Der Irrtum über die Kreditwürdigkeit des Vertragspartners und die Verschlechterungseinrede. Anwendbarkeit des BGB neben dem UN-Kaufrecht (CISG)/Auslegung des § 321 BGB, BB 1994, 873–879

Flesch, Karin: Mängelhaftung und Beschaffenheitsirrtum beim Kauf, Baden-Baden: Nomos (1994)

Flessner, Axel: Befreiung vom Vertrag wegen Nichterfüllung, ZEuP 1997, 255–320

Flessner, Axel: Einstweilige Zurückhaltung der Gegenleistung nach europäischem Vertragsrecht, in: *Neumeyer* (Hrsg.), Emptio – venditio inter nationes: Wiener Übereinkommen über den internationalen Warenkauf: Festgabe für Karl Heinz Neumayer, Basel: Recht und Gesellschaft (1997)

Flessner, Axel/Kadner, Thomas: CISG? Zur Suche nach einer Abkürzung für das Wiener Übereinkommen über Verträge über den internationalen Warenkauf, ZEuP 1995, 347–350

Flume, Werner: Allgemeiner Teil des bürgerlichen Rechts, Bd. 2: Das Rechtsgeschäft, 4. Aufl., Berlin, Heidelberg, New York: Springer (1992) (Kurztitel: Das Rechtsgeschäft)

Flume, Werner: Eigenschaftsirrtum und Kauf, Münster: Regensberg (1948) (Kurztitel: Eigenschaftsirrtum)

Fogt, Morten M.: Einheitlicher Vertrag oder Aufspaltung gemäß Art. 3 Abs. 2 CISG bei einem Mietkauf, IPRax 2003, 364–369

Fogt, Morten M.: Konkludente Vertragsannahme und grenzüberschreitendes kaufmännisches Bestätigungsschreiben nach CISG, IPRax 2007, 417–422

Fogt, Morten M.: Rechtzeitige Rüge und Vertragsaufhebung bei Waren mit raschem Wertverlust nach UN-Kaufrecht, ZEuP 2002, 580–596

Fogt, Morten M./Rosch, Wolfgang: Habitudes entre les parties et clause d'arbitrage, D. 2003, somm. 2369–2370

Fontaine, Marcel: Das Recht des internationalen Warenkaufs, in: *Bauer u. a.* (Hrsg.), Festschrift für Ernst Steindorff zum 70. Geburtstag, Berlin: de Gruyter (1990), S. 1193–1209 (Kurztitel: Recht des internationalen Warenkaufs)

Fontaine, Marcel: La formation des contrats, Codifications récentes et besoins de la pratique, in: Festschrift zum 40. Geburtstag der Commission Droit et Vie des Affaires, Bruxelles: Bruylant (1998), S. 681–695 (Kurztitel: FS Commission Droit et Vie des Affaires)

Fontaine, Marcel: Le processus de formation du contrat: Contributions comparatives et interdisciplinaires à l'harmonisation du droit européen, Brüssel: Bruylant (2002)

Literatur

Fontaine, Marcel: Les clauses de force majeure dans les contrats internationaux, Dr. prat. com. int. 1979, 469–506

Fontaine, Marcel: Les clauses de hardship – aménagement conventionnel de l'imprévision dans les contrats internationaux à long terme, Dr. prat. com. int. 1976, 7–49

Fontaine, Marcel: Les dispositions relatives au hardship et à la force majeure, in: *Bonell/Bonelli* (Hrsg.), Contratti commerciali internazionali e principi UNIDROIT, Mailand: Giuffrè (1997), S. 183–191 (Kurztitel: Les dispositions relatives au hardship)

Fontaine, Marcel: Offre et acceptation, approche dépassée du processus de formation des contrats?, in: Mélanges offerts à Pierre Van Ommeslaghe, Bruxelles: Bruylant (2000), S. 115–133 (Kurztitel: Offre et acceptation)

Fortier, Vicente: Le prix dans la Convention de Vienne sur la vente internationale de marchandises: les articles 14 et 55, J. D. I. 1990, 381–391

Fountoulakis, Christiana: Das Verhältnis von Nacherfüllungsrecht des Verkäufers und Vertragsaufhebungsrecht des Käufers im UN-Kaufrecht – Unter besonderer Berücksichtigung der Rechtsprechung der Schweizer Gerichte, IHR 2003, 160–168

Fountoulakis, Christiana: Remedies for Breach of Contract Under the United Nations Convention on the International Sale of Goods, ERA Forum (2011), 12, 7–23 (Kurztitel: *Fountoulakis,* ERA Forum (2011) 12)

Fountoulakis, Christiana: Set-off Defences in International Arbitration – A Comparative Analysis, Oxford: Hart Publishing (2011) (Kurztitel: *Fountoulakis,* Set-off Defences)

Fountoulakis, Christiana: The parties' choice of 'neutral law' in international commercial sales contracts, 7 EJLR (2005), 303–329

Fountoulakis, Christiana: Zurückbehaltungsrecht bei nicht ausgestellter Quittung im UN-Kaufrecht, IHR 2005, 244–249

Frécon, Alain: Practical Considerations in Drafting F. O. B. Terms in International Sales, 3 Int'l Tax. & Bus. Law (1986), 346–367

Fötschl, Andreas: Das neue dänische Verjährungsrecht, RIW 2011, 696–702

Freiburg, Nina: Das Recht auf Vertragsaufhebung im UN-Kaufrecht: unter besonderer Berücksichtigung der Ausschlussgründe (Diss. Münster 2000), Berlin: Duncker & Humblot (2001)

Freiburg, Nina: Die Rügeobliegenheit des Käufers bei grenzüberschreitendem Warenverkehr, IHR 2005, 56–64

Freitag, Robert: Kollisionsrecht, in: *Leible/Sosnitza* (Hrsg.), Versteigerungen im Internet, Heidelberg: Recht und Wirtschaft (2004), S. 326–389 (Kurztitel: Kollisionsrecht)

Frense, Astrid: Grenzen der formularmäßigen Freizeichnung im einheitlichen Kaufrecht, Heidelberg: Recht und Wirtschaft (1993)

Fridman, Gerald Henry Louis: The Law of Contract in Canada, 3. Aufl., Toronto 1994 (Kurztitel: Contracts)

Friedmann, Daniel: Restitutions of Profits Gained by Party in Breach of Contract, 104 L. Q. R. 1988, 383–388

Friedmann, Daniel: The Efficient Breach Fallacy, 18 J. Leg. Stud. (1989), 1–24

Friehe, Heinz Albert: Die Setzung der unangemessen kurzen Nachfrist im CISG mit einem Ausblick auf das BGB (Teil 1), IHR 2010, 230–249

Friehe, Heinz Albert: Die Setzung der unangemessen kurzen Nachfrist im CISG mit einem Ausblick auf das BGB (Teil 2), IHR 2011, 16–37

Friehe, Heinz Albert/Huck, Winfried: Das UN-Kaufrecht in sieben Sprachen, IHR 2008, 14–26

Frigge, Bettina: Externe Lücken und internationales Privatrecht nach dem UN-Kaufrecht (Art. 7 Abs. 2) (Diss. Heidelberg), Frankfurt a. M.: Lang (1994)

Frignani, Aldo: Compravendita internazionale: la Convenzione di Vienna del 1980, la Convenzione sulla prescrizione, in Il diritto del commercio internazionale: Manuale teorico-pratico per la redazione dei contratti, Milano (1985), 169–181

Frignani, Aldo: Il Contratto Internazionale, Padua: CEDAM (1990) (Kurztitel: Contratto Internazionale)

Frignani, Aldo/Torsello, Marco: Il Contratto Internazionale Diritto Comparato e Prassi Commerciale Vol.12, 2. Aufl., Padua: Cedam (2010) (Kurztitel: Il contratto internazionale)

Frisch, David: Commercial Common Law, the United Nations Convention on the International Sale of Goods, and the Inertia of Habit, 74 Tul. L. Rev. (1999–2000), 495–559

Fritzemeyer, Wolfgang/Heun, Sven-Erik: Rechtsfragen des EDI, CR 1992, 129–133

Frohn, E. N.: Toepassing Weens Koopverdrag 1980 door de nederlandse rechter, Molengrafica 1995, 199–221

Fuchs, Annick: Anmerkung zu LG Mönchengladbach, Urt. v. 15.7.2003 – 7 O 221/02, IHR 2003, 229–231, IHR 2003, 231–233

Literatur

Furrer, Andreas/Schramm, Dorothee: Zuständigkeitsprobleme im europäischen Vertragsrecht – Die neuesten Entwicklungen zu Art. 5 Ziff. 1 LugÜ/euGVÜ, SJZ 2003, 105–117

Furrer, Andreas/Schramm, Dorothee: Zuständigkeitsprobleme im europäischen Vertragsrecht (Fortsetzung), SJZ 2003, 137–142

Furtak, Oliver: UN-Kaufrecht und EKG: Gefahrtragung beim Versendungskauf, Jb. It. R. 3 (1990), 127–133

Gabor, Francis A.: Stepchild of the New Lex Mercatoria: Private International Law from the United States Perspective (Symposium Reflections), 8 Nw. J. Int'l L. & Bus. (1988), 538–569

Gabriel, Henry D.: Contracts for the Sale of Goods, Dobbs Ferry, New York: Oceana Publications (2004) (Kurztitel: Sale of Goods)

Gabriel, Henry D.: How International is the Sales Law of the United States, Centro di studi e ricerche di diritto comparato e straniero, Rom (1999) (Kurztitel: Sales Law of the U. S.)

Gabriel, Henry D.: The Battle of the Forms: A Comparison of the United Nations Convention for the International Sale of Goods and the Uniform Commercial Code, 49 Bus. Law. (1994), 1053–1064

Gabriel, Henry D.: The Buyer's Performance Under the CISG: Articles 53–60. Trends in the Decisions, 25 J. L. & Com. (2005), 273–283

Gabriel, Henry D.: The United Nations Convention on the Use of Electronic Communications in International Contracts: An Overview and Analysis, 11 Uniform L. Rev. (2006/2), 285–304

Gabuardi, Carlos A.: Open Price Terms in the CISG, the UCC and Mexican Commercial Law, in: *Maggi* (Hrsg.), Review of the Convention on Contracts for the International Sale of Goods (CISG), Boston: Kluwer (2004), S. 101–126

Galgano, Francesco: Diritto civile e diritto commerciale, in: *Galgano/Ferrari* (Hrsg.), Atlante di diritto privato comparato, 2. Aufl., Bologna: Zanichelli (1993), S. 35–44 (Kurztitel: Diritto civile e diritto commerciale)

Galgano, Francesco: Il diritto uniforme: la vendita internazionale, in: *Galgano/Ferrari* (Hrsg.), Atlante di diritto privato comparato, 3. Aufl., Bologna: Zanichelli (1999), S. 211–220

Galgano, Francesco: Il trasferimento della proprietà mobiliare per atto fra vivi, in: *Galgano/Ferrari* (Hrsg.), Atlante di diritto privato comparato, 3. Aufl., Bologna: Zanichelli (1999), S. 103–108 (Kurztitel: Trasferimento della proprietà)

Galston, Nina M./Smit, Hans (Hrsg.): International Sales: The United Nations Convention on Contracts for the International Sale of Goods. Conference held by the Parker School of Foreign and Comparative Law, Columbia University, October 1983, New York: Matthew Bender (1984) (Kurztitel: International Sales)

Garro, Alejandro: Cases, analyses and unresolved issues in Articles 25–34, 45–52, in: *Ferrari/Flechtner/Brand* (Hrsg.): The Draft UNCITRAL Digest and Beyond: Cases, Analysis and Unresolved Issues in the U. N. Sales Convention. München/London: Sellier. European Law Publishers (2004), S. 362–376 (Kurztitel: Draft Digest)

Garro, Alejandro M.: La formación del contrato en la Convención de Viena sobre compraventas internacionales y en el proyecto de unificación, Der. comp. 1988, Nr. 7, 227

Gargagni, Alessandro: Mancanza dell'autorizzazione valutaria al pagamento del prezzo: inadepimento del compratore o invalidità del contratto?, in: La Vendita Internazionale, Milano: Giuffrè (1981), S. 383–384

Garro, Alejandro: Some Misunderstandings about the U. N. Sales Convention in Latin America, in: *Ferrari* (Hrsg.), Quo Vadis CISG? Celebrating the 25th anniversary of the United Nations Convention on Contracts for the International Sale of Goods, München: Sellier (2005), S. 113–127 (Kurztitel: Misunderstandings)

Garro, Alejandro M.: The Buyer's „Safety Valve" Under Article 40: What is the Seller Supposed to Know and When?, 25 J. L. & Com. (2005), 253–260

Garro, Alejandro M.: The Gap-Filling Role of the UNIDROIT Principles in International Sales Law: Some Comments on the Interplay between the Principles and the CISG, 69 Tul. L. Rev. (1995), 1149–1190

Garro, Alejandro M.: The U. N. Sales Convention in the Americas: Recent Developments, 17 J. L. & Com. (1998), 219–244

Garro, Alejandro M./Zuppi, Alberto: Compraventa internacional de mercaderías, Buenos Aires: La Rocca (1990) (Kurztitel: Compraventa internacional)

Gauch, Peter: Von der konstitutiven Wirkung des kaufmännischen Bestätigungsschreibens, SZW/RSDA 1991, 177–188

Gauch, Peter/Schluep, Walter R./Schmid, Jörg/Rey, Heinz: Schweizerisches Obligationenrecht: Allgemeiner Teil ohne ausservertragliches Haftpflichtrecht, 8. Aufl., Zürich: Schulthess (2003) (Kurztitel: Obligationenrecht)

Gaudemet-Tallon, Hélène: Le nouveau droit international privé des contrats, Rev. trim. dr. euro. (1981), 215–285
Gaudemet-Tallon, Hélène: Les conventions de Bruxelles et de Lugano, 2. Aufl., Paris: L. D. J. G. (1996) (Kurztitel: Les Conventions)
Gebauer, Martin: Neuer Klägergerichtsstand durch Abtretung einer dem UN-Kaufrecht unterstehenden Zahlungsforderung?, IPRax (1999), 432–435
Gebauer, Martin: Uniform Law, Gensal Principles and Autonomous Interpretation, Uniform L. Rev. 2000, 683–705
Gehri, Myriam A.: Neuerungen bei den internationalen Vertragsgerichtsständen, in: *Spühler* (Hrsg.), Internationales Zivilprozess- und Verfahrensrecht II, Zürich: Schulthess (2003), S. 5–49
Geimer, Reinhold/Schütze, Rolf A.: Europäisches Zivilverfahrensrecht, 2. Aufl., München: Beck (2004) (Kurztitel: EUZPR)
Geist, Reinhard: Die Gefahrtragung nach dem UN-Übereinkommen über den internationalen Warenkauf, Wi. Bl. 1989, 349–356
Geldsetzer, Anette: Einvernehmliche Änderung und Aufhebung von Verträgen (Diss. Freiburg), Baden-Baden: Nomos (1993)
Gernhuber, Joachim: Die Erfüllung und ihre Surrogate sowie das Erlöschen der Schuldverhältnisse aus anderen Gründen, Handbuch des Schuldrechts, Band 3, 2. Aufl., Tübingen: Mohr (1994)
Gerny, Michael Georg: Untersuchungs- und Rügepflichten beim Kauf nach schweizerischem, französischem und US-amerikanischem Recht sowie nach CISG, Basel/Genf/München: Helbing & Lichtenhahn (1999)
Gesang, Jochen: Force majeure und ähnliche Entlastungsgründe im Rahmen der Lieferverträge von Gattungsware, Königstein: Athenäum (1980)
Ghestin, Jacques: La fusion des actions, in: *Ghestin*, Conformité et Garanties dans la Vente, Paris: L. G. D. J. (1983), nos. 227–245, 219–228 (Kurztitel: Fusion des actions)
Ghestin, Jacques: Les obligations du vendeur selon la Convention de Vienne du 11. Avril 1980 sur les contrats de vente internationale de marchandises, R. D. A. I. 1988, 5–26 = Int'l Bus. L. J. 1988, 5–26
Ghestin, Jacques: Les obligations du vendeur, in: *Derains/Ghestin* (Hrsg.), La Convention de Vienne et les incoterms, Paris: L. G. D. J. (1990), S. 83–115 (Kurztitel: Obligations du vendeur)
Ghestin, Jacques: Rapport de Synthèse – Harmonisation des droits nationaux en matière de conformité et de garanties, in: Les Ventes Internationales de Marchandises, Paris: Economica (1981), S. 369–388 (Kurztitel: Harmonisation)
Ghestin, Jacques: Traité de droit civil, La formation du contrat, 3. Aufl., Paris: L. G. D. J. (1993) (Kurztitel: La formation du contrat)
Ghestin, Jacques: Traité de droit civil, Les obligations, Les effets du contrat, 2. Aufl., Paris: L. G. D. J. (1994) (Kurzitel: Les effets du contrat)
Ghestin, Jacques/Desché, Bernard: Traité des Contrats, La Vente, Paris: L. G. D. J. (1990) (Kurztitel: Traité des Contrats)
Giancotti, Gianandrea: La determinazione del foro competente, in tema di vendita internazionale di beni mobili, in caso di cumulo di domande relativo ad obbligazioni da eseguirsi in Stati diversi, Giur. it. 2001, 233–236
Gianuzzi, Karen B.: The Convention on Contracts for the International Sale of Goods: Temporarily Out of „Service"?, 28 L. & Pol'cy Int'l Bus. (1997), 991–1035
Giardina, Andrea: I Principi Unidroit quale legge regolatrice dei contratti internazionali (i principi ed il diritto internazionale privato), in: *Bonell/Bonelli* (Hrsg.), Contratti commerciali internazionali e Principi Unidroit, Milano: Giuffrè (1997), 55–70 (Kurztitel: I Principi Unidroit)
Giardina, Andrea: Les Principes UNIDROIT sur les contrats internationaux, J. D. I. 1995, 547–558
Gillette, Clayton P.: Can Transaction Costs Reconcile the Differences Between the UCC and the CISG?, in: *Blaurock/Hager* (Hrsg.), Obligationenrecht im 21. Jahrhundert, Baden-Baden: Nomos (2010), S. 89–98 (Kurztitel: Transaction Costs)
Gillette, Clayton P.: Harmony and Stasis in Trade Usages for International Sales, Va. J. Int'l L. (1999), 707–741
Gillette, Clayton P./Scott, Robert E.: The Political Economy of International Sales, 25 Int'l Rev. L. & Econ. (2005), 446–486
Gillette, Clayton P./Walt, Steven D.: Sales Law – Domestic and International, 2. Aufl., New York: Fondation Press (2002)
Ginatta, Franco: Spunti sui criteri di collegamento e le riserve alla convenzione, in: La Vendita Internazionale, Mailand: Giuffrè (1981), S. 385–388
Girsberger, Daniel: The Time Limits of Article 39 CISG, 25 J. L. & Com. (2005), 241–251
Girsberger, Daniel: Verjährung und Verwirkung im internationalen Obligationenrecht, Zürich: Schulthess (1989) (Kurztitel: Verjährung und Verwirkung)

Girsberger, Daniel: Was hat Thurgauer Ahorn mit Ananas aus Afrika gemeinsam? Die schleichende Internationalisierung des schweizerischen Mängelrügerechts, in: *Schmid/Seiler* (Hrsg.), Recht des ländlichen Raums: Festgabe der Rechtswissenschaftlichen Fakultät der Universität Luzern für Paul Richli zum 60. Geburtstag, Zürich: Schulthess (2006), S. 225–241 (Kurztitel: FS Richli)

Giuliano, Adam M.: Nonconformity in the Sale of Goods between the United States and China: The new Chinese Contract Law, the Uniform Commercial Code, and the Convention on Contracts for the International Sale of Goods, 18 Fla. J. Int'l L. (2006), 331–358

Gliha, Igor: Überblick der Gesetzgebung Kroatiens im Bereich des Schuld-, Sachen- und Erbrechts, ZfRVgl 1993, 116–122

Godenhielm, Berndt: Some Views on the System of Remedies in the Uniform Law of International Sales, 10 Scand. Stud. L. (1966), 9–35

Goderre, Diane Madeline: International Negotiations Gone Sour: Precontractual Liability under the United Nations Sales Convention, 66 U. Cin. L. Rev. (1997), 258–281

Goger: Labor Disputes as Excusing. Under UCC § 2–615, Failure to deliver Goods sold, 70 A. L. B. 3d (1974), 1266–1269

Goldstajn, Aleksandar: The Contract of Goods Inspection, 14 Am. J. Comp. L. (1965), 383–394

Goldstajn, Aleksandar: The Formation of Contract, in: *Honnold* (Hrsg.), Unification of the Law Governing International Sales, Paris: Dalloz (1966), 41–54 (Kurztitel: Formation)

Goldstajn, Aleksandar: Usages of Trade and Other Autonomous Rules of International Trade According to the UN (1980) Sales Convention, in: *Šarkičevič/Volken* (Hrsg.), Dubrovnik Lectures, New York: Oceana (1986), S. 55–110 (Kurztitel: Usages of Trade)

Gomard, Bernhard/Rechnagel, Hardy: International Købelov (International Sales Law), Kopenhagen: Jurist- og Økonomforbundet (1990)

Goode, Roy M.: Commercial Law, 3. Aufl., London: Penguin (2004)

Goode, Roy M.: Litigation or Arbitration? The Influence of the Dispute Resolution Procedure in Substantive Rights, 19 Pace Int'l L. Rev. (2007), 53–62

Goode, Roy M.: Reflections on the Harmonisation of Commercial Law, Uniform L. Rev. 1991, 54–74

Goode, Roy M.: Usage and its reception in transnational commercial law, 46 Int'l. & Comp. L. Q. (1997), 1–36

Goodfriend, Douglas E.: After the Damage is Done: Risk of Loss Under the United Nations Convention on Contracts for the International Sale of Goods, 22 Colum. J. Transnat'l L. (1984), 575–606

Göritz, Andreas: Zur wesentlichen Vertragsverletzung beim Warenkauf – Wechselbeziehungen zwischen dem nordischen und dem international einheitlichen Recht. Vorträge, Reden und Berichte aus dem Europa-Institut Nr. 149, Saarbrücken: Europa-Institut (1988) (Kurztitel: Wesentliche Vertragsverletzung beim Warenkauf)

Gotanda, John Yukio: A Study of Interest, Villanova University School of Law Working Paper 83/2007, http://law.bepress.com/villanovalwps/papers/art83

Gotanda, John Yukio: Awarding Costs and Attorneys' Fees in International Commercial Arbitrations, 21 Mich. J. Int'l L. (1999), 1–50

Gotanda, John Yukio: Awarding Damages under the United Nations Convention on the International Sale of Goods: A Matter of Interpretation, 37 Geo. J. Int'l. L. (2005), 95–140

Gotanda, John Yukio: Awarding Interest in International Arbitration, 90 Am. J. Int'l L. (1996), 40–63

Gotanda, John Yukio: Conflict of interest: Article 78 CISG and Post-Judgement Interest Statutes, in: *Büchler/Müller-Chen* (Hrsg.), Private Law, national – global – comparative, Festschrift für Ingeborg Schwenzer zum 60. Geburtstag, Bern: Stämpfli (2011), S. 597–607 (Kurztitel: FS Schwenzer)

Gotanda, John Yukio: Using the UNIDROIT Principles to Fill Gaps in the CISG, in: *Saidov/Cunnington* (Hrsg.), Contract Damages: Domestic and International Perspectives, Oxford: Hart (2008), S. 107–122 (Kurztitel: Using PICC to Fill Gaps)

Gotanda, John Yukio: When Recessions Create Windfalls: The Problems of Using Domestic Law to Fix Interest Rates under Article 78 CISG, 13 VJ (2009), 300–325

Göttig, Triin: Estnisches und deutsches Leistungsstörungsrecht im Vergleich zum UN-Kaufrecht und den Grundregeln des Europäischen Vertragsrechts, ZfRV 2006, 138–152

Gottwald, Peter: Internationale Gerichtsstandsvereinbarungen: Verträge zwischen Prozessrecht und materiellem Recht, in: *Gerhardt/Diederichsen/Rimmelspacher/Costede* (Hrsg.), Festschrift für Wolfram Henckel zum 70. Geburtstag am 21. April 1995, Berlin, New York: de Gruyter (1995), S. 295–309 (Kurztitel: FS Henckel)

Graffi, Leonardo: Die Anwendung des CISG in einigen neueren italienischen Urteilen, EuLF 2000/2001, 240–244

Graffi, Leonardo: Divergences in the Interpretation of the CISG: The Concept of „Fundamental Breach", in: *Ferrari* (Hrsg.), The 1980 Uniform Sales Law. Old Issues Revisited in the Light of

Recent Experien-ces, Mailand/München: Giuffrè/Sellier European Law Publishers (2003), S. 305–323 (Kurztitel: Divergences)
Graffi, Leonardo: L'interpretazione autonoma della Convenzione di Vienna: rilevanza del precedente straniero e disciplina della lacune, Giur. merito 2004, 873–882
Graffi, Leonardo: Securing Harmonized Effects of Arbitration Agreements under the New York Convention, 28 Hous. J. Int'l L. (2006), 663–769
Graffi Leonardo: Spunti in tema di vendita internazionale e forum shopping, Dir. com. int. 2003, 807–828
Gränicher, Dieter: Die kollisionsrechtliche Anknüpfung ausländischer Devisenmassnahmen, Basel/Frankfurt a. M.: Helbing & Lichtenhahn (1984)
Graves, Jack: CISG Article 6 and Issues of Formation: The Problem of Circularity, Belgr. L. Rev. (2011), 124–139
Graveson, R. H./Cohn, Ernst Joseph/Graveson, Diana M.: The Uniform Laws on International Sales Act, 1967, London: Butterworths (1968) (Kurztitel: Uniform Laws on International Sales Act)
Grebler, Eduardo: Fundamental Breach of Contract Under the CISG: A Controversial Role, 101 ASIL Proc. (2007), 407–413
Greene, Sarah/Saidov, Djakhongir: Software as Goods, J. Bus. L. (2007), 161–181
Grewal, Shivbir S.: Risk of loss in Goods Sold During Transit: A Comparative Study of the United Nations Convention on Contracts for the International Sale of Goods, the Uniform Commercial Code, and the British Sale of Goods Act, 14 Loy. L. A. Int'l & Comp. L. J. (1991), 93–119
Grieser, Simon G.: Die Behandlung von atypischen Kaufverträgen im UN-Kaufrecht: Eine Untersuchung der Anwendbarkeit des UN-Kaufrechts auf den Leasing-, Mietkauf-, Vertriebsvertrag und andere Vertragstypen (Diss. Hamburg), Frankfurt a. M.: Peter Lang Verlag (2004)
Grigera Naón, Horacio A.: The UN Convention on Contracts for the International Sale of Goods, in: *Horn/Schmitthoff* (Hrsg.), The Transnational Law of International Commercial Transactions: Studies in Transnational Economic Law, Deventer: Kluwer Law and Taxation (1982), Bd. 2, S. 89–124 (Kurztitel: UN Convention on Contracts)
Griß, Irmgard: Akkreditiv und Wiener Kaufrecht, in: *Hoyer/Posch* (Hrsg.), Das Einheitliche Wiener Kaufrecht, Wien: Orac (1992), S. 207–213
Gröning, Jochem: Die Grundlagen des neuen Vergaberechtsschutzes, ZIP 1999, 52–59
Gros, Wolfgang: Bookbuilding, ZHR 162 (1998), 318–339
Grossfeld, Bernhard/Winship, Peter: The Law Professor Refugee, 18 Syracuse J. Int'l L. & Com. (1992), 3–20
Großmann-Doerth, Hans: Das Recht des Überseekaufs, Bd. I, Berlin, Leipzig: Bensheimer (1930) (Kurztitel: Überseekauf)
Großmann-Doerth, Hans: Die Rechtsfolgen vertragswidriger Andienung, Marburg: Elwert (1934) (Kurztitel: Andienung)
Grube, Lars: Verzugszinsen in Spanien, RIW 1992, 634–638
Gruber, Georg: Bemessung von Bereicherungsansprüchen bei schwankendem Geldwert, in: *Schwenzer/Hager* (Hrsg.), Festschrift für Peter Schlechtriem zum 70. Geburtstag, Tübingen: Mohr (2003), S. 721–741 (Kurztitel: FS Schlechtriem)
Gruber, Georg: Geldwertschwankungen und handelsrechtliche Verträge in Deutschland und Frankreich – Bestandsaufnahme und Aussichten für das europäische Währungs- und Privatrecht (Diss. Freiburg 2000), Berlin: Duncker & Humblot (2002)
Gruber, Urs Peter: Methoden des internationalen Einheitsrechts, Tübingen: Mohr Siebeck (2004) (Kurztitel: Methoden)
Grundmann, Stefan: Europäisches Schuldvertragsrecht: Das Europäische Recht der Unternehmensgeschäfte, Berlin, New York: de Gruyter (1999)
Grundmann, Stefan: Verbraucherrecht, Unternehmensrecht, Privatrecht – warum sind sich UN-Kaufrecht und EU-Kaufrechts-Richtlinie so ähnlich?, AcP 202 (2002), 40–71
Grunewald, Barbara: Der Verdacht als Mangel, in: *Dauner-Lieb/Hommelhoff/Jacobs/Kaise/Weber* (Hrsg.), Festschrift für Horst Konzen, Tübingen (2006), S. 131–140 (Kurztitel: FS Konzen)
Grunewald, Barbara: Die Grenzziehung zwischen der Rechts- und Sachmängelhaftung beim Kauf, Bonn: Stollfuß (1980)
Grunewald, Barbara: Kaufrecht, Handbuch des Schuldrechts, Band 6, Tübingen: Mohr (2006) (Kurztitel: Kaufrecht)
Grunsky, Wolfgang: Anwendbares Recht und gesetzlicher Zinssatz, in: *Gerhardt* (Hrsg.), Festschrift für Franz Merz, Köln: Verlag Kommunikationsforum, Recht, Wirtschaft, Steuern (1992), S. 147–157 (Kurztitel: FS Merz)
Grunsky, Wolfgang: Verzugsschaden und Geldentwertung, in: *Blatzer* (Hrsg.), Gedächtnisschrift für Rudolf Bruns, München: Vahlen (1980), S. 19–34 (Kurztitel: GS Bruns)

Literatur

Grüter, Karl: Die Auftragsbestätigung nach einheitlichem Kaufrecht, RIW 1975, 611–616
Gsell, Beate: Autonom bestimmter Gerichtsstand am Erfüllungsort nach der Brüssel I-Verordnung, IPRax 2002, 484–491
Gstoehl, Matthias: Das Verhältnis von Gewährleistung nach UN-Kaufrecht und Irrtumsanfechtung nach nationalem Recht, östZRVgl 1998, 1–10
Guhl, Theo/Koller, Alfred/Schnyder, Anton K./Druey, Jean Nicolas: Das Schweizerische Obligationenrecht mit Einschluss des Handels- und Wertpapierrechts, Zürich: Schulthess (2002) (Kurztitel: *Guhl/Bearbeiter*)
Gustin, Manuel: Le transfert des risques et l'impossibilité d'exécution dans la CVIM, R. D. A. I. 2001, 379–400
Gutknecht, Uta: Das Nacherfüllungsrecht des Verkäufers bei Kauf- und Werklieferungsverträgen. Rechtsvergleichende Untersuchung zum CISG, zum US-amerikanischen Uniform commercial code, zum deutschen Recht und zu dem Vorschlag der Kommission zur Überarbeitung des deutschen Schuldrechts (Diss. Hamburg), Frankfurt a. M.: Lang (1996)

Haack, Hansjörg: Erfüllung oder Schadenersatz? (Diss. Osnabrück 1990), Aachen: Shaker (1994)
Haage, Hans: Das Abladegeschäft, 4. Aufl., Hamburg: Cram/de Gruyter (1958)
Hachem, Pascal: Agreed Sums in CISG Contracts, Belgrade Law Review 2011, 140–149
Hachem, Pascal: Agreed Sums Payable Upon Breach of an Obligation – Rethinking Penalty And Liquidated Damages Clauses, Den Hague: Eleven International Publishing (2011) (Kurztitel: Agreed Sums)
Hachem, Pascal: Die Konturen des Prinzips *Pacta Sunt Servanda*, in: *Bühler/Müller-Chen* (Hrsg.), Festschrift für Ingeborg Schwenzer zum 60. Geburtstag, Bern: Stämpfli (2011), S. 647–668 (Kurztitel: FS Schwenzer)
Hachem, Pascal: Fixed Sums in CISG Contracts, 13 VJ (2009), 217–229
Hachem, Pascal: Prävention und Punitive Damages, in: *Wolf/Mona/Hürzeler* (Hrsg.), Prävention im Recht, Basel: Helbing Lichtenhahn (2008), 196–220 (Kurztitel: Punitive Damages)
Hachem, Pascal: Property Damages Under the CISG, in: *Schwenzer/Spagnolo* (Hrsg.), State of Play, The 3rd Annual MAA Peter Schlechtriem CISG Conference, The Hague: Eleven International Publishing (2012), S. 17–27 (Kurztitel: Property Damages)
Hachem, Pascal/Mohs, Florian: Verjährung von Ansprüchen des Käufers wegen Nichtlieferung und Lieferung vertragswidriger Ware aus CISG nach internem Schweizer Recht – Zugleich eine Urteilsanmerkung zum Entscheid des Bundesgerichts vom 18. Mai 2009, CISG-online 1900, AJP 2009, 1541–1549
Hackenberg, Ulf: Der Erfüllungsort von Leistungspflichten unter Berücksichtigung des Wirkungsortes von Erklärungen im UN-Kaufrecht und der Gerichtsstand des Erfüllungsortes im deutschen und europäischen Zivilprozessrecht, Hamburg: Kovac (2000)
Hackney, Philip: Is the United Nations Convention on the International Sale of Goods Achieving Uniformity?, 61 La. L. Rev. (2001), 473–486
Hadding, Walther/Schneider, Uwe H. (Hrsg.): Recht der Kreditsicherheiten in europäischen Ländern, Berlin: Duncker & Humblot, Teil III: Belgien, bearb. v. *Stranart-Thilly/Hainz* (1979); Teil IV: England, bearb. v. *Brink/Habel* (1980); Teil V: Schweiz, bearb. v. *Mühl/Petereit* (1983); Teil VI: Österreich, bearb. v. *Habel* (1986); Teil VII/1: Spanien, bearb. v. *Reichmann* (1988); Teil VIII: Griechenland, bearb. v. *Hamouzopoulos* (1999); Teil IX: Polen, bearb. v. *Brockhuis* (2000)
Hafez Mohamed: Modern Contract and Sales Law in the Middle Eastern and Arab Countries, a Comparativ Study (Diss. Basel), Köln: Lambert LAP Academic Publishing (2011)
Hager, Günter: Die Gefahrtragung beim Kauf – Eine rechtsvergleichende Untersuchung, Frankfurt a. M.: Metzner (1982) (Kurztitel: Gefahrtragung)
Hager, Günter: Die Rechtsbehelfe des Verkäufers wegen Nichtnahme der Ware nach amerikanischem, deutschem und einheitlichem Haager Kaufrecht (Diss. Freiburg), Frankfurt a. M.: Metzner (1975) (Kurztitel: Rechtsbehelfe des Verkäufers)
Hager, Günter: Gefahrtragung nach UN-Kaufrecht im Vergleich zu EKG und BGB, in: *Schlechtriem* (Hrsg.), Einheitliches Kaufrecht und nationales Obligationenrecht, Baden-Baden: Nomos (1987), S. 387–411 (Kurztitel: Gefahrtragung nach UN-Kaufrecht)
Hager, Günter: Schadenersatz bei antizipiertem Vertragsbruch, in: *Bühler/Müller-Chen* (Hrsg.), Festschrift für Ingeborg Schwenzer zum 60. Geburtstag, Bern: Stämpfli (2011), S. 681–696 (Kurztitel: FS Schwenzer)
Hager, Günter: Zur Auslegung des UN-Kaufrechts – Grundsätze und Methoden, in: *Baums u. a.* (Hrsg.), Festschrift für Ulrich Huber zum siebzigsten Geburtstag, Tübingen: Mohr Siebeck (2006), S. 319–339 (Kurztitel: FS U. Huber)
Hager, Günter/Bentele, Florian: Der Lieferort als Gerichtsstand – zur Auslegung des Art. 5 Nr. 1 lit. b EuGVO, IPRax 2004, 73–77
Hagstrøm, Viggo: CISG – Implementation in Norway, an approach not advisable, IHR 2006, 246–248

Hahnkamper, Wolfgang: Acceptance of an Offer in Light of Electronic Communications, 25 J. L. & Com. (2005–06), 147–151
Hammer, Wolf-Henning: Das Zurückbehaltungsrecht gemäss Art. 71 CISG im Vergleich zu den Kaufgesetzen der nordischen Staaten unter Einbeziehung transportrechtlicher Aspekte, Eine rechtsvergleichende Studie, Frankfurt a. M.: Lang (1999)
Hammerschmidt, Jana: Kollision Allgemeiner Geschäftsbedingungen im Geltungsbereich des UN-Kaufrechts (Diss. Göttingen 2004), Göttingen: Cuvillier (2004) (Kurztitel: Kollidierende AGB)
Han, Shiyuan: China, in: *Ferrari* (Hrsg.), The CISG and Its Impact on National Legal Systems, München: Sellier. European Law Publishers (2008), S. 71–91
Hancock, William A.: Special Report on the U. N. Convention on Contracts for the International Sale of Goods, Corporate Counsel's International Adviser, Issue No. 32 (January 1988) (Kurztitel: UN Convention)
Hancock, William A.: The Convention on Contracts for the International Sale of Goods and the Uniform Commercial Code, in: *Hancock* (Hrsg.), Guide to the International Sale of Goods Convention, Chesterland, Ohio: Business Laws (1992), 106.01–106.21 (Kurztitel: Convention on Contracts)
Hanisch, Hans: Das Genfer Abkommen über die Stellvertretung beim internationalen Warenkauf von 1983, in: *Habscheid* (Hrsg.), Festschrift zum 60. Geburtstag von Professor Dr. iur. Dr. phil Hans Giger, Bern: Stämpfli (1989), S. 251–267 (Kurztitel: FS Giger)
Happ, Richard: Anwendbarkeit völkerrechtlicher Auslegungsmethoden auf das UN-Kaufrecht, RIW 1997, 376–380
Happ, Richard/Roth, Marianne: Interpretation of uniform law instruments according to Principles of International Law, Uniform L. Rev. (1997), 702–711
Harjani, Sunil R.: The Convention on Contracts for the International Sale of Goods in United States Courts, 23 Houst. J. Int'l L. (2000), 49–90
Hart, Dieter: Alternativen zum Vertragsschluß – Begründung von vertraglichen Schuldverhältnissen durch Nicht-Willenserklärungen, in: *Brüggemeier/Hart*, Soziales Schuldrecht, Bremen: Universität Bremen (1987), S. 63–97
Hartkamp, A. S.: Das neue niederländische Bürgerliche Gesetzbuch aus europäischer Sicht, RabelsZ 57 (1993), 664–684
Hartkamp, A. S.: Einführung in das neue Niederländische Schuldrecht, Teil I: Rechtsgeschäfte und Verträge, AcP 191 (1991), 396–410
Hartkamp, A. S.: Einführung in das niederländische Schuldrecht, AcP 191 (1991), 396–410
Hartley, Trevor/Dogauchi, Masato: Explanatory Report on the 2005 Hague Choice of Court Agreements Convention, Den Haag: Haager Konferenz für Internationales Privatrecht (2007) (Kurztitel: Explanatory Report)
Hartmann, Felix: Ersatzherausgabe und Gewinnhaftung beim internationalen Warenkauf: Zugleich ein Beitrag zum Einfluss des UN-Kaufrechts auf die Entwicklung eines künftigen europäischen Vertragsrechts, IHR 2009, 189–201
Hartmann, Felix: Ungeschriebene Zurückbehaltungsrechte im UN-Kaufrecht, IHR 2006, 181–191
Hartmann, Stephan: Die Rückabwicklung von Schuldverträgen, Zürich: Schulthess (2005)
Hartnell, Helen Elizabeth: Rousing the Sleeping Dog: The Validity Exception to the Convention on Contracts for the International Sale of Goods, 18 Yale J. Int'l L. (1993), 1–93
Hartwieg, Oskar: Prozessuale Aspekte einheitlicher Anwendung der Wiener UN-Konvention über den Internationalen Warenkauf (CISG). Eine komparative Fall-Studie zur einheitlichen Rechtsanwendung, ZVerglRW 1993, 282–325
Hascher, Dominique: Anmerkung zu ICC-Schiedsspruch 6281/1989, J. D. I. 1991, 1056–1059
Hascher, Dominique: Anmerkung zu ICC-Schiedsspruch 7153/92, J. D. I. 1992, 1009
Hau, Wolfgang: Der Vertragsgerichtsstand zwischen judizieller Konsolidierung und legislativer Neukonzeption, IPRax 2000, 354–361
Hauschildt, Jürgen/Stahrenberg, Cora: Zur Effektivität von Inkasso-Unternehmen, BB 1991, 3–7
Häusler, Christoph: Das UNIDROIT Übereinkommen über internationales Factoring (Ottawa 1988) unter besonderer Berücksichtigung seiner Anwendbarkeit, zugleich ein Beitrag zur Lehre vom internationalen Einheitsrecht (Diss. Regensburg 1997), Frankfurt a. M.: Lang (1998)
Hausmann, Rainer: Zum teilweisen Ausschluß der Einheitlichen Kaufgesetze durch Allgemeine Geschäftsbedingungen, WM 1980, 726–737
Hay, Peter/Müller-Freienfels, Wolfram: Agency in the Conflict of Laws and The 1978 Hague Convention, 29 Am. J. Comp. L. (1979), 1–49
Hayward, Benjamin: The CISG in Australia – The Jigsaw Puzzle Missing A Piece, 14 VJ (2010), 193–222
Hayward, Benjamin/Perlen, Patricia: The CISG in Australia – The Jigsaw Puzzle That Doesn't Quite Fit, 15 VJ (2011), 119–156

Literatur

Heck, Philipp: Grundriß des Schuldrechts, Tübingen: Mohr (1929)
Heidrich, Joerg/Tschoepe, Sven: Rechtsprobleme der E-Mail-Filterung, MMR 2004, 75–80
Heiderhoff, Bettina/Skamel, Frank: Teilleistung im Kaufrecht, JZ 2006, 383–392
Heilmann, Jan: Mängelgewährleistung im UN-Kaufrecht – Voraussetzungen und Rechtsfolgen im Vergleich zum deutschen internen Kaufrecht und zu den Haager Einheitlichen Kaufgesetzen (Diss. Hamburg 1992), Berlin: Duncker & Humblot (1994)
von Hein, Jan: Die culpa in contrahendo im europäischen Privatrecht: Wechselwirkungen zwischen IPR und Sachrecht, GPR 2007, 54–61
Heinrichs, Helmut: AGB-Gesetz und Kreditwirtschaft – ausgewählte Probleme der Inhaltskontrolle, in: Hadding/Hopt (Hrsg.), Verbraucherkreditrecht, AGB-Gesetz und Kreditwirtschaft, Frankfurt a. M.: de Gruyter (1991), S. 101–117
Heinrichs, Helmut: Das Transparenzgebot und die EG-Richtlinie über mißbräuchliche Klauseln in Verbraucherverträgen, in: *Graf von Westphalen/Sandrock* (Hrsg.), Lebendiges Recht: von den Sumerern bis zur Gegenwart, Festschrift für Reinhold Trinkner zum 65. Geburtstag, Heidelberg: Recht und Wirtschaft (1995), S. 157–177 (Kurztitel: FS Trinkner)
Heiz, Christoph R.: Validity of Contracts Under the United Nations Convention on Contracts for the International Sale of Goods, April 11, 1980, and Swiss Contract Law, 20 Vand. J. Transnat'l L. (1987), 639–663
Heldrich, Andreas: Persönlichkeitsverletzungen im Internationalen Privatrecht, in: *von Caemmerer* (Hrsg.), Vorschläge und Gutachten zur Reform des deutschen internationalen Privatrechts der außervertraglichen Schuldverhältnisse, Tübingen: Mohr (1983), S. 380–439
Hellner, Jan: Das internationale Kaufrecht im Blickwinkel der Gesetzgebungstechnik, ZG 1988, 249–266
Hellner, Jan: Ipso facto avoidance, in: *Ehmann* (Hrsg.), Privatautonomie, Eigentum und Verantwortung, Festgabe für Hermann Weitnauer zum 70. Geburtstag, Berlin: Duncker & Humblot (1980), S. 85–99 (Kurztitel: Ipso facto avoidance)
Hellner, Jan: Sales and other contracts, in: *Tiberg* (Hrsg.), Swedish Law: A Survey, Stockholm: Juristförlaget (1994), 193–212 (Kurztitel: Swedish Law)
Hellner, Jan: The limits of Contractual Damages in the Scandinavian Law of Sales, 10 Scand. Stud. L. (1966), 37–79
Hellner, Jan: The Structure of Law in a Legislative Perspective, in: *Frändberg/van Höcke* (Hrsg.), The Structure of Law, Uppsala (1987), S. 101–114 (Kurztitel: Structure of Law)
Hellner, Jan: The UN Convention on International Sales of Goods – an Outsider's View, in: *Jayme* (Hrsg.), Ius inter nationes, Festschrift für Stefan Riesenfeld, Heidelberg: C. F. Müller (1983), S. 71–102 (Kurztitel: UN Convention)
Hellner, Jan: The Vienna Convention and Standard Form Contracts, in: *Šarčević/Volken* (Hrsg.), Dubrovnik Lectures, New York: Oceana (1986), S. 335–363 (Kurztitel: Standard Form Contracts)
Hellner, Jan: Unification of Sales Law at the Regional and International Level: A Scandinavian View, in: Ziegel/Foster (Hrsg.), Aspects of Comparative Commercial Law: Consumer Sales, Credit and Secured Transactions, New York: Oceana (1969), S. 90–109 (Kurztitel: Unification of Sales Law)
Hellwege, Phillip: Die Rückabwicklung gegenseitiger Verträge als einheitliches Problem, Tübingen: Mohr Siebeck (2004)
Helm, Johann Georg: Das Dokument des kombinierten Transports – ein neues Wertpapier, in: *Fischer* (Hrsg.), Strukturen und Entwicklungen im Handels-, Gesellschafts- und Wirtschaftsrecht. Festschrift für Wolfgang Hefermehl, München: Beck (1976), S. 57–73 (Kurztitel: FS Hefermehl)
Hennecke, Rudolf: Gefahrtragung beim Rücktransport der Ware, IHR 2003, 268–275
Hennemann, Marc Samuel: AGB-Kontrolle im UN-Kaufrecht aus deutscher und französischer Sicht (Diss. Tübingen 2001)
Henninger, Michael: Die Frage der Beweislast im Rahmen des UN-Kaufrechts: zugleich eine rechtsvergleichende Grundlagenstudie zur Beweislast, München: VVF (1995)
Henschel, René Franz: Conformity of Goods Governed by CISG Article 35: Caveat Venditor, Caveat Emptor and Contract Law as background Law and as a Competing Set of Rules, 1 Nordic J. Com. L. (2004), 1–21
Henschel, René Franz: The Conformity of Goods in International Sales – An analysis of Article 35 in the United Nations Convention on Contracts for the International Sale of Goods (CISG), Kopenhagen: Forlaget Thomson A/S (2005) (Kurztitel: Conformity of Goods)
Hepting, Reinhard: Die ADSp im internationalen Speditionsverkehr, RIW 1975, 457–464
Herber, Rolf: Anmerkung zu OLG Düsseldorf I-23 U 70/03 und LG Trier 7 HKO 134/03, IHR 2004, 117–118

Herber, Rolf: Anwendungsbereich des UNCITRAL-Kaufrechtsübereinkommens, in: *Doralt* (Hrsg.), Das UNCITRAL-Kaufrecht im Vergleich zum österreichischen Recht, Wien: Manz (1985), S. 28–45 (Kurztitel: Anwendungsbereich)

Herber, Rolf: Anwendungsvoraussetzungen und Anwendungsbereich des Einheitlichen Kaufrechts, in: *Schlechtriem* (Hrsg.), Einheitliches Kaufrecht und nationales Obligationenrecht, Baden-Baden: Nomos (1987), S. 97–105 (Kurztitel: Anwendungsvoraussetzungen)

Herber, Rolf: CLOUT, UNILEX und andere Veröffentlichungen zum internationalen Kaufrecht, RIW 1995, 502–504

Herber, Rolf: Das Arbeiten des Ausschusses der Vereinten Nationen für internationales Handelsrecht (UNCITRAL), RIW 1974, 577–584; RIW 1976, 125–133; RIW 1977, 314–320; RIW 1980, 81–87

Herber, Rolf: Das Verhältnis des CISG zu anderen Übereinkommen und Rechtsnormen, insbesondere zum Gemeinschaftsrecht der EU, IHR 2004, 89–94

Herber, Rolf: Das VN-Übereinkommen über internationale Kaufverträge, RIW 1980, 601–608

Herber, Rolf: Deutsche Einheit und internationales Kaufrecht, BB 1990, Beil. 37, 1–5

Herber, Rolf: Deutsche Einheit und internationales Kaufrecht. Eine Replik, BB 1991, Beil. 14, 7–10

Herber, Rolf: Eine neue Institution: Der CISG Advisory Council, IHR 2003, 201–202

Herber, Rolf: Einführung zum Wiener UNCITRAL-Kaufrecht, in: Bundesstelle für Aussenhandelsinformation (Hrsg.), Wiener UNCITRAL-Übereinkommen über internationale Warenkaufverträge vom 11. April 1980, 3. Aufl., Köln (1991), S. 1–57 (Kurztitel: Einführung)

Herber, Rolf: Gedanken zum Inkrafttreten des VN-Kaufrechtsübereinkommens, RIW 1987, 340–342

Herber, Rolf: Gesetzgebungsprobleme bei der internationalen Zivilrechtsvereinheitlichung, ZG 1987, 17–42

Herber, Rolf: Internationales Handelsrecht – ein für die Praxis wichtiges, doch für sie bisher zu wenig erschlossenes Rechtsgebiet, IHR 1999, 1–6

Herber, Rolf: „Lex mercatoria" und „Principles" – gefährliche Irrlichter im internationalen Kaufrecht, IHR 2003, 1–10

Herber, Rolf: Mangelfolgeschäden nach dem CISG und nationales Deliktsrecht – Zugleich Besprechung von Dirk Schneider, UN-Kaufrecht und Produktehaftpflicht, IHR 2001, 187–191

Herber, Rolf: Möglichkeiten der Vertragsgestaltung, in: *Bucher* (Hrsg.), Wiener Kaufrecht, Bern: Stämpfli (1991), S. 215–236 (Kurztitel: Möglichkeiten der Vertragsgestaltung)

Herber, Rolf: UN-Kaufrechtsübereinkommen: Produkthaftung -Verjährung, MDR 1993, 105–107

Herber, Rolf: Wiener UNCITRAL-Übereinkommen über internationale Warenkaufverträge vom 11. April 1980, 3. Aufl., Köln: Bundesstelle für Außenhandelsinformation (1991) (Kurztitel: UNCITRAL-Übereinkommen)

Herber, Rolf: Zum Verhältnis von UN-Kaufrechtsübereinkommen und deliktischer Haftung, in: *Schwenzer/Hager* (Hrsg.), Festschrift für Peter Schlechtriem zum 70. Geburtstag, Tübingen: Mohr (2003), S. 207–222 (Kurztitel: FS Schlechtriem)

Herber, Rolf/Czerwenka, Beate: Internationales Kaufrecht, Kommentar zu dem Übereinkommen der Vereinten Nationen vom 11. April 1980 über Verträge über den internationalen Warenkauf, München: Beck (1991)

Herbert, R.: La Convention Interamericana sobre el derecho aplicable a los contratos internacionales, Rev. Ur. Der. Int. Priv. 1995, 45 ff.

Herbots, Jacques H.: La responsabilité du fait d'auxiliaires dans la Convention de Vienne d'un point de vue droit comparé, in: *Majoros* (Hrsg.), Emptio – venditio inter nationes: Wiener Uebereinkommen über den internationalen Warenkauf: Festgabe, Basel: Recht und Gesellschaft (1997), S. 335–353 (Kurztitel: FS Neumayer)

Hermann, A. H.: International Trade Terms: Standard Terms for Contracts for the International Sale of Goods, London: Graham & Trotman (1993)

Herrmann, Gerold: Anwendbarkeit des Einheitskaufrechts auf Kaufvertrag mit Zweigniederlassung (Art. 1 Abs. 1 EKG), IPRax 1983, 212–215

Herrmann, Gerold: Anwendungsbereich des Wiener Kaufrechts – Kollisionsrechtliche Probleme, in: *Bucher* (Hrsg.), Wiener Kaufrecht, Bern: Stämpfli (1991), S. 83–99 (Kurztitel: Anwendungsbereich)

Herrmann, Gerold: Einheitliches Kaufrecht für die Welt: UN-Übereinkommen über internationale Warenkäufe, IPRax 1981, 109–113

Heß, Burkhard: Gerichtsstandsvereinbarungen zwischen EuGVÜ und ZPO, IPRax 1992, 358–361

Heuzé, Vincent: De quelques infirmités congénitales du droit uniforme: l'exemple de l'article 5.1 de la Convention de Bruxelles du 27 septembre 1968, Rev. crit. dr. int. privé 2000, 595–639

Heuzé, Vincent: La formation du contrat selon la CVIM: quelques difficultés, R. D. A. I. 2001, 277–291

Heuzé, Vincent: La vente internationale de marchandises – Droit uniforme, 2. Aufl., Paris: L. G. D. J. (2000)

Literatur

Heuzé, Vincent: Note Com. 1.3.1994, Rev. crit. dr. int. privé 1994, 673–680
Heymann, Ernst: Handelsgesetzbuch (ohne Seerecht), Band 4: Viertes Buch, §§ 343–475h, 2. Aufl., Berlin: de Gruyter Recht (2005) (Kurztitel: *Heymann/Bearbeiter*)
Heynen, Peter: Die Klausel „Kasse gegen Lieferschein", Hamburg: Hansa (1955)
Hilberg, Söntje Julia: Das neue UN-Übereinkommen zum elektronischen Geschäftsverkehr und dessen Verhältnis zum UN-Kaufrecht – Wegweiser in Sachen E-Commerce? (Teil I), IHR 2007, 12–24
Hilger, Norbert: Die verspätete Annahme – Eine vergleichende Betrachtung der §§ 149, 150 BGB und des Art. 9 EAG, AcP 185 (1985), 559–600
Hill, Anita F.: A comparative study of the United Nations Convention on the Limitation Period in the International Sale of Goods and section 2–725 of the Uniform Commercial Code, 25 Tex. Int'l L. J. (1990), 1–22
Hillman, Robert A.: Applying the United Nations Convention on Contracts for the International Sale of Goods: The Elusive Goal of Uniformity, 1 Rev. CISG (1995), 21–49
Hillman, Robert A.: Article 29 (2) of the United Nations Convention on Contracts for the International Sale of Goods: A New Effort at Clarifying the Legal Effect of „No Oral Modification" Clauses, 21 Cornell Int'l L. J. (1988), 449–466
Himmen, Tatjana: Die Lückenfüllung anhand allgemeiner Grundsätze im UN-Kaufrecht (Diss. Bielefeld), München (2007) (Kurztitel: Lückenfüllung)
Hirner, Matthias: Der Rechtsbehelf der Minderung nach dem UN-Kaufrecht (CISG) (Diss. Freiburg 1998), Frankfurt a. M.: Lang (2000)
Hoeren, Thomas: Der Softwareüberlassungsvertrag als Sachkauf, CR 1988, 908–917
Hoeren, Thomas/Martinek, Michael/Malzer, Matthias: Systematischer Kommentar zum Kaufrecht, Recklinghausen: Verlag für Rechts- und Anwaltspraxis (2002)
von Hoffmann, Bernd: Gewährleistungsansprüche im UN-Kaufrecht – verglichen mit dem EKG und BGB, in: *Schlechtriem* (Hrsg.), Einheitliches Kaufrecht und nationales Obligationenrecht, Baden-Baden: Nomos (1987), S. 293–303 (Kurztitel: Gewährleistungsansprüche)
von Hoffmann, Bernd: „Lex mercatoria" vor internationalen Schiedsgerichten, IPRax 1984, 106–108
von Hoffmann, Bernd: Passing of Risk in International Sales of Goods, in: *Šarčević/Volken* (Hrsg.), Dubrovnik Lectures, New York: Oceana (1986), S. 265–303 (Kurztitel: Passing of Risk)
von Hoffmann, Bernd: Staatsunternehmen im internationalen Privatrecht, Berichte der Deutschen Gesellschaft für Völkerrecht 25 (1984), 35–74
von Hoffmann, Bernd: Vertraglicher Ausschluß des UN-Übereinkommens über internationale Warenkaufverträge, RIW 1989, 513–518
von Hoffmann, Bernd: Zur Auslegung von Formularbedingungen des internationalen Handelsverkehrs, RIW 1970, 247–253
Hoffmann, Nadja: Die Koordination des Vertrags- und Deliktsrechts in Europa (Diss. Berlin 2004), Tübingen: Mohr Siebeck (2006) (Kurztitel: Koordination)
Hoffmann, Stefan-Georg/Ratajczak, Ines/Wiebusch, Martina: Exportverträge, Juristischer Wegweiser zum UN-Kaufrecht, Bonn: DIHT (1999)
Hofmann, Nathalie: Interpretation Rules and Good Faith as Obstacles to the UK's Ratification of the CISG and to the Harmonization of Contract Law in Europe, 22 Pace Int'l L. Rev. (2010), 145–182
Hohloch, Gerhard: Entlastung des Verkäufers nach Art. 79 CISG und Zulässigkeit eines Grundurteils, JuS 1999, 1235–1236
Holl, Volker H./Keßler, Oliver: „Selbstgeschaffenes Recht der Wirtschaft" und Einheitsrecht – Die Stellung der Handelsbräuche und Gepflogenheiten im Wiener UN-Kaufrecht, RIW 1995, 457–460
Holthausen, Rüdiger: Die wesentliche Vertragsverletzung nach Art. 25 UN-Kaufrecht, RIW 1990, 101–107
Holthausen, Rüdiger: Vertraglicher Ausschluß des UN-Übereinkommens über internationale Warenkaufverträge, RIW 1989, 513–518
Hondius, Ewoud: CISG and a European Civil Code, RabelsZ 71 (2007), 99–114
Honka, Hannu: Harmonization of Contract Law through International Trade: A Nordic Perspective, 11 Tul. Civ. L. F. (1996), 111–184
Honnold, John O. (Hrsg.): Documentary history of the uniform law for international sales. The studies, deliberations and decisions that led to the 1980 United Nations Convention with introductions and explanations, Deventer: Kluwer Law and Taxation (1989) (Kurztitel: Documentary history)
Honnold, John O. (Hrsg.): Unification of the Law Governing International Sales of Goods – The Comparison and Possible Harmonization of National and Regional Unifications (Colloquium IALS), Paris: Dalloz (1966) (Kurztitel: Unification of Law)
Honnold, John O.: International Sales Law and Open-Price Contract, in: Instituto de Investigaciones Jurídicas (Hrsg.), Estudios en Homenaje a Jorge Barrera Graf, Vol. II, Mexico: Universidad Nacional Autónoma de México (1989), 915–933 (Kurztitel: Open-Price Contract)

Honnold, John O.: Risk of Loss, in: *Galston/Smit* (Hrsg.), International Sales, New York: Matthew Bender (1984), Kap. 8, S. 1–15 (Kurztitel: Risk of Loss)
Honnold, John O.: The 1980 Sales Convention – Can Uniform Words Give Us Uniform Results?, JT 1990–91, 3–14
Honnold, John O.: The Draft Convention on Contracts for the International Sale of Goods: An Overview, 27 Am. J. Comp. L. (1979), 223–230
Honnold, John O.: The Sales Convention in Action – Uniform International Words: Uniform Application?, 8 J. L. & Com. (1988), 207–212
Honnold, John O.: The Sales Convention: Background, Status, Application, 8 J. L. & Com. (1988), 1–10
Honnold, John O.: UN Convention on Contracts for the International Sale of Goods 1980, 15 J. World Trade L. (1981), 265–267
Honnold, John O.: Uniform Law and Uniform Trade Terms – Two Approaches to a Common Goal, in: *Horn* (Hrsg.), The transnational law of international commercial transactions, Deventer: Kluwer (1982), S. 161–172 (Kurztitel: Uniform Law and Trade Terms)
Honnold, John O.: Uniform Law for International Sales Under the 1980 United Nations Convention, 2. Aufl., Deventer: Kluwer Law and Taxation (1991)
Honnold, John O.: Uniform Law for International Sales Under the 1980 United Nations Convention, 3. Aufl., The Hague: Kluwer International Law (1999) (Kurztitel: *Honnold*)
Honnold, John O.: Uniform Law for International Trade – Progress and Prospects, 20 Int'l Law. (1986), 635–639
Honnold, John O.: Uniform Words and Uniform Application. The 1980 Sales Convention and International Juridicial Practice, in: *Schlechtriem* (Hrsg.), Einheitliches Kaufrecht und nationales Obligationenrecht, Baden-Baden: Nomos (1987), S. 115–146 (Kurztitel: Uniform Words)
Honnold, John O./Flechtner, Harry M.: Uniform Law for International Sale under the 1980 United Nations Convention, 4. Aufl., The Hague: Kluwer Law International (2009) (Kurztitel: *Honnold/ Flechtner*)
Honsell, Heinrich: Das Übereinkommen über den internationalen Warenkauf (Wiener Kaufrecht), plädoyer 2/1990, 38–44
Honsell, Heinrich: Der Vermögensschaden bei der Geldschuld, in: *Medicus* (Hrsg.), Festschrift für Hermann Lange zum 70. Geburtstag, Stuttgart: Kohlhammer (1992), S. 509–521 (Kurztitel: FS Lange)
Honsell, Heinrich: Die Vertragsverletzung des Verkäufers nach dem Wiener Kaufrecht, SJZ 1992, 345–354, 361–365
Honsell, Heinrich (Hrsg.): Kommentar zum UN-Kaufrecht. Übereinkommen der Vereinten Nationen über Verträge über den Internationalen Warenkauf (CISG), Berlin/New York: Springer (1997) (Kurztitel: Honsell/Bearbeiter)
Honsell, Heinrich: Kommentar zum UN-Kaufrecht, 2. Auflage, Berlin/Heidelberg: Springer (2010) (Kurztitel: Honsell/Bearbeiter)
Honsell, Heinrich: Schweizerisches Obligationenrecht, Besonderer Teil, 7. Aufl., Bern: Stämpfli (2003) (Kurztitel: OR BT)
Horn, Norbert: Die Anpassung langfristiger Verträge im internationalen Wirtschaftsverkehr – Vertragsklauseln und Schiedspraxis, in: *Kötz/von Bieberstein* (Hrsg.): Die Anpassung langfristiger Verträge – Vertragsklauseln und Schiedspraxis, Verhandlungen der Vereinigten Fachgruppen für Zivilrechtsvergleichung und für vergleichendes Handels- und Wirtschaftsrecht anläßlich der Tagung für Rechtsvergleichung im Bonn vom 21. bis zum 24.9.1983, Frankfurt a. M.: Metzner (1984), S. 9–71 (Kurztitel: Anpassung langfristiger Verträge)
Horn, Norbert: Standard Clauses on Contract and Adaptation in international Commerce, in: *Horn* (Hrsg.), Adaptation and Renegotiation of Contracts in International Trade and Finance, Deventer: Kluwer (1985), S. 111–140
Horn, Norbert: Vertragsdauer: Die Vertragsdauer als schuldrechtliches Regelungsproblem: Empfiehlt sich eine zusammenfassende Regelung der Sonderprobleme von Dauerschuldverhältnissen und langfristigen Verträgen?, in: Bundesministerium der Justiz (Hrsg.), Gutachten und Vorschläge zur Überarbeitung des Schuldrechts, Köln: Bundesanzeiger (1981), S. 551–645 (Kurztitel: Vertragsdauer)
Hornung, Rainer: Die Rückabwicklung gescheiterter Verträge nach französischem, deutschem und nach Einheitsrecht: Gemeinsamkeiten, Unterschiede, Wechselwirkungen (Diss. Freiburg), Baden-Baden: Nomos (1998)
Horowitz, Andrew J.: Revisiting Barter under the CISG, 29 J. L. & Com. (2010), 99–116
van Houtte, Hans: The Law of International Trade, London: Sweet & Maxwell (2002) (Kurztitel: International Trade)
Hoyer, Hans: Der Anwendungsbereich des Einheitlichen Wiener Kaufrechts, in: *Hoyer/Posch* (Hrsg.), Das Einheitliche Wiener Kaufrecht, Wien: Orac (1992), S. 31–42 (Kurztitel: Anwendungsbereich)

Literatur

Hoyer, Hans: Der Anwendungsbereich des UNCITRAL-Einheitskaufrechts, WBl. 1988, 70–72
Hoyer, Hans/Posch, Willibald (Hrsg.): Das Einheitliche Wiener Kaufrecht. Neues Recht für den internationalen Warenkauf, Wien: Orac (1992) (Kurztitel: Das Einheitliche Wiener Kaufrecht)
Huber, Peter: CISG – the Structure of Remedies, RabelsZ 71 (2007), 13–34
Huber, Peter: Die Konkurrenz von Irrtumsanfechtung und Sachmängelhaftung im neuen Schuldrecht, in: *Häuser/Hammen/Hennrichs/Steinbeck/Siebel/Walter* (Hrsg.), Festschrift für Walter Hadding zum 70. Geburtstag am 8. Mai 2004, Berlin: De Gruyter Recht (2004), S. 105–119 (Kurztitel: FS Hadding)
Huber, Peter: Internationales Deliktsrecht und Einheitskaufrecht (zu BGH, 28.11.1994 – VIII ZR 44/94, IPRax 1996, 124), IPRax 1996, 91–95
Huber, Peter: Irrtumsanfechtung und Sachmängelhaftung, Tübingen: Mohr (2001) (Kurztitel: Irrtumsanfechtung)
Huber, Peter: On the beaten track – the European DCFR and the CISG, in: *Büchler/Müller-Chen* (Hrsg.), Private Law, national – global – comparative, Festschrift für Ingeborg Schwenzer zum 60. Geburtstag, Bern: Stämpfli (2011), S. 807–826 (Kurztitel: FS Schwenzer)
Huber, Peter: Rügeversäumnis nach UN-Kaufrecht (zu OGH, 19.12.2007 – 9 Ob 75/07f), IPRax 2009, 89–90
Huber, Peter: Some introductory remarks on the CISG, IHR 2006, 228–238
Huber, Peter: Standard Terms under the CISG, 13 VJ (2009), 123–134
Huber, Peter: Typically German? – Two Contentious German Contributions to the CISG, 3 Belgr. L Rev. 2011, 150–161
Huber, Peter: UN-Kaufrecht und Irrtumsanfechtung. Die Anwendung nationalen Rechts bei einem Eigenschaftsirrtum des Käufers, ZEuP 1994, 585–602
Huber, Peter: Vertragswidrigkeit und Handelsbrauch im UN-Kaufrecht – zu OGH, 27.2.2003 – 2 Ob 48/02a, IPRax 2004, 358–360
Huber, Peter: Zug-um-Zug-Verurteilung, Annahmeverzug und UN-Kaufrecht, IPRax 2001, 557–561
Huber, Peter/Bach, Ivo: Cover Purchase Without Avoidance: Welcome When Worthwile, in: *Kröll/Mistelis/Perales Viscasillas/Roger* (Hrsg.), International Arbitration and International Commercial Law: synergy, convergence, and evolution: liber amicorum Eric Bergsten, Alphen aan den Rijn: Kluwer Law International (2011), S. 585–595 (Kurztitel: FS Bergsten)
Huber, Peter/Kröll, Stefan: Deutsche Rechtsprechung zum UN-Kaufrecht in den Jahren 2001/2002, IPRax 2003, 309–317
Huber, Peter/Mullis, Alastair: The CISG, A new textbook for students and practitioners, München: Sellier (2007) (Kurztitel: Huber/Mullis)
Huber, Ulrich: Das Einheitliche Gesetz über den internationalen Kauf beweglicher Sachen, DB 1975, 1205–1211
Huber, Ulrich: Der UNCITRAL-Entwurf eines Übereinkommens über internationale Warenkaufverträge, RabelsZ 43 (1979), 413–526
Huber, Ulrich: Die Haftung des Verkäufers für Verzug und Sachmängel nach dem Wiener Kaufrechtsübereinkommen, östJBl 1989, 273–284
Huber, Ulrich: Die Haftung des Verkäufers nach dem Kaufrechtsübereinkommen der Vereinten Nationen und nach deutschem Recht, Berlin: de Gruyter (1991) (Kurztitel: Haftung des Verkäufers)
Huber, Ulrich: Die Rechtsbehelfe der Parteien, insbesondere der Erfüllungsanspruch, die Vertragsaufhebung und ihre Folgen nach UN-Kaufrecht im Vergleich zu EKG und BGB, in: *Schlechtriem* (Hrsg.), Einheitliches Kaufrecht und nationales Obligationenrecht, Baden-Baden: Nomos (1987), S. 199–223 (Kurztitel: Rechtsbehelfe der Parteien)
Huber, Ulrich: Leistungsstörungen: Empfiehlt sich die Einführung eines Leistungsstörungsrechts nach dem Vorbild des Einheitlichen Kaufgesetzes? Welche Änderungen im Gesetzestext und welche praktischen Auswirkungen im Schuldrecht würden sich dabei ergeben?, in: Bundesminister der Justiz (Hrsg.), Gutachten und Vorschläge zur Überarbeitung des Schuldrechts, Köln: Bundesanzeiger (1981), Bd. 1, S. 647–909 (Kurztitel: Leistungsstörungen)
Huber, Ulrich: Leistungsstörungen, in: *Gernhuber* (Hrsg.), Handbuch des Schuldrechts in Einzeldarstellungen, Band 9 Teilband 1: Die allgemeinen Grundlagen; der Tatbestand des Schuldnerverzuges; die vom Schuldner zu vertretenden Umstände; Teilband 2: Die Folgen des Schuldnerverzuges; Die Erfüllungsverweigerung und die vom Schuldner zu vertretende Unmöglichkeit, Tübingen: Mohr (1999) (Kurztitel: Handbuch/Leistungsstörungen)
Huber, Ulrich: Modellregeln für ein Europäisches Kaufrecht, ZEuP 2008, 708–744
Huber, Ulrich: Probleme des Rechts der Leistungsstörungen im Lichte des Haager Einheitlichen Kaufrechts, JZ 1974, 433–446

Huber, Ulrich: Right of Stoppage in Transitu und deutsches Konkursrecht, in: *Bökelmann/Henckel/Jahr* (Hrsg.), Festschrift für Friedrich Weber zum 70. Geburtstag am 19. Mai 1975, Berlin: de Gruyter (1975), S. 253–273 (Kurztitel: FS Weber)
Hudson, A. H.: Exemptions and Impossibility under The Vienna Convention, in: *McKendrick* (Hrsg.), Force Majeure and Frustration of Contract, 2. Aufl., London: Lloyd's of London Press (1995), S. 175–194
Hutter, Max: Die Haftung des Verkäufers für Nichtlieferung bzw. Lieferung vertragswidriger Ware nach dem Wiener UNCITRAL-Übereinkommen über internationale Warenkaufverträge vom 11. April 1980 (Diss. Regensburg 1988)
Huwiler, Bruno: Die „Vertragsmäßigkeit der Ware", Romanistische Gedanken zu Art. 35 und 45 ff. des Wiener Kaufrechts, in: *Bucher* (Hrsg.), Wiener Kaufrecht, Bern: Stämpfli (1991), S. 249–274
Hyland, Richard: Conformity of Goods to the Contract Under the United Nations Sales Convention and the Uniform Commercial Code, in: *Schlechtriem* (Hrsg.), Einheitliches Kaufrecht und nationales Obligationenrecht, Baden-Baden: Nomos (1987), S. 305–341 (Kurztitel: Conformity of Goods)
Hyland, Richard: Draft, 97 Colum. L. Rev. (1997), S. 1343–1362

Illescas Ortiz, De Rafael/Perales Viscasillas, Pilar: Derecho Mercantil Internacional. El Derecho Uniforme, Madrid: Centro de Estudios Ramon Areces (2003)
Imberg, Alexander: Die Verteilung der Beweislast beim Gefahrübergang nach UN-Kaufrecht (Diss. Mainz 1997), Frankfurt a. M.: Lang (1998)
Imberg, Alexander P./Grijalva Ernesto: The Economic Impact of International Trade on San Diego and the Application of the United Nations Convention on the International Sale of Goods to San Diego/Tijuana Commercial Transactions, 35 San Diego L. Rev. (1998), 769–782

Jäckle, Wolfgang: Effektivität und Erstattungsfähigkeit der Kosten eines Inkassounternehmens, BB 1993, 2463–2467
Jäckle, Wolfgang: Erstattung der Inkassokosten, NJW 1995, 2767–2769
Jacobs, Christopher M.: Notice of Avoidance Under the CISG: A Practical Examination of Substance and Form Considerations, the Validity of Implicit Notice, and the Question of Revocability, 64 U. Pitt. L. Rev. (2003)
Jafarzadeh, Mirghasem: Buyer's Right to Withhold Performance and Termination of Contract – A Comparative Study Under English Law, Vienna Convention on Contract fort he International Sale of Goods 1980, Iranian and Shi'ah Law, http://cisgw3.law.pace.edu/cisg/biblio/jafarzadeh1.html (2001) (Kurztitel: Termination)
Jaffé, Michael: Die Anknüpfung der Verjährung im deutsch-amerikanischen Rechtsverkehr sowie das Institut der Verjährung beim Handelskauf beweglicher Sachen im Staate New York (Diss. Regensburg 1994)
Jäger, Markus: Reimbursement for Attorney's Fees – A comparative study of the laws of Switzerland, Germany, France, England and the United States of America; International Arbitration Rules and the United Nations Convention on Contracts for the International Sale of Goods (CISG) (Diss. Basel 2009), The Hague: Eleven International Publishing (2010) (Kurztitel: Attorney's Fees)
Jakobs, Horst Heinrich: Unmöglichkeit und Nichterfüllung, Bonn: Röhrscheidt (1969) (Kurztitel: Unmöglichkeit und Nichterfüllung)
Jametti Greiner, Monique: Der Vertragsabschluß – Zeitpunkt, Formvorschriften, rechtsgeschäftliche Erklärungen, in: *Hoyer/Posch* (Hrsg.), Das Einheitliche Wiener Kaufrecht, Wien: Orac (1992), S. 43–57 (Kurztitel: Vertragsabschluß)
Jametti Greiner, Monique: Neues Lugano-Übereinkommen: Stand der Arbeiten, in: *Spühler* (Hrsg.), Internationales Zivilprozess- und Verfahrensrecht II, Zürich: Schulthess (2003), S. 113–126 (Kurztitel: Neues Lugano-Übereinkommen)
Jan, Sheng-Lin: Die Erfüllungsverweigerung im deutschen und im UN-Kaufrecht (Diss. Frankfurt a. M. 1992), Frankfurt a. M.: Lang (1992)
Janal, Ruth M.: Sanktionen und Rechtsbehelfe bei der Verletzung verbraucherschützender Informations- und Dokumentationspflichten im elektronischen Geschäftsverkehr, (Diss. Freiburg 2003), Berlin: Tenea Verlag für Medien (2003)
Janal, Ruth M.: The Seller's Responsibility for Third Party Intellectual Property Rights under the Vienna Sales Convention, in: *Andersen/Schroeter* (Hrsg.), Sharing International Commercial Law across National Boundaries: Festschrift for Albert H. Kritzer on the Occasion of his 80th Birthday, London: Wildy, Simmonds & Hill (2008), S. 203–231 (Kurztitel: FS Kritzer)
Jansen, Nils/Zimmermann, Reinhard: Contract Formation and Mistake in European Contract Law: A Genetic Comparison of Transnational Model Rules, Oxford J. Legal Stud. 2011, 1–38

Literatur

Janssen, André: Das Verhältnis nationaler Verjährungsvorschriften zur Ausschlussfrist des Art. 39 Abs. 2 CISG in der Schweiz, IPRax 2003, 369–372

Janssen, André: Die Einbeziehung von allgemeinen Geschäftsbedingungen in internationale Kaufverträge und die Bedeutung der UNIDROIT- und der Lando-Principles, IHR 2004, 194–200

Janssen, André: Die Untersuchungs- und Rügepflichten im deutschen, niederländischen und internationalen Kaufrecht, Eine rechtsvergleichende Darstellung der Gemeinsamkeiten und Unterschiede, Baden-Baden: Nomos (2001)

Janssen, André: Kollidierende Allgemeine Geschäftsbedingungen im internationalen Kaufrecht (CISG), wbl 2002, 453–457

Janssen, André: Nach welchem Recht richtet sich die Einbeziehung von Allgemeinen Geschäftsbedingungen in den Niederlanden?, IHR 2005, 155–158

Janssen, André: The Application of the CISG in Dutch Courts, in: *Ferrari* (Hrsg.), Quo Vadis CISG? Celebrating the 25th anniversary of the United Nations Convention on Contracts for the International Sale of Goods, München: Sellier (2005), S. 129–165 (Kurztitel: Application)

Janssen, André/Kiene, Sören Claas: The CISG and Its General Principles, in: *Janssen/Meyer* (Hrsg.), CISG Methodology, München: Sellier. European Law Publishers (2009), S. 261–285 (Kurztitel: General Principles)

Jauernig, Othmar (Hrsg.): Bürgerliches Gesetzbuch, erl. v. *Jauernig, Schlechtriem, Stürner, Teichmann, Vollkommer*, 10. Aufl., München: Beck (2002) (Kurztitel: *Jauernig/Bearbeiter*)

Jauernig, Othmar: Zeitliche Grenzen für die Genehmigung von Rechtsgeschäften eines falsus procurator?, in: *Jayme* (Hrsg.), Festschrift für Hubert Niederländer zum siebzigsten Geburtstag am 10. Februar 1991, Heidelberg: Winter (1991), S. 285–294 (Kurztitel: FS Niederländer)

Jayme, Erik: Ein Klägergerichtsstand für den Verkäufer – Der EuGH verfehlt den Sinn des EuGVÜ, IPRax 1995, 13–14

Jayme, Erik: Tagung der Deutsch-Italienischen Juristenvereinigung in Fulda, IPRax 1989, 332–333

Jegher, Gion: Luganer Gerichtsstand am Erfüllungsort – Quo vadis?, in: *Berti/Girsberger* (Hrsg.), „nur, aber immerhin": Beiträge zum nationalen und internationalen Wirtschaftsrecht: Festgabe für Anton K. Schnyder zum 50. Geburtstag, Zürich: Schulthess (2002), S. 117–129 (Kurztitel: FS Schnyder)

Jenkins, Sarah: Exemption for Nonperformance: UCC, CISG, UNIDROIT-Principles – A Comparative Assessment, 72 Tul. L. Rev. (1998), 2015–2030

Jentsch, Armin: Die Erhaltungspflichten des Verkäufers und des Käufers im UN-Kaufrecht im Vergleich zum US-amerikanischen Uniform Commercial Code und zum deutschen Recht (Diss. Hamburg 2002), Frankfurt a. M. u. a.: Peter Lang (2002) (Kurztitel: Erhaltungspflichten)

Johannsen, Sandra: Der Vorbehalt der skandinavischen Staaten gemäss Art. 92 CISG (Diss. Kiel 2003), Baden-Baden: Nomos (2004) (Kurztitel: Vorbehalt)

John, Uwe: Grundsätzliches zum Wirksamwerden empfangsbedürftiger Willenserklärungen, AcP 184 (1984), 385–412

Johnson, William P: Understanding Exclusion oft he CISG: A New Paradigm of Determining Party Intent, 59 Buff. L. Rev. (2011), 213–292

Jokela, Heikki: The Role of Usages in the Uniform Law on International Sales, 10 Scand. Stud. L. (1966), 81–96

Jones, Gareth: Must the Party in Breach Account for Profits from his Breach of Contract?, in: *Schwenzer/Hager* (Hrsg.), Festschrift für Peter Schlechtriem zum 70. Geburtstag, Tübingen: Mohr (2003), S. 763–774 (Kurztitel: FS Schlechtriem)

Jones, Gareth H./Schlechtriem, Peter: Breach of Contract (Deficiences in a party's performance), in: Int. Enc. Comp. L., Under the Auspices of the I. A. L. S., Vol. VII: Contracts in General, ch. 15, Tübingen: Mohr (1999) (Kurztitel: Breach of Contract)

Jörs, Paul/Kunkel, Wolfgang/Wenger, Leopold: Römisches Recht, bearb. v. *Honsell, Mayer-Maly, Selb*, 4. Aufl., Berlin: Springer (1987) (Kurztitel: *Jörs/Kunkel/Bearbeiter*)

Joseph, James Edward: Contract Formation Under the United Nations Convention on Contracts for the International Sale of Goods and the Uniform Commercial Code, 3 Dick. J. Int'l L. (1984), 107–138

Juan Yang, Sophia: The Modern Sales Contract Law in Asia (Diss. Basel 2010)

Jung, Reinhard: Die Beweislastverteilung im UN-Kaufrecht, insbesondere bei Vertragsabschluß, bei Vertragsverletzungen des Käufers, bei allgemeinen Bestimmungen sowie bei gemeinsamen Bestimmungen über Verkäufer- und Käuferpflichten (Diss. Mainz), Frankfurt a. M.: Lang (1996)

Junge, Werner: Das Kammergutachten, in: Wirtschaft und Verwaltung (1987), 195–206

Junker, Abbo: Die einheitliche Auslegung nach dem EG-Schuldvertragsübereinkommen, RabelsZ 55 (1991), 674–696

Junker, Abbo: Vom Brüsseler Übereinkommen zur Brüsseler Verordnung – Wandlungen des Internationalen Zivilprozessrechts, RIW 202, 569–577

Jurewicz, Aleksandra: A Milestone in Polish CISG Jurisprudence and Its Significance to the World Trade Community, 28 J. L. & Com. (2009), 63–74

Kabik, Michael: Through the Looking Glass: International Trade in the „Wonderland" of the United Nations Convention on Contracts for the International Sale of Goods, 9 Int'l Tax & Bus. Law. (1992), 408–430

Kaczorowska, Alina: Règles uniformes d'interpétation d'un contrat international, R. D. I. D. C. 1991, 294–313

Kadner, Thomas: Gerichtsstand des Erfüllungsortes im EuGVÜ, Einheitliches Kaufrecht und international-zivilprozessuale Gerechtigkeit, Jura 1997, 240–248

Käerdi, Martin: Abgrenzung der vertraglichen und außervertraglichen Haftungssysteme im deutschen, estnischen und im Einheitsrecht, Nomos: Baden-Baden (2006)

Kahn, Philippe: Anmerkung zu CA Grenoble 29.3.1995, J. D. I. 1995, 969–971

Kahn, Philippe: Convention de Vienne du 11 avril 1980 – Caractères et domaine d'application des règles conventionelles, Dr. prat. com. int. 1989, 385–399

Kahn, Philippe: Etude comparée des Conventions de la Haye du 1er juillet 1964 sur la vente internationale des objets mobiliers corporels et la formation du contrat de vente, et projet de Convention sur les contrats de vente internationale de marchandises préparée par la CNUDCI, Brüssel: Commission des Communautés Européennes (1979) (Kurztitel: Etude comparée)

Kahn, Philippe: La Convention de Vienne du 11 avril 1980 sur les contrats de vente internationale de marchandises, Rev. int. dr. comp. 1981, 951–986

Kahn, Philippe: La vente commerciale internationale (Diss. Dijon), Paris: Sirey (1961)

Kahn, Philippe: Qu'est-ce que la vente?, Int'l Bus. L. J. 2001, 241–252

Kaiser, Dagmar: Die Rückabwicklung gegenseitiger Verträge wegen Nicht- und Schlechterfüllung nach BGB (Rücktritts-, Bereicherungs- und Schadenersatzrecht), unveröffentlichte Freiburger Habilitationsschrift

Kamanabrou, Sudabeh: Vertragliche Anpassungsklauseln, München: Beck (2004)

Kampf, Achim: UN-Kaufrecht und Kollisionsrecht, RIW 2009, 297–301

Kanda, Antonín: Nichterfüllung eines internationalen Kaufvertrages: Die Regelungen des tschechoslowakischen Gesetzes über den internationalen Handel und des Haager Einheitlichen Kaufgesetzes, RabelsZ 34 (1970), 315–335

Kanning, Arnold J.: Het Weense Koopverdrag, Een transactiekosten-benadering, TvP 1996, 883–907

Kantor, Mark: The Convention on Contracts for the International Sale of Goods: An International Sales Law, 1 Int'l law pract. (NYSBA) (1988), 8–14

Kappus, Andreas: „Lex mercatoria" in Europa und Wiener UN-Kaufrechtskonvention 1980. „Conflict avoidance" in Theorie und Praxis. Schiedsrichterliche und ordentliche Rechtsprechung in Konkurrenz zum Einheitskaufrecht der Vereinten Nationen (Diss. Innsbruck), Frankfurt a. M.: Lang (1990) (Kurztitel: Lex Mercatoria)

Kappus, Andreas: Rechtsvergleichende Aspekte zur Vertragsaufhebung wegen Sachmangels nach UN-Kaufrecht, RIW 1992, 528–533

Kappus, Andreas: Vertragsaufhebung nach UN-Kaufrecht in der Praxis, NJW 1994, 984–985

Karollus, Martin: Anmerkung zu BGH, Urt. v. 31.10.2001 – VIII ZR 60/01, LM 3/2002 CISG Nr. 9

Karollus, Martin: Der Anwendungsbereich des UN-Kaufrechts im Überblick, JuS 1993, 378–382

Karollus, Martin: Judicial interpretation and application of the CISG in Germany 1988–1994, 1 Rev. CISG (1995), 51–94

Karollus, Martin: OGH: Vertragsabschluss, Nichtlieferung und Schadenersatz nach dem UN-Kaufrecht, RdW 1996, 197–199

Karollus, Martin: UN-Kaufrecht, Wien/New York: Springer (1991)

Karollus, Martin: UN-Kaufrecht: Hinweise für die Vertragspraxis, östJBl 1993, 23–33

Karollus, Martin: UN-Kaufrecht: Vertragsaufhebung und Nacherfüllungsrecht bei Lieferung mangelhafter Ware, ZIP 1993, 490–497

Karton, Joshua: Contract Law in International Commercial Arbitration: The Case of Suspension of Performance, 58 Int'l & Comp. L. Q. (2009), 863–896

Karton, Joshua D. H./de Germiny, Lorraine: Has the CISG Advisory Council Come of Age?, 27 Berkeley J. Int'l L. (2009), 448–495

Kaser, Max: Das römische Privatrecht, Bd. 1, 2. Aufl., München: Beck (1971) (Kurztitel: Kaser I); Bd. 2, 2. Aufl., München: Beck (1975) (Kurztitel: Kaser II)

Kaser, Max/Knütel, Rolf: Römisches Privatrecht, 18. Aufl., München: Beck (2005)

Literatur

Kastely, Amy H.: The Right to Require Performance in International Sales: Towards an International Interpretation of the Vienna Convention, 63 Wash. L. Rev. (1988), 607–651

Kastely, Amy H.: Unification and Community: A Rhetorical Analysis of the United Nations Sales Convention, 8 Nw. J. Int'l L. & Bus. (1988), 574–622

Kathrein, Reed R./Magraw, Daniel Barstow (Hrsg.): The Convention for the International Sale of Goods: A Handbook of Basic Materials, Washington, D. C.: A. B. A. Section of International Law and Practice (1990)

Katzarov, Konstantin: Katzarov's Manual on Industrial Property: All over the World, 9. Aufl., Genf: Katzarov SA (1981)

Kaufmann, Sebastian: Parol Evidence Rule und Merger Clauses im internationalen Einheitsrecht, (Diss. Frankfurt 2004), Frankfurt a. M.: Lang (2004) (Kurztitel: Parol Evidence Rule)

Kaye, Peter: Civil Jurisdiction and Enforcement of Foreign Judgments, Abindon, Oxon: Professional Books Limited (1987) (Kurztitel: Civil Jurisdiction)

Kaye, Peter: The new privat international law of contract of the European Community, Implementation of the EEC's contractual obligations convention in England and Wales under the contracts (applicable law) act 1990, Aldershot: Dartmouth (1993)

Kazimierska, Anna: The Remedy of Avoidance under the Vienna Convention on the International Sale of Goods, Pace Int'l L. Rev. (1999–2000), 79–192

Kee, Christopher: Remedies for breach of contract where only part of the contract has been performed – Comparison between provisions of CISG (Articles 51, 73) and counterpart provisions of the Principles of European Contract Law, 6 VJ (2002–2), 281–286

Kegel, Gerhard: Empfiehlt es sich, den Einfluß grundlegender Veränderungen des Wirtschaftslebens auf Verträge gesetzlich zu regeln und in welchem Sinn? – Gutachten für den 40. Juristentag, Tübingen: Mohr (1953) (Kurztitel: Gutachten)

Kegel, Gerhard/Rupp, Hans/Zweigert, Konrad: Die Einwirkung des Krieges auf Verträge, Berlin: de Gruyter (1941)

Kegel, Gerhard/Schurig, Klaus: Internationales Privatrecht, 9. Aufl., München: Beck (2004)

Keil, Andreas: Die Haftungsbefreiung des Schuldners im UN-Kaufrecht im Vergleich mit dem deutschen und US-amerikanischen Recht, Frankfurt a. M.: Lang (1993)

Keily, Ttoy: Good Faith & the Vienna Convention on Contracts for the International Sale of Goods (CISG), 3 VJ (1999), 15–40

Keinath, Steffen: Der gute Glauben im UN-Kaufrecht, Konstanz: Hartung-Gorre (1997)

Keller, Bertram: Early delivery and Seller's Right to Cure Lack of Conformity: Article 37 CISG and UNIDROIT Principles Comparative, www.cisg.law.pace.edu/cisg/text/anno-art-37.html. (Kurztitel: Right to Cure)

Keller, Bertram: Favor Contractus – Reading the CISG in Favor of the Contract, in: *Andersen/Schroeter* (Hrsg.), Sharing International Commercial Law across National Boundaries: Festschrift for Albert H. Kritzer on the Occasion of his Eightseth Birthday, London: Wildy, Simmonds & Hill (2008), S. 247–266 (Kurztitel: FS Kritzer)

Keller, Max/Siehr, Kurt: Kaufrecht, 3. Aufl., Zürich: Schulthess (1995)

Kelso, J. Clark: The United Nations Convention on Contracts for the International Sale of Goods: Contract Formation and the Battle of Forms, 21 Colum. J. Transnat'l L. (1982/83), 529–556

Kennedy, Andrew J.: Recent Developments: Nonconforming Goods Under the CISG – What's a Buyer to Do?, 16 Dick. J. Int'l L. (1998), 319–341

Kern, Christoph: Ein einheitliches Zurückbehaltungsrecht im UN-Kaufrecht?, ZEuP 2000, 837–859

Kern, Christoph: Leistungsverweigerungsrechte im UN-Kaufrecht, in: *Will* (Hrsg.), Rudolf Meyer zum Abschied – Beiträge zum UN-Kaufrecht, zum internationalen Privatrecht und zur Rechtsvergleichung, Genève: Faculté de droit, Université de Genève (1999), S. 73–111 (Kurztitel: FS R. Meyer)

Kessedjian, Catherine: Competing Approaches to Force Majeure and Hardship, Int'l Rev. L. & E. 25 (2005), 641–670

Kessler, Friedrich/Gilmore, Grant/Kronman, Anthony T.: Contracts: Cases und Materials, 3. Aufl., Boston/Toronto: Little, Brown and Company (1986) (Kurztitel: Contracts)

Khadjavi-Gontard, Bardia/Hausmann, Rainer: Zurechenbarkeit von Hoheitsakten und subsidiäre Staatshaftung bei Verträgen mit ausländischen Staatsunternehmen, RIW 1980, 533–544 und RIW 1983, 1–15

Kiene, Sörren C.: Rechtsmängel im UN-Kaufrecht und das Verhältnis von Art. 30 CISG zu Art. 41, 43 CISG. Zugleich Anmerkung zum Urteil des BGH vom 11.1.2006 (IHR 2006, 82), IHR 2006, 93–97

Kieninger, Eva Maria: Der Richtlinienvorschlag der Europäischen Kommission zur Bekämpfung des Zahlungsverzugs im Handelsverkehr, WM 1998, 2213–2221

Kieninger, Eva Maria: Mobiliarsicherheiten im Europäischen Binnenmarkt: zum Einfluß der Warenverkehrsfreiheit auf das nationale und internationale Sachenrecht der Mitgliedstaaten, Baden-Baden: Nomos (1996)
Killian, Monica: CISG and the Problem with Common Law Jurisdictions, 10 J. Transnat'l L. & Pol'y (2001), 217–243
Kim, Jee J.: Federal Courts Required to Examine Parol Evidence when Interpreting Contracts Governed by the United Nations Convention on Contracts for the International Sale of Goods (CISG), 12 N.Y. Int'l L. R. (1999), 105–110
Kimbel, Ericson P.: Nachfrist notice and avoidance under the CISG, 18 J. L. & Com. (1999), 301–331
Kindler, Peter: Die Anwendungsvoraussetzungen des Wiener Kaufrechtsübereinkommens der Vereinten Nationen im deutsch-italienischen Rechtsverkehr, RIW 1988, 776–782
Kindler, Peter: Einige Hauptfragen des CISG im Spiegel der neueren deutschen Kommentarliteratur, Jb. It. R. 5 (1992), 201–224
Kindler, Peter: Gesetzliche Zinsansprüche im Zivil- und Handelsrecht: Plädoyer für einen kreditmarktorientierten Fälligkeitszins (Habil. Konstanz 1995), Tübingen: Mohr (1996)
Kindler, Peter: Ob Walzfräsmaschine oder Schreibtischsessel: Keine Obliegenheit zur AGB-Übersendung beim Vertragsschluss nach CISG!, in: *Lorenz/Trunk/Eidenmüller/Wendehorst/Adolff* (Hrsg.), Festschrift für Andreas Heldrich zum 70. Geburtstag, München: Beck (2005), S. 225–234 (Kurztitel: FS Heldrich)
Kindler, Peter: Sachmängelhaftung, Aufrechnung und Zinssatzbemessung: Typische Fragen des UN-Kaufrechts in der gerichtlichen Praxis, IPRax 1996, 16–22
Kindler, Peter: Zur Anhebung des gesetzlichen Zinssatzes in Italien, RIW 1991, 304–305
King, Colin: The CISG – Another One of Equity's Darlings?, 8 VJ (2004), 249–268
Kirby, Amy: Punitive Damages in Contract Actions: The Tensions Between the United Nations Convention on Contracts for the International Sale of Goods and U. S. Law, 16 J. L. & Com. (1997), 215–231
Kircher, Wolfgang: Die Voraussetzungen der Sachmängelhaftung beim Warenkauf, Eine vergleichende Darstellung des deutschen und englischen Rechts unter Berücksichtigung des UN-Kaufrechts und aktueller Reformbestrebungen, Tübingen: Mohr (1998)
Kjelland, Cecilie: Das neue Kaufrecht der nordischen Länder im Vergleich mit dem Wiener Kaufrecht und dem deutschen Kaufrecht, Aachen: Shaker (2000)
Klaas, Christoph: Formelle Dokumentenstrenge im Recht der Bankgarantie, ZIP 1997, 1098–1102
Klapsa, Krzysztof: Die Auswirkungen des Gesetzes über die polnische Sprache auf die Vertragspraxis, WiRO 2000, 233–236
Kleineman, Jan (Hrsg.): CISG Part II Conference, Stockholm, 4–5 September 2008, Uppsala: Iustus (2009)
Klepper, Caroline Delisle: The Convention for the International Sale of Goods: a Practical Guide for the State of Maryland and its Trade Community, 15 Md. J. Int'l L. & Trade (1992), 235–261 (Kurztitel: Practical Guide)
Klindt, Thomas: Öffentlich-rechtliches Warenvertriebsrecht im Binnenmarkt am Beispiel des Maschinenhandels – zugleich Besprechung zu österr. OGH, Beschluß vom 13.4.2000 – 2 Ob 100/00w, IHR 2001, 103–106
Klingsporn, Burkhard: Das europäische Übereinkommen über den Ort der Zahlung von Geldschulden, WM 1972, 1262–1274
Klotz, James M./Barret, John A.: International Sales Agreement – An annotated Drafting and Negotiating Guide, The Hague/London/Boston: Kluwer Law International (1998)
Klotz, James M./Mazzacano, Peter/Pribetic, Antonin I.: All Quiet on the CISG Front: Guiliani v. Invar Manufacturing, the Battle of the Forms, and the Elusive Concept of Terminus Fixus, 46 Can. Bus. L. J. (2008), 430–442
Knobbe-Keuk, Brigitte: Möglichkeiten und Grenzen abstracter Schadensberechnung, VersR 1976, 401–411
Koch, Raphael: Anmerkung zu R. J. & A. M. Smallmon v. Transport Sales Ltd. And Grant Alan Miller, High Court of New Zealand, Urteil vom 30.7.2010, IHR 2011, 129–130
Koch, Raphael: Vertragsmäßigkeit der Ware bei Divergenz öffentlich-rechtlicher Vorgaben, IHR 2009, 233–236
Koch, Robert: Der besondere Gerichtsstand des Klägers/Verkäufers im Anwendungsbereich des UN-Kaufrechts, Zugleich Anmerkung zum Urteil des EuGH vom 29.6.1994 – Rs. C-288/92 – Custom Made Commercial Ltd./Stawa Metallbau GmbH, RIW 1994, 676 f., RIW 1996, 687 f.
Koch, Robert: „Fundamental breach": Commentary on whether the UNIDROIT Principles of International Commercial Contracts may be used to interpret or supplement Article 25 CISG, in: *Felemegas* (Hrsg.), An International Approach to the Interpretation of the United Nations Convention on Contracts for the International Sale of Goods (1980) as Uniform Sales Law, Cambridge: Cambridge University Press (2007), S. 124–133 (Kurztitel: Art. 25 CISG–PICC)

Literatur

Koch, Robert: Surprising Terms in Standard Contracts under the CISG, in: *Kröll/Mistelis/Perales Viscasillas/Rogers* (Hrsg.), International Arbitration and International Commercial Law: Synergy, Convergence and Evolution, Liber Amicorum Eric Bergsten, Alphen aan den Rijn: Kluwer Law International (2011), S. 597–612 (Kurztitel: FS Bergsten)

Koch, Robert: The CISG as the Law Applicable to Arbitration Agreements?, in: *Andersen/Schroeter* (Hrsg.), Sharing International Commercial Law across National Boundaries: Festschrift for Albert H. Kritzer on the Occasion of his Eightseth Birthday, London: Wildy, Simmonds & Hill (2008), S. 267–2686 (Kurztitel: FS Kritzer)

Koch, Robert: Wider den formularmäßigen Ausschluß des UN-Kaufrechts, NJW 2000, 910–915

Koch, Robert: Zur Bestimmung des Begriffs der wesentlichen Vertragsverletzung im UN-Kaufrecht im Falle der Lieferung nicht vertragsgemäßer Ware, RIW 1995, 98–100

Kock, Anette: Nebenpflichten im UN-Kaufrecht (Diss. Hamburg), Regensburg: Roderer Verlag (1995)

Köck, Heribert Franz: Vertragsinterpretation und Vertragsrechtskonvention: zur Bedeutung der Artikel 31 und 32 der Wiener Vertragsrechtskonvention 1969, Berlin: Duncker & Humblot (1976)

Koerner, Dörthe: Fakultatives Kollisionsrecht in Frankreich und Deutschland (Diss. Hamburg 1894), Tübingen: Mohr (1995)

Köhler, Helmut: Die Problematik automatisierter Rechtsvorgänge, insbesondere von Willenserklärungen, AcP 182 (1982), 126–171

Köhler, Martin: Die Haftung nach UN-Kaufrecht im Spannungsverhältnis zwischen Vertrag und Delikt, (Diss. Saarbrücken), Tübingen: Mohr-Siebeck 2003 (Kurztitel: Spannungsverhältnis)

Koller, Ingo: Die Dokumentenstrenge im Licht von Treu und Glauben bei Dokumentenakkreditiv, WM 1990, 293–303

Koller, Ingo: Transportrecht: Kommentar zu Spedition, Straßen- und Lufttransport, 5. Aufl., München: Beck (2004)

Koller, Thomas: AGB-Kontrolle und UN-Kaufrecht (CISG) – Probleme aus schweizerischer Sicht, in: *Harrer/Portmann/Zäch* (Hrsg.), Besonderes Vertragsrecht – aktuelle Probleme, Festschrift für Heinrich Honsell zum 60. Geburtstag, Zürich: Schulthess (2002), S. 223–245 (Kurztitel: FS Honsell)

Koller, Thomas: Das Regressrecht des CISG-Importeurs gegen den CISG-Verkäufer bei Produkthaftungsfällen mit Körperschäden, in: *Bucher u. a.* (Hrsg.), Norm und Wirkung – Beiträge zum Privat- und Wirtschaftsrecht aus heutiger und historischer Perspektive. Festschrift für Wolfgang Wiegand zum 65. Geburtstag, S. 421–447 (Kurztitel: FS Wiegand)

Koller, Thomas: Die Verjährung von Ansprüchen aus der Lieferung nicht vertragsgemässer Ware nach UN-Kaufrecht (CISG) – Keine Anwendung der Einjahresfrist von Art. 210 Abs. 1 OR, Jusletter 20.7.2009

Koller, Thomas: Die Verjährung von Ansprüchen des Käufers aus der Lieferung nicht vertragskonformer Ware im Spannungsfeld zwischen UN-Kaufrecht (CISG) und nationalem Partikularrecht, recht 2003, 41–54

Koller, Thomas/Mauerhofer, Marc André: Das Beweismass im UN-Kaufrecht (CISG), in: *Bühler/Müller-Chen* (Hrsg.), Festschrift für Ingeborg Schwenzer zum 60. Geburtstag, Bern: Stämpfli (2011), S. 963–980 (Kurztitel: FS Schwenzer)

Koller, Ingo/Roth, Wulf-Henning/Morck, Winfried: Kommentar zum Handelsgesetzbuch (HGB), 7. Aufl., München: Beck (2011) (Kurztitel: *Koller/Roth/Morck/Bearbeiter*)

Kolter, Martin: Zur rechtlichen Einordnung typischer Handelsklauseln unter besonderer Berücksichtigung des EAG, EKG und UN-Kaufrechts (Diss. Marburg 1991)

Kokoruda, Christopher C.: The U. N. Convention on Contracts for the International Sale of Goods - It's Not Your Father's Uniform Commercial Code, 85-JUN Fla. B. J. (2011), 103–109

Komarov, Alexander S.: Internationality, Uniformity and Observance of Good Faith as Criteria in Interpretation of CISG: Some Remarks on Article 7(1), 25 J. L. & Com. (2006), 75–85

Köndgen, Johannes: Kommentar zu Hart, Alternativen zum Vertragsschluß – Begründung von vertraglichen Schuldverhältnissen durch Nicht-Willenserklärungen, in: *Brüggemeier/Hart,* Soziales Schuldrecht, Bremen: Universität Bremen (1987), S. 98–182

Koneru, Phanesh: The International Interpretation of the UN Convention on Contracts for the International Sale of Goods: An Approach Based on General Principles, 6 Minn. J. Global Trade (1997), 105–152

König, Detlev: Voraussehbarkeit des Schadens als Grenze vertraglicher Haftung, in: *Leser/Marschall von Bieberstein* (Hrsg.), Das Haager Einheitliche Kaufgesetz und das Deutsche Schuldrecht, Kolloquium zum 65. Geburtstag von Ernst v. Caemmerer, Karlsruhe: C. F. Müller (1973), S. 75–130 (Kurztitel: Voraussehbarkeit des Schadens)

König, Wolfgang/Reichel-Holzer, Claudia: Das Unternehmensgesetzbuch: UGB – HGB im Vergleich, Wien: Linde (2006)

Literatur

Königer, Ursula: Die Bestimmung der gesetzlichen Zinshöhe nach dem deutschen Internationalen Privatrecht: eine Untersuchung unter besonderer Berücksichtigung der Art. 78 und 84 I UN-Kaufrecht (CISG) (Diss. Freiburg), Berlin: Duncker & Humblot (1997)
Kötz, Hein: Europäisches Vertragsrecht, Bd. I, Tübingen: Mohr (1996) (Kurztitel: Europäisches Vertragsrecht I)
Kötz, Hein: Rechtsvereinheitlichung – Nutzen, Kosten, Methoden, Ziele, RabelsZ 50 (1986), 1–18
Koziol, Helmut: Rechtsfolgen der Verletzung einer Schadensminderungspflicht – Rückkehr der archaischen Culpakompensation, ZEuP 1998, 593–601
Koziol, Helmut/Bydlinski, Peter/Bollenberger, Raimund (Hrsg.), Kurzkommentar zum ABGB, 2. Aufl., Wien, New York: Springer (2007) (Kurztitel: *Koziol/Bydlinski/Bollenberger*)
Koziol, Helmut/Welser, Rudolf/Kletečka, Andreas: Bürgerliches Recht, Band I, 13. Aufl., Wien: Manzsche Verlags- und Universitätsbuchhandlung (2006) (Kurztitel: *Koziol/Welser/Kletečka*)
Koziol, Helmut/Welser, Rudolf/Kletečka, Andreas: Bürgerliches Recht, Band II, 13. Aufl., Wien: Manzsche Verlags- und Universitätsbuchhandlung (2007) (Kurztitel: *Koziol/Welser/Kletečka*)
Kramer, Ernst A.: Abschied von der Aliud-Lieferung?, in: *Harrer/Portmann/Zäch* (Hrsg.), Besonderes Vertragsrecht – aktuelle Probleme, FS für Heinrich Honsell zum 60. Geburtstag, Zürich: Schulthess (2002), S. 247–260 (Kurztitel: FS Honsell)
Kramer, Ernst A.: „Battle of the Forms", in: *Tercier/Amstutz/Koller/Schmid/Stöckli* (Hrsg.), Gauchs Welt. Festschrift für Peter Gauch zum 65. Geburtstag, Zürich: Schulthess (2004), S. 493–506 (Kurztitel: FS Gauch)
Kramer, Ernst A.: Der Irrtum beim Vertragsschluss. Eine weltweit rechtsvergleichende Bestandsaufnahme, Zürich: Schulthess (1998) (Kurztitel: Irrtum beim Vertragsschluss)
Kramer, Ernst A.: Die Gültigkeit der Verträge nach den UNIDROIT Principles of International Commercial Contracts, ZEuP 1999, 209–228
Kramer, Ernst A.: Europäische Privatrechtsvereinheitlichung, östJBl 1998, 477–489
Kramer, Ernst A.: Konsensprobleme im Rahmen des UN-Kaufrechts, in: *Fischer-Czermak/Kletečka/Schauer/Zankl* (Hrsg.), Festschrift für Rudolf Welser zum 65. Geburtstag, Wien: Manz (2004), S. 539–558 (Kurztitel: FS Welser)
Kramer, Ernst A.: Konvergenz und Internationalisierung der juristischen Methode, in: *Meier-Schatz* (Hrsg.), Die Zukunft des Rechts, Basel/Genf/München: Helbing & Lichtenhahn (1999), S. 71–88
Kramer, Ernst A.: Neues aus Gesetzgebung, Praxis und Lehre zum Vertragsschluß, BJM 1995, 1–24
Kramer, Ernst A.: Rechtzeitige Untersuchung und Mängelanzeige bei Sachmängeln nach Art. 38 und 39 UN-Kaufrecht – eine Zwischenbilanz, in: *Kramer/Schuhmacher* (Hrsg.), Beiträge zum Unternehmensrecht, Festschrift für Hans-Georg Koppensteiner zum 65. Geburtstag, Wien: Orac Verlag (2001), S. 617–629 (Kurztitel: FS Koppensteiner)
Kramer, Ernst A.: Uniforme Interpretation von Einheitsprivatrecht – mit besonderer Berücksichtigung von Art. 7 UNKR, östJBl 1996, 137–151
Kramer, Ernst A.: Uniforme Interpretation von Einheitsprivatrecht – mit besonderer Berücksichtigung von Art. 7 UNKR, in: *Kramer* (Hrsg.), Zur Theorie und Politik des Privat- und Wirtschaftsrechts: Beiträge aus den Jahren 1969–1996, München: Beck (1997), S. 401–432 (Kurztitel: Uniforme Interpretation)
Krämer, Rosa-Maria: Der „kleine" und der „große Schadenersatz" beim Kauf mangelhafter Waren im amerikanischen und deutschen Recht, Frankfurt a. M.: Lang (1989)
Krämer, Rosa-Maria: Die Berechnung des Nichterfüllungsschadens bei der Sachmängelhaftung im amerikanischen Recht des Warenkaufs, RIW 1994, 115–126
Kranz, Norbert: Die Schadensersatzpflicht nach den Haager Einheitlichen Kaufgesetzen und dem Wiener UN-Kaufrecht (Diss. Hamburg), Frankfurt a. M.: Lang (1989)
Krapp, Thea: Die Abkommen der Vereinten Nationen über den Kauf und über die Verjährung beim internationalen Warenkauf, ZSR 1984, 289–317
Krapp, Thea: Die Verjährung von Käuferansprüchen bei vertragswidrigen Leistungen: Analyse der kurzen Frist des § 477 BGB und Änderungsvorschläge unter Mitberücksichtigung des schweizerischen und französischen Rechts sowie des Einheitlichen Kaufgesetzes und der UN-Abk., München: Florentz (1983) (Kurztitel: Verjährung)
Krapp, Thea: The Limitation Convention for the International Sale of Goods, 19 J. World Trade L. (1985), 343–372
Krätzschmar, Tobias: Öffentlichrechtliche Beschaffenheitsvorgaben und Vertragsmässigkeit der Ware im UN-Kaufrecht (CISG) (Diss. Dresden 2008), München: Sellier. European Law Publishers (2008)
Krebs, Markus: Die Rückabwicklung im UN-Kaufrecht, Baden-Baden: Nomos (2000) (Kurztitel: Rückabwicklung)

Literatur

Krebs, Markus: L'article 28 CVIM peut-il empêcher la restitution en nature après la résolution du contrat de vente? in: *Will* (Hrsg.), Schriftenreihe deutscher Jura-Studenten in Genf, Bd. 17 – Marc Mounier zum Abschied, Genf: Selbstverlag (1997), S. 157–162 (Kurztitel: L'article 28 CVIM)

Krejci, Heinz (Hrsg.): Kommentar zu den durch das HaRÄG 2005 eingeführten Neuerungen im Unternehmensgesetzbuch und im Allgemeinen bürgerlichen Gesetzbuch, Wien: Manzsche Verlags- und Universitätsbuchhandlung (2007)

Kremer, Ralf Bodo, Das Persönlichkeitsrecht – Geistiges Eigentum im Sinne des Art. 42 CISG? (Diss. Bielefeld 2008), Jena: JWV (2009) (Kurztitel: Persönlichkeitsrecht)

Krenz, Roland: Bestimmbarkeit des Preises und der Leistung bei Sukzessivlieferungsverträgen und ähnlichen Verträgen nach französischem Recht, RIW 1997, 201–206

Kreuzer, Karl Friedrich: Internationale Mobiliarsicherungsrechte an Luftfahrzeugen, Zu der Convention on International Interests in Mobile Equipment und dem Protocol to the Convention on International Interests in Mobile Equipment on Matters Specific to Aircraft Equipment, in: *Schwenzer/Hager* (Hrsg.), Festschrift für Peter Schlechtriem zum 70. Geburtstag, Tübingen: Mohr (2003), S. 869–902 (Kurztitel: FS Schlechtriem)

Kreuzer, Karl Friedrich: Mobiliarsicherheiten – Vielfalt oder Einheit?, Verhandlungen der Fachgruppe für Vergleichendes Handels- und Wirtschaftsrecht anlässlich der Tagung der Gesellschaft für Rechtsvergleichung in Jena am 20.–22. März 1996, Baden-Baden: Nomos (1999) (Kurztitel: Mobiliarsicherheiten)

Kritzer, Albert H.: CISG: Pace University School of Law Internet World Wide Web Site Excerpt, 9 Pace Int'l L. Rev. (1997), 187–222

Kritzer, Albert H.: Guide to Practical Applications of the United Nations Convention on Contracts for the International Sale of Goods, Deventer: Kluwer Law and Taxation (1989) (Kurztitel: Guide to Practical Applications)

Kritzer, Albert H.: ICM-Guide to Practical Applications of the UN Convention on Contracts for the International Sale of Goods, Deventer: Kluwer (1994) (Kurztitel: ICM-Guide)

Kritzer, Albert H.: The Convention on Contracts for the International Sale of Goods: Scope, Interpretation, and Resources, 1 Rev. CISG (1995), 147–207

Kritzer, Albert H./Rogers, Vikky M.: A Uniform International Sales Law Terminology, in: *Schwenzer/Hager* (Hrsg.), Festschrift für Peter Schlechtriem zum 70. Geburtstag, Tübingen: Mohr (2003), S. 223–254 (Kurztitel: FS Schlechtriem)

Kröll, Stefan: Burden of Proof for the Non-Conformity of Goods under Art. 35 CISG, Annals Fac. L. Belgrade 2011, 162-180

Kröll, Stefan: Gerichtsstandsvereinbarungen aufgrund Handelsbrauchs im Rahmen des GVÜ, ZZP 113 (2000), 135–159

Kröll, Stefan: Selected Problems Concerning the CISG's Scope of Application, 25 J. L. & Com. (2005), 39–57

Kröll, Stefan: The Burden of Proof for the Non-Conformity of the Goods under Art. 35 CISG, 15 VJ (2011), 33–50

Kröll, Stefan/Hennecke, Rudolf: Kaufmännische Bestätigungsschreiben beim internationalen Warenkauf, RabelsZ 67 (2003), 448–493

Kröll, Stefan/Hennecke, Rudolf: Kollidierende Allgemeine Geschäftsbedingungen in internationalen Kaufverträgen, RIW 2001, 736–743

Kröll, Stefan/Mistelis, Loukas/Perales Viscasillas, Pilar (Hrsg.): UN Convention on Contracts for the International Sale of Goods (CISG), München: C. H. Beck (2011) (Kurztitel: *Kröll u. a./Autor*)

Kromer, Ulrich: Der Begriff der Lieferung im Haager Einheitlichen Kaufrecht: Entstehungsgeschichte, Bedeutung und Funktion in rechtsvergleichender Sicht (Diss. Freiburg 1986), Pfaffenweiler: Centaurus (1987)

Kronke, Herbert: Zur Verwendung von allgemeinen Geschäftsbedingungen im Verkehr mit Auslandsberührung, NJW 1977, 992–993

Kropholler, Jan: Der „Ausschluß" des internationalen Privatrechts im einheitlichen Kaufgesetz, RabelsZ 38 (1974), 372–387

Kropholler, Jan: Europäisches Zivilprozeßrecht, 8. Aufl., Frankfurt a. M.: Verlag Recht und Wirtschaft (2005) (Kurztitel: EUZPR)

Kropholler, Jan: Europäisches Zivilprozeßrecht: Kommentar zu EuGVO und Lugano-Übereinkommen, 87. Aufl., Heidelberg: Recht und Wirtschaft (2005) (Kurztitel: EUZPR)

Kropholler, Jan: Internationales Einheitsrecht – Allgemeine Lehren, Tübingen: Mohr (1975) (Kurztitel: Internationales Einheitsrecht)

Kropholler, Jan: Internationales Privatrecht, 5. Aufl., Tübingen: Mohr (2004) (Kurztitel: IPR)

Kropholler, Jan/von Hein, Jan: Europäisches Zivilprozessrecht, Kommentar zu EuGVO, Lugano-Übereinkommen 2007, EuVTVO, EuMVVO und EuGFVO, 9. Aufl., Frankfurt a. M.: Deutscher Fachverlag (2011) (Kurztitel: *Kropholler/von Hein,* EUZPR)

Kropholler, Jan/von Hinden, Michael: Die Reform des europäischen Gerichtsstands am Erfüllungsort (Art. 5 Nr. 1 EuGVÜ), in: *Schack* (Hrsg.), Gedächtnisschrift für Alexander Lüderitz, München: Beck (2000), S. 401–414

Krüger, Kai: Norsk kjøpsrett, 4. Aufl., Bergen: Alma Mater (1999)

Krüger, Ulrich: Modifizierte Erfolgshaftung im UN-Kaufrecht, Frankfurt a. M./Bern: Lang (1999)

Kruisinga, Sonja: Non-conformity in the 1980 UN-Convention for the International Sale of Goods: A Uniform Concept?, Antwerp: Intersentia (2004) (Kurztitel: Non-conformity)

Kruisinga, Sonja A.: The Impact of Uniform Law on National Law: Limits and Possibilities – CISG and Its Incidence in Dutch Law, 13.2 Electr. J. Comp. L. (Mai 2009), 1–20

Kruisinga, Sonja A.: The Seller's Right to Cure in the CISG and the Common European Sales Law, Vol. 19/Nr. 6 ERPL (2011), 907–919

Kubis, Sebastian: Gerichtsstand am Erfüllungsort: Erneute Enttäuschung aus Luxemburg, ZEuP 2001, 737–752

Kühl, Sebastian/Hingst, Kai-Michael: Das UN-Kaufrecht und das Recht der AGB, in: *Karl-Heinz Thume* (Hrsg.), Transport- und Vertriebsrecht 2000, Festgabe für Rolf Herber, Neuwied: Luchterhand (1999), S. 50–63 (Kurztitel: FS Herber)

Kuhlen, Dydra: Produkthaftung im internationalen Kaufrecht. Entstehungsgeschichte, Anwendungsbereich und Sperrwirkung des Art. 5 des Wiener UN-Kaufrechts (CISG) (Diss. Augsburg 1996), Augsburg: Wittmann (1997)

Kull, Irene: Reform of Contract Law in Estonia: Influences of Harmonisation of European Contract Law, Juridica Int. 2008, 122–129

Kuoppala, Saana: Examination of the Goods under the CISG and the Finnish Sale of Goods Act, www.cisg.law.pace.edu/cisg/biblio/kuoppala.html. (Kurztitel: Examination)

Küpper, Wolfgang: Das Scheitern von Vertragsverhandlungen als Fallgruppe der culpa in contrahendo (Diss. Köln 1987), Berlin: Duncker & Humblot (1988)

La China, Sergio: La convenzione di Vienna sulla vendita internazionale di diritto uniforme. Profili processuali: la giurisdizione (Seminar, Mailand, 26.11.1989), Riv. trim. dir. proced. civ. 1990, 769–783

La Vendita Internazionale: La Convenzione di Vienna dell' 11 Aprile 1980, atti del Convegno di Studi di S. Margherita Ligure (26–28 settembre 1980), Mailand: Giuffrè (1981) (Kurztitel: La Vendita Internazionale)

Lacasse, Nicole: Le champ d'application de la Convention des Nations Unies sur les contrats de vente internationale de marchandises, in: *Perret/Lacasse* (Hrsg.), Actes du colloque sur la vente internationale, Montréal: Wilson & Lafleur (1989), 23–45 (Kurztitel: Le champ d'application)

Ladas, Dimitrios: Die Wirksamkeit der Willenserklärungen gegenüber Sprachunkundigen (Diss. Berlin 1993)

Lagergren, Gunnar K. A.: Formation of Contract, in: *Honnold* (Hrsg.), Unification of the Law Governing International Sales, Paris: Dalloz (1966), 55–73

Laimer, Simon: Durchführung und Rechtsfolgen der Vertragsaufhebung bei nachträglichen Erfüllungsstörungen, Tübingen: Mohr Siebeck (2009)

Lake, Ralph B./Draetta, Ugo: Letters of Intent and Other Precontractual Documents, London: Butterworths (1989)

Lanciotti, Alessandra: Norme uniformi di conflitto e materiali nella disciplina convenzionale della compravendita, Neapel: Ed. Scientifiche Italiane (1992)

Landfermann, Hans-Georg: AGB-Gesetz und Auslandsgeschäfte, RIW 1977, 445–453

Landfermann, Hans-Georg: Anmerkung zu BGH, 28.3.1979 – VIII ZR 37/78, NJW 1979, 1782–1783

Landfermann, Hans-Georg: Das UNCITRAL-Übereinkommen über die Verjährung beim internationalen Warenkauf, RabelsZ 39 (1975), 253–277

Landfermann, Hans-Georg: Die Auflösung des Vertrages nach richterlichem Ermessen als Rechtsfolge der Nichterfüllung im französischen Recht, Frankfurt a. M.: Metzner (1968) (Kurztitel: Die Auflösung des Vertrages)

Landfermann, Hans-Georg: Neues Recht für den internationalen Kauf, NJW 1974, 385–391

Lando, Ole: CISG and Its Followers: A Proposal to Adopt Some International Principles of Contract Law, 53 Am. J. Comp. L. (2005), 379–401

Lando, Ole: Contracts, in: Int. Enc. Comp. L., Vol. III: Private International Law, chap. 24, Tübingen/Den Haag/Paris: Mohr/Monton (1976) (Kurztitel: Private International Law)

Lando, Ole: Principles on European Contract Law – An Alternative or a Precursor of European Legislation, RabelsZ 56 (1992), 261–273

Lando, Ole: Salient Features of the Principles of European Contract Law: A Comparison with the UCC, 13 Pace Int'l L. Rev. (2001), 339–369

Literatur

Lando, Ole: The 1955 and 1985 Hague Conventions on the Law Applicable to the International Sale of Goods, RabelsZ 57 (1993), 155–174

Lando, Ole: The 1985 Hague Convention on the Law Applicable to Sales, RabelsZ 51 (1987), 60–85

Lando, Ole/Beale, Hugh: Principles of European Contract Law, Part I and II, prepared by The Commission of European Contract Law, The Hague/London/Boston: Kluwer Law International (2000) (Kurztitel: *Lando/Beale,* Part I and II)

Lando, Ole/Clive, Eric/Prüm, André/Zimmerman, Reinhart: Principles of European Contract Law, Part III, The Hague/London/Boston: Kluwer Law International (2003) (Kurztitel: *Lando/Clive/Prüm/Zimmerman,* Part III)

Langenecker, Josef: UN-Einheitskaufrecht und Immaterialgüterrechte. Die Rechtsmängelhaftung bei internationalen Kaufverträgen nach dem UN-Kaufrechtsübereinkommen unter besonderer Berücksichtigung von Immaterialgüterrechten (Diss. München 1993), München: VVF (1993)

Lapiashvili, Natia: Modern Sales Law in Eastern Europe and Central Asia (Diss. Basel 2010), The Hague: Eleven International Publishing (2011)

Larenz, Karl: Geschäftsgrundlage und Vertragserfüllung, 3. Aufl., München: Beck (1963)

Larenz, Karl: Lehrbuch des Schuldrechts, Bd. I: Allgemeiner Teil, 14. Aufl., München: Beck (1987) (Kurztitel: SchR I)

Larson, Marcus G.: Applying Uniform Sales Law to International Software Transactions: The Use of the CISG, its Shortcomings, and a Comparative Look at How the Proposed U. C. C. Article 2 B Would Remedy Them, 5 Tul. J. Int'l & Comp. L. (1997), 445–488

Lautenbach, Boris R.: Die Haftungsbefreiung im internationalen Warenkauf nach dem UN-Kaufrecht und dem schweizerischen Kaufrecht (Diss. Zürich 1990)

Lautenschlager, Felix: Current Problems regarding the Interpretation of Statements and Party Conduct under the CISG – Reasonable Third Person, Language Problems and Standard Terms and Conditions, 11 VJ (2007), 259–290

Law Student, Unification and Certainty: The United Nations Convention on Contracts for the Intertional Sale of Goods, (1984) 97 Harv. L. Rev., 1984–2000, www.cisg.law.pace.edu/cisg/biblio/harvard-note.html

Lee, Robert G. R.: The UN Convention on Contracts for the International Sale of Goods: OK for the UK?, J. Bus. L. (1993), 131–148

Lee, Wanki W.: Exemptions of Contract Liability Under the 1980 United Nations Convention, 8 Dick. J. Int'l L. (1990), 375–394

Leenen, Detlef: Abschluß, Zustandekommen und Wirksamkeit des Vertrages, AcP 188 (1988), 381–418

Lehmkuhl, Heiko: Das Nacherfüllungsrecht des Verkäufers im UN-Kaufrecht (Diss. Heidelberg 2001), Frankfurt a. M. u. a.: Peter Lang (2002)

Lehner, Dominik: Erfüllungsort und Gerichtsstand für Geldschulden im nationalen Recht und im internationalen Einheitsrecht (Diss. Basel 1990)

Lehr, Wolfgang: Die neuen Incoterms 2000, VersR 2000, 548–557

Leisinger, Benjamin K.: Fundamental Breach Considering Non-Conformity of the Goods (Diss. Basel, 2007), München: Sellier (2007) (Kurztitel: Fundamental Breach)

Leisinger, Benjamin K.: Some Thoughts About Art. 39(2) CISG, IHR 2006, 76–81

Les Ventes Internationales de Marchandises: Problèmes juridiques d'actualité. Colloque de la Fondation internationale pour l'enseignement du droit des affaires à la Faculté de droit d'Aix-en-Provence, 7 et 8 mars 1980, Paris: Economica (1981) (Kurztitel: Les Ventes Internationales de Marchandises)

Leser, Hans G.: Der Rücktritt vom Vertrag, Abwicklungsverhältnis und Gestaltungsbefugnisse bei Leistungsstörungen, Tübingen: Mohr (1975) (Kurztitel: Rücktritt vom Vertrag)

Leser, Hans G.: Die Erfüllungsweigerung, in: *von Caemmerer/Mentschikott/Zweigert* (Hrsg.), Ius privatum gentium: Festschrift für Max Rheinstein zum 70. Geburtstag am 5. Juli 1989, Bd. 2, Tübingen: Mohr (1969), S. 643–650 (Kurztitel: Erfüllungsweigerung)

Leser, Hans G.: Die Vertragsaufhebung im Einheitlichen Kaufgesetz, in: *Leser/Marschall von Bieberstein* (Hrsg.), Kolloquium zum 65. Geburtstag von Ernst v. Caemmerer, Karlsruhe: Müller (1973), S. 1–19 (Kurztitel: Vertragsaufhebung im Einheitl. Kaufgesetz)

Leser, Hans G.: Lösung vom Vertrag, in: *Bickel* (Hrsg.), Festschrift Ernst Wolf – Recht und Rechtserkenntnis, Köln: Heymanns (1985), S. 373–394 (Kurztitel: Lösung vom Vertrag)

Leser, Hans G.: Sind Rücktritt und Schadensersatz Alternativen? Eine Skizze zum BGB und zum internationalen Einheitskaufrecht, in: *Chuo University* (Hrsg.), Conflict and Integration: Comparative Law in the World Today, The 40th Anniversary of the Institute of Comparative Law in Japan, Tokio: Chuo University Press (1989), S. 577–588 (Kurztitel: Sind Rücktritt und Schadensersatz Alternativen?)

Leser, Hans G.: Strukturen von Schadensersatz und Vertragsaufhebung im deutschen und UN-Kaufrecht, in: *Leser/Isomura* (Hrsg.), Wege zum japanischen Recht, Festschrift für Zentaro Kitagawa zum 65. Geburtstag, Berlin: Duncker & Humblot (1992), S. 455–470 (Kurztitel: FS Kitagawa)
Leser, Hans G.: Vertragsaufhebung und Rückabwicklung unter dem UN-Kaufrecht, in: *Schlechtriem* (Hrsg.), Einheitliches Kaufrecht und nationales Obligationenrecht, Baden-Baden: Nomos (1987), S. 225–255 (Kurztitel: Vertragsaufhebung und Rückabwicklung)
Leser, Hans G./Marschall von Bieberstein, Wolfgang (Hrsg.): Das Haager Einheitliche Kaufgesetz und das Deutsche Schuldrecht, Kolloquium zum 65. Geburtstag von Ernst von Caemmerer, Karlsruhe: C. F. Müller (1973) (Kurztitel: Das Haager Einheitliche Kaufgesetz)
Lesguillons, Henry: Frustration, Force Majeure, Imprévision, Wegfall der Geschäftsgrundlage, Dr. prat. com. int. 1979, 507–532
Lessiak, Rudolf: UNCITRAL-Kaufrechtsabkommen und Irrtumsanfechtung, östJBl 1989, 487–496
Leumann Liebster, Pascal: Reputationsschaden im UN-Kaufrecht (CISG), in: *Bühler/Müller-Chen* (Hrsg.), Festschrift für Ingeborg Schwenzer zum 60. Geburtstag, Bern: Stämpfli (2011), S. 1031-1048 (Kurztitel: FS Schwenzer)
LEXIS: hrsg. v. Lexis-nexis (Datenbank zum U. S.-amerikanischen Recht): http://www.lexis-nexis.com
Lichtsteiner, René A.: Convention des Nations Unies sur les contrats de vente internationale de marchandises: présentation et comparaison avec le droit suisse, in: *Dessemontet* (Hrsg.), Contrats de vente internationale, Lausanne: CEDIDAC (1991), S. 181–294 (Kurztitel: Convention)
Liebscher, Marc/Zoll, Frederyk: Einführung in das polnische Recht, München: Beck (2005)
Liesecke, Rudolf: Die neuere Rechtsprechung, insbesondere des Bundesgerichtshofes, auf dem Gebiete des Überseekaufs, WM 1966, 174–183
Liesecke, Rudolf: Die typischen Klauseln des internationalen Handelsverkehrs, WM 1978, Sonderbeilage Nr. 3 zu Nr. 15 vom 15. April 1978
Liguori, Fabio: Il diritto uniforme della vendita internazionale: prassi e tendenze applicative della convenzione di Vienna del 1980, Riv. dir. civ. 1999, 143–177
Liguori, Fabio: La convenzione di Vienna sulla vendita internazionale di beni mobili nella pratica: un'analisi critica delle prime cento decisioni, Foro it. 1996, IV, 145–183
Liguori, Fabio: UNILEX: a means to promote uniformity in the application of CISG, ZEuP 1996, 600–609
Limbach, Francis: Lieu de paiement. Applicabilité de la CVIM, formation du contrat et notion d'établissement, D. 2002, Jur. 315–317
Lindacher, Walter F.: Der Topos der Transparenz im Rahmen der Einbeziehungs- und Inhaltskontrolle Allgemeiner Geschäftsbedingungen, in: Juristische Gesellschaft Osnabrück-Emsland (Hrsg.), Vorträge zur Rechtsentwicklung der achtziger Jahre, Köln: Heymanns (1991), S. 347–363 (Kurztitel: Transparenz)
Lindacher, Walter F.: Gefahrtragung und Gefahrübergang, in: *Hoyer/Posch* (Hrsg.), Das Einheitliche Wiener Kaufrecht, Wien: Orac (1992), S. 165–176 (Kurztitel: Gefahrtragung und Gefahrübergang)
Lindbach, Jochen: Rechtswahl im Einheitsrecht am Beispiel des Wiener UN-Kaufrechts (Diss. Augsburg), Aachen: Shaker (1996)
Lindström, Niklas: Changed Circumstances and Hardship in the International Sale of Goods, 1 Nordic J. Com. L. (2006), 1–29
Linhart Karin: Internationales Einheitsrecht und einheitliche Auslegung (Diss. Würzburg 2003), Tübingen: Mohr Siebeck (2005) (Kurztitel: Einheitliche Auslegung)
Linke, Hartmut: Sonderanknüpfung der Willenserklärung? Auflösungstendezen im internationalen Schuldrecht, ZVerglRW 1980, 1–58
Linne, Anna L.: Burden of Proof under Article 35 CISG, 20 Pace Int'l L. Rev. (2008) 31–44
Linnerz, Markus: Die Untersuchungs- und Rügefrist des Käufers nach dem UN-Kaufrecht (Magisterarbeit Saarbrücken 2000)
Liu, Chengwei: Additional Period (Nachfrist) for Late Performance: Perspectives from the CISG, UNIDROIT Principles, PECL and Case Law, 2. Aufl., www.cisg.law.pace.edu/cisg/biblio/liu4.html (Kurztitel: Additional Period)
Liu, Chengwei: Force Majeure: Perspectives from the CISG, UNIDROIT Principles, PECL and Case Law, 2. Aufl., Case annotated update (April 2005), www.cisg.law.pace.edu/cisg/biblio/liu6.html#fmiv (Kurztitel: Force Majeure)
Liu, Chengwei: Suspension or Avoidance Due to Anticipatory Breach: Perspectives from Arts. 71/72 CISG, the UNIDROIT Principles, PECL and Case Law (2005), http://cisgw3.law.pace.edu/cisg/biblio/liu9.html (Kurztitel: Suspension)
Lobinger, Thomas: Rechtsgeschäftliche Verpflichtung und autonome Bindung (Diss. Tübingen), Tübingen: Mohr (1999)

Literatur

Lockhardt, Thomas L./McKenna, Richard J.: Software Licence Agreements in Light of the UCC and the Convention on the International Sale of Goods, 70 Mich. B. J. (1991), 646

Loewe, Roland: Anwendungsgebiet, Auslegung, Lücken und Handelsgebräuche, in: Schweizerisches Institut für Rechtsvergleichung (Hrsg.), Lausanner Kolloquium 1984, Zürich: Schulthess (1985), S. 11–20 (Kurztitel: Anwendungsgebiet)

Loewe, Roland: Der Übereinkommensentwurf der Vereinten Nationen über die Verjährung in internationalen Kaufsachen, in: *von Caemmerer* (Hrsg.), Festschrift für Pan. J. Zepos anlässlich seines 65. Geburtstages, Bd. II, Athen/Freiburg/Köln: Katsikalis (1973), S. 409–420 (Kurztitel: FS Zepos II)

Loewe, Roland: Internationales Kaufrecht, Wien: Manz (1989)

Loewe, Roland: Kaufrechtsübereinkommen – Lückenfüllung durch nichtamtliche Kodifikationen, in: *Thume* (Hrsg.): Transport- und Vertriebsrecht 2000, Festgabe für Rolf Herber, Neuwied: Luchterhand (1999), S. 7–20 (Kurztitel: FS Herber)

Lohmann, Arnd: Parteiautonomie und UN-Kaufrecht: zugleich ein Beitrag zum Anwendungsbereich des Wiener Kaufrechtsübereinkommens der Vereinten Nationen vom 11. April 1980 (Diss. Heidelberg 2003), Tübingen: Mohr Siebeck (2005) (Kurztitel: Parteiautonomie)

Lohs, Marcel Martin/Nolting, Norbert: Regelung der Vertragsverletzung im UN-Kaufrechtsübereinkommen, ZVerglRW 1998, 4–29

Longobardi, Laura E.: Disclaimers of Implied Warranties: The 1980 United Nations Convention on Contracts for the International Sale of Goods, 53 Fordham L. Rev. (1985), 863–887

Lookofsky, Joseph M.: Alive and well in Scandinavia: CISG Part II, 18 J. L. & Com. (1999), 289–299

Lookofsky, Joseph M.: CISG foreign case law: how much regard should we have?, in: *Ferrari u. a.* (Hrsg.), The Draft UNCITRAL Digest and Beyond: Cases, Analysis and Unresolved Issues in the U. N. Sales Convention, München/London: Sellier. European Law Publishers/Sweet&Maxwell (2004), S. 216–234 (Kurztitel: Foreign Case Law)

Lookofsky, Joseph M.: Consequential Damages in Comparative Context: From Breach of Promise to Monetary Remedy in the American, Scandinavian and International Law of Contracts and Sales, Kopenhagen: Jurist-og Økonomforbundets (1989)

Lookofsky, Joseph M.: Digesting CISG Case Law: How Much Regard Should We Have?, 8 VJ (2004), 181–195

Lookofsky, Joseph M.: Fault and No-Fault in Danish, American and International Sales Law. The Reception of the 1980 United Nations Sales Convention, 27 Scand. Stud. L. (1983), 107–138

Lookofsky, Joseph M., Impediments and Hardship in International Sales: A Commentary on Catherine Kessedjian's „Competing Approaches to Force Majeure and Hardship", Int'l Rev. L. & E. 25 (2005), 434–445

Lookofsky, Joseph M.: Loose Ends and Contorts in International Sales: Problems in the Harmonization of Private Law Rules, 39 Am. J. Comp. L. (1991), 403–416

Lookofsky, Joseph M.: In Dubio pro Conventione? Some thoughts about opt-outs, computer programs and preëmptions under the 1980 Vienna Sales Convention (CISG), 13 Duke J. of Comp. & Int'l L. (2003), 263–289

Lookofsky, Joseph M.: Loose Ends and Contorts in International Sales: Problems in the Harmonization of Private Law Rules, 39 Am. J. Comp. L. (1991), 403–416

Lookofsky, Joseph M.: The 1980 United Nations Convention on Contracts for the International Sale of Goods, in: *Blanpain* (Hrsg.), International Encyclopedia of Laws – Contracts, Deventer: Kluwer (2007) (Kurztitel: The 1980 United Nations Convention)

Lookofsky, Joseph: The CISG in Denmark and Danish Courts, The Special Issue: The Internationalisation of Danish Law, 80 Nordic J. Int'l L. (2011), 295–320

Lookofsky, Joseph M.: The Scandinavian Experience, in: *Ferrari* (Hrsg.): The 1980 Uniform Sales Law. Old Issues Revisited in the Light of Recent Experience, Milano/München: Giuffrè/Sellier European Law Publishers, S. 95–127 (Kurztitel: Scandinavian Experience)

Lookofsky, Joseph M.: Understanding the CISG: A Compact Guide to the 1980 United Nations Convention on Contracts for the International Sale of Goods, 3. Aufl., Alphen an den Rijn: Kluwer (2008) (Kurztitel: *Lookofsky*, Understanding the CISG)

Lookofsky, Joseph M.: Understanding the CISG in Scandinavia, Kopenhagen: DJOF Publishing (1996) (Kurztitel: Understanding the CISG in Scandinavia)

Lookofsky, Joseph M.: Understanding the CISG in the USA: A Compact Guide to the 1980 United Nations Convention on Contracts for the International Sale of Goods, 3. Aufl., The Hague: Kluwer 2008 (Kurztitel: Understanding the CISG in the USA)

Lookofsky, Joseph M./Flechtner, Harry M.: Zapata Retold: Attorneys Fees Are (Still) Not Governed by the CISG, 26 J. L. & Com. (2006-07), 1–9

Literatur

Lopez de Gonzalo, Marco: La vendita intenazionale, in: *Alpa/Bessone* (Hrsg.), I contratti in generale, Turin: UTET (1991), S. 901–920 (Kurztitel: Vendita intenazionale)

Lopez de Gonzalo, Marco: Vendita internazionale, Contr. Imp. 1988, 255–275

López Rodríguez, Ana M.: The Duty To Pay Interest on Advance Payments Under Art. 84(1) CISG, 2 Nordic J. Com. L. (2005), 1–9

López Rodríguez, Ana M.: The Effects of Avoidance on Obligations: The Modes of Restitution Under the 1980 U. N. Convention on the International Sale of Goods, 9 VJ (2005), 291–302

Lorenz, Stephan/Riehm, Thomas: Lehrbuch zum neuen Schuldrecht, München: Beck (2002)

Lorenz, Werner: Konsensprobleme bei international-schuldrechtlichen Distanzverträgen, AcP 159 (1960), 193–235

Lorenz, Werner: Vom alten zum neuen internationalen Schuldvertragsrecht, IPRax 1987, 269–276

Löwisch, Manfred: Arbeitskampf und Vertragserfüllung, AcP 174 (1974), 202–264

Lubbe, Gerhard: Fundamental breach under the CISG: A source of fundamentally divergent results, RabelsZ 68 (2004), 444–472

Lüderitz, Alexander: Pflichten der Parteien nach UN-Kaufrecht im Vergleich zu EKG und BGB, in: Schlechtriem (Hrsg.), Einheitliches Kaufrecht und nationales Obligationenrecht, Baden-Baden: Nomos (1987), S. 179–195 (Kurztitel: Pflichten der Parteien)

Ludwig, Katharina: Der Vertragsabschluß nach UN-Kaufrecht im Spannungsverhältnis von Common Law und Civil Law, dargestellt auf der Grundlage der Rechtsordnungen Englands und Deutschlands (Diss. Heidelberg), Frankfurt a. M.: Lang (1994)

Luig, Eva: Der internationale Vertragsschluß: Ein Vergleich von UN-Kaufrecht, UNIDROIT-Principles und Principles of European Contract Law (Diss. Heidelberg 2002), Frankfurt a. M. u. a.: Lang (2003)

Lurger, Brigitta: Die Anwendung des Wiener UNCITRAL-Kaufrechtsübereinkommens 1980 auf den internationalen Tauschvertrag und sonstige Gegengeschäfte, östZRVgl 1991, 415–431

Lurger, Brigitta: Die wesentliche Vertragsverletzung nach Art. 25 CISG, IHR 2001, 91–102

Lurger, Brigitta: Überblick über die Judikaturentwicklung zu ausgewählten Fragen des CISG (Teil 1), IHR 2005, 177–188

Lutz, Henning: The CISG and Common Law Courts: Is there really a Problem?, 35 Vic. U. Well. L. Rev. (2004), 711–733

Luzzatto, Riccardo: Vendita (dir. internaz.), in: 46 Enc. D. (1993), 502–515

Magnus, Ulrich: 25 Jahre UN-Kaufrecht, ZEuP 2006, 96–123

Magnus, Ulrich: Aktuelle Fragen des UN-Kaufrechts, ZEuP 1993, 79–99

Magnus, Ulrich: Aufhebungsrecht des Käufers und Nacherfüllungsrecht des Verkäufers im UN-Kaufrecht, in: *Schwenzer/Hager* (Hrsg.), Festschrift für Peter Schlechtriem zum 70. Geburtstag, Tübingen: Mohr (2003), S. 599–612 (Kurztitel: FS Schlechtriem)

Magnus, Ulrich: CISG and Force Majeure, in: *Šarčevič/Volken* (Hrsg.), Dubrovnik Lectures, New York u. a.: Oceana (2001), S. 1–33 (Kurztitel: CISG and Force Majeure)

Magnus, Ulrich: CISG in the German Federal Civil Court, in: *Ferrari* (Hrsg.), Quo Vadis CISG? Celebrating the 25th anniversary of the United Nations Convention on Contracts for the International Sale of Goods, München: Sellier (2005), S. 211–234 (Kurztitel: CISG in the German Federal Civil Court)

Magnus, Ulrich: Comparative editorial remarks on the provisions regarding good faith in CISG Article 7 (1) and the UNIDROIT Principles Article 1.7, in: *Felemegas* (Hrsg.), An International Approach to the Interpretation of the United Nations Convention on Contracts for the International Sale of Goods (1980) as Uniform Sales Law, Cambridge: Cambridge University Press (2007), S. 45–48 (Kurztitel: Art. 7 CISG-UP)

Magnus, Ulrich: Das Recht der vertraglichen Leistungsstörungen und der Common Frame of Reference, ZEuP 2007, 260–279

Magnus, Ulrich: Das Schadenskonzept des CISG und transportrechtliche Konventionen, in: *Thume* (Hrsg.), Transport- und Vertriebsrecht 2000, Festgabe für Rolf Herber, Neuwied: Luchterhand (1999), S. 27–36 (Kurztitel: FS Herber)

Magnus, Ulrich: Das UN-Kaufrecht – aktuelle Entwicklungen und Rechtsprechungspraxis, ZEuP 2002, 523–541

Magnus, Ulrich: Das UN-Kaufrecht – bereit für die nächste Dekade, ZEuP 2010, 881–903

Magnus, Ulrich: Das UN-Kaufrecht: Fragen und Probleme seiner praktischen Bewältigung, ZEuP 1997, 823–846

Magnus, Ulrich: Das UN-Kaufrecht: stete Weiterentwicklung der Praxis, ZEuP 2008, 318–333

Magnus, Ulrich: Das UN-Kaufrecht tritt in Kraft!, RabelsZ 51 (1987), 123–129

Literatur

Magnus, Ulrich: Das UN-Kaufrecht und die Erfüllungszuständigkeiten in der neuen EuGVO, IHR 2002, 45–52
Magnus, Ulrich: Delays in Performance Under CISG, in: *Flechtner/Brand/Walter* (Hrsg.), Drafting Contracts under the CISG, Oxford: Oxford University Press (2008), S. 459–480 (Kurztitel: Drafting Contracts)
Magnus, Ulrich: Die allgemeinen Grundsätze im UN-Kaufrecht, RabelsZ 59 (1995), 469–494
Magnus, Ulrich: Die Rügeobliegenheit des Käufers im UN-Kaufrecht, TranspR-IHR 1999, 29–34
Magnus, Ulrich: Erfahrungen mit dem Haager Waren-Kaufrecht, Erwartungen von der UNCITRAL-Konvention, in: *Hoyer/Posch* (Hrsg.), Das Einheitliche Wiener Kaufrecht, Wien: Orac (1992), S. 5–29 (Kurztitel: Erfahrungen und Erwartungen)
Magnus, Ulrich: Europäische Kaufrechtsvereinheitlichung, RabelsZ 45 (1981), 144–168
Magnus, Ulrich: Incorporation of Standard Contract Terms under the CISG, in: *Andersen/Schroeter* (Hrsg.), Sharing International Commercial Law across National Boundaries: Festschrift for Albert H. Kritzer on the Occasion of his Eightieth Birthday, London: Wildy, Simmonds & Hill (2008), S. 303–325 (Kurztitel: FS Kritzer)
Magnus, Ulrich: Internationale Aufrechnung, in: *Leible* (Hrsg.), Das Grünbuch zum Internationalen Vertragsrecht, München: Sellier (2004), S. 209–233 (Kurztitel: Aufrechnung)
Magnus, Ulrich: Konventionsübergreifende Interpretation internationaler Staatsverträge privatrechtlichen Inhalts, in: *Basedow u. a.* (Hrsg.), Aufbruch nach Europa, 75 Jahre Max-Planck-Institut für Privatrecht, Tübingen: Mohr (2001), S. 571–582 (Kurztitel: Konventionsübergreifende Interpretation)
Magnus, Ulrich: Mangelverdacht als Mangel im CISG?, in: *Heldrich/Koller/Prölls/Langenbucher/Grigoleit/Hager, J./Hey/Neuner/Petersen/Singer* (Hrsg.), Festschrift für Claus-Wilhelm Canaris zum 70. Geburtstag, München, C. H. Beck (2007), S. 257–270 (Kurztitel: FS Canaris)
Magnus, Ulrich: Reform des Haager Einheitskaufrechts, ZRP 1978, 129–133
Magnus, Ulrich: Remarks on Good Faith: The United Nations Convention on Contracts for the International Sale of Goods, 10 Pace Int'l L. Rev. (1998), 89–95
Magnus, Ulrich: Stand und Entwicklung des UN-Kaufrechts, ZEuP 1995, 202–215
Magnus, Ulrich: The Remedy of Avoidance of Contract under CISG – General Remarks and Special Cases, 25 J. L. & Com. (2005), 423–436
Magnus, Ulrich: Tracing Methodology in the CISG: Dogmatic Foundations, in: *Janssen/Meyer* (Hrsg.), CISG Methodology, München: Sellier European Law Publishers (2009), S. 33–60 (Kurztitel: CISG Methodology)
Magnus, Ulrich: Unbestimmter Preis und UN-Kaufrecht, zu OGH, 10.11.1994 – 2 Ob 547/93, IPRax 1996, 145–148
Magnus, Ulrich: UN-Kaufrecht und neues Verjährungsrecht des BGB – Wechselwirkungen und Praxisfolgen, RIW 2002, 577–584
Magnus, Ulrich: Währungsfragen im Einheitlichen Kaufrecht. Zugleich ein Beitrag zu seiner Lückenfüllung und Auslegung, RabelsZ 53 (1989), 116–143
Magnus, Ulrich: Wesentliche Fragen des UN-Kaufrechts, ZEuP 1999, 642–666
Magnus, Ulrich: Zum räumlichen internationalen Anwendungsbereich des UN-Kaufrechts und zur Mängelrüge, IPRax 1993, 390–392
Magnus, Ulrich/Lüsing, Jan: CISG und INCOTERMS, Leistungsverzug und Fixgeschäft, IHR 2007, 1–12
Majoros, Ferenc (Hrsg.): Emptio – venditio inter nationes: Convention de Vienne sur la vente internationale de marchandises: Wiener Uebereinkommen über den internationalen Warenkauf, Festgabe für Karl Heinz Neumayer, Basel: Recht und Gesellschaft (1997)
Majoros, Ferenc: Konflikte zwischen Staatsverträgen auf dem Gebiete des Privatrechts, RabelsZ 46 (1982), 84–117
Majoros, Ferenc: Le droit international privé, 4. Aufl., Paris: Presses Universitaires de France (1997) (Kurztitel: Droit privé)
Malaurie, Philippe/Aynès, Laurent: Cours de droit civil, Bd. VI: Les obligations, 7. Aufl., Paris: Cujas (1997) (Kurztitel: Les obligations)
Malaurie, Philippe/Aynès, Laurent: Cours de droit civil, Bd. VIII: Les contrats spéciaux civils et commerciaux, 14. Aufl., Paris: Éditions Cujas (2001) (Kurztitel: Les contrats spéciaux)
Maley, Kristian: The Limits to the Conformity of Goods in the United Nations Convention on Contracts for the International Sale of Goods (CISG), 12 Int'l Trade & Bus. L. Rev. (2009), 82–126
Malik, Shahdeen: Offer: Revocable or Irrevocable. Will Art. 16 of the Convention on Contracts for the International Sale Ensure Uniformity?, 25 Indian J. Int'l L. (1985), 26–49
Mallmann, Dankwart: Die Regelung der Allgemeinen Geschäftsbedingungen in Portugal, RIW 1987, 111–114
Mankowski, Peter: Anmerkung zu BGH 1.6.2005 – VIII ZR 256/04, RIW 2005, 776

Literatur

Mankowski, Peter: Der Erfüllungsortbegriff unter Art. 5 Nr. 1 lit. b EuGVVO – ein immer größer werdendes Rätsel?, IHR 2009, 46–62

Mankowski, Peter: Die Qualifikation der culpa in contrahendo – Nagelprobe für den Vertragsbegriff des europäischen IZPR und IPR, IPRax 2003, 127–135

Mankowski, Peter: Überlegungen zur sach- und interessengerechten Rechtswahl für Verträge des internationalen Wirtschaftsverkehrs, RIW 2003, 2–15

Mankowski, Peter: Zum Nachweis des Zugangs bei elektronischen Erklärungen, NJW 2004, 1901–1907

Mann, Francis A.: Anmerkung zu BGH, 4.12.1985 – VIII ZR 17/85, JZ 1986, 647

Mann, Francis A.: The Interpretation of Uniform Statutes, L. Q. R. 1946, 278–291

Mansel, Heinz-Peter/Budzikiewicz, Christine: Das neue Verjährungsrecht, Bonn: Dt. Anwaltsverlag (2002)

Marchand, Sylvain: Les limites de l'uniformisation materielle du droit de la vente internationale: mise en oeuvre de la Convention des Nations Unies du 11 avril 1980 sur la vente internationale de marchandises dans le contexte juridique suisse (Diss. Genf), Basel: Helbing & Lichtenhahn (1994) (Kurztitel: Limites de l'uniformisation materielle)

Mari, Luigi: Le prime decisioni arbitrali in applicazione dei Pricipi UNIDROIT, Dir. com. int. 1995, 487–501

Mari, Luigi: Problemi di giurisdizione in tema di rappresentanza: la convenzione di Ginevra del 1983 sulla rappresentanza nella compravendita internazionale di merci, Foro Pad. 1997, 9–25

Markel, Asa: American, English and Japanese Warranty Law Compared: Should the U. S. Reconsider Her Article 95 Declaration to the CISG, 21 Pace Int'l L. Rev. (2009), 163–204

Markus, Alexander R.: Schwerpunkte des neuen LugÜ, in: *Spühler* (Hrsg.), Aktuelle Probleme des nationalen und internationalen Zivilprozessrechts, Zürich: Schulthess (2000), S. 35–79

Markus, Alexander R.: Tendenzen beim materiellrechtlichen Vertragserfüllungsort im internationalen Zivilverfahrensrecht (Habil. Luzern 2009), Basel: Helbing Lichtenhahn (2009) (Kurztitel: Vertragserfüllungsort)

Markus, Alexander R.: Vertragsgerichtsstände nach Art. 5 Ziff. 1 RevLugÜ/EuGVVO – ein EuGH zwischen Klarheit und grosser Komplexität, AJP/PJA 8/2010, 971–986

Marly, Jochen: Softwareüberlassungsverträge, 3. Aufl., München: Beck (2000)

Martí, Juan Hernández: Spanien, in: *Graf von Westphalen* (Hrsg.), Handbuch des Kaufvertragsrechts in den EG-Staaten, Köln: O. Schmidt (1992), S. 977–1040 (Kurztitel: Handbuch des Kaufvertragsrechts)

Martin-Davidson, Susan J.: Selling Goods Internationally: Scope of the U. N. Convention on Contracts for the International Sale of Goods, 17 Mich. St. J. Int'l L. (2008), 657–702

Martinek, Michael: Die Lehre von den Neuverhandlungspflichten – Bestandsaufnahme, Kritik ... und Ablehnung, AcP 198 (1998), 329–400

Martinek, Michael: Sind Rügeverzichtsklauseln in Just-in-time-Verträgen AGB-rechtlich wirksam?, in: *Martinek* (Hrsg.), Festschrift für Günther Jahr zum siebzigsten Geburtstag: restigia iuris, Tübingen: Mohr (1993), S. 305–338 (Kurztitel: FS Jahr)

Martinez Canellas, Anselmo M.: La Interpretación y la Integración de la Convención de Viena. Sobre la Compraventa International de Mercaderías de 11 de Abril de 1980, Albolote: Editorial Comares (2004) (Kurztitel: Interpretaciòn y Integraciòn)

Martinez-Lopez, Manuel/Alfonso, Lucia: UN-Kaufrecht in Spanien, Münster: Alpmann Intern. (2000)

Martiny, Dieter: Autonome und einheitliche Auslegung im Europäischen Internationalen Zivilprozeßrecht, RabelsZ 45 (1981), 427–447

Martiny, Dieter: Europäisches Internationales Vertragsrecht – Ausbau und Konsolidierung, ZEuP 1999, 246–270

Maskow, Dietrich: Hardship and Force Majeure, 40 Am. J. Comp. L. (1992), 657–669

Maskow, Dietrich: The Convention on the International Sale of Goods from the Perspective of the Socialist Countries, in: La Vendita Internazionale, Mailand: Giuffrè (1981), S. 39–59 (Kurztitel: Perspective of the Socialist Countries)

Maskow, Dietrich: Zur Auslegung des Einheitskaufrechts der UNO-Kaufrechtskonvention von 1980 (Topic I. C. 1), in: Nationales Komitee für Rechtswissenschaft der DDR (Hrsg.), Nationalberichte zum XII. Internationalen Kongreß für Rechtsvergleichung (Sydney/Melbourne, 18.–26.8.1986), Potsdam-Babelsberg: Akademie für Staats- und Rechtswissenschaft der DDR (1986), S. 5–18 (Kurztitel: Auslegung)

Mather, Henry: Choice of Law for International Sales Issues Not Resolved by the CISG, 20 J. L. & Com. (2001), 155–208

Mather, Henry: Firm Offers Under the UCC and the CISG, 105 Dick. L. Rev. (2000–01), 31–56

Mattera, Joseph D.: The United Nations Convention on Contracts for the International Sale of Goods (CISG) and Geneva Pharmaceuticals Technology Corp. v. Barr Laboratories, Inc./Apothecon, Inc.

Literatur

v. Barr Laboratories, Inc.: The U. S. District Court for the Southern District of New york's Application and Interpretation of the Scope of the CISG, 16 Pace Int'l L. Rev. (2004), 165–191
Maultzsch, Felix: Die Rechtsnatur des Art. 1 Abs. 1 lit. b CISG zwischen internationaler Abgrenzungsnorm und interner Verteilungsnorm, in: *Bühler/Müller-Chen* (Hrsg.), Festschrift für Ingeborg Schwenzer zum 60. Geburtstag, Bern: Stämpfli (2011), S. 1213–1228 (Kurztitel: FS Schwenzer)
Maxl, Martin J.: Zur Sonderanknüpfung des Schweigens im rechtsgeschäftlichen Verkehr, IPRax 1989, 398–401
Mayer, Pierre: Les conflits de lois en matière de réserve de propriété après la loi du 12 mai 1980, J. C. P. 1981, II, 13.481
Mayer, Ulrich: Die Vereinbarung Allgemeiner Geschäftsbedingungen bei Geschäften mit ausländischen Kontrahenten (Diss. Tübingen 1984)
Mazeaud, Henri/Mazeaud, Jean/Mazeaud, Léon/Chabas, François: Leçons de Droit Civil, Bd. II/1, Obligations, Théorie Générale, 98. Aufl., Paris: Montchrestien (19981) (Kurztitel: *Mazeaud/Chabas*)
Mazeaud, Henri/Mazeaud, Jean/Mazeaud, Léon/de Juglart, Michel: Leçons de Droit Civil, Bd. III/2, Vente et Échange, 7. Aufl., Paris: Montchrestien (1987)
Mazzacano, Peter J.: Force Majeure, Impossibility, Frustration & the Like: Excuses for Non-Performance; the Historical Origins and Development of an Autonomous Commercial Norm in the CISG,, 2 Nordic J. Com. L. (2011), 1–54
Mazzoni, Alberto: CISG Article 78: Endless disagreement among commentators, much less among the courts, www.cisg.law.pace.edu/cisg/biblio/mazzotta78.html (Kurztitel: Article 78)
Mazzoni, Alberto: Cause di esonero nella Convenzione di Vienna sulla vendita internazionale di cose mobili „force majeure" nei contratti internazionali, Riv. dir. com. 1991, 539–573
Mazzotta, Francesco G.: Effects of avoidance: Comparison between the provisions of CISG Article 81 and its PECL counterparts, in: *Felemegas, John:* An International Approach to the Interpretation of the United Nations Convention on Contracts for the International Sale of Goods (1980) as Uniform Sales Law, New York: Cambridge University Press (2007), S. 518–524 (Kurztitel: Comparison)
Mazzotta, Francesco G.: Notes on the United Nations Convention on the Use of Electronic Communications in International Contracts and its Effects on the United Nations Convention on Contracts for the International Sale of Goods, 33 Rutgers Computer & Tech. L. J. (2007), 251–298
Mazzotta Francesco G.: Restitution of the Goods: Comparison between the provisions of CISG Article 82 and the counterpart provisions of PECL 9:309, in: *Felemegas, John:* An International Approach to the Interpretation of the United Nations Convention on Contracts for the International Sale of Goods (1980) as Uniform Sales Law, New York: Cambridge University Press (2007), S. 514–519 (Kurztitel: Restitution)
Mazzotta Francesco: Why Do Some American Courts Fail to Get it Right?, 3 Loyola U. Chi. Int'l L. Rev. (2005), 85–115
McCreery, John H.: Continuity of Contracts and the Euro, N. Y. Int'l L. Rev. (1999), 58–77
McGregor, Harvey: McGregor On Damages, 17. Aufl., London: Sweet & Maxwell (2003)
McKendrick, Ewan (Hrsg.): Goode on Commercial Law, 4. Aufl., London: Penguin (2010) (Kurztitel: Goode On Commercial Law)
McKendrick, Ewan (Hrsg.): Sale of Goods, London/Hong Kong: LLP (2000)
McMahon, Anthony J.: Differentiating between Internal and External Gaps in the U. N. Convention on Contracts for the International Sale of Goods: A Proposed Method for Determining „Governed by" in the Context of Article 7(2), 44 Colum. J. Trans'l L. (2006), 992–1032
McMahon, John P.: Coping with Nonconforming Tender and Insecurity Under UCC Article 2 and the CISG, 39 UCC L. J. 4 Art. 3 (2007)
McMahon, John P.: Is a Post-Breach Decline in the Value of Currency an Article 74 CISG 'Loss'?, in: *Andersen/Schroeter* (Hrsg.), Sharing International Commercial Law across National Boundaries: Festschrift for Albert H. Kritzer on the Occasion of his Eightieth Birthday, London: Wildy, Simmonds & Hill (2008), S. 347–360 (Kurztitel: FS Kritzer)
McQuillen, Marlyse: The Development of a Federal CISG Common Law in US Courts: Patterns of Interpretation and Citation, 61 U. Miami L. Rev. (2007), 509–537
Medicus, Dieter: Allgemeiner Teil des BGB, 8. Aufl., Heidelberg: C. F. Müller (2002) (Kurztitel: *Medicus, AT*)
Medwedew, Jewgeni/Rosenberg, Michail: UNO-Konferenz für internationale Kaufverträge, Außenhandel – UdSSR (Moskau) 1981 Nr. 1, 31–39
von Mehren, Arthur Taylor: The „Battle of the Forms": A Comparative View, 38 Am. J. Comp. L. (1990), 265–298
von Mehren, Arthur Taylor: The Formation of Contracts, in: Int. Enc. Comp. L., Vol. VII: Under the Auspices of the I. A. L. S., Contracts in General, Chap. 9, Tübingen/Dordrecht: Mohr/Nijhoff (1992)

Mehrings, Josef: Verbraucherschutz im Cyberlaw: Zur Einbeziehung von AGB im Internet, BB 1998, 2373–2380
Meier-Hayoz, Arthur/von der Crone, Hans Caspar: Wertpapierrecht, 2. Aufl., Bern: Stämpfli (2000)
Melin, Patrick: Gesetzesauslegung in den USA und in Deutschland: Historische Entwicklung, moderne Methodendiskussion und die Auswirkungen für das internationale Einheitskaufrecht (CISG) (Diss. Bonn), Tübingen: Mohr Siebeck (2005)
Melville, M. L.: The Nature of Fundamental Breach, 130 N. L. J. (1980), 307–310
Memmo, Daniela: Il contratto di vendita internazionale nel diritto uniforme, Riv. trim. dir. proced. civ. 1983, 180–214
Memmo, Daniela: La „sede d'affari" secondo la disciplina uniforme sulla vendita internazionale nella più recente giurisprudenza della Corte federale tedesca, Riv. trim. dir. proced. civ. 1983, 755–761
Mendes, Errol P.: The U. N. Sales Convention and U. S.-Canada Transactions. Enticing the World's Largest Trading Bloc to Do Business Under a Global Sales Law, 8 J. L. & Com. (1988), 109–144
Merkt, Hanno: Internationaler Unternehmenskauf, Köln: RWS-Verl. Kommunikationsforum (1997)
Merkt, Hanno: Internationaler Unternehmenskauf und Einheitskaufrecht, ZVglRWiss 1994, 353–378
Merrett, Louise: Article 23 of the Brussels I Regulation: A Comprehensive Code for Jurisdiction Agreements?, 58 Int'l & Comp. L. Q. (2009), 545–564
van der Mersch, Murielle/Phillippe, Denis: L'inexécution dans les contrats du commerce internationale, in: Fontaine/Viney (Hrsg.), Les Sanctions de l'inexécution des obligation contractuelle, édudes de droit comparé, Paris: LGDJ (2001), S. 701–788
Merschformann, Ulrike: Die objektive Bestimmung des Vertrasstatuts beim internationalen Warenkauf nach Art. 28 EGGBGB unter Berücksichtigung der Haager IPR-Abkommen von 1955 und 1986 (Diss. Freiburg 1990), Baden-Baden: Nomos (1991)
Mertens, Hans-Joachim/Rehbinder, Eckard: Internationales Kaufrecht: Kommentar zu den Einheitlichen Kaufgesetzen, Frankfurt a. M.: Metzner (1975)
Mestre, Jacques: Jurisprudence fran aise en matière de droit civil, B. Obligations et contrats spéciaux, 1. Obligations en général, Rev. trim. dr. civ. 1990, 462–480
Metzger, Axel: Die Haftung des Verkäufers für Rechtsmängel gemäss Artt. 41, 42 CISG, RabelsZ 73 (2009), 842–865
Metzler, Ewald: Zur Substitution, insbesondere zu ihrer Abgrenzung von der Erfüllungsgehilfenschaft, AcP 159 (1960), 143–161
Meyer, Justus: UN-Kaufrecht in der deutschen Anwaltspraxis, RabelsZ 69 (2005), 457–486
Meyer, Justus: Verbraucherverträge im UN-Kaufrecht und EU-Vertragsrecht, in: *Rasmussen-Bonne/Freer/Lüke/Weitnauer* (Hrsg.), Balancing of Interests: Liber amicorum Peter Hay zum 70. Geburtstag, Frankfurt a. M.: Recht und Wirtschaft (2005), S. 297–322 (Kurztitel: FS Hay)
Meyer, Lars: Soft Law for Solid Contracts? A Comparative Analysis of the Value of the UNIDROIT Principles of International Commercial Contracts and the Principles of European Contract Law to the Process of Contract Law Harmonization, 34 Denv. J. Int'l L. & Pol'y (2006), 119–143
Meyer, Olaf: Constructive Interpretation – Applying the CISG in the 21st Century, in: *Janssen/Meyer* (Hrsg.), CISG Methodology, München: Sellier. European Law Publishers (2009), S. 319–342 (Kurztitel: Interpretation)
Meyer, Olaf: Die Anwendung des UN-Kaufrechts in der US-amerikanischen Gerichtspraxis, IPRax 2005, 462–467
Michida, Shinichiro: Cancellation of Contract, 27 Am. J. Comp. L. (1979), 279–289
Micklitz, Hans-Wolfgang: Verbraucherschutz und Bildschirmtext, NJW 1982, 263–265
Micklitz, Hans-W./Rott, Peter: Vergemeinschaftung des EuGVÜ in der Verordnung (EG) Nr. 44/2001, EuZW 2001, 325–334
Mistelis, Loukas: Art. 55 CISG: The Unknown Factor, 25 J. L. & Com. (2005–06), 285–297
Mistelis, Loukas: CISG and Arbitration, in: *Janssen/Meyer* (Hrsg.), CISG Methodology, München: Sellier (2009), S. 375–395 (Kurztitel: CISG Methodology)
Mistelis, Loukas: CISG-AC publishes first opinion, IHR 2003, 243–244
Mittmann, Alexander: Zur Einbeziehung von Allgemeinen Geschäftsbedingungen in einen dem CISG unterliegenden Vertrag, IHR 2006, 103–106
Moecke, Hans Jürgen: Gewährleistungsbedingungen und Allgemeine Lieferbedingungen nach dem UNCITRAL-Übereinkommen über den Warenkauf, RIW 1983, 885–895
Mohs, Florian: Anmerkung zu BGer, 13.11.2003, CISG-online 840 = BGE 130 III 258, IHR 2004, 219–221
Mohs, Florian: Bundesgericht, I. zivilrechtliche Abteilung, Urteil vom 17.12.2009, BGE 136 III 56 (4A_440/2009), A. gegen B. SA, Beschwerde in Zivilsachen, AJP 2011, 425–429
Mohs, Florian: Die Vertragswidrigkeit im Rahmen des Art. 82 Abs. 2 lit. c CISG, IHR 2002, 59–66

Literatur

Mohs, Florian: Drittwirkung von Schieds- und Gerichtsstandsvereinbarungen, Frankfurt a. M./München: QUADIS/Sellier.ELP (2006) (Kurztitel: Schieds- und Gerichtsstandsvereinbarungen)

Mohs, Florian: Effects of avoidance and restitution of the goods: Remarks on the manner in which Articles 7.3.5 and 7.3.6 of the UNIDROIT Principles compare with Articles 81 and 82 of the CISG, in: *Felemegas, John* (Hrsg.): An International Approach to the Interpretation of the United Nations Convention on Contracts for the International Sale of Goods (1980) as Uniform Sales Law, Cambridge/New York u. a.: Cambridge University Press (2007), S. 252–259 (Kurztitel: Effects of Avoidance)

Mohs, Florian: The CISG and the Commodities Trade, in: *Büchler/Müller-Chen* (Hrsg.), Private Law, national – global – comparative, Festschrift für Ingeborg Schwenzer zum 60. Geburtstag, Bern: Stämpfli (2011), S. 1285–1302 (Kurztitel: FS Schwenzer)

Mohs, Florian/Zeller, Bruno: Commentary: Penalty and Liquidated Damages Clauses in CISG Contracts Revisited, 21 Mealey's Int'l Arb. Rep. (2006), 1–5

Moore, David H.: The Parol Evidence Rule and the United Nations Convention on Contracts for the International Sale of Goods: Justifying Beijing Metals & Minerals Import/Export Corp. v. American Business Center, Inc., B. Y. U. L. Rev. (1995), 1347–1376

Morrissey, Joseph/Graves, Jack M.: International Sales Law and Arbitration, Austin/Boston/Chicago/New York/Alphen aan den Rijn: Wolters Kluwer (2008)

Morscher, Thomas: Staatliche Rechtssetzungsakte als Leistungshindernisse im internationalen Warenkauf. Ihre kollisionsrechtliche Behandlung im schweizerischen IPR-Gesetz und im UN-Kaufrecht (Diss. Basel 1991), Basel: Helbing u. Lichtenhahn (1992)

Moses, Margaret L.: The Principles and Practice of International Commercial Arbitration, Cambridge (Mass): Cambridge University Press (2008) (Kurztitel: Commercial Arbitration)

Moses, Margaret L.: United Nations Convention on Contracts for the International Sale of Goods, N. J. Law. (1992), 36–39

Mosimann, Peter/Müller-Chen, Markus: Kauf eines Originals der bildenden Kunst, insbesondere einer Fotografie, in: *Büchler/Müller-Chen* (Hrsg.), Festschrift für Ingeborg Schwenzer zum 60. Geburtstag, Bern: Stämpfli (2011), S. 1303–1324 (Kurztitel: FS Schwenzer)

Mouly, Christian: La Convention de Genève sur la représentation en matière de vente internationale de marchandises, Rev. int. dr. comp. 1983, 829–839

Mouly, Christian: Que change la Convention de Vienne sur la vente internationale par rapport au droit français interne?, D. 1991, Chron., 77–79

Mugdan, Benno: Die gesammten Materialien zum Bürgerlichen Gesetzbuch für das Deutsche Reich, Bd. II, Berlin: Decker's Verlag (1899)

Muir Watt, Horatia: Anmerkung zu Civ. 1, 23.1.1996, J. C. P. (1996), éd. G, II, 22.734

Muir Watt, Horatia: L'applicabilité de la Convention des Nations Unies sur les contrats de vente internationale de marchandises devant l'arbitre international, R. D. A. I. 1996, 401–406

Müller Holger/Otto Hans-Hermann: Allgemeine Geschäftsbedingungen im internationalen Wirtschaftsverkehr, Berlin: Luchterhand (1994)

Müller, Hans-Friedrich: Europäische Vertragsrechtskodifikation und UN-Kaufrecht, GPR 2006, 168–174

Müller, Hans-Friedrich: Unternehmensregress im internationalen Geschäftsverkehr, IHR 2005, 133–138

Müller, Tobias Malte: Ausgewählte Fragen der Beweislastverteilung im UN-Kaufrecht im Lichte der aktuellen Rechtsprechung (Diss. Frankfurt a. M), München (2005) (Kurztitel: Beweislast)

Müller, Tobias Malte: Die Beweislastverteilung im UN-Kaufrecht im Spiegel der aktuellen weltweiten Rechtsprechung, RIW 2007, 673–681

Müller, Tobias Malte/Togo, Federica: Die Berücksichtigung der Überzeugungskraft ausländischer Präzedenzfälle bei der Auslegung des CISG – Die neuere italienische Rechtsprechung als Vorreiter und Vorbild, IHR 2005, 102–107

Müller-Chen, Markus: Abtretungsverbote im internationalen Rechts- und Handelsverkehr, in: *Hager/Schwenzer* (Hrsg.), Festschrift für Peter Schlechtriem zum 70. Geburtstag, Tübingen: Mohr Siebeck (2003), S. 903–921 (Kurztitel: FS Schlechtriem)

Müller-Chen, Markus: Folgen der Vertragsverletzung, Zürich: Schulthess (1999) (Kurztitel: Vertragsverletzung)

Müller-Chen, Markus/Pair, Lara M.: Avoidance for non-conformity of goods under Art. 49(1)(A) CISG, in: *Kröll/Mistelis/Perales/Rogers* (Hrsg.), Liber Amicorum Eric Bergsten. International Arbitration and International Commercial Law: Synergy Convergence and Evolution, Alphen aan den Rijn: Kluwer Law International (2011), S. 655–676

Müller-Hengstenberg, Claus D.: Computersoftware ist keine Sache, NJW 1994, 3128–3134

Mullis, Alastair: Avoidance for Breach under the Vienna Convention: A Critical Analysis of Some of the Early Cases, in: *Andenas/Jareborg* (Hrsg.), Anglo-Swedish Studies in Law, Uppsala: Iustus Förlag (1998), S. 326–355 (Kurztitel: Avoidance)

Mullis, Alastair: Termination for Breach of Contract in C. I. F. Contracts Under the Vienna Convention and English Law: Is There a Substantial Difference?, in: *Lomnicka/Morse* (Hrsg.), Contemporary Issues in Commercial Law: Essays in Honour of Professor A. G. Guest, London: Sweet & Maxwell (1997), S. 137–160 (Kurztitel: FS Guest)
Mullis, Alastair: U. K., Damages and the Vienna Sales Convention, RabelsZ 71 (2007), 35–51
Münchener Kommentar zum Bürgerlichen Gesetzbuch: hrsg. v. *Säcker/Rixecker,* 6. Aufl. (2012 ff.), teilweise noch 5. Aufl. (2006 ff.), München: Beck (Kurztitel: MünchKomm/*Bearbeiter*)
Münchener Kommentar zum Handelsgesetzbuch: hrsg. v. *K. Schmidt* Bd. 7, redigiert v. *Basedow,* 21. Aufl., München: Beck/Vahlen (2007) (Kurztitel: MünchKommHGB/*Bearbeiter*)
Münchener Kommentar zum Handelsgesetzbuch: hrsg. v. *Schmidt, K.,* 2. Aufl., München: Beck/Vahlen (2005 ff.) (Kurztitel: MünchKommHGB/*Bearbeiter*)
Münchener Kommentar zur Zivilprozessordnung: hrsg. v. *Lüke/Wax,* Bd. 3, 2. Aufl., München: Beck (2001) (Kurztitel: MünchKommZPO/*Bearbeiter*)
Münchener Vertragshandbuch: 6. Aufl., München: Beck (2005 ff.), teilweise noch 5. Aufl. 2000 ff.
Muñoz, Edgardo: Impossibility, Hardship and Exemption under Ibero-American Contract Law, 14 VJ (2010), 175–192
Muñoz, Edgardo: Modern Law of Contracts and Sales in Latin-America, Spain and Portugal, Utrecht: eleven publishing (2010)
Munz, Martin: Allgemeine Geschäftsbedingungen in den USA und Deutschland im Handelsverkehr: eine rechtsvergleichende Untersuchung der richterlichen Kontrolle vorformulierter Vertragsklauseln, Heidelberg: Recht und Wirtschaft (1992)
Murphey, Arthur G. Jr.: Consequential Damages in Contracts for the International Sale of Goods and the Legacy of Hadley, 23 Geo. Wash. J. Int'l L. & Econ. (1989), 415–474
Murphy, Maureen T.: United Nations Convention on Contracts for the International Sale of Goods: Creating Uniformity in International Sales Law, 12 Fordham Int'l L. J. (1989), 727–750
Murray, Daniel E.: The „Open Price" Sale of Goods Contract in a Worldwide Setting, 89 Com. L. J. (1984), 491–500
Murray, Carole/Cleave, Barbara: Schmitthoff's Export Trade. The Law and Practice of International Trade, 11. Aufl., London: Sweet and Maxwell (2007) (Kurztitel: International Trade)
Murray, Daniel E.: The „Open Price" Sale of Goods Contract in a Worldwide Setting, 89 Com. L. J. (1984), 491–500
Murray, Grant G.: A Corporate Counsel's Perspective of the „Battle of the Forms", 4 Can. Bus. L. J. (1979–80), 290–296
Murray, John Edward Jr.: An Essay on the Formation of Contracts and Related Matters Under the United Nations Convention on Contracts for the International Sale of Goods, 8 J. L. & Com. (1988), 11–51
Murray, John Edward Jr.: Buyer's obligations under the CISG, in: *Ferrari/Flechtner* (Hrsg.), The Draft UNCITRAL Digest and Beyond. Cases, Analysis and Unresolved Issues in the UN Sales Convention, München: Sellier, London: Sweet & Maxwell (2003), S. 440–467 (Kurztitel: Draft Digest)
Murray, John Edward Jr.: The Definitive „Battle of the Forms": Chaos Revisited, 20 J. L. & Com. (2000), 1–48
Murray, John Edward Jr.: United Nations Convention on Contracts for the International Sale of Goods: a Primer, in: Murray on Contracts, 3. Aufl., Charlottesville, Va.: Michie Co. (1990), Kap. 14, S. 871–903
Muscheler, Karlheinz/Schewe, Markus: Die invitatio ad offerendum auf dem Prüfstand, Jura 2000, 565–570
Musger, Gottfried: Die wesentliche Vertragsverletzung – Probleme des Art. 25 WKR und Parallelen im österreichischen Recht: Vorträge, Reden und Berichte aus dem Europa-Institut Nr. 168, Saarbrücken: Europa-Institut (1989)

Nabati, Mikaël F. : Les règles d'interprétation des contrats dans les Principes d'UNIDROIT et la CVIM: entre unité structurelle et diversité fonctionnelle, Rev. dr. unif. 2007, 247–263
Nadelmann, Kurt H.: The Uniform Law on the International Sale of Goods: A conflict of Laws Imbroglio, 74 Yale L. J. (1964–65), 449–464
Najork, Eike Nikolai: Treu und Glauben im CISG (Diss. Bonn 2000)
Nakamura, Hideo: Conformity of Goods with Regulatory Restrictions – BGH Decisions in the Mussels and the Pork Case, 15 VJ (2011), 53–64
Nakata, Gary Kenji: Sounds of Silence Bellow Forth Under the CISG's International Battle of Forms, 7 Transnat'l Law. (1994), 141–163
Naumann, Hanno: Der Regelungsbereich des UN-Kaufrechts im Spannungsfeld zwischen Einheitsrecht und Kollisionsrecht, Frankfurt a. M.: Lang (2000)

Literatur

Navas Navarro, Susana: UN-Kaufrecht: Anwendungsbereich und Vertragsschluss in der spanischen Rechtsprechung, IHR 2006, 74–76

Nemeczek, Heinrich: Die Vertragsübernahme als Regelungsgegenstand des UN-Kaufrechts, IHR 2011, 49–56

Ndulo, Muna: The Vienna Sales Convention 1980 and the Hague Uniform Laws on International Sale of Goods 1964: A Comparative Analysis, 38 Int'l & Comp. L. Q. (1989), 1–25

Nelson, Steven C.: A. B. A., Convention on the Limitation Period in the International Sale of Goods, 24 Int'l Law. (1990), 583–599

Nestor, Ion I.: Commission des Nations Unies pour le droit commercial international: projet de convention sur la prescription en matière de vente internationale d'objets mobiliers corporels, in: *Fabricius* (Hrsg.), Law and international trade, Festschrift für Clive M. Schmitthoff zum 70. Geburtstag, Frankfurt a. M.: Athenaeum (1973), S. 291–309 (Kurztitel: FS Schmitthoff)

Neufang, Paul: Erfüllungszwang als „remedy" bei Nichterfüllung. Eine Untersuchung zu Voraussetzungen und Grenzen der zwangsweisen Durchsetzung vertragsgemäßen Verhaltens im US-amerikanischen Recht im Vergleich mit der Rechtslage in Deutschland (Diss. Freiburg 1997), Baden-Baden: Nomos (1998)

Neuhaus, Paul Heinrich/Drobnig, Ulrich/von Hoffmann, Bernd/Martiny, Dieter: Die Immaterialgüterrechte im künftigen internationalen Privatrecht der Europäischen Gemeinschaften, RabelsZ 40 (1976), 189–232

Neumayer, Karl H.: Das Wiener Kaufrechtsübereinkommen und die sogenannte „Battle of Forms", in: *Habscheid u. a.* (Hrsg.), Freiheit und Zwang – rechtliche, wirtschaftliche und gesellschaftliche Aspekte, Festschrift zum 60. Geburtstag von Hans Giger, Bern: Stämpfli (1989), S. 501–526 (Kurztitel: Battle of Forms)

Neumayer, Karl H.: Der Vertragsschluß nach dem Recht des internationalen Warenkaufs (Wiener Übereinkommen von 1980), in: *Pfister/Will* (Hrsg.), Festschrift für Werner Lorenz zum 70. Geburtstag, Tübingen: Mohr (1991), S. 747–762 (Kurztitel: Vertragsschluß)

Neumayer, Karl H.: Les contrats d'adhésion dans les pays industrialisés, Genève: Droz (1999)

Neumayer, Karl H.: Offene Fragen zur Anwendung des Abkommens der Vereinten Nationen über den internationalen Warenkauf, RIW 1994, 99–109

Neumayer, Karl H.: Rechtsgestaltende Erklärungen im Wiener Einheitlichen Kaufrecht, in: *Basedow u. a.* (Hrsg.), Festschrift für Ulrich Drobnig zum siebzigsten Geburtstag, Tübingen: Mohr (1998), S. 97–118 (Kurztitel: FS Drobnig)

Neumayer, Karl H.: Vertragsschluß durch Kreuzofferten?, in: *Aubin u. a.* (Hrsg.), Festschrift für Otto Riese aus Anlaß seines 70. Geburtstages, Karlsruhe: Müller (1964), S. 309–328 (Kurztitel: FS Riese)

Neumayer, Karl H.: Wiener Kaufrechtsübereinkommen und Anfechtung wegen Eigenschaftsirrtums, in: Studi in memoria di Gino Gorla, Tomo II, Mailand: Giuffrè (1994), S. 1285–1277 (Kurztitel: Anfechtung wegen Eigenschaftsirrtums)

Neumayer, Karl H.: Zu Art. 8 des neuen UWG – Eine rechtsvergleichende Analyse, in: *Forstmoser* (Hrsg.), Beiträge zum Familien- und Vormundschaftsrecht, Schuldrecht, internationalen Privatrecht, Verfahrens-, Banken-, Gesellschafts-, und Unternehmensrecht, zur Rechtsgeschichte und zum Steuerrecht: Festschrift für Max Keller zum 65. Geburtstag, Zürich: Schulthess (1989), S. 727–741 (Kurztitel: FS Keller)

Neumayer, Karl H.: Zur Revision des Haager Einheitlichen Kaufrechts: Gefahrtragung, Gehilfenhaftung, fait du vendeur und Lückenproblem, in: *Ficker*, Festschrift für Ernst v. Caemmerer zum 70. Geburtstag, Tübingen: Mohr (1978), S. 955–986 (Kurztitel: FS von Caemmerer)

Neumayer, Karl H./Ming, Catherine: Convention de Vienne sur les contrats de vente internationale de marchandises. Commentaire, Lausanne: CEDIDAC (1993)

Neuvians, Nicole/Mensler, Stefan: Die Kündigung durch Einschreiben nach Einführung der neuen Briefzusatzleistungen, BB 1998, 1206–1207

Nicholas, Barry: Force Majeure and Frustration, 27 Am. J. Comp. L. (1979), 231–245

Nicholas, Barry: Impracticability and Impossibility in the U. N. Convention on Contracts for the International Sale of Goods, in: *Galston/Smit* (Hrsg.), International Sales, New York: Matthew Bender (1984), Kap. 5, S. 1–23 (Kurztitel: Impracticability)

Nicholas, Barry: Prerequisites and Extent of Liability for Breach of Contract under the U. N. Convention, in: *Schlechtriem* (Hrsg.), Einheitliches Kaufrecht und nationales Obligationenrecht, Baden-Baden: Nomos (1987), S. 283–288 (Kurztitel: Prerequisites)

Nicholas, Barry: The Vienna Convention on International Sales Law, 105 L. Q. R. (1989), 201–243

Nickel, Friedhelm G./Saenger, Ingo: Die warranty-Haftung des englischen Rechts, JZ 1991, 1050–1057

Nicoll, C. C.: Can Computers Make Contracts?, J. B. L. (1998), 35–49

Nielsen, Jens, Anmerkung zu BGH, 3.4.1996 – VIII ZR 51/95, WuB I H 1.–1.97, 131–132

Literatur

Niemann, Christopher: Einheitliche Anwendung des UN-Kaufrechts in italienischer und deutscher Rechtsprechung und Lehre (Diss. Bochum), Frankfurt a. M.: Peter Lang (2006) (Kurztitel: Einheitliche Anwendung)

Niggemann, Friedrich: Die Bedeutung des Inkrafttretens des UN-Kaufrechts für den deutsch-französischen Wirtschaftsverkehr, RIW 1991, 372–378

Niggemann, Friedrich: Die Pflichten des Verkäufers und die Rechtsbehelfe des Käufers, in: Hoyer/Posch (Hrsg.), Das Einheitliche Wiener Kaufrecht, Wien: Orac (1992), S. 77–110 (Kurztitel: Pflichten des Verkäufers)

Niggemann, Friedrich: Erreur sur une qualité substantielle de la chose et application de la C. V. I. M., R. D. A. I. 1994, 397–415 = Error about a Substantial Quality of the Goods and Application of the CISG, Int'l Bus. L. J. (1994), 397–415

Niggemann, Friedrich: Les obligations de l'acheteur sous la convention des Nations Unies sur les contrats de vente internationale de marchandises, R. D. A. I. 1988, 27–43 = Buyer's Obligations under the United Nations Convention on Contracts for the International Sale of Goods, Int'l Bus. L. J. (1988), 27–43

(Note): Unification and Certainty: The United Nations Convention on Contracts for the International Sale of Goods, 97 Harv. L. Rev. (1984), 1984–2000

Nottage, Luke: Changing Contract Lenses: Unexpected Supervening Events in English, New Zealand, U. S., Japanese, and International Sales Law and Practice, 14 Ind. J. Global Legal Stud. (2007), 385–418

Nottage, Luke: Who's Afraid of the CISG? A New Zealander's View from Australia and Japan, 36 Vict. U. Well. L. Rev. (2005), 815–845

Noussias, Konstantinos: Die Zugangsbedürftigkeit von Mitteilungen nach den Einheitlichen Haager Kaufgesetzen und nach dem UN-Kaufgesetz (Diss. Freiburg 1981), Heidelberg: Winter (1983) (Kurztitel: Zugangsbedürftigkeit von Mitteilungen)

Nyer, Damien: Withholding Performance for Breach in International Transactions: An Exercise in Equations, Proportions or Coercion, 18 Pace Int'l L. Rev. (2006), 29–81

O'Malley, Stephen/Layton, Alexander: European Civil Practice, London: Sweet & Maxwell (1989)

Oertmann, Paul: Bürgerliches Gesetzbuch, Bd. 2, 3./4. Auflage, Berlin: Heymanns (1910)

Oetiker, Christian/Weibel, Thomas (Hrsg.): Basler Kommentar zum Lugano Übereinkommen, Basel: Helbing & Lichtenhahn (2011)

Oliver, Geoffrey D.: Future Interpretations of Article 17 of the Convention on Jurisdiction and the Enforcement of Judgments in the European Communities, 70 Cornell L. Rev. (1985), 289–315

Oly, G. G.: Algemene beschouwingen over de Eenvormige wet op de internationale koop van goederen in historisch perspectief (Diss. Amsterdam), Deventer: Kluwer (1982) (Kurztitel: Algemene beschouwingen)

van Ommeslaghe, Pierre: Les clauses de force majeure et d'imprévision (hardship) dans les contrats internationaux, Rev. dr. int. 1980, 7–59

Opie, Elisabeth: Bergsten's Mark on the Law's International Reasonable Person, in: Kröll/Mistelis/Perales Viscasillas/Rogers (Hrsg.), International Arbitration and International Commercial Law: synergy, convergence, and evolution: liber amicorum Eric Bergsten, Alphen aan den Rijn, Kluwer Law International (2011), S. 677–683 (Kurztitel: FS Bergsten)

Oppetit, Bruno: L'adaptation des contrats internationaux aux changements de circonstances: la clause de „hardship", J. D. I. 1974, 794–814

Orlandi, Chiara Giovannucci: Procedural Law Issues and Law Conventions, Uniform L. Rev. 2000, 23–41

Oschmann, Friedrich: Calvo-Doktrin und Calvo-Klauseln: wechselnde Realitäten im internationalen Wirtschaftsrecht Lateinamerikas (Diss. Münster 1992/93), Heidelberg: Recht und Wirtschaft (1993)

Osman, Filali: Les principes généraux de la Lex Mercatoria – Contribution à l'étude d'un ordre juridique anational, Paris: L. G. D. J. (1992)

Ostendorf, Patrick: Noch einmal: Führt die Vereinbarung einer CIF-Klausel zum Fixgeschäft?, IHR 2009, 100–103

Osuna-González, Alejandro: Buyer's Enabling Steps to Pay the Price: Article 54 of the United Nations Convention on Contracts for the International Sale of Goods, 25 J. L. & Com. (2005–06), 299–323

Osuna-González, Alejandro: Dealing with Avoidance and its Consequences: Articles 49(2), 64(2), and 81 through 88, in: Flechtner/Walter (Hrsg.), Drafting Contracts Under the CISG, Oxford: University Press (2008), S. 481–503 (Kurztitel: Dealing with Avoidance)

Osuna-González, Alejandro: The Sixth Civil Court in Tijuana issues its Second CISG Judgment; Superior Court of Baja California Hands Down its First CISG Decision on Appeal, July 2006, www.cisg.law.pace.edu/cisg/biblio/osuna.html (Kurztitel: Tijuana CISG Judgment)

Otto, Dirk: Neues Zinsrecht in Pakistan?, RIW 1992, 854–855

Literatur

Otto, Dirk: Nochmals – UN-Kaufrecht und EG-Produkthaftungsrichtlinie, MDR 1993, 306
Otto, Dirk: Produkthaftung nach dem UN-Kaufrecht, MDR 1992, 533–538

Paal, Boris P.: Methoden der Lückenfüllung: UN-Kaufrecht und BGB im Vergleich, ZVglRWiss 2011, 64–89
Padovini, Fabio: Der internationale Kauf: Von den Haager Konventionen zur Wiener Konvention – Erfahrungen und Aussichten, ZfRVgl 1987, 87–96
Padovini, Fabio: La vendita internazionale dalle convenzioni dell'Aja alla convenzione di Vienna, Riv. dir. int. priv. proc. 1987, 47–58
Paefgen, Thomas Christian: Forum: Bildschirmtext – Herausforderung zum Wandel der allgemeinen Rechtsgeschäftslehre?, JuS 1988, 592–598
Paisant, Gilles: La loi du 6 janvier 1988 sur les opérations de vente à distance et le „télé-achat", J. C. P. (1988), éd. G, I, 3350
Palandt, Otto: Bürgerliches Gesetzbuch, 71. Aufl., München: Beck (2012) (Kurztitel: *Palandt/Bearbeiter*)
Palandt, Otto: Bürgerliches Gesetzbuch mit Einführungsgesetz, etc., 68. Aufl., München: Beck (2009) (Kurztitel: *Palandt/Bearbeiter*)
Palandt, Otto: Bürgerliches Gesetzbuch mit Einführungsgesetz, etc., 67. Aufl., München: Beck (2008) (Kurztitel: *Palandt/Bearbeiter*)
Pamboukis, Ch.: The Concept and Function of Usages in the United Nations Convention on Contracts for the International Sale of Goods, 25 J. L. & Com. (2005–06), 107–131
Papandréou-Deterville, Marie-France: La Convention de Vienne l'emporte sur le Statute of Frauds, D. 2002, Jur., 398–399
Papandréou-Deterville, Marie-France: Note sur Delchi Carrier v. Rotorex (U. S. Circuit Court of Appeals 6 December 1995), D. 1997, 226
Papandréou-Deterville, Marie-France: Note sur Hermanos Sucesores, S. A. v. Hearthside Baking Co., U. S. Ct. App. (7th Cir.), 19.11.2002, D. 2003, Somm. 2372–2373
Patterson, Elizabeth Hayes: United Nations Convention on Contracts for the International Sale of Goods: Unification and the Tension Between Compromise and Domination, 22 Stan. J. Int'l L. (1986), 263–303
Pattison, Patricia/Herron, Daniel: The Mountains Are High and the Emperor Is Far Away: Sanctity of Contract in China, 40 Am. Bus. L. J. (2003), 459–510
Pavic, Vladimir/Djordjevic, Milena: Application of the CISG before the Foreign Trade Court of Arbitration at the Serbian Chamber of Commerce – Looking Back at the Latest 100 Cases, 28 J. L. & Com. (2009), 1–62
Peacock, Darren: Avoidance and the Notion of Fundamental Breach Under the CISG: An English Perspective, 8 Int'l Trade & Bus. L. Ann. (2003), 95–133
Pearce, David/Halson, Roger: Damages for Breach of Contract: Compensation, Restitution and Vindication, 28 Oxford J. Legal Stud. (2008), 73–98
Pelichet, Michel: La vente internationale de marchandises et le conflit de lois, 201 Rec. des Cours (1988), 1987–I, 9–210 (Kurztitel: Vente internationale)
Penda Matipé, Jean Alain: Modern Sales Law in Sub-Sahara Africa (Diss. Basel 2011)
Perales Viscasillas, Maria del Pilar: Battle of Forms and the Burden of Proof: An Analysis of BGH 9 January 2002, 6 VJ (2002), 217–228
Perales Viscasillas, Maria del Pilar: CISG Articles 14 Through 24, in: *Flechtner/Brand/Walter* (Hrsg.), Drafting Contracts under the CISG, Oxford: Oxford University Press (2008), S. 295–327 (Kurztitel: Drafting Contracts)
Perales Viscasillas, Maria del Pilar: Contract Conclusion under CISG, 16 J. L. & Com. (1997), 315–344
Perales Viscasillas, Maria del Pilar: La formación del contrato en la compraventa international de mercaderías, Valencia: Tirant Lo Blanch (1996) (Kurztitel: Formación del contrato)
Perales Viscasillas, Maria del Pilar: La perfección por silencio de la compraventa internationcal en la Convención de Viena de 1980, Der. neg. 1995 (52), 9–14
Perales Viscasillas, Maria del Pilar: Late Payment Directive 2000/35/EC and the CISG, 19 Pace Int'l L. Rev., 125–142
Perales Viscasillas, Maria del Pilar: Modification and Termination of the Contract (Art. 29 CISG), 25 J. L. & Com. (2005–06), 167–178
Perales Viscasillas, Pilar: Spanish Case Law on the CISG, in: *Ferrari* (Hrsg.), Quo Vadis CISG? Celebrating the 25th anniversary of the United Nations Convention on Contracts for the International Sale of Goods, München: Sellier (2005), S. 235–261 (Kurztitel: Spanish Case Law)
Perales Viscasillas, Maria del Pilar: The Role of the UNIDROIT Principles and the PECL, in: *Janssen/Meyer* (Hrsg.), CISG Methodology, München: Sellier European Law Publishers (2009), S. 287–318 (Kurztitel: CISG Methodology)

Literatur

Perea, Trevor: Treibacher Industrie, A. G. v. Allegheny Technologies, Inc.: A Perspective on the Lacluster Implementation of the CISG by American Courts, 20 Pace Int'l L. Rev. (2008), 191–213

Perillo, Joseph M.: Damages, in: *Corbin, Arthur Linton:* Corbin on Contracts. A Comprehensive Treatise on the Rules of Contract Law, Vol. XI, Newark/San Francisco: Lexis Law Pub. (2005) (Kurztitel: Damages)

Perovic, Jelena: Selected Critical Issues regarding the Sphere of Application of the CISG, Annals Fac. L. Belgrade 2011, 181–195

Perret, Louis/Lacasse, Nicole (Hrsg.): Actes du colloque sur la vente internationale (Ottawa 14.10.1987), Montréal: Wilson & Lafleur (1989) (Kurztitel: Actes du colloque sur la vente internationale)

Peter, Alexander F.: Ersatz der Inkassokosten im grenzüberschreitenden Rechtsverkehr nach UN-Kaufrecht?, IPRax 1999, 159–161

Petrikic, Radivoje: Das Nacherfüllungsrecht im UN-Kaufrecht, Wien: Manzsche Verlags- und Universitätsbuchhandlung (1999)

Petrochilos, Georgios C.: Arbitration Conflict of Laws Rules and the 1980 International Sales Convention, 52 Rev. Hell. Dr. Int'l (1999), 191–218

Petzinger, Walter F.: „Battle of Forms" und AGB im amerikanischen Recht, RIW 1988, 673–680

Pfeiffer, Thomas: Die Entwicklung des Internationalen Vertrags-, Schuld- und Sachenrechts in den Jahren 1997–1999, NJW 1999, 3674–3687

Pfeiffer, Thomas/Batereau, Lutz: Handbuch der Handelsgeschäfte, Köln: RWS (1999)

Pfund, Peter H.: Overview of the Codification Process, 15 Brooklyn J. Int'l L. (1989), 8–22

Pichonnaz, Pascal: Impossibilité et exorbitance. Etude analytique des obstacles à l'exécution des obligations en droit suisse, Fribourg: Éditions Universitaires Fribourg Suisse (1997)

Piliounis, Peter A.: The Remedies of Specific Performance, Price Reduction and Additional Time (Nachfrist) under the CISG: Are these worthwhile changes or additions to English Sales Law?, 12 Pace Int'l L. Rev. (2000), 1–46

Piltz, Burghard: AGB in UN-Kaufverträgen, IHR 2004, 133–138

Piltz, Burghard: Anmerkung zu LG Darmstadt, Urteil vom 29.5.2001, IHR 2001, 162–163

Piltz, Burghard: Anmerkung: Einbeziehung von AGB, IHR 2007, 121–123

Piltz, Burghard: Der Anwendungsbereich des UN-Kaufrechts, AnwBl 1991, 57–62

Piltz, Burghard: Entscheidungen des BGH zum CISG, IHR 1999, 13–18

Piltz, Burghard: Export- und Importgeschäfte (UN-Kaufrecht und Incoterms), in: *Pfeiffer* (Hrsg.), Handbuch der Handelsgeschäfte, RWS (1999), S. 475–562 (Kurztitel: Export- und Importgeschäfte)

Piltz, Burghard: Gerichtsstand des Erfüllungsortes in UN-Kaufverträgen, IHR 2006, 53–59

Piltz, Burghard: Gestaltung von Exportverträgen nach der Schuldrechtsreform, IHR 2002, 2–7

Piltz, Burghard: Incoterms 2000 – ein Praxisüberblick, RIW 2000, 485–489

Piltz, Burghard: Incoterms 2010, EJCCL 2011, 1–10

Piltz, Burghard: Incoterms und UN-Kaufrecht, in: *Thume* (Hrsg.), Transport- und Vertriebsrecht 2000, Festgabe für Rolf Herber, Neuwied: Luchterhand (1999), S. 20–27 (Kurztitel: FS Herber)

Piltz, Burghard: Internationales Kaufrecht, NJW 1989, 615–621

Piltz, Burghard: Internationales Kaufrecht. Das UN-Kaufrecht in praxisorientierter Darstellung, München: Beck (1993) (Kurztitel: Internationales Kaufrecht)

Piltz, Burghard: Internationales Kaufrecht. Das UN-Kaufrecht in praxisorientierter Darstellung, 2. Aufl., München: Beck (2008) (Kurztitel: Internationales Kaufrecht)

Piltz, Burghard: Lieferverträge: Exportvertrag – Maschine, in: *Schütze/Weipert* (Hrsg.), Münchener Vertragshandbücher, Band 4: Wirtschaftsrecht III, München: Beck (2007), 6. Aufl., S. 319–390 (Kurztitel: Lieferverträge)

Piltz, Burghard: Neue Entwicklungen im UN-Kaufrecht, NJW 1994, 1101–1106

Piltz, Burghard: Neue Entwicklungen im UN-Kaufrecht, NJW 1996, 2768–2773

Piltz, Burghard: Neue Entwicklungen im UN-Kaufrecht, NJW 2000, 553–560

Piltz, Burghard: Neue Entwicklungen im UN-Kaufrecht, NJW 2003, 2056–2063

Piltz, Burghard: Neue Entwicklungen im UN-Kaufrecht, NJW 2007, 2159–2163

Piltz, Burghard: Neue Entwicklungen im UN-Kaufrecht, NJW 2009, 2258–2264

Piltz, Burghard: Neue Entwicklungen im UN-Kaufrecht, NJW 2011, 2261–2266

Piltz, Burghard: Rechtsverfolgungskosten als ersatzfähiger Schaden, in: *Bühler/Müller-Chen* (Hrsg.), Festschrift für Ingeborg Schwenzer zum 60. Geburtstag, Bern: Stämpfli (2011), S. 1387–1398 (Kurztitel: FS Schwenzer)

Piltz, Burghard: UN-Kaufrecht, in: *Graf von Westphalen* (Hrsg.), Handbuch des Kaufvertragsrechts in den EG-Staaten (einschl. Österreich, Schweiz und UN-Kaufrecht), Köln: O. Schmidt (1990), S. 1–64 (Kurztitel: UN-Kaufrecht)

Literatur

Piltz, Burghard: UN-Kaufrecht: Anwendungsbereich und Strukturen, IStR 1993, 475–481
Piltz, Burghard: UN-Kaufrecht. Wegweiser für die Praxis. Gestaltung von Export- und Importverträgen, 3. Aufl., Bonn: Economica (2000) (Kurztitel: Export- und Importverträge)
Piltz, Burghard: Urteilsanmerkung zur Entscheidung des EuGH vom 3.5.2007 – C-386/05 – zur EuGVO, NJW 2007, 1801–1802
Piltz, Burghard: Vom EuGVÜ zur Brüssel I-Verordnung, NJW 2002, 789–794
Planck, Gottlieb: Planck's Kommentar zum bürgerlichen Gesetzbuch, hrsg. v. *Strohal, Emil/Planck, Gottlieb,* 4. Aufl., Berlin/Leipzig: de Gruyter (1928) (Kurztitel: *Planck/Bearb.*)
Plantard, Jean-Pierre: Droits et obligations de l'acheteur, in: Schweizerisches Institut für Rechtsvergleichung (Hrsg.), Lausanner Kolloquium 1984, Zürich: Schulthess (1985), S. 111–117 (Kurztitel: Droits et obligations de l'acheteur)
Plantard, Jean-Pierre: Un nouveau droit uniforme de la vente internationale: La Convention des Nations Unies du 11 avril 1980, J. D. I. 1988, 311–367
Posch, Willibald: Die Pflichten des Käufers und die Rechtsbehelfe des Verkäufers, in: *Hoyer/Posch* (Hrsg.), Das Einheitliche Wiener Kaufrecht, Wien: Orac (1992), S. 143–163 (Kurztitel: Pflichten des Käufers und Rechtsbehelfe des Verkäufers)
Posch, Willibald: Kommentar zu OGH, 12.2.1998, ZfRVgl 1999, 68–70
Posch, Willibald: Pflichten des Käufers, Rechtsbehelfe des Verkäufers, Gefahrenübergang und Schadenersatz, in: *Doralt* (Hrsg.), Das UNCITRAL-Kaufrecht im Vergleich zum österreichischen Recht, Wien: Manz (1985), S. 153–183 (Kurztitel: Pflichten des Käufers)
Posch, Willibald/Kandut, Gabriele: Die allgemeinen Bestimmungen über den Warenkauf: Art. 25–29, in: *Hoyer/Posch* (Hrsg.), Das Einheitliche Wiener Kaufrecht, Wien: Orac (1992), S. 59–76
Posch, Willibald/Petz, Thomas: Austrian Cases on the UN Convention on Contracts for the International Sale of Goods (CISG), 6 VJ (2002), 1–24
Posch, Willibald/Terlitza, Ulfried: Entscheidungen des österreichischen Obersten Gerichtshof zur UN-Kaufrechtskonvention (CISG), IHR 2001, 47–56
Posch, Willibald/Terlitza, Ulfried: The CISG before Austrian Courts, in: *Ferrari* (Hrsg.), Quo Vadis CISG? Celebrating the 25th anniversary of the United Nations Convention on Contracts for the International Sale of Goods, München: Sellier (2005), S. 263–292 (Kurztitel: The CISG before Austrian Courts)
Potocki, André M.: Rapport zu Com., 16.9.2008, abrufbar unter CISG-france.org
Potzmann, Dietmar: Internationaler Kauf und IPR, ÖRiZ 1989, 262–267
Prager, Martin: Verkäuferhaftung und ausländische gewerbliche Schutzrechte. Die Haftung des Verkäufers beweglicher Sachen für deren Freiheit von gewerblichen Schutzrechten oder Urheberrechten nach dem UN-Kaufrechtsübereinkommen vom 11. April 1980 (Diss. Bremen 1986), Pfaffenweiler: Centaurus (1987)
Pribetic, Antonin I.: „Bringing Locus into Focus": A Choice-of-Law Methodology for CISG-based Concurrent Contract and Product Liability Claims, Rev. CISG (2004/2005), 179–223
Primak, L. Scott: Computer Software: Should the U. N. Convention on Contracts for the International Sale of Goods Apply? A Contextual Approach to the Question, 11 Computer L. J. (1991), 197–231
Problems of Unification of International Sales Law: Working Papers Submitted to the Colloquium of the International Association of Legal Science Potsdam, August 1977, New York: Oceana (1980) = 7 Dig. Com. L. (1980) (Kurztitel: Problems of Unification)
Prosser, William Lloyd: Prosser and Keeton on the law of torts, 5. Aufl., St. Paul (Minn.): West Publ. Comp. (1984)
Prütting, Hanns/Wegen, Gerhard/Weinreich, Gerd: BGB: Kommentar, 4. Aufl., Köln: Luchterhand (2009) (Kurztitel: *PWW/Bearbeiter*)
Pünder, Hermann: Das Einheitliche UN-Kaufrecht – Anwendung kraft kollisionsrechtlicher Verweisung nach Art. 1 Abs. 1 lit. b UN-Kaufrecht, RIW 1990, 869–873

Rabel, Ernst: A Draft of an International Law of Sales, 5 U. Chic. L. Rev. (1938), 543–565 = Ges. Aufs. Bd. 3, Tübingen: Mohr (1967), 613–636
Rabel, Ernst: Aufgabe und Notwendigkeit der Rechtsvergleichung, in: *Leser* (Hrsg.), Gesammelte Aufsätze, Vol. 3: Arbeiten zur Rechtsvergleichung und zur Rechtvereinheitlichung 1919–1945, Tübingen: Mohr Siebeck (1967), S. 1–21 (Kurztitel: Aufgabe und Notwendigkeit der Rechtsvergleichung)
Rabel, Ernst: Das Recht des Warenkaufs, Bd. 1, Berlin: de Gruyter (1957) (Kurztitel: Recht des Warenkaufs, Bd. 1)
Rabel, Ernst: Der Entwurf eines einheitlichen Kaufgesetzes, RabelsZ 9 (1935), 1–79, 339–363 = Ges. Aufs. Bd. 3, Tübingen: Mohr (1967), 522–612
Rabel, Ernst: Die eigene Handlung des Schuldners und des Verkäufers, RheinZ 1 (1909), 187–226

Literatur

Rabel, Ernst: Recht des Warenkaufs, Bd. 1 (unveränderter Nachdruck der Ausgabe von 1936) und Bd. 2, Berlin: de Gruyter (1957, 1958) (Kurztitel: Recht des Warenkaufs, Bd. 1/2)

Rabel, Ernst: Gesammelte Aufsätze, hrsg. v. *Leser,* Bd. 1, Arbeiten zum Privatrecht 1907–1930, Tübingen: Mohr (1965); Bd. 3, Arbeiten zur Rechtsvergleichung und zur Rechtsvereinheitlichung 1919–1954, Tübingen: Mohr (1967) (Kurztitel: Ges. Aufs. Bd. 1/3)

Rabel, Ernst: The Conflict of Laws. A Comparative Study, Bd. 2, 2. Aufl., Michigan: Michigan Legal Studies (1960) (Kurztitel: The Conflict of Laws)

Rabel, Ernst: The Hague Conference on the Unification of Sales Law, 1 Am. J. Comp. L. (1952), 58–69

Rade, Christophe: L'autonomie de l'action en garantie des vices cachés, Anmerkung zu Civ. 1, 14.5.1996, J. C. P. (1997), éd G, I, 4009

Rajski, Jerzy: Method of Unification of Law for the International Sale of Goods, National Report: Poland (Topic I. C. 1), 12th Congress, International Academy of Comparative Law, Sydney/Melbourne (18.–26.8.1986), in: Rapports polonais présentés au douzième Congrès International de Droit Comparé, Warschau 1986, S. 45–54

Ramberg, Christina Hultmark: The E-Commerce Directive and formation of contract in a comparative perspective, European L. Rev. 2001, 429–450

Ramberg, Jan: International Commercial Transactions, 3. Auflage. Stockholm 2004. (Kurztitel: International Transactions)

Ramberg, Jan: The Law of Freight Forwarding, Zürich: FIATA (2002)

Ramberg, Jan: Unification of the Law of International Freight Forwarding, ULR 1998, 5–14

Ramos Muñoz, David: The Rules on Communication of Defects in the CISG: Static Rules and Dynamic Environments. Different Scenarios for a Single Player, http://www.cisg.law.pace.edu/cisg/biblio/munoz.html (Kurztitel: Communication of Defects)

Ramos Muñoz, David: Modern Law of Contracts and Sales in Latin America, Spain and Portugal (International Commerce and Arbitration), Den Haag, 2011

Randall, Kenneth C./Norris, John E.: A New Paradigm for International Business Transactions, 71 Wash. U. L. Q. (1993), 599

Ranieri, Filippo: Europäisches Obligationenrecht, 3. Auflage, Berlin u. a.: Springer (2009) (Kurztitel: Europ. Obligationenrecht)

Rapsomanikis, Michael G.: Frustration of Contract in International Trade Law and Comparative Law, 18 Duq. L. Rev. (1980), 551–573

Rathjen, Peter: Haftungsentlastung des Verkäufers oder Käufers nach Art. 79, 80 CISG, RIW 1999, 561–565

Rauda, Christian/Etier, Guillaume: Warranty for Intellectual Property Rights in the International Sale of Goods, 4 VJ (2000), 30–61

Rauscher, Thomas: Europäisches Zivilprozeßrecht, 2. Aufl., München: Sellier. European Law Publishers (2006) (Kurztitel: *Rauscher/Bearbeiter*)

Rauscher, Thomas: Verpflichtung und Erfüllungsort in Art. 5 Nr. 1 EuGVÜ (Diss. München 1983), München: Florentz (1984) (Kurztitel: Verpflichtung und Erfüllungsort)

Rauscher, Thomas: Zuständigkeitsfragen zwischen CISG und Brüssel I, in: *Lorenz/Trunk/Eidenmüller/Wendehorst/Adolff* (Hrsg.), Festschrift für Andreas Heldrich zum 70. Geburtstag, München: Beck (2005), S. 933–953 (Kurztitel: FS Heldrich)

Recknagel, Christian: Die Trennung von Zivil- und Handelsrecht unter besonderer Berücksichtigung der Untersuchungs- und Rügepflicht nach § 377 HGB. Eine rechtsvergleichende Untersuchung unter Einbeziehung internationaler Einheitsrechte (EKG, UN-Kaufrecht) und des französischen, englischen, amerikanischen und schweizerischen Rechts (Diss. Giessen 1984), Frankfurt a. M.: Lang (1985)

Réczei, László: The Area of Operation of the International Sales Conventions, 29 Am. J. Comp. L. (1981), 513–522

Réczei, László: The Rules of the Convention Relating to its Field of Application and to its Interpretation, in: Problems of Unification of International Sales Law, New York: Oceana (1980), S. 53–103 = 7 Dig. Com. L. (1980), S. 53–103 (Kurztitel: Rules of the Convention)

Redeker, Helmut: Geschäftsabwicklung mit externen Rechnern im Bildschirmtextdienst, NJW 1984, 2390–2394

Rehbinder, Eckard: Vertragsschluß nach UN-Kaufrecht im Vergleich zu EAG und BGB, in: *Schlechtriem* (Hrsg.), Einheitliches Kaufrecht und nationales Obligationenrecht, Baden-Baden: Nomos (1987), S. 149–170 (Kurztitel: Vertragsschluß)

Reich, Norbert/Micklitz, Hans-Wolfgang: Verbraucherschutzrecht in den EG-Staaten, New York/Cincinnatti: van Nostrand Reinhold Company (1981)

Reichsgerichtsrätekommentar: Das Bürgerliche Gesetzbuch mit besonderer Berücksichtigung der Rechtsprechung des Reichsgerichts und des Bundesgerichtshofes, hrsg. v. den Mitgliedern des

Bundesgerichtshofes, 7 Bände, 12. Aufl., Berlin: de Gruyter (1974–1999) (Kurztitel: RGRK/*Bearbeiter*)

Reidt, Olaf/Stickler, Thomas/Glahs, Heike: Vergaberecht, 2. Aufl., Köln: O. Schmidt (2003) (Kurztitel: Reidt/Stickler/Glahs/*Bearbeiter*)

Reifner, Claire: Stillschweigender Ausschluss des UN-Kaufrechts im Prozess?, IHR 2002, 52–58

Reimers-Zocher, Birgit: Beweislastfragen im Haager und Wiener Kaufrecht (Diss. Hamburg 1994), Frankfurt a. M.: Lang (1995)

Reinhart, Gert: Die weltweite Vereinheitlichung des Kaufrechts im 20. Jahrhunderts, in: *Peter Müller-Graf/Roth* (Hrsg.), Recht und Rechtswissenschaft, Signaturen und Herausforderungen zum Jahrtausendbeginn, Heidelberg: Müller (2001), S. 329–349

Reinhart, Gert: Erschwerter Ausschluß der Anwendung des Einheitlichen Kaufrechts, IPRax 1986, 288–290

Reinhart, Gert: Fälligkeitszinsen und UN-Kaufrecht, IPRax 1991, 376–379

Reinhart, Gert: UN-Kaufrecht. Kommentar zum Übereinkommen der Vereinten Nationen vom 11. April 1980 über Verträge über den internationalen Warenkauf, Heidelberg: C. F. Müller (1991)

Reinhart, Gert: Vom Haager zum Wiener Einheitlichen Kaufrecht. Italien und die Bundesrepublik Deutschland auf gleichem Weg in unterschiedlichem Tempo, Jb. It. R. 2 (1989), 65–75

Reinhart, Gert: Zehn Jahre deutsche Rechtsprechung zum Einheitlichen Kaufrecht, IPRax 1985, 1–5

Reinhart, Gert: Zum Inkrafttreten des UN-Kaufrechts für die Bundesrepublik Deutschland. Erste Entscheidungen deutscher Gerichte, IPRax 1990, 289–292

Reinhart, Gert: Zum Sprachenproblem im grenzüberschreitenden Handelsverkehr, IPRax 1982, 226–229

Reinhart, Gert: Zur nachträglichen Änderung des Vertragsstatuts nach Art. 27 Abs. 2 EGBGB durch Parteivereinbarung im Prozeß, Anm. zu OLG Köln, IPRax 1995, 365–371

Reinhart, Gert: Zurückbehaltungsrecht und Unsicherheitseinrede nach UN-Kaufrecht im Vergleich zu EKG und BGB, in: *Schlechtriem* (Hrsg.), Einheitliches Kaufrecht und nationales Obligationenrecht, Baden-Baden: Nomos (1987), S. 361–383 (Kurztitel: Zurückbehaltungsrecht)

Reinicke, Dietrich/Tiedtke, Klaus: Kreditsicherung: durch Schuldbeitritt, Bürgschaft, Patronatserklärung, Garantie, Pfandrecht an beweglichen Sachen und Rechten, Hypothek und Grundschuld, 4. Aufl., Neuwied: Luchterhand (2000)

Reischauer, Rudolph: Der Entlastungsbeweis des Schuldners (§ 1298 ABGB). Ein Beitrag zum Recht der Leistungsstörungen mit rechtsvergleichenden Bezügen (Habil. Linz), Berlin: Duncker & Humblot (1975)

Reithmann, Christoph/Martiny, Dieter (Hrsg.): Internationales Vertragsrecht: Das internationale Privatrecht der Schuldverträge, 6. Aufl., Köln: O. Schmidt (2004) (Kurztitel: Reithmann/Martiny/*Bearbeiter*)

Remien, Oliver: Die Währung von Schaden und Schadensersatz – Grundlagen und vertragsrechtliche Besonderheiten, RabelsZ 53 (1989), 245–292

Remien, Oliver: Zwingendes Vertragsrecht und Grundfreiheiten des EG-Vertrages (Habil. Hamburg 1999/2000), Tübingen: Mohr Siebeck (2003) (Kurztitel: Zwingendes Vertragsrecht)

Renck, Andreas W.: Der Einfluß der Incoterms 1990 auf das UN-Kaufrecht. Eine Untersuchung zu den rechtlichen Wirkungen der Incoterms 1990 im Recht des internationalen Warenkaufs, Münster: Lit (1995)

Report of the A. B. A. Committee on International Energy Transactions, 8 Energy L. J. (1987), 147–158

Report of the A. B. A. House of Delegates, 18 Int'l Law (1984), 39 ff.

Resch, Reinhard: Zur Rüge bei Sachmängeln nach UN-Kaufrecht, ÖJZ 1992, 470–479

Rheinstein, Max: Die Struktur des vertraglichen Schuldverhältnisses im anglo-amerikanischen Recht, Berlin: de Gruyter (1932)

Richardi, Reinhard: Auswirkungen eines Arbeitskampfes auf Schuldverhältnisse mit Dritten, JuS 1984, 825–836

Richards, Bradley J.: Contracts for the International Sale of Goods: Applicability of the United Nations Convention, 69 Iowa L. Rev. (1983), 209–240

Riese, Otto: Der Entwurf zur internationalen Vereinheitlichung des Kaufrechts, RabelsZ 22 (1957), 16–116

Riese, Otto: Die Haager Konferenz über die internationale Vereinheitlichung des Kaufrechts, RabelsZ 29 (1965), 1–100

Riesenkampff, Philipp: Die Beweisbarkeit des Zugangs beim Telefax in Deutschland und England, ZVglRWiss 107 (2008), 428–449

Rigaux, François: Le domaine d'application de la loi uniforme sur la vente internationale des objets mobiliers corporels et de la loi uniforme sur la formation de ces contrats de vente, Journal des Tribunaux 1972, 561–572

Literatur

Rimke, Joern: Force majeure and hardship: Application in international trade practice – with specific regard to the CISG and the UNIDROIT Principles of International Commercial Contracts, CISG Rev. 2000, 197–243

Rivista trimestrale di diritto e procedura civile: Seminario „Obbligazioni del venditore e del compratore" in Milano (26.11.1989), Riv. trim. dir. proced. civ. 1990, 715–810

Rizzi, A.: Interpretazione e integrazione della legge uniforme sulla vendita internazionale di cose mobili, Riv. di diritto privato 1997, 237–285

Robertson, R.J.Jr.: The Right to Demand Adequate Assurance of Due Performance: Uniform Commercial Code Section 2–609 and Restatement (Second) of Contracts Section 251, 38 Drake L. Rev. (1988–89), 305

Rodière, René: La Formation du Contrat, Paris: A. Pedone (1976)

Rohwer, Claude D./Coe, Jack D.: The 1980 Vienna Convention on the International Sale of Goods and the UCC – Peaceful Coexistence?, in: *Campbell/Rohwer* (Hrsg.), Legal Aspects of International Business Transactions, Amsterdam, New York, Oxford: North-Holland (1984), S. 225–378

Rolland, Walter: Vorschläge zur Schuldrechtsreform auf dem Hintergrund internationaler Entwicklungen, in: *Schwenzer/Hager* (Hrsg.), Festschrift für Peter Schlechtriem zum 70. Geburtstag, Tübingen: Mohr Siebeck (2003), S. 629–655 (Kurztitel: FS Schlechtriem)

Romein, Annemieke: Gefahrtragung nach UN-Kaufrecht im Vergleich zu deutschem Recht (Diss. Heidelberg 1999)

Romito, Angela Maria/Sant'Elia, Charles: CISG: Italian Court and Homeward Trend, 14 Pace Int'l L. Rev. (2002), 179–203

Rosati, Francesca: Anmerkung zu Trib. Vigevano, 12.7.2000, IHR 2001, 78–81

Rosch, Wolfgang: Anm. zu Tribunal Supremo, 28.1.2000, D. 2002, Somm. 322–323

Rosch, Wolfgang: Pactum de non cedendo im französischen Recht: Totgesagte leben länger!, RIW 2001, 604–609

Rosch, Wolfgang/Spiegel, Nico: Consentement à la vente et interprétation de la volonté des parties, D. 2002, Jur. 396–398

Rosenberg, Leo: Die Beweislast auf der Grundlage des BGB und der ZPO, 5. Aufl., München: Beck (1965)

Rosenberg, Mark N.: The Vienna Convention: Uniformity in Interpretation for Gap-Filling – An Analysis and Application, 20 Aust. Bus. L. Rev. (1992), 442–459

Rosett, Arthur: Critical Reflections on the United Nations Convention on Contracts for the International Sale of Goods, 45 Ohio St. L.J. (1984), 265–305

Rösler, Hannes: Hardship in German Codified Private Law – In Comparative Perspective to English, French and International Contract Law, ERPL 2007, 483–513

Roßmeier, Daniela: Schadensersatz und Zinsen nach UN-Kaufrecht – Artt. 74–78 CISG, RIW 2000, 407–415

Roßnagel, Alexander/Pfitzmann, Andreas: Der Beweiswert von E-Mail, NJW 2003, 1209–1214

Roth, Marianne/Happ, Richard: Interpretation of Uniform Law Instruments According to Principles of International Law, Uniform L. Rev. 1997, 700–711

Roth, Marianne/Zenker, Wolfgang: UN-Kaufrecht und internationale Schiedsverfahren: the Third Annual Willem C. Vis International Commercial Arbitration Moot 1995/96, ZEuP 1997, 190–194

Roth, P. M.: The Passing of Risk, 27 Am. J. Comp. L. (1979), 291–310

Roth, Wulf-Henning/Kunz, Christian: Zur Bestimmbarkeit des Preises im UN-Kaufrecht, RIW 1997, 17–21

Rott, Thilo: Vereinheitlichung des Rechts der Mobiliarsicherheiten: Möglichkeiten und Grenzen im Kollisions-, Europa-, Sach- und Vollstreckungsrecht unter Berücksichtigung des US-amerikanischen Systems der Kreditsicherheiten (Diss. Freiburg 1999), Tübingen: Mohr (2000)

Rovelli, Luigi: Conflitti tra norme della Convenzione e norme di diritto internazionale privato, in: La Vendita Internazionale, Mailand: Giuffrè (1981), 89–112 (Kurztitel: Conflitti)

Rowley, Keith A.: A Brief History of Anticipatory Repudiation in American Contract Law, 69 U. Cin. L. Rev. (2001), 565–639

Rubanov, A./Tschikvadse, V.: Some Aspects of the Unification of the Law of Sales, in: *Honnold* (Hrsg.), Unification of the Law Governing International Sales, Paris: Dalloz (1966), S. 333–361 (Kurztitel: Some Aspects)

Rudolph, Helga: Kaufrecht der Export- und Importverträge: Kommentierung des UN-Übereinkommens über internationale Warenkaufverträge mit Hinweisen für die Vertragspraxis, Freiburg: Haufe (1996)

Rummel, Peter (Hrsg.): Kommentar zum Allgemeinen bürgerlichen Gesetzbuch, 3. Auflage, Wien: Manz (2004 ff.)

Literatur

Rummel, Peter: Schadenersatz, höhere Gewalt und Fortfall der Geschäftsgrundlage, in: *Hoyer/Posch* (Hrsg.), Das Einheitliche Wiener Kaufrecht, Wien: Orac (1992), S. 177–193 (Kurztitel: Schadenersatz)

Rummel, Peter: Telefax und Schriftform, in: *Aicher* (Hrsg.), Beiträge zum Zivil- und Handelsrecht, Festschrift für Rolf Ostheim zum 65. Geburtstag, Wien: Orac (1990), S. 211–224 (Kurztitel: FS Ostheim)

Rummer, Hans: Die Verteilung bei knappen Kontingenten, NJW 1988, 225–235

Rüetschi, David: Substanziierung der Mängelrüge – Bundesgericht, I. Zivilabteilung, Urteil 4C.395/2001 vom 28. Mai 2002, Recht 2003, 115–121

Rütten, Wilhelm: Zur Entstehung des Erfüllungszwangs im Schuldverhältnis, in: *Lange u. a.* (Hrsg.), Festschrift für Joachim Gernhuber, Tübingen: Mohr (1993), S. 939–959 (Kurztitel: FS Gernhuber)

Ryan, Lisa M.: The Convention on Contracts on the International Sale of Goods, Divergent Interpretations, 4 Tul. J. Int'l & Comp. L. (1995), 99–118

Ryffel, Gritli: Die Schadenersatzhaftung des Verkäufers nach dem Wiener Übereinkommen über internationale Warenkaufverträge vom 11. April 1980 (Diss. Zürich), Bern: Lang (1992)

Sabbagh-Farshi, Fariba: Die vorvertragliche Haftung im UN-Kaufrecht und in den Unidroit- und Lando-Prinzipien unter Einbeziehung des deutschen und englischen Rechts (Diss. Hamburg), Frankfurt a. M.: Lang (2008)

Sacerdoti, Giorgio: I criteri di applicazione della convenzione di Vienna sulla vendita internazionale: diritto uniforme, diritto internazionale privato e autonomia dei contraenti, Riv. trim. dir. proced. civ. 1990, 733–748

von Sachsen Gessaphe, Karl August: Internationales Privatrecht und UN-Kaufrecht, 2. Aufl., Berlin: Berliner Wissenschafts-Verlag (2007) (Kurztitel: IPR und UN-Kaufrecht)

Saenger, Ingo/Sauthoff, Elisabeth: Die Aufrechnung im Anwendungsbereich des CISG, IHR 2005, 189–195

Saidov, Djakhongir: Anticipatory Non-Performance and Underlying Values of the UNIDROIT Principles, Rev. dr. unif. 2006, 795–823

Saidov, Djakhongir: Cases on CISG decided in the Russian Federation, 7 VJ (2003), 1–62

Saidov, Djakhongir: Damages: The Need for Uniformity, 25 J. L. & Com. (2006), 393–403

Saidov, Djakhongir: Damage to Business Reputation and Goodwill under the Vienna Sales Convention, in: *Saidov/Cunnington* (Hrsg.), Contract Damages: Domestic and International Perspectives, Oxford: Hart (2008), S. 389–418

Saidov, Djakhongir: Documentary Performance and the CISG, in: *Schwenzer/Spagnolo* (Hrsg.), State of Play, The 3rd Annual MAA Peter Schlechtriem CISG Conference, The Hague: Eleven International Publishing (2012), S. 49–88 (Kurztitel: Documentary Performance)

Saidov, Djakhongir: Methods of Limiting Damages under the Vienna Convention on Contracts for the International Sale of Goods, www.cisg.law.pace.edu/cisg/biblio/saidov.html. (Kurztitel: Limiting Damages)

Saidov, Djakhongir: Standards of Proving Loss and Determining the Amount of Damages, 22 J. Cont. L. (2006), 1–76

Saidov, Djakhongir: The Law of Damages in International Sales: The CISG and other International Instruments, Oxford: Hart Publishing (2008) (Kurztitel: Damages in Int'l Sales)

Saidov, Djakhongir: The Present State of Damages under the CISG: A Critical Assessment, 13 VJ (2009), 197–216

Saiegh, Sandra: Avoidance Under the CISG and Its Challenges Under International Organizations Commercial Transactions, 25 J. L. & Com. (2005), 443–449

Salama, Shani: Pragmatic Responses to Interpretive Impediments: Article 7 of the CISG – An Inter-American Application, 38 U. Miami Inter-Am. L. Rev. (2006), 225–250

Salger, Hanns-Christian: Beschaffung und Beschaffenheit. Zur vertraglichen Haftung des Warenverkäufers für seine Lieferquelle unter Betrachtung insbesondere des deutschen und amerikanischen Rechts als Beitrag zum UN-Kaufrecht (Diss. Freiburg 1984), Köln: Heymanns (1985)

Sampson, Herbert M.: Title-Passage Rule: Applicable Law Under the CISG, 16 Int'l Tax J. (1990), 137–152

Samson, Claude: Etude comparative de certaines dispositions de la Convention de Vienne et les règles du droit québécois en la matière, in: *Perret/Lacasse* (Hrsg.), Actes du colloque sur la vente internationale, Montréal: Wilson & Lafleur (1989), S. 105–135 (Kurztitel: Etude comparative)

Samson, Claude: La Convention des Nations Unies sur les contrats de vente internationale de marchandises. Etude comparative des dispositions de la Convention et des règles de droit québécois en la matière, 23 Cah. de Dr. (1982), 919–980

Sandrock, Otto: Die kollisionsrechtliche Behandlung der Deliktshaftung bei der Verletzung von gewerblichen Schutzrechten und Urheberrechten, in: *von Caemmerer* (Hrsg.), Vorschläge und Gutachten zur

Reform des deutschen internationalen Privatrechts der außervertraglichen Schuldverhältnisse, Tübingen: Mohr (1983), S. 380–439

Sanilevici, Renée: Die Rechtsprechung des israelischen Obersten Gerichts betreffend das Gesetz über den Internationalen Kaufvertrag, RIW 1988, 346–349

Sannini, Ilaria: L'applicazione della Convenzione di Vienna sulla vendita internazionale negli Stati Uniti, Padua: Cedam (2006) (Kurztitel: L'applicazione)

Šarčević, Petar: Articles 53–65 CISG, in: *Ferrari/Flechtner* (Hrsg.), The Draft UNCITRAL Digest and Beyond. Cases, Analysis and Unresolved Issues in the UN Sales Convention, München: Sellier/ London: Sweet & Maxwell (2003), S. 482–495 (Kurztitel: Draft Digest)

Šarčević, Petar: The CISG and Regional Unification, in: *Ferrari* (Hrsg.), The 1980 Uniform Sales Law. Old issues revisited in the light of recent experiences. Verona Conference 2003, Mailand/München: Giuffrè/Sellier European Law Punlishers (2003), S. 3–17 (Kurztitel: Regional Unification)

Šarčević, Petar/Volken, Paul (Hrsg.): International Sale of Goods: Dubrovnik Lectures (11.–23.3.1985), New York: Oceana (1986) (Kurztitel: Dubrovnik Lectures)

Sargeant, Malcolm: An amended Acquired Rights Directive, J. Bus. L. (1998), 577–590

Sauthoff, Elisabeth: Auslegung der Art. 75, 76 CISG nach Treu und Glauben?, IHR 2005, 151–154

Sauthoff, Elisabeth: Lieferverzug als wesentliche Vertragsverletzung bei Vereinbarung sofortiger Lieferung und wirksame Einbeziehung fremdsprachiger AGB, IHR 2005, 21–24

Schaaf, Robert W.: Entry Into Force in 1988 of UN Convention on Contracts for the International Sale of Goods, 15 Int'l J. Leg. Inf. (1987), 56–59

Schack, Haimo: Der Erfüllungsort im deutschen, ausländischen und internationalen Privat- und Zivilprozeßrecht, Frankfurt a. M.: Metzner (1985) (Kurztitel: Erfüllungsort)

Schack, Haimo: Der internationale Klägergerichtsstand des Verkäufers, IPRax 1986, 82–85

Schack, Haimo: Internationales Zivilverfahrensrecht, 4. Aufl., München: Beck (2006) (Kurztitel: Zivilverfahrensrecht)

Schack, Haimo: Stare decisis ohne Rücksicht auf die Zuständigkeitsgerechtigkeit, ZEuP 1995, 659–668

Schackel, Torsten: Der Anspruch auf Ersatz des negativen Interesses bei Nichterfüllung von Verträgen, ZEuP 2001, 248–275

Schackmar, Rainer: Die Lieferpflicht des Verkäufers in internationalen Kaufverträgen, Berlin: Schmidt (2001)

Schäfer, Frederike: Die Wahl nicht-staatlichen Rechts nach Art. 3 Abs. 2 des Entwurfs einer Rom-I-VO – Auswirkungen auf das optionale Instrument des europäischen Vertragsrechts, GPR 2006, 54–60

Schäfer, Frederike: Failure of performance caused by other party: Editorial remarks on wether and the extent to which the UNIDROIT Principles may be used to help interpret Article 80 of the CISG, in: *Felemegas* (Hrsg.), An International Approach to the Interpretation of the United Nations Convention on Contracts for the International Sale of Goods (1980) as Uniform Sales Law, Cambridge: Cambridge University Press (2003), S. 246–252 (Kurztitel: Failure of performance caused by other party)

Schäfer, Frederike: Zur Anwendbarkeit des UN-Kaufrechts auf Werklieferungsverträge, IHR 2003, 118–121

Scheifele, Bernd: Die Rechtsbehelfe des Verkäufers nach deutschem und UN-Kaufrecht (Diss. Freiburg), Rheinfelden: Schäuble (1986)

Scherner, Karl Otto: Rücktrittsrecht wegen Nichterfüllung. Untersuchungen zur deutschen Privatrechtslehre der Neuzeit (Diss. Mainz 1962), Wiesbaden: Steiner (1965)

von Scheven, Michael: Der Sukzessivlieferungsvertrag – Eine rechtsvergleichende Untersuchung zum deutschen Recht, zum Haager Einheitlichen Kaufrecht und zum UN-Kaufrecht (Diss. Giessen), Frankfurt a. M.: Lang (1984)

Schilf, Sven: Writing in confirmation: valid evidence of a sales contract? Reflections on a Danish case regarding usages, CISG and the UNIDROIT-Principles, Uniform L. Rev. 1999, 1004–1009

Schlechtriem, Peter (Hrsg.): Einheitliches Kaufrecht und nationales Obligationenrecht. Fachtagung Einheitliches Kaufrecht der Gesellschaft für Rechtsvergleichung, Freiburg i. Br. 16./17.2.1987, Baden-Baden: Nomos (1987) (Kurztitel: Einheitliches Kaufrecht und nationales Obligationenrecht)

Schlechtriem, Peter (Hrsg.): Kommentar zum Einheitlichen UN-Kaufrecht: Das Übereinkommen der Vereinten Nationen über Verträge über den internationalen Warenkauf – (CISG-Kommentar), 3. Aufl., München: Beck (2000)

Schlechtriem, Peter: 10 Jahre CISG – Der Einfluß des UN-Kaufrechts auf die Entwicklung des deutschen und des internationalen Schuldrechts, IHR 2001, 12–18

Schlechtriem, Peter: Anmerkung zu BGH, 2.3.2005, CISG-online 999 = JZ 2005, 844–848

Schlechtriem, Peter: Anmerkung zu BGH, 24.3.1999, VIII ZR 121/98, JZ 1999, 794–797

Literatur

Schlechtriem, Peter: Anmerkung zu den Schiedssprüchen SCH-4366 (15.6.1994) und SCH-4318 (15.6.1994) des Internationalen Schiedsgerichts der gewerblichen Wirtschaft in Österreich, RIW 1995, 592–594

Schlechtriem, Peter: Anmerkung zu OLG Köln, Urteil vom. 22.2.1994, EWiR 1994, 867–868

Schlechtriem, Peter: Anmerkung zu OLG München, Urteil vom 11.3.1998, EWiR 1998, 549–550

Schlechtriem, Peter: Anwaltskosten als Teil des ersatzfähigen Schadens, IPRax 2002, 226–227

Schlechtriem, Peter: Anwendungsvoraussetzungen und Anwendungsbereich des UN-Übereinkommens über Verträge über den internationalen Warenkauf (CISG), AJP 1992, 339–357

Schlechtriem, Peter: Aufhebung des Vertrages als Rechtsbehelf bei Leistungsstörungen, in: *Dieckmann/Frank/Hanisch/Simitis* (Hrsg.), Festschrift für Wolfram Müller-Freienfels, Baden-Baden: Nomos (1986), S. 525–545 (Kurztitel: FS Müller-Freienfels)

Schlechtriem, Peter: Aufhebung von CISG-Kaufverträgen wegen vertragswidriger Beschaffenheit der Ware, in: *Baums/Wertenbruch/Lutter/Schmidt* (Hrsg.), Festschrift für Ulrich Huber zum siebzigsten Geburtstag, Tübingen: Mohr Siebeck (2006), S. 563–574 (Kurztitel: FS U. Huber)

Schlechtriem, Peter: Auslegung und Lückenfüllung im internationalen Einheitsrecht: „Erfüllungsort" für Rückabwicklungspflichten in EuGVÜ und EKG, IPRax 1981, 113–116

Schlechtriem, Peter: Bemerkungen zur Geschichte des Einheitskaufrechts, in: *Schlechtriem* (Hrsg.), Einheitliches Kaufrecht und nationales Obligationenrecht, Baden-Baden: Nomos (1987), S. 27–36 (Kurztitel: Geschichte)

Schlechtriem, Peter: Beweis des Abschlusses eines Vertrages nach UN-Kaufrecht durch kaufmännisches Bestätigungsschreiben, Anm. zu OLG Köln v. 22.2.1994, EWiR 1994, 867–868

Schlechtriem, Peter: Bindung an Erklärungen nach dem Einheitlichen Kaufrecht, in: *Majoros* (Hrsg.), Emptio – venditio inter nationes, Basel: Recht und Gesellschaft (1997), S. 259–277 (Kurztitel: Bindung an Erklärungen)

Schlechtriem, Peter: Calculation of Damages in the Event of Anticipatory Breach under the CISG, in: *Cranston/Ramberg/Ziegel* (Hrsg.), Commercial Law Challenges in the 21st Century, Jan Hellner in memoriam, Stockholm Centre for Commercial law (2007), S. 229–248 (Kurztitel: GS Hellner)

Schlechtriem, Peter: CISG – Auslegung, Lückenfüllung und Weiterentwicklung, in: *Christ/Kramer* (Hrsg.), Symposium für Frank Vischer, Basel: Helbing & Lichtenhahn (2005), S. 47–72 (Kurztitel: Symposium Vischer)

Schlechtriem, Peter: Das „Sprachrisiko" – ein neues Problem?, in: *Ehmann/Hefermehl/Laufs* (Hrsg.), Privatautonomie, Eigentum und Verantwortung, Festschrift für Hermann Weitnauer zum 70. Geburtstag, Berlin: Duncker & Humblot (1980), S. 129–143 (Kurztitel: FS Weitnauer)

Schlechtriem, Peter: Das Wiener Kaufrechtsübereinkommen von 1980 (Convention on the International Sale of Goods), IPRax 1990, 277–283

Schlechtriem, Peter: Der Staat als Partei in CISG-Verträgen, in: Towards Europeanization of Private Law – Essays in Honour of Professor Jerzey Rajski, Warschau: Beck (2007), S. 549–562 (Kurztitel: FS Rajski)

Schlechtriem, Peter: Deutsche Grundsätze zum „Sprachrisiko" als „Datum" unter italienischem Vertragsstatut, zu OLG Hamm, 8.2.1995 – 11 U 206/93, IPRax 1996, 184

Schlechtriem, Peter: Die Kollision von Standardbedingungen nach BGB und Einheitlichem Kaufabschlußgesetz, BB 1974, 1309–1311

Schlechtriem, Peter: Die Pflichten des Verkäufers und die Folgen ihrer Verletzung, insbesondere bezüglich der Beschaffenheit der Ware, in: *Bucher* (Hrsg.), Wiener Kaufrecht, Bern: Stämpfli (1991), S. 103–135 (Kurztitel: Pflichten des Verkäufers)

Schlechtriem, Peter: Die Unmöglichkeit – ein Wiedergänger, in: *Coester/Martiny/Gessaphe* (Hrsg.), Privatrecht in Europa: Vielfalt, Kollision, Kooperation, Festschrift für Hans Jürgen Sonnenberger zum 70. Geburtstag, München: Beck (2004), S. 125–133 (Kurztitel: FS Sonnenberger)

Schlechtriem, Peter: Effectiveness and Binding Nature of Declarations (Notices, Requests and Other Communications) under Part II and Part III of the CISG, Rev. CISG (1995), 95–114

Schlechtriem, Peter: Einheitliches Kaufrecht und nationales Obligationenrecht, Fachtagung Einheitliches Kaufrecht der Gesellschaft für Rechtsvergleichung, Freiburg i. Br. 16.–17. Februar 1987, Baden-Baden: Nomos (1987) (Kurztitel: Einheitliches Kaufrecht und nationales Obligationenrecht)

Schlechtriem, Peter: Einheitliches Kaufrecht: Erfahrungen mit den Haager Kaufgesetzen – Folgerungen für das Wiener UN-Kaufrecht, RdW 1989, 41–52

Schlechtriem, Peter: Einheitliches UN-Kaufrecht. Das Übereinkommen der Vereinten Nationen über internationale Warenkaufverträge – Darstellung und Texte, Tübingen: Mohr (1981) (Kurztitel: Einheitliches UN-Kaufrecht)

Schlechtriem, Peter: Einheitliches UN-Kaufrecht. Das Übereinkommen der Vereinten Nationen vom 11. April 1980 über Verträge über den internationalen Warenkauf (CISG), JZ 1988, 1037–1048

Schlechtriem, Peter: Einheitskaufrecht in der Rechtsprechung des Bundesgerichts, in: *Canaris u. a.* (Hrsg.), 50 Jahre Bundesgerichtshof: Festgabe aus der Wissenschaft, München: Beck (2000), Band I, S. 407–441 (Kurztitel: 50 Jahre BGH)

Schlechtriem, Peter: Erfüllung von Zahlungsansprüchen nach CISG am Ort der Niederlassung des Gläubigers, EWiR 1993, 1075–1076

Schlechtriem, Peter: Fristsetzungen bei Leistungsstörungen im Einheitlichen UN-Kaufrecht (CISG) und der Einfluß des § 326 BGB, in: *von Westphalen/Sandrock* (Hrsg.), Lebendiges Recht: von den Sumerern bis zur Gegenwart, Festschrift für Reinhold Trinkner zum 65. Geburtstag, Heidelberg: Recht und Wirtschaft (1995), S. 321–335 (Kurztitel: Fristsetzungen)

Schlechtriem, Peter: From the Hague to Vienna – Progress in Unification of the Law of International Sales Contracts?, in: *Horn/Schmitthoff* (Hrsg.), The Transnational Law of International Commercial Transactions: Studies in Transnational Economic Law, Deventer: Kluwer Law and Taxation (1982), vol. 2, S. 125–135 (Kurztitel: From Hague to Vienna)

Schlechtriem, Peter: Gemeinsame Bestimmungen über Verpflichtungen des Verkäufers und des Käufers, in: Schweizerisches Institut für Rechtsvergleichung (Hrsg.), Lausanner Kolloquium 1984, Zürich: Schulthess (1985), S. 149–171 (Kurztitel: Gemeinsame Bestimmungen)

Schlechtriem, Peter: Haager Einheitliches Kaufrecht und AGB-Gesetz, in: *Klug u. a.* (Hrsg.), Gesetzgebungstheorie, Juristische Logik, Zivil-und Prozeßrecht, Gedächtnisschrift für Jürgen Rödig, Berlin: Springer (1978), S. 255–260 (Kurztitel: Haager Einheitliches Kaufrecht)

Schlechtriem, Peter: International Einheitliches Kaufrecht und neues Schuldrecht, in: *Dauner-Lieb/Konzen/Schmidt, K.* (Hrsg.), Das neue Schuldrecht in der Praxis, Köln: Heymanns (2003), S. 71–86 (Kurztitel: Neues Schuldrecht)

Schlechtriem, Peter: Internationales UN-Kaufrecht. Ein Studien- und Erläuterungsbuch zum Übereinkommen der Vereinten Nationen über Verträge über den internationalen Warenkauf (CISG), 4. Aufl. Tübingen: Mohr (2007) (Kurztitel: Internationales UN-Kaufrecht)

Schlechtriem, Peter: Interpretation, gap filling and further development of the UN Sales Convention, Pace Int'l L. Rev. (2004), 279–306

Schlechtriem, Peter: Kollidierende Geschäftsbedingungen im internationalen Vertragsrecht, in: *Thume* (Hrsg.), Festschrift für Rolf Herber zum 70. Geburtstag, Neuwied: Luchterhand (1999), S. 36–49 (Kurztitel: FS Herber)

Schlechtriem, Peter: Kollidierende Standardbedingungen und Eigentumsvorbehalt, in: *Schlechtriem/Leser* (Hrsg.), Zum Deutschen und Internationalen Schuldrecht. Kolloquium aus Anlaß des 75. Geburtstages von Ernst von Caemmerer, Tübingen: Mohr (1983), S. 1–25 (Kurztitel: Kollidierende Standardbedingungen)

Schlechtriem, Peter: Kurzkommentar zu OLG Düsseldorf vom 2.7.1993, EWiR 1993, 1075–1076

Schlechtriem, Peter: Noch einmal: Vertragsgemäße Beschaffenheit der Ware bei divergierenden öffentlich-rechtlichen Qualitätsvorgaben, IPRax 2001, 161–163

Schlechtriem, Peter: Non-Material Damages – Recovery Under the CISG, 19 Pace Int'l L. Rev. (2007), 89–102

Schlechtriem, Peter: Opting out of Merger and Form Clauses under the CISG – Second thoughts on *TeeVee Toons, Inc. & Steve Gottlieb, Inc. v. Gerhard Schubert GmbH,* in: *Andersen/Schroeter* (Hrsg.), Sharing International Commercial Law across National Boundaries: Festschrift for Albert H. Kritzer on the Occasion of his Eightieth Birthday, London: Wildy, Simmonds & Hill (2008), S. 416–424 (Kurztitel: FS Kritzer)

Schlechtriem, Peter: Recent Developments in International Sales Law, 18 Israel L. Rev. (1983), 309–326

Schlechtriem, Peter: Rechtsvereinheitlichung und Schuldrechtsreform in Deutschland, ZEuP 1993, 217–246

Schlechtriem, Peter: Requirements of Application and Sphere of Applicability of the CISG, 36 Vict. U. Well. L. Rev. (2005), 781–794

Schlechtriem, Peter: Restitution und Bereicherungsausgleich in Europa – Eine rechtsvergleichende Darstellung, Bd. 1, Tübingen: Mohr (2000) (Kurztitel: Restitution), Bd. 2, Tübingen: Mohr (2001) (Kurztitel: Restitution II)

Schlechtriem, Peter: Richterliche Kontrolle von Schadenersatzpauschalierungen und Vertragsstrafen, in: *Leser/Marschall von Bieberstein* (Hrsg.), Das Haager Einheitliche Kaufgesetz und das Deutsche Schuldrecht, Kolloquium zum 65. Geburtstag von Ernst von Caemmerer, Karlsruhe: C. F. Müller (1973), S. 51–74 (Kurztitel: Das Haager Einheitliche Kaufgesetz)

Schlechtriem, Peter: Schadenersatz und Erfüllungsinteresse, in: *Stathopoulos u. a.* (Hrsg.), Festschrift für Apostolos Georgiades zum 70. Geburtstag, München: Beck (2006), S. 383–402 (Kurztitel: FS Georgiades)

Schlechtriem, Peter: Schuldrecht Besonderer Teil, 6. Aufl., Tübingen: Mohr (2003) (Kurztitel: SchuldR BT)

Literatur

Schlechtriem, Peter: Schuldrecht Besonderer Teil, 7. Aufl., Tübingen: Mohr (2008) (Kurztitel: SchuldR BT)
Schlechtriem, Peter: Subsequent Performance and Delivery Deadlines – Avoidance of CISG Sales Contracts Due to Non-conformity of the Goods, 18 Pace Int'l L. Rev. (2006), 83–93
Schlechtriem, Peter: The Borderline of Tort and Contract – Opening a New Frontier?, 21 Cornell Int'l L. J. (1988), 467–476
Schlechtriem, Peter: The New Law of Obligations in Estonia and the Developments towards Unification and Harmonisation of Law in Europe, Juridica Int. 2001, 16–22
Schlechtriem, Peter: The Sale of Goods: Do Regions Matter ? – An Overview, Uniform L. Rev. 2003, 173–175
Schlechtriem, Peter: The Seller's Obligations under the United Nations Convention on Contracts for the International Sale of Goods, in: *Galston/Smit* (Hrsg.), International Sales, New York: Matthew Bender (1984), Kap. 6, S. 1–35 (Kurztitel: Seller's Obligations)
Schlechtriem, Peter: Ultra Vires-Geschäfte von Bürgermeistern, in: *Diederichsen/Fischer u. a.* (Hrsg.), Festschrift für Walter Rolland zum 70. Geburtstag, Köln: Bundesanzeiger (1999), S. 317–325 (Kurztitel: FS Rolland)
Schlechtriem, Peter: Uniform Sales Law – The Experience with Uniform Sales Laws in the Federal Republic of Germany, 3 JT (1991/92), 1–28
Schlechtriem, Peter: Uniform Sales Law: The UN-Convention on Contracts for the International Sale of Goods, Wien: Manz (1986) (Kurztitel: Uniform Sales Law)
Schlechtriem, Peter: Verfahrenskosten als Schaden in Anwendung des UN-Kaufrechts, IHR 2006, 49–53
Schlechtriem, Peter: Verjährung von Ansprüchen und Rechten aus einem Kaufvertrag nach CISG, in: *Mansel u. a.* (Hrsg.), Festschrift für Erik Jayme, Bd. 2, München: Sellier European Law Publishers (2004), S. 1353–1360 (Kurztitel: FS Jayme)
Schlechtriem, Peter: Vertragsmäßigkeit der Ware als Frage der Beschaffenheitsvereinbarung, IPRax 1996, 12–16
Schlechtriem, Peter: Vertragsmäßigkeit der Ware und öffentlich-rechtliche Vorgaben, IPRax 1999, 388–390
Schlechtriem, Peter: Vertragsordnung und außervertragliche Haftung (Habil. Freiburg 1971), Frankfurt a. M.: Metzner (1972) (Kurztitel: Vertragsordnung)
Schlechtriem, Peter: Vienna Sales Convention 1980: developed countries' perspectives, in: *Rao Penna* (Hrsg.), Current Developments in International Transfers of Goods and Services, (6th Singapore Conference on International Business Law, Sept. 1992), Singapur: Butterworths Asia (1994), S. 103–137
Schlechtriem, Peter: Zuständigkeit deutscher Gerichte für Zahlungsklage eines deutschen Lieferanten bei Erfüllungsort nach Einheitskaufrecht. Kommentierung des EuGH-Urteils vom 29.6.1994, Rs C-288/92, EWiR 1995, 55–56
Schlechtriem, Peter/Butler, Petra: UN Law on International Sales, Berlin: Springer (2009)
Schlechtriem, Peter/Coen, Christoph/Hornung, Rainer: Restitution and Unjust Enrichment in Europe, 2/3 European Review of Private Law (2001), 377–415
Schlechtriem, Peter/Magnus, Ulrich: Internationale Rechtsprechung zu EKG und EAG, Baden-Baden: Nomos (1987)
Schlechtriem, Peter/Perales Viscasillas, Pilar: Case note on decision of Court of First Instance of Tudela (Spain), http://cisgw3.law.pace.edu/cisg/biblio/perales4.html
Schlechtriem, Peter/Schmidt-Kessel, Martin: Anmerkung zu BGH VIII ZR 306/95, 4.12.1996, EWiR 1997, 653–654
Schlechtriem, Peter/Schmidt-Kessel, Martin: Anmerkung zu BGH, 23.7.1997 – VII ZR 134/96, EWiR 1997, 985–986
Schlechtriem, Peter/Schmidt-Kessel, Martin: Schuldrecht Allgemeiner Teil, 6. Aufl., Tübingen: Mohr (2005) (Kurztitel: SchuldR AT)
Schlechtriem, Peter/Witz, Claude: Convention de Vienne sur les Contrats de Vente Internationale de Marchandises, Paris: Dalloz (2008)
Schlegelberger, Franz: Handelsgesetzbuch, Kommentar v. *Geßler, Hefermehl, Hildebrandt u. Schröder,* 5. Aufl., München: Vahlen (1973 ff.) (Kurztitel: *Schlegelberger/Bearbeiter*)
Schlesinger, Rudolf B. (Hrsg.): Formation of Contracts. A Study of the Common Core of Legal Systems, 2 Bde., Dobbs Ferry, NY: Oceana (1968) (Kurztitel: *Schlesinger/Bearbeiter,* Bd. 1/2)
von Schlieffen, Albrecht Graf: Besondere Fragen: Verspätungshaftung, Gefahrübergang, Vertragsstrafe, Höhere Gewalt, in: Zur Vertragsgestaltung im Auslandsgeschäft nach UNCITRAL-Kaufrecht, Bundesstelle für Aussenhandelsinformation, Berichte und Dokumente zum ausländischen Wirtschafts- und Steuerrecht Nr. 179, Köln: Bundesstelle für Außenhandelsinformation (1984), S. 21–37

Literatur

Schlosser, Peter: Rechtszersplitterung durch internationales Einheitsrecht?, in: *Beuthien u. a.* (Hrsg.), Festschrift für Dieter Medicus: Zum 70. Geburtstag, Köln: Heymann (1999), S. 543–554 (Kurztitel: FS Medicus)
Schlosser, Peter: Schiedsklauseln in AGB, ZEuP 1994, 682–693
Schluchter, Anne-Kathrin: Die Gültigkeit von Kaufverträgen unter dem UN-Kaufrecht. Wie gestaltet sich die Ergänzung des Einheitsrechts mit deutschen und französischen Nichtigkeitsnormen? (Diss. Freiburg 1995), Baden-Baden: Nomos (1996)
Schmid, Christoph: Das Verhältnis von Einheitlichem Kaufrecht und nationalem Deliktsrecht am Beispiel des Ersatzes von Mangelfolgeschäden, RIW 1996, 904–913
Schmid, Christoph: Das Zusammenspiel von Einheitlichem UN-Kaufrecht und nationalem Recht. Lückenfüllung und Normenkonkurrenz (Diss. München 1995), Berlin: Duncker & Humblot (1996) (Kurztitel: Lückenfüllung und Normenkonkurrenz)
Schmid, Gudrun: Einheitliche Anwendung von internationalem Einheitsrecht (Diss. Augsburg), Baden-Baden: Nomos (2004) (Kurztitel: Einheitliche Anwendung)
Schmid, Petra: Der Schuldnerverzug: Voraussetzungen und Rechtsfolgen nach BGB und UN-Kaufrecht (Diss. Augsburg), Aachen: Shaker (1996) (Kurztitel: Schuldnerverzug)
Schmidlin, Bruno: Frustration of Contract and clausula rebus sic stantibus, Basel: Helbing und Lichterhahn (1985)
Schmidt, Detlef: Qualitätssicherungsvereinbarungen und ihr rechtlicher Rahmen, NJW 1991, 144–152
Schmidt, Folke: The International Contract Law in the context of some of its Sources, 14 Am. J. Comp. L. (1965), 1–37
Schmidt, Hubert: Einbeziehung von AGB im Verbraucherverkehr, NJW 2011, 1633–1639
Schmidt, Karsten: Die Praxis zum sog. kaufmännischen Bestätigungsschreiben: ein Zankapfel der Vertragsrechtsdogmatik, in: *Harrer* (Hrsg.), Besonderes Vertragsrecht: aktuelle Probleme, Festschrift für Heinrich Honsell zum 60. Geburtstag, Zürich: Schulthess (2002), S. 100–118 (Kurztitel: FS Honsell)
Schmidt, Karsten: Handelsrecht, 4. Auflage, Köln: Heymanns (1994) (Kurztitel: Handelsrecht)
Schmidt, Lutz: Die Vertragsaufhebung durch den Warenkäufer: eine rechtsvergleichende Untersuchung mit Interessenanalyse und Ausblicken auf ein mögliches europäisches Schuldvertragsrecht (Diss. Berlin 2003), Baden-Baden: Nomos (2003) (Kurztitel: Vertragsaufhebung)
Schmidt, Mareike: Profiting from Substitute Transactions? – Offsetting Losses and Benefits under the CISG, in: *Bühler/Müller-Chen* (Hrsg.), Festschrift für Ingeborg Schwenzer zum 60. Geburtstag, Bern: Stämpfli (2011), S. 1499–1512 (Kurztitel: FS Schwenzer)
Schmidt, Michael Johannes: Kann Schweigen auf eine Gerichtsstandsklausel in AGB einen Gerichtsstand nach Art. 17 EuGVÜ/LuganoÜ begründen?, RIW 1992, 173–179
Schmidt-Ahrendts, Nils: Das Verhältnis von Erfüllung, Schadensersatz und Vertragsaufhebung im CISG (Diss. Freiburg 2007), Tübingen: Mohr Siebeck (2008), (Kurztitel: Rechtsbehelfe)
Schmidt-Ahrendts, Nils: Der Ersatz „frustrierter Aufwendungen" im Fall der Rückabwicklung gescheiterter Verträge im UN-Kaufrecht, IHR 2006, 67–73
Schmidt-Ahrendts, Nils: Disgorgement of Profits under the CISG, in: *Schwenzer/Spagnolo* (Hrsg.), State of Play, The 3rd Annual MAA Peter Schlechtriem CISG Conference, The Hague: Eleven International Publishing (2012), S. 89–102 (Kurztitel: Disgorgement of Profits)
Schmidt-Kessel, Martin: CISG-Verträge in der Insolvenz – eine Skizze, in: *Schwenzer/Hager* (Hrsg.), Festschrift für Peter Schlechtriem zum 70. Geburtstag, Tübingen: Mohr (2003), S. 255–274 (Kurztitel: FS Schlechtriem)
Schroeter, Ulrich G.: Das einheitliche Kaufrecht der afrikanischen OHADA-Staaten im Vergleich zum UN-Kaufrecht, Recht in Afrika (2001), 163–176
Schmidt-Kessel, Martin: Die Zahlungsverzugsrichtlinie und ihre Umsetzung, NJW 2001, 97–103
Schmidt-Kessel, Martin (Hrsg.): Ein einheitliches europäisches Kaufrecht? Eine Analyse des Vorschlags der Kommission, München: Sellier (2012) (Kurztitel: *Schmidt-Kessel/Bearbeiter*, Europäisches Kaufrecht)
Schmidt-Kessel, Martin: Einbeziehung von Allgemeinen Geschäftsbedingungen unter UN-Kaufrecht, NJW 2002, 3444–3446
Schmidt-Kessel, Martin: Entwurf der Richtlinie zum Zahlungsverzug und die Folgen für die Vertragsgestaltung, ZNotP 1999, 95–104
Schmidt-Kessel, Martin: Haftungsstandards im internationalen Warenkauf, in: *Bühler/Müller-Chen* (Hrsg.), Festschrift für Ingeborg Schwenzer zum 60. Geburtstag, Bern: Stämpfli (2011), S. 1513-1528 (Kurztitel: FS Schwenzer)
Schmidt-Kessel, Martin: Implied Term – auf der Suche nach dem Funktionsäquivalent, ZVerglRW 96 (1997), 101–155
Schmidt-Kessel, Martin: Standards vertraglicher Haftung nach englischem Recht, Limits of Frustation (Diss. Freiburg 2001), Baden-Baden: Nomos (2003) (Kurztitel: Standards)

Literatur

Schmidt-Kessel, Martin: Urteilsanmerkung zu BGH NJW 1995, 2101, RIW 1996, 60–65
Schmidt-Kessel, Martin: Vertragsaufhebung nach UN-Kaufrecht, RIW 1996, 60–65
Schmidt-Kessel, Martin/Meyer, Linus: Allgemeine Geschäftsbedingungen und UN-Kaufrecht, IHR 2008, 177–180
Schmitt, Hansjörg: Intangible Goods in Online-Kaufverträgen und der Anwendungsbereich des CISG, CR 2001, 145–155
Schmitthoff, Clive M.: Das neue Recht des Welthandels, RabelsZ 28 (1964), 47–77
Schmitthoff, Clive M.: Export Trade. The Law and Practice of International Trade, 10. Aufl., London: Stevens & Sons (2000) (Kurztitel: Export Trade)
Schmittmann, Jens M.: Zur Telefaxübermittlung im Geschäftsverkehr und den Gefahren der Manipulation, DB 1993, 2575–2579
Schmitz, Dirk: UN-Kaufrecht (CISG) und Datentransfer via Internet, MMR 2000, 256–260
Schmutz, Pascal: Die Gefahrtragung beim Kaufvertrag nach schweizerischem und UNCITRAL-Kaufrecht (Diss. Basel), Basel: Econom (1983)
Schneider, Dirk: UN-Kaufrecht und Produkthaftpflicht. Zur Auslegung von Art. 4 Satz 1 und Art. 5 CISG und zur Abgrenzung vertraglicher und außervertraglicher Haftung aus der Sicht des CISG (Diss. Basel), Basel: Helbing und Lichtenhahn (1995)
Schneider, Eric C.: Consequential Damages in the International Sale of Goods: Analysis of two decisions, J. Int'l Bus. L. 1995, 615–668
Schneider, Eric C.: Measuring Damages under the CISG: Article 74 of the United Nations Convention on Contracts for the International Sale of Goods, 9 Pace Int'l L. Rev., 223–237
Schneider, Eric C.: The Seller's Right to Cure under the Uniform Commercial Code and the United Nations Convention on Contracts for the International Sale of Goods, 7 Ariz. J. Int'l L. (1989), 69–103
Schnyder, Anton K.: Das neue IPR-Gesetz, 2. Aufl., Zürich: Schulthess Polygraphischer Verlag (1990)
Schnyder, Anton K./Grolimund, Pascal: „Opting-in" oder „opting-out"? Anwendung der UNIDROIT Principles of International Commercial Contracts in schiedsgerichtlichen Verfahren, in: *Schwenzer/Hager* (Hrsg.), Festschrift für Peter Schlechtriem zum 70. Geburtstag, Tübingen: Mohr (2003), S. 395–411 (Kurztitel: FS Schlechtriem)
Schönenberger, Beat: Sach- und Rechtsgewährleistung – eine zeitgemässe Unterscheidung?, BJM 2009, 173–191
Schoibl, Norbert A.: Vom Brüsseler Übereinkommen zur Brüssel-I-Verordnung: Neuerungen im europäischen Zivilprozessrecht, östJBl 2003, 149–173
Scholz, Ingo: Das Problem der autonomen Auslegung des EuGVÜ, Tübingen: Mohr (1998)
Schoop, Jan: Die Haftungsbefreiung für arbeitskampfbedingte Vertragsverletzungen im UN-Kaufrecht (CISG) (Diss. Hamburg), Münster/Hamburg/London: Lit (2000)
Schroeter, Ulrich G.: Backbone or Backyard of the Convention? The CISG's Final Provisions, in: *Andersen/Schroeter* (Hrsg.), Sharing International Commercial Law Across National Boundaries: Festschrift in Honour of Albert H. Kritzer on the Occasion of his Eightieth Birthday, London: Wildly, Simmons & Hill (2008), S. 425–469 (Kurztitel: FS Kritzer)
Schroeter, Ulrich G.: Das einheitliche Kaufrecht der afrikanischen OHADA-Staaten im Vergleich zum UN-Kaufrecht, RiAfr 2001, 163–176
Schroeter, Ulrich G.: Die Anwendbarkeit des UN-Kaufrechts auf grenzüberschreitende Versteigerungen und Internet-Auktionen, ZEuP 2004, 20–35
Schroeter, Ulrich G.: Die Fristenberechnung im Bürgerlichen Recht, JuS 2007, 29–35
Schroeter, Ulrich G.: Die Vertragsstaateneigenschaft Hongkongs und Macaus unter dem UN-Kaufrecht, IHR 2004, 7–17
Schroeter, Ulrich G.: Freedom of contract: Comparison between provisions of the CISG (Article 6) and counterpart provisions of the Principles of European Contract Law, 6 VJ (2002), 257–266
Schroeter, Ulrich G.: Freedom of contract: Comparison between provisions of the CISG (Article 6) and the counterpart provisions of the Principles of European Contract Law, in: *Felemegas* (Hrsg.), An International Approach to the Interpretation of the United Nations Convention on Contracts for the International Sale of Goods (1980) as Uniform Sales Law, Cambridge: Cambridge University Press (2007), S. 261–268 (Kurztitel: Art. 6 CISG-PECL)
Schroeter, Ulrich G.: Interpretation of „Writing": Comparison between provisions of the CISG (Art. 13) and the counterpart provisions of the PECL, 6 VJ (2002), 267–274
Schroeter, Ulrich G.: Interpretation of „writing": Comparison between provisions of CISG (Article 13) and counterpart provisions of the Principles of European Contract Law, in: *Felemegas* (Hrsg.): An International Approach to the Interpretation of the United Nations Convention on Contracts for the International Sale of Goods (1980) as Uniform Sales Law, Cambridge: Cambridge University Press (2007), S. 288–295 (Kurztitel: Art. 13 CISG-PECL)

Schroeter, Ulrich G.: Kurzkommentar zu BGH, Urt. v. 27.11.2007 – X ZR 111/04 (OLG München), IHR 2008, 49 EWiR 2008, 303–304
Schroeter, Ulrich G.: The Status of Hong Kong and Macao under the United Nations Convention on Contracts for the International Sale of Goods, 16 Pace Int'l L. Rev. (2004), 307–332
Schroeter, Ulrich G.: UN-Kaufrecht und Europäisches Gemeinschaftsrecht: Verhältnis und Wechselwirkungen, München: Sellier (2005) (Kurztitel: UN-Kaufrecht)
Schroeter, Ulrich G.: Vienna Sales Convention: Applicability to „Mixed Contracts" and Interaction with the 1968 Brussels Convention, 5 VJ (2001), 74–86
Schubert, Reinhard: Der Einfluß des Einheitskaufrechts auf die Schuldrechtsreform in der Bundesrepublik Deutschland, in: *Schlechtriem* (Hrsg.), Einheitliches Kaufrecht und nationales Obligationenrecht, Baden-Baden: Nomos (1987), 415–436
Schultheiß, Jörg: Allgemeine Geschäftsbedingungen im UN-Kaufrecht: eine vergleichende Analyse des Einheitsrechts mit dem Recht Deutschlands, Österreichs, der Schweiz, Frankreichs und der USA (Diss. Saarbrücken 2003), Frankfurt a. M. u. a.: Lang (2004)
Schultz, Rob: Rolling Contract Formation under the UN Convention on Contracts for the International Sale of Goods, 35 Cornell Int'l L. J. (2002), 263–289
Schulz, Florian: Der Ersatzlieferungs- und Nachbesserungsanspruch des Käufers im internen deutschen Recht, im UCC und im CISG, Frankfurt a. M.: Lang (2002)
Schulze, Rainer/Zuleeg, Manfred (Hrsg.): Europarecht: Handbuch für die deutsche Rechtspraxis, Baden-Baden: Nomos (2006)
Schumacher, Florian: Kaufoptionsvertrag und Verwendungsrisiko im UN-Kaufrecht, IHR 2005, 147–151
Schütz, Markus: UN-Kaufrecht und culpa in contrahendo (Diss. Heidelberg 1995), Frankfurt a. M.: Lang (1996)
Schütze, Rolf A.: Das Dokumentenakkreditiv im Internationalen Handelsverkehr, 5. Aufl., Heidelberg: Verlag Recht und Wirtschaft (1999) (Kurztitel: Dokumentenakkreditiv)
Schütze, Rolf A.: Die Bedeutung des Wiener Kaufrechtsübereinkommen für das internationale Zivilprozeßrecht, in: *Ballon/Hagen* (Hrsg.), Verfahrensgarantien im nationalen und internationalen Zivilprozeßrecht: Festschrift für Franz Matscher zum 65. Geburtstag, Wien: Manz (1993), S. 423–433
Schwartz, Alan: The Case of Specific Performance, 89 Yale L. J. (1979), 271–306
Schwartze, Andreas: Europäische Sachmängelgewährleistung beim Warenkauf, Optionale Rechtsangleichung auf der Grundlage eines funktionalen Rechtsvergleichs, Tübingen: Mohr (2000)
Schweizerischer Bundesrat: Botschaft betreffend das Wiener Übereinkommen über Verträge über den internationalen Warenkauf, Bbl. 1989 I, 745–840 (Kurztitel: Botschaft des Schweizerischen Bundesrats)
Schwenzer, Ingeborg: Anmerkung zu BGer, Urteil vom 18.1.1996 – 4 C.75/1995, AJP 1996, 1050–1052
Schwenzer, Ingeborg: Aufwendungsersatz bei nicht durchgeführten Verträgen, in: *Schwenzer/Hager* (Hrsg.), Festschrift für Peter Schlechtriem zum 70. Geburtstag, Tübingen: Mohr (2003), S. 657–676 (Kurztitel: FS Schlechtriem)
Schwenzer, Ingeborg: Avoidance of the Contract in Case of Non-Conforming Goods (Artikel 49(1)(A) CISG), 25 J. L. & Com. (2005–06), 437–442
Schwenzer, Ingeborg: Besprechung von *Stern,* Erklärungen im UNCITRAL-Kaufrecht, NJW 1991, 1402
Schwenzer, Ingeborg: Buyer's Remedies in the Case of Non-conforming Goods: Some Problems in a Core Area of the CISG, (2007) 101 ASIL Proc (2007), 416–422
Schwenzer, Ingeborg: Conformity of the Goods – Physical Features on the Wane?, in: *Schwenzer/Spagnolo* (Hrsg.), State of Play, The 3rd Annual MAA Peter Schlechtriem CISG Conference, The Hague: Eleven International Publishing (2012), S. 103–112 (Kurztitel: Physical Features)
Schwenzer, Ingeborg: Das UN-Abkommen zum internationalen Warenkauf, NJW 1990, 602–607
Schwenzer, Ingeborg: Das UN-Abkommen zum internationalen Warenkauf, recht 1991, 113–121
Schwenzer, Ingeborg: Development of Comparative Law in Germany, Switzerland and Austria, in: *Reimann/Zimmermann* (Hrsg.), The Oxford Handbook of Comparative Law, Oxford: Oxford University Press (2006), S. 69–106 (Kurztitel: Development of Comparative Law)
Schwenzer, Ingeborg: Die clausula und das CISG, in: *Wiegand/Koller, T/Walter* (Hrsg.), Tradition mit Weitsicht, Festschrift für Eugen Bucher zum 80. Geburtstag, Bern/Zürich: Stämpfli/Schulthess (2009), S. 723–741 (Kurztitel: FS Bucher)
Schwenzer, Ingeborg: Die Freizeichnung des Verkäufers von der Sachmängelhaftung im amerikanischen und deutschen Recht, Frankfurt a. M.: Metzner (1979) (Kurztitel: Freizeichnung)
Schwenzer, Ingeborg: Force Majeure and Hardship in International Sales Contracts, 39 Vict. U. Well. L. Rev. (2009), 709–725
Schwenzer, Ingeborg: Internationaler Gerichtsstand für die Kaufpreisklage, IPRax 1989, 274–276

Literatur

Schwenzer, Ingeborg: National Preconceptions that Endanger Uniformity, 19 Pace Int'l L. Rev. (2007), 103–124
Schwenzer, Ingeborg: Products Liability and Property Damages, 9 Tel Aviv University Studies in Law (1989), 127–145
Schwenzer, Ingeborg: Rechtsbehelfe und Rückabwicklungsmodelle im CISG, in den European und UNIDROIT-Principles, im Gandolfi-Entwurf sowie im Entwurf eines Schuldrechtsmodernisierungsgesetzes, in: *Schlechtriem* (Hrsg.), Wandlungen des Schuldrechts, Baden-Baden: Nomos (2002), S. 223–227 (Kurztitel: Rückabwicklungsmodelle)
Schwenzer, Ingeborg: Rechtsverfolgungskosten als Schaden?, in: *Gauch/Werro/Pichonnaz* (Hrsg.), Mélanges en l'honneur de Pierre Tercier, Genève: Schulthess (2008), S. 417–426 (Kurztitel: FS Tercier)
Schwenzer, Ingeborg: Sachgüterschutz im Spannungsfeld deliktischer Verkehrspflichten und vertraglicher Leistungspflichten, JZ 1988, 525–531
Schwenzer, Ingeborg (Hrsg.): Schlechtriem & Schwenzer, Commentary on the UN Convention on the International Sale of Goods (CISG), 3. Aufl., Oxford: Oxford University Press 2010 (Kurztitel: Schlechtriem/Schwenzer/Bearbeiter, CISG Commentary)
Schwenzer, Ingeborg: Schweizerisches Obligationenrecht. Allgemeiner Teil, 6. Aufl., Bern: Stämpfli (2012) (Kurztitel: OR AT)
Schwenzer, Ingeborg: The Application of the CISG in Light of National Law, IHR 2010, 45–56
Schwenzer, Ingeborg: „The Battle of the Forms" und das EAG, IPRax 1988, 212–214
Schwenzer, Ingeborg: The CISG Advisory Council, Nederlands Tijdschrift voor Handelsrecht 2012, 46–51
Schwenzer, Ingeborg: The Danger of Domestic Pre-Conceived Views with Respect to the Uniform Interpretation of the CISG: The Question of Avoidance in the Case of Non-Conforming Goods and Documents, Vict. U. Well. L. Rev. 36 (2005/4), 795–807
Schwenzer, Ingeborg: The Noble Month (Articles 38, 39 CISG) – The Story Behind the Scenery, European Journal of Law Reform, 353–356
Schwenzer, Ingeborg/Fountoulakis, Christiana (Hrsg.): International Sales Law, London: Routledge (2007) (Kurztitel: International Sales Law)
Schwenzer, Ingeborg/Hachem, Pascal: The CISG – Successes and Pitfalls, (2009) 57 Am. J. Comp. L. (2009), 457–478
Schwenzer, Ingeborg/Hachem, Pascal: The Scope of the CISG Provisions on Damages, in: *Saidov/Cunnington* (Hrsg.), Contract Damages: Domestic and International Perspectives, Oxford (2008), S. 91–105 (Kurztitel: Scope of Damages)
Schwenzer, Ingeborg/Hachem, Pascal/Kee, Christopher: Global Sales and Contract Law, Oxford: Oxford University Press (2012)
Schwenzer, Ingeborg/Leisinger, Benjamin K.: Ethical Values and International Sales Contracts, in: *Cranston/Ramberg/Ziegel* (Hrsg.), Commercial Law Challenges in the 21st Century – Jan Hellner in memoriam, Stockholm Centre for Commercial Law (2007), 249–276 (Kurztitel: GS Hellner)
Schwenzer, Ingeborg/Manner, Simon: „The Claim is Time-Barred": The Proper Limitation Regime for International Sales Contracts in International Commercial Arbitration, 23 Arb. Int'l (2007), 293–307
Schwenzer, Ingeborg/Manner, Simon: The Pot Calling the Kettle Black: The Impact of the Non-Breaching Party's (Non-) Behavior in its CISG-Remedies, in: *Andersen/Schroeter* (Hrsg.): Sharing International Commercial Law across National Boundaries: Festschrift for Albert H. Kritzer on teh Occasion of his Eightieth Birthday, London: Wildy, Simmonds & Hill (2008), S. 470–488 (Kurztitel: FS Kritzer)
Schwenzer, Ingeborg/Mohs, Florian: Arbitration Clauses in Chains of Contracts, 27 ASA Bulletin (2009) 213–235
Schwenzer, Ingeborg/Mohs, Florian: Old Habits Die Hard: Traditional Contract Formation in a Modern World, IHR 2006, 239–246
Schwenzer, Ingeborg/Muñoz, Edgardo (Hrsg.), Schlechtriem & Schwenzer; Comentario sobre la convención de las naciones unidas sobre los contratos de compraventa internacional de mercaderías, Cizur Menor (Navarra): Thomson Reuters (2011) (Kurztitel: *Schwenzer/Muñoz/Bearbeiter*)
Schwenzer, Ingeborg/Schmidt, Mareike: Extending the CISG to Non-Privity Parties, 13 VJ (2009) 100–125
Schwenzer, Ingeborg/Tebel, David: Produktpiraterie und internationals Kaufrecht, Jusletter 17.9.2012 (Kurztitel: Produktpiraterie)
Schwerha, Joseph J.: Warranties against Infringement in the Sale of Goods: A comparison of UCC 2–312 (3) and Article 42 of the UN Convention on Contracts for the International Sale of Goods, 16 Mich. J. Int'l L. (1995), 441–483
Schwimann, Michael: ABGB Praxiskommentar, Bd. 4: §§ 859–1089 ABGB, WucherG, UN-Kaufrecht, 3. Aufl., Wien: LexisNexis (2006) (Kurztitel: *Schwimann/Bearbeiter*)

Schwind, Fritz: Internationales Privatrecht: Lehr- und Handbuch für Theorie und Praxis, Wien: Manz (1990)
Schwintowski, Hans-Peter: Informationspflichten und effet utile – Auf der Suche nach einem effektiven und effizienten europäischen Sanktionensystem, in: *Schulze/Ebers/Grigoleit* (Hrsg.), Informationspflichten und Vertragsschluß im Acquis communitaire, Tübingen: Mohr (2003), S. 267–290 (Kurztitel: Sanktionen)
Scoles, Eugene F./Hay, Peter/Borchers, Patrick J./Symeonides, Symeon C.: Conflict of Laws, 4. Aufl., St. Paul (Minn.): West (2004) (Kurztitel: Conflict of Laws)
Sebert, John A. Jr.: Punitive Damages and Nonpecuniary Damages in Actions Based upon Contract: Toward Achieving the Objective of Full Compensation, 33 UCLA L. Rev. (1986), 1565–1677
Seckel, Emil: Die Gestaltungsrechte des Bürgerlichen Rechts, in: Festgabe der juristischen Gesellschaft zu Berlin zum 50 jährigen Dienstjubiläum ihres Vorsitzenden Richard Koch, Berlin: Liebmann (1903), S. 205–253, (Kurztitel: Gestaltungsrechte)
Secomb, Matthew: A Uniform, Three-step Approach to Interest Rates in International Arbitration, in: *Kröll/Mistelis/Perales Viscasillas/Rogers* (Hrsg.), International Arbitration and International Commercial Law: Synergy, Convergence and Evolution, Alphen aan den Rijn: Kluwer Law International (2011), S. 431–450 (Kurztitel: FS Bergsten)
Sein, Karin/Kull, Irene: Die Bedeutung des UN-Kaufrechts im estnischen Recht, IHR 2005, 138–142
von der Seipen, Christoph: Zum Ausschluß des Einheitlichen Kaufrechts im deutsch-englischen Rechtsverkehr, IPRax 1984, 244–246
Seliazniova, Tatsiana: Prospective Non-Performance or Anticipatory Breach of Contract (Comparison of the Belarusian Approach to CISG Application and Foreign Legal Experience), 24 J. L. & Com. (2004), 111–140
Sevón, Leif: Obligations of the Buyer Under the UN Convention on Contracts for the International Sale of Goods, in: *Šarčević/Volken* (Hrsg.), Dubrovnik Lectures, New York: Oceana (1986), S. 203–238 (Kurztitel: Obligations of the Buyer)
Sevón, Leif: Passing of Risk, in: Schweizerisches Institut für Rechtsvergleichung (Hrsg.), Lausanner Kolloquium 1984, Zürich: Schulthess (1985), S. 191–206 (Kurztitel: Passing of Risk)
Sevón, Leif: The New Scandinavian Codification on the Sale of Goods and the 1980 United Nations Convention on Contracts for the International Sale of Goods, in: *Schlechtriem* (Hrsg.), Einheitliches Kaufrecht und nationales Obligationenrecht, Baden-Baden: Nomos (1987), S. 343–357 (Kurztitel: Scandinavian Codification)
Shanker, Morris G.: „Battle of the Forms": A Comparison and Critique of Canadian, American and Historical Common Law Perspectives, 4 Can. Bus. L. J. (1979–80), 263–276
Shariff, Mary J./de Carteret, Kevin Marechal: Revisiting the Battle of the Forms: A Case Study Approach to Legal Strategy Development, 9 Asper Rev. Int'l Bus. & Trade L. (2009), 21–64
Sheehy, Benedict C.: Good Faith in the CISG: Interpretation Problems in Article 7, Rev. CISG (2005/2006), 153–193
Shen, Jianming: The Remedy of Requiring Performance Under the CISG and the Relevance of Domestic Rules, 13 Ariz. J. Int'l & Comp. L. (1996), 253–306
Shin, Chang-Sop: Declaration of Price Reduction under the CISG Article 50 Price Reduction Remedy, 25 J. L. & Com. (2005), 349–352
Shinn, Allen M. jr.: Liabilities under Article 42 of the U. N.-Convention on the International Sale of Goods, 2 Minn. J. Global Trade (1993), 115–143
Sieg, Oliver: Allgemeine Geschäftsbedingungen im grenzüberschreitenden Geschäftsverkehr, RIW 1997, 811–819
Siehr, Kurt: Der internationale Anwendungsbereich des UN-Kaufrechts, RabelsZ 52 (1988), 587–616
Siehr, Kurt: Internationales Privatrecht, Heidelberg: C. F. Müller (2001) (Kurztitel: IPR)
Siehr, Kurt: UN-Kaufrecht von 1980 und der Handel mit Kulturgütern, in: *Bühler/Müller-Chen* (Hrsg.), Festschrift für Ingeborg Schwenzer zum 60. Geburtstag, Bern: Stämpfli (2011), S. 1593–1604 (Kurztitel: FS Schwenzer)
Sieveking, Robert: Die Geschäftsbedingungen des Waren-Vereins der Hamburger Börse e. V., Berlin/New York: de Gruyter (1979)
Silva Ruiz, Pedro F.: La buena fe en la Convención de las Naciones Unidas sobre los Contratos de Compraventa Internacional de Mercaderías, Libro centenario del código civil (Vol. 1), Madrid: Complutense (1989), 111–119 (Kurztitel: Buena fe)
Sinay-Cytermann, Anne: Comments on Cour d'appel de Grenoble 23 October 1996, Rev. Crit. Dr. Int. privé 1997, 762–771
Singh, Lachmi/Leisinger, Benjamin: A Law for International Sale of Goods: A Reply to Michael Bridge, 20 Pace Int'l L. Rev. (2008), 161–190

Literatur

Sivesand, Hanna: The Buyer's Remedies for Non-Conforming Goods (Diss. Uppsala), München: Sellier (2006) (Kurztitel: Buyer's Remedies)

Skelton, James W.: Potential Effects of the International Sales Convention on U. S. Crude Oil Traders, 9 Houst. J. Int'l L. (1986), 95–110

Slater, Scott D.: Overcome by Hardship: The Inapplicability of the UNIDROIT Principles' Hardship Provisions to CISG, 12 Fla. Int'l L. J. (1998), 231–262

Smit, Hans: The Convention on the Limitation Period in the International Sale of Goods: UNCITRAL's First-Born, 23 Am. J. Comp. L. (1975), 337–362

Smith, John C./Thomas, Joseph A.: Casebook on Contract, London: Sweet & Maxwell (1992)

Smith, Stephan A.: Performance, Punishment and the Nature of Contractual Obligation, 60 Mod. L. Rev. (1997), 360–377

Smythe, Donald J.: The Road to Nowhere: *Caterpillar v. Usinor* and CISG Claims by Downstream Buyers Against Remote Sellers, 2 Geo. Mason J. Int,l Comm. L. (Spring 2011), 123–150

Soergel, Hans Th.: Bürgerliches Gesetzbuch mit Einführungsgesetz und Nebengesetzen, begr. v. *Soergel*, neu hrsg. v. *Siebert*, 12. Aufl., (1987 ff.), teilweise 13. Aufl. (1999 ff.), Stuttgart u. a.: Kohlhammer (Kurztitel: *Soergel/Bearbeiter*)

Soergel, Hans Th.: Bürgerliches Gesetzbuch mit Einführungsgesetz und Nebengesetzen, begr. v. *Soergel*, neu hrsg. v. *Siebert*, Bd. 13: Schuldrechtliche Nebengesetze 2: Übereinkommen der Vereinten Nationen über Verträge über den internationalen Warenkauf (CISG), 13. Aufl. (2000) (Kurztitel: *Soergel/Lüderitz/Bearbeiter*)

Sollund, Marius: The U. N. Convention on the International Sale of Goods, Article 7(1) – The Interpretation of the Convention and the Norwegian Approach, Nordic J. Com. L. (2007), 1–35

Sondahl, Erika: Understanding the Remedy of Price Reduction – A Means to Fostering a More Uniform Application of the United Nations Convention on Contracts for the International Sale of Goods, 7 VJ (2003), 255–276

Song, Yang-Ho: Vertragsaufhebung und Rückabwicklung nach deutschem und koreanischem Recht und internationalem Einheitskaufrecht. Eine Analyse der Folgen des Untergangs oder einer Beeinträchtigung der Kaufsache vor oder nach Erklärung der Aufhebung, Frankfurt a. M.: Lang (1999)

Sonnenberger, Hans Jürgen: Französisches Handels- und Wirtschaftsrecht, 2. Aufl., Heidelberg: Recht und Wirtschaft (1991)

Sonnenberger, Hans Jürgen: Leistungsstörung, positive Forderungsverletzung und Beweislast – rechtsvergleichende Bemerkungen, in: *Beuthien/Fuchs/Roth/Schiemann/Wache* (Hrsg.), Festschrift Dieter Medicus, Köln: Heymann (1999), S. 621–636 (Kurztitel: FS Medicus)

Sono, Hiroo: The Applicability of the CISG to Software Sales Transactions, in: *Andersen/Schroeter* (Hrsg.), Sharing International Commercial Law across National Boundaries: Festschrift for Albert H. Kritzer on the Occasion of his Eightieth Birthday, London: Wildy, Simmonds & Hill (2008), S. 512–526 (Kurztitel: FS Kritzer)

Sono, Kazuaki: Formation of International Contracts under the Vienna Convention: A Shift Above the Comparative Law, in: *Šarčević/Volken* (Hrsg.), Dubrovnik Lectures 1985, New York: Oceana (1986), S. 111–131 (Kurztitel: Formation of International Contracts)

Sono, Kazuaki: Japan's Accession to the CISG: The Asia Factor, 20 Pace Int'l L. Rev. (2008), 105–114

Sono, Kazuaki: Restoration of the Rule of Reason in Contract Formation: Has There Been Civil and Common Law Disparity?, 21 Cornell Int'l L. J. (1988), 477–486

Sono, Kazuaki: Unification of Limitation Period in the International Sale of Goods, 35 Lou. L. Rev. (1975), 1127–1138

Spagnolo, Lisa: Opening Pandora's Box: Good Faith and Precontractual Liability in the CISG, 21 Temp. Int'l & Comp. L. J. (2007), 262–310

Spagnolo, Lisa: The Last Outpost: Automatic CISG Opt Outs, Misapplications and the Costs of Ignoring the Vienna Sales Convention for Australian Lawyers, 10 Melb. J. Int'l L. (2009), 141–216

Spaic, Aneta: Approaching Uniformity in International Sales Law: Comparative Analysis of the Concept of Fundamental Breach under the UN Convention on Contracts for the International Sale of Goods (CISG), http://cisgw3.law.pace.edu/cisg/biblio/spaic.html, besucht am 12.7.2007 (Kurztitel: Fundamental Breach)

Spellenberg, Ulrich: Doppelter Gerichtsstand in fremdsprachigen AGB, IPRax 2007, 98–105

Spellenberg, Ulrich: Fremdsprache und Rechtsgeschäft, in: *Heldrich/Sonnenberger* (Hrsg.), Festschrift für Murad Ferid zum 80. Geburtstag, Frankfurt a. M.: Verlag für Standesamtswesen (1988), S. 463–494 (Kurztitel: Fremdsprache und Rechtsgeschäft)

Spickhoff, Andreas: Internationales Handelsrecht vor Schiedsgerichten und staatlichen Gerichten, RabelsZ 56 (1992), 116–141

Spiro, Karl: Befristung und Verjährung der Ansprüche aus dem Wiener Kaufrechtsübereinkommen, in: Hoyer/Posch (Hrsg.), Das Einheitliche Wiener Kaufrecht, Wien: Orac (1992), S. 195–206

Spiro, Karl: Die Begrenzung privater Rechte durch Verjährungs-, Verwirkungs- und Fatalfristen, Bd. 1: Die Verjährung der Forderungen, Bern: Stämpfli (1975) (Kurztitel: Begrenzung privater Rechte)

Spiro, Karl: Die Haftung für Erfüllungsgehilfen, Bern: Stämpfli (1984)

Spoorenberg, Frank/Fellrath, Isabelle: Offsetting losses and profits in case of breach of commercial sales/purchase agreements under Swiss law and the Vienna Convention on the International Sale of Goods, IPRax 2009, 357–362

Stadie, Volker/Nietzer, Wolf, M: CISG – Das UN-Kaufrecht in der Anwaltspraxis, MDR 2002, 428–433

Stadler, Hans-Jörg: Allgemeine Geschäftsbedingungen im internationalen Handel, Heidelberg: Verlag Recht und Wirtschaft (2003) (Kurztitel: AGB)

Stadler, Hans-Jörg: Internationale Einkaufsverträge, Heidelberg: Verlag Recht und Wirtschaft (1998)

Stalder, Michael: Die Beweislast und wichtige Rügemodalitäten bei vertragswidriger Warenlieferung nach UN-Kaufrecht (CISG), AJP 2004, 1472–1482

Stanton, Heidi: How to Be or Not to Be. The United Nations Convention on Contracts for the International Sale of Goods, Article 6, 4 Cardozo J. Int'l & Comp. L. (1996), 400–430

Starck, Boris/Roland, Henri/Boyer, Laurent: Droit civil – Obligations, Bd. 2, Contrat et Quasi-contrat. Régime général, 6. Aufl., Paris: litec (1998)

Staub, Hermann: Handelsgesetzbuch, Großkommentar, begr. v. Staub, hrsg. v. Canaris, Schilling u. Ulmer, 4. Aufl. (1995 ff.), teilweise noch 3. Aufl. (1967 ff.), Berlin/New York: de Gruyter (Kurztitel: Staub/Bearbeiter)

Stauder, Dieter: Grenzüberschreitende Verletzungsverbote im gewerblichen Rechtsschutz und das EuGVÜ, IPRax 1998, 317–322

Staudinger, Ansgar: Schadensersatzrecht – Wettbewerb der Ideen und Rechtsordnungen, NJW 2006, 2433–2439

Staudinger, Julius: Julius von Staudingers Kommentar zum Bürgerlichen Gesetzbuch mit Einführungsgesetz und Nebengesetzen, 12. Aufl., teilweise schon 13. Aufl., Berlin: Sellier/de Gruyter (1997 ff.) (Kurztitel: Staudinger/Bearbeiter)

Staudinger, Julius: Julius von Staudingers Kommentar zum Bürgerlichen Gesetzbuch mit Einführungsgesetz und Nebengesetzen, 13. Aufl., teilweise schon 16. Aufl., Berlin: Sellier/de Gruyter (1994 ff.) (Kurztitel: Staudinger/Bearbeiter)

Steensgaard, Kasper: Standardbetingelser i internationale kontrakter: Saerligt om vedtagelse under CISG og andre internationale regelsaet (Diss. Aarhus), Kopenhagen: Thomson Reuters (2010)

Steindorff, Ernst: Abstrakte und konkrete Schadensberechnung, AcP 158 (1959/1960), 431–469

Steindorff, Ernst: Gewinnentgang und Schadensberechnung des Verkäufers, JZ 1961, 12–15

Steinmann, Christina: Qualitätssicherungsvereinbarungen zwischen Endproduktherstellern und Zulieferern, Heidelberg: v. Decker (1992)

Steinmetzler, Ulrich: Recht und Ökonomie der Grundstrukturen des Leistungsstörungsrechts im UN-Kaufrecht, Hamburg: Kovac (2001)

Steltmann, Isabel: Die Vertragsstrafe in einem Europäischen Privatrecht – Möglichkeiten einer Rechtsvereinheitlichung auf Basis eines Rechtsvergleichs der Rechtsordnungen Deutschlands, Frankreichs, Englands und Schwedens (Diss. Mannheim 1998/99), Berlin: Duncker und Humblot (2000) (Kurztitel: Vertragsstrafe)

Stephan, Paul B.: The Futility of Unification and Harmonization of International Commercial Law, 39 Va. J. Int'l L. (1999), 743–797

Stern, Elisabeth: Erklärungen im UNCITRAL-Kaufrecht, Wien: Manz (1990) (Kurztitel: Erklärungen)

Stiegle, Andreas/Halter, Rudolf: Nochmals: Einbeziehung von Allgemeinen Geschäftsbeziehungen im Rahmen des UN-Kaufrechts – Zugänglichmachung im Internet, IHR 2003, 169

Stöcker, Hans A.: Das Genfer Übereinkommen über die Vertretung beim internationalen Warenkauf, WM 1983, 778–785

Stoffel, Walter A.: Ein neues Recht des internationalen Warenkaufes in der Schweiz, SJZ 1990, 169–179

Stoffel, Walter A.: Formation du contrat, in: Schweizerisches Institut für Rechtsvergleichung (Hrsg.), Lausanner Kolloquium 1984, Zürich: Schulthess (1985), S. 55–76 (Kurztitel: Formation du contrat)

Stoffel, Walter A.: Le droit applicable aux contrats de vente internationale de marchandises, in: Dessemontet (Hrsg.), Contrats de vente internationale, Lausanne: CEDIDAC (1991), S. 15–46 (Kurztitel: Droit applicable)

Stoffels, Markus: AGB-Recht, München: Beck (2003) (Kurztitel: AGB-Recht)

Stoffer, André: Gegenstand und Normzweck des Art. 50 CISG, IHR 2007, 221–231

Stoll, Hans: Anmerkung zu BGH, 24.3.1999, VIII ZR 121/98, LM CISG Nr. 6/7, 1749–1753

Literatur

Stoll, Hans: Das Statut der Rechtswahlvereinbarung – eine irreführende Konstruktion, in: *Meier/Siehr* (Hrsg.), Rechtskollisionen, Festschrift für Anton Heini zum 65. Geburtstag, Zürich: Schulthess (1995), S. 429–444 (Kurztitel: FS Heini)
Stoll, Hans: Die bei der Nichterfüllung nutzlosen Aufwendungen des Gläubigers als Maßstab der Interessenbewertung. Eine rechtsvergleichende Studie zum Vertragsrecht, in: *Pawlowski/Wiese/Wüst* (Hrsg.), Festschrift für Konrad Duden zum 70. Geburtstag, München: Beck (1977), S. 641–660 (Kurztitel: FS Duden)
Stoll, Hans: Ersatz für Vertrauensschaden nach dem Einheitlichen Kaufrecht, in: *Majoros* (Hrsg.), Emptio – venditio inter nationes, Basel: Recht und Gesellschaft (1997), S. 313–333 (Kurztitel: FS Neumayer)
Stoll, Hans: Haftungsfolgen fehlerhafter Erklärungen beim Vertragsschluß, in: *Jayme* (Hrsg.), Ius inter nationes, Festschrift für Stefan Riesenfeld, Heidelberg: C. F. Müller (1983), S. 275–299 (Kurztitel: FS Riesenfeld)
Stoll, Hans: Haftungsfolgen im Bürgerlichen Recht, Eine Darstellung auf rechtsvergleichender Grundlage, Heidelberg: C. F. Müller (1993) (Kurztitel: Haftungsfolgen)
Stoll, Hans: Inhalt und Grenzen der Schadensersatzpflicht sowie Befreiung von der Haftung im UN-Kaufrecht im Vergleich zu EKG und BGB, in: *Schlechtriem* (Hrsg.), Einheitliches Kaufrecht und nationales Obligationenrecht, Baden-Baden: Nomos (1987), S. 257–281 (Kurztitel: Schadensersatzpflicht)
Stoll, Hans: Internationalprivatrechtliche Fragen bei der landesrechtlichen Ergänzung des Einheitlichen Kaufrechts, in: *Heldrich/Sonnenberger* (Hrsg.), Festschrift für Murad Ferid zum 80. Geburtstag, Frankfurt a. M.: Verlag für Standesamtswesen (1988), S. 495–518 (Kurztitel: Internationalprivatrechtliche Fragen)
Stoll, Hans: Notizen zur Neuordnung des Rechts der Leistungsstörungen, JZ 2001, 589–597
Stoll, Hans: Rechtliche Inhaltskontrolle bei internationalen Handelsgeschäften, in: *Musielak* (Hrsg.), Festschrift für Gerhard Kegel zum 75. Geburtstag, Stuttgart: Kohlhammer (1987), S. 626–662 (Kurztitel: FS Kegel II)
Stoll, Hans: Regelungslücken im Einheitlichen Kaufrecht und IPR, IPRax 1993, 75–79
Stoll, Hans: Zur Haftung bei Erfüllungsverweigerung im Einheitlichen Kaufrecht, RabelsZ 52 (1988), 617–643
Stone, Bradford: Uniform commercial code in a nutshell, 4. Aufl., St. Paul (Minn.): West Publishing (1995) (Kurztitel: UCC in a Nutshell)
Stötter, Viktor: Der stillschweigende Ausschluß der Anwendbarkeit des EKG nach Art. 3 Satz 2 EKG, RIW 1978, 578–581
Stötter, Viktor: Internationales Einheits-Kaufrecht, München: Goldmann (1975)
Straatmann, Kuno/Ulmer, Peter: Handelsrechtliche Schiedsgerichts-Praxis, Bd. 1, 2, Köln: O. Schmidt (1975, 1982), fortgef. unter d. Titel: Rechtsprechung kaufmännischer Schiedsgerichte, Bd. 3, Hamburg: Handelskammer (1984), Bd. 4, Baden-Baden: Nomos (1988) (Kurztitel: HSG)
Straube, Manfred (Hrsg.): Kommentar zum Handelsgesetzbuch mit einschlägigen Rechtsvorschriften, Bd. 1, §§ 1–188, §§ 343–453, 3. Aufl., Wien: Manz (2003) (Kurztitel: *Straube/Bearbeiter*)
Stringer, Dana: Choice of Law and Choice of Forum in Brazilian International Commercial Contracts, 44 Col. J. Trans'l L. (2005–6), 959–991
Strömer, Tobias H./Le Fevre, Anne-Marie: Gesetzliche Zinsen in Frankreich, EuZW 1992, 210–213
Strub, M. Gilbey: The Convention on the International Sale of Goods: Anticipatory Repudiation Provisions and Developing Countries, 38 Int'l & Comp. L. Q. (1989), 475–501
Stumpf, Herbert: Der Know-How-Vertrag, 3. Aufl., Heidelberg: Verlag Recht und Wirtschaft (1977)
Stumpf, Herbert: Einheitliches Gesetz über den internationalen Kauf beweglicher Sachen, RIW 1964, 305–310
Stumpf, Herbert: Schutz vor ungerechtfertigten Schadenersatzansprüchen bei Exportgeschäften durch richtige Vertragsgestaltung. Im Blickpunkt: die Rechtsbeziehung zu den USA, RIW 1999, 411–417
Stürner, Michael: Mängeleinrede und Aufrechnung bei verjährtem Gewährleistungsanspruch nach italienischem Recht im Verhältnis zum UN-Kaufrecht, RIW 2006, 338–344
Su, Yingxia: Die Rechtsmängelhaftung des Verkäufers nach UN-Kaufrecht und im chinesischen Recht, IPRax 1997, 284–290
Su, Yingxia: Die vertragsgemäße Beschaffenheit der Ware im UNCITRAL-Kaufrecht im Vergleich zum deutschen und chinesischen Recht (Diss. Bonn), Münster: Lit (1996)
Sukurs, Charles: Harmonizing the battle of the forms: A comparison of the United States, Canada, and the United Nations Convention on Contracts for the International Sale of Goods, 34 Vand. J. Transnat'l L. (2001), 1481–1515
Sundermann, Stefan: Probleme der autonomen Auslegung des UN-Kaufrechts: Auslegungsmethoden nach Art. 7 CISG anhand der Rechtsprechung der USA und Deutschlands (Diss. Bielefeld, 2009/2010), Hamburg: Kovač, (2010) (Kurztitel: Probleme der autonomen Auslegung)

Literatur

Sumulong, Victor A.: International Trade Law and the United Nations Convention on the Limitation Period in the International Sale of Goods, 50 Philippine L. J. (1975), 318–371
Sutton, Jeffrey S.: Measuring Damages under the United Nations Convention on the International Sale of Goods, 50 Ohio St. L. J. (1989), 737–752
Sutton, Kenneth C. T.: Formation of Contract: Unity in International Sales of Goods, 16 U. W. Ont. L. Rev. (1977), 113–162
Szász, Iván: The CMEA Uniform Law for International Sales, 2. Aufl., Dordrecht: Nijhoff (1985)

Tacheva, Maia: Rechtsbehelfe des Käufers im Warenkaufrecht (Diss. Osnabrück), Frankfurt a. M.: Peter Lang (2005) (Kurztitel: Rechtsbehelfe des Käufers)
Takawira, Admire: Departing from mere compromise: Reformulating the remedy of specific performance under the Convention on the International Sale of Goods (CISG) in line with the Convention's underlying goals, November 2007, www.cisg.law.pace.edu/cisg/biblio/takawira.html
Tallon, Denis: La révision du contrat pour imprévision au regard des enseignements récents du droit comparé, in Droit et vie des affaires, Études à la mémoire d'Alain Sayag, Paris: Litecc (1997), 403–417 (Kurztitel: Études Sayag)
Tallon, Denis: The Buyer's Obligations under the Convention on Contracts for the International Sale of Goods, in: *Galston/Smit* (Hrsg.), International Sales, New York: Matthew Bender (1984), Kap. 7, S. 1–20 (Kurztitel: Buyer's Obligations)
Tannò, Patrick: Die Berechnung der Rügefrist im schweizerischen, deutschen und UN-Kaufrecht, St. Gallen: Dike (1993)
Taschner, Hans Claudius: Anmerkung zu BGH, Urteil vom 3.11.1999 – VIII ZR 287/98, TranspR-IHR 2003, 3–4
Taschner, Hans Claudius: Produkthaftung: Richtlinie d. Rates vom 25. Juli 1985 zur Angleichung d. Rechts- u. Verwaltungsvorschriften d. Mitgliedstaaten über d. Haftung für fehlerhafte Produkte (85/374/EWG), Beck: München (1986)
Taschner, Martin: Die Darlegung von Mängeln und der richtige Mängeladressat – Zugleich Anmerkung zu der Entscheidung des LG Köln vom 30.11.1999 – 89 O 20/99, IHR 2001, 69, IHR 2001, 61–63
Teichert, Ulrike: Lückenfüllung im CISG mittels UNIDROIT-Prinzipien – Zugleich ein Beitrag zur Wählbarkeit nichtstaatlichen Rechts (Diss. Köln), Frankfurt a. M.: Lang (2006) (Kurztitel: Lückenfüllung)
Teitz, Louise Ellen: The Hague Choice of Court Convention: Validating Party Autonomy and Providing an Alternative to Arbitration, 53 Am. J. Comp. L. (2005), 543–558
Teiling, Annabel: CISG: U. S. Court Relies on Foreign Case Law and the Internet: A note on the decision in Chicago Prime Packers v. Northam Food Trading [21 May 2004] United States District Court, N. D. Illinois, Eastern Division, Uniform L. Rev. 2004, 431–435
Teklote, Stephan: Die Einheitlichen Kaufgesetze und das deutsche AGB-Gesetz. Probleme bei der Verwendung Allgemeiner Geschäftsbedingungen im CISG und im EKG/EAG (Diss. Münster 1993), Baden-Baden: Nomos (1994)
Tercier, Pierre: Droits et obligations de l'acheteur, in: Schweizerisches Institut für Rechtsvergleichung (Hrsg.), Lausanner Kolloquium 1984, Zürich: Schulthess (1985), S. 119–142 (Kurztitel: Droits et obligations)
Tescaro, Mauro: Il concorso tra rimedi contrattuali di cui alla Convenzone di Vienna sulla vendita internazionale di beni mobili (CISG) e i rimedi domestici, Contr. Imp. E. 2007, 319–341
Teske, Wolfgang: Schriftformklauseln in Allgemeinen Geschäftsbedingungen (Diss. Erlangen-Nürnberg 1988/89), Köln: Heymanns (1990)
Tessitore, Michael A.: The U. N. Convention on International Sales and the Seller's Ineffective Right of Reclamation under the U. S. Bankruptcy Code, 35 Willamette L. Rev. (1999), 367–391
The Principles of European Contract Law (PECL), www.storme.be/PECL2en.html (PECL)
Thieffry, Jean: Arbitration and New Rules Applicable to International Sales Contracts under the United Nations Convention, 4 Arb. Int'l (1988), 52–61
Thieffry, Jean: La Convention de Vienne et les contrats de distribution, Dr. prat. com. int. 1993, 62–68
Thieffry, Jean: L'arbitrage, les usages et les nouvelles règles conventionnelles de la vente, in: *Perret/Lacasse* (Hrsg.), Actes du colloque sur la vente internationale, Montréal: Wilson & Lafleur (1989), S. 93–104 (Kurztitel: Arbitrage, usages et nouvelles règles conventionnelles)
Thieffry, Jean: Les nouvelles règles de la vente internationale, Dr. prat. com. int. 1989, 369–384
Thiele, Christian: Anmerkung zu OLG Koblenz, Urteil vom 18.11.1999 – 2 U 1556/98, IHR 2001, 111–112
Thiele, Christian: Das UN-Kaufrecht vor US-amerikanischen Gerichten, IHR 2002, 8–14
Thiele, Christian: Erfüllungsort bei der Rückabwicklung von Vertragspflichten nach Art. 81 UN-Kaufrecht – ein Plädoyer gegen die herrschende Meinung, RIW 2000, 892–895

Literatur

Thomas, Heinz/Putzo, Hans: Zivilprozessordnung, 33. Aufl., München: Beck (2012) (Kurztitel: *Thomas/Putzo/Bearbeiter*)
Thorn, Karsten: Die UN-Verjährungskonvention und ihre Geltung in Deutschland, IPRax 1993, 215–216
Thorn, Karsten: Termingeschäfte auf Auslandsmärkten und internationale Schiedsgerichtsbarkeit, IPrax 1997, 98–106
von Tuhr, Andreas: Der allgemeine Teil des Deutschen Bürgerlichen Rechts, Bd. II/2, Neudruck Berlin: Duncker & Humblot (1957) (Kurztitel: AT II/2)
Tiedemann, Stefan: Kollidierende AGB-Rechtswahlklauseln im österreichischen und deutschen IPR, IPrax 1991, 424–427
Tiedtke, Klaus: Ablieferung der Kaufsache und Verjährungsbeginn der Gewährleistungsansprüche, NJW 1988, 2578–2581
Tiling, Johann: Haftungsbefreiung, Haftungsbegrenzung und Freizeichnung im Einheitlichen Gesetz über den internationalen Kauf beweglicher Sachen, RabelsZ 32 (1968), 258–283
Timpano, Francesco: Vendita internazionale e problemi di giurisdizione, iContr. 2000, 664–667
Torsello, Marco: Common Features of Uniform Commercial Law Conventions, A Comparative Study Beyond the 1980 Uniform Sales Law, München: Sellier. ELP (2004) (Kurztitel: Common Features)
Torsello, Marco: Preliminary Agreements and CISG Contracts, in: *Fletchner/Brand/Walter* (Hrsg.), Drafting Contracts under the CISG, Oxford: Oxford University Press (2008), S. 191–252 (Kurztitel: Preliminary Agreements)
Torsello, Marco: Remedies for Breach of Contract under the 1980 U. N. Convention on Contracts for the International Sale of Goods, 9 VJ 2005, 253–290
Torsello, Marco: Remedies for Breach of Contract, in: *Ferrari* (Hrsg.), Quo Vadis CISG? Celebrating the 25th anniversary of the United Nations Convention on Contracts for the International Sale of Goods, München: Sellier (2005), S. 43–87 (Kurztitel: Remedies)
Torsello, Marco: The CISG's Impact on Legislators: The Drafting of International Commercial Law Conventions, in: *Ferrari* (Hrsg.), The 1980 Uniform Sales Law. Old Issues Revisited in the Light of Recent Experiences, Mailand/München: Giuffrè/Sellier European Law Publishers (2003), S. 199–275 (Kurztitel: The CISG's Impact)
Torzilli, Paolo: The Aftermath of MCC-Marble: Is This the Death Knell for the Parol Evidence Rule?, 74 St. John's L. Rev. (2000), 843–873
Trachsel, Heribert: Die vollständige und teilweise Haftungsbefreiung sowie die Haftungsreduktion nach UN-Kaufrecht (Art. 79, 80 und 77 CISG), in: *Baudenbacher* (Hrsg.), Aktuelle Entwicklungen des Europäischen und Internationalen Wirtschaftsrechts, Basel: Helbing & Lichtenhahn (2003), S. 345–418 (Kurztitel: Haftungsbefreiung)
Treitel, Guenter H.: Remedies for Breach of Contract. Courses of action open to the party aggrieved, in: Int. Enc. Comp. L., Under the Auspices of the I. A. L. S., Vol. VII: Contracts in General, Kap. 16, Tübingen: Mohr (1989) (Kurztitel: Remedies for Breach)
Treitel, Guenter H.: The Law of Contract, 10. Aufl., London: Stevens (1999) (Kurztitel: Law of Contract)
Treitel, Guenter H.: Unmöglichkeit, „Impracticability" und „Frustration" im anglo-amerikanischen Recht, Baden-Baden: Nomos (1991) (Kurztitel: Unmöglichkeit)
Triebel, Volker/Balthasar, Stephan: Auslegung englischer Vertragstexte unter deutschem Vertragsstatut– Fallstricke des Art. 32 I Nr. 1 EGBGB, NJW 2004, 2189–2196
Troiano, Stefano: The CISG's Impact on EU Legislation, IHR 2008, 221–249
Troller, Alois: Immaterialgüterrecht, Bd. I, 3. Aufl., Basel/Frankfurt a. M.: Helbing & Lichtenhahn (1989)
Trommler, Andreas: Die Auslegung des Begriffes „wesentliche Vertragsverletzung" in Art. 25 CISG (Diss. Konstanz 2001), Frankfurt a. M.: Lang (2002) (Kurztitel: wesentliche Vertragsverletzung)
Trompenaars, Bernardine W. M.: Interpretatie-clausules in het eenvormig recht (Interpretation Clauses in the Uniform Law), in: *Kokkini-Iatridou/Van der Velden* (Hrsg.), Eenvormig en vergelijkend privaatrecht, Lelystad: Koninklijke Vermande (1989), S. 25–49 (Kurztitel: Interpretatie-clausules)
Trompenaars, Bernardine W. M.: Pluriforme unificatie en eniforme interpretatie – in het bijzonder de bijdrage van UNCITRAL aan de internationale unificatie van het privaatrecht, (Pluriform Unification and Uniform Interpretation), Deventer: Kluwer (1989) (Kurztitel: Unificatie en interpretatie)
Trunk, Alexander: Erste deutsche Rechtsprechung zum Lugano-Übereinkommen, IPrax 1996, 249–254
Tuggey, T. N.: The 1980 United Nations Convention on Contracts for the International Sale of Goods: Will a Homeward Trend Emerge?, 21 Tex. Int'l L. J. (1986), 540–557

Literatur

Tunc, André: Commentaire des Conventions de la Haye du 1er juillet 1964 sur la vente internationale des objets mobiliers corporels et sur la formation des contrats de vente. Actes et Documents de la Conférence diplomatique sur l'unification du droit en matière de vente internationale, tome II: Actes, 355–391; in deutscher Übersetzung abgedruckt in BT-Drs. VI/3722, 78–118 (Kurztitel: Actes)

Tunc, André: Commentary on the Hague Conventions of the 1st of July 1964 on International Sale of Goods and the Formation of the Contract of Sale, in: Ministry of Justice of the Netherlands (Hrsg.), Diplomatic Conference on the Unification of Law Governing the International Sale of Goods (The Hague, 2.–25.4.1964) – Records and Documents of the Conference, Vol. 1 – Records, The Hague (Government) (1966), S. 355–391 (Kurztitel: Commentary)

Ubertaite, Edita: Application of the CISG in the United States, 7 EJLR (2005), 277–301

Ulmer, Eugen: Int. Enc. Comp. L., Vol. XIV: Copyright and Industrial Property, chap. 1: General Questions – The International Conventions, Tübingen: Mohr (1987)

Ulmer, Eugen: General Questions – The International Conventions, in: *David* (Hrsg.), International Encyclopedia of Comparative Law, Vol. XIV, Kap. 1, Tübingen: Mohr/Dordrecht u. a.: Nijhoff (1987)

Ulmer, Peter: Die Immaterialgüterrechte im internationalen Privatrecht, Köln/Berlin/Bonn/München: Heymanns (1975)

Ulmer, Peter: Gewerbliche Schutzrechte und Urheberrechte im internationalen Privatrecht, RabelsZ 41 (1977), 479–512

Ulmer, Peter/Brandner, Hans Erich/Hensen, Horst-Diether: AGB-Gesetz, Kommentar zum Gesetz zur Regelung des Rechts der Allgemeinen Geschäftsbedingungen, hrsg. v. *Ulmer, Brandner, Hensen u. H. Schmidt,* 8. Aufl., Köln: O. Schmidt (1997) (Kurztitel: *Ulmer/Brandner/Hensen*)

Ulmer, Peter/Brandner, Hans Erich/Hensen, Horst-Diether: AGB-Recht, Kommentar zu den §§ 305–310 BGB und zum Unterlassungsklagengesetz, 10. Aufl., Köln: Otto Schmidt (2006) (Kurztitel: *Ulmer/Brandner/Hensen/Bearbeiter*)

UNCITRAL Digest of Case Law on the United Nations Convention on the International Sale of Goods, New York (2008) (Kurztitel: UNCITRAL Digest 2008)

UNIDROIT (Hrsg.): International Uniform Law in Practice/Le droit uniforme international dans la pratique. International Congress Rome 7.–10.9.1987, New York/Rom: Oceana: UNIDROIT (1988) (Kurztitel: International Uniform Law in Practice)

UNCITRAL (Hrsg.): Model Law on Electronic Commerce with Guide to Enactment 1996, New York (1997) (Kurztitel: UNCITRAL, Electronic Commerce)

UNIDROIT (Hrsg.): Principles of International Commercial Contracts, Rome: UNIDROIT (1994/2004)

Unification and Certainty: The United Nations Conventions on Contracts for the International Sale of Goods, 97 Harv. L. Rev. (1984), 1984–2000

United Nations Conference on Prescription (Limitation) in the International Sale of Goods: New York, 20 May – 14 June 1974; official records; documents of the conference and summary records of the plenary meetings and of the meetings of the main committee, New York: United Nations (1975)

Vahle, Oliver: Der Erfüllungsanspruch des Käufers nach UN-Kaufrecht im Vergleich mit dem deutschen Kaufrecht, ZVerglRW 1999, 54–73

Valcárcel Schnüll, Dagmar: Die Haftung des Verkäufers für Fehler und zugesicherte Eigenschaften im europäischen Rechtsvergleich (Diss. Bonn 1994)

Valloni, Lucien William: Der Gerichtsstand des Erfüllungsortes nach Lugano- und Brüsseler Übereinkommen, Zürich: Schulthess (1998)

Vanwijk-Alexandre, Michèle: Contravention Anticipée et contrats à livraisons successives dans la CVIM, R. D. A. I. 2001, 353–378

Varul, Paul: CISG: a Source of Inspiration for the Estonian Law of Obligations, Uniform L. Rev. 2003, 209–210

Vázquez Lepinette, Tomás: La compraventa internacional de mercaderias. Una vision Jurisprudencial, Pamplona: Aranzandi (2000) (Kurztitel: La compraventa internacional)

Vázquez Lepinette, Tomás: The interpretation of the 1980 Vienna Convention on International Sales, Dir. com. int. 1995, 377–399

Vékás, Lajos: The Foreseeability Doctrine in Contractual Damage Cases, 43 Acta Juridica Hungarica (2002), 145–174 = http://www.cisg.law.pace.edu/cisg/biblio/vekas.html (Kurztitel: Foreseeability)

Vékás, Lajos: Zum persönlichen und räumlichen Anwendungsbereich des UN-Einheitskaufrechts, IPRax 1987, 342–346

Literatur

van der Velden, Frans J. A.: The Law of International Sales, The Hague Conventions 1964 and the UNCITRAL Uniform Sales Code 1980 – Some Main Items Compared, in: *Voskuil/Wade* (Hrsg.), Hague-Zagreb Essays 4, Den Haag: Asser Instituut/Martinus Nijhoff (1983), S. 46–106 (Kurztitel: Main Items)

van der Velden, Frans J. A.: Uniform International Sales Law and the Battle of Forms, in: Unification and Comparative Law in Theory and Practice: Liber amicorum Jean Georges Sauveplanne, Deventer: Kluwer (1984), S. 233–249 (Kurztitel: Battle of Forms)

Veneziano, Anna: Mancanza di conformità delle merci ed onere della prova nella vendita internazionale: un esempio di interpretazione autonoma del diritto uniforme alla luce dei precedenti stranieri, Dir. com. int. 2001, 509–518

Veneziano, Anna: Nonconformity of goods in international sales: a survey of current caselaw on CISG = Non-conformité des marchandises dans les ventes internationales: étude de la jurisprudence atctuelle sur la CVIM, R. D. A. I. 1997, 39–65

Veneziano, Anna: Uniform Interpretation: What is Being Done? Unofficial Efforts and Their Impact, in: *Ferrari* (Hrsg.), The 1980 Uniform Sales Law. Old Issues Revisited in the Light of Recent Experiences, Mailand/München: Giuffrè/Sellier European Law Publishers (2003), S. 325–333 (Kurztitel: Uniform Interpretation)

Ventsch, Verena/Kluth, Peter: Die Einbeziehung von Allgemeinen Geschäftsbedingungen im Rahmen des UN-Kaufrechts, IHR 2003, 61–66

Ventsch, Verena/Kluth, Peter: UN-Kaufrecht: Keine Einbeziehung von AGB durch Abrufmöglichkeit im Internet, IHR 2003, 224–225

Venturi, Silvio: La reduction du prix de vente en cas de défaut ou de non-conformité de lachose. Le code suisse des obligations et la Convention de Nations Unies sur les contrats de vente internationale de marchandises (Diss. Fribourg), Fribourg: Editions Universitaires (1994)

Vergne, François: The „Battle of Forms" Under the 1980 United Nations Convention on Contracts for the International Sale of Goods, 33 Am. J. Comp. L. (1985), 233–258

Verweyen, Urs: Die Käuferrechtsbehelfe des UN-Kaufrechts im Vergleich zu denen des neuen internen deutschen Handelskaufrechts aus Sicht eines deutschen Warenexporteurs (Diss. Hamburg), Frankfurt a. M.: Peter Lang (2005) (Kurztitel: Internationaler Warenkauf)

Verweyen, Urs/Foerster, Viktor/Toufar, Oliver: Handbuch des Internationalen Warenkaufs, UN-Kaufrecht (CISG), 2. Aufl., Stuttgart/München: Richard Boorberg Verlag (2008) (Kurztitel: Handbuch)

Vida, Sándor Alexander: Alapvető szerződésszegés a nemzetközi adásvételnél: Német bírói gyakorlat, J. Közlöny 1993, 169–175

Vida, Sándor Alexander: Differenzierte Rechtsanwendung beim internationalen Kaufvertrag, IPRax 2002, 146–147

Vida, Sándor Alexander: Garantie du vendeur et popriété industrielle: les „vices juridiques" dans la vente internationale de marchandises (convention de vienne), RTD com. 1994, 21–36

Vida, Sándor Alexander: Keine Anwendung des UN-Kaufrechtsübereinkommens bei Übertragung des Geschäftsanteils einer GmbH, IPRax 1995, 52–53

Vida, Sándor Alexander: Unwirksamkeit der Offerte wegen Unbestimmtheit nach UN-Kaufrecht, IPRax 1995, 261–264

Vida, Sándor Alexander: Zur Anwendung des UN-Kaufübereinkommens in Ungarn (zu Hauptstadtgericht Budapest, Urteil v. 24.3.1992, AZ 12. G.41.471/1991), IPRax 1993, 263–264

Vilus, Jelena: Komentar Konvencije Ujedinjenih nacija o medjunarodnoj prodaji robe, 1980, uvod i redakcija Aleksandar Goldstajn, (Commentary on the United Nations Convention on the International Sale of Goods) (English Summary 193–199), Zagreb: Informator (1981)

Vilus, Jelena: Provisions Common to the Obligations of the Seller and the Buyer, in: *Šarčević/Volken* (Hrsg.), Dubrovnik Lectures 1985, New York: Oceana (1986), S. 239–264 (Kurztitel: Provisions)

Viney, Geneviève: Exécution de l'oblitagtion, faculté de remplacement et reparation en nature en droit français, in: *Fontaine/Viney* (Hrsg.), Les Sanctions de l'inexécution des obligation contractuelle, études de droit comparé, Paris: L. G. D. J. (2001), S. 167–203

Vischer, Frank: Die kollisionsrechtliche Bedeutung der Wahl einer nichtstaatlichen Ordnung für den staatlichen Richter am Beispiel der Unidroit Principles of International Commercial Contracts, in: *Schwenzer/Hager* (Hrsg.), Festschrift für Peter Schlechtriem zum 70. Geburtstag, Tübingen: Mohr (2003), S. 445–454 (Kurztitel: FS Schlechtriem)

Vischer, Frank: Gemeinsame Bestimmungen über Verpflichtungen des Verkäufers und des Käufers, in: Schweizerisches Institut für Rechtsvergleichung (Hrsg.), Lausanner Kolloquium 1984, Zürich: Schulthess (1985), S. 173–184 (Kurztitel: Gemeinsame Bestimmungen)

Vischer, Frank/Huber, Lucius/Oser, David: Internationales Vertragsrecht, 2. Aufl, Bern: Stämpfli (2000)

Literatur

Vogel, Hans-Josef: Die Untersuchungs- und Rügepflicht im UN-Kaufrecht (Diss. Bonn 2000)

Vogenauer, Stefan/Kleinheisterkamp, Jan (Hrsg.), Commentary on the UNIDROIT Principles of International Commercial Contracts (PICC), Oxord: University Press (2009) (Kurztitel: *Vogenauer/Kleinheisterkamp/Autor*)

Volken, Paul: Champ d'application, interprétation, lacunes, usages, in: Schweizerisches Institut für Rechtsvergleichung (Hrsg.), Lausanner Kolloquium 1984, Zürich: Schulthess (1985), S. 21–33 (Kurztitel: Champ d'application)

Volken, Paul: Das Wiener Übereinkommen über den internationalen Warenkauf. Anwendungsvoraussetzungen und Anwendungsbereich, in: *Schlechtriem* (Hrsg.), Einheitliches Kaufrecht und nationales Obligationenrecht, Baden-Baden: Nomos (1987), S. 81–96 (Kurztitel: Anwendungsvoraussetzungen)

Volken, Paul: Konventionskonflikte im internationalen Privatrecht, Zürich: Schulthess (1977) (Kurztitel: Konventionskonflikte)

Volken, Paul: The Vienna Convention: Scope, Interpretation and Gap-Filling, in: *Šarčević/Volken* (Hrsg.), Dubrovnik Lectures 1985, New York: Oceana (1986), S. 19–53 (Kurztitel: Scope)

Voser, Nathalie/Boog, Christopher: Die Wahl des Schweizer Rechts – Was man wissen sollte, RIW 2009, 126–139

Voskuil, C. C. A./Wade, J. A. (Hrsg.): Hague-Zagreb Essays 4: On the Law of International Trade. Hague-Zagreb Colloquium, 4th, Eernewoude-NL 12.–15.5.1981, Den Haag: Asser Instituut/Martinus Nijhoff (1983) (Kurztitel: Hague-Zagreb Essays 4)

de Vries, H.: Disengaging Sales Law from the Sale Construct: a Proposal to Extend the Scope of Article 2 of the UCC, 96 Harv. L. Rev. (1982), 470–491

de Vries, H.: The Passing of Risk in International Sales under the Vienna Sales Convention 1980 as compared with Traditional Trade Terms, 17 Eur. Transp. L. (1982), 495–528

van Vuuren, Elbi Janse: Termination of international commercial contracts for breach of contract: The provision of the UNIDROIT Principles of international commercial contracts, 15 Ariz. J. Int'l and Comp. L., (1998), 583–634

Wagner, Gerhard: Gutachten zum 66. Deutschen Juristentag, in: Verhandlungen des sechsundsechzigsten Deutschen Juristentages, Band 1 – Gutachten, A 11 – A 135, Stuttgart 2006. (Kurztitel: Gutachten)

Wagner-von Papp, Florian: European Contract Law: Are No Oral Modification Clauses Not Worth the Paper They Are Written On? DCFR II.-4:105 v. CISG 29(2), UNIDROIT Principles 2.1.18, UCC § 2–209, and Comparative Law, 63 CLP (2010), 511–596

Wahl, Eduard: Vertragsansprüche Dritter im französischen Recht unter Vergleich mit dem deutschen Recht, dargestellt an Hand der Fälle der action directe, Berlin/Leipzig: de Gruyter (1935)

Waldenberger, Arthur: Grenzen des Verbraucherschutzes beim Abschluß von Verträgen im Internet, BB 1996, 2365–2371

Walker, Janet: Agreeing to Disagree: Can We Just Have Words? CISG Article 11 and the Model Law Writing Requirement, 25 J. L. & Com. (2005–06), 153–165

Walt, Steven: For Specific Performance Under the United Nations Sales Convention, 26 Tex. Int'l L. J. (1991), 211–251

Walt, Steven: Novelty and the Risks of Uniform Sales Law, 39 Va. J. Int'l L. (1999), 671–705

Walt, Steven: The CISG's expansion bias: A comment on Franco Ferrari's 'What Sources of Law for Contracts for the International Sale of Goods', 25 Int'l Rev. L. & Econ. (2005), 342–349

Walter, Gerhard: Das UN-Kaufrechtsübereinkommen und seine prozessualen Folgen für die Schweiz, in: *Schwander/Stoffel* (Hrsg.), Beiträge zum schweizerischen und internationalen Zivilprozessrecht, Festschrift für Oscar Vogel, Freiburg (Schweiz): Universitätsverlag (1991), S. 317–335 (Kurztitel: FS Vogel)

Walter, Gerhard: Kaufrecht, Tübingen: Mohr (1987) (Kurztitel: Kaufrecht)

Walter, Mark S.: Drafting Contracts to Deal with Insecurity and Propective Breach (Articles 71, 72, 73 (2)), in: *Flechtner/Brand/Walter* (Hrsg.), Drafting Contracts under the CISG, Oxford: Oxford University Press (2008), S. 413–428 (Kurztitel: Drafting Contracts)

Walther, Lena/Morawietz, Matthias: Declaration according to Article 96 CISG – Senseless?, IHR 2006, 252–254

Wang, Peter Jen-Huong: Das Wiener Übereinkommen über internationale Warenkaufverträge vom 11. April 1980. Unter besonderer Berücksichtigung des Aussenhandels, ZVerglRW 1988, 184–202

Wang, Xiaolin/Andersen, Camilla Baasch: The Chinese Declaration as to Form of Contracts under CISG- Time to Withdraw?, Uniform L. Rev 2004, 870–873

Wartenberg, Konrad: CISG und deutsches Verbraucherschutzrecht: Das Verhältnis der CISG insbesondere zum VerbrKrG, HaustürWG und ProdHaftG, Baden-Baden: Nomos (1998)

Wasmer, Wolfgang: Vertragsfreiheit und UN-Kaufrecht, Hamburg: Kovac (2004)

Literatur

Weber, Johann-Ahrend: Warenpapiere ohne Traditionsfunktion (Diss. Bonn 1978)
Weber, Rolf H.: Vertragsverletzungsfolgen: Schadenersatz, Rückabwicklung, vertragliche Gestaltungsmöglichkeiten, in: *Bucher* (Hrsg.), Wiener Kaufrecht, Bern: Stämpfli (1991), S. 165–210 (Kurztitel: Vertragsverletzungsfolgen)
Wegen, Gerhard/Wilske, Stephan: Die anwendbare Zeitzone für Fristen in internationalen Schiedsverfahren, SchiedsVZ 2003, 124–125
Weill, Alex/Terré, François: Droit civil, Les obligations, 4. Aufl., Paris: Dalloz (1986) (Kurztitel: Droit civil)
Weitnauer, Hermann: Nichtvoraussehbarkeit eines Schadens nach Art. 82 S. 2 des Einheitlichen Gesetzes über den internationalen Kauf beweglicher Sachen, IPRax 1981, 83–85
Weitnauer, Hermann: Vertragsaufhebung und Schadenersatz nach dem Einheitlichen Kaufgesetz und nach geltendem deutschen Recht, in: *Wahl* (Hrsg.), Rechtsvergleichung und Rechtsvereinheitlichung, Festschrift zum 50 jährigen Bestehen des Instituts für Ausländisches und Internationales Privat- und Wirtschaftsrecht der Universität Heidelberg, Heidelberg: Winter (1967), S. 71–114
Weitnauer, Hermann: Zum Vorrang der „Gepflogenheiten" zwischen den Vertragsparteien vor den Bestimmungen des Einheitlichen Kaufrechts, IPRax 1984, 185–186
Weizuo, Chen: The Conflict of Laws in the Context of the CISG: A Chinese Perspective, 20 Pace Int'l L. Rev. (2008), 115–128
Weller, Marc-Philippe: Stillschweigende Einbeziehung der AGB-Banken im internationalen Geschäftsverkehr?, IPRax 2005, 428–431
Weller, Matthias: Die UNIDROIT-Konvention von Ottawa über internationales Factoring, RIW 1999, 161–167
Welser, Rudolf: Die Verbrauchsgüterkauf-Richtlinie und ihre Umsetzung in Österreich und Deutschland, in: *Schlechtriem* (Hrsg.), Wandlungen des Schuldrecht, Baden-Baden: Nomos (2002), S. 83–96
Welser, Rudolf: Die Vertragsverletzung des Verkäufers und ihre Sanktion, in: *Doralt* (Hrsg.), Das UNCITRAL-Kaufrecht im Vergleich zum österreichischen Recht. Referate und Diskussionen des Symposiums in Baden bei Wien, 17.–19. April 1983, Wien: Manz (1985), S. 105–132 (Kurztitel: Vetragsverletzung des Verkäufers)
Welser, Rudolf/Jud, Brigitta: Die neue Gewährleistung: Kurzkommentar zu sämtlichen Bestimmungen des ABGB und des KSchG, Wien: Manz (2001)
Wenner, Wolfgang/Schödel, Christoph: Kaufvertragsrecht in Frankreich, in: *Graf von Westphalen* (Hrsg.), Handbuch des Kaufvertragsrechts in den EG-Staaten, Köln: Schmidt (1992), S. 417–479
Werro, Franz: La responsabilité du vendeur dans le commerce international et dans le marché intérieur européen, Sem. Jud. (2002), 289–323
Wertenbruch, Johann: Das Wahlrecht des Gläubigers zwischen Erfüllungsanspruch und den Rechten aus § 326 BGB nach einer Erfüllungsverweigerung des Schuldners, AcP 193 (1993), 191–203
Westermann, Harm Peter: Zum Anwendungsbereich des UN-Kaufrechts bei internationalen Kaufverträgen, DZWir 1995, 1–10
Graf von Westphalen, Friedrich (Hrsg.): Handbuch des Kaufvertragsrechts in den EG-Staaten, Köln: O. Schmidt (1992) (Kurztitel: Handbuch des Kaufvertragsrechts)
Graf von Westphalen, Friedrich: Allgemeine Geschäftsbedingungen und Einheitliches Kaufgesetz, in: *Schlechtriem* (Hrsg.), Einheitliches Kaufrecht und nationales Obligationenrecht, Baden-Baden: Nomos (1987), S. 49–74 (Kurztitel: AGB und Einheitliches Kaufgesetz)
Graf von Westphalen, Friedrich: Anwendung des AGB-Rechts im Export, in: *Heinrichs u. a.* (Hrsg.), Zehn Jahre AGB-Gesetz, Köln: RWS Kommunikationsforum (1987), S. 175–199 (Kurztitel: Anwendung des AGB-Rechts)
Wey, Marc: Der Vertragsabschluß beim internationalen Warenkauf nach UNCITRAL- und schweizerischem Recht (Diss. Basel 1984)
White, James J./Summers, Robert S.: Uniform Commercial Code, 5. Aufl., St. Paul (Minn).: West Publishing (2000)
Whitlock, Alicia Jurney/Abbey, Boris S.: Who's Afraid of the CISG – Why North Carolina Practitioners Should Learn a Thing or Two about the 1980 United Nations Convention on Contracts for the International Sale of Goods, 30 Campbell L. Rev. (2007), 275–296
Whittington, Nicholas: Reconsidering Domestic Sale of Goods Remedies in Light of the CISG, 37 Vict. U. Well. L. Rev. (2006), 421–449
Wichard, Johannes Christian: Die Anwendung der UNIDROIT-Prinzipien für internationale Handelsverträge durch Schiedsgerichte und staatliche Gerichte, RabelsZ 60 (1996), 269–302
Widmer, Corinne/Hachem, Pascal: The CISG in Switzerland, in: *Ferrari* (Hrsg.), The CISG and its Impact on National Legal Systems, München: Sellier (2008), S. 281–302 (Kurztitel: CISG in Switzerland)

Widmer, Pierre: Droits et obligations du vendeur, in: Schweizerisches Institut für Rechtsvergleichung (Hrsg.), Lausanner Kolloquium 1984, Zürich: Schulthess (1985), S. 91–104 (Kurztitel: Droits et obligations du vendeur)
Wiegand, Wolfgang (Hrsg.): Mobiliarsicherheiten, Berner Bankrechtstag, Bd. 5, Bern: Stämpfli (1998)
Wiegand, Wolfgang: Die Pflichten des Käufers und die Folgen ihrer Verletzung, in: *Bucher* (Hrsg.), Wiener Kaufrecht, Bern: Stämpfli (1991), S. 143–164 (Kurztitel: Pflichten des Käufers)
Wietzorek, Michael: Der Beweis des Zugangs von Anhängen in E-Mails, MMR 2007, 156–159
Wildner, Kaia: Art. 19 CISG: The German Approach to the Battle of the Forms in International Contract Law: The Decision of the Federal Supreme Court of Germany of 9 January 2002, 20 Pace Int'l L. Rev. (2008), 1–30
Wilhelm, Georg: UN-Kaufrecht: Einführung und Gesetzestext, Wien: Manz (1993)
Wilhelmsson, Thomas: Private Law Remedies against Breach of Information Requirements of EC Law, in: *Schulze/Ebers/Grigoleit* (Hrsg.), Informationspflichten und Vertragsschluß im Acquis communitaire, Tübingen: Mohr (2003), S. 245–265
Will, Michael R.: Conflits entre conditions générales de vente, in: Les Ventes Internationales de Marchandises, Paris: Economica (1981), S. 99–109 (Kurztitel: Conflits)
Will, Michael R.: „Meine Großmutter in der Schweiz . . .": Zum Konflikt von Verjährung und Rügefrist nach UN-Kaufrecht, in: *Rauscher/Mansel* (Hrsg.): FS für Werner Lorenz zum 80. Geburtstag, München: Sellier (2001), S. 623–642 (Kurztitel: FS Lorenz)
Will, Michael R.: Twenty years of international sales law under the CISG, The Hague: Kluwer Law International (2000) (Kurztitel: Twenty years)
Williams, Adam: Limitations on Uniformity in International Sales Law: A Reasoned Argument for the Application of a Standard Limitation Period under the Provisions of the CISG, 10 VJ (2006), 229–262
Williston, Samuel: A Treatise on the Law of Contracts, 3. Aufl., Mount Kisco, N. Y.: Baker, Voorhis & 38; Co. (1968)
von Wilmowsky, Peter: Europäisches Kreditsicherungsrecht, Sachenrecht und Insolvenzrecht unter dem EG-Vertrag, Tübingen: Mohr (1996)
Wilting, Wilhelm Heinrich: Vertragskonkurrenz im Völkerrecht, Köln u. a.: Heymanns (1996)
Windbichler, Christine: Neue Vertriebsformen und ihr Einfluß auf das Kaufrecht, AcP 198 (1998), 261–286
Winship, Peter: Aircraft and International Sales Conventions, 50 J. Air L. & Com. (1985), 1053–1066
Winship, Peter: Changing Contract Practices in the Light of the United Nations Convention: A Guide for Practitioners, 29 Int'l Law. (1995), 525–554
Winship, Peter: Changing Contract Practices in the Light of the United Nations Sales Convention: A Guide for Practitioners, 9 Int'l Quarterly (1997), 110–148
Winship, Peter: Commentary on Professor Kastely's Rhetorical Analysis (Symposium Reflections), 8 Nw. J. Int'l L. & Bus. (1988), 623–639
Winship, Peter: Energy Contracts and the United Nations Sales Convention, 25 Tex. Int'l L. J. (1990), 365–379
Winship, Peter: Export-Import Sales under the 1980 United Nations Sales Convention, 8 Hastings Int'l & Comp. L. Rev. (1985), 197–211
Winship, Peter: Formation of International Sales Contracts under the 1980 Vienna Convention, 17 Int'l Law. (1983), 1–18
Winship, Peter: International Sales Contracts Under the 1980 Vienna Convention, 17 UCC L. J. (1984), 55–71
Winship, Peter: Private International Law and the U. N. Sales Convention, 21 Cornell Int'l L. J. (1988), 487–533
Winship, Peter: The Convention on the Limitation Period in the International Sale of Goods, the United States adopts UNCITRAL's firstborn, 28 Int'l Law. (1994), 1071–1081
Winship, Peter: The Scope of the Vienna Convention on International Sales Contracts, in: *Galston/Smit* (Hrsg.), International Sales, New York: Matthew Bender (1984), Kap. 1, S. 1–53 (Kurztitel: Scope)
Winship, Peter: The U. N. Sales Convention and the emerging Caselaw, in: *Majoros* (Hrsg.), Emptio – venditio inter nationes, Basel: Recht und Gesellschaft (1997), S. 227–237 (Kurztitel: FS Neumayer)
Winsor, Katrina: The Applicability of the CISG to Govern Sales of Commodity Type Goods, 14 VJ (2010), 83–116
Wittinghofer, Mathias/Becker, Anja: Zur Berechnung des Schadensersatzes nach Art. 76 UN-Kaufrecht, IHR 2010, 225–230
Witz, Claude: A Raw Nerve in Disputes relating to the Vienna Sales Convention: The Reasonable Time for the Buyer to Give Notice of a Lack of Conformity, ICC Ct. Bull. 11/2, 2000, 15–21
Witz, Claude: Anmerkung zu CA Colmar, 24.10.2000, D 2002, Somm. 393

Literatur

Witz, Claude: Anmerkung zu CA Paris, 6.11.2001, D. 2002, 2795–2799
Witz, Claude: Anmerkung zu Cass. 26.6.2001, D. 2001, 3608–3614
Witz, Claude: Anmerkung zu Civ. 1, 16.7.1998, D. 1999, 117–120
Witz, Claude: Anmerkung zu Civ. 1, 19.3.2002, CISG-online 662, D. 2003, Somm. 2361–2373
Witz, Claude: Anmerkung zu Civ 1, 26.5.1999, D 2000, 788
Witz, Claude: Anmerkung zu Civ. 1, 23.1.1996, D. 1996, 334–338
Witz, Claude: Anmerkung zu OLG Köln, 21.8.1997, D. 1998, Somm. 311–312
Witz, Claude: Beyond the Digest: Articles 53–65, in: *Ferrari/Flechtner* (Hrsg.), The Draft UNCITRAL Digest and Beyond. Cases, Analysis and Unresolved Issues in the UN Sales Convention, München: Sellier/London: Sweet & Maxwell (2003), S. 424–439 (Kurztitel: Draft Digest)
Witz, Claude: CVIM: interprétation et questions non couvertes, Int'l Bus. L.J. 2001, 253–275
Witz, Claude: Droit uniforme de la vente internationale de marchandises, Receuil Dalloz 2007, 530–540
Witz, Claude: L'interprétation de la CVIM: divergences dans l'interprétation de la Convention de Vienne, in: *Ferrari* (Hrsg.), The 1980 Uniform Sales Law. Old Issues Revisited in the Light of Recent Experiences, Mailand/München: Giuffrè/Sellier European Law Publishers (2003), S. 279–304 (Kurztitel: L'interprétation)
Witz, Claude: L'exclusion de la Convention des Nations unies sur les contrats de vente internationale de marchandises par la volonté des parties (Convention de Vienne du 11 avril 1980), D. 1990, Chron. 107–112
Witz, Claude: La Convention de Vienne sur la vente internationale de marchandises a l'epreuve de la jurisprudence naissante, D. 1995, Chron. 143–146
Witz, Claude: L'application de la Convention de Vienne sur la vente internationale de marchandises par les jurisdiction fran aises – Premier bilan, in: *Majoros* (Hrsg.), Emptio – venditio inter nationes, Basel: Recht und Gesellschaft (1997), S. 425–456 (Kurztitel: FS Neumayer)
Witz, Claude: Les nouveaux délais de prescription du droit allemand applicables aux ventes internationals de merchandises régies par la Convention de Vienne, D. 2002, Chron. 2860–2862
Witz, Claude: Les premières applications jurisprudentielles du droit uniforme de la vente internationale (Convention des Nations Unies du 11 avril 1980), Paris: LGDJ (1995) (Kurztitel: Les premières applications)
Witz, Claude/Hlawon, Martin: Der neueste Beitrag der französischen Cour de Cassation zur Auslegung des CISG (2007–2010), IHR 2011, 93–109
Witz, Claude/Wolter, Gerhard: Die ersten Entscheidungen französischer Gerichte zum Einheitlichen UN-Kaufrecht, RIW 1995, 810–815
Witz, Claude/Wolter, Gerhard: Die neuere Rechtsprechung französischer Gerichte zum Einheitlichen UN-Kaufrecht, RIW 1998, 278–285
Witz, Wolfgang: Der unbestimmte Kaufpreis – ein rechtsvergleichender Beitrag zur Bedeutung des pretium certum, Neuwied: Metzner (1989)
Witz, Wolfgang: Die Liquidation des «Konzernschadens», in: *Bühler/Müller-Chen* (Hrsg.), Festschrift für Ingeborg Schwenzer zum 60. Geburtstag, Bern: Stämpfli (2011), S. 1795–1808 (Kurztitel: FS Schwenzer)
Witz, Wolfgang: The First Decision of France's Court of Cassation Applying the U.N. Convention on Contracts for the International Sale of Goods, 16 J. L. & Com. (1997), 345–356
Witz, Wolfgang: Zurückbehaltungsrechte im internationalen Kauf – Eine praxisorientierte Analyse zur Durchsetzung des Kaufpreisanspruchs im CISG, in: *Schwenzer/Hager* (Hrsg.), Festschrift für Peter Schlechtriem zum 70. Geburtstag, Tübingen: Mohr (2003), S. 291–307 (Kurztitel: FS Schlechtriem)
Witz, Wolfgang/Salger, Hanns-Christian/Lorenz, Manuel: International Einheitliches Kaufrecht, Heidelberg: Verlag Recht und Wirtschaft (2000)
Wolf, Eckhard: Die Rechtsprechung des Gerichtshofs zum Kaufrecht, WM 1998, Sonderbeilage Nr. 2, 1–48
Wolf, Eckhard: Rücktritt, Vertretenmüssen und Verschulden, AcP 153 (1954), 97–144
Wolf, Manfred: Auslegung und Inhaltskontrolle von AGB im internationalen kaufmännischen Verkehr, ZHR 153 (1989), 300–321
Wolf, Manfred/Horn, Norbert/Lindacher, Walter F.: AGB-Gesetz, Gesetz zur Regelung des Rechts der Allgemeinen Geschäftsbedingungen, Kommentar v. *Wolf, Horn* u. *Lindacher,* 4. Aufl., München: Beck (1999) (Kurztitel: *Wolf/Horn/Lindacher*)
Wolf, Manfred/Lindacher, Walter F./Pfeiffer, Thomas (Hrsg.): AGB-Recht – Kommentar, 5. Auflage, München: Beck (2009) (Kurztitel: *Wolf/Lindacher/Pfeiffer/Bearbeiter*)
Wolff, Katharina: Die Rechtsmängelhaftung nach dem Uniform Commercial Code und dem UN-Kaufrecht (Diss. Bonn 1989)

Woltier: Limitations of Liability in Commercial Contracts, in: *Campell* (Hrsg.): Structuring International Contracts, Den Haag: Kluwer Law International (1996), S. 219–230 (Kurztitel: Limitations of Liability)

Wortley, B. A.: Mercantile Usage and Custom, RabelsZ 24 (1959), 259–269

Woschnagg, Karl: Das neue schwedische Kaufrecht, RIW 1992, 117–121

Wu, Dong: The Effect of Fundamental Breach on Passage of Risk in the International Sale of Goods under the United Nations Convention on Contracts for the International Sale of Goods: Comparative Analysis with the Contract Law of the People's Republic of China, 7 VJ (2003), 233–254

Wulf, Hans Markus: UN-Kaufrecht und eCommerce (Diss. Hamburg 2003), Frankfurt a. M.: Lang (2003) (Kurztitel: UN-Kaufrecht und eCommerce)

Yang, Sophia Juan: Force Majeure and Hardship in Chinese Contract Law – The Latest Developement in Theory and Practice, in: *Bühler/Müller-Chen* (Hrsg.), Festschrift für Ingeborg Schwenzer zum 60. Geburtstag, Bern: Stämpfli (2011), S. 1809–1820 (Kurztitel: FS Schwenzer)

Yang, Sophia Juan: The Modern Sales Contract Law in Asia – From a Comparative Perspective (Diss. Basel 2010)

Yang, Yinghao: Suspension Rules under Chinese Contract Law, the UCC and the CISG: Some Comparative Perspectives, 18 China Law & Practice (2004), 23–27

Yasseen, Mustafa Kamil: L'interprétation des traités d'aprés la Convention de Vienne sur le droit des traités, 151 Rec. des Cours (1976), 2–114

Yorio, Edward: Contract Enforcement: Specific Performance and Injunctions, Boston: Little, Brown (1989 und Supplement 1995, hrsg. v. *Thiel*) (Kurztitel: Contract Enforcement)

Zahn, Johannes C./Ehrlich, Dietmar/Neumann, Kerstin: Zahlung und Zahlungssicherung im Außenhandel, 7. Aufl., Berlin, New York: De Gruyter Recht (2001) (Kurztitel: Zahlung)

Zamir, Eyal: The Missing Interest: Restoration of the Contractual Equivalence, 93 Va. L. Rev. (2007), 59

Zeller, Bruno: CISG and the Unification of International Trade Law, Oxford: Routledge-Cavendish (2007) (Kurztitel: CISG and the Unification)

Zeller, Bruno: Commodity Sales and the CISG, in: *Andersen/Schroeter* (Hrsg.), Sharing International Commercial Law Across National Boundaries: Festschrift in Honour of Albert H. Kritzer on the Occasion of his 80th Birthday, London: Wildly, Simmons & Hill (2008), S. 627–639 (Kurztitel: FS Kritzer)

Zeller, Bruno: Damages under the Convention on Contracts for the International Sale of Goods, New York: Oceana (2005) (Kurztitel: Damages)

Zeller, Bruno: International Commercial Law for Business, Sydney: Federation Press (1999)

Zeller, Bruno: International Trade Law – Problems of Language and Concepts?, 23 J. L. & Com. (2003), 39–51

Zeller, Bruno: Penalty Clauses: Are They Governed by the CISG?, 23 Pace Int'l L. Rev. (2011), 1–14

Zeller, Bruno: The CISG in Australasia – An Overview, in: *Ferrari* (Hrsg.), Quo Vadis CISG? Celebrating the 25th anniversary of the United Nations Convention on Contracts for the International Sale of Goods, München: Sellier (2005), S. 293–323 (Kurztitel: The CISG in Australasia)

Zeller, Bruno: The UN Convention on Contracts for the International Sale of Goods (CISG) – a leap forward towards unified international sales laws, 12 Pace Int'l L. Rev. (2000), 79–106

Zeller, Bruno: The UNIDROIT Principles of Hardship and the Application of Article 79 CISG: Are They Compatible?, in: *Schwenzer/Spagnolo* (Hrsg.), State of Play, The 3rd Annual MAA Peter Schlechtriem CISG Conference, The Hague: Eleven International Publishing (2012), S. 113–127 (Kurztitel: Hardship)

Zeno-Zencovich, Vincenzo: Il luogo del pagamento del prezzo nella vendita internazionale, G. it. 1987, I, 1, 911–922

Zhang, Xi: Die Rechtsmängelhaftung des Verkäufers nach UN-Kaufrecht im Vergleich mit deutschem, englischem, US-amerikanischem und Haager Einheitlichem Kaufrecht (Diss. Tübingen 1994)

Ziegel, Jacob S.: Canada and the Vienna Sales Convention, 12 Can. Bus. L. J. (1986–87), 367–375

Ziegel, Jacob S.: Comment on Roder Zelt- und Hallenkonstruktionen GmbH v. Rosedown Park Pty Ltd., CISG Rev. 1999, 53–62

Ziegel, Jacob S.: The Remedial Provisions in the Vienna Sales Convention: Some Common Law Perspectives, in: *Galston/Smit* (Hrsg.), International Sales, New York: Matthew Bender (1984), Kap. 9, S. 1–43 (Kurztitel: Remedial Provisions)

Ziegel, Jacob S.: The Scope of the Convention: Reaching out to Article One and Beyond, 25 J. L. & Com. (2005/06), 59–73

Literatur

Ziegel, Jacob S.: The Vienna International Sales Convention, in: *Ziegel/Graham* (Hrsg.), New Dimensions in International Trade Law: A Canadian Perspective, Toronto: Butterworths (1982), S. 38–57 (Kurztitel: Vienna Convention)

Ziegel, Jacob S.: Uniformity in Applying the 1980 U. N. Convention, National Report: Canada (Topic I. C.1), 12th Congress, International Academy of Comparative Law, Sydney/Melbourne (18.–26.8.1986) (Kurztitel: Uniformity)

Ziegler, Alexander von: The Right of Suspension and Stoppage in Transit (and Notification Thereof), 25 J. L. & Com. (2005), 353–374

Ziegler, Ulrich: Leistungsstörungsrecht nach dem UN-Kaufrecht (Diss. München 1994), Baden-Baden: Nomos (1995)

Zimmermann, Reinhard: Historische Verbindungen zwischen civil law and common law, in: *Müller-Graff* (Hrsg.), Gemeinsames Privatrecht in der Europäischen Gemeinschaft, 2. Aufl., Baden-Baden: Nomos (1999), S. 103–125 (Kurztitel: Historische Verbindungen)

Zimmermann, Reinhard: The Law of Obligations, München: Beck (1993)

Zmij, Grzegorz: Währungsrechtliche Probleme des vertraglichen Schadensersatzes unter besonderer Berücksichtigung der UNIDROIT-Grundregeln der Internationalen Handelsverträge, ZfRVgl 1998, 21–34

Zoll, Fryderyk: The Impact of the Vienna Convention on the International Sale of Goods on Polish Law, With Some References to Other Central and Eastern European Countries, RabelsZ 71 (2007), 81–98

Zoll, Fryderyk: UN-Kaufrecht und Common Frame of Reference im Bereich der Leistungsstörungen: Ein Beitrag aus der Perspektive der Acquis Group, ZEuP 2007, 229–246

Zöller, Richard: Zivilprozessordnung, 28. Aufl., Köln: Otto Schmidt (2010) (Kurztitel: *Zöller/Bearbeiter*)

Zuppi, Alberto L.: A Comparison of Buyer's Remedies Under the CISG with the Latin American Legal Tradition, CISG Rev. 1999, 3–39

Zuppi, Alberto L.: Die Rechtsbehelfe des Käufers im UN-Kaufrecht im Vergleich mit den lateinamerikanischen Rechten, in: *Majoros* (Hrsg.), Emptio – venditio inter nationes, Basel: Recht und Gesellschaft (1997), S. 113–150 (Kurztitel: FS Neumayer)

Zwart, Sara G.: The New International Law of Sales: A Marriage Between Socialist, Third World, Common, and Civil Law Principles, 13 N. C. J. Int'l L. & Com. Reg. (1988), 109–128

Zweigert, Konrad/Drobnig, Ulrich: Einheitliches Kaufgesetz und internationales Privatrecht, RabelsZ 29 (1965), 146–165

Zweigert, Konrad/Kötz, Hein: Einführung in die Rechtsvergleichung auf dem Gebiete des Privatrechts, 3. Aufl., Tübingen: Mohr (1996) (Kurztitel: *Zweigert/Kötz*)

Zweigert, Konrad/Kötz, Hein: Introduction to Comparartive Law, 3. Aufl., Oxford: Clarendon Press (1998)

Zwilling-Pinna, Claudia: Update wichtiger Handelsklauseln: Neufassung der Incoterms ab 2011, BB 2010, 2980–2983

Einleitung

I.

Das Übereinkommen der Vereinten Nationen über Verträge über den internationalen Warenkauf, das in diesem Buch erläutert wird, hat sich durchgesetzt. Seit seinem Inkrafttreten am 1. Januar 1988 und der ersten Bearbeitung dieses Kommentars ist die Zahl der Vertragsstaaten auf 79 gestiegen,[1] so dass heute ca. 80% des Welthandels in Waren vom Übereinkommen erfasst werden (können). Jüngst trat auch Brasilien dem CISG bei; das CISG tritt dort am 1.4.2014 in Kraft. Für Deutschland bedeutet dies, dass dann 19 seiner 20 wichtigsten Handelspartner Vertragsstaaten sind.[2] Das CISG hat den Bemühungen um eine Vereinheitlichung des Rechts für den grenzüberschreitenden Warenverkehr, die in den zwanziger Jahren begonnen wurden, einen grossen und erhofften, aber so nicht zu erwartenden Erfolg gebracht. Als erster Schritt wird zumeist die Anregung berichtet, die *Ernst Rabel* im Jahre 1928 dem Präsidenten des am 3. September 1926 gegründeten und am 30. Mai 1928 eingeweihten Internationalen Instituts für die Vereinheitlichung des Privatrechts, *Vittorio Scialoja,* im Zusammenhang mit der Aufstellung des ersten Arbeitsplanes des Instituts gegeben hatte, sich um die Vereinheitlichung des Rechts des grenzüberschreitenden Warenkaufs zu bemühen.[3] Sie führte zu dem am 21. Februar 1929 von *Ernst Rabel* – „the master mind behind the draft Uniform International Sales Law"[4] – dem Direktionsrat des römischen Instituts erstatteten (ersten) vorläufigen Bericht über die Möglichkeiten der Kaufrechtsvereinheitlichung,[5] dann zu dem im gleichen Jahr vorgelegten berühmten „Blauen Bericht",[6] zur Berufung eines Komitees aus Vertretern des englischen, französischen, skandinavischen und deutschen Rechtskreises am 29. April 1930, zu dem ersten Entwurf aus dem Jahre 1935 und schliesslich zu den auf der Haager Konferenz im Jahre 1964 erarbeiteten Haager Kaufgesetzen EAG und EKG.[7]

Gemessen an der Erwartung, dass sie eine weltweite Vereinheitlichung des Kaufrechts für den grenzüberschreitenden Warenverkehr bringen würden, war diesen von nur neun Staaten eingeführten Haager Kaufgesetzen[8] kein Erfolg beschieden. Die Zahl der Ratifikationen ist allein jedoch kein geeigneter Massstab. Zunächst ist darauf hinzuweisen, dass das Haager Einheitliche Kaufrecht in der Praxis der Gerichte in Deutschland, den Benelux-Staaten und Italien erhebliche Bedeutung gewonnen hatte. Bei der Weiterentwicklung der internen Kaufrechte haben nationale Reformer und Gesetzgeber das Einheitskaufrecht zunehmend als Vorbild und Modell verwendet.[9] Vor allem aber war das Haager Kaufrecht von Anfang an die Grundlage für das von UNCITRAL erarbeitete „neue"

---

[1] Liste der Vertragsstaaten mit Stand vom 11.4.2013 s. Anhang I.
[2] Vgl. die Fakten zum deutschen Außenhandel 2011 des Bundesministeriums für Wirtschaft und Technologie, abrufbar unter http://www.bmwi.de/BMWi/Redaktion/PDF/F/fakten-zum-deutschen-aussenhandel-2011,property=pdf,bereich=bmwi2012,sprache=de,rwb=true.pdf
[3] S. *Rabel,* RabelsZ 9 (1935), 1–79, abgedr. in *ders.,* Ges. Aufs. Bd. 3, S. 522–612; s. zur Vorgeschichte und *Rabels* Einfluss *Kindler,* Jb. It. R. 5 (1992), 201.
[4] S. *Grossfeld/Winship,* 18 Syracuse J. Int'l L. & Com. (1992), 3, 11.
[5] S. Sitzungsbericht A des römischen Instituts, RabelsZ 3 (1929), 402, 406.
[6] Rapport sur le droit comparé de vente par l' „Institut für ausländisches und internationales Privatrecht" de Berlin, Rom: Pallotta (1929), abgedr. u. a. in *Rabel,* Ges. Aufs. Bd. 3, S. 381–476.
[7] Für Einzelheiten dieser Entwicklung s. *Riese,* RabelsZ 22 (1957), 16–116; *ders.,* RabelsZ 29 (1965), 1–100; *von Caemmerer,* RabelsZ 29 (1965), 101–145; sowie *Schlechtriem,* Geschichte, S. 27.
[8] In Kraft gesetzt haben EKG und EAG Belgien am 18.8.1972, Gambia am 5.9.1974, Israel am 18.8.1972 (EKG) und am 30.11.1980 (EAG), Italien am 23.8.1972, Luxemburg am 6.8.1979, die Niederlande am 18.8.1972, San Marino am 18.8.1972 und Grossbritannien (freilich mit dem Vorbehalt, dass das Einheitskaufrecht von den Parteien gewählt werden muss) am 18.8.1972. In der Bundesrepublik waren die Haager Kaufgesetze am 16.4.1974 in Kraft getreten.
[9] Vgl. unten sub III. 4.

einheitliche Kaufrecht und hat nicht nur die Grundstrukturen und Schlüsselbegriffe, sondern auch viele Detaillösungen des schliesslich 1980 geschlossenen Übereinkommens (CISG) geprägt.

Die Arbeit der im Jahre 1966 als ständiger Ausschuss der UN eingesetzten Kommission für internationales Handelsrecht (UNCITRAL), die sich seit 1968 der Kaufrechtsvereinheitlichung gewidmet hatte, ist auch in deutscher Sprache genau berichtet worden,[10] so dass hier die Entstehungsgeschichte des CISG nicht in Einzelheiten nachgezeichnet werden muss. Man begann mit einer Aufforderung an die Mitgliedsstaaten, zu den Haager Kaufgesetzen Stellung zu nehmen, und einer Auswertung der eingehenden Antworten. Die jährlichen UNCITRAL-Konferenzen wurden von einer Arbeitsgruppe vorbereitet, die, beginnend im Januar 1970, in Auseinandersetzung mit den Haager Kaufgesetzen Entwürfe für die Plenarsitzungen von UNCITRAL vorbereitete.[11] Die Arbeitsgruppe ihrerseits setzte Unterarbeitsgruppen (working parties) ein, die jeweils spezielle Probleme, etwa die Definition und Umschreibung internationaler Warenkäufe oder die Frage, ob Kollisionsregeln vorgeschaltet werden sollten, besonders behandelten.[12] Im Jahre 1976 hatte die Arbeitsgruppe den Entwurf eines Kaufrechtsübereinkommens fertiggestellt, den die UNCITRAL-Kommission auf ihrer 10. Sitzung 1977 überarbeitete.[13] Die Vorschriften für den Vertragsschluss, die von der Arbeitsgruppe auf ihrer 9. Sitzung im September 1977 vorbereitet worden waren,[14] wurden von der Kommission auf ihrer 11. Sitzung 1978 in New York beraten und mit den Vorschriften des materiellen Kaufrechts zum „New Yorker Entwurf" verschmolzen. Dieser „New Yorker Entwurf" wurde dann den Regierungen der UN-Mitgliedsstaaten zur Stellungnahme zugeleitet und war mit den eingegangenen Antworten Grundlage der Wiener Konferenz im Frühjahr 1980.[15]

Für die Arbeit von UNCITRAL und der Arbeitsgruppe(n), vor allem aber für die Ergebnisse war ihre Zusammensetzung von grosser Bedeutung. Zum einen war die Zahl der Mitglieder limitiert auf zunächst 29, dann 36 Staaten, zum anderen hatte man eine repräsentative Vertretung der verschiedenen Regionen der Welt dadurch zu erreichen versucht, dass in der Satzung der Kommission eine bestimmte regionale Verteilung für die Mitglieder vorgeschrieben war. Danach standen Afrika 9, Asien 7, Osteuropa 5, Lateinamerika 6 und den westlichen Staaten 9 Sitze zu.[16] Die UNCITRAL-Satzung sah weiter vor, dass die Delegierten der Mitgliedsstaaten möglichst grosse Erfahrungen auf dem Gebiet des internationalen Handels haben sollten. Erwähnung verdient die Kontinuität im Verhältnis zu den Haager Kaufgesetzen, die dadurch ermöglicht wurde, dass eine Reihe von Staaten Vertreter entsandten, die bereits die Haager Kaufgesetze mit erarbeitet hatten, so Professor *Honnold* aus den USA, Professor *Eörsi* aus Ungarn und Professor *Loewe* aus Österreich. Gleichwohl war nicht nur die Diskrepanz der juristisch-technischen Begriffe, in denen nationale Rechtsordnungen ihre Lösungen jeweils verschlüsseln, noch grösser als auf der Haager Konferenz

---

[10] Vgl. vor allem *Herber,* RIW 1974, 577–584; RIW 1976, 125–133; RIW 1977, 314–320; *Huber,* RabelsZ 43 (1979), 413–526; ferner die (Schweizer) Botschaft betreffend das Wiener Übereinkommen über Verträge über den internationalen Warenkauf, Bbl. 1989 I, 745 ff., 748.

[11] Insgesamt wurden neun Arbeitsgruppensitzungen von 1970 bis 1977 abgehalten, die im Einzelnen dokumentiert sind in: YB I (1968–1970), S. 176 ff., II (1971), S. 50 ff., III (1972), S. 77 ff., IV (1973), S. 61 ff., V (1974), S. 29 ff., VI (1975), S. 49 ff., VII (1976), S. 87 ff., VIII (1977), S. 73 ff., IX (1978), S. 61 ff., 83 ff.; auch die verdienstvolle Dokumentation in *Honnold,* Documentory History, gibt genau Aufschluss über die Arbeitsverfahren der Arbeitsgruppen und die Abfolge der Entwürfe, Beratungen etc.

[12] Vgl. hierzu YB I (1968–1970), S. 177 ff.; *Farnsworth,* 20 Am. J. Comp. L. (1972), 314–322; *Honnold,* 27 Am. J. Comp. L. (1979), 223–230; *Patterson,* 22 Stan. J. Int'l L. (1986), 263, 271 ff.

[13] Zum sog. „Genfer Entwurf" oder „Genfer Arbeitsgruppenentwurf" s. YB VII (1976), S. 89–96; zur weiteren Behandlung s. YB VIII (1977), S. 25–65; der von der Kommission verabschiedete sog. „Wiener Entwurf" ist abgedr. in YB VIII (1977), S. 15–21.

[14] S. hierzu unten *Schroeter,* Vor Artt. 14–24 Rn. 2.

[15] Zur Dokumentation im Einzelnen s. Anhang III.

[16] Für die Satzung von UNCITRAL s. die Resolution der Generalversammlung 2205 (XXI) v. 17.12.1966, YB I (1968–1970), S. 65, durch die UNCITRAL gegründet wurde. Zum Beschluss der Generalversammlung über die Erweiterung von 29 auf 36 Mitglieder s. YB V (1974), S. 10–12.

und in den Kommissionen, in denen die Entwürfe für die Haager Kaufgesetze vorbereitet worden waren, sondern vor allem auch die Unterschiede in den Interessen, als deren Vertreter sich die Repräsentanten der verschiedenen Länder und Weltregionen empfanden. Insbesondere die Interessengegensätze zwischen Industriestaaten und den Ländern der Dritten und Vierten Welt waren gravierender als in den Gremien, die EKG und EAG erarbeitet hatten.[17]

Die Bundesrepublik Deutschland gehörte seit Ende 1973 zu den Mitgliedern von UNCITRAL und nahm zum ersten Mal an der 7. Tagung im Jahre 1974 teil; in der Arbeitsgruppe war die Bundesrepublik zunächst nur als Beobachter beteiligt.[18]

Auf der Grundlage des New Yorker Entwurfs fanden dann die Beratungen der UN-Konferenz im März und April 1980 in Wien statt, an der 62 Staaten teilnahmen. In der Schlussabstimmung votierten 42 Staaten für die auf der Konferenz erarbeitete Fassung des CISG. Die nach Art. 99 des Übereinkommens erforderliche Hinterlegung von zehn Ratifikations-, Annahme-, Genehmigungs- oder Beitrittsurkunden wurde am 11. Dezember 1986 erreicht. Das Übereinkommen ist deshalb am 1. Januar 1988 in Kraft getreten. Da Deutsch nicht Abkommenssprache ist, musste eine amtliche Übersetzung erstellt werden. Um grösstmögliche Übereinstimmung der Fassungen zu erzielen, wurde dazu eine Übersetzungskonferenz der deutschsprachigen Länder im Januar 1982 in Bonn abgehalten, auf der allerdings aus teils sprachlichen, teils rechtlichen Gründen keine völlige Textidentität erreicht werden konnte. Die verbliebenen Unterschiede werden in diesem Kommentar in den durch * gekennzeichneten Fussnoten kenntlich gemacht.

In der Bundesrepublik wurde das CISG zusammen mit dem dazugehörigen Vertragsgesetz (Zustimmungsgesetz) vom Bundesrat durch die Beschlüsse vom 23. September 1988 und 12. Mai 1989 gebilligt, vom Bundestag am 20. April 1989 angenommen. Die Ausfertigung durch den Bundespräsidenten erfolgte am 5. Juli 1989. Die Ratifikationsurkunde wurde am 21. Dezember 1989 hinterlegt, die Haager Übereinkommen mit Wirkung zum 1. Januar 1991 gekündigt. Das CISG ist in der Bundesrepublik am 1. Januar 1991 in Kraft getreten, und zwar auch in den neuen Bundesländern. In der früheren DDR war das Übereinkommen bereits seit dem 1. März 1990 bis zum Beitritt der ehemaligen DDR zum Geltungsbereich des Grundgesetzes am 3. Oktober 1990 in Kraft. In der Schweiz ist das CISG seit 1. März 1991, in Österreich bereits seit dem 1. Januar 1989 in Geltung.

II.

Das CISG ist in vier Teile gegliedert: Teil I enthält die Regeln zum Anwendungsbereich und allgemeine Bestimmungen, Teil II die Vorschriften über den Vertragsschluss, Teil III das materielle Kaufrecht, also Pflichten und Rechte, insbesondere Rechtsbehelfe, der Parteien, Teil IV die völkerrechtlichen Schlussklauseln. Art. 92 I erlaubt es den Vertragsstaaten, das Übereinkommen auch ohne Teil II oder Teil III einzuführen.

Die Abweichungen in Struktur und Regelungstechnik von den Haager Kaufgesetzen sind in der 1. und 2. Aufl. skizziert worden. Für diese Einleitung muss ein Hinweis auf einige wenige Besonderheiten genügen. Zu erwähnen ist zunächst die „horizontale" Regelung des materiellen Kaufrechts. Das CISG regelt zuerst alle Verpflichtungen des Verkäufers und sodann die Rechtsbehelfe des Käufers, ebenso alle Verpflichtungen des Käufers und dann die korrespondierenden Rechtsbehelfe des Verkäufers, und es formuliert schliesslich – im Anschluss an Vorschriften zur Gefahrtragung – allgemeine Regeln, die für beide Teile gleichermassen gelten (Artt. 71–88),[19] was den Überblick erleichtert, die Beurteilung ein-

---

[17] Informativ hierzu *Plantard,* J. D. I. 1988, 311–367; *Zwart,* 13 N. C. J. Int'l L. & Com. Reg. (1988), 109, 113–123.
[18] Vgl. *Herber,* RIW 1974, 577, 579.
[19] Vgl. zu diesen unterschiedlichen Kodifikationstechniken *Hellner,* Structure of Law, S. 107–109; *ders.,* ZG 1988, 249, 257 f.

zelner Rechtsfragen jedoch erschweren kann.[20] Dem deutschen Juristen dürfte freilich die mit einer solchen Gliederung erreichte Abstrahierung allgemeiner Regeln keine Schwierigkeiten bereiten.[21] Eher wird er die häufige Verwendung unbestimmter Rechtsbegriffe wie „angemessen" (angemessene Frist) oder „vernünftig" (als Massstab für ein bestimmtes gebotenes Verhalten) als Schwäche empfinden, lassen sie doch Rechtsunsicherheit und in der Sache divergierende Entscheidungen befürchten. Zweifellos enthält das CISG mehr solche unbestimmten Rechtsbegriffe als noch das Haager Einheitliche Kaufrecht, und es hat teilweise die Wertungsrahmen vergrössert, so, wenn etwa an Stelle der „kurzen" Frist für die Rüge eine „angemessene" Frist getreten ist, Art. 39.[22] Aber der durch solche wertungsoffenen Begriffe den Gerichten eingeräumte Spielraum ist vielfach durch die Natur der Sache geboten: Eine feste Frist für die Erhebung der Rüge lässt sich angesichts der Vielfalt der möglichen Situationen und Kaufgegenstände kaum normativ festlegen.[23] Teils war freilich die Verwendung unbestimmter Rechtsbegriffe auch ein Kompromiss zwischen unüberbrückbaren Interessengegensätzen, um ein Scheitern der Konferenz zu vermeiden, so z. B. die „vernünftige Entschuldigung" für die Rügeversäumung nach Art. 44. Im Übrigen dürfte der Verzicht auf scharf zugeschnittene, „hard and fast rules" ein Teil des Preises für die weltweite Akzeptanz des Übereinkommens durch Juristen sein, die in ganz unterschiedlichen Traditionen und Begriffswelten aufgewachsen sind – ebenso wie der Verzicht auf hochgezüchtete und multifunktionale Begriffe wie die „Lieferung" des Art. 19 EKG, die durch eine deskriptive Festlegung der Voraussetzungen für richtige Erfüllung, Gefahrübergang und Fälligkeit der Gegenleistung ersetzt worden ist.[24] Hier ist es nicht zuletzt Aufgabe der Rechtswissenschaft, auf eine behutsame Annäherung der unterschiedlichen Systeme hinzuwirken.

Grundsätzlich verlangt das CISG für seine Anwendung Niederlassung der Parteien in Vertragsstaaten,[25] jedoch erreicht es[26] eine Erweiterung seines Anwendungsbereichs auf Parteien in Nichtvertragsstaaten durch Art. 1 I b).[27] Der deutsche Gesetzgeber hat von der durch Art. 95 eröffneten Möglichkeit, Art. 1 I b) nicht in Geltung zu setzen, keinen Gebrauch gemacht. Da die meisten Vertragsstaaten ebenfalls die Vorbehaltsmöglichkeit nicht genutzt haben, war das CISG in zahlreichen Fällen bereits vor seinem Inkrafttreten anzuwenden, wenn das IPR des Forums auf das Recht eines solchen Vertragsstaates verwies.[28] Der Streit um Reichweite und Tauglichkeit des Art. 1 I b), der vielfach auf einem Missverständnis über seine Funktion beruht,[29] verliert mit der wachsenden Zahl von Vertragsstaaten an Bedeutung, da auch Vorbehaltsstaaten Vertragsstaaten i. S. d. Art. 1 I a) sind. Wo ein Vorbehaltsstaat das CISG auch als nationales Handelsrecht übernommen hat wie die ehemalige Tschechoslowakei[30] – und jetzt ihre Nachfolgestaaten –, führt die Anwendung seines Rechts trotz Vorbehalts ebenfalls zur Anwendung von CISG-Regeln.

Da sich bereits bei Ausarbeitung der Einheitskaufrechte die Bedeutung des Verbraucherschutzrechts als einer weithin als *ius strictum* ausgestalteten Sondermaterie abzeichnete, will

---

[20] S. *Hellner*, ZG 1988, 249, 257.

[21] Krit. dagegen *Lüderitz*, Pflichten der Parteien, S. 195 (zur Regelung der Pflichten der Parteien): „... mehr Hülle und Verpackung als Inhalt".

[22] Hierzu informativ *Patterson*, 22 Stan. J. Int'l L. (1986), 263, 288 ff.

[23] Hierzu unten Art. 39 Rn. 16.

[24] Vgl. weiter zur Begriffsbildung in EKG und CISG noch *Hellner*, ZG 1988, 249, 259 ff.; zur Schwierigkeit, Regelungen zu treffen, die sich nationalen Rechtsordnungen einfügen lassen, s. *Herber*, ZG 1987, 26.

[25] Vgl. hierzu *Czerwenka*, Rechtsanwendungsprobleme, S. 93 ff. (EKG), 136 ff. (CISG) sowie die Kommentierung zu Art. 1.

[26] Anders als EKG/EAG, s. hierzu OLG Köln, 16.10.1992, CISG-online 50 = CR 1993, 211 ff.

[27] S. hierzu unten *Ferrari*, Art. 1 Rn. 69–81; Art. 2 VertragsG Rn. 1, 2.

[28] Z. B. OLG Karlsruhe, 20.11.1992, CISG-online 54 = NJW-RR 1993, 1316; Art. 2 VertragsG, der (nur) bei Verweisung auf das Recht eines Vorbehaltsstaates die Anwendung des CISG ausschliesst, regelt nur, was ohnehin gelten würde, s. Art. 2 VertragsG Rn. 1.

[29] Ein solches Missverständnis liegt m. E. der Auffassung zugrunde, Art. 1 I b) sei selbst IPR-Norm, so wohl *Honsell/Siehr*, Art. 1, Rn. 17; *Keller/Siehr*, S. 169.

[30] *Bednarikova*, S. 61 ff.

das CISG generell auf Konsumentenkäufe nicht angewendet werden, Art. 2a). Die – freilich unvollkommene – Ausnahme für die Produktehaftung, Art. 5, belegt ebenfalls die Berücksichtigung der Rechtsentwicklung zum Konsumentenschutz ausserhalb des Kaufrechts.

Grosse Bedeutung für die Bewahrung der Rechtseinheit dürften die in Art. 7 festgelegten Richtlinien für die Auslegung und Lückenfüllung des Übereinkommens haben. Auch wenn für den Fall, dass allgemeine Grundsätze, die zur Lückenfüllung herangezogen werden können, im Übereinkommen nicht zu finden sind, deutlicher auf das über IPR berufene nationale Recht verwiesen wird, dürfte Art. 7 in der Sache dem umstrittenen Art. 17 EKG entsprechen. Er wird m. E. auch grosse Bedeutung für die Fortentwicklung des CISG gewinnen (hierzu unten III. 1.).

Die in Teil II getroffene Regelung des Vertragsschlusses durch Angebot und Annahme entspricht traditionellen Auffassungen. Sie überbrückt ähnlich wie Art. 5 EKG den Graben zwischen (vor allem) dem englischen Recht und anderen Rechtsordnungen in der Frage der Widerruflichkeit einer Offerte durch einen Kompromiss und schweigt, wie schon das EAG, zu solchen für die Praxis zentralen Fragen wie Einbeziehung und Kollision von Allgemeinen Geschäftsbedingungen.[31] Obwohl es an Vorstössen zur Regelung dieser Probleme in Wien nicht fehlte, hat man sich gescheut, diese vielfach auch in den nationalen Rechten noch nicht geklärten Fragen zu entscheiden.

Im materiellen Kaufrecht ist die bereits im EKG vorgezeichnete Konzeption eines einheitlichen Tatbestandes des Vertragsbruchs, in dem Fälle der Nichtleistung, verzögerten Leistung oder Schlechtleistung weitgehend aufgehen, konsequent durchgeführt worden, wenngleich bestimmte Eigenheiten dieser unterscheidbaren Modalitäten eines Vertragsbruchs bei den Rechtsbehelfen doch wieder zu berücksichtigen waren. Das dem schweizerischen OR und dem deutschen Recht entlehnte Nachfristmodell, das in Zweifelsfällen Klärung der Voraussetzung „wesentlicher Vertragsbruch" für eine Vertragsaufhebung ermöglicht, ist auf die Leistungsstörungen Nichtlieferung, Nichtzahlung und Nichtabnahme zurückgeschnitten worden, so dass in den wichtigen Fällen einer vertragswidrigen Beschaffenheit der Ware oder der Verletzung anderer Pflichten, z. B. zur Montage, zum Unterlassen eines Reimports usw., nur dann, wenn dadurch ein wesentlicher Vertragsbruch bewirkt worden ist, aufgehoben werden kann. Wie schon im EKG werden peius und aliud als vertragswidrige Beschaffenheit gleichbehandelt. Die Rechtsbehelfe für Sach- und Rechtsmängel sind weitgehend angeglichen; in diesem Zusammenhang wurde die Belastung mit gewerblichen oder intellektuellen Schutzrechten als Vertragswidrigkeit mit geregelt (Artt. 42, 43). Auch der dem deutschen Juristen selbstverständliche Erfüllungsanspruch als Rückgrat der Obligation und primärer Rechtsbehelf wurde nicht nur beibehalten – für die Common Law-Länder freilich durch Art. 28 erträglich gemacht –, sondern noch dadurch verstärkt, dass er selbst bei nicht zu vertretenden Leistungshindernissen wie Unmöglichkeit auf Grund höherer Gewalt bestehen bleiben soll (Art. 79 V).[32]

Die Praxis in Deutschland hat mit dem CISG keine Schwierigkeiten. Aufnahme und Anwendung des neuen Einheitskaufrechts dürften nicht nur durch den bestandenen Probelauf der Haager Kaufgesetze erheblich erleichtert worden sein, sondern auch durch die breite wissenschaftliche Behandlung in der deutschsprachigen Literatur und auf Fachtagungen in Deutschland, der Schweiz und Österreich; die zahlreichen im Literaturverzeichnis aufgelisteten Beiträge in deutscher Sprache sind dafür Zeugnis.

III.

Trotz der oben sub I. erwähnten Gegensätze der Interessen, die bei der Abfassung des CISG nicht immer im Sinne der sachgerechtesten Lösung zu überbrücken waren, darf das Übereinkommen im ganzen als wohlgelungen und zukunftsweisend bewertet werden. In

---

[31] Vgl. hierzu unten *Schroeter*, Art. 19 Rn. 19 ff.
[32] Vgl. hierzu aber unten Art. 79 Rn. 52 ff.; *Müller-Chen*, Art. 28 Rn. 10, 13 f.

die Regeln des Einheitskaufrechts sind Lösungen aus vielen Rechtsordnungen eingegangen, die von den Verfassern in abwägender Rechtsvergleichung ausgewählt und fortentwickelt worden sind. Insbesondere dürfte durch die enge und vorurteilsfreie Zusammenarbeit von Juristen aus dem Rechtskreis des Common Law einerseits und aus den kontinentalen Rechten und ihren Tochterrechten andererseits erreicht worden sein, was die frühe Zusammenarbeit von *Ernst Rabel* und *Karl Llewellyn* bereits in den vierziger Jahren für den UCC und später für das EKG und EAG erhoffen liess, aber nicht tatsächlich erreicht wurde:[33] eine Symbiose von Common Law und kontinentalem Recht, die den mit Kaufrecht befassten Juristen wieder eine einheitliche Sprache und ein Instrumentarium einheitlicher Begriffe für die Bezeichnung von Sachfragen und Lösungen zur Verfügung stellt. Im Übrigen dürfte die Vereinheitlichung des Kaufrechts für grenzüberschreitende Kaufverträge auch zu einer erheblichen Verminderung der Transaktionskosten führen, die sonst bei grenzüberschreitenden Rechtsgeschäften entstehen bzw. zu erwarten sind, falls Streit entsteht.[34]

1. Die Aufgabe, den Rechtsverkehr bei grenzüberschreitenden Warenkäufen einheitlichen Regeln zu unterstellen, ist freilich mit Einführung des CISG allein noch nicht gelöst. Sie verlangt vielmehr ständig, in der Anwendung, Auslegung und Lückenfüllung, vor allem aber bei der Fortentwicklung des Übereinkommens die verbal erreichte Vereinheitlichung zu bewahren und zu fördern. Das macht nicht nur in Anwendung des CISG Vergegenwärtigung seines internationalen Charakters und der Richtlinien des Art. 7 für Auslegung und Lückenfüllung erforderlich,[35] sondern verlangt auch eine genaue Beobachtung der wissenschaftlichen Aufarbeitung und der Anwendungspraxis in anderen Ländern. Insoweit kommt einem Kommentar wie dem hier in 6. Auflage vorgelegten besondere Bedeutung zu, da die in Wissenschaft und Praxis im Ausland vertretenen Lösungen dem deutschen Juristen oft nicht oder nur schwer zugänglich sind.[36]

Bewahrung der Rechtseinheit muss dabei vor allem durch möglichst einheitliche und autonome Auslegung der im CISG verwandten Begriffe und durch konkretisierende Typenbildung bei unbestimmten Rechtsbegriffen, etwa dem zu ersetzenden „voraussehbaren" Schaden oder der „angemessenen Frist" für eine Mängelrüge, versucht werden. Auch muss bei den Einzelregelungen der oft komplexe Hintergrund ihrer Entstehung mit bedacht werden, so dass man nicht vorschnell auf scheinbar glatte, auf den Wortlaut gestützte und stimmig in Strukturvorstellungen des jeweils eigenen Rechts eingepasste Lösungen zurückgreifen kann.[37] Wo die Gerichte in Auslegung unbestimmter Rechtsbegriffe zu unterschiedlichen Ergebnissen kommen, muss das nicht notwendig eine ernsthafte Gefährdung der Rechtsvereinheitlichung bedeuten, sondern kann sachnahe und deshalb unterschiedliche

---

[33] S. zu dieser Zusammenarbeit *Grossfeld/Winship*, 18 Syracuse J. Int'l L. & Com. (1992), 3, 11.
[34] S. hierzu *Kanning*, TvP 1996, 883–907, der allerdings davon ausgeht, dass internationale Handelsbräuche, an die sich Kaufleute regelmässig halten, im Wettbewerb mit dem Einheitlichen Kaufrecht überlegen sind.
[35] *Ferrari*, 24 Ga. J. Int'l & Comp. L. (1994), 183–228.
[36] Zur Bewahrung der Rechtseinheit als Informationsproblem s. vor allem *Honnold*, Uniform Words, S. 115 ff., dort auch zur Notwendigkeit eines Zentrums für Dokumentation von Entscheidungen und wissenschaftlichem Schrifttum (S. 145), eine Aufgabe, der sich UNCITRAL inzwischen durch Aufbau des Informationssystems „Case Law on Uncitral Texts (CLOUT)" angenommen hat. Daneben gibt es inzwischen zahlreiche nationale und übernationale Datenbanken, die Gerichts- und Schiedsurteile über Internet zugänglich machen, ferner sog. „Digests" u. ä., die Rechtsprechung zu bestimmten Sachfragen aufarbeiten, vgl. *Ferrari*, Art. 7 Rn. 18–20. Vor allem will die hier als Fundstelle für die zitierten und ausgewerteten Entscheidungen durchgehend zugrundegelegte Datenbank www.cisg-online.ch Zugang zu wichtigen Entscheidungen und damit die erforderliche Information über die Rechtsentwicklung in den deutschsprachigen, aber auch in den nicht-deutschsprachigen Vertragsstaaten ermöglichen. Schliesslich soll dieser Kommentar selbst durch Aufarbeitung der internationalen Rechtsprechung diese für die Bewahrung der Rechtseinheit unerlässliche Informationsquelle eröffnen.
[37] Als Beispiel vgl. *Roth/Kunz*, RIW 1997, 17–21, die im Erfordernis eines bestimmten oder bestimmbaren Preises in Art. 14 I 2 CISG nur ein Abgrenzungskriterium zwischen Offerte und Invitatio ad offerendum sehen wollen, das bei Vertragsschlüssen durch Einigwerden ohne Angebot und Annahme keine Rolle spiele (weshalb auch kein Widerspruch zwischen Art. 14 I 2 und Art. 55 CISG bestehe). S. dazu die Kommentierung zu Art. 14 Rn. 8–11.

Beurteilung konkreter und verschieden liegender Fälle sein. Grössere Gefahren für die erreichte Rechtsvereinheitlichung drohen m. E. in zwei Bereichen, die auf den ersten Blick weit auseinander liegen: Zum einen könnte bei nicht ganz eindeutigen Regelungen im CISG und der gebotenen lückenfüllenden Auslegung zweifelhaft sein, ob das Übereinkommen allgemeine Grundsätze enthält, die eine Lückenfüllung erlauben, oder ob auf nationales Recht zurückgegriffen werden muss. Zum anderen droht den Lösungen des CISG Gefahr durch nationale Rechtsregeln, die nach der lex fori anders als kaufrechtlich oder als Gültigkeitsvorschrift qualifiziert werden. Gefährlich scheinen mir z. B. die Entscheidungen U. S.-amerikanischer Gerichte zu sein, in der die Berufung auf „negligent misrepresentation" parallel zu den Regeln des CISG für möglich gehalten wurde.[38] Wenn nationale Gerichte die Ersatzfähigkeit von Rechtsverfolgungskosten einfach als prozessrechtliche Frage qualifizieren und deshalb vom Anwendungsbereich der Artt. 74 ff. ausnehmen, entstehen schnell sich vergrössernde Enklaven der Anwendung nationalen Rechts, die dem entscheidenden Richter vielleicht selbstverständlich und seinen historisch geprägten Rechtsüberzeugungen entsprechend „richtig" erscheinen mögen, die aber die erreichte Rechtsvereinheitlichung erheblich gefährden und ausserhalb des Wirkungskreises dieser historischen Überzeugungen kaum auf Zustimmung oder Gefolgschaft hoffen dürfen.[39] Würden diese Beispiele der Anwendung konkurrierender Regeln, die nach der lex fori nicht als kaufrechtliche qualifiziert werden, Schule machen, dann wäre nationalen Rechtsregeln bald Tür und Tor geöffnet. Mit Deliktsansprüchen, die (ausnahmsweise) auf das Vertragsinteresse gerichtet sein können, wäre das Rügeerfordernis oder die Begrenzung des ersatzfähigen Schadens zu unterlaufen. Ansprüche aus culpa in contrahendo könnten das System der Vertragsschlussvorschriften oder der Rechtsbehelfe wegen vertragswidriger Beschaffenheit, die Irrtumsanfechtung die Voraussetzungen der Unsicherheitseinrede nach Art. 71 aus den Angeln heben, und die Einordnung von Beschaffungsverträgen staatlicher Stellen als „öffentlichrechtliche Materien" könnte die Anwendung des CISG oder seiner Einzelregeln fast willkürlich beschneiden oder verdrängen. Entschiedenen Widerspruch verdient auch die Ansicht, dass die Frage, was „Gültigkeit" i. S. v. Art. 4 S. 2a) sei, vom nationalen Recht entschieden werde: Da in den nationalen Rechten bei Leistungsstörungen in verschiedenen Fällen Rechtsbehelfe zur Verfügung stehen, die die Gültigkeit des Vertrages berühren – Nichtigkeit ipso iure bei anfänglicher Unmöglichkeit, Vertragsauflösung durch Gestaltungserklärung oder richterliche Entscheidung bei Nichterfüllung, unterstellte Verabredung einer auflösenden Bedingung der Durchführbarkeit des Vertrages –, wäre die Rechtsvereinheitlichung für Kaufverträge in ihrem Kernbereich gefährdet, wenn es insoweit bei (konkurrierendem oder gar ausschliesslich massgeblichem) nationalem Recht bliebe.[40] Auch Irrtumsanfechtung wegen vertragswidriger Beschaffenheit darf deshalb nicht als Gültigkeitsfrage nationalen Rechts behandelt werden, sondern hat den speziellen Rechtsbehelfen des CISG zu weichen.[41] Beide Probleme – Lückenfüllung und genaue Abgrenzung des Anwendungsbereichs – führen freilich auf die gleiche Frage zurück: Was ist in diesem Übereinkommen geregelte Materie, „matters governed by this Convention", Art. 7 II? Entscheiden muss darüber eine autonome und funktionale Qualifikation der in Betracht kommenden Regeln, nicht dagegen ihre Einordnung nach der lex fori. Ist die zu entscheidende Sachfrage bei funktionaler Qualifikation eine solche des Kaufrechts und enthält das CISG eine explizite oder durch

---

[38] *Miami Valley Paper, LLC v. Lebbing Eng'g GmbH*, U. S. Dist. Ct. (S. D. Ohio), 10.10.2006, CISG-online 1362; *Sky Cast, Inc. v. Global Direct Distribution, LLC*, U. S. Dist. Ct. (E. D. Kent), 18.3.2008, CISG-online 1652 = IHR 2009, 24, 27. Für Vorrang des CISG hingegen neuerdings *Electrocraft Arkansas, Inc. v. Super Electric Motors, Ltd. et al.*, U. S. Dist. Ct. (E. D. Ark.), 23.12.2009, CISG-online 2045. Vgl. dazu auch unten Art. 35 Rn. 47.
[39] Vgl. zu dieser durch die amerikanischen Entscheidungen in der Sache *Zapata Hermanos Sucesores, S. A. v. Hearthside Baking Company, Inc.* (CISG-online 599, 663, 684) veranlassten Bemerkung die Darstellung des Streitstands unten in Art. 74 Rn. 28 ff. und als Beispiel für solche nationalen Voreingenommenheiten *Flechtner/Lookofsky*, 7 VJ (2003), 93 ff.
[40] Vgl. *Hartnell*, 18 Yale J. Int'l L. (1993), 1, 69 ff.; *Kindler*, Jb. It. R. 5 (1992), 201, 209 ff.
[41] Überzeugend hierzu *Flesch*, S. 140 ff., s. a. *P. Huber*, ZEuP 1994, 585–602.

Anwendung seiner Grundsätze zu ermittelnde Lösung, dann sollte die Regelung der Sachfrage durch das CISG auch als abschliessend angesehen und nicht durch nationale Rechtsbehelfe verändert oder ergänzt werden. Eine besondere Bedrohung für die weltweit erreichte Rechtsvereinheitlichung für grenzüberschreitende Warenkäufe wäre gegeben, wenn man der Auffassung folgte, Richtlinien der EU verdrängten wie völkerrechtliche Verträge nach Art. 90 das an sich anwendbare CISG. Die Überschneidungsbereiche zwischen Richtlinien und Einheitskaufrecht waren früher gering, sind aber durch Richtlinien etwa zum Zahlungsverzug oder zum E-Commerce erheblich grösser geworden und machen eine grundsätzliche Entscheidung unausweichlich. Sie darf m. E. nicht zugunsten eines Vorrangs der Richtlinien fallen,[42] da sonst die für den grenzüberschreitenden Warenverkehr erreichte Rechtsvereinheitlichung durch die Inkonsistenz einzelner auf Richtlinien zurückgehender Regeln mit den Pflichten und Rechtsbehelfen nach CISG nicht nur in Europa, sondern weltweit schwer beeinträchtigt würde.[43] Wünschenswert wäre jedenfalls, wenn Richtlinien die Zentralbegriffe und Grundstrukturen des CISG übernehmen würden, wie in der „Richtlinie des Europäischen Parlaments und des Rates über den Verbrauchsgüterkauf und -garantien"[44] für die „vertragsgemässe Beschaffenheit" geschehen – zwar ist der Überschneidungsbereich gering, da das CISG Verbraucherkäufe nur in Ausnahmefällen erfasst, doch trägt eine solche Anlehnung dazu bei, europaweit und international einheitliches Kaufrecht zu schaffen bzw. zu bewahren.

2. Kodifikationen altern und werden von Schichten um Schichten von Fallrecht und wissenschaftlicher Exegese überlagert. Bei einem erst 1980 endgültig ausgearbeiteten Regelwerk scheint es unpassend, daran zu erinnern. Aber die Grundstrukturen des CISG sind, wie oben skizziert, viel älter, und auch in seinen Einzelregelungen schreibt das CISG oft einen Erkenntnisstand fest, der heute bereits gealtert, um nicht zu sagen veraltet erscheint. So wie man als Beispiele für antiquierte Modelle der BGB-Verfasser auf den „Auszug eines Bienenschwarms" oder auf das Inventar von „Mühle, Schmiede, Brauhaus" verweist, so könnte man für das CISG auf das in Art. 13 als schriftformäquivalent aufgeführte „Telex" hinweisen. Wichtigere Beispiele sind die Orientierung am vertragskonstitutiven Austausch von „Angebot" und „Annahme", die nicht nur andere Vertragsschlussformen vernachlässigt, sondern für den Dissens über unterschiedliche Geschäftsbedingungen nur das untaugliche Lösungsmodell des Art. 19 CISG zur Verfügung stellt, oder das dem Begriff „Ware" zugrunde liegende Verständnis als bewegliche Sache, welches die Anwendung des CISG auf Verträge über Software[45] erschwert. Bei komplexen Verträgen, z. B. turnkey-contracts oder Lieferverträgen mit Montageverpflichtung, die nach Art. 3 II CISG vom Einheitskaufrecht erfasst sein können, lassen sich Leistungsstörungen nicht ohne weiteres den auf Verletzung von Lieferpflichten bezogenen Vorschriften für die Rechtsbehelfe des Käufers subsumieren, etwa, wenn der Lieferant mit der Montageverpflichtung in Verzug gerät und der Käufer deshalb den Vertrag durch Nachfristsetzung aufheben will. Die Fixierung auf traditionelle Formen des Vertriebs und Erwerbs von Gütern, die in der Regelung des punktuellen Austauschs Ware gegen Geld zum Ausdruck kommt, vernachlässigt komplexere, netzartige Beziehungen zwischen Zulieferer, Hersteller und Grosshändler für die Ordnung ihrer langfristigen Lieferbeziehungen und kann insbesondere auch keine Massstäbe für die Inhaltskontrolle einseitig vorformulierter Verträge in diesem Bereich bieten. Nicht einmal der gute alte Vertragshändlervertrag, der viele Einzelheiten der in seinem Rahmen vorgesehenen und erwarteten Lieferungen regelt, wird richtig erfasst, sondern muss entweder als Rahmen*kauf*vertrag oder als eine vom CISG streng zu unterscheidende Geschäftsbesorgungsform behandelt werden, so dass Auseinandersetzungen zwischen Vertragshändler und

---

[42] So aber *Herber*, 2. Aufl., Art. 90 Rn. 12; wie hier jetzt unten *Ferrari*, Art. 90 Rn. 3.

[43] Vgl. zum Einheitskaufrecht als Quasi-Acquis communitaire *Schlechtriem*, Internationales UN-Kaufrecht, Rn. 345a.

[44] ABlEG Nr. L 171 vom 7.7.1999, S. 12–16.

[45] S. *Müller-Hengstenberg*, NJW 1994, 3128–3134.

Lieferant möglicherweise nach zwei verschiedenen Rechtsordnungen beurteilt werden müssen.

Aufgabe eines solchen Kommentars muss es deshalb auch und in zunehmendem Masse sein, die erwünschte und unvermeidbare Weiterentwicklung des Einheitskaufrechts in solchen Bereichen wissenschaftlich und rechtsvergleichend zu begleiten, vielleicht sogar zu beeinflussen, und deutlich die Grenzen zu markieren, jenseits derer das subsidiär berufene nationale, unvereinheitlichte Recht gilt. Darüber hinaus gilt es, Entwicklungstendenzen in nationalen Rechten zu beobachten und gegebenenfalls eine Hereinnahme in das CISG zu ermöglichen, um ein Ausweichen auf nationales Recht und damit ein Aufweichen des CISG in seinen Kernbereichen zu verhindern.[46]

3. Die Einfügung des CISG in die nationalen Kaufrechtsordnungen kann aber auch nicht ohne Rückwirkungen auf Auslegung und Weiterentwicklung des internen Kaufrechts bleiben. Das Gebot der inneren Konsistenz einer Rechtsordnung verlangt eine Berücksichtigung sowohl der Grundprinzipien als auch der Detaillösungen des CISG bei der Interpretation aller kaufrechtlichen Regeln des nationalen Rechts, insbesondere dort, wo durch Gewohnheitsrecht und richterrechtliche Schöpfungen Lücken gefüllt und Regelungskomplexe ergänzt worden sind, aber u. U. auch in offener Korrektur vom Gesetzgeber normierter Lösungen, wenn diese nicht mehr zeitgemäss sind. Es sollte auch nur eine Frage der Zeit sein, dass und wann das Einheitskaufrecht durch seine wissenschaftliche Berücksichtigung in Lehrbüchern und Kommentaren sowie auf Grund der Vertrautheit der Gerichte mit seinen Regeln dazu führt, dass auch ohne eine legislatorische Reform bestimmte Strukturen und Prinzipien der nationalen Obligationenrechte neu interpretiert werden und – mit allgemeingültigen Sinngehalten versehen – überlebensfähig bleiben;[47] freilich darf man dabei den Widerstand nationaler Dogmen und Dogmatiker nicht unterschätzen.

4. Die damit Wissenschaft und Praxis überantwortete Aufgabe ist nicht leicht. Die Auseinandersetzung mit diesen Fragen wie der Umgang mit dem Einheitskaufrecht überhaupt können freilich die bisher zu wenig beachtete Chance des Einheitskaufrechts deutlich machen, die mit der Hoffnung auf eine lex mercatoria verfolgte Utopie doch noch zu realisieren. Für die Entstehung der im 13. bis 18. Jahrhundert in Europa durchaus lebendigen Überzeugung einer einheitlichen Rechtskultur, die erst mit den grossen nationalstaatlichen Kodifikationen des 19. und 20. Jahrhunderts wenn nicht aufgegeben worden, so doch im Bewusstsein der meisten Juristen verloren gegangen ist,[48] könnte das Einheitskaufrecht ein neuer Kristallisationskern sein. Für diese Hoffnung gibt es gute Gründe: Das Einheitskaufrecht hat grossen Einfluss auf moderne Kodifikationen wie das Obligationenrecht des niederländischen Wetboeks[49] und die deutsche Schuldrechtsreform gehabt.[50] Die skandinavischen Kaufrechte sind nach dem Vorbild des CISG neu kodifiziert worden und bilden ihrerseits die Grundlage für den – nicht kodifizierten – allgemeinen Teil des Schuldrechts.[51] Die Reformstaaten Mittel- und Osteuropas, die OHADA-Staaten sowie die Nachfolgestaaten der früheren Sowjetunion und Jugoslawiens haben sich bei der Wiederherstellung ihrer Privatrechtsordnung am Einheitskaufrecht orientiert und es teilweise als internes Kaufrecht oder Handelskaufrecht rezipiert.[52] Vor allem ist das neue chinesische Obligationenrecht, das auf Dauer für den Welthandel immer wichtiger werden dürfte, auf der Basis des

---

[46] Vgl. unten Art. 74 Rn. 35.
[47] Vgl. für Lateinamerika *Zuppi,* FS Neumayer 1997, S. 147, der darauf hinweist, der Erfolg bestehe in „der tatsächlichen Vereinheitlichung der Hauptbegriffe des Kaufrechts von verschiedenen Rechtskulturen".
[48] Vgl. *Kramer,* östJBl 1988, 477 ff.
[49] Vgl. hierzu *Hartkamp,* AcP 191 (1991), 396, 407.
[50] Vgl. hierzu Abschlussbericht der Kommission zur Überarbeitung des Schuldrechts, hrsg. vom Bundesminister der Justiz, 1992, 26; *Schubert,* S. 415 ff., sowie *Schlechtriem,* ZEuP 1993, 217–246.
[51] Vgl. *Lookofsky,* The Scandinavian Experience, S. 110 ff.; *Hellner,* Swedish Law, S. 193–212; ferner *Sévon,* Scandinavian Codification, S. 343 ff.
[52] Vgl. für die ehemalige Tschechoslowakei *Bednarikova,* S. 61 ff.; zum Einfluss des UN-Kaufrechts auf das kroatische Schuldrecht s. *Gliha,* östZRVgl 1993, 116, 118; zu den OHADA-Staaten vgl. *Schroeter,* RiA 2001, 163 ff.

CISG geschaffen worden. Auch die von UNIDROIT erarbeiteten „Principles for International Commercial Contracts" wie der von einer von *Ole Lando* geleiteten Arbeitsgruppe erarbeitete Entwurf für „Principles of European Contract Law", die sich jeweils als Modelle eines europäischen oder internationalen Obligationenrechts verstehen, sind in den Grundstrukturen stark vom CISG beeinflusst.[53] Auch die Richtlinie der EG zum Verbrauchsgüterkauf und Garantien für Verbrauchsgüter lehnt sich, wie oben erwähnt, an Grundstrukturen des CISG an, etwa bei Regelung der vertragswidrigen Beschaffenheit. Der jüngste Entwurf eines Gemeinsamen Europäischen Kaufrechts (CESL)[54] basiert ebenfalls zu weiten Teilen auf dem Einheitskaufrecht. Allerdings wurden teilweise empfindliche Änderungen an der systematischen Stimmigkeit des CISG vorgenommen.[55] Schliesslich setzt sich immer mehr die Auffassung durch, dass das Einheitskaufrecht Teil – vielleicht sogar der einzig wirklich funktionsfähige Teil – der internationalen lex mercatoria ist.[56] Die zunehmende internationale Überlegenheit des CISG spiegelt sich nicht zuletzt in der Tatsache wider, dass immer mehr Vertragsparteien nicht nur das an sich anwendbare CISG nicht abwählen, sondern umgekehrt im Wege des opting-in ihren Vertrag dem CISG unterstellen. Anwendung und wissenschaftliche Aufarbeitung des CISG machen es nicht nur unabweisbar, mit international vereinheitlichten Begriffen und Strukturen vertraut zu werden,[57] sondern erfordern, sie aus sich selbst heraus zu verstehen und der oben sub III.1 durch Beispiele belegten Gefahr zu begegnen, dass sie im Lichte der aus dem eigenen Sachrecht vertrauten Lösungen interpretiert werden. Besondere Schwierigkeiten dürften dabei die zentralen Schlüsselbegriffe des Einheitskaufrechts bereiten, die verschiedene, in den nationalen Rechten mit unterschiedlichen Rechtsbegriffen besetzte Sachfragen abdecken. So betrifft „Aufhebung des Vertrages" („avoidance") die durch nationale Begriffe wie „Rücktritt", „Wandelung", auch „Kündigung" und teilweise „Irrtumsanfechtung", „termination", „cancellation", „rescission"[58], „rédhibition", „résolution" (durch Gericht oder – ausnahmsweise – Parteierklärung) geregelten Fragen. Auch die für die Anwendung des CISG zu klärende Frage, was „Waren" – „goods, marchandises" – sind, also die oben erwähnte Sachfrage, ob z. B. Software dazugehört, kann nicht unter Rückgriff auf nationale Anschauungen entschieden, sondern muss autonom und unter Berücksichtigung der Tauglichkeit und Sachgerechtigkeit der Lösungen des CISG für Softwareverträge und Softwaremängel – etwa bei nicht verkörperten, sondern elektronisch übermittelten Programmen – gelöst werden. „Wesentlicher Vertragsbruch" (fundamental breach) umfasst Unmöglichkeit, schwerwiegende Säumnis, gravierende Rechts- oder Sachmängel, u. U. teilweise Nichterfüllung, „frustration", „impossibility" usw., so dass nationale Lösungen nicht mehr – auch nicht als Gültigkeitsfrage, als Dichotomie von warranty oder condition[59] oder im Gewand prozessualer Normen der lex fori – berücksichtigt werden dürfen. Die Festlegung der Verantwortungsvoraussetzungen für den Schuldner in Art. 79 entspricht in der Funktion der verkehrserforderlichen Sorgfalt nach § 276 BGB, der Garantiehaftung für die Beschaffungsfähigkeit bei Gattungswaren, der verschuldensunabhängigen Einstandspflicht für Erfüllungshilfen nach § 278 BGB, der Verantwortung für Mängel nach §§ 434 ff. BGB, Art. 1645 frz. Cc. Dabei wird es zuweilen unvermeidlich sein, dass diese neuen und

---

[53] Vgl. hierzu die Einleitung zu den UNIDROIT-Principles, S. VIII; *Schlechtriem*, ZEuP 1993, 217, 219 m. w. N.; der Text der UNIDROIT-Principles findet sich unten in Anhang V.
[54] Vorschlag für eine Verordnung des Europäischen Parlaments und des Rates über ein Gemeinsames Europäisches Kaufrecht, 11.10.2011, KOM (2011) 635.
[55] Dazu im Einzelnen unten im Rahmen der Kommentierung der jeweiligen Artikel des CISG.
[56] Vgl. hierzu *Blaurock*, ZEuP 1993, 247–267; zum ganzen *Kappus*, Lex Mercatoria, mit einer genauen und informativen Analyse der Geschichte der lex mercatoria und dem Nachweis, dass sie vor allem in der Schiedsgerichtsbarkeit deshalb Bedeutung erlangt hat, weil die Schiedsrichter damit von der Ermittlung und Anwendung nationaler Rechte, die zuweilen auch veraltet und für den konkreten Fall unpassend waren, entbunden sind. Dass dagegen das moderne CISG den Schiedsgerichten und auch staatlichen Gerichten passender erscheint, zeigen Entscheidungen, die es als Handelsbrauch anwenden.
[57] Vgl. hierzu die interessante Studie von *Kastely*, 8 Nw. J. Int'l L. & Bus. (1988), 574, 591–607.
[58] Vgl. hierzu *Crawford*, 8 J. L. & Com. (1988), 187, 190.
[59] Vgl. *Nickel/Saenger*, JZ 1991, 1050–1057.

weitreichenden Begriffe im Verständnis von Juristen, deren Rechtsdenken durch ein bestimmtes nationales Recht geprägt ist, eine entsprechende Färbung annehmen. Sie zu vermeiden oder jedenfalls wieder „auszubleichen", verlangt eine bewusste Distanzierung, dazu aber auch einen ständigen Vergleich mit den begrifflich oft ganz anders gefassten, vielleicht sogar in der Sache verschieden geregelten Lösungen des eigenen Rechts. Damit wird auch die Weiterentwicklung der Regelungen des internen Rechts gefördert: Sie erscheinen in einem neuen Licht, können – wie aus der Rechtsvergleichung vertraut – auf neue und sachnähere Begründungen gestützt und von dogmatischen Verkrustungen befreit werden.

Eine herausragende Rolle in der Herstellung und Bewahrung einheitlicher Auslegung kommt dabei dem CISG-AC zu, der in Form von Gutachten (Opinions) zu aktuellen umstrittenen Fragen des CISG Stellung nimmt.[60] Bereits jetzt berufen sich auch staatliche Gerichte auf die in diesen Opinions vertretenen Auffassungen.[61]

Die Vielfalt der Rechtskulturen soll mit dem Einheitsrecht nicht den Rechtshistorikern überantwortet werden. Doch sie gewinnt an Legitimation, wo sie sich in Auseinandersetzung mit einem allen Juristen vertrauten Grundbestand an Regeln und Vorstellungen auseinandersetzen muss und kann. So sollen auch die in diesem Kommentar oft unternommenen Vergleiche mit dem schweizerischen und deutschen Recht nicht nur der Erläuterung des CISG, sondern auch der Vergewisserung über das Recht des OR, des BGB und des HGB dienen.

---

[60] Vgl. dazu *Schwenzer*, Nederlands Tijdschrift voor Handelsrecht 2012, 46 ff.
[61] Vgl. *TeeVee Toons, Inc. (d/b/a TVT Records) & Steve Gottlieb, Inc. (d/b/a Biobox) v. Gerhard Schubert GmbH*, U. S. Dist. Ct. (S. D. N. Y.), 23.8.2006, CISG-online 1272: „The Court thus turns to the text of the CISG, as interpreted by the CISG Advisory Council."; Gerechtshof Arnhem, 9.3.2010, CISG-online 2095; vgl. auch *Cedar Petrochemicals, Inc. v. Dongbu Hannong Chemical Co., Ltd.*, U. S. Dist. Ct. (S. D. N. Y.), 28.9.2011, CISG-online 2338.

Übereinkommen der Vereinten Nationen über Verträge über den internationalen Warenkauf
United Nations Convention on Contracts for the International Sale of Goods
Convention des Nations Unies sur les contrats de vente internationale de marchandises

Vom 11. April 1980

(BGBl. II S. 588)

Präambel

Die Vertragsstaaten dieses Übereinkommens –

im Hinblick auf die allgemeinen Ziele der Entschließungen, die von der Sechsten Außerordentlichen Tagung der Generalversammlung der Vereinten Nationen über die Errichtung einer neuen Weltwirtschaftsordnung angenommen worden sind,

in der Erwägung, daß die Entwicklung des internationalen Handels auf der Grundlage der Gleichberechtigung und des gegenseitigen Nutzens ein wichtiges Element zur Förderung freundschaftlicher Beziehungen zwischen den Staaten ist,

in der Meinung, daß die Annahme einheitlicher Bestimmungen, die auf Verträge über den internationalen Warenkauf Anwendung finden und die verschiedenen Gesellschafts-, Wirtschafts- und Rechtsordnungen berücksichtigen, dazu beitragen würde, die rechtlichen Hindernisse im internationalen Handel zu beseitigen und seine Entwicklung zu fördern –

haben folgendes vereinbart:

The States parties to this Convention,

bearing in mind the broad objectives in the resolutions adopted by the sixth special session of the General Assembly of the United Nations on the establishment of a New International Economic Order,

considering that the development of international trade on the basis of equality and mutual benefit is an important element in promoting friendly relations among States,

being of the opinion that the adoption of uniform rules which govern contracts for the international sale of goods and take into account the different social, economic and legal systems would contribute to the removal of legal barriers in international trade and promote the development of international trade,

have agreed as follows:

Les Etats parties à la présente Convention

ayant présents à l'esprit les objectifs généraux inscrits dans les résolutions relatives à l'instauration d'un nouvel ordre économique international que l'Assemblée générale a adoptées à sa sixième session extraordinaire,

considérant que le développement du commerce international sur la base de l'égalité et des avantages mutuels est un élément important dans la promotion de relations amicales entre les Etats,

estimant que l'adoption de règles uniformes applicables aux contrats de vente internationale de marchandises et compatibles avec les différents systèmes sociaux, économiques et juridiques contribuera à l'élimination des obstacles juridiques aux échanges internationaux et favorisera le développement du commerce international,

sont convenus de ce qui suit:

I. Vorgeschichte

1 Dem Text der 101 Artikel des CISG ist, wie bei internationalen Übereinkommen üblich,[1] eine Präambel vorangestellt, die unter wesentlicher Mitwirkung des UNCITRAL-Sekretariats anlässlich der Diplomatischen Konferenz entworfen und ohne eingehende sachliche Diskussion beschlossen wurde.[2]

2 Inhaltlich nimmt die Präambel einige der bereits im ersten[3] von UNCITRAL erarbeiteten Übereinkommen, der Verjährungskonvention von 1974, niedergelegten Gedanken auf (Abs. 2 und 3), ohne sich jedoch auf diese zu beschränken (Abs. 1). An dieser ausführlicheren Präambel[4] orientieren sich wiederum die (kürzere) Präambel des Haager Übereinkommens über die Vertretung beim internationalen Warenkauf[5] von 1983,[6] sowie die Prämbeln anderer, auch viel neuerer Übereinkommen.[7]

II. Bedeutung der Präambel

3 Streitig ist, welche **Bedeutung der Präambel** zugesprochen werden muss, vor allem weil in verschiedenen Rechtsordnungen die Bedeutung von Präambeln unterschiedlich beurteilt wird.[8] Die größte Bedeutung scheint Präambeln dabei in den (ehemals) sozialistischen Ländern zuzukommen,[9] da dort „in Präambeln im Allgemeinen eine verbindliche Bestimmung der sozialen Funktion des betreffenden Rechtsaktes vorgenommen [wird]".[10] Dies bedeutet jedoch nicht, dass in nicht sozialistischen Ländern die Präambeln als unbeachtlich anzusehen seien. Mit Bezug auf die Präambel des CISG führt dies m. E. dazu, dass man trotz einiger Auffassungen, die in der Präambel eine bloße rechtspolitische Äußerung sehen,[11] die für die **Auslegung** einzelner Bestimmungen nicht relevant sein kann,[12] davon ausgehen muss, dass die Präambel des Übereinkommens, genauso wie die anderer Übereinkommen, bei der Auslegung desselben heranzuziehen ist,[13] was die Vorschriften einiger neuerer Übereinkommen, wie zum Beispiel des UNCITRAL Übereinkommens über die Abtretung von Forderungen im internationalen Handel,[14] des

---

[1] Vgl. MünchKomm/*Westermann*, Präambel, Rn. 1.
[2] Vgl. O. R., S. 219 f.; *Schlechtriem/Schwenzer/Schwenzer/Hachem*, CISG Commentary, Preamble, Rn. 1.
[3] Siehe hierzu statt aller *Boele-Woelki*, Molengrafica 1996, 99–146; *Winship*, 28 Int'l Law (1994), 1071–1081.
[4] So *Herber*, 2. Aufl., Präambel Rn. 3; *Schlechtriem/Schwenzer/Schwenzer/Hachem*, CISG Commentary, Preamble, Rn. 1.
[5] Übereinkommen vom 17.2.1983 über die Vertretung beim internationalen Warenkauf, Uniform L. Rev. 1983, I, 161.
[6] So *Bianca/Bonell/Evans*, Präambel, Anm. 2.4.; *Staudinger/Magnus*, Präambel, Rn. 5.
[7] Vgl. etwa die Prämbel der UN-Konvention über Verträge über die internationale Beförderung von Gütern ganz oder teilweise auf See von 2008, sowie die des Übereinkommens zur Nutzung elektronischer Kommunikationsmittel in internationalen Verträgen von 2005.
[8] So *Herber*, 2. Aufl., Präambel, Rn. 2; *Schlechtriem/Schwenzer/Schlechtriem*, CISG Commentary, 2. Aufl., Preamble, Rn. 2; *Schlechtriem/Schwenzer/Schwenzer/Hachem*, CISG Commentary, Preamble, Rn. 2.
[9] Vgl. auch MünchKomm/*Westermann*, Präambel, Rn. 1 und dort auch Fn. 1.
[10] *Enderlein/Maskow/Strohbach*, Präambel, Anm. 1.
[11] *Honnold/Flechtner*, Rn. 475.
[12] So *Loewe*, Präambel.
[13] Wie hier *Enderlein/Maskow/Strohbach*, Präambel, Anm. 1; *Grieser*, S. 84; *Herber/Czerwenka*, Präambel, Rn. 2; *Frohn*, Molengrafica 1995, 199, 204, Fn. 30; *Kastely*, 8 Nw.J. Int'l L. & Bus. (1988), 574, 594; MünchKomm/*Westermann*, Präambel, Rn. 1; *Reinhart*, Präambel, Rn. 1; *Staudinger/Magnus*, Präambel, Rn. 7, 8, will die Präambel sogar bei der Lückenfüllung heranziehen; ebenso nunmehr *Schlechtriem/Schwenzer/Schwenzer/Hachem*, CISG Commentary, Preamble, Rn. 4; m. E. ist dies nicht möglich
[14] Vgl. Art. 7 des UNCITRAL Übereinkommens vom 12.12.2001 über die Abtretung von Forderungen im internationalen Handel.

Factoring-Übereinkommens[15] oder des Leasing-Übereinkommens,[16] ausdrücklich festlegen.

Auch die **Wiener Vertragsrechtskonvention**[17] schreibt ausdrücklich vor, dass Präambeln bei der Auslegung internationaler Übereinkommen heranzuziehen sind (Art. 31 II). Vielfach wird die Anwendbarkeit der in dieser Konvention vorgesehenen Auslegungsregeln (Artt. 31–33)[18] jedoch auf die Teile I–III des CISG ausgeschlossen.[19] M. E. ist dies aber nicht zwingend.[20]

III. Die Präambel im Einzelnen

Abs. 1 sieht eine in der Präambel der Verjährungskonvention,[21] an der sich die des CISG orientiert,[22] nicht enthaltene Bezugnahme auf die Mitte der siebziger Jahre erreichten Ergebnisse der Bemühungen der Generalversammlung der Vereinten Nationen zur **Schaffung einer Neuen Weltwirtschaftsordnung** vor.[23] Es handelt sich dabei zum einen um die am 1.5.1974 erlassene Entschließung über die Errichtung einer Neuen Weltwirtschaftsordnung (3201 S-VI) und das Aktionsprogramm über die Errichtung einer Neuen Weltwirtschaftsordnung (3202 S-VI)[24] und, zum anderen, um die Resolution 3281 vom 12.12.1974 über die Charta der ökonomischen Rechte und Pflichten von Staaten,[25] mit denen das Ziel der **schrittweisen Überwindung der wirtschaftlichen Rückständigkeit** der sogenannten Entwicklungsländer verfolgt wurde.[26] Diesbezüglich kann das CISG aber lediglich einen geringen Beitrag leisten, da die mehr technischen Vorschriften des CISG den wirtschaftlichen Warenstrom zwischen den Staaten weit weniger beinflussen als etwa außenwirtschaftliche, devisenrechtliche, zollrechtliche Bestimmungen und Übereinkommen.[27] Daraus folgt, dass die Bezugnahme auf die Neue Weltwirtschaftsordnung mehr politischen als normativen Charakter hat.[28] Gleichwohl finden sich in der Entstehungsgeschichte des CISG Nachweise dafür, dass sich die Konventionsgeber beim Verfassen einzelner Vorschrif-

---

[15] Vgl. Art. 4 I des UNIDROIT-Übereinkommens vom 28.5.1988 über das internationale Factoring, BGBl. 1998 II 178: „Bei der Auslegung dieses Übereinkommens sind sein Zweck und Ziel, wie in der Präambel dargelegt, sein internationaler Charakter und die Notwendigkeit zu berücksichtigen, seine einheitliche Anwendung und die Wahrung des guten Glaubens im internationalen Handel zu fördern."

[16] Vgl. den mit dem in der vorigen Fn. zitierten Vorschrift wortgleichen Art. 6 I des UNIDROIT-Übereinkommens vom 28.5.1988 über das internationale Finanzierungsleasing, in deutscher Übersetzung abgedruckt in *Dageförde*, S. 162 ff.

[17] BGBl. 1990 II 1414.

[18] Vgl. hierzu etwa *Köck*, Vertragsinterpretation und Vertragsrechtskonvention: zur Bedeutung der Artikel 31 und 32 der Wiener Vertragsrechtskonvention 1969; *Yasseen*, Rec. des Cours (1976), 2–114.

[19] So etwa *Diedrich*, Autonome Auslegung, S. 133; *Herber*, 2. Aufl., Art. 7 Rn. 12; *Honnold/Flechtner*, Art. 7, Rn. 103; *Karollus*, S. 13; *Staudinger/Magnus*, Präambel, Rn. 7.

[20] Wie hier *Czerwenka*, Rechtsanwendungsprobleme, S. 34; *Roth/Happ*, Uniform L. Rev. 1997, 702, 710.

[21] Siehe oben Fn. 3.

[22] So *Staudinger/Magnus*, Präambel, Rn. 6.

[23] Siehe auch *Honsell/Siehr*, Präambel, Rn. 8, mit Hinweis darauf, dass „aus dieser neuen Weltwirtschaftsordnung [...] bislang nichts geworden" ist; in der Tat ist heute bisweilen vom „New New International Economic Order" die Rede.

[24] Beide sind abgedruckt in: Resolutionen zu Grundfragen der internationalen Wirtschaftsbeziehungen. Die Vereinten Nationen und ihre Spezialorganisationen, Dokumente, Bd. 5, Berlin: Springer (1978), S. 220 ff. und 234 ff.

[25] Abgedruckt in YB (1974), 402 ff.

[26] So auch *Honsell/Siehr*, Präambel, Rn. 8; *Rudolph*, Präambel, Rn. 2 f.; MünchKomm/*Westermann*, Präambel, Rn. 3; *Schlechtriem/Schwenzer/Schlechtriem*, CISG Commentary, 2. Aufl., Preamble, Rn. 4; *Schlechtriem/Schwenzer/Schwenzer/Hachem*, CISG Commentary, Preamble, Rn. 5 a. E.

[27] In diesem Sinn auch *Enderlein/Maskow/Strohbach*, Präambel, Anm. 2.2., mit Hinweis auf *Date-Bah*, Problems of Unification, S. 40.

[28] So schon *Herber*, 2. Aufl., Präambel Rn. 4; *Staudinger/Magnus*, Präambel, Rn. 9; siehe auch *Bianca/Bonell/Evans*, Präambel, Anm. 3., und *Rudolph*, Präambel, Rn. 2, die von einer „allgemeinen politischen Deklaration" sprechen; vgl. neuerdings auch *Schlechtriem/Schwenzer/Schwenzer/Hachem*, CISG Commentary, Preamble, Rn. 6.

ten am erwähnten entwicklungspolitischen Ziel orientiert haben: Als Beispiel sei hier nur Art. 44 genannt, der eine Ausnahme von der Rügeobliegenheit vorsieht. Diese Ausnahme ist bekanntermaßen[29] auf Betreiben einer Gruppe von Entwicklungsländern anlässlich der Diplomatischen Konferenz[30] aufgenommen worden,[31] um den harten Folgen einer unterlassenen Mängelanzeige entgegenzuwirken, die sich vor allem für die Käufer ergeben, die, wie etwa die Käufer aus Entwicklungsländern, mangels Sachkunde den Mangel entweder nicht entdecken oder nicht genau bezeichnen können, oder die mit dem Erfordernis der Untersuchung und der alsbaldigen Anzeige nicht vertraut sind.[32] Es sei außerdem angemerkt, dass einem Teil der Lehre nach die genannte Überwindung der wirtschaftlichen Rückständigkeit der sogenannten Entwicklungsländer notwendigerweise einhergeht mit der Stärkung der Menschenrechte in ebendiesen Entwicklungsländern, mit Folgen u. a. für die Anwendung des CISG.[33]

6   **Abs. 2 der Präambel** geht davon aus, dass die Entwicklung des internationalen Handels auf der Grundlage der Gleichberechtigung und des gegenseitigen Nutzens der Förderung freundschaftlicher Beziehungen zwischen den Staaten dient.[34] Beim Aufbauen internationaler Handelsbeziehungen muss demnach die Schlechter- bzw. Besserstellung bestimmter Interessen bzw. Interessenvertreter zugunsten einer **ausgewogenen wertneutralen Lösung** vermieden werden.[35] Ein solches Ergebnis ist zum Beispiel in Bezug auf die bereits erwähnte Problematik der Mängelanzeige erreicht worden. Die harten Folgen der Rügepflichtverletzung sind durch die Einführung des Art. 44 aufgeweicht worden, der im Falle entschuldigter Rügeversäumnis dem Käufer das Recht auf Minderung und Schadensersatz – außer für Gewinnausfall – belässt.[36] Auch die Ansicht, prozessuale Rechtsverfolgungskosten seien nicht als Schadenersatz im Sinne von Ar.t 74 anzusehen,[37] wird zum Teil mit dem Berstreben nach wertneutralen Lösungen gerechtfertigt:[38] „die schadenersatzrechtliche Lösung [würde] einseitig den obsiegenden Kläger bevorzugen, während der obsiegende Beklagte mangels schadenersatzrechtlicher Anspruchsgrundlagen leer ausgehen würde."[39]

7   **Abs. 3 umschreibt das Übereinkommen** als Summe einheitlicher Bestimmungen, die auf Verträge über den internationalen Warenkauf Anwendung finden und die verschiedene Gesellschafts-, Wirtschafts- und Rechtsordnungen berücksichtigen.[40] Aus dieser Definition (m. E. aber auch aus Abs. 2) lässt sich leicht der **Kompromisscharakter** des Übereinkommens ableiten,[41] der bei der Auslegung des Übereinkommens zu berücksichtigen ist und

---

[29] Siehe *Díez-Picazo/Miquel Gonzalez*, Art. 44, S. 399; *Schlechtriem*, Einheitliches UN-Kaufrecht, S. 60; *Staudinger/Magnus*, Art. 44, Rn. 3 f.
[30] Vgl. O. R., S. 107 f., 320 ff., 345 ff.
[31] In diesem Sinne auch *Ferrari*, La vendita internazionale, S. 229, mit weiteren Nachweisen.
[32] So *Date-Bah*, Problems of Unification, S. 47 f.; *Schwenzer*, Art. 44 Rn. 2.
[33] Vgl. hierzu *Schwenzer/Leisinger*, GS Hellner, S. 249 ff.; *Schlechtriem/Schwenzer/Schwenzer/Hachem*, CISG Commentary, Preamble, Rn. 7.
[34] Vgl. hierzu auch *Hartwieg*, ZVerglRW 1993, 282, 324 f.
[35] Ähnlich auch Brunner, Präambel, Rn. 1 (Streben nach einem auf Gleichberechtigung basierenden, wirtschaftspolitisch neutralen System); *Honsell/Siehr*, Präambel, Rn. 10, (Protektionismus und Diskriminierung sollen vermieden werden); *Schlechtriem/Schwenzer/Schwenzer/Hachem*, CISG Commentary, Preamble, Rn. 8 („strictly neutral set of rules that does not grant preferred treatment t one or the other side").
[36] So *Schwenzer*, Art. 39 Rn. 2.
[37] Vgl. in der Rechtsprechung *Zapata Hermanos Sucesores, S. A. v. Hearthside Baking Company, Inc. d/b/a Maurice Lenell Cooky Company*, U. S. Ct. App. (7th Cir.), 19.11.2002, CISG-online 684.
[38] Vgl. *Schlechtriem/Schwenzer/Schwenzer/Hachem*, CISG Commentary, Preamble, Rn. 8.
[39] *Schwenzer*, Art. 74 Rn. 29.
[40] Dieser Absatz der Präambel ist in der Rechtsprechung verschiedentlich zitiert worden, um zu rechtfertigen, dass das CISG im Rahmen seines Geltungsbereichs nationales Recht verdrängt; vgl. *Geneva Pharmaceuticals Tech. Corp. v. Barr Labs. Inc.*, U. S. District Court, S. D. of New York, 10.5.2002, CISG-online 653; *Asante Technologies, Inc. v. PMC-Sierra, Inc.*, U. S. District Court, N. D. of California, 27.7.2001, CISG-online 616; vgl. auch *Kröll u. a. /Mistelis*, Preamble.
[41] Ähnlich *Bell*, FS Schwenzer, S. 143, 144; *Herber*, 2. Aufl., Präambel Rn. 8; *Jurewicz*, 28 J. L. & Com. (2009), 63, 68; *Karton/de Germiny*, 27 Berkeley J. Int'l L. (2009), 448, 449; *Kokoruda*, 85-JUN Fla. B. J. (2011), 103, 103; *Markel*, 21 Pace Int'l L. Rev. (2009) 163, 167; *Martin-Davidson*, 17 Mich. St. J. Int'l L. (2008), 657,

dazu führt, dass die einzelnen Begriffe bzw. Bestimmungen **in der Regel**[42] also nicht vor dem Hintergrund und vom Verständnis her interpretiert werden sollten, die sie in der Rechtsordnung haben, aus der sie entnommen worden sind.[43] Abs. 3 bekräftigt somit lediglich einen das gesamte Einheitsrecht durchdringenden Gedanken: Einheitsrecht, zumindest wenn es sich spezifisch „nationalen" Vorstellungen verschließt, erhöht die Rechtssicherheit und trägt somit zur Förderung des internationalen Handels bei.[44] International tätige Geschäftsleute werden sich nicht länger vor dem Abschluss von Verträgen deshalb scheuen müssen, weil sie die rechtliche Basis ihrer Vertragsbeziehungen nicht kennen (bzw. nicht kennen können). Die Vereinheitlichung der Grundbegriffe des Kaufrechts zum Beispiel, ihre offizielle Formulierung in sechs verschiedenen Sprachen[45] und ihre Übersetzung in mindestens ebenso viele fördern ohne Zweifel den Abschluss von Verträgen, da sie es den international tätigen Kaufleuten erleichtern, zumindest nach einer gewissen Eingewöhnungszeit, die m. E. in Bezug auf das CISG als bereits verstrichen angesehen werden muss, die auf ihre Vertragsbeziehungen anwendbaren Rechtsvorschriften zu bestimmen. Darin liegt ein sehr großer Vereinfachungseffekt, der sich selbst dann noch auswirkt, wenn für die Bedürfnisse einzelner Handelsbeziehungen Sonderbestimmungen zusätzlich zu den Regeln des CISG oder auch in Abweichung von diesen formuliert werden.[46]

Gemäß Abs. 3 sieht es so aus, als könnten die angestrebten Ziele durch bloße „Annahme einheitlicher Bestimmungen" – so der Text – erreicht werden. Dies ist jedoch auszuschließen. Es genügt nicht, einheitliche Texte auszuarbeiten und „anzunehmen";[47] um Einheitsrecht zu schaffen, denn darum geht es hier, müssen diese Texte auch einheitlich angewendet und ausgelegt werden.[48] Auf diese Problematik wird jedoch andernorts näher eingegangen werden.[49]

658; *Perea,* 20 Pace Int'l L. Rev. (2008), 191, 205; *Schlechtriem/Schwenzer/Schlechtriem,* CISG Commentary, , 2. Aufl., Preamble, Rn. 8; *Schlechtriem/Schwenzer/Schwenzer/Hachem,* CISG Commentary, Preamble, Rn. 9.

[42] Vgl. aber Art. 7 Rn. 12 f.
[43] Vgl. *Brunner,* Präambel, Rn. 2; *Flechtner,* FS Schwenzer, S. 493, 502; *Hartnell,* 18 Yale J. Int'l L. (1993), 1, 46 ff.; *Honnold/Flechtner,* Rn. 475.
[44] Vgl. RB Amsterdam, 3.6.2009, CISG-online 2065.
[45] Die sechs offiziellen Fassungen des CISG sind u. a. abgedruckt in *Bianca/Bonell,* S. 683 ff.
[46] So *Herber,* 2. Aufl., Präambel Rn. 6.
[47] So auch *Martiny,* RabelsZ 45 (1981), 427 (mit Bezug auf Gerichtsstands- und Vollstreckungsübereinkommen vom 27.9.1968); *Ryan,* 4 Tul. J. Int'l & Comp. L. (1995), 99, 101 („textual uniformity […] is insufficient").
[48] Vgl. auch *Ferrari,* Applicabilità ed applicazioni, S. 8 f.; *Vázquez Lepinette,* Dir. com. int. 1995, 377, 387.
[49] Vgl. Art. 7 Rn. 1 ff.

Teil I. Anwendungsbereich und allgemeine Bestimmungen

Kapitel I. Anwendungsbereich

Part I	Première partie
Sphere of application and general provisions	Champ d'application et dispositions générales
Chapter I	Chapitre I
Sphere of application	Champ d'application

Vorbemerkungen zu Artt. 1–6

Übersicht

	Rn.
I. Vorgeschichte	1
II. Grundzüge	3
1. Gegenstand des Kapitels	3
2. Praktische Bedeutung der Vorschriften	5
3. Internationales Privatrecht und Anwendungsbereich	6
III. Anwendungsbereich und Vorbehaltsmöglichkeiten	8
1. Allgemeines	8
2. Ratifikationen und Vorbehalte	13
IV. Bedeutung der einzelnen Vorbehalte	15
1. Art. 92 – Nichtanwendung des Teiles II oder III	15
2. Art. 93 – Nichtanwendung in gespaltener Rechtsordnung	17
3. Art. 94 – Vorrang regionaler Rechtsvereinheitlichung bzw. -angleichung	19
4. Art. 95 – Nichtanwendung des Art. 1 I lit. b)	21
5. Art. 96 – Formfreiheit	23
V. Anwendung des CISG	24
1. CISG und Haager Kaufgesetze	24
2. Die deutsche Übersetzung des CISG in der Praxis	27
3. UN-Kaufrecht und nationales Recht	29
4. UN-Kaufrecht und IPR	34

I. Vorgeschichte

Obwohl der Anwendungsbereich des CISG mit dem des EKG und EAG übereinzustimmen scheint – sowohl das CISG, als auch das EKG und EAG regeln „internationale Warenkaufverträge"[1] – unterscheiden sich die Anwendungsbereiche doch stark voneinander.[2] Bisweilen ist sogar behauptet worden, der Anwendungsbereich des CISG sei der am stärksten gegenüber dem EKG und EAG veränderte Teil des Übereinkommens.[3] Dies

---

[1] Vgl. *Ferrari*, Applicabilità ed applicazioni, S. 39.
[2] In diesem Sinne auch *Barbic*, Uniform Law, S. 4; *Ferrari*, The Sphere of Application, S. 7.
[3] So ausdrücklich *Herber*, 2. Aufl., Vor Artt. 1–6 Rn. 1; *Schlechtriem/Schwenzer/Schlechtriem*, CISG Commentary, 2. Aufl., Intro to Arts 1–6, Rn. 1; *Schlechtriem/Schwenzer/Schwenzer/Hachem*, CISG Commentary, Intro to Arts 1–6, Rn. 1.

kann nicht weiter überraschen, wurde doch der **Anwendungsbereich des EKG** und EAG schon sehr früh wegen seiner **Unübersichtlichkeit** kritisiert,[4] die sich aus der Möglichkeit ergab, verschiedene Vorbehalte einzulegen.[5] In der Tat war die Kompliziertheit der Regelung und die Uneinheitlichkeit des Anwendungsbereichs zwischen den (wenigen) Vertragsstaaten infolge Ausübung verschiedener Vorbehalte ein wesentlicher Grund für eine Reihe praktischer Schwierigkeiten bei der Anwendung des EKG und EAG.[6] Dies hat dazu geführt, dass von Beginn der Arbeiten in UNCITRAL an allgemein die Auffassung vertreten wurde, die Vorschriften über den Anwendungsbereich sollten vereinfacht werden,[7] unter anderem durch Begrenzung der Anzahl der Vorbehaltsmöglichkeiten.[8]

2   Das Ziel der **Vereinfachung des Anwendungsbereichs** ist erreicht worden.[9] Allerdings mussten auch die Konventionsgeber einige (wenige) Vorbehalte zulassen.[10] Von diesen ist der Vorbehalt, wonach die Vertragsstaaten die Ausdehnung des Anwendungsbereichs ex Art. 1 I lit. b) ausschließen können, wohl der problematischste.[11]

II. Grundzüge

1. Gegenstand des Kapitels

3   Kapitel I, das den persönlich-räumlichen und sachlichen Anwendungsbereich des dispositiven[12] Übereinkommens umschreibt,[13] enthält verschiedene Gruppen von Bestimmungen:[14] Während einige Bestimmungen festlegen, **ob Verträge** dem Übereinkommen unterliegen (Artt. 1–3, 6),[15] bestimmen andere Vorschriften (Artt. 4 und 5 und, in einem gewissen Maße, auch Art. 6, zumindest insoweit als er es den Parteien ermöglicht, das Übereinkommen auszuschließen)[16] **inwieweit** diese Verträge dem CISG unterfallen.[17] Dabei fällt auf, dass einige Bestimmungen **positiv** formuliert sind (Artt. 1, 3 I, 4 S. 1),

---

[4] Vgl. statt aller *Rigaux*, Journal des Tribunaux 1972, 561, 564.
[5] Vgl. *Lohmann*, Parteiautonomie, S. 32.
[6] So *Herber*, 2. Aufl, Vor Art. 1–6 Rn. 1.
[7] *Schlechtriem/Schwenzer/Schlechtriem*, CISG Commentary, 2. Aufl., Intro to Arts 1–6, Rn. 1; *Schlechtriem/ Schwenzer/Schwenzer/Hachem*, CISG Commentary, Intro to Arts 1–6, Rn. 1.
[8] YB I (1968–1970), S. 132, Nr. 19; S. 162, Nr. 14, 18, 19; S. 180, Nr. 37.
[9] So auch *Herber*, Anwendungsbereich, S. 31; *Magnus*, ZRP 1978, 129 f.; *J. Meyer*, RabelsZ 69 (2005), 457, 476; *Schlechtriem/Schwenzer/Schwenzer/Hachem*, CISG Commentary, Intro to Arts 1–6, Rn. 1 a. E.
[10] *Schlechtriem/Schwenzer/Schlechtriem*, CISG Commentary, 2. Aufl., Intro to Arts 1–6, Rn. 2.
[11] Vgl. hierzu ausführlich Art. 1 Rn. 77 ff.; vgl. auch *Ferrari*, NIPR 13 (1995), 317; *ders.*, IHR 2006, 248.
[12] So auch *Bamberger/Roth/Saenger*, Artt. 6, Rn. 1; *Borisova*, CISG-UP, S. 40; *Carbone*, S. 78; *Carbone/ Luzzatto*, S. 131; *Diéz-Picazo/Calvo Caravaca*, Art. 6, S. 92; *Ferrari*, Applicabilità ed applicazioni, S. 201; *ders.*, Int. Bus. L.J. 2003, 221, 227; *Herber*, IHR 2003, 1; *Lanciotti*, S. 146; *Lindbach*, S. 67; *Lohmann*, Privatautonomie, S. 193; *Piltz*, Rn. 2–190; *Reifner*, IHR 2002, 52, 54; *Sacerdoti*, Riv. trim. dir. proced. civ. 1990, 733, 744; *Volken*, Anwendungsvoraussetzungen, S. 92; *Witz*, D. 1990, Chron. 107; für Hinweise in der Rechtsprechung auf den dispositiven Charakter des CISG, vgl. Cass. 19.6.2000, CISG-online 1317 = Corr. Giur. 2002, 369, 371; OGH, 21.3.2000, CISG-online 641 = IHR 2001, 41; OGH, 27.8.1999, CISG-online 485 = IHR 2001, 81, 83; OGH, 15.10.1998, CISG-online 380 = TranspR-IHR 1999, 25; HGer Wien, 4.3.1997, CISG-online 743; KG Wallis, 29.6.1994, CISG-online 134 = Zeitschrift für Walliser Rechtsprechung 1994, 126.
[13] Siehe MünchKommHGB/*Benicke*, Art. 1, Rn. 1; *Enderlein/Maskow/Strohbach*, Vorbem. Art. 1, Anm. 1.
[14] Vgl. hierzu auch *Schlechtriem/Schwenzer/Schlechtriem*, CISG Commentary, 2. Aufl., Intro to Arts 1–6, Rn. 3.
[15] Vgl. hierzu auch *Schmid*, Lückenfüllung und Normenkonkurrenz, S. 29.
[16] So auch *Herber*, 2. Aufl., Vor Artt. 1–6 Rn. 3; *Kröll u. a./Djordjevic*, Art. 4, Rn. 2; *Schlechtriem/Schwenzer/ Schlechtriem*, CISG Commentary, 2. Aufl., Intro to Arts 1–6 Rn. 3; *Schlechtriem/Schwenzer/Schwenzer/Hachem*, CISG Commentary, Intro to Arts 1–6, Rn. 2.
[17] In der Lehre sind verschiedene Bezeichnungen benutzt worden, um die im Text erwähnte Unterscheidung hervorzuheben; für einen Überblick, vgl. statt aller *Schluchter*, S. 25.

Vorbemerkungen zu Artt. 1–6   4, 5   **Vor Artt. 1–6**

andere hingegen **negativ** (Artt. 2, 3 II, 4 S. 2, 5),[18] was sich unter anderem auf die Beweislast auswirkt.[19]

Bei der Bestimmung des Anwendungsbereichs des Übereinkommens sind jedoch auch in 4 anderen Kapiteln enthaltene Vorschriften zu berücksichtigen;[20] als Beispiel sei hier nur Art. 10 erwähnt,[21] der, hat eine Vertragspartei mehrere Niederlassungen, bei der Identifizierung der (unter anderem für die Internationalität des Vertrages) relevanten Niederlassung heranzuziehen ist. Was den zeitlichen Anwendungsbereich angeht, so ergibt sich dieser aus Art. 100.[22]

2. Praktische Bedeutung der Vorschriften

Die Vorschriften dieses Kapitels haben eine zweifache Bedeutung:[23] Zum einen **redu-** 5 **zieren** sie (in Vertragsstaaten) die Notwendigkeit der **herkömmlichen Erarbeitung** des für internationale Kaufverträge maßgeblichen Rechts[24] anhand von Kollisionsnormen,[25] die oft problematisch ist.[26] Gänzlich ausgeschlossen ist die Zwischenschaltung des Kollisionsrechts (für die Anwendbarkeit) aber nur, wenn das Übereinkommen kraft Art. 1 I lit. a) zur Anwendung kommt,[27] also „direkt"[28] bzw. auf „autonomem Anwendungsweg",[29] und die Fragen, die es zu lösen gilt, im Übereinkommen (ausdrücklich oder implizit) geregelt sind.[30] Zum anderen grenzen die Vorschriften des Kapitels I die internationalen, vom Übereinkommen erfassten Sachverhalte von den nationalen Sachverhalten ab,[31] für die weiterhin das nationale Recht des im konkreten Fall berufenen Vertragsstaates anwendbar bleibt.[32]

---

[18] Vgl. *Enderlein/Maskow/Strohbach,* Vorbem. Art. 1, Anm. 2. („the sphere of application is defined positively and negatively by way of inclusion and exclusion").
[19] Zur Beweislast, vgl. Art. 4 Rn. 48 ff.; Art. 7 Rn. 56.
[20] *Bamberger/Roth/Saenger,* Art. 1, Rn. 1a; *Schlechtriem/Schwenzer/Schwenzer/Hachem,* CISG Commentary, Intro to Arts 1–6, Rn. 2.
[21] Siehe aber auch Art. 99, aus dem sich der Begriff des Vertragsstaates ergibt, der für den räumlichen Anwendungsbereich relevant ist, und Art. 73, aus dem hervorgeht, dass auch Sukzessivlieferungsverträge dem CISG unterliegen.
[22] Vgl. *Bamberger/Roth/Saenger,* Art. 1, Rn. 1a; *Enderlein/Maskow/Strohbach,* Vorbem. Art. 1, Anm. 1; *Schlechtriem/Schwenzer/Schlechtriem,* CISG Commentary, 2. Aufl., Intro to Arts 1–6, Rn. 3.
[23] Vgl. *Lohmann,* Parteiautonomie, S. 38; *Schlechtriem/Schwenzer/Schlechtriem,* CISG Commentary, 2. Aufl., Intro to Arts 1–6, Rn. 4; *Schlechtriem/Schwenzer/Schwenzer/Hachem,* CISG Commentary, Intro to Arts 1–6, Rn. 5; allgemein hierzu *Kropholler,* Internationales Einheitsrecht, S. 190.
[24] Vgl. hierzu statt aller *Palandt/Heldrich,* Art. 27 EGBGB, Rn. 3 ff.
[25] Ähnlich *Bianca/Bonell/Jayme,* Art. 1, Anm. 1.2; *Schlechtriem/Schwenzer/Schwenzer/Hachem,* CISG Commentary, Intro to Arts 1–6, Rn. 5.
[26] Hierzu *Piltz,* Rn. 1–33.
[27] Vgl. Art. 1 Rn. 63 ff.
[28] Vgl. *Chiomenti,* EuLF 2005, 141, 143; *Díez-Picazo/Calvo Caravaca,* Art. 1, S. 54; *Ferrari,* Applicabilità ed applicazioni, S. 70; *Frignani/Torsello,* Il contratto internazionale, S. 452; *Kröll u. a./Perales Viscasillas,* Art. 1, Rn. 47; *Magnus,* IPRax 1993, 390; *Niemann,* Einheitliche Anwendung, S. 70; *Ragno,* Convenzione di Vienna e Diritto europeo, S. 82; *Sannini,* L'applicazione, S. 64; *Pavic/Djordjevic,* 28 J. L. & Com. (2009), 1, 15; *Perovic,* Annals Fac. L. Belgrade 2011, 181, 182; *Spagnolo,* 10 Melb. J. Int'l L. (2009), 141, 143; *Weizuo,* 20 Pace Int'l L. Rev. (2008), 115, 115.
[29] *Staudinger/Magnus,* Art. 1, Rn. 85 ff.; in der Rechtsprechung auf diesen „autonomen" Anwendungsweg hinweisend etwa KG Wallis, 2.2.2005, CISG-online 1193 = IHR 2006, 155, 156; OGH, 20.3.1997, CISG-online 269 = ZfRVgl 1997, 204 ff.; KG Waadt, 29.6.1994, CISG-online 134 = ZWR 1994, 125; sich gegen die Verwendung des Begriffs der „autonomen" Anwendung aussprechend, um die Lösung des Art. 1 I lit. a) zu beschreiben, etwa *Lohmann,* Parteiautonomie, S. 37, Fn. 95, mit der Begründung, „der Geltungsanspruch des UN-Kaufrechts [ergebe sich] auch im Falle des Art. 1 Abs. 1 lit. CISG unmittelbar aus der Konvention".
[30] *Ferrari u. a./Saenger,* Internationales Vertragsrecht, Art. 4, Rn. 1 a. E.; *Schlechtriem/Schwenzer/Schlechtriem,* CISG Commentary, 2. Aufl., Intro to Arts 1–6, Rn. 6; vgl. aber in der Rechtsprechung OLG Linz, 23.3.2005, CISG-online 1376 = IHR 2007, 123, 125, wonach das internationale Kaufrecht „als (durch Staatsvertrag) vereinheitlichtes spezielles Sachrecht die Anwendung des IPR im entsprechenden Bereich überflüssig macht".
[31] So auch *Kropholler,* Internationales Einheitsrecht, S. 190; *Schlechtriem,* Internationales Kaufrecht, Rn. 17; *Schlechtriem/Schwenzer/Schwenzer/Hachem,* CISG Commentary, Intro to Arts 1–6, Rn. 5; *Schmid,* Lückenfüllung und Normenkonkurrenz, S. 30.
[32] So schon *Herber,* 2. Aufl., Vor Artt. 1–6 Rn. 4.

3. Internationales Privatrecht und Anwendungsbereich

6   Obwohl die Vorschriften dieses Kapitels eine autonome Umschreibung des Anwendungsbereichs des Übereinkommens enthalten (Art. 1 I lit. a)), darf die Bedeutung des Internationalen Privatrechts nicht unterschätzt werden.[33] Dies ergibt sich unschwer zum Beispiel aus Art. 1 I lit. b), wonach das Übereinkommen auch dann zur Anwendung kommen kann, wenn die Regeln des Internationalen Privatrechts zur Anwendung des Rechts eines Vertragsstaates führen.[34] Mit der Einführung dieses alternativen[35] Anwendungsweges haben die Konventionsgeber den Anwendungsbereich auch auf Fälle ausgedehnt,[36] in denen nur eine oder unter besonderen Umständen gar keine Partei ihre Niederlassung in einem Vertragsstaat hat.[37]

7   Das Internationale Privatrecht kann aber selbst dann relevant sein, wenn das Übereinkommen aufgrund autonomer Anwendungsvoraussetzungen[38] (Art. 1 I lit. a)) zum Zuge kommt.[39] Dies hängt zum einen mit den verschiedenen Vorbehalten zusammen, es sei hier nur Art. 96 erwähnt, zum anderen damit, dass das Übereinkommen **keine abschließende Kaufrechtsordnung** darstellt,[40] also nicht alle Rechtsfragen regelt.[41] Für die ausgeschlossenen Materien muss das anwendbare Recht bestimmt werden, dem sodann die Lösung entnommen werden muss,[42] sofern natürlich kein anderes Einheitssachrecht vorgeht. Gleiches gilt auch für die Fragen, die im Übereinkommen geregelte Materien betreffen, in diesem aber nicht ausdrücklich geregelt sind, zumindest dann, wenn diese nicht nach

---

[33] Vgl. zum Verhältnis von CISG und IPR neuerdings *Ferrari*, J. D. I. 2006, 27 ff.
[34] Vgl. Art. 1 Rn. 69 ff.
[35] So auch *Goode*, Uniform L. Rev. 1991-I, 54, 67; *Memmo*, Riv. trim. dir. proced. civ. 1983, 180, 205.
[36] Vgl. *Diez-Picazo/Calvo Caravaca*, Art. 1, S. 57; *Schlechtriem/Schwenzer/Schlechtriem*, CISG Commentary, 2. Aufl., Intro to Arts 1–6, Rn. 7; MünchKomm/*Westermann*, Vor Art. 1, Rn. 2.
[37] Siehe *Schlechtriem*, Internationales UN-Kaufrecht, Rn. 16; *Schlechtriem/Schwenzer/Schwenzer/Hachem*, CISG Commentary, Intro to Arts 1–6, Rn. 8.
[38] Zu dieser Terminologie, vgl. *Schlechtriem*, Einheitliches UN-Kaufrecht, S. 9.
[39] A. A. *Douglas*, 13 U. Miami Int'l & Comp. L. Rev. (2006), 367, 376.
[40] A. A. aber BGer, 15.9.2000, CISG-online 770: „La CVIM est d'application exhaustive; elle régit l'ensemble du contrat"; ebenso BezG Laufen, 7.5.1993, CISG-online 136 (das CISG ist eine „einheitliche, abschließende und autonome Kaufrechtsordnung"); a. A. in der Lehre *Fitzgerald*, 27 J. L. & Com. (2008), 1, 2 („comprehensive code"); ebenso *Perea*, 20 Pace Int'l L. Rev. (2008), 191, 191 der sich aber dann selbst widerspricht, 192; *Shariff/de Carteret*, 9 Asper Rev. Int'l Bus. & Trade L. (2009) 21, 55.
[41] So ausdrücklich auch *Andreason*, B.Y.U.L.Rev. (1999), 351, 376; *Bamberger/Roth/Saenger*, Art. 4, Rn. 1; *G. Bell*, 9 Singapore Y.B. Int'l L. (2005), 55, 67; *Brunner*, Art. 4, Rn. 1; *Cetiner*, S. 19; *Cuniberti*, 39 Vand. J. Transnat'l L. (2006), 1511, 1544; *De Ly*, 25 J.L. & Com. (2005), 1; *Ferrari*, IHR 2006, 1, 2 und 11; *Ferrari u. a./Saenger*, Internationales Vertragsrecht, Art. 4, Rn. 1; *Frignani/Torsello*, Il contratto internazionale, S. 444; *Gianuzzi*, 28 L. & Pol'y Int'l Bus. (1997), 991, 1016; *Gstoehl*, östZfRvgl 1998, 1; *Hayward*, 14 VJ (2010), 193, 219; *Niemann*, Einheitliche Anwendung, S. 30; *Ragno*, Convenzione di Vienna e Diritto europeo, S. 23; *Sannini*, L'applicazione, S. 121 f.; *Schlechtriem/Schwenzer/Schlechtriem*, CISG Commentary, 2. Aufl., Art. 4, Rn. 3; *Schlechtriem/Schwenzer/Schwenzer/Hachem*, CISG Commentary, Preamble, Rn. 2 und Art. 4, Rn. 2; *Schwenzer/Hachem/Kee*, Rn. 3.19; *Schroeter*, 6 VJ (2002), 257, 263; *ders.*, 5 VJ (2001), 74; *Spagnolo*, 21 Temp. Int'l & Comp. L. J. (2007), 261, 305; *Tescaro*, Contr. Imp. E. 2007, 319; *Torsello*, The CISG's Impact, S. 214 ff.; *Trompenaars*, S. 18 f.; *Vida*, IPRax 2002, 146, 147; *Walt*, 35 UCC L. J. (2002), 43; *ders.*, 25 Int'l Rev. L. & Econ. (2005), 342, 343; *C. Witz*, Int. Bus. L. J. 2001, 253, 261; so auch ein Teil der Rechtsprechung: Tribunale di Modena, 9.12.2005, CISG-online 1398 = Riv. dir. int. priv. proc. 2007, 387, 390; KG Nidwalden, 23.5.2005, CISG-online 1086 = IHR 2005, 253, 254; KG Schaffhausen, 20.10.2003, CISG-online 957 = IHR 2005, 206, 207; OGH, 22.10.2001, CISG-online 613 = IHR 2002, 24, 27; a.A. BGer, 15.9.2000, CISG-online 770: „La CVIM est d'application exhaustive; elle régit l'ensemble du contrat, c'est-à-dire la formation de celui-ci, ainsi que les droits et obligations des parties, de même que les conséquences d'une inexécution. En principe, l'application supplétive du droit national est exclue". Ebenso BGer, 19.2.2004, CISG-online 839, 3.2.2.; Cour de Justice de Génève, 15.11.2002, CISG-online 853, 2b); BezG Laufen, 7.5.1993, CISG-online 136; a. A. in der Lehre *Shariff/de Carteret*, 9 Asper Rev. Int'l Bus. & Trade L. (2009) 21, 55; zu den nicht geregelten Rechtsfragen eingehend vgl. Art. 4 Rn. 3 ff.
[42] Vgl. hierzu allgemein *Ferrari*, Int. Bus. L. J. (1998), 835 ff.; *Mather*, 20 J. L. & Com. (2001), 155 ff.; *Witz*, Int. Bus. L. J. 2001, 253 ff.

den dem Übereinkommen zugrunde liegenden Grundsätzen entschieden werden können.[43]

III. Anwendungsbereich und Vorbehaltsmöglichkeiten

1. Allgemeines

Da die Erklärung durch viele (wenn auch nicht alle)[44] der wenigen Vertragsstaaten des Haager Kaufrechts eines oder mehrerer Vorbehalte[45] den Anwendungsbereich des EKG – und mittelbar durch Verweisung auf diesen auch den des EAG[46] – uneinheitlich und vor allem unübersichtlich hatte werden lassen,[47] was auch zum geringen Erfolg des Haager Kaufrechts beigetragen hat,[48] haben die Konventionsgeber des CISG der Einheitlichkeit und Übersichtlichkeit halber versucht, ähnlich weitgehende Vorbehalte zu vermeiden.[49] Dennoch sieht auch das CISG eine Reihe von Vorbehaltsmöglichkeiten vor, von denen einige durchaus auch Probleme für die Praxis aufwerfen. 8

Trotz einiger Widerstände anlässlich der Diplomatischen Konferenz in Wien,[50] vor allem der australischen Delegation,[51] wurde der Vorbehalt nach Art. V des Kaufübereinkommens von 1964 nicht übernommen, der auf englischen Wunsch anlässlich der Diplomatischen Konferenz in Den Haag eingeführt worden war.[52] Danach reduzierte sich die Pflicht eines Vertragsstaates zur Einführung des EKG und EAG darauf, die Regeln des Übereinkommens lediglich im Falle der Vereinbarung der Parteien anzuerkennen (opting-in).[53] 9

Der praktisch wichtigste Vorbehalt des Haager Kaufrechts war der nach Art. III des Kaufübereinkommens,[54] mittels dessen dem oft kritisierten[55] **„erga omnes approach"**[56] des Übereinkommens entgegengewirkt werden sollte.[57] Danach konnten die Vertragsstaaten die Anwendbarkeit des Haager Kaufrechts auf die Fälle beschränken, in denen die Vertragsparteien ihre Niederlassung oder ihren gewöhnlichen Aufenthalt in Vertragsstaaten hatten.[58] Dieser Vorbehalt ist (in seiner alten Form) im CISG nicht übernommen worden. Dies hängt damit zusammen, dass die Konventionsgeber von vorneherein den erwähnten „erga omnes approach" aufgegeben[59] und für die Anwendbarkeit des CISG neben der Internationalität des Kaufvertrages auch auf eine Beziehung zu (mindestens) einem Vertragsstaat beharrt haben.[60] Die anlässlich der Diplomatischen Konferenz in Wien an dieser 10

---

[43] Siehe *Ferrari*, JZ 1998, 9, 15; *Schlechtriem/Schwenzer/Schwenzer/Hachem*, CISG Commentary, Intro to Arts 1–6, Rn. 10.
[44] Statt aller, vgl. hierzu *Carbone/Luzzatto*, S. 137.
[45] Einen Überblick über die von den verschiedenen Vertragsstaaten erklärten Vorbehalte geben u. a. *Boschiero*, Le Convenzioni, S. 267; *Ferrari*, La vendita internazionale, S. 35, Fn. 46; *Frignani*, Contratto internazionale, S. 263; *Herber*, Anwendungsbereich, S. 31 f.
[46] Vgl. Art. 1 EAG.
[47] Für eine Kritik an der großen Anzahl von Vorbehaltsmöglichkeiten, vgl. statt aller *Réczei*, 29 Am. J. Comp. L. (1981), 513, 516, Fn. 10.
[48] Vgl. *Luzzatto*, 46 Enc. D. (1993), 502, 507.
[49] *Schlechtriem/Schwenzer/Schlechtriem*, CISG Commentary, 2. Aufl., Intro to Arts 1–6, Rn. 1 und 12.
[50] Vgl. hierzu die Diskussion im Ersten und Zweiten Ausschuß der Diplomatischen Konferenz, O. R., S. 247 f., Nr. 37 ff.; O. R., S. 436 ff., Nr. 40 ff.
[51] Vgl. O. R., S. 144.
[52] Siehe *Dölle/Herber*, Vor Artt. 1–8 EKG, Rn. 14 f.
[53] So *Herber*, 2. Aufl., Vor Artt. 1–6 Rn. 13; *Schlechtriem/Schwenzer/Schlechtriem*, CISG Commentary, 2. Aufl., Intro to Arts 1–6, Rn. 13.
[54] *Schlechtriem/Schwenzer/Schlechtriem*, CISG Commentary, 2. Aufl., Intro to Arts 1–6, Rn. 14.
[55] Vgl. *Nadelmann*, 74 Yale L. J. (1964-65), 449, 456.
[56] Vgl. *Ragno*, Convenzione di Vienna e Diritto europeo, S. 70 f.
[57] Vgl. Art. 1 Rn. 1.
[58] Von den 9 Vertragsstaaten der Haager Kaufrechtsübereinkommen haben 6 Staaten von dem Vorbehalt nach Art. III Gebrauch gemacht; vgl. BGBl. 1974 II 146, 1122; BGBl. 1979 II 646.
[59] Vgl. YB VI (1975), S. 89, Nr. 10 ff.; YB VIII (1977), S. 13, Nr. 18; S. 26, Nr. 17, 23.
[60] Vgl. Art. 1 Rn. 61 ff.

Lösung geübte Kritik hat zu der in Art. 95 eingeräumten Vorbehaltsmöglichkeit geführt, die einen ähnlichen Zweck verfolgt wie die in Art. III des EKG eingeräumte Vorbehaltsmöglichkeit.[61]

11   In Bezug auf die anderen Vorbehaltsmöglichkeiten muss angemerkt werden, dass diese nur teilweise übernommen wurden.[62] Während der in Art. II des Kaufübereinkommens eingeräumte Vorbehalt – Vorbehaltmöglichkeit zugunsten regionaler Rechtseinheit bzw. -angleichung – auch im CISG Niederschlag gefunden hat (Art. 94), wurde der Vorbehalt des Art. IV des Kaufübereinkommens – Vorrang der Regeln kollisionsrechtlicher Übereinkommen vor den Regeln über den Anwendungsbereich des Kaufübereinkommens[63] – m. E. nicht übernommen,[64] auch nicht in Art. 90, da dieser sich lediglich auf materielle Vorschriften bezieht.[65]

12   Gemäß Art. 98 sind nur solche Vorbehalte zulässig, die im Übereinkommen ausdrücklich für zulässig erklärt worden sind.[66] Das Übereinkommen geht demnach von einer abschließenden Aufzählung der Vorbehalte aus.[67] Dies führt dazu, dass auch solche Vorbehalte, die eventuell nach Art. 19 Wiener Vertragsrechtskonvention möglich wären, nicht zulässig sind.[68] Dies bedeutet jedoch nicht, und dies ergibt sich auch aus der Diskussion anlässlich der Diplomatischen Konferenz,[69] dass Staaten nicht auch andere Erklärungen abgeben könnten,[70] deren Wirkungen sodann am allgemeinen Völkerrecht gemessen werden müssten.

2. Ratifikationen und Vorbehalte

13   Während einige Vorbehalte nur bei der Unterzeichnung, der Ratifikation, der Annahme, der Genehmigung oder dem Beitritt erklärt werden können, was sich unschwer aus dem Text einiger die Vorbehalte einräumenden Bestimmungen ergibt,[71] können sowohl der in Art. 94 eingeräumte Vorbehalt zugunsten regionaler Rechtseinheit bzw. -angleichung als auch der in Art. 96 eingeräumte Vorbehalt zugunsten der Schriftform jederzeit – also auch zu einem späteren Zeitpunkt – erklärt werden.[72]

14   Die Rücknahme einer Vorbehaltserklärung kann jederzeit erfolgen. Das Wirksamwerden der Rücknahme bestimmt sich nach Art. 97.

IV. Bedeutung der einzelnen Vorbehalte

1. Art. 92 – Nichtanwendung des Teiles II oder III

15   Jeder Vertragsstaat hat die Möglichkeit, Teil II oder III auszuschließen. Dieser Vorbehalt hat in den Haager Übereinkommen kein Pendant, da die in Teil II (Vertragsabschluß) und Teil III (Rechte und Pflichten der Parteien) des CISG geregelten Fragen in zwei getrennten

---

[61] Siehe auch *Staudinger/Magnus*, Art. 95, Rn. 2 („ähnliche, jedoch nicht identische Vorbehaltsmöglichkeit").
[62] A. A. *Herber*, 2. Aufl., Vor Artt. 1–6 Rn. 15, der davon ausgeht, dass sie alle „in ähnlicher Form in das CISG übernommen worden" seien; so auch *Schlechtriem/Schwenzer/Schlechtriem*, CISG Commentary, 2. Aufl., Intro to Arts 1–6, Rn. 15.
[63] Vgl. *Dölle/Herber*, Vor Artt. 1–8 EKG, Rn. 13.
[64] A. A. *Herber*, 2. Aufl., Vor Artt. 1–6 Rn. 15.
[65] So auch *Kindler*, RIW 1988, 776, 780; a. A. *Staudinger/Magnus*, Art. 90, Rn. 5; *Schlechtriem/Schwenzer/Hachem*, CISG Commentary, Intro to Arts 1–6, Rn. 6.
[66] *Schlechtriem/Schwenzer/Schlechtriem*, CISG-Commentary, 2. Aufl., Intro to Arts 1–6, Rn. 16.
[67] Siehe *Herber*, 2. Aufl., Vor Artt. 1–6 Rn. 16; *Schlechtriem/Schwenzer/Hachem*, CISG Commentary, Intro to Arts 1–6, Rn. 18.
[68] So *Staudinger/Magnus*, Art. 98, Rn. 1.
[69] Vgl. O. R., S. 459, Nr. 13 ff.
[70] Vgl. *Bianca/Bonell/Evans*, Art. 98, Anm. 2.3.
[71] Vgl. Artt. 92 I, 93 I, 95 I.
[72] Vgl. *Herber*, 2. Aufl., Art. 94 Rn. 8; Art. 96 Rn. 2; *Staudinger/Magnus*, Art. 94, Rn. 4; Art. 96, Rn. 3.

Einheitsgesetzen geregelt wurden, und es somit den Staaten möglich war, das eine oder das andere oder beide Kaufgesetze in Kraft treten zu lassen.[73] Mit dem Vorbehalt ist demnach – trotz äußerlicher Zusammenfassung der Vorschriften in einem Übereinkommen – praktisch der frühere Zustand, im Sinne der Trennung der erwähnten Rechtsmaterien, beibehalten worden.[74]

Dieser Vorbehalt hat durchaus praktische Bedeutung, da der Staat, der einen solchen Vorbehalt erklärt hat (bislang sind dies die skandinavischen Staaten), in Bezug auf den ausgeschlossenen Teil nicht als Vertragsstaat angesehen werden kann.[75] Dies führt, wie auch in der Rechtsprechung bereits hervorgehoben wurde,[76] dazu, dass auch wenn beide Vertragsparteien ihre Niederlassung in verschiedenen Vertragsstaaten haben, von denen einer aber einen Vorbehalt gemäß Art. 92 erklärt hat, der ausgeschlossene Teil des Übereinkommens nicht über Art. 1 I lit. a) Anwendung finden kann.[77]

2. Art. 93 – Nichtanwendung in gespaltener Rechtsordnung

Diese in vielen neueren Einheitsprivatrechtskonventionen[78] enthaltene Vorbehaltsmöglichkeit erlaubt Staaten ohne bundeseinheitliche Rechtsordnung (weil sie etwa in Mitgliedsstaaten, Bundesländer, Unionsrepubliken, Kantone, Provinzen oder Regionen mit eigener Rechtsordnung gegliedert sind),[79] das Übereinkommen nur auf einzelne seiner Gebietseinheiten zu erstrecken. Erklärt ein Staat einen solchen Vorbehalt, so führt dies – wie beim Vorbehalt des Art. 92 – dazu, dass die Gebietseinheit, auf die das Übereinkommen nicht erstreckt worden ist, nicht als Vertragsstaat angesehen werden kann; eine in dieser Gebietseinheit gelegene Niederlassung ist mithin nicht als eine solche in einem Vertragsstaat anzusehen.[80] Demnach kann das Übereinkommen nie ex Art. 1 I lit. a) auf Verträge Anwendung finden, die zwischen Vertragsparteien geschlossen worden sind, von denen mindestens eine ihre Niederlassung in einem solchen Teilgebiet hat.[81]

Bislang haben folgende Staaten einen Vorbehalt nach Art. 93 erklärt: Australien, Dänemark, die Niederlande und Kanada; Kanada hat den Vorbehalt jedoch später zurückgenommen.

---

[73] Siehe *Enderlein/Maskow/Strohbach*, Art. 92, Anm. 1.
[74] So *Herber*, 2. Aufl., Vor Artt. 1–6 Rn. 18; *Schlechtriem/Schwenzer/Schlechtriem*, CISG Commentary, 2. Aufl., Intro to Arts 1–6, Rn. 18; *Schlechtriem/Schwenzer/Schwenzer/Hachem*, CISG Commentary, Intro to Arts 1–6, Rn. 19.
[75] *Achilles*, Art. 92, Rn. 1; *Herber/Czerwenka*, Art. 92, Rn. 3; *Honsell/Siehr*, Art. 92, Rn. 1; *Kröll u. a./Herre*, Art. 92, Rn. 1 und 3; *Lookofsky*, 80 Nordic J. Int'l L. (2011), 295, 299; *Piltz*, Rn. 2–89; *Schlechtriem/Schwenzer/Schwenzer/Hachem*, CISG Commentary, Intro to Arts 1–6, Rn. 19.
[76] In der Rechtsprechung haben sich u. a. mit der Frage der Auswirkungen eines nach Art. 92 erklärten Vorbehalts beschäftigt: *Mitchell Aircraft Spares, Inc. v. European Aircraft Service AB*, U. S. Dist. Ct. (N. D. Ill.), 28.10.1998, CISG-online 444 = 1998 WL 754 801 (amerikanischer Käufer und schwedischer Verkäufer); Stadtgericht Budapest, 21.5.1996, CISG-online 252 (schwedisch-ungarischer Kaufvertrag); OLG Rostock, 27.7.1995, CISG-online 209 = OLG-Rp (Brandenburg u. a.) 1996, 50 (dänischer Verkäufer und deutscher Käufer); OLG München, 8.3.1995, CISG-online 145 = RIW 1996, 854 (schwedisch-deutscher Kaufvertrag); BezG Laufen, 7.5.1993, CISG-online 136 (schwedisch-schweizerischer Kaufvertrag).
[77] *Ferrari u. a./Mankowski*, Internationales Vertragsrecht, Art. 92, Rn. 5; *Lookofsky*, 20 J. L. & Com. (1999), 289, 292; *Mather*, 20 J. L. & Com. (2001), 155, 165–166; *Torsello*, Uniform L. Rev. (2000), 85, 98; falsch daher OLG Naumburg, 27.4.1999, CISG-online 512: Anwendung auch der Artt. 14–24 kraft Art. 1 I lit. a), obwohl eine Vertragspartei ihre Niederlassung in einem Vorbehaltsstaat hatte.
[78] Siehe u. a. Art. 92 der UN-Konvention über Verträge über die internationale Beförderung von Gütern ganz oder teilweise auf See; Art. 18 des UNCITRAL Übereinkommens zur Nutzung elektronischer Kommunikationsmittel in internationalen Verträgen; Art. 35 des UNCITRAL Übereinkommens über die Abtretung von Forderungen im internationalen Handel; Art. 16 des UNIDROIT-Übereinkommens über Internationales Factoring; Art. 18 des UNIDROIT-Übereinkommens über Internationales Finanzierungsleasing.
[79] Vgl. *Herber*, 2. Aufl., Vor Artt. 1–6 Rn. 19; *Schlechtriem/Schwenzer/Schwenzer/Hachem*, CISG Commentary, Intro to Arts 1–6, Rn. 20.
[80] *Schlechtriem/Schwenzer/Schlechtriem*, CISG Commentary, 2. Aufl., Intro to Arts 1–6, Rn. 20.
[81] So auch *Staudinger/Magnus*, Art. 93, Rn. 7.

3. Art. 94 – Vorrang regionaler Rechtsvereinheitlichung bzw. -angleichung

19 Diese auf Beharren der skandinavischen Staaten zurückgehende[82] und dem Art. II des Haager Kaufübereinkommens entsprechende Vorbehaltsmöglichkeit, mit der die Konventionsgeber (implizit) dem Ergebnis eventueller **regionaler Rechtsvereinheitlichungsbestrebungen** (unter bestimmten Bedingungen) **Vorrang** eingeräumt haben,[83] erlaubt **Staaten mit gleichen oder einander sehr nahekommenden Rechtsvorschriften** die Anwendung des CISG für die Fälle auszuschließen, in denen die Parteien ihre Niederlassung in diesen Staaten haben. Gemäß Art. 94 müssen zwei Fälle unterschieden werden:[84] Art. 94 I geht von dem Fall aus, dass die betroffenen Staaten mit gleichen oder einander sehr nahekommenden Rechtsvorschriften ausnahmslos Vertragsstaaten des CISG sind. Solche Staaten können **jederzeit** durch gemeinsame oder aufeinander bezogene einseitige Erklärungen die Anwendung des CISG für die Fälle ausschließen (wobei auch ein teilweiser Ausschluss zulässig ist),[85] in denen die Parteien beide ihre Niederlassung in einem solchen Staat haben.

20 Abs. 2 regelt hingegen den Fall, dass die Rechtsvorschriften eines **Vertragsstaates** mit denen eines oder mehrerer **Nichtvertragsstaaten** verwandt sind.[86] Mittels einer einseitigen Erklärung kann der Vertragsstaat die Anwendung des CISG für die Fälle ausschließen, in denen die Parteien in rechtsverwandten Vorbehalts- und Nichtvertragsstaaten niedergelassen sind. Tritt das CISG sodann in einem solchen Nichtvertragsstaat in Kraft, so wird die gemäß Abs. 3 gemachte Erklärung in Bezug auf ihre Wirkungen in eine solche nach Abs. 1 übergeleitet,[87] „vorausgesetzt, dass sich der neue Vertragsstaat einer solchen Erklärung anschließt oder eine auf eine darauf bezogene einseitige Erklärung abgibt".[88]

4. Art. 95 – Nichtanwendung des Art. 1 I lit. b)

21 Die in Art. 95 vorgesehene (bisweilen kritisierte)[89] Vorbehaltsmöglichkeit erlaubt Vertragsstaaten, die **Ausdehnung des Anwendungsbereichs** auf Vertragsbeziehungen zwischen Parteien, die nicht alle ihre Niederlassung in Vertragsstaaten haben, **einzuschränken.**[90] Verschiedene Vertragsstaaten haben die Erklärung dieses Vorbehalts mit der Begründung gerechtfertigt, „eine allzu große Einschränkung des Anwendungsbereichs ihrer internen Vorschriften müsse vermieden werden".[91] Ob die Erklärung dieses Vorbehalts ausreicht, um das erwähnte Ziel zu erreichen, ist streitig und soll andernorts näher untersucht werden.[92]

22 Unstrittig ist, dass sich dieser **Vorbehalt nicht** auf die Anwendbarkeit des Übereinkommens ex **Art. 1 I lit. a)** auswirkt, d. h., haben die Parteien ihre Niederlassung in verschiedenen Vertragsstaaten, so kann das Übereinkommen durchaus ex Art. 1 I lit. a) Anwendung finden,[93]

---

[82] Siehe O. R., S. 436.
[83] *Schroeter*, UN-Kaufrecht, S. 346; vgl. auch *Ferrari u. a./Mankowski*, Internationales Vertragsrecht, Art. 94, Rn. 2; *H.-F. Müller*, GPR 2006, 168, 173; allgemein zum Verhältnis von CISG und regionaler Rechtsvereinheitlichung auf dem Gebiet des Kaufrechts, vgl. *Ferrari*, Uniform L. Rev. 2003, 177 ff.; *ders.*, Rev. dr. aff. int. 2004, 445 ff.; *Šarčević*, Regional Unification, S. 3 ff.; *Schlechtriem*, Uniform L. Rev. 2003, 173 ff.
[84] So schon *Herber*, 2. Aufl., Vor Artt. 1–6 Rn. 22; vgl. auch *Schlechtriem/Schwenzer/Schlechtriem*, CISG Commentary, 2. Aufl., Intro to Arts 1–6, Rn. 22.
[85] So *Staudinger/Magnus*, Art. 94, Rn. 4.
[86] *Schlechtriem/Schwenzer/Schwenzer/Hachem*, CISG Commentary, Intro to Arts 1–6, Rn. 21.
[87] Vgl. *Herber*, 2. Aufl., Vor Artt. 1–6 Rn. 22.
[88] Art. 94 III.
[89] Siehe *Hermmann*, IPRax 1981, 109, 111; *Pelichet*, Vente internationale, S. 41.
[90] Vgl. hierzu *Ferrari*, Applicabilità ed applicazioni, S. 98 ff.
[91] *Luzzatto*, 46 Enc. D. (1993), 502, 510; ausführlich zu den Gründen, die zur Einführung dieser Vorschrift geführt haben, vgl. neuerdings *Bell*, 9 Singapore YB Int'l L. (2005), 55, 58 ff.
[92] Vgl. hierzu Art. 1 Rn. 77 ff.
[93] *Bell*, 9 Singapre YB Int'l L. (2005), 55, 56; *Ferrari*, IHR 2006, 248, 249; *Ferrari u. a./Mankowski*, Internationales Vertragsrecht, Art. 95, Rn. 4; *Sannini*, L'applicazione, S. 75.

Vorbemerkungen zu Artt. 1–6

unabhängig davon, ob eine[94] oder beide[95] Parteien in Vorbehaltsstaaten niedergelassen sind, und dies auch dann, wenn die berufenen Gerichte die eines Vorbehaltsstaates sind.[96]

---

[94] Für Fälle, in denen staatliche Gerichte und Schiedsgerichte das Übereinkommen ex Art. 1 I lit. a) auf Kaufverträge angewendet haben, die zwischen Parteien mit Sitz in verschiedenen Vertragsstaaten hatten, von denen einer Vorbehaltsstaat im Sinne von Art. 95 war, vgl. neuerdings District Court Trnava, 19.5.2011, CISG-online 2190 (slovakisch-österreichischer Vertrag); District Court Trnava, 13.5.2011, CISG-online 2191 (deutsch-slovakischer Vertrag); *Castel Electronics Pty. Ltd. v. Toshiba Singapore Pte. Ltd.*, Federal Court of Australia, 20.4.2011, CISG-online 2219 (Vertrag zwischen Partein mit Niederlassung in Singapur und Australien); District Court Trnava, 9.3.2011, CISG-online 2210 (italienisch-slovakischer Vertrag); *CSS Antenna, Inc. v. Amphenol-Tuchel Electronics, GmbH*, U. S. Dist. Ct. (D. Md.), 8.2.2011, CISG-online 2177 (deutsch-amerikanischer Vertrag); *Hanwha Corporation v. Cedar Petrochemicals, Inc.*, U. S. Dist. Ct. (S. D. N. Y.), 18.1.2011, CISG-online 2178 (amerikanisch-koreanischer Vertrag); OLG Jena, 10.11.2010, CISG-online 2226 (deutsch-amerikanischer Vertrag); *Forestal Guarani S. A. v. Daros International, Inc.*, U. S. Ct. App. (3rd Cir.), 21.7.2010, CISG-online 2112 (argentinisch-amerikanischer Vertrag); District Court Namestovo, 13.7.2010, CISG-online 2189; OLG Dresden, 27.5.2010, CISG-online 2182 (deutsch-slovakischer Vertrag); *Pasta Zara S. p. A. v. United States, American Italian Pasta Company, et al.*, U. S. Ct. Int'l Trade, 7.4.2010, CISG-online 2094 (italienisch-amerikanischer Vertrag); *Belcher-Robinson, L. L. C. v. Linamar Corporation, et al.*, U. S. Dist. Ct. (M. D. Ala., Eastern Division), 31.3.2010, CISG-online 2092 (amerikanisch-kanadischer Vertag); *Semi-Materials Co., Ltd v. MEMC Electronic Materials, Inc., et al.*, U. S. Dist. Ct. (E. D. Mo.), 10.1.2010, CISG-online 2169 (amerikanisch-koreanischer Vertrag); Audiencia Provincial de Madrid, 14.7.2009; CISG-online 2087 (spanisch-amerikanischer Vertrag); CA de Poitiers, 26.2.2009, CISG-online 2208 (französisch-amerikanischer Vertrag); Tribunal Supremo, 9.12.2008, CISG-online 2100 (spanisch-amerikanischer Vertrag); *Ajax Tool Works, Inc. v. Can-Eng Manufacturing Ltd.*, U. S. Dist. Ct. (N. D. Ill.), 29.1.2003, 2003 U. S. Dist. LEXIS 1306 (kanadisch-amerikanischer Vertrag); *Schmitz-Werke GmbH & Co. v. Rockland Industries, Inc.*, U. S. Ct. App. (4th Cir.), 21.6.2002, CISG-online 625 = 37 Fed. Appx. 687 (deutsch-amerikanischer Vertrag); *Magellan International v. Salzgitter Handel*, U. S. Dist. Ct. (N. D. Ill.), 7.12.1999, CISG-online 439 = 76 F. Supp. 2d 919 = UCC Rep. Serv. 2d 321 (deutsch-amerikanischer Vertrag); *KSTP-FM, LLC v. Specialized Communications, Inc. and Adtronics Signs, Ltd.*, U. S. Dist. Ct. (Minn.), 9.3.1999, CISG-online 471 (kanadisch-amerikanischer Vertrag); *Mitchell Aircraft Spares, Inc. v. European Aircraft Service AB*, U. S. Dist. Ct. (N. D. Ill.), 28.10.1998, CISG-online 444 = 1998 WL 754 801 (amerikanisch-schwedischer Kaufvertrag); CA Grenoble, 22.2.1995, CISG-online 151 = J. D. I. 1995, 632 ff. (französisch-amerikanischer Kaufvertrag); *Delchi Carrier SpA v. Rotorex Corp.*, U. S. Dist. Ct. (N. D. N. Y.), 9.9.1994, (ISG-online 113 = 1994 WL 495 787, (amerikanisch-italienischer Kaufvertrag); *S. V. Braun Inc. v. Alitalia- Linee Aeree Italiana SpA*, U. S. Dist. Ct. (S. D. N. Y.), 6.4.1994, CISG-online 112 = 1994 WL 121 680 (amerikanisch-ungarischer Kaufvertrag); ICC, 7399/1994, ICC Ct. Bull. 2/1995, 68 f. (amerikanisch-schweizerischer Vertrag); *José Luis Morales y/o Son Export, S. A. de C. V., de Hermosillo Sonora, México v. Nez Marketing de Los Angeles California, E. U. A.*, Comisión para la Protección del Comercio Exterior de México, 4.5.1993, CISG-online 75 = Diario oficial de 27.5.1993, 17–19 (mexikanisch-amerikanischer Vertrag); ICC, 7531/1994, CISG-online 565 = ICC Ct. Bull. 2/1995, 67 (chinesisch-österreichischer Kaufvertrag); LG Heidelberg, 3.7.1992, CISG-online 38 (amerikanisch-deutscher Kaufvertrag); *Filanto SpA v. Chilewich International Corp.*, U. S. Dist. Ct. (S. D. N. Y.), 14.4.1992, CISG-online 45 = 789 F. Supp. 1229 (italienisch-amerikanischer Kaufvertrag).

[95] Vgl. District Court Trnava, 20.10.2010, CISG-online 2188; District Court Namestovo, 13.7.2010, CISG-online 2189; *Guangxi Nanning Baiyang Food Co. Ltd. v. Long River International, Inc.*, U. S. Dist. Ct. (S. D. N. Y.), 30.3.2010, CISG-online 2091 (amerikanisch-chinesischer Vertrag); District Court Zvolen, 5.11.2009, CISG-online 2194; District Court Brezno, 21.7.2009, CISG-online 2195; Shanghai No. 1 Intermediate People's Court, 19.3.2009, CISG-online 2060; District Court Komarno, 24.2.2009, CISG-online 1992; District Court Nitra, 15.1.2009, CISG-online 2212; District Court Trnava, 17.12.2008, CISG-online 2203; District Court Dolny Kubin, 24.11.2008, CISG-online 1879; District Court Trnava, 17.11.2008, CISG-online 2136; Supreme Court Slovak Republic, 12.12.2008, CISG-online 1955; Regional Court Nitra, 15.10.2008, CISG-online 1877; District Court Brezno, 24.6.2008, CISG-online 2198; CIETAC Schiedsspruch, 1995 Law YB China, 922 ff.; *Beijing Metals & Minerals Import-Export Corp. v. American Business Center Inc.*, U. S. Ct. App. (5th Cir.), 15.6.1993, CISG-online 89 = 993 F. 2d. 1178.

[96] Vgl. in der neueren Rechtsprechung etwa District Court Trnava, 19.5.2011, CISG-online 2190; District Court Trnava, 13.5.2011, CISG-online 2191; District Court Trnava, 9.3.2011, CISG-online 2210; *CSS Antenna, Inc. v. Amphenol-Tuchel Electronics, GmbH*, U. S. Dist. Ct. (D. Md.), 3.2.2011, CISG-online 2177; *Hanwha Corporation v. Cedar Petrochemicals, Inc.*, U. S. Dist. Ct. (S. D. N. Y.), 18.1.2011, CISG-online 2178; *Electrocraft Arkansas, Inc. v. Super Electric Motors, Ltd et al.*, U. S. Dist. Ct. (E. D. Ark., Western Division), 2.4.2010, CISG-online 2093; District Court Dolny Kubin, 1.4.2010, CISG-online 2192; *Guangxi Nanning Baiyang Food Co. Ltd. v. Long River International, Inc.*, U. S. Dist. Ct. (S. D. N. Y.), 30.3.2010, CISG-online 2091; District Court Nitra, 29.10.2008, CISG-online 2213; District Court Trnava, 17.9.2008, CISG-online 1991; Supreme Court Slovak Republic, 19.6.2008, CISG-online 1875; District Court Dolny Kubin, 17.6.2008, CISG-online 1874; District Court Nitra, 29.5.2008, CISG-online 1766; *Zhejiang Shaoxing Yongli Printing and Dyeing Co., Ltd v. Microflock Textile Group Corporation*, U. S. Dist. Ct. (S. D. Fl.), 19.5.2008, CISG-online 1771; *China North Chemical Industries Corporation v. Beston Chemical Corporation*, U. S. Dist. Ct. (S. D. Tex., Houston Division),

5. Art. 96 – Formfreiheit

23 Art. 96 schafft eine Vorbehaltsmöglichkeit zugunsten solcher Vertragsstaaten, nach deren Rechtsvorschriften Kaufverträge schriftlich geschlossen oder nachgewiesen werden müssen, mit der Folge, dass die die Formfreiheit bestimmenden Vorschriften des Übereinkommens immer dann nicht gelten, wenn eine Vertragspartei ihre Niederlassung in einem Vorbehaltsstaat hat und das Internationale Privatrecht des Forums auf das Recht eines Vorbehaltsstaats verweist. Obwohl diese Vorbehaltsmöglichkeit aber nur für Vertragsstaaten mit Formzwang besteht,[97] haben auch einige Vertragsstaaten, namentlich Argentinien und Chile, deren Recht auf dem Prinzip der Formfreiheit basiert, von ihr Gebrauch gemacht.[98] Welche Konsequenzen sich daraus ergeben können, muss dem Völker(vertrags)recht entnommen werden.

V. Anwendung des CISG

1. CISG und Haager Kaufgesetze

24 Das CISG stellt, im Gegensatz zu den als „lois uniformes" konzipierten EAG und EKG,[99] eine sog. „convention intégrale"[100] dar.[101] Im Gegensatz zum EAG und zum EKG, sind die vereinheitlichten Vorschriften des CISG nicht einem völkerrechtlichen Trägerübereinkommen als Anlage beigefügt, das die Vertragsstaaten „lediglich" dazu verpflichtet, die Anlage in Kraft zu setzen.[102] Sie sind vielmehr im Übereinkommen selbst eingearbeitet.[103] Das CISG ist also ein „self-executing treaty",[104] mit der Folge, dass **Rechte und Pflichten unmittelbar aus dem Übereinkommen** abgeleitet werden können,[105] soweit dessen Anwendungsvoraussetzungen vorliegen,[106] die der Richter von Amts wegen zu untersuchen hat.[107]

7.2.2006, CISG-online 1177; Shanghai No. I. Intermediate People's Court, 23.3.2004, CISG-online 1497; vgl. auch die in den vorigen Fn. zitierten Entscheidungen der Gerichte der Vereinigten Staaten und der Slowakei.
[97] Vgl. *Herber/Czerwenka*, Art. 96, Rn. 2; *Staudinger/Magnus*, Art. 96, Rn. 4.
[98] Siehe *Garro*, 17 J. L. & Com. (1998), 219, 228 f.
[99] Zu den Unterschieden zwischen EAG und EKG auf der einen und dem CISG auf der anderen Seite, vgl. etwa *Barbic*, Uniform Law, S. 3 ff.; *Kahn*, Etude comparée, S. 1 ff.; *Ndulo*, 38 Int'l & Comp. L. Q. (1989), 1–25; *van der Velden*, Main Items, S. 46 ff.
[100] Vgl. YB VI (1975), S. 50, Nr. 13.
[101] So schon *Herber*, 2. Aufl., Vor Art. 1–6 Rn. 25; vgl. auch *Schlechtriem/Schwenzer/Schlechtriem*, CISG Commentary, 2. Aufl., Intro to Arts 1–6, Rn. 25; *Schlechtriem/Schwenzer/Schwenzer/Hachem*, CISG Commentary, Intro to Arts 1–6, Rn. 15; MünchKomm/*Westermann*, Vor Art. 1, Rn. 7.
[102] Vgl. *Volken*, Anwendungsvoraussetzungen, S. 83.
[103] Zu dieser Kodifikationstechnik, vgl. *Czerwenka*, Rechtsanwendungsprobleme, S. 124; *Lebedev*, Uniform L. Rev. 1981, I, 2, 15 ff.
[104] *Bailey*, 32 Cornell Int'l L. J. (1999), 273, 280–281; *Butler*, 76 Fla. B. J. (2002), 24; *Hackney*, 61 La. L. Rev. (2001), 473, 474; *Lohmann*, Privatautonomie, S. 124; *Martin-Davidson*, 17 Mich. St. J. Int'l L. (2008), 657, 658; *Niemann*, Einheitliche Anwendung, S. 28; *Sannini*, L'applicazione, S. 29 und 55; *Schlechtriem/Schwenzer/Schwenzer/Hachem*, CISG Commentary, Intro to Arts 1–6, Rn. 15; *Schmid*, Einheitliche Anwendung, S. 31; *Speidel*, 16 Nw. J. Int'l L. & Bus. (1995), 165, 166; *Tessitore*, 35 Willamette L. Rev. (1999), 367, 368; *Ubertaite*, 7 (EJLR), 2005, 277, 283 f.; MünchKomm/*Westermann*, Vor Art. 1, Rn. 7; vgl. in der Rechtsprechung *American Mint LLC v. GOSoftware, Inc.*, U. S. Dist. Ct. (M. D. Pa.), 16.8.2005, CISG-online 1104 = 2005 WL 2021248; *Chicago Prime Packers, Inc. v. Northam Food Trading Co.*, U. S. Ct. App. (7th Cir.), 23.5.2005, CISG-online 1026 = 2005 WL 1 243 344 (7th Cir. (Ill.)); *Genpharm Inc. v. Pliva-Lachema A. S., Pliva d. d.*, U. S. Dist. Ct. (N. D. N. Y.), 19.3.2005, CISG-online 1006 = 361 F. Supp. 2d 49; *Usinor Industeel v. Leeco Steel Products, Inc.*, U. S. Dist. Ct. (N. D. Ill.), 28.3.2002, CISG-online 696 = 2002 WL 655 540; *Asante Technologies, Inc. v. PMC-Sierra, Inc.*, U. S. Dist. Ct. (N. D. Cal.), 27.7.2001, CISG-online 616 = 164 F. Supp. 2d 1142, 1147; vgl. allgemein zu self-executing treaties *Henckaerts*, 26 Int'l J. Leg. Inf. (1998), 56 ff.
[105] Vgl. hierzu auch *Melin*, Gesetzesauslegung, S. 344; *Volken*, Scope, S. 21 f.
[106] So auch *Ferrari*, Applicabilità ed applicazioni, S. 36; *Schmidt-Kessel*, FS *Schlechtriem*, S. 255, 269.
[107] *Achilles*, Art. 1, Rn. 11; *Délebecque/Jacquet*, RTD com. 2002, 210, 211; *Muir Watt*, Rev. crit. dr. int. priv. 2002, 94, 96; *Schlechtriem/Schwenzer/Schwenzer/Hachem*, CISG Commentary, Intro to Arts 1–6, Rn. 3; *Schwenzer/Hachem/Kee*, Rn. 3.23; *Witz*, D. 2001, Jur. 3608, 3609 f.; *ders.*, D. 2002, Chron. 2796, 2797; vgl. in der

Nach deutschem Staatsrecht ergibt sich aus dieser veränderten Konzeption aber kein 25 grundsätzlicher Unterschied,[108] da auch die Haager Einheitsgesetze – wenn auch nur infolge eines selbständigen Gesetzgebungsaktes des deutschen Gesetzgebers – unmittelbar anwendbares deutsches Recht wurden, genauso wie die Vorschriften des CISG heute unmittelbar anwendbares deutsches Recht sind.[109]

Diese Gemeinsamkeit darf jedoch nicht über einen für die Rechtsanwendung durchaus 26 **wesentlichen Unterschied** gegenüber den Haager Kaufgesetzen hinwegtäuschen:[110] Während letztere in der BR Deutschland infolge des eigenständigen deutschen Gesetzesbefehls durch die Einheitlichen Kaufgesetze vom 17. Juli 1973[111] in der darin enthaltenen deutschen Fassung galten, ist das **CISG in seiner Originalfassung** anwendbar.[112] Diesbezüglich ist die Unterzeichnungsklausel zu erwähnen, die ausdrücklich festlegt, dass sein Text gleichrangig in arabischer, chinesischer, englischer, französischer, russischer und spanischer Sprache[113] verbindlich ist.[114] Bei Nichtübereinstimmung der verschiedenen sprachlichen Versionen sind, genauso wie bei Auslegungszweifeln, die Vorschriften des Wiener Vertragrechtsübereinkommens heranzuziehen,[115] was dazu führt, dass – da anlässlich sowohl der Vorarbeiten als auch der Diplomatischen Konferenz die vorwiegend benutzte Sprache die englische war[116] – in Zweifelsfällen der **englischen Fassung besonderes Gewicht** zukommt.[117]

2. Die deutsche Übersetzung des CISG in der Praxis

Die wie auch anlässlich anderer Übereinkommen ausgearbeitete deutsche, zwischen den 27 deutschsprachigen Ländern abgestimmte **Übersetzung**[118] des Übereinkommens stellt **lediglich eine unverbindliche Anwendungshilfe** für die Gerichte dieser Länder dar,[119] ist also nicht verbindlich,[120] weshalb nicht primär auf die deutsche Version abgestellt werden

---

Rechtsprechung OGer Zug, 16.12.2006, CISG-online 1565; OGH, 8.11.2005, CISG-online 1156; Tribunale di Padova, 11.1.2005, CISG-online 967 = Riv. dir. int. priv. proc. 2005, 791 ff.; CA Paris, 6.11.2001, CISG-online 677; Civ., 26.6.2001, CISG-online 598 = D. 2001, Jur. 3607.

[108] *Schlechtriem/Schwenzer/Schlechtriem*, CISG Commentary, 2. Aufl., Intro to Arts 1–6, Rn. 26.
[109] *Lohmann*, Parteiautonomie, S. 124; MünchKomm/*Westermann*, Vor Art. 1, Rn. 7; vgl. in der Rechtsprechung OLG Schleswig, 29.10.2002, CISG-online 717 = IHR 2003, 67: „Der Inhalt des CISG ist unmittelbar anwendbares deutsches Recht".
[110] So schon *Herber*, 2. Aufl., Vor Artt. 1–6 Rn. 26.
[111] Vgl. Einheitliches Gesetz über den internationalen Kauf beweglicher Sachen vom 17. Juli 1973, BGBl. 1973 I 856; Einheitliches Gesetz über den Abschluss von internationalen Kaufverträgen über bewegliche Sachen vom 17. Juli 1973, BGBl. 1973 I 868.
[112] *Schlechtriem/Schwenzer/Schlechtriem*, CISG Commentary, 2. Aufl., Intro to Arts 1–6, Rn. 27; MünchKomm/*Westermann*, Vor Art. 1, Rn. 3.
[113] Die verbindlichen Fassungen des CISG sind abgedruckt in: *Kathrein/Magrau*, S. 169 ff.
[114] Siehe *Herber*, 2. Aufl., Unterzeichnungsklausel Rn. 1; *Schlechtriem/Schwenzer/Schwenzer/Hachem*, CISG Commentary, Intro to Arts 1–6, Rn. 16; *Schwenzer/Hachem/Kee*, Rn. 3.17; *Staudinger/Magnus*, Unterzeichnungsklausel, Rn. 1.
[115] Näher hierzu Art. 7 Rn. 33 ff.
[116] Siehe diesbezüglich die Bemerkungen des schwedischen Delegierten anlässlich der Diplomatischen Konferenz: „English had been more or less the working language", O.R., S. 272.
[117] So auch *Achilles*, Art. 7, Rn. 4; *Brunner*, Art. 7, Rn. 5; *Gruber*, Methoden, S. 142; *Honsell/Melis*, Art. 7, Rn. 10; MünchKomm/*Westermann*, Art. 7, Rn. 7; *Piltz*, Internationales Kaufrecht, Rn. 2–183; *Staudinger/Magnus*, Art. 7, Rn. 17 und 33; a.A. *Flechtner*, 17 J.L. & Com. (1998), 187, 208, der sich gegen die Bevorzugung, auch im Falle eines Widerspruchs der verschiedenen verbindlichen Textfassungen, der englischen Originalfassung ausspricht; ebenso nunmehr auch *Martinez Canellas*, S. 178. Auch die Rechtsprechung spricht sich im Zweifel für den Vorrang der englischen (und französischen) Fassung aus; vgl. BGer, 13.11.2003, CISG-online 840: „Bei Unklarheiten über den Wortlaut ist auf die Originaltexte abzustellen, wobei der englischen und sekundär der französischen Fassung eine erhöhte Bedeutung zukommt, da Englisch und Französisch die offiziellen Konferenzsprachen waren und die Verhandlungen hauptsächlich auf Englisch geführt wurden".
[118] Vgl. die Denkschrift, S. 38; *Schlechtriem/Schwenzer/Schwenzer/Hachem*, CISG Commentary, Intro to Arts 1–6, Rn. 15.
[119] So auch *Schwenzer/Hachem/Kee*, Rn. 3.17; *Staudinger/Magnus*, Art. 7, Rn. 15.
[120] MünchKomm/*Westermann*, Vor Art. 1, Rn. 16; *Schroeter*, VJ (2001), 74, 76, Fn. 4.

sollte, unter anderem auch, weil der unverbindlichen deutschen Übersetzung die Vermutung der Richtigkeit m. E. nicht ohne weiteres beigemessen werden kann.[121]

28 Ein Teil der Lehre[122] hat diesbezüglich nicht nur hervorgehoben, dass sich bei verschiedenen Vorschriften **Ungenauigkeiten** finden[123] (so wird etwa in Art. 46 III die Wendung „may require", „peut exiger", mit „kann auffordern" und nicht – was wohl richtiger wäre – mit „kann verlangen" übersetzt);[124] er hat auch festgestellt, dass die Übersetzung einiger **Formulierungen unrichtig** ist. So ist zum Beispiel[125] die Wendung „that may be known to him", „dont il peut avoir connaissance", in Art. 65 I mit „soweit ihm diese bekannt sind" übersetzt worden. Diese Übersetzung ist jedoch unrichtig.[126] Der Text hätte mit der Formulierung „soweit er diese kennen kann" übersetzt werden müssen. Diese Auffassung wird *impliciter* von der h. L. bestätigt, wenn diese dem Verkäufer auferlegt, bei der Durchführung der Spezifikation die Bedürfnisse des Käufers zu berücksichtigen, die der Verkäufer „kennen kann".[127]

3. UN-Kaufrecht und nationales Recht

29 Wie erwähnt,[128] dienen die Vorschriften zum Anwendungsbereich unter anderem der Abgrenzung gegenüber dem innerstaatlichen Recht.[129] Dies schließt aber nicht aus, dass letzteres auch dann relevant sein kann, wenn das CISG zur Anwendung kommt.[130]

30 Dies ergibt sich auch aus dem Übereinkommen selbst.[131] Diesbezüglich sei beispielhaft Art. 28 erwähnt, der statuiert, dass eine Entscheidung auf **Erfüllung in Natur** („specific performance") vom einem Gericht nur dann gefällt werden muss, wenn es dies auch nach **seinem eigenen Recht** bei gleichartigen Kaufverträgen täte.[132] Insoweit hängt das Verurteilenmüssen (zur Leistung in Natur) also von innerstaatlichem Recht ab (und welchem in diesem Fall daher „limitative" Wirkung zukommt).[133] Als weiteres Beispiel einer **ausdrücklichen Bezugnahme auf innerstaatliches Recht** in einer Vorschrift des CISG sei Art. 96 erwähnt:[134] Dieser lässt die Möglichkeit eines Vorbehalts nach Art. 96 von den innerstaatlichen Formvorschriften abhängen.

31 Innerstaatliches Recht ist aber auch in anderen, von einer ausdrücklichen Bezugnahme auf dieses unabhängigen Fällen durchaus relevant. Dies ergibt sich bereits aus der **nicht abschließenden Natur**[135] des CISG: Das Übereinkommen erfasst weder alle Kaufverträge[136] noch

---

[121] MünchKomm/*Westermann,* Vor Art. 1, Rn. 16; a. A. *Herber,* 2. Aufl., Vor Artt. 1–6 Rn. 30, der der deutschen Übersetzung „zumindest" die Vermutung der Richtigkeit beimisst.

[122] Vgl. *Honsell/Siehr,* Art. 7, Rn. 10; *Staudinger/Magnus,* Art. 7, Rn. 19.

[123] Dies wird etwa von *Schmid,* Lückenfüllung und Normenkonkurrenz, S. 23, übersehen, was diesen Autor zur (unrichtigen) Schlussfolgerung veranlasst, es bestehe kein Anlass, auf die Originalfassungen zurückzugreifen.

[124] Vgl. außerdem die Übersetzung der Formulierung „for a period of time" in Art. 36 II mit der Wendung „für eine bestimmte Zeit"; gemeint war aber „für eine gewisse Zeit".

[125] Vgl. auch die Übersetzung der in Art. 79 I enthaltenen Wendung „beyond his control" mit der Formulierung „außerhalb ihres Einflussbereichs"; diese Formulierung scheint schwächer zu sein, d. h. gemäß der deutschen Übersetzung wird sich die nicht erfüllende Partei eher entlasten können.

[126] So ausdrücklich *Staudinger/Magnus,* Art. 65, Rn. 3.

[127] Vgl. *Mohs,* Art. 65, Rn. 6; *Herber/Czerwenka,* Art. 65, Rn. 5.

[128] Vgl. oben Rn. 5.

[129] So auch *Herber,* 2. Aufl., Vor Artt. 1–6 Rn. 4.

[130] Ebenso *Andreason,* B. Y. U. L. Rev. (1999), 351, 378; *Frignani/Torsello,* Il contratto itnernazionale, S. 443.

[131] Vgl. hierzu etwa *Ferrari,* RIW 2002, 169, 176.

[132] Vgl. zu Art. 28 etwa *Catalano,* 71 Tul. L. Rev. (1997), 1807 ff.; *Piliounis,* 12 Pace Int'l L. Rev. (2000), 1 ff.; *Shen,* 13 Ariz. J. Int'l & Comp. L. (1996), 253 ff.; *Walt,* 26 Texas Int'l L. J. (1991), 211 ff.

[133] So *Marchand,* Limites de l'uniformisation matérielle, S. 29.

[134] So auch *Schmid,* Lückenfüllung und Normenkonkurrenz, S. 51.

[135] Vgl. *De Ly,* 25 J. L. & Com. (2005), 1; *Ferrari,* Int. Bus. L. J. 2003, 221, 226; *Witz,* D. 2002, Chron. 2796, 2797; a. A. aber BGer, 15.9.2000, CISG-online 770, das das CISG als „abschließende Regelung" bezeichnet; ebenso BezG Laufen, 7.5.1993, CISG-online 136, der das CISG als „abschließende […] Kaufrechtsordnung" definiert; in der Lehre ebenso *Shariff/de Carteret,* 9 Asper Rev. Int'l Bus. & Trade L. (2009) 21, 55.

[136] Vgl. etwa Art. 2.

alle sich aus internationalen Kaufgeschäften ergebenden Rechtsfragen.[137] Diese Kaufverträge und die nicht erfassten Rechtsfragen müssen anhand des in üblicher Weise bestimmten anwendbaren Rechts geregelt werden,[138] weshalb ein Teil der Lehre auch vom **„suppletiven"** bzw. „ergänzenden" Charakter des innerstaatlichen Rechts gesprochen hat.[139]

Innerstaatliches Recht kann aber auch zur Regelung von vom Übereinkommen erfasster **32** Fragen herangezogen werden, und zwar dann, wenn die Parteien die Vorschriften des Übereinkommens ausgeschlossen haben[140] (**substitutive Wirkung** des innerstaatlichen Rechts).[141]

Ferner muss erwähnt werden, dass innerstaatliches Recht auch **„ausfüllenden"** Cha- **33** rakter hat. Dies gilt immer dann, wenn ein Begriff nicht autonom, d. h., aus sich selbst heraus, sondern anhand des anwendbaren nationalen Rechts ausgelegt werden muss. Als Beispiel eines solchen Begriffs, der auch für die Anwendbarkeit des CISG relevant ist, sei hier lediglich auf den der „Vertragspartei" hingewiesen.[142] Wer „Vertragspartei" ist, bestimmt sich nach innerstaatlichem Recht.[143] Welche anderen Begriffe „national" ausgefüllt werden, wird an entsprechender Stelle hervorgehoben.[144]

4. UN-Kaufrecht und IPR

Genauso wie die Haager Kaufgesetze, im Gegensatz jedoch zu anderen Einheitssach- **34** rechtskonvention, wie etwa die CMR[145] oder das UNCITRAL Übereinkommen über die Abtretung von Forderungen im internationalen Handel; die auch Kollisionsnormen enthenhalten,[146] enthält das CISG selbst keine IPR Vorschriften,[147] sondern nur materielles Vertragsrecht.[148] Ein Konflikt mit der Rom-I VO und dem Römischen Übereinkommen der EG-Staaten über das auf vertragliche Schuldverhältnisse anwendbare Recht vom 19. Juni 1980, das in verschiedenen Vertragsstaaten des CISG in Kraft ist, und das trotz Inkrafttretens der Rom-I VO auch weiterhin auf vor dem 18.12.2009 geschlossene Verträge

---

[137] So ausdrücklich etwa *Staudinger/Magnus*, Art. 4, Rn. 1; vgl. auch *Andreason*, B. Y. U. L. Rev. (1999), 351, 375; *Bamberger/Roth/Saenger*, Art. 4, Rn. 1; *G. Bell*, 9 Singapore Y. B. Int'l L. (2005), 55, 67; *Brunner*, Art. 4, Rn. 1; *Cetiner*, S. 19; *Cuniberti*, 39 Vand. J. Transnat'l L. (2006), 1511, 1544; *De Ly*, 25 J. L. & Com. (2005), 1; *Ferrari*, IHR 2006, 1, 2 und 11; *Ferrari u. a./Saenger*, Internationales Vertragsrecht, Art. 4, Rn. 1; *Frignani/Torsello*, Il contratto itnernazionale, S. 444; *Gianuzzi*, 28 L. & Pol'y Int'l Bus. (1997), 991, 1016; *Gstoehl*, östZfRvgl 1998, 1; *Hayward*, 14 VJ (2010), 193, 219; *Kröll u. a./Perales Viscasillas*, Art. 1, Rn. 6; *Niemann*, Einheitliche Anwendung, S. 30; *Ragno*, Convenzione di Vienna e Diritto europeo, S. 23; *Sannini*, L'applicazione, S. 121 f.; *Schlechtriem*, 36 Vict. U. Well. L. Rev. (2005), 781, 784; *Schlechtriem/Schwenzer/Schlechtriem*, CISG Commentary, 2. Aufl., Art. 4, Rn. 3; *Schwenzer/Hachem/Kee*, Rn. 3.19; *Schroeter*, 6 VJ (2002), 257, 263; *ders.*, 5 VJ (2001), 74; Spagnolo, 21 Temp. Int'l & Comp. L. J. (2007), 261, 305; *Tescaro*, Contr. Imp. E. 2007, 319; *Torsello*, The CISG's Impact, S. 214 ff.; *Trompenaars*, S. 18 f.; *Vida*, IPRax 2002, 146, 147; *Walt*, 35 UCC L. J. (2002), 43; *ders.*, 25 Int'l Rev. L. & Econ. (2005), 342, 343; *C. Witz*, Int. Bus. L. J. 2001, 253, 261.

[138] *Frignani/Torsello*, Il contratto itnernazionale, 444; *Kröll u. a./Perales Viscasillas*, Art. 1, Rn. 6; *Schlechtriem*, 36 Vict. U. Well. L. Rev. (2005), 781, 784.

[139] Vgl. ausführlich hierzu *Marchand*, Limites de l'uniformisation matérielle, S. 26 f.; a. A. BGer, 15.9.2000, CISG-online 770, das ausschließt, dass das CISG suppletiven Charakter haben kann.

[140] Vgl. auch *Ferrari*, IHR 2006, 1, 14 ff.; *Frignani/Torsello*, Il contratto itnernazionale, S. 443; *Torsello*, Common Features, S. 115.

[141] Vgl. *Marchand*, Limites de l'uniformisation matérielle, S. 28.

[142] Allgemein zur Frage, ob und welche Begriffe des Übereinkommens nicht autonom, sondern im Lichte innerstaatlichen Rechts auszulegen sind, siehe *Ferrari*, Int'l Contr. Adviser (1998), 33 ff.

[143] So schon *Ferrari*, Applicabilità ed applicazioni, S. 50, Fn. 74 m. w. N.

[144] Vgl. etwa zur Streitfrage, ob der Begriff der „Gültigkeit" autonom ausgelegt werden muss, Art. 4 Rn. 15 ff.

[145] Vgl. BGBl. 1961 II 1119.

[146] Vgl. hierzu MünchKommHGB/*Basedow*, Einleitung CMR, Rn. 38; *Koller*, Vor Art. 1 CMR, Rn. 3.

[147] MünchKomm/*Westermann*, Vor Art. 1, Rn. 6; so ausdrücklich in der Rechtsprechung Tribunal cantonal du Jura, 3.11.2004, CISG-online 965.

[148] So auch Trib. Com. Bruxelles, 5.10.1994, CISG-online 447; vgl. auch KG Jura, 3.11.2004, CISG-online 965; Tribunale di Padova, 25.2.2004, CISG-online 819; Cass., 20.4.2004, CISG-online 927; OGH, 23.5.2005, CISG-online 1041; *McDowell Valley Vineyards, Inc. v. Sabaté USA Inc. et al.*, U. S. Dist. Ct. (N. D. Cal.), 2.11.2005, 2005 WL 2893848 (N. D. Cal.); Tribunale di Padova, 10.1.2006, CISG-online 1157; Tribunale di Forlì, 16.2.2009, CISG-online 1780; OGer Aargau, 3.3.2009, CISG-online 2013; Cass., 5.10.2009, CISG-online 2105.

anwendbar ist, ist dennoch möglich, da auch diese Instrumente zwischenparteiliche Beziehungen bei internationalen Kaufverträgen betreffen, diese allerdings durch Verweisung auf nationales Vertragsrecht regeln.[149] Fraglich ist jedoch, ob dieser Konflikt, ex Art. 25 der Rom-I VO bzw. Art. 21 des EVÜ gelöst werden muss,[150] wonach diese Instrumente „nicht die Anwendung internationaler Übereinkommen, denen ein Vertragsstaat angehört oder angehören wird"[151] berühren.[152] Im Verhältnis zum EVÜ, das in Deutschland durch Übernahme seines wesentlichen Inhalts in das EGBGB in Kraft gesetzt wurde, ergab sich der Vorrang des CISG – so auch die Rechtsprechung –[153] aus Art. 3 II EGBGB a. F.[154] M. E.[155] muss man aber nicht nur in Bezug auf das Verhältnis des CISG zum EVÜ vom Vorrang des CISG ausgehen; auch mit Bezug auf das Rangverhältnis zwischen dem CISG und dem Haager IPR-Übereinkommen von 1955, das in verschiedenen europäischen Ländern in Kraft ist, muss vom Vorrang des CISG ausgegangen werden,[156] und dies selbst dann, wenn die Lösung dieses Konventionskonflikts[157] auf den ersten Blick dem Haager IPR-Übereinkommen Vorrang zukommen lassen müsste, sieht doch nur das CISG (Art. 90) – und nicht auch das Haager IPR-Übereinkommen – eine dem Art. 21 EVÜ bzw. Art. 25 Rom-I VO ähnliche Regel vor,. M. E. ist das CISG in Bezug auf IPR-Vorschriften nämlich immer vorrangig anwendbar,[158] und zwar kraft des Grundsatzes, wonach „der unbedingte Vorrang einer vereinheitlichten Sachnorm vor jeder konkurrierenden Kollisionsnorm [...] sich im Rangverhältnis der scheinbar kollidierenden völkerrechtlichen Abkommen nieder(schlägt), und zwar derart, dass den materiellen Abkommen als den weit gewichtigeren der Vorrang gebührt".[159] Aus diesem Grund ist auch vom Vorrang des CISG gegenüber der Rom-I VO auszugehen,[160] den ein Teil der Lehre hingegen damit rechtfertigen will, dass die Rom-I VO eine dem Art. 90 CISG ähnliche Regel, nämlich Art. 25, enthalte.[161] Die hier vertretene

---

[149] Vgl. hierzu *Ferrari*, Corr. giur. 2000, 932 ff.

[150] Vgl. zur Lösung des Konfliktes zwischen dem CISG und dem Übereinkommen der EG-Staaten über das auf vertragliche Schuldverhältnisse anwendbare Recht ex Art. 21 desselben, Cass. civ., 18.10.2002, Nr. 14 837, nicht veröffentlicht.

[151] Art. 21 EuIPRÜ.

[152] So, mit Bezug jedoch auf die CMR und das Übereinkommen der EG-Staaten über das auf vertragliche Schuldverhältnisse anwendbare Recht, MünchKommHGB/*Basedow*, Einleitung CMR, Rn. 26.

[153] OLG Schleswig, 29.10.2002, CISG-online 717 = IHR 2003, 67.

[154] Vgl. *T. M. Müller*, Beweislast, S. 3; MünchKommHGB/*Basedow*, Einleitung CMR, Rn. 26; *Schmidt-Kessel*, FS *Schlechtriem*, S. 269.

[155] Vgl. hierzu *Ferrari*, Corr. giur. 2002, 372, 374 f.

[156] Vgl. in der Lehre statt aller *Fallon/Philippe*, Journal des Tribunaux, 1998, 17, 19; a. A. *Naumann*, S. 18; *Schwenzer/Hachem/Kee*, Rn. 3.25.

[157] Siehe hierzu allgemein *Majoros*, Les conventions internationales en matière de droit privé, Paris: Pédone (Bd. I, 1976), (Bd. II, 1980); *ders.*, RabelsZ 46 (1982), 84; *Volken*, Konventionskonflikte; *Wilting*, Vertragskonkurrenz im Völkerrecht.

[158] Vgl. hierzu auch *Ragno*, Convenzione di Vienna e Diritto europeo, S. 76 ff.; *Veneziano*, Dir. comm. int. 2001, 509, 513; vgl. in der Rechtsprechung LG Krefeld, 20.9.2006, CISG-online 1459: „Das UN-Kaufrecht hat als vereinheitlichtes Recht vor jeder konkurrierenden Kollisionsnorm und internationalen Privatrecht Vorrang"; ebenso Tribunale di Forlì, 16.2.2009, CISG-online 1780; Court of First Instance of Athens, Aktenzeichen 4505/2009 (ohne Datum), CISG-online 2228; Tribunale di Forlì, 11.12.2008, CISG-online 1729; OLG Schleswig, 24.10.2008, CISG-online 2020; Tribunale di Rovereto, 21.11.2007, CISG-online 1590; Tribunale di Padova, 31.3.2004, CISG-online 823; Tribunale di Padova, 25.2.2004, CISG-online 819; Kantonsgericht Schaffhausen, 20.10.2003, CISG-online 957; Obergericht des Kantons Thurgau, 11.9.2003, CISG-online 1810; OGH, 18.12.2002, CISG-online 1279; Tribunale di Rimini, 26.11.2002, CISG-online 737; Tribunale di Vigevano, 12.7.2000, CISG-online 493; Tribunale di Pavia, 29.12.1999, CISG-online 678.

[159] *Zweigert/Drobnig*, RabelsZ 29 (1965), 146, 161; vgl. neuerdings auch *Chiomenti*, EuLF 2005, 141, 142; *Lohmann*, Parteiautonomie, S. 41; in der Rechtsprechung gehen vom Vorrang des CISG im Verhältnis zu IPR-Vorschriften, neben den in der vorigen Fn. zitierten Urteilen, auch folgende Urteile aus: HGer Zürich, 30.11.1998, CISG-online 415 = SZIER 1999, 186 ff.; OLG Dresden, 9.7.1998, CISG-online 559 = IHR 2001, 18 f.; LG Heilbronn, 15.9.1997, CISG-online 562; OLG Frankfurt a. M., 20.4.1994, CISG-online 125 = RIW 1995, 593 f.

[160] Kritisch zu diesem Ansatz *Schroeter*, UN-Kaufrecht, § 14, Rn. 87 ff.

[161] So etwa *Schlechtriem/Schwenzer/Schwenzer/Hachem*, CISG Commentary, Intro to Arts 1–6, Rn. 6, die freilich nicht erklären, wie der Konflikt zwischen Art. 90 CISG und Art. 25 Rom-I VO gelöst werden soll, in Bezug auf das Verhältnis zwischen CISG und EuIPRÜ aber den Vorrang des CISG damit begründen, dass das

Ansicht ist mittlerweile auch von verschiedenen (italienischen) Gerichten herangezogen worden, um das Verhältnis zwischen CISG und IPR-Vorschriften zu klären. In einem Urteil des Tribunale di Pavia[162] heißt es ausdrücklich, dass „dem Rückgriff auf die Vorschriften des internationalen Privatrechts der auf Vorschriften des (durch Übereinkommen gesetzten) internationalen Einheitssachrechts vorzuziehen ist, da diese Vorschriften aufgrund ihrer Spezialität den Kollisionsnormen vorgehen". In neueren Urteilen sind andere italienische Gerichte[163] sogar weiter gegangen als der Tribunale di Pavia, auf dessen Urteil sich die neuere Entscheidungen auch ausdrücklich beziehen, indem sie festgelegt haben, worin das erwähnte „Spezialitätsverhältnis" besteht: „Dieses Spezialitätsverhältnis ergibt sich nicht nur daraus, dass der Anwendungsbereich des Wiener Kaufrechts enger gefasst ist (dieses ist nur auf Kaufverträge anwendbar, bei denen der internationale Bezug sich aus dem Standort der Niederlassung der Vertragsparteien in unterschiedlichen Staaten ergibt, während – wie allgemein bekannt – das [in Italien anwendbare] Haager-Übereinkommen jeden Typ ‚internationalen' Kaufvertrags betrifft), sondern insbesondere daraus, dass die Anwendung von vereinheitlichten Normen materiellen Rechts gegenüber der Anwendung von Vorschriften des Internationalen Privatrechts (unabhängig von ihrer Quelle) immer Vorrang haben muss. Denn die ersten sind *per definitionem* spezieller als die zweiten, da sie auf direktem Wege das materielle Rechtsproblem lösen und dabei den zweifachen Schritt, erst das anwendbare Recht zu bestimmen, um dieses sodann anzuwenden, entfallen lassen. Dieser Vorgang ist immer notwendig, wenn auf die Vorschriften des Internationalen Privatrechts Bezug genommen wird".[164] Damit hat das italienische Gericht die von der Lehre vorgeschlagene Lösung[165] übernommen und die Frage nach dem Verhältnis zwischen CISG und nationalem IPR hoffentlich endgültig gelöst.[166]

Im Gegensatz zu den Verfassern der Haager Kaufgesetze, die (zu Unrecht)[167] davon **35** ausgegangen sind, es sei möglich, ein Einheitskaufrecht zu schaffen,[168] das einen Rekurs auf Kollisionsnormen überflüssig mache,[169] reflektiert das CISG die gegenteilige Meinung der Konventionsgeber von 1980, wonach ein Rückgriff auf Kollisionsnormen nicht gänzlich ausgeschlossen werden kann.[170] Diese zweifelsfrei realistischere Einstellung[171] hat unter anderem dazu geführt, dass die „internen" Lücken des CISG, d. h., die im CISG geregelten Gegenstände, auf die das Übereinkommen jedoch unmittelbar keine Antwort gibt, nunmehr – und insoweit abweichend von den Haager Kaufgesetzen –[172] gemäß Art. 7 II nach

---

CISG *lex specialis* gegenüber dem EuIPRÜ sei, und zwar insoweit, als das CISG nur auf Warenkaufverträge, das EuIPRÜ auch auf andere Vertragstypen anwendbar sei. Die Autoren verkennen, dass der im Text vertretene Ansatz (ausdrücklich) auf das Verhältnis zwischen *lex specialis – lex generalis* als Rechtfertigungsgrund für den Vorrang des CISG abstellt; auf das Verhältnis *lex specialis – lex generalis* abstellend, um den Vorrang des CISG zu rechtfertigen, neuerdings auch *Maultzsch*, FS Schwenzer, S. 1213, 1218.
[162] Tribunale di Pavia, 29.12.1999, CISG-online 678 = Corr. giur. 2000, 932, 932, m. Anm. *Ferrari*.
[163] Tribunale di Vigevano, 12.7.2000, CISG-online 493 = IHR 2001, 72 ff.; Tribunale di Rimini, 26.11.2002, CISG-online 737 = Giur. it. 2003, 896 ff., m. Anm. *Ferrari*; Tribunale di Padova, 25.2.2004, CISG-online 819 = Giur. it. 2004, 1405 ff., m. Anm. *Ferrari*; Tribunale di Padova, 31.3.2004, CISG-online 823 = Giur. merito 2004, 1065 ff., m. Anm. *Ferrari*; Tribunale di Padova, 11.1.2005, CISG-online 967 = Riv. dir. int. priv. proc. 2005, 791 ff.; Tribunale di Rovereto, 21.9.2007, CISG-online 1590; Tribunale di Forlì, 11.12.2008, CISG-online 1729.
[164] Tribunale di Vigevano, 12.7.2000, CISG-online 493 = IHR 2001, 72, 73.
[165] Vgl. hierzu schon *Ferrari*, Corr. giur. 2000, 933, 935; *Majoros*, Droit international privé, S. 6.
[166] In der Rechtsprechung anderer Länder, vgl. vor allem BezG Sissach, 5.11.1998, CISG-online 1466.
[167] Vgl. *Zweigert/Drobnig*, RabelsZ 29 (1965), 146–165.
[168] Vgl. Art. 2 EAG: „Soweit dieses Gesetz nicht etwas anderes bestimmt, sind bei seiner Anwendung die Regeln des internationalen Privatrechts ausgeschlossen."
[169] Vgl. kritisch hierzu auch *Kropholler*, RabelsZ 38 (1974), 372–387.
[170] So auch *Melin*, Gesetzesauslegung, S. 332; *Schlechtriem*, 36 Vict. U. Well. L. Rev. (2005), 781, 784; vgl. auch OLG Schleswig, 29.10.2002, CISG-online 717 = IHR 2003, 67; wohl a. A. *Niemann*, Einheitliche Anwendung, S. 25 f.
[171] *Frignani/Torsello*, Il contratto itnernazionale, S. 443.
[172] Ein Teil der Lehre hatte sich jedoch bereits unter den Haager Kaufgesetzen für die im CISG aufgenomme Lösung ausgesprochen; vgl. *Kropholler*, RabelsZ 38 (1974), 372–387.

Vor Artt. 1–6 35   Teil I. Kapitel I. Anwendungsbereich

dem Recht zu schließen sind, das nach den Regeln des IPR anzuwenden ist (aber nur insoweit sie nicht nach den dem CISG zugrunde liegenden allgemeinen Grundsätzen geschlossen werden können).[173]

---

[173] Siehe zur Frage der Lückenfüllung nach CISG (und anderen Einheitsvertragsrechtskonventionen) zuletzt Ferrari, JZ 1998, 9 ff.

Art. 1 [Anwendungsbereich]

(1) Dieses Übereinkommen ist auf Kaufverträge über Waren zwischen Parteien anzuwenden, die ihre Niederlassung in verschiedenen Staaten haben,
a) wenn diese Staaten Vertragsstaaten sind oder
b) wenn die Regeln des internationalen Privatrechts zur Anwendung des Rechts eines Vertragsstaats führen.

(2) Die Tatsache, daß die Parteien ihre Niederlassung in verschiedenen Staaten haben, wird nicht berücksichtigt, wenn sie sich nicht aus dem Vertrag, aus früheren Geschäftsbeziehungen oder aus Verhandlungen oder Auskünften ergibt, die vor oder bei Vertragsabschluß zwischen den Parteien geführt oder von ihnen erteilt worden sind.

(3) Bei Anwendung dieses Übereinkommens wird weder berücksichtigt, welche Staatsangehörigkeit die Parteien haben, noch ob sie Kaufleute oder Nichtkaufleute sind oder ob der Vertrag handelsrechtlicher oder bürgerlich-rechtlicher* Art ist.

Art. 1

(1) This Convention applies to contracts of sale of goods between parties whose places of business are in different States:

(a) when the States are Contracting States; or
(b) when the rules of private international law lead to the application of the law of a Contracting State.

(2) The fact that the parties have their places of business in different States is to be disregarded whenever this fact does not appear either from the contract or from any dealings between, or from information disclosed by, the parties at any time before or at the conclusion of the contract.

(3) Neither the nationality of the parties nor the civil or commercial character of the parties or of the contract is to be taken into consideration in determining the application of this Convention.

Art. 1

1) La présente Convention s'applique aux contrats de vente de marchandises entre des parties ayant leur établissement dans des Etats différents:

a) lorsque ces Etats sont des Etats contractants; ou
b) lorsque les règles du droit international privé mènent à l'application de la loi d'un Etat contractant.

2) Il n'est pas tenu compte du fait que les parties ont leur établissement dans des Etats différents lorsque ce fait ne ressort ni du contrat, ni de transactions antérieures entre les parties, ni de renseignements „donnés par elles à un moment quelconque avant la conclusion ou lors de la conclusion du contrat.

3) Ni la nationalité des parties ni le caractère civil ou commercial des parties ou du contrat ne sont pris en considération pour l'application de la présente" Convention.

Übersicht

	Rn.
I. Vorgeschichte	1
II. Allgemeines	8
1. Internationalität des Kaufvertrages	8
2. Eingrenzung auf Verträge mit Beziehungen zu einem oder mehr Vertragsstaaten	10
3. Beziehungen zwischen Art. 1 und anderen Vorschriften	11
III. Der sachliche Anwendungsbereich	12
1. Kaufvertrag und andere vom Übereinkommen geregelte Verträge	12
2. Nicht in den sachlichen Anwendungsbereich fallende Verträge	25
3. Waren im Sinne des CISG	34
IV. Der persönlich-räumliche Anwendungsbereich	40
1. Die Internationalität des Kaufvertrages	40
2. Der Begriff der Niederlassung	44
3. Die Erkennbarkeit der Internationalität des Kaufvertrages	48

---

* Österreich, Schweiz: zivilrechtlicher.

    4. Unerheblichkeit der Staatsangehörigkeit und der
Kaufmannseigenschaft 59
V. Die Beziehung zu einem oder mehreren Vertragsstaaten als
Anwendungsvoraussetzung des Übereinkommens 61
    1. Allgemeines 61
    2. Die autonome Anwendung des Übereinkommens 63
    3. Anwendung kraft kollisionsrechtlicher Verweisung auf Vertragsstaatenrecht 69
    4. Der Vorbehalt nach Art. 95 und dessen Wirkung 77
    5. Anwendung des Übereinkommens durch Schiedsgerichte 82
    6. Parteiwille und Anwendung des CISG bei fehlender
Anwendungsvoraussetzung 85

Vorläufer und **Entwürfe:** Art. 1 I, III, V; Artt. 2, 7 EKG; Art. 1 I, II, III EAG; Genfer E 1976 Artt. 1, 6; Wiener E 1977 Art. 1; New Yorker E 1978 Art. 1.

I. Vorgeschichte

1   Der Anwendungsbereich des Haager Kaufrechts ist oft kritisiert worden. Es wurde hervorgehoben, dass er zu weit sei,[1] da er sich auch auf Kaufverträge zwischen Vertragsparteien ohne Beziehung zu Vertragsstaaten ausdehne[2] und daher die Zulassung verschiedener Vorbehalte durch die Konferenz von 1964 erforderlich gemacht habe, deren Ausübung durch die meisten Vertragsstaaten die Einheitlichkeit des Anwendungsbereichs kompliziert und unübersichtlich gemacht habe.[3] Diese Kritik ist durchaus angebracht, bedenkt man, wie unterschiedlich die verschiedenen Vorbehaltsmöglichkeiten waren:[4] Gemäß Art. III der Einführungskonventionen zu EKG und EAG konnten die Vertragsstaaten zum Beispiel die Anwendbarkeit des Übereinkommens auf Verträge zwischen Vertragsparteien mit Niederlassung in verschiedenen Vertragsstaaten beschränken (eine Vorbehaltsmöglichkeit, von der auch die BR Deutschland Gebrauch gemacht hat),[5] während sie sich gemäß einer anderen Vorschrift, Art. VI der genannten Einführungskonventionen, die Vorschaltung von Kauf-IPR-Konventionen vorbehalten konnten.[6]

2   Die an der Kompliziertheit und der durch verschiedene Vorbehaltsmöglichkeiten eröffnete Uneinheitlichkeit des Anwendungsbereichs des Haager Kaufrechts geäußerte Kritik[7] hat die Konventionsgeber dazu veranlasst, den Anwendungsbereich durch Abweichungen[8] vom Haager Vorbild zu vereinfachen.[9]

3   Aus diesem Grund haben die Konventionsgeber auch auf die in den Haager Übereinkommen vorgesehenen (alternativen) objektiven Merkmale verzichtet.[10] Zwar wollte man zu Beginn der Ausarbeitung des Übereinkommens noch auf den grenzüberschreitenden Transport der Ware als internationalitätsbestimmendes Merkmal abstellen,[11] im Interesse der **Vereinfachung und Erweiterung des Anwendungsbereichs** beschloss man aber schon

---

    [1] Vgl. hierzu bereits *Dölle/Herber,* Art. 1 EKG, Rn. 2, 15 ff.; siehe neuerdings *Ferrari,* Vendita internazionale, S. 20 f.; *Sacerdoti,* Riv. trim. dir. proced. civ. 1990, 733, 736.
    [2] *Schlechtriem/Schwenzer/Schwenzer/Hachem,* CISG Commentary, Art. 1, Rn. 1.
    [3] Siehe MünchKomm/*Westermann,* Art. 1, Rn. 1; *Reczei,* 29 Am.J. Comp. L. (1981), 513, 515, Fn. 10; *Schlechtriem/Schwenzer/Schlechtriem,* CISG Commentary, 2. Aufl., Intro to Arts 1–6, Rn. 12.
    [4] Für einen detaillierteren Überblick über die verschiedenen Vorbehaltsmöglichkeiten, siehe *Frignani,* Contratto internazionale, S. 263.
    [5] Vgl. *Dölle/Herber,* Einf. vor Artt. 1–8 EKG, Rn. 10.
    [6] *Staudinger/Magnus,* Art. 1, Rn. 7 f.
    [7] YB I (1968–1970), S. 164, Nr. 25 ff.
    [8] Die Abweichungen des CISG vom Haager Kaufrecht wurden oft untersucht; vgl. statt aller *Ndulo,* 38 Int'l & Comp. L. Q. (1989), 1–25; *van der Velden,* Main Items, S. 46–106.
    [9] So auch *Luzzatto,* 46 Enc. D. (1993), 502, 507; *Schlechtriem/Schwenzer/Schlechtriem,* CISG Commentary, 2. Aufl., Art. 1, Rn. 2 ff.; *Schlechtriem/Schwenzer/Schwenzer/Hachem,* CISG Commentary, Intro to Arts 1–6, Rn. 1.
    [10] *Boschiero,* Le convenzioni, S. 268; *Staudinger/Magnus,* Art. 1, Rn. 7.
    [11] So schon *Herber,* 2. Aufl., Art. 1 Rn. 3.

sehr früh, die Internationalität des Vertrages allein durch die Niederlassung oder eventuell den gewöhnlichen Aufenthalt der Vertragsparteien zu bestimmen.[12] Gestützt wurde diese Entscheidung unter anderem auch darauf, dass es den Verkäufer bei einem Verkauf „FOB" oder „ex works" regelmäßig kaum interessiere, ob ein grenzüberschreitender Transport vorliege oder nicht.[13] Für die Internationalität ist nunmehr lediglich die Lokalisierung der Niederlassungen der Parteien relevant.[14]

Anstelle der objektiven internationalitätsbestimmenden Merkmale der Haager Übereinkommen haben die Konventionsgeber, um eine zu weite Ausweitung des Anwendungsbereichs zu vermeiden, in Abs. 2 jedoch das Erfordernis eingeführt, wonach das (subjektive)[15] internationalitätsbestimmende Merkmal, d. h. die Niederlassung der Parteien in verschiedenen Staaten, dann unberücksichtigt bleibt, wenn die **Internationalität** den Parteien vor oder bei Vertragsabschluss nicht **erkennbar** ist.[16]

Vor allem aber der Umstand, dass die Konventionsgeber vom sogenannten „**erga omnes approach**"[17] – oder „**Universalitätsprinzip**"[18] – abgegangen sind und daher auf die Vielzahl der in den Haager Übereinkommen vorgesehenen Vorbehaltsmöglichkeiten verzichten konnten, hat zur Vereinfachung des Anwendungsbereichs geführt.[19] Daran ändert auch der Umstand, dass die Konventionsgeber, zumindest der Meinung einiger Autoren nach,[20] das Universalitätsprinzip durch Art. 1 I lit. b) in gewissem Umfang wieder eingeführt haben,[21] nichts. Art. 1 I lit. b) hat den Vorteil, den Anwendungsbereich, der ohne diese Vorschrift zu eng ausgefallen wäre, auszudehnen,[22] ohne jedoch so weit wie das Universalitätsprinzip zu gehen;[23] dass es sich dabei um eine Vereinfachung handelt, geht unter anderem auch daraus hervor, dass die Einführung des Art. 1 I lit. b) lediglich eine Vorbehaltsmöglichkeit erforderlich gemacht hat.[24]

Dies bedeutet jedoch nicht, dass Art. 1 I lit. b) keine Probleme aufwirft. Dies hat die Delegation der BR Deutschland bereits anlässlich der Ausarbeitung des Übereinkommens hervorgehoben. Sie hat insbesondere beanstandet, dass die in Art. 1 I lit. b) enthaltene (kollisionsrechtliche) Anwendungsalternative zu Auslegungs- und Anwendungsproblemen führen könnte, da sie die Gefahr hervorriefe, infolge einer Sonderanknüpfung von Teilfragen nach dem IPR der lex fori nur zur teilweisen Anwendung des Übereinkommens zu führen,[25] und dass es schließlich nicht sachgerecht sei, wenn in einem internationalen Übereinkommen das Gegenseitigkeitsprinzip verlassen werde und die Vertragsstaaten verpflichtet seien, das Übereinkommen auch im Verhältnis zu Vertragsparteien aus Nichtvertragsstaaten anzuwenden.[26]

---

[12] YB II (1971), S. 52, Nr. 12 ff., insbesondere Nr. 14 ff.

[13] YB II (1971), S. 52, Nr. 17.

[14] So ausdrücklich auch OGH, 15.10.1998, CISG-online 380 = ZfRVgl 1999, 63; vgl. auch *Piltz*, NJW 2000, 553, 555.

[15] So qualifiziert das internationalitätsbestimmende Merkmal des CISG zum Beispiel *Reczei*, 29 Am. J. Comp. L. (1981), 513, 517; *Schlechtriem/Schwenzer/Schwenzer/Hachem*, CISG Commentary, Art. 1, Rn. 3 Fn. 14.

[16] YB II (1971), S. 52, Nr. 17.

[17] *Bianca/Carbone/Lopez de Gonzalo*, Art. 1, S. 4; *Sacerdoti*, Riv. trim. dir. proced. civ. 1990, 733, 738.

[18] Vgl. *Honnold/Flechtner*, Art. 1, Rn. 45; *Honnold*, 8 J.L. & Com. (1988), 1, 6; *Lohmann*, Privatautonomie, S. 30; *Schlechtriem/Schwenzer/Schwenzer/Hachem*, CISG Commentary, Art. 1, Rn. 2; *Tuggey*, 21 Texas Int'l L.J. (1986), 540, 542; *Winship*, 21 Cornell Int'l L.J. (1988), 487, 501.

[19] *Schlechtriem/Schwenzer/Schlechtriem*, CISG Commentary, 2. Aufl., Art. 1, Rn. 5.

[20] So *Herber*, 2. Aufl., Art. 1 Rn. 6.

[21] *Schlechtriem/Schwenzer/Schlechtriem*, CISG Commentary, 2. Aufl., Art. 1, Rn. 6.

[22] Positiv zu dieser Ausdehnung *U. Huber*, RabelsZ 43 (1979), 413, 424; *Pelichet*, Vente internationale, S. 39; *Volken*, Anwendungsvoraussetzungen, S. 96; kritisch hingegen *Grigera Naón*, S. 98; *Herber*, Anwendungsbereich, S. 36 f.; *Karollus*, JuS 1993, 378, 379.

[23] Vgl. *Ferrari*, Vendita internazionale, S. 38; *Schlechtriem/Schwenzer/Schwenzer/Hachem*, CISG Commentary, Art. 1, Rn. 5.

[24] *Czerwenka*, Rechtsanwendungsprobleme, S. 155 ff.

[25] Vgl. zu dieser Kritik auch *Schlechtriem*, Einheitliches UN-Kaufrecht, S. 10 f.; Botschaft des Schweizerischen Bundesrats, S. 758 f.

[26] O.R., S. 236 f., Nr. 9 ff.

7 Diese Beanstandungen haben zu einem deutschen, auf die Streichung des Art. 1 I lit. b) gerichteten Antrag geführt, der jedoch erfolglos geblieben ist. Die Mehrzahl der Delegationen hat sich dafür ausgesprochen, den Anwendungsbereich des Übereinkommens im Zweifel eher weit zu erstrecken.[27] Als Kompromiss[28] wurde jedoch die Möglichkeit eingeführt, die durch die in Art. 1 I lit. b) vorgesehene Anwendungsalternative erzeugte Ausdehnung des Anwendungsbereichs durch Erklärung eines Vorbehaltes ex Art. 95 einzuschränken.[29]

II. Allgemeines

1. Internationalität des Kaufvertrages

8 Nach Art. 1 I unterliegen die vom Übereinkommen erfassten Verträge nur dann demselben, wenn sie international sind, d. h., wenn die Vertragsparteien – bei Vertragsschluss –[30] ihre **Niederlassung in verschiedenen Staaten** haben.[31] Neben diesem subjektiven[32] Erfordernis verlangt das Übereinkommen kein weiteres Erfordernis,[33] anders noch als das Haager Kaufrecht, welches außerdem entweder einen zwischenstaatlichen Transport oder einen Vertragsabschluss über die Grenze oder ein Auseinanderfallen der Staaten des Vertragsabschlusses und der Lieferung erforderte.[34]

9 Die Reichweite der **Definition** der Internationalität wird allerdings durch Abs. 2 **eingeschränkt:**[35] Demnach muss die Internationalität des Vertrages für jede Vertragspartei bei Vertragsschluss aus den Umständen ersichtlich gewesen sein.[36]

2. Eingrenzung auf Verträge mit Beziehungen zu einem oder mehr Vertragsstaaten

10 Kumulativ zum erwähnten Internationalitätserfordernis verlangt das Übereinkommen, dass die Vertragsparteien oder der Vertrag einen Bezug zu einem oder mehreren Vertragsstaaten haben. Dieser Bezug besteht gemäß Art. 1 I lit. a) dann, wenn die Vertragsparteien ihre **Niederlassung in verschiedenen Vertragsstaaten** haben.[37] Gemäß Art. 1 I lit. b) liegt der notwendige Bezug aber auch dann vor, wenn die Vorschriften des Internationalen Privatrechts auf das Recht eines Vertragsstaates verweisen.[38] Ob man heute bezüglich dieser Alternative[39] noch von „einer ungewöhnlichen Konstruktion einer autonomen Anwendungsvorschrift" sprechen kann,[40] muss angezweifelt werden. Verschiedene neuere Einheitsprivatrechtskonventionen[41] umschreiben ihren räumlichen Anwendungsbereich anhand einer ähnlichen Regelung. Dies darf m. E. aber (noch) nicht dazu führen, von der Anwendbarkeit des Übereinkommens auf Grund kollisionsrechtlicher Verweisung auf Vertragsstaatenrecht als dem Ergebnis eines „klassischen Anwendungskriteriums" zu sprechen.[42]

---

[27] So *Staudinger/Magnus*, Art. 1, Rn. 11.
[28] Vgl. auch *Ferrari u. a./Saenger*, Internationales Vertragsrecht, Art. 1, Rn. 16.
[29] Siehe *Czerwenka*, Rechtsanwendungsprobleme, S. 156 f.; vgl. hierzu auch unten Rn. 77–81.
[30] Vgl. statt aller RB Hasselt, 20.9.2005, CISG-online 1496; OLG Dresden, 27.12.1999, CISG-online 511 = TranspR-IHR 2000, 20 ff.
[31] Vgl. zuletzt hierzu OLG Rostock, 10.10.2001, CISG-online 671; OLG Köln, 21.5.1996, CISG-online 254.
[32] So auch *Enderlein/Maskow/Strohbach*, Art. 1, Anm. 4.; *Ferrari*, Vendita internazionale, S. 22.
[33] *Ferrari u. a./Saenger*, Internationales Vertragsrecht, Art. 1, Rn. 9; *Herber/Czerwenka*, Art. 1, Rn. 9; *Rudolph*, Art. 1, Rn. 2.
[34] *Bamberger/Roth/Saenger*, Art. 1, Rn. 9.
[35] Vgl. auch *Herber*, Anwendungsbereich, S. 35; *Schlechtriem/Schwenzer/Schlechtriem*, CISG Commentary, 2. Aufl., Art. 1, Rn. 7.
[36] Vgl. *Hoyer*, Anwendungsbereich, S. 35.
[37] Vgl. unten Rn. 63–68.
[38] Vgl. unten Rn. 69–76.
[39] Dass es sich bei Art. 1 I lit. a) und lit. b) um Alternativen handelt, ist oft hervorgehoben worden; vgl. *Memmo*, Riv. trim. dir. priv. proced. 1983, 180, 205; *Pünder*, RIW 1990, 869.
[40] So noch *Herber*, 2. Aufl., Art. 1 Rn. 10.
[41] Vgl. Art. 2 I lit. b) des UNIDROIT Übereinkommens über Internationales Factoring.
[42] So aber *Cassoni*, Riv. dir. int. priv. proc. 1982, 429, 434.

Anwendungsbereich   11–13 **Art. 1**

3. Beziehungen zwischen Art. 1 und anderen Vorschriften

Der Zweck des Art. 1 liegt darin, den Anwendungsbereich des CISG festzulegen.⁴³ Dies **11** bedeutet jedoch nicht, dass Art. 1 allein für die genaue Bestimmung des Anwendungsbereichs des Übereinkommens ausreiche.⁴⁴ Dies ergibt sich einerseits daraus, dass einige der in Art. 1 zur Bestimmung des Anwendungsbereichs verwendeten Begriffe in anderen Vorschriften präzisiert werden.⁴⁵ Als Beispiel sei hier lediglich auf die Vertragsstaateneigenschaft hingewiesen, die sich aus in dem den Schlussbestimmungen gewidmeten Teil IV des Übereinkommens enthaltenen Vorschriften ergibt.⁴⁶ Andererseits ergibt sich dies auch daraus, dass der in Art. 1 umschriebene Anwendungsbereich durch einige Vorschriften eingeengt,⁴⁷ durch andere hingegen erweitert wird.⁴⁸

III. Der sachliche Anwendungsbereich

1. Kaufvertrag und andere vom Übereinkommen geregelte Verträge

Wie in den Haager Übereinkommen⁴⁹ fehlt auch in dem CISG eine ausdrückliche **12** Definition des Kaufvertrages. Dies ist sowohl durch die Rechtsprechung⁵⁰ als auch durch die Lehre⁵¹ immer wieder hervorgehoben worden. Das Fehlen einer ausdrücklichen Definition wurde bisweilen damit begründet, dass die in den verschiedenen Rechtsordnungen existierenden Definitionen sich nicht sehr voneinander unterscheiden, eine ausdrückliche Definition demnach unnötig sei.⁵² Bisweilen wurde das Fehlen einer ausdrücklichen Begriffsbestimmung aber gerade darauf zurückgeführt, dass diese auf Grund der Verschiedenheit der Definition unmöglich sei.⁵³

Das Fehlen einer ausdrücklichen Definition ist jedoch nicht mit der Unmöglichkeit **13** gleichzustellen, eine – autonome –⁵⁴ Definition auf der Grundlage des CISG erarbeiten zu

---

⁴³ In diesem Sinne *Staudinger/Magnus*, Art. 1, Rn. 1 ff.
⁴⁴ *Ferrari*, Vendita internazionale, S. 44; *Ferrari u. a./Saenger*, Internationales Vertragsrecht, Art. 1, Rn. 1; *Kröll u. a./Perales Viscasillas*, Art. 1, Rn. 1; *Schlechtriem*, Uniform Sales Law, S. 28.
⁴⁵ *Schlechtriem/Schwenzer/Schwenzer/Hachem*, CISG Commentary, Art. 1, Rn. 7.
⁴⁶ Vgl. Art. 92 II, 93 II, 99.
⁴⁷ Vgl. Art. 2.
⁴⁸ Vgl. Art. 3.
⁴⁹ Hierzu *Frignani*, Contratto internazionale, S. 264.
⁵⁰ Vgl. Hof 's-Hertogenbosch, 18.1.2011, CISG-online 2179; Tribunale di Forlì, 11.12.2008, CISG-online 1729; High Commercial Court, 19.12.2006, CLOUT 916; Tribunale di Padova, 11.1.2005, CISG-online 967; Tribunale di Padova, 25.2.2004, CISG-online 819; Tribunale di Rimini, 26.11.2002, CISG-online 737 = Giur. it. 2003, 896 ff., m. Anm. *Ferrari*; KG Schaffhausen, 25.2.2002, CISG-online 723; CA Colmar, 12.6.2001, CISG-online 694; KG Waadt, 11.3.1996, CISG-online 333 = SZIER 1998, 82; OGH, 10.11.1994, CISG-online 117 = östJBl 1995, 253 f.
⁵¹ *Chiomenti*, EuLF 2005, 141, 142; *Fairlie*, S. 46; *Ferrari u. a./Saenger*, Internationales Vertragsrecht, Art. 1, Rn. 2; *Frignani/Torsello*, Il contratto internazionale, S. 456; *P. Huber/Mullis/P. Huber*, S. 43; *Gillette/Walt*, Sales Law, S. 50; *Grieser*, S. 35; *Heuzé*, Anm. 88.; *Kahn*, Rev. dr. aff. int. 2001, 241, 242; *Kröll u. a./Perales Viscasillas*, Art. 1, Rn. 2 und 25; MünchKomm/*Westermann*, Art. 1, Rn. 6; MünchKommHGB/*Benicke*, Art. 1, Rn. 7; *Niemann*, Einheitliche Anwendung, S. 82; *Padovini*, ZfRVgl 1987, 87, 91; *Pavic/Djordjevic*, 28 J. L. & Com. (2009), 1, 22; *Perovic*, Annals Fac. L. Belgrade 2011, 181, 182; *Piltz*, Internationales Kaufrecht, Rn. 2–20; *Ragno*, Convenzione di Vienna e Diritto europeo, S. 11 f.; *Rudolph*, Art. 1, Rn. 3; *Schlechtriem/Schwenzer/Schlechtriem*, CISG Commentary, 2. Aufl., Art. 1, Rn. 14; *Schlechtriem/Schwenzer/Schwenzer/Hachem*, CISG Commentary, Art. 1, Rn. 8; *Schmitt*, CR 2001, 145, 147; *Schumacher*, IHR 2005, 147, 147; *Thiele*, IHR 2002, 8, 10; *Wulf*, S. 12.
⁵² So etwa *Luzzatto*, 46 Enc. D. (1993), 502, 503, Fn. 4; *Memmo*, Riv. trim. dir. proced. civ. 1983, 180, 189; *Padovini*, Riv. dir. int. priv. proc. 1987, 47, 52.
⁵³ *Lopez de Gonzalo*, Vendita internazionale, S. 906.
⁵⁴ *Brunner*, Art. 2, Rn. 1; *Chiomenti*, EuLF 2005, 141, 143; *Ferrari u. a./Saenger*, Internationales Vertragsrecht, Art. 1, Rn. 2; *Ragno*, Convenzione di Vienna e Diritto europeo, S. 12; *Reinhart*, Art. 1, Rn. 1; *Staudinger/Magnus*, Art. 1, Rn. 4; ebenso in der Rechtsprechung Hof 's-Hertogenbosch, 18.1.2011, CISG-online 2179; HGer Aargau, 10.3.2010, CISG-online 2176; Tribunale di Forlì, 16.2.2009, CISG-online 1780; Tribunale di Padova, 11.1.2005, CISG-online 967.

können. Wie auch die Rechtsprechung neuerdings ausdrücklich hervorgehoben hat,[55] lässt sich eine **Definition aus den dispositiven**[56] **Artt. 30 und 53** ableiten:[57] Danach ist Kaufvertrag im Sinne des CISG der Vertrag, durch den die eine Partei, der Verkäufer, zur Lieferung der Ware sowie zur Übertragung des Eigentums daran (und gegebenenfalls zur Aushändigung der die Ware betreffenden Urkunden), die andere Partei zur Annahme der Ware sowie zur Zahlung des Kaufpreises verpflichtet wird.[58] Demnach muss es sich „um einen Austausch von Ware gegen Geld handeln".[59]

14 Diese Definition entspricht sachlich der des § 433 BGB n. F., sogar mehr als sie der Definition des § 433 BGB a. F. entsprach; während nämlich die a. F. auch den Rechtskauf umfasste (der vom Anwendungsbereich des CISG ausgeschlossen ist), ist der Rechtskauf nunmehr in einer eigenständigen Vorschrift (§ 453 BGB n. F.) geregelt (die die entsprechende Anwendung der Vorschriften über den Sachkauf anordnet).[60] Auf den ersten Blick scheint sie jedoch der Definition des Kaufvertrages, die in Rechtsordnungen vorzufinden ist, die – wie etwa die französische und italienische[61] – bezüglich der Eigentumsübertragung an beweglichen Sachen vom Konsensualprinzip ausgehen,[62] nicht zu entsprechen.[63] Dies hängt damit zusammen, dass in diesen Rechtsordnungen der (gültige) Kaufvertrag in der Regel[64] selbst das Eigentum an den Käufer übergehen lässt, die Pflicht zur Übertragung des

---

[55] Vgl. Tribunale di Padova, 25.2.2004, CISG-online 819; KG Schaffhausen, 25.2.2002, CISG-online 723; RB Rotterdam, 1.11.2001, NIPR 2001, Nr. 114; CA Colmar, 12.6.2001, CISG-online 694; KG Waadt, 11.3.1996, CISG-online 333 = SZIER 1998, 82.

[56] Der Umstand, dass sowohl Art. 30 als auch Art. 53 dispositiv sind, kann dazu führen, dass die Parteien das im Text erwähnte Pflichtenprogramm modifizieren können. Dies ermöglicht es den Parteien etwa, auch den Kauf unter Eigentumsvorbehalt, der eine Modifizierung des in Art. 30 vorgesehenen Pflichtenprogramms voraussetzt, dem CISG zu unterstellen, zumindest hinsichtlich der schuldrechtlichen Aspekte; so *Schlechtriem*, Internationales UN-Kaufrecht, Rn. 37.

[57] Vgl. in der Lehre *Achilles*, Art. 1, Rn. 2; *Brunner*, Art. 2, Rn. 7; *Chiomenti*, EuLF 2005, 141, 143; *Díez-Picazo/Calvo Caravaca*, Art. 1, S. 47; *Endler/Daub*, CR 1993, 601; *Fairlie*, S. 46; *Ferrari*, Vendita internazionale, S. 45; *Ferrari u. a./Saenger*, Internationales Vertragsrecht, Art. 1, Rn. 3; *Frignani/Torsello*, Il contratto internazionale, S. 456; *P. Huber/Mullis/P. Huber*, S. 43; *Grieser*, S. 35; *Kröll u. a./Djordjevic*, Art. 4, Rn. 11; *Lohmann*, Parteiautonomie, S. 12; MünchKomm/*Westermann*, Vor Art. 1, Rn. 4; *Niemann*, Einheitliche Anwendung, S. 83; *Pavic/Djordjevic*, 28 J. L. & Com. (2009), 1, 22; *Perovic*, Annals Fac. L. Belgrade 2011, 181, 182; *Piltz*, Internationales Kaufrecht, Rn. 2–20; *Ragno*, Convenzione di Vienna e Diritto europeo. S. 12; *Sannini*, L'applicazione, S. 92; *Schlechtriem/Schwenzer/Schlechtriem*, CISG Commentary, 2. Aufl., Art. 1, Rn. 14; *Schlechtriem/Schwenzer/Schwenzer/Hachem*, CISG Commentary, Art. 1, Rn. 8; *Schmitt*, CR 2001, 145, 149; *Schumacher*, IHR 2005, 147, 147; *Soergel/Lüderitz/Fenge*, Art. 1, Rn. 22; *Wulf*, S. 21; vgl. in der Rechtsprechung Hof 's-Hertogenbosch, 18.1.2011, CISG-online 2179; Tribunale di Forlì, 16.2.2009, CISG-online 1780; Tribunale di Forlì, 11.12.2008, CISG-online 1729; High Commercial Court, 19.12.2006, CLOUT 916; KG Wallis, 27.10.2006, CISG-1563; Tribunale di Padova, 10.1.2006, CISG-online 1157; Tribunale di Padova, 11.1.2005, CISG-online 967; Tribunale di Padova, 25.2.2004, CISG-online 819.

[58] Ebenso *Bamberger/Roth/Saenger*, Art. 1, Rn. 3; *Frignani/Torsello*, Il contratto internazionale, S. 456 und 549; *Herber/Czerwenka*, Art. 1, Rn. 3; *P. Huber/Mullis/P. Huber*, S. 43; MünchKomm/*Westermann*, Art. 1, Rn. 6; MünchKommHGB/*Benicke*, Art. 1, Rn. 7; *Ragno*, Convenzione di Vienna e Diritto europeo, S. 12; *Sannini*, L'applicazione, S. 93; *Schwenzer/Hachem/Kee*, Rn. 8.1; *Thiele*, IHR 2002, 8, 10; vgl. in der Rechtsprechung auch Hof 's-Hertogenbosch, 18.1.2011, CISG-online 2179; Tribunale di Forlì, 16.2.2009, CISG-online 1780; KG Wallis, 28.1.2009, CISG-online 2025; Tribunale di Forlì, 11.12.2008, CISG-online 1729; High Commercial Court, 19.12.2006, CLOUT 916; KG Wallis, 27.10.2006, CISG-1563; Tribunale di Padova, 10.1.2006, CISG-online 1157; Tribunale di Padova, 11.1.2005, CISG-online 967; Tribunale di Padova, 25.2.2004, CISG-online 819; KG Wallis, 3.8.2003, CISG-online 895; Tribunale di Rimini, 26.11.2002, CISG-online 737 = Giur. it. 2003, 896 ff., m. Anm. *Ferrari*; KG Schaffhausen, 25.2.2002, CISG-online 723; Audiencia Provincial de Navarra, 27.3.2000, CISG-online 575; für eine ähnliche Definition auch OGH, 10.11.1994, CISG-online 117 = östJBl 1995, 253 f.
Die im Text vorgeschlagene Definition entspricht der vieler nationaler Rechtsordnungen; vgl. hierzu etwa *E. Muñoz*, S. 65 f. (zum Recht Spaniens und Portugals sowie der Staaten Lateinamerikas).

[59] KG Zug, 21.10.1999, CISG-online 491 = IHR 2001, 45.

[60] *Palandt/Weidenkaff*, § 433 BGB, Rn. 1.

[61] So schon *Staudinger/Magnus*, Art. 1, Rn. 13.

[62] Ein Überblick über die bezüglich der Eigentumsübertragung vom Konsensualprinzip ausgehenden Rechtsordnungen findet sich bei *Galgano*, Trasferimento della proprietà, S. 102 f.

[63] Vgl. zum Folgenden auch *Ferrari*, Vendita internazionale, S. 46 f.

[64] Es gibt Fälle, in denen auch in den vom Konsensualprinzip ausgehenden Rechtsordnungen die Eigentumsübertragung nicht solo consensu erfolgt bzw. erfolgen kann; vgl. hierzu etwa *Ferrari*, ZEuP 1993, 52–78.

Eigentums an den Käufer also überhaupt nicht erwächst.[65] Dies ist jedoch irrelevant, da das die Definition des Kaufvertrages nach dem CISG kennzeichnende Merkmal die Pflicht zur entgeltlichen und endgültigen Übertragung des Eigentums am Kaufgegenstand ist, unabhängig davon, ob „der Eigentumsübergang schon durch den Kauf selbst oder erst durch spätere Erfüllungsakte erreicht wird"[66] (was sich unschwer daraus ergibt, dass Art. 4 lit. b) ausdrücklich „die Wirkungen, die der Vertrag auf das Eigentum an der verkauften Waren haben kann" vom sachlichen Geltungsbereich des CISG ausnimmt).[67]

Auch die meisten Unterformen des Kaufs,[68] der auch **bedingt** sein kann,[69] werden vom Übereinkommen erfasst,[70] was sich bezüglich einiger Vertragstypen aus dem Übereinkommen selbst ergibt. Dies trifft zum Beispiel für den **Sukzessivlieferungsvertrag** zu,[71] der in Art. 73 CISG eigenen Regeln unterstellt ist;[72] dies ist auch durch die Rechtsprechung bestätigt worden.[73] 15

Gleiches gilt auch für den **Kauf nach Muster**[74] oder **Probe:**[75] Das Übereinkommen erwähnt den Kauf nach Muster oder Probe im Abschnitt über die Vertragsmäßigkeit der Ware.[76] Art. 35 II lit. c) statuiert, dass die Ware nur dann dem Vertrag entspricht, wenn sie die gleichen Eigenschaften besitzt wie die Ware, die dem Käufer als Probe oder Muster vorgelegt wurde.[77] 16

Auch der **Spezifikationskauf,** wonach es dem Käufer zusteht, die Form, Maße, etc., der Ware zu bestimmen, ist im Übereinkommen ausdrücklich geregelt;[78] diesbezüglich ist Art. 65 relevant.[79] 17

---

[65] Vgl. auch *Niemann,* Einheitliche Anwendung, S. 82.
[66] *Staudinger/Magnus,* Art. 1, Rn. 14.
[67] Vgl. *Frignani/Torsello,* Il contratto internazionale, S. 457; *Heuzé,* Anm. 94.; *Schlechtriem/Schwenzer/Schwenzer/Hachem,* CISG Commentary, Art. 1, Rn. 8 Fn. 23 a. E.; *Schwenzer/Hachem/Kee,* Rn. 8.6.
[68] Ein Vertrag, der Kaufvertrag im Sinne des CISG ist, unterliegt dem CISG unabhängig davon, wie die Parteien den Vertrag qualifizieren; so ausdrücklich in der Rechtsprechung Serbian Chamber of Commerce, 15.7.2008, CISG-online 1795; vgl. auch *Kröll u. a./Djordjevic,* Art. 4, Rn. 11 a. E.; *Pavic/Djordjevic,* 28 J. L. & Com. (2008), 1, 22 f.
[69] In der Lehre vgl. *Brunner,* Art. 2, Rn. 8; *Schlechtriem/Schwenzer/Schwenzer/Hachem,* CISG Commentary, Art. 1, Rn. 10; *Staudinger/Magnus,* Art. 1, Rn. 14; in der Rechtsprechung siehe OLG Schleswig, 29.10.2002, CISG-online 717 = IHR 2003, 67 (aufschiebend bedingter Kaufvertrag); OLG Graz, 7.3.2002, CISG-online 669 (aufschiebend bedingter Kaufvertrag); ICC, 7884/1994, CISG-online 567.
[70] So ausdrücklich *Staudinger/Magnus,* Art. 1, Rn. 15; vgl. neuerdings auch *Bamberger/Roth/Saenger,* Art. 1, Rn. 3; *Brunner,* Art. 2, Rn. 8; *Grieser,* S. 35; *Schlechtriem/Schwenzer/Schwenzer/Hachem,* CISG Commentary, Art. 1, Rn. 9.
[71] Wie hier auch *Achilles,* Art. 1, Rn. 2; *Bamberger/Roth/Saenger,* Art. 1, Rn. 3; *Brunner,* Art. 2, Rn. 8; *Chiomenti,* EuLF 2005, 141, 143; *Crucelaegui,* S. 48; *De Nova,* Riv. trim. dir. proced. civ. 1990, 749; *Ferrari u. a./Saenger,* Internationales Vertragsrecht, Art. 1, Rn. 3; *Flambouras,* 29 J. L. & Com. (2011), 171, 189 f.; *Grieser,* S. 35; *Herber/Czerwenka,* Art. 1, Rn. 4; *Kröll u. a./Perales Viscasillas,* Art. 1, Rn. 26; *Lohmann,* Parteiautonomie, S. 13; *Navas Navarro,* IHR 2006, 74, 75; *Ortiz/Perales Viscasillas,* S. 101 f.; *Sannini,* L'applicazione, S. 93 f.; *Schlechtriem/Schwenzer/Schlechtriem,* CISG Commentary, 2. Aufl., Art. 1, Rn. 15; *Schlechtriem/Schwenzer/Schwenzer/Hachem,* CISG Commentary, Art. 1, Rn. 9; *Schmitt,* CR 2001, 145, 149, Fn. 96; *Witz/Salger/Lorenz/Lorenz,* Art. 1, Rn. 6.
[72] A. A. *Padovini,* ZfRVgl 28 (1987), 87, 91.
[73] Vgl. HGer Zürich, 22.11.2010, CISG-online 2160; OLG Düsseldorf, 9.7.2010, CISG-online 2171; HGer Aargau, 10.3.2010, CISG-online 2176; Court of First Instance of Athens, Aktenzeichen 4505/2009 (ohne Datum), CISG-online 2228; OLG Frankfurt a. M., 6.10.2004, CISG-online 919; CA Colmar, 12.6.2001, CISG-online 694; HGer Zürich, 30.11.1998, CISG-online 415 = TranspR-IHR 2000, 12; LG Ellwangen, 21.8.1995, CISG-online 279; zum Haager Kaufrecht vgl. BGH, NJW 1979, 1779 m. Anm. *Landfermann.*
[74] *Brunner,* Art. 2, Rn. 8.
[75] *Achilles,* Art. 1, Rn. 2; *Bamberger/Roth/Saenger,* Art. 1, Rn. 3; *Ferrariu. a./Saenger,* Internationales Vertragsrecht, Art. 1, Rn. 3; *Niemann,* Einheitliche Anwendung, S. 85; *Staudinger/Magnus,* Art. 1, Rn. 17; *Schmitt,* CR 2001, 145, 149.
[76] Botschaft des Schweizerischen Bundesrats, S. 762 f.
[77] Vgl. hierzu LG München I, 8.2.1995, CISG-online 203; *Delchi Carrier SpA v. Rotorex Corp.,* U. S. Ct. App. (2nd Cir.), 6.12.1995, CISG-online 140 = 10 F. 3d 1024.
[78] Vgl. *Achilles,* Art. 1, Rn. 2; *Brunner,* Art. 2, Rn. 8; *Ferrari u. a./Saenger,* Internationales Vertragsrecht, Art. 1, Rn. 3; *Schmitt,* CR 2001, 145, 149, Fn. 96; *Staudinger/Magnus,* Art. 1, Rn. 16.
[79] *Grieser,* S. 35.

Art. 1 18–24 Teil I. Kapitel I. Anwendungsbereich

18 Dem Übereinkommen können auch der **Versendungskauf**[80] und das **Streckengeschäft**[81] unterliegen; dies ergibt sich unzweifelhaft aus Art. 31.[82]

19 Aus Art. 29 ergibt sich, und dies ist nicht nur in der Lehre[83] sondern auch in der Rechtsprechung hervorgehoben worden,[84] dass die Vorschriften des Übereinkommens auch auf **Vereinbarungen über die Änderung** und die **Aufhebung**[85] eines dem CISG unterstehenden Kaufvertrages Anwendung finden können.[86]

20 Das Übereinkommen bezieht sich nicht ausdrücklich auf den **Fixkauf**. Wie die Lehre aber festgestellt hat,[87] ergibt sich mittelbar aus Art. 33 und Art. 49, dass auch diese Unterform des Kaufs dem CISG unterliegen kann (was neuerdings auch durch die Rechtsprechung bestätigt worden ist).[88]

21 Aufgrund der engen Verknüpfung zwischen Vorvertrag und Hauptvertrag muss man davon ausgehen, dass auch der einen vom Übereinkommen erfassten Vertragstyp betreffende **Vorvertrag** vom CISG geregelt werden kann.[89] Entsprechendes gilt für **Kaufoptionen**,[90] so auch der französische Kassationshof.[91]

22 Die Lehre, die sich mit der Frage beschäftigt hat, ob das Übereinkommen auch auf **Kaufgeschäfte mit der Zusatzabrede,** die dem Käufer das Recht gibt, **unverkaufte Ware zurückzugeben,** Anwendung finden könne, hat dies – unter Bezugnahme auf zum Haager Kaufrecht ergangene Rechtsprechung – bejaht.[92]

23 Was den **Kauf auf Probe** angeht, der es dem Käufer erlaubt, die Ware auch dann zurückzuweisen, wenn diese keine Mängel aufweist, ist anzumerken, dass dieser nur dann dem CISG unterliegen kann, wenn die Parteien einverständlich von Art. 35 abweichen. Dies ist notwendig, da kraft dieser Vorschrift der Käufer die Ware nur ablehnen kann, wenn sie vertragswidrig im Sinne von Art. 35 ist. „Liegt eine solche Parteivereinbarung vor, so untersteht der Kauf auf Probe im Übrigen dem Wiener Übereinkommen."[93]

24 Soweit der Besteller herzustellender Waren nicht einen „wesentlichen Teil" der für die Herstellung notwendigen Stoffe selbst zur Verfügung stellt, sind **Werklieferungsverträge** Kaufverträgen gleichzusetzen[94] und können somit dem Übereinkommen unterliegen.[95] Auch

---

[80] So auch *Achilles*, Art. 1, Rn. 2; *Bamberger/Roth/Saenger*, Art. 1, Rn. 3; *Ferrari u. a./Saenger*, Internationales Vertragsrecht, Art. 1, Rn. 3; *Schlechtriem/Schwenzer/Schlechtriem*, CISG Commentary, 2. Aufl., Art. 1, Rn. 15; vgl. in der Rechtsprechung zum CISG BGH, 12.2.1998, CISG-online 343 = WM 1998, 2077, 2079; vgl. zum EKG BGH, 4.4.1979, BGHZ 74, 136.

[81] Vgl. zum CISG *Achilles*, Art. 1, Rn. 2; *Brunner*, Art. 2, Rn. 8; *Ferrari u. a./Saenger*, Internationales Vertragsrecht, Art. 1, Rn. 3; MünchKomm/*Westermann*, Art. 1, Rn. 6; *Posch/Terlitza*, IHR 2001, 47, 49; *Witz/Salger/Lorenz/Lorenz*, Art. 1, Rn. 3; in der Rechtsprechung zum CISG, vgl. OGH, 24.10.1995, CISG-online 166 = ZfRVgl 1996, 76; vgl. zum EKG BGH, 24.10.1980, IPRax 1981, 96, m. Anm. *Weitnauer*.

[82] *Grieser*, S. 35; *Staudinger/Magnus*, Art. 1, Rn. 18.

[83] *Ferrari*, Vendita internazionale, S. 47; *Kröll u. a./Perales Viscasillas*, Art. 1, Rn. 26; *Schlechtriem/Schwenzer/Schwenzer/Hachem*, CISG Commentary, Art. 1, Rn. 15.

[84] Vgl. AG Sursee, 12.9.2008, CISg-online 1728; OLG Hamburg, 5.10.1998, CISG-online 473; OLG München, 8.2.1995, CISG-online 143; ICC, 7331/1994, CISG-online 106 = ICC Ct. Bull. 2/1995, 73; LG Hamburg, 26.9.1990, CISG-online 21 = IPRax 1991, 400.

[85] *Schlechtriem/Schwenzer/Schlechtriem*, CISG Commentary, 2. Aufl., Art. 1, Rn. 19.

[86] So bereits nach Haager Kaufrecht; vgl. OLG Hamburg, RIW 1982, 435.

[87] *Brunner*, Art. 2, Rn. 8; *Schlechtriem/Schwenzer/Schwenzer/Hachem*, CISG Commentary, Art. 1, Rn. 9; *Staudinger/Magnus*, Art. 1, Rn. 20.

[88] Vgl. LG München II, 20.2.2002, CISG-online 712 = IHR 2003, 24, 26; AG Oldenburg i. H., 24.4.1990, CISG-online 20 = IPRax 1991, 336 f.

[89] Wie hier *Achilles*, Art. 1, Rn. 2; *Ferrari*, Vendita internazionale, S. 48; *Memmo*, Riv. trim. dir. proced. civ. 1983, 180, 193; a. A. *Padovini*, Riv. dir. int. priv. proced. 1987, 47, 54.

[90] Vgl. *Achilles*, Art. 1, Rn. 2; *Bamberger/Roth/Saenger*, Art. 1, Rn. 3; *Ferrari u. a./Saenger*, Internationales Vertragsrecht, Art. 1, Rn. 3; *Schumacher*, IHR 2005, 147, 148 f.; *Staudinger/Magnus*, Art. 1, Rn. 41.

[91] Civ. 30.6.2004, CISG-online 870.

[92] *Ferrari*, Applicabilità ed applicazioni, S. 133 f.; a. A. *Winship*, Scope, S. 1–24.

[93] Botschaft des Schweizerischen Bundesrats, S. 763; vgl. auch *Ferrari u. a./Saenger*, Internationales Vertragsrecht, Art. 1, Rn. 3.

[94] Vgl. detailliert hierzu Art. 3 Rn. 4 ff.

[95] Vgl. zuletzt OLG Dresden, 30.10.2010, CISG-online 2183; HGerZürich, 25.6.2010, CISG-online 2161; KG St. Gallen, 15.6.2010, CISG-online 2159; OLG Saarbrücken, 12.5.2010, CISG-online 2155; KG Zug,

Verträge, bei denen neben die Verpflichtung zur Eigentumsverschaffung und Übergabe der Ware die Verpflichtung zur **Leistung oder Verschaffung von Arbeit oder anderen Dienstleistungen** tritt, unterstehen dem CISG, solange letztere Verpflichtung nicht den überwiegenden Teil der Pflichten der Partei ausmacht, welche die Ware liefern muss.

2. Nicht in den sachlichen Anwendungsbereich fallende Verträge

Das Übereinkommen selbst schließt (mittelbar oder unmittelbar) einige Verträge von seinem Anwendungsbereich aus. So zum Beispiel sind neben den in Art. 2 ausgeschlossenen Kaufverträgen **(Konsumentenkäufe, „amtliche" Veräußerungen, Käufe bestimmter Gegenstände)** auch Verträge dem Anwendungsbereich entzogen, in denen die **arbeits- oder dienstvertraglichen Pflichten überwiegen.** Auch auf Verträge über die **Lieferung herzustellender Waren** finden die Vorschriften des CISG keine Anwendung, zumindest dann, wenn der Besteller einen „wesentlichen Teil" der zur Herstellung notwendigen Stoffe liefert. 25

Da **Abzahlungsgeschäfte** grundsätzlich Verbrauchergeschäfte sein werden, die vom Anwendungsbereich ausgenommen sind,[96] werden diese in der Regel nicht dem CISG unterstehen. Greift der Ausschluss nach Art. 2 lit. a) jedoch nicht ein, so kann auch ein Abzahlungsgeschäft unter das Übereinkommen fallen.[97] 26

Ein Teil der Lehre hat sich für die Anwendbarkeit des CISG auf **Mietkaufverträge** ausgesprochen,[98] zumindest dann, wenn das Interesse am Kauf oder das an der vorangehenden Gebrauchsüberlassung wirtschaftlich größer ist.[99] Da der Mietkaufvertrag aber ein Mietvertrag ist, bei dem dem Mieter lediglich ein Recht zum Erwerb der Sache eingeräumt wird, der Vermieter also nicht notwendigerweise zur entgeltlichen und endgültigen Übertragung der Sache verpflichtet ist – eine Pflicht, die jedoch die Definition des Kaufvertrags nach dem Übereinkommen kennzeichnet –,[100] fällt der **Mietkaufvertrag nicht unter das CISG.**[101] 27

Gleiches gilt auch in Bezug auf **Leasingverträge,**[102] selbst wenn ein Teil der Lehre zumindest das Finanzierungsleasing mit Kaufoption dem CISG unterstellen will, weil der Kauferfolg bei dieser Art des Leasings im Vordergrund stehe.[103] Leasingverträge unterstehen dem CISG nicht,[104] unabhängig davon, ob es sich um ein operating oder financial leasing (selbst mit Kaufoption) handelt,[105] da das Nutzungsinteresse des Leasingnehmers gegenüber 28

14.12.2009, CISG-online 2026; OGer Aargau, 3.3.2009, CISG-online 2013; HGer Aargau, 25.1.2005, CISG-online 1091 = IHR 2006, 34; HGer St. Gallen, 29.4.2004, CISG-online 962; KG Schaffhausen, 27.1.2004, CISG-online 960; LG München I, 27.2.2002, CISG-online 654; OLG Saarbrücken, 14.2.2001, CISG-online 610 = IHR 2001, 64; OLG Stuttgart, 28.2.2000, CISG-online 583 = IHR 2001, 65.

[96] Botschaft des Schweizerischen Bundesrats, S. 763.
[97] *Staudinger/Magnus*, Art. 1, Rn. 25.
[98] So *Grieser*, S. 124, *Honsell/Siehr*, Art. 2, Rn. 5.
[99] So etwa *Achilles*, Art. 1, Rn. 3; *Díez-Picazo/Calvo Caravaca*, Art. 1, S. 48; *Ferrari u. a./Saenger*, Internationales Vertragsrecht, Art. 1, Rn. 4; *Herber/Czerwenka*, Art. 1, Rn. 4; *Reinhart*, Art. 1, Rn. 2; *Grunewald*, Kaufrecht, S. 655, 658.
[100] So auch *Karollus*, S. 20.
[101] Gegen jegliche Einbeziehung des Mietkaufvertrags auch *Czerwenka*, Rechtsanwendungsprobleme, S. 146; *Enderlein/Maskow/Strohbach*, Art. 1, Anm. 1.; *Piltz*, Internationales Kaufrecht, Rn. 2–27; *ders.*, AnwBl. 1991, 57, 59; *Schlechtriem/Schwenzer/Schlechtriem/Schwenzer/Hachem*, CISG Commentary, Art. 3, Rn. 22; vgl. aber *Honsell/Siehr*, Art. 1, Rn. 5, die den Mietkauf immer dem CISG unterstellen; a. A. auch *Schwenzer/Hachem/Kee*, Rn. 8.24.
[102] Vgl. *Ferrari*, Vendita internazionale, S. 50.
[103] In diesem Sinne *Díez-Picazo/Calvo Caravaca*, Art. 1, S. 48, Fn. 8; *Grieser*, S. 98; *Karollus*, JuS 1993, 378, 380.
[104] *P. Huber/Mullis/P. Huber*, S. 48; *Kröll u. a./Djordjevic*, Art. 4, Rn. 11; MünchKommHGB/*Benicke*, Art. 1, Rn. 11; *Perovic*, Annals Fac. L. Belgrade 2011, 181, 193; a. A. *Achilles*, Art. 1, Rn. 3; *Ferrari u. a./Saenger*, Internationales Vertragsrecht, Art. 1, Rn. 4; *Rudolph*, Art. 1, Rn. 3; *Schlechtriem/Schwenzer/Schwenzer/Hachem*, CISG Commentary, Art. 1, Rn. 13 und Art. 3, Rn. 22; *Staudinger/Magnus*, Art. 1, Rn. 34.
[105] Wie hier *Brunner*, Art. 2, Rn. 9; *Czerwenka*, Rechtsanwendungsprobleme, S. 146; *Enderlein/Maskow/Strohbach*, Art. 1, Anm. 1.; *Ferrari*, Applicabilità ed applicazioni, S. 130 f.; *Honsell/Siehr*, Art. 2, Rn. 6; *Staudinger/Magnus*, Art. 1, Rn. 34; a. A. *Grieser*, S. 98 f., der zwischen Finanzierungsleasingverträge mit Kaufoption

etwaigen Erwerbsabsichten überwiegt.[106] Dies schließt jedoch nicht aus, dass die Vertragsbeziehungen zwischen Leasinggeber und dem Lieferanten des Leasing-Objekts durch das Übereinkommen geregelt sein können.[107] Nach leasing-typischer Abtretung der Gewährleistungsrechte des Leasinggebers an den Leasingnehmer richtet sich auch dessen Rechtstellung nach dem Übereinkommen;[108] gleiches galt bereits unter dem Haager Kaufrecht.[109] Auch Joint-Venture-Verträge fallen nicht in den sachlichen Anwendungsbereich des CISG.[110]

29 Da ein **sale-and-lease-back Geschäft** in der Regel aus zwei rechtlich selbstständigen Verträgen besteht, aus einem Kaufvertrag, durch den der Leasinggeber das Leasinggut vom Leasingnehmer erwirbt, und einem Leasingvertrag, auf der Grundlage dessen der Leasinggeber dem -nehmer das Leasinggut zurückverleast, muss zwischen dem Leasingvertrag und dem Kaufvertrag unterschieden werden. Während das Übereinkommen aus den genannten Gründen nicht für den Leasingvertrag gelten kann, kann der Kaufvertrag durchaus dem Übereinkommen unterstehen.[111]

30 Ein weiterer vom Übereinkommen – wie schon vom Haager Kaufrecht[112] – nicht erfasster Vertrag ist der **Tauschvertrag**.[113] Dafür spricht auch der Wortlaut des Übereinkommens. Art. 53 statuiert unter anderem die Pflicht des Käufers, den Kaufpreis zu zahlen,[114] „unter dem eine in gängigen Zahlungsmitteln ausgedrückte Geldsumme zu

---

oder Andienungsrecht und Operating Leasingverträge unterscheidet, und erstere dem CISG unterstellt (S. 98), leztere hingegen nicht (S. 99).

[106] So auch *Schlechtriem/Schwenzer/Schlechtriem,* CISG Commentary, 2. Aufl., Art. 1, Rn. 16; *von Westphalen,* RIW 1992, 257, 258; a. A. *Schlechtriem,* Internationales UN-Kaufrecht, Rn. 25, der auch in Bezug auf Mietkäufe die Anwendbarkeit des CISG davon abhängen lassen will, ob „im wirtschaftlichen Ergebnis die Sache erworben werden soll, insbesondere, ob die vereinbarten Zahlungen des Erwerbers (einschließlich Anzahlung und Abschlusszahlung) den Sachwert und die Finanzierungskosten decken, der Vertrag also im Ergebnis entweder auf die Übertragung der Sachsubstanz gerichtet ist oder jedenfalls während seiner Laufzeit die Nutzungsmöglichkeit dem ‚Erwerber' so vollständig zugeordnet ist, dass der Gebrauchswert der Sache während der Vertragsdauer vollständig aufgezehrt ist". Vgl. in diesem Sinne neuerdings auch *P. Huber/Mullis/ P. Huber,* S. 48; *Kröll u. a./Perales Viscasillas,* Art. 1, Rn. 35.

[107] *Enderlein/Maskow/Strohbach,* Art. 1, Anm. 1.; *Grieser,* S. 109; *Herber,* 2. Aufl., Art. 1 Rn. 16; MünchKommHGB/*Benicke,* Art. 1, Rn. 13; *Perovic,* Annals Fac. L. Belgrade 2011, 181, 193; *Schlechtriem/Schwenzer/ Schwenzer/Hachem,* CISG Commentary, Art. 1, Rn. 13; *Schwenzer/Hachem/Kee,* Rn. 8.25; *Soergel/Lüderitz/ Fenge,* Art. 3, Rn. 6; *Vischer/L. Huber/Oser,* Rn. 354; *von Westphalen,* RIW 1992, 257, 258; ebenso zum EKG, vgl. BGH, 14.3.1984, NJW 1984, 2034; BGH, 28.11.1990, NJW 1991, 639.

[108] *Herber,* 2. Aufl., Art. 1, Rn. 16; *Staudinger/Magnus,* Art. 1, Rn. 35.

[109] BGH, 28.11.1990, NJW 1991, 639.

[110] *Kröll u. a./Djordjevic,* Art. 4, Rn. 11; vgl. in der Rechtsprechung *Amco Ukrservice & Promriladamco v. American Meter Company,* U. S. Dist. Ct. (E. D. Pa.), 29.3.2004, CISG-online 1664; Tribunale d'Appello Ticinio, 15.12.1999, CISG-online 422.

[111] Ebenso *Schlechtriem/Schwenzer/Schwenzer/Hachem,* CISG Commentary, Art. 1, Rn. 13; *Schwenzer/Hachem/Kee,* Rn. 8.25; *Staudinger/Magnus,* Art. 1, Rn. 36.

[112] Vgl. *Dölle/Herber,* Art. 1 EKG, Rn. 7.

[113] Wie hier auch *Achilles,* Art. 1, Rn. 3; *Bamberger/Roth/Saenger,* Art. 1, Rn. 4; *Brunner,* Art. 2, Rn. 9; *Czerwenka,* Rechtsanwendungsprobleme, S. 141; *Ferrari,* Vendita internazionale, S. 49; *Ferrari u. a./Saenger,* Internationales Vertragsrecht, Art. 1, Rn. 4; *Frignani/Torselli,* Il contratto internazionale, S. 458; *Grieser,* S. 148; *Herber/Czerwenka,* Art. 1, Rn. 5; *Honsell/Siehr,* Art. 2, Rn. 4; *Karollus,* S. 25; *Kröll u. a./Djordjevic,* Art. 4, Rn. 11; *Kröll u. a./Perales Viscasillas,* Art. 1, Rn. 30; MünchKomm/*Westermann,* Art. 1, Rn. 6; MünchKommHGB/*Benicke,* Art. 1, Rn. 8; *Niemann,* Einheitliche Anwendung, S. 100 f.; *Piltz,* Internationales Kaufrecht, Rn. 2–23; *Reinhart,* Art. 1, Rn. 2; *Rudolph,* Art. 1, Rn. 3; Botschaft des Schweizerischen Bundesrats, S. 763; *Schlechtriem,* Uniform Sales Law, S. 24; *ders.,* 36 Vict. U. Well. L. Rev. (2005), 781, 787; *Schlechtriem/ Schwenzer/Schlechtriem,* CISG Commentary, 2. Aufl., Art. 1, Rn. 18; *Schmitt,* CR 2001, 145, 149, Fn. 96; *Soergel/Lüderitz/Fenge,* Art. 1, Rn. 22; *Staudinger/Magnus,* Art. 1, Rn. 29; *Winship,* Scope, S. 1–24; ebenso in der Rechtsprechung Tribunal of International Commercial Arbitration at the Russian Federation Chamber of Commerce and Industry, 9.3.2004, CISG-online 1184; Federal Arbitration Court for the Moscow Region, 26.5.2003, CISG-online 836; a. A. *Horowitz,* 29 J. L. & Com. (2010), 99, 100 ff.; *Schlechtriem/Schwenzer/ Schwenzer/Hachem,* CISG Commentary, Art. 1, Rn. 11; *Schwenzer/Hachem/Kee,* Rn. 818; *Schwenzer/Kee,* IHR 2009, 229, 232 f.; a. A. in der Rechsprechung Tribunal of International Commercial Arbitration at the Ukraine Chamber of Commerce and Trade, 10.10.2003, CISG-online 1268; die Frage ansprechend, ohne jedoch eine eigene Lösung vorzuschlagen, *Perovic,* Annals Fac. L. Belgrade 2011, 181, 191 f.

[114] Vgl. auch Art. 2 lit. (i) des Vorschlags für eine Verordnung des Europäischen Parlaments und des Rates über ein Gemeinsames Europäisches Kaufrecht vom 11.10.2011, KOM(2011) 635 endgültig, S. 26, wonach

Anwendungsbereich 31 **Art. 1**

verstehen ist. Zahlung durch Warenlieferung sieht die Konvention nicht vor."[115] Auch **Gegengeschäfte oder Kompensationsgeschäfte** fallen nicht unter das Übereinkommen,[116] zumindest dann nicht,[117] wenn es sich bei diesen Geschäften um ein **einheitliches Geschäft** handelt.[118] Wenn diese Gegengeschäftsvereinbarungen aber aus zwei rechtlich unterscheidbaren, jedoch miteinander verknüpften Kaufverträgen bestehen, kann das Übereinkommen auf die einzelnen Kaufverträge Anwendung finden.[119]

Eine weitere Gruppe vom Anwendungsbereich des Übereinkommens ausgeschlossener **31** Verträge ist die der **Vertriebsverträge**[120] (zu denen unter anderem Alleinvertriebsverträge und Eigenhändlerverträge zählen).[121] Diese stellen in der Regel Rahmenvereinbarungen dar,[122] die „auf die Ausgestaltung des Vertriebskonzepts, die Fixierung globaler Liefer- und Abnahmeverpflichtungen gerichtet sind",[123] und fallen nicht in den Anwendungsbereich des CISG.[124] Dies ist nicht nur in der Lehre vertreten worden;[125] auch die Rechtsprechung hat wiederholt darauf hingewiesen, dass Vertriebsverträge bzw. Rahmenverträge[126] nicht vom Übereinkommen erfasst werden,[127] zumindest dann, wenn „nach den Vorstellungen

---

„Preis" „Geld" ist, „das im Austausch für eine gekaufte Ware, für bereitgestellte digitale Inhalte oder eine erbrachte verbundene Dienstleistung geschuldet ist".

[115] *Staudinger/Magnus,* Art. 1, Rn. 29; ebenso *Frignani/Torsello,* Il contratto internazionale, S. 458; a. A. *Bianca/Bonell/Maskow,* Art. 53, Anm. 2.3.; *Fairlie,* S. 46; *Honnold/Flechtner,* Art. 2, Rn. 56.1; *Horowitz,* 29 J. L. & Com. (2010), 99, 102; *Schlechtriem/Schwenzer/Schwenzer/Hachem,* CISG Commentary, Art. 1, Rn. 1.

[116] *Ferrari u. a./Saenger,* Internationales Vertragsrecht, Art. 1, Rn. 4; *Schlechtriem,* Internationales UN-Kaufrecht, Rn. 24; *Staudinger/Magnus,* Art. 1, Rn. 30.

[117] *Czerwenka,* Rechtsanwendungsprobleme, S. 141; a. A. *Lurger,* östZRVgl 1991, 415, 431.

[118] *Schlechtriem/Schwenzer/Schlechtriem,* CISG Commentary, 2. Aufl., Art. 1, Rn. 18.

[119] So auch *Bamberger/Roth/Saenger,* Art. 1, Rn. 4; *Enderlein/Maskow/Strohbach,* Art. 1, Anm. 1.; *Ferrari u. a./Saenger,* Internationales Vertragsrecht, Art. 1, Rn. 4; *Karollus,* S. 25; MünchKommHGB/*Benicke,* Art. 1, Rn. 9; *Piltz,* Internationales Kaufrecht, Rn. 2–24; *Schlechtriem,* Internationales UN-Kaufrecht, Rn. 24; a. A. *Czerwenka,* Rechtsanwendungsprobleme, S. 141.

[120] Vgl. hierzu eingehend *Ferrari,* EuLF 2000/2001, 7 ff.; *ders.,* Giust. Civ. 2000, 2334 ff.

[121] Vgl. HGer Aargau, 10.3.2010, CISG-online 2176; HGer Zürich, 8.4.1999, CISG-online 489 = SZIER 2000, 113, 114.

[122] So ausdrücklich auch *Bamberger/Roth/Saenger,* Art. 1, Rn. 5; *Ferrari u. a./Saenger,* Internationales Vertragsrecht, Art. 1, Rn. 5.

[123] OGer Luzern, 8.1.1997, CISG-online 228.

[124] Vgl. zum Haager Kaufrecht BGH, 4.4.1979, BGHZ 74, 136; BGH, 26.11.1980, NJW 1981, 1156.

[125] Vgl. *Achilles,* Art. 1, Rn. 3; *Bonell/Liguori,* Uniform L. Rev. 1996, 147, 149; *Brunner,* Art. 3, Rn. 13; *Corvaglia,* S. 15; *Ferrari u. a./Saenger,* Internationales Vertragsrecht, Art. 1, Rn. 5; *Gillette/Walt,* Sales Law, S. 50; *Grieser,* S. 139, *Honnold/Flechtner,* Art. 2, Rn. 56.2; *Honsell/Siehr,* Art. 2, Rn. 7; *Janssen,* The Application of the CISG in Dutch Courts, S. 129, 132; *Kahn,* Rev. dr. aff. int. 2001, 241, 250; *Klima,* RIW 1996, 1035, 1036; *Kritzer,* Guide to Practical Applications, S. 18; *Kröll u. a./Djordjevic,* Art. 4, Rn. 11; *Lohmann,* Parteiautonomie, S. 13 f.; *Magnus,* CISG in the German Federal Civil Court, S. 211, 214 f.; *ders.,* ZEuP 2002, 523, 528; MünchKommHGB/*Benicke,* Art. 1, Rn. 14; *Perovic,* Annals Fac. L. Belgrade 2011, 181, 188; *Piltz,* Internationales Kaufrecht, Rn. 2–41; *ders.,* NJW 2000, 553, 555; *Sannini,* L'applicazione, S. 94 f.; *Schlechtriem,* Internationales UN-Kaufrecht, Rn. 24a; *Schlechtriem/Schwenzer/Schlechtriem,* CISG Commentary, 2. Aufl., Art. 1, Rn. 16a; *Schlechtriem/Schwenzer/Schwenzer/Hachem,* CISG Commentary, Art. 1, Rn. 14; *Soergel/Lüderitz/Fenge,* Art. 1, Rn. 22; *Witz/Salger/Lorenz/Lorenz,* Art. 1, Rn. 7; z. T. a. A. *P. Huber/Mullis/P. Huber,* S. 48; *Kröll u. a./Perales Viscasillas,* Art. 1, Rn. 28; *Thieffry,* Dr. prat. com. int. 1993, 62, 68.

[126] Zum Ausschluss von Rahmenverträgen vom Anwendungsbereich des CISG, vgl. HGer Aargau, 10.3.2010, CISG-online 2176; Supreme Court of the People's Republic of China, 21.9.2005, CISG-online 1611; *Amco Ukrservice & Promriladamco v. American Meter Company,* U. S. Dist. Ct. (E. D. Pa.), 29.3.2004, CISG-online 1664; OLG Hamm, 3.11.1997, CISG-online 381; a. A. ICC, 12713, CISG-online 2066.

[127] Vgl. *Gruppo Essenziero Italiano, S. P. A. v. Aromi D'Italia, Inc.,* U. S. Dist. Ct. (D. Md.), 27.7.2011, CISG-online 2223; Serbian Chamber of Commerce, 28.1.2009, CISG Pace; High Commercial Court, Serbia, 22.4.2008, CISG-online 1990; Serbian Chamber of Commerce, 13.11.2007, CISG-online 1794; Cass. com., 20.2.2007, CISG-online 1492; ICC, 11 849/2003, CISG-online 1421; *Amco Ukrservice & Promriladamco v. American Meter Company,* U. S. Dist. Ct. (E. D. Pa.), 13.4.2004, CISG-online 1409; ICC, 11849, CISG-online 1429; KG Schaffhausen, 23.4.2002, CISG-online 731; *Viva Vino Import v. Farnese Vini,* U. S. Dist. Ct. (E. D. Pa.), 29.8.2000, CISG-online 675 = 2000 U. S. Dist. LEXIS 12 347 = IHR 2002, 28; OLG Dresden, 27.12.1999, CISG-online 511 = TranspR-IHR 2000, 20; OLG Hamburg, 5.10.1998, CISG-online 473 = TranspR-IHR 1999, 37 f.; *Helen Kaminski Pty. Ltd. v. Marketing Austrialian Products Inc.,* U. S. Dist. Ct. (S. D. N. Y.), 23.6.1997, CISG-online 297 = 1998 WL 414 137; BGH, 23.7.1997, CISG-online 285 = NJW 1997, 3304 ff.; OGer Luzern, 8.1.1997, CISG-online 228; OLG Düsseldorf, 11.7.1996, CISG-online 201 =

der Parteien andere als die typisch kaufrechtlichen Elemente" überwiegen.[128] Die in Durchführung von Vertriebsverträgen abgeschlossenen **einzelnen Kaufverträge** können – bei Vorliegen aller anderen Anwendungsvoraussetzungen – aber durchaus dem CISG unterliegen,[129] selbst dann, wenn die Rahmenvereinbarung vor dessen Inkrafttreten abgeschlossen worden ist.[130]

32 Ausgeschlossen vom Anwendungsbereich des CISG sind auch **Franchiseverträge**,[131] die auch Rahmenvereinbarungen darstellen, in denen die kauffremden Pflichten im Vordergrund stehen.[132] Auf die in Durchführung eines Franchisevertrags geschlossenen einzelnen Kaufverträge kann das Übereinkommen aber Anwendung finden,[133] und dies selbst dann, wenn der Franchisevertrag nichtig ist – zum Beispiel weil er gegen nationales oder europäisches Kartellrecht verstößt. Dies gilt zumindest dann, wenn nach dem anwendbaren nationalen Recht, an dem ex Art. 4 lit. a) die Gültigkeit der Kaufverträge gemessen werden muss,[134] die Nichtigkeit des Franchisevertrages nicht zur Nichtigkeit der einzelnen Kaufverträge führt.[135]

RIW 1996, 958; Stadtgericht Budapest, 19.3.1996, CISG-online 289; OLG Koblenz, 17.9.1993, CISG-online 91 = RIW 1993, 934; Hof Amsterdam, 16.7.1992, CISG-online 48 = NIPR 10 (1992), Nr. 420; Polnischer Oberster Gerichtshof, 27.1.2006, CISG-online 1399; a. A. Cass. civ., 14.12.1999, Giust. Civ. 2000, 2333 ff., mit krit. Anm. *Ferrari* = EuLF 2000/2001, 11, mit krit. Anm. *Ferrari*.

[128] OGer Luzern, 8.1.1997, CISG-online 228; Vgl. aber OLG München, 22.9.1995, CISG-online 208 = RIW 1996, 1035, mit abl. Anm. *Klima*, wonach „die Frage, ob das Klägerin eine Lieferpflicht unter Einhaltung eines Alleinvertriebsrechts der Beklagten hat, dem CISG [unterliegt]", da im konkreten Fall das Alleinvertriebsrecht nicht nur das Recht gibt, „ein Produkt eines anderen in einem bestimmten Gebiet zu vertreiben, sondern den Hersteller/Lieferanten dazu [verpflichtet], die hierzu erforderliche Ware unter bestimmten Voraussetzungen zur Verfügung zu stellen". Vgl. aber auch Polnischer Oberster Gerichtshof, 27.1.2006, CISG-online 1399: Anwendung des CISG auf Rahmenverträge; OLG Graz, 28.9.2000, CISG-online 798: Anwendung des CISG „auf Rahmenverträge kaufrechtlichen Inhaltes".

[129] Vgl. in der Lehre *Bamberger/Roth/Saenger*, Art. 1, Rn. 5; *Brunner*, Art. 3, Rn. 13, *Butler*, 76 Fla. B.J. (2002), 24, 26; *Ferrari*, Giust. civ. 2000, 2333, 2338–2339; *ders.*, EuLF 2000/01, 7, 10; *Ferrari u. a./Saenger*, Internationales Vertragsrecht, Art. 1, Rn. 5; *Honsell/Siehr*, Art. 1, Rn. 7; *Janssen*, The Application of the CISG in Dutch Courts, S. 129, 132 f.; *Kahn*, Rev. dr. aff. int. 2001, 241, 250; *Kröll u. a./Perales Viscasillas*, Art. 1, Rn. 33; *Lohmann*, Parteiautonomie, S. 15; MünchKomm/*Westermann*, Art. 1, Rn. 6; MünchKommHGB/*Benicke*, Art. 1, Rn. 14; *Perovic*, Annals Fac. L. Belgrade 2011, 181, 188; *Piltz*, Internationales Kaufrecht, Rn. 2–41 a. E.; *ders.*, NJW 2000, 553, 555; *ders.*, NJW 2003, 2056, 2058; *Sannini*, L'applicazione, S. 95; *Schlechtriem*, Internationales UN-Haufrecht, Rn. 24a; *Schlechtriem/Schwenzer/Schlechtriem*, CISG Commentary, 2. Aufl., Art. 1, Rn. 16a; *Staudinger/Magnus*, Art. 1, Rn. 37; *Witz/Salger/Lorenz/Lorenz*, Art. 1, Rn. 7; vgl. in der Rechtsprechung *Gruppo Essenziero Italiano, S. P. A. v. Aromi D'Italia, Inc.*, U. S. Dist. Ct. (D. Md.), 27.7.2011, CISG-online 2223; HGer Aargau, 10.3.2010, CISG-online 2176; Yugoslav Chamber of Commerce, 28.1.2009, CISG-online 1856; High Commercial Court of Serbia, 24.4.2008, CISG-online 1990; Serbian Chamber of Commerce, 13.11.2007, CISG-online 1794; OLG Köln, 15.9.2004, CISG-online 1057 = IHR 2005, 161, 162; *Amco Ukrservice & Promriladamco v. American Meter Company*, U. S. Dist. Ct. (E. D. Pa.), 29.3.2004, CISG-online 1664; ICC, 11849, CISG-online 1429; OLG Köln, 28.5.2001, CISG-online 681 = IHR 2002, 21, 23; HGer Zürich, 8.4.1999, CISG-online 489 = SZIER 2000, 113, 114; OLG München, 9.7.1997, CISG-online 282 = Forum Int. R. 1998, 29 ff.; HGer Zürich, 26.4.1995, CISG-online 248 = TranspR-IHR 1999, 54; OLG Düsseldorf, 11.7.1996, CISG-online 201 = NJW-RR 1997, 822.

[130] Vgl. in der Rechtsprechung zum CISG OLG Koblenz, 17.9.1993, CISG-online 91 = RIW 1993, 936; Hof Amsterdam, 16.7.1992, CISG-online 48 = NIPR 1992, Nr. 420; zum EKG, siehe BGH, 4.4.1979, BGHZ 74, 136; BGH, 26.11.1980, NJW 1981, 1156; in der Lehre est verwiesen auf *Honnold/Flechtner*, Art. 2, Rn. 56.2; *Kahn*, Dr. prat. com. int. 1989, 385, 389; *Kritzer*, Guide to Practical Applications, S. 71; *Staudinger/Magnus*, Art. 1, Rn. 37.

[131] Vgl. *Achilles*, Art. 1, Rn. 3; *Bamberger/Roth/Saenger*, Art. 1, Rn. 5; *Brunner*, Art. 2, Rn. 9 und Art. 3, Rn. 14; *Fairlie*, S. 46; *Ferrari u. a./Saenger*, Internationales Vertragsrecht, Art. 1, Rn. 5; *Gillette/Walt*, Sales Law, S. 50; *Kröll u. a./Djordjevic*, Art. 4, Rn. 11; *Piltz*, Internationales Kaufrecht, Rn. 2–41; *Staudinger/Magnus*, Art. 1, Rn. 39; *Vischer/L. Huber/Oser*, Rn. 357; a. A. *Kröll u. a./Perales Viscasillas*, Art. 1, Rn. 28 (vgl. aber dort Rn. 34).

[132] So ausdrücklich BGH, 23.7.1997, CISG-online 285 = NJW 1997, 3304, 3309; auch OGer Luzern, 8.1.1997, CISG-online 228, schließt Franchiseverträge vom Anwendungsbereich aus.

[133] *Brunner*, Art. 2, Rn. 9.

[134] Vgl. Art. 4 Rn. 15 ff.

[135] BGH, 23.7.1997, CISG-online 276 = NJW 1997, 3309.

Anwendungsbereich 33, 34 **Art. 1**

Schenkungen fallen unzweifelhaft nicht unter das Übereinkommen.[136] Ein Teil der 33 Lehre hat jedoch darauf hingewiesen, dass Käufe, „bei denen ein unangemessen niedriger (Freundschafts-)Preis oder ein nur symbolischer Preis („1 Dollar", „1 Euro") berechnet wird",[137] problematisch sein können. M. E. kann das Übereinkommen auf diese Kaufverträge durchaus Anwendung finden, aber nur, wenn diese nicht nach dem anwendbaren Recht ungültig sind.[138]

3. Waren im Sinne des CISG

Das Übereinkommen definiert den Begriff der „Ware" genauso wenig wie es den des 34 Kaufvertrages definiert.[139] Dies bedeutet jedoch nicht, dass zu dessen Bestimmung auf nationales Recht zurückgegriffen werden kann.[140] Der Begriff ist **autonom** zu bestimmen.[141] Dies scheint keine zu großen Schwierigkeiten aufzuwerfen, unter anderem auch deshalb, weil man auf die Erfahrungen mit dem Haager Kaufrecht zurückgreifen kann, obwohl das Haager Kaufrecht nicht vom Begriff der „Ware" ausgeht, sondern von dem der „Sache". Dieser sprachliche Unterschied ergibt sich nicht so sehr aus den englischen Originalfassungen, die beide denselben Ausdruck, „goods", verwenden,[142] sondern aus den französischen Originaltexten.[143] Während das Wiener Übereinkommen auf einen „unverbrauchteren Ausdruck",[144] dem der „marchandises", abstellt, spricht das Haager Kaufrecht präziser von „objets mobiliers corporels". Mit der Abweichung von der Haager Terminologie ist jedoch keine grundsätzliche Änderung verbunden.[145] Als „Waren" sind demnach auch nach dem CISG grundsätzlich nur **(zur Zeit der Lieferung)**[146] **bewegliche kör-**

---

[136] *Brunner*, Art. 2, Rn. 9; *Fairlie*, S. 46; *Lacasse*, Le champ d'application, S. 27; MünchKommHGB/*Benicke*, Art. 1, Rn. 10; *Schmitt*, CR 2001, 145, 149; *Vischer/L. Huber/Oser*, Rn. 350.

[137] *Staudinger/Magnus*, Art. 1, Rn. 32.

[138] *Staudinger/Magnus*, Art. 1, Rn. 32, geht davon aus, dass wenn man bei diesen Verträgen nicht zwischen einem entgeltlichen Kauf und einer unentgeltlichen Schenkung trennen kann, die Konvention grundsätzlich anzuwenden sei, da sie auch sonst nicht nach der Ausgewogenheit der gegenseitigen Leistungen differenziere; a. A. MünchKommHGB/*Benicke*, Art. 1, Rn. 10: CISG sei nicht anwendbar, „wenn der Kaufpreis nur symbolische Bedeutung hat (1 Dollar oder 1 Euro) und es sich daher in der Sache um eine Schenkung handelt".

[139] *Bailey*, 32 Cornell Int'l L. J. (1999), 273, 306; *Bamberger/Roth/Saenger*, Art. 1, Rn. 2; Botschaft des Schweizerischen Bundesrats, S. 759; *Esslinger*, ALI-ABA (1999), 69, 80; *Fairlie*, S. 43; *Gillette/Walt*, Sales Law, S. 49; *Kröll u. a./Perales Viscasillas*, Art. 1, Rn. 36; *Martin-Davidson*, 17 Mich. St. J. Int'l L. (2008), 657, 669; *Maley*, 12 Int'l Trade & Bus. L. Rev. (2009), 82, 84; *Niemann*, Einheitliche Anwendung, S. 89; *Perovic*, Annals Fac. L. Belgrade 2011, 181, 193; *Rudolph*, Art. 1, Rn. 3; *Sannini*, L'applicazione, S. 103; *Schmitt*, CR 2001, 145, 147; *Schwenzer/Hachem/Kee*, Rn. 7.5; *Wulf*, S. 37; ebenso in der Rechtsprechung Tribunale di Padova, 10.1.2006, CISG-online 1157.

[140] So schon *Ferrari*, Applicabilità ed applicazioni, S. 163; vgl. nun auch *Kröll u. a./Perales Viscasillas*, Art. 1, Rn. 36; *Schwenzer/Hachem/Kee*, Rn. 7.5.

[141] Vgl. *Bamberger/Roth/Saenger*, Art. 1, Rn. 2; *Brunner*, Art. 2, Rn. 1; *Diedrich*, RIW 1993, 441, 443 f.; *Ferrari u. a./Saenger*, Internationales Vertragsrecht, Art. 1, Rn. 2; *Kee*, FS Schwenzer, S. 925, 934; *Kröll u. a./Perales Viscasillas*, Art. 1, Rn. 36; MünchKommHGB/*Benicke*, Art. 1, Rn. 2; *Niemann*, Einheitliche Anwendung, S. 89; *Perovic*, Annals Fac. L. Belgrade 2011, 181, 193; *Piltz*, Internationales Kaufrecht, Rn. 2–49; *Reinhart*, Art. 1, Rn. 1; *Schlechtriem/Schwenzer/Schwenzer/Hachem*, CISG Commentary, Art. 1, Rn. 16; ebenso in der Rechtsprechung Tribunale di Forlì, 11.12.2008, CISG-online 1729; Tribunale di Padova, 11.1.2005, CISG-online 967; Tribunale di Padova, 25.2.2004, CISG-online 819; a. A. *Garro/Zuppi*, Compraventa internacional, S. 78 f.

[142] Vgl. hierzu neuerdings auch *Schlechtriem/Schwenzer/Schwenzer/Hachem*, CISG Commentary, Art. 1, Rn. 16.

[143] Vgl. *Herber*, 2. Aufl., Art. 1 Rn. 20.

[144] *Staudinger/Magnus*, Art. 1, Rn. 43 a. E.

[145] Vgl. *Ferrari*, Applicabilità ed applicazioni, S. 156; *Herber*, 2. Aufl., Art. 1 Rn. 20; *Kahn*, Rev. int. dr. comp. 1981, 951, 956; *Niemann*, Einheitliche Anwendung, S. 90; *Schlechtriem/Schwenzer/Schlechtriem*, CISG Commentary, 2. Aufl., Art. 1, Rn. 20; a. A. *Karollus*, S. 21, den die neue Terminologie zur „Ausdehnung des Waren-Begriffs auf alle Sachen, die Gegenstand von Handelskäufen sind", führt.

[146] Siehe *Bamberger/Roth/Saenger*, Art. 1, Rn. 6; *Brunner*, Art. 2, Rn. 2 und Art. 3, Rn. 4; *Ferrari u. a./Saenger*, Internationales Vertragsrecht, Art. 1, Rn. 6; *Herber/Czerwenka*, Art. 1, Rn. 7; *Karollus*, S. 21; *Kröll u. a./Perales Viscasillas*, Art. 1, Rn. 37; MünchKommHGB/*Benicke*, Art. 1, Rn. 16; *Schlechtriem*, Internationales Kaufrecht, Rn. 31; *Schlechtriem/Schwenzer/Schlechtriem*, CISG Commentary, 2. Aufl., Art. 1, Rn. 23; *Schlechtriem/Schwenzer/Schwenzer/Hachem*, CISG Commentary, Art. 1, Rn. 16; *Schwenzer/Hachem/Kee*, Rn. 7.6;

Art. 1 35   Teil I. Kapitel I. Anwendungsbereich

perliche Sachen zu verstehen,[147] was nicht nur durch die deutsche[148] und ausländische Lehre,[149] sondern auch durch die neuere Rechtsprechung hervorgehoben worden ist.[150] Irrelevant ist nicht nur die Form der Waren,[151] sondern auch ob es sich dabei um bereits **existierende, herzustellende** oder **entstehende** Sachen handelt.[152] Auch **lebende Tiere**[153] oder **Sachgesamtheiten** können „Waren" im Sinne des Übereinkommens sein.[154]

35   Aus dieser Definition ergibt sich unter anderem, dass **Immobilien,** also unbewegliche Sachen, nicht unter den Warenbegriff fallen.[155] Demnach sind Grundstücke keine „Waren" im Sinne des CISG.[156] Unter den Warenbegriff des Übereinkommens fallen jedoch **Bestandteile,** die zwar mit einem Grundstück verbunden werden sollen (oder mit diesem verbunden sind), aber bei der Übergabe beweglich sind,[157] und dies, da der Warenbegriff

---

Witz/Salger/Lorenz/Lorenz, Art. 1, Rn. 6; vgl. in der Rechtsprechung OGer Aargau, 3.3.2009, CISG-online 2013; Tribunale di Forlì, 16.2.2009, CISG-online 1780; Tribunale di Padova, 25.2.2004, CISG-online 819; Tribunale di Rimini, 26.11.2002, CISG-online 737; CA Grenoble, 26.4.1995, CISG-online 154; unklar *Martin-Davidson,* 17 Mich. St. J. Int'l L. (2008), 657, 679 f.

[147] Vgl. auch Art. 2 lit. (h) des Vorschlags für eine Verordnung des Europäischen Parlaments und des Rates über ein Gemeinsames Europäisches Kaufrecht vom 11.10.2011, KOM(2011) 635 endgültig, S. 26, wonach „Waren" „bewegliche körperliche Gegenstände" sind.

[148] Vgl. *Achilles,* Art. 1, Rn. 4; *Czerwenka,* Rechtsanwendungsprobleme, S. 147; *Lohmann,* Parteiautonomie, S. 12; *Ragno,* Convenzione di Vienna e Diritto europeo, S. 15 f.; *Schlechtriem/Schwenzer/Schwenzer/Hachem,* CISG Commentary, Art. 1, Rn. 16; *Wasmer,* S. 14; weniger eindeutig *Staudinger/Magnus,* Art. 1, Rn. 43 f., wonach auch bestimmte unkörperliche Gegenstände unter den Warenbegriff einzuordnen sind; so auch *Piltz,* Internationales Kaufrecht, Rn. 2–48; *Schlechtriem,* Internationales UN-Kaufrecht, Rn. 32a; *Witz/Salger/Lorenz/Lorenz,* Art. 1, Rn. 5.

[149] *Brunner,* Art. 2, Rn. 2; *Díez-Picazo/Calvo Caravaca,* Art. 1, S. 48; *P. Huber/Mullis/P. Huber,* S. 41; *Gillette/Walt,* Sales Law, S. 49; *Kahn,* Rev. dr. aff. int. 2001, 241, 243; *Kröll u. a./Perales Viscasillas,* Art. 1, Rn. 37; *Perovic,* Annals Fac. L. Belgrade 2011, 181, 193; *Sannini,* L'applicazione, S. 104; vgl. auch *Maley,* 12 Int'l Trade & Bus. L. Rev. (2009), 82, 86, der jedoch etwas weitergeht: „goods does not include things that are entirely intagible property but does include things comprising dominant physical aspects and subsidiary non-physical characteristics".

[150] So ausdrücklich HGer Aargau, 10.3.2010, CISG-online 2176; Tribunale di Forlì, 16.2.2009, CISG-online 1780; Tribunale di Forlì, 11.12.2008, CISG-online 1729; HGer Aargau, 20.9.2007, CISG-online 1742; Tribunale di Padova, 10.1.2006, CISG-online 1157; Tribunale di Padova, 11.1.2005, CISG-online 967; Tribunale di Padova, 25.2.2004, CISG-online 819; Tribunale di Rimini, 26.11.2002, CISG-online 737 = Giur. it. 2003, 896 f., m. Anm. *Ferrari;* KG Zug, 21.10.1999, CISG-online 491 = IHR 2001, 45; Tribunale di Pavia, 29.12.1999, CISG-online 678 = Corr. giur. 2000, 932, 932; OLG Köln, 21.5.1996, CISG-online 254; OGH, 10.11.1994, CISG-online 117 = ZfRVgl 1995, 79 ff.; OLG Köln, 26.8.1994, CISG-online 132 = RIW 1994, 970, in dem außerdem statuiert wird, dass „Waren" im Sinne des Übereinkommens nur „körperliche bewegliche Sachen [sind], die typischerweise den Gegenstand eines Handelskaufs bilden".

[151] So ausdrücklich Tribunale di Forlì, 16.2.2009, CISG-online 1780; Tribunale di Forlì, 11.12.2008, CISG-online 1729.

[152] *Brunner,* Art. 2, Rn. 2; *Ferrari u. a./Saenger,* Internationales Vertragsrecht, Art. 1, Rn. 6; *Kröll u.a / Mistelis/Raymond,* Art. 3, Rn. 1; *Nottage,* 36 Vic. U. Well. L. Rev. (2005), 815, 819; *Piltz,* NJW 2000, 553, 554.

[153] So ausdrücklich Tribunale di Forlì, 16.2.2009, CISG-online 1780; Tribunale di Forlì, 11.12.2008, CISG-online 1729; District Court Copenhagen, 19.10.2007, CISG-online 2150; Tribunale di Padova, 11.1.2005, CISG-online 967; OLG Schleswig-Holstein, 29.10.2002, CISG-online 717 = IHR 2003, 67; LG Flensburg, 19.1.2001, CISG-online 619 = IHR 2001, 67; CA Paris, 14.1.1998, CISG-online 347; Hof Arnhem, 22.8.1995, CISG-online 317.

[154] *Achilles,* Art. 1, Rn. 4; *Bamberger/Roth/Saenger,* Art. 1, Rn. 6; *Brunner,* Art. 2, Rn. 2; *Ferrari u. a./Saenger,* Internationales Vertragsrecht, Art. 1, Rn. 6; *Staudinger/Magnus,* Art. 1, Rn. 51; einen Überblick in den verschiedenen Kategorien von Waren, deren Kauf zu dem CISG unterliegt, geben neuerdings; *Schwenzer/Hachem/Kee,* Rn. 5.46.

[155] *Enderlein/Maskow/Strohbach,* Art. 1, Anm. 2.; *Ferrari,* Applicabilità ed applicazioni, S. 162 f.; *Gillette/Walt,* Sales Law, S. 49; *Hafez,* S. 44; *Honsell/Siehr,* Art. 2, Rn. 9; *Karollus,* JuS 1993, 378, 380; MünchKomm/*Westermann,* Vor Art. 1, Rn. 4; *Penda Matipé,* S. 38; *Reinhart,* Art. 1, Rn. 3; *Rudolph,* Art. 1, Rn. 4; *Schlechtriem,* 36 Vict. U. Well. L. Rev. (2005), 781, 784; *Schwenzer/Hachem/Kee,* Rn. 7.5; *Wasmer,* S. 14; *Witz/Salger/Lorenz/Lorenz,* Art. 1, Rn. 5.

[156] So Botschaft des Schweizerischen Bundesrats, S. 760; vgl. in der Rechsprechung OGer Aargau, 3.3.2009, CISG-online 2013.

[157] *Herber,* 2. Aufl., Art. 1 Rn. 23; *Herber/Czerwenka,* Art. 1, Rn. 7; MünchKomm/*Westermann,* Art. 1, Rn. 8; *Schlechtriem/Schwenzer/Schwenzer/Hachem,* CISG Commentary, Art. 1, Rn. 17; ebenso in der Rechsprechung OGer Aargau, 3.3.2009, CISG-online 2013.

Anwendungsbereich   36–38   **Art. 1**

autonom auszulegen ist, selbst dann, wenn diese nach nationalem Sachenrecht nicht selbstständig verkehrsfähig sind.[158]

Aus der Definition der „Waren" ergibt sich auch, dass **unkörperliche Sachen** in der Regel nicht unter den Warenbegriff fallen.[159] **Rechte,**[160] wie etwa Forderungen,[161] Patente,[162] Lizenzen[163] etc., können, genauso wenig wie **Sendezeit oder -raum** in einem Medium, daher nicht als „Waren" im Sinne des Übereinkommens angesehen werden[164] (Sachen aber, an denen Schutzrechte bestehen, fallen unter den Warenbegriff, wobei irrelevant ist, ob das Schutzrecht mitveräußert wird oder einem Dritten zusteht).[165] Daher ist es nicht verwunderlich, dass der Kauf eines Geschäftsanteils einer GmbH vom Anwendungsbereich des Übereinkommens ausgeschlossen worden ist.[166] Was den **Unternehmenskauf** angeht, muss wohl davon ausgegangen werden, dass er nicht unter das Übereinkommen fällt, unabhängig davon, ob es sich um einen asset deal oder share deal handelt.[167] 36

Der **Dokumentenkauf,** insbesondere das sogenannte **Abladegeschäft,**[168] bei dem der Verkäufer die Verpflichtung zur Verschiffung übernimmt, auch wenn im Vertrag ein Traditionspapier als Kaufgegenstand angegeben ist, unterfällt aber dem Übereinkommen,[169] da hier nicht das Wertpapier oder sonstige Dokumente, sondern die Sache selbst Kaufgegenstand ist.[170] 37

Das Merkmal der Körperlichkeit erlaubt es außerdem nicht, **„Know-how"** als Ware im Sinne des Übereinkommens zu qualifizieren,[171] zumindest sofern es nicht Bestandteil eines 38

---

[158] A. A. *Staudinger/Magnus,* Art. 1, Rn. 54.
[159] *Kröll u. a./Perales Viscasillas,* Art. 1, Rn. 38; *Maley,* 12 Int'l Trade & Bus. L. Rev. (2009), 82, 84; *Sannini,* L'applicazione, S. 104 f.; a. A. *Schmitt,* CR 2001, 145, 149: „Waren i. S. des Art. 1 I CISG sind sowohl bewegliche als auch unkörperliche, abgrenzbare, bewegliche Gegenstände".
[160] Vgl. *Achilles,* Art. 1, Rn. 4; *Ferrari u. a./Saenger,* Art. 1, Rn. 6; *Gillette/Walt,* Sales Law, S. 49; *Karollus,* S. 21; *Kröll u. a./Perales Viscasillas,* Art. 1, Rn. 38; *Merkt,* Internationaler Unternehmenskauf, Rn. 841; MünchKomm/*Westermann,* Art. 1, Rn. 6; MünchKommHGB/*Benicke,* Art. 1, Rn. 16; *Schlechtriem,* 36 Vict. U. Well. L. Rev. (2005), 781, 786; *Schlechtriem/Schwenzer/Schwenzer/Hachem,* CISG Commentary, Art. 1, Rn. 22; *Witz/Salger/Lorenz/Lorenz,* Art. 1, Rn. 5.
[161] Vgl. in der Lehre *Schlechtriem,* Internationales UN-Kaufrecht, Rn. 31.
[162] *Brunner,* Art. 2, Rn. 3.
[163] *Bamberger/Roth/Saenger,* Art. 1, Rn. 7; *Ferrari u. a./Saenger,* Internationales Vertragsrecht, Art. 1, Rn. 4; MünchKommHGB/*Benicke,* Art. 1, Rn. 18.
[164] *Díez-Picazo/Calvo Caravaca,* Art. 1, S. 48.
[165] So ausdrücklich *Brunner,* Art. 2, Rn. 3; *Staudinger/Magnus,* Art. 1, Rn. 57.
[166] Vgl. *Achilles,* Art. 1, Rn. 4; *Honnold/Flechtner,* Art. 2, Rn. 56.5; *Merkt,* ZVglRW 1994, 353, 359; *Schlechtriem,* Internationales UN-Kaufrecht, Rn. 31; *Soergel/Lüderitz/Fenge,* Art. 1, Rn. 21; *Vida,* IPRax 1995, 52 f.
[167] So im Ergebnis auch *Merkt,* Internationaler Unternehmenskauf, Rn. 875, der jedoch hervorhebt, dass die amerikanische Praktikerliteratur eine andere Auffassung vertritt; ders., ZVglRW 1994, 353, 361 und 370; den Unternehmenskauf vom Anwendungsbereich generell ausschließend auch *Achilles,* Art. 1, Rn. 4; *Bamberger/Roth/Saenger,* Art. 1, Rn. 6; *Ferrari u. a./Saenger,* Internationales Vertragsrecht, Art. 1, Rn. 6; *Herber/Czerwenka,* Art. 1, Rn. 7; *Kröll u. a./Perales Viscasillas,* Art. 1, Rn. 39; MünchKomm/*Westermann,* Art. 1, Rn. 6; *Vischer/L. Huber/Oser,* Rn. 359; *Witz/Salger/Lorenz/Lorenz,* Art. 1, Rn. 8; z. T. a. A. *Schlechtriem,* Internationales UN-Kaufrecht, Rn. 31, der bei einem asset deal das CISG dann für anwendbar erklärt, wenn das Betriebsvermögen überwiegend aus beweglichen Sachen besteht; ebenso *Brunner,* Art. 2, Rn. 5; *P. Huber/Mullis/P. Huber,* S. 42; *Schlechtriem/Schwenzer/Schlechtriem,* CISG Commentary, 2. Aufl., Art. 1, Rn. 24; vgl. hingegen *Schlechtriem/Schwenzer/Schwenzer/Hachem,* CISG Commentary, Art. 1, Rn. 21.
[168] MünchKomm/*Westermann,* Art. 1, Rn. 6.
[169] Vgl. etwa CISG-AC, Op. 5 *(Schwenzer),* Comment 4.12; *P. Huber/Mullis/P. Huber,* S. 49; *Kröll u. a./Perales Viscasillas,* Art. 1, Rn. 41; *Mohs,* FS Schwenzer, S. 1285, 1297; *Schlechtriem,* 36 Vict. U. Well. L. Rev. (2005), 781, 784; *Zeller,* FS Kritzer, S. 627, 632.
[170] Vgl. *Bailey,* 32 Cornell Int'l L. J. (1999), 273, 309; *Bianca/Carbone/Lopez de Gonzalo,* Art. 1, S. 3; *Ferrari,* Applicabilità ed applicazioni, S. 188; *Karollus,* S. 21; *Lacasse,* Le champ d'application, S. 33; *Schlechtriem,* Einheitliches UN-Kaufrecht, S. 15; *Schlechtriem/Schwenzer/Schlechtriem,* CISG Commentary, 2. Aufl., Art. 1, Rn. 22; *Schlechtriem/Schwenzer/Schwenzer/Hachem,* CISG Commentary, Art. 1, Rn. 20; *Schwenzer/Hachem/Kee,* Rn. 7.22; Sekretariatskommentar, Art. 2, Nr. 8; *Staudinger/Magnus,* Art. 1, Rn. 47; *Witz/Salger/Lorenz/Lorenz,* Art. 1, Rn. 6.
[171] *P. Huber/Mullis/P. Huber,* S. 42; *Maley,* 12 Int'l Trade & Bus. L. Rev. (2009), 82, 84; *Sannini,* L'applicazione, S. 105; *Schlechtriem/Schwenzer/Schwenzer/Hachem,* CISG Commentary, Art. 1, Rn. 19.

körperlichen Mediums ist.[172] Gleiches gilt auch in Bezug auf **Computerprogramme** (Software):[173] Programme, die über einen Träger nutzbar sind, müssen als „Waren" angesehen werden.[174] Dies bedeutet jedoch nicht, dass der Kauf von Computerprogrammen selbst bei Vorliegen der zeitlichen und territorialen Anwendungsvoraussetzungen dem Übereinkommen immer unterliegen muss.[175] Dies hängt damit zusammen, dass bei einem Vertrag über die Ausarbeitung eines Computerprogramms **(Individualsoftware)** die arbeits- bzw. dienstvertraglichen Pflichten durchaus überwiegen können, was kraft Art. 3 II zum Ausschluss vom Anwendungsbereich des CISG führt.[176] Handelt es sich bei den über einen Träger nutzbar gemachten Computerprogrammen jedoch um **Standardsoftware,** ist Art. 3 II in der Regel nicht anwendbar; das Übereinkommen kann demnach Anwendung finden.[177] Diese Meinung ist nicht nur in der (deutschen[178] und ausländischen)[179] Lehre vertreten worden; sie ist neuerdings auch von der Rechtsprechung aufgegriffen worden.[180] Es muss jedoch darauf hingewiesen werden, dass selbst bei Verträgen, die Standardsoftware zum Gegenstand haben, das CISG nicht immer Anwendung finden kann. Dies hängt aber weniger von dem Gegenstand des Vertrages ab, als von dem Vertrag selbst. Wird nämlich die Standardsoftware nur auf Zeit überlassen, endet „am Ende der Laufzeit [...] die Nutzungsberechtigung und der Lizenznehmer muss zurückgeben, was zurückgebbar ist".[181] Auf

---

[172] Vgl. auch *Achilles,* Art. 1, Rn. 4; *Fairlie,* S. 48; *Ferrari u. a./Saenger,* Internationales Vertragsrecht, Art. 1, Rn. 7; *Magnus,* ZEuP 1995, 202, 206; *Schlechtriem,* AJP 1992, 339, 346; *Schlechtriem/Schwenzer/Schlechtriem,* CISG Commentary, 2. Aufl., Art. 1, Rn. 21a; a. A. *Enderlein/Maskow/Strohbach,* Art. 1, Anm. 2.; MünchKommHGB/*Benicke,* Art. 1, Rn. 18 a. E.

[173] Keine Sorgen bereitet die Anwendbarkeit des CISG auf den Verkauf von Hardware; vgl. etwa LG München I, 29.5.1995, CISG-online 235 = NJW 1996, 401 f.; LG Heidelberg, 3.7.1992, CISG-online 38; vgl. in der Lehre statt aller *Honnold/Flechtner,* Art. 2, Rn. 56.4.

[174] *Achilles,* Art. 1, Rn. 4; *Diedrich,* RIW 1993, 441, 451 f.; *Hoeren,* CR 1988, 908, 916; *Maley,* 12 Int'l Trade & Bus. L. Rev. (2009), 82, 85; *Niemann,* Einheitliche Anwendung, S. 89; *H. Sono,* FS Kritzer, S. 512, 517 f.; *Staudinger/Magnus,* Art. 1, Rn. 44; in der Rechtsprechung vgl. OGH, 21.6.2005, CISG-online 1047 = IHR 2005, 195 ff.: Anwendbarkeit des CISG auf dauerhafte Überlassung einer auf Datenträgern verkörperten Standardsoftware; vgl. aber *Bamberger/Roth/Saenger,* Art. 1, Rn. 7 und *Karollus,* S. 21 (Anwendung des CISG auf Kauf von Computerprogrammen, ohne dass es dafür auf einen mitverkauften Datenträger ankomme); ebenso *Brunner,* Art. 2, Rn. 4; *P. Huber/Mullis/P. Huber,* S. 43; *Schlechtriem/Schwenzer/Schlechtriem,* CISG Commentary, 2. Aufl., Art. 1, Rn. 21; *Schlechtriem/Schwenzer/Hachem,* CISG Commentary, Art. 1, Rn. 18; *Witz/Salger/Lorenz/Lorenz,* Art. 1, Rn. 6; *Wulf,* S. 42 ff., insb. S. 47 ff.; a. A. wohl auch *Schmitt,* CR 2001, 145, 150: „Die Online-Überlassung von Audio-, Bild-, Text- und Videoinhalten ist ebenfalls ein [dem CISG unterliegender] Kaufvertrag". Den Kauf von Software ohne jegliche Differenzierung dem CISG unterstellend hingegen RB Arnhem, 28.6.2006, CISG-online 1265.

[175] So aber *Honnold/Flechtner,* Art. 2, Rn. 56.4; *Schlechtriem/Schwenzer/Schwenzer/Hachem,* CISG Commentary, Art. 1, Rn. 18; so wohl auch *American Mint LLC v. GOSoftware, Inc.,* U. S. Dist. Ct. (M. D. Pa.), 6.1.2006, CISG-online 1175.

[176] Siehe auch *Brunner,* Art. 2, Rn. 4; *Diedrich,* RIW 1993, 441, 452; *Ferrari u. a./Saenger,* Internationales Vertragsrecht, Art. 1, Rn. 7; *Kröll u. a./Perales Viscasillas,* Art. 1, Rn. 40; *Kröll u. a./Mistelis/Raymond,* Art. 3, Rn. 25; *Maley,* 12 Int'l Trade & Bus. L. Rev. (2009), 82, 86; *Mankowski,* FS Schwenzer, S. 1175, 1183; *Schmitt,* CR 2001, 145, 150; *Soergel/Lüderitz/Fenge,* Art. 1, Rn. 21; *Wulf,* S. 30 ff.; kritisch hierzu *Schlechtriem/Schwenzer/Schlechtriem,* CISG Commentary, 2. Aufl., Art. 1, Rn. 21, Fn. 37b; *Schlechtriem/Schwenzer/Schwenzer/Hachem,* CISG Commentary, Art. 1, Rn. 18 Fn. 61; vgl. auch *Schwenzer/Hachem/Kee,* Rn. 7.29.

[177] Im Ergebnis auch *Bamberger/Roth/Saenger,* Art. 1, Rn. 7; *Bazinas,* Uniformity, S. 25; MünchKommHGB/*Benicke,* Art. 1, Rn. 18; *Piltz,* IHR 2005, 197; *Sannini,* L'applicazione, S. 109 ff.; *Witz/Salger/Lorenz/Lorenz,* Art. 1, Rn. 6; vgl. aber *Schlechtriem,* Internationales Kaufrecht, Rn. 32, der sich gegen die im Text erwähnte Unterscheidung ausspricht.

[178] Vgl. *Endler/Daub,* CR 1993, 601, 605; *Ferrari u. a./Saenger,* Internationales Vertragsrecht, Art. 1, Rn. 7; *Herrmann,* Anwendungsbereich, S. 92; *Magnus,* ZEuP 1995, 202, 206; MünchKomm/*Westermann,* Art. 1, Rn. 6; *Piltz,* AnwBl 1991, 57, 59; *Soergel/Lüderitz,* Art. 1, Rn. 16.

[179] *Ferrari,* Applicabilità ed applicazioni, S. 159 ff.; *Kahn,* Rev. dr. aff. int. 2001, 241, 244; *Liguori,* Foro it. 1996, IV, 145, 153.

[180] So OGH, 21.6.2005, CISG-online 1047 = IHR 2005, 195, 196; LG München I, 8.2.1995, CISG-online 203; obiter in diesem Sinne auch OLG Köln, 26.8.1994, CISG-online 132 = RIW 1994, 971; OLG Koblenz, 17.9.1993, CISG-online 91 = RIW 1993, 936; a. A. Hof 's-Hertogenbosch, 19.11.1996, CISG-online 323 = NIPR 1997, Nr. 123: Anwendung des CISG ohne Unterscheidung zwischen Standard- und Individualsoftware.

[181] *Schlechtriem,* Internationales Kaufrecht, Rn. 32b.

Anwendungsbereich   39, 40   **Art. 1**

diesen Vertrag findet das CISG keine Anwendung,[182] selbst wenn der Vertrag Standardsoftware zum Gegenstand hat.[183] Eine **wissenschaftliche Studie,** die auf Anfrage erstellt wird, wird aber selbst dann nicht als „Ware" angesehen werden können, wenn sie in bestimmter Form fixiert werden soll.[184]

Für den Warenbegriff irrelevant sind **Verkehrsfähigkeit** der Sachen[185] und besondere   39 Verkehrsbeschränkungen. Diese berühren lediglich die kraft Art. 4 lit. a) vom CISG nicht erfasste Frage der Gültigkeit des Kaufvertrages.[186] Bedeutungslos für den Warenbegriff ist ferner, ob eine Sache **neu** oder **gebraucht** ist,[187] ob sie bereits existiert oder noch hergestellt beziehungsweise produziert werden muss.[188]

IV. Der persönlich-räumliche Anwendungsbereich

1. Die Internationalität des Kaufvertrages

Wie nach dem Haager Kaufrecht unterfallen dem CISG lediglich „internationale" Kauf-   40 verträge. Im Gegensatz zum Haager Kaufrecht kommt diese (bisweilen kritisierte, weil nicht mehr der Realität entsprechende)[189] Internationalität aber nicht darin zum Ausdruck, dass neben einem subjektiven Erfordernis – wonach die Vertragsparteien ihre Niederlassung in verschiedenen Staaten haben müssen – auch ein objektives Erfordernis – zwischenstaatlicher Transport oder Vertragsabschluss über die Grenze oder Auseinanderfallen der Staaten des Vertragsabschlusses und der Lieferung – verlangt wird.[190] Im Sinne des CISG ist ein Kaufvertrag immer dann international, wenn die Parteien zum **Zeitpunkt des Vertragsschlusses,**[191] so nunmehr auch die Rechtsprechung,[192] ihre Niederlassung in **verschiedenen Staaten** haben.[193] Ein weiteres (objektives) Element ist nicht notwendig,[194] weshalb die

---

[182] Ebenso *Fairlie,* S. 45; *H. Sono,* FS Kritzer, S. 512, 516 ff.; vgl. auch OGH, 21.6.2005, CISG-online 1047 = IHR 2005, 195, 196: „Die dauerhafte Überlassung einer auf Datenträgern verkörperten Standardsoftware gegen Zahlung eines einmaligen Entgelts wird als Kauf einer beweglichen Sache qualifiziert".

[183] Vgl. auch *Schlechtriem,* 36 Vict. U. Well. L. Rev. (2005), 781, 786.

[184] Vgl. OLG Köln, 26.8.1994, CISG-online 132 = RIW 1994, 971; vgl. auch *Kröll u. a./Perales Viscasillas,* Art. 1, Rn. 38; *Maley,* 12 Int'l Trade & Bus. L. Rev. (2009), 82, 84; MünchKommHGB/*Benicke,* Art. 1, Rn. 18; *Schlechtriem/Schwenzer/Schwenzer/Hachem,* CISG Commentary, Art. 1, Rn. 19; *Soergel/Lüderitz/Fenge,* Art. 1, Rn. 21; *Staudinger/Magnus,* Art. 1, Rn. 46.

[185] Vgl. *Schlechtriem/Schwenzer/Schwenzer/Hachem,* CISG Commentary, Art. 1, Rn. 16: „Even if items are *extra commercium* or trade with them is otherwise restricted, they remain ‚goods' in the sense of Article 1".

[186] So *Staudinger/Magnus,* Art. 1, Rn. 49.

[187] Vgl. Tribunale di Forlì, 16.2.2009, CISG-online 1780; Tribunale di Forlì, 11.12.2008, CISG-online 1729; LG Köln, 16.11.1995, CISG-online 265; vgl. in der Lehre *Schlechtriem/Schwenzer/Schwenzer/Hachem,* CISG Commentary, Art. 1, Rn. 16.

[188] Vgl. Art. 3 Rn. 1 ff.

[189] Vgl. *Bonell,* Riv. trim. dir. proced. civ. 1990, 715, 717; *Rosett,* 45 Ohio St. L. J. (1984), 265, 269.

[190] Hierzu, vgl. *Dölle/Herber,* Art. 1 EKG, Rn. 15 ff.

[191] *Bamberger/Roth/Saenger,* Art. 1, Rn. 13; *Ferrari,* Applicabilità ed applicazioni, S. 46; *Ferrari u. a./Saenger,* Internationales Vertragsrecht, Art. 1, Rn. 13; *Honsell/Siehr,* Art. 1, Rn. 10; *Kröll u. a./Perales Viscasillas,* Art. 1, Rn. 2 und 42; MünchKomm/*Westermann,* Art. 1, Rn. 11; MünchKommHGB/*Benicke,* Art. 1, Rn. 20; *Rovelli,* S. 93 f.; *Rudolph,* Art. 1, Rn. 5; *Schlechtriem/Schwenzer/Schlechtriem,* CISG Commentary, 2. Aufl., Art. 1, Rn. 25; *Schlechtriem/Schwenzer/Schwenzer/Hachem,* CISG Commentary, Art. 1, Rn. 26.

[192] OLG Dresden, 30.10.2010, CISG-online 2183; Tribunale di Forlì, 11.12.2008, CISG-online 1729; RB Hasselt, 20.9.2005, CISG-online 1496; Tribunale di Padova, 25.2.2004, CISG-online 819; OLG Dresden, 27.12.1999, CISG-online 511 = TranspR-IHR 2000, 20 ff.

[193] Vgl. *Bamberger/Roth/Saenger,* Art. 1, Rn. 9; *K. Bell,* 8 Pace Int'l L. Rev. (1996), 237, 244; *Boschiero,* Le convenzioni, S. 268; *Díez-Picazo/Calvo Caravaca,* Art. 1, S. 48; *Ferrari,* Riv. trim. dir. proced. civ. 1994, 893, 910; *Ferrari u. a./Saenger,* Internationales Vertragsrecht, Art. 1, Rn. 9; *Frignani/Torsello,* Il contratto internazionale, S. 450; *Gillette/Walt,* Sales Law, S. 40; *Kindler,* RIW 1988, 776, 777; *Martin-Davidson,* 17 Mich. St. J. Int'l L. (2008), 657, 662 f.; *Nicholas,* 105 L. Q. R. (1989), 201, 205; *Sannini,* L'applicazione, S. 58.

[194] So auch *Frignani/Torsello,* Il contratto internazionale, S. 450; *Herber/Czerwenka,* Art. 1, Rn. 9; *Heuzé,* Anm. 102.; *P. Huber/Mullis/P. Huber,* S. 49 f.; MünchKommHGB/*Benicke,* Art. 1, Rn. 20; *Piltz,* NJW 2000, 553, 555; *Rudolph,* Art. 1, Rn. 2; *Witz/Salger/Lorenz/Lorenz,* Art. 1, Rn. 9; vgl. in der Rechtsprechung Tribunale di Vigevano, 12.7.2000, CISG-online 493 = IHR 2001, 72 ff.; OGH, 15.10.1998, CISG-online 380 = ZfRVgl 1999, 63; OLG Köln, 21.5.1996, CISG-online 254; OGH, 10.11.1994, CISG-online 117 =

Meinung des Teils der Lehre, die die Internationalität davon abhängen lassen will, dass die Parteien ihre Niederlassung in verschiedenen Vertragsstaaten haben,[195] falsch ist.[196] Diese – auch für die Alternative des Abs. 1 lit. b) (Vorschaltung des internationalen Privatrechts) geltende[197] – Voraussetzung ist nicht gegeben, wenn die Niederlassungen der Parteien – bei mehreren Niederlassungen eines oder beider Vertragsparteien die jeweils nach Art. 10 lit. a) maßgebende Niederlassung, die nicht unbedingt mit der Hauptniederlassung übereinstimmen muss[198] – in demselben Staatsgebiet liegen.[199] Dies gilt auch dann, wenn der Vertrag in einem anderen Staat geschlossen wurde und wenn er dort oder über die Grenze zu erfüllen ist, was nicht nur durch die Lehre,[200] sondern auch durch die Rechtsprechung hervorgehoben worden ist.[201] Auch der Umstand, dass die Parteien unterschiedliche Staatsangehörigkeit haben, führt nicht dazu, dass ein zwischen Parteien mit Niederlassung in ein und demselben Staat geschlossener Vertrag zu einem internationalen Vertrag im Sinne von Art. 1 I CISG wird.[202]

41 Ob in den Fällen der **Stellvertretung** auf die Niederlassung des Stellvertreters oder des Vertretenen abzustellen ist, hängt von den Vorschriften des durch das **IPR** des Forumsstaates berufenen Rechts ab,[203] da der Begriff der Vertragspartei nicht autonom auszulegen ist,[204] ist die Stellvertretung im CISG doch nicht geregelt.[205] Ist deutsches oder italienisches Stellvertretungsrecht nach den Vorschriften des IPR anwendbar, dann kommt es darauf an, in wessen Namen der Stellvertreter auftritt.[206] Handelt der Stellvertreter im Namen des Vertretenen und schließt er den Vertrag mit unmittelbarer Wirkung für und gegen diesen (offene Vertretung), so ist allein die Niederlassung des Vertretenen bedeutsam,[207] der von vorneherein Vertragspartei ist.[208] Bei verdeckter Vertretung wird es hingegen, zumindest nach deutschem und italienischem Recht, auf die Niederlassung des Vertreters ankommen.[209]

ZfRVgl 1995, 79 ff.; OLG Köln, 26.8.1994, CISG-online 132 = NJW 1995, 245, 246; a. A. *Wang*, ZVglRW 1988, 184, 186 f.; völlig unverständlich MünchKomm/*Westermann*, Art. 1, Rn. 5: „Die Internationalität setzt allgemein voraus, dass es sich um einen Warenkauf iS des Art. 1 handelt"; siehe aber auch *ders.*, Art. 1, Rn. 10; krit. gegenüber dem erwähnten Zitat neuerdings auch *Schlechtriem/Schwenzer/Schwenzer/Hachem*, CISG Commentary, Art. 1, Rn. 2 Fn. 10.

[195] So etwa *Butler*, 76 Fla. B. J. (2002), 24, 26; *Kröll u. a./Perales Viscasillas*, Art. 1, Rn. 2 a E.; MünchKomm/*Westermann*, Art. 1, Rn. 5.

[196] So ausdrücklich auch LG Hamburg, 26.9.1990, CISG-online 21 = IPRax 1991, 401.

[197] MünchKomm/*Westermann*, Art. 1, Rn. 15.

[198] *A. A. ECEM European Chemical Marketing B. V. v. The Purolite Company*, U. S. Dist. Ct. (E. D. Pa.), 29.1.2010, CISG-online 2090.

[199] *Vision Systems, Inc. v. EMC Corporation*, Superior Court of Massachusetts, 28.2.2005, CISG-online 1005.

[200] Vgl. *Gillette/Walt*, Sales Law, S. 40; *Herber/Czerwenka*, Art. 1, Rn. 11; *Heuzé*, Anm. 102.; *Kröll u. a./Perales Viscasillas*, Art. 1, Rn. 44; MünchKomm/*Westermann*, Art. 1, Rn. 5; *Schlechtriem*, From Hague to Vienna, S. 127; *Schlechtriem/Schwenzer/Schlechtriem*, CISG Commentary, 2. Aufl., Art. 1, Rn. 29; *Schlechtriem/Schwenzer/Schwenzer/Hachem*, CISG Commentary, Art. 1, Rn. 26.

[201] Vgl. *Kliff et al. v. Grace Label, Inc.*, U. S. Dist. Ct. (S. D. Iowa), 25.1.2005, CISG-online 1666; *Asante Technologies, Inc. v. PMC-Sierra, Inc.*, U. S. Dist. Ct. (N. D. Cal.), 27.7.2001, CISG-online 616; OLG Köln, 27.11.1991, CISG-online 31.

[202] *Kröll u. a./Perales Viscasillas*, Art. 1, Rn. 44.

[203] So auch *Ferrari u. a./Saenger*, Internationales Vertragsrecht, Art. 1, Rn. 12; *Honsell/Siehr*, Art. 1, Rn. 7; *Schlechtriem/Schwenzer/Schwenzer/Hachem*, CISG Commentary, Art. 1, Rn. 27; *Staudinger/Magnus*, Art. 1, Rn. 68; a. A. *Martin-Davidson*, 17 Mich. St. J. Int'l L. (2008), 657, 664, freilich ohne Begründung.

[204] Vgl. näher hierzu *Ferrari*, Int'l Bus. L. J. 1998, 495, 496 f.; vgl. auch *Bamberger/Roth/Saenger*, Art. 1, Rn. 9: „Wer Vertragspartei ist, regelt das CISG nicht"; ebenso *Ferrari u. a./Saenger*, Internationales Vertragsrecht, Art. 1, Rn. 9; *Honsell/Siehr*, Art. 1, Rn. 7; *Lohmann*, Parteiautonomie, S. 29; so in der Rechtsprechung ausdrücklich Tribunale di Padova, 25.2.2004, CISG-online 819.

[205] *Schlechtriem/Schwenzer/Schwenzer/Hachem*, Art. 4 Rn. 2; *Schwenzer/Hachem/Kee*, Rn. 3.19.

[206] So nunmehr auch die Rechtsprechung; vgl. OLG Köln, 13.11.2000, CISG-online 657.

[207] Eine Bestätigung der im Text erwähnten Regel scheint sich – in Bezug auf französisches Recht – zu finden in CA Paris, 22.4.1992, in: *Witz*, Les premières applications, S. 135 f.; vgl. neuerdings in der deutschen Rechtsprechung OLG Köln, 13.11.2000, CISG-online 657.

[208] So zum deutschen Recht *Herber/Czerwenka*, Art. 1, Rn. 13; *Schlechtriem/Schwenzer/Schlechtriem*, CISG Commentary, 2. Aufl., Art. 1, Rn. 30; *Staudinger/Magnus*, Art. 1, Rn. 68; *Witz/Salger/Lorenz/Lorenz*, Art. 1, Rn. 10; zum italienischen Recht, vgl. *Ferrari*, Applicabilità ed applicazioni, S. 49 ff.

[209] *Rudolph*, Art. 1, Rn. 5; *Schlechtriem/Schwenzer/Schlechtriem*, CISG Commentary, 2. Aufl., Art. 1, Rn. 31; *Witz/Salger/Lorenz/Lorenz*, Art. 1, Rn. 10.

Die **Internationalität** ist von der Partei zu **beweisen,** die sich auf die Anwendung des CISG beruft.[210] 42

Handelt es sich dagegen – wie etwa regelmäßig bei der **Einkaufs- und Verkaufskommission** – um eine sogenannte verdeckte oder mittelbare Stellvertretung, so wird allein der „Vertreter" Vertragspartei des Kaufvertrages, d. h. allein auf dessen Niederlassung kommt es an.[211] Es ist irrelevant, dass er im Innenverhältnis verpflichtet ist, das aus dem Geschäft Erlangte herauszugeben; in welcher Weise das Eigentum an den gekauften oder verkauften Gegenständen von dem Dritten auf den „Vertretenen" übergeht oder umgekehrt, kann dabei nicht entscheidend sein: Für die Anwendung des CISG kommt es allein auf den Kaufvertrag an. Dieser aber wird bei einer bloß mittelbaren Stellvertretung nicht mit dem wirtschaftlich interessierten Hintermann, sondern allein mit dem „Vertreter" geschlossen. Daher muss in diesen Fällen – namentlich bei der Kommission – die Niederlassung des im Außenverhältnis unmittelbar Handelnden (also des Kommissionärs) allein entscheiden,[212] selbst wenn der wirtschaftlich letztlich Interessierte (der Kommittent) seine Niederlassung in einem anderen Staat hat.[213] Dieses Ergebnis mag auf den ersten Blick wirtschaftlich unzweckmäßig erscheinen, doch entspricht es der – sich nach bisher unvereinheitlichtem, jeweils anwendbarem Stellvertretungsrecht richtenden – schuldrechtlichen Situation. 43

2. Der Begriff der Niederlassung

Der für den Anwendungsbereich (genauso wie für andere Fragen)[214] äußerst wichtige Begriff der „Niederlassung" wird im Übereinkommen leider[215] nicht ausdrücklich definiert.[216] Das Übereinkommen versucht, genauso wie andere Einheitsprivatrechtskonventionen,[217] lediglich für die Fälle Vorsorge zu treffen, in denen eine Vertragspartei mehr als eine oder gar keine Niederlassung hat: Im ersten Fall ist die Niederlassung maßgeblich, die die engste Verbindung zu dem Vertrag und seiner Erfüllung aufweist; im zweiten Fall hingegen ist der gewöhnliche Aufenthalt maßgebend. 44

Das Fehlen einer Definition ist darauf zurückzuführen, dass sich die Vertreter der verschiedenen Regierungen nicht auf eine Definition einigen konnten.[218] Während einige Delegationen zum Beispiel jeder mit autonomen Befugnissen ausgestatteten Einrichtung, die auf Dauer angelegt ist, die Niederlassungseigenschaft zuerkennen wollten, haben andere 45

---

[210] Ebenso *Ferrari u. a./Saenger,* Internationales Vertragsrecht, Art. 1, Rn. 27; *Jung,* S. 195; *Schlechtriem/Schwenzer/Schlechtriem,* CISG Commentary, 2. Aufl., Art. 1, Rn. 25; *Schlechtriem/Schwenzer/Schwenzer/Hachem,* CISG Commentary, Art. 1, Rn. 26 a.E.; ebenso in der Rechtsprechung Tribunale di Vigevano, 12.7.2000, CISG-online 493 = IHR 2001, 72 ff.

[211] Vgl. *Ferrari,* Applicabilità ed applicazioni, S. 51; MünchKommHGB/*Benicke,* Art. 1, Rn. 24.

[212] MünchKomm/*Westermann,* Art. 1, Rn. 11.

[213] A. A. offenbar der Sekretariatskommentar, Art. 1, Nr. 9; Denkschrift, S. 40 (zu Art. 1) und *Schlechtriem,* Einheitliches UN-Kaufrecht, S. 12, Fn. 57; der dort als Beispiel für die Nichterkennbarkeit des Auslandsbezugs nach Abs. 2 genannte Fall eines im Inland für einen Ausländer als mittelbarer Stellvertreter handelnden Agenten fällt nach der hier vertretenen Auffassung schon nicht unter Abs. 1, da der Auslandsbezug völlig fehlt. Wie hier *Enderlein/Maskow/Strohbach,* Art. 1, Anm. 7.2. unter Differenzierung zwischen common law und civil law.

[214] Vgl. etwa Art. 12, 20 II, 24, 31 lit. c), 42 I, 57, 69 II, 90, 93 III, 94, 96; vgl. auch *Butler,* VJ (2002), 275, 276, Fn. 5.

[215] Kritisch zum Fehlen einer Definition der „Niederlassung", *Grigera Naón,* S. 97.

[216] *Bamberger/Roth/Saenger,* Art. 1, Rn. 9; *K. Bell,* 8 Pace Int'l L. Rev. (1996), 237, 245; *Ferrari u. a./Saenger,* Internationales Vertragsrecht, Art. 1, Rn. 9; *Frignani/Torsello,* Il contratto internazionale, S. 450; *Honsell/Siehr,* Art. 1, Rn. 11; *Kröll u. a./Perales Viscasillas,* Art. 1, Rn. 42; *Martin-Davidson,* 17 Mich. St. J. Int'l L. (2008), 657, 663; MünchKomm/*Westermann,* Art. 1, Rn. 9; MünchKommHGB/*Benicke,* Art. 1, Rn. 22; *Niemann,* Einheitliche Anwendung, S. 71; *Rudolph,* Art. 1, Rn. 5; *Schlechtriem/Schwenzer/Schwenzer/Hachem,* CISG Commentary, Art. 1, Rn. 23; *Schmitt,* CR 2001, 145, 147; *Staudinger/Magnus,* Art. 1, Rn. 62; *Stephan,* 39 Va. J. Int'l L. (1999), 743, 775; *Wulf,* S. 55; in der Rechtsprechung ausdrücklich auf das Fehlen einer Definition der Niederlassung hinweisend etwa KG Wallis, 23.5.2006, CISG-online 1532; KG Wallis, 3.8.2003, CISG-online 895.

[217] Vgl. Art. 2 II des Unidroit Übereinkommens über internationales Factoring.

[218] Vgl. auch *Sannini,* L'applicazione, S. 59.

Art. 1 46

vorgeschlagen, auch die auf Dauer angelegte Einrichtung, die keine selbstständigen Befugnisse hat, als Niederlassung anzusehen.²¹⁹ Aus dem Fehlen einer ausdrücklichen Definition darf jedoch nicht auf die Notwendigkeit des Rückgriffs auf nationales Recht geschlossen werden:²²⁰ Dem Rückgriff auf national-rechtlich gebundene Vorstellungen ist im Lichte einer Förderung der einheitlichen Anwendung des UN-Kaufrechts eine **autonome Auslegung** vorzuziehen.²²¹

46 Als Kriterien, die bei der näheren Umschreibung des Begriffs der „Niederlassung", dessen Vorhandensein aber immer anhand der tatsächlichen Gegebenheiten des jeweiligen Falles untersucht werden muss,²²² hilfreich sein können, müssen vor allem die **Stabilität**²²³ sowie das Vorhandensein einer gewissen **Selbstständigkeit** erwähnt werden.²²⁴ Dies führt dazu, dass die Niederlassung definiert werden kann als der Ort, von dem die selbstständige, tatsächliche,²²⁵ auf Dauer angelegte Teilnahme am Wirtschaftsverkehr erfolgt;²²⁶ mittlerweile hat auch die Rechtsprechung auf ebendiesen Grundlagen die Niederlassung definiert als „Ort, von dem aus die geschäftliche Tätigkeit tatsächlich und schwerpunktmäßig betrieben wird [...], wofür eine gewisse Dauer und Stabilität der Einrichtung und eine gewisse selbstständige Handlungskompetenz erforderlich sind."²²⁷ Nicht erforderlich ist, dass sich dort auch der Mittelpunkt der geschäftlichen Tätigkeit oder der Sitz der Geschäftsleitung befindet.²²⁸ Diese Definition schließt unter anderem aus, dass man ein **liaison-office**, d. h., ein rechtlich unselbstständiges, lediglich für das eigene Unternehmen werbend auftretendes Außenbüro, als Niederlassung ansehen kann, was nicht nur durch die Lehre,²²⁹ sondern

---

²¹⁹ Vgl. hierzu *Bianca/Carbone/Lopez de Gonzalo*, Art. 1, S. 5.
²²⁰ Ebenso *Schlechtriem/Schwenzer/Schwenzer/Hachem*, CISG Commentary, Art. 1, Rn. 23.
²²¹ So ausdrücklich *Bamberger/Roth/Saenger*, Art. 1, Rn. 10 und Art. 10, Rn. 2; *Brunner*, Art. 1, Rn. 1, Fn. 49; *Ferrari u. a./Saenger*, Internationales Vertragsrecht, Art. 1, Rn. 10; *Honsell/Siehr*, Art. 1, Rn. 11; *Lohmann*, Parteiautonomie, S. 26; *Piltz*, Internationales Kaufrecht, Rn. 2–77; *Schlechtriem/Schwenzer/Schlechtriem*, CISG Commentary, 2. Aufl., Art. 10, Rn. 2; *Schlechtriem/Schwenzer/Schwenzer/Hachem*, CISG Commentary, Art. 1, Rn. 23; ebenso in der Rechtsprechung Tribunale di Forlì, 11.12.2008, CISG-online 1729; Tribunale di Padova, 11.1.2005, CISG-online 967; teilweise anders *Garro/Zuppi*, Compraventa internacional, S. 89 f.
²²² So schon *Ferrari*, Applicabilità ed applicazioni, S. 54; *Bianca/Ferretti*, Art. 10, S. 43; *Niemann*, Einheitliche Anwendung, S. 71; *Sannini*, L'applicazione, S. 59.
²²³ Vgl. *K. Bell*, 8 Pace Int'l L. Rev. (1996), 237, 245; *Rosett*, 45 Ohio St. L. J. (1984), 265, 279; *Schlechtriem*, Uniform Sales Law, S. 42; *Schlechtriem/Schwenzer/Schwenzer/Hachem*, CISG Commentary, Art. 1, Rn. 23; *Winship*, Scope, S. 1–22; in der Rechtsprechung, vgl. OGH, 10.11.1994, CISG-online 117 = ZfRVgl 1995, 79 ff.
²²⁴ Vgl. statt aller *Bamberger/Roth/Saenger*, Art. 1, Rn. 10 und Art. 10, Rn. 2; *Bianca/Carbone/Lopez de Gonzalo*, Art. 1, S. 5; *Butler*, Art. 10 CISG-UP, S. 60; *dies.*, VJ (2002), 275, 277; *Ferrari*, Int. Bus. L. J. 2002, 961, 963; *Ferrari u. a./Saenger*, Internationales Vertragsrecht, Art. 1, Rn. 10; *Frignani/Torsello*, Il contratto internazionale, S. 450; *Honnold/Flechtner*, Art. 1, Rn. 43; *Honsell/Siehr*, Art. 1, Rn. 11; *MünchKommHGB/Benicke*, Art. 1, Rn. 23; *Piltz*, Internationales Kaufrecht, Rn. 2–78 f.; *Schlechtriem/Schwenzer/Schlechtriem*, CISG Commentary, 2. Aufl., Art. 1, Rn. 27; *Witz/Salger/Lorenz/Lorenz*, Art. 1, Rn. 9; *Wulf*, S. 55.
²²⁵ So AG Duisburg, 13.4.2000, CISG-online 659 = IHR 2001, 114, 115.
²²⁶ So auch *Hilberg*, IHR 2007, 12, 23; *Limbach*, D. 2002, Jur. 315, 316; *Lohmann*, Privatautonomie, S. 26; *Karollus*, S. 29; *MünchKomm/Westermann*, Art. 1, Rn. 9; *Niemann*, Einheitliche Anwendung, S. 71; *Schmitt*, CR 2001, 145, 147; ähnlich *Staudinger/Magnus*, Art. 1, Rn. 63; wie im Text auch OLG Hamm, 2.4.2009, CISG-online 1978; so zum EKG schon BGH, 2.6.1982, NJW 1982, 2730: „Mittelpunkt der geschäftlichen Tätigkeit der nach außen gerichteten Teilnahme am Wirtschaftsverkehr".
²²⁷ OLG Stuttgart, 28.2.2000, CISG-online 583 = IHR 2001, 65, 66; wortgleich auch (unter ausdrücklicher Bezugnahme auf das Urteil des OLG Stuttgart), Tribunale di Rimini, 26.11.2002, CISG-online 737 = Giur. it. 2003, 896 ff., m. Anm. *Ferrari*; ebenso, unter Hinweis auf die erwähnten Urteile, Tribunale di Padova, 11.1.2005, CISG-online 967; Tribunale di Padova, 25.2.2004, CISG-online 819; ähnlich auch OLG Hamm, 2.4.2009, CISG-online 1978; Tribunale di Forlì, 11.12.2008, CISG-online 1729; Tribunal cantonal du Jura, 3.11.2004, CISG-online 965; OLG Graz, 29.7.2004, CISG-online 1627; OGH, 10.11.1994, CISG-online 117 = ZfRVgl 1995, 79 ff.; vgl., die Notwendigkeit der Selbstständigkeit hervorhebend, OLG Köln, 13.11.2000, CISG-online 657; die Niederlassung ohne Bezugnahme auf die Selbstständigkeit definierend aber KG Wallis, 3.8.2003, CISG-online 895; völlig unverständlich daher *Niemann*, Einheitliche Anwendung, S. 72: die italienische Rechtsprechung „ha[be] bisher bezüglich der Definition des Begriffs der Niederlassung geschwiegen".
²²⁸ *Wulf*, S. 55 f.; so aber anscheinend *Bernardini*, S. 89.
²²⁹ *Bamberger/Roth/Saenger*, Art. 1, Rn. 10; *Bonell/Liguori*, Uniform L. Rev. 1996, 147, 153; *Butler*, Art. 10 CISG-UP, S. 61; *dies.*, VJ (2002), 275, 277; *Esslinger*, ALI-ABA (1999), 69, 77; *Ferrari*, The CISG's Sphere of Application, S. 21, 27 f.; *Ferrari u. a./Saenger*, Internationales Vertragsrecht, Art. 1, Rn. 10; *Honnold/Flechtner*,

Anwendungsbereich   47, 48 **Art. 1**

neuerdings auch durch die Rechtsprechung hervorgehoben worden ist.[230] Die erwähnte Definition schließt ferner aus, dass die nur auf vorübergehender Teilnahme am Wirtschaftsverkehr gerichteten Tätigkeiten, wie zum Beispiel die Ausstellung von Waren anlässlich einer Messe[231] oder das Mieten eines Konferenzzimmers,[232] keine Niederlassung begründen.[233] Auch der bloße Aufenthalt am Ort der Vertragsverhandlungen oder des Vertragsabschlusses begründet keine Niederlassung.[234]

Werden Kaufverträge von **Tochtergesellschaften** abgeschlossen, so kommt es in der 47 Regel auf die Niederlassung dieser Gesellschaften, nicht die der Muttergesellschaft, an.[235] Auch die konzernmässige Verbundenheit mit der Muttergesellschaft ändert nichts an der Zurechnung des Vertrages zu der Tochtergesellschaft,[236] weshalb auch zwischen Tochter- und Muttergesellschaften abgeschlossene Kaufverträge dem CISG unterstehen können.[237]

3. Die Erkennbarkeit der Internationalität des Kaufvertrages

Mit Rücksicht auf den durch den Verzicht auf objektive Internationalitätserfordernisse 48 weiten räumlichen Anwendungsbereich des CISG, der – hinsichtlich der Internationalität des Vertrages – allein von dem subjektiven Erfordernis der Niederlassung der Parteien in verschiedenen Staaten abhängt,[238] sieht Abs. 2 eine Einschränkung[239] subjektiver Art[240] vor, die für beide Anwendungsalternativen des Abs. 1 gilt:[241] Demnach ist die Tatsache, dass der Kaufvertrag international ist, dann nicht zu berücksichtigen, wenn die Niederlassung der Parteien in verschiedenen Staaten nicht spätestens[242] bei Vertragsschluss[243] **beiden Partei-**

Art. 1, Rn. 43; *Kröll u. a./Perales Viscasillas,* Art. 1, Rn. 43; *Lohmann,* Parteiautonomie, S. 27, Fn. 57; MünchKommHGB/*Benicke,* Art. 1, Rn. 23; *Niemann,* Einheitliche Anwendung, S. 72 f.; *Piltz,* Internationales Kaufrecht, Rn. 2–80; a. A. *De Ly,* 25 J. L. & Com. (2005), 1, 6 f.

[230] Vgl. Civ., 4.1.1995, D. 1995, Jur. 289; ICC, 7531/1994, CISG-online 565 = ICC Ct. Bull. 1995, 67 f.; CA Paris, 22.4.1992, CISG-online 222.

[231] Ähnlich *Ferrari u. a./Saenger,* Internationales Vertragsrecht, Art. 1, Rn. 10; *Siehr,* RabelsZ 52 (1988), 587, 590, Fn. 1; vgl. in der Rechtsprechung KG Wallis, 23.5.2006, CISG-online 1532; KG Wallis, 3.8.2003, CISG-online 895.

[232] So auch *Butler,* Art. 10 CISG-UP, S. 61; *Ferrari,* Applicabilità ed applicazioni, S. 55 f.; *Rosett,* 45 Ohio St. L. J. (1984), 265, 279; vgl. auch *Schlechtriem/Schwenzer/Schwenzer/Hachem,* CISG Commentary, Art. 1, Rn. 23.

[233] Vgl. *Bamberger/Roth/Saenger,* Art. 1, Rn. 10; *Honnold/Flechtner,* Art. 1, Rn. 43; *Honsell/Siehr,* Art. 1, Rn. 11; *Schlechtriem/Schwenzer/Schwenzer/Hachem,* CISG Commentary, Art. 1, Rn. 23.

[234] *Lacasse,* Le champ d'application, S. 31; *Staudinger/Magnus,* Art. 1, Rn. 64; vgl. in der Rechtsprechung ICC, 9781/2000, CISG-online 1202.

[235] So auch *Bamberger/Roth/Saenger,* Art. 1, Rn. 11; *Ferrari u. a./Saenger,* Internationales Vertragsrecht, Art. 1, Rn. 11; *Herrmann,* Anwendungsbereich, S. 86; *Honnold/Flechtner,* Art. 1, Rn. 43; *Honsell/Siehr,* Art. 1, Rn. 13; MünchKomm/*Westermann,* Art. 1, Rn. 9; MünchKommHGB/*Benicke,* Art. 1, Rn. 24; *Schlechtriem/Schwenzer/Schwenzer/Hachem,* CISG Commentary, Art. 1, Rn. 25; *Staudinger/Magnus,* Art. 1, Rn. 66; *Witz/Salger/Lorenz/Lorenz,* Art. 1, Rn. 9.

[236] Ebenso *Staub/Koller,* vor § 373 HGB, Rn. 623; *Honnold/Flechtner,* Art. 1, Rn. 42; vgl. auch *Achilles,* Art. 1, Rn. 5; MünchKomm/*Westermann,* Art. 1, Rn. 9; *Schlechtriem/Schwenzer/Schlechtriem,* CISG Commentary, 2. Aufl., Art. 1, Rn. 28.

[237] MünchKommHGB/*Benicke,* Art. 1, Rn. 24; *Staudinger/Magnus,* Art. 1, Rn. 66.

[238] *Achilles,* Art. 1, Rn. 5.

[239] So auch *Boschiero,* Le convenzioni, S. 268; *Herber,* Anwendungsbereich, S. 35.

[240] Vgl. auch *Bamberger/Roth/Saenger,* Art. 1, Rn. 21; *Ferrari u. a./Saenger,* Internationales Vertragsrecht, Art. 1, Rn. 22; *Karollus,* S. 29; *Reinhart,* Art. 1, Rn. 11; *Schlechtriem/Schwenzer/Schlechtriem,* CISG Commentary, 2. Aufl., Art. 1, Rn. 48; *Schlechtriem/Schwenzer/Schwenzer/Hachem,* CISG Commentary, Art. 1, Rn. 39.

[241] So auch *Brunner,* Art. 1, Rn. 5; *Czerwenka,* Rechtsanwendungsprobleme, S. 160; *Schlechtriem/Schlechtriem,* CISG Commentary, 2. Aufl., Art. 1, Rn. 35; *Schlechtriem/Schwenzer/Schwenzer/Hachem,* CISG Commentary, Art. 1, Rn. 30 und 39; *Siehr,* RabelsZ 52 (1988), 587, 591; *Staudinger/Magnus,* Art. 1, Rn. 72; a. A. *Hoyer,* WBl. 1988, 70, 72 (Abs. 2 gelte nur für die in Abs. 1 lit. a) vorgesehene Anwendungsalternative); ebenso *Soergel/Lüderitz/Fenge,* Art. 1, Rn. 17.

[242] Vgl. auch *Schlechtriem,* IPRax 1990, 277, 278, der hervorhebt, dass wenn die Internationalität erst nach Vertragsabschluss erkennbar wird, die Konvention nicht zum Zug kommt.

[243] *Achilles,* Art. 1, Rn. 6; *Schlechtriem/Schwenzer/Schlechtriem,* CISG Commentary, 2. Aufl., Art. 1, Rn. 35; *Schlechtriem/Schwenzer/Schwenzer/Hachem,* CISG Commentary, Art. 1, Rn. 39; *Witz/Salger/Lorenz/Lorenz,* Art. 1, Rn. 14.

en[244] erkennbar war[245] (bisweilen ist diesbezüglich vom Offenheitsprinzip gesprochen worden),[246] mit der Folge, dass bei mangelnder Erkennbarkeit der Internationalität immer nur das über das IPR des Gerichtsstaates berufene nationale, unvereinheitlichte Recht Anwendung finden kann.[247] In Bezug auf die **Beweislast** führt dies dazu, dass – da es sich bei der Erkennbarkeit der Internationalität nicht um eine positive Anwendungsvoraussetzung, sondern um einen negativen Ausschlussgrund handelt[248] – die Vertragspartei, die die Nichterkennbarkeit behauptet, diese zu beweisen hat,[249] was auch von der neueren Rechtsprechung bestätigt worden ist.[250]

49 Die Beurteilung, ob die Tatsache, dass die Parteien ihre Niederlassung in verschiedenen Staaten haben, unerkennbar war, ist anhand **objektiver Kriterien** vorzunehmen.[251] Eine ursprünglich von der UNCITRAL-Arbeitsgruppe in Aussicht genommene Formulierung, in der auf die Kenntnis oder fahrlässige Unkenntnis abgestellt wurde,[252] ist im Laufe der Vorarbeiten bewusst mit dem Hinweis auf die durch dieses subjektive Element bedingten Anwendungsschwierigkeiten aufgegeben worden.[253]

50 Wichtigster Anwendungsfall, der in den Beratungen eine Rolle gespielt hat, ist der Abschluss des Vertrages durch einen „Vertreter" im Inland, der den ausländischen „Vertretenen" nicht offenbart.[254] Regelmäßig wird in solchen Fällen aus den bereits erwähnten Gründen[255] – zumindest wenn deutsches oder italienisches Stellvertretungsrecht anwendbar ist –[256] nicht der „Vertretene" vertraglich gebunden werden, d. h. es kommt auf die Niederlassung des „Vertreters" an,[257] weshalb die Anwendung des CISG im erwähnten Fall mangels Internationalität ausscheidet.[258]

---

[244] *Ferrari*, Applicabilità ed applicazioni, S. 63; *Schlechtriem/Schwenzer/Schlechtriem*, CISG Commentary, 2. Aufl., Art. 1, Rn. 50; *Staudinger/Magnus*, Art. 1, Rn. 75.
[245] Vgl. *U. Huber*, RabelsZ 43 (1979), 413, 421; für bloße Verweise auf Art. 1 II CISG, ohne weitere Stellungnahmen, vgl. etwa LG Stuttgart, 29.10.2009, CISG-online 2017; Tribunale di Forlì, 16.2.2009, CISG-online 1780; Court of First Instance of Athens, Aktenzeichen 4505/2009 (ohne Datum), CISG-online 2228; High Commercial Court of Serbia, 22.4.2008, CISG-online 1990; *American Mint LLC v. GOSoftware, Inc.*, U. S. Dist. Ct. (M. D. Pa.), 16.8.2005, CISG-online 1104; Tribunale di Padova, 11.1.2005, CISG-online 967; Tribunale di Padova, 25.2.2004, CISG-online 819; OLG Köln, 13.11.2000, CISG-online 657; Tribunale di Vigevano, 12.7.2000, CISG-online 493 = IHR 2001, 72, 73.
[246] *Soergel/Lüderitz/Fenge*, Art. 1, Rn. 5.
[247] A. A. *MünchKommHGB/Benicke*, Art. 1, Rn. 28.
[248] Vgl. *T. M. Müller*, Beweislast, S. 44.
[249] Vgl. *Achilles*, Art. 1, Rn. 11; *Bamberger/Roth/Saenger*, Art. 1, Rn. 26; *Baumgärtel/Laumen/Hepting/Müller*, Art 1, Rn. 7; *Brunner*, Art. 1, Rn. 5 a. E.; *Czerwenka*, Rechtsanwendungsprobleme, S. 136; *Ferrari u. a./Saenger*, Internationales Vertragsrecht, Art. 1, Rn. 23; *Herber/Czerwenka*, Art. 1, Rn. 20; *Heuzé*, Anm. 103.; *P. Huber/Mullis/P. Huber*, Art. 1, Rn. 50; *Jung*, S. 197; *Kröll u. a. /Perales Viscasillas*, Art. 1, Rn. 46; *T. M. Müller*, Beweislast, S. 45; *MünchKommHGB/Benicke*, Art. 1, Rn. 27; *Pünder*, RIW 1990, 869, Fn. 13; *Reimers-Zocher*, S. 173; *Schlechtriem/Schwenzer/Schlechtriem*, CISG Commentary, 2. Aufl., Art. 1, Rn. 49; *Witz/Salger/Lorenz/Lorenz*, Art. 1, Rn. 15.
[250] Tribunale di Vigevano, 12.7.2000, CISG-online 493 = IHR 2001, 72, 77.
[251] *Achilles*, Art. 1, Rn. 7; *Bamberger/Roth/Saenger*, Art. 1, Rn. 26; *Czerwenka*, Rechtsanwendungsprobleme, S. 136; *Ferrari*, Applicabilità ed applicazioni, S. 66; *Ferrari u. a./Saenger*, Internationales Vertragsrecht, Art. 1, Rn. 23; *Karollus*, S. 29; *Lohmann*, Privatautonomie, S. 28; *Piltz*, Internationales Kaufrecht, Rn. 2–85; *Schlechtriem/Schwenzer/Schlechtriem*, CISG Commentary, 2. Aufl., Art. 1, Rn. 50; *Schlechtriem/Schwenzer/Hachem*, CISG Commentary, Art. 1, Rn. 42; *Soergel/Lüderitz/Fenge*, Art. 1, Rn. 6; *Wulf*, S. 57; a. A. *Audit*, Vente internationale, S. 19.
[252] YB II (1971), S. 52, Nr. 13.
[253] YB III (1972), S. 83, Nr. 9 f.
[254] Vgl. *Czerwenka*, Rechtsanwendungsprobleme, S. 135; *Esslinger*, ALI-ABA (1999), 69, 78; *Herrmann*, Anwendungsbereich, S. 85; *MünchKomm/Westermann*, Art. 1, Rn. 12 a. E.; *MünchKommHGB/Benicke*, Art. 1, Rn. 27; *Reinhart*, Art. 1, Rn. 11; *Schlechtriem*, Einheitliches UN-Kaufrecht, S. 12, Fn. 57; *Schlechtriem/Schwenzer/Schlechtriem*, CISG Commentary, 2. Aufl., Art. 1, Rn. 51; *Schlechtriem/Schwenzer/Hachem*, CISG Commentary, Art. 1, Rn. 45.
[255] Vgl. oben Rn. 41 ff.
[256] Vgl. *Ferrari*, Applicabilità ed applicazioni, S. 50.
[257] So auch *Enderlein/Maskow/Strohbach*, Art. 1, Anm. 7.2.; vgl. auch *Ferrari u. a./Saenger*, Internationales Vertragsrecht, Art. 1, Rn. 12.
[258] Sekretariatskommentar, Art. 1, Nr. 9; im Ergebnis ebenso *Brunner*, Art. 1, Rn. 5.

Anwendungsbereich 51–54 **Art. 1**

Nach dem Wortlaut der Vorschrift genügt es, wenn Anhaltspunkte für eine Niederlassung 51 des Vertragspartners in einem anderen, nicht notwendig in einem bestimmten Staat bestehen. Eine positive Kenntnis der Verschiedenheit der Niederlassungen ist nicht notwendig;[259] da die **objektive Erkennbarkeit** der Internationalität des Vertrages ausreicht,[260] müssen die Parteien den Vertrag also nicht im Bewusstsein geschlossen haben, dass es sich um einen internationalen Vertrag im Sinne des Übereinkommens handle.[261] Daraus ergibt sich, dass auch das Bewusstsein der Anwendbarkeit des Übereinkommens nicht notwendig ist,[262] was leider von einem neueren US-amerikanischen Urteil verkannt worden ist.[263]

Streitig ist, ob die in Abs. 2 enthaltene Aufzählung der Erkenntnisquellen, aus der sich die 52 objektive Erkennbarkeit ergeben muss, abschließend ist.[264] Letztendlich ist die Beantwortung dieser Frage aber nicht sehr relevant, da die erwähnte Aufzählung wegen ihrer Bezugnahme auf weite Begriffe praktisch alle wesentlichen Umstände einschließen dürfte, zumindest alle Umstände, die mit dem konkreten Geschäftsverhältnis der Parteien verbunden sind. Andere, mit diesem Geschäftsverhältnis nicht verbundene Umstände, die zur Kenntnis der Internationalität führen können (wie zum Beispiel Auskünfte Dritter), dürfen dem Wortlaut des Abs. 2 nach nicht in Betracht gezogen werden.[265]

Abs. 2 zählt drei (alternative)[266] Arten von Erkenntnisquellen auf, aus denen sich die 53 Internationalität des Vertrages ergeben muss: **Frühere Geschäftsbeziehungen** der Parteien können auf die Verschiedenheit der Niederlassung hindeuten; dies bedeutet jedoch nicht, dass es sich dabei um aus Kaufverträgen hervorgehenden Beziehungen handeln muss.[267]

Der von der Konvention verlangte Auslandsbezug kann sich auch aus dem **Vertrag** und 54 den diesen **vorbereitenden Verhandlungen** ergeben.[268] Dies schließt nicht nur Korrespondenz und unmittelbare Vertragserklärungen ein,[269] sondern auch die Verwendung einer fremden Sprache, die Angabe einer ausländischen Adresse, an die die Lieferung der Ware zu erfolgen hat, etc.[270] Beim Vertragsschluss über Internet reicht m. E.[271] für die Erkennbarkeit der Internationalität des Vertrages die Verwendung einer bestimmten Toplevel-Domain[272] aus; demnach ist der Vertrag bereits dann als international erkennbar, wenn sich die von den

---

[259] Wie hier *Díez-Picazo/Calvo Caravaca*, Art. 1, S. 52; *Honsell/Siehr*, Art. 1, Rn. 28; *Wulf*, S. 57; a. A. *Audit*, Vente internationale, S. 19; *Lacasse*, Le champ d'application, S. 32; *Siehr*, RabelsZ 52 (1988), 587, 591.
[260] *Schlechtriem/Schwenzer/Schwenzer/Hachem*, CISG Commentary, Art. 1, Rn. 42; *Staudinger/Magnus*, Art. 1, Rn. 74.
[261] Ebenso *Bamberger/Roth/Saenger*, Art. 1, Rn. 22; *MünchKomm/Westermann*, Art. 1, Rn. 12; *Ragno*, Convenzione di Vienna e Diritto europeo, S. 81; *Schlechtriem/Schwenzer/Schlechtriem*, CISG Commentary, 2. Aufl., Art. 1, Rn. 50; *Schlechtriem/Schwenzer/Schwenzer/Hachem*, CISG Commentary, Art. 1, Rn. 41 und 44; a. A. *Audit*, Vente internationale, S. 19.
[262] *Honsell/Siehr*, Art. 1, Rn. 28; *Piltz*, IHR 2002, 2, 4; *MünchKommHGB/Benicke*, Art. 1, Rn. 26; *Schlechtriem/Schwenzer/Schlechtriem*, CISG Commentary, 2. Aufl., Art. 1, Rn. 50; *Schlechtriem/Schwenzer/Schwenzer/Hachem*, CISG Commentary, Art. 1, Rn. 42.
[263] *Impuls I. D. Internacional, S. L., Impuls I. D. Systems, Inc., and PSIAR, S. A., v. Psion-Teklogix Inc.*, U. S. Dist. Ct. (S. D. Fla.), 22.11.2002, CISG-online 783 = 2002 U. S. Dist. LEXIS 22 977 (Schutz nicht des Vertrauens auf den nationalen Charakter des Kaufvertrags, sondern des Bewusstseins der Anwendbarkeit des CISG); kritisch zu diesem Urteil *Sannini*, L'applicazione, S. 60.
[264] Bejahend *Herber*, 2. Aufl., Art. 1 Rn. 53; Botschaft des Schweizerischen Bundesrats, S. 757; a. A. *MünchKommHGB/Benicke*, Art. 1, Rn. 26; *Soergel/Lüderitz/Fenge*, Art. 1, Rn. 7; *Schlechtriem/Schwenzer/Schlechtriem*, CISG Commentary, 2. Aufl., Art. 1, Rn. 53; *Schlechtriem/Schwenzer/Schwenzer/Hachem*, CISG Commentary, Art. 1, Rn. 43.
[265] *Achilles*, Art. 1, Rn. 7; a. A. *Brunner*, Art. 1, Rn. 5; *Staudinger/Magnus*, Art. 1, Rn. 76.
[266] Vgl. Botschaft des Schweizerischen Bundesrats, S. 757.
[267] *Herber*, 2. Aufl., Art. 1 Rn. 54; *MünchKomm/Westermann*, Art. 1, Rn. 13; *Schlechtriem/Schwenzer/Schlechtriem*, CISG Commentary, 2. Aufl., Art. 1, Rn. 54; *Staudinger/Magnus*, Art. 1, Rn. 79.
[268] Vgl. *Boschiero*, Le convenzioni, S. 268; *Schlechtriem/Schwenzer/Schlechtriem*, CISG Commentary, 2. Aufl., Art. 1, Rn. 55; *Siehr*, RabelsZ 52 (1988), 587, 590 f.; vgl. in der Rechtsprechung OLG Stuttgart, 31.3.2008, CISG-online 1658.
[269] Vgl. *Schlechtriem/Schwenzer/Schwenzer/Hachem*, CISG Commentary, Art. 1, Rn. 43.
[270] So auch *Ferrari*, Applicabilità ed applicazioni, S. 66, Fn. 155 f.; *Staudinger/Magnus*, Art. 1, Rn. 77.
[271] *Ferrari*, EuLF 2001, 301, 301 f.
[272] Etwa „.de", „.us", „.it".

Art. 1 55–60   Teil I. Kapitel I. Anwendungsbereich

Parteien verwendeten Toplevel-Domains unterscheiden, da die Parteien in diesem Fall nicht davon ausgehen können, dass der Vertrag ein rein nationaler Vertrag ist.[273]

55   Die Tatsache, dass die erwähnten Umstände auf einen nur vorübergehenden Aufenthalt im Inland hindeuten, dürfte in der Regel ausreichen, die Nichterkennbarkeit der Internationalität auszuschließen, obwohl der vorübergehende Aufenthalt, wie erwähnt,[274] keine Niederlassung begründet. Unabhängig hiervon begründet sie aber sicher keine Pflicht zu Rückfragen.[275]

56   Schließlich sind auch **Auskünfte** der anderen Vertragspartei zu berücksichtigen. Diesbezüglich können zum Beispiel Werbeanzeigen von Bedeutung sein, die dem Vertragspartner gegenüber abgegeben wurden.[276] Nicht notwendig ist, dass die Auskünfte ausdrücklich auf die ausländische Niederlassung hinweisen.[277]

57   Obwohl dem Wortlaut des Abs. 2 nach lediglich auf die Erkennbarkeit der ausländischen Niederlassung abgestellt wird, findet auch im Rahmen des hier besprochenen Absatzes Art. 10 lit. b) Anwendung;[278] demzufolge ist auch bezüglich Art. 1 II bei Fehlen einer Niederlassung auf den gewöhnlichen Aufenthalt abzustellen.[279]

58   Um zu vermeiden, dass die Anwendbarkeit des Übereinkommens zu sehr durch die Vorschrift eingeschränkt wird, muss man diese m. E. **eng auslegen**.[280] Dies darf aber nicht dazu führen, dass der **Zweck der Vorschrift** umgangen wird, der darin liegt, zu vermeiden, dass eine Partei, die einen Vertrag für ein reines Inlandsgeschäft gehalten hat, plötzlich mit der Anwendung des Übereinkommens konfrontiert wird.[281]

4. Unerheblichkeit der Staatsangehörigkeit und der Kaufmannseigenschaft

59   Abs. 3 statuiert, dass sowohl die Staatsangehörigkeit der Parteien[282] als auch ihre Kaufmannseigenschaft[283] genauso wie die kaufrechtliche Natur des Vertrages für die Anwendung des Übereinkommens unbedeutsam sind.[284] Diese Klarstellung ist aus Art. 1 III und Art. 7 EKG in das CISG übernommen worden.

60   Die Unbeachtlichkeit der Staatsangehörigkeit wirft keine Probleme auf,[285] da ein Auslandsbezug durch die Niederlassung oder den gewöhnlichen Aufenthalt ausreichend begründet wird.[286] Bedenklicher erscheint hingegen die Unbeachtlichkeit der Kaufmanns-

---

[273] *Ferrari*, EuLF 2001, 301, 302; *Staudinger/Magnus*, Art. 1. Rn. 77; so neuerdings auch *Schlechtriem/Schwenzer/Schwenzer/Hachem*, CISG Commentary, Art. 1, Rn. 43; krit. zu dieser Ansicht *Wulf*, S. 59; vgl. auch Art. 6 Abs. 5 des UNECIC: „The sole fact that a party makes use of a domain name or electronic mail address connected to a specific country does not create a presumption that its place of business is located in that country"; zu diesem Übereinkommen vgl. *Faria*, 39 UCC L.J. (2006), 25; *ders.*, 55 Int'l & Comp. L. Q. (2006), 689; *Gabriel*, Uniform L. Rev. 2006, 285; *Hilberg*, IHR 2007, 12 und 56.
[274] Vgl. oben Rn. 46.
[275] So aber *Herber*, 2. Aufl., Art. 1 Rn. 55.
[276] *Staudinger/Magnus*, Art. 1, Rn. 78.
[277] *Schlechtriem/Schwenzer/Schlechtriem*, CISG Commentary, 2. Aufl., Art. 1, Rn. 56.
[278] *Schlechtriem/Schwenzer/Schwenzer/Hachem*, CISG Commentary, Art. 1, Rn. 40.
[279] So auch *Loewe*, Art. 1; Botschaft des Schweizerischen Bundesrats, S. 757; ungenau *Herber*, 2. Aufl., Art. 1 Rn. 58, der es im Hinblick auf die Erkennbarkeit der Internationalität anscheinend genügen lässt, „wenn ein Auslandsbezug durch einen ‚gewöhnlichen Aufenthalt' erkennbar war." Der gewöhnliche Aufenthalt kann jedoch ex Art. 10 lit. b) nur bei Fehlen einer Niederlassung in Betracht gezogen werden.
[280] So schon *Herber*, 2. Aufl., Art. 1 Rn. 57; vgl. auch *Schlechtriem/Schwenzer/Schlechtriem*, CISG Commentary, 2. Aufl., Art. 1, Rn. 57; *Schlechtriem/Schwenzer/Schwenzer/Hachem*, CISG Commentary, Art. 1, Rn. 44.
[281] Vgl. *Díez-Picazo/Calvo Caravaca*, Art. 1, S. 52. *Enderlein/Maskow/Strohbach*, Art. 1, Anm. 7.1.; ähnlich neuerdings auch *MünchKomm/Westermann*, Art. 1, Rn. 12.
[282] Zur Unbeachtlichkeit der Staatsangehörigkeit vgl. in der Rechtsprechung etwa OLG Graz, 29.7.2004, CISG-online 1627; RB Hasselt, 13.5.2003, CISG Belgium; BGH, 31.10.2001, CISG-online 617 = IHR 2002, 14 f.; RB Veurne, 25.4.2001, CISG-online 765; Int. Ct. Bulgarian CCI, 24.4.1996, CISG-online 435; vgl. auch *Sollund*, Nordic L.J. (2007), 1, 6.
[283] Vgl. OLG Düsseldorf, 21.4.2004, CISG-online 914 = IHR 2005, 24, 27: „Das CISG unterscheidet […] nicht zwischen Kaufleuten und Nichtkaufleuten".
[284] Vgl. zur Unbeachtlichkeit der Kaufmannseigenschaft neuerdings etwa BGH, 31.10.2001, CISG-online 617 = IHR 2002, 14, 16; RB Veurne, 25.4.2001, CISG-online 765.
[285] Ebenso *Schlechtriem/Schwenzer/Schwenzer/Hachem*, CISG Commentary, Art. 1, Rn. 46.
[286] Die Unerheblichkeit der Nationalität hat auch den Vorteil, dass „sie von der Frage entbindet, welche ‚Nationalität' etwa eine juristische Person hat", *Schlechtriem*, Internationales UN-Kaufrecht, Rn. 12.

eigenschaft der Parteien und der kaufrechtlichen Natur des Vertrages, ist das CISG in seiner Regelung doch vielfach auf den gewerblichen Warenaustausch zugeschnitten. Ein Abstellen auf Kaufleute, wie es der Zweiteilung von bürgerlich-rechtlichem Kaufrecht und Handelskauf in einigen Rechten (unter anderem dem deutschen Recht) entspricht,[287] musste aber international ausscheiden, da der Anwendungsbereich der Sonderregeln für Kaufleute international nicht einheitlich definiert ist[288] und in vielen Rechtsordnungen solche Regeln völlig unbekannt sind[289] – dies trifft zum Beispiel in der Schweiz und in Italien zu. Eine Einschränkung des Anwendungsbereichs auf den gewerblichen Warenaustausch ergibt sich de facto aber aus dem in Art. 2 lit. a) vorgesehenen Ausschluss – vom Anwendungsbereich des CISG – der Warenkäufe für den persönlichen Gebrauch.[290] Dadurch werden die Einwände gegen eine mögliche Überforderung nichtkaufmännischer Vertragspartner weitgehend gegenstandslos.[291]

V. Die Beziehung zu einem oder mehreren Vertragsstaaten als Anwendungsvoraussetzung des Übereinkommens

1. Allgemeines

Die Internationalität des Kaufvertrages allein reicht für die Anwendbarkeit des Übereinkommens nicht aus.[292] Das Übereinkommen verlangt außerdem, dass entweder die Parteien oder der Kaufvertrag eine **bestimmte Beziehung** zu einem oder mehreren Vertragsstaaten aufweisen.[293] Mit der Einführung dieses Erfordernisses, das heute in verschiedenen Einheitsprivatrechtskonventionen vorgesehen ist,[294] ist dem oft kritisierten „Universalitätsprinzip"[295] des Haager Kaufrechts eine Absage erteilt worden.[296]   61

Die für die Anwendbarkeit nötige Verbindung zu einem oder mehreren Vertragsstaaten   62
liegt vor, wenn die Parteien ihre Niederlassung in verschiedenen Staaten haben, die Vertragsstaaten sind – diesbezüglich ist von einer **autonomen Anwendungsalternative** gesprochen worden[297] –, **oder**[298] wenn die Vorschriften des Internationalen Privatrechts auf

---

[287] Einen Überblick über Länder, die zwischen bürgerlichem Recht und Handelsrecht unterscheiden, gibt *Galgano*, Diritto civile e diritto commerciale, S. 35 ff.

[288] *Schlechtriem/Schwenzer/Schwenzer/Hachem*, CISG Commentary, Art. 1, Rn. 47.

[289] Dazu schon *Dölle/Herber*, Art. 7 EKG, Rn. 1.

[290] So auch *Date-Bah*, 11 Rev. Ghana L. (1979), 50, 53; *Ferrari*, Applicabilità ed applicazioni, S. 170; *Garro/Zuppi*, Compraventa internacional, S. 80; *P. Huber/Mullis/P. Huber*, S. 49; *Kröll u. a./Spohnheimer*, Art. 2, Rn. 7; *Schlechtriem/Schwenzer/Schwenzer/Hachem*, CISG Commentary, Art. 1, Rn. 47 und Art. 2, Rn. 4; *Wang*, ZVerglRW 1988, 184, 186; ebenso neuerdings auch *Schwenzer/Hachem/Kee*, Rn. 6.16, die auch darauf hinweisen, dass OHADA eine dem Art. 2 lit. a) ähnliche Vorschrift eingeführt hat.

[291] *Herber*, 2. Aufl., Art. 1 Rn. 60.

[292] So ausdrücklich neuerdings Tribunale di Forlì, 11.12.2008, CISG-online 1729; Tribunale di Rimini, 26.11.2002, CISG-online 737 = Giur. it. 2003, 896 ff.; Tribunale di Vigevano, 12.7.2000, CISG-online 493 = IHR 2001, 72, 73; vgl. auch *Chiomenti*, EuLF 2005, 141, 143; *Ferrari*, IHR 2006, 1, 10; *Frignani/Torsello*, Il contratto internazionale, S. 452; *Kröll u. a./Perales Viscasillas*, Art. 1, Rn. 47; *Ragno*, Convenzione di Vienna e Diritto europeo, S. 79 f.; *Sannini*, L'applicazione, S. 63; völlig falsch *Perea*, 20 Pace Int'l L. Rev. (2008), 191, 192: „The treaty itself becomes the governing domestic law once ratified by a member state, making it the applicable contract law to all international transactions falling under its internationality requirements".

[293] So ausdrücklich auch *Honnold/Flechtner*, Art. 1, Rn. 44; vgl. auch *Achilles*, Art. 1, Rn. 8; *Frignani/Torsello*, Il contratto itnernazionale, 443; *P. Huber/Mullis/P. Huber*, S. 50; *Torsello*, Common Features, S. 16; *Pavic/Djordjevic*, 28 J.L. & Com. (2009), 1, 5 und 7; ebenso in der Rechtsprechung Tribunale di Vigevano, 12.7.2000, CISG-online 493; Tribunale di Rimini, 26.11.2002, CISG-online 737.

[294] Siehe statt aller Art. 2 I des UNIDROIT-Übereinkommens über internationales Factoring; Art. 3 I des UNIDROIT-Übereinkommens über internationales Finanzierungsleasing.

[295] Vgl. auch oben Rn. 5.

[296] *Díez-Picazo/Calvo Caravaca*, Art. 1, S. 58.

[297] Vgl. statt aller *Bamberger/Roth/Saenger*, Art. 1, Rn. 14; *Karollus*, S. 30; *Schlechtriem*, Internationales UN-Kaufrecht, Rn. 11.

[298] Dass es sich um Alternativen handelt, ist in der Lehre oft hervorgehoben worden; vgl. etwa *Ferrari*, Applicabilità ed applicazioni, S. 70; *Frignani/Torsello*, Il contratto internazionale, S. 452 f.; *Gillette/Walt*, Sales Law, S. 40; *Goode*, Uniform L. Rev. 1991-I, 54, 67; *Kröll u. a./Perales Viscasillas*, Art. 1, Rn. 4; *Memmo*, Riv.

das Recht eines Vertragsstaates verweisen **(kollisionsrechtliche Anwendungsalternative)**.[299]

2. Die autonome Anwendung des Übereinkommens

63 Die Konvention kommt gemäß lit. a) „direkt",[300] unmittelbar[301] beziehungsweise „autonom"[302] zur Anwendung, d. h., „ohne weitere Zwischenschaltung des Kollisionsrechts",[303] wenn die relevanten Niederlassungen[304] der Vertragsparteien in **verschiedenen Vertragsstaaten** liegen.[305] Das IPR des Forumstaates ist demnach nur soweit relevant, als das Übereinkommen keine Regelung trifft[306] (beziehungsweise die vom Übereinkommen getroffene Regelung auf Grund Parteiwillens nicht zur Anwendung kommt).[307] „Voraussetzung ist allerdings, dass der angerufene Richter seinerseits in einem Vertragsstaat tätig ist"[308] und dass die Parteien das CISG nicht kraft Art. 6 CISG[309] ausgeschlossen haben.[310] Nicht notwendig ist jedoch, dass sich die Niederlassung einer Partei im Forumstaat befindet;[311] dies wird aus Zuständigkeitsgründen aber häufig der Fall sein.[312]

---

trim. dir. proced. civ. 1983, 180, 205; *Pünder,* RIW 1990, 869; *Ragno,* Convenzione di Vienna e Diritto europeo, S. 82.

[299] Völlig unverständlich die Anwendungsalternative, die vorgeschlagen wird bei *Kröll u. a./Perales Viscasillas,* Art. 1, Rn. 7: „the CISG will apply by effect of […] direct choice of law rules of the Convention by the contracting parties".

[300] *Chiomenti,* EuLF 2005, 141, 143; *Díez-Picazo/Calvo Caravaca,* Art. 1, S. 54; *Ferrari,* Sphere of Application, S. 13; *Frignani/Torsello,* Il contratto internazionale, S. 452; *Kröll u. a./Perales Viscasillas,* Art. 1, Rn. 47; *Magnus,* IPRax 1993, 390; *Niemann,* Einheitliche Anwendung, S. 70; *Ragno,* Convenzione di Vienna e Diritto europeo, S. 82; *Sannini,* L'applicazione, S. 64; *Pavic/Djordjevic,* 28 J. L. & Com. (2009), 1, 15; *Perovic,* Annals Fac. L. Belgrade 2011, 181, 182; *Spagnolo,* 10 Melb. J. Int'l L. (2009), 141, 143; *Weizuo,* 20 Pace Int'l L. Rev. (2008), 115, 115; in der Rechtsprechung auf die „direkte" Anwendbarkeit des CISG hinweisend auch HGer Aargau, 10.3.2010, CISG-online 2176; AG Sursee, 12.9.2008, CISG-online 1728; HGer Aargau, 19.6.2007, CISG-online 1741; KG Wallis, 21.2.2005, CISG-online 1193 = IHR 2006, 155, 156; BGer, 11.7.2000, CISG-online 627.

[301] MünchKommHGB/*Benicke,* Art. 1, Rn. 29; *Navas Navarro,* IHR 2006, 74; *Sannini,* L' applicazione, S. 64.

[302] *Achilles,* Art. 1, Rn. 8; Botschaft des Schweizerischen Bundesrats, S. 758; *Brunner,* Art. 1, Rn. 1; *Ferrari u. a./Saenger,* Internationales Vertragsrecht, Art. 1, Rn. 14; *P. Huber/Mullis/P. Huber,* S. 51; *Kröll u. a./Perales Viscasillas,* Art. 1, Rn. 5; MünchKomm/*Westermann,* Art. 1, Rn. 1; *Posch/Terlitza,* IHR 2001, 47, 49; *Ragno,* Convenzione di Vienna e Diritto europeo, S. 82; *Schlechtriem/Schwenzer/Schlechtriem,* CISG Commentary, 2. Aufl., Art. 1, Rn. 32; *Schlechtriem/Schwenzer/Schwenzer/Hachem,* CISG Commentary, Art. 1, Rn. 28; vgl. in der Rechtsprechung etwa OGer Aargau, 3.3.2009, CISG-online 2013; AG Sursee, 12.9.2008, CISG-online 1278; KG Wallis, 21.2.2005, CISG-online 1193 = IHR 2006, 155, 156; OGH, 20.3.1997, CISG-online 269 = ZfRVgl 1997, 204 ff.; KG Waadt, 29.6.1994, CISG-online 134 = ZWR 1994, 125; sich gegen die Verwendung des Begriffs der „autonomen" Anwendung, um die Lösung des Art. 1 I lit. a) zu beschreiben, aussprechend etwa *Lohmann,* Parteiautonomie, S. 37, Fn. 95, mit der Begründung, „der Geltungsanspruch des UN-Kaufrechts [ergebe sich] auch im Falle des Art. 1 Abs. 1 lit. a CISG unmittelbar aus der Konvention".

[303] *Staudinger/Magnus,* Art. 1, Rn. 85; vgl. auch *Herber/Czerwenka,* Art. 1, Rn. 16; *Lohmann,* Privatautonomie, S. 37; *Witz/Salger/Lorenz/Lorenz,* Art. 1, Rn. 11; so auch in der Rechtsprechung AG Sursee, 12.9.2008, CISG-online 1278; Cass., 20.9.2004, CISG-online 1015; OGH, 10.9.1998, CISG-online 409 = RdW 1999, 210; BGH, 11.12.1996, CISG-online 225 = NJW 1997, 870 ff.

[304] Falsch daher *Sky Cast, Inc. v. Global Direct Distribution, LLC,* U. S. Dist. Ct. (E. D. Ky.), 18.3.2008, CISG-online 1652, wonach das CISG Anwendung findet auf Kaufverträge zwischen „parties whose *principal* places of business are in different nations if those nations are signatories to the treaty" (Hervorhebung durch den Autor).

[305] Es ist irrelevant, ob die Vertragsparteien bei Vertragsabschluss von der Vertragsstaateneigenschaft wussten; vgl. *Siehr,* RabelsZ 52 (1988), 587, 591 f.

[306] Vgl. *Soergel/Lüderitz,* Art. 1, Rn. 14; *Schlechtriem/Schwenzer/Schlechtriem,* CISG Commentary, 2. Aufl., Art. 1, Rn. 32; *Schlechtriem/Schwenzer/Schwenzer/Hachem,* CISG Commentary, Art. 1, Rn. 28; vgl. auch HGer Aargau, 10.3.2010, CISG-online 2176.

[307] Zur Funktion des IPR und des innerstaatlichen Rechts, vgl. Vor Artt. 1–6 Rn. 29 ff.

[308] So ausdrücklich Botschaft des Schweizerischen Bundesrats, S. 758; in diesem Sinne auch *P. Huber/Mullis/ P. Huber,* S. 51; MünchKommHGB/*Benicke,* Art. 1, Rn. 29.

[309] Vgl. hierzu ausführlich Art. 6 Rn. 1 ff.

[310] So ausdrücklich in der Rechtsprechung Tribunale di Vigevano, 12.2.2000, CISG-online 493 = IHR 2001, 72, 73; OGH, 9.3.2000, CISG-online 573 = IHR 2001, 39 f.; Schiedsgericht der Zürcher Handelskammer, 31.5.1996, YB. Comm. Arb. 1998, 128 ff.; Int. Ct. Hungarian CCI, 5.12.1995, CISG-online 163.

Anwendungsbereich 64, 65 **Art. 1**

Aus dem bisher Gesagten ergibt sich unschwer die Bedeutung der genauen Definition des 64
„Vertragsstaates" für die Anwendbarkeit des Übereinkommens kraft Art. 1 I lit. a); dies gilt
aber auch für die Anwendbarkeit ex Art. 1 I lit. b). **Vertragsstaat** ist[313] in der Regel jeder
Staat, in dem die Konvention im Anschluss an das Verstreichen einer bestimmten Zeitspanne
nach Hinterlegung eines vom Übereinkommen selbst vorgesehenen Instruments (Ratifikations-, Annahme-, Genehmigungs- oder Beitrittsurkunde) in Kraft getreten ist.[314] Die bloße
Ratifikation reicht genauso wie der bloße Beitritt nicht aus.[315]

Ob ein Staat Vertragsstaat ist, hängt aber auch davon ab, ob er einen **Vorbehalt** erklärt 65
hat, der sich auf die **Vertragsstaateneigenschaft** auswirkt.[316] Erklärt ein Vertragsstaat
gemäß Art. 92, dass Teil II oder III des CISG für ihn nicht verbindlich ist, so gilt er – für die
Gerichte aller Veertragsstaaten –[317] insoweit nicht als Vertragsstaat.[318] Dies hat zur Folge, dass
zum Beispiel[319] auf einen Vertrag zwischen einem in Dänemark niedergelassenen Verkäufer
und einem Käufer mit Niederlassung in Deutschland das Übereinkommen nicht gänzlich
kraft Art. 1 I lit. a) Anwendung finden kann,[320] da Dänemark, genauso wie Finnland,
Norwegen und Schweden, Teil II des Übereinkommens ausgeschlossen hat.[321] Ob die Vor-

---

[311] Vgl. *Vékás*, IPRax 1987, 342.
[312] *Staudinger/Magnus*, Art. 1, Rn. 91.
[313] Ob ein Staat Vertragsstaat ist, hat das Gericht von Amts wegen zu ermitteln; vgl. *T. M. Müller*, Beweislast, S. 43 f.; *Staudinger/Magnus*, Art. 1, Rn. 128.
[314] *Bamberger/Roth/Saenger*, Art. 1, Rn. 14; *Ferrari*, Applicabilità ed applicazioni, S. 75; *Ferrari u. a./Saenger*, Internationales Vertragsrecht, Art. 1, Rn. 14; *Schlechtriem/Schwenzer/Schlechtriem*, CISG Commentary, 2. Aufl., Art. 1, Rn. 32; zur Vertragsstaateneigenschaft von Hongkong, vgl. in der Rechtsprechung *Electrocraft Arkansas, Inc. v. Super Electric Motors, Ltd and Raymond O'Gara*, U. S. Dist. Ct. (E. D. Ark., Western Division), 19.8.2010, CISG-online 2149 (die Vertragsstaateneigenschaft bejahend); *Electrocraft Arkansas, Inc. v. Super Electric Motors, Ltd et al.*; U. S. Dist. Ct. (E. D. Ark., Western Division), 23.12.2009, CISG-online 2045 (die Vertragsstaateneigenschaft bejahend); *Innotex Precision Limited v. Horei Image Products, Inc., et al.*, U. S. Dist. Ct. (N. D. Ga., Atlanta Division), 17.12.2009, CISG-online 2044 (die Vertragsstaateneigenschaft verneinend); *Hannaford (trading as Torrens Valley Orchards) v Australian Farmlink*, Federal Court of Australia (South Australia Registry), 24.10.2008, CISG-online 1743 (die Vertragsstaateneigenschaft verneinend); *CNA Int'l Inc. v. Guangdong Kelon Electronical Holdings et al.*, U. S. Dist. Ct. (N. D. Ill.), 3.9.2008, CISG-online 2043 (die Vertragsstaateneigenschaft bejahend); Civ., 2.4.2008, CISG-online 1651 (die Vertragsstaateneigenschaft verneinend); OGH, 31.8.2005, CISG-online 1093 (die Vertragsstaateneigenschaft bejahend); OGH, 17.12.2003, CISG-online 828 = IHR 2004, 148, 155 f. (die Vertragsstaateneigenschaft weder bejahend noch verneinend); Hof van Beroep Antwerpen, 14.2.2002, CISG-online 995 (die Vertragsstaateneigenschaft bejahend); OLG Hamm, 12.11.2001, CISG-online 1430 (die Vertragsstaateneigenschaft bejahend); RB Turnhout, 18.1.2001, CISG-online 994 (die Vertragsstaateneigenschaft bejahend); in der Lehre vgl. hierzu (sowie zur Vertragsstaateneigenschaft von Macao) *Schroeter*, FS Kritzer, S. 425, 462 f.; *ders.*, IHR 2004, 2 ff., *ders.*, 16 Pace Int'l L. Rev. (2004), 307 ff.; vgl. auch Art. 93, Rn. 4.
[315] So aber *Herber*, 2. Aufl., Art. 1 Rn. 32.
[316] Vgl. *Díez-Picazo/Calvo Carava*, Art. 1, S. 53.
[317] Vgl. *Schroeter*, FS Kritzer, S. 425, 444: „erga omnes effect".
[318] So auch *Honnold/Flechtner*, Art. 1, Rn. 46.1; *MünchKommHGB/Benicke*, Art. 1, Rn. 30; *Ragno*, Convenzione di Vienna e Diritto europeo, S. 118; *Sannini*, L'applicazione, S. 69; *Schlechtriem/Schwenzer/Schwenzer/Hachem*, CISG Commentary, Art. 1, Rn. 29; *Schroeter*, FS Kritzer, S. 425, 444.
[319] OLG Rostock, 27.7.1995, CISG-online 209 = OLG-Rp. (Brandenburg u. a.) 1996, 50; vgl. auch Stadtgericht Budapest, 21.5.1996, CISG-online 252 (schwedischer Verkäufer und ungarischer Käufer); OLG München, 8.3.1995, CISG-online 145 = RIW 1996, 854 ff. (finnischer Verkäufer und deutscher Käufer); ICC, 7585/1992, CISG-online 105 (italienischer Verkäufer und finnischer Käufer).
[320] Falsch daher OLG Naumburg, 27.4.1999, CISG-online 512 = TranspR-IHR 2000, 22 f.: „Nach Art. 1 Abs. 1 lit. a CISG ist das Übereinkommen bei Kaufverträgen über Waren anzuwenden, wenn die Parteien ihren Sitz in Vertragsstaaten haben. Sowohl Deutschland (Sitz der Beklagten), als auch Dänemark (Sitz jedenfalls der Verkaufsniederlassung der Klägerin – vgl. Art. 28 Abs. 2 S. 2 EGBGB –) sind Vertragsstaaten des Übereinkommens [...]. Damit ist das Abkommen anzuwenden und geht den Vorschriften des BGB vor"; falsch auch RB Arnhem, 17.1.2007, CISG-online 1455 (Anwendung des CISG i. E. auf der Grundlage von Art. 1 I lit. a), obwohl einer der Parteien ihre Niederlassung in Schweden hatte);falsch daher RB Arnhem, 17.1.2007, CISG-online 1455 (schwedisch-holländischer Kaufvertrag, den das Gericht ex Art. 1(1)(a) dem CISG unterstellt hat); OLG Schleswig, 22.8.2002, CISG-online 710 = IHR 2003, 20 ff. (Anwendung des CISG ex Art. 1 I lit. a)), ohne jeglichen Hinweis auf den Umstand, dass eine der Parteien ihre Niederlassung in einem Vorbehaltsstaat – Dänemark – hatte; vgl. auch OLG Frankfurt a. M., 4.3.1994, CISG-online 110 (schwedisch-deutscher Kaufvertrag, der dem Gericht nach ex Art. 1 I lit. a) dem CISG unterliegt); kritisch zu diesem Urteil auch *Fogt*, ZEuP 2002, 580, 587, Fn. 22.

schriften des Teil II zur Anwendung kommen können, wird davon abhängen, ob das IPR des Forumsstaates auf das Recht eines Vertragsstaates[322] oder auf das dänische Recht,[323] d. h., das Recht des Vorbehaltsstaates, verweist.[324] Dies gilt auch für den Fall, dass das berufene Gericht das Gericht eines Vorbehaltsstaates ist.[325]

66 Gemäß Art. 93 kann ein **Vertragsstaat mit territorial gespaltenem** Kaufrecht auch erklären, dass das Übereinkommen für bestimmte Gebietseinheiten nicht gilt; dies führt dazu, dass wenn eine Vertragspartei ihre Niederlassung in einer dieser Gebietseinheiten hat, die Niederlassung von den Gerichten aller Vertragsstaaten[326] als nicht in einem Vertragsstaat liegend angesehen werden muss.[327] Auf jeden Fall kann das CISG nicht über Art. 1 I lit. a) Anwendung finden, wenn eine Vertragspartei ihre Niederlassung in einem Staat hat, der einen Vorbehalt gemäß Art. 93 erklärt hat.[328]

67 Vertragsstaaten mit **(partieller) Rechtseinheit** können gemäß Art. 94 mit Bezug zueinander eine Erklärung abgeben, wonach das Übereinkommen dann nicht Anwendung findet – auch nicht kraft Abs. 1 lit. b) –[329] wenn die Vertragsparteien ihre Niederlassung in diesen Staaten haben. Dies wirkt sich m. E. aber **nicht auf die Vertragsstaateneigenschaft** aus.[330]

68 Sonstige von den Vertragsstaaten erklärte Vorbehalte haben auf die Vertragsstaateneigenschaft keine Auswirkung.[331]

3. Anwendung kraft kollisionsrechtlicher Verweisung auf Vertragsstaatenrecht

69 Kraft der in Art. 1 Abs. 1 lit. b) vorgesehenen Anwendungsalternative,[332] die sich an die Gerichte der Vertragsstaaten richtet, also nur von diesen zwingend zu beachten ist,[333] kann das Übereinkommen selbst dann Anwendung finden, wenn eine oder sogar beide Parteien[334] ihre Niederlassung in einem Nichtvertragsstaat haben, sofern die Vorschriften des IPR des Forumsstaates[335] auf das Recht eines Vertragsstaates verweisen (und alle anderen Anwen-

---

[321] So *Honsell/Siehr*, Art. 1, Rn. 22 f.; ebenso *P. Huber/Mullis/P. Huber*, S. 51; *Magnus*, ZEuP 1997, 823, 827.

[322] Vgl. hierzu etwa OLG München, 8.3.1995, CISG-online 145 = RIW 1996, 854 (Verweisung auf deutsches Recht, mit der Folge der Anwendbarkeit auch des Teil II des CISG); ICC, 7585/1992, CISG-online 105 = J. D. I. 1995, 1015 ff. (Verweisung auf italienisches Recht und Anwendung der Art. 144 ff. CISG); a. A. – ohne Begründung – LG Bielefeld, 12.12.2003, CISG-online 905: Anwendung der BGB-Vorschriften zum Vertragsschluss, obwohl der deutsch-dänische Vertrag aufgrund einer Rechtswahl deutschem Recht, also dem Recht eines Vertragsstaates, unterstellt worden war.

[323] So etwa OLG Rostock, 27.7.1995, CISG-online 209 = OLG-Report Rostock 1996, 50 f.

[324] Vgl. *Ferrari*, Applicabilità ed applicazioni, S. 80 f.; *Fogt*, ZEuP 2002, 580, 587; *P. Huber/Mullis/P. Huber*, S. 51 f.; *Ragno*, Convenzione di Vienna e Diritto europeo, S. 118 f.; vgl. neben dem in der vorigen Fn. zitierten Urteil auch Stadtgericht Budapest, 21.5.1996, CISG-online 252: Verweis auf schwedisches Recht, mit der Folge der bloß teilweisen Anwendbarkeit des CISG.

[325] Østre Landsret Kopenhagen, 23.4.1998, CISG-online 486; vgl. hierzu *Lookofsky*, 18 J. L. & Com. (1999), 289 ff.

[326] Vgl. *Schroeter*, FS Kritzer, S. 425, 444: „erga omnes effect"

[327] *Ragno*, Convenzione di Vienna e Diritto europeo, S. 119; *Schroeter*, FS Kritzer, S. 425, 444.

[328] MünchKommHGB/*Benicke*, Art. 1, Rn. 31; *Ragno*, Convenzione di Vienna e Diritto europeo, S. 119.

[329] So ausdrücklich *Honsell/Siehr*, Art. 1, Rn. 25.

[330] So aber *Staudinger/Magnus*, Art. 1, Rn. 89.

[331] *Herber*, 2. Aufl., Art. 1 Rn. 33; *Schlechtriem/Schwenzer/Schlechtriem*, CISG Commentary, 2. Aufl., Art. 1, Rn. 33; *Staudinger/Magnus*, Art. 1, Rn. 90; a. A. MünchKommHGB/*Benicke*, Art. 1, Rn. 31.

[332] Zur Rechtsnatur des Art. 1 Abs. 1 lit. b), vgl. *Maultzsch*, FS Schwenzer, S. 1213 ff.

[333] So ausdrücklich *Staudinger/Magnus*, Art. 1, Rn. 95; vgl. auch *Mosimann/Müller-Chen*, FS Schwenzer, S. 1303, 1314, Fn. 44.

[334] So auch *Ferrari*, Applicabilità ed applicazioni, S. 84; *Ferrari u. a./Saenger*, Internationales Vertragsrecht, Art. 1, Rn. 16; *Kröll u. a./Perales Viscasillas*, Art. 1, Rn. 5 und 51; *Ragno*, Convenzione di Vienna e Diritto europeo, S. 86; *Sannini*, L'applicazione, S. 72; *Schlechtriem*, Internationales UN-Kaufrecht, Rn. 14; *Schwenzer/Hachem/Kee*, Rn. 3.27; *Vischer*, FS Schlechtriem, S. 445, 447–450; a. A. anscheinend *Martin-Davidson*, 17 Mich. St. J. Int'l L. (2008), 657, 699.

[335] So ausdrücklich Tribunale di Vigevano, 12.7.2000, CISG-online 493 = IHR 2001, 72, 73.

Anwendungsbereich 70, 71 **Art. 1**

dungsvoraussetzungen – von der erkennbaren Internationalität[336] bis hin zu den sachlichen und zeitlichen Anwendungserfordernissen – vorliegen).[337]

Die Einführung dieser Anwendungsalternative war bis zuletzt unsicher,[338] weil sich anlässlich der Diplomatischen Konferenz verschiedene Delegationen, unter anderem auch die der BR Deutschland,[339] gegen diese Lösung ausgesprochen haben,[340] da sie Rechtsunsicherheit und eine zu weite Ausdehnung des Anwendungsbereichs des Übereinkommens mit sich bringe.[341] Diese Kritik hat dazu geführt, dass die Vorbehaltsmöglichkeit des Art. 95 eingeführt worden ist.[342] Die BR Deutschland hat von der erwähnten Vorbehaltsmöglichkeit keinen Gebrauch gemacht; demzufolge ist der deutsche Richter an Art. 1 I lit. b) gebunden. Eine Einschränkung ergibt sich in Deutschland aber aus Art. 2 des Vertragsgesetzes.[343] 70

Voraussetzung für die „indirekte"[344] Anwendbarkeit des Übereinkommens kraft Art. 1 I lit. b) – die Anwendungsalternative, die zumindest in den Anfangsjahren öfter zur Anwendung des Übereinkommens geführt hat[345] als die autonome Anwendungsalternative, die hingegen heute überwiegt[346] – ist, dass die **Regeln des Internationalen Privatrechts zum Recht eines Vertragsstaates** führen.[347] Mit diesen Regeln sind die Kollisionsnormen des Gerichtsstaates gemeint, was immer wieder hervorgehoben worden ist.[348] Dies bedeutet aber, dass der Begriff des Internationalen Privatrechts nicht autonom auszulegen 71

---

[336] Ebenso MünchKomm/*Westermann*, Art. 1, Rn. 15 Fn. 63; a. A. *Soergel/Lüderitz/Fenge*, Art. 1, Rn. 13, der die Erkennbarkeit der Internationalität nur auf die „autonome Anwendungsalternative" bezieht.

[337] So auch *Herber*, 2. Aufl., Art. 1 Rn. 35; *Schlechtriem/Schwenzer/Schwenzer/Hachem*, CISG Commentary, Art. 1, Rn. 30; *Staudinger/Magnus*, Art. 1, Rn. 97.

[338] Vgl. hierzu *Czerwenka*, Rechtsanwendungsprobleme, S. 155 ff.; *Eörsi*, 31 Am. J. Cop. L. (1983), 333, 353; *Herber*, RIW 1987, 340, 341 f.; *Goode*, Uniform L. Rev. 1991-I, 54, 67; *Neumayer*, RIW 1994, 99, 101; *Sacerdoti*, Riv. trim. dir. proced. civ. 1990, 733, 739 f.; *Schlechtriem*, JZ 1988, 1037, 1039; *Volken*, Scope, S. 29.

[339] Vgl. O. R., S. 236 f., Nr. 9–12 Schlechtriem/Schwenzer/*Schlechtriem/Schwenzer/Hachem*, CISG Commentary, Art. 95, Rn. 1.

[340] Auch die Delegationen verschiedener sogenannter „sozialistischer Länder" haben sich gegen diese Anwendungsalternative ausgesprochen; vgl. *Boschiero*, Le convenzioni, S. 271; *Cassoni*, Riv. dir. int. priv. proc. 1982, 429, 435; *Réczei*, 29 Am. J. Comp. L. (1981), 513, 520 f.; *Winship*, 21 Cornell Int'l L. J. (1988), 487, 508.

[341] Vgl. auch *Schlechtriem*, Internationales UN-Kaufrecht, Rn. 16; *Staudinger/Magnus*, Art. 1, Rn. 108.

[342] Vgl. statt aller *Díez-Picazo/Calvo Caravaca*, Art. 1, S. 58.

[343] Siehe hierzu Rn. 79.

[344] *Frignani/Torsello*, Il contratto internazionale, S. 453; *Spagnolo*, 10 Melb. J. Int'l L. (2009), 141, 143.

[345] Für neuere Anwendungen des CISG kraft Art. 1 I lit. b), vgl. OLG Saarbrücken, 30.5.2011, CISG-online 2225; Tribunale di Reggio Emilia, 12.4.2011, CISG-online 2229; BGer, 16.9.2010, CISG-online 2220; Cámara Nacional de Apelaciones en lo Commercial, 7.10.2010, CISG-online 2156; BGH, 11.5.2010, CISG-online 2125; OGer Zug, 21.6.2004, IHR 2006, 112 ff.; OLG Düsseldorf, 21.4.2004, CISG-online 915 = IHR 2005, 24 ff.; OLG Karlsruhe, 10.12.2003, CISG-online 911 = IHR 2004, 62 ff.; AppGer Basel-Stadt, 22.8.2003, CISG-online 943 = IHR 117 ff.; HGer St. Gallen, 3.12.2002, CISG-online 727; LG Braunschweig, 30.7.2001, CISG-online 689 = IHR 2002, 71; Civ., 26.6.2001, CISG-online 600; *Downs Investment Pty Ltd. v. Perwaja Stell SDN BHD*, Supreme Court of Queensland, 17.11.2000, CISG-online 587; Cámara Nacional de Apelaciones en lo Comercial, 24.4.2000, CISG-online 699; Tribunale di Pavia, 29.12.1999, CISG-online 678 = Corr. giur. 2000, 932 f.; OLG Hamburg, 26.11.1999, CISG-online 515 = IHR 2001, 19 ff.; OLG Bamberg, 13.1.1999, CISG-online 516 = TranspR-IHR 2000, 17 f.; HGer Zürich, 30.11.1998, CISG-online 415 = TranspR-IHR 2000, 12; OLG Celle, 11.11.1998, CISG-online 507 = TranspR-IHR 2000, 18 ff.

[346] Siehe *Ferrari u. a./Saenger*, Internationales Vertragsrecht, Art. 1, Rn. 14 a. E.: „Die Anwendung des CISG gem. Abs. 1 lit. a hat mit der steigenden Zahl der Vertragsstaaten an Bedeutung gewonnen und stellt den Regelfall dar"; ebenso neuerdings *Kröll u. a./Perales Viscasillas*, Art. 1, Rn. 47; *Ragno*, Convenzione di Vienna e Diritto europeo, S. 83; *Schlechtriem/Schwenzer/Schwenzer/Hachem*, CISG Commentary, Art. 1, Rn. 30 a. E.

[347] *Reifner*, IHR 2002, 52, 53; *Schlechtriem/Schwenzer/Schlechtriem*, CISG Commentary, 2. Aufl., Art. 1, Rn. 37.

[348] Vgl. *Bamberger/Roth/Saenger*, Art. 1, Rn. 16; *Ferrari*, Applicabilità ed applicazioni, S. 84; *P. Huber/Mullis/P. Huber*, S. 52; *Lohmann*, Parteiautonomie, S. 139; *Niemann*, Einheitliche Anwendung, S. 73; *Ragno*, Convenzione di Vienna e Diritto europeo, S. 74 ff. und 86; *Rudolph*, Art. 1, Rn. 8; *Schlechtriem/Schwenzer/Schwenzer/Hachem*, CISG Commentary, Art. 1, Rn. 32; *Schmid*, Einheitliche Anwendung, S. 54; *Staudinger/Magnus*, Art. 1, Rn. 10; *Siehr*, RabelsZ 52 (1988), 587, 592 f.; vgl. in der Rechtsprechung Tribunale di Padova, 25.2.2004, CISG-online 819 = Giur. it. 2004, 1403; Tribunale di Rimini, 26.11.2002, CISG-online 737 = Giur. it 2003, 896, 902; Tribunale di Vigevano, 12.7.2000, CISG-online 493 = IHR 2001, 72, 73; überraschend daher *Kröll u. a./Perales Viscasillas*, Art. 1, Rn. 51: „It is not always clear which rules of private international law would be relevant, but it is reasonable to assume that they will be those of the forum".

ist,[349] was zum einen dazu führt, dass in den Staaten, in denen – wie etwa in Österreich vor Inkrafttreten des EVÜ[350] – ein **Renvoi** nicht ausgeschlossen ist, eine Rück- oder Weiterverweisung durchaus zu beachten ist.[351] Zum anderen führt dies dazu, dass in den Staaten, in denen der Grundsatz der Parteiautonomie nicht zu den Regeln des IPR zählt,[352] eine Rechtswahl unbeachtlich ist.[353] Schließlich führt dies auch dazu, dass wenn das IPR des Gerichtsstaates den Vertrag nicht einheitlich anknüpft, weil es etwa Vertragsabschluss und -wirkungen verschiedenen Rechten unterstellt, diese gespaltene Anknüpfung **(dépecage)** durchaus zu beachten ist.[354] Aus dem Gesagten folgt, dass die Aussage, wonach das CISG *forum shopping* vermeidet,[355] nicht haltbar ist.[356]

72 Ist das maßgebende **Internationale Privatrecht das deutsche,** oder das anderer Staaten, deren relevante Kollisionsnormen den Vorschriften der Rom-I VO bzw. denen des EVÜ entsprechen, so kann eine zulässige **Rechtswahl,** die dann notwendigerweise vom Richter zu beachten ist[357] und sowohl ausdrücklich als auch stillschweigend[358] vorgenommen werden kann,[359] durchaus zur Anwendung des CISG führen,[360] selbst dann, wenn keine der Vertragsparteien ihre Niederlassung in einem Vertragsstaat hat[361] beziehungsweise auch dann, wenn nach objektiver Anknüpfung das Recht eines Nichtvertragsstaates an-

---

[349] Hierzu eingehend *Ferrari*, ZEuP 1998, 162 ff.; vgl. auch *Ferrari u. a./Saenger*, Internationales Vertragsrecht, Art. 1, Rn. 17; in der Rechtsprechung so ausdrücklich Tribunale di Padova, 25.2.2004, CISG-online 819.

[350] So *Karollus*, S. 33; *Potzmann*, ÖRiZ 1989, 262, 263; *Schmidt-Kessel*, ZEuP 2002, 682, 685. Zur für die Anwendbarkeit des CISG relevanten Berücksichtigung des Renvoi in Österreich, vgl. BezG Wien, RdW 1992, 239.

[351] Wie hier *Czerwenka*, Rechtsanwendungsprobleme, S. 161 f.; *Ferrari*, Applicabilità ed applicazioni, S. 84 f., Fn. 68; a. A. MünchKommHGB/*Benicke*, Art. 1, Rn. 36; *Schlechtriem/Schwenzer/Schlechtriem*, CISG Commentary, 2. Aufl., Art. 1, Rn. 39; *Schlechtriem/Schwenzer/Schwenzer/Hachem*, CISG Commentary, Art. 1, Rn. 34; *Staudinger/Magnus*, Art. 1, Rn. 106.

[352] Ungerechtfertigt *Weizuo*, 20 Pace Int'l L. Rev. (2008), 115, 118 und 121, der in der Tat behauptet, das IPR aller Staaten erlaube eine Rechtswahl.

[353] So schon *Ferrari*, ZEuP 1998, 162, 169; vgl. neuerdings auch *Schlechtriem/Schwenzer/Schwenzer/Hachem*, CISG Commentary, Art. 1, Rn. 33; a. A. wohl *Rudolph*, Art. 1, Rn. 8, die von der „allgemeinen Anerkennung des Grundsatzes der Parteiautonomie" ausgeht; in diesem Sinne auch *Herber*, 2. Aufl., Art. 1 Rn. 38.

[354] *Schlechtriem/Schwenzer/Schlechtriem*, CISG Commentary, 2. Aufl., Art. 1, Rn. 39; *Schlechtriem/Schwenzer/Schwenzer/Hachem*, CISG Commentary, Art. 1, Rn. 34; *Staudinger/Magnus*, Art. 1, Rn. 107.

[355] So etwa *Kröll u.a./Perales Viscasillas*, Art. 1, Rn. 3.

[356] Vgl. hierzu etwa *Ferrari*, 23 J. L. & Com. (2004), 169; *ders.*, RIW 2002, 169; vgl. in der Rechtsprechung Tribunale di Rimini, 26.11.2002, CISG-online 737 = Giur. it. 2003, 896 ff., m. Anm. *Ferrari*.

[357] Ebenso, mit Bezug auf Art. 27 EGBGB a. F. bzw. Art. 3 EVÜ, *Brunner*, Art. 1, Rn. 3; *Ferrari u. a./Saenger*, Internationales Vertragsrecht, Art. 1, Rn. 18; MünchKomm/*Westermann*, Art. 1, Rn. 16; MünchKommHGB/*Benicke*, Art. 1, Rn. 37; a. A. *Lohmann*, Parteiautonomie, S. 156 ff., insb. aber S. 169 ff., der sich entschieden gegen „die Einordnung der Parteiautonomie als ,Regel des internationalen Privatrechts'" ausspricht.

[358] Vgl. Schiedsgericht der Handelskammer Hamburg, 21.3.1996, CISG-online 187 = NJW 1996, 3229 ff.: „aus der Schiedsklausel mit der Vereinbarung eines deutschen Schiedsgerichts – hier des Schiedsgerichts der Handelskammer Hamburg – [ist] auf die Wahl deutschen Rechts zu schließen"; ebenso Hamburger Freundschaftliche Arbitrage, 30.8.1996, YCA 1997, 57: Wahl der Hamburger freundlichen Arbitrage wird als stillschweigende Vereinbarung des am Sitz des Schiedsgerichts geltenden, deutschen Rechts angesehen.

[359] Vgl. zu Art. 3 Rom-I VO *Ferrari u. a./Ferrari*, Internationales Vertragsrecht, Art. 3 Rom-I VO, Rn. 26 ff.; *Rauscher/von Hein*, Art. 3 Rom-I VO, Rn. 10 ff.; *Staudinger/Magnus*, Art. 3 Rom-I VO, Rn. 70 ff.; vgl. zur Situation vor dem Inkrafttreten der Rom-I VO *Achilles*, Art. 1, Rn. 9; *Piltz*, NJW 2000, 553, 555.

[360] Vgl. etwa BGH, 11.5.2010, CISG-online 2125; Hof van Beroep Gent, 15.5.2002, CISG-online 746 (Wahl französischen Rechts); OGH, 12.2.1998, CISG-online 349 = TranspR-IHR 1999, 25 (Wahl österreichischen Rechts); KG Bern-Laupen, 29.1.1999, CISG-online 701 (Wahl deutschen Rechts); LG Kassel, 15.2.1996, CISG-online 191 = NJW-RR 1996, 1146 (Wahl deutschen Rechts); Schiedsgericht der Handelskammer Hamburg, 21.3.1996, CISG-online 187 = MDR 1996, 781 ff. (Wahl deutschen Rechts); ICC, 8324/1995, CISG-online 569 = J.D.I. 1996, 1019 (Wahl französischen Rechts); CA Grenoble, 13.9.1995, CISG-online 157 (Wahl französischen Rechts); RB Gravenhage, 7.6.1995, CISG-online 369 = NIPR 13 (1995), Nr. 524 (Wahl niederländischen Rechts); OLG Düsseldorf, 8.1.1993, CISG-online 76 = RIW 1993, 325 (Wahl deutschen Rechts); OLG Koblenz, 17.9.1993, CISG-online 91 = RIW 1993, 934 (Wahl französischen Rechts). Unzutreffend Tribunale di Monza, 29.3.1993, CISG-online 102 = Foro ital. 1994, 921, wonach die Wahl des Rechts eines Vertragsstaates die Anwendbarkeit des Art. 1 I lit. b) ausschließe; kritisch zu diesem Urteil *Ferrari*, Riv. dir. civ. 1995, II, 669–685; *ders.*, 14 J. L. & Com. (1995), 159–174.

[361] *Niemann*, Einheitliche Anwendung, S. 74.

Anwendungsbereich 73, 74 **Art. 1**

zuwenden wäre,³⁶² sofern natürlich das Recht eines Vertragsstaates berufen ist. Dies gilt selbst dann, wenn die Parteien das Übereinkommen nicht erwähnt haben,³⁶³ aber nur soweit die Vertragsparteien mit der Wahl des Rechts des Vertragsstaates nicht dessen unvereinheitlichtes Kaufrecht berufen haben;³⁶⁴ eine solche Wahl könnte durchaus als kraft Art. 6 zugelassener Ausschluss des Übereinkommens angesehen werden.³⁶⁵

Bei Fehlen einer zulässigen Rechtswahl hängt die Anwendung des Übereinkommens kraft **73** Art. 1 I lit. b) davon ab, ob die **objektive Anknüpfung** zum Recht eines Vertragsstaates führt (wobei bezüglich der Vertragsstaateneigenschaft das oben Gesagte gilt).³⁶⁶ Bei einem Verfahren vor einem deutschen Gericht (beziehungsweise vor einem Gericht, dessen maßgebende Kollisionsnormen mit den Vorschriften der Rom-I VO bzw. des EVÜ übereinstimmen) führt dies zur Anwendung der Art. 4 ff. Rom-I VO bzw. der Art. **28 ff. EGBGB a. F.**³⁶⁷). Diesen Vorschriften zufolge kommt das Übereinkommen grundsätzlich dann zur Anwendung, wenn das Recht am Verkäufersitz,³⁶⁸ d. h., das Recht, das entweder kraft Art. 4 I lit. a) Rom-I VO oder kraft Art. 28 EGBGB a. F. (bzw. oder Art. 4 EVÜ) zur Anwendung kommt,³⁶⁹ oder das Recht, mit dem der Vertrag eine engere (so Art. 28 V EGBGB bzw. Art. 4 V EVÜ)³⁷⁰ bzw. offensichtlich engere (so Art. 4 III Rom-I VO) Beziehung aufweist, das Recht eines Vertragsstaates ist.

Unabhängig davon, ob das **Recht eines Vertragsstaates** in deutschen Gerichten an- **74** zuwenden ist, weil dort der Vertrag seinen Schwerpunkt hat oder weil die Vertragsparteien

---

³⁶² Vgl. *Bamberger/Roth/Saenger*, Art. 1, Rn. 17; *Czerwenka*, Rechtsanwendungsprobleme, S. 160 f.; *Ferrari u. a./Saenger*, Internationales Vertragsrecht, Art. 1, Rn. 18; *MünchKomm/Westermann*, Art. 1, Rn. 16.

³⁶³ In der Lehre vgl. *Achilles*, Art. 6, Rn. 4; *G. Bell*, 9 Singapore YB. Int'l L. (2005), 55, 56 und 68; *K. Bell*, 8 Pace Int'l L. Rev. (1996), 237, 255; *Boggiano*, 13 Rev. der. com. oblig. (1980), 355, 357; *Cuniberti*, 39 Vand. J. Transnat'l L. (2006), 1511, 1536; *Enderlein/Maskow/Strohbach*, Art. 6, Anm. 1.3.; *Esslinger*, ALI-ABA (1999), 69, 79; *Herber*, Möglichkeiten der Vertragsgestaltung, S. 221; *ders.*, Anwendungsvoraussetzungen, S. 104; *Herber/Czerwenka*, Art. 6, Rn. 15; *Holthausen*, RIW 1989, 513, 516; *Honsell/Siehr*, Art. 6, Rn. 7; *Muir Watt*, Rev. crit. dr. int. priv. 2002, 94, 97; *Imberg*, 35 San Diego L. Rev. (1998), 769, 777; *Kritzer*, Guide to Practical Applications, S. 100 f.; *Lando*, RabelsZ 51 (1987), 60, 84; *Lindbach*, S. 308; *Magnus*, ZEuP 1997, 823, 827; *Niemann*, Einheitliche Anwendung, S. 74; *Staudinger/Magnus*, Art. 1, Rn. 104; *Witz*, D. 1990, Chron. 107, 109.

³⁶⁴ So auch *Bianca/Bonell/Bonell*, Art. 6, S. 18; *Capuccio*, Dir. com. int. 1994, 861, 867, 873; *Ferrari*, Applicabilità ed applicazioni, S. 215 ff.; *Honsell/Siehr*, Art. 6, Rn. 6.

³⁶⁵ Vgl. näher hierzu Art. 6 Rn. 21 ff.

³⁶⁶ Vgl. oben Rn. 64 f.

³⁶⁷ Monographisch hierzu *Merschformann*.

³⁶⁸ Siehe hierzu *Achilles*, Art. 1, Rn. 9; *Bamberger/Roth/Saenger*, Art. 1, Rn. 16; *Ferrari*, Int. Bus. L. J. 2002, 961, 967; *Magnus*, ZEuP 2002, 523, 527; *H.-F. Müller*, IHR 2005, 133, 134; *MünchKomm/Westermann*, Art. 1, Rn. 16; *Navas Navarro*, IHR 2006, 74, 75; *Piltz*, NJW 2000, 553, 555; *Ragno*, Convenzione di Vienna e Diritto europeo, S. 96; *Reifner*, IHR 2002, 52, 54; *Schillo*, IHR 2003, 257, 259; *Staudinger/Magnus*, Art. 1, Rn. 104; *Witz/Salger/Lorenz/Lorenz*, Art. 1, Rn. 12.

³⁶⁹ Verschiedene Urteile haben ausdrücklich darauf hingewiesen, dass der Verkäufer die für den Kaufvertrag charakteristische Leistung erbringt; vgl. etwa AG Geldern, 17.8.2011, CISG-online 2302; OLG Stuttgart, 30.5.2011, CISG-online 2225; LG Bielefeld, 9.11.2010, CISG-online 2204; OLG Saarbrücken, 12.5.2010, CISG-online 2155; RB Harleem, 3.12.2008, CISG-online 1816; Hof van Beroep Antwerpen, 22.1.2007, CISG Belgium; Tribunale di Modena, 9.12.2005, CISG-online 1398; Finnish Supreme Court, 14.10.2005, CISG Pace; OGH, 8.11.2005, CISG-online 1156; OLG Düsseldorf, 20.12.2004, CISG-online 997; OLG Frankfurt a. M., 6.10.2004, CISG-online 996; LG Düsseldorf, 28.5.2004, CISG-online 850 = IHR 2004, 203, 207; LG Möchengladbach, 15.7.2003, CISG-online 813; Hof van Beroep Gent, 15.5.2002, CISG-online 746; LG Berlin, 24.3.1998, CISG-online 742; LG München I, 6.5.1997, CISG-online 341; LG Kassel, 15.2.1996, CISG-online 191 = NJW-RR 1996, 1146; ICC, 8324/1995, CISG-online 569 = J. D. I. 1996, 1019 ff.; OLG Düsseldorf, 10.2.1994, CISG-online 116 = RIW 1995, 53 (Anwendung des Rechts des Verkäufers kraft Art. 28 II EGBGB); RB Roermond, 6.5.1993, CISG-online 454 (Anwendung des Rechts des Verkäufers kraft Art. 4 II EVÜ); OLG Koblenz, 27.9.1991, CISG-online 30 (Anwendung des Rechts des italienischen Verkäufers kraft Art. 28 II EGBGB); OLG Frankfurt a. M., 13.6.1991, CISG-online 23 = NJW 1991, 3102 (Anwendung kraft Art. 28 II EGBGB des französischen Rechts, da der Verkäufer in Frankreich seine Niederlassung hatte).

³⁷⁰ Vgl. LG Kassel, 22.6.1995, CISG-online 370 (Anwendung des Übereinkommens auf einen Kaufvertrag zwischen einem in San Marino – einem Nichtvertragsstaat – niedergelassenen Verkäufer und einem deutschen Käufer; in diesem Fall hat das Gericht nicht auf die in Art. 28 II EGBGB niedergelegte widerlegbare Vermutung abgestellt, da „sich aus der Gesamtheit der Umstände des Vertragsabschlusses in Kassel objektiv ergibt, dass der Vertrag engere Verbindung mit deutschem Recht aufweist", die sich ferner auch daraus ergab, dass der Kaufpreis in DM bezahlt werden musste und Deutsch Vertragssprache war).

eine entsprechende Rechtswahl vorgenommen haben, ist festzuhalten, dass damit immer nur das **Sachrecht** berufen ist, da, wie auch die Rechtsprechung hervorgehoben hat,[371] eine Rück- oder Weiterverweisung in Deutschland kraft Art. 20 Rom-I VO bzw. Art. 35 EGBGB a. F. nicht zu beachten ist.[372]

75 Auch in den Vertragsstaaten, in denen das **Haager Übereinkommen vom 15.6.1955** über das auf internationale Warenkaufverträge anzuwendende Recht in Kraft ist,[373] wie etwa in Dänemark, Finnland, Frankreich, Italien, Norwegen, Schweden und der Schweiz,[374] ist eine Rechtswahl durchaus zu beachten[375] und kann über Art. 1 I lit. b) zur Anwendung des Übereinkommens führen.[376] Gemäß Art. 3 des Haager Kauf-IPR-Übereinkommens kommt bei fehlender Rechtswahl das Recht des Verkäufers zur Anwendung, so sowohl die Lehre,[377] als auch die Rechtsprechung[378], sofern die Bestellung vom Verkäufer nicht im Käuferland entgegengenommen worden ist.[379]

---

[371] Vgl. LG Aachen, 3.4.1990, CISG-online 12 = RIW 1990, 491 („die Anwendung des italienischen Rechts führt zu den Vorschriften des UN-Kaufrechts. Gemäß Art. 35 EGBGB sind die Sachnormen des italienischen Rechts anzuwenden, eine Rück- oder Weiterverweisung ist ausgeschlossen"); in diesem Sinne auch LG Hamburg, 26.9.1990, CISG-online 21 = RIW 1990, 1016 („die Verweisung auf das italienische Recht ist abschließend, da sie als Sachnormverweisung ausgesprochen wird (Art. 35 EGBGB)"); ähnlich auch OLG Koblenz, 23.2.1990, CISG-online 19 = RIW 1990, 316; OLG Koblenz, 27.9.1991, CISG-online 30.

[372] So auch *Ferrari*, ZEuP 1998, 162, 171 ff.; MünchKomm/*Westermann*, Art. 1, Rn. 16; *Staudinger/Magnus*, Art. 1, Rn. 105; *Witz/Salger/Lorenz/Lorenz*, Art. 1, Rn. 12.

[373] Abgedruckt in *Staudinger/Firsching*, Vorbem. zu Art. 27–37 n. F., Rn. 42b.

[374] In Dänemark, Finnland, Frankreich, Italien, Norwegen und Schweden ist das auf internationale Warenkaufverträge anzuwendende Recht nicht mittels der Vorschriften des EVÜ, die auch dort gelten, sondern mittels der Regeln des Haager Übereinkommens zu ermitteln, da das zuletzt erwähnte Übereinkommen kraft Art. 21 des EVÜ diesem vorgeht; hierzu in der Rechtsprechung, siehe Tribunale di Rimini, 26.11.2002, CISG-online 737; Tribunale di Vigevano, 12.7.2000, CISG-online 493; Tribunale di Pavia, 29.12.1999, CISG-online 678 = Corr. giur. 2000, 932, 932–933; Trib. com. Bruxelles, 5.10.1994, CISG-online 447; übersehen von Cass., 5.10.2009, CISG-online 2105; Tribunale di Modena, 9.12.2005, CISG-online 1398; in der Lehre, vgl. hierzu *Conetti*, ZfRVgl. 1987, 83 ff.; *Ferrari*, Applicabilità ed applicazioni, S. 86 ff., Fn. 72; *ders.*, Corr. giur. 2000, 933, 934; *Fogt*, ZEuP 2002, 580, 584; *Graffi*, EuLF 2000/2001, 240, 241; *Kaye*, S. 367; *Kindler*, RIW 1988, 778 ff.; *Magnus*, ZEuP 2002, 523, 527; *Ragno*, Convenzione di Vienna e Diritto europeo, S. 97; *Reifner*, IHR 2002, 52, 54; a. A. *Kahn*, J. D. I. 1990, 421: Vorrang des EVÜ; *Naumann*, S. 18, der zwar vom Vorrang des Haager Übereinkommens gegenüber dem EVÜ ausgeht, diesem gegenüber dem CISG aber dann den Vorrang einräumt, wenn beide Vertragsparteien ihre Niederlassung in Vertragsstaaten des Haager Übereinkommens haben.

[375] Vgl. *Brunner*, Art. 1, Rn. 3; *Heuzé*, Anm. 24.; *Kröll u. a./Perales Viscasillas*, Art. 1, Rn. 52.

[376] Vgl. Trib. com. Bruxelles, 13.11.1992, CISG-online 458 (die kraft Art. 2 des Haager Kauf-IPR-Übereinkommens relevante Wahl italienischen Rechts führte zur Anwendung des Übereinkommens).

[377] *Magnus*, ZEuP 2002, 523, 527; *Niemann*, Einheitliche Anwendung, S. 75 f.; *Ragno*, Convenzione di Vienna e Diritto europeo, S. 98 f.; *Romito/Sant'Elia*, 14 Pace Int'l L. Rev. (2002), 179, 188.

[378] Siehe BG, 16.12.2008, CISG-online 1800; KG Wallis, 27.10.2006, CISG-1563 (Anwendung des Rechts des Verkäufers kraft Art. 3 I des Haager Übereinkommens); KG Nidwalden, 23.5.2005, CISG-online 1086 = IHR 2005, 253, 256 („Art. 3 Abs. 1 des [Haager] Übereinkommens bestimmt, dass bei fehlender Rechtswahl durch die Parteien der Vertrag dem innerstaatlichen Recht des Landes untersteht, in dem der Verkäufer zum Zeitpunkt, an dem er die Bestellung empfängt, seinen gewöhnlichen Aufenthalt hat"); Tribunal cantonal du Jura, 3.11.2004, CISG-online 965 (Anwendung des Rechts des Verkäufers, der in einem Vertragsstaat CISG niedergelassen war); ICC, 8908/1999, CISG-online 751 = ICC Ct. Bull. 1999, 83 ff.; RB Hasselt, 9.10.1996, CISG-online 361 (Haager Kauf-IPR-Übereinkommen führte zur Anwendung des in einem Vertragsstaat niedergelassenen Verkäufers); RB Hasselt, 8.11.1995, CISG-online 363 (Anwendung des CISG über Anwendung des Rechts am Verkäufersitz); RB Hasselt, 18.10.1995, CISG-online 364 = Rechtskundig Weekblad 1995, 1378 (Anwendung des Rechts des in einem Vertragsstaat niedergelassenen Verkäufers); CA Grenoble, 26.4.1995, CISG-online 154 (Anwendung des CISG über Art. 1 I lit. b), da die Vorschriften des Haager Kauf-IPR-Übereinkommens auf das Recht des in einem Vertragsstaat niedergelassenen Verkäufers verweisen); RB Hasselt, 24.1.1995, CISG-online 375 = Rechtskundig Weekblad 1996, 444 (Anwendung des CISG über Art. 1 I lit. b) des CISG und Art. 3 I des Haager Kauf-IPR-Übereinkommens); Trib. com. Bruxelles, 5.10.1994, CISG-online 447 (Verweisung auf das Rechts des italienischen Verkäufers); RB Hasselt, 23.2.1994, CISG-online 456 (Anwendung deutschen Verkäuferrechts und demzufolge des Übereinkommens); KG Waadt, 6.12.1993, CISG-online 457 (Anwendung kraft Art. 3 I des Haager Kauf-IPR-Übereinkommens französischen Rechts, da es das am Verkäufersitz geltende Recht war); BezG Laufen, 7.5.1993, CISG-online 136 (Anwendung finnischen Verkäuferrechts – und daher des Übereinkommens); Pretura Locarno-Campagna, 27.4.1992, CISG-online 68 (Anwendung kraft Art. 3 I des Haager Kauf-IPR-Übereinkommens des Rechts des italienischen Verkäufers).

[379] Vgl. in der Rechtsprechung zum CISG KG Obwalden, 16.8.2005, CISG-online 1727; Cass., 26.6.2001, CISG-online 598; Tribunale di Verona, 17.12.1997, Riv. vr. giur. ec. impr. 1998, 22 ff.; CA Grenoble,

Anwendungsbereich 76, 77 **Art. 1**

An dieser Stelle sei darauf hingewiesen, dass unabhängig davon, ob das **Übereinkommen** 76
auf Grund der kollisionsrechtlichen oder der autonomen Anwendungsalternative zur Anwendung kommt, Gerichte von Vertragsstaaten es immer als nationales – und **nicht als ausländisches – Recht** anwenden.[380] Die Anwendung des Übereinkommens ist daher auch in diesen Fällen in der Revisionsinstanz in vollem Umfang zu überprüfen.[381]

4. Der Vorbehalt nach Art. 95 und dessen Wirkung

Die Ausdehnung des Anwendungsbereiches des Übereinkommens durch Einführung der 77
kollisionsrechtlichen Anwendungsalternative ist rechtspolitisch umstritten gewesen.[382] Dies
hat, sozusagen als Kompromiss,[383] zur Einführung einer in Art. 95 enthaltenen Vorbehaltsmöglichkeit geführt, wonach jeder Staat erklären kann, dass Art. 1 I lit. b) für ihn nicht
verbindlich ist.[384] Welche Auswirkungen ein gemäß Art. 95 erklärter Vorbehalt hat, hängt
davon ab, ob das Gericht eines Vertragsstaates, das eines Vorbehaltsstaates oder das eines
Nichtvertragsstaates berufen ist.[385] Die Anwendbarkeit des CISG kraft Art. 1 I lit. a) beeinträchtigt einen nach Art. 95 erklärten Vorbehalt nicht.[386]

23.10.1996, CISG-online 305 = Rev. crit. 1997, 756 (das Haager Kauf-IPR-Übereinkommen hat zur Anwendung des Rechts des französischen Käufers geführt – und somit zur Anwendung des CISG –, da der in einem Nichtvertragsstaat niedergelassene Verkäufer die Bestellung im Käuferland entgegengenommen hat); CA Paris, 22.4.1992, CISG-online 222 (Anwendung kraft Art. 3 II des Haager Kauf-IPR-Übereinkommens des Rechts am französischen Käufersitz, da der in einem Nichtvertragsstaat niedergelassene Verkäufer die Bestellung im Käuferland erhalten hat).

[380] So zutreffend *Czerwenka*, Rechtsanwendungsprobleme, S. 162; *Herber/Czerwenka*, Art. 1, Rn. 17; *Maultzsch*, FS Schwenzer, S. 1213, 1218; *Pünder*, RIW 1990, 869, 873; *Ragno*, Convenzione di Vienna e Diritto europeo, S. 80; *Schlechtriem/Schwenzer/Schlechtriem*, CISG Commentary, 2. Aufl., Art. 1, Rn. 38; *Schlechtriem/Schwenzer/Schwenzer/Hachem*, CISG Commentary, Art. 1, Rn. 35; *Staudinger/Magnus*, Art. 1, Rn. 84; *Wey*, Rn. 70; *Witz/Salger/Lorenz/Lorenz*, Art. 1, Rn. 12; vgl. in der neueren Rechtsprechung *Castel Electronics Pty Ltd. v. Toshiba Singapore Pte Ltd*; Federal Court of Australia, CISG-online 2158: „The Convention is not to be treated as a foreign law which requires proof as a fact"; zu dieser Problematik, vgl. auch OLG Schleswig-Holstein, 29.10.2002, CISG-online 717; KG Bern-Laupen, 29.1.1999, CISG-online 701; BezG Laufen, 7.5.1993, CISG-online 136.

[381] So auch *Escher*, RIW 1999, 495, 500 f.; *Schlechtriem/Schwenzer/Schwenzer/Hachem*, CISG Commentary, Art. 1, Rn. 35 Fn. 119; *Soergel/Lüderitz/Fenge*, Art. 1, Rn. 19; *Herber*, 2. Aufl., Art. 1 Rn. 42.

[382] Vgl. *Czerwenka*, Rechtsanwendungsprobleme, S. 157 ff.; *Eörsi*, 31 Am. J. Comp. L. (1983), 333, 353; *Ragno*, Convenzione di Vienna e Diritto europeo, S. 112; *Réczei*, 7 Dig. Com. L. (1980), 53, 66 f.; *Rudolph*, Art. 95, Rn. 1; *Vékás*, IPRax 1987, 342; *Volken*, Scope, S. 29.

[383] *Piltz*, Internationales Kaufrecht, Rn. 2–103.

[384] Ausführlich zu den Gründen, die zur Einführung dieser Vorschrift geführt haben, vgl. neuerdings *G. Bell*, 9 Singapore YB. Int'l L. (2005), 55, 58 ff.; *Markel*, 21 Pace Int'l L. Rev. (2009), 163, 170 ff.

[385] Vgl. zu dieser Unterscheidung auch *Ferrari*, Applicabilità ed applicazioni, S. 100 ff.; *Ferrari u. a./Mankowski*, Internationales Vertragsrecht, Art. 95, Rn. 4 ff.; a. A. ohne Begründung *Harjani*, 23 Houst. J. Int'l L. (2000), 49, 55, der davon ausgeht, das UN-Kaufrecht könne nie Anwendung finden, wenn eine Partei ihre Niederlassung in einem Vorbehaltsstaat hat, und dies „even though the conflict of law rules lead to the application of the law of the Contracting State".

[386] Ebenso *G. Bell*, 9 Singapore YB. Int'l L. (2005), 55, 56; *Ferrari*, IHR 2006, 248, 249; *Ferrari u. a./ Mankowski*, Internationales Vertragsrecht, Art. 95, Rn. 4; MünchKomm/*Westermann*, Art. 1, Rn. 19; *Piltz*, Internationales Kaufrecht, Rn. 2–104; *Sannini*, L'applicazione, S. 75; *Schlechtriem*, Internationales UN-Kaufrecht, Rn. 18; *ders.*, 36 Vict. U. Well. L. Rev. (2005), 781, 783; *Schlechtriem/Schwenzer/Schlechtriem/Schwenzer/ Hachem*, CISG Commentary, Art. 95, Rn. 2; *Whitlock/Abbey*, 30 Campbell L. Rev. (2007), 275 281; zur Anwendbarkeit des CISG ex Art. 1 I lit. a) in Fällen, in denen mindestens eine der Parteien in einem Vertragsstaat niedergelassen ist, der einen Vorbehalt nach Art. 95 erklärt hat, vgl. in der Rechtsprechung District Court Trnava, 19.5.2011, CISG-online 2190; District Court Trnava, 13.5.2011, CISG-online 2191; *Castel Electronics Pty Ltd v Toshiba Singapore Pte Ltd.*, Federal Court of Australia, 20.4.2011, CISG-online 2219; District Court Trnava, 9.3.2011 CISG-online 2210; *CSS Antenna, Inc. v. Amphenol-Tuchel Electronics, GmbH*, U. S. Dist. Ct. (D. Md.), 8.2.2011, CISG-online 2177 (deutsch-amerikanischer Vertrag); *Hanwha Corporation v. Cedar Petrochemicals, Inc.*, U. S. Dist. Ct. (S. D. N. Y.), 18.1.2011, CISG-online 2178; OLG Jena, 10.11.2010, CISG-online 2216 (deutsch-amerikanischer Vertrag); *Forestal Guarani S. A. v. Daros International, Inc.*, U. S. Ct. App. (3rd Cir.), 21.7.2010, CISG-online 2112 (argentinisch-amerikanischer Vertrag); District Court Namestovo, 13.7.2010, CISG-online 2189 (tschechisch-slowakischer Vertrag); OLG Dresden, 27.5.2010, CISG-online 2182 (deutsch-slowakischer Vertrag); *Pasta Zara S. p. A. v. United States, American Italian Pasta Company, et al.*, U. S. Court of International Trade, 7.4.2010, CISG-online 2094 (italienisch-

78 Verweisen die **Kollisionsnormen eines Vertragsstaates,** der keine Erklärung gemäß Art. 95 abgegeben hat, auf das **Recht eines Vorbehaltsstaates,** so muss man davon ausgehen, dass das Übereinkommen Anwendung findet,[387] da die Voraussetzungen der Anwendbarkeit des Übereinkommens ex Art. 1 I lit. b) gegeben sind[388] und der Vorbehalt nur die Gerichte des Vorbehaltsstaates von der Beachtung des Art. 1 I lit. b) befreit.[389] Dies entspricht der Rechtsprechung des Bundesgerichtshofs zum EKG,[390] gegen deren Übertragung auf das CISG auch angesichts dessen keine Bedenken bestehen, dass deren Umsetzung in nationales Recht in anderer Weise erfolgt ist als die des EKG.[391]

---

amerikanischer Vertrag); *Belcher-Robinson, L. L. C. v, Linamar Corporation, et al.,* U. S. Dist. Ct. (M. D. Ala.), Eastern Division, 31.3.2010, CISG-online 2092 (amerikanisch-kanadischer Vertrag); *Golden Valley Grape Juice and Wine, LLC v. Centrisys Corporation et al.,* U. S. Dist. Ct. (E. D. Cal.), 21.1.2010, CISG-online 2089 (amerikanisch-australischer Vertrag); *Semi-Materials Co., Ltd v. MEMC Electronic Materials, Inc., et al.,* U. S. Dist. Ct. (E. D. Mo.), 10.1.2010, CISG-online 2169 (amerikanisch-koreanischer Vertrag); *Electrocraft Arkansas, Inc. v. Electric Motors, Ltd et al.,* U. S. Dist. Ct. (E. D. Ark., Western Division), 23.12.2009, CISG-online 2045 (chinesisch-amerikanischer Vertrag); Audiencia Provincial de Madrid, 14.7.2009; CISG-online 2087 (spanischamerikanischer Vertrag); Cour d'appel de Poitiers, 26.2.2009, CISG-online 2208 (französisch-amerikanischer Vertrag); Tribunal Supremo, 9.12.2008, CISG-online 2100 (spanisch-amerikanischer Vertrag); *Cedar Petrochemicals, Inc. v. Dongbu Hannong Chemical Co., Ltd.,* U. S. Dist. Ct. (S. D. N. Y.), 19.7.2007, CISG-online 1509 = 2007 WL 2 059 239 (S. D. N. Y. Jul 19, 2007) (amerikanisch-koreanischer Vertrag); *TeeVee Toons, Inc. et al v. Gerhard Schubert GmbH,* U. S. Dist. Ct. (S. D. N. Y.), 23.8.2006, CISG-online 1272 = 2006 WL 2 463 537 (S. D. N. Y.) (deutsch-amerikanischer Vertrag); *Ajax Tool Works, Inc. v. Can-Eng Manufacturing Ltd.,* U. S. Dist. Ct. (N. D. Ill.), 29.1.2003, CISG-online 772 = 2003 U. S. Dist. LEXIS 1306 (kanadisch-amerikanischer Vertrag); *Schmitz-Werke GmbH & Co., v. Rockland Industries, Inc.,* U. S. Ct. App. (4th Cir.), CISG-online 625 (deutsch-amerikanischer Vertrag); Audiencia Provincial de Granada, 2.3.2000, IHR 2002, 82 f. (spanischamerikanischer Kaufvertrag); *Magellan International v. Salzgitter Handel,* U. S. Dist. Ct. (N. D. Ill.), 7.12.1999, CISG-online 439 = UCC Rep. Serv. 2d 321 (deutsch-amerikanischer Vertrag); *KSTP-FM, LLC v. Specialized Communications, Inc. and Adtronics Signs, Ltd.,* U. S. Dist. Ct. (Minn.), 9.3.1999, CISG-online 471 (kanadischamerikanischer Vertrag); *Mitchell Aircraft Spares, Inc. v. European Aircraft Service AB,* U. S. Dist. Ct. (N. D. Ill.), 28.10.1998, CISG-online 444 = 1998 WL 754 801 (amerikanisch-schwedischer Kaufvertrag); CA Grenoble, 22.2.1995, CISG-online 151 = J. D. I. 1995, 632 ff. (französisch-amerikanischer Kaufvertrag); *Delchi Carrier SpA v. Rotorex Corp.,* U. S. Ct. App. (2nd Cir.), 6.12.1995, CISG-online 140 = 10 F. 3d 1024 (amerikanischitalienischer Kaufvertrag); *S. V. Braun Inc. v. Alitalia Linee Aeree Italiane SpA,* U. S. Dist. Ct. (S. D. N. Y.), 6.4.1994, CISG-online 112, 1994 WL 495 787 (amerikanisch-ungarischer Kaufvertrag); ICC, 7399/1994, CISG-online 106 = ICC Ct. Bull. 2/1995, 68 f. (amerikanisch-schweizerischer Vertrag); *José Luis Morales y/o Son Export, S. A., de C. V., de Hermosillo Sonora, México v. Nez Marketing de Los Angeles California, E. U. A.,* Comisión para la Protección del Comercio Exterior de México, 4.5.1993, CISG-online 75 = Diario oficial de 27.5.1993, 17 ff. (mexikanisch-amerikanischer Vertrag); ICC, 7531/1994, CISG-online 565 = ICC Ct. Bull. 2/1995, 67 f. (chinesisch-österreichischer Kaufvertrag); LG Heidelberg, 3.7.1992, CISG-online 38 (amerikanisch-deutscher Kaufvertrag); *Filanto SpA v. Chilewich International Corp.,* U. S. Dist. Ct. (S. D. N. Y.), 14.4.1992, CISG-online 45 = 789 F. Supp. 1229 ff. (italienisch-amerikanischer Kaufvertrag).

[387] So auch *Czerwenka,* Rechtsanwendungsprobleme, S. 159; *Herber,* Anwendungsvoraussetzungen, S. 101 f.; *Herrmann,* Anwendungsbereich, S. 89; *Honsell/Siehr,* Art. 1, Rn. 17; *P. Huber/Mullis/P. Huber,* S. 55; *Lanciotti,* S. 117; *Lando,* RabelsZ 51 (1987), 60, 82; *Lohmann,* S. 62; *Piltz,* Internationales Kaufrecht, Rn. 2–104; *Kröll u. a./Herre,* Art. 95, Rn. 8; *Maultzsch,* FS Schwenzer, S. 1213, 1218 f.; *Ragno,* Convenzione di Vienna e Diritto europeo, S. 115; *Schlechtriem/Schwenzer/Schlechtriem/Schwenzer/Hachem,* CISG Commentary, 2. Aufl., Art. 95, Rn. 3. *Schlechtriem/Schwenzer/Schwenzer/Hachem,* CISG Commentary, Art. 1, Rn. 38; *Schroeter,* FS Kritzer, S. 425, 446; *Siehr,* RabelsZ 52 (1988), 587, 601 ff.; a. A. *Bamberger/Roth/Saenger,* Art. 1, Rn. 19; *Bianca/Bonell/Evans,* Art. 95, Anm. 3.4.; *Ferrari u. a./Saenger,* Internationales Vertragsrecht, Art. 1, Rn. 20; *Heuzé,* Anm. 118.; *Kritzer,* Guide to Practical Applications, S. 78; MünchKommHGB/*Benicke,* Art. 1, Rn. 39; *Neumayer,* RIW 1994, 99, 101; *Neumayer/Ming,* Art. 1, Anm. 8.; *Pünder,* RIW 1990, 869, 871; *Schlechtriem,* AJP 1992, 339, 345; ders., Internationales UN-Kaufrecht, Rn. 18; *Schmidt-Kessel,* ZEuP 2002, 682, 684; *Staudinger/Magnus,* Art. 1, Rn. 110; *Vékás,* IPRax 1987, 342, 345 f.; die Frage offen lassend *G. Bell,* 9 Singapore YB. Int'l L. (2005), 55, 63.
[388] *Ferrari,* Applicabilità ed applicazioni, S. 104; *Ragno,* Convenzione di Vienna e Diritto europeo, S. 116.
[389] Vgl. auch *Czerwenka,* RIW 1986, 293, 294; *Schroeter,* FS Kritzer, S. 425, 447.
[390] Vgl. BGHZ 96, 313, 317 mit zustimmenden Anmerkungen von *Czerwenka,* RIW 1986, 293, 295; *Herber,* EWiR 1986, 155, 156; *Piltz,* NJW 1986, 1405, 1406.
[391] Der Unterschied zwischen der innerstaatlichen Inkraftsetzung des Einheitsgesetzes und der Transformation mit unmittelbarer Anwendung des Übereinkommens ist ein rein formaler: In beiden Fällen beruht die innerstaatliche Geltung auf autonomen deutschen Gesetzgebungsakt, beim CISG allerdings dem Vertragsgesetz i. V. m. Art. 59 GG.

Deutsche Gerichte werden auf Grund des **Art. 2 des Vertragsgesetzes** zum gegenteiligen Schluss gelangen müssen.[392] Gemäß dieser Vorschrift müssen deutsche Gerichte – wenn deutsches Internationales Privatrecht zur Anwendung des Rechts eines Vorbehaltstaates führt – das unvereinheitlichte Kaufrecht dieses Vertragsstaates anwenden.[393] Wie diese anlässlich des Beitritts der BR Deutschland abgegebene Interpretationserklärung[394] zu verstehen ist, ist umstritten. Sicher ist jedoch, dass sie keinen „Vorbehalt",[395] auch nicht einen „Teilvorbehalt",[396] darstellt, der gemäß Art. 98 auch nicht zulässig wäre.[397] Die Regierung der BR Deutschland wollte nämlich – wie sich unschwer sowohl aus dem Text der Erklärung als auch aus der Gesetzesbegründung ergibt – nicht die Geltung des Art. 1 I lit. b) einschränken.[398] „Art. 2 VertragsG und die Erklärung zu Art. 95 finden natürlich keine Anwendung, wenn auf das Recht eines Nichtvorbehaltsstaates verweisen wird".[399] 79

Befindet sich das berufene **Gericht in einem Vorbehaltsstaat,** dann führt der Vorbehalt dazu, dass der Richter Art. 1 I lit. b) nicht anwenden wird.[400] Dies bedeutet m. E. aber nicht notwendigerweise, dass das Übereinkommen in Vorbehaltsstaaten nur über Art. 1 I lit. a) Anwendung finden kann,[401] also nur dann, wenn beide Vertragsparteien ihre Niederlassung in verschiedenen Vertragsstaaten haben.[402] Unzweifelhaft ist, dass die Richter eines Vorbehaltsstaates das Übereinkommen dann nicht anwenden werden, wenn die Kollisionsnormen auf die lex fori verweisen,[403] da dies mit der ratio der Vorbehaltserklärung nicht vereinbar wäre.[404] Führen aber die Kollisionsnormen zum Recht eines anderen Vertragsstaates, unabhängig davon, ob Vorbehaltsstaat oder Nichtvorbehaltsstaat, dann kann das 80

---

[392] *Piltz,* Internationales Kaufrecht, Rn. 2–105; *Schlechtriem/Schwenzer/Schlechtriem/Schwenzer/Hachem,* CISG Commentary, Art. 95, Rn. 3.

[393] Vgl. *Bamberger/Roth/Saenger,* Art. 1, Rn. 20; *Ferrari u. a./Mankowski,* Internationales VertragsrechtR, Art. 95, Rn. 8; *Ferrari u. a./Saenger,* Internationales Vertragsrecht, Art. 1, Rn. 21; *Manz/Padmann-Reich,* 19 Int'l Bus. Law. (1991), 300, 302; MünchKomm/*Westermann,* Vor Art. 1, Rn. 2; *Niemann,* Einheitliche Anwendung, S. 76; *Schroeter,* IHR 2004, 7, 15; *Soergel/Lüderitz/Fenge,* Art. 1, Rn. 16; *Witz/Salger/Lorenz/Lorenz,* Art. 1, Rn. 13.

[394] Vgl. allgemein hierzu *Heymann,* Einseitige Interpretationserklärungen zu multilateralen Verträgen, Berlin: Dunker & Humblot (2005).

[395] *Schroeter,* FS Kritzer, S. 425, 454.

[396] So jedoch *Reinhart,* Art. 1, Rn. 5.

[397] *Ferrari u. a./Mankowski,* Internationales Vertragsrecht, Art. 95, Rn. 8.

[398] Siehe auch *Staudinger/Magnus,* Art. 1, Rn. 112.

[399] *Ferrari u. a./Mankowski,* Internationales Vertragsrecht, Art. 95, Rn. 8; in der Rechtsprechung vgl. OLG Düsseldorf, 21.4.2004, CISG-online 915 = IHR 2005, 24, 25: „Die Parteien haben unstreitig die Geltung deutschen Rechts vereinbart, weswegen dieses Recht nach Art. 27 I EGBGB gilt. Soweit Deutschland eine Erklärung zu Art. 95 CISG zu Art. 1 I b) CISG abgegeben hat, führt dies nicht zur Nichtanwendbarkeit des CISG. Denn Art. 1 I b) CISG bleibt nur dann außer Betracht, wenn das (deutsche) Kollisionsrecht zum Nachteil eines Vorbehaltsstaats führt".

[400] Vgl. *G. Bell,* 9 Singapore YB. Int'l L. (2005), 55, 63; *Ferrari u. a./Mankowski,* Internationales Vertragsrecht, Art. 95, Rn. 5; *Ragno,* Convenzione di Vienna e Diritto europeo, S. 114; *Schlechtriem/Schwenzer/Schwenzer/Hachem,* CISG Commentary, Art. 1, Rn. 37.

[401] Ebenso *Ragno,* Convenzione di Vienna e Diritto europeo, S. 114.

[402] So aber *Bamberger/Roth/Saenger,* Art. 1, Rn. 18; *Dore,* 77 Am.J. Int'l l. (1983), 521, 537; *Gabor,* 8 Nw.J. Int'l L. & Bus. (1988), 538, 539; *Markel,* 21 Pace Int'l L. Rev. (2009), 163, 173; *Piltz,* Internationales Kaufrecht, Rn. 2–104; *Pünder,* RIW 1990, 869, 872; *Richards,* 69 Iowa L. Rev. (1983), 209, 222; *Schlechtriem,* Internationales UN-Kaufrecht, Rn. 18; *Staudinger/Magnus,* Art. 1, Rn. 108; *S.J.Yang,* S. 8, Fn. 25; *Whitlock/Abbey,* 30 Campbell L. Rev. (2007), 275 280; auch einige neuere Urteile scheinen die hier verworfene Ansicht zu vertreten; vgl. *Prime Start Ltd. v. Maher Forest Products Ltd. et al.,* U. S. Dist. Ct. (W.D. Wash.), 17.7.2006, CISG-online 1242 = IHR 2006, 259, 260, m. krit. Anm. Ferrari (248 ff.); *Impuls I. D. Internacional, S. L., Impuls I. D. Systems, Inc., and PSIAR, S. A. v. Psion-Teklogix Inc.,* U. S. Dist. Ct. (S. D. Fa.), 22.11.2002, CISG-online 783 = 2002 U. S. Dist. LEXIS 22 977.

[403] So auch *G. Bell,* 9 Singapore YB. Int'l L. (2005), 55, 63; *Ferrari u. a./Saenger,* Internationales Vertragsrecht, Art. 1, Rn. 19; *Frignani/Torsello,* Il contratto internazionale, S. 454 Fn. 71; *Karollus,* S. 32; *Kröll u. a./Herre,* Art. 95, Rn. 3 und 7; *Maultzsch,* FS Schwenzer, S. 1213, 1220; MünchKommHGB/*Benicke,* Art. 1, Rn. 38; *Pelichet,* Vente internationale, S. 43 f.; *Ragno,* Convenzione di Vienna e Diritto europeo, S. 114; *Siehr,* RabelsZ (1988), 587, 608 f.

[404] Vgl. hierzu *Ferrari,* Applicabilità ed applicazioni, S. 102 f.

Art. 1 81   Teil I. Kapitel I. Anwendungsbereich

CISG durchaus Anwendung finden,[405] und zwar als Bestandteil der ausländischen Rechtsordnung, auf die die Kollisionsnormen verweisen[406] (im Gegensatz zur Anwendung des CISG kraft Art. 1 I lit. b), die zur Anwendung des Übereinkommens als nationales Recht führt).[407]

81   Auch in **Gerichten eines Nichtvertragsstaates** kann das Übereinkommen zur Anwendung kommen, und zwar dann, wenn die Kollisionsnormen der lex fori auf das Recht eines Vertragsstaates verweisen.[408] Dies ist nicht nur in der Lehre hervorgehoben worden;[409] viele deutsche,[410] niederländische,[411] belgische[412] und schweizerische[413] Gerichte haben das Übereinkommen als materielles (ausländisches) Sachrecht auf Sachverhalte aus der Zeit vor Inkrafttreten des CISG im Forumsstaat angewendet. M. E. muss diese Lösung auch für den Fall gelten, dass der Vertragsstaat, auf dessen Recht verwiesen wird, ein Vorbehaltsstaat ist.[414]

---

[405] *G. Bell*, 9 Singapore YB. Int'l L. (2005), 55, 65; *Frignani/Torsello*, Il contratto internazionale, S. 454 Fn. 71; *Maultzsch*, FS Schwenzer, S. 1213, 1221; MünchKommHGB/*Benicke*, Art. 1, Rn. 40; *Ragno*, Convenzione di Vienna e Diritto europeo, S. 114; *Schlechtriem/Schwenzer/Schlechtriem*, CISG Commentary, 2. Aufl., Art. 1, Rn. 41; *Schlechtriem/Schwenzer/Schwenzer/Hachem*, CISG Commentary, Art. 1, Rn. 37; a. A. *Ferrari u. a./Saenger*, Internationales Vertragsrecht, Art. 1, Rn. 19; *P. Huber/Mullis/P. Huber*, S. 56; *Kröll u. a./Herre*, Art. 95, Rn. 4.
Maultzsch, FS Schwenzer, S. 1213, 1220 f., hingegen, lässt die Anwendbarkeit des CISG davon abhängen, welchen Zweck der Vorbehalt befolgt. Dies schließt die im Text vorgeschlagene Lösung der Anwendbarkeit des CISG dann nicht aus, wenn der Vorbehalt den Zweck verfolgt, die Anwendung des Rechts des Vorbehaltsstaates zu schützen.

[406] *Ferrari u. a./Mankowski*, Internationales Vertragsrecht, Art. 95, Rn. 5; *Honsell/Siehr*, Art. 95, Rn. 4 f.

[407] Wie hier *Behr*, 12 J. L. & Com. (1993), 271, 272 f.; *Ferrari*, Sphere of Application, S. 16; *Karollus*, S. 32; vorsichtiger, ohne jedoch die Möglichkeit der Anwendung des Übereinkommens auszuschließen, *Winship*, Scope, S. 1–32.

[408] Dies darf aber nicht dazu verleiten, in Art. 1 I lit. b) CISG den Grund für die Anwendbarkeit des CISG in Nichtvertragsstaaten zu sehen, ist in diesen Staaten Art. 1 I lit. b) CISG doch überhaupt nicht in Kraft; ebenso *Maultzsch*, FS Schwenzer, S. 1213, 1221; *Ragno*, Convenzione di Vienna e Diritto europeo, S. 116; falsch daher *Cetiner*, S. 18, Fn. 5; *Gillette/Walt*, Sales Law, S. 44 f.; MünchKommHGB/*Benicke*, Art. 1, Rn. 35; *Nottage*, 36 Vic. U. Well. L. Rev. (2005), 815, 819; *Schlechtriem/Schwenzer/Schwenzer/Hachem*, CISG Commentary, Art. 1, Rn. 32 a. E.; *Schwenzer/Hachem/Kee*, Rn. 3.26; a. A. auch *Ferrari u. a./Saenger*, Internationales Vertragsrecht, Art. 1, Rn. 15 a. E.

[409] *De Ly*, Bus. L. Int'l (2003), 241, 241; *Ferrari*, Applicabilità ed applicazioni, S. 105 f.; *Karollus*, S. 32; *Kröll u. a./Perales Viscasillas*, Art. 1, Rn. 11; *Plantard*, J. D. I. (1988), 321; *Pünder*, RIW 1990, 869, 872; *Schlechtriem*, Internationales UN-Kaufrecht, Rn. 13 und 14; *Schlechtriem/Schwenzer/Schlechtriem*, CISG Commentary, 2. Aufl., Art. 1, Rn. 37 und 40; *Schlechtriem/Schwenzer/Schwenzer/Hachem*, CISG Commentary, Art. 1, Rn. 32; *Schroeter*, VJ (2002), 257, 259, Fn. 4; *Schwenzer/Hachem/Kee*, Rn. 3.26; a. A. *Gillette/Walt*, Sales Law, S. 42 f.; *P. Huber/Mullis/P. Huber*, S. 55 f.

[410] Vgl. OLG Düsseldorf, 2.7.1993, CISG-online 74 = RIW 1993, 845; OLG Frankfurt a. M., 13.6.1991, CISG-online 23 = NJW 1991, 3102; OLG Koblenz, 23.2.1990, CISG-online 19 = IPRax 1991, 241, 243; LG Aachen, 3.4.1990, CISG-online 12 = RIW 1990, 491, 492; LG Baden-Baden, 14.8.1991, CISG-online 24 = RIW 1992, 62; LG Hamburg, 26.9.1990, CISG-online 21 = IPRax 1991, 400, 401; LG München I, 3.7.1989, CISG-online 4 = IPRax 1990, 316; LG Stuttgart, 31.8.1989, CISG-online 11 = IPRax 1990, 317; AG Oldenburg i. H., 24.4.1990, CISG-online 20 = IPRax 1991, 336.

[411] Vgl. HR, 20.2.1998, CISG-online 313 = NIPR 16 (1998), Nr. 214; RB Amsterdam, 5.10.1994, CISG-online 446 = NIPR 13 (1995), Nr. 231; RB Arnhem, 30.12.1993, CISG-online 104 = NIPR 12 (1994), Nr. 268; RB Arnhem, 25.2.1993, CISG-online 98 = NIPR 11 (1993), Nr. 445; Hof 's-Hertogenbosch, 26.2.1992, CISG-online 65 = NIPR 10 (1992), Nr. 374; RB Roermond, 19.12.1991, CISG-online 29 = NIPR 10 (1992), Nr. 394; RB Dordrecht, 21.11.1990, CISG-online 16 = NIPR 9 (1991), Nr. 159; vgl. zu dieser Rechtsprechung auch *Frohn*, Molengrafica 1995, 199–221.

[412] Siehe RB Hasselt, 21.1.1997, CISG-online 360; RB Hasselt, 9.10.1995, CISG-online 361; RB Hasselt, 8.11.1995, CISG-online 363; RB Hasselt, 18.10.1995, CISG-online 364; Trib. com. Nivelles, 19.9.1995, CISG-online 366; RB Hasselt, 2.5.1995, CISG-online 371; RB Hasselt, 1.3.1995, CISG-online 373; RB Hasselt, 24.1.1995, CISG-online 375; RB Hasselt, 16.3.1994, CISG-online 455; RB Hasselt, 23.2.1994, CISG-online 456; Trib. com. Bruxelles, 13.11.1992, CISG-online 458.

[413] Vgl. HGer Zürich, 9.9.1993, CISG-online 79; BezG Laufen, 7.5.1993, CISG-online 136; ZGer Basel-Stadt, 21.12.1992, CISG-online 55 = BJM 1993, 310; Pretura Locarno-Campagna, 27.4.1992, CISG-online 68; Pretura Locarno-Campagna, 16.12.1991, CISG-online 27.

[414] Ebenso *Sannini*, L'applicazione, S. 77; vgl. hierzu aber OLG Frankfurt a. M., 13.6.1991, CISG-online 23 = NJW 1991, 3102; OLG Frankfurt a. M., 17.9.1991, CISG-online 28 = NJW 1992, 633, 634; LG Hamburg, 26.9.1990, CISG-online 21 = IPRax 1991, 400, 401, die obiter darauf hinweisen, dass das CISG vor Gerichten von Nichtvertragsstaaten im Falle des Verweises auf das Recht eines Vorbehaltsstaates nicht anwendbar sei.

5. Anwendung des Übereinkommens durch Schiedsgerichte[415]

Seit seinem Inkrafttreten ist das Übereinkommen auch in Schiedsgerichten bereits oft zur Anwendung gekommen.[416] Dabei ist zwischen der Anwendbarkeit kraft Art. 1 I lit. a) einerseits,[417] und der Anwendung kraft kollisionsrechtlicher Verweisung andererseits[418] unterschieden worden.[419] Bezüglich letzterer Fälle stellt sich bei Schiedsgerichten die Frage, welches Internationale Privatrecht Anwendung findet. Im Grundsatz ist dies wohl das am Schiedsort geltende,[420] selbst wenn auch eine Wahl seitens des Schiedsgerichts zwischen mehreren Kollisionsrechten in Betracht kommen kann.[421] 82

Während die Anwendung des Übereinkommens kraft autonomer oder kollisionsrechtlicher Anknüpfung in Schiedsgerichten (bei Vorliegen aller anderer Anwendungsvoraussetzungen) nicht überrascht, überrascht, dass das Übereinkommen in einigen Schiedsverfahren auch auf Sachverhalte aus der Zeit vor seinem Inkrafttreten, also trotz Fehlens zumindest der zeitlichen Anwendungsvoraussetzungen, angewendet worden ist.[422] Das CISG hätte in diesen Fällen[423] nicht zur Anwendung gebracht werden sollen.[424] Auch in Schiedsgerichten sollte das Übereinkommen nur bei Vorliegen aller Anwendungsvoraussetzungen zum Zuge kommen. 83

Ob das CISG als Bestandteil der sogenannten **lex mercatoria** Anwendung finden kann, darf m. E. nicht pauschal bejaht oder verneint werden.[425] Es wird unter anderem darauf ankommen, ob das Schiedsgericht nach Billigkeit entscheiden kann,[426] ob die Schiedsordnung es den Schiedsrichtern erlaubt, auf der Grundlage der lex mercatoria zu richten, 84

---

[415] Siehe zum Verhältnis von CISG und Schiedsrecht, die Frage der Anwendung des CISG durch Schiedsgerichte jedoch nicht behandelnd, *Perales Viscasillas/Ramos Muñoz,* FS Schwenzer, S. 1355 ff.

[416] Vgl. diesbezüglich *Béraudo,* 5 I. C. A. B. (1994), 60–64; *Muir Watt,* R. D. A. I. 1996, 401–406.

[417] Vgl. etwa Serbian Chamber of Commerce, 15.7.2008, CISG-online 1795; CIETAC, 18.4.2008, CISG-online 2057; Serbian Chamber of Commerce, 23.1.2008, CISG-online 1946; Serbian Chamber of Commerce, 1.10.2007, CISG-online 1793; CIETAC, 24.7.2007, CISG-online 2055; CIETAC, 30.6.2007, CISG-online 1930; CIETAC, 1.5.2007, CISG-online 1975; CIETAC, 14.2.2007, CISG-online 1929; Int. Ct. Russian CCI, 30.1.2007, CISG-online 1886; CIETAC, 1.12.2006, CISG-online 1927; CIETAC, 1.11.2006, CISG-online 1925; CIETAC, 1.11.2006, CISG-online 1926; Serbian Chamber of Commerce, 30.10.2006, CISG-online 2081; CIETAC, 20.9.2006, CISG-online 1473; CIETAC, 18.9.2006, CISG-online 2053; CIETAC, 1.9.2006, CISG-online 1924; CIETAC, 3.8.2006, CISG-online 1919; CIETAC, 1.6.2006, CISG-online 1918; Int. Ct. Russian CCI, 19.5.2006, CISG-online 2006; CIETAC, 1.5.2006, CISG-online 1917; Int. Ct. Russian CCI, 7.4.2006, CISG-online 1943; CIETAC, 1.4.2006, CISG-online 1967; CIETAC, 1.3.2006, CISG-online 2051; CIETAC, 23.2.2006, CISG-online 2050; Int. Ct. Ukranian, 15.2.2006, CISG-online 1961; Int. Ct. Hungarian CCI, 8.5.1997, CISG-online 307; Int. Ct. Russian CCI, 17.10.1995, CISG-online 207; Int. Ct. Russian CCI, 25.4.1995, CISG-online 206; Int. Ct. Russian CCI, 16.3.1995, CISG-online 205; Int. Ct. Russian CCI, 3.3.1995, CISG-online 204; Int. Ct. Hungarian CCI, 17.1.1994, CISG-online 251; ICC, 7153/1992, CISG-online 35 = J. D. I. 1992, 1005.

[418] Siehe Serbian Chamber of Commerce, 28.1.2009, CISG-online 1856; ICC, 10303, CISG-online 2137; Int. Ct. Russian CCI, 13.4.2006, 1944; ICC, 12173, CISG-online 2066; ICC, 11 333/2003, CISG-online 1420; CIETAC, 24.3.1998, CISG-online 930; Schiedsgericht der Handelskammer Hamburg, 21.3.1996, CISG-online 187 = RIW 1996, 766; ICC, 7197/1992, CISG-online 36 = J. D. I. 1993, 1028; Internationales Schiedsgericht der Bundeskammer der gewerblichen Wirtschaft Wien, SCH-4366, CISG-online 121 = RIW 1995, 590; Internationales Schiedsgericht der Bundeskammer der gewerblichen Wirtschaft Wien, 15.6.1994, SCH-4318, CISG-online 120 = RIW 1995, 591; ICC, 6653/1993, CISG-online 71 = J. D. I. 1993, 1040.

[419] Vgl. hierzu auch *Ferrari,* Applicabilità ed applicazioni, S. 108 ff.

[420] So ausdrücklich *Staudinger/Magnus,* Art. 1, Rn. 121, mit Hinweis auch auf ICC, 6281/1989, J. D. I. 1989, 1114.

[421] *Staudinger/Magnus,* Art. 1, Rn. 121.

[422] Näher hierzu *Ferrari,* Applicabilità ed applicazioni, S. 110 f.

[423] Vgl. ICC, 5713/1989, YB Comm. Arb. 15 (1990), 70 (Anwendung des Übereinkommens auf verschiedene 1979 geschlossene Verträge); *Watkins-Johnson CO Watkins Johnson Ltd. v. The Islamic Republic of Iran & Bank Saderat Iran,* Schiedsspruch des Iran-US Claims Tribunal Nr. 370, 28.7.1989, YB Comm. Arb. 15 (1990), 220, 226 (Anwendung auf vor dem Inkrafttreten des Übereinkommens geschlossene Kaufverträge).

[424] Vgl. *Ferrari,* Applicabilità ed applicazioni, S. 111 f. m. w. N.

[425] A. A. *Del Duca/Del Duca,* 27 UCC Code L. J. (1995), 331, 342 f., die die Frage nach der Möglichkeit der Anwendung des CISG als Teil der lex mercatoria pauschal bejahen; vgl. auch *Kilian,* 10 J. Transnat'l L. (2001), 217, 224 f., die die Frage hingegen pauschal zu verneinen scheint.

[426] Vgl. *Staudinger/Magnus,* Art. 1, Rn. 122.

und ob die Schiedsrichter überhaupt glauben, dass das Übereinkommen einen Teil der lex mercatoria ausmacht,[427] etc.

6. Parteiwille und Anwendung des CISG bei fehlender Anwendungsvoraussetzung

85 Das Übereinkommen kann kraft Parteiwillens auch dann Anwendung finden, wenn Anwendungsvoraussetzungen fehlen.[428] Auf diese Fragen wird detailliert anlässlich der Kommentierung des Art. 6 eingegangen.

---

[427] Bejahend hierzu ICC, 7331/1994, CISG-online 106 („the general principles of law [...], trade usages [...] and accepted usages are most aptly contained in the United Nations Convention on Contracts for the International Sale of Goods"); ICC, 5713/1989, YB Comm. Arb. 15 (1990), 70 („there is no better source to determine the prevailing trade usages than the terms of the United Nations Convention on the International Sale of Goods"); *Watkins-Johnson CO. Watkins Johnson Ltd. v. The Islamic Republic of Iran & Bank Saderat Iran,* Schiedsspruch des Iran-US Claims Tribunal Nr. 370, 28.7.1989, YB Comm. Arb. 15 (1990), 220, 226 (die Vorschriften des CISG „are relevant trades usages"); kritischer hierzu aber ICC, 6149/1990, YB Comm. Arb. 20 (1995), 41, 56 f.

[428] Vgl. neuerdings etwa Arbitration Institute of the Stockholm Chamber of Commerce, 5.4.2007, CISG online 1521: Anwendung des CISG aufgrund der Wahl desselben als von den Parteien gewähltes „Recht"; vgl. auch CIETAC, 9.2.2008, CISG-online 2056.

Art. 2 [Anwendungsausschlüsse]

Dieses Übereinkommen findet keine Anwendung auf den Kauf
a) von Ware für den persönlichen Gebrauch oder den Gebrauch in der Familie oder im Haushalt, es sei denn, daß der Verkäufer vor oder bei Vertragsabschluß weder wußte noch wissen mußte, daß die Ware für einen solchen Gebrauch gekauft wurde,
b) bei Versteigerungen,
c) aufgrund von Zwangsvollstreckungs- oder anderen gerichtlichen Maßnahmen,
d) von Wertpapieren oder Zahlungsmitteln,
e) von Seeschiffen, Binnenschiffen, Luftkissenfahrzeugen oder Luftfahrzeugen,
f) von elektrischer Energie.

Art. 2

This Convention does not apply to sales:
(a) of goods bought for personal, family or household use, unless the seller, at any time before or at the conclusion of the contract, neither knew nor ought to have known that the goods were bought for any such use;
(b) by auction;
(c) on execution or otherwise by authority of law;
(d) of stocks, shares, investment securities, negotiable instruments or money;
(e) of ships, vessels, hovercraft or aircraft;
(f) of electricity.

Art. 2

La présente Convention ne régit pas les ventes:
a) de marchandises achetées pour un usage personnel, familial ou domestique, à moins que le vendeur, à un moment quelconque avant la conclusion ou lors de la conclusion du contrat, n'ait pas su et n'ait pas été censé savoir que ces marchandises étaient achetées pour un tel usage;
b) aux enchères;
c) sur saisie ou de quelque autre manière par autorité de justice;
d) de valeurs mobilières, effets de commerce et monnaies;
e) de navires, bateaux, aéroglisseurs et aéronefs;
f) d'électricité.

Übersicht

	Rn.
I. Vorgeschichte	1
II. Allgemeines	4
III. Aufgrund des Verwendungszwecks ausgenommene Verträge	7
1. Konsumentenkäufe (lit. a))	7
a) Persönlicher Gebrauch	7
b) Gebrauch in Familie und Haushalt	13
2. Erkennbarkeit des persönlichen Gebrauchs	15
3. Beweislast	22
4. Verhältnis zum Verbraucherschutzrecht	24
IV. Ausschluss auf Grund der Art und Weise des Zustandekommens des Kaufvertrages	27
1. Versteigerungen (lit. b))	27
2. Zwangsvollstreckungen oder andere gerichtliche Maßnahmen (lit. c))	31
V. Art der erworbenen Ware als Ausschlusskriterium	34
1. Wertpapiere und Zahlungsmittel (lit. d))	34
2. Kauf von Wasser- und Luftfahrzeugen (lit. e))	38
3. Elektrische Energie (lit. f))	46

Vorläufer und **Entwürfe:** Art. 5 EKG; Art. 1 VI EAG; Genfer E 1976 Art. 2; Wiener E 1977 Art. 2; New Yorker E 1978 Art. 2.

I. Vorgeschichte

1 Die Vorschrift hat in lit. c)–f) im Wesentlichen[1] die Ausnahmetatbestände aus Art. 5 I EKG[2] übernommen;[3] einige Änderungen wurden jedoch auch bezüglich der ex lit. c)–f) ausgeschlossenen Käufe vorgenommen;[4] so schließt zum Beispiel Art. 2 lit. e) den Kauf aller Schiffe und Flugzeuge vom Anwendungsbereich aus,[5] während die entsprechende Vorschrift des EKG, Art. 5 I lit. b), nur die eingetragenen Schiffe und Flugzeuge ausschloss;[6] außerdem ist ex Art. 2 lit. e) nunmehr auch der Kauf von Luftkissenfahrzeugen ausgeschlossen.[7]

2 **Neu** in den Katalog der vom Übereinkommen nicht erfassten Käufe[8] aufgenommen worden sind sowohl **Konsumentengeschäfte**[9] als auch **Versteigerungen** (wobei sich die Neuerung darauf beschränkt, Käufe bei Versteigerungen privater Natur vom Anwendungsbereich ausgeschlossen zu haben).[10] Die Aufnahme dieser Anwendungsausschlüsse wurde insbesondere deshalb für notwendig gehalten, weil der Geltungsbereich des Art. 1 gegenüber dem EKG durch den Verzicht auf objektive Momente in der Begriffsbestimmung des internationalen Kaufs[11] wesentlich erweitert und infolgedessen befürchtet wurde,[12] dass Kaufverträge in die Regelung einbezogen würden, die, obgleich die Vertragsparteien Niederlassung und ständigen Aufenthalt in verschiedenen Staaten haben, wirtschaftlich nur von lokaler Bedeutung sind.[13]

3 Bezüglich des Ausschlusses von Konsumentengeschäften ist zu Recht darauf hingewiesen worden, dass dieser in gewissem Umfang an die Stelle des Art. 5 II EKG trete.[14] Diese Vorschrift sah einen Vorrang zwingender nationaler Bestimmungen vor.[15] Schon zu Beginn der Redaktionsarbeiten wurde kritisiert, dass diese Vorschrift zu eng sei und zu Auslegungsfragen bei dem Begriff „zwingende nationale Bestimmungen" führe.[16] Es wurde daher vorgeschlagen, eine Regelung einzuführen, die über den Begriff der Abzahlungsgeschäfte hinaus sonstige Verbraucherverträge erfasse[17] oder die Übereinkommensgeltung auf Handelsgeschäfte einschränke.[18] Trotz verschiedener Versuche[19] gelang es nicht, eine positive, allgemein akzeptable Umschreibung der auszuschließenden „Verbrauchergeschäfte" zu fin-

---

[1] Ebenso *Schlechtriem/Schwenzer/Schlechtriem/Schwenzer/Hachem,* CISG Commentary, Art. 2, Rn. 1; *Lanciotti,* S. 123, hingegen, geht unrichtig von einer gänzlichen Übereinstimmung der Anwendungsausschlüsse aus.
[2] Zu dessen Entstehungsgeschichte vgl. *Dölle/Herber,* Art. 5 EKG, Rn. 3.
[3] *Schlechtriem/Schwenzer/Schlechtriem,* CISG Commentary, 2. Aufl., Art. 2, Rn. 1.
[4] Vgl. *Bianca/Carbone/Lopez de Gonzalo,* Art. 2, S. 7.
[5] Anders, etwa, als der Einheitliche Akt zum Allgemeinen Handelsrecht, der keinen entsprechenden Ausschluß vorsieht; vgl. *Penda Matipé,* S. 44.
[6] So auch *Staudinger/Magnus,* Art. 2, Rn. 3.
[7] Vgl. *Ferrari,* Applicabilità ed applicazioni, S. 191.
[8] *Herber,* 2. Aufl., Art. 1 Rn. 1, spricht von nicht erfassten „Gegenständen"; Art. 2 bezieht sich aber nicht auf „Gegenstände", sondern auf Käufe, wie sich eindeutig aus dem Einleitungssatz ergibt.
[9] Vgl. unten Rn. 7 ff.
[10] Ein Teil der Lehre hat zu Recht darauf hingewiesen, dass Art. 5 EKG zumindest die Versteigerungen, die durch gerichtliche Maßnahmen oder auf Grund einer Beschlagnahme geschahen, ausnahm; vgl. *Ferrari,* Applicabilità ed applicazioni, S. 167, Fn. 12; *Herber/Czerwenka,* Art. 2, Rn. 9; *Schmitt,* CR 2001, 145, 146, Fn. 16.
[11] Vgl. hierzu Art. 1 Rn. 3.
[12] Vgl. auch *Schlechtriem/Schwenzer/Schlechtriem/Schwenzer/Hachem,* CISG Commentary, Art. 2, Rn. 1.
[13] YB II (1971), S. 56, Nr. 56 ff.; Sekretariatskommentar, Art. 2, Nr. 3; kritisch hierzu *Réczei,* Rules of the Convention, S. 70.
[14] Vgl. *Ferrari,* Vendita internazionale, S. 59; *Memmo,* Riv. trim. dir. proced. civ. 1983, 180, 196; *Schlechtriem,* Einheitliches UN-Kaufrecht, S. 13 („Art. 2 (a) entspricht in der Funktion […] Art. 5 II EKG"); ebenso *Schlechtriem/Schwenzer/Schlechtriem,* CISG Commentary, 2. Aufl., Art. 2, Rn. 2.
[15] Vgl. *Dölle/Herber,* Art. 5 EKG, Rn. 15 ff.
[16] Vgl. YB I (1968–1970), S. 168, Nr. 71 ff.; YB II (1971), S. 44, Nr. 48 ff.; eingehend hierzu *Czerwenka,* Rechtsanwendungsprobleme, S. 148.
[17] YB I (1968–1970), S. 187, Nr. 120.
[18] YB I (1968–1970), S. 169, Nr. 77; S. 187, Nr. 121.
[19] Vgl. etwa YB II (1971), S. 55; weitere Nachweise in *Bianca/Bonell/Khoo,* Art. 2, Anm. 1.1. ff.

den,[20] weshalb die Idee im Laufe der Vorarbeiten aufgegeben wurde.[21] Auf der Basis eines norwegischen Vorschlags[22] und unter Berücksichtigung der Formulierungen des Verjährungsübereinkommens von 1974[23] wurde stattdessen zur Umschreibung des Begriffs „Konsumentenvertrag" auf die Verwendung des Kaufgegenstandes abgestellt.[24] Für den Konsumentenvertrag in diesem Sinne wurde nicht nur – wie beim EKG – der Vorrang zwingenden Rechts, sondern eine vollständige Bereichsausnahme vorgesehen.[25] Damit sollte zum einen die Rechtsanwendung erleichtert,[26] zum anderen das Problem umgangen werden, das sich bei der Präzisierung des Begriffs „zwingend" gestellt hatte.[27]

II. Allgemeines

Die Vorschrift schließt bestimmte Arten von Veräußerungsgeschäften vom Anwendungsbereich des Übereinkommens aus (und engt somit den Anwendungsbereich desselben ein).[28] Ein einheitlicher Rechtfertigungsgrund für die verschiedenen Ausschlüsse ist jedoch nicht erkennbar,[29] weshalb bezüglich des Ausschlusskatalogs auch von einer „etwas willkürlichen Sammlung von Ausnahmen" gesprochen worden ist.[30]

Die als **abschließend**[31] **(und nicht analogiefähig)**[32] anzusehende Aufzählung der vom Anwendungsbereich ausgenommenen Kaufverträge[33] erfolgt auf der Grundlage **dreier**

---

[20] Vgl. zuletzt die Anregung von UNIDROIT auf der Diplomatischen Konferenz, den Begriff „Verbraucherverträge" positiv zu definieren als „retail sales" oder „sales in shops accessible to the public" und die Erwiderung Norwegens hierauf, O. R., S. 238, Nr. 40; S. 239, Nr. 54.
[21] Vgl. *Ferrari*, Applicabilità ed applicazioni, S. 172 m. w. N.; *Schlechtriem/Schwenzer/Schlechtriem/Schwenzer/Hachem*, CISG Commentary, Art. 2, Rn. 2.
[22] Vgl. YB II (1971), S. 44, Nr. 51: „The present law shall not affect the application of any mandatory provisions of national law for the protecton of a party which contemplates the purchase of (consumer) goods by that party (primarily) for personal, family or household purposes."
[23] Siehe YB VI (1975), S. 51, Nr. 21 ff.; vgl. auch *Bianca/Bonell/Khoo*, Art. 2, Anm. 1.2. f.; *Schlechtriem/Schwenzer/Schlechtriem*, CISG Commentary, 2. Aufl., Art. 2, Rn. 2.
[24] Vgl. zu den Vorentwürfen insbesondere YB II (1971), S. 55, Nr. 51 („The present Law shall not apply to sales: (a) Of goods of a kind and in a quantity ordinarily bought by an individual for personal, family, household or similar use, unless the seller knew that the goods were bought for a different use; [...]"); YB III (1972), S. 79, Art. 2 („The present Law shall not apply to sales: (a) Of goods of a kind and in a quantity ordinarily bought by an individual for personal, family or household use, unless it appears from the contract (or from any dealings between, or from information disclosed by the parties at any time before or at the conclusion of the contract) that they are bought for a different use; [...]"); YB VII (1976), S. 89, Art. 2 („This Convention does not apply to sales: (a) Of goods bought for personal, family or household use, unless the seller, at the time of the conclusion of the contract, did not know and had no reason to know that the goods were bought for any such use; [...]").
[25] Vgl. YB II (1971), S. 53, Nr. 22; S. 56, Nr. 57; Sekretariatskommentar, Art. 2, Nr. 3.
[26] Vgl. YB II (1971), S. 56, Nr. 57.
[27] YB II (1971), S. 56, Nr. 59; die Definition „zwingenden" Rechts wurde bereits in der zu Art. 5 II EKG vorgebrachten Kritik als problematisch angesehen, vgl. YB I (1968–1970), S. 168, Nr. 71 ff.
[28] So schon *Boschiero*, Le convenzioni, S. 276; *Bianca/Carbone/Lopez de Gonzalo*, Art. 2, S. 7; *Schlechtriem*, Uniform Sales Law, S. 28; vgl. neuerdings hierzu auch *Schlechtriem/Schwenzer/Schlechtriem/Schwenzer/Hachem*, CISG Commentary, Art. 2, Rn. 3.
[29] Vgl. *Díez-Picazo/Laporta*, Art. 2, S. 59; MünchKomm/*Westermann*, Art. 2, Rn. 1.
[30] *Staudinger/Magnus*, Art. 2, Rn. 9.
[31] Vgl. *Achilles*, Art. 2, Rn. 1; *Bamberger/Roth/Saenger*, Art. 2, Rn. 1; *Czerwenka*, Rechtsanwendungsprobleme, S. 155; *Kröll u. a./Spohnheimer*, Art. 2, Rn. 4; MünchKomm/*Westermann*, Art. 2, Rn. 1; *Schlechtriem/Schwenzer/Schlechtriem/Schwenzer/Hachem*, CISG Commentary, Art. 2, Rn. 3; *Soergel/Lüderitz/Fenge*, Art. 1, Rn. 1; in der Rechtsprechung vgl. OLG Schleswig, 29.10.2002, CISG-online 717.
[32] *Ferrari u. a./Saenger*, Internationales Vertragsrecht, Art. 2, Rn. 1; *Kröll u. a./Spohnheimer*, Art. 2, Rn. 4; MünchKomm/*Westermann*, Art. 2, Rn. 1; *Schlechtriem/Schwenzer/Schlechtriem/Schwenzer/Hachem*, CISG Commentary, Art. 2, Rn. 3; a. A. MünchKommHGB/*Benicke*, Art. 2, Rn. 10.
[33] In verschiedenen Urteilen wird ausdrücklich darauf hingewiesen, dass keine der in Art. 2 aufgezählten Ausnahmen der Anwendbarkeit des CISG im Wege stehen; vgl. etwa *Doolim Corp. v. R Doll, LLC.*, U. S. Dist. Ct. (S. D. N. Y.), 29.5.2009, CISG-online 1892; OLG München, 14.1.2009, CISG-online 2011; LG Landshut, 12.6.2008, CISG-online 1703; *TeeVee Toons, Inc. & Steve Gottlieb, Inc. v. Gerhard Schubert GmbH*, U. S. Dist. Ct. (S. D. N. Y.), 23.8.2006, CISG-online 1272; LG Gera, 29.6.2006, CISG-online 1852; Tribunal cantonal Vaud, 11.4.2002, CISG-online 899; OLG Hamm, 12.11.2001, CISG-online 1430; CA Colmar, 12.6.2001, CISG-online 694; LG Landshut, 5.4.1995, CISG-online 193; AG Cloppenburg, 14.4.1993, CISG-online 85.

Art. 2 6, 7   Teil I. Kapitel I. Anwendungsbereich

Kriterien:[34] „Verwendungszweck der Ware (lit.a)) – Art und Weise des Zustandekommens des Kaufvertrages (lit. b) und c)), – Art der Ware (lit. d), e) und f))."[35]

6   Soweit die Bestimmungen des Übereinkommens mit denen des Haager Kaufrechts übereinstimmen, kann auf die Ergebnisse zurückgegriffen werden, zu denen man anlässlich der Diskussion um letztere gelangt ist.[36]

III. Aufgrund des Verwendungszwecks ausgenommene Verträge

1. Konsumentenkäufe (lit. a))

7   **a) Persönlicher Gebrauch.** Gemäß Art. 2 lit. a) sind vom Anwendungsbereich des Übereinkommens diejenigen Geschäfte ausgenommen, mit denen der Käufer persönliche, „familiäre" oder dem Haushalt eigene Bedürfnisse befriedigen will,[37] wie etwa der Kauf eines Wagens für den persönlichen Gebrauch.[38] Der Ausschlussgrund ist vor allem[39] darin zu suchen, dass ein Konflikt mit nationalen Verbraucherschutzbestimmungen, die es mittlerweile doch in den meisten, aber eben nicht allen Staaten[40] gibt,[41] vermieden werden sollte.[42] Die Ausklammerung nationalen Konsumentenschutzrechts ist aber nicht voll gelungen,[43] was mittlerweile auch von der Rechtsprechung hervorgehoben worden ist.[44] Dies ist nicht verwunderlich, muss man doch davon ausgehen, was auch anlässlich der Vorarbeiten her-

---

[34] So auch *Bianca/Bonell/Khoo*, Art. 2, Anm. 2.1.; *Enderlein/Maskow/Strohbach*, Art. 2, Anm. 1.; *Díez-Picazo/Laporta*, Art. 2, S. 59; *Ferrari*, Applicabilità ed applicazioni, S. 166 f.; *Ferrari u. a./Saenger*, Internationales Vertragsrecht, Art. 2, Rn. 1; *Karollus*, JuS 1993, 378, 380; *Kröll u. a./Spohnheimer*, Art. 2, Rn. 2; *Samson*, 23 Cah. de Dr. (1982), 919, 928; *Sannini*, L'applicazione, S. 112. Einige Autoren teilen die Ausnahmen hingegen lediglich in zwei Kategorien ein; vgl. *K. Bell*, 8 Pace Int'l L. Rev. (1996), 237, 250; *Honnold/Flechtner*, Art. 2, Rn. 50; *Jung*, S. 198; *Lanciotti*, S. 123; *Volken*, Anwendungsvoraussetzungen, S. 91.
[35] *Enderlein/Maskow/Strohbach*, Art. 2, Anm. 1.
[36] *Herber*, 2. Aufl., Art. 2 Rn. 4.
[37] Für Hinweise in der Rechtsprechung darauf, dass das CISG Anwendung findet, da kein ex Art. 2 lit. a) ausgeschlossener Konsumentenkauf vorliegt, weshalb das fehlende Vorliegen des Ausnahmestatbestandes des Art. 2 lit. a) auch als negative Anwendungsvoraussetzung gesehen werden kann, vgl. etwa OLG Hamm, 2.4.2009, CISG-online 1978 = IHR 2010, 61; OGer Aargau, 3.3.2009, CISG-online 2013; Hof 's-Gravenhage, 17.2.2009, unveröff.; Court of First Instance of Athens, Aktenzeichen 4505/2009 (ohne Datum), CISG-online 2228; BG, 16.12.2008, CISG-online 1800; RB Arnhem, 5.11.2008, CISG-online 1751; LG Bamberg, 23.10.2006, 1400 = IHR 2007, 113, 115; RB Arnhem, 1.3.2006, CISG-online 1475; LG Neubrandenburg, 3.8.2005, CISG-online 1190; LG Kiel, 27.7.2004, CISG-online 1534; LG Saarbrücken, 1.6.2004, CISG-online 1228; Audiencia Provincial de Valencia, 7.6.2003, CISG-online 948; Hof 's-Hertogenbosch, 25.2.2003, unveröff.; LG Saarbrücken, 25.11.2002, CISG-online 718; LG Saarbrücken, 2.7.2002, CISG-online 713; LG München II, 20.2.2002, CISG-online 712; AG Alsfeld, 12.5.1995, CISG-online 170; LG Oldenburg, 15.2.1995, CISG-online 197 LG Oldenburg, 9.11.1994, CISG-online 114; KG Wallis, 29.6.1994 CISG-online 134; BG Laufen, 7.5.1993, CISG-online 136.
[38] Vgl. KG Nidwalden, 5.6.1996, CISG-online 332 = SZIER 1999, 82.
[39] Vgl. den Sekretariatskommentar, Art. 3, Nr. 2, wonach der Ausschluss der Konsumentenkäufe auch damit gerechtfertigt wurde, dass diese vor allem reine Inlandsgeschäfte beziehungsweise Geschäfte mit lediglich lokaler Bedeutung seien.
[40] So etwa Bolivien und Kuba; vgl. *E. Muñoz*, S. 46.
[41] Vgl. diesbezüglich *E. Muñoz*, S. 46 ff. (zum Recht Spaniens und Portugals sowie der Staaten Lateinamerikas).
[42] Vgl. *Achilles*, Art. 2, Rn. 1; *K. Bell*, 8 Pace Int'l L. Rev. (1996), 237, 251; *Díez-Picazo/Laporta*, Art. 2, S. 60; *Dore*, 77 Am.J. Int'l L. (1983), 521, 532; *U. Huber*, RabelsZ 43 (1979), 413, 421; *Karollus*, S. 26 f.; *Memmo*, Riv. trim. dir. proced. civ. 1983, 180, 193 f.; *Plantard*, J. D. I. 1988, 311, 325; *Reinhart*, Art. 2, Rn. 3; *Sannini*, L'applicazione, S. 113 f.; *Schlechtriem*, Internationales UN-Kaufrecht, Rn. 29; ders., IPRax 1990, 277, 278; *Schlechtriem/Schwenzer/Schlechtriem*, CISG Commentary, 2. Aufl., Art. 2, Rn. 17; *Schmitt*, CR 2001, 145, 145; *Schwenzer/Hachem/Kee*, Rn. 6.38; *Staudinger/Magnus*, Art. 2, Rn. 10; *Wasmer*, S. 14 und 70.
[43] So ausdrücklich *Schlechtriem*, Einheitliches UN-Kaufrecht, S. 13; vgl. auch MünchKomm/*Westermann*, Art. 2, Rn. 3; *Schmitt*, CR 2001, 145, 146; *Wartenberg*, S. 24 ff.; a. A., freilich ohne Begründung, *Ferrari*, FS Frignani, S. 243, 251.
[44] So ausdrücklich BGH, 31.10.2001, CISG-online 617 = IHR 2002, 14, 16.

vorgehoben worden ist, dass „die Aufgabe, zu den unterschiedlichen Anwendungsvoraussetzungen nationaler Konsumentenschutzgesetze deckungsgleiche Ausgrenzungsmerkmale im Einheitskaufrecht zu finden, [...] unlösbar sein [dürfte]."[45]

Art. 2 lit. a) stellt auf den persönlichen beziehungsweise auf den diesem Gebrauch gleichgestellten Gebrauch in der Familie und im Haushalt ab. Es kommt demnach allein auf die zum **Zeitpunkt des Vertragsabschlusses**[46] **beabsichtigte Nutzung**,[47] nicht die wirkliche,[48] an,[49] was mittlerweile auch von der (höchstrichterlichen) Rechtsprechung bestätigt worden ist.[50] Verwendet der Käufer die Ware später anders als geplant, bleibt das für die Ausnahme demnach ohne Einfluss.[51] **8**

Der **persönliche Gebrauch**[52] (beziehungsweise der diesem gleichgestellte Gebrauch in der Familie und im Haushalt)[53] bildet den Gegensatz zum Gebrauch im Rahmen einer **Berufs- oder Geschäftstätigkeit.**[54] Nicht maßgebend ist, ob der Gebrauch zu gewerblichen Zwecken erfolgt.[55] Auch der zu freiberuflichen Zwecken bestimmte Gebrauch,[56] genauso wie der landwirtschaftliche Gebrauch,[57] sind nicht von der in Art. 2 lit. a) geregelten Ausnahme erfasst. Daher unterfallen dem Übereinkommen etwa – bei Vorliegen aller Anwendungsvoraussetzungen – der Kauf eines Konversationslexikon durch einen Schriftsteller oder von Wetterkleidung durch einen Lotsen, der Kauf einer Kamera durch einen Berufsfotografen oder der Kauf von Seife seitens eines Unternehmens,[58] genauso wie der **9**

---

[45] *Schlechtriem*, Einheitliches UN-Kaufrecht, S. 13, Fn. 62.
[46] Vgl. *Audit*, Vente internationale, S. 28; *Bianca/Bonell/Khoo*, Art. 2, Anm. 2.2.; *Bianca/Carbone/Lopez de Gonzalo*, Art. 2, S. 7; *Brunner*, Art. 2, Rn. 10; *Enderlein/Maskow/Strohbach*, Art. 2, Anm. 3.1. a. E.; *Ferrari u. a./Saenger*, Internationales Vertragsrecht, Art. 2, Rn. 3; *Honsell/Siehr*, Art. 2, Rn. 13; *Kröll u. a./Spohnheimer*, Art. 2, Rn. 8 und 10; *Rudolph*, Art. 2, Rn. 2 a. E.; *Schlechtriem/Schwenzer/Schlechtriem/Schwenzer/Hachem*, CISG Commentary, Art. 2, Rn. 12; *Schroeter*, UN-Kaufrecht, § 6, Rn. 87; *Witz/Salger/Lorenz/Lorenz*, Art. 2, Rn. 5; vgl. in der Rechtsprechung Tribunal cantonal du Jura, 3.11.2004, CISG-online 965; BGH, 31.10.2001, CISG-online 617, E. III.4.
[47] So auch *Achilles*, Art. 2, Rn. 2; *Bernardini*, Compravendita internazionale, S. 87; *Díez Piacazo/Laporta*, Art. 2, S. 61; *Enderlein/Maskow/Strohbach*, Art. 2, Anm. 2.; *Honnold/Flechtner*, Art. 2, Rn. 50; *Honsell/Siehr*, Art. 2, Rn. 13; *Lanciotti*, S. 126; *Memmo*, Riv. trim. dir. proced. civ. 1983, 180, 194; *Mosimann/Müller-Chen*, FS Schwenzer, S. 1303, 1314; *MünchKommHGB/Benicke*, Art. 2, Rn. 2; *Schmitt*, CR 2001, 145, 145; *Staudinger/Magnus*, Art. 2, Rn. 11.
[48] *Sannini*, L'applicazione, S. 114 f.; *Schlechtriem/Schwenzer/Schlechtriem/Schwenzer/Hachem*, CISG Commentary, Art. 2, Rn. 4.
[49] *Karollus*, S. 25; *Piltz*, NJW 2000, 553, 554; *Schlechtriem/Schwenzer/Schlechtriem*, CISG Commentary, 2. Aufl., Art. 2, Rn. 5; *Soergel/Lüderitz/Fenge*, Art. 2, Rn. 3.
[50] OGH, 11.2.1997, CISG-online 298: es kommt „auf den beabsichtigten, nicht auf den tatsächlichen Gebrauch an".
[51] *Ferrari u. a./Saenger*, Internationales Vertragsrecht, Art. 2, Rn. 3; *MünchKommHGB/Benicke*, Art. 2, Rn. 5; *Schlechtriem/Schwenzer/Schlechtriem*, CISG Commentary, 2. Aufl., Art. 2, Rn. 8a; *Staudinger/Magnus*, Art. 2, Rn. 11.
[52] Obwohl der Text nur vom Gebrauch spricht, ist auch der Kauf zum persönlichen Verbrauch vom Anwendungsbereich ausgenommen; vgl. *Kröll u. a./Spohnheimer*, Art. 2, Rn. 8; *Lohmann*, Parteiautonomie, S. 21; *Schlechtriem/Schwenzer/Schlechtriem*, CISG Commentary, 2. Aufl., Art. 2, Rn. 8a; *Soergel/Lüderitz/Fenge*, Art. 2, Rn. 2.
[53] *Schlechtriem/Schwenzer/Schlechtriem/Schwenzer/Hachem*, CISG Commentary, Art. 2, Rn. 6.
[54] So auch *Achilles*, Art. 2, Rn. 2; *Brunner*, Art. 2, Rn. 10; *Kröll u. a./Spohnheimer*, Art. 2, Rn. 8; *Lohmann*, Parteiautonomie, S. 21; *MünchKommHGB/Benicke*, Art. 2, Rn. 3; *Witz/Salger/Lorenz/Lorenz*, Art. 2, Rn. 3; vgl. in der Rechtsprechung KG Jura, 3.11.2004, CISG-online 965: „but commercial ou professionel".
[55] *Herber*, 2. Aufl., Art. 2, Rn. 4; *Schlechtriem/Schwenzer/Schlechtriem*, CISG Commentary, 2. Aufl., Art. 2, Rn. 5.
[56] So auch *Achilles*, Art. 2, Rn. 2; *Bamberger/Roth/Saenger*, Art. 2, Rn. 3; *Ferrari*, Applicabilità ed applicazioni, S. 175; *Karollus*, JuS 1993, 378, 380; *Rudolph*, Art. 2, Rn. 2; *Schlechtriem/Schwenzer/Schlechtriem/Schwenzer/Hachem*, CISG Commentary, Art. 2, Rn. 4; vgl. in der neueren Rechtsprechung LG Bamberg, 13.4.2005, CISG-online 1402: Kauf von Möbeln für Kanzleiräume fällt unter das CISG.
[57] *Piltz*, Internationales Kaufrecht, Rn. 2–60.
[58] Für diese Beispiele siehe schon *Herber/Czerwenka*, Art. 2, Rn. 6; *Schlechtriem/Schwenzer/Schlechtriem*, CISG Commentary, 2. Aufl., Art. 2, Rn. 6; *Staudinger/Magnus*, Art. 2, Rn. 15; vgl. neuerdings auch *Schlechtriem/Schwenzer/Schlechtriem/Schwenzer/Hachem*, CISG Commentary, Art. 2, Rn. 4.

Art. 2 10–12 Teil I. Kapitel I. Anwendungsbereich

Kauf einer Schreibmaschine durch einen Rechtsanwalt.[59] Dies ergibt sich auch aus dem Sekretariatskommentar.[60]

10   Das Übereinkommen scheint zu verlangen, dass der Käufer die für den persönlichen Gebrauch erworbenen **Waren selbst benutzt**.[61] Dies ist nur insoweit zutreffend, als man damit nicht aussagen will, dass der Käufer der „Endverbraucher" sein muss: Ein Fall persönlicher Nutzung ist nämlich auch dann gegeben, wenn „der Käufer die Ware erwirbt, um sie privat (und nicht etwa als Firmenwerbung) weiterzuverschenken."[62]

11   Vom Anwendungsbereich des Übereinkommens ausgeschlossen sind grundsätzlich, da in der Regel unter den Ausnahmetatbestand subsumierbar, Käufe von **zur Befriedigung privater Bedürfnisse dienender Waren** wie etwa Kleidung, Lebensmittel, Toilettenartikel, Bücher, etc.[63] Da jedoch nicht Konsumgüter als solche von der Ausgrenzung des Art. 2 lit. a) erfasst sind,[64] sondern der Kauf derselben, kann es durchaus vorkommen, dass auch der Kauf der genannten Waren vom Übereinkommen geregelt wird,[65] und zwar dann, wenn die Käufer keine Privatleute sind.[66] Mit anderen Worten, **„nur private Käufe, nicht private Verkäufe [sind] ausgenommen."**[67] Aus diesem Grund hat etwa ein Gericht Kauf von Schuhen für das Gewerbe dem CISG unterstellt.[68]

12   An dieser Stelle muss man sich fragen, ob der beabsichtigte private Gebrauch, der zum Ausschluss des Kaufs vom Anwendungsbereich des Übereinkommens führt, ein **ausschließlicher** sein muss. Der norwegische Antrag, auf den die Bestimmung zurückgeht,[69] versuchte zunächst, die Ausnahme schon bei „primär" für den persönlichen Gebrauch bestimmten Käufen eingreifen zu lassen. Diese Einschränkung wurde jedoch von der Konferenz nicht übernommen; die Vorschrift ist deshalb als Ausnahmebestimmung und im Interesse der Rechtssicherheit eng auszulegen,[70] d. h., so auch die Rechtsprechung,[71] nur der für einen **ausschließlich** persönlichen Zwecken dienende Kauf fällt unter die Ausnahme des lit. a).[72] Daher hat die Rechtsprechung auch den Kauf eines ausschließlich dem

---

[59] Zu diesem Beispiel vgl. auch *Schlechtriem*, Einheitliches UN-Kaufrecht, S. 14; *Piltz*, Internationales Kaufrecht, Rn. 2–61; *Schlechtriem/Schwenzer/Schlechtriem/Schwenzer/Hachem*, CISG Commentary, Art. 2, Rn. 4; vgl. in der Rechtsprechung LG Bamberg, 13.4.2005, CISG-online 1402 (Einrichtung für Anwaltsbüro).

[60] Vgl. Sekretariatskommentar, Art. 2, Nr. 2.

[61] *Staudinger/Magnus*, Art. 2, Rn. 14.

[62] *Staudinger/Magnus*, Art. 2, Rn. 14 ähnlich auch *Ferrari u. a./Saenger*, Internationales Vertragsrecht, Art. 2, Rn. 3; *Schlechtriem*, Einheitliches UN-Kaufrecht, S. 14; *Schlechtriem/Schwenzer/Schlechtriem*, CISG Commentary, 2. Aufl., Art. 2, Rn. 8a.; *Schlechtriem/Schwenzer/Schlechtriem/Schwenzer/Hachem*, CISG Commentary, Art. 2, Rn. 4.

[63] *Bamberger/Roth/Saenger*, Art. 2, Rn. 2; *Schlechtriem/Schwenzer/Schlechtriem/Schwenzer/Hachem*, CISG Commentary, Art. 2, Rn. 4.

[64] A. A. wohl AG Duisburg, 13.4.2000, CISG-online 659 = IHR 2001, 114, 115, das darauf hinweist, dass die Anwendbarkeit des CISG auf den zu bewertenden Kaufvertrag nicht gemäß Art. 2 ausgeschlossen war, „weil Gegenstand des Kaufvertrags keine *Verbrauchsgüter* etc. waren" (Hervorhebung durch den Autor).

[65] Vgl. *Bianca/Carbone/Lopez de Gonzalo*, Art. 2, S. 7; *Enderlein/Maskow/Strohbach*, Art. 2, Anm. 3.1.; *Schlechtriem*, Internationales UN-Kaufrecht, Rn. 29; *Schlechtriem/Schwenzer/Schlechtriem*, CISG Commentary, 2. Aufl., Art. 2, Rn. 5; *Schlechtriem/Schwenzer/Schlechtriem/Schwenzer/Hachem*, CISG Commentary, Art. 2, Rn. 4; vgl. in der Rechtsprechung OLG Stuttgart, 31.3.3008, CISG-online 1658 (Autokauf).

[66] Vgl. *Ferrari u. a./Saenger*, Internationales Vertragsrecht, Art. 2, Rn. 3, Fn. 3; vgl. auch *Karollus*, S. 26, der hervorhebt, dass es immer nur um die Käuferseite gehe: „Verkäufe von Privaten (z. B. Verkauf eines Gebrauchtwagens an einen Händler) fallen nicht unter den Ausnahmetatbestand." Ähnlich auch *Mosimann/Müller-Chen*, FS Schwenzer, S. 1303, 1314; *Staudinger/Magnus*, Art. 2, Rn. 18.

[67] *Witz/Salger/Lorenz/Lorenz*, Art. 2, Rn. 2; vgl. auch MünchKommHGB/*Benicke*, Art. 2, Rn. 6 a. E.

[68] LG München II, 20.2.2002, CISG-online 712 = IHR 2003, 24, 25.

[69] Vgl. YB II (1971), S. 44, Nr. 51.

[70] So auch *Czerwenka*, Rechtsanwendungsprobleme, S. 151 f.; *Karollus*, S. 26; *Schlechtriem/Schwenzer/Schlechtriem/Schwenzer/Hachem*, CISG Commentary, Art. 2, Rn. 7; vgl. auch Finnish Supreme Court, 14.10.2005, CISG Pace.

[71] District Court Copenhagen, 19.10.2007, CISG-online 2150; Finnish Supreme Court, 14.10.2005, CISG Pace.

[72] *Achilles*, Art. 2, Rn. 2; *Baumgärtel/Laumen/Hepting/Müller*, Art 2, Rn. 3; *Brunner*, Art. 2, Rn. 10; *Ferrari*, Applicabilità ed applicazioni, S. 178; *Ferrari u. a./Saenger*, Internationales Vertragsrecht, Art. 2, Rn. 3; *Honsell/*

persönlichen Gebrauch dienenden Wagens,[73] Motorrads[74] sowie eines Wohnwagens[75] dem Anwendungsbereich des CISG entzogen. Ein griechisches Gericht hat auch den Kauf eines Sportbootes dem Anwendungsbereich des Art. 2 lit. a) unterstellt, und nationales Recht statt CISG zur Anwendung kommen lassen.[76]

b) Gebrauch in Familie und Haushalt. Dem privaten Gebrauch ist, wie bereits **13** erwähnt, der Gebrauch in der **Familie** oder im **Haushalt** gleichgesetzt.[77] Da der Begriff der Familie autonom und weit[78] auszulegen ist, sind Familienangehörige im Sinne des Übereinkommens nicht nur Verwandte und Verschwägerte im Sinne nationalen Familienrechts,[79] sondern alle Personen, die unter einen eher an soziologischen Befunden orientierten Begriff fallen.[80]

Diese Ausnahme führt, trotz der gemäß Art. 1 III bei der Anwendung des Übereinkom- **14** mens nicht zu berücksichtigenden Kaufmannseigenschaft der Vertragsparteien beziehungsweise der handelsrechtlichen oder bürgerlich-rechtlichen Natur des Vertrages, de facto zu einer Beschränkung des Anwendungsbereichs auf Handelskäufe.[81]

2. Erkennbarkeit des persönlichen Gebrauchs

Der zweite Halbsatz von Art. 2 lit. a) enthält eine **Unterausnahme**,[82] wonach der **15** beabsichtigte persönliche Gebrauch der erworbenen Waren außer Betracht bleibt, wenn der Verkäufer diesen zum Zeitpunkt des Vertragsschlusses[83] nicht kannte beziehungsweise nicht kennen musste.[84] Demzufolge erfasst das Übereinkommen bei fehlender Kenntnis und Erkennbarkeit auch Verbraucherverträge.[85]

Siehr, Art. 2, Rn. 12; *Karollus*, S. 25 f.; MünchKommHGB/*Benicke*, Art. 2, Rn. 4; *Piltz*, Internationales Kaufrecht, Rn. 2–61; *Schlechtriem/Schwenzer/Schlechtriem*, CISG Commentary, 2. Aufl., Art. 2, Rn. 8; *Schlechtriem/Schwenzer/Schlechtriem/Schwenzer/Hachem*, CISG Commentary, Art. 2, Rn. 7; *Witz/Salger/Lorenz/Lorenz*, Art. 2, Rn. 4; a. A. *Soergel/Lüderitz/Fenge*, Art. 2, Rn. 3; differenzierend, und daher nur unter bestimmten Bedingungen die Ausnahme auf zu ausschließlich persönlichen Zwecken geschlossene Kaufverträge limitierend, *Kröll u. a./Spohnheimer*, Art. 2, Rn. 14.

[73] OGH, 11.2.1997, CISG-online 298; KG Nidwalden, 5.6.1996, CISG-online 332.
[74] RB Harleem, 15.12.2005, CISG-online 1696.
[75] RB Arnhem, 27.5.1993, CISG-online 99.
[76] Court of Appeals of Piraeus, Aktenzeichen 520/2008 (ohne Datum), CISG Pace. Das Gericht hat außerdem statuiert, dass der Kauf auch kraft Art. 2 lit. e) nicht dem CISG unterliegen konnte.
[77] *Kröll u. a./Spohnheimer*, Art. 2, Rn. 13; *Schlechtriem/Schwenzer/Schlechtriem/Schwenzer/Hachem*, CISG Commentary, Art. 2, Rn. 6.
[78] *Ferrari u. a./Saenger*, Internationales Vertragsrecht, Art. 2, Rn. 3; *Piltz*, Internationales Kaufrecht, Rn. 2–60; *Witz/Salger/Lorenz/Lorenz*, Art. 2, Rn. 4.
[79] Vgl. *Bamberger/Roth/Saenger*, Art. 2, Rn. 2 („Auch entferntere Verwandte und nichteheliche Lebenspartner werden davon erfasst"); vgl. auch *Kröll u. a./Spohnheimer*, Art. 2, Rn. 13.
[80] So auch *Schlechtriem*, Einheitliches UN-Kaufrecht, S. 15; *Schlechtriem/Schwenzer/Schlechtriem*, CISG Commentary, 2. Aufl., Art. 2, Rn. 7; *Schlechtriem/Schwenzer/Schlechtriem/Schwenzer/Hachem*, CISG Commentary, Art. 2, Rn. 6; ähnlich *Czerwenka*, Rechtsanwendungsprobleme, S. 152, die hinzufügt, dass auch die Erwähnung des Gebrauchs in der Familie nur ein Beispielsfall für den persönlichen Gebrauch darstellt; ebenso *Ferrari*, Applicabilità ed applicazioni, S. 176; *U. Huber*, RabelsZ 43 (1979), 413, 422.
[81] Vgl. *Date-Bah*, 11 Rev. Ghana L. (1979), 50, 53; *Ferrari*, Applicabilità ed applicazioni, S. 170; *P. Huber/Mullis/P. Huber*, S. 49; *Garro/Zuppi*, Compraventa internacional, S. 80; *Kröll u. a./Spohnheimer*, Art. 2, Rn. 7; *Schlechtriem/Schwenzer/Schwenzer/Hachem*, CISG Commentary, Art. 1, Rn. 47 und Art. 2, Rn. 4; *Wang*, ZVerglRW 1988, 184, 186; ebenso neuerdings auch *Schwenzer/Hachem/Kee*, Rn. 6.16, die auch darauf hinweisen, dass OHADA eine dem Art. 2 lit. a) ähnliche Vorschrift eingeführt hat.
[82] So auch *Ferrari*, Art. 2, Rn. 2; *Schlechtriem/Schwenzer/Schlechtriem*, CISG Commentary, 2. Aufl., Art. 2, Rn. 9; ähnlich auch *Kröll u. a./Spohnheimer*, Art. 2, Rn. 11 und 15 („counter-exception"); *Schlechtriem/Schwenzer/Schlechtriem/Schwenzer/Hachem*, CISG Commentary, Art. 2, Rn. 8 („counter-exception").
[83] OLG Stuttgart, 31.3.2008, CISG-online 1658.
[84] Diese Unterausnahme zunächst völlig übersehend *Martin-Davidson*, 17 Mich. St. J. Int'l L. (2008), 657, 668 f.; vgl. aber 689.
[85] *Enderlein/Maskow/Strohbach*, Art. 2, Anm. 3.1.; *Staudinger/Magnus*, Art. 2, Rn. 20.

16 **Positive Kenntnis** vom beabsichtigten persönlichen Gebrauch erlangt der Verkäufer in der Regel durch Mitteilungen des Käufers; daher hat es dieser auch in der Hand, der Meinung zumindest eines Teils der Lehre nach, das Übereinkommen anhand einer entsprechenden Erklärung **einseitig auszuschließen**.[86] Der erwähnte Halbsatz verlangt jedoch nicht, dass sich die Kenntnis des Verkäufers notwendigerweise aus vom Käufer gemachten Mitteilungen ergibt. Erlangt der Verkäufer vor dem relevanten Zeitpunkt, d. h., vor Vertragsabschluss, Kenntnis vom privaten Verwendungszweck, auch durch Dritte, reicht dies aus.

17 Die **Erkennbarkeit** kann sich aus verschiedenen Anhaltspunkten ergeben. Häufig wird schon der **Gegenstand des Kaufvertrages** auf den beabsichtigten persönlichen Gebrauch hindeuten,[87] und zwar dann, wenn „die Sache typischerweise dem persönlichen Gebrauch dient."[88] So etwa beim Kauf von Bekleidung, Sport- oder Hobbyausrüstung. In diesen Fällen ist von einem Verbraucherkauf auszugehen,[89] zumindest dann, wenn der Kauf auf Grund der begrenzten Menge[90] oder des limitierten Wertes der Bestellung den Zuschnitt eines Verbraucherkaufs hat.[91] Erwirbt der Käufer hingegen mehrere gleiche Gegenstände,[92] etwa drei gleiche Fotoapparate, wird regelmäßig nicht von einem privaten Verwendungszweck auszugehen sein,[93] d. h., das Übereinkommen kann durchaus Anwendung finden,[94] genauso wie es Anwendung finden kann, wenn der Käufer die Ware entgegen dem Anschein für geschäftliche Zwecke verwendet,[95] „da objektiv kein Verbraucherkauf vorliegt."[96]

18 Dient der Kaufgegenstand **typischerweise geschäftlichen oder beruflichen Zwecken**, muss von einem dem Anwendungsbereich nicht entzogenem Kaufvertrag ausgegangen werden.[97] Unter den Ausnahmetatbestand kann ein solcher Kaufvertrag nur fallen, wenn der Verkäufer zum Zeitpunkt des Vertragsabschlusses positive Kenntnis vom beabsichtigten persönlichen Gebrauch hatte oder wenn dieser auf Grund anderer Anhaltspunkte erkennbar war.

19 Anhaltspunkte, die auf den persönlichen Verwendungszweck hindeuten, kann auch die **Person des Käufers** beziehungsweise dessen Auftreten liefern.[98] Kauft etwa ein Berufsfotograf einen Fotoapparat, so muss man davon ausgehen, dass es sich bei dem Kauf nicht um einen Verbraucherkauf handelt.[99] Gleiches gilt, wenn der Käufer Vertragsverhandlungen auf Geschäftspapier[100] oder in den Geschäftsräumen führt.[101]

---

[86] Vgl. hierzu *Ferrari*, Applicabilità ed applicazioni, S. 178, Fn. 73; *Ferrari u. a./Saenger*, Internationales Vertragsrecht, Art. 2, Rn. 5; *Loewe*, Art. 2; kritisch hierzu *Schlechtriem/Schwenzer/Schlechtriem*, CISG Commentary, 2. Aufl., Art. 2, Rn. 11: „A notice, however, is strong evidence of the intended use"; ebenso nun auch *Schlechtriem/Schwenzer/Schlechtriem/Schwenzer/Hachem*, CISG Commentary, Art. 2, Rn. 10.

[87] Vgl. *Ferrari*, Applicabilità ed applicazioni, S. 182; MünchKommHGB/*Benicke*, Art. 2, Rn. 7; *Schlechtriem/Schwenzer/Schlechtriem*, CISG Commentary, 2. Aufl., Art. 2, Rn. 10; *Schlechtriem/Schwenzer/Hachem*, CISG Commentary, Art. 2, Rn. 9.

[88] *U. Huber*, RabelsZ 43 (1979), 413, 421; so neuerdings auch KG Jura, 3.11.2004, CISG-online 965.

[89] Vgl. *Herber*, 2. Aufl., Art. 2 Rn. 10.

[90] So auch *Ferrari*, Sphere of Application, S. 28.

[91] *Staudinger/Magnus*, Art. 2, Rn. 22.

[92] *Kröll u. a./Spohnheimer*, Art. 2, Rn. 18; *Schlechtriem/Schwenzer/Schlechtriem/Schwenzer/Hachem*, CISG Commentary, Art. 2, Rn. 9.

[93] *Schlechtriem/Schwenzer/Schlechtriem*, CISG Commentary, 2. Aufl., Art. 2, Rn. 10.

[94] Vgl. *Ferrari*, Sphere of Application, S. 28.

[95] So *Enderlein/Maskow/Strohbach*, Art. 2, Anm. 3.1.; *Karollus*, S. 26; *Loewe*, Art. 2.

[96] *Staudinger/Magnus*, Art. 2, Rn. 22; zustimmend *Ferrari u. a./Saenger*, Internationales Vertragsrecht, Art. 2, Rn. 5 a. E.

[97] So auch *Soergel/Lüderitz/Fenge*, Art. 2, Rn. 3.

[98] *Ferrari*, Vendita internazionale, S. 66; *Kröll u. a./Spohnheimer*, Art. 2, Rn. 18; *Schlechtriem/Schwenzer/Schlechtriem*, CISG Commentary, 2. Aufl., Art. 2, Rn. 10.

[99] So schon *Herber*, 2. Aufl., Art. 2 Rn. 10; vgl. auch *Schlechtriem/Schwenzer/Schlechtriem/Schwenzer/Hachem*, CISG Commentary, Art. 2, Rn. 9.

[100] *Schlechtriem/Schwenzer/Schlechtriem/Schwenzer/Hachem*, CISG Commentary, Art. 2, Rn. 9.

[101] Vgl. hierzu auch *Bamberger/Roth/Saenger*, Art. 2, Rn. 4; *Memmo*, Riv. trim. dir. proced. civ. 1983, 180, 198.

Zweifel des Verkäufers an der Zweckbestimmung begründen **keine Erkundungspflicht**,[102] so auch die Rechtsprechung.[103] Will der Verkäufer sich jedoch Klarheit über den Nutzungszweck verschaffen, sollte er dennoch nachfragen.[104] Fragt er nicht nach, wird es darauf ankommen, ob ein vernünftiger Verkäufer in der gleichen Lage den beabsichtigten persönlichen Gebrauch erkannt hätte. Was dies bedeutet, ist umstritten. Während ein Teil der Lehre die Ansicht vertritt, der Ausdruck „wissen musste" bezeichne Unkenntnis infolge grober Fahrlässigkeit,[105] geht ein anderer Teil davon aus, dass **jede vorwerfbare Unkenntnis** beachtlich ist.[106] M. E. ist auf Grund des Wortlautes der Vorschrift letztere Ansicht vorzuziehen.[107]

In Fällen der **Stellvertretung** kommt es auf die Kenntnis oder die vorwerfbare Unkenntnis des Vertreters an, zumindest dann, wenn deutsches[108] oder italienisches Recht[109] Vertragsstatut ist.

3. Beweislast

Zweifelhaft – weil nicht ausdrücklich geregelt – ist, wen die Beweislast hinsichtlich der Kenntnis beziehungsweise der vorwerfbaren Unkenntnis trifft. Die Ansicht, die Beweislast sei hier – wie auch an anderen Stellen des CISG – überhaupt nicht geregelt und daher nationalem Recht überlassen,[110] wird unter Bezugnahme auf den Wortlaut des Halbsatzes[111] und der Konferenzgeschichte[112] ganz überwiegend abgelehnt.[113] Dies bedeutet jedoch nicht, dass Einigkeit darüber bestehe, wen die Beweislast letztendlich trifft. Zum Teil wird die Ansicht vertreten, der Käufer müsse das Bestehen des Verbrauchervertrages beweisen, während der Verkäufer die Beweislast für das Vorliegen des Gegenausnahmetatbestandes

---

[102] Wie hier schon *Staudinger/Magnus*, Art. 2, Rn. 25; *Achilles*, Art. 2, Rn. 3; *Bamberger/Roth/Saenger*, Art. 2, Rn. 4; *Piltz*, Internationales Kaufrecht, Rn. 2–64; ebenso neuerdings auch *Kröll u. a./Spohnheimer*, Art. 2, Rn. 17; *Schlechtriem/Schwenzer/Schlechtriem/Schwenzer/Hachem*, CISG Commentary, Art. 2, Rn. a. A. aber *Karollus*, S. 26, zumindest dann, wenn Zweifel am kommerziellen Charakter des Geschäfts bestehen.

[103] OLG Hamm, 2.4.2009, CISG-online 1978; „Den Verkäufer trifft keine Erkundigungspflicht hinsichtlich des Verwendungszwecks".

[104] Vgl. auch *Honnold/Flechtner*, Art. 2, Rn. 50.

[105] So etwa *Herber*, 2. Aufl., Art. 2 Rn. 12; *Herber/Czerwenka*, Art. 2, Rn. 6; *P. Huber/Mullis/P. Huber*, S. 49; *Karollus*, S. 26; *Schlechtriem/Schwenzer/Schlechtriem*, CISG Commentary, 2. Aufl., Art. 2, Rn. 12; *Schlechtriem/Schwenzer/Schlechtriem/Schwenzer/Hachem*, CISG Commentary, Art. 2, Rn. 11.

[106] Vgl. *Achilles*, Art. 2, Rn. 3; *Bamberger/Roth/Saenger*, Art. 2, Rn. 4; *Bianca/Bonell/Khoo*, Art. 2, Anm. 2.2.; *Ferrari u. a./Saenger*, Internationales Vertragsrecht, Art. 2, Rn. 5; *Lohmann*, Parteiautonomie, S. 22; MünchKommHGB/*Benicke*, Art. 2, Rn. 6; *Schlechtriem*, Einheitliches UN-Kaufrecht, S. 13; a. A. *Kröll u. a./Spohnheimer*, Art. 2, Rn. 17: abstellend darauf, ob eine vernünftige Person in der Position des Verkäufers hätte erkennen können, ob die Waren zum persönlichen Gebrauch gekauft wurden.

[107] Im Ergebnis auch *Staudinger/Magnus*, Art. 2, Rn. 22, der dies damit begründet, dass die Konvention den Maßstab der groben Fahrlässigkeit durchgehend mit der Formulierung „nicht in Unkenntnis sein konnte" bezeichnet.

[108] *Schlechtriem/Schwenzer/Schlechtriem*, CISG Commentary, 2. Aufl., Art. 2, Rn. 14.

[109] Vgl. § 166 BGB und Art. 1391 Cc.

[110] So etwa *Bianca/Bonell/Khoo*, Art. 2, Anm. 3.2.; *Lichtsteiner*, Convention, S. 186.

[111] Vgl. statt aller *Honnold/Flechtner*, Art. 2, Rn. 50.

[112] So ist bei der Einfügung der Formulierung „unless the seller [...] did not realize or had no reason to realize" ausdrücklich darauf hingewiesen worden (ohne dass dieser Auffassung widersprochen wurde), dass hierdurch klargestellt würde, dass die Beweislast beim Verläufer läge; vgl. YB VI (1975), S. 51, Nr. 25. Siehe auch die Diskussion auf der Diplomatischen Konferenz zu einem Antrag der ehemaligen CSSR, Art. 2 lit. a) wie folgt zu formulieren: „of goods bought for personal, family or household use, if the seller at any time before or at the conclusion of the contract, knew or ought to have known that the goods where bought for such a use", Sekretariatskommentar, O. R., S. 83, Art. 2, Nr. 3. Anlass für diesen Änderungsantrag war, dass die Formulierung „unless the seller knew" für nicht praktikabel gehalten wurde, da sie dem Verkäufer die Last auferlege, mangelnde Kenntnis zu beweisen; O. R., S. 238, Nr. 40 ff. Vgl. hierzu in der Lehre *Memmo*, Riv. trim. dir. proced. civ. 1983, 180, 197.

[113] Vgl. in diesem Sinne etwa *Baumgärtel/Laumen/Hepting/Müller*, Vor Art 1, Rn. 16; *Czerwenka*, Rechtsanwendungsprobleme, S. 150; *Enderlein/Maskow/Strohbach*, Art. 2, Anm. 3.2.; *Ferrari*, Applicabilità ed applicazioni, S. 181; *Karollus*, S. 26; *Kröll u. a./Spohnheimer*, Art. 2, Rn. 45; *Schlechtriem*, Einheitliches UN-Kaufrecht, S. 13; *Schlechtriem/Schwenzer/Schlechtriem*, CISG Commentary, 2. Aufl., Art. 2, Rn. 15; *Schlechtriem/Schwenzer/Schlechtriem/Schwenzer/Hachem*, CISG Commentary, Art. 2, Rn. 13; *Staudinger/Magnus*, Art. 2, Rn. 28.

Art. 2 23, 24   Teil I. Kapitel I. Anwendungsbereich

trage, d. h., für die mangelnde Kenntnis beziehungsweise die nicht vorwerfbare Unkenntnis.[114]

23   Dieser Auffassung ist ohne weiteres beizupflichten, aber nur insoweit, als sie sich auf den statistischen Normalfall bezieht (Käufer beruft sich auf einen Konsumentenkauf, der Verkäufer auf seine nicht vorwerfbare Unkenntnis).[115] Es kann aber durchaus vorkommen, dass der Käufer sich auf die Anwendbarkeit des Übereinkommens beruft,[116] etwa weil das CISG diesem bessere Rechte (etwa auf Gewährleistung) gibt als das nationale Recht. In solchen Fällen wird man dem Verkäufer zubilligen müssen, die Nichtanwendbarkeit des CISG wegen beabsichtigten persönlichen Gebrauchs des Käufers darzulegen und zu beweisen;[117] gelingt ihm dies, so mag andererseits der Käufer daran interessiert sein, nachzuweisen, dass diese Absicht dem Verkäufer unbekannt und unerkennbar war.[118] Demzufolge muss für die Beweislastverteilung gelten, dass die Partei, die sich auf die **Anwendbarkeit** des Übereinkommens beruft, die (nicht vorwerfbare) **Unkenntnis beweisen** muss.[119]

4. Verhältnis zum Verbraucherschutzrecht

24   Wie bereits erwähnt,[120] ist die Ausnahme des lit. a) wesentlich damit begründet worden, dass eine Kollision mit nationalem Verbraucherschutzrecht vermieden werden sollte.[121] Dies ist jedoch nur hinsichtlich der innerstaatlichen Schutzgesetze gelungen, deren Anwendungsvoraussetzungen mit denen des lit. a) deckungsgleich sind.[122] Hängt die Anwendung nationaler Verbraucherschutzvorschriften hingegen von Anwendungsvoraussetzungen ab, die nicht mit denen des Ausnahmetatbestandes überstimmen,[123] dann kann, was neuerdings auch von der höchstrichterlichen Rechtsprechung hervorgehoben worden ist,[124] es durchaus **zu Überschneidungen** kommen,[125] d. h. zu Fällen, „in denen sowohl das Einheitliche Kaufrecht als auch nationale Konsumentenschutzvorschriften mit zwingendem Inhalt Anwendung finden".[126] Eine solche Überschneidung kann sich zum Beispiel dann ergeben,

---

[114] So etwa *Bamberger/Roth/Saenger*, Art. 2, Rn. 12; *Czerwenka*, Rechtsanwendungsprobleme, S. 150; *Enderlein/Maskow/Strohbach*, Art. 2, Anm. 3.2.; *Honnold/Flechtner*, Art. 2, Rn. 50; *P. Huber/Mullis/P. Huber*, S. 48 f.; *Neumayer/Ming*, Art. 4, Anm. 13., Fn. 44; *Loewe*, Anwendungsgebiet, S. 40; *Lohmann*, Parteiautonomie, S. 22; *Schlechtriem*, Internationales UN-Kaufrecht, Rn. 29 a. E.
[115] So auch *Jung*, S. 198 f.; MünchKomm/*Westermann*, Art. 2, Rn. 6; vgl. auch MünchKommHGB/*Benicke*, Art. 2, Rn. 25; *Schlechtriem/Schwenzer/Schlechtriem/Schwenzer/Hachem*, CISG Commentary, Art. 2, Rn. 15.
[116] Vgl. auch *Baumgärtel/Laumen/Hepting/Müller*, Vor Art 1, Rn. 43 und Art 1, Rn. 2.
[117] *Schlechtriem/Schwenzer/Schlechtriem*, CISG Commentary, 2. Aufl., Art. 2, Rn. 16; *Schlechtriem/Schwenzer/Schlechtriem/Schwenzer/Hachem*, CISG Commentary, Art. 2, Rn. 15.
[118] So auch *Herber/Czerwenka*, Art. 2, Rn. 7.
[119] Ebenso *Baumgärtel/Laumen/Hepting/Müller*, 1. Aufl., Art. 2, Rn. 2; *Ferrari*, Applicabilità ed applicazioni, S. 181; MünchKommHGB/*Benicke*, Art. 2, Rn. 24; *Sannini*, L'applicazione, S. 116; *Schlechtriem*, Einheitliches UN-Kaufrecht, S. 13; *Soergel/Lüderitz/Fenge*, Art. 2, Rn. 4.
[120] Vgl. oben Rn. 7.
[121] Vgl. *Bianca/Bonell/Khoo*, Art. 2, Anm. 3.2.; *Czerwenka*, Rechtsanwendungsprobleme, S. 148 f.; *U. Huber*, RabelsZ 43 (1979), 413, 421; *Kröll u. a./Spohnheimer*, Art. 2, Rn. 21; *Réczei*, Rules of the Convention, S. 69; *Schlechtriem*, Einheitliches UN-Kaufrecht, S. 13; *Schlechtriem/Schwenzer/Schlechtriem*, CISG Commentary, 2. Aufl., Art. 2, Rn. 17; *Schlechtriem/Schwenzer/Schlechtriem/Schwenzer/Hachem*, CISG Commentary, Art. 2, Rn. 16; *Schmitt*, CR 2001, 145, 145.
[122] A. A. *Enderlein/Maskow/Strohbach*, Art. 2, Anm. 2., wonach nationale Verbraucherschutzgesetze „meet the very definition of the contracts excluded here. Insofar the relationship between the CISG and the mandatory domestic consumer protection rules does not have to be determined."
[123] Vgl. *Schlechtriem/Schwenzer/Schlechtriem/Schwenzer/Hachem*, CISG Commentary, Art. 2, Rn. 5 und 16, die auf nationale Bestimmungen verweisen; vgl. auch, mit Bezug auf die Länder des subsaharischen Afrikas, *Penda Matipé*, S. 34 f., der jedoch nicht immer den Unterschied zwischen den nationalen Vorschriften und dem CISG sieht (so etwa auf S. 34).
[124] So ausdrücklich BGH, 31.10.2001, CISG-online 617 = IHR 2002, 14, 16.
[125] Vgl. auch *Bamberger/Roth/Saenger*, Art. 2, Rn. 6; *Díez-Picazo/Laporta*, Art. 2, S. 63; *Ferrari*, Applicabilità ed applicazioni, S. 172; *Ferrari u. a./Saenger*, Internationales Vertragsrecht, Art. 2, Rn. 7; *Garro/Zuppi*, Compraventa internacional, S. 82, Fn. 17; *Schlechtriem/Schwenzer/Schlechtriem*, CISG Commentary, 2. Aufl., Art. 2, Rn. 17; *Schlechtriem/Schwenzer/Schlechtriem/Schwenzer/Hachem*, CISG Commentary, Art. 2, Rn. 5 und 16 ff.; *Schmitt*, CR 2001, 145, 145; *Wartenberg*, S. 24 ff.
[126] *Schlechtriem*, Einheitliches UN-Kaufrecht, S. 13 f.; a. A. *Enderlein/Maskow/Strohbach*, Art. 2, Anm. 2.

wenn nationale Konsumentenschutzvorschriften im Gegensatz zu Art. 2 lit. a) nicht verlangen, dass der Verkäufer den beabsichtigten persönlichen Gebrauch der Waren kannte oder kennen musste.[127]

Es stellt sich somit die Frage, in welchem Verhältnis Einheitskaufrecht und innerstaatliches Konsumentenschutzrecht zueinander stehen. Da Art. 4 lit. a) des Übereinkommens die **Gültigkeit des Vertrages** von seinem Regelungsbereich ausdrücklich ausschließt, kommen die in nationalen Verbraucherschutzgesetzen enthaltenen, zur Nichtigkeit des Vertrages oder einzelner Klauseln führenden Vorschriften – wie etwa §§ 308, 309 BGB – ohne weiteres zur Anwendung.[128] Dies gilt auch hinsichtlich besonderer verbraucherrechtlicher Rechtsbehelfe,[129] deren unterlassene Geltendmachung als negative Gültigkeitsvoraussetzungen für den Kaufvertrag anzusehen sind;[130] konkret bedeutet dies, dass dem Verbraucher diese Rechtsbehelfe „**auch dann erhalten bleiben,** wenn der Vertrag im Übrigen an dem UN-Kaufrecht zu messen ist."[131] 25

Andere zwingende Verbraucherschutzvorschriften treten jedoch nach überwiegender Auffassung hinter das Übereinkommen zurück.[132] Dies wird zum Teil damit begründet, dass die Nichtanwendung des Übereinkommens einer Verletzung völkerrechtlicher Pflichten gleichkomme,[133] bisweilen damit, dass das Übereinkommen im Verhältnis zu bereits vorhandenen innerstaatlichen Verbraucherschutzgesetzen das jüngere und speziellere Gesetz darstelle.[134] Auch die analoge Anwendung des in Art. 3 II EGBGB a. F. enthaltenen Gedankens ist zur Rechtfertigung des Vorrangs des CISG aufgeführt worden.[135] 26

IV. Ausschluss auf Grund der Art und Weise des Zustandekommens des Kaufvertrages

1. Versteigerungen (lit. b))

Die Lehre hat verschiedentlich darauf hingewiesen, dass lit. b) zu den innovativen Vorschriften zu zählen sei, da es Versteigerungen dem Anwendungsbereich des Einheitskaufrechts entziehe, die nicht vom Anwendungsbereich des EKG ausgenommen waren.[136] Diese Vorschrift ist jedoch weniger innovativ, als es den Anschein hat. Dies liegt daran, dass Versteigerungen auch vom Anwendungsbereich des EKG ausgenommen waren, zumindest sofern sie durch gerichtliche Maßnahmen oder zumindest auf Grund einer Beschlagnahme geschahen,[137] d. h., sofern sie vom Ausnahmetatbestand des Art. 5 lit. d) EKG erfasst 27

---

[127] So auch *Karollus,* S. 26; MünchKommHGB/*Benicke,* Art. 2, Rn. 8 a. E.; *Schlechtriem/Schwenzer/Schlechtriem,* CISG Commentary, 2. Aufl., Art. 2, Rn. 17; *Schlechtriem/Schwenzer/Schlechtriem/Schwenzer/Hachem,* CISG Commentary, Art. 2, Rn. 5.
[128] Vgl. *Frense,* S. 47; *Herber/Czerwenka,* Art. 2, Rn. 8; *Piltz,* Internationales Kaufrecht, Rn. 2–70; *Schlechtriem/Schwenzer/Schlechtriem,* CISG Commentary, 2. Aufl., Art. 2, Rn. 17; *Schlechtriem/Schwenzer/Schwenzer/Hachem,* CISG Commentary, Art. 2, Rn. 17.
[129] Vgl. §§ 355, 495 BGB.
[130] So auch MünchKommHGB/*Benicke,* Art. 4, Rn. 7; *Schlechtriem,* Einheitliches UN-Kaufrecht, S. 14; *ders.,* AJP 1992, 339, 352.
[131] *Piltz,* Internationales Kaufrecht, Rn. 2–70.
[132] Vgl. *Lohmann,* Privatautonomie, S. 390; *Schlechtriem/Schwenzer/Schlechtriem/Schwenzer/Hachem,* CISG Commentary, Art. 2, Rn. 18; *Staudinger/Magnus,* Art. 2, Rn. 30 m. w. N.; a. A. *Kröll u. a./Spohnheimer,* Art. 2, Rn. 23, immer sowohl europarechtlichen als auch nationalen Verbraucherschutzvorschriften den Vorrang einräumend.
[133] *Czerwenka,* Rechtsanwendungsprobleme, S. 151; *Piltz,* Internationales Kaufrecht, Rn. 70; *Schlechtriem/Schwenzer/Schlechtriem,* CISG Commentary, 2. Aufl., Art. 2, Rn. 18.
[134] Vgl. etwa *Audit,* Vente internationale, S. 28; *Schlechtriem,* Einheitliches UN-Kaufrecht, S. 14.
[135] *Staudinger/Magnus,* Art. 2, Rn. 30.
[136] Vgl. *Bianca/Bonell/Khoo,* Art. 2, Anm. 1.12.; *Bianca/Carbone/Lopez de Gonzalo,* Art. 2, S. 7.
[137] Dazu im Einzelnen *Dölle/Herber,* Art. 5 EKG, Rn. 13 f.

waren.[138] Die Innovation des lit. b) liegt demnach darin, auch **private Versteigerungen** dem Anwendungsbereich entzogen zu haben.[139]

28 Als Versteigerung im autonomen[140] Sinne des CISG kann der „öffentliche, publik gemachte Verkauf durch Zuschlag an den Meistbietenden"[141] angesehen werden,[142] d. h. ein Verkauf, der ein Überbieten möglich macht; da auch Online-Auktionen dieses Überbieten möglich machen, findet das CISG auch auf sie keine Anwendung.[143] Da das **Einholen mehrerer Angebote,** um das günstigste anzunehmen, gegenseitiges Überbieten ausschließt, kann es nicht als Versteigerung im Sinne des CISG angesehen werden.[144]

29 **Gerichtliche Versteigerungen** sind natürlich auch weiterhin Versteigerungen im Sinne des Übereinkommens, doch fallen diese unter den Ausnahmetatbestand der lit. c);[145] keine Versteigerungen im Sinne des CISG sind dagegen Verkäufe an einer **Warenbörse,**[146] da es sich hier lediglich um eine bestimmte Form des – weitgehend von Gebräuchen geregelten – Vertragsabschlusses handelt.[147]

30 Der **Ausschluss** von Versteigerungen[148] ist unterschiedlich **begründet** worden: Im Sekretariatskommentar[149] wird diesbezüglich darauf hingewiesen, dass Versteigerungen häufig nationalen Sonderregelungen unterstehen.[150] Richtiger ist, dass die Regelungen für Versteigerungen zumeist von den Institutionen selbst aufgestellt werden, diese also selbstgeschaffenen Regeln und Gebräuchen unterliegen.[151] Als Rechtfertigungsgrund ist auch der Umstand genannt worden, dass der Verkäufer sehr häufig den Käufer nicht kennen wird,

---

[138] So auch schon *Ferrari,* Applicabilità ed applicazioni, S. 167, Fn. 12; vgl. auch *Schlechtriem/Schwenzer/ Schlechtriem/Schwenzer/Hachem,* CISG Commentary, Art. 2, Rn. 19.

[139] Vgl. *Kröll u. a./Spohnheimer,* Art. 2, Rn. 25; MünchKomm/*Westermann,* Art. 2, Rn. 7; *Piltz,* Internationales Kaufrecht, Rn. 2–29; *Schlechtriem/Schwenzer/Schlechtriem,* CISG Commentary, 2. Aufl., Art. 2, Rn. 19; *Schlechtriem/Schwenzer/Schlechtriem/Schwenzer/Hachem,* CISG Commentary, Art. 2, Rn. 19; *Schmitt,* CR 2001, 145, 146; *Schwenzer/Hachem/Kee,* Rn. 8.14; *Soergel/Lüderitz/Fenge,* Art. 2, Rn. 6; *Witz/Salger/ Lorenz/Lorenz,* Art. 2, Rn. 6; a. A. *Schroeter,* ZEuP 2004, 20, 29 f.

[140] *Schlechtriem/Schwenzer/Schlechtriem/Schwenzer/Hachem,* CISG Commentary, Art. 2, Rn. 20.

[141] So *Staudinger/Magnus,* Art. 2, Rn. 33; für eine ähnliche Definition, vgl. auch *Brunner,* Art. 2, Rn. 11; MünchKommHGB/*Benicke,* Art. 2, Rn. 9; *Ferrari u. a./Saenger,* Internationales VertragsrechtR, Art. 2, Rn. 8; *Kröll u. a./Spohnheimer,* Art. 2, Rn. 25; *Schlechtriem/Schwenzer/Schlechtriem/Schwenzer/Hachem,* CISG Commentary, Art. 2, Rn. 20.

[142] Zum Ausschluss von Versteigerungen aus dem sachlichen Anwendungsbereich des CISG, vgl. in der Rechtsprechung BGH, 2.10.2002, CISG-online 700 = IHR 2003, 28.

[143] *Schmitt,* CR 2001, 145, 146; a. A. *Kröll u. a./Spohnheimer,* Art. 2, Rn. 27; *Piltz,* Internationales Kaufrecht, Rn. 2–29; *Schlechtriem/Schwenzer/Schlechtriem/Schwenzer/Hachem,* CISG Commentary, Art. 2, Rn. 21; *Schroeter,* ZEuP 2004, 20, 31 f.

[144] *Díez-Picazo/Laporta,* Art. 2, S. 64; *Schmitt,* CR 2001, 145, 146, Fn. 17; *Staudinger/Magnus,* aaO.

[145] *Kröll u. a./Spohnheimer,* Art. 2, Rn. 25; *Schwenzer/Hachem/Kee,* Rn. 8.14; *Witz/Salger/Lorenz/Lorenz,* Art. 2, Rn. 6.

[146] Ebenso *Achilles,* Art. 2, Rn. 5; *Audit,* Vente internationale, S. 29; *Bamberger/Roth/Saenger,* Art. 2, Rn. 7; *Brunner,* Art. 2, Rn. 11, Fn. 106; *Ferrari,* Applicabilità ed applicazioni, S. 167 f. Fn. 12; *Ferrari u. a./ Saenger,* Internationales Vertragsrecht, Art. 2, Rn. 8; *Honnold/Flechtner,* Art. 2, Rn. 51, Fn. 10; *U. Huber,* RabelsZ 43 (1979), 413, 422; *Kantor,* 1 Int'l law pract. (NYSBA) (1988), 8, 10; *Karollus,* S. 27; *Kröll u. a./ Spohnheimer,* Art. 2, Rn. 26; *Schlechtriem/Schwenzer/Schlechtriem,* CISG Commentary, 2. Aufl., Art. 2, Rn. 20; *Schmitt,* CR 2001, 145, 146; *Schroeter,* ZEuP 2004, 20, 25; *Staudinger/Magnus,* Art. 2, Rn. 35; a. A. MünchKommHGB/*Benicke,* Art. 2, Rn. 10, den Ausschluss von Verkäufen an Warenbörsen mit der Begründung befürwortend, dass, wie hinsichtlich der Versteigerungen, auch im Rahmen dieser Verkäufe „die Identität des Vertragspartners erst nachträglich bekannt wird […], so dass eine analoge Anwendung von lit. b) gerechtfertigt ist".

[147] *Herber,* 2. Aufl., Art. 2 Rn. 20; *Schlechtriem/Schwenzer/Schlechtriem/Schwenzer/Hachem,* CISG Commentary, Art. 2, Rn. 20 a. E.

[148] Für einen neueren Fall des Ausschlusses des CISG auf Grund von Art. 2 lit. b), vgl. BGH, 2.10.2002, CISG-online 700.

[149] Sekretariatskommentar, Art. 2, Nr. 5.

[150] So auch *Bamberger/Roth/Saenger,* Art. 2, Rn. 7; *Brunner,* Rn. 11; *Fairlie,* S. 47; *Reinhart,* Art. 2, Rn. 5; *Sannini,* L'applicazione, S. 116; *Schlechtriem/Schwenzer/Schlechtriem/Schwenzer/Hachem,* CISG Commentary, Art. 2, Rn. 19.

[151] Ebenso *Enderlein/Maskow/Strohbach,* Art. 2, Anm. 4.; *Honnold/Flechtner,* Art. 2, Rn. 51; *Réczei,* Rules of the Convention, S. 70; YB II (1971), S. 56, Nr. 58.

die Anwendung des Übereinkommens also schon wegen Art. 1 II unsicher sein würde.[152] Ferner ist auch angeführt worden, dass erst mit Zuschlag an den Meistbietenden und damit für den Verkäufer unzumutbar spät feststehe, ob der Kauf dem Übereinkommen unterliege oder nicht.[153]

2. Zwangsvollstreckungen oder andere gerichtliche Maßnahmen (lit. c))

Trotz einer geringfügigen Änderung der Formulierung,[154] die lediglich dem Umstand Rechnung trägt, dass die Beschlagnahme nur ein Sonderfall der gerichtlichen Maßnahme ist, entspricht die Vorschrift sachlich unverändert dem Art. 5 I lit. d) EKG,[155] der die Käufe auf Grund gerichtlicher Zwangsvollstreckungs- oder anderen gerichtlichen Maßnahmen vom Anwendungsbereich auch ausgeschlossen hatte.[156] Die Frage, wann ein solcher Kauf vorliegt, ist **autonom** zu beantworten,[157] also nicht auf der Grundlage des Recht jeden einzelnen Staates.[158] 31

Sicher vom Anwendungsbereich des Einheitskaufrechts ausgeschlossen sind, genauso wie unter dem EKG,[159] **Zwangsversteigerungen.**[160] Dies gilt sowohl dann, wenn sie in der Einzelvollstreckung erfolgt, als auch bei der Versteigerung auf Betreiben eines Insolvenzverwalters.[161] Dies entspricht auch der herrschenden Anschauung im deutschen Recht,[162] nach welchem bei der Zwangsversteigerung kein privatrechtlicher Kaufvertrag abgeschlossen wird, sondern nur hoheitliche Maßnahmen vorgenommen werden.[163] 32

Auch der **freihändige Verkauf** von gepfändeten Sachen durch den Gläubiger[164] fällt unter den Ausnahmetatbestand,[165] ebenso wie der von Nutzungen eines Grundstücks durch den Zwangsverwalter[166] oder von Gegenständen aus der Insolvenzmasse durch den Insolvenzverwalter, da auch diese Verkäufe „auf Grund von gerichtlichen Maßnahmen" erfolgen,[167] 33

---

[152] *Herber*, 2. Aufl., Art. 2 Rn. 21; so neuerdings auch *Achilles*, Art. 2, Rn. 1; MünchKommHGB/*Benicke*, Art. 2, Rn. 9.

[153] So *Bianca/Bonell/Khoo*, Art. 2, Anm. 2.3.; *Díez-Picazo/Laporta*, Art. 2, S. 63; *Heuzé*, Anm. 90.; *Honnold/Flechtner*, Art. 2, Rn. 51; *Staudinger/Magnus*, Art. 2, Rn. 26.

[154] YB II (1971), S. 56, Nr. 54.

[155] Vgl. zum Verhältnis zwischen Art. 2 lit. c) und EKG etwa *Bianca/Carbone/Lopez de Gonzalo*, Art. 2, S. 7.

[156] Zur Begründung des Ausschlusses wird in der Regel angeführt, dass es den Parteien kaum möglich sei, auf die anwendbaren Vorschriften Einfluss zu nehmen; vgl. etwa *Audit*, Vente internationale, S. 29; *Carbone/Lopez de Gonzalo*, Art. 2, S. 7; *Heuzé*, Anm 90.

[157] So *Ferrari u. a./Saenger*, Internationales Vertragsrecht, Art. 2, Rn. 9; *Honsell/Siehr*, Art. 2, Rn. 15; a. A. *Audit*, Vente internationale, S. 29; *Staudinger/Magnus*, Art. 2, Rn. 36.

[158] In diesem Sinne aber *Díez-Picazo/Laporta*, Art. 2, S. 64; *Kröll u. a./Spohnheimer*, Art. 2, Rn. 31; MünchKommHGB/*Benicke*, Art. 2, Rn. 11.

[159] Vgl. *Dölle/Herber*, Art. 5 EKG, Rn. 13.

[160] *Díez-Picazo/Laporta*, Art. 2, S. 64; *Rudolph*, Art. 2, Rn. 4; *Schlechtriem/Schwenzer/Schlechtriem*, CISG Commentary, 2. Aufl., Art. 2, Rn. 23; *Schlechtriem/Schwenzer/Schlechtriem/Schwenzer/Hachem*, CISG Commentary, Art. 2, Rn. 22.
Vgl. auch Art. 2 lit. (k) des Vorschlags für eine Verordnung des Europäischen Parlaments und des Rates über ein Gemeinsames Europäisches Kaufrecht vom 11.10.2011, KOM(2011) 635 endgültig, S. 26, der den Kauf zwangsversteigerter Waren vom Anwendungsbereich des Vorschlags ausnimmt.

[161] So auch *Ferrari*, Applicabilità ed applicazioni, S. 184; *Ferrari u. a./Saenger*, Internationales Vertragsrecht, Art. 2, Rn. 9; MünchKomm/*Martiny*, 2. Aufl., Art. 28 EGBGB, Anh. II., Rn. 42; vgl. auch *Schmidt-Kessel*, FS Schlechtriem, S. 255, 256.

[162] Für eine ausführliche, sich auf das italienische Recht beziehende Liste ex Art. 2 lit. c) CISG ausgeschlossener Käufe siehe *La China*, Riv. trim. dir. proced. civ. 1990, 769, 771.

[163] Vgl. *Herber*, 2. Aufl., Art. 2 Rn. 23 m. w. N.

[164] Vgl. § 817a III, §§ 821, 825 ZPO.

[165] Ebenso *Achilles*, Art. 2, Rn. 6; *Bamberger/Roth/Saenger*, Art. 2, Rn. 8; *Ferrari u. a./Saenger*, Internationales Vertragsrecht, Art. 2, Rn. 9; MünchKomm/*Westermann*, Art. 2, Rn. 7; *Piltz*, Rn. 2–29; *Schlechtriem/Schwenzer/Schlechtriem*, CISG Commentary, 2. Aufl., Art. 2, Rn. 24; *Schlechtriem/Schwenzer/Schlechtriem/Schwenzer/Hachem*, CISG Commentary, Art. 2, Rn. 22; *Schmidt-Kessel*, FS Schlechtriem, S. 255; *Soergel/Lüderitz/Fenge*, Art. 2, Rn. 7.

[166] Vgl. § 152 I ZVG.

[167] Vgl. zum EKG – unter Hinweis auf dessen Entstehungsgeschichte – *Dölle/Herber*, Art. 5 EKG, Rn. 14.

soweit es sich um Verwertungsmaßnahmen handelt.[168] Der **privatrechtliche Pfandverkauf** durch den einzelnen Gläubiger fällt jedoch nicht unter den Ausnahmetatbestand.[169]

V. Art der erworbenen Ware als Ausschlusskriterium

1. Wertpapiere und Zahlungsmittel (lit. d))

34 Dieser auf Art. 5 I lit. a) EKG zurückgehende Ausschluss[170] ist vor allem durch das Bestreben begründet, Überschneidungen mit zwingenden nationalen Rechtsvorschriften zu vermeiden.[171] Ein Teil der Lehre hat jedoch darauf hingewiesen, dass der ausdrückliche Ausschluss zumindest hinsichtlich der Wertpapiere überflüssig sei, da diese in der Regel Rechte verbriefen, deren Kauf sowieso nicht unter den Anwendungsbereich des Übereinkommens falle.[172] Demzufolge fällt aber der Kauf eines die Ware vertretenden Wertpapiers **(Dokumentenkauf, Abladegeschäft)**[173] nicht unter den Ausnahmetatbestand, da in Wahrheit die Ware selbst den Kaufgegenstand bildet.[174]

35 Im Sinne des Übereinkommens sind **Wertpapiere,** deren Kauf vom Anwendungsbereich des CISG ausgeschlossen ist, die Papiere, die einen Anspruch verbriefen und hinsichtlich derer ein selbstständiger Erwerb in Betracht kommt.[175] Beispielhaft seien diesbezüglich erwähnt: Aktien,[176] Schuldverschreibungen,[177] Investmentzertifikate,[178] Wechsel[179] und Schecks.[180]

36 **Namens- und Rektapapiere** fallen nicht unter den Wertpapierbegriff des Übereinkommens.[181] Deshalb sind der Kauf von Hypotheken-, Grundschuld- und Rentenschuldbrie-

---

[168] MünchKommHGB/*Benicke,* Art. 2, Rn. 13.
[169] *Brunner,* Art. 2, Rn. 12 a. E. ; *Ferrari/ u. a./Saenger,* Internationales Vertragsrecht, Art. 2, Rn. 9; *Karollus,* S. 27; *Piltz,* Internationales Kaufrecht, Rn. 2–29; differenzierend *Staudinger/Magnus,* Art. 2, Rn. 37.
[170] Vgl. *Schlechtriem,* Einheitliches UN-Kaufrecht, S. 15.
[171] *Díez Piaczo/Laporta,* Art. 2, S. 64; *Enderlein/Maskow/Strohbach,* Art. 2, Anm. 6.; *Ferrari u. a./Saenger,* Internationales Vertragsrecht, Art. 2, Rn. 10; *Memmo,* Riv. trim. dir. proced. civ. 1983, 180, 196; MünchKommHGB/*Benicke,* Art. 2, Rn. 14; *Reinhart,* Art. 2, Rn. 6; *Schlechtriem/Schwenzer/Schlechtriem,* CISG Commentary, 2. Aufl., Art. 2, Rn. 25; *Schlechtriem/Schwenzer/Schlechtriem/Schwenzer/Hachem,* CISG Commentary, Art. 2, Rn. 23; Sekretariatskommentar, Art. 2, Nr. 7.
[172] Siehe hierzu etwa *Audit,* Vente internationale, S. 29; *Ferrari,* Applicabilità ed applicazioni, S. 188.
[173] Vgl. statt aller *Ferrari u. a./Saenger,* Internationales VertragsrechtR, Art. 2, Rn. 10; *Kröll u. a./Spohnheimer,* Art. 2, Rn. 33; *Schlechtriem,* Internationales UN-Kaufrecht, Rn. 30.
[174] H. M.; vgl. *Bianca/Carbone/Lopez de Gonzalo,* Art. 2, S. 7; *Brunner,* Art. 2, Rn. 13; *Czerwenka,* Rechtsanwendungsprobleme, S. 100; Denkschrift, S. 40; *Díez-Picazo/Laporta,* Art. 2, S. 65; *Enderlein/Maskow/Strohbach,* Art. 2, Anm. 6.; *Ferrari,* Applicabilità ed applicazioni, S. 188 f.; *Honnold/Flechtner,* Art. 2, Rn. 53; *U. Huber,* RabelsZ 43 (1979), 413, 419; *P. Huber/Mullis/P. Huber,* S. 49 Fn. 169; *Karollus,* S. 22; MünchKomm/*Westermann,* Art. 2, Rn. 8; MünchKommHGB/*Benicke,* Art. 2, Rn. 17; *Reinhart,* Art. 2, Rn. 7; *Sannini,* L'applicazione, S. 118; *Schlechtriem,* Uniform Sales Law, S. 30; *Schlechtriem/Schwenzer/Schlechtriem/Schwenzer/Hachem,* CISG Commentary, Art. 2, Rn. 25; Sekretariatskommentar, Art. 2, Nr. 8; *Soergel/Lüderitz/Fenge,* Art. 2, Rn. 8; vgl. zum EKG: *Dölle/Herber,* Art. 5 EKG, Rn. 6; *Mertens/Rehbinder,* Art. 5 EKG, Rn. 4.
[175] So auch *Bamberger/Roth/Saenger,* Art. 2, Rn. 9; *Ferrari u. a./Saenger,* Internationales Vertragsrecht, Art. 2, Rn. 10.
[176] Vgl. in der Lehre statt aller *Brunner,* Art. 2, Rn. 12; *Enderlein/Maskow/Strohbach,* Art. 2, Anm. 6; *Kröll u. a./Spohnheimer,* Art. 2, Rn. 34; MünchKommHGB/*Benicke,* Art. 2, Rn. 15; *Piltz,* NJW 2000, 553, 554; *Schlechtriem/Schwenzer/Schlechtriem,* CISG Commentary, 2. Aufl., Art. 2, Rn. 27; *Schlechtriem/Schwenzer/Schlechtriem/Schwenzer/Hachem,* CISG Commentary, Art. 2, Rn. 23; vgl. in der Rechtsprechung Cour de Justice Genève, 9.10.1998, CISG-online 424 = SZIER 1999, 195; Schiedsgericht der Handelskammer Zürich, 31.5.1996, CISG-online 1291.
[177] Siehe u. a. *Piltz,* Internationales Kaufrecht, Rn. 2–50.
[178] *Staudinger/Magnus,* Art. 2, Rn. 40.
[179] Vgl. etwa *Ferrari,* Applicabilità ed applicazioni, S. 188; *Rudolph,* Art. 2, Rn. 5.
[180] Siehe *Bamberger/Roth/Saenger,* Art. 2, Rn. 9; *Brunner,* Art. 2, Rn. 12; *Díez-Picazo/Laporta,* Art. 2, S. 65; *Kröll u. a./Spohnheimer,* Art. 2, Rn. 34; MünchKommHGB/*Benicke,* Art. 2, Rn. 15; *Reinhart,* Art. 2, Rn. 6; *Witz/Salger/Lorenz/Lorenz,* Art. 2, Rn. 7.
[181] *Ferrari u. a./Saenger,* Internationales Vertragsrecht, Art. 2, Rn. 10, *Schlechtriem/Schwenzer/Schlechtriem,* CISG Commentary, 2. Aufl., Art. 2, Rn. 29; *Staudinger/Magnus,* Art. 2, Rn. 42: *Witz/Salger/Lorenz/Lorenz,* Art. 2, Rn. 7.

Anwendungsausschlüsse

fen,[182] wie auch der von Sparkassenbüchern nicht vom Anwendungsbereich ausgenommen; diese bilden aber in der Regel nicht den Gegenstand eines gesonderten Kaufvertrages. Vielmehr folgt das Recht am Papier dem übertragenen Recht.

Art. 2 lit. d) schließt auch den Kauf von jeglichen (d. h., in- oder ausländischen) **gesetz- 37 lichen Zahlungsmitteln** aus.[183] Der Kauf von Zahlungsmitteln, die lediglich **künstlerische oder historische Bedeutung** haben,[184] kann, gleichwie nur noch historisch oder artistisch bedeutsame Wertpapiere, dem Übereinkommen unterliegen,[185] sofern alle anderen Anwendungsvoraussetzungen vorliegen.[186]

2. Kauf von Wasser- und Luftfahrzeugen (lit. e))

Art. 5 I lit. b) EKG enthielt bereits eine Ausnahme für den Kauf von Schiffen und **38** Luftfahrzeugen.[187] Dort war die Ausnahme jedoch auf den Kauf von eingetragenen beziehungsweise eintragungspflichtigen Schiffen und Luftfahrzeugen beschränkt. Die mit dieser Voraussetzung verknüpfte Rechtsunsicherheit, die sich einerseits daraus ergab, dass die Voraussetzungen für die Eintragung in den verschiedenen Ländern zum Teil unterschiedlich geregelt sind, und andererseits daraus, dass unklar war, nach welchem innerstaatlichen Recht die Eintragungspflicht bemessen werden musste,[188] hat dazu geführt, dass auf die Registrierungspflicht verzichtet wurde.[189] Eine anderweitige Beschränkung des Ausnahmetatbestandes ist trotz einiger Versuche nicht geglückt.[190] Daraus ergibt sich, dass der Anwendungsbereich des vom Übereinkommen vorgesehenen Ausnahmetatbestandes weiter gefasst ist, als der des Art. 5 I lit. b) EKG.[191]

Grundsätzlich ist der Kauf **aller Schiffe** vom Anwendungsbereich des CISG ausgenom- **39** men.[192] In Anlehnung vor allem an den französischen Originaltext stellt die deutsche Übersetzung klar, dass es keinen Unterschied macht, ob der Kauf See- oder Binnenschiffe zum Gegenstand hat.[193] Irrelevant ist ferner, ob die Wasserfahrzeuge durch Wind- oder Motorkraft betrieben werden.[194] Sie müssen jedoch **zur dauernden Fortbewegung** bestimmt sein;[195]

---

[182] *Achilles*, Art. 2, Rn. 7; *Bamberger/Roth/Saenger*, Art. 2, Rn. 9.
[183] So ausdrücklich *Honsell/Siehr*, Art. 2, Rn. 17; *Schlechtriem/Schwenzer/Schlechtriem/Schwenzer/Hachem*, CISG Commentary, Art. 2, Rn. 26.
[184] Vgl. *Plantard*, J. D. I. 1988, 311, 325; *Soergel/Lüderitz/Fenge*, Art. 2, Rn. 8.
[185] Siehe hierzu auch *Ferrari*, Applicabilità ed applicazioni, S. 190; *Ferrari u. a./Saenger*, Internationales Vertragsrecht, Art. 2, Rn. 10; *Kröll u. a./Spohnheimer*, Art. 2, Rn. 36; *Martin-Davidson*, 17 Mich. St. J. Int'l L. (2008), 657, 688; MünchKomm/*Westermann*, Art. 2, Rn. 8; MünchKommHGB/*Benicke*, Art. 2, Rn. 16; *Rudolph*, Art. 2, Rn. 5; *Schlechtriem/Schwenzer/Schlechtriem*, CISG Commentary, 2. Aufl., Art. 2, Rn. 30; *Schlechtriem/Schwenzer/Schlechtriem/Schwenzer/Hachem*, CISG Commentary, Art. 2, Rn. 26; *Schwenzer/Hachem/Kee*, Rn. 7.11.
[186] Ähnlich, mit Bezug jedoch lediglich auf Zahlungsmittel, *Honsell/Siehr*, Art. 2, Rn. 17.
[187] Vgl. *Dölle/Herber*, Art. 5 EKG, Rn. 9 ff.
[188] Siehe YB VI (1975), S. 51, Nr. 28; S. 90, Nr. 26; vgl. auch *Loewe*, Art. 2; *Schlechtriem/Schwenzer/Schlechtriem*, CISG Commentary, 2. Aufl., Art. 2, Rn. 31.
[189] Vgl. Sekretariatskommentar, Art. 2, Nr. 9; vgl. auch *Bailey*, 32 Cornell Int'l L. J. (1999), 273, 306; *Kröll u. a./Spohnheimer*, Art. 2, Rn. 37; MünchKommHGB/*Benicke*, Art. 2, Rn. 19; *Schlechtriem/Schwenzer/Schlechtriem/Schwenzer/Hachem*, CISG Commentary, Art. 2, Rn. 27.
[190] YB VIII (1977), S. 27, Nr. 29 ff.; vgl. in der Lehre *Czerwenka*, Rechtsanwendungsprobleme, S. 153; *Honnold/Flechtner*, Art. 2, Rn. 54.
[191] So auch *Audit*, Vente internationale, S. 30; *Loewe*, Art. 2.
[192] Die Anwendbarkeit des CISG wurde bereits in verschiedenen Fällen von Käufen von Schiffen ausgeschlossen; vgl. etwa Int. Ct. Russian CCI, 6.4.1998, CISG-online 778; Schiedsgericht der Jugoslawischen Handelskammer, 15.4.1999, CISG-online 1587.
[193] So ausdrücklich *Herber*, 2. Aufl., Art. 2, Rn. 31.
[194] *Achilles*, Art. 2, Rn. 8; *Schlechtriem/Schwenzer/Schlechtriem/Schwenzer/Hachem*, CISG Commentary, Art. 2, Rn. 28; *Staudinger/Magnus*, Art. 2, Rn. 45.
[195] So auch *Bamberger/Roth/Saenger*, Art. 2, Rn. 10; *Ferrari u. a./Saenger*, Internationales Vertragsrecht, Art. 2, Rn. 11; *Schlechtriem/Schwenzer/Schlechtriem*, CISG Commentary, 2. Aufl., Art. 2, Rn. 33; *Schlechtriem/Schwenzer/Schlechtriem/Schwenzer/Hachem*, CISG Commentary, Art. 2, Rn. 28.

Pontonbrücken, Bohrinseln, Gaststättenschiffe und Schwimmdocks sind daher nicht Schiffe im Sinne des Übereinkommens.[196]

40 Umstritten ist, ob man nach dem Wegfall der Registrierungspflicht davon ausgehen muss, dass nunmehr der Kauf von Wasserfahrzeugen (beziehungsweise Luftfahrzeugen) jeder Größe dem Anwendungsbereich des CISG entzogen ist.[197] Während einige Autoren auch den Kauf kleinster Boote vom Anwendungsbereich des CISG ausnehmen[198] (und dies teilweise damit begründen, dass ein Vorschlag, nur Schiffe einer bestimmten Größe dem Anwendungsbereich zu entziehen, nicht angenommen wurde),[199] wollen einige Autoren den Ausnahmetatbestand nur auf Käufe von „größeren Schiffeinheiten" erstrecken,[200] beziehungsweise auf Schiffe von „nicht ganz unbedeutender Größe".[201] Als Begründung wird zum Teil „die Entstehung der Vorschrift sowie das Interesse an einer einheitlichen, von der Praxis in den einzelnen Vertragsstaaten losgelösten[n] Bestimmung des Anwendungsbereiches des UN-Kaufrechts" angeführt.[202]

41 Eine Beschränkung des Ausnahmetatbestandes auf Käufe von Schiffen einer gewissen Größe ist m. E. nicht nur nicht angebracht,[203] sondern auch nicht zwingend, gibt es doch durchaus ein von der Größe verschiedenes, die in Art. 7 I angesprochene Einheitlichkeit der Auslegung gewährleistendes Kriterium, anhand dessen die Wasserfahrzeuge bestimmt werden können, deren Kauf unter den Ausnahmetatbestand fällt, nämlich die **Funktion des Wasserfahrzeuges:**[204] Handelt es sich bei einem Wasserfahrzeug eher um ein Transportmittel als um ein Sportgerät, dann fällt dessen Kauf unter den Ausnahmetatbestand, andernfalls kann das Übereinkommen Anwendung finden.[205] Beispiele hierfür sind Kanus, Ruder-, Paddel- und Schlauchboote Wasserfahrzeuge,[206] weshalb deren Kauf dem CISG unterstehen kann,[207] während der Kauf eines Segelbootes, so zumindest die neuere Rechtsprechung, nicht dem CISG untersteht.[208] Auch der Kauf einer Yacht unterliegt ex Art. 2 lit. e) nicht dem CISG.[209] Aus dem Gesagten geht aber auch hervor, dass auch der Verkauf eines nicht

---

[196] Vgl. *Achilles,* Art. 2, Rn. 8; *Schlechtriem/Schwenzer/Schlechtriem,* CISG Commentary, 2. Aufl., Art. 2, Rn. 33; *Schlechtriem/Schwenzer/Schlechtriem/Schwenzer/Hachem,* CISG Commentary, Art. 2, Rn. 28.

[197] Zum Folgenden vgl. auch *Ferrari,* Applicabilità ed applicazioni, S. 192 ff.

[198] Vgl. *Audit,* Vente internationale, S. 30; *Honnold/Flechtner,* Art. 2, Rn. 54; *Réczei,* Rules of the Convention, S. 71.

[199] *Honnold/Flechtner,* Art. 2, Rn. 54.

[200] So etwa *Czerwenka,* Rechtsanwendungsprobleme, S. 154; *Enderlein/Maskow/Strohbach,* Art. 2, Anm. 7.2.; *Schlechtriem,* Einheitliches UN-Kaufrecht, S. 16; Botschaft des Schweizerischen Bundesrats, S. 760; so neuerdings auch *Brunner,* Art. 2, Rn. 14.

[201] *Herber,* 2. Aufl., Art. 2 Rn. 33.

[202] *Piltz,* Internationales Kaufrecht, Rn. 2–52.

[203] So nunmehr grundsätzlich auch *Schlechtriem/Schwenzer/Schlechtriem,* CISG Commentary, 2. Aufl., Art. 2, Rn. 33; *Schlechtriem/Schwenzer/Schlechtriem/Schwenzer/Hachem,* CISG Commentary, Art. 2, Rn. 30.

[204] Auch die Anwendung dieses Kriteriums kann dazu führen, dass die vom Begriff des „Schiffes" im Sinne des Übereinkommens umfassten Wasserfahrzeuge letztendlich alle eine gewisse Größe aufweisen; dies ist jedoch nur eine Konsequenz der Anwendung des vorgeschlagenen Kriteriums und nicht Unterscheidungskriterium; vgl. aber *Soergel/Lüderitz/Fenge,* Art. 2, Rn. 9, die sich gegen das im Text vorgeschlagene Kriterium aussprechen; ebenso MünchKommHGB/*Benicke,* Art. 2, Rn. 19, Fn. 45; vgl. auch *Schlechtriem/Schwenzer/Schlechtriem,* CISG Commentary, 2. Aufl., Art. 2, Rn. 33: subsidiäre Anwendung des im Text erwähnten Kriteriums; *Schlechtriem/Schwenzer/Schlechtriem/Schwenzer/Hachem,* CISG Commentary, Art. 2, Rn. 30; neuerdings auf das im Text vorgeschlagene Kriterium abstellend auch *Schwenzer/Hachem/Kee,* Rn. 7.21.

[205] So schon *Ferrari,* Applicabilità ed applicazioni, S. 193 f.; vgl. nun auch *Bamberger/Roth/Saenger,* Art. 2, Rn. 10; vgl. in der Rechtsprechung RB Arnhem, 12.9.2006, CISG Pace: Anwendung des CISG auf Verkauf eines Plattbodenschiffes, da es dem Vergnügen diene.

[206] *Ferrari u. a./Saenger,* Internationales Vertragsrecht, Art. 2, Rn. 11.

[207] Zu diesem Ergebnis gelangen, wenn auch mit anderer Begründung, auch *Enderlein/Maskow/Strohbach,* Art. 2, Anm. 7.2.; *Kröll u. a./Spohnheimer,* Art. 2, Rn. 39; MünchKommHGB/*Benicke,* Art. 2, Rn. 19; *Piltz,* Internationales Kaufrecht, Rn. 2–52; *Rudolph,* Art. 2, Rn. 6; *Schlechtriem/Schwenzer/Schlechtriem,* CISG Commentary, 2. Aufl., Art. 2, Rn. 33. Vgl. auch Hof Leeuwarden, 31.8.2005, CISG-online 1700: Anwendung des CISG auf Kauf eines Motorbootes.

[208] RB Middelburg, 2.4.2008, CISG-online 1737.

[209] Hof Arnhem, 12.9.2006, CISG-online 1736.

mehr funktionsfähigen, ehemals der Marine gehörenden Unterseebootes durchaus dem CISG unterliegen kann.[210]

Für **Luftfahrzeuge** gilt Ähnliches: Demnach sind Luftfahrzeuge, deren Kauf vom An- 42 wendungsbereich des Übereinkommens ausgeschlossen ist,[211] solche Luftfahrzeuge, die dauernd zum Transport in der Luft bestimmt sind,[212] unabhängig von ihrer Größe.[213] Dies schließt notwendigerweise den Kauf von Modellflugzeugen,[214] Satelliten, Raumstationen, Raketen, Hängegleitern und Drachen vom Ausnahmetatbestand aus.[215]

Der Kauf von **Luftkissenfahrzeugen** ist neu in den Ausnahmenkatalog aufgenommen 43 worden. Diese Neuerung ist darauf zurückzuführen, dass klargestellt werden sollte, dass Luftkissenfahrzeuge Schiffen gleichstehen.[216]

Da die Aufzählung der Ausnahmetatbestände **abschließend** ist, erstreckt sich die Nicht- 44 anwendbarkeit des Übereinkommens nicht auf den Kauf von Landfahrzeugen.

Bezüglich aller in Art. 2 lit. e) aufgezählten Ausnahmen muss hervorgehoben werden, 45 dass nur wenn ein Kauf die **Fahrzeuge als fertige Einheit** zum Gegenstand hat, dieser unter den Ausnahmetatbestand fällt.[217] Werden Einzelteile veräußert, findet Art. 2 lit. e) keine Anwendung,[218] selbst dann nicht, wenn es sich beim Kaufgegenstand um wesentliche Bestandteile der aufgezählten Fahrzeuge handelt.[219] Diese Auffassung entspricht nicht nur der herrschenden (deutschen[220] und ausländischen)[221] Lehre; sie ist auch von der Rechtsprechung übernommen worden.[222]

3. Elektrische Energie (lit. f))

Der Kauf elektrischer Energie war auch vom Anwendungsbereichs des EKG ausgeschlos- 46 sen (Art. 5 I lit. c)).[223] Er wäre wohl ohnehin vom Anwendungsbereich des Übereinkommens ausgeschlossen, da der Warenbegriff des Übereinkommens elektrische Energie nicht erfassen dürfte.[224] Der Grund für die Ausnahme liegt, so der Sektretariatskommentar[225] und

---

[210] Schiedsgericht der Russischen Marinekommission, 18.12.1998, CISG Pace.
[211] Zum Ausschluss der Anwendbarkeit des CISG auf den Kauf eines Luftfahrzeuges, vgl. Schiedsgericht der Industrie- und Handelskammer der Russischen Föderation, 255/1996, CISG Pace.
[212] Ebenso *Bamberger/Roth/Saenger*, Art. 2, Rn. 10.
[213] So auch *Ferrari*, 10 Preadviezen (1995), 81, 141; a. A. *Herber*, 2. Aufl., Art. 2 Rn. 35.
[214] Den Verkauf von Modellflugzeugen ausschließend auch *Ferrari u. a./Saenger*, Internationales Vertragsrecht, Art. 2, Rn. 11 a. E.; *Schlechtriem/Schwenzer/Schlechtriem*, CISG Commentary, 2. Aufl., Art. 2, Rn. 35; ebenso MünchKommHGB/*Benicke*, Art. 2, Rn. 20.
[215] So auch *Staudinger/Magnus*, Art. 2, Rn. 48; vgl. hierzu auch *Kröll u. a./Spohnheimer*, Art. 2, Rn. 41; *Schlechtriem/Schwenzer/Schlechtriem/Schwenzer/Hachem*, CISG Commentary, Art. 2, Rn. 32.
[216] Vgl. den Vorschlag Indiens, A/CONF. 97/C.1/L.12, O. R., S. 83, Art. 2 lit. e), sowie die Diskussion auf der Diplomatischen Konferenz hierzu, O. R., S. 241, Nr. 18 ff.
[217] *Kröll u. a./Spohnheimer*, Art. 2, Rn. 42; MünchKomm/*Westermann*, Art. 2, Rn. 9; *Schlechtriem/Schwenzer/Schlechtriem/Schwenzer/Hachem*, CISG Commentary, Art. 2, Rn. 32; a. E. *Herber*, 2. Aufl., Art. 2 Rn. 35.
[218] *Achilles*, Art. 2, Rn. 9; *Brunner*, Art. 2, Rn. 14; MünchKommHGB/*Benicke*, Art. 2, Rn. 21; *Schlechtriem/Schwenzer/Schlechtriem*, CISG Commentary, 2. Aufl., Art. 2, Rn. 35; *Soergel/Lüderitz/Fenge*, Art. 2, Rn. 9; *Witz/Salger/Lorenz/Lorenz*, Art. 2, Rn. 9.
[219] A. A. *Audit*, Vente internationale, S. 30.
[220] Vgl. *Bamberger/Roth/Saenger*, Art. 2, Rn. 10; *Magnus*, ZEuP 1993, 79, 84 f.; *Piltz*, Internationales Kaufrecht, Rn. 2–54; *Reinhart*, Art. 2, Rn. 7.
[221] Siehe *Ferrari*, Applicabilità e applicazioni, S. 195; *Heuzé*, Anm. 91.; *Karollus*, S. 22; *Lanciotti*, S. 124, Fn. 16; *Sannini*, L'applicazione, S. 118 f.; letztendlich auch *Audit*, Vente internationale, S. 30.
[222] Vgl. das Urteil des Obersten Gerichtshofs der Ungarischen Republik, 29.9.1992, W3 No. 920 925 h1, zitiert u. a. in *Magnus*, ZEuP 1993, 79, 84 f.
[223] Vgl. zum EKG *Dölle/Herber*, Art. 5 EKG, Rn. 12.
Es sei hier angemerkt, dass Art. 2 lit. (h), der Vorschlags für eine Verordnung des Europäischen Parlaments und des Rates über ein Gemeinsames Europäisches Kaufrecht vom 11.10.2011, KOM(2011) 635 endgültig, S. 26, zwar nicht den Kauf von Strom seinem Anwendungsbereich entzieht, aber Strom – sowie Erdgas – vom Warenbegriff ausnimmt.
[224] Vgl. hierzu auch *Fairlie*, S. 43; kritisch hierzu *Reinhart*, Art. 2, Rn. 8, der hervorhebt, dass der Ausschluss des Kaufs elektrischer Energie „ein Ausdruck der veralteten rechtlichen Konzeption, Strom könne – anders als Gas – nicht als körperliche Sache angesehen werden, ist."
[225] Sekretariatskommentar, Art. 2, Nr. 10.

ein Teil der Lehre, darin, „dass Stromlieferungsverträge häufig besonderen Bedingungen unterliegen, für welche die Regeln des CISG nicht passen."[226] Dieser Rechtfertigungsgrund verkennt aber, dass – wie verschiedentlich hervorgehoben worden ist[227] – auch Kaufverträge bezüglich anderer Energieträger „besonderen Bedingungen" unterliegen, diese aber trotzdem nicht vom Anwendungsbereich ausgenommen sind.[228] Dies gilt etwa für Gas-[229] und Erdöllieferungsverträge,[230] auf die, genauso wie auf Kaufverträge, die andere Energieträger zum Gegenstand haben, wie etwa Brennelemente für Kernkraftwerke, die Vorschriften des Übereinkommens durchaus Anwendung finden können, da der Ausschlusstatbestand nicht im Wege der Analogie auf andere Energieträger ausgedehnt werden kann.[231]

---

[226] So etwa *Bamberger/Roth/Saenger*, Art. 2, Rn. 11; *Ferrari u. a./Saenger*, Internationales Vertragsrecht, Art. 2, Rn. 12; *Herber*, 2. Aufl., Art. 2 Rn. 37; ähnlich *Heuzé*, Anm. 91.; *Schlechtriem/Schwenzer/Schlechtriem*, CISG Commentary, 2. Aufl., Art. 2, Rn. 37; *Schmitt*, CR 2001, 145, 148 Fn. 50; *Schwenzer/Hachem/Kee*, Rn. 7.19.
[227] Vgl. etwa *Sannini*, L'applicazione, S. 119 f.; *Winship*, Scope, S. 1–25.
[228] Ebenso *Fairlie*, S. 43; *Ferrari*, Applicabilità ed applicazioni, S. 196.
[229] *Brunner*, Art. 2, Rn. 15; MünchKommHGB/*Benicke*, Art. 1, Rn. 18; *Schlechtriem/Schwenzer/Schlechtriem*, CISG Commentary, 2. Aufl., Art. 2, Rn. 37; *Schlechtriem/Schwenzer/Schlechtriem/Schwenzer/Hachem*, CISG Commentary, Art. 2, Rn. 33; *Soergel/Lüderitz/Fenge*, Art. 2, Rn. 10; vgl. auch OGH, 6.2.1996, CISG-online 224 (Anwendung des CISG auf Gaslieferungsvertrag).
[230] Vgl. *Achilles*, Art. 2, Rn. 10; *Bamberger/Roth/Saenger*, Art. 2, Rn. 11; *Czerwenka*, Rechtsanwendungsprobleme, S. 155; *Garro/Zuppi*, Compraventa internacional, S. 80; *Honnold/Flechtner*, Art. 2, Rn. 56; *Honsell/Siehr*, Art. 2, Rn. 19; *Penda Matipé*, S. 46 f.; *Piltz*, Internationales Kaufrecht, Rn. 2–54; *Rudolph*, Art. 2, Rn. 7; *Schwenzer/Hachem/Kee*, Rn. 7.19; *Skelton*, 9 Houst. J. Int'l L. (1986), 95, 101; *Soergel/Lüderitz/Fenge*, Art 2, Rn. 10; *S. J. Yang*, S. 35; *Witz/Salger/Lorenz/Lorenz*, Art. 2, Rn. 10.
[231] So ausdrücklich *Staudinger/Magnus*, Art. 2, Rn. 50; ebenso *Bridge*, The International Sale of Goods, Rn. 2, 17; *Ferrari u. a./Saenger*, Internationales Vertragsrecht, Art. 2, Rn. 12; *Kröll u. a./Spohnheimer*, Art. 2, Rn. 44; MünchKommHGB/*Benicke*, Art. 2, Rn. 22; *Schlechtriem/Schwenzer/Schlechtriem*, CISG Commentary, 2. Aufl., Art. 2, Rn. 37; *Schmitt*, CR 2001, 145, 148; die Frage der Anwendbarkeit des CISG auf Lieferung von Gas und Öl spricht MünchKomm/*Westermann*, Art. 2, Rn. 9 a. E. an, ohne sie jedoch zu lösen.

Art. 3 [Verträge über herzustellende Waren oder Dienstleistungen]

(1) **Den Kaufverträgen stehen Verträge über die Lieferung herzustellender oder zu erzeugender Ware gleich, es sei denn, daß der Besteller einen wesentlichen Teil der für die Herstellung oder Erzeugung notwendigen Stoffe selbst zur Verfügung zu stellen* hat.**

(2) **Dieses Übereinkommen ist auf Verträge nicht anzuwenden, bei denen der überwiegende Teil der Pflichten der Partei, welche die Ware liefert, in der Ausführung von Arbeiten oder anderen Dienstleistungen besteht.**

Art. 3

(1) Contracts for the supply of goods to be manufactured or produced are to be considered sales unless the party who orders the goods undertakes to supply a substantial part of the materials necessary for such manufacture or production.

(2) This Convention does not apply to contracts in which the preponderant part of the obligations of the party who furnishes the goods consists in the supply of labour or other services.

Art. 3

1) Sont réputés ventes les contrats de fourniture de marchandises à fabriquer ou à produire, à moins que la partie qui commande celles-ci n'ait à fournir une part essentielle des éléments matériels nécessaires à cette fabrication ou production.

2) La présente Convention ne s'applique pas aux contrats dans lesquels la part prépondérante de l'obligation de la partie qui fournit les marchandises consiste en une fourniture de main-d'oeuvre ou d'autres services.

Übersicht

	Rn.
I. Vorgeschichte	1
II. Werklieferungsverträge (Abs. 1)	4
III. Lieferverträge mit arbeits- oder dienstvertraglichen Pflichten (Abs. 2)	12
1. Einheitlichkeit des Vertrages und deren Rechtsfolgen	12
2. Der „überwiegende Teil" der Pflichten des Lieferanten	13
3. Rechtsfolgen der Anwendbarkeit des Übereinkommens	16
4. Einzelfälle	17
5. Beweislast	20

Vorläufer und **Entwürfe:** Art. 6 EKG; Art. 1 VII EAG; Genfer E 1976 Art. 3; Wiener E 1977 Art. 3; New Yorker E 1978 Art. 3.

I. Vorgeschichte

Art. 6 EKG und Art. 1 VII EAG enthielten eine dem **Abs. 1** entsprechende Vorschrift,[1] deren Geschichte sogar bis zum Entwurf von 1935 zurückverfolgt werden kann.[2] Die (weite)[3] Ausdehnung des Anwendungsbereichs auf Werklieferungsverträge, denn auf diese bezieht sich Abs. 1,[4] zeichnet auch alle anderen Entwürfe aus,[5] beziehungsweise ist 1

---

* Schweiz: zu liefern.

[1] *Schlechtriem/Schwenzer/Schlechtriem*, CISG Commentary, 2. Aufl., Art. 3, Rn. 1; *Schlechtriem/Schwenzer/ Schlechtriem/Schwenzer/Hachem*, CISG Commentary, Art. 3, Rn. 1.

[2] Vgl. Art. 2 des Entwurfes von 1935; siehe zu dieser Vorschrift *Rabel*, RabelsZ 9 (1935), 1, 47.

[3] So *De Nova*, Riv. trim. dir. proced. civ. 1990, 749, 751.

[4] *Soergel/Lüderitz/Fenge*, Art. 3, Rn. 2; *Witz/Salger/Lorenz/Lorenz*, Art. 3, Rn. 3.

[5] Vgl. etwa Art. 2 des Entwurfes von 1939; Art. 10 der Entwürfe von 1956 und 1963; Art. 3 der Entwürfe von Genf (1976), Wien (1977) und New York (1978).

Art. 3 2–4

vom Anfang der Vereinheitlichungsbestrebungen an durchgehalten worden und wurde auch anlässlich der Diplomatischen Konferenz nicht ernsthaft in Frage gestellt.[6] Dies kann aber nicht weiter überraschen, finden die Vorschriften des Kaufrechts doch auch nach dem innerstaatlichen Recht verschiedener Länder auf Werklieferungsverträge Anwendung.[7] Das Übereinkommen stellt aber nur solche Werklieferungsverträge Kaufverträgen gleich, im Rahmen derer der Käufer nicht einen wesentlichen Teil der für die Herstellung beziehungsweise die Produktion notwendigen Stoffe selbst zur Verfügung stellen muss.[8]

2   Eine dem **Abs. 2** entsprechende Vorschrift war nicht im EKG enthalten. Sie geht zurück auf einen Vorschlag Spaniens,[9] wonach das Übereinkommen nicht auf Verträge Anwendung finden sollte, die die Vertragsparteien im Wesentlichen zu anderen Leistungen als der Zahlung und Lieferung der Ware verpflichteten.[10] Obwohl dieser Vorschlag als zu allgemein verworfen wurde,[11] blieb sein Grundgedanke leitend. Dies ergibt sich unschwer daraus, dass die endgültige Fassung, die auf Art. 6 I des Verjährungsübereinkommens zurückgeht,[12] die ursprünglich als zu allgemein gehaltene Fassung eigentlich nur beschränkt hat, und zwar auf die Fälle, in denen die geschuldeten Leistungen Arbeits- oder Dienstleistungen sind.[13]

3   Anlässlich der Diplomatischen Konferenz wurde lediglich eine redaktionelle Änderung vorgenommen:[14] Der im Verjährungsübereinkommen verwendete Begriff „Verkäufer" wurde durch „Partei, welche die Ware liefert" ersetzt; denn die Vorschrift hat gerade Verträge im Auge, die nicht als Kaufverträge im Sinne der Konvention angesehen werden können.[15]

II. Werklieferungsverträge (Abs. 1)

4   Zweck des Abs. 1 ist es, den Anwendungsbereich des Übereinkommens auch auf Verträge auszudehnen, deren Gegenstand noch erzeugt oder hergestellt werden muss.[16] Ein modernes Kaufrecht kommt nicht umhin,[17] solche Verträge mit Kaufverträgen – also auch fertiggestellte Waren mit noch fertigzustellenden Waren[18] – gleichzustellen.[19]

---

[6] Siehe O. R., S. 84 f. und S. 241 ff.
[7] So auch *Ferrari*, Applicabilità ed applicazioni, S. 136 f.; *P. Huber/Mullis/P. Huber*, S. 45; *Staudinger/Magnus*, Art. 3, Rn. 2; vgl. hierzu auch schon *Rabel*, Recht des Warenkaufs, Bd. 1, S. 54.
[8] Vgl. Rn. 6 f.
[9] Siehe YB III (1972), S. 79: „The present Law shall not apply to contracts where the obligations of the parties are substantially other than the delivery of and the payment for money."
[10] Vgl. *Czerwenka*, Rechtsanwendungsprobleme, S. 142; *Schlechtriem/Schwenzer/Schlechtriem/Schwenzer/Hachem*, CISG Commentary, Art. 3, Rn. 1.
[11] YB VIII (1977), S. 28.
[12] YB V (1974), S. 211.
[13] So *Herber*, 2. Aufl., Art. 3 Rn. 1.
[14] *Schlechtriem/Schwenzer/Schlechtriem/Schwenzer/Hachem*, CISG Commentary, Art. 3, Rn. 1.
[15] Vgl. O. R., S. 242, Nr. 39 f.; S. 245, Nr. 5.
[16] Vgl. *Bamberger/Roth/Saenger*, Art. 3, Rn. 1; *Kröll u. a./Mistelis/Raymond*, Art. 3, Rn. 1; *Perovic*, Annals Fac. L. Belgrade 2011, 181, 183; *Schlechtriem/Schwenzer/Schlechtriem/Schwenzer/Hachem*, CISG Commentary, Art. 3, Rn. 3; *Staudinger/Magnus*, Art. 3, Rn. 5; *Wasmer*, S. 13.
[17] Siehe auch *Honnold/Flechtner*, Art. 3, Rn. 58: „A modern sales law must include transactions, which call for the manufacture or production of goods".
[18] Vgl. auch *Brunner*, Art. 3, Rn. 3; *Ferrari u. a./Saenger*, Internationales Vertragsrecht, Art. 3, Rn. 2; *Grieser*, S. 35 f.; MünchKomm/*Westermann*, Art. 3, Rn. 2; *Piltz*, Internationales Kaufrecht, Rn. 2–31; *Schlechtriem/Schwenzer/Schlechtriem/Schwenzer/Hachem*, CISG Commentary, Art. 3, Rn. 3; Sekretariatskommentar, Art. 3, Nr. 4; vgl. OLG Saarbrücken, 14.2.2001, CISG-online 610 = IHR 2001, 64.
[19] Vgl. diesbezüglich auch schon *Rabel*, Recht des Warenkaufs, Bd. 1, S. 54, der bereits 1936 auf die Notwendigkeit hinwies, dem Einheitskaufrecht auch Werklieferungsverträge zu unterstellen: „würde man Werklieferungsverträge […] ausscheiden, so wäre diese Regelung recht unvollständig." Vgl. auch Art. 2 lit. (k) des Vorschlags für eine Verordnung des Europäischen Parlaments und des Rates über ein Gemeinsames Europäisches Kaufrecht vom 11.10.2011, KOM(2011) 635 endgültig, S. 26.

Verträge über herzustellende Waren oder Dienstleistungen   5, 6 **Art. 3**

Diese **Gleichstellung** von Verträgen, wonach der Lieferant die versprochene Ware noch 5 herzustellen oder zu erzeugen hat,[20] also von Werklieferungsverträgen,[21] mit Kaufverträgen entspricht weitgehend der Regelung des deutschen Rechts (**§ 651 BGB**),[22] genauso wie der des **schweizerischen Rechts**.[23] Anders als nach § 651 BGB findet eine Differenzierung danach, ob die Ware vertretbar ist oder nicht, jedoch nicht statt.[24]

Die bisweilen kritisierte[25] Gleichstellung ebendieser Verträge mit Kaufverträgen gilt „aber 6 nur insoweit der Besteller nicht einen **wesentlichen Teil** der für die **Erzeugung oder Herstellung notwendigen Stoffe**[26] selbst zu Verfügung stellen muss.[27] Obwohl anhand des Einzelfalles zu entscheiden ist, was als „wesentlich" angesehen werden muss,[28] lassen sich m. E. dennoch einige für die – autonome –[29] **Bestimmung der „Wesentlichkeit"** nützliche, allgemein gültige Anmerkungen machen: Der Gebrauch zweier voneinander verschiedener Ausdrücke in ein und derselben Vorschrift, „wesentlich" in Abs. 1 und „überwiegend" in Abs. 2, lässt darauf schließen, dass der Unterschied nicht nur terminologischer Natur ist.[30] Daher ist der Ansicht der Lehre zuzustimmen, die auf der Grundlage des

---

[20] Vgl. in der Rechtsprechung hierzu KG Zug, 14.12.2009, CISG-online 2026; OG Aargau, 3.3.2009, CISG-online 2013; Hof van Beroep Gent, 14.11.2008, CISG-online 1908; CA Colmar, 26.2.2008, CISG-online 1657; OLG Oldenburg, 20.12.2007, CISG-online 1644; OLG Innsbruck, 18.12.2007, CISG-online 1735; OLG Linz, 24.9.2007, CISG-online 1583; KG Aargau, 20.9.2007, CISG-online 1742; HGer Zürich, 25.6.2007, CISG-online 1564 = IHR 2008, 31; OGer Zug, 16.12.2006, CISG-online 1565; RB Arnhem, 28.6.2006, CISG-online 1265; Cour de Justice de Genève, 20.1.2006, CISG-online 1504; OGH, 8.11.2005, CISG-online 1156; CIETAC, 13.6.2005, CISG-online 1707; HGer Aargau, 25.1.2005, CISG-online 1091; RB Koophandel Hasselt, 14.9.2004, CISG Pace; HGer St. Gallen, 29.4.2004, CISG-online 962; OGH, 21.4.2004, CISG-online 1048; KG Schaffhausen, 27.1.2004, CISG-online 960; Szegedi Itelotabla, (ohne datum), CISG Pace; HGer St. Gallen, 3.12.2002, CISG-online 727; HGer Aargau, 5.11.2002, CISG-online 715; Hof van Beroep Gent, 15.5.2002, CISG-online 746; Int. Ct. Hungarian CCI, 5.12.1995, CISG-online 163 = NJW-RR 1996, 1145; LG Oldenburg, 15.2.1995, CISG-online 197 = NJW 1995, 2101; LG Memmingen, 1.12.1993, CISG-online 73 = IPRax 1995, 251; ICC, 7660/JK, CISG-online 129 = ICC Ct. Bull. 2/1995, 69; ICC, 7844/1994, CISG-online 567 = ICC Ct. Bull. 2/1995, 72; HGer Zürich, 9.9.1993, CISG-online 79.

[21] Werklieferungsverträge wurden ausdrücklich den in Art. 3 I angesprochenen Verträgen und somit den Kaufverträgen im Sinne des Übereinkommens gleichgestellt in OLG Dresden, 30.10.2010, CISG-online 2183; HaGer Zürich, 25.6.2010, CISG-online 2161; KG St. Gallen, 15.6.2010, CISG-online 2159; OLG Saarbrücken, 12.5.2010, CISG-online 2155; HGer Aargau, 10.3.2010, CISG-online 2176; OGer Aargau, 3.3.2009, CISG-online 2013; KG Zug, 14.12.2009, CISG-online 2026; HGer Aargau, 20.9.2007, CISG-online 1742; Cour de Justice de Genève, 20.1.2006, CISG-online 1504; HGer Aargau, 25.1.2005, CISG-online 1091 = IHR 2006, 34; HGer St. Gallen, 29.4.2004, CISG-online 962; KG Schaffhausen, 27.1.2004, CISG-online 960; HGer Zürich, 9.7.2002, CISG-online 726; LG München I, 27.2.2002, CISG-online 654; OLG Saarbrücken, 14.2.2001, CISG-online 610 = IHR 2001, 64; OLG Stuttgart, 28.2.2000, CISG-online 583 = IHR 2001, 65; BGH, 4.12.1996, CISG-online 260 = NJW-RR 1997, 690; OLG München, 8.2.1995, CISG-online 142; OLG Köln, 26.8.1994, CISG-online 132 = RIW 1994, 970; OLG Saarbrücken, 13.1.1993, CISG-online 83; OLG Frankfurt a. M., 17.9.1991, CISG-online 28 = RIW 1991, 950.

[22] *Bamberger/Roth/Saenger*, Art. 3, Rn. 2; MünchKommHGB/*Benicke*, Art. 3, Rn. 2; *Schlechtriem*, Internationales UN-Kaufrecht, Rn. 26.

[23] So die Botschaft des Schweizerischen Bundesrats, S. 762; vgl. auch *Achilles*, Art. 3, Rn. 1; gemäß *Honnold/Flechtner*, Art. 3, Rn. 58, stellt die im Text erwähnte Gleichstellung lediglich „the necessary premise [of] a modern sales law" dar.

[24] MünchKommHGB/*Benicke*, Art. 3, Rn. 2; vgl. auch *Ferrari u. a./Saenger*, Internationales Vertragsrecht, Art. 3, Rn. 2; *Schlechtriem/Schwenzer/Schlechtriem/Schwenzer/Hachem*, CISG Commentary, Art. 3, Rn. 3; CISG-AC, Op. 4 *(Perales Viscasillas)*, Comment 1.6.

[25] Vgl. *Rosett*, 45 Ohio St. L. J. (1984), 265, 280.

[26] Art. 3 I findet keine Anwendung, wenn die vom Besteller zur Verfügung gestellten Stoffe einen „wesentlichen Teil" der Stoffe darstellen, die zu anderen als den genannten Zwecken (Herstellung und Erzeugung) dienen, wie etwa der Verpackung, dem Transport, etc.; so schon *Achilles*, Art. 3, Rn. 2; CISG-AC, Op. 4 *(Perales Viscasillas)*, Comment 2.11; *Ferrari*, Applicabilità ed applicazioni, S. 145, Fn. 149; *P. Huber/Mullis/P. Huber*, S. 44; *Schlechtriem/Schwenzer/Schlechtriem/Schwenzer/Hachem*, CISG Commentary, Art. 3, Rn. 4; *Schroeter*, VJ (2001), 74, 76; *Staudinger/Magnus*, Art. 3, Rn. 20.

[27] Ist der Besteller nicht vertraglich dazu verpflichtet, die Stoffe zur Verfügung zu stellen, ist der Eigenanteil beziehungsweise dessen Wesentlichkeit hinsichtlich der Anwendung von Art. 3 I unbedeutsam.

[28] *Herber*, 2. Aufl., Art. 3 Rn. 3; *P. Huber/Mullis/P. Huber*, S. 44 f.; *Rudolph*, Art. 3, Rn. 3; Botschaft des Schweizerischen Bundesrats, S. 762.

[29] CISG-AC, Op. 4 *(Perales Viscasillas)*, Comment 1.6.

[30] *Sannini*, L'applicazione, S. 101 f.

„allgemeinen Sprachverständnisses"[31] an einen Begriff, den des „wesentlichen Teils", geringere Anforderungen stellt als an den anderen, den des „überwiegenden Teils".[32] Demzufolge kann der „wesentliche Teil" unter der Hälfte liegen,[33] liegt doch der „überwiegende Teil" sicher darüber.[34]

7   Umstritten ist jedoch, woran sich die „Wesentlichkeit" der vom Besteller kostenlos[35] beziehungsweise ohne rechtlich unterscheidbaren Kaufvertrag[36] dem Lieferanten zur Verfügung gestellten Stoffe[37] bemisst,[38] d. h., ob zur Bestimmung der „Wesentlichkeit" allein ein quantitativ-wertmässiges Kriterium heranzuziehen ist[39], oder ob auch andere Elemente eine Rolle spielen können.[40] Vielfach wird auf das **Wertverhältnis** der von den Vertragsparteien beizutragenden Stoffe abgestellt, die der Lieferant zur Herstellung beziehungsweise Erzeugung der Waren benutzt.[41] Gemäß einer anderen Auffassung kommt es hingegen darauf an, ob der **Beitrag** des Bestellers **als solcher,** also unter Berücksichtigung auch der vom Besteller geleisteten Arbeits- beziehungsweise Dienstleistungen, den Vertrag prägt.[42]

8   M. E. spricht der Wortlaut dafür, dass neben dem Wertverhältnis **auch** ein **qualitatives Element** bei der Bestimmung der Wesentlichkeit Berücksichtigung finden muss.[43] Ob der Vertrag dem Übereinkommen unterliegt, kann demnach auch von der Natur der vom Besteller zur Verfügung gestellten Stoffe abhängen.[44] Dies ergibt sich m. E. aus dem Wortlaut des französischen Textes, in dem auf die „part essentielle", also auf die „Wesentlichkeit"

---

[31] *Czerwenka,* Rechtsanwendungsprobleme, S. 144.
[32] Vgl. auch *Bianca/Bonell/Khoo,* Art. 3, Anm. 2.2.; *Bridge,* Draft Digest, S. 235, 242; *Honnold/Flechtner,* Art. 3, Rn. 59; *Heuzé,* Anm. 89.; *Kröll u. a./Mistelis/Raymond,* Art. 3, Rn. 5; MünchKommHGB/*Benicke,* Art. 3, Rn. 4; *Schlechtriem/Schwenzer/Schlechtriem/Schwenzer/Hachem,* CISG Commentary, Art. 3, Rn. 5.
[33] So schon *Bianca/Carbone/Lopez de Gonzalo,* Art. 3, S. 8; *Brunner,* Art. 3, Rn. 3; *Staudinger/Magnus,* Art. 3, Rn. 16.
[34] Ebenso *Enderlein/Maskow/Strohbach,* Art. 3, Anm. 3.
[35] *Enderlein/Maskow/Strohbach,* Art. 3, Anm. 3.; MünchKommBGB/*Westermann,* Art. 3, Rn. 3; *Rudolph,* Art. 3, Rn. 3; *Schlechtriem/Schwenzer/Schlechtriem/Schwenzer/Hachem,* CISG Commentary, Art. 3, Rn. 4; *Staudinger/Magnus,* Art. 3, Rn. 19.
[36] *Piltz,* Internationales Kaufrecht, Rn. 2–33.
[37] Liefert der Käufer den (unwesentlichen) Teil der für die Herstellung oder Erzeugung notwendigen Stoffe nicht, haftet er nach den Vorschriften des CISG; vgl. *Schlechtriem/Schwenzer/Schlechtriem/Schwenzer/Hachem,* CISG Commentary, Art. 3, Rn. 10. Die Nicht- bzw. Schlechtlieferung seitens des Käufers kann sich auch auf dessen Ansprüche auswirken; vgl. Schwenzer, Art. 80, Rn. 9 (zur beidseitigen Verursachung der Nichterfüllung).
[38] Vgl. zum Stand der Diskussion auch *Schlechtriem/Schwenzer/Schlechtriem,* CISG Commentary, 2. Aufl., Art. 3, Rn. 3a; *Schlechtriem/Schwenzer/Schlechtriem/Schwenzer/Hachem,* CISG Commentary, Art. 3, Rn. 5 ff.
[39] Vgl. CISG-AC, Op. 4 *(Perales Viscasillas),* Comment 2.6-2.7: „The „economic value" criterion should prevail in the interpretation of the words „substantial part" in Article 3.1 CISG […]. An „essential" criterion should only be considered where the „economic value" is impossible or inappropriate to apply, i. e., when the comparison of the materials provided for by both parties amounts to nearly the same value".
[40] Vgl. auch *Niemann,* Einheitliche Anwendung, S. 92 ff.; die Frage ansprechend, ohne jedoch eine Lösung vorzuschlagen, *Martin-Davidson,* 17 Mich. St. J. Int'l L. (2008), 657, 675 ff.
[41] So etwa *Achilles,* Art. 3, Rn. 3; *Audit,* Vente internationale, S. 25; *Bamberger/Roth/Saenger,* Art. 3, Rn. 3; *Brunner,* Art. 3, Rn. 3; *Ebenroth,* östJBl 1986, 681, 684; *Enderlein/Maskow/Strohbach,* Art. 3, Anm. 3.; *Garro/Zuppi,* Compraventa internacional, S. 74; *Herber,* 2. Aufl., Art. 3 Rn. 3; *Honnold/Flechtner,* Art. 3, Rn. 59; *Honsell/Siehr,* Art. 3, Rn. 3; *Lacasse,* Le champ d'application, S. 29 f.; *Lohmann,* Parteiautonomie, S. 17 f.; MünchKommHGB/*Benicke,* Art. 3, Rn. 4; MünchKommBGB/*Westermann,* Art. 3, Rn. 3; *Neumayer/Ming,* Art. 3, Anm. 3.; *Perovic,* Annals Fac. L. Belgrade 2011, 181, 185; *Piltz,* Internationales Kaufrecht, Rn. 2–32; *Reinhart,* Art. 3, Rn. 1; *Schlechtriem,* Internationales UN-Kaufrecht, Rn. 26; *Soergel/Lüderitz/Fenge,* Art. 3, Rn. 3; *Witz/Salger/Lorenz/Lorenz,* Art. 3, Rn. 3; CISG-AC, Op. 4 *(Perales Viscasillas),* Comment 2.6; vgl. in der Rechtsprechung OLG Innsbruck, 18.12.2007, CISG-online 1735; Int. Ct. Hungarian CCI, 5.12.1995, CISG-online 163 = NJW-RR 1996, 1145.
[42] So etwa *Karollus,* S. 23.
[43] Vgl. hierzu *Audit,* Vente internationale, S. 26; *Ferrari,* Applicabilità ed applicazioni, S. 142 ff.; *Sannini,* L'applicazione, S. 101; *Schlechtriem/Schwenzer/Schlechtriem,* CISG Commentary, 2. Aufl., Art. 3, Rn. 3a; *Schlechtriem/Schwenzer/Schlechtriem/Schwenzer/Hachem,* CISG Commentary, Art. 3, Rn. 7; *Schwenzer/Hachem/Kee,* Rn. 8.38; *Winship,* Scope, S. 1–24; a. A. ausdrücklich MünchKomm/*Westermann,* Art. 3, Rn. 3, Fn. 9; a. A. wohl auch *Kröll u. a./Mistelis/Raymond,* Art. 3, Rn. 11 ff.
[44] So auch *Richards,* 69 Iowa L. Rev. (1983), 209, 231 („The nature of the materials supplied will be a factor in deciding whether a 'substantial' amount of the material will be supplied").

abgestellt wird.[45] Der Umstand, dass in der englischen Fassung lediglich von der „substantial part" die Rede ist, steht der hier vorgeschlagenen Lösung nicht im Weg,[46] weshalb es nicht verwundert, dass verschiedene Autoren die Auffassung vertreten haben, auch 15% könnten einen „wesentlichen Teil" im Sinne des Abs. 1 ausmachen.[47] In der Rechtsprechung findet sich jedoch ein Urteil, wonach bei Zulieferungen des Käufers unter 20% des Gesamtwertes ein „wesentlicher Teil" und damit eine Ausnahme im Sinne von Art. 3 I nicht vorliegt.[48] Das aprioristische Abstellen auf bestimmte Prozentsätze ist m. E. zugunsten einer Einzelfallanalyse abzulehnen.[49] Sicher ist lediglich, dass bei Lieferung aller für die Herstellung notwendigen Stoffe das CISG keine Anwendung findet.[50]

Auf **Veredelungsverträge** findet das Übereinkommen in der Regel keine Anwendung,[51] so auch die Rechtsprechung,[52] da normalerweise die vom Besteller zur Verfügung gestellten Stoffe einen „wesentlichen Teil" ausmachen werden, unabhängig davon, welche der zur Bestimmung der Wesentlichkeit vorgeschlagenen Kriterien herangezogen werden.[53] Ähnliches gilt auch in Bezug auf Reparaturverträge, Besserungsverträge, Generalüberholungsverträge, etc.[54] **9**

Pläne, Anweisungen, Know-how, etc., sind keine **Stoffe** bzw. kein Material im Sinne der Konvention,[55] weshalb eine französische Entscheidung[56] kritisiert werden muss: Sie hat vom Besteller gegebene Anweisungen den im Abs. 1 erwähnten für die Herstellung und **10**

---

[45] Für einen Hinweis auf die im Text zitierte französische Fassung bei dem Versuch, die angesprochene Frage zu lösen, vgl. *Sannini*, L'applicazione, S. 101; in der Rechtsprechung vgl. OLG München, 3.12.1999, CISG-online 585 = RIW 2000, 712, 713.

[46] Auch *Herber*, 2. Aufl., Art. 3 Rn. 3, stellt die französische Fassung mit der englischen gleich (um jedoch zu einem anderen Ergebnis hinsichtlich des Elementes zu gelangen, anhand dessen die „Wesentlichkeit" beurteilt werden muss); zu den durch die verschiedenen Wortlaute des Abs. 1 geschaffenen Auslegungsproblemen vgl. auch *Kritzer*, Guide to Practical Applications, S. 73.

[47] *Honnold/Flechtner*, Art. 3, Rn. 59; a. A. *Bamberger/Roth/Saenger*, Art. 3, Rn. 4; *Brunner*, Art. 3, Rn. 3; *Enderlein/Maskow/Strohbach*, Art. 3, Anm. 3.; *Lacasse*, Le champ d'application, S. 30; *Niemann*, Einheitliche Anwendung, S. 95; *Staudinger/Magnus*, Art. 3, Rn. 16; a. A. auch MünchKommHGB/*Benicke*, Art. 3, Rn. 4 a. E., der vorschlägt als Richtwert einen Wert von mindestens einem Drittel zu verlangen; noch anders *Ferrari u. a./Saenger*, Internationales Vertragsrecht, Art. 3, Rn. 4: „Die Wesentlichkeitsgrenze dürfte in der Nähe der 50% einzuordnen sein".

[48] Int. Ct. Hungarian CCI, 5.12.1995, CISG-online 163 = NJW-RR 1996, 1145.

[49] Vgl. auch CISG-AC, Op. 4 *(Perales Viscasillas)*, Comment 2.9: „It does not seem to be advisable to quantify the word 'substantial' *a priori* in percentages. A case-by-case analysis is preferable and thus it should be determined on the basis of an overall assessment"; sich gegen das Abstellen auf bestimmte Prozentsätze aussprechend auch *P. Huber/Mullis/P. Huber*, S. 45; *Lapiashvili*, S. 56; *E. Muñoz*, S. 69.

[50] OGH, 27.10.1994, CISG-online 133 = ZfRVgl 1995, 159 ff.; vgl. auch *Perovic*, Annals Fac. L. Belgrade 2011, 181, 183; *Schlechtriem/Schwenzer/Schlechtriem/Schwenzer/Hachem*, CISG Commentary, Art. 3, Rn. 4.

[51] Vgl. *Achilles*, Art. 3, Rn. 3; *Bamberger/Roth/Saenger*, Art. 3, Rn. 4; *Enderlein/Maskow/Strohbach*, Art. 3, Anm. 4.; *U. Huber*, RabelsZ 43 (1979), 413, 418 f.; *Lohmann*, Parteiautonomie, S. 18; *Magnus*, ZEuP 1997, 823, 829; *Posch/Terlitza*, IHR 2001, 47, 49; *Reinhart*, Art. 3, Rn. 1; *Schlechtriem*, Internationales UN-Kaufrecht, Rn. 27a; *Schlechtriem/Schwenzer/Schlechtriem/Schwenzer/Hachem*, CISG Commentary, Art. 3, Rn. 4; *Staudinger/Magnus*, Art. 3, Rn. 15.

[52] Vgl. OGH, 27.10.1994, CISG-online 133 = ZfRVgl 1995, 159, 161.

[53] Es sei angemerkt, dass OGH, 27.10.1994, CISG-online 133 = ZfRVgl 1995, 159, 161, den Veredelungsvertrag deshalb vom Anwendungsbereich ausgenommen hat, weil die Veredelungsleistung im Vordergrund steht, der Vertrag also ex Art. 3 II nicht in den Anwendungsbereich fallen kann.

[54] So auch *Lohmann*, Privatunternehmen, S. 18; *Rudolph*, Art. 3, Rn. 3; *Schlechtriem/Schwenzer/Schlechtriem*, CISG Commentary, 2. Aufl., Art. 3, Rn. 3.

[55] *Bamberger/Roth/Saenger*, Art. 3, Rn. 3; *Brunner*, Art. 3, Rn. 4; CISG-AC, Op. 4 *(Perales Viscasillas)*, Comment 2.12 f.; *Fairlie*, S. 48; *Ferrari u. a./Saenger*, Internationales Vertragsrecht, Art. 3, Rn. 3; *Karollus*, S. 22; *Kröll u. a./Mistelis/Raymond*, Art. 3, Rn. 14; *Magnus*, ZEuP 1997, 823, 829; MünchKommHGB/ *Benicke*, Art. 3, Rn. 4; *Schlechtriem*, Internationales UN-Kaufrecht, Rn. 26; *Schlechtriem/Schwenzer/Schlechtriem/Schwenzer/Hachem*, CISG Commentary, 2. Aufl., Art. 3, Rn 3b; *Schlechtriem/Schwenzer/Schlechtriem/Schwenzer/Hachem*, CISG Commentary, Art. 3, Rn. 8; *Soergel/Lüderitz/Fenge*, Art. 3, Rn. 3; *Vischer/L. Huber/Oser*, Rn. 342; *Witz/Wolter*, RIW 1995, 810, 811; *Wulf*, S. 29 f.; vgl. in der Rechtsprechung HGer Zürich, 10.2.1999, CISG-online 488; OLG Frankfurt a. M., 17.9.1991, CISG-online 28 = NJW 1991, 633 f.; a. A.: *Schmitt*, CR 2001, 145, 153: Informationen und Anweisungen des Bestellers seien als „Stoffe" i. S. v. Art. 3 CISG anzusehen; die Frage ansprechend, ohne sie jedoch zu lösen, *P. Huber/Mullis/P. Huber*, S. 44.

[56] CA Chambéry, 25.5.1993, CISG-online 223 = Rev. jur. com. 1995, 242.

Art. 3 11, 12   Teil I. Kapitel I. Anwendungsbereich

Erzeugung notwendigen Stoffen gleichgesetzt.[57] Ferner ist auch ein Grundstück, auf dem eine vom Verkäufer zu liefernde Industrieanlage zu errichten ist, kein „notwendiger Stoff" im Sinne des CISG,[58] denn auch „wenn sie mit Errichtung wesentlicher Bestandteil des Grundstücks wird, entscheidet über die Wertverhältnisse nach Art. 3 I CISG der Zeitpunkt des Vertragsschlusses, nicht der eines späteren Einbaus oder einer anderen Verwendung."[59]

11   In Bezug auf die **Beweislast** ist zu Recht darauf hingewiesen worden, dass die Partei, die sich auf die Ausnahme beruft, d. h., darauf, dass der Besteller einen wesentlichen Teil für die Herstellung oder Erzeugung notwendigen Stoffe zur Verfügung gestellt hat, diese beweisen muss.[60]

III. Lieferverträge mit arbeits- oder dienstvertraglichen Pflichten (Abs. 2)

1. Einheitlichkeit des Vertrages und deren Rechtsfolgen

12   Abs. 2, der keinen Vorläufer im EKG hat,[61] erweitert den sachlichen Anwendungsbereich des Übereinkommens auf Lieferverträge mit arbeits- oder dienstvertraglichen Pflichten[62] (wie etwa Montage, Überwachung, Kontrolle, Lagerung, Kundendienst),[63] sofern diese Pflichten nicht den überwiegenden Teil der Pflichten des „Verkäufers" darstellen,[64] d. h., sofern die kauffremden Pflichten nicht eine übergeordnete Rolle spielen.[65] Bei dem Vertrag muss es sich um einen **einheitlichen Vertrag** handeln.[66] Liegen hingegen zwei **getrennte**

---

[57] Kritisch zur zitierten Entscheidung auch *Bonell/Liguori*, Uniform L. Rev. 1996, 147, 151; *Magnus*, ZEuP 1997, 823, 829; *Schlechtriem*, Internationales UN-Kaufrecht, Rn. 26; *Witz*, Les Premières applications, S. 34; *ders.*, Rev. dr. aff. int. 2001, 253, 256; *Witz/Wolter*, RIW 1995, 810, 811.

[58] *Schlechtriem/Schwenzer/Schlechtriem*, CISG Commentary, 2. Aufl., Art. 3, Rn. 3c; *Schlechtriem/Schwenzer/Schlechtriem/Schwenzer/Hachem*, CISG Commentary, Art. 3, Rn. 9.

[59] *Schlechtriem*, Internationales UN-Kaufrecht, Rn. 26.

[60] Vgl. *Achilles*, Art. 3, Rn. 9; *Bamberger/Roth/Saenger*, Art. 3, Rn. 5; *Baumgärtel/Hepting/Laumen*, 1. Aufl., Art. 3 Rn. 5; *Baumgärtel/Laumen/Hepting/Müller*, Art. 3, Rn. 2; *Droste*, S. 161; *Ferrari u. a./Saenger*, Internationales Vertragsrecht, Art. 3, Rn. 5; *Herber/Czerwenka*, Art. 3, Rn. 7; *Henninger*, S. 205; *P. Huber/Mullis/P. Huber*, S. 44; *Jung*, S. 201; *Kröll u. a./Mistelis/Raymond*, Art. 3, Rn. 2 und 26; *Reimers-Zocher*, S. 177; *Schlechtriem*, Uniform Sales Law, S. 17; *Schlechtriem/Schwenzer/Schlechtriem*, CISG Commentary, 2. Aufl., Art. 3, Rn. 3d; *Schlechtriem/Schwenzer/Schlechtriem/Schwenzer/Hachem*, CISG Commentary, Art. 3, Rn. 23; *Witz/Salger/Lorenz/Lorenz*, Art. 3, Rn. 8.

[61] So auch *Richards*, 69 Iowa L. Rev. (1983), 209, 233.

[62] Zu den Kriterien, die in den verschiedenen Rechtsordnungen herangezogen werden, um Kaufverträge von Lieferverträge mit arbeits- oder dienstvertraglichen Pflichten zu unterscheiden, vgl. CISG-AC, Op. 4 (Perales Viscasillas), Comment 1.4.

[63] Zu dieser Aufzählung, vgl. *Enderlein/Maskow/Strohbach*, Art. 3, Anm. 7.; vgl. auch *Niemann*, Einheitliche Anwendung, S. 95; *Schlechtriem/Schwenzer/Schlechtriem*, CISG Commentary, 2. Aufl., Art. 3, Rn. 6a; *Schlechtriem/Schwenzer/Schlechtriem/Schwenzer/Hachem*, CISG Commentary, Art. 3, Rn. 13.

[64] Für Urteile, in denen auf Art. 3 II CISG hingewiesen wurde, in denen die nicht kaufvertraglichen Pflichten aber nicht überwogen, vgl. Hof Arnhem, 27.4.1999, CISG-online 741 = NIPR 1999, Nr. 245; KG Zug, 25.2.1999, CISG-online = IHR 2001, 45; OLG München, 9.7.1997, CISG-online 281 = BB 1998, 2295; OGer Luzern, 8.1.1997, CISG-online 228 = SJZ 1998, 515 ff.; HGer Zürich, 26.4.1995, CISG-online 248 = TranspR-IHR 1999, 54; CA Grenoble, 26.4.1995, CISGonline 154; OGH, 27.10.1994, CISG-online 133; BezG Laufen, 7.5.1993, CISG-online 136 = SZIER 1995, 277; ein Hinweis auf Art. 3 II CISG findet sich auch in RB Hasselt, 19.9.2001, CISG-online 604, wo jedoch die Frage nur angesprochen worden ist, ohne näher auf sie einzugehen.

[65] Vgl. auch *Enderlein/Maskow/Strohbach*, Art. 3, Anm. 7; *Esslinger*, ALI-ABA (1999), 69, 81; *Lacasse*, Le champ d'application, S. 31; für Fälle der Nichtanwendbarkeit des CISG aufgrund des Überwiegens der kauffremden Pflichten vgl. Hof van Beroep Antwerpen, 3.1.2005, CISG-online 1001; Hof van Beroep Gent, 24.11.2004, CISG-online 966; Hof van Beroep Gent, 29.10.2003, CISG-online 1654; Cass., 6.6.2002, CISG-online 1679.

[66] So auch *Bianca/Bonell/Khoo*, Art. 3, Anm. 3.1.; CISG-AC, Op. 4 (Perales Viscasillas), Comment 3.1; *P. Huber/Mullis/P. Huber*, S. 46; *Kröll u. a./Mistelis/Raymond*, Art. 3, Rn. 15; *Lohmann*, Parteiautonomie, S. 16; MünchKomm/*Westermann*, Art. 3, Rn. 6; MünchKommHGB/*Benicke*, Art. 3, Rn. 10; *Perovic*, Annals Fac. L. Belgrade 2011, 181, 186; *Schlechtriem*, Einheitliches UN-Kaufrecht, S. 17 f.; *ders.*, Internationales UN-Kaufrecht, Rn. 27a; *Schlechtriem/Schwenzer/Schlechtriem*, CISG Commentary, 2. Aufl., Art. 3, Rn. 5; *Schlechtriem/Schwenzer/Schlechtriem/Schwenzer/Hachem*, CISG Commentary, Art. 3, Rn. 12; *Witz/Salger/Lorenz/Lorenz*, Art. 3, Rn. 5; in der Rechtsprechung vgl. LG Mainz, 21.11.1998, CISG-online 563, A. 1.

Verträge über herzustellende Waren oder Dienstleistungen 13 **Art. 3**

Verträge vor, so wird der Arbeits- oder Dienstleistungsvertrag nationalem Recht, der Kaufvertrag dem Einheitskaufrecht unterliegen.[67] Die Frage, ob zwei getrennte Verträge oder ein einheitlicher Vertrag vorliegen, ist nach verbreiteter Auffassung – die sich unter anderem auf den Sekretariatskommentar stützen kann[68] – anhand nationalen Rechts zu beantworten.[69] Dies widerspricht jedoch der in Art. 7 I festgeschriebenen Notwendigkeit, das Übereinkommen autonom auszulegen. Daher muss das **Übereinkommen selbst darüber bestimmen,** ob ein Vertrag als einheitliches Geschäft anzusehen ist.[70] Da letztendlich der (ausdrückliche oder stillschweigende) **Parteiwille** über Einheit oder Trennung entscheiden wird,[71] gehen die erwähnten Positionen jedoch nicht so stark auseinander, wie dies auf den ersten Blick den Anschein hat.[72]

2. Der „überwiegende Teil" der Pflichten des Lieferanten

Liegt ein einheitlicher Vertrag vor, kommt das Übereinkommen ex Abs. 2[73] dann nicht 13 zur Anwendung, wenn die Pflichten des Lieferanten überwiegend arbeits- oder dienstvertraglicher Natur sind.[74] Ob diese negative Anwendungsvoraussetzung[75] gegeben ist, richtet sich – anders als nach Abs. 1[76] – **vor allem** nach der **Relation des Wertes der beiden Leistungsteile**[77] **zum Zeitpunkt des Vertragsschlusses.**[78] „Zu vergleichen ist der isolierte Preis der zu liefernden Gegenstände mit der Vergütung für Arbeit und Dienste, so als

---

[67] Ebenso *Audit*, Vente internationale, S. 26 f.; *Brunner*, Art. 3, Rn. 8; *Herber*, 2. Aufl., Art. 3, Rn. 7; *P. Huber/Mullis/P. Huber*, S. 46; MünchKommHGB/*Benicke*, Art. 3, Rn. 10; *Perovic*, Annals Fac. L. Belgrade 2011, 181, 186; *Piltz*, Internationales Kaufrecht, Rn. 2–35; *Schlechtriem/Schwenzer/Schlechtriem*, CISG Commentary, 2. Aufl., Art. 3, Rn. 7; *Walter*, S. 655 ff.; a. A., d. h., gegen jede Aufspaltung, *Reinhart*, Art. 3, Rn. 4.
[68] Sekretariatskommentar, Art. 3, Nr. 3.
[69] Vgl. etwa *Garro/Zuppi*, Compraventa internacional, S. 77; *Honnold/Flechtner*, Art. 3, Rn. 60.2; *Lacasse*, Le champ d'application, S. 31; *Reimers-Zocher*, S. 177; *Schlechtriem*, Einheitliches UN-Kaufrecht, S. 17.
[70] So auch *Bamberger/Roth/Saenger*, Art. 3, Rn. 1; *Brunner*, Art. 3, Rn. 8; *Czerwenka*, Rechtsanwendungsprobleme, S. 146, Fn. 696; *Ferrari*, Applicabilità ed applicazioni, S. 154 f.; *Ferrari u. a./Saenger*, Internationales Vertragsrecht, Art. 3, Rn. 1; *Herber*, 2. Aufl., Art. 3 Rn. 6; *Herber/Czerwenka*, Art. 3, Rn. 4; *Kahn*, Rev. int. dr. comp. 1981, 951, 956; *Schlechtriem/Schwenzer/Schlechtriem/Schwenzer/Hachem*, CISG Commentary, Art. 3, Rn. 12; *Soergel/Lüderitz/Fenge*, Art. 3, Rn. 3; a. A. *Fogt*, IPRax 2003, 364, 368; *Lohmann*, Parteiautonomie, S. 16.
[71] Vgl. auch *Schlechtriem/Schwenzer/Schlechtriem/Schwenzer/Hachem*, CISG Commentary, Art. 3, Rn. 12.
[72] So auch *P. Huber/Mullis/P. Huber*, S. 46; *Piltz*, Internationales Kaufrecht, Rn. 2–36; *Schlechtriem*, Einheitliches UN-Kaufrecht, S. 17 f.; *ders.*, AJP 1992, 339, 347; *Schlechtriem/Schwenzer/Schlechtriem*, CISG Commentary, 2. Aufl., Art. 3, Rn. 5 a. E.; *Staudinger/Magnus*, Art. 3, Rn. 10.
[73] Abs. 2 hat ein Gegenstück in verschiedenen nationalen Rechten, wie etwa im peruvianischen Recht; vgl. *E. Muñoz*, S. 70.
[74] Unter den Begriff der arbeits- oder dienstvertraglichen Pflichten darf man wohl kaum Patentlizenzen oder die Vermittlung von Know-how subsumieren; so schon *Herber*, Anwendungsbereich, S. 40.
[75] Vgl. in der Rechtsprechung *TeeVee Toons, Inc. & Steve Gottlieb, Inc. v. Gerhard Schubert GmbH*, U. S. Dist. Ct. (S. D. N. Y.), 23.8.2006, CISG-online 1272 (Fehlen des Ausnahmetatbestands als Anwendungsvoraussetzung); vgl. auch HGer Zürich, 17.2.2000, CISG-online 637; Hof Arnhem, 27.4.1999, CISG-online 741 = NIPR 1999, Nr. 245.
[76] A. A. *Schlechtriem*, Internationales UN-Kaufrecht, Rn. 27, wonach „Art. 3 II CISG *ähnlich wie Abs. 1* darauf ab[stellt], ob der *überwiegende Teil* der Leistungen auf die Dienste oder Arbeiten entfällt" (Hervorhebung durch den Autor).
[77] So auch *Achilles*, Art. 3, Rn. 5; *Bamberger/Roth/Saenger*, Art. 3, Rn. 6; *Brunner*, Art. 3, Rn. 7; *Ferrari*, Applicabilità ed applicazioni, S. 147 ff.; *Grieser*, S. 36; *Honnold/Flechtner*, Art. 3, Rn. 60.1; *Honsell/Siehr*, Art. 3, Rn. 5; *P. Huber/Mullis/P. Huber*, S. 46; *Karollus*, S. 24; MünchKommHGB/*Benicke*, Art. 3, Rn. 9; *Perovic*, Annals Fac. L. Belgrade 2011, 181, 187; *Schlechtriem/Schwenzer/Schlechtriem*, CISG Commentary, 2. Aufl., Art. 3, Rn. 7a; *Schmitt*, CR 2001, 145, 150; *Schroeter*, 5 VJ (2001), 74, 77 f.; vgl. in der Rechtsprechung KG Zug, 14.12.2009, CISG-online 2026; OGer Aargau, 3.3.2009, CISG-online 2013; Hof van Beroep Gent, 14.11.2008, CISG-online 1908; BGH, 9.7.2008, CISG-online 1717; OGer Zug, 19.12.2006, CISG-online 1427; OLG Wien, 1.6.2004, CISG-online 954; RB Koophandel Hasselt, 4.2.2004, CISG-online 863; ICC, 9781/2000, CISG-online 1202; KG Bern-Laupen, 29.1.1999, CISG-online 701; OLG München, 3.12.1999, CISG-online 585 = RIW 2000, 712, 713; KG Zug, 15.2.1999, CISG-online 490; LG Mainz, 21.11.1998, CISG-online 563, A. 1.
[78] CISG-AC, Op. 4 *(Perales Viscasillas)*, Comment 3.3; *Martin-Davidson*, 17 Mich. St. J. Int'l L. (2008), 657, 678; *Schlechtriem/Schwenzer/Schlechtriem*, CISG Commentary, 2. Aufl., Art. 3, Rn. 7a a. E.; *Staudinger/Magnus*, Art. 3, Rn. 25.

Art. 3 14, 15   Teil I. Kapitel I. Anwendungsbereich

ob zwei getrennte Verträge abgeschlossen worden wären."[79] Legt man dieses Abgrenzungskriterium zugrunde, kann es nicht überraschen, dass ein deutsches Gericht[80] die Anwendbarkeit des Übereinkommens auf das Erstellen einer in schriftlicher Form abzuliefernden Marktstudie ausgeschlossen hat,[81] überwogen doch unzweifelhaft die Dienstleistungen.

14   Aus der Entstehungsgeschichte ergibt sich aber, dass die Wertrelation nicht das einzige Kriterium sein kann,[82] wurde doch ein englischer Antrag, die Formulierung „major part in value" einzuführen, verworfen.[83] Als weitere Kriterien wurden zu Recht der **Parteiwille**[84] genauso wie das **Parteiinteresse**,[85] unter anderem auch von der Rechtsprechung,[86] vorgeschlagen.[87] Es sei ferner angemerkt, dass ein deutsches Gericht außerdem statuiert hat, dass, „da eine reine wertmäßige Herausdifferenzierung der jeweiligen Vertragsleistungen rechnerisch nicht möglich"[88] sei, auch „die Vertragsgrundlagen und die sonstigen für das Zustandekommen des Vertrages maßgeblichen Umstände bei der Bewertung herangezogen werden" müssen. Ob, wie von einem schweizerischem Gericht statuiert,[89] die Qualifizierung der Arbeitsleistung als charakteristische Leistung ausreicht, um zum Ausschluss der Anwendung des CISG zu führen, ist zu bezweifeln.

15   Während bezüglich der Kriterien, anhand derer die Rolle der kauffremden Pflichten[90] des Lieferanten bestimmt werden muss, keine Einigkeit besteht, ist sich die Lehre einig darüber, dass der (zum Zeitpunkt des Vertragsschlusses)[91] **„überwiegende Teil"** ein Anteil von

---

[79] *Schlechtriem,* Einheitliches UN-Kaufrecht, S. 18; ähnlich auch *Enderlein/Maskow/Strohbach,* Art. 3, Anm. 7.; *Memmo,* Riv. trim. dir. proced. civ. 1983, 180, 192; vgl. in der Rechtsprechung KG Zug, 14.12.2009, CISG-online 2026: „Ob dieser Ausschlussgrund gegeben ist, richtet sich vor allem nach der Relation des Wertes der beiden Leistungsteile"; KG Zug, 25.2.1999, CISG-online 490 = IHR 2001, 45: „entscheidendes Kriterium für die Anwendbarkeit des Wiener Kaufrechts liegt im Verhältnis zwischen der Sachlieferung und der Arbeitsleistung"; vgl. auch OGH, 8.11.2005, CISG-online 1156 = IHR 2006, 87, 90: „Entscheidend ist das Verhältnis kaufvertragsfremder zu kaufvertragstypischen Pflichten im Einzelfall".

[80] OLG Köln, 26.8.1994, CISG-online 132 = RIW 1994, 970.

[81] Zustimmend auch *Brunner,* Art. 3, Rn. 5; *Schlechtriem,* Internationales UN-Kaufrecht, Rn. 27.

[82] So auch *Schlechtriem/Schwenzer/Schlechtriem/Schwenzer/Hachem,* CISG Commentary, Art. 3, Rn. 18 f.; *Staudinger/Magnus,* Art. 3, Rn. 21; ausdrücklich darauf verweisend, dass die Wertrelation nicht das einzige Kriterium ist, ohne jedoch anderen Kriterien ausdrücklich zu erwähnen, vgl. OGer Aargau, 3.3.2009, CISG-online 2013; a. A. *Maley,* 12 Int'l Trade & Bus. L. Rev. (2009), 82, 87.

[83] Vgl. Sekretariatskommentar, O. R., S. 84 und 241 ff.

[84] Vgl. diesbezüglich etwa *Richards,* 69 Iowa L. Rev. (1983), 209, 233; ebenso in der Rechtsprechung KG Zug, 14.12.2009, CISG-online 2026; OLG Dresden, 11.6.2007, CISG-online 1720; zurückhaltender jedoch *Schlechtriem/Schwenzer/Schlechtriem,* CISG Commentary, 2. Aufl., Art. 3, Rn. 7a; *Schlechtriem/Schwenzer/Schlechtriem/Schwenzer/Hachem,* CISG Commentary, Art. 3, Rn. 18.

[85] *Czerwenka,* Rechtsanwendungsprobleme, S. 144; *Kahn,* Rev. int. dr. comp. 1981, 951, 955; *Karollus,* S. 24; *Kröll u. a./Mistelis/Raymond,* Art. 3, Rn. 19; *Schroeter,* 5 VJ (2001), 74, 78.

[86] KG Zug, 14.12.2009, CISG-online 2026: „Weitere Kriterien sind der Parteiwille und das Parteiinteresse"; OLG Karlsruhe, 12.6.2008, CISG-online 1716" das „Interesse des Kunden" als Kriterium heranziehend; OLG Innsbruck, 18.12.2007, CISG-online 1735: auch auf das Parteiinteresse abstellend: OGH, 5.11.2005, CISG-online 1156: „Typengemischte Verträge unterliegen dann nicht dem Anwendungsbereich des UN-Kaufrechtsübereinkommens, wenn der Anteil der kauffremden Vertragspflichten wertmäßig oder nach dem Parteiinteresse deutlich überwiegt"; OLG München, 3.12.1999, CISG-online 585 = RIW 2000, 712, 713: „Das Überwiegen eines Teils der Pflichten ist dabei in erster Linie nach der Relation des Werts der einzelnen Verpflichtungen zu bestimmen. Darüber hinaus kommt es aber auch auf das besondere Interesse des Auftraggebers am jeweiligen Leistungsbereich, also der vertragscharakteristische Leistung, an"; vgl. auch LG Mainz, 21.11.1998, CISG-online 563, A. 1: „Da eine reine wertmäßige Herausdifferenzierung der jeweiligen Vertragsleistungen rechnerisch nicht möglich ist […], müssen die Vertragsgrundlagen und die sonstigen für das Zustandekommen des Vertrages maßgeblichen Umstände bei der Bewertung herangezogen werden".

[87] Vgl. auch MünchKommHGB/*Benicke,* Art. 3, Rn. 9 a. E. ; *Niemann,* Einheitliche Anwendung, S. 97.

[88] LG Mainz, 26.11.1998, CISG-online 563.

[89] KG Bern-Laupen, 29.1.1999, CISG-online 701.

[90] Verschiedenen Urteilen nach gehört die Produktion der Waren nicht zu den kauffremden Pflichten; vgl. OLG Karlsruhe, 12.6.2008, CISG-online 1716; CA Colmar, 26.2.2008, CISG-online 1657; OGH, 14.1.2002, CISG-online 643; CA Paris, 14.6.2001, CISG-online 693; ebenso *Schlechtriem/Schwenzer/Schlechtriem/Schwenzer/Hachem,* CISG Commentary, Art. 3, Rn. 11; vgl. aber OLG Karlsruhe, 12.6.2008, CISG-online 1716, wonach Entwicklung und Hestellung durchaus überwiegen können, und zwar wenn es um die Probemodelle geht; ebenso OLG Köln, OLGR 2005, 380.

[91] *Achilles,* Art. 3, Rn. 8; *Bamberger/Roth/Saenger,* Art. 3, Rn. 6; *Honsell/Siehr,* Art. 3, Rn. 5.

mehr als 50% sein muss.[92] Ob hingegen ein **deutliches Überwiegen** der kauffremden Leistungen zu verlangen ist, wie vielfach – u. a. auch in der Rechtsprechung[93] – behauptet wird,[94] ist fraglich (und im Lichte des Wortlautes nicht zwingend).[95]

3. Rechtsfolgen der Anwendbarkeit des Übereinkommens

Fällt der Liefervertrag mit arbeits- oder dienstvertraglichen Pflichten nicht unter die vom Übereinkommen ex Art. 3 II ausgeschlossenen Verträge, so ist das Übereinkommen im Grunde auf den **gesamten Vertrag** anwendbar.[96] Hinsichtlich der Anwendung der **nicht kaufspezifischen Vorschriften** des CISG auf die kauffremden Pflichten wirft dies keine Probleme auf.[97] Die Vorschriften zum Vertragsabschluss und zur Auslegung der Verträge sind demnach auch auf die kauffremden Elemente anzuwenden, genauso wie „die allgemeinen Leistungsstörungsvorschriften des Übereinkommens, vor allem die Schadensersatzsanktion bei Vertragsverletzung".[98] Die Regelung **spezifisch arbeits- oder dienstvertraglicher Fragen**, die im Übereinkommen keine Regelung finden, müssen mittels Rückgriff auf nationales Recht gelöst werden.[99] Widersprechen sich die Vorschriften des Übereinkommens und die für die kauffremden Elemente geltenden nationalen Regelungen „(wenn z. B. das nationale Recht für Montageverträge eine einseitige ordentliche Kündigung zulässt, die [das CISG] nicht kennt)",[100] geht das Übereinkommen vor. Gerade hierin liegt der Sinn der Ausdehnung des Anwendungsbereiches des Übereinkommens.

4. Einzelfälle

Lieferverträge mit Montage-, Schulungs- oder Wartungsverpflichtung werden in der Regel in den Anwendungsbereich des Übereinkommens fallen,[101] da die Montage, wie nicht nur die Rechtsprechung zum EKG,[102] sondern auch die zum CISG,[103] zeigt, meist nur

---

[92] Vgl. statt aller *Bianca/Bonell/Khoo*, Art. 3, Anm. 2.3.; *Brunner*, Art. 3, Rn. 7; MünchKommHGB/*Benicke*, Art. 3, Rn. 9; *Maley*, 12 Int'l Trade & Bus. L. Rev. (2009), 82, 87; *Rudolph*, Art. 3, Rn. 6; *Sannini*, L'applicazione, S. 103; *Schwenzer/Hachem/Kee*, Rn. 8.45; *Witz/Salger/Lorenz/Lorenz*, Art. 3, Rn. 4; vgl. in der Rechtsprechung KG Zug, 14.12.2009, CISG-online 2026; die im Text vertretene Ansicht falsch verstehend *Ferrari u. a./Saenger*, Internationales Vertragsrecht, Art. 3, Rn. 6.

[93] OLG Innsbruck, 18.12.2007, CISG-online 1735; OGer Zug, 19.12.2006, CISG-online 1427; OGH, 5.11.2005, CISG-online 1156; KG Zug, 25.2.1999, CISG-online 490 = IHR 2001, 45; KG Bern-Laupen, 29.1.1999, CISG-online 701.

[94] So *Honnold/Flechtner*, Art. 3, Rn. 60.1; *Kröll u. a./Mistelis/Raymond*, Art. 3, Rn. 3; *Lookofsky*, Foreign Case Law, S. 214, 224 f.; *Schlechtriem*, Einheitliches UN-Kaufrecht, S. 17; *Schwenzer/Hachem/Schlechtriem/Schwenzer/Hachem*, CISG Commentary, Art. 3, Rn. 20; *Schroeter*, 5 VJ (2001), 74, 77; *Soergel/Lüderitz/Fenge*, Art. 3, Rn. 4; die Frage ansprechend, ohne jedoch Stellung zu nehmen, *Kröll u. a./Mistelis/Raymond*, Art. 3, Rn. 18, die im Text verworfene „standard is not widely followed".

[95] Die im Text vertretene Ansicht völlig falsch verstehend *Schlechtriem/Schwenzer/Schlechtriem*, CISG Commentary, 2. Aufl., Art. 3, Rn. 7b, Fn. 57.

[96] Ebenso *Achilles*, Art. 3, Rn. 6; *Bamberger/Roth/Saenger*, Art. 3, Rn. 7; *Ferrari u. a./Saenger*, Internationales Vertragsrecht, Art. 3, Rn. 7; *Honnold/Flechtner*, Art. 3, Rn. 60.1; *Käerdi*, S. 89.

[97] So auch *Enderlein/Maskow/Strohbach*, Art. 3, Anm. 7.

[98] *Schlechtriem/Schwenzer/Schlechtriem/Schwenzer/Hachem*, CISG Commentary, Art. 3, Rn. 17; *Staudinger/Magnus*, Art. 3, Rn. 29.

[99] A. A. *Staudinger/Magnus*, Art. 3, Rn. 29, der dann, wenn es um Sonderfragen des arbeits- oder dienstvertraglichen Teils geht, für die im CISG Regeln fehlen oder nicht passen, zunächst eine Anpassung der nächstliegenden Regeln des Übereinkommens vorschlägt und nur danach auf das anwendbare nationale Recht zurückgreifen will; ähnlich auch *Achilles*, Art. 3, Rn. 6; *Bamberger/Roth/Saenger*, Art. 3, Rn. 7; *Ferrari u. a./Saenger*, Internationales Vertragsrecht, Art. 3, Rn. 7; MünchKommHGB/*Benicke*, Art. 3, Rn. 8; *Schlechtriem/Schwenzer/Schlechtriem/Schwenzer/Hachem*, CISG Commentary, Art. 3, Rn. 17; *Schmidt-Kessel*, FS Schwenzer, S. 1513, 1525.

[100] *Enderlein/Maskow/Strohbach*, Art. 3, Anm. 7.

[101] Vgl. auch *Schmidt-Kessel*, FS Schwenzer, S. 1513, 1525.

[102] BGH, NJW 1991, 639; OLG Celle, RIW 1985, 571; OLG Stuttgart, NJW 1978, 545.

[103] Vgl. neben dem in der folgenden Fn. zitierten Urteil auch Tribunale di Forlì, 16.2.2009, CISG-online 1780; Hof Beroep Gent, 14.11.2008, CISG-online 1908; OGer Zug, 19.12.2006, CISG-online 1427; ZG Basel, 8.11.2006, CISG-online 1731; Tribunale di Padova, 10.1.2006, CISG-online 1157; OGH, 8.11.2005,

eine (wertmäßig) untergeordnete Rolle spielt.[104] Fälle, in denen die kauffremden Pflichten überwiegen, sind aber nicht von vorneherein auszuschließen.[105]

18 Abs. 2 regelt auch – und ist in erster Linie bestimmt zur Regelung der – **Anlagenlieferverträge**.[106] Da beim echten Anlagenbau kaufvertragliche Elemente aber selten im Vordergrund stehen,[107] wird Abs. 2 bei Anlagenlieferverträgen in der Regel zur Nichtanwendung des CISG führen.[108] Dies entspricht auch der Einschätzung während der Ausarbeitung des Übereinkommens.

19 Bezüglich **anderer gemischter Verträge,** d. h., Verträge, bei denen zwar die kauffremden Pflichten des Lieferanten überwiegen, diese aber nicht arbeits- oder dienstvertraglicher Natur sind, gilt Abs. 2 analog.[109] Positiv ausgedrückt bedeutet dies, dass das Übereinkommen auch für Verträge gilt, „die etwa miet- oder gesellschaftsrechtliche Zusatzpflichten oder Elemente sonstiger Vertragsverhältnisse enthalten, sofern die kauffremden Anteile nicht überwiegen."[110]

5. Beweislast

20 Was die **Beweislast** angeht, so gilt auch hier, so auch der OGH,[111] das bereits zu Abs. 1 Gesagte:[112] Diejenige Partei, die die Nichtanwendbarkeit des Übereinkommens behauptet, muss diese beweisen.[113]

CISG-online 1156; Tribunale d'appello Ticinio, 29.10.2003, CISG-online 912; KG Schaffhausen, 25.2.2002, CISG-online 723; OLG München, 3.12.1999, CISG-online 585, 1.b; ICC, 23.8.1994, CISG-online 129; Gerichtskommission Oberrheintal, 30.6.1995, CISG-online 425 = TranspR-IHR 2000, 11; HGer Zürich, 26.4.1995, CISG-online 248.

[104] *Achilles,* Art. 3, Rn. 6; *Bamberger/Roth/Saenger,* Art. 3, Rn. 8; *Ferrari u. a./Saenger,* Internationales Vertragsrecht, Art. 3, Rn. 8; *Honsell/Siehr,* Art. 3, Rn. 6; *Staudinger/Magnus,* Art. 3, Rn. 26; vgl. in der Rechtsprechung OGer Zug, 19.12.2006, CISG-online 1427 = IHR 2007, 129: „die Klägerin hatte nebst der Lieferpflicht eine Montageverpflichtung. Solche Verträge fallen in der Regel in den Anwendungsbereich des Übereinkommens, da die Montage meist nur eine – wertmässig – untergeordnete Rolle spielt".

[105] Siehe Grieser, S. 153; *Piltz,* Rn. 2–38; eine Einzelfallanalyse vorziehend CISG-AC, Op. 4 *(Perales Viscasillas),* Comment 3.5; vgl. in der Rechtsprechung Foreign Trade Court of Arbitration attached to the Yugoslav Chamber of Commerce, 9.5.2003, CISG Pace (Überwiegen der Montageverpflichtung).

[106] Dies ist oft hervorgehoben worden; vgl. statt aller YB VII (1976), S. 98, Nr. 2; *Schlechtriem/Schwenzer/ Schlechtriem,* CISG Commentary, 2. Aufl., Art. 3, Rn. 8; *Schlechtriem/Schwenzer/Schlechtriem/Hachem,* CISG Commentary, Art. 3, Rn. 21.

[107] *Czerwenka,* Rechtsanwendungsprobleme, S. 145; *Fairlie,* S. 49; vgl. auch KG Zug, 14.12.2009, CISG-online 2026; OGH, 8.11.2005, CISG-online 1156.

[108] *Bamberger/Roth/Saenger,* Art. 3, Rn. 8; *Ferrari u. a./Saenger,* Internationales Vertragsrecht, Art. 3, Rn. 8; Grieser, S. 153 f.; *P. Huber/Mullis/P. Huber,* S. 47; *Kröll u. a./Mistelis/Raymond,* Art. 3, Rn. 16; MünchKomm/ Westermann, Art. 3, Rn. 7; *Piltz,* Internationales Kaufrecht, Rn. 2–38; *Rudolph,* Art. 3, Rn. 7; *Schlechtriem/ Schwenzer/Schlechtriem,* CISG Commentary, 2. Aufl., Art. 3, Rn. 8; *Schlechtriem/Schwenzer/Schwenzer/Hachem,* CISG Commentary, Art. 3, Rn. 21; *Schwenzer/Hachem/Kee,* Rn. 8.47; vgl. in der Rechtsprechung HGer Zürich, 9.7.2002, CISG-online 726: „In Übereinstimmung mit der Lehre ist daher […] davon auszugehen, dass das UN-Kaufrecht auf Anlagelieferungsverträge, welche nicht so sehr ein Austauschverhältnis von Ware gegen Geld, sondern vielmehr ein Geflecht von gegenseitigen Mitwirkungs- und Hilfspflichten darstellen, keine Anwendung finden soll"; vgl. neuerdings auch OGer Aargau, 3.3.2009, CISG-online 2013.

[109] So *Czerwenka,* Rechtsanwendungsprobleme, S. 146; *Honnold/Flechtner,* Art. 3, Rn. 60.4; *Schlechtriem,* Internationales UN-Kaufrecht, Rn. 28; *Schlechtriem/Schwenzer/Schlechtriem,* CISG Commentary, 2. Aufl., Art. 3, Rn. 9; *Schlechtriem/Schwenzer/Schlechtriem/Schwenzer/Hachem,* CISG Commentary, Art. 3, Rn. 22.

[110] Staudinger/Magnus, Art. 3, Rn. 30; i. E. auch *Schlechtriem,* Internationales UN-Kaufrecht, Rn. 28.

[111] OGH, 8.11.2005, CISG-online 1156 = IHR 2006, 87, 90.

[112] Vgl. oben Rn. 11.

[113] Ebenso *Achilles,* Art. 3, Rn. 9; *Bamberger/Roth/Saenger,* Art. 3, Rn. 9 f.; *Baumgärtel/Laumen/Hepting/ Müller,* Art 3, Rn. 3; *Ferrari u. a./Saenger,* Internationales Vertragsrecht, Art. 3, Rn. 10; *Herber/Czerwenka,* Art. 3, Rn. 7; *P. Huber/Mullis/P. Huber,* S. 45; *Jung,* S. 201; *Kröll u. a./Mistelis/Raymond,* Art. 3, Rn. 26; MünchKomm/Westermann, Art. 3, Rn. 8; MünchKommHGB/Benicke, Art. 3, Rn. 12; *Piltz,* Internationales Kaufrecht, Rn. 2–37; *Schlechtriem/Schwenzer/Schlechtriem,* CISG Commentary, 2. Aufl., Art. 3, Rn. 10; *Schlechtriem/Schwenzer/Schlechtriem/Schwenzer/Hachem,* CISG Commentary, Art. 3, Rn. 23; *Staudinger/Magnus,* Art. 3, Rn. 32; ebenso in der Rechtsprechung OLG Oldenburg, 20.12.2007, CISG-online 1644; a. A. *Czerwenka,* Rechtsanwendungsprobleme, S. 144; ihr folgend auch *Reimers-Zocher,* S. 177.

Art. 4 [Sachlicher Geltungsbereich]

Dieses Übereinkommen regelt ausschließlich den Abschluß des Kaufvertrages und die aus ihm erwachsenden Rechte und Pflichten des Verkäufers und des Käufers. Soweit in diesem Übereinkommen nicht ausdrücklich etwas anderes bestimmt ist, betrifft es insbesondere nicht
a) die Gültigkeit des Vertrages oder einzelner Vertragsbestimmungen oder die Gültigkeit von Gebräuchen,*
b) die Wirkungen, die der Vertrag auf das Eigentum an der verkauften Ware haben kann.

Art. 4

This Convention governs only the formation of the contract of sale and the rights and obligations of the seller and the buyer arising from such a contract. In particular, except as otherwise expressly provided in this Convention, it is not concerned with:
(a) the validity of the contract or of any of its provisions or of any usage;
(b) the effect which the contract may have on the property in the goods sold.

Art. 4

La présente Convention régit exclusivement la formation du contrat de vente et les droits et obligations qu'un tel contrat fait naître entre le vendeur et l'acheteur. En particulier, sauf disposition contraire expresse de la présente Convention, celle-ci ne concerne pas:
a) la validité du contrat ni celle d'aucune de ses clauses non plus que celle des usages;
b) les effets que le contrat peut avoir sur la propriété des marchandises vendues.

Übersicht

	Rn.
I. Vorgeschichte	1
II. Allgemeines	3
III. Vom Übereinkommen ausdrücklich erfasste Rechtsfragen (S. 1)	8
1. Allgemeines	8
2. Vertragsabschluss	9
3. Rechte und Pflichten der Kaufvertragsparteien	10
IV. Ausdrücklich ausgeschlossene Rechtsfragen (S. 2)	12
1. Allgemeines	12
2. Gültigkeit	15
3. Gültigkeit und AGB	20
4. Gültigkeit und Willensmängel	22
5. Gültigkeit von Gebräuchen	26
6. Eigentumsfragen	29
V. Weitere vom Regelungsbereich ausgeschlossene Rechtsfragen	32
VI. Vom Übereinkommen erfasste Rechtsfragen	42
VII. Beweislast	48

Vorläufer und **Entwürfe:** Artt. 4, 5 II, 8 EKG; Genfer E 1976 Art. 7; Wiener E 1977 Art. 6; New Yorker E 1978 Art. 4.

I. Vorgeschichte

Die Vorschrift entspricht im wesentlichen Art. 8 EKG, der ebenfalls die Gültigkeit des **1** Vertrages (sowie von Gebräuchen) und die Eigentumsfragen ausdrücklich dem Regelungsbereich des Einheitskaufrechts entzog.[1] In redaktioneller Hinsicht weicht die Vorschrift

---
* Schweiz: Handelsbräuchen, Österreich: Bräuchen.
[1] Vgl. hierzu *Dölle/Herber*, Art. 8 EKG, Rn. 1 ff.

Art. 4 2, 3   Teil I. Kapitel I. Anwendungsbereich

jedoch in zwei Punkten vom Haager Vorläufer ab: Zum einen sind wegen der Aufnahme der Bestimmungen zum Vertragsabschluss in das CISG, die vormals im EAG geregelt waren, die sich auf diesen beziehenden Fragen nicht mehr als ausgenommen aufgeführt;[2] zum anderen sind nicht mehr nur die Pflichten der Vertragsparteien als Regelungsgegenstand genannt, sondern auch die (diesen jeweils entsprechenden) Rechte derselben. Sachlich hat sich damit jedoch nichts geändert.[3]

2 Während der Vorarbeiten hat es an Versuchen, die Vorschrift zu streichen, nicht gefehlt;[4] diese waren jedoch nicht erfolgreich, da man sich letztendlich der Nützlichkeit der in der Vorschrift beinhalteten Klarstellung bewusst geworden ist.[5] Es wurde auch ein Versuch gemacht, die Liste der ausdrücklich vom Regelungsbereich ausgeschlossen Fragen zu erweitern: So sah der Genfer Entwurf zum Beispiel vor, dass auch Fragen des geistigen Eigentums ausgeschlossen seien.[6] Auf Betreiben vor allem der deutschen Delegation[7] entschied sich UNCITRAL aber dafür, auch Fragen der Haftung für gewerbliche Schutzrechte oder andere auf geistigem Eigentum beruhende Rechte dem Übereinkommen zu unterstellen,[8] weshalb der jetzige Art. 42 eingeführt wurde.[9]

II. Allgemeines

3 Das Übereinkommen **regelt nicht alle Rechtsfragen,** die im Zusammenhang mit einem Kaufvertrag aufkommen können,[10] genauso wenig wie andere Einheitsvertragsrechts-

---

[2] Siehe Art. 8 EKG: „Dieses Gesetz regelt ausschließlich die aus dem Kaufvertrag entstehenden Pflichten des Verkäufers und des Käufers. Insbesondere befasst es sich, soweit es nicht ausdrücklich etwas anderes bestimmt, weder mit dem Abschluss des Vertrages noch mit dessen Wirkungen in Bezug auf das Eigentum an der verkauften Sache noch mit der Gültigkeit des Vertrages oder der in diesem enthaltenen Bestimmungen noch mit der Gültigkeit von Gebräuchen".

[3] Ebenso *Schlechtriem/Schwenzer/Schlechtriem,* CISG Commentarty, 2. Aufl., Art. 4, Rn. 1; *Schlechtriem/Schwenzer/Schwenzer/Hachem,* CISG Commentary, Art. 4, Rn. 1; *Staudinger/Magnus,* Art. 4, Rn. 6.

[4] Vgl. YB III (1972), S. 74, Nr. 37; YB VI (1975), S. 52, Nr. 32 f.; S. 92, Nr. 49 f.

[5] Siehe *Bianca/Bonell/Khoo,* Art. 4, Anm. 1.2.; *Hoffmann,* Koordination, S. 295.

[6] Art. 7 II Genfer E 1976 lautete: „This Convention does not govern the rights and obligations which might arise between the seller and the buyer because of the existence in any person of rights or claims which relate to industrial or intellectual property or the like." YB VII (1976), S. 90.

[7] Vgl. YB VIII (1977), S. 147, Nr. 5.

[8] YB VIII (1977), S. 31, Nr. 78.

[9] *Schlechtriem/Schwenzer/Schlechtriem,* CISG Commentary, 2. Aufl., Art. 4, Rn. 2.

[10] *Andreason,* B. Y. U. L. Rev. (1999), 351, 376; *Bamberger/Roth/Saenger,* Art. 4, Rn. 1; *G. Bell,* 9 Singapore YB. Int'l L. (2005), 55, 67; *Brunner,* Art. 4, Rn. 1; *Cetiner,* S. 19; *Cuniberti,* 39 Vand. J. Transnat'l L. (2006), 1511, 1544; *De Ly,* 25 J. L. & Com. (2005), 1; *Ferrari,* IHR 2006, 1, 2 und 11; *ders.,* Scope of Application, S. 96, 96; *Ferrari u. a./Saenger,* Internationales Vertragsrecht, Art. 4, Rn. 1; *Frignani/Torsello,* Il contratto internazionale, S. 444; *Gianuzzi,* 28 L. & Pol'y Int'l Bus. (1997), 991, 1016; *Gsothl,* östZfRvgl 1998, 1; *Hayward,* 14 VJ (2010), 193, 219; *Kröll,* 25 J. L. & Com. (2005), 39, 39; *Kröll u. a./Djordjevic,* Art. 4, Rn. 1; *Markel,* 21 Pace Int'l L. Rev. (2009), 163, 167; *Niemann,* Einheitliche Anwendung, S. 30; *Ragno,* Convenzione di Vienna e Diritto europeo, S. 444; *Sannini,* L'applicazione, S. 121 f.; *Schlechtriem/Schwenzer/Schlechtriem,* CISG Commentary, 2. Aufl., Art. 4, Rn. 3; *Schlechtriem/Schwenzer/Schwenzer/Hachem,* CISG Commentary, Preamble, Rn. 2 und Art. 4, Rn. 2; *Schwenzer/Hachem/Kee,* Rn. 3.19; *Schroeter,* 6 VJ (2002), 257, 263; *ders.,* 5 VJ (2001), 74; Spagnolo, 21 Temp. Int'l & Comp. L. J. (2007), 261, 305; *Tescaro,* Contr. Imp. E. 2007, 319; *Torsello,* The CISG's Impact, S. 214 ff.; *Trompenaars,* S. 18 f.; *Vida,* IPRax 2002, 146, 147; *Walt,* 35 UCC L. J. (2002), 43; *ders.,* 25 Int'l Rev. L. & Econ. (2005), 342, 343; *Winsor,* 14 VJ (2010), 83, 88; *C. Witz,* Int. Bus. L. J. 2001, 253, 261; so auch ein Teil der Rechtsprechung: AG Sursee, 12.9.2008, CISG-online 1728; Tribunale di Modena, 9.12.2005, CISG-online 1398 = Riv. dir. int. priv. proc. 2007, 387, 390; KG Nidwalden, 23.5.2005, CISG-online 1086 = IHR 2005, 253, 254; KG Schaffhausen, 20.10.2003, CISG-online 957 = IHR 2005, 206, 207; OGH, 22.10.2001, CISG-online 614 = IHR 2002, 24, 27; a. A. BGer, 15.9.2000, CISG-online 770: „La CVIM est d'application exhaustive; elle régit l'ensemble du contrat, c'est-à-dire la formation de celui-ci, ainsi que les droits et obligations des parties, de même que les conséquences d'une inexécution. En principe, l'application supplétive du droit national est exclue"; ebenso BGer, 19.2.2004, CISG-online 839, 3.2.2.; Cour de Justice de Genève, 15.11.2002, CISG-online 853, 2b); BezG Laufen, 7.5.1993, CISG-online 136; a. A. in der Lehre *Fitzgerald,* 27 J. L. & Com. (2008), 1, 2 („comprehensive code"); ebenso *Perea,* 20 Pace Int'l L. Rev. (2008), 191, 191, der sich aber dann selbst widerspricht, 192; *Shariff/de Carteret,* 9 Asper Rev. Int'l Bus. & Trade L. (2009) 21, 55.

konventionen alle Rechtsfragen beantworten,[11] die sich im Zusammenhang mit den von diesen geregelten Verträgen ergeben können.[12] Nach eigenem Wortlaut beschränkt sich das Übereinkommen darauf, das Zustandekommen des Vertrages[13] und die Rechte und Pflichten der Kaufvertragsparteien[14] zu regeln. Diese Vorschrift hat also – genauso wie Art. 5 – den Zweck, den **Regelungsbereich** des Übereinkommens abzustecken, nicht den Anwendungsbereich:[15] Der Regelungs- oder Geltungsbereich[16] ist vom Anwendungsbereich zu unterscheiden.[17] Während letzterer sich mit der Frage beschäftigt, **ob** das Übereinkommen anwendbar ist, beantwortet ersterer die Frage, „in welcher Tiefe Verträge vom CISG erfasst werden",[18] d. h., **inwieweit** es Anwendung findet.[19]

Dieser (anscheinend abschließenden)[20] positiven[21] Auszählung der geregelten Gegenstände in S. 1 wird in S. 2 eine (beispielhafte)[22] Aufzählung nicht geregelter Fragen gegenübergestellt. Demnach regelt das Übereinkommen zweifelsfrei weder die Anforderungen an die **Wirksamkeit des Vertrages,** was auch in der Rechtsprechung hervorgehoben worden ist,[23] die etwa wegen mangelnder Geschäftsfähigkeit eines Vertragspartners, wegen Verstoßes gegen ein gesetzliches Verbot oder gegen die guten Sitten[24] oder auch im Hinblick auf eine Anfechtung wegen Willensmängel[25] zweifelhaft sein kann, noch die **Gültigkeit von Gebräuchen.**[26] Das Übereinkommen befasst sich auch nicht mit Fragen der Übertragung des **Eigentums** an den verkauften Waren.[27] Der Ausschluss der erwähnten Rechtsfragen vom Regelungsbereich des Übereinkommens ist zum einen darauf zurückzuführen, dass die Ausarbeitung einheitlicher Regeln den Abschluss des Übereinkommens unangemessen verzögert hätte,[28] zum anderen darauf, dass eine Einigung auf Grund nationaler Verschiedenheiten kaum erreichbar, im Hinblick auf den Übereinkommenszweck aber auch nicht erforderlich erschien.[29] 4

Die Abgrenzung zwischen den vom Übereinkommen geregelten und nicht geregelten Rechtsfragen führt bezüglich der ausdrücklich aufgezählten Aspekte zu keinen großen 5

---

[11] Für einen Hinweis auf die Unmöglichkeit von Einheitsprivatrechtskonventionen, alle Fragenkomplexe zu regeln, vgl. auch *Frigge,* S. 4; *Mather,* 20 J. L. & Com. (2001), 155, 156; *Schluchter,* S. 21.
[12] So auch *De Nova,* Riv. trim. dir. proced. civ. 1990, 749, 752; *Melin,* S. 399; *Reinhart,* Art. 4, Rn. 1.
[13] Vgl. unten Rn. 9.
[14] Vgl. unten Rn. 10 ff.
[15] Vgl. *Staudinger/Magnus,* Art. 4, Rn. 1, der hervorhebt, dass Art. 4 „einen wichtigen Teil des sachlichen Anwendungsbereichs" regelt, damit also den „sachlichen Anwendungsbereich" dem Regelungsbereich gleichsetzt; vgl. neuerdings auch *Kröll u. a./Djordjevic,* Art. 4, Rn. 2.
[16] Diesen Ausdruck verwendet etwa der OGH, Forum International 1997, 93.
[17] Vgl. hierzu auch *Schluchter,* S. 25 (Unterscheidung zwischen Regelungsbereich und generellem Anwendungsbereich); *Schlechtriem,* AJP 1992, 337, 340 f. (Unterscheidung zwischen Anwendungsbereich und Regelungsbereich).
[18] *Kröll u. a./Djordjevic,* Art. 4, Rn. 2; *Schmid,* Lückenfüllung und Normenkonkurrenz, S. 29.
[19] Siehe auch Vor Artt. 1–6 Rn. 3.
[20] *Wasmer,* S. 15, Fn. 17, geht doch in der Tat davon aus, dass die Aufzählung eine abschließende sei.
[21] *P. Huber,* IHR 2006, 228, 231; MünchKommHGB/*Benicke,* Art. 4, Rn. 1.
[22] Vgl. statt aller *Flesch,* S. 145; MünchKommHGB/*Benicke,* Art. 4, Rn. 1; *Schlechtriem/Schwenzer/Schwenzer/Hachem,* CISG Commentary, Art. 4, Rn. 3; *Staudinger/Magnus,* Art. 4, Rn. 4.
[23] Vgl. etwa BGer, 22.12.2000, CISG-online 628; Civ. 1, 1.4.1995, CISG-online 138 = D. 1995, 289, nit Anm. *C. Witz.*
[24] Vgl. OLG Stuttgart, 30.5.2011, CISG-online 2225: „Die Inhaltskontrolle von Kaufverträgen unter dem Gesichtspunkt der Vereinbarkeit mit den guten Sitten ist im CISG nicht vereinheitlicht".
[25] *Piltz,* NJW 2000, 553, 556; vgl. in der Rechtsprechung RB Almelo, 28.1.1998, nicht veröffentlicht; HGer St. Gallen, 24.8.1995, CISG-online 247 = SZIER 2000, 116.
[26] Vgl. detaillierter hierzu unten Rn. 26 ff.
[27] Siehe Rn. 29 ff.
[28] So für die Gültigkeit YB IX (1978), S. 65 f., Nr. 48 ff.; YB VIII (1977), S. 93, Nr. 27; für die Fragen der Gültigkeit war ein eigenständiges Übereinkommen erarbeitet worden, vgl. UNIDROIT-Draft of a Law for the Unification of Certain Rules relating to the Validity of Contracts of International Sale of Goods, 1972, YB VIII (1977), S. 104 ff.; vgl. auch *Ferrari,* Scope of Application, S. 96, 99; *Kröll u. a./Djordjevic,* Art. 4, Rn. 5.
[29] So für die Eigentumsübertragung Sekretariatskommentar, Art. 4, Nr. 4. An dieser Stelle muss erwähnt werden, dass während zur Zeit der Ausarbeitung des CISG die hierauf bezüglichen Unterschiede zwischen den nationalen Rechtsordnungen noch unüberbrückbar erschienen, diese heute durchaus als überwindbar angesehen werden; vgl. hierzu etwa *Drobnig,* Transfer of Property, S. 495–542; *Ferrari,* ZEuP 1993, 52–78.

Schwierigkeiten.[30] Schwieriger ist die Einordnung nicht ausdrücklich erwähnter Rechtsfragen,[31] zu denen etwa die Regelung der Beweislast, der positiven Forderungsverletzung, der culpa in contrahendo, der Zinsfrage, etc., gehören, die im Folgenden genauer untersucht werden. Auf welcher Grundlage die Unterscheidung der geregelten von den nicht geregelten Rechtsfragen zu erfolgen hat, ist umstritten. Sicher ist jedoch, dass nicht auf nationale Kriterien abgestellt werden kann, würde dies doch dem Vereinheitlichungsgedanken des CISG widersprechen.[32]

6 Die vom Übereinkommen **nicht geregelten Fragen** müssen entweder anhand der Anwendung **nationalen Rechts** beantwortet werden,[33] das auf der Grundlage der Kollisionsnormen des Forumsstaates zu bestimmen ist,[34] oder anhand anderen **Einheitsrechts**.[35] Diesbezüglich sei beispielhaft erwähnt, dass die Abtretung internationaler Forderungen, wie Lehre[36] und Rechtsprechung[37] hervorgehoben haben, nicht durch das Übereinkommen geregelt ist. Dies schließt jedoch die Anwendbarkeit des UNIDROIT Übereinkommens über Internationales Factoring, dessen Anwendbarkeit vor dem Rückgriff auf das Internationale Privatrecht untersucht werden muss, nicht aus.[38]

7 Das Gesagte gilt (als „ultima ratio")[39] auch für vom Übereinkommen geregelte, aber in diesem nicht ausdrücklich entschiedene Fragen, sofern diese nicht mittels Rückgriff auf die

---

[30] So schon *Herber*, 2. Aufl., Art. 4, Rn. 5.

[31] So nunmehr auch *Kröll u. a./Djordjevic*, Art. 4, Rn. 4; *Niemann*, Einheitliche Anwendung, S. 60; *Schlechtriem/Schwenzer/Schwenzer/Hachem*, CISG Commentary, Art. 4, Rn. 4.

[32] Vgl. *Schlechtriem/Schwenzer/Schwenzer/Hachem*, CISG Commentary, Art. 4, Rn. 5: „The relevant test has to be whether the provisions of the CISG aim at regulating a certain matter or not." Vgl. auch CISG-AC, Op. 6 (*Gotanda*), Comment 2.5.

[33] Vgl. *Schlechtriem/Schwenzer/Schlechtriem*, CISG Commentary, 2. Aufl., Art. 4, Rn. 5; siehe aber BGer, 15.9.2000, CISG-online 770: „En principe, l'application supplétive du droit national est exclue".

[34] Vgl. diesbezüglich etwa OGH, 13.4.2000, CISG-online 576 = IHR 2001, 117, 118; AG Duisburg, 13.4.2000, CISG-online 659 = IHR 2001, 114, 115.

[35] Die meisten Autoren weisen auch die Möglichkeit hin, dass anderes Einheitsrecht auf die vom Übereinkommen ausgenommenen Rechtsfragen Anwendung finden kann; vgl. etwa *Reinhart*, Art. 4, Rn. 3; *Rudolph*, Art. 4, Rn. 3; *Schmid*, Lückenfüllung und Normenkonkurrenz, S. 23; *Soergel/Lüderitz/Fenge*, Art. 4, Rn. 2; siehe aber *Honsell/Siehr*, Art. 4, Rn. 1, der auf das „anwendbare Recht außerhalb des WKR" abstellt, und auch Einheitsrecht darunter fallen lässt; vgl. neuerdings auch *Schlechtriem/Schwenzer/Schwenzer/Hachem*, CISG Commentary, Art. 4, Rn. 6; *Teichert*, Lückenfüllung, S. 5 f.; *Wasmer*, S. 15.

[36] Vgl. *Achilles*, Art. 4, Rn. 9; *Bamberger/Roth/Saenger*, Art. 4, Rn. 21; *Brunner*, Art. 4, Rn. 34; *Ferrari*, Applicabilità ed applicazioni, S. 242; *ders.*, Scope of Application, S. 96, 106; *ders.*, Forum International 1997, 89, 92; *Ferrari u. a./Saenger*, Internationales Vertragsrecht, Art. 4, Rn. 22; *Janssen*, The Application of the CISG in Dutch Courts, S. 129, 137; *Karollus*, S. 45; *Kröll u. a./Djordjevic*, Art. 4, Rn. 46; *Lurger*, IHR 2005, 177, 180; *Martin-Davidson*, 17 Mich. St. J. Int'l L. (2008), 657, 691; *Mather*, 20 J. L. & Com. (2001), 155, 160; MünchKomm/*Westermann*, Art. 4, Rn. 15; MünchKommHGB/*Benicke*, Art. 4, Rn. 15; *Piltz*, Internationales Kaufrecht, Rn. 2–163; *ders.*, NJW 2000, 553, 556; *Posch/Terlitza*, IHR 2001, 47, 49; *Rosch*, D. 2000, Jur. 437, 438; *Schlechtriem*, Internationales UN-Kaufrecht, Rn. 41; *Schlechtriem/Schwenzer/Schlechtriem*, CISG Commentary, 2. Aufl., Art. 4, Rn. 23; *Schlechtriem/Schwenzer/Schlechtriem/Schwenzer/Hachem*, CISG Commentary, Art. 4, Rn. 22; *Schwenzer/Schmidt*, 13 VJ (2009), 109, 115 f.; *Soergel/Lüderitz/Fenge*, Art. 4, Rn. 9; *Staudinger/Magnus*, Art. 4, Rn. 57; *Stoll*, Internationalprivatrechtliche Fragen, S. 506; *Teichert*, Lückenfüllung, S. 19; *C. Witz*, Rev. dr. aff. int. 2001, 253, 265 f.

[37] Vgl. HGer Aargau, 26.11.2008, CISG-online 1739; District Court Trnava, 17.9.2008, CISG-online 1991; OLG Hamburg, 25.1.2008, CISG-online 1681; Regional Court Kosice, 22.5.2007, CISG-online 1989; Tribunal of International Commercial Arbitration at the Russian Federation Chamber of Commerce and Industry, 27.5.2005, CISG-online 1456; Tribunale di Padova, 25.2.2004, CISG-online 819; Supreme Court of Poland, 19.12.2003, CISG-online 1222; Trib. com. Nivelles, 19.9.1995, CISG-online 366; OLG Hamm, 9.6.1995, CISG-online 146 = IPRax 1996, 197; BezG Arbon, 9.12.1994, CISG-online 376; ebenso zum EKG OLG Hamm, 20.6.1983, RIW 1983, 952.

[38] Vgl. CA Grenoble, 13.9.1995, CISG-online 157 (Anwendung des Factoring Übereinkommens auf die vom Übereinkommen nicht geregelte Forderungsabtretung).

[39] Vgl. hierzu *Ferrari*, 24 Ga J. Int'l & Comp. L. (1994), 183, 228; *ders.*, Uniform L. Rev. 1997, 451, 470; *Herber*, 2. Aufl., Art. 4, Rn. 6; *Pavic/Djordjevic*, 28 J. L. & Com. (2009), 1, 28 f.; *Ragno*, Convenzione di Vienna e Diritto europeo, S. 124; *Schlechtriem/Schwenzer/Schlechtriem*, CISG Commentary, 2. Aufl., Art. 4, Rn. 6; *Schlechtriem/Schwenzer/Schwenzer/Hachem*, CISG Commentary, Art. 4, Rn. 6; *Stoll*, Internationalprivatrechtliche Fragen, S. 498; *Sundermann*, Probleme der autonomen Auslegung, S. 21, Fn. 21; vgl. in der Rechtsprechung ICC, 8611/HV/JK, CISG-online 236.

allgemeinen, dem Übereinkommen zugrundeliegenden Grundsätze entschieden werden können.

III. Vom Übereinkommen ausdrücklich erfasste Rechtsfragen (S. 1)

1. Allgemeines

Gemäß S. 1 erfasst das Übereinkommen „nur" („only", „exclusivement") den Vertragsabschluss sowie die Rechte und Pflichten der Parteien; die **Aufzählung** der geregelten Rechtsfragen scheint demnach abschließend zu sein.[40] Dass sie aber **nicht abschließend** ist,[41] ergibt sich unschwer aus dem Übereinkommen selbst, regelt dieses doch ausdrücklich auch andere Fragen.[42] Diesbezüglich sei etwa auf die Fragen der Vertragsauslegung hingewiesen, die in Art. 8 eine Regelung finden und weder dem Bereich des (autonom zu qualifizierenden) Vertragsabschlusses[43] noch dem der Rechte und Pflichten der Parteien angehören. Auch die Vertragsaufhebung beziehungsweise -änderung, die in Art. 29 geregelt ist, fällt aus den erwähnten Bereichen heraus.[44] Aus dem Gesagten folgt, dass der Ausdruck „nur" im Sinne von „zweifelsfrei" zu verstehen ist.[45]

2. Vertragsabschluss

Das Übereinkommen regelt, gemäß Art. 4 S. 1, „ausschließlich"[46] den Vertragsabschluss und die Rechte und Pflichten der Parteien.[47] In Bezug auf diese – von der Rechtsprechung zum Teil unkritisch wiederholte[48] – Aussage muss man sich zunächst fragen, was mit „Abschluss des Kaufvertrages" gemeint ist. Diesbezüglich ist zu Recht sowohl in der Lehre,[49]

---

[40] Es fehlt leider nicht an Entscheidungen, die ausdrücklich statuieren, dass das CISG ausschließlich Fragen des Vertragsabschlusses und die Rechte und Pflichten der Parteien regelt; vgl. etwa KG Wallis, 27.5.2005, CISG-online 1137; Civ. 1, 5.1.1999, Rev. crit. dr. int. priv. 1999, 519; CA Paris, 22.4.1992, CISG-online 222.
[41] A. A. aber BGer, 15.9.2000, CISG-online 770: „La CVIM est d'application exhaustive; elle régit l'ensemble du contrat"; ebenso BezG Laufen, 7.5.1993, CISG-online 136 (das CISG ist eine „einheitliche, abschließende und autonome Kaufrechtsordnung").
[42] *Bamberger/Roth/Saenger*, Art. 4, Rn. 1; *Ferrari u. a./Saenger*, Internationales Vertragsrecht, Art. 4, Rn. 1; *Kröll u. a./Djordjevic*, Art. 4, Rn. 6; MünchKomm/*Westermann*, Art. 4, Rn. 1; *Schlechtriem/Schwenzer/Schwenzer/Hachem*, CISG Commentary, Art. 4, Rn. 2 und 7; *Soergel/Lüderitz/Fenge*, Art. 4, Rn. 2; *Staudinger/Magnus*, Art. 4, Rn. 13.
[43] Vgl. hierzu etwa *Schluchter*, S. 30 und 40.
[44] Vgl. *Schlechtriem/Schwenzer/Schlechtriem*, CISG Commentary, 2. Aufl., Art. 4, Rn. 3; *Schluchter*, S. 27; *Teichert*, Lückenfüllung, S. 17.
[45] *Ferrari*, Scope of Application, S. 96, 97; *Kröll u. a./Djordjevic*, Art. 4, Rn. 6; *Schlechtriem/Schwenzer/Schlechtriem* CISG Commentary, 2. Aufl., Art. 4, Rn. 3; *Schlechtriem/Schwenzer/Schwenzer/Hachem*, CISG Commentary, Art. 4, Rn. 2; *Staudinger/Magnus*, Art. 4, Rn. 13.
[46] Vgl. oben Rn. 8.
[47] Verschiedene Entscheidungen haben auf Art. 4 I verwiesen, ohne jedoch näher auf diese Vorschrift einzugehen; vgl. etwa *Golden Valley Grape Juice and Wine, LLC v. Centris Corporation*, U. S. Dist. Ct. (E. D. Cal.), 21.1.2010, CISG-online 2089; KG Wallis, 28.1.2009, CISG-online 2025; District Court Nitra, 29.5.2008, CISG-online 1766; *Zhejiang Shaoxing Yongli Printing and Dyeing Co., Ltd v. Microflock Textile Group Corporation*, U. S. Dist. Ct. (S. D. Fl.), 19.5.2008, CISG-online 1771; CA Paris, 10.9.2003, CISG-online 788.
[48] Vgl. *MSS, Inc. v. Maser Corporation*, U. S. Dist. Ct. (D. Md.), 18.7.2011, CISG-online 2222; Hof van Cassatie, 19.6.2009, CISG-online 1963; CA Paris, 22.4.1992, CISG-online 222.
[49] *Achilles*, Art. 3, Rn. 2; *Bamberger/Roth/Saenger*, Art. 4, Rn. 2; *Brunner*, Art. 4, Rn. 1; *Bydlinski*, Allgemeines Vertragsrecht, S. 57, 60; *Ferrari*, RabelsZ 71 (2007), 52, 60; *ders.*, Formazione, S. 10; *Ferrari u. a./Saenger*, Internationales Vertragsrecht, Art. 4, Rn. 2; *Herber/Czerwenka*, Vor Art. 14, Rn. 6; *P. Huber*, IHR 2006, 228, 231; *ders.*, ZEuP 1994, 585, 593 und 601; *P. Huber/Mullis/P. Huber*, S. 21f; MünchKomm/*Gruber*, Vor Art. 14, Rn. 1; MünchKommHGB/*Benicke*, Art. 4, Rn. 5; *Piltz*, Internationales Kaufrecht, Rn. 3-2; *Karollus*, S. 55; *Piltz*, IHR 2004, 133; *Schlechtriem*, Internationales UN-Kaufrecht, Rn. 33; *ders.*, Voraufl., Vor Art. 14–24, Rn. 1; *Schlechtriem/Schwenzer/Schlechtriem*, CISG Commentary, 2. Aufl., Art. 4, Rn. 3 und 7; *Schlechtriem/Schwenzer/Schwenzer/Hachem*, CISG Commentary, Art. 4, Rn. 8; *Schlechtriem/Schwenzer/Schroeter*, CISG Commentary, Intro to Artt. 14–24, Rn. 24; *Stoffel*, Formation du contrat, S. 55, 56; *Staudinger/Magnus*, Vorbem. zu Art. 14 ff., Rn. 2; *Teichert*, Lückenfüllung, S. 15; *Wasmer*, S. 15; *Witz/Salger/Lorenz/Witz*, Vor Artt. 14–24, Rn. 6 und Art. 4, Rn. 8.

als auch in der Rechtsprechung[50] darauf hingewiesen worden, dass damit der **„äußere Konsens"** gemeint ist, d. h., die „Mechanik, nach der zwischen zwei oder mehr Parteien eine bindende, auf dem Parteiwillen beruhende Vereinbarung zustande kommt."[51] Ob hingegen diese Vereinbarung **irrtumsfrei** zustande gekommen ist, regelt sich hingegen nicht nach dem Übereinkommen, sondern nach dem anwendbaren Recht,[52] zumindest in der Regel. Nationale Regeln zur Irrtumsanfechtung werden aber von denen des Übereinkommens verdrängt, wenn das Übereinkommen abschließende, das Sachproblem regelnde Vorschriften vorsieht,[53] wie dies etwa bezüglich der Fragen des **Irrtums über Sacheigenschaften**[54] oder die **Leistungsfähigkeit** der Gegenpartei[55] der Fall ist.[56]

3. Rechte und Pflichten der Kaufvertragsparteien

10 Aus der ausdrücklichen Bezugnahme auf die „Rechte und Pflichten des Verkäufers und des Käufers" ergibt sich unschwer, dass sich die Vertragswirkungen nicht per se auf Dritte erstrecken können.[57]

11 Die Rechte und Pflichten der Vertragsparteien im Sinne des Übereinkommens sind vor allem die **primären gegenseitigen Ansprüche**[58] sowie die zusätzlich vereinbarten Pflichten,[59] die sich aus wirksamen Kaufverträgen ergeben und die Rechte, die bei Vertragsverletzungen entstehen. Diesbezüglich sind vor allem Artt. 30 und 53 relevant, aus denen sich die Pflichten des Verkäufers (Lieferpflicht und Pflicht zur Übertragung des Eigentums) und die des Käufers ergeben (Annahme- und Preiszahlungspflicht), und die Vorschriften, die die verschiedenen Rechtsbehelfe vorsehen. Ob sich andere Pflichten ableiten lassen, etwa aus allgemeinen Grundsätzen, ist umstritten, aber letzendlich zu bejahen.[60] Beispielhaft seien nur die sich aus Art. 7 II ergebenden Informationspflichten erwähnt.[61]

---

[50] Vgl. OLG München, 11.7.2011, Aktenzeichen 34 Sch 15/10, unveröff.; AG Sursee, 12.9.2008, CISG-online 1728; CA Liège, 28.4.2003, CISG-online 944; OGH, 22.10.2001, CISG-online 613; OGH, 6.2.1996, CISG-online 224; ZGer Basel-Stadt, 21.12.1992, CISG-online 55.

[51] *Staudinger/Magnus*, Art. 4, Rn. 13; see also *Ferrari*, Scope of Application, S. 96, 98; *Kröll*, 25 J. L. & Com. (2005), 39, 42; *Kröll u. a./Djordjevic*, Art. 4, Rn. 7; *Schlechtriem/Schwenzer/Schwenzer/Hachem*, CISG Commentary, Art. 4, Rn. 8.

[52] So ausdrücklich die neuere Rechtsprechung; vgl. HGer St. Gallen, 24.8.1995, CISG-online 247; Cámara Nacional de Apelaciones en lo Commercial, 14.10.1993, CISG-online 87 = El Derecho 2.4.1994.

[53] So ausdrücklich LG Aachen, 14.5.1993, CISG-online 86 = RIW 1993, 760 f. Vgl. hierzu monographisch *Flesch*, Mängelhaftung und Beschaffenheitsirrtum, die auch zu der im Text vertretenen Ansicht gelangt, genauso wie *Schluchter*, S. 98 ff.; vgl. neuerdings auch *P. Huber/Mullis/P. Huber*, S. 22 f.; *Kröll u. a./Djordjevic*, Art. 4, Rn. 7; *Piltz*, IHR 2002, 2, 5.

[54] *Honnold/Flechtner*, Art. 35, 41, Rn. 240, 266.1; *Kröll u. a./Djordjevic*, Art. 4, Rn. 21; *Loewe*, S. 29; *Schlechtriem*, Internationales UN-Kaufrecht, Rn. 36.

[55] Vgl. *Enderlein/Maskow/Strohbach*, Art. 4, Anm. 3.1.; *Kröll u. a./Djordjevic*, Art. 4, Rn. 21.

[56] A. A. *Ebenroth*, östJBl 1986, 681, 688; *Karollus*, S. 42 (mit ausdrücklichen Bezug auf das österreichische Recht, in dem von der Konkurrenz zwischen Irrtums- und Leistungsstörungsrecht ausgegangen wird); ebenso *Lessiak*, östJBl 1989, 487 ff.; *Reinhart*, Art. 4, Rn. 23.

[57] *Achilles*, Art. 1, Rn. 4 a. E. und Art. 4, Rn. 3; *Bamberger/Roth/Saenger*, Art. 4, Rn. 2; *Ferrari*, Scope of Application, S. 96, 98; *Ferrari u. a./Saenger*, Internationales Vertragsrecht, Art. 4, Rn. 2; *Hoffmann*, Koordination, S. 270; *Kröll*, 25 J. L. & Com. (2005), 39, 47; *Kröll u. a./Djordjevic*, Art. 4, Rn. 8; *Kröll u. a./Ribeiro*, Art. 5, Rn. 10; *Mather*, 20 J. L. & Com. (2001), 155, 159 f.; MünchKommHGB/*Benicke*, Art. 4, Rn. 3; *Schlechtriem/Schwenzer/Schlechtriem*, CISG Commentary, 2. Aufl., Art. 4, Rn. 3; *Schwenzer/M. Schmidt*, 13 VJ (2009), 109, 116; vgl. auch *Cedar Petrochemicals, Inc. v. Dongbu Hannong Chemical Co., Ltd.*, U. S. Dist. Ct. (S. D. N. Y.), 19.7.2007, CISG-online 1509 = 2007 WL 2059 239 (S. D. N. Y.); CA Rouen, 19.12.2006, CISG-online 1933; *American Mint LLC v. GOSoftware, Inc.*, U. S. Dist. Ct. (M. D. Pa.), 16.8.2005, CISG-online 1104 = 2005 WL 2021248; Hof van Beroep Gent, 24.6.2004, CISG-online 987; *Usinor Industeel v. Leeco Steel Products, Inc.*, U. S. Dist. Ct. (N. D. Ill.), 28.3.2002, CISG-online 696 = 209 F. Supp. 2d 880; BGH, 12.2.1998, CISG-online 343 = NJW 1998, 3205.

[58] MünchKomm/*Westermann*, Art. 4, Rn. 4, der von „typischen", aus dem Kaufvertrag erwachsenden Rechte und Pflichten der Parteien spricht; vgl. auch *Schlechtriem/Schwenzer/Schlechtriem/Schwenzer/Hachem*, CISG Commentary, Art. 4, Rn. 14.

[59] So *Staudinger/Magnus*, Art. 4, Rn. 16.

[60] Ebenso *Schlechtriem/Schwenzer/Schlechtriem/Schwenzer/Hachem*, CISG Commentary, Art. 4, Rn. 15; *Staudinger/Magnus*, Art. 4, Rn. 17.

[61] Vgl. Art. 7, Rn. 54; vgl. monographisch zu den Informationspflichten *Benedick*, Die Informationspflichten im UN-Kaufrecht (CISG) und Ihre Verletzung, Bern: Stämpli (2008).

IV. Ausdrücklich ausgeschlossene Rechtsfragen (S. 2)

1. Allgemeines

Wie schon oben incidenter erwähnt,[62] handelt es sich bei der Aufzählung der nicht **12** geregelten Rechtsfragen in S. 2 um eine lediglich **beispielhafte Aufzählung**,[63] d. h., „S. 2 charakterisiert nur einen Ausschnitt des weiten Bereichs, welcher vom Regelungsbereich des CISG (sprich Art. 4 S. 1 CISG) sowieso nicht erfasst wird."[64] Dies geht unzweideutig aus dem Begriff „insbesondere" hervor.[65] Welche Rechtsfragen neben den ausdrücklich vom Regelungsbereich ausgenommenen nicht in den Regelungsbereich fallen, wird andernorts erörtert.[66]

Die Tatsache, dass eine Rechtsfrage in Art. 4 S. 2 ausdrücklich erwähnt wird, führt nicht **13** notwendigerweise dazu, dass deren Beantwortung dem anwendbaren Recht überlassen ist.[67] Vielmehr muss zunächst untersucht werden, ob das spezifische Problem nicht doch im CISG geregelt ist.[68] Diesbezüglich sieht das Übereinkommen vor, dass die in Art. 4 S. 2 erwähnten Rechtsfragen dem Regelungsbereich nur insoweit dem Übereinkommen entzogen sind, als „in diesem Übereinkommen nicht **ausdrücklich etwas anderes bestimmt** ist." Dies ist jedoch nicht wörtlich zu verstehen.[69] An keiner Stelle bestimmt das Übereinkommen ausdrücklich, dass es entgegen dem Wortlaut von Art. 4 S. 2 Fragen der Gültigkeit des Vertrages (oder von Gebräuchen) oder der Eigentumsübertragung doch regelt.[70] Daraus muss gefolgert werden, dass das CISG immer dann „ausdrücklich" etwas anderes bestimmt, wenn es einen Sachverhalt, der die Gültigkeit des Vertrages (oder von Gebräuchen) oder die Eigentumsübertragung betrifft, die grundsätzlich vom Regelungsbereich ausgenommen sind,[71] abschließend regelt. Eine solche „ausdrückliche Bestimmung" sieht das Übereinkommen hinsichtlich der **Formfrage** vor,[72] die durchaus als Gültigkeitsfrage angesehen werden kann und daher eigentlich vom Regelungsbereich ausgeschlossen

---

[62] Vgl. oben Rn. 4.
[63] Siehe auch *Achilles*, Art. 4, Rn. 7; *Bamberger/Roth/Saenger*, Art. 4, Rn. 1; *Ferrari*, Vendita internazionale, S. 101, Fn. 1; *ders.*, Int'l Bus. L.J. 1998, 835, 836; *P. Huber*, IHR 2006, 228, 231; *Kröll u. a./Djordjevic*, Art. 4, Rn. 12; MünchKommHGB/*Benicke*, Art. 4, Rn. 1; *Niemann*, Einheitliche Anwendung, S. 59; *Rudolph*, Art. 4, Rn. 11; Botschaft des Schweizerischen Bundesrats, S. 764; *Schlechtriem/Schwenzer/Schlechtriem*, CISG Commentary, 2. Aufl., Art. 4, Rn. 4; *Soergel/Lüderitz/Fenge*, Art. 4, Rn. 2; *Wasmer*, S. 16.
[64] *Schluchter*, S. 26.
[65] *Flesch*, S. 145; *Kröll u. a./Djordjevic*, Art. 4, Rn. 12; *T.M. Müller*, Beweislast, S. 27; *Staudinger/Magnus*, Art. 4, Rn. 4; *C. Witz*, Rev. dr. aff. int. 2001, 253, 261.
[66] Vgl. unten Rn. 32 ff.
[67] Ebenso *Ferrari*, Int'l Bus. L.J. 1998, 835, 836; *Kröll u. a./Djordjevic*, Art. 4, Rn. 12; *Schlechtriem/Schwenzer/Hachem*, CISG Commentary, Art. 4, Rn. 29; *Staudinger/Magnus*, Art. 4, Rn. 18.
[68] Vgl. auch *Leyens*, Rev. CISG (2003–2004), 3, 15; *Schroeter*, VJ (2002), 257, 264; *Staudinger/Magnus*, Art. 4, Rn. 18.
[69] Hierzu auch *Schlechtriem*, Einheitliches UN-Kaufrecht, S. 19; *Schlechtriem/Schwenzer/Schwenzer/Hachem*, CISG Commentary, Art. 4, Rn. 29; *Tescaro*, Contr. Imp. E. 2007, 319, 323 f.
[70] So auch *Enderlein/Maskow/Strohbach*, Art. 4, Anm. 3.1. („Ganz offensichtlich kann dabei nicht verlangt werden, dass eine ausdrückliche, wenn auch anonyme Zurückweisung bestimmter nationaler Konzepte erfolgt").
[71] Für Urteile, die etwa die Gültigkeit des Vertrages als eine vom Regelungsbereich ausgenommene Materie qualifizieren, ohne darauf einzugehen, dass das CISG diese nicht doch „ausdrücklich" regelt, vgl. *Geneva Pharmaceuticals Tech. Corp. v. Barr Labs. Inc.*, U.S. Dist. Ct. (S.D.N.Y.), 10.5.2002, CISG-online 653 = 2002 U.S. Dist. LEXIS 8411; *Asante Technologies, Inc. v. PMC-Sierra, Inc.*, U.S. Dist. Ct. (N.D. Cal.), 27.7.2001, CISG-online 616 = 2001 WL 1182 401; OGH, 7.9.2000, CISG-online 642; Hof van Beroep Antwerpen, 18.6.1996, CISG-online 758.
[72] Siehe *Achilles*, Art. 4, Rn. 3; *Bamberger/Roth/Saenger*, Art. 4, Rn. 4; *Brunner*, Art. 4, Rn. 1; *Diez-Picazo/Rojo Ajuria*, Art. 4, S. 82; *Ferrari*, IHR 2004, 1, 2; *ders.*, Vendita internazionale, S. 97; *ders.*, RabelsZ 71 (2007), 52, 66; *Ferrari u. a./Saenger*, Internationales Vertragsrecht, Art. 4, Rn. 4; *Karollus*, S. 41; MünchKomm/*Westermann*, Art. 4, Rn. 6; MünchKommHGB/*Benicke*, Art. 4, Rn. 10; *Schlechtriem*, 36 Vict. U. Well. L. Rev. (2005), 781, 788; *Schlechtriem/Schwenzer/Schlechtriem*, CISG Commentary, 2. Aufl., Art. 4, Rn. 8; *Soergel/Lüderitz/Fenge*, Art. 4, Rn. 4; *Tescaro*, Contr. Imp. E. 2007, 319, 323; *Witz/Salger/Lorenz/Lorenz*, Art. 4, Rn. 10.

Art. 4 14–16 Teil I. Kapitel I. Anwendungsbereich

sein sollte.[73] Nach Art. 11 sind internationale Kaufverträge formfrei, zumindest wenn die Parteien ihre Niederlassung in keinem Vertragsstaat haben, der von dem Vorbehalt des Art. 96 Gebrauch gemacht hat.[74] Hat eine Partei ihre Niederlassung in einem solchen Vorbehaltsstaat, dann haben Gerichte des Vorbehaltsstaates (genauso wie Gerichte eines anderen Vertragsstaates)[75] nach ihrem Internationalen Privatrecht zu beurteilen, welche nationalen Formvorschriften anwendbar sind.[76] Ist das anzuwendende Recht das eines Vertragsstaates ohne Vorbehalt, ist das Übereinkommen – letztendlich also der Grundsatz der Formfreiheit – anzuwenden;[77] ist das anzuwendende Recht hingegen das eines Vorbehaltsstaates, so werden die Gerichte dessen Formvorschriften zu beachten haben.[78] Der Umstand, dass die Formfrage im CISG geregelt, führt etwa dazu, dass ein dem CISG unterliegender Vertrag der als formäquivalente Gültigkeitsvoraussetzung ausgestalteten **„consideration"** nicht bedarf, um gültig zu sein.[79]

14 Das Gesagte bezieht sich jedoch lediglich auf kaufvertragliche Abreden;[80] mit dem Kaufvertrag verbundene **Kartellabreden** sind, genauso wie **Gerichtsstands- und Schiedsgerichtsklauseln,** in Bezug auf die einzuhaltenden Formerfordernisse nationalem Recht unterstellt.[81]

2. Gültigkeit

15 Wie erwähnt, regelt das Übereinkommen den für das Zustandekommen eines Vertrages nötigen **äußeren Konsens.**[82] Die anderen die Gültigkeit des Vertrages berührenden Fragen sind **in der Regel** nach dem anwendbaren nationalen Recht zu beantworten.[83]

16 Wann eine Frage eine Gültigkeitsfrage ist, ist umstritten.[84] Verschiedentlich wurde die Auffassung vertreten, der Begriff der „Gültigkeit" müsse dem anwendbaren Recht ent-

---

[73] So ausdrücklich Tribunale di Padova, 31.3.2004, CISG-online 823; vgl. auch *Schlechtriem/Schwenzer/Schwenzer/Hachem,* CISG Commentary, Art. 4, Rn. 29.
[74] Vgl. auch *Enderlein/Maskow/Strohbach,* Art. 4, Anm. 5.1.
[75] Ebenso *Czerwenka,* Rechtsanwendungsprobleme, S. 166.
[76] Vgl. hierzu *Ferrari,* IHR 2004, 1, 5 f.
[77] Vgl. MünchKommHGB/*Ferrari,* Art. 11, Rn. 11.
[78] Vgl. auch Vor Artt. 1–6, Rn. 23.
[79] So etwa *Audit,* S. 74; Bianca/Bonell/*Date-Bah,* Art. 29 Anm. 2.1.; *Enderlein/Maskow/Strohbach,* Art. 29, Anm. 1.1.; *Ferrari,* Vendita internazionale, S. 222; ders., Writing Requirements: Article 11–13, in: Ferrari/Flechtner/Brand (Hrsg.), The Draft UNCITRAL Digest and Beyond: Cases, Analyses and Unresolved Issues in the U.N. Sales Convention, München, 2004, S. 206, 211; *Ferrari u. a./Saenger,* Int. VertragsR, Art. 11, Rn. 4; *U. Huber,* RabelsZ 43 (1979), 413, 435; *P. Huber/Mullis/P. Huber,* S. 38; *Jametti Greiner,* Der Vertragsabschluß, in: Hoyer/Posch (Hrsg.), Das Einheitliche Wiener Kaufrecht, Wien, 1992, S. 43, 46; *Kröll u. a. Perales Viscasillas,* Art. 4, Rn. 4 und 8; *Lando,* FS Schwenzer, S. 1001, 1006; MüKommBGB/*Westermann,* Rn. 2; *Piltz,* Internationales Kaufrecht, Rn. 3–132; *Schlechtriem,* Einheitliches UN-Kaufrecht, S. 52; *Schlechtriem/Schwenzer/Schlechtriem/Schmidt-Kessel,* Rn. 12; *Schlechtriem/Schwenzer/Schlechtriem/Schmidt-Kessel,* Rn. 12; *Staudinger/Magnus,* Rn. 13; *Wey,* Rn. 411.
[80] *Herber,* 2. Aufl., Art. 4, Rn. 8, Fn. 11a.
[81] *Herber/Czerwenka,* Art. 11, Rn. 5; *Neumayer/Ming,* Art. 11, Anm. 1.; *Schlechtriem/Schmidt-Kessel,* Art. 11, Rn. 7; a. A. *Piltz,* Internationales Kaufrecht, Rn. 3–130; *Schluchter,* S. 89 ff.
[82] So in der Rechtsprechung ausdrücklich AG Sursee, 12.9.2008, CISG-online 1728; OGH, 22.10.2001, CISG-online 613 = IHR 2002, 24; OGH, 6.2.1996, CISG-online 224; ZGer Basel-Stadt, 21.12.1992, CISG-online 55.
[83] Vgl. *MSS, Inc. v. Maser Corporation,* U. S. Dist. Ct. (D. Md.), 18.7.2011, CISG-online 2222; HGer Aargau, 10.3.2010, CISG-online 2176; KG Wallis, 28.1.2009, CISG-online 2025; RB Arnhem, 14.11.2007, unveröff.; *Barbara Berry, S. a. de C. V. v. Ken M. Spooner Farms, Inc.,* U. S. Dist. Ct. (W. D. Wash.), 13.4.2006, CISG-online 1354; CIETAC, 1.6.2005, CISG-online 1909; Tribunal of International Commercial Arbitration at the Russian Federation Chamber of Commerce and Industry, 3.2.2004, CISG-online 1180; CIETAC, 3.12.2003, CISG-online 1469; CA Liège, 28.4.2003, CISG-online 944; *Geneva Pharmaceuticals Tech. Corp. v. Barr Labs. Inc.,* U. S. Dist. Ct. (S. D. N. Y.), 10.5.2002, CISG-online 653; BGH, 31.10.2001, CISG-online 617; BGer, 22.12.2000, CISG-online 628; zum Ausschluss der Fragen der Gültigkeit vom Geltungsbereich des CISG; vgl. auch *Geneva Pharmaceuticals Tech. Corp. v. Barr Labs. Inc.,* U. S. Dist. Ct. (S. D. N. Y.), 10.5.2002, CISG-online 653 = 2002 U. S. Dist. LEXIS 8411 = 201 F. Supp. 2d 236.
[84] Unstreitig ist jedoch, dass irrelevant ist, ob die Ungültigkeit ipso iure eintritt oder auf Grund rechtsgeschäftlicher Gestaltung; so ausdrücklich *Schlechtriem,* Internationales UN-Kaufrecht, Rn. 35.

Sachlicher Geltungsbereich 17 **Art. 4**

nommen werden.[85] Dies hätte aber zur Folge, dass die angestrebte Vereinheitlichung aufgrund der Unterschiedlichkeit der nationalen Definitionen[86] gefährdet werden würde,[87] weshalb die herrschende Lehre zu Recht den **Begriff autonom interpretiert**.[88] In zwei neueren US-amerikanischen Urteilen ist als Gültigkeitsfrage definiert worden „any issue by which the domestic law would render the contract void, voidable, or unenforceable".[89]

Als die Gültigkeit des Vertrages betreffende Fragen, die nicht im Übereinkommen 17 geregelt werden, sind die **Rechts-** und **Geschäftsfähigkeit** und die Folgen des Fehlens derselben einzustufen.[90] Die Rechtsfähigkeit juristischer Personen richtet sich entweder nach dem Gründungsstatut, wie etwa in der Schweiz, den Niederlanden, den USA, oder nach dem am effektiven Verwaltungssitz geltenden Recht, wie etwa in Deutschland und Österreich.[91] Was die Rechts- und Geschäftsfähigkeit natürlicher Personen angeht, so unterstehen sie entweder dem Heimatrecht, wie etwa in der BR Deutschland[92] und Italien,[93] oder dem Wohnsitzrecht, wie etwa in der Schweiz[94] und den USA.[95]

---

[85] Für eine nationale Auslegung sprechen sich aus: *Bianca/Bonell/Tallon*, Art. 79, Anm. 2.4.3.; *Bydlinski*, Allgemeines Vertragsrecht, S. 85 f.; *Grigera Naón*, S. 101, 123; *Heuzé*, Anm. 94.; *Lessiak*, östJBl 1989, 487, 492 f.; *Longobardi*, 53 Fordham L. Rev. (1985), 863, 874; *Neumayer/Ming*, Art. 4, Anm. 2., 6. f.; *Reinhart*, Art. 4, Rn. 5; *Ziegel*, Vienna Convention, S. 43.
[86] Vgl. *Ferrari*, Scope of Application, S. 96, 100.
[87] *Sannini*, L'applicazione, S. 126 f.
[88] So auch *Bianca/Bonell/Khoo*, Art. 4, Anm. 3.3.5.; *Bridge*, Draft Digest, S. 235, 243; *Brunner*, Art. 4, Rn. 5; *Diéz-Picazo/Rojo Ajura*, Art. 4, S. 77; *Enderlein/Maskow/Strohbach*, Art. 4, Anm. 3.1.; *Ferrari*, RabelsZ 71 (2007), 52, 63 f.; *ders.*, Scope of Application, S. 94, 100; *Gruber*, Methoden, S. 86 und 285; *Heiz*, 20 Vand. J. Transnat'l L. (1987), 639, 660 f.; *Herber/Czerwenka*, Art. 4, Rn. 13; *Honnold/Flechtner*, Art. 4, Rn. 65, Art. 29, Rn. 204.2 und Rn. 234; *P. Huber*, IHR 2006, 228, 231; *ders.*, ZEuP 1995, 585, 594 ff.; *Leyens*, Rev. CISG (2003–2004), 3, 26 ff.; *Kröll*, 25 J. & Com. (2005), 39, 40; *Kröll u. a./Djordjevic*, Art. 4, Rn. 14; *MünchKomm/Westermann*, Art. 4, Rn. 2 a. E.; *Piltz*, FS Schwenzer, S. 1387, 1393; *ders.*, Rn. 2–147 f.; *ders.*, IHR 2002, 2, 5; *Schlechtriem/Schwenzer/Schlechtriem*, CISG Commentary, 2. Aufl., Art. 4, Rn. 7; *Schlechtriem/Schwenzer/Schwenzer/Hachem*, CISG Commentary, Art. 4, Rn. 31; *Schwenzer/Hachem*, 57 Am. J. Comp. L. (2009), 457, 472; *Schluchter*, S. 45; *Tescaro*, Contr. Imp. E. 2007, 319, 321; *Winship*, 8 Nw. J. Int'l L. & Bus. (1988), 623, 637; a. A. *Lessiak*, östJBl (1989), 487, 492 f.; *Longobardi*, 53 Fordham L. Rev. (1985), 863, 867 f.
[89] *Barbara Berry, S. A. de C. V. v. Ken M. Spooner Farms, Inc.*, U. S. Dist. Ct. (W. D. Wash.), 13.4.2006, CISG-online 1354 = 2006 WL 1 009 299; *Geneva Pharmaceuticals Tech. Corp. v. Barr Labs. Inc.*, U. S. Dist. Ct. (S. D. N. Y.), 10.5.2002, CISG-online 653 = 2002 U. S. Dist. LEXIS 8411 = 201 F. Supp. 2d 236; vgl. auch KG Wallis, 27.5.2005, CISG-online 1137; diese Definition findet sich bereits bei *Hartnell*, 18 Yale J. Int'l L. (1993), 1, 45; krit. zu dieser Definition jedoch *Schlechtriem/Schwenzer/Schwenzer/Hachem*, CISG Commentary, Art. 4, Rn. 31, Fn. 115 a. E.
[90] Ebenso *Achilles*, Art. 4, Rn. 3; *Audit*, Vente internationale, S. 31; *Bamberger/Roth/Saenger*, Art. 4, Rn. 4 und 25; *Bonell*, 56 Am. J. Comp. L. (2008), 1, 3; *Brunner*, Art. 4, Rn. 6; *Bucher*, Neuerungen, S. 45 f.; *Czerwenka*, Rechtsanwendungsprobleme, S. 165; *Fairlie*, S. 50; *Ferrari*, Vendita internazionale, S. 97; *Garro/Zuppi*, Compraventa internacional, S. 82; *Ferrari u. a./Saenger*, Internationales Vertragsrecht, Art. 4, Rn. 26; *Honnold/Flechtner*, Art. 4, Rn. 66; *Honsell/Siehr*, Art. 4, Rn. 7; *P. Huber*, IHR 2006, 228, 231; *P. Huber/Mullis/P. Huber*, S. 22; *Kabik*, 9 Int'l Tax Bus. Law. (1992), 408, 413; *Karollus*, S. 41; *Kröll u. a./Djordjevic*, Art. 4, Rn. 17; *Lurger*, IHR 2005, 177, 180; *Martin-Davidson*, 17 Mich. St. J. Int'l L. (2008), 657, 681; *Mather*, 20 J. L. & Com. (2001), 155, 162; *MünchKomm/Westermann*, Art. 4, Rn. 3; *MünchKommHGB/Benicke*, Art. 4, Rn. 5; *Sannini*, L'applicazione, S. 133; *Schlechtriem*, Einheitliches UN-Kaufrecht, S. 18; *ders.*, Internationales Kaufrecht, Rn. 34 und 41; *ders.*, 36 Vict. U. Well. L. Rev. (2005), 781, 788; *Schlechtriem/Schwenzer/Schlechtriem*, CISG Commentary, 2. Aufl., Art. 4, Rn. 11; *Schlechtriem/Schwenzer/Schwenzer/Hachem*, CISG Commentary, Art. 4, Rn. 32; *Soergel/Lüderitz/Fenge*, Art. 4, Rn. 8; *Teichert*, Lückenfüllung, S. 18; *Wasmer*, S. 17; *Witz/Salger/Lorenz/Lorenz*, Art. 4, Rn. 8; vgl. in der Rechtsprechung HG Aargau, 26.11.2008, CIS-online 1739; KG Wallis, 27.4.2007, CISG-online 1721; KG Wallis, 27.5.2005, CISG-online 1137; Tribunal of International Commercial Arbitration at the Russian Federation Chamber of Commerce and Industry, 9.6.2004, CISG-online 1239; CIETAC, 15.7.2002, CISG-online 1553; OGH, 22.10.2001, CISG-online 613.
[91] So ausdrücklich *Honsell/Siehr*, Art. 4, Rn 4.
[92] Vgl. Art. 7 I 1 EGBGB.
[93] Siehe *Annibale*, S. 134 und 140 f.
[94] Vgl. *Schnyder*, S. 46 (in Bezug auf die Handlungsfähigkeit; die Rechtsfähigkeit untersteht kraft Art. 34 I des IPR-Gesetzes vom 18.12.1987 schweizerischem Recht).
[95] *Honsell/Siehr*, Art. 4, Rn. 4.

Art. 4 18–20   Teil I. Kapitel I. Anwendungsbereich

18   Auch die Frage, welche Wirkungen ein nationales **gesetzliches Verbot** oder ein **Verstoß gegen die guten Sitten** entfaltet, ist als Gültigkeitsfrage einzustufen[96] und, da das Übereinkommen nicht „ausdrücklich" etwas anderes bestimmt, nationalem Recht überlassen.[97] Dies bedeutet etwa, sollte deutsches Recht anwendbar sein, dass § 134 BGB und § 138 BGB uneingeschränkt zur Anwendung kommen.[98] Gleiches gilt für ausländische, dem § 138 BGB entsprechende Vorschriften, wie etwa Art. 1418 des italienischen Cc.

19   Auch die Verletzung **wirtschaftslenkender Vorschriften**,[99] etwa des Devisenrechts,[100] sowie von **Verbraucherschutzgesetzen**,[101] wird, sofern sie Nichtigkeit zur Folge hat, als Gültigkeitsfrage angesehen, die im Übereinkommen nicht „ausdrücklich" geregelt ist.[102] „Allerdings ist in solchen Fällen zu prüfen, ob solche nationalen Vorschriften überhaupt Anwendung auf grenzüberschreitende Warenkaufverträge beanspruchen."[103]

3. Gültigkeit und AGB

20   Auch die Frage, **inwieweit** Vorschriften hinsichtlich allgemeiner Geschäftsbedingungen zu beachten sind, wird von Art. 4 lit. a) erfasst.[104] Diesbezüglich gilt, dass sich die Inhaltskontrolle von Klauseln nach dem kollisionsrechtlich anwendbaren Recht richtet,[105] wie etwa nach §§ 308, 309 BGB,[106] was nicht nur in der Lehre,[107] sondern auch in der Rechtsprechung hervorgehoben worden ist.[108] Ob hingegen die AGB Bestandteil des Vertrages geworden sind, bemisst sich nach dem CISG.[109] Umstritten ist, welcher **Maßstab** bei der

---

[96] *Herber*, 2. Aufl., Art. 4 Rn. 9; *P. Huber/Mullis/P. Huber*, S. 22; *Karollus*, S. 41; *Kabik*, 9 Int'l Tax & Bus. Law. (1992), 408, 413; *Schlechtriem*, Internationales UN-Kaufrecht, Rn. 34; *Schlechtriem/Schwenzer/Schwenzer/Hachem*, CISG Commentary, Art. 4, Rn. 39; *Soergel/Lüderitz/Fenge*, Art. 4, Rn. 5; Botschaft des Schweizerischen Bundesrats, S. 764; *Herber*, 2. Aufl., Art. 4, Rn. 15.
[97] Vgl. auch *Achilles*, Art. 3, Rn. 4; *Bamberger/Roth/Saenger*, Art. 4, Rn. 24; *Mather*, 20 J. L. & Com. (2001), 155, 162; MünchKomm/*Westermann*, Art. 4, Rn. 8; *Schlechtriem/Schwenzer/Schwenzer/Hachem*, CISG Commentary, Art. 4, Rn. 39; *Teichert*, Lückenfüllung, S. 18.
[98] Vgl. *Herber/Czerwenka*, Art. 4, Rn. 10 ff.; *Schluchter*, S. 231 (in Bezug lediglich auf § 138 BGB; die Anwendbarkeit des § 134 BGB sei zwar nicht ausgeschlossen, jedoch nur in modifizierter Form möglich).
[99] So auch *Enderlein/Maskow/Strohbach*, Art. 4, Anm. 5.1.; *P. Huber*, IHR 2006, 228, 231; MünchKomm/*Westermann*, Art. 4, Rn. 8; MünchKommHGB/*Benicke*, Art. 4, Rn. 6; *Piltz*, Internationales Kaufrecht, Rn. 2–152.
[100] *Achilles*, Art. 4, Rn. 4; *Rudolph*, Art. 4, Rn. 10; *Schlechtriem/Schwenzer/Schlechtriem*, CISG Commentary, 2. Aufl., Art. 4, Rn. 9; *Staudinger/Magnus*, Art. 4, Rn. 22.
[101] Vgl. etwa *Schlechtriem*, Internationales UN-Kaufrecht, Rn. 34; vgl. hierzu aber auch die Ausführungen zu Art. 2, Rn. 24 ff.
[102] *Herber*, 2. Aufl., Art. 4, Rn. 9.
[103] *Schlechtriem*, Internationales UN-Kaufrecht, Rn. 34.
[104] *Staudinger/Magnus*, Art. 4, Rn. 24.
[105] Vgl. aber *Stoll*, Internationalprivatrechtliche Fragen, S. 512, der für die Maßgeblichkeit des Rechts der zu schützenden Partei eintritt; kritisch hierzu *Staudinger/Magnus*, Art. 4, Rn. 5.
[106] Vgl. *Schlechtriem*, Internationales UN-Kaufrecht, Rn. 34.
[107] So auch *Bamberger/Roth/Saenger*, Art. 4, Rn. 22; *Ferrari*, Scope of Application, S, 96, 101; *Honsell/Siehr*, Art. 4, Rn. 5; *P. Huber*, 13 VJ (2009), 123, 131; *P. Huber/Mullis/P. Huber*, S. 30; *Kröll u. a./Djordjevic*, Art. 4, Rn. 25; *Lurger*, IHR 2001, 91, 93; *Magnus*, Incorporation of Standard Contract Terms, S. 303, 306; MünchKommHGB/*Benicke*, Art. 4, Rn. 5; *Schlechtriem/Schwenzer/Schlechtriem/Schwenzer/Hachem*, CISG Commentary, Art. 4, Rn. 12; *Schluchter*, S. 192; zum EKG, vgl. *von Westphalen*, AGB und Einheitliches Kaufgesetz, S. 57 ff. und 65 ff.
Für *Koch*, FS Bergsten, S. 597, 606, handelt es sich bei der Frage, ob bestimmte Klauseln überraschend sind, nicht um eine Frage der Inhaltskontrolle, weshalb ein Rückgriff auf nationales Recht auch diesbezüglich zu verneinen sei.
[108] Vgl. OLG Jena, 10.11.2010, CISG-online 2216; LG Landshut, 12.6.2008, CISG-online 1703; LG Neubrandenburg, 3.8.2005, CISG-online 1190; OLG Düsseldorf, 21.4.2004, CISG-online 915; OGH, 7.9.2000, CISG-online 642 = IHR 2001, 42 ff.; RB Zutphen, 29.5.1997, CISG-online 546 = NIPR 1998, Nr. 110; AG Nordhorn, 14.6.1994, CISG-online 259; vgl. zum EKG OLG Hamm, IPRax 1983, 231 f.
[109] Vgl. statt aller *Brunner*, Art. 4, Rn. 16; *Ferrari u. a./Mankowski*, Vor Art. 14, Rn. 21; *Honsell/Dornis*, Vor Art. 14, Rn. 6; *Koch*, FS Bergsten, S. 597, 598 f.; *Kröll u. a./Ferrari*, pre Artt. 14–24, Rn. 5; *Magnus*, FS Kritzer, S. 303, 305 ff.; MünchKomm/*Westermann*, Art. 4, Rn. 5; MüchKommHGB/*Ferrari*, vor Art. 14, Rn. 5; *Schlechtriem*, FS Kritzer, S. 416, 418 f.; *Schlechtriem/Schwenzer/Schlechtriem/Schwenzer/Hachem*, CISG Commentary, Art. 4, Rn. 12; *Schlechtriem/Schwenzer/Schroeter*, CISG Commentary, Intro to Artt. 14–24,

Inhaltskontrolle anzulegen ist. Ein Teil der Lehre vertritt die Auffassung, Prüfungsmaßstab sei das unvereinheitlichte, nationale Recht. Die wohl herrschende Lehre[110] sowie die Rechtsprechung[111] gehen jedoch zu Recht davon aus, dass „bei der inhaltlichen Kontrolle von AGB-Klauseln, [...] den Wertungen Rechnung zu tragen [ist], die dem UN-Kaufrecht zugrunde liegen und in dessen Bestimmungen ihren Niederschlag gefunden haben."[112] Soweit das BGB anwendbar ist, bedeutet dies, dass **Kontrollmaßstab** im Sinne des § 307 BGB das **Übereinkommen**,[113] nicht das BGB, ist.[114]

An dieser Stelle muss jedoch erwähnt werden, dass nicht nationales Recht die Frage regelt, ob die allgemeinen Geschäftsbedingungen **Vertragsbestandteil** geworden sind, sondern das Übereinkommen.[115] Dies ist auch von der neueren Rechtsprechung hervorgehoben worden.[116]

4. Gültigkeit und Willensmängel

Die Frage, ob ein Kaufvertrag wegen **Willensmängel** anfechtbar ist, kann ohne weiteres als Gültigkeitsfrage qualifiziert werden.[117] Fraglich ist, ob dies notwendigerweise dazu führt,

---

Rn. 5 f.; *Schwenzer/Hachem,* 57 Am. J. Comp. L. (2009), 457, 473; *Soergel/Lüderitz/Fenge,* Art. 4, Rn. 6; vgl. neuerdings hierzu Hof 's-Hertogenbosch, 18.1.2011, CISG-online 2179; LG Neubrandenburg, 3.8.2005, CISG-online 1190; HR, 28.1.2005, CISG-online 1002; OLG Düsseldorf, 21.4.2004, CISG-online 915; OGH, 17.12.2003, CISG-online 828; BGH, 31.10.2001, CISG-online 617; OLG Zweibrücken, 31.3.1998, CISG-online 481.

[110] Kritisch aber *Schluchter,* S. 195 ff.
[111] Vgl. OGH, 7.9.2000, CISG-online 642 = TranspR-IHR 2001, 42 ff.: „Wie bereits von den Vorinstanzen zutreffend ausgeführt, können die Parteien die Rechte des Käufers grundsätzlich abändern. Solche Vereinbarungen unterliegen allerdings gemäß Art. 4 lit. a) UN-Kaufrecht einer Gültigkeitskontrolle des nach den Regeln des internationalen Privatrechts jeweils anwendbaren nationalen – hier deutschen – Rechts, das diesen Ausschluss – wie erwähnt – bei beidseitigen Handelsgeschäften gestattet. Diese Regelung widerspricht auch nicht den Grundwertungen des UN-Kaufrechts; nur diesen Grundwertungen widersprechende nationale Bestimmungen könnten als unzulässig angesehen werden." Ähnlich auch OLG Linz, 23.3.2005, CISG-online 1376 = IHR 2007, 123, 127.
[112] *Piltz,* Internationales Kaufrecht, Rn. 2–153; so auch *Schlechtriem/Schwenzer/Schwenzer/Hachem,* CISG Commentary, Art. 4, Rn. 38; *von Westphalen,* EWS 1990, 105, 107.
[113] Vgl. OLG Düsseldorf, 21.4.2004, CISG-online 915.
[114] So ausdrücklich auch *Schlechtriem,* Internationales UN-Kaufrecht, Rn. 34; vgl. auch *Bamberger/Roth/Saenger,* Art. 4, Rn. 22; *Ferrari u. a./Saenger,* Internationales Vertragsrecht, Art. 6, Rn. 8 a. E.; *Magnus,* FS Schwenzer, S. 1153, 1167 f.; MünchKomm/*Westermann,* Art. 4, Rn. 6; MünchKommHGB/*Benicke,* Art. 4, Rn. 5; *Ostendorf/Neumann/Ventsch,* IHR 2006, 21; *Piltz,* IHR 2004, 133, 138; *Schillo,* IHR 2003, 257, 258; *Wasmer,* S. 59; so ebenfalls, in Bezug jedoch auf das AGBG, *Frense,* S. 47; *Herber/Czerwenka,* Art. 6, Rn. 17; *Müller-Chen,* Art. 45 Rn. 37; *Karollus,* östJBl 1993, 23, 30; *Koch,* NJW 2000, 910, 910; *Piltz,* IStR 1993, 475, 478; *ders.,* Internationales Kaufrecht, § 2, Rn. 140; *Schlechtriem,* JZ 1988, 1037, 1040, Fn. 28; *ders.,* IPRax 1990, 277, 279; *Schroeter,* 6 VJ (2002), 257, 264–265; *von Westphalen,* AGB und Einheitliches Kaufgesetz, S. 67; *Witz/Salger/Lorenz/Lorenz,* Art. 4, Rn. 17; vgl. zum EKG in diesem Sinne auch *von Caemmerer,* Vertragspflichten und Vertragsgültigkeit, S. 40; *ders.,* AcP 178 (1978), 121, 128; *Schlechtriem,* Haager Einheitliches Kaufrecht, S. 257.
[115] So auch *Hartnell,* 18 Yale J. Int'l L. (1993), 1, 83 f.; *Hellner,* Standard Form Contracts, S. 355 ff.; *Honnold/Flechtner,* Art. 4, Rn. 235 f.; *P. Huber,* 13 VJ (2009), 123, 125; *P. Huber/Mullis/P. Huber,* S. 30; *Kröll,* 25 J. L. & Com. (2005), 39, 47; *Kröll u. a./Djordjevic,* Art. 4, Rn. 24; *Magnus,* Incorporation of Standard Contract Terms, S. 303, 305 f.; MünchKommHGB/*Benicke,* Art. 4, Rn. 5; *Piltz,* NJW 1996, 2768, 2770; *Schlechtriem,* Einheitliches UN-Kaufrecht, S. 18; *Schlechtriem/Schwenzer/Schlechtriem/Schwenzer/Hachem,* CISG Commentary, Art. 4, Rn. 12; *Schlechtriem/Schwenzer/Schroeter,* CISG Commentary, Intro to Artt. 14–24, Rn. 5 f.; *Soergel/Lüderitz/Fenge,* Art. 14, Rn. 10; *Staudinger/Magnus,* Art. 4, Rn. 25.
[116] Vgl. BGH, 31.10.2001, CISG-online 617 = IHR 2002, 14, 16: „Nach allgemeiner Ansicht richtet sich die Einbeziehung von Allgemeinen Geschäftsbedingungen in einen dem UN-Kaufrecht unterliegenden Vertrag nach den für diesen geltenden Vertragsabschlussvorschriften (Art. 14, 18 CISG)"; vgl. auch OLG Düsseldorf, 23.3.2011, CISG-online 2218; OLG Oldenburg, 20.12.2007, CISG-online 1644; LG Neubrandenburg, 3.8.2005, CISG-online 1190; OLG Linz, 23.3.2005, CISG-online 1376; HR, 28.1.2005, CISG-online 1002; OLG Karlsruhe, 20.7.2004, CISG-online 858; AG Nordhorn, 14.6.1994, CISG-online 259; a. A. RB Arnhem, 17.3.2004, CISG Pace.
[117] Siehe etwa *Czerwenka,* Rechtsanwendungsprobleme, S. 165; *Ferrari,* Vendita internazionale, S. 98; *Garro/Zuppi,* Compraventa internacional, S. 82; Botschaft des Schweizerischen Bundesrats, S. 763; *Leyens,* Rev. CISG (2003–2004), 3, 37; *Rosch/Spiegel, D.* 2002, Jur. 396, 397; *Staudinger/Magnus,* Art. 4, Rn. 20.

dass stets nationales Recht Anwendung findet. Dies hängt davon ab, „ob eine bestimmte Sachfrage von den Verfassern des CISG gesehen und im CISG deutlich geregelt worden ist",[118] beziehungsweise ob das Übereinkommen eine **„funktional äquivalente Lösung"** bereithält.[119] Hält das Übereinkommen eine solche Lösung bereit, so muss man vom Vorrang der Vorschriften des Übereinkommens ausgehen,[120] eine Lösung, die durchaus auch der vom Übereinkommen angestrebten Rechtseinheit entspricht.[121]

23   Dieser bisweilen kritisierte **funktionale Ansatz**[122] ist so verstanden worden, dass zunächst die für die Lückenfüllung maßgebliche nationale Rechtsordnung über das anwendbare Internationale Privatrecht ermittelt werden muss, um daraufhin die vergleichende Überprüfung anstellen zu können, ob die im nationalen Recht als Gültigkeitsproblem ausgestaltete Frage im Übereinkommen eine abschließende Regelung erfahren hat.[123] Dieser Ansatz hat den Verdienst, die von der herrschenden Lehre[124] geforderte **„vertragsautonome" Auslegung** des Begriffs „Gültigkeit" zu fördern, da er auf die sachliche Funktion des Rechtsinstituts – und nicht auf dessen „label" – abstellt.[125]

23a   Relevant ist der erwähnte funktionale Ansatz auch, um zu entscheiden, ob im Rahmen von dem CISG unterliegenden Verträgen nationale **Widerrufs- bzw. Rückgaberechte** relevant sein können,[126] wie etwa die, die das BGB in §§ 355, 356 Verbrauchern einräumt. Obwohl diese Vorschriften nur Verbrauchern Widerrufs- bzw. Rückgaberechte einräumen, also sich nur auf Verträge zu beziehen scheinen, die vom Anwendungsbereich des CISG ex Art. 2 lit. a) ausgenommen sind, ist die Frage dennoch relevant; dies ist darauf zurückzuführen, dass die Anwendung der nationalen Verbraucherschutzvorschriften von Anwendungsvoraussetzungen abhängt, die nicht mit denen des Ausnahmetatbestands des Art. 2 lit. a) übereinstimmen, es demnach durchaus zu Überschneidungen kommen kann,[127] was neuerdings auch von der höchstrichterlichen Rechtsprechung hervorgehoben worden ist.[128] Eine solche Überschneidung kann sich zum Beispiel dann ergeben, wenn nationale Konsumentenschutzvorschriften im Gegensatz zu Art. 2 lit. a) nicht verlangen, dass der Verkäufer den beabsichtigten persönlichen Gebrauch der Waren kannte oder kennen musste.[129] Was die erwähnten Widerrufs- bzw. Rückgaberechte angeht, hängt deren Relevanz davon ab, ob das CISG **funktional äquivalente Lösungen** für die Situationen vorsieht, die mittels der Widerrufs- bzw. Rückgaberechte geregelt werden sollen; ist dem so, geht das CISG kraft Art. 4 S. 2 CISG ohne weiteres vor. Haben die Widerrufs- bzw. Rückgaberechte hingegen im CISG kein funktionales Pendant (weil sie etwa den Verbraucher vor übereilten vertraglichen Bindungen schützen wollen), können sie durchaus relevant sein.[130]

---

[118] *Schlechtriem*, Internationales UN-Kaufrecht, Rn. 36.

[119] A. A. *Reinhart*, Art. 4, Rn. 5, der sich gegen die Verdrängung nationalen Gültigkeitsrechts durch funktional äquivalente Lösungen ausspricht; vgl. auch *Gstoehl*, östZfRVgl 1998, 1, 8, der sich sprachlich auf das Kriterium der funktionalen Äquivalenz bezieht, im Grunde aber auf „inhaltliche Identität" abstellt.

[120] Vgl. *Bock*, FS Schwenzer, S. 175, 184; *Enderlein/Maskow/Strohbach*, Art. 4, Anm. 3.1.; *Ferrari*, Vendita internazionale, S. 99; *Gruber*, Methoden, S. 235 ff.; *Honnold/Flechtner*, Art. 4, Rn. 65; *Schluchter*, S. 40 m. w. N.; Sekretariatskommentar, Art. 4, Nr. 2; *Tescaro*, Contr. Imp. E. 2007, 319, 324.

[121] So auch *Herber*, 2. Aufl., Art. 4, Rn. 13; *Honsell/Siehr*, Art. 4, Rn. 6.

[122] Den im Text vertretenen Ansatz kritisieren vor allem Autoren, deren nationales Recht – wie etwa das österreichische Recht – das Nebeneinander von kaufrechtlichen Bestimmungen und Nichtigkeitsgründen zulässt: *Karollus*, S. 41 f.; *Lessiak*, östJBl 1989, 487 ff.; dagegen aber *Loewe*, Art. 45.

[123] So ausdrücklich *Schluchter*, S. 45; vgl. neuerdings auch *Tescaro*, Contr. Imp. E. 2007, 319, 323 f.

[124] Statt aller vgl. *Heiz*, 20 Vand. J. Transnat'l L. (1987), 639, 660 f.; *Herber/Czerwenka*, Art. 4, Rn. 13.

[125] So *Honnold/Flechtner*, Art. 4, Rn. 65: „The substance rather than the label or characterization of the competing rule of domestic law determines whether it is displaced by the Convention"; ebenso *Ferrari*, RabelsZ 71 (2007), 52, 66 ff.; vgl. auch *Lutz*, 35 Vic. U. Well. L. Rev. (2004), 711, 723.

[126] Vgl. hierzu *Schlechtriem*, Internationales UN-Kaufrecht, Rn. 36b.

[127] Vgl. auch *Díez-Picazo/Laporta*, Art. 2, S. 63; *Ferrari*, Applicabilità ed applicazioni, S. 172 f.; *Garro/Zuppi*, Compraventa internacional, S. 82, Fn. 17; *Schmitt*, CR 2001, 145, 145; *Wartenberg*, S. 24 ff.

[128] So ausdrücklich BGH, 31.10.2001, CISG-online 617 = IHR 2002, 14, 16.

[129] So auch *Herber*, 2. Aufl., Art. 2, Rn. 17; *Karollus*, S. 26.

[130] *Schlechtriem*, Internationales UN-Kaufrecht, Rn. 36b.

Der beschriebene Ansatz der „funktionalen Äquivalenz" führt dazu, dass das Übereinkommen die nationalen, die **Anfechtung wegen Irrtums über Eigenschaften** der Sache zulassenden Vorschriften verdrängt,[131] da es eine abschließende Regelung der Haftung für nicht vertragsgemäße Beschaffenheit der Ware bereithält;[132] diese Auffassung ist auch in der Rechtsprechung vertreten worden.[133] Gleiches gilt auch hinsichtlich der nationalen Regeln über die Anfechtung wegen **Irrtums über die Leistungsfähigkeit einer Person und deren Bonität:**[134] Da das Übereinkommen auch diesbezüglich eine abschließende Regelung vorsieht, nämlich Art. 71, werden die nationalen Vorschriften vom Einheitskaufrecht verdrängt.[135] Da das Übereinkommen auch eine Regelung, Art. 27, für den Fall vorsieht, dass eine Erklärung falsch übermittelt worden ist, bleibt auch für nationale Vorschriften zum **Übermittlungsirrtum** kein Platz.[136] Kein Raum ist ferner für die Anwendung von nationalen Vorschriften zur **objektiven anfänglichen Unmöglichkeit,** da sie im Übereinkommen „eindeutig als Fall einer Leistungsstörung gesehen und bei den Gefahrtragungsregeln ausdrücklich berücksichtigt worden [ist]."[137] 24

Die Anfechtung wegen **Inhaltsirrtums** untersteht aber, da nicht im CISG geregelt, nationalem Recht.[138] Gleiches gilt – so auch die Rechtsprechung[139] – auch hinsichtlich des 25

---

[131] Vgl. etwa *Bamberger/Roth/Saenger*, Art. 4, Rn. 23; *Bock*, FS Schwenzer, S. 175, 184; *Brunner*, Art. 4, Rn. 10; *Ferrari*, RabelsZ 71 (2007): 52, 68 ff.; *P. Huber*, IHR 2006, 228, 231 f.; *P. Huber/Mullis/P. Huber*, S. 22 f.; *Kröll*, 25 J.L. & Com. (2005), 39, 55 f.; *Kröll u. a./Djordjevic*, Art. 4, Rn. 21; *Leyens*, Rev. CISG (2003–2004), 3, 43 ff.; MünchKommHGB/*Benicke*, Art. 4, Rn. 8; *Schlechtriem/Schwenzer/Schlechtriem/Schwenzer/Hachem*, CISG Commentary, Art. 4, Rn. 19; *Staudinger/Magnus*, Art. 4, Rn. 48; *Teichert*, Lückenfüllung, S. 18; so im Ergebnis nunmehr auch *Schlechtriem*, Internationales UN-Kaufrecht, Rn. 36a; *Schroeter*, VJ (2002), 257, 264; a.A. *Fairlie*, S. 50.

[132] So auch *Achilles*, Art. 4, Rn. 4; *Ferrari*, RabelsZ 71 (2007), 52, 68 f.; *Herber/Czerwenka*, Art. 4, Rn. 13, 22; *Heuzé*, Anm. 282., 307.; *P. Huber*, ZEuP 1994, 585, 597 ff., 602; *Kindler*, Jb.I.R. 5 (1992), 201, 224; *Rosch/Spiegel*, D. 2002, Jur. 396, 397; *Ryffel*, S. 128 ff.; *Schlechtriem*, Einheitliches UN-Kaufrecht, S. 19; *Schlechtriem/Schwenzer/Schlechtriem*, CISG Commentary, 2. Aufl., Art. 4, Rn. 13; *Schluchter*, S. 102 f.; *Schwenzer*, NJW 1990, 602, 603; *Soergel/Lüderitz/Fenge*, Art. 4, Rn. 8; *Tescaro*, Contr. Imp. E. 2007, 319, 324; a.A. *Bydlinski*, Allgemeines Vertragsrecht, S. 86; *Ebenroth*, östJBl 1986, 681, 688; so im Ergebnis auch *Gstoehl*, östZfRVgl 1998, 1–10, zumindest was das österreichische Recht angeht.

[133] Vgl. RB Hasselt, 19.4.2006, CISG-online 1389; LG Aachen, 14.5.1993, CISG-online 86 = RIW 1993, 761.

[134] *Bamberger/Roth/Saenger*, Art. 4, Rn. 23; *Brunner*, Art. 4, Rn. 10; *Ferrari*, RabelsZ 71 (2007), 52, 69; *ders.*, Scope of Application, S. 96, 98; *P. Huber*, IHR 2006, 228, 232; *Kröll u. a./Djordjevic*, Art. 4, Rn. 21; *Leyens*, Rev. CISG (2003–2004), 3, 48 ff.; MünchKommHGB/*Benicke*, Art. 4, Rn. 8; MünchKommHGB/*Mankowski*, Art. 71, Rn. 25; *Schlechtriem/Schwenzer/Schlechtriem*, CISG Commentary, 2. Aufl., Art. 4, Rn. 13.

[135] *Bamberger/Roth/Saenger*, Art. 4, Rn. 23; *Enderlein/Maskow/Strohbach*, Art. 4, Anm. 3.1.; *Flesch*, BB 1994, 873, 876 f.; *Herber/Czerwenka*, Art. 4, Rn. 22; *P. Huber*, ZEuP 1994, 585, 601; *P. Huber/Mullis/P. Huber*, S. 24; MünchKommHGB/*Benicke*, Art. 4, Rn. 8; *Piltz*, Internationales Kaufrecht, Rn. 2–136; *Reinhart*, Art. 71, Rn. 10 (sich selbst aber widersprechend, vgl. Art. 4, Rn. 5); *Schlechtriem*, Einheitliches UN-Kaufrecht, S. 85; *Schluchter*, S. 116; *Witz/Salger/Lorenz/Lorenz*, Art. 4, Rn. 23; a.A. *Bydlinski*, Das allgemeine Vertragsrecht, S. 85 f.; kritisch hinsichtlich der im Text erwähnten Begründung neuerdings MünchKomm/*Westermann*, Art. 4, Rn. 10: Art. 71 keine Rechtsfertigungsgrund darstellen, da er sich lediglich auf Sukzessivlieferungsverträge beziehe. „Entscheidend sollte unter diesen Umständen die Besorgnis sein, dass durch Eingehen auf zahlreiche nationale Instrumente zur Lockerung oder Beseitigung der Bindung an den Vertrag die eigenständige Lösung des Leistungsstörungsproblems durch das CISG unterlaufen werden könnte".

[136] *Ferrari*, RabelsZ 71 (2007), 52, 70; *Ferrari u. a./Saenger*, Internationales Vertragsrecht, Art. 4, Rn. 24; MünchKomm/*Gruber*, Art. 27, Rn. 15; *Schlechtriem/Schwenzer/Schmidt-Kessel*, CISG Commentary, Art. 8, Rn. 6; *Schlechtriem/Schwenzer/Hachem*, CISG Commentary, Art. 4, Rn. 36; *Staudinger/Magnus*, Art. 4, Rn. 51.

[137] *Schlechtriem*, Internationales UN-Kaufrecht, Rn. 36; ebenso *Enderlein/Maskow/Strohbach*, Art. 79, Anm. 5.2.; *Ferrari u. a./Saenger*, Internationales Vertragsrecht, Art. 4, Rn. 14; *Herber/Czerwenka*, Art. 4, Rn. 13, Art. 68, Rn. 8, Art. 79, Rn. 1; *P. Huber/Mullis/P. Huber*, S. 24; *Karollus*, S. 43; MünchKommHGB/*Benicke*, Art. 4, Rn. 9; *Schlechtriem*, Einheitliches UN-Kaufrecht, S. 82; *Schlechtriem/Schwenzer/Hachem*, CISG Commentary, Art. 4, Rn. 33; *Stoll*, 2. Aufl., Art. 79, Rn. 21; a.A. *Bianca/Bonell/Tallon*, Art. 79, Anm. 2.4.3.

[138] *Bianca/Bonell/Farnsworth*, Art. 8, Anm. 3.4.; *Heuzé*, Anm. 233.; *Hoyer*, WBl. 1988, 70, 71; *Rosch/Spiegel*, D. 2002, Jur. 396, 397; *Schluchter*, S. 99.

[139] Schiedsgericht der Handelskammer Zürich, 31.5.1996, UNILEX.

Art. 4 25a, 26 Teil I. Kapitel I. Anwendungsbereich

Kalkulationsirrttums[140] und der **arglistigen Täuschung**, die, wie sich auch aus der Entstehungsgeschichte ergibt,[141] im Übereinkommen nicht geregelt ist,[142] auch dann nicht, wenn es sich um Täuschung durch **Unterlassen** handelt.[143] Auch die Anfechtung wegen **Irrtums über die Identität** der Person untersteht nationalem Recht,[144] genauso wie die Anfechtung wegen **Drohung**.[145]

25a Auch die Frage, ob die Verletzung von **Informationspflichten** oder anderen im Rahmen eines Vertragsschlusses relevanten Pflichten zu Irrtümern geführt hat, die die Möglichkeit einer Anfechtung eröffnen, bestimmt sich ex Art. 4 S. 2 lit. a) nach **nationalem Recht**.[146] Diesbezüglich sind vor allem die Informationspflichten relevant, die, wie § 312c Abs. 1 Nr. 1 BGB i. V. m. § 1 Nr. 1 InfoVO, die Willensbildung einer Partei, im Falle des § 312c BGB des Verbrauchers, schützen: Welche Folgen eventuelle Willensmängel haben, ergibt sich demnach aus dem über das IPR des Forums zu bestimmenden nationalen Recht. Von diesen Pflichten sind die Pflichten zu unterscheiden, die sich etwa ex § 312e I BGB i. V. m. § 3 InfoVO in Bezug auf den elektronischen Geschäftsverkehr ergeben. Auch diesbezüglich ist natürlich das Verhältnis zwischen CISG und nationalem Recht ausschlaggebend: Regelt das CISG – irgendwie, also auch durch Rückgriff auf allgemeine Grundsätze[147] – Fragen des elektronischen Geschäftsverkehrs (wie etwa Gültigkeit eines über Internet geschlossenen Vertrages, Zugang einer elektronisch übermittelten Nachricht, etc.),[148] dann haben die Vorschriften des CISG Vorrang; fehlt es jedoch an einer – auch nur funktional äquivalenten – Lösung, dann können die erwähnten Pflichten im Rahmen des Vertragsstatuts durchaus Bedeutung erlangen.

5. Gültigkeit von Gebräuchen

26 Die Beurteilung der Gültigkeit von Gebräuchen muss von den Fragen, wie Gebräuche im Sinne des Übereinkommens zu definieren sind, unter welchen Umständen sie für die Parteien verbindlich sind, und in welchem Verhältnis sie zu den Regelungen des Über-

---

[140] BGH, 27.11.2007, CISG-online 1617.
[141] YB V (1974), S. 46, Nr. 196 f.; YB VIII (1977), S. 42, Nr. 233 f.
[142] So auch *Audit*, Vente internatinoale, S. 117; *Bamberger/Roth/Saenger*, Art. 4, Rn. 23; *Bianca/Bonell/Bonell*, Art. 6, Anm. 3.3.; *Díez-Picazo/Rojo Ajuria*, Art. 4, S. 78; *Esslinger*, ALI-ABA (1999), 69, 79; *Ferrari*, Scope of Application, S. 96, 98; *Ferrari u. a./Saenger*, Internationales Vertragsrecht, Art. 4, Rn. 24; *Hartnell*, 18 Yale J. Int'l L. (1993), 1, 70; *Heiz*, 20 Vand. J. Transnat'l L. (1987), 639, 654; *Henschel*, Conformity of Goods, S. 131; *Honnold/Flechtner*, Atr. 4, Rn. 65; *P. Huber*, IHR 2006, 228, 232; *ders.*, ZEuP 1994, 585, 601; *P. Huber/Mullis/P. Huber*, S. 23; *Karollus*, S. 41; *Kastely*, 8 Nw. J. Int'l L. & Bus. (1988), 574, 590; *Kröll u. a./Djordjevic*, Art. 4, Rn. 23; *Loewe*, Art. 35; *Mather*, 20 J. L. & Com. (2001), 155, 162; *MünchKomm/Westermann*, Art. 4, Rn. 8; *MünchKommHGB/Benicke*, Art. 4, Rn. 19; *Neumayer/Ming*, Art. 4, Anm. 6.; *Piltz*, Internationales Kaufrecht, Rn. 2–149; *Reinhart*, Art. 35, Rn. 11; *Schlechtriem*, Seller's Obligation, S. 6–29; *Schlechtriem/Schwenzer/Schlechtriem/Schwenzer/Hachem*, CISG Commentary, Art. 4, Rn. 19; *Staudinger/Magnus*, Art. 4, Rn. 52; *Winship*, Scope, S. 1–37; vgl. in der Rechtsprechung *Electrocraft Arkansas, Inc. v. Super Electric Motors, Ltd et al.*, U. S. Dist. Ct. (E. D. Ark.), Western Division, 23. 12 2009, CISG-online 2045; *Miami Valley Paper, LLC v. Lebbing Engineering & Consulting GmbH*, U. S. Dist. Ct. (S. D. Ohio), 26.3.2009, CISG-online 1880; KG St. Gallen, 13.5.2008, CISG-online 1768; *Miami Valley Paper, LLC v. Lebbing Engineering & Consulting GmbH*, U. S. Dist. Ct. (S. D. Ohio), 10.10.2006, CISG-online 1362; *TeeVee Toons, Inc. et al v. Gerhard Schubert GmbH*, U. S. Dist. Ct. (S. D. N. Y.), 23.8.2006, CISG-online 1272; CIETAC, 21.10.2005, CISG-online 1472; *Sonox Sia v. Albury Grain Sales Inc. et al.*, Quebec Superior Court, District of Montreal, 29.7.2005, CISG Pace; *Treibacher Industrie, A. G. v. TDY Industries, Inc.*, U. S. Dist. Ct. (N. D. Ala.), 27.4.2005, CISG-online 1178.
[143] So auch *Enderlein/Maskow/Strohbach*, Art. 40, Anm. 1.; *Honnold/Flechtner*, Artt. 39, 40, 44, Rn. 260, Fn. 33; vgl. aber *Schluchter*, S. 107, die eine Anfechtung wegen Täuschung durch Unterlassen nur dann zulassen will, wenn der Verkäufer eine Vertragswidrigkeit nach Art. 35 verschwiegen hat.
[144] *Tescaro*, Contr. Imp. E. 2007, 319, 324.
[145] *Achilles*, Art. 4, Rn. 4; *Esslinger*, ALI-ABA (1999), 69, 79; *Martin-Davidson*, 17 Mich. St. J. Int'l L. (2008), 657, 681; *Staudinger/Magnus*, Art. 4, Rn. 52; *Witz/Salger/Lorenz/Lorenz*, Art. 4, Rn. 24.
[146] *Schlechtriem*, Internationales UN-Kaufrecht, Rn. 42a; *Schlechtriem/Schwenzer/Schwenzer/Hachem*, CISG Commentary, Art. 4, Rn. 34.
[147] Vgl. Art. 7 Rn. 48 ff.
[148] Vgl. hierzu *Ferrari*, VJ (2002), 289 ff.; *ders.*, EuLF 2001, 301 ff.

einkommens stehen, unterschieden werden.[149] Diese Fragen sind in Art. 9 geregelt,[150] So nunmehr auch die (höchstrichterliche) Rechtsprechung.[151]

Mit der „Gültigkeit" von Gebräuchen, die in Art. 4 lit. a) angesprochen und dem 27 anwendbaren Recht überlassen ist,[152] ist nur eine **Inhaltskontrolle** gemeint,[153] d. h., „die Prüfung der inhaltlichen Vereinbarkeit des Brauchs mit den zwingenden Bestimmungen des nationalen Rechts."[154] Irrelevant ist jedoch, wegen des Prinzips der Formfreiheit, ob der Brauch gegen nationale Formvorschriften verstößt, zumindest dann, wenn keine der Parteien ihre Niederlassung in einem Staat hat, der einen Vorbehalt nach Art. 96 erklärt hat.[155]

Abschließend ist noch zu erwähnen, dass dann, wenn eine Willenserklärung durch einen 28 Brauch, den die erklärende Partei nicht kennt, einen anderen als den gewollten Sinn erhält, ein Problem der Gültigkeit des Vertrages vorliegt, nicht der Gültigkeit des Brauchs, was zur Anfechtung führen kann.[156]

6. Eigentumsfragen

Das Übereinkommen schließt, wie vor ihm bereits das Haager Kaufrecht,[157] Eigentums- 29 fragen ausdrücklich von seinem Regelungsbereich aus.[158] Demnach richten sich die dinglichen Wirkungen des Vertrages auf die Eigentumslage nicht nach dem CISG,[159] sondern nach dem anwendbaren nationalen Recht, meist also nach der **lex rei sitae**,[160] auch wenn es nicht an IPR Regeln fehlt, die, wie etwa die schweizerische Regel, den Eigentumsübergang bei Exportgeschäften dem Recht des Bestimmungslandes unterstellen.[161] Dieser Ausschluss vom Regelungsbereich ist – u. a. auch im Sekretariatskommentar[162] – damit begründet worden, dass es unmöglich sei, die „unüberbrückbaren Differenzen zwischen jenen Staaten, die für die Übereignung ein besonderes dingliches Rechtsgeschäft verlangen (z. B. Deutschland, Österreich), und jenen, die bereits mit Abschluss des Kaufvertrages den Eigentumsübergang vollziehen (z. B. Frankreich, Großbritannien)"[163] zu beseitigen.[164] Ob

---

[149] So schon *Ferrari*, Vendita internazionale, S. 95, Fn. 1; *Herber*, 2. Aufl., Art. 4, Rn. 15; vgl. hierzu neuerdings auch *Ferrari*, EuLF 2002, 272 ff.; *Schlechtriem/Schwenzer/Schlechtriem*, CISG Commentary, 2. Aufl., Art. 4, Rn. 15; *Schlechtriem/Schwenzer/Schwenzer/Hachem*, CISG Commentary, Art. 4, Rn. 45.

[150] So auch *Díez-Picazo/Rojo Ajuria*, Art. 4, S. 86; *Ferrari u. a./Saenger*, Internationales Vertragsrecht, Art. 4, Rn. 6; *Piltz*, Internationales Kaufrecht, Rn. 2–154; Botschaft des Schweizerischen Bundesrats, S. 764; *Schlechtriem/Schwenzer/Schwenzer/Hachem*, CISG Commentary, Art. 4, Rn. 45; *Staudinger/Magnus*, Art. 4, Rn. 30.

[151] OGH, 15.10.1998, CISG-online 380 = östZfRVgl 1999, 63 f.

[152] Vgl. OGH, 21.3.2000, CISG-online 641 = IHR 2001, 40 ff.

[153] Ebenso *Bonell*, östJBl 1985, 385, 393 f.; *Babusiaux*, D. 2002, Jur. 320, 321.

[154] *Karollus*, S. 43; in diesem Sinne auch *Ferrari u. a./Saenger*, Internationales Vertragsrecht, Art. 4, Rn. 5; *Herber*, 2. Aufl., Art. 4, Rn. 16; *MünchKommHGB/Benicke*, Art. 4, Rn. 11; *Piltz*, Internationales Kaufrecht, Rn. 2–154.

[155] So auch *Czerwenka*, Rechtsanwendungsprobleme, S. 180; *Staudinger/Magnus*, Art. 4, Rn. 29.

[156] Vgl. hierzu auch *Bonell*, östJBl 1985, 385, 393; *Schlechtriem/Schwenzer/Schlechtriem*, CISG Commentary, 2. Aufl., Art. 4, Rn. 17; *Staudinger/Magnus*, Art. 4, Rn. 31.

[157] Vgl. *Dölle/Herber*, Art. 8 EKG, Rn. 4.

[158] Vgl. in der Rechtsprechung etwa OLG München, 5.3.2008, CISG-online 1686; CIETAC, 18.4.2008, CISG-online 2057; *Usinor Industeel v. Leeco Steel Products*, U. S. Dist. Ct. (N. D. Ill.), 28.3.2002, CISG-online 696 = 2002 WL 655 540; *St. Paul Guardian Insurance Co., et al. v. Neuromed Medical Systems & Support, et al.*, U. S. Dist. Ct. (S. D. N. Y.), 26.3.2002, CISG-online 615 = 2002 U. S. Dist. LEXIS 5096; LG Freiburg, 22.8.2002, CISG-online 711 = IHR 2003, 22, 23; kritisch zum Ausschluss *Padovini*, östZfRVgl 1987, 87, 93.

[159] *Kröll u. a./Djordjevic*, Art. 4, Rn. 28; *Schlechtriem/Schwenzer/Schwenzer/Hachem*, CISG Commentary, Art. 4, Rn. 3 a. E. und 46.

[160] *Bamberger/Roth/Saenger*, Art. 4, Rn. 8; *Brunner*, Art. 4, Rn. 17; *P. Huber/Mullis/P. Huber*, S. 25; *Schlechtriem*, Internationales UN-Kaufrecht, Rn. 37; *Soergel/Lüderitz/Fenge*, Art. 4, Rn. 3; *Staudinger/Magnus*, Art. 4, Rn. 32.

[161] *Honsell/Siehr*, Art. 4, Rn. 28, unter Bezugnahme auf Art. 130 des schweizerischen IPR-Gesetzes.

[162] Sekretariatskommentar, Art. 4, Nr. 4.

[163] *Karollus*, S. 44.

[164] Ähnlich auch *Audit*, Vente internationale, S. 34 f.; *Czerwenka*, Rechtsanwendungsprobleme, S. 165; *Díez-Picazo/Rojo Ajuria*, Art. 4, S. 86; *Herber*, 2. Aufl., Art. 4, Rn. 18; *MünchKommHGB/Benicke*, Art. 4, Rn. 12; *Reinhart*, Art. 4, Rn. 6.

Art. 4 30–32

jedoch heute noch von „unüberbrückbaren Differenzen" gesprochen werden kann,[165] ist fragwürdig, da in der neueren Lehre immer öfter von der Möglichkeit einer **Vereinheitlichung auch des Mobiliarsachenrechts** gesprochen wird.[166]

30 Die neuere Rechtsprechung[167] hat, genauso wie die Lehre,[168] hervorgehoben, dass nicht nur die Eigentumsübertragung,[169] sondern auch der **Eigentumsvorbehalt** von Art. 4 lit. b) erfasst wird;[170] das Übereinkommen regelt also nicht „die Frage, ob und auf welche Art und Weise bei grenzüberschreitendem Warenkauf ein Eigentumsvorbehalt rechtswirksam getroffen werden kann."[171] Ferner regelt das CISG nicht die sachrechtlichen Fragen, ob dem Käufer bereits bei Besitzerwerb ein dingliches Anwartschaftsrecht zusteht, ob der Erwerb des Vollrechts automatisch mit Zahlung des Restkaufpreises geschieht oder ob es zum vollständigen Eigentumserwerb weiterer Voraussetzungen bedarf.[172] Die Beantwortung dieser Frage wird vom anwendbaren Recht abhängen, genauso wie die Frage, ob ein **gutgläubiger Erwerb** der verkauften Waren möglich ist.[173]

31 Vom Übereinkommen werden Eigentumsfragen in Artt. 41 und 42 angesprochen:[174] Der Verkäufer hat gemäß Art. 41 Ware ohne Rechtsmängel zu liefern; Art. 42 regelt hingegen den Fall, dass die Ware mit Rechten Dritter belastet ist, die auf „gewerblichem oder anderem geistigen Eigentum beruhen."

V. Weitere vom Regelungsbereich ausgeschlossene Rechtsfragen

32 Durch die Verwendung des Wortes „insbesondere" wird deutlich zum Ausdruck gebracht, dass die Aufzählung der nicht vom Regelungsbereich erfassten Rechtsfragen **nicht abschließend** ist.[175]

---

[165] Vgl. auch *Staudinger/Magnus*, Art. 4, Rn. 32, der hervorhebt, dass sich Konsensualprinzip und Traditionsprinzip „bislang unversöhnt gegenüberstehen".

[166] Vgl. etwa *Drobnig*, Transfer of Property, S. 495 ff.; *Ferrari*, ZEuP 1993, 52 ff.; ders., Riv. dir. civ. 1993, 729 ff.

[167] Siehe *Usinor Industeel v. Leeco Steel Products*, U. S. Dist. Ct. (N. D. Ill.), 28.3.2002, CISG-online 696 = 2002 WL 655 540; *Roder Zelt- und Hallenkonstruktionen v. Rosedown Park Pty Ltd. and Reginald R Eustace*, FCA (Adelaide, SA), 28.4.1995, CISG-online 218 = 1995 Federal Court Reports (Australia) 216; OLG Koblenz, 16.1.1992, CISG-online 47 = RIW 1992, 1019.

[168] Vgl. *Ferrari*, Forum International 1997, 89, 91; *Ferrari u. a./Saenger*, Internationales Vertragsrecht, Art. 4, Rn. 8; *P. Huber/Mullis/P. Huber*, S. 25; *Sannini*, L'applicazione, S. 138 f.; *Schlechtriem*, 36 Vict. U. Well. L. Rev. (2005), 781, 789; *Schlechtriem/Schwenzer/Schlechtriem*, CISG Commentary, 2. Aufl., Art. 4, Rn. 18; *Soergel/Lüderitz/Fenge*, Art. 4, Rn. 3; *Staudinger/Magnus*, Art. 4, Rn. 32.

[169] *Kröll u. a./Djordjevic*, Art. 4, Rn. 28; *Schlechtriem/Schwenzer/Schwenzer/Hachem*, CISG Commentary, Art. 4, Rn. 46; zum Ausschluß der Eigentumsübertragung vom Geltungsbereich des CISG vgl. in der Rechtsprechung etwa CIETAC, 18.4.2008, CISG-online 2057; OLG München, 5.3.2008, CISG-online 1686; LG Freiburg, 22.8.2002, CISG-online; *Usinor Industeel v. Leeco Steel Products*, U. S. Dist. Ct. (N. D. Ill.), 28.3.2002, CISG-online 696 = 2002 WL 655 540; *St. Paul Guardian Insurance Co., et al. v. Neuromed Medical Systems & Support, et al.*, U. S. Dist. Ct. (S. D. N. Y.), 26.3.2002, CISG-online 615 = 2002 U. S. Dist. LEXIS 5096; vgl. jedoch *Victoria Alloys, Inc. v. Fortis Bank SA/NV*, U. S. Bankruptcy Ct. (N. D. Ohio), 10.4.2001, CISG-online 589.

[170] Vgl. auch *Achilles*, Art. 4, Rn. 6; *Bamberger/Roth/Saenger*, Art. 4, Rn. 8; *Brunner*, Art. 4, Rn. 17; *Fairlie*, S. 50 ff.; *Martin-Davidson*, 17 Mich. St. J. Int'l L. (2008), 657, 691; MünchKomm/*Westermann*, Art. 4, Rn. 9; MünchKommHGB/*Benicke*, Art. 4, Rn. 12; *Schlechtriem/Schwenzer/Schwenzer/Hachem*, CISG Commentary, Art. 4, Rn. 3 a. E. und 47; *Spagnolo*, 10 Melb. J. Int'l L. (2009), 141, 173; *Witz/Salger/Lorenz/Lorenz*, Art. 4, Rn. 26.

[171] OLG Koblenz, 16.1.1992, CSIG-online 47 = RIW 1992, 1019; see also Serbian Chamber of Commerce, 15.7.2008, CISG-online 1795; *Usinor Industeel v. Leeco Steel Products*, U. S. Dist. Ct. (N. D. Ill.), 28.3.2002, CISG-online 696 = 2002 WL 655 540.

[172] *Schlechtriem*, Internationales UN-Kaufrecht, Rn. 37.

[173] MünchKomm/*Westermann*, Art. 4, Rn. 15; *Schlechtriem/Schwenzer/Schlechtriem*, CISG Commentary, 2. Aufl., Art. 4, Rn. 18 a. E.; *Schlechtriem/Schwenzer/Hachem*, CISG Commentary, Art. 4, Rn. 3 a. E. und 46; vgl. auch LG Freiburg, 22.8.2002, CISG-online 711 = IHR 2003, 22, 23.

[174] Vgl. auch *Enderlein/Maskow/Strohbach*, Art. 4, Rn. 8.

[175] So ausdrücklich *Ferrari*, Forum International 1997, 89, 90; *Herber*, 2. Aufl., Art. 4, Rn. 19; Botschaft des Schweizerischen Bundesrats, S. 764; *Teichert*, Lückenfüllung, S. 17; widersprüchlich *Schlechtriem/Schwenzer/Schlechtriem*, CISG Commentary, 2. Aufl., Art. 4, Rn. 19 und 22.

Nicht in den Regelungsbereich fallen **verfahrensrechtliche Fragen**.[176] Daher kann es nicht weiter überraschen, dass Lehre[177] und Rechtsprechung die Frage, ob ein Gericht örtlich zuständig sei, dem Regelungsbereich des CISG entzogen haben.[178] Dies schließt jedoch nicht aus, dass Vorschriften des Übereinkommens, wie etwa Art. 31, für die Frage der Zuständigkeit relevant sein können.[179] Ferner schließt dies auch nicht aus, dass bestimmte mit der **Insolvenz** einer Partei zusammenhängende Fragen vom CISG erfasst werden;[180] diesbezüglich sei etwa darauf hingewiesen, dass ein in bestimmter Weise ausgeübtes, auf Grund nationalen Insolvenzrechts dem Verwalter zustehendes Wahlrecht zu einem wesentlichen Vertragsbruch i. S. v. Art. 25 CISG führen kann, nämlich dann, wenn der Verwalter die Erfüllung ablehnt, ist darin doch eine endgültige Erfüllungsverweigerung zu sehen.[181] Das CISG wirkt sich außerdem auf etwaige, zum Schutz des Verwalterwahlrechts im nationalen Recht vorgesehene **Aufhebungssperren** aus: Da das CISG die Voraussetzungen der Vertragsaufhebung abschließend regelt, bleibt dem Gläubiger bei wesentlichem Vertragsbruch durch die Nichterfüllungswahl die Möglichkeit, den Vertrag aufzulösen.[182]

Zu den nicht ausdrücklich erwähnten Rechtsfragen, die vom Regelungsbereich ausgeschlossen sind, gehört die **Stellvertretung**,[183] was auch in der Rechtsprechung wiederholt hervorgehoben worden ist.[184] Da das Genfer Übereinkommen über die Stellvertretung

---

[176] *Ferrari*, Scope of Application, S. 96, 107; *Herber*, 2. Aufl., Art. 4, Rn. 20; *Honsell/Siehr*, Art. 4, Rn. 29; MünchKomm/*Westermann*, Art. 4, Rn. 17; *Schlechtriem/Schwenzer/Schlechtriem*, CISG Commentary, 2. Aufl., Art. 4, Rn. 20; *Schwenzer/Hachem*, 57 Am. J. Comp. L. (2009), 457, 471; vgl. hierzu auch KG Wallis, 21.2.2005, CISG-online 1193 = IHR 2006, 155, 156: „Dagegen regelt das CISG selbst keine prozessualen Fragen"; siehe auch BGer, 11.7.2000, CISG-online 627; sich gegen eine Unterscheidung zwischen materiellrechtlichen und prozessualrechtlichen Fragen aussprechend jedoch *Gotanda*, 13 VJ (2009), 229, 234; *Kröll u. a./Djordjevic*, Art. 4, Rn. 31 („counterproductive"); *Orlandi*, Uniform L. Rev. 2000, 23, 26.

[177] Vgl. statt aller *Ferrari*, Choice of Forum and CISG, S. 103, 104; *Kröll*, 25 J. L. & Com. (2005), 39, 43; *Kröll u. a./Djordjevic*, Art. 4, Rn. 32; *Magnus*, Incorporation of Standard Contract Terms, S. 303, 308; *Piltz*, NJW 2000, 553, 556.

[178] HGer Zürich, 26.4.1995, CISG-online 248.

[179] Vgl. in Bezug auf das Verhältnis von EuGVÜ bzw. LuganoÜ und CISG *De Cristofaro*, Uniform L. Rev. 2000, 43 ff.; *Ferrari*, Corr. giur. 2002, 372 ff.; *Fiumara*, Rass. Avv. Stato 1994, I, 282 ff.; *Giancotti*, Giur. it. 2001, 233 ff.; *Kadner*, Jura 1997, 240 ff.; *Magnus*, IHR 2002, 45 ff.; *Mari*, Foro pad. 1997, 9 ff.; *Schütze*, S. 423 ff.; *Timpano*, iContr. 2000, 664 ff. Zum Verhältnis von CISG und EuGVO vgl. hingegen *Ferrari*, ecolex 2007, 303 ff.; *ders.*, IPRax 2007, 61 ff.; *ders.*, Int'l Bus. L. J. 2007, 83 ff.; *Piltz*, IHR 2006, 53 ff.; *Ragno*, Giur. merito 2006, 1413 ff.

[180] Vgl. hierzu *Schmidt-Kessel*, FS Schlechtriem, S. 255 ff.; a. A. *Schlechtriem/Schwenzer/Schlechtriem*, CISG Commentary, 2. Aufl., Art. 4, Rn. 20.

[181] *Schmidt-Kessel*, FS Schlechtriem, S. 255, 272.

[182] So *Schmidt-Kessel*, FS Schlechtriem, S. 255, 274.

[183] Vgl. *Achilles*, Art. 4, Rn. 3 und Rn. 4; *Bamberger/Roth/Saenger*, Art. 4, Rn. 26; *Brunner*, Art. 4, Rn. 33; *Ferrari*, Vendita internazionale, S. 97; *ders.*, Applicabilità ed applicazioni, S. 241; *ders.*, Scope of Application, S. 96, 101; *Ferrari u. a./Saenger*, Internationales Vertragsrecht, Art. 4, Rn. 27; *Hartnell*, 18 Yale Int'l L. J. (1993), 1, 64; *Honnold/Flechtner*, Art. 4, Rn. 66; *Kröll u. a./Djordjevic*, Art. 4, Rn. 18; *Lohmann*, Parteiautonomie, S. 29, Fn. 66; *Martin-Davidson*, 17 Mich. St. J. Int'l L. (2008), 657, 691; *Mather*, 20 J. L. & Com. (2001), 155, 162; MünchKomm/*Westermann*, Vor Art. 1, Rn. 17 und Art. 4, Rn. 8; MünchKommHGB/*Benicke*, Art. 4, Rn. 14; *Papandréou-Deterville*, D. 2002, Jur. 398, 398; *Piltz*, NJW 2000, 553, 556; *Posch/Terlitza*, IHR 2001, 47, 49; *Rosenberg*, 20 Aust. Bus. L. Rev. (1992), 442, 447; *Schlechtriem*, Internationales UN-Kaufrecht, Rn. 41; *ders.*, 36 Vict. U. Well. L. Rev. (2005), 781, 788; *Schlechtriem/Schwenzer/Schwenzer/Hachem*, CISG Commentary, Art. 4, Rn. 2 und 9; *Schwimann/Posch*, Art. 4, Rn. 11; *Soergel/Lüderitz/Fenge*, Art. 4, Rn. 8; *Stoll*, Internationalprivatrechtliche Fragen, S. 497; *Wasmer*, S. 17; *Witz/Salger/Lorenz/Lorenz*, Art. 4, Rn. 29.

[184] Vgl. etwa OLG Schleswig, 24.10.2008, CISG-online 2020; LG Landshut, 12.6.2008, CISG-online 1703; CIETAC, 10.12.2007, CISG-online 1932; KG Wallis, 27.4.2007, CISG-online 1721; CA Versailles, 13.10.2005, CISG-online 1433; CIETAC, 1.10.2005, CISG-online 1914; KG Wallis, 27.5.2005, CISG-online 1137; CIETAC, CISG/2005/22 (ohne Datum), CISG-online 1912; CIETAC, 28.2.2005, CISG-online 1580; CIETAC, 1.9.2004, CISG-online 1910; Shanghai No. I. Intermediate People's Court, 23.3.2004, CISG-online 1497; CIETAC, 12.3.2004, CISG-online 1599; Tribunale di Padova, 25.2.2004, CISG-online 819 = Giur. it. 2004, 1405; OGH, 22.10.2001, CISG-online 613; Tribunale di Vigevano, 12.7.2000, CISG-online 493 = IHR 2001, 72, 76; HGer Aargau, 11.6.1999, CISG-online 494 = SZIER 2000, 117 f.; KG Zürich, 30.11.1998, CISG-online 415 = SZIER 1999, 186 ff.; LG Berlin, 24.3.1998, CISG-online 742; OGH, 20.3.1997, CISG-online 269; App. Tessin, 12.2.1996, CISG-online 233 = SZIER 1996, 135; LG Kassel,

Art. 4 35   Teil I. Kapitel I. Anwendungsbereich

auf dem Gebiet des internationalen Warenkaufs vom 17.2.1983 noch nicht in Kraft getreten ist,[185] also kein materielles Einheitsrecht auf dem Gebiet der Stellvertretung existiert, wird diese Frage immer anhand des über die IPR Vorschriften des Forumsstaates berufenen nationalen Rechts zu entscheiden sein:[186] In Deutschland gilt insoweit das Statut der jeweiligen gesetzlichen Vertretung,[187] bei rechtsgeschäftlicher Vertretung das Recht des Wirkungslandes.[188] Ob eine Erklärung überhaupt auf eine andere Person als möglichen Vertragspartner zielt, muss jedoch zunächst anhand der im Übereinkommen festgelegten Auslegungsregeln entschieden werden.[189]

35 Dem Regelungsbereich des Übereinkommens ist, so auch die Rechtsprechung,[190] auch die **Verjährung** entzogen.[191] Dies führt aber nicht notwendigerweise dazu, dass das über das IPR des Forumsstaates berufene Recht zur Anwendung kommt.[192] Ist der Forumsstaat

---

22.6.1995, CISG-online 370; AG Alsfeld, 12.5.1995, CISG-online 170 = NJW-RR 1996, 120; KG Berlin, 24.1.1994, CISG-online 130 = RIW 1994, 683; LG Hamburg, 26.9.1990, CISG-online 21 = EuZW 1991, 188.

[185] Vgl. hierzu etwa *Bonell*, Riv. dir. comm. 1983, I, 273 ff.; *Stöcker*, WM 1983, 778 ff.

[186] So auch *Honsell/Siehr*, Art. 4, Rn. 7; *Kröll/Mistelis/Perales Viscasillas/Djordjevic*, Art. 4, Rn. 18; in der Rechtsprechung vgl. LG Kassel, 22.6.1995, CISG-online 370 („Stellvertretungsfragen sind nach dem materiellen Recht zu entscheiden, das vom IPR [...] berufen wird"); vgl. auch AG Sursee, 12.9.2008, CISG-online 1728: „So sind sowohl die gesetzliche als auch die rechtsgeschäftliche Stellvertretung nach dem kollisionsrechtlich berufenen Recht zu beurteilen".

[187] *Kropholler*, IPR, § 42 I 1.

[188] *Herber*, 2. Aufl., Art. 4, Rn. 11; *Staudinger/Magnus*, Art. 4, Rn. 37; in der Rechtsprechung, vgl. BGH, 13.5.1982, NJW 1982, 2733; BGH, 15.4.1975, BGHZ 64, 183; BGH, 3.12.1964, BGHZ 43, 21.

[189] So LG Hamburg, 26.9.1990, CISG-online 21 = RIW 1990, 1015, 1016; zustimmend *Karollus*, S. 41; *ders.*, RdW 1991, 319; *Reinhart*, IPRax 1991, 376.

[190] Vgl. BGer, 18.5.2009, CISG-online 1900; AppGer Basel-Stadt, 26.9.2008, CISG-online 1732; Court of First Instance of Athens, Aktenzeichen 4505/2009 (ohne Datum), CISG-online 2228; Suprene Court Slovak Republic, 30.4.2008, CISG-online 1873; Audiencia Provincial de Valencia, 13.3.2007, CISG-online 1719; OLG Köln, 13.2.2006, CISG-online 1219 = IHR 2006, 145, 147; CA Versailles, 13.10.2005, CISG-online 1433; Regional Court Bratislava, 11.10.2005, CISG-online 1858 (dort aber mit falschem Datum); OLG Linz, 8.8.2005, CISG-online 1087; Tribunal of International Commercial Arbitration at the Russian Federation Chamber of Commerce and Industry, 2.6.2005, CISG-online 1501; KG Nidwalden, 23.5.2005, CISG-online 1086 = IHR 2005, 253, 256; LG Bamberg, 13.4.2005, CISG-online 1402; Hof van Bereop Gent, 4.10.2004, CISG-online 985; OLG Karlsruhe, 20.7.2004, CISG-online 858 = IHR 2004, 246, 250; Tribunal of International Commercial Arbitration at the Russian Federation Chamber of Commerce and Industry, 9.6.2004, CISG-online 1239; Hof van Beroep Gent, 17.5.2004, CISG-online 990; Tribunal of International Commercial Arbitration at the Ukraine Chamber of Commerce and Trade, 15.4.2004, CISG-online 1270; Tribunale di Padova, 25.2.2004, CISG-online 819; KG Schaffhausen, 27.1.2004, CISG-online 960; OLG Karlsruhe, 10.12.2003, CISG-online 911 = IHR 2004, 62, 65; ICC, 11 849/2003, CISG-online 1421; OLG Zweibrücken, 26.7.2002, CISG-online 688 = IHR 2002, 67, 69; OGH, 14.1.2002, CISG-online 643 = IHR 2002, 77, 79; ICC, 11 333/2002, CISG-online 1420; OGH, 22.10.2001, CISG-online 613; RB Ieper, 29.1.2001, CISG-online 606; OGH, 7.9.2000, CISG-online 642 = IHR 2001, 42 ff.; Tribunale di Vigevano, 12.7.2000, CISG-online 493 = IHR 2001, 72, 76; OGH, 26.5.1998, östZfRVgl 2000, 77; OLG München, 21.1.1998, CISG-online 536; LG Heilbronn, 15.9.1997, CISG-online 562; OGH, 24.10.1995, CISG-online 166 = östZfRVgl 1996, 76; LG Düsseldorf, 11.10.1995, CISG-online 180; OLG Hamm, 9.6.1995, CISG-online 146 = IPRax 1996, 269 f.; ICC, 7660/JK, CISG-online 129 = ICC Ct. Bull. 2/1995, 69.

[191] *Achilles*, Art. 4, Rn. 14; *Bamberger/Roth/Saenger*, Art. 4, Rn. 29; *Bonell*, 56 Am. J .Comp. L. (2008), 1, 3; *Brunner*, Art. 4, Rn. 18; *Enderlein/Maskow/Strohbach*, Art. 4, Anm. 4.1.; *Esslinger*, ALI-ABA (1999), 49, 69; *Ferrari*, Scope of Application, S. 96, 106; *ders.*, Forum International 1997, 89, 91; *Ferrari u. a./Saenger*, Internationales Vertragsrecht, Art. 4, Rn. 31; *Flambouras*, 29 J. L. & Com. (2011), 171, 217; *P. Huber*, IHR 2006, 228, 234; *P. Huber/Mullis/P. Huber*, S. 29; *Janssen*, The Application of the CISG in Dutch Courts, S. 129, 137; *Kuhlen*, S. 97; *Markel*, 21 Pace Int'l L. Rev. (2009), 163, 190 f.; *Martin-Davidson*, 17 Mich. St. J. Int'l L. (2008), 657, 691; *Mather*, 20 J. L. & Com. (2001), 155, 161; MünchKomm/*Westermann*, Vor Art. 1, Rn. 17 und Art. 4, Rn. 16; MünchKommHGB/*Benicke*, Art. 4, Rn. 13; *Piltz*, NJW 2003, 2056, 2059; *ders.*, NJW 2000, 553, 556; *Posch/Terlitza* IHR 2001, 47, 49; *Schillo*, IHR 2003, 257, 258; *Schlechtriem*, Internationales UN-Kaufrecht, Rn. 41; *Schlechtriem/Schwenzer/Schlechtriem*, CISG Commentary, 2. Aufl., Art. 4, Rn. 21; *Schlechtriem/Schwenzer/Schwenzer/Hachem*, CISG Commentary, Art. 4, Rn. 50; *Schwenzer/Manner*, Arb. Int'l (2007), 293, 294 und 302; *Soergel/Lüderitz/Fenge*, Art. 4, Rn. 10; *Wasmer*, S. 17; *C.Witz*, Rev. dr. aff. int. 2001, 253, 265; *ders.*, D. 2002, Chron. 2796, 2797 f.; *ders.*, D. 2000, Jur. 442, 443; *Witz/Salger/Lorenz/Lorenz*, Art. 4, Rn. 29.

[192] So aber LG Düsseldorf, 11.10.1995, CSIG-online 180.

Sachlicher Geltungsbereich   36, 37 **Art. 4**

Vertragsstaat des UNCITRAL Verjährungsübereinkommens von 1974 (oder der 1980 dem CISG angepassten Version), so muss zunächst geprüft werden, ob dessen Anwendungsvoraussetzungen vorliegen.[193] Nur wenn das Übereinkommen nicht zur Anwendung kommt, ist auf das über das IPR berufene nationale Recht abzustellen;[194] ist der Forumsstaat Nichtvertragsstaat des Verjährungsübereinkommens, kann dagegen unmittelbar auf die IPR Vorschriften zurückgegriffen werden, um das anwendbare Recht zu bestimmen.[195] Bei einem **deutschen Forum** bedeutet dies sowohl kraft Art. 32 I 4 EGBGB in Verbindung mit Art. 27 ff. EGBGB[196] als auch kraft Art. 12 I lit. d) Rom-I VO in Verbindung mit Art. 3 ff. Rom-I VO, dass die Verjährung dem Recht untersteht, dem der Kaufvertrag unterliegen würde, fände nicht das CISG Anwendung,[197] bei fehlender Rechtswahl also in der Regel dem Recht des Verkäufers, d. h., der Partei, die im Rahmen des Kaufvertrages die charakteristische Leistung zu vollbringen hat.[198] Zu diesem Ergebnis gelangt man selbstverständlich auch in den anderen Rechtsordnungen, in denen die relevanten IPR Normen mit denen des Römischen Vertragrechtsübereinkommens übereinstimmen.[199]

Kommt **deutsches Verjährungsrecht** zur Anwendung, so muss neben den einschlägi‑ 36 gen, nunmehr neu gefassten Vorschriften des BGB[200] auch die neue Fassung des **Art. 3 des Vertragsgesetzes** beachtet werden. Gleich wie sein Vorgänger, bezieht sich Art. 3 VertragsG n. F. nur auf Sachmängel, d. h., er erfasst alle Ansprüche, die Art. 45 CISG dem Käufer nicht vertragsgemäßer Ware einräumt, also den Anspruch auf Nachlieferung oder Nachbesserung, das Recht auf Vertragsaufhebung, Preisminderung sowie den Anspruch auf Schadenersatz. Genauso wie die alte Fassung bezieht sich Art. 3 VertragsG nicht auf Rechtsmängel.[201] Anders als die alte Fassung sieht die neue Fassung jedoch keinen eigenständigen Verjährungsbeginn vor; vielmehr entspricht nunmehr der Verjährungsbeginn von CISG-Ansprüchen dem von BGB-Ansprüchen[202] – was nur auf Grund der Verlängerung der kaufrechtlichen Verjährungsfrist auf zwei Jahre (also der in Art. 39 II CISG vorgesehenen Frist) möglich geworden ist.[203]

Zu den vom Regelungsbereich des Übereinkommens ausgeschlossenen Rechtsfragen 37 zählt nicht nur die Lehre,[204] sondern auch die Rechtsprechung[205] auch die **Schuldüber-**

---

[193] Vgl. *Ferrari*, IHR 2006, 1, 13 f.; zum Verjährungsübereinkommen vgl. die Kommentierung des Verjährungsübereinkommens von *Müller-Chen;* sowie *Boele-Woelki,* Molengrafica 1996, 99–146; *Krapp,* 19 J. World Trade L. (1985), 343–372; *Landfermann,* RabelsZ 39 (1975), 253–277; *Smit,* 23 Am. J. Comp. L. (1975), 337–362; *Winship,* 28 Int'l Law. (1994), 1071–1081.
[194] *P. Huber,* IHR 2006, 228, 234.
[195] *Staudinger/Magnus,* Art. 4, Rn. 39, spricht vom „üblichen kollisionsrechtlichen Weg".
[196] Vgl. auch *Ferrari u. a./Ferrari,* 1. Aufl., Art. 32 EGBGB, Rn. 24 f.; *Kuhlen,* S. 99; *Magnus,* RIW 2002, 577, 578 f.; *Piltz,* Internationales Kaufrecht, Rn. 2–165; in der Rechtsprechung vgl. LG Bamberg, 13.4.2005, CISG-online 1402.
[197] *Herber,* 2. Aufl., Art. 4, Rn. 21.
[198] So auch *Magnus,* RIW 2002, 577, 578 f.; *Rudolph,* Art. 4, Rn. 21.
[199] Vgl. auch *Honsell/Siehr,* Art. 4, Rn. 25.
[200] Zum Verhältnis zwischen neuem Verjährungsrecht und UN-Kaufrecht, vgl. *Magnus,* RIW 2002, 577 ff.; *C. Witz,* D. 2002, Chron. 2860 ff.
[201] Vgl. *Magnus,* RTW 2002, 577, 581; a. A. *Schroeter,* Art. 3 VertragsG, Rn. 6.
[202] *C. Witz,* D. 2002, Chron. 2860, 2861.
[203] Vgl. Begründung BT-Drs. 14/6040, S. 284.
[204] Vgl. *Achilles,* Art. 4, Rn. 9; *Bamberger/Roth/Saenger,* Art. 4, Rn. 27; *Brunner,* Art. 4, Rn. 34; *Ferrari,* IHR 2006, 1, 13; *ders.,* Scope of Application, S. 96, 107; *Ferrari u. a./Saenger,* Internationales Vertragsrecht, Art. 4, Rn. 28; *Honsell/Siehr,* Art. 4, Rn. 19; *Karollus,* S. 45; *Kröll u. a./Djordjevic,* Art. 4, Rn. 46; *Magnus,* ZEuP 2002, 523, 529; *MünchKomm/Westermann,* Art. 4, Rn. 16; *MünchKommHGB/Benicke,* Art. 4, Rn. 15; *Piltz,* Internationales Kaufrecht, Rn. 2–161; *Piltz,* NJW 2000, 553, 556; *Posch/Terlitza,* IHR 2001, 47, 49; *Schlechtriem,* Internationales UN-Kaufrecht, Rn. 41; *Schlechtriem/Schwenzer/Schlechtriem,* CISG Commentary, 2. Aufl., Art. 4, Rn. 23; *Schlechtriem/Schwenzer/Schlechtriem/Schwenzer/Hachem,* CISG Commentary, Art. 4, Rn. 22; *Soergel/Lüderitz/Fenge,* Art. 4, Rn. 9; *Vida,* IPRax 2002, 146, 147; *Witz/Salger/Lorenz/Lorenz,* Art. 4, Rn. 29.
[205] So ausdrücklich OGH, 24.4.1997, CISG-online 291 = Forum International 1997, 93, m. zust. Anm. *Ferrari;* vgl. auch Hauptstadtgericht Budapest, zitiert und angemerkt von *Vida,* IPRax 2002, 146 ff.

Art. 4 38, 39   Teil I. Kapitel I. Anwendungsbereich

nahme. Gleiches gilt auch hinsichtlich des **Schuldbeitritts,**[206] des Schuldanerkenntnisses[207] und der Vertragsübernahme.[208]

38 Das Übereinkommen regelt auch die **Abtretung** nicht;[209] dies ist sowohl von der deutschen,[210] der österreichischen[211] als auch der schweizerischen,[212] belgischen[213] Rechtsprechung als auch der Rechtsprechung der Gerichte anderer Staaten[214] bestätigt worden.[215] Dies bedeutet jedoch nicht, dass notwendigerweise auf das IPR des Forumsstaates zurückgegriffen werden muss, um das anwendbare Recht zu bestimmen.[216] Da in verschiedenen Staaten das Ottawa Übereinkommen über Internationales Factoring in Kraft getreten ist,[217] müssen die Gerichte jener Staaten zunächst untersuchen, ob die Abtretung als Factoring in Sinne des Übereinkommens qualifiziert werden kann, und ob die anderen Anwendungsvoraussetzungen vorliegen.[218] Sollte dem so sein,[219] ist auf das IPR nur zur Schließung von Lücken zurückzugreifen oder dann, wenn die Parteien die Anwendbarkeit des Übereinkommens ausgeschlossen haben.

39 Problematischer ist die Frage, ob die **Aufrechnung** im Übereinkommen geregelt ist, also nationale Vorschriften verdrängt werden.[220] Dies hängt damit zusammen, dass ein Teil der Lehre und der Rechtsprechung[221] die **Geldansprüche** der Vertragsparteien eines dem

---

[206] *Lurger*, IHR 2005, 177, 180; *Staudinger/Magnus*, Art. 4, Rn. 57.

[207] *Ferrari*, Scope of Application, S. 96, 107; *Ferrari u. a./Saenger*, Internationales Vertragsrecht, Art. 4, Rn. 29; *Kröll u. a./Djordjevic*, Art. 4, Rn. 46; *Lurger*, IHR 2005, 177, 180; *Magnus*, ZEuP 2002, 523, 529, mit Hinweis auf BGH, 9.1.2002, CISG-online 651 = RIW 2002, 396 ff.; *Soergel/Lüderitz/Fenge*, Art. 4, Rn. 9; vgl. auch LG Hamm, 23.6.1998, CISG-online 434 = TranspR-IHR 2000, 7, 9.

[208] *Bamberger/Roth/Saenger*, Art. 4, Rn. 27; *Lurger*, IHR 2005, 177, 180.

[209] *Achilles*, Art. 4, Rn. 9; *Bamberger/Roth/Saenger*, Art. 4, Rn. 21; *Brunner*, Art. 4, Rn. 34; *Ferrari*, Applicabilità ed applicazioni, S. 242; *ders.*, Scope of Application, S. 96, 106; *ders.*, Forum International 1997, 89, 92; *Ferrari u. a./Saenger*, Internationales Vertragsrecht, Art. 4, Rn. 22; *Janssen*, The Application of the CISG in Dutch Courts, S. 129, 137; *Karollus*, S. 45; *Kröll u. a./Djordjevic*, Art. 4, Rn. 46; *Lurger*, IHR 2005, 177, 180; *Martin-Davidson*, 17 Mich. St. J. Int'l L. (2008), 657, 691; *Mather*, 20 J. L. & Com. (2001), 155, 160; MünchKomm/*Westermann*, Art. 4, Rn. 15; MünchKommHGB/*Benicke*, Art. 4, Rn. 15; *Piltz*, Internationales Kaufrecht, Rn. 2–163; *ders.*, NJW 2000, 553, 556; *Posch/Terlitza*, IHR 2001, 47, 49; *Rosch*, D. 2000, Jur. 437, 438; *Schlechtriem*, Internationales UN-Kaufrecht, Rn. 41; *Schlechtriem/Schwenzer/Schlechtriem*, CISG Commentary, 2. Aufl., Art. 4, Rn. 23; *Schlechtriem/Schwenzer/Schlechtriem/Schwenzer/Hachem*, CISG Commentary, Art. 4, Rn. 22; *Schwenzer/Schmidt*, 13 VJ (2009), 109, 115 f.; *Soergel/Lüderitz/Fenge*, Art. 4, Rn. 9; *Staudinger/Magnus*, Art. 4, Rn. 57; *Stoll*, Internationalprivatrechtliche Fragen, S. 506; *Teichert*, Lückenfüllung, S. 19; *C. Witz*, Rev. dr. aff. int. 2001, 253, 265 f.

[210] OLG Hamburg, 25.1.2008, CISG-online 1681; BGH, 12.2.1998, CISG-online 343 = TranspR-IHR 1999, 125 ff.; OLG Hamm, 9.6.1995, CISG-online 146 = IPRax 1996, 297; KG Berlin, 24.1.1994, CISG-online 130 = RIW 1994, 683.

[211] OGH, 7.9.2000, CISG-online 642 = IHR 2001, 42 ff.; OGH, 26.5.1998, östZfRVgl 2000, 77.

[212] HGer Aargau, 26.11.2008, CISG-online 1739; OGer Thurgau, 19.12.1995, CISG-online 496; BezG Arbon, 9.12.1994, CISG-online 376.

[213] Vgl. Trib. com. Nivelles, 19.9.1995, CISG-online 366.

[214] District Court Trnava, 17.9.2008, CISG-online 1991; Regional Court Kosice, 22.5.2007, CISG-online 1989; Tribunal of International Commercial Arbitration at the Russian Federation Chamber of Commerce and Industry, 27.5.2005, CISG-online 1456; Tribunale di Padova, 25.2.2004, CISG-online 819; Supreme Court of Poland, 19.12.2003, CISG-online 1222.

[215] Es sei angemerkt, dass der Zessionar, sollte das Verhältnis zwischen Zedenten und Schuldner dem CISG unterliegen, grundsätzlich nur insoweit Ansprüche geltend machen kann, als ihm diese auf der Grundlage des CISG zustehen; vgl. *Schwenzer/M. Schmidt*, 13 VJ (2009), 109, 119 ff., die aber auch hervorheben, dass in Bezug auf „claims based on express warranties or guarantees, on the other hand, the remote purchaser's claim is independent of any earlier contracts in the chain and must be determined solely based on the relationship between the manufacturer and the sub-purchaser." Vgl. auch *Schlechtriem/Schwenzer/Schlechtriem/Schwenzer/Hachem*, CISG Commentary, Art. 4, Rn. 24.

[216] So aber *Magnus*, ZEuP 1995, 202, 208.

[217] Seit dem 1.12.1998 ist das Factoring Übereinkommen auch in der BR Deutschland in Kraft.

[218] Siehe diesbezüglich *Ferrari*, RIW 1996, 181–188; *ders.*, 31 Int'l Law. (1997), 41–63; *ders.*, Riv. trim. dir. proced. civ. 1996, 196–218; *Häusler*, Das UNIDROIT Übereinkommen über internationales Factoring.

[219] Vgl. etwa CA Grenoble, 13.9.1995, CISG-online 157.

[220] Ausführlich hierzu neuerdings *Saenger/Sauthoff*, IHR 2005, 189 ff.

[221] AG Duisburg, 13.4.2000, CISG-online 659 = IHR 2001, 114, 115: „Das Übereinkommen der Vereinten Nationen über Verträge über den internationalen Warenkauf (CISG) enthält keine ausdrückliche Regelung über die Aufrechnung. Anerkannt ist, dass eine Aufrechnung mit wechselseitigen Ansprüchen aus demselben

Sachlicher Geltungsbereich 39 **Art. 4**

Übereinkommen unterliegenden Vertragsverhältnisses für **(konventionsintern) aufrechenbar** erklärt,²²² auf der Grundlage entweder des Art. 84 II, der eine Aufrechnung des zurückzuzahlenden Kaufpreises mit dem Wert der Gebrauchsvorteile anordnet,²²³ oder auf der Grundlage des Grundsatzes, wonach Leistungen Zug-um-Zug zu erfüllen sind.²²⁴ Dieser Auffassung ist m. E.²²⁵ nicht zuzustimmen,²²⁶ da man kaum vertreten kann, dass die erwähnten Bestimmungen die Frage der Aufrechnung abschließend regeln.²²⁷ Diesbezüglich sei lediglich darauf hingewiesen, dass „sich aus dem Übereinkommen keine Antwort zur Frage entnehmen lässt, ob (und unter welchen Voraussetzungen) die Aufrechnung ipso iure oder durch Erklärung erfolgt."²²⁸ Ob hingegen Ansprüche aufrechenbar sind, die sich nicht lediglich aus einem dem Übereinkommen unterliegenden Vertragsverhältnis ergeben, ist aber ohne Zweifel auf der Grundlage des über das IPR berufenen Rechts zu entscheiden,²²⁹ also sicher nicht konventionsintern.²³⁰ Ein bloßes Abstellen auf die lex fori ist jedoch nicht zulässig.²³¹

Kaufvertrag i. S. d. CISG möglich ist (*Staudinger/Magnus*, Art. 4, Rn. 47)". Vgl. auch OLG Hamburg, 26.11.1999, CISG-online 515 = IHR 2001, 19 ff.: „Die Aufrechnung gilt als allgemeines Prinzip im Sinne von Art. 7 Abs. 2 CISG jedenfalls insoweit, als sich, wie hier, gegenseitige Ansprüche aus der Konvention gegenüberstehen". Die Aufrechnung von sich aus demselben Vertrag ergebenden Ansprüche nicht von vornherein ausschließend auch BGer, 20.12.2006, CISG-online 1426 = IHR 2007, 127, 128, OLG Karlsruhe, 20.7.2004, CISG-online 858 = IHR 2004, 246, 251.

²²² Vgl. etwa *Achilles*, Art. 4, Rn. 10; *Bridge,* Draft Digest, S. 235, 251 f.; *Brunner*, Art. 4, Rn. 52; CISG-AC, Op. 9 (*Bridge*), Comment 3.23; *Enderlein/Maskow/Strohbach*, Art. 84, Anm. 1.; *Kröll*, 25 J. L. & Com. (2005), 39, 48; *Kröll u. a./Djordjevic*, Art. 4, Rn. 41; *Magnus*, ZEuP 1995, 202, 207 f.; *Martin-Davidson*, 17 Mich. St. J. Int'l L. (2008), 657, 691; *Schlechtriem/Schwenzer/Schwenzer/Hachem*, CISG Commentary, Art. 4, Rn. 28; *Weber*, Vertragsverletzungsfolgen, S. 186.

²²³ *Staudinger/Magnus*, Art. 4, Rn. 46.

²²⁴ *Piltz*, Internationales Kaufrecht, Rn. 5–326; a. A. *Frigge*, S. 79, die diesbezüglich statuiert, dass „das Rechtsinstitut der Aufrechnung [...] nicht aus den allgemeinen Grundsätzen abgeleitet werden [kann]."

²²⁵ Vgl. auch *Ferrari*, IHR 2006, 1, 13; *ders.*, Applicabilità ed applicazioni, S. 242; *ders.*, Scope of Application, S. 96, 108.

²²⁶ Ebenso *Bamberger/Roth/Saenger*, Art. 4, Rn. 19; *Bazinas*, Uniformity, S. 26; *Bonell*, 56 Am. J. Comp. L. (2009), 1, 3; *Ferrari u. a./Saenger*, Internationales Vertragsrecht, Art. 4, Rn. 20; *Flambouras*, 29 J. L. & Com. (2011), 171, 203; *Fuchs*, IHR 2003, 231 f.; *Honnold/Flechtner*, Art. 4, Rn. 70; *P. Huber*, IHR 2006, 228, 234; *P. Huber/Mullis/P. Huber*, S. 30; *Janssen*, The Application of the CISG in Dutch Courts, S. 129, 134; *T. M. Müller*, Beweislast, S. 32; MünchKomm/*Westermann*, Art. 4, Rn. 12; *Piltz*, NJW 2000, 553, 556; *Saenger/Sauthoff*, IHR 2005, 189, 190; *Schlechtriem*, Internationales UN-Kaufrecht, Rn. 42e; *ders.*, 36 Vict. U. Well. L. Rev. (2005), 781, 791; *Schlechtriem/Schwenzer/Schlechtriem*, CISG Commentary, 2. Aufl., Art. 4, Rn. 22a; *Witz/Salger/Lorenz/Lorenz*, Art. 4, Rn. 29.

²²⁷ So auch in der Rechtsprechung LG Bamberg, 23.10.2006, CISG-online 1400.

²²⁸ *Schlechtriem*, Internationales UN-Kaufrecht, Rn. 42; ebenso *Bianca/Bonell/Tallon*, Art. 81, Anm. 2.6.; ebenso in der Rechtsprechung etwa OGer Thurgau, 19.12.1995, CISG-online 496.

²²⁹ *Honsell/Siehr*, Art. 4, Rn. 21; *Saenger/Sauthoff*, IHR 2005, 189; *Soergel/Lüderitz/Fenge*, Art. 4, Rn. 10; so in der Rechtsprechung ausdrücklich OGH, 22.10.2001, CISG-online 613 = IHR 2002, 24, 27: „Mangels einer im UN-Kaufrecht getroffenen Regelung über die Aufrechnung mit konventionsfremden Ansprüchen, also mit solchen, die sich nicht aus einem dem UN-Kaufrecht unterworfenen Vertragsverhältnis ergeben, ist für die Wirkungen der Aufrechnung und deren Zulässigkeit einschließlich etwaiger Aufrechnungshindernisse allein das nach Maßgabe des nach IPR-Regeln berufene nationale Recht maßgebend"; ebenso BGer, 20.12.2006, CISG-online 1426 = IHR 2007, 127, 128 f.; OLG Karlsruhe, 20.7.2004, CISG-online 858 = IHR 2004, 246, 251.

²³⁰ Dass die Aufrechnung überhaupt nicht in den Regelungsbereich des Übereinkommens fällt, ist in der Rechtsprechung oft hervorgehoben worden; vgl. zum CISG BGH, 23.6.2010, CISG-online 2129 = IHR 2010, 217, 221; AppGer Basel-Stadt, 26.9.2008, CISG-online 1732; OLG Köln, 19.5.2008, CISG-online 1700; Single-Member Court of First Instance of Thessalonika, Aktenzeichen 43945/2007 (ohne Datum), CISG Pace; BGer, 20.12.2006, CISG-online 1426, 2.2.1; LG Bamberg, 23.10.2006, CISG-online 1400; OLG Köln, 13.2.2006, CISG-online 1219 = IHR 2006, 145, 147; HGer Zürich, 22.12.2005, CISG-online 1195 = IHR 2006, 161, 164; OLG Linz, 23.3.2005, CISG-online 1376; OLG Düsseldorf, 20.12.2004, CISG-online 997; OLG Düsseldorf, 22.7.2004, CISG-online 916 = IHR 2005, 29, 30; BGer, 7.7.2004, CISG-online 848 = IHR 2004, 252, 253; OLG Düsseldorf, 28.5.2004, CISG-online 850 = IHR 2004, 203, 207 und 212; Tribunale di Padova, 25.2.2004, CISG-online 819 = IHR 2005, 31, 33; LG Mönchengladbach, 15.7.2003, CISG-online 813 = IHR 2003, 229, 230, m. Anm. *Fuchs;* OGH, 22.10.2001, CISG-online 613 = IHR 2002, 27; OLG Köln, 28.1.2001, IHR 2002, 21, 24; Tribunale di Vigevano, CISG-online 493 = 12.7.2000, IHR 2001, 72, 76; AG Duisburg, 13.4.2000, CISG-online 659 = IHR 2001, 114 f.; OLG Koblenz, 18.11.1999,

Art. 4 40, 41   Teil I. Kapitel I. Anwendungsbereich

40   Auch die inhaltliche **Gültigkeit beziehungsweise Zulässigkeit von Vertragsstrafenvereinbarungen** bzw. **liquidated damage clauses** bestimmt sich nach nationalem Recht,[232] nicht nach dem Übereinkommen.[233] Das Zustandekommen dieser Vereinbarungen richtet sich jedoch, sofern diese als Nebenbestimmungen eines dem Übereinkommen unterliegenden Vertrages vereinbart werden, nach dem Übereinkommen,[234] genauso wie sich auch das Zustandekommen einer in einem dem Übereinkommen unterliegenden Vertrag enthaltenen **Gerichtstands- oder Schiedsgerichtsvereinbarung** nach dem Übereinkommen richtet,[235] selbst wenn sich die inhaltliche Gültigkeit nach nationalem Recht bemisst.[236]

41   Auch die Frage, ob jemand **gesamtschuldnerisch haftet,** ist nicht im Übereinkommen geregelt.[237] Gleiches gilt auch für den Anspruch auf Unterlassung der Inanspruchnahme einer Bankgarantie,[238] sowie für die Frage, in welcher **Währung** Zahlungen zu erfolgen haben.[239]

CISG-online 570 = IHR 2001, 110, 111; OLG München, 11.3.1998, CISG-online 310, Anm. *Schlechtriem,* EWiR 1998, 549; LG Hagen, 15.10.1997, CISG-online 311; OLG Düsseldorf, 11.7.1996, CISG-online 201 = RIW 1996, 958; LG Duisburg, 17.4.1996, CISG-online 186 = RIW 1996, 774; OLG Stuttgart, 21.8.1995, CISG-online 150 = IPRax 1996, 139; AG München, 23.6.1995, CISG-online 368; OLG Hamm, 9.6.1995, CISG-online 146 = NJW-RR 1996, 179; RB Middelburg, 25.1.1995, CISG-online 374 = NIPR 14 (1996), Nr. 127; OLG Düsseldorf, 10.2.1994, CISG-online 116 = DB 1994, 2494; LG Frankfurt a. M., 13.7.1994, CISG-online 118 = NJW-RR 1994, 1265; OLG Koblenz, 17.9.1993, CISG-online 91 = RIW 1993, 934; RB Roermond, 6.5.1993, CISG-online 454; RB Arnhem, 25.2.1993, CISG-online 98 = NIPR 11 (1993), Nr. 445; anscheinend gehen aber OLG Düsseldorf, 10.2.1994, CISG-online 115 = NJW-RR 1994, 507 und OLG München, 2.3.1994, CISG-online 108 = RIW 1994, 596 inzident davon aus, dass eine „konventionsinterne" Aufrechnungsmöglichkeit besteht; vgl. hierzu *Magnus,* ZEuP 1995, 202, 208.
[231] So aber AG Frankfurt a. M., 31.1.1991, CISG-online 34 = IPRax 1991, 345, mit abl. Anm. *Jayme;* kritisch hierzu auch *Staudinger/Magnus,* Art. 4, Rn. 47.
[232] So auch die Rechtsprechung; vgl. Serbian Chamber of Commerce, 15.7.2008, CISG-online 1795; OLG Hamburg, 25.1.2008, CISG-online 1681; Tribunal of International Commercial Arbitration at the Russian Federation Chamber of Commerce and Industry, 1.3.2006, CISG-online 1941; Tribunal of International Commercial Arbitration at the Russian Federation Chamber of Commerce and Industry, 13.1.2006, CISG-online 1622; CIETAC, 7.12.2005, CISG-online 2124; CIETAC, 9.11.2005, CISG-online 1444; Tribunal of International Commercial Arbitration at the Russian Federation Chamber of Commerce and Industry, 27.4.2005, CISG-online 1500; CIETAC, 1.9.2004, CISG-online 1910; Tribunal of International Commercial Arbitration at the Russian Federation Chamber of Commerce and Industry, 9.6.2004, CISG-online 1239; Tribunal of International Commercial Arbitration at the Russian Federation Chamber of Commerce and Industry, 24.5.2004, CISG-online 1210; RB Hasselt, 17.6.1998, CISG-online 760; Hof van Beroep Antwerpen, 18.6.1996, CISG-online 758; Hof Arnhem, 22.8.1995, CISG-online 317 = NIPR 13 (1995), Nr. 514; ICC, 7197/1992, CISG-online 36 = J. D. I. 1993, 1028.
[233] *Brunner,* Art. 4, Rn. 37; *Czerwenka,* Rechtsanwendungsprobleme, S. 167; *Farnsworth,* 27 Am. J. Comp. L. (1979), 247; *Ferrari,* Forum International 1997, 89, 91; *Hachem.* 13 VJ (2009), 217, 222; *Janssen,* The Application of the CISG in Dutch Courts, S. 129, 137; *Kröll u. a./Djorjevic,* Art. 4, Rn. 26; *Reinhart,* Art. 4, Rn. 7 und Art. 79, Rn. 12; *Schlechtriem/Schwenzer/Schlechtriem,* CISG Commentary, 2. Aufl., Art. 4, Rn. 23; *Schlechtriem/Schwenzer/Hachem,* CISG Commentary, Art. 4, Rn. 44; *Soergel/Lüderitz/Fenge,* Art. 4, Rn. 9; *Witz/Salger/Lorenz/Lorenz,* Art. 4, Rn. 29; a. A. *Koneru,* 6 Minn. J. Global Trade (1997), 105, 142; *Zeller,* 23 Pace In'tl L. Rev. (2011), 1, 5 ff.
[234] *Achilles,* Art. 4, Rn. 11; *Honsell/Siehr,* Art. 4, Rn. 22; *Schlechtriem/Schwenzer/Schlechtriem/Schwenzer/Hachem,* CISG Commentary, Art. 4, Rn. 17; *Staudinger/Magnus,* Art. 4, Rn. 61; *Teichert,* Lückenfüllung, S. 20.
[235] So ausdrücklich *Koch,* FS Kritzer, S. 267, 282; *Kröll u. a./Djorjevic,* Art. 4, Rn. 32; *Mistelis,* CISG Methodology, S. 365, 394; *Piltz,* Internationales Kaufrecht, Rn. 2–128; *Schlechtriem/Schwenzer/Schwenzer/Hachem,* CISG Commentary, Art. 4, Rn. 11; *Schroeter,* UN-Kaufrecht, § 6, Rn. 25; in der Rechtsprechung vgl. *Golden Valley Grape Juice and Wine, LLC v. Centris Corporation,* U. S. Dist. Ct. (E. D. Cal.), 21.1.2010, CISG-online 2089; LG Trier, 8.1.2004, CISG-online 910; *Filanto SpA v. Chilewich International Corp.,* U. S. Dist. Ct. (S. D. N. Y.), 14.4.1992, CISG-online 45 = 789 F. Supp. 1229; a. A. *Staudinger/Magnus,* Art. 14, Rn. 41c.
[236] Vgl. hierzu etwa HGer Zürich, 26.4.1995, CISG-online 248 = TranspR-IHR 1999, 54.
[237] *Ferrari,* Scope of Application, S. 96, 107; *Schlechtriem/Schwenzer/Schlechtriem,* CISG Commentary, 2. Aufl., Art. 4, Rn. 23; *Teichert,* Lückenfüllung, S. 20; in der Rechtsprechung vgl. LG München I, 25.1.1996, CISG-online 278.
[238] *Posch/Terlitza,* IHR 2001, 47, 49; in der Rechtsprechung vgl. OGH, 29.7.1999, CISG-online 483.
[239] KG Wallis, 27.4.2007, CISG-online 1721; KG Wallis, 27.10.2006, CISG-online 1563; KG Wallis, 3.8.2003, CISG-online 895; Juzgado Commercial No. 26, 17.3.2003, CISG-online 1844; OGH, 22.10.2001,

VI. Vom Übereinkommen erfasste Rechtsfragen

Ein Teil der Rechtsprechung hat dem Regelungsbereich des Übereinkommens auch die **Verwirkung** entzogen.[240] Diese Ansicht ist m. E. aber nicht haltbar,[241] so auch der überwiegende Teil der Rechtsprechung,[242] da die Verwirkung im Übereinkommen geregelt ist, wenn auch nicht „ausdrücklich":[243] Für das Einheitskaufrecht ist die Verwirkung (ex Art. 7 II) aus dem Grundsatz des Verbotes des „venire contra factum proprium" zu entwickeln.[244] 42

Auch die **Haftung für** vom Schuldner zur Vertragserfüllung eingesetzte **Dritte** ist nach dem Übereinkommen zu beurteilen.[245] Dies geht unschwer auf Art. 79 II hervor,[246] weshalb ein Rückgriff auf das über das IPR berufene Recht nicht nötig bzw. zulässig ist.[247] 43

Das Übereinkommen verdrängt auch die nationalen Vorschriften zum **Wegfall der Geschäftsgrundlage,**[248] da das Übereinkommen abschließend regelt, wann veränderte Umstände die Pflichten der Vertragsparteien ändern,[249] das Übereinkommen also auch diesbezüglich eine „ausdrückliche" Bestimmung bereithält.[250] 44

Aus den gleichen Gründen sind auch nationale Vorschriften zum **Erlass**[251] und zur **Stundung** nicht anwendbar:[252] Da diese im Grunde einer Vertragsänderung gleichkommen, für die das Übereinkommen aber eine Regelung, nämlich Art. 29, vorsieht, werden die entsprechenden nationalen Vorschriften verdrängt.[253] Aus diesem Grund sind auch auf die **vergleichsweise Bereinigung** von sich aus einem dem Übereinkommen unterliegen- 45

CISG-online 613; HGer Zürich, 30.11.1998, CISG-online 415 = SZIER 1999, 186 ff.; KG Waadt, 30.6.1998, CISG-online 419 = SZIER 1999, 192 f.; a. A. KG Berlin, 24.1.1994, CISG-online 130 = RIW 1994, 683 f.; a. A. auch *Brunner*, Art. 4, Rn. 54.

[240] Vgl. RB Middelburg, 1.12.1999, 1343 = NIPR 18 (2000), Nr. 188; RB Amsterdam, 5.10.1994, CISG-online 446 = NIPR 13 (1995), Nr. 231m. krit. Anm. *Ferrari*; krit. zu den erwähnten Urteilen auch *Janssen*, The Application of the CISG in Dutch Courts, S. 129, 134 f.

[241] *Ferrari*, Forum International 1997, 89, 92, Fn. 27; ebenso *Bamberger/Roth/Saenger*, Art. 4, Rn. 16; *Ferrari u. a./Saenger*, Internationales Vertragsrecht, Art. 4, Rn. 17; a. A. *Soergel/Lüderitz/Fenge*, Art. 4, Rn. 9; *Teichert*, Lückenfüllung, S. 31; *Witz/Salger/Lorenz/Lorenz*, Art. 4, Rn. 29.

[242] OLG Karlsruhe, 25.6.1997, CISG-online 263 = RIW 1998, 235 ff.; Internationales Schiedsgericht der Bundeskammer der gewerblichen Wirtschaft in Österreich, 15.6.1994, SCH-4318, CISG-online 120 = RIW 1995, 591 f.; Internationales Schiedsgericht der Bundeskammer der gewerblichen Wirtschaft in Österreich, 15.6.1994, SCH-4366, CISG-online 121 = RIW 1995, 590 f.; Hof 's-Hertogenbosch, 26.2.1992, CISG-online 65 = NIPR 1992, Nr. 354.

[243] Vgl. auch *Achilles*, Art. 4, Rn. 14; *Schlechtriem*, Internationales UN-Kaufrecht, Rn. 48.

[244] *Staudinger/Magnus*, Art. 4, Rn. 53, schließt die Verwirkung in den Regelungsbereich des CISG ein, wobei er sich auf den Grundsatz von Treu und Glauben stützt; a. A. *Frigge*, S. 82, 86 f.

[245] *Bamberger/Roth/Saenger*, Art. 4, Rn. 13; *Ferrari u. a./Saenger*, Internationales Vertragsrecht, Art. 4, Rn. 13; *MünchKommHGB/Benicke*, Art. 4, Rn. 16; *Schlechtriem/Schwenzer/Schlechtriem*, CISG Commentary, 2. Aufl., Art. 4, Rn. 24; *Soergel/Lüderitz/Fenge*, Art. 4, Rn. 11.

[246] Vgl. auch *Honsell/Siehr*, Art. 4, Rn. 13.

[247] *Schlechtriem*, östJBl 1989, 45.

[248] So ausdrücklich LG Aachen, 14.5.1993, RIW 1993, 760, 761.

[249] *MünchKomm/Westermann*, Art. 4, Rn. 11; *MünchKommHGB/Benicke*, Art. 4, Rn. 9 a. E.; *Schlechtriem/Schwenzer/Schlechtriem*, CISG Commentary, 2. Aufl., Art. 4, Rn. 14; *Soergel/Lüderitz/Fenge*, Art. 4, Rn. 11; *Staudinger/Magnus*, Art. 4, Rn. 59; *Stoll*, Internationalprivatrechtliche Fragen, S. 505; ebenso zur entsprechenden Problematik im EKG *von Caemmerer*, AcP 178 (1978), 121, 127; a. A. *Vischer*, Gemeinsame Bestimmungen, S. 177.

[250] Ebenso *Achilles*, Art. 4, Rn. 8; *Bamberger/Roth/Saenger*, Art. 4, Rn. 17; *Soergel/Lüderitz/Fenge*, Art. 4, Rn. 11; z. T. a. A. *Witz/Salger/Lorenz/Lorenz*, Art. 4, Rn. 13.

[251] *Bamberger/Roth/Saenger*, Art. 4, Rn. 12.

[252] Vgl. *Achilles*, Art. 4, Rn. 8; *Bamberger/Roth/Saenger*, Art. 4, Rn. 17; *Brunner*, Art. 4, Rn. 50; *Ferrari u. a./Saenger*, Internationales Vertragsrecht, Art. 4, Rn. 12; *Magnus*, ZEuP 1993, 79, 85; *MünchKommHGB/Benicke*, Art. 4, Rn. 16; *Schlechtriem*, Internationales UN-Kaufrecht, Rn. 41 a. E.; *Schlechtriem/Schwenzer/Schlechtriem*, CISG Commentary, 2. Aufl., Art. 4, Rn. 25; *Staudinger/Magnus*, Art. 4, Rn. 55 f.; *Teichert*, Lückenfüllung, S. 17.

[253] Zur Stundung vgl. in diesem Sinne auch HGer Zürich, 10.2.1999, CISG-online 488 = SZIER 2000, 111 f.; LG Hamburg, 26.9.1990, CISG-online 21 = IPRax 1991, 400, 402.

Art. 4 45a, 46 Teil I. Kapitel I. Anwendungsbereich

den Vertragverhältnis ergebenden Streitfragen nationale Vorschriften nicht anwendbar.[254] Die Gültigkeit eines Vergleichs untersteht jedoch nationalem Recht.[255]

45a   Auch **Zurückbehaltungsmöglichkeiten** sind im CISG geregelt;[256] diesbezüglich sei etwa an die in Art. 58 I CISG vorgesehene Zug-um-Zug Abwicklung der Hauptleistung[257] oder die nach Art. 71 I CISG erlaubte Zurückhaltung der eigenen Leistung gedacht.[258] Da diese Vorschriften, so sowohl die herrschende Lehre[259] als auch die Rechtsprechung,[260] einen allgemeinen Grundsatz verankern, muss davon ausgegangen werden, dass alle nationalen Vorschriften hierzu verdrängt werden (Art. 7 II CISG), mit Ausnahme derer, die die dinglichen Sicherungswirkungen, Verwertungsrechte mit Wirkung gegenüber Drittgläubigern, etc., regeln.[261]

46   Da das Übereinkommen die Ansprüche aus jedweder Vertragsverletzung abschliessend regelt (mit Ausnahme der sich aus Personenschäden ergebenden Ansprüche), bleibt (im soeben gesteckten Rahmen) für nationale Vorschriften zur **positiven Vertragsverletzung** kein Raum.[262] Gleiches gilt auch in Bezug auf die **culpa in contrahendo**,[263] zumindest dann, wenn es trotz dieses Verschuldens zum **Vertragsabschluss** gekommen ist.[264] In diesen Fällen richtet sich die Haftung nach den maßgeblichen Vorschriften des Übereinkommens, ein Rückgriff auf nationales Recht ist ausgeschlossen.[265] Hat die culpa in contrahendo den **Abbruch der Vertragshandlungen** zur Folge, führt dies m. E. nicht notwendigerweise zur Verdrängung des über das IPR berufenen nationalen Rechts.[266] Es kommt vielmehr darauf an, welche vorvertraglichen Pflichten verletzt worden sind.[267] In einigen Fällen, „etwa vorvertraglicher Pflichten zum Schutz der Sachgüter des künftigen Vertragspartners

---

[254] Ebenso *Brunner*, Art. 4, Rn. 50; *Geldsetzer*, S. 31; *Schlechtriem*, Internationales UN-Kaufrecht, Rn. 41; in der Rechtsprechung vgl. OLG Karlsruhe, 10.12.2003, CISG-online 911 = IHR 2004, 62, 64; HGer Zürich, 24.10.2003, CISG-online 857; anders aber LG Aachen, 14.5.1993, RIW 1993, 760.
[255] LG Aachen, 14.5.1993, CISG-online 86 = RIW 1993, 760 f.
[256] Vgl. eingehend hierzu neuerdings *Hartmann*, IHR 2006, 181 ff.; *W. Witz*, FS Schlechtriem, S. 291 ff.; in der Rechtsprechung von einem „allgemeinen Zurückbehaltungsrecht" ausgehend etwa OGH, 8.11.2005, CISG-online 1156 = IHR 2006, 87, 90; a. A. OLG Stuttgart, 20.12.2004, CISG-online 997: „Das Zurückbehaltungsrecht ist im CISG nicht geregelt. Ob überhaupt ein Zurückbehaltungsrecht besteht, richtet sich nach dem Recht, welches nach dem internationalen Privatrecht zur Beurteilung berufen wäre".
[257] Vgl. *P. Huber*, IPRax 2001, 557 ff.; vgl. auch *Hartmann*, IHR 2006, 181; in der Rechtsprechung wird das Zug-um-Zug Prinzip als ein auch unter dem CISG geltendes Prinzip anerkannt etwa vom OGH, 30.11.2006, CISG-online 1417 = IHR 2007, 74, 75; OGH, 8.11.2005, CISG-online 1156 = IHR 2006, 87, 91.
[258] *Schlechtriem*, Internationales UN-Kaufrecht, Rn. 42d; *Schlechtriem/Schwenzer/Schlechtriem*, CISG Commentary, 2. Aufl., Art. 4, Rn. 22a; a. A. *Bamberger/Roth/Saenger*, Art. 4, Rn. 20; a. A. in der Rechtsprechung OLG Stuttgart, 20.10.2004, CISG-online 997.
[259] Vgl. auch CISG-AC, Op. 5 (*Schwenzer*), Comment 4.19; *Fountoulakis*, IHR 2005, 244, 247 f.; *Hartmann*, IHR 2006, 181; *Kern*, ZEuP 2000, 837; MünchKomm/*Westermann*, Art. 4, Rn. 12; *Nyer*, 18 Pace Int'l L. Rev. (2006), 29, 72 ff.; *Schlechtriem*, 18 Pace Int'l L. Rev. (2006), 83, 92; *ders.*, 36 Vict. U. Well. L. Rev. (2005), 781, 791; *Schlechtriem/Schwenzer/Schlechtriem*, CISG Commentary, 2. Aufl., Art. 7, Rn. 34; *Schlechtriem/Schwenzer/Schlechtriem/Schwenzer/Hachem*, CISG Commentary, Art. 4, Rn. 20; *Teichert*, Lückenfüllung, S. 33; *Witz*, FS Schlechtriem, S. 291.
[260] OGH, 8.11.2005, CISG-online 1156 = IHR 2006, 87, 90.
[261] So ausdrücklich *Schlechtriem*, Internationales UN-Kaufrecht, Rn. 42d.
[262] Ebenso *Achilles*, Art. 4, Rn. 15; *Bamberger/Roth/Saenger*, Art. 4, Rn. 15; *Bock*, FS Schwenzer, S. 175, 184; *Müller-Chen*, Art. 45 Rn. 32 Fn. 70; *Honsell/Siehr*, Art. 4, Rn. 17; *Witz/Salger/Lorenz/Lorenz*, Art. 4, Rn. 12; a. A. *Karollus*, S. 45, der die positive Vertragsverletzung zu den vom Übereinkommen nicht geregelten Fragen zählt; a. A. auch MünchKommHGB/*Benicke*, Art. 4, Rn. 18, der die Ansicht vertritt, dass, „soweit eine Rechtsordnung, wie die deutsche, funktional deliktische Schutzpflichten vertraglich ausgestaltet, [...] die Regeln der positiven Forderungsverletzung des nationalen Rechts anwendbar sein" können.
[263] *Brunner*, Art. 4, Rn. 48; a. A. *Karollus*, S. 45; eher zweifelnd auch *Diéz-Picazo/Rojo Ajuria*, Art. 4, S. 80.
[264] *Bamberger/Roth/Saenger*, Art. 4, Rn. 15a; *Bock*, FS Schwenzer, S. 175, 184.
[265] So auch *Honsell/Siehr*, Art. 4, Rn. 8; z. T. a. A. *Gruber*, Methoden, S. 241.
[266] Ebenso *P. Huber/Mullis/P. Huber*, S. 28 f.; MünchKommHGB/*Benicke*, Art. 4, Rn. 17; *Witz/Salger/Lorenz/Lorenz*, Art. 4, Rn. 12; a. A. wohl *Bonell*, RIW 1990, 693, 701.
[267] *Schlechtriem/Schwenzer/Schlechtriem*, CISG Commentary, 2. Aufl., Art. 4, Rn. 23a; *Schlechtriem/Schwenzer/Schlechtriem/Schwenzer/Hachem*, CISG Commentary, Art. 4, Rn. 18.

oder einer Sachwalterhaftung eines Vertragsmittlers, bleibt es [daher] bei dem über Kollisionsrecht berufenen nationalen Recht."[268]

Außerhalb des Regelungsbereichs des Einheitskaufrechts liegen auch **Ansprüche aus Frachtverträgen,** die der Verkäufer in Zusammenhang mit seiner Lieferung, insbesondere der Versendung der Ware, abschließt. Auch die im deutschen Recht in **§ 421 HGB** vorgesehene Ermächtigung für den Käufer, solche Schadenersatzansprüche im eigenen Namen gegen den Frachtführer geltend zu machen, ist – wohl – eine **Prozessstandschaft,** die nicht die vom Übereinkommen geregelte Materie betrifft. Sie kann jedoch mittelbar die Rechtsstellung des Käufers berühren, der bei Beschädigung oder Verlust der Ware den wirtschaftlichen Schaden, den er durch den Gefahrübergang und seine fortbestehende Kaufpreiszahlungspflicht erleidet, beim Frachtführer liquidieren kann, falls deutsches Recht als lex fori anzuwenden ist. 47

VII. Beweislast

Ob die Beweislast in den Regelungsbereich des Übereinkommens fällt, ist umstritten. Verschiedene Autoren vertreten die Auffassung, das Übereinkommen regele die Beweislastfragen nicht, man müsse – von Ausnahmen abgesehen –[269] in Bezug auf die Beweislast demnach an nationales Recht anknüpfen,[270] eine Auffassung, die auch in der Rechtsprechung vertreten worden ist.[271] Welches nationale Recht anzuwenden sei, ist jedoch nicht klar. Während einige Autoren die Ansicht vertreten, es müsse auf die lex fori Rückgriff genommen werden, also auf das am Gerichtsort geltende Recht,[272] vertreten andere die Meinung, die Beweislast richte sich nach dem über das IPR des Forumstaates berufenen Recht.[273] 48

Die wohl überwiegende Lehre geht jedoch – zu Recht[274] – davon aus, dass Fragen der **Beweislast**[275] **im Übereinkommen** (zumindest implizit,[276] mittelbar[277] oder „autonom"[278]) **geregelt** seien.[279] Dies wird zum Teil damit begründet, dass das Übereinkommen 49

---

[268] *Schlechtriem,* Internationales UN-Kaufrecht, Rn. 42; vgl. auch *Schlechtriem/Schwenzer/Schlechtriem/Schwenzer/Hachem,* CISG Commentary, Art. 4, Rn. 18.
[269] Vgl. etwa *Hutter,* S. 44, bezüglich Art. 35 II lit. b) Hs. 2.
[270] *Bianca/Bonell/Khoo,* Art. 2, Anm. 3.2.; *Flechtner,* 13 VJ (2009), 91, 102 ff.; *Müller-Chen,* Art. 46 Rn. 22; *U. Huber,* RabelsZ 43 (1979), 413, 479 f.; *Hutter,* S. 54; *Reinhart,* Art. 36, Rn. 2; *Rosett,* 45 Ohio St. L. J. (1984), 265, 281; *Ryffel,* S. 59.
[271] Vgl. Arbitration Chamber of Paris, 9926/2007, CISG-online 1850; Serbian Chamber of Commerce, 21.2.2005, CISG-online 2038; Cour de Justice de Genève, 15.11.2002, CISG-online 853; Helsinki Court of Appeals, 26.10.2000, CISG-online 748; ICC, 6653/1993, CISG-online 71 = J.D.I. 1993, 1040, 1044.
[272] Vgl. *Bianca/Bonell/Khoo,* Art. 2, Anm. 3.2.; *Otto,* MDR 1992, 533, 534; *Ryffel,* S. 59.
[273] So *Grewal,* 14 Loy. L. A. Int'l & Comp. L. J. (1991), 93, 102.
[274] Vgl. hierzu auch *Ferrari,* IPRax 2001, 354, 357 f.
[275] Zur Definition der „Beweislast" anlässlich der Diskussion des CISG, vgl. *Kröll,* 2011 Annals Fac. L. Belgrade 2011, 162, 166 ff.; vgl. in der Rechtsprechung AppHof Bern, 11.2.2004, CISG-online 1191.
[276] *Achilles,* Art. 4, Rn. 15; *Herber,* 2. Aufl., Art. 4, Rn. 22; *Honsell/Dornis* Vorbem. Artt. 14–24, Rn. 28; *T. M. Müller,* IHR 2005, 16; so auch ausdrücklich HGer Zürich, 9.9.1993, CISG-online 79.
[277] *Neumayer/Ming,* Art. 4, Anm. 13.
[278] *Hartwieg,* ZVerglRW 1993, 282, 321.
[279] Vgl. *Aue,* Mängelgewährleistung im UN-Kaufrecht, S. 110 ff.; *Bamberger/Roth/Saenger,* Art. 4, Rn. 11; *Baumgärtel u. a./Müller,* Vor Art. 1, Rn. 16; *Bianca/Bonell/Bianca,* Art. 36, Anm. 3.1.; *Bianca/Bonell/Knapp,* Art. 74, Anm. 2.8.; *Bianca/Bonell/Sono,* Art. 44, Anm. 3.1.; CISG-AC, Op. 6 (*Gotanda*), Comment 2; *Ferrari,* Vendita internazionale, S. 102; *Ferrari u. a./Saenger,* Internationales Vertragsrecht, Art. 4, Rn. 11; *Herber,* Anwendungsbereich, S. 41; *Herber/Czerwenka,* Art. 4, Rn. 8, Art. 35, Rn. 9; *Honsell/Siehr,* Art. 4, Rn. 10; *P. Huber/Mullis/P. Huber,* S. 36 f.; *Jung,* S. 40; *Koller/Mauerhofer,* FS Schwenzer, S. 963, 964 f.; *Kröll,* 2011 Annals Fac. L. Belgrade 2011, 162, 169; *ders.,* 25 J. L. & Com. (2005), 39, 48; *Kröll u. a./Djordjevic,* Art. 4, Rn. 34; *Magnus,* CISG in the German Federal Civil Court, S. 211, 216 ff.; *ders.,* ZEuP 1995, 202, 207; *ders.,* ZEuP 2002, 523, 530; *Mohs,* IHR 2004, 219; MünchKomm/*Westermann,* Art. 4, Rn. 17; *Noussias,* Zugangsbedürftigkeit von Mitteilungen, S. 105 f.; *Orlandi,* Uniform L. Rev. 2000, 23, 27 f.; *Reimers-Zocher,* S. 148;

selbst eine ausdrückliche Beweislastregel vorsieht,[280] nämlich in Art. 79 I,[281] also ein völliger Ausschluss der Beweislastfragen vom Regelungsbereich des Übereinkommens auch von den Konventionsgebern nicht gewollt sein kann, zum Teil damit, dass so enge Beziehungen der Beweislast zum materiellen Recht bestehen, dass eine Beweislastregel nur aus dem Übereinkommen selbst ermittelt werden kann.[282]

50 Das Übereinkommen regelt also die **Beweislast;** diese Ansicht ist auch in der Rechtsprechung zum CISG vertreten worden.[283] Fraglich ist jedoch, wie diese **konkret verteilt** werden muss.[284] Eine Untersuchung der einzelnen Vorschriften auf der Grundlage sowohl ihrer Entstehungsgeschichte als auch ihres Wortlautes[285] hat die Lehre dazu gebracht, eine dem römisch-rechtlichen Grundsatz „ei incumbit probatio, qui dicit, non qui negat" ähnliche Regel der Frage der konventionsinternen Beweislastverteilung zugrunde zu legen.[286] Demnach ist jede Partei für die tatsächlichen Voraussetzungen der Vorschriften, auf denen sie ihre Ansprüche gründet, beweispflichtig.[287] Aus der erwähnten Grundregel ergibt sich aber auch, dass die Partei, die sich auf eine Ausnahmeregel beruft, die tatsächlichen Voraussetzungen derselben zu beweisen hat.[288]

Schlechtriem/Schwenzer/Schlechtriem, CISG Commentary, 2. Aufl., Art. 4, Rn. 22; *Schlechtriem/Schwenzer/ Schwenzer/Hachem,* CISG Commentary, Art. 4, Rn. 25; *Schwenzer/Hachem,* 57 Am.J. Comp. L. (2009), 457, 471 f.; *Soergel/Lüderitz/Fenge,* Art. 4, Rn. 11; *Spiegel,* D. 2000, Jur. 445, 445; *ders.,* D. 2002, Jur. 395, 396; *Teichert,* Lückenfüllung, S. 16; *Veneziano,* Dir. com. int. 2001, 509, 515–516; *Witz/Salger/Lorenz/Lorenz,* Art. 4, Rn. 11.

[280] Vgl. statt aller *Soergel/Lüderitz/Fenge,* Art. 4, Rn. 11; *Staudinger/Magnus,* Art. 4, Rn. 64; *C. Witz,* Rev. dr. aff. int. (2001), 253, 269.

[281] Vgl. auch *Graffi,* EuLF (2000/2001), 240, 244; *Kröll,* 2011 Annals Fac. L. Belgrade 2011, 162, 170; *Reimers-Zocher,* S. 146 ff.; *C.Witz,* D. 2002, Chron. 2796, 2797; vgl. in der Rechtsprechung AppHof Bern, 11.2.2004, CISG-online 1191; BGH, 9.1.2002, CISG-online 651 = RIW 2002, 396 ff.; Tribunale di Vigevano, 12.7.2000, CISG-online 493 = IHR 2001, 72, 76 f.; Tribunale di Pavia, 29.12.1999, CISG-online 678 = Corr. giur. 2000, 932, 933.

[282] So ausdrücklich *Jung,* S. 38, 40; ebenso auch *Janssen,* The Application of the CISG in Dutch Courts, S. 129, 135; *Hartwieg,* ZVerglRW 1993, 282, 288 f.; *Neumayer/Ming,* Art. 4, Anm. 13.

[283] Vgl. HGer Zürich, 25.6.2010, CISG-online 2161; KG Wallis, 28.1.2009, CISG-online 2025; OGH, 12.9.2006, CISG-online 1364 = IHR 39, 41; Cour de Justice de Genève, 20.1.2006, CISG-online 1504; KG Nidwalden, 23.5.2005, CISG-online 1086; KG Wallis, 27.5.2005, CISG-online 1137; BGer, 7.7.2004, CISG-online 848; Tribunale di Padova, 25.2.2004, CISG-online 819; AppHof Bern, 11.2.2004, CISG-online 1191; KG Schaffhausen, 13.11.2003, CISG Pace; Tribunale di Rimini, 26.11.2002, CISG-online 737 = Giur. it. 2003, 896 ff., m. Anm. *Ferrari;* BGH, 9.1.2002, CISG-online 651 = IHR 2002, 16, 19; Tribunale di Vigevano, 12.7.2000, CISG-online 493 = IHR 2001, 72, 76 f.; Tribunale di Pavia, 29.12.1999, CISG-online 678 = Corr. giur. 2000, 932, 933; HGer Zürich, 26.4.1995, CISG-online 248 (das CISG sieht keine speziellen Regeln zur Beweislastverteilung vor, ein allgemeiner Grundsatz lässt sich aber ableiten); HGer Zürich, 9.9.1993, CISG-online 79 (Beweislast ist implizit geregelt).

[284] Vgl. auch *Baumgärtel u. a./Müller,* Vor Art. 1, Rn. 20 ff.

[285] Vgl. etwa *Jung,* S. 52 ff.

[286] *Graffi,* EuLF 2000/2001, 240, 244; *Jung,* S. 44, *Kröll,* 2011 Annals Fac. L. Belgrade 2011, 162, 171; *Kröll u. a./Djordjevic,* Art. 4, Rn. 35; *Magnus,* ZEuP 1995, 202, 207; *T.M. Müller,* Beweislast, S. 36; *Piltz,* IHR 2006, 154; *C. Witz,* D. 2002, Chron. 2796, 2797; ebenso *Linne,* 20 Pace Int'l L. Rev. (2008) 31, 33 ff., die jedoch auch darauf hinweist, der im Text erwänte Grundsatz reiche nicht aus (43 f.).

[287] *Achilles,* Art. 4, Rn. 15; *Brunner,* Art. 4, Rn. 56; *Ferrari,* Int'l Bus. L. Rev. 2000, 665, 667; *Ferrari u. a./ Saenger,* Internationales Vertragsrecht, Art. 4, Rn. 11; *Honsell/Dornis* Vorbem. Artt. 14–24, Rn. 28; *P. Huber,* IHR 2006, 228, 235; *P. Huber/Mullis/P. Huber,* S. 37; *Kröll,* 2011 Annals Fac. L. Belgrade 2011, 162, 171; *Kröll u. a./Djordjevic,* Art. 4, Rn. 35; *Mohs,* IHR 2004, 219; *T.M. Müller,* IHR 2005, 16; MünchKomm/*Westermann,* Art. 4, Rn. 17; MünchKommHGB/*Benicke,* Art. 4, Rn. 20; *Schlechtriem/Schwenzer/Schlechtriem,* CISG Commentary, 2. Aufl., Art. 4, Rn. 22; *Schlechtriem/Schwenzer/Schwenzer/Hachem,* CISG Commentary, Art. 4, Rn. 25; *Sein/Kull,* IHR 2005, 138, 142; *Staudinger/Magnus,* Art. 4, Rn. 67, der hervorhebt, dass diese Beweislastvorstellung ersichtlich Art. 79 I als Modellvorstellung zugrundeliege; vgl. zur Beweislastverteilung in Art. 79 I auch *Reimers-Zocher,* S. 146 ff.

[288] Vgl. *Jung,* S. 44; *Kröll u. a./Djordjevic,* Art. 4, Rn. 35; *T.M. Müller,* Beweislast, S. 36; *Schlechtriem/Schwenzer/Schwenzer/Hachem,* CISG Commentary, Art. 4, Rn. 25; *Staudinger/Magnus,* Art. 4, Rn. 68, der den im Text erwähnten Grundsatz den Art. 79 I 2 lit. a) und 35 II lit. b) entnimmt; ähnlich neuerdings auch *C. Witz,* L'interprétation, S. 279, 289 f.; *ders.,* Rev. dr. aff. int. 2001, 253, 271; *Witz/Salger/Lorenz/Lorenz,* Art. 4, Rn. 11; vgl. in der Rechtsprechung KG Wallis, 28.1.2009, CISG-online 2025; Tribunale di Rimini, 26.11.2002, CISG-online 737 = Giur. it. 2003, 896 ff., m. Anm. *Ferrari.*

Sachlicher Geltungsbereich   51, 52 **Art. 4**

Auch Billigkeitserwägungen sind, so sowohl der BGH[289], das schweizerische Bundes- 51
gericht[290] als auch der OGH,[291] bei der Beweislastverteilung zu berücksichtigen.[292] Dies
führt zum Beispiel dazu, dass Tatsachen aus dem eigenen Zuständigkeitsbereich, die einer
Partei deutlich besser als der anderen Partei bekannt sein müssen, von der Partei bewiesen
werden müssen, die die Herrschaft über diesen Bereich hat.[293]

Die von der herrschenden Lehre vertretene Auffassung ist von einem Großteil der 52
Rechtsprechung bestätigt worden.[294] So hat etwa der OGH in einem neueren Urteil
statuiert, dass „nach allgemeinen Regeln des UN-K grundsätzlich derjenige Vertragspartner
die tatsächlichen Voraussetzungen jener Vorschrift zu behaupten und zu beweisen hat, aus
der er einen Vorteil für sich herleitet".[295] Ein ähnlicher Grundsatz findet sich auch in der
deutschen Rechtsprechung; so hat etwa in einer neueren Entscheidung der BGH statuiert,[296] dass „das CISG die Beweislast ausdrücklich (etwa in Art. 79 I) oder konkludent (mit
Art. 2 lit. a) regelt, dass infolgedessen ein Rückgriff auf das nationale Recht insofern verwehrt ist und dass das CISG dabei dem Regel-Ausnahme-Prinzip folgt",[297] mit der Folge,
dass die Klägerin „die Tatsachen nachweisen [muss], die regelmäßig gegeben sein müssen,
um einen Anspruch zu begründen."[298] Verschiedene italienische Gerichte haben in neueren
Entscheidungen ausdrücklich den von der Lehre vorgeschlagenen Grundsatz „ei incumbit
probatio, qui dicit, non qui negat" ihren Entscheidungen zugrunde gelegt.[299] Konkret
bedeutet dies etwa, dass „auch nach Wiener Kaufrecht der geschädigte Käufer die Beweislast
für die objektiven **Voraussetzungen des Schadenersatzanspruchs** [trägt]. Er hat demnach den Schaden und den Kausalzusammenhang zwischen Vertragsverletzung und Schaden
sowie die **Voraussehbarkeit des Schadens** im Sinne von Art. 74 S. 2 CISG nachzuweisen."[300] Aus dem oben erwähnten allgemeinen Grundsatz ergibt sich aber auch, dass der
Nachweis der Vertragswidrigkeit nach der rügelosen Annahme der Ware vom Käufer

---

[289] BGH, 30.6.2004, CISG-online 847 = NJW 2004, 3181, 3182 = IHR 2004, 201, 202.
[290] BGer, 7.7.2004, CISG-online 848 = IHR 2004, 252, 253; BGer, 13.11.2003, CISG-online 846 = IHR 2004, 215, 218.
[291] OGH, 12.9.2006, CISG-online 1364 = IHR 2007, 39, 41.
[292] Vgl. auch *Ferrari u. a./Saenger*, Internationales Vertragsrecht, Art. 4, Rn. 11; *Kröll*, 2011 Annals Fac. L. Belgrade 2011, 162, 171; *Mohs*, IHR 2004, 219, 220; *Reimers-Zocher*, S. 154 ff.; *Schlechtriem/Schwenzer/Schwenzer/Hachem*, CISG Commentary, Art. 4, Rn. 25.
[293] So ausdrücklich *Staudinger/Magnus*, Art. 4, Rn. 69; vgl. auch *Baumgärtel u. a./Müller*, Vor Art. 1, Rn. 33; *T. M. Müller*, Beweislast, S. 39 f.; vgl. in der Rechtsprechung Cour de Justice de Genève, 20.1.2006, CISG-online 1504.
[294] Vgl. neben den in den folgenden Fußnoten zitierten Urteilen auch HGer Zürich, 25.6.2010, CISG-online 2161; Cour de Justice de Genève, 20.1.2006, CISG-online 1504; HGer Zürich, 22.12.2005, CISG-online 1195 = IHR 2006, 161, 162; KG Wallis, 27.5.2005, CISG-online 1137; BGer, 7.7.2004, CISG-online 848 = IHR 2004, 252, 253; AG Bern, 11.2.2004, CISG-online 1191 = IHR 2006, 149, 151; BGer, 13.11.2003, CISG-online 846 = IHR 2004, 215, 218; HGer Zürich, 10.2.1999, CISG-online 488 = SZIER 2000, 111, 112; a. A. BGer Saane, 20.2.1997, CISG-online 426 = SZIER 1999, 195 ff.; „Das WKR enthält keine Beweislastregeln, somit muss nach Art. 7 Abs. 2 Halbsatz 2 WKR auf das internationale Privatrecht des Forums zurückgegriffen werden"; a. A. auch Cour de Justice Genève, 15.11.2002, SZIER 2004, 106; die Frage offen lassend hingegen RB Zwolle, 21.5.2003, CISG-online 993 = IHR 2005, 34, 36.
[295] OGH, 12.9.2006, CISG-online 1364 = IHR 2007, 39, 41; ebenso KG Nidwalden, 23.5.2005, CISG-online 1086 = IHR 2005, 253, 254; BGer, 13.11.2003, CISG-online 846 = IHR 2004, 215, 218; OLG Innsbruck, 1.7.1994, CISG-online 107.
[296] BGH, 9.1.2002, CISG-online 651 = IHR 2002, 16, 19, der außerdem statuiert, dass „die Beweislastregeln des CISG nicht weiter reichen können als sein materieller Geltungsbereich".
[297] Vgl. auch BGH, 30.6.2004, CISG-online 847 = NJW 2004, 3181, 3182.
[298] LG Frankfurt a. M., 6.7.1994, CISG-online 257 vgl. auch KG Wallis, 28.1.2009, CISG-online 2025; KG Schaffhausen, 20.10.2003, CISG-online 957; BGH, 9.1.2002, CISG-online 651; Tribunale di Vigevano, 12.7.2000, CISG-online 493.
[299] Vgl. etwa Tribunale di Padova, 25.2.2004, CISG-online 819; Tribunale di Rimini, 26.11.2002, CISG-online 737 = Giur. it. 2003, 896 ff., m. Anm. *Ferrari*; Tribunale di Vigevano, 12.7.2000, CISG-online 493 = IHR 2001, 72, 77; vgl. auch AG Bern, 11.2.2004, CISG-online 1191 = IHR 2006, 149, 151.
[300] HGer Zürich, 26.4.1995, CISG-online 248; ebenso Tribunale di Vigevano, 12.7.2000, CISG-online 493 = IHR 2001, 72, 77.

Art. 4 53   Teil I. Kapitel I. Anwendungsbereich

geführt werden muss.[301] Ferner hat der erwähnte Grundsatz in der Rechtsprechung dazu geführt, dass „diejenige Partei, die die mangelnde Anwendbarkeit des CISG wegen der Nichterkennbarkeit des internationalen Bezugs des Vertragsverhältnisses vorträgt, diese Nichterkennbarkeit nachweisen muss; die Partei, die die Unanwendbarkeit des Übereinkommens wegen Ausschlusses gem. Art. 6 CISG vorträgt, muss das Vorliegen einer Ausschlussvereinbarung nachweisen."[302] Der erwähnte Grundsatz hat auch dazu geführt, dass der derjenigen Partei, die die Nichtanwendbarkeit des CISG kraft Art. 3 II behauptet, beweisenn muss, dass der überwiegende Teil der Pflichten der Partei, welche die Ware liefert, in der Ausführung von Arbeiten oder anderen Dienstleistungen besteht.[303]

53   Obwohl die Frage der Beweislastverteilung als vom Übereinkommen geregelt angesehen werden kann, fällt die **Frage, wann der Beweis** konkret als geführt anzusehen ist,[304] so die herrschende Lehre[305] und ein Teil der Rechtsprechung,[306] nicht in den Regelungsbereich des Übereinkommens und unterliegt, da Verfahrensfrage, der lex fori.[307] Dennoch wird – vor allem, aber nicht eben nicht nur, anlässlich der Diskussion um Art. 74 – auch die Ansicht vertreten, die erwähnte Frage müsse, zum Zwecke der Förderung der Rechtseinheit,[308] auf der Grundlage einer einheitlichen, dem CISG selbst zu entnehmenden Regel beantwortet werden,[309] und zwar anhand der auf den allgemeinen Grundsatz, wonach die Parteien sich wie „vernünftige Personen" verhalten müssen,[310] zurückgehenden Regel der „reasonable certainty",[311] mit der Folge etwa, dass „[g]iven the need to promote the Convention's international character and the need to promote uniformity in the Convention's application, and in light of the purposes and policies of Article 74, the aggrieved party bears the burden of proving with reasonable certainty such party has suffered a loss as a result of the breach".[312]

---

[301] BGer, 7.7.2004, CISG-online 848 = IHR 2004, 252, 253; AG Bern, 11.2.2004, CISG-online 1191 = IHR 2006, 149, 152; BGer, 13.11.2003, CISG-online 846 = IHR 2004, 215, 218; Tribunale di Vigevano, 12.7.2000, CISG-online 493 = IHR 2001, 72, 77; BGH, 8.5.1995, CISG-online 144 = BGHZ 129, 75, 81; OLG Frankfurt a. M., 13.6.1991, CISG-online 23 = NJW 1991, 3102; vgl. auch *Mohs*, IHR 2004, 219, 220, der zu Recht die im Text vertretene Ansicht so versteht, „dass der Verkäufer die Beweislast trägt, wenn der Käufer die Ware sofort, d. h. mit physischer Entgegennahme, rügt"; a. A. *Kruisinga*, S. 174.

[302] Tribunale di Vigevano, 12.7.2000, CISG-online 493 = IHR 2001, 72, 77.

[303] Vgl. OLG Oldenburg, 20.12.2007, CISG-online 1644.

[304] Vgl. hierzu neuerdings *Koller/Mauerhofer*, FS Schwenzer, S. 963 ff.

[305] Vgl. auch *Brunner*, Art. 4, Rn. 57; *Ferrari u. a./Saenger*, Internationales Vertragsrecht, Art. 4, Rn. 1; *Fountoulakis*, IHR 2005, 244, 245; *Kröll*, 2011 Annals Fac. L. Belgrade 2011, 162, 170; *Kruisinga*, Non-conformity, S. 167; *T. M. Müller*, Beweislast, S. 3; MünchKomm/*Westermann*, Art. 4, Rn. 17 a. E.; *Orlandi*, Uniform L. Rev. 2000, 23, 28; *Rosati*, IHR 2001, 78, 81; *Staudinger/Magnus*, Art. 4, Rn. 70.

[306] KG Nidwalden, 23.5.2005, CISG-online 1086 = IHR 2005, 253, 254: „Fragen des Beweismasses, der notwendige Grad der richterlichen Überzeugung, sind dagegen der lex fori, in casu dem Schweizerischen Privatrecht, zu entnehmen".

[307] Diese Fragen ansprechend, ohne jedoch Stellung zu beziehen, BGer, 17.12.2009, CISG-online 2022.

[308] Vgl. CISG-AC, Op. 6 *(Gotanda)*, Comment 2.3: „The existence of differing rules concerning the proof of damage could lead to the differential treatment of similarly situated parties [...]. This result would be unfair and undermine the goal of the Convention to provide a uniform law on the sale of goods"; vgl. auch *Koller/Mauerhofer*, FS Schwenzer, S. 963, 975 ff.; *Schlechtriem/Schwenzer/Schwenzer*, CISG Commentary, Art. 74, Rn. 65.

[309] Vgl. auch *Kröll u. a./Djordjevic*, Art. 4, Rn. 27; *Saidov*, The Law of Damages, S. 168 f.; *Schlechtriem/Schwenzer/Schwenzer/Hachem*, CISG Commentary, Art. 4, Rn. 26; *Schwenzer/Hachem*, 57 Am. J. Comp. L. (2009), 457, 472.

[310] Vgl. zu diesem allgemeinen Grundsatz *Colligan*, 6 VJ (2002), 40, 49; *Diesse*, J. D. I. 2002, 55, 60 f.; *Ferrari*, 24 Ga. J. Int'l & Comp. L. (1994), 183, 224 f.; *Frignani*, S. 308; *Hackney*, 61 La. L. Rev. (2001), 473, 478; *Harjani*, 23 Hous. J. Int'l L. (2000), 49, 64; *Hoffmann*, Koordination, S. 283; *Honnold*, Uniform Words, S. 139; *Karollus*, S. 16 f.; *Najork*, S. 99; *Schlechtriem*, Internationales UN-Kaufrecht, Rn. 48; *Whittington*, 37 Vict. U. Wellington L. Rev. (2006), 421, 432; *Witz/Salger/Lorenz/Witz*, Art. 7, Rn. 31.

[311] Vgl. in der Rechtsprechung *TeeVee Toons, Inc. et al v. Gerhard Schubert GmbH*, U. S. Dist. Ct. (S. D. N. Y.), 23.8.2006, CISG-online 1272 = 2006 WL 2 463 537 (S. D. N. Y.), wo jedoch nicht auf „reasonable certainty" abgestellt wird, unrichtig daher CISG-AC, Op. 6 *(Gotanda)*, Comment 2.8, sondern auf die Möglichkeit, dass „a reasonable inference [can] be drawn".

[312] CISG-AC, Op. 6 *(Gotanda)*, Comment 2.6; vgl. auch *Th. Koller/Mauerhofer*, FS Schwenzer, S. 963, 975 ff.; *Leumann Liebster*, FS Schwenzer, S. 1031, 1042; *Schlechtriem/Schwenzer/Schwenzer*, CISG Commentary, Art. 74, Rn. 65.

Art. 5 [Ausschluß der Haftung für Tod oder Körperverletzung]

Dieses Übereinkommen findet keine Anwendung auf die Haftung des Verkäufers für den durch die Ware verursachten Tod oder die Körperverletzung einer Person.

Art. 5
This Convention does not apply to the liability of the seller for death or personal injury caused by the goods to any person.

Art. 5
La présente Convention ne s'applique pas à la responsabilité du vendeur pour décès ou lésions corporelles causés à quiconque par les marchandises.

Übersicht

	Rn.
I. Vorgeschichte	1
II. Die Vorschrift im Einzelnen	3
1. Ausschluss von Ansprüchen wegen Personenschäden	3
2. Rückgriffsansprüche wegen Personenschäden	8
3. Produkthaftung wegen Sachschäden	9
III. Produkthaftung und Art. 90	14

I. Vorgeschichte

Die Vorschrift hat **kein Vorbild im EKG**.[1] Die Frage, ob sich UNCITRAL überhaupt mit Fragen der Produkthaftung befassen solle, ist erstmals 1974 aufgeworfen worden.[2] Die diesbezügliche Diskussion hat zur Verfassung eines Berichts seitens des Generalsekretariats geführt,[3] der sich ausführlich mit der Frage befasste, von wem, unter welchen Umständen und in welchem Ausmaß eine Person Ersatz für entstandene Körper- oder Sachschäden verlangen kann, die durch den Gebrauch mangelhafter Waren eingetreten sind.[4] Obwohl sich aus dem erwähnten Bericht ergab, dass eine einheitliche Regelung auch der Produkthaftung durchaus machbar und dem internationalen Handel förderlich sei, entschied man sich anlässlich der 10. Sitzung von UNCITRAL, eine Regelung der Produkthaftungsfragen nicht weiter zu verfolgen, „um die Kräfte des Sekretariats nicht mit einer wenig aussichtsreichen Materie zu binden, die zudem nur mittelbare Auswirkungen auf den Handel habe."[5] 1

Auf der Wiener Konferenz wurde die Frage der Produkthaftung erneut angesprochen, wobei es aber nicht darum ging, einheitliche Vorschriften für die Produkthaftung zu erarbeiten, sondern darum, die Produkthaftung aus dem Regelungsbereich des Übereinkommens auszunehmen. Die heutige Fassung der Vorschrift geht auf einen gemeinsamen Vorschlag der Delegationen Frankreichs, Finnlands und der USA zurück[6] und ist darauf zurückzuführen, dass **Überschneidungen zwischen dem Übereinkommen und nationalen Produkt-** 2

---

[1] *Ferrari*, Vendita internazionale, S. 103; *Hoffmann*, Koordination, S. 298; *Honnold/Flechtner*, Art. 5, Rn. 71, Fn. 1; *Kröll u. a./Ribeiro*, Art. 5, Rn. 3; *Kuhlen*, S. 22; *Schlechtriem/Schwenzer/Schwenzer/Hachem*, CISG Commentary, Art. 5, Rn. 1.
[2] Vgl. *Herber*, RIW 1974, 577, 582.
[3] YB VIII (1977), 235 ff.
[4] So ausdrücklich *Kuhlen*, S. 23; vgl. auch *Schlechtriem/Schwenzer/Schwenzer/Hachem*, CISG Commentary, Art. 5, Rn. 1.
[5] *Herber*, RIW 1980, 81, 84.
[6] Zu den Anträgen, die die im Text erwähnten Delegationen vor ihrem gemeinsamen Antrag gestellt hatten, vgl. A/CONF. 97/C.1/L.4 (USA), A/CONF. 97/C.1/L.20 (Frankreich) und A/CONF. 97/C.1/L.51 (Finnland); zum gemeinsamen Antrag vgl. O. R., S. 85, sowie die Diskussion hierzu, O. R., S. 245, Nr. 11.

haftungsregelungen vermieden werden sollten.[7] Dies ist jedoch nicht gänzlich geglückt. Da der Begriff der Produkthaftung nicht eindeutig definiert werden konnte,[8] ist nicht die Produkthaftung als solche, sondern nur die Haftung für Personenschäden dem Regelungsbereich des CISG entzogen worden.[9] Die Haftung für Sachschäden kann aber – trotz Fehlens eines ausdrücklichen Vorschrift[10] – dem Übereinkommen unterstehen.[11]

II. Die Vorschrift im Einzelnen

1. Ausschluss von Ansprüchen wegen Personenschäden

3   Die Haftung des Verkäufers für **Tod oder Körperverletzung**, also Personenschäden, ist ganz allgemein ausgenommen.[12] Dies bedeutet nicht, dass für Tod oder Körperverletzung nicht gehaftet werden müsse.[13] Vielmehr hat dies lediglich zur Folge, dass über die maßgeblichen Kollisionsnormen das anwendbare Recht bestimmt werden muss.[14] Dabei muss zwischen **deliktischen** und vertraglichen Ansprüchen unterschieden werden. Sind die Ansprüche als deliktische zu qualifizieren, wie dies regelmäßig der Fall sein wird, so kommt es für die Bestimmung des anwendbaren Rechts wiederum darauf an, ob zwischen Geschädigten und Schädiger vertragliche Beziehungen bestehen. Ist diese Frage zu bejahen, werden in Deutschland – zumindest in der Lehre[15] – deliktsrechtliche Schadenersatzansprüche akzessorisch an das Vertragsstatut angeknüpft.[16] Besteht zwischen den Parteien kein vertragliches Verhältnis, wird es in der Regel auf das Recht des Tatortes ankommen.[17] Handelt es sich dagegen um **vertragliche Ansprüche** wegen durch die Ware verursachter Personenschäden, ist dagegen das Recht des Staates berufen, dem der Vertrag unterliegen würde, wäre das Übereinkommen nicht anwendbar.[18]

---

[7] Vgl. O. R., S. 245, Nr. 12; *P. Huber*, IHR 2006, 228, 233; *P. Huber/Mullis/P. Huber*, S. 25; MünchKomm/*Westermann*, Art. 5, Rn. 1; *Sannini*, L'applicazione, S. 125; *Schlechtriem*, Internationales UN-Kaufrecht, Rn. 39; *Schneider*, S. 33; siehe aber *Date-Bah*, 11 Rev. Ghana L. (1979), 50, 53, und *Honnold/Flechtner*, Art. 5, Rn. 71, die die Ausnahme damit begründen, dass „the Convention (shall not) collide with the special protection that some domestic rules provide for the noncommercial comsumer".
[8] Siehe Denkschrift, S. 41 (zu Art. 5); *Hoffmann*, Koordination, S. 269; MünchKomm/*Westermann*, Art. 5, Rn. 1; *Schlechtriem/Schwenzer/Schlechtriem*, CISG Commentary, 2. Aufl., Art. 5, Rn. 1.
[9] *Ferrari*, Vendita internazionale, S. 104; *Hackney*, 61 La. L. Rev. (2001), 473, 476; *Käerdi*, S. 92; *Staudinger/Magnus*, Art. 5, Rn. 3; *Tessitore*, 35 Willamette L. Rev. (1999), 367, 369.
[10] Vgl. *Schneider*, S. 37 ff.
[11] *Bianca/Carbone/Lopez de Gonzalo*, Art. 5, S. 16; *Brunner*, Art. 5, Rn. 1; *Enderlein/Maskow/Strohbach*, Art. 5, Anm. 1.2.
[12] *Gruber*, Methoden, S. 248; MünchKommHGB/*Benicke*, Art. 5, Rn. 1; *Schlechtriem/Schwenzer/Schlechtriem*, CISG Commentary, 2. Aufl., Art. 5, Rn. 2; so ausdrücklich auch HGer Zürich, 26.4.1995, CISG-online 248 = TranspR-IHR 1999, 54.
[13] So ausdrücklich *Honsell/Siehr*, Art. 5, Rn. 2; vgl. auch *Gruber*, Methoden, S. 248; *Lohmann*, Parteiautonomie, S. 23; *Reinhart*, Art. 5, Rn. 3; *Schlechtriem/Schwenzer/Schlechtriem*, CISG Commentary, 2. Aufl., Art. 5 Rn. 7, Fn. 10; *Schlechtriem/Schwenzer/Schwenzer/Hachem*, CISG Commentary, Art. 5, Rn. 5, Fn. 11; *Staudinger/Magnus*, Art. 5, Rn. 16; *Tescaro*, Contr. Imp. E. 2007, 319, 325; a. A. wohl *Niggemann*, RIW 1991, 372, 377, der für die Vorschrift eine Sperrwirkung beizumessen scheint.
[14] Vgl. *Bamberger/Roth/Saenger*, Art. 5, Rn. 2; *Ferrari u. a./Saenger*, Art. 5, Rn. 2; *Herber*, 2. Aufl., Art. 5, Rn. 6; *ders.*, MDR 1993, 105; *Honsell/Siehr*, Art. 5, Rn. 2; *Mather*, 20 J. L. & Com. (2001), 155, 160; *Otto*, MDR 1992, 533, 537; *Rudolph*, Art. 5, Rn. 4; *Schlechtriem/Schwenzer/Schlechtriem*, CISG Commentary, 2. Aufl., Art. 5, Rn. 6; *Witz/Salger/Lorenz/Lorenz*, Art. 5, Rn. 1.
[15] Die deutsche Rechtsprechung hat die akzessorische Anknüpfung bislang nicht anerkannt, vgl. BGH, 12.11.2003, NJW-RR 2004, 308, 309.
[16] Siehe statt aller *Kropholler*, IPR, § 53 V; vgl. auch *Bamberger/Roth/Saenger*, Art. 5, Rn. 2; an der Möglichkeit der vertragsakzessorischen Anknüpfung hat sich mit dem Inkrafttretens der Rom-II VO nicht geändert; vgl. Art. 4 III; vgl. hierzu ErmannBGB/*Hochloch*, Anh. Art 42 EGBGB, Art. 4 Rom-II VO, Rn. 17.
[17] *Rudolph*, Art. 5, Rn. 5; *Schlechtriem/Schwenzer/Schwenzer/Hachem*, CISG Commentary, Art. 5, Rn. 5; vgl. auch Art. 5 Rom-II VO.
[18] So auch *Ferrari u. a./Saenger*, Art. 5, Rn. 2; *Kuhlen*, S. 47 f.; MünchKomm/*Westermann*, Art. 5, Rn. 2; *Schlechtriem/Schwenzer/Schwenzer/Hachem*, CISG Commentary, Art. 5, Rn. 5.

Ausschluß der Haftung für Tod oder Körperverletzung 4–8 **Art. 5**

Ob zur Bestimmung des anwendbaren Rechts in den Vertragsstaaten des **Haager Pro-** 4 **dukthaftungsübereinkommens** vom 2.10.1973 dessen Vorschriften einschlägig sein können,[19] ist wohl auszuschließen,[20] da dieses gemäß Art. 1 II keine Anwendung findet,[21] wenn der Geschädigte das Eigentum oder das Nutzungsrecht an der Sache vom Schädiger erhalten hat.[22]

Auch durch Schlechtlieferung verursachter **Ärger** oder andere **immaterielle Beschwer** 5 ist als Personenschaden eingeordnet worden;[23] ob dieser zu ersetzen ist, hängt demnach vom anwendbaren Recht ab; gleiches gilt für **Ansprüche auf Schmerzensgeld**.[24]

Das Übereinkommen beschränkt sich nicht darauf, die Haftung des Verkäufers für vom 6 Käufer erlittene Personenschäden auszuschließen. Vielmehr bezieht sich der **Haftungsausschluss auf sämtliche Personen.**[25] „Demnach ist völlig belanglos, ob der Personenschaden bei dem Vertragspartner des CISG-Verkäufers, bei einem in den Vertrag einbezogenen Dritten oder bei einem sog. „innocent bystander" eingetreten ist."[26]

Ausgeschlossen ist die Haftung für **„durch die Ware"** verursachte Personenschäden. 7 Dazu gehören, so die Lehre, auch die Fälle, in denen die Ware „erst auf Grund falscher Instruktion Schaden stiftet oder wenn ein erster, durch zweite Andienung später korrigierter Erfüllungsversuch schadensursächlich war."[27] Der bei der Anlieferung der Ware mit dem LKW entstandene Personenschaden kann jedoch nicht als ein „durch die Ware" verursachter Körperschaden angesehen werden,[28] weshalb sich die Haftung in diesem Fall nach dem CISG richtet.[29] Der Begriff „durch die Ware" ist vielmehr eng auszulegen.[30]

2. Rückgriffsansprüche wegen Personenschäden

Als „durch die Ware" verursachter Personenschaden muss jedoch der angesehen werden, 8 der dem Käufer dadurch entsteht, dass er eigene Abnehmer für erlittene Körperverletzungen entschädigen muss,[31] d. h., dass zu den ausgeschlossenen Ansprüchen auch Regressansprüche des Käufers gehören, der seinen Abnehmern wegen Tod oder Körperverletzung Ersatz

---

[19] Zu den Vertragsstaaten des CISG, in denen das Produkthaftungsübereinkommen in Kraft getreten ist, zählen Finnland, Frankreich, (das ehemalige) Jugoslawien, Luxemburg, Norwegen, Spanien und Slowenien.
[20] A. A. *Honsell/Siehr*, Art. 5, Rn. 2.
[21] Vgl. Art. 1 II: „Where the property in, or the right to use, the product was transferred to the person suffering the damage by the person claimed to the liable, the Convention shall not apply to their liability inter se".
[22] So schon *Kuhlen*, S. 45 f.
[23] *Kröll* u. a./*Ribeiro*, Art. 5, Rn. 5; *Staudinger/Magnus*, Art. 5, Rn. 5, unter Hinweis auf O. R., S. 201 f.; *Tescaro*, Contr. Imp. E. 2007, 319, 327.
[24] *Ferrari* u. a./*Saenger*, Art. 5, Rn. 3.
[25] So auch *Audit*, Vente internationale, S. 36; *Bamberger/Roth/Saenger*, Art. 5, Rn. 3; *Brunner*, Art. 5, Rn. 1; *Enderlein/Maskow/Strohbach*, Art. 5, Anm. 1.1.; *Ferrari*, Vendita internazionale, S. 104; *ders.*, Scope of Application, S. 96, 103; *Ferrari* u. a./*Saenger*, Internationales Vertragsrecht, Art. 5, Rn. 3; *Herber/Czerwenka*, Art. 5, Rn. 4; *Hoffmann*, Koordination, S. 270; *Plantard*, J. D. I. 1988, 311, 327; *Reinhart*, Art. 5, Rn. 3; *Sannini*, L'applicazione, S. 140 f.; *Schlechtriem/Schwenzer/Schlechtriem*, CISG Commentary, 2. Aufl., Art. 5, Rn. 4; *Staudinger/Magnus*, Art. 5, Rn. 7; *Witz/Salger/Lorenz/Lorenz*, Art. 5, Rn. 4; a. A. *Kröll* u. a./*Ribeiro*, Art. 5, Rn. 13; *Schlechtriem/Schwenzer/Schwenzer/Hachem*, CISG Commentary, Art. 5, Rn. 10.
[26] *Kuhlen*, S. 61; ebenso *Schlechtriem/Schwenzer/Schwenzer/Hachem*, CISG Commentary, Art. 5, Rn. 4.
[27] *Staudinger/Magnus*, Art. 5, Rn. 6; vgl. auch MünchKomm/*Westermann*, Art. 5, Rn. 3.
[28] *Audit*, Vente internationale, S. 36; *Bamberger/Roth/Saenger*, Art. 5, Rn. 3; *Ferrari*, Vendita internazionale, S. 105 f.; *Ferrari* u. a./*Saenger*, Art. 5, Rn. 3.
[29] *Achilles*, Art. 5, Rn. 2; *Brunner*, Art. 5, Rn. 1; *Herber/Czerwenka*, Art. 5, Rn. 2; *Kröll* u. a./*Ribeiro*, Art. 5, Rn. 7; *Magnus*, ZEuP 1993, 79, 95; MünchKomm/*Westermann*, Art. 5, Rn. 4; weniger eindeutig *Schlechtriem/Schwenzer/Schlechtriem*, CISG Commentary, 2. Aufl., Art. 5, Rn. 5: „such liability for breach of an ancillary duty may be subject to the CISG"; ähnlich auch *Schlechtriem/Schwenzer/Schwenzer/Hachem*, CISG Commentary, Art. 5, Rn. 6; a. A. MünchKommHGB/*Benicke*, Art. 5, Rn. 6: Anwendung nationalen Rechts.
[30] *Schlechtriem*, 21 Cornell Int'l L. J. (1988), 467, 473; *Bamberger/Roth/Saenger*, aaO.
[31] So auch *Achilles*, Art. 5, Rn. 2; *Audit*, Vente internationale, S. 36; *Brunner*, Art. 5, Rn. 1; *Ferrari*, Vendita internazionale, S. 105, Fn. 13; *Herber/Czerwenka*, Art. 5, Rn. 4; MünchKommHGB/*Benicke*, Art. 5, Rn. 3; *Schlechtriem/Schwenzer/Schlechtriem*, CISG Commentary, 2. Aufl., Art. 5, Rn. 7.

schuldet.³² Dieser Fall ist durch den Wortlaut des Übereinkommens gedeckt, der auf den Tod oder die Körperverletzung „jeder" Person, also nicht nur des Vertragspartners,³³ abstellt.³⁴ Die Erstreckung der Ausnahme auf diesen Fall ist auch gewollt und sachgerecht, weil nur so die Weiterleitung des Schadenersatzanspruchs durch die Abnehmerkette bis zurück zum Produzenten ermöglicht wird.³⁵ Leider ist dies vom OLG Düsseldorf in einem neueren Urteil³⁶ übersehen worden:³⁷ Das Gericht hat das Übereinkommen für anwendbar erklärt auf Ersatzansprüche der deutschen Käuferin, die ihr dadurch entstanden waren, dass die von der amerikanischen Verkäuferin gelieferte Ware bei der russischen Abnehmerin einen Unfall verursacht hatte, bei dem Arbeiter der Abnehmerin verletzt worden waren, für deren Verletzung sie gehaftet hatte.³⁸

3. Produkthaftung wegen Sachschäden

9 Die Vorschrift schließt lediglich die Produkthaftung wegen Personenschäden (im oben gesteckten Rahmen) aus.³⁹ Die Haftung für **Sachschäden** ist nicht per se ausgeschlossen.⁴⁰ Ob und inwieweit sie dem Übereinkommen unterliegt, hängt vom Regelungsbereich des Übereinkommens ab.⁴¹

10 Bei **vertraglichen Ansprüchen** wegen durch die Ware verursachter Sach- und Vermögensschäden ist das Übereinkommen ausschließlich⁴² anwendbar,⁴³ auch auf Ansprüche, die sich aus Schäden an der Ware selbst ergeben.⁴⁴

11 Umstritten ist, wie sich aus nationalem Deliktsrecht ergebende **deliktische Ansprüche** angesichts der vertraglichen CISG-Haftung zu behandeln sind. Die Beantwortung dieser **Frage** ist, trotz gegenteiliger Auffassung eines Teils der Lehre,⁴⁵ **durchaus praxisrelevant**,⁴⁶ etwa dann, „wenn das CISG anwendbar ist, aber im konkreten Fall keinen Schaden-

---

³² *Bamberger/Roth/Saenger*, Art. 5, Rn. 3; *Bianca/Bonell/Khoo*, Art. 5, Anm. 2.; *Enderlein/Maskow/Strohbach*, Art. 5, Anm. 1.1.; *P. Huber/Mullis/P. Huber*, S. 26; *Kuhlen*, S. 61; *Reinhart*, Art. 5, Rn. 3; *MünchKomm/Westermann*, Art. 5, Rn. 3; *Rudolph*, Art. 5, Rn. 3; *Schlechtriem*, Einheitliches UN-Kaufrecht, S. 20; *Schlechtriem/Schwenzer/Schlechtriem*, CISG Commentary, 2. Aufl., Art. 5, Rn. 3; *Soergel/Lüderitz/Fenge*, Art. 5, Rn. 1, *Witz/Salger/Lorenz/Lorenz*, Art. 5, Rn. 5; a. A. nunmehr *Schlechtriem*, Internationales UN-Kaufrecht, Rn. 39; a. A. auch *Koller*, FS Wiegand, S. 422, 425; *Schlechtriem/Schwenzer/Schwenzer*, CISG Commentary, Art. 74, Rn. 32.
³³ Vgl. hierzu schon oben Rn. 6.
³⁴ Vgl. auch *P. Huber*, IHR 2006, 228, 233; *MünchKomm/Westermann*, Art. 5, Rn. 3; *Staudinger/Magnus*, Art. 5, Rn. 7.
³⁵ So auch *Kuhlen*, S. 61; *Schlechtriem*, Einheitliches UN-Kaufrecht, S. 20.
³⁶ OLG Düsseldorf, 2.7.1993, CISG-online 74 = RIW 1993, 845 mit Anm. *Schlechtriem*, EWiR 1993, 1076.
³⁷ Kritisch zum erwähnten Urteil auch *Schlechtriem*, Internationales UN-Kaufrecht, Rn. 39, Fn. 72.
³⁸ Vgl. auch *Kuhlen*, S. 61; das im Text zitierte Urteil befürwortend, hingegen, *MünchKomm/Westermann*, Art. 5, Rn. 3 a. E.
³⁹ Vgl. HGer Zürich, 26.4.1995, CISG-online 248 = TranspR-IHR 1999, 54.
⁴⁰ Vgl. *Bridge*, Draft Digest, S. 235, 246; *Brunner*, Art. 5, Rn. 2; *Ferrari*, Vendita internazionale, S. 106; ders., Scope of Application, S. 96, 103; *Kröll u. a./Ribeiro*, Art. 5, Rn. 2 und 15; *Kritzer*, Guide to Practical Applications, S. 95; *Lohmann*, Parteiautonomie, S. 24; *MünchKommHGB/Benicke*, Art. 5, Rn. 7; *Schlechtriem*, Internationales UN-Kaufrecht, Rn. 40; *Schlechtriem/Butler*, Rn. 40; *Schlechtriem/Schwenzer/Schlechtriem*, CISG Commentary, 2. Aufl., Art. 5, Rn. 8; *Schlechtriem/Schwenzer/Hachem*, CISG Commentary, Art. 5, Rn. 11; *Staudinger/Magnus*, Art. 5, Rn. 9; *Witz/Salger/Lorenz/Lorenz*, Art. 5, Rn. 2 und Rn. 7; a. A. *Ndulo*, 38 Int'l & Comp. L. Q. (1989), 1, 5. An dieser Stelle sei erwähnt, dass „Schadenersatzansprüche wegen Sachschäden [...], die durch Fehler am Produkt entstanden sind, nach dem Wiener Kaufrecht nur nach rechtzeitiger Rüge geltend gemacht werden [können]", HGer Zürich, 26.4.1995 CISG-online 248 = TranspR-IMR 1999, 54.
⁴¹ *Herber*, 2. Aufl., Art. 5, Rn. 8; *Käerdi*, S. 95.
⁴² Vgl. *Honnold/Flechtner*, Art. 5, Rn. 73; *Rudolph*, Art. 5, Rn. 12 a. E. ; *Staudinger/Magnus*, Art. 5, Rn. 10.
⁴³ *Bamberger/Roth/Saenger*, Art. 5, Rn. 4; *Ferrari u. a./Saenger*, Art. 5, Rn. 5; *Karollus*, S. 44; *Piltz*, Rn. 2–156; *Rudolph*, Art. 5, Rn. 11; *Ryffel*, S. 134; *Soergel/Lüderitz/Fenge*, Art. 5, Rn. 5; a. A. *Schlechtriem/Schwenzer/Hachem*, CISG Commentary, Art. 5, Rn. 15.
⁴⁴ So auch *Audit*, Vente internationale, S. 36; *Ferrari*, Vendita internazionale, S. 106 f.
⁴⁵ Vgl. etwa *Herber/Czerwenka*, Art. 5, Rn. 6; *Otto*, MDR 1992, 533, 537.
⁴⁶ *Ferrari*, Vendita internazionale, S. 107; so auch *Bamberger/Roth/Saenger*, Art. 5, Rn. 5; *Käerdi*, S. 91; *Schlechtriem*, 36 Vict. U. Well. L. Rev. (2005), 781, 793; *Staudinger/Magnus*, Art. 5, Rn. 11; *Tescaro*, Contr. Imp. E. 2007, 319, 325.

ersatzanspruch gewährt, während das nationale Produkthaftungsrecht ihn konkurrierend gerade vorsieht",[47] oder wenn die nach dem Übereinkommen für die Geltendmachung der Schadensersatzansprüche nötige Rüge nicht rechtzeitig gemacht worden ist:[48] Da es nach nationalem Deliktsrecht keiner Mängelrüge bedarf, kann ein Anspruch also auch bei verpasster Rüge noch geltend gemacht werden.[49] Die praktische Bedeutung der Antwort auf die Frage ergibt sich aber auch aus der Tatsache, dass das Übereinkommen ex Art. 74 nur zum Ersatz des voraussehbaren Schadens verpflichtet, nationales Deliktsrecht aber durchaus großzügiger sein kann.[50]

Ein Teil der Lehre geht, was die Beziehungen zwischen nationalem Deliktsrecht und Einheitskaufrecht angeht, in Bezug auf Schadensersatzansprüche des Käufers wegen Sachschäden von der **Exklusivität des Einheitskaufrechts**[51] aus,[52] wonach das Übereinkommen innerstaatliches Produkthaftungsrecht verdrängt.[53] Der vorzuziehenden Auffassung zufolge verdrängt Einheitskaufrecht nationales Deliktsrecht jedoch nicht unbedingt.[54] Dies hängt zum einen damit zusammen, dass in diesem Fall – anders als etwa in Bezug auf den Eigenschaftsirrtum und den Irrtum über die Leistungsfähigkeit der Vertragspartei – das Übereinkommen **keine abschließende funktional äquivalente Lösung** bereithält,[55] zum anderen damit, dass „die Deliktshaftung auf anderen Wertungen [beruht] – sie lässt vor allem regelmäßig keine Abdingbarkeit zu – und führt zu anderen Ergebnissen".[56] Aus dem Gesagten folgt, dass das über das IPR des Gerichtsstaates berufene nationale Deliktsrecht[57] insoweit anwendbar bleibt, als es „– wie regelmäßig – das Integritätsinteresse des Geschädigten, also etwa seine Rechtsgüter vor Schäden durch fehlerhafte Ware, schützen [will]".[58]

---

[47] *Staudinger/Magnus*, Art. 5, Rn. 11.
[48] Siehe HGer Zürich, 26.4.1995, CISG-online 248 = TranspR-IHR 1999, 54, und den oben in Fn. 40 zitierten Text.
[49] So auch *Rudolph*, Art. 5, Rn. 11.
[50] Vgl. *Ferrari*, Vendita internazionale, S. 107.
[51] Vgl. zu diesem Begriff *Schneider*, S. 229.
[52] So auch *Bianca/Bonell/Khoo*, Art. 5, Anm. 3.3.5.; *Enderlein/Maskow/Strohbach*, Art. 5, Anm. 1.2.; *Herber*, MDR 1993, 105, 105 f.; *Honnold/Flechtner*, Art. 5, Rn. 73; *Köhler*, Die Haftung nach UN-Kaufrecht, S. 142 ff. und 152 ff.; *Kröll u. a./Ribeiro*, Art. 5, Rn. 25; *Kuhlen*, S. 114 f.; *Mather*, 20 J.L. & Com. (2001), 155, 161; *Otto*, MDR 1992, 533, 537; *Piltz*, Internationales Kaufrecht, Rn. 2–141; *Ryffel*, S. 136; *Schmid*, S. 55 ff. Für eine ähnliche Lösung in der Rechtsprechung, vgl. HGer Zürich, 26.4.1995, CISG-online 248 = TranspR-IHR 1999, 54: „Auch bezüglich der Folgeschäden findet das Wiener Kaufrecht Anwendung und geht dem schweizerischen und deutschen Recht vor".
[53] *Herber*, FS Schlechtriem, S. 207, 212 ff.; *ders.*, IHR 2001, 187, 189; *ders.*, MDR 1993, 105, 105 f.; *Herber/Czerwenka*, Art. 5, Rn. 5.
[54] So auch *Achilles*, Art. 5, Rn. 1; *Bamberger/Roth/Saenger*, Art. 5, Rn. 8; *Brunner*, Art. 5, Rn. 2; *Czerwenka*, Rechtsanwendungsprobleme, S. 168 f.; *Ferrari u. a./Saenger*, Internationales Vertragsrecht, Art. 5, Rn. 8; *Hoffmann*, Koordination, S. 311; *Honsell/Siehr*, Art. 5, Rn. 4; *P. Huber*, IPRax 1997, 23 (mit Bezug auf das EKG); *Lohmann*, Parteiautonomie, S. 24; *Magnus*, ZEuP 1993, 79, 95 f.; *MünchKomm/Martiny*, 2. Aufl., Art. 28 Anh. II, Rn. 54; *MünchKommHGB/Benicke*, Art. 5, Rn. 8; *Plantard*, J.D.I. 1988, 311, 327; *Sannini*, L'applicazione, S. 142 ff.; *Schlechtriem*, Internationales UN-Kaufrecht, Rn. 40; *ders.*, JZ 1988, 1037, 1040; *ders.*, 21 Cornell Int'l L.J. (1988), 467, 473 f.; *ders.*, 36 Vict. U. Well. L. Rev. (2005), 781, 793; *Schlechtriem/Schwenzer/Schlechtriem*, CISG Commentary, 2. Aufl., Art. 5, Rn. 9; *Soergel/Lüderitz/Fenge*, Art. 5, Rn. 4; *Stoffel*, SJZ 1990, 169, 171; *Stoll*, Internationalprivatrechtliche Fragen, S. 510 f.; *Tescaro*, Contr. Imp. E. 2007, 319, 329; *Thiele*, IHR 2002, 8, 12; *Witz/Salger/Lorenz/Lorenz*, Art. 4, Rn. 28; vgl. in der Rechtsprechung *Electrocraft Arkansas, Inc. v. Super Electric Motors, Ltd et al.*, U.S. Dist. Ct. (E.D. Ark., Western Division), 23.12.2009, CISG-online 2045; *Geneva Pharmaceuticals Tech. Corp. v. Barr Labs. Inc.*, U.S. Dist. Ct. (S.D.N.Y.), 10.5.2002, CISG-online 653 = 2002 U.S. Dist. LEXIS 8411; die im Text ausgedrückte Meinung falsch verstehend *Hoffmann*, Koordination, S. 269, Fn. 10; unverständlich *Pribetic*, Rev. CISG (2004/2005), 179 ff.
[55] So auch *Staudinger/Magnus*, Art. 5, Rn. 14; *Tescaro*, Contr. Imp. E. 2007, 319, 329 f.
[56] *Magnus*, ZEuP 1993, 79, 96; ähnlich auch *Schlechtriem*, 21 Cornell Int'l L.J. (1988), 467, 473 ff.; *Schlechtriem/Schwenzer/Schlechtriem*, CISG Commentary, 2. Aufl., Art. 5, Rn. 10.
[57] Das über das IPR des Gerichtsstaates berufene nationale Deliktsrecht entscheidet auch darüber, ob eine konkurrierende Anwendung des Deliktsrechts überhaupt zulässig ist; vgl. *Bridge*, Draft Digest, S. 235, 246; *Ferrari*, RabelsZ 71 (2007), 52, 76; *Schlechtriem/Schwenzer/Schlechtriem*, CISG Commentary, 2. Aufl., Art. 5, Rn. 10; *Tescaro*, Contr. Imp. E. 2007, 319, 331.
[58] *Staudinger/Magnus*, Art. 5, Rn. 14; vgl. hierzu auch *Ferrari*, RabelsZ 71 (2007), 52, 74 f.; *Schlechtriem/Schwenzer/Schwenzer/Hachem*, CISG Commentary, Art. 5, Rn. 14; a. A. jedoch *Gruppo Essenziero Italiano*,

"Wo dagegen mit deliktsrechtlichen Regeln das Erfüllungsinteresse des Käufers wegen der vertragswidrigen Beschaffenheit geltend gemacht [wird], [hat] das CISG Vorrang".[59] Das Gesagte gilt aber nur insoweit, als die geschädigten Rechtsgüter nur zufällig mit der fehlerhaften Ware in Kontakt gekommen sind, etwa weil sie im gleichen Lager abgestellt waren. Bei notwendigem Kontakt, wie etwa bei der Vermengung mit der fehlerhaften Ware, kommt ausschließlich das CISG zur Anwendung.

13 Die hier vertretene Auffassung ist auch mit der Möglichkeit, die Haftung nach dem Übereinkommen auszuschließen, eher vereinbar,[60] da bei Abbedingung der Haftung ex Art. 6 der Geschädigte nicht gänzlich schutzlos bleibt.[61]

III. Produkthaftung und Art. 90

14 Nach der hier vertretenen Auffassung schließt das Übereinkommen auf nationalem Produkthaftungsrecht gründende Ansprüche nicht aus. Zu dem gleichen Ergebnis gelangen auch einige der Autoren, die die gegenteilige Auffassung vertreten (Exklusivität des Übereinkommens), zumindest in Bezug auf Fälle, in denen beide Vertragsparteien in **EU-Staaten** niedergelassen sind,[62] die die **Produkthaftungs-Richtlinie** vom 25. Juli 1985[63] umgesetzt haben. Dies ist darauf zurückzuführen, dass diese Autoren[64] auf der Grundlage einer Anwendung des Art. 90 des CISG Rechtsetzungsakten der Europäischen Gemeinschaft, wie etwa den Richtlinien, die auf eine völkerrechtliche Übereinkunft zurückgehen, dem EG-Vertrag, Vorrang vor dem Übereinkommen einräumen.[65] Da es sich bei diesen Rechtsetzungsakten nicht um Völkerrecht handele, auf das sich die erwähnte Vorschrift aber ausdrücklich bezieht, könne die erwähnte Vorschrift aber nur analoge Anwendung finden.[66]

15 M. E.[67] ist es nicht möglich, den ex Art. 90 völkerrechtlichen Übereinkünften gewährten Vorrang auf Richtlinien beziehungsweise sekundäres Gemeinschaftsrecht als solches auszudehnen.[68] Dies hängt nicht nur damit zusammen, dass Richtlinien – wie auch von den Vertretern der hier abgelehnten Auffassung zugestanden wird[69] – keine „völkerrechtliche Übereinkünfte" sind,[70] sondern auch damit, dass die Vorschrift (Art. 90) eine Ausnahmeregel vorsieht (Zurücktreten des Übereinkommens) und daher keine analoge Anwendung finden sollte.

S. P. A. v. Aromi D'Italia, Inc., U. S. Dist. Ct. (D. Md.), 27.7.2011, CISG-online 2223, wonach deliktsrechtliche Ansprüche immer nationalen Recht zu unterstellen seien.

[59] *Schlechtriem*, Internationales UN-Kaufrecht, Rn. 40 a. E.; vgl. auch *Käerdi*, S. 96 f.; *Schlechtriem/Schwenzer/Schwenzer/Hachem*, CISG Commentary, Art. 5, Rn. 14

[60] Vgl. auch *Ferrari*, RabelsZ 71 (2007), 52, 77; *Staudinger/Magnus*, Art. 5, Rn. 14 a. E.

[61] Vgl. *Bamberger/Roth/Saenger*, Art. 5, Rn. 7; *Honsell/Siehr*, Art. 5, Rn. 4; *Tescaro*, Contr. Imp. E. 2007, 319, 330; a. A. *Herber*, 2. Aufl., Art. 5, Rn. 13.

[62] Vgl. *Kuhlen*, S. 122.

[63] Richtlinie 85/374/EWG des Rates der EG, AblEG Nr. L 210v. 7.8.1985, S. 29.

[64] Vgl. statt aller *Herber*, FS Schlechtriem, S. 207, 220 ff.

[65] *Honsell/Siehr*, Art. 90, Rn. 7; *Ryffel*, S. 137; *Herber*, 2. Aufl., Art. 90, Rn. 12; *Witz/Salger/Lorenz/Lorenz*, Art. 5, Rn. 8 und Art. 90, Rn. 3.

[66] *Herber*, MDR 1993, 105, 105 f.; *Kuhlen*, S. 122.

[67] Anders hierzu noch *Ferrari*, Vendita internazionale, S. 109.

[68] So auch *P. Huber*, IHR 2006, 228, 233; *Otto*, MDR 1993, 306, 306; *Rudolph*, Art. 5, Rn. 12 a. E.; *Schlechtriem*, Internationales UN-Kaufrecht, Rn. 36b; *Taschner*, Art. 22, Rn. 2.

[69] Vgl. *Herber*, FS Schlechtriem, S. 207, 220.

[70] Ebenso *P. Huber/Mullis/P. Huber*, S. 28; MünchKomm/*Westermann*, Vor Art. 1, Rn. 17; *Piltz*, IHR 2002, 2, 4.

Art. 6 [Ausschluß, Abweichung oder Änderung durch Parteiabrede]

Die Parteien können die Anwendung dieses Übereinkommens ausschließen oder, vorbehaltlich des Artikels 12, von seinen Bestimmungen abweichen oder deren Wirkung ändern.

Art. 6
The parties may exclude the application of this Convention or, subject to article 12, derogate from or vary the effect of any of its provisions.

Art. 6
Les parties peuvent exclure l'application de la présente Convention ou, sous réserve des dispositions de l'article 12, déroger à l'une quelconque de ses dispositions ou en modifier les effets.

Übersicht

	Rn.
I. Vorgeschichte	1
II. Allgemeines	5
1. Die dispositive Natur des CISG und seine Grenzen	5
2. Voraussetzungen der Abwahl beziehungsweise der Änderung des CISG	12
III. Die Vorschrift im Einzelnen	15
1. Ausdrückliche Abbedingung mit oder ohne Wahl des anwendbaren Rechts	15
2. Stillschweigender Ausschluss des CISG	18
a) Grundsatz	18
b) Einzelfälle	19
3. Modifikation und teilweiser Ausschluss des CISG	33
a) Grundsatz	33
b) Teilweiser Ausschluss und Lückenfüllung	34
4. Ergänzende vertragliche Vereinbarung	36
5. Beweislast	38
IV. Opting-in des Übereinkommens	39

Vorläufer und **Entwürfe:** Art. 3 EKG; Art. 2 EAG; Genfer E 1976 Art. 5; Wiener E 1977 Art. 4; New Yorker E 1978 Art. 5.

I. Vorgeschichte

Die Vorschrift geht auf Art. 3 EKG zurück,[1] weicht jedoch in verschiedener Hinsicht von diesem ab.[2] So fällt etwa auf, dass die in Art. 3 S. 2 EKG ausdrücklich vorgesehene Möglichkeit, das Einheitsgesetz auch stillschweigend auszuschließen,[3] im CISG nicht übernommen wurde.[4] Das Fehlen eines ausdrücklichen Hinweises auf die Möglichkeit eines **stillschweigenden Ausschlusses** bedeutet jedoch nicht, dass die Vorschriften inhaltlich verschieden seien,[5] d. h., dass den Vertragsparteien die Möglichkeit des stillschweigenden Ausschlusses genommen sei.[6] Dies geht unschwer aus der Entstehungsgeschichte hervor: **1**

---

[1] Vgl. *Bianca/Bonell/Bonell*, Art. 6, Anm. 1.
[2] *Ferrari*, Applicabilità ed applicazioni, S. 200 f.; *Kröll u. a./Mistelis*, Art. 6, Rn. 4; MünchKomm/*Westermann*, Art. 6, Rn. 2; *Schlechtriem/Schwenzer/Schlechtriem*, CISG Commentary, 2. Aufl., Art. 6, Rn. 1.
[3] Vgl. Art. 3 S. 2 EKG: „Der Ausschluss kann ausdrücklich oder stillschweigend erfolgen".
[4] Siehe auch *Bureau*, Rev. crit. dr. int. privé 2006, 374, 378; *Rudolph*, Art. 6, Rn. 4; *Schlechtriem/Schwenzer/Hachem*, CISG Commentary, Art. 6, Rn. 1.
[5] So auch *Staudinger/Magnus*, Art. 6, Rn. 5; vgl. auch *Schlechtriem/Schwenzer/Schlechtriem*, CISG Commentary, 2. Aufl., Art. 6, Rn. 1.
[6] Ebenso *Borisova*, Art. 6 CISG-UP, S. 41; *Chiomenti*, EuLF 2005, 141, 143; *Ferrari*, Applicabilità ed applicazioni, S. 207 f.; *Ferrari u. a./Saenger*, Internationales Vertragsrecht, Art. 6, Rn. 2; MünchKommHGB/

Während der Vorarbeiten in UNCITRAL wurde vorgeschlagen, einen stillschweigenden Ausschluss nicht zuzulassen.[7] Schon auf der zweiten Sitzung der UNCITRAL-Arbeitsgruppe einigte man sich indes darauf, den in Art. 3 EKG festgelegten Grundsatz beizubehalten.[8] Dass ein stillschweigender Ausschluss auch weiterhin, d. h., nach neuem Einheitskaufrecht, zulässig ist, ergibt sich auch daraus, dass verschiedene Vorschläge abgelehnt wurden, die darauf zielten, nur eine ausdrückliche Abbedingungsmöglichkeit zuzulassen.[9] Das Fehlen eines ausdrücklichen Hinweises auf die stillschweigende Abbedingungsmöglichkeit ist – trotz einiger weniger Stimmen, die die gegenteilige Auffassung vertreten[10] – demnach nicht so zu verstehen, dass den Vertragsparteien diese Möglichkeit nicht gegeben sei. Die Streichung des Wortes „implied" sollte „[lediglich] allzu großzügigen Unterstellungen eines Ausschlusses des Einheitskaufrechts durch die Gerichte vorbeugen".[11] Aus diesem Grund wurde auch ein Antrag, den Hinweis auf die Möglichkeit einer stillschweigender Abbedingung wieder einzufügen,[12] abgelehnt.[13]

2   Die Vorschrift unterscheidet sich aber auch in anderer Hinsicht von Art. 3 EKG: Während Art. 6 CISG einen ausdrücklichen Hinweis auf die Möglichkeit vorsieht, dass die Parteien von den Bestimmungen des Gesetzes „abweichen oder deren Wirkung ändern" können,[14] fehlt ein solcher Hinweis im Haager Kaufrecht. Aber auch diese Änderung ist nur als eine redaktionelle Änderung zu verstehen.[15]

3   Wie hingegen die fehlende Bezugnahme auf die in Art. 4 EKG vorgesehene Möglichkeit der Vertragsparteien, das Einheitskaufrecht auch bei Fehlen der räumlichen Anwendungsvoraussetzungen durch ausdrückliche Wahl zur Anwendung zu bringen, einzuschätzen ist, soll andernorts untersucht werden.[16]

4   Schließlich sei auch erwähnt, dass für den Abschluss von Kaufverträgen zunächst in dem UNCITRAL-Entwurf für den Kaufabschluss von 1977 – ähnlich wie in Art. 2 I EAG – eine Sonderregelung vorgeschlagen wurde.[17] Anlässlich der Zusammenführung dieses Entwurfs mit dem Wiener E 1977 wurde die Vorschrift jedoch gestrichen,[18] um zu vermeiden,

---

Benicke, Art. 6, Rn. 10; *Niemann,* Einheitliche Anwendung, S. 79; *Reifner,* IHR 2002, 52, 55; *Wasmer,* S. 20; a. A. *Murphy,* 12 Fordham Int'l L. J. (1989), 727, 749.

[7] YB I (1968–1970), S. 168, Nr. 70.

[8] YB II (1971), S. 55, Nr. 44 f.

[9] Vgl. den Vorschlag der Philippinen zu Art. 5 Genfer E 1976, YB VIII (1977), S. 127, sowie den auf der Diplomatischen Konferenz in Wien von der pakistanischen Delegation unterbreiteten Vorschlag, O. R., S. 86.

[10] Vgl. in der Rechtsprechung LG Landshut, 5.4.1995, CISG-online 193 („die Parteien können die Anwendung des CISG nur ausdrücklich ausschließen"); *Orbisphere Corp. v. United States,* Ct. Int'l Trade, 24.10.1989, CISG-online 7 = 726 F. Supp. 1344 (das CISG sei anwendbar „unless the parties expressly contract out of the Convention's coverage"); widersprüchlich OGH, 17.12.2003, CISG-online 828 = IHR 2004, 148, 153: während der OGH an einer Stelle statuiert, dass, „ist das UN-K anwendbar, [müssen] die Parteien, die seine Anwendung nicht wollen, eine entsprechende ausdrückliche oder stillschweigende Ausschlussvereinbarung treffen", statuiert es an anderer Stelle, dass das CISG „nach h. M. [...] nur unter ausdrücklicher Nennung desselben abbedungen werden [kann]"; vgl. ferner die in Fn. 76 zitierten Urteile.

[11] *Schlechtriem,* Einheitliches UN-Kaufrecht, S. 21; so auch *Bianca/Bonell/Bonell,* Art. 6, Anm. 1.2.; *Dokter,* RabelsZ 68 (2004), 430, 433; *Ebenroth,* östJBl 1986, 681, 684; *Ferrari,* ZEuP 2002, 737, 742; *ders.,* Applicabilità ed applicazioni, S. 210; *ders.,* 10 Preadviezen (1995), 81, 145 f.; *Kröll u. a./Mistelis,* Art. 6, Rn. 6; *Lindbach* S. 253; Sekretariatskommentar, Art. 5, Nr. 2; *Schlechtriem,* Internationales UN-Kaufrecht, Rn. 19; *Soergel/Lüderitz/Fenge,* Art. 6, Rn. 1; *Staudinger/Magnus,* Art. 6, Rn. 5; *C. Witz,* D. 1995, Chron. 143, 144.

[12] Vgl. den auf der Diplomatischen Konferenz in Wien von der britischen Delegation unterbreiteten Antrag (A/CONF. 97/C.1/L.8), O. R., S. 85, und den der belgischen Delegation (A/CONF. 97/ C.1/L.41), O. R., S. 86.

[13] Siehe O. R., S. 248 ff., Nr. 4 ff.

[14] Vgl. *Lohmann,* Parteiautonomie, S. 128.

[15] Vgl. *Herber,* 2. Aufl., Art. 6, Rn. 3.

[16] Vgl. unten Rn. 39 ff.

[17] Vgl. Art. 2 des Entwurfs, YB VIII (1977), S. 88, sowie die Anmerkungen hierzu in YB IX (1978), S. 108 f., Art. 2.

[18] Vgl. Art. 5 New Yorker E 1978, YB IX (1978), S. 15.

dass hierin die Möglichkeit einseitiger Abbedingung gesehen werden könnte, die mit den Grundsätzen des Übereinkommens nicht vereinbar erschien.[19]

II. Allgemeines

1. Die dispositive Natur des CISG und seine Grenzen

Die Vorschrift stellt klar, dass das Übereinkommen, genauso wie sein Vorgänger, das Haager Einheitskaufrecht, **dispositiver Natur** ist,[20] d. h., „la convention fait de la volonté des parties la source première du contrat de vente".[21] 5

Art. 6 CISG ist aber nicht die einzige Vorschrift, aus der sich die nachgiebige Natur ableiten lässt.[22] Vielmehr lässt sich diese auch aus verschiedenen anderen Vorschriften ableiten. Diesbezüglich sind etwa die Vorschriften hinsichtlich der Pflichten der Vertragsparteien relevant: Sowohl Art. 30 als auch Art. 53 CISG, die jeweils einleitend die sich aus einem Kaufvertrag ergebenden Hauptpflichten des Verkäufers bzw. des Käufers regeln, stellen fest, dass diese Pflichten „nach Maßgabe des Vertrages und dieses Übereinkommens" zu erfüllen sind und damit eine vertragliche, von den Konventionsregelungen abweichende Absprache der Parteien vorrangig zu beachten ist.[23] 6

Trotz des erwähnten nachgiebigen Charakters „ist das CISG aber nicht nur Modellgesetz oder Empfehlung, sondern **geltendes Recht**, das stets anzuwenden ist,"[24] und zwar **ex officio**,[25] zumindest in civil-law-Ländern,[26] wenn alle Anwendungsvoraussetzungen vor- 7

---

[19] Vgl. YB IX (1978), S. 32, Nr. 12; vgl. zur Frage der einseitigen Abbedingung auch die Zusammenfassung der Stellungnahmen zu Art. 2 des UNCITRAL-Entwurfs für den Kaufabschluss von 1977, YB IX (1978), S. 130 f., Nr. 40.

[20] So auch *Bamberger/Roth/Saenger*, Art. 6, Rn. 1; *Borisova*, Art. 6 CISG-UP, S. 40; *Brunner*, Art. 6, Rn. 8; *Carbone*, S. 78; *Carbone/Luzzatto*, S. 131; *Díez-Picazo/Calvo Caravaca*, Art. 6, S. 92; *Dokter*, RabelsZ 68 (2004), 430; *Ferrari*, Applicabilità ed applicazioni, S. 201; *ders.*, Int. Bus. L.J. 2003, 221, 227; *Ferrari u. a./Saenger*, Internationales Vertragsrecht, Art. 6, Rn. 1; *Herber*, IHR 2003, 1; *Kröll u. a./Mistelis*, Art. 6, Rn. 7 und 8; *Lanciotti*, S. 146; *Lindbach*, S. 67; *Lohmann*, Parteiautonomie, S. 193; MünchKommHGB/*Benicke*, Art. 6, Rn. 19; *Piltz*, Rn. 2–190; *Reifner*, IHR 2002, 52, 54; *Sacerdoti*, Riv. trim. dir. proced. civ. 1990, 733, 744; *Sannini*, L'applicazione, S. 79; *D. Schäfer*, S. 2; *Volken*, Anwendungsvoraussetzungen, S. 92; *C. Witz*, D. 1990, Chron. 107, 107; für ausdrückliche Hinweise in der Rechtsprechung auf den dispositiven bzw. nicht zwingenden Charakter des CISG, vgl. OGer Bern, 19.5.2008, CISG-online 1738; Shanghai Higher People's Court, 17.5.2007, CISG-online 1976; Tribunal cantonal de Vaud, 24.11.2004, CISG-online 1842; KG Jura, 3.11.2004, CISG-online 965; Tribunal cantonal du Vaud, 11.4.2002, CISG-online 899; Cass. civ., 19.6.2000, Corr. giur. 2002, 369, 371; OGH, 21.3.2000, CISG-online 641 = IHR 2001, 41; OGH, 27.8.1999, CISG-online 485 = IHR 2001, 81, 83; OGH, 15.10.1998, CISG-online 380 = TranspR-IHR 1999, 25; HGer Wien, 4.3.1997, CISG Austria; KG Wallis, 29.6.1994, CISG-online 134 = Zeitschrift für Walliser Rechtsprechung 1994, 126.

[21] *Audit*, Vente internationale, S. 37; ebenso *Ferrari*, Vendita internazionale, S. 110; *Hoyer*, Anwendungsbereich, S. 41; *Kröll u. a./Mistelis*, Art. 6, Rn. 1; MünchKommHGB/*Benicke*, Art. 6, Rn. 1; ausdrücklich auf die zentrale Rolle des Parteiwillens für das CISG hinweisend LG Stendal, 12.10.2000, CISG-online 592 = IHR 2001, 32; Juzgado Nacional de Primera Instancia en lo Comercial No. 10, 6.10.1994, CISG-online 378.

[22] Vgl. *Dokter*, RabelsZ 68 (2004), 430, 433; *Ferrari*, ZEuP 2002, 737, 738, Fn. 12; *Schlechtriem/Schwenzer/Schlechtriem*, CISG Commentary, 2. Aufl., Art. 6, Rn. 15; *Schlechtriem/Schwenzer/Schwenzer/Hachem*, CISG Commentary, Art. 6, Rn. 8.

[23] So auch *Bamberger/Roth/Saenger*, Art. 6, Rn. 1; *Lindbach*, S. 68; MünchKommHGB/*Benicke*, Art. 6, Rn. 19.

[24] *Staudinger/Magnus*, Art. 6, Rn. 2; vgl. auch *Lohmann*, Parteiautonomie, S. 120; *Kröll u. a./Mistelis*, Art. 6, Rn. 2; *Wasmer*, S. 27.

[25] Vgl. *Bureau*, Rev. crit. dr. int. privé 2006, 374, 375; *Délebecque/Jacquet*, RTDcom. 2002, 210, 211; MünchBGB/*Westermann*, Vor Art. 1, Rn. 1; *Piltz*, Rn. 2–6; *Schlechtriem/Schwenzer/Schwenzer/Hachem*, CISG Commentary, Intro to Arts 1–6, Rn. 3 und Art. 6, Rn. 2; *Sinay-Cytermann*, Gaz. Pal. 2003, 234; *C. Witz*, L'interprétation, S. 279, 289; vgl. auch *Fountoulakis*, 7 EJLR (2005), 303, 314: „It is a Convention applying automatically"; ähnlich *Cuniberti*, 39 Vand. J. Transnat'l L. (2006), 1511, 1515; *Lohmann*, Parteiautonomie, S. 2; *Lookofsky*, Case Law Scandinavia, S. 167, 170 f.; *Niemann*, Einheitliche Anwendung, S. 26.

[26] *Achilles*, Art. 1, Rn. 11; *Muir Watt*, Rev. crit. dr. int. priv. 2002, 94, 96; *dies.*, Rev. crit. dr. int. priv. 2002, 344, 345; *C. Witz*, D. 2001, Jur. 3608, 3609 f.; *ders.*, D. 2002, Chron. 2796, 2797; vgl. in der Rechtsprechung

Art. 6 8   Teil I. Kapitel I. Anwendungsbereich

liegen und die Parteien es nicht wirksam ausgeschlossen haben.[27] Das Übereinkommen stellt demnach kein Einheitsrecht dar, das nur auf Grund der Wahl der Vertragsparteien (sog. opting-in Lösung, die durchaus vorgeschlagen wurde) zur Anwendung kommen kann;[28] die Konventionsgeber haben vielmehr die sog. opting-out Lösung bevorzugt,[29] mit der Folge, dass der fehlende Ausschluss zur negativen Anwendungsvoraussetzung erhoben wird.[30]

8   **Eine Ausnahme** hinsichtlich der dispositiven Natur des CISG bildet Art. 12,[31] die Bestimmung, wonach die Formvorschrift des Art. 11 dann keine Anwendung findet, wenn eine der Vertragsparteien ihre Niederlassung in einem Vertragsstaat hat, der gemäß Art. 96 einen Vorbehalt gegen diese Vorschrift eingelegt hat.[32] Damit soll verhindert werden, dass

---

OGH, 8.11.2005, CISG-online 1156; Tribunale di Padova, 25.2.2004, CISG-online 819; CA Paris, 6.11.2001.

[27] So ausdrücklich auch *Barrière-Brousse*, S. 133, 138; vgl. auch *Achilles*, Art. 6, Rn. 1; *Johnson*, 59 Buff. L. Rev. (2011), 213, 218; *Schlechtriem/Schwenzer/Schwenzer/Hachem*, CISG Commentary, Art. 6, Rn. 2; *Spagnolo*, 10 Melb. J. Int'l L. (2009), 141, 143; *Whittington*, 37 Vict. U. Wellington L. Rev. (2006), 421, 428.

[28] Vgl. auch MünchKommHGB/*Benicke*, Art. 1, Rn. 5 und Art. 6, Rn. 1; *Navas Navarro*, IHR 2006, 74, 75; *Schlechtriem*, Einheitliches UN-Kaufrecht, S. 21; *C. Witz*, D. 2002, Chron. 2796, 2797.

[29] *Brunner*, Art. 6, Rn. 1; *Bureau*, Rev. crit. dr. int. privé 2006, 374, 379; *Lohmann*, Parteiautonomie, S. 120 ff.; MünchKomm/*Westermann*, Art. 6, Rn. 1; *Muir Watt*, Rev. crit. dr. int. priv. 2002, 94, 97; *Schlechtriem/Schwenzer/Schwenzer/Hachem*, CISG Commentary, Art. 6, Rn. 2; *Schwenzer/Hachem/Kee*, Rn. 3.24; *Wasmer*, S. 27; a. A. *C. Witz*, L'interprétation, S. 279, 289, der jedoch dann, S. 292, hervorhebt, dass das CISG auf der opting-out Lösung basiert.

[30] So etwa *Ferrari*, ZEuP 2002, 737, 739; ebenso neuerdings auch MünchKomm/*Westermann*, Art. 1, Rn. 5; auch verschiedene Gerichte haben darauf hingewiesen, dass das CISG trotz Vorliegen aller anderen Anwendungsvoraussetzungen nur dann zur Anwendung kommt, wenn es von den Parteien nicht ausgeschlossen worden ist; vgl. RB Rotterdam, 29.12.2010, CISG-online 2180; Hof Arnhem, 9.3.2010, CISG-online 2095; KG St. Gallen, 15.1.2010, CISG-online 2159; OLG Hamm, 2.4.2009, CISG-online 1978; Tribunale di Forlì, 16.2.2009, CISG-online 1780; RB Breda, 16.1.2009, CISG-online 1789; Multi-Member Court of First Instance of Athens, Aktenzeichen 2282/2009 (ohne Datum), CISG Pace; Court of First Instance of Athens, Aktenzeichen 4505/2009 (ohne Datum), CISG-online 2228; Tribunale di Forlì, 11.12.2008, CISG-online 1729; KG Zug, 27.11.2008, CISG-online 2024; Hof van Beroep Gent, 14.11.2008, CISG-online 1819; Forestal Guarani, S. A. v. Daros International, Inc., U. S. Dist. Ct. (D. N. J.), 7.10.2008, CISG-online 1779; U Zhejiang Shaoxing Yongli Printing and Dyeing Co., Ltd v. Microflock Textile Group Corporation, U. S. Dist. Ct. (S. D. Fl.), 19.5.2008, CISG-online 1771; OLG Innsbruck, 18.12.2007, CISG-online 1735; OLG Linz, 24.9.2007, CISG-online 1583; HGer Aargau, 20.9.2007, CISG-online 1742; Audiencia Provincial de Valencia, 13.3.2007, CISG-online 1719; Cass., 20.2.2007, CISG-online 1492; Property Casualty Company of America et al. v. Saint-Gobain Technical Fabrics Canada Limited, U. S. Dist. Ct. (Minn.), 31.1.2007, CISG-online 1435 = 2007 WL 313 591 (D. Minn.); BGer, 20.12.2006, CISG-online 1426; RB Arnhem, 28.6.2006, CISG-online 1265; OLG Köln, 24.5.2006, CISG-online 1232 = IHR 2006, 147, 148; OLG Köln, 3.4.2006, CISG-online 1218; HGer Zürich, 22.12.2005, CISG-online 1195 = IHR 2006, 161; *American Mint LLC v. GOSoftware, Inc.*, U. S. Dist. Ct. (M. D. Pa.), 16.8.2005, CISG-online 1104 = 2005 WL 2021248; OLG Linz, 8.8.2005, CISG-online 1087 = IHR 2006, 249, 251; LG Neubrandenburg, 3.8.2005, CISG-online 1190 = IHR 2006, 26, 27; OGH, 21.6.2005, CISG-online 1047 = IHR 2005, 195, 196; OGH, 24.5.2005, CISG-online 1046 = IHR 2005, 249; KG Wallis, 21.2.2005, CISG-online 1193 = IHR 2006, 155, 156; OGH, 26.1.2005, CISG-online 1045; = IHR 2005, 199, 203; OLG Karlsruhe, 20.7.2004, CISG-online 858 = IHR 2004, 246, 249; OLG Celle, 10.3.2004, CISG-online 824 = IHR 2004, 106, 107; OGH, 17.12.2003, CISG-online 828 = IHR 2004, 148, 153; Tribunale di Padova, 25.2.2004, CISG-online 819; HGer Zürich, 24.10.2003, CISG-online 857; HGer St. Gallen, 3.12.2002, CISG-online 727; Civ. 1, 26.6.2001, CISG-online 695 = D. 2001, 2591, 2591; Tribunale di Vigevano, 12.7.2000, CISG-online 493 = IHR 2001, 72, 73; OGH, 9.3.2000, CISG-online 573 = IHR 2001, 39 f.; OLG Hamm, 23.6.1998, CISG-online 434; CA Paris, 15.10.1997, CISG-online 293; OLG München, 9.7.1997, CISG-online 281; OLG Karlsruhe, 25.6.1997, CISG-online 263; OGH, 11.2.1997, CISG-online 298; LG Trier, 12.10.1995, CISG-online 160 = NJW-RR 1996, 564 ff.; LG Landshut, 5.4.1995, CISG-online 193; LG Oldenburg, 15.2.1995, CISG-online 197; OGH, 10.11.1994, CISG-online 117 = ZfRVgl 1995, 79 f.

[31] A. A. *Herber*, 2. Aufl., Art. 6, Rn. 5, der als Ausnahme „lediglich" Art. 12 ansieht; ähnlich *Rudolph*, Art 6, Rn. 8, die Art. 12 als „einzige Vorschrift" bezeichnet, die der Dispositionsfreiheit entzogenen ist; so neuerdings auch *Graves*, Annals Fac. L. Belgrade 2011, 124, 125, Fn. 3; *Schroeter*, VJ (2002), 257, 261; ebenso *Lohmann*, Parteiautonomie, S. 193, aber dann (Fn. 8) hervorhebt, dass es auch andere Vorschriften gibt, die nicht abgedungen werden können.

[32] Auf Art. 12 als Begrenzung der Abdingbarkeit des CISG hinweisend etwa OLG Linz, 23.1.2006, CISG-online 1377.

zwingende Formvorschriften eines Vorbehaltsstaates, auf dessen Recht die Kollisionsnormen des Forumsstaates verweisen,[33] mit Hilfe des Art. 6 CISG abbedungen werden.[34]

Den Parteien ist es auch nicht erlaubt, die **Vorschriften** des Übereinkommens abzubedingen, die sich nicht an die Parteien, sondern **an die Vertragsstaaten richten,**[35] wie etwa die Vorschriften des Teil IV.[36] Gleiches gilt, so zu Recht die herrschende Lehre,[37] für **Art. 28,** wonach ein Gericht eine Entscheidung auf Erfüllung in Natur nur zu fällen hat, wenn es dies auch nach seinem eigenen Recht bei gleichartigen Kaufverträgen täte.[38] **9**

Im Gegensatz zu einigen Autoren, die **Art. 7** für unabdingbar halten,[39] muss man m. E. von dessen **Abdingbarkeit** ausgehen.[40] Hinsichtlich der in **Art. 7 I** geregelten Frage der Auslegung führt die Abbedingung dazu, dass das Übereinkommen im Lichte der im Forumsstaat geltenden Regeln zur Auslegung von Konventionen interpretiert werden muss. Dies führt aber grundsätzlich nicht zu Ergebnissen, die denen widersprechen, zu denen man anhand einer auf der Grundlage des Art. 7 I erfolgten Auslegung gelangen würde, da auch im nationalen Recht, etwa durch Anwendbarkeit der Wiener Vertragsrechtskonvention, durchaus die gleichen Grundsätze gelten.[41] Was **Art. 7 II** angeht, so führt dessen Abbedingung dazu, dass nicht versucht werden muss, „interne Lücken"[42] anhand der dem Übereinkommen zugrunde liegenden allgemeinen Grundsätze zu schließen; vielmehr kann bzw. muss „sofort" auf das über die Kollisionsnormen des Forums zu bestimmende anwendbare Recht abgestellt werden. **10**

Verschiedentlich ist die Auffassung vertreten worden, auch **Art. 4** sei unabdingbar.[43] Dies ist aber nicht nur nicht haltbar,[44] da kein Anhaltspunkt für dessen zwingende Natur vorliegt, sondern auch nicht praktisch,[45] da dies zu keinem anderen Ergebnis führen würde, als dem, das Art. 4 sowieso vorsieht, d. h., Anwendbarkeit des nationalen Rechts auf die nicht geregelten Fragen. „Eine vertragliche Modifikation des Art. 4, die etwa die Gültigkeit der **11**

---

[33] Vgl. hierzu auch Vor Artt. 1–6 Rn. 23.
[34] So auch *Brunner*, Art. 6, Rn. 8; vgl. auch *Staudinger/Magnus*, Art. 6, Rn. 52, der ferner darauf hinweist, dass Art. 12 bei einem gänzlichen Ausschluss unbeachtlich ist; ebenso neuerdings auch *Niemann*, Einheitliche Anwendung, S. 77.
[35] So in der neueren Rechtsprechung Tribunale di Padova, 11.1.2005, CISG-online 967; Tribunale di Vigevano, 12.7.2000, CISG-online 493 = IHR 2001, 72, 74; a. A., ohne jegliche Begründung, *Schroeter*, 6 VJ (2002), 257, 261.
[36] *Czerwenka*, Rechtsanwendungsprobleme, S. 172; *Ferrari*, IHR 2004, 1, 6; *ders.*, Rev. gén. der. 2002, 335, 340; *Ferrari u. a./Saenger*, Internationales Vertragsrecht, Art. 6, Rn. 1; *Kröll u. a./Mistelis*, Art. 6, Rn. 9; *Lindbach*, S. 76; *MünchKomm/Westermann*, Art. 6, Rn. 9; *Schlechtriem/Schwenzer/Schlechtriem*, CISG Commentary, 2. Aufl., Art. 6, Rn. 4; *Schroeter*, 6 VJ (2002), 261, 262, Fn. 14; *Wasmer*, S. 59.
[37] *Achilles*, Art. 6, Rn. 9; *Audit*, Vente internationale, S. 123 f.; *Brunner*, Art. 6, Rn. 8; *Lohmann*, Parteiautonomie, S. 193 Fn. 8; *MünchKomm/Gruber*, Art. 28, Rn. 13; *MünchKommHGB/Benicke*, Art. 6, Rn. 19; *Neumayer/Ming*, Art. 28, Anm. 6.; *Reinhart*, Art. 28, Rn. 3; *Schlechtriem/Schwenzer/Schlechtriem*, CISG Commentary, 2. Aufl., Art. 6, Rn. 3 Fn. 16a; *Schlechtriem/Schwenzer/Hachem*, CISG Commentary, Art. 6, Rn. 9; *Staudinger/Magnus*, Art. 6, Rn. 57; *Torsello*, Remedies, S. 43, 75 ff.; ebenso zum Vorläufer des Art. 28, Art. 16 EKG, *Mertens/Rehbinder*, Art. 16 EKG, Anm. 5.; *Dölle/Reinhart*, Art. 16 EKG, Rn. 21; a. A. zum CISG *Bianca/Bonell/Lando*, Art. 28, Anm. 3.1.; *Kastely*, 63 Wash. L. Rev. (1988), 607, 642 f.
[38] Vgl. auch *Müller-Chen*, Art. 28 Rn. 24; ebenso in der Rechtsprechung Tribunale di Padova, 11.1.2005, CISG-online 967.
[39] So etwa *Bianca/Bonell/Bonell*, Art. 6, Anm. 2.; *Lohmann*, Parteiautonomie, S. 193; *Schlechtriem/Schwenzer/Schlechtriem*, CISG Commentary, 2. Aufl., Art. 6, Rn. 3; *Schmid*, Einheitliche Anwendung, S. 64 f.; *Teichert*, Lückenfüllung, S. 11; *Wasmer*, S. 77 f.; ebenso in der Rechtsprechung etwa Comisión para la Protección del Comercio Exterior de México (Compromex), 30.11.1998, CISG-online 504 = Diario oficial v. 29.1.1999, I, 69 f.
[40] Vgl. *Bamberger/Roth/Saenger*, Art. 6, Rn. 1; *Burkart*, S. 203; *Ferrari*, Rev. gén. dr. 2002, 335, 340; *Herber*, IHR 2003, 1, 9; *Rosch, D.* 2000, Jur. 449, 450; *Staudinger/Magnus*, Art. 6, Rn. 55.
[41] Vgl. statt aller Art. 2 des italienischen Gesetzes zur Reform des IPR vom 31.5.1995.
[42] Vgl. hierzu Art. 7 Rn. 43.
[43] *Bianca/Bonell/Bonell*, Art. 6, Anm. 3.4.; *MünchKomm/Westermann*, Art. 6, Rn. 9.
[44] So auch *Bamberger/Roth/Saenger*, Art. 6, Rn. 1.
[45] So neuerdings auch *Schlechtriem/Schwenzer/Schwenzer/Hachem*, CISG Commentary, Art. 6, Rn. 9.

Konvention auch auf Gültigkeitsfragen erstrecken wollte, scheitert [demnach] daran, dass Bestimmungen hierüber im CISG fehlen."[46]

2. Voraussetzungen der Abwahl beziehungsweise der Änderung des CISG

12 Voraussetzung für den Ausschluss (und die Änderung) ex Art. 6 des Übereinkommens – genauso wie des Haager Kaufrechts[47] – ist eine, auch formlose,[48] **Vereinbarung**[49] (beziehungsweise eine „vertragliche Einigung")[50] der Parteien.[51] Dies ergibt sich unschwer aus dem Wortlaut des Art. 6, der statuiert, dass „die Parteien" das Übereinkommen ausschließen beziehungsweise abändern können.[52]

13 Problematisch erscheint vor allem die Frage, nach welchem Recht sich der Abschluss eines internationalen Warenkaufvertrages bemisst, wenn der Anbietende in seinem **Angebot das Übereinkommen einseitig ausschließt**.[53] Ein Teil der Lehre vertritt die Auffassung, die Frage müsse auf der Grundlage des vom Anbietenden bestimmten Rechts oder, bei Fehlen einer Angabe des anzuwendenden Rechts, auf der Grundlage des objektiv anwendbaren Rechts entschieden werden.[54] Dieser Auffassung ist jedoch nicht zuzustimmen.[55] Ob es sich bei der Erklärung des die Initiative zum Vertragsschluss Ergreifenden überhaupt um ein Angebot handelt, muss genauso anhand der in Teil II des CISG enthaltenen Regeln entschieden werden, wie die Frage, ob die Erklärung der Partei, an die das Angebot gerichtet ist, eine Annahme darstellt.[56] Gibt der Annehmende eine dem Angebot entsprechende Erklärung ab, liegt ohne Zweifel eine **Ausschlussvereinbarung** vor;[57] entspricht die vom Oblaten gemachte Erklärung insoweit nicht dem Angebot, als dieser nicht mit dem Ausschluss einverstanden ist, dann ergibt sich aus Art. 19, dass die Ausschlussvereinbarung nicht zustande gekommen ist.[58] Gleiches gilt auch, wenn nicht der Anbietende, sondern der **Oblat das Übereinkommen ausschließen will:** Da es sich dabei ohne weiteres um eine

---

[46] *Staudinger/Magnus*, Art. 6, Rn. 54.
[47] Siehe hierzu *Czerwenka*, Rechtsanwendungsprobleme, S. 113; *Dölle/Herber*, Art. 3 EKG, Rn. 2; *ders.*, Art. 1 EAG, Rn. 7 ff.; *Mertens/Rehbinder*, Art. 3 EKG, Rn. 7; in der Rechtsprechung, vgl. BGH, 4.12.1985, BGHZ 96, 320, 322; OLG Hamm, 20.6.1983, NJW 1984, 1307; LG Braunschweig, 16.11.1982, RIW 1983, 372.
[48] *Bamberger/Roth/Saenger*, Art. 6, Rn. 2; *Ferrari u. a./Saenger*, Internationales Vertragsrecht, Art. 6, Rn. 2; *Johnson*, 59 Buff. L. Rev. (2011), 213, 259 ff.; *Kröll u. a./Mistelis*, Art. 6, Rn. 10; *Martin-Davidson*, 17 Mich. St. J. Int'l L. (2008), 657, 699; vgl. in der Rechtsprechung HGer Aargau, 10.3.2010, CISG-online 2176; HGer Aargau, 20.9.2007, CISG-online 1742.
[49] Vgl. *Bianca/Bonell/Bonell*, Art. 6, Anm. 4.; *Ferrari*, Vendita internazionale, S. 123; *U. Huber*, RabelsZ 43 (1979), 413, 426; *Lohmann*, Parteiautonomie, S. 197; MünchKomm/*Westermann*, Art. 6, Rn. 3; *Niemann*, Einheitliche Anwendung, S. 77; Schlechtriem/Schwenzer/*Schlechtriem*, CISG Commentary, 2. Aufl., Art. 6, Rn. 6; Schlechtriem/Schwenzer/Schwenzer/*Hachem*, CISG Commentary, Art. 6, Rn. 10; *Wasmer*, S. 28; *Winship*, Scope, S. 1–33.
[50] *Czerwenka*, Rechtsanwendungsprobleme, S. 169; *De Ly*, Opting-Out, S. 25, 35; *Holthausen*, RIW 1989, 513, 513; *Reifner*, IHR 2002, 52, 54.
[51] Einen Überblick über die in der Lehre für den die Abwahl begründenden Akt benutzten Formulierungen gibt *Lindbach*, S. 218 f.
[52] *Lohmann*, Parteiautonomie, S. 197, Fn. 23; *Staudinger/Magnus*, Art. 6, Rn. 10; missverständlich *TeeVee Toons, Inc. et al v. Gerhard Schubert GmbH*, U. S. Dist. Ct. (S. D. N. Y.), 23.8.2006, CISG-online 1272 = 2006 WL 2 463 537 (S. D. N. Y.): „neither party chose, by express provision in the contract at issue, to opt out of the application of the CISG".
[53] Siehe zum Folgenden auch *Ferrari*, Applicabilità ed applicazioni, S. 233 ff.
[54] *Bamberger/Roth/Saenger*, Art. 6, Rn. 2; *Herber*, 2. Aufl., Art. 6, Rn. 23; *Honsell/Siehr*, Art. 6, Rn. 4; *Kröll u. a./Mistelis*, Art. 6, Rn. 10; *Piltz*, Internationales Kaufrecht, Rn. 2–112; *Rehbinder*, Vertragsschluss, S. 151; Schlechtriem/Schwenzer/*Schlechtriem*, CISG Commentary, 2. Aufl., Art. 6, Rn. 7.
[55] So auch *Brunner*, Art. 6, Rn. 5; *Hager*, FS Huber, S. 319, 327; *Karollus*, JuS 1993, 378, 381; *Lohmann*, Privatautonomie, S. 199 ff.; *Niemann*, Einheitliche Anwendung, S. 78 f.; Schlechtriem/Schwenzer/Schwenzer/*Hachem*, CISG Commentary, Art. 6, Rn. 4; *Staudinger/Magnus*, Art. 6, Rn. 11 f.
[56] Ebenso *Czerwenka*, Rechtsanwendungsprobleme, S. 169; *Ferrari u. a./Saenger*, Internationales Vertragsrecht, Art. 6, Rn. 2; *Piltz*, IHR 2004, 133, 136; *Reifner*, IHR 2002, 52, 54; Schlechtriem/Schwenzer/*Schmidt-Kessel*, CISG Commentary, Art. 8, Rn. 1; Schlechtriem/Schwenzer/Schwenzer/*Hachem*, CISG Commentary, Art. 6, Rn. 4.
[57] *Lohmann*, Parteiautonomie, S. 202.
[58] *Lohmann*, Parteiautonomie, S. 202; *Staudinger/Magnus*, Art. 6, Rn. 12.

"wesentliche" Abweichung vom Angebot im Sinne des Art. 19 II handelt, muss die Erklärung des Oblaten als Gegenangebot angesehen werden.[59]

Die Regeln des Teil II des Übereinkommens sind auch auf die Frage anwendbar, ob trotz **widerstreitender Allgemeiner Geschäftsbedingungen** eine Ausschlussvereinbarung zustande gekommen ist,[60] was in der Regel dazu führt, dass von einer Vereinbarung nicht gesprochen werden kann: „Eine Einigung über den Ausschluss des CISG fehlt hier in der Regel, da eine vom Angebot abweichende Rechtswahlklausel als wesentliche Abweichung und damit als neues Angebot anzusehen ist."[61] **14**

III. Die Vorschrift im Einzelnen

1. Ausdrückliche Abbedingung mit oder ohne Wahl des anwendbaren Rechts

Anlässlich der Vorbereitungsarbeiten in UNCITRAL wurde versucht, wie zuvor schon während der Ausarbeitung des EKG,[62] die Möglichkeit der Abbedingung des Einheitskaufrechts davon abhängig zu machen, dass die Vertragsparteien das Recht gewählt haben, das an die Stelle der ausgeschlossenen Regeln tritt.[63] Dieser Vorschlag wurde abgelehnt;[64] demnach kann man heute davon ausgehen,[65] dass eine **ausdrückliche Abwahl**[66] des CISG, die, so zumindest ein Gericht, auch dann vorliegt, wenn die Parteien das „UNCITRAL law" ausschließen,[67] auch dann zulässig ist, wenn die Parteien **keine Rechtswahl** getroffen haben;[68] das **stattdessen anwendbare Recht** muss in einem solchen Fall mittels Rückgriff auf das Kollisionsrecht des Forums ermittelt werden.[69] Verweist dieses auf das Recht eines Vertragsstaates, ist das unvereinheitlichte Recht dieses Staates anzuwenden.[70] **15**

---

[59] So auch *Baumgärtel u. a./Müller*, Art 6, Rn. 3; *Herber*, 2. Aufl., Art. 6, Rn. 23; *Jung*, S. 78.

[60] Ebenso *Hellner*, Standard Form Contracts, S. 339; *Lindbach*, S. 246; *Karollus*, S. 70 f.; *Ostendorf/Neumann/Ventsch*, IHR 2006, 21, 22.

[61] *Staudinger/Magnus*, Art. 6, Rn. 13.

[62] Vgl. *Dölle/Herber*, Art. 3 EKG, Rn. 2.

[63] YB I (1968-170), S. 166, Nr. 50 f.; S. 168, Nr. 68 f.
Für einen ausdrücklichen Ausschluss des CISG mit Rechtswahl vgl. etwa LG Hamburg, 6.9.2011, Aktenzeichen 312 O 316/11, unveröff.; KG St. Gallen, 15.6.2010, CISG-online 2159.

[64] *Herber*, 2. Aufl., Art. 6, Rn. 3.

[65] Anders noch *Rabel*, RabelsZ 9 (1935), 1, 53.

[66] Eine ausdrückliche Abwahl des CISG lag etwa in folgenden Fällen vor: LG Hamburg, 6.9.2011, Aktenzeichen 312 O 316/11, unveröff.; KG St. Gallen, 15.6.2010, CISG-online 2159; Serbian Chamber of Commerce, 17.8.2009, CISG-online 2039; RB Utrecht, 15.4.2009, CISG Pace; Tribunal of International Commercial Arbitration at the Russian Federation Chamber of Commerce and Industry, 5.11.2004, CISG-online 1360.
Für Hinweise auf die den Parteien ohne weiteres gegebene Möglichkeit das CISG auszuschließen, vgl. zuletzt OGH, 2.4.2009, CISG-online 1889; OLG Hamm, 2.4.2009, CISG-online 1978; Tribunale di Forlì, 11.12.2008, CISG-online 1729.

[67] Vgl. *Olivaylle Pty Ltd. v. Flotweg GmbH & Co KGAA*, Federal Court of Australia (Queensland Registry), 20.5.2009, CISG-online 1902.

[68] So auch *Bonell*, RabelsZ 58 (1994), 20, 28; *Ferrari*, Vendita internazionale, S. 122; *Ferrari u. a./Saenger*, Internationales Vertragsrecht, Art. 6, Rn. 3; *Honnold/Flechtner*, Art. 6, Rn. 75; *Karollus*, S. 38; *Kröll u. a./Mistelis*, Art. 6, Rn. 22; *Lohmann*, Parteiautonomie, S. 243; *MünchKomm/Westermann*, Art. 6, Rn. 4; *Sacerdoti*, Riv. trim. dir. proced. civ. 1990, 733, 746; *Schlechtriem*, Internationales UN-Kaufrecht, Rn. 19; *ders.*, Einheitliches UN-Kaufrecht, S. 21; *Schlechtriem/Schwenzer/Schwenzer/Hachem*, CISG Commentary, Art. 6, Rn. 10 a. E.; *Wasmer*, S. 21; a. A. anscheinend *Klotz/Mazzacano/Pribetic*, 46 Can. Bus. L. J. (2008), 430, 435.

[69] Vgl. *Achilles*, Art. 6, Rn. 3; *Bamberger/Roth/Saenger*, Art. 6, Rn. 3; *Bianca/Bonell/Bonell*, Art. 6, Anm. 4.; *Ferrari*, Applicabilità ed applicazioni, S. 233; *Ferrari u. a./Saenger*, Internationales Vertragsrecht, Art. 6, Rn. 3; *Imberg*, 35 San Diego L. Rev. (1998), 769, 776; MünchKommHGB/*Benicke*, Art. 6, Rn. 3; *Rudolph*, Art. 6, Rn. 2; *Schlechtriem/Schwenzer/Schwenzer/Hachem*, CISG Commentary, Art. 6, Rn. 19; *Schlechtriem/Schwenzer/Schlechtriem*, CISG Commentary, 2. Aufl., Art. 6, Rn. 7; *Wasmer*, S. 21; *Witz/Salger/Lorenz/Lorenz*, Art. 6, Rn. 4.

[70] *Borisova*, Art. 6 CISG-UP, S. 43; *Herber*, 2. Aufl., Art. 6, Rn. 9; *Sannini*, L'applicazione, S. 80 f.; *Staudinger/Magnus*, Art. 6, Rn. 17.

Art. 6 16–18   Teil I. Kapitel I. Anwendungsbereich

16 Um die mit der Bestimmung des anwendbaren Rechts auf den üblichen kollisionsrechtlichen Weg zusammenhängenden Probleme zu vermeiden, sollten die Parteien das an die Stelle des ausgeschlossenen Kaufrechts tretende Recht anlässlich der Abbedingung des Übereinkommens wählen.[71] Ob die **positive Rechtswahl** zulässig und wirksam ist, bestimmt sich jedoch nicht nach dem Übereinkommen:[72] die Wirksamkeit bemisst sich – zumindest dort wo die Rom-I VO und das EVÜ (staatsvertraglich oder autonom) gelten – nach dem von den Parteien gewählten Recht,[73] während sich die Zulässigkeit der Rechtswahl aus dem IPR des Gerichtsstaates ergibt.[74] Das Übereinkommen lässt lediglich eine Abbedingung zu, ohne jedoch zu bestimmen, was an deren Stelle vereinbart werden kann.[75]

17 Die Abbedingungsvereinbarung mit der Wahl des stattdessen anwendbaren Rechts muss, wie bereits erwähnt, nicht durch **individuelle Abrede** getroffen werden, sondern kann auch auf **allgemeinen Geschäftsbedingungen** gründen,[76] sofern diese wirksam Vertragsbestandteil geworden sind.[77] „Allerdings liegt es insoweit besonders nahe, eine entsprechende Abwahl als überraschende Klausel im Sinne von § 305c BGB zu sehen, insbesondere, wenn die Parteien zuvor schon auf der Grundlage des CISG Verträge geschlossen und abgewickelt haben."[78]

2. Stillschweigender Ausschluss des CISG

18 **a) Grundsatz.** Obwohl die Konventionsgeber darauf verzichtet haben, den im EKG enthaltenen ausdrücklichen Hinweis auf die Möglichkeit eines stillschweigenden Ausschlusses zu übernehmen,[79] darf dies nicht zur Annahme führen, diese Möglichkeit sei den Vertragsparteien nach dem Übereinkommen nicht gegeben.[80] Die **Parteien können**

---

[71] Eine ähnliche Empfehlung findet sich auch bei *Lohmann*, Privatautonomie, S. 244; *Rudolph*, Art. 6, Rn. 2; *Staudinger/Magnus*, Art. 6, Rn. 16; vgl. in der Rechtsprechung BGH, 23.7.1997, CISG-online 276: positive Rechtswahl unter Ausschluss des CISG.

[72] *Herber*, 2. Aufl., Art. 6, Rn. 11; *Wasmer*, S. 49.

[73] Ebenso *Boele-Woelki*, FS Schwenzer, S. 191, 195; *Ferrari*, Applicabilità ed applicazioni, S. 213; *Kröll u. a./Mistelis*, Art. 6, Rn. 22, Fn. 42; *Sacerdoti*, Riv. trim. dir. proced. civ. 1990, 733, 746; *Sannini*, L'applicazione, S. 80; vgl. in der Rechtsprechung Serbian Chamber of Commerce, 17.8.2009, CISG-online 2039.

[74] Vgl. statt aller *Lohmann*, Parteiautonomie, S, 244; MünchKommHGB/*Benicke*, Art. 6, Rn. 4; *Schlechtriem/Schwenzer/Schwenzer/Hachem*, CISG Commentary, Art. 6, Rn. 4; unklar MünchKomm/*Westermann*, Art. 6, Rn. 4, der die Wirksamkeit der Rechtswahlvereinbarung mit der Zulässigkeit gleichzusetzen scheint.

[75] So ausdrücklich *Herber*, 2. Aufl., Art. 6, Rn. 11; vgl. auch *Czerwenka*, Rechtsanwendungsprobleme, S. 173 f.

[76] Vgl. OLG Oldenburg, 20.12.2007, CISG-online 1644; OGH, 4.7.2007, CISG-online 1560; KG Jura, 3.11.2004, CISG-online 965; BGH, 9.1.2002, CISG-online 651 = IHR 2002, 16, 17–18; BGH, 4.12.1996, CISG-online 260 = NJW-RR 1997, 690.

[77] Vgl. auch *Ferrari u. a./Saenger*, Internationales Vertragsrecht, Art. 6, Rn. 3; *U. Huber*, RabelsZ 43 (1979), 413, 427; *Lohmann*, Privatautonomie, S. 208 ff.; *Piltz*, IHR 2002, 2, 6; *Schlechtriem/Schwenzer/Schwenzer/Hachem*, CISG Commentary, Art. 6, Rn. 10; *Staudinger/Magnus*, Art. 6, Rn. 18; ebenso die Rechtsprechung zum EKG: OLG Bamberg, 23.2.1979, RIW 1979, 566.

[78] *Schlechtriem*, Internationales UN-Kaufrecht, Rn. 21; *Witz/Salger/Lorenz/Lorenz*, Art. 6, Rn. 3; vgl. in der Rechtsprechung OLG Düsseldorf, NJW-RR 1994, 1232, wonach die Klausel „Diese Vereinbarung unterliegt unter Ausschluss der internationalen Kaufgesetze englischem Recht" überraschend im Sinne von § 3 AGB-Gesetz ist; a. A. *Lindbach*, S. 249, der die Ansicht vertritt, § 3 AGBG sei nicht neben dem CISG anwendbar, da der Überraschungseffekt, der durch die Vorschrift verhindert werden solle, die äußere Konsensfindung betreffe, die jedoch dem Regelungsbereich des Übereinkommens vorbehalten sei.

[79] Zur Entstehungsgeschichte dieser Vorschrift, vgl. oben Rn. 1; vgl. auch *Imberg*, 35 San Diego L. Rev. (1998), 769, 776.

[80] So aber in der Tat *Dore*, 77 Am. J. Int'l L. (1983), 521, 532; *Dore/DeFranco*, 23 Harv. Int'l L. J. (1982), 49, 53 f.; *Dutton*, 7 (EJLR), 2005, 239, 246; *Ostendorf/Neumann/Ventsch*, IHR 2006, 21, 22; in der Rechtsprechung haben die Möglichkeit einer stillschweigenden Abbedingung ausgeschlossen: *Cedar Petrochemicals, Inc. v. Dongbu Hannong*, U. S. Dist. Ct. (S. D. N. Y.), 28.9.2011, 2011 WL 4494602 (S. D. N. Y.); *Forestal Guarani, S. A. v. Daros International, Inc.*, U. S. Dist. Ct. (D. N. J.), 7.10.2008, CISG-online 1779; *Easom Automation Systems, Inc. v. Thyssenkrupp Fabco, Corp.*, U. S. Dist. Ct. (E. D. Mich.), 28.9.2007, CISG-online 1601; *Cedar Petrochemicals, Inc. v. Dongbu Hannong Chemical Co., Ltd.*, U. S. Dist. Ct. (S. D. N. Y.), 19.7.2007, CISG-online 1509 = 2007 WL 2 059 239 (S. D. N. Y.); *Property Casualty Company of America et al. v. Saint-Gobain Technical Fabrics Canada Limited*, U. S. Dist. Ct. (Minn.), 31.1.2007, CISG-online 1435 = 2007 WL 313 591 (D. Minn.); *TeeVee Toons*,

– so zu Recht sowohl die herrschende Lehre[81] als auch die Rechtsprechung[82] – das Übereinkommen durchaus auch **stillschweigend ausschließen;** die Streichung des Hinweises hatte lediglich den Zweck, einen Ausschluss nur bei hinreichend deutlichem Parteiwillen zuzulassen.[83] Dies ist verständlich, wenn man bedenkt, in welchem Umfang

---

Inc. et al. v. Gerhard Schubert GmbH, U. S. Dist. Ct. (S. D. N. Y.), 23.8.2006, CISG-online 1272 = 2006 WL 2 463 537 (S. D. N. Y.); *American Mint LLC v. GOSoftware, Inc.,* U. S. Dist. Ct. (M. D. Pa.), 16.8.2005, CISG-online 1104 = 2005 WL 2021248; *Valero Marketing & Supply Company v. Greeni Oy & Greeni Trading Oy,* U. S. Dist. Ct. (D. N. J.), 15.6.2005, CISG-online 1028; KG Zug, 11.12.2003, CISG-online 958; RB Zwolle, 21.5.2003, IHR 2005, 34, 35; *Ajax Tool Works, Inc. v. Can-Eng Manufacturing Ltd.,* U. S. Dist. Ct. (N. D. Ill.), 29.1.2003, CISG-online 772, 2003 U. S. Dist. LEXIS 1306; *St. Paul Insurance Company et al. v. Neuromed Medical Systems & Support et al.,* U. S. Dist. Ct. (S. D. N. Y.), 26.3.2002, CISG-online 615 = 2002 U. S. Dist. LEXIS 5096; RB Hasselt, 4.10.1999, CISG-online 763; *Helen Kaminski PTY, Ltd. v. Marketing Australian Products, Inc.,* U. S. Dist. Ct. (S. D. N. Y.), 23.7.1997, CISG-online 297 = 1997 WL 414 137; *Delchi Carrier, SpA v. Rotorex Corp.,* U. S. Ct. App. (2nd Cir.), 6.12.1995, CISG-online 140 = 71 F. 3rd. 1024, 1027-28; LG Landshut, 5.4.1995, CISG-online 193; *Orbisphere Corp. v. United States,* Ct. Int'l Trade, 24.10.1989, CISG-online 7 = 726 F. Supp. 1344; vgl. jedoch *Ho Myung Moolsan, Co. Ltd. v. Manitou Mineral Water, Inc.,* U. S. Dist. Ct. (S. D. N. Y.), 2.12.2010, CISG-online 2170: der Umstand, dass die Parteien auf der blossen Grundlage des Uniform Commercial Code verhandelt haben, sei als Ausschluss des CISG zu bewerten, der aber nicht ein ausdrücklicher Ausschluss ist.
[81] In diesem Sinne auch *Achilles,* Art. 6, Rn. 2; *Audit,* Vente internationale, S. 38; *Bamberger/Roth/Saenger,* Art. 6, Rn. 2; *K. Bell,* 8 Pace Int'l L. J. (1996), 237, 255; *Borisova,* Art. 6 CISG-UP, S. 41; *Brunner,* Art. 6, Rn. 1; *Cappuccio,* Dir. com. int. 1994, 867, 868 f.; *Carbone/Luzzatto,* Art. 6, Rn. 2; *Chiomenti,* EuLF 2005, 141, 143; *Czerwenka,* Rechtsanwendungsprobleme, S. 170; *Date-Bah,* 11 Rev. Ghana L. (1979), 50, 54; *Diéz-Picazo/ Calvo Caravaca,* Art. 6, S. 94; *Ferrari,* ZEuP 2002, 737, 741 f.; *ders.,* 10 Preadviezen (1995), 81, 145; *Ferrari u. a./Saenger,* Internationales Vertragsrecht, Art. 6, Rn. 2; *Garro/Zuppi,* Compraventa internacional, S. 98; *Graffi,* EuLF 2000/2001, 240, 241; *Hager,* FS Huber, S. 319, 325; *Hoffmann,* Koordination, S. 272; *Holthausen,* RIW 1989, 513, 515; *Honsell/Siehr,* Art. 6, Rn. 6; *P. Huber/Kröll,* IPRax 2003, 309, 310; *Muir Watt,* Rev. crit. dr. int. priv. 2002, 94, 98; *Imberg,* 35 San Diego L. Rev. (1998), 769, 776; *Karollus,* S. 38; *Kennedy,* 16 Dick. J. Int'l L. (1998), 319, 321 f.; *Klotz/Mazzacano/Pribetic,* 46 Can. Bus. L. J. (2008), 430, 436 f.; *Kröll u. a./Mistelis,* Art. 6, Rn. 15; *Lacasse,* Le champ d'application, S. 37; *Liguori,* Foro it. 1996, IV, 145, 158; *ders.,* Riv. dir. civ. 1999, 143, 154; *Lindbach,* S. 253; *Lohmann,* Parteiautonomie, S. 248 ff.; *T. M. Müller,* Beweislast, S. 45; MünchKomm/*Westermann,* Art. 6, Rn. 5; MünchKommHGB/*Benicke,* Art. 6, Rn. 10; *Nicholas,* 105 L. Q. R. (1989), 201, 208; *Niemann,* Einheitliche Anwendung, S. 79; *Pavic/Djordjevic,* 28 J. L. & Com. (2009), 1, 9; *Piltz,* IHR 2007, 35; *Reifner,* IHR 2002, 52, 55; *Richards,* 69 Iowa L. Rev. (1983), 209, 237; *Sannini,* L'applicazione, S. 83; *Schlechtriem,* Internationales UN-Kaufrecht, Rn. 19; *ders.,* Einheitliches UN-Kaufrecht, S. 21; *Schlechtriem/Schwenzer/Schlechtriem,* CISG Commentary, 2. Aufl., Art. 6, Rn. 8; *Schlechtriem/Schwenzer/ Schwenzer/Hachem,* CISG Commentary, Art. 6, Rn. 3; *Schwenzer/Hachem/Kee,* Rn. 4.33; *Soergel/Lüderitz/ Fenge,* Art. 6, Rn. 1; *Thiele,* IHR 2002, 8, 9; *Veneziano,* Dir. comm. int. 2001, 509, 514; *Wasmer,* S. 28 ff.; *C. Witz,* L'interprétation, S. 279, 286; *ders.,* D. 1990, Chron. 107, 108; *ders.,* D. 1995, Chron. 143, 144; *ders.,* D. 2001, Jur. 3608, 3608; *Witz/Salger/Lorenz/Lorenz,* Art. 6, Rn. 2; a. A. neuerdings jedoch *Ostendorf/ Neumann/Ventsch,* IHR 2006, 21, 22: „UN-Kaufrecht kann gem. Art. 6 CISG grundsätzlich durch vertragliche Vereinbarung zwischen den Parteien ausgeschlossen werden. Ein solcher Ausschluss muss allerdings ausdrücklich erfolgen".
[82] Vgl. statt aller HGer Aargau, 10.3.2010, CISG-online 2176; OGH, 2.4.2009, CISG-online 1889; OLG Hamm, 2.4.2009, CISG-online 1978; OGer Aargau, 3.3.2009, CISG-online 2013; Tribunale di Forlì, 16.2.2009, CISG-online 1780; Serbian Chamber of Commerce, 28.1.2009, CISG Pace; Court of First Instance of Athens, Aktenzeichen 4505/2009 (ohne Datum), CISG-online 2228; Tribunale di Forlì, 11.12.2008, CISG-online 1729; OGer Bern, 19.5.2008, CISG-online 1738; OGH, 4.7.2007, CISG-online 1560; LG Bamberg, 23.10.2006, CISG-online 1400; OLG Linz, 23.1.2006, CISG-online 1377; Civ. 1, 25.10.2005, CISG-online 1226 = Rev. crit. dr. int. privé 2006, 373, 374; OLG Linz, 8.8.2005, CISG-online 1087; RB Tongeren, 25.1.2005, CISG-online 1106; KG Jura, 3.11.2004, CISG-online 965; Tribunale di Padova, 25.2.2004, CISG-online 819; OGH, 17.12.2003, CISG-online 828; ICC, 11 849/2003, CISG-online 1421; HGer St. Gallen, 3.12.2002, CISG-online 727; ICC, 11 333/2002, CISG-online 1420; OGH, 22.10.2001, CISG-online 614 = IHR 2002, 24, 26; Civ. 1, 26.6.2001, CISG-online 598 = D. 2001, Jur. 3607, 3607; Tribunale di Vigevano, 12.7.2000, CISG-online 493 = IHR 2001, 72, 73–74; OLG Dresden, 27.12.1999, CISG-online 511 = TranspR-IHR 2000, 20; OLG München, 9.7.1997, CISG-online 282; LG München I, 29.5.1995, CISG-online 235; OLG Celle, 24.5.1995, CISG-online 152.
[83] So ausdrücklich *Staudinger/Magnus,* Art. 6, Rn. 20; ebenso *Bianca/Bonell/Bonell,* Art. 6, Anm. 1.3.; *Enderlein/Maskow/Strohbach,* Art. 6, Anm. 1.2.; *Ferrari,* Applicabilità ed applicazioni, S. 210; *Lohmann,* Privatautonomie, S. 248; MünchKomm/*Westermann,* Art. 6, Rn. 5; *Niemann,* Einheitliche Anwendung, S. 79; *Piltz,* Rn. 2–114; *Reifner,* IHR 2002, 52, 55; *Schlechtriem,* Internationales UN-Kaufrecht, Rn. 19; *Schlechtriem/Schwenzer/Schwenzer/Hachem,* CISG Commentary, Art. 6, Rn. 3; Sekretariatskommentar, Art. 5, Nr. 2.

schon unter der Geltung des EKG versucht wurde, den Ausschluss des Einheitsrechts auf Grund hypothetischen Parteiwillens – also einer Interessensabwägung auf objektiver Grundlage – ohne Rücksicht auf einen realen Parteiwillen anzunehmen.[84] Ein hypothetischer Parteiwille genügt – so auch die neuere Rechtsprechung[85] – also nach dem CISG[86] ebenso wenig wie nach dem Haager Kaufrecht.[87] Es muss ein **„klar"**[88] **und unmissverständlich**[89] **bzw. unzweideutig**[90] – wenn auch implizit – **ausgedrückter wirklicher Wille** der Parteien hinsichtlich des Ausschlusses des CISG vorliegen.[91] Wann dieser vorliegt,[92] bemisst sich, wie schon hinsichtlich des Haager Kaufrechts,[93] nicht nach nationalem, über die Kollisionsnormen des Forumsstaates berufenem Recht,[94] sondern nach dem Übereinkommen.[95] Dies führt dazu, dass für die Auslegung der Erklärungen der Parteien (genauso wie für die Auslegung des Verhaltens derselben) die in Art. 8 festgelegten Maßstäbe zu beachten sind.[96]

---

[84] Vgl. die Nachweise bei *Dölle/Herber*, Art. 3 EKG, Rn. 11, sowie OLG Hamm, 3.10.1979, RIW 1980, 662, 663, das die Verdrängung des Einheitskaufrechts auf Grund eines hypothetischen Parteiwillens dann für gerechtfertigt hält, wenn die „Anwendung des EKG für eine Partei zu völlig unerträglichen Ergebnissen" führt; ebenso *v. d. Seipen*, IPRax 1984, 244, 245.

[85] Vgl. zum CISG KG Berlin, 24.1.1994, CISG-online 130 = RIW 1994, 683: „Zum Ausschluss der Anwendung des Einheitlichen UN-Kaufrechts ist es notwendig, dass das im wirklichen Willen der Parteien und nicht in deren hypothetischen Parteiwillen zum Ausdruck kommt." Siehe auch OLG Linz, 23.1.2006, CISG-online 1377: „es [kommt] auf den wirklichen und nicht auf den hypothetischen Parteiwillen an"; ebenso KG Jura, 3.11.2004, CISG-online 965.

[86] Vgl. *Diéz-Picazo/Calvo Caravaca*, Art. 6, S. 96; *Enderlein/Maskow/Stargardt*, Art. 6, Anm. 1.2.; *Ferrari u. a./Saenger*, Internationales Vertragsrecht, Art. 6, Rn. 4; *Herber/Czerwenka*, Art. 6, Rn. 10; *Magnus*, RabelsZ 51 (1987), 116, 127; *Reinhart*, Art. 6, Rn. 5; *Soergel/Lüderitz/Fenge*, Art. 6, Rn. 4; *Wasmer*, S. 34; *Witz/Salger/Lorenz/Lorenz*, Art. 6, Rn. 7.

[87] Siehe zum EKG in der Rechtsprechung: BGHZ 96, 313, 319, mit zust. Anm. *Herber*, EWiR 1986, 155, 156; ebenso *Piltz*, NJW 1986, 1405, und *Czerwenka*, RIW 1986, 293, 295; OLG Hamburg, RIW 1980, 263 mit zust. Anm. *Kronke*; OLG Karlsruhe, RIW 1978, 544; vgl. in der Lehre *Dölle/Herber*, Art. 3 EKG, Rn. 6; *Hausmann*, WM 1980, 726, 727; *Mertens/Rehbinder*, Art. 3 EKG, Rn. 8; *Reinhart*, IPRax 1985, 1, 3.

[88] *Hanwha Corporation v. Cedar Petrochemicals, Inc.*, U. S. Dist. Ct. (S. D. N. Y.), 18.1.2011, CISG-online 2178; Cour Cass., 3.11.2009, CISG-online 2004; OLG Linz, 23.1.2006, CISG-online 1377; KG Jura, 3.11.2004, CISG-online 965; *BP International, Ltd. and BP Exploration & Oil, Inc., v. Empresa Estatal Petroleos de Ecuador, et al.*, U. S. Ct. App. (5th Circuit), 11.6.2003, CISG-online 730; Tribunal de Commerce Namur, 15.1.2002, CISG-online 759; *Asante Technologies v. PMC-Sierra*, U. S. Dist. Ct. (N. D. Cal.), 27.7.2001, CISG-online 616.

[89] So ausdrücklich *Hanwha Corporation v. Cedar Petrochemicals, Inc.*, U. S. Dist. Ct. (S. D. N. Y.), 18.1.2011, CISG-online 2178.

[90] Vgl. OGH, 4.7.2007, CISG-online 1560: „Das UN-K [kann] auch stillschweigend ausgeschlossen sein, wenn die diesbezügliche Absicht unzweideutig zum Ausdruck kommt"; ebenso OLG Linz, 23.1.2006, CISG-online 1377.

[91] Ebenso *Bamberger/Roth/Saenger*, Art. 6, Rn. 4; *Brunner*, Art. 6, Rn. 1; *Muir Watt*, Rev. crit. dr. int. priv. 2002, 94, 102; *Imberg*, 35 San Diego L. Rev. (1998), 769, 777; *Lindbach*, S. 256; *Lohmann*, Parteiautonomie, S. 249; *MünchKomm/Westermann*, Art. 6, Rn. 3; *Piltz*, IHR 2007, 35; *Reifner*, IHR 2002, 52, 55; vgl. auch Tribunal Namur, 15.1.2002, CISG-online 759 (der Umstand, dass der Vertrag in deutscher Sprache gehalten ist, reicht für die Annahme eines stillschweigenden Ausschlusses nicht aus); krit. gegenüber der Verwendung des Ausdrucks „wirklicher Wille" *Dokter*, RabelsZ 68 (2004), 430, 434. Falsch daher *Golden Valley Grape Juice and Wine, LLC v. Centrisys Corporation et al.*, U. S. Dist. Ct. (E. D. Cal.), 21.1.2010, CISG Pace, wonach das CISG zur Anwendung komme, „unless the subject contract contains a choice-of-law provision"; krit. dieser Entscheidung gegenüber auch *Johnson*, 59 Buff. L. Rev. (2011), 213, 215.

[92] Zum Zwecke des Ausschlusses des CISG kann es daher nicht ausreichen, dass eine Partei sich gegen die Anwendung des CISG ausspricht; so jedoch Shanghai Higher People's Court, 17.5.2007, CISG-online 1976.

[93] Vgl. in der Rechtsprechung BGH, 28.3.1979, BGHZ 74, 193, 197; BGHZ 96, 313, 319; in der Lehre, vgl. *Czerwenka*, RIW 1986, 293, 295.

[94] So aber *Schlechtriem/Schwenzer/Schlechtriem*, CISG Commentary, 2. Aufl., Art. 6, Rn. 8.

[95] So auch *Bianca/Bonell/Bonell*, Art. 6, Anm. 2.3.1.; *Lohmann*, Privatautonomie, S. 250; *Staudinger/Magnus*, Art. 6, Rn. 20; *Winship*, Scope, S. 1–35; ebenso in der Rechtsprechung OLG Linz, 23.1.2006, CISG-online 1377.

[96] Vgl. *Lohmann*, Parteiautonomie, S. 250 f.; MünchKommHGB/*Benicke*, Art. 6, Rn. 10 a. E.; *C. Witz*, L'interprétation, S. 279, 290.

b) Einzelfälle. Das Vorliegen des Parteiwillens bezüglich des Ausschlusses des Übereinkommens muss von Fall zu Fall untersucht werden.[97] Dennoch ist es möglich, eine Reihe von Fallgruppen herauszubilden, bei denen eine stillschweigende Abbedingung des Übereinkommens nahe liegt.[98]

Ein typischer Fall[99] des stillschweigenden Ausschlusses des CISG wird sowohl von der Lehre[100] als auch von der Rechtsprechung[101] darin gesehen, dass die Parteien das **Recht eines Nichtvertragsstaates wählen**,[102] sofern die Parteien dieses Recht nicht lediglich als ergänzende Rechtsordnung gewählt haben.[103] Die Wahl einer bestimmten Rechtsordnung ist natürlich nur dann zu beachten, wenn die Kollisionsnormen des Forumstaates den dementsprechenden Parteiwillen für relevant erklären,[104] und wenn die Rechtswahl den Anforderungen des Rechts entspricht, das nach den Regeln des IPR des angerufenen Gerichts berufen ist, nach deutschem IPR[105] des Rechts, dessen Anwendung vereinbart worden ist.[106] Ist danach die Rechtswahl unwirksam, so darf nicht davon ausgegangen werden, dass das Übereinkommen nicht anwendbar sei,[107] denn es kann – mangels näherer Anhaltspunkte – nicht ohne weiteres davon ausgegangen werden, dass die Parteien den Ausschluss des Übereinkommens ungeachtet der Wirksamkeit der Rechtswahlvereinbarung gewollt haben,[108] sich also bei Nichtigkeit ihrer Rechtswahl dem nationalen Recht ausliefern wollten, das nach den Regeln des IPR kraft objektiver Anknüpfung berufen ist.[109]

Problematischer ist, ob die **Wahl des Rechts eines Vertragsstaates** zum Ausschluss des Übereinkommens führt.[110] Dies hängt davon ab, ob die Parteien auf das unvereinheitlichte Recht des Staates abgestellt haben oder nicht.[111] Eine Bezugnahme auf das **unvereinheit-**

---

[97] *Lohmann*, Parteiautonomie, S. 255; *Wasmer*, S. 29; ebenso in der Rechtsprechung OLG Linz, 23, 1, 2006, CISG-online 1377; KG Jura, 3.11.2004, CISG-online 965.

[98] So auch OLG Linz, 23.1.2006, CISG-online 1377.

[99] So auch *Ferrari*, Applicabilità ed applicazioni, S. 213; ähnlich *Cappuccio*, Dir. com. int. 1994, 867, 868; a. A. *Schlechtriem/Schwenzer/Schlechtriem*, CISG Commentary, 2. Aufl., Art. 6, Rn. 5 Fn. 17 a: „This is not a ‚typical case of implicit derogation' […], but a most explicit derogation".

[100] Ebenso *Achilles*, Art. 6, Rn. 3; *Audit*, Vente internationale, S. 39; *Bamberger/Roth/Saenger*, Art. 6, Rn. 4; *Bianca/Bonell/Bonell*, Art. 6, Anm. 2.3.2.; *Carbone*, Riv. dir. int. priv. proc. 1980, 513, 527; *Carbone/Luzzatto*, S. 132; *Chiomenti*, EuLF 2005, 141, 144; *Enderlein/Maskow/Strohbach*, Art. 6, Anm. 1.3.; *Ferrari*, ZEuP 2002, 737, 743; *ders.*, Vendita internazionale, S. 116; *Ferrari u. a./Saenger*, Internationales Vertragsrecht, Art. 6, Rn. 4; *Garro/Zuppi*, Compraventa internacional, S. 95; *Hoffmann*, Koordination, S. 273; *Holthausen*, RIW 1989, 513, 515; *Honsell/Siehr*, Art. 6, Rn. 6; *Lando*, RabelsZ 51 (1987), 60, 84; *Liguori*, Foro it. 1996, IV, 145, 158; *T. M. Müller*, Beweislast, S. 46; *MünchKommHGB/Benicke*, Art. 6, Rn. 7; *Piltz*, Internationales Kaufrecht, Rn. 2–114; *Reifner*, IHR 2002, 52, 55; *Reithmann/Martiny/Martiny*, Rn. 645; *Sacerdoti*, Riv. trim. dir. proced. civ. 1990, 733, 746; *Sannini*, L'applicazione, S. 83; *Schlechtriem/Schwenzer/Schwenzer/Hachem*, CISG Commentary, Art. 6, Rn. 12; *Schwenzer/Hachem/Kee*, Rn. 4.39; *Thiele*, IHR 2002, 8, 9; *Wasmer*, S. 29; *Winship*, Scope, S. 1–35.

[101] Vgl. OLG Düsseldorf, 2.7.1993, CISG-online 74 = RIW 1993, 845; *Ajax Tool Works, Inc. v. Can-Eng Manufacturing Ltd.*, U. S. Dist. Ct. (N. D. Ill.), 29.1.2003, CISG-online 772, 2003 U. S. Dist. LEXIS 1306; KG Jura, 3.11.2004, CISG-online 965; Tribunale di Padova, 11.1.2005, CISG-online 967; OLG Linz, 23.1.2006, CISG-online 1377.

[102] *Borisova*, Art. 6 CISG-UP, S. 42; *Kröll u. a./Mistelis*, Art. 6, Rn. 12 und 17; *Lohmann*, Parteiautonomie, S. 256; *MünchKomm/Westermann*, Art. 6, Rn. 5; *Niemann*, Einheitliche Anwendung, S. 80; *Pavic/Djordjevic*, 28 J. L. & Com. (2009), 1, 9; *Schlechtriem/Schwenzer/Schlechtriem*, CISG Commentary, 2. Aufl., Art. 6, Rn. 5.

[103] *Lindbach*, S. 306; *Schlechtriem/Schwenzer/Schwenzer/Hachem*, CISG Commentary, Art. 6, Rn. 12; *Staudinger/Magnus*, Art. 6, Rn. 23; *Witz/Salger/Lorenz/Lorenz*, Art. 6, Rn. 8.

[104] So auch *Schlechtriem*, Internationales UN-Kaufrecht, Rn. 21; *Schlechtriem/Schwenzer/Schlechtriem*, CISG Commentary, 2. Aufl., Art. 6, Rn. 3 und 7.

[105] Vgl. diesbezüglich Art. 3 V Rom-I VO; Art. 27 IV EGBGB a. F.; Art. 3 IV EVÜ; vgl. hierzu auch *Ferrari*, Applicabilità ed applicazioni, S. 213.

[106] *Herber*, 2. Aufl., Art. 6, Rn. 14; unklar MünchKomm/*Westermann*, Art. 6, Rn. 5.

[107] So aber *Bianca/Bonell/Bonell*, Art. 6, Anm. 3.3.2.

[108] MünchKommHGB/*Benicke*, Art. 6, Rn. 9.

[109] Anders verhält es sich m. E. im Falle eines ausdrücklichen Ausschlusses des Übereinkommens mit Rechtswahl: In diesem Fall führt eine unwirksame Rechtswahl nicht per se zur Unwirksamkeit des Ausschlusses; Rechtswahl und Ausschluss sind in diesem Fall voneinander zu trennen; vgl. auch *Ferrari*, Applicabilità ed applicazoni, S. 213.

[110] Ebenso *Borisova*, Art. 6 CISG-UP, S. 42, jedoch ohne jegliche Stellungnahme.

[111] Vgl. auch *Lohmann*, Parteiautonomie, S. 257.

lichte Recht („Der Vertrag unterliegt dem Kaufrecht des BGB") kann durchaus als Ausschluss bewertet werden,[112] was nunmehr auch von der Rechtsprechung bestätigt worden ist.[113] Gleiches galt in Bezug auf das Haager Kaufrecht.[114]

22 Die **Wahl** des Rechts eines Vertragsstaates **ohne Verweisung auf das unvereinheitlichte Recht** ist, so die herrschende Lehre[115] sowie die (staatliche[116]

---

[112] *Bamberger/Roth/Saenger*, Art. 6, Rn. 4; *Bianca/Bonell/Bonell*, Art. 6, S. 18; *Brunner*, Art. 6, Rn. 3; *Capuccio*, Dir. com. int. 1994, 861, 867, 873; *Chiomenti*, EuLF 2005, 141, 144; *Ferrari*, Vendita internazionale, S. 117; *Ferrari u. a./Saenger*, Internationales Vertragsrecht, Art. 6, Rn. 4; *Kröll u. a./Mistelis*, Art. 6, Rn. 12; *Lohmann*, Parteiautonomie, S. 257; MünchKommHGB/*Benicke*, Art. 6, Rn. 5; *Niemann*, Einheitliche Anwendung, S. 81; *Reifner*, IHR 2002, 52, 56; *Sannini*, L'applicazione, S. 85; *Soergel/Lüderitz/Fenge*, Art. 6, Rn. 3; *Staudinger/Magnus*, Art. 6, Rn. 30; *Wasmer*, S. 31; *C. Witz*, L'interprétation, S. 279, 294 f.; *Witz/Salger/Lorenz/Lorenz*, Art. 6, Rn. 11.

[113] *Doolim Corp. v. R Doll, LLC.*, U.S. Dist. Ct. (S.D.N.Y.), 29.5.2009, CISG-online 1892; OGH, 2.4.2009, CISG-online 1889; OGer Aargau, 3.3.2009, CISG-online 2013; OLG Stuttgart, 31.3.2008, CISG-online 1658; OGH, 4.7.2007, CISG-online 1560; OLG Linz, 23.1.2006, CISG-online 1377; Tribunale di Padova, 11.1.2005, CISG-online 967; OLG Rostock, 10.10.2001, CISG-online 671 = IHR 2003, 17, 18; *Asante Technologies v. PMC-Sierra*, U.S. Dist. Ct. (N.D.Cal.), 27.7.2001, CISG-online 616 = 2001 U.S. Dist. LEXIS 16 000; OLG Frankfurt a.M., 30.8.2000, CISG-online 594 = RIW 2001, 383 f.; vgl. auch OLG Celle, 24.5.1995, CISG-online 152.

[114] Vgl. BGH, 4.12.1985, BGHZ 96, 323; BGH, 26.10.1983, RIW 1984, 151; BGH, 26.11.1980, NJW 1981, 2641, BGH NJW 1981, 1157; a. A. OLG Koblenz, 9.1.1981, IPRax 1982, 20 f.

[115] *Achilles*, Art. 6, Rn. 4; *G. Bell*, 9 Singapore YB. Int'l L. (2005), 55, 56 und 68; *K. Bell*, 8 Pace Int'l Rev. (1996), 237, 255; *Boggiano*, 13 Rev. der. com. oblig. (1980), 355, 357; *Brunner*, Art. 6, Rn. 1; *Chiomenti*, EuLF 2005, 141, 144; *Cuniberti*, 39 Vand. J. Transnat'l L. (2006), 1511, 1536; *Enderlein/Maskow/Strohbach*, Art. 6, Anm. 1.3.; *Esslinger*, ALI-ABA (1999), 69, 79; *Herber*, Möglichkeiten der Vertragsgestaltung, S. 221; *ders.*, Anwendungsvoraussetzungen, S. 104; *Herber/Czerwenka*, Art. 6, Rn. 15; *Hoffmann*, Koordination, S. 273 f.; *Honsell/Siehr*, Art. 6, Rn. 7; *Johnson*, 59 Buff. L. Rev. (2011), 213, 285; *Kröll u. a./Mistelis*, Art. 6, Rn. 18; *Lurger*, IHR 2005, 177, 178; MünchKommHGB/*Benicke*, Art. 6, Rn. 6; *Muir Watt*, Rev. crit. dr. int. priv. 2002, 94, 97; *Imberg*, 35 San Diego L. Rev. (1998), 769, 777; *Kritzer*, Guide to Practical Applications, S. 100 f.; *Lando*, RabelsZ 51 (1987), 60, 84; *Lindbach*, S. 308; *Lohmann*, Privatautonomie, S. 261; *Magnus*, ZEuP 1997, 823, 827; *Maultzsch*, FS Schwenzer, S. 1213, 1214, Fn. 4; *Mazzacano*, Rev. CISG (2005/2006), 85, 124 f.; *J. Meyer*, RabelsZ 69 (2005), 457, 471 f.; *Niemann*, Einheitliche Anwendung, S. 74; *Papandréou-Deterville*, D. 2002, Jur. 398, 399; *Piltz*, Rn. 2–116; *ders.*, IHR 2002, 2, 6; *ders.*, NJW 2000, 553, 555; *Plantard*, J.D.I. 1988, 311, 321; *Posch/Terlitza*, IHR 2001, 47; *Reifner*, IHR 2002, 52, 55; *Rémery*, Rev. crit. dr. int. privé 1997, 73, 74; *Sannini*, L'applicazione, S. 84 f.; *Schillo*, IHR 2003, 257, 258, Fn. 8; *Schlechtriem*, Internationales UN-Kaufrecht, Rn. 15 und 20; *Schlechtriem/Schwenzer/Schlechtriem*, CISG Commentary, 2. Aufl., Art. 6, Rn. 5; *Schwenzer*, NJW 1990, 602, 603; *Schlechtriem/Schwenzer/Schwenzer/Hachem*, CISG Commentary, Art. 6, Rn. 14; *Schwenzer/Hachem/Kee*, Rn. 3.28 und 4.33; *Schwimann/Posch*, Art. 6, Rn. 8; *Soergel/Lüderitz/Fenge*, Art. 6, Rn. 2; *Thiele*, IHR 2002, 8, 10; *Wasmer*, S. 29 ff.; *Winship*, Scope, S. 1–35; *ders.*, 17 UCC L.J. (1984), 55, 65; *C. Witz*, D. 1990, Chron. 107, 109; *ders.*, D. 1995, Chron. 143, 144 f.; *ders.*, D. 2001, Jur. 2608, 3610; *ders.*, L'interprétation, S. 279, 290; *Witz/Salger/Lorenz/Lorenz*, Art. 6, Rn. 9; a. A. *Karollus*, S. 39, *ders.*, östJBl 1993, 23, 27; *ders.*, JuS 1993, 378, 381; *Neumayer/Ming*, Art. 6, Anm. 5.; *Stoffel*, SJZ 1990, 169, 174; a. A. auch *Flambouras*, 29 J.L. & Com. (2011), 171, 184 f., der in der Wahl des Rechts eines Vertragsstaates immer einen Fall der Anwendbarkeit des CISG ex Art. 1 I lit. b) sieht.

[116] Für Fälle, in denen die Wahl des Rechts eines Vertragsstaates nicht als Ausschluss des CISG bewertet wurde, vgl. OLG Hamm, 30.11.2010, CISG-online 2217; BGH, 11.5.2010, CISG-online 2125; RB Rotterdam, 3.2.2010, CISG-online 2097; OGH, 2.4.2009, CISG-online 1889; OLG Hamm, 2.4.2009, CISG-online 1978; OGer Aargau, 3.3.2009, CISG-online 2013; Court of First Instance of Athens, Aktenzeichen 4505/2009 (ohne Datum), CISG-online 2228; RB Rotterdam, 5.11.2008, CISG-online 1817; RB Middelburg, 2.4.2008, CISG-online 1737; OLG Stuttgart, 31.3.2008, CISG-online 1658; *Easom Automation Systems, Inc. v. Thyssenkrupp Fabco, Corp.*, U.S. Dist. Ct. (E.D. Mich), 28.9.2007, CISG-online 1601; BGer, 17.7.2007, CISG-online 1515; *Property Casualty Company of America et al. v. Saint-Gobain Technical Fabrics Canada Limited*, U.S. Dist. Ct. (Minn.), 31.1.2007, CISG-online 1435 = 2007 WL 313 591 (D. Minn.); RB Hasselt, 28.6.2006, CISG Belgium; RB Arnhem, 28.6.2006, CISG-online 1265; Hof van Beroep Antwerpen, 24.4.2006, CISG-online 1258; RB Hasselt, 15.2.2006, CISG-online 1257; OLG Linz, 23.1.2006, CISG-online 1377; RB Hasselt, 14.9.2005, CISG Belgium; Hof Leeuwarden, 31.8.2005, CISG-online 1100; OLG Linz, 8.8.2005, CISG-online 1087 = IHR 2005, 249, 251; OLG Linz, 23.3.2005, CISG-online 1376 = IHR 2007, 123, 127; CA Lyon, 18.12.2003, CISG-online 871; KG Zug, 11.12.2003, CISG-online 958 = IHR 2005, 119, 120; HGer St. Gallen, 3.12.2002, CISG-online 727; OLG Zweibrücken, 26.7.2002, CISG-online 688 = IHR 2002, 67, 68; HGer Zürich, 9.7.2002, CISG-online 726; CA Paris, 6.11.2001, CISG-online 677; OGH, 22.10.2001, CISG-online 614 = IHR 2002, 24, 26; OLG Rostock, 10.10.2001, CISG-online 671 = IHR 2003, 17, 18; *Asante Technologies v. PMC-Sierra*, U.S. Dist. Ct. (N.D. Cal.), 27.7.2001, CISG-online 616 = 2001 U.S. Dist. LEXIS 16 000; OLG Hamburg, 26.1.2001, IHR 2001, 109; OLG Graz, 28.9.2000, CISG-online 798; OLG Frankfurt a.M., 30.8.2000, CISG-online 594 = RIW 2001, 383 f.; Int. Ct. Russian CCI, 24.1.2000, CISG-online 1042 = IHR 2006, 114, 115; RB Hasselt, 4.10.1999, CISG-online 763; BGH,

und schiedsgerichtliche[117]) Rechtsprechung, per se nicht als Ausschluss des Übereinkommens zu bewerten,[118] denn der allgemeine Verweis auf das Recht des Vertragsstaates[119] muss „dahin verstanden werden, dass dieses insgesamt, also unter Einschluss des auch nach diesem vorrangig anwendbaren CISG, zur Anwendung komme".[120] Die Ansicht des Teils der

---

25.11.1998, CISG-online 353 = RIW 1999, 385; OGH, 12.2.1998, CISG-online 349 = östJBl 1999, 54 f.; RB 's-Gravenhage, NIPR 17 (1999), Nr. 15; OLG Karlsruhe, 25.6.1997, CISG-online 263 = RIW 1998, 235; ICC, 8324/1995, CISG-online 569 = J. D. I. 1996, 1019; LG Kassel, 15.2.1996, CISG-online 191 = NJW-RR 1996, 1146; Hof Arnhem, 7.5.1996, NIPR 14 (1996), Nr. 397; Hof Leuwarden, 3.6.1996, NIPR 14 (1996), Nr. 404; CA Grenoble, 13.9.1995, CISG-online 157; OLG Hamm, 9.6.1995, CISG-online 146 = IPRax 1996, 269; RB 's-Gravenhage, 7.6.1995, CISG-online 369 = NIPR 13 (1995), Nr. 524; OLG Celle, 24.5.1995, CISG-online 152; OLG Köln, 22.2.1994, CISG-online 127 = RIW 1994, 972; OLG Koblenz, 17.9.1993, CISG-online 91 = RIW 1994, 936; OLG Düsseldorf, 8.1.1993, CISG-online 76 = IPRax 1993, 412, mit Anm. *Magnus*, IPRax 1993, 390; a. A. BezG Weinfelden, 23.11.1998, CISG-online 428 = SZIER 1999, 198 f.: „Nach den Verkaufs- und Lieferbedingungen (kläg.act. 35) ist das Recht der Bundesrepublik Deutschland anwendbar [...]. b) Zu prüfen ist nun in einem zweiten Schritt, ob zum anwendbaren Recht der Bundesrepublik Deutschland auch das – auf den vorliegenden Sachverhalt grundsätzlich anwendbare – Wiener Kaufrecht zähle. Die BRD hat ebenso wie die Schweiz das Übereinkommen der Vereinten Nationen über Verträge über den internationalen Warenkauf (kurz: Wiener Kaufrecht) unterzeichnet. Es zählt damit zum in internationalen Belangen anwendbaren Recht in Deutschland. Nun dürften aber die Parteien, als sie das Recht der Bundesrepublik Deutschland für anwendbar erklärt haben, das dem Kläger bekannte BGB (Bürgerliche Gesetzbuch) gemeint haben, nicht aber das Wiener Kaufrecht"; a. A. auch HR, 21.5.2010, CISG-online 2096 (Wahl holländischen Rechts als Ausschluss des CISG bewertet); KG Aargau, 20.9.2007, CISG-online 1742 (Wahl schweizerischen Rechts wurde als Ausschluss des CISG angesehen).

[117] Yugoslav Chamber of Commerce, 28.1.2009, CISG-online 1856; Tribunal of International Commercial Arbitration at the Russian Federation Chamber of Commerce and Industry, Russia, 22.10.2004, CISG-online 1359; Tribunal of International Commercial Arbitration at the Russian Federation Chamber of Commerce and Industry, 17.9.2003, CISG-online 979; Tribunal of International Commercial Arbitration at the Russian Federation Chamber of Commerce and Industry, 25.6.2003, CISG-online 978; Tribunal of International Commercial Arbitration at the Russian Federation Chamber of Commerce and Industry, Russia, 16.6.2003, CISG-online 97; ICC, 11 333/2002, CISG-online 1420; ICC, 9187/1999, CISG-online 705; Schiedsgericht der Börse für Landwirtschaftliche Produkte – Wien, 10.12.1997, CISG-online 351 = ZfRVgl 1998, 211 ff.; Schiedsgericht der Handelskammer Hamburg, 21.3.1996, CISG-online 187 = MDR 1996, 781 ff.; Int. Ct. Hungarian CCI, 17.11.1995, CISG-online 250; ICC, 8324/1995, CISG-online 569 = J. D. I. 1996, 1019 ff.; ICC, 7844/1994, CISG-online 567 = ICC Ct. Bull. 1995, 72 f.; ICC, 7660/JK, CISG-online 129 = ICC Ct. Bull. 1995, 68; ICC, 7565/1994, CISG-online 566 = ICC Ct. Bull. 1995, 64 ff.; Schiedssprüche des Internationalen Schiedsgericht der gewerblichen Wirtschaft in Österreich, 15.6.1994, SCH-4366 und 4318, CISG-online 121 und 120 = RIW 1995, 590 f.; ICC, 6653/1993, CISG-online 71 = J. D. I. 1993, 1040 ff.

[118] Dies gilt auch in Bezug auf die Wahl des Rechts eines Teilgebietes eines Vertragsstaates; vgl. in der Rechtsprechung *Property Casualty Company of America et al. v. Saint-Gobain Technical Fabrics Canada Limited,* U. S. Dist. Ct. (Minn.), 31.1.2007, CISG-online 1435 = 2007 WL 313 591 (D. Minn.) (Wahl des Rechts von Minnesota); *American Mint LLC v. GOSoftware, Inc.,* U. S. Dist. Ct. (M. D. Pa.), 16.8.2005, CISG-online 1104 = 2005 WL 2 021 248 (Wahl des Rechts von Georgia); *Ajax Tool Works, Inc. v. Can-Eng Manufacturing Ltd.,* U. S. Dist. Ct. (N. D. Ill.), 29.1.2003, 2003 U. S. Dist. LEXIS 1306 (Wahl des Rechts von Ontario); vgl. in der Lehre *Honnold/Flechtner,* Art. 6, Rn. 77.1; *Staudinger/Magnus,* Art. 6, Rn. 28; *Winship,* Scope, S. 1–35 f.; a. A. *American Biophysics v. Dubois Marine Specialties, a/k/a Dubois Motor Sports,* U. S. Dist. Ct. (D. R. I.), 30.1.2006, CISG-online 1176; krit. hierzu *Johnson,* 59 Buff. L. Rev. (2011), 213, 214 f., und 230 f.

[119] In einem Fall hat ein deutsches Gericht (OLG Hamburg, 5.10.1998, CISG-online 473 = TranspR-IHR 1999, 37 ff.) das CISG sogar auf Grund folgender Rechtswahlklausel auf einen Vertrag zwischen einer chinesischen und einer deutschen Partei zur Anwendung kommen lassen: „the law governing this agreement as per European common market (EU)", mit der Begründung, dass dieser Klausel „der eindeutige Parteiwille zu entnehmen [sei], dass jedenfalls nicht chinesisches Recht, sondern in der EU geltendes Recht maßgebend sein soll. Hieraus könnte abgeleitet werden, dass das in der EU oder jedenfalls in den Staaten des vertraglichen Vertriebsgebietes einheitliche Recht vereinbart werden sollte. Doch gibt es ein allgemeines einheitliches Vertragsrecht, insbesondere für Alleinvertriebsverträge, in der EU bisher nicht – selbst das CISG gilt nicht in allen EU-Staaten und erfasst auch grundsätzlich nicht Vertriebsverträge [...]. Die hier vereinbarte Rechtswahlklausel ist nach Auffassung des Senats deshalb dahin auszulegen, dass das mit dem Sachverhalt am stärksten verbundene europäische Recht gewählt werden sollte. Dies ist das deutsche Recht, in dessen Geltungsbereich der Beklagte seine geschäftliche Niederlassung hat und dessen Geltungsbereich auch den Großteil des Vertriebsgebietes ausmacht. Für die Geltung deutschen Rechts hat sich auch die Kl. im Verfahren ausgesprochen; der Beklagte ist dem nicht entgegengetreten. Die Wahl des deutschen Rechts schließt das CISG als Teil der deutschen Rechtsordnung ein."

[120] OLG Dresden, 27.12.1999, CISG-online 511 = TranspR-IHR 2001, 20 ff.; vgl. auch OGH, 2.4.2009, CISG-online 1889; OGH, 26.1.2005, CISG-online 1045; OGH, 21.4.2004, CISG-online 1048.

Art. 6 23, 24 Teil I. Kapitel I. Anwendungsbereich

Lehre[121] und der Rechtsprechung,[122] die vom Gegenteil ausgehen, kann nicht geteilt werden. Dies hängt zum einen damit zusammen, dass auch das CISG, gleiches galt aber auch hinsichtlich des EKG,[123] Bestandteil des Rechts des Vertragsstaates ist, dessen Recht die Parteien gewählt haben,[124] zum anderen damit, dass „eine Ergänzung des Art. 6 dahin, dass die Wahl des Rechts eines Vertragsstaates das CISG ausschließe, auf der Wiener Konferenz ausdrücklich abgelehnt [wurde] und der Vorschrift deshalb nicht unterstellt werden [darf]."[125] Um bei Wahl des Rechts eines Vertragsstaates von einem Ausschluss ausgehen zu können, bedarf es demnach „zusätzlicher, über den bloßen Text der Rechtswahlklausel hinausgehender Anhaltspunkte".[126]

23 Zum erwähnten Ergebnis muss man unabhängig davon gelangen, ob den Parteien bewusst war, dass ohne ihre Vereinbarung das Übereinkommen zur Anwendung gekommen wäre.[127] Die handelnden Kaufleute werden sich oft keine Gedanken darüber machen, welche Rechtsvorschriften in concreto anzuwenden sind, vielmehr eine bestimmte Rechtsordnung allgemein wählen.[128]

24 Die Frage, ob auch die Wahl des Rechts eines **Vertragsstaates, der den Vorbehalt nach Art. 95** eingelegt hat, zum Ausschluss des Übereinkommens führt, kann nicht pauschal beantwortet werden;[129] die Antwort hängt vielmehr davon ab, ob die berufenen Gerichte die Gerichte des Staates sind, dessen Recht die Parteien gewählt haben, und ob das Übereinkommen nicht schon ex Art. 1 I lit. a) anwendbar ist. In einem solchen Fall kann die Rechtswahl nur als Ausschluss des Übereinkommens interpretiert werden.[130] Gleiches muss m. E. ex Art. 2 Vertragsgesetz auch dann gelten, wenn die

---

[121] Vgl. etwa *Karollus*, S. 38; *ders.*, JuS 1993, 378, 381; *Mann*, JZ 1986, 647; *Stoffel*, SJZ 1990, 169, 173; *Vékás*, IPRax 1987, 342, 346; ebenso, jedoch nur in Bezug auf die Wahl des Rechts eines Teilstaates, *Honnold*, 3. Aufl., Rn. 77.

[122] Siehe Hof 's-Hertogenbosch, 13.11.2007, CISG Pace; Netherlands Arbitration Institute, 17.5.2005, CISG-online 1422; Tribunal of International Commercial Arbitration at the Russian Federation Chamber of Commerce and Industry, 16.3.2005, CISG-online 1480; KG Jura, 3.11.2004, CISG-online 965; Tribunal of International Commercial Arbitration at the Russian Federation Chamber of Commerce and Industry, 12.4.2004, CISG-online 1208; Tribunal of International Commercial Arbitration at the Russian Federation Chamber of Commerce and Industry, 11.10.2002, CISG-online 893; Tribunal of International Commercial Arbitration at the Russian Federation Chamber of Commerce and Industry, 6.9.2002, CISG-online 892; CA Colmar, 26.9.1995, CISG-online 226; KG Zug, 16.3.1995, CISG-online 230 = IHR 2000, 44; Corte Arbitrale ad hoc di Firenze, 19.4.1994, CISG-online 124 = Dir. com. int. 1994, 861 ff.

[123] Vgl. in der Rechtsprechung BGH, 4.12.1985, BGHZ 96, 313, 323 = NJW 1986, 1429 = RIW 1986, 214 mit zust. Anm. *Piltz*, und *Czerwenka*, RIW 1986, 294; OLG Celle, 2.3.1984, IPRax 1985, 283, 284 mit zust. Anm. *Duintjer Tebbens*, IPRax 1985, 262, 263; OLG Hamm, 29.4.1982, IPRax 1983, 231 und OLG Hamm, 20.6.1983, NJW 1984, 1307; OLG Hamburg, 9.7.1980, RIW 1981, 262, 263; vgl. im Schrifttum *Dölle/Herber*, Art. 3 EKG, Rn. 9; *Lindbach*, S. 301 f.; *Rehbinder*, IPRax 1982, 7, 8; *Reinhart*, IPRax 1985, 1; *v. d. Seipen*, IPRax 1984, 244, 245; *Zweigert/Drobnig*, RabelsZ 29 (1965), 146, 162 f.

[124] So ausdrücklich in der Rechtsprechung vgl. auch OGH, 2.4.2009, CISG-online 1889; OGH, 26.1.2005, CISG-online 1045; OGH, 26.1.2005, CISG-online 1045 = IHR 2005, 199, 203; OGH, 21.4.2004, CISG-online 1048; Tribunal Namur, 15.1.2002, CISG-online 759; OGH, 22.10.2001, CISG-online 614 = IHR 2002, 24, 26; OLG Hamburg, 26.1.2001, IHR 2001, 109; BGH, 25.11.1998, CISG-online 353 = RIW 1999, 385; BGH, 23.7.1997, CISG-online 276 = NJW 1997, 3309; LG Kassel, 15.2.1996, CISG-online 191 = NJW-RR 1996, 1146; OLG Celle, 24.5.1995, CISG-online 152; ICC, 7565/1994, CISG-online 566 = ICC Ct. Bull. 2/1995, 64. Vgl. in der Lehre *Achilles*, Art. 1, Rn. 9; *Dokter*, RabelsZ 68 (2004), 430, 435; *Ferrari u. a./Saenger*, Internationales Vertragsrecht, Art. 6, Rn. 4; *Lookofsky*, Case Law Scandinavia, S. 167, 181; *Magnus*, CISG in the German Federal Civil Court, S. 211, 213; *ders.*, Erfahrungen und Erwartungen, S. 25; *Mittmann*, IHR 2006, 103, 104; *Reifner*, IHR 2002, 52, 56; *C. Witz*, D. 2002, Chron. 2796, 2797.

[125] *Staudinger/Magnus*, Art. 6, Rn. 26; vgl. auch O. R., S. 250.

[126] *Piltz*, NJW 2000, 553, 556; vgl. in der Rechtsprechung OLG Karlsruhe, 25.6.1997, CISG-online 263 = RIW 1998, 235.

[127] Vgl. *Lohmann*, Privatautonomie, S. 263 f. und 269; *Reifner*, IMR 2002, 52, 56; *Schlechtriem/Schwenzer/Schwenzer/Hachem*, CISG Commentary, Art. 6, Rn. 14 a. E. ; *Schroeter*, Art. 6 CISG-PECL, S. 263; ebenso zum EKG BGH, 26.11.1980, NJW 1981, 1156, 1157; BGH, 4.12.1985, BGHZ 96, 313, 319.

[128] Vgl. auch *Piltz*, IHR 2002, 2, 4.

[129] Vgl. aber *Schlechtriem/Schwenzer/Schwenzer/Hachem*, CISG Commentary, Art. 6, Rn. 18; *Staudinger/Magnus*, Art. 6, Rn. 27; *Tiehle*, IHR 2002, 8, 10.

[130] Vgl. auch *Ferrari*, Rev. gén. dr. 2002, 335, 341.

Ausschluß, Abweichung oder Änderung durch Parteiabrede   25   **Art. 6**

berufenen Gerichte deutsche Gerichte sind. In allen anderen Fällen ist das Übereinkommen selbst bei Wahl des Rechts eines Vertragsstaates mit Vorbehalt nicht per se ausgeschlossen.[131]

Von der stillschweigenden kollisionsrechtlichen Abwahl des Übereinkommens zugunsten 25 des Rechts eines Nichtvertragsstaates oder des unvereinheitlichten Rechts eines Vertragsstaates, die, zumindest in Deutschland, auch nachträglich[132] – und sogar im Prozess[133] (spätestens bis zum Abschluss der letzten mündlichen Tatsachenverhandlung)[134] – erfolgen kann,[135] ist das **bloße Verhandeln auf der Grundlage des BGB/HGB** vor einem deutschen Gericht deutlich zu unterscheiden.[136] Dies hängt damit zusammen, dass insoweit keine Rechtswahl, sondern allenfalls eine Ausgestaltung der kaufvertraglichen Beziehungen vorliegt,[137] die im Rahmen der materiell-rechtlichen Parteiautonomie durchaus zulässig ist. Als Ausschluss des Übereinkommens kann ein Verhandeln der Parteien auf der Grundlage des BGB/HGB aber nur angesehen werden, wenn „die Parteien wirklich Erklärungsbewusstsein und Erklärungswillen für eine derart vertragsmodifizierende Vereinbarung hatten. Ein Fehler im Prozess, d. h. Verhandeln auf der Grundlage nicht anwendbarer Normen, kann sicher nicht als eine solche Vertragsänderung verstanden werden"[138] und führt demnach **nicht per se zum Ausschluss des CISG**[139] (er kann aber zur **Haftung der Anwälte**

---

[131] Kritisch hierzu *Lindbach,* S. 308; von einem Ausschluss des CISG ausgehend *Achilles,* Art. 6, Rn. 4; *Soergel/Lüderitz/Fenge,* Art. 1, Rn. 16.

[132] Ebenso *Bianca/Bonell/Bonell,* Art. 6, Anm. 3.1.; *Czerwenka,* Rechtsanwendungsprobleme, S. 170; *Diez-Picazo/Calvo Caravaca,* Art. 6, S. 99; *Hager,* FS Huber, S. 319, 325; *Hoffmann,* Koordination, S. 272; *Holthausen,* RIW 1989, 513, 515; *Karollus,* S. 38; *Lohmann,* Parteiautonomie, S. 287; *Soergel/Lüderitz/Fenge,* Art. 1, Rn. 10 und Art. 6, Rn. 4; *C. Witz,* L'interprétation, S. 279, 291; *ders.,* D. 1990, Chron. 107, 108; ebenso die Rechtsprechung zum CISG: OLG Celle, 24.5.1995, CISG-online 152; zum EKG siehe BGH, 26.10.1983, RIW 1984, 151; OLG Koblenz, 9.1.1981, IPRax 1982, 20; BGH, 26.11.1980, WM 1981, 169, 170. Zu Fällen, in denen ein Ausschluss vor Abschluss des eigentlichen Kaufvertrages denkbar und nützlich ist, vgl. *Ferrari,* Applicabilità ed applicazioni, S. 234, Fn. 156; *Lindbach,* S. 240 f.; *Rehbinder,* Vertragsschluss, S. 151.

[133] *Achilles,* Art. 6, Rn. 7; *Dokter,* RabelsZ 68 (2004), 430, 435; *Ferrari u. a./Saenger,* Internationales Vertragsrecht, Art. 6, Rn. 2; *Reifner,* IHR 2002, 52, 57; *Rosati,* IHR 2001, 78, 80; *Schlechtriem,* Internationales UN-Kaufrecht, Rn. 21; *Wasmer,* S. 48.

[134] Vgl. *Neumayer/Ming,* Art. 6, Anm. 2.; *Staudinger/Magnus,* Art. 6, Rn. 51; *Grunewald,* Kaufrecht, S. 632; *Witz/Salger/Lorenz/Lorenz,* Art. 6, Rn. 5; zum EKG vgl. LG Braunschweig, 16.11.1982, RIW 1983, 372; BGH, 26.11.1980, WM 1981, 170.

[135] Siehe hierzu OLG Rostock, 10.10.2001, CISG-online 671 = IHR 2003, 17; OLG Köln, 22.2.1994, CISG-online 127 = RIW 1994, 970.

[136] Ebenso *Wasmer,* S. 31 f.

[137] *Schlechtriem,* Internationales UN-Kaufrecht, Rn. 21.

[138] *Schlechtriem,* IPRax 1996, 256; ebenso *Honsell/Siehr,* Art. 6, Rn. 3, der hervorhebt, dass neben der Bezugnahme der Parteien auf dasselbe nationale Recht auch „das Bewusstsein der Parteien [hinzutreten muss], dass sie hiermit ein bisher anwendbares Recht (WKR) durch ein neues Recht (nationales Recht) ersetzen". In diesem Sinne auch *Bamberger/Roth/Saenger,* Art. 6, Rn. 4b; *Ferrari u. a./Saenger,* Internationales Vertragsrecht, Art. 6, Rn. 6; *Imberg,* 35 San Diego L.Rev. (1998), 769, 776; *Piltz,* NJW 2000, 553, 555; *Reifner,* IHR 2002, 52, 57; *Rosati,* IHR 2001, 78, 80; *Soergel/Lüderitz/Fenge,* Art. 6, Rn. 4; *Spiegel,* D. 2002, Jur. 395, 395; vgl. in der Rechtsprechung Civ. 1, 25.10.2005, CISG-online 1226 = Rev. crit. dr. int. privé 2006, 373, 374: „il résulte de la procédure et de l'arrêt attaqué qu'en invoquant et en discutant sans aucune réserve la garantie de la chose vendue définie par les articles 1641 et suivants du Code civil, toutes les parties ont, en connaissance du caractère international des ventes qu'elles avaient conclues, *volontairement* placé la solution de leurs différends sous le régime du droit interne français de la vente".

[139] So auch *Bazinas,* Uniformity, S. 26; *Brunner,* Art. 6, Rn. 1; *Bureau,* Rev. crit. dr. int. privé 2006, 374, 379; *Kröll u. a./Mistelis,* Art. 6, Rn. 19; *Magnus,* ZEuP 1997, 823, 827; *ders.,* ZEuP 2002, 523, 530; MünchKommHGB/*Benicke,* Art. 6, Rn. 12; *Reifner,* IMR 2002, 52, 57; *Schlechtriem/Schwenzer/Schlechtriem,* CISG Commentary, 2. Aufl., Art. 6, Rn. 14; *Schwenzer/Hachem/Kee,* Rn. 4.34; *Veneziano,* Dir. com. int. 2001, 509, 514; missverständlich *Wolf,* WM 1998, Sonderbeilage Nr. 2, 1, 41 f.; vgl. in der neueren Rechtsprechung LG Bamberg, 23.10.2006, CISG-online 1400: Der Anwendung des CISG „steht nicht entgegen, dass die Parteien zunächst in ihren Schriftsätzen unter Bezugnahme auf Bestimmungen des deutschen Rechts argumentiert haben, weil diese Handhabung noch nicht zu einem stillschweigenden Ausschluss des UN-Kaufrechts nach Art. 6 führt"; vgl. auch OLG Hamm, 2.4.2009, CISG-online 1978; a. A. *Ho Myung Moolsan, Co. Ltd. v. Manitou Mineral Water, Inc.,* U. S. Dist. Ct. (S. D. N. Y.), 2.12.2010, CISG-online 2170; Regional Court Bratislava, 10.10.2007, CISG-online 1828; Civ. 1, 25.10.2005, CISG-online 1226.

führen,[140] die den entsprechenden Fehler gemacht haben),[141] da auch diesbezüglich – so nunmehr auch die Rechtsprechung[142] – zumindest in civil-law Ländern das Prinzip iura novit curia gilt,[143] d. h., es ist Sache des Richters, das richtige, auf den Sachverhalt anzuwendende Sachrecht zu ermitteln.[144]

26 Dies ist auch von (einem Teil) der **Rechtsprechung** erkannt worden,[145] die zwar das Verhandeln auf der Grundlage des unvereinheitlichten Rechts als zulässige Art der Abbedingung des Übereinkommens anerkennt, aber hervorhebt, dass „ein solches Verhalten stets Ausdruck eines gemeinsamen Willens sein [muss]".[146] Wenn „das Prozessverhalten [...] also nicht auf einer bewussten Wahl des deutschen Kaufrechts [beruht], sondern auf der Rechtsmeinung, es sei ohnehin anwendbar",[147] kann das Übereinkommen bei Vorliegen aller Anwendungsvoraussetzungen durchaus zur Anwendung kommen.[148]

27 Diesbezüglich muss darauf hingewiesen werden, dass nach **deutschem Prozessrecht ex § 139 ZPO** den Richter die Pflicht trifft, zum Zweck der vollständigen Klärung aller entscheidungserheblichen Umstände das Streitverhältnis mit den Parteien in tatsächlicher und rechtlicher Hinsicht zu erörtern. Daraus – und **ex § 278 III ZPO** – ergibt sich eine **Fragebeziehungsweise Hinweispflicht des Richters** immer dann, wenn die Parteien, trotz Vorliegen aller Anwendungsvoraussetzungen des Übereinkommens, auf der Grundlage des deutschen Rechts argumentieren.[149] Ein Hinweis auf die Anwendbarkeit des Übereinkommens wurde zu Recht in einem Fall gegeben, in dem die Vertragsparteien pauschal deutsches Recht gewählt hatten, was zur Anwendbarkeit des Übereinkommens ex Art. 1 I lit. b) geführt hat.[150]

28 Eine stillschweigende Abbedingung des Übereinkommens wird im Zweifel auch dann nicht anzunehmen sein, wenn die Vertragsparteien nach dem Außerkrafttreten des Haager Kaufrechts nur auf „**internationales Einheitsrecht**" Bezug nehmen. Im Zweifel wird in solchen Fällen der Wille anzunehmen sein, nicht das EKG sondern das CISG als die neuere Fassung eines materiell nur fortentwickelten internationalen Einheitsrechts anzuwenden. Der vertragliche Ausschluss des Haager Kaufrechts (etwa in vorgefertigten Allgemeinen Geschäftsbedingungen) führt, nachdem das CISG das Haager Kaufrecht ersetzt hat, nicht per se zum Ausschluss desselben, so nicht nur die Lehre,[151] sondern auch die Rechtsprechung.[152]

---

[140] Vgl. zu eventueller Haftung bei Ausschluss des CISG *Koch*, NJW 2000, 910 ff.

[141] Vgl. auch *Wasmer*, S. 32.

[142] Tribunale di Padova, 25.2.2004, CISG-online 819; Tribunale di Vigevano, 12.7.2000, CISG-online 493 = IHR 2001, 72, 74.

[143] *Graffi*, EuLF 2000/20 001, 240, 242; *Schlechtriem*, Internationales UN-Kaufrecht, Rn. 21; *Schlechtriem/Schwenzer/Schwenzer/Hachem*, CISG Commentary, Art. 6, Rn. 21; *C. Witz*, L'interprétation, S. 279, 293 f.

[144] Vgl. *Reifner*, IHR 2002, 52, 57; *Schlechtriem/Schwenzer/Schlechtriem*, CISG Commentary, 2. Aufl., Art. 6, Rn. 14 a. E.

[145] Vgl. etwa OLG Hamm, 2.4.2009, CISG-online 1978; LG Saarbrücken, 2.7.2002, CISG-online 713 = IHR 2003, 27; OLG Rostock, 10.10.2001, CISG-online 671 = IHR 2003, 17, 18; KG Nidwalden, 3.12.1997, CISG-online 331 = SZIER 1999, 81 f.; OLG Hamm, 9.6.1995, CISG-online 146 = RIW 1996, 689; LG Landshut, 5.4.1995, CISG-online 193; a. A. Civ. 1, 26.6.2001, CISG-online 598 = D. 2001, Jur. 3607, 3607, mit krit. Anm. *C. Witz*; zu Recht krit. auch *Dokter*, RabelsZ 68 (2004), 430, 436 f.; *C. Witz*, L'interprétation, S. 279, 292 ff.; weniger krit. hingegen *Hager*, FS U. Huber, S. 319, 327.

[146] OLG Celle, 24.5.1995, CISG-online 152; vgl. auch OLG Hamm, 2.4.2009, CISG-online 1978; OLG Stuttgart, 31.3.2008, CISG-online 1658.

[147] OLG Celle, 24.5.1995 CISG-online 152.

[148] So auch *Staudinger/Magnus*, Art. 6, Rn. 51; vgl. auch OLG Linz, 23.1.2006, CISG-online 1377: „Kein hinreichend deutlich gewordener vollkommener Ausschluss des UN-Kaufrechts liegt etwa vor, wenn die Parteien [...] im Prozess sich übereinstimmend auf nationales Recht berufen, ohne sich einer nachträglichen Rechtswahl bewusst zu sein"; vgl. auch OLG Hamm, 2.4.2009, CISG-online 1978; OLG Stuttgart, 31.3.2008, CISG-online 1658; Tribunale di Padova, 25.2.2004, CISG-online 819; Tribunale di Vigevano, 12.7.2000, CISG-online 493 = IHR 2001, 72, 74; OLG Dresden, 27.12.1999, CISG-online 511 = TranspR-IHR 2001, 20 ff.

[149] Vgl. auch *Lindbach*, S. 296 f.; *Lohmann*, Parteiautonomie, S. 293; *Schlechtriem*, Internationales UN-Kaufrecht, Rn. 21.

[150] Vgl. OLG Düsseldorf, 2.7.1993, CISG-online 74 = NJW-RR 1993, 1000.

[151] *Piltz*, NJW 2000, 553, 555.

[152] LG Düsseldorf, 11.10.1995, CISG-online 180: „Gemäß Art. 6 CISG können die Parteien die Anwendung des Übereinkommens zwar ausschließen, und zwar grundsätzlich auch durch allgemeine Geschäfts-

Auch die **Vereinbarung von Incoterms®** deutet nicht notwendigerweise auf die 29
Abbedingung des CISG hin,[153] weil diese nur einzelne Aspekte des Kaufvertrages regeln und deshalb nicht die Anwendung eines bestimmten, vom CISG abweichenden Kaufrechts als Basis voraussetzen.[154] Dies ist nunmehr auch von der (höchstrichterlichen) Rechtsprechung bestätigt worden.[155]

Fraglich ist, ob die **Vereinbarung kollidierender Regelungen** als Ausschluss gewertet 30
werden muss.[156] Der Ansicht, die Vereinbarung **einzelner Vorschriften** eines unvereinheitlichten Rechts deute auf den Ausschluss des CISG als Ganzes hin, wenn es sich um zentrale Bestimmungen handele,[157] ist m. E. nicht zu folgen,[158] da abweichende Abreden mit dem Übereinkommen durchaus verträglich sind.[159] Ergibt sich aus dem Vertragsinhalt und dem System des Vertrages[160] jedoch, dass diese so sehr vom Recht eines bestimmten Staates beeinflusst sind, weil etwa die **allgemeinen Geschäftsbedingungen** sich auf ein bestimmtes Recht beziehen,[161] dass der Vertragsinhalt unvereinbar ist mit dem Übereinkommen als Ganzem, dann muss, waren sich die Parteien der Anwendbarkeit des Übereinkommens bewusst, von einem Ausschluss ausgegangen werden.[162]

Auch **Gerichtsstandsvereinbarungen** können zum stillschweigenden Ausschluss des 31
Übereinkommens führen. Diesbezüglich reicht es jedoch nicht aus, dass der Gerichtsstand in einem Nichtvertragsstaat vereinbart wird,[163] da mit der Gerichtsstandwahl nicht notwendigerweise die Wahl des Rechts des Forums verbunden ist.[164] Liegt der vereinbarte Gerichts-

---

bedingungen, sofern diese wirksam vereinbart sind [...]. Durch die allgemeinen Liefer- und Geschäftsbedingungen der Beklagten wird die Anwendung des CISG jedoch nicht ausgeschlossen [...]. Ziffer X C) der Geschäftsbestimmungen der Beklagten bestimmt im Übrigen lediglich, dass das einheitliche Gesetz über den Kauf beweglicher Sachen (EKG) vom 17.7.1973 nicht anwendbar sein soll. Dieses Gesetz ist indes ohnehin durch das am 1.1.1991 in Kraft getretene CISG ersetzt worden. Die Anwendung des CISG wird daher durch die allgemeinen Geschäfts- und Lieferbedingungen der Beklagten nicht ausgeschlossen." Siehe auch OLG München, 19.10.2006, CISG-online 1394 = IHR 2007, 30, 32; OGH, 10.3.1998, CISG-online 356.

[153] So auch *Dokter*, RabelsZ 68 (2004), 430, 440; *Kröll u. a./Mistelis*, Art. 6, Rn. 20; *Lohmann*, Parteiautonomie, S. 278; MünchKomm/*Westermann*, Art. 6, Rn. 6; MünchKommHGB/*Benicke*, Art. 6, Rn. 13; *Schlechtriem/Schwenzer/Schlechtriem*, CISG Commentary, 2. Aufl., Art. 6, Rn. 12; *Schlechtriem/Schwenzer/Hachem*, CISG Commentary, Art. 6, Rn. 26; *Wasmer*, S. 32; *Witz/Salger/Lorenz/Lorenz*, Art. 6, Rn. 16.

[154] Ebenso *Ebenroth*, östJBl 1986, 681, 684 f.; *Honsell/Siehr*, Art. 6, Rn. 7; *Magnus/Lüsing*, IHR 2007, 1, 6; *Staudinger/Magnus*, Art. 6, Rn. 46, sowie – zum EKG – *Dölle/Herber*, Art. 3 EKG, Rn. 10.

[155] OGH, 22.10.2001, CISG-online 614 = IHR 2002, 24, 26: „Auch die Vereinbarung von Incoterms – wie hier – deutet nicht notwendigerweise auf die Abbedingung des UN-Kaufrechts hin, weil diese nur einzelne Aspekte des Kaufvertrags regeln und deshalb nicht die Anwendung eines bestimmten, vom UN-Kaufrecht abweichenden Kaufrechts als Basis voraussetzen"; i. E. neuerdings ebenso Hof Beroep Antwerpen, 22.1.2007, CISG Belgium.

[156] Vgl. hierzu neuerdings auch *Lohmann*, Parteiautonomie, S. 276 ff.

[157] *Herber*, 2. Aufl., Art. 6, Rn. 18; *Schlechtriem/Schwenzer/Schlechtriem*, CISG Commentary, 2. Aufl., Art. 6, Rn. 12; *Schlechtriem/Schwenzer/Hachem*, CISG Commentary, Art. 6, Rn. 26; vgl. jedoch OGer Bern, 19.5.2008, CISG-online 1738.

[158] Anders noch *Ferrari*, Applicabilità ed applicazioni, 1. Aufl., 1997, S. 175.

[159] So auch *Enderlein/Maskow/Strohbach*, Art. 6, Anm. 1.3.; *Lohmann*, Parteiautonomie, S. 276; MünchKomm/*Westermann*, Art. 6, Rn. 4; MünchKommHGB/*Benicke*, Art. 6, Rn. 11; *Wasmer*, S. 32 und 49.

[160] *Enderlein/Maskow/Strohbach*, Art. 6, Anm. 1.3.

[161] Vielfach ist hervorgehoben worden, dass das Übereinkommen auch durch kollidierende AGB ausgeschlossen werden kann; vgl. statt aller *Audit*, Vente internationale, S. 39; *U. Huber*, RabelsZ 43 (1979), 413, 427.

[162] *Bianca/Bonell/Bonell*, Art. 6, S. 18; *Chiomenti*, EuLF 2005, 141, 144; *Ferrari*, Applicabilità ed applicazioni, S. 224 f.; *Lohmann*, Privatautonomie, S. 278; MünchKomm/*Westermann*, Art. 6, Rn. 7; *Schlechtriem/Schwenzer/Schlechtriem*, CISG Commentary, 2. Aufl., Art. 6, Rn. 12; *Schlechtriem/Schwenzer/Hachem*, CISG Commentary, Art. 6, Rn. 26; *Staudinger/Magnus*, Art. 6, Rn. 42; a. A. *Witz/Salger/Lorenz/Lorenz*, Art. 6, Rn. 13.

[163] Ebenso *Schlechtriem/Schwenzer/Hachem*, CISG Commentary, Art. 6, Rn. 20; a. A. *Bamberger/Roth/Saenger*, Art. 6, Rn. 4; *Kröll u. a./Mistelis*, Art. 6, Rn. 12; *Schlechtriem/Schwenzer/Schlechtriem*, CISG Commentary, 2. Aufl., Art. 6, Rn. 8 a. E.; a. A. auch OLG Linz, 23.1.2006, CISG-online 1377.

[164] *Ferrari*, Applicabilità ed applicazioni, S. 226; *Schlechtriem/Schwenzer/Hachem*, CISG Commentary, Art. 6, Rn. 20; ebenso in der Rechtsprechung OLG Stuttgart, 31.3.2008, CISG-online 1658; a. A. *Staudinger/Magnus*, Art. 6, Rn. 36, der davon ausgeht, dass „wenn ein Gerichtsstand in einem Nichtvertragsstaat vereinbart wird [...] hieraus – wie üblich – die Wahl des Rechts dieses Staates hergeleitet werden kann"; ebenso *Wasmer*, S. 33; ebenso in der neueren Rechtsprechung OLG Hamm, 2.4.2009, CISG-online 1978.

stand aber in einem Vertragsstaat, so kann dies für sich allein sicher nicht als Ausschluss bewertet werden.[165]

32 Gleiches gilt auch hinsichtlich **Schiedsgerichtsvereinbarungen:** Die Vereinbarung eines Schiedsgerichts führt nicht notwendigerweise zum Ausschluss des Übereinkommens.[166] Davon auszugehen, dass in der Regel aus der Wahl des Schiedsorts auf das anwendbare Recht geschlossen werden könne,[167] ist nicht haltbar, da nicht alle Schiedsgerichte das Recht anwenden, das im Staat gilt, in dem der Schiedsort liegt.[168]

3. Modifikation und teilweiser Ausschluss des CISG

33 a) **Grundsatz.** Art. 6 enthält den Grundsatz, der – wie auch die Vorarbeiten zeigen – von Anfang an nicht zweifelhaft war,[169] wonach die Parteien – im oben bereits gesteckten Rahmen[170] – von den Bestimmungen des CISG abweichen oder dessen Wirkung ändern können. Damit wird noch deutlicher als nach dem EKG, der keinen ausdrücklichen Hinweis darauf vorsah, dass die Parteien von den Bestimmungen des Gesetzes „abweichen oder deren Wirkung ändern" können,[171] dass den Parteien im Rahmen des Anwendungs- und Regelungsbereichs des Übereinkommens eine **Vertragsfreiheit** gewährt wird, die etwa entgegenstehendes – auch **zwingendes – Recht** der Vertragsstaaten **zurücktreten** lässt.[172]

34 b) **Teilweiser Ausschluss und Lückenfüllung.** Wie bereits erwähnt,[173] führt die **Abwahl einzelner Vorschriften** nicht notwendigerweise zum Ausschluss des Übereinkommens als Ganzes, selbst dann nicht, wenn es sich um „zentrale Bestimmungen"[174] handelt.

35 Wird das Übereinkommen teilweise ausgeschlossen,[175] weil einzelne Vorschriften oder ganze Teile (etwa der Abschlussteil oder der materiell-rechtliche Teil) ausgeschlossen werden, muss man sich fragen, anhand welcher Regeln die nicht mehr von den Vorschriften des Übereinkommens erfassten Fragen zu regeln sind. Ein Teil der Lehre vertritt die Ansicht, es sei, bei Fehlen einer Vereinbarung der Parteien hinsichtlich des anwendbaren Rechts[176] oder der Ersetzung der ausgeschlossenen Vorschriften durch von den Parteien einvernehmlich vereinbarte Regeln, im Zweifel anzunehmen, dass die Parteien den Rückgriff auf nationales Recht nicht wünschen,[177] und demnach die Lücken ex Art. 7 II anhand der allgemeinen Grundsätze des Übereinkommens auszufüllen seien.[178] M. E. ist diese Meinung nicht haltbar.[179] Dies folgt zum einen daraus, dass ein Rückgriff auf die allgemeinen Grundsätze notwendigerweise zu dem Ergebnis führt, das die Parteien durch ihre Abbedingung vermeiden wollten, da sich die allgemeinen Grundsätze, die sich auf die ausgeschlossenen Fragen beziehen, aus den von den Parteien abgedungenen Vorschriften bezüglich ebendieser

---

[165] Ebenso *Holthausen*, RIW 1989, 513, 518; *Lohmann*, Parteiautonomie, S. 279; *Grunewald*, Kaufrecht, S. 632; ebenso in der Rechtsprechung HGer Aargau, 10.3.2010, CISG-online 2176.
[166] Siehe auch *Ferrari*, Applicabilità ed applicazioni, S. 226; *Lohmann*, Parteiautonomie, S. 286.
[167] So *Bamberger/Roth/Saenger*, Art. 6, Rn. 4a; *Staudinger/Magnus*, Art. 6, Rn. 37.
[168] Vgl. auch *Chiomenti*, EuLF 2005, 141, 144: Ausschluss des CISG bei Wahl des Schiedsorts nur dann, wenn sich dieser in einem Nichtvertragsstaat befindet und sich aus dem Vertrag ergibt, dass die Parteien auch das Recht dieses Staates zur Anwendung kommen lassen wollten.
[169] So ausdrücklich *Lindbach*, S. 67.
[170] Vgl. oben Rn. 5 ff.
[171] *Herber*, 2. Aufl., Art. 6, Rn. 3.
[172] *Enderlein/Maskow/Strohbach*, Art. 6, Anm. 3.1.; *Piltz*, IHR 2002, 2, 4; *Schroeter*, VJ (2002), 257, 263; *Wasmer*, S. 60.
[173] Vgl. oben Rn. 30.
[174] So aber *Herber*, 2. Aufl., Art. 6, Rn. 18.
[175] Auf die Möglichkeit eines teilweisen Ausschlusses hinweisend etwa BGH, 9.1.2002, CISG-online 651 = IHR 2002, 16, 18.
[176] Ob die Wahl des Rechts hinsichtlich bestimmter Fragen relevant ist, wird davon abhängen, ob das IPR des Forumsstaates dépeçage zulässt.
[177] So *Herber*, 2. Aufl., Art. 6, Rn. 26.
[178] So *Heuzé*, Anm. 100.; *Wey*, S. 50, Rn. 147.
[179] Vgl. hierzu schon *Ferrari*, 10 Preadviezen (1995), 81, 151; so neuerdings auch MünchKommHGB/ *Benicke*, Art. 6, Rn. 21; *Wasmer*, S. 49 f.

Fragen ergeben.[180] Zum anderen steht auch der Wortlaut des Art. 7 II der hier widersprochenen Ansicht entgegen: Auf die allgemeinen Grundsätze ist ex Art. 7 II nur zurückzugreifen, um im CISG zwar geregelte, aber in diesem nicht ausdrücklich entschiedene Frage zu entscheiden, um die es hier aber überhaupt nicht geht, da die von den Parteien abbedungenen Vorschriften sicher „ausdrücklich geregelte" Fragen betreffen. Daher ist diesbezüglich auf das **über den üblichen kollisionsrechtlichen Weg anwendbare nationale Recht** abzustellen.[181]

4. Ergänzende vertragliche Vereinbarung

Die Parteien können durchaus ergänzende Vereinbarungen treffen. Deren Zustandekommen richtet sich nach den Vorschriften des Teil II des Übereinkommens. **Ob diese Vereinbarungen jedoch wirksam** sind, muss, unter Berücksichtigung der anlässlich der Kommentierung des Art. 4 gemachten Einschränkungen,[182] auf der Grundlage des anwendbaren Rechts entschieden werden,[183] da das Übereinkommen die Gültigkeit des Vertrages oder einzelner Vertragsbestimmungen (grundsätzlich) nicht regelt. Maßgebend ist das Recht des Staates, dem der Vertrag unterläge, wäre nicht das Übereinkommen anzuwenden. Führt dieses Recht – wie etwa das deutsche Recht nach § 138 BGB oder nach §§ 305 ff. BGB – im Einzelfall zur Nichtigkeit der Vereinbarung, so muss die in Frage stehende Vereinbarung außer Betracht bleiben. 36

Bei der **Anwendung der §§ 305 ff. BGB** ist zu prüfen, ob die von den Parteien getroffene Regelung „mit wesentlichen Grundgedanken der gesetzlichen Regelung, von der abgewichen wird, nicht zu vereinbaren ist" (§ 307 Abs. 2 Nr. 1 BGB). Diese gesetzliche Regelung ist heute[184] das **CISG,** so dass dessen **Leitgedanken** nicht essentiell verletzt werden dürfen.[185] 37

5. Beweislast

Auf der Grundlage des dem Übereinkommens zugrunde liegenden Prinzips, wonach diejenige Partei, die sich auf das Eingreifen einer Ausnahmeregel beruft, im Zweifelsfall die tatsächlichen Voraussetzungen derselben zu beweisen hat,[186] muss man davon ausgehen, dass denjenigen, der **vorträgt, das CISG sei** von den Parteien **ausgeschlossen** worden, die Beweislast trifft[187] – so nunmehr auch die Rechtsprechung[188] – stellt Art. 6 doch eine den Anwendungsbereich betreffende Ausnahmevorschrift dar.[189] 38

---

[180] Vgl. auch *Ferrari,* Applicabilità ed applicazioni, S. 232 f.
[181] So auch *Bianca/Bonell/Bonell,* Art. 6, Anm. 7.; *Teichert,* Lückenfüllung, S. 10 f.; *Wasmer,* S. 49 f.; so nunmehr auch *Staudinger/Magnus,* Art. 6, Rn. 60.
[182] Siehe Art. 4 Rn. 15 ff.
[183] MünchKomm/*Westermann,* Art. 6, Rn. 8; *Piltz,* IHR 2002, 2, 6; *Schluchter,* S. 180 und 183.
[184] Ebenso zum EKG Denkschrift zum EKG, BT-Drs. 7/115, 55 a. E.; *von Caemmerer,* Vertragspflichten und Vertragsgültigkeit, S. 40; *ders.,* AcP 178 (1978), 121, 128; *Czerwenka,* Rechtsanwendungsprobleme, S. 107 f.; *Dölle/Stoll,* Art. 74 EKG, Rn. 145 m. w. N.; *Hausmann,* WM 1980, 726, 735; *Schlechtriem,* Haager Einheitliches Kaufrecht und AGB-Gesetz, S. 257.
[185] So auch *Bamberger/Roth/Saenger,* Art. 6, Rn. 5; *Ferrari u. a./Saenger,* Internationales Vertragsrecht, Art. 6, Rn. 8 a. E.; MünchKomm/*Westermann,* Art. 4, Rn. 6; MünchKommHGB/*Benicke,* Art. 4, Rn. 5; *Ostendorf/Neumann/Ventsch,* IHR 2006, 21; *Piltz,* IHR 2004, 133, 138; *Schillo,* IHR 2003, 257, 258; *Wasmer,* S. 59.
[186] Vgl. *Staudinger/Magnus,* Art. 4, Rn. 68.
[187] So auch *Achilles,* Art. 6, Rn. 10; *Bamberger/Roth/Saenger,* Art. 6, Rn. 6; *Baumgärtel u. a./Müller,* Art 6, Rn. 1; *Brunner,* Art. 6, Rn. 12; *Dokter,* RabelsZ 68 (2004), 430, 437 f.; *Ferrari u. a./Saenger,* Internationales Vertragsrecht, Art. 6, Rn. 9; *Jung,* S. 203 ff.; *Lohmann,* Parteiautonomie, S. 254; *T. M. Müller,* Beweislast, S. 45; MünchKomm/*Westermann,* Art. 6, Rn. 13; *Reimers-Zocher,* S. 166 f.; *Schlechtriem,* Internationales UN-Kaufrecht, Rn. 20; *C. Witz,* L'interprétation, S. 279, 290; *ders.,* D. 2002, Chron. 2796, 2797.
[188] OLG Linz, 23.1.2006, CISG-online 1377; CA Paris, 6.11.2001, CISG-online 677 = D. 2002, Chron. 2795.
[189] Ebenso *Lindbach,* S. 300.

IV. Opting-in des Übereinkommens

39 Im Gegensatz zum Haager Kaufrecht, das eine Vorschrift vorsah (Art. 4 EKG), die den Parteien ausdrücklich die Möglichkeit zuerkannte, dieses auch bei Fehlen der räumlich-internationalen[190] (nicht aber bei Fehlen der sachlichen[191]) Anwendungsvoraussetzungen zur Anwendung kommen zu lassen,[192] enthält das CISG keine derartige Vorschrift.[193] Der Wegfall des ausdrücklichen Hinweises geht darauf zurück, dass man die in Art. 4 EKG enthaltene Begrenzung auf den räumlichen Anwendungsbereich als zu eng und seinen Vorbehalt des „zwingenden Rechts" als zu unbestimmt ansah.[194] Dies bedeutet jedoch nicht, dass den Parteien die Wahl des Kaufrechts, etwa durch die Klausel „Das Vertragsverhältnis unterliegt dem Wiener Übereinkommen über Verträge über den internationalen Warenkauf von 1980",[195] verschlossen sei.[196] Die Gründe, die zur Wahl des CISG als „anwendbares Recht" führen können, allen voran die Neutralität des CISG,[197] so auch ein Schiedsurteil,[198] sind in der Lehre bereits oft untersucht worden. Auf diese Untersuchungen sei hier verwiesen.[199]

40 Diesbezüglich muss aber zwischen der **kollisionsrechtlichen und der materiellrechtlichen Wahl** des Übereinkommens in Fällen, in denen es nicht per se anwendbar ist, unterschieden werden.[200] Um welche Art der Wahl es sich bei einer Vereinbarung des Übereinkommens handelt, muss anhand der **Auslegungsregeln des anwendbaren nationalen Rechts,** nicht des Übereinkommens, entschieden werden.[201]

41 Was die **materiellrechtliche Wählbarkeit** angeht, so wird diese nicht in Frage gestellt.[202] Die Vorschriften des Übereinkommens werden durch diese Art der Wahl wie AGB in den Vertrag inkorporiert;[203] daher muss diese Art der Wahl des Übereinkommens auch die **Schranken der vom maßgeblichen nationalen Recht eingeräumten Parteiautonomie** respektieren.[204] Dies führt etwa dazu, dass der in Art. 11 festgelegte Grundsatz der

---

[190] So auch *Czerwenka,* Rechtsanwendungsprobleme, S. 102 f.

[191] So *Mertens/Rehbinder,* Art. 4 EKG, Rn. 8.

[192] Für einen Bezug auf Fälle, in denen das EKG als maßgeblich vereinbart wurde, *Piltz,* Praktische Erfahrungen, S. 47 f.

[193] *Lohmann,* Parteiautonomie, S. 128; *Wasmer,* S. 68; *C. Witz,* D. 2002, Jur. 323, 324.

[194] So ausdrücklich *Staudinger/Magnus,* Art. 6, Rn. 62.

[195] Vgl. für weitere Formulierungsvorschläge *Allmendinger,* S. 33; *Lindbach,* S. 178.

[196] Dass die Parteien das CISG vereinbaren können, ist in der Lehre oft hervorgehoben worden; vgl. *Bamberger/Roth/Saenger,* Art. 6, Rn. 1; *K. Bell,* 8 Pace Int'l L. Rev. (1996), 237, 250; *Bianca/Bonell/Bonell,* Art. 6, Anm. 3.5.; *Ferrari,* Applicabilità ed applicazioni, S. 235 ff.; *Heuzé,* Anm. 125.; *Rovelli,* Conflitti, S. 98; *Schlechtriem,* Einheitliches UN-Kaufrecht, S. 22; *ders.,* 36 Vict. U. Well. L. Rev. (2005), 781, 785; *Wasmer,* S. 69; vgl. in der Rechtsprechung ICC, 11849, CISG-online 1421: Anwendung des CISG auf einen Vertriebsvertrag aufgrund ausdrücklicher Wahl der Vertragsparteien.

[197] Vgl. etwa *Dutton,* 7 (EJLR), 2005, 239, 243 ff.; *Ferrari u. a./Saenger,* Internationales Vertragsrecht, Art. 6, Rn. 1.

[198] ICC, 11 849/2003, CISG-online 1421.

[199] Vgl. *De Ly,* Opting-Out, S. 25, 36 ff.; *Fountoulakis,* 7 (EJLR), 2005, 303, 313 ff.; *J. Meyer,* RabelsZ 69 (2005), 457, 479 ff.

[200] *Schlechtriem/Schwenzer/Schwenzer/Hachem,* CISG Commentary, Art. 6, Rn. 31; a. A. *Schlechtriem,* Internationales UN-Kaufrecht, 3. Aufl., Rn. 23, der nur von der materiellrechtlichen Wählbarkeit des CISG auszugehen scheint; anders nunmehr *Schlechtriem,* Internationales Kaufrecht, 4. Aufl., Rn. 23a, und *ders.,* 36 Vict. U. Well. L. Rev. (2005), 781, 785 f., wo auch der Autor die im Text erwähnte Unterscheidung vornimmt.

[201] So neuerdings auch *Schlechtriem/Schwenzer/Schwenzer/Hachem,* CISG Commentary, Art. 6, Rn. 31; *Wasmer,* S. 69.

[202] Vgl. statt aller *Bamberger/Roth/Saenger,* Art. 6, Rn. 4c; *Ferrari u. a./Saenger,* Internationales Vertragsrecht, Art. 6, Rn. 7; *Schlechtriem/Schwenzer/Schlechtriem,* CISG Commentary, 2. Aufl., Art. 6, Rn. 13; *Schlechtriem/Schwenzer/Schwenzer/Hachem,* CISG Commentary, Art. 6, Rn. 31.

[203] So ausdrücklich *Staudinger/Magnus,* Art. 6, Rn. 64.

[204] *Bamberger/Roth/Saenger,* Art. 6, Rn. 4c; *Ferrari u. a./Saenger,* Internationales Vertragsrecht, Art. 6, Nr. 7; *Lindbach,* S. 180; *H.-F. Müller,* IHR 2005, 133, 136; *MünchKomm/Westermann,* Art. 6, Rn. 12; *Schlechtriem,* Einheitliches UN-Kaufrecht, S. 22; *ders.,* 36 Vict. U. Well. L. Rev. (2005), 781, 785; *Schlechtriem/Schwenzer/Schlechtriem,* CISG Commentary, 2. Aufl., Art. 6, Rn. 13; *Schlechtriem/Schwenzer/Schwenzer/Hachem,* CISG Commentary, Art. 6, Rn. 31; *Schroeter,* Art. 6 CISG-PECL, S. 267.

Formfreiheit unbeachtlich ist, wenn das maßgebliche nationale Recht bestimmte Formerfordernisse vorschreibt.

In Bezug auf die **kollisionsrechtliche Wählbarkeit** des Übereinkommens muss zunächst hervorgehoben werden, dass diese nicht pauschal ausgeschlossen oder bejaht werden darf.[205] Die Möglichkeit der kollisionsrechtlichen Wahl des CISG hängt vielmehr davon ab, ob die maßgeblichen **Kollisionsnormen des Forumstaates** eine derartige „Rechtswahl" zulassen.[206] Sowohl das EVÜ als auch die Rom-I VO und das Haager IPR-Übereinkommen von 1955 schließen dies m. E. aus,[207] so nunmehr auch die neuere Rechtsprechung.[208]

Hinsichtlich des **deutschen Kollisionsrechts** vertritt ein Teil der Lehre die Ansicht, das CISG sei durchaus kollisionsrechtlich wählbar,[209] unter anderem mit der Begründung, dem CISG komme trotz seiner formalen Geltung als innerstaatliches Recht der Vertragsstaaten eine von den staatlichen Rechtssystemen abgehobene und eigenständige Qualität zu, die vom Kollisionsrecht verlangt werde.[210] Ob dies wirklich zutrifft (und ob dies ausreichen würde), ist zweifelhaft. Sowohl die Rom-I VO als auch das EGBGB a. F. schließen die kollisionsrechtliche Wählbarkeit des CISG aus.[211] Dies ist von der neuesten Rechtsprechung bestätigt worden.[212]

---

[205] Ebenso *Lohmann*, Parteiautonomie, S. 322; vgl. aber *Herber*, 2. Aufl., Art. 6, Rn. 31, der sich bei seinen Erläuterungen lediglich auf die materiellrechtliche Wahl bezieht, die kollisionsrechtliche Wählbarkeit also wohl ausschließt; so im Ergebnis auch *Honnold/Flechtner*, Art. 6, Rn. 84; vgl. auch *Schroeter*, VJ (2002), 257, 266, der die Möglichkeit der kollisionsrechtlichen Wahl des CISG als anwendbares Recht pauschal ausschließt; a. A. *Witz/Salger/Lorenz/Lorenz*, Art. 6, Rn. 21, die der Meinung vertreten, dass „vom Fall des Art. 34 EGBGB einmal abgesehen, [...] kein Grund ersichtlich [ist], weshalb die Wahl des UN-Kaufrechts nicht, wie jede andere Rechtswahl auch, zur Nichtanwendbarkeit zwingender Vorschriften des Forumstaats führt."

[206] Ebenso *Bianca/Bonell/Bonell*, Art. 6, Anm. 3.5.; *Ferrari u. a./Saenger*, Internationales Vertragsrecht, Art. 6, Rn. 7; *Karollus*, S. 39; *Lindbach*, S. 193; *Lohmann*, Privatautonomie, S. 310; *Merkt*, ZVerglRW 1994, 353, 377; MünchKommHGB/*Benicke*, Art. 1, Rn. 21; MünchKommHGB/*Benicke*, Art. 6, Rn. 17; *Schlechtriem*, Internationales UN-Kaufrecht, Rn. 23a; *Schlechtriem/Schwenzer/Schlechtriem*, CISG Commentary, 2. Aufl., Art. 6, Rn. 11 a. E.; *Schlechtriem/Schwenzer/Schwenzer/Hachem*, CISG Commentary, Art. 6, Rn. 34; *Siehr*, RabelsZ 52 (1988), 587, 612.; a. A. hinsichtlich des EVÜ bzw. EGBGB aber *Lohmann*, Parteiautonomie, S. 327 ff. und 352.

[207] Vgl. *Ferrari u. a./Ferrari*, 1. Aufl., Art. 27 EGBGB, Rn. 17; *Ferrari u. a./Ferrari*, Art. 3 Rom-I VO, Rn. 19; ebenso zum EVÜ bzw. EGBGB *Mankowski* RIW 2003, 2, 10 f.; MünchKommHGB/*Benicke*, Art. 6, Rn. 17; ebenso zum Rom-I VO *Gardella*, Nuove Leggi civ. commentate 2009, 611, 624; a. A. *Fountoulakis*, 7 EJLR, 2005, 303, 314: „From a conflict of law rules perspective, the choice of the CISG does not raise any difficulties [...]. It is a Convention and, as such, ‚hard law' of the same authoritative quality as any chosen domestic law". A. A. zur Rom-I VO auch *Schlechtriem/Schwenzer/Schwenzer/Hachem*, CISG Commentary, Art. 6, Rn. 34, wo die Autoren jedoch auf den Entwurf der Rom-I VO von 2005 verweisen, vom dem der europäische Gesetzgeber aber bezüglich gerade der im Text angesprochenen Frage radikal abgewandt hat.

[208] Vgl. Trib. Padova, 11.1.2005, CISG-online 967; a. A., in Bezug auf Art. 27 EGBGB, OLG Jena, 26.5.1998, CISG-online 513.

[209] Vgl. *Piltz*, NJW 1989, 615, 617; *Schlechtriem/Schwenzer/Schwenzer/Hachem*, CISG Commentary, Art. 6, Rn. 34; *Siehr*, RabelsZ 52 (1988), 587, 612.

[210] *Lindbach*, S. 203.

[211] So wohl auch *Staudinger/Magnus*, Art. 6, Rn. 65.

[212] Vgl. Tribunale di Padova, 11.1.2005, CISG-online 967.

Kapitel II. Allgemeine Bestimmungen

Art. 7 [Auslegung des Übereinkommens]

(1) Bei der Auslegung dieses Übereinkommens sind sein internationaler Charakter und die Notwendigkeit zu berücksichtigen, seine einheitliche Anwendung und die Wahrung des guten Glaubens im internationalen Handel zu fördern.

(2) Fragen, die in diesem Übereinkommen geregelte Gegenstände betreffen, aber in diesem Übereinkommen nicht ausdrücklich entschieden werden, sind nach den allgemeinen Grundsätzen, die diesem Übereinkommen zugrunde liegen, oder mangels solcher Grundsätze nach dem Recht zu entscheiden, das nach den Regeln des internationalen Privatrechts anzuwenden ist.

Art. 7

(1) In the interpretation of this Convention, regard is to be had to its international character and to the need to promote uniformity in its application and the observance of good faith in international trade.

(2) Questions concerning matters governed by this Convention which are not expressly settled in it are to be settled in conformity with the general principles on which it is based or, in the absence of such principles, in conformity with the law applicable by virtue of the rules of private international law.

Art. 7

1) Pour l'interprétation de la présente Convention, il sera tenu compte de son caractère international et de la nécessité de promouvoir l'uniformité de son application ainsi que d'assurer le respect de la bonne foi dans le commerce international.

2) Les questions concernant les matières régies par la présente Convention et qui ne sont pas expressément tranchées par elle seront réglées selon les principes généraux dont elle s'inspire ou, à défaut de ces principes, conformément à la loi applicable en vertu des règles du droit international privé.

Übersicht

	Rn.
I. Vorgeschichte	1
II. Allgemeines	4
III. Die Auslegung des Übereinkommens	8
1. Auslegungsgrundsätze	8
a) Internationaler Charakter und „autonome" Auslegung	9
b) Kritisches zur „autonomen" Auslegung	11
c) Die Notwendigkeit der Förderung der einheitlichen Anwendung und die Rechtsprechung anderer Staaten	15
d) Kritisches zur Beachtung ausländischer Rechtsprechung	18
e) Die Wahrung des guten Glaubens im internationalen Handel	25
2. Auslegungsmethoden	28
a) Wortlaut des Übereinkommens	30
b) Historische Auslegung	36
c) Systematische Auslegung	37
d) Rechtsvergleichung	40
IV. Lückenfüllung	41
1. Im Übereinkommen geregelte Gegenstände	42
2. Alternativen interner Lückenfüllung	44
3. Die allgemeinen Grundsätze des Übereinkommens	48
V. Rückgriff auf nationales Recht	57
VI. Lückenfüllung und UNIDROIT Principles	59
1. UNIDROIT Principles als objektiv anwendbares Recht	59
2. UNIDROIT Grundsätze, „interne" Lücken und Vertragsfreiheit	62

Vorläufer und **Entwürfe:** Art. 17 EKG; Genfer E 1976 Art. 13; Wiener E 1997 Art. 13; New Yorker E 1978 Art. 6.

I. Vorgeschichte

Art. 7 CISG hat keinen direkten Vorläufer im Haager Kaufrecht. Das EKG enthält zwar **1** eine sich mit der Lückenfüllung beschäftigende Vorschrift, Art. 17 EKG, die Art. 7 II CISG ähnelt,[1] da sie statuiert, dass die vom EKG erfassten, in diesem aber nicht ausdrücklich entschiedenen Fragen „nach den allgemeinen Grundsätzen zu entscheiden [sind], die diesem Gesetz zugrunde liegen", es enthält aber keine Vorschrift zur Auslegung des Einheitsrechts, d. h., keine Vorschrift, die sich mit den in Art. 7 I CISG angesprochenen Fragen beschäftigt.[2] Die heutige Fassung des Art. 7 I geht auf eine frühe Entscheidung zurück, zunächst nur einen allgemeinen Hinweis auf das Erfordernis der Rücksichtnahme auf den internationalen Charakter der Vorschriften des Übereinkommens bei ihrer Auslegung und Anwendung einzuführen.[3] Dieser Hinweis fand als Art. 13 Eingang in den Genfer E 1976.[4]

Im New Yorker E 1978 (Art. 6) wurde die Notwendigkeit der „Wahrung des guten **2** Glaubens im internationalen Handel" hinzugefügt.[5] Dieser Aufnahme des Hinweises auf den „guten Glauben", die erst spät erfolgte, obwohl ein Vorschlag zur Einbeziehung desselben bereits 1972 gemacht worden war,[6] war eine ausführliche Diskussion vorangegangen, da in der Arbeitsgruppe sowohl Gegner als auch Befürworter einer Einbeziehung des „guten Glaubens" stark vertreten waren.[7]

Auf der Diplomatischen Konferenz blieb dieser Teil der Vorschrift, der heutige Art. 7 I, **3** unverändert, mit Ausnahme der Streichung des Hinweises auf die „Anwendung" des Übereinkommens.[8] Es wurde jedoch nach längerer Diskussion[9] der Abs. 2 angefügt.[10] Diese Vorschrift geht auf einen Vorschlag der DDR zurück,[11] der, nachdem die Vorschläge Bulgariens,[12] der Tschechoslowakei[13] und Italiens[14] keine Zustimmung gefunden hatten,[15] diese kombinierte und schließlich mit knapper Mehrheit[16] angenommen wurde.[17]

II. Allgemeines

Diese Vorschrift, die sich fast wortgleich auch in den meisten neueren Einheitsvertrags- **4** rechtskonventionen findet,[18] enthält zwei anscheinend einfache Regeln, die wechselweise

---

[1] Vgl. auch *Sundermann*, Probleme der autonomen Auslegung, S. 30.
[2] So auch *Ferrari*, Vendita internazionale, S. 130; *Honnold/Flechtner*, Art. 7, Rn. 86, Fn. 1; *Melin*, S. 352.
[3] Der Entwurf lautete: „In interpreting and applying the provision of this law, regard shall be had to its international character and to the need to promote uniformity (in its interpretation and application)." Vgl. YB II (1971), S. 62.
[4] Vgl. YB VII (1976), S. 90.
[5] Dass die (Kaufvertrags-)Parteien „must observe the principles of fair dealing and act in good faith", war in dem – zunächst selbstständigen – Entwurf von Vorschriften für den Abschluss von Kaufverträgen vorgesehen (vgl. YB IX (1978), S. 67), der 1978 mit den materiellen Vorschriften vereinigt wurde.
[6] Vgl. YB III (1972), S. 76.
[7] Siehe *Keinath*, S. 82.
[8] Auf Antrag der USA und Frankreichs; vgl. O. R., S. 87; vgl. hierzu auch *Honsell/Melis*, Art. 7, Rn. 3.
[9] O. R., S. 255 ff.
[10] *Frigge*, S. 39.
[11] *Staudinger/Magnus*, Art. 7, Rn. 7.
[12] Der bulgarische Vorschlag ging dahin, bei nicht lösbaren Fragen immer auf das nationale Recht des Verkäufers zurückzugreifen; vgl. O. R., S. 255, Nr. 7 ff.
[13] Die Delegation der Tschechoslowakei schlug vor, auf das nationale, über den üblichen kollisionsrechtlichen Weg anwendbare Recht Rückgriff zu nehmen; O. R., S. 255, Nr. 10 ff.
[14] Der italienische Vorschlag ging dahin, zunächst auf die allgemeinen Grundsätze des Übereinkommens und bei Fehlen solcher auf das nationale Recht beider Vertragsparteien abzustellen; vgl. O. R., S. 256, Nr. 17; eine andere Interpretation des italienischen Vorschlags gibt *Herber*, 2. Aufl., Art. 6, Rn. 4, Fn. 10.
[15] *Frigge*, S. 39.
[16] Die Vorschrift wurde mit 17 : 14 Stimmen bei 11 Enthaltungen angenommen; siehe O. R., S. 257.
[17] *Herber*, 2. Aufl., Art. 7, Rn. 4.
[18] Vgl. *Kröll u. a./Perales Viscasillas*, Art. 7, Rn. 11; *MünchKommHGB/Ferrari*, Art. 4 FactÜ, Rn. 1; *Schlechtriem/Schwenzer/Schwenzer/Hachem*, CISG Commentary, Art. 7, Rn. 6; *Torsello*, Common Features, S. 157 ff.;

Art. 7 5
Teil I. Kapitel II. Allgemeine Bestimmungen

aufeinander einwirken,[19] anhand derer die angestrebte Rechtssicherheit sichergestellt werden soll,[20] die sich jedoch bei der Anwendung im Einzelfall als problematisch erweisen.[21]

5   Hinsichtlich der **Auslegung** stellt Abs. 1 **drei** – grundsäzlich gleichrangige –[22] **Auslegungsgrundsätze** auf:[23] Es soll auf die Herkunft der Normen („**internationaler Charakter**"),[24] auf den **Vereinheitlichungszweck** und schließlich auf die Förderung des „**guten Glaubens**" im Handelsverkehr Bedacht genommen werden. Die in Bezug auf diese Grundsätze von *Herber* geäußerte Ansicht,[25] dass die beiden ersten Grundsätze allen internationalen rechtsvereinheitlichenden Übereinkommen gemeinsam seien – und daher in gleicher Formulierung auch in anderen von UNCITRAL erarbeiteten Übereinkommen festgelegt seien,[26] während der Hinweis auf den „guten Glauben" eine Besonderheit des CISG sei, ist nicht haltbar. Dies ergibt sich unschwer aus der Tatsache, dass sich die Vorschrift in ihrer jetzigen Formulierung (also einschließlich der Bezugnahme auf den „guten Glauben"), wie bereits erwähnt,[27] in verschiedenen Konventionen entweder wortgleich[28] oder mit nur geringen Änderungen[29] findet.[30] Auch der Ansicht, die Bezugnahme auf den „guten Glauben" richte sich nicht nur auf die Auslegung der Vorschriften, sondern auch auf das Verhalten der Parteien, und könne daher mit § 242 BGB verglichen werden,[31] ist nicht ohne weiteres zuzustimmen.[32] Hierauf soll jedoch andernorts näher eingegangen werden.[33] Diese Meinungsverschiedenheit zeigt aber bereits, dass die anscheinend einfache Regel zu Problemen führen kann;[34] auf diese wird unten eingegangen.

---

vgl. in der Rechtsprechung Audiencia Provincial de Valencia, 7.6.2003, CISG-online 948, wonach die in Art. 7 festgeschriebenen Auslegungsgrundsätze einen „Standard" für internationales Handelsrecht darstellen.

[19] So ausdrücklich *Kröll u. a. /Perales Viscasillas*, Art. 7, Rn.; *Magnus*, CISG Methodology, S. 33, 39; *Sollund*, Nordic L.J. (2007), 1, 5; *Schlechtriem/Schwenzer/Schlechtriem*, CISG Commentary, 2. Aufl., Art. 7, Rn. 5; *Staudinger/Magnus*, Art. 7, Rn. 9.

[20] *Bailey*, 32 Cornell Int'l L.J. (1999), 273, 292; *Ferrari u. a./Saenger*, Art. 7, Rn. 1 f.; *Honsell/Siehr*, Art. 7, Rn. 2, *Schmid*, Einheitliche Anwendung, S. 30.

[21] *Herber*, 2. Aufl., Art. 7, Rn. 5; *Paal* ZVglRWiss (2011), 64, 66; *Schlechtriem/Schwenzer/Schwenzer/Hachem*, CISG Commentary, Art. 7, Rn. 5.

[22] So *Flechtner*, FS Schwenzer, S. 493, 503 ff., der aber auch hervorhebt, dass die einzelnen Auslegungsgrundsätze zu unterschiedlichen Ergebnissen führen können.

[23] Vgl. *Diez-Picazo/Calvo Caravaca*, Art. 7, S. 103; *Felemegas*, Introduction, S. 10; *Flechtner*, FS Schwenzer, S. 493, 503; *Hoffmann*, Koordination, S. 278; *Honsell/Melis*, Art. 7, Rn. 3; *P. Huber/Mullis/P. Huber*, S. 7; *Melin*, S. 353; *T. M. Müller*, Beweislast, S. 12; *Pribetic*, Rev. CISG (2004/2005), 179, 189; *Rudolph*, Art. 7, Rn. 4; *Schlechtriem/Schwenzer/Schwenzer/Hachem*, CISG Commentary, Art. 7, Rn. 7; *Sollund*, Nordic L.J. (2007), 1, 6; *Witz/Salger/Lorenz/Witz*, Art. 7, Rn. 7; für eine ausdrückliche Erwähnung der drei im Text aufgezählten Auslegungsgrundsätze in der Rechtsprechung vgl. BGH, 2.3.2005, CISG-online 999 = IHR 2005, 158, 159.

[24] Für ausdrückliche Hinweise in der Rechtsprechung auf die Notwendigkeit, den internationalen Charakter des CISG zu berücksichtigen, vgl. *Forestal Guarani S. A. v. Daros International, Inc.*, U. S. Ct. App. (3rd Cir.), 21.7.2010, CISG-online 2112; Hof van Cassatie, 19.7.2009, CISG-online 1963; RB Breda, 27.2.2008, CISG Pace; BGH, 2.3.2005, CISG-online 999 = IHR 2005, 158; *Chicago Prime Packers, Inc. v. Northam Food Trading Co., et al.*, U. S. Dist. Ct. (N.D. Ill.), 21.5.2004, CISG-online 851; Netherlands Arbitration Institute, 15.10.2002, CISG-online 780; *Medical Marketing v. Internazionale Medico Scientifica*, U. S. Dist. Ct. (E.D. La.), 17.5.1999, CISG-online 387; *Delchi Carrier v. Rotorex*, U. S. Ct. App. (2nd Cir.), 6.12.1995, CISG-online 140; OLG Frankfurt a. M., 20.4.1994, CISG-online 125; BezG Laufen, 7.5.1993, CISG-online 136.

[25] *Herber*, 2. Aufl., Art. 7, Rn. 6 f.; ähnlich auch *Honsell/Melis*, Art. 7, Rn. 3.

[26] Siehe Art. 9 des Verjährungsübereinkommens und Art. 3 der Hamburg-Regeln von 1978.

[27] Vgl. oben Rn. 1.

[28] Vgl. Art. 6 des Genfer Übereinkommens über die Stellvertretung beim internationalen Warenkauf vom 17.2.1983, abgedruckt in Uniform L. Rev. 1983, 133 ff.

[29] Vgl. Art. 4 des UNIDROIT Übereinkommens über Internationales Factoring; Art. 6 des UNIDROIT Übereinkommens über Internationales Finanzierungsleasing; vgl. hierzu *Torsello*, Common Features, S. 165.

[30] Vgl. auch *Ferrari*, 17 J. L. & Com. (1998), 245, 246; *Hartwieg*, ZVerglRW 1993, 282, 285; *Schlechtriem/Schwenzer/Schlechtriem*, CISG Commentary, 2. Aufl., Art. 7, Rn. 7; *Staudinger/Magnus*, Art. 7, Rn. 8.

[31] *Herber*, 2. Aufl., Art. 7, Rn. 7; so neuerdings aber auch *Bamberger/Roth/Saenger*, Art. 7, Rn. 6.

[32] Vgl. *Ferrari*, Vendita internazionale, S. 145 ff.

[33] Siehe unten Rn. 25 ff.

[34] Vgl. zu den Problemen, die sich aus Art. 7 I ergeben, *Ferrari*, 17 J. L. & Com. (1998), 245.

Was die in **Abs. 2** enthaltene Regel für die **Lückenfüllung** angeht, so ist auch diese auf 6 den ersten Blick einfach: Die im Übereinkommen geregelten, aber nicht ausdrücklich entschiedenen „Gegenstände"[35] sind anhand der dem Übereinkommen zugrunde liegenden „allgemeinen Grundsätze" zu entscheiden.[36] Nur dann, wenn solche Grundsätze nicht festgestellt werden können, ist auf das nach dem anwendbaren Internationalen Privatrecht berufene nationale Recht zurückzugreifen.[37] Die Vorschrift stellt also eine **Rangfolge** auf:[38] Zunächst ist nach den **allgemeinen Grundsätzen** zu entscheiden; fehlen diese, kann auf **nationales Recht** zurückgegriffen werden.

So einfach diese Regel auf den ersten Blick erscheint, so schwer ist ihre praktische 7 Anwendung.[39] Dies hängt zum einen damit zusammen, dass nicht leicht festgestellt werden kann, welche Fragen vom Übereinkommen erfasst sind, ohne in diesem aber ausdrücklich entschieden zu sein.[40] Zum anderen ist dies darauf zurückzuführen, dass die Herausarbeitung der dem Übereinkommen zugrunde liegenden „allgemeinen Grundsätze" nicht unproblematisch ist.[41]

III. Die Auslegung des Übereinkommens

1. Auslegungsgrundsätze

Abs. 1, der im Verhältnis zum Haager Kaufrecht innovativ ist,[42] da dieses zwar eine dem 8 Abs. 2 ähnelnde Vorschrift enthält, aber keine, die sich mit Fragen der Auslegung beschäftigt,[43] die sich bei internationalen Übereinkommen wie dem CISG unweigerlich ergeben,[44] sieht einige Gesichtspunkte vor, die bei der Auslegung des Übereinkommens zu beachten sind. Sie betreffen allerdings nur die **Grundsätze** der Auslegung,[45] nicht deren **Methode**,[46] die deshalb ebenso wie im EKG[47] zu Problemen führen kann.[48] Im Folgenden soll erläutert werden, was die Grundsätze im Einzelnen bedeuten.

a) Internationaler Charakter und „autonome" Auslegung. Der Hinweis auf die 9 notwendige Rücksichtnahme auf den „internationalen Charakter" des Übereinkommens als Element, das bei der Auslegung zu berücksichtigen ist, wird in der Lehre[49] zu Recht so

---

[35] Der deutsche Text des EKG sprach – bei gleichem englischen und französischen Wortlaut („matters"/ „matières") von „Rechtsgebieten".
[36] *Schlechtriem/Schwenzer/Schlechtriem*, CISG Commentary, 2. Aufl., Art. 7, Rn. 8; vgl. auch Hof van Cassatie, 19.6.2009, CISG-online 1963.
[37] *Andreason*, B. Y. U. L. Rev. (1999), 351, 377.
[38] *Staudinger/Magnus*, Art. 7, Rn. 2.
[39] *Herber*, 2. Aufl., Art. 7, Rn. 8; zur Anwendung dieser Regel in der Praxis vgl. neuerdings *Ferrari*, Rev. dr. aff. int. 2003, 221 ff.; ders., 7 VJ 2003, 63 ff.; ders., FS Kritzer, S. 134 ff.
[40] *Schlechtriem/Schwenzer/Schlechtriem*, CISG Commentary, 2. Aufl., Art. 7, Rn. 9; vgl. hierzu auch *Ferrari*, Scope of Application, S. 96, 96 ff.
[41] Ähnlich auch *Ferrari*, JZ 1998, 9, 10.
[42] *Kröll u. a. /Perales Viscasillas*, Art. 7, Rn. 6; *Witz/Salger/Lorenz/Witz*, Art. 7, Rn. 3.
[43] Vgl. *Ferrari*, IPRax 1997, 64, Fn. 4.
[44] Siehe hierzu etwa *Bonell*, Riv. dir. civ. 986, II, 221, 223; *Ferrari*, Vendita internazionale, S. 128.
[45] So auch *Eörsi*, General Provisions, S. 2–1, 2–5; *P. Huber/Mullis/P. Huber*, S. 9 („guidelines").
[46] Ebenso *Amato*, 13 J. L. & Com. (1993), 1, 21; *Audit*, Vente internationale, S. 47; *Bamberger/Roth/Saenger*, Art. 7, Rn. 2; *Burkart*, S. 178; *Diez-Picazo/Calvo Caravaca*, Art. 7, S. 103; *Eiselen*, CISG Methodology, S. 61, 61; *Ferrari*, Vendita internazionale, S. 132; *Ferrari u. a./Saenger*, Internationales Vertragsrecht, Art. 7, Rn. 2; *Gruber*, Methoden, S. 119; *Happ*, RIW 1997, 376 f.; *Honsell/Melis*, Art. 7, Rn. 3; *Kindler*, Jb. I. R. 5 (1992), 201, 205; *Magnus*, CISG Methodology, S. 33, 40; *Melin*, S. 357; MünchKomm/*Westermann*, Art. 7, Rn. 3; *Roth/Happ*, Rev. dr. unif. 1997, 700; *Schmid*, Einheitliche Anwendung, S. 40; *Sundermann*, Probleme der autonomen Auslegung, S. 21; *Teichert*, S. 22; i. E. auch Staudinger/*Magnus*, Art. 7, Rn. 11; *Witz/Salger/Lorenz/Witz*, Art. 7, Rn. 7.
[47] Vgl. zur Auslegung des EKG eingehend *Dölle*, Bemerkungen zu Art. 17 des EKG, S. 138 ff.; *Dölle/Wahl*, Art. 17 EKG, Rn. 20 ff.; *Mertens/Rehbinder*, Art. 17 EKG, Rn. 7 ff.
[48] Siehe auch *Volken*, Scope, S. 19, 39.
[49] Auch in der Rechtsprechung ist auf die Notwendigkeit, den „internationalen Charakter" des Übereinkommens zu beachten, abgestellt worden; vgl. *Forestal Guarani S. A. v. Daros International, Inc.*, U. S. Ct App.

verstanden, dass bei Anwendung jeder Auslegungsmethode zu bedenken ist, dass das Übereinkommen das Ergebnis internationaler Vereinheitlichungsbestrebungen ist,[50] dass es also **nicht,** wie ein **nationales Gesetz,** auf dem Hintergrund einer einheitlichen nationalen Rechtsordnung, auf Grund eines meist klar erkennbaren Willens des Gesetzgebers und in einer durch bestehende Definitionen der verwendeten Begriffe und Formulierungen vorgezeichneten Gesetzessprache zustande gekommen ist.[51] Dies hat die Lehre – und die Rechtsprechung[52] – dazu geführt, von der Notwendigkeit einer **„autonomen Auslegung"** zu sprechen,[53] d. h., von der Notwendigkeit, „die Begriffe des CISG aus sich selbst heraus zu interpretieren [...]. Ein Rückgriff auf das nationale Recht des Anwenders oder auf bestimmte nationale Begriffe oder Verständnisse verbietet sich".[54] Gleiches gilt für

(3rd Cir.), 21.7.2010, CISG-online 2112; Hof van Cassatie, 19.7.2009, CISG-online 1963; RB Breda, 27.2.2008, CISG Pace; BGH, 2.3.2005, CISG-online 999 = IHR 2005, 158, 159; *Medical Marketing Internationl Inc. v. Interazionale Medico Scientifica S. r. l.,* U. S. Dist. Ct. (E. D. La.), 17.5.1999, CISG-online 387 = 1999 U. S. Dist. LEXIS 7380; *Rotorex Corp. v. Delchi Carrier S. p. A.,* U. S. Ct. App. (2nd Cir.), 6.12.1995, CISG-online 140 = 71 F. 3d 1024 ff.; OLG Frankfurt a. M., RIW 1994, 593; BezG Laufen, 7.5.1993, CISG-online 136 = SZIER 1995, 277.
[50] Vgl. auch *Bianca/Bonell/Bonell,* Art. 7, Anm. 2.2.2.; *Ferrari,* IHR 2001, 56, 57; *Honsell/Melis,* Art. 7, Rn. 5; *Loewe,* S. 32.
[51] *Bailey,* 32 Cornell Int'l L. J. (1999), 273, 288; *Felemegas,* Introduction, S. 10; *Hager,* FS Huber, S. 319, 320; *Herber,* TransportR-IHR 1999, 2; *Karollus,* S. 11; *Romito/Sant'Elia,* 14 Pace Int'l L. Rev. (2002), 179, 186; *Herber,* 2. Aufl., Art. 7, Rn. 11; *Sannini,* L'applicazione, S. 3; *Schlechtriem/Schwenzer/Schlechtriem,* CISG Commentary, 2. Aufl., Art. 7, Rn. 11; *Sundermann,* Probleme der autonomen Auslegung, S. 34 f.
[52] So ausdrücklich etwa *RJ & AM Smallmon v. Transport Sales Limited,* Court of Appeal New Zealand, 22.7.2011, CISG-online 2215; *RJ & AM Smallmon v. Transport Sales Limited,* High Court of New Zealand, 30.7.2010, CISG-online 2113; Tribunale di Forlì, 16.2.2009, CISG-online 1780; Court of First Instance of Athens, Aktenzeichen 4505/2009 (ohne Datum); Tribunale di Modena, 9.12.2005, CISG-online 1398 = Riv. dir. int. priv. proc. 2007, 387, 390; OGH, 23.5.2005, CISG-online 1041 = 2005 IHR, 165, 167; BGH, 2.3.2005, CISG-online 999 = IHR 2005, 158, 159; Tribunale di Padova, 11.1.2005, CISG-online 967; OLG München, 15.9.2004, CISG-online 1013 = IHR 2005, 70, 71; OLG Düsseldorf, 21.4.2004, CISG-online 915; OLG Düsseldorf, 21.4.2004, CISG-online 914 = IHR 2005, 24, 27; Tribunale di Padova, 25.2.2004, CISG-online 819 = Giur. it. 2004, 1402, 1403; KG Schaffhausen, 27.1.2004, CISG-online 960; BGH, 24.3.1999, CISG-online 396 = NJW 1999, 2440 ff.; HGer Aargau, 26.9.1997, CISG-online 329.
[53] Vgl. etwa *Achilles,* Art. 7, Rn. 3; *Audit,* Vente internationale, S. 47; *Bamberger/Roth/Saenger,* Art. 7, Rn. 2; *Bazinas,* Uniformity, S. 19; *Bianca/Bonell/Bonell,* Art. 7, Anm. 2.2.2.; *Bonell,* Dr. prat. comm. int. 1981, 7, 14; *ders.,* Nuove leggi civ. comm. 1989, 21; *Bridge,* Draft Digest, S. 235, 249; *Brunner,* Art. 7, Rn. 2; *Butler,* Annals Fac. L. Belgrade 2011, 7, 7 f.; *Dejaco,* S. 42; *Diedrich,* 8 Pace Int'l L. Rev. (1996), 303, 303; *Eiselen,* CISG Methodology, S. 61, 74; *Felemegas,* Interpretation, S. 11; *ders.,* Rev. CISG (2000/2001), 115, 235; *Ferrari,* Rev. int. dr. comp. 1996, 813, 827; *Ferrari u. a./Saenger,* Internationales Vertragsrecht, Art. 7, Rn. 2 und 4; *Frignani/Torsello,* Il contratto internazionale, S. 464; *Gebauer,* Uniform L. Rev. 2000, 683, 686; *Graffi,* Giur. merito 2004, 873, 874 f.; *Grieser,* S. 75; *Gruber,* Methoden, S. 79 ff.; *Hackney,* 61 La. L. Rev. (2001), 473, 475; *Hager,* FS Huber, S. 319, 320; *Hagstrøm,* IHR 2006, 246; *Hoffmann,* Koordination, S. 279; *P. Huber,* IHR 2006, 228, 229; *P. Huber/Mullis/P. Huber,* S. 7; *Jametti Greiner,* Der Vertragsabschluß, S. 43, 57; *Janssen,* IHR 2004, 194, 199; *Jurewicz,* 28 J. L. & Com. (2009), 63, 68; *Karollus,* S. 11; *Komarov,* 25 J. L. & Com. (2006), 75, 78; *Kröll u. a./Perales Viscasillas,* Art. 7, Rn. 13; *Leisinger,* Fundamental Breach, S. 1; *Leyens,* Rev. CISG (2003–2004), 3, 26; *Loewe,* S. 32; *Lohmann,* Parteiautonomie, S. 3; *Magnus,* Konventionsübergreifende Interpretation, S. 571, 572; *ders.,* CISG Methodology, S. 33, 40; *Markel,* 21 Pace Int'l L. Rev. (2009), 163, 196; *Mazzotta,* 3 Loy. Univ. Chi. Int'l L. Rev. (2005), 85, 101; *Martinez Canellas,* S. 119 ff.; *McMahon,* 44 Colum. J. Transnat'l L. (2006), 992, 993 und 1000; *Melin,* S. 355; *T. M. Müller,* Beweislast, S. 12; MünchKomm/*Westermann,* Vor Art. 1, Rn. 1 und Art. 7, Rn. 1; *T. M. Müller/Togo,* IHR 2005, 102, 102; *Najork,* S. 53; *Naumann,* S. 166; *Niemann,* S. 41; *Pavic/Djordjevic,* 28 J. L. & Com. (2009), 1, 24; *Perea,* 20 Pace Int'l L. Rev. (2008), 191, 201 f.; *Piltz,* FS Schwenzer, S. 1387, 1393; *ders.,* IHR 2005, 160; *ders.,* Rn. 2–185; *Reinhart,* Art. 7, Rn. 2; *Sannini* L'applicazione, S. 3; *Sauthoff,* IHR 2005, 151, 153; *Schlechtriem/Schwenzer/Schwenzer/Hachem,* CISG Commentary, Art. 7, Rn. 8; *Schmid,* Einheitliche Anwendung, S. 42; *Teichert,* S. 21; *Vazquez Lepinette,* Dir. comm. int. 1995, 377, 387 f.; *Schlechtriem,* Internationales UN-Kaufrecht, Rn. 43; *Schlechtriem/Schwenzer/Schlechtriem,* CISG Commentary, 2. Aufl., Art. 7, Rn. 11; *Schmitt,* CR 2001, 145, 147; *Schwenzer/Hachem/Kee,* Rn. 3.54; *Soergel/Lüderitz/Fenge,* Art. 7, Rn. 2; *Sollund,* Nordic L. J. (2007), 1, 6; *Sundermann,* Probleme der autonomen Auslegung, S. 17 und 25 ff.; *Ubartaite,* 7 (EJLR), 2005, 277, 292; *Witz/Salger/Lorenz/Witz,* Art. 7, Rn. 8.
[54] *Staudinger/Magnus,* Art. 7, Rn. 12; vgl. diesbezüglich auch *Babiak,* 6 Temp. Int'l & Comp. L. J. (1992), 113, 117; *Basedow,* 50 Jahre BGH, S. 779 f.; *Brunner,* Art. 7, Rn. 2; *Cetiner,* S. 28; *Dejaco,* S. 42; *Diedrich,* Autonome Auslegung, S. 77 ff.; *Eiselen,* CISG Methodology, S. 61, 74; *Ferrari,* IPRax 1997, 64, 65; *Ferrari u. a./Saenger,* Art. 7, Rn. 4; *Flechtner,* FS Schwenzer, S. 493, 497 f.; *Graffi,* Giur. merito 2004, 873, 875; *ders.,* Dir. comm. int. 2003, 807, 810; *Hackney,* 61 La. L. Rev. (2001), 473, 477; *Heuzé,* Anm. 95.; *Honsell/Melis,* Art. 7,

nationale Auslegungskriterien:[55] Das Übereinkommen darf nicht anhand nationaler Kriterien ausgelegt werden,[56] da dies der angestrebten Vereinheitlichung abträglich wäre,[57] unterscheiden sich die Auslegungskriterien in den verschiedenen Staaten doch stark voneinander.[58] Diesbezüglich kann der **Rückgriff auf die Lehre,** der sowohl von Vertretern des civil law[59] als auch des common law[60] immer wieder vorgeschlagen worden ist, durchaus hilfreich sein, zumindest dann, wenn sich diese nicht auf eine Beschreibung des Übereinkommens im Lichte rein nationalen Rechts beschränkt.[61]

Das Prinzip, das heute allgemein für die Auslegung von internationalen Einheitsrechtskonventionen (sowohl materiell-,[62] als auch kollisions-[63] und prozessrechtlichen In-

---

Rn. 5; *Lookofsky,* 13 Duke J. Comp. & Int'l L. (2003), 263, 265; *Markel,* 21 Pace Int'l L. Rev. (2009), 163, 196; *Martinez Canellas,* S. 120; *Mattera,* 16 Pace Int'l L. Rev. (2004), 165, 190; *Mazzotta,* 3 Loy. Univ. Chi. Int'l L. Rev. (2005), 85, 93; *Melin,* S. 355; MünchKomm/ *Westermann,* Art. 7, Rn. 4; *Niemann,* S. 30; *Piltz,* Internationales Kaufrecht, Rn. 2–185; *Schlechtriem,* Internationales UN-Kaufrecht, Rn. 43; *Schmid,* Einheitliche Anwendung, S. 41 f.; *Spagnolo,* 10 Melb. J. Int'l L. (2009), 141, 165; *Sundermann,* Probleme der autonomen Auslegung, S. 25 f. Und 30 f.; *Torzilli,* 74 St. John's L. Rev. (2000), 843, 859.

Vgl. in der Rechtsprechung *RJ & AM Smallmon v. Transport Sales Limited,* Court of Appeal New Zealand, 22.7.2011, CISG-online 2215 („In reading and understanding the provisions, concepts and words of the Convention, recourse to the understanding of these words and the like in domestic systems, in particular the domestic legal system of the reader, must be avoided"); *RJ & AM Smallmon v. Transport Sales Limited and Grant Alan Miller,* High Court of New Zealand, 30.7.2010, CISG-online 2113 („[to interpret the CISG autonomously], means [that] the Convention must be applied and interpreted exclusively on its own terms, having regard to the principles of the Convention and Convention-related decisions in overseas jurisdictions. Recourse to domestic case law is to be avoided"); American Arbitration Association, 23.10.2007, CISG-online 1645 („[m]aterial for interpretation of the Convention unless [the Convention] expressly provides otherwise, must be taken from the Convention itself"); BGH, 2.3.2005, CISG-online 999 = IHR 2005, 158, 159: „Die Vorschriften des CISG sind autonom, […] ohne Rückgriff auf die zu den Normen des unvereinheitlichten nationalen Rechts entwickelten Regeln auszulegen"; OLG Karlsruhe, 25.6.1997, CISG-online 263: „deutschrechtliche Begriffe wie ‚Fehler' bzw. ‚zugesicherte Eigenschaften' sind […] auf das CISG nicht übertragbar"; BezG Laufen, 7.5.1993, CISG-online 136 = SZIER 1995, 277: „[Das Übereinkommen] soll aus sich heraus ausgelegt werden, und nicht aus der Sicht des jeweils nationalen Rechts des Rechtsanwenders." Sehr kritisch gegenüber der Möglichkeit, das CISG effektiv nicht im Lichte des nationalen Rechts auszulegen, *Cuniberti,* 39 Vand. J. Transnat'l L. (2006), 1511, 1517.

A. etwa *Hilaturas Miel, S. L. v. Republic of Iraq,* U. S. Dist. Ct. (S. D. N. Y.), 20.8.2008, CISG-online 1777; *Macromex Srl. v. Globex International, Inc.,* U. S. Dist. Ct. (S. D. N. Y.), 16.4.2008, CISG-online 1653; *Genpharm Inc. v. Pliva-Lachema A.S,* U. S. Dist. Ct. (E. D. N. Y.), 19.3.2005, CISG-online 1006; *Raw Materials Inc. v. Manfred Forberich GmbH & Co., KG,* U. S. Dist. Ct., (N. D. Ill.), 6.7.2004, CISG-online 1665.

[55] *Bariatti,* S. 160; *Bazinas,* Uniformity, S. 18; *Bianca/Bonell/Bonell,* Art. 7, Anm. 2.2.; *Bonell,* Nuove legg civ. comm. 1989, 20, 20; *Burkart,* S. 127 ff.; *de Lucowicz,* S. 24; *Dejaco,* S. 42; *Felemegas,* Introduction, S. 11; *Ferrari,* Vendita internazionale, S. 134; *ders.,* Int. Bus. L. J. 2003, 221, 222; *Frigge,* S. 107; *Gruber,* Methoden, S. 80; *P. Huber/Mullis/P. Huber,* S. 9; *Kröll u. a./Perales Viscasillas,* Art. 7, Rn. 18; MünchKomm/*Westermann,* Art. 7, Rn. 4; *Romito/Sant'Elia,* 14 Pace Int'l L. Rev. (2002), 179, 185; *Schlechtriem/Schwenzer/Schlechtriem,* CISG Commentary, 2. Aufl., Art. 7, Rn. 12; *Schlechtriem/Schwenzer/Schmidt-Kessel,* CISG Commentary, Art. 8, Rn. 1; *Schmid,* Einheitliche Anwendung, S. 41; *Spagnolo,* 10 Melb. J. Int'l L. (2009), 141, 166; *Teichert,* S. 22; *Zeller,* 12 Pace Int'l L. Rev. (2000), 79, 85; für einen Überblick der nationalen Auslegungskriterien, vgl. *Gruber,* Methoden, S. 114 ff.

[56] So ausdrücklich auch (in Bezug jedoch auf eine vom Übereinkommen verschiedene Konvention) Cass. civ., 24.6.1968, Nr. 2106, Riv. dir. int priv. proc. 1969, 914; vgl. zu diesem Urteil *Bonell,* Riv. dir. civ. 1986, II, 221, 225; in verschiedenen Staaten hat die Rechtsprechung aber auf nationale Auslegungskriterien Rückgriff genommen, um internationale Übereinkommen zu interpretieren; vgl. hierzu *Bayer,* RabelsZ 20 (1955), 603 ff.; *Mann,* L. Q. R. (1946), 279 ff.

[57] *Gruber,* Methoden, S. 62; zu den Gefahren, die eine nicht „autonome" Auslegung internationalen Einheitsrechts mit sich bringt, vgl. statt aller *Sturley,* 27 Va. J. Int'l L. (1986), 729, 733 ff.

[58] Vgl. diesbezüglich *Diedrich,* Autonome Auslegung, S. 59 ff.; *Kötz,* RabelsZ 50 (1986), 1, 8; *Gorriz Lopez,* Contr. imp. E 1998, 467, 467 f.; *Gruber,* Methoden, S. 6 ff.; *Magnus,* RabelsZ 53 (1989), 116, 122.

[59] *Ferrari,* Vendita internazionale, S. 143; *ders.,* Int. Bus. L. J. 2003, 221, 222; *Herber/Czerwenka,* Art. 7, Rn. 5; *Witz/Salger/Lorenz/Witz,* Art. 7, Rn. 10.

[60] Vgl. *Amato,* 13 J. L. & Com. (1993), 1, 28; *Hackney,* 61 La. L. Rev. (2001), 473, 478; *Honnold,* Uniform Words, S. 126; *ders.,* 8 J. L. & Com. (1988), 207, 208 f.; *Schultz,* 35 Cornell Int'l L. J. (2002), 263, 268; *Spagnolo,* 10 Melb. J. Int'l L. (2009), 141, 166.

[61] *Ferrari,* IPRax 1997, 64 f.

[62] Siehe etwa Art. 4 I des UNIDROIT Übereinkommens über Internationales Factoring; Art. 6 I des UNIDROIT Übereinkommens über Internationales Finanzierungsleasing.

[63] Vgl. Art. 18 des EG-Übereinkommens über das auf vertragliche Schuldverhältnisse anzuwendende Recht.

Art. 7 10 Teil I. Kapitel II. Allgemeine Bestimmungen

halts[64]) gilt,[65] wonach eine sich an „nationalen" Begriffen oder Auslegungskriterien orientierende Interpretation zu vermeiden ist,[66] ist grundsätzlich, so auch die Rechtsprechung,[67] ebenfalls in Bezug auf die (wenigen) Fälle zu beachten, in denen die Originalfassungen des Übereinkommens[68] **Ausdrücke** verwenden, mit denen **in einer bestimmten Rechtsordnung ein spezifisches juristisches Konzept** verbunden wird[69] (man denke nur an die Ausdrücke „dommages-intérêts", „breach of contract", „good faith",[70] etc.),[71] zumindest soweit Rechtsinstitute nicht gezielt aus einer Rechtsordnung übernommen wurden.[72] Ergibt sich aus der Entstehungsgeschichte aber, dass nationale Vorstellungen hinter bestimmten Begriffen stehen, „darf für ihr Verständnis und die Auslegung der entsprechenden Vorschriften berücksichtigt werden, welchem Zweck sie im Herkunftsrecht dienen".[73]

---

[64] Auch in Bezug auf das EuGVÜ geht die Lehre trotz Fehlens einer entsprechenden Vorschrift von der Notwendigkeit der „autonomen" Auslegung aus; vgl. *Kropholler*, EUZPR, Rn. 45; vgl. in der Rechtsprechung *Shearson/TVB*, EuGH Slg. 1993, I, 186, Rn. 13; *Mulox./.Geels*, EuGH Slg. 1993, I, 4102, Rn. 10.

[65] Ebenso *Ferrari*, ZEuP 1998, 162, 165; *Hartwieg*, ZVerglRW 1993, 282, 285; *Niemann*, S. 41 f.; *Schlechtriem*, Internationales UN-Kaufrecht, Rn. 43; *Schmid*, Einheitliche Anwendung, S. 58 ff.

[66] Vgl. auch *Babiak*, 6 Temp. Int'l & Comp. L. J. (1992), 113, 117; *Ferrari u. a./Saenger*, Art. 7, Rn. 4; *Kröll u. a./Perales Viscasillas*, Art. 7, Rn. 12; *Graffi*, Divergences, S. 305, 307 f.; MüKommBGB/*Westermann*, Art. 7, Rn. 4; *Niemann*, S. 30 f.; *Plantard*, J. D. I. 1988, 311, 329; vgl. in der Rechtsprechung Tribunale di Padova, 25.2.2004, CISG-online 819 = Giur. it. 2004, 1402, 1403.

[67] Vgl. *Orbisphere Corp. v. United States*, Ct. Int'l Trade, 24.10.1989, CISG-online 7 = 726 F. Supp. 1344, 1355, wo darauf hingewiesen wird, dass, obwohl der UCC und das CISG sich zum Teil sehr ähneln, „UCC caselaw is not per se applicable"; so auch *Delchi Carrier S. p. A. v. Rotorex Corp.*, U. S. Ct. App. (2nd Cir.), 6.12.1995, CISG-online 140 = 71 F. 3d 1024, 1028; vgl. ferner *Calzaturificio Claudia S. n. c. v. Olivieri Footwear Ltd.*, U. S. Dist. Ct. (S. D. N. Y.), 6.4.1998, CISG-online 440 = 1998 WL 164 824: „although the CISG is similar to the UCC with respect to certain provisions, [...] it would be inappropriate to apply UCC case law in construing contracts under the CISG". Eine ähnliche, sich aber auf das deutsche Recht beziehende Feststellung findet sich auch in einem Urteil des BGH, 3.4.1996, CISG-online 135 = JZ 1997, 35 ff.: demnach „unterscheidet sich das CISG vom deutschen Recht, dessen Vorschriften und spezielle Prinzipien bei der Auslegung des UN-Kaufrechts grundsätzlich unanwendbar sind". A. A. jedoch *Chicago Prime Packers, Inc. v. Northam Food Trading Co.*, U. S. Ct. App. (7th Cir.), 23.5.2005, CISG-online 1026 = 2005 WL 1 243 344 (7th Cir. (Ill.)): „Many provisions of the UCC and the CISG are the same or similar, and ‚[c]aselaw interpreting analogous provisions of Article 2 of the [UCC], may [...] inform a court where the language of the relevant CISG provision tracks that of the UCC"; ebenso *Hilaturas Miel, S. L. v. Republic of Iraq*, U. S. Dist. Ct. (S. D. N. Y.), 20.8.2008, CISG-online 1777; *Macromex Srl. v. Globex International, Inc.*, U. S. Dist. Ct. (S. D. N. Y.), 16.4.2008, CISG-online 1653; American Arbitration Association, 23.10.2007, CISG-online 1645; *Genpharm Inc. v. Pliva-Lachema A.S*, U. S. Dist. Ct. (E. D. N. Y.), 19.3.2005, CISG-online 1006; *Raw Materials Inc. v. Manfred Forberich GmbH & Co., KG*, U. S. Dist. Ct. (N. D. Ill., E. D.) 6.7.2004, CISG-online 925 = 2004 WL 1 535 839 (N. D. Ill.); vgl. auch *Travelers Property Casualty Company of America et al. v. Saint-Gobain Technical Fabrics Canada Limited*, U. S. Dist. Ct. (Minn.), 31.1.2007, CISG-online 1435 = 2007 WL 313 591 (D. Minn.); *Schmitz-Werke GmbH/Co. v. Rockland Industries, Inc., Rockland International FS C, Inc.*, U. S. Ct. App. (4th Cir.), 21.6.2002, CISG-online 625 = 2002 U. S. App. LEXIS 12 336; krit. hierzu etwa *Ferrari*, IHR 2009, 8, 14 ff.; *Lookofsky/Flechtner*, 9 VJ (2005), 199 ff.; *Mazzotta*, 3 Loy. Univ. Chi. Int'l L. Rev. (2005), 85, 89 ff.

[68] Die (sechs gleichwertigen) Originalfassungen des Übereinkommens sind abgedruckt in *Bianca/Bonell*, S. 683 ff.

[69] So auch *Bailey*, 32 Cornell Int'l L. J. (1999), 273, 289; *Diedrich*, Autonome Auslegung, S. 74; *Ferrari*, ZEuP 1998, 162, 166; *ders.*, IHR 2001, 56, 57–58; *Gruber*, Methoden, S. 193; *Hager*, FS Huber, S. 319, 320; *Kropholler*, Internationales Einheitsrecht, S. 265; *Mazzotta*, 3 Loy. Univ. Chi. Int'l L. Rev. (2005), 85, 93; *Mertens/Rehbinder*, Art. 17 EKG, Rn. 13; *T. M. Müller*, Beweislast, S. 17; *Niemann*, S. 31 und 42; *Sauthoff*, IHR 2005, 151, 153; *Schlechtriem/Schwenzer/Schlechtriem*, CISG Commentary, 2. Aufl., Art. 7, Rn. 13; *Schlechtriem/Schwenzer/Schwenzer/Hachem*, CISG Commentary, Art. 7, Rn. 9; *Sollund*, Nordic L. J. (2007), 1, 7; *Stephan*, 39 Va. J. Int'l L. (1999), 743, 774; vgl. in der Rechtsprechung *MCC-Marble Ceramic Inc. v. Ceramica Nuova d'Agostino S. p. A.*, U. S. Ct. App. (11th Cir.), 29.6.1998, CISG-online 342 = 144 F. 3d 1384, 1391; a. A. jedoch *Andreason*, B. Y. U. L. Rev. (1999), 351, 355; *Dimatteo*, 23 Syracuse J. Int'l L. & Com. (1997), 67, 79.

[70] Vgl. hierzu bereits *Ferrari*, 29 Loy. L. A. L. Rev. (1996), 1021, 1026.

[71] *Burkart*, S. 146; *Ferrari*, ZEuP 1998, 162, 166; *Honnold/Flechtner*, Art. 7, Rn. 87.

[72] Vgl. RB Zwolle, 5.3.1997, CISG-online 545, wonach der „gute Glaube" des französischen Rechts nicht mit dem des CISG übereinstimme.

[73] *Staudinger/Magnus*, Art. 7, Rn. 13; im Ergebnis ebenso *Achilles*, Art. 7, Rn. 3; *Bamberger/Roth/Saenger*, Art. 7, Rn. 4; *Ferrari*, ZEuP 1998, 162, 166; *Ferrari u. a./Saenger*, Art. 7, Rn. 4; *Herber*,

Auslegung des Übereinkommens   11, 12 **Art. 7**

b) Kritisches zur „autonomen" Auslegung. Aus dem im vorigen Absatz Gesagten 11
ergibt sich unschwer, dass trotz der anscheinend einfachen Regel die „autonome" Auslegung des Übereinkommens problematisch ist: Die Konventionsgeber haben versucht, um der Gefahr der „nationalen" Auslegung so weit als möglich vorzubeugen,[74] immer neutrale,[75] nicht auf bestimmte Rechtsordnungen gründende Termini zu benutzen,[76] was neuerdings auch von der Rechtsprechung hervorgehoben worden ist[77] (und weshalb auch vom CISG als einer „lingua franca" gesprochen worden ist).[78] Dies ist jedoch nicht immer möglich gewesen,[79] was angesichts der Vielzahl der an der Ausarbeitung beteiligten Delegationen durchaus verständlich ist. Dies führt unweigerlich zu Rechtsunsicherheit. Als Beispiel sei diesbezüglich der um die Auslegung des Begriffs der „Gültigkeit" entstandene Meinungsstreit erwähnt:[80] Während ein Teil der Lehre – zu Recht[81] – davon ausgeht, dass der Begriff „autonom" auszulegen sei,[82] vertritt ein anderer Teil der Lehre die Ansicht, man müsse auf nationales Recht abstellen.[83]

Art. 7 sieht jedoch keine absolute Pflicht vor, alle Termini autonom auszulegen.[84] Die 12
meisten Begriffe sind autonom auszulegen;[85] es gibt jedoch durchaus Begriffe, die „na-

---

[2]. Aufl., Art. 7, Rn. 13; *Hoffmann*, Koordination, S. 280; *Niemann*, S. 42; vgl. auch *Gruber*, Methoden, S. 85: „‚Autonom auszulegen' ist ein Begriff des internationalen Einheitsrechts [...] nur dann, wenn er im Ergebnis der Auslegung inhaltlich von dem (in Hinblick auf Wortlaut oder Funktion vergleichbaren) Begriff der nationalen Rechtsordnung des Richters abweicht". Vgl. auch *Schlechtriem/Schwenzer/Schwenzer/Hachem*, CISG Commentary, Art. 7, Rn. 9, wo jedoch zumindest ein falsches Beispiel genannt wird (Fn. 24). So verkennen *Schwenzer/Hachem* etwa, dass Art. 74 CISG nicht nach der *Hadley v. Baxendale*-Regel modelliert ist; ebenso *Sundermann*, Probleme der autonomen Auslegung, S. 35; vgl. hierzu ausführlich *Ferrari*, Foreseeability, S. 305 ff.

[74] Vgl. diesbezüglich *Honnold*, 8 J. L. & Com. (1988), 207, 208, der hervorhebt, dass die im Text erwähnte Gefahr der nationalen Auslegung unausweichlich ist: „One threat to international uniformity in interpretation is a natural tendency to read the international text through the lenses of domestic law"; vgl. hierzu auch *Bayer*, RabelsZ 20 (1955), 603, 635; *Diedrich*, Autonome Auslegung. S. 58; *Ferrari*, Vendita internazionale, S. 133; ders., 17 J. L. & Com. (1998), 245, 246; *Flechtner*, 17 J. L. & Com. (1998), 187, 204; *Rizzi*, Riv. dir. priv. 1997, 237, 239.

[75] So auch *Honnold/Flechtner*, Art. 7, Rn. 87, der von „plain language" spricht; vgl. auch *Ferrari*, Uniform Interpretation, S. 3, 9; ders., Int. Bus. L. J. 1998, 495, 497; *Martinez Canellas*, S. 127; *Walt*, 39 Va. J. Int'l L. (1999), 671, 699; *Zeller*, 23 J. L. & Com. (2004), 39, 39; vgl. auch *Melin*, S. 333 (ohne spezifischen Bezug auf das CISG). Zur Neutralität des CISG als einer der Gründe, warum es als „neutral law" in internationalen Kaufverträgen gewählt werden sollte, vgl. *Fountoulakis*, 7 (EJLR), 2005, 303, 314.

[76] *Crawford*, 8 J. L. & Com. (1988), 187, 190; *Ferrari*, IPRax 1997, 64; *Plantard*, J. D. I. 1988, 311, 328; *Zeller*, CISG and the Unification, S. 17.

[77] *St. Paul Guardian Insurance Co., et al. v. Neuromed Medical Systems & Support, et al.*, U. S. Dist. Ct. (S. D. N. Y.), 26.3.2002, CISG-online 615 = 2002 U. S. Dist. LEXIS 5096 = IHR 2005, 256, 257, wo von „non-nation specific language" die Rede ist.

[78] Vgl. *Andersen*, Global Jurisconsultorium, S. 37; *Schlechtriem*, 36 Vict. U. Well. L. Rev. (2005), 781, 782.

[79] Vgl. auch *Niemann*, S. 42.

[80] Näher hierzu Art. 4 Rn. 15 ff.

[81] Vgl. *Ferrari*, Vendita internazionale, S. 96.

[82] So etwa *Bonell*, Nuove leggi civ. comm. 1989, 20, 21; *Diéz-Picazo/Rojo Ajura*, Art. 4, S. 77; *Enderlein/Maskow/Strohbach*, Art. 4, Anm. 3.1.; *Heiz*, 20 Vand. J. Transnat'l L. (1987), 639, 660 f.; *Herber/Czerwenka*, Art. 4, Rn. 13; *Honnold/Flechtner*, Art. 4, Rn. 65, 204.2 und 234; *Piltz*, Internationales Kaufrecht, Rn. 2–147 f.; ders., IHR 2002, 2, 5; *Winship*, 8 Nw. J. Int'l L. & Bus. (1988), 623, 637.

[83] Für eine nationale Auslegung sprechen sich aus: *Bianca/Bonell/Tallon*, Art. 79 Anm. 2.4.3.; *Bydlinski*, Allgemeines Vertragsrecht, S. 57, 85 f.; 123; *Heuzé* Anm. 94.; *Lessiak*, JBl. 1989, 487, 492 f.; *Longobardi*, 53 Fordham L. Rev. (1985), 863, 874; *Neumayer/Ming*, Art. 4, Anm. 2., 6. f.; *Reinhart*, Art. 4, Rn. 5; *Ziegel*, Vienna Convention, S. 38, 43.

[84] Vgl. *Ferrari*, Uniform Interpretation, S. 3, 9 ff.; ders., Int. Bus. L. J. 1998, 495, 497; *Melin*, S. 357; *Romito/Sant'Elia*, 14 Pace Int'l L. Rev. (2002), 179, 185; *Sundermann*, Probleme der autonomen Auslegung, S. 35.

[85] Vgl. hierzu in der Rechtsprechung Tribunale di Forlì, 16.2.2009, CISG-online 1780 (autonome Auslegung der Begriffe des Kaufvertrages, der Waren und der Niederlassung); Tribunale di Forlì, 11.12.2008, CISG-online 1729 (autonome Auslegung der Begriffe des Kaufvertrages, der Waren und der Niederlassung); BGH, 2.3.2005, CISG-online 999 = IHR 2005, 158 ff. (autonome Auslegung des Begriffs des Kaufvertrags); Tribunale di Padova, 11.1.2005, CISG-online 967 (autonome Auslegung der Begriffe der Waren, des Kaufvertrags und der Niederlassung); Tribunale di Padova, 25.2.2004, CISG-online 819 (autonome Auslegung der Begriffe des Kaufvertrags und der Waren).

tional" ausgelegt werden müssen. Die Aufgabe, die verschiedenen **nicht autonom auszulegenden Begriffe** herauszuarbeiten,[86] ist demnach der Lehre überlassen worden. Diese hat, genauso wie die neuere Rechtsprechung,[87] bereits einige dieser Begriffe herausgearbeitet: Zu diesen gehören der der **„Vertragspartei"** und der des „Internationalen Privatrechts".[88] Was ersteren angeht, so geht die herrschende Lehre, genauso wie die Rechtsprechung,[89] zu Recht davon aus, dass das anhand der Kollisionsnormen des Forumstaates zu bestimmende anwendbare Recht darüber entscheidet, wer Vertragspartei ist.[90] Dies bedeutet jedoch, dass der Begriff nicht „autonom" auszulegen ist.

13   Ähnliches gilt auch hinsichtlich des Begriffs des **„Internationalen Privatrechts".**[91] Die herrschende Lehre vertritt zu Recht die Ansicht, dass die das „Internationale Privatrecht" erwähnenden Vorschriften des Übereinkommens (Art. 1 I lit. b) und Art. 7 II) auf das IPR des Forums abstellen.[92] Gleiches geht auch aus verschiedenen Urteilen hervor.[93] Dies bedeutet jedoch, dass das Übereinkommen keinen „autonomen" Begriff des „Internationalen Privatrecht" geschaffen hat.[94]

14   Aus dem Gesagten geht unschwer hervor, so auch die Rechtsprechung,[95] dass zur Verwirklichung des vom Übereinkommen angestrebten Zieles eine „autonome" Auslegung allein nicht ausreicht.[96] Es genügt, mit anderen Worten, nicht, dass der Rechtsanwender den „internationalen Charakter" des Übereinkommens berücksichtigt, da dies allein nicht alle Auslegungsprobleme löst.[97] Im Gegenteil, derselbe „internationale Charakter" des Übereinkommens wirft neue Auslegungsprobleme auf: So ist zum Beispiel die Existenz der verschiedenen offiziellen Fassungen des CISG auf ebendiesen „internationalen Charakter" zurückzuführen;[98] diese Koexistenz an sich gleichwertiger Versionen[99] kann aber selbst

---

[86] Auch *Flechtner*, 17 J. L. & Com. (1998), 187, 205, hebt hervor, dass nicht alle Begriffe autonom ausgelegt werden können bzw. müssen.
[87] Vgl. etwa Tribunale di Padova, 25.2.2004, CISG-online 819 = Giur. it. 2004, 1402, 1403.
[88] Vgl. hierzu ausführlicher *Ferrari*, 17 J. L. & Com. (1998), 245, 249 ff.
[89] Tribunale di Padova, 25.2.2004, CISG-online 819 = Giur. it. 2004, 1402, 1403.
[90] Vgl. hierzu *Ferrari*, Vendita internazionale, S. 24; *Herber/Czerwenka*, Art. 1, Rn. 13.
[91] Spezifisch zum Begriff des IPR im UN-Kaufrecht siehe *Ferrari*, ZEuP 1998, 162 ff.; zum Verhältnis zwischen CISG und IPR vgl. neuerdings *Ferrari*, J. D. I. 2006, 27 ff.; *ders.*, CISG and PIL, S. 19; *Kampf*, RIW 2009, 297.
[92] So etwa *Bamberger/Roth/Saenger*, Art. 1, Rn. 16; *Ferrari*, Uniform Interpretation, S. 3, 10 f.; *Flechtner*, 17 J. L. & Com. (1998), 187, 199; *Gruber*, Methoden, S. 85 f.; *Lohmann*, Parteiautonomie, S. 139; *Niemann*, S. 73; *Schmid*, Einheitliche Anwendung, S. 54; *Siehr*, RabelsZ 52 (1988), 587, 592 f.
[93] Vgl. diesbezüglich die in *Ferrari*, ZEuP 1998, 162 ff., angemerkten Entscheidungen: OLG Düsseldorf, 8.1.1993, CISG-online 76 = IPRax 1993, 412 ff.; BezG Wien, 20.2.1992, CISG-online 53 = RdW 1992, 239; LG Aachen, 30.4.1990, CISG-online 12 = RIW 1990, 491 f.; vgl. neuerdings auch Tribunale di Padova, 11.1.2005, CISG-online 967; Tribunale di Padova, 25.2.2004, CISG-online 819 = Giur. it. 2004, 1402, 1403; Tribunale di Rimini, 26.11.2002, CISG-online 737 = Giur. it. 2003, 896, 902; Tribunale di Vigevano, 12.7.2000, CISG-online 493 = Giur. it. 2001, 280, 286.
[94] So auch *Ferrari u. a./Saenger*, Internationales Vertragsrecht, Art. 7, Rn. 4 a. E.; *Niemann*, S. 73; *Schmid*, Einheitliche Anwendung, S. 54; *Staudinger/Magnus*, Art. 7, Rn. 14; *Zeller*, CISG and the Unification, S. 17; vgl. in der Rechtsprechung Tribunale di Padova, 11.1.2005, CISG-online 967 (ausdrücklich darauf hinweisend, dass der Begriff des IPR kein autonom auszulegender Begriff ist); ebenso Tribunale di Padova, 25.2.2004, CISG-online 819; a. A. *Gruber*, Methoden, S. 86: aus dem Umstand, dass das CISG auf die Regeln des IPR des Gerichtsstaats abstellt, „lässt sich nicht der Schluss ziehen, dass das CISG an dieser Stelle nicht autonom auszulegen sei. Die Verweisungsnorm des Art. 1 Abs. 1 lit. b CISG ist, was den Inhalt ihrer Verweisung im einzelnen anbelangt, nach den autonomen Maßstäben des internationalen Einheitsrechts auszulegen".
[95] Tribunale di Padova, 25.2.2004, CISG-online 819 = Giur. it. 2004, 867, 869.
[96] Ebenso im Ergebnis *Enderlein/Maskow/Strohbach*, Art. 7, Anm. 4.; *Ferrari*, Uniform Interpretation, S. 3, 12; *Graffi*, Giur. merito 2004, 873, 875 f.; *Kritzer/Rogers*, FS Schlechtriem, S. 223, 224; *Martinez Canellas*, S. 126 f.; *Sannini*, L'applicazione, S. 4.
[97] So ausdrücklich Tribunale di Padova, 25.2.2004, CISG-online 819 = Giur it. 2004, 1402, 1403; vgl. auch *Schmid*, Einheitliche Anwendung, S. 57 f.
[98] Vgl. zuletzt hierzu *Flechtner*, 17 J. L. & Com. (1998), 187, 190; *Sukurs*, 34 Vand. J. Transnat'l L. (2001), 1481, 1504; allgemein von in mehreren Sprachen verfasster Übereinkommen, *Shelton*, 20 Hastings Int'l & Comp. L. Rev. (1997), 611 ff.
[99] So auch *Staudinger/Mangus*, Art. 7, Rn. 17.

Auslegungsprobleme mit sich bringen,[100] da nur sehr selten selbst bei von den Konventionsgebern gewollter Identität der authentischen Fassungen diese wirklich identisch sein werden.[101]

c) Die Notwendigkeit der Förderung der einheitlichen Anwendung und die Rechtsprechung anderer Staaten. Neben dem Gebot, dem „internationalen Charakter" 15 des Übereinkommens Rechnung zu tragen, stellt Abs. 1 auch das Gebot auf, die Notwendigkeit der Förderung der einheitlichen Anwendung zu beachten.[102] Dies kann nicht weiter überraschen, sind die erwähnten **Grundsätze** doch **miteinander verbunden:**[103] Beide zielen auf die Schaffung von Einheitsrecht ab, im Bewusstsein, dass die bloße Ausarbeitung eines einheitlichen Textes allein noch kein Einheitsrecht schafft.[104]

Aus dem Gebot der Förderung der einheitlichen Anwendung, die heute, wie oft hervorgehoben worden ist, noch nicht erreicht worden ist,[105] wird zum einen die Forderung 16 abgeleitet, „dass sich der Rechtsanwender von vornherein bei Auslegungsfragen stets um **internationalisierungsfähige Lösungen** zu bemühen hat, die auch in anderen Vertragsstaaten auf Befolgung rechnen können".[106] Dies fällt umso leichter, desto „autonomer" die Begriffe ausgelegt werden, woraus sich auch der enge Zusammenhang zwischen dem Gebot der Rücksichtnahme auf den „internationalen Charakter" und dem Postulat einer die Förderung der einheitlichen Anwendung dienenden Auslegung ergibt.[107]

Zum anderen wird der erwähnte Auslegungsgrundsatz sowohl von der deutschen[108] 17 und ausländischen[109] Lehre – und neuerdings auch von einem Teil der Rechtspre-

---

[100] Siehe *Crawford*, 8 J. L. & Com. (1988), 187, 191; *Diedrich*, 8 Pace Int'l L. Rev. (1996), 303, 316; *Nicholas*, 105 L. Q. R. (1989), 201, 206 und 242; *Niemann*, S. 42.

[101] Siehe auch *Crawford*, 8 J. L. & Com. (1988), 187, 190 f.; *Diedrich*, Autonome Auslegung, S. 66; *Flechtner*, 17 J. L. & Com. (1998), 187, 189 f.

[102] *Ferrari u. a./Saenger*, Internationales Vertragsrecht, Art. 7, Rn. 5; *Staudinger/Magnus*, Art. 7, Rn. 20; bezüglich eines Hinweises der Rechtsprechung auf die im Text erwähnten Gebote, vgl. BGH, 2.3.2005, CISG-online 999 = IHR 2005, 158, 159, *Medical Marketing International, Inc. v. Internazionale Medico Scientifica s. r. l.*, U. S. Dist. Ct. (E. D. La.), 17.5.1999, CISG-online 387 = 1999 U. S. Dist. LEXIS 7380; OLG Frankfurt a. M., 20.4.1993, CISG-online 125.

[103] So schon *Ferrari*, Vendita internazionale, S. 135 f.; *ders.*, Int. Bus. L. J. 2003, 221, 226; vgl. neuerdings auch *Felemegas*, Introduction, S. 10, 12, 356; *van Alstine*, 146 U. Pa. L. Rev. (1998), 687, 732.

[104] In diesem Sinne auch *Felemegas*, Introduction, S. 15; *Ferrari*, Uniform Interpretation, S. 3; *ders.*, IHR 2001, 56, 57; *ders.*, IPRax 1997, 64; *Ferrari u. a./Saenger*, Internationales Vertragsrecht, Art. 7, Rn. 5; *Graffi*, Divergences, S. 305, 306; *Gruber*, Methoden, S. 79; *Karollus*, S. 11; *Martiny*, RabelsZ (1981), 427; *Melin*, S. 333; *Munday*, 27 Int'l & Comp. L. Q. (1978), 450; *Niemann*, S. 43; *Reifner*, IHR 2002, 52, 58; *Ryan*, 4 Tul. J. Int'l & Comp. L. (1995), 99, 101; *Sannini*, L'applicazione, S. 10; *Schmid*, Einheitliche Anwendung, S. 17 f.; *Zeller*, CISG and the Unification, S. 19.

[105] Vgl. etwa *Flechtner*, FS Schwenzer, S. 493, 494; *Schwenzer/Hachem*, 57 Am. J. Com. L. (2009), 457, 457.

[106] *Staudinger/Magnus*, Art. 7, Rn. 20; vgl. auch *Achilles*, Art. 7, Rn. 5; *Bailey*, 32 Cornell Int'l L. J. (1999), 273, 293; *Calleo*, 28 Hofstra L. Rev. (2000), 799, 826; *Ferrari u. a./Saenger*, Internationales Vertragsrecht, Art. 7, Rn. 5; *Frignani/Torsello*, Il contratto internazionale, S. 464; *Gruber*, Methoden, S. 104 ff.; *Naumann*, S. 166; *Niemann*, S. 44; *Piltz*, Internationales Kaufrecht, Rn. 2–185; *Reifner*, IHR 2002, 52, 58; *Schlechtriem/Schwenzer/Schwenzer/Hachem*, CISG Commentary, Art. 7, Rn. 10; *Schmid*, Einheitliche Anwendung, S. 50; *Sukurs*, 34 Vand. J. Transnat'l L. (2001), 1481, 1505; *Sundermann*, Probleme der autonomen Auslegung, S. 24; *C. Witz*, D. 2002, Jur. 788, 788; ähnlich – aber in Bezug auf das EVÜ – *Junker*, RabelsZ 55 (1991), 674, 680: „Lege so aus, dass deine Auslegung in allen Staaten der Gemeinschaft gebilligt werden kann".

[107] Zu der Wechselbeziehung zwischen dem Gebot der „autonomen" Auslegung und dem im Text erwähnten Auslegungsgrundsatz vgl. auch *Bonell*, Nuove leggi civ. comm. 1989, 20, 21; *Ferrari*, IPRax 1997, 64, 65.

[108] Vgl. *Dejaco*, S. 42 f.; *Enderlein/Masow/Strohbach*, Art. 7, Anm. 4.; *Grieser*, S. 36; *Happ*, RIW 1997, 376, 380; *Hager*, FS Huber, S. 319, 320; *Herber/Czerwenka*, Art. 7, Rn. 5; *Magnus*, CISG Methodology, S. 33, 41; *ders.*, RabelsZ 53 (1989), 116, 123; *Maskow*, Perspective of the Socialist Countries, S. 54; *Melin*, S. 358; *T. M. Müller*, Beweislast, S. 12; *Piltz*, Internationales Kaufrecht, Rn. 2–185; *Reifner*, IMR 2002, 52, 58; *Schlechtriem/Schwenzer/Schlechtriem*, CISG Commentary, 2. Aufl., Art. 7, Rn. 14; *Schlechtriem/Schwenzer/Schwenzer/Hachem*, CISG Commentary, Art. 7, Rn. 10; *Schmid*, Einheitliche Anwendung, S. 19 und 56 ff.; *Soergel/Lüderitz/Fenge*, Art. 7, Rn. 6; *Staudinger/Magnus*, Art. 7, Rn. 21 m. w. N; *Sundermann*, Probleme der autonomen Auslegung, S. 36; *Teichert*, S. 85; *Witz/Salger/Lorenz/Witz*, Art. 7, Rn. 9.

[109] So etwa *Amato*, 13 J. L. & Com. (1993), 1, 25; *Bailey*, 32 Cornell Int'l L. J. (1999), 273, 290; *Bazinas*, Uniformity, S. 19; *Bianca/Bonell/Bonell*, Art. 7, Anm. 3.1.3.; *Bonell*, Nuove leggi civ. comm. 1989, 20, 22;

chung[110] – so verstanden, dass die das CISG anwendenden Gerichte die **Rechtsprechung der Gerichte anderer Staaten** berücksichtigen sollen, um auf diese

Brand/Flechtner, 12 J. L. & Com. (1992), 239, 241; *Bridge,* Draft Digest, S. 235, 250; *Brunner,* Art. 7, Rn. 3; *Cook,* 50 U. Pitt. L. Rev. (1988), 197, 226; *dies.,* 16 J. L. & Com. (1997), 261; *Darkey,* 15 J. L. & Com. (1995), 139, 142; *Diesse,* J. D. I. 2002, 55, 76; *DiMatteo,* CISG Methodology, 2009, S. 113 ff.; *Esslinger,* ALI-ABA (1999), 69, 73; *Felemegas,* Introduction, S. 15 ff.; *ders.,* Rev. CISG (2000/2001), 115, 249; *Ferrari,* Do Courts Interpret the CISG Uniformly?, S. 3, 5 f.; *ders.,* Int. Bus. L. J. 2003, 221, 222–223; *Hartnell,* 18 Yale J. Int'l L. (1993), 1, 7; *Heuzé,* Anm. 95.; *Honnold/Flechtner,* Art. 7, Rn. 92; *Janssen,* IHR 2004, 194, 199; *Jurewicz,* 28 J. L. & Com. (2009), 63, 68; *Kritzer,* Guide to Practical Applications, S. 109; *Liguori,* Foro it. 1996, IV, 145, 150; *Lookofsky,* 8 VJ (2004), 181, 184 ff.; *Lurger,* IHR 2005, 177; *Mazzotta,* 3 Loy. Univ. Chi. Int'l L. Rev. (2005), 85, 91; *Moccia,* 13 Fordham Int'l L. J. (1990), 649, 676; *MünchKomm/Westermann,* Art. 7, Rn. 2; *Patterson,* 22 Stanford J. Int'l L. (1986), 263, 283; *Pavic/Djordjevic,* 28 J. L. & Com. (2009), 1, 25; *Romito/Sant'Elia,* 14 Pace Int'l L. Rev. (2002), 179, 203; *Sannini,* L'applicazione, S. 6 f.; *Schultz,* 35 Cornell Int'l L. J. (2002), 263, 268; *Sollund,* Nordic L. J. (2007), 1, 9; *Veneziano,* Dir. comm. int. 2001, 509, 512; *Winship,* 29 Int'l Law. (1995), 525, 528; *Zeller,* 12 Pace Int'l L. Rev. (2000), 79, 85.

[110] Ausländische Rechtsprechung ist etwa in folgenden Urteilen berücksichtigt worden: Tribunale di Forlì, 26.3.2012, CISG-online 2336 (Bezugnahme auf ca. 40 ausländische Urteile und Schiedssprüche); *RJ & AM Smallmon v. Transport Sales Limited,* Court of Appeal New Zealand, 22.7.2011, CISG-online 2215 (Bezugnahme auf acht ausländische Urteile); OLG Stuttgart, 30.5.2011, CISG-online 2225 (Bezugnahme auf eine Entscheidung des Court de Cassation); Tribunale di Reggio Emilia, 12.4.2011, CISG-online 2229 (Bezugnahme auf 8 ausländische Entscheidungen); *RJ & AM Smallmon v. Transport Sales Limited,* High Court of New Zealand, 30.7.2010, CISG-online 2113 (Bezugnahme auf ein deutsches, ein französisches und ein us-amerikanisches Urteil); *Innotex Precision Limited v. Horei, Inc., et al.,* U. S. Dist. Ct. (N. D. Ga., Atlanta Division), 17.12.2009, CISG-online 2044 (Bezugnahme auf eine französische und eine chinesische Entscheidung); RB Arnhem, 29.7.2009, CISG-online 1939 (Bezugnahme auf eine österreichische Entscheidung); RB Amsterdam, 3.6.2009, CISG-online 2065 (Bezugnahme auf eine Entscheidung des BGH); OLG Hamm, 2.4.2009, CISG-online 1978 (Bezugnahme auf eine in den USA ergangene Entscheidung); Audiencia Provinciale de Zaragoza, 31.3.2009, CISG-online 2085 (Bezugnahme auf ein deutsches Urteil); RB Rotterdam, 25.2.2009, CISG-online 1812 (Bezugnahme auf ein vom BGH erlassenes Urteil); Tribunale di Forlì, 16.2.2009, CISG-online 1780 (Bezugnahme auf mehr als 30 ausländische Urteile und Schiedssprüche); RB Utrecht, 21 January 2009, CISG-online 1814 (Bezugnahme auf ein deutsches Urteil); Tribunale di Forlì, 11.12.2008, CISG-online 1729 (Bezugnahme auf mehr als 40 ausländische Urteile und Schiedssprüche); *Hannaford v. Australian Farmlink Pty Ltd.,* Federal Court of Australia, South Australia District Registry, 24.10.2008, CISG-online 1743 (Bezugnahme auf ein Urteil der Cour de Cassation); *CNA Int'l, Inc. v. Guangdong Kelon Electronical Holdings et al.,* U. S. Dist. Ct. (N. D. Ill.), 3.9.2008, CISG-online 2043 (Bezugnahme auf ein französisches Urteil); OLG Stuttgart, 31.3.2008, CISG-online 1658 (Bezugnahme auf ein französisches und ein holländisches Urteil); Tribunale di Rovereto, 21.11.2007, CISG-online 1590 (Bezugnahme auf zwei deutsche Entscheidungen); Supreme Court of Poland, 11.5.2007, CISG-online 1790 (Bezugnahme auf eine österreichische Entscheidung); *Barbara Berry, S. A. de C. V. v. Ken M. Spooner Farms, Inc.,* U. S. Dist. Ct. (W. D. of Wash.), 13.4.2006, CISG-online 1354 = 2006 WL 1 009 299 (W. D. Wash.) (Bezugnahme auf ein schweizerisches Urteil); KG Appenzell Ausserrhoden, 9.3.2006, CISG-online 1375 (Bezugnahme auf eine deutsches und ein österreichisches Urteil); OLG Karlsruhe, 8.2.2006, CISG-online 1328 (Bezugnahme auf ein österreichisches und ein US-amerikanisches Urteil); OGH, 25.1.2006, CISG-online 1223 (Bezugnahme auf ein Urteil des BGH); Tribunale di Padova, 10.1.2006, CISG-online 1157 = (Bezugnahme auf etwa 10 ausländische Urteile); LG Neubrandenburg, 3.8.2005, CISG-online 1190 = IHR 2006, 26 ff. (Bezugnahme auf einen russischen Schiedsspruch); BGH, 2.3.2005, CISG-online 999 = IHR 2005, 158 ff. (Bezugnahme auf zwei österreichische Urteile); LG Salzburg, 2.2.2005, CISG-online 1189 (Bezugnahme auf Urteil des BGH); Tribunale di Padova, 11.1.2005, CISG-online 967 = Riv. dir. int. priv. proc. 2005, 791 ff. (Bezugnahme auf etwa 20 ausländische Entscheidungen); OLG Karlsruhe, 20.7.2004, CISG-online 858 = IHR 2004, 246, 250 (Bezugnahme auf ein österreichisches Urteil); BGH, 30.6.2004, CISG-online 847 = IHR 2004, 201 (Bezugnahme auf zwei ausländische Urteile und zwei Schiedssprüche); *Chicago Prime Packers, Inc. v. Northam Food Trading Co., et al.,* U. S. Dist. Ct. (N. D. Ill., E. D.), 21.5.2004, CISG-online 851 = IHR 2004, 156 ff. (Bezugnahme auf sieben ausländische Urteile); Tribunale di Padova, 31.3.2004, CISG-online 823 = Giur. merito 2004, 1065 ff. (Bezugnahme auf ungefähr 30 ausländische Urteile); *Amco Ukrservice et al. v. American Meter Company,* U. S. Dist. Ct. (E. D. Pa.), 29.3.2004, CISG-online 1664 = 2004 WL 692 233 (E. D. Pa.) (Bezugnahme auf zwei deutsche Entscheidungen); Tribunale di Padova, 25.2.2004, CISG-online 819 = Giur. it. 2004, 1402 ff. (Bezugnahme auf ungefähr 30 ausländische Urteile); LG Mannheim, 16.2.2004, IHR 2006, 106, 107 (Bezugnahme auf ein US-amerkanisches und ein schweizerisches Urteil); LG Trier, 8.1.2004, IHR 2004, 115, 116 (Bezugnahme auf ein US-amerikanisches Urteil); BGer, 13.11.2003, CISG-online 840 (Bezugnahme auf 4 ausländische Urteile); HG Zürich, 24. 10 2003, CISG-online 857 (Bezugnahme auf ein Urteil des BGH); Audiencia Provincial Valencia, 7.6.2003, CISG-online 948 (Bezugnahme auf 3 ausländische Entscheidungen); Tribunale di Rimini, 26.11.2002, CISG-online 737 = Giur. it. 2003, 896 ff., m. Anm. *Ferrari* (Bezugnahme auf 35 ausländische Urteile); HG Aargau, 5.11.2002, CISG-online 715 (Bezugnahme auf eine deutsche Entscheidung); *Usinor Industeel v. Leeco Steel Products, Inc.,* U. S. Dist. Ct (N. D. Ill.), 28.3.2002, CISG-online 696 = 2002 WL 655 540 (Bezugnahme auf ein australisches

Weise – wie im innerstaatlichen Bereich – eine gemeinsame Interpretation herauszubilden.[111]

d) Kritisches zur Beachtung ausländischer Rechtsprechung. Die Beachtung aus- 18 ländischer **Rechtsprechung** entspricht unzweifelhaft dem Ziel der Schaffung eines Einheitsrechts. Dies bedeutet jedoch nicht, dass sie unproblematisch ist.[112] Ein erstes – **praktisches** – **Problem** hängt mit der Kenntnisnahme ausländischer Entscheidungen zusammen:[113] Ausländische Urteile sind zum einen nicht leicht zugänglich,[114] zum anderen sind sie in der Regel in Fremdsprachen abgefasst.[115] Aus diesem Grund kann nicht verwundern, dass sich in den ersten Jahren nach Inkrafttreten des CISG nicht allzu viele Entscheidungen finden liessen, in denen ausländische Urteile zur Entscheidungsfindung herangezogen wurden.[116] Hervorzuheben sind jedoch verschiedene italienische Urteile: in einem Urteil aus dem Jahr 2000, das zu Recht große Beachtung gefunden hat,[117] hat der Einzelrichter 40 ausländische Schieds- und Gerichtsurteile zitiert;[118] in neueren Urteilen (u. a. auch desselben Einzelrichters) sind bis zu 35 ausländische Urteile zitiert worden.[119]

Urteil); *St. Paul Guardian Insurance Company et al. v. Neuromed Medical Systems & Support et al.*, U. S. Dist. Ct. (S. D. N. Y.), 26.3.2002, CISG-online 615 = IHR 2005, 256 ff. (Bezugnahme auf 3 deutsche Entscheidungen); RB Hasselt, 6.3.2002, CISG-online 622 (Bezugnahme auf ein schweizerisches Urteil); Tribunale di Vigevano, 12.7.2000, CISG-online 493 = IHR 2001, 72 ff. (Bezugnahme auf 40 ausländische Urteile); Tribunale di Pavia, 29.12.1999, CISG-online 678 = Corr. giur. 2000, 932 f. (Bezugnahme auf ein schweizerisches Urteil); RB Hasselt Belgium, 28.4.1999, CISG belgium (Bezugnahme auf ein Urteil des OGH und ein Urteil des AG Kehl); *Medical Marketing v. Internazionale Medico Scientifica*, U. S. Dist. Ct. (E. D. La), 17.5.1999, CISG-online 387 = 1999 WL 311 945 (E. D. La.); RB Hasselt, 2.12.1998, CISG-online 761 (Bezugnahme auf ein deutsches und ein österreichisches Urteil); CA Grenoble, 23.10.1996, CISG-online 305 (Bezugnahme auf ein deutsches Urteil); Tribunale di Cuneo, 31.1.1996, CISG-online 268 (Bezugnahme auf ein schweizerisches und ein deutsches Urteil); für einen neueren Überblick vgl. neuerdings *Ferrari*, Uniform Interpretation, S. 3 ff.; *ders.*, 9 VJ (2005), 233 ff.; vgl. auch, in Bezug auf die US-amerikanische Rechtsprechung, *Flechtner*, The CISG in U. S. Courts, S. 91 ff.

[111] So auch *Brunner*, Art. 7, Rn. 3; *Ferrari*, Rev. int. dr. comp. 1996, 813, 831 f.; *ders.*, Vendita internazionale, S. 138; *Graffi*, Giur. merito 2004, 873, 876 f.; *Hartnell*, 18 Yale J. Int'l L. (1993), 1, 7; *P. Huber/Mullis/P. Huber*, S. 8; *Lookofsky*, 8 VJ 2004, 181, 184; vgl. auch *Sollund*, Nordic L. J. (2007), 1, 9; vgl. in der Rechtsprechung Serbian Chamber of Commerce, 28.1.2009, CISG Pace; Serbian Chamber of Commerce, 15.7.2008, CISG-online 1795; Trib.unale di Padova, 25.2.2004, CISG-online 819; Audiencia Provincial de Valencia, 7.6.2003, CISG-online 948, Tribunale di Rimini, 26.11.2002, CISG-online 737; *Usinor Industeel v. Leeco Steel Products, Inc.*, U. S. Dist. Ct. (N. D. Ill.), 28.3.2002, CISG-online 1326.

[112] Ebenso *Harjani*, 23 Hous. J. Int'l L. (2000), 49, 65–66; *T. M. Müller*, Beweislast, S. 20 ff.; *Witz/Salger/Lorenz/Witz*, Art. 7, Rn. 9; ausführlich hierzu *Ferrari*, 17 J. L. & Com. (1998), 245 ff.

[113] Vgl. *Ferrari*, Uniform Interpretation, S. 3, 13 ff.; *Kritzer/Rogers*, FS Schlechtriem, S. 223, 239; *Magnus*, CISG Methodology, S. 33, 41; *Melin*, S. 388; *Niemann*, S. 44; *Schmid*, Einheitliche Anwendung, S. 187 ff.

[114] *Gruber*, Methoden, S. 327.

[115] Ebenso nunmehr auch *Frigge*, S. 327; *Sollund*, Nordic L. J. (2007), 1, 10; dies scheint vor allem für die nordamerikanische Rechtsprechung Probleme darzustellen, haben doch verschiedene Urteile ausdrücklich auf das „Fehlen von Rechtsprechung" zum CISG hingewiesen, zu einem Zeitpunkt, als es aber bereits sehr viel (ausländische und nicht in englischer Sprache verfasste) Rechtsprechung gab; vgl. statt aller *Helen Kaminski PTY LTD. v. Marketing Australian Products, INC.*, U. S. Dist. Ct. (S. D. N. Y.), 23.7.1997, CISG-online 297 = 1997 WL 414 137; krit. zu dieser Rechtsprechung auch krit. zum erwähnten Trend in der us-amerikanischen Rechtsprechung *Ferrari*, IHR 2009, 8 ff.; *Kröll u. a./Perales Viscasillas*, Art. 7, Rn. 19; *T. M. Müller/Togo*, IHR 2005, 102, 103.

[116] Vgl. Tribunale di Cuneo, 31.1.1996, CISG-online 268, das zur Entscheidungsfindung sowohl auf ein deutsches (LG Stuttgart, 31.8.1989, CISG-online 11 = IPRax 1990, 317) als auch ein schweizerisches Urteil (Pretura Locarno-Campagna, 27.4.1992, CISG-online 68) Bezug genommen hat; siehe auch CA Grenoble, 23.10.1996, CISG-online 305, das ohne weiter darauf einzugehen, OLG Düsseldorf, 2.7.1993, CISG-online 74 = RIW 1993, 845, zitiert hat.

[117] Für Anmerkungen vgl. *Ferrari*, IPRax 2001, 354 ff.; *ders.*, Giur. it. 2002, 281 ff.; *ders.*, IHR 2001, 56 ff.; *ders.*, Uniform L. Rev. 2001, 203 ff.; *ders.*, 21 J. L. & Com. 2001, 225 ff.; *Graffi*, EuLF 2001, 240 ff.; *Rosati*, IHR 2001, 78 ff.; *Spiegel*, D. 2002, 395 f.; *Veneziano*, Dir. comm. int. 2001, 497 ff.

[118] Tribunale di Vigevano, 12.7.2000, CISG-online 493 = Giur. it. 2001, 280 ff. (Bezugnahme auf insgesamt 40 ausländische Urteile und Schiedssprüche).

[119] Tribunale di Reggio Emilia, 12.4.2011, CISG-online 2229; Tribunale di Forlì, 16.2.2009, CISG-online 1780; Tribunale di Forlì, 11.12.2008, CISG-online 1729; Tribunale di Rovereto, 21.11.2007, CISG-online 1590; Tribunale di Padova, 10.1.2006, CISG-online 1157; Tribunale di Padova, 11.1.2005, CISG-online 967;

19 Um diesem (praktischen) Hindernis entgegenzuwirken, sind verschiedene offizielle Initiativen unternommen worden.[120] UNCITRAL selbst gibt – auf Grund eines anlässlich der 21. Sitzung gefassten Beschlusses[121] – seit längerem „**CLOUT**" („Case Law on UNCITRAL Texts"),[122] eine Sammlung von Zusammenfassungen von Entscheidungen zu UNCITRAL-Texten, heraus, also auch von Entscheidungen zum Übereinkommen.[123] Ferner ist ein weiteres UNCITRAL-Projekt zu erwähnen, das das angestrebte Ziel der einheitlichen Anwendung sicher fördern wird: UNCITRAL hat eine nach Artikeln geordnete Sammlung („**Digest**") von Urteilen durch fünf Experten erarbeiten lassen,[124] deren endgültige Fassung[125] im Jahr 2004 erschienen ist[126] – eine Neuauflage ist im Jahre 2012 erschienen – und die bereits von verschiedenen Gerichten zur Entscheidungsfindung herangezogen worden ist.[127]

19a Neuerdings ist von privater Seite[128] auch ein sog. **CISG-Advisory Council** geschaffen worden,[129] dem verschiedene Professoren aus unterschiedlichen Rechtskreisen angehören, der auch das Ziel hat, die einheitliche Anwendung zu fördern, u. a. durch Veröffentlichung von „Opinions" zu bestimmten Sachfragen. Mittlerweile hat der CISG-Advisory Council „Opinions" veröffentlicht zu folgenden Fragen: *Electronic issues* (Op. 1), Untersuchung- und Rügeobliegenheit nach Artt. 38 und 39 CISG (Op. 2), *Parol Evidence Rule, Plain Meaning Rule, Contractual Merger Clause and the CISG* (Op. 3), Fragen des Art. 3 CISG (Op. 4), wesentliche Vertragsverletzung (Op. 5), Schaden nach Art. 74 CISG (Op. 6), Entlastung nach Art. 79 CISG (Op. 7), Berechnung des Schadensersatzes nach Artt. 75 und 76 (Op. 8) und Rechtsfolgen der Vertragsaufhebung (Op. 9). Eine dieser „Opinions" ist von der US-amerikanischen Rechtsprechung auch bereits zitiert worden.[130]

20 Unter der Leitung von *Bonell* veröffentlicht das Centro di studi e ricerche di diritto comparato e straniero eine Datenbank, **UNILEX**,[131] die auch über Internet gratis abrufbar

---

Tribunale di Padova, 31.3.2004, CISG-online 823; Tribunale di Padova, 25.2.2004, CISG-online 819 = Giur. it. 2004, 1402 ff., m. Anm. *Ferrari*; Tribunale di Rimini, 26.11.2002, CISG-online 737 = Giur it. 2003, 896 ff., m. Anm. *Ferrari*.
Sehr krit. diesen Urteilen gegenüber (und z. T. den Sinn dieser Entscheidungen missverstehend) *Schlechtriem/ Schwenzer/Schwenzer/Hachem*, CISG Commentary, Art. 7, Rn. 13 Fn. 38.
[120] Siehe hierzu *Bergsten*, CISG Methodology, S. 5, 30 f.; *De Ly*, Uniform Interpretation, S. 335 ff.; *Ferrari u. a./Saenger*, Art. 7, Rn. 3; *Magnus*, CISG Methodology, S. 33, 37 ff.; *Schlechtriem/Schwenzer/Schwenzer/ Hachem*, CISG Commentary, Art. 7, Rn. 11 f.; vgl. auch *Bazinas*, Uniformity, S. 18 ff. und dort vor allem S. 20 ff.
[121] Vgl. Report of the United Nations Commission on International Trade Law on the work of its twenty-first session, 11–22 April 1988, UNCITRAL YB XIX (1988), S. 98 ff.; siehe auch das den Beratungen zugrunde liegende Dokument A/CN.9/312.
[122] Diese Sammlung von Zusammenfassungen ist auch über das Internet zugänglich; vgl. unter der folgenden Adresse: http://www.uncitral.org; vgl. hierzu *Bazinas*, Uniformity, S. 18 ff.
[123] Vgl. detaillierter hierzu auch *Ferrari*, Vendita internazionale, S. 139 f.
[124] Neben dem Autor, der auch Koordinator des Werkes war, waren folgende Experten eingeladen worden, den Digest zu verfassen: Harry *Flechtner*, Ulrich *Magnus*, Peter *Winship*, Claude *Witz*.
[125] Der Entwurf ist – samt einer kritischen Würdigung – abgedruckt bei *Ferrari u. a.* (Hrsg.), The Draft UNCITRAL Digest and Beyond: Cases, Analyses and Unresolved Issues, München: Sellier, (2004), S. 501 ff.
[126] Die endgültige Fassung kann unter folgender Internet-Adresse abgerufen werden: http://www.uncitral. org/uncitral/en/case_law/digests/cisg.html; vgl. hierzu etwa *Lookofsky*, 8 VJ (2004), 181 ff.
[127] Vgl. *Forestal Guarani S. A. v. Daros International, Inc.*, U. S. Ct. App. (3rd Cir.), 21.7.2010, CISG-online 2112; *Valero Marketing & Supply Company v. Greeni Trading Oy*, U. S. Ct. App. (3rd Cir.), 19.7.2007, CISG-online 1510 = 2007 WL 2 064 219 (C. A. 3 (N. J.)); *Multi-Juice, S. A. v. Snapple Beverage Corp.*, U. S. Dist. Ct. (S. D. N. Y.), 1.6.2006, CISG-online 1229 = 2006 WL 1 519 981 (S. D. N. Y.).
[128] Vgl. ausführlich zu den „privaten" bzw. „inoffiziellen" Initiativen *Veneziano*, Uniform Interpretation: What is Being Done? Unofficial Efforts and Their Impact, S. 325 ff.
[129] Vgl. hierzu *Herber*, IHR 2003, 201 f.; *Karton/de Germiny*, 27 Berkeley J. Int'l L. (2009), 683 ff.; *Mistelis*, IHR, 2003, 243 f. = 15 Pace Int'l L. Rev. (2003), 453 ff.
[130] Vgl. *TeeVee Toons, Inc. et al v. Gerhard Schubert GmbH*, U. S. Dist. Ct. (S. D. N. Y.), 23.8.2006, CISG-online 1272 = 2006 WL 2 463 537 (S. D. N. Y.).
[131] Zu dieser Datenbank, vgl. den Aufsatz eines der Mitarbeiter des die Datenbank veröffentlichenden Instituts *Liguori*, ZEuP 1996, 600 ff.

ist,[132] und die ebenfalls das Ziel hat, die Kenntnisnahme von Entscheidungen von Gerichten der verschiedensten Staaten zu fördern.[133]

Schließlich sei darauf hingewiesen, dass man über **verschiedene Internet-Adressen** 21 eine Vielzahl von belgischen,[134] deutschen,[135] österreichischen,[136] schweizerischen,[137] französischen[138] und amerikanischen Entscheidungen[139] abrufen kann; auf einige dieser Adressen hat auch die Rechtsprechung zurückgegriffen, als es darum ging, ausländische Entscheidungen ausfindig zu machen.[140]

An dieser Stelle muss man sich jedoch fragen, ob die bloße Kenntnisnahme ausländischer 22 Rechtsprechung alle materiellen Fragen lösen kann. Hätte die bloße Kenntnis der in den verschiedenen Ländern ergangenen Urteile zur Frage, ob die Wahl des Rechts eines Vertragsstaates zur Anwendung des Übereinkommens oder zu dessen Ausschluss führt, die aus der Rechtsprechung und Lehre bekannten Widersprüche[141] vermeiden können? Hätte die Kenntnis ausländischer Rechtsprechung den Meinungsstreit bezüglich der Bestimmung der Höhe des Zinssatzes bei Zahlungsverzug vermeiden können? Dies ist auszuschließen.[142] Die Kenntnis der Rechtsprechung ausländischer Gerichte führt per se nicht zum gewollten Ziel der einheitlichen Anwendung des Übereinkommens,[143] genauso wenig wie die Kenntnis der Rechtsprechung eines Staates in den Gerichten dieses Staates notwendigerweise zur einheitlichen Anwendung nationaler Vorschriften dieses Staates führt. Die gegenteilige Ansicht würde zu einem absurden Ergebnis führen: Würde die Kenntnis ausländischer Rechtsprechung immer ausreichen, dann würde die Lösung einer Frage letztendlich davon abhängen, wie das Gericht, das sich zuerst mit einer Frage zu beschäftigen hat, diese Frage entscheidet.[144]

Die Kenntnis ausländischer Rechtsprechung löst aber nicht nur nicht alle Probleme, sie 23 wirft auch neue – zumindest eines – auf:[145] das der **Bindungswirkung ausländischer Rechtsprechung.** Ein Teil der Lehre vertritt die Ansicht, ausländischer Rechtsprechung komme bindende Wirkung zu, zumindest wenn „there is already a body of international case law".[146] Ein Autor geht sogar weiter und fordert ein „supranational stare decisis".[147] Diese Ansichten sind, so mittlerweile auch die Rechtsprechung,[148] nicht haltbar.[149] Was die

---

[132] Vgl. http://www.unilex.info.
[133] Vgl. auch *Herber,* RIW 1995, 502 ff.
[134] Siehe CISG Belgium: http://www.law.kuleuven.be/ipr/eng/cisg/index.php?language=en.
[135] Siehe http://www.jura.uni-freiburg.de/ipr1/cisg, nunmehr übernommen von Frau Professor Schwenzer, Universität Basel, vgl. http://www.globalsaleslaw.org/.
[136] Siehe Austria: http://www.cisg.at/.
[137] Siehe CISG-online: http://www.globalsaleslaw.org/.
[138] Vgl. CISG France: http://www.cisg-france.org/.
[139] Siehe die Website des Institute of International Commercial Law der Pace University: http://cisg.law.pace.edu; vgl. zu dieser Website *Kritzer,* 9 Pace Int'l L. Rev. (1997), 187 ff.
[140] Vgl. etwa HGer Zürich, 10.11.2010, CISG-online 2160: Verweis auf die CISG-online Datenbank; *RJ & AM Smallmon v. Transport Sales Limited,* High Court of New Zealand, 30.7.2010, CISG-online 2113: Verweis auf die Datenbank der Pace University; KG Appenzell Ausserrhoden, 9.3.2006, CISG-online 1375: Verweis auf die CISG-online Datenbank; ebenso OLG Karlsruhe, 20.7.2004, CISG-online 858 = IHR 2004, 246 ff.; BGer, 13.11.2003, CISG-online 840.
[141] Vgl. hierzu Art. 6 Rn. 21 ff.
[142] Ebenso *Ferrari,* Riv. dir. civ. 1998, II, 93 ff.
[143] So nunmehr auch *Niemann,* S. 44.
[144] So auch *Amato,* 13 J. L. & Com. (1993), 1, 26.
[145] Vgl. hierzu auch *Ferrari,* Uniform Interpretation, S. 3, 19 ff.; *Frigge,* S. 341 ff.; *Lookofsky,* 8 VJ (2004), 181, 184 ff.
[146] *Bianca/Bonell/Bonell,* Art. 7, Anm. 3.1.3.
[147] *Dimatteo,* 23 Syracuse J. Int'l L. & Com. (1997), 79; vgl. auch *Mazzacano,* Rev. CISG (2005/2006), 85, 89, der von einer „form of ipso facto stare decisis or supranational stare decisis" spricht.
[148] Vgl. Tribunale di Vigevano, 12.7.2000, CISG-online 493 = IHR 2001, 72, 73: „[Die ausländische Rechtsprechung] bindet zwar das Gericht nicht (die Bindungswirkung wird nur von einer Mindermeinung vertreten), sie ist jedoch zur Sicherung und Förderung der einheitlichen Auslegung des UN-Kaufrechts zu berücksichtigen, wie nun Art. 7 Abs. 1 CISG selbst vorgesehen."
[149] In diesem Sinne auch *Andersen,* Uniform Application, S. 50; *Bailey,* 32 Cornell Int'l L. J. (1999), 273, 293; *Baumgärtel u. a./Müller,* Vor Art. 1, Rn. 46; *Bazinas,* Uniformity, S. 19; *De Ly,* Uniform Interpretation,

Art. 7 24, 25 Teil I. Kapitel II. Allgemeine Bestimmungen

erste Meinung angeht, so muss diese abgelehnt werden, da sie (mehr oder weniger) konstante Rechtsprechung mit der Richtigkeit des Ergebnisses dieser Rechtsprechung gleichsetzt. Die Forderung nach einem System des „supranational stare decisis"[150] ist abzulehnen,[151] weil sie völlig verkennt, dass das Übereinkommen nicht in eine hierarchische und rigide Struktur der Gerichte eingebettet ist, die gerade Voraussetzung des „stare decisis" ist.[152]

24 Der ausländischen **Rechtsprechung** kann daher, so auch die neuere Rechtsprechung,[153] immer „inspirational"[154] aber nie mehr[155] als **„persuasive authority"** zukommen.[156]

25 **e) Die Wahrung des guten Glaubens im internationalen Handel.** Die Einführung des Gebotes, bei der Auslegung auch die Notwendigkeit der Förderung des guten Glaubens im internationalen Handel zu berücksichtigen, war **umstritten.**[157] Einerseits wurde die Ansicht vertreten, der Begriff sei zu vage und führe zu Rechtsunsicherheit;[158] diese aber

---

S. 335, 357; *Espinassous,* L'uniformisation du droit substantiel, S. 166 ff.; *Ferrari,* IHR 2001, 56, 59; *ders.,* Int. Bus. L. J. 1998, 495, 503; *Flechtner,* 17 J. L. & Com. (1998), 187, 211; *Graffi,* EuLF 2000/2001, 240; *Hackney,* 61 La. L. Rev. (2001), 473, 475 und 479; *Hager,* FS Huber, S. 319, 320; *Harjani,* 23 Hous. J. Int'l L. (2000), 49, 66; *Jurewicz,* 28 J. L. & Com. (2009), 63, 68; *Markel,* 21 Pace Int'l L. Rev. (2009), 163, 196; *Melin,* S. 389 f.; *Lookofsky,* 8 VJ (2004), 181, 186; *Mazzotta,* 3 Loy. Univ. Chi. Int'l L. Rev. (2005), 85, 91; *Schlechtriem/ Schwenzer/Schlechtriem,* CISG Commentary, 2. Aufl., Art. 7, Rn. 14; *Schlechtriem/Schwenzer/Schwenzer/Hachem,* CISG Commentary, Art. 7, Rn. 13; i. E. ebenso *Gruber,* Methoden, S. 343.

[150] Siehe neben dem in Fn. 145 genannten Aufsatz auch *DiMatteo,* 22 Yale Int'l L. J. (1997), 133; kritisch gegenüber der Forderung nach einem „supranational stare decisis" auch *DiMatteo u. a./Pagnattaro,* International Sales Law, S. 4, mit dem Hinweis darauf, dass der zuletzt genannte Aufsatz sich jedoch nicht bloß auf ein „supranantional stare decisis" beziehe, sondern auf ein „informal supranational stare decisis"; diese Klarstellung löst m. E. aber kaum das im Text angesprochene Problem der Bindunswirkung ausländischer Rechtsprechung.

[151] Auch die Rechtsprechung hat diese Ansicht ausdrücklich verworfen; vgl. Tribunale di Padova, 25.2.2004, CISG-online 819 = Giur. it. 2004, 1402, 1403; Tribunale di Vigevano, 12.7.2000, CISG-online 493 = IHR 2001, 72, 73.

[152] So bereits *Ferrari,* 17 J. L. & Com. (1998), 245, 259 f.; *ders.,* Int. Bus. L. J. 2003, 221, 224; vgl. neuerdings auch *Andersen,* Uniform Applicatation, S. 50; *Gruber,* Methoden, S. 344 f.; *Hager,* FS Huber, S. 319, 320.

[153] *TeeVee Toons, Inc. et al v. Gerhard Schubert GmbH,* U. S. Dist. Ct. (S. D. N. Y.), 23.8.2006, CISG-online 1272 = 2006 WL 2 463 537 (S. D. N. Y.); *Chicago Prime Packers, Inc. v. Northam Food Trading Co., et al.,* U. S. Dist. Ct. (N. D. Ill., E. D.), 21.5.2004, CISG-online 851 = IHR 2004, 156, 158, Fn. 11; Tribunale di Padova, 25.2.2004, CISG-online 819 = Giur. it. 2004, 1402, 1403; Tribunale di Rimini, 26.11.2002, CISG-online 737 = Giur. it. 2003, 896, 902; Tribunale di Vigevano, 12.7.2000, CISG-online 493 = IHR 2001, 72, 73; Tribunale di Pavia, 29.12.1999, CISG-online 678 = Corr. Giur. 2000, 932, 933.

[154] *Andersen,* Uniform Applicatation, S. 51 f.

[155] So ausdrücklich *Gilette/Scott,* 25 Int'l Rev. L. & Econ. (2005), 446, 479: „,foreign court decisions at most must have ,persuasive' (non-binding) value"; ebenso *Lookofsky,* Foreign case law, S. 216, 218; *ders.,* 8 VJ (2004), 181, 186.

[156] Ausländischer Rechtsprechung „persuasive value" zusprechend etwa *Amato,* 13 J. L. & Com. (1993), 1, 25; *Bamberger/Roth/Saenger,* Art. 7, Rn. 5; *Burkart,* S. 152 f.; *Ferrari,* Uniform Interpretation, S. 3, 21 f.; *ders.,* Int. Bus. L. J. 1998, 495, 503; *Ferrari u. a./Saenger,* Art. 7, Rn. 2; *Frigge,* S. 347; *Frignani/Torsello,* Il contratto internazionale, S. 464; *Gebauer,* Uniform L. Rev. 2000, 683, 690; *Graffi,* 28 Hous. J. Int'l L. (2006), 663, 769; *ders.,* Divergences, S. 305, 308 f.; *ders.,* Giur. merito 2004, 873, 876; *ders.,* Dir. comm. int. 2003, 807, 812; *Gruber,* Methoden, S. 347; *Harjani,* 23 Hous. J. Int'l L. (2000), 49, 65; *Honnold/ Flechtner,* Art. 7, Rn. 92; *Honsell/Melis,* Art. 7, Rn. 7; *P. Huber,* IHR 2006, 228, 229; *P. Huber/Mullis/P. Huber,* S. 8; *Janssen,* IHR 2004, 194, 199; *Kramer,* östJBl. 1996, 137, 146; *Kröll u. a./Perales Viscasillas,* Art. 7, Rn. 41; *Lookofsky,* 8 VJ. (2004), 181, 184 ff.; *Magnus,* CISG Methodology, S. 33, 42; *ders.,* RabelsZ 53 (1989), 116, 123; *Mazzotta,* 3 Loy. Univ. Chi. Int'l L. Rev. (2005), 85, 91; *Melin,* S. 390; *T. M. Müller,* Beweislast, S. 12; *ders.,* IHR 2005, 16, 20; *T. M. Müller/Togo,* IHR 2005, 102, 103; MünchKomm/*Westermann,* Art. 7, Rn. 1; *Niemann,* S. 46; *Schlechtriem,* Internationales UN-Kaufrecht, Rn. 43; *ders.,* 36 Vict. U. Well. L. Rev. (2005), 781, 790; *Schlechtriem/Schwenzer/Schlechtriem,* CISG Commentary, 2. Aufl., Art. 7, Rn. 14; *Schmid,* Einheitliche Anwendung, S. 110 ff.; *Sollund,* Nordic L. J. (2007), 1, 10; *Spagnolo,* 10 Melb. J. Int'l L. (2009), 141, 165; *Staudinger/Magnus,* Art. 7, Rn. 21; *Sundermann,* Probleme der autonomen Auslegung, S. 200; *Teichert,* S. 25; *Zeller,* 12 Pace Int'l L. Rev. (2000), 79, 90; unverständlich jedoch *Zeller,* CISG and the Unification, S. 18; zum Begriff der „persuasive authority" neuerdings *DiMatteo,* CISG Methodology, S. 113, 119.

[157] Vgl. neuerdings *Lando,* FS Schwenzer, S. 1001, 1001 f.; zum guten Glauben im CISG vgl. neuerdings *G. Bell,* Rev. CISG (2005/2006), 5 ff.; *Magnus,* Art. 7 CISG-UP, S. 45 ff.; *Sheehy,* Rev. CISG (2005/2006), 153 ff.

[158] Vgl. UNCITRAL YB IX (1978), S. 35, Nr. 44.

stünde gerade im Gegensatz zu den vom CISG verfolgten Zielen[159] und dürfe daher nicht im CISG übernommen werden. Andererseits wurde die ausdrückliche Bezugnahme auf das Prinzip des guten Glaubens mit der Begründung abgelehnt, sie sei unnötig, da dieses Prinzip jeder Rechtsordnung immanent sei.[160] Die Befürworter der Einführung eines ausdrücklichen Hinweises auf den guten Glauben begründeten ihre Meinung unter anderem damit, dass die Streichung einer allgemein anerkannten Verhaltensnorm, deren Anwendbarkeit im internationalen Handel (vor allem mit den sogenannten Entwicklungsländern) verhindere.[161]

Da der Hinweis auf den „guten Glauben" in Art. 7 I aufgenommen worden ist,[162] d. h., **26** in der sich mit der Auslegung des Übereinkommens beschäftigenden Vorschrift, muss man sich fragen, ob der „gute Glaube" **lediglich für die Auslegung** des Übereinkommens oder auch in Bezug auf die **Parteierklärungen und -pflichten** relevant sein kann.[163] Ein Teil der Lehre betrachtet den Gutglaubensgrundsatz (unter anderem weil lediglich in Art. 7 I angesprochen) als bloße Auslegungsmaxime,[164] während ein anderer Teil der Lehre, und der Rechtsprechung,[165] trotz des nur in Art. 7 I enthaltenen Hinweises die Ansicht vertritt, er stelle sogar ein Mittel zur Herstellung der materiellen Gerechtigkeit zwischen den Parteien dar.[166] Der Gutglaubensgrundsatz ist sowohl **Auslegungsmaxime**, was sich unschwer aus **Art. 7 I** ergibt,[167] als auch Element, das sich auf die **Parteibeziehungen** auswirkt.[168] Letzteres aber **nur ex Art. 7 II**, d. h., nur insoweit, als es sich bei den zu lösenden Fragen um im Übereinkommen geregelte, aber nicht ausdrücklich entschiedene Fragen handelt,[169] und als der Gutglaubensgrundsatz als dem Übereinkommen zugrunde liegender allgemeiner Grundsatz Niederschlag gefunden hat.[170]

Dass **nationale Gutglaubensmaßstäbe** irrelevant sind,[171] außer wenn „sie auch als **27** Maßstäbe für den internationalen Handel anerkannt sind",[172] ergibt sich aus dem Gebot, dem internationalen Charakter des Übereinkommens und der Notwendigkeit seiner einheitlichen Anwendung Rechnung zu tragen.[173]

---

[159] Siehe auch *Keinath*, S. 83.
[160] UNCITRAL YB IX (1978), S. 35, Nr. 44.
[161] UNCITRAL YB IX (1978), S. 35, Nr. 46.
[162] Siehe zum guten Glauben auch *Magnus*, 10 Pace Int'l L. Rev. (1998), 89 ff.
[163] Vgl. hierzu auch *G. Bell*, Rev. CISG (2005/2006), 5, 12 ff.; *Ferrari*, Vendita internazionale, S. 145 ff.; *Schlechtriem*, Internationales UN-Kaufrecht, Rn. 44; *Sheehy*, Rev. CISG (2005/2006), 153, 154 ff.
[164] So wohl *Farnsworth*, Convention, S. 18; *Honnold/Flechtner*, Art. 7, Rn. 94; *Jurewicz*, 28 J. L. & Com. (2009), 63, 70; *Schlechtriem/Schwenzer/Schlechtriem*, CISG Commentary, 2. Aufl., Art. 7, Rn. 7; *Winship*, 8 Nw. J. Int'l L. & Bus. (1988), 623, 631; ebenso die Rechtsprechung s. ICC, 8611/HV/JK, CISG-online 236: „Aus der Förderung des guten Glaubens in Artikel 7 Absatz 1 Kaufrechtsübereinkommen lassen sich keine Nebenpflichten ableiten, denn diese Bestimmung betrifft nur die Auslegung des Übereinkommens".
[165] Vgl. etwa Comisión para la Protección del Comercio Exterior de México (Compromex), 30.11.1998, CISG-online 504 = Diario Oficial, 29.1.1999, I, 69 f.
[166] So etwa *King*, 8 VJ (2004), 249, 259; *Kock*, S. 30 und 132; *Schmid*, S. 249 und 257; kritisch *Enderlein/Maskow/Strohbach*, Art. 7, Anm. 5.: „Jedoch kann [durch Bezugnahme auf den Gutglaubensgrundsatz] ein eindeutiger Wortlaut des Vertrages nicht verändert werden"; kritisch auch *Schroeter*, 6 VJ (2002), 257, 260.
[167] In diesem Sinne wurde auf den Grundsatz von Treu und Glauben zurückgegriffen etwa in Schiedsgericht der Hamburger Freundschaftlichen Arbitrage, 21.6.1996, CISG-online 465.
[168] *Ferrari*, Vendita internazionale, S. 150; *Lando*, FS Schwenzer, S. 1001, 1002; *Magnus*, Art. 7 CISG-UP, S. 45; *Sannini*, L'applicazione, S. 42 f.; *Schroeter*, VJ (2002), 257, 260.
[169] *Ferrari*, 24 Ga. J. Int'l & Comp. L. (1994), 183, 215; so nunmehr auch *Felemegas*, Rev. CISG (2000/2001), 115, 249; so wohl auch *Hofmann*, 22 Pace Int'l L. Rev. (2010), 145, 167.
[170] Vgl. *Ferrari*, Int. Bus. L. J. 2003, 221, 225; *Ferrari u. a./Saenger*, Internationales Vertragsrecht, Art. 7, Rn. 6; so wohl auch *Schlechtriem*, Internationales UN-Kaufrecht, Rn. 44.
[171] In diesem Sinne auch *Bianca/Bonell/Bonell*, Art. 7, Anm. 2.4.2.; *Ferrari u. a./Saenger*, Internationales Vertragsrecht, Art. 7, Rn. 6; *P. Huber/Mullis/P. Huber*, S. 8; *Magnus*, Art. 7 CISG-UP, S. 46; *Niemann*, S. 50; *Rudolph*, Art. 7, Rn. 8; *Sauthoff*, IHR 2005, 151, 153; *Schlechtriem/Schwenzer/Schlechtriem*, CISG Commentary, 2. Aufl., Art. 7, Rn. 18; *Schlechtriem/Schwenzer/Schwenzer/Hachem*, CISG Commentary, Art. 7, Rn. 18; *Zeller*, 12 Pace Int'l L. Rev. (2000), 79, 93; vgl. in der Rechtsprechung RB Zwolle, 5.3.1997, CISG-online 545; a. A. OLG Brandenburg, 18.11.2008, CISG-online 1734 (Bezugnahme auf deutsche Gutglaubensstandards); vgl. auch OLG München, 15.9.2004, IHR 2005, 70, 71; OLG Oldenburg, 5.12.2000, CISG-online 618.
[172] *Enderlein/Maskow/Strohbach*, Art. 7, Anm. 6.
[173] Vgl. auch *Bamberger/Roth/Saenger*, Art. 7, Rn. 6; *Ferrari*, Vendita internazionale, S. 148, Fn. 1; *Ferrari u. a./Saenger*, Internationales Vertragsrecht, Art. 7, Rn. 6; *Piltz*, Internationales Kaufrecht, Rn. 2–186; *Soergel/*

2. Auslegungsmethoden

28 Wie erwähnt, enthält Art. 7 I keine Auslegungsmethoden,[174] sondern nur Auslegungsgrundsätze bzw. -ziele,[175] von denen sich der Rechtsanwender bei der Auslegung des Übereinkommens leiten lassen muss.[176]

29 Was die Auslegungsmethoden angeht, führt die Beachtung des internationalen Charakters einerseits und die Notwendigkeit der Förderung der einheitlichen Anwendung andererseits dazu, dass, wie bereits erwähnt,[177] **nationale Interpretationsmethoden nicht** herangezogen werden sollten.[178] Auf welche Methoden aber konkret zurückgegriffen werden kann, ist nicht ganz klar, da sich eine einheitliche Vorgehensweise bei der Auslegung von Einheitsrecht, trotz beachtlicher Annäherung[179] noch nicht herausgebildet hat.[180] Dies schließt jedoch **einige Gemeinsamkeiten und Übereinstimmungen** nicht aus,[181] auf die im Folgenden eingegangen werden soll.

30 a) **Wortlaut des Übereinkommens.** Wie generell hinsichtlich Einheitsrecht,[182] ist auch hinsichtlich des Übereinkommens **vor allem**[183] auf den **Wortlaut der Vorschriften** abzustellen.[184] Die Textinterpretation steht demnach im Vordergrund,[185] was dazu führt, dass – so der BGH in Bezug auf das Haager Kaufrecht – eine vom Wortlaut abweichende

---

Lüderitz/Fenge, Art. 7, Rn. 7; *Staudinger/Magnus*, Art. 7, Rn. 24; *Wasmer*, S. 81; a. A., jedoch ohne Begründung, *Note*, 97 Harv. L. Rev. (1984), 1984, 1991 („In applying the [good faith] rule, national courts remain free to draw on domestic – and hence diverse – conceptions of good faith").

[174] Siehe *Burkart*, S. 140; *Eiselen*, CISG Methodology, S. 61, 61; *Ferrari u. a./Saenger*, Internationales Vertragsrecht, Art. 7, Rn. 2; *Flechtner*, FS Schwenzer, S. 493, 502f.; *Hager*, FS Huber, S. 319, 322; *Schlechtriem/Schwenzer/Schlechtriem*, CISG Commentary, 2. Aufl., Art. 7, Rn. 19; *Schlechtriem/Schwenzer/Schwenzer/Hachem*, CISG Commentary, Art. 7, Rn. 20; *Sundermann*, Probleme der autonomen Auslegung, S. 40; *Vogel*, S. 10; *Witz/Salger/Lorenz/Witz*, Art. 7, Rn. 7 und 18.

[175] Vgl. *Frigge*, S. 113; *Flechtner*, FS Schwenzer, S. 493, 503; *Schmid*, Einheitliche Anwendung, S. 40; *Veneziano*, Dir. comm. int. 2001, 509, 510.

[176] Siehe auch *Karollus*, S. 11; *Magnus*, RabelsZ 53 (1989), 116, 122; *Schmitt*, CR 2001, 145, 147.

[177] Vgl. hierzu oben Rn. 9.

[178] *Burkart*, S. 141; *Dejaco*, S. 42; *Herber*, 2. Aufl., Art. 6, Rn. 19; *Hoffmann*, Koordination, S. 278; *Kramer*, Konvergenz und Internationalisierung der juristischen Methode, S. 71, 84; *Martinez Canellas*, S. 163; *Niemann*, S. 40 und 53; *Schlechtriem/Schwenzer/Schwenzer/Hachem*, CISG Commentary, Art. 7, Rn. 20.

[179] Diesbezüglich sei statt aller verwiesen auf *Honnold*, Uniform Words, S. 119 ff.

[180] So *Staudinger/Magnus*, Art. 7, Rn. 30; von einer wohl größeren Annäherung geht wohl *Herber*, 2. Aufl., Art. 6, Rn. 19, aus: „[Die Methoden der Auslegung] weichen von denen des deutschen Rechts nicht wesentlich ab." Ebenso neuerdings auch *Gruber*, Methoden, S. 108 ff.; *Hoffmann*, Koordination, S. 277.

[181] Vgl. *Melin*, S. 370: „weitreichende Übereinstimmung"; *Teichert*, S. 22: „Grundkonsens"; *van Alstine*, 146 U. Pa. l. Rev. (1998), 687, 740: „substantial agreement"; siehe auch *Gruber*, Methoden, S. 82: „Ziel der Auslegungslehre des internationalen Einheitsrechts muss es zunächst sein, eine Grundübereinstimmung im Hinblick auf das maßgebliche Auslegungsziel sowie die maßgeblichen Auslegungskriterien im Allgemeinen und ihre Anwendung im Einzelnen herzustellen".

[182] Vgl. *Kropholler*, Internationales Einheitsrecht, S. 258 ff.

[183] So auch OGH, 23.5.2005, CISG-online 1041 = IHR 2005, 165, 167: „Das UN-Kaufrecht schafft materielles Recht [...] und ist nach Art. 7 UN-K autonom auszulegen, weshalb hier Erörterungen zur österreichischen Rechtslage [...] unterbleiben müssen und vorrangig vom Wortsinn [...] auszugehen ist". Vgl. auch *Forestal Guarani S. A. v. Daros International, Inc.*, U. S. Ct. App. (3rd Cir.), 21.7.2010, CISG-online 2112 (The interpretation of a treaty, like the interpretation of a statute, begins with its text"); *Genpharm Inc. v. Pliva-Lachema A. S*, U. S. Dist. Ct. (E. D. N. Y.), 19.3.2005, CISG-online 1006 („[i]n deciding issues under the treaty, courts generally look to its language"); ähnlich auch *Schmitz-Werke GmbH & Co. v. Rockland Industries, Inc.; Rockland International FSC, Inc.*, U. S. Ct. App. (4th Circ.), 21.6.2002, CISG-online 625.

[184] *Brunner*, Art. 7, Rn. 5; *de Lukowicz*, S. 26; *Ferrari u. a./Saenger*, Internationales Vertragsrecht, Art. 7, Rn. 2; *Gruber*, Methoden, S. 125 ff.; *Hackney*, 61 La. L. Rev. (2001), 473, 477; *Hoffmann*, Koordination, S. 279; *P. Huber/Mullis/P. Huber*, S. 9; *Karollus*, S. 13; *Kröll u. a./Perales Viscasillas*, Art. 7, Rn. 33; *Lookofsky*, 13 Duke J. Comp. & Int'l L. (2003), 263, 266; *Markel*, 21 Pace Int'l L. Rev. (2009), 163, 195; MünchKomm/*Westermann*, Art. 7, Rn. 7; *Niemann*, S. 53 f.; *Piltz*, Internationales Kaufrecht, Rn. 2–185; *Schlechtriem/Schwenzer/Schlechtriem*, CISG Commentary, 2. Aufl., Art. 7, Rn. 20; *Schlechtriem/Schwenzer/Schwenzer/Hachem*, CISG Commentary, Art. 7, Rn. 21; *Schultz*, 35 Cornell Int'l L. J. (2002), 263, 268; *Soergel/Lüderitz/Fenge*, Art. 7, Rn. 9; *Staudinger/Magnus*, Art. 7, Rn. 32; *Teichert*, S. 22 f.; *Vogel*, S. 10.

[185] So schon *Eiselen*, CISG Methodology, S. 61, 61; *Herber/Czerwenka*, Art. 6, Rn. 7; *Magnus*, CISG Methodology, S. 33, 53; *Rudolph*, Art. 7, Rn. 7.

Gesetzesauslegung nur gerechtfertigt werden kann, wenn „schwerwiegende, am Gerechtigkeitsdenken orientierte Gründe vorliegen."[186]

Die Textinterpretation ist aber nicht unproblematisch, da der allein **maßgebende Text** der **des Originals** ist, und zwar – mit gleicher Verbindlichkeit – in allen Vertragssprachen[187] (Arabisch, Chinesisch, Englisch, Französisch, Russisch und Spanisch).[188] Die anderen existierenden Fassungen sind lediglich als **unverbindliche Hilfsmittel** anzusehen.[189] Dies gilt selbstverständlich auch für die **deutsche Übersetzung,**[190] obwohl sie von Sachverständigen der (zurzeit ihrer Erarbeitung) vier deutschsprachigen Ländern – Bundesrepublik Deutschland, Österreich, Schweiz und DDR –, die an der Konferenz beteiligt waren, gemeinsam ausgearbeitet wurde.[191] Daher ist es falsch davon auszugehen, praktisch werde die deutsche Übersetzung für die innerstaatliche Anwendung für sich die Vermutung beanspruchen müssen und können, sie übertrage zutreffend in die deutsche Rechtsterminologie den Inhalt des CISG.[192] Die Unrichtigkeit der erwähnten Vermutung ergibt sich auch aus einer einfachen Gegenüberstellung der deutschen Übersetzung mit der englischen und der französischen Textfassung, enthält die deutsche Übersetzung doch einige Fehler und Ungenauigkeiten.[193] **31**

Dass die deutsche Übersetzung lediglich als unverbindliches Hilfsmittel beziehungsweise als Anwendungshilfe[194] zu qualifizieren ist, steht in scharfem **Gegensatz** zu den **Haager Kaufgesetzen,** die in der Bundesrepublik Deutschland in der Fassung der deutschen Übersetzung Gesetzeskraft hatten. **32**

Zur Auslegung des CISG müssen eigentlich **alle authentischen Fassungen** miteinander verglichen werden;[195] dass dies wohl kaum geschehen wird, wird wohl niemanden überraschen.[196] Bleiben auch danach noch Auslegungszweifel, ist auf die Vorschriften zur Auslegung mehrsprachiger völkerrechtlicher Instrumente der **Wiener Vertragsrechtskonven-** **33**

---

[186] BGH, 25.9.1991, WM 1991, 2108; vgl. auch MünchKomm/*Westermann*, Art. 7, Rn. 7: „Eine Abweichung der Interpretation vom Wortlaut muss eigens begründet werden"; vorsichtiger *Melin*, S. 396 f.

[187] Vgl. auch die Unterzeichnungsklausel des CISG und die Bemerkungen dazu; kritisch *Bell*, FS Schwenzer, S. 143, 144 ff.

[188] Der Text des CISG in allen Vertragssprachen ist abgedruckt in Bianca/Bonell, S. 683 ff.

[189] *Achilles*, Art. 7, Rn. 4; *Burkart*, S. 181; *de Lukowicz*, S. 26; *Diedrich*, Autonome Auslegung, S. 66; *Ferrari u. a./Saenger*, Internationales Vertragsrecht, Art. 7, Rn. 2; *Piltz*, Internationales Kaufrecht, Rn. 2–193; *Schillo*, IHR 2003, 257, 258; *Teichert*, S. 23; vgl. auch Vor Artt. 1–6 Rn. 26 ff.; weniger zurückhaltend *Gruber*, Methoden, S. 147.

[190] *Niemann*, S. 54.

[191] Zur Unterscheidung von verschiedenen Arten von – nicht verbindlichen – Übersetzungen (offizielle Texte, amtliche Übersetzungen, private Übersetzungen) vgl. *Gruber*, Methoden, S. 146 ff.

[192] So aber *Herber*, 2. Aufl., Art. 6, Rn. 21; krit. zu dieser Ansicht auch *Melin*, S. 371, Fn. 231.

[193] Siehe diesbezüglich *Honsell/Melis*, Art. 7, Rn. 10, und vor allem *Staudinger/Magnus*, Art. 7, Rn. 19, wo verschiedene Fehler und Ungenauigkeiten der deutschen Übersetzung hervorgehoben werden.

[194] *Staudinger/Magnus*, Art. 7, Rn. 15.

[195] *Bell*, FS Schwenzer, S. 143, 151 ff.; *de Lukowicz*, S. 27; *Ferrari u. a./Saenger*, Internationales Vertragsrecht, Art. 7, Rn. 2; *Flechtner*, 17 J. L. & Com. (1998), 187, 207 f.; *Gebauer*, Uniform L. Rev. 2000, 683, 687; *Hager*, FS Huber, S. 319, 323; *Niemann*, S. 54; *Schmid*, Einheitliche Anwendung, S. 24; *Teichert*, S. 23; kritisch diesbezüglich MünchKomm/*Westermann*, Art. 7, Rn. 7.

[196] Es sei an dieser Stelle jedoch darauf hingewiesen, dass bislang zwar noch kein Gericht auf alle sechs Fassungen zurückgegriffen hat; das OLG München hat aber in seinem Urt. v. 3.12.1999, CISG-online 585 = RIW 2000, 712, 713, auf zwei offizielle Fassungen (die englische und die französische) verwiesen, um die Frage zu lösen, wann von einem „wesentlichen Teil" der für die Herstellung notwendigen Stoffe im Sinne von Art. 3 I gesprochen werden kann. Auf für die Praxis relevante Unterschiede zwischen der englischen und französischen Fassung einerseits und der deutschen Fassung andererseits hinweisend etwa BGer, 13.11.2003, CISG-online 840: „Nach der deutschen Übersetzung von Art. 39 Abs. 1 des Übereinkommens der Vereinten Nationen über Verträge über den internationalen Warenkauf […] hat der Käufer bei der Anzeige der Vertragswidrigkeit deren Art genau zu bezeichnen. Der englische und französische Konventionstext sprechen von ‚specifying the nature of the lack of conformity' bzw. von ‚en précisant la nature de ce défaut'. Die Anzeige muss damit die Natur, d. h. die Art oder Wesensart, das Wesen bzw. den Charakter der Vertragswidrigkeit spezifizieren (vgl. Merriam-Webster Dictionary, der ‚nature' als Synonym von ‚essence' als ‚the inherent character of a person or thing' definiert; vgl. auch Le Grand Robert de la langue française, der ‚nature' mit ‚essence' gleichsetzt). Zu beachten ist, dass die Verben ‚specify' bzw. ‚préciser' nicht nur mit ‚genau bezeichnen', sondern auch mit ‚bezeichnen' bzw. ‚angeben' übersetzt werden können. Die Original-

tion von 1969 zurückzugreifen,[197] und dies unabhängig davon, ob es sich bei den auszulegenden Vorschriften um in Teil IV des CISG enthaltene Vorschriften handelt, auf die ein Teil der Lehre die Möglichkeit der direkten Anwendung der Auslegungsregeln der Wiener Vertragsrechtskonvention beschränken möchte.[198] Die in der Wiener Vertragsrechtskonvention enthaltenen Vorschriften sind zur Auslegung auch auf die anderen Teile des CISG anwendbar,[199] genauso wie sie auf die Auslegung etwa der Vorschriften der CMR anwendbar sind,[200] und dies, obwohl das CISG ein law-making treaty ist, auf das ein Teil der Lehre die Wiener Vertragsrechtskonvention nicht angewandt sehen will:[201] Eine Unterscheidung zwischen law-making treaty einerseits und contract-treaties andererseits wird nämlich für Fragen der Auslegung in Bezug auf die Wiener Vertragsrechtskonvention abgelehnt.[202]

34 Die Vorschriften kollidieren auch nicht mit den Geboten des Art. 7 I: Letztere stellen vielmehr nur eine Zusammenfassung der verschiedenen Vorschriften der Wiener Vertragsrechtskonvention dar. Daraus folgt, dass man auch bei Fehlen des Art. 7 I zu den gleichen Auslegungsresultaten gelangen würde.[203]

35 Bei sich aus der **Vielfalt der authentischen Textfassungen** des CISG ergebenden Auslegungszweifeln führt die Anwendung der Vorschriften der Wiener Vertragsrechtskonvention dazu, dass – da anlässlich sowohl der Vorarbeiten als auch der Diplomatischen Konferenz die vorwiegend benutzte Sprache die englische war[204] – in Zweifelsfällen der **englischen** (bisweilen aber auch der französischen)[205] **Fassung besonderes Gewicht** zukommt,[206] so mittlerweile auch die (höchstrichterliche) Rechtsprechung.[207]

---

texte stellen daher an die Genauigkeit der Bezeichnung weniger hohe Anforderungen, als dies die deutsche Übersetzung erwarten lässt".

[197] A. A. *Kröll u. a./Perales Viscasillas,* Art. 7, Rn. 9; *Lohmann,* Parteiautonomie, S. 6; *Schlechtriem/Schwenzer/Schwenzer/Hachem,* CISG Commentary, Art. 7, Rn. 22.

[198] So etwa *Burkart,* S. 156 f.; *Diedrich,* Autonome Auslegung, S. 133; *ders.,* RIW 1995, 352, 357; *Enderlein/Maskow/Strohbach,* Art. 7, Anm. 2.2.; *Grieser,* S. 73; MünchKomm/*Westermann,* Art. 7, Rn. 2; *Niemann,* S. 55; *Reinhart,* Art. 7, Rn. 8; *Piltz,* Internationales Kaufrecht, Rn. 2–184; *Schlechtriem/Schwenzer/Schlechtriem,* CISG Commentary, 2. Aufl., Art. 7, Rn. 12; *Staudinger/Magnus,* Art. 7, Rn. 16; *Wey,* Rn. 383; *Witz/Salger/Lorenz/Witz,* Art. 7, Rn. 19; *Zeller,* 12 Pace Int'l L. Rev. (2000), 79, 85–86; *Schmid,* Einheitliche Anwendung, S. 39, schließt sogar die Anwendung von Art. 7 CISG auf die Schlussbestimmungen aus und will ausschließlich die Wiener Vertragsrechtskonvention zur Anwendung kommen lassen.

[199] Ebenso *Bammarny,* Treu und Glauben, S. 129 ff.; *Diez-Picazo/Calvo Caravaca,* Art. 89, S. 700; *Happ,* RIW 1997, 376, 377; *Magnus,* CISG Methodology, S. 33, 47; a. A. *Melin,* S. 361 f.

[200] Vgl. hierzu *MünchKommHGB/Basedow,* Einl. CMR, Rn. 18 ff.

[201] Siehe etwa *Karollus,* S. 13.

[202] So *Gruber,* Methoden, S. 122; *Happ,* RIW 1997, 376, 379, m. w. N.; a. A. *Lohmann,* Parteiautonomie, S. 6.

[203] A. A. wohl *Reinhart,* Art. 7, Rn. 8.

[204] Siehe diesbezüglich die Bemerkungen des schwedischen Delegierten anlässlich der Diplomatischen Konferenz: „English had been more or less the working language", O. R., S. 272.

[205] *Bell,* FS Schwenzer, S. 143, 144; *Ferrari u. a./Saenger,* Internationales Vertragsrecht, Art. 7, Rn. 2; *Hager,* FS Huber, S. 319, 324.

[206] Sich im Zweifelsfalle für den Vorrang der englischen Fassung aussprechend auch *Achilles,* Art. 7, Rn. 4; *Brunner,* Art. 7, Rn. 5; *Ferrari u. a./Saenger,* Internationales Vertragsrecht, Art. 7, Rn. 2; *Gruber,* Methoden, S. 142; *Honsell/Melis,* Art. 7, Rn. 10; *Melin,* S. 372; *J. Meyer,* RabelsZ 69 (2005), 457, 480; *Piltz,* Internationales Kaufrecht, Rn. 2–183; *Schlechtriem/Schwenzer/Schlechtriem,* CISG Commentary, 2. Aufl., Art. 7, Rn. 22; *Schlechtriem/Schwenzer/Schlechtriem,* CISG Commentary, Art. 7, Rn. 4; *Schroeter,* UN-Kaufrecht, S. 299, Fn. 4; *Staudinger/Magnus,* Art. 7, Rn. 17 und 33; *Vogel,* S. 8; *Wulf,* S. 38; a. A. *Flechtner,* 17 J. L. & Com. (1998), 187, 208, der sich gegen die Bevorzugung, auch im Falle eines Widerspruchs der verschiedenen verbindlichen Textfassungen, der englischen Originalfassung ausspricht; so auch *Bell,* FS Schwenzer, S. 143, 151; *Kröll u. a./Perales Viscasillas,* Art. 7, Rn. 34; a. A. auch MünchKomm/*Westermann,* Art. 7, Rn. 7, der immer vom „Übergewicht der englischen Fassung" ausgeht.

[207] Vgl. BGer, 13.11.2003, CISG-online 840: „Bei Unklarheiten über den Wortlaut ist auf die Originaltexte abzustellen, wobei der englischen und sekundär der französischen Fassung eine erhöhte Bedeutung zukommt, da Englisch und Französisch die offiziellen Konferenzsprachen waren und die Verhandlungen hauptsächlich auf Englisch geführt wurden".

b) Historische Auslegung. Die Textinterpretation reicht jedoch nicht immer aus, um 36 alle Auslegungszweifel zu bereinigen, weshalb sie der Ergänzung durch weitere Interpretationsmethoden bedarf.[208] Zu den bezüglich des CISG sowohl von der Lehre aus dem civil law Bereich[209] als auch der aus dem common law Bereich[210] (die bekanntlich lange Zeit vor einem Rückgriff auf die Entstehungsgeschichte scheute),[211] allgemein anerkannten Interpretationsmethoden zählt auch die **historische Auslegung**;[212] demnach ist die Entstehungsgeschichte der auszulegenden Vorschrift heranzuziehen,[213] so mittlerweile auch die (deutsche) Rechtsprechung.[214] Dies ist nicht weiter schwierig, da die **Materialien** bei dem CISG **zugänglich** sind wie bei kaum einem anderen internationalen Übereinkommen.[215] Konferenzverlauf und Konferenzdokumente sind in den ausführlichen Official Records, aber auch in *Honnolds* Werk „Documentary History",[216] die Vorberatungen in UNCITRAL und seiner Arbeitsgruppe in den UNCITRAL-Yearbooks wiedergegeben.[217] Hinzu kommt, dass viele Vorschriften auf die Haager Kaufübereinkommen zurückgehen, über die in Deutschland in erheblichem Umfang Rechtsprechung und Literatur vorhanden ist.[218]

c) Systematische Auslegung. Bei der Auslegung des Übereinkommens muss auch die 37 systematische Stellung der jeweiligen Vorschrift sowie die Behandlung des Problems in anderen Vorschriften beachtet werden.[219] Dies kann durchaus dazu führen, dass einem auf der Grundlage der Textinterpretation erzielten Resultat zu widersprechen ist, und dies selbst dann, wenn die Textinterpretation keine Zweifel läßt. Als Beispiel sei hier nur auf die Einleitungsworte von Art. 4 verwiesen, wonach das CISG „ausschließlich" den Vertragsschluss und die Rechte und Pflichten der Parteien regelt. Die systematische Auslegung erlaubt jedoch, obwohl die Bedeutung des Wortes „ausschließlich" unzweifelhaft ist, zu einem anderen Resultat zu gelangen, regelt das CISG doch auch die Auslegung von Verträgen, Fragen der Formfreiheit, etc., also auch Fragen, die nicht unter die in Art. 4

---

[208] So ausdrücklich *Diedrich*, Autonome Auslegung, S. 68.
[209] *Audit*, Vente internationale, S. 48; *Bonell*, Nuove leggi civ. comm. 1989, 20, 22; *Enderlein/Maskow/Strohbach*, Art. 7, Anm. 3.; *Ferrari*, Vendita internazionale, S. 140 ff.; *Ferrari u. a./Saenger*, Internationales Vertragsrecht, Art. 7, Rn. 2; *P. Huber*, IHR 2006, 228, 230; *Karollus*, S. 11 f.; *Kramer*, östJBl. 1996, 137, 144; *Kröll u. a./Perales Viscasillas*, Art. 7, Rn. 35; *Lohmann*, Parteiautonomie, S. 4; *Lutz*, 35 Vic. U. Well. L. Rev. (2004), 771, 715; *Piltz*, Internationales Kaufrecht, Rn. 2–185; *Sannini*, L'applicazione, S. 14; *Schlechtriem/Schwenzer/Schlechtriem*, CISG Commentary, 2. Aufl., Art. 7, Rn. 24; *Witz/Salger/Lorenz/Witz*, Art. 7, Rn. 18; vgl. auch *Schlechtriem/Schwenzer/Schwenzer/Hachem*, CISG Commentary, Art. 7, Rn. 22, die jedoch suggerieren, dass mit dem Vergehen der Zeit die Bedeutung der historischen Auslegung abzunehmen hat.
[210] *Bailey*, 32 Cornell Int'l L. J. (1999), 273, 290; *Eiselen*, CISG Methodology, S. 61, 89; *Esslinger*, ALI-ABA (1999), 69, 73; *Felemegas*, Introduction, S. 18 f.; *Gruber*, Methoden, S. 164 ff.; *Rosenberg*, 20 Austr. Bus. L. Rev. (1992), 442, 447; *Schultz*, 35 Cornell Int'l L. J. (2002), 263, 268; *Zeller*, 12 Pace Int'l L. Rev. (2000), 79, 85.
[211] Vgl. hierzu auch *Ferrari*, Rev. int. dr. comp. (1996), 813, 834 f.; *Honnold*, Uniform Words, S. 131 ff.
[212] Vgl. auch *Melin*, S. 378 ff.
[213] *Amato*, 13 J. L. & Com. (1993), 1, 28; *Burkart*, S. 182; *Ferrari*, Int. Bus. L. J. 2003, 221, 222; *ders.*, Rev. int. dr. comp. 1996, 813, 833; *Gruber*, Methoden, S. 163 ff.; *Hackney*, 61 La. L. Rev. (2001), 478–479; *Harjani*, 23 Hous. J. Int'l L. (2000), 49, 64–65; *Honnold/Flechtner*, Art. 7, Rn. 88; *P. Huber/Mullis/P. Huber*, S. 9; *Lutz*, 35 Vic. U. Well. L. Rev. (2004), 711, 715; *Martinez Canellas*, S. 168 ff.; *Mazzotta*, 3 Loy. Univ. Chi. Int'l L. Rev. (2005), 85, 107; MünchKomm/*Westermann*, Art. 7, Rn, 7; *Nakata*, 7 Transnat'l Law. (1994), 141, 163; *Romito/Sant'Elia*, 14 Pace Int'l L. Rev. (2002), 179, 203; Soergel/*Lüderitz/Fenge*, Art. 7, Rn. 5; Staudinger/*Magnus*, Art. 7, Rn. 35; *Teichert*, S. 23; *Witz/Salger/Lorenz/Witz*, Art. 7, Rn. 22.
[214] Für einen Rückgriff auf die Entstehungsgeschichte, siehe etwa LG Aachen, 20.7.1995, CISG-online 169; OLG Frankfurt a. M., 20.4.1994, CISG-online 125 = RIW 1994, 593 f.
[215] *Schlechtriem/Schwenzer/Schlechtriem*, CISG Commentary, 2. Aufl., Art. 7, Rn. 24; *Sundermann*, Probleme der autonomen Auslegung, S. 195, Fn. 896.
[216] *Honnold*, Documentary History.
[217] Vgl. auch *Witz/Salger/Lorenz/Witz*, Art. 7, Rn. 22.
[218] *Herber/Czerwenka*, Art. 7, Rn. 8; *Karollus*, S. 15; *Magnus*, RabelsZ 53 (1989), 116, 123 f.; *Niemann*, S. 56.
[219] So Staudinger/*Magnus*, Art. 7, Rn. 34; vgl. auch *de Lukowicz*, S. 27; *Ferrari u. a./Saenger*, Internationales Vertragsrecht, Art. 7, Rn. 2; *Gebauer*, Uniform L. Rev. 2000, 683, 687; *Grieser*, S. 75; *Gruber*, Methoden, S. 148 ff.; *Hager*, FS Huber, S. 319, 324; *Hoffmann*, Koordination, S. 279; *Karollus*, S. 14; *Magnus*, RabelsZ 53 (1989), 116, 124; *ders.*, CISG Methodology, S. 33, 54 f.; MünchKomm/*Westermann*, Art. 7, Rn. 5; *Perea*, 20 Pace Int'l L. Rev. (2008), 191, 205; Soergel/*Lüderitz/Fenge*, Art. 7, Rn. 9; *Teichert*, S. 24.

erwähnten Rechtsmaterien subsumiert werden können, auf die sich der Geltungsbereich des CISG kraft Art. 4 zu beschränken scheint.[220]

38   Die Ansicht, eine **weitergehende systematische Auslegung** durch einen Rückgriff auf Lösungen **anderer Einheitsrechtskonventionen** zur Vermeidung von Wertungswidersprüchen wäre nur dann zulässig, wenn die vergleichend heranzuziehenden Übereinkommen auch von derselben internationalen Organisation oder denselben Staaten ausgearbeitet und verabschiedet worden seien,[221] ist nicht vertretbar.[222] Die etwa hinsichtlich des Factoring-Übereinkommens erarbeiteten Lösungen sollten durchaus bei der Auslegung des CISG herangezogen werden, gründen doch beide Übereinkommen auf derselben ratio conventionis und denselben Auslegungsgrundsätzen.[223] Außerdem kann nur eine **interkonventionelle Auslegung**[224] Einheitsrecht schaffen, das über die Grenzen einer reinen Teilrechtsvereinheitlichung hinausgeht.[225] Natürlich gilt das Gesagte nur insoweit, als den verschiedenen Konventionen die gleichen gesetzgeberischen Intentionen zugrunde liegen, weshalb etwa die Übernahme von anlässlich der Diskussion um IZPR-Konventionen erarbeiteten Ergebnisse nicht per se für die Auslegung von Einheitsprivatrechtskonvention (wie etwa das CISG) zu bejahen ist. Sind die gesetzgeberischen Intentionen, wie bei den verschiedenen Einheitsvertragsrechtskonventionen, jedoch identisch, dann darf eine interkonventionelle Auslegung nicht a priori abgelehnt werden.[226] Dies gilt auch in Bezug auf Konventionen, die keinen materiellrechtlichen Inhalt haben. Aus diesem Grund hat ein italienisches Gericht[227] – m. E. zu Recht[228] – die Ansicht vertreten, das CISG könne zur Bestimmung des Begriffs des „Warenkaufvertrages" der Verordnung (EG) Nr. 44/2001 des Rates vom 22.12.2000 über die gerichtliche Zuständigkeit und die Anerkennung und Vollstreckung von Entscheidungen in Zivil- und Handelssachen[229] herangezogen werden, handelt es sich doch auch bei diesem Begriff um einen „materiellrechtlichen" Begriff.[230]

39   Dies führt dazu, dass etwa zur Definition der „Niederlassung" im Sinne des CISG die anlässlich der Definition des Begriffs der „Niederlassung" im Sinne des Factoring-Übereinkommens erarbeiteten Lösungen benutzt werden können und vice versa.

40   **d) Rechtsvergleichung**[231]. Die Rechtsvergleichung kann bei der Auslegung und Anwendung des Übereinkommens nur beschränkt von Nutzen sein.[232] Abgesehen von prakti-

---

[220] Vgl. aber *P. Huber/Mullis/P. Huber*, S. 20: „As a general rule, one can assume that the terms ‚formation' and ‚rights and obligations of the parties' have to be understood as covering everything that the Convention actually deals with, in particular in Art. 14–24 CISG and in Art. 25–88, but also in Art. 11–13 CISG (concerning form which can also be regarded as a matte rof ‚formation' in its widest sense)".
[221] So *Diedrich*, Autonome Auslegung, S. 69; sich gegen die Berücksichtigung anderen Einheitsrechts aussprechend auch *Botzenhardt*, S. 130 f.; *Niemann*, S. 54; *Trommler*, S. 21; *Witz/Salger/Lorenz/Witz*, Art. 7, Rn. 21.
[222] Zum Folgenden eingehend *Ferrari*, Riv. dir. int. priv. proc. 2000, 669 ff.; i. E. ebenso neuerdings *Lohmann*, Parteiautonomie, S. 5, Fn. 11; *Melin*, S. 376; die hier vertretene Meinung völlig falsch verstehend MünchKomm/*Westermann*, Art. 7, Rn. 7, Fn. 33.
[223] Vgl. (jedoch vorsichtiger) auch *Magnus*, Konventionsübergreifende Interpretation, S. 571, 579 ff.
[224] Vgl. hierzu *Ferrari*, Riv. dir. int. priv. proc. 2000, 669 ff.; *Torsello*, Common Features, S. 271 ff.
[225] Vgl. hierzu auch *Ferrari*, Uniform L. Rev. 2000, 69 ff.
[226] Einschränkender *Gruber*, Methoden, S. 161: „Maßgeblich ist vielmehr der Wille des Regelungsgebers des zu einem späteren Zeitpunkt geschaffenen Regelungssystems, ein mit dem früher geschaffenen Regelungssystem inhaltlich abgestimmtes bzw. inhaltsgleiches Regelungssystem zu schaffen. Eine systematische Auslegung i. e. S. ist daher nur insoweit möglich, als es sich um die Bestimmung des Inhalts des später geschaffenen Regelungssystems handelt".
[227] Vgl. Trib. Padova, Urt. v. 10.1.2006, CISG-online 1157.
[228] Vgl. *Ferrari*, Giur. it. 2006, 1016 ff.; ders., IPRax 2007, 61 ff.
[229] Siehe Amtsblatt 2001 Nr. L 12, S. 1; berichtigt in Amtsblatt 2001 Nr. L 307, S. 28; ergänzt in Amtsblatt 2002 Nr. L 225, S. 13.
[230] Zustimmend auch *Ragno*, Giur. merito 2006, 1413 ff.
[231] Vgl. auch *Gruber*, Methoden, S. 196 ff.
[232] So ausdrücklich *Herber/Czerwenka*, Art. 7, Rn. 9; *Schlechtriem/Schwenzer/Schlechtriem*, CISG Commentary, 2. Aufl., Art. 7, Rn. 27; vorsichtig hinsichtlich der Verwendung der Rechtsvergleichung als Auslegungsmethode auch *Ferrari*, Rev. int. dr. comp. 1996, 813, 836; *Ferrari u. a./Saenger*, Internationales Vertragsrecht,

schen Schwierigkeiten, die der Berücksichtigung fremden Rechts – theoretisch aller Vertragsstaaten – namentlich durch die Gerichte im Wege stehen, entspricht die Berücksichtigung der Auslegung bestimmter Begriffe, die sich in nationalen Rechtsordnungen finden, auch nicht dem Ziel des Übereinkommens. Der **Vergleich mit der Auslegungspraxis** anderer Staaten[233] zum CISG wirft hingegen keine Probleme auf[234] und ist zwingend, um dem Gebot der Förderung der einheitlichen Anwendung gerecht zu werden,[235] ist aber wohl kaum als „echte Rechtsvergleichung" zu qualifizieren.[236]

IV. Lückenfüllung

Wie nach dem EKG, sind auch nach dem CISG Gegenstände, die im Übereinkommen **41** geregelt, in diesem aber nicht ausdrücklich entschieden sind, nach den **allgemeinen Grundsätzen** zu entscheiden, die dem Übereinkommen zugrunde liegen.[237] Lassen sich solche Grundsätze jedoch nicht feststellen, ist als **ultima ratio**[238] und insoweit abweichend vom EKG – auf über das IPR des Gerichtsstaates zu ermittelndes nationales Recht zurückzugreifen.[239]

1. Im Übereinkommen geregelte Gegenstände

Aus dem Wortlaut des Art. 7 II ergibt sich eindeutig, dass der Rückgriff auf die **42** allgemeinen Grundsätze des CISG nur in Bezug auf vom Übereinkommen geregelte, selbst wenn nicht ausdrücklich entschiedene Gegenstände vorgeschrieben ist.[240] Daraus folgt unter anderem, dass die Ansicht, wonach auch bei der Entscheidung von sich auf nicht geregelte Gegenständen beziehende Fragen auf die allgemeinen Grundsätze ab-

---

Art. 7, Rn. 2; *Honsell/Melis*, Art. 7, Rn. 11; *P. Huber/Mullis/P. Huber*, S. 9; *Najork*, S. 52; *Niemann*, S. 56; *Staudinger/Magnus*, Art. 7, Rn. 37; weniger zögernd *Burkart*, S. 142 ff.; ebenso *Schlechtriem/Schwenzer/Schwenzer/Hachem*, CISG Commentary, Art. 7, Rn. 24: „[t]he value of the comparative law method for the interpretation cannot be overestimated".

[233] Für neuere Überblicke zur CISG-Rechtsprechung verschiedener Staaten bzw. Regionen vgl. etwa *Bach* IPRax 2009, 299 ff.; *Ferrari*, International Sales Law. Applicability and Application of the 1980 Vienna Sales Convention, Boston/Leiden, 2. Aufl. 2012; *Flechtner*, The CISG in U. S. Courts, S. 91 ff.; *Garro*, Misunderstandings, S. 113 ff.; *Janssen*, The Application of the CISG in Dutch Courts, S. 129 ff.; *Lookofsky*, CISG Case Law in Scandinavia, S. 167 ff.; *Magnus*, CISG in the German Federal Civil Court, S. 211 ff.; *O. Meyer*, IPRax 2005, 462 ff.; *Navas Navarro*, IHR 2006, 74 ff.; *Perales Viscasillas*, Spanish Case Law on the CISG, S. 235 ff.; *Posch/Terlitza*, The CISG before Austrian Courts, S. 263 ff.; *Zeller*, The CISG in Australasia – An Overview, S. 293 ff.

[234] So auch *Bariatti*, S. 163; *Burkart*, S. 145; *Diedrich*, Autonome Auslegung, S. 75; *Ferrari*, Rev. int. dr. comp. 1996, 813, 831; vgl. zum Wert der „rechtsvergleichenden Auslegung" im CISG auch *Schmid*, Einheitliche Anwendung, S. 26 ff.

[235] *Diedrich*, Autonome Auslegung, S. 76; *Niemann*, S. 57.

[236] Vgl. auch *Brunner*, Art. 7, Rn. 5; *Diedrich*, RIW 1995, 352, 356; *Melin*, S. 387; *Schlechtriem*, Unification, S. 146 ff.; a. A. *Frignani/Torsello*, Il contratto internazionale, S. 465; *Witz/Salger/Lorenz/Witz*, Art. 7, Rn. 24.

[237] Dem Art. 7 Abs. 2 CISG ähnelnde Vorschriften finden sich auch in anderen Einheitssachrechtskonventionen; für eine neuere Liste vgl. *Schlechtriem/Schwenzer/Schwenzer/Hachem*, CISG Commentary, Art. 7, Rn. 27, Fn. 85.

[238] Vgl. American Arbitration Association, 23.10.2007, CISG-online 1645; Federal Arbitration Court for the Moscow Region, 25.6.2001, CISG Pace; vgl. auch *Dejaco*, S. 44 („extrema ratio"); *Kröll u. a./Perales Viscasillas*, Art. 7, Rn. 48 („ultima ratio").

[239] Dazu *Enderlein*, DDR-AW 1987/RiA Nr. 98, 1 ff.; *Hartwieg*, ZVerglRW 1993, 282, 285; *Janssen/Kiene*, CISG Methodology, S. 261, 261; *Magnus*, RabelsZ 53 (1989), 116, 120; *Niemann*, S. 59; *Paal*, ZVglRWiss (2011), 64, 77 f.; *Rosenberg*, 20 Austr. Bus. L. Rev. (1992), 442, 446; in der Rechtsprechung vgl. OG Kanton Thurgau, 12.12.2006, CISG-online 1566; Tribunal of International Commercial Arbitration at the Russian Federation Chamber of Commerce and Industry, 28.5.2004, CISG-online 1513; Juzgado Comercial No. 26, 2.7.2003, CISG Pace; BezG Sissach, 5.11.1998, CISG-online 1466.

[240] *Bock*, FS Schwenzer, S. 175, 183; *Ferrari*, JZ 1998, 9, 10; *ders.*, Int. Bus. L. J. 2003, 221, 226; *McMahon*, 44 Colum. J. Transnat'l L. (2006), 992, 992; *Paal*, ZVglRWiss (2011), 64, 65 f.

Art. 7 43   Teil I. Kapitel II. Allgemeine Bestimmungen

zustellen sei, nicht geteilt werden kann.[241] Diese überhaupt nicht geregelten Gegenstände[242] sind anhand des über das IPR des Forumsstaates zu ermittelnden anwendbaren Rechts zu entscheiden.[243]

43   Der Rückgriff auf die allgemeinen Grundsätze ist also nur vorgesehen, um die sogenannten „internen"[244] beziehungsweise „versteckten Lücken"[245] oder Lücken praeter legem[246] zu füllen,[247] **Rechtsfragen** also, die **in den Regelungsbereich des Übereinkommens** fallen,[248] auf die die Vorschriften desselben aber keine unmittelbare Antwort geben.[249] Die Frage, ob es sich um eine derartige Rechtsfrage handelt, muss demnach immer zuerst entschieden werden[250] und ist nicht immer leicht zu beantworten.[251] Fällt eine Frage nicht in den Regelungsbereich des Übereinkommens,[252] so liegt eine „nicht geregelte Frage" (beziehungsweise eine „externe Lücke"[253] oder Lücke intra legem[254]) vor, die sich entweder

---

[241] Vgl. hierzu *Diedrich*, RIW 1995, 352, 358 f., der bezüglich der nicht geregelten Fragen von der Unanwendbarkeit der im Art. 7 II festgelegten Vorgehensweise ausgeht, aber nicht schon deswegen das IPR des Forumsstaates zum Zuge kommen lassen will. Er schlägt vor, „nach einer mit der lex fori und lex causae zu vereinbarenden international einheitlichen kollisionsrechtlichen Anknüpfung zu suchen und das hiernach berufene Sachrecht in Hinblick auf die ratio conventionis des Einheitsrechts supranational auszulegen". Leider gibt es für diese Vorgehensweise keinen Rechtfertigungsgrund im Übereinkommen. Kritisch gegenüber der erwähnten Ansicht neuerdings auch *Melin*, S. 401; *Naumann*, S. 9 f.
[242] Ein Überblick der nicht geregelten Gegenstände findet sich neuerdings bei *Ferrari*, Forum International 1997, 89 ff.; *ders.*, Int. Bus. L.J. 1998, 835 ff.; *Mather*, 20 J.L. & Com. (2001), 155 ff.; *C. Witz*, Int. Bus. L.J. 2001, 253 ff.
[243] *Enderlein/Maskow/Strohbach*, Art. 7, Anm. 11.; *Hoffmann*, Koordination, S. 319; *Janssen/Kiene*, CISG Methodology, S. 261, 261; *Pfeiffer*, NJW 1997, 1207, 1212; *Staudinger/Magnus*, Art. 4, Rn. 19; *Teichert*, S. 7 ff.
[244] *Bammarny*, Treu und Glauben, S. 160; *Basedow*, Uniform L.Rev. 2000, 129, 135; *Brunner*, Vor Artt. 2–5, Rn. 1, Art. 7, Rn. 7; *Dejaco*, S. 43; *Ferrari u.a./Saenger*, Internationales Vertragsrecht, Art. 7, Rn. 7; *P. Huber/Mullis/P. Huber*, S. 34; *Karollus*, S. 16; *Kröll u.a./Perales Viscasillas*, Art. 7, Rn. 52; *Magnus*, RabelsZ 59 (1995), 469, 475; *ders.*, CISG Methodology, S. 33, 44; *McMahon*, 44 Colum. J. Trans'l L. (2006), 992, 993; *Melin*, S. 399; MünchKommHGB/*Benicke*, Art. 4, Rn. 4; *Niemann*, S. 59; *Paal*, ZVglRWiss (2011), 64, 79; *Schlechtriem/Schwenzer/Schwenzer/Hachem*, CISG Commentary, Art. 7, Rn. 27; *Schmid*, Einheitliche Anwendung, S. 173; *Sundermann*, Probleme der autonomen Auslegung, S. 29; *C. Witz*, D. 2002, Chron. 2796, 2798; vgl. in der Rechtsprechung AG Sursee, 12.9.2008, CISG-online 1728; OLG Frankfurt a.M., 6.10.2004, CISG-online 996.
[245] *Bammarny*, Treu und Glauben, S. 160; *Diedrich*, RIW 1995, 352, 353.
[246] *Colligan*, 6 VJ (2002), 40, 48; *Felemegas*, Rev. CISG (2000/2001), 115, 276 f.; *Ferrari*, Rev. int. dr. comp. 1996, 813, 842 f.; *Graffi*, Giur. merito 2004, 873, 879; *Hackney*, 61 La.L.Rev. (2001), 473, 478; *Kröll u.a./Perales Viscasillas*, Art. 7, Rn. 6; *Markel*, 21 Pace Int'l L.Rev. (2009), 163, 196; *McMahon*, 44 Colum. J. Trans-nat'l L. (2006), 992, 1002; *Pavic/Djordjevic*, 28 J.L. & Com. (2009), 1, 28; *Ragno*, Convenzione di Vienna e Diritto europeo, S. 123; in der Rechtsprechung zum CISG wird dieser Ausdruck etwa vom Tribunale di Padova, 25.2.2004, CISG-online 819 = Giur. it. 2004, 1402, 1405, verwendet.
[247] *Bock*, FS Shwenzer, S. 175, 183.
[248] *Schlechtriem*, Internationales UN-Kaufrecht, Rn. 45; vgl. auch *Frigge*, S. 5; *Gruber*, Methoden, S. 282 f., *Mather*, 20 J.L. & Com. (2001), 155, 156; MünchKomm/*Westermann*, Art. 7, Rn. 10; *Schmid*, Lückenfüllung und Normenkonkurrenz, S. 26 f.
[249] *Bamberger/Roth/Saenger*, Art. 7, Rn. 8; *Herber/Czerwenka*, Art. 7, Rn. 10.
[250] So auch *Janssen/Kiene*, CISG Methodology, S. 261, 265; *Magnus*, CISG Methodology, S. 33, 44; *Paal*, ZVglRWiss (2011), 64, 79; *Staudinger/Magnus*, Art. 7, Rn. 38.
[251] Vgl. auch *Paal*, ZVglRWiss (2011), 64, 66; *Schlechtriem/Schwenzer/Schwenzer/Hachem*, CISG Commentary, Art. 7, Rn. 28.
[252] Detailliert zur Abgrenzung der vom Übereinkommen erfassten Rechtsfragen von den nicht geregelten Rechtsfragen, vgl. die in *Ferrari*, Rev. dr. aff. int. 1998, 835 ff.; Art. 4 Rn. 12 ff.; *C. Witz*, Rev. dr. aff. int. 2000, 253 ff.
[253] Diesen Begriff verwenden etwa *Basedow*, Uniform L.Rev. 2000, 129, 135; *Brunner*, Vor. Artt. 2–5, Rn. 3, Art. 4, Rn. 3; *Naumann*, S. 1; *Ragno*, Convenzione di Vienna e Diritto europeo, S. 124; *Schlechtriem*, Internationales UN-Kaufrecht, Rn. 41; *Sundermann*, Probleme der autonomen Auslegung, S. 29; vgl. in der Rechtsprechung AG Sursee, 12.9.2008, CISG-online 1728; kritisch hierzu *Kramer*, östJBl. 1996, 137, 147, Fn. 90.
[254] *Colligan*, 6 VJ (2002), 40, 48; *Felemegas*, Rev. CISG (2000/2001), 115, 277; *Ferrari*, Uniform L.Rev. 1997, 451, 454 f.; *Graffi*, Giur. merito 2004, 873, 879; *Hackney*, 61 La.L.Rev. (2001), 473, 478; *Markel*, 21 Pace Int'l L.Rev. (2009), 163, 196; *McMahon*, 44 Colum. J. Transnat'l L. (2006), 992, 1002; *Melin*, S. 399; *Pavic/Djordjevic*, 28 J.L. & Com. (2009), 1, 28.

nach dem anwendbaren nationalen Recht[255] oder der im gegebenen Fall anwendbaren Einheitsrechtskonvention beurteilt.[256]

2. Alternativen interner Lückenfüllung

Um interne Lücken von Einheitsrechtskonventionen zu schließen, können **grundsätz-** 44 **lich drei verschiedene Methoden** in Betracht kommen:[257] (a) die Füllung von Lücken allein durch Rückgriff auf die allgemeinen Grundsätze der Konvention, also allein von innen heraus;[258] diese Methode ist vergleichbar mit der, die in vielen civil-law-Ländern herangezogen wird, um Lücken in Zivilgesetzbüchern zu füllen;[259] (b) Lückenfüllung durch „externe" Vorschriften, eine Methode, die offensichtlich im Bereich des Common Law bevorzugt wird;[260] (c) Lückenfüllung durch Kombination der unter (a) und (b) erwähnten Methoden,[261] wobei zuerst auf die allgemeinen Grundsätze zurückgegriffen werden soll und nur in Ermangelung solcher auf ein mittels IPR näher bestimmtes nationales Recht.[262]

Während sich die Verfasser des Haager Kaufrechts klar für die erste Methode entschieden 45 haben, wiesen die Verfasser des CISG (genauso wie anderer neuerer Einheitsvertragsrechtskonventionen) diese Methode – da „kaum akzeptabel" – zurück,[263] was sich unschwer aus dem Text des Art. 7 II ableiten lässt. Damit haben die Verfasser auch die Idee verworfen, es sei möglich, ein vom nationalen Recht unabhängiges Einheitsrecht zu schaffen.[264]

Die in Art. 7 II statuierte **„gemischte" Methode**[265] hat aber nicht nur den Vorteil, 46 realistischer zu sein, als die, wonach lediglich auf interne Regeln abzustellen ist,[266] sondern

---

[255] So auch *Achilles*, Art. 7, Rn. 7; *Bianca/Bonell/Bonell*, Art. 7, Anm. 2.3.1.; *Brunner*, Art. 7, Rn. 7 a. E.; *Ferrari*, Int. Bus. L. J. 2003, 221, 226; *Ferrari u. a./Saenger*, Internationales Vertragsrecht, Art. 7, Rn. 8; *Honsell/ Melis*, Art. 7, Rn. 12; *Janssen/Kiene*, CISG Methodology, S. 261, 261 und 264; *Magnus*, CISG Methodology, S. 33, 44; MünchKomm/*Westermann*, Art. 7, Rn. 10; *Paal*, ZVglRWiss (2011), 64, 80; *Thiele*, RIW 2000, 892, 894.
Vgl. in der Rechtsprechung RB Rotterdam, 17.3.2010, CISG-online 2098; RB Zwolle, 9.12.2009, CISG-online 2069; LG München I, 18.5.2009, CISG-online 1998; San Lucio, S. r. l. et al. v. Import & Storage Services, LLC et al., U. S. Dist. Ct. (D. N. J.), 15.4.2009, CISG-online 1836; Court of First Instance of Athens, Aktenzeichen 4505/2009 (ohne Datum), CISG-online 2228; AG Sursee, 12.9.2008, CISG-online 1728; LG Landshut, 12.6.2008, CISG-online 1703; Audiencia Provincial de Pontevedra, 19.12.2007, CISG-online 1688; KG Wallis, 27.4.2007, CISG-online 1721; Hof 's-Hertogenbosch, 2.1.2007, CISG-online 1434; District Court Galanta, 15.12.2006, CISG-online 1863; OG Kanton Thurgau, 12.12.2006, CISG-online 1566; Tribunale di Modena, 9.12.2005, CISG-online 1398; Tribunal of International Commercial Arbitration at the Russian Federation Chamber of Commerce and Industry, 15.11.2006, CISG-oline 2008; Tribunal of International Commercial Arbitration at the Russian Federation Chamber of Commerce and Industry, 7.3.2006, CISG-online 1942; RB Arnhem, 1.3.2006, CISG-online 1475; Tribunal of International Commercial Arbitration at the Russian Federation Chamber of Commerce and Industry, 13.2.2006, CISG-online 1623; Tribunal of International Commercial Arbitration at the Russian Federation Chamber of Commerce and Industry, 13.1.2006, CISG-online 1622; Tribunale di Modena, 9.12.2005, CISG-online 1398.
Sich vehement gegen die Qualifikation der nicht geregelten Fragen als „Lücken" aussprechend *Gebauer*, Uniform L. Rev. 2000, 683, 696 f.
[256] OG Kanton Thurgau, 12.12.2006, CISG-online 1566.
[257] Siehe zum Folgenden *Ferrari*, JZ 1998, 9, 10 f.; *ders.*, 24 Ga. J. Int'l & Comp. L. (1994), 183, 217 f.; diese Ausführungen oft – und fast immer wortgleich übernehmend – *Felemegas*, Interpretation, S. 24 ff.; *ders.*, Rev. CISG (2000/2001), 115, 277 f.
[258] Vgl. *Kritzer*, Guide to Practical Applications, S. 117; *Sannini*, L'applicazione, S. 45.
[259] Vgl. *Bianca/Bonell/Bonell*, Art. 7, Anm. 2.3.2.; *Ferrari*, Int. Bus. L. J. 2003, 221, 226–227; *Hackney*, 61 La. L. Rev. (2001), 473, 478; *Ubartaite*, 7 (EJLR), 2005, 277, 290.
[260] So *Dore/Defranco*, 23 Harv. Int'l L. J. (1982), 49, 63 f.; *Hackney*, 61 La. L. Rev. (2001), 473, 478.
[261] *Sannini*, L'applicazione, S. 45 f.
[262] Vgl. zu den im Text angesprochenen drei Methoden *Kropholler*, RabelsZ (1974), 382; es sei angemerkt, dass zumindest ein Autor lediglich zwei Methoden ((a) und (b)) anerkennt: *Honka*, 11 Tul. Eur. & Civ. L. Forum (1996), 142 f.
[263] *Dore/Defranco*, 23 Harv. Int'l L. J. (1982), 49, 63.
[264] Ähnlich auch *Frignani*, S. 308.
[265] *Ferrari*, JZ 1998, 9, 11.
[266] So neuerdings auch *Melin*, S. 406.

auch den, die durch die Konvention angestrebte Rechtseinheit zu fördern:[267] Wird nämlich bei der Lückenfüllung zuerst eine Lösung innerhalb des Übereinkommens gesucht und nur subsidiär auf „externe" Vorschriften zurückgegriffen, auf die das IPR verweist, so kommt dies der Rechtseinheit unweigerlich zugute.[268]

47 Die Berufung auf die allgemeinen Grundsätze stellt lediglich eine Art dar, Lücken aus der Konvention – also von innen – heraus, denn darum geht es in Art. 7 II,[269] zu schließen.[270] Man muss sich daher fragen ob Art. 7 II in einem weiten Sinn zu verstehen ist, d. h., ob Art. 7 II etwa auch das **Analogieverfahren** als Mittel der Lückenschließung zulässt,[271] oder ob er restriktiv auszulegen ist, also dahingehend, dass er nur einen Rückgriff auf die allgemeinen Grundsätze der Konvention zulässt. Meiner Meinung nach ist das Analogieverfahren nicht nur **zulässig,**[272] sondern es ist sogar davon auszugehen, dass „es bei einer Lücke in der Konvention erforderlich ist, als erstes den Fall de quo durch eine analoge Anwendung der einzelnen Bestimmungen zu lösen".[273] Wenn allerdings die zu beantwortende Frage sich von den ausdrücklich geregelten so unterscheidet, dass es nicht ungerechtfertigt erscheint, eine abweichende Lösung zu wählen, muss man die erwähnten allgemeinen Grundsätze zur Lückenfüllung heranziehen[274] und folglich auf ein Vorgehen zurückgreifen, das sich von der analogen Anwendung insoweit unterscheidet,[275] als die konkrete Frage nicht mittels einer bloßen Erweiterung der einzelnen Vorschriften beantwortet wird, „sondern auf der Basis der Grundsätze und Bestimmungen, die Kraft ihres Allgemeincharakters in einem viel weiteren Umfang angewandt werden können".[276]

3. Die allgemeinen Grundsätze des Übereinkommens

48 Einige allgemeine Grundsätze lassen sich leicht herausarbeiten, da sie sich – mehr oder weniger klar – im CISG ausdrücklich formuliert finden.[277] Zu diesen gehört, so auch die Rechtsprechung,[278] ohne Zweifel das **Prinzip des Vorranges des Parteiwil-**

---

[267] So schon *Kramer,* Uniforme Interpretation, S. 423; ebenso in der Rechtsprechung Hof van Cassatie, 19.6.2009, CISG-online 1963.
[268] So auch *Bianca/Bonell/Bonell,* Art. 7, Anm. 2.3.; *Garro/Zuppi,* S. 57 f.; *Teichert,* S. 5.
[269] *Enderlein/Maskow/Strohbach,* Art. 7, Anm. 9.1.
[270] *Kramer,* östJBl 1996, 137, 148.
[271] Vgl. hierzu auch *Adame Goddard,* Compraventa internacional, S. 77.
[272] So etwa *Felemegas,* Rev. CISG (2000/2001), 115, 280 ff.; *Ferrari,* Int. Bus. L. J. 2003, 221, 227; *Ferrari u. a./Saenger,* Internationales Vertragsrecht, Art. 7, Rn. 7; *Gebauer,* Uniform L. Rev. 2000, 683, 697 f.; *Hackney,* 61 La. L. Rev. (2001), 473, 478; *Herber/Czerwenka,* Art. 7, Rn. 11; *Jurewicz,* 28 J. L. & Com. (2009), 63, 69; *Loewe,* S. 33; *Najork,* S. 47; *Paal,* ZVglRWiss (2011), 64, 88; *Schlechtriem,* Internationales UN-Kaufrecht, Rn. 47; *Schlechtriem/Schwenzer/Schlechtriem,* CISG Commentary, 2. Aufl., Art. 7, Rn. 30; *Schlechtriem/Schwenzer/Schwenzer/Hachem,* CISG Commentary, Art. 7, Rn. 31; *Soergel/Lüderitz/Fenge,* Art. 7, Rn. 10; *Teichert,* S. 27; a. A. MünchKomm/*Westermann,* Art. 7, Rn. 36 a. E.; vgl. in der Rechtsprechung Supreme Court of Poland, 11.5.2007, CISG-online 1790; OGH, 18.12.2002, CISG-online 1279.
[273] *Bianca/Bonell/Bonell,* Art. 7, Anm. 2.3.2.1.; so auch *Adame Goddard,* Compraventa internacional, S. 77; *Melin,* S. 411 f.; *Sannini,* L'applicazione, S. 47; *van Alstine,* 146 U. Pa. L. Rev. (1998), 687, 749; i. E. ebenso *Gruber,* Methoden, S. 288; *Hartmann,* IHR 2006, 181, 183.
[274] Vgl. hierzu *Herber,* 2. Aufl., Art. 7, Rn. 34, der anlässlich der Diskussion um die allgemeinen Grundsätze hervorhebt, dass es nicht unbedingt notwendig sei, eine Grenze zur Analogie zu ziehen, da auch diese zugelassen sei; kritisch hierzu *Rosenberg,* 20 Austr. Bus. L. Rev. (1993), 442, 451.
[275] Zur Trennung zwischen dem Analogieverfahren und der Anwendung allgemeiner Grundsätze, siehe statt aller *Kropholler,* Internationales Einheitsrecht, S. 292 ff.
[276] *Bianca/Bonell/Bonell,* Art. 7, Anm. 2.3.2.2.
[277] So auch *Adame Goddard,* Compraventa internacional, S. 78; *Bammarny,* Treu und Glauben, S. 160; *Ferrari,* JZ 1998, 9, 11; *Melin,* S. 413; *Sannini,* L'applicazione, S. 48; *Teichert,* S. 28; zurückhaltender *Herber/Czerwenka,* Art. 7, Rn. 11: „Allgemeine Grundsätze sind im Kaufübereinkommen kaum ausdrücklich niedergelegt"; ähnlich *Hoffmann,* Koordination, S. 281.
[278] Vgl. RB Tongeren, 25.1.2005, CISG-online 1106; Tribunale di Rimini, 26.11.2002, CISG-online 737 = Giur. it. 2003, 896, 903, m. Anm. *Ferrari;* Hof van Beroep Gent, 15.5.2002, CISG-online 746; RB Ieper, 18.2.2002, CISG-online 747; RB Ieper, 29.1.2001, CISG-online 606 = Rechtskundig Weekblad 2001, 1396 ff. m. Anm. *Roox;* LG Stendal, 12.10.2000, CISG-online 592 = IHR 2001, 32; Juzgado Nacional de Primera Instancia en lo Comercial No. 10, 6.10.1994, CISG-online 378.

lens,²⁷⁹ das generell als der wichtigste allgemeine Grundsatz betrachtet wird,²⁸⁰ mit der Folge, dass man davon ausgehen muss, dass das Übereinkommen selbst nur eine subsidiäre Rolle spielt, dessen Vorschriften also nur dann relevant sind, wenn die Vertragsparteien keine andere Absprache getroffen haben.²⁸¹ Daraus folgt wiederum, dass im Fall eines Konflikts zwischen dem Prinzip der Parteiautonomie und irgendeinem anderen allgemeinen Grundsatz ersteres vorgeht.²⁸²

Ob das **Gebot von Treu und Glauben,** das bereits unter dem EKG zu den allgemeinen 49 Grundsätzen gerechnet wurde,²⁸³ als echter Grundsatz angesehen werden kann, ist lange Zeit umstritten gewesen,²⁸⁴ wird heute aber sowohl von der herrschenden Lehre²⁸⁵ als auch von der Rechtsprechung²⁸⁶ nicht mehr in Frage gestellt.²⁸⁷ Da sich ein Hinweis auf das

---

²⁷⁹ Vgl. *Achilles,* Art. 7, Rn. 8; *Bamberger/Roth/Saenger,* Art. 7, Rn. 7; *Bammarny,* Treu und Glauben, S. 162 f.; *Burkart,* S. 194; *Dejaco,* S. 44; *Felemegas,* Rev. CISG (2000/2001), 115, 284; *Ferrari,* Int. Bus. L. J. 2003, 221, 227; *Ferrari u. a./Saenger,* Internationales Vertragsrecht, Art. 7, Rn. 7; *Frigge,* S. 294; *Frignani/Torsello,* Il contratto internazionale, S. 463; *Garro/Zuppi,* S. 58, Fn. 10; *Graves,* Annals Fac. L. Belgrade 2011, 124, 127 f.; *Gruber,* Methoden, S. 294; *Hackney,* 61 La. L. Rev. (2001), 473, 478; *Hager,* FS Huber, S. 319, 321; *Honsell/Melis,* Art. 7, Rn. 13; *P. Huber/Mullis/P. Huber,* S. 34; *Hyland,* Conformity of Goods, S. 305, 329 ff.; *Janssen/Kiene,* CISG Methodology, S. 261, 271 f.; *Karollus,* S. 16 f.; *Kramer,* östJBl. 1996, 137, 149; *Kröll u. a./Perales Viscasillas,* Art. 7, Rn. 58; *Mather,* 20 J. L. & Com. (2001), 155, 158 und 165; *Mohs,* FS Schwenzer, S. 1285, 1290; *Niemann,* S. 61; *Paal,* ZVglRWiss (2011), 64, 78 und 82; *Piltz,* Internationales Kaufrecht, Rn. 2–190; *Reifner,* IHR 2002, 52, 54; *Sannini,* L'applicazione, S. 48; *Schlechtriem,* Internationales UN-Kaufrecht, Rn. 49; *Schlechtriem/Schwenzer/Schlechtriem,* CISG Commentary, 2. Aufl., Art. 7, Rn. 30; *Schlechtriem/Schwenzer/Schwenzer/Hachem,* CISG Commentary, Art. 7, Rn 32; *Schroeter,* 6 VJ (2002), 257, 258; *Sein/Kull,* IHR 2005, 138, 139; *Soergel/Lüderitz/Fenge,* Art. 7, Rn. 10; *Staudinger/Magnus,* Art. 7, Rn. 42; *Teichert,* S. 29; *Veneziano,* Dir. comm. int. 2001, 509, 514; *Vogel,* S. 12; vgl. in der Rechtsprechung Court of First Instance of Athens, Aktenzeichen 4505/2009 (ohne Datum), CISG-online 2228; Tribunale di Padova, 25.2.2004, CISG-online 819; Yugoslav Chamber of Commerce, 9.12.2002, CISG-online 2123; Tribunale di Rimini, 26.11.2002, CISG-online 737; Hof Beroep Gent, 15.5.2002, CISG-online 746; RB van Koophandel Ieper, 18.2.2002, CISG-online 764.

²⁸⁰ Vgl. *Honnold/Flechtner,* Art. 7, Rn. 2; *P. Huber,* IHR 2006, 228, 234; *Melin,* S. 413; *Wasmer,* S. 21.

²⁸¹ So etwa *Farnsworth,* Rights and Obligations, S. 84; *Magnus,* RabelsZ 59 (1995), 469, 480; *Niemann,* S. 63.

²⁸² *Ferrari,* Int. Bus. L. J. 2003, 221, 227; *Janssen/Kiene,* CISG Methodology, S. 261, 272; *Kritzer,* Guide to Practical Applications, S. 115.

²⁸³ Vgl. *Dölle/Wahl,* Art. 17 EKG, Rn. 55 f.

²⁸⁴ Vgl. *Ferrari,* Vendita internazionale, S. 150.

²⁸⁵ *Achilles,* Art. 7, Rn. 8; *G. Bell,* Rev. CISG (2005/2006), 5, 16 ff.; *Bock,* FS Schwenzer, S. 175, 185; *Burkart,* S. 194; *Dejaco,* S. 44; *Diesse,* J. D. I. 2002, 55, 58 ff.; *Frignani/Torsello,* Il contratto internazionale, S. 463; *Herber/Czerwenka,* Art. 7, Rn. 11; *Honnold/Flechtner,* Art. 7, Rn. 94; *Honsell/Melis,* Art. 7, Rn. 13; *Janssen/Kiene,* CISG Methodology, S. 261, 272; *Karollus,* S. 12; *Lando,* FS Schwenzer, S. 1001, 1002; *Magnus,* Art. 7 CISG-UP, S. 45 ff.; *Mather,* 20 J. L. & Com. (2001), 155, 157; *Niemann,* S. 64; *Paal,* ZVglRWiss (2011), 64, 82; *Sannini,* L'applicazione, S. 42; *Schlechtriem,* Internationales UN-Kaufrecht, Rn. 48; *Thiele,* RIW 2000, 892, 894; *Vogel,* S. 12; *Witz/Salger/Lorenz/Witz,* Art. 7, Rn. 31; zurückhaltender *Loewe,* S. 33.

²⁸⁶ So in der neueren Rechtsprechung OLG Celle, 24.7.2009, CISG-online 1906; RB Rotterdam, 25.2.2009, CISG-online 1812; OLG München, 14.1.2009, CISG-online 2011; OLG Brandenburg, 18.11.2008, CISG-online 1734; Tribunal of International Commercial Arbitration at the Russian Federation Chamber of Commerce and Industry, 8.2.2008, CISG-online 2102; Audiencia Provincial de Navarra, 27.12.2007, CISG-online 1798; Tribunale di Rovereto, 21.11.2007, CISG-online 1590; American Arbitration Association, 23.10.2007, CISG-online 1645; OLG Köln, 21.12.2005, CISG-online 1201; LG Neubrandenburg, 3.8.2005, CISG-online 1190; Tribunal of International Commercial Arbitration at the Russian Federation Chamber of Commerce and Industry, 2.6.2005, CISG-online 1501; Tribunal of International Commercial Arbitration at the Russian Federation Chamber of Commerce and Industry, 27.5.2005, CISG-online 1456; Primer Tribunal Colegiado en Materia Civil del Primer Circuito, 10.3.2005, CISG-online 1004; Tribunale di Padova, 25.2.2004, CISG-online 819 = Giur. it. 2004, 1402, 1404; Hof 's-Gravenhage, 23.4.2003, CISG-online 903; ICC, 11849, CISG-online 1421; Hof van Beroep Gent, 15.5.2002, CISG-online 746; BGH, 9.1.2002, CISG-online 651 = IHR 2002, 16, 19; BGH, 31.10.2001, CISG-online 617 = IHR 2002, 14 f.; Hof Arnhem, 9.2.1999, CISG-online 1338 = NIPR 17 (1999), Nr. 244; CA Milano, 11.12.1998, CISG-online 430; BGH, 25.11.1998, CISG-online 353 = RIW 1999, 385; HGer Zürich, 30.11.1998, CISG-online 415; Comisión para la Protección del Comercio Exterior de México (Compromex), 30.11.1998, CISG-online 504 = Diario Oficial, 29.1.1999, 69 ff.; OLG Hamburg, 28.2.1997, CISG-online 261; Schiedsspruch des Int. Ct. Hungarian CCI, 17.11.1995, CISG-online 250; OLG Celle, 24.5.1995, CISG-online 152; CA Grenoble, 22.2.1995, CISG-online 151.

²⁸⁷ Siehe aber RB Zwolle, 5.3.1997, NIPR 15 (1997), Nr. 230; krit. hierzu *Janssen,* The Application of the CISG in Dutch Courts, S. 129, 140 f.

Gebot von Treu und Glauben lediglich in der die Auslegung des Übereinkommens betreffenden Vorschrift findet,[288] muss man aber vorsichtig sein, das **Gebot nicht** zu einer dem § 242 BGB ähnlichen **Generalklausel** werden zu lassen.[289] Daher muss man eine neuere deutsche Entscheidung kritisieren,[290] die auf der Grundlage des Gebotes der „Wahrung des guten Glaubens im internationalen Handel" eine Ausnahme vom Grundsatz der Erforderlichkeit der Aufhebungserklärung zugelassen hat, obwohl im CISG keine Ausnahme vorgesehen ist.[291]

50 In Bezug auf diesen Grundsatz ergeben sich auch praktische Probleme, da er zu **vage** ist, um dem Richter handhabbare Entscheidungshilfe geben zu können.[292] Er bedarf demnach **näherer Ausfüllung** durch genauer bestimmte Grundsätze,[293] zu denen, so auch die Rechtsprechung,[294] nach h. L. das Verbot des **venire contra factum proprium**[295] und das **Verbot missbräuchlicher Rechtsausübung**[296] zählen,[297] die sich auch aus einzelnen Vorschriften des CISG ergeben:[298] Relevant sind diesbezüglich vor allem Art. 16 II und, so auch die Rechtsprechung,[299] Art. 29 II.[300]

51 Auch das Institut der **Verwirkung** stellt zumindest in einem gewissen Maße eine Ausprägung des Gebotes von Treu und Glauben dar und muss als allgemeiner Grundsatz des Übereinkommens betrachtet werden,[301] trotz einiger Stimmen, die vom Gegenteil ausgehen.[302]

52 Zu den allgemeinen (mehr oder weniger ausdrücklich formulierten) Grundsätzen des Übereinkommens zählen auch: der Grundsatz der **Formfreiheit** (Art. 11),[303] der nur durch

---

[288] Vgl. oben Rn. 26.
[289] So aber ausdrücklich *Herber,* 2. Aufl., Art. 7, Rn. 17; vgl. jedoch *Soergel/Lüderitz/Fenge,* Art. 7, Rn. 8, die die im Text vertretene Ansicht befürworten.
[290] OLG Hamburg, 28.2.1997, CISG-online 261 = OLG-Rp. Hamburg 1997, 149 ff.
[291] Krit. auch *Ferrari,* Interpretation of the Convention and gap-filling: Art. 7, S. 138, 156; *ders.,* Int. Bus. L. J. 2003, 221, 226.
[292] So ausdrücklich *Magnus,* RabelsZ 59 (1989), 469, 480.
[293] *Staudinger/Magnus,* Art. 7, Rn. 25.
[294] Vgl. OLG München, 15.9.2004, CISG-online 1013 = IHR 2005, 72 ff.; Tribunale di Padova, 31.3.2004, CISG-online 823 = Giur. merito 2004, 1065, 1067; Tribunale di Padova. 25.2.2004, CISG-online 819 = Giur. it. 2004, 1402, 1405; Tribunale di Rimini, 26.11.2002, CISG-online 737 = Giur. it 2003, 896, 903; ICC, 8786/1997, CISG-online 749= ICC Ct. Bull. 2000, 70 ff.
[295] *Achilles,* Art. 7, Rn. 8; *Bamberger/Roth/Saenger,* Art. 7, Rn. 6; *Brunner,* Art. 7, Rn. 4; *Burkart,* S. 195; *Diesse,* J. D. I. 2002, 55, 62 und 83; *Escher,* RIW 1999, 495, 500; *Felemegas,* 13 Pace Int'l L. Rev. (2001), 399, 402; *Ferrari,* Uniform L. Rev. 1997, 451, 464; *Hoffmann,* Koordination, S. 287; *Magnus,* Art. 7 CISG-UP, S. 46; *Najork,* S. 105; *Niemann,* S. 64; *Sannini,* L'applicazione, S. 49; *Sauthoff,* IHR 2005, 151, 153; *Schlechtriem/Schwenzer/Schlechtriem,* CISG Commentary, 2. Aufl., Art. 7, Rn. 30; *Soergel/Lüderitz/Fenge,* Art. 7, Rn. 10; *Teichert,* S. 30; *Vogel,* S. 12; *Witz/Salger/Lorenz/Witz,* Art. 7, Rn. 14; vgl. in der Rechtsprechung etwa ICC, 8786/1997, CISG-online 749 = ICC Ct. Bull. 2000, 70 ff.
[296] *Achilles,* Art. 7, Rn. 8; *Audit,* Vente internationale, S. 51 f.; *Dejaco,* S. 44; *Escher,* RIW 1999, 495, 500; *Ferrari,* JZ 1998, 9, 12; *Frignani,* S. 308; *Herber/Czerwenka,* Art. 7, Rn. 6; *Honnold,* Uniform Words, S. 144; *Kröll u. a./Perales Viscasillas,* Art. 7, Rn. 58; *Najork,* S. 52 und 98; *Piltz,* Internationales Kaufrecht, Rn. 2–186; *Rudolph,* Art. 7, Rn. 14; *Schlechtriem/Schwenzer/Schwenzer/Hachem,* CISG Commentary, Art. 7, Rn. 32; *Teichert,* S. 30; *Thiele,* RIW 2000, 892, 894; vgl. in der Rechtsprechung etwa OLG München, 15.9.2004, CISG-online 1013 = IHR 2005, 70, 71; ICC, 8786, CISG-online 749 = ICC Ct. Bull. 2000, 70 ff.
[297] Vgl. diesbezüglich BGH, 25.11.1998, CISG-online 353 = RIW 1999, 385; CA Grenoble, 22.2.1995, CISG-online 151.
[298] *Magnus,* RabelsZ 59 (1989), 469, 481.
[299] Tribunale di Padova, 31.3.2004, CISG-online 823 = Giust. merito 2004, 1065, 1067.
[300] So auch *Ferrari,* JZ 1998, 9, 12; *Najork,* S. 105; *Staudinger/Magnus,* Art. 7, Rn. 44.
[301] *Bammarny,* Treu und Glauben, S. 166 f.; *Hoffmann,* Koordination, S. 287; *King,* 8 VJ (2004), 249, 264 ff.; *Magnus,* RabelsZ 59 (1995), 469, 482; *Mather,* 20 J. L. & Com. (2001), 155, 157; *MünchKomm/Westermann,* Art. 7, Rn. 9; *Niemann,* S. 64; *Schlechtriem,* Internationales UN-Kaufrecht, Rn. 48; *Teichert,* S. 31; vgl. in der Rechtsprechung etwa OLG Karlsruhe, 25.6.1997, CISG-online 263 = RIW 1998, 235 ff.; Internationales Schiedsgericht der Bundeskammer der gewerblichen Wirtschaft, Schiedssprüche SCH-4366 und SCH-4318, CISG-online 121 und 120 = RIW 1995, 590 ff.; Hof 's-Hertogenbosch, 26.2.1992, CISG-online 65 = NIPR 1992, Nr. 354.
[302] *Frigge,* S. 82; ebenso in der Rechtsprechung *Caterpillar, Inc. and Caterpillar Mexico, S. A. v. Usinor Industeel, Usinor Industeel (U. S. A.), Inc. and Leeco Steel Products, Inc.;* U. S. Dist. Ct. (N. D. Ill.), 30.3.2005, CISG-online 1007.
[303] *Achilles,* Art. 7, Rn. 8; *Bamberger/Roth/Saenger,* Art. 7, Rn. 7; *Bammarny,* Treu und Glauben, S. 167; *Bianca/Bonell/Bonell,* Art. 7, Anm. 2.3.2.2.; *Dejaco,* S. 44; *Felemegas,* Rev. CISG (2000/2001), 115, 285; *Ferrari,*

Art. 12 eingeschränkt wird;[304] der Grundsatz der **Pflicht zur Schadensminderung** (Art. 77),[305] auf Grund dessen der Schadensgläubiger den Schaden so gering als möglich halten muss;[306] der Grundsatz der **Verbindlichkeit** von im internationalen Handel allgemein bekannten und regelmäßig beachteten **Gebräuchen** (Art. 9);[307] der Grundsatz, wonach der Gläubiger bei Zahlungsverzug **Anspruch auf Zinsen** hat,[308] und zwar vom Tag ihrer Fälligkeit an (Art. 78);[309] der Grundsatz kontinentalen Ursprungs,[310] dass nur der **voraussehbare Schaden** ersetzt wird,[311] der sich, genauso wie der der **Totalreparation**, aus Art. 74 ergibt;[312] der Grundsatz, „dass für die Wirksamkeit von Erklärungen und Mitteilungen ihre Absendung genügt [...], soweit nicht die Konvention ausdrücklich

---

[304] IHR 2004, 1, 2; *ders.*, Int. Bus. L. J. 2003, 221, 228; *Ferrari u. a./Saenger*, Internationales Vertragsrecht, Art. 7, Rn. 7; *Herber/Czerwenka*, Art. 7, Rn. 12; *P. Huber*, IHR 2006, 228, 234; *P. Huber/Mullis/P. Huber*, S. 34; *Janssen/Kiene*, CISG Methodology, S. 261, 276 f.; *Kröll u. a./Perales Viscasillas*, Art. 7, Rn. 58; *Magnus*, RabelsZ 59 (1995), 469, 483; *Mather*, 20 J. L. & Com. (2001), 155, 158; *Melin*, S. 413; *Niemann*, S. 61; *Posch/Terlitza*, IHR 2001, 47, 50; *Reinhart*, Art. 7, Rn. 7; *Sannini*, L'applicazione, S. 48; *Schlechtriem*, Internationales UN-Kaufrecht, Rn. 49 a. E.; *Schlechtriem/Schwenzer/Schlechtriem*, CISG Commentary, 2. Aufl., Art. 7, Rn. 30; *Schlechtriem/Schwenzer/Schwenzer/Hachem*, CISG Commentary, Art. 7, Rn. 32; *Sein/Kull*, IHR 2005, 138, 139; *Teichert*, S. 31; *Thiele*, RIW 2000, 892, 894; a. A. *Jametti Greiner*, Vertragsabschluss, S. 43, 46 f.; vgl. in der Rechtsprechung RB Arnhem, 17.1.2007, CISG-online 1455; Tribunale di Padova, 31.3.2004, CISG-online 823; Tribunale di Padova, 25.2.2004, CISG-online 81 = Giur. it. 2004, 1402, 1405; AG Bern, 11.2.2004, CISG-online 1191; Tribunale di Rimini, 26.11.2002, CISG-online 737 = Giur. it. 2003, 896 ff., m. Anm. *Ferrari;* OGH, 9.3.2000, CISG-online 573 = IHR 2001, 39 f.; Comisión para la Protección del Comercio Exterior de México (Compromex), 29.4.1996, CISG-online 350 = Diario Oficial, 16.7.1996, 12 ff., wo der Grundsatz der Formfreiheit ausdrücklich als einer der allgemeinen Grundsätze des CISG bezeichnet wird.

[304] *Staudinger/Magnus*, Art. 7, Rn. 46.

[305] So ausdrücklich in der Rechtsprechung Tribunale di Padova. 25.2.2004, CISG-online 819 = Giur. it. 2004, 1402, 1405; Tribunale di Rimini, 26.11.2002, CISG-online 737 = Giur. it. 2003, 896, 903, m. Anm. *Ferrari;* LG Zwickau, 19.3.1999, CISG-online 519; ICC, 8817/ 1997, CISG-online 776.

[306] *Achilles*, Art. 7, Rn. 8; *Audit*, Vente internationale, S. 52; *Botzenhardt*, S. 151; *Ferrari;* Uniform L. Rev. 1997, 451, 464; *ders.*, Int. Bus. L. J. 2003, 221, 229; *Frigge*, S. 294; *Gruber*, Methoden, S. 294; *Heuzé*, Anm. 95.; *Honnold/Flechtner*, Art. 7, Rn. 101; *Kröll u. a./Perales Viscasillas*, Art. 7, Rn. 58; *Magnus*, RabelsZ 59 (1995), 469, 483; *Maskow/Enderlein/Strohbach*, Art. 7, Anm. 9.1.; *Mather*, 20 J. L. & Com. (2001), 155, 157; MünchKomm/*Westermann*, Art. 7, Rn. 8; *Niemann*, S. 63; *Sannini*, L'applicazione, S. 49; *Schlechtriem/Schwenzer/Schlechtriem*, CISG Commentary, 2. Aufl., Art. 7, Rn. 30; *Sein/Kull*, IHR 2005, 138, 139; *Thiele*, RIW 2000, 892, 894; *Witz/Salger/Lorenz/Witz*, Art. 7, Rn. 31.

[307] So auch *Achilles*, Art. 7, Rn. 8; *Dore/Defranco*, 23 Harv. Int'l L. J. (1982), 49, 63; *Felemegas*, Rev. CISG (2000/2001), 115, 284; *Ferrari*, Int. Bus. L. J. 2003, 221, 229; *Ferrari u. a./Saenger*, Art. 7, Rn. 7; *Karollus*, S. 17; *Kröll u. a./Perales Viscasillas*, Art. 7, Rn. 58; *Melin*, S. 414; *Niemann*, S. 61; *Plantard*, J. D. I. 1988, 311, 332; *Sein/Kull*, IHR 2005, 138, 139; *Teichert*, S. 31; in diesem Sinne auch die neuere Rechtsprechung: Tribunale di Padova, 25.2.2004, CISG-online 819 = Giur. it. 2004, 1402, 1405, m. Anm. *Ferrari;* Tribunale di Rimini, 26.11.2002, CISG-oline 737 = Giur. it. 2003, 896, 903, m. Anm. *Ferrari;* RB Ieper, 29.1.2001, CISG-online 606 = Rechtskundig Weekblad 2001, 1396 ff. mit Anm. *Roox*.

[308] MünchKomm/*Westermann*, Art. 7, Rn. 13; in der Rechtsprechung vgl. etwa ICC, 8908/1998, CISG-online 751.

[309] *Magnus*, RabelsZ 59 (1989), 469, 489; *Sannini*, L'applicazione, S. 48 f.; *Teichert*, S. 35. Das CISG enthält jedoch keinen allgemeinen Grundsatz bezüglich des Zinssatzes; vgl. statt aller San Lucio S. r. l.; San Lucio USA v. Import & Storage Services, LLC., U. S. Dist. Ct. (D. N. J.), 15.4.2009, CISG-online 1836; a. A. statt aller Yugoslav Chamber of Commerce, 28.1.2009, CISG-online 1856.

[310] Vgl. zur Geschichte der Voraussehbarkeitsregel *Ferrari*, Contr. impr. 1993, 760 ff.; *ders.*, 53 La. L. Rev. (1993), 1257 ff.

[311] *Achilles*, Art. 7, Rn. 8; *Enderlein/Maskow/Strohbach*, Art. 7, Anm. 9.1.; *Frignani*, S. 308; *Maskow*, Perspective of the Socialist Countries, S. 39, 57; *Teichert*, S. 32; *Witz/Salger/Lorenz/Witz*, Art. 7, Rn. 31.

[312] Zum Prinzip der Totalreparation bzw. der vollständigen Schadensreparation als allgemeiner Grundsatz des CISG, vgl. etwa Yugoslav Chamber of Commerce, 28.1.2009, CISG-online 1856; Tribunale di Padova, 25.2.2004, CISG-online 819 = Giur. it 2004, 1402, 1405, m. zust. Anm. *Ferrari;* Tribunale di Rimini, 26.11.2002, CISG-online 737 = Giur. it. 2003, 896, 903, m. Anm. *Ferrari;* OGH, 14.1.2002, CISG-online 643 = IHR 2002, 77, 80; OGH, 9.3.2000, CISG-online 573; vgl. in der Lehre etwa *Bock*, FS Schwenzer, S. 175, 186 f.; *Callaghan*, 14 J. L. & Com. (1995), 183, 200; *Colligan*, 6 VJ (2002), 40, 50 f.; *Darkey*, 15 J. L. & Com. (1995), 139, 150; *Ferrari*, Int. Bus. L. J. 2003, 221, 228; *Flambouras*, 13 Pace Int'l L. Rev. (2001), 261, 289; *Hager*, FS Huber, S. 319, 321; *P. Huber*, IHR 2006, 228, 234; *P. Huber/Mullis/P. Huber*, S. 34; *Koneru*, 6 Minn. J. Global Trade (1997), 105, 125; *Kröll u. a./Perales Viscasillas*, Art. 7, Rn. 58; *Leumann Liebster*, FS Schwenzer, S. 1031, 1031; *Piltz*, FS Schwenzer, S. 1387, 1388; *Roßmeier*, RIW 2000, 407, 408; *Schlechtriem/Schwenzer/Schlechtriem*, CISG Commentary, 2. Aufl., Art. 7, Rn. 30; *Schlechtriem/Schwenzer/Schwenzer/Hachem*,

Zugang verlangt",[313] sowie der Grundsatz, wonach **Feiertage in Fristen** einzurechnen, diese bei Zustellungsunmöglichkeit aber zu verlängern sind (Art. 20 II).[314] Auch Art. 84 I CISG statuiert, so die neuere Lehre, einen allgemeinen Grundsatz, nämlich das Gebot der Erstattung von Bereicherung, das eingesetzt werden kann, um Wertersatzansprüche für den Fall der Aufhebung des Vertrages für enthaltene Dienstleistungen zu begründen.[315] Auch Art. 40 CISG scheint einen allgemeinen Grundsatz zu enthalten:[316] diesem Grundsatz nach erscheint „selbst der grob fahrlässig unwissende Käufer [...] schutzwürdiger als der arglistig handelnde Verkäufer".[317]

53   Zu den allgemeinen **Grundsätzen,** die sich im Gegensatz zu den oben erwähnten aus einem einheitlichen, **übergreifenden Gedanken mehrerer** Vorschriften ergeben,[318] ist derjenige zu zählen, wonach die Parteien sich wie „vernünftige Personen" verhalten müssen.[319] Auf den **„Maßstab des Vernünftigen"**[320] verweist das Übereinkommen in der Tat des Öfteren:[321] Bisweilen stellt es auf die Parteien als Subjekte mit den Qualitäten „vernünftiger Personen" ab;[322] an anderen Stellen wird den Parteien vom Übereinkommen auferlegt, innerhalb eines „angemessenen" Zeitraums eine bestimmte Handlung vorzunehmen oder ein bestimmte Mitteilung zu machen.[323]

54   Zu den allgemeinen Grundsätzen, die aus den verschiedenen Bestimmungen des CISG abgeleitet werden können, zählen auch: der Grundsatz des **Vertrauensschutzes,** der sich unter anderem aus Art. 16 II und Art. 29 II ergibt;[324] der Grundsatz des **favor contractus,**[325]

CISG Commentary, Art. 7, Rn. 35; *Smythe,* 2 Geo. Mason J. Int'l Com. L. (2011), 123, 133; *Thiele,* IHR 2001, 111, 112; *van Alstine,* 146 Univ. Pa. L. Rev. (1998), 687, 752.

[313] *Staudinger/Magnus,* Art. 7, Rn. 51; ebenso *Bianca/Bonell/Bonell,* Art. 7, Anm. 2.3.2.2.; *Botzenhardt,* S. 143 f.; *Enderlein/Maskow/Strohbach,* Art. 7, Anm. 9.1.; *Magnus,* RabelsZ 59 (1995), 469, 487; *Mather,* 20 J. L. & Com. (2001), 155, 158; *Teichert,* S. 34; vgl. in der Rechtsprechung Tribunale di Padova, 25.2.2004, CISG-online 819 = Giur. it. 2004, 1402, 1405; Tribunale di Rimini, 26.11.2002, CISG-online 737 = Giur. it. 2003, 896, 903.

[314] *Bammarny,* Treu und Glauben, S. 160; *Herber/Czerwenka,* Art. 7, Rn. 7; *Melin,* S. 414; *Niemann,* S. 63; *Schlechtriem/Schwenzer/Schwenzer/Hachem,* CISG Commentary, Art. 7, Rn. 33; *Teichert,* S. 33 f.

[315] So ausdrücklich *Schlechtriem,* Internationales UN-Kaufrecht, Rn. 49.

[316] So auch *T. M. Müller,* Beweislast, S. 14; *Witz/Salger/Lorenz/Witz,* Art. 7, Rn. 14.

[317] OLG Köln, 21.5.1996, CISG-online 254; vgl. auch Arbitration Institute of the Stockholm Chamber of Commerce, 5.6.1998, CISG-online 379: „Thus, the Article 40 is an expression of the principles of fair trading that underlie also many other provisions of CISG, and it is by its very nature a codification of a general principle".

[318] Zu dieser Vorgehensweise zur Erarbeitung allgemeiner Grundsätze, vgl. *Audit,* Vente internationale, S. 51; *Magnus,* RabelsZ 59 (1995), 469, 478; *Sannini,* L'applicazione, S. 49; kritisch hierzu *Rizzi,* Riv. di diritto privato 1997, 237, 283.

[319] *Colligan,* 6 VJ (2002), 40, 49; *Diesse,* J. D. I. 2002, 55, 60 f.; *Ferrari,* 24 Ga. J. Int'l & Comp. L. (1994), 183, 224 f.; *Frignani,* S. 308; *Hackney,* 61 La. L. Rev. (2001), 473, 478; *Harjani,* 23 Hous. J. Int'l L. (2000), 49, 64; *Hoffmann,* Koordination, S. 283; *Honnold,* Uniform Words, S. 139; *Karollus,* S. 16 f.; *Najork,* S. 99; *Opie,* FS Bergsten, S. 677, 678 ff.; *Schlechtriem,* Internationales UN-Kaufrecht, Rn. 48; *Whittington,* 37 Vict. U. Wellington L. Rev. (2006), 421, 432; *Witz/Salger/Lorenz/Witz,* Art. 7, Rn. 31.

[320] Vgl. *Bamberger/Roth/Saenger,* Art. 7, Rn. 7; *Bammarny,* Treu und Glauben, S. 165; *Bock,* FS Schwenzer, S. 175, 185; *Felemegas,* Rev. CISG (2000/2001), 115, 285; *Ferrari u. a./Saenger,* Internationales Vertragsrecht, Art. 7, Rn. 7; *Frignani/Torselli,* Il contratto internazionale, S. 463; *Hager,* FS Huber, S. 319, 321; *Th. Koller/Mauerhofer,* FS Schwenzer, S. 963, 977; *Niemann,* S. 63; *Soergel/Lüderitz/Fenge,* Art. 7, Rn. 10; *Staudinger/Magnus,* Art. 7, Rn. 45; *Sannini,* L'applicazione, S. 49; *Teichert,* S. 30; *Witz/Salger/Lorenz/Witz,* Art. 7, Rn. 31.

[321] Es sei hier angemerkt, dass das Übereinkommen sich verschiedentlich auch auf den Standard des „Unvernünftigen" bezieht; vgl. Art. 86 II; Art. 87; Art. 88 I; Art. 88 II; siehe hierzu auch *Adame Goddard,* Compraventa internacional, S. 78; *Ferrari,* JZ 1998, 9, 13, Fn. 69; *Teichert,* S. 30, Fn. 19.

[322] Vgl. hierzu Art. 8; Art. 25; Art. 35 Abs. 2 lit. b); Art. 60 lit. a); Art. 79 I; Art. 85; 86 I; 88 II.

[323] Siehe Art. 18 II; Art. 33 lit. c); Art. 39; Art. 43; Art. 47; Art. 49 II lit. a); Art. 63 I; Art. 64 II lit. b); Art. 65 I; Art. 65 II; Art. 75.

[324] *Magnus,* RabelsZ 59 (1995), 469, 481; *Schlechtriem/Schwenzer/Schwenzer/Hachem,* CISG Commentary, Art. 7, Rn. 33.

[325] So auch *Audit,* Vente internationale, S. 51; *Bammarny,* Treu und Glauben, S. 164 f.; *Dejaco,* S. 44; *Dimsey,* Consequences of Avoidence, S. 525, 529; *Djordjevic,* FS Bergsten, S. 551, 553; *Ferrari,* Uniform L. Rev. 1997, 451, 464; *ders.,* Int. Bus. L. J. 2003, 221, 229; *Felemegas,* Rev. CISG (2000/2001), 115, 285; *Heuzé,* Anm. 95.; *Honnold,* Uniform Words, S. 140; *P. Huber/Mullis/P. Huber,* S. 34; *Kröll u. a./Perales Viscasillas,* Art. 7, Rn. 59; *Janssen/*

Auslegung des Übereinkommens 55 **Art. 7**

wonach „die Lösung bevorzugt werden muss, die die Existenz der vertraglichen Bindung gegen ein vorzeitiges, von einer Partei herbeigeführtes Erlöschen schützt";[326] der Grundsatz, nach dem jede Partei mit der anderen **zusammenarbeiten** muss,[327] um ihr die Erfüllung zu ermöglichen und um das Vertragsziel nicht zu gefährden,[328] ein Grundsatz, der m. E.[329] – so aber neuerdings auch die höchstrichterliche Rechsprechung[330] – auch eine generelle **Informationspflicht** umfasst,[331] bei der es sich auch um ein allgemeines Prinzip handelt.[332]

Als allgemeiner Grundsatz muss auch angesehen werden, dass die **Fälligkeit** von Zahlungsansprüchen **ohne Mahnung** eintritt.[333] Gleiches gilt auch hinsichtlich des Grundsatzes, dass bei **Teilbarkeit eines Vertrages die Aufhebung** des Vertrages auf den Teil beschränkt ist, der von der Leistungsstörung betroffen ist.[334] Ferner sieht, so auch die Rechtsprechung,[335] das CISG auch ein **allgemeines Zurückbehaltungsrecht** vor,[336] dass sich etwa aus der in Art. 58 I vorgesehenen Zug-um-Zug Abwicklung der Hauptleistun-

---

Kiene, CISG Methodology, S. 261, 273 f.; *Magnus,* RabelsZ 59 (1995), 469, 483; *Melin,* S. 414; *Niemann,* S. 63; *Plantard,* J. D. I. 1988, 311, 333; *Rosenberg,* 20 Austr. Bus. L. Rev. (1993), 442, 452; *Sannini,* L'applicazione, S. 49; *Schlechtriem/Schwenzer/Schlechtriem,* CISG Commentary, 2. Aufl., Art. 7, Rn. 30; *Schlechtriem/Schwenzer/Schwenzer/Hachem,* CISG Commentary, Art. 7, Rn. 35; *Teichert,* S. 31; *Torsello,* Remedies, S. 43, 55.

[326] *Bonell,* Nuove leggi civ. comm. 1989, 20, 25; siehe auch *Achilles,* Art. 7, Rn. 8; *Burkart,* S. 197; vgl. in der Rechtsprechung American Arbitration Association, 23.10.2007, CISG-online 1645; vgl. auch OGH, 7.9.2000, CISG-online 642, wo auch von der Auflösung des Vertrages als „ultmia ratio" die Rede ist; BGer, 28.10.1998, CISG-online 413, wo vom Grundsatz des „Vorrangs der Vertragserhaltung" die Rede ist. Vgl. auch *Lurger,* IHR 2001, 91, 94, die statuiert, die „Möglichkeit der Aufhebung als ultima ratio bei wesentlichen Vertragsbrüchen zähle zu den Grundwertungen des CISG"; ebenso auch *Posch/Terlitza,* IHR 2001, 47, 50.

[327] In diesem Sinne auch *Achilles,* FS Schwenzer, S. 1, 16; *Audit,* Vente internationale, S. 51; *Bamberger/Roth/Saenger,* Art. 7, Rn. 7; *Béraudo,* ICC Ct. Arb. Bull. 1994, 63, 65; *Bianca/Bonell/Bonell,* Art. 7, Anm. 2.3.2.2.; *Burkart,* S. 196; *Diesse,* J. D. I: 2002, 55, 61 ff.; *Enderlein/Maskow/Strohbach,* Art. 7, Anm. 9.1.; *Felemegas,* 13 Pace Int'l L. Rev. (2001), 399, 402; *Ferrari u. a./Saenger,* Internationales Vertragsrecht, Art. 7, Rn. 7; *Hager,* FS Huber, S. 319, 321; *Honnold/Flechtner,* Art. 7, Rn. 101; *Karollus,* S. 16, Fn. 88; *Kritzer,* Guide to Practical Applications, S. 115; *Linne,* 20 Pace Int'l L. Rev. (2008), 31, 40; *Magnus,* CISG in the German Federal Civil Court, S. 211, 215 f.; *Mather,* 20 J. L. & Com. (2001), 155, 157; *Melin,* S. 415; MünchKomm/*Westermann,* Art. 7, Rn. 8; *Najork,* S. 63 ff.; *Sannini,* L'applicazione, S. 49 f.; *Soergel/Lüderitz/Fenge,* Art. 7, Rn. 10; *Teichert,* S. 32; *C. Witz,* J. D. I. 2000, 1020, 1024 f.; *ders.,* D. 2000, 441, 442; *Witz/Salger/Lorenz/Witz,* Art. 7, Rn. 15; vgl. zu dieser Kooperationspflicht in der Rechtsprechung OLG Celle, 24.7.2009, CISG-online 1906; Tribunale di Rovereto, 21.11.2007, CISG-online 1590; Tribunal of International Commercial Arbitration at the Russian Federation Chamber of Commerce and Industry, 9.12.2002, CISG Pace; BGH, 31.10.2001, CISG-online 617 = IHR 2002, 14, 15; BGH, 23.7.1997, CISG-online = 276 NJW 1997, 3304; OLG Köln, 21.12.2005, CISG-online 1201 = IHR 2006, 86 f.; LG Neubrandenburg, 3.8.2005, CISG-online 1190 = IHR 2006, 26 ff.; LG Mönchengladbach, 25.7.2003, CISG-online 919.

[328] So ausdrücklich *Staudinger/Magnus,* Art. 7, Rn. 47.

[329] Hierzu schon *Ferrari,* Vendita internazionale, S. 162.

[330] BGH, 31.10.2001, CISG-online 617 = IHR 2002, 14, 15; vgl. auch OLG Köln, 21.12.2005, CISG-online 1201 = IHR 2006, 86 f.; LG Neubrandenburg, 3.8.2005, CISG-online 1190 = IHR 2006, 26 ff.

[331] Ebenso *Achilles,* FS Schwenzer, S. 1, 16; *Botzenhardt,* S. 149 f.; *Honnold/Flechtner,* Art. 7, Rn. 100; *Mather,* 20 J. L. & Com. (2001), 155, 157; *Niemann,* S. 63; *Witz/Salger/Lorenz/Witz,* Art. 7, Rn. 15; a. A. *Staudinger/Magnus,* Art. 7, Rn. 48; vgl. auch OLG Celle, 24.7.2009, CISG-online 1906.

[332] So auch *Audit,* Vente internationale, S. 51; *Bockenhardt,* S. 149 f.; *Hyland,* Conformity of Goods, S. 305, 331 f.; *Vogel,* S. 12; vorsichtiger jedoch *Najork,* S. 66 ff., der zwar eine Informationspflicht aus dem CISG herleitet, aber diese dahingehend begrenzt, als dass sich nicht um eine „rein altruistische Informationspflicht", die nicht in unmittelbarem Zusammenhang mit der Vertragsdurchführung steht", handelt (S. 69).

[333] *Burkart,* S. 199; *Janssen/Kiene,* CISG Methodology, S. 261, 280; *Melin,* S. 414; *Niemann,* S. 63; *Schlechtriem/Schwenzer/Schwenzer/Hachem,* CISG Commentary, Art. 7, Rn. 35; *Staudinger/Magnus,* Art. 7, Rn. 52; *Teichert,* S. 34; ebenso in der Rechtsprechung HGer Aarau, 26.9.1997, CISG-online 329; KG Berlin, 24.1.1994, CISG-online 130 = RIW 1994, 683; Pretore Locarno-Campagna, 27.4.1992, CISG-online 68 = SZIER 1993, 665; a. A. Int. Ct. Bulgarian CCI, 11/1996, CISG-online 436.

[334] Hierzu etwa *Coen,* S. 189, 200 f.

[335] OGH, 8.11.2005, CISG-online 1156 = IHR 2006, 87, 90.

[336] Vgl. auch *Fountoulakis,* IHR 2005, 244, 247 f.; *Hartmann,* IHR 2006, 181; *Nyer,* 18 Pace Int'l L. Rev. (2006), 29, 72 ff.; *Schlechtriem,* 18 Pace Int'l L. Rev. (2006), 83, 92; *ders.,* 36 Vict. U. Well. L. Rev. (2005), 781, 791; *Schlechtriem/Schwenzer/Schlechtriem,* CISG Commentary, 2. Aufl., Art. 7, Rn. 34; *Teichert,* S. 33; a. A. OLG Stuttgart, 20.12.2004, CISG-online 997 „Das Zurückbehaltungsrecht ist im CISG nicht geregelt. Ob überhaupt ein Zurückbehaltungsrecht besteht, richtet sich nach dem Recht, welches nach dem internationalen Privatrecht zur Beurteilung berufen wäre".

Art. 7 55

gen[337] und der nach Art. 71 I erlaubten Zurückhaltung der eigenen Leistung entwickeln lässt.[338] Neuerdings ist vorgeschlagen worden, auch den **"functional equivalence approach"**, mittels dessen etwa das Verhältnis des CISG zum nationalen Anfechtungsrecht geklärt werden kann,[339] als allgemeinen Grundsatz des CISG anzusehen.[340] Gleiches ist auch in Bezug auf den sich aus dem Rechtsgedanken des Art. 46 Abs. 1 Hs. 2 entnehmenden Grundsatz **"impossibilia nulla est obligatio"** vorgeschlagen worden.[341] M. E.[342] enthält das CISG jedoch keinen allgemeinen Grundsatz, aus dem sich die **Währung** ergibt, in der die Zahlung zu erfolgen hat.[343] Gleiches gilt m. E. auch hinsichtlich des **Erfüllungsorts für Zahlungsansprüche:**[344] die Existenz von Art. 57 I lit. a), der die Kaufpreiszahlungspflicht als Bringschuld qualifiziert, darf nicht dazu verleiten, darin einen allgemeinen Grundsatz für jedweden Zahlungsanspruch zu sehen.[345] M. E.[346] gründet das CISG auch nicht auf dem allgemeinen Grundsatz, wonach sich aus dem CISG unterliegenden Verträgen ergebende Forderungen konventionsintern kompensiert werden können,[347] regelt das CISG die Aufrechnung doch überhaupt nicht.[348] Als allgemeine Grundsätze des CISG dürfen auch nicht die **UNIDROIT Principles** angesehen werden,[349] was bisweilen aber übersehen worden ist.[350] Auf das Verhältnis zwischen CISG und UNIDROIT Principles wird im Folgenden näher eingegangen.[351]

---

[337] Vgl. *P. Huber,* IPRax 2001, 557 ff.; vgl. auch *Hartmann,* IHR 2006, 181; in der Rechtsprechung wird das Zug-um-Zug Prinzip als ein auch unter dem CISG geltendes Prinzip anerkannt etwa vom OGH, 30.11.2006, CISG-online 1417 = IHR 2007, 74, 75; OGH, 8.11.2005, CISG-online 1156 = IHR 2006, 87, 91; vgl. auch Supreme Court of Poland, 11.5.2007, CISG-online 1790.

[338] *Hartmann,* IHR 2006, 181,183 f.; *Kröll u. a./Perales Viscasillas,* Art. 7, Rn. 58; *Schlechtriem,* Internationales UN-Kaufrecht, Rn. 42d; *Schlechtriem/Schwenzer/Schwenzer/Hachem,* CISG Commentary, Art. 7, Rn. 35; ebenso in der Rechtsprechung HGer Aargau, 10.3.2010, CISG-online 2176; OGH, 8.11.2005, CISG-online 1156; a. A. OLG Stuttgart, 20.12.2004, CISG-online 997.

[339] Siehe Art. 4 Rn. 22 ff.

[340] *Tescaro,* Contr. Imp. E. 2007, 319, 337 f.

[341] Vgl. *Bach/Stieber,* IHR 2006, 59 ff.

[342] *Ferrari,* Interpretation of the Convention and gap-filling: Article 7, S. 138, 163 f.

[343] Vgl. in der Rechtsprechung OLG Frankfurt a. M., 20.4.1994, CISG-online 125; vgl. auch LG Berlin, 24.3.1998, CISG-online 742, in der die Frage zwar angesprochen, letztendlich aber nicht beantwortet wird.

[344] *Ferrari,* Int. Bus. L. J. 2003, 221, 228; vgl. auch *Thiele,* RIW 2000, 892, 894 f., der zwar die Meinung vertritt, Art. 57 könne nicht herangezogen werden, um einen allgemeinen Grundsatz zu rechtfertigen, wonach jede Zahlungspflicht am Ort des Gläubigers zu erfüllen sei, aber dennoch in Bezug auf den Erfüllungsort bei Rückabwicklung von Vertragspflichten nach Art. 81 einen allgemeinen Grundsatz aufstellt, auf dessen Grundlage alle Rückabwicklungspflichten nach Art. 81 am Ort der Niederlassung des vertragstreuen Teils zu erfüllen sind; ebenso nunmehr auch *Hackenberg,* S. 170 ff.

[345] Ebenso CA Paris, 14.1.1998, CISG-online 347 = SZIER 1999, 201; a. A. in der Rechtsprechung OGH, 29.6.1998, CISG-online 483 = TranspR-IHR 1999, 48; CA Grenoble, 23.10.1996, CISG-online 305 = Rev. crit. dr. int. priv. 1997, 756 (mit Hinweis auch auf die UNIDROIT Principles, die – so das Gericht – einen ähnlichen Grundsatz enthalten); OLG Düsseldorf, 2.7.1993, CISG-online 74 = RIW 1993, 845 f.; a. A. in der Lehre *Bamberger/Roth/Saenger,* Art. 7, Rn. 7; *Ferrari u. a./Saenger,* Internationales Vertragsrecht, Art. 7, Rn. 7.

[346] Vgl. *Ferrari,* Int. Bus. L. J. 2003, 221, 229.

[347] A. A. OLG Hamburg, 26.11.1999, CISG-online 515 = IHR 2001, 19 ff.: „Die Aufrechnung gilt als allgemeines Prinzip im Sinne von Artikel 7 II CISG jedenfalls insoweit, als sich, wie hier, gegenseitige Ansprüche aus der Konvention gegenüberstehen"; in der Lehre vertreten diese Ansicht etwa *Enderlein/Maskow/Strohbach,* Art. 84, Anm. 1.; *Magnus,* ZEuP 1995, 202, 207 f.; *Weber,* Vertragsverletzungsfolgen, S. 186.

[348] Ebenso auch *Bamberger/Roth/Saenger,* Art. 4, Rn. 19; *Bazinas,* Uniformity, S. 26; *Bonell,* 56 Am. J. Comp. L. (2009), 1, 3; *Ferrari u. a./Saenger,* Internationales Vertragsrecht, Art. 4, Rn. 20; *Flambouras,* 29 J. L. & Com. (2011), 171, 203; *Fuchs,* IHR 2003, 231 f.; *Honnold/Flechtner,* Art. 4, Rn. 70; *P. Huber,* IHR 2006, 228, 234; *P. Huber/Mullis/P. Huber,* S. 30; *Janssen,* The Application of the CISG in Dutch Courts, S. 129, 134; *T. M. Müller,* Beweislast, S. 32; MünchKomm/*Westermann,* Art. 4, Rn. 12; *Piltz,* NJW 2000, 553, 556; *Saenger/Sauthoff,* IHR 2005, 189, 190; *Schlechtriem,* Internationales UN-Kaufrecht, Rn. 42e; *ders.,* 36 Vict. U. Well. L. Rev. (2005), 781, 791; *Schlechtriem/Schwenzer/Schlechtriem,* CISG Commentary, 2. Aufl., Art. 4, Rn. 22a; *Witz/Salger/Lorenz/Lorenz,* Art. 4, Rn. 29.

[349] Vgl. *Bamberger/Roth/Saenger,* Art. 7, Rn. 7 a E.; *Ferrari,* Int. Bus. L. J. 2003, 221, 230; *Flechtner,* The CISG's Impact, S. 190; *Sabourin,* S. 237, 247; a. A. *Burkart,* S. 215; *Garro,* 69 Tul. L. Rev. (1994), 1149, 1133 und 1156; *M. E. Storme,* Rev. dr. int. dr. comp. 1995, 309, 317.

[350] Vgl. ICC, 8128/1995, CISG-online 526 = J. D. I. 1996, 1024 ff.: „L'arbitre considère justifié d'appliquer au litige les règles identiques contenues dans les principes UNIDROIT […] en tant que principes généraux au sens de l'article 7(2) de la Convention"; ähnlich neuerdings Hof van Cassatie, 19.6.2009, CISG-online 1963.

[351] Vgl. Rn. 59 ff.

Ob es möglich ist, auch mit Bezug auf die **Beweislast** eine oder mehrere allgemeine 56
Grundsätze aufzustellen, ist umstritten.[352] Obwohl verschiedene Autoren dies ablehnen, da
sie davon ausgehen, dass die Beweislast im CISG überhaupt nicht geregelt sei,[353] kann man
(auf Grund des Textes von Art. 79 und Art. 2 lit. a) CISG)[354] durchaus davon ausgehen, dass
das UN-Kaufrecht auch in diesem Bereich einen allgemeinen **Grundsatz** vorsieht:[355]
Grundsätzlich hat derjenige die tatsächlichen Voraussetzungen derjenigen Vorschrift zu
beweisen, aus der er einen Vorteil für sich herleitet,[356] d. h. „ei incumbit probatio, qui dicit,
non qui negat".[357] Auch die Regel, wonach derjenige, der sich auf eine Ausnahmeregel
beruft, die tatsächlichen Voraussetzungen derselben zu beweisen hat, muss als allgemeiner
Grundsatz des CISG angesehen werden können,[358] was neuerdings auch von der Rechtsprechung bestätigt worden ist.[359]

V. Rückgriff auf nationales Recht

In Ermangelung allgemeiner Grundsätze, ist – so ausdrücklich der Text der Vorschrift – 57
nach dem Recht zu entscheiden, das nach den **Regeln des IPR** anzuwenden ist.[360] Dies ist

---

[352] Monographisch zu Fragen des Verhältnisses zwischen UN-Kaufrecht und Prozessrecht im Allgemeinen und der Beweislast im Besonderen vgl. *Antweiler; Hepting; Henninger; Imberg; Jung; T. M. Müller; Reimers-Zocher.*
[353] So zum Beispiel *Bianca/Bonell/Khoo*, Art. 2, Anm. 3.2.; MünchKomm/*Westermann*, Art. 7, Rn. 9.
[354] Die im Text zitierten Vorschriften sind verschiedentlich herangezogen worden, um die Existenz eines allgemeinen Grundsatzes zu rechtfertigen; vgl. zuletzt *Ferrari*, Int. Bus. L. J. 2003, 221, 228; vgl. in der Rechtsprechung BGH, 9.1.2002, CISG-online 651 = NJW 2002, 1651 ff.; Tribunale di Vigevano, 12.7.2000, CISG-online 493 = IHR 2001, 72, 76; Tribunale di Pavia, 29.12.1999, CISG-online 678 = Corr. giur. 2000, 932 f.
[355] Vgl. auch *Aue*, Mängelgewährleistung im UN-Kaufrecht, S. 110 ff.; *Bamberger/Roth/Saenger*, Art. 4, Rn. 11; *Baumgärte u. a./Müller*, Vor Art. 1, Rn. 16; *Bianca/Bonell/Bianca*, Art. 36, Anm. 3.1.; *Bianca/Bonell/Knapp*, Art. 74, Anm. 2.8.; *Bianca/Bonell/Sono*, Art. 44, Anm. 3.1.; CISG-AC, Op. 6 (*Gotanda*), Comment 2; *Ferrari*, Rev. CISG (2000/2001), 1 ff.; *Ferrari u. a./Saenger*, Internationales Vertragsrecht, Art. 4, Rn. 11; *Honsell/Siehr*, Art. 4, Rn. 10; *P. Huber*, IHR 2006, 228, 235; *P. Huber/Mullis/P. Huber*, S. 36 f.; *Jung*, S. 40; *Koller/Mauerhofer*, FS Schwenzer, S. 963, 964 f.; *Kröll*, 2011 Annals Fac. L. Belgrade 2011, 162, 169; *ders.*, 25 J. L. & Com. (2005), 39, 48; *Kröll u. a./Djordjevic*, Art. 4, Rn. 34; *Magnus*, CISG in the German Federal Civil Court, S. 211, 216 ff.; *ders., ZEuP* 1995, 202, 207; *ders.*, ZEuP 2002, 523, 530; *Mohs*, IHR 2004, 219; MünchKomm/*Westermann*, Art. 4, Rn. 17; *Noussias*, Zugangsbedürftigkeit von Mitteilungen, S. 105 f.; *Orlandi*, Uniform L. Rev. 2000, 23, 27 f.; *Reimers-Zocher*, S. 148; *Schlechtriem/Schwenzer/Schlechtriem*, CISG Commentary, 2. Aufl., Art. 4, Rn. 22; *Schlechtriem/Schwenzer/Schwenzer/Hachem*, CISG Commentary, Art. 4, Rn. 25; *Schwenzer/Hachem*, 57 Am. J. Comp. L. (2009), 457, 471 f.; *Soergel/Lüderitz/Fenge*, Art. 4, Rn. 11; *Spiegel*, D. 2000, Jur. 445, 445; *ders.*, D. 2002, Jur. 395, 396; *Teichert*, Lückenfüllung, S. 16; *Veneziano*, Dir. comm. int. 2001, 509, 515–516; *Witz/Salger/Lorenz/Lorenz*, Art. 4, Rn. 11; ebenso in der Rechtsprechung HGer Zürich, 25.6.2010, CISG-online 2161; KG Wallis, 28.1.2009, CISG-online 2025; OGH, 12.9.2006, CISG-online 1364 = IHR 2007, 39, 41; KG Nidwalden, 23.5.2005, CISG-online 1086 = IHR 2005, 253, 254; BGer, 7.7.2004, CISG-online 848 = IHR 2004, 252, 253; Tribunale di Padova, 31.3.2004, CISG-online 823 = Giur. merito 2004, 1065, 1068; Tribunale di Padova, 25.2.2004, CISG-online 819 = Giur. it. 2004, 1402, 1405; BGer, 13.11.2003, CISG-online 846 = IHR 2004, 215, 218; Tribunale di Rimini, 26.11.2002, CISG-online 737 = Giur. it. 2003, 896 ff., m. Anm. *Ferrari*; Tribunale di Vigevano, 12.7.2000, CISG-online 493 = IHR 2001, 72 ff.; Tribunale di Pavia, 29.12.1999, CISG-online 678 = Corr. giur. 2000, 932 f., m. Anm. *Ferrari*; HGer Zürich, 26.4.1995, CISG-online 248 = TranspR-IHR 1999, 54; HGer Zürich, 9.9.1993, CISG-online 79; a. A. ICC, 6653/1993, CISG-online 71 = J. D. I. 1993, 1040, das zwar das Übereinkommen anwendet, aber die Frage der Beweislast anhand französischen unvereinheitlichten Rechts löst.
[356] Ebenso *Brunner*, Art. 4, Rn. 56; *P. Huber*, IHR 2006, 228, 235; *Koller/Mauerhofer*, FS Schwenzer, S. 963, 965; *Magnus*, RabelsZ 59 (1995), 469, 489; *Mohs*, IHR 2004, 219; *T. M. Müller*, IHR 2005, 16; MünchKomm/*Westermann*, Art. 4, Rn. 17; MünchKommHGB/*Benicke*, Art. 4, Rn. 20; *Neumayer/Ming*, Art. 4, Rn. 13; *Sannini*, L'applicazione, S. 50; *Schlechtriem*, Internationales UN-Kaufrecht, Rn. 50; *Sein/Kull*, IHR 2005, 138, 142; vgl. in der Rechtsprechung OGH, 12.9.2006, CISG-online 1364 = IHR 2007, 39, 41; BGer, 13.11.2003, CISG-online 846 = IHR 2004, 215, 218.
[357] Vgl. etwa Tribunale di Padova, 31.3.2004, CISG-online 823 = Giur. merito 2004, 1065, 1068; Tribunale di Padova, 25.2.2004, CISG-online 819 = Giur. it. 2004, 1402, 1405; Tribunale di Rimini, 26.11.2002, CISG-online 737 = Giur. it. 2003, 896 ff., m. Anm. *Ferrari*; Tribunale di Vigevano, 12.7.2000, CISG-online 493 = IHR 2001, 72, 77.
[358] So auch *Ferrari*, Int. Bus. L. J. 2003, 221, 228; *Staudinger/Magnus*, Art. 4, Rn. 64.
[359] Tribunale di Vigevano, 12.7.2000, CISG-online 493 = IHR 2001, 72, 77.
[360] Der Vorschlag, das deutsche IPR so auszulegen, dass für Rest- und Randfragen „ohne Wertungsprobleme von einiger Bedeutung" stets das Sachrecht der lex fori gelte (so *Stoll*, Internationalprivatrechtliche Fragen,

nicht weiter problematisch, handelt es sich doch um eine Bezugnahme auf den üblichen kollisionsrechtlichen Weg.

58   Der Rückgriff auf „externe" Regeln, denn auf diese wird abgestellt, ist, so auch die Rechtsprechung,[361] nur als **ultima ratio** zulässig,[362] der übrigens auch ohne ausdrückliche Ermächtigung schon nach dem EKG für zulässig gehalten wurde.[363]

VI. Lückenfüllung und UNIDROIT Principles

1. UNIDROIT Principles als objektiv anwendbares Recht

59   An dieser Stelle muss man sich aber fragen, ob für die vielfach von der Lehre als Mittel zur Lückenfüllung des CISG angepriesenen **UNIDROIT Principles** bei der Schließung von Lücken des Übereinkommens Raum bleibt[364] (die UNIDROIT Principles sehen dies übrigens ausdrücklich vor):[365] „Externe" Lücken sind nämlich, wie erwähnt, durch das IPR des Forums berufene Recht zu schließen,[366] während „interne" Lücken soweit als möglich durch die allgemeinen Grundsätze zu füllen sind, auf denen das Übereinkommen beruht (in Ermangelung derselben, sind auch diese Lücken mittels des über die Regeln des IPR anzuwendenden Rechts zu schließen).[367] Um diese Frage beantworten zu können, muss man – wenn auch nur kurz – auf den Anwendungsbereich der UNIDROIT Principles eingehen; Ausgangspunkt soll dabei der weite Anwendungsbereich sein, den sich die UNIDROIT Principles, trotz Fehlen formaler Bindungswirkung,[368] selbst zuerkannt haben.[369] Demzufolge sind diese vor allem dann anzuwenden, wenn „die Parteien vereinbart haben, dass ihr Vertrag diesen Principles unterliegt. Sie können [ferner] angewendet werden, wenn die Parteien vereinbart haben, dass ihr Vertrag „Allgemeinen Rechtsgrundsätzen", der „Lex mercatoria" oder dergleichen unterliegt."[370] Bedeutet dies, dass die Richter in den soeben genannten Fällen an die Principles gebunden sind und diese daher als Lückenfüller herangezogen werden können und/oder müssen? Bedeutet dies ferner, dass

---

S. 498, 499; *ders.,* IPRax 1993, 75, 75), ist auf der Grundlage kritisiert worden, dass die Abgrenzung zu wertungsbedürftigen Fragen kaum überzeugend und praktikabel zu vollziehen wäre; kritisch zu dem Vorschlag *Stolls* etwa *Staudinger/Magnus,* Art. 7, Rn. 59.

[361] ICC, 8611/HV/JK, CISG-online 236.

[362] Ebenso *Bacher,* FS Schlechtriem, S. 155, 162; *Bonell,* Nuove leggi civ. comm. 1989, 20, 25; *Brunner,* Art. 7, Rn. 6; *Burkart,* S. 202; *Ferrari,* JZ 1998, 9, 15; *ders.,* Rev. int. dr. comp. 1996, 852; *Frigge,* S. 306; *Gruber,* Methoden, S. 306; *Melin,* S. 407; *T. M. Müller,* Beweislast, S. 13; MünchKomm/*Westermann,* Art. 7, Rn. 12; *Niemann,* S. 27; *Sannini,* L'applicazione, S. 52; *Schlechtriem/Schwenzer/Schlechtriem,* CISG Commentary, 2. Aufl., Intro to Artt. 1–6, Rn. 10 und Art. 7, Rn. 35; *Schlechtriem/Schwenzer/Schwenzer/Hachem,* CISG Commentary, Art. 7, Rn. 42; *Schmid,* Einheitliche Anwendung, S. 53; *Staudinger/Magnus,* Art. 7, Rn. 58; *Sundermann,* Probleme der autonomen Auslegung, S. 21, Fn. 12; *Thiele,* IHR 2001, 111, 112; *ders.,* RIW 2000, 892, 894.

[363] Vgl. *Mertens/Rehbinder,* Art. 17 EKG, Rn. 26.

[364] Vgl. eingehend zum Verhältnis zwischen CISG und UNIDROIT Principles *Bonell,* Uniform L. Rev. 2006, 305 ff.; *ders.,* Rev. jur. Thémis 2002, 335 ff.; *ders.,* Bus. L. Int. 2000, 89 ff.; *Burkart,* S. 202; *Flechtner,* The CISG's Impact, S. 169 ff.; *Guillemard,* Rev. CISG (2000/2001), 83 ff.; *Lando,* 53 Am. J. Comp. L. (2005), 379 ff.; *Perales Viscasillas,* CISG Methodology, S. 287 ff.

[365] Siehe Präambel Abs. 5 der UNIDROIT Principles: „Sie können benutzt werden, um Regelwerke des internationalen Einheitsrechts auszulegen oder zu ergänzen".

[366] Vgl. auch *Gruber,* Methoden, S. 302 f.

[367] Vgl. neuerdings hierzu auch *McMahon,* 44 Colum. J. Transnat'l L. (2006), 992 ff.

[368] *Burkart,* S. 35; *Frigge,* S. 303; *Herber,* IHR 2003, 1, 6 f.; *Schnyder/Grolimund,* FS Schlechtriem, S. 395, 397; in der Rechtsprechung wurde die fehlende Bindunswirkung der UNIDROIT Principles hervorgehoben in Tribunale di Padova, 10.1.2006, CISG-online 1157.

[369] Vgl. zu dieser Feststellung, *Basedow,* Uniform L. Rev. 2000, 129, 131 f.; *Boele-Woelki,* IPRax 1995, 161, 162.

[370] So die Präambel, die ferner vorschreibt, dass die Principles auch eine Lösung eines aufgeworfenen Problems bieten können, wenn es sich als unmöglich erweist, die maßgebende Regel des anzuwendenden Rechts zu ermitteln. Sie können, so die Präambel, außerdem als Modell für nationale und internationale Gesetzgeber dienen.

bei Fehlen eines solchen Hinweises auf die Grundsätze, diese nicht zur Anwendung kommen können?[371]

Letztere Frage soll im Folgenden zuerst beantwortet werden, da sie, statistisch gesehen, **60** sicher am häufigsten aufkommt. Dies hängt damit zusammen, dass die (erste Fassung der) Principles erst 1994 veröffentlicht wurden,[372] und, trotz vieler Publikationen[373] und Seminare,[374] unter der Mehrheit der Praktiker noch nicht sehr verbreitet sind, selbst wenn man ihnen einen gewissen Bekanntheitsgrad nicht absprechen kann, was sich auch daraus ergibt, dass es bereits zu den UNIDROIT Principles ergangene (Schieds-)Entscheidungen gibt.[375] Man muss sich also fragen, ob die UNIDROIT Principles zur Anwendung kommen können, wenn jeglicher Hinweis auf dieselben im Vertrag fehlt.

Um in einem solchen Fall vor **staatlichen Gerichten**[376] zur Anwendung gelangen zu **61** können, müssten die UNIDROIT Principles als Bestandteil des durch die objektiven Anknüpfungskriterien des IPR des Forumstaates berufenen Rechts Anwendung finden. **De lege lata** ist dies zumindest in den Ländern, in denen das EVÜ (unabhängig davon, ob staatsvertraglich oder autonom) gilt, **auszuschließen.**[377] Die relevante Vorschrift normiert nämlich, dass in Ermangelung einer gültigen Rechtswahl, der Vertrag dem „Recht des Staates" unterliegt, mit dem er die engsten Verbindungen aufweist.[378] Diese Vorschrift „schließt jede Anknüpfung an nichtstaatliches Recht eindeutig aus",[379] da sie die Anwendung eines staatlichen Rechts diktiert.[380] Für die Schließung von Lücken internationaler Einheitsprivatrechtskonventionen bedeutet dies, dass zumindest bei Fehlen eines Hinweises auf die UNIDROIT Grundsätze die mittels Rückgriff auf das durch das IPR des Forumstaates berufene Recht zu schließenden Lücken, namentlich die „externen Lücken" sowie die „internen", die nicht mittels Rückgriff auf die allgemeinen Grundsätze der jeweiligen Konvention gefüllt werden können, in staatlichen Gerichten nicht anhand der UNIDROIT Principles geschlossen werden können,[381] zumindest nicht dort, wo das EVÜ gilt.[382] **De lege ferenda** kann dies nur **kritisiert** werden. Ein Rückgriff auf ein eigens für internationale (vertragliche) Sachverhalte konzipiertes Regelwerk ist in der Regel[383] dem Rückgriff auf ein für nationale Situationen geschaffenes Recht vorzuziehen.[384] Einen ersten Schritt in diese Richtung scheint, so einige Autoren, die inter-amerikanische Konvention über das auf Verträge anwendbare Recht[385] gegangen zu sein. Verschiedene Autoren

---

[371] Vgl. hierzu neuerdings auch *Drobnig*, Uniform L. Rev. 1998, 385 ff.

[372] Zur Geschichte, vgl. *Bonell*, Codice internazionale, S. 27 ff.

[373] Vgl. hierzu nur die im Anhang des Buches von *Bonell*, Codice internazionale, abgedruckte Bibliographie (S. 685 ff.).

[374] Eine Liste dieser Seminare findet sich unter anderem bei *Bonell*, Uniform L. Rev. 1997, 34, 35.

[375] Zu den ersten Anwendungen der UNIDROIT Grundsätze, vgl. *Berger*, 46 Am. J. Comp. L. (1998), 129 ff.; *Bonell*, 1 (EJLR), 1998, 193 ff.; *Mari*, Dir. comm. int. 1995, 487 ff.; *Veneziano*, Rev. dr. aff. int 2001, 477 ff.

[376] Zur Beantwortung dieser Frage in Bezug auf Schiedsgerichte, vgl. zuletzt *Boele-Woelki*, IPRax 1995, 161, 168–169, deren Anmerkungen aber etwas zu unkritisch erscheinen; vgl. auch *Bonell*, Codice internazionale, S. 204 ff.; *Wichard*, RabelsZ 60 (1996), 291–294.

[377] *Drobnig*, Uniform L. Rev. 1998, 385, 392 f.; *Ferrari*, JZ 1998, 9, 15; *Frigge*, S. 304; *Herber*, IHR 2003, 1, 7 ff.

[378] Vgl. Art. 4 Abs. 1 EVÜ und Art. 28 I EGBGB; siehe hierzu auch Art. 117 I des schweizerischen IPRG vom 18.12.1987.

[379] So auch *Wichard*, RabelsZ 60 (1996), 294.

[380] In diesem Sinne auch *Bonell*, Codice internazionale, S. 193 f.; *Lorenz*, IPRax 1987, 272 ff.; *Spickhoff*, RabelsZ 56 (1992), 116 ff.

[381] Siehe auch *Herber*, IHR 2003, 1, 9; *Schlechtriem*, Internationales UN-Kaufrecht, Rn. 52, Fn. 80; a. A., freilich ohne Begründung, *L. Meyer*, 34 Denv. J. Int'l L. & Pol'y (2006), 119, 136.

[382] *Drobnig*, Uniform L. Rev. 1998, 385, 392 f., m. w. N.

[383] An dieser Stelle kann nicht unerwähnt bleiben, dass es bekanntlich einige Staaten gibt, die ein eigens für internationale Handelsverträge geschaffenes Gesetz erlassen haben, das der Internationalität des Sachverhalts genauso Rechnung trägt wie die UNIDROIT Principles und daher nicht unbedingt nachsteht.

[384] So auch *Boele-Woelki*, IPRax 1995, 161, 169; *Frigge*, S. 305.

[385] Der englische Text ist abgedruckt in ILM 1994, 732 ff.; monographisch zu diesem Übereinkommen *Gebele*, Konvention von Mexiko.

nehmen diesbezüglich an,³⁸⁶ dass Art. 9 II dieser Konvention eine objektive kollisionsrechtliche Anknüpfung an die Principles zulasse, da er vorsehe, dass in Ermangelung einer gültigen Rechtswahl bei der Feststellung des anwendbaren Rechts die von internationalen Organisationen anerkannten allgemeinen Grundsätze des internationalen Handelsrechts zu berücksichtigen sind. Vielfach wird aber nicht erwähnt,³⁸⁷ dass Art. 9 I ausdrücklich normiert, dass in Ermangelung einer gültigen Rechtswahl „der Vertrag durch das Recht desjenigen Staates geregelt wird, mit dem er die engsten Verbindungen aufweist",³⁸⁸ und der Richter die erwähnten allgemeinen Grundsätze nur zu berücksichtigen hat, nachdem er das Recht mit den engsten Verbindungen zum Vertrag ausgemacht hat. Auch die interamerikanische Konvention hält demnach an der Staatlichkeit des objektiv berufenen Rechts fest,³⁸⁹ was sich auch aus Art. 17 derselben ergibt, der festlegt, dass „im Sinne dieses Übereinkommens unter dem Begriff des „Rechts" dasjenige zu verstehen ist, das in einem Staat in Kraft ist."³⁹⁰ Dies schließt zwar nicht aus, dass die **UNIDROIT Principles** in Betracht kommen können, aber **nicht Kraft objektiver Anknüpfung.**

2. UNIDROIT Grundsätze, „interne" Lücken und Vertragsfreiheit

62 Was die „internen" Lücken des CISG angeht, so muss man davon ausgehen, dass diese in Ermangelung eines entsprechenden Hinweises³⁹¹ durch die Vertragsparteien **de lege lata leider nicht durch die UNIDROIT Principles** geschlossen werden können.³⁹² Dies hängt aber nicht notwendigerweise mit dem soeben Gesagten zusammen, sondern vielmehr mit der durch Art. 7 II vorgeschriebenen Vorgehensweise bei der Lückenfüllung. Diese sind durch die allgemeinen Grundsätze, die dem Übereinkommen zugrunde liegen, zu schließen. Demnach ist ein Rückgriff auf „externe" Grundsätze, wie sie die UNIDROIT Principles darstellen, ausdrücklich ausgeschlossen.³⁹³ Staatliche Gerichte müssen sich bei der Antwort auf eine zwar nicht ausgeschlossene, aber nicht ausdrücklich geregelte Frage nur auf die allgemeinen Grundsätze stützen, die dem Übereinkommen zugrunde liegen,³⁹⁴ zu denen die UNIDROIT Principles m. E. nicht zählen.³⁹⁵

63 Dies soll aber nicht heißen, dass den UNIDROIT Grundsätzen auch in Ermangelung eines jeglichen Hinweises auf dieselben bei der Schließung interner Lücken überhaupt keine Rolle zugesprochen werden kann. So können sie zum Beispiel angesichts ihrer **„persuasive authority"**³⁹⁶ helfen, eine auf einen allgemeinen Grundsatz gestützte **Lösung zu bekräftigen.**³⁹⁷

---

³⁸⁶ Vgl. *Boele-Woelki*, IPRax 1995, 161, 170.
³⁸⁷ So zum Beispiel *Boele-Woelki*, IPRax 1995, 161, 169.
³⁸⁸ Vgl. hierzu allgemein *Bonell*, Codice internazionale, S. 195 f.
³⁸⁹ Siehe auch Art. 9 II der inter-amerikanischen Konvention: „The Court will take into account all objective and subjective elements of the contract to determine the law of the State with which it has the closest ties. It shall also take into account the general principles of international commercial law recognized by international organizations".
³⁹⁰ In diesem Sinne auch schon *Herbert*, Rev. Ur. Der. Int. Priv. (1995), 45; a. A. *Burkart*, S. 73.
³⁹¹ Bei einem Hinweis der Parteien hat der Richter die Lücken ohne weiteres nach den UNIDROIT Principles zu füllen (vgl. *Bonell*, Uniform L. Rev. 2000, 199, 210; *Teichert*, S. 112), aber nur insoweit als diese nicht dem zwingenden Vorschriften des anwendbaren Rechts widersprechen; vgl. auch Rn. 66 ff.
³⁹² *Ferrari*, JZ 1998, 9, 16; *Gruber*, Methoden, S. 304; *P. Huber*, IHR 2006, 228, 235; *P. Huber/Mullis/ P. Huber*, S. 35; *Melin*, S. 416; *Paal*, ZVglRWiss (2011), 64, 82 f.; a. A. *Basedow*, Uniform L. Rev. 2000, 129, 135 ff.; *ders.*, FS Drobnig, S. 19, 23 f.; *Brunner*, Art. 7, Rn. 9; a. A. auch, jedoch anlässlich der Untersuchung des FactÜ, *Staudinger/Hausmann*, Anh. zu Art. 33 EGBGB, Rn. 10 a. E.; *Weller*, RIW 1999, 169.
³⁹³ So auch *Rizzi*, Riv. dir. priv. 1997, 237, 278 f., Fn. 129; vgl. auch *Bamberger/Roth/Saenger*, Art. 7, Rn. 7 a. E.; *P. Huber/Mullis/P. Huber*, S.35 f.
³⁹⁴ Vgl. Hierzu auch *Bonell*, Codice internazionale, 193 ff., m. w. N.
³⁹⁵ Vgl. *Ferrari*, Interpretation of the Convention and gap-filling: Article 7, S. 138, 169 f.; *ders.*, JZ 1997, 9, 16; siehe auch *Ferrari u. a./Saenger*, Internationales Vertragsrecht, Art. 7, Rn. 7; *Melin*, S. 419 f.; a. A. ICC, 8128/1995, CISG-online 526.
³⁹⁶ *Burkart*, S. 215; *Wichard*, RabelsZ 60 (1996), 271.
³⁹⁷ So etwa ICC, 9117/1998, CISG-online 777; ICC, 8817/1997, CISG-online 776; vgl. in der Lehre zuletzt *Ferrari*, Int. Bus. L. J. 2003, 221, 230; *P. Huber*, IHR 2006, 228, 235; *P. Huber/Mullis/P. Huber*, S. 36; *Schlechtriem/Schwenzer/Schwenzer/Hachem*, CISG Commentary, Art. 7, Rn. 26.

Zum anderen können die UNIDROIT Principles, so auch die staatliche Rechtspre- **64** chung,[398] auch helfen, einen **allgemeinen Grundsatz,** auf den eine Einheitsprivatrechtskonvention basiert, näher zu **umschreiben**.[399] Aber auch hier ist Voraussetzung, dass ein solcher Grundsatz im Übereinkommen überhaupt Niederschlag gefunden hat.[400] Fehlt ein allgemeiner Grundsatz, so muss auf das durch das IPR des Forumsstaates berufene staatliche Recht zurückgegriffen werden, zumindest de lege lata.

Quid iuris, jedoch, wenn die Vertragsparteien die Anwendung der UNIDROIT Grund- **65** sätze vereinbaren? Können die UNIDROIT Grundsätze dann als Lückenfüller herangezogen werden? Bei der Beantwortung dieser Frage muss man zwei Fälle unterscheiden: (A) Die Parteien erklären, dass ausschließlich die Principles ihre internationalen Vertragsbeziehungen regeln;[401] (B) sie vereinbaren, dass die Principles neben einem staatlichen Recht auf ihren internationalen Vertrag anzuwenden sind.

Im zuletzt genannten Fall ist der **Hinweis** auf die Principles der herrschenden Meinung **66** nach ohne weiteres als **materiellrechtliche Verweisung** zu verstehen,[402] mit der Folge, dass die zwingenden Vorschriften des anwendbaren staatlichen Rechts beachtet werden müssen.[403] Mit der Feststellung, bei dem genannten Hinweis handle es sich um eine materiellrechtliche Verweisung, sind aber längst nicht alle Probleme gelöst;[404] so muss man sich zum Beispiel fragen, ob im Falle eines Kontrastes zwischen dem anwendbaren (dispositiven) staatlichen Recht und den UNIDROIT Principles diese oder die Vorschriften des anwendbaren Rechts vorgehen. Lässt sich aus dem Hinweis selbst (oder auf andere Weise) der diesbezügliche Parteiwille nicht ermitteln, so muss man m. E.[405] davon ausgehen, dass die Principles generell Vorrang haben. Dies hängt damit zusammen, dass sie speziell auf internationale Sachverhalte zugeschnitten sind,[406] und daher im Verhältnis zum auf nationale Sachverhalte zugeschnittenen staatlichen Recht als lex specialis vorzuziehen sind. Dies gilt aber dann nicht, wenn das CISG als Teil des anwendbaren Rechts auf das internationale Vertragsverhältnis anzuwenden ist. In diesem Fall muss das **CISG vorrangig zum Zug** **kommen,** da es im Verhältnis zu den UNIDROIT Principles als lex specialis anzusehen ist.

---

[398] Vgl. RB Zwolle, 5.3.1997, CISG-online 545: der Begriff des guten Glaubens könne durch die UNIDROIT Principles näher umschrieben werden.
[399] In diesem Sinne auch *Carbone,* Principi, S. 32, mit einigen Beispielen; vgl. auch *Bonell,* Codice internazionale, S. 138 ff.; *Brunner,* Art. 7, Rn. 9; *Burkart,* S. 219; *Gruber,* Methoden, S. 303; *Ferrari,* JZ 1998, 9, 16; *Harjani,* 23 Hous. J. Int'l L. (2000), 49, 68–69; *Michaels,* RabelsZ 62 (1998), 580, 606; *Schlechtriem,* Internationales UN-Kaufrecht, Rn. 52, Fn. 106; *Veneziano,* Rev. dr. aff. int. 2001, 477, 479; *Wichard,* RabelsZ 60 (1996), 269, 298.
[400] Z. T. a. A. *Brunner,* Art. 7, Rn. 9: „aufgrund von Abs. 2 ist an sich vorausgesetzt, dass der entscheidungsrelevante allgemeine Grundsatz im CISG selbst enthalten ist, weshalb zur Lückenfüllung des CISG nur jene Bestimmungen der Unidroit Prinzipien in Frage kommen, die im Einklang mit den Grundsätzen des CISG stehen. Dieser Einklang wird jedoch, obwohl im Detail Unterschiede bestehen können, aufgrund der Verwandtschaft beider Instrumente zumeist gegeben sein".
[401] Ob der Wahl der Principles der Hinweis auf die Anwendbarkeit „allgemeiner Rechtsgrundsätze" oder der „lex mercatoria" gleichkommt, muss bezweifelt werden (so im Grunde auch *Honka,* 11 Tulane European and Civil Law Forum (1996), 111, 171) und kann nicht ohne weiteres damit begründet werden, dass die Präambel dies ausdrücklich vorsieht; so zum Beispiel aber *Boele-Woelki,* IPRax 1995, 161, 165. Der staatliche Richter, der überhaupt einen solchen Hinweis beachten, muss nämlich erst feststellen, ob die Principles überhaupt den „allgemeinen Grundsätzen" oder der „lex mercatoria" entsprechen; er kann ohne weiteres zu dem Ergebnis gelangen, dass die Principles diesen nicht oder nicht mehr entsprechen.
[402] Vgl. statt aller *Boele-Woelki,* IPRax 1995, 161, 165; *Drobnig,* Vereinheitlichung durch soft law, S. 745, 753; *Vischer,* FS Schlechtriem, S. 445, 447–448.
[403] Vgl. auch *Bonell,* Codice internazionale, S. 194; zur Problematik, welche zwingenden Normen zu beachten sind, vgl. *Giardina,* I principi Unidroit, S. 64 ff.; *Wichard,* RabelsZ 60 (1996), 282 ff.
[404] Davon aber scheint *Boele-Woelki,* IPRax 1995, 161, 165, auszugehen, da sie lediglich feststellt, es handle sich um eine materiellrechtliche Verweisung, ohne weiter auf die Fragen einzugehen, die diese Qualifikation mit sich bringt.
[405] *Ferrari,* JZ 1998, 9, 16 f.
[406] Vgl. *Wichard,* RabelsZ 60 (1996), 289, der hervorhebt, dass „anders als die nationalen Rechtsordnungen, deren Normen für den Binnenverkehr konzipiert sind und die daher häufig auf internationale Sachverhalte nicht recht passen, sich die PIH ausschließlich an den Bedürfnissen des internationalen Handelsverkehrs [orientieren]".

Was die Schließung von Lücken des (vorrangigen) Übereinkommens angeht, so schließt dies aber nicht aus, dass zumindest „externe" Lücken im oben gesteckten Rahmen, d. h., bei Hinweis auf die Principles, durch ebendiese zu füllen sind. Was die „internen" Lücken angeht, so muss man aber davon ausgehen, dass diese durch die allgemeinen Grundsätze des CISG gefüllt werden müssen.[407]

67 Was aber, wenn die **Parteien ausschließlich die UNIDROIT Principles für anwendbar erklärt haben?** Eine solche Wahl der UNIDROIT Grundsätze ist, zumindest in den Staaten, in denen entweder das EVÜ,[408] die Rom-VO[409] oder die Haager-Kauf-IPR-Übereinkommen von 1955 gilt,[410] nicht als kollisionsrechtliche Verweisung,[411] sondern, so auch die neueste Rechtsprechung,[412] lediglich als Bestimmung des Vertragsinhalts per relationem zu verstehen,[413] weshalb auch in diesem Fall zwingendes Recht vorzugehen hat.[414] Der staatliche Richter ist nämlich bei der Bestimmung des anwendbaren Rechts an seine Kollisionsnormen gebunden. Die erwähnten Übereinkommen erlauben es Richtern nicht, die Wahl der UNIDROIT Principles als kollisionsrechtliche Verweisung zu qualifizieren,[415] da die Wahl nichtstaatlicher Normen, und um solche Normen handelt es sich bei den UNIDROIT Principles, als Vertragsstatut bislang nicht für zulässig gehalten wird.[416]

68 Die materiellrechtliche (ausschließliche) Verweisung auf die UNIDROIT Grundsätze ist aber von der oben erwähnten (nicht ausschließlichen) Verweisung zu unterscheiden: Während nämlich im letztgenannten Fall die **Vorschriften des CISG** den UNIDROIT Principles vorgehen, gehen bei einer ausschließlichen Verweisung die UNIDROIT Principles den Vorschriften des CISG vor. Die Frage, ob bei der Füllung von Lücken des CISG die UNIDROIT Grundsätze herangezogen werden können, stellt sich bei dieser Fallkonstellation demnach überhaupt nicht, da es – kraft Parteiwillens – keine Lücken des CISG zu füllen gibt.

69 Die soeben angestellten Überlegungen beziehen sich auf die Anwendung der UNIDROIT Principles in staatlichen Gerichten. In **Schiedsgerichten** können diese durchaus Anwendung finden,[417] zumindest dann, wenn die vom Schiedsgericht anzuwendenden

---

[407] Natürlich nur, sofern diese überhaupt existieren; in Ermangelung derselben erscheint ein Rückgriff auf die UNIDROIT Grundsätze durchaus gerechtfertigt, aber natürlich nur soweit sie nicht mit zwingendem Recht kollidieren.

[408] So *Ferrari u. a./Ferrari*, Internationales Vertragsrecht, 1. Aufl., Art. 27 EGBGB, Rn. 17; a. A. *Basedow*, Germany, S. 146; *Boele-Woelki*, IPRax 1997, 161, 166 ff.; *Grundmann*, General Principles, S. 216; *Vischer*, 1 (EJLR), 1998, 203, 211 ff.; *Wichard*, RabelsZ 60 (1996), 269, 282 ff.

[409] *Ferrari u. a./Ferrari*, Internationales Vertragsrecht, Art. 3 Rom-I VO, Rn. 21.

[410] So zu Recht in der Rechtsprechung Tribunale di Padova, 11.1.2005, CISG-online 967; vgl. zu Art. 3 EVÜ bzw. zu Art. 27 EGBGB a. F. auch *Ferrari u. a./Ferrari*, Internationales Vertragsrecht, 1. Aufl., Art. 27 EGBGB, Rn. 17; *Mankowski*, RIW 2003, 2, 11 f.; *Michaels*, RabelsZ 62 (1998), 580, 610; MünchKomm/*Martiny*, Art. 28 EGBGB, Rn. 33; *Staudinger/Magnus*, Art. 27 EGBGB, Rn. 48; *von Bar/Mankowski*, IPR I, § 2, Rn. 86.

[411] Vgl. zum bisherigen Recht auch *Bamberger/Roth/Spickhoff*, Art 27 EGBGB, Rn. 10; *Ferrari* JZ 1998, 9, 17; *Giardina* J. D. I. 1995, 547, 549 f.; *Herber* IHR 2003, 1, 8; *Looschelders*, Art. 27 EGBGB, Rn. 12; *Mankowski*, RIW 2003, 2, 11 f.; *Michaels*, RabelsZ 62 (1998), 580, 610; MüKommBGB/*Martiny*, 4. Aufl., Art. 28 EGBGB, Rn. 33; *Staudinger/Magnus*, Art. 27 EGBGB, Rn. 48; *von Bar/Mankowski*, IPR I, § 2, Rn. 86; a. A. AnwK-BGB/*Leible*, Art. 27 EGBGB, Rn. 33; *Grundmann*, in: FS Rolland, 1999, S. 145, 151 f.; *Kappus* IPRax 1993, 137; *Leible* ZvergIRW 97 (1998), 286, 313 ff.; *Vischer*, FS Schecehtriem, S. 445, 451–452; *Wichard* RabelsZ 60 (1996), 269, 282 f.; zum neuen Recht vgl. *Schinkels*, GPR 2007, 106 ff.

[412] Vgl. Tribunale di Padova, 11.1.2005, CISG-online 967 = Riv. dir. int priv. proc. (2005), 791, 798, m. zust. Anmerkung *Chiomenti*, EuLF 2005, 141 ff.

[413] So auch *Giardina*, I principi Unidroit, S. 58 f.

[414] Vgl. in diesem Sinne auch *Bonell*, Riv. dir. civ. (1997), I, 231, 244; *Drobnig*, Unidroit Principles, S. 225; MünchKomm/*Martiny*, Art. 27 EGBGB, Rn. 33.

[415] *Herber*, IHR 2003, 1, 8.

[416] So auch *Drobnig*, Vereinheitlichung von Zivilrecht durch soft law, S. 745, 753–754; *ders.*, Uniform L. Rev. 1998, 385, 386; *Herber*, IMR 2003, 1, 8; *Mankowski*, RIW 2003, 2, 12; a. A. *Vischer*, FS Schlechtriem, S. 445, 451–452, der davon ausgeht, dass „dem Einbezug nichtstaatlichen Rechts durch ein staatliches Gericht im Falle einer Rechtswahl [...] der Wortlaut des EVÜ [...] nicht entgegen" stehe.

[417] Vgl. hierzu ausführlich *Schnyder/Grolimund*, FS Schlechtriem, S. 395, 397.

Regeln dies zulassen.[418] Da diese in den letzten Jahren „liberalisiert" worden sind,[419] ist die Anwendung der UNIDROIT Principles in Schiedsgerichten durchaus möglich, weshalb es nicht überraschen kann, dass verschiedene Schiedsgerichte diese bereits zur Anwendung haben kommen lassen.[420]

---

[418] *Drobnig,* Uniform L. Rev. 1998, 385, 390; *Giardina,* J. D. I. 1995, 552; MünchKomm/*Martiny,* Art. 27 EGBGB, Rn. 33.
[419] *Drobnig,* Uniform L. Rev. 1998, 385, 390.
[420] Vgl. UNILEX, das über 100 Schiedssprüche zu den UNIDROIT Principles aufzählt.

Art. 8 [Auslegung von Erklärungen und Verhalten]

(1) Für die Zwecke dieses Übereinkommens sind Erklärungen und das sonstige Verhalten einer Partei nach deren Willen auszulegen, wenn die andere Partei diesen Willen kannte oder darüber nicht in Unkenntnis sein konnte.

(2) Ist Absatz 1 nicht anwendbar, so sind Erklärungen und das sonstige Verhalten einer Partei so auszulegen, wie eine vernünftige Person der gleichen Art* wie die andere Partei sie unter den gleichen Umständen aufgefaßt hätte.

(3) Um den Willen einer Partei oder die Auffassung festzustellen, die eine vernünftige Person gehabt hätte, sind alle erheblichen Umstände zu berücksichtigen, insbesondere die Verhandlungen zwischen den Parteien, die zwischen ihnen entstandenen Gepflogenheiten, die Gebräuche** und das spätere Verhalten der Parteien.

Art. 8

(1) For the purposes of this Convention statements made by and other conduct of a party are to be interpreted according to his intent where the other party knew or could not have been unaware what that intent was.

(2) If the preceding paragraph is not applicable, statements made by and other conduct of a party are to be interpreted according to the understanding that a reasonable person of the same kind as the other party would have had in the same circumstances.

(3) In determining the intent of a party or the understanding a reasonable person would have had, due consideration is to be given to all relevant circumstances of the case including the negotiations, any practices which the parties have established between themselves, usages and any subsequent conduct of the parties.

Art. 8

1) Aux fins de la présente Convention, les indications et les autres comportements d'une partie doivent être interprétés selon l'intention de celle-ci lorsque l'autre partie connaissait ou ne pouvait ignorer cette intention.

2) Si le paragraphe précédent n'est pas applicable, les indications et autres comportements d'une partie doivent être interprétés selon le sens qu'une personne raisonnable de même qualité que l'autre partie, placée dans la même situation, leur aurait donné.

3) Pour déterminer l'intention d'une partie ou ce qu'aurait compris une personne raisonnable, il doit être tenu compte des circonstances pertinentes, notamment des négociations qui ont pu avoir lieu entre les parties, des habitudes qui se sont établies entre elles, des usages et de tout comportement ultérieur des parties.

Übersicht

	Rn.
I. Regelungsgegenstand	1
1. Auslegung und Ergänzung von Erklärungen und Verhalten	1
2. Bestimmung des Vertragsinhalts	3
3. Auslegung und Willensmängel	6
4. Auslegung und Teilnichtigkeit	7a
5. Grenze zur Geschäftsgrundlage	8
II. Leitideen von Auslegung und Ergänzung	9
1. Parteiwille und Verkehrsschutz	9
2. Vervollständigung des Vertrags	11
III. Auslegung nach dem Willen des Erklärenden (Art. 8 I)	12
1. Feststellung des Parteiwillens	12
2. Kenntnis oder zurechenbare Unkenntnis des Erklärungsempfängers	14
IV. Auslegung nach dem vernünftigen Verständnis (Art. 8 II)	19
V. Bestimmung des Vertragsinhalts	21
1. Stufenleiter der Bestimmung des Vertragsinhalts	21
2. Feststellbarer gemeinsamer Parteiwille und erkennbarer Wille eines Teils	22

---

* Schweiz: in gleicher Stellung.
** Schweiz: Handelsbräuche, Österreich: Bräuche.

3. Objektive Dritte	24
4. Richterliche Vertragsergänzung	25
VI. Einzelfragen der Auslegung	28
1. Ausrichtung am Vertragsgegenstand	28
2. Auslegung des Vertrags als Ganzem	29
3. Treu und Glauben als Auslegungsleitlinie	30
4. Berücksichtigung der Verhandlungen und der Umstände des Vertragsschlusses	31
a) Allgemeines	31
b) Parol Evidence Rule und Vermutung der Richtigkeit und Vollständigkeit	32
c) Behandlung von merger clauses	35
5. Schweigen und Rückfrageobliegenheit	36
6. Vorhersehbarkeit und Erkennbarkeit als Umstände	39
7. Üblicher Wortsinn	40
8. Sprachrisiken	41
9. Gepflogenheiten	44
10. Gebräuche	45
11. Contra proferentem	47
12. Favor negotii und wirksamkeitsorientierte Auslegung	49
13. Späteres Verhalten der Parteien	50
14. Favor debitoris	51a
VII. Behandlung allgemeiner Geschäftsbedingungen	52
1. Einbeziehung allgemeiner Geschäftsbedingungen	52
2. Überraschende Klauseln	57
3. Vorrang der Individualabrede	58
4. Auslegung allgemeiner Geschäftsbedingungen	59
VIII. Behandlung im Verfahren	60
1. Rechts- oder Tatfrage	60
2. Beweislast	61

Entwürfe: New Yorker E 1978 Art. 7.

I. Regelungsgegenstand[1]

1. Auslegung und Ergänzung von Erklärungen und Verhalten

Art. 8 regelt die Auslegung von Erklärungen der Parteien eines dem CISG unterfallenden Kaufvertrags sowie die Auslegung von deren sonstigem Verhalten. Die Regelung schließt den Rückgriff auf nationale Auslegungsregeln aus.[2] Gegenstand der Auslegung sind insbesondere diejenigen Erklärungen, welche zum Vertragsschluss führen[3] einschließlich von Rechtswahlklauseln.[4] Ebenfalls erfasst sind Parteierklärungen, welche zur Aufhebung des Vertrags führen und zwar sowohl die einseitigen i. S. d. Art. 26,[5] als auch solche, die auf den Abschluss eines Aufhebungsvertrags[6] oder eine Vereinbarung über die

---

[1] Zur Vorgeschichte vgl. *Junge*, 3. Aufl., Rn. 1 sowie *Staudinger/Magnus*, Art. 8, Rn. 4–6.
[2] *Witz/Salger/Lorenz/Witz*, Art. 8, Rn. 1 („nationale Auslegungsdogmen"). Offenbar übersehen von OLG Frankfurt a. M., 31.3.1995, CISG-online 137, wo auf deutsche Auslegungsregeln Bezug genommen wird.
[3] Ausdrücklich etwa OGer Kanton Thurgau, 19.12.1995, CISG-online 496; *Witz/Salger/Lorenz/Witz*, Art. 8, Rn. 3. Das gilt insbesondere bei Art. 8 II auch für gleich lautende Erklärungen, vgl. unten Rn. 19.
[4] HR, 28.1.2005, CISG-online 1002; *Kingston Estate Wines Pty Ltd.* v. *Vetreria Etrusca S. r. l.*, Supreme Court of South Australia, 14.3.2008, CISG-online 1891; *Dokter*, RabelsZ 68 (2004), 430, 435 ff. Zu Rechtswahlklauseln in AGB s. unten Rn. 55.
[5] SchiedsG der Handelskammer Hamburg, 21.3.1996, CISG-online 187; OLG Koblenz, 31.1.1997, CISG-online 256; Audiencia Provincial de Navarra, 27.12.2007, CISG-online 1798; Außenhandelsschiedsgericht der Serbischen Handelskammer, 15.7.2008, CISG-online 1795.
[6] OLG Düsseldorf, 12.3.1993, CISG-online 82; *Perales Viscasillas*, 25 J. L. & Com. (2005–06), 167, 171; *Witz/Salger/Lorenz/Witz*, Art. 8, Rn. 3.

Rücksendung mangelhafter Ware[7] gerichtet sind. Dasselbe gilt für Fristsetzungen nach Art. 47 CISG.[8]

2   Darüber hinaus steuert Art. 8 die Auslegung jedes rechtlich relevanten Verhaltens der am Vertrag Beteiligten:[9] Das gilt etwa für die Frage, ob in dem Verhalten eines Teils eine Erfüllungsverweigerung zu sehen ist.[10] Auch die nach Art. 71[11] und Art. 72[12] erforderlichen Prognosen über die künftige Leistungsfähigkeit und -willigkeit des Vertragspartners sind an den in Art. 8 aufgestellten Maßstäben zu messen und ebenso die Frage, ob eine Partei zur Entgegennahme elektronischer Erklärungen (E-Mail etc.) bereit ist.[13] Ob dem Verhalten einer Partei überhaupt ein Erklärungswert zukommt, richtet sich ebenfalls nach der Vorschrift: Von praktischer Bedeutung ist dies insbesondere bei Passivität gegenüber vertragswidrigem Verhalten des anderen Teils, etwa bei Schweigen des Gläubigers nach verspätetem Zahlungseingang[14] oder wenn der Verkäufer die Abstandnahme vom Vertrag durch den anderen Teil mit Bedauern hinnimmt.[15] Hier steht jeweils der stillschweigende Verzicht auf eigene Rechtspositionen im Raum.[16] Umgekehrt kann der Zahlung des Kaufpreises respektive der Eröffnung oder Auszahlung eines Akkreditivs Erklärungsbedeutung im Sinne einer Annahmeerklärung bei Vertragsschluss zukommen.[17] Gelegentlich wird auch die unterlassene oder verfristete Mängelrüge (Artt. 39, 43) hierher gerechnet.[18] Dem ist im Grundsatz zuzustimmen; allerdings sind die einschlägigen Vorschriften sowohl hinsichtlich der Anforderungen an die Rüge,[19] als auch hinsichtlich der Rechtsfolgen *leges speciales*.

2. Bestimmung des Vertragsinhalts

3   Während die PECL in Art. 5:101 eine ausdrückliche Regelung der Auslegung von Verträgen enthalten[20] und die PICC zwischen Vertragsauslegung (Art. 4.1) und der Auslegung einzelner Erklärungen (Art. 4.2) differenzieren, behandelt Art. 8 seinem Wortlaut nach nur die Auslegung einzelner Erklärungen. Gleichwohl ist es nahezu unbestritten, dass die Vorschrift auch die Auslegung von Verträgen regelt.[21] Auch insoweit ist der Rückgriff auf nationales Recht also ausgeschlossen. Eine Begründung für die Anwendung von Art. 8 wird freilich selten gegeben. Gelegentlich wird darauf verwiesen, dass Art. 19 den Inhalt des Angebots zum Vertragsinhalt erhebt und Vertragsauslegung also letztlich Angebotsauslegung ist.[22]

---

[7] Audiencia Provincial de Madrid, 10.3.2009, CISG-online 2084.
[8] Hof Arnhem, 7.10.2008, CISG-online 1749.
[9] *Bamberger/Roth/Saenger*, Art. 8, Rn. 1; *Enderlein/Maskow/Strohbach*, Art. 8, Anm. 1.; *Staudinger/Magnus*, Art. 8, Rn. 8. Viel zu begrifflich hingegen *Kröll u. a/Zuppi*; Art. 8, Rn. 7–10.
[10] Vgl. SchiedsG der Handelskammer Hamburg, 21.3.1996, CISG-online 187; SchiedsG Hamburger freundschaftliche Arbitrage, 29.12.1998, CISG-online 638.
[11] *Staudinger/Magnus*, Art. 8, Rn. 19.
[12] Der Sache nach LG Krefeld, 28.4.1993, CISG-online 101.
[13] CISG-AC, Op. 1 *(Ramberg)*, Comment 15.4 und 15.6 = IHR 2003, 244–252.
[14] Der Sache nach LG Mönchengladbach, 22.5.1992, CISG-online 56. Allgemein zum Erklärungswert des Schweigens s. unten Rn. 36–38.
[15] OLG Celle, 24.5.1995, CISG-online 152.
[16] S. unten Rn. 37.
[17] HGer St. Gallen, 15.6.2010, CISG-online 2159 (AGB-Einbeziehung zum Ausschluß des CISG).
[18] *Bianca/Bonell/Farnsworth*, Art. 8, Anm. 2.1.; *Honnold/Fletchner*, Art. 8, Rn. 105.
[19] Vgl. BGH, 4.12.1996, CISG-online 260 sowie *Schwenzer*, Art. 39 Rn. 6 ff.
[20] Vgl. Comment A zu Art. 5:101 PECL.
[21] Hof Arnhem, 14.10.2008, CISG-online 1818; HGer Zürich, 25.6.2010, CISG-online 2161, Nr. 4.2.6; *Bianca/Bonell/Farnsworth*, Art. 8, Anm. 2.1.; *Enderlein/Maskow/Strohbach*, Art. 8, Anm. 2.3.; *Honnold/Fletchner*, Art. 8, Rn. 105; *Kröll u. a./Zuppi*, Art. 8, Rn. 2; *Leisinger*, Fundamental Breach, S. 145; *Najork*, S. 14; *Schwenzer/Hachem/Kee*, Rn. 26.6; *Soergel/Lüderitz/Fenge*, Art. 8, Rn. 10; *Staudinger/Magnus*, Art. 8, Rn. 7; *Witz/Salger/Lorenz/Witz*, Art. 8, Rn. 3. A. A. jedoch *Heuzé*, Anm. 235. ohne Bezugnahme auf sonstige Stimmen.
[22] So – jedenfalls für den Vertragsschluss in der klassischen Form durch Angebot und Annahme – *Najork*, S. 14. Ähnlich *Witz/Salger/Lorenz/Witz*, Art. 8, Rn. 3, der die Beschränkung von Art. 8 auf das überkommene Dogma des Vertragsschlusses durch Angebot und Annahme zurückführt.

Jedenfalls aber begründet Art. 8 (insbesondere zusammen mit Artt. 6, 11) allgemeine Grundsätze des Übereinkommens, welche nach Art. 7 II Alt. 1 eine eventuelle – interne – Lücke füllen.[23] Für die Vertragsauslegung ist Art. 8 auch insoweit maßgebend, als es um die Anwendungsvoraussetzungen der Konvention geht.[24] Ebenfalls erfasst werden die Auslegung einer Reihe von (CISG-)Verträgen und deren Verhältnis zueinander[25] sowie die Bestimmung der richtigen Parteien des Vertrags.[26]

Für die Anwendung auf die Auslegung von Verträgen bedarf Art. 8 freilich einer diesem **4** Zweck entsprechenden Anpassung.[27] Die Vertragsauslegung unterscheidet sich nämlich von der Auslegung einzelner Erklärungen dadurch, dass sie den Konsens der Parteien voraussetzt und diesen daher nicht verlassen darf.[28] Die Grenzen dieses *sufficient agreement* ergeben sich aus Art. 19.[29] Für die vorgelagerte Feststellung des Konsenses sind die jeweiligen Parteierklärungen noch getrennt auszulegen.[30]

Im Rahmen der Vertragsauslegung kommt Art. 8 auch im Hinblick auf solche **Fragen** **5** zur Anwendung, welche **nicht Regelungsgegenstand des CISG** sind.[31] Abgesehen davon, dass die Konvention selbst in Art. 19 III auf Vereinbarungen über Fragen verweist, die im Übrigen nicht Regelungsgegenstand der Konvention sind, ergibt sich dies bereits aus dem Gebot der Auslegung des Vertrags als Ganzem.[32] Vor allem aber ist die Auslegung eines CISG-Vertrags ausweislich von Art. 8 ein von der Konvention behandelter Gegenstand, ohne dass die Vorschrift insoweit eine Beschränkung erkennen ließe. So erfolgt etwa die Feststellung eines nicht ausdrücklich vereinbarten Aufrechnungsverbots[33] oder einer Parteiauswechslung[34] im Wege der Auslegung nach den Regeln der Konvention. Auch für die Bestimmung des genauen Inhalts vertraglicher Wettbewerbsverbote und Vertriebsbeschränkungen[35] oder Exklusivlieferungsvereinbarungen[36] ist Art. 8 heranzuziehen und ebenso für die Frage, ob die Parteien einen Eigentumsvorbehalt vereinbart haben.[37] Eine schiedsgerichtliche Entscheidung hat unter Berufung auf Art. 8 auch die Frage entschieden, ob die Voraussetzungen einer Novation vorliegen.[38] Ebenso erfolgt auch die Auslegungen eines aus Streitigkeiten über einen CISG-Vertrag hervorgegangenen Vergleichs nach Art. 8.[39] Maß-

---

[23] So in der Sache auch der zweite Begründungsweg von *Najork*, S. 14; zu weit gehend *Brunner*, Art. 8, Rn. 1, der sogar eine hilfsweise Anwendung von Artt. 4.1–4.8 PICC befürwortet.
[24] Vgl. HGer Aargau, 5.2.2008, CISG-online 1740, Nr. 3.4.1 (Qualifikation des Vertrags als Kauf und nicht als Kommission am Maßstab von Art. 8); HGer Aargau, 5.2.2008, CISG-online 1739, 4.2 (Abgrenzung Kauf / Kommission).
[25] *Norfolk Southern Railway Company v. Power Source Supply, Inc.*, U.S. Dist. Ct. (W.D. Pen.), 25.7.2008, CISG-online 1776.
[26] Hof Arnhem, 9.3.2010, CISG-online 2095, Nr. 4.5 f.; für die Situation bei Stellvertretung s. auch unten Rn. 5.
[27] *Staudinger/Magnus*, Art. 8, Rn. 7. Zu den Einzelheiten unten Rn. 21–27.
[28] Vgl. Comment A zu Art. 6:102 PECL.
[29] Vgl. Art. 2.11 PICC; Art. 2:103 PECL.
[30] Comment 1 zu Art. 4.2 PICC.
[31] *Staudinger/Magnus*, Art. 8, Rn. 7. A. A. *Ferrari*, IHR 2003, 10.
[32] Dazu unten Rn. 29.
[33] OLG Hamburg, 5.10.1998, CISG-online 473 (Nettoklausel begründet nach Art. 8 einen Aufrechnungsausschluss); OLG Linz, 23.3.2005, CISG-online 1376 (wirksame Einbeziehung der AGB); *Staudinger/Magnus*, Art. 8, Rn. 7. Anders hingegen OLG München, 28.1.1998, CISG-online 339 (ohne Begründung).
[34] So unausgesprochen BGer, 4.8.2003, CISG-online 804 = IHR 2004, 28, 30 ff. A. A. zu Unrecht OGH, 24.4.1997, CISG-online 291 (ohne weitere Auseinandersetzung mit der Frage); zur Vertragsübernahme als Regelungsgegenstand des UN-Kaufrechts vgl. *Schmidt-Kessel*, RIW 1996, 60 ff.
[35] CA Grenoble, 22.2.1995, CISG-online 151; vgl. *Staudinger/Magnus*, Art. 8, Rn. 7.
[36] *Staudinger/Magnus*, Art. 8, Rn. 7.
[37] *Roder Zelt- und Hallenkonstruktionen GmbH v. Rosedown Park Pty Ltd and Reginald R Eustace*, FCA (Adelaide, SA), 28.4.1995, CISG-online 218.
[38] ICC, 7331/1994, UNILEX (zur Feststellung des vom Schiedsgericht – m. E. zu Unrecht – für erforderlich gehaltenen gesonderten *animus novandi*). Allerdings ist die Novation richtigerweise als ein von der Konvention geregelter Gegenstand aufzufassen, soweit der Inhalt der neuen Vereinbarung nicht außerhalb des Anwendungsbereichs der Konvention liegt: *Schroeter*, Art. 29 Rn. 2 (Mietvertrag anstelle des Kaufvertrags).
[39] HGer Zürich, 24.10.2003, CISG-online 857.

geblich ist die Vorschrift weiterhin für die Auslegung der Vertretererklärung im Hinblick darauf, ob dieser in eigenem oder in fremdem Namen handelt,[40] des Verhaltens eines Lieferanten, der bislang für den Verkäufer geliefert hat und nun selbst Vertragspartei sein will,[41] sowie überhaupt für die Ermittlung der richtigen Vertragsparteien im Wege der Auslegung.[42] Auch steuerrechtliche Fragen, insbesondere die Verteilung von Steuerbelastungen, können unter Rückgriff auf Art. 8 zu entscheiden sein, etwa die Frage der Überwälzbarkeit der Umsatzsteuer auf den Käufer.[43] Schließlich ist Art. 8 – wie bereits die Bezugname in Art. 19 III zeigt – für die Auslegung von Gerichtsstandsvereinbarungen und Schiedsklauseln heranzuziehen.[44] Dasselbe gilt für die die internationale Zuständigkeit steuernden Erfüllungsortsvereinbarungen.[45]

3. Auslegung und Willensmängel

6   Nach ganz herrschender Auffassung ist die Anfechtung von Erklärungen wegen Willensmängeln eine Gültigkeitsfrage und bleibt daher nach Art. 4 S. 2 lit. a) dem nationalen Recht überlassen.[46] Die Folgen der Diskrepanz von wirklichem Willen und Erklärungsinhalt nach Art. 8 II seien, so die Begründung, in der Konvention nicht geregelt.[47] Die damit erforderliche Abgrenzung zwischen Auslegung und Willensmängeln ist allerdings problematisch, da die Auslegungskriterien auch die Beachtlichkeit bestimmter Irrtümer ansprechen[48] und damit Irrtumsrisiken zuweisen: Insbesondere erklärt Art. 8 das tatsächlich Gewollte auch bei falscher Formulierung für maßgeblich, wenn der Erklärungsempfänger den richtigen Willen kennen muss;[49] dieser trägt mithin das Irrtumsrisiko. Ein Beispiel für diese Konstellation wäre der offene Kalkulationsirrtum, welcher nach Art. 8 und nicht nach nationalem Irrtumsrecht zu behandeln ist.[50] Erkennbare Fehler bei der Erklärungshandlung oder bei der Willensformulierung sind in diesen Fällen also bereits nach Einheitsrecht unbeachtlich.[51] Des Weiteren wird für den Vertragsschluss das Irrtumsrisiko des Anbietenden durch die Widerrufsmöglichkeit nach Art. 16 wenigstens zeitweilig minimiert. Schließlich stellt sich angesichts von Art. 19 die Frage, ob es mit den Wertungen der Konvention vereinbar wäre, einen Vertrag wegen eines Irrtums zu beseitigen, der die Wesentlichkeits-

---

[40] Vgl. LG Hamburg, 26.9.1990, CISG-online 21; OGer Kanton Thurgau, 19.12.1995, CISG-online 496; Hof 's-Hertogenbosch, 2.1.2007, CISG-online 1434; *Soergel/Lüderitz/Fenge*, Art. 8, Rn. 1. Im Übrigen ist das Vertretungsrecht nicht Gegenstand der Konvention: *Ferrari*, Art. 4 Rn. 27; die Auslegungsregel kann freilich den Rückgriff auf das Vertretungsstatut entbehrlich machen, so in OGer Kanton Thurgau, 19.12.1995. CISG-online 496.
[41] BGer, 4.8.2003, CISG-online 804, E. 4.4.
[42] LG Hamburg, 26.9.1990, CISG-online 21; OGer Kanton Thurgau, 19.12.1995, CISG-online 496; OLG Stuttgart, 28.2.2000, CISG-online 583; OLG Frankfurt a. M., 30.8.2000, CISG-online 594; vgl. auch Hof Arnhem, 9.3.2010, CISG-online 2095, Nr. 4.5 f.
[43] OLG Köln, 3.4.2006, CISG-online 1218 (Auslegung führt i. d. R. zur Maßgeblichkeit der einschlägigen steuerlichen Vorschriften des Verkäuferlandes); AG Geldern, 17.8.2011, CISG-online 2302.
[44] *Château des Charmes Wines Ltd. v. Sabate USA Inc., Sabate S. A.*, U. S. Ct. App. (9th Cir.), 5.5.2003, CISG-online 767; RB Arnheim, 17.1.2007, CISG-online 1476, Nr. 2.5; OLG Stuttgart, 15.5.2006, CISG-online 1414; OLG Düsseldorf, 30.1.2004, CISG-online 821; vgl. Art. 9 Rn. 4.
[45] *Rauscher*, FS Heldrich, S. 933, 938.
[46] OGH, 20.3.1997, CISG-online 269; Ungarisches Hauptstadtgericht, 1.7.1997, CISG-online 306; OLG Hamburg, 5.10.1998, CISG-online 473; *Bianca/Bonell/Farnsworth*, Art. 8, Anm. 3.4.; *Ferrari*, Art. 4 Rn. 24.; *Heuzé*, Anm. 235.; *Schroeter*, Vor Artt. 14–24 Rn. 1; *Soergel/Lüderitz/Fenge*, Art. 8, Rn. 4; *Staudinger/Magnus*, Art. 8, Rn. 21; *Witz/Salger/Lorenz/Witz*, Art. 8, Rn. 4.
[47] *Schlechtriem*, Internationales UN-Kaufrecht, Rn. 55.
[48] Vgl. Note 1 zu Art. 5:101 PECL.
[49] S. unten Rn. 22. Übersehen von BGH, 27.11.2007, CISG-online 1617, Rn. 18 (Anwendung des „deutschen allgemeinen Privatrechts" möglich).
[50] So mit Recht *Schroeter*, EWiR 2007, 303 gegen BGH, 27.11.2007, CISG-online 1617, Rn. 18. Vgl. *Schwenzer/Hachem/Kee*, Rn. 17.36.
[51] Wie hier jetzt auch *Schwenzer/Hachem*, 57 Am. J. Comp. L. (2009), 472; *Schwenzer/Hachem/Kee*, Rn. 17.34. Ebenso schon früher *Soergel/Lüderitz/Fenge*, Art. 8, Rn. 4 (für den Erklärungsirrtum). Anders *Enderlein/Maskow/Strohbach*, Art. 8, Anm. 3.4.; *Ferrari*, IHR 2003, 10, 13 (jeweils Gültigkeitsfrage).

schwelle dieser Vorschrift nicht erreicht.[52] Die Beachtlichkeit nationaler Regeln der Irrtumsanfechtung ist also zumindest in Teilen zweifelhaft.[53]

Auch im Übrigen enthält die Konvention für eine ganze Reihe an Willensmängeln abschließende Regelungen: Soweit etwa Übermittlungsrisiken nach nationalem Recht ebenfalls durch das Irrtumsrecht zugewiesen werden, geht Art. 27 dem vor.[54] Nicht zu beachten sind ferner nationale Regeln zum Scheingeschäft: Art. 8 begründet die Geltung des verdeckten Geschäfts; das Scheingeschäft entfaltet als nicht gewollt nach Art. 8 I keine Wirkungen.[55] Ebenfalls irrelevant ist ein geheimer Vorbehalt:[56] Art. 8 I HS. 2 und II schließen dessen Beachtlichkeit aus. Soweit nationales Recht einen Dissens über einzelne Punkte nach Regeln über Willensmängel löst, tritt Art. 19 an deren Stelle.[57] Schließlich sind auch die Folgen fehlenden Erklärungsbewusstseins richtigerweise keine Gültigkeitsfrage i. S. d. Art. 4 S. 2 lit. a);[58] vielmehr ist Art. 8 I, II die Wertung zu entnehmen, dass es unter dem CISG auf das Bewusstsein des Handelnden, eine rechtserhebliche Erklärung abzugeben, nicht ankommt.[59] **7**

4. Auslegung und Teilnichtigkeit

Gemäß Art. 4 S. 2 lit. a) regelt die Konvention die Fragen der Gültigkeit des Vertrages nicht, soweit sich nicht aus der Konvention ein anderes ergibt. Diese Regel bereitet Schwierigkeiten, wo kollisionsrechtlich berufene Nichtigkeitsanordnungen nur Teile eines Vertrags betreffen. Dann stellt sich nämlich die Frage, nach welchen Regeln über das Schicksal des Vertrags im übrigen zu entscheiden ist. Richtigerweise ergibt sich aus Art. 4 S. 2 lit. a), dass primär auf die die Nichtigkeit anordnende Norm selbst abzustellen ist: verlangt diese – etwa zum Zwecke der Abschreckung – die Nichtigkeit des gesamten Vertrags, geht diese Entscheidung vor. Bislang ungeklärt sind hingegen die verbleibenden Fälle, in denen die Norm die Wirksamkeit der übrigen Vertragsteile nicht tangiert. Teilweise wird insoweit vertreten, es komme auch insoweit auf das Recht an, welches die Teilnichtigkeit herbeigeführt habe.[60] Art. 4 S. 2 lit. a) gebietet dies jedoch nicht, so daß ein Rückgriff auf nationale Regelungen zur Teilnichtigkeit nur in Betracht kommt, soweit die Konvention keine Regelung enthält. Eine solche Regelung lässt sich aber Art. 8 entnehmen: **Maßstab der Auslegung** wird jeweils die hypothetische Frage sein, ob die Parteien den kaufrechtlichen Teil des Geschäfts auch ohne den formbedürftigen anderen Teil abgeschlossen hätten.[61] Das über Kollisionsnormen der lex fori berufene, für die Gültigkeit eines Rechtsgeschäfts maßgebende Recht ist bei internationalen Verträgen vielfach schon deshalb nicht geeignet, auch über Reichweite (und Folgen) der Teilnichtigkeit zu entscheiden, weil diese nicht selten auf Eingriffsnormen des Forums und nicht auf der lex contractus beruhen wird.[62] An einer die Anwendbarkeit nationalen Rechts rechtfertigenden Lücke fehlt es mithin. **7a**

---

[52] Zur etwa in England anzutreffenden Auffassung vom Irrtum als Problem des Konsenses vgl. *Anson/Beatson*, S. 321 ff. Vgl. auch *Heuzé*, Anm. 235.

[53] Nach HGer Aargau, 5.2.2008, CISG-online 1740, Nr. 3.2.1 soll sogar fehlendes Erklärungsbewußtsein unschädlich sein. Anders möglicherweise *Miami Valley Paper v. Lebbing Engineering & Consulting*, U. S. Dist. Ct. (S. D. Oh), 26.3.2009, CISG-Online 1880 (kein summary judgment).

[54] *Staudinger/Magnus*, Art. 8, Rn. 21.

[55] *Schlechtriem*, Internationales UN-Kaufrecht, Rn. 55; *Witz/Salger/Lorenz/Witz*, Art. 8, Rn. 6. Die Gültigkeit des verdeckten Geschäfts ist über Art. 4 S. 2 lit. a) nach nationalem Recht zu beurteilen: *Enderlein/Maskow/Strohbach*, Art. 8, Anm. 3.1.

[56] *Schlechtriem*, Internationales UN-Kaufrecht, Rn. 55; *Witz/Salger/Lorenz/Witz*, Art. 8, Rn. 5.

[57] *Junge*, 3. Aufl., Rn. 4a; *Witz/Salger/Lorenz/Witz*, Art. 8, Rn. 4; enger offenbar *Schlechtriem*, Internationales UN-Kaufrecht, Rn. 55 und *Schroeter*, Vor Artt. 14–24 Rn. 6.

[58] In diesem Sinne aber LG Hamburg, 19.6.1997, CISG-online 283; *Schroeter*, Art. 14 Rn. 12.

[59] Missverständlich insoweit *Magnus*, ZEuP 523, 530, der tatsächlich das Fehlen des Parteiwillens meint.

[60] So für die partielle Formnichtigkeit *Schlechtriem*, 4. Aufl., Art. 11 Rn 7.

[61] Vgl. *Schlechtriem*, Einheitliches UN-Kaufrecht, S. 31 Fn. 138; *Wey*, Rn. 304 und (speziell zum Schweizer Kartellrecht) Rn. 421.

[62] S. für die partielle Formnichtigkeit Art. 11 Rn. 7.

5. Grenze zur Geschäftsgrundlage

8 Schwierigkeiten kann auch die Abgrenzung der Vertragsauslegung von der – in ihrer Beachtlichkeit umstrittenen[63] – Idee einer Entlastung durch *hardship*, Unerschwinglichkeit, Störung der Geschäftsgrundlage oder ähnliches bereiten: Grundsätzlich verbietet die Konvention eine Modifikation des durch Auslegung und gegebenenfalls Ergänzung ermittelten Vertragsinhalts durch den Richter.[64] Aber auch soweit von vielen Autoren im Rahmen von Art. 79 die – seltene – Möglichkeit einer Entlastung vom Schadensersatz[65] wegen „Unerschwinglichkeit" angenommen wird,[66] ist vorrangig auf die durch Auslegung zu ermittelnde Risikoverteilung zu sehen.[67]

II. Leitideen von Auslegung und Ergänzung

1. Parteiwille und Verkehrsschutz

9 Auch die offenbar erste rechtskreisübergreifende Regelung der Auslegung von Verträgen unter Privatrechtssubjekten[68] entkommt dem Standarddilemma von Auslegungsregeln einer auf Privatautonomie aufbauenden Vertragsrechtsordnung nicht: Einerseits wird die Durchsetzung der vertraglichen Bindung nur durch den Willen des betroffenen Schuldners legitimiert, andererseits muss dieser seinen Willen kommunizieren, also aus der Sphäre der eigenen Willensbildung heraus mit dem anderen Teil in Verbindung treten; von wenigen Ausnahmen abgesehen ist er dabei gezwungen, sich einschlägiger Codes zu bedienen: Um eine Bindung eingehen zu können, muss der Einzelne daher bereit sein, die Herrschaft seines Willens durch die Begrenztheiten von Kommunikation zu relativieren. Auslegungsregeln dienen in erster Linie dazu, die regelmäßig auftretenden Differenzen zwischen Wille und Kommunikation zu bewältigen.[69]

10 Entsprechend ihrer Betonung der Privatautonomie in Art. 6 stellt die Konvention den Willen des Erklärenden in Art. 8 I an die erste Stelle; bezogen auf den Vertragsschluss entspricht dem die Forderung nach einem (subjektiven) *meeting of minds*. Dieser an sich herrschenden Willenstheorie[70] zieht freilich bereits in demselben Absatz der in den Standards des *could not have been unaware* verschlüsselte Verkehrsschutz eine Grenze[71]. Praktisch überwiegt die – in Art. 8 II formaliter als nachrangig festgeschriebene – sogenannte objektive Auslegung nach dem hypothetischen Verständnis einer vernünftigen Person „in den Schuhen" des Erklärungsempfängers.[72] Der Grund für dieses Übergewicht liegt in der Art der prozessualen Ermittlung des Erklärungsinhalts, bei welcher der äußere Erklärungstatbestand – und unausgesprochen oder uneingestanden dessen objektive Auslegung nach

---

[63] Vgl. *Schlechtriem*, Internationales UN-Kaufrecht, Rn. 291 sowie RB, 25.1.2005, CISG-online 1106.

[64] Vgl. Comment B zu Art. 5:101 PECL.

[65] Das Schicksal des Erfüllungsanspruchs richtet sich bei Störungen dieser Art nach dem nationalen Recht des Forums (Art. 28).

[66] *Stoll*, 3. Aufl., Art. 79 Rn. 39 f.; *Schwenzer*, Art. 79 Rn. 49, jeweils m. w. N.

[67] Vgl. *Najork*, S. 157 f.

[68] Vgl. *Staudinger/Magnus*, Art. 8, Rn. 3; *Soergel/Lüderitz/Fenge*, Art. 8, Rn. 1. Zur bereits früher angegangenen Auslegung völkerrechtlicher Verträge vgl. Artt. 31 f. Wiener Vertragsrechtskonvention und dazu *Baldus*, Regelhafte Vertragsauslegung, S. 139–152 *et passim*.

[69] Grundlegend zum Vorrang des Willens vor heteronomen Elementen *Lobinger*, Rechtsgeschäftliche Verpflichtung und autonome Bindung, Tübingen 1999, S. 66 ff., 336 *et passim*.

[70] *Honnold/Fletchner*, Art. 8, Rn. 106; *Junge*, 3. Aufl., Rn. 1, 2; *Staudinger/Magnus*, Art. 8, Rn. 17; vgl. Note 2 zu Art. 5:101 PECL.

[71] *Honnold/Fletchner*, Art. 8, Rn. 106; vgl. *Tjittes*, R. M. Themis 2005, 2, 7 („subjectief-objectieve uitleg").

[72] *MCC-Marble Ceramic Center, Inc. v. Ceramica Nuova D'Agostino S. P. A.*, U. S. Ct. App. (11th Cir.), 29.6.1998, CISG-online 342 = 144 F. 3d 1384, 1391; *Honnold/Fletchner*, Art. 8, Rn. 107; *Witz/Salger/Lorenz/Witz*, Art. 8, Rn. 5; vgl. Note 4 zu Art. 5:101 PECL. Das Bild von den Schuhen des Empfängers findet sich etwa bei *Schroeter*, Art. 14 Rn. 16.

Art. 8 II – regelmäßig ein unverzichtbares Indiz für die Feststellung des tatsächlichen Parteiwillens darstellt.[73]

2. Vervollständigung des Vertrags

Die Auslegungsregeln der Konvention haben zudem bei der Auslegung von Verträgen eine zweite Funktion zu erfüllen: Regelmäßig konzentriert sich der ermittelbare Parteiwille auf einige Kernfragen des Vertragsschlusses; über weitere Punkte haben sich die Parteien keinerlei Gedanken gemacht. Der Vertrag ist dadurch letztlich nicht unvollständig: Er weist das Risiko schlicht derjenigen Partei zu, die sich auf einen bestimmten Vertragsinhalt beruft, dessen Bestand aber nicht nachweisen kann; ein dem deutschen Recht vergleichbares Lückenerfordernis kennt die Konvention also nicht.[74] Dass die Konvention es nicht notwendig bei diesem Ergebnis belässt, zeigt sich bereits an ihrer Geltung als dispositives Recht und der Möglichkeit ihrer Fortentwicklung nach den Regeln von Art. 7 II Alt. 1, an der Einbeziehung von Gepflogenheiten und Gebräuchen nach Art. 9 und insbesondere an Art. 8 II. Die Vorschrift erfüllt daher auch Aufgaben bei der Ergänzung „unvollständiger" Verträge;[75] offen ist lediglich wo die Grenzen dieser heteronomen Vertragsergänzung verlaufen.[76] Mechanismen der Vertragsergänzung nach nationalem Recht werden verdrängt.[77]

III. Auslegung nach dem Willen des Erklärenden (Art. 8 I)

1. Feststellung des Parteiwillens

Art. 8 I erfordert grundsätzlich die Aufklärung des Parteiwillens auch insoweit, als er im objektiven Erklärungsinhalt keinen Niederschlag gefunden hat.[78] Eine allgemeine materielle Vermutung dafür, dass der Parteiwille einer Auslegung nach Art. 8 II entspricht,[79] begründet Abs. I nicht.[80] Die Konvention gibt den Gerichten statt dessen auf, bei der Ermittlung des Willens eine Reihe von Umständen zu berücksichtigen (Art. 8 III)[81], nämlich die Verhandlungen zwischen den Parteien,[82] die zwischen ihnen entstandenen Gepflogenheiten[83] und Gebräuche[84] sowie das spätere Parteiverhalten.[85] Diese Liste, welche auch auf weitere

---

[73] Zu weit geht freilich die von einem US-Bundesappellationsgericht gezogene Konsequenz einer materiellrechtlichen Vermutung, dass der Parteiwille nach Art. 8 I einer Auslegung nach Art. 8 II entspreche (*MCC-Marble Ceramic Center, Inc. v. Ceramica Nuova D'Agostino S. P. A.,* U. S. Ct. App. (11th Cir.), 29.6.1998, CISG-online 342 = 144 F. 3d 1384, 1388: Sie ist offenbar der für US-Gerichte ungewöhnlichen Situation geschuldet, den subjektiven Parteiwillen tatsächlich ermitteln zu müssen. Vgl. 144 F. 3d 1384, 1387: Das Gericht betont ausdrücklich die darin liegende Abweichung von der üblichen US-amerikanischen Praxis.

[74] Anders offenbar *Schwenzer/Hachem/Kee*, Rn. 26.65, 26.69, jedoch ohne Begründung.

[75] Wie hier jetzt auch *Kröll u. a./Zuppi,* Art. 8, Rn. 29 (unter Berufung auf *favor contractus,* vgl. Rn. 49); der Sache nach ebenso OLG Köln, 2.7.2007, CISG-online 1811, Rn. 28.

[76] S. Rn. 25–27.

[77] *Schwenzer/Hachem/Kee*, Rn. 26.4, 26.71 sowie unten Rn. 25–27. Vgl. OLG Köln, 2.7.2007, CISG-online 1811, Rn. 37. Anders Schiedsgericht der Börse für landwirtschaftliche Produkte in Wien, 10.12.1997, CISG-online 351.

[78] *MCC-Marble Ceramic Center, Inc. v. Ceramica Nuova D'Agostino S. P. A.,* U. S. Ct. App. (11th Cir.), 29.6.1998, CISG-online 342 = 144 F. 3d 1384, 1387; *Supermicro Computer Inc. v. Digitechnic, S. A.,* U. S. Dist. Ct. (N. D. Cal.), 30.1.2001, CISG-online 612 = 145 F. 2d 1147, 1151; BGer, 5.4.2005, CISG-online 1012, E. 3.2.

[79] So *MCC-Marble Ceramic Center, Inc. v. Ceramica Nuova D'Agostino S. P. A.,* U. S. Ct. App. (11th Cir.), 29.6.1998, CISG-online 342 = 144 F. 3d 1384, 1388.

[80] S. oben Rn. 10.

[81] A. A. *Witz/Salger/Lorenz/Witz,* Art. 8, Rn. 5 (Abs. 3 diene bei Abs. 1 nur der Ermittlung der gebotenen Sorgfalt). Abs. 3 bezieht sich gerade auf den Willen und ist allenfalls insoweit missglückt, als dieser nicht ausdrücklich außerdem zur Konkretisierung des „*could not have been unaware"* herangezogen wird.

[82] S. u. Rn. 31–35.

[83] S. u. Rn. 44.

[84] S. u. Rn. 45 f.

[85] S. u. Rn. 50 f.

Unternehmungen zur Vertragsrechtsvereinheitlichung ausgestrahlt hat,[86] ist nicht abschließend.[87] Vielmehr sind, wie Art. 8 III ausdrücklich betont, alle denkbaren Umstände zu berücksichtigen.[88] Zweck dieser Regelung ist der Ausschluss formeller Beschränkungen des vom Gericht zu beachtenden Auslegungsmaterials: Die Konvention kennt keine formellen Schranken für die Auslegung und verdrängt damit gegenteilige nationale Regeln.[89] Vorrangiger Ausgangspunkt muss allerdings der – in Abs. 3 nicht ausdrücklich genannte – Wortlaut der Erklärung sein.[90]

13 Art. 8 III verallgemeinert die in Art. 11 für den Kaufvertrag niedergelegte Regel in zweierlei Hinsicht: Zum einen bedarf keine Erklärung, auf welche die Konvention Anwendung findet, der schriftlichen Form und kann auf jede Weise bewiesen werden; zum anderen richtet sich die materielle wie beweisrechtliche Formfreiheit nicht nur gegen Schriftformerfordernisse, sondern gegen jede materielle oder formelle Beschränkung des Auslegungsmaterials. Auf die Gewichtung desselben und auf den Vorgang der Tatsachenfeststellung als solchen nimmt die Konvention hingegen keinen Einfluss. Ebenfalls zulässig ist die Nichtbeachtung an sich einschlägigen Materials wegen prozessualer Fehler einer Partei, etwa auf Grund einer Präklusion.

2. Kenntnis oder zurechenbare Unkenntnis des Erklärungsempfängers

14 Der Frage nach der Kenntnis oder zurechenbaren Unkenntnis des Erklärungsempfängers ist zunächst eine andere vorgelagert, nämlich diejenige, auf wessen Kenntnis abzustellen ist. Wichtig ist dies insbesondere bei der Abgrenzung der Vertragsparteien von Vermittlern, etwa Warenmaklern. Maßgebend ist hier der vom Erklärenden bestimmte Adressat der Erklärung.[91] Erkennt dieser seine Adressatenstellung nicht und musste er dies auch nicht, scheidet eine Anwendung von Art. 8 I jedenfalls hinsichtlich der Bestimmung der Vertragsparteien aus. Für die Ermittlung des übrigen Vertragsinhalts kommt eine Anwendung von Abs. 1 jedoch auch in diesem Falle in Betracht.

15 Abgesehen von dem angesprochenen Auslegungsmaterial enthält die Konvention naturgemäß **keine Regel**, wann der Erklärungsempfänger positive Kenntnis vom Willen des Erklärenden hatte. Soweit diese in einzelnen Entscheidungen ausdrücklich angenommen wird, lässt sich nicht leicht sagen, ob sich hinter den Urteilsformulierungen vielleicht doch nur der Sorgfaltsverstoß des Erklärungsempfängers verbirgt: Das gilt etwa für die in einem Fall angenommene Kenntnis von der Bedeutung einer Vertriebsbeschränkung,[92] den ausdrücklichen Schluss von der käuferseitigen Kenntnis vom Verwendungszweck auf die Kenntnis vom Willen zur entsprechenden Eignung[93] oder die festgestellte Kenntnis eines belgischen Unternehmers von den Standardbedingungen der Vereinigung der Schweizer Maschinenbauindustrie.[94]

16 Als **Maßstab zurechenbarer Unkenntnis** enthält Art. 8 I die Formel *could not have been unaware*, welche in der Konvention noch an weiteren Stellen Verwendung findet (Artt. 35 III, 40, 42 I, II lit. a) und auch in die Auslegungsbestimmungen weiterer Schritte internationaler Rechtsvereinheitlichung Eingang gefunden hat (Art. 4.2 I PICC; Art. 5:101 II PECL). Üblicherweise wird darunter – im Unterschied zu der etwa ebenfalls

---

[86] Vgl. Art. 4.3 PICC und Art. 5:102 PECL.
[87] *Bianca/Bonell/Farnsworth*, Art. 8, Anm. 2.6.; *Kröll u. a./Zuppi*, Art. 8, Rn. 25; *Staudinger/Magnus*, Art. 8, Rn. 24; *Witz/Salger/Lorenz/Witz*, Art. 8, Rn. 11; vgl. Comment 1 zu Art. 4.3 PICC; Comment zu Art. 5:102 PECL.
[88] *Staudinger/Magnus*, Art. 8, Rn. 2.
[89] *Staudinger/Magnus*, Art. 8, Rn. 23. Vgl. Rn. 35 *(merger clauses)*, 32 f. *(parol evidence rule)*.
[90] *Witz/Salger/Lorenz/Witz*, Art. 8, Rn. 11; *Schwenzer/Hachem/Kee*, Rn. 26.16.
[91] OGH, 18.6.1997, CISG-online 292; *Staudinger/Magnus*, Art. 8, Rn. 11.
[92] CA Grenoble, 22.2.1995, CISG-online 151 (Vertrieb der verkauften Kleidung nur in Südamerika).
[93] CA Grenoble, 13.9.1995, CISG-online 157.
[94] Trib. com. Nivelles (Belgien), 19.9.1995, CISG-online 366.

zu findenden Formulierung *ought to have known*[95] – ein gesteigertes Maß an Sorgfaltswidrigkeit verstanden,[96] welches in der deutschsprachigen Literatur regelmäßig mit grober Fahrlässigkeit gleichgesetzt wird.[97] Besser als diese Anknüpfung an nationale Begrifflichkeiten ist freilich die schlichte Formulierung, dass der Wille besonders leicht zu erkennen war respektive eine Rückfrage sich geradezu aufdrängte.[98] Soweit in dieser Anknüpfung an die Sorgfalt des Erklärungsempfängers ein Funktionsäquivalent zur Lehre vom Empfängerhorizont gesehen wird,[99] ist jedenfalls darauf zu achten, dass es in Art. 8 I allenfalls um einen subjektiven Empfängerhorizont gehen kann.[100]

Bei der **Konkretisierung des Maßstabs** im Rahmen von Art. 8 I ist zu beachten, dass es 17 in der Praxis auf diesen nur selten ankommt:[101] Von Interesse ist die Prüfung der erhöhten Sorgfaltswidrigkeit nämlich nur dann, wenn der Wille des Erklärenden nicht schon mit der Auslegung nach Abs. 2 übereinstimmt, dieser also nicht dem Verständnis einer vernünftigen Person in den Schuhen des Erklärungsempfängers entspricht. Das gilt insbesondere für den in der Rechtsprechung behandelten Fall des unmissverständlichen Wortlauts der Erklärung,[102] in welchem sich der richtige Kern der – überkommenen und unter der Konvention schon wegen Abs. III unanwendbaren[103] – Regel *in claris non fit interpretatio* respektive der *plain meaning rule* widerspiegelt.[104] Relevant wird Abs. 1 zudem im Falle eines besonderen, zuvor zwischen den Parteien geklärten Verständnishintergrunds, der von einem vernünftigen Verständnis bewusst abweicht.[105]

Eine über den Maßstab des Abs. 2 hinaus erhöhte, besondere Sorgfaltswidrigkeit im Sinne von Abs. 1 kann sich jedoch im Einzelfall etwa aus dem Einsatz eines sprachunkundigen Mitarbeiters,[106] aus der besonderen Fachkunde des Erklärungsempfängers oder aus dessen vertrautem rechtlichen Umfeld[107] ergeben.

Umstritten ist der für die Kenntnis und ihr Äquivalent **maßgebliche Zeitpunkt**: Über- 18 wiegend wird wohl auf den Erklärungszeitpunkt abgestellt,[108] während es nach einer Gegenauffassung auf das Wirksamwerden der Erklärung ankommen soll.[109] In der Sache geht es vor allem um die Bewertung nachträglichen Erkenntnisfortschritts beim Erklärungsempfänger und dessen zeitliches Verhältnis zu den Wirkungen der Erklärung. Diese Sachfrage lässt sich jedoch nicht abschließend entscheiden: Kommt es etwa vor Eintritt der Bindung an das Angebot nach Art. 16 zu einem Erkenntnisfortschritt des Empfängers, ist dieser zu berücksichtigen. Sollte Aufhebung des Vertrags erklärt werden und war dies zunächst nicht deutlich genug, werden spätere Erkenntnisse des Aufhebungsgegners hingegen nicht zu einer rückwirkenden Aufhebung führen.

---

[95] Artt. 2 lit. a), 9 II, 38 III, 49 II lit. b) Nr. i, 64 II lit. b) Nr. i, 68 III, 74 S. 2, 79 IV 2. Entsprechend Art. 39 I sowie 82 II lit. c) („ought to have discovered"), Art. 43 I („ought to have become aware of") und 74 S. 2 („ought to have foreseen").
[96] *Witz/Salger/Lorenz/Witz*, Art. 8, Rn. 5.
[97] *Honsell/Melis*, Art. 8, Rn. 6; *Staudinger/Magnus*, Art. 8, Rn. 12. Mit Recht kritisch dazu *Witz/Salger/Lorenz/Witz*, Art. 8, Rn. 5.
[98] LG Kassel, 15.2.1996, CISG-online 190; *Bamberger/Roth/Saenger*, Art. 8, Rn. 2; *Staudinger/Magnus*, Art. 8, Rn. 12; *Witz/Salger/Lorenz/Witz*, Art. 8, Rn. 5.
[99] *Junge*, 3. Aufl., Rn. 4; *Bamberger/Roth/Saenger,* Art. 8, Rn. 2; *Staudinger/Magnus*, Art. 8, Rn. 11.
[100] LG Hamburg, 26.9.1990, CISG-online 21; *Junge*, 3. Aufl., Rn. 5. Zu undifferenziert daher LG Oldenburg, 28.2.1996, CISG-online 189 und OLG Schleswig, 29.10.2002, CISG-online 717.
[101] *Dokter*, RabelsZ 68 (2004), 430, 434.
[102] ICC, 8324/1995, CISG-online 569 („prix provisoire" ist keine engültige Preisvereinbarung; „facture provisoire" ist keine endgültige Rechnung). Vgl. auch Audiencia Provincial de Cáceres, 14.7.2010, CISG-online 2131.
[103] CISG-AC, Op. 3 (*Hyland*). Verkannt durch Hof van Beroep Antwerpen, 24.4.2006, CISG-online 1258 (klare vertragliche Regel habe Vorrang vor Art. 8 und (insoweit zutreffend) Art. 9).
[104] *Baldus*, Regelhafte Vertragsauslegung, S. 117 f.
[105] BGH, CISG-online 1617, Rn. 14 (Vertragsänderung dient der Verschleierung des wahren Kaufpreises gegenüber Dritten).
[106] *Staudinger/Magnus*, Art. 8, Rn. 13.
[107] *Junge*, 3. Aufl., Rn. 5.
[108] *Enderlein/Maskow/Strohbach*, Art. 8, Anm. 3.1.; *Staudinger/Magnus*, Art. 8, Rn. 15.
[109] *Bianca/Bonell/Farnsworth*, Art. 8, Anm. 2.2.; *Ferrari*, IHR 2003, 10, 12.

IV. Auslegung nach dem vernünftigen Verständnis (Art. 8 II)

19 Der formaliter nachrangige[110] Art. 8 II enthält den praktischen Kernsatz der Auslegung unter der Konvention: Erklärungen sind so auszulegen, wie sie von einer vernünftigen Person in den Schuhen des Empfängers aufgefasst worden wären. Maßgebend ist also das hypothetische Verständnis einer vernünftigen Person der gleichen Art, die sich – wie hinzuzusetzen ist – in der gleichen äußeren Situation befindet.[111] Art. 8 II stellt also von vornherein auf den Empfängerhorizont ab,[112] im Unterschied zu Abs. 1 allerdings auf den objektiven.[113] Die Vorschrift schützt somit das Vertrauensprinzip.[114] Dieser Maßstab kann bei Bedeutungsunterschieden zwischen den Sphären von Vertragsschließenden zum Dissens führen,[115] welcher allerdings nicht dadurch vermieden werden kann, dass man den Anwendungsbereich von Art. 8 II bei zwei gleich lautenden Erklärungen auf die Erste beschränkt.[116] Die Möglichkeit einer derartigen Einschränkung lässt die Konvention nicht erkennen. Ob in solchen Fällen der Vertrag an den unterschiedlichen Verständnissen scheitert, entscheidet sich vielmehr – abgesehen von vorrangig zu prüfenden Rückfrage- und Klärungsobliegenheiten – nach dem Maßstab von Art. 19.

20 Bei der Feststellung des hypothetischen Empfängerverständnisses sind wiederum die in Art. 8 III genannten Gesichtspunkte zu berücksichtigen.[117] Diese doppelte Anwendung der Kriterien des Abs. 3 zur Feststellung des tatsächlichen Willens des Erklärenden einerseits und zur Ermittlung des hypothetischen Verständnisses des Empfängers andererseits hat zweifellos mit dazu beigetragen, dass die Absätze 1 und 2 vielfach nicht unterschieden werden. Neben den in Abs. 3 benannten Gesichtspunkten findet sich auch zu Abs. 2 der Hinweis, abzustellen sei auf einen Fachmann der betreffenden Branche.[118] Zudem wird dem Wortlaut der Erklärung wiederum ein besonderes Gewicht zugemessen.[119]

V. Bestimmung des Vertragsinhalts

1. Stufenleiter der Bestimmung des Vertragsinhalts

21 Im Rahmen der Anwendung von Art. 8 bei der Auslegung abgeschlossener Verträge kommt es zu einigen Modifikationen und Akzentverschiebungen: Ausgangspunkt ist immer der hinreichende Konsens der Parteien.[120] Von diesem ausgehend gilt die von Art. 8 begründete Rangordnung auch für die Auslegung von Verträgen:[121] Primär maßgeblich ist

---

[110] AppGer Basel-Stadt, 26.9.2008, CISG-online 1732, Nr. 4.2; *Staudinger/Magnus*, Art. 8, Rn. 17.

[111] *Bianca/Bonell/Farnsworth*, Art. 8, Anm. 2.4.; *Honnold/Fletchner*, Art. 8, Rn. 107.1; *Staudinger/Magnus*, Art. 8, Rn. 17. Vgl. auch die schweizerische Fassung: „in gleicher Stellung".

[112] HGer Aargau, 5.2.2008, CISG-online 1740, Nr. 3.1.2; *Bamberger/Roth/Saenger*, Art. 8, Rn. 3; *Schlechtriem*, Internationales UN-Kaufrecht, Rn. 54; *Staudinger/Magnus*, Art. 8, Rn. 17; *Witz/Salger/Lorenz/Witz*, Art. 8, Rn. 7.

[113] LG Hamburg, 26.9.1990, CISG-online 21; *Junge*, 3. Aufl., Rn. 7; *Ferrari*, IHR 2003, 10, 13; *Soergel/Lüderitz/Fenge*, Art. 8, Rn. 5. Ein subjektives Verständnis im Sinne von Art. 8 II findet sich hingegen etwa bei OLG Hamm, 22.9.1992, CISG-online 57. Zu den Schwierigkeiten ibero-amerikanischer Rechtsordnungen mit dieser Regel vgl. *Schlechtriem/Schwenzer/Muñoz*, Sec. Comp. Ibero, Arts. 7–13, Rn. 4, 8.

[114] AppGer Lugano, 29.10.2003, CISG-online 912, Nr. 3.2; KG Freiburg, 11.10.2004, CISG-online 964.

[115] *Bianca/Bonell/Farnsworth*, Art. 8, Anm. 3.2.; *Heuzé*, Anm. 235. Insoweit zutreffend auch *Witz/Salger/Lorenz/Witz*, Art. 8, Rn. 8.

[116] So aber *Witz/Salger/Lorenz/Witz*, Art. 8, Rn. 8.

[117] *Staudinger/Magnus*, Art. 8, Rn. 17.

[118] *Junge*, 3. Aufl., Rn. 7.

[119] OLG Dresden, 27.12.1999, CISG-online 511 (vorrangig heranzuziehen); *Witz/Salger/Lorenz/Witz*, Art. 8, Rn. 11.

[120] S. oben Rn. 4.

[121] *Ferrari*, IHR 2003, 10, 11; *Staudinger/Magnus*, Art. 8, Rn. 7; s. auch ICC, 8324/1995, CISG-online 569 (système à trois étages).

nach Art. 8 I Alt. 1 auch hier der Parteiwille, freilich in Gestalt einer *common intention* der Parteien.[122] Ist nur der Wille einer Seite feststellbar, genügt entsprechend Art. 8 I Alt. 2, dass die andere Seite diesen nicht verkennen konnte.[123] Des Weiteren ist dann auf das hypothetische Verständnis vernünftiger Personen derselben Art zurückzugreifen (Art. 8 II)[124] und außerdem kommt darüber hinaus auch unter der Konvention eine richterliche Vertragsergänzung in Betracht.[125] Nur hilfsweise greifen dann die Regelungen der Konvention ein (Grundsatz der Subsidiarität der Konvention).

2. Feststellbarer gemeinsamer Parteiwille und erkennbarer Wille eines Teils

Wie allgemein Art. 8 I darf die praktische Bedeutung der *common intention* der Parteien – schon allein wegen der Beweisschwierigkeiten – nicht überschätzt werden.[126] Immerhin hat ihr Vorrang zur Konsequenz, dass eine *falsa demonstratio* nicht schadet.[127] Das Fallmaterial zu diesem Punkt ist freilich wiederum eher dürftig: So hat man die einseitige Regelung in einer Vorausrechnung für die Feststellung eines gemeinsamen Parteiwillens nicht ausreichen lassen.[128] Ein festgestelltes gemeinsames Verständnis von frei- und franco-Klauseln ersetzt gegebenenfalls die übliche Bedeutung.[129] Schließlich kann die *common intention* sogar Art. 19 III überspielen.[130]

Der *common intention* ist der unverkennbare Wille eines Teils gleichgestellt.[131] Die ausdrückliche Aufnahme dieser – Art. 8 I Alt. 2 entsprechenden – Regel war bei der Entstehung der Konvention zeitweise vorgesehen gewesen.[132] Darin liegt wieder ein Ausfluss des gesetzlich vorgegebenen Vorrangs des Parteiwillens.[133] In der Auslegungspraxis ist diese Konstellation schon deshalb eher anzutreffen, weil sie für das entscheidende Gericht die schwierige Feststellung eines zweiten Parteiwillens entbehrlich macht.

3. Objektive Dritte

Praktischer Regelfall der Vertragsauslegung ist wiederum die Anknüpfung an das hypothetische Verständnis eines vernünftigen Dritten; er bestimmt die prozessuale Ausgangslage. Maßgebend ist die Figur des vernünftigen Geschäftsteilnehmers bei Geschäften derselben Art.[134] Diese offene Bezugnahme auf die *reasonableness* vermeidet die sonst unweigerlich eintretende Versuchung der Gerichte, einen tatsächlichen Parteiwillen zu fingieren.[135] Der tatsächlich festgestellte Wille der Parteien kann daher als Auslegungsgrenze dienen.[136] Für

---

[122] So ausdrücklich BGer, 5.4.2005, CISG-online 1012, E. 3.2 und AppGer Basel-Stadt, 26.9.2008, CISG-online 1732, Nr. 4.2; HGer Zürich, 25.6.2010, CISG-online 2161, Nr. 4.2.6; ebenso Art. 4.1 I PICC; Art. 5:101 I PECL. Die Willensübereinstimmung ersetzt also die ansonsten nach Art. 8 I Alt. 1 erforderliche Kenntnis des anderen Teils.
[123] Art. 5:101 II PECL; vgl. Art. 4.2 II PICC.
[124] Art. 4.1 II PICC; Art. 5:101 III PECL.
[125] ICC, 8324/1995, CISG-online 569 („les techniques habituelles de raisonnement qui relèvent de la logique générale [raisonnement par analogie, a contrario, etc.]"); vgl. Artt. 4.8, 5.2 PICC; Art. 6:102 PECL.
[126] Comment 1 zu Art. 4.1 PICC.
[127] *Schwenzer/Hachem/Kee*, Rn. 17.37; *Bamberger/Roth/Saenger*, Art. 8, Rn. 2; *Soergel/Lüderitz/Fenge*, Art. 8, Rn. 4; *Staudinger/Magnus*, Art. 8, Rn. 16; *Witz/Salger/Lorenz/Witz*, Art. 8, Rn. 6; Comment 1 zu Art. 4.1 PICC; Comment B zu Art. 5:101 PECL.
[128] RB Hasselt, 18.10.1995, CISG-online 364 (Ausschluss des CISG).
[129] BGH, 11.12.1996, CISG-online 225.
[130] OGH, 20.3.1997, CISG-online 269.
[131] BGer 5.4.2005, CISG-online 1012, E. 3.3.
[132] Art. 3 II UNIDROIT-Entwurf zum Vertragsschluss.
[133] *Heuzé*, Anm. 235.; Comment C zu Art. 5:101 PECL.
[134] Schiedsgericht der Börse für landwirtschaftliche Produkte in Wien, 10.12.1997, CISG-online 351; BGer 4.8.2003, CISG-online 804, E. 4.3; BGer 5.4.2005, CISG-online 1012, E. 3.3; *Ferrari*, IHR 2003, 10, 13; *Staudinger/Magnus*, Art. 8, Rn. 17.
[135] Comment D zu Art. 5:101 PECL; vgl. Schiedsgericht der Börse für landwirtschaftliche Produkte in Wien, 10.12.1997, CISG-online 351.
[136] Comment D zu Art. 5:101 PECL.

bestimmte Regelungen wird freilich bisweilen subjektive Einvernehmlichkeit für unabdingbar gehalten; dies ist insbesondere für den stillschweigenden Ausschluss der Konvention so entschieden worden.[137]

4. Richterliche Vertragsergänzung

25   Jüngere Vorhaben zur Rechtsvereinheitlichung sehen heute regelmäßig neben den Regeln der Vertragsauslegung besondere Vorschriften für die Vertragsergänzung durch den Richter vor, welche sich – bei in Teilen abweichenden Maßstäben – der anglo-amerikanischen Konzeption der *implied terms* bedienen.[138] Weder diese, noch die kontinentale Tradition der „ergänzenden Vertragsauslegung" oder der *clause tacite* haben in der Konvention ausdrückliche allgemeine Übernahme gefunden; in Literatur und Rechtsprechung finden sich immer wieder Stimmen, welche eine richterliche Vertragsergänzung unter der Konvention überhaupt ablehnen[139] und die einschlägigen nationalen Regeln der Vertragsergänzung zur Anwendung bringen wollen.[140] Bisweilen wird der Rückgriff auf entsprechende Instrumente sogar als entbehrlich bezeichnet, weil sich im internationalen Warenhandel entsprechende Praktiken und Gebräuche entwickelt hätten, welche bereits in die Vertragsauslegung eingingen; zudem sei in Musterverträgen hinreichend Vorsorge getroffen.[141] Der durch die bislang ergangene Rechtsprechung vermittelte Eindruck spricht allerdings nicht dafür, dass die Konvention vornehmlich auf derart gut organisierten Märkten Anwendung findet. Der außerdem denkbare Rückschluss aus den vorhandenen Sonderregeln in den Unidroit-Principles und die European Principles, entsprechende Regeln gebe es unter der Konvention nicht, würde deren deutlich spätere Entstehung vernachlässigen.

26   Tatsächlich eröffnet die Konvention die Möglichkeit richterlicher Vertragsergänzung für den Einzelfall und verdrängt insoweit die betreffenden nationalen Mechanismen.[142] Das ergibt sich aus ihrem Gesamtbild: Die Konvention kennt ausweislich Art. 35 II die Konzeption der *implication of terms* sehr wohl,[143] und das Schweizer Bundesgericht hat unlängst im Blick auf beide Artt. 8, 35 – funktional treffend – von objektiver Auslegung gesprochen.[144] Ebenfalls auf die Technik der *implication* greift zudem Art. 9 II zurück.[145] Art. 35 konkretisiert dabei die beiden anderen Vorschriften. Die Konvention kennt also die Vertragsergänzung unabhängig vom Parteiwillen;[146] fraglich sind nur deren Grenzen. Unproblematisch ist dabei zunächst die Ergänzung durch dispositives Recht (vgl. Art. 6)[147] sowie durch Gepflogenheiten und Gebräuche (Art. 9).[148] Möglich ist auch eine explizite Ermächtigung des (Schieds-)Gerichts zur Vertragsergänzung *ex aequo et bono* durch Parteivereinbarung.[149] Wie Art. 7 II zeigt, ergänzen – bei internen Lücken – außerdem die aus den allgemeinen Grundsätzen der Konvention rechtsfortbildend entwickelten Regeln den jeweiligen Vertrag. Im Blick auf Artt. 6, 8 I ist daher erst recht davon auszugehen, dass den Gerichten grundsätzlich eine am individuellen Vertrag orientierte Ergänzung möglich ist. Dies ergibt sich, sofern *in concreto* die

---

[137] RB Hasselt, 18.10.1995, CISG-online 364; der Sache nach auch *Magnus*, ZEuP 2002, 523, 530. Vgl. auch *Neumayer/Ming*, Art. 6, Anm. 3.
[138] Vgl. Artt. 4.8, 5.2 PICC, Art. 6:102 PECL sowie Comment A zu Art. 5:101 PECL. Zur Konzeption im englischen Recht s. *Schmidt-Kessel*, ZVerglRW 96 (1997), 101, 101–133.
[139] Schiedsgericht der Börse für landwirtschaftliche Produkte in Wien, 10.12.1997, CISG-online 351; *Junge*, 3. Aufl., Rn. 3; *Najork*, S. 61 f.
[140] Schiedsgericht der Börse für landwirtschaftliche Produkte in Wien, 10.12.1997, CISG-online 351.
[141] So insbesondere *Junge*, 3. Aufl., Rn. 3.
[142] Siehe bereits oben Rn. 11 (mit Nachweisen) sowie Fn. 147.
[143] Audiencia Provincial de Madrid, 20.2.2007, CISG-online 1637; wie hier jetzt auch *Schwenzer/Hachem/Kee*, Rn. 26.4, 26.71.
[144] BGer, 22.12.2000, CISG-online 628.
[145] *Najork*, S. 46 f. S. Art. 9 Rn. 2, 12.
[146] OLG Köln, 2.7.2007, CISG-online 1811, Rn. 28; *Brunner*, Art. 8, Rn. 21; *Kröll u. a./Zuppi*, Art. 8, Rn. 29; *Witz/Salger/Lorenz/Witz*, Art. 8, Rn. 5.
[147] *Najork*, S. 44. Vgl. Comment 2 zu Art. 4.8 PICC.
[148] Vgl. Artt. 1.8, 5.2 lit. b) PICC; in diesem Sinne auch Comment zu Art. 5:102 PECL.
[149] *Najork*, S. 44.

Grenzen des Art. 8 II überschritten sind, aus einem allgemeinen Grundsatz der Konvention, welcher vor allem in Artt. 6, 7, 8, 9, 35 II seinen Niederschlag und zugleich in Artt. 4.8, 5.2 PICC eine hilfreiche Aufzeichnung gefunden hat.[150] Die Steuerung individueller Vertragsergänzung durch die Konvention ist schließlich auch im Hinblick auf die Einheitlichkeit ihrer Auslegung (Art. 7 I) geboten: Da sich die Grenzen der sog. objektiven Auslegung zur richterlichen Vertragsergänzung nicht hinreichend präzise bestimmen lassen, drohten ansonsten divergierende Auslegungen von Art. 8.[151]

Die Vertragsergänzung ist insbesondere dann geboten, wenn andernfalls der Parteiwille 27 leerzulaufen droht.[152] Im Blick auf Art. 8 II hat sich diese insbesondere am hypothetischen Parteiwillen zu orientieren:[153] Hypothetisch ist die Inhaltsbestimmung bereits bei der schlichten Anwendung von Art. 8 II auf einzelne Erklärungen; geht es um die Bestimmung des Vertragsinhalts, steht dem hypothetischen Verständnis dessen hypothetische Billigung gegenüber. Das Kriterium der *reasonableness*[154] spielt daneben keine eigenständige Rolle.[155] Eine unüberwindliche Grenze der Vertragsergänzung bildet in jedem Falle der festgestellte Wille der Parteien.[156] Ob unter der Konvention eine allgemeine Pflicht besteht, die Interessen des Vertragspartners bei der Vertragsabwicklung zu wahren, ist bislang offen.[157]

VI. Einzelfragen der Auslegung

1. Ausrichtung am Vertragsgegenstand

Die Auslegung eines Vertrags und der auf ihn bezogenen Erklärungen muss sich an dessen 28 Gegenstand orientieren.[158] Unter der Konvention geht es selbstverständlich primär um die klassischen kaufvertraglichen Pflichten der Lieferung ordnungsgemäßer Ware, der Übereignung und der Zahlung. Soweit sich aus einem Vertrag auch sonstige Pflichten ergeben, muss sich die auf sie bezogene Auslegung daneben auch an diesen orientieren. Soweit der Vertrag in gewissem Umfang auch zu Dienstleistungen verpflichtet (vgl. Art. 3) kommt etwa eine Qualifikation dieser Pflichten als bloße Verhaltenspflichten *(obligations de moyens)*[159] und damit eine Haftungsentlastung auch unterhalb der hohen Anforderungen von Art. 79 in Betracht.[160]

2. Auslegung des Vertrags als Ganzem

Die Konvention verlangt, dass bei der Auslegung der Vertrag als Ganzer in den Blick 29 genommen wird.[161] Einzelne Bestimmungen sind als integraler Bestandteil des Vertrags

---

[150] Zum gegenteiligen Ergebnis kommt *Najork*, S. 61 f.; Grund dafür ist, dass er nicht einen allgemeinen Grundsatz richterlicher Vertragsergänzung, sondern lediglich zwei – tatsächlich nicht einschlägige – Maßstäbe derselben (Treu und Glauben sowie *reasonableness*) untersucht.
[151] Siehe die insoweit überaus problematische Entscheidung des Schiedsgerichts der Börse für landwirtschaftliche Produkte in Wien, 10.12.1997, CISG-online 351.
[152] Wie hier jetzt auch *Kröll u. a./Zuppi*, Art. 8, Rn. 29 (efficiancy of the contract). Vgl. *Baldus*, Regelhafte Vertragsauslegung, S. 135.
[153] Comment C zu Art. 6:102 PECL. Dagegen *Junge*, 3. Aufl., Rn. 3 sowie *Ferrari*, IHR 2003, 10, 11 f. (jeweils ohne Begründung). Vgl. Art. 4.8 II lit. d) PICC; 6:102 lit. a) PECL.
[154] Vgl. Artt. 4.8 II lit. d), 5.2 lit. d) PICC sowie die kritischen Hinweise von *Najork*, S. 56–60.
[155] Zu *good faith and fair dealing* und Art. 7 I vgl. Rn. 30 (Treu und Glauben keine allgemeine Auslegungsleitlinie) sowie *Najork*, S. 52–56, dem insoweit beizutreten ist. Siehe außerdem Artt. 4.8 II lit. c), 5.2 lit. c) PICC; Artt. 5:102 lit. g), 6:102 lit. c) PECL.
[156] *Staudinger/Magnus*, Art. 9, Rn. 17 (für Handelsbräuche). Vgl. Art. 4.8 II lit. a) PICC; 6:102 lit. a) PECL.
[157] OLG Köln, 2.7.2007, CISG-online 1811, Rn. 28 ff. (*in concreto* jedenfalls keine Pflichtverletzung).
[158] Vgl. Artt. 4.3 lit. d), 4.8 II lit. b), 5.2 lit. a) PICC; Artt. 5:102 lit. c), 6:102 lit. b) PECL.
[159] Comment A zu Art. 5:101 PECL; Comment D zu Art. 6:102 PECL; vgl. Art. 5.4, 5.5 PICC.
[160] Entsprechendes gilt etwa für die besonderen Pflichten nach Artt. 85–88; siehe zu beiden Punkten *Schmidt-Kessel*, Standards, S. 294.
[161] Internationales SchiedsG der Industrie- und Handelskammer der Russischen Föderation, 27.5.2005, CISG-online 1456, Nr. 3.3.3; *Brunner*, Art. 8, Rn. 13; *Nabati*, Rev. dr. unif. 2007, 247, 254; *Schwenzer/Hachem/Kee*, Rn. 26.25; vgl. Art. 4.4 PICC, Art. 5:105 PECL; *Tjittes*, R. M. Themis 2005, 2, 16.

aufzufassen; sie sind aus dem Gesamtzusammenhang des Vertrags heraus und nicht isoliert zu betrachten.[162] Dazu gehört auch die Berücksichtigung der Interessenlage der Parteien.[163] Es gilt grundsätzlich keine Hierarchie vertraglicher Klauseln, etwa nach ihrer Reihenfolge;[164] Abweichungen davon begründen die explizit vereinbarte Hierarchie,[165] der Vorrang der Individualabrede vor allgemeinen Geschäftsbedingungen,[166] die restriktive Auslegung von Ausnahmetatbeständen[167] sowie unter Umständen der Vorrang einer spezielleren Regelung.[168] Besonderes Gewicht kommt zudem der Präambel sowie etwaigen Definitionsnormen zu; letzteres korrespondiert teilweise mit der Vermutung für eine einheitliche Terminologie im Vertrag.[169] Das Gebot der Auslegung des Vertrags als Ganzem kann darüber hinaus auch auf Gruppen von Verträgen anzuwenden sein,[170] etwa auf einen Rahmenvertrag und die zugehörigen Ausführungsgeschäfte[171] oder auf eine Abfolge mehrerer Verträge.

3. Treu und Glauben als Auslegungsleitlinie

30 Auf Schwierigkeiten stößt die Annahme, Treu und Glauben böten eine allgemeine Auslegungsleitlinie für Verträge. Obwohl Art. 8 im Gegensatz zu Art. 7 I keinen Bezug auf dieses Prinzip nimmt, wird eine solche Leitlinie vielfach ausdrücklich vertreten.[172] Dem ist freilich nicht zuzustimmen. Die Konvention hat dem Prinzip von Treu und Glauben über Art. 7 I hinaus bewusst keinen Raum gegeben, sondern sich mit der Übernahme partieller Funktionsäquivalente – im Blick auf die Auslegung vor allem der sog. objektiven Vertragsauslegung und die Vertragsergänzung – begnügt.[173] Insbesondere gestattet die Konvention keine Begründung einer Inhaltskontrolle auf der Basis von Treu und Glauben und Art. 8.[174] Auch die Reduktion einer Vertragsstrafe aus Billigkeitsgründen kann nicht auf Art. 8 gestützt werden.[175]

4. Berücksichtigung der Verhandlungen und der Umstände des Vertragsschlusses

31 **a) Allgemeines.** Zu den in Art. 8 III genannten Umständen, welche bei der Ermittlung des Parteiwillens (Abs. 1) wie auch bei der Bestimmung des hypothetischen Verständnisses des Empfängers (Abs. 2) zu beachten sind, zählen auch die Verhandlungen und die Umstände des Vertragsschlusses.[176] Auf diese Weise kann sich etwa die Bedeutung unklarer Währungsangaben (z. B. Dollar bei Kontakten mit Kanada oder Australien) klären lassen.[177]

---

[162] Comment 1 zu Art. 4.2 PICC; Comment zu Art. 5:105 PECL. Der Sache nach auch BGH, 3.4.1996, CISG-online 135 sowie CIETAC, 7.12.2005, CISG Online 1445. Vgl. HGer Zürich, 30.11.1998, CISG-online 415.
[163] OLG Dresden, 27.12.1999, CISG-online 511.
[164] Comment 2 zu Art. 4.4 PICC; Comment zu Art. 5:105 PECL.
[165] Comment 2 zu Art. 4.4 PICC.
[166] S. oben Rn. 58.
[167] Vgl. *Baldus*, Regelhafte Vertragsauslegung, S. 120 f.
[168] Vgl. Comment 2 zu Art. 4.4 PICC; *Baldus*, Regelhafte Vertragsauslegung, S. 127.
[169] Entsprechend Comment zu Art. 4.4 PICC; Comment zu Art. 5:105 PECL.
[170] Comment zu Art. 5:105 PECL.
[171] OLG Hamburg, 5.10.1998, CISG-online 473 (Rechtswahl); *Junge*, 3. Aufl., Rn. 2; Comment zu Art. 5:105 PECL. Vgl. Rn. 44.
[172] Civ. 1, 30.6.2004, CISG-online 870 (kritisch dazu *Remy-Corlay*, RTDciv 2005, 354, 355); OGer Zug, 5.7.2005, CISG-online 1155; OGer Kanton Thurgau, 19.12.1995, CISG-online 496; *Junge*, 3. Aufl., Rn. 9; *Brunner*, Art. 8, Rn. 14; *Staudinger/Magnus*, Art. 8, Rn. 10. Zurückhaltender *Schlechtriem*, Internationales UN-Kaufrecht, Rn. 54: „durch das Prinzip von Treu und Glauben ausgeleuchtet".
[173] Dazu die Arbeit von *Najork* (auch zur Verortung weiterer Funktionen).
[174] Vgl. Art. 9 Rn. 5, 20.
[175] So Hof Arnhem, 22.8.1995, CISG-online 317, welcher diese Frage mit Recht nach nationalem Recht löst.
[176] Vgl. Art. 4.3 lit. a) PICC; Art. 5:102 lit. a) PECL.
[177] Illustration 2 zu Art. 4.3 PICC.

Auch bei der Untersuchung des Vertrags auf die Vereinbarung eines Eigentumsvorbehalts, dessen Vereinbarung in den Verhandlungen immer wieder eine Rolle spielte,[178] kann der Rückgriff auf dieses Material helfen.

b) *Parol Evidence Rule*[179] und Vermutung der Richtigkeit und Vollständigkeit. Von 32 Bedeutung ist der Verweis auf die Verhandlungen und sonstigen bei Vertragsschluss erheblichen Umstände insbesondere im Blick auf die *parol evidence rule*, wie sie viele angloamerikanische Rechtsordnungen kennen.[180] Dabei geht es um zwei Sachfragen, nämlich zum einen um die Beweisbarkeit – und somit funktional: Beachtlichkeit – mündlicher Nebenabreden und zum anderen um die Heranziehung weiterer Auslegungsmaterials zur Klärung des Inhalts eines schriftlich niedergelegten Vertrags. Beide Punkte sind freilich nicht vollständig voneinander zu trennen; die Konvention behandelt sie – wenn auch nicht ausdrücklich[181] – in den Artt. 8, 11.[182] Danach gilt unter dem UN-Kaufrecht keine *parol evidence rule*:[183] Zum einen ist Art. 8 III mit einem generellen Ausschluss des dort angesprochenen Auslegungsmaterials unvereinbar;[184] der generellen Unbeachtlichkeit mündlicher Nebenabreden steht außerdem[185] Art. 11 entgegen.[186] Den Parteien steht ferner grundsätzlich der Zeugenbeweis darüber offen, dass sie an bestimmte Klauseln des schriftlichen Vertrags nicht gebunden sein wollten.[187] Die gelegentlich vertretene Gegenauffassung[188]

---

[178] *Roder Zelt- und Hallenkonstruktionen GmbH v. Rosedown Park Pty Ltd. and Reginald R Eustace*, FCA (Adelaide, S. A.), 28.4.1995, CISG-online 218.

[179] Zentral hierzu CISG-AC, Op. 3 (*Hyland*). Zur Ausweitung des Auslegungsmaterials im englischen Recht unter Einfluss des CISG s. *Rugby Group Ltd. v. ProForce Recruit Ltd.* [2006], EWCA Civ 69 (C. A.), 17.2.2006, CISG-online 1424 und *The Square Mile Partnership Ltd. v. Fitzmaurice McCall Ltd.* (C. A.), 18.12.2006, CISG-online 1423, Rz. 61 f. (per L. J. *Arden*).

[180] S. insbesondere § 2–202 UCC; s. die rechtsvergleichenden Darstellungen bei *Baumann*, Auslegung, S. 88–98, *Kaufmann*, Parol Evidence Rule, S. 23–145 sowie *Schwenzer/Hachem/Kee*, Rn. 26.28, 26.45 ff.

[181] *MCC-Marble Ceramic Center, Inc. v. Ceramica Nuova D'Agostino S. P. A.*, U. S. Ct. App. (11th Cir.), 29.6.1998, CISG-online 342 = 144 F. 3d 1384, 1389; *Honnold/Fletchner*, Art. 8, Rn. 110.

[182] S. dementsprechend *Schroeter*, Art. 11 Rn. 11 ff.

[183] *Filanto, S. p. A. v. Chilewich Intern. Corp.*, U. S. Dist. Ct. (S. D. N. Y.), 14.4.1992, CISG-online 45 = 789 F. 1229, 1238 Fn. 7; *Calzaturificio Claudia v. Olivieri Footwear Ltd.*, U. S. Dist. Ct. (S. D. N. Y.), 6.4.1998, CISG-online 440 = 1998 WL 164824; *MCC Marble Ceramic Center, Inc. v. Ceramica Nuova D'Agostino S. P. A.*, U. S. Ct. App. (11th Cir.), 29.6.1998, CISG-online 342 = 144 F. 3d 1384, 1389 f.; *Mitchell Aircraft Sparse Inc. v. European Aircraft Service AB*, U. S. Dist. Ct. (N. D. Ill.), 28.10.1998, CISG-online 444 = 23 F. 2d 915, 920; *TeeVee Tunes, Inc. v. Gerhard Schubert GmbH*, U. S. Dist. Ct. (S. D. N. Y.), 12.8.2006, CISG-online 1272; *Miami Valley Paper, LLC v. Lebbing Engineering & Consulting GmbH*, U .S. Dist. Ct. (S. D. Ohio), 26.3.2009, CISG-online 1880; *ECEM European Chemical Marketing B. V. v. The Purolite Company*, U .S. Dist. Ct. (E. D. Pen.), 29.1.2010, CISG-online 2090; *Andreason*, 1999 B. Y. U. L. Rev., 351, 364 ff.; *Del Duca*, 25 J. L. & Com. (2005–06), 133, 136, 142 ff.; *Honold/Fletchner*, Art. 8, Rn. 110; *Soergel/Lüderitz/Fenge*, Art. 8, Rn. 8; *Staudinger/Magnus*, Art. 8, Rn. 23; *Witz/Salger/Lorenz/Witz*, Art. 8, Rn. 1. Gegen eine Rezeption dieser Regel durch das autonome neuseeländische Recht wegen Bindung an den Privy Council *Hideo Yoshimoto v. Canterbury Golf International Ltd.*, 27.11.2000, CISG-online 1078, Nr. 88 ff.

[184] *Filanto, S. p. A. v. Chilewich Internat. Corp.*, U. S. Dist. Ct. (S. D. N. Y.), 14.4.1992, CISG-online 45 = 789 F. 1229, 1238 Fn. 7; *MCC Marble Ceramic Center, Inc. v. Ceramica Nuova D'Agostino S. P. A.*, U. S. Ct. App. (11th Cir.), 29.6.1998, CISG-online 342 = 144 F. 3d 1384, 1389 f.; *Mitchell Aircraft Spares Inc. v. European Aircraft Service AB*, U. S. Dist. Ct. (N. D. Ill.), 28.10.1998, CISG-online 444 = 23 F. 2d 915, 920 f.; *Schwenzer/Hachem/Kee*, Rn. 26.50; *Staudinger/Magnus*, Art. 8, Rn. 23; missverständlich daher *Kaufmann*, Parol Evidence Rule, S. 272: „Das CISG befasst sich an keiner Stelle ausdrücklich mit der Zulässigkeit von vertragsexternen Beweismitteln zur Ermittlung des Vertragsinhalts".

[185] Zum Verhältnis s. oben Rn. 13.

[186] *Calzaturificio Claudia v. Olivieri Footwear Ltd.*, U. S. Dist. Ct. (S. D. N. Y.), 6.4.1998, CISG-online 440 = 1998 WL 164824; *MCC Marble Ceramic Center, Inc. v. Ceramica Nuova D'Agostino S. P. A.*, U. S. Ct. App. (11th Cir.), 29.6.1998, CISG-online 342 = 144 F. 3d 1384, 1389.

[187] *ECEM European Chemical Marketing B. V. v. The Purolite Company*, U .S. Dist. Ct. (E. D. Pen.), 29.1.2010, CISG-online 2090.

[188] *Beijing Metals & Minerals Import/Export Corp. v. American Business Center, Inc.*, U. S. Ct. App. (5th Cir.), 15.6.1993, CISG-online 89 = 993 F. 2d 1178, 1183; *Moore*, 1995 B. Y. U. L. Rev., 1347, 1351. Die in diesem Punkt nicht begründete Entscheidung *Beijing Metals* gilt als überholt: *MCC Marble Ceramic Center, Inc. v. Ceramica Nuova D'Agostino S. P. A.*, U. S. Ct. App. (11th Cir.), 29.6.1998, CISG-online 342 = 144 F. 3d 1384, 1390: „not particularly persuasive on this point" (zustimmend *Mitchell Aircraft Spares Inc. v. European Aircraft Service AB*, U. S. Dist. Ct. (N. D. Ill.), 28.10.1998, CISG-online 444 = 23 F. 2d 915, 920); *ECEM European*

würde die Einheitlichkeit der Auslegung der Konvention gefährden.[189] Sie läßt sich auch nicht mit dem Hinweis auf den Empfängerhorizont des andern Teils rechtfertigen; diesen prägen nämlich auch die weiteren in Abs. III genannten Umstände.

33 Bei der *parol evidence rule* handelt es sich funktional um eine materiellrechtliche Regel, die ein nationales Gericht auch nicht als Teil seines – grundsätzlich unbeschränkt anzuwendenden – Prozessrechts anwenden kann;[190] gleichwohl prägt sie noch das Prozessverhalten US-amerikanischer Parteien[191] und gegebenenfalls auch die Aufgabenverteilung zwischen Richter und Jury.[192] Ein berechtigtes Vertrauen in die Anwendbarkeit heimischer Rechtsregeln gibt es insoweit zwar nicht,[193] die Konvention beansprucht jedoch keine Einflussnahme auf die prozessuale Aufgabenverteilung.[194]

34 In gleicher Weise stellen Artt. 8, 11 entsprechende Instrumente anderer Rechtsordnungen wie etwa die deutsche **Vermutung der Richtigkeit und Vollständigkeit**[195] oder die widerlegliche Vermutung der *parol evidence rule* nach englischem Verständnis[196] in Frage. Als Rechtsregel ließe sich diese im Anwendungsbereich der Konvention nur aufrecht erhalten, soweit sie sich in Art. 8 wiederfindet. Für die Vereinbarkeit mit der Konvention spricht immerhin die Widerleglichkeit der Vermutung, die also die weiteren nach Art. 8 III zu berücksichtigenden Umstände nicht unbefragt lässt.[197] Gleichwohl lässt sich eine solche Privilegierung schriftlicher Erklärungen den Artt. 8, 11 gerade nicht entnehmen; dem Regelungszweck dieser Normen widerspricht jede formale Verstärkung des tatsächlich ohnehin bereits gegebenen Beweisgefälles.[198] Denkbar und im Zweifelsfalle realiter zu überprüfen wäre freilich die Annahme eines entsprechenden Handelsbrauchs, welcher die Grundregeln der Artt. 8, 11 zu überspielen geeignet wäre[199]. Angesichts der Verbreitung des tatsächlichen Beweisgefälles ist auch nicht ausgeschlossen, dass insoweit die Schwelle des Art. 9 II überwunden wird.

35 **c) Behandlung von *merger clauses*[200].** Die Anordnung umfassender Berücksichtigung des gesamten verfügbaren Auslegungsmaterials durch Art. 8 III ist dispositiv.[201] Die Konvention nimmt daher die Vereinbarung von *merger clauses*[202] (auch *„four corner clause"*,[203]

Chemical Marketing B. V. v. The Purolite Company, U.S. Dist. Ct. (E. D. Pen.), 29.1.2010, CISG-online 2090 Fn. 5: „not ... particularly persuasive on this point".

[189] *MCC Marble Ceramic Center, Inc. v. Ceramica Nuova D'Agostino S. P. A.*, U.S. Ct. App. (11th Cir.), 29.6.1998, CISG-online 342 = 144 F. 3d 1384, 1391 (zustimmend zitiert von *Zapata Hermanos Sucesores, S. A. v. Heartside Baking Co., Inc.*, U.S. Dist. Ct. (N. D. Ill.), 28.8.2001, CISG-online 599 = 2001 WL 1000 927).

[190] *MCC Marble Ceramic Center, Inc. v. Ceramica Nuova D'Agostino S. P. A.*, U.S. Ct. App. (11th Cir.), 29.6.1998, CISG-online 342 = 144 F. 3d 1384, 1389 unter Hinweis auf Art. 11.

[191] *Calzaturificio Claudia v. Olivieri Footwear Ltd.*, U.S. Dist. Ct. (S.D. N. Y.), 6.4.1998, CISG-online 440 = 1998 WL 164, 824.

[192] CISG-AC, Op. 3 (*Hyland*) Comment 1.2.2; *Flechtner*, 18 J. L. & Com. (1999), 259, 275.

[193] *MCC Marble Ceramic Center, Inc. v. Ceramica Nuova D'Agostino S. P. A.*, U.S. Ct. App. (11th Cir.), 29.6.1998, CISG-online 342 = 144 F. 3d 1384, 1391.

[194] *Flechtner*, 18 J. L. & Com. (1999), 259, 275.

[195] Angewandt etwa von OLG Hamm, 22.9.1992, CISG-online 57. S. Nachweise entsprechender Regeln in Japan und Skandinavien bei CISG-AC, Op. 3 (*Hyland*) Comment 1.2.8.

[196] S. CISG-AC, Op. 3 (*Hyland*) Comment 1.2.4.

[197] In diesem Sinne für das deutsche Recht ausdrücklich BGH, 18.7.2002, NJW 2002, 3254.

[198] *Kaufmann*, Parol Evidence Rule, S. 294; In diesem Sinne auch *Flechtner*, 18 J. L. & Com. (1999), 259, 278 f. Für ein „Beweisgefälle" zugunsten schriftlicher Erklärungen im Sinne einer widerleglichen (Art. 8 III) Vermutung der Vollständigkeit und Richtigkeit hingegen *Schlechtriem*, 4. Aufl., Art. 11 Rn. 13. Vgl. CISG-AC, Op. 3 (*Hyland*) Comment 2.7.

[199] Zur Dispositivität der Vorschriften in diesem Punkt sogleich Rn. 35.

[200] Hierzu CISG-AC, Op. 3 (*Hyland*).

[201] *Flechtner*, 18 J. L. & Com. (1999), 259, 275; *Honsell/Melis*, Art. 8, Rn. 4; *Kaufmann*, Parol Evidence Rule, S. 298 f.; *Schlechtriem*, FS Kritzer, 416, 420; *Schwenzer/Hachem/Kee*, Rn. 26.53; *Soergel/Lüderitz/Fenge*, Art. 8, Rn. 9; *Witz/Salger/Lorenz/Witz*, Art. 8, Rn. 1.

[202] S. *TeeVee Tunes, Inc. v. Gerhard Schubert GmbH*, U.S. Dist. Ct. (S. D. N. Y.), 12.8.2006, CISG-online 1272 mit einem Beispiel aus einem CISG-Vertrag.

[203] People's Supreme Court, Appeal Division in Ho Chi Minh City, 5.4.1996, UNILEX.

entire agreement clause[204] oder *integration clause*[205]) ohne weiteres hin.[206] Klauseln dieser Art sind darauf gerichtet, den Vertrag auf die Vertragsurkunde zu reduzieren; dahinter steht das Bild, die vorherigen Verhandlungen verschmölzen *(merge)* in dem schriftlich niedergelegten Text. Von amerikanischen Stimmen werden solche Klauseln als Ausgleich für das Fehlen der *parol evidence rule* empfohlen.[207] Die unter schlichten Hinweis auf ein schriftliches Vertragsdokument erfolgende Annahme einer *implied merger clause* genügt den Anforderungen des Art. 8 III allerdings nicht.[208] Die Gültigkeit solcher Klauseln richtet sich nach Art. 4 S. 2 lit. a)[209] und ist damit nicht immer gewährleistet.[210] Teilweise wird die wirksame Einbeziehung einer solchen Klausel sehr eingehend geprüft.[211] Im Einzelfall ist durch Auslegung ferner zu ermitteln, ob solche Klauseln lediglich mündliche Nebenabreden beseitigen oder ob sie auch den Rückgriff auf weiteres Auslegungsmaterial neben der Vertragsurkunde verschließen;[212] letzteres wird ganz überwiegend als Regelfall angesehen.[213] Etwa hat der People's Supreme Court, Appeal Division in Ho Chi Minh Stadt die Heranziehung einer Klausel zur Auslegung des Vertrags verweigert, welche in einem nachträglich eröffneten Akkreditiv enthalten war; darin liege lediglich das Angebot zum Abschluss eines Änderungsvertrags.[214]

5. Schweigen und Rückfrageobliegenheit

Das Schweigen einer Partei wird unter der Konvention allgemein als bei der Auslegung **36** zu berücksichtigender Umstand anerkannt.[215] Obwohl es nach der ausdrücklichen Anordnung des Art. 18 I 2 allein als Annahmeerklärung nicht ausreicht, wird es – im Zusammenspiel mit weiteren Umständen – von den Gerichten vielfach als Zustimmung eingeordnet, welcher als Komplement eine *duty to alert*, eine Rückfrageobliegenheit der betreffenden Partei gegenübersteht.[216] Das gilt insbesondere bei Eingreifen entsprechender Gepflogenheiten und Gebräuche,[217] etwa den Regeln über das kaufmännische Bestätigungsschreiben,[218] und es gilt im Sinne einer *last shot rule* vielfach bei Vertragsdurchführung ohne

---

[204] *Rugby Group Ltd. v. ProForce Recruit Ltd.* [2006], EWCA Civ 69 (C. A.), 17.2.2006, CISG-online 1424.
[205] *Witz/Salger/Lorenz/Witz*, Art. 8, Rn. 17.
[206] Unrichtig *Kröll u. a./Zuppi*, Art. 8, Rn. 26: Abs. 3 überwinde jede *merger clause*.
[207] *Kim*, 12 N. Y. Int'l L. R. (1999), 105; *Murray*, 8 J. L. & Com. (1988), 11 (bei Fn. 155). Skeptisch hingegen *Andreason*, 1999 B. Y. U. L. Rev., 351, 370–372; vgl. für einige empfohlene Klauseln *Kaufmann*, Parol Evidence Rule, S. 299–302.
[208] *Flechtner*, 18 J. L. & Com. (1999), 259, 278; *Schwenzer/Hachem/Kee*, Rn. 26.53.
[209] *Bianca/Bonell/Farnsworth*, Art. 8, Anm. 3.3.; *Kaufmann*, Parol Evidence Rule, S. 313 f.; *Staudinger/Magnus*, Art. 8, Rn. 9; *Witz/Salger/Lorenz/Witz*, Art. 8, Rn. 17.
[210] Vgl. *Bianca/Bonell/Farnsworth*, Art. 8, Anm. 3.3.; *Witz/Salger/Lorenz/Witz*, Art. 8, Rn. 17; zurückhaltend hinsichtlich des Spielraumes zur Vereinbarung von *merger clauses* im deutschen Recht *Kaufmann*, Parol Evidence Rule, S. 314–316.
[211] *TeeVee Tunes, Inc. v. Gerhard Schubert GmbH*, U. S. Dist. Ct. (S. D. N. Y.), 12.8.2006, CISG-online 1272 (unter Bezugnahme auf CISG-AC, Op. 3 (*Hyland*)).
[212] Wie hier jetzt auch *Schwenzer/Hachem/Kee*, Rn. 26.53. Vgl. *Witz/Salger/Lorenz/Witz*, Art. 8, Rn. 17.
[213] People's Supreme Court, Appeal Division in Ho Chi Minh City, 5.4.1996, UNILEX; *MCC-Marble Ceramic Center, Inc. v. Ceramica Nuova D'Agostino S. P. A.*, U. S. Ct. App. (11th Cir.), 29.6.1998, CISG-online 342 = 144 F. 3d 1384, 1391; *Honnold/Fletchner*, Art. 8, Rn. 110; *Schwenzer/Hachem/Kee*, Rn. 26.53; *Staudinger/Magnus*, Art. 8, Rn. 9; wohl auch CISG-AC, Op. 3 (*Hyland*) Comment 4.5; anders für das englische Recht *Rugby Group Ltd. v. ProForce Recruit Ltd.* [2006], EWCA Civ 69 (C. A.), 17.2.2006, CISG-online 1424, Nr. 57 unter Berufung auf PICC und CISG.
[214] People's Supreme Court, Appeal Division in Ho Chi Minh City, 5.4.1996, UNILEX.
[215] Civ. 1, 27.1.1998, CISG-online 309; OLG Jena, 10.11.2010, CISG-online 2216, Rn. 31; *Junge*, 3. Aufl., Rn. 10; *Bamberger/Roth/Saenger*, Art. 8, Rn. 4; *Staudinger/Magnus*, Art. 8, Rn. 27.
[216] *Filanto, S. p. A. v. Chilewich Intern. Corp.*, U. S. Dist. Ct. (S. D. N. Y.), 14.4.1992, CISG-online 45 = 789 F. 1229, 1240; der Sache nach auch etwa LG Mönchengladbach, 22.5.1992, CISG-online 56; LG Augsburg, 12.7.1994, CISG-online 390; CA Grenoble, 26.4.1995, CISG-online 153. Allgemein zu Rückfrageobliegenheiten Rn. 38.
[217] OLG Innsbruck, 1.2.2005, CISG-online 1130; s. Rn. 44–46 und vgl. Art. 9 Rn. 12.
[218] S. unten Art. 9 Rn. 22–24.

Widerspruch gegen die letzte Äußerung des anderen Teils.[219] Entsprechende Entscheidungen sind durchaus zahlreich: So wird bisweilen das Zustandekommen einer Gerichtsstandsvereinbarung durch Schweigen auf eine zum Vertragsschluss führende „pro forma"-Rechnung angenommen.[220] Verlangt in einer dauerhaften Lieferbeziehung der Lieferant ab einem bestimmten Zeitpunkt einen höheren Preis und nimmt der Käufer weitere Lieferungen widerspruchslos an, kann darin nach Art. 8 II eine Zustimmung zur Preiserhöhung gesehen werden.[221] Ebenso lässt sich der vorbehaltlosen Zustimmung zu einem – auf Wunsch des Käufers – geänderten Konstruktionsplan das Einverständnis mit den damit verbundenen technischen Spezifikationen entnehmen.[222] Gleiches gilt für die widerspruchslos gebliebene Mitteilung der Käufererwartungen an die Leistungsfähigkeit einer verkauften Maschine.[223] Schließlich kann die widerspruchslose Einlösung eines Schecks, der gutgläubig über einen geringeren Betrag als den geschuldeten ausgestellt und als Restzahlung gekennzeichnet wird, zum Erlass des überschießenden Betrags nach Art. 29 führen.[224] Im Regelfalle wird jedoch das schlichte Schweigen auf ein Angebot zur Vertragsänderung nicht ausreichen.[225]

37 Grundsätzlich möglich ist unter der Konvention ein stillschweigender Verzicht auf eigene Rechtspositionen.[226] Das mehrmonatige Verhandeln über eine Schadensregulierung spricht nach Auffassung des Bundesgerichtshofs etwa für Verzicht auf den Verspätungseinwand nach Art. 39.[227] Der Verzicht ist bei solchen Rechten ausgeschlossen, welche dem Erklärenden unbekannt sind und mit deren Bestehen er nicht rechnet.[228] Daran fehlt es allerdings, wenn sich die Rechte aus Grundregeln des Handelsverkehrs ergeben.[229] Auch anwaltliche Beratung spricht gegen die Unkenntnis des Berechtigten.[230]

38 Immer wieder wird die Passivität eines Teils auch unter dem Gesichtspunkt einer Rückfrageobliegenheit diskutiert[231]: Bejaht wurde sie etwa bei Verständnisschwierigkeiten auf Grund mangelnder Sprachkenntnisse.[232] Hingegen hält der Bundesgerichtshof die Rückfrage des Erklärungsempfängers bei Verweis auf nicht übersandte Geschäftsbedingungen für unzumutbar.[233] Schließlich ist instanzgerichtlich etwa die Hinnahme einer verspäteten Zahlung unter Skontoabzug ohne entsprechende Rückfrage als Einverständnis gewertet worden.[234]

6. Vorhersehbarkeit und Erkennbarkeit als Umstände

39 Individuelle Umstände berücksichtigt die Auslegung auch dort, wo sie die Vorhersehbarkeit und Erkennbarkeit bestimmter Risikolagen heranzieht. Dahinter steht die Überlegung, dass derjenige, der bei Vertragsschluss bestimmte Umstände vorgesehen oder erkannt hat, diese in seine Überlegungen auch einbezogen hat. Letztlich geht es wieder um die Bewertung von Passivität: Wer einen Umstand vorhersieht oder erkennt und sich davon nicht

---

[219] In diesem Sinne etwa *Filanto, S. p. A. v. Chilewich Intern. Corp.*, U. S. Dist. Ct. (S. D. N. Y.), 14.4.1992, CISG-online 45 = 789 F. 1229, 1240; BGer, 5.4.2005, CISG-online 1012, E. 4.2, 4.3; *Staudinger/Magnus*, Art. 8, Rn. 27. Zur Problematik kollidierender AGB s. *Schroeter*, Art. 19 Rn. 19–36.
[220] Cámara Nacional de Apelaciones en lo Comercial, 14.10.1993, CISG-online 87.
[221] CA Grenoble, 26.4.1995, CISG-online 153.
[222] Civ. 1, 27.1.1998, CISG-online 309.
[223] AppGer Basel-Stadt, 26.9.2008, CISG-online 1732, Nr. 4.3.
[224] LG Kassel, 15.2.1996, CISG-online 190.
[225] OLG Jena, 10.11.2010, CISG-online 2216, Rn. 31 (nachträgliche Einbeziehung von AGB).
[226] Vgl. BGH, 25.11.1998, CISG-online 353 (auf Rechte aus Art. 39).
[227] BGH, 25.11.1998, CISG-online 353.
[228] BGH, 25.11.1998, CISG-online 353.
[229] BGH, 25.11.1998, CISG-online 353.
[230] BGH, 25.11.1998, CISG-online 353.
[231] Vgl. *Heuzé*, Anm. 235.; *Soergel/Lüderitz/Fenge*, Art. 8, Rn. 5. Außer den im Folgenden angesprochenen Entscheidungen etwa auch *Filanto, S. p. A. v. Chilewich Intern. Corp.*, U. S. Dist. Ct. (S. D. N. Y.), 14.4.1992, CISG-online 45 = 789 F. 1229, 1240.
[232] OLG Hamm, 8.2.1995, CISG-online 141; *Junge*, 3. Aufl., Rn. 4a; *Staudinger/Magnus*, Art. 8, Rn. 29.
[233] BGH, 31.10.2001, CISG-online 617; dazu unten Rn. 54.
[234] LG Mönchengladbach, 22.5.1992, CISG-online 56.

durch Vereinbarung schützt, übernimmt das betreffende Risiko. Durch die Objektivierung der Auslegung wird diese Überlegung auch auf die mangelnde Sorgfalt der Vergewisserung erstreckt. Entsprechende Überlegungen haben in großer Zahl in gesetzliche Tatbestände Eingang gefunden, die sich dadurch letztlich als – Art. 8 nicht selten modifizierende – Auslegungsregeln offenbaren.[235] So kommt es für die Erheblichkeit der Störung für die verletzte Seite nach Art. 25 auch auf deren Vorhersehbarkeit an;[236] insoweit begründet Art. 25 a. E. eine von Art. 8 I abweichende, aber Art. 8 II entsprechende Beweislast[237] des verletzenden Teils. Ein weiteres Beispiel ist etwa der Ausschluss der Vertragswidrigkeit nach Art. 42 II lit. a), wenn der Käufer das Bestehen des Schutzrechts hätte erkennen können.[238]

7. Üblicher Wortsinn

Besonderes Gewicht wird angesichts der Objektivierung durch Art. 8 III und den **40** Maßstäben der Empfängersorgfalt nach Abs. 2 dem üblichen Sinn der von den Parteien verwandten Worte zugemessen.[239] Eine Vermutung, dass der Parteiwille einer Auslegung nach Art. 8 II entspricht,[240] wird dadurch freilich nicht begründet.[241] Der im Einzelfall gewollte Wortsinn geht vor.[242] Bei Bezugnahme auf Standardklauseln oder -bedingungen spricht hingegen eine Vermutung für den Parteiwillen, dass die übliche Auslegung dieser Klauseln maßgeblich sein soll.[243] Eine gelegentlich angesprochene Wortlautgrenze[244] besteht – wegen der Möglichkeiten richterlicher Vertragsergänzung und der Vorrangigkeit des Parteiwillens – nicht. Auch ein genereller Vorrang eines „klaren Wortlaut[s]"[245] läßt sich Art. 8 nicht entnehmen.

Der übliche Wortsinn bestimmt sich regelmäßig nach derjenigen **Rechtsordnung,** **40a** **deren Sprache verwendet wird**.[246] Dazu können auch gerichtliche und schiedsgerichtliche Entscheidungen zu bestimmten Klauseln[247] oder verbreitete Auslegungsregeln wie die Incoterms® 1990, 2000 oder 2010[248] zählen. Allerdings ist bei letzteren immer zu fragen, ob die jeweils vorgenommenen Auslegungen tatsächlich den „üblichen" Sinn widerspiegeln. So können etwa Frei- und franco-Klauseln auch – in Abweichung vom Verständnis von FCA, FAS und FOB nach den Incoterms® – als reine Kostenklauseln ohne Auswirkung auf den Erfüllungsort zu verstehen sein.[249] Dies ist nur ein Beispiel dafür, dass die Anknüpfung an den üblichen Wortsinn auf ganz erhebliche Schwierigkeiten stößt, wenn Termini einer Sprache in unterschiedlichen Rechtsordnungen oder Märkten verschiedene Bedeu-

---

[235] Außer den folgenden die oben Rn. 16 genannten Vorschriften der Konvention.
[236] Vgl. OLG Frankfurt a. M., 17.9.1991, CISG-online 28; LG Berlin, 30.9.1992, CISG-online 70.
[237] Dazu Rn. 61.
[238] Vgl. Civ. 1, 19.3.2002, CISG-online 662.
[239] HGer Zürich, 24.10.2003, CISG-online 857 (allgemeines Sprachverständnis des Worts Austausch schließe die Rücknahme mit ein); *Junge*, 3. Aufl., Rn. 8; *Staudinger/Magnus*, Art. 9, Rn. 32. Kritisch *Bonell*, JBl. 1985, 385, 391 f. Vgl. Art. 9 III EKG; Art. 4.3 lit. e) PICC; Art. 5:102 lit. e) PECL.
[240] Dafür *MCC-Marble Ceramic Center, Inc. v. Ceramica Nuova D'Agostino S. P. A.,* U.S. Ct. App. (11th Cir.), 29.6.1998, CISG-online 342 = 144 F. 3d 1384, 1388.
[241] S. oben Rn. 10.
[242] *Treibacher Industrie, A. G. v. Allegheny Technologies, Inc.,* U. S. Ct. App. (11th Cir.), 12.9.2006, CISG-online 1278.
[243] Vgl. *Staudinger/Magnus*, Art. 8, Rn. 20.
[244] S. OLG Stuttgart, 15.5.2006, CISG-online 1414.
[245] Dafür HGer Zürich, 24.10.2003, CISG-online 857.
[246] OLG Karlsruhe, 20.11.1992, CISG-online 54; vgl. zum deutschen Recht *Triebel/Balthasar*, NJW 2004, 2189–2196 (mit vielen Differenzierungen).
[247] *Junge*, 3. Aufl., Rn. 8; Comment zu Art. 5:102 PECL.
[248] BGH, 7.11.2012, CISG-online 2374, Rn. 20, 22; *Bianca/Bonell/Farnsworth*, Art. 9, Anm. 3.5.; *Junge*, 3. Aufl., Rn. 8. Die Frage der Bindung an die Erläuterungen der Incoterms® ist eine andere Frage (vgl. Art. 9 Rn. 26), die von der Heranziehung zur Auslegung freilich nicht immer hinreichend unterschieden wird: vgl. *Witz/Salger/Lorenz/Witz*, Art. 8, Rn. 11.
[249] BGH, 11.12.1996, CISG-online 225. Vgl. auch OLG Karlsruhe, 20.11.1992, CISG-online 54 („frei Haus, verzollt, unversteuert" als Regelung auch der Gefahrtragung); OGH, 10.9.1998, CISG-online 409 („frei Haus" üblicherweise Lieferklausel).

tungen haben.²⁵⁰ Ein zwischen den Parteien üblicher Wortsinn überspielt selbstverständlich einen sonst üblichen ebenso wie Gebräuche i. S. v. Art. 9.²⁵¹

8. Sprachrisiken

41 Ein besonderes Problem des internationalen Rechtsverkehrs ist die Zuweisung der durch die Verwendungen unterschiedlicher Sprachen entstehenden Risiken.²⁵² Das Risiko einer fehlerhaften Erklärungsformulierung trägt dabei nach den Wertungen von Art. 8 durchgehend der Erklärende; insoweit kommen ihm allenfalls nationale Gültigkeitsnormen zur Hilfe²⁵³. Die wichtigeren Risiken falschen Verstehens werden vielfach dadurch verteilt, dass sich die Parteien auf eine Vertragssprache festlegen. Dies geschieht nicht selten im Wege einer Gepflogenheit²⁵⁴ oder des Einlassens auf eine Verhandlungssprache durch eine Seite.²⁵⁵ Die Festlegung auf eine Vertragssprache weist das Risiko von Missverständnissen demjenigen zu, der diese falsch versteht.²⁵⁶ Das gilt insbesondere für die Auslegung von AGB.²⁵⁷ Verwendet eine Seite in der weiteren Kommunikation eine andere Sprache, tut sie dies auf ihr Risiko,²⁵⁸ wenn es sich nicht ausnahmsweise um eine Heimatsprache des Empfängers – also eine am Ort seiner Niederlassung gesprochene Sprache – handelt; dann nämlich trägt der Empfänger das Risiko des Missverstehens.²⁵⁹ Die Einbeziehung von AGB in einer abweichenden Sprache oder durch fremdsprachigen Hinweis scheitert vielfach.²⁶⁰ **Nationale Sprachregelungen**, welche die Verwendung bestimmter Sprachen vorschreiben,²⁶¹ begründen hingegen keine für die Auslegung maßgebliche Vertragssprache, weil sie im Anwendungsbereich der Konvention von Art. 11 CISG verdrängt werden.²⁶²

42 Lässt sich **keine besondere Vertragssprache** feststellen, trägt der Verwender einer Sprache grundsätzlich das Risiko, dass ihn der Erklärungsempfänger mangels Sprachbeherrschung nicht oder nicht richtig versteht.²⁶³ Dieses Risiko kann freilich durch die Maßstäbe des Art. 8 begrenzt sein, wenn der Erklärungsempfänger die Standards nach Abs. 1, 2 verletzt, insbesondere wenn er erklärt hat, der betreffenden Sprache mächtig zu sein,²⁶⁴ oder sich nicht in zumutbarer Weise über den Inhalt der Erklärung vergewissert.²⁶⁵ Dies ist etwa dann der Fall, wenn eine Partei ein Dokument unterzeichnet, dessen Sprache sie nicht versteht.²⁶⁶

---

²⁵⁰ *Bianca/Bonell/Farnsworth*, Art. 9, Anm. 3.5.; *Honnold/Fletchner*, Art. 8, Rn. 107.1 (er nennt *warranty, condition, disclaimer, trust*); *Witz/Salger/Lorenz/Witz*, Art. 8, Rn. 10.

²⁵¹ *Treibacher Industrie, A. G. v. Allegheny Technologies, Inc.,* U. S. Ct. App. (11th Cir.), 12.9.2006, CISG-online 1278.

²⁵² Grundlegend *Schlechtriem*, FS Weitauer, S. 129. Irreführend *Ferrari*, IHR 2003, 10, 13 f., der von der Wirkungslosigkeit der betreffenden Erklärungen spricht.

²⁵³ Zu den Einschränkungen bei der Anwendbarkeit der Regeln über Willensmängel s. oben Rn. 6 f. Normen, welche Sprachrisiken als solche zuweisen (vgl. etwa die inzwischen aufgehobene französische Loi 75–1349), sind durch Art. 8 verdrängt.

²⁵⁴ *Witz/Salger/Lorenz/Witz*, Art. 8, Rn. 9; vgl. LG Augsburg, 12.7.1994, CISG-online 390; OGH 17.12.2003, CISG-online 828; LG Aachen, 22.6.2010, CISG-online 2161, Rn. 49.

²⁵⁵ LG Kassel, 15.2.1996, CISG-online 190; *Enderlein/Maskow/Strohbach*, Art. 8, Anm. 3.2.; *Witz/Salger/Lorenz/Witz*, Art. 8, Rn. 9.

²⁵⁶ LG Augsburg, 12.7.1994, CISG-online 390; OLG Hamm, 8.2.1995, CISG-online 141; LG Kassel, 15.2.1996, CISG-online 190; *Junge*, 3. Aufl., Rn. 4a.

²⁵⁷ Vgl. Comment 4 zu Art. 4.1 PICC; Comment 3 zu Art. 2.20 PICC.

²⁵⁸ *Witz/Salger/Lorenz/Witz*, Art. 8, Rn. 9.

²⁵⁹ *Staudinger/Magnus*, Art. 8, Rn. 28.

²⁶⁰ Vgl. Rn. 54a.

²⁶¹ Etwa das Gesetz über die polnische Sprache vom 7.10.1999 (dazu *Klapsa*, WiRO 2000, 233 ff.), ferner Art. 671 Handelsgesetzbuch von Guatemala (zitiert nach *Schwenzer/Hachem/Kee*, Rn. 26.18).

²⁶² S. *Schmidt-Kessel*, Art. 11 Rn. 14a.

²⁶³ Der Sache nach bereits LG Frankfurt a. M., 2.5.1990, CISG-online 183. Ebenso die Literatur *Junge*, 3. Aufl., Rn. 4a; *Staudinger/Magnus*, Art. 8, Rn. 29; *Witz/Salger/Lorenz/Witz*, Art. 8, Rn. 9.

²⁶⁴ LG Kassel, 15.2.1996, CISG-online 190; *Witz/Salger/Lorenz/Witz*, Art. 8, Rn. 9.

²⁶⁵ Vgl. OLG Hamm, 8.2.1995, CISG-online 141.

²⁶⁶ *MCC-Marble Ceramic Center, Inc. v. Ceramica Nuova D'Agostino S. P. A.,* U. S. Ct. App. (11th Cir.), 29.6.1998, CISG-online 342 = 144 F. 3d 1384, 1387 (die Entscheidung spricht von einem „*reckless behavior*" der betreffenden Partei); *Schlechtriem*, FS Weitauer, S. 129, 138.

Ferner wird die Sprache des Niederlassungs- und – soweit eine Zweigniederlassung handelt – auch des Zweigniederlassungsstaats als verständlich vorausgesetzt werden können; das gilt um so mehr, wenn die Berufszulassung einer Partei Kenntnisse in der – verwendeten – Sprache seines Niederlassungsstaats voraussetzt.[267] Über die Auswirkungen der Verwendung der englischen Sprache besteht keine Einigkeit: Bisweilen wird die These vertreten, die Kenntnis dieser Sprache könne im grenzüberschreitenden Handel generell erwartet werden.[268] Richtiger erscheint freilich der Standpunkt, dass sich insoweit eine generalisierende Betrachtungsweise verbietet.[269] Längst nicht auf jedem grenzüberschreitenden Markt wird Englisch gesprochen und verstanden. Allerdings dürften die Anforderungen an die Verständnismöglichkeiten der Parteien bei dieser Sprache typischerweise erheblich höher sein als bei anderen. Denkbar ist auch, dass auf bestimmten Märkten das Verständnis des Englischen als Gebrauch vorausgesetzt werden kann.[270] Schließlich dürfte es auch vorkommen, dass sich eine Partei aus Imagegründen nicht auf mangelnde Sprachkenntnisse berufen mag.[271]

Werden von einem Vertrag **mehrere Sprachfassungen** erstellt und ergeben sich Differenzen zwischen diesen, kommt der Fassung in der Sprache des ursprünglichen Entwurfs ein besonderes Gewicht zu.[272] Allerdings ist auch diese Regel abdingbar: Sieht der Vertrag die Verbindlichkeit aller Sprachfassungen gleichermaßen vor, scheidet das Kriterium der Originalfassung aus.[273] Abweichungen von der Grundregel liegen zudem bei Bezugnahmen auf internationale Standardbedingungen nahe.[274]

9. Gepflogenheiten

Zwischen den Parteien entstandene Gepflogenheiten[275] gehören zu den in Art. 8 III ausdrücklich angesprochenen Umständen.[276] Dazu zählt insbesondere auch eine Bedeutung, welche die Parteien bereits zuvor ähnlichen Klauseln gegeben haben.[277] Gepflogenheiten sind auch geeignet, das Verständnis nach internationalem Handelsbrauch zu überspielen.[278] In der bisherigen Entscheidungspraxis haben Gepflogenheiten besonders häufig eine Rolle gespielt: So wurden etwa Wirkungen von Rahmenverträgen auf die Ausführungsgeschäfte so eingeordnet.[279] Umgekehrt sprach die Ablehnung des Angebots zu einem Rahmenvertrag gegen die Annahme einer Gepflogenheit bezüglich der darin enthaltenen Geschäftsbedingungen.[280] Nicht selten geht es auch um die Fortschreibung von Regelungen aus vorangegangenen Verträgen unter den nachfolgenden. Dies ist etwa für zuvor besonders vereinbarte Rügefristen[281], Lieferklauseln[282] oder Fälligkeiten[283] und gelegentlich

---

[267] Vgl. Art. 53 der EG-Richtlinie 2005/36/EG über die Anerkennung von Berufsqualifikationen, ABlEG Nr. L 255 vom 30.9.2005, 22.
[268] *Schlechtriem*, 3. Aufl., Art. 24 Rn. 16; zurückhaltender nunmehr *Schroeter*, Art. 24 Rn. 38 („meist"); vgl. OGH, 17.12.2003, CISG-online 828 („Deutsch nach Englisch und Französisch wohl auch ... Weltsprache").
[269] OLG Hamm, 8.2.1995, CISG-online 141; *Ferrari*, IHR 2003, 10, 13.
[270] In diese Richtung *Schlechtriem*, FS Weitauer, S. 129, 133 (für den Seetransport); *Witz/Salger/Lorenz/Witz*, Art. 8, Rn. 9.
[271] *Schlechtriem*, FS Weitauer, S. 129, 133.
[272] Vgl. *Kingston Estate Wines Pty Ltd.* v. *Vetreria Etrusca S. r. l.*, Supreme Court of South Australia, 14.3.2008, CISG-online 1891 (ausdrückliche Anordnung des Vorrangs im Vertrag). Ebenso Comment zu Art. 4.7 PICC; Comment zu Art. 5:107 PECL.
[273] Comment zu Art. 5:107 PECL.
[274] Comment zu Art. 4.7 PICC.
[275] Zum Begriff Art. 9 Rn. 8.
[276] Vgl. auch Art. 4.3 lit. b) PICC; Art. 5:102 lit. d) PECL.
[277] Vgl. Art. 5:102 lit. d) PECL.
[278] *Treibacher Industrie, A. G.* v. *Allegheny Technologies, Inc.*, U. S. Ct. App. (11th Cir.), 12.9.2006, CISG-online 1278; *Magnus*, ZEuP 2008, 318, 327.
[279] OLG Hamburg, 5.10.1998, CISG-online 473 (Rechtswahl); *Junge*, 3. Aufl., Rn. 2.
[280] OGH, 6.2.1996, CISG-online 224.
[281] Vgl. *MCC-Marble Ceramic Center, Inc.* v. *Ceramica Nuova D'Agostino S. P. A.*, U. S. Ct. App. (11th Cir.), 29.6.1998, CISG-online 342 = 144 F. 3d 1384, 1392.
[282] OLG Karlsruhe, 20.11.1992, CISG-online 54 („frei Haus, verzollt, unversteuert").
[283] Oberstes Gericht der Slowakischen Republik, 30.4.2008, CISG-online 1873; CA Québec, 12.4.2011, CISG-online 2278, Nr. 24.

sogar für allgemeine Geschäftsbedingungen insgesamt[284] angenommen worden. Außerdem kann ein nachfolgender Vertrag *ex works* zu verstehen sein, wenn die vorherigen dementsprechend durchgeführt wurden und der Käufer nicht widersprochen hat.[285] War es zwischen den Parteien einer dauernden Geschäftsbeziehung üblich, dass der Verkäufer auf Bestellung des Käufers immer sofort lieferte, ohne diese zu bestätigen, kann sein Schweigen auf weitere Bestellungen – entgegen Art. 18 I 2 – als Annahme zu bewerten sein.[286] War die Vereinbarung einer Vorleistungspflicht zwischen den Parteien üblich, ließ sich daraus nicht deren Verfall als Vertragsstrafe für den Fall ableiten, dass die Ware nicht abgenommen wird.[287] Hatte der Schuldner bei einer vereinbarten Zahlungsfrist von zehn Tagen bislang immer innerhalb von zehn Arbeitstagen gezahlt, bedurfte es in einem Folgevertrag deutlicher Hinweise, wenn für diesen auf Kalendertage umgestellt werden soll.[288] War es schließlich zwischen den Parteien einer Dauerlieferbeziehung über Rohöl üblich, kleinere Mengenabweichungen mit „+/– 10%" zu umschreiben, sprach dies gegen eine Auslegung der Formulierung „bis zu" im Sinne von annähernd.[289] War die Ersatzlieferung bei mangelhafter Ware bislang immer auch mit deren Rücknahme verbunden, streitet dies für ein Verständnis des Wortes „Austausch", welches die Rücknahme durch den Verkäufer einschließt.[290]

10. Gebräuche

45   Auch Gebräuche[291] zählen zu dem nach Art. 8 III zu berücksichtigenden Auslegungsmaterial.[292] Allerdings ist insoweit das Verhältnis der Vorschrift zu Art. 9 II nicht völlig gesichert; die zu entscheidende Frage lautet, ob auch im Rahmen von Art. 8 III die Voraussetzungen von Art. 9 II vorliegen müssen.[293] Dies wird nicht selten bezweifelt.[294] Richtigerweise sind mit *Schlechtriem* auch örtliche oder nationale Gebräuche berücksichtigungsfähig.[295] Art. 8 III erfüllt nämlich eine von Art. 9 II sehr verschiedene Funktion, denn in jenem geht es nicht um die Ergänzung des Vertrages „oder" bzw. „und" um den Inhalt von Gebräuchen, sondern lediglich um die Sammlung des Auslegungsmaterials.[296] Die gegenteilige Auffassung führt zudem durch die Hintertür systematischer Auslegung eine – nach Art. 8 III gerade abzulehnende – Beschränkung des Auslegungsmaterials ein. Letztlich kommt es daher auch nicht auf die Geltung am Ort des Vertragsschlusses an,[297] sondern darauf, ob der betreffende Gebrauch einen Schluss auf den Willen des Erklärenden i. S. d. Art. 8 I ermöglicht respektive Teil des objektiven Empfängerhorizonts i. S. d. Abs. 2 ist. Letzteres wird nicht selten – aber nicht „zumindest"[298] – erfordern, dass der Gebrauch

---

[284] ICC, 8611/1997, CISG-online 236; LG Coburg, 12.12.2006, CISG-online 1447; vgl. *Bianca/Bonell/Farnsworth*, Art. 9, Anm. 2.1.1.

[285] *Calzaturificio Claudia v. Olivieri Footwear Ltd.*, U. S. Dist. Ct. (S. D. N. Y.), CISG-online 440 = 1998 WL 164, 824 (*in casu* abgelehnt, weil Gepflogenheit nicht hinreichend substantiiert vorgetragen).

[286] CA Grenoble, 21.10.1999, CISG-online 574.

[287] OLG München, 8.2.1995, CISG-online 143.

[288] S. Illustration 1 zu Art. 5:102 PECL.

[289] Int. Ct. Russian CCI, 21.2.1997, CISG-online 781.

[290] HGer Zürich, 24.10.2003, CISG-online 857.

[291] Zum Begriff Art. 9 Rn. 11.

[292] Vgl. Artt. 4.3 lit. f), 1.8 PICC, Art. 5:102 lit. f) PECL.

[293] In diesem Sinne etwa OLG Hamm, 30.11.2010, CISG-online 2217; *Soergel/Lüderitz/Fenge*, Art. 8, Rn. 6; *Witz/Salger/Lorenz/Witz*, Art. 8, Rn. 12. Vgl. die Differenzierung zwischen Art. 4.3 lit. e) und f) sowie dazu Comment 2 zu Art. 4.3 PICC und außerdem Comment zu Art. 5:102 PECL.

[294] *Staudinger/Magnus*, Art. 8, Rn. 24. Implizit offen gelassen in BGH, 11.12.1996, CISG-online 225, da Parteiwille feststellbar. Jetzt BGH, 7.11.2012, CISG-online 2374, Rn. 24: „Selbst wenn daraus noch kein den Anforderungen des Art. 9 Abs. 2 CISG entsprechender Handelsbrauch erwachsen ist".

[295] *Schlechtriem*, Internationales UN-Kaufrecht, Rn. 56. In der Sache ebenso *Kröll u. a./Zuppi*, Art. 8, Rn. 27; *Witz/Salger/Lorenz/Witz*, Art. 8 Rn. 11 (ausdrücklich anders allerdings Rn. 12).

[296] *Schlechtriem*, Internationales UN-Kaufrecht, Rn. 56. Beide Funktionen unterscheiden auch *Najork*, S. 46 und *Pamboukis*, 25 J. L. & Com. (2005-06), 107, 108.

[297] So aber Comment zu Art. 5:102 PECL.

[298] So aber *Junge*, 3. Aufl., Rn. 10.

auch im Heimatstaat des Empfängers gilt.[299] Gibt es jedoch Anzeichen für ein abweichendes Verständnis des Erklärenden, wird der Empfänger nicht ohne weiteres davon ausgehen dürfen, dass der Erklärungsinhalt seinem gewohnten Verständnis entspricht.[300] Richtigerweise ist mit dieser Abweichung von Art. 9 II auch die besondere Bedeutung solcher international verbreiteter Regelwerke wie der Incoterms® zu erklären,[301] die als solche nicht als Handelsbräuche anzuerkennen sind.

Eine Auslegung unter Rückgriff auf Gebräuche hat die Rechtsprechung etwa bei der **46** Klausel Lieferung „*prima ferie non dopo*" vorgenommen und darauf verwiesen, dass diese Klausel im deutsch-italienischen Schuhhandel Lieferung vor August verlange.[302] Von zwei Schiedsgerichten ist des Weiteren eine Vorkassevereinbarung dahingehend ausgelegt worden, dass diese üblicherweise nicht bedeute, dass der Käufer vor der Lieferung noch Beträge aus anderen Verträgen ausgleichen muss.[303] Eine weitere schiedsgerichtliche Entscheidung hat die Auffassung, zwischen den Parteien seien die Kaufpreise noch nicht abschließend festgelegt worden, außer auf den Wortlaut der Vereinbarungen auch auf die Üblichkeit vorläufiger Preise auf dem Magnesiummarkt gestützt.[304] Ferner ist der Deckungsgleichheit von Handelsbrauch und Wortlaut der Parteivereinbarung besonderes Gewicht beigemessen worden.[305] Werden üblicherweise keine Kommissionsgeschäfte, sondern Kaufverträge geschlossen, ist die Schwelle für eine Abweichung von dieser „Usanz" hoch.[306] Für den deutsch-niederländischen unternehmerischen Geschäftsverkehr wird im Regelfalle davon ausgegangen, dass vereinbarte Preise bezogen auf die Umsatzsteuer Nettopreise sind.[307]

11. Contra proferentem

Die international weit verbreitete Regel, dass unklare Erklärungen *contra proferentem* **47** auszulegen seien,[308] gilt als einer der Ursprünge der sog. objektiven Auslegung.[309] Die Regel ist auch unter der Konvention anzuwenden.[310] Sie ist dort – in Umkehrung der Genealogie – eine Konsequenz aus der Maßgeblichkeit des Empfängerverständnisses.[311] *Contra proferentem* beruht auf dem Grundgedanken, dass diejenige Partei, welche die betreffende Formulierung entworfen oder durchgesetzt hat, das Risiko ihrer Unklarheit tragen muss;[312] für die Konvention ergibt sich diese Risikoverteilung als allgemeiner Grundsatz (Art. 7 II Alt. 1) aus Art. 8 sowie aus weiteren Vorschriften, in welchen dieser seinen Niederschlag gefunden hat.[313] In Anwendung dieses Grundsatzes lassen sich auch

---

[299] In diesem Sinne etwa OLG Karlsruhe, 20.11.1992, CISG-online 54 („frei Haus, verzollt, unversteuert" bezogen auf die Regelung der Gefahrtragung). Kritisch zu dieser Entscheidung *Witz/Salger/Lorenz/Witz*, Art. 8, Rn. 11.
[300] Insoweit treffend *Witz/Salger/Lorenz/Witz*, Art. 8, Rn. 11; ebenso *Soergel/Lüderitz/Fenge*, Art. 8, Rn. 6.
[301] Vgl. *Leisinger*, Fundamental Breach, S. 145.
[302] AG Nordhorn, 14.6.1994, CISG-online 259.
[303] SchiedsG der Handelskammer Hamburg, 21.3.1996, CISG-online 187; SchiedsG Hamburger freundschaftliche Arbitrage, 29.12.1998, CISG-online 638 = NJW-RR 1999, 780, 782.
[304] ICC, 8324/1995, CISG-online 569.
[305] OLG Hamm, 30.11.2010, CISG-online 2217 (zum Gesundheits- und Infektionszustand von Schweinen).
[306] HGer Aargau, 5.2.2008, CISG-online 1740, Nr. 3.4.1 (Obsthandel).
[307] AG Geldern, 17.8.2011, CISG-online 2302.
[308] Für weitere Formulierungen dieser Regel siehe *Baldus*, Regelhafte Vertragsauslegung, S. 118.
[309] *Honnold/Fletchner*, Art. 8, Rn. 107.1.
[310] OLG Stuttgart, 31.3.2008, CISG-online 1658, Rn. 37; *Honnold/Fletchner*, Art. 8, Rn. 107.1; *Brunner*, Art. 8, Rn. 20; *Kröll u.a./Zuppi*, Art. 8, Rn. 24; *Schwenzer/Hachem/Kee*, Rn. 26.61; *Staudinger/Magnus*, Art. 8, Rn. 18. Der Sache nach auch OLG Frankfurt a. M., 31.3.1995, CISG-online 137; OLG Celle, 24.5.1995, CISG-online 152. Vgl. Art. 4.6 PICC; Art. 5:103 PECL. Zweifelnd hingegen *Witz/Salger/Lorenz/Witz*, Art. 8, Rn. 15, weil Art. 8 II nicht über verbleibende Mehrdeutigkeiten hinweghelfe. Abweichend auch *Ferrari*, IHR 2003, 10, 14.
[311] *Staudinger/Magnus*, Art. 8, Rn. 18.
[312] Comment zu Art. 4.6 PICC; Comment zu Art. 5:103 PECL. Zur Person des *proferens Baldus*, Regelhafte Vertragsauslegung, S. 118–120.
[313] Artt. 14, 35 II lit. b), 39 I, 43 I.

solche Mehrdeutigkeiten auflösen, welche nach Art. 8 möglicherweise[314] nicht zu beseitigen wären. Dabei ist die Auslegung allgemeiner Geschäftsbedingungen zwar der wichtigste, nicht aber der einzige Anwendungsbereich; die Regel gilt auch für den von einer Seite formulierten Entwurf eines Individualvertrags oder für entsprechende Vertragsteile respektive -klauseln. *Contra proferentem* begründet keinen absoluten Vorrang der Auslegung gegen den Verwender, sondern setzt die Offenheit des Auslegungsergebnisses voraus.[315] Bei feststellbarem und erkennbarem Parteiwillen scheidet ihre Anwendung daher aus.[316] Zu den systematischen Konsequenzen der Regel gehört, dass Art. 8 insoweit eine Ausnahme von Art. 4 S. 2 lit. a) begründet, als – anders als gelegentlich nach nationalen Rechten – die Unbestimmtheit einer einseitig gestellten Klausel nicht deren Nichtigkeit nach sich zieht, wenn eine Auslegung zu Lasten des Erklärenden möglich ist[317]; das gilt insbesondere für AGB-rechtliche Transparenzgebote wie § 307 I 2 BGB.[318] Allerdings kann die Anwendung von *contra proferentem* ergeben, dass eine Parteierklärung kein hinreichend bestimmtes Angebot i. S. d. Art. 14 enthält.[319]

48 Anwendung findet *contra proferentem* etwa bei divergierenden Sprachfassungen, wenn diese oder die Ursprungsfassung einseitig entworfen wurden.[320] Die Unbeachtlichkeit einer nicht hinreichend bestimmten Rüge nach Art. 39 ist ein gesetzlich geregelter Anwendungsfall.[321] Die Regel gilt erst recht dann, wenn der Erklärende trotz Rückfrage nicht für Klarheit sorgt.[322] Die Gerichte haben es, gestützt auf diesen Gedanken, etwa abgelehnt, einem vereinbarten Ausschluss des Haager Kaufrechts eine Abwahl der Konvention zu entnehmen.[323] Weiter kann eine Vertragsaufhebung unwirksam sein, wenn die Erklärungen des Berechtigten widersprüchlich sind.[324] Schließlich lässt etwa die Klausel Lieferung „*prima ferie non dopo*"[325] einen möglicherweise beabsichtigten Fixcharakter nicht hinreichend erkennen.[326]

12. *Favor negotii* und wirksamkeitsorientierte Auslegung

49 In Übereinstimmung mit den besonderen Regeln der *Principles*[327] lässt sich Art. 8 eine allgemeine Auslegungsleitlinie des *favor negotii* entnehmen.[328] Ihr liegt die letztlich in Artt. 6, 8 I wurzelnde Erwägung zugrunde, dass die Parteien einen sinnvollen Vertrag schließen wollen. Das Prinzip schützt den übereinstimmenden Parteiwillen und damit die Vertragsziele.[329] Der *favor negotii* hat vor allem drei Spielarten: Die Auslegung soll erstens die Unwirksamkeit des Vertrags vermeiden[330] oder, bei Ungültigkeit oder Sinnlosigkeit einzelner Vertragsteile, auf diese minimieren.[331] Die Konvention kennt daher das Gebot einer

---

[314] Vgl. *Witz/Salger/Lorenz/Witz*, Art. 8, Rn. 15.
[315] Comment zu Art. 5:103 PECL.
[316] In der Sache ebenso BGH, 11.12.1996, CISG-online 225.
[317] Vgl. *Witz/Salger/Lorenz/Witz*, Art. 8, Rn. 1.
[318] A. A. *Schroeter*, Vor Artt. 14–24 Rn. 4.
[319] Vgl. OGH, 10.11.1994, CISG-online 117; *Magellan International Corp. v. Salzgitter Handel GmbH*, U. S. Dist. Ct. (N. D. Ill), 17.12.1999, CISG-online 439 = 76 F. 2d 919, 924; *Geneva Pharmaceutical Technology Corp. v. Barr Laboratories, Inc.*, U. S. Dist. Ct. (S. D. N. Y.), 10.5.2002, CISG-online 653 = 201 F. 2d 236, 282 (*in casu* aber jeweils hinreichende Bestimmtheit angenommen); *Schroeter*, Art. 14 Rn. 2. A. A.: offenbar OGH, 20.3.1997, CISG-online 269.
[320] Comment zu Art. 5:107 PECL.
[321] Der Sache nach OLG Saarbrücken, 13.1.1993, CISG-online 83; BGH, 4.12.1996, CISG-online 260. Zu Rügeobliegen und Auslegung s. oben Rn. 37.
[322] Vgl. OLG Frankfurt a. M., 31.3.1995, CISG-online 137.
[323] LG Düsseldorf, 11.10.1995, CISG-online 180; a. A. *Wolf/Horn/Lindacher/Lindacher*, Anh. zu § 2, Rn. 73.
[324] OLG Koblenz, 31.1.1997, CISG-online 256.
[325] S. oben Rn. 46.
[326] AG Nordhorn, 14.6.1994, CISG-online 259.
[327] Vgl. Art. 5:106 PECL; Art. 4.5 PICC und dazu *Nabati*, Rev. dr. unif. 2007, 247, 254.
[328] *Brunner*, Art. 8, Rn. 20; *Kröll u. a./Zuppi*, Art. 8, Rn. 29; *Schwenzer/Hachem/Kee*, Rn. 26.56.
[329] *Baldus*, Regelhafte Vertragsauslegung, S. 131.
[330] Wie hier jetzt auch *Schwenzer/Hachem/Kee*, Rn. 26.58. Comment zu Art. 5:105 PECL.
[331] Vgl. OLG Stuttgart, 15.5.2006, CISG-online 1414 (gegen eine Auslegung, welche einer Schiedsklausel keinen relevanten Anwendungsbereich belässt).

geltungserhaltenden Reduktion unwirksamer Klauseln; dieses findet freilich seine Grenze in den gleichfalls nach Art. 4 S. 2 lit. a) zu berücksichtigenden nationalen Verboten einer solchen Auslegung. Zweitens dient der *favor negotii* der Vermeidung absurder Auslegungsergebnisse.[332] So sind insbesondere Widersprüche zwischen einzelnen Klauseln dem Vertragszweck entsprechend sinnvoll aufzulösen; die Regel gemahnt also, in solchen Fällen nicht am Wortlaut festzuhalten. Grundsätzlich unvereinbar mit Art. 8 wäre die Annahme der Nichtigkeit beider Klauseln. Ferner resultiert aus dem *favor negotii* die – widerlegliche – Vermutung, dass die Parteien die einzelnen Klauseln nicht ohne Grund vereinbart haben.[333] Einen Nichtigkeitsgrund der Perplexität von Erklärungen kennt die Konvention dementsprechend nicht und lässt dafür auch keinen Raum.

13. Späteres Verhalten der Parteien

Der vierte nach ausdrücklicher Anordnung durch Art. 8 III zu beachtende Umstand ist **50** das spätere Verhalten der Parteien. Dessen – trotz der Schwierigkeiten einer logischen Rechtfertigung[334] verbreitete[335] – Beachtlichkeit beruht darauf, dass das spätere Verhalten **Rückschlüsse auf den ursprünglichen Willen** respektive das ursprüngliche Verständnis der Parteien erlauben kann.[336] Zugleich verweist Art. 8 III insoweit auf allgemeine Grundsätze der Konvention, nämlich auf das Verbot des *venire contra factum proprium*[337] sowie auf die Möglichkeit der Verwirkung von Rechtspositionen.[338] Schwierigkeiten kann allerdings die fließende Grenze[339] zwischen Auslegung anhand späteren Parteiverhaltens und der Vertragsänderung i. S. d. Art. 29 bereiten. Insbesondere ist der Gefahr vorzubeugen, dass durch entsprechendes Verhalten einseitig eine nachträgliche Vertragsänderung herbeigeführt wird.[340]

Späteres Parteiverhalten spielt besonders in solchen Fällen eine Rolle, in denen die **51 Bindung an den Vertrag** insgesamt in Frage stand. So belegt etwa eine spätere **vorbehaltlose Bezugnahme** auf den Vertragstext, dass sich die betreffende Partei an den Vertrag gebunden fühlt.[341] Der Weiterverkauf der Ware belegt die Auffassung, einen wirksamen Vertrag geschlossen zu haben.[342] Akzeptiert eine Partei auf den Vertrag bezogene Rechnungen der anderen, spricht dies dafür, den Vertrag als zwischen ihnen geschlossen anzusehen.[343] Hingegen zeigt die Forderung nach einer Bestätigung des Vertrags Zweifel an der vertraglichen Bindung.[344] Des Weiteren spricht die Fortsetzung der Vertragsdurchführung durch eine Partei gegen deren Annahme, sie habe eine wirksame Vertragsaufhebung

---

[332] Comment zu Art. 5:105 PECL; vgl. *Baldus*, Regelhafte Vertragsauslegung, S. 116 f.
[333] Vgl. Illustration zu Art. 4.5 PICC; sowie jetzt auch *Schwenzer/Hachem/Kee*, Rn. 26.59.
[334] *Schlechtriem*, Internationales UN-Kaufrecht, Rn. 57; skeptisch auch *Baldus*, Regelhafte Vertragsauslegung, S. 137 f.
[335] Vgl. Art. 4.3 lit. c) PICC; Art. 5:102 lit. b) PECL sowie *Schwenzer/Hachem/Kee*, Rn. 26.40.
[336] HGer Aargau, 5.2.2008, CISG-online 1740, Nr. 3.1.1; *Schlechtriem*, Internationales UN-Kaufrecht, Rn. 57. So für das deutsche Recht BGH, 7.12.2006, NJW-RR 2007, 529, 530.
[337] OLG Linz, 23.3.2005, CISG-online 1376, Nr. 5.1. Vgl. *Junge*, 3. Aufl., Rn. 6; *Enderlein/Maskow/Strohbach*, Art. 8, Anm. 11.; *Najork*, S. 47; zurückhaltender *Staudinger/Magnus*, Art. 8, Rn. 26 (Präferenz für Verhalten).
[338] Vgl. Internationales SchiedsG der Bundeskammer d. gewerblichen Wirtschaft (Wien), 15.6.1994, CISG-online 120. Zum stillschweigenden Verzicht s. oben Rn. 37.
[339] Vgl. *Staudinger/Magnus*, Art. 8, Rn. 25; *Schlechtriem*, Internationales UN-Kaufrecht, Rn. 57; *Witz/Salger/Lorenz/Witz*, Art. 8, Rn. 13. Zu weit aber OLG Linz, 23.3.2005, CISG-online 1376, Nr. 5.1: umfaßt auch Änderungen des Vertragsinhalts.
[340] *Staudinger/Magnus*, Art. 8, Rn. 25; vgl. People's Supreme Court, Appeal Division in Ho Chi Minh City, 5.4.1996, UNILEX (Ablehnung der Berücksichtigung einer Klausel aus einem später gestellten Akkreditiv; Qualifikation als Angebot zur Vertragsänderung); *Château de Charmes Wines Ltd. v. Sabate USA Inc., Sabate S. A.*, U. S. Ct. App. (9th Cir.), 5.5.2003, CISG-online 767 (keine wirksame Vereinbarung eines Gerichtsstands durch Klausel in späteren Rechnungen). Zu undifferenziert daher *Ferrari*, IHR 2003, 10, 14.
[341] *Filanto, S. p. A. v. Chilewich Intern. Corp.*, U. S. Dist. Ct. (S. D. N. Y.), 14.4.1992, CISG-online 45 = 789 F. 1229, 1240; BGer 5.4.2005, CISG-online 1012, E. 4.3.
[342] OGH, 10.11.1994, CISG-online 117.
[343] OLG Stuttgart, 28.2.2000, CISG-online 583.
[344] OLG Frankfurt a. M., 30.8.2000, CISG-online 594.

erklärt.³⁴⁵ Und ebenso widerstreitet das vorbehaltlose Verlangen des Käufers nach der Rechnung für die gesamte Lieferung in Kenntnis des Umstandes, dass nur ein Teil der Ware gebraucht werden würde, einem vereinbarten Rückgaberecht.³⁴⁶

14. Favor debitoris

51a Andere Handlungen lassen auf den **Vertragsinhalt** schließen. So geht diejenige Partei, welche ohne eine entsprechende vertragliche Regelung eine Transportversicherung abschließt, offenbar davon aus, selbst das Transportrisiko zu tragen.³⁴⁷ Hingegen belegt eine von Art. 57 abweichende Praxis nicht notwendig eine abweichende Zahlungsortvereinbarung; sie kann auch eine Großzügigkeit des Gläubigers darstellen.³⁴⁸ Weiter kann die rügelose Annahme für die Vertragsgemäßheit der Ware sprechen;³⁴⁹ allerdings ist diese Überlegung nicht unproblematisch, weil Artt. 38 ff. insoweit eine besondere Regelung enthalten. Basis dieser Regelung ist gerade der Erklärungswert der rügelosen Annahme. Dieser Erklärungswert findet auch sonst Beachtung: So lassen sich gegen die Annahme eines Fixgeschäfts die Annahme der verspäteten Lieferung³⁵⁰ wie auch die Hinnahme einer Frist nach Art. 48 III, II ins Treffen führen.³⁵¹ Auch wenn die Annahme der Leistung nur zum Zwecke der Schadensminderung i. S. d. Art. 77 geschieht, kann dies gegen die Wesentlichkeit des Vertragsbruchs sprechen.³⁵² Die widerspruchslose Entgegennahme einer nachträglichen Mitteilung des Käufers, er werde die Kaufsache in einer bestimmten Art und Weise verwenden, kann den Schluss rechtfertigen, diese konkrete Verwendung sei von Anfang an Teil eines weniger bestimmt formulierten Verwendungszwecks i. S. v. Art. 35 II lit. b) gewesen. Die Vorlegung eines vom Verkäufer auf den Preis einer Teillieferung ausgestellten Wechsels zum Akzept durch den Käufer spricht gegen eine sofortige Fälligkeit des gesamten Kaufpreises.³⁵³

Eine generelle Leitlinie der Auslegung zugunsten des Schuldners beruht auf der Erfahrung, dass sich jede Partei so wenig wie möglich verpflichten will. Sie kann mit *contra proferentem* konform gehen oder dieser Leitlinie entgegen wirken, weil der Anknüpfungspunkt nicht die Vorgabe der vertraglichen Formulierung, sondern die vertragliche Verpflichtung selbst ist. Ob sich dieser Erfahrungssatz unter der Konvention in eine allgemeine Auslegungsregel ummünzen lässt,³⁵⁴ ist offen. Der objektive Auslegungsansatz von Art. 8 II spricht jedoch sehr dagegen; dementsprechend wird der Erfahrungssatz allenfalls bei der Konkretisierung der Sorgfaltserwartung nach Abs. 1 Berücksichtigung finden können.

VII. Behandlung allgemeiner Geschäftsbedingungen

1. Einbeziehung allgemeiner Geschäftsbedingungen

52 Die Konvention enthält keine besonderen Regeln zur Behandlung allgemeiner Geschäftsbedingungen. Art. 8 bestimmt daher – zusammen mit Artt. 14 ff. – die Voraussetzungen wirksamer Einbeziehung von Bedingungen in den Vertrag.³⁵⁵ Diese setzt zumindest einen

---

³⁴⁵ OLG Koblenz, 31.1.1997, CISG-online 256.
³⁴⁶ BezG St. Gallen, 3.7.1997, CISG-online 336.
³⁴⁷ OLG Karlsruhe, 20.11.1992, CISG-online 54.
³⁴⁸ Vgl. Cass., 7.8.1998, CISG-online 538.
³⁴⁹ Vgl. OLG Frankfurt a. M., 31.3.1995, CISG-online 137.
³⁵⁰ AG Nordhorn, 14.6.1994, CISG-online 259; für ein gegenteiliges Parteiverhalten vgl. etwa CA Milano, 20.3.1998.
³⁵¹ AG Nordhorn, 14.6.1994, CISG-online 259.
³⁵² OLG Hamburg, 5.10.1998, CISG-online 473.
³⁵³ Int. Ct. Russian CCI, 27.5.2005, CISG-online 1456, Nr. 3.3.3.2.
³⁵⁴ Dafür offenbar *Schwenzer/Hachem/Kee*, Rn. 26.62.
³⁵⁵ OLG Saarbrücken, 13.1.1993, CISG-online 83; OGH, 6.2.1996, CISG-online 224; OLG Zweibrücken, 31.3.1998, CISG-online 481; BGH, 31.10.2001, CISG-online 617; OGH, 17.12.2003, CISG-online 828; HR, 28.1.2005, CISG-online 1002; *Honnold/Fletchner*, Art. 8, Rn. 109; *Lurger*, IHR 2005, 177, 182; *Schlech-*

ausdrücklichen Verweis auf die allgemeinen Geschäftsbedingungen voraus.[356] Dieser muss hinreichend klar sein.[357] Ohne einen solchen Verweis ergibt sich weder die Einbeziehung aus Art. 8 II noch besteht Kenntnis oder eine zu vertretende Unkenntnis nach Art. 8 I.[358] Die ausdrückliche Zurückweisung übersandter AGB schließt jedenfalls deren Einbeziehung aus,[359] während die individuelle und ausdrückliche Billigung der Einbeziehung die AGB auch ohne Kenntnis des anderen Teils zur Anwendung bringt.[360] Praktisch bedeutsam sind diejenigen Fälle, in denen der **andere Teil** mit **Stillschweigen** reagiert hat. Möglich ist ferner die Einbeziehung aufgrund einer Gepflogenheit der Parteien gem. Art. 9 I[361] oder Handelsbrauch nach Art. 9 II; eine solche könnte die Einbeziehung im Einzelfall auch ausschließen.[362] Die Anwendbarkeit von Artt. 8, 9, 14 ff. schließt den Rückgriff auf nationales Recht aus.[363] Eine Schutznorm vergleichbar Art. 31 II EGBGB[364] oder Art. 8 II Rom I-Übk/Art. 10 II Rom I-VO ist weder vorhanden noch erforderlich.[365] Soweit das CISG über Art. 1 I lit. b) zur Anwendung gelangt, sind diese – gegebenenfalls zu einer gespaltenen Beurteilung des Vertrags führenden[366] – Regeln allerdings beachtlich. Die Frage der **Gültigkeit von AGB** ist der Konvention nach Art. 4 S. 2 lit. a) ausdrücklich entzogen.[367] Hingegen erfolgt die Behandlung **kollidierender AGB** nach den Maßstäben der Artt. 8, 9, 14 ff.[368]

Umstritten ist die Frage, ob sich Art. 8 eine **allgemeine Übersendungsobliegenheit** 53 für den Verwender allgemeiner Geschäftsbedingungen entnehmen lässt oder ob auch ein Verweis auf die nicht übersandten Bedingungen ausreichen kann.[369] Der deutsche Bundesgerichtshof hat sich – im Anschluss an eine verbreitete Auffassung in der deutschen Literatur – für ein generelles Übersendungserfordernis ausgesprochen.[370] Begründet wird dies vor allem mit dem Hinweis, der Verzicht des deutschen Rechts auf eine Übersendung recht-

---

triem, Internationales UN-Kaufrecht, Rn. 58; *Schroeter*, Art. 14 Rn. 33; *Schwenzer/Mohs*, IHR 2006, 239, 241; *Wolf/Horn/Lindacher/Lindacher*, Anh. zu § 2, Rn. 73, 77. Vgl. Art. 2:104 PECL; anders Cámara Nacional de Apelaciones en lo Commercial (Argentinien), 14.10.1993, CISG-online 87 (für eine Gerichtsstandsklausel) sowie Entscheidungen einiger niederländischer Instanzgerichte, s. RB Arnhem, 17.4.2004, CISG-online 946 sowie die Nachweise bei *Janssen*, Uniform L. Rev. 2005, 901, 904 f. Ferner *Barbara Berry, S. A. de C. V. v. Ken M. Spooner Farms Inc.*, U. S. Dist. Ct. (W. D. W. T.), 13.4.2006, CISG-online 1354 (Anwendung von Art. 4).
[356] So ausdrücklich nunmehr RB Zwolle, 9.12.2009, CISG-online 2069, Nr. 4.6. Zur Frage der Übersendungsobliegenheit siehe sogleich ab Rn. 53.
[357] *CSS Antenna, Inc. v. Amphenol-Tuchel Electronics, GmbH*, U. S. Dist. Ct. (Maryland), 8.2.2011, CISG-online 2177 („This language is ambiguous at best.") für die zu höflich geratene Formulierung „May we point out that for all deliveries and services only the known general conditions of supply and delivery for products and services of the electrical industry (ZVEI) in their latest editions are valid.".
[358] Für letzteres s. *CSS Antenna, Inc. v. Amphenol-Tuchel Electronics, GmbH*, U. S. Dist. Ct. (Maryland), 8.2.2011, CISG-online 2177.
[359] OLG Linz, 23.3.2005, CISG-online 1376, Nr. 6.2.
[360] S. Rn. 53a.
[361] OGH, 31.8.2005, CISG-online 1093; OLG Hamm, 6.12.2005, CISG-online 1221, Rn. 33 (zu Art. 23 Brüssel I-VO, aber CISG-Fall); OLG Linz, 23.3.2005, CISG-online 1376, Nr. 5.2; OLG Innsbruck, 1.2.2005, CISG-online 1130. Ebenso für das deutsche Recht BGH, 1.6.2005, NJW-RR 2005, 1518, 1520.
[362] S. RB Zwolle, 22.1.2003, CISG-online 1023 (in casu verneint).
[363] OLG Zweibrücken, 31.3.1998, CISG-online 481; BGH, 31.10.2001, CISG-online 617; *Schroeter*, Vor Artt. 14–24 Rn. 3.
[364] Vgl. zu den Wirkungen dieser Norm auf die Einbeziehung von AGB *Weller*, IPRax 2005, 428 ff.
[365] S. OLG Innsbruck, 1.2.2005, CISG-online 1130. Vgl. auch HR, 28.1.2005, CISG-online 1002.
[366] Vgl. *Ferrari*, Art. 1 Rn. 8; *Staudinger/Magnus*, Art. 1 Rn. 107.
[367] S. *Ferrari*, Art. 4 Rn. 20.
[368] Dazu *Schroeter*, Art. 19 Rn. 19–36 sowie *Junge*, 3. Aufl., Rn. 11.
[369] Eine Übersendungsobliegenheit ergibt sich etwa aus Art. 2:104 II PECL; anders die UNIDROIT-Principles: Comment 3 zu Art. 2.19 PICC; beide Artikel werden in Hof 's-Hertogenbosch, 16.10.2002, CISG-online 816 (Urteil zum CISG) erwogen.
[370] BGH, 31.10.2001, CISG-online 617; OLG München, 14.1.2009, CISG-online 2011, Rn 37; OLG Celle, 24.7.2009, CISG-online 1906, Rn. 17; OLG Jena, 10.11.2010, CISG-online 2216, Rn. 27; OLG Düsseldorf, 23.3.2011, CISG-online 2218; LG Neubrandenburg, 3.8.2005, CISG-online 1190; LG Trier, 8.12.2004, CISG-online 910; Hof 's-Hertogenbosch, 16.10.2002, CISG-online 816 (unter ausdrücklichem Bezug auf Art. 2:104 PECL); Rb Utrecht, 21. 1 2009, CISG-online 1814, Nr. 4.10; *Holthausen*, RIW 1989, 513, 517; *Magnus*, ZEuP 2002, 523, 532; *ders.*, ZEuP 2008, 318, 325; *Piltz*, NJW 1996, 2768, 2770 f.; *ders.*,

fertige sich aus der Inhaltskontrolle.[371] Zu den anerkannten Ausnahmen zählen die bereits zuvor vorhandene Kenntnis der AGB[372] sowie die Befolgung von Gepflogenheiten oder die Befolgung eines internationalen Handelsbrauchs durch die Einbeziehung;[373] sind die AGB selbst bereits einschlägiger internationaler Handelsbrauch erfolgt die Einbeziehung nicht nach Art. 8, sondern nach Art. 9.[374] Eine Übersendung an die Abrechnungsabteilung des Vertragspartners wird diesen Maßstäben jedenfalls nicht gerecht.[375]

53a Richtigerweise ist eine solche **generelle Übersendungsobliegenheit** allerdings **abzulehnen**.[376] Da der BGH offenbar vorherige Urteile des OGH sowie des Tribunal commercial de Nivelles (Belgien)[377] übersehen hat, besitzt sein Urteil noch nicht einmal *persuasive authority* als Präzendenzfall.[378] Die US-amerikanische Rechtsprechung neigt dazu, die Frage ohne Eingehen auf den europäischen Streitstand anhand der Maßstäbe des Art. 8 zu entscheiden.[379] Positive Kenntnis vom Inhalt der Bedingungen ist danach ohnehin nicht erforderlich, Art. 8 II.[380] Erforderlich ist vielmehr eine differenzierte Betrachtung, wie sie der Offenheit von Art. 8 entspricht: In Betracht kommt nämlich sogar die stillschweigende Einbeziehung auf Grund der Verhandlungen oder qua Gepflogenheit;[381] erst recht kann der schlichte Verweis genügen.[382] Entscheidend ist dabei, dass dieser Verweis so deutlich ist, dass eine vernünftige Partei i. S. d. Art. 8 II ihn versteht.[383] Außerdem muss auf Rückfrage die Möglichkeit gegeben werden, von den Bedingungen in zumutbarer Weise Kenntnis zu nehmen. Eine solche Rückfrage ist dem Erklärungsempfänger auch nicht durchweg unzumutbar;[384] selbst suchen muss er freilich nicht.[385] Die durch ihre Notwendigkeit entstehende Verzögerung geht freilich zu Lasten des Verwenders und ist gegebenenfalls im Rahmen von Art. 16 II zu sanktionieren.

53b Grundsätzlich setzt die Einbeziehung der AGB voraus, dass der Verweis während der Verhandlungen über den konkreten Vertrag,[386] das heißt **spätestens mit Vertragsschluss** erfolgt. Schwierigkeiten bereitet vielfach die nachträgliche Übersendung von Rechnungen

---

IHR 2004, 133, 134; *ders.*, IHR 2007, 121, 122; *Ventsch/Kluth*, IHR 2003, 61, 62; *Wolf/Horn/Lindacher/Lindacher*, Anh. zu § 2, Rn. 77.

[371] BGH, 31.10.2001, CISG-online 617; OLG Celle, 24.7.2009, CISG-online 1906, Rn. 17; OLG Jena, 10.11.2010, CISG-online 2216, Rn. 27; *Magnus*, ZEuP 2002, 523, 532; *Wolf/Horn/Lindacher/Lindacher*, Anh. zu § 2, Rn. 77.

[372] *Magnus*, ZEuP 2008, 318, 326.

[373] *Magnus*, ZEuP 2008, 318, 326 (der damit die abweichenden OGH-Entscheidungen zu erklären versucht); *Schwenzer/Hachem/Kee*, Rn. 12.13 f.

[374] *Schwenzer/Hachem/Kee*, Rn. 12.15; s. *Schmidt-Kessel*, Art. 9 Rn. 6.

[375] Vgl. *CSS Antenna, Inc. v. Amphenol-Tuchel Electronics, GmbH*, U.S. Dist. Ct. (Maryland), 8.2.2011, CISG-online 2177.

[376] Vgl. Trib. com. Nivelles (Belgien), 19.9.1995, CISG-online 366; OGH, 6.2.1996, CISG-online 224; LG Heilbronn, 15.9.1997, CISG-online 562; OLG Zweibrücken, 31.3.1998, CISG-online 481; OLG Linz, 8.8.2005, CISG-online 1087; *Berger*, FS Horn, 17; *Kindler*, FS Heldrich, 225 ff.; *Mittmann*, IHR 2006, 103, 105; *Schmidt-Kessel*, NJW 2002, 3444 ff. Offen gelassen von Trib. Rovereto, 24.8.2006, CISG-online 1374.

[377] S. OGH, 6.2.1996, CISG-online 224 (gefolgt von OGH, 17.12.2003, CISG-online 828); Trib. com. Nivelles (Belgien), 19.9.1995, CISG-online 366.

[378] Vgl. *Janssen*, IHR 2004, 194, 199–200.

[379] *CSS Antenna, Inc. v. Amphenol-Tuchel Electronics, GmbH*, U.S. Dist. Ct. (Maryland), 8.2.2011, CISG-online 2177.

[380] Missverständlich RB Tongeren, 25.1.2005, CISG-online 1106.

[381] OGH, 6.2.1996, CISG-online 224; OLG Zweibrücken, 31.3.1998, CISG-online 481; OGH, 17.12.2003, CISG-online 828; OGH, 31.8.2005, CISG-online 1093; LG Coburg, 12.12.2006, CISG-online 1447; *Kramer*, FS Welser, 539, 550 f.; *Schwenzer/Mohs*, IHR 2006, 239, 241. Zu den Anforderungen an eine solche Gepflogenheit jetzt LG Aachen, 22.6.2010, CISG-online 2161, Rn. 51.

[382] OLG Zweibrücken, 31.3.1998, CISG-online 481 (obiter für individuelle AGB); OGH, 17.12.2003, CISG-online 828 ; LG Coburg, 12.12.2006, CISG-online 1447.

[383] OLG Zweibrücken, 31.3.1998, CISG-online 481 (obiter für individuelle AGB); OGH, 17.12.2003, CISG-online 828; LG Coburg, 12.12.2006, CISG-online 1447.

[384] Generell anders BGH, 31.10.2001, CISG-online 617.

[385] *Schwenzer/Mohs*, IHR 2006, 239, 241.

[386] LG Coburg, 12.12.2006, CISG-online 1447; RB Kortrijk, 8.12.2004, CISG-online 1511 = IHR 2005, 114 (mit irreführendem Leitsatz von *Piltz*); *Piltz*, IHR 2007, 121.

oder Lieferscheinen mit Verweisen auf AGB. Diese führt in der Regel nicht zur Einbeziehung.[387] Davon gibt es zwei **Ausnahmen**: Die Einbeziehung kraft Verweises in nachträglich übersandten Lieferscheinen und Rechnungen kann in seltenen Fällen im Wege einer Vertragsänderung erfolgen, allerdings wird es zum Beleg eines entsprechenden Parteiwillens schon für den Übersender zusätzlicher Hinweise bedürfen; die schlichte Übersendung reicht dafür nicht aus.[388] Auch an den Willen des anderen Teils sind hohe Anforderungen zu stellen: insbesondere lässt sich aus der schlichten Begleichung der Rechnung keine Zustimmung zur Vertragsänderung entnehmen[389] und erst recht nicht aus schlichtem Schweigen.[390] Eine zweite Ausnahme kann sich bei laufenden Geschäftsbeziehungen dadurch ergeben, dass die regelmäßig übersandten Rechnungen oder Lieferscheine mit dem Verweis auf AGB für später abgeschlossene Verträge Wirkungen entfalten. So haben einige Instanzgerichte die regelmäßige Übersendung von Rechnungen oder ähnlichen Unterlagen mit Verweisen auf AGB für die Einbeziehung ausreichen lassen, wenn die Hinweise auch für den flüchtigen Leser ohne weiteres erkennbar waren.[391] Ob dies ohne Vorliegen weiterer Indizien für die Annahme ausreicht, dass die Parteien ihre Geschäfte auf Basis der AGB abwickeln wollten,[392] ist Sache des Tatrichters.[393] Jedenfalls sollte es für die Einbeziehung ausreichen, dass die Parteien andere, lediglich in den Rechnungen oder Lieferscheinen enthaltene Klauseln – etwa eine Skontoklausel – bei der Vertragsdurchführung beachtet haben.[394]

Neben diesem grundsätzlichen Punkt finden sich Entscheidungen zu vielen **Einzelfragen**: So genügt etwa der Verweis auf die auf der Rückseite des Vertrags abgedruckten Bedingungen,[395] während der schlichte Abdruck auf der Rückseite ohne einen solchen Verweis unter Umständen nicht genügt.[396] Ausreichend kann auch der Verweis in einer zum Vertragsschluss führenden „pro forma"-Rechnung sein.[397] In der Literatur umstritten ist, ob bei Vertragsschlüssen im Internet die Bereitstellung der AGB auf der Homepage des Verwenders genügt;[398] den – zu strengen – Anforderungen des deutschen Bundesgerichtshofs dürfte dies kaum genügen. Von einer – beiderseits – stillschweigenden oder durch Gepflogenheit erfolgenden Einbeziehung kann nur ausgegangen werden, wenn der andere Teil die Bedingungen positiv kennt.[399] Der schlichte Verweis auf „übliche Konditionen" respektive die „Vertragsbasis" genügt für die Einbeziehung hingegen nicht, wenn zwischen den Parteien nicht klar ist, dass davon die Geschäftsbedingungen erfasst sind.[400] Die Abgrenzung solcher Bedingungen zu aufgezeichneten Gebräuchen kann Schwierigkeiten bereiten.[401] Die Allgemeinen Lieferbedingungen des Rats für gegenseitige Wirtschaftshilfe (ALB RGW)

---

[387] Ontario Superior Court of Justice, 28.10.2005, CISG-online 1139, Nr. 29 („*unreasonable*"); RB Hasselt, 2.6.1999, CISG-online 762; Hof Arnhem, 21.10.2000, CISG-online 1533 = NIPR 2001, Nr. 14; RB Rotterdam, 14.10.1999, CISG-online 1312; *Mittmann*, IHR 2006, 103, 105 f.

[388] Wie hier jetzt OLG Jena, 10.11.2010, CISG-online 2216, Rn. 30; LG Aachen, 22.6.2010, CISG-online 2161, Rn. 50.

[389] Ontario Superior Court of Justice, 28.10.2005, CISG-online 1139, Nr. 29; RB Kortrijk, 8.12.2004, CISG-online 1511 = IHR 2005, 114 (mit irreführendem Leitsatz von Piltz); insoweit zutreffend *Piltz*, IHR 2007, 121 f.

[390] OLG Jena, 10.11.2010, CISG-online 2216, Rn. 31.

[391] OLG Zweibrücken, 31.3.1998, CISG-Online 481; LG Coburg, 12.12.2006, CISG-online 1447; kritisch dazu *Piltz*, IHR 2007, 121, 122.

[392] Verneinend *Piltz*, IHR 2007, 121, 122; vgl. *Rauscher*, FS Heldrich, 933, 941.

[393] S. Rn. 60.

[394] Vgl. BGer, 5.4.2005, CISG-online 1012, E. 4.2.

[395] OLG Saarbrücken, 13.1.1993, CISG-online 83; AG Nordhorn, 14.6.1994, CISG-online 259.

[396] *MCC-Marble Ceramic Center, Inc. v. Ceramica Nuova D'Agostino S.P.A.*, U.S. Ct. App. (11th Cir.), 29.6.1998, CISG-online 342 = 144 F. 3d 1384, 1391 f.; LG Göttingen, 31.7.1997, CISG-online 564.

[397] Cámara Nacional de Apelaciones en lo Comercial (Argentinien), 14.10.1993, CISG-online 87 (für Gerichtsstandsklausel).

[398] Dafür *Stiegele/Halter*, IHR 2003, 169; dagegen *Ventsch/Kluth*, IHR 2003, 224 f.

[399] OGH, 6.2.1996, CISG-online 224; Trib. Rovereto, 24.8.2006, CISG-online 1374. Bei der einseitig stillschweigenden Einbeziehung genügt hingegen die zumutbare Möglichkeit der Kenntnisnahme, s. Rn. 52 ff.

[400] OGH, 6.2.1996, CISG-online 224.

[401] Vgl. OGH, 15.10.1998, CISG-online 380 (österreichische Holzhandelsusancen).

jedenfalls werden seit dem Verlust ihrer normativen Kraft nur noch dann Vertragsbestandteil, wenn die Parteien diese ausdrücklich einbezogen haben.[402]

54a Sind die Bedingungen in einer **Sprache** abgefasst, die dem Erklärungsempfänger nicht verständlich und auch nicht ohnehin Vertragssprache ist und nach den Umständen auch nicht sein muss, kann dies die Kenntnisnahme unzumutbar sein lassen und ebenfalls die Einbeziehung hindern.[403] Dasselbe gilt in der Regel für einen fremdsprachigen Verweis auf AGB, wenn es sich nicht um die Vertragssprache handelt und die verwendete Sprache dem Empfänger nicht verständlich ist.[404] Welche Sprache dem Erklärungsempfänger verständlich sein muss, richtet sich nach den Umständen des Einzelfalles. Je verbreiteter eine Sprache ist, desto eher wird die Einbeziehung gelingen;[405] dafür ist die Verwendung des Englischen weder erforderlich[406] noch immer ausreichend.[407] Der Verwender muss die Verständlichkeit nachweisen; verbleibende Zweifel gehen zu seinen Lasten.[408] Verständlich ist der Erklärungsempfänger jedenfalls eine Sprache, derer ein von ihm eingesetzter Vertreter mächtig ist.[409] Trotz Unverständlichkeit sind auch solche AGB einbezogen, deren Geltung die unverständige Seite ausdrücklich und individualvertraglich akzeptiert hat.[410]

55 Die allgemeinen Regeln der Einbeziehung gelten auch für **Rechtswahlklauseln**:[411] Artt. 1 I lit. b), 6 weisen die Frage dem Regelungsbereich der Konvention zu; Artt. 8, 14 ff. kontrollieren daher die Einbeziehung.[412] Dies gilt im Grundsatz auch für die schlichte Abwahl der Konvention respektive die Wahl des Rechts eines Vertragsstaats unter Ausschluss der Konvention.[413] Die verbreitete kollisionsrechtliche Grundregel der Maßgeblichkeit des Zielrechts[414] findet hingegen keine Anwendung, weil es sich jeweils nicht um eine kollisionsrechtliche Rechtswahl handelt.[415] Erst Recht finden besondere kollisionsrechtliche Schutzmechanismen,[416] welche auf das Recht am Sitz des Erklärungsempfängers verweisen, keine Anwendung.[417] Zwei praktisch wenig relevante Ausnahmen davon sind der Fall, dass der Forumstaat kein Vertragsstaat der Konvention ist und dessen internationales Privatrecht Art. 1 I lit. b) nicht anerkennt und die Konstellation, dass der Forumstaat Vorbehaltsstaat nach Art. 95 ist und Art. 1 I lit. b) auch im Übrigen nicht anerkennt. Praktisch erheblich wichtiger ist die Wahl des Rechts eines Nichtvertragsstaats; in diesem Falle richtet sich die

---

[402] Int. Ct. Bulgarian CCI, 12.2.1998, CISG-online 317.
[403] OLG Düsseldorf, 21.4.2004, CISG-online 915; LG Heilbronn, 15.9.1997, CISG-online 562; LG Aachen, 22.6.2010, CISG-online 2162, Rn. 49; AG Kehl, 6.10.1995, CISG-online 162; *Witz/Salger/Lorenz/Witz*, Art. 8, Rn. 16; *Schwenzer/Hachem/Kee*, Rn. 12.18; vgl. AG Nordhorn, 14.6.1994, CISG-online 259 (*in casu* zweisprachige AGB ausreichend); OLG Linz, 8.8.2005, CISG-online 1087 (Verhandlungssprache ausreichend).
[404] OGH, 6.11.2008, CISG-online 1833; OLG Düsseldorf, 21.4.2004, CISG-online 915; LG Göttingen, 31.7.1997, CISG-online 564; vgl. OLG Stuttgart, 16.6.1987, IPRax 1988, 293 f.; OGH, 17.12.2003, CISG-online 828 und OGH, ÖJZ 2004, 837 (zum österreichischen Recht); zu undifferenziert *Piltz*, NJW 2005, 2126, 2128.
[405] S. OGH, 17.12.2003, CISG-online 828 („Deutsch nach Englisch und Französisch wohl auch … Weltsprache") und nachfolgend OLG Innsbruck, 1.2.2005, CISG-online 1130.
[406] Zu eng daher *Schwenzer/Mohs*, IHR 2006, 239, 241.
[407] Man denke nur an Verträge zwischen Partnern aus verschiedenen Nachfolgestaaten der früheren Sowjetunion, für die regelmäßig Russisch als AGB-Sprache ausreichen muss, während das Englische ggf. die Einbeziehung hindert.
[408] OLG Düsseldorf, 21.4.2004, CISG-online 915; LG Aachen, 22.6.2010, CISG-online 2161, Rn. 49.
[409] OGH, 17.12.2003, CISG-online 828; OLG Innsbruck, 1.2.2005, CISG-online 1130.
[410] S. Rn. 42.
[411] S. Rn 1.
[412] *Wolf/Horn/Lindacher/Lindacher*, Anh. zu § 2, Rn. 73; offengelassen von OLG Düsseldorf, 30.1.2004, CISG-online 821; offenbar übersehen von OLG Celle, 2.9.1998, CISG-online 506.
[413] HGer St. Gallen, 15.6.2010, CISG-online 2159; LG Aachen, 22.6.2010, CISG-online 2162.
[414] Vgl. Art. 8 I EuIPRÜ; Art. 31 I EGBGB.
[415] *Schlechtriem*, 50 Jahre BGH, S. 407, 410 f.; *Schmidt-Kessel*, NJW 2002, 3444 f.; i. E. ebenso *Ventsch/Kluth*, IHR 2003, 61.
[416] Vgl. Art. 8 II EuIPRÜ; Art. 31 II EGBGB.
[417] Offenbar nicht gesehen von LG Duisburg, 17.4.1996, CISG-online 186.

wirksame Einbeziehung nicht nach der Konvention, sondern das gewählte Zielrecht entscheidet über die Wirksamkeit der Rechtswahl.

Schwierigkeiten bereitet die Behandlung von **Gerichtsstands- und Schiedsklauseln**.[418] 56 Deren Geltungsvoraussetzungen liegen grundsätzlich außerhalb des Regelungsbereichs der Konvention.[419] Unsicherheit besteht freilich darüber, ob der Konsens über die betreffende Klausel und damit auch insbesondere ihre Einbeziehung zum Regelungsbereich der Konvention gehört[420] oder nicht.[421] Entscheidend für die Anwendung der Artt. 8, 14 ff. auf Gerichtsstands- und Schiedsklauseln spricht Art. 19 III:[422] Die Vorschrift erklärt Klauseln dieser Art sogar zum wesentlichen Vertragsinhalt und lässt den Vertragsschluss im Zweifel scheitern, wenn Differenzen über diesen Punkt bestehen. Die Konvention verdrängt insoweit sämtliche nationalen Einbeziehungsregeln; hingegen finden Sonderregeln über den Konsens, welche sich aus völkerrechtlichen Verträgen ergeben, nach Art. 90 vorrangig Anwendung.[423]

2. Überraschende Klauseln

Enthalten allgemeine Geschäftsbedingungen überraschende Klauseln, so werden diese 57 auch dann nicht Vertragsbestandteil, wenn die Einbeziehung im Übrigen glückt.[424] Insoweit darf nämlich der andere Teil den Willen des Erklärenden verkennen (Art. 8 I). Ferner entspricht die Klausel nicht demjenigen Vertragsinhalt, den eine vernünftige Person in den Schuhen des Vertragspartners angenommen hätte. Voraussetzung für die Nichteinbeziehung ist daher zunächst die Unkenntnis des Vertragspartners von der Klausel.[425] Außerdem muss diese Klausel für ihn – nach Inhalt, Sprache und äußerer Gestaltung des Vertrags – vernünftigerweise nicht zu erwarten gewesen sein. Diese zweite Schwelle ist recht hoch und wird umso weniger überschritten, je weiter verbreitet die verwandten Bedingungen sind.[426] Im Blick auf Art. 4 S. 2 lit. a) ist jeweils darauf zu achten, dass einschlägige Klauseln nur im Hinblick auf ihren Überraschungscharakter untersucht werden, weil nur dessen Beurteilung von den Artt. 8, 14 ff. erfasst wird.

3. Vorrang der Individualabrede

Die Konvention kennt den Vorrang der Individualabrede vor einbezogenen Geschäfts- 58 bedingungen.[427] Ausnahmsweise kommt es daher zu einer Hierarchie von Klauseln. Diese ergibt sich aus dem Gesamtzusammenhang des Vertrags[428] und aus der vorrangigen Beachtlichkeit des Parteiwillens, welchem die individuelle Vereinbarung – nach einer widerleglichen Vermutung – näher steht als die allgemeinen Geschäftsbedingungen.[429] Diese Vermutung gilt auch für mündliche Abreden.[430]

---

[418] Vgl. OLG Köln, 8.1.1997, CISG-online 217; *Wolf/Horn/Lindacher/Lindacher*, Anh. zu § 2, Rn. 81–124; ausführlich zu diesen Fragen *Rauscher*, FS Heldrich, 933 ff.
[419] *Schlechtriem*, Internationales UN-Kaufrecht, Rn. 58.
[420] So Trib. com. Nivelles (Belgien), 19.9.1995, CISG-online 366; LG Trier, 8.1.2004, CISG-online 910; offengelassen von OLG Düsseldorf, 30.1.2004, CISG-online 821.
[421] In diesem Sinne Cámara Nacional de Apelaciones en lo Comercial (Argentinien), 14.10.1993, CISG-online 87; *Schlechtriem*, 3. Aufl., Vor Artt. 14–24 Rn. 1.
[422] Wie hier jetzt *Mittmann*, IHR 2006, 103, 104.
[423] *Schlechtriem*, Internationales UN-Kaufrecht, Rn. 58.
[424] OLG Düsseldorf, 21.4.2004, CISG-online 915 (mit unklarer Grenzziehung zwischen Art. 8 und § 3 AGBG a. F.); *Junge*, 3. Aufl., Rn. 8a Fn. 24; *Schwenzer/Mohs*, IHR 2006, 239, 241; *Wolf/Horn/Lindacher/Lindacher*, Anh. zu § 2, Rn. 77. A. A. (Anwendung nationalen Rechts, da Gültigkeitsfrage) *Schlechtriem*, JZ 1988, 1037, 1040 Fn. 28; *Staudinger/Magnus*, Art. 4, Rn. 25. Vgl. Art. 2.20 PICC.
[425] Vgl. Comment 4 zu Art. 2.20 PICC.
[426] *Junge*, 3. Aufl., Rn. 9. Zu verschiedenen Kriterien s. *Schwenzer/Hachem/Kee*, Rn. 12.24.
[427] *Witz/Salger/Lorenz/Witz*, Art. 8, Rn. 14; *Wolf/Horn/Lindacher/Lindacher*, Anh. zu § 2, Rn. 77; *Schwenzer/Hachem/Kee*, Rn. 12.25. Vgl. Art. 2.21 PICC; Art. 5:104 PECL.
[428] S. oben Rn. 29.
[429] Comment zu Art. 2.21 PICC; Comment zu Art. 5:104 PECL.
[430] Comment zu Art. 5:104 PECL.

4. Auslegung allgemeiner Geschäftsbedingungen

59 Insgesamt richtet sich die Auslegung allgemeiner Geschäftsbedingungen nach den allgemeinen Regeln der Konvention.[431] Allerdings wird vielfach eine Berücksichtigung des individuellen Willens des Verwenders nach Art. 8 I für unangebracht gehalten.[432] Besondere Bedeutung entfaltet hingegen die Regel einer Auslegung *contra proferentem*;[433] allerdings gilt dies umso weniger, je weiter verbreitet die verwandten Bedingungen sind.[434] Bei besonders verbreiteten Standardbedingungen sind gerichtliche Entscheidungen zu bestimmten Klauseln bei der Auslegung mit zu berücksichtigen.[435] Insgesamt kommt Art. 8 damit in gewissem Umfang auch die Funktion einer inhaltlichen Kontrolle allgemeiner Geschäftsbedingungen zu; daher verdrängt die Vorschrift auch solche nationalen Regeln zur Auslegung allgemeiner Geschäftsbedingungen, die funktional der Inhaltskontrolle zuzuordnen sind.[436] Art. 4 S. 2 lit. a) findet insoweit wegen der anderweitigen Regelung in Art. 8 keine Anwendung. Bei der Ausgestaltung ihrer Inhaltskontrolle haben die Vertragsstaaten vielmehr ihre völkerrechtlichen Verpflichtungen zu beachten, die sich in der durch beide Vorschriften gezogenen Grenze konkretisieren: Im Anwendungsbereich der Konvention kann das Instrumentarium der Vertragsauslegung – jenseits des Art. 8 – nicht zum Zwecke der Inhaltskontrolle eingesetzt werden.

VIII. Behandlung im Verfahren

1. Rechts- oder Tatfrage

60 Für die prozessuale Behandlung der Vertragsauslegung hat vielerorts die Differenzierung nach Rechts- und Tatfragen Bedeutung: Danach kann sich etwa richten, ob die Entscheidung über die Auslegung dem Richter oder der *jury* zugewiesen ist.[437] Wichtig ist die Grenzziehung auch für die Zulässigkeit von auf Rechtsfragen beschränkten Rechtsmitteln wie Revision oder Kassationsbeschwerde:[438] So hat etwa der niederländische *Hoge Raad* eine berufungsgerichtliche Entscheidung zur Auslegung nur auf ihre *onbegrijpelijkheid* geprüft und diese verneint.[439] Das schweizerische Bundesgericht hat die Überprüfung von Feststellungen zum wirklichen Willen einer Partei abgelehnt, die Fragen des Erkennenmüssens dieses Willens und des Verständnisses eines vernünftigen Dritten hingegen als Rechtsfrage eingeordnet und damit der bundesgerichtlichen Kontrolle zugänglich gemacht; tatsächliche Feststellungen zu den nach Art. 8 III beachtlichen Umständen hat es für sich als bindend angesehen.[440] Dahinter steht letztlich die Frage nach der Reichweite der völkervertraglichen Bindung der Vertragsstaaten und konkret diejenige, ob die Konvention in die prozessualen Aufgabenteilungen der einzelnen Staaten eingreift. Obwohl dies grundsätzlich zu verneinen ist[441] und die Vertragsauslegung ganz überwiegend als Tatfrage eingeordnet

---

[431] *Wolf/Horn/Lindacher/Lindacher*, Anh. zu § 2, Rn. 79; *Brunner*, Art. 8, Rn. 9. Übersehen von HR, 28.1.2005, CISG-online 1002.
[432] *Witz/Salger/Lorenz/Witz*, Art. 8, Rn. 14; Comment 4 zu Art. 4.1 PICC.
[433] *Staudinger/Magnus*, Art. 8, Rn. 18. S. oben Rn. 47 f.
[434] *Junge*, 3. Aufl., Rn. 9.
[435] S. oben Rn. 40.
[436] A. A. *Teklote*, S. 156–159; *Wolf/Horn/Lindacher/Lindacher*, Anh. zu § 2, Rn. 79. Zur Verdrängung nationaler Transparenzgebote Rn. 47.
[437] *Calzaturificio Claudia v. Olivieri Footwear Ltd.*, U. S. Dist. Ct. (S. D. N. Y.), 6.4.1998, CISG-online 440 = 1998 WL 164, 824 (Auslegung als Frage des *trials*); *Honnold/Fletchner*, Art. 8, Rn. 110.
[438] OGH, 9.3.2000, CISG-online 573 (Bindung des OGH an die erstinstanzlichen Feststellungen hinsichtlich der Auslegung).
[439] HR, 7.11.1997, CISG-online 551.
[440] BGer, 5.4.2005, CISG-online 1012, E. 3.2, 3.4.
[441] *Honnold/Fletchner*, Art. 8, Rn. 110.

wird,⁴⁴² verlangt die effiziente Durchführung der Konvention immerhin die vollständige Berücksichtigung des von Art. 8 III vorgegebenen Auslegungsmaterials und deren hinreichende Überprüfbarkeit. Jedenfalls ist die Auslegung – auch fremdsprachiger Texte – selbst Aufgabe des Richters und nicht von Sachverständigen.⁴⁴³

2. Beweislast

Die von der Konvention in aller Regel mitbehandelte Beweislast⁴⁴⁴ trifft bei der Auslegung nach Art. 8 I den Erklärenden und zwar sowohl hinsichtlich seines Willens als auch dessen Unverkennbarkeit.⁴⁴⁵ Daran knüpfen sich in der Regel auch entsprechende Vortrags- oder Darlegungslasten.⁴⁴⁶ Hingegen bleibt es bei der Auslegung nach Abs. 2 und bezüglich der Umstände nach Abs. 3 bei der Grundregel, dass deren Beweis derjenigen Partei obliegt, der sie günstig sind.⁴⁴⁷ Die wertende Beurteilung der Erklärungen und ihrer Umstände ist hingegen Rechtsfrage und daher dem Beweis nicht zugänglich.⁴⁴⁸

61

---

⁴⁴² *Calzaturificio Claudia v. Olivieri Footwear Ltd.*, U. S. Dist. Ct. (S. D. N. Y.), 6.4.1998, CISG-online 440 = 1998 WL 164 824; OGH, 9.3.2000, CISG-online 573; BGH, 11.12.1996, CISG-online 225; HR, 7.11.1997, CISG-online 551.
⁴⁴³ Zur Aufgabenteilung s. OLG Stuttgart, 15.5.2006, CISG-online 1414.
⁴⁴⁴ Siehe etwa HGer Zürich, 10.2.1999, CISG-online 488; HGer Zürich, 25.6.2010, CISG-online 2161, Nr. 4.2.7; *Ferrari*, Art. 4 Rn. 11; *Antweiler*, S. 197 *et passim*; *Henninger*, 181 ff.
⁴⁴⁵ *Ferrari*, IHR 2003, 10, 15; *Staudinger/Magnus*, Art. 8, Rn. 31; *Witz/Salger/Lorenz/Witz*, Art. 8, Rn. 5. Nur letzteres spricht *T. M. Müller*, Beweislast, S. 53 an.
⁴⁴⁶ Etwa HGer Zürich, 25.6.2010, CISG-online 2161, Nr. 4.2.12 (fehlender Vortrag zum eigenen Erklärungswillen).
⁴⁴⁷ *T. M. Müller*, Beweislast, S. 50; *Staudinger/Magnus*, Art. 8, Rn. 31; der Sache nach auch OLG Koblenz, 31.1.1997, CISG-online 256; sowie KG Zug, 2.12.2004, CISG-online 1194, Nr. 3.1 (für Gepflogenheiten mit Bedeutung für die Auslegung). Zu undifferenziert hingegen HGer Aargau, 5.2.2008, CISG-online 1739, 6.2.1.3.1 (Beweislast für behaupteten Vertragsinhalt).
⁴⁴⁸ *T. M. Müller*, Beweislast, S. 48. Zur Aufgabenteilung zwischen Gericht und Sachverständigen in diesem Zusammenhang s. KG Zug, 21.6.2004, CISG-online 1213.

Art. 9 [Handelsbräuche und Gepflogenheiten]

(1) Die Parteien sind an die Gebräuche,* mit denen sie sich einverstanden erklärt haben, und an die Gepflogenheiten gebunden, die zwischen ihnen entstanden sind.

(2) Haben die Parteien nichts anderes vereinbart, so wird angenommen, daß sie sich in ihrem Vertrag oder bei seinem Abschluß stillschweigend auf Gebräuche* bezogen haben, die sie kannten oder kennen mußten und die im internationalen Handel den Parteien von Verträgen dieser Art in dem betreffenden Geschäftszweig weithin bekannt sind und von ihnen regelmäßig beachtet werden.

Art. 9

(1) The parties are bound by any usage to which they have agreed and by any practices which they have established between themselves.

(2) The parties are considered, unless otherwise agreed, to have impliedly made applicable to their contract or its formation a usage of which the parties knew or ought to have known and which in international trade is widely known to, and regularly observed by, parties to contracts of the type involved in the particular trade concerned.

Art. 9

1) Les parties sont liées par les usages auxquels elles ont consenti et par les habitudes qui se sont établies entre elles.

2) Sauf convention contraire des parties, celles-ci sont réputées s'être tacitement référées dans le contrat et pour sa formation à tout usage dont elles avaient connaissance ou auraient dû avoir connaissance et qui, dans le commerce international, est largement connu et régulièrement observé par les parties à des contrats de même type dans la branche commerciale considérée.

Übersicht

	Rn.
I. Regelungsgegenstand	1
1. Gebräuche, Gepflogenheiten und Bestimmung des Vertragsinhalts	1
2. Anwendbarkeit auf Vertragsschlussregeln	3
3. Konventionsfremde Materien	4
4. „Gültigkeit" von Gebräuchen	5
II. Gebräuche und Gepflogenheiten (Art. 9 I)	6
1. Einigung auf Gebräuche	6
2. Gepflogenheiten	8
III. Gebräuche des internationalen Handels (Art. 9 II)	11
1. Beachtlichkeit von internationalen Handelsbräuchen	11
a) Begriff des Handelsbrauchs	11
b) Beachtlichkeit internationaler Handelsbräuche und ihr Grund	12
2. Voraussetzungen der Beachtlichkeit	15
a) Bekanntheit und Beachtung	16
b) Internationalität	18
c) Kenntnis oder Kennenmüssen der Parteien	19
3. Ermittlung und prozessuale Behandlung	20
IV. Einzelfälle	21
1. Kaufmännisches Bestätigungsscheiben	22
2. Gerichtsstandsvereinbarungen und Schiedsklauseln	25
3. Behandlung von Regelwerken	26

Vorläufer und **Entwürfe**: Art. 2 I und 13 EAG; Art. 9 EKG; jeweils Art. 9 Genfer E 1976, Wiener E 1977, New Yorker E 1978.

---

* Schweiz: Handelsbräuche, Österreich: Bräuche.

I. Regelungsgegenstand[1]

1. Gebräuche, Gepflogenheiten und Bestimmung des Vertragsinhalts

Art. 9 stellt klar, dass die rechtlichen Beziehungen der Vertragsparteien auch durch 1 Gebräuche und Gepflogenheiten bestimmt werden. Insbesondere bewirkt die Vorschrift eine entsprechende Ergänzung des jeweiligen Vertragsinhalts.[2] In den Fällen des Abs. 1 erfolgt die Berücksichtigung von Gebräuchen und Gepflogenheiten auf der Basis des nach Art. 8 festzustellenden Parteiwillens.[3] Letztlich ist die Vorschrift insoweit nur deklaratorisch, weil sich ihre Regeln bereits aus Artt. 6, 8 ergeben.[4] Abs. 2 belegt hingegen die Möglichkeit der vom tatsächlichen Parteiwillen unabhängigen Ergänzung des Vertrags.[5] Bei *Honnold* findet sich eine der im anglo-amerikanischen Recht dafür typischen Formeln: „*it goes without saying*".[6] Gegenstand einer solchen Ergänzung nach Abs. 2 sind freilich nur solche internationalen Handelsbräuche, welche die Parteien zumindest kennen mussten.[7]

In Art. 9 geht es nicht um die Anerkennung von Rechtsnormen gar von Gewohnheits- 2 recht[8] oder gar einer *lex mercatoria*[9], sondern um die Ermittlung des Inhalts der betreffenden Parteivereinbarungen. Insbesondere Art. 9 II begründet daher keine normative Geltung der einschlägigen internationalen Handelsbräuche, sondern lediglich *terms implied by usage*.[10] Dementsprechend kommt es unter der Konvention auf eine kollisionsrechtliche Anerkennung von Gebräuchen nicht an.[11] Jenseits von Art. 4 S. 2 lit. a)[12] ist es folglich unschädlich, wenn Gebräuchen nach einer nationalen *lex causae* zwingendes Recht entgegenstünde:[13] Artt. 6, 9 verdrängen dieses im Anwendungsbereich der Konvention.

2. Anwendbarkeit auf Vertragsschlussregeln

Die von Art. 9 erfassten Regeln beschränken sich nicht auf den Vertragsinhalt.[14] Vielmehr 3 kommen auch solche Gebräuche und Gepflogenheiten zur Anwendung, welche sich auf den Abschluss von Verträgen beziehen.[15] Für Abs. 2 ergibt sich dies bereits aus dem Wortlaut der Vorschrift, und erst recht muss es für die Fälle des Abs. 1 gelten. Bei den vereinbarten Gebräuchen ist dies allerdings – abgesehen von Rahmenvereinbarungen – ohne Aufweichung der Anforderungen an die Einigung der Parteien schwer vorstellbar.[16] Der Rückgriff auf Gepflogenheiten aus früheren Verträgen steht hingegen ohne weiteres auch für den Vertragsschluss offen. Ein wichtiges Beispiel dafür ist – neben der Problematik des Vertragsschlusses durch Schweigen auf ein kaufmännisches Bestätigungsschreiben[17] – der Verzicht auf eine ausdrückliche Annahmeerklärung qua Gebrauch oder Gepflogenheit.

---

[1] Zur Vorgeschichte vgl. *Junge*, 3. Aufl., Rn. 1 sowie *Staudinger/Magnus*, Art. 9, Rn. 3–5.
[2] SchiedsG der Börse für landwirtschaftliche Produkte in Wien, 10.12.1997, CISG-online 351; *Junge*, 3. Aufl., Rn. 2; *Staudinger/Magnus*, Art. 9, Rn. 1. Zum Einfluss auf den Vertragsschluss s. Rn. 3.
[3] *Staudinger/Magnus*, Art. 9, Rn. 6. Ebenso für Gebräuche *Junge*, 3. Aufl., Art. 9, Rn. 8.
[4] Zweifelnd am Regelungsgehalt der Norm auch *Witz/Salger/Lorenz/Witz*, Art. 9, Rn. 1. Vgl. *Schlechtriem*, Internationales UN-Kaufrecht, Rn. 59.
[5] *Witz/Salger/Lorenz/Witz*, Art. 9, Rn. 1. Vgl. Art. 8 Rn. 26.
[6] *Honnold*, Rn. 112, 121; ähnlich *Bianca/Bonell/Farnsworth*, Art. 9, Anm. 2.1.2. Vgl. *Schmidt-Kessel*, ZVerglRW 96 (1997), 101, 126–129.
[7] Zu den Einzelheiten ab Rn. 11.
[8] So aber offenbar *Pamboukis*, 25 J. L. & Com. (2005-06), 107, 121 f. Bedenklich *Ferrari*, IHR 2006, 1, 16 („*other sources of law*").
[9] So *Kröll u. a./Perales Viscasillas*, Art. 9, Rn. 17.
[10] S. Rn. 12.
[11] Irreführend daher *Junge*, 3. Aufl., Rn. 5 und *Soergel/Lüderitz/Fenge*, Art. 9, Rn. 6.
[12] Zur Gültigkeit von Gebräuchen s. Rn. 5.
[13] Anders offenbar *Junge*, 3. Aufl., Rn. 5.
[14] Irreführend daher *Treibacher Industrie, A. G. v. Allegheny Technologies, Inc.*, U. S. Ct. App. (11th Cir.), 12.9.2006, CISG-online 1278 („*provides rules for interpreting the contracts*").
[15] So ausdrücklich jetzt auch *Kröll u. a./Perales Viscasillas*, Art. 9 Rn. 1.
[16] Insoweit richtig *Witz/Salger/Lorenz/Witz*, Art. 9, Rn. 5.
[17] S. unten Rn. 22–24.

3. Konventionsfremde Materien

4 Wie die Regeln über die Vertragsinhaltsbestimmung allgemein[18] findet Art. 9 auch auf solche Vertragsinhalte Anwendung, welche nicht zum Anwendungsbereich der Konvention gehören,[19] etwa bei der Frage, ob ein Aufrechnungsausschluss[20] oder ein Abtretungsverbot[21] Vertragsbestandteil geworden sind. Art. 9 beansprucht daher grundsätzlich auch Geltung für die Vereinbarung von Gerichtsstands- und Schiedsklauseln. Von Interesse für die Auslegung der Vorschrift und für die Ermittlung von Handelsbräuchen im Sinne von Abs. 2 ist freilich umgekehrt auch die Rechtsprechung zu Art. 17 I 2 lit. b), c) EuGVÜ/LugÜ und Art. 23 I 3 lit. b), c) EuGVO,[22] zumal diese Vorschriften die Regelung des Art. 9 bewusst für das Gemeinschaftsrecht rezipiert haben.[23] Ebenfalls zu berücksichtigen ist die Rechtsprechung zu Art. 1.8 PICC, welcher ebenfalls auf Art. 9 zurückgeht.

4. „Gültigkeit" von Gebräuchen

5 Unter der Gültigkeit von Gebräuchen, wie sie in Art. 4 S. 2 lit. a) ausdrücklich angesprochen wird, versteht die Konvention nicht etwa das tatsächliche Bestehen von Gebräuchen[24] oder das Vorliegen der Voraussetzungen nach Art. 9. Auch geht es bei Art. 4 nicht um Geltung in einem normativen Sinne,[25] weil sonst ein Widerspruch zu Art. 9 entstünde. Vielmehr meint die verkürzende Formulierung die Gültigkeit der durch Gebräuche in den Vertrag eingestellten Regelungen. Diese richtet sich nach den allgemeinen Regeln der Konvention, wegen Art. 4 S. 2 lit. a) also regelmäßig nach nationalem Recht.[26] Eine eigenständige abstrakte Inhaltskontrolle von Handelsbräuchen durch das Gebot der *reasonableness* kennt die Konvention nicht[27] und zwar auch nicht unter Art. 7 II.[28]

II. Gebräuche und Gepflogenheiten (Art. 9 I)

1. Einigung auf Gebräuche

6 Die Parteien sind nach Abs. 1 Alt. 1 an solche Gebräuche gebunden, mit welchen sie sich einverstanden erklärt haben. Der Frage, was genau unter dem Begriff des Gebrauchs im Sinne des Abs. 1 zu verstehen ist, kommt dabei letztlich keine Bedeutung zu, da nach Art. 8 kraft Vereinbarung ohnehin jede Regel gilt, auf welche die Parteien – mit hinreichender

---

[18] Art. 8 Rn. 5.
[19] *Kröll u. a./Perales Viscasillas*, Art. 9, Rn. 35; *Staudinger/Magnus*, Art. 9, Rn. 18. A. A. *Enderlein/Maskow/Strohbach*, Art. 9, Anm. 6.; *Honsell/Melis*, Art. 9, Rn. 2.
[20] OLG Dresden, 9.7.1998, CISG-online 559; *Staudinger/Magnus*, Art. 9, Rn. 18.
[21] *Staudinger/Magnus*, Art. 9, Rn. 18.
[22] So mit Recht *Witz/Salger/Lorenz/Witz*, Art. 9, Rn. 3. Vgl. etwa LG Duisburg, 17.4.1996, CISG-online 186; ZGer Basel-Stadt, 3.12.1997, CISG-online 346.
[23] S. *Rauscher*, FS Heldrich, 933, 952 f.
[24] Dies betont auch *Ferrari*, Art. 4 Rn. 5. Missverständlich hingegen OGH, 15.10.1998, CISG-online 380; OGH, 21.3.2000, CISG-online 641 (jeweils Geltung: nationales Recht; Art. 9: Anwendbarkeit); *Junge*, 3. Aufl., Rn. 5; *Soergel/Lüderitz/Fenge*, Art. 9, Rn. 6 (jeweils: „Anerkennung" durch nationales Recht) sowie *Staudinger/Magnus*, Art. 9, Rn. 20 („Geltungsvoraussetzungen").
[25] Auf diesem Unterschied zum herrschenden Verständnis von § 346 öHGB (Handelsbrauch mittelbar zum gesetzlichen Inhalt erhoben) beruhen die erwähnten missverständlichen Äußerungen des OGH, 15.10.1998, CISG-online 380; OGH, 21.3.2000, CISG-online 641.
[26] *Ferrari*, Art. 4 Rn. 6; *Bianca/Bonell/Farnsworth*, Art. 9, Anm. 3.4.; *Honnold/Flechtner*, Art. 9, Rn. 121; *Staudinger/Magnus*, Art. 9, Rn. 10. Anders *Kröll u. a./Perales Viscasillas*, Art. 9, Rn. 7 (allein durch Art. 9 bestimmt). Zur Behandlung von Willensmängeln s. unten Rn. 13.
[27] *Bianca/Bonell/Farnsworth*, Art. 9, Anm. 3.4.2.; *Enderlein/Maskow/Strohbach*, Art. 9, Anm. 7.; *Kröll u. a./Perales Viscasillas*, Art. 9, Rn. 26; *Schwenzer/Hachem/Kee*, Rn. 27.44; *Witz/Salger/Lorenz/Witz*, Art. 9, Rn. 13. Anders etwa für den Fall des unbekannten Handelsbrauchs das englische Recht: *Schmidt-Kessel*, ZVerglRW 96 (1997), 101, 128.
[28] Anders *Bianca/Bonell/Farnsworth*, Art. 9, Anm. 3.4.2.

Deutlichkeit[29] aber nicht notwendig ausdrücklich[30] – Bezug nehmen oder verweisen.[31] Die Vorschrift hat insoweit allein deklaratorische Funktion.[32] Hinter Abs. 1 Alt. 1 steht allerdings die verbreitete Praxis, dass die Parteien auf schriftlich aufgezeichnete Gebräuche verweisen,[33] wie etwa die Tegernseer Gebräuche für den Holzhandel[34] oder die österreichischen Holzhandelsusancen,[35] die Bedingungen der Bremer Baumwollbörse, die Usancen der Börse für landwirtschaftliche Produkte in Wien[36] oder auf Regelwerke wie die Incoterms®.[37] Die einseitige Ausarbeitung durch eine Partei wird freilich in aller Regel mit einem Handelsbrauch unvereinbar sein.[38] Abs. 1 Alt. 1 erfasst dabei auch rein nationale oder lokale Gebräuche[39] sowie solche anderer Branchen.[40]

Ob sich die Parteien i. S. v. Abs. 1 Alt. 1 über den Verweis auf einen Gebrauch geeinigt haben, richtet sich nach den allgemeinen Regeln (Artt. 8, 14 ff.).[41] Die Parteien müssen sich dafür auch tatsächlich geeinigt haben.[42] Der von *Witz* vertretenen Gegenauffassung, dass es darauf nicht ankommen könne, da sonst die Anwendbarkeit von Abs. 1 auf den Vertragsschluss leerliefe,[43] ist diese Konsequenz weitgehend einzuräumen. Sie beruht letztlich auf der durch Artt. 8, 14 ff. gesteuerten Herrschaft der Parteien über den Vertragsinhalt, welche durch Abs. 1 Alt. 1 nicht beschnitten werden soll. Das Fehlen einer Einigung schließt freilich eine großzügige Berücksichtigung des betreffenden Gebrauchs bei der Erklärungsauslegung nicht aus; das ergibt sich aus Art. 8 III, wo eine Einigung über den zu berücksichtigenden Gebrauch nicht verlangt wird. Für Abs. 1 Alt. 1 genügt jedenfalls eine stillschweigende Einigung.[44] Auch nach Vertragsschluss ist sie noch möglich, unterliegt dann aber zusätzlich den Regeln des Art. 29.[45] Der Vorrang eines solcherart vereinbarten Gebrauchs vor den Regeln der Konvention[46] ergibt sich ohne weiteres aus Art. 6.[47] Er kann bei Geschäftsbeziehungen aus der Zeit vor dem Inkrafttreten der Konvention auch ihre – materiellrechtliche – Abwahl beinhalten.[48]

7

---

[29] Vgl. Art. 8 Rn. 40.
[30] *Treibacher Industrie, A. G. v. Allegheny Technologies, Inc.*, U. S. Ct. App. (11th Cir.), 12.9.2006, CISG-online 1278; *Leisinger*, Fundamental Breach, S. 135.
[31] *Honsell/Melis*, Art. 9, Rn. 2; *Pamboukis*, 25 J. L. & Com. (2005-06), 107, 111; *Staudinger/Magnus*, Art. 9, Rn. 7; *Witz/Salger/Lorenz/Witz*, Art. 9, Rn. 4. Mit Nachdruck abweichend *Kröll u. a./Perales Viscasillas*, Art. 9, Rn. 16, die außerhalb des Begriffs Art. 6 anwenden will, ohne freilich praktische Folgen aufzuzeigen. Zur Einbeziehung von AGB s. Art. 8 Rn. 52–56.
[32] *Leisinger*, Fundamental Breach, S. 135.
[33] Vgl. *Bianca/Bonell/Farnsworth*, Art. 9, Anm. 2.1.2.
[34] Vgl. BGH, 23.4.1986, BB 1986, 1395 (zum deutschen Recht); OGH, 21.3.2000, CISG-online 641. Dazu auch *Kröll u. a./Perales Viscasillas*, Art. 9, Rn. 21.
[35] S. OGH, 21.3.2000, CISG-online 641.
[36] Dazu SchiedsG der Börse für landwirtschaftliche Produkte in Wien, 10.12.1997, CISG-online 351 sowie *Leisinger*, Fundamental Breach, S. 136.
[37] *Bamberger/Roth/Saenger*, Art. 9, Rn. 2; *Honnold/Flechtner*, Art. 9, Rn. 114; *Kröll u. a./Perales Viscasillas*, Art. 9, Rn. 15. Vgl. auch die Entscheidung des Xiamen Intermediate People's Court (VR China), 9.5.1994, UNILEX (abstract).
[38] *Schwenzer/Hachem/Kee*, Rn. 12.15.
[39] OGH, 15.10.1998, CISG-online 380; OGH, 21.3.2000, CISG-online 641; *Ferrari*, IHR 2006, 1, 17; *Junge*, 3. Aufl., Rn. 8; *Bianca/Bonell/Farnsworth*, Art. 9, Anm. 2.1.2.; *Bamberger/Roth/Saenger*, Art. 9, Rn. 2; *Kröll u. a./Perales Viscasillas*, Art. 9, Rn. 14; *Staudinger/Magnus*, Art. 9, Rn. 8.
[40] *Kröll u. a./Perales Viscasillas*, Art. 9, Rn. 14.
[41] *Honnold/Flechtner*, Art. 9, Rn. 114.
[42] *Pamboukis*, 25 J. L. & Com. (2005-06), 107, 112 f.; *Staudinger/Magnus*, Art. 9, Rn. 9.
[43] *Witz/Salger/Lorenz/Witz*, Art. 9, Rn. 5.
[44] *Bamberger/Roth/Saenger*, Art. 9, Rn. 2; *Bianca/Bonell/Farnsworth*, Art. 9, Anm. 2.1.2.; *Kröll u. a./Perales Viscasillas*, Art. 9, Rn. 14; *Soergel/Lüderitz/Fenge*, Art. 9, Rn. 3; *Staudinger/Magnus*, Art. 9, Rn. 9; *Witz/Salger/Lorenz/Witz*, Art. 9, Rn. 5.
[45] Unscharf *Ferrari*, EuLF 2002, 272, 273.
[46] Allgemeine Meinung: OGH, 15.10.1998, CISG-online 380; OGH, 21.3.2000, CISG-online 641; RB Brüssel, 24.3.2004, CISG-online 1568 = R. W. 2005, 629; *Junge*, 3. Aufl., Rn. 2; *Bamberger/Roth/Saenger*, Art. 9, Rn. 1; *Ferrari*, IHR 2006, 1, 17; *Staudinger/Magnus*, Art. 9, Rn. 2, 11; *Witz/Salger/Lorenz/Witz*, Art. 9, Rn. 1.
[47] *Junge*, 3. Aufl., Rn. 2; *Bamberger/Roth/Saenger*, Art. 9, Rn. 1; *Bianca/Bonell/Farnsworth*, Art. 9, Anm. 1.3.1.; *Kröll u. a./Perales Viscasillas*, Art. 9, Rn. 4; *Witz/Salger/Lorenz/Witz*, Art. 9, Rn. 1.
[48] RB Brüssel, 24.3.2004, CISG-online 1568 = R. W. 2005, 629.

Art. 9 8, 9   Teil I. Kapitel II. Allgemeine Bestimmungen

2. Gepflogenheiten

8   Nach Abs. 1 Alt. 2 sind die Parteien auch an Gepflogenheiten gebunden, welche sich zwischen ihnen entwickelt haben.[49] Dabei kommt es nur auf deren Beachtung zwischen den Parteien an;[50] eine weitere Verbreitung ist freilich unschädlich.[51] Gegenstand des Gebrauchs können auch AGB sein.[52] Erforderlich ist in jedem Falle eine gewisse Häufigkeit und Dauer,[53] also mehr als eine nur einmalige Wiederholung des betreffenden Umstandes durch die Parteien;[54] mehrfach ist auch die zweimalige Wiederholung für nicht ausreichend gehalten worden,[55] insbesondere wenn sich der Umstand nur bei für die Geschäftsbeziehung atypischen Konstellationen ergab.[56] Soweit Gepflogenheiten auch den Vertragsschlußprozess beeinflussen, kommt auch eine Bindung nach Abs. 1 Alt. 2 an Verhandlungsgepflogenheiten in Betracht.[57] Möglich ist aber eine Bindung durch ein auf Kulanz beruhendes Verhalten.[58] Jedenfalls können sich Gepflogenheiten nicht ohne vorangehenden Geschäftskontakt bilden.[59] Erforderlich ist zudem, dass die Übung das berechtigte Vertrauen begründet hat, dass auch in Zukunft entsprechend verfahren werde.[60] Dazu ist erforderlich, dass die Parteien ihr Verhalten als Übung erkennen.[61] Letztlich handelt es sich um eine Ausprägung des – in der Konvention auch an weiteren Stellen aufzufindenden – allgemeinen Verbots des *venire contra factum proprium*.[62] Beweisbelastet hinsichtlich der Voraussetzungen ist derjenige, der sich auf eine Gepflogenheit beruft.[63]

9   Die **Beendigung oder Änderung von Gepflogenheiten** ist möglich,[64] und zwar auch durch Änderung der zugrundeliegenden Verhältnisse.[65] Die Wirkung einer einseitigen Beendigung beschränkt sich allerdings auf künftige Verträge. Für laufende Verträge ist Einvernehmen erforderlich.[66]

---

[49] Vgl. die Beispiele Art. 8 Rn. 44.
[50] *Witz/Salger/Lorenz/Witz*, Art. 9, Rn. 17.
[51] *Junge*, 3. Aufl., Art. 9, Rn. 7; *Witz/Salger/Lorenz/Witz*, Art. 9, Rn. 17. Unscharf daher *Bamberger/Roth/Saenger*, Art. 9, Rn. 3; *Soergel/Lüderitz/Fenge*, Art. 9, Rn. 2; *Staudinger/Magnus*, Art. 9, Rn. 13.
[52] *Schwenzer/Hachem/Kee*, Rn. 12.14; s. Art. 8 Rn. 53.
[53] Stadtgericht Budapest, 24.3.1992, CISG-online 61; HGer Aargau, 26.9.1997, CISG-online 329; CA Grenoble, 13.9.1995, CISG-online 157 *("plusieurs mois")*; LG Frankenthal, 17.4.1997, CISG-online 479; *Bamberger/Roth/Saenger*, Art. 9, Rn. 3; *Ferrari*, IHR 2006, 1, 17; *Kröll u. a./Perales Viscasillas*, Art. 9, Rn. 11; *Schlechtriem*, Internationales UN-Kaufrecht, Rn. 60; *Staudinger/Magnus*, Art. 9, Rn. 13. Zu weitgehend *Pamboukis*, 25 J. L. & Com. (2005-06), 107, 116: *„various contracts"*.
[54] HGer Aargau, 26.9.1997, CISG-online 329; ZGer Basel-Stadt, 3.12.1997, CISG-online 346; *Schwenzer/Hachem/Kee*, Rn. 27.12; *Witz/Salger/Lorenz/Witz*, Art. 9, Rn. 17. Für eine bislang eher theoretische Ausnahme für wesentliche Vorgänge, deren Wiederholung zu erwarten ist *Schwenzer/Hachem/Kee*, Rn. 27.12.
[55] ZGer Basel-Stadt, 3.12.1997, CISG-online 346; AG Duisburg, 13.4.2000, CISG-online 659 (bei insgesamt längerer Geschäftsbeziehung); anders aber Hof 's-Hertogenbosch, 24.4.1996, CISG-online 321 (zwei kleinere vorangehende Geschäftskontakte genügen; allerdings differenziert das Gericht nicht zwischen Abs. 1 und Abs. 2); i. d. S. auch *Pamboukis*, 25 J. L. & Com. (2005-06), 107, 116. Vgl. OGH, 31.8.2005, CISG-online 1093 (vier vorherige Verträge; Gepflogenheit hinsichtlich der sonst verwandten AGB bejaht).
[56] OLG Düsseldorf, 30.1.2004, CISG-online 821.
[57] Etwas zu strikt daher *Kröll u. a./Perales Viscasillas*, Art. 9, Rn. 9.
[58] HGer Zürich, 24.10.2003, CISG-online 857.
[59] Anders offenbar OGH, 6.2.1996, CISG-online 224, der freilich nicht klar zwischen Gepflogenheiten und vereinbarten Gebräuchen unterscheidet.
[60] LG Frankenthal, 17.4.1997, CISG-online 479; *Pamboukis*, 25 J. L. & Com. (2005-06), 107, 113; *Soergel/Lüderitz/Fenge*, Art. 9, Rn. 2; *Staudinger/Magnus*, Art. 9, Rn. 13; ähnlich *Honnold/Flechtner*, Art. 9, Rn. 116.
[61] OGH, 6.2.1996, CISG-online 224. Skeptisch offenbar *Schwenzer/Hachem/Kee*, Rn. 27.15.
[62] HGer Zürich, 24.10.2003, CISG-online 857; *Junge*, 3. Aufl., Rn. 7; *Kröll u. a./Perales Viscasillas*, Art. 9, Rn. 12; *Witz/Salger/Lorenz/Witz*, Art. 9, Rn. 16.
[63] HGer Aargau, 26.9.1997, CISG-online 329; *Claudia v. Olivieri Footwear Ltd.*, U. S. Dist. Ct. (S. D. N. Y.), 6.4.1998, CISG-online 440; AG Duisburg, 13.4.2000, CISG-online 659; *Pamboukis*, 25 J. L. & Com. (2005-06), 107, 118.
[64] ICC, 8817/1997, UNILEX; *Kröll u. a./Perales Viscasillas*, Art. 9, Rn. 12; *Pamboukis*, 25 J. L. & Com. (2005-06), 107, 113 f.; *Schwenzer/Hachem/Kee*, Rn. 27.17, 27.24; *Staudinger/Magnus*, Art. 9, Rn. 14; *Witz/Salger/Lorenz/Witz*, Art. 9, Rn. 17.
[65] *Witz/Salger/Lorenz/Witz*, Art. 9, Rn. 17.
[66] ICC, 8817/1997, UNILEX; *Pamboukis*, 25 J. L. & Com. (2005-06), 107, 113 f.

Vertragsinhalte, welche sich aus Gepflogenheiten nach Abs. 1 Alt. 2 ergeben, haben **Vor-** 10
rang vor den Regeln der Konvention;[67] dies ergibt sich wiederum ohne weiteres aus
Art. 6;[68] das kann bei ständigen Geschäftsbeziehungen aus der Zeit vor dem Inkrafttreten
der Konvention auch deren – materiellrechtliche – Abwahl bedeuten.[69] Das Verhältnis zu
vereinbarten Gebräuchen (Abs. 1 Alt. 1), welche von den Gepflogenheiten abweichen, ist
eine Frage des durch Auslegung festzustellenden Parteiwillens;[70] eine dogmatisch abgeleitete
generelle Regel über das Rangverhältnis[71] wäre mit Artt. 6, 8 unvereinbar. Gegenüber
Handelsbräuchen nach Abs. 2 ist ein die Gepflogenheiten vorziehender Parteiwille hingegen
zu vermuten;[72] abstrakt klären lässt sich das Verhältnis jedoch nicht.

III. Gebräuche des internationalen Handels (Art. 9 II)

1. Beachtlichkeit von internationalen Handelsbräuchen

a) Begriff des Handelsbrauchs. Für die Vertragsergänzung nach Abs. 2 kommt es – 11
anders als für die Vereinbarung nach Abs. 1 Alt. 1 – darauf an, wie der Begriff des Handelsbrauchs aufzufassen ist. Richtigerweise ist er autonom, also ohne Rückgriff auf nationale
Vorverständnisse auszulegen.[73] Handelsbräuche sind danach Regeln des geschäftlichen Verkehrs, die von den beteiligten Handelskreisen in einer Branche oder an einem Marktort
üblicherweise eingehalten werden.[74] Eine subjektive Überzeugung von der Verbindlichkeit
wird hingegen nicht gefordert.[75] Die örtliche Geltung als Rechtsnorm schadet nicht,[76]
ebenso wenig die schriftliche Aufzeichnung als Handelsbrauch.[77] Bei der Anknüpfung der
geschuldeten Qualität der Ware an den gewöhnlichen Gebrauch in Art. 35 II lit. a) handelt
es sich um einen Spezialfall zu Art. 9 II,[78] weshalb es dort auf die weiteren Voraussetzungen
der Vertragsergänzung nicht ankommt; vielmehr ist Art. 35 II lit. a) in seinen Voraussetzungen unabhängig von der allgemeinen Regel.

b) Beachtlichkeit internationaler Handelsbräuche und ihr Grund. Art. 9 II begrün- 12
det – entgegen einer vor allem im romanischen Raum vertretenen Ansicht[79] – keine normative Geltung der betreffenden Handelsbräuche.[80] Vielmehr geht es um eine Vertragsergänzung

---

[67] Allgemeine Ansicht: OGH, 15.10.1998, CISG-online 380; OGH, 21.3.2000, CISG-online 641; RB Brüssel, 24.3.2004, CISG-online 1568 = R. W. 2005, 629; *Bamberger/Roth/Saenger*, Art. 9, Rn. 1; *Schwenzer/Hachem/Kee*, Rn. 27.16; *Witz/Salger/Lorenz/Witz*, Art. 9, Rn. 1.
[68] *Bamberger/Roth/Saenger*, Art. 9, Rn. 1; *Bianca/Bonell/Farnsworth*, Art. 9, Anm. 1.3.1.; *Witz/Salger/Lorenz/Witz*, Art. 9, Rn. 1.
[69] So jedenfalls Rechtsbank van KB Brüssel, 24.3.2004, CISG-online 1568 = R. W. 2005, 629.
[70] So treffend *Staudinger/Magnus*, Art. 9, Rn. 15.
[71] So etwa für den Vorrang von Gepflogenheiten: *Junge*, 3. Aufl., Rn. 7; für den Vorrang der Gebräuche: *Ferrari*, EuLF 2002, 272, 274; *ders.*, IHR 2006, 1, 17.
[72] Weitergehend HGer Zürich, 24.10.2003, CISG-online 857; *Ferrari*, IHR 2006, 1, 17; *Kröll u. a./Perales Viscasillas*, Art. 9, Rn. 4; *Schwenzer/Hachem/Kee*, Rn. 27.19; *Staudinger/Magnus*, Art. 9, Rn. 19 (jeweils genereller Vorrang der Gepflogenheit).
[73] *Kröll u. a./Perales Viscasillas*, Art. 9, Rn. 20; *Pamboukis*, 25 J. L. & Com. (2005-06), 107, 111; *Staudinger/Magnus*, Art. 9, Rn. 7; *Witz/Salger/Lorenz/Witz*, Art. 9, Rn. 4.
[74] *Bianca/Bonell/Farnsworth*, Art. 9, Anm. 3.2.; *Kröll u. a./Perales Viscasillas*, Art. 9, Rn. 20; *Staudinger/Magnus*, Art. 9, Rn. 7; vgl. Art. 13 I EAG.
[75] Anders *Kröll u. a./Perales Viscasillas*, Art. 9, Rn. 20.
[76] Vgl. *Bianca/Bonell/Farnsworth*, Art. 9, Anm. 3.2.; *Schlosser*, FS Medicus, S. 543, 550; *Staudinger/Magnus*, Art. 9, Rn. 27 (für das Bestätigungsschreiben); sowie *Honnold/Flechtner*, Art. 9, Rn. 121.
[77] *Bianca/Bonell/Farnsworth*, Art. 9, Anm. 3.2.; *Kröll u. a./Perales Viscasillas*, Art. 9, Rn. 21; *Soergel/Lüderitz/Fenge*, Art. 9, Rn. 2. S. die Beispiele oben Rn. 6.
[78] Vgl. ICC, 8213/1995, UNILEX; *Schwenzer*, Art. 35 Rn. 16.
[79] *Ferrari*, EuLF 2002, 272, 275; *Holl/Keßler*, RIW 1995, 457, 459; *Honsell/Melis*, Art. 9, Rn. 2; *Kröll u. a./Perales Viscasillas*, Art. 9, Rn. 24; *Pamboukis*, 25 J. L. & Com. (2005-06), 107, 108 f.; *Soergel/Lüderitz/Fenge*, Art. 9, Rn. 1. Siehe den Überblick bei *Muñoz*, Modern Law of Contracts and Sales in Latin America, Spain and Portugal, S. 252–259.
[80] *Honnold/Flechtner*, Art. 9, Rn. 117; *Schlechtriem*, Internationales UN-Kaufrecht, Rn. 61. Unklar *Staudinger/Magnus*, Art. 9, Rn. 1, 16. Die Rede von den „Geltungsvoraussetzungen" (*Staudinger/Magnus*, Art. 9,

auf der Basis eines hypothetischen Parteiwillens[81] respektive um die Annahme einer *implied term*, aus welcher sich eine Vereinbarung im Sinne von Abs. 1 ergibt.[82] Insoweit hat sich das anglo-amerikanische Verständnis bezüglich der Beachtlichkeit von Handelsbräuchen gegenüber dem auf dem Kontinent herrschenden durchgesetzt.[83] Abs. 2 begründet keine Fiktion des Parteiwillens[84] und schon gar nicht geht es um einen willensunabhängigen Vertragsbestandteil;[85] vielmehr entspricht die Vorschrift den durch Art. 8 II gesetzten Standards der Vertragsauslegung, welche die legitimen Parteierwartungen schützen.[86] Die positive Feststellung eines tatsächlichen Parteiwillens im Sinne des Handelsbrauchs ist daher entbehrlich.

13 Mit der Begründung des Rückgriffs auf Handelsbräuche ist die Sachfrage nach der Beachtlichkeit von Irrtümern hinsichtlich Bestand und Inhalt von Handelsbräuchen verbunden. Sie ist richtigerweise ohne Entscheidung des Streits um den Grund der Beachtlichkeit zu klären: Abs. 2 weist seinem Zweck nach das **Irrtumsrisiko** gerade dem sorgfaltswidrig Irrenden zu.[87] Die Anwendung von Art. 4 S. 2 lit. a) und der dadurch mögliche Rückgriff auf nationales Recht sind folglich ausgeschlossen. Weiter als Abs. 2 reicht der Schutz von Außenseitern nicht.

14 Bei Vorliegen der weiteren Voraussetzungen von Abs. 2 ist – auf der Basis von Art. 6 – der Vorrang der dadurch herangezogenen Handelsbräuche vor den Regeln der Konvention[88] selbstverständlich.[89] Im Übrigen ergibt er sich aus dem Regelungszweck von Art. 9[90] und gilt auch für dispositives nationales Recht, das zur Füllung externer oder interner Lücken der Konvention zur Anwendung gelangt.[91] Umgekehrt stellen Artt. 6, 9 II den Vorrang abweichender Parteivereinbarungen klar,[92] welcher auch für vom Handelsbrauch abweichende AGB[93] oder Gepflogenheiten[94] sowie für einen davon abweichenden Wortgebrauch der Parteien[95] gilt. Auch im Rahmen von Art. 9 II kommt daher die Vereinbarung einer *merger clause* in Betracht, die den Rückgriff auf Gebräuche und Gepflogenheiten

---

Rn. 20) deutet freilich auf ein normatives Verständnis hin. Rein deskriptiv und ohne eigene Stellungnahme *Junge*, 3. Aufl., Rn. 3.

[81] Vgl. *Honnold/Flechtner*, Art. 9, Rn. 117.

[82] In diesem Sinne auch *Bianca/Bonell/Farnsworth*, Art. 9, Anm. 2.2.1.; *Honsell/Melis*, Art. 9, Rn. 8; *Schlechtriem*, Internationales UN-Kaufrecht, Rn. 61; *Schwenzer/Hachem/Kee*, Rn. 27.28; *Witz/Salger/Lorenz/Witz*, Art. 9, Rn. 1.

[83] Vgl. *Schmidt-Kessel*, ZVerglRWiss 1997, 101, 126–129.

[84] So aber OGH, 15.10.1998, CISG-online 380; OGH, 21.3.2000, CISG-online 641; *Ferrari*, EuLF 2002, 272, 275; *Pamboukis*, 25 J. L. & Com. (2005-06), 107, 119; *Staudinger/Magnus*, Art. 9, Rn. 16. Unklar *Witz/Salger/Lorenz/Witz*, Art. 9, Rn. 6 („kommt … Fiktion gleich" und „widerlegbare Vermutung").

[85] So aber *Bamberger/Roth/Saenger*, Art. 9, Rn. 5; *Pamboukis*, 25 J. L. & Com. (2005-06), 107, 109.

[86] *Pamboukis*, 25 J. L. & Com. (2005-06), 107, 119.

[87] Im Ergebnis ebenso *Bianca/Bonell/Farnsworth*, Art. 9, Anm. 3.4.1.; *Witz/Salger/Lorenz/Witz*, Art. 9, Rn. 6.

[88] OLG Saarbrücken, 13.1.1993, CISG-online 83; OGH, 15.10.1998, CISG-online 380; OGH, 21.3.2000, CISG-online 641; *Junge*, 3. Aufl., Rn. 2; *Bamberger/Roth/Saenger*, Art. 9, Rn. 1; *Bianca/Bonell/Farnsworth*, Art. 9, Anm. 1.3.1.; *Enderlein/Maskow/Strohbach*, Art. 9, Anm. 1.2.; *Kröll u. a./Perales Viscasillas*, Art. 9, Rn. 4; *Pamboukis*, 25 J. L. & Com. (2005-06), 107, 109, 122; *Soergel/Lüderitz/Fenge*, Art. 9, Rn. 1; *Staudinger/Magnus*, Art. 9, Rn. 2, 17; *Witz/Salger/Lorenz/Witz*, Art. 9, Rn. 1.

[89] Wer der These von der Normativität der erfassten Handelsbräuche folgt, muss in Art. 9 hingegen die Anordnung eines normativen Vorrangs sehen. Widersprüchlich daher *Pamboukis*, 25 J. L. & Com. (2005-06), 107, 109.

[90] *Witz/Salger/Lorenz/Witz*, Art. 9, Rn. 1.

[91] LG Saarbrücken, 25.11.2002, CISG-online 718 (Vorrang vor gesetzlichen Zinssätzen des nationalen Rechts).

[92] Juzgado Nacional de Primera Instancia en lo Comercial No. 7, 20.5.1991, CISG-online 461; OLG Saarbrücken, 13.1.1993, CISG-online 83; *Honnold/Flechtner*, Art. 9, Rn. 121; *Kröll u. a./Perales Viscasillas*, Art. 9, Rn. 4, 19; *Pamboukis*, 25 J. L. & Com. (2005-06), 107, 119; *Soergel/Lüderitz/Fenge*, Art. 9, Rn. 1; *Staudinger/Magnus*, Art. 9, Rn. 17; *Witz/Salger/Lorenz/Witz*, Art. 9, Rn. 1.

[93] S. OLG Saarbrücken, 13.1.1993, CISG-online 83.

[94] So zurecht *Kröll u. a./Perales Viscasillas*, Art. 9, Rn. 5 (die freilich meine Überlegungen zu Kollision von Handelsbrauch und *merger clause* im gegenteiligen Sinne missversteht).

[95] *Treibacher Industrie, A. G. v. Allegheny Technologies, Inc.*, U. S. Ct. App. (11th Cir.), 12.9.2006, CISG-online 1278.

ausschließt;[96] allerdings wird dies nicht die regelmäßige Bedeutung einer solchen Klausel sein;[97] vielmehr wird es regelmäßig zusätzlicher Hinweise in der Klausel bedürfen.[98] Die Behandlung einer Kollision einer solchen Klausel mit einem Einvernehmen nach Art. 9 I lässt sich hingegen nur für den Einzelfall durch Auslegung klären. Eine Rechtswahlklausel als solche ist hingegen keine anderweitige Vereinbarung, die einen Handelsbrauch zu überspielen geeignet ist; nur wenn und soweit die Rechtswahl zur Unanwendbarkeit der Konvention insgesamt führt, wird ein nach Art. 9 I beachtlicher Handelsbrauch überspielt.

2. Voraussetzungen der Beachtlichkeit

Anders als bei ausdrücklichem Verweis nach Abs. 1 Alt. 1 auf ganze Regelwerke, erfasst Abs. 2 gewöhnlich nur einzelne Regeln. Für die richtige Anwendung der Vorschrift ist es daher wichtig, grundsätzlich für jede angesprochene Regel einzeln zu prüfen, ob die Voraussetzungen vorliegen. Die Schwelle für die Berücksichtigung von Regelwerken und entsprechenden Aufzeichnungen von Gebräuchen ist hingegen sehr viel höher, weil die Voraussetzungen von Abs. 2 für sämtliche enthaltenen Regeln vorliegen müssen.[99] Diese Voraussetzungen müssen auch bereits bei Vertragsschluss vorliegen; eine nachträgliche Vertragsänderung durch einen entstehenden Handelsbrauch[100] kann nur durch Vertragsänderung, also unter den Voraussetzungen von Art. 29, erfolgen, soweit nicht ausnahmsweise ein auch nachträgliche Änderungen von Handelsbräuchen umfassender Parteiwille feststellbar ist; letzteres mag etwa bei sich ändernden Ortsbräuchen eines internationalen Containerterminals der Fall sein können. Die in Art. 9 II genannten Voraussetzungen sind abschließend; insbesondere ist nicht zusätzlich erforderlich, dass der betreffende Handelsbrauch vernünftig (*„reasonable"*) ist;[101] eine – über dieses Erfordernis üblicherweise organisierte – Inhaltskontrolle findet vielmehr allenfalls nach nationalem Recht statt.[102]

a) Bekanntheit und Beachtung. Art. 9 II setzt voraus, dass die betreffende Regel Parteien, welche an gleichartigen Verträgen regelmäßig beteiligt sind, weitgehend bekannt ist und von ihnen eingehalten wird.[103] Universelle Bekanntheit ist nicht erforderlich.[104] Soweit es sich nicht ausnahmsweise um einen universellen Handelsbrauch handelt, muss diese Voraussetzung gerade für den betroffenen Handelszweig erfüllt sein.[105] Diese Abhängigkeit von der jeweiligen Branche ergibt sich bereits aus dem Zweck der Regelung, nämlich die Anwendbarkeit der von der Praxis entwickelten spezifischen Regeln zu sichern.[106] Sie macht vielfache Differenzierungen in sachlicher, persönlicher und räumlicher Hinsicht erforderlich.[107] In der betreffenden Branche muss der Handelsbrauch der Mehrheit der einschlägigen Verkehrsteilnehmer bekannt und von ihr beachtet sein;[108] es darf keine

---

[96] CISG-AC, Op. 3 (*Hyland*); *Kröll u. a./Perales Viscasillas*, Art. 9, Rn. 19; *Witz/Salger/Lorenz/Witz*, Art. 9, Rn. 19. Zu *merger clauses* s. Art. 8, Rn. 35.
[97] CISG-AC, Op. 3 (*Hyland*) Comment 4.7; *Kröll u. a./Perales Viscasillas*, Art. 9, Rn. 19.
[98] Vgl. *Kröll u. a./Perales Viscasillas*, Art. 9, Rn. 19 (besonders angesprochene Gebräuche oder Hinweis auf Art. 9).
[99] Zur teilweise problematischen Entscheidungspraxis im Hinblick auf die Incoterms® und die PICC s. Rn. 26.
[100] In Ansätzen etwa RB Tongeren, 25.1.2005, CISG-online 1106.
[101] *Schwenzer/Hachem/Kee*, Rn. 27.44.
[102] S. Rn. 5.
[103] *Schlechtriem*, Internationales UN-Kaufrecht, Rn. 61; *Staudinger/Magnus*, Art. 9, Rn. 21 f.
[104] *Ferrari*, IHR 2006, 1, 17.
[105] OGH, 6.2.1996, CISG-online 224 (Mineralölbranche); OGH, 21.3.2000, CISG-online 641 (Holzhandel); *Staudinger/Magnus*, Art. 9, Rn. 22; *Witz/Salger/Lorenz/Witz*, Art. 9, Rn. 8; der Sache nach auch Int. Ct. Russian CCI, 16.2.2004, CISG-online 1181; entsprechend für Art. 23 EuGVO: EuGH, 20.2.1997, Slg. 1997, I-911 Nr. 23 (*MSG*) (Kiestransporte auf dem Oberrhein); EuGH, 16.3.1999, Slg. 1999, I-1597, Nr. 25 (*Castelletti*) (Gerichtsstandsklausel auf der Rückseite des Konnossements); *Kropholler*, EUZPR, Art. 23, Rn. 55.
[106] *Honnold/Flechtner*, Art. 9, Rn. 112; vgl. *Staudinger/Magnus*, Art. 9, Rn. 2.
[107] *Junge*, 3. Aufl., Rn. 4, 10; *Kröll u. a./Perales Viscasillas*, Art. 9, Rn. 27; *Pamboukis*, 25 J. L. & Com. (2005-06), 107, 120; *Witz/Salger/Lorenz/Witz*, Art. 9, Rn. 8.
[108] OGH, 15.10.1998, CISG-online 380; OGH, 21.3.2000, CISG-online 641; *Staudinger/Magnus*, Art. 9, Rn. 22.

erhebliche Gruppe von „Nichtkennern" geben.[109] Gelegentliche Abweichungen schaden allerdings nicht („weithin") und können sogar als Beleg für den Handelsbrauch dienen, wenn die Parteien die Notwendigkeit einer ausdrücklichen Vereinbarung sehen.[110] Auf eine langdauernde Übung kommt es nicht an.[111] Neu entstehende Handelsbräuche etablieren sich freilich nur langsam; allein der Umstand, dass bereits mehrere Vertragspartner eines Lieferanten wegen der Erhöhung der Rohstoffpreise einer nachträglichen Preiserhöhung zugestimmt haben, begründet noch keinen Handelsbrauch.[112] Branchen, die ohnehin grenzüberschreitend organisiert sind – wie die Rohstoffmärkte[113] – weisen allerdings schon wegen dieser Organisation regelmäßig eine große Zahl von Handelsbräuchen auf. Kenntnis von der rechtlichen Bedeutung des Handelsbrauchs verlangt Art. 9 nicht.[114] Beruht die überwiegende Einhaltung eines Handelsbrauchs tatsächlich auf den Vorgaben eines Monopolisten, ist dieses ordnungspolitische Problem nicht mit den Maßstäben des Art. 7 I zu lösen.[115] Richtigerweise geht es insoweit nicht um den tatsächlichen Bestand des Handelsbrauchs, sondern um eine Gültigkeitsfrage i. S. v. Art. 4 S. 2 lit. a),[116] welche nach den Regeln des Wettbewerbsrechts zu entscheiden ist.[117]

17 Mit diesen Kriterien ist auch der gelegentlich diskutierte Fall **kollidierender Handelsbräuche**[118] zu bewältigen: Unterschiedliche Praktiken innerhalb derselben Branche und in demselben räumlichen Zusammenhang schließen die hinreichende Beachtung des Handelsbrauchs und damit eine Anwendung von Abs. 2 aus, soweit sich keine deutlichen Mehrheiten feststellen lassen.[119] Andere Lösungen im Sinne von Rangentscheidungen sind nur auf Basis eines – unzutreffenden[120] – normativen Verständnisses von Handelsbräuchen unter Art. 9 II denkbar.[121]

18 **b) Internationalität.** Das Erfordernis der Internationalität schließt solche Handelsbräuche aus dem Anwendungsbereich von Abs. 2 aus, welche sich nur für Inlandsgeschäfte entwickelt haben.[122] Eine weltweite Verbreitung ist jedoch nicht erforderlich.[123] Vielmehr können lokale Handelsbräuche und Platzusancen genügen.[124] Allerdings sind in diesem Falle der erforderliche Bezug auf internationalen Handel[125] sowie die hinreichende Bekanntheit

---

[109] *Witz/Salger/Lorenz/Witz*, Art. 9, Rn. 8.
[110] Wie hier jetzt auch *Schwenzer/Hachem/Kee*, Rn. 27.32.
[111] *Staudinger/Magnus*, Art. 9, Rn. 23.
[112] S. RB Tongeren, 25.1.2005, CISG-online 1106. Zum maßgebenden Zeitpunkt s. Rn. 15.
[113] Vgl. die Darstellung bei *Leisinger*, Fundamental Breach, S. 137 ff.
[114] *Schlosser*, FS Medicus, S. 543, 552.
[115] So aber *Witz/Salger/Lorenz/Witz*, Art. 9, Rn. 13.
[116] S. o. Rn. 5.
[117] Vgl. etwa BGH, 21.12.1973, BGHZ 62, 71, 82. In der Europäischen Gemeinschaft sind insbesondere Artt. 101 f. AEUV zu beachten, zumal einer Vernachlässigung der Anerkennungsfähigkeit von staatlichen schiedsgerichtlichen Entscheidungen entgegenstehen kann: EuGH, 1.6.1999, Slg. 1999, I-3055 *(Eco Swiss China Time Ltd v. Benetton International NV)*.
[118] *Kröll u. a./Perales Viscasillas*, Art. 9, Rn. 32; *Pamboukis*, 25 J. L. & Com. (2005-06), 107, 121 f.; *Staudinger/Magnus*, Art. 9, Rn. 19.
[119] *Junge*, 3. Aufl., Rn. 12; *Bamberger/Roth/Saenger*, Art. 9, Rn. 5; im Ergebnis ebenso *Staudinger/Magnus*, Art. 9, Rn. 19.
[120] *Kröll u. a./Perales Viscasillas*, Art. 9, Rn. 30; S. oben Rn. 2.
[121] So etwa konsequent *Kröll u. a./Perales Viscasillas*, Art. 9, Rn. 32.
[122] OLG Graz, 9.11.1995, CISG-online 308; *Schlechtriem*, Internationales UN-Kaufrecht, Rn. 61; *Staudinger/Magnus*, Art. 9, Rn. 21; *Witz/Salger/Lorenz/Witz*, Art. 9, Rn. 8.
[123] *Honnold/Flechtner*, Art. 9, Rn. 120.1; *Junge*, 3. Aufl., Rn. 9; *Kröll u. a./Perales Viscasillas*, Art. 9, Rn. 27; *Staudinger/Magnus*, Art. 9, Rn. 22.
[124] OLG Graz, 9.11.1995, CISG-online 308; *Honnold/Flechtner*, Art. 9, Rn. 120.1; *Bianca/Bonell/Farnsworth*, Art. 9, Anm. 2.2.3.; *Kröll/Hennecke*, RabelsZ 67 (2003), 448, 472; *Kröll u. a./Perales Viscasillas*, Art. 9, Rn. 27; *Schwenzer/Hachem/Kee*, Rn. 27.34; *Staudinger/Magnus*, Art. 9, Rn. 22; *Witz/Salger/Lorenz/Witz*, Art. 9, Rn. 9. Entsprechend *Kropholler*, EUZPR, Art. 23, Rn. 55. Zu eng daher LG Frankfurt a. M., 6.7.1994, CISG-online 257.
[125] OLG Graz, 9.11.1995, CISG-online 308; *Kröll u. a./Perales Viscasillas*, Art. 9, Rn. 27; *Schwenzer/Hachem/Kee*, Rn. 27.34; *Soergel/Lüderitz/Fenge*, Art. 9, Rn. 4; *Staudinger/Magnus*, Art. 9, Rn. 22; *Witz/Salger/Lorenz/Witz*, Art. 9, Rn. 9. Problematisch hingegen Hof 's-Hertogenbosch, 24.4.1996, CISG-online 321 (Anwen-

und Beachtung[126] besonders kritisch zu prüfen. Zu weit geht daher die Auffassung,[127] Abs. 2 könne auch rein interne Gebräuche zur Anwendung bringen, wenn der auswärtige Teil sich nur hinreichend intensiv in dem betreffenden Staat betätige. In solchen Fällen können Gebräuche nur nach den Regeln der Artt. 8 III, 9 I beachtlich sein. Erforderlich ist schließlich in jedem Falle ein hinreichender Bezug des Geschäfts zum örtlichen oder sachlichen Verbreitungsbereich des Handelsbrauchs; der Bezug nur einer Partei zum Verbreitungsbereich genügt nicht.[128]

c) Kenntnis oder Kennenmüssen der Parteien. Abs. 2 setzt für die Vertragsergänzung 19 voraus, dass der Handelsbrauch den Parteien – richtigerweise im Zeitpunkt des Vertragsschlusses – bekannt ist oder bekannt sein muss. Anders als nach Art. 8 I ist aber kein gesteigerter Sorgfaltsverstoß erforderlich.[129] Das Erfordernis hat daher auch nur geringe praktische Bedeutung, zumal sich aus der objektiven Bekanntheit regelmäßig der Sorgfaltsverstoß ableiten lässt.[130] Es dient lediglich dazu, sicherzustellen, dass zwischen dem Handelsbrauch und den Parteien eine hinreichende Verbindung besteht;[131] eine Bindung einer Partei an ihr gänzlich unbekannte Handelsbräuche ist daher möglich.[132] Die Kriterien für die Sorgfalt der Parteien bei ihrer Selbstvergewisserung sind nicht eben zahlreich: Das Kennenmüssen ergibt sich regelmäßig aus der Ansässigkeit der betreffenden Partei im (örtlichen) Verbreitungsbereich.[133] Es genügt freilich auch die regelmäßige Betätigung im betreffenden (örtlichen oder sachlichen) Verbreitungsbereich.[134]

3. Ermittlung und prozessuale Behandlung

Das Bestehen eines Handelsbrauchs ist Tatfrage,[135] ebenso die Bestimmung seines genauen 20 Inhalts. Die Konvention verlangt keine Beachtung von Amts wegen,[136] schließt eine solche aber auch nicht aus. Nach einer verbreiteten Auffassung soll Art. 7 I und nicht Art. 8 Maßstab der Auslegung von Handelsbräuchen sein.[137] In der Sache führt dieser – letztlich auf einem normativen Verständnis beruhende – Hinweis jedoch in die Irre: Gleich wie Handelsbräuche auszulegen sind, sie können nach Art. 9 II nur insoweit Vertragsinhalt werden, als die Parteien sie zumindest kennen mussten. Damit entspricht der Maßstab demjenigen des Art. 8 II.[138] Erst recht findet unter der Konvention keine auf Art. 7 I gestützte Inhaltskontrolle des Handelsbrauchs statt.[139] Maßgebender Inhalt des Handels-

---

dung des deutschen Garnkontrakts gegenüber einem Niederländer), wenn die Entscheidung auf Art. 9 II zu beziehen ist.

[126] *Kröll u. a./Perales Viscasillas,* Art. 9, Rn. 27; *Staudinger/Magnus,* Art. 9, Rn. 22; *Witz/Salger/Lorenz/Witz,* Art. 9, Rn. 9.

[127] OLG Graz, 9.11.1995, CISG-online 308; der Entscheidung folgend *Kröll u. a./Perales Viscasillas,* Art. 9, Rn. 27; *Pamboukis,* 25 J. L. & Com. (2005-06), 107, 120 f.

[128] OLG Frankfurt a. M., 5.7.1995, CISG-online 257; vgl. *Staudinger/Magnus,* Art. 9, Rn. 28.

[129] *Staudinger/Magnus,* Art. 9, Rn. 30; *Witz/Salger/Lorenz/Witz,* Art. 9, Rn. 7.

[130] *Leisinger,* Fundamental Breach, S. 139; *Soergel/Lüderitz/Fenge,* Art. 9, Rn. 5.

[131] *Pamboukis,* 25 J. L. & Com. (2005-06), 107, 119.

[132] *Kröll u. a./Perales Viscasillas,* Art. 9, Rn. 25.

[133] ZGer Basel-Stadt, 21.12.1992, CISG-online 55; OGH, 15.10.1998, CISG-online 380; OGH, 21.3.2000, CISG-online 641; *Staudinger/Magnus,* Art. 9, Rn. 25. Nicht etwa ist die Ansässigkeit Anwendungsvoraussetzung, richtig: *Kröll u. a./Perales Viscasillas,* Art. 9, Rn. 26.

[134] OGH, 15.10.1998, CISG-online 380; OGH, 21.3.2000, CISG-online 641; *Staudinger/Magnus,* Art. 9, Rn. 25. Vgl. auch Hof 's-Hertogenbosch, 24.4.1996, CISG-online 321.

[135] OGH, 15.10.1998, CISG-online 380; OGH, 21.3.2000, CISG-online 641; OGH, 27.2.2003, CISG-online 794; *Junge,* 3. Aufl., Rn. 13; *Bamberger/Roth/Saenger,* Art. 9, Rn. 6; *Bianca/Bonell/Farnsworth,* Art. 9, Anm. 3.3.; *T. M. Müller,* Beweislast, S. 53; *Kröll u. a./Perales Viscasillas,* Art. 9, Rn. 34. Entsprechend für Art. 23 EuGVO: EuGH, 20.2.1997, Slg. 1997, I-911 Nr. 23 *(MSG);* EuGH, 16.3.1999, Slg. 1999, I-1597, Nr. 25 *(Castelletti);* Kropholler, EUZPR, Art. 23, Rn. 55.

[136] Insoweit zutreffend *Bianca/Bonell/Farnsworth,* Art. 9, Anm. 3.3.; *Kröll u. a./Perales Viscasillas,* Art. 9, Rn. 33.

[137] *Junge,* 3. Aufl., Rn. 6; *Schlechtriem,* Internationales UN-Kaufrecht, Rn. 63; *Witz/Salger/Lorenz/Witz,* Art. 9, Rn. 12.

[138] S. Art. 8 Rn. 17, 19.

[139] S. schon oben Rn. 5.

brauchs ist derjenige, welchen die beteiligten Handelskreise ihm üblicherweise beilegen.[140] Er ist gegebenenfalls unter Heranziehung bisheriger Rechtsprechung zu ermitteln.[141] Weil es sich dabei lediglich um die Ermittlung von Tatsachen handelt, sind auch Entscheidungen aus Nichtvertragsstaaten zu berücksichtigen.[142] Die Feststellung eines Handelsbrauchs ist folgerichtig in aller Regel nicht mit solchen Rechtsmitteln angreifbar, welche auf eine Rechtsprüfung beschränkt sind.[143] Beweisbelastet für die tatsächlichen Voraussetzungen von Abs. 2 ist wiederum derjenige, der sich auf einen streitigen Handelsbrauch beruft, und zwar sowohl hinsichtlich des Bestehens, als auch hinsichtlich der Umstände, aus denen sich das Kennenmüssen ergibt.[144] Vom Handelsbrauch abweichende Vereinbarungen muss wiederum derjenige beweisen, der sich darauf stützen will.[145] Die zulässigen Beweismittel ergeben sich aus dem nationalen Verfahrensrecht;[146] dabei ist allerdings darauf zu achten, dass Art. 9 nicht durch große Restriktionen in diesem Bereich – etwa Beschränkungen auf durch eine Handelskammer festgestellte Bräuche – die praktische Wirksamkeit genommen wird.

IV. Einzelfälle

21 Für die einzelnen Handelsbräuche ist grundsätzlich auf die einzelnen Kommentierungen zu den betreffenden Sachfragen zu verweisen. So haben Gerichte etwa in der Einigung über die Begebung eines Wechsels eine zinslose Stundung des Kaufpreises gesehen[147] oder die Prime rate der Federal Reserve Bank New York[148] oder schlicht den Satz von 12%[149] als Verzinsung für Dollarschulden zum internationalen Handelsbrauch erklärt.[150] Im Bereich des Geldrechts wird außerdem vielfach eine § 244 BGB entsprechende Ersetzungsbefugnis hinsichtlich der Währung am Zahlungsort in Betracht kommen.[151] Für viele Bereiche werden ferner die Regeln der EAN-Identsysteme[152] sowie die durch Normungsorganisationen entwickelten technischen Standards als Handelsbräuche zur Anwendung gelangen.[153] In anderen Fällen sind Auswirkungen auf die Vertragssprache[154] oder die Modifizierung des Mechanismus von Art. 39 durch das Recht des Verkäufers angenommen worden, bei der Untersuchung durch den Käufer anwesend zu sein.[155] Internationale Handelsbräuche können ferner die Pflicht zur Anzeige eines Deckungsgeschäfts i. S. v. Art. 75 begründen[156] sowie die Standards der Schadensminderung nach Art. 77 determinieren.[157] Die Vertrags-

---

[140] *Staudinger/Magnus*, Art. 9, Rn. 31.
[141] *Staudinger/Magnus*, Art. 9, Rn. 31.
[142] *Staudinger/Magnus*, Art. 9, Rn. 31. Zu eng daher *Herber/Czerwenka*, Art. 9, Rn. 13.
[143] Vgl. AppGer Helsinki, 29.1.1998, UNILEX (ohne Angriff auf die Feststellung des erstinstanzlichen Gerichts keine Prüfung); OGH, 15.10.1998, CISG-online 380 (Berufungsgericht muss Handelsbrauch ermitteln). Eine Ausnahme kann sich freilich ergeben, wenn ein internationaler Handelsbrauch nach der *lex fori* zugleich als Rechtsnorm gilt. Zwar verdrängt die Konvention die nationale *lex fori*. Die Rechtsmittelfähigkeit bestimmter Fragen wird davon jedoch nicht tangiert. Den Vertragsstaaten steht es frei, Revision oder Kassation gerade in solchen Fällen zuzulassen, in denen aus Sicht von Art. 9 II nur Tatfragen zu klären sind.
[144] ZGer Basel-Stadt, 3.12.1997, CISG-online 346; OLG Dresden, 9.7.1998, CISG-online 559; *Bamberger/Roth/Saenger*, Art. 9, Rn. 6; *Lurger*, IHR 2005, 177, 181; *T. M. Müller*, Beweislast, S. 54; *Pamboukis*, 25 J. L. & Com. (2005-06), 107, 124 f.; *Schlechtriem*, Internationales UN-Kaufrecht, Rn. 63; *Staudinger/Magnus*, Art. 9, Rn. 33; *Witz/Salger/Lorenz/Witz*, Art. 9, Rn. 11.
[145] *T. M. Müller*, Beweislast, S. 54.
[146] OGH, 27.2.2003, CISG-online 794 (alle Beweismittel der öZPO).
[147] LG Hamburg, 26.9.1990, CISG-online 21; Juzgado Nacional de Primera Instancia en lo Comercial No. 7, 20.5.1991, CISG-online 461. Vgl. *Witz/Salger/Lorenz/Witz*, Art. 9, Rn. 8, Fn. 31.
[148] Juzgado Nacional de Primera Instancia en lo Comercial No. 10, 23.10.1991, CISG-online 460.
[149] Juzgado Nacional de Primera Instancia en lo Comercial No. 10, 6.10.1994, CISG-online 378.
[150] S. *Bacher*, Art. 78 Rn. 38.
[151] *Prütting/Wegen/Weinreich/Schmidt-Kessel*, § 244, Rn. 17.
[152] S. www.gs1-germany.de.
[153] S. *Schulze/Zuleeg/Schmidt-Kessel*, § 19, Rn. 145.
[154] Vgl. OLG Hamm, 8.2.1995, CISG-online 141 sowie Art. 8 Rn. 41 f.
[155] Vgl. AppGer Helsinki, 29.1.1998, UNILEX (Stahlhandel); vgl. *Schwenzer*, Art. 38 Rn. 31, Art. 39 Rn. 34 f.
[156] *Stoll/Gruber*, 4. Aufl., Art. 75 Rn. 3.
[157] *Schlechtriem*, Internationales UN-Kaufrecht, Rn. 315.

gemäßheit von Ware kann durch auf bestimmten öffentlich-rechtlichen Vorgaben beruhende Handelsbräuche bestimmt sein.[158] Hingegen ist die Annahme eines Handelsbrauchs abgelehnt worden, wonach im Importhandel die bargeldlose Zahlung mittels Banküberweisung auf das Konto des Verkäufers üblich sei.[159] Von allgemeiner Bedeutung sind vor allem die Frage nach den Wirkungen des Schweigens auf ein kaufmännisches Bestätigungsschreiben,[160] die Auswirkungen von Art. 9 auf Gerichtsstandsvereinbarungen und Schiedsklauseln[161] und die Möglichkeiten der Behandlung ganzer Regelwerke insgesamt als Handelsbrauch.[162] Zudem wird zunehmend die Auffassung vertreten, die Einhaltung grundlegender ethischer Standards sei kraft internationalen Handelsbrauchs Gegenstand eines jeden internationalen Kaufvertrags.[163]

1. Kaufmännisches Bestätigungsschreiben[164]

Viele Rechtsordnungen messen dem Schweigen auf ein kaufmännisches Bestätigungsschreiben eine besondere Bedeutung bei.[165] Dabei reicht die Spanne von der konstitutiven Wirkung für den – zuvor noch fehlenden – Vertragsschluss über die Konstitution des Vertragsinhalts bis hin zur Berücksichtigung des Schreibens als schlichtes Beweismittel oder Auslegungsindiz. Letzteres ergibt sich unter der Konvention bereits aus Art. 8.[166] Ebenso ist eine konstitutive Wirkung nach Abs. 1 kraft Gepflogenheit[167] oder vereinbartem Gebrauch möglich.[168] Ein unmittelbarer Rückgriff auf nationales Recht ist hingegen ausgeschlossen;[169] insbesondere ergibt sich insoweit **weder** eine **interne**[170] **noch** eine **externe**[171] **Lücke** der Konvention. Vielmehr kann das – bis auf Gültigkeitsfragen – als umfassend geregelt anzusehende Vertragsschlussrecht der Artt. 14 ff. lediglich durch nach Art. 9 zu berücksichtigende Gebräuche oder Gepflogenheiten überlagert werden.[172] 22

Da die konstitutiven Wirkungen des Schweigens auf ein Bestätigungsschreiben keine universelle Anerkennung finden, muss das Vorliegen eines Handelsbrauchs im Sinne von Abs. 2 **jeweils gesondert geprüft** werden. Üblicherweise wird darauf abgestellt, dass beide Parteien im räumlichen Verbreitungsbereich entsprechender Regeln niedergelassen sind.[173] Nach einer zurückhaltenderen Auffassung liegt im Bestehen paralleler Gebräuche nur ein starkes Indiz für das Vorliegen der Voraussetzungen von Abs. 2.[174] Die Geltung nur am Sitz des Schweigenden 23

---

[158] OGH, 27.2.2003, CISG-online 794 (aktuelle Fangquote als Handelsbrauch im internationalen Fischhandel).
[159] ZGer Basel-Stadt, 3.12.1997, CISG-online 346.
[160] Sogleich Rn. 22–24.
[161] Rn. 25.
[162] Rn. 26.
[163] *Schwenzer/Leisinger*, FS Hellner, S. 267; *Kröll u. a./Perales Viscasillas*, Art. 9, Rn. 18.
[164] Zur Vorgeschichte s. *Schroeter*, Art. 19 Rn. 4.
[165] Vgl. Art. 2.12 PICC, Art. 2:210 PECL sowie EuGH, 20.2.1997, Slg. 1997, I-911 *(MSG)* sowie rechtsvergleichend etwa *Ebenroth*, ZVglRWiss 77 (1978), 161, 164–180; *Esser*, öStZRVgl 1988, 167–193; *Schlosser*, FS Medicus, S. 543, 546 ff.
[166] S. OLG Frankfurt a. M., 5.7.1995, CISG-online 258; LG Neubrandenburg, 3.8.2005, CISG-online 1190.
[167] S. BGer, 5.4.2005, CISG-online 1012, E. 4.1 sowie die Hilfsbegründung des ZGer Basel-Stadt, 21.12.1992, CISG-online 55.
[168] Wie hier jetzt auch *Schwenzer/Mohs*, IHR 2006, 239, 245.
[169] *Kramer*, FS Welser, 539, 546; a. A. *Fogt*, ZEuP 2002, 580, 584 f.
[170] Die von *Fogt*, ZEuP 2002, 580, 584 f. behauptete herrschende Ansicht einer internen Lücke vermag sich in der Literatur so nicht aufzufinden. Siehe immerhin nunmehr *Kröll/Hennecke*, RabelsZ 67 (2003), 448, 456.
[171] So jedoch die problematische Auffassung *Fogt*, IPRax 2001, 358, 361; *Fogt*, ZEuP 2002, 580, 585.
[172] *Kröll u. a./Perales Viscasillas*, Art. 9, Rn. 30.
[173] ZGer Basel-Stadt, 21.12.1992, CISG-online 55; LG Saarbrücken, 23.3.1993, CISG-online 60; *Kröll/Hennecke*, RabelsZ 67 (2003), 448, 475 ff. (auch zu weiteren Kriterien); *Perales Viscasillas*, 25 J. L. & Com. (2005-06), 167, 174; *Schwenzer/Mohs*, IHR 2006, 239, 245; *Staudinger/Magnus*, Art. 9, Rn. 27.
[174] *Schlechtriem*, Internationales UN-Kaufrecht, Rn. 62; wohl auch *Soergel/Lüderitz/Fenge*, Art. 9, Rn. 7.

genügt nicht;[175] die Gegenauffassung[176] beruht wiederum auf einem normativen Verständnis von Abs. 2. Neben der Niederlassung kann – wegen der international durchaus beachtlichen Verbreitung des Handelsbrauchs[177] – auch die ständige Tätigkeit im örtlichen Verbreitungsbereich die Anwendung der Regeln über das kaufmännische Bestätigungsschreiben rechtfertigen. Die Verbindung beider Parteien zum Verbreitungsbereich genügt freilich dann nicht für die Annahme eines internationalen Handelsbrauchs im Sinne von Abs. 2, wenn dieser nicht auch für den konkreten Handelszweig gilt.[178] Dies ist insbesondere so bei einzelnen, gut organisierten Märkten, in welchen Bestätigungsschreiben üblicherweise nicht versandt werden.[179] Soweit die **PICC** als einschlägiger internationaler Handelsbrauch einzuordnen sind, ergibt sich die Möglichkeit einer konstitutiven Wirkung aus Art. 2.1.12 PICC.[180]

24 Zum **örtlichen Verbreitungsbereich** des Handelsbrauchs, der einem kaufmännischen Bestätigungsschreiben konstitutive Wirkungen beimisst, zählen etwa Dänemark,[181] Deutschland,[182] Polen[183], die Türkei[184], die Schweiz[185], Spanien (mit Einschränkungen)[186] sowie – in beschränktem Umfang – die USA.[187] Bei Beteiligung von Parteien aus folgenden Staaten ist die Anwendung hingegen nicht gewährleistet: Frankreich[188], Italien[189], Österreich[190] und Vereinigtes Königreich[191]. Daran ändert auch die Rechtsprechung zu Art. 23 EuGVO nichts, weil diese ebenfalls das tatsächliche Bestehen eines entsprechenden Handelsbrauchs voraussetzt und nicht etwa einen solchen fingiert.[192] Soweit die Konvention über Art. 1 I lit. b) zur Anwendung gelangt, sind – selbst bei Bestehen eines internationalen Handelsbrauchs für eine bestimmte Branche – zusätzlich Schutzklauseln wie Art. 8 II Rom I-Übk und Art. 31 II EGBGB zu beachten.

2. Gerichtsstandsvereinbarungen und Schiedsklauseln

25 Abs. 2 verhilft auch solchen Handelsbräuchen zur Anwendung, welche Gerichtsstandsvereinbarungen oder Schiedsklauseln in den Vertrag implizieren.[193] Die Vorschrift erfasst als

---

[175] *Fogt*, IPRax 2007, 417, 420; *Soergel/Lüderitz/Fenge*, Art. 9, Rn. 7.
[176] *Ebenroth*, JBl. 1986, 681, 687; *U. Huber*, RabelsZ 43 (1979), 413, 449. Ebenso der Sache nach LG Kiel, 27.7.2004, CISG-online 1534 (offenbar irrtümlich für einen deutsch-niederländischen Fall; dazu die Anm. von *Fogt*, IPRax 2007, 417).
[177] Vgl. Rn. 24.
[178] LG Landshut, 12.6.2008, CISG-online 1703 (Lieferung von Deckenplatten; sehr streng); *Schlechtriem*, Internationales UN-Kaufrecht, Rn. 62.
[179] Darin liegt der richtige Kern der bei *Witz/Salger/Lorenz/Witz*, Art. 9, Rn. 10 geäußerten Bedenken.
[180] So zutreffend *Schwenzer/Mohs*, IHR 2006, 239, 245.
[181] *Witz/Salger/Lorenz/Witz*, Art. 9, Rn. 10.
[182] *Schlechtriem*, Internationales UN-Kaufrecht, Rn. 62; *Soergel/Lüderitz/Fenge*, Art. 9, Rn. 7; *Staudinger/Magnus*, Art. 9, Rn. 27.
[183] *Enderlein/Maskow/Strohbach*, Art. 18, Anm. 3. m. w. N.
[184] Art. 23 Handelsgesetzbuch; *Schwenzer/Mohs*, IHR 2006, 239, 245.
[185] BGer, 27.10.1988, BGE 114 II 250 ff.; ZGer Basel-Stadt, 21.12.1992, CISG-online 55; BernerKomm/Schmidlin, Art. 6 OR, Rn. 81 ff.; *Witz/Salger/Lorenz/Witz*, Art. 9, Rn. 10.
[186] S. *Kröll u. a./Perales Viscasillas*, Art. 9, Rn. 30 Fn. 97.
[187] Siehe *Kröll/Hennecke*, RabelsZ 67 (2003), 448, 480 ff. Vgl. *Barbara Berry, S. A. de C. V. v. Ken M. Spooner Farms, Inc.*, U. S. Dist. Ct. (Washington), 13.4.2006, CISG-online 1354 (mit Verweis auf die unrichtige Entscheidung ZGer Basel-Stadt, 21.12.1992, CISG-online 55).
[188] OLG Frankfurt a. M., 5.7.1995, CISG-online 258; *Witz/Salger/Lorenz/Witz*, Art. 9, Rn. 10. Anders LG Saarbrücken, 23.3.1993, CISG-online 60 unter Hinweis auf Req., 22.3.1920, S. 1920, Somm. 77; Com., 7.11.1950, Bull. Civ. III, S. 228, Nr. 321; Civ., 6.5.1954, Bull. Civ. II, S. 118, Nr. 165 (bei den ersten beiden Entscheidungen wurde das Schreiben freilich nur zur Auslegung herangezogen, bei der dritten ging es um die nachträgliche Einbeziehung einer Gerichtsstandsklausel); *Schwenzer/Mohs*, IHR 2006, 239, 245. Differenzierend *Kröll/Hennecke*, RabelsZ 67 (2003), 448, 479 f. Anders offenbar Belgien: BGH, 9.3.1994, EuZW 1994, 635.
[189] OLG Köln, 16.3.1988, NJW 1988, 2182 f.
[190] OGH, 26.6.1974, JBl. 1975, 89; OGH, 28.4.1993, CISG-online 100 = JBl. 1993, 782; OGH, 22.12.1993, ecolex 1994, 316; OLG Graz, 7.3.2002, CISG-online 669; *Koziol/Welser*, I 94 f.; *Rummel/Rummel*, § 861, Rn. 13. Unrichtig daher ZGer Basel-Stadt, 21.12.1992, CISG-online 55, siehe die Kritik von *Kramer*, FS Welser, 539, 548 f.
[191] *Kröll u. a./Perales Viscasillas*, Art. 9, Rn. 30, Fn. 97.
[192] Vgl. EuGH, 20.2.1997, Slg. 1997, I-911 *(MSG)*; *Kropholler*, EUZPR, Art. 23, Rn. 61.
[193] RB Breda 27.2.2008, CISG-online 2252, Nr. 2.7.

Regelung zur Vertragsinhaltsbestimmung auch diese an sich konventionsfremde Materie.[194] Für Gerichtsstandsvereinbarungen werden allerdings nach Art. 90 vielfach die Anforderungen des vereinheitlichten internationalen Zuständigkeitsrechts (EuGVO, EuGVÜ, LugÜ) vorrangig zu beachten sein.[195] Von größerer praktischer Relevanz ist freilich die Einbeziehung von Schiedsklauseln. So enthalten etwa Platzusancen nicht selten auch Schiedsklauseln,[196] und auch für bestimmte Branchen kommt eine Schiedsvereinbarung qua Handelsbrauch in Betracht.[197]

3. Behandlung von Regelwerken

Schwierigkeiten bereitet die Behandlung ganzer Regelwerke, etwa der Incoterms®, der ERA/ERI oder der PICC. Sie sind – regelmäßig und bislang – jedenfalls nicht in vollem Umfang Handelsbrauch,[198] während einzelnen Bestimmungen dieser Werke diese Qualität ohne weiteres zukommen kann.[199] Freilich finden sich hinsichtlich der Incoterms®[200] wie auch der PICC[201] Entscheidungen, welche diese *in toto* als Handelsbrauch qualifizieren. Daher ist nicht ausgeschlossen, dass sich beide Regelwerke dauerhaft als „verlässliche Quelle" internationaler Handelsbräuche etablieren. Insbesondere die PICC sind mit dieser Begründung bereits mehrfach von Schiedsgerichten herangezogen worden.[202] Bei den Incoterms® liegt hingegen das tatsächliche Problem vornehmlich in der regelmäßigen Beachtung innerhalb des betreffenden Geschäftszweigs,[203] an der Zweifel bereits aufgrund der wiederkehrenden Neufassungen[204] angebracht sind. Recht weit geht daher der Vorschlag einer tatsächlichen Vermutung der Geltung als Handelsbrauch.[205] Bei sonstigen Regelwerken wird vielfach sowohl die regelmäßige Beachtung[206] als auch schon die Bekanntheit[207] problematisch sein. Die zuverlässige Anwendbarkeit solcher Regelwerke insgesamt kann daher nur durch eine ausdrückliche und präzise Vereinbarung sichergestellt werden.[208] Ohne die Anwendbarkeit kraft Vereinbarung oder kraft Handelsbrauchs bleibt ihnen allerdings die Funktion des nach Art. 8 III zu berücksichtigenden Auslegungsmaterials.[209]

---

[194] S. o. Rn. 4 sowie Art. 8 Rn. 5.
[195] Vgl. EuGH, 20.2.1997, Slg. 1997, I-911; BGH, 3.12.1992, NJW 1993, 1798; *Junge*, 3. Aufl., Art. 8, Rn. 10.
[196] *Junge*, 3. Aufl., Rn. 2.
[197] Vgl. BGH, 3.12.1992, NJW 1993, 1798 (zu § 346 HGB für den internationalen Fellhandel).
[198] ICC, 8873/1997, J. D. I. 1998, 1017, 1019 (für PICC); ICC, 9029/1998, UNILEX (für PICC); *Brunner*, Art. 9; Rn. 2 (für UCP 500); *Staudinger/Magnus*, Art. 9, Rn. 8 (für Incoterms®); *Magnus/Lüsing*, IHR 2007, 1, 7 (für Incoterms®); ähnlich *Bianca/Bonell/Farnsworth*, Art. 9, Anm. 3.5.).
[199] *Honnold/Flechtner*, Art. 9, Rn. 117; *Kröll u. a./Perales Viscasillas*, Art. 9, Rn. 36; *Soergel/Lüderitz/Fenge*, Art. 9, Rn. 4. Offen die Formulierung bei *Witz/Salger/Lorenz/Witz*, Art. 9, Rn. 4 („Unter Art. 9 können auch ... fallen"). Vgl. etwa ICC, 9029/1998, UNILEX (zu Artt. 3.10, 6.2.2 PICC).
[200] Juzgado Nacional de Primera Instancia en lo Comercial No. 7, 20.5.1991, CISG-online 461 (obiter dictum); *St. Paul Guardian Insurance Company et al. v. Neuromed Medical Systems & Support et al.*, U. S. Dist. Ct. (S. D. N. Y.), 26.3.2002, CISG-online 615 unter Hinweis auf BGH, 18.6.1975, WM 1975, 917; *BP International, Ltd. and BP Exploration & Oil Inc. v. Empressa Estatal Petroleos de Ecuador, et al.*, U. S. Ct. App. (5th Cir.), 11.6.2003, CISG-online 730; *China North Chemical Industries Corp. v. Beston Chemical Corp.*, U. S. Dist. Ct. (S. D. T. H.), 7.2.2006, CISG-online 1177; KG Wallis, 28.1.2009, CISG-online 2025; ebenso *Pamboukis*, 25 J. L. & Com. (2005-06), 107, 129.
[201] Int. Ct. Russian CCI, 5.6.1997, CISG-online 1247; zustimmend *Janssen*, IHR 2004, 194, 199; *Pamboukis*, 25 J. L. & Com. (2005-06), 107, 130; *Rauscher*, FS Heldrich, 933, 942.
[202] Vgl. ICC, 9875/1999, UNILEX; ICC, 9479/1999, UNILEX; Int. Ct. Russian CCI, 27.7.1999, CISG-online 779; ICC, 10 022/2000, UNILEX.
[203] *Witz/Salger/Lorenz/Witz*, Art. 9, Rn. 14. Bejaht etwa für FOB durch die Corte d'appello di Genova, 24.3.1995, CISG-online 315 (aber ohne ausdrückliche Bezugnahme auf die Incoterms®).
[204] Zu den Incoterms® 2010 s. etwa *Zwilling-Pinna*, BB 2010, 2980 ff.
[205] So *Leisinger*, Fundamental Breach, S. 144 ff.
[206] *Witz/Salger/Lorenz/Witz*, Art. 9, Rn. 15 (für ERA/ERI).
[207] *Witz/Salger/Lorenz/Witz*, Art. 9, Rn. 15 (für ERA/ERI).
[208] *Staudinger/Magnus*, Art. 9, Rn. 8; *Witz/Salger/Lorenz/Witz*, Art. 9, Rn. 14.
[209] BGH, 7.11.2012, CISG-online 2374, Rn. 24. Für diese Funktion auch *Kröll u. a./Perales Viscasillas*, Art. 9, Rn. 38.

Art. 10 [Mehrere Niederlassungen; gewöhnlicher Aufenthalt]

Für die Zwecke dieses Übereinkommens ist,
a) falls eine Partei mehr als eine Niederlassung hat, die Niederlassung maßgebend, die unter Berücksichtigung der vor oder bei Vertragsabschluß den Parteien bekannten oder von ihnen in Betracht gezogenen Umstände die engste Beziehung zu dem Vertrag und zu seiner Erfüllung hat;
b) falls eine Partei keine Niederlassung hat, ist ihr gewöhnlicher Aufenthalt maßgebend.

Art. 10

For the purposes of this Convention:

(a) if a party has more than one place of business, the place of business is that which has the closest relationship to the contract and its performance, having regard to the circumstances known to or contemplated by the parties at any time before or at the conclusion of the contract;
(b) if a party does not have a place of business, reference is to be made to his habitual residence.

Art. 10

Aux fins de la présente Convention:

a) si une partie a plus d'un établissement, l'établissement à prendre en considération est celui qui a la relation la plus étroite avec le contrat et son exécution eu égard aux circonstances connues des parties ou envisagées par elles à un moment quelconque avant la conclusion ou lors de la conclusion du contrat;
b) si une partie n'a pas d'établissement, sa résidence habituelle en tient lieu.

Übersicht

	Rn.
I. Allgemeines	1
II. Die Vorschrift im Einzelnen	4
1. Relevante Niederlassung (lit. a))	4
a) Das Haager Kaufrecht	4
b) CISG	5
2. Der gewöhnliche Aufenthalt (lit. b))	9
III. Beweislast	11

Vorläufer und **Entwürfe:** Art. 1 II EKG; Art. 1 II EAG; Genfer E 1976 Art. 6; Wiener E 1977 Art. 5; New Yorker E 1978 Art. 9.

I. Allgemeines

1   Während die Gleichsetzung des gewöhnlichen Aufenthaltsortes mit der Niederlassung ein Vorbild in Art. 1 II EKG hat,[1] ist die mehrere Niederlassungen betreffende Lösung des lit. a) im Verhältnis zum EKG neu.[2] Ursprünglich war vorgesehen, grundsätzlich die Hauptniederlassung als maßgebliche Niederlassung zu bestimmen.[3] Letztendlich wurde aber eine auf Art. 2 lit. c) des Verjährungsübereinkommens von 1974 zurückgehende Lösung bevorzugt.[4]

---

[1] *Honsell/Melis,* Art. 10, Rn. 1.
[2] Vgl. *Bamberger/Roth/Saenger,* Art. 10, Rn. 3; *Bianca/Bonell/Rajski,* Art. 10, Anm. 1.2.; *Diez Picazo/Calvo Caravaca,* Art. 10, S. 146; *Schlechtriem/Schwenzer/Schlechtriem,* CISG Commentary, 2. Aufl., Art. 10, Rn. 1; *Schlechtriem/Schwenzer/Schwenzer/Hachem,* CISG Commentary, Art. 10, Rn. 1.
[3] Siehe UNCITRAL YB II (1971), S. 52, Art. 2 lit. b), Nr. 12: „Where a party has places of business in more than one State, his place of business shall be his principal place of business, unless another place of business has a closer relationship to the contract and its performance, having regard to the circumstances known to or contemplated by the parties at the time of the conclusion of the contract", S. 53, Nr. 23 f.
[4] Vgl. UNCITRAL YB VI (1975), S. 52, Nr. 31; siehe auch *Bianca/Bonell/Rajski,* Art. 10, Anm. 1.2.; *Honsell/Melis,* Art. 10, Rn. 1; *Herber,* 2. Aufl., Art. 10, Rn. 1; *Witz/Salger/Lorenz/Witz,* Art. 10, Rn. 1.

Art. 10 **definiert den „autonomen"**[5] **Begriff** „Niederlassung", der im CISG – wie oft 2
hervorgehoben worden ist[6] – an zahlreichen Stellen benutzt wird,[7] **nicht**.[8] Die Vorschrift
setzt die Existenz verschiedener Niederlassungen vielmehr voraus,[9] d. h., die Frage, ob
Niederlassungen vorliegen, muss bereits positiv beantwortet worden sein, bevor die Vorschrift überhaupt Anwendung finden kann.

Die Vorschrift verfolgt also „lediglich" den Zweck, die bereits von *Rabel* aufgeworfene[10] – 3
im EKG aber nicht geregelte[11] – Frage nach der im Falle verschiedener Niederlassungen
eines Rechtssubjektes **maßgeblichen Niederlassung** zu beantworten.[12] Die in der Vorschrift gegebenen Anhaltspunkte werfen aber dennoch zahlreiche Zweifel auf.[13] So ist zum
Beispiel die Definition der „engsten Beziehung", auf die die Vorschrift zur Bestimmung der
relevanten Niederlassung abstellt, nicht unproblematisch.

II. Die Vorschrift im Einzelnen

1. Relevante Niederlassung (lit. a))

a) Das Haager Kaufrecht. Unter dem Haager Kaufrecht hat die Frage nach der 4
relevanten Niederlassung im Falle mehrerer Niederlassungen eines Rechtssubjektes zu
einem Meinungsstreit geführt:[14] Während einerseits die Meinung vertreten wurde, die
relevante Niederlassung sei immer die Hauptniederlassung,[15] wurde andererseits auf die
Niederlassung mit der engsten Beziehung zum Vertrag abgestellt.[16] Diesen Meinungsstreit
hat eine auch im Ausland[17] beachtete Entscheidung des BGH[18] in der Folge beigelegt und
zwar zugunsten der zuletzt genannten Lösung.[19]

b) CISG. Der unter dem Haager Kaufrecht entstandene Meinungsstreit kann unter dem 5
CISG überhaupt nicht aufkommen, da dieses nunmehr verbindlich klarstellt, dass dort, wo

---

[5] Vgl. statt aller *Bamberger/Roth/Saenger*, Art. 1, Rn. 10 und Art. 10, Rn. 2; *Brunner*, Art. 1, Rn. 1 Fn. 49; *Ferrari u. a./Saenger*, Internationales Vertragsrecht, Art. 1, Rn. 10; *Honsell/Siehr*, Art. 1, Rn. 11; *Kröll u. a./Brekoulakis*, Art. 10, Rn. 10; *Lohmann*, Parteiautonomie, S. 26; *Piltz*, Internationales Kaufrecht, Rn. 2–77; *Schlechtriem/Schwenzer/Schlechtriem*, CISG Commentary, 2. Aufl., Art. 10, Rn. 2; *Schlechtriem/Schwenzer/Schwenzer/Hachem*, CISG Commentary, Art. 1, Rn. 23; ebenso in der Rechtsprechung Tribunale di Forlì, 11.12.2008, CISG-online 1729; KG Wallis, 23.5.2006, CISG-online 1532; Tribunale di Padova, 11.1.2005, CISG-online 967; teilweise anders *Garro/Zuppi*, Compraventa internacional, S. 89 f.

[6] *Diez-Picazo/Calvo Caravaca*, Art. 10, S. 145 Fn. 1; *Ferrari*, Vendita internazionale, S. 206 Fn. 7 m. w. N.

[7] Siehe Artt. 1 I, 12, 20 II 2, 24, 31 lit. c), 42 I lit. b), 57 I lit. a) und II, 69 II, 90, 93 III, 94 I 1 und II, 96; vgl. auch *Ferrari u. a./Saenger*, Internationales Vertragsrecht, Art. 10, Rn. 1; *Kröll u. a./Brekoulakis*, Art. 10, Rn. 3 ff.; *Schlechtriem/Schwenzer/Schwenzer/Hachem*, CISG Commentary, Art. 10, Rn. 2.

[8] Ebenso *Ferrari u. a./Saenger*, Internationales Vertragsrecht, Art. 1, Rn. 10 und Art. 10, Rn. 1; MünchKomm/*Westermann*, Art. 10, Rn. 1; *Neumayer/Ming*, Art. 10, Anm. 1; *Rudolph*, Art. 10, Rn. 2; a. A. *Achilles*, Art. 1, Rn. 5; *Butler*, VJ (2002), 275, 277; *Herber*, 2. Aufl., Art. 10, Rn. 2; *Honnold/Flechtner*, Art. 1, Rn. 43; *Schlechtriem/Schwenzer/Schlechtriem*, CISG Commentary, 2. Aufl., Art. 10, Rn. 2; kritisch zur Ansicht, Art. 10 definiere die „Niederlassung", vgl. *Richards*, 69 Iowa L. Rev. (1983), 209, 220 und dort Fn. 90.

[9] *Baumgärtel/Laumen/Prütting/Hepting/Müller*, Art. 10, Rn. 1; *Ferrari u. a./Saenger*, Internationales Vertragsrecht, Art. 10, Rn. 1; *Schlechtriem/Schwenzer/Schwenzer/Hachem*, CISG Commentary, Art. 10, Rn. 1; *Soergel/Lüderitz/Fenge*, Art. 10, Rn. 1; so nunmehr auch *Schlechtriem/Schwenzer/Schlechtriem*, CISG Commentary, 2. Aufl., Art. 10, Rn. 2, wo aber auch statuiert wird, dass „Article 10 defines the relevant 'place of business'".

[10] *Rabel*, Recht des Warenkaufs, Bd. 1, S. 51.

[11] Siehe auch *Diez-Picazo/Calvo Caravaca*, Art. 10, S. 146.

[12] *Esslinger*, ALI-ABA (1999), 69, 77; MünchKomm/*Westermann*, Art. 10, Rn. 1; Sekretariatskommentar, O. R., S. 19; *Staudinger/Magnus*, Art. 10, Rn. 1.

[13] Darauf weist auch *Bianca/Bonell/Rajski*, Art. 10, Anm. 3., hin.

[14] Vgl. hierzu *Ferrari*, The CISG's Sphere of Application, S. 21, 28 f.; ders., Vendita internazionale, S. 206 f.; *Herrmann*, IPRax 1983, 212, 214.

[15] So etwa *U. Huber*, DB 1975, 1205, 1205; *Landfermann*, NJW 1974, 385, 388.

[16] *Stötter*, Internationales Einheitskaufrecht, S. 132.

[17] Vgl. hierzu *Memmo*, Riv. trim. dir. proc. civ. 1983, 755 ff.

[18] BGH, IPRax 1983, 228 f.

[19] *Ferrari*, Vendita internazionale, S. 207.

Art. 10 6, 7 Teil I. Kapitel II. Allgemeine Bestimmungen

auf die Niederlassung einer Vertragspartei abgestellt wird, bei mehreren Niederlassungen **nicht notwendigerweise die Hauptniederlassung** maßgebend ist,[20] sondern vielmehr diejenige, die – gemäß Vertrag[21] – zum Vertrag und seiner Erfüllung die **engste Beziehung** aufweist;[22] Haupt- und Zweigniederlassung werden demnach gleichgestellt.[23] Worin diese Beziehung zum Ausdruck kommt, hängt vom Einzelfall ab.[24]

6   Die Vorschrift wirft insofern eine neue Zweifelsfrage auf,[25] als sie die **Erfordernisse** der engsten Beziehung zu dem Vertrag und zu seiner Erfüllung **kumulativ** nebeneinander stellt.[26] Denn es wird durchaus nicht selten sein, dass der Vertrag durch eine Niederlassung einer Partei abgeschlossen wird, seine Erfüllung jedoch von oder zugunsten einer anderen Niederlassung dieser Partei erfolgt.[27]

7   Bei der Bestimmung der „engsten Beziehung", die nach **objektiven Maßstäben** zu erfolgen hat,[28] sind die von den Parteien[29] **vor oder bei Vertragsschluss** bekannten oder von ihnen in Betracht gezogenen **Umstände**,[30] wie zum Beispiel Anschrift, Briefkopf,[31] Fax-Adresse,[32] genauso wie eine eventuelle Parteivereinbarung,[33] so auch die

---

[20] Vgl. *Bamberger/Roth/Saenger*, Art. 10, Rn. 3; *Brunner*, Art. 10, Rn. 1; *Ferrari*, The CISG's Sphere of Application, S. 21, 29; *Ferrari u. a./Saenger*, Internationales Vertragsrecht, Art. 1, Rn. 10; *Herrmann*, IPRax 1983, 212, 215; *P. Huber/Mullis/P. Huber*, S. 50; Sekretariatskommentar, O. R., S. 19; *Loewe*, S. 35; Münch-Komm/*Westermann*, Art. 10, Rn. 2; *Schlechtriem*, Einheitliches UN-Kaufrecht, S. 29; *Schlechtriem/Schwenzer/Schlechtriem*, CISG Commentary, 2. Aufl., Art. 1, Rn. 27 und Art. 10, Rn. 4; *Soergel/Lüderitz/Fenge*, Art. 10, Rn. 5; *Staudinger/Magnus*, Art. 10, Rn. 5; a. A. *Hackney*, 61 La. L. Rev. (2001), 473, 473; a. A. auch *Cedar Petrochemicals, Inc. v. Dongbu Hannong Chemical Co., Ltd.*, U. S. Dist. Ct. (S. D. N. Y.), 19.7.2007, CISG-online 1509 = 2007 WL 2 059 239 (S. D. N. Y.): „The CISG governs the sale of goods between parties whose principal places of business are in different nations as long as those nations are signatories to the treaty".
[21] *Bianca/Bonell/Rajski*, Art. 10, Anm. 2.1.
[22] *Brunner*, Art. 10, Rn. 1; *Ferrari u. a./Saenger*, Internationales Vertragsrecht, Art. 10, Rn. 3; *Nakata*, 7 Transnat'l Law. (1994), 141, 157; so ausdrücklich in der Rechtsprechung neuerdings vgl. neuerdings auch *American Mint LLC v. GOSoftware, Inc.*, U. S. Dist. Ct. (M. D. Pa.), 6.1.2006, CISG-online; OLG Stuttgart, 28.2.2000, CISG-online 583 = IHR 2001, 65, 67; für ein Anwendungsbeispiel s. BezG Saane, 20.2.1997, CISG-online 426 = SZIER 1999, 195 ff.
[23] *Bamberger/Roth/Saenger*, Art. 1, Rn. 10; *Diez Picazo/Calvo Caravaca*, Art. 10, S. 146; *Honsell/Melis*, Art. 10, Rn. 3; *Witz/Salger/Lorenz/Witz*, Art. 1, Rn. 9; a. A. *Cedar Petrochemicals, Inc. v. Dongbu Hannong Chemical Co., Ltd.*, U. S. Dist. Ct. (S. D. N. Y.), 19.7.2007, CISG-online 1509: „The CISG governs the sale of goods between parties whose principal places of business are in different nations as long as those nations are signatories to the treaty".
[24] Ebenso *Bianca/Bonell/Rajski*, Art. 10, Anm. 3.1.; *Czerwenka*, S. 133 f.; *Ferrari u. a./Saenger*, Internationales Vertragsrecht, Art. 10, Rn. 3; *Schlechtriem/Schwenzer/Schwenzer/Hachem*, CISG Commentary, Art. 10, Rn. 4; ein Anwendungsbeispiel findet sich in RB Hasselt, 2.6.1999, CISG-online 762.
[25] So ausdrücklich *Herber*, 2. Aufl., Art. 10, Rn. 3; vgl. auch *Ferretti*, Nuove leggi civ. comm. 1989, 43, 44.
[26] Das beanstanden auch *Bianca/Bonell/Rajski*, Art. 10, Anm. 3.1.; *Schlechtriem/Schwenzer/Schlechtriem*, CISG Commentary, 2. Aufl., Art. 10, Rn. 3; *Schlechtriem/Schwenzer/Schwenzer/Hachem*, CISG Commentary, Art. 10, Rn. 4.
[27] Ähnlich auch *G. Bell*, 8 Pace Int'l L. Rev. (1996), 237, 245; *Ferrari*, Vendita internazionale, S. 208; *Herber/Czerwenka*, Art. 10, Rn. 4; *Schlechtriem*, Uniform Sales Law, S. 43.
[28] Ebenso *Achilles*, Art. 10, Rn. 2; *Ferrari u. a./Saenger*, Internationales Vertragsrecht, Art. 10, Rn. 3; *Herber/Czerwenka*, Art. 10, Rn. 3; *Honsell/Melis*, Art. 10, Rn. 5; *Neumayer/Ming*, Art. 10, Anm. 2.; *Piltz*, Rn. 2–82; *Herber*, 2. Aufl., Art. 10, Rn. 7; *Rudolph*, Art. 10, Rn. 3; *Schlechtriem/Schwenzer/Schlechtriem*, CISG Commentary, 2. Aufl., Art. 10, Rn. 7; *Schlechtriem/Schwenzer/Schwenzer/Hachem*, CISG Commentary, Art. 10, Rn. 10; *Soergel/Lüderitz/Fenge*, Art. 10, Rn. 2; a. A. aber wohl *Czerwenka*, S. 134.
[29] Zu Recht ist darauf hingewiesen worden, dass „die Kenntnis oder Annahme bei beiden Vertragsparteien bestanden haben muss. Praktisch wird es allerdings in der Regel maßgeblich auf die Kenntnis des Vertragspartners ankommen, der mit der Partei Vertragsverhandlungen aufgenommen hat, die mehrere Niederlassungen hat; denn letzterer sind die internen Umstände bekannt". *Herber*, 2. Aufl., Art. 10, Rn. 6.
[30] Vgl. auch *Baumgärtel/Laumen/Hepting/Müller*, Art. 10, Rn. 6; *Ferrari u. a./Saenger*, Internationales Vertragsrecht, Art. 10, Rn. 3; *Herber*, 2. Aufl., Art. 10, Rn. 5; *Kröll u. a./Brekoulakis*, Art. 10, Rn. 38; *Piltz*, Internationales Kaufrecht, Rn. 2–82.
[31] Vgl. *McDowell Valley Vineyards, Inc. v. Sabaté USA Inc. et al.*, U. S. Dist. Ct. (N. D. Cal.), 2.11.2005, CISG Pace = 2005 WL 2893848 (N. D. Cal.).
[32] MünchKomm/*Westermann*, Art. 10, Rn. 3; *Staudinger/Magnus*, Art. 10, Rn. 5.
[33] Vgl. *Ferrari*, Vendita internazionale, S. 209, Fn. 12; *Ferrari u. a./Saenger*, Internationales Vertragsrecht, Art. 10, Rn. 1; *Kritzer*, Guide to Practical Applications, S. 75; *Kröll u. a./Brekoulakis*, Art. 10, Rn. 27; *Witz/Salger/Lorenz/Witz*, Art. 10, Rn. 6.

Rechtsprechung zum EKG,[34] **zu berücksichtigen**.[35] Daraus folgt etwa, dass die bloß nach Vertragsschluss bekannt gewordenen Umstände unbeachtlich sind,[36] genauso wie Umstände, die nicht nach außen sichtbar gemacht worden sind.[37] Maßgebend ist daher allein „das äußere Erscheinungsbild des Vertragspartners, der mehrere Niederlassungen hat".[38]

Aus dem Gesagten folgt die h. L., dass im Zweifel auf die für den **Vertragsabschluss** 8 **verantwortliche Niederlassung** abzustellen sei.[39] Dies trifft aber nur dann zu, wenn die für die **Erfüllung verantwortliche Niederlassung** nicht beiden Parteien bekannt oder von ihnen nicht in Betracht gezogen worden ist, da andernfalls diese Niederlassung als relevante Niederlassung zu betrachten ist.[40]

2. Der gewöhnliche Aufenthalt (lit. b))

Hat eine Vertragspartei keine Niederlassung, was wohl nur bei natürlichen Personen 9 denkbar ist[41] und nur selten relevant sein wird, da Geschäfte zwischen Privaten grundsätzlich[42] vom Anwendungsbereich des Übereinkommens ausgenommen sind,[43] so muss auf den „gewöhnlichen Aufenthalt" derselben abgestellt werden. Für den autonomen[44] Begriff des „gewöhnlichen Aufenthaltes", der ein häufiger Anknüpfungspunkt im internationalen Privatrecht ist,[45] sind die **tatsächlichen Verhältnisse** entscheidend[46] (was per se zur Reduktion der Möglichkeiten von Auslegungsdivergenzen führen dürfte).[47]

Obwohl es auch in Bezug auf diesen Begriff auf den Einzelfall ankommt, kann man doch 10 eine für die Bestimmung des „gewöhnlichen Aufenthaltes" nützliche Regel aufstellen: Eine

---

[34] Vgl. OLG Hamburg, 30.12.1980, in: *Schlechtriem/Magnus*, Internationale Rechtsprechung zu EKG und EAG, S. 113.

[35] Das bloße Kennenkönnen der im Text erwähnten Umstände ist nicht relevant.

[36] *Diez Picazo/Calvo Caravaca*, Art. 10, S. 147; *Ferrari*, Vendita internazionale, S. 208 f.; *Ferrari u. a./Saenger*, Internationales Vertragsrecht, Art. 10, Rn. 3; *Ferretti*, Nuove leggi civ. comm. 1989, 43, 44; *Witz/Salger/Lorenz/Witz*, Art. 10, Rn. 4.

[37] *Ferrari u. a./Saenger*, Internationales Vertragsrecht, Art. 10, Rn. 3; *Herber*, 2. Aufl., Art. 10, Rn. 7.

[38] *Honsell/Melis*, Art. 10, Rn. 5; so auch *Herber/Czerwenka*, Art. 10, Rn. 3; *Schlechtriem/Schwenzer/Schwenzer/Hachem*, CISG Commentary, Art. 10, Rn. 10.

[39] Vgl. *Bamberger/Roth/Saenger*, Art. 10, Rn. 3; *Brunner*, Art. 10, Rn. 1; *Enderlein/Maskow/Strohbach*, Art. 10, Anm. 3.; *Ferrari u. a./Saenger*, Internationales Vertragsrecht, Art. 10, Rn. 4; *Herber/Czerwenka*, Art. 10, Rn. 4; MünchKomm/*Martiny*, Art. 28 EGBGB Anh. II, Rn. 68; *Soergel/Lüderitz/Fenge*, Art. 10, Rn. 2; *Staudinger/Magnus*, Art. 10, Rn. 5; *Witz/Salger/Lorenz/Witz*, Art. 10, Rn. 3; a. A. *Achilles*, Art. 10, Rn. 2 (im Zweifel auf die Hauptniederlassung abstellend); a. A. auch *Schlechtriem/Schwenzer/Schwenzer/Hachem*, CISG Commentary, Art. 10, Rn. 6: „prevalence to that place of business which has the most power to exert influence upon the contractual relationship", unter Bezugnahme auf *Asante Technologies, Inc. v. PMC-Sierra, Inc.*, U. S. Dist. Ct. (N. D. Cal.), 27.7.2001, CISG-online 616; so auch *Piltz*, Internationales Kaufrecht, Rn. 2–82.

[40] So *Kröll u. a./Brekoulakis*, Art. 10, Rn. 30 f.; a. A. *Herrmann*, IPRax 1983, 212, 214 (immer auf die für die Erfüllung verantwortliche Niederlassung abzustellend); die Frage bloß ansprechend, ohne jedoch eine eigene Lösung vorzuschlagen, *Martin-Davidson*, 17 Mich. St. J. Int'l L. (2008), 657, 667 f.

[41] So ausdrücklich *Witz/Salger/Lorenz/Witz*, Art. 10, Rn. 5; vgl. auch *Bamberger/Roth/Saenger*, Art. 10, Rn. 4; *Ferrari u. a./Saenger*, Internationales Vertragsrecht, Art. 10, Rn. 4; *Rudolph*, Art. 10, Rn. 4.

[42] Siehe hierzu ausführlich Art. 2 Rn. 7 ff.

[43] Vgl. diesbezüglich auch *Enderlein/Maskow/Strohbach*, Art. 10, Anm. 5.; *Reinhart*, Art. 10, Rn. 5; *Schlechtriem*, Einheitliches UN-Kaufrecht, S. 30; *Staudinger/Magnus*, Art. 10, Rn. 8.

[44] So *Schlechtriem/Schwenzer/Schlechtriem*, CISG Commentary, 2. Aufl., Art. 10, Rn. 8; *Witz/Salger/Lorenz/Witz*, Art. 10, Rn. 5.

[45] So auch *Bamberger/Roth/Saenger*, Art. 10, Rn. 4; *Bianca/Bonell/Rajski*, Art. 10, Anm. 2.3.; *Diez Picazo/Calvo Caravaca*, Art. 10, S. 147; *Ferrari*, Vendita internazionale, S. 210 und dort auch Fn. 3; *Herber*, 2. Aufl., Art. 10, Rn. 8; MünchKomm/*Westermann*, Art. 10, Rn. 4.

[46] *Bianca/Bonell/Rajski*, Art. 10, Anm. 3.2.; *Ferrari*, The CISG's Sphere of Application, S. 21, 30; ders., Vendita internazionale, S. 210; *Ferrari u. a./Saenger*, Internationales Vertragsrecht, Art. 10, Rn. 4; *Neumayer/Ming*, Art. 10, Anm. 4.; *Piltz*, Rn. 2–84; *Reinhart*, Art. 10, Rn. 5; *Schlechtriem/Schwenzer/Schlechtriem*, CISG Commentary, 2. Aufl., Art. 10, Rn. 8; *Staudinger/Magnus*, Art. 10, Rn. 8; *Witz/Salger/Lorenz/Witz*, Art. 10, Rn. 5.

[47] In diesem Sinne auch *Ferrari u. a./Saenger*, Internationales Vertragsrecht, Art. 10, Rn. 4 a. E.; *Herber/Czerwenka*, Art. 10, Rn. 5; *Herber*, 2. Aufl., Art. 10, Rn. 8; *Schlechtriem/Schwenzer/Hachem*, CISG Commentary, Art. 10, Rn. 11.

bloß **kurzfristige physische Präsenz ist nicht ausreichend**,[48] vielmehr wird ein tatsächlicher Aufenthalt von gewisser Dauer vorausgesetzt.[49] Aus diesem Grund ist ausgeschlossen worden, dass ein angemietetes Hotelzimmer, von dem aus Vertragsverhandlungen geführt werden, als gewöhnlicher Aufenthaltsort angesehen werden kann.[50]

III. Beweislast

11   Auf der Grundlage des dem CISG zugrundeliegenden Regel-Ausnahme-Verhältnisses,[51] muss diejenige Partei, die sich auf die Maßgeblichkeit einer bestimmten Niederlassung beruft, diese beweisen.[52] Hingegen muss diejenige Partei, die sich auf die Maßgeblichkeit des gewöhnlichen Aufenthaltes stützt, die Voraussetzungen von lit. b) beweisen. „Dazu gehört der Nachweis, dass keine Niederlassung besteht".[53]

---

[48] So ausdrücklich *Piltz,*Internationales Kaufrecht, Rn. 2–84; vgl. auch MünchKomm/*Westermann,* Art. 10, Rn. 4.
[49] *Bamberger/Roth/Saenger,* Art. 10, Rn. 4; *Baumgärtel/Laumen/Hepting/Müller,* Art. 10, Rn. 11; *Bianca/Bonell/Rajski,* Art. 10, Anm. 3.2.; *Ferrari,* Vendita internazionale, S. 210; *Ferrari u. a./Saenger,* Internationales Vertragsrecht, Art. 10, Rn. 4; *Herber/Czerwenka,* Art. 10, Rn. 5; *Honsell/Melis,* Art. 10, Rn. 6; *Kröll u. a./Brekoulakis,* Art. 10, Rn. 42; MünchKomm/*Westermann,* Art. 10, Rn. 4; *Schlechtriem/Schwenzer/Schlechtriem,* CISG Commentary, 2. Aufl., Art. 10, Rn. 8; *Schlechtriem/Schwenzer/Schwenzer/Hachem,* CISG Commentary, Art. 10, Rn. 11; *Staudinger/Magnus,* Art. 10, Rn. 8.
[50] *Rudolph,* Art. 10, Rn. 4.
[51] Vgl. ausführlich *Ferrari,* Rev. dr. aff. int. 2000, 665 ff.; *ders.* Art. 4 Rn. 48 ff.; vgl. auch *Baumgärtel/Laumen/Hepting/Müller,* Art. 10, Rn. 2.
[52] *Achilles,* Art. 10, Rn. 4; *Bamberger/Roth/Saenger,* Art. 10, Rn. 5; *Ferrari u. a./Saenger,* Internationales Vertragsrecht, Art. 10, Rn. 5; *Schlechtriem/Schwenzer/Schwenzer/Hachem,* CISG Commentary, Art. 10, Rn. 7; *Staudinger/Magnus,* Art. 10, Rn. 9; vgl. aber *Vision Systems, Inc. v. EMC Corporation,* Superior Court of Massachusetts, 28.2.2005, CISG-online 1005 = 19 Mass. L. Rptr. 139 (2005): „Similarly, CISG does not apply to the sale of goods between parties if one party has 'multiple business locations' unless it is shown that that party's international location 'has the closest relationship to the contract and its performance'".
[53] *Ferrari u. a./Saenger,* Internationales Vertragsrecht, Art. 10, Rn. 5.

Art. 11 [Formfreiheit]

Der Kaufvertrag braucht nicht schriftlich geschlossen oder nachgewiesen zu werden und unterliegt auch sonst keinen Formvorschriften. Er kann auf jede Weise bewiesen werden, auch durch Zeugen.

Art. 11

A contract of sale need not be concluded in or evidenced by writing and is not subject to any other requirement as to form. It may be proved by any means, including witnesses.

Art. 11

Le contrat de vente n'a pas à etre conclu ni constaté par écrit et n'est soumis à aucune autre condition de forme. Il peut etre prouvé par tous moyens, y compris par témoins.

Übersicht

	Rn.
I. Vorgeschichte	1
II. Allgemeines: Funktionen und Prinzip der Formfreiheit	3
1. Prinzip	3
2. Bedeutung der Formfreiheit bei internationalen Verträgen	4
III. Anwendungsbereich	5
1. Vertragsschluss und Änderung	5
a) Vertragsschluss nach Art. 14 ff.	5
b) Vertragsschluss nach anderen Regeln	6
c) Verträge mit nicht-kaufrechtlichen Teilen	7
d) Vertragsänderungen	8
2. Andere Willenserklärungen und Mitteilungen	9
a) Andere Erklärungen und Mitteilungen	9
b) Im CISG nicht vorgesehene Mitteilungen	10
IV. Verdrängte Regeln	11
1. Nationale Formvorschriften als Gültigkeits- oder Beweisvoraussetzungen	11
a) Form als Gültigkeitsvoraussetzung	11
b) Form als Voraussetzung für Beweis und prozessuale Durchsetzung	12
c) „parol evidence rule"	13
d) Verbraucherschützende Formvorschriften	14
e) Vorgaben zur Sprachverwendung	14a
f) Manifestationspflichten	14b
2. Qualifikationsprobleme	15
V. Vereinbarte Form	16

Vorläufer und **Entwürfe:** Art. 15 EKG, Art. 3 EAG; Genfer E 1976 Art. 11, Wiener E 1977 Art. 11 I, New Yorker E 1978 Art. 10.

I. Vorgeschichte

Die deutschen Juristen seit Art. 317 ADHGB vertraute **Formfreiheit** für Handels- 1 geschäfte hatte sich bereits in den Haager Einheitlichen Kaufgesetzen, allerdings gegen Widerstände, durchgesetzt.[1] Auch bei den Vorarbeiten zum CISG wurde von einzelnen Delegationen gegen die Übernahme des Grundsatzes der Formfreiheit aus den Haager

---

[1] Vgl. zur Vorgeschichte des Art. 3 EAG *von Caemmerer*, RabelsZ 29 (1965), 101, 114 ff.; zu den Vorläufern von Art. 15 EKG *Riese*, RabelsZ 29 (1965), 1, 26 ff.; sowie *Rabel*, RabelsZ 9 (1935), 1, 55 f.; abgedr. in *ders.*, Ges. Aufs. Bd. 3, S. 560; ferner zur Entstehungsgeschichte *Dölle/Reinhart*, Art. 15 EKG, Rn. 27 ff., Art. 3 EAG, Rn. 6 ff.; ferner *Riese*, RabelsZ 29 (1965), 1, 27 und *Dölle/Reinhart*, Art. 15 EKG, Rn. 29 zu den Vorschlägen, den Grundsatz der Formfreiheit aufzugeben oder jedenfalls zugunsten der Staaten, in denen Formvorschriften für Kaufverträge gelten, einzuschränken, um die Ratifikation der (Haager) Kaufrechtsübereinkommen nicht zu gefährden.

Kaufgesetzen noch entschieden Stellung bezogen.[2] Zwar wurde schließlich auf der Wiener Konferenz der Grundsatz der Formfreiheit mit Mehrheit angenommen, doch wurde für die sog. „Schriftformstaaten" als Kompromiss ein Vorbehalt vorgesehen.[3]

2   Im Abkommen ist dieser Kompromiss in Artt. 12, 96 geregelt worden. Ist eine Partei in einem Vorbehaltsstaat niedergelassen, dann entscheidet das IPR des Forums, welches nationale Recht für Formbedürftigkeit oder Formfreiheit maßgebend ist; nicht etwa gelten ohne weiteres die Formvorschriften des Vorbehaltsstaates.[4] Das gilt auch, wenn eine Partei ein Staat, eine Untergliederung eines Staates oder ein Unternehmen im Staatseigentum ist.[5] Die Vorbehaltsmöglichkeit nach Art. 92 I für Teil II der Konvention erfasst den Grundsatz der Formfreiheit nicht.[6]

2a Die Regelungen für Formfreiheit sowie mögliche Ausnahmen (s. Artt. 12, 13) sind am Modell der Alternative „schriftliche oder mündliche" Vertragsschlusserklärungen orientiert. Die modernen elektronischen Kommunikationsmöglichkeiten konnten von den Verfassern des CISG noch nicht berücksichtigt werden. Soweit es beim Grundsatz der Formlosigkeit bleibt, sind auch die durch **elektronische Kommunikation** übermittelten Erklärungen zweifelsfrei gültig;[7] die Konvention ist damit der neueren Tendenz nach medienneutraler Ausgestaltung (s. Rn 4) von Vertragsrecht gefolgt. Die weiteren Fragen zu Zugang, Zeitpunkt und Ort des Wirksamwerdens solcher Erklärungen bei Verwendung elektronischer Kommunikationsmittel sind nicht unter Art. 11 zu behandeln.

II. Allgemeines: Funktionen und Prinzip der Formfreiheit

1. Prinzip

3   Obwohl wichtige Rechtsordnungen (auch) für Kaufverträge an Formen oder formäquivalenten Erfordernissen als Voraussetzung für Gültigkeit und (oder) Beweisbarkeit des Vertragsschlusses und Vertragsinhaltes festhalten, darf man Formfreiheit für Vertragsschlusserklärungen und andere Mitteilungen im Zusammenhang mit dem Abschluss und der Durchführung von Kaufverträgen über bewegliche Sachen als ein anerkanntes, in einer großen Zahl von Rechtsordnungen zu Grunde gelegtes Prinzip sehen.[8] Es setzt die in Art. 6 niedergelegte Parteiautonomie konsequent fort. Allerdings hat das Prinzip Beweisschwierigkeiten zur Folge und prozessrechtlich als Beweisverbote formulierte Regeln werfen trotz der klaren Entscheidung in S. 2 immer wieder Zweifelsfragen auf.[9] Die Vorschrift begründet eine Gegenausnahme zur Herausnahme der Gültigkeitsfragen aus der Konvention durch Art. 4 S. 2 lit. a).[10]

---

[2] Zur entschiedenen Ablehnung des Art. 15 EKG vor allem durch die Vertreter der ehemaligen UdSSR s. YB I (1968–1970), S. 137, Nr. 65 ff.; S. 170, Nr. 90 ff.; S. 187, Nr. 123 f.; YB II (1971), S. 48 f., Nr. 81 ff.; ferner die Diskussionen in YB II (1971), S. 20 f., Nr. 70 ff.; YB III (1972), S. 74 ff., Nr. 41 ff.; YB VI (1975), S. 73 ff.; YB VIII (1977), S. 33 f., Nr. 115 ff.; S. 109 ff. Verständnis für diese Haltung noch bei *Enderlein/Maskow/Strohbach*, Art. 11, Anm. 1.1.: Internationaler Handel sei ohne Dokumentation von Informationen außerhalb der Köpfe der Beteiligten nicht möglich. Das ist richtig, rechtfertigt aber nicht, solche Dokumentation – die im Übrigen heute oft als elektronische Speicherung geschieht – zum Wirksamkeitserfordernis zu machen.
[3] Zu Einzelheiten der Vorgeschichte s. *Schlechtriem*, 1. Aufl., Art. 11 Rn. 1, 2. Zur Liste der Vorbehaltsstaaten s. Anh. I.
[4] Str., s. hierzu Art. 12 Rn. 2.
[5] S. Rn. 7.
[6] *Del Duca*, 25 J. L. & Com. (2005-06), 133, 140 f.; vgl. OLG München, 8.3.1995, CISG-online 145.
[7] S. CISG-AC, Op. 1 (*Chr. Ramberg*), Comment 11.1.
[8] Vgl. die rechtsvergleichenden Übersichten bei *Dölle/Reinhart*, Art. 15 EKG, Rn. 10–25 und *Lando/Beale*, Part I and II, PECL Art. 2:102, Comment 4 (a); neuere Kodifikationen s. NBW 3:37; estnisches Obligationenrecht § 11 I; chinesisches Vertragsgesetz Art. 10 I.
[9] Zu Beweismitteln und -erleichterungen nach der lex fori s. unten Rn. 13.
[10] Etwa *Kröll*, 25 J. L. & Com. (2005), 39, 54.

2. Bedeutung der Formfreiheit bei internationalen Verträgen

Formfreiheit ist auch im grenzüberschreitenden Warenverkehr wichtig. Zwar werden 4 Verträge wohl zumeist irgendwann schriftlich fixiert, Vertragsschlusserklärungen oft durch Fax oder elektronisch übermittelt, doch kann unsicher sein, ob eine zur Dokumentation erfolgte Fixierung des Vertragsinhalts, z. B. Ausdruck einer E-Mail- oder Internet-Korrespondenz, die konstitutiven Vertragsschlusserklärungen enthält, ob ein Fax Schriftformerfordernissen entspricht, usw.[11] Zulässigkeit formfreier Einigung entbindet von der Klärung solcher Zweifelsfragen (s. Rn. 2). Vor allem für **Vertragsänderungen**, deren Notwendigkeit sich „vor Ort" bei Durchführung eines Kaufvertrages zeigen kann – z. b. bei Montage des Kaufgegenstandes –, ist die Verbindlichkeit von Vereinbarungen im Wege direkter Kommunikationsmittel – mündliche und telefonische Erklärungen, Fernschreiben, Telekopien (Fax), E-Mail und andere elektronische Kommunikation etc. – unverzichtbar.[12] Auch Vertragsschlüsse geschehen häufig durch derart mitgeteilte Erklärungen. Soweit die Parteien korrespondiert und mündlich erklärt haben, entlastet der Grundsatz der Formfreiheit davon, Vorkorrespondenz, Vertragsschlusserklärungen und dem Vertragsschluss nachfolgende Kommunikation, etwa zusammenfassende und bestätigende Memoranda, **aus Formgründen** klar abgrenzen zu müssen.[13] Art. 8 III schreibt dies für die Auslegung fort, wenngleich Artt. 14, 18, 19 – anders als Art. 2.1.1 PICC („conduct of the parties that is sufficient to show agreement") – für den Vertragsschluss eine Identifizierung der erforderlichen Erklärungen fordern. Schließlich aber entbindet das Prinzip der Formfreiheit von der Notwendigkeit, die Formvorschriften fremder Rechtsordnungen zu ermitteln und zu beachten. Dies wird auch deshalb zunehmend wichtiger, weil mit der schnellen Entwicklung neuer Kommunikationsmöglichkeiten immer wieder fraglich wird, ob und inwieweit ihre Nutzung den – zumeist – auf einem früheren Stand der Entwicklung stehengebliebenen Formvorschriften in nationalen Rechten entspricht.[14] Die Konvention folgt hier dem rechtspolitischen Gebot der **Medienneutralität** des Vertragsrechts.

III. Anwendungsbereich

1. Vertragsschluss und Änderung

a) **Vertragsschluss nach Art. 14 ff.** Art. 11 ordnet Formfreiheit für den **Vertrags-** 5 **schluss**, d. h. die vertragskonstitutiven Willenserklärungen „Angebot" (Art. 14 I) und „Annahme" (Artt. 18, 19 II) an. Die Vorgeschichte zu Art. 3 EAG[15] macht deutlich, dass Formfreiheit nicht Ausdrücklichkeit voraussetzt, sondern dass die Möglichkeit stillschweigender, konkludent durch Verhalten zum Ausdruck gebrachter Vertragsschlusserklärungen, wie Art. 18 I 1 für die Annahme verdeutlicht („other conduct", „Verhalten"), offengehalten werden sollte.[16] Art. 11 gilt direkt nur für die Vertragsschlusserklärungen der Parteien,

---

[11] S. hierzu Fn. 14 sowie Art. 13 Rn. 5 ff.

[12] S. Art. 29 Rn. 2 f.

[13] Hat bei Aufgabe einer Bestellung auf einem Bestellformular nur eine der beiden Parteien unterschrieben, dann braucht nicht geprüft zu werden, ob eine solche „einseitige" Unterschrift auf einem Bestellformular der Verkäuferin in den Betracht kommenden nationalen Formvorschriften entspricht, vgl. zu Art. 3 EAG, LG Heidelberg, 30.1.1979, in: *Schlechtriem/Magnus*, Art. 22 EKG, Nr. 2; OLG Hamm, 25.6.1984, daselbst Art. 3 EAG, Nr. 5.

[14] Vgl. zur Behinderung zügiger Geschäftsabwicklung durch die Notwendigkeit eigenhändiger Unterschrift nach § 126 BGB, die den Bedürfnissen neuzeitlicher Bürotechnik nicht entspricht, MünchKomm/*Einsele*, § 126 BGB, Rn. 23 f.; ferner *Köhler*, AcP 182 (1982), 126, 147 ff. zu Faksimile-Unterschriften. Zur Frage, ob ein Fax der Schriftform des § 126 BGB entspricht, s. BGH NJW 1993, 1126; *Prütting/Wegen/Weinreich/Ahrens*, § 126, Rn. 13 (verneinend); anders für das Prozessrecht GmS-OGB NJW 2000, 2340, 2341.

[15] S. *Dölle/Reinhart*, Art. 3 EAG, Rn. 10 f.; ferner *von Caemmerer*, RabelsZ 29 (1965), 101, 138 f. zu den Vorschlägen, konkludente Vertragsschlüsse besonders zu regeln.

[16] Formfreiheit bedeutet freilich nicht völlige Formlosigkeit, vgl. *Wey*, Rn. 409. Auch Zugangserfordernisse verlangen eine gewisse Förmlichkeit, s. zu ihrer Notwendigkeit für die Vertragsschlusserklärungen Artt. 15 I, 18 II, 24. Zur juristischen Form i. w. S. s. *Flume*, Allgemeiner Teil, Bd. 2, § 15 I 5, S. 249 f.

Schmidt-Kessel

Art. 11 6, 7 Teil I. Kapitel II. Allgemeine Bestimmungen

jedoch ist die Vorschrift nicht anzuwenden, soweit die Parteien zusätzlich zu Angebot und Annahme weitere Erklärungen vorsehen, etwa eine „Billigung", „Letztentscheidung" u. ä. nach einer Bedenkzeit, und Formfreiheit erleichtert die Möglichkeit des Zustandekommens eines Vertrages ohne identifizierbare Erklärungen „Angebot" und „Annahme".[17] Hingegen gilt Art. 11 **nicht** für sonstige vertragskonstitutive Erklärungen, etwa die Zustimmung des Vertretenen zu einem Vertretergeschäft,[18] der gesetzlichen Vertreter eines Minderjährigen[19] oder eines Ehegatten,[20] die Genehmigung einer Behörde.[21] Diese Erklärungen sind auch nicht Regelungsgegenstand der Konvention i. S. v. Art. 7.

6 b) **Vertragsschluss nach anderen Regeln.** Soweit auf Grund von Parteivereinbarungen, Übung der Parteien oder nach Art. 9 I oder II zu berücksichtigenden **Handelsbräuchen** der Vertragsschluss[22] anders als durch korrespondierende und als Angebot und Annahme zu qualifizierende Erklärungen geschieht, müssen die insoweit vereinbarten, durch Übung der Parteien etablierten oder auf Grund Internationalität eines Handelsbrauchs geltenden Regeln für die maßgeblichen Formen Beachtung finden: Sollten die deutschen Regeln zu **kaufmännischen Bestätigungsschreiben** auf Grund einer dieser Geltungsmöglichkeiten anwendbar[23] und ein an Dissens gescheiterter Vertragsschluss durch ein Bestätigungsschreiben heilbar sein, so muss die Bestätigung schriftlich erfolgen;[24] Berufung auf Art. 11, um einer mündlichen (z. B. telefonischen) Bestätigung vertragskonstitutive Wirkung über die Voraussetzungen für eine solche Wirkung nach den insoweit maßgeblichen Bräuchen hinaus zu verschaffen, ist nicht möglich.

7 c) **Verträge mit nicht-kaufrechtlichen Teilen.** Art. 11 gilt bei gemischten Verträgen nur für den kaufrechtlichen Teil. Dieser schließt grundsätzlich auch Verträge mit staatlichen Stellen ein und verdrängt damit nationales **Vergaberecht**.[25] Die Formbedürftigkeit von **Wettbewerbsabreden**,[26] die mit dem Kaufvertrag verbunden sind, sowie von im Zusammenhang mit einem Warenkauf vereinbarten **Grundstücksgeschäften, Gerichtsstands-** und **Schiedsgerichtsklauseln** richtet sich nach den anwendbaren nationalen oder einheitsrechtlichen Formvorschriften;[27] für letztere ergibt sich dies schon aus Art. 90.[28] Ist Folge ihrer Verletzung Nichtigkeit eines (Teils des) Rechtsgeschäfts, so bestimmt zunächst die die Nichtigkeit anordnende Norm auch die Folgen einer solchen **Teilnichtigkeit** für das Gesamtgeschäft (Art. 4 S. 2 lit. a)). Soweit dieses keine Nichtigkeit des Gesamtgeschäfts

---

[17] S. hierzu auch unten Rn. 10.
[18] Zur Maßgeblichkeit des über IPR berufenen nationalen Rechts für die Vertretung s. OLG Koblenz, 16.3.1984 in: *Schlechtriem/Magnus*, Art. 1 EAG, Nr. 11.
[19] S. *Dölle/Reinhart*, Art. 3 EAG, Rn. 25; *Wey*, Rn. 414; dagegen muss die Erklärung des Minderjährigen selbst stets formfrei sein; zweifelnd *Wey*, Rn. 107 f., 414.
[20] *Wey*, Rn. 414.
[21] Vgl. *Dölle/Reinhart*, Art. 3 EAG, Rn. 25; *Wey*, Rn. 415, 416 (auch zur Form einer Kompetenzbegründung für Organe und Vertreter öffentlich-rechtlicher Organisationen; dazu noch Rn. 15).
[22] Zur Geltung des Art. 9 auch für das Vertragsschlussverfahren s. *Schlechtriem*, Einheitliches UN-Kaufrecht, S. 28; zum Ganzen *Schroeter*, Vor Artt. 14–24 Rn. 2–5 und Art. 9 Rn. 3, 22–24.
[23] Hierzu Art. 9 Rn. 22–24; *Schlechtriem*, Einheitliches UN-Kaufrecht, S. 29; *Schlosser*, FS Medicus, S. 550 f.
[24] S. auch das ZGer Basel-Stadt, 21.12.1992, CISG-online 55 = BJM 1993, 310, 312 f.: Anwendung österreichischer und schweizer Regeln zu kaufmännischen Bestätigungsschreiben – Vertragskonstitutiv war in Schriftform bestätigt worden. Im Blick auf das österreichische Recht ist die Entscheidung freilich unzutreffend, s. Art. 9 Rn. 25. Unrichtig für den Fall der Maßgeblichkeit der Situation in Deutschland *Kröll u. a./Perales Viscasillas*, Art. 9, Rn. 31: ausnahmsweise auch mündlich.
[25] Für die Anwendbarkeit im Vergabekontext *Ziegel*, 25 J. L. & Com. (2005), 59, 62. Zum Sonderfall der Begrenzung der Vertretungsmacht von Amtsinhabern durch Formvorschriften s. Rn 15.
[26] *Ferrari*, Draft Digest, S. 206, 208. Zur Streichung von § 35 GWB s. *Bunte*, BB 1998, 1600–1601.
[27] *Herber/Czerwenka*, Art. 11, Rn. 5; *Neumayer/Ming*, Art. 11, Anm. 1.; für Schiedsklausel s. OLG München, 8.3.1995, CISG-online 145 = NJW-RR 1996, 1532; BGH, 23.7.1997, CISG-online 276 = NJW 1997, 3309, m. Anm. *Schlechtriem/Schmidt-Kessel*, EWiR 1997, 985 f.; *Witz/Salger/Lorenz/Witz*, Art. 11, Rn. 7; *Bamberger/Roth/Saenger*, Art. 11, Rn. 6; a. A. *Kröll u. a./Perales Viscasillas*, Art. 11, Rn. 13; *Piltz*, Internationales Kaufrecht, 1. Aufl., § 3, Rn. 119.
[28] *Schwenzer/Hachem/Kee*, Rn. 3.33; insoweit zutreffend auch *Kröll u. a./Perales Viscasillas*, Art. 13, Rn. 10; *Del Duca*, 25 J. L. & Com. (2005-06), 133, 141 f.

fordert, sind die Folgen der Teilnichtigkeit im Wege der Auslegung nach Art. 8 der Konvention zu bewältigen;[29] Art. 4 S. 2 lit. a) fordert richtigerweise keine Anwendung der allgemeinen Regeln des nationalen Rechts zur Teilnichtigkeit.[30] Maßstab der Auslegung wird jeweils sein, ob die Parteien den kaufrechtlichen Teil des Geschäfts auch ohne den formbedürftigen anderen Teil abgeschlossen hätten.[31] Ein Rückgriff auf nationale Regeln wie § 139 BGB kommt nicht in Betracht.[32]

d) Vertragsänderungen. Formfreiheit auf Grund Art. 11 gilt auch für **Vertragsänderungen**, **-ergänzungen** und **-aufhebung**.[33] Art. 29 I, der die Möglichkeit von Vertragsänderung und -aufhebung vorsieht, ihr Zustandekommen jedoch selbst nicht regelt, geht von der Anwendbarkeit der Art. 14 ff. auf derartige Vereinbarungen aus.[34] Die Anwendbarkeit des Art. 11 wird in der Regelung des Art. 29 II 1 erkennbar vorausgesetzt, wie auch die Bezugnahme auf die Artt. 11 und 29 in Art. 12 zeigt. Möglich ist insbesondere eine konkludente Aufhebung des Vertrags.[35] Richtigerweise erfasst Art. 11 damit auch die Vertragsübernahme.[36]

2. Andere Willenserklärungen und Mitteilungen

a) Andere Erklärungen und Mitteilungen. Auch andere im Abkommen vorgesehene Erklärungen der Parteien, die im Vertragsschlussverfahren,[37] für die Durchführung des Vertrages[38] oder als Reaktion auf Leistungsstörungen[39] erforderlich werden, sind formfrei.[40] Art. 11 regelt die Formfreiheit dieser Erklärungen freilich nicht ausdrücklich, doch muss m. E. eine Auslegung des Abkommens auf Grund der in Art. 7 II festgehaltenen Maxime die Formfreiheit als einen der maßgebenden Grundsätze beachten, sodass ihre Geltung für diese Erklärungen, Mitteilungen usw. vorbehaltlich einer abweichenden Vereinbarung der Parteien anzunehmen ist. Auf die international nicht einheitlich beurteilten Voraussetzungen einer Analogie kommt es daher nicht an.[41]

b) Im CISG nicht vorgesehene Mitteilungen. Für andere als die im Abkommen geregelten Erklärungen, Mitteilungen, Anzeigen usw. ist dagegen zunächst zu entscheiden, ob sie „in diesem Abkommen geregelte Gegenstände" i. S. d. Art. 7 II betreffen und deshalb nach den Grundsätzen des Abkommens zu behandeln, also formfrei sind,[42] oder ob sie als nicht-kaufrechtliche Materie einem der in Betracht kommenden nationalen Rechte unterstehen. Werden z. B. im Zuge der Rückabwicklung eines aufgehobenen Kaufvertrages Mitteilungen erforderlich, so dürfen sie formfrei vorgenommen werden,

---

[29] Anders noch die Vorauflage.
[30] S. Art. 8 Rn. 7a.
[31] Vgl. *Schlechtriem*, Einheitliches UN-Kaufrecht, S. 31 Fn. 138; *Wey*, Rn. 304 und (speziell zum Schweizer Kartellrecht) Rn. 421.
[32] S. Art. 8 Rn. 7a.
[33] *Kröll u. a./Perales Viscasillas*, Art. 11, Rn. 1.
[34] Vgl. *Enderlein/Maskow/Strohbach*, Art. 29, Anm. 1.2.; *Honsell/Karollus*, Art. 29, Rn. 9 f.; *Staudinger/Magnus*, Art. 29, Rn. 9 f.; *Rudolph*, Art. 29, Rn. 2; *Wey*, Rn. 411, 413; *Ferrari*, Draft Digest, S. 206, 207 f.; s. auch *Schroeter*, Art. 29 Rn. 2.
[35] *Ferrari*, Draft Digest, S. 206, 208.
[36] Dafür nachdrücklich *Nemeczek*, IHR 2011, 49, 54.
[37] Z. B. Rücknahmeerklärungen, Artt. 15 II, 22; Angebotswiderruf, Art. 16 I; Beanstandung einer abweichenden Annahme, Art. 19 II 1; Unterrichtungen bei verspäteter Annahme nach Art. 21 I, II.
[38] Z. B. Aufforderung oder Anzeige des Verkäufers nach Art. 48 I, III; Spezifikation der Warenmerkmale, Art. 65 I; Mitteilung, Art. 65 II; Zuordnungsanzeige, Art. 67 II.
[39] Z. B. Aufhebungserklärung, Artt. 26, 49, 64, 72 I, 73; Anzeigen und Aufforderungen oder sonstige Mitteilungen, Art. 27; Mängelrüge, Artt. 39, 43 I; Nachfristsetzung, Art. 47, 63 I; Minderungserklärung, Art. 50; Zurückbehaltungsanzeige, Art. 71 III; Aufhebungswarnung, Art. 72 II; Anzeige beabsichtigten Selbsthilfeverkaufs, Art. 88 II.
[40] *Enderlein/Maskow/Strohbach*, Art. 11, Anm. 1.3.; *Wey*, Rn. 404; *Bamberger/Roth/Saenger*, Art. 11, Rn. 4; *Kröll u. a./Perales Viscasillas*, Art. 11, Rn. 1; *Staudinger/Magnus*, Art. 11, Rn. 7; *Ferrari*, Draft Digest, 206, 207.
[41] Für eine Analogie etwa *Witz/Salger/Lorenz*, Art. 11, Rn. 4.
[42] *Kröll u. a./Perales Viscasillas*, Art. 11, Rn. 6.

denn insoweit geht es um eine – wenn auch lückenhaft geregelte – Kaufrechtsmaterie. Erklärungen zur Bewirkung oder Durchführung von Erfüllungs- oder Sicherungsgeschäften unterliegen dagegen nationalen Formvorschriften.[43]

IV. Verdrängte Regeln

1. Nationale Formvorschriften als Gültigkeits- oder Beweisvoraussetzungen

11 a) **Form als Gültigkeitsvoraussetzung.** Art. 11 bedarf – auch hinsichtlich des Begriffs der Form – einer **autonomen Auslegung**, die einem **funktionalen** Ansatz folgt.[44] Die Vorschrift verdrängt daher zunächst diejenigen Regeln in nationalen Rechten, die Form als Gültigkeitsvoraussetzung einsetzen, bei Formlosigkeit oder Formverletzungen also Ungültigkeit, Nichtigkeit (wie nach § 125 S. 1 BGB) oder Vernichtbarkeit und evtl. Heilbarkeit eintreten lassen. Art. 4 S. 2 lit. a) gilt insoweit nicht. Welche Form i. e. das nationale Recht vorschreibt – Schriftlichkeit, eigenhändige Unterschrift einer oder beider Seiten, Zeugenunterschriften usw. –, ist unerheblich.[45] Auch **„consideration"** als formäquivalentes Gültigkeitserfordernis ist nicht erforderlich,[46] etwa für als bindend ausgestaltete Erklärungen (Angebot), vor allem aber bei Vertragsänderungen und -ergänzungen (Art. 29). Unberührt bleiben freilich andere, d. h. Gültigkeit und Durchsetzbarkeit des Vertrages nicht berührende und von dem nationalen Recht, das die Form vorschreibt, verhängte **Sanktionen** gegen den formlos Erklärenden, z. B. dienstrechtliche Maßregeln gegen Mitarbeiter wegen Verletzung zur Kontrolle dienender Gegenzeichnungsvorschriften, Strafvorschriften für die Nichtbeachtung von zur Devisenbewirtschaftung erlassenen Formvorschriften usw.[47]

12 b) **Form als Voraussetzung für Beweis und prozessuale Durchsetzung.** Art. 11 S. 2 entbindet von nationalen Formvorschriften, die zwar nicht die Gültigkeit, aber die Beweisbarkeit des Vertrages bzw. einzelner Erklärungen von bestimmten Formen abhängig machen, wie etwa Statutes of Frauds oder entsprechende kontinentale Regelungen.[48] Auch wenn das nationale Recht solche **Beweisformvorschriften** prozessual qualifiziert, geht Art. 11 vor. Auch Art. 8 III beruht auf dem Grundsatz der beweisrechtlichen Zulässigkeit jeglichen Auslegungsmaterials.[49] Allerdings bleiben nationale Verfahrensvorschriften über Beweismittel und ihre Beschränkung, etwa für den Urkundenprozess oder für die Parteivernehmung, unberührt.[50] Auch der Beweiswert, d. h. die Beweiswürdigung, bleibt Sache nationalen Verfahrensrechts.[51] Entscheidend für die Abgrenzung „echter" Prozessnormen

---

[43] Vgl. für die Übereignung Art. 4 S. 2 lit. b); gleiches muss für Zahlung und Zahlungssicherung gelten.

[44] S. Rn. 15.

[45] So ausdrücklich für den Fall einer fehlenden schriftlichen Auftragsbestätigung nach telefonischem Vertragsschluss RB Arnheim, 5.11.2008, CISG-online 1751, Nr. 4.5 und KreisG St. Gallen, 16.10.2009, CISG-online 2023. Zu den Vorteil, damit auch von Zweifelsfragen in nationalen Rechten zu veralteten Formvorschriften entlastet zu sein, s. o. Rn. 4.

[46] *Ferrari*, Draft Digest, S. 206, 211; *ders.*, IHR 2004, 1, 4; vgl. zunächst *Wey*, Rn. 410 Fn. 1098. Entsprechend für kontinentale *causa*-Lehren *Kröll u. a./Perales Viscasillas*, Art. 11, Rn. 8.

[47] *Enderlein/Maskow/Strohbach*, Art. 11, Anm. 1.2.; *Honnold/Flechtner*, Art. 11, Rn. 127; *Lookofsky*, The 1980 United Nations Convention, Anm. 93.; s. a. Sekretariatskommentar, Art. 10, Nr. 2 f.

[48] S. § 2–201 UCC, auch in der geänderten Fassung 2006 (*Calzaturificio Claudia v. Olivieri Footwear Ltd.*, U. S. Dist. Ct. (S. D. N. Y.), 6.4.1998, CISG-online 440; *Solae, LLC v. Hershey Canada, Inc.*, U. S. Dist. Ct. (Del.), 9.5.2008, CISG-online 1769; *Miami Valley Paper, LLC v. Lebbing Engineering & Consulting GmbH*, U. S. Dist. Ct. (S. D. Ohio), 26.3.2009, CISG-online 1880; *Honnold/Flechtner*, Art. 11, Rn. 126; *Del Duca*, 25 J. L. & Com. (2005-06), 133; übergangen von der Mehrheit der Richter in *GPL Treatment Ltd. v. Louisiana-Pacific Corp.*, U. S. Ct. App. (9th Cir.), 12.4.1995, CISG-online 147. Ferner Art. 1341 Code civil und Art. 2721 Codice civile (*Del Duca*, 25 J. L. & Com. (2005-06), 133; s. außerdem *Lando/Beale*, PECL, Art. 2:102 Anm. 4 (b).

[49] *Schmidt-Kessel*, Art. 8 Rn. 13.

[50] Vgl. *Dölle/Reinhart*, Art. 15 EKG, Rn. 58, 59; *Staudinger/Magnus*, Art. 11, Rn. 17; *Wey*, Rn. 410; unklar *Honsell/Melis*, Art. 11, Rn. 6.

[51] *Schmidt-Kessel*, Art. 8 Rn. 13: Gewichtung des Auslegungsmaterials. Wie hier auch *Ferrari*, Draft Digest, S. 206, 212 sowie *Kröll u. a./Perales Viscasillas*, Art. 11, Rn. 18.

von Formvorschriften ist die Funktion der Norm: Soweit bei Nichteinhaltung der Form der Beweis und damit die Durchsetzbarkeit völlig abgeschnitten werden, wirkt die Beweisform wie eine Gültigkeitsvoraussetzung[52] und ist deshalb als sachrechtliche Formvorschrift zu qualifizieren, fällt also unter Art. 11.[53] Soweit Urkunden nur Beweiserleichterungen bewirken, gilt das Verfahrensrecht der lex fori.[54] Die Formulierung in Art. 11, dass „auf jede Weise bewiesen werden" kann, lässt also vor deutschen Gerichten bei Streitigkeiten aus CISG-Verträgen nicht uneingeschränkt Parteivernehmung oder im Urkundenprozess sogar Zeugen als Beweismittel zu.

c) „parol evidence rule". Soweit nationale Vorschriften bei Auslegung eines Vertrages dokumentierten Erklärungen und ihrem Inhalt Ausschließlichkeit einräumen und den Beweis, dass mündlich anderes vereinbart oder eine andere Bedeutung gemeint war, nicht zulassen, haben sie ebenfalls zurückzutreten: Mündliche (Zusatz)vereinbarungen sind nach Art. 11 gültig, die Ermittlung des von den Parteien gewollten oder gemeinten Inhalts ihrer Erklärungen richtet sich nach Art. 8 III und kann nicht durch nationales Recht – etwa eine **„parol evidence rule"** wie in § 2–202 UCC – beschränkt werden.[55] Ein „Beweisgefälle" zugunsten schriftlicher Erklärungen wird dadurch jedoch nicht verhindert.[56] Ob eine schriftliche Niederlegung des Vertrages eine Vermutung der Vollständigkeit und Richtigkeit begründen kann, ist umstritten.[57] Jedenfalls kann zur Widerlegung dieser Vermutung nach Art. 8 (insbesondere Abs. 3) auf außerhalb der Urkunde liegende Umstände zurückgegriffen werden.[58]

d) **Verbraucherschützende Formvorschriften.** Im Anschluss an entsprechende Erörterungen zu Artt. 15 EKG, 3 EAG[59] könnte zweifelhaft sein, ob **verbraucherschützende Formvorschriften** nationaler Rechte – in Italien z. B. Art. 1341 II Cc – von Art. 11 unberührt bleiben. M. E. sollte Art. 11 auch von Formvorschriften, die vielleicht im na-

---

[52] *Wey*, Rn. 410: würde zur Entstehung von unvollkommenen Obligationen führen.
[53] Pauschaler *Kröll u. a./Perales Viscasillas*, Art. 11, Rn. 18.
[54] LG Memmingen, 1.12.1993, CISG-online 73 = IPRax 1995, 251 m. Anm. *Ranker*; s. a. OLG München, 8.3.1995, CISG-online 145 = NJW-RR 1996, 1532 f.; früher so schon *Dölle/Reinhart*, Art. 15 EKG, Rn. 58.
[55] CISG-AC, Op. 3 (*Hyland*), Comment 1; *Honnold/Flechtner*, Art. 8, Rn. 110; *Wey*, Rn. 407; *Schmidt-Kessel*, Art. 8 Rn. 32 ff. Bedenklich deshalb das obiter dictum in *Beijing Metals & Minerals Import/Export Corp. v. American Business Center, Inc.*, U. S. Ct. App. (5th Cir.), 15.6.1993, CISG-online 89 = 993 F. 2d. 1178, 1182, die „parol evidence rule applies regardless", d. h. sie sei ohne Rücksicht auf die Anwendbarkeit des CISG zu berücksichtigen; kritisch dazu *Flechtner*, 14 J. L. & Com. (1995), 153–176; *Moore*, B. Y. U. L. Rev. (1995), 1347; überwiegend verneinen US-amerikanische Gerichte die Anwendbarkeit dieser Regel im Geltungsbereich des CISG, s. *Calzaturificio Claudia s. n. c. v. Olivieri Footwear Ltd.*, U. S. Dist. Ct. (S. D. N. Y.), 6.4.1998, CISG-online 440; *Fercus S. r. l. v. Mario Palazzo and others*, U. S. Dist. Ct. (S. D. N. Y.), 8.8.2000, CISG-online 588 = 2000 U. S. Dist. LEXIS 11 086; *MCC-Marble Ceramic Center, Inc. v. Ceramica Nuova D'Agostino S. p. A.*, U. S. Ct. App. (11th Cir.), 29.6.1998, CISG-online: „It should also be noted that (…) the Convention essentially rejects both the Statute of Frauds and the parol evidence rule, Sale of Goods Convention Article 11, Article 8 (3)"; s. ferner *Filanto S. p. A. v. Chilewich International Corp.*, U. S. Dist. Ct. (S. D. N. Y.), 14.2.1992, CISG-online 45 = 789 F. Supp. 1229, 1238 Fn. 7, m. Anm. *Brand/Flechtner*, 12 J. L. & Com. (1993), 239–240; *L. F. Del Duca/P. Del Duca*, 27 UCC L. J. (1995), 331; *Kröll u. a./Perales Viscasillas*, Art. 11, Rn. 16; *Nakata*, 7 Transnat'l Law. (1994), 141–163; *Bundesamt für Justiz (Schweiz)*, SZIER 1993, 653; *Magnus*, ZEuP 1993, 79; *Piltz*, NJW 1994, 1101–1106; *Perales*, Der. neg. 1995, 9–14; die Sachfrage ignoriert *GPL Treatment Ltd. v. Louisiana-Pacific Corp.*, U. S. Ct. App. (9th Cir.), 12.4.1995, CISG-online 147.
[56] Vgl. *Honnold/Flechtner*, Art. 8, Rn. 110: „Jurists interpreting agreements subject to the Convention can be expected to continue to give special and, in most cases, controlling effect to detailed written agreements." S. a. *José Luis Morales y/o Son Export, S. A. de C. V., de Hermosillo Sonora, México v. Nez Marketing de Los Angeles California, E. U. A.*, Comisión para la Protección del Comercio Exterior de México, 4.5.1993, CISG-online 75, Diario oficial de 27.5.1993, 17–19: Existenz eines Vertrages hinreichend durch die Rechnung des Verkäufers und die Lieferdokumente, die den Käufer als Abnehmer auswiesen, belegt; ferner RB Hasselt, 22.5.2002, CISG-online 703.
[57] Dafür die 4. Auflage. Dagegen *Schmidt-Kessel*, Art. 8 Rn. 34.
[58] Vgl. BGH, 5.7.2002, NJW 2002, 3164 (nicht zum CISG); *Prütting/Wegen/Weinreich/Ahrens*, § 125, Rn. 26 (zum deutschen Recht).
[59] Vgl. *Dölle/Reinhart*, Art. 15 EKG, Rn. 55, einerseits, *Dölle/Stoll*, Art. 74 EKG, Rn. 145, 147, andererseits.

tionalen Recht zeitweise einen besonders hohen rechtspolitischen Stellenwert hatten oder haben, nicht verdrängt werden.⁶⁰ Zuweilen kann fraglich sein, ob Vorschriften als Formvorschriften, als Gültigkeitsnormen oder anders zu qualifizieren sind: § 305c I BGB (früher § 3 AGBG) regelt an sich eine Frage der Gestaltung des Vertragsinhalts beim Vertragsschluss und müsste im Anwendungsbereich des CISG den Artt. 14 ff. weichen; *Drobnig*⁶¹ qualifiziert ihn dagegen als Formvorschrift, die (deshalb) hinter Art. 11 zurückzustehen habe. M. E. ist § 305c I BGB jedoch Gültigkeitsnorm.⁶²

14a **e) Vorgaben zur Sprachverwendung.** Ebenfalls als Formvorschriften i. S. v. Art. 11 sind Vorgaben über die **Sprachverwendung** zu qualifizieren. Diese werden ebenfalls durch das CISG verdrängt;⁶³ auch ein Vorbehalt nach Art. 96 ändert daran nichts, weil diese Vorschrift allein die Möglichkeit der Etablierung zusätzlicher Schriftformerfordernisse erfasst. Verdrängt wird damit etwa das Gesetz über die polnische Sprache,⁶⁴ soweit es im Anwendungsbereich des CISG Vorgaben für die Gestaltung von Verträgen macht. Hingegen sind Gebote der Verständlichkeit und Transparenz, die evtl. auch zur Beschränkung in der Verwendung von Sprachen führen können, nicht als Formproblem zu behandeln,⁶⁵ sondern eine Frage des Zugangs von Erklärungen und ihrer Auslegung.⁶⁶

14b **f) Manifestationspflichten.** Zunehmend auferlegt der nationale Gesetzgeber bestimmten Vertragsparteien – vor allem, aber nicht nur dem Vertragspartner eines Verbrauchers – im Zusammenhang des Vertragsschlusses Pflichten zur **Manifestation** oder **Manifestationsmöglichkeit** von Vertragsschlusserklärungen und Vertragstexten, vgl. § 312e I Ziff. 2 BGB i. V. m. § 3 Ziff. 2 Informationspflichten-VO, § 312e I Ziff. 4 BGB,⁶⁷ § 312c II BGB i. V. m. § 1 II und III Informationspflichten-VO.⁶⁸ Die Einhaltung solcher Pflichten ist zwar nicht wie bei „echten" Formvorschriften Gültigkeitsvoraussetzung, sodass sie eindeutig durch Art. 11 S. 1 verdrängt würden, und die zu manifestierenden Erklärungen und Texte sind auch nicht ausschließliche Beweismittel i. S. v. Art. 11 S. 2. Aber diese Vorschriften normieren nicht nur unverbindliche Appelle, auch wenn die Sanktionen für Pflichtverletzungen und damit der Überschneidungsbereich zum CISG vielfach unklar sind.⁶⁹ Jedenfalls kann die Erfüllung dieser Manifestationspflichten erzwungen werden, etwa durch (teilweise)

---

⁶⁰ Wie hier Cass., 16.5.2007, CISG-online 1404 (für Art. 1341 Cc). Ebenso *Frense*, S. 45; *Kröll u. a./Perales Viscasillas*, Art. 11, Rn. 10; *Neumayer/Ming*, Art. 11, Anm. 1.; *Rehbinder*, Vertragsschluss, S. 155; zum ital. Recht *Bonell*, ZVerglRW 1979, 1–20; *Staudinger/Magnus*, Art. 11, Rn. 14; *Padovini*, 23 Riv. dir. int. priv. proc. 1987, 47–58; zur Anknüpfung von zwingenden verbraucherschützenden Vorschriften s. jedoch auch *Stoll*, Internationalprivatrechtliche Fragen, S. 511 f. Wo auf Grund einer Widerrufsmöglichkeit Gültigkeitsfragen, die nach Art. 4 S. 2 lit. a) nationalem Recht vorbehalten bleiben, geregelt sind, und der Lauf einer Widerrufsfrist von einer schriftlichen Belehrung des Widerrufsberechtigten abhängt, dürfen solche nationalen Formvorschriften im Anwendungsbereich des CISG auch nicht mittelbare Wirkung haben; der Fristbeginn muss deshalb durch eine am Einheitsrecht ausgerichtete Auslegung anders angesetzt werden. Zum VerbrKrG vertrat jedoch *Herber* in der 2. Aufl., Art. 2 Rn. 18, generell Vorrang auf Grund Art. 90, da es auf eine EG-Richtlinie zurückgeht.
⁶¹ *Drobnig*, FS Mann, S. 614 f.
⁶² S. Vor Artt. 14–24 Rn. 9.
⁶³ Zutreffend *Piltz*, NJW 2003, 2056, 2061.
⁶⁴ Etwa das Gesetz über die polnische Sprache vom 7.10.1999; dazu *Klapsa*, WiRO 2000, 233 ff.
⁶⁵ Vgl. *Freitag*, IPRax 1999, 142, 146 ff.; *Spellenberg*, Fremdsprache und Rechtsgeschäft, S. 465 (zu Art. 11 EGBGB).
⁶⁶ Vgl. zu AGB Art. 14 Rn. 16 f.; zur Sprache Art. 24 Rn. 16, Art. 27 Rn. 8.
⁶⁷ Die Regelung dieser Vorschrift geht auf Art. 10 III E-Commerce-RL zurück und ist deshalb auch in anderen europäischen Rechtsordnungen zu finden.
⁶⁸ Die Vorschrift, die auf die Fernabsatzrichtlinie zurückgeht und deshalb auch in anderen europäischen Rechtsordnungen in dieser oder inhaltsähnlicher Form zu finden ist, wendet sich zwar an den Vertragspartner eines Verbrauchers, doch sind Verbraucherverträge auf Grund der subjektiven Komponente des Art. 2 lit. a) HS. 2 nicht stets vom Anwendungsbereich des CISG ausgeschlossen; auch ist nicht auszuschließen, dass solche Regelungen für Verträge getroffen werden, an denen nicht (nur) Konsumenten als Besteller beteiligt sind.
⁶⁹ Einzelheiten hierzu *Janal*, S. 144 ff.; *Schwintowski*, Sanktionen, S. 270 („chronisches Rechtsfolgendefizit"), 271 ff.; *Wilhelmsson*, Remedies, S. 247 („…in most cases the contractual consequences of breaching such information requirements have not been expressly regulated").

Zurückhaltung der eigenen Leistung.[70] Sie sollen die Rechtsstellung der jeweils geschützten Partei verbessern, indem sie Beweisführungsmöglichkeiten sichern und Belehrung über vertragliche und gesetzliche Rechte erreichen sollen; auch soll das Vertragsschlussverfahren für die geschützte Partei transparenter werden. Damit verschieben sie aber die Interessengewichtung des CISG zugunsten der geschützten Partei und entsprechen in der Funktion den in Art. 11 S. 2 erfassten Vorschriften für Beweismittel; der Quasi-Formcharakter solcher Regeln sollte ihre Anwendung allein auf Grund des hilfsweise berufenen Formstatuts ausschließen.[71] Etwas anderes kann nur zwischen Partnern in Mitgliedsstaaten der EG, die die entsprechenden Richtlinien umgesetzt haben, gelten, wenn sie sich bei ihren Abschlüssen an diese Vorgaben gehalten haben und sie deshalb zwischen ihnen zu Parteigepflogenheiten i. S. d. Art. 9 I, wenn nicht sogar zu stillschweigend konsentierten Bräuchen geworden sind, s. Rn. 6. Gegenüber Partnern, die nicht in Staaten niedergelassen sind, die solche Regeln entweder in Umsetzung oder freiwilligem Nachvollzug der zugrundeliegenden Richtlinien in Kraft gesetzt haben, können sie aber keine Geltung beanspruchen: Der US-amerikanische Verkäufer eines deutschen Käufers, der Maßgeblichkeit deutschen Rechts durchsetzen konnte – ohne das CISG ausgeschlossen zu haben –, ist m. E. nicht an die Manifestationspflichten aus §§ 312c, 312e BGB gebunden. Die dabei entstehenden Konflikte mit dem Gemeinschaftsrecht sind gegebenenfalls durch einen nachträglichen Vorbehalt nach Art. 94 zu beseitigen.

2. Qualifikationsprobleme

Nicht nur bei der Abgrenzung prozessualer und sachrechtlicher Formvorschriften[72] oder bei verbraucherschützenden Normen[73] können **Qualifikationsprobleme** entstehen, sondern auch hinsichtlich anderer Normen des nationalen Rechts: Sieht eine Rechtsnorm, die die Befugnisse der Organe juristischer Personen des öffentlichen Rechts (Bürgermeister, Landräte etc.) oder anderer Beamter regelt, vor, dass sie Rechtsgeschäfte nur in bestimmter Form, mit Gegenzeichnung durch andere Organe oder Beamte usw. wirksam abschließen können, so ist fraglich, ob insoweit Formerfordernisse oder Voraussetzungen wirksamer Vertretungsmacht normiert werden. Will man i. S. v. Art. 7 I verhindern, dass durch Qualifikationen nach der lex fori Formvorschriften so umqualifiziert werden, dass sie als Stellvertretungsregeln oder andere, vom CISG nicht erfasste Rechtsgebiete – etwa einfach als „öffentliches Recht" – dem Art. 11 entzogen werden, muss man **funktional** qualifizieren. Vorschriften für Dokumentation und Unterzeichnung von Kaufverträgen sind danach m. E. Formvorschriften i. S. d. Art. 11. Ob sie zusätzlich Wirksamkeitsvoraussetzung für Vertretungsmacht oder die „Rechtsmacht" einer Gemeinde sind, muss freilich das nationale Recht entscheiden.[74] Dieses herrscht auch über die Folgen entsprechender Verstöße: (Nur) interne

---

[70] Vgl. *Janal*, S. 269 f.; zur Frage, ob entsprechende Zurückbehaltungsrechte in Lückenfüllung nach Art. 7 II aus Grundsätzen des CISG entwickelt oder nur unter Rückgriff auf das durch IPR berufene Vertragsstatut geltend gemacht werden können, s. *W. Witz*, FS Schlechtriem, S. 291 ff., 295 m. w. N.

[71] Zu dem grundsätzlichen Problem, ob solche Rechtsregeln als Richtlinienrecht Vorrang oder Nachrang zum CISG haben, s. *Schroeter*, UN-Kaufrecht, *passim*; *Ferrari*, Art. 90 Rn. 8 ff.; *Schlechtriem*, Internationales UN-Kaufrecht, Rn. 345a.

[72] S. o. Rn. 12.

[73] S. o. Rn. 14, 14a.

[74] Vgl. etwa § 54 GemO Baden-Württemberg, § 56 GemO Nordrhein-Westfalen; die Kommentare machen deutlich, dass diese Vorschriften nur deshalb als Regelung der Vertretungsmacht angesehen werden, weil sonst dem Landesgesetzgeber die Kompetenz gefehlt hätte, s. *Kunze/Bronner/Katz/v. Rotberg*, Gemeindeordnung für Baden-Württemberg, 4. Aufl., Stuttgart: Kohlhammer (1988), § 54 GemO, Rn. 14; MünchKomm/*Einsele*, § 125 BGB, Rn. 22, 30. Bei funktionaler Qualifikation handelt es sich um eine „echte" Formvorschrift. Anders BGH ZfBR 1994, 123 zu § 71 II Hess. GemO: Materielle Vorschrift über Beschränkung der Vertretungsmacht; BGH, 10.5.2001, NJW 2001, 2626, 2628 weist auf die Verschränkung von materiellrechtlichen und Formelementen hin und verneint Formcharakter, entscheidet in concreto aber gegen Anwendbarkeit des § 179 BGB; BGH, 4.12.2003, WM 2004, 182, 185 verneint wegen Fehlens kommunalaufsichtsrechtlicher „Rechtsmacht" (ultra vires-Lehre in Deutschland?) und bejaht Haftung aus cic; zum Ganzen *Schluchter*, S. 93 ff.; zur Entwicklung der Rspr., die zunächst Formerfordernis, später aber materielle Wirksamkeitsvoraussetzung angenommen hat, s. *Schlechtriem*, FS Rolland, 1999, S. 319 f.

Sanktionen, z. B. Maßregelung von Mitarbeitern, berühren die Gültigkeit nicht.[75] Fehlen materieller Gültigkeitserfordernisse wie förmliche Zustimmung einer Behörde oder eines Gerichts oder von formbedürftiger Vertretungsmacht bewirkt dagegen Unwirksamkeit.

V. Vereinbarte Form

16 Eine von den Parteien **vereinbarte Form** geht Art. 11 vor.[76] Das ergibt sich aus Art. 6 und wird in Art. 29 II vorausgesetzt. Abweichungen von Art. 11 können ausdrücklich oder konkludent[77] vereinbart worden sein oder sich aus **Handelsbräuchen** oder **Gepflogenheiten** ergeben, die auf Grund der in Art. 9 geregelten Voraussetzungen für die Parteien Verbindlichkeit haben.[78] Die Formvereinbarung ist auch maßgebend dafür, was im Einzelnen als „Form" einzuhalten ist, d. h. ob „Schriftform" eigenhändige Unterschrift entsprechend § 126 I BGB, eine elektronische Signatur oder andere Authentizität und Beweisbarkeit sichernde Anforderungen verlangt. Auch kann nur die Formvereinbarung selbst bzw. ihre Auslegung ergeben, ob bei sukzessivem Vertragsschluss beide Erklärungen formbedürftig sind, ob Unterschriften auf der gleichen Urkunde oder Angebot und Annahme in verschiedenen Urkunden zur Einhaltung der Form ausreichen, usw.[79] Insbesondere wird hier (d. h. bei der Vereinbarung einer Form oder bei entsprechenden Handelsbräuchen oder Gepflogenheiten, die sich zwischen den Parteien gebildet haben) Bedeutung gewinnen, ob bestimmte Formen der elektronischen Kommunikation von den Parteien vorgesehen worden sind und deshalb Formcharakter haben. Schließlich entscheidet die Formvereinbarung und ihre ggf. erforderliche Auslegung auch darüber, ob sie mündliche Nebenabreden völlig ausschließen soll oder nur eine Vermutung der Vollständigkeit begründet.[80] Die Parteien können eine Formvereinbarung auch rückgängig machen, doch ist für die Form einer solchen Vereinbarung Art. 29 II zu beachten. Die **Beweislast** für eine Formvereinbarung und ihre Reichweite trägt die Partei, die sie geltend macht, für die Wahrung der unstreitig vereinbarten Form die Partei, die sich auf die Wirksamkeit des Vertrages beruft.[81]

17 Auch formularmäßig oder in **Standardbedingungen** vorgesehene Schriftformerfordernisse sind wirksam, wenn zu diesen vorformulierten Bedingungen kontrahiert wird.[82] Ein einseitiges Formverlangen kann jedoch Art. 11 nicht verdrängen,[83] und stillschweigendes Einverständnis dürfte eine seltene Ausnahme sein. Auch können sich Schriftformklauseln an nationalen Verboten solcher Klauseln über Art. 4 S. 2 lit. a) brechen. Eine unangemessene Benachteiligung i. S. v. § 307 II 1 BGB wegen Abweichung von Art. 11 ist nicht anzunehmen, da Art. 29 II 1 die Zulässigkeit von Schriftformklauseln voraussetzt.[84] Die Formabrede

---

[75] S. o. Rn. 11.
[76] *Bianca/Bonell/Rajski*, Art. 11, Anm. 3.1.; *Del Duca*, 25 J. L. & Com. (2005-06), 133, 137; umfassend *Breitling*, S. 59 ff.
[77] *Bianca/Bonell/Rajski*, Art. 11, Anm. 3.1.; ferner zur Möglichkeit impliziter Abweichungen vom Abkommen *Schlechtriem*, Einheitliches UN-Kaufrecht, S. 21; s. a. OGH, 6.2.1996, CISG-online 224 = östZRVgl 1996, 248–254 (Hinweis auf Informationsmappe reicht nicht aus, Schriftform als vereinbart anzunehmen).
[78] Wie hier jetzt auch *Schwenzer/Hachem/Kee*, Rn. 22.20.
[79] Vgl. BGH, 18.10.2000, NJW 2001, 221, 222 (Gegen-)Annahme eines (Gegen-)Angebots in einem anderen Schriftstück nicht ausreichend für § 126 II BGB.
[80] Entsprechende Klauseln, die nicht-formgerechten, insbesondere mündlichen Nebenabreden jegliche Verbindlichkeit nehmen, können Ersatz für die *parol evidence rule* (oben Rn. 13) sein; s. a. *Schmidt-Kessel*, Art. 8 Rn. 35 zu *merger clauses*.
[81] *Baumgärtel/Laumen/Hepting*, Art. 11 WKR, Rn. 1.
[82] Vgl. *Enderlein/Maskow/Strohbach*, Art. 29, Anm. 2. Bsp.: Standardbedingungen der Europäischen Wirtschaftskommission der Vereinten Nationen (E. C. E.) für verschiedene Wirtschaftszweige wie die Allgemeinen Liefer- und Montagebedingungen für den Import und Export von Maschinen und Anlagen, Nr. 188 und 188 A, ferner Nr. 574 A 1957, oder die Allgemeinen Verkaufsbedingungen für den Import und Export von langlebigen Konsumgütern und anderen Serienerzeugnissen der metallverarbeitenden Industrie (Nr. 730 1961); Textbeispiele u. 2. Aufl.
[83] Vgl. *Wey*, Rn. 424.
[84] Zu Vollständigkeits- und Bestätigungsklauseln s. Art. 29 Rn. 6.

der Parteien kann über die Art der Form und die Folgen ihrer Verletzung bestimmen.[85] Vereinbaren die Parteien nur „Schriftform", so bestimmt Art. 13, mit welchen Mitteln die Schriftform der einzelnen Erklärungen[86] eingehalten werden kann. I. Ü. wird eine Auslegung der Schriftformabrede nach Art. 8 II und III oft ergeben, dass sich Wille und Vorstellung der Partei(en) am eigenen Umweltrecht orientiert haben, bei in der Bundesrepublik niedergelassener Partei also an den §§ 127, 126 BGB.

---

[85] Vgl. zum EKG *Dölle/Reinhart,* Art. 15 EKG, Rn. 63.
[86] Hierzu *Wey,* Rn. 430; s. a. Art. 13 Rn. 2.

Art. 12 [Wirkungen eines Vorbehaltes hinsichtlich der Formfreiheit]

Die Bestimmungen der Artikel 11 und 29 oder des Teils II dieses Übereinkommens, die für den Abschluß eines Kaufvertrages, seine Änderung oder Aufhebung durch Vereinbarung oder für ein Angebot, eine Annahme oder eine sonstige Willenserklärung eine andere als die schriftliche Form gestatten, gelten nicht, wenn eine Partei ihre Niederlassung in einem Vertragsstaat hat, der eine Erklärung nach Artikel 96 abgegeben hat. Die Parteien dürfen von dem vorliegenden Artikel weder abweichen noch seine Wirkung ändern.

Art. 12

Any provision of article 11, article 29 or Part II of this Convention that allows a contract of sale or its modification or termination by agreement or any offer, acceptance or other indication of intention to be made in any form other than in writing does not apply where any party has his place of business in a Contracting State which has made a declaration under article 96 of this Convention. The parties may not derogate from or vary the effect of this article.

Art. 12

Toute disposition de l'article 11, de l'article 29 ou de la deuxième partie de la présente Convention autorisant une forme autre que la forme écrite, soit pour la conclusion ou pour la modification ou la résiliation amiable d'un contrat de vente, soit pour toute offre, acceptation ou autre manifestation d'intention, ne s'applique pas dès lors qu'une des parties a son établissement dans un Etat contractant qui a fait une déclaration conformément à l'article 96 de la présente Convention. Les parties ne peuvent déroger au présent article ni en modifier les effets.

Übersicht

	Rn.
I. Vorgeschichte	1
II. Bedeutung des Vorbehalts	2
III. Reichweite	4

Vorläufer und **Entwürfe**: Wiener E 1977 Art. 11 II, New Yorker E 1978 Art. 11.

I. Vorgeschichte

1   Die Vorschrift, die kein Vorbild in EAG und EKG hat,[1] geht auf das Drängen vor allem der Delegation der ehemaligen UdSSR zurück.[2] Bei Nutzung der Vorbehaltsmöglichkeit aus Art. 96[3] werden Artt. 11 und 29 unanwendbar, und nationale Formvorschriften können in bestimmtem, i. e. freilich streitigem Umfang[4] maßgebend werden. Die Zahl der Vorbehaltsstaaten ist beschränkt.[5]

II. Bedeutung des Vorbehalts

2   Die Bundesrepublik hat den Vorbehalt aus Art. 96 nicht eingelegt. Deutsche Gerichte haben unter den in Art. 12 genannten Voraussetzungen – (mindestens) eine der Parteien hat

---

[1] S. jedoch Art. 11 Rn. 1 Fn. 1.
[2] S. Art. 11 Rn. 1 Fn. 2 f.; *Eörsi*, General Provisions, § 2.08, S. 2–31; *Honnold/Flechtner*, Art. 12, Rn. 128; *Kröll u. a./Perales Viscasillas*, Art. 12, Rn. 2; *Schlechtriem*, Einheitliches UN-Kaufrecht, S. 30 Fn. 135; ferner zur Rechtslage in der ehemaligen UdSSR *Goldštajn*, Formation, S. 43 f.; *Rubanov/Tschikvadse*, Some Aspects, S. 349 f., sub Nr. 17.
[3] Zu den Versuchen, die Vorbehaltsmöglichkeit einzuschränken oder zu konkretisieren s. Art. 11 Rn. 2.
[4] S. u. Rn. 2, 3.
[5] S. die im Anhang I aufgeführten Vorbehalte.

ihre (evtl. nach Art. 10 maßgebliche) Niederlassung in einem Vorbehaltsstaat – das Formstatut nach Art. 11 EGBGB zu bestimmen.[6] Abzulehnen ist die Mindermeinung, dass sich die Formvorschriften eines Vorbehaltsstaates, in dem eine Partei niedergelassen ist, stets durchsetzen,[7] da danach der Vorbehaltsstaat mit der allseitig beanspruchten Geltung seiner Formvorschriften das IPR anderer (Vertrags)Staaten verdrängen und seine Formvorschriften zu international geltendem Einheitsrecht machen würde; die abweichenden unterinstanzlichen Entscheidungen hierzu sind durchweg ohne Begründung geblieben.[8] Haben z. B. die Parteien eines deutsch-russischen Vertrages deutsches Recht (ohne Ausschluss des CISG) gewählt, dann ist der Vertrag formfrei gültig.[9] So hat ein ungarisches Gericht in einem deutsch-ungarischen Fall zutreffend deutsches Recht als Formstatut angewendet und einen telefonisch geschlossenen Vertrag als wirksam beurteilt, obwohl Ungarn Vorbehaltsstaat ist.[10] Entsprechend hat der United States Court of Appeals, Third Circuit entschieden, dass die Anwendbarkeit des Rechts eines Vorbehaltsstaats von den Vorgaben des autonomen Kollisionsrechts abhängt.[11]

Soweit angenommen wird, dass IPR das maßgebliche Formstatut bestimmt, ist weiter streitig, ob bei Berufung des Rechts eines Nicht-Vorbehaltsstaates dessen nationale Formvorschriften oder CISG, also Art. 11, anzuwenden sind.[12] M. E. sollte bei Berufung des Rechts eines Vertragsstaates als Formstatut Art. 11 (wieder) anwendbar werden. Andernfalls käme man zu Formvorschriften, die ohne Vorbehalt überhaupt nicht anwendbar wären.[13]

---

[6] Wie hier jetzt auch *Forestal Guarani S. A. v. Daros International, Inc.*, U. S. Ct. App. (3rd Cir.), 21.7.2010, CISG-online 2112 (Argentinien / New Jersey). Entsprechend die bereits zuvor herrschende Auffassung in der Literatur: *Bernstein/Lookofsky*, § 2–14; *Bianca/Bonell/Rajski*, Art. 12, Anm. 2.3.; *Czerwenka, Drobnig,* Diskussionsbeiträge in: *Schlechtriem (Hrsg.)*, Einheitliches Kaufrecht und nationales Obligationenrecht, S. 170 f., 175 f.; *Enderlein/Maskow/Strohbach*, Art. 12, Anm. 2.2.; *Eörsi,* General Provisions, § 2.08, S. 2–33; *Herber/Czerwenka,* Art. 12, Rn. 4; *Honnold/Flechtner,* Art. 12, Rn. 129; *Jametti Greiner,* Vertragsabschluss, S. 47; *Honsell/Melis,* Art. 12, Rn. 4; *Karollus,* S. 80; *Staub/Koller,* Vor § 373 HGB, Rn. 638; *Kröll u. a./Perales Viscasillas,* Art. 12, Rn. 8; *Lookofsky,* The 1980 United Nations Convention, Anm. 96.; *Loewe,* Art. 11, S. 37; *Neumayer/Ming,* Art. 12, Anm. 1.; *Nicholas,* 105 L. Q. R. (1989), 201, 212; *Piltz,* Export- und Importgeschäfte, § 12, Rn. 70; *Wey,* Rn. 475; *Rudolph,* Art. 12, Rn. 3; *Staudinger/Magnus,* Art. 12, Rn. 8; *Witz/Salger/Lorenz/Witz,* Art. 12, Rn. 12; *Ferrari,* Draft Digest, S. 206, 213.

[7] Für Beachtung der Formvorschriften eines Vorbehaltsstaates in jedem Fall *Reinhart,* Art. 12, Rn. 3; *Rehbinder,* Vertragsschluss, S. 155: „Wirtschaftspolitisch motivierte Formvorschriften eines anderen Vertragsstaates (verlangen) Respekt", deshalb entweder Sonderanknüpfung oder extensive Auslegung des Art. 12, die zu allseitiger Geltung der Formvorschriften von Vorbehaltsstaaten führt. Ähnlich *Stoffel,* Formation du contrat, S. 60; wohl auch *Piltz,* Internationales Kaufrecht, 1. Aufl., § 3, Rn. 114; s. ferner *Medwedew/Rosenberg,* Internationale Kaufverträge, S. 34; zum allseitigen Geltungsanspruch der entsprechenden Norm der ehemaligen UdSSR *Goldštajn,* Formation, S. 44.

[8] S. RB Hasselt (Belgien), 2.5.1995, CISG-online 371 (Behauptungen des Käufers zufolge hatten die Parteien den Kaufpreis nachträglich geändert. Da jedoch Chile eine Erklärung nach Art. 96 CISG abgegeben hat und sich der Sitz des Verkäufers in Chile befand, hätte nach Ansicht des Gerichts der Vertrag schriftlich abgeändert werden müssen); entsprechend *Zhejiang Shaoxing Yongli Printing and Dyeing Co., Ltd. v. Microflock Textile Group Corporation,* U. S. Dist. Ct. (S. D. Flo.), 19.5.2008, CISG-online 1771 (Vertragsänderung in chinesisch-US-amerikanischem Vertrag abgelehnt; overruled durch *Forestal Guarani S. A. v. Daros International, Inc.*, U. S. Ct. App. (3rd Cir.), 21.7.2010, CISG-online 2112); *Forestal Guarani S. A. v. Daros International, Inc.*, U. S. Dist. Ct. (N. J.), 7.8.2008, CISG-online 1779 (argentinisch-US-amerikanischer Fall; overruled durch *Forestal Guarani S. A. v. Daros International, Inc.*, U. S. Ct. App. (3rd Cir.), 21.7.2010, CISG-online 2112); offenbar auch Int. Ct. Russian CCI, 9.6.2004, CISG-online 1239, Nr. 3.3 a. E. (Anwendbarkeit von Art. 162 Russ. Zivilgesetzbuch, wenn eine Partei in Russland ihren Sitz hat).

[9] S. auch zur Maßgeblichkeit der Formvorschriften des gewählten Rechts BGH, 22.1.1997, WM 1997, 1713, 1715 (kein CISG-Fall).

[10] Fovárosi Biróság (Hauptstadtgericht) Budapest, 24.3.1992, CISG-online 61, dazu Bericht *Vida,* IPRax 1993, 263 f., der auch über die Gründe Ungarns für die Einlegung eines Vorbehalts berichtet.

[11] *Forestal Guarani S. A. v. Daros International, Inc.*, U. S. Ct. App. (3rd Cir.), 21.7.2010, CISG-online 2112.

[12] Für nationale Formvorschriften *Staudinger/Magnus,* Art. 12, Rn. 9; *Wey,* Rn. 475; *Honnold/Flechtner,* Art. 12, Rn. 129; Fovárosi Biróság (Hauptstadtgericht) Budapest, 24.3.1992, CISG-online 61; anders die wohl jetzt h. A., s. *Honsell/Melis,* Art. 12, Rn. 4; *U. Huber,* RabelsZ 43 (1979), 413, 434 f.; *Schlechtriem,* Einheitliches UN-Kaufrecht, S. 32; *Soergel/Lüderitz/Fenge,* Art. 12, Rn. 2; *Witz/Salger/Lorenz/Witz,* Art. 12, Rn. 12; zuweilen wird nicht eindeutig Stellung genommen, vgl. *Karollus,* S. 80.

[13] Vgl. *Wey,* Rn. 476, der deshalb eine „teleologische Reduktion" des Art. 12 befürwortet. Anders das ungarische Gericht im berichteten Fall (Rn. 2), das Formfreiheit nach BGB beurteilt hat.

Dem Vorbehaltsstaat wird damit nichts Unbilliges zugemutet, denn er müsste ja auch Formfreiheit hinnehmen, wenn über das IPR des Forumstaates nationale Regeln, die Formfreiheit vorsehen, zur Anwendung kämen. Kaufmännische Vorsicht dürfte freilich gebieten, bei Verträgen mit Partnern in Vorbehaltsstaaten deren Schriftformvorschriften zu beachten, falls nicht ausgeschlossen werden kann, dass ein Gericht im Vorbehaltsstaat mit der Sache befasst wird.

III. Reichweite

4   Art. 12 ist **zwingend**. Die Parteien können ihn weder abbedingen noch modifizieren, Art. 12 S. 2. Die Parteien können, soweit das CISG nach Art. 1 I lit. a) zur Anwendung gelangt, der Vorschrift auch nicht ausweichen, weil sich die Wirksamkeit der Abwahlvereinbarung nach den Regeln der Konvention und mithin auch nach Art. 12 richtet.[14] Nur in den Fällen des Art. 1 I lit. b) lässt sich Art. 12 im Wege der Rechtswahl vermeiden. In den Fällen der Anwendbarkeit Kraft internationalen Privatrechts können Art. 12 und nationale Formvorschriften allerdings über Schutzklauseln wie Art. 8 II Rom I-Übk. und Art. 31 II EGBGB zur Anwendung gelangen.[15] Inwieweit dann das statt dessen geltende Recht, insbesondere das maßgebliche Formstatut, sich an Formvorschriften von Vorbehaltsstaaten „bricht", ist eine Frage des anzuwendenden IPR.

5   Die Entstehungsgeschichte der Vorschrift, die auf das Bedürfnis der ehemaligen UdSSR zurückgeht, ihre für Außenhandelsgeschäfte vorgesehene Schriftform beizubehalten,[16] sowie der Wortlaut von Artt. 12 und 96 verdeutlichen, dass nur Wahrung der in den nationalen Rechten der Vorbehaltsstaaten – bei deren Maßgeblichkeit als Formstatut (oben Rn. 2) – geregelten **„Schriftform"** gemeint sein kann. Weitergehende Formvorschriften (notarielle Beurkundung, Beglaubigung durch Konsulate, Anbringung von Stempelmarken usw.) dürften nicht gedeckt sein.[17] Auch andersartige Formvorgaben, etwa die Verwendung einer bestimmten Sprache, werden von der Vorbehaltsmöglichkeit nicht gedeckt; insoweit verbleibt es bei Artt. 11.[18] Wenn das maßgebliche Recht sie als Schriftform(en) regelt, ist fraglich, ob „schriftliche Form" i. S. d. Art. 12 autonome Qualifikation zulässt oder eine solche nach der lex fori gebotet; ersteres wäre sinnvoll, letzteres ist jedenfalls in Vorbehaltsstaaten zu erwarten. Art. 13 kann dieses Problem entschärfen.

6   Art. 12 erzwingt Berücksichtigung nationaler Formerfordernisse **nur** für **Abschluss**, **Änderung** oder **Aufhebung** des Vertrages sowie für die dazu erforderlichen einzelnen Erklärungen; das ergibt sich aus dem enumerativ gefassten Wortlaut der Vorschrift. Er gilt nicht für andere Mitteilungen und Erklärungen innerhalb und außerhalb des Teils II der Konvention, z. B. Vertragsaufhebung, Mängelrüge usw.,[19] aber auch Rücknahme eines Angebots.[20]

---

[14] Anders die Vorauflage sowie *Enderlein/Maskow/Strohbach*, Art. 12, Anm. 4.; *Wey*, Rn. 477, 478; *Borisova*, 9 VJ (2005), 153, 159.
[15] Vgl. dazu Art. 8 Rn 52.
[16] Dazu Rn. 1.
[17] *Witz/Salger/Lorenz/Witz*, Art. 12, Rn. 12; a. A. *Enderlein/Maskow/Strohbach*, Art. 13, Anm. 1.
[18] S. Art. 11 Rn. 14a.
[19] H. A., vgl. *Bianca/Bonell/Rajski*, Art. 12, Anm. 2.2.; *Enderlein/Maskow/Strohbach*, Art. 12, Anm. 1.; *Kröll u. a./Perales Viscasillas*, Art. 11, Rn. 5; *Wey*, Rn. 480; *Witz/Salger/Lorenz/Witz*, Art. 12, Rn. 11; zu weiteren Erklärungen usw. s. Art. 11 Rn. 9, 10.
[20] Dagegen *Kröll u. a./Perales Viscasillas*, Art. 12, Rn. 3.

Art. 13 [Schriftlichkeit]

Für die Zwecke dieses Übereinkommens umfaßt der Ausdruck „schriftlich" auch Mitteilungen durch Telegramm oder Fernschreiben.

Art. 13

For the purposes of this Convention „writing" includes telegram and telex.

Art. 13

Aux fins de la présente Convention, le terme „écrit" doit s'entendre également des communications adressées par télégramme ou par télex.

Übersicht

	Rn.
I. Vorgeschichte	1
II. Bedeutung und Funktionen	2
1. Vereinbarte Schriftform	2
2. Verspätete Annahme	3
3. Schriftform auf Grund Art. 12	4
III. Ausweitungen der Vorschrift	5
1. Allgemeiner Grundsatz i. S. v. Art. 7 II	5
2. Telefax	6
3. Elektronische Kommunikation	7

I. Vorgeschichte

Die Vorschrift ist erst auf der Wiener Konferenz auf Antrag der Bundesrepublik eingefügt worden.[1] Der Antrag wurde ohne weitere Diskussion angenommen, da eine gleich lautende Bestimmung bereits im Verjährungsübereinkommen (Art. 1 III lit. g)) vorgesehen war. Die Möglichkeit, der Schriftform durch die in Art. 13 genannten Kommunikationsmittel zu genügen, entsprach seinerzeit dem Trend moderner Gesetzgebung für den internationalen Handel.[2] Heute muss die Vorschrift mangels Medienneutralität als unzureichend angesehen werden, weshalb in mehrerlei Hinsicht Analogien und auf Art. 7 II gestützte Ausweitungen diskutiert werden (s. Rn. 5–7). 1

II. Bedeutung und Funktionen

1. Vereinbarte Schriftform

Art. 13 stellt die **autonome Auslegung** des Begriffs „schriftlich" sicher.[3] Art. 13 hat vor allem Bedeutung für die Auslegung einer von den Parteien **vertraglich vereinbarten Schriftformklausel** einschließlich einer solchen nach Art. 29 II.[4] Entscheidend ist zunächst, was die Parteien selbst als Schriftform vorgeschrieben haben; ggf. ist durch Auslegung nach Art. 8 zu ermitteln, was gewollt und gemeint war. Haben die Parteien nichts anderes bestimmt, dann wird der vereinbarten Schriftform auch durch **Telex** oder **Telegramm** genügt; zu beachten ist jedoch, dass die Parteien in der Auswahl bestimmter Kommunikationsformen frei sind und diesen – etwa elektronischen Kommunikationsmitteln – auch den Rang von Formerfordernissen einräumen können, etwa, wenn eine 2

---
[1] S. O. R., S. 74, Art. 9, Nr. 3; Antrag s. A/Conf. 97/C. 1/L. 18, O. R., S. 90, Art. 9, Nr. 2 f.
[2] Vgl. die Nachweise bei *Bianca/Bonell/Rajski*, Art. 13, Anm. 2.1.
[3] *Kröll u. a./Perales Viscasillas*, Art. 12, Rn. 5.
[4] S. Art. 11 Rn. 16.

elektronische Signatur vereinbart worden ist.[5] Art. 13 ist selbstverständlich abdingbar (Art. 6), sodass eine vereinbarte Schriftform auch strenger sein kann, indem sie etwa eigenhändige Unterschrift verlangt. Entsprechendes gilt für Schriftformerfordernisse auf Grund von **Bräuchen oder Parteigepflogenheiten**: Zunächst entscheidet der Inhalt des Brauchs oder der zwischen den Parteien etablierten Gepflogenheiten – Art. 9 I – über die genauen Anforderungen der dadurch festgelegten Form; soweit auslegungsoffen nur Schriftform verlangt ist, gilt Art. 13.

2. Verspätete Annahme

3   Eine schriftliche Mitteilung nach Art. 21 II kann ebenfalls fernschriftlich oder telegraphisch erfolgen.[6]

3. Schriftform auf Grund Art. 12

4   Über die Bedeutung des Art. 13 im Falle der Maßgeblichkeit der **Formvorschriften eines Vorbehaltsstaates** (s. Art. 12) gehen die Ansichten auseinander. Teilweise wird dieser Fall nicht behandelt.[7] Einige Autoren interpretieren Art. 13 als eine Norm des Einheitsrechts, die bei Maßgeblichkeit nationaler Formvorschriften sicherstellt, dass ihnen jedenfalls auch durch Telex und Telegramm genügt werden kann.[8] Andere vertreten, dass diese Vorschrift „Interpretation eines Schriftformerfordernisses gemäß nationalem Recht" erlaube; sie könne „be applied also to writing requirements provided for by the provisions of domestic law exceptionally applied according to relevant conflict-of-law rules", sei aber jedenfalls keine Sachnorm des Einheitsrechts.[9]

Von manchen Autoren wird die Anwendbarkeit des Art. 13 jedoch auf die (wenigen) Fälle einer im CISG selbst vorgesehenen Schriftlichkeit (Artt. 21 II, 29 I) sowie – als Auslegungsregel – auf von den Parteien verwendete Schriftformklauseln beschränkt.[10] Das ist zu eng. Der Antrag der Bundesrepublik[11] war damit begründet worden, die vorgeschlagene Vorschrift solle „make clear that the requirement of 'writing' shall be fulfilled by telegram and telex"; allerdings war auch auf „the application of some provisions of the draft Convention, such as article 29, paragraph 2" abgehoben worden.[12] Die (unveröffentlichten) Protokolle des Deutschen Rats für Internationales Privatrecht, auf dessen Stellungnahme der Antrag der Bundesrepublik zurückgeht, machen aber deutlich, dass man eine Definition der Schriftform gerade auch zur Vermeidung von Unsicherheiten bei Maßgeblichkeit nationaler Formvorschriften für erforderlich gehalten hat.

Ein solches Verständnis des Art. 13 entspricht auch der Möglichkeit eines Vorbehalts nach Art. 96 und dem darauf aufbauenden Wortlaut des Art. 12: Einlegung eines Vorbehalts führt

---

[5] Strikter *Kröll u. a./Perales Viscasillas*, Art. 12, Rn. 5, die eine Abweichung von Art. 13 durch Auslegung der Formvereinbarung offenbar ausschließen will. Zur digitalen Signatur auf der Basis kryptographischer Systeme nach deutschem Recht s. § 126a BGB i. V. m. SigG.
[6] Zur Geltung des Art. 13 im Falle des Art. 21 II s. *Schroeter*, 6 VJ (2002), 268.
[7] Vgl. etwa *Honnold/Flechtner*, Art. 13, Rn. 130; *Eörsi*, General Provisions, S. 34: „Needs no comment".
[8] *Bydlinski*, Allgemeines Vertragsrecht, S. 83; *Herber/Czerwenka*, Art. 13, Rn. 2; *Jametti Greiner*, S. 47; *Honsell/Melis*, Art. 13, Rn. 5; *Karollus*, S. 81; *Loewe*, Art. 13, S. 38; *Rudolph*, Art. 13, Rn. 2; *Schlechtriem*, Einheitliches UN-Kaufrecht, S. 32 f.; *Stoffel*, Formation du contrat, S. 60; *Wey*, Rn. 483 ff., 486; *Bamberger/Roth/Saenger*, Art. 13, Rn. 2; *Witz/Salger/Lorenz/Witz*, Art. 13, Rn. 1; wohl auch *Sono*, Formation of International Contracts, S. 130; *Schroeter*, 6 VJ (2002), 270: „Primary role ... interpretation of contractual form requirements". Die gleiche Ansicht wird auch in der Botschaft des (Schweizer) Bundesrats zu Grunde gelegt, BBl. 1989 I, 769; eine eigene Stellungnahme *Staudinger/Magnus*, Art. 13, Rn. 8, 9 (referierend); unklar insoweit Comisión para la Protección del Comercio Exterior de México, 29.4.1996, CISG-online 350 = Diario oficial de 16.7.1996, 12 (dazu *Rosch* in D. 1998, Somm. 317).
[9] Vgl. *Bianca/Bonell/Rajski*, Art. 13, Anm. 3.1.; ähnlich *Enderlein/Maskow/Strohbach*, Art. 13, Anm. 1.
[10] *Audit*, Vente internationale, Anm. 77.; *Lookofsky*, The 1980 United Nations Convention, Anm. 98.; *Neumayer/Ming*, Art. 13, Anm. 2.; *Soergel/Lüderitz/Fenge*, Art. 13, Rn. 2.
[11] S. Fn. 1.
[12] S. auch den Abdruck des deutschen Antrags bei *Kritzer*, Guide to Practical Applications, S. 121.

nach Art. 12 S. 1 zur Unanwendbarkeit von Artt. 11 und 29 und zur Maßgeblichkeit nationaler Formvorschriften, (nur) soweit sie „schriftliche Form" vorschreiben. Diese vom Abkommen ausnahmsweise ermöglichte Geltung von Schriftformerfordernissen nationalen Rechts kann und sollte das Abkommen selbst durch eine verbindliche Regel zur Schriftform eingrenzen und konkretisieren. Richter und Parteien werden dadurch bei Verwendung von Telex oder Telegramm von der Notwendigkeit entlastet, fremde Formvorschriften, insbesondere solche von Vorbehaltsstaaten zu ermitteln und ihre genaue Bedeutung zu erforschen. Gleichwohl ist den Parteien bei Verträgen mit Partnern in Vorbehaltsstaaten auch hier (vgl. Art. 12 Rn. 3) zu raten, die Schriftform entsprechend den Regeln des Vorbehaltsstaates zu beachten.

III. Ausweitungen der Vorschrift

1. Allgemeiner Grundsatz i. S. v. Art. 7 II

Die mangelnde Medienneutralität der Vorschrift hat diese schnell veralten lassen und Fragen nach einer Ausweitung hervorgerufen. Teilweise wird vorgeschlagen, das Verständnis des Wortes „writing" auszudehnen.[13] Dagegen spricht freilich die Entstehungsgeschichte und vor allem die Systematik: Art. 13 wäre dann entbehrlich. Die damit verbleibende Lücke hinsichtlich der Einordnung sonstiger moderner Kommunikationsformate bedarf der Füllung. Zwar steht dafür die Analogie mangels einheitlichen Methodenverständnisses im Einheitsrecht nicht zur Verfügung, jedoch stellt die Konvention mit der Lückenfüllung über allgemeine Grundsätze der Konvention gem. Art. 7 II ein funktionsäquivalentes Instrument der Lückenfüllung bereit: Art. 13 lässt sich nämlich ein allgemeiner Grundsatz der Konvention dergestalt entnehmen, dass diese der Verwendung anderer Formate offensteht, so diese dieselbe Funktionalität wie die klassische Schriftform, das Telegramm und das Telex aufweisen. Das entspricht auch dem – verallgemeinerungsfähigen – Regelungszweck von Art. 13: Die Vorschrift will sichern, dass eine rechtserhebliche Kommunikation jedenfalls manifest ist oder werden, d. h. ausgedruckt werden kann (*possibility to retrieve*) und damit sicherer aufnehmbar, verstehbar und ggf. beweisbar wird.[14] Die Funktionalität der drei von Art. 13 erfassten Formate ist – wie der CISG-AC zutreffend annimmt – gegeben, wenn die **dauerhafte Abrufbarkeit in einer greifbaren Form** gewährleistet ist.[15] Formen, welche diese beiden Anforderungen erfüllen, sind im Anwendungsbereich der Konvention der Schriftform gleichzustellen, und zwar auch soweit es um Fälle des Art. 12 geht (s. Rn. 4); die national vorgeschriebene Form wird insoweit durch das CISG modifiziert. Jedenfalls empfiehlt sich jedoch bei Vereinbarung von Schriftform klarzustellen, ob und welche elektronischen Kommunikationsmittel das Schriftformerfordernis erfüllen.

2. Telefax

Das Telefax **steht der Schriftform** unter der Konvention **gleich**.[16] Die zum BGB h. A., dass ein Fax nicht der Schriftform des § 126 BGB entspricht, kann für Art. 13 nicht

---

[13] So jedenfalls der Wortlaut der Opinion zu Art. 13 des CISG-AC, Op. 1 (*Chr. Ramberg*), Comment 13.1, 13.2.
[14] S. 4. Aufl. Rn 2a; *Schroeter*, 6 VJ (2002), 272 f.; zurückhaltend hingegen *Witz/Salger/Lorenz/Witz*, Art. 13, Rn. 2.
[15] CISG-AC, Op. 1 (*Chr. Ramberg*), Comment 13.1.
[16] Wie hier – wenngleich vielfach auf das Instrument der Analogie zurückgreifend – *Audit*, Vente internationale, Anm. 77.; *Enderlein/Maskow/Strohbach*, Art. 13, Anm. 1. mit Hinweis auf die 1988 erarbeitete Factoring Convention; *Herber/Czerwenka*, Art. 13, Rn. 4; *Honnold/Flechtner*, Art. 13, Rn. 130; *Honsell/Melis*, Art. 13, Rn. 4 (differenzierend); *Karollus*, S. 81; *Schroeter*, 6 VJ (2002), 271 f.; *Staub/Koller*, Vor § 373 HGB, Rn. 638; *Lookofsky*, The 1980 United Nations Convention, Anm. 98.; *Neumayer/Ming*, Art. 13, Anm. 1.; *Reinhart*, Art. 13, Rn. 5; *Soergel/Lüderitz/Fenge*, Art. 13, Rn. 1; *Staudinger/Magnus*, Art. 13, Rn. 6; *Witz/Salger/Lorenz/Witz*, Art. 13, Rn. 3; *Ferrari*, Draft Digest, S. 206, 209. Zur Möglichkeit entsprechender Lückenfüllung s. *Schlechtriem*, 3 JT (1991/92), 1, 18.

herangezogen werden, da auch bei Telex oder Telegramm keine Erklärung *mit Unterschrift* übermittelt wird.[17] Für das von Computer zu Computer übermittelte gilt Art. 13 (nur), wenn es vom Empfänger ausgedruckt werden kann;[18] ob tatsächlich ausgedruckt worden ist, spielt keine Rolle.[19] Bei Beurteilung des Beweiswerts sind freilich die Manipulationsmöglichkeiten bei Faxübertragungen zu berücksichtigen.[20]

3. Elektronische Kommunikation

7   Ob und inwieweit Vertragsschlüsse per E-Mail oder anderen elektronischen Kommunikationsmitteln als schriftformäquivalent gesehen werden können, ist nicht gesichert. Hier ist das CISG behutsam neuen Entwicklungen anzupassen.[21] Sieht man die Funktion einer vereinbarten Schriftform in der Sicherung der Beweisbarkeit des Erklärten bzw. Vereinbarten und auch (obwohl bei Telex nicht gewährleistet) in der Authentizität des Erklärten, dann wird man jedenfalls mit elektronischer Signatur versehene Mitteilungen als der klassischen Schriftform gleichwertig behandeln können; dies gilt – abgesehen von den Fällen des Art. 12 – selbstverständlich erst recht, wenn die Parteien sich auf solche Kommunikationsmittel geeinigt haben oder entsprechende Gepflogenheiten zwischen ihnen etabliert worden sind (s. Art. 11 Rn. 16).[22] Man wird aber noch einen Schritt weitergehen und elektronische Kommunikation, die die wesentlichen Funktionen der klassischen Schriftform i. S. d. Art. 13 gleichwertig erfüllen kann, als genügend sehen müssen, sofern die Parteien mit der Vereinbarung von Schriftform nichts anderes gemeint haben.[23] Das entspricht Art. 23 II EuGVO.[24] Es entspricht auch der noch nicht in Kraft befindlichen United Nations Convention on the Use of Electronic Communications in International Contracts von 2005, die zwischen Vertragsstaaten nach Art. 90 CISG Vorrang hätte;[25] ob diese Konvention über Art. 7 II auch Art. 13 modifizieren würde, wenn die Parteien ihren Sitz nicht in deren Vertragsstaaten haben,[26] ist bislang völlig offen.

---

[17] Generell zu elektronischer Datenübermittlung s. *Honnold/Flechtner*, Art. 13, Rn. 130; *Lookofsky*, The 1980 United Nations Convention, Anm. 98.; *Rummel*, FS Ostheim, S. 222.

[18] *Witz/Salger/Lorenz/Witz*, Art. 13, Rn. 3. Dagegen unter knappem Verweis auf die Analogie *Kröll u. a./ Perales Viscasillas*, Art. 13, Rn. 7 (anders aber offenbar Rn. 8: „It is the possibility to make the electronic data tangible – wether by paper or not – that ought to be considered when interpreting Art. 13.").

[19] Anders noch die 4. Auflage.

[20] Vgl. *Schmittmann*, DB 1993, 2575, 2576 f.; vgl. auch BGH ZIP 1997, 1694 (nicht zum CISG, aber grundsätzlich zu Fax und Schriftformerfordernis).

[21] Vgl. nunmehr Art. 9 UNECIC vom 23.11.2005 (http://www.uncitral.org/pdf/english/texts/electcom/ 06–57452_Ebook.pdf), dessen Abs. 2 lautet: „Where the law requires that a communication or a contract should be in writing, or provides consequences for the absence of a writing, that requirement is met by an electronic communication if the information contained therein is accessible so as to be usable for subsequent reference."

[22] Haben die Parteien Schriftform vereinbart und ist deutsches Recht als Formstatut anzuwenden, dann muss eine digitale Signatur nach § 126a BGB ausreichen, da Art. 13 das Schriftformerfordernis auflockert: Wenn schon Telex (und nach h. L. Fax) dem Schriftformerfordernis genügen, dann muss das erst recht für eine mit elektronischer Signatur versehene Erklärung gelten.

[23] In diesem Sinne auch *Ferrari*, Draft Digest, S. 206, 209; *Schwenzer/Mohs*, IHR 2006, 239, 245.

[24] Vgl. statt aller *Kropholler*, EUZPR, Art. 23, Rn. 41.

[25] Dazu *Kröll u. a./Perales Viscasillas*, Art. 13, Rn. 10.

[26] So verstehe ich *Kröll u. a./Perales Viscasillas*, Art. 13, Rn. 10.

Teil II. Abschluss des Vertrages

Part II
Formation of the Contract

Deuxième partie
Formation du contrat

Vorbemerkungen zu Artt. 14–24

Übersicht

	Rn.
I. Geltungsbereich: Äußerer Konsens und Gültigkeit	1
1. Nicht geregelte Fragen	2
2. Kontrolle von Vertragsbestimmungen, insbes. standardisierter Klauseln	3
a) Inhaltskontrolle	3
b) Einbeziehungskontrolle	4
c) Kontrolle überraschender Klauseln	5
aa) Überraschender Klauselinhalt	5
bb) Überraschende sprachliche Fassung oder Präsentation	5
cc) Kombination mehrerer Faktoren; Rechtsprechung	5
3. Dissens	6
4. Widerrufsrechte	7
5. Einbeziehung von Streitbeilegungsklauseln	9
a) Äußerer Konsens	10
b) Formgültigkeit	11
c) Normenkonkurrenzen und -konflikte	12
6. Einigung über Ausschluss oder Wahl des CISG	14a
a) Ausschluss der Anwendung des CISG nach Art. 6 („opting out")	14b
b) Wahl des CISG („opting in")	14d
II. Geltungsbereich: Andere Vertragsschlussformen	15
1. Grundsätzliche Position des CISG	16
2. Vertragsschluss durch Schweigen auf kaufmännisches Bestätigungsschreiben	18
3. Vertragsschluss ohne eindeutige Angebots- bzw. Annahmeerklärung	23
4. Vertragsschluss im elektronischen Geschäftsverkehr (e-commerce)	25
a) Anwendbarkeit des CISG	25
b) Autonome Auslegung der Artt. 14–24	26
c) Einverständnis der Parteien mit der Verwendung elektronischer Kommunikationsmittel	27
5. Internet-Auktionen	28
6. Käufe an Warenbörsen	29
7. Internationale Ausschreibungen	30
III. Vertragsschluss bei Mehrparteienverträgen	30a
1. Mehrparteienkaufverträge	30a
2. Anwendbarkeit der Artt. 14–24	30b
3. Problemlagen	30d
IV. Verhandlungen und vorvertragliche Pflichten	31
1. Vorvertragliche Pflichten nach dem CISG	32
2. Anwendbarkeit vorvertraglicher Pflichten nach nationalem Recht neben dem CISG	34
a) Allgemeine Pflichten zum Schutz von Leib, Leben, Eigentum etc	35
b) Schutz vor fraudulösem Parteiverhalten	36
c) Schutz vor fahrlässiger Fehlinformation, insbesondere *negligent misrepresentation*	37
d) Abbruch von Vertragsverhandlungen	38
e) Vorvertragliche Aufklärungs- und Informationspflichten	39
3. Vorverträge etc	41

V. Vertragsschluss und Vertragsinhalt 42
VI. Vorbehalt nach Art. 92 44
VII. Ausstrahlungswirkung des Teil II 46
   1. Vorbildfunktion der Artt. 14–24 für andere Einheitsrechte und nationale Rechtsreformen 46
   2. Folgen für die Auslegung 50
      a) Ausstrahlung des Teil II auf die Auslegung anderer Rechtsakte 51
      b) Verbot der Auslegung des Teil II im Lichte anderer Rechtsakte (Art. 7 I) 52

I. Geltungsbereich: Äußerer Konsens und Gültigkeit

1   Das CISG regelt von den Voraussetzungen für das wirksame Zustandekommen eines Kaufvertrages in seinem Teil II (Artt. 14–24)[1] nur den **äußeren Konsens,** der durch Angebot und Annahme hergestellt wird.[2] Wichtig für den **Vertragsschluss** sind aber auch die allgemeinen Bestimmungen der Artt. 7–13, insbesondere Art. 8 zur Auslegung der Vertragsschlusserklärungen und Art. 11 zur Formfreiheit, ferner Art. 6 zur Möglichkeit parteiautonomer Ausgestaltung des Vertragsschlussverfahrens. Soweit das Übereinkommen für Fragen des Vertragsschlusses eine Regelung bereithält – sei es in Gestalt einer ausdrücklichen Bestimmung oder aber eines allgemeinen Grundsatzes, der nach Art. 7 II zur Lückenfüllung heranzuziehen ist – regelt es **abschließend** und lässt keinen Raum für die parallele Anwendung anderer (vor allem nationaler) Vorschriften und Rechtsgrundsätze, welche dieselbe Sachfrage betreffen. Dies gilt unabhängig davon, ob diese ihr jeweiliges Regelungsziel durch materielle Vertragsschlussnormen, die Statuierung von Nebenpflichten und daran anknüpfende Haftungsanordnungen (etwa *culpa in contrahendo*)[3] oder auf andere Weise verfolgen.

1. Nicht geregelte Fragen

2   Für **Gültigkeitsfragen, die nicht äußeren Konsens oder Form betreffen,** bleibt das vom IPR des Forums berufene unvereinheitlichte Recht zuständig, Art. 4 S. 2 lit. a). Ungültigkeit des Vertrages oder einzelner Bestimmungen kann bei Maßgeblichkeit deutschen Rechts wegen Verstoßes gegen ein Verbotsgesetz i. S. v. § 134 BGB oder gegen § 138 BGB, aber auch bei nach dem AGB-Recht (§§ 305c ff. BGB) verbotenen Klauseln gegeben sein. Ob ein **Verbotsgesetz** ipso iure vernichtet oder die Ungültigkeitsfolge durch private Erklärung, Gerichtsentscheidung oder anderen Staatsakt zu bewirken ist, richtet sich ebenfalls nach dem maßgebenden Recht. Unwirksamkeit oder Vernichtbarkeit wegen **Willensmängeln, arglistiger Täuschung,**[4] Verstoß gegen die **guten Sitten,**[5] **fehlender** oder **beschränkter Geschäftsfähigkeit,**[6] **mangelnder Rechtsfähigkeit**[7] oder Unzulässigkeit **missbräuchlicher Klauseln**[8] ist ebenso nach dem über IPR jeweils berufenen nationalen Recht – ggf. auch nach in anderen Übereinkommen, EG-Verordnungen oder auf Grund

---

[1] Beachte, dass der Vertragsschlussteil der Konvention nicht in Staaten gilt, die einen Vorbehalt nach Art. 92 eingelegt haben (s. näher unten Rn. 44; Liste der CISG-Vertragsstaaten mit erklärten Vorbehalten in Anhang I).

[2] Zur Vorgeschichte des Teils II s. *Ludwig*, S. 287 ff. sowie die Darstellung und Nachweise in der 1. Aufl., *Schlechtriem*, Vor Artt. 14–24 Rn. 1 f.

[3] Zur Haftung wegen Verletzung vorvertraglicher Pflichten nach nationalem Recht s. unten Rn. 34 ff.

[4] S. noch unten Rn. 36.

[5] KG Jura, 3.11.2004, CISG-online 965: „le régime des contrats contraires aux bonnes mœurs est aussi exclu de la Convention"; *Neumayer/Ming*, Art. 4, Anm. 5. (mit Hinweis auf § 879 III ABGB); *Schlechtriem/Witz*, Convention de Vienne, Anm. 52.

[6] *Kröll u. a./Ferrari*, pre Arts 14–24, Rn. 4.

[7] *Rudolph*, Art. 4, Rn. 5; *Schwenzer/Mohs*, IHR 2006, 239; umfassend *Hartnell*, 18 Yale J. Int'l L. (1993), 1, 63 ff.

[8] S. sogleich Rn. 3.

von EG-Richtlinien usw. vereinheitlichten Regeln[9] – zu beurteilen wie die Voraussetzungen wirksamer **Stellvertretung** durch bevollmächtigte Agenten oder **Organe juristischer Personen**.[10] Dagegen können solche nationalen Vorschriften auf den CISG-Vertragsschluss **keine Anwendung** finden, die für den Fall der Vereinbarung eines **Scheingeschäfts** dessen Nichtigkeit anordnen, weil Art. 8 diesbezüglich eine vorrangige Regelung bereithält.[11] Entsprechendes gilt auch für das Erfordernis einer „**consideration**" nach Common Law, denn hierbei handelt es sich um eine formäquivalente Gültigkeitsanforderung, die durch Art. 11 verdrängt wird.[12]

2. Kontrolle von Vertragsbestimmungen, insbes. standardisierter Klauseln

Die Vertragsschlussregeln in Teil II des CISG bestimmen auch über die Einbeziehung 3 standardisierter Vertragsinhalte (Allgemeiner Geschäftsbedingungen (AGB), Formularbedingungen, Incoterms®, Standardkontrakte) in internationale Kaufverträge; ihre diesbezügliche Anwendung hat zu einem umfangreichen Rechtsprechungskorpus geführt (s. dazu ausführlich unten Art. 14 Rn. 32 ff.). Bei der erforderlichen Abgrenzung ihres Geltungsbereiches gegenüber demjenigen unvereinheitlichter (nationaler) Rechtsregeln ist anhand der geregelten **Sachfrage** zu differenzieren:

a) Inhaltskrontolle. Inhaltliche Klauselkontrolle ist nicht Sache des CISG. Soweit nationale Gesetze oder Rechtsregeln bestimmte Klauseln aufgrund von deren **Inhalt** als unzulässig, d. h. nichtig (oder auch vernichtbar) bewerten, gehen diese Vorschriften dem CISG vor, vgl. Art. 4 S. 2 lit. a).[13] Wo wertungsoffene Normen wie etwa §§ 307 I 1, II, 310 BGB standardisierte Vertragsbedingungen oder andere Klauseln an gesetzlichen Maßstäben messen, sind diese nationalen Vorschriften ebenfalls über Art. 4 S. 2 lit. a) anzuwenden,[14] doch sind die anzuwendenden Wertungsmaßstäbe der gesetzlichen Regelung des CISG und nicht etwa dem nationalen Recht zu entnehmen.[15]

---

[9] Zum Verhältnis des EG-Sekundärrechts zum CISG s. umfassend *Schroeter*, UN-Kaufrecht, § 6, Rn. 83 ff., § 9, Rn. 22 ff., § 10, Rn. 11 f. und § 15, Rn. 3 (Zusammenfassung).

[10] OLG Graz, 24.2.1999, CISG-online 797; oben *Ferrari*, Art. 4 Rn. 34; *Honsell/Siehr*, Art. 4, Rn. 11; *Rudolph*, Art. 4, Rn. 13; *Soergel/Lüderitz/Fenge*, Art. 4, Rn. 5; *Staudinger/Magnus*, Art. 4, Rn. 37; *Witz/Salger/Lorenz/Lorenz*, Art. 4, Rn. 29–31.

[11] KG Zug, 14.12.2009, CISG-online 2026: Art. 18 OR auf CISG-Verträge unanwendbar; *Schlechtriem*, Internationales UN-Kaufrecht, Rn. 55; oben *Schmidt-Kessel*, Art. 8 Rn. 7; *Witz/Salger/Lorenz/Witz*, Art. 8, Rn. 6; a. A. OLG Graz, 24.2.1999, CISG-online 797: österreichisch-slowenischer Kaufvertrag über Autoersatzteile, durch den angeblich ein Waffenverkauf verdeckt werden sollte – § 916 Abs. 1 ABGB angewandt.

[12] *Audit*, Vente internationale, Anm. 36.; *Bridge*, Int'l Sale of Goods, Rn. 3.02; *Ferrari*, RabelsZ 71 (2007), 52, 79 f.; *Honnold/Flechtner*, Art. 29, Rn. 204.4; *Mattera*, 16 Pace Int'l L. Rev. (2004), 165, 186 f.; *McQuillen*, 61 U. Miami L. Rev. (2007), 509, 525; *Schlechtriem*, Internationales UN-Kaufrecht, Rn. 64; oben *Schmidt-Kessel*, Art. 11 Rn. 11; *Schultz*, 35 Cornell Int'l L. J. (2002), 263, 273 Fn. 91; *van Alstine*, 37 Va. J. Int'l L. (1996), 1, 16 Fn. 47. Anders jedoch *Geneva Pharmaceuticals Technology Corp. v. Barr Laboratories, Inc.*, U. S. Dist. Ct. (S. D. N. Y.), 10.5.2002, CISG-online 653 = 201 F. Supp. 2d 236, 282 ff.: Notwendigkeit einer „consideration" als Gültigkeitsfrage i. S. d. Art. 4 S. 2 lit. a) eingeordnet und nach dem Recht New Jerseys beurteilt; dazu mit Recht kritisch *Mattera*, aaO., 181: „clearly flawed"; *McQuillen*, 61 U. Miami L. Rev. (2007), 509, 525.

[13] Com., 13.2.2007, CISG-online 1561 = IHR 2011, 105, 106; *Barbara Berry, S. A. de C. V v. Ken M. Spooner Farms, Inc.*, U. S. Dist. Ct. (W. D. Wash.), 13.4.2006, CISG-online 1354: Frage, ob Haftungsausschlussklausel in CISG-Vertrag *unconscionable* und daher undurchsetzbar ist, bestimmt sich nach dem durch das IPR berufenen Recht (hier: des U. S.-Staates Washington); OLG Köln, 21.5.1996, CISG-online 254: individualvertraglicher Gewährleistungsausschluss bei arglistigem Verhalten des Gebrauchtwagenverkäufers nach § 476 BGB a. F. nichtig.

[14] OGH, 7.9.2000, CISG-online 642 = IHR 2001, 42, 43; RB Zutphen, 29.5.1997, CISG-online 546 = NIPR 1998, Nr. 110; oben *Ferrari*, Art. 4 Rn. 20 ff.; *Kühl/Hingst*, FS Herber, S. 59; *Lookofsky*, 13 Duke J. Comp. & Int'l L. (2003), 263, 281; *Magnus*, FS Kritzer, S. 307; *Staudinger/Coester*, Vorbem zu §§ 307–309, Rn. 11; *Witz/Hlawon*, IHR 2011, 93, 98; *Wolf/Lindacher/Pfeiffer/Hau*, IntGV, Rn. 76; zur Anknüpfung s. *Stoll*, Internationalprivatrechtliche Fragen, S. 512.

[15] OGH, 7.9.2000, CISG-online 642 = IHR 2001, 42, 43; OLG Linz, 23.3.2005, CISG-online 1376 = IHR 2007, 123, 127; OLG Düsseldorf, 21.4.2004, CISG-online 915 = IHR 2005, 24, 27; LG Heilbronn,

4 b) Einbeziehungskontrolle. Über die Einbeziehung Allgemeiner Geschäftsbedingungen und anderer standardisierter Vertragsinhalte entscheiden hingegen die Vertragsschlussregeln des CISG, d. h. Artt. 14 ff. i. V. m. Art. 8.[16] Der Regelungsbereich des Übereinkommens kann sich deshalb mit dem Regelungsbereich nationaler Vorschriften schneiden, welche die Einbeziehung von AGB in Verträge regeln. Die Anwendbarkeit nationaler **AGB-Kontrollnormen** auf CISG-Verträge hängt davon ab, ob die betreffenden Vorschriften Fragen des Vertragsschlusses oder der Form (dann werden sie durch Artt. 14 ff. i. V. m. Art. 8 bzw. Art. 11 verdrängt) oder aber solche der Gültigkeit der AGB-Klauseln regeln (die außerhalb des Regelungsbereiches des CISG liegen). Entscheidend ist eine **funktionale Qualifikation:** Danach sind solche Normen nicht neben dem CISG anwendbar, die besondere Einbeziehungsvoraussetzungen für AGB (wie etwa die Hinweis- und Kenntnisverschaffungserfordernisse des § 305 II, III BGB,[17] der Art. 6:233 f. niederländisches NBW und des Art. 384 § 1 polnischer Kodeks cywilny,[18] das Vorlageerfordernis des portugiesischen AGB-Rechts[19] oder das Hinweis- und Erläuterungserfordernis in Art. 39 I chinesisches Vertragsgesetz) oder aber Formerfordernisse wie z. B. dasjenige eines schriftlichen Einverständnisses des anderen Teils[20] aufstellen,[21] während die materielle **Transparenz** von AGB-Klauseln als Gültigkeitsfrage einzuordnen[22] und daher bei Anwendbarkeit deutschen Rechts an § 307 I 2 BGB zu messen ist.[23]

5 c) Kontrolle überraschender Klauseln. Hinsichtlich der Kontrolle „überraschender" oder „ungewöhnlicher" Klauseln in AGB ist zu **unterscheiden:**[24]

aa) Überraschender Klauselinhalt. Die Kontrolle überraschender Klauseln betrifft deren Gültigkeit und richtet sich daher nach dem anwendbaren **nationalen Recht,** wenn und soweit die Kontrollnorm ihre Sanktionswirkung zumindest primär an die **inhaltliche Ausgestaltung** der AGB-Klausel anknüpft.[25] In diesem Fall ist es unerheblich, ob die

---

15.9.1997, CISG-online 562; oben *Ferrari,* Art. 4 Rn. 20 m. w. N.; *Honsell/Dornis,* Art. 14, Rn. 4; *Koller,* FS Honsell, S. 243; *Staudinger/Coester,* § 307, Rn. 238; *Wolf/Lindacher/Pfeiffer/Hau,* IntGV, Rn. 76.

[16] S. dazu unten Art. 14 Rn. 33 m. ausf. Nachw.

[17] OLG Jena, 10.11.2010, CISG-online 2216 = IHR 2011, 79, 81 (zu § 305 BGB); OLG Zweibrücken, 31.3.1998, CISG-online 481 (zu § 2 AGBG); *Lohmann,* Parteiautonomie, S. 223; *Piltz,* IHR 2004, 133; *Staudinger/Schlosser,* § 305, Rn. 103; *Ulmer/Brandner/Hensen/H. Schmidt,* Anh. § 305 BGB, Rn. 10; anders und bedenklich *Kramer,* FS Welser, S. 549 f.: § 305 II BGB sei „via Art. 8 II" auch für das UN-Kaufrecht beherzigenswert – dies liefe auf eine Auslegung des Einheitskaufrechts anhand nationalen Rechts hinaus und dürfte daher mit Art. 7 I unvereinbar sein; ebenfalls die Berücksichtigung einzelner nationaler Einbeziehungsregeln befürwortend aber *Neumayer/Ming,* Art. 8, Anm. 6.

[18] S. dazu *Liebscher/Zoll,* in: *dies.,* § 5, Rn. 43.

[19] Zum Vorlageerfordernis nach Art. 5 der portugiesischen Gesetzesverfügung Nr. 446/85 vgl. *Mallmann,* RIW 1987, 111.

[20] So etwa Art. 1341 II ital. Cc (deutschsprachige Übersetzung der Norm bei *Ranieri,* Europ. Obligationenrecht, S. 334); wie hier Cass., 13.10.2006, CISG-online 1404; *Asam,* Jb. It. R. 3 (1990), 3, 20, 24; *Hammerschmidt,* S. 33; *Kröll u. a./Ferrari,* pre Arts 14–24, Rn. 5; MünchKommHGB/*Ferrari,* Vor Art. 14, Rn. 5, Art. 14, Rn. 41; *Padovini,* Riv. dir. int. priv. proc. 1987, 47, 55; a. A. RB Zwolle, 1.3.1995, CISG-online 372 = NIPR 1996, Nr. 95; *Witz/Salger/Lorenz/Witz,* Vor Artt. 14–24, Rn. 11: vom CISG nicht erfasste Gültigkeitsfrage.

[21] *Koller,* FS Honsell, S. 236.

[22] In diesem Sinne auch *Armbrüster,* Standard Contract Terms, S. 169; *Heinrichs,* S. 101 ff., 106; *ders.,* FS Trinkner, S. 157, 161 ff.; *Lindacher,* Transparenz, S. 347 ff., 358, 362; *H. Schmidt,* NJW 2011, 1633, 1634: die in § 307 I 2 BGB kodifizierte materielle Transparenz sei „inhaltlich determiniert".

[23] *Jungemeyer,* RIW 2010, 166, 167; *Ulmer/Brandner/Hensen/Fuchs,* § 307 BGB, Rn. 330 f. A. A. MünchKomm/*Gruber,* Art. 14, Rn. 33, der für eine konventionsautonom zu entwickelnde Transparenzkontrolle eintritt; in diese Richtung auch *Koch,* FS Bergsten, S. 612.

[24] Zu pauschal daher LG Landshut, 12.6.2008, CISG-online 1703 = IHR 2008, 184, 187; ebenso wohl *Koch,* FS Bergsten, S. 607 ff. Wie hier *Schwenzer/Hachem/Kee,* Rn. 12.24; *Steensgaard,* Standardbetingelser, § 8, Rn. 92 ff. u. § 10, Rn. 1 ff.

[25] S. *Bamberger/Roth/Saenger,* Art. 14, Rn. 7; *Hammerschmidt,* S. 34; *Kühl/Hingst,* FS Herber, S. 61; MünchKomm/*Westermann,* Art. 4, Rn. 5; *Piltz,* IHR 2004, 133, 138; *Sauthoff,* IHR 2005, 21, 23; *Schlechtriem,* JZ 1988, 1037, 1040; *Staudinger/Magnus,* Art. 14, Rn. 42; *Stoffels,* AGB-Recht, Rn. 252; *Witz/Salger/Lorenz/Witz,* Vor Artt. 14–24, Rn. 11; a. A. *Brunner,* Art. 4, Rn. 46; *Drasch,* S. 6, 11 ff.; *Koch,* FS Bergsten, S. 611;

betreffende Kontrollnorm – wie etwa § 305c I BGB und § 864a ABGB – als Rechtsfolge anordnet, dass ungewöhnliche Klauseln „nicht Vertragsbestandteil" werden. Neben dem CISG anwendbar bleibt nach diesen Grundsätzen § 305c I BGB,[26] in dessen Rahmen von der Rechtsprechung vorrangig (wenn auch nicht ausschließlich) auf den Grad der Abweichung vom dispositiven Gesetzesrecht abgestellt wird[27] und der in seiner maßgeblichen praktischen Regelungswirkung daher §§ 307 ff. BGB ähnelt,[28] sowie bei Geltung österreichischen Rechts § 864a ABGB,[29] der ebenfalls die Frage der Einbeziehung mit einer Inhaltskontrolle verknüpft.[30] Auch die durch die Rechtsprechung entwickelte **Ungewöhnlichkeitsregel** des **schweizerischen Rechts** lässt sich funktional als Inhaltskontrolle einordnen,[31] kann jedoch auf CISG-Verträge deshalb nicht angewandt werden, weil sie durch die dortigen Gerichte eindeutig dem Konsensbereich zugeordnet wird und es ihr daher an einem eigenen Geltungswillen als inhaltliche Gültigkeitskontrollnorm mangelt.[32] Soweit bei der Beurteilung der Ungewöhnlichkeit einer Klausel im Rahmen der AGB-Kontrolle die Abweichung vom Gesetzesrecht eine Rolle spielt, ist im Übrigen auch hier die Abweichung von den Regelungen des CISG entscheidend[33] – eine Klausel, die in innerstaatlichen Verträgen eines bestimmten Landes gängig ist, mag gleichwohl für ausländische Vertragspartner überraschend sein, wenn diese sich berechtigterweise auf die einheitlichen Bestimmungen des UN-Kaufrechts eingestellt haben.

bb) Überraschende sprachliche Fassung oder Präsentation. Soweit nationale Normen zur Kontrolle überraschender Klauseln deren „überraschende" Natur hingegen im konkreten Fall anhand ihrer Sprachfassung oder ihrer Präsentation gegenüber der anderen Partei (wie z. B. der versteckten Stellung der Klausel im Vertragswerk) beurteilen würden, werden sie durch das CISG **verdrängt**: In diesem Fall ist nach dem **(insoweit vorrangig anwendbaren)** Art. 8 II zu prüfen, ob die Berücksichtigung des Empfängerhorizontes eines vernünftigen Adressaten in der gleichen Stellung wie des Empfängers und unter den gleichen Umständen dazu führt, dass überraschende oder intransparente Klauseln in den AGB, die durch Verweisung Bestandteil der Offerte werden sollen, von ihm nicht „aufgefasst" werden können und bereits deshalb nicht in den Vertrag einbezogen werden.[34]

Lohmann, Parteiautonomie, S. 224; MünchKomm/*Gruber*, Art. 14, Rn. 34; *Schmidt-Kessel*, oben Art. 8 Rn. 57; *Stadler*, AGB, S. 99; *Wolf/Lindacher/Pfeiffer/Hau*, IntGV, Rn. 73.

[26] OLG Düsseldorf, 21.4.2004, CISG-online 915 = IHR 2005, 24, 28 (zu § 3 AGBG); a. A. *Schmidt-Kessel/Meyer*, IHR 2008, 177, 180.

[27] BGH, 30.10.1987, BGHZ 102, 152, 159; BGH, 21.11.1991, NJW 1992, 1234, 1235; *Palandt/Grüneberg*, § 305c, Rn. 3; PWW/*K. P. Berger*, § 305c, Rn. 5; *Ranieri*, Europ. Obligationenrecht, S. 371.

[28] Vgl. MünchKomm/*Basedow*, § 305c, Rn. 3; MünchKomm/*Westermann*, Art. 4, Rn. 5: es sei inhaltlich eine Wertungsfrage zu entscheiden; MünchKommHGB/*Benicke*, Art. 4, Rn. 5: die Missbilligung des Klauselinhalts stehe im Vordergrund. S. als Beispiel für die funktionale Austauschbarkeit beider Kontrollansätze OLG Zweibrücken, 31.3.1998, CISG-online 481: AGB-Klausel in CISG-Vertrag am Maßstab des § 9 AGBG geprüft und dabei als „überraschend und daher unwirksam" eingestuft; bestätigt durch BGH, 24.3.1999, CISG-online 396 = BGHZ 141, 129, 135.

[29] *Hammerschmidt*, S. 33; a. A. *Stadler*, AGB, S. 186.

[30] Vgl. *Rummel/Rummel*, § 864a ABGB, Rn. 4; *Schwimann/Apathy/Riedler*, § 864a ABGB, Rn. 7.

[31] Berner Komm/*Kramer*, Art. 19–20 OR, Rn. 279: „verdeckte (verkappte) Inhaltskontrolle"; *Koller*, FS Honsell, S. 241: „im Ergebnis eine Art Inhaltskontrolle von krass einseitigen AGB"; BaslerKomm/*Huguenin*, Art. 19/20 OR, Rn. 27: „Je unbilliger die AGB sind, umso höher werden die Anforderungen an das Zustandekommen einer ‚Einigung' geschraubt."

[32] Vgl. *Brunner*, Art. 4, Rn. 46. Die im Jahre 2011 neu gefasste AGB-Kontrollnorm des Art. 8 schw. UWG schützt bewusst nur Konsumenten und ist daher bei CISG-Verträgen regelmäßig nicht einschlägig.

[33] Unstr., s. OLG Düsseldorf, 21.4.2004, CISG-online 915 = IHR 2005, 24, 28; *Staudinger/Magnus*, Art. 14, Rn. 42.

[34] Vgl. LG Landshut, 12.6.2008, CISG-online 1703 = IHR 2008, 184, 187; OLG Düsseldorf, 21.4.2004, CISG-online 915 = IHR 2005, 24, 28: da in den Vertragsverhandlungen schnellstmögliche Lieferung zugesagt worden und deren Bedeutung „nach den gemäß Art. 8 CISG zu berücksichtigenden Umständen" ersichtlich war, war AGB-Klausel ungewöhnlich und überraschend, die (außer bei schriftlicher Zusage eines genauen Liefertermins) eine Vertragsauflösung wg. Lieferverzögerung von einer Nachfristsetzung mit Ablehnungsandrohung abhängig machte (hier allerdings nach § 3 AGBG geprüft). Vgl. auch *Kramer*, FS Welser, S. 550; *Steensgaard*, Standardbetingelser, § 8, Rn. 92 ff.

cc) Kombination mehrerer Faktoren; Rechtsprechung. Ergibt sich der Überraschungscharakter einer AGB-Klausel sowohl aus deren Inhalt als auch deren Sprachfassung und Präsentation, so ist auf den im konkreten Fall ausschlaggebenden Faktor abzustellen. Zur Kontrolle überraschender Klauseln in der **bisherigen Rechtsprechung** zum CISG s. unten Art. 14 Rn. 35.

3. Dissens

6   Das CISG enthält keine Vorschriften über die Auswirkungen eines offenen oder versteckten Dissenses auf Gültigkeit und Inhalt des Vertrages. Ob insoweit auf nationale Vorschriften, ggf. also die §§ 154, 155 BGB zurückgegriffen werden kann, ist zweifelhaft. Einseitige Irrtümer unterstehen grundsätzlich[35] nationalem Recht. Soweit ein Dissens zu einzelnen Punkten des Vertrages durch Erklärungsdivergenzen entstanden ist, gilt Art. 19. Falls ein offener oder ein unerkannter Dissens geblieben ist, der nicht durch Divergenzen von Angebot und Annahme entstanden und deshalb nach Art. 19 zu beurteilen ist, sollte m. E. auf der Grundlage von Art. 7 II eine **einheitsrechtliche Lösung** gefunden und der Rückgriff auf nationales Recht vermieden werden.[36] Als tragender Grundsatz für eine Lösung darf gelten, dass das CISG für das Zustandekommen eines Vertrages entscheidend auf den Konsens der Parteien abstellt, gebunden sein zu wollen (s. unten Rn. 15, 24). Soweit einzelne Punkte offen geblieben sind, hängt der Vertragsschluss deshalb davon ab, ob die Parteien gleichwohl gebunden sein wollten, sei es, dass sie die offenen Punkte später klären oder unentschieden lassen wollten, sei es, dass sie diese Punkte gar nicht bemerkt haben (versteckter Dissens), den Vertrag aber auch in Kenntnis des Einigungsmangels über diese Punkte geschlossen hätten.[37] Bei Nichteinigung über den Kaufpreis[38] gelten Artt. 14 I 2, 55.[39] In der Sache dürfte damit eine den §§ 154, 155 BGB entsprechende Lösung erreichbar sein, die einen Rückgriff auf nationales Recht entbehrlich macht.

4. Widerrufsrechte

7   Ob Widerrufs- und Rückgaberechte nationaler Rechtsordnungen oder anderer internationaler Rechtsakte neben dem CISG angewandt werden können, bemisst sich danach, ob das betreffende Widerrufsrecht an eine **Sachfrage** anknüpft, welche bereits funktional äquivalent im CISG geregelt ist:[40] Ist dies der Fall, wird das Lösungsrecht durch das Übereinkommen verdrängt, während bei einem abweichenden Regelungsgegenstand einer parallelen Anwendung nichts im Wege steht. Ohne Bedeutung ist dabei, ob das Widerrufsrecht – wie heute weitgehend üblich – allein nach nationalem Recht (und innerhalb der EU vielfach durch Vorgaben des Unionsrechts) näher definierten „Verbrauchern" zusteht,[41] denn das Erkennbarkeitserfordernis in Art. 2 lit. a), bei dessen fehlender Erfüllung Käufe zu privaten Zwecken dem CISG unterliegen können,[42] soll gerade sicherstellen, dass der Verkäufer in solchen Konstellationen auf die ungeschmälerte Anwendung der Übereinkom-

---

[35] S. jedoch oben *Ferrari*, Art. 4 Rn. 24.
[36] Zustimmend *Honsell/Dornis*, Vorbem 14–24, Rn. 4; *Kramer*, FS Welser, S. 541.
[37] Anders MünchKomm/*Gruber*, Art. 19, Rn. 29.
[38] Vgl. BGH, 26.2.1999, NJW-RR 1999, 927 (unklare Verrechnungsabrede als Einigungsmangel nach § 154 BGB – kein CISG-Fall).
[39] S. unten Art. 14 Rn. 16 ff.
[40] *Benedick*, Informationspflichten, Rn. 933; oben *Ferrari*, Art. 4 Rn. 23a; *Schlechtriem*, Internationales UN-Kaufrecht, Rn. 36b; *Schroeter*, UN-Kaufrecht, § 6, Rn. 156; *Wartenberg*, S. 64; allgemein bereits oben Rn. 1.
[41] Wie hier *Benedick*, Informationspflichten, Rn. 930; a. A. *Honsell/Dornis*, Vorbem 14–24, Rn. 4.
[42] BGH, 31.10.2001, CISG-online 617 = BGHZ 149, 113, 119; oben *Ferrari*, Art. 4 Rn. 23a; *Schroeter*, UN-Kaufrecht, § 6, Rn. 111; a. A. und unzutreffend *Staudinger/Thüsing*, Vorbem zu §§ 312 b-f, Rn. 36. Das UN-Kaufrecht kann zudem auch dann nur einen objektiv vorliegenden Verbraucherkauf anzuwenden sein, wenn sich keine der Parteien auf die Ausnahmevorschrift des Art. 2 lit. a beruft; vgl. in diesem Sinne OGH, 18.12.2002, CISG-online 1279.

mensregeln vertrauen kann.[43] Ebenfalls kein tauglicher Maßstab ist die Einordnung von Widerrufsrechten als Gültigkeitsfrage i. S. des Art. 4 S. 2 lit. a),[44] denn durch letztere Vorschrift werden Fragen der Vertragsgültigkeit weder ausschließlich noch in jedem Fall vom Regelungsanspruch des Übereinkommens ausgenommen („Soweit in diesem Übereinkommen nicht ausdrücklich etwas anderes bestimmt ist ...").[45]

Nach der somit differenzierend und mit Blick auf das einzelne Widerrufsrecht vorzunehmenden Beurteilung[46] sind solche Widerrufsrechte neben dem CISG anwendbar, durch welche dem Verbraucher eine zusätzliche **Überlegungsfrist** („cooling-off period") eingeräumt werden soll, bevor in als **risikobehaftet eingestuften Situationen** abgeschlossene Verträge endgültig bindend werden.[47] Dies gilt bei Anwendbarkeit deutschen Rechts für das Widerrufs- bzw. Rückgaberecht nach § 312 I i. V. m. §§ 355 f. BGB,[48] bei Anwendbarkeit österreichischen Rechts für das Rücktrittsrecht nach § 3 I KSchG, schweizerischen Rechts für das Widerrufsrecht nach Art. 40b OR und französischen Rechts für das *droit de renoncer* nach Art. L. 121-25 C. consom.[49] Dasselbe gilt für das Rücktrittsrecht, welches § 3a I, II öst. KSchG dem Verbraucher für den Fall gewährt, dass ohne seine Veranlassung für seine **Einwilligung maßgebliche Umstände,** die der Unternehmer im Zuge der Vertragsverhandlungen als wahrscheinlich dargestellt hat, **nicht** oder nur in erheblich geringerem Ausmaß **eintreten,** weil Eigenschaften der Ware nicht zu den tatbestandlichen Umständen zählen[50] und das CISG in Art. 35 II lit. b) nur diesbezüglich eine Regelung enthält. Ebenfalls parallel zum CISG anwendbar sind Widerrufsrechte, die eine Überlegungsfrist aufgrund der **wirtschaftlichen Bedeutung** eines in Verbindung mit einem Kauf abgeschlossenen **Finanzierungsgeschäftes** verwirklichen sollen, wie dies etwa bei §§ 495 I, 499 I, 501, 505, 507 i. V. m. §§ 355, 358 I BGB[51] und §§ 16 I 1, 21 schweiz. KKG[52] der Fall ist. Funktional mit Regelungen des CISG **unvereinbar** und daher **nicht** neben dem Übereinkommen anwendbar sind hingegen Widerrufsrechte, welche es dem kaufenden (auch dem nicht als solchen erkennbaren) Verbraucher erlauben sollen, frei darüber zu entscheiden, ob ihm der im Fernabsatz erworbene Kaufgegenstand subjektiv gefällt und sich ggf. wieder vom Vertrag zu lösen, ohne dass es dabei darauf ankäme, ob die gelieferte Ware objektiv vertragswidrig ist oder nicht – hierin liegt eine offenkundige Inkompatibilität mit dem eng begrenzten Vertragsaufhebungsrecht des Art. 49 I.[53] Durch das CISG **verdrängt**

---

[43] *Schroeter,* UN-Kaufrecht, § 6, Rn. 152 ff.
[44] Wie hier *Grunewald,* Kaufrecht, § 2, Rn. 59; a. A. *Audit,* Vente internationale, Anm. 37.; *Béraudo/Kahn,* Vente Internationale, S. 36; *Piltz,* Internationales Kaufrecht, Rn. 2–70; MünchKomm/*Ulmer,* Vor §§ 491–495, Rn. 46; *Staudinger/Magnus,* Art. 4, Rn. 21.
[45] *Schlechtriem/Witz,* Convention de Vienne, Anm. 57.; *Schroeter,* UN-Kaufrecht, § 6, Rn. 144 ff.; *Wartenberg,* S. 61 ff.
[46] Wie hier *Benedick,* Informationspflichten, Rn. 933. Pauschal für eine Anwendbarkeit aller Widerrufsrechte neben dem CISG hingegen *Bamberger/Roth/Saenger,* Art. 2, Rn. 6; *Grunewald,* Kaufrecht, § 2, Rn. 59; *Honsell/Dornis,* Vorbem 14–24, Rn. 4; *Kröll u. a./Ferrari,* pre Arts 14–24, Rn. 6; MünchKomm/*Gruber,* Vor Art. 14, Rn. 10; MünchKomm/*Westermann,* Art. 2, Rn. 3; MünchKommHGB/*Benicke,* Art. 4, Rn. 7; MünchKommHGB/*Ferrari,* Vor Art. 14, Rn. 6; *Piltz,* Internationales Kaufrecht, Rn. 2–70; *Soergel/Lüderitz/ Fenge,* Art. 4, Rn. 5; pauschal dagegen *Daun,* JuS 1997, 811, 813; *Meyer,* FS Hay, S. 304.
[47] Oben *Ferrari,* Art. 4 Rn. 23a.
[48] *Staudinger/Magnus,* Art. 4, Rn. 21; *Wartenberg,* S. 78 (zu § 1 I HaustürWG).
[49] *Schlechtriem/Witz,* Convention de Vienne, Anm. 57.
[50] *Schwimann/Apathy,* § 3a KSchG, Rn. 1. Die Aufzählung maßgeblicher Umstände in § 3a II KSchG ist abschließend; *Kathrein,* in: *Koziol/Bydlinski/Bollenberger,* § 3a KSchG, Rn. 2; *Schwimann/Apathy,* § 3a KSchG, Rn. 6; kritisch *Rummel/Krejci,* § 3a KSchG, Rn. 2.
[51] *Bamberger/Roth/Möller,* § 491, Rn. 8; *Bülow/Artz,* 3. Teil, Rn. 21; *Erman/Saenger,* Vor §§ 491–507, Rn. 20; MünchKomm/*Ulmer,* Vor §§ 491–495, Rn. 46; MünchKomm/*Westermann,* Art. 2, Rn. 3; *Staudinger/Kessal-Wulf,* Einl. zu §§ 491 ff., Rn. 49; *Staudinger/Magnus,* Art. 4, Rn. 21; *Wartenberg,* S. 78 (zu §§ 7, 9 II VerbrKrG); a. A. *Erman/Rebmann,* 10. Aufl., § 1 VerbrKrG, Rn. 52; *Herber/Czerwenka,* Art. 2, Rn. 8 (zu § 1b AbzG).
[52] A. A. *Benedick,* Informationspflichten, Rn. 938 ff.
[53] *Schroeter,* UN-Kaufrecht, § 15, Rn. 78 ff.; vgl. auch *Schlechtriem,* Internationales UN-Kaufrecht, Rn. 36b, der eine Unvereinbarkeit mit Artt. 35, 45 für Widerrufsrechte konstatiert, die dem Käufer für den Fall von Mängeln ein *erleichtertes* Lösungsrecht geben (ebenso *Staudinger/Magnus,* Art. 4, Rn. 21) – der im Text

werden daher etwa das Widerrufs- bzw. Rückgaberecht gemäß § 312d I i. V. m. §§ 355 f. BGB,[54] das Rücktrittsrecht gemäß § 5e I öst. KSchG sowie die Widerrufsrechte anderer nationaler Rechtsordnungen, die der Umsetzung der Vorgaben des Art. 6 I EG-Fernabsatzrichtlinie dienen.[55]

5. Einbeziehung von Streitbeilegungsklauseln

9 Vertragsschlusserklärungen, durch die ein dem CISG unterliegender Kaufvertrag zustande kommen soll, enthalten neben Klauseln zu im engeren Sinne kaufrechtlichen Regelungsgegenständen häufig auch Klauseln über die Beilegung etwaiger Streitigkeiten zwischen den Parteien, namentlich **Gerichtsstands- oder Schiedsklauseln**. Ihre wirksame Vereinbarung wirft zum einen Fragen nach der materiellen Einigung der Parteien über die Streitbeilegungsklausel und zum anderen nach deren Gültigkeit auf. Beides ist **streng zu trennen**:

10 a) **Äußerer Konsens.** Soweit die Streitbeilegungsklausel Bestandteil einer Parteierklärung ist, die sich auf Abschluss eines CISG-Kaufvertrages richtet, bestimmt sich ihre Einbeziehung in den Kaufvertrag und damit das Zustandekommen der materiellen Einigung zwischen den Vertragsparteien nach Artt. 14–24.[56] Die Anwendbarkeit der Vertragsschlussregeln des Übereinkommens erschließt sich deutlich aus Art. 19 III, denn wenn nach dieser Vorschrift eine abweichende Streitbeilegungsklausel in der Annahmeerklärung das Zustandekommen des Kaufvertrages verhindert, müssen diesbezüglich übereinstimmende Parteierklärungen eine solche Klausel im Umkehrschluss zum Bestandteil des Vertrages werden lassen.[57] Daneben zeigt auch Art. 81 I 2, dass das CISG Klauseln über die Beilegung von Streitigkeiten als Bestandteil des dem Übereinkommen unterliegenden Vertragsbandes behandelt.[58] In Übereinstimmung damit hat die Rechtsprechung das Zustandekommen von **Gerichtsstands-**[59]

---

behandelte Widerrufsrechtstyp setzt hingegen überhaupt keinen Mangel voraus und führt damit in der Sache zu einem Kauf auf Probe.

[54] *Benedick,* Informationspflichten, Rn. 960; a. A. *Kindler,* FS Heldrich, S. 231.

[55] Nachw. zur Umsetzung des Widerrufsrechts nach Art. 6 I EG-Fernabsatzrichtlinie in anderen EG-Staaten bei *Staudinger/Thüsing,* Vorbem zu §§ 312 b–f, Rn. 45 ff.

[56] *Brunner,* Art. 4, Rn. 39, Art. 90, Rn. 4; *Fogt,* IPRax 2003, 364, 365; *Gottwald,* FS Henckel, S. 301; *Herber,* IHR 2004, 117 f.; *Koch,* FS Kritzer, S. 282; *Perales Viscasillas/Ramos Muñoz,* FS Schwenzer, S. 1366; *Piltz,* Internationales Kaufrecht, Rn. 2–128; *ders.,* NJW 2007, 2159, 2160; *Schlosser,* EuZPR, Art. 23 EuGVVO, Rn. 19; *Schroeter,* UN-Kaufrecht, § 6, Rn. 25; a. A. MünchKomm/*Westermann,* Art. 4, Rn. 7; *Staudinger/Magnus,* Art. 14, Rn. 41c; *Witz,* D. 1999, 117, 119; ähnlich auch *Magnus,* ZEuP 2006, 96, 112; *ders.,* FS Kritzer, S. 309 f.: nur, soweit keine anderweitigen speziellen Vertragsabschlussregeln eingreifen; ebenso *Schlechtriem,* Internationales UN-Kaufrecht, Rn. 58; *Schlechtriem/Witz,* Convention de Vienne, Anm. 69.

[57] *Chateau des Charmes Wines Ltd. v. Sabaté USA Inc., Sabaté S. A.,* U. S. Ct. App. (9th Cir.), 5.5.2003, CISG-online 767 = IHR 2003, 295, 296; *Piltz,* Internationales Kaufrecht, Rn. 2–128; *Schlosser,* EuZPR, Art. 23 EuGVVO, Rn. 19; *Schroeter,* UN-Kaufrecht, § 6, Rn. 25.

[58] *Schroeter,* UN-Kaufrecht, § 6, Rn. 25; *Winship,* FS Neumayer, S. 234; a. A. *Garro,* 17 J. L. & Com. (1998), 219, 238.

[59] Civ. 1, 16.7.1998, CISG-online 344 = D. 1998, 222; *Chateau des Charmes Wines Ltd. v. Sabaté USA Inc., Sabaté S. A.,* U. S. Ct. App. (9th Cir.), 5.5.2003, CISG-online 767 = IHR 2003, 295, 296; OLG Braunschweig, 28.10.1999, CISG-online 510 = TranspR-IHR 2000, 4 f.; OLG Düsseldorf, 30.1.2004, CISG-online 821 = IHR 2004, 108, 111; OLG Düsseldorf, 23.3.2011, CISG-online 2218; OLG Köln, 24.5.2006, CISG-online 1232 = IHR 2006, 147, 148; OLG Oldenburg, 20.12.2007, CISG-online 1644 = IHR 2008, 112, 117; OGer Bern, 19.5.2008, CISG-online 1738; *CSS Antenna, Inc. v. Amphenol-Tuchel Electronics GmbH,* U. S. Dist. Ct. (D. Md.), 8.2.2011, CISG-online 2177; *Belcher-Robinson, L. L. C. v. Linamar Corporation, et al.,* U. S. Dist. Ct. (M. D. Ala.), 31.3.2010, CISG-online 2092; *Golden Valley Grape Juice and Wine, LLC v. Centrisys Corp. et al.,* U. S. Dist. Ct. (E. D. Cal.), 21.1.2010, CISG-online 2089; *Solae, LLC v. Hershey Canada, Inc.,* U. S. Dist. Ct. (D. Del.), 9.5.2008, CISG-online 1769 = 557 F. Supp. 2d 452, 456; Gerechtshof's-Hertogenbosch, 19.11.1996, CISG-online 323 = NIPR 1997, Nr. 123; CA Paris, 13.12.1995, CISG-online 312 = J. C. P., II, Nr. 22 772; LG Gießen, 17.12.2002, CISG-online 766 = IHR 2003, 276, 277; auch Audiencia Provincial de Navarra, 27.12.2007, CISG-online 1798 (gestützt auf Art. 7 I). Unklar Cámara Nacional de Apelaciones en lo Comercial de Buenos Aires, 14.10.1993, CISG-online 87: nach Art. 4 „es claro que no se halla destinada a reglar de manera inmediata cuestiones de competencia internacional, sin prejuicio de que de alguna de sus disposiciones pudieran extraerse pautas para resolver el caso", wo sodann die Einbeziehung der auf einer Rechnung aufgedruckten Gerichtsstandsklausel verneint und dabei Art. 18 zitiert wird.

wie auch **Schiedsvereinbarungen**[60] mit großer Selbstverständlichkeit den Artt. 14–24 unterstellt, einschließlich solcher Konstellationen, in denen die Streitbeilegungsklausel – wie häufig – Bestandteil von AGB war und deren Einbeziehung in den Vertrag in Rede stand (dazu näher unten Art. 14 Rn. 32 ff.). Selbiges gilt auch für die nachträgliche Einbeziehung von Streitbeilegungsklauseln im Wege der Vertragsänderung oder –ergänzung (Art. 29).[61] Die Vertragsschlussregeln des CISG sind daneben aber auch anwendbar, soweit es um die Einbeziehung von Mediationsvereinbarungen oder „hybriden" bzw. „multi-tiered" Streitbeilegungsklauseln in Kaufverträge geht.

b) Formgültigkeit. Die Formgültigkeit von in CISG-Verträgen enthaltenen Gerichtsstandsvereinbarungen bemisst sich vor europäischen Gerichten hingegen vorrangig nach Art. 23 I 3 **EuGVO** und Art. 23 I 3 rev. **LuganoÜ**,[62] während für Schiedsvereinbarungen Art. 2 II **NYC** gilt; daneben bestehen parallele Formvorschriften der nationalen Prozess- und Schiedsverfahrensrechte. Der Grundsatz der Formfreiheit des Art. 11 ist insoweit nach zutreffender, aber nicht unbestrittener h. M. nicht einschlägig,[63] wie sich aus einer historisch-systematischen Auslegung des Art. 11 mit Blick auf die Vorbehaltsmöglichkeit der Artt. 12, 96 erschließt: Da die Erklärung eines solchen Vorbehalts nach dem Übereinkommen die einzige Möglichkeit darstellt, die Wirkung des Art. 11 auszuschließen, ist offenkundig, dass die Verfasser des UN-Kaufrechts Streitbeilegungsklauseln von vornherein als nicht vom Anwendungsbereich der Vorschrift erfasst ansahen[64] – andernfalls wäre es nur Vorbehaltsstaaten möglich gewesen, die verbreiteten Schriftformanforderungen an Gerichtsstands- und Schiedsvereinbarungen weiterhin anwenden zu können.[65]

Auch das bislang nicht in Kraft getretene **Haager Übereinkommen über Gerichtsstandsvereinbarungen** vom 30. Juni 2005 stellt in Art. 3 lit. c) Formerfordernisse für Gerichtsstandsvereinbarungen auf. Gemäß Art. 3 lit. a) wird dabei das Vorliegen einer „Vereinbarung" vorausgesetzt, deren Zustandekommen sich nach dem Willen der Übereinkommensverfasser jedoch nach dem anwendbaren materiellen Recht (und damit potentiell Art. 14–24 CISG) richten soll,[66] während das Haager Übereinkommen selbst insoweit keine Regelungen enthält.

---

[60] Tribunal Supremo, 17.2.1998, CISG-online 1333; OLG Frankfurt a. M., 26.6.2006, CISG-online 1385 = IHR 2007, 42, 44; Lietuvos Apeliacinio teismo Civiliniu, 27.3.2000, CISG-online 1505 m. zust. Anm. *Fogt/Rosch*, D. 2003, som., 2369, 2370; *Filanto, S. p. A. v. Chilewich International Corp.*, U. S. Dist. Ct. (S. D. N. Y.), 14.4.1992, CISG-online 45 = 789 F. Supp. 1229, 1237; RB Arnhem, 17.1.2007, CISG-online 1455; RB Utrecht, 21.1.2009, CISG-online 1814; LG Hamburg, 19.6.1997, CISG-online 283 = RIW 1997, 873; Netherlands Arbitration Institute, 10.2.2005, CISG-online 1621 = YB. Comm. Arb. 2007, 93, 99 ff.; s. auch OLG Stuttgart, 15.5.2006, CISG-online 1414 = NJOZ 2006, 2836, 2838 (Auslegung einer Schiedsvereinbarung nach A.).
[61] *BTC-USA Corp. v. Novacare et al.*, U. S. Dist. Ct. (D. Minn.), 16.6.2008, CISG-online 1773; vgl. auch unten Art. 29, Rn. 2, 6.
[62] KG Zug, 11.12.2003, CISG-online 958 = IHR 2005, 119, 120 (zu Art. 17 I LuganoÜ a. F.).
[63] KG Zug, 11.12.2003, CISG-online 958 = IHR 2005, 119, 120; *Brunner*, Art. 11, Rn. 1, Art. 90, Rn. 4; *Herber/Czerwenka*, Art. 11, Rn. 5; *Honsell/Melis*, Art. 11, Rn. 5; *Koch*, FS Kritzer, S. 276 ff. mit ausf. Begründung; MünchKommHGB/*Ferrari*, Art. 11, Rn. 4; *Neumayer/Ming*, Art. 11, Anm. 1.; oben *Schmidt-Kessel*, Art. 11 Rn. 7; *Schroeter*, UN-Kaufrecht, § 6, Rn. 31; *Staudinger/Magnus*, Art. 11, Rn. 7; *Witz/Salger/Lorenz/Witz*, Art. 11–12, Rn. 7; a. A. Tribunal Supremo, 17.2.1998, CISG-online 1333; *Chateau des Charmes Wines Ltd. v. Sabaté USA Inc., Sabaté S. A.*, U. S. Ct. App. (9th Cir.), 5.5.2003, CISG-online 767 = IHR 2003, 295, 296; MünchKomm/*Westermann*, Art. 4, Rn. 7; *Perales Viscasillas/Ramos Muñoz*, FS Schwenzer, S. 1366; *Piltz*, Internationales Kaufrecht, Rn. 2–130; *Schlucher*, S. 90 ff.; *Walker*, 25 J. L. & Com. (2005-06), 153, 163 ff.
[64] *Schroeter*, UN-Kaufrecht, § 6, Rn. 32. Dieses Argument ablehnend *Perales Viscasillas/Ramos Muñoz*, FS Schwenzer, S. 1367; im Ergebnis wie hier, aber mit abw. Begründung *Koch*, FS Kritzer, S. 282 ff.
[65] Im Gegenteil war man auf der Diplomatischen Konferenz in Wien peinlich bemüht, Übergriffe des CISG auf das Zuständigkeitsrecht zu vermeiden; vgl. (freilich in anderem Zusammenhang) O. R., S. 369: „... the undesirable effect of impinging upon national rules on jurisdiction ...".
[66] *Hartley/Dogauchi*, Explanatory Report, Anm. 94.; *Teitz*, 53 Am. J. Comp. L. (2005), 543, 552 (mit Hinweis darauf, dass Vorschläge zur Schaffung materiellrechtlicher Regelungen im Haager Übereinkommen selbst keine ausreichende Zustimmung fanden).

12 c) Normenkonkurrenzen und -konflikte. Zu Überschneidungen der auf die Formgültigkeit von Streitbeilegungsklauseln anwendbaren Regelwerke mit Artt. 14–24 und daraus resultierenden Schwierigkeiten in der Rechtsanwendung kommt es zum einen dann, wenn man annimmt, dass die erstgenannten **Formregelungen implizit** auch für den Bereich der **materiellen Einigung Regelungsanspruch** erheben. So wird in der Tat verbreitet vertreten, Art. 23 I 1 EuGVO stelle in Gestalt des darin enthaltenen Wortes „vereinbart" eine einheitliche und abschließende Vertragsschlussregelung auf,[67] wobei man (zu Unrecht) meint, sich auf die Rechtsprechung des EuGH stützen zu können.[68] Der referierten Ansicht kann allerdings nicht gefolgt werden,[69] weil sie mit der durch den EuGH konkretisierten Grundkonzeption des Art. 23 I 1 EuGVO nicht im Einklang steht und vor allem zu erheblicher Rechtsunsicherheit führen würde, müssten doch komplexe Vertragsschlussprobleme anhand einer Norm gelöst werden, die zu diesem Fragenkomplex schlicht keinerlei greifbare Aussage bereit hält. Soweit etwa aus Art. 23 I 3 lit. c) EuGVO abgeleitet wird, dass bei Erfüllung der dort geregelten Formanforderungen die zudem notwendige Willenseinigung der Parteien bezüglich des Gerichtsstands *vermutet* wird,[70] gerät diese Regelung mit dem CISG hingegen schon deshalb nicht in Konflikt, weil sie eine im Übereinkommen nicht geregelte[71] Frage des Beweismaßes betrifft.[72]

13 Zum anderen besteht – unabhängig von der soeben genannten Streitfrage – bei einzelnen **Sachfragen** die latente Gefahr, dass sie einerseits als Problem der materiellen Einigung, andererseits hingegen als Formfrage eingeordnet werden können und daher insoweit (jedenfalls auf den ersten Blick) mehrere, jeweils autonom auszulegende Regelwerke Regelungsanspruch erheben. Entsprechende Schwierigkeiten sind bislang vor allem bei der Behandlung von in AGB enthaltenen Streitbeilegungsklauseln aufgetreten: So wird die zu fordernde Kenntnisverschaffung (auch) bei entsprechenden Klauseln überwiegend als Frage des äußeren Konsens eingeordnet und daher Artt. 14 ff. i. V. m. Art. 8 unterstellt,[73] während andere Stimmen sie als Formfrage verstanden und daher Art. 2 II NYC,[74] Art. 23 I 3 EuGVO[75] oder Art. 17 I LuganoÜ[76] angewandt haben, wobei hier insbesondere die Formalternative der „halben Schriftlichkeit" (Art. 23 I 3 lit. a) Alt. 1 EuGVO) schwierige Abgrenzungsfragen aufwirft. Desgleichen werden Anforderungen betreffend die Sprache, in der AGB-

---

[67] *Burgstaller/Burgstaller/Ritzberger*, Rn. 2.140; *Fogt*, IPRax 2003, 364, 365; *Geimer/Schütze*, EUZPR, 1. Aufl., Art. 23, Rn. 75; *Kröll*, ZZP 113 (2000), 135, 144; *Merrett*, 58 Int'l & Comp. L. Q. (2009), 545, 554 ff.; *Rauscher*, FS Heldrich, S. 948; *Ulmer/Brandner/Hensen/H. Schmidt*, Anh. § 305 BGB, Rn. 23; *Witz*, D. 1999, 117, 118; *Zöller/Geimer*, Anh. I Art. 23 EuGVVO, Rn. 21. Andere wollen Art. 23 I EuGVVO immerhin Mindesterfordernisse an die materielle Einigung entnehmen; so etwa *Magnus*, FS Kritzer, S. 309; *Rauscher/Mankowski*, Art. 23 Brüssel I-VO, Rn. 39; *Reithmann/Martiny/Hausmann*, Rn. 2983 ff.; *Steensgaard*, Standardbetingelser, § 11, Rn. 44 ff.
[68] S. dazu *Schroeter*, UN-Kaufrecht, § 15, Rn. 11 ff.
[69] Wie hier OLG Düsseldorf, 6.1.1989, NJW-RR 1989, 1330, 1332; OLG Saarbrücken, 2.10.1991, NJW 1992, 987 f.; *Gaudemet-Tallon*, Les Conventions, Anm. 131.; *Gottwald*, FS Henckel, S. 301 ff.; *Kaye*, Civil Jurisdiction, S. 1032 f.; *MünchKommZPO/Gottwald*, Art. 17 EuGVÜ, Rn. 14; *Oliver*, 70 Cornell L. Rev. (1985), 289, 302 ff.; *O'Malley/Layton*, Rn. 21.33; *Schlosser*, EuZPR, Art. 23 EuGVVO, Rn. 3; *Schroeter*, UN-Kaufrecht, § 15, Rn. 23; *Thomas/Putzo/Hüßtege*, Art. 23 EuGVVO, Rn. 4.
[70] EuGH, 20.2.1997, Rs. C-106/95 *(MSG Mainschiffahrts-Genossenschaft/Les Gravières Rhénanes)*, NJW 1997, 1431, Rn. 19; OLG Hamm, 20.9.2005, IPRax 2007, 125, 126.
[71] KG Nidwalden, 23.5.2005, CISG-online 1086 = IHR 2005, 253, 254: „Fragen des Beweismasses, der notwendige Grad der richterlichen Überzeugung, sind dagegen der lex fori, in casu dem Schweizerischen Privatrecht, zu entnehmen"; KG Zug, 14.12.2009, CISG-online 2026; *Ferrari*, oben Art. 4 Rn. 53; *MünchKomm/Westermann*, Art. 4, Rn. 17; *Staudinger/Magnus*, Art. 4, Rn. 70; anders nunmehr – für Anwendung des Maßstabs der *reasonableness – Schwenzer*, unten Art. 74 Rn. 65, Art. 35 Rn. 55.
[72] Vgl. CA Liège, 28.4.2003, CISG-online 944.
[73] OLG Braunschweig, 28.10.1999, CISG-online 510 = TranspR-IHR 2000, 4 f.; OLG Köln, 21.12.2005, CISG-online 1201 (insoweit nicht abgedr. in IHR 2006, 86 ff.); LG Gießen, 17.12.2002, CISG-online 766 = IHR 2003, 276, 277.
[74] OLG München, 8.3.1995, CISG-online 145 = NJW-RR 1996, 1532.
[75] LG Aachen, 22.6.2010, CISG-online 2162 = IHR 2011, 82, 83 f.
[76] KG Zug, 11.12.2003, CISG-online 958 = IHR 2005, 119, 121; zustimmend *Fountoulakis*, IHR 2005, 122, 124.

Klauseln formuliert sein müssen, auch für Gerichtsstandsvereinbarungen aus Artt. 14 ff. i. V. m. Art. 8 entnommen,[77] während andererseits verbreitet postuliert wird, vom nationalen Gesetzgeber aufgestellte Vorschriften über die Verwendung bestimmter Sprachen seien im Anwendungsbereich des Art. 23 EuGVO unbeachtlich.[78]

In einer solchen Konstellation ist zunächst zu untersuchen, ob die scheinbare Überschneidung der Regelungsbereiche durch eine **CISG-konforme Auslegung** von EuGVO, LuganoÜ, NYC bzw. der betroffenen nationalen Normen ausgeräumt werden kann. Eine einschränkende Interpretation des CISG im Lichte eines konkurrierenden Rechtsaktes kommt hingegen von vornherein nicht in Frage, weil diese Vorgehensweise mit den Vorgaben des Art. 7 I unvereinbar wäre.[79] Lässt sich die Überschneidung durch eine harmonisierende Auslegung nicht beseitigen und führen beide Regelungen im konkreten Fall auch zu unterschiedlichen Ergebnissen,[80] so liegt ein **Normenkonflikt** vor,[81] der sodann, soweit das Verhältnis zu einem internationalen Rechtsakt in Rede steht, anhand der einschlägigen Relationsnormen[82] und – subsidiär – der allgemeinen Rechtsanwendungsregeln (wie etwa *lex specialis derogat legi generali*) aufzulösen ist.[83] Ergeben sich die mit dem CISG konfligierenden Anforderungen hingegen aus einer rein nationalen Norm, so genießt das Übereinkommen ohne Weiteres Vorrang.

6. Einigung über Ausschluss oder Wahl des CISG

Die Vertragsparteien haben die Möglichkeit, die Anwendbarkeit des Übereinkommens auf ihren Kaufvertrag partei- bzw. privatautonom zu beeinflussen, indem sie die Anwendung des UN-Kaufrechts gem. Art. 6 ausschließen („opting out") oder – in gleichsam umgekehrter Stoßrichtung – dessen Anwendung vereinbaren, obgleich Anwendungsvoraussetzungen der Artt. 1 ff. in concreto nicht erfüllt sind („opting in"). Beide Vorgänge setzen eine **materielle Einigung** der Kaufvertragsparteien über den Ausschluss der Anwendung des UN-Kaufrechts bzw. (umgekehrt) deren Herbeiführung voraus. Ob sich das Zustandekommen auch solcher Parteivereinbarungen nach Artt. 14–24 oder aber nach anderen Regeln bestimmt, bedarf einer differenzierten Beurteilung:[84]

a) Ausschluss der Anwendung des CISG nach Art. 6 („opting out"). Dass ein vollständiger Ausschluss des Übereinkommens, der Ausschluss lediglich seines Teil II (oder anderer Teile[85]) ebenso wie die Abweichung von einzelnen seiner Vorschriften grundsätzlich **zulässig** ist, wird in Art. 6 ausdrücklich klargestellt. Art. 6 legt allerdings nicht fest, nach welchen Vertragsschlussregeln sich die hierzu erforderliche Einigung zwischen den Parteien bemisst. In der Sache geht es um die rechtliche Behandlung von Vertragsangeboten, die

---

[77] S. im Einzelnen unten Art. 14 Rn. 61 ff.; *Stadler*, AGB, S. 96.
[78] OLG Köln, 24.5.2006, CISG-online 1232 = IHR 2006, 147, 148; OLG Hamm, 20.9.2005, IPRax 2007, 125, 126 m. Anm. *Spellenberg*, aaO., S. 98 ff.; *Reithmann/Martiny/Hausmann*, Rn. 2984; a. A. OLG Hamm, 10.10.1988, IPRax 1991, 324, 326; *Schlosser*, EuZPR, Art. 23 EuGVVO, Rn. 3.
[79] *Schroeter*, UN-Kaufrecht, § 20, Rn. 5 ff., 8 ff. m. w. N.; vorsichtig für eine harmonisierende Auslegung des CISG aber *Meyer*, FS Hay, S. 318 f.
[80] Häufig wird die Anwendung beider Vorschriften nämlich zum selben Ergebnis führen; so etwa in OGH, 6.11.2008, CISG-online 1833: Gerichtsstandsklausel in fremdsprachigen AGB – Anforderungen an sprachliche Verständlichkeit sind unter Art. 23 I EuGVO und Art. 8 CISG identisch; OLG Oldenburg, 20.12.2007, CISG-online 1644 = IHR 2008, 112, 117: wg. mangelnder Übersendung der AGB waren weder die Anforderungen an die materielle Einigung (Artt. 14 ff. CISG) noch an die Form (Art. 23 I 3 lit. a) EuGVO) erfüllt; OLG Dresden, 11.6.2007, CISG-online 1720 = IHR 2008, 162, 166: „Denn hier wie dort ist nötig ...".
[81] *Rauscher*, FS Heldrich, S. 949.
[82] S. unten *Ferrari*, Art. 90 Rn. 3 f., Art. 94 Rn. 5; *Staudinger/Magnus*, Art. 90, Rn. 11. Zum Begriff der Relationsnorm *Schroeter*, UN-Kaufrecht, § 7, Rn. 27 ff.
[83] Danach gehen LuganoÜ und NYC dem CISG im Ergebnis vor, während die EuGVO hinter das Kaufrechtsübereinkommen zurücktritt; vgl. *Schroeter*, UN-Kaufrecht, § 15, Rn. 3 ff.
[84] Vgl. *Honnold/Flechtner*, Intro to Art. 14–24, Rn. 132.2: „presents special conceptual challenges" (ohne eigene Stellungnahme zur Frage, ob und in welchem Umfang Artt. 14–24 Anwendung finden).
[85] Zu Teil IV vgl. insoweit *Schroeter*, 6 VJ (2002), 257, 262 Fn. 14 a. E.

Vor Artt. 14–24 14c

(typischerweise in einer AGB-Klausel) den Ausschluss des UN-Kaufrechts vorsehen,[86] sowie deren Annahme. Die praktisch wichtige Frage ist konzeptionell höchst **umstritten**: Nach einer Auffassung sind insoweit nicht Artt. 14–24 CISG, sondern diejenigen Vorschriften maßgeblich, die anwendbar wären, wenn die angestrebte Rechtswahl wirksam zustande gekommen wäre (sog. *bootstrap principle*;[87] normiert etwa in Artt. 3 V, 10 I Rom I-VO); ersatzweise soll das nationale Recht eingreifen, das durch eine objektive Anknüpfung nach dem IPR des Forums berufen wird.[88] Dies läuft regelmäßig auf eine Beurteilung nach nationalem, unvereinheitlichten Recht hinaus, weil Parteien in ihren Rechtswahlklauseln fast durchweg positiv ihr nationales „Heimatrecht" wählen. Eine weitere, differenzierende Ansicht will das Zustandekommen der Ausschlussvereinbarung dann nach dem über das Kollisionsrecht berufenen nationalen Recht bestimmen, wenn die Anwendung des Übereinkommens insgesamt ausgeschlossen wird, während bei einem lediglich teilweisen Ausschluss Artt. 14–24 CISG maßgeblich sein sollen.[89] Die wohl herrschende Auffassung im Schrifttum wendet auf das Zustandekommen jeglicher Parteieinigungen über einen Ausschluss der Anwendung des CISG dagegen Artt. 14–24 an.[90] Ihr hat sich auch die überwiegende Rechtsprechung angeschlossen.[91]

14c Zustimmung verdient der letztgenannte Ansatz, dem zufolge sich die materielle Einigung der Parteien auf ein **„opting out"** aus dem UN-Kaufrecht **ausschließlich nach Artt. 14–24 CISG** bestimmt; nationale Rechtsvorschriften werden verdrängt. Dies gilt unabhängig davon, ob die Parteien die Anwendung des gesamten Übereinkommens, die Anwendung nur seines Teils II (in der Praxis selten) oder lediglich einzelner CISG-Bestimmungen ausschließen wollen. Artt. 14–24 entscheiden auch darüber, ob **AGB** (in denen sich Rechtswahlklauseln einschließlich etwaiger CISG-Ausschlüsse üblicherweise befinden) in den Vertrag zwischen den konkreten Parteien einbezogen wurden;[92] für die Auslegung von „opt out"-Angeboten und Annahmen gilt Art. 8.[93]

Gedanklich sind in diesem Zusammenhang **drei Schritte** zu **unterscheiden**, unter denen der zweite das „opt out" aus dem UN-Kaufrecht betrifft: Der erste Schritt ist die Bestimmung der **Anwendbarkeit des CISG**, die sich ausschließlich nach dessen autonomen

---

[86] Zur erforderlichen Deutlichkeit des Parteiwillens zum Ausschluss des CISG ausführlich *Ferrari*, oben Art. 6 Rn. 19 ff.

[87] So benannt nach dem berühmten Ausspruch von Judge *Learned Hand* in E. Gerli & Co. v. Cunard S. S. Co., 48 F. 2d 115, 117 (2nd Cir. 1931): „But an agreement is not a contract, except as the law says it shall be, and to try to make it one is to pull on one's bootstraps. Some law must impose the obligation, and the parties have nothing whatever to do with that …".

[88] RB Rotterdam, 13.10.2010, CISG-online 2297; *Ferrari u. a./Mankowski*, Internationales Vertragsrecht, Vor Art. 14, Rn. 48, der das *bootstrap principle* dem CISG „unterlegen" will (ohne freilich deutlich zu machen, worin die methodische Grundlage für eine solche „Unterlegung" bestehen soll); *Graves*, Belgr. L. Rev. 2011, 124, 129; *Honsell/Siehr*, Art. 6, Rn. 4; *Schlechtriem/Schwenzer/Schlechtriem*, CISG Commentary, 2. Aufl., Art. 6, Rn. 7.

[89] *Baumgärtel/Laumen/Hepting*, Art. 6, Rn. 3 und Art. 14, Rn. 19; *Honsell/Dornis*, Vorbem 14–24, Rn. 27; *Rehbinder*, Vertragsschluß, S. 151; *Steensgaard*, Standardbetingelser, § 12, Rn. 64 ff.

[90] *Bamberger/Roth/Saenger*, Art. 6, Rn. 2 (anders noch in der Voraufl.); *Brunner*, Art. 6, Rn. 5; *Ferrari*, oben Art. 6 Rn. 13; *Hager*, FS Huber, S. 319, 327; *Karollus*, JuS 1993, 378, 381; *Kröll u. a./Ferrari*, pre Arts 14–24, Rn. 11; *Lindbach*, S. 235 ff.; *Lohmann*, Parteiautonomie, S. 199 ff.; MünchKomm/*Westermann*, Art. 6, Rn. 3; MünchKommHGB/*Benicke*, Art. 6, Rn. 2; *Niemann*, Einheitliche Anwendung, S. 78 f.; *Piltz*, Internationales Kaufrecht, Rn. 2–112 (anders noch in der Voraufl.); ders., NJW 2011, 2261, 2262; *Schlechtriem/Schwenzer/Schwenzer/Hachem*, CISG Commentary, Art. 6, Rn. 4; *Schwenzer/Hachem/Kee*, Rn. 4.39; *Staudinger/Magnus*, Art. 6, Rn. 11 f.

[91] OLG Frankfurt a. M., 24.3.2009, CISG-online 2165 = IHR 2010, 250, 253; OLG Oldenburg, 20.12.2007, CISG-online 1644 = IHR 2008, 112, 117; HGer St. Gallen, 15.6.2010, CISG-online 2159 = IHR 2011, 149, 150; RB Rotterdam, 25.2.2009, CISG-online 1812 = EJCL 2009, 105; LG Aachen, 22.6.2010, CISG-online 2162 = IHR 2011, 82, 85.

[92] OLG Frankfurt a. M., 24.3.2009, CISG-online 2165 = IHR 2010, 250, 253; OLG Oldenburg, 20.12.2007, CISG-online 1644 = IHR 2008, 112, 117; HGer St. Gallen, 15.6.2010, CISG-online 2159 = IHR 2011, 149, 150; LG Aachen, 22.6.2010, CISG-online 2162 = IHR 2011, 82, 85; *Jungemeyer*, RIW 2010, 166; *Piltz*, Internationales Kaufrecht, Rn. 2–113.

[93] OLG Linz, 23.1.2006, CISG-online 1377 sub. 2.2; *Johnson*, 59 Buff. L. Rev. (2011), 213, 266 ff.; MünchKomm/*Westermann*, Art. 6, Rn. 3; *Schlechtriem/Schwenzer/Schwenzer/Hachem*, CISG Commentary, Art. 6, Rn. 4.

Anwendungsvoraussetzungen in Artt. 1–3 richtet.[94] Auf eine positive Einigkeit der Parteien bezüglich der Anwendbarkeit des Übereinkommens, dessen „Anerkennung"[95] durch die Partei(en) oder auch nur deren diesbezügliches Bewusstsein kommt es in diesem Zusammenhang nicht an.[96] Ebensowenig ist Voraussetzung für die Anwendung der Artt. 14–24, dass ein Kaufvertrag zwischen den Parteien zustande gekommen ist,[97] denn Teil II regelt selbstverständlich auch Fälle, in denen der Vertragsschluss letztlich scheitert. Wenn die Anwendbarkeit des Übereinkommens auf einen bestimmten Kaufvertrag (einschließlich dessen Abschlusses) danach feststeht, stellt sich in einem zweiten Schritt die Frage nach einem parteiautonomen **Ausschluss** von dessen Anwendung (Art. 6), dessen Zustandekommen sich – soweit der hierfür nötige materielle Parteikonsens in Rede steht – nach Artt. 14–24 bestimmt. Dies erschließt sich schon daraus, dass die Anwendbarkeit des Übereinkommens bereits feststeht und dessen Vertragsschlussregeln folglich über deren Beseitigung entscheiden müssen; ein irgendwie gearteter Zirkelschluss[98] liegt darin keineswegs. Hinzutreten kann in einem dritten Schritt schließlich eine **positive Rechtswahlvereinbarung** zugunsten eines (an Stelle des abbedungenen CISG eingreifenden) nationalen Rechts, die aber nicht zwingend erfolgen muss; nach Art. 6 ist auch ein „isolierter" Ausschluss des CISG zulässig.[99] (Nur) das Zustandekommen dieser Rechtswahlvereinbarung untersteht dem nationalen Recht, das nach Maßgabe des IPR (ggfs. nach dem *bootstrap principle*) bestimmt wird.

b) Wahl des CISG („opting in"). Anders stellt sich die Rechtslage in Situationen dar, **14d** in denen der konkrete Vertrag **nicht** in den originären Anwendungsbereich des Übereinkommens fällt, der in Artt. 1 ff. definiert wird: Auf eine Vereinbarung der Parteien, ihren Vertrag gleichwohl den Regeln des Übereinkommens oder Teilen von diesen zu unterstellen („opting in"),[100] finden Artt. 14–24 unmittelbar **keine** Anwendung.[101] Das insoweit einschlägige materielle Vertragsschlussrecht muss vielmehr über das anwendbare Kollisionsrecht ermittelt werden,[102] das auch über die Zulässigkeit einer kollisionsrechtlichen Wahl des CISG entscheidet.[103] Verweist dieses nun seinerseits – etwa mittels des *bootstrap principles* entsprechend Artt. 3 V, 10 I Rom I-VO – auf das UN-Kaufrecht, so findet dessen Teil II infolge dieser kollisionsrechtlichen Verweisung, also gleichsam mittelbar Anwendung.

II. Geltungsbereich: Andere Vertragsschlussformen

Artt. 14–24 regeln den Vertragsschluss entsprechend „traditioneller Theorie"[104] mit den **15** Bausteinen „Angebot" und „Annahme", durch die Konsens der Parteien hergestellt wird.

---

[94] Darüber hinaus kann es auf Vorbehalte gem. Artt. 92 ff. ankommen, welche die Anwendung der Artt. 1 ff. beeinflussen können; vgl. dazu *Schroeter*, FS Kritzer, S. 437 ff. Die Rom I-VO tritt ihrerseits schon deshalb hinter das CISG zurück, weil sie diesem durch die Relationsnorm in Art. 25 I Rom I-VO Vorrang einräumt; *Ferrari u. a./Schulze*, Internationales Vertragsrecht, Art. 26 Rom I-VO, Rn. 4; *Palandt/Thorn*, Art. 25 Rom I (IPR), Rn. 2.
[95] So aber *Rehbinder*, Vertragsschluß, S. 151.
[96] *Schroeter*, 6 VJ (2002), 257, 259. Erst recht irrelevant ist, ob der Offerent (wie etwa in einer einseitigen Ausschlussklausel in seinem Angebot zum Ausdruck kommend) dem Übereinkommen „nicht unterstehen will"; a. A. *Baumgärtel/Laumen/Hepting*, Art. 6, Rn. 3.
[97] A. A., aber unzutreffend *Graves*, Belgr. L. Rev. 2011, 124, 127.
[98] So *Graves*, Belgr. L. Rev. 2011, 124, 125: „The problem, of course, is one of circularity."
[99] *Herber/Czerwenka*, Art. 6, Rn. 5; *Honnold/Flechtner*, Art. 6, Rn. 75; *Schlechtriem*, Internationales UN-Kaufrecht, Rn. 19.
[100] Vgl. *Schroeter*, 6 VJ (2002), 257, 265 f.
[101] *Staudinger/Magnus*, Art. 6, Rn. 62.
[102] *Bianca/Bonell/Bonell*, Art. 6, Anm. 3.5.; *MünchKommHGB/Benicke*, Art. 6, Rn. 17; *Schlechtriem*, Internationales UN-Kaufrecht, Rn. 23; *Staudinger/Magnus*, Art. 6, Rn. 62.
[103] *Lindbach*, S. 192 ff.; *Schlechtriem/Schwenzer/Schwenzer/Hachem*, CISG Commentary, Art. 6, Rn. 34. Diese Zulässigkeit wird unter Art. 3 I Rom I-VO überwiegend verneint mit der Folge, dass eine (isolierte) Wahl des UN-Kaufrechts als lediglich materiellrechtliche Wahl eingestuft wird; vgl. in diesem Sinne statt vieler MünchKomm/*Martiny*, Art. 3 VO (EG) 593/2008, Rn. 31.
[104] *Lagergren*, S. 55.

Das entspricht, wie die von *Schlesinger* geleiteten und herausgegebenen Forschungen zum Vertragsschluss,[105] *Ernst Rabels* Arbeiten[106] und die Ergebnisse *von Mehrens*[107] belegen, Vorstellungen, die allen Rechtsordnungen gemeinsam sind.[108] Gleichwohl ist bereits von *Schlesinger*[109] und aus Anlass der wissenschaftlichen Aufarbeitung des EAG[110] sowie zu Problemen des CISG[111] darauf hingewiesen worden, dass das Modell eines Vertragsschlusses durch Angebot und Annahme – eine Denkfigur des 19. Jahrhunderts – nicht allen Vertragsschlusssituationen und -problemen gerecht werden kann.[112] So dürfte heute kaum noch zweifelhaft sein,[113] dass ein Vertrag durch Einigwerden der Parteien, das sich nicht in deutlich identifizierbaren Einigungserklärungen „Angebot" und „Annahme" manifestiert, zustande kommen kann, etwa durch eine in Verhandlungen oder längerem Schriftwechsel Punkt für Punkt erreichte Übereinstimmung, für die ein „Herausschneiden" einzelner Erklärungen als Offerte und Annahme eine willkürliche juristische Operation wäre.[114] **Kreuzofferten** oder Schweigen auf ein **kaufmännisches Bestätigungsschreiben**[115] als Möglichkeiten, zu einer bindenden Vereinbarung zu kommen, lassen sich ebenfalls nicht ohne weiteres mit dem Schema Angebot/Annahme erfassen, während Vertragsschlüsse im elektronischen Geschäftsverkehr (**e-commerce**) im Allgemeinen[116] und über **Internet-Auktionen** im Besonderen[117] bei Schaffung des Übereinkommens aufgrund des damaligen technischen Entwicklungsstandes noch unbekannt waren und daher nicht bedacht werden konnten. Käufe an **Warenbörsen**[118] und aufgrund internationaler **Ausschreibungen**[119] stellen schließlich weitere Sonderformen von Vertragsschluss bzw. -anbahnung dar, die auch im internationalen Warenhandel vorkommen und die Frage der Anwendbarkeit des CISG aufwerfen.

1. Grundsätzliche Position des CISG

16 Bereits auf der Haager Konferenz war erwogen worden, eine Vorschrift aufzunehmen, die ein Einigsein der Parteien aus ihrem Verhalten abzuleiten erlaubt hätte; der Vorschlag fand keine Zustimmung, da er die Gesamtsystematik des Gesetzes geändert hätte.[120] Auch zum CISG wurden noch einmal Vorschriften vorgeschlagen, die Vertragsschluss durch den Nachweis des Einigseins (statt durch Angebot und Annahme) und auch durch Kreuzofferten regeln sollten; die Anträge wurden schließlich – auch wegen der „extreme difficulty of

---

[105] *Schlesinger, passim*; ebenso das von *Rodière* geleitete und publizierte Projekt, *passim*.
[106] *Rabel*, Recht des Warenkaufs, Bd. 1, S. 69–116.
[107] Sec. 117 ff.
[108] Zur historischen Tiefe dieser Tradition s. jedoch *Bucher*, FS Piotet, S. 387 ff. („Denkfiguren der letzten Minute", d. h. des 19. Jahrhunderts).
[109] *Schlesinger*, Bd. 2, S. 1584 f.
[110] Vgl. *Dölle/Schlechtriem*, Art. 4 EAG, Rn. 2; *Lagergren*, S. 72.
[111] S. *Bucher*, FS Piotet, S. 390 ff.; *Farnsworth*, FS von Overbeck, S. 657 f.: Die Regeln zum Vertragsschluss durch Angebot und Annahme entsprächen „the measured cadence of contracting in the nineteenth century".
[112] Vgl. statt aller *Fontaine*, FS Commission Droit et Vie des Affaires, S. 681–695; *ders.*, Offre et acceptation, S. 115–133: Gleichwohl blieben Offerte und Annahme „des outils de travail adéquate pour l'analyse du processus de formation de la plupart des contrats", S. 133.
[113] Vgl. etwa § 2–204(1), § 2–207 UCC (2003) sowie zu den (ausführlicheren) Normvorschlägen der Vorentwürfe *Schlechtriem*, FS Herber, S. 42 ff.
[114] Ein Beispiel bietet der Fall *Filanto, S. p. A. v. Chilewich International Corp.*, U. S. Dist. Ct. (S. D. N. Y.), 14.4.1992, CISG-online 45 = 789 F. Supp. 1229; bestätigt in 984 F. 2d. 58 (2nd Cir. 1993), bei dessen Entscheidung die New Yorker Gerichte in Anwendung des CISG ein Schriftstück aus der umfangreichen, monatelangen Korrespondenz der Parteien als Offerte der amerikanischen Käuferin qualifizierten, die von der italienischen Verkäuferin durch schlüssiges Verhalten angenommen worden sei – ein mögliches, aber sicherlich nicht zwingendes Ergebnis; vgl. die kritische Analyse von *Brand/Flechtner*, 12 J. L. & Com. (1993), 239. S. näher unten Rn. 23 f.
[115] Rn. 18 ff.
[116] Rn. 25 ff.
[117] Rn. 28.
[118] Rn. 29.
[119] Rn. 30.
[120] *Von Caemmerer*, RabelsZ 29 (1965), 101, 138 f.

formulating an acceptable text" – zurückgezogen,[121] wobei man davon ausging, dass entsprechende Fälle mit dem Instrumentarium der Konvention gelöst werden könnten.[122]

Bei der Beurteilung **nicht ausdrücklich geregelter Einigungsvorgänge** nach CISG ist 17 daher zunächst zu klären, ob seine Regelung des Vertragsschlusses durch Angebot und Annahme, obwohl fragmentarisch, abschließend sein will, so dass für andere Formen des Einigwerdens wieder unvereinheitlichtes nationales, über IPR berufenes Recht anzuwenden ist,[123] oder ob Art. 7 II erlaubt, ja gebietet, zunächst eine Lösung auf der Grundlage der Prinzipien, die dem Übereinkommen zugrunde liegen, zu versuchen, und in behutsamer Weiterentwicklung des Einheitskaufrechts entsprechende Regeln zu entwickeln. Die vorstehend referierte Entstehungsgeschichte des Übereinkommens streitet dabei nach ganz überwiegender Ansicht generell für die Entwicklung **einheitsrechtlicher Lösungen.**[124] Sodann ist zu prüfen, ob es für das konkrete Vertragsschlussproblem tragfähige Grundsätze im CISG gibt.

2. Vertragsschluss durch Schweigen auf kaufmännisches Bestätigungsschreiben

Der Vertragsschluss durch Schweigen auf ein **kaufmännisches Bestätigungsschreiben** 18 gehört im weiteren Sinne zu den Möglichkeiten, einen vertraglichen Konsens herzustellen.[125] Er war bereits im Haag Verhandlungs- und Regelungsgegenstand, und man hat die Sachfrage durch die den deutschen Wünschen entsprechende Berücksichtigung normativer Handelsbräuche auch zum Vertragsschluss als erfasst gesehen.[126] In Wien wurde das kaufmännische Bestätigungsschreiben ebenfalls angesprochen, wobei das Ziel eines Antrags, Lückenfüllung auf Grund der Prinzipien des Übereinkommens großzügiger zu gestatten, u. a. damit begründet wurde, dass so die Anwendbarkeit der deutschen Regeln über kaufmännisches Bestätigungsschreiben als nationales, über IPR berufenes Recht verhindert (!) werden könne.[127] Aus dieser und anderen Erwähnungen des kaufmännischen Bestätigungsschreibens ist zu schließen, dass man es als ein evtl. zum Vertragsschluss einsetzbares Instrument zu den **nach CISG zu beurteilenden Fragen gerechnet**[128] und die Sachfrage dahin entschieden hat, dass die deutschen Regeln allenfalls als **Handelsbräuche** Berücksichtigung finden, falls und soweit Handelsbräuche nach Art. 9 I oder II Geltung beanspruchen können.[129]

---

[121] S. YB IX (1978), S. 38 f., Nr. 94 ff., 104, 108.
[122] S. YB IX (1978), S. 39, Nr. 103, 107, dazu noch unten Art. 19 Rn. 4.
[123] So zum UNCITRAL-E 1978 *Huber*, RabelsZ 43 (1979), 413, 445, 447–450, vor allem für das kaufmännische Bestätigungsschreiben; generell nationales Recht bevorzugend auch *Heuzé*, Anm. 174.
[124] OLG München, 8.3.1995, CISG-online 145 = NJW-RR 1996, 1532, 1533; *Bonell*, International Restatement, S. 75 ff.; *Brunner*, Vorbem. Art. 14–24, Rn. 4; *Bydlinski*, Allgemeines Vertragsrecht, S. 61; *Kröll u. a./Ferrari*, pre Arts 14–24, Rn. 7; MünchKommHGB/*Ferrari*, Vor Art. 14, Rn. 7; *Rehbinder*, Vertragsschluß, S. 166; *Soergel/Lüderitz/Fenge*, Vor Art. 14, Rn. 3; *Schlechtriem*, Einheitliches UN-Kaufrecht, S. 34 f.; *Staudinger/Magnus*, Vor Art. 14 ff., Rn. 5; auch *Witz/Salger/Lorenz/Witz*, Vor Artt. 14–24, Rn. 5.
[125] Rechtsvergleichend zu Regeln und Funktionen kaufmännischer Bestätigungsschreiben *Ebenroth*, ZfRVgl 1978, 161, 164–180 (England, USA, Italien, Frankreich, Belgien, Schweiz); *Esser*, östZRVgl 1988, 167 ff. (zur Funktion als Beweismittel s. S. 193, zur analogen Anwendung des Art. 19 II auf vertragsmodifizierende Bestätigungen, S. 190 f.); *Kröll/Hennecke*, RabelsZ 67 (2003), 448, 477 ff. (Schweiz, Österreich, Frankreich, USA, England).
[126] Vgl. *von Caemmerer*, RabelsZ 29 (1965), 101, 114 („Darüber war man sich ... einig"), ferner 139 f. („dringendes deutsches Anliegen").
[127] S. O. R., S. 256, Nr. 18 *(Bonell)*. Weitere Nachw. s. unten Art. 19 Rn. 4.
[128] *Brunner*, Vorbem. Art. 14–24, Rn. 4; *Kröll/Hennecke*, RabelsZ 67 (2003), 448, 456; *Wey*, Rn. 239 ff.; a. A. *Steensgaard*, Standardbetingelser, § 4, Rn. 95 ff.
[129] OLG Dresden, 30.11.2010, CISG-online 2183 = IHR 2011, 142, 144; *Esser*, östZRVgl 1988, 167, 186 ff.; *Grunewald*, Kaufrecht, § 2, Rn. 55; *Herber/Czerwenka*, Vor Art. 14, Rn. 18; *Janssen*, IHR 2004, 194, 197; *Kröll/Ferrari*, pre Arts 14–24, Rn. 2; MünchKommHGB/*Ferrari*, Vor Art. 14, Rn. 7; *Neumayer/Ming*, Art. 9 Anm. 4., aber auch Art. 18, Anm. 3.; *Perales Viscasillas*, 25 J. L. & Com. (2005-06), 167, 174; *Piltz*, Internationales Kaufrecht, Rn. 2–127; *Reinhart*, Art. 9, Rn. 3; *Schwenzer/Mohs*, IHR 2006, 239, 245; *Soergel/Lüderitz/Fenge*, Art. 9, Rn. 7; *Staudinger/Magnus*, Vor Artt. 14 ff., Rn. 6; *Witz/Salger/Lorenz/Witz*,

19 Für eine kollisionsrechtliche Verweisung auf deutsches materielles Recht und seine Regeln zu kaufmännischen Bestätigungsschreiben ist nach alledem grundsätzlich[130] kein Raum.[131] Im Übrigen würde bei Maßgeblichkeit deutschen Rechts eine Vertragspartei, deren Aufenthaltsrecht dem Schweigen auf ein kaufmännisches Bestätigungsschreiben nicht die gleiche Wirkung wie das deutsche Recht beimisst, durch Art. 10 II Rom I-VO geschützt, so dass die Voraussetzungen für die Berücksichtigung deutscher Regeln als Handelsbräuche über Art. 9 II und die Maßgeblichkeit deutschen Rechts gegenüber abweichendem Aufenthaltsrecht zu weitgehend konvergierenden Ergebnissen führen dürften.[132] Eine autonome Regel, die als Lückenfüllung nach Art. 7 II zu entwickeln und anzuwenden wäre, kommt nicht in Betracht, da die ausdrückliche Ablehnung entsprechender Vorschläge in Wien – soweit nicht Parteigepflogenheiten oder Handelsbräuche nach Art. 9 einer solchen Regel Geltung verschaffen – gerade keine Lücke gelassen hat.[133]

20 Die damit maßgeblichen Geltungsvoraussetzungen nach **Art. 9 I oder II** dürften am ehesten dann vorliegen, wenn die Parteien in Staaten niedergelassen sind, in denen – jedenfalls im jeweiligen Handelszweig – ähnliche Regeln zum kaufmännischen Bestätigungsschreiben und den Wirkungen eines Schweigens des Adressaten gelten wie im deutschen Recht.[134] Allerdings reicht – und dies wird häufig übersehen – die „Parallelität" der Bräuche allein nicht aus, sondern es müssen auch die weiteren – einschränkenden – Voraussetzungen des Art. 9 II gegeben sein, insbesondere „Verträge dieser Art", „im betreffenden Geschäftszweig", „bekannt" und „beachtet".[135] Das Bestehen eines nationalen Handelsbrauchs bezüglich des kaufmännischen Bestätigungsschreibens am Sitz lediglich einer der beteiligten Parteien genügt für die Zwecke des Art. 9 II jedenfalls nicht.[136] Zu **beweisen** ist der einschlägige internationale Handelsbrauch durch die Partei, die sich auf ihn beruft.[137]

21 Die bisherige **Rechtsprechung** hat den Vertragsschluss durch Schweigen auf ein kaufmännisches Bestätigungsschreiben nur **ganz vereinzelt** als internationalen Handelsbrauch i. S. von Art. 9 I oder II anerkannt: Verneint wurde dies für den Handel mit Chemikalien zwischen Parteien in Deutschland und der Schweiz,[138] für den dänisch-deutschen Handel mit Dessous,[139] für den deutsch-französischen Handel mit Schokoladewaren, weil eine

---

Art. 9, Rn. 10; zurückhaltend *Karollus*, S. 72; s. auch *K. Schmidt*, FS Honsell, S. 117. Zur Form s. oben *Schmidt-Kessel*, Art. 11 Rn. 6; „in engen Grenzen" (nämlich nach Art. 8 II, III) für eine Einordnung von Schweigen auf ein kaufmännisches Bestätigungsschreiben als konkludente Annahme *Kramer*, FS Welser, S. 546 ff.; s. dazu noch unten Art. 29 Rn. 7 f.

[130] Etwas anderes gilt nur, wenn eine der Vertragsparteien in einem Staat niedergelassen ist, der – wie bis zum Jahre 2012 die skandinavischen Länder – auf Grund Vorbehalts nach Art. 92 den Vertragsschlussteil des CISG nicht übernommen hat. Dadurch kann auch Art. 9 II CISG nicht zur „Einfallspforte" vereinheitlichter Vertragsschlussregeln auf der Grundlage entsprechender Bräuche werden; vgl. *Schroeter*, FS Kritzer, S. 439.

[131] OLG Dresden, 30.11.2010, CISG-online 2183 = IHR 2011, 142, 144; OLG Köln, 22.2.1994, CISG-online 127 = RIW 1994, 972 m. Anm. *Schlechtriem*, EWiR 1994, 867; LG Kiel, 27.7.2004, CISG-online 1534 = IPRax 2007, 451, 452; LG Landshut, 12.6.2008, CISG-online 1703 = IHR 2008, 184, 187; LG Neubrandenburg, 3.8.2005, CISG-online 1190 = IHR 2006, 26, 29; *Kramer*, FS Welser, S. 546; *Kröll u. a./Ferrari*, pre Arts 14–24, Rn. 8; a. A. RB Hasselt, 24.1.1995, CISG-online 375: deutsches unvereinheitlichtes Recht angewandt.

[132] Vgl. zu EAG/EKG OLG Köln, 16.3.1988, RIW 1988, 555, 557.

[133] Anders wohl *Kröll/Hennecke*, RabelsZ 67 (2003), 448, 456 ff., die solche Regeln aus dem Konsensprinzip entwickeln wollen.

[134] KG Zug, 14.12.2009, CISG-online 2026; s. auch *K. Schmidt*, FS Honsell, S. 117; *Kröll/Hennecke*, RabelsZ 67 (2003), 448, 464 ff.

[135] S. LG Landshut, 12.6.2008, CISG-online 1703 = IHR 2008, 184, 187: „Es wäre vorzutragen gewesen, dass ein spezifischer Handelsbrauch für die Lieferung von Deckenplatten zwischen Deutschland und Italien vorliegt, welcher […] die Grundsätze des Schweigens auf ein kaufmännisches Bestätigungsschreiben beinhaltet"; *Kröll u. a./Ferrari*, pre Arts 14–24, Rn. 9.

[136] OLG Frankfurt a. M., 5.7.1995, CISG-online 258; *Herber/Czerwenka*, Art. 9, Rn. 12; a. A. LG Kiel, 27.7.2004, CISG-online 1534 = IPRax 2007, 451, 452 mit zu Recht krit. Anm. *Fogt*, IPRax 2007, 417, 420.

[137] OLG Dresden, 9.7.1998, CISG-online 559 = IHR 2001, 18, 19: etwa durch Auskunft der int. Handelskammer.

[138] KG Freiburg, 11.10.2004, CISG-online 964 = IHR 2005, 72, 76.

[139] OLG Dresden, 30.11.2010, CISG-online 2183 = IHR 2011, 142, 144.

derartige Bestätigung in der französischen Handelspraxis unüblich sei,[140] für den österreichisch-deutschen Handel mit Schweinefleisch, denn in Österreich habe die Bestätigung keine konstitutive Wirkung;[141] offen gelassen wurde die Frage für den belgisch-deutschen Obsthandel (Sauerkirschen).[142] Dagegen hat das Zivilgericht Basel-Stadt im Falle eines Kaufvertrages zwischen Parteien, die in Österreich und der Schweiz niedergelassen waren, einem kaufmännischen Bestätigungsschreiben der österreichischen Lieferantin vertragskonstitutive Bedeutung zuerkannt, weil sowohl in Österreich als auch in der Schweiz das kaufmännische Bestätigungsschreiben eine solche Wirkung haben könne und deshalb davon auszugehen sei, dass beide Parteien die rechtlichen Wirkungen gekannt haben mussten.[143] Diese Entscheidung ist in der Sache unzutreffend und hat daher zu Recht Kritik erfahren.[144] Keinesfalls darf sie als Grundlage für eine pauschale Einstufung dieser Vertragsschlussform als internationalen Handelsbrauch benutzt werden, ohne in irgendeiner Form darauf einzugehen, ob die Anforderungen des Art. 9 II in der konkreten Fallkonstellation erfüllt sind.[145] Bejaht worden ist ein Handelsbrauch hinsichtlich des kaufmännischen Bestätigungsschreibens auch für den Warenverkehr zwischen der Bundesrepublik Deutschland und Frankreich,[146] wobei die Begründung durch das Gericht hier ebenfalls erhebliche Zweifel aufwirft.[147] Ob die fortschrittlichere Regel des Art. 2.12 PICC ihrerseits bereits als Handelsbrauch gelten kann, ist zweifelhaft[148] und m. E. abzulehnen.[149]

Unberührt bleibt in jedem Fall die Bedeutung des kaufmännischen Bestätigungsschreibens **22** als **Beweismittel** nach nationalem Prozessrecht,[150] wobei hier nach dem Gegenstand des Beweises unterschieden werden muss: Das von einer Partei vorgelegte kaufmännische Bestätigungsschreiben kann Beweis für den genauen Inhalt eines abgeschlossenen Kaufvertrages sein,[151] der freilich unter dem CISG schon wegen Art. 11 S. 2 durch gegenteiligen (Zeugen-)Beweis widerlegt werden kann; insofern bleibt seine Wirkung wesentlich hinter der materiellrechtlichen Wirkung des Schweigens auf das Bestätigungsschreiben nach deutschem unvereinheitlichtem Recht zurück.[152] Kein ausreichender Beweiswert kommt dem von einer Partei erstellten kaufmännischen Bestätigungsschreiben allein hingegen für das – logisch vorgelagerte – Zustandekommen des Vertrages, namentlich die Annahme des

---

[140] OLG Frankfurt a. M., 5.7.1995, CISG-online 258; a. A. LG Saarbrücken, 23.3.1992, CISG-online 60.
[141] OLG Graz, 7.3.2002, CISG-online 669 = IHR 2003, 71, 72.
[142] LG Neubrandenburg, 3.8.2005, CISG-online 1190 = IHR 2006, 26, 29.
[143] ZGer Basel-Stadt, 21.12.1992, CISG-online 55 = BJM 1993, 310, 312 f. mit der weiteren Erwägung, aufgrund eines früheren Bestätigungsschreibens sei auch eine zwischen den Parteien geübte Gepflogenheit i. S. d. Art. 9 I anzunehmen.
[144] Sie begegnet jedenfalls insoweit Zweifeln, als sie in Österreich geltende Regeln des Inhalts annimmt, dass Schweigen auf ein kaufmännisches Bestätigungsschreiben konstitutiv wirke. Rspr. und h. L. lehnen das dort aber grundsätzlich ab; nur in den Ausnahmefällen, in denen ein Bestätigungsschreiben als Offerte und als konkludent „angenommen" angesehen werden könne, sei eine vertragskonstitutive Wirkung möglich (vgl. OGH, 28.4.1993, CISG-online 100 = östJBl 1993, 782, 784 ff.; wie hier OLG Graz, 7.3.2002, CISG-online 669 = IHR 2003, 71, 72). In der Literatur kritisch insbes. *Kramer*, BJM 1995, 1, 9; *ders.*, FS Welser, S. 548: „nicht haltbar"; *Steensgaard*, Standardbetingelser, § 4, Rn. 112 ff.
[145] So aber geschehen in *Barbara Berry, S. A. de C. V. v. Ken M. Spooner Farms, Inc.,* U. S. Dist. Ct. (W. D. Wash.), 13.4.2006, CISG-online 1354 bezüglich eines U. S.-amerikanisch-mexikanischen (!) Kaufvertrages über Himbeerpflanzen.
[146] LG Saarbrücken, 23.3.1992, CISG-online 60.
[147] S. *Schmidt-Kessel*, Art. 9 Rn. 24; a. A. für den deutsch-französischen Warenverkehr auch OLG Frankfurt a. M., 5.7.1995, CISG-online 258.
[148] So *Schilf*, Uniform L. Rev. 1999, 1004 ff. in Besprechung eines dänischen Urteils, das Vertragsschluss durch Schweigen auf ein Bestätigungsschreiben abgelehnt hat; für eine Übertragung der in Art. 2.12 PICC vorgesehenen Lösung auf das CISG hingegen *Brunner*, Vorbem. Art. 14–24, Rn. 7; auch KG Zug, 14.12.2009, CISG-online 2026.
[149] Wie hier *Kröll/Hennecke*, RabelsZ 67 (2003), 448, 489 f.; MünchKomm/*Gruber*, Art. 18, Rn. 24.
[150] OLG Frankfurt a. M., 5.7.1995, CISG-online 258; OLG Köln, 22.2.1994, CISG-online 127 = RIW 1994, 972; Cour de Justice Genève, 13.9.2002, CISG-online 722; KG Zug, 14.12.2009, CISG-online 2026; LG Neubrandenburg, 3.8.2005, CISG-online 1190 = IHR 2006, 26, 29; *Brunner*, Vorbem. Art. 14–24, Rn. 9; *Steensgaard*, Standardbetingelser, § 4, Rn. 124 ff.; *Stoffel*, Formation du contrat, S. 68, sowie hier Art. 18 Rn. 4.
[151] *Kröll/Hennecke*, RabelsZ 67 (2003), 448, 462; MünchKomm/*Gruber*, Art. 18, Rn. 26.
[152] S. dazu MünchKommHGB/*K. Schmidt*, § 346, Rn. 145, 165.

(typischerweise mündlich erfolgten) Angebotes durch die andere Partei zu,[153] die im Bestreitensfalle nur auf andere Weise bewiesen werden kann.[154] Es kann allerdings zum Beweis der Vertragsschlusserklärung derjenigen Partei dienen, die das Bestätigungsschreiben selbst versandt hat, sofern diese den Vertragsschluss ihrerseits später bestreitet.[155] Auf die **Verteilung der** (dem CISG unterliegenden) **Beweislast** hat die Verwendung eines kaufmännischen Bestätigungsschreibens – anders als nach manchem nationalen Recht, etwa in der Schweiz[156] – von vornherein keinerlei Auswirkungen.[157]

3. Vertragsschluss ohne eindeutige Angebots- bzw. Annahmeerklärung

23   **Einigungen ohne** eindeutig als **Offerte und Annahme** identifizierbare Elemente gehören, wie die Regelungsversuche zu EAG und CISG zeigen,[158] ebenfalls zum Bereich des vom CISG geregelten äußeren Konsenses.[159] Aus der Aufgabe entsprechender Regelungsabsichten lässt sich das Gegenteil schon deshalb nicht ableiten, weil man sich nicht gegen eine Geltung des einheitlichen Abschlussrechts für derartige Einigungsmöglichkeiten entschieden, sondern vor allem vor den Schwierigkeiten der Formulierung einer entsprechenden Regel kapituliert hat. Es ist deshalb eine den Grundzügen des CISG entsprechende Lösung zu finden.[160] Vielfach werden sich in den zum Einigsein führenden Vorgängen doch Angebot und Annahme ausmachen lassen,[161] auch wenn dazu ein wenig Konstruktionsjurisprudenz erforderlich ist. Auch können sich die Parteien in einem Vorvertrag, der m. E. bei Vorliegen der Voraussetzungen der Artt. 1 ff. ebenfalls dem CISG unterliegen dürfte, auf ein anderes Vertragsschlussverfahren verständigt haben, etwa auf eine Schritt für Schritt über die Sachfragen herzustellende Verständigung; auch die Vorschriften zum Vertragsschluss unterliegen der Parteidisposition, Art. 6. Vom traditionellen Vertragsschlussmodell abweichende Gepflogenheiten der Parteien sind schon nach Art. 9 I nicht nur beachtlich, sondern als einheitsrechtlicher Vertragsschluss, der Rückgriff auf IPR und nationales Recht ausschließt, zu sehen[162] – auch und gerade, wenn unvereinheitlichtes Recht derartigen Konsens nicht kennt.

24   Die Grundzüge, die zur Beurteilung solcher und anderer Fälle heranzuziehen sind und eine Lösung tragen können, sind **Konsensprinzip**[163] und Feststellbarkeit eines – in den

---

[153] Vgl. in diesem Sinne *Calzaturificio Claudia s. n. c. v. Olivieri Footwear Ltd.*, U. S. Dist. Ct. (S. D. N. Y.), 6.4.1998, CISG-online 440: „plaintiff relies on invoices which it prepared unilaterally and which do not contain language evidencing, either explicitly or implicitly, that the invoices reflect the parties' final agreement".

[154] S. etwa Cour de Justice Genève, 13.9.2002, CISG-online 722 (Annahme bewiesen u. a. durch nachfolgende Korrespondenz der die Annahme bestreitenden Partei bzgl. Akkreditiveröffnung); LG Neubrandenburg, 3.8.2005, CISG-online 1190 = IHR 2006, 26, 29 (Annahme bewiesen anhand späterer Schreiben der die Annahme bestreitenden Partei, in denen auf abgeschlossenen Kaufvertrag Bezug genommen wurde).

[155] So in OLG Köln, 22.2.1994, CISG-online 127 = RIW 1994, 972; OLG Frankfurt a. M., 5.7.1995, CISG-online 258.

[156] Selbst dort scheidet eine Beweislastumkehr allerdings aus, wenn das Bestätigungsschreiben inhaltlich mehrdeutig ist; s. OGer Basel-Land, 5.10.1999, CISG-online 492 = SZIER 2000, 115.

[157] *Kröll/Hennecke*, RabelsZ 67 (2003), 448, 461; a. A. *Brunner*, Vorbem. Art. 14–24, Rn. 9, der eine Beweislastumkehr für denkbar erachtet.

[158] Oben Rn. 16.

[159] Hof van Beroep Gent, 15.5.2002, CISG-online 746; *Bonell*, RIW 1990, 693, 695; *Brunner*, Vorbem. Art. 14–24, Rn. 4; *Ludwig*, S. 294 f.; MünchKomm/*Gruber*, Vor Art. 14, Rn. 3; *Schwenzer/Mohs*, IHR 2006, 239; *Staudinger/Magnus*, Vor Artt. 14 ff., Rn. 5; *Wey*, Rn. 576 ff., 727 ff.; unklar *Grunewald*, Kaufrecht, § 2, Rn. 56.

[160] *Bonell*, RIW 1990, 693, 695 ff.

[161] Vgl. zum EAG LG Heidelberg, 30.1.1979, in: *Schlechtriem/Magnus*, Art. 3 EAG, Nr. 2 (Unterzeichnung eines Antragsformulars durch Käufer in Gegenwart eines Vertreters des Verkäufers).

[162] So mag auf Grundlage von Art. 9 im Einzelfall auch unter dem CISG ein „gestreckter" Vertragsschluss nach dem Vorbild einer (im U. S.-amerikanischen Recht teilweise befürworteten) „rolling contract formation" in Frage kommen – freilich werden die Anforderungen des Art. 9 hierbei sorgfältig zu prüfen sein, weil von einem entsprechenden internationalen Handelsbrauch z. Zt. kaum ausgegangen werden kann; vgl. zum Ganzen *Schultz*, 35 Cornell Int'l L. J. (2001–2002), 263, 273 f., 279, 286 f.

[163] Ebenso *Fontaine*, FS Commission Droit et Vie des Affaires, S. 689 ff.; *Perales Viscasillas*, Formacíon del contrato, S. 389 f.; *Rehbinder*, Vertragsschluß, S. 166: Das zugrunde liegende materielle Konsensprinzip erlaube

Anforderungen an eine Offerte in Art. 14 umschriebenen – **Mindestinhaltes**[164] für den Vertrag. Bei Beteiligung von Parteien aus Formvorbehaltsstaaten (Artt. 12, 96) müssen Konsens und Mindestinhalt ggf. formgerecht dokumentiert sein. Entspricht eine erreichte Einigung diesen grundsätzlichen Anforderungen, sei es, dass sie sukzessive und punktuell hergestellt worden ist, sei es, dass man ein Schriftstück gleichzeitig abgezeichnet hat oder dass sich unwiderrufliche Offerten mit identischem Inhalt gekreuzt haben,[165] dann wird man einen Vertragsschluss nach Artt. 7 II, 14 ff. annehmen können mit der Folge, dass Rekurs auf IPR und unvereinheitlichtes Recht nicht nur nicht erforderlich, sondern ausgeschlossen ist.[166] Die eigentlichen Schwierigkeiten bei solchen vom geregelten Vertragsschlussverfahren abweichenden Vertragsschlüssen liegen natürlich im Nachweis, dass, wann genau und – sofern es darauf ankommt – wo[167] der Vertragsschluss geschehen ist.[168] Deshalb ist den Parteien, die solche vom geregelten Verfahren abweichende Einigungsprozesse befolgen, dringend zu raten, in einem Schlussdokument eindeutig festzuhalten, wann, wo und inwieweit man sich einig geworden ist, gebunden zu sein.

4. Vertragsschluss im elektronischen Geschäftsverkehr (e-commerce)

a) Anwendbarkeit des CISG. Der Vertragsschluss im elektronischen Geschäftsverkehr ist 25 eine moderne Spielart des Zustandekommens internationaler Kaufverträge, der in der heutigen Praxis des internationalen Warenkaufs eine erhebliche Bedeutung zukommt.[169] Dass die Regelungen des CISG auch auf Vertragsschlüsse im elektronischen Geschäftsverkehr **anwendbar** sind,[170] ergibt sich dabei schon aus Art. 11, der Angebot- und Annahmeerklärungen von sämtlichen Formanforderungen freistellt.[171] Die technischen Besonderheiten moderner Kommunikationsformen konnten bei Schaffung des Übereinkommens allerdings naturgemäß noch nicht im Einzelnen berücksichtigt werden. Sich in diesem Bereich ergebende Fragen sind vorrangig durch **Auslegung der Artt. 14 ff.** und subsidiär unter Rückgriff auf Prinzipien zu lösen, die eine **lückenfüllende Regelbildung** nach Art. 7 II erlauben.[172] Die Regeln des Einheitskaufrechts haben sich als ausreichend flexibel erwiesen, um in diesem Zusammenhang aufgeworfene Problemstellungen zu bewältigen,[173] gleich ob diese den

---

die Annahme eines Vertragsschlusses, wenn Einigsein feststehe; *Schwenzer/Mohs*, IHR 2006, 239; *Staudinger/Magnus*, Vor Artt. 14 ff., Rn. 5; *Steensgaard*, Standardbetingelser, § 4, Rn. 12 ff.

[164] Zustimmung *Staudinger/Magnus*, Vor Artt. 14 ff., Rn. 5; natürlich sind die Parteien auch insoweit in der Lage, auf der Grundlage von Art. 6 zu disponieren und den Mindestinhalt zu beschränken.

[165] Vgl. die von *Mestre* berichteten französischen Fälle sich kreuzender „promesses unilatérales croisées", Rev. trim. dr. civ. 1990, 462–480.

[166] Im Ergebnis ebenso *Wey*, Rn. 578 f., der vor allem auf die mit Art. 8 ermöglichte Auslegung der Parteierklärungen und den durch Art. 6 eröffneten Weg, parteiautonom andere Vertragsschlussverfahren zu vereinbaren, abstellt; a. A. *Huber/Mullis*, S. 101 f.

[167] Hierzu unten Art. 23 Rn. 7.

[168] *Perales Viscasillas*, Formación del contrato, S. 389 f.

[169] S. *Borges*, Verträge im elektronischen Geschäftsverkehr, S. 302: „Das CISG ist für den Vertragsabschluss per Internet von großer Bedeutung".

[170] LG Freiburg, 22.8.2002, CISG-online 711 = IHR 2003, 22: CISG auf Vertragsschluss im Internet angewandt; OLG Dresden, 30.11.2010, CISG-online 2183 = IHR 2011, 142, 144: CISG auf Vertragsschluss nach Angebot per E-mail angewandt; *Chwee Kin Keong and Others v. Digilandmall.com Pte Ltd.*, High Ct. Sing., 12.4.2004, CISG-online 1641 = [2004] 2 SLR 594, Rn. 100: das CISG „ought to be taken into consideration in determining the appropriate default rule in e-commerce transactions" (obiter, zu innerstaatlicher Transaktion); CISG-AC, Op. 1 (*Ramberg*), Comment 11.1 = IHR 2003, 244; *Benedick*, Informationspflichten, Rn. 968; *Borges*, Verträge im elektronischen Geschäftsverkehr, S. 302 ff.; *Eiselen*, 6 VJ (2002), 305, 308 f.; *Ferrari*, EuLF 2001, 301, 305; *Honsell/Dornis*, Vorbem 14–24, Rn. 2; *Mazzotta*, 33 Rutgers Computer & Tech. L. J. (2007), 251, 260, 271; *Schlechtriem/Witz*, Convention de Vienne, Anm. 72.; *Schwenzer/Mohs*, IHR 2006, 239; *Wulf*, UN-Kaufrecht und eCommerce, S. 85 ff.

[171] CISG-AC, Op. 1 (*Ramberg*), Comment 11.1 = IHR 2003, 244; *Eiselen*, 6 VJ (2002), 305, 308 f.

[172] *Benedick*, Informationspflichten, Rn. 968; *Eiselen*, 6 VJ (2002), 305, 308 f.; *Schlechtriem*, Internationales UN-Kaufrecht, Rn. 42b.

[173] *Hahnkamper*, 25 J. L. & Com. (2005-06), 147, 151; *O. Meyer*, Interpretation, S. 338 f.; *Schwenzer/Mohs*, IHR 2006, 239.

elektronischen Vertragsschluss durch E-Mail, im World Wide Web[174] oder durch Electronic Data Interchange (EDI)[175] betreffen.[176] Soweit sich dem CISG auf diesem Wege Aussagen entnehmen lassen, regelt das Übereinkommen den Vertragsschluss im elektronischen Geschäftsverkehr **abschließend**;[177] sachlich einschlägige nationale Vorschriften wie etwa § 312g III, IV BGB (sog. „Buttonlösung") oder Art. 384 § 4 polnischer Kodeks cywilny[178] werden daher verdrängt. Vom Einheitskaufrecht nicht abgedeckte Sachfragen wie etwa die Sicherung der Transparenz des elektronischen Vertragsschlusses durch spezifische Informationspflichten (s. etwa § 312g I BGB) unterliegen hingegen dem nationalen Recht.[179]

26 b) Autonome Auslegung der Artt. 14–24. Demgegenüber wird im Schrifttum verschiedentlich vorgeschlagen, Lösungen, die in **neueren internationalen Regelwerken** zum Recht des elektronischen Geschäftsverkehrs vorgesehen sind, auf das CISG zu **übertragen**. Genannt werden in diesem Zusammenhang etwa die e-Commerce-Richtlinie der EG, die ICC eTerms 2004,[180] das UNCITRAL-Modellgesetz zum elektronischen Geschäftsverkehr[181] sowie das ebenfalls von UNCITRAL entwickelte UN-Übereinkommen zum elektronischen Geschäftsverkehr (UNECIC).[182] Einer systematischen Interpretation des CISG anhand anderer Regelwerke steht jedoch schon der Grundsatz der autonomen Auslegung (Art. 7 I) entgegen.[183] Weitere Probleme ergeben sich aus der Tatsache, dass die bestehenden internationalen Regelwerke zum e-commerce gerade zu Fragen des Vertragsschlusses vielfach untereinander divergierende Lösungen vorsehen[184] und die Auslegung des CISG daher entscheidend von der Auswahl des maßgeblichen Regelwerkes durch den Auslegenden abhängen würde,[185] was in einer Beeinträchtigung von Vorhersehbarkeit und Rechtssicherheit resultierte. Die besseren Gründe sprechen somit dafür, die neueren (und weitere, künftig entstehende) Regelwerke als lediglich **unverbindliche Inspirationsquel-**

---

[174] Vgl. LG Freiburg, 22.8.2002, CISG-online 711 = IHR 2003, 22.

[175] S. dazu *Behling*, S. 80 ff.; *Fritzemeyer/Heun*, CR 1992, 129 ff.; *Nicoll*, J. B. L. (1998), 35 ff.

[176] S. im Einzelnen zu automatisierten Erklärungen in World Wide Web und Electronic Data Interchange (EDI) Art. 14 Rn. 24; zur Angebotsqualität von Internet-Websites Art. 14 Rn. 28; zur Einbeziehung von AGB durch elektronische Erklärungen Art. 14 Rn. 44, 49 f.; zur „Widerrufssperre" durch Absendung einer elektronischen Annahmeerklärung Art. 16 Rn. 4; zur Annahmeerklärung per E-Mail und EDI Art. 18 Rn. 5 f. und zu Annahmefristen im elektronischen Geschäftsverkehr Art. 18 Rn. 14 f., 17; zum Widerspruch gegen abweichende Annahmeerklärungen (Art. 19 II 1) Art. 19 Rn. 15; zu Annahmefristen in elektronischen Angebotserklärungen Art. 20 Rn. 3a; zu elektronischen Kommunikationsmitteln im Zusammenhang mit verspäteten Annahmeerklärungen Art. 21 Rn. 9, 16, 20; zum Zugang elektronischer Erklärungen Art. 24 Rn. 6, 24 f., 34 f. Zu Internet-Auktionen s. sogleich Rn. 28.

[177] *Benedick*, Informationspflichten, Rn. 968; so wohl auch *Mazzotta*, 33 Rutgers Computer & Tech. L. J. (2007), 251, 260; unklar *Ferrari*, EuLF 2000/01, 301, 306.

[178] S. dazu *Liebscher/Zoll*, in: *dies.*, § 5, Rn. 44.

[179] So *Benedick*, Informationspflichten, Rn. 969; *Schlechtriem*, Internationales UN-Kaufrecht, Rn. 42b (ebenso zur – nicht mit vertragskonstitutiver Wirkung versehenen – Empfangsbestätigung nach Art. 11 kompatiblen – Empfangsbestätigung nach § 312g I Nr. 3 BGB); MünchKomm/*Gruber*, Vor Art. 14 CISG, Rn. 12; skeptisch hingegen *Meyer*, FS Hay, S. 303; a. A. *Piltz*, Internationales Kaufrecht, Rn. 1–27 (für Verdrängung des § 312e a. F. BGB durch das CISG).

[180] *Schwenzer/Mohs*, IHR 2006, 239, 241.

[181] *Ferrari*, EuLF 2000/01, 301, 307; *Wulf*, UN-Kaufrecht und eCommerce, S. 20. Die Umsetzung des Modellgesetzes geschah in den verschiedenen Staaten allerdings sehr unterschiedlich; vgl. *Chong/Chao*, 18 SAcLJ (2006), 116, 117; *Wulf*, UN-Kaufrecht und eCommerce, S. 19.

[182] *Hilberg*, IHR 2007, 12, 23; *Wulf*, UN-Kaufrecht und eCommerce, S. 20; wohl auch *Hahnkamper*, 25 J. L. & Com. (2005-06), 147, 148. Aus Art. 20 UNECIC ergibt sich, dass dieses Übereinkommen im Falle eines Normenkonflikts jedenfalls gegenüber dem CISG zurücktritt; vgl. *Mazzotta*, 33 Rutgers Computer & Tech. L. J. (2007), 251, 254.

[183] Ebenso O. *Meyer*, Interpretation, S. 338 (zu UNECIC); vgl. des Weiteren *Schlechtriem*, Internationales UN-Kaufrecht, Rn. 43; *Schroeter*, UN-Kaufrecht, § 20, Rn. 10, 43; *Witz/Salger/Lorenz/Witz*, Art. 7, Rn. 21; a. A. wohl *Wulf*, UN-Kaufrecht und eCommerce, S. 20, der in Frage stellt, ob die Vorschriften des CISG angesichts ihres Alters auf Fragen des e-Commerce „noch immer uneingeschränkt anwendbar sind".

[184] Vgl. *Chong/Chao*, 18 SAcLJ (2006), 116, 118 (zu UNCITRAL-Modellgesetz und e-Commerce-Richtlinie der EG), 131 (zu UNCITRAL-Modellgesetz und UNECIC); *Ramberg*, European L. Rev. 2001, 429, 431 (zu UNCITRAL-Modellgesetz und e-Commerce-Richtlinie); *Schwenzer/Mohs*, IHR 2006, 239, 241 Fn. 31 (zu ICC eTerms und UNECIC).

[185] Vgl. etwa *Schwenzer/Mohs*, IHR 2006, 239, 241 Fn. 31.

len im Rahmen der Auslegung des CISG zu verwenden, die „within the four corners" des Übereinkommens stattzufinden hat.

c) Einverständnis der Parteien mit der Verwendung elektronischer Kommunikationsmittel. Dass das Übereinkommen als Regelwerk auf elektronische Vertragsabschlüsse anwendbar ist, bedeutet allein noch nicht, dass auch jede Vertragspartei elektronische Erklärungen im Rahmen der Vertragsanbahnung, des -abschlusses und der -abwicklung akzeptieren muss. Grundvoraussetzung ist insoweit vielmehr, dass der konkrete Adressat – die Position des Erklärenden ist unproblematisch, da dieser die elektronische Kommunikationsform gewählt hat – ausdrücklich (etwa durch Angabe einer E-Mail-Adresse auf Briefpapier, Visitenkarte oder Homepage[186]) oder implizit sein **Einverständnis** zum Ausdruck gebracht hat, elektronische Erklärungen in der jeweils vom Erklärenden verwendeten Form und an die betreffende Adresse zu erhalten.[187] Implizite Zustimmung ist – in Anwendung von Art. 8 – insbesondere auf Grund einer Verwendung des elektronischen Kommunikationsmittels (dieser Art und dieses Formats) in früheren Verträgen, Vorverhandlungen oder eigenen Erklärungen zum Abschluss des jeweiligen Vertrages anzunehmen,[188] kann aber auch in Parteigepflogenheiten oder Bräuchen etabliert worden sein, Art. 9 I, II. Dieses Erfordernis gilt dabei unabhängig davon, ob die betroffene Erklärung nach dem CISG zugangsbedürftig ist oder nicht. 27

5. Internet-Auktionen

Eine weitere alternative Vertragsschlussform stellen schließlich grenzüberschreitende Vertragsabschlüsse über Internet-Auktionen dar, die außerhalb des Anwendungsbereiches des Art. 2 lit. b) liegen und daher durch das **CISG erfasst** werden.[189] Das Zustandekommen des einzelnen Kaufvertrages richtet sich hier vorrangig nach den Bedingungen der jeweiligen Auktionsplattform, die regelmäßig durch den Plattformbetreiber vorgegeben werden und denen die Auktionsteilnehmer vor Durchführung der Auktion üblicherweise durch einen Mausklick zustimmen (sog. Click-wrap-Einbindung[190]). Sofern es an entsprechenden parteiautonomen Regelungen fehlt, ist anhand des Maßstabs des Art. 8 II, III zu ermitteln, ob die Präsentation der Ware im Internet im konkreten Fall als bloße invitatio ad offerendum zu verstehen ist, auf die das elektronische Gebot als Angebot i. S. d. Art. 14 I und sodann eine (ggf. konkludente) Annahme durch den Verkäufer (Art. 18 I) folgt, oder ob bereits die Präsentation der Ware auf der Auktionsplattform durch einen verständigen Dritten in der Situation des Bieters (Art. 8 II) als Angebot zum Vertragsschluss mit dem Meistbietenden bzw. als antizipierte Annahme des Höchstgebots aufgefasst werden kann.[191] 28

6. Käufe an Warenbörsen

Eine vergleichbare Rechtslage besteht bezüglich Käufen an Warenbörsen, die unter die Vorschriften des CISG fallen[192] und auf die folglich auch die Vertragsschlussregelungen des 29

---

[186] Vgl. unten Art. 24 Rn. 26.
[187] S. CISG-AC, Op. 1 (*Ramberg*), Comments 15.4 ff., IHR 2003, 244, 245 u. öfter; *Borges*, Verträge im elektronischen Geschäftsverkehr, S. 319; *Coetzee*, 11 VJ (2007), 11, 18 f.; *Hahnkamper*, 25 J. L. & Com. (2005-06), 147, 150; *Schlechtriem*, Internationales UN-Kaufrecht, Rn. 71; *Steensgaard*, Standardbetingelser, § 8, Rn. 49; s. auch Art. 8 II UNECIC.
[188] Vgl. LG Hamburg, 23.11.2003, CISG-online 875: Annahmeerklärung per E-Mail, nachdem der Offerent sein Angebot per E-Mail gemacht hatte; *Schwenzer/Hachem/Kee*, Rn. 11.14.
[189] *Freitag*, Kollisionsrecht, Rn. 809; *Piltz*, Internationales Kaufrecht, Rn. 2–29; *Schlechtriem*, Internationales UN-Kaufrecht, Rn. 30; *Schlechtriem/Schwenzer/Schwenzer/Hachem*, CISG Commentary, Art. 2, Rn. 21; ausführlich *Schroeter*, ZEuP 2004, 20, 30 ff.; a. A. *Borges*, Verträge im elektronischen Geschäftsverkehr, S. 305; *Staudinger/Magnus*, Art. 2, Rn. 33. S. auch hier *Ferrari*, Art. 2 Rn. 28.
[190] *Dannemann*, FS Rudden, S. 191 f; *Wulf*, UN-Kaufrecht und eCommerce, S. 86.
[191] S. näher unten Art. 14 Rn. 28 sowie *Dannemann*, FS Rudden, S. 183 ff.
[192] Oben *Ferrari*, Art. 2 Rn. 29; *Heuzé*, S. 78; *Honnold/Flechtner*, Art. 2, Rn. 51; *Kantor*, 1 Int'l law pract. (NYSBA) (1988), 8, 10; *Schroeter*, ZEuP 2004, 20, 26; *Staudinger/Magnus*, Art. 2, Rn. 35; a. A. MünchKommHGB/*Benicke*, Art. 2, Rn. 10 (analoge Anwendung von Art. 2 lit. b)).

Einheitskaufrechts Anwendung finden können. In der Praxis kommt den Artt. 14 ff. auch insoweit allerdings nur ausnahmsweise Bedeutung zu, weil das Zustandekommen der Kontrakte an Warenbörsen vorrangig durch Börsenbedingungen und Gebräuche geregelt wird.[193]

7. Internationale Ausschreibungen

30   Das CISG erfasst auch Kaufverträge, bei denen der Verkäufer über eine internationale Ausschreibung ausgewählt wird,[194] was bei Einkäufen durch private Unternehmen, besonders häufig aber dann der Fall ist, wenn als Käufer die **öffentliche Hand** selbst[195] oder aber ein Unternehmen agiert, welches seinerseits einen Auftrag der öffentlichen Hand zu bedienen hat.[196] Hier sieht das nationale Vergaberecht, das innerhalb Europas häufig auf gemeinschaftsrechtliche Vorgaben zurückgeht, vielfach Schutzpflichten – Gleichbehandlung, Bevorzugung des wirtschaftlichsten Angebots, s. § 97 II, V GWB – vor, die auch und gerade zugunsten ausländischer Bieter wirken.[197] Da die Ausschreibung typischerweise nur den Zeitabschnitt bis zur Auswahl des erfolgreichen Bieters betrifft, können die Artt. 14 ff. auf den darauf folgenden Vertragsschlussvorgang aber regelmäßig unproblematisch Anwendung finden, ohne mit die Ausschreibung regelnden vergaberechtlichen Bestimmungen in Konflikt zu geraten.[198] Die Angebote der Bieter stellen danach Offerten i. S. d. Art. 14 I 1 dar, wobei das erfolgreiche Angebot durch den Zuschlag des Ausschreibenden angenommen wird, der damit die vertragsrechtliche Annahme (Art. 18 I) darstellt.[199] Vorschriften wie § 13 S. 6 VgV, welche die Nichtigkeit unter Verletzung vergaberechtlicher Informationspflichten und -fristen abgeschlossener Verträge anordnen, können über Art. 4 S. 2 lit. a) auf CISG-Verträge Anwendung finden.[200] Sollte das öffentliche Vergaberecht oder das auf private Ausschreibungen anwendbare nationale Zivilrecht allerdings im Einzelfall Vorgaben enthalten, die mit dem CISG unvereinbar sind – zu denken ist hier etwa an Schadensersatzansprüche aufgrund nicht erfolgten Vertragsabschlusses (etwa nach § 97 ff., 126 GWB bei Aufhebung der Ausschreibung) in Situationen, in denen nach dem CISG ein frei widerrufliches Angebot vorliegt – so werden die entsprechenden Regelungen durch das Übereinkommen verdrängt.[201]

---

[193] *Magnus*, FS Kritzer, S. 316 f.; *Schroeter*, ZEuP 2004, 20, 25; *Staudinger/Magnus*, Art. 2, Rn. 35.

[194] *Hilaturas Miel, S. L. v. Republic of Iraq*, U. S. Dist. Ct. (S. D. N. Y.), 20.8.2008, CISG-online 1777 = 573 F. Supp. 2d 781, 789; *Bamberger/Roth/Saenger*, Art. 2, Rn. 7; oben *Ferrari*, Art. 2 Rn. 28; *Heuzé*, S. 78; *Piltz*, Internationales Kaufrecht, Rn. 2–29; *Schroeter*, ZEuP 2004, 20, 26; *Staudinger/Magnus*, Art. 2, Rn. 34.

[195] *Hilaturas Miel, S. L. v. Republic of Iraq*, U. S. Dist. Ct. (S. D. N. Y.), 20.8.2008, CISG-online 1777 = 573 F. Supp. 2d 781, 787 ff.: Ausschreibung im Rahmen des „Oil for Food"-Programms der U. N. – auf Kaufvertrag zwischen spanischer Bieterin und irakischem Staatsunternehmen fand CISG Anwendung. Auch durch die öffentliche Hand oder ihren Einrichtungen abgeschlossene Kaufverträge können ohne weiteres in den Anwendungsbereich des Übereinkommens fallen; *Honnold/Flechtner*, Art. 11, Rn. 127; *Neumayer/Ming*, Art. 1, Anm. 11.; *Schlechtriem*, FS Rajski, S. 549 ff.; *Schroeter*, ZEuP 2004, 20, 26; *Ziegel*, 25 J. L. & Com. (2005/06), 59, 62.

[196] So etwa in *Diversitel Communications, Inc. v. Glacier Bay Inc.*, Ontario Superior Court of Justice, 6.10.2003, CISG-online 1436: Käufer, der seinerseits einen Vertrag mit dem kanadischen Verteidigungsministerium zu erfüllen hatte, suchte über einen „request for quotation" Angebote für die Lieferung von Isolierpanelen.

[197] *Byok/Jaeger/Hailbronner*, Rn. 203 ff.; *Reidt/Stickler/Glahs/Stickler*, § 97, Rn. 9; *Schroeter*, UN-Kaufrecht, § 4, Rn. 31.

[198] *Krüger*, Norsk kjøpsrett, S. 717; *Schlechtriem*, FS Rajski, S. 553; *Schroeter*, ZEuP 2004, 20, 26.

[199] BGH, 9.2.2004, BGHZ 158, 43, 48 (kein CISG-Fall); *Byok/Jaeger/Werner*, Rn. 611; *Gröning*, ZIP 1999, 52, 57. Zur regelmäßigen Qualifikation der Ausschreibung selbst als bloße invitatio ad offerendum s. unten Art. 14 Rn. 30.

[200] Oben Rn. 2.

[201] S. unten Rn. 38 sowie Art. 14 Rn. 29.

III. Vertragsschluss bei Mehrparteienverträgen

1. Mehrparteienkaufverträge

Warenkaufverträge kommen typischerweise zwischen zwei Vertragsparteien zustande, einem Verkäufer und einem Käufer. Die Regelungen des Übereinkommens beruhen stillschweigend auf diesem **Modell** eines **bilateralen Kaufvertrages**, wie sich aus dem Sprachgebrauch zahlreicher Vorschriften erschließt, in denen „der Verkäufer" und „der Käufer" oder „beide Parteien"[202] genannt werden. In der **Praxis** kommen demgegenüber auch Kaufverträge in Form von **Mehrparteienverträgen** (genauer: Verträgen mit mehr als zwei Parteien) vor, an denen mehrere Verkäufer[203] und/oder mehrere Käufer[204] beteiligt sind. Daneben finden sich gelegentlich Kaufverträge unter Beteiligung sonstiger Vertragsparteien, wie etwa Bürgen, Warenproduzenten, die eine Herstellergarantie gewähren,[205] oder Lizenzgeber. 30a

2. Anwendbarkeit der Artt. 14–24

Die Vertragsschlussregeln in Teil II des Übereinkommens entscheiden **auch** über den Abschluss von Kaufverträgen, an denen **mehrere** Verkäufer und/oder Käufer beteiligt sind,[206] und sind in der Vergangenheit ohne erkennbare Schwierigkeiten auf solche Mehrparteienverträge angewandt worden. Artt. 14–24 setzen nicht zwingend voraus, dass Verkäufer und Käufer einzelne Individuen oder Gesellschaften sind. Schwierigkeiten können freilich entstehen, sofern die verschiedenen Parteien, die auf derselben Transaktionsseite an einem Warenkauf beteiligt sind, während des Vertragsschlussprozesses divergierende und sich inhaltlich widersprechende Erklärungen abgeben. Obwohl das traditionelle, die Bausteine „Angebot und „Annahme" verwendende Vertragsschlussmodell des CISG sich einfacher auf den Austausch einzelner Vertragserklärungen anwenden lässt, ist es **hinreichend flexibel**, um auch die Kommunikation zwischen mehr als zwei Akteuren rechtlich zu erfassen.[207] 30b

Die Regeln des Übereinkommens zum Vertragsschluss finden allerdings nur insoweit direkte Anwendung, als es um den materiellen Konsens zwischen solchen Parteien geht, die als Verkäufer oder Käufer agieren. Die Begründung vertraglicher Pflichten für **sonstige Personen** wie Gutachter, Warenprüfer oder Bürgen liegt **außerhalb** des persönlichen Anwendungsbereiches von Teil II des UN-Kaufrechts, selbst wenn diese dasselbe Vertragsdokument unterzeichnen wie Verkäufer und Käufer.[208] Die vertragliche Bindung solcher 30c

---

[202] So in Art. 81 I, II.
[203] ICC, 20.12.1999, CISG-online 1646 = IHR 2004, 21: deutsches Handelsunternehmen, das den Kaufvertrag vermittelt hatte, und deutscher Warenhersteller waren beide als Verkäufer an Kaufvertrag mit jugoslawischer Käuferin beteiligt; OLG Graz, 29.7.2004, CISG-online 1627: ein deutsches und ein österreichisches Bauunternehmen, die beide gemeinsam eine Tunnelbaustelle in Deutschland betrieben, verkauften einen gebrauchten Tunnelbagger an einen österreichischen Käufer – das Gericht ging von einem Dreiparteien-Kaufvertrag aus und wandte das CISG an (bezüglich der österreichischen Verkäuferin wurde die Baustelle in Deutschland als relevante Niederlassung i. S. d. Art. 10 lit. a) angesehen), obgleich die beiden Verkäuferinnen eine BGB-Gesellschaft deutschen Rechts bildeten und daher richtigerweise nur *ein* Verkäufer beteiligt war; vgl. die krit. Anm. von *Bach*, IPRax 2009, 299, 300.
[204] Vgl. Schiedsgericht der Handelskammer Zürich, 31.5.1996, CISG-online 1291 = YB. Comm. Arb. 1998, 128 ff.: CISG-Kontrakt zwischen russischem Verkäufer und Käufern aus Argentinien und Ungarn, die beide demselben Konzern angehörten.
[205] Vgl. *Honnold/Flechtner*, Art. 4, Rn. 63.
[206] Vgl. *Ferrari u. a./Mankowski*, Internationales Vertragsrecht, Vor Art. 14, Rn. 11; *Staudinger/Magnus*, Art. 4, Rn. 13, der von Vereinbarungen zwischen „zwei oder mehr Parteien" spricht.
[207] S. *Nemeczek*, IHR 2011, 49, 55 ff. zu trilateralen Parteieinigungen zum Zweck einer Vertragsübernahme (vgl. dazu aber unten Art. 29 Rn. 10); zu potentiellen Problemstellungen unten Rn. 30d, 30e.
[208] *Ferrari u. a./Mankowski*, Internationales Vertragsrecht, Vor Art. 14, Rn. 12; *Honsell/Dornis*, Vorbem 14–24, Rn. 21. Nach hier vertretener Ansicht liegen spätere Vertrags*änderungen* unter Beteiligung Dritter (wie z. B. Abtretung, Vertrags- oder Schuldübernahme sowie Schuldbeitritt) ebenfalls außerhalb des Anwendungsbereiches des UN-Kaufrechts (namentlich seines Art. 29 I), weil solche Transaktionen Fragen nach der

Parteien muss über die Anwendung des Kollisionsrechts des Forums ermittelt werden, welches seinerseits zu einer „indirekten" Anwendbarkeit der Artt. 14–24 führen kann, sofern es z. B. das Recht des „Hauptvertrages" (d. h. des Kaufvertrages) auch auf akzessorische Vertragsbeziehungen erstreckt (s. § 194 Restatement (Second) of Conflict of Laws hinsichtlich Bürgschafts- und Garantieverträgen; vgl. auch Artt. 10 I, 4 IV Rom I-VO).[209] Ob ein **Warenhersteller**, der eine Garantie oder *warranty* für die Qualität der produzierten Ware abgibt, für die Zwecke der Artt. 14–24 als Verkäufer zu behandeln ist, bestimmt sich vorrangig nach der Auslegung der vom Warenhersteller abgegebenen Erklärung sowie den Umständen des Falles.[210] M. E. wird die Stellung eines Produzenten gegenüber Verkäufern und (End-)Käufern nur selten derjenigen eines „Verkäufers" i. S. d. UN-Kaufrechts entsprechen, sodass die Begründung vertraglicher Beziehungen in diesem Verhältnis sich nicht unmittelbar nach Artt. 14–24 richtet.

3. Problemlagen

30d   Die Anwendung der Artt. 14–24 auf den Abschluss von Mehrparteienverträgen verursacht **keine** besonderen **Schwierigkeiten**, sofern die Parteien auf der Verkäufer- wie auch der Käuferseite der Transaktion entweder jeweils nur eine einheitliche Vertragsschlusserklärung abgeben oder die unterschiedlichen Parteierklärungen derselben Seite keine inhaltlichen Widersprüche aufweisen: In diesen Fällen bestimmen die Vertragsschlussregeln in Teil II des Übereinkommens wie auch sonst, ob und wann ein materieller Konsens zwischen beiden Seiten zustande gekommen ist (Artt. 14, 18) oder nicht (Art. 19). Keine zusätzlichen Probleme ergeben sich, wenn mehrerer Verkäufer (respektive Käufer) gemeinsame Erklärungen abgeben.[211] Werden Angebot oder Annahme dagegen nur durch einen unter mehreren Verkäufern/Käufern abgegeben, so entscheidet das nationale Stellvertretungsrecht[212] darüber, ob die handelnde Person ihre beabsichtigten Mitkontrahenten rechtlich wirksam binden konnte.

30e   Das Vertragsschlussmodell der Konvention passt weniger gut für solche Mehrparteienkonstellationen, in denen unterschiedliche Akteure derselben Vertragsseite **uneinheitlich** agieren, namentlich durch die Abgabe untereinander inkompatibler Vertragsschlusserklärungen. Die Lösung für entsprechende Problemlagen liegt zuvörderst im Prinzip der **Privatautonomie**: Gerichte und Schiedsgerichte haben zunächst zu prüfen, ob die Parteierklärungen selbst Bestimmungen zu dieser Sachlage aufweisen[213] oder nach Art. 8 II, III so ausgelegt werden können, dass die scheinbaren Widersprüche entfallen. In den verbleibenden Fällen wird eine Anwendung des Art. 14 entweder ergeben, dass **zwei separate Angebote** vorliegen oder – sofern die Person des Offerenten endgültig nicht bestimmbar ist – **keine wirksame Offerte** gemacht wurde.[214] Sollten dagegen Widersprüche zwischen mehreren Annahmeerklärungen auftreten, so wird Art. 19 üblicherweise zu ihrer Bewertung als **Gegenofferte(n)** führen, weil eine Abweichung hinsichtlich der Person des

---

notwendigen Mitwirkungen des Dritten und den genauen Rechtsfolgen dieser Vorgänge aufwerfen, für die das Übereinkommen keine Antworten bereithält. S. noch näher unten Art. 29 Rn. 10.

[209] Vgl. zur *„doctrine of infection"* nach englischem Kollisionsrecht *Wahda Bank v. Arab Bank plc*, 7.11.1995, [1996] 1 Lloyd's Rep 470, 473; zum Konzept der „zusammenhängenden Verträge" nach deutschem IPR *Reithmann/Martiny/Martiny*, Rn. 162 ff.; zur Rechtslage nach dem (früheren) österreichischen Kollisionsrecht OGH, 12.6.1986, ZfRVgl 1988, 126, 130: „Bürgschaft als abhängiges Rechtsgeschäft".

[210] Vgl. auch *Honnold/Flechtner*, Art. 4, Rn. 63; *Schlechtriem/Schwenzer/Schwenzer/Hachem*, CISG Commentary, Art. 4, Rn. 24.

[211] Vgl. ICC, 20.12.1999, CISG-online 1646 = IHR 2004, 21 ff.: Kaufvertrag wurde durch die beiden Verkäufer und den Käufer unterzeichnet.

[212] Vgl. oben Rn. 3 sowie *Ferrari*, oben Art. 4 Rn. 34.

[213] ICC, 20.12.1999, CISG-online 1646 = IHR 2004, 21, 23: Kaufvertrag bestimmte ausdrücklich, dass durch einen der zwei Verkäufer mit dem Käufer getroffene Preisabsprachen auch für den anderen Verkäufer bindend sein sollten.

[214] Die Bestimmbarkeit der Identität des Anbietenden zählt unter dem UN-Kaufrecht zu den Mindestvoraussetzungen für eine wirksame Offerte; s. unten Art. 14 Rn. 4.

Annehmenden immer als „wesentliche" Abweichung i. S. d. Art. 19 II, III zu bewerten sein wird.[215]

IV. Verhandlungen und vorvertragliche Pflichten

Art. 8 III, eine auch für das Vertragsschlussverfahren wichtige Vorschrift,[216] nimmt auf Verhandlungen zwischen den Parteien Bezug. Damit wird jedoch nur ein Umstand für die Auslegung bezeichnet, nicht das Verhandlungsstadium vor Vertragsschluss zu den vom Übereinkommen geregelten Fragen gezogen.[217] Bei der Behandlung vorvertraglicher Pflichtenbeziehungen ist aus Perspektive des CISG daher zu differenzieren: **31**

1. Vorvertragliche Pflichten nach dem CISG

Ob es überhaupt nach CISG entstehende und zu beurteilende vorvertragliche Pflichten (entsprechend § 311 II BGB) gibt, ist umstritten.[218] Ein auf der Wiener Konferenz von der DDR gestellter Antrag, eine allgemeine **culpa in contrahendo-Haftung** einzuführen, ist abgelehnt worden.[219] Damit liegt eine ausdrückliche Entscheidung der Übereinkommensverfasser gegen eine Einbeziehung vorvertraglicher Pflichtenverhältnisse in das Übereinkommen und die von ihm geregelte Materie vor; gesteigerte Pflichtenbeziehungen in diesem Stadium, der Inhalt entsprechender Pflichten und die Folgen ihrer Verletzung sind daher grundsätzlich nach unvereinheitlichtem **nationalen Recht** zu beurteilen.[220] **32**

Damit ist allerdings nicht generell ausgeschlossen, dass in vorsichtiger, das in Art. 7 I und II verfügbare Instrumentarium nutzender Weiterentwicklung des CISG[221] **einzelne Sachfragen** aus vorvertraglichen Beziehungen aus dem Anwendungsbereich nationaler Vorschriften herausgenommen und **einheitsrechtlich** gelöst werden können. In der Literatur sind insoweit mit hier nicht im Einzelnen nachzuzeichnenden Begründungen folgende vorvertragliche Pflichten aus dem CISG abgeleitet worden: Die Pflicht, die Vertragsverhandlungen jedenfalls in den Fällen des Art. 16 II lit. b) nicht abzubrechen[222] oder – allgemeiner – einen Vertragsschluss nicht treuwidrig zu verhindern,[223] Aufklärungspflichten, soweit der Pflichtengegenstand nicht bereits durch Artt. 35 II lit. b) oder 71 erfasst ist,[224] sowie einzelne Schutzpflichten.[225] Zu Recht wird aber darauf hingewiesen, dass die Kon- **33**

---

[215] Vgl. unten Art. 19 Rn. 9 a. E.
[216] S. oben *Schmidt-Kessel*, Art. 8 Rn. 31 sowie hier Rn. 1.
[217] Art. 8 III als Anknüpfungspunkt für eine vorvertragliche Haftung nach CISG nennend hingegen *Goderre*, 66 U. Cin. L. Rev. (1997), 258, 280.
[218] Befürwortend *Bonell*, RIW 1990, 693, 700 f.; *Goderre*, 66 U. Cin. L. Rev. (1997), 258, 280 f.; *Schmid*, Lückenfüllung und Normenkonkurrenz, S. 261 ff.; a. A. MünchKomm/*Gruber*, Vor Art. 14, Rn. 6; *Spagnolo*, 21 Temp. Int'l & Comp. L.J. (2007), 262, 291 u. 309; *Staudinger/Magnus*, Art. 4, Rn. 42.
[219] S. O. R., S. 294 f.; zu diesem Vorgang auch *Schlechtriem*, Einheitliches UN-Kaufrecht, S. 45. Bereits die Arbeitsgruppe hatte entsprechende Vorschläge abgelehnt, s. YB IX (1978), S. 66 f., Nr. 85: „... too vague and uncertain to be usefully included in the draft Convention". Eingehend zur Behandlung der *culpa in contrahendo* in der Entstehungsgeschichte *Kritzer*, Guide to Practical Applications, S. 198 ff.
[220] *Bridge*, Int'l Sale of Goods, Rn. 304; *Grunewald*, Kaufrecht, § 6, Rn. 54; *Honsell/Dornis*, Vorbem 14–24, Rn. 21; MünchKomm/*Gruber*, Vor Art. 14, Rn. 2; *Spagnolo*, 21 Temp. Int'l & Comp. L.J. (2007), 262, 291 u. 309; *Staudinger/Magnus*, Art. 4, Rn. 42; *Stoll*, Internationalprivatrechtliche Fragen, S. 504 f.; *Torsello*, Preliminary Agreements, S. 219; *Witz/Salger/Lorenz/Witz*, Vor Artt. 14–24, Rn. 17; sowie im Folgenden die Rechtsprechungsnachw. in Rn. 34 ff.
[221] Vgl. *Schmid*, Lückenfüllung und Normenkonkurrenz, S. 265 ff. sowie in jüngerer Zeit *Benedick*, Informationspflichten, Rn. 985 ff.
[222] S. unten Rn. 14; *Heuzé*, R.D.A.I. 2001, 277, 284; *Köhler*, Spannungsverhältnis, S. 222 f.; *Staudinger/Magnus*, Art. 4, Rn. 42 f.; wohl auch *Goderre*, 66 U. Cin. L. Rev. (1997), 258, 281.
[223] *Bonell*, RIW 1990, 693, 700 f. (auf der Grundlage von Art. 7 I); *Sabbagh-Farshi*, S. 112 f.; *Schmid*, Lückenfüllung und Normenkonkurrenz, S. 266 f.; *Staudinger/Magnus*, Art. 4, Rn. 43; a. A. *Köhler*, Spannungsverhältnis, S. 224 ff. S. auch hier Rn. 38.
[224] *Schmid*, Lückenfüllung und Normenkonkurrenz, S. 267 ff.; vgl. auch *Benedick*, Informationspflichten, Rn. 1072 ff.
[225] *Schmid*, Lückenfüllung und Normenkonkurrenz, S. 270 ff.; vgl. auch *Magnus*, ZEuP 1993, 79, 95 (für allg. Schutzpflicht *während* der Vertragserfüllung); a. A. *Schütz*, S. 204.

struktion eines allgemeinen Schutzpflichtennetzes – wie etwa im deutschen unvereinheitlichten Recht bekannt – im Anwendungsbereich des CISG nicht möglich ist.[226]

2. Anwendbarkeit vorvertraglicher Pflichten nach nationalem Recht neben dem CISG

34 Vorvertragliche Pflichten der Parteien und eine sich an deren Verletzung möglicherweise anknüpfende *culpa in contrahendo*-Haftung nach dem durch IPR berufenen nationalen Recht[227] sind nicht unterschiedslos neben dem CISG anwendbar. Entsprechende Rechtsinstitute können vielmehr ganz unterschiedliche **Funktionen und Schutzzwecke** haben, die über ihre funktionale Qualifikation und damit ihr Verhältnis zum CISG und seinem Anwendungsbereich bestimmen: Wo eine an sich auch mit der Rechtsfigur der *culpa in contrahendo* lösbare Detailfrage bereits im CISG geregelt ist, kommt ein Rückgriff auf unvereinheitlichtes nationales Recht danach nicht in Betracht.[228] Im Einzelnen ist zu unterscheiden:

35 **a) Allgemeine Pflichten zum Schutz von Leib, Leben, Eigentum etc.** Vorvertragliche Pflichten können Pflichten der außervertraglichen Schutzordnung, insbesondere allgemeine Verkehrs(sicherungs)pflichten zum Schutz von Leib, Leben, Eigentum und anderen Rechtsgütern sein, die durch die Situation der Vertragsanbahnung konkretisiert und verschärft werden können. Sie gehören nicht zur Regelungsmaterie des CISG – Art. 5 macht das für den Schutz von Leib und Leben ganz deutlich – und sind deshalb nach nationalem Recht zu beurteilen,[229] mag dieses sie als außervertragliche oder quasivertragliche Pflichten einordnen.[230]

36 **b) Schutz vor fraudulösem Parteiverhalten.** Das Recht kann sich unterschiedlicher Mechanismen bedienen, wo es um den Schutz vor fraudulösem, also **arglistigem** oder **vorsätzlich sittenwidrigem** Verhalten geht: Erklären nationale Vorschriften durch Arglist erschlichene Verträge für nichtig oder unwirksam, so finden sie schon deshalb auf CISG-Verträge Anwendung, weil das Übereinkommen deren Gültigkeit ausweislich Art. 4 Satz 2 lit. a) nicht regelt.[231] Nationales Recht bleibt aber auch dort anwendbar, wo es Opfer fraudulösen Verhaltens auf andere Art und Weise (wie namentlich durch Schadensersatzpflichten) schützt.[232] Dies kam in der ausdrücklichen Ausnahme in Art. 89 EKG[233] deutlich zum Ausdruck, deren Regelungsgehalt auch im Anwendungsbereich des CISG gilt[234] – entscheidend ist, dass das Einheitskaufrecht zu dieser Sachfrage keine abschließende Rege-

---

[226] *Benedick,* Informationspflichten, Rn. 1001; *Schmid,* Lückenfüllung und Normenkonkurrenz, S. 276, dazu auch S. 106 ff.

[227] Die unterschiedliche Qualifikation der verschiedenen cic-Haftungsfälle kann dabei unterschiedliche Anknüpfungen erforderlich machen; vgl. *Stoll,* Internationalprivatrechtliche Fragen, S. 504 f. sowie hier Rn. 36, 38. Innerhalb der EU ist durch Art. 12 Rom II-VO in dieser Hinsicht eine (allerdings nicht umfassende) Vereinheitlichung des Kollisionsrechts bewirkt worden; vgl. *von Hein,* GPR 2007, 54, 59.

[228] *Karollus,* S. 216; *Köhler,* Spannungsverhältnis, S. 214 f.; MünchKomm/*Gruber,* Vor Art. 14, Rn. 13; *Schwenzer/Mohs,* IHR 2006, 239; *Witz/Salger/Lorenz/Witz,* Vor Artt. 14–24, Rn. 17 sowie unten Art. 14 Rn. 29.

[229] *Bonell,* RIW 1990, 693, 700; *Honsell/Dornis,* Vorbem 14–24, Rn. 22; *Schütz,* S. 205; *Witz/Salger/Lorenz/Witz,* Vor Artt. 14–24, Rn. 17.

[230] Hierzu *Schmid,* Lückenfüllung und Normenkonkurrenz, S. 271 f.

[231] S. oben Rn. 3 sowie *Schlechtriem/Schwenzer/Schwenzer/Hachem,* CISG Commentary, Art. 4, Rn. 37.

[232] OLG Hamm, 2.4.2009, CISG-online 1978 = IHR 2010, 59, 63; *Miami Valley Paper, LLC v. Lebbing Engineering & Consulting GmbH,* U. S. Dist. Ct. (S.D. Ohio), 10.10.2006, CISG-online 1362; Schiedsgericht der Handelskammer Zürich, 31.5.1996, CISG-online 1291 = YB. Comm. Arb. 1998, 128 ff., Rn. 149; *Hartnell,* 18 Yale J. Int'l L. (1993), 1, 70 ff.; *Honnold/Flechtner,* Art. 4, Rn. 65; *Honsell/Dornis,* Vorbem 14–24, Rn. 22; *Lookofsky,* 13 Duke J. Comp. & Int'l L. (2003), 263, 280; MünchKommHGB/*Benicke,* Art. 4, Rn. 19.

[233] "Im Falle absichtlicher Schädigung oder arglistiger Täuschung bestimmt sich der Schadenersatz nach den Vorschriften, die für nicht diesem Gesetz unterliegende Kaufverträge gelten".

[234] S. *Schlechtriem,* Einheitliches UN-Kaufrecht, S. 19; vgl. zu Art. 89 EKG auch die Erläuterungen von *Tunc,* abgedruckt in Actes, S. 114: Rechtsfolgen von Arglist und Betrug könnten nicht einheitsrechtlich geregelt werden, da sie zu eng mit der öffentlichen Ordnung der einzelnen Staaten zusammenhingen.

lung aufstellt.²³⁵ Entsprechende Bestimmungen der nationalen Rechtsordnungen, die dort vielfach Teil der außervertraglichen Haftungsordnung sind, greifen dabei auch dort ein, wo der Schutz reiner Vermögensinteressen in Rede steht. Praktische Bedeutung hat dies etwa für Klagen erlangt, die auf den Vorwurf bei dem Abschluss von CISG-Verträgen erfolgten *fraudulent inducements, fraudulent misrepresentation, common law fraud* oder absichtlicher Täuschung gestützt wurden.²³⁶

Nationale Regelungen der vorstehend genannten Art verdrängen das CISG dabei nicht, sondern finden neben dem Übereinkommen Anwendung,²³⁷ weshalb dasselbe fraudulöse Parteiverhalten u. U. zu **parallelen** Schadenersatzverpflichtungen nach nationalem Recht und nach CISG führen kann.²³⁸

c) **Schutz vor fahrlässiger Fehlinformation, insbesondere *negligent misrepresentati-* 37 *on*.** Anders ist hingegen dort zu entscheiden, wo nationales Recht die (lediglich) **fahrlässige** Verletzung vorvertraglicher Pflichten sanktioniert, die – wie etwa die Grundsätze der *negligent misrepresentation* in U. S.-amerikanischen Rechtsordnungen – auf die Aufklärung des Käufers über bestimmte Wareneigenschaften gerichtet sind und dem Käufer die nachträgliche Loslösung vom Vertrag und/oder das Verlangen von Schadenersatz erlauben: Da hier die Gefahr der Aushebelung sowohl der Informationsrisikoverteilung der Artt. 35 ff. als auch der Untersuchungs- und Rügeobliegenheiten des Übereinkommens (Artt. 38 ff.) droht, ohne dass dieses durch einen gesonderten Verhaltensunwert auf Seiten der pflichtverletzenden Partei gerechtfertigt wäre, ist für die Anwendung entsprechender Regelungen neben dem insoweit abschließend normierenden CISG nach richtiger Ansicht **kein Raum**.²³⁹ Eine Reihe U. S.-amerikanischer Gerichte hat freilich (unreflektiert) anders entschieden und Ansprüche wegen *negligent misrepresentation* ohne weitere Differenzenierungen auch bei CISG-Verträgen zugelassen.²⁴⁰

d) **Abbruch von Vertragsverhandlungen.**²⁴¹ Der Abbruch von Vertragsverhandlungen 38 sollte, sofern nicht fraudulöses Verhalten vorliegt, keine Ansprüche nach nationalem Recht und, wie die grundsätzliche Rücknehmbarkeit und Widerruflichkeit einer Offerte (Artt. 15 II, 16 I) sowie die Widerspruchs- bzw. Verwahrungsrechte nach Art. 19 II, 21 II

---

²³⁵ *Honnold/Flechtner*, Art. 4, Rn. 65.
²³⁶ *Dingxi Longhai Dairy, Ltd. v. Becwood Technology Group, L. L. C.*, U. S. Dist. Ct. (D. Minn.), 1.7.2008, CISG-online 1774 (zu *fraudulent misrepresentation* nach dem Recht des U. S.-Bundesstaates Minnesota); *Miami Valley Paper, LLC v. Lebbing Engineering & Consulting GmbH*, U. S. Dist. Ct. (S. D. Ohio), 10.10.2006, CISG-online 1362 (zu *fraudulent inducement* nach dem Recht des U. S.-Bundesstaates Ohio); *TeeVee Toons, Inc. & Steve Gottlieb, Inc. v. Gerhard Schubert GmbH*, U. S. Dist. Ct. (S. D. N. Y.), 23.8.2006, CISG-online 1272 (zu *common law fraud* nach New Yorker Recht); *Beijing Metals & Minerals v. American Business Center, Inc.*, U. S. Ct. App. (5th Cir.), 15.6.1993, CISG-online 89 (zu *duress* und *fraudulent inducement* nach dem Recht des U. S.-Bundesstaates Texas); KG St. Gallen, 13.5.2008, CISG-online 1768 = IHR 2009, 161 (zu Schadenersatz gemäß Art. 41 I OR und *culpa in contrahendo* nach absichtlicher Täuschung (Art. 28 OR)); OLG Hamm, 2.4.2009, CISG-online 1978 = IHR 2010, 59, 63 (zum Anspruch aus § 812 I 1 Alt. 1 BGB nach Anfechtung wg. arglistiger Täuschung gem. § 123 I BGB).
²³⁷ KG St. Gallen, 13.5.2008, CISG-online 1768 = IHR 2009, 161. Auch nach Art. 89 EKG fand das nationale Recht *neben* dem Einheitskaufrecht Anwendung, verdrängte Letzteres also nicht; vgl. *Dölle/Weitnauer*, Art. 89 EKG, Rn. 3.
²³⁸ KG St. Gallen, 13.5.2008, CISG-online 1768 = IHR 2009, 161: Schadenersatzansprüche wg. absichtlicher Täuschung gemäß Schweizer Recht *und* nach Artt. 61 I lit. b), 74 CISG, weil die Käuferin zugleich eine ausdrückliche vertragliche Nebenpflicht (Unterlassung der Weiterveräußerung der Ware an Abnehmer in bestimmten Drittstaaten) verletzt hatte.
²³⁹ *Bridge*, Int'l Sale of Goods, Rn. 12.21 (zum englischen Recht); MünchKomm/*Huber*, Art. 45, Rn. 24; *Schlechtriem*, Internationales UN-Kaufrecht, Rn. 42; unten *Schwenzer*, Art. 35 Rn. 47; *dies.*, IHR 2010, 45, 52.
²⁴⁰ *Sky Cast, Inc. v. Global Direct Distribution, LLC*, U. S. Dist. Ct. (E. D. Ky.), 18.3.2008, CISG-online 1652 = IHR 2009, 24; *Miami Valley Paper, LLC v. Lebbing Engineering & Consulting GmbH*, U. S. Dist. Ct. (S. D. Ohio), 10.10.2006, CISG-online 1362; *Geneva Pharmaceuticals Technology Corp. v. Barr Laboratories, Inc.*, U. S. Dist. Ct. (S. D. N. Y.), 10.5.2002, CISG-online 653 = 201 F. Supp. 2d 236, 286; *Lookofsky*, 13 Duke J. Comp. & Int'l L. (2003), 263, 280 ff., 286.
²⁴¹ S. auch unten Art. 14 Rn. 29.

zeigen, keine Haftung auslösen können, weder auf das negative noch auf das positive Interesse.[242] Die deutsche Rechtsprechung zum unvereinheitlichten deutschen Recht, die das Scheitern von Vertragsverhandlungen u. U. einer Seite aus *culpa in contrahendo* zurechnet und nach §§ 280 I, 241, 311 II BGB Schadensersatz sogar auf das Erfüllungsinteresse zuspricht,[243] ist auf die Anbahnung von CISG-Verträgen nicht übertragbar.[244] Dasselbe muss für Rechtsbehelfe gelten, die auf die U. S.-amerikanische Rechtsfigur des *promissory estoppel* gestützt werden, weil die Behandlung des Vertrauens auf vorvertragliche Äußerungen insoweit in Art. 16 II lit. b) eine abschließende Regelung erfahren hat.[245] Auch die mögliche Qualifikation solcher (Schadenersatz)ansprüche als deliktisch[246] macht sie, falls ein im Anwendungsbereich der Artt. 14 ff. liegender Vertrag angebahnt wurde, nicht anwendbar.

39   e) **Vorvertragliche Aufklärungs- und Informationspflichten.** Vorvertragliche Aufklärungs- und Informationspflichten können unterschiedliche Schutzzwecke haben: Soweit sie – wie insbesondere Informationspflichten, die auf EG-Richtlinien wie die Fernabsatz- und die E-Commerce-Richtlinie zurückgehen – die **Freiheit der Willensbildung** einer Partei schützen sollen, bleiben sie neben dem CISG anwendbar, und zwar unabhängig davon, welche Folgen (etwa Unwirksamkeit, Vernichtbarkeit oder auch Widerrufbarkeit einer Vertragsschlusserklärung) das nationale Recht für den Fall ihrer Verletzung anordnet. Beispiele sind § 312c I BGB i. V. m. Art. 246 § 1 I Nr. 1–12 EGBGB.[247] Soweit Manifestations- und Dokumentationspflichten – wie etwa die (nicht zwingend vor Vertragsschluss zu erfüllenden[248]) Pflichten zur Informationsübermittlung in Textform nach § 312c I BGB i. V. m. Art. 246 § 2 I 1 Nr. 2 EGBGB – auf **Sicherung der Rechtsposition einer Seite** abzielen, können sie im Anwendungsbereich des CISG Geltung beanspruchen, soweit ihre Beachtung weder für das Zustandekommen des Kaufvertrages konstitutiv ist[249] (weil in diesem Fall eine Unvereinbarkeit mit Art. 11 bestünde[250]) noch durch ein Vertragslösungsrecht sanktioniert wird.[251] Auch die dokumentationsbezogene Pflicht des § 312g I Nr. 4

---

[242] *Benedick,* Informationspflichten, Rn. 686, 689; *Karollus,* S. 216; *Köhler,* Spannungsverhältnis, S. 226; *Sabbagh-Farshi,* S. 104 f.; *Schütz,* S. 287; *Schwenzer/Mohs,* IHR 2006, 239; *Soergel/Lüderitz/Fenge,* Art. 16, Rn. 2; *Staudinger/Magnus,* Art. 16, Rn. 14; *Witz/Salger/Lorenz/Witz,* Art. 16, Rn. 16; a. A. *Heuzé,* R. D. A. I. 2001, 277, 284 ff.; MünchKomm/*Gruber,* Art. 15, Rn. 9. Zur funktionalen Vergleichbarkeit von „Bindung an das Angebot" und „Vertrauen auf einen als sicher hingestellten Vertragsschluss" s. *Küpper,* S. 236 Fn. 273; *Schlechtriem,* EWiR 1989, 443 f.; *Sono,* 21 Cornell Int'l L. J. (1988), 477, 480 Fn. 12.

[243] Vgl. für Verletzung von Pflichten bei Ausschreibungen OLG Celle, 9.5.1996, NJW-RR 1997, 662; BGH, 6.2.2002, WM 2002, 2381 ff. und BGH, 16.4.2002, WM 2002, 2383 ff.; für die ungerechtfertigte Aufhebung öffentlicher Ausschreibungen BGH, 8.9.1998, NJW 1998, 3636, 3638. Dazu bereits oben Rn. 30 sowie unten Art. 14 Rn. 29.

[244] Vgl. aber OLG Frankfurt a. M., 4.3.1994, CISG-online 110 (nach paralleler Vertragsschlussprüfung nach BGB und CISG nur *in concreto* Voraussetzungen der cic verneint); ähnlich auch Fovárosi Biróság Budapest, 17.6.1997, CISG-online 288 (zu Schadensersatzansprüchen nach ungarischem Recht).

[245] Vgl. *Geneva Pharmaceuticals Technology Corp. v. Barr Laboratories, Inc.,* U. S. Dist. Ct. (S. D. N. Y.), 10.5.2002, CISG-online 653 = 201 F. Supp. 2d 236, 286 f. (wo allerdings im konkreten Fall – mit unglücklicher Argumentation – ein *promissory estoppel claim* zugelassen wurde; zu Recht krit. *Mattera,* 16 Pace Int'l L. Rev. (2004), 165, 190); *Malik,* 25 Indian J. Int'l L. (1985), 26, 42 ff., 47.

[246] Vgl. EuGH, 17.9.2002, Rs. C-334/00 *(Fonderie Officine Meccaniche Tacconi/Heinrich Wagner Sinto Maschinenfabrik),* NJW 2002, 3159, Rn. 23, 26; krit. dazu *Mankowski,* IPRax 2003, 127 f.; s. auch Com., 7.4.1998, J. C. P. 1999, ed. E, 579 (Schadensersatzansprüche wegen Abbruch von Vertragsverhandlungen „sans motif légitime" auf der Grundlage von Art. 1382 Cc gebilligt).

[247] *Schroeter,* UN-Kaufrecht, § 6, Rn. 130 ff.; a. A. *Benedick,* Informationspflichten, Rn. 956.

[248] Vgl. *Staudinger/Thüsing,* § 312c, Rn. 100.

[249] Die Erfüllung der Pflichten nach § 312c I BGB i. V. m. Art. 246 § 2 EGBGB ist für die Wirksamkeit des Vertragsschlusses bedeutungslos; s. *Staudinger/Thüsing,* § 312c, Rn. 93.

[250] S. oben *Schmidt-Kessel,* Art. 11 Rn. 14a.

[251] *Schroeter,* UN-Kaufrecht, § 6, Rn. 134 (zu Art. 5 I EG-Fernabsatzrichtlinie); a. A. (für generelle Unvereinbarkeit mit dem CISG) *Benedick,* Informationspflichten, Rn. 950; *Schlechtriem,* Internationales UN-Kaufrecht, Rn. 42c. Bei den Informationspflichten nach § 312c I BGB i. V. m. Art. 246 § 2 EGBGB wird ein Vertragslösungsrecht ausnahmsweise auf Grundlage von §§ 280, 241 II BGB für denkbar gehalten; vgl. MünchKomm/*Wendehorst,* § 312c, Rn. 144. Die zudem aus § 312d II BGB resultierende Erweiterung des Widerrufsrechts im Fernabsatz wirkt sich bei CISG-Verträgen hingegen schon deshalb nicht aus, weil das Widerrufsrecht des § 312d I 1 BGB neben dem Übereinkommen keine Anwendung findet; s. oben Rn. 8.

Vorbemerkungen zu Artt. 14–24 **40, 41 Vor Artt. 14–24**

BGB fällt in diese Kategorie, kann aber schon deshalb neben dem CISG angewandt werden, weil ihre Anforderungen inhaltlich mit Artt. 14 ff. kompatibel sind.[252]

Soweit vorvertragliche Aufklärungs- und Informationspflichten auf eine **Konkretisie-** 40 **rung** der mit Vertragsschluss für die Parteien, insbesondere den Verkäufer entstehenden **Pflichten** abzielen (wie z. B. § 312c I BGB i. V. m. Art. 246 § 1 I Nr. 4, 9 EGBGB), sind sie mit dem CISG kompatibel, doch darf ihre Verletzung nicht zu Ansprüchen oder Rechten führen, welche die Voraussetzungen entsprechender Ansprüche und Rechte nach dem Übereinkommen – etwa zur Aufhebung des Vertrages – unterlaufen würden. Das Gleiche gilt für den wichtigen Bereich sonstiger, gesetzlich angeordneter oder von der Rechtsprechung entwickelter **Aufklärungspflichten,** etwa über sachliche oder rechtliche **Eigenschaften der Ware** oder die auf sie bezogenen Dokumente:[253] Die unterlassene Aufklärung über eine auch im CISG geregelte Sachfrage kann weder ein Vertragslösungsrecht wegen Verletzung einer vorvertraglichen Pflicht noch einen auf Vertragsaufhebung oder auf Geldzahlung zielenden Schadenersatzanspruch wegen *culpa in contrahendo* auslösen,[254] weil eine Mangelhaftigkeit andernfalls nach nationalem Recht Folgen für die Parteien zeitigen könnte, die im konkreten Fall nach CISG nicht einträten, etwa weil nach dem Übereinkommen eine Aufhebung des Vertrages aufgrund mangelnden Erreichens der Schwelle des wesentlichen Vertragsbruchs (Art. 25) nicht möglich oder der Schadenersatzanspruch in seinem Umfang durch die Vorhersehbarkeitsregel (Art. 74 S. 2) begrenzt wäre.

3. Vorverträge etc.

Das CISG schweigt zur Frage seiner Anwendung auf **Vorverträge, Rahmenverein-** 41 **barungen, Vertragshändler- und Agenturverträge, Vor-, Rück-** und **Wiederkaufverträge, Kaufoptionen, promesses de vente** etc.[255] M. E. ist das Zustandekommen derartiger Vereinbarungen nach dem CISG zu beurteilen, wenn sie der Sache nach bereits Verpflichtungen zwischen Vertragspartnern in verschiedenen Staaten zur Lieferung beweglicher Güter begründen und die weiteren Voraussetzungen für die Anwendung des CISG gegeben sind.[256] **Bedarfsdeckungsverträge,** die zur Lieferung auf Abruf des Berechtigten verpflichten, fallen deshalb ebenso unter das CISG[257] wie **output-contracts,** in denen sich jemand zur Abnahme von im Einzelnen noch zu vereinbarenden oder einseitig zu bestimmenden Mengen verpflichtet. Auch „la promesse de vente vaut vente" (vgl. Art. 1589 Cc), falls die Parteien über Preis und Ware einig sind, und unterfällt dem CISG. **Vertriebs-, Vertragshändler-** oder **Eigenhändlerverträge, Joint Venture-Verträge, Agenturverträge** usw. können dagegen nur dann als – im Wesentlichen – Kaufverträge beurteilt werden, wenn mit ihrem Abschluss bereits konkrete Lieferungs- und Abnahmepflichten zwischen den Parteien begründet werden[258] und die sonstigen Pflichten, etwa zu Dienstleistungen (Werbung, Kundenbetreuung, Bevorratung von Ersatzteilen, usw.) daneben

---

[252] *Schroeter,* UN-Kaufrecht, § 6, Rn. 317 f.
[253] Dabei kommt es nicht darauf an, ob die betreffende Aufklärungspflicht fahrlässig (dazu bereits Rn. 37) oder aber ohne Verschulden verletzt wurde. Neben dem CISG anwendbar bleiben allerdings Rechte infolge fraudulösen Parteiverhaltens; s. oben Rn. 36.
[254] Vgl. RB Hasselt, 19. 4, 2006, CISG-online 1389; *Honsell/Siehr,* Art. 4, Rn. 9; *Köhler,* Spannungsverhältnis, S. 256; *Schlechtriem,* Internationales UN-Kaufrecht, Rn. 42; *Witz/Salger/Lorenz/Lorenz,* Art. 4, Rn. 12.
[255] Zur Abgrenzung von Option, Vorvertrag und bindendem Angebot s. OLG Hamburg, 15.2.1991, EWiR 1991, 547 *(Kramer).*
[256] Wie hier *Grunewald,* Kaufrecht, § 2, Rn. 60 f.; *Honsell/Dornis,* Vorbem 14–24, Rn. 2; MünchKomm/ *Gruber,* Vor Art. 14, Rn. 5, Art. 14, Rn. 3; *Schwenzer/Mohs,* IHR 2006, 239, 240; s. auch *Torsello,* Preliminary Agreements, S. 233 ff.
[257] Civ. 1, 30.6.2004, CISG-online 870 m. Anm. *Schumacher,* IHR 2005, 147 ff.
[258] *Viva Vino Import Corp. v. Farnese Vini S. r. l.,* U. S. Dist. Ct. (E. D. Pa.), 29.8.2000, CISG-online 675 = IHR 2002, 28: für Exklusivvertriebsvereinbarung und Kommissionsvereinbarung im konkreten Fall verneint, weil Warenmenge und Preis darin nicht bestimmt waren; zu Recht kritisch *Thiele,* IHR 2002, 8, 11.

geringes Gewicht – s. Art. 3 II – haben;[259] ansonsten ist der Rahmenvertrag nach dem vom IPR bestimmten nationalen Recht zu beurteilen, während die einzelnen Lieferverträge zwischen Händler und Hersteller dem CISG unterliegen können.[260] Fällt ein Rahmen- oder Vorvertrag unter das CISG, dann werden die Mindesterfordernisse an die Offerte nach Art. 14 I 2, insbes. Menge und Preis, erst in den auf Grund des Rahmenvertrages abzuschließenden Einzelvereinbarungen bzw. im Hauptvertrag in Vollzug des Vorvertrages festgelegt, doch genügt eine solche von den Parteien selbst vorgesehene spätere Konkretisierung dem Bestimmtheitserfordernis.[261]

V. Vertragsschluss und Vertragsinhalt

42 Die in Artt. 14 ff. geregelten Erklärungen bewirken nicht nur den Abschluss des Vertrages, sondern sind auch die Instrumente zur Gestaltung seines Inhalts; sie sind Akt und Regelung.[262] Die Anforderungen an die Offerte sind gleichzeitig Anforderungen an den Mindestinhalt des Vertrages; die Vorschriften über die modifizierende Annahme (Art. 19) regeln, auf welchem Wege der Annehmende den Vertragsinhalt beeinflussen bzw. zu beeinflussen versuchen kann. Diese Gleichsetzung von vertragsschlusskonstituierenden Erklärungen und Inhaltsgestaltung des Vertrages stellt eine Schwäche des auf „Angebot" und „Annahme" beruhenden Regelungsmodells dar: Werden Vertragsschluss und Ausgestaltung des Vertragsinhalts grundsätzlich an die gleichen Erklärungen gebunden, dann wird bei Divergenzen in den Erklärungen – etwa durch Verwendung unterschiedlicher Standardbedingungen – ein entsprechender Dissens stets zum Gültigkeitsproblem, wie Art. 19 CISG zeigt, der nur bei einem Dissens über unwesentliche Punkte Erleichterungen für den Vertragsschluss vorsieht (Art. 19 II).[263]

43 Grundlage für die in Offerte und Annahme genutzten Gestaltungsmöglichkeiten ist die in Art. 6 verankerte und in anderen Vorschriften ausdrücklich vorausgesetzte **Parteiautonomie**.[264] Damit gewinnen auch die nach Art. 4 S. 2 lit. a) zu berücksichtigenden materiellen Gültigkeitsvorschriften Bedeutung: Verbietet eine – anwendbare – nationale Rechtsregel Zahlungsverpflichtungen in Fremdwährung, dann kann daran schon eine Offerte scheitern, die eine unwirksame bzw. nicht wirksam zu vereinbarende Preisfestsetzung in Devisen enthält. Parteiautonomie gestattet, wie oben in Rn. 23 f. festgehalten, auch ein Abweichen von den geregelten Vertragsschlusserfordernissen und für die Inhaltsgestaltung maßgebenden Regeln, doch unterliegen entsprechende Abreden natürlich eben-

---

[259] Zuweilen wenden Gerichte das CISG auch unreflektiert auf Vertriebsverträge an, s. *Medical Marketing International, Inc. v. Internazionale Medico Sientifica S. R. L.*, U. S. Dist. Ct. (E. D. La.), 17.5.1999, CISG-online 387 m. Anm. *Schlechtriem*, IPRax 1999, 388; Fővárosi Bíróság Budapest, 17.6.1997, CISG-online 288.

[260] *Amco Ukrservice & Promriladamco v. American Meter Company*, U. S. Dist. Ct. (E. D. Pa.), 29.3.2004, CISG-online 1409 = 312 F. Supp. 2d 681, 687 (Joint Venture-Vertrag); BGH, 23.7.1997, CISG-online 276 = NJW 1997, 3309 ff. („Benetton II" – Franchisevertrag); *Helen Kaminski Pty. Ltd. v. Marketing Australian Products Inc.*, U. S. Dist. Ct. (S. D. N. Y.), 23.7.1997, CISG-online 297 (Vertragshändlervertrag); OLG Düsseldorf, 11.7.1996, CISG-online 201 = EWiR 1996, 843 *(Schlechtriem)* (Alleinvertriebsvertrag); OLG München, 22.9.1995, CISG-online 208 = RIW 1996, 1035 (Vertragshändlervertrag); *Soergel/Lüderitz/Fenge*, Art. 1, Rn. 22; *Staudinger/Magnus*, Art. 1, Rn. 37; *Witz/Salger/Lorenz/Lorenz*, Art. 1, Rn. 7; zum Ganzen s. oben *Ferrari*, Art. 1 Rn. 31; *Schlechtriem*, Internationales UN-Kaufrecht, Rn. 24a.

[261] S. unten Art. 14 Rn. 9; Civ. 1, 30.6.2004, CISG-online 870; im Ergebnis ebenfalls wie hier, aber in der Begründung bedenklich *Genpharm Inc. v. Pliva-Lachema A. S.*, U. S. Dist. Ct. (E. D. N. Y.), 19.3.2005, CISG-online 1006 = 361 F. Supp. 2d 49, 55 (Auslegung des CISG anhand von Rspr. zur Art. 2 UCC – zur Unvereinbarkeit dieser Vorgehensweise mit Art. 7 I s. oben *Ferrari*, Art. 7 Rn. 9 f.). A. A. *Viva Vino Import Corp. v. Farnese Vini S. r. l.*, U. S. Dist. Ct. (E. D. Pa.), 29.8.2000, CISG-online 675 = IHR 2002, 28; *Gruppo Essenziero Italiano, S. p. A. v. Aromi D'Italia, Inc.*, U. S. Dist. Ct. (D. Md.), 27.7.2011, CISG-online 2223.

[262] Hierzu *Flume*, Das Rechtsgeschäft, § 6 I, S. 78 f.

[263] S. dazu näher unten Art. 19 Rn. 25.

[264] Vgl. z. B. Artt. 30, 53 („... nach Maßgabe des Vertrages ..."), Art. 35 („Anforderungen des Vertrages ...").

falls der Gültigkeitskontrolle des über Art. 4 S. 2 lit. a) zu berücksichtigenden nationalen Rechts.[265]

VI. Vorbehalt nach Art. 92

Die Aufspaltung des Haager Einheitskaufrechts in zwei Abkommen ermöglichte es, entweder nur den Abschlussteil oder nur das materielle Kaufrecht zu übernehmen. Entsprechende Bedürfnisse wurden auch für das CISG geltend gemacht, als man sich für eine Integration der Abschlussregeln in das geplante Einheitskaufrecht entschloss.[266] In Wien wurde deshalb in Art. 92 I eine Vorbehaltsmöglichkeit aufgenommen, die Staaten den Beitritt zum Übereinkommen bzw. dessen Ratifikation ohne Teil II gestattet. Sie wurde anfänglich von den **skandinavischen Staaten** genutzt, sodass das Übereinkommen für diese Staaten zunächst ohne Teil II in Kraft trat. Nachdem Zweifel an der Sinnhaftigkeit dieser Vorbehaltserklärungen aufgekommen waren,[267] haben sich die skandinavischen Staaten zwischenzeitlich allerdings übereinstimmend entschlossen, ihre Art. 92-Vorbehalte in Übereinstimmung mit Art. 97 IV, V **zurückzunehmen**. Die entsprechenden Formalitäten wurden überwiegend im Jahre 2012 abgeschlossen, sodass die praktische Bedeutung des Vorbehalts mittelfristig entfallen wird. Für eine **Übergangszeit** behält Art. 92 jedoch zunächst seine Relevanz; der für die Beurteilung des Vertragsstaatenstatus (Rn. 45) entscheidende Zeitpunkt bestimmt sich nach Art. 100 I.[268] **44**

Da **Vorbehaltsstaaten** gemäß Art. 92 II **nicht als Vertragsstaaten** nach Art. 1 I lit. a) gelten, ist bei einem Kaufvertrag zwischen deutschen oder anderen Parteien in Vertragsstaaten und Partnern in Vorbehaltsstaaten Teil II nicht anzuwenden.[269] Wenn freilich der Forumstaat – auch dann, wenn es sich um einen Vorbehaltsstaat handelt – das CISG auf Grund einer Verweisung nach Art. 1 I lit. b) als Recht eines Vertragsstaates anwendet, muss auch der Vertragsschlussteil des Übereinkommens angewendet werden, falls dieser Vertragsstaat nicht selbst Vorbehaltsstaat ist:[270] Wenn Art. 1 I b) zur Anwendung des CISG sogar gegenüber Partnern in Nichtvertragsstaaten führen kann, muss Teil II auch gegenüber Parteien in Vorbehaltsstaaten anwendbar sein. Der Partei im Vorbehaltsstaat geschieht damit kein Nachteil, denn für sie fremdes Abschlussrecht muss sie ohnehin – auf Grund des IPR des Forums – hinnehmen, und bei der Wahl zwischen unvereinheitlichtem oder vereinheitlichtem Recht dürfte für sie das vereinheitlichte Recht, weil im Zweifel leichter zu erschließen, zudem vorzugswürdig sein. Bei einem Kaufvertrag zwischen in der Bundesrepublik und – z. B. – Norwegen niedergelassenen Parteien haben deutsche Gerichte also auch dann Teil II des CISG anzuwenden, wenn zum Zeitpunkt des Kaufvertragsabschlusses (Art. 100 I) für Norwegen noch der Art. 92-Vorbehalt galt, und zwar nicht auf Grund von Art. 1 I lit. a), sondern auf Grund von Art. 1 I lit. b), falls auf deutsches Recht – etwa als Verkäuferrecht nach Art. 4 I lit. a) Rom I-VO – verwiesen wird,[271] nicht dagegen die §§ 145 ff. BGB. **45**

---

[265] Zum Zusammenspiel nationaler Vorschriften mit den Vertragsschlussregelungen des Übereinkommens bei der Einbeziehungs- und Inhaltskontrolle Allgemeiner Geschäftsbedingungen s. bereits oben Rn. 3 ff. sowie unten Art. 14 Rn. 33 ff.
[266] S. YB IX (1978), S. 13, Nr. 17.
[267] S. hierzu umfassend die Beiträge in *Kleineman*, CISG Part II Conference (2009).
[268] Zu den Vorbehaltsstaaten s. unten Anhang I.
[269] *Valero Marketing & Supply Company v. Greeni Oy*, U. S. Dist. Ct. (D. N. J.), 15.6.2005, CISG-online 1028 = 373 F. Supp. 2d 475, 480 (U. S.-amerikanisch-finnischer Kaufvertrag). Unzutreffend OLG Dresden, 30.11.2010, CISG-online 2183 = IHR 2011, 142, 144: Teil II des CISG angewandt auf dänisch-deutschen Kaufvertrag.
[270] Vgl. *Schroeter*, FS Kritzer, S. 439; zur Anwendung von Teil II durch Gerichte in skandinavischen (Vorbehalts-)Staaten *Lookofsky*, 18 J. L. & Com. (1999), 289 ff.; *Steensgaard*, Standardbetingelser, § 7, Rn. 1 ff.
[271] Wie hier (zur Situation skandinavischer Länder) *Lookofsky*, 39 Am. J. Comp. L. (1991), 403, 405; *Schroeter*, FS Kritzer, S. 439; unklar OLG München, 8.3.1995, CISG-online 145 = NJW-RR 1996, 1532 f. (deutsch-finnischer Kaufvertrag): Auf das anwendbare nationale Rechts sei nicht zurückzugreifen, da das CISG andere Formen des Vertragsschlusses zulasse (also doch anwendbar ist?); im Übrigen sei auch nach finnischem Recht ein wirksamer Vertragsschluss anzunehmen.

VII. Ausstrahlungswirkung des Teil II

1. Vorbildfunktion der Artt. 14–24 für andere Einheitsrechte und nationale Rechtsreformen

46 Über seine Rolle im Rahmen des UN-Kaufrechts hinaus ist dem Vertragsschlussrecht des Übereinkommens dadurch noch eine weitere Funktion zugewachsen, dass es seit seiner Annahme im Jahre 1980 verschiedenen neueren Vertragsschlussregelungen zum Vorbild gedient hat. Diese **Vorbildfunktion**[272] der Artt. 14–24 ist zum einen durch ihre legislative Qualität und zum anderen durch den Umstand erklärbar, dass Teil II des CISG – obgleich als Bestandteil eines kaufrechtlichen Übereinkommens geschaffen – Bestimmungen enthält, die in der Sache zur Beurteilung jeglichen materiellen Parteikonsenses taugen.[273] Sie eignen sich daher auch als Modell für allgemeine, d. h. vertragstypenübergreifend konzipierte Vertragsschlussrechte, die nach deutschem Vorverständnis systematisch dem allgemeinen Schuldrecht oder sogar dem Allgemeinen Teil des Bürgerlichen Rechts zugeordnet würden,[274] und sind verschiedentlich in diesem Sinne verwandt worden.

47 So haben die Artt. 14–24 zunächst verschiedenen **einheitsrechtlichen Texten** zum Vorbild gedient. Dies gilt etwa für die PICC, die als Vertragsgrundsätze mit globalem Geltungsbereich formuliert wurden; Artt. 2.1.1 ff. PICC übernehmen zahlreiche Bestimmungen wörtlich aus Teil II des UN-Kaufrechts.[275] Innerhalb Europas ist das Vertragsschlussrecht des CISG sodann bei Schaffung der PECL als „besonders ergiebige Inspirationsquelle" genutzt worden.[276] Die inhaltlich auf den PECL aufbauenden Vertragsschlussregeln in Artt. II–4:101 ff. DCFR sowie Artt. 30 ff. des Vorschlags für ein „Gemeinsames Europäisches Kaufrecht" der EU (CESL) orientieren sich ebenfalls auffallend eng an Artt. 14–24 CISG und sehen nur in ganz vereinzelten Punkten eine abweichende Lösung vor. Aus dem afrikanischen Raum ist schließlich das Vertragsschlussrecht für Handelskäufe des einheitlichen allgemeinen Handelsrechts der OHADA (Artt. 241 ff. AUDCG) zu nennen, das sich in seiner Struktur wie im Detail am UN-Kaufrecht ausrichtet.[277]

48 Darüber hinaus haben die Regelungen in Teil II Einfluss auf verschiedene **nationale Rechte** gehabt,[278] deren Bestimmungen zum Vertragsschluss den Artt. 14–24 im Zuge jüngerer Rechtsreformen ganz oder zum Teil nachgebildet wurden.[279] Zu nennen sind aus dem europäischen Raum etwa das niederländische Recht mit seinem NBW aus dem Jahre 1992 (dessen Artt. 6:217 ff. freilich bereits durch das EAG, den Vorgänger des CISG, beeinflusst wurden),[280] das estnische Recht in Gestalt der §§ 9 ff. des estnischen Schuldrechtsgesetzes aus dem Jahre 2001[281] und das polnische Recht, dessen im Kodeks civilny niedergelegte Vertragsschlussregeln in enger Anlehnung an das UN-Kaufrecht reformiert wur-

---

[272] *Schlechtriem*, IHR 2001, 12 stuft den Einfluss des UN-Kaufrechts auf die legislatorische Rechtsentwicklung sogar als den „langfristig vielleicht bedeutendsten" Teil der Erfolgsgeschichte des Einheitskaufrechts ein; *Schroeter*, UN-Kaufrecht, § 18, Rn. 25.

[273] *Enderlein/Maskow/Strohbach*, Vor Art. 14, Anm. 8.; *Magnus*, ZEuP 1993, 79, 80; *Ramberg*, European L. Rev. 2001, 429, 431; *Schroeter*, UN-Kaufrecht, § 18, Rn. 30.

[274] *Schlechtriem*, Juridica Int. 2001, 16, 19.

[275] Vgl. dazu (mit gelegentlich kritischen Untertönen) *Vogenauer/Kleinheisterkamp/Kleinheisterkamp*, Art. 2.1.3, Rn. 2, Art. 2.1.5, Rn. 1 und öfter: „The PICC, sticking literally to the CISG…"; *Jansen/Zimmermann*, Oxford J. Legal Stud. 2011, 1, 13.

[276] Vgl. *von Bar/Zimmermann*, Grundregeln des Europäischen Vertragsrechts, S. XXVII. Hinzu tritt eine mittelbare Beeinflussung der PECL, weil diese auf die (ihrerseits durch das CISG beeinflussten) PICC aufbauen; vgl. *Jansen/Zimmermann*, Oxford J. Legal Stud. 2011, 1, 14.

[277] *Schroeter*, RiAfr 2001, 163, 167.

[278] Vgl. allgemein zur Bedeutung des CISG für nationale Rechtsreformen *Ferrari*, CISG and Its Impact, S. 471 ff.

[279] *Ranieri*, Europ. Obligationenrecht, S. 176.

[280] *Hartkamp*, AcP 191 (1991), 396, 403; *ders.*, RabelsZ 57 (1993), 664, 674; *Kruisinga*, 13.2 Electr. J. Comp. L. (May 2009), 1, 2 und 8 f.

[281] *Kull*, Juridica Int. 2008, 122, 128; *Sein/Kull*, IHR 2005, 138, 139 f.; *Varul*, Uniform L. Rev. 2003, 209.

den.²⁸² In Asien gilt dasselbe für das Recht der Volksrepublik China, wo der Inhalt der Artt. 9 ff. des Vertragsgesetzes an Teil II des CISG ausgerichtet wurde.²⁸³

Die enge Orientierung der neueren Gesetzestexte am Teil II belegt zunächst die **Sachgerechtigkeit** der Lösungen, die im Vertragsschlussrecht des Übereinkommens niedergelegt wurden. Soweit jenem nachgebildete Einheitsrechtstexte und nationale Rechte **inhaltliche Abweichungen** von dem Wortlaut der Artt. 14–24 aufweisen, beziehen diese sich regelmäßig auf isolierte Gegenstände, deren Regelung im Übereinkommenstext allgemein als verbesserungswürdig eingestuft wird. Dies sind namentlich die Anforderungen des Art. 14 I 2 an die Bestimmbarkeit des Preises bei Angebotsabgabe *(pretium certum)*,²⁸⁴ von denen außerhalb des UN-Kaufrechts regelmäßig zugunsten der Lösung in Art. 55 (hilfsweiser Rückgriff auf den unter vergleichbaren Umständen üblicherweise berechneten Preis) abgewichen wird,²⁸⁵ weil so von vornherein ein Konflikt zwischen beiden Vorschriften vermieden wird²⁸⁶ und die *pretium certum*-Vorgabe des Art. 14 I 2 als für heutige internationale Handelsverträge nicht angemessen gilt,²⁸⁷ sowie der im CISG nicht gesondert geregelte Konflikt zwischen Standardbedingungen („battle of the forms"),²⁸⁸ für den neuere Texte überwiegend ausdrückliche Lösungen i. S. der sog. „knock-out rule" (Restgültigkeitslösung) anordnen.²⁸⁹ Der Unterschied zum Teil II des UN-Kaufrechts besteht dabei vielfach nur in dem abweichenden Wortlaut der Vorschriften, wohingegen die betreffenden Sachlösungen auch unter dem Übereinkommen bereits durch die Literatur entwickelt und in der Rechtsprechung angewandt wurden;²⁹⁰ die neueren Texte vollziehen daher den bestehenden Rechtszustand unter der *„Convention in action"* regelmäßig nur nach.

2. Folgen für die Auslegung

Die beschriebene Vorbildfunktion des UN-Kaufrechts wirft die Frage auf, ob und inwieweit sich auch die Auslegung der inhaltsähnlichen Regelwerke wechselseitig beeinflussen darf. Bei ihrer Beantwortung muss zwischen zwei Ausstrahlungsrichtungen unterschieden werden:

a) **Ausstrahlung des Teil II auf die Auslegung anderer Rechtsakte.** Vor dem Hintergrund des Umstands, dass der Wortlaut neuerer Rechtsakte bewusst am Vorbild der Artt. 14–24 ausgerichtet wurde, will die Literatur²⁹¹ diese Vorbildfunktion auf die **Interpretation** der Rechtsakte **erstrecken**. Dabei wird auch dort für eine Orientierung am CISG eingetreten, wo das Übereinkommen zu einzelnen Sachfragen gar keine ausdrückliche Vorschrift enthält, aber Rechtsprechung und Schrifttum in dessen Interpretation und Fortbildung vorbildtaugliche Lösungen entwickelt haben.²⁹² Die Rechtsprechung ist diesem Ansatz gefolgt und hat etwa bei Auslegung des Vertragsschlussrechts des niederländischen

---

²⁸² *Zoll*, RabelsZ 71 (2007), 81, 83 ff.: „… the main ideas were taken directly from the Convention."
²⁸³ *Han*, S. 84 f.
²⁸⁴ S. unten Art. 14 Rn. 16 ff.
²⁸⁵ So in Art. 2.1.2 PICC; Artt. 2:101, 2:201 PECL; Art. II–4:103 DCFR; Artt. 30 f. CESL-Entwurf; Art. 9 I estnisches SchuldrechtsG. Anders dagegen Art. 241 II AUDCG, wo am Erfordernis eines bestimmbaren Preises festgehalten wird; kritisch dazu *Schroeter*, RiAfr 2001, 163, 168.
²⁸⁶ So zu Art. 9 I und Art. 28 estnisches SchuldrechtsG *Sein/Kull*, IHR 2005, 138, 139.
²⁸⁷ So zu Art. 2.1.2 PICC *Vogenauer/Kleinheisterkamp/Kleinheisterkamp*, Art. 2.1.2, Rn. 24; zu Art. 2:101 PECL *Luig*, S. 75.
²⁸⁸ S. unten Art. 19 Rn. 19 ff.
²⁸⁹ So in Art. 2.1.22 PICC; Art. 2:209 PECL; Art. II–4:209 DCFR; Art. 39 CESL-Entwurf; § 21 III estnisches SchuldrechtsG (dazu *Sein/Kull*, IHR 2005, 138, 139); Art. 385 polnischer Kodeks civilny (dazu *Liebscher/Zoll*, in: *dies.*, § 5, Rn. 35). Anders aber das niederländische Recht, das in Art. 6:225 III NBW eine „first shot rule" vorsieht; vgl. dazu *Hartkamp*, AcP 191 (1991), 396, 403.
²⁹⁰ Dies gilt sowohl für den Konflikt zwischen Art. 14 I 2 und Art. 55 (s. dazu unten Art. 14 Rn. 20 ff.) als auch die Restgültigkeitslösung für das Problem des „battle of the forms" (dazu unten Art. 19 Rn. 25 ff.).
²⁹¹ Zum estnischen Recht *Sein/Kull*, IHR 2005, 138 f.; zum niederländischen Recht *Kruisinga*, 13.2 Electr. J. Comp. L. (May 2009), 1, 20.
²⁹² In diesem Sinne (zu den PICC) *Vogenauer/Kleinheisterkamp/Naudé*, Intro to Arts 2.1.9–2.1.22, Rn. 3.

NBW auf Vorschriften des UN-Kaufrechts zurückgegriffen.[293] Dem ist zuzustimmen, weil auf diese Weise im Wege einer historisch-systematischen Interpretation der nachgebildeten Einheits- und nationalen Rechte[294] sichergestellt werden kann, dass die angestrebte inhaltliche Parallelität mit dem CISG erhalten bleibt. Richter und Schiedsrichter haben entsprechende Vorschriften, die bestimmten Normen im Teil II des UN-Kaufrechts ähneln, daher im Zweifel identisch zu verstehen.[295]

52 **b) Verbot der Auslegung des Teil II im Lichte anderer Rechtsakte (Art. 7 I).** Des Weiteren wird in Teilen des Schrifttums dafür eingetreten, die Vertragsschlussbestimmungen der PICC,[296] der PECL[297] sowie nationaler Rechte – gleichsam umgekehrt – auch im Rahmen der Auslegung der Artt. 14–24 als Interpretationshilfen heranzuziehen. Dieser Ansatz ist **abzulehnen**, weil er mit den Vorgaben des Art. 7 I unvereinbar ist:[298] Das Gebot der autonomen Auslegung des Übereinkommens, das Art. 7 I in Übereinstimmung mit der ganz h. M.[299] zu entnehmen ist, bedeutet zugleich ein Verbot der Auslegung (auch) der Artt. 14–24 „im Lichte", „in Anlehnung an" oder „anhand" mutmaßlich vergleichbarer anderer Rechtsakte. Dieses Verbot, das der interpretativen Ausstrahlung sowohl von Einheitsrechtsakten und -prinzipien als auch nationaler Vertragsschlussrechte gleichermaßen entgegensteht, ist **streng** durchzuhalten. Es darf keinesfalls durch die Unterstellung ausgehebelt werden, in zeitlich später entstandenen Regelwerken seien die dem UN-Kaufrecht zugrunde liegenden allgemeinen Grundsätze (Art. 7 II) kodifiziert worden, sodass über die Konstruktion einer angeblichen „internen Lücke" im Vertragsschlussrecht des CISG ein Rückgriff auf konkurrierende (und inhaltlich nicht immer kongruente) Einheitsrechtstexte eröffnet wäre.[300] Andere Vertragsschlussregeln können daher ausschließlich in den seltenen Fällen zur Anwendung gelangen, in denen Teil II des UN-Kaufrechts für eine bestimmte Sachfrage weder ausdrückliche Bestimmungen noch allgemeine Grundsätze bereit hält,[301] also eine „externe Lücke" vorliegt.

---

[293] RB Utrecht, 1.8.2001, CISG-online 2299 = NJ 2002, 157: Übertragung des Angebotsbegriffs des Art. 14.
[294] S. dazu *Schroeter*, UN-Kaufrecht, § 17, Rn. 26.
[295] Vgl. *Schroeter*, UN-Kaufrecht, § 17, Rn. 26.
[296] *Bonell*, 10 Wuhan U. Int'l L. Rev. (2008/09), 100, 110 ff.; *Vogenauer/Kleinheisterkamp/Michaels*, Preamble I, Rn. 99 ff.; *Luig*, S. 20 ff., 247.
[297] *Luig*, S. 30 f., 247.
[298] Wie hier *Janssen*, IHR 2004, 194, 198; *Sein/Kull*, IHR 2005, 138, 139; *Steensgaard*, Standardbetingelser, § 2, Rn. 46 ff.
[299] S. nur *Schlechtriem/Schwenzer/Schwenzer/Hachem*, CISG Commentary, Art. 7, Rn. 8 m. w. N.
[300] Vgl. dazu *Schroeter*, UN-Kaufrecht, § 20, Rn. 8 ff.
[301] S. bereits oben Rn. 17.

Art. 14 [Begriff des Angebots]

(1) Der an eine oder mehrere bestimmte Personen gerichtete Vorschlag zum Abschluß eines Vertrages stellt ein Angebot dar, wenn er bestimmt genug ist und den Willen des Anbietenden zum Ausdruck bringt, im Falle der Annahme gebunden zu sein. Ein Vorschlag ist bestimmt genug, wenn er die Ware bezeichnet und ausdrücklich oder stillschweigend die Menge und den Preis festsetzt oder deren Festsetzung ermöglicht.

(2) Ein Vorschlag, der nicht an eine oder mehrere bestimmte Personen gerichtet ist, gilt nur als Aufforderung, ein Angebot abzugeben,* wenn nicht die Person, die den Vorschlag macht, das Gegenteil deutlich zum Ausdruck bringt.

Art. 14

(1) A proposal for concluding a contract addressed to one or more specific persons constitutes an offer if it is sufficiently definite and indicates the intention of the offeror to be bound in case of acceptance. A proposal is sufficiently definite if it indicates the goods and expressly or implicitly fixes or makes provision for determining the quantity and the price.

(2) A proposal other than one addressed to one or more specific persons is to be considered merely as an invitation to make offers, unless the contrary is clearly indicated by the person making the proposal.

Art. 14

1) Une proposition de conclure un contrat adressée à une ou plusieurs personnes déterminées constitue une offre si elle est suffisamment précise et si elle indique la volonté de son auteur d'être lié en cas d'acceptation. Une proposition est suffisamment précise lorsqu'elle désigne les marchandises et, expressément ou implicitement, fixe la quantité et le prix ou donne des indications permettant de les déterminer.

2) Une proposition adressée à des personnes indéterminées est considérée seulement comme une invitation à l'offre, à moins que la personne qui a fait la proposition n'ait clairement indiqué le contraire.

Übersicht

	Rn.
I. Grundlagen	1
II. Bestimmtheit bzw. Bestimmbarkeit des Mindestinhalts	2
1. Mindestinhalt	3
a) Ware, Menge und Preis	3
b) Identität der Vertragsparteien	4
c) Sonstige Vertragsdetails	5
d) Fehlendes Mindesterfordernis	6
e) Beweislast	7
2. Bestimmtheit bzw. Bestimmbarkeit	8
a) Ausdrückliche oder stillschweigende Bestimmung	8
b) Willensmängel	10
c) Bestimmbarkeit	12
3. Bestimmungsbefugnisse	13
a) Bestimmung durch Dritten oder die Parteien	13
b) Bestimmung durch eine Partei	14
c) Tagespreisklauseln	15
III. Unbestimmter Preis	16
1. Bestimmbarkeitserfordernis des Art. 14 I 2	16
2. Entstehungsgeschichtlicher Hintergrund	17
3. Spektrum der Lösungsansätze	19
4. Stellungnahme	20
IV. Bindungswille	23
1. Bindungswille des Offerenten	23

---

* Schweiz: gilt nur als Einladung zu einem Angebot.

2. Maßgeblichkeit der objektiven Erklärungsbedeutung	24
3. Einzelfälle	25
a) „Freibleibend" etc.	25
b) Letters of intent o. ä.	26
c) Fehlender Bindungswille	27
d) Präsentationen im Internet	28
4. Unverbindlichkeit der invitatio ad offerendum, konkurrierende vorvertragliche Pflichten	29
V. Publikumsofferte	30
VI. Bedingtes Angebot	31a
1. Bedingungen bei Vertragsschluss	31a
2. Erfassung durch das CISG	31b
3. Auslegung von Bedingungen	31c
4. Beweislast	31d
VII. Einbeziehung standardisierter Vertragsbedingungen	32
1. Maßgebliche Rechtsvorschriften	33
2. AGB als Bestandteil des Angebots	36
a) Hinweis auf AGB in Angebotserklärung	37
b) Kenntnisnahme des Adressaten vom AGB-Text	39
3. Anforderungen an die Kenntnisverschaffung bezüglich des Inhalts der AGB	43
a) Übersendung	44
b) Anderweitiges Zugänglichmachen	47
aa) Bei Vertragsschluss unter Anwesenden	48
bb) Zurverfügungstellung im Internet	49
cc) Laufende Geschäftsbeziehungen	51
dd) International übliche Standardbedingungen	53
ee) Nicht ausreichend	55
c) Gestaltung des AGB-Textes	56
d) Änderung des AGB-Textes	58
4. Zeitpunkt der Kenntnis	59
5. Sprache der AGB	61
a) Verhandlungssprache	62
b) Vertragssprache	63
c) Sonstige, dem Adressaten verständliche Sprache	64
d) „Weltsprache"	65
e) AGB in mehreren Sprachfassungen	67
6. Einbeziehung der AGB in das Angebot nach Artt. 8 III, 9	68
a) Einbeziehung bestimmter AGB als Parteigepflogenheit	69
b) AGB als internationaler Handelsbrauch	73
7. Annahme des Angebots	74
8. Beweislast	76

Vorläufer und **Entwürfe:** Art. 4 EAG, New Yorker E 1977 Art. 4, Genfer E 1977 Art. 8, New Yorker E 1978 Art. 12.

I. Grundlagen

1 Wie in den Vorbemerkungen zu Artt. 14–24 (Rn. 15) kritisch angemerkt, beruht der Vertragsschluss nach CISG auf den beiden Willenserklärungen „Angebot" und „Annahme", die deshalb eine eingehende Regelung erfahren haben, während andere Vertragsschlussmöglichkeiten ungeregelt geblieben sind. Die Offerte ist **Willenserklärung,** so dass sie nicht nur den in Art. 14 geregelten Voraussetzungen entsprechen muss, sondern auch den Vorschriften unvereinheitlichten, durch IPR berufenen nationalen Rechts zur Wirksamkeit von Willenserklärungen, also zur Geschäftsfähigkeit, Irrtumsfreiheit, Vertretungsmacht.[1] Das Personalstatut des Erklärenden bestimmt über seine Geschäftsfähigkeit, das Vollmachtsstatut

---

[1] S. oben Vor Artt. 14–24 Rn. 2.

über seine wirksame Vertretung kraft Vollmacht, das Gesellschaftsstatut über die Rechtsmacht des erklärenden Organs.

Als entscheidende Voraussetzungen für die Willenserklärung „**Offerte**" regelt Art. 14 I **Verpflichtungswillen** und einen erforderlichen **Mindestinhalt**.[2] Aus der Vorschrift werden darüber hinaus auch die Anforderungen an die praktisch wichtige Einbeziehung standardisierter Vertragsbedingungen (AGB) in CISG-Verträge abgeleitet (Rn. 32 ff.).

II. Bestimmtheit bzw. Bestimmbarkeit des Mindestinhalts

Der Vorschlag zum Vertragsschluss muss, um Offerte sein zu können, bestimmt genug 2 sein, um im Falle der Annahme einen durchführbaren Vertrag mit Pflichten, die Grundlage gerichtlicher Urteile sein können, zustande kommen zu lassen.[3] Bezeichnung als „Angebot", „Offerte" usw. ist nicht erforderlich;[4] auch eine Auftragsbestätigung,[5] ein sonstiges Bestätigungsschreiben,[6] eine sog. Pro-forma-Rechnung[7] oder eine Rechnung[8] können ein Angebot sein.

1. Mindestinhalt

a) Ware, Menge und Preis. Die „**essentialia contractus**" müssen so vorgeschlagen 3 worden sein, dass die positive Gegenerklärung des Adressaten und die ergänzend eingreifenden Bestimmungen des Gesetzes einen Vertrag mit durchführbarem Inhalt zustande bringen können. Als Mindestbestandteile legt Art. 14 I 2 dabei die **Ware**, ihre **Menge** und den **Preis** fest.[9] Nicht zwingend erforderlich ist die Spezifizierung einzelner Wareneigenschaften, wie die Regelung des Art. 65 zeigt;[10] ein Angebot zur Veräußerung von KfZ, das die zu liefernden Fahrzeugmodelle benennt, aber deren Farbe und Ausstattung explizit offen lässt[11] oder eine Offerte zum Kauf von Damendessous, die Klärungsbedarf hinsichtlich der Größe der zu produzierenden Teile signalisiert,[12] sind daher ausreichend bestimmt.

b) Identität der Vertragsparteien. Das kann freilich immer noch zu wenig sein:[13] In 4 Art. 14 I 2 nicht ausdrücklich angesprochen, aber stillschweigend vorausgesetzt ist etwa auch, dass die **Person** des **Anbietenden** – also dessen, der durch das Angebot rechtlich gebunden sein soll – bestimmbar ist.[14] Problematisch kann dies in Konstellationen sein, in denen derselbe Vertreter für verschiedene Unternehmen (sowie ggf. im eigenen Namen)

---

[2] Zur Vorgeschichte *Schlechtriem*, 1. und 2. Aufl., Art. 14 Rn. 1.
[3] Vgl. *Bianca/Bonell/Eörsi*, Art. 14, Anm. 2.2.2.: „This requirement has its roots in English court practice."
[4] *Honsell/Dornis*, Art. 14, Rn. 6; *Perales Viscasillas*, Formación del contrato, S. 271.
[5] OLG Jena, 27.8.2008, CISG-online 1820 = NJW 2009, 689.
[6] Tallinna Ringkonnakohus, 19.2.2004, CISG-online 826/827. Zum Vertragsschluss durch Schweigen auf ein kaufmännisches Bestätigungsschreiben s. oben Vor Artt. 14–24 Rn. 18 ff.
[7] *MünchKomm/Gruber*, Art. 14, Rn. 6; *Piltz*, NJW 1996, 2768, 2770; s. auch die Nachw. unten in Rn. 26.
[8] OLG Jena, 27.8.2008, CISG-online 1820 = NJW 2009, 689.
[9] Keine Rolle spielt in diesem Zusammenhang hingegen der Katalog des Art. 19 III, der allein von einem Angebot abweichende Annahmeerklärungen, nicht hingegen den Mindestinhalt eines Angebots betrifft; unzutreffend daher *Kolmar Petrochemicals Americas v. Idesa Petroquímica*, Primer Tribunal Colegiado en Materia Civil del Primer Cicuito, 10.3.2005, CISG-online 1004.
[10] Unten *Mohs*, Art. 65 Rn. 1; *Brunner*, Art. 14, Rn. 5; *Staudinger/Magnus*, Art. 14, Rn. 19.
[11] CIETAC, 23.4.1997, CISG-online 1151.
[12] OLG Dresden, 30.11.2010, CISG-online 2183 = IHR 2011, 142, 144: Produktion der im Angebot genannten Ware sollte erst „nach OK vom Größensatz" beginnen.
[13] Vgl. *Enderlein/Maskow/Strohbach*, Art. 14, Anm. 7.; *MünchKomm/Gruber*, Art. 14, Rn. 14; a. A. *Herber/Czerwenka*, Art. 14, Rn. 7.
[14] Vgl. BGer, 4.8.2003, CISG-online 804 = IHR 2004, 28, 31; KG Jura, 3.11.2004, CISG-online 965: Die Frage, ob der Betreiber eines Bauernhofes oder ein Handwerker, der aufgrund eines Werkvertrages Bauarbeiten am Hof vornahm und zu diesem Zweck Baumaterial bestellte, durch den Kaufvertrag gegenüber dem Verkäufer gebunden wurde, betrifft nicht Wirksamkeit i. S. d. Art. 4 lit. a), sondern ist nach Maßgabe der Artt. 14 ff. zu beantworten; OGer Thurgau, 19.12.1995, CISG-online 496 = SZIER 2000, 118 ff.: Bestimmung des Offerenten bemisst sich ausschließlich nach Art. 14 I i. V. m. Art. 8, ohne dass für das Vertretungs-

auftritt,[15] in denen mehrere rechtlich selbstständige Unternehmen mit ähnlicher Firma (häufig Konzernunternehmen) in Frage kommen[16] oder in denen in einer kettenartigen Lieferbeziehung Unklarheit über die Person des Verkäufers[17] bzw. bei Zahlungen durch Dritte Zweifel über die Identität des Käufers auftreten;[18] hier ist die Angebotserklärung nach Art. 8 auszulegen.[19] Zusätzliche Informationen über den Offerenten, wie sie (sofern ausnahmsweise anwendbar) § 312c I 2, II BGB und § 1 I Nr. 1, 2 BGB-InfoV verlangen,[20] sind hingegen nicht Wirksamkeitsvoraussetzung einer Offerte nach CISG.[21]

Zudem muss im Zweifel auch der **Adressat** bestimmt oder bestimmbar sein[22] (vgl. auch Rn. 30 zur Publikumsofferte). Dem in Art. 14 I 1 verwendeten Begriff der „Personen" kommt in diesem Zusammenhang allerdings keine einschränkende Funktion zu; er umfasst natürliche ebenso wie juristische Personen[23] und sonstige Vereinigungen und Verbände.

5   c) **Sonstige Vertragsdetails.** Lieferzeit[24] und Lieferort, selbst die Art der Verpackung[25] können im konkreten Fall ebenfalls „essentialia negotii" sein. Beim Softwarekauf können Lizenzbedingungen wesentlich sein.[26] Ergibt sich aus den Vorverhandlungen oder Gepflo-

---

statut Raum bleibt; *Schwenzer/Mohs,* IHR 2006, 239, 240 (mit dem zutreffenden Hinweis, es müsse zudem erkennbar sein, ob der Anbietende kaufen oder verkaufen wolle).

[15] Vgl. HGer St. Gallen, 5.12.1995, CISG-online 245: Vertreter der Käuferin hatte im Rahmen telefonischer Verhandlungen nicht klar geäußert, für welches Unternehmen er handelte, und den Eindruck erweckt, aufgrund von deren wirtschaftlicher Verflechtung komme diesem Umstand auch keine Bedeutung zu – Käuferin anhand späterer Fax-Bestellung ermittelt; Gerechtshof Arnhem, 14.10.2008, CISG-online 1818 = EJCL 2009, 40 f.: ob der Kaufvertrag im eigenen Namen oder in Vertretung einer juristischen Person geschlossen wurde, wurde durch Auslegung der betreffenden Parteierklärung bestimmt.

[16] OLG Stuttgart, 28.2.2000, CISG-online 583 = IHR 2001, 65, 66: Deutsches Mutter- und spanisches Tochterunternehmen mit identischem Firmenkern („D. AG" bzw. „D. S. A.") und teilweiser Identität der Vorstandsmitglieder – Übersendung von Ware und Rechnungen nach Art. 8 als Angebot des deutschen Mutterunternehmens ausgelegt, weil die Rechnungen in dessen Namen ausgestellt waren; OLG Frankfurt a. M., 30.8.2000, CISG-online 594 = RIW 2001, 383: kein wirksames Angebot eines schweizerischen Garnhandelsunternehmens, weil unklar war, ob im eigenen Namen oder auf Anweisung und im Namen des rechtlich selbstständigen Mutterunternehmens mit identischem Firmenkern und Sitz in Indien gehandelt wurde; OLG Koblenz, 1.3.2010, CISG-online 2126 = NJW-RR 2010, 1004 f.: deutsche Muttergesellschaft (und nicht deren frz. Tochtergesellschaft) durch Auslegung des Angebots als Offerentin identifiziert; LG Hamburg, 26.9.1990, CISG-online 21 = RIW 1990, 1015, 1016 f.: Käuferin unter mehreren in Frage kommenden Unternehmen nach Art. 8 ermittelt.

[17] BGer, 4.8.2003, CISG-online 804 = IHR 2004, 28, 31: Weinlieferung durch italienischen Weinproduzenten an schweizerische Endabnehmerin war kein konkludentes Angebot auf Abschluss eines Kaufvertrages, weil der Produzent bislang stets in Erfüllung von Kaufverträgen mit einem schweizerischen Zwischenhändler geliefert hatte und daher nicht ersichtlich war, dass er nunmehr die Endabnehmerin ein Angebot im eigenen Namen abgeben wollte; *Guang Dong Light Headgear Factory Co., Ltd. v. ACI International, Inc.,* U. S. Dist. Ct. (D. Kan.), 28.9.2007, CISG-online 1602: nach Art. 8 ermittelt, dass Vertrag der U. S.-amerikanischen Käuferin direkt mit der chinesischen Produzentin (und nicht mit einer Vermittlerin) zustande gekommen war.

[18] HR, 7.11.1997, CISG-online 551 = NIPR 1998, Nr. 91: Niederländische Wodkaproduzentin erhielt von der russischen Firma Nordstream per Fax Bestellung mit der Ankündigung, die Überweisung des Kaufpreises werde in Kürze erfolgen. Nachdem Kaufpreis durch einen Dritten überwiesen worden war, behauptete dieser, die Überweisung selbst habe konkludentes Kaufangebot dargestellt, und verlangte Lieferung an sich – das Gericht qualifizierte nach Art. 8 II (nur) Nordstream als Offerentin, weil der Dritte der Verkäuferin bis dato unbekannt gewesen und seine Überweisung zudem mit dem Hinweis „Contract Nordstream Moscow" erfolgt war.

[19] Gerechtshof Arnhem, 14.10.2008, CISG-online 1818 = EJCL 2009, 40 f. ließ offen, ob Art. 8 CISG oder Auslegungsregeln des niederländischen Rechts (Art. 3:35 BW) maßgeblich waren.

[20] Dazu *Janal,* S. 51 f.

[21] S. oben Vor Artt. 14–24 Rn. 39 f.

[22] OGH, 18.6.1997, CISG-online 292 = östJBl. 1998, 255: Angebot gegenüber Handelsvertreter, der für verschiedene Unternehmen tätig war; OGer Thurgau, 19.12.1995, CISG-online 496 = SZIER 2000, 118 ff.; MünchKomm/*Gruber,* Art. 14, Rn. 13.

[23] *Schultz,* 35 Cornell Int'l L. J. (2001-02), 263, 271 Fn. 69.

[24] *Geneva Pharmaceuticals Technology Corp. v. Barr Laboratories, Inc.,* U. S. Dist. Ct. (S. D. N. Y.), 10.5.2002, CISG-online 653 = 201 F. Supp. 2d 236, 282 Fn. 28.

[25] *Neumayer/Ming,* Art. 14, Anm. 4. Fn. 14; s. a. *Audit,* Vente internationale, Anm. 63.

[26] *Witz/Salger/Lorenz/Witz,* Art. 14, Rn. 28.

genheiten der Parteien, dass über solche zusätzlichen, in Art. 14 I 2 nicht genannten Details konkrete Angaben in der Offerte gemacht und durch Annahme vereinbart werden müssen, dann ist ein Vorschlag ohne solche Details ebenfalls keine Offerte.[27] Auch kann, wenn solche weiteren Details von den Parteien als wesentlich bewertet worden sind, einem Vorschlag ohne diese Details noch der Bindungswille[28] fehlen. Regelmäßig werden sich jedoch die für den Vertrag erforderlichen weiteren Einzelheiten durch Auslegung der Offerte nach Art. 8[29] und auf Grund ihrer Ergänzung durch die Vorschriften der Konvention, etwa zum Lieferort oder zur Lieferzeit, vervollständigen lassen.

d) Fehlendes Mindesterfordernis. Fehlt ein Mindesterfordernis, dann kann der Vorschlag grundsätzlich nicht als Offerte gelten und deshalb auch nicht Grundlage eines Vertrages sein. Dies gilt etwa in Fällen, in denen der Vorschlag alternativ zwei unterschiedliche Kaufgegenstände nennt und keinerlei Anhaltspunkte dafür vorliegen, welche Ware bei Abschluss eines Kaufvertrages mit diesem Inhalt verkauft wäre,[30] oder bei Übersendung einer bloßen Warenprobe.[31] Ein Mindesterfordernis fehlt auch dann, wenn es im Vorschlag enthalten, aber nach einem anwendbaren nationalen Recht mit Nichtigkeitsfolge verboten ist,[32] z. B. die verbotene Vereinbarung eines Preises in fremder Währung,[33] aber auch, wenn die Bedeutung eines Details unklar ist und durch Auslegung nicht geklärt werden kann, z. B. bei Verwendung mehrdeutiger Worte.[34] 6

Parteiautonomie nach Art. 6 erlaubt aber auch, von Art. 14 I 2 abzuweichen.[35] Die Parteien können deshalb z. B. einvernehmlich einen Vorschlag als Offerte gelten lassen, der den Preis offen lässt; die Lücke im Vertrag ist dann durch Art. 55 zu schließen.[36]

e) Beweislast. Die Beweislast für das Vorliegen einer wirksamen Offerte trägt, wer sich darauf beruft.[37] 7

2. Bestimmtheit bzw. Bestimmbarkeit

a) Ausdrückliche oder stillschweigende Bestimmung. Bestimmtheit von Ware, Menge und Preis liegt bei **ausdrücklicher Festsetzung** vor. Die Bezeichnung der Ware kann dabei individuell oder gattungsmäßig erfolgen.[38] Abs. 1 Satz 2 erlaubt aber auch „**stillschweigende Festsetzung**".[39] Da Stillschweigen selbst die Ware, ihre Menge oder den Preis nicht angeben kann, sind damit Anhaltspunkte gemeint, die eine Auslegung ermöglichen, die zu einem bestimmten Preis, einer bestimmten Ware oder (und) ihrer 8

---

[27] Vgl. *Bianca/Bonell/Eörsi*, Art. 14, Anm. 2.2.2.; MünchKomm/*Gruber*, Art. 14, Rn. 15; MünchKommHGB/*Ferrari*, Art. 14, Rn. 5.
[28] Hierzu unten Rn. 23.
[29] S. oben *Schmidt-Kessel*, Art. 8 Rn. 11; Soergel/*Lüderitz/Fenge*, Art. 14, Rn. 4; *Witz/Salger/Lorenz/Witz*, Art. 14, Rn. 30.
[30] Dies wurde in CIETAC, 25.12.1998, CISG-online 1135 angenommen für einen Vertrag über „10.000 MT basic pig iron or foundry pig iron as to be mutually agreed, price to be mutually agreed as well" – wegen mangelnder Bestimmbarkeit (nur) der Ware kein wirksamer Vertragsschluss.
[31] Hof van Beroep Gent, 8.11.2004, CISG-online 982: kein Angebot, da weder Warenmenge noch Preis bestimmbar.
[32] A. A. *Honsell/Dornis*, Art. 14, Rn. 12.
[33] MünchKomm/*Gruber*, Art. 14, Rn. 13.
[34] S. hierzu unten Rn. 16.
[35] Ebenso *Honnold/Flechtner*, Art. 14, Rn. 137.6; *Staudinger/Magnus*, Art. 14, Rn. 3; *Rudolph*, Vor Art. 14, Rn. 7, Art. 14, Rn. 4; MünchKomm/*Gruber*, Art. 14, Rn. 16; Soergel/*Lüderitz/Fenge*, Art. 14, Rn. 4; *Witz/Salger/Lorenz/Witz*, Art. 14, Rn. 13.
[36] S. hierzu unten Rn. 20.
[37] LG Bamberg, 13.4.2005, CISG-online 1402; *Achilles*, Art. 14, Rn. 7; *Bamberger/Roth/Saenger*, Art. 14, Rn. 4; *Baumgärtel/Laumen/Hepting*, Art. 14 WKR, Rn. 1 ff. Für die Behauptung einer vertragsschlusshindernden Lücke ist dagegen der Behauptende beweispflichtig, *Baumgärtel/Laumen/Hepting*, Art. 19 WKR, Rn. 17 f.
[38] *Enderlein/Maskow/Strohbach*, Art. 14, Anm. 7.; *Heuzé*, Anm. 165. f., insbes. zur Verwendung eindeutiger Maßeinheiten zur Vermeidung (versteckter) Dissense.
[39] S. Fovárosi Biróság (Hauptstadtgericht) Budapest, 24.3.1992, CISG-online 61 = IPRax 1993, 263 (Bericht *Vida*).

Menge führt.⁴⁰ Diese Anhaltspunkte können und werden zumeist verbal erklärt werden; so kann unter langjährigen Geschäftspartnern die Angabe einer Zahl genügen, um die Ware und ihre Menge, u. U. auch den Preis zu bezeichnen.⁴¹ Ein auslegungsfähiges Erklärungsverhalten kann aber auch in anderer Form „geäußert" werden, z. B. durch die Übersendung der Ware mit einem Preisschild, die eine entsprechende Offerte zum Ausdruck bringen soll.⁴²

9 Auslegungsmöglichkeiten zur Ermittlung der Mindestanforderungen oder entsprechende Ergänzungen der Erklärung können sich insbes. auf Grund von **Bräuchen** oder **Gepflogenheiten** zwischen den Parteien,⁴³ ihres späteren Verhaltens oder auf Grund von **Rahmenvereinbarungen,** die Einzelne der Mindestbestandteile einer Offerte bereits festlegen und nur noch durch Bezugnahme in Kurzformeln aufgegriffen werden, ergeben.⁴⁴ Haben die Parteien in ihrer mehrjährigen Geschäftsbeziehung stets denselben Stückpreis für die gehandelte Ware zugrunde gelegt, so ist dieser Preis infolge der entstandenen Gepflogenheit (Art. 8 III) auch Bestandteil weiterer Angebote, selbst wenn diese nichts Ausdrückliches zum Preis sagen.⁴⁵ Eine Ziffer allein als Preis wäre an sich ohne Währungsangabe im grenzüberschreitenden Verkehr zu unbestimmt, doch wird sich zumeist durch Auslegung ergeben, in welcher Währung fakturiert werden soll.⁴⁶ Selbiges gilt, wenn die Währung nicht zweifelsfrei benannt worden ist, wie etwa bei einer Preisangabe in Dollar – hier ist durch Auslegung zu ermitteln, ob U. S.-amerikanische, kanadische, australische oder andere Dollar gemeint sind.⁴⁷

10 **b) Willensmängel.** Annahmefähig ist eine Offerte auch dann, wenn der erforderliche Mindestinhalt von „einer vernünftigen Person der gleichen Art" wie der Empfänger „unter gleichen Umständen" ausreichend konkret aufgefasst werden kann, Art. 8 II.⁴⁸ War sie vom Erklärenden nicht so gemeint, dann können nationale Regeln über Willensmängel eingreifen, also etwa **Irrtumsanfechtung.** War dagegen eine Bezeichnung für die oder einzelne

---

⁴⁰ Zustimmend *Honsell/Dornis,* Art. 14, Rn. 15.
⁴¹ Vgl. *Neumayer/Ming,* Art. 14, Anm. 7. Informativ zur Auslegung einer Ausschreibung, um einen ausreichend bestimmten Vertragsinhalt zu ermitteln, BGH, 27.6.1996, WM 1996, 2208, 2209 (kein CISG-Fall).
⁴² Nationales Recht kann freilich diese Angebotsform verbieten, um Konsumenten vor unerwünschten Zusendungen zu schützen, vgl. § 241a I BGB. Ein Verbot mit Nichtigkeitsfolge wäre über Art. 4 S. 2 lit. a) zu beachten. Für Inhalt und Wirkung eines Vertragsangebots geht m. E. das CISG vor, doch kann ein solches nationales Gesetz den Verständnishorizont des Empfängers nach Art. 8 II beeinflussen.
⁴³ Vgl. Fovárosi Biróság (Hauptstadtgericht) Budapest, 24.3.1992, CISG-online 61 = IPRax 1993, 263 (Bericht *Vida*); OGH, 6.2.1996, CISG-online 224 = ZfRVgl 1996, 248, 252: Mengenvereinbarung über „ca. 700–800 t" Flüssiggas entspricht „den im Erdgasgeschäft üblichen Usancen"; *Geneva Pharmaceuticals Technology Corp. v. Barr Laboratories, Inc.,* U. S. Dist. Ct. (S. D. N. Y.), 10.5.2002, CISG-online 653 = 201 F. Supp. 201, 236, 282: „commercial quantities" Clathrat auf Grundlage eines Brauches der betroffenen Branche hinreichend bestimmt.
⁴⁴ Vgl. auch OGH, 10.11.1994, CISG-online 117 = östJBl 1995, 253 m. Anm. *Karollus*; *Magnus,* IPRax 1996, 145: „größere Menge von Chinchilla-Fellen" als hinreichend bestimmt gesehen; Cir. 1, 30.4.2004, CISG-online 870 m. Anm. *Schumacher,* IHR 2005, 147 ff.: Rahmenvereinbarung, die prognostizierte Lieferquoten nannte, die Warenmenge aber vom Bedarf des Käufers abhängig machte – hinreichend bestimmt; *Solae, LLC v. Hershey Canada, Inc.,* U. S. Dist. Ct. (D. Del.), 9.5.2008, CISG-online 1769 = 557 F. Supp. 2d. 452, 456: Rahmenvereinbarung, die angestrebte Jahresabnahme („up to 250,000 pounds") sowie Pfundpreis festlegte – hinreichend bestimmt.
⁴⁵ CA Paris, 18.11.2009, CISG-online 2237: italienisch-französische Kaufverträge über Mandeln waren während der vergangenen zwei Jahre stets zum Stückpreis von 0,019056 €/Mandel abgerechnet worden – weil bei neuer Bestellung keiner der Parteien den Preis ansprach, kam auch neuer Kaufvertrag zum bisherigen Preis zustande.
⁴⁶ Vgl. zum EAG/EKG LG Heidelberg, 21.4.1981, in: *Schlechtriem/Magnus,* Art. 56 EKG, Nr. 3; OLG Koblenz, 21.1.1983, daselbst Art. 56 EKG, Nr. 7; OLG Koblenz, 1.3.1985, daselbst Art. 56 EKG, Nr. 10.
⁴⁷ MünchKomm/*Gruber,* Art. 14, Rn. 18.
⁴⁸ S. schon oben Rn. 4, 8, ferner unten Rn. 20 sowie LG Oldenburg, 28.2.1996, CISG-online 189: „3 LKW-Ladungen Eier" bei Auslegung hinreichend bestimmt; *Geneva Pharmaceuticals Technology Corp. v. Barr Laboratories, Inc.,* U. S. Dist. Ct. (S. D. N. Y.), 10.5.2002, CISG-online 653 = 201 F. Supp. 2d 236, 282: „commercial quantities" Clathrat ausreichend bestimmt; OLG Hamburg, 4.7.1997, CISG-online 1299: „20 LKW-Ladungen Tomatenmark" bezeichnet bezüglich der Ladefähigkeit eines LKW eine branchenübliche Menge.

Mindestbestandteile so mehrdeutig, dass auch klärende Auslegung nach Art. 8 ausscheidet, dann liegt keine annahmefähige Offerte vor; eines Rückgriffs auf nationale Regeln über **Dissens** bedarf es dann m. E. nicht.[49]

Fehlen von Mindestbestandteilen und damit der Annahmefähigkeit kann auch gegeben **11** sein, wenn ein Verkäufer verschiedene Waren anbietet, aber nur für einzelne einen Preis nennt und für die übrigen der Preis nicht bestimmbar ist; zumindest hinsichtlich der Gegenstände, für die ein Preis weder bestimmt noch bestimmbar ist, ist die Qualifikation der Erklärung als Offerte wegen fehlender Mindestbestandteile zweifelhaft.[50]

c) **Bestimmbarkeit.** Die **Mindestbestandteile** müssen nicht durch eindeutige oder **12** auslegungsfähige Bezeichnungen bestimmt sein, sondern es genügt, wenn ihre „**Festsetzung ermöglicht**" wird, d. h. wenn sie **bestimmbar** sind. Soweit die zur Bestimmung erforderlichen Faktoren bei Abgabe des Angebots bereits vorliegen, wird es meist um Auslegung bzw. Einbeziehung von Erklärungen außerhalb des Angebots in dieses gehen, z. B. beim Verweis auf aktuelle Preislisten des Anbietenden[51] oder Bezugnahmen auf eine detaillierte invitatio z. B. einer Ausschreibung.[52] „Bestimmbar" sind Mindesterfordernisse eines Angebots aber auch dann, wenn die Faktoren erst später, etwa im Lieferzeitpunkt, entstehen oder feststehen, z. B. beim Verweis auf Börsen- oder Marktpreise im Lieferzeitpunkt[53] oder bei Angebot des Verkaufs der gesamten künftigen Ernte oder Jahresproduktion.[54] Bei einer Preisspanne von DM 35,– bis DM 65,– hat der österreichische OGH Bestimmbarkeit angenommen, wenn (und weil) auf Grund der Qualitätsunterschiede der verkauften Felle eine Konkretisierung des Preises möglich war.[55]

3. Bestimmungsbefugnisse

a) **Bestimmung durch Dritten oder die Parteien.** Bestimmbarkeit und damit eine **13** Erfüllung der Mindestanforderungen nach Art. 14 I 2 ist auch gegeben, wenn konkrete **Bestimmung durch einen Dritten**[56] oder **beide Parteien**[57] vereinbart bzw. in der

---

[49] Vgl. auch oben *Schmidt-Kessel*, Art. 8 Rn. 7 (bei Dissens über Einzelpunkte: Art. 19); ferner *Dölle/Schlechtriem*, Art. 4 EAG, Rn. 6.

[50] Vgl. hierzu unten Rn. 16 ff.

[51] Vgl. OLG Rostock, 10.10.2001, CISG-online 671 = IHR 2003, 17, 18: stillschweigende Bezugnahme auf bei Vertragsschluss geltende Preislisten des Verkäufers, nach denen bereits eine Vielzahl von Verträgen abgewickelt worden war (aber zusätzlich Art. 55 angeführt). Zu Tagespreisklauseln s. noch unten Rn. 15

[52] Vgl. BGH, 27.6.1996, WM 1996, 2208, 2209 (kein CISG-Fall).

[53] OLG München, 19.10.2006, CISG-online 1394 = IHR 2007, 30, 35: bei Verkauf von PKW Verweis auf Listenpreis des Herstellers am Tag der Lieferung.

[54] Vgl. zu solchen Fällen der Bestimmbarkeit Sekretariatskommentar, Art. 12, Nr. 11–13; ferner *Bianca/Bonell/Eörsi*, Art. 14, Anm. 2.2.4.2.: Quantität entsprechend einem Preis von 5000 SFR im Lieferzeitpunkt sei bestimmbar; *Enderlein/Maskow/Strohbach*, Art. 14, Anm. 9. (Bezugnahme auf den gesamten Bedarf oder die gesamte Produktion eines Erzeugnisses); *Neumayer/Ming*, Art. 14, Anm. 7.; a. A. MünchKommHGB/*Ferrari*, Art. 14, Rn. 24: Menge nicht ausreichend bestimmt.

[55] OGH, 10.11.1994, CISG-online 117 = östJBl 1995, 253 m. Anm. *Karollus*; zustimmend *Kramer*, FS Welser, S. 544; *Schwimann/Posch*, Art. 14, Rn. 9; dazu auch *Magnus*, IPRax 1996, 145.

[56] *Bamberger/Roth/Saenger*, Art. 14, Rn. 4; *Bianca/Bonell/Eörsi*, Art. 14, Anm. 2.2.4.3.; MünchKomm/*Gruber*, Art. 14, Rn. 20; *Neumayer/Ming*, Art. 14, Anm. 8.; *Schwimann/Posch*, Art. 14, Rn. 6; für Preisbestimmung *Witz/Salger/Lorenz/Witz*, Art. 14, Rn. 49; a. A. *Audit*, Vente internationale, Anm. 63.; *Heuzé*, Anm. 174.

[57] *Solae, LLC v. Hershey Canada, Inc.*, U. S. Dist. Ct. (D. Del.), 9.5.2008, CISG-online 1769 = 557 F. Supp. 2d. 452, 456: Abnahme von „up to 250,000 pounds" vorgesehen – hinreichend bestimmt; HGer Zürich, 10.7.1996, CISG-online 227 = SZIER 1997, 131 f.: Vertraglicher Vorbehalt, nach welchem die Verkäuferin berechtigt sein soll, von der bestellten Menge um bis zu 10% abzuweichen, hindert Bestimmtheit nicht; *Bydlinski*, Allgemeines Vertragsrecht, S. 62; *Enderlein/Maskow/Strohbach*, Art. 14, Anm. 12.; *Lookofsky*, The 1980 United Nations Convention, Anm. 102.; MünchKomm/*Gruber*, Art. 14, Rn. 20; *Sono*, Formation of International Contracts, S. 120; ferner Sekretariatskommentar, Art. 12, Nr. 12 zu „requirement contracts", bei denen der Käufer nach Bedarf abruft, also die Menge noch zu bestimmen hat; *Joseph*, 3 Dick. J. Int'l L. (1984), 107, 121: „Output and requirement contracts" seien anerkannt, doch dürften die entsprechenden Bestimmungsbefugnisse nur im Rahmen von Treu und Glauben – Art. 7 I – ausgeübt werden: Die Bestimmungsbefugnis könne nicht über die benötigte oder für den anderen Teil verfügbare Menge hinaus genutzt werden; hierzu auch *von Mehren*, Sec. 93.

Offerte vorgeschlagen wird. Das gilt grundsätzlich auch für den **Preis**. Eine Vereinbarung bzw. ein Vorschlag in der Offerte zur Festsetzung des Preises durch Dritte, etwa Sachverständige, aber auch durch die Parteien gemeinsam („price to be mutally agreed"),[58] ist möglich und macht die Offerte bestimmt genug. Weigert sich der vertraglich vorgesehene Dritte allerdings, die ihm übertragene Bestimmung vorzunehmen, so muss bei Fehlen einer vertraglichen Regelung für diesen Fall das nationale Recht über die subsidiär anzuwendende Regelung entscheiden;[59] ist hingegen eine einvernehmliche Preisfestsetzung durch die Parteien vereinbart und scheitert eine entsprechende Einigung später, so wird man häufig auf Art. 55 zurückgreifen können.[60]

14 **b) Bestimmung durch eine Partei.** Hinreichende Bestimmbarkeit i. S. d. Art. 14 I 2 liegt ebenfalls vor, wenn das Angebot eine **Bestimmungsbefugnis** zugunsten **einer der Parteien** vorsieht.[61] Eine solche einseitige Befugnis kann sich sachlich auf jeden der Mindestbestandteile einer Offerte beziehen, auch auf mehrere. In der Praxis kommen vor allem Klauseln vor, die einer Partei die Festsetzung der zu liefernden **Menge** überlassen, wobei dieses Recht teilweise dem Käufer nach dessen Bedarf *(requirement contract)*[62] oder innerhalb bestimmter Grenzen[63], teilweise dem Verkäufer eingeräumt wird (ohne Beschränkung *(output contract)*[64] oder als begrenzte Abweichungsbefugnis[65]). Auch eine vereinbarte Befugnis zur einseitigen Festsetzung des **Preises** genügt den Anforderungen des Art. 14 I 2[66] (s. zu Tagespreisklauseln noch Rn. 15). Zudem kann die Bestimmung der **(Art der) Ware** einer Partei überlassen werden, obgleich Art. 14 I 2 insofern einen strengeren Maßstab aufzustellen scheint („bezeichnen" im Gegensatz zum bloßen „Festsetzung ermöglichen"), denn die Parteien können nach Art. 6 – auch konkludent – von diesen Vorgaben abweichen.[67]

Ob und inwieweit **nationale Nichtigkeitsvorschriften** (s. Art. 4 S. 2 lit. a)) eine entsprechende Klausel **unwirksam** machen und dem Vorschlag damit die Qualität einer Offerte nehmen können, hängt von sachlichem Bezugspunkt und Regelungsziel der Nichtigkeitsvorschrift ab:[68] Nationale Normen, die aus der unzureichenden Bestimmtheit von Vertragsbestandteilen bei Vertragsschluss oder dem bloßen Bestehen eines einseitigen Parteieinflusses auf deren Festsetzung die Nichtigkeit von Angebot oder Vertrag herleiten, werden

---

[58] CIETAC, 25.12.1998, CISG-online 1135: Angebot mit Klausel „price to be mutually agreed" ist hinreichend bestimmt; skeptisch zu dieser Bestimmungsart *Tallon*, Buyer's Obligations, § 7.03 sub 7–13. Schwierigkeiten entstehen freilich dann, wenn die Parteien sich später nicht auf einen Preis einigen können, so in Int. Ct. Russian CCI, 9.4.2004, 129/2003, CISG-online 1207.
[59] MünchKomm/*Gruber*, Art. 14, Rn. 21. Dies deshalb, weil sich die Parteien durch Übertragung der Preisbestimmung auf einen Dritten deutlich gegen eine Anwendung des üblichen (Markt-)Preises (Art. 55) entschieden haben, der in solchen Fällen häufig ohnehin nicht bestehen wird; a. A. *Bridge*, Int'l Sale of Goods, Rn. 3.09: Pflicht der Parteien zur gemeinsamen Bestimmung eines anderen Dritten sei aus Art. 7 I bzw. Art. 7 II ableitbar.
[60] Anders entschieden in Int. Ct. Russian CCI, 9.4.2004, 129/2003, CISG-online 1207, wo Scheitern des Vertragsschlusses angenommen und eine Anwendung des Art. 55 abgelehnt wurde.
[61] *Solae, LLC v. Hershey Canada, Inc.,* U. S. Dist. Ct. (D. Del.), 9.5.2008, CISG-online 1769 = 557 F. Supp. 2d. 452, 456; HGer Zürich, 10.7.1996, CISG-online 227 = SZIER 1997, 131 f.; *Enderlein/Maskow/Strohbach*, Art. 14, Anm. 12.; *Lookofsky*, The 1980 United Nations Convention, Anm. 102.; MünchKomm/*Gruber*, Art. 14, Rn. 20; *Piltz*, Internationales Kaufrecht, Rn. 3–23.
[62] Sekretariatskommentar, Art. 12, Nr. 12; *Joseph*, 3 Dick. J. Int'l L. (1984), 107, 121 (zu „output and requirement contracts"); hierzu auch *von Mehren*, Sec. 93 sowie oben Rn. 12.
[63] *Solae, LLC v. Hershey Canada, Inc.,* U. S. Dist. Ct. (D. Del.), 9.5.2008, CISG-online 1769 = 557 F. Supp. 2d. 452, 456: Abnahme von „up to 250,000 pounds" Sojalezithin vorgesehen – hinreichend bestimmt.
[64] S. auch oben Rn. 12.
[65] HGer Zürich, 10.7.1996, CISG-online 227 = SZIER 1997, 131 f.: Vertraglicher Vorbehalt, nach welchem die Verkäuferin berechtigt sein soll, von der bestellten Menge um bis zu 10% abzuweichen, hindert Bestimmtheit nicht.
[66] *Achilles*, Art. 14, Rn. 5; *Brunner*, Art. 14, Rn. 4 Fn. 469; im Ergebnis auch *Honsell/Dornis*, Art. 14, Rn. 19: wg. Art. 6; a. A. *Heuzé*, Anm. 174.; MünchKommHGB/*Ferrari*, Art. 14, Rn. 29; *Witz/Salger/Lorenz/Witz*, Art. 14, Rn. 45. S. auch unten Rn. 21.
[67] S. schon oben Rn. 6.
[68] Ohne die folgende Differenzierung noch *Schlechtriem/Schroeter* in der Vorauflage.

verdrängt, weil Art. 14 I 2 die Anforderungen an Bestimmtheit und Bestimmbarkeit des Offerteninhalts abschließend regelt. **Anwendbar** bleiben hingegen nationale Regelungen, die Anforderungen an Art und Weise der Festsetzung durch eine Partei, an den zulässigen Umfang einseitiger vertraglicher Bestimmungsbefugnisse oder die inhaltliche Billigkeit einer Festsetzung aufstellen und sanktionieren, weil diesbezügliche übereinkommensautonome Maßstäbe (Art. 7 II Alt. 1) bislang noch nicht entwickelt wurden.[69] Im deutschen Recht ist für Bestimmungsvorbehalte in AGB daher an §§ 308 Nr. 4, 309 Nr. 1 BGB zu denken, deren Grundwertungen u. U. im Rahmen des § 307 BGB auch bei Verträgen im kaufmännischen grenzüberschreitenden Verkehr zur Geltung kommen können.[70] Im Übrigen kann zur Überprüfung § 315 III BGB herangezogen werden.[71] Nach schweizerischem Recht kann eine nicht nach billigem Ermessen vorgenommene Bestimmung nach Art. 20 I OR bzw. Art. 27 ZGB unwirksam sein.[72]

c) Tagespreisklauseln. Ein Angebot ist auch dann hinsichtlich des **Preises** i. S. d. Art. 14 I 2 ausreichend **bestimmbar**, wenn es eine Tagespreisklausel (z. B. „Verkaufspreis ist der am Liefertag gültige Listenpreis") enthält.[73] Der in Bezug genommene Tagespreis kann je nach Klauselgestaltung „objektiv" (durch unabhängige Dritte oder anhand allgemeiner Faktoren, etwa Markt- oder Börsenpreisen[74]) oder „subjektiv" (von einer der Parteien, i. d. R. dem Verkäufer) festzusetzen sein; dem Bestimmbarkeitserfordernis des Art. 14 I 2 wird beides gerecht.[75] Sofern die Offerte eine Tagespreisklausel nicht ausdrücklich vorsieht, muss bei der **Auslegung** des Angebots (Art. 8 II, III) angesichts der starken Widerstände auf der Wiener Konferenz und bei den Vorarbeiten[76] sowohl gegen im Preis „offene" Verträge als auch Preisbestimmungsmöglichkeiten des Verkäufers allerdings ein strenger Maßstab angelegt werden; insbesondere bezüglich einer Herleitung von Tagespreisklauseln aus Umständen des Vertragsschlusses und Vorverhandlungen (Art. 8 III) ist Zurückhaltung geboten.[77] Hinsichtlich der **Kontrolle** von Tagespreisklauseln nach **nationalem Recht** ist wiederum anhand der oben in Rn. 14 genannten Maßstäbe zu **unterscheiden**: Vorgaben bzgl. der Preisbestimmtheit bei Vertragsschluss wie etwa des französischen Rechts (Artt. 1108, 1591 Cc)[78] können daher auf CISG-Verträge keine Anwendung finden,[79] während Vorschriften zu den Grenzen von einseitigen Preisbestimmungsmöglichkeiten oder der Billigkeit erfolgter Preisfestsetzungen anwendbar bleiben. Aus diesem Grund können Tagespreisklauseln in AGB an § 307 BGB scheitern.[80]

---

[69] Erste Ansätze bei *Joseph*, 3 Dick. J. Int'l L. (1984), 107, 121: einseitige Bestimmungsbefugnisse dürften nur im Rahmen von Treu und Glauben – Art. 7 I – ausgeübt werden; ebenso *Brunner*, Art. 14, Rn. 4.
[70] MünchKomm/*Gruber*, Art. 14, Rn. 21.
[71] *Brunner*, Art. 14, Rn. 4; *Heuzé*, Anm. 174.; MünchKomm/*Gruber*, Art. 14, Rn. 21.
[72] *Brunner*, Art. 14, Rn. 4: sofern die Bestimmungsbefugnis nicht nach Treu und Glauben (Art. 7 I) ausgeübt werde.
[73] OLG München, 19.10.2006, CISG-online 1394 = IHR 2007, 30, 35: bei Verkauf von PKW Verweis auf Listenpreis des Herstellers am Tag der Lieferung; *Brunner*, Art. 14, Rn. 7; MünchKomm/*Gruber*, Art. 14, Rn. 21.
[74] S. bereits oben Rn. 12.
[75] MünchKomm/*Gruber*, Art. 14, Rn. 19 f.
[76] Dazu noch unten Rn. 17 f.
[77] In der Tendenz wohl toleranter OLG Rostock, 10.10.2001, CISG-online 671 = IHR 2003, 17, 18: „stillschweigende" Bezugnahme auf Preislisten des Verkäufers angenommen.
[78] In Frankreich hat die Rechtsprechung des Kassationshofs früher wiederholt auf der Grundlage von Artt. 1108, 1591 Cc Verträge verworfen, die dem Verkäufer die Preisbestimmung im Lieferzeitpunkt überließen (s. *Schlechtriem*, 2. Aufl., Rn. 7 in Fn. 24). Civ. 1, 29.11.1994, J. C. P. 1995, II, 22 371, m. Anm. *Ghestin* brachte insoweit jedoch eine Wende; ferner Ass. plén., 1.12.1995, J. C. P. 1996, II, 22 565 m. Anm. *Ghestin* sowie *Witz* zu Civ. 1, 4.1.1995, CISG-online 138 = D. 1995, 289 und *ders./Wolter*, RIW 1995, 810.
[79] *Lookofsky*, The 1980 United Nations Convention, Anm. 102.; *Witz*, Les premières applications, S. 68 ff.
[80] *Bamberger/Roth/Saenger*, Art. 14, Rn. 5; *Witz/Salger/Lorenz/Witz*, Art. 14, Rn. 62 (Vorsicht bei einseitigen Preisbestimmungsrechten); zu intransparenten Preisanpassungsklauseln s. BGH, 19.11.2002, NJW 2003, 507 (kein CISG-Fall); zur Kontrolle von Preisanpassungsklauseln im deutschen Recht umfassend *Kamanabrou*, S. 273 ff.

III. Unbestimmter Preis

1. Bestimmbarkeitserfordernis des Art. 14 I 2

16 Nach Art. 14 I 2 ist ein Vorschlag keine Offerte, wenn er weder einen Preis – evtl. auch „stillschweigend"[81] – enthält noch – wieder evtl. „stillschweigend" – eine Preisbestimmungsmöglichkeit vorsieht.[82] Ausreichend ist jedoch die Angabe von Stück- oder Mengenpreisen, wenn dem anderen Teil die Bestimmung der Stückzahl oder Menge überlassen bleibt wie bei Bedarfsdeckungsverträgen (requirement contracts).[83] Enthält jedoch auch die Gegenerklärung weder einen bestimmten noch einen bestimmbaren Preis, so dass sie ebenfalls nicht als Offerte aufgefasst und nach Art. 18 angenommen werden kann, dann scheitert jedenfalls der Vertragsschluss nach Artt. 14 ff. an der fehlenden Preisbestimmung.[84] Das Gleiche gilt, falls eine Preisbestimmung oder ein Preisbestimmungsvorbehalt zugunsten einer Partei nach einem anwendbaren nationalen Recht nichtig[85] oder so unklar ist, dass auch Auslegung keinen festgesetzten oder festsetzbaren Preis ergibt.[86]

2. Entstehungsgeschichtlicher Hintergrund

17 Ob bei fehlender Preisbestimmung gleichwohl ein Vertrag zustande kommen kann und welcher Preisbestimmungsmechanismus zur Lückenfüllung eingesetzt werden soll, war bei der Erarbeitung des CISG eine heftig umstrittene Frage, wobei wesentlich die Unterschiede in den jeweiligen nationalen Rechtsordnungen bestimmend waren. Während der erste Entwurf der Arbeitsgruppe für ausreichend hielt, dass die Offerte vorsah „that a price is to be paid", und für den Fall fehlender Preisbestimmung eine Art. 57 EKG entsprechende Regel aufgestellt hatte,[87] enthielt Art. 12 I 2 New Yorker E 1978 bereits eine Art. 14 I 2 entsprechende Regel, aber in Art. 51 New Yorker E für den Fall fehlender Preisbestimmung bzw. Preisbestimmbarkeit eine Verweisung auf die Verkäuferpreise im Zeitpunkt des Vertragsschlusses (entsprechend Art. 57 EKG), hilfsweise auf die üblichen Preise zur Zeit des Vertragsschlusses für Güter, die unter vergleichbaren Umständen gehandelt werden.[88]

18 Auf der **Wiener Konferenz** standen sich wieder zwei Lager gegenüber: Während eine Gruppe von Ländern verschiedene Vorschläge und Anträge einbrachte, die letztlich alle

---

[81] S. oben Rn. 8.
[82] Zu einer solchen Situation kann es auch bei Divergenzen zwischen Offerte und Annahme (= Gegenofferte) und anderen Erklärungen kommen, vgl. OLG Frankfurt a. M., 4.3.1994, CISG-online 110, wo eine bestimmte Offerte durch eine zu Preisen u. a. unbestimmte Gegenerklärung beantwortet worden war. In einem vom Obersten Ungarischen Gericht (Legfelsóbb Birósag) am 25.9.1992 entschiedenen, bekannten CISG-Fall (CISG-online 63 = 13 J. L. & Com. (1993), 31 ff.) hatte die amerikanische Flugzeugmotorenherstellerin *Pratt & Whitney* der ungarischen Fluglinie *Malev* in einer „Absichtserklärung" verschiedene Flugzeugmotoren und Triebwerkssysteme „angeboten" – nachdem *Malev* in einem Telex mitgeteilt hatte, dass man für die Erstausstattung einen bestimmten Motor ausgewählt habe und sich auf die künftige Zusammenarbeit freue, verneinte das Oberste Gericht im Rahmen einer Schadenersatzklage von *Pratt & Whitney* einen gültigen Vertragsschluss nach CISG, weil für den von der ungarischen Fluglinie gewählten Motortyp in der Erklärung der Lieferantin noch kein vollständiger Preis für das gesamte System, d. h. Düsentriebwerke und Ergänzungsteile wie Nascellen usw., sondern nur für die Motoren selbst angegeben war und auf dem Markt für Düsentriebwerkssysteme Marktpreise fehlten, deshalb auch eine Preisbestimmung nach Art. 55 nicht möglich sei. Die Entscheidung wird zu Recht kritisiert von *Amato*, 13 J. L. & Com. (1993), 1, 16 ff.
[83] S. oben Rn. 14. Ob insoweit nur ein Rahmenvertrag oder schon ein Kaufvertrag mit Bestimmungsbefugnis des Käufers geschlossen worden ist, muss durch Auslegung ermittelt werden (s. auch oben Vor Artt. 14–24 Rn. 41).
[84] S. jedoch unten Rn. 20 f.
[85] S. oben Rn. 6 sowie zu Preisbestimmungsvorbehalten Rn. 13 f.
[86] S. hierzu oben Rn. 10.
[87] S. Art. 4 III, IV; YB VIII (1977), S. 78, Nr. 50.
[88] Der Sekretariatskommentar machte dazu deutlich, dass man einerseits für die Offerte großzügig von stillschweigenden Preisfestsetzungsmöglichkeiten ausgehen wollte, andererseits die Hilfsregel des Art. 51 E Bedeutung nur für solche Staaten haben sollte, die den Vertragsschlussteil der Konvention nicht ratifizieren würden; Art. 12 E (= Art. 14) sollte also Vorrang vor Art. 51 E (= Art. 55) haben, s. O. R., S. 45.

darauf abzielten, eine Offerte und damit einen Vertrag auch ohne bestimmten oder bestimmbaren Preis, also den ihnen vertrauten open price term contract, zuzulassen, wollten andere Staaten aus unterschiedlichen Gründen strikt am Erfordernis des bestimmten oder jedenfalls bestimmbaren Preises festhalten.[89] Die Differenzen wurden zunächst bei Behandlung des Art. 14 (Art. 12 E) deutlich und brachen erneut bei Behandlung des Art. 55 (Art. 51 E) auf, wobei wiederholt darauf hingewiesen wurde, dass zwischen beiden Vorschriften ein Widerspruch bestünde.[90] Im Ergebnis kam es zur geltenden Regelung, weil eine Reihe von Teilnehmern davon ausging, dass ihre Staaten das Übereinkommen ohne Teil II ratifizieren würden, so dass ihr nationales Kaufabschlussrecht, das kein Erfordernis eines **pretium certum** enthält, anwendbar sei; bei der Abstimmung über Art. 55 unterstützten sie dann jedoch entschieden die Delegationen, die einen hilfsweisen Preisbestimmungsmechanismus für unverzichtbar hielten.

3. Spektrum der Lösungsansätze

Zur **Lösung** des Konflikts zwischen Artt. 14 und 55 werden **verschiedene Ansichten** 19 vertreten.[91] Manche Autoren nehmen grundsätzlich Vorrang des Art. 55 an, so dass das Preisbestimmtheitserfordernis in Art. 14 I 2 weitgehend leer läuft.[92] Andere gehen prinzipiell davon aus, dass ein bindender Vertrag unabhängig von den Erfordernissen an eine Offerte nach Art. 14 I 2 zustande kommen könne, so dass in solchen Fällen Art. 55 eine sinnvolle ergänzende Funktion habe;[93] ein Überschneidungsbereich sei dann gar nicht gegeben.[94] Eine Variante dieser Ansicht behauptet, dass Art. 14 I 2 überhaupt nur die Abgrenzung von Offerte und invitatio ad offerendum erleichtern soll.[95] Teilweise wird ein offener Widerspruch angenommen, der nur aus den Entstehungsbedingungen zu erklären[96] und mit unterschiedlichen Techniken aufzulösen sei; überhaupt wird der jeweilige Ausgangspunkt fast immer für bestimmte Fälle eingeschränkt, für die in der Sache dann doch weitgehend Einigkeit besteht (s. unten Rn. 20 f.). Manche Autoren schließlich behaupten absoluten Vorrang des Art. 14 I 2.[97] In der **Rechtsprechungspraxis** ist die Sachfrage vielfach in Fällen zu entscheiden gewesen, in denen vor allem Divergenzen und Unklarhei-

---

[89] S. zu den Anträgen und der Debatte O.R., S. 275 ff.; unten *Mohs*, Art. 55 Rn. 2; ferner zur Geschichte *Bianca/Bonell/Eörsi*, Art. 14, Anm. 1.2. und Art. 55, Anm. 1.1.–1.3.3.; *Schlechtriem*, Einheitliches UN-Kaufrecht, S. 37 f.; *Witz/Salger/Lorenz/Witz*, Art. 14, Rn. 3 ff.

[90] S. O.R., S. 363 ff., dort zu Hinweisen auf den Widerspruch z. B. Nr. 22, 36, 51.

[91] Umfassend *Perales Viscasillas*, Formacíon del contrato, S. 353 ff. (Stand 1996).

[92] *Corbisier*, Rev. int. dr. comp. 1988, 767, 828 ff.; *Fortier*, J.D.I. 1990, 381, 390; *Honnold/Flechtner*, Art. 14, Rn. 137.4 ff.; *Joseph*, 3 Dick. J. Int'l L. (1984), 107, 122; *Karollus*, S. 62; *Kritzer*, Guide to Practical Applications, S. 139 ff.; *Loewe*, Art. 55, S. 76; s. dagegen *Nicholas*, 105 L.Q.R. (1989), 201, 213; *Farnsworth*, Formation of Contract, § 3.04 sub 3–9 Fn. 5 und weitere Gegenstimmen in Fn. 6.

[93] *Bianca/Bonell/Eörsi*, Art. 55, Anm. 2.2.2.; *Bucher*, FS Piotet, S. 371 ff., 404 f.; *Herber*, RIW 1980, 601, 604; *Neumayer/Ming*, Art. 14, Anm. 11.; *Steensgaard*, Standardbetingelser, § 4, Rn. 24 ff. Zum New Yorker E 1978 *Huber*, RabelsZ 43 (1979), 413, 439, 511.

[94] *Honsell/Schnyder/Straub*, 1. Aufl., Art. 14, Rn. 54.

[95] So *Neumayer/Ming*, Art. 14, Anm. 11.; *Roth/Kunz*, RIW 1997, 17, 19; die qualifizierten Juristen, die auf der Wiener Konferenz ihre Staaten vertreten und über das Verhältnis von Art. 14 und Art. 55 lange und engagiert diskutiert haben, müssten dann diesen einfachen Lösungsweg übersehen haben. Dass die Konferenzteilnehmer es aber anders gesehen haben und für sie die Offerte nur das technische Instrument war, um die erwünschte Qualifizierung des pretium certum als Gültigkeitsvoraussetzung eines *Vertrages* (und nicht nur einer Offerte) zu erreichen, zeigt ein Blick auf Art. 1591 Cc, der für die französischen Juristen und andere Delegierte, deren Rechtsordnung vom französischen Code civil beeinflusst ist, damals Richtschnur für ihre Stellungnahme war.

[96] Vgl. *Bydlinski*, Allgemeines Vertragsrecht, S. 63; *Ebenroth*, östJBl 1986, 681, 685; *Hondius*, RabelsZ 71 (2007), 99, 102, der zwischenzeitlichen Übergang der ehemals sozialistischen Staaten zur Marktwirtschaft und die neuere Rechtsprechungsentwicklung der frz. Cour de Cassation als Argument für einen nunmehrigen Vorrang des Art. 55 anführt; *Loewe*, Diskussionsbeitrag in: *Doralt* (Hrsg.), Das UNCITRAL-Kaufrecht im Vergleich zum österreichischen Recht, S. 77 („zugegebenermaßen vorhandener Widerspruch"); unten *Mohs*, Art. 55 Rn. 2 f.; *Neumayer*, Diskussionsbeitrag daselbst; zum Ganzen *Wey*, Rn. 686 ff.

[97] *Ghestin*, R.D.A.I. 1988, 5, 6; besonders engagiert gegen jede Abschwächung des „pretium certum" *Heuzé*, Anm. 169. ff., 173. f.

ten in den von den Parteien gewechselten Erklärungen aufgetreten waren.[98] Im Übrigen sind die Unterschiede in den Entscheidungsergebnissen wesentlich auf die jeweiligen Besonderheiten des Falles zurückzuführen und erlauben deshalb keine generalisierende Zusammenfassung; überwiegend wurde ein wirksamer Vertragsschluss angenommen,[99] seltener im Ergebnis verneint.[100]

4. Stellungnahme

20 M. E. muss man verschiedene **Möglichkeiten** und **Fallgestaltungen** unterscheiden.[101] Zunächst hat Art. 55 natürlich Bedeutung, falls das CISG ohne Teil II anzuwenden ist (Art. 92)[102] und unvereinheitlichtes Recht einen wirksamen Vertragsschluss ohne Preisbestimmung zulässt. Im Übrigen wird in vielen Fällen unterbliebener Preisangabe von einem „stillschweigend"[103] bestimmten Preis, der durch Auslegung zu ermitteln ist, auszugehen sein.[104] Bei der erforderlich werdenden Auslegung kann mangels konkreter anderer Anhaltspunkte oft der in Art. 55 bezeichnete Preis als gewollt angenommen werden.[105] Vor allem in den als Beispiel für die Notwendigkeit einer hilfsweisen Preisbestimmung kraft Gesetzes genannten Fällen der Bestellung dringend benötigter Ersatzteile wird der Offerent von dem üblichen Preis solcher Teile im Zeitpunkt des Vertragsschlusses ausgehen. Art. 55 greift hier nicht direkt ein, ist aber bei der Ermittlung des „stillschweigend" Vorgeschlagenen Auslegungsrichtlinie.[106] Das dürfte auch für diejenigen akzeptabel sein, die Machtmiss-

---

[98] S. Legfelsóbb Biróság, 25.9.1992, CISG-online 63 = 13 J. L. & Com. (1993), 31 ff.; OLG Frankfurt a. M., 4.3.1994, CISG-online 110.

[99] Vgl. BezG St. Gallen, 3.7.1997, CISG-online 336 = SZIER 1998, 84: „aufgrund der bereits erfolgten Vertragsdurchführung" vermöge fehlende Kaufpreisbestimmung das Zustandekommen des Vertrages nicht zu hindern – Art. 55 angewandt; HGer Aargau, 26.9.1997, CISG-online 329 = SZIER 1998, 78 ff.: wirksamer Vertrag trotz ungeklärten Kaufpreises; ICC, 8324/1995, CISG-online 569 = J. D. I. 1996, 1019 ff.: offener Kaufpreis, gleichwohl Gültigkeit des Vertrages, das sich aus dem Parteiverhalten ergebe, unter der endgültige Preis von dem vom Käufer bei seinen Abnehmern erzielten Preis abhängen solle; OLG Rostock, 10.10.2001, CISG-online 671 = IHR 2003, 17, 18: Art. 55 genannt, um den Preis (für Langusten) der Preisliste der Verkäuferin zu entnehmen, nach welcher „die Vielzahl" der Bestellungen zwischen den Parteien abgerechnet worden war; KG Freiburg, 11.10.2004, CISG-online 964 = IHR 2005, 72, 74 f.: „Offerte" der Verkäuferin mangels Preisangabe kein wirksames Angebot, jedoch wies Antwortschreiben Preis aus, das sodann konkludent angenommen wurde.

[100] Int. Ct. Russian CCI, 9.4.2004, 129/2003, CISG-online 1207: kein wirksamer Vertragsschluss, weil Vertrag gemeinsame Preisfestlegung durch die Parteien binnen bestimmter Frist vorsah, die jedoch nicht erfolgte (Anwendung des Art. 55 abgelehnt); Int. Ct. Russian CCI, 3.3.1995, 309/1993, CISG-online 204: mangels Einigung über Kaufpreis kein Vertrag; ähnlich OLG Frankfurt a. M., 4.3.1994, CISG-online 110.

[101] Im Wesentlichen wie hier *Honsell/Dornis*, Art. 14, Rn. 23.

[102] S. dazu unten Rn. 44 f.

[103] Dazu oben Rn. 8; speziell zum Preis noch *Winship*, 17 Int'l Law. (1983), 1, 5 f.: „dealings" oder „recognized custom in the trade" können zu Katalogpreisen des Verkäufers führen.

[104] Vgl. Sekretariatskommentar, Art. 12, Nr. 16: Bezugnahme auf Verkäuferkatalog schließt dessen Preise ein; *Sono*, Formation of International Contracts, S. 120: Bestellt der Käufer Ersatzteile ohne Preisangabe in seiner Offerte, dann nimmt er stillschweigend auf die vom Verkäufer gegenwärtig berechneten Preise Bezug; *Piltz*, Internationales Kaufrecht, Rn. 3–26.

[105] So in LG Neubrandenburg, 3.8.2005, CISG-online 1190 = IHR 2006, 26, 30: Durch Vertragsklausel „Price: To be fixed during the season" sei für Saisonware (Sauerkirschen) konkludent Festsetzung nach den Maßstäben der Art. 55 vereinbart worden und der Preis daher bestimmbar; Arb. Ct. Bulgarian CCI, 30.11.1998, CISG-online 1832: obwohl der Kaufvertrag ausdrücklich nur einen vorläufigen, ungefähren Preis angab, war der Vertrag wirksam geschlossen worden und der Preis nach Art. 55 zu bestimmen; *Hager/Maultzsch*, 5. Aufl., Art. 55 Rn. 7; *Sono*, Formation of International Contracts, S. 120; *Šarcevic*, Diskussionsbeitrag in: *Doralt* (Hrsg.), Das UNCITRAL-Kaufrecht im Vergleich zum österreichischen Recht, S. 77; a. A. *Roth/Kunz*, RIW 1997, 17, 19.

[106] Vgl. *Wey*, Rn. 688, 692: Normativ betriebene Auslegung. In diesem Sinne auch *Brunner*, Art. 14, Rn. 9; *Jametti Greiner*, S. 49; *Loewe*, Art. 55, S. 76; *Murray*, 8 J. L. & Com. (1988), 11, 17; *Stern*, Erklärungen, Rn. 39; sowie die amtlichen Erläuterungen zum österreichischen Gesetz, Nr. 94 der Beilagen zu den stenografischen Protokollen des Nationalrates, XVII. Gesetzgebungsperiode, S. 63: Art. 55 sei als „Hilfsmittel für die Bestimmbarkeit eines Preises zu deuten, den die Parteien zwar nicht genannt, aber für dessen Bestimmung sie eine dem Geschäftsleben entsprechende Erwartung gehegt haben oder gehegt hätten". A. A. *Honsell/Dornis*, Art. 14, Rn. 23.

Begriff des Angebots

brauch ökonomisch stärkerer Verkäufer fürchteten,[107] da – anders als Art. 51 New Yorker E 1978 – Art. 55 nicht mehr auf die vom Verkäufer üblicherweise im Zeitpunkt des Vertragsschlusses verlangten Preise abstellt, sondern einen objektiven Maßstab verwendet.

In vielen anderen Fällen wird ein Vertrag durch Einigsein angenommen werden können, ohne dass eine Offerte, die den Anforderungen des Art. 14 I 2 entspricht, gegeben war, sei es, dass die Parteien Art. 14 I 2 stillschweigend derogiert haben,[108] sei es, dass ein Vertrag – mit den sonst erforderlichen essentialia negotii – überhaupt anders als durch Angebot und Annahme gültig geschlossen worden ist.[109] Auch Gepflogenheiten, die sich zwischen den Parteien gebildet haben, sowie (ausnahmsweise) internationale Bräuche können Bestimmbarkeit oder stillschweigende Bestimmung des Preises ergeben.[110] Vor allem bei zunächst unbeanstandeter Vertragsdurchführung sollte die spätere, vielleicht erst nach Rügeversäumung oder anderen Leistungsstörungen vorgebrachte „Entdeckung" fehlender Preisbestimmung keine Auswirkungen auf die Gültigkeit des Vertragsschlusses mehr haben.[111]   21

Nur in den verbleibenden, vermutlich eher seltenen Fällen, in denen die Offerte ohne Preis unersetzbarer Baustein der Einigung ist, Auslegung weder zu einem bestimmten noch einem bestimmbaren Preis führt und die Parteien auch nicht durch Vertragsdurchführung ihr Einigsein manifestiert haben, oder in denen es trotz Einigseins keinen nach Art. 55 feststellbaren Preis gibt,[112] wird man einen wegen mangelnder Einigungsgrundlage gescheiterten Vertragsschluss anzunehmen haben.[113] Ein Rückgriff auf unvereinheitlichtes nationales Recht über IPR kommt jedenfalls nicht in Betracht,[114] da sonst die Regeln des CISG ausgehöhlt würden.[115]   22

IV. Bindungswille

1. Bindungswille des Offerenten

Bindungswille des Offerenten ist begriffswesentliches Merkmal der Offerte,[116] das aufgrund der Natur der Sache, d. h. der Funktion der Offerte, auch der Parteidisposition   23

---

[107] Vgl. *Date-Bah*, Problems of Unification, S. 51: Käufer in Entwicklungsländern könnten sich mit Verkäuferpreisen weit über Marktpreisen konfrontiert sehen, falls Art. 51 E in Geltung gesetzt würde; *Enderlein/Maskow/Strohbach*, Art. 14, Anm. 11.

[108] So *Kramer*, FS Welser, S. 544 f.; *Loewe*, Diskussionsbeitrag in: *Doralt* (Hrsg.), Das UNCITRAL-Kaufrecht im Vergleich zum österreichischen Recht, S. 77; s. auch *Piltz*, Internationales Kaufrecht, Rn. 3–27; *Wey*, Rn. 699; *Staudinger/Magnus*, Art. 14, Rn. 33; wohl auch *Perales Viscasillas*, Formación del contrato, S. 354 ff. Zu weitgehend *Dilger*, RabelsZ 45 (1981), 169, 191, der davon ausgeht, dass „in Deutschland, wo ein Vertrag auch ohne einen bestimmten Preis zustande kommen kann (vgl. § 316 BGB), der Ausschluss der Vorschrift (Art. 14 I 2) im Zweifel von den Gerichten bejaht werden" wird.

[109] S. zu dieser Möglichkeit oben Vor Artt. 14–24 Rn. 15, 23; *Brunner*, Art. 14, Rn. 11; *Bucher*, FS Piotet, S. 371, 390 ff.; *Honnold/Flechtner*, Art. 14, Rn. 137.5, 137.8; *Lookofsky*, The 1980 United Nations Convention, Anm. 102.; *Steensgaard*, Standardbetingelser, § 4, Rn. 29; sehr viel enger und grundsätzlich nationale Regeln bevorzugend jedoch *Heuzé*, Anm. 174.; *Stoffel*, Formation du contrat, S. 63 f.; a. A. auch MünchKomm/*Gruber*, Art. 14, Rn. 24.

[110] Vgl. Fovárosi Bíróság (Hauptstadtgericht) Budapest, 24.3.1992, CISG-online 61 = IPRax 1993, 263 (Bericht *Vida*).

[111] Überzeugend *Bucher*, FS Piotet, S. 371, 398 ff.; *Kramer*, FS Welser, S. 545 (der zusätzlich auf Art. 7 I – Verbot des *venire contra factum proprium* – verweist); aus der Rspr. BezG St. Gallen, 3.7.1997, CISG-online 336 = SZIER 1998, 84: „aufgrund der bereits erfolgten Vertragsdurchführung" Art. 55 angewandt.

[112] So Legfelsóbb Bíróság, 25.9.1992, CISG-online 63 = 13 J. L. & Com. (1993), 31 ff. für Düsentriebwerke.

[113] Vgl. zum Haager Einheitskaufrecht BGH, 27.6.1990, RIW 1990, 749: kein Rückgriff auf § 316 BGB.

[114] So aber *Ebenroth*, östJBl 1986, 681, 685; *Jametti Greiner*, S. 49, die entsprechende nationale Vorschriften wie Art. 1591 Cc sogar auf Grund von Art. 4 S. 2 lit. a) als Gültigkeitsnormen berücksichtigen will. So wohl auch *Audit*, Vente internationale, Anm. 63.; *Heuzé*, Anm. 169. ff., 173. f.

[115] *Kramer*, FS Welser, S. 545 f. will daher über Art. 7 II zunächst auf die Prinzipien der Parteiautonomie und des *favor negotii* als dem CISG zugrunde liegende allgemeine Grundsätze zurückgreifen und erst subsidiär nationales Recht anwenden.

[116] S. *Wey*, Rn. 722.

entzogen ist.[117] Er markiert die Grenze zwischen unverbindlichen Vorverhandlungen und erster Bindung, jedenfalls in Bezug auf das Vertragsinteresse.[118] Art. 14 I 1 entspricht Art. 4 I EAG; hinzugekommen ist nur die klärende Zweifelsregel für Vorschläge an einen unbestimmten Personenkreis, Abs. 2.[119] Bindungswille bedeutet, im Falle der Annahme gebunden zu sein, und hat nichts mit einer Bindung an die Offerte zu tun.[120] Auch ist der Bindungswille nicht Voraussetzung der durch Vertragsanbahnung und mit einer Offerte im deutschen Recht bewirkten gesteigerten Pflichtenbeziehung, die zu Ansprüchen aus *culpa in contrahendo* führen kann.[121]

2. Maßgeblichkeit der objektiven Erklärungsbedeutung

24   Die Fassung des Art. 14 I 1 macht deutlich, dass es auf die objektive Erklärungsbedeutung ankommt.[122] Wo ein von der objektiven Erklärungsbedeutung abweichender subjektiver Wille der anderen Partei nicht bekannt oder erkennbar war – Art. 8 I –, ist also auf den Empfängerhorizont einer vernünftigen Person „der gleichen Art" wie der Adressat unter gleichen Umständen abzustellen, Art. 8 II.[123] Nachträgliches Verhalten – Bsp.: Der Erklärende sendet die offerierte Ware ab – ist zu berücksichtigen, ebenso Gebräuche und Gepflogenheiten, Art. 8 III.[124] Ist zwischen den Parteien die Gepflogenheit entstanden, bei Vertragsschlüssen in einem zweischrittigen Verfahren zunächst eine Einigung über die essentialia negotii (sog. „firm bid") und sodann über die weiteren Details des Vertragsinhalts zu erzielen, so erfolgt der Vorschlag zur Verabredung eines „firm bid" noch ohne Bindungswille.[125] Fehlen Abschlusswille oder auch Erklärungsbewusstsein, kann ggf. nach nationalem Irrtumsrecht angefochten werden.[126] Auch eine Scherzerklärung, wenn es sie im grenzüberschreitenden Handel überhaupt geben sollte, kann deshalb Offerte sein.[127] Da nach Art. 14 I 1 allein auf die objektive Erklärungsbedeutung abzustellen ist, kommt unter dem CISG schließlich auch eine durch ein **vollautomatisiertes Computersystem** abgegebene elektronische Vertragsschlusserklärung[128] – sei sie nun im World Wide Web erfolgt[129] oder durch EDI übermittelt[130] – unproblematisch als Angebot mit erforderlichem Bindungswillen in Frage.[131]

3. Einzelfälle

25   a) **„Freibleibend" etc.** Vorschläge **„freibleibend", „sans engagement", „without obligation"** werden generell als invitationes ad offerendum qualifiziert,[132] können aber

---

[117] *Wey*, Rn. 722; zu „freibleibenden" Offerten s. unten Rn. 25.
[118] *Von Mehren*, Sec. 130; zu vorvertraglichen Bindungen s. oben Vor Artt. 14–24 Rn. 31 ff., 34 ff.
[119] Hierzu unten Rn. 30.
[120] *Enderlein/Maskow/Strohbach*, Art. 14, Anm. 6.; zur Bindung an das Angebot s. unten Art. 16 Rn. 2 ff.
[121] S. dazu oben Vor Artt. 14–24 Rn. 31 ff., 34 ff.
[122] OGer Thurgau, 19.12.1995, CISG-online 496 = SZIER 2000, 118 ff.; *Honsell/Dornis*, Art. 14, Rn. 26.
[123] MünchKomm/*Gruber*, Art. 14, Rn. 6.
[124] S. *Murray*, 8 J.L. & Com. (1988), 11, 13; *Neumayer/Ming*, Art. 14, Anm. 3.; *Wey*, Rn. 725; *Witz/Salger/Lorenz/Witz*, Art. 14, Rn. 50.
[125] *Hanwha Corporation v. Cedar Petrochemicals, Inc.*, U.S. Dist. Ct. (S.D.N.Y.), 18.1.2011, CISG-online 2178: „two-step process", der zwischen der koreanischen Käuferin und der U.S.-amerikanischen Verkäuferin von Chemikalien während der zurückliegenden 20 Vertragsschlüsse praktiziert worden war.
[126] Unabhängig von der Behandlung des fehlenden Erklärungsbewusstseins im nationalen Recht – zum BGB s. *Bydlinski*, JZ 1975, 1 f. – und der Frage Nichtigkeit oder Anfechtbarkeit wird man jedenfalls für die allein nach CISG zu beurteilende Voraussetzung einer Offerte zur Feststellung des „Bindungswillens" auf die objektive Erklärungsbedeutung abstellen müssen.
[127] *Dölle/Schlechtriem*, Art. 4 EAG, Rn. 20; *Wey*, Rn. 726.
[128] Dazu *Schwenzer/Hachem/Kee*, Rn. 11.17 ff.; *Steensgaard*, Standardbetingelser, § 8, Rn. 56.
[129] *Chong/Chao*, 18 SAcLJ (2006), 116, 126 nennen als Beispiel die Amazon.com-Website.
[130] *Nicoll*, J.B.L. (1998), 35, 41 f.
[131] *Mazzotta*, 33 Rutgers Computer & Tech.L.J. (2007), 251, 285; *Wulf*, S. 101. Dies entspricht der Regelung in § 2–204 UCC (2003), vgl. dazu *Flechtner*, IHR 2004, 225, 229.
[132] KG Zug, 2.12.2004, CISG-online 1194 = IHR 2006, 158, 159 zur Angabe „freibleibend"; LG Hannover, 21.4.2009, CISG-online 2298 = IHR 2012, 59, 60 zur Angabe „without engagement"; *Bamberger/Roth/Saenger*, Art. 14, Rn. 6.; *Enderlein/Maskow/Strohbach*, Art. 14, Anm. 5.; MünchKomm/*Gruber*, Art. 14,

ausnahmsweise auch einen Widerrufsvorbehalt hinsichtlich der Offerte oder gar des bereits geschlossenen Vertrages bedeuten.[133] Für die Auslegung derartiger Klauseln ist deshalb Art. 8 zu berücksichtigen, wobei der objektive Erklärungswert regelmäßig gegen Bindungswillen sprechen wird. Freilich kann aus den nach Art. 8 III zu berücksichtigenden Umständen, insbes. den Verhandlungen der Parteien und zwischen ihnen entstandenen Gepflogenheiten eine andere Bedeutung der Klausel folgen.

b) Letters of intent o. ä. Eine „Absichtserklärung",[134] ein **„letter of intent"**[135] oder vergleichbare Erklärungen („memoranda of understanding", „agreements in principle", „heads of agreement"[136]) müssen ebenfalls durch Auslegung nach Art. 8 II und insbesondere III qualifiziert werden.[137] Sie können je nach Wortlaut und zu berücksichtigenden Umständen eine bloße Fixierung des im Rahmen der Vertragsverhandlungen bereits erzielten Zwischenergebnisses sein, welche die Parteien nicht zum Abschluss eines endgültigen Vertrages verpflichtet (sog. Punktation),[138] eine bereits bindende Niederlegung der wesentlichen Vertragspunkte darstellen, die später nochmals schriftlich fixiert und bei der Gelegenheit um Nebenpunkte ergänzt werden soll[139] oder aber – weniger weitgehend – zwar noch keine kaufvertragliche Bindung sein, aber nach dem Willen der Parteien eine Haftung für etwaige Schäden aus dem Abbruch der Vertragsverhandlungen begründen.[140] Eine **Pro-Forma-Rechnung** stellt in der internationalen Praxis häufig ein Angebot dar.[141]

c) Fehlender Bindungswille. Bindungswille fehlt bei Vorschlägen, Vertragsverhandlungen aufzunehmen, und vor allem bei der **invitatio ad offerendum,** die deshalb von der Offerte abzugrenzen ist. Zeitungsinserate, Werbung in Rundfunk und Fernsehen, Prospekte, Kataloge, Preislisten, Rundbriefe u. ä. sind, auch wenn an einen bestimmten Kundenkreis gerichtet, generell als invitationes ad offerendum anzusehen.[142] Nur ausnahmsweise können solche an einen größeren bestimmten oder unbestimmten Personenkreis gerichteten Adressen als **Publikumsofferten** und damit als echte Angebote zu verstehen sein.[143] Bindungswille kann auch fehlen, wo trotz Bestimmung oder Bestimmbarkeit von Ware, Menge und Preis andere, für den vorgeschlagenen Vertrag essentielle Details noch nicht geklärt oder sogar ausdrücklich als klärungsbedürftig bezeichnet worden sind. Im Übrigen hängt es von den Umständen des Einzelfalles ab, ob ein Bindungswille zum Ausdruck kommt: Eine detaillierte Mitteilung, die Frist für eine Rückäußerung setzt, kann

---

Rn. 8; *Neumayer/Ming,* Art. 14, Anm. 3.; *Piltz,* NJW 2007, 2159, 2161; *Schlesinger,* Bd. 1, S. 78; *Schwimann/Posch,* Art. 14, Rn. 4; *Staudinger/Magnus,* Art. 14, Rn. 14.

[133] Vgl. *Brunner,* Art. 14, Rn. 2; MünchKomm/*Gruber,* Art. 14, Rn. 8; *Soergel/Lüderitz/Fenge,* Art. 14, Rn. 8; *Witz/Salger/Lorenz/Witz,* Art. 14, Rn. 23 („subject to contract" ist unverbindliche Absichtserklärung).

[134] S. den ungarischen Flugzeugmotorenfall Legfelsóbb Birósag, 25.9.1992, CISG-online 63 = 13 J. L. & Com. (1993), 31 ff.; *Schwimann/Posch,* Art. 14, Rn. 5: mangels Bindungswille kein Angebot.

[135] Hof van Beroep Gent, 15.5.2002, CISG-online 746: Bezeichnung „letter of intent" habe keine feststehende rechtliche Bedeutung.

[136] Vgl. *Brunner,* Art. 14, Rn. 3.

[137] S. hierzu *Torsello,* Preliminary Agreements, S. 214 ff.

[138] *Brunner,* Art. 14, Rn. 3; *Schwimann/Posch,* Art. 14, Rn. 5 (zum „letter of intent"); zu „letter of intent" und „memorandum of understanding" MünchKommHGB/*Ferrari,* Art. 14, Rn. 14: i. d. R. kein Bindungswille.

[139] Ausführlich *Bonell,* RIW 1990, 693, 697.

[140] MünchKomm/*Gruber,* Art. 14, Rn. 9; *Staudinger/Magnus,* Art. 14, Rn. 15.

[141] OLG Frankfurt a. M., 4.3.1994, CISG-online 110; BezG Saane, 20.2.1997, CISG-online 426 = SZIER 1999, 195; *Achilles,* Art. 14, Rn. 3.

[142] Vgl. *Brunner,* Art. 14, Rn. 2; *Enderlein/Maskow/Strohbach,* Art. 14, Anm. 4.; *Honnold/Flechtner,* Art. 14, Rn. 135; MünchKomm/*Gruber,* Art. 14, Rn. 8; *Schlesinger,* Bd. 1, S. 79; *Schwimann/Posch,* Art. 14, Rn. 4; s. a. *Staudinger/Magnus,* Art. 14, Rn. 37 („Empfängerkreis nicht genau überschaubar"); ferner Art. 337 ADHGB. Die abweichende Einstellung des französischen Rechts wird in ihrer Wirkung durch die Widerruflichkeit der Offerte, vor allem aber durch die solchen Offerten implizierten Vorbehalte stark eingeschränkt, s. *Schlesinger/Bonassies,* Bd. 1, S. 361 ff. Zur Abgrenzung von Offerten und Werbung s. rechtsvergleichend *von Mehren,* Sec. 130.

[143] Hierzu unten Rn. 30.

als Offerte zu verstehen sein; ein vom Vertreter des Verkäufers dem Käufer vorgelegtes Auftragsformular ist nicht nur invitatio, sondern Offerte, so dass die Unterschrift des Käufers bereits Vertragsschluss bewirkt.[144] Auch im Falle der Übersendung des Kaufgegenstandes mit Preisangabe sind regelmäßig nicht nur die essentialia negotii,[145] sondern auch der Bindungswille schlüssig erklärt. Gleiches gilt, wenn eine „Order" des Kaufinteressenten Ware, Menge und Preis nennt, aber bezüglich Details der Ware weiteren Abstimmungsbedarf vorsieht.[146]

28   **d) Präsentationen im Internet.** Präsentationen im Internet, etwa auf einer eigenen Firmenwebsite, können **je nach Inhalt** invitatio oder Offerte sein.[147] Sofern der Bindungswille oder – häufiger – sein Fehlen auf der Website nicht ausdrücklich klargestellt wird, wird man hier im Allgemeinen aufgrund der gesetzlichen Wertung des Art. 14 II,[148] dem Interesse des Verkäufers an der Sicherstellung seiner Lieferfähigkeit und der auch im Übrigen bestehenden funktionalen Vergleichbarkeit von Warenverzeichnissen im Internet mit traditionellen Katalogen[149] vom Vorliegen einer invitatio auszugehen haben;[150] eine Position, die auch Art. 11 UNECIC bezieht. Etwas anderes gilt hingegen für Internetwebsites, auf denen die Stückzahl der aktuell noch vorrätigen Produkte angezeigt wird, weil hierin ein Bindungswille zum Ausdruck kommt.[151] Auch Warenpräsentationen auf Websites Dritter, etwa bei Internet-Auktionen auf der Plattform eines entsprechenden Veranstalters, sind nach Art. 8 auszulegen.[152]

4. Unverbindlichkeit der invitatio ad offerendum, konkurrierende vorvertragliche Pflichten

29   Nationales Recht kann für bestimmte Formen der invitatio – etwa eine Ausschreibung für die Lieferung einer Anlage,[153] die nach Art. 3 unter das CISG fallen kann – bestimmte Regeln vorsehen, deren Verletzung Schadenersatzansprüche auslösen kann;[154] darüber hinaus wird im deutschen Recht vertreten, dass Aufforderung zur Abgabe von Angeboten und ein daraufhin abgegebenes Angebot zwischen den Parteien vorvertragliche Schuldbeziehungen entstehen lässt.[155] Welche Rechtsfolgen aus der Annahme eines solchen vorvertraglichen Schuldverhältnisses bei CISG-Verträgen entstehen, ist unklar. M. E. muss die

---

[144] Vgl. LG Heidelberg, 30.1.1979, in: *Schlechtriem/Magnus,* Art. 22 EKG, Nr. 2.
[145] Oben Rn. 3.
[146] OLG Dresden, 30.11.2010, CISG-online 2183 = IHR 2011, 142, 144: Order über Damendessous mit der Maßgabe, dass die Produktion der Teile durch die Verkäuferin erst „nach OK vom Größensatz" beginnen solle – Angebot mit Bindungswille bejaht.
[147] S. dazu oben Vor Artt. 14–24 Rn. 25 ff., 28; LG Freiburg, 22.8.2002, CISG-online 711 = IHR 2003, 22: Anzeige eines zu verkaufenden Gebrauchtwagens im Internet ohne nähere Begründung als Angebot gewertet. Vgl. auch *Schwenzer/Hachem/Kee,* Rn. 11.11.
[148] Gegen die Anwendung von Art. 14 II auf Websites im WWW hingegen *Borges,* Verträge im elektronischen Geschäftsverkehr, S. 316.
[149] Oben Rn. 27.
[150] *Brunner,* Art. 14, Rn. 2; *Ferrari,* EuLF 2000/01, 301, 306; *Schlechtriem,* Internationales UN-Kaufrecht, Rn. 73; *Schroeter,* UN-Kaufrecht, § 6, Rn. 298; *Schwenzer/Mohs,* IHR 2006, 239, 240 f.; *Wulf,* S. 91 f.; vorsichtiger MünchKomm/*Gruber,* Art. 14, Rn. 8 (nur für „bloße Werbeseiten" im Internet); gegen eine Vermutung zugunsten einer bloßen invitatio O. *Meyer,* Interpretation, S. 340. Im Einzelnen differenzierend *Borges,* Verträge im elektronischen Geschäftsverkehr, S. 317.
[151] *Schwenzer/Mohs,* IHR 2006, 239, 241.
[152] Dazu bereits oben Vor Artt. 14–24 Rn. 28.
[153] Zur Vertragsanbahnung durch internationale Ausschreibungen bereits oben Vor Artt. 14–24 Rn. 30.
[154] Vgl. BGH, 8.9.1998, NJW 1998, 3636 und 3640 zu Ansprüchen eines Bieters bei Aufhebung einer Ausschreibung (§ 26 VOB/A); OLG München, 17.1.2007, OLGR München 2007, 597, 598 f. Auch gesetzliche Vorschriften wie die für die Vergabe von Aufträgen der öffentlichen Hand in §§ 97 ff. GWB festgelegten Regeln können deutsche (öffentliche) Auftraggeber verpflichten, so dass auch zugunsten ausländischer Bieter Schutzpflichten anzunehmen sind (oben Vor Artt. 14–24 Rn. 30), deren Verletzung Schadenersatzansprüche aus c. i. c. auslösen kann.
[155] OLG München, 17.1.2007, OLG-Rp. München 2007, 597 f. m. w. N.; *Staudinger/Bork,* § 145 BGB, Rn. 30, 37, § 146 BGB, Rn. 10.

Änderung oder Zurückziehung einer nicht bindenden invitatio jederzeit zulässig sein.[156] Ob der zur Abgabe von Angeboten Auffordernde informieren muss, wenn keine Vertragsbereitschaft mehr besteht, und ggf. schadenersatzpflichtig wird, wenn der Anbietende im Vertrauen auf die invitatio Aufwendungen gemacht hat, ist – wie oben Vor Artt. 14–24 Rn. 30, 32, 38 festgehalten – grundsätzlich eine nationalem Recht vorbehaltene Frage, die mit Regeln zur *culpa in contrahendo,* aber auch auf der Grundlage einer generalklauselartigen Fassung deliktsrechtlicher Normen gelöst werden kann. Im Anwendungsbereich des CISG muss jedoch beachtet werden, dass das Übereinkommen vom Grundsatz der völligen Unverbindlichkeit einer invitatio ad offerendum ausgeht und dieser Grundsatz nicht durch weitergehende Bindungen nach nationalem Recht ausgehöhlt werden darf, da insoweit eine Regelungsmaterie des Einheitskaufrechts und eine entsprechende Entscheidung seiner Verfasser vorliegt.[157] Das schließt natürlich nicht aus, dass Handelsbräuche oder zwischen den Parteien etablierte Gepflogenheiten Grundlage für die Annahme entsprechender vorvertraglicher Pflichten zwischen den Parteien sein können. Eine Weiterentwicklung des CISG auf der Grundlage des Art. 7 I und II – etwa in Richtung einer Verpflichtung, Vertragsverhandlungen nicht bösgläubig und grundlos abzubrechen – ist ebenfalls nicht auszuschließen, doch wird man diese Prinzipien heute noch nicht ohne weiteres, d. h. ohne die engen Voraussetzungen in Art. 9 II, als anwendbar sehen können.[158] Bei fraudulösem Verhalten bleibt jedenfalls der Rückgriff auf nationales Recht offen.[159]

V. Publikumsofferte

Die zum EAG auf Grund der Formulierung „an eine oder mehrere bestimmte Personen **30** gerichtet" umstrittene Frage der Publikumsofferte,[160] d. h. ob Vorschläge an einen unbestimmten Personenkreis überhaupt Offerte sein können, hat Art. 14 II geregelt.[161] Im **Zweifel** sind Vorschläge an einen unbestimmten Personenkreis **invitationes ad offerendum.** Das gilt für Preislisten, Zirkulare, Inserate in Zeitungen, Spots in Rundfunk und Fernsehen (auch wenn Preis und Warendetails entsprechend Art. 14 I 2 genau vorgestellt werden), Prospekte,[162] evtl. „Angebote" an einen unbestimmten Personenkreis über Internet[163] (zu Internet-Auktionen s. aber oben Rn. 28 und Vor Artt. 14–24 Rn. 28), aber auch für öffentliche Ausschreibungen[164] oder Schaufensterauslagen.[165] Art. 14 lässt jedoch zu, dass ein Vorschlag an einen unbestimmten Personenkreis als Offerte wirkt, wenn der Vorschlagende dies deutlich zum Ausdruck bringt. Beispiele sind Angebote an einen Kreis

---

[156] Vgl. hierzu *Gros,* ZHR 162 (1998), 319, 326.
[157] Oben Vor Artt. 14–24 Rn. 38.
[158] S. oben Vor Artt. 14–24 Rn. 32 f. (auch zu Ansätzen in der Literatur, die bereits heute für die Geltung entsprechender vorvertraglicher Pflichten nach CISG eintreten).
[159] S. oben Vor Artt. 14–24 Rn. 36.
[160] Zu den Klärungsversuchen s. *von Caemmerer,* RabelsZ 29 (1965), 101, 118 f.
[161] Eingefügt auf der 9. Sitzung der Arbeitsgruppe, s. YB IX (1978), S. 73, Nr. 155 ff.; zur Geschichte auch *Bianca/Bonell/Eörsi,* Art. 14, Anm. 1.3. Zur Abgrenzung „bestimmter" und „unbestimmter" Personenkreis, die über die Qualifikation als Offerte in Anwendung von Art. 14 I 1 entscheidet, s. *Wey,* Rn. 733 ff.: Nicht Mehrzahl der Personen, sondern Zufälligkeit und Beliebigkeit des Empfängerkreises entscheiden; ähnlich *Honnold/Flechtner,* Art. 14, Rn. 136. Zur Frage der Bestimmtheit des *Offerenten* s. oben Rn. 4.
[162] S. oben Rn. 27.
[163] S. oben Rn. 28.
[164] *Enderlein/Maskow/Strohbach,* Art. 14, Anm. 4. Zur Vertragsanbahnung über Ausschreibungen s. bereits oben Vor Artt. 14–24 Rn. 30.
[165] Wessen Schuldrecht Schaufensterauslage als Offerte kennt – vgl. Art. 7 III OR –, wird seine Auslage regelmäßig auch als Angebot qualifizieren, denn „der Inhalt einer rechtserheblichen Erklärung lässt sich in vielen Fällen nur vor dem Hintergrund der Rechtsordnung richtig verstehen, in deren Rahmen sie abgegeben worden ist", BGH, 28.11.1994, RIW 1995, 157; vgl. *Joseph,* 3 Dick. J. Int'l L. (1984), 107, 119; *Wey,* Rn. 739; s. auch *Honsell/Schnyder/Straub,* 1. Aufl., Art. 14, Rn. 21, vor dem Hintergrund schweizerischen Rechts: Gleiche Gültigkeitsvoraussetzungen wie für jeden anderen Abschlussvorschlag, falls Bindungswille zum Ausdruck gebracht.

von Stammkunden oder Sonderangebote unter dem Vorbehalt „solange der Vorrat reicht",[166] Internetwebsites, auf denen die Stückzahl aktuell noch vorrätiger Produkte angezeigt werden,[167] eine Fristsetzung für erwartete Antworten,[168] die Aufforderung, Vorleistungen auf einen bestimmten Vorschlag zu erbringen,[169] oder das Versprechen einer Belieferung bis zu einem bestimmten Datum zu einem besonders günstigen Preis.[170]

31 Auch ein Vorschlag an einen unbestimmten Personenkreis muss, um Offerte zu sein, grundsätzlich die Mindestbestandteile nach Art. 14 I 2 enthalten.[171] Das schließt ebenso wie bei der Individualofferte jedoch nicht aus, dass die Parteien auf der Grundlage der Parteiautonomie von Art. 14 I 2 abweichen.[172]

VI. Bedingtes Angebot

1. Bedingungen bei Vertragsschluss

31a Der Offerent hat die Möglichkeit, sein Angebot unter einer **aufschiebenden** oder **auflösenden Bedingung** abzugeben, indem er die Bedingung zum Bestandteil seiner Angebotserklärung i. S. d. Art. 14 macht. Entsprechende Sachbedingungen haben nichts mit dem Bindungswillen nach Art. 14 I a. E.[173] zu tun; sie schließen ihn nicht aus,[174] sondern setzen ihn voraus. **Beispiele** aus der Rechtsprechung sind Kaufangebote unter der Bedingung, dass der Käufer durch einen (dritten) Generalunternehmer beauftragt wird,[175] dass die jeweils vorangegegangene Teillieferung unter einem Sukzessivlieferungsvertrag nicht durch Veterinär- und Zollbehörden beanstandet[176] oder die Kaufsache an einen Abnehmer weiterverkauft wird,[177] sowie Verkaufsangebote unter der Bedingung, dass der annehmende Käufer bis zu einem bestimmten Datum eine Anzahlung und/oder den (Rest-)Kaufpreis leistet.[178] Nimmt der Oblat das so ausgestaltete Angebot in Übereinstimmung mit Artt. 18 ff. an, so kommt es zu einem bedingten Vertragsschluss (bei Einigung auf eine aufschiebende Bedingung) oder einer bedingten Vertragsbindung (bei Vereinbarung einer auflösenden Bedingung).[179]

2. Erfassung durch das CISG

31b Der Vertragsschluss unter aufschiebenden oder auflösenden Bedingungen hat ebenso wie die Behandlung entsprechend bedingter Angebote im UN-Kaufrecht keine ausdrückliche Regelung erfahren. Das Übereinkommen stimmt darin mit jüngeren kaufrechtsvereinheitlichenden Texten[180] überein, während breiter angelegte Einheitsrechtsprojekte hierzu Be-

---

[166] *Neumayer/Ming*, Art. 14, Anm. 13.; *Witz/Salger/Lorenz/Witz*, Art. 14, Rn. 23; a. A. MünchKomm/*Gruber*, Art. 14, Rn. 12; *Staudinger/Magnus*, Art. 14, Rn. 14.
[167] *Schwenzer/Mohs*, IHR 2006, 239, 241; s. auch oben Rn. 28.
[168] Vgl. zum amerikanischen Recht *Schlesinger/Macneil*, Bd. 1, S. 332 f.; ferner den schottischen Fall *Philip & Co. v. Knoblauch* (1907), Sess. Cas. 994, 997.
[169] Vgl. die Fälle bei *Schlesinger/Macneil*, Bd. 1, S. 331 f.
[170] Zuweilen werden solche Mitteilungen deshalb als Offerte bewertet, um Lockvogelangebote zu verhindern, s. BGer, 2.2.1954, BGE 80 II 26, 36: dictum zu Art. 7 III OR; amerikanische Entscheidungen bei *Schlesinger/Macneil*, Bd. 1, S. 334 f.
[171] Vgl. zum insoweit missverständlichen Wortlaut von Art. 14 II *Bianca/Bonell/Eörsi*, Art. 14, Anm. 2.2.5.2., 3.3.; *Murray*, 8 J. L. & Com. (1988), 11, 18 f.; *Schultz*, 35 Cornell Int'l L. J. (2001-02), 263, 272.
[172] S. oben Vor Artt. 14–24 Rn. 1 sowie hier Rn. 21.
[173] Zu diesem bereits oben in Rn. 23 ff.
[174] S. demgegenüber zu Angeboten „unter Vorbehalt" *Ferrari u. a./Mankowski*, Art. 14, Rn. 7 f.
[175] ICC, 7844/1994, CISG-online 567 (Kaufvertrag über Fernkommunikationsausrüstung).
[176] OLG Hamm, 22.9.1992, CISG-online 57 (Kaufvertrag über Schweinespeck) – Bedingtheit des Kaufangebots vom Käufer behauptet, aber in concreto nicht bewiesen.
[177] OLG Schleswig, 29.10.2002, CISG-online 717 = IHR 2003, 67, 69 (Kaufvertrag über einen Hengst).
[178] Audiencia Provincial de Murcia, 15.7.2010, CISG-online 2130 (Kaufvertrag über einen Kran).
[179] S. dazu noch sogleich in Rn. 31b sowie unten Art. 23 Rn. 3.
[180] Auch der CESL-Entwurf behandelt aufschiebende und auflösende Bedingungen nicht.

stimmungen enthalten.[181] Aus der Entstehungsgeschichte des UN-Kaufrechts ergibt sich jedoch, dass man die bedingte Ausgestaltung von Angeboten als **Frage** angesehen hat, die vom sachlichen Anwendungsbereich des Übereinkommens **erfasst** ist;[182] man hielt eine gesonderte Regelung für überflüssig, weil bereits Art. 6 die Aufnahme von Bedingungen in Vertragserklärungen ermöglicht.[183] Die Einbeziehung einer Bedingung in einen CISG-Vertrag bestimmt sich daher **nach Artt. 14 ff.**;[184] jede bedingte Parteierklärung enthält dabei zugleich das Angebot, insoweit i. S. d. Art. 6 von der sachlich einschlägigen Vorschrift im Übereinkommen – das selbst, wie namentlich in Art. 14, durchgehend unbedingte Erklärungen vorsieht – abzuweichen[185] bzw. deren Wirkung zu ändern.

3. Auslegung von Bedingungen

Die Auslegung bedingter Parteierklärungen und Verträge einschließlich der Fragen, auf **31c** den Eintritt welchen Ereignisses sich die Bedingung inhaltlich bezieht und ob es sich typologisch um eine aufschiebende oder auflösende Bedingung handelt, richtet sich nach **Art. 8**.[186] Sorgfalt ist bei der Beurteilung von als Bedingung formulierten Vertragsklauseln geboten, die sich inhaltlich auf Gegenstände beziehen, die auch in Teil III des Übereinkommens eine detaillierte Regelung erfahren haben (wie namentlich Art, Qualität und Menge der Ware, oder Zeitpunkt und Modalitäten der Kaufpreiszahlung): Hier wird im Zweifel davon auszugehen sein, dass die Parteien lediglich privatautonome Festlegungen zum Inhalt der betreffenden Parteipflichten treffen wollten (s. etwa Art. 35 I), die Rechtsfolgen von deren Verletzung sich jedoch nach dem Rechtsbehelfssystem des Übereinkommens (einschließlich der Schwelle einer „wesentlichen" Vertragsverletzung (Art. 25) für Vertragsaufhebungen, Artt. 49 I lit. a), 64 I lit. a)) richten sollen, wohingegen eine von vornherein nur auflösend bedingte Parteibindung aus Sicht einer vernünftigen Person i. S. d. Art. 8 II[187] nur bei klaren Indikatoren anzunehmen sein wird.

4. Beweislast

Die Beweislast für die Vereinbarung einer aufschiebenden oder auflösenden Bedingung **31d** sowie für deren Eintreten trägt diejenige Partei, die sich darauf beruft.[188]

VII. Einbeziehung standardisierter Vertragsbedingungen

Die Offerte ist unerlässlicher Baustein beim Abschluss des Vertrages und regelmäßig auch **32** Grundlage seines Inhalts. Sie lässt nicht nur die Mindestbestandteile, die Art. 14 I 2 nennt, sondern auch weitere Details des Vertrages, die entweder von den gesetzlichen Vorschriften abweichen oder im CISG nicht geregelte Punkte vertraglich regeln sollen, zum Vertragsinhalt werden.[189] Solche inhaltlichen Ausgestaltungen des Vertrages können nicht nur in der

---

[181] Artt. 5.3.1 ff. PICC; Artt. 16:101 ff. PECL; Art. III–1:106 DCFR.
[182] *Honsell/Dornis,* Art. 23, Rn. 3; MünchKomm/*Gruber,* Art. 23, Rn. 4; *Staudinger/Magnus,* Art. 23, Rn. 4; *Witz/Salger/Lorenz/Witz,* Art. 23, Rn. 4; a. A. *Honsell/Schnyder/Straub,* 1. Aufl., Art. 23, Rn. 5; *Karollus,* S. 76: Rückgriff auf das durch IPR berufene interne Recht.
[183] Vgl. YB IX (1978), S. 80 f.; Nr. 268, 269 ff. Aus der Rspr. in diesem Sinne ICC, 7844/1994, CISG-online 567.
[184] Audiencia Provincial de Murcia, 15.7.2010, CISG-online 2130; OLG Hamm, 22.9.1992, CISG-online 57; *Ferrari u. a./Mankowski,* Art. 23, Rn. 8; MünchKomm/*Gruber,* Art. 23, Rn. 4.
[185] Vgl. Audiencia Provincial de Murcia, 15.7.2010, CISG-online 2130: „… que el artículo 14 de la Convención de Viena no excluye la posibilidad de que la oferta esté sometida a condición" (Art. 14 schließe nicht aus, dass ein Angebot unter einer Bedingung abgegeben wird).
[186] OLG Schleswig, 29.10.2002, CISG-online 717 = IHR 2003, 67, 69; *Staudinger/Magnus,* Art. 23, Rn. 4.
[187] Vgl. OLG Hamm, 22.9.1992, CISG-online 57.
[188] OLG Hamm, 22.9.1992, CISG-online 57; *Ferrari u. a./Mankowski,* Art. 23, Rn. 8; *Honsell/Dornis,* Art. 23, Rn. 7; *Jung,* S. 144 f.; MünchKomm/*Gruber,* Art. 23, Rn. 7.
[189] Vgl. hierzu oben Vor Artt. 14–24 Rn. 42.

Offerte selbst geschehen bzw. vorgeschlagen werden, sondern auch durch Verweis auf Rahmenvereinbarungen, Vorverhandlungen, Incoterms®, standardisierte Musterverträge,[190] technische Normen[191] oder **Allgemeine Geschäftsbedingungen**. Die praktische Bedeutung standardisierter Vertragsbedingungen im Bereich des internationalen Warenhandels ist immens,[192] und der Vertragsschluss unter (jedenfalls angestrebter) Einbeziehung von AGB dürfte unter dem UN-Kaufrecht heute nicht mehr die Ausnahme, sondern den Regelfall darstellen.[193]

1. Maßgebliche Rechtsvorschriften

33   Besondere Voraussetzungen für die Einbeziehung standardisierter Geschäftsbedingungen in einen Vertrag stellt das CISG nicht auf; man hielt die Aufnahme einer speziellen Regelung für nicht erforderlich, weil das Übereinkommen bereits Regeln für die Auslegung des Vertragsinhalts enthält.[194] Da die Sachfrage somit vom CISG erfasst wird, sind die entsprechenden Regeln nach ganz h. A. aus **Artt. 14 ff. i. V. m. Art. 8** zu entwickeln;[195] vereinzelt wird – ohne Unterschiede im Ergebnis – gemäß Art. 7 II auf die dem Übereinkommen zugrunde liegenden allgemeinen Grundsätze rekurriert.[196] Die gelegentlich vertretene Gegenauffassung, die insoweit auf unvereinheitlichtes nationales Recht zurückgreifen will,[197] hat sich zu Recht nicht durchsetzen können.

34   Nationale **AGB-Kontrollnormen** sind auf CISG-Verträge daneben nur anwendbar, sofern sie funktional qualifiziert die Gültigkeit der AGB-Klauseln betreffen, während konkurrierende Anforderungen an den Vertragsschluss oder die Form durch Artt. 14 ff. i. V. m. Art. 8 bzw. durch Art. 11 verdrängt werden.[198] Nicht neben dem CISG anwend-

---

[190] Hierzu *Fontaine*, Recht des internationalen Warenkaufs, S. 1197 f. mit zahlreichen Beispielen.
[191] Vgl. *Heuzé*, Anm. 167. (zur Qualitätsbestimmung).
[192] *Schwenzer/Hachem/Kee*, Rn. 12.01.
[193] Vgl. dazu *Koller*, FS Honsell, S. 225; *Schultz*, 35 Cornell Int'l L. J. (2001-02), 263, 287.
[194] Ein Vorschlag in der Arbeitsgruppe, die Einbeziehung von Allgemeinen Geschäftsbedingungen des Offerenten ausdrücklich zu regeln, ist auf der 9. Sitzung mit diesem Argument abgelehnt worden, s. YB IX (1978), S. 81, Nr. 278.
[195] BGH, 31.10.2001, CISG-online 617 = BGHZ 149, 113, 117; OGH, 31.8.2005, CISG-online 1093 = IHR 2006, 31, 32; OGH, 17.12.2003, CISG-online 828 = IHR 2004, 148, 153; OGH, 6.2.1996, CISG-online 224 = ZfRVgl 1996, 248, 251; Gerechtshof 's-Hertogenbosch, 29.5.2007, CISG-online 1550; Gerechtshof 's-Hertogenbosch, 16.10.2002, CISG-online 816 = IHR 2004, 194, 195 m. Anm. *Janssen*, 196 ff.; OGer Bern, 19.5.2008, CISG-online 1738; *Travelers Property Casualty Company of America et al. v. Saint-Gobain Technical Fabrics Canada Ltd.*, U. S. Dist. Ct. (D. Minn.), 31.1.2007, CISG-online 1435 = IHR 2007, 240, 243; OLG Celle, 24.7.2009, CISG-online 1906 = NJW-RR 2010, 136, 138; OLG Frankfurt a. M., 26.6.2006, CISG-online 1395 = IHR 2007, 42, 44; OLG Jena, 10.11.2010, CISG-online 2216 = IHR 2011, 79, 80; KG Zug, 11.12.2003, CISG-online 958 = IHR 2005, 119, 120; Trib. Rovereto, 24.8.2006, CISG-online 1374; *Achilles*, Art. 14, Rn. 6; *Honsell/Dornis*, Vorbem. 14–24, Rn. 6; *Kindler*, FS Heldrich, S. 227; *Koller*, FS Honsell, S. 236; *Kramer*, FS Welser, S. 549; *Kröll u. a./Ferrari*, pre Arts 14–24, Rn. 5; *Kruisinga*, 13.2 Electr. J. Comp. L. (May 2009), 1, 19; *Lautenschlager*, 11 VJ (2007), 259, 275 ff.; *Lohmann*, Parteiautonomie, S. 184; *Magnus*, FS Kritzer, S. 305 f.; *Mittmann*, IHR 2006, 103, 104; MünchKomm/*Gruber*, Art. 14, Rn. 27; *Neumayer/Ming*, Art. 8, Anm. 6.; *Piltz*, IHR 2004, 133, 134: unmittelbar Artt. 14 ff., nicht primär Art. 8; *ders.*, NJW 2007, 2159, 2160; *Reithmann/Martiny/Martiny*, Rn. 738; *Schmidt-Kessel*, oben Art. 8 Rn. 52 ff. *Schwenzer/Hachem/Kee*, Rn. 12.05; *Staudinger/Magnus*, Art. 14, Rn. 41; *Staudinger/Schlosser*, § 305, Rn. 103; *Steensgaard*, Standardbetingelser, § 8, Rn. 4 ff.; *Ventsch/Kluth*, IHR 2003, 61, 62; *Wey*, Rn. 1328 f.; *Wolf/Lindacher/Pfeiffer/Hau*, IntGV, Rn. 72.
[196] HR, 28.1.2005, CISG-online 1002 = Uniform L. Rev. 2005, 901 m. Anm. *Janssen*, IHR 2005, 155; RB Arnhem, 17.1.2007, CISG-online 1455, wo als Quelle „allgemeiner Grundsätze" auf Artt. 8, 11, 14–24 verwiesen wird; RB Breda, 27.2.2008, CISG-online 2252.
[197] Hof van Beroep Gent, 4.10.2004, CISG-online 985; RB Arnhem, 17.3.2004, CISG-online 946 (beachte, dass diese und die folgenden instanzgerichtlichen Entscheidungen aus den Niederlanden durch die zwischenzeitlich ergangene höchstrichterliche Entscheidung HR, 28.1.2005, CISG-online 1002 = Uniform L. Rev. 2005, 901 überholt sind); RB Zutphen, 29.5.1997, CISG-online 546 = NIPR 1998, Nr. 110; RB Zwolle, 21.5.2003, CISG-online 993 = IHR 2005, 34 (dazu *Janssen*, IHR 2005, 155, 157); RB Zwolle, 1.3.1995, CISG-online 372 = NIPR 1996, Nr. 95; OLG Celle, 2.9.1998, CISG-online 506; LG Duisburg, 17.4.1996, CISG-online 186 = RIW 1996, 774; LG München I, 29.5.1995, CISG-online 235 = NJW 1996, 401, 402; in der Literatur in diesem Sinne allein *Ebenroth*, östJBl 108 (1986), 686 f.
[198] Vgl. schon oben Vor Artt. 14–24 Rn. 3 ff.

bar sind daher etwa die Hinweis- und Kenntnisverschaffungserfordernisse des § 305 II, III BGB, das Vorlageerfordernis nach Art. 5 der portugiesischen Gesetzesverfügung Nr. 446/85, das Hinweis- und Erläuterungserfordernis nach Art. 39 I chinesisches Vertragsgesetz und das Erfordernis eines schriftlichen Einverständnisses des anderen Teils nach Art. 1341 II ital. Cc.[199]

Auch die Kontrolle **überraschender Klauseln** in AGB stellt sich funktional weithin als Gültigkeitsfrage dar und richtet sich nach dem nationalen Recht;[200] neben dem CISG überwiegend anwendbar bleiben daher etwa § 305c I BGB und § 864a öst. ABGB. In deren Anwendung sind in der Rechtsprechung etwa AGB-Klauseln aufgrund ihres Inhalts für „überraschend" und daher nicht wirksam in den CISG-Vertrag einbezogen gehalten worden, welche vor Geltendmachung von Käuferrechtsbehelfen die Setzung einer Nachfrist mit Ablehnungsandrohung verlangen (weil das CISG das Erfordernis einer Ablehnungsandrohung nicht kennt)[201] oder Schadensersatzansprüche ohne Einschränkung hinsichtlich des Verschuldens (Vorsatz, grobe Fahrlässigkeit) vollständig ausschließen[202]; ebenso wurde für eine Rechtswahlklausel entschieden, durch welche (auch) das Einheitskaufrecht in seiner Gesamtheit zugunsten eines nationalen (hier: englischen) Rechts abbedungen werden sollte.[203] Andere Klauseln stellten sich hingegen aufgrund ihrer Präsentation und Unvereinbarkeit mit den übrigen Umständen des konkreten Vertrags als „überraschend" dar und wurden nach Art. 8 nicht in den Kaufvertrag einbezogen,[204] wie etwa eine Erfüllungsortsklausel, die in kleiner Schrift am Ende der Seite aufgedruckt war und in unerwartetem Widerspruch zu einer Erfüllungsortsvereinbarung stand, auf die sich die Parteien zuvor geeinigt hatten.[205] 35

2. AGB als Bestandteil des Angebots

Um in den Vertrag einbezogen werden zu können, müssen die AGB nach dem Willen der erklärenden Partei, der für den Adressaten erkennbar gewesen sein muss (Art. 8 I, II), Bestandteil des Angebots sein.[206] Dies setzt regelmäßig sowohl einen Hinweis des Offerenten auf die AGB als auch die Kenntnisnahme des Angebotsempfängers von deren Inhalt voraus, sofern die Geschäftsbedingungen nicht ausnahmsweise bereits aufgrund der Verhandlungen zwischen den Parteien oder der zwischen ihnen entstandenen Gepflogenheiten Bestandteil der Offerte sind (Art. 8 III; dazu unten Rn. 68 ff.) oder als Handelsbrauch zur Anwendung gelangen (unten Rn. 73). 36

a) **Hinweis auf AGB in Angebotserklärung.** Standardbedingungen werden nicht immer in ihrem vollständigen Wortlaut in der Angebotserklärung selbst wiedergegeben.[207] Um sie gleichwohl zum rechtlichen Bestandteil der Offerte zu machen, bedarf es in der 37

---

[199] S. oben Vor Artt. 14–24 Rn. 4 m. w. N.
[200] S. oben Vor Artt. 14–24 Rn. 5.
[201] OLG Düsseldorf, 21.4.2004, CISG-online 915 = IHR 2005, 24, 28.
[202] OLG Zweibrücken, 31.3.1998, CISG-online 481: „überraschend und daher unwirksam" (obwohl als Kontrollmaßstab § 9 AGBG genannt wird); bestätigt durch BGH, 24.3.1999, CISG-online 396 = BGHZ 141, 129, 135.
[203] OLG Düsseldorf, 14.1.1994, NJW-RR 1994, 1132; OLG Düsseldorf, 8.3.1996, WM 1996, 1489, 1492; so auch BuB/*Nielsen*, Rn. 5/30; *Schlechtriem*, Internationales UN-Kaufrecht, Rn. 21. (In den vom OLG Düsseldorf entschiedenen Fällen dürfte freilich die Abbedingung des unvereinheitlichten deutschen Rechts und nicht des internationalen Kaufrechts entscheidend gewesen sein, da es sich um Börsentermingeschäfte handelte.)
[204] S. zu dieser Differenzierung oben Vor Artt. 14–24 Rn. 5.
[205] LG Landshut, 12.6.2008, CISG-online 1703 = IHR 2008, 184, 187.
[206] OGH, 31.8.2005, CISG-online 1093 = IHR 2006, 31, 32; OGH, 17.12.2003, CISG-online 828 = IHR 2004, 148, 153; BGH, 31.10.2001, CISG-online 617 = BGHZ 149, 113, 117; OGH, 6.2.1996, CISG-online 224 = ZfRVgl 1996, 248, 251. Zur ebenfalls notwendigen Annahme siehe unten Rn. 74 f.
[207] Die Aufnahme „entscheidender Regelungen" in den Individualvertrag empfehlen *Ventsch/Kluth*, IHR 2003, 61, 64 f.

Angebotserklärung daher eines Hinweises auf die AGB, der deren Einbeziehung in den Inhalt der Offerte deutlich macht.[208] Formelle Anforderungen an den Hinweis und dessen Deutlichkeit (wie etwa Schriftform, Fettdruck, Abfassung in einer gesonderten Urkunde oder ein Unterzeichnungserfordernis) kennt das Einheitskaufrecht nicht;[209] er muss so **deutlich** sein, dass eine vernünftige Person „in den Schuhen des Empfängers" – Art. 8 II – ihn versteht.[210] Daran kann es fehlen, wenn der Einbeziehungshinweis zu vage formuliert ist; die Rechtsprechung hat etwa den formularmäßigen Hinweis mit dem Wortlaut „May we point out that for all deliveries and services only the known [AGB] in their latest editions are valid" in einer englischsprachigen Auftragsbestätigung als unzureichend angesehen.[211] Erforderlich ist zudem die Abfassung des Hinweises in einer **Sprache**, die der Adressat versteht oder verstehen muss.[212]

Fand sich die Bezugnahme auf AGB lediglich in einer vorvertraglichen Erklärung, aber nicht in der Vertragserklärung des Verwenders selbst, so kann Letzterer jedenfalls dann gem. Art. 8 II, III **kein** aktueller Einbeziehungswille entnommen werden, wenn zwischen beiden Erklärungen ein erheblicher Zeitraum verstrichen ist.[213] Ebensowenig genügt, dass der AGB-Verwender bei Abschluss eines früheren Kaufvertrages mitgeteilt hatte, er liefere stets „nur zu seinen AGB", sofern die AGB im späteren Angebot auf Abschluss eines neuen Vertrages keinerlei Erwähnung fanden.[214] Ein ausreichender Hinweis muss sowohl klar stellen, dass die in Bezug genommenen AGB für diesen konkreten Kaufvertrag gelten sollen[215] als auch, sofern unterschiedliche Standardbedingungen existieren, welche dieser AGB mit dem Hinweis gemeint sind.[216] Diese Grundsätze gelten auch für elektronische Angebotserklärungen.[217] Sind die AGB auf der Rückseite eines übersandten Formulars

---

[208] OGH, 31.8.2005, CISG-online 1093 = IHR 2006, 31, 32; OLG Dresden, 11.6.2007, CISG-online 1720 = IHR 2008, 162, 166: „... ist nötig, dass der Geschäftspartner des Verwenders erkennen kann, dass dieser seine Bedingungen in den Vertrag einbeziehen will"; OLG Saarbrücken, 13.1.1993, CISG-online 83; OLG Zweibrücken, 31.3.1998, CISG-online 481; Audiencia Provincial de Navarra, 27.12.2007, CISG-online 1798 (gestützt auf Art. 7 I – guter Glaube); Hof van Beroep Antwerpen, 4.11.1998, CISG-online 1310; RB Utrecht, 21.1.2009, CISG-online 1814; RB Veurne, 25.4.2001, CISG-online 765; *Koller*, FS Honsell, S. 237; *Kramer*, FS Welser, S. 549; *Magnus*, FS Kritzer, S. 315; MünchKomm/*Gruber*, Art. 14, Rn. 32; *Piltz*, IHR 2004, 133, 134; *Stadler*, AGB, S. 91; *Ulmer/Brandner/Hensen/H. Schmidt*, Anh. § 305 BGB, Rn. 12.

[209] Vgl. Trib. Rovereto, 24.8.2006, CISG-online 1374: CISG verlangt keinen hervorgehobenen Hinweis auf AGB; Trib. com. Nivelles, 19.9.1995, CISG-online 366: Hinweis in fett gedruckten Buchstaben ausreichend; a. A. *Stadler*, AGB, S. 92, der durchgehend eine grafische Hervorhebung des Hinweises fordert.

[210] OLG Düsseldorf, 30.1.2004, CISG-online 821 = IHR 2004, 108, 111; OLG Karlsruhe, 20.7.2004, CISG-online 858 = IHR 2004, 246, 250: „deutlicher" Hinweis in Angebotserklärung genügt jedenfalls; Hof van Beroep Antwerpen, 4.11.1998, CISG-online 1310: ausdrücklicher *(uitdrukkelijk)* Hinweis ausreichend; RB Utrecht, 21.1.2009, CISG-online 1814; LG Coburg, 12.12.2006, CISG-online 1447 = IHR 2007, 117, 118; *Berger*, FS Horn, S. 17; *Brunner*, Art. 4, Rn. 41; *Koller*, FS Honsell, S. 237; *Kramer*, FS Welser, S. 549; *Lohmann*, Parteiautonomie, S. 212; *Piltz*, IHR 2004, 133, 136; *Stoffels*, Rn. 253.

[211] *CSS Antenna, Inc. v. Amphenol-Tuchel Electronics GmbH*, U. S. Dist. Ct. (D. Md.), 8.2.2011, CISG-online 2177: „This language is ambiguous at best. The phrase 'may we point out' is neither clear nor specific regarding [des deutschen Verkäufer]'s intent that the General Conditions should control the terms of the sale. The ambiguity of the language referencing the General Conditions is further highlighted by the specificity of the surrounding language in the purchase confirmation form ...".

[212] S. hierzu näher unten Rn. 61 ff.

[213] OLG Jena, 10.11.2010, CISG-online 2216 = IHR 2011, 79, 80: *Sourcing Conformation Letter* mit Hinweis auf AGB war knapp 10 Monate vor Vertragsschluss übersandt worden – kein ausreichendes Anzeichen für aktuellen Einbeziehungswillen bei Vertragsschluss.

[214] OLG Düsseldorf, 23.3.2011, CISG-online 2218.

[215] *Piltz*, IHR 2004, 133, 135.

[216] OGH, 6.2.1996, CISG-online 224 = ZfRVgl 1996, 248, 252: im Laufe der Verhandlungen zwischen deutschem und österreichischem Erdgashändler waren von AGB für Tagesgeschäfte und einem Rahmenvertrag für Tendergeschäfte die Rede gewesen – spätere Verweise in der Korrespondenz auf „übliche Konditionen" bzw. „auf Vertragsbasis" führten nicht zur Einbeziehung von Standardbedingungen in den Kaufvertrag, weil die Hinweise nicht deutlich machten, welche der Bedingungen gemeint war.

[217] *Magnus*, FS Kritzer, S. 316; zu elektronischen Kommunikationsmitteln unter dem CISG s. allgemein oben Vor Artt. 14–24 Rn. 25 ff.

aufgedruckt, **ohne** dass dieses auf der Vorderseite einen Hinweis auf die AGB enthält, so werden sie **nicht** in das Angebot einbezogen.[218]

Soweit in der Rechtsprechung des österreichischen OHG gelegentlich pauschal behauptet wird, die Einbeziehung von AGB könne auch **stillschweigend** geschehen,[219] wird man dem unter dem UN-Kaufrecht nur unter der Bedingung zustimmen können, dass die AGB bereits Gegenstand der Verhandlungen zwischen den Parteien waren (Art. 8 III) oder eine Gepflogenheit bzw. ein Handelsbrauch eingreift (dazu unten Rn. 68 ff.).[220] **38**

b) Kenntnisnahme des Adressaten vom AGB-Text. Ein Hinweis auf die Einbeziehung von AGB in den Inhalt des Angebots reicht in denjenigen Konstellationen unbestritten aus, in denen der Inhalt der betreffenden AGB dem Erklärungsempfänger bei Übermittlung des Angebots bereits positiv **bekannt** ist, Art. 8 I.[221] **39**

Schwierigkeiten machen die weit häufigeren Fälle, in denen eine solche positive Kenntnis nicht vorliegt oder vom AGB-Verwender nicht bewiesen werden kann.[222] Hier war in Rechtsprechung und Literatur zunächst umstritten, ob für die Einbeziehung der AGB schon die Möglichkeit des Angebots**empfängers** ausreicht, vom Inhalt der AGB in zumutbarer Weise Kenntnis zu nehmen und es daher im Zweifelsfall ihm überlassen bleibt, sich danach **zu erkundigen** (**Kenntnisnahmemöglichkeit** des Adressaten),[223] oder ob es Aufgabe des anbietenden **Verwenders** der AGB und Voraussetzung für deren Einbeziehung in das Angebot ist, dem Erklärungsgegner ungefragt Kenntnis vom Inhalt seiner Standardbedingungen zu **verschaffen** (**Kenntnisverschaffungsobliegenheit** des Offerenten).[224] **40**

Der BGH hatte die Frage im Jahre 2001 als erstes Höchstgericht eines CISG-Vertragsstaates zu entscheiden. Er schloss sich der letztgenannten, in Rechtsprechung und Literatur

---

[218] Audiencia Provincial de Navarra, 27.12.2007, CISG-online 1798; CA Paris, 13.12.1995, CISG-online 312 = J. C. P. 1997, éd. G, II, Nr. 22 772; LG Hannover, 21.4.2009, CISG-online 2298 = IHR 2012, 59, 61; vgl. auch OLG Düsseldorf, 30.1.2004, CISG-online 821 = IHR 2004, 108, 111 f.: Geschäftsformular enthielt auf der Vorderseite den Hinweis: „Rücksenden an: siehe Rückseite", und auf der Rückseite waren neben der auf der Vorderseite in Bezug genommenen Adresse Lieferbedingungen aufgedruckt – keine Einbeziehung der AGB mangels ausreichend eindeutigen Hinweises; *Magnus*, FS Kritzer, S. 315 f.; MünchKomm/*Gruber*, Art. 14, Rn. 32; *Schwenzer/Hachem/Kee*, Rn. 12.07; *Steensgaard*, Standardbetingelser, § 8, Rn. 9 f.; a. A. *Rudolph*, Art. 14, Rn. 7.

[219] OGH, 17.12.2003, CISG-online 828 = IHR 2004, 148, 153 unter Hinweis auf die zum unvereinheitlichten österreichischen Recht ergangene (!) Entscheidung OGH, 15.1.1997, IPRax 1998, 294 ff.; dem folgend OGH, 31.8.2005, CISG-online 1093 = IHR 2006, 31, 32; so auch bereits OGH, 6.2.1996, CISG-online 224 = ZfRVgl 1996, 248, 251.

[220] *Kramer*, FS Welser, S. 551.

[221] OGH, 29.11.2005, CISG-online 1227: Aushändigung der AGB vor Aufnahme der Geschäftsbeziehung; *Magnus*, FS Kritzer, S. 322; MünchKomm/*Gruber*, Art. 14, Rn. 30; *Steensgaard*, Standardbetingelser, § 8, Rn. 32, 39 ff.; *Ventsch/Kluth*, IHR 2003, 61, 62: bei ausdrücklicher Einigung über den AGB-Inhalt.

[222] Zur Beweislast s. oben Rn. 76.

[223] Aus der Rspr. Trib. com. Nivelles, 19.9.1995, CISG-online 366 (dem Sachverhalt lassen sich keine Anzeichen dafür entnehmen, dass der belgischen Käuferin der Inhalt der „conditions générales de l'association suisse des industriels en machines", auf die in den zahlreichen Angebotsschreiben der schweizerischen Verkäuferin verwiesen wurde, tatsächlich bekannt waren); LG Coburg, 12.12.2006, CISG-online 1447 = IHR 2007, 117, 118; LG Heilbronn, 15.9.1997, CISG-online 562; aus der Literatur *Berger*, FS Horn, S. 9 ff.; *Hammerschmidt*, S. 36; *Holthausen*, RIW 1989, 513, 517; *Kindler*, FS Heldrich, S. 228 ff., 233; *Luig*, S. 222; *Schmidt-Kessel*, zu Art. 8 Rn. 53; *ders.*, NJW 2002, 3444, 3445; *Soergel/Lüderitz/Fenge*, Art. 14, Rn. 10; *Stadler*, AGB, S. 94 f.; *Staudinger/Schlosser*, § 305, Rn. 157.

[224] Aus der Rspr. *Mansonville Plastics (B. C.) Ltd. v. Kurtz GmbH*, Sup. Ct. BC, 21.8.2003, CISG-online 1017; OGer Bern, 19.5.2008, CISG-online 1738; Gerechtshof 's-Hertogenbosch, 16.10.2002, CISG-online 816 = IHR 2004, 194, 196 unter Verweis auf Art. 2.220 PICC und Art. 2:104 PECL (zu diesem Begründungsansatz mit Recht kritisch *Janssen*, IHR 2004, 194, 198); OLG Koblenz, 4.10.2002, CISG-online 716 = IHR 2003, 66; LG Trier, 8.1.2004, CISG-online 910 = IHR 2004, 115, 116; aus der Literatur *Brunner*, Art. 4, Rn. 41; *Drasch*, S. 5 ff.; *Hennemann*, S. 72 ff.; *Jungemeyer*, RIW 2010, 166 f.; *Lohmann*, Parteiautonomie, S. 215; *Magnus*, FS Kritzer, S. 320; *O. Meyer*, Interpretation, S. 342; MünchKomm/*Basedow*, § 305, Rn. 95; MünchKomm/*Gruber*, Art. 14, Rn. 29; MünchKomm/*Westermann*, Art. 4, Rn. 5; *Piltz*, NJW 2003, 2056, 2060 m. w. N.; *ders.*, NJW 2007, 2159, 2161; *Schroeter*, UN-Kaufrecht, § 6, Rn. 317; *Stoffels*, Rn. 253; *Teklote*, S. 112 ff.; *Ventsch/Kluth*, IHR 2003, 61, 62 f.; *Witz/Salger/Lorenz/Witz*, Vor Artt. 14–24, Rn. 12; *Wolf/Lindacher/Pfeiffer/Hau*, IntGV, Rn. 73; zum EAG *Drobnig*, Standard Forms, S. 123, der „actual knowledge and nothing less" verlangt.

herrschenden Auffassung an und stellte mit ausführlicher Begründung im Ergebnis **zu Recht** fest, dass unter dem UN-Kaufrecht vom AGB-Verwender zu fordern ist, dass er dem Erklärungsgegner deren Text unaufgefordert **übersendet** oder **anderweitig zugänglich** macht.[225] Die **neuere Rechtsprechung** sowohl deutscher Instanzgerichte[226] als auch der Gerichte anderer Vertragsstaaten (Italien,[227] Niederlande,[228] Schweiz[229]) ist dem in Übereinstimmung mit dem Postulat international einheitlicher Auslegung des Übereinkommens (Art. 7 I) **gefolgt**. Die Frage ist damit jedenfalls für die praktische Rechtsanwendung **geklärt**.

41   Die nach Art. 14 i. V. m. Art. 8 II, III für Zwecke der Einbeziehung standardisierter Bedingungen in den Vertrag bestehende **Kenntnisverschaffungsobliegenheit** hat zur Folge, dass die diesbezüglichen Anforderungen im Ausgangspunkt schärfer ausfallen als im innerdeutschen kaufmännischen Verkehr,[230] wo die bloße Möglichkeit der Kenntnisnahme als hinreichend erachtet wird.[231] Die Haltung des UN-Kaufrechts steht damit anderen nationalen Vertragsrechten näher, die in ihren Einbeziehungsanforderungen vielfach ebenfalls strenger sind als das deutsche Recht.[232] Sie begründet sich dadurch, dass es nach den Vertragsschlussregeln des Einheitskaufrechts Aufgabe des Offerenten ist, seine AGB, deren Einbeziehung in seinem Interesse liegt, an den Verhandlungstisch zu bringen und nicht Aufgabe der Gegenseite, danach zu fragen.[233] Wenn danach also der Offerent den Inhalt seines Angebots zu definieren und verständlich auszugestalten hat, lässt sich eine (gegenläufige) Erkundigungsobliegenheit des Adressaten konsequenterweise allenfalls in den Fällen begründen, in denen der Inhalt des Klauselwerks für diesen – in Abweichung vom Horizont des „üblichen" Erklärungsempfängers (Art. 8 II, III) – im konkreten Fall *ausnahmsweise* nicht erkennbar ist.[234] Eine grundsätzliche Kenntnis des Empfängers vom typischen Inhalt verwandter AGB kann dagegen allein bei innerstaatlichen Geschäften angenommen werden, weil hier die Klauseln innerhalb einer Branche vielfach ähnlich ausgestaltet sind;[235] für eine entsprechende Vermutung ist demgegenüber im internationalen Rechtsverkehr kein Raum, weil dort in Anbetracht der unterschiedlichen nationalen Rechtsordnungen und Gepflogenheiten typischerweise erhebliche Unterschiede zwischen den jeweiligen Klauselwerken bestehen.[236]

---

[225] BGH, 31.10.2001, CISG-online 617 = BGHZ 149, 113, 117; *Janssen,* IHR 2004, 194, 199 f.; MünchKommHGB/*Ferrari,* Art. 14, Rn. 39; *Ventsch/Kluth,* IHR 2003, 61, 62.

[226] OLG Celle, 24.7.2009, CISG-online 1906 = NJW-RR 2010, 136, 138; OLG Düsseldorf, 25.7.2003, CISG-online 919; OLG Düsseldorf, 30.1.2004, CISG-online 821 = IHR 2004, 108, 112; OLG Düsseldorf, 21.4.2004, CISG-online 915 = IHR 2005, 24, 27; OLG Düsseldorf, 23.3.2011, CISG-online 2218; OLG Jena, 10.11.2010, CISG-online 2216 = IHR 2011, 79, 81; OLG Köln, 21.12.2005, CISG-online 1201 (insoweit nicht abgedr. in IHR 2006, 86 ff.); OLG München, 14.1.2009, CISG-online 2211 = IHR 2009, 201, 203; OLG Oldenburg, 20.12.2007, CISG-online 1644 = IHR 2008, 112, 117; LG Gießen, 17.12.2002, CISG-online 766 = IHR 2003, 276, 277; LG Landshut, 12.6.2008, CISG-online 1703 = IHR 2008, 184, 186; LG Neubrandenburg, 3.8.2005, CISG-online 1190 = IHR 2006, 26, 27.

[227] Trib. Rovereto, 21.12.2007, CISG-online 1590; Trib. Rovereto, 24.8.2006, CISG-online 1374.

[228] RB Rotterdam, 25.2.2009, CISG-online 1812 = EJCL 2009, 105; RB Utrecht, 21.1.2009, CISG-online 1814.

[229] OGer Bern, 19.5.2008, CISG-online 1738.

[230] *Piltz,* IHR 2004, 133, 136; *Schmidt-Kessel,* NJW 2002, 3444, 3445; *Staudinger/Magnus,* Art. 14, Rn. 41; *Ventsch/Kluth,* IHR 2003, 224; so schon LG Oldenburg, 28.2.1996, CISG-online 189: nach Artt. 14–19 CISG „eher strengere" Einbeziehungsvoraussetzungen.

[231] BGH, 12.2.1992, BGHZ 117, 190, 198; BGH, 30.6.1976, NJW 1976, 1886; MünchKomm/*Basedow,* § 305, Rn. 91 f. m. w. N.

[232] Vgl. die Nachw. bei *Reithmann/Martiny/Martiny,* Rn. 227.

[233] *Mittmann,* IHR 2006, 103, 105; wohl auch Gerechtshof 's-Hertogenbosch, 16.10.2002, CISG-online 816 = IHR 2004, 194, 195.

[234] A. A. *Kindler,* FS Heldrich, S. 228 ff., 233: ein Kunde handele i. S. d. Art. 8 I „grob sorgfaltswidrig", wenn er sich nicht über den Inhalt der AGB vergewissere; *Schmidt-Kessel,* NJW 2002, 3444, 3445: in Art. 8 sei eine „generelle Rückfrageobliegenheit" verankert.

[235] MünchKomm/*Basedow,* § 305, Rn. 92 will die AGB-Einbeziehung durch bloßen Hinweis daher unter dem BGB zu Recht auf branchenübliche AGB beschränkt wissen.

[236] BGH, 31.10.2001, CISG-online 617 = BGHZ 149, 113, 117 f.; OLG Düsseldorf, 25.7.2003, CISG-online 919; *Magnus,* FS Kritzer, S. 320 f.; MünchKomm/*Basedow,* § 305, Rn. 95; MünchKomm/*Gruber,*

Verschiedene der sonstigen, zur **Begründung** der Kenntnisverschaffungsobliegenheit er- 42
gänzend angeführten Argumente überzeugen hingegen kaum: So ist der Grundsatz von Treu
und Glauben (Art. 7 I)[237] deshalb kein geeigneter Ansatzpunkt, weil zum einen die Auslegung des Art. 14 i. V. m. Art. 8 schon ohne dessen ergänzende Berücksichtigung zum hier
vertretenen Ergebnis führt[238] und zum anderen zweifelhaft ist, ob Treu und Glauben darüber
hinaus unter dem CISG überhaupt unmittelbare Parteipflichten begründen kann;[239] und auch
eine pauschal und ohne Nennung einer Rechtsgrundlage angeführte „allgemeine Kooperations- und Informationspflicht der Parteien"[240] dürfte die Vertragsschlussregelungen des
Einheitskaufrechts jedenfalls nicht ohne weiteres modifizieren können, sofern man eine
erhebliche Rechtsunsicherheit in diesem Bereich vermeiden will. Ob und in welcher Intensität eine Inhaltskontrolle von AGB nach nationalem Recht erfolgt (Art. 4 S. 2 lit. a)), überlässt das CISG im Übrigen der Entscheidung der nationalen Gesetzgeber; ein unter manchen
Rechtsordnungen insoweit vermutetes unzureichendes Schutzniveau[241] darf schon deshalb
nicht durch eine Erhöhung der Einbeziehungsanforderungen ausgeglichen werden, weil
diese Problematik außerhalb des Regelungsbereiches des CISG liegt.[242] Schließlich lässt sich
eine Kenntnisverschaffungsobliegenheit nicht mit der Schutzbedürftigkeit von Verbrauchern
i. S. d. § 13 BGB begründen,[243] deren Kaufgeschäft bei Vorliegen eines „verdeckten" Verbraucherkaufes in der Tat unter das CISG fallen kann,[244] weil dem Käufer in diesen Fallgestaltungen, in denen sein privater Erwerbszweck dem Verkäufer nicht erkennbar war, eben
gerade dieselben Rechte und Pflichten wie jedem anderen Käufer zukommen sollen.[245]

3. Anforderungen an die Kenntnisverschaffung bezüglich des Inhalts der AGB

Sofern der Offerent – wie im Regelfall[246] – dem Adressaten den Inhalt der Standard- 43
bedingungen zur Kenntnis bringen muss, unter deren Geltung er zu kontrahieren wünscht,
so kann er dieser Obliegenheit durch die Übersendung der AGB oder deren anderweitiges
Zugänglichmachen genügen. Die Kenntnisverschaffung hat dabei **unaufgefordert** zu erfolgen; eine Erkundigungsobliegenheit des Angebotsempfängers besteht unter dem UN-Kaufrecht nicht.[247]

Art. 14, Rn. 29; a. A. *Berger*, FS Horn, S. 9 f. unter Hinweis auf von internationalen Verbänden oder
Organisationen formulierte AGB (deren Verwendung freilich nicht den Regelfall darstellen dürfte).
[237] BGH, 31.10.2001, CISG-online 617 = BGHZ 149, 113, 118; Gerechtshof 's-Hertogenbosch,
16.10.2002, CISG-online 816 = IHR 2004, 194, 195; Trib. Rovereto, 21.12.2007, CISG-online 1590;
Ventsch/Kluth, IHR 2003, 61, 63.
[238] *Kindler*, FS Heldrich, S. 228: „methodisch ein Sündenfall".
[239] Vgl. *Schlechtriem*, Internationales UN-Kaufrecht, Rn. 44; *Steensgaard*, Standardbetingelser, § 8, Rn. 26.
[240] BGH, 31.10.2001, CISG-online 617 = BGHZ 149, 113, 118; Trib. Rovereto, 21.12.2007, CISG-online
1590; *Koller*, FS Honsell, S. 238; *Ventsch/Kluth*, IHR 2003, 61, 63.
[241] Darauf abstellend BGH, 31.10.2001, CISG-online 617 = BGHZ 149, 113, 117 f.; *Soergel/Lüderitz/Fenge*,
Art. 14, Rn. 10.
[242] *Schmidt-Kessel*, NJW 2002, 3444, 3445. Im Übrigen muss es den Parteien frei stehen, ihren Vertrag im
Wege der Rechtswahl bewusst einer nationalen Rechtsordnung zu unterstellen, die keine umfassende AGB-Inhaltskontrolle kennt, worin etwa ein Grund für die häufige Wahl des schweizerischen Rechts gesehen wird
(*Berger*, FS Horn, S. 10).
[243] So aber BGH, 31.10.2001, CISG-online 617 = BGHZ 149, 113, 119; wieder anders MünchKomm/
Gruber, Art. 14, Rn. 29, der die Schutzbedürftigkeit „unerfahrener Marktteilnehmer etwa aus Entwicklungsländern" anführt; wie hier *Kindler*, FS Heldrich, S. 231; *O. Meyer*, Interpretation, S. 335 Fn. 52.
[244] KG Jura, 3.11.2004, CISG-online 965; *Schroeter*, UN-Kaufrecht, § 6, Rn. 108.
[245] *Schmidt-Kessel*, NJW 2002, 3444, 3445; a. A. *Berger*, FS Horn, S. 17 und *Kindler*, FS Horn, S. 232, die
im Rahmen von Art. 8 zwischen unternehmerischen und nicht unternehmerischen Erklärungsempfängern
differenzieren wollen.
[246] S. zur Einbeziehung bestimmter AGB als Parteigepflogenheit oder Handelsbrauch unten Rn. 68 ff.
MünchKomm/*Gruber*, Art. 14, Rn. 32 will auf eine Kenntnisverschaffung in den (wohl wenig praxisnahen)
Fällen verzichten, in denen der Vertragsgegner des AGB-Verwenders die Geltung der AGB verlangt hat.
[247] BGH, 31.10.2001, CISG-online 617 = BGHZ 149, 113, 118; OLG Jena, 10.11.2010, CISG-online
2216 = IHR 2011, 79, 81; OLG München, 14.1.2009, CISG-online 2211 = IHR 2009, 201, 203; Trib.
Rovereto, 21.12.2007, CISG-online 1590; *Karollus*, LM 3/2002 CISG Nr. 9; MünchKomm/*Gruber*, Art. 14,

44 a) Übersendung. Eine ausreichende Kenntnisverschaffung im Wege der Übersendung der AGB liegt zum einen dann vor, wenn die AGB in ihrem Volltext unmittelbar in der **Angebotserklärung selbst** enthalten sind; so etwa dann, wenn das Angebotsschreiben auf seiner Vorderseite einen deutlichen Hinweis auf die AGB aufweist, die auf der **Rückseite** aufgedruckt sind.[248] Erforderlich ist dabei natürlich, dass (etwa im Rahmen einer Übersendung per Telefax) auch die Rückseite des Schreibens dem Erklärungsempfänger übermittelt wird, nicht etwa nur die Vorderseite.[249] Bei einem per **E-Mail** unterbreiteten Angebot genügt es, wenn die AGB der E-Mail als Anhang (attachment) beigefügt sind.[250]

45 Der Anbietende kann den AGB-Text dem Angebotsschreiben alternativ auch in sonstiger Weise beifügen[251] oder die Übersendung des AGB-Textes außerhalb der Angebotserklärung in einem **gesonderten Übersendungsakt** vornehmen, der in diesem Fall allerdings **rechtzeitig** vor Abschluss des Vertragsschlussvorganges erfolgen muss.[252] Die Zurverfügungstellung während der vorangegangenen Vertragsverhandlungen kann dabei nach Maßgabe des Art. 8 III ausreichen.[253]

46 Scheitert die Übermittlung der AGB an **technischen Problemen,** etwa an der Unleserlichkeit des durch Fax übersandten AGB-Textes, der fehlenden Lesbarkeit einer Datei[254] oder an der Funktionsunfähigkeit eines Hyperlinks im Internet, so bestimmen sich die Rechtsfolgen nach Art. 24. Sofern das Fax danach richtig abgesandt und empfangen worden ist, gehört die Lesbarkeit des Ausdrucks des Empfängergeräts zum Risiko des Adressaten, weil die Funktionsfähigkeit dieses Geräts zur Sphäre des Empfängers zählt.[255]

47 b) Anderweitiges Zugänglichmachen. Der Inhalt der AGB wird mit den Worten des BGH zudem dann Inhalt der Offerte des Verwenders, wenn dieser dem Adressaten den AGB-Text **anderweitig zugänglich gemacht** hat.[256] Unter diesen Obergriff lassen sich zahlreiche derjenigen Konstellationen fassen, in denen eine „Übersendung" des Klauseltextes im engeren Sinne nicht erfolgt ist, wobei die Zuordnung hier freilich nicht immer zweifelsfrei ist:

Rn. 29; *Piltz,* IHR 2007, 121, 122; *Reithmann/Martiny/Martiny,* Rn. 738; *Staudinger/Magnus,* Art. 14, Rn. 41; teilweise a. A. *Honsell/Dornis,* Vorbem. 14–24, Rn. 8.

[248] OGH, 31.8.2005, CISG-online 1093 = IHR 2006, 31, 33; OLG Karlsruhe, 20.7.2004, CISG-online 858 = IHR 2004, 246, 250; CA Colmar, 24.10.2000, CISG-online 578; OLG Saarbrücken, 13.1.1993, CISG-online 83; Hof van Beroep Antwerpen, 4.11.1998, CISG-online 1310; AG Nordhorn, 14.6.1994, CISG-online 259; MünchKommHGB/*Ferrari,* Art. 14, Rn. 39; *Staudinger/Magnus,* Art. 14, Rn. 41; a. A. RB Rotterdam, 14.10.1999, CISG-online 1312 = NIPR 2000, Nr. 29.

[249] So in Gerechtshof 's-Hertogenbosch, 16.10.2002, CISG-online 816 = IHR 2004, 194, 195: Übersendung einer Kopie der Rechnungsvorderseite genügte nicht; Netherlands Arbitration Institute, 10.2.2005, CISG-online 1621 = YB. Comm. Arb. 2007, 93, 104; *Schwenzer/Hachem/Kee,* Rn. 12.07; *Ventsch/Kluth,* IHR 2003, 61, 65.

[250] *Golden Valley Grape Juice and Wine, LLC v. Centrisys Corp. et al.,* U. S. Dist. Ct. (E. D. Cal.), 21.1.2010, CISG-online 2089; *Brunner,* Art. 4, Rn. 42; *Karollus,* LM 3/2002 CISG Nr. 9; *Lohmann,* Parteiautonomie, S. 219; *Magnus,* FS Kritzer, S. 323; *Piltz,* NJW 2011, 2261, 2263; *Schwenzer/Mohs,* IHR 2006, 239, 241 (die darin jedoch begrifflich anscheinend keine „Übersendung" sehen); *Staudinger/Magnus,* Art. 14, Rn. 41a. Unter dem Gesichtspunkt der Beweisbarkeit hiervon abratend *Jungemeyer,* RIW 2010, 166, 168.

[251] *TeeVee Toons, Inc. & Steve Gottlieb, Inc. v. Gerhard Schubert GmbH,* U. S. Dist. Ct. (S. D. N. Y.), 23.8.2006, CISG-online 1272; *Schlechtriem,* FS Kritzer, S. 418 f.

[252] S. dazu noch näher unten Rn. 59.

[253] Vgl. OGH, 29.11.2005, CISG-online 1227; OLG Linz, 8.8.2005, CISG-online 1087 = IHR 2005, 249, 251: Übergabe der AGB zu Beginn der Geschäftsbeziehung im Rahmen eines Gesprächs, in dem die Rahmenbedingungen für die künftige, als längerfristig geplante Geschäftsbeziehung abgesprochen wurden; OLG Frankfurt a. M., 24.3.2009, CISG-online 2165 = IHR 2010, 250, 253 f.

[254] Vgl. OLG Düsseldorf, 21.4.2004, CISG-online 915 = IHR 2005, 24, 27: Text der AGB, die per E-Mail übersandt worden waren, soll „teilweise nicht lesbar" gewesen sein – ausreichende Kenntnisverschaffung bejaht, denn der Adressatin habe in diesem Fall ein Hinweis an die Absenderin obliegen.

[255] S. unten Art. 24 Rn. 23, 25.

[256] BGH, 31.10.2001, CISG-online 617 = BGHZ 149, 113, 117. Dies übersehen *Schmidt-Kessel/Meyer,* IHR 2008, 177, 178.

aa) Bei Vertragsschluss unter Anwesenden. Bei einem Vertragsschluss unter Anwe- **48** senden reicht es aus, wenn die AGB, auf die der Offerent hingewiesen hat, dem Adressaten übergeben werden[257] oder aber im Geschäftslokal ausliegen bzw. -hängen und der Offertenempfänger Gelegenheit hat, sie zu lesen,[258] wohingegen eine bloßes Vorzeigen des AGB-Textes anlässlich der Vertragsverhandlungen nicht genügt, sofern keine Zeit für dessen Lektüre war und er der Gegenpartei auch nicht ausgehändigt wurde.[259]

bb) Zurverfügungstellung im Internet. Umstritten ist, ob das Zurverfügungstellen **49** des AGB-Textes im **Internet,** namentlich auf der Homepage des AGB-Verwenders, zur Erfüllung der Kenntnisverschaffungsobliegenheit ausreicht. Insoweit ist zu differenzieren: Wird der **Kaufvertrag** selbst **über das Internet** (etwa ein Bestellformular auf einer Homepage[260]) abgeschlossen, so genügt es, wenn die AGB über einen Hyperlink auf der Homepage abruf- und herunterladbar sind.[261] Der Zugang zum AGB-Text muss dabei so gestaltet sein, dass dieser für eine vernünftige Person der gleichen Art wie die andere Partei (Art. 8 II) unschwer auffindbar und zugänglich ist;[262] hieran kann es fehlen, sofern auf eine andere Website verlinkt wird, auf welcher die AGB erst unter mehreren AGB-Fassungen oder anderen Inhalten gesucht werden müssen. Eine ausreichende Kenntnisnahmemöglichkeit stellen AGB im Internet auch dar, wenn bei einem Vertragsschluss durch **individuelle E-Mails** mittels eines Hyperlinks in der E-Mail des Verwenders auf die AGB-Datei verwiesen wird.[263] In jedem Fall ist erforderlich, dass sich der im Internet abrufbare AGB-Text **ausdrucken** lässt.[264] Die **Beweislast** für die Auffindbarkeit der AGB sowie deren technische Abruf- und Ausdruckbarkeit trifft den AGB-Verwender, aus dessen Perspektive es daher ratsam ist, sich die erfolgte Kenntnisnahme vom AGB-Text etwa durch das Anklicken eines Bestätigungsfeldes (sog. „Click-wrap"[265]) nachweisbar bestätigen zu lassen.

Sofern der Vertragsschluss hingegen **außerhalb des Internets** mit Hilfe anderer Kom- **50** munikationsmittel (mündlich, schriftlich, Telefax etc., aber auch bei Verwendung sonstiger elektronischer Kommunikationsformen wie EDI) erfolgt, reicht die Abrufbarkeit der AGB im Internet **nicht** aus, um der Kenntnisverschaffungsobliegenheit des Verwenders zu genügen.[266] Dies gilt unabhängig davon, ob die Gegenpartei im konventionellen Schriftverkehr mit eigener E-Mail-Adresse auftritt[267] oder der AGB-Verwender in seinem nicht-elektronischen Einbeziehungshinweis die genaue Internetadresse angegeben hat,[268] weil dem

---

[257] *Karollus,* LM 3/2002 CISG Nr. 9.
[258] *Staudinger/Magnus,* Art. 14, Rn. 41b.
[259] OGH, 6.2.1996, CISG-online 224 = ZfRVgl 1996, 248 f.; *Lohmann,* Parteiautonomie, S. 218 f.; *Staudinger/Magnus,* Art. 14, Rn. 41b.
[260] S. dazu *Dannemann,* FS Rudden, S. 181 ff.
[261] *Berger,* FS Horn, S. 18; *Brunner,* Art. 4, Rn. 42; *Karollus,* LM 3/2002 CISG Nr. 9; *Kindler,* FS Heldrich, S. 234; *Lohmann,* Parteiautonomie, S. 219; *O. Meyer,* Interpretation, S. 342; MünchKomm/*Gruber,* Art. 14, Rn. 30; *Schwenzer/Mohs,* IHR 2006, 239, 241; *Steensgaard,* Standardbetingelser, § 8, Rn. 53; *Stiegele/Halter,* IHR 2003, 169; *Wolf/Lindacher/Pfeiffer/Hau,* IntGV, Rn. 73; möglicherweise strenger *Staudinger/Magnus,* Art. 14, Rn. 41a.
[262] Dies stimmt mit den Grundsätzen überein, die der BGH, 14.6.2006, NJW 2006, 2976, 2977 in Anwendung des (auf CISG-Verträge nicht anwendbaren) § 305 II Nr. 2 BGB aufgestellt hat.
[263] *Berger,* FS Horn, S. 18; *Schwenzer/Mohs,* IHR 2006, 239, 241; *Steensgaard,* Standardbetingelser, § 8, Rn. 51.
[264] *Koller,* FS Honsell, S. 238; *Magnus,* FS Kritzer, S. 323; *Ventsch/Kluth,* IHR 2003, 224, 225; *Wolf/Lindacher/Pfeiffer/Hau,* IntGV, Rn. 73.
[265] S. *Eiselen,* 6 VJ (2002), 305, 317.
[266] OLG Celle, 24.7.2009, CISG-online 1906 = NJW-RR 2010, 136, 138; *Bamberger/Roth/Saenger,* Art. 14, Rn. 7; *Honsell/Dornis,* Vorbem. 14–24, Rn. 12; *Jungemeyer,* RIW 2010, 166, 167; *Magnus,* FS Kritzer, S. 323; *Piltz,* IHR 2007, 121, 122; ders., NJW 2011, 2261, 2263; *Schwenzer/Mohs,* IHR 2006, 239, 241; *Staudinger/Magnus,* Art. 14, Rn. 41a; *Ventsch/Kluth,* IHR 2003, 224; a. A. *Berger,* FS Horn, S. 18; *Karollus,* LM 3/2002 CISG Nr. 9; *Kindler,* FS Heldrich, S. 234; *Lautenschlager,* 11 VJ (2007), 259, 282; *O. Meyer,* Interpretation, S. 342; *Stadler,* AGB, S. 95; *Wolf/Lindacher/Pfeiffer/Hau,* IntGV, Rn. 73; differenzierend *Brunner,* Art. 4, Rn. 42.
[267] A. A. MünchKomm/*Gruber,* Art. 14, Rn. 30; *Stiegele/Halter,* IHR 2003, 169.
[268] Für diesen Fall a. A. *Berger,* FS Horn, S. 18; *Stiegele/Halter,* IHR 2003, 169.

Adressaten andernfalls die Beschaffung des AGB-Textes seines Vertragspartners aufgebürdet würde, was durch dessen Kenntnisverschaffungsobliegenheit gerade verhindert werden soll.[269] Obgleich eine Erkundigung nach den AGB über das Internet einfacher sein mag als auf sonstigem Wege, kann im territorialen Anwendungsbereich eines auf weltweite Geltung angelegten Übereinkommens zudem keineswegs von einer unterschiedslosen Zugänglichkeit des Internets ausgegangen werden,[270] weshalb es als Informationsmedium in der hier interessierenden Frage nur in den Fällen genügt, in denen die Vertragsparteien durch seine übereinstimmende Verwendung eine diesbezügliche Einigkeit gezeigt haben.

51 cc) **Laufende Geschäftsbeziehungen.** In **laufenden Geschäftsbeziehungen** zwischen zwei Parteien kann es zur Kenntnisverschaffung ausreichen, dass die AGB dem Vertragspartner bereits bei in der Vergangenheit getätigten Vertragsabschlüssen zugänglich gemacht wurden.[271] Voraussetzung für die Annahme einer fortdauernden Kenntnis vom AGB-Inhalt (mit der Folge, dass die Standardbedingungen in später geschlossene Kaufverträge ohne nochmalige Zugänglichmachung einbezogen werden können) ist jedenfalls, dass die AGB in die **zurückliegenden Kaufverträge** tatsächlich **wirksam einbezogen** worden waren;[272] nicht ausreichend ist demgegenüber, dass die AGB in der Vergangenheit gelegentlich oder häufig auf Rechnungsrückseiten, d. h. nach den jeweiligen Vertragsschlüssen übersandt[273] oder bereits früher in einer Sprachfassung übergeben wurden, die für eine wirksame Einbeziehung nach CISG nicht geeignet ist,[274] denn an den Inhalt von Standardbedingungen, die nie rechtliche Bindungswirkung erlangten, muss sich niemand erinnern.[275] Ob insoweit schon ein bei erstmaliger Einbeziehung der AGB gegebener Hinweis ausreicht, dem zufolge die AGB „für den vorliegenden und alle künftigen Verträge" gelten sollen, ist unsicher, aber letztlich wohl zu verneinen, weil andernfalls der Adressat durch einseitige Erklärung einer unbegrenzten Aufbewahrungsobliegenheit unterworfen werden könnte und zudem der Unterschied zu einem Rahmenvertrag eingeebnet würde.

52 Im Übrigen hängt es von den **Umständen des Einzelfalles** ab, ob man bei Zugang einer Angebotserklärung nach dem Maßstab des Art. 8 von einer Kenntnis der darin in Bezug genommenen AGB ausgehen kann; insofern werden Faktoren wie die Dauer der Geschäftsbeziehung,[276] die Beteiligung unterschiedlicher Organisationseinheiten auf Seiten des Empfängers,[277] die Anzahl der Geschäfte und deren zeitlicher Abstand eine Rolle

---

[269] *Bamberger/Roth/Saenger*, Art. 14, Rn. 7; *Ventsch/Kluth*, IHR 2003, 224; a. A. *Stiegele/Halter*, IHR 2003, 169.

[270] Wie hier *Ventsch/Kluth*, IHR 2003, 224, 225; wohl auch *Berger*, FS Horn, S. 18; a. A. *Karollus*, LM 3/2002 CISG Nr. 9; *Lautenschlager*, 11 VJ (2007), 259, 282; *Stiegele/Halter*, IHR 2003, 169.

[271] Netherlands Arbitration Institute, 10.2.2005, CISG-online 1621 = YB. Comm. Arb. 2007, 93, 103; RB Breda, 27.2.2008, CISG-online 2252; *Honsell/Dornis*, Vorbem. 14–24, Rn. 13; *Karollus*, LM 3/2002 CISG Nr. 9; *Lohmann*, Parteiautonomie, S. 218; MünchKomm/*Gruber*, Art. 14, Rn. 31; *Piltz*, IHR 2004, 133, 134; ders., IHR 2007, 121, 122; *Steensgaard*, Standardbetingelser, § 8, Rn. 32; *Witz/Salger/Lorenz/Witz*, Vor Artt. 14–24, Rn. 12.

[272] LG Hannover, 21.4.2009, CISG-online 2298 = IHR 2012, 59, 61; *Piltz*, IHR 2007, 121, 122. Großzügiger Netherlands Arbitration Institute, 10.2.2005, CISG-online 1621 = YB. Comm. Arb. 2007, 93, 104 f. A. A., aber unzutreffend OLG München, 14.1.2009, CISG-online 2211 = IHR 2009, 201, 203.

[273] Vgl. OLG Düsseldorf, 23.3.2011, CISG-online 2218; *Chateau des Charmes Wines Ltd. v. Sabaté USA Inc., Sabaté S. A.*, U. S. Ct. App. (9th Cir.), 5.5.2003, CISG-online 767 = IHR 2003, 295, 296; *C9 Ventures v. SVC West L. P.*, Cal. App. 4 Dist., 27.1.2012, CISG-online 2307; a. A. RB Breda, 27.2.2008, CISG-online 2252. Zum Kriterium der Rechtzeitigkeit der Kenntnis vom AGB-Inhalt s. unten Rn. 59.

[274] RB Mechelen, 18.1.2002, CISG-online 1432 = R. W. 2002/03, 1351, 1352: Wenn AGB aufgrund Formulierung in dem Adressaten unverständlicher Sprache und Verwendung von Kleindruck nicht Vertragsbestandteil werden, spielt es keine Rolle, dass die Parteien bereits seit einiger Zeit Geschäftsbeziehungen unterhalten. Zur Sprachenfrage bei der AGB-Einbeziehung i. e. unten Rn. 61.

[275] Vgl. LG Neubrandenburg, 3.8.2005, CISG-online 1190 = IHR 2006, 26, 27. Abwegig OLG München, 14.1.2009, CISG-online 2211 = IHR 2009, 201, 203 f.

[276] MünchKomm/*Gruber*, Art. 14, Rn. 31.

[277] Vgl. *Huber/Kröll*, IPRax 2003, 309, 311; *Karollus*, LM 3/2002 CISG Nr. 9: keine Kenntnis dann, wenn AGB zuvor einer anderen Abteilung im Unternehmen des Empfängers übermittelt worden waren und kein interner Informationsaustausch erwartet werden kann.

Begriff des Angebots   53, 54 **Art. 14**

spielen.[278] Eine äußere zeitliche Grenze wird man der Wertung des Art. 39 II entnehmen können, der zufolge es den Parteien spätestens zwei Jahre nach Lieferung erlaubt sein soll, das Geschäft „endgültig zur Seite zu legen"[279] – länger braucht daher auch die Kenntnis von AGB des damaligen Vertragspartners nicht vorgehalten zu werden.

dd) International übliche Standardbedingungen. Daneben wird eine Kenntnisverschaffung von einem Teil des Schrifttums auch dann für entbehrlich erachtet, wenn es sich bei dem konkret betroffenen Bedingungswerk um **international übliche Standardbedingungen** handelt,[280] weil in diesem Fall die vorhandene Kenntnis unterstellt werden könne[281] und es hier zudem an einer Prägung durch nationale Besonderheiten fehle, mit der die Kenntnisverschaffungsobliegenheit begründet wird.[282] Welchen Grad der Bekanntheit und Verbreitung eines Klauselwerkes man dabei für erforderlich hält, bleibt freilich unklar und wird von den einzelnen Autoren wohl auch unterschiedlich gesehen; im Einzelnen genannte Anwendungsfälle reichen von den häufig angeführten Incoterms®[283] über weitere ICC-Regelwerke wie die Einheitlichen Richtlinien und Gebräuche für Dokumentenakkreditive[284] und den Model International Contract for Sale[285] bis zu branchenspezifischen Standardbedingungen wie die Allgemeinen Lieferbedingungen für den Export von Anlagegütern der ECE,[286] die General Conditions for the Supply of Mechanical, Electrical and Electronic Products der europäischen Maschinenbau-Vereinigung ORGALIME, die GAFTA 100 und die Regeln der Sugar Association of London.[287] 53

M. E. kann die Kenntnisverschaffungsobliegenheit außerhalb der Fälle, in denen der Vertragspartner vom Inhalt des Bedingungswerkes bereits positive (und beweisbare) Kenntnis hat,[288] auch bei international verbreiteten Standardbedingungen **nur** entfallen, sofern deren Verwendung den Gepflogenheiten der Parteien oder einem **Handelsbrauch** entspricht, weil unter dieser Voraussetzung die Angebotserklärung nach **Art. 8 III** als den Inhalt des Klauselwerkes umfassend ausgelegt werden kann. Erforderlich ist daher auch hier, dass die in Bezug genommenen Bedingungen in dem betreffenden Geschäftszweig weithin bekannt sind und von den dort tätigen Parteien regelmäßig beachtet werden.[289] Unabhängig davon, ob man die im Rahmen des Art. 8 III berücksichtigungsfähigen Bräuche grundsätzlich nicht auf im internationalen Handel beachtete Usancen beschränken, sondern (insofern über Art. 9 II hinaus) auch auf nationale und örtliche Bräuche erstrecken möchte,[290] ist im vorliegenden Zusammenhang jedenfalls zu fordern, dass die betroffenen Standardbedingungen auch im Heimatstaat des Angebotsempfängers bekannt sind und beachtet werden.[291] 54

---

[278] *Huber/Kröll*, IPRax 2003, 309, 311 wollen auf „zeitnahe" Geschäftsabschlüsse nach Übersendung beschränken.
[279] So *Schwenzer*, unten Art. 39 Rn. 22.
[280] *Berger*, FS Horn, S. 9 f.; *Honsell/Dornis*, Vorbem. 14–24, Rn. 10; *Huber/Kröll*, IPRax 2003, 309, 311; *Karollus*, LM 3/2002 CISG Nr. 9; *Kindler*, FS Heldrich, S. 229; *Magnus*, FS Kritzer, S. 322; *Schmidt-Kessel*, NJW 2002, 3444, 3446; *Steensgaard*, Standardbetingelser, § 8, Rn. 39 ff.; a. A. MünchKomm/*Gruber*, Art. 14, Rn. 31; *Ventsch/Kluth*, IHR 2003, 61, 62 f.
[281] *Kindler*, FS Heldrich, S. 229; *Magnus*, FS Kritzer, S. 322; wohl auch *Schmidt-Kessel*, NJW 2002, 3444, 3446; a. A. MünchKomm/*Gruber*, Art. 14, Rn. 31; *Ventsch/Kluth*, IHR 2003, 61, 62 f.
[282] *Berger*, FS Horn, S. 9 f.; wohl auch *Huber/Kröll*, IPRax 2003, 309, 311; vgl. bereits oben Rn. 41.
[283] *Huber/Kröll*, IPRax 2003, 309, 311; *Kindler*, FS Heldrich, S. 229; *Lautenschlager*, 11 VJ (2007), 259, 280; *Magnus*, FS Kritzer, S. 322: unwiderlegbare Vermutung der Kenntnis; *Schmidt-Kessel*, NJW 2002, 3444, 3446; *Steensgaard*, Standardbetingelser, § 8, Rn. 44 ff.
[284] *Magnus*, FS Kritzer, S. 322.
[285] *Berger*, FS Horn, S. 9 f.
[286] *Berger*, FS Horn, S. 9; *Schmidt-Kessel*, NJW 2002, 3444, 3446.
[287] *Schmidt-Kessel*, NJW 2002, 3444, 3446; a. A. *Magnus*, FS Kritzer, S. 322 Fn. 74: Bei lediglich branchenüblichen Bedingungen sei positive Kenntnis erforderlich und zu beweisen.
[288] Oben Rn. 39.
[289] S. oben *Schmidt-Kessel*, Art. 9 Rn. 16 sowie hier Rn. 73.
[290] So *Schlechtriem*, Internationales UN-Kaufrecht, Rn. 56; oben *Schmidt-Kessel*, Art. 8 Rn. 45; zurückhaltend Staudinger/*Magnus*, Art. 8, Rn. 24; a. A. *Soergel/Lüderitz/Fenge*, Art. 8, Rn. 6; *Witz/Salger/Lorenz/Witz*, Art. 8, Rn. 12.
[291] Vgl. auch oben *Schmidt-Kessel*, Art. 8 Rn. 45. Aus diesem Grund hätte in dem viel zitierten Fall des Trib. com. Nivelles, 19.9.1995, CISG-online 366 die Bekanntheit der „conditions générales de l'association suisse

55 **ee) Nicht ausreichend.** Nicht ausreichend ist nach dem CISG die Einsehbarkeit von AGB in den Geschäftsräumen des Verwenders, sofern der Vertrag nicht dort geschlossen wird,[292] oder das bloße Angebot des AGB-Verwenders, den Text der AGB auf Wunsch kostenlos zur Verfügung zu stellen.[293] Auch die in den Niederlanden übliche Praxis, die AGB bei einem **Gericht** oder einer **Handelskammer** zu **hinterlegen,** genügt gegenüber ausländischen Vertragspartnern nicht.[294]

56 **c) Gestaltung des AGB-Textes.** Spezifische Anforderungen an die Gestaltung und das Format der AGB kennt das CISG nicht; es kommt insoweit darauf an, dass eine vernünftige Person der gleichen Art wie der Angebotsgegner von ihrem Inhalt Kenntnis nehmen kann **(Art. 8 II).** Zur in diesem Zusammenhang vielfach problematischen Sprachenfrage s. unten Rn. 61.

57 Die Rechtsprechung hat die Einbeziehung von AGB gelegentlich daran scheitern lassen, dass deren Text umfangreich und sehr klein gedruckt und daher **nicht lesbar** war.[295] Abzulehnen ist die auf einer gegenteiligen Tendenz liegende Ansicht, der zufolge die bloße Übermittlung der „rechtlich erheblichen Eckpunkte" der AGB in manchen Konstellationen zur Einbeziehung der gesamten AGB genügen soll[296] – dies wird man nur anerkennen können, soweit sich Entsprechendes aus Gepflogenheiten oder Gebräuchen ergibt, während ansonsten nur die übermittelten AGB-Teile Vertragsbestandteil werden können.

58 **d) Änderung des AGB-Textes.** Wird ein einmal zur Kenntnis gebrachter AGB-Text durch den Verwender später teilweise geändert oder vollständig neu gefasst, so ist dies für bereits unter Bezugnahme auf die AGB abgeschlossene Kaufverträge ohne Belang; für diese gelten die AGB in der Fassung, die dem Vertragspartner zum **Zeitpunkt** des **jeweiligen Vertragsschlusses**[297] zugänglich war. Soll die neue AGB-Fassung in künftige Einzelverträge einbezogen werden, so ist hierzu notwendig, dass ihr Inhalt dem Adressaten nach den oben beschriebenen Grundsätzen zur Kenntnis gebracht wird, und zwar auch dann, wenn der Hinweis in den Angebotserklärungen sich auf die AGB des Verwenders „in ihrer geltenden Fassung" bezieht. Zudem wird man zu fordern haben, dass der Verwender seinen Vertragspartner bei erstmaliger Einbeziehung der neuen AGB in ein Angebot **ausdrücklich** auch auf den Umstand **hinweist,** dass sich deren Inhalt gegenüber den bislang verwandten Standardbedingungen geändert hat.

---

des industriels en machines" in belgischen Branchenkreisen geprüft werden müssen, bevor deren Einbeziehung in den Kaufvertrag bejaht wurde.

[292] OLG Celle, 24.7.2009, CISG-online 1906 = NJW-RR 2010, 136, 138. Zur Zugänglichmachung des AGB-Textes beim Vertragsschluss unter Anwesenden s. oben Rn. 48.

[293] RB Utrecht, 21.1.2009, CISG-online 1814; LG Landshut, 12.6.2008, CISG-online 1703 = IHR 2008, 184, 186 f.; LG Neubrandenburg, 3.8.2005, CISG-online 1190 = IHR 2006, 26, 27; *Piltz*, IHR 2007, 121, 122; a. A. LG Coburg, 12.12.2006, CISG-online 1447 = IHR 2007, 117, 119.

[294] Gerechtshof Arnhem, 27.4.1999, CISG-online 741 = NIPR 1999, Nr. 245 zur Hinterlegung der AGB bei der Kanzlei eines niederländischen Landgerichts (*Griffie van de Arrondissementsrechtsbank te Almelo*); RB Hasselt, 2.12.1998, CISG-online 761 zur Hinterlegung der AGB bei einer niederländischen *Kamer van Koophandel* (Handelskammer); LG Göttingen, 31.7.1997, CISG-online 564 zur Hinterlegung der AGB bei einem niederländischen Landgericht; RB Utrecht, 21.1.2009, CISG-online 1814 (dto.); *Janssen*, IHR 2004, 194, 199 Fn. 37; *Lohmann*, Parteiautonomie, S. 218; *MünchKomm/Gruber*, Art. 14, Rn. 29 Fn. 66; *Piltz*, NJW 2003, 2056, 2060; *ders.*, IHR 2004, 133, 134; *Staudinger/Magnus*, Art. 14, Rn. 41; a. A. RB Arnhem, 8.7.1999, CISG-online 1431 = NIPR 1999, Nr. 251 zur Hinterlegung der AGB bei einer niederländischen Handelskammer.

[295] RB Mechelen, 18.1.2002, CISG-online 1432 = R. W. 2002/03, 1351, 1352: AGB-Text nicht einbezogen, da „met het blote oog nauwelijks te lezen" (mit bloßem Auge kaum lesbar); CA Colmar, 24.10.2000, CISG-online 578: „Il s'agit en effet de l'énoncé compact d'un nombre important de conditions (39 articles) rédigées en petits caractères à peine distincts …".

[296] *Piltz*, IHR 2004, 133, 135; *ders.*, IHR 2007, 121, 122.

[297] Zum insoweit maßgeblichen Zeitpunkt s. genau oben Rn. 59.

4. Zeitpunkt der Kenntnis

Der Wille des Offerenten, unter Einbeziehung von AGB zu kontrahieren, muss für den Adressaten so rechtzeitig erkennbar sein, dass dessen Annahme sich auf das Angebot unter Einschluss der Standardbedingungen beziehen kann. Wenn vielfach davon gesprochen wird, der Hinweis des Anbietenden auf die AGB und das Zugänglichmachen des AGB-Textes müsse spätestens bis Vertragsabschluss erfolgen,[298] so ist dies mindestens unpräzise, weil der Kaufvertrag gemäß Artt. 18 II 1, III und 23 f. im Regelfall zum Zeitpunkt des Zugangs der Annahmeerklärung beim Offerenten zustande kommt; tatsächlich müssen die Voraussetzungen für eine Einbeziehung der AGB daher **vor** dem Zeitpunkt der **Erklärung der Vertragsannahme durch die andere Partei** gegeben sein.[299] Erfolgt der Hinweis auf die AGB bzw. das Zugänglichmachen des AGB-Textes hingegen erst **nach** diesem Zeitpunkt („**nachgeschobene AGB**"), so genügt dies zur Einbeziehung nicht;[300] die AGB bleiben daher für den konkreten Vertrag **unbeachtlich**. Dies gilt insbesondere für Standardbedingungen, deren Einführung – wie in der Praxis häufig – erstmals anlässlich der Rechnungserteilung versucht wird.[301] 59

Nur in sehr seltenen, ungewöhnlich gelagerten Fällen wird man darin ein Angebot auf Vertragsänderung sehen können, das von der anderen Vertragspartei konkludent oder im Wege einer annahmeäquivalenten Handlung angenommen wird und damit zur nachträglichen Einbeziehung der AGB im Wege der Vertragsänderung gemäß Art. 29 I führt[302] (s. dazu näher unten Art. 29 Rn. 7 f.). Im Regelfall kann vor allem nicht unterstellt werden, die Rechnungsadressatin stimme erstmals mit der Rechnung übermittelten AGB dadurch konkludent zu, dass sie die Ware entgegennimmt oder die Rechnung bezahlt.[303] Dasselbe gilt, wenn die Käuferin einen Lieferschein unterschreibt, auf dessen Rückseite die AGB des Verkäufers abgedruckt sind, denn dadurch bestätigt sie lediglich den Empfang der Ware (Art. 8), nicht aber ihr Einverständnis mit den „nachgeschobenen" AGB.[304] 60

---

[298] Gerechtshof 's-Hertogenbosch, 16.10.2002, CISG-online 816 = IHR 2004, 194, 196; OLG Oldenburg, 20.12.2007, CISG-online 1644 = IHR 2008, 112, 117; RB Kortrijk, 8.12.2004, CISG-online 1511 = IHR 2005, 114, 115: spätestens bei Zustandekommen des Vertrages; RB Veurne, 25.4.2001, CISG-online 765; LG Neubrandenburg, 3.8.2005, CISG-online 1190 = IHR 2006, 26, 28; *Lohmann*, Parteiautonomie, S. 218; *Magnus*, FS Kritzer, S. 324; *Piltz*, NJW 2007, 2159, 216; *Schmidt-Kessel/Meyer*, IHR 2008, 177, 179; *Steensgaard*, Standardbetingelser, § 8, Rn. 57 ff.

[299] *Honsell/Dornis*, Vorbem. 14–24, Rn. 9; *Karollus*, LM 3/2002 CISG Nr. 9; *Piltz*, IHR 2004, 133, 134; ähnlich LG Coburg, 12.12.2006, CISG-online 1447 = IHR 2007, 117, 118: grundsätzlich während der Verhandlungen über den konkreten Vertrag.

[300] CA Paris, 13.12.1995, CISG-online 312 = J. C. P. 1997, éd. G, II, Nr. 22 772; LG Neubrandenburg, 3.8.2005, CISG-online 1190 = IHR 2006, 26, 28; *Mittmann*, IHR 2006, 103, 106; a. A. *Jungemeyer*, RIW 2010, 166, 167.

[301] Gerechtshof 's-Hertogenbosch, 29.5.2007, CISG-online 1550; Gerechtshof 's-Hertogenbosch, 16.10.2002, CISG-online 816 = IHR 2004, 194, 196; *Chateau des Charmes Wines Ltd. v. Sabaté USA Inc., Sabaté S. A.*, U. S. Ct. App. (9th Cir.), 5.5.2003, CISG-online 767 = IHR 2003, 295, 296; KG Zug, 11.12.2003, CISG-online 958 = IHR 2005, 119, 121; KG Jura, 3.11.2004, CISG-online 965; OLG Düsseldorf, 23.3.2011, CISG-online 2218; RB Hasselt, 2.6.1999, CISG-online 762; RB Kortrijk, 8.12.2004, CISG-online 1511 = IHR 2005, 114, 115; RB Rotterdam, 14.10.1999, CISG-online 1312 = NIPR 2000, Nr. 29; RB Veurne, 25.4.2001, CISG-online 765; LG Neubrandenburg, 3.8.2005, CISG-online 1190 = IHR 2006, 26, 28; LG Trier, 8.1.2004, CISG-online 910 = IHR 2004, 115, 116; *Lohmann*, Parteiautonomie, S. 218; *Magnus*, FS Kritzer, S. 324; *Mittmann*, IHR 2006, 103, 106; *Piltz*, NJW 2003, 2056, 2060; *ders.*, IHR 2004, 133, 135; a. A. nur LG Coburg, 12.12.2006, CISG-online 1447 = IHR 2007, 117, 118: Hinweis auf AGB in Rechnung ausreichend.

[302] Wie hier OGer Bern, 19.5.2008, CISG-online 1738: „… une modification tacite ne doit pas être admise sans retenue"; *Magnus*, FS Kritzer, S. 324; *Piltz*, IHR 2007, 121.

[303] RB Kortrijk, 8.12.2004, CISG-online 1511 = IHR 2005, 114, 115; KG Zug, 11.12.2003, CISG-online 958 = IHR 2005, 119, 121; *Janssen*, IHR 2004, 194, 197; *Magnus*, FS Kritzer, S. 324; *Piltz*, IHR 2007, 121 f.

[304] OLG Düsseldorf, 23.3.2011, CISG-online 2218.

5. Sprache der AGB

61 Für die Aufnahmemöglichkeit des Adressaten wird regelmäßig auch die Sprache, in der auf AGB verwiesen wird und in der sie abgefasst sind, von Bedeutung sein.[305] Die im Folgenden darzustellenden Grundsätze greifen ein, sofern im konkreten Fall keine einschlägigen Gebräuche oder Gepflogenheiten (Art. 9) zur Einbeziehung fremdsprachiger Standardbedingungen bestehen.[306] Sie gelten insoweit gleichermaßen für die Anforderungen an die Sprache des Hinweises auf die Einbeziehung der AGB[307] wie für die (nicht notwendigerweise identische[308]) Sprache des AGB-Textes selbst.[309]

62 **a) Verhandlungssprache.** Der Einbeziehung von AGB in den Kaufvertrag steht nichts entgegen, wenn sie in der zwischen den Parteien praktizierten **Verhandlungssprache** abgefasst sind,[310] weil gemäß Art. 8 II, III insbesondere die Verhandlungen zwischen den Parteien für das Verständnis der Angebotserklärung durch eine vernünftige Person maßgeblich sind. Um eine Verhandlungssprache in diesem Sinne handelt es sich dabei allerdings nicht schon dann, wenn im Einzelfall kurze schriftliche Mitteilungen in dieser Sprache erfolgt sind, im Übrigen aber durchgehend eine andere Sprache verwandt wurde.[311] Schwierigkeiten wirft die Frage auf, nach welchen Rechtsregeln zu bestimmen ist, ob eine Partei sich die Sprachkenntnis ihres während der Vertragsverhandlung für sie aufgetretenen **Repräsentanten** zurechnen lassen muss: Hier spricht auf den ersten Blick manches für eine Qualifikation als Frage der Stellvertretung, die sich nach dem über IPR zu ermittelnden nationalen Recht richtet, wohingegen die bisherige Rechtsprechung die maßgeblichen Regeln anscheinend dem CISG selbst entnehmen will.[312]

---

[305] OGH, 17.12.2003, CISG-online 828 = IHR 2004, 148, 153; allgemein zur Bedeutung der Sprachenfrage bei der Beurteilung des Erklärungszugangs unten Art. 24 Rn. 36.

[306] *Schwenzer/Mohs,* IHR 2006, 239, 241.

[307] RB Utrecht, 21.1.2009, CISG-online 1814: in im Übrigen deutschsprachiger Auftragsbestätigung enthaltener Satz „N. Z. V. Condities – gedeponeerd Arr.rechtbank A'dam no. 233/1933. Condities liggen bij ons ter inzage en worden op verzoek onverwijld kosteloos toegezonden" stellt gegenüber deutschem Käufer keinen hinreichend verständlichen Hinweis auf AGB dar; im selben Sinne RB Rotterdam, 25.2.2009, CISG-online 1812 = EJCL 2009, 105.

[308] S. *Spellenberg,* IPRax 2007, 98, 102: Entsprechendes komme „nicht selten" vor.

[309] In diesem Sinne LG Göttingen, 31.7.1997, CISG-online 564; *Piltz,* IHR 2004, 133, 135; *Sauthoff,* IHR 2005, 21, 23; im Hinblick auf die Sprache des AGB-Textes großzügiger *Magnus,* FS Kritzer, S. 325; ähnlicher Ansatz in OGH, 6.11.2008, CISG-online 1833.

[310] OGH, 6.11.2008, CISG-online 1833; OGH, 29.11.2005, CISG-online 1227; OLG Linz, 8.8.2005, CISG-online 1087 = IHR 2005, 249, 251: Verhandlungssprache zwischen den Repräsentanten der Parteien; LG Göttingen, 31.7.1997, CISG-online 564; LG Memmingen, 13.9.2000, CISG-online 820; *Berger,* FS Horn, S. 18; *Kühl/Hingst,* FS Herber, S. 53; *Piltz,* NJW 2007, 2159, 2161; *Schultheiß,* S. 16; *Ventsch/Kluth,* IHR 2003, 61, 65; *Witz/Salger/Lorenz/Witz,* Vor Artt. 14–24, Rn. 13. Dies gilt auch, wenn jede der Parteien einseitig eine Verhandlungssprache benutzt hat; so auch *Stadler,* AGB, S. 85.

[311] LG Memmingen, 13.9.2000, CISG-online 820: Verhandlungen über Kaufvertrag zwischen deutscher Verkäuferin und italienischer Käuferin fast durchgehend in englischer Sprache geführt, aber gelegentlich deutschsprachige Mitteilungen der Käuferin – deutschsprachige AGB der Verkäuferin aus Sprachgründen nicht wirksam einbezogen. Großzügiger *Schultheiß,* S. 17; *Witz/Salger/Lorenz/Witz,* Vor Artt. 14–24, Rn. 13: Verwendung mehrerer Sprachen macht jede dieser Sprachen zur Verhandlungssprache.

[312] Der OGH, 31.8.2005, CISG-online 1093 = IHR 2006, 31, 33 stellt ohne Nennung des angewandten Maßstabs lapidar fest, dass der Partei „Verhalten und Kenntnisse" ihrer beim Vertragsschluss eingesetzten Agentin „selbstredend zuzurechnen sind"; vgl. auch *MCC-Marble Ceramic Center, Inc. v. Ceramica Nuova D'Agostino S. p. A.,* U. S. Ct. App. (11th Cir.), 29.6.1998, CISG-online 342 = 144 F. 3d 1384, 1385 f.: Verhandlungen zwischen italienischer Verkäuferin und U.S.-amerikanischer Käuferin fanden während einer Messe in Bologna statt, wobei ein Agent der Verkäuferin als Übersetzer auftrat, weil der Präsident der Käuferin der italienischen Sprache nicht mächtig war. Der Vertrag wurde noch auf der Messe auf einem Formular der Verkäuferin unterzeichnet, das vollständig in italienischer Sprache abgefasst war und auf der Rückseite italienischsprachige AGB enthielt, auf die auf der Vorderseite (in italienischer Sprache) hingewiesen wurde – das Gericht hielt die Einbeziehung der AGB für unproblematisch.

Begriff des Angebots 63, 64 **Art. 14**

b) Vertragssprache. Der vielfach ebenfalls genannten Vertragssprache[313] kann daneben **63** nur dann eigene Bedeutung zukommen, wenn sie von der Verhandlungssprache abweicht.[314] Zum gesonderten Anknüpfungspunkt für die Frage der Kenntnisnahmemöglichkeit taugt sie deshalb nicht, weil zum einen das Zustandekommen des Vertrages trotz bestehender Sprachdivergenzen und dessen Inhalt ja gerade zu klären ist – vielfach wird der Kaufvertrag nämlich bereits mündlich geschlossen worden sein – und zum anderen das Verstehen der in einer fremden Sprache ausgedrückten *essentialia negotii*, über die zuvor in einer abweichenden Sprache bereits verhandelt wurde, nicht ohne weiteres mit dem Verstehen eines erstmals beigefügten umfangreichen AGB-Textes gleichzusetzen ist.[315]

c) Sonstige, dem Adressaten verständliche Sprache. Für eine Einbeziehung in den **64** Vertrag ausreichend ist auch eine Übermittlung der AGB in der **Heimatsprache** der anderen Partei (Art. 8 II)[316] oder in einer **sonstigen Sprache,** die der Adressat hinreichend **versteht** (Art. 8 I).[317] Im letztgenannten Fall kommt es für die Einbeziehung der AGB in einen mit einem Unternehmen abzuschließenden Kaufvertrag darauf an, ob die mit dem konkreten Vertrag befassten Mitarbeiter des Vertragspartners der betreffenden Sprache mächtig sind;[318] das Vertrauen auf diese Verständnismöglichkeit ist dabei für den AGB-Verwender freilich riskant, weil er nicht nur das Vorhandensein der Sprachkenntnisse darlegen und beweisen muss,[319] sondern auch den Umstand, dass die betreffenden Mitarbeiter bereits zum Zeitpunkt des Vertragsschlusses für seinen Vertragspartner tätig waren.[320]

---

[313] OGH, 17.12.2003, CISG-online 828 = IHR 2004, 148, 154; CA Colmar, 24.10.2000, CISG-online 578; RB Hasselt, 2.6.1999, CISG-online 762; AG Kehl, 6.10.1995, CISG-online 162 = NJW-RR 1996, 565, 566; *Sauthoff,* IHR 2005, 21, 23; *Steensgaard,* Standardbetingelser, § 8, Rn. 71; *Ventsch/Kluth,* IHR 2003, 61, 65.

[314] Zwischen Verhandlungs- und Vertragssprache wird hingegen nicht getrennt von LG Heilbronn, 15.9.1997, CISG-online 562; *Brunner,* Art. 4, Rn. 41; *Lohmann,* Parteiautonomie, S. 220; *Piltz,* NJW 2003, 2056, 2060; anders und zutreffend *Spellenberg,* IPRax 2007, 98, 103.

[315] Wie hier OGH, 6.11.2008, CISG-online 1833: wo Verhandlungs- und Vertragssprache nicht dieselbe ist, muss wenigstens die Hinweis auf die AGB zwingend in der Verhandlungssprache erfolgen; OLG Stuttgart, 16.6.1987, IPRax 1988, 293, 294; *Spellenberg,* FS Ferid, S. 481; *ders.,* IPRax 2007, 98, 103 f.; strenger hingegen *MCC-Marble Ceramic Center, Inc. v. Ceramica Nuova D'Agostino S. p. A.,* U. S. Ct. App. (11th Cir.), 29.6.1998, CISG-online 342 = 144 F. 3d 1384, 1387, Fn. 9: „[Die U. S.-amerikanische Käuferin] MCC makes much of the fact that the written order form is entirely in Italian and that Monzon [ihr Präsident], who signed the contract on MCC's behalf directly below this provision incorporating the terms on the reverse of the form, neither spoke nor read Italian. This fact is of no assistance to MCC's position. We find it nothing short of astounding that an individual, purportedly experienced in commercial matters, would sign a contract in a foreign language and expect not to be bound simply because he could not comprehend its terms. We find nothing in the CISG that might counsel this type of reckless behavior and nothing that signals any retreat from the proposition that parties who sign contracts will be bound by them regardless of whether they have read them or understood them"; a. A. auch *Asam,* Jb. It. R. 3 (1990), 3, 16; *Stadler,* AGB, S. 85.

[316] OGH, 17.12.2003, CISG-online 828 = IHR 2004, 148, 154; OLG Karlsruhe, 20.7.2004, CISG-online 858 = IHR 2004, 246, 250; CA Colmar, 24.10.2000, CISG-online 578; LG Memmingen, 13.9.2000, CISG-online 820; AG Nordhorn, 14.6.1994, CISG-online 259: bei italienisch-deutschem Kaufvertrag entsprechend zweisprachiger AGB-Text ausreichend; *Berger,* FS Horn, S. 18; *Piltz,* IHR 2004, 133, 135; *ders.,* NJW 2007, 2159, 2161; *Sauthoff,* IHR 2005, 21, 23; *Schultheiß,* S. 17: Muttersprache; *Spellenberg,* FS Ferid, S. 480; *Stadler,* AGB, S. 85.

[317] OGH, 17.12.2003, CISG-online 828 = IHR 2004, 148, 154; *Koller,* FS Honsell, S. 237; *Piltz,* IHR 2004, 133, 135; *Schultheiß,* S. 17; *Soergel/Lüderitz/Fenge,* Art. 14, Rn. 10; *Spellenberg,* FS Ferid, S. 480; *Staudinger/Magnus,* Art. 14, Rn. 41; *Steensgaard,* Standardbetingelser, § 8, Rn. 73; *Wilhelm,* S. 10. Im konkreten Fall verneint etwa in RB Mechelen, 18.1.2002, CISG-online 1432 = R. W. 2002/03, 1351, 1352: belgisch-französischer Kaufvertrag – deutschsprachige AGB der belgischen Verkäuferin nicht wirksam einbezogen. Anders, aber unhaltbar OLG München, 14.1.2009, CISG-online 2211 = IHR 2009, 201, 204 („Der Wirksamkeit der Vereinbarung steht nicht entgegen, dass die AGB nicht in der Verhandlungssprache, sondern in englischer Sprache abgefasst sind, wobei bedeutungslos ist, ob die andere Partei diese Sprache beherrscht").

[318] OLG Düsseldorf, 21.4.2004, CISG-online 915 = IHR 2005, 24, 28 („die mit der Vertragsabwicklung befassten Mitarbeiter"); zustimmend *Sauthoff,* IHR 2005, 21, 23.

[319] *Schmidt-Kessel/Meyer,* IHR 2008, 177, 179; *Spellenberg,* FS Ferid, S. 480.

[320] OLG Düsseldorf, 21.4.2004, CISG-online 915 = IHR 2005, 24, 28: Bei israelisch-deutschem Kaufvertrag war Verhandlungs- und Vertragssprache englisch, die von der deutschen Käuferin übersandten AGB

65 d) „**Weltsprache**". Daneben wird von manchen auch die Einbeziehung solcher AGB in den Vertrag für möglich gehalten, die in einer **Weltsprache** abgefasst sind, sofern der Vertragspartner nicht unverzüglich wegen mangelnder Sprachkenntnis widerspreche.[321] Zur Begründung wird angeführt, dass es international tätigen Unternehmen unter Berücksichtigung der Länge, Intensität und Bedeutung der geschäftlichen Beziehung zuzumuten sein könne, sich entweder selbst um eine Übersetzung des AGB-Textes zu bemühen oder den Verwender zur Übermittlung auch einer Übersetzung aufzufordern.[322]

66 Der referierte Ansatz ist für die Einbeziehung von Standardbedingungen in dem CISG unterliegende Kaufverträge **abzulehnen**.[323] Zu erinnern ist zunächst daran, dass der AGB-Abfassung in einer „Weltsprache" nur unter der Voraussetzung Relevanz zukommen kann, dass es sich bei dieser Sprache weder um die Verhandlungssprache noch eine dem Adressaten sonst geläufige Sprache handelt, weil andernfalls bereits die oben in Rn. 62 ff. dargestellten, aus Art. 8 abgeleiteten Grundsätze eingreifen. Jenseits dieser, mit Blick auf die **Besonderheiten der konkreten Vertragskonstellation** vorgenommenen Verteilung des Sprachrisikos, in deren Rahmen im Welthandel weithin verbreiteten Sprachen (wie namentlich Englisch) schon aufgrund ihrer häufigen Verwendung in der internationalen Vertragsanbahnung zweifelsohne eine herausgehobene Bedeutung zukommen wird, besteht weder Anlass noch Grundlage für eine generelle Privilegierung von pauschal als „Weltsprache" qualifizierten Sprachen. Dies gilt vor allem, weil unklar bleibt, nach welchen Kriterien diese Einordnung erfolgen soll,[324] weshalb im Ergebnis auch keinerlei Einigkeit über den Kreis der insoweit anzuerkennenden Weltsprachen besteht.[325] Keine herausgehobene Bedeutung kann insoweit den Sprachen zukommen, in denen der Übereinkommenstext des CISG authentisch niedergelegt wurde,[326] weil es nicht auf die für Zwecke des diplomatischen Verkehrs herausgehobenen Amtssprachen der UN, sondern allenfalls auf die im grenzüberschreitenden Handelsverkehr zwischen Kaufleuten „Weltrang" besitzenden Sprachen ankommen kann,[327] wobei freilich bereits die Anerkennung der *lingua franca* des Welthandels Englisch in dieser Hinsicht bezweifelt wird.[328] Da anhand der bisherigen Rechtsprechung zudem deutlich wird, dass die Gerichte im Einzelfall regelmäßig eben doch die Verständlichkeit der „Weltsprache" für den konkreten Adressa-

---

aber in deutscher Sprache abgefasst – die Einbeziehung der AGB scheiterte an der Sprachenfrage, weil die israelische Verkäuferin zwar eine für die Vertragsabwicklung zuständige Mitarbeiterin beschäftigte, die deutsch sprach und mit der deutschen Käuferin auch auf deutsch korrespondierte, aber erst nach Vertragsschluss in das Unternehmen eingetreten war; *Sauthoff*, IHR 2005, 21, 23.

[321] OGH, 17.12.2003, CISG-online 828 = IHR 2004, 148, 154 unter Bezugnahme auf *Stadler*, AGB, S. 86; OLG Innsbruck, 1.2.2005, CISG-online 1130; OLG Linz, 8.8.2005, CISG-online 1087 = IHR 2005, 249, 251; LG Göttingen, 31.7.1997, CISG-online 564; *Asam*, Jb. It. R. 3 (1990), 3, 16; *Schwenzer/Mohs*, IHR 2006, 239, 241; *Soergel/Lüderitz/Fenge*, Art. 24, Rn. 6.
[322] OGH, 17.12.2003, CISG-online 828 = IHR 2004, 148, 154.
[323] Wie hier *Jungemeyer*, RIW 2010, 166, 167; *Schultheiß*, S. 18; *Steensgaard*, Standardbetingelser, § 8, Rn. 75 ff.; ebenso zu einer formularmäßigen Abtretungsanzeige OLG Hamm, 8.2.1995, CISG-online 141 = NJW-RR 1996, 1271, 1272.
[324] *Schultheiß*, S. 17.
[325] OGH, 17.12.2003, CISG-online 828 = IHR 2004, 148, 154: nach Englisch und Französisch sei wohl auch Deutsch als Weltsprache anzusehen; OLG Düsseldorf, 30.1.2004, CISG-online 821 = IHR 2004, 108, 112: jedenfalls Englisch; OLG Innsbruck, 1.2.2005, CISG-online 1130: Deutsch; OLG Linz, 8.8.2005, CISG-online 1087 = IHR 2005, 249, 251: Deutsch; LG Göttingen, 31.7.1997, CISG-online 564: die niederländische Sprache zähle „bei allem Respekt" nicht zu den Weltsprachen; *Asam*, Jb. It. R. 3 (1990), 3, 16: nur Englisch und Französisch; *Schwenzer/Mohs*, IHR 2006, 239, 241: nur Englisch.
[326] Vgl. aber *Schultheiß*, S. 17. Zur späteren Korrektur einzelner authentischer Sprachfassungen des CISG s. *Schroeter*, FS Kritzer, S. 429 f.
[327] Vgl. *Soergel/Lüderitz/Fenge*, Art. 14, Rn. 10: Ein deutscher Vertragspartner muss nicht ohne weiteres mit der Einbeziehung chinesisch oder arabisch verfasster AGB rechnen, auch wenn diese beigelegt sind.
[328] OLG Hamm, 8.2.1995, CISG-online 141 = NJW-RR 1996, 1271, 1272 (zu formularmäßiger Abtretungsanzeige); MünchKommHGB/*Ferrari*, Art. 24, Rn. 8; *Schmidt-Kessel/Meyer*, IHR 2008, 177, 179; *Ventsch/Kluth*, IHR 2003, 61, 65; *Wilhelm*, S. 10: „Juristenenglisch (-amerikanisch) ist in diesem Sinne nicht ohne weiteres eine allgemein verständliche Sprache"; a. A. *Berger*, FS Horn, S. 18; *Kühl/Hingst*, FS Herber, S. 53; *Soergel/Lüderitz/Fenge*, Art. 14, Rn. 10.

ten fordern,[329] sollte letzterer Aspekt konsequent als entscheidend angesehen werden. Der Einordnung einer bei der AGB-Einbeziehung verwandten Sprache als „Weltsprache" kommt daher unter dem CISG **keine Bedeutung** zu.

e) AGB in mehreren Sprachfassungen. Sofern die AGB in mehreren Sprachfassungen 67 zugänglich gemacht wurden, unter denen nur eine Fassung dem Adressaten nach den vorstehenden Grundsätzen verständlich war, so kann nur diese Sprachfassung Vertragsbestandteil werden. In diesem Fall ist es unzulässig, die andere, nicht wirksam einbezogene Sprachfassung zur Auslegung der einbezogenen Sprachfassung zu verwenden.[330] Sind mehrere Sprachfassungen wirksam einbezogen worden, so empfiehlt sich eine klarstellende Klausel zur Frage, welche Sprachfassung im Streitfall gelten soll.[331] Fehlt eine solche Festlegung, so wird regelmäßig den in der Verhandlungssprache abgefassten AGB der Vorrang einzuräumen sein.

6. Einbeziehung der AGB in das Angebot nach Artt. 8 III, 9

Geschäftsbedingungen einer Seite können zudem schon auf Grund der Verhandlungen 68 zwischen den Parteien oder der zwischen ihnen entstandenen Gepflogenheiten – Art. 8 III – Bestandteil der Offerte sein[332] oder als internationaler Handelsbrauch zur Geltung kommen.

a) Einbeziehung bestimmter AGB als Parteigepflogenheit. Zwischen den Kaufver- 69 tragsparteien entstandene Gepflogenheiten, die sich auch auf Fragen des Vertragsschlusses[333] einschließlich der Einbeziehung von AGB[334] beziehen können, sind gemäß Art. 9 I für die Parteien bindend und können zudem im Rahmen der Auslegung von Vertragsschlusserklärungen eine Rolle spielen (Art. 8 III).[335] Welche **genauen Folgen** aus ihnen für die Einbeziehung von AGB in die Kaufverträge zwischen den Vertragsparteien resultieren, hängt vom Inhalt der im konkreten Parteiverhältnis entstandenen Gepflogenheiten ab, deren Ermittlung Tatfrage ist: Es ist sowohl denkbar, dass nach einer Gepflogenheit der Hinweis auf die Einbeziehung der AGB in das Angebot,[336] deren Übermittlung im Rahmen des konkreten Vertragsschlusses[337] oder aber beides[338] entbehrlich ist.

Gepflogenheiten i. S. des Art. 9 I[339] sind dabei Verhaltensweisen, die mit einer gewissen 70 **Häufigkeit** und während eines gewissen **Zeitraums** von den Parteien gesetzt werden und

---

[329] Vgl. OGH, 17.12.2003, CISG-online 828 = IHR 2004, 148, 154: Einbeziehung in „Weltsprache" Deutsch abgefasster AGB in österreichisch-chinesischen Kaufvertrag, wobei als Vertreterin der hongkong-chinesischen Käuferin ein Schweizer mit deutscher Muttersprache aufgetreten war; LG Göttingen, 31.7.1997, CISG-online 564: „Weltsprache, deren Beherrschung vorausgesetzt werden kann, wenn ein deutscher Unternehmer mit einem ausländischen Unternehmen kontrahiert". Aus dem Schrifttum in diesem Sinne *Sauthoff*, IHR 2005, 21, 23: Bei Abfassung der AGB in einer Weltsprache habe Verwender entsprechende Sprachkenntnisse des Erklärungsgegners zu beweisen.
[330] LG Memmingen, 13.9.2000, CISG-online 820.
[331] *Ventsch/Kluth*, IHR 2003, 61, 65.
[332] OGH, 31.8.2005, CISG-online 1093 = IHR 2006, 31, 32; OGH, 17.12.2003, CISG-online 828 = IHR 2004, 148, 153; BGH, 31.10.2001, CISG-online 617 = BGHZ 149, 113, 117; OGH, 6.2.1996, CISG-online 224 = ZfRVgl 1996, 248, 251; *MCC-Marble Ceramic Center, Inc. v. Ceramica Nuova D'Agostino S. p. A.*, U. S. Ct. App. (11th Cir.), 29.6.1998, CISG-online 342 = 144 F. 3d 1384, 1392; OLG Innsbruck, 1.2.2005, CISG-online 1130; OLG Linz, 8.8.2005, CISG-online 1087 = IHR 2005, 249, 251; OLG Zweibrücken, 31.3.1998, CISG-online 481; *Kramer*, FS Welser, S. 551; *Mittmann*, IHR 2006, 103, 105.
[333] Oben *Schmidt-Kessel*, Art. 9 Rn. 3.
[334] OLG München, 14.1.2009, CISG-online 2211 = IHR 2009, 201, 203; *Berger*, FS Horn, S. 18: „in vielen Fällen".
[335] S. dazu bereits oben Rn. 54.
[336] *Karollus*, LM 3/2002 CISG Nr. 9; *Schwenzer/Hachem/Kee*, Rn. 12.14.
[337] So in OGH, 31.8.2005, CISG-online 1093 = IHR 2006, 31, 33; OLG Innsbruck, 1.2.2005, CISG-online 1130; OLG Linz, 8.8.2005, CISG-online 1087 = IHR 2005, 249, 251; Netherlands Arbitration Institute, 10.2.2005, CISG-online 1621 = YB. Comm. Arb. 2007, 93, 104 f.
[338] ICC, 8611/1997, CISG-online 236; *Magnus*, FS Kritzer, S. 321.
[339] Die strikte Beachtung der Anforderungen des Art. 9 anmahnend *Kruisinga*, 13.2 Electr. J. Comp. L. (May 2009), 1, 20.

von denen nach Treu und Glauben angenommen werden kann, dass sie in einem gleich gelagerten Fall wieder beachtet würden.[340] Nach h. A. ist damit jedenfalls mehr als eine nur einmalige Wiederholung der betreffenden Verhaltensweisen gefordert,[341] während die Rechtsprechung verschiedentlich auch eine zweimalige Wiederholung als noch nicht ausreichend erachtet hat.[342] Demgegenüber haben österreichische Gerichte es für denkbar gehalten, dass Vorstellungen einer Partei, die sich allenfalls aus Vorgesprächen ergeben und nicht ausdrücklich vereinbart wurden, schon bei Beginn der Geschäftsbeziehung als „Gepflogenheiten" i. S. des Art. 9 I Inhalt auch bereits des ersten Vertrages werden können, sofern dem Vertragspartner gemäß Art. 8 aus den Umständen klar sein musste, dass die andere Partei grundsätzlich nur bereit ist, derartige Geschäfte aufgrund ganz bestimmter Bedingungen abzuschließen.[343] Dem wird man nicht folgen können, weshalb es in Konstellationen, in denen es an der erforderlichen Mindestzahl durchgeführter Geschäfte fehlt, mit den Anforderungen an die AGB-Einbeziehung in laufenden Geschäftsbeziehungen (oben Rn. 51) sein Bewenden hat.

71 Unstreitig ist, dass das Entstehen einer einschlägigen Gepflogenheit i. S. des Art. 9 I jedenfalls voraussetzt, dass der **Inhalt der AGB** zu Beginn der Geschäftsbeziehung **wirksam** in die Kaufverträge **einbezogen** wurde, welche die Gepflogenheit begründeten;[344] vergangene einseitige Versuche zur Einbeziehung von AGB reichen hierzu nicht aus.[345] Der AGB-Text muss der anderen Vertragspartei durch den AGB-Verwender daher in jenem Zusammenhang zur Kenntnis gebracht worden sein, weshalb die oben zur Kenntnisverschaffungsobliegenheit ausgeführten Einzelheiten (oben Rn. 43 ff.) insoweit auch hier gelten. Wurde diese Voraussetzung erfüllt, so kann die entstandene Gepflogenheit von der Notwendigkeit einer wiederholten Zugänglichmachung des AGB-Textes im Rahmen jedes einzelnen Vertragsschlusses dispensieren;[346] ist eine Kenntnisverschaffung hingegen in der Vergangenheit zu keinem Zeitpunkt erfolgt, so scheidet eine Gepflogenheit aus.

72 Durch Parteigepflogenheiten können die Anforderungen für eine Einbeziehung von AGB im Ergebnis vor allem in den Fällen gesenkt werden, in denen es in der Angebotserklärung an einem **Hinweis** auf die AGB **fehlt;**[347] das Zugänglichmachen des AGB-Textes kann demgegenüber auch außerhalb einer den Anforderungen des Art. 9 I genügenden Gepflogenheit entbehrlich sein, sofern er dem Adressaten in der Vergangenheit zur Kenntnis gebracht wurde (Art. 8 I, II).

73 **b) AGB als internationaler Handelsbrauch.** Eines ausdrücklichen Hinweises in der Angebotserklärung und einer Kenntnisverschaffung bezüglich des Inhalts von Standard-

---

[340] OGH, 31.8.2005, CISG-online 1093 = IHR 2006, 31, 33; RB Arnhem, 17.1.2007, CISG-online 1455: „regelmatig zaken met elkaar doen" (regelmäßig Geschäfte miteinander machen); *Pamboukis,* 25 J. L. & Com. (2005-06), 107, 113.

[341] HGer Aargau, 26.9.1997, CISG-online 329 = SZIER 1998, 78; LG Zwickau, 19.3.1999, CISG-online 519; *Pamboukis,* 25 J. L. & Com. (2005-06), 107, 117; oben *Schmidt-Kessel,* Art. 9 Rn. 8; *Witz/Salger/Lorenz/Witz,* Art. 9, Rn. 17.

[342] ZGer Basel-Stadt, 3.12.1997, CISG-online 346 = SZIER 1999, 190; AG Duisburg, 13.4.2000, CISG-online 659 = IHR 2001, 114, 115.

[343] OGH, 31.8.2005, CISG-online 1093 = IHR 2006, 31, 33; OGH, 6.2.1996, CISG-online 224 = ZfRVgl 1996, 248, 251 f.; OLG Graz, 7.3.2002, CISG-online 669 = IHR 2003, 71, 72 (jeweils ohne Begründung).

[344] ICC, 8611/1997, CISG-online 236: „Die ersten" einzelnen Kaufverträge waren unter Einbeziehung der Verkaufs- und Lieferbedingungen geschlossen worden, die dann zu Gepflogenheiten wurden; OGH, 31.8.2005, CISG-online 1093 = IHR 2006, 31, 33: AGB wurden bei der ersten Bestellung von Gegenpartei unterzeichnet und zurückgeschickt, die damit „ihre Unterwerfung unter die Einkaufsbedingungen der Beklagten augenfällig zum Ausdruck gebracht" hatte; OGH, 6.2.1996, CISG-online 224 = ZfRVgl 1996, 248, 252; OLG Linz, 8.8.2005, CISG-online 1087 = IHR 2005, 249, 251; *Kramer,* FS Welser, S. 551.

[345] Vgl. *Piltz,* IHR 2007, 121, 122; großzügiger wohl Netherlands Arbitration Institute, 10.2.2005, CISG-online 1621 = YB. Comm. Arb. 2007, 93, 104 f.

[346] OGH, 31.8.2005, CISG-online 1093 = IHR 2006, 31, 33; OLG Linz, 8.8.2005, CISG-online 1087 = IHR 2005, 249, 251.

[347] Wie hier *Schwenzer/Hachem/Kee,* Rn. 12.14.

Begriff des Angebots 74, 75 **Art. 14**

bedingungen bedarf es schließlich auch dort nicht, wo die betreffenden Bedingungen den Rang eines **internationalen Handelsbrauches** besitzen,[348] weil – über Art. 8 III hinaus[349] – gemäß Art. 9 II angenommen wird, dass die Parteien sich beim Abschluss ihres Vertrages stillschweigend auf entsprechende Gebräuche bezogen haben. Bei AGB, die von einer der beteiligten Kaufvertragsparteien vorformuliert wurden, dürfte eine Einordnung als internationaler Handelsbrauch allerdings kaum denkbar sein,[350] während dies bei von unabhängiger dritter Seite entwickelten Standardbedingungen durchaus möglich ist und insbesondere für die **Incoterms®** verschiedentlich bejaht wurde.[351] Da die Incoterms® allerdings insgesamt 13 alternativ wählbare Klauseln umfassen,[352] kann es bei der Frage der Einbeziehung der Incoterms® über Art. 9 II von vornherein nicht um die unterschiedslose Maßgeblichkeit des gesamten Regelwerkes für die Vertragsbeziehung der konkreten Parteien gehen, sondern allein darum, dass die Parteien sich nicht auf die **fehlende Kenntnis** des Inhalts der Incoterms® und damit auch der daraus konkret gewählten Klausel berufen können.[353] Als internationalen Handelsbrauch hat die Rechtsprechung daneben die **„Tegernseer Gebräuche"** im Holzhandel[354] sowie (mit allerdings unklarer Begründung) den **„Deutschen Garnkontrakt"**[355] anerkannt.

7. Annahme des Angebots

Für die erforderliche Annahme des die AGB umfassenden Angebots gelten die allgemeinen Regeln der Artt. 18 ff.;[356] nach Art. 19 bestimmt sich insbesondere die Behandlung von Annahmeerklärungen, die unter Einbeziehung kollidierender Standardbedingungen abgegeben werden („battle of the forms").[357] 74

Keine Voraussetzung für eine wirksame Annahme ist, dass die AGB tatsächlich gelesen wurden,[358] dass ihre Geltung für den Vertrag ausdrücklich bestätigt wird[359] oder dass sie gar durch beide Parteien unterschrieben oder abgezeichnet werden.[360] Eine schriftliche An- 75

---

[348] Vgl. OGH, 6.2.1996, CISG-online 224 = ZfRVgl 1996, 248, 252; *Berger*, FS Horn, S. 18; *Magnus*, FS Kritzer, S. 321; *Piltz*, IHR 2004, 133, 134; *Soergel/Lüderitz/Fenge*, Art. 14, Rn. 11; *Steensgaard*, Standardbetingelser, § 8, Rn. 46; *Witz/Salger/Lorenz/Witz*, Vor Artt. 14–24, Rn. 12; übersehen von *Schmidt-Kessel*, NJW 2002, 3444, 3446, der daher zu Unrecht eine „Zugangsschranke" für Marktneulinge befürchtet.
[349] S. dazu bereits oben Rn. 54.
[350] *Schwenzer/Hachem/Kee*, Rn. 12.15; *Soergel/Lüderitz/Fenge*, Art. 14, Rn. 11; in diesem Sinne auch *Rummel/Rummel*, § 864a AGBG, Rn. 3.
[351] *BP Oil International, Ltd. v. Empressa Estatal Petroleos de Ecuador (PetroEcuador)*, U. S. Ct. App. (5th Cir.), 11.6.2003, CISG-online 730 = 332 F. 3d 333, 337 f.; *China North Chemical Industries Corporation v. Beston Chemical Corporation*, U. S. Dist. Ct. (S. D. Tex.), 7.2.2006, CISG-online 1177; *St. Paul Guardian Insurance Company v. Neuromed Medical Systems & Support GmbH*, U. S. Dist. Ct. (S. D. N. Y.), 26.3.2002, CISG-online 615 = IHR 2005, 256, 257; KG Wallis, 28.1.2009, CISG-online 2025; *Lohmann*, Parteiautonomie, S. 219; *Pamboukis*, 25 J. L. & Com. (2005-06), 107, 127.
[352] S. im Einzelnen Anhang IV.
[353] Vgl. KG Wallis, 28.1.2009, CISG-online 2025: Vertragsinhalt anhand vereinbarter Klausel „Incoterms: DDU ..." ermittelt.
[354] OGH, 21.3.2000, CISG-online 641 = IHR 2001, 40, 41: Maßgeblichkeit der Tegernseer Gebräuche für deutsch-österreichischen Holzkaufvertrag bejaht (wobei *in casu* eine Partei ausdrücklich auf die Gebräuche hingewiesen hatte).
[355] Gerechtshof 's-Hertogenbosch, 24.4.1996, CISG-online 321 = NIPR 1996, Nr. 235: bei deutsch-niederländischem Kaufvertrag unter Verweis auf Art. 9 Anwendung des „Deutschen Garnkontrakt – Kartellfassung vom 24. November 1976", auf den die deutsche Verkäuferin angeblich in ihren AGB (deren Übermittlung allerdings streitig blieb) hingewiesen hatte.
[356] Trib. Rovereto, 24.8.2006, CISG-online 1374.
[357] S. dazu näher unten Art. 19 Rn. 19 ff.
[358] *Drasch*, S. 8; *Koller*, FS Honsell, S. 238; *Piltz*, IHR 2004, 133, 135; missverständlich CA Colmar, 24.10.2000, CISG-online 578; a. A. *Drobnig*, Standard Forms, S. 123: „actual knowledge by the other party and nothing less" (zum EAG).
[359] *Lohmann*, Parteiautonomie, S. 221; *Magnus*, FS Kritzer, S. 318; *Piltz*, IHR 2004, 133, 135; unklar *Witz/Salger/Lorenz/Witz*, Vor Artt. 14–24, Rn. 14.
[360] *Golden Valley Grape Juice and Wine, LLC v. Centrisys Corp. et al.*, U. S. Dist. Ct. (E. D. Cal.), 21.1.2010, CISG-online 2089: „Pursuant to the CISG, acceptance does not require a signature or formalistic adoption of the offered terms"; *Piltz*, IHR 2004, 133, 134.

erkennung der AGB durch die Gegenseite³⁶¹ stellt freilich die sicherste und vor allem im Streitfall auch beweisbare Form der Einbeziehung dar und ist daher aus praktischer Perspektive zu empfehlen.

8. Beweislast

76 Die Beweislast für die erfolgte Einbeziehung der AGB in den Kaufvertrag einschließlich der notwendigen Kenntnisverschaffung bezüglich deren Inhalts trifft die Partei, die sich auf die AGB stützt,³⁶² also praktisch immer den **Verwender**.³⁶³ Beruft sich der AGB-Verwender auf Handelsbräuche, Gepflogenheiten zwischen den Parteien oder eine laufende Geschäftsbeziehung, aufgrund derer die Einbeziehung der Standardbedingungen erfolgt oder wenigstens eine Kenntnisverschaffung entbehrlich gewesen sei, so trifft ihn die Beweislast für das Vorliegen dieser Umstände.³⁶⁴ Bei Abfassung der AGB in einer Sprache, die nicht die zwischen den Parteien praktizierte Verhandlungssprache ist, hat der Verwender entsprechende Sprachkenntnisse des Erklärungsgegners zu beweisen,³⁶⁵ und zwar auch, wenn es sich bei der Sprache der Standardbedingungen um eine „Weltsprache" handelt.³⁶⁶

---

³⁶¹ Dazu *Kühl/Hingst*, FS Herber, S. 53.
³⁶² OLG Düsseldorf, 25.7.2003, CISG-online 919; OLG Jena, 10.11.2010, CISG-online 2216 = IHR 2011, 79, 80; CA Colmar, 24.10.2000, CISG-online 578; LG Memmingen, 13.9.2000, CISG-online 820; AG Kehl, 6.10.1995, CISG-online 162 = NJW-RR 1996, 565, 566; MünchKomm/*Gruber*, Art. 14, Rn. 38; *Schlechtriem*, FS Kritzer, S. 419.
³⁶³ Ausnahmen können freilich vorkommen, sofern sich im Einzelfall die AGB der Gegenseite für eine Partei als günstiger erweisen als die eigenen Standardbedingungen; so etwa im „Milchpulver-Fall" des BGH, 9.1.2002, CISG-online 651 = NJW 2002, 1651, 1652, wo die AGB der Käuferin, über deren Einbeziehung in den Kaufvertrag gestritten wurde, „erhebliche Haftungsbeschränkungen für den Verkäufer" (!) vorsahen.
³⁶⁴ *Piltz*, IHR 2004, 133, 134.
³⁶⁵ S. bereits oben Rn. 64; OLG Düsseldorf, 21.4.2004, CISG-online 915 = IHR 2005, 24, 28; *Spellenberg*, FS Ferid, S. 480.
³⁶⁶ *Sauthoff*, IHR 2005, 21, 23.

Art. 15 [Wirksamwerden des Angebots; Rücknahme]

(1) Ein Angebot wird wirksam, sobald es dem Empfänger zugeht.

(2) Ein Angebot kann, selbst wenn es unwiderruflich ist, zurückgenommen werden, wenn die Rücknahmeerklärung dem Empfänger vor oder gleichzeitig mit dem Angebot zugeht.

Art. 15

(1) An offer becomes effective when it reaches the offeree.

(2) An offer, even if it is irrevocable, may be withdrawn if the withdrawal reaches the offeree before or at the same time as the offer.

Art. 15

1) Une offre prend effet lorsqu'elle parvient au destinataire.

2) Une offre, même si elle est irrévocable, peut être rétractée si la rétractation parvient au destinataire avant ou en même temps que l'offre.

Übersicht

	Rn.
I. Funktion	1
II. Zugangswirkungen und Rücknahme	2
1. Wirksamkeit	2
a) Mit Zugang	2
b) Publikumsofferten	3
2. Rücknahme	4
a) Zugangsbedürftigkeit	4
b) Publikumsofferten	5
c) Rechtsfolge	6
3. Tod, Geschäftsunfähigkeit, Konkurs des Erklärenden vor Zugang der Erklärung	7

Vorläufer und **Entwürfe:** Art. 5 I EAG, New Yorker E 1977 Art. 9, New Yorker E 1978 Art. 13.

I. Funktion

Art. 15 entspricht sachlich § 130 I BGB, unterscheidet aber „Rücknahme" (bis zum Zugang) vom „Widerruf" (nach Zugang, Art. 16).[1]   **1**

II. Zugangswirkungen und Rücknahme

1. Wirksamkeit

a) Mit Zugang. Die Offerte wird (erst) mit **Zugang** und nur mit dem zugegangenen   **2** Inhalt wirksam; zum Zugang s. Art. 24. Weicht der nach Art. 15 I maßgebliche Angebotsinhalt bei Zugang vom Inhalt des Angebots bei Absendung infolge falscher Übermittlung ab, so ist nationales Irrtumsrecht maßgeblich, Art. 4 S. 2 lit. a).[2] Zugang schließt zwar nicht grundsätzlich, aber doch vielfach Widerruf aus – vgl. Art. 16 I einerseits, II andererseits –, so dass der Zugangszeitpunkt für die Widerruflichkeit wichtig ist.[3] Zugang setzt voraus, dass

---

[1] Zur Vorgeschichte s. *Schlechtriem*, 1. und 2. Aufl., Art. 15 Rn. 1; zu EAG und den Entwürfen zu Art. 5 EAG s. *Dölle/Schlechtriem*, Art. 5 EAG, Rn. 1; zur Entwicklung von Art. 15 *Bianca/Bonell/Eörsi*, Art. 15, Anm. 1.2., 1.3.; zur Terminologie daselbst Anm. 2.1.1.; ferner *Wey*, Rn. 791.
[2] MünchKomm/*Gruber*, Art. 15, Rn. 8; *Staudinger/Magnus*, Art. 15, Rn. 6; s. schon oben Vor Artt. 14–24 Rn. 2.
[3] *Staudinger/Magnus*, Art. 15, Rn. 3.

mit Willen des Autors abgesandt worden ist. Eine vom zuständigen Gremium beschlossene und abgefasste, aber noch nicht abgesandte Offerte, die der in Aussicht genommene Empfänger auf unbefugte Weise erlangt, ist nicht zugegangen und deshalb nicht wirksam;[4] Ansprüche auf Schadenersatz nach nationalem Recht (wie etwa nach § 122 BGB analog) kommen in dieser Situation neben dem CISG nicht in Frage.[5] Fehlende Wirksamkeit vor Zugang bedeutet, dass die Offerte noch nicht angenommen werden kann, auch wenn der Adressat sie schon kennt. Eine bereits vorsorglich abgesandte Annahmeerklärung muss aber Wirkung entfalten, wenn die Offerte später zugeht und damit wirksam wird.[6] Auch Vertragsschluss durch Kreuzofferten scheitert nicht daran, dass die vom Übereinkommen grundsätzlich vorausgesetzte Abfolge „Erklärung der Offerte", „Zugang der Offerte", „Gegenerklärung" nicht eingehalten worden ist.[7] Die **Beweislast** für den Zugang des Angebots trägt derjenige, der sich hierauf beruft.[8]

3   b) Publikumsofferten. Bei Erklärungen an die Öffentlichkeit, die ausnahmsweise **Publikumsofferte** sind,[9] ist Zugangsbedürftigkeit zweifelhaft und hat zu in Nuancen divergierenden Ansichten in der Literatur geführt.[10] Je nach Art der an einen unbestimmten Personenkreis gerichteten Vorschläge kommt Zugang i. S. d. Art. 24 in Betracht, z. B. bei Versendung von Preislisten, Katalogen, oder ist schwer konstruierbar, z. B. bei Zeitungsinseraten, Schaufensterauslagen, Angeboten im Fernsehen, über Internet etc. Sachfragen sind der Zeitpunkt des Wirksamwerdens und die Rücknahmemöglichkeit. Sind Vorschläge in Katalogen, Preislisten usw., die an einen großen, aber doch durch die Anschriften der Empfänger abgegrenzten Interessentenkreis übersandt werden, ausnahmsweise als Publikumsofferte gemeint, dann werden sie erst mit Zugang nach Art. 15 I wirksam. In anderen Fällen der Vorschläge ad incertas personas sollte der Zeitpunkt ihres Wirksamwerdens genauso wie ihre Qualität als Publikumsofferte vom Willen des Erklärenden abhängen.[11] Denkbar ist eine Datierung des Wirksamwerdens („ab 15. 8. bieten wir an …"). Fehlt eine solche Bestimmung, so ist von der Absicht auszugehen, dass der Vorschlag bereits mit der Veröffentlichung und nicht erst mit Vernehmung durch potentielle Adressaten wirksam sein soll.

2. Rücknahme

4   Fehlende Wirksamkeit vor Zugang bedeutet vor allem, dass der Erklärende bis zum Zugang der Erklärung, spätestens mit ihrem Zugang („gleichzeitig") zurücknehmen kann, Art. 15 II. Praktische Bedeutung kommt dieser Regelung vor allem dann zu, wenn der Offerent für die Rücknahme ein schnelleres Kommunikationsmittel als für das Angebot selbst einsetzt (etwa Angebot durch Brief, Rücknahme per Telefax) und die Rücknahmeerklärung die Offerte daher zu „überholen" vermag.

---

[4] Vgl. die Fälle bei *Schlesinger/Macneil,* Bd. 1, S. 683 Fn. 1; RG, 22.5.1908, RGZ 68, 407, 409 f. Wie hier *Witz/Salger/Lorenz/Witz,* Art. 15, Rn. 5; andere Begründung bei MünchKomm/*Gruber,* Art. 15, Rn. 9; *Soergel/Lüderitz/Fenge,* Art. 15, Rn. 3. Beweislast für fehlende Absendung trägt jedoch der Erklärende, *Baumgärtel/Laumen/Hepting,* Art. 14 WKR, Rn. 10.

[5] S. hierzu bereits oben Vor Artt. 14–24 Rn. 1; a. A. MünchKomm/*Gruber,* Art. 15, Rn. 9.

[6] Wohl auch *Honsell/Dornis,* Art. 15, Rn. 2; differenzierend *Witz/Salger/Lorenz/Witz,* Art. 15, Rn. 5 für den Fall der Rücknahme des Angebots.

[7] S. hierzu oben Vor Artt. 14–24 Rn. 15, 23 sowie unten Art. 18 Rn. 10; MünchKomm/*Gruber,* Art. 15, Rn. 7; umfassend *Perales Viscasillas,* Formación del contrato, S. 385 ff. (nationale Lösungen), 388 ff. (zum CISG).

[8] *Baumgärtel/Laumen/Hepting,* Art. 15 WKR, Rn. 1.

[9] S. oben Art. 14 Rn. 30.

[10] Vgl. MünchKomm/*Gruber,* Art. 15, Rn. 5 (Zugang auch hier stets erforderlich); *Soergel/Lüderitz/Fenge,* Art. 15, Rn. 5; *Staudinger/Magnus,* Art. 15, Rn. 5 (Zugang, anders bei Inseraten: Veröffentlichung); *Witz/Salger/Lorenz,* Art. 15, Rn. 7.

[11] Wie hier *Honsell/Dornis,* Art. 15, Rn. 3.

Wirksamwerden des Angebots; Rücknahme 5 **Art. 15**

a) Zugangsbedürftigkeit. Auch die **Rücknahmeerklärung** ist, wie schon der Wortlaut des Art. 15 II besagt, zugangsbedürftig;[12] Voraussetzungen und Zeitpunkt ihrer Wirkung bestimmen sich nach Art. 24. Das Zusammenspiel von Art. 15 II und Art. 24 ermöglicht bei schriftlichen Erklärungen den „gleichzeitigen" Zugang von Angebot und Rücknahme, etwa wenn beide durch Brief erklärt werden und mit derselben Post beim Adressaten eintreffen.[13] Bei **elektronischen Erklärungen,** deren technische Besonderheiten bei Schaffung des Art. 15 II noch nicht in Rechnung gestellt werden konnten, kann diese Konstellation hingegen deshalb nicht auftreten, weil E-Mails i. S. des Art. 24 mit Eingang der einzelnen Nachricht im Server des Empfängers sowie deren möglicher Abrufbarkeit zugehen[14] und mehrere E-Mails daher nicht „gleichzeitig" zugehen können.[15] Es ist daher vorgeschlagen worden, insoweit auf die Kenntnisnahmemöglichkeit des Adressaten abzustellen mit der Folge, dass ein durch am Samstag zugegangene E-Mail gemachtes Angebot und die durch am Sonntag zugegangene E-Mail erklärte Rücknahme als „gleichzeitig" zugegangen zu behandeln sind, wenn der Adressat beide Nachrichten am Montagmorgen liest[16] – dem kann nicht gefolgt werden, weil es nach Art. 15 II auf den Zeitpunkt der tatsächlichen Kenntnisnahme gerade nicht ankommen soll[17] und der in ihrer Geschwindigkeit liegende Vorteil der elektronischen Kommunikation keiner Ergänzung durch eine erweiterte Rücknahmemöglichkeit bedarf.

Rücknahme ist **Willenserklärung;** wie bei der Offerte bestimmen sich Geschäftsfähigkeit, Folgen von Willensmängeln, Voraussetzungen wirksamer Vertretung nach dem durch IPR berufenen unvereinheitlichten Recht. Sie kann formlos erfolgen,[18] auch wenn Schriftform für den Vertrag selbst in der Offerte vorgesehen ist,[19] und muss nicht mit dem gleichen Erklärungsmittel wie die Offerte erfolgen.[20] Bei Verträgen mit Parteien in Vorbehaltsstaaten – Artt. 12, 96 – entscheidet aber das berufene Formstatut,[21] da Rücknahme eine „sonstige" Willenserklärung i. S. von Art. 12 ist.[22] Eine Qualifikation der Erklärungsmittel wie in Art. 12 II EAG sieht das CISG für Vertragsschluss-, Rücknahme- und Widerrufserklärungen nicht mehr vor; Art. 27 bezieht sich nur auf die – lediglich absendebedürftigen – Erklärungen in Teil III. Eine Beschränkung der möglichen Erklärungsmittel ergibt sich aber aus der Zugangsbedürftigkeit der Erklärung und ihren Voraussetzungen.[23] **Beweislast** für Rücknahme trägt, wer Unwirksamkeit der Offerte behauptet, d. h. regelmäßig der Offerent.[24]

b) Publikumsofferten. Für die **Rücknahme** einer **Publikumsofferte** könnte die 5 Geltung des Zugangsprinzips zweifelhaft sein.[25] M. E. sollte die Wirksamkeit der Rücknahme einer Publikumsofferte von den gleichen Voraussetzungen abhängen wie das Wirksamwerden der Offerte selbst: Soweit die Publikumsofferte erst mit Zugang wirksam wird,

---

[12] *Stern,* Erklärungen, Rn. 49; *Soergel/Lüderitz/Fenge,* Art. 15, Rn. 4; Ausnahmen sollen nach *Heuzé,* Anm. 177., möglich sein.
[13] *Staudinger/Magnus,* Art. 15, Rn. 9.
[14] S. CISG-AC, Op. 1 *(Chr. Ramberg),* Comments 15.2 ff., IHR 2003, 244, 245 f.; *Eiselen,* 6 VJ (2002), 305, 310 f.; hier unten Art. 24 Rn. 24.
[15] *Schwenzer/Mohs,* IHR 2006, 239, 241.
[16] So *Schwenzer/Mohs,* IHR 2006, 239, 241 f.
[17] S. MünchKomm/*Gruber,* Art. 15, Rn. 10.
[18] RB Tongeren, 25.1.2005, CISG-online 1106.
[19] *Honsell/Dornis,* Art. 15, Rn. 8; *Soergel/Lüderitz/Fenge,* Art. 15, Rn. 4; *Witz/Salger/Lorenz/Witz,* Art. 15, Rn. 5.
[20] *Enderlein/Maskow/Strohbach,* Art. 15, Anm. 6.; *Honsell/Dornis,* Art. 15, Rn. 8; MünchKomm/*Gruber,* Art. 15, Rn. 11.
[21] Dazu oben *Schmidt-Kessel,* Art. 12 Rn. 2, 3.
[22] *Honsell/ Dornis,* Art. 15, Rn. 8; MünchKomm/*Gruber,* Art. 15, Rn. 11; a. A. *Reinhart,* Art. 15, Rn. 3.
[23] Dazu unten Art. 24 Rn. 16, 19 ff.
[24] OLG Dresden, 10.11.2006, CISG-online 1625; *Baumgärtel/Laumen/Hepting,* Art. 15 WKR, Rn. 2; dagegen Rn. 4, 5 zur Beweislast für behauptete Rechtzeitigkeit (Zugangszeitpunkte).
[25] Ein englischer Antrag, Rücknahme durch bloße Publikation einer entsprechenden Erklärung in der gleichen Weise wie die Offerte genügen zu lassen, wurde auf Grund des Missverständnisses, dass es Publikumsofferten nicht gebe, zurückgewiesen, s. Sekretariatskommentar, Art. 14, Nr. 3, 5; dazu auch *Schlechtriem,* Einheitliches UN-Kaufrecht, S. 39 Fn. 170.

Art. 15 6–8   Teil II. Abschluss des Vertrages

kann vom Offerenten, der Wirksamkeit durch Rücknahme verhindern will, erwartet werden, dass er die Rücknahmeerklärung ebenfalls zugehen lässt. Wo dagegen die Publikumsofferte ohne Zugang wirksam wird, sollte auch eine Rücknahme in der gleichen Weise wie die Publikation der Offerte erfolgen können.[26] Diese Wertung liegt dem § 658 I 2 BGB zugrunde und lässt sich in den Rechtsordnungen, die die Publikumsofferte kennen, nachweisen.[27] Rücknahme durch individuelle Erklärung, die freilich zur Wirksamkeit des Zugangs nach Art. 24 bedarf, bleibt daneben stets möglich.

6   c) **Rechtsfolge.** Rechtsfolge der Rücknahme ist vollständiger Wegfall der Offerte, die folglich nicht mehr angenommen werden kann.[28] Die Rücknahme kann nicht ihrerseits wieder zurückgenommen werden, die Offerte ist vielmehr neu vorzunehmen.[29] Eine trotz rechtzeitiger Rücknahme der Offerte erklärte Annahme kann jedoch u. U. als Offerte gedeutet werden und so eine Wiederaufnahme des Vertragsschlussverfahrens bewirken.

3. Tod, Geschäftsunfähigkeit, Konkurs des Erklärenden vor Zugang der Erklärung

7   Eine Vorschrift zu der in § 130 II BGB geregelten Sachfrage enthält das CISG nicht. Art. 11 EAG enthielt noch eine vergleichbare Regel; ihre Beibehaltung wurde jedoch von der Arbeitsgruppe auf der 9. Sitzung schließlich abgelehnt.[30] Bereits Art. 11 EAG war im Verlauf seiner Entstehungsgeschichte umstritten,[31] da manche Rechtsordnungen Tod oder Geschäftsunfähigkeit einer Person in bestimmten Situationen als Parallele zum wirksamen Widerruf der Offerte behandeln.[32] Die Arbeitsgruppe bemängelte, dass eine auf die Fälle Tod und Geschäftsunfähigkeit beschränkte Regelung unzureichend sei, da sie die für die Praxis des grenzüberschreitenden Warenkaufs viel wichtigeren Fälle des Konkurses oder der Auflösung einer juristischen Person nicht erfasse.[33]

8   Der bewusste Verzicht auf eine Regelung des Einflusses von **Tod, Wegfall von Geschäftsfähigkeit** oder **Rechtsfähigkeit** sowie **Insolvenz** auf eine im Lauf befindliche Offerte lässt den Schluss zu, dass es sich insoweit um außerhalb des Regelungsanspruchs des Übereinkommens liegende Materien handelt.[34] Dafür spricht auch, dass Rechts- und Geschäftsfähigkeit und die Folgen ihres Fehlens für Willenserklärungen grundsätzlich vom unvereinheitlichten, über IPR berufenen nationalen Recht geregelt werden.[35] Anhaltspunkt für eine vom Übereinkommen geregelte Materie könnte lediglich die Formulierung des Art. 15 I sein, wonach für die Wirksamkeit einer Offerte (allein?) entscheidend ihr Zugang ist. Das würde, da es sich um nicht ausdrücklich entschiedene Fragen handelt, zu Art. 7 II führen. Als allgemeiner Grundsatz lässt sich jedoch aus Art. 15 I allenfalls ableiten, dass der

---

[26] Wie hier *Soergel/Lüderitz/Fenge*, Art. 15, Rn. 5; *Staudinger/Magnus*, Art. 15, Rn. 10; *Honsell/Dornis*, Art. 15, Rn. 7.
[27] S. *Schlesinger*, Bd. 1, S. 113.
[28] RB Tongeren, 25.1.2005, CISG-online 1106.
[29] *Bianca/Bonell/Eörsi*, Art. 15, Anm. 2.1.2.; a. A. *Honsell/Dornis*, Art. 15, Rn. 16; MünchKomm/*Gruber*, Art. 15, Rn. 14.
[30] YB IX (1978), S. 81 f., Nr. 279–283. Auf der 8. Sitzung sollte zunächst Art. 11 EAG übernommen werden; auch gab es Vorschläge zur Regelung des Konkursfalles, s. YB VIII (1977), S. 85.
[31] S. *Dölle/Schlechtriem*, Art. 11 EAG, Rn. 1, 10; *Wey*, Rn. 913 ff.
[32] Vgl. *Schlesinger*, Bd. 1, S. 117; *Schlesinger/Leyser*, Bd. 1, S. 880 ff.; *Schlesinger/Bonassies*, Bd. 1, S. 889 ff.; *Schlesinger/Gorla*, Bd. 1, S. 904 ff.; aus jüngerer Zeit rechtsvergleichend *Christandl*, ERCL 2011, 463, 468 ff.
[33] YB IX (1978), S. 81, Nr. 281; umfassend zu den Beratungen der UNCITRAL-Arbeitsgruppe *Ludwig*, S. 382; zur Gleichbehandlung von Geschäftsunfähigkeit und Konkurs als „incapacité", „incapacity" und die Behandlung dieser Fragen bei den Vorarbeiten zu Art. 11 EAG s. *von Caemmerer*, RabelsZ 29 (1965), 101, 132; *Dölle/Schlechtriem*, Art. 11 EAG, Rn. 8.
[34] So eindeutig die Entscheidung der Verfasser des EAG für den Fall des Konkurses, s. *von Caemmerer*, RabelsZ 29 (1965), 101, 132; zum CISG *Honsell/Dornis*, Vorbem. 14–24, Rn. 23; *Jametti Greiner*, S. 51; MünchKomm/*Gruber*, Art. 15, Rn. 17; *Staub/Koller*, Vor § 373 HGB, Rn. 641; ebenso für den Konkursfall *Herber/Czerwenka*, Art. 15, Rn. 6, anders aber für Tod und Geschäftsunfähigkeit: kein Einfluss auf Wirksamkeit des Angebots.
[35] S. oben Vor Artt. 14–24 Rn. 2.

Anbietende bis zum Zugang des Angebots Herr der Offerte bleibt und deshalb Änderungen in seinen persönlichen Verhältnissen wie eine Rücknahme Einfluss auf das Wirksamwerden der Offerte haben können. Allgemeine Grundsätze zu den Auswirkungen einer nach Abgabe der Erklärung eintretenden Rechts- oder Geschäftsunfähigkeit, des Todes oder der Eröffnung eines Insolvenzverfahrens lassen sich dagegen aus dem Übereinkommen nicht mehr ableiten. Gleichwohl wird vielfach vertreten, dass auf Grund allgemeiner Rechtstradition und des Inhalts der meisten nationalen Rechte Tod und Geschäftsunfähigkeit auf die Wirksamkeit abgesandter Erklärungen ohne Einfluss bleiben müssen.[36] M. E. bleibt aber nur, diese Fragen dem nationalen Recht vorzubehalten.[37]

---

[36] *Soergel/Lüderitz/Fenge,* Art. 17, Rn. 3; wie hier *Achilles,* Art. 17, Rn. 2; *Bamberger/Roth/Saenger,* Art. 15, Rn. 2, Art. 17, Rn. 2; *Witz/Salger/Lorenz/Witz,* Vor Artt. 14–24, Rn. 8.

[37] Wie hier *Brunner,* Art. 15, Rn. 1; *Honnold/Flechtner,* Vor Artt. 14–24, Rn. 132; *Honsell/Dornis,* Art. 15, Rn. 19; *Schlechtriem,* Internationales UN-Kaufrecht, Rn. 78. A. A. *Staudinger/Magnus,* Art. 15, Rn. 14: CISG sei abschließende Regelung, deshalb kein Erlöschen bei Tod, Geschäftsunfähigkeit oder Insolvenz des Erklärenden; *Bianca/Bonell/Eörsi,* Art. 16, Anm. 1.2.1., der aus dem Schweigen von CISG ableitet, dass Art. 11 EAG übernommen werden könne; ähnlich *Herber/Czerwenka,* Art. 15, Rn. 6; *Neumayer/Ming,* Art. 15, Anm. 3. S. auch *Huber,* RabelsZ 43 (1979), 413, 441, der Tod und Geschäftsunfähigkeit Bedeutung für die abgesandte Offerte abspricht, alternativ aber auch Behandlung als Gültigkeitsfrage erwägt.

Art. 16 [Widerruf des Angebots]

(1) **Bis zum Abschluß des Vertrages kann ein Angebot widerrufen werden, wenn der Widerruf dem Empfänger zugeht, bevor dieser eine Annahmeerklärung abgesandt hat.**

(2) **Ein Angebot kann jedoch nicht widerrufen werden,**
a) **wenn es durch Bestimmung einer festen Frist zur Annahme oder auf andere Weise zum Ausdruck bringt, daß es unwiderruflich ist, oder**
b) **wenn der Empfänger vernünftigerweise darauf vertrauen konnte, daß das Angebot unwiderruflich ist, und er im Vertrauen auf das Angebot gehandelt hat.**

Art. 16

(1) Until a contract is concluded an offer may be revoked if the revocation reaches the offeree before he has dispatched an acceptance.

(2) However, an offer cannot be revoked:
(a) if it indicates, whether by stating a fixed time for acceptance or otherwise, that it is irrevocable; or
(b) if it was reasonable for the offeree to rely on the offer as being irrevocable and the offeree has acted in reliance on the offer.

Art. 16

1) Jusqu'à ce qu'un contrat ait été conclu, une offre peut être révoquée si la révocation parvient au destinataire avant que celui-ci ait expédié une acceptation.

2) Cependant, une offre ne peut être révoquée:
a) si elle indique, en fixant un délai déterminé pour l'acceptation, ou autrement, qu'elle est irrévocable; ou
b) s'il était raisonnable pour le destinataire de considérer l'offre comme irrévocable et s'il a agi en conséquence.

Übersicht

	Rn.
I. Sachfrage und Grundzüge der Lösung	1
1. Sachfrage	1
2. Grundzüge	2
II. Ausübung des Widerrufs; zeitliche Grenzen der Widerrufsmöglichkeit – Abs. 1	3
1. Widerruf durch empfangsbedürftige Willenserklärung	3
2. Ende der Widerrufsmöglichkeit	4
3. Folgen unwirksamen Widerrufs	5
4. Abweichende Ausgestaltung der Widerrufssperre	6
5. Beweislast	7
III. Bindung an das Angebot – Abs. 2	8
1. Bindung durch Ausgestaltung der Offerte als unwiderruflich – Abs. 2 lit. a)	8
a) Ausdruck des Bindungswillens	8
b) Annahmefrist als Vermutung der Unwiderruflichkeit	9
c) Widerlegung der Vermutung	10
2. Bindung aufgrund tätigen Vertrauens – Abs. 2 lit. b)	11
IV. Rechtsfolgen von Widerruflichkeit oder Widerrufssperre und Rechtsbehelfe nach nationalem Recht	13
1. Bei widerruflichem Angebot	13
2. Bei Widerrufssperre	14

Vorläufer und **Entwürfe:** Art. 5 EAG, New Yorker E 1977 Art. 5, Genfer E 1977 Art. 10, New Yorker E 1978 Art. 14.

I. Sachfrage und Grundzüge der Lösung

1. Sachfrage

1 Das in Art. 16 geregelte Problem der Bindung an die Offerte und ihrer Widerruflichkeit war eine der schwierigsten Fragen der Vereinheitlichung des Vertragsschlussrechts, da eine

Brücke zwischen verschiedenen Auffassungen zu schlagen war: Während sich im deutschen Rechtskreis, aber auch in den skandinavischen Rechten die seit Art. 319 ADHGB bekannte Bindung des Offerenten an sein Angebot durchgesetzt hat, nehmen die romanischen und angelsächsischen Rechtsordnungen eine Gegenposition ein, wobei im Einzelnen wieder Unterschiede in der Möglichkeit des Offerenten bestehen, sich für eine bestimmte Zeit zu binden, und zudem Unterschiede auch hinsichtlich einer Schadenersatzverpflichtung bei Widerruf gelten.[1] Art. 5 EAG war bereits ein mühsam errungener Kompromiss;[2] die Entwürfe der Arbeitsgruppe und von UNCITRAL wie die schließlich gefundene Fassung des Art. 16 lassen ebenfalls erkennen, dass man unterschiedlichen Konzeptionen Rechnung zu tragen versucht hat.[3] In der Endfassung war freilich der Kompromiss nur noch um den Preis einer Unklarheit zu erlangen.[4]

Das bis heute andauernde fast völlige Fehlen von Gerichtsurteilen oder Schiedssprüchen, in denen Art. 16 CISG entscheidungserheblich gewesen wäre, lassen freilich den Schluss zu, dass die tiefgreifenden Unterschiede der Rechtssysteme im Grundsätzlichen und die reichhaltige wissenschaftliche Diskussion keine Entsprechung in praktischen Bedürfnissen haben,[5] und dass – vor allem – die an Kommunikation durch Briefpost orientierten Regeln durch moderne Kommunikationsmittel, die unmittelbare Kontakte wie unter Anwesenden ermöglichen, an Bedeutung verloren haben.[6] Im Ergebnis dürfte Art. 16 II lit. b) daher eher als Steinbruch für Grundsätze zur Lückenfüllung i. S. v. Art. 7 II genutzt werden, so, wenn es gilt, das Verbot widersprüchlichen Verhaltens oder „promissory estoppel" als solche Prinzipien zu begründen.[7]

2. Grundzüge

Art. 16 I geht vom **Grundsatz** der **Widerruflichkeit** der Offerte aus, schränkt diesen aber bereits dadurch ein, dass nicht nur der Vertragsschluss, sondern bereits die Absendung der Annahmeerklärung die Widerrufsmöglichkeit abschneidet.[8] Der Offerent kann seine Offerte aber auch als bindende ausgestalten, ohne dass es dafür einer „consideration" – z. B. einer Gegenleistung oder Gegenverpflichtung – oder Einhaltung besonderer Formen – wie in § 2–205 UCC – bedarf[9] oder eine zeitliche Grenze für solche Selbstbindung vorgeschrieben wäre.[10] Setzen einer Frist für die Annahme ist als Ausdruck einer solchen Bindungs-

---

[1] Vgl. zu den verschiedenen Systemen *Dilger*, RabelsZ 45 (1981), 169, 175 ff.; *von Mehren*, Sec. 134 ff.; *Rabel*, Recht des Warenkaufs, Bd. 1, S. 86 ff.; *Rodière*, sub B VI; *Schlesinger*, Bd. 1, S. 109 ff.; *Zweigert/Kötz*, S. 37 ff., 350 ff.; *Malik*, 25 Indian J. Int'l L. (1985), 26–49.
[2] Vgl. *von Caemmerer*, RabelsZ 29 (1965), 101, 119 ff.; *Schmidt*, 14 Am. J. Comp. L. (1965), 1, 10; *Dölle/Schlechtriem*, Art. 5 EAG, Rn. 20; *Perales Viscasillas*, Formación del contrato, S. 392 ff. *Eörsi*, der von Anfang an zu den Mitgestaltern des Einheitlichen Kaufrechts gehörte, nennt die Geschichte der Artt. 5 EAG, 16 CISG „dramatic" (in: *Bianca/Bonell*, Art. 16, Anm. 1.2.).
[3] S. schon 8. Sitzung der Arbeitsgruppe, YB VIII (1977), S. 80, Nr. 77: „The basic compromise of ULF (= EAG) should be retained."
[4] Vgl. zur Geschichte von Art. 16 CISG *Bianca/Bonell/Eörsi*, Art. 16, Anm. 1.3.–1.7.2.; *Honnold/Flechtner*, Art. 16, Rn. 143, 143.1 („tempest in a teapot"); *Perales Viscasillas*, Formación del contrato, S. 392 ff.; *Schlechtriem*, Einheitliches UN-Kaufrecht, S. 39.
[5] In diesem Sinne auch *Flechtner*, FS Schwenzer, S. 498.
[6] So auch *Schwenzer/Mohs*, IHR 2006, 239, 242.
[7] Vgl. Internationales Schiedsgericht des Bundeskammer der gewerblichen Wirtschaft (Wien), 15.6.1994, CISG-online 120 = RIW 1995, 590, 592; mit ähnlicher Zielrichtung auch *Geneva Pharmaceuticals Technology Corp. v. Barr Laboratories, Inc.*, U. S. Dist. Ct. (S. D. N. Y.), 10.5.2002, CISG-online 653 = 201 F. Supp. 2d 236, 286 f.: aus Art. 16 II lit. b) folge, dass *promissory estoppel claims* nach nationalem Recht nicht neben dem CISG geltend gemacht werden können, soweit diese an andere (und möglicherweise geringere) Anforderungen für die Bindung an eine Offerte anknüpfen; s. schon oben Vor Artt. 14–24 Rn. 38.
[8] S. zu dieser aus der sog. „mailbox rule" des Common Law (dazu *Treitel*, Law of Contract, S. 23–29) entwickelten Einschränkung *Farnsworth*, Formation of Contract, § 3.04 sub 3–12 (3); *Honnold/Flechtner*, Art. 16, Rn. 140; *Stern*, Erklärungen, Rn. 54.
[9] *Honnold/Flechtner*, Art. 16, Rn. 142; zur Irrelevanz der „consideration" unter dem Vertragsschlussmodell des CISG bereits oben Vor Artt. 14–24 Rn. 2.
[10] So aber § 2–205 UCC: drei Monate; zum Erlöschen einer bindenden Offerte ohne zeitliche Befristung s. unten Art. 17 Rn. 5.

absicht zu verstehen, Abs. 2 lit. a). Bindung tritt aber auch ein, wenn der Offertenempfänger im vernünftigen Vertrauen auf die Unwiderruflichkeit „gehandelt" hat, Abs. 2 lit. b). Der Möglichkeit für den Offerenten, sein Angebot als bindend auszugestalten, entspricht es, dass er auch die Widerrufssperre des Art. 16 I in der Ausgestaltung seiner Offerte ausdrücklich abbedingen kann.[11]

Es versteht sich, dass Art. 16 unmittelbar nur den Widerruf solcher Offerten regelt, die im Falle ihrer Annahme zu einem Kaufvertrag führen würden, der sachlich dem Übereinkommen untersteht. Darüber hinaus kann das Kollisionsrecht des Forums allerdings bestimmen, dass Art. 16 auch auf materielle Einigungen außerhalb des Regelungsbereichs des UN-Kaufrechts Anwendung findet, wie etwa auf die Abtretung einer Forderung,[12] die unter einem CISG-Vertrag entstanden ist (vgl. Art. 14 I Rom I-VO oder Art. 145 I 1 schw. IPRG); Art. 16 greift in diesem Fall aufgrund kollisionsrechtlichen Verweises als Teil der *lex causae* ein.[13]

II. Ausübung des Widerrufs; zeitliche Grenzen der Widerrufsmöglichkeit – Abs. 1

1. Widerruf durch empfangsbedürftige Willenserklärung

3   **Widerruf** hat – wie Rücknahme der Offerte[14] – durch **zugangsbedürftige Willenserklärung** zu erfolgen;[15] für den Zugang gilt Art. 24. Kenntnis des Angebotsempfängers von einer Widerrufsabsicht des Offerenten, die er vielleicht von einem Dritten erlangt hat, bewirkt noch keinen Widerruf.[16] Geschäftsfähigkeit, Vertretungsmacht eines widerrufenden Vertreters und andere Wirksamkeitsvoraussetzungen bestimmen sich nach nationalem Recht.[17] Zulässig ist auch ein **teilweiser** Widerruf der Offerte;[18] eine Rücknahmeerklärung, die zeitlich erst nach dem Angebot und damit für Art. 15 II nicht mehr rechtzeitig zugeht, wird regelmäßig nach Art. 8 als Widerruf ausgelegt werden können.[19] Die **Beweislast** für den Widerruf trägt, wer sich auf das Erlöschen des Angebotes beruft.[20] Für den Widerruf der Publikumsofferte wie etwa eines Angebots im World Wide Web (WWW)[21] muss jedoch das Gleiche gelten wie für ihre Rücknahme: Soweit sie in Abweichung von Art. 15 I bereits mit Publikation wirksam wird, muss auch in gleicher Form widerrufen werden können.[22] Bindung des Widerrufenden an seine Erklärung tritt grundsätzlich (erst) mit Zugang ein, doch sollte ausnahmsweise **Widerruf des Widerrufs** möglich sein, solange der Adressat sich noch nicht darauf eingestellt hat, insbes. solange er noch keine Kenntnis erlangt hat.[23] Beweislast hierfür trägt der Widerrufende.

---

[11] S. unten Rn. 6.
[12] Die Abtretung wird vom UN-Kaufrecht nicht geregelt; s. *Ferrari*, oben Art. 4 Rn. 23.
[13] Vgl. OLG Hamburg, 25.1.2008, CISG-online 1681 = IHR 2008, 98, 102: auf Grundlage von Artt. 27 ff. EGBGB wurde Art. 16 CISG auf Angebot zum Abschluss einer Abtretungsvereinbarung über eine Vertragsstrafenforderung aus CISG-Vertrag angewandt.
[14] S. oben Art. 15 Rn. 4.
[15] *Enderlein/Maskow/Strohbach*, Art. 16, Anm. 3.; MünchKomm/*Gruber*, Art. 16, Rn. 3; *Stern*, Erklärungen, Rn. 58; *Staudinger/Magnus*, Art. 16, Rn. 5; *Wey*, Rn. 886; *Witz/Salger/Lorenz/Witz*, Art. 16, Rn. 7. Zu möglichen anderen Lösungen in nationalen Rechten umfassend *von Mehren*, Sec. 147 ff.
[16] *Wey*, Rn. 886; anders im englischen Recht *Dickinson v. Dodds* [1876] 2 Ch. D. 463; krit. dazu *Treitel*, Law of Contract, S. 41.
[17] S. oben Vor Artt. 14–24 Rn. 2.
[18] MünchKomm/*Gruber*, Art. 16, Rn. 3.
[19] Sekretariatskommentar, Art. 13, Nr. 4; MünchKomm/*Gruber*, Art. 16, Rn. 3; *Piltz*, Internationales Kaufrecht, Rn. 3–44.
[20] OLG Dresden, 10.11.2006, CISG-online 1625; *Baumgärtel/Laumen/Hepting*, Art. 16 WKR, Rn. 2.
[21] *Borges*, Verträge im elektronischen Geschäftsverkehr, S. 310.
[22] S. *Witz/Salger/Lorenz/Witz*, Art. 16, Rn. 17; ferner hier oben Art. 15 Rn. 5; *Wey*, Rn. 888.
[23] Str., a. A. *Honsell/Dornis*, Art. 16, Rn. 25; MünchKomm/*Gruber*, Art. 16, Rn. 4; zum allgemeinen Problem des Widerrufs oder der Rücknahme zugegangener Erklärungen, solange der Empfänger noch keine Kenntnis hatte, s. unten Art. 27 Rn. 14; *Schlechtriem*, Bindung an Erklärungen, S. 259 ff., 275 f.

2. Ende der Widerrufsmöglichkeit

Die **Widerrufsmöglichkeit endet** nach Art. 16 I **mit Abschluss des Vertrages,** d. h. **4** mit wirksamer Annahme nach Art. 18 II.[24] Es kommt nicht darauf an, ob der Akzeptant zusätzlich bereits mit der Erfüllung des Vertrages (etwa durch Absenden der Ware) begonnen hat.[25] Mit der Entstehung des Vertrages als solchem werden die Willenserklärungen, die für seinen Abschluss erforderlich waren, endgültig der Parteidisposition entzogen;[26] sie gehen im Vertrag auf. Ein Vorbehalt, der jetzt noch Widerruf ermöglichen soll, ist der Sache nach Vorbehalt einer Befugnis zur rückwirkenden Auflösung des geschlossenen Vertrages und muss deshalb als solcher deutlich ausgedrückt oder durch Auslegung zweifelsfrei zu ermitteln sein.

Art. 16 I schränkt Widerruf aber bereits durch „**Absenden**" der **Annahmeerklärung** ein. Da die Annahme nur in den Ausnahmefällen des Art. 18 III ohne Zugang wirksam und damit grundsätzlich – d. h. vorbehaltlich eines weitergehenden Widerrufsvorbehalts – eine Widerrufssperre schon durch einen solchen Vertragsschluss bewirkt werden kann, schneidet Absendung der Annahmeerklärung die Widerrufsmöglichkeit in den anderen Fällen regelmäßig zeitlich früher ab. Die Widerrufssperre durch Absenden der Annahmeerklärung stammt aus dem Common Law[27] und war bereits in Art. 5 EAG Teil des Kompromisses zwischen grundsätzlicher Widerruflichkeit und dem Bedürfnis, den Antragsempfänger zu schützen.[28] Die Widerrufssperre nach Art. 16 I geht allerdings über die „mailbox rule" des Common Law hinaus, da nicht nur Absenden der Annahmeerklärung durch Postbrief oder Telegramm, sondern auch durch andere Kommunikationsmittel, z. B. Fernschreiber, Telefax, EDI, per E-Mail[29] etc. ausreicht.[30] Die Widerrufssperre durch Absenden einer Annahmeerklärung gilt auch für eine Publikumsofferte.[31]

3. Folgen unwirksamen Widerrufs

Ein Widerruf nach Absenden der Annahmeerklärung ist unwirksam,[32] ein Vertrag gleich- **5** wohl bis zum Zugang der Annahmeerklärung regelmäßig noch nicht geschlossen. Bis zum Zugang der Annahmeerklärung besteht ein Schwebezustand. Falls die Annahmeerklärung überhaupt nicht zugeht, scheitert der Vertragsschluss, es sei denn, es liegt der Fall einer nicht zugangsbedürftigen Annahmeerklärung nach Art. 18 III vor. Die Bindung des Offerenten darf jedoch nicht ewig dauern. Falls er kein Datum für das Erlöschen seiner Offerte gesetzt hat, kann eine Befristung durch Auslegung nach Art. 8 ermittelt werden; äußersten Falles gilt die in Art. 18 II 2 vorgesehene Frist.[33]

---

[24] BerufungsG Lujubljana, 9.4.2008, CISG-online 2238 = EJCL 2010, 143 f.
[25] BerufungsG Lujubljana, 9.4.2008, CISG-online 2238 = EJCL 2010, 143 f.
[26] OLG Hamburg, 25.1.2008, CISG-online 1681 = IHR 2008, 98, 102 (betraf die Abtretung einer Forderung); *Schlechtriem*, FS Kritzer, S. 420.
[27] Vgl. hierzu *Farnsworth,* Formation of Contract, § 3.04 sub 3–12 (3); *Honnold/Flechtner,* Art. 16, Rn. 140; s. auch *Zweigert/Kötz,* S. 352, 358; umfassend *Ludwig,* S. 249 ff.
[28] S. *von Caemmerer,* RabelsZ 29 (1965), 101, 122; *Dölle/Schlechtriem,* Art. 5 EAG, Rn. 37.
[29] *Borges,* Verträge im elektronischen Geschäftsverkehr, S. 309.
[30] *Farnsworth,* Formation of Contract, § 3.04 sub 3–12 (3), weist darauf hin, dass „practical importance has diminished in the electronic age". Zeitdifferenz zur Wirksamkeit der Annahme kann jedoch bei Verwendung solch elektronischer, unmittelbar übermittelter Erklärungen entstehen, deren Eingang oder Ausdruck beim Empfänger ausnahmsweise noch nicht Zugang bewirkt, sondern die dem eigentlichen Adressaten noch übermittelt werden müssen, s. unten Art. 24 Rn. 23.
[31] *Dölle/Schlechtriem,* Art. 5 EAG, Rn. 42: Der Offerent muss das damit verbundene Risiko durch entsprechende Vorbehalte in seiner Offerte eingrenzen, wenngleich dann zumeist der Bindungswille und damit die Qualität einer Offerte fehlen wird.
[32] Zu den Rechtsfolgen eines wirksamen Widerrufs unten Rn. 13.
[33] S. unten Art. 17 Rn. 5.

4. Abweichende Ausgestaltung der Widerrufssperre

6 **Widerrufssperre** durch Absendung ist **dispositiv**. Der Offerent kann sich also mehr Dispositionsfreiheit vorbehalten, etwa mit der Formel „freibleibend bis zum Eingang Ihrer Antwort".[34]

5. Beweislast

7 Die Beweislast für Absendung der Annahmeerklärung vor Eintreffen des Widerrufs (also insbesondere den Zeitpunkt der Absendung) trägt der Akzeptant, da sich dieser Vorgang allein in seiner Sphäre abspielt.[35] Der Offerent hat dagegen den Zugang des Widerrufs sowie den Zugangszeitpunkt zu beweisen.

III. Bindung an das Angebot – Abs. 2

1. Bindung durch Ausgestaltung der Offerte als unwiderruflich – Abs. 2 lit. a)

8 **a) Ausdruck des Bindungswillens.** Der Offerent kann seine Offerte als unwiderrufliche qualifizieren. Dazu genügt sein Wille und eine entsprechende Erklärung („zum Ausdruck bringt"); einer Gegenleistung, consideration oder Einhaltung bestimmter Formen bedarf es nicht.[36] **Bindungswille** kann zum Ausdruck gebracht werden durch insoweit eindeutige Worte („fest",[37] „unwiderruflich bis …", „firm offer", „will be held open")[38] oder im jeweiligen Verkehrskreis als Ausdruck eines Bindungswillens verstandene Worte, z. B. „open offer", „option", „guarantee".[39] Entscheidend für eine Auslegung ist wieder Art. 8. Auch außerhalb der Offerte liegende Umstände, z. B. entsprechende Erwartungen in der invitatio oder den Ausschreibungsbedingungen, die Einräumung von Sicherheiten durch den Offerenten,[40] Vorverhandlungen, Gepflogenheiten zwischen den Parteien usw. können nach Art. 8 III Bindungswillen verdeutlichen.

9 **b) Annahmefrist als Vermutung der Unwiderruflichkeit.** Bindungswille wird nach Abs. 2 lit. a) insbesondere durch eine **Fristsetzung** zum Ausdruck gebracht. Die Bedeutung einer Fristsetzung war noch auf der Wiener Konferenz umstritten, da in den Common Law-Ländern eine Frist regelmäßig nur die Bedeutung hat, dass die Offerte nach Fristablauf erlischt („lapse").[41] Während die Entwürfe und entsprechende Anträge in Wien einer Fristsetzung stets die Bedeutung der Unwiderruflichkeit der Offerte für die gesetzte Frist zukommen lassen wollten, ohne dass es auf einen entsprechenden Bindungswillen des Offerenten ankommen sollte, setzten sich am Ende die Gegenansichten mit der Formulierung durch, wonach Fristsetzung nur ein für Bindungswillen sprechender Umstand sei. Allerdings waren in Wien Delegationen auch noch nach Verabschiedung dieser Formulie-

---

[34] S. MünchKomm/*Gruber*, Art. 16, Rn. 2; zum EAG *von Caemmerer*, RabelsZ 29 (1965), 101, 122; zur üblichen Bedeutung von „freibleibend" s. jedoch oben Art. 14 Rn. 25.

[35] *Baumgärtel/Laumen/Hepting*, Art. 16 WKR, Rn. 4.

[36] S. oben Rn. 2.

[37] S. *Enderlein/Maskow/Strohbach*, Art. 16, Anm. 6.

[38] *Lookofsky*, The 1980 United Nations Convention, Anm. 107.; weitere Klauselbeispiele bei *Rudolph*, Art. 16, Rn. 9; *Honsell/Dornis*, Art. 16, Rn. 17; *Mather*, 105 Dick. L. Rev. (2000-01), 31, 55; *Staudinger/Magnus*, Art. 16, Rn. 11; *Witz/Salger/Lorenz/Witz*, Art. 16, Rn. 8. Umfassend (rechtsvergleichend) *Perales Viscasillas*, Formación del contrato, S. 425 ff.

[39] Vgl. zu Vorschlägen in der Vorbereitung des EAG, solche Termini im Text zu nennen, *Dölle/Schlechtriem*, Art. 5 EAG, Rn. 30.

[40] S. zu den unterschiedlichen Bewertungsmöglichkeiten solcher „Reugelder" *Dölle/Schlechtriem*, Art. 5 EAG, Rn. 31; bei Ausschreibungen der öffentlichen Hand (dazu oben Vor Artt. 14–24 Rn. 30) gelten in manchen Rechten derartige „bid bonds" oder „deposits" als Ausdruck des Bindungswillens, s. *Schlesinger/Macneil*, Bd. 1, S. 758.

[41] S. *Farnsworth*, Formation of Contract, § 3.04 sub 3–11 (2); *Feltham*, J. Bus. L. (1981), 346, 352; *Flechtner*, FS Schwenzer, S. 498; überzeugend gegen eine solche Auslegung im Zweifelsfalle *Malik*, 25 Indian J. Int'l L. (1985), 26, 34 ff., 38 f.

rung der Ansicht, dass Fristsetzung schlechthin Unwiderruflichkeit bedeute.[42] Dementsprechend wird auch heute noch in der Literatur vertreten, dass eine befristete Offerte bis zum Ablauf der Frist unwiderruflich sei.[43] Dagegen spricht die Entstehungsgeschichte; auch sollte im Interesse einer einheitlichen Auslegung nach Art. 7 I kein Konflikt mit der für Juristen aus bestimmten Rechtskreisen maßgebenden Rechtsüberzeugung provoziert werden. Fristsetzung sollte daher als **widerlegliche Vermutung** des Bindungswillens gelten.[44] Die Bestimmung einer solchen „festen Frist zur Annahme" (Art. 16 II lit. a)) kann dabei durch Nennung eines Zeitraumes oder aber eines Endtermins bzw. -zeitpunkts geschehen.[45] **Beispiele** sind etwa „wir halten uns bis zum ... gebunden", „dieses Angebot kann bis zum ... angenommen werden", „our offer is at any rate good until ...", „we stand by this offer until ...",[46] „wir erwarten Ihre Bestätigung bis morgen bei unserer Eröffnung"[47] oder „acceptance must be received before:...".[48] Die durch Fristsetzung indizierte Auslegung, dass Bindung an die Offerte bis zum Ablauf der Frist gewollt sei, kann aber durch den Nachweis ausgeräumt werden, dass der genannte Termin im konkreten Fall nur die Bedeutung haben sollte, die Offerte nach Fristablauf erlöschen zu lassen.[49] Die **Beweislast** trifft den Widerrufenden.[50]

c) **Widerlegung der Vermutung.** Abs. 2 lit. a) ist **Auslegungsregel** und ergänzt insoweit Art. 8.[51] Bei Partnern aus Rechtsordnungen, die eine befristete Offerte als bindende regeln, wird man auch einen entsprechenden Willen des Erklärenden (Art. 8 I) und ein solches Verständnis des Empfängers annehmen können.[52] Bei Partnern aus Common Law-Ländern dürfte dagegen eine Befristung auf der Grundlage von Artt. 8 II, 16 II lit. a) allein noch nicht stets Bindungswillen zum Ausdruck bringen, sofern nicht zusätzliche Anhaltspunkte dafür gegeben sind.[53] Ein Offerent aus einem solchen Land, der auf dem Kontinent oder in einem anderen Land mit kontinentaler Rechtstradition anbietet, muss sich freilich regelmäßig auf Grund der Auslegungsregel des Art. 16 II lit. a) und des nach Art. 8 II zu berücksichtigenden Empfängerhorizonts an der durch Fristsetzung zum Ausdruck gebrachten, wenn auch vielleicht fehlenden Bindungsabsicht festhalten lassen.[54] Gleichwohl ist

---

[42] Zum Ablauf der Konferenz s. O. R., S. 278–280; *Bianca/Bonell/Eörsi*, Art. 16, Anm. 1.7.2.: „few delegations were unaware that the rule in sub-paragraph 2(a) was, due to differing legal backgrounds, ambiguous", ferner Anm. 2.2.1.; s. a. *Farnsworth*, Formation of Contract, § 3.04 sub 3–11 (2); *Honnold/Flechtner*, Art. 16, Rn. 143.1; *Schlechtriem*, Einheitliches UN-Kaufrecht, S. 39; *Winship*, 17 Int'l Law. (1983), 1, 7 mit Fn. 17.
[43] *Neumayer*, RIW 1994, 99, 103; *Neumayer/Ming*, Art. 16, Anm. 5a. mit zahlreichen weiteren Nachweisen; *Reinhart*, Art. 16, Rn. 3; wohl auch *Soergel/Lüderitz/Fenge*, Art. 16, Rn. 5.
[44] S. *Audit*, Vente internationale, Anm. 64.; *Baumgärtel/Laumen/Hepting*, Art. 16 WKR, Rn. 7, 8; Botschaft des (Schweizer) Bundesrats, Bbl. 1989 I 773; *Enderlein/Maskow/Strohbach*, Art. 16, Anm. 7.; *Heuzé*, Anm. 179.; *Honnold/Flechtner*, Art. 16 I Rn. 143.1; *Honsell/Dornis*, Art. 16, Rn. 18; *Jametti Greiner*, S. 51; *Karollus*, S. 65; MünchKomm/*Gruber*, Art. 16, Rn. 13; *Staub/Koller*, Vor § 373 HGB, Rn. 642; *Loewe*, Art. 16, S. 40; *Piltz*, Internationales Kaufrecht, Rn. 3–48; *Staudinger/Magnus*, Art. 16, Rn. 12; *Wey*, Rn. 857; a. A. *Mather*, 105 Dick. L. Rev. (2000-01), 31, 46: weder Vermutung für noch gegen Unwiderruflichkeit.
[45] Dies ergibt sich aus einem Vergleich des englischsprachigen Normwortlauts des Art. 16 II lit. a) („time for acceptance") mit demjenigen des Art. 20 I („period of time for acceptance").
[46] S. *Bianca/Bonell/Eörsi*, Art. 16, Anm. 2.2.1.; *Staudinger/Magnus*, Art. 16, Rn. 12.
[47] LG Hamburg, 23.11.2003, CISG-online 875: „Bindungsfrist".
[48] Vgl. *Lookofsky*, The 1980 United Nations Convention, Anm. 108.
[49] *Staudinger/Magnus*, Art. 16, Rn. 12; s. auch sogleich Rn. 10.
[50] S. *Baumgärtel/Laumen/Hepting*, Art. 16 WKR, Rn. 7; *Malik*, 25 Indian J. Int'l L. (1985), 26, 38 f.
[51] S. *Honnold/Flechtner*, Art. 16, Rn. 143.1; *Wey*, Rn. 859.
[52] Vgl. zur Bedeutung der Herkunft der Parteien *Wey*, Rn. 862. S. a. BGH, 28.11.1994, RIW 1995, 157: „Der Inhalt einer rechtserheblichen Erklärung lässt sich in vielen Fällen nur vor dem Hintergrund der Rechtsordnung richtig verstehen, in deren Rahmen sie abgegeben worden ist."
[53] S. *Bianca/Bonell/Eörsi*, Art. 16, Anm. 2.2.1. mit dem Beispiel: „Our offer is not good after May 13"; *Flechtner*, FS Schwenzer, S. 499 f.
[54] Vgl. den Rat von *Farnsworth*, Formation of Contract, § 3.04 sub 3–12 (2): „An offeror wishing to fix a time for lapse but not for irrevocability should make his intention plain"; ähnlich warnend *Feltham*, 24 J. Bus. L. (1981), 346, 352. Zur Vorsicht vor der gegenteiligen Überzeugung rät *Wey*, Rn. 862: Der Oblat habe nicht ohne weiteres Grund zur Annahme, der Offerent wolle sich einheitsrechtlich völlig ungewohnt binden. S. a. *Wang*, ZVerglRW 87 (1988), 184, 193, nach dem schon der Gebrauch des Wortes „lapse" auf die

Empfängern von Offerten aus Common Law-Ländern zu raten, einer bloßen Fristsetzung nicht blind als Ausdruck von Bindung zu vertrauen.[55] Jedenfalls ist der Praxis zu empfehlen, Bindungswillen für die gesetzte Frist unzweideutig zum Ausdruck zu bringen bzw. rechtzeitig Klarstellung zu verlangen.[56]

2. Bindung aufgrund tätigen Vertrauens – Abs. 2 lit. b)

11   Abs. 2 lit. b) enthält das schon in Art. 5 II EAG normierte Verbot widersprüchlichen Verhaltens und hält den Offerenten an dem von ihm geschaffenen Vertrauenstatbestand fest.[57] **Zwei Voraussetzungen** – Vertrauen und eine dadurch veranlasste Disposition des Vertrauenden – müssen gegeben sein. Das **Vertrauen** muss im konkreten Fall gerechtfertigt, d. h. „vernünftig" sein, und der Angebotsempfänger muss im Vertrauen auf die Bindung an die Offerte „gehandelt" haben; Vertrauen ist dabei kausales Bindeglied zwischen Offerte und „Handlung". Wo die Offerte selbst mangelnde Bindung zum Ausdruck bringt, kann Art. 16 II lit. b) nicht eingreifen. **Verhalten** im Vertrauen auf die Bindung kann im Beginn der Produktion, im Erwerb von Materialien, Abschluss entsprechender Verträge, kostenträchtiger Preiskalkulation,[58] aufwändiger Vorklärungen, Einholung von Subunternehmer- oder Zuliefererangeboten,[59] Anmietung von Lagerflächen, Weiterverkauf der Ware, Abschluss von Beförderungsverträgen, Eröffnung eines Akkreditivs,[60] u. U. Einstellung von Leuten liegen, immer vorausgesetzt, ein solches Verhalten war durch „vernünftiges" Vertrauen in der Situation des Angebotsempfängers[61] veranlasst. „Handeln" bedeutet nicht nur aktives Handeln, sondern auch Unterlassen,[62] z. B. der sonst nachweisbar erfolgten Einholung weiterer Angebote. Nicht erforderlich ist, dass dem Vertrauenden durch einen Widerruf ein nachweisbarer Schaden entstünde, denn Art. 16 II lit. b) ist nicht auf Fälle einer *detrimental reliance* beschränkt.[63] Die **Beweislast** für Bindungsvoraussetzungen trägt, wer sich auf Unwiderruflichkeit beruft.[64]

12   Das **Verhältnis** von Abs. 2 lit. a) und Abs. 2 lit. b) ist theoretisch unsicher,[65] dürfte aber praktisch keine Schwierigkeiten bereiten: Der kontinentale Jurist wird bei befristeten Offerten regelmäßig Variante a) zugrunde legen können, für die es auf ein Verhalten auf Grund „vernünftigen Vertrauens" nicht mehr ankommt.[66] Wo die Bedeutung einer Fristsetzung unsicher ist oder überhaupt keine Frist gesetzt ist, so dass Streit über einen

---

Common Law-Bedeutung einer Frist hinweisen soll. Gegen die hier vertretene Auffassung *Flechtner*, FS Schwenzer, S. 501.
[55] Vgl. *Wey*, Rn. 863.
[56] *Staudinger/Magnus*, Art. 16, Rn. 12; *Witz/Salger/Lorenz/Witz*, Art. 16, Rn. 18.
[57] S. zum insoweit gleichen U. S.-amerikanischen Recht *Farnsworth*, Formation of Contract, § 3.04 sub 3–12 (2); *Honnold/Flechtner*, Art. 16, Rn. 144; Restatement (2d) of Contracts, § 87 (2); *von Mehren*, Sec. 139; zur Herkunft des Art. 16 II lit. b) aus dem Common Law s. *Ludwig*, S. 378; *Bianca/Bonell/Eörsi*, Art. 16, Anm. 2.2.: lit. a) sei Konzession an Civil Law-Staaten, lit. b) dagegen Übernahme eines Grundsatzes des Common Law; aber auch Anm. 2.2.2.: Die Regelung in lit. b) sei vergleichbar dem Prinzip von „Treu und Glauben" des BGB. Zur Verwandtschaft zum „estoppel"-Prinzip *Wey*, Rn. 868.
[58] *Schwimann/Posch*, Art. 16, Rn. 5.
[59] Vgl. zu solchen Beispielsfällen *Bianca/Bonell/Eörsi*, Art. 16, Anm. 2.2.2.; *Enderlein/Maskow/Strohbach*, Art. 16, Anm. 8.; *Joseph*, 3 Dick. J. Int'l L. (1984), 107, 126; *Staudinger/Magnus*, Art. 16, Rn. 13; *Witz/Salger/Lorenz/Witz*, Art. 16, Rn. 13.
[60] *Köhler*, S. 218.
[61] Hierzu *Malik*, 25 Indian J. Int'l L. (1985), 26, 40 f.
[62] Zweifelnd *Mather*, 105 Dick. L. Rev. (2000-01), 31, 49.
[63] *Geneva Pharmaceuticals Technology Corp. v. Barr Laboratories, Inc.*, U. S. Dist. Ct. (S. D. N. Y.), 10.5.2002, CISG-online 653 = 201 F. Supp. 2d 236, 287; *Herber/Czerwenka*, Art. 16, Rn. 10; *Honsell/Dornis*, Art. 16, Rn. 22.
[64] *Baumgärtel/Laumen/Hepting*, Art. 16 WKR, Rn. 9 f.; *Bamberger/Roth/Saenger*, Art. 16, Rn. 6.
[65] S. *Rehbinder*, Vertragsschluss, S. 159; *Ludwig*, S. 379 f.; umfassend *Wey*, Rn. 842 ff.: Art. 16 II lit. b) sei bedingte Variante von Abs. 1.
[66] Eine (bedenkenswerte) Kombinationslösung schlägt *Flechtner*, FS Schwenzer, S. 510 vor, der Vorliegen oder Fehlen von „tätigem Vertrauen" auch im Rahmen der Widerlegung der Vermutung des Art. 16 II lit. a) berücksichtigen will.

Bindungswillen entstehen könnte, kann jedenfalls Variante b) eingreifen und eine unsichere Beweiserhebung über das Gewollte vermeiden.[67]

IV. Rechtsfolgen von Widerruflichkeit oder Widerrufssperre und Rechtsbehelfe nach nationalem Recht

1. Bei widerruflichem Angebot

Ist der Offerent im konkreten Fall an sein Angebot **nicht** gebunden, so kann er das Angebot durch einen rechtzeitigen und wirksamen Widerruf zum Erlöschen bringen. Der Zugang der Widerrufserklärung hat zur Folge, dass das Angebot nicht mehr angenommen werden kann.[68] Daneben darf Rücknahme vor Zugang nach Art. 15 I oder Widerruf nach Zugang grundsätzlich keine Schadenersatzansprüche nach nationalem Recht auslösen: Soweit und solange Widerruf „berechtigt", d. h. nach dem CISG zulässig ist, darf er nicht mit Schadensersatzpflichten sanktioniert und damit faktisch weiter eingeschränkt werden.[69] Der mühsam errungene Kompromiss in Art. 16 würde gefährdet, wenn durch die Hintertür von Schadenersatzansprüchen nach unvereinheitlichtem nationalen Recht unterschiedlicher Zwang, eine nach dem CISG frei widerrufbare Offerte in Geltung zu lassen, ausgeübt würde. Ebenfalls versperrt ist daher der Rückgriff auf die Rechtsfigur des „promissory estoppel" der Common Law-Rechtsordnungen.[70] Grenze muss allerdings auch hier die fraudulöse Schädigung des anderen Teils sein, da Deliktsansprüche wegen arglistiger Interessenverletzung grundsätzlich vom Geltungsbereich des einheitlichen Kaufrechts ausgenommen sind.[71]

2. Bei Widerrufssperre

Rechtsfolge einer **Widerrufssperre** ist Bindung an das Angebot und damit die Möglichkeit für den Oblaten, anzunehmen und einen Vertrag zustande zu bringen;[72] ein gleichwohl erklärter Widerruf entfaltet keine Wirkungen. Auch insoweit liegt eine **abschließende Regelung** durch das CISG vor, die keinen Raum für Rechtsbehelfe nach nationalem (unvereinheitlichten) Recht lässt. Der Angebotsempfänger kann deshalb zum einen nicht den widerrufenden Offerenten beim Wort nehmen, den unwirksamen Widerruf als wirksam behandeln und Schadenersatz, z. B. des negativen Interesses in Form von Aufwendungen oder Verpflichtungen aus Deckungsgeschäften, verlangen.[73] Zum anderen haben Schadenersatzansprüche nach unvereinheitlichten nationalen Recht aus culpa in contrahendo, auf der Grundlage von „promissory estoppel"-Rechtsbehelfen nach Common Law[74] oder auf Grund einer deliktischen Generalklausel auszuscheiden, soweit nicht die Schwelle

---

[67] Zutreffend deshalb die positive Bewertung von *Herber*, Einführung, S. 16; wohl auch *Ludwig*, S. 380 f.; skeptisch dagegen *Rehbinder*, Vertragsschluss, S. 160.
[68] MünchKomm/*Gruber*, Art. 16, Rn. 9.
[69] Vgl. MünchKomm/*Gruber*, Art. 16, Rn. 9; *Staudinger/Magnus*, Art. 16, Rn. 14; weitere Nachweise s. oben Vor Artt. 14–24 Rn. 34, 38.
[70] *Geneva Pharmaceuticals Technology Corp. v. Barr Laboratories, Inc.*, U. S. Dist. Ct. (S. D. N. Y.), 10.5.2002, CISG-online 653 = 201 F. Supp. 2d 236, 286 f.; s. bereits oben Vor Artt. 14–24 Rn. 38.
[71] S. oben Vor Artt. 14–24 Rn. 36.
[72] *Brunner*, Art. 16, Rn. 3.
[73] *Köhler*, S. 222 f. Zu Vorschlägen im Schrifttum, für diese Fälle eine übereinkommensautonome vorvertragliche Haftung herzuleiten, s. oben Vor Artt. 14–24 Rn. 33.
[74] *Geneva Pharmaceuticals Technology Corp. v. Barr Laboratories, Inc.*, U. S. Dist. Ct. (S. D. N. Y.), 10.5.2002, CISG-online 653 = 201 F. Supp. 2d 236, 286 f.; mit eingehender Begründung und sorgfältiger Auseinandersetzung mit der Common Law-Doktrin des „promissory estoppel" auch *Malik*, 25 Indian J. Int'l L. (1985), 26, 42 ff., 47: Im Interesse der Einheitlichkeit in der Anwendung des Übereinkommens sei es besser, Ersatz des Vertrauensschadens in solchen Fällen wegen Bruchs des (geschlossenen) Vertrages zu gewähren; in diesem Sinne bereits oben Vor Artt. 14–24 Rn. 38.

fraudulösen Verhaltens überschritten worden ist.[75] Der Angebotsempfänger kann vielmehr durch Annahme den Vertrag zustande bringen und den Widerruf als ernsthafte Erfüllungsverweigerung behandeln, die ein Vorgehen nach Art. 72 ermöglicht.[76]

---

[75] Wie hier *Brunner*, Art. 16, Rn. 3; *Staudinger/Magnus*, Art. 16, Rn. 14; s. auch oben Vor Artt. 14–24 Rn. 34, 36. Zweifelnd *Honnold/Flechtner*, Art. 16, Rn. 148–150: insoweit bestehe eine Lücke im Übereinkommen, die durch Lückenfüllung nach Art. 7 II, offenbar mit dem Ergebnis eines Schadensersatzanspruchs, geschlossen werden soll. Für eine Konkurrenz nationaler Rechtsbehelfe auch *Honsell/Dornis*, Art. 16, Rn. 27; *Neumayer/Ming*, Art. 16, Anm. 6.; *Wey*, Rn. 883. S. ferner *Sono*, 21 Cornell Int'l L.J. (1988), 477, 480 ff., sowie *Heuzé*, Anm. 180., der eine Annahme der (unwirksam widerrufenen) Offerte als möglicherweise treuwidrig sieht, gleichwohl aber im Ergebnis Schadensersatz wegen Bruchs eines geschlossenen Vertrages zugesteht.

[76] *Brunner*, Art. 16, Rn. 3; *Staudinger/Magnus*, Art. 16, Rn. 15.

Art. 17 [Erlöschen des Angebots]

Ein Angebot erlischt, selbst wenn es unwiderruflich ist, sobald dem Anbietenden eine Ablehnung zugeht.

Art. 17
An offer, even if it is irrevocable, is terminated when a rejection reaches the offeror.

Art. 17
Une offre, meme irrévocable, prend fin lorsque son rejet parvient à l'auteur de l'offre.

Übersicht

	Rn.
1. Zugang der Ablehnung	1
2. Fristablauf	4
3. Sonstige Erlöschensgründe	6

Vorläufer und **Entwürfe:** New Yorker E 1977 Art. 7, Genfer E 1977 Art. 11, New Yorker E 1978 Art. 15.

1. Zugang der Ablehnung

Nach Art. 17 **erlischt** das **Angebot** mit Zugang der Ablehnung – Art. 24 – durch den Angebotsempfänger.[1] Auch bei Unwiderruflichkeit, etwa während einer noch nicht abgelaufenen Frist, tritt diese Folge einer Ablehnung ein. Ein Vertragsschlussverfahren kann dann nur durch eine neue Offerte in Gang gesetzt werden.

Die **Ablehnung** kann **ausdrücklich**[2] oder **implizit**, z. B. durch Verlangen anderer Bedingungen, das nicht nur modifizierende Annahme nach Art. 19 I sein soll,[3] erklärt werden.[4] Ob eine Erklärung des Angebotsempfängers als Zurückweisung der Offerte gemeint und zu verstehen ist oder – z. B. – als Nachfrage, richtet sich nach Art. 8.[5] Die Ablehnung zum Ausdruck bringende Erklärung muss aber jedenfalls zugegangen sein.[6] Ein Kaufangebot wird nicht dadurch wirksam zurückgewiesen, dass der Angebotsempfänger den Kaufgegenstand an einen Dritten verkauft.

Als Ablehnung gilt auch eine Annahmeerklärung mit wesentlichen Modifikationen, Art. 19 I.[7] Sie stellt gleichzeitig eine neue Offerte des Angebotsempfängers dar.

Eine **Ablehnung** des Angebots kann auch noch **nach Absendung der Annahme** erfolgen, hindert aber den Vertragsschluss nur, wenn sie dem Offerenten vor oder gleichzeitig mit der Annahme zugeht. Zwar regelt Art. 22 diesen Fall nicht direkt, doch ist auf der Grundlage von Art. 7 II Ablehnung des Angebots einer Rücknahme der Annahme gleichzustellen.[8] Geht die Ablehnung vor der Annahme zu, scheitert der Vertragsschluss und kann auch nicht über Art. 21 gerettet werden.[9] In diesem Fall bleibt dem vormaligen Angebotsempfänger die Möglichkeit, nunmehr seinerseits dem ursprünglichen Anbietenden ein Angebot zu machen.[10]

---

[1] Das EAG enthielt noch keine entsprechende Regel, s. hierzu und zur Vorgeschichte *Schlechtriem*, 2. Aufl., Rn. 1; *von Caemmerer*, RabelsZ 29 (1965), 101, 111 f.; *Dölle/Schlechtriem*, Art. 5 EAG, Rn. 44. Nach *Schwimann/Posch*, Art. 17, Rn. 1 stellt Art. 17 „nicht viel mehr als einen juristischen Gemeinplatz dar".

[2] So etwa in *Key Safety Systems, Inc. v. Invista*, S. A. R. L., L. L. C., U. S. Dist. Ct. (E. D. Mich.), 16.9.2008, CISG-online 1778, wo der Verkäufer auf jede Bestellung routinemäßig mit den Worten reagierte: „Unable to accept your order, however, we are able to offer the Products on the following terms …".

[3] Vgl. *Heuzé*, Anm. 181.

[4] S. Sekretariatskommentar, Art. 15, Nr. 2; *Neumayer/Ming*, Art. 17, Anm. 2.

[5] MünchKomm/*Gruber*, Art. 17, Rn. 2, 4; *Staudinger/Magnus*, Art. 17, Rn. 7.

[6] *Witz/Salger/Lorenz/Witz*, Art. 17, Rn. 6.

[7] MünchKomm/*Gruber*, Art. 17, Rn. 2.

[8] *Staudinger/Magnus*, Art. 17, Rn. 10; ähnlich MünchKomm/Gruber, Art. 17, Rn. 4: Artt. 15 II, 22 analog; differenzierend *Honsell/Dornis*, Art. 17, Rn. 11.

[9] *Honnold/Flechtner*, Art. 17, Rn. 152 f.; *Neumayer/Ming*, Art. 16, Anm. 2.

[10] *Schwimann/Posch*, Art. 17, Rn. 3.

Die **Beweislast** für eine wirksame Ablehnung einschließlich des Zugangszeitpunktes trägt, wer sich auf Erlöschen des Angebots beruft.[11]

2. Fristablauf

4 Eine befristete Offerte erlischt regelmäßig entsprechend § 146 BGB mit Fristablauf.[12] Das ist zwar nicht ausdrücklich geregelt, ergibt sich aber aus Artt. 18 II 2, 20, 21. Allerdings kann der Offerent auch insoweit sein Angebot anders ausstatten, z. B. die Frist nur auf die Bindung beziehen, so dass nach Fristablauf die Offerte zwar widerruflich wird, aber offen bleibt. Die Bedeutung einer Fristsetzung ist durch Auslegung zu ermitteln; als Regelfolge ist mangels anderer Anhaltspunkte Erlöschen anzunehmen.[13]

5 Fehlt eine Fristsetzung, dann bleibt die Offerte nicht ewig in Kraft. Es gilt vielmehr eine angemessene Frist, Art. 18 II 2, nach deren Ablauf die Offerte erlischt.[14]

3. Sonstige Erlöschensgründe

6 Ob **Tod, Verlust** (voller) **Geschäftsfähigkeit** oder **Rechtsfähigkeit,** Eröffnung des **Insolvenzverfahrens** oder ähnlicher, die rechtlichen Befugnisse einschränkender Verfahren eine bereits abgesandte Offerte erlöschen lassen, ist im CISG anders als in Art. 11 EAG nicht geregelt worden. M. E. bleibt für die Auswirkungen solcher Ereignisse auf eine bereits im Lauf befindliche Offerte grundsätzlich nationales Recht maßgebend.[15] Allenfalls für die durch Absendung der Annahmeerklärung bereits bindend gewordene Offerte könnte entsprechend der im Rechtsvergleich als herrschend bestätigten Überzeugung[16] vertreten werden, dass sie damit „so entpersönlicht" worden ist, dass jedenfalls Tod oder Geschäftsunfähigkeit ihres Urhebers den Vertragsschluss nicht mehr hindern können. Aber Art. 7 II lässt den Rückgriff auf allgemeine, rechtsvergleichend gewonnene Grundsätze gerade nicht zu, sondern nur auf solche, die dem Übereinkommen zugrunde liegen. Das CISG enthält aber nicht nur keine Grundsätze zu diesem Problem, sondern geht prinzipiell davon aus, dass Fragen der Rechts-, Geschäfts- und Handlungsfähigkeit dem unvereinheitlichten nationalen Recht unterstellt bleiben.[17] Für das Schicksal der unwiderruflich gewordenen Offerte in diesen Fällen kann nichts anderes gelten.

---

[11] *Baumgärtel/Laumen/Hepting,* Art. 17 WKR, Rn. 1, 4; *Jung,* S. 105; MünchKomm/*Gruber,* Art. 17, Rn. 7.
[12] *Enderlein/Maskow/Strohbach,* Art. 17, Anm. 1.; *Schwimann/Posch,* Art. 17, Rn. 2; *Staudinger/Magnus,* Art. 17, Rn. 6; a. A. *Honsell/Dornis,* Art. 14, Rn. 33.
[13] S. zum EAG *Dölle/Schlechtriem,* Art. 5 EAG, Rn. 12, 28.
[14] *Staudinger/Magnus,* Art. 17, Rn. 6; *Witz/Salger/Lorenz/Witz,* Art. 17, Rn. 4.
[15] S. oben Art. 15 Rn. 7, 8; *Wey,* Rn. 910 ff., 916: vollkommen außerhalb des CISG-Regelungsbereichs liegender Problemstoff; a. A. für Tod und Geschäftsunfähigkeit *Herber/Czerwenka,* Art. 15, Rn. 6, sowie die oben in Art. 15 Rn. 8 zitierten Autoren; umfassend *Ludwig,* S. 381 ff.
[16] S. *Schlesinger,* Bd. 1, S. 116.
[17] S. bereits oben Vor Artt. 14–24 Rn. 2.

Art. 18 [Begriff der Annahme]

(1) Eine Erklärung oder ein sonstiges Verhalten des Empfängers, das eine Zustimmung zum Angebot ausdrückt, stellt eine Annahme dar. Schweigen oder Untätigkeit allein stellen keine Annahme dar.

(2) Die Annahme eines Angebots wird wirksam, sobald die Äußerung der Zustimmung dem Anbietenden zugeht. Sie wird nicht wirksam, wenn die Äußerung der Zustimmung dem Anbietenden nicht innerhalb der von ihm gesetzten Frist oder, bei Fehlen einer solchen Frist, innerhalb einer angemessenen Frist zugeht; dabei sind die Umstände des Geschäfts einschließlich der Schnelligkeit der vom Anbietenden gewählten Übermittlungsart zu berücksichtigen. Ein mündliches Angebot muß sofort angenommen werden, wenn sich aus den Umständen nichts anderes ergibt.

(3) Äußert jedoch der Empfänger aufgrund des Angebots, der zwischen den Parteien entstandenen Gepflogenheiten oder der Gebräuche* seine Zustimmung dadurch, daß er eine Handlung vornimmt,** die sich zum Beispiel auf die Absendung der Ware oder die Zahlung des Preises bezieht, ohne den Anbietenden davon zu unterrichten, so ist die Annahme zum Zeitpunkt der Handlung wirksam, sofern diese innerhalb der in Absatz 2 vorgeschriebenen Frist vorgenommen wird.

Art. 18

(1) A statement made by or other conduct of the offeree indicating assent to an offer is an acceptance. Silence or inactivity does not in itself amount to acceptance.

(2) An acceptance of an offer becomes effective at the moment the indication of assent reaches the offeror. An acceptance is not effective if the indication of assent does not reach the offeror within the time he has fixed or, if no time is fixed, within a reasonable time, due account being taken of the circumstances of the transaction, including the rapidity of the means of communication employed by the offeror. An oral offer must be accepted immediately unless the circumstances indicate otherwise.

(3) However, if, by virtue of the offer or as a result of practices which the parties have established between themselves or of usage, the offeree may indicate assent by performing an act, such as one relating to the dispatch of the goods or payment of the price, without notice to the offeror, the acceptance is effective at the moment the act is performed, provided that the act is performed within the period of time laid down in the preceding paragraph.

Art. 18

1) Une déclaration ou autre comportement du destinataire indiquant qu'il acquiesce à une offre constitue une acceptation. Le silence ou l'inaction à eux seuls ne peuvent valoir acceptation.

2) L'acceptation d'une offre prend effet au moment où l'indication d'acquiescement parvient à l'auteur de l'offre. L'acceptation ne prend pas effet si cette indication ne parvient pas à l'auteur de l'offre dans le délai qu'il a stipulé ou, à défaut d'une telle stipulation, dans un délai raisonnable, compte tenu des circonstances de la transaction et de la rapidité des moyens de communication utilisés par l'auteur de l'offre. Une offre verbale doit être acceptée immédiatement, à moins que les circonstances n'impliquent le contraire.

3) Cependant, si, en vertu de l'offre, des habitudes qui se sont établies entre les parties ou des usages, le destinataire de l'offre peut indiquer qu'il acquiesce en accomplissant un acte se rapportant, par exemple, à l'expédition des marchandises ou au paiement du prix, sans communication à l'auteur de l'offre, l'acceptation prend effet au moment où cet acte est accompli, pour autant qu'il le soit dans les délais prévus par le paragraphe précédent.

Übersicht

	Rn.
I. Grundzüge	1
II. Annahme	3
1. Annahme durch Erklärung	4

---

* Österreich: Bräuche.
** Österreich, Schweiz: durch eine Handlung.

a) Bindungswille und Wortlaut	4
b) Erklärungsmittel	5
2. Annahme durch Verhalten	7
a) Formen erklärungsäquivalenten Verhaltens	7
b) Rollenwechsel nach Art. 19 I	8
c) Schweigen	9
d) Kreuzofferten	10
III. Wirksamkeit der Annahmeerklärung	11
1. Zeitpunkt der Wirksamkeit: Bedeutung	11
a) Vertragsschluss	11
b) Rücknehmbarkeit der Annahme	12
2. Rechtzeitigkeit und Wirkung der zugangsbedürftigen Äußerung der Zustimmung (Annahme)	13
a) Zugangsprinzip	13
b) Rechtzeitigkeit bei Fristsetzung	14
c) Rechtzeitigkeit bei angemessener Frist	15
d) Rechtzeitige Annahme einer mündlichen Offerte	16
e) „Mündlich", Abgrenzung zu anderen Kommunikationsmitteln	17
3. Rechtzeitigkeit und Wirkung der nicht zugangsbedürftigen Äußerung der Zustimmung (Annahme)	18
a) Handlungen	18
b) Nicht zugangsbedürftige Erklärungen?	19
c) Rechtzeitigkeit	19a
4. Voraussetzungen der Annahme ohne Zugang einer entsprechenden Äußerung	20
a) Ausgestaltung der Offerte	20
b) Gepflogenheiten, Bräuche, Rahmenvereinbarungen	21
c) Wirkung	22
IV. Mitteilungsobliegenheit oder -nebenpflicht	23

Vorläufer und **Entwürfe**: Art. 2 II, 6, 8 I EAG, New Yorker E 1977 Art. 8, Genfer E 1977 Art. 12, New Yorker E 1978 Art. 16.

I. Grundzüge

1   Art. 18 fasst eine Reihe von Bestimmungen des EAG[1] zusammen; die wesentlichen Sachentscheidungen sind dabei bereits in der Arbeitsgruppe getroffen worden. In Wien wurde nur noch geringfügig geändert und „Schweigen" durch „Untätigkeit" ergänzt.[2]

2   Verträge werden nach dem CISG grundsätzlich durch die korrespondierenden Willenserklärungen „Angebot" und „Annahme" geschlossen (s. oben Vor Artt. 14–24 Rn. 15). Die Annahme wird jedoch häufig konkludent zum Ausdruck gebracht; Art. 18 I 1 berücksichtigt deshalb die Möglichkeiten sowohl verbaler Erklärung als auch schlüssigen Verhaltens[3] und darf deshalb auch als Beleg für den Grundsatz – i. S. des Art. 7 II – gesehen werden, dass Verträge auch durch konkludentes Verhalten geschlossen werden können. Ferner unterscheidet Art. 18 für beide Erklärungsformen die Zugangsbedürftigkeit einerseits von der Wirkung bereits auf Grund der Äußerung andererseits: Grundsätzlich setzt wirksame Annahme rechtzeitigen Zugang der Zustimmung zum Vertragsangebot voraus, Art. 18 II, doch berücksichtigt Abs. 3 die Möglichkeit, dass der Annahmewille bereits mit Äußerung wirksam wird, und regelt die Voraussetzungen dafür. Insgesamt sind also drei Annahmeformen zu unterscheiden: 1. Ausdrücklich erklärte und zugangsbedürftige Annah-

---

[1] Zur Vorgeschichte dieser Bestimmungen des EAG s. *von Caemmerer*, RabelsZ 29 (1965), 101, 123 ff.
[2] S. O. R., S. 280; zur Entwicklung im Einzelnen s. *Bianca/Bonell/Farnsworth*, Art. 18, Anm. 1.–1.4.; *Kritzer*, Guide to Practical Applications, S. 160 f.
[3] Vgl. *Golden Valley Grape Juice and Wine, LLC v. Centrisys Corp. et al.*, U. S. Dist. Ct. (E. D. Cal.), 21.1.2010, CISG-online 2089: „Pursuant to the CISG, acceptance does not require a signature or formalistic adoption of the offered terms."

me, 2. konkludent erklärte und zugangsbedürftige Annahme und 3. konkludent erklärte und nicht zugangsbedürftige, d. h. mit dem konkludenten Verhalten wirksame Annahme.[4] Art. 18 findet dabei auch Anwendung, wenn es um die Annahme eines Angebots zur Vertragsänderung oder -aufhebung (Art. 29 I) geht.[5]

II. Annahme

Die **Annahme** geschieht durch **Willenserklärung** oder erklärungsäquivalentes Verhalten. 3 Unabhängig davon, ob sie zugangsbedürftig ist oder nicht,[6] ob sie verbal erklärt oder konkludent zum Ausdruck gebracht wird, müssen die nach unvereinheitlichtem nationalen Recht zu beurteilenden Voraussetzungen für eine wirksame Willenserklärung oder ein rechtsgeschäftlich wirkendes Verhalten gegeben sein, also **Geschäftsfähigkeit,** Freiheit von **Willensmängeln,** ggf. **Vertretungsmacht** des Erklärenden. Keinen Einfluss auf die Auslegung und Anwendung der Begriffe „Annahmeerklärung" und „annahmeäquivalentes Verhalten" haben Regeln der nationalen Rechte, die Annahme oder erklärungsäquivalentes Verhalten mit anderen Kategorien, z. B. „Willensgeschäft", „Willensbetätigung" (statt „Willenserklärung") erfassen[7] und evtl. geringere Wirksamkeitsanforderungen stellen.[8] Auch von einem nicht voll Geschäftsfähigen kann ein Angebot angenommen werden, doch muss für ihn eine dazu befugte Person (gesetzlicher Vertreter) handeln bzw. zustimmen.[9] Das CISG regelt für die Annahme nur die Möglichkeiten, den Annahmewillen zum Ausdruck zu bringen, sowie Wirksamkeit und Rechtzeitigkeit durch, soweit erforderlich, Zugang oder annahmeäquivalentes Verhalten. Die Rechtsprechung hat die Regeln des Art. 18 dabei vereinzelt auch auf die Vereinbarung von Vertragsbestandteilen angewandt, die dem CISG in ihrer Wirkung nicht unterliegen, wie etwa Eigentumsvorbehaltsklauseln (s. Art. 4 S. 2 lit. b)).[10]

1. Annahme durch Erklärung

a) Bindungswille und Wortlaut. Die Annahmeerklärung muss Zustimmung des An- 4 gebotsadressaten[11] zum Angebot ausdrücken, d. h. einen entsprechenden **Bindungswillen,**[12] der auch die Bedingungen des Angebots umfasst. Bloße Bestätigung des Eingangs des Angebots, Dank für die Offerte, Bekundung von Interesse sind noch nicht dem Angebot zustimmender Ausdruck eines entsprechenden Annahmewillens.[13] Die Auslegung entsprechender Erklärung und ihrer Bedeutung geschieht wie bei der Offerte nach Art. 8.[14] Wo Vorbehalte hinsichtlich einzelner Punkte, über die noch verhandelt werden soll, gemacht

---

[4] S. *Ludwig*, S. 318 ff.
[5] S. unten Art. 29 Rn. 2, 8.
[6] Hierzu unten Rn. 18.
[7] Vgl. zu § 151 BGB *Flume*, Das Rechtsgeschäft, § 35 II 3, S. 654 ff.; BGH, 18.12.1985, NJW-RR 1986, 415 f. (Vertretungsmacht erforderlich).
[8] Vgl. zur Anfechtung und Rücknahme der „Betätigung" nach § 151 BGB *Bydlinski*, JuS 1988, 36–38. Anfechtung offen gelassen in BGH, 18.12.1985, NJW-RR 1986, 415 f., doch soll bei einem geheimen Vorbehalt § 116 BGB anwendbar sein.
[9] Zum Zugang einer Offerte an einen nicht voll geschäftsfähigen Adressaten s. unten Art. 24 Rn. 2.
[10] *Roder Zelt- und Hallenkonstruktionen GmbH v. Rosedown Park Pty Ltd. and Reginald R Eustace*, FCA (SA, Adelaide), 28.4.1995, CISG-online 218 = 1995 F. C. R. (Aus.) 216 ff. (Vereinbarung einer *retention of title clause*).
[11] OGH, 18.6.1997, CISG-online 292 = östJBl. 1998, 255; zum Angebotsadressaten s. oben Art. 14 Rn. 4, 30 (Publikumsofferte).
[12] Vgl. *Wey*, Rn. 950: „Wie beim Angebot müssen bei der Annahmeerklärung der Geschäfts- und Erklärungswille wenigstens nach objektivierter Auslegung (Art. 8 II) zum Erscheinen kommen"; ferner *Brunner*, Art. 18, Rn. 1; *Honsell/Dornis*, Art. 18, Rn. 11; *Perales Viscasillas*, Formación del contrato, S. 495; *Rudolph*, Art. 18, Rn. 5; *Staudinger/Magnus*, Art. 18, Rn. 7.
[13] RB Tongeren, 25.1.2005, CISG-online 1106; *Bianca/Bonell/Farnsworth*, Art. 18, Anm. 2.1.
[14] LG Aurich, 8.5.1998, CISG-online 518; MünchKomm/*Gruber*, Art. 18, Rn. 2; *Staudinger/Magnus*, Art. 18, Rn. 7; *Witz/Salger/Lorenz/Witz*, Art. 18, Rn. 5.

Art. 18 5   Teil II. Abschluss des Vertrages

werden, fehlt regelmäßig Annahmewille; zur Gegenerklärung mit Abweichungen vom Angebot s. Art. 19.

Auf den Wortlaut oder die Sprache[15] der Annahmeerklärung kommt es nicht an; sie braucht insbesondere nicht ausdrücklich den Begriff der „Annahme" zu verwenden.[16] Der Annehmende kann sich auf schlichte Zustimmung beschränken oder die Offerte ganz oder teilweise wiederholen. Bei Auftragsvergabe durch Ausschreibung stellt regelmäßig die Zuschlagserteilung durch den Ausschreibenden die Annahme dar.[17] Das Wort **„Auftragsbestätigung"** wird häufig Annahme zum Ausdruck bringen,[18] kann aber auch ein **kaufmännisches Bestätigungsschreiben** bedeuten.[19] Die Unterzeichnung eines „Bestätigungsformulars" des Verkäufers, das seine Offerte zum Ausdruck bringen soll, kann ebenso Annahmeerklärung sein[20] wie die Rücksendung eines Bestellformulars des Käufers, das durch den Verkäufer gegengezeichnet[21] bzw. mit einer im betriebsinternen Geschäftsablauf des Verkäufers verwandten Erfassungsnummer versehen wurde;[22] gleiches gilt für die Übersendung einer E-Mail, in der für die Auftragsbestätigung gedankt wird[23] oder die Übersendung einer Pro-forma-Rechnung durch den Verkäufer.[24] Ob eine „Bestätigung" o ä. Annahmeerklärung oder kaufmännisches Bestätigungsschreiben sein soll, ist aber in jedem Einzelfall durch Auslegung nach Art. 8 zu klären. Bezugnahme auf einen bereits geschlossenen Vertrag in der Bestätigung muss ein Adressat nach Art. 8 II regelmäßig als kaufmännisches Bestätigungsschreiben – das auch nach dem CISG ausnahmsweise die dem deutschen Juristen vertrauten konstitutiven Wirkungen erzeugen kann[25] – und nicht als Ausdruck eines Annahmewillens verstehen. Ebenso ist durch Auslegung nach Art. 8 II zu klären, ob eine Antwort nur den Eingang der Offerte bestätigt oder Annahme zum Ausdruck bringen soll. Die **Beweislast** für eine wirksame und rechtzeitige Annahme trägt, wer sich auf den Vertragsschluss beruft.[26]

5   **b) Erklärungsmittel.** Die Annahmeerklärung kann sich prinzipiell jedes **Kommunikationsmittels** bedienen. Der Annehmende muss nicht das gleiche Erklärungsmittel benutzen wie der Offerent:[27] Eine schriftliche Offerte kann mündlich,[28] per Telex, E-Mail[29] oder mit einem anderen Kommunikationsmittel angenommen werden. Wirksame

---

[15] Die verwendete Sprache kann jedoch für den Zugang wichtig werden, s. unten Art. 24 Rn. 36; teilweise anders *Staudinger/Magnus*, Art. 18, Rn. 9.
[16] RB Tongeren, 25.1.2005, CISG-online 1106.
[17] S. bereits oben Vor Artt. 14–24 Rn. 30.
[18] Vgl. Tribunal Supremo, 28.1.2000, CISG-online 503 („Confirmamos el pedido…" als Annahme); OLG Saarbrücken, 13.1.1993, CISG-online 83 („Auftragsbestätigung" als Annahme); KreisG St. Gallen, 16.10.2009, CISG-online 2023 (dto.); LG Aurich, 8.5.1998, CISG-online 518 („confirmation of order" als Annahme).
[19] S. hierzu oben Vor Artt. 14–24 Rn. 18 ff.; unten Art. 19 Rn. 4. Die theoretisch klare Abgrenzung des kaufmännischen Bestätigungsschreibens von einer als Annahme gemeinten Auftragsbestätigung ist freilich in der Praxis nicht immer leicht, da sie davon abhängt, was der „Bestätigung" vorausgegangen ist bzw. vom Vorausgegangenen bewiesen werden kann, vgl. *von Caemmerer*, RabelsZ 29 (1965), 101, 128: „… faktisch ist der Tatbestand der abändernden Antwort, die eine Annahme sein will, damit – d. h. mit dem Tatbestand, der Grundlage eines Bestätigungsschreibens ist – eng verwandt, und die Fälle werden im Bewusstsein der Parteien und im Inhalt des Briefes nicht selten ineinander übergehen".
[20] S. OLG Koblenz, 23.12.1983, in: *Schlechtriem/Magnus*, Art. 6 EAG, Nr. 14.
[21] CA Paris, 13.12.1995, CISG-online 312 = J. C. P. 1997, éd. G., II, 22 772 m. Anm. *de Vareilles-Sommières*.
[22] RB Tongeren, 25.1.2005, CISG-online 1106.
[23] LG Hamburg, 23.11.2003, CISG-online 875.
[24] Okresný súd Nitra, 27.2.2006, CISG-online 1755.
[25] S. oben Vor Artt. 14–24 Rn. 18 ff. In Betracht kommt auch seine Verwertung als Beweismittel, denn insoweit gilt nationales Prozessrecht, vgl. oben Vor Artt. 14–24 Rn. 22.
[26] OLG Dresden, 10.11.2006, CISG-online 1625; CA Paris, 10.9.2003, CISG-online 788 (allerdings auf Grundlage von Art. 1315 frz. Cc); *Baumgärtel/Laumen/Hepting*, Art. 18 WKR, Rn. 1, zum Zugang hier Rn. 5.
[27] *Bridge*, Int'l Sale of Goods, Rn. 12.05.
[28] *Easom Automation Systems, Inc. v. Thyssenkrupp Fabco. Corp.*, U. S. Dist. Ct. (E. D. Mich.), 28.9.2007, CISG-online 1601 = IHR 2008, 34, 35.
[29] *Borges*, Verträge im elektronischen Geschäftsverkehr, S. 311.

Annahme mit einem elektronischen Kommunikationsmittel setzt aber voraus, dass der Offerent/Adressat sich mit der Verwendung dieser Art elektronischer Kommunikation ausdrücklich oder implizit einverstanden erklärt hat,[30] was zweifelsfrei der Fall ist, wenn er seine Offerte mit *diesem* elektronischen Kommunikationsmittel gemacht hat.[31] Die Freiheit in der Wahl des Erklärungsmittels kann jedoch **eingeschränkt** sein. Der Offerent darf ein bestimmtes Erklärungsmittel vorschreiben, z. B. Brief, Telex, E-Mail, EDI etc., und dabei sogar die Anforderungen des Art. 18 i. V. m. Art. 24 verschärfen, so dass Zugang allein nicht ausreicht, sondern – z. B. – Annahme durch eingeschriebenen Brief, gegen Empfangsbestätigung, Rückschein usw. erforderlich wird.[32] Eine Annahme, die entsprechende Vorgaben in der Offerte nicht einhält, entspricht nicht den Bedingungen des Angebots und ist nach Art. 19 zu beurteilen. Bei geringfügigen Abweichungen gilt deshalb auch Art. 19 II, z. B. wenn für die Annahme nicht ein der Offerte anhängendes Formblatt verwendet wird, sondern die Annahme – inhaltlich dem Formblatt voll entsprechend – gesondert niedergeschrieben wird. Wo für die Annahme Schriftform ohne weitere Qualifikation vorgeschrieben wird, muss in entsprechender Anwendung des Art. 13 auch Telex, Fax oder eine elektronische Erklärung[33] genügen. Allerdings muss nicht jede Erwähnung eines Kommunikationsmittels im Angebot eine bindende Anweisung für Form oder Kommunikationsmittel der Annahme bedeuten. Der Hinweis in der Offerte auf ein bestimmtes, besonders schnelles Erklärungsmittel für die Annahme kann auch Fristsetzung zum Ausdruck bringen.[34]

Die Parteien können auch **einvernehmlich** von den Anforderungen der Artt. 18, 24 abweichen – Art. 6 – und bestimmte Kommunikationsformen vereinbaren[35] oder auf Grund von Bräuchen, die nach Art. 9 I oder II gelten, auf bestimmte Erklärungsmittel verwiesen sein. So kann zwischen den Parteien Einigkeit bestehen, dass bei stark fluktuierendem Markt telegraphische Angebote nur telegraphisch, per Fax oder Telex angenommen werden können;[36] heute dürften freilich elektronische Kommunikationsmittel wie E-Mail oder EDI weithin an die Stelle solch überholter Kommunikationsinstrumente wie Telegraph oder Telex getreten sein.

Häufig werden Vorgaben in der Offerte oder Abreden der Parteien **Erleichterungen** für die Erklärung der Annahme ermöglichen, so insbes. für den Zugang;[37] die Offerte kann jedoch Schweigen oder Untätigkeit allein nicht die Bedeutung einer Annahmeerklärung verleihen, Art. 18 I 2.[38]

Eine Art. 12 II EAG[39] entsprechende Einschränkung der Erklärungsmittel sieht das CISG **6** nicht vor. Sie ist zugunsten der jetzt in Art. 24 festgehaltenen Fassung, dass eine Erklärung mündlich gemacht oder „delivered by any other means" werden könne,[40] aufgegeben worden. Die Annahme kann also – vorbehaltlich anders lautender Vorgaben des Offerenten

---

[30] S. bereits generell oben or Artt. 14–24 Rn. 27 sowie CISG-AC, Op. 1 *(Chr. Ramberg)*, Comment 18.3 i. V. m. 15.6, IHR 2003, 244, 246: "He [d. h. der Adressat] must have consented to receiving electronic messages of that type, in that format, and to that address."
[31] LG Hamburg, 23.11.2003, CISG-online 875: Angebot und Annahme per E-Mail.
[32] S. *Bianca/Bonell/Farnsworth*, Art. 18, Anm. 2.2.: Offerent kann Annahme durch Telex oder persönliche Aushändigung des Annahmeschreibens verlangen. Generell zur Vereinbarung von bestimmten Formen für die Kommunikation und Kommunikationsmittel s. oben *Schmidt-Kessel*, Art. 11 Rn. 16.
[33] S. oben *Schmidt-Kessel*, Art. 13 Rn. 7; Schroeter, Interpretation of „writing", S. 293 m. w. N.
[34] Vgl. *Flume*, Das Rechtsgeschäft, § 35 II 1, S. 649; s. auch *Tinn v. Hoffmann & Co.* (1873), 29 L. T. 271: „Your reply by return of post".
[35] S. oben *Schmidt-Kessel*, Art. 11 Rn. 16; MünchKomm/*Gruber*, Art. 18, Rn. 6.
[36] Vgl. RG, 17.2.1922, Recht 1922, Nr. 1391 – dictum –; ferner *Quenerduaine v. Cole* [1883] 32 W. R. 185.
[37] Zu Art. 18 III s. unten Rn. 18.
[38] S. noch unten Rn. 9.
[39] "Mitteilungen sind mit den nach den Umständen üblichen Mitteln zu bewirken".
[40] S. YB VIII (1977), S. 86, Nr. 151 sowie den Bericht des Generalsekretärs in YB VIII (1977), S. 103, der auf eine entsprechende Formulierung in Art. 6 I EAG hinweist.

(s. oben Rn. 5) – mit jedem möglichen Erklärungsmittel erfolgen;[41] Einschränkungen können sich nur noch aus dem Begriff des Zugangs ergeben.[42]

2. Annahme durch Verhalten

7   **a) Formen erklärungsäquivalenten Verhaltens.** Art. 18 I 1 lässt **Annahme** auch durch „**sonstiges Verhalten**" zu. Die Vorschrift trennt deutlich die Möglichkeit einer konkludenten Erklärung durch entsprechendes Verhalten von der Frage der Zugangsbedürftigkeit: Auch bei einem Verhalten, das Annahme zum Ausdruck bringt, muss prinzipiell die darin liegende Erklärung zugehen, sofern nicht Abs. 3 eingreift.[43] Art. 18 II 1 verdeutlicht das für beide in Abs. 1 S. 1 genannten Zustimmungsformen mit der Formulierung, dass die „Äußerung der Zustimmung" erst mit Zugang wirksam wird.[44]

7a **Beispiele** solchen Erklärungsverhaltens sind Absenden der Ware durch den Verkäufer[45] – auch von Teillieferungen[46] –, Verpackung der Ware zum Versand an den oder entsprechend der Wünsche des offerierenden Käufer(s),[47] ihre Abholung auf Veranlassung des Käufers[48] oder Anlieferung durch den Verkäufer;[49] ihre Entgegennahme[50] und (oder) Verarbeitung durch den Käufer,[51] Übersendung von Rechnungen und Packlisten durch den Verkäufer[52] oder anderer auf die Ware bezogener Dokumente,[53] Zahlung[54] oder Leistung einer An-[55] oder Teilzahlung,[56] Eröffnung eines Akkreditivs für den Kaufpreis,[57] Leistungsvorbereitungen durch Abschluss von Deckungsgeschäften oder Produktionsbeginn,[58] das Drängen auf Lieferung der Ware durch den Käufer,[59] die Mitteilung des Liefertermins durch den Ver-

---

[41] *Soergel/Lüderitz/Fenge,* Art. 18, Rn. 1; *Staudinger/Magnus,* Art. 18, Rn. 8.

[42] S. unten Art. 24 Rn. 16, 19 ff.

[43] *Honnold/Flechtner,* Art. 18, Rn. 163. Zu abweichenden Regeln in anderen Rechten *Soergel/Lüderitz/Fenge,* Art. 18, Rn. 4.

[44] Vgl. KG Freiburg, 11.10.2004, CISG-online 964 = IHR 2005, 72, 76: Lieferung der Ware als Annahme einer entsprechenden Offerte (Bestellung) führt grundsätzlich erst mit Zugang der Ware zum Vertragsschluss; Sekretariatskommentar, Art. 16, Nr. 3. Zu Art. 18 III s. unten Rn. 18 ff.

[45] OGH, 31.8.2005, CISG-online 1093 = IHR 2006, 31, 33; CA Rennes, 27.5.2008, CISG-online 1746; LG Bamberg, 13.4.2005, CISG-online 1402; *Bianca/Bonell/Farnsworth,* Art. 18, Anm. 2.2.

[46] RB Tongeren, 25.1.2005, CISG-online 1106.

[47] *Brunner,* Art. 18, Rn. 5; *Heuzé,* Anm. 184.

[48] Schleswig-Holsteinisches OLG, 29.10.2002, CISG-online 717 = IHR 2003, 67, 68.

[49] OLG Dresden, 10.11.2006, CISG-online 1625.

[50] *Barbara Berry, S. A. de C. V. v. Ken M. Spooner Farms, Inc.,* U. S. Dist. Ct. (W. D. Wash.), 13.4.2006, CISG-online 1354: Öffnen der Warenverpackung, auf der eine gut sichtbare Haftungsausschlussklausel aufgedruckt war, stellt Zustimmung des Käufers zu dieser Klausel dar; OLG Linz, 23.3.2005, CISG-online 1376 = IHR 2007, 123, 126; KG Zug, 2.12.2004, CISG-online 1194 = IHR 2006, 159, 160; HGer Zürich, 10.7.1996, CISG-online 227 = SZIER 1997, 131 f.: Widerspruchslose Entgegennahme und Weiterverkauf von 61.900 gelieferten Jetons stellt Annahme des entsprechenden Angebots (richtigerweise wohl: auf Vertragsänderung) dar, obgleich zunächst nur 60.000 Jetons bestellt gewesen waren; OLG Saarbrücken, 13.1.1993, CISG-online 83; ICC, 8611/1997, CISG-online 236; enger RB Tongeren, 25.1.2005, CISG-online 1106: widerspruchslose Annahme der Ware.

[51] OLG Saarbrücken, 13.1.1993, CISG-online 83.

[52] *Zhejiang Shaoxing Yongli Printing and Dyeing Co. v. Microflock Textile Group Corp.,* U. S. Dist. Ct. (S. D. Fla.), 19.5.2008, CISG-online 1771.

[53] BGer, 5.4.2005, CISG-online 1012 = IHR 2005, 204, 206: Übersendung einer Spezifikationsanalyse des verkauften Triethylen-Tetramins sowie von EG-Sicherheitsdatenblättern durch den Verkäufer.

[54] *Barbara Berry, S. A. de C. V. v. Ken M. Spooner Farms, Inc.,* U. S. Dist. Ct. (W. D. Wash.), 13.4.2006, CISG-online 1354; OLG Linz, 23.3.2005, CISG-online 1376 = IHR 2007, 123, 126; RB Tongeren, 25.1.2005, CISG-online 1106; *Bianca/Bonell/Farnsworth,* Art. 18, Anm. 2.2.

[55] HGer St. Gallen, 29.4.2004, CISG-online 962.

[56] OLG Jena, 27.8.2008, CISG-online 1820 = NJW 2009, 689: Teilzahlung in Höhe von USD 200.000.

[57] *Magellan International Corp. v. Salzgitter Handel GmbH,* U. S. Dist. Ct. (N. D. Ill.), 7.12.1999, CISG-online 439 = 76 F. Supp. 2d 919; HGer St. Gallen, 15.6.2010, CISG-online 2159 = IHR 2011, 149, 151.

[58] RB Tongeren, 25.1.2005, CISG-online 1106; *Bianca/Bonell/Farnsworth,* Art. 18, Anm. 2.2.; *Enderlein/Maskow/Strohbach,* Art. 18, Anm. 2.; freilich haben diese Fälle vor allem Bedeutung für die weitergehende Möglichkeit, Annahmewirkung auch ohne Zugang nach Art. 18 III entstehen zu lassen; dazu unten Rn. 18 ff.

[59] OLG Düsseldorf, 21.4.2004, CISG-online 915 = IHR 2005, 24, 26.

Begriff der Annahme   7b–8 Art. 18

käufer.⁶⁰ Auch die Zusendung der Rechnung oder ihre Abzeichnung durch den Käufer,⁶¹ der Weiterverkauf vom Verkäufer angebotener⁶² oder auch unbestellt zugesandter⁶³ Ware durch den Käufer, die Einlösung eines mit der Offerte übersandten Schecks⁶⁴ oder die Nutzung einer Abbuchungsermächtigung im Lastschriftverfahren können als Ausdruck der Annahme verstanden werden.⁶⁵ Maßgebend ist der Verständnishorizont des (potentiellen) Empfängers, Art. 8 II.⁶⁶ Die Vorbereitung der Annahmeerklärung bringt deshalb im Regelfall nicht schon Annahmewillen zum Ausdruck, selbst wenn der Fall des Art. 18 III gegeben sein sollte (unten Rn. 20 ff.).⁶⁷ Auch die Herstellung von Ware durch den Adressaten einer Bestellung wird man allein nur dann ausreichen lassen können, wenn es sich dabei um Spezialanfertigungen o. ä. handelt, die sich der konkreten Bestellung zuordnen lassen.⁶⁸

Der deutliche Grundsatz, dass die durch Verhalten zum Ausdruck gebrachte Zustimmung **zugehen** muss, sofern nicht die Voraussetzungen des Abs. 3 vorliegen, verschiebt den Eintritt der Perfektionierung des Vertrages: Der absendende Verkäufer kann durch Rückruf oder Stoppung seine Annahme zurücknehmen – Art. 22 –, ohne vertragsbrüchig zu werden, der Käufer ist noch nicht gebunden (und zahlungspflichtig), wenn die die Annahme ausdrückende Ware untergeht, d. h. nicht ankommt.⁶⁹ **7b**

Die **Absendung fehlerhafter Güter** kann Annahme sein.⁷⁰ Für das EAG war die Frage in der Wortwahl („Absendung" statt „Lieferung") bewusst entschieden worden.⁷¹ Da auch Art. 18 III von „Absendung" spricht, kann es auf vertragsmäßige Beschaffenheit nicht ankommen.⁷² Bei einem aliud wird man unterscheiden müssen: Im Falle einer Verwechslung ist die Absendung Ausdruck des Annahmewillens.⁷³ Bei bewusster Übersendung einer anderen Sache als „Ersatzangebot" ist dagegen ein zugangsbedürftiges Gegenangebot gemeint, das freilich nach Art. 8 II gleichwohl als Annahme verstanden werden kann.⁷⁴ Um die Deutung der Absendung als Annahme nach Art. 8 II zu verhindern, muss der Verkäufer sie deutlich als Gegenofferte deklarieren. **7c**

b) Rollenwechsel nach Art. 19 I. Nicht selten dürfte, wie die Rechtsprechung zeigt, Annahme durch erklärungsäquivalentes Verhalten in den Fällen eines **Rollenwechsels** nach Art. 19 I geschehen, d. h. auf eine als Gegenofferte bewertete Annahme mit Modifikatio- **8**

---

⁶⁰ BGer, 5.4.2005, CISG-online 1012 = IHR 2005, 204, 206; *Piltz,* NJW 2007, 2159, 2161.
⁶¹ OLG Linz, 23.3.2005, CISG-online 1376 = IHR 2007, 123, 126; Cámara Nacional de Apelaciones en lo Comercial de Buenos Aires, 14.10.1993, CISG-online 87: Abzeichnung der Rechnung durch den Käufer, um sie einem Finanzierungsinstitut vorzulegen, als implizite Annahme.
⁶² *Golden Valley Grape Juice and Wine, LLC v. Centrisys Corp. et al.,* U. S. Dist. Ct. (E. D. Cal.), 21.1.2010, CISG-online 2089.
⁶³ LG Köln, 5.12.2006, CISG-online 1440.
⁶⁴ S. *Honsell/Dornis,* Art. 18, Rn. 30; LG Kassel, 15.2.1996, CISG-online 190 (zu Art. 29); vgl. aber BGH, 28.3.1990, BGHZ 111, 97, 102 zur Einreichung eines übersandten Schecks: keine Annahme eines Abfindungsangebots (zum BGB).
⁶⁵ Vgl. *Honsell/Dornis,* Art. 18, Rn. 30; ferner zur Rechnung RG, 20.12.1921, RGZ 103, 312 ff., wo freilich schon in der Offerte Rechnung und Lieferung verlangt worden waren.
⁶⁶ OLG Frankfurt a. M., 30.8.2000, CISG-online 594 = RIW 2001, 383, 384.
⁶⁷ *Brunner,* Art. 18, Rn. 5; *Piltz,* Internationales Kaufrecht, Rn. 3–60.
⁶⁸ *Brunner,* Art. 18, Rn. 5; *Schwenzer/Mohs,* IHR 2006, 239, 242 Fn. 47.
⁶⁹ Vgl. *Wey,* Rn. 963.
⁷⁰ S. CA Rennes, 27.5.2008, CISG-online 1746; *Brunner,* Art. 18, Rn. 5; *Honsell/Dornis,* Art. 18, Rn. 31; MünchKomm/*Gruber,* Art. 18, Rn. 5; *Staudinger/Magnus,* Art. 18, Rn. 11. Zu den Problemen, dass durch nicht dem Angebot entsprechende Ware ein Vertrag zustande kommt, obwohl der Inhalt der Annahme mit der Offerte nicht korrespondiert, s. *Stern,* Erklärungen, Rn. 83; *Wey,* Rn. 960, 1229.
⁷¹ S. *von Caemmerer,* RabelsZ 29 (1965), 101, 124.
⁷² A. A. OLG Frankfurt a. M., 23.5.1995, CISG-online 185 (Absendung einer Mindermenge als Gegenangebot); *Perales Viscasillas,* Formación del contrato, S. 552 ff. (mit ausführlicher Darstellung der Entwicklungsgeschichte und Rechtsvergleichung): Gegenofferte.
⁷³ MünchKomm/*Gruber,* Art. 18, Rn. 5.
⁷⁴ Vgl. *Achilles,* Art. 18, Rn. 2; *Wey,* Rn. 1069; *Schmidt,* 14 Am. J. Comp. L. (1965), 1, 19: Der Offerent könne die Übersendung stets als Annahme behandeln und Vertragsbruch geltend machen. M. E. kann der Lieferant jedoch deutlich machen, dass ein Gegenangebot gewollt war, so dass Art. 8 I eingreift. Im Übrigen liegt ein Willensmangel vor, der nach BGB, sofern anwendbar, zur Anfechtung berechtigte.

nen hin, die der ursprüngliche Offerent jetzt in der Rolle des Annehmenden durch Leistungen oder anderes annahmeäquivalentes Verhalten beantwortet.[75] Häufig geht es dabei um Gegenofferten, durch die Standardbedingungen (**AGB**) in den Vertrag einbezogen werden sollen, weshalb die insoweit durch Rechtsprechung und Literatur entwickelten besonderen Einbeziehungsvoraussetzungen (insbes. die Kenntnisverschaffungsobliegenheit des Anbietenden)[76] zu beachten sind;[77] für die Qualifizierung des darauf folgenden Empfängerverhaltens gilt Art. 8 II, III.[78]

8a   Schließlich kommt eine Annahme durch erklärungsäquivalentes Verhalten auch dort in Betracht, wo das Angebot auf **Änderung eines** bereits geschlossenen **Vertrages (Art. 29 I)** gerichtet ist;[79] eine Konstellation, die wiederum vielfach bei Versuchen zur Einbeziehung von (hier: „nachgeschobenen") AGB eine Rolle gespielt hat.[80] In der letztgenannten Situation wird das Verhalten des Adressaten im Rahmen der Vertragsdurchführung allerdings durch eine vernünftige Person unter den gleichen Umständen (Art. 8 II) nur ausnahmsweise als Annahme des (regelmäßig konkludent, etwa durch Aufdruck auf einer Rechnung erklärten) Vertragsänderungsangebotes aufgefasst werden können; vgl. hierzu noch näher Art. 29 Rn. 7 f.

9   **c) Schweigen.** Auch **Schweigen** oder **Untätigkeit** können prinzipiell Ausdruck eines Annahmewillens sein; freilich kommt Zugang nicht in Betracht. Allerdings **müssen** zum Schweigen oder zur Untätigkeit **weitere Umstände** hinzukommen, um solchem Verhalten die Bedeutung, Zustimmung zum Ausdruck zu bringen, zu geben.[81] Die Möglichkeit, einen Vertrag durch Schweigen auf eine Offerte hin zustande kommen zu lassen, darf freilich **nicht** dazu genutzt werden, dass der Offerent durch eine entsprechende **Bedingung des Angebots** den Empfänger auf Grund seines Schweigens verpflichten kann.[82] Art. 18 I 2 bestimmt, dass Schweigen allein oder Unterbleiben jeglicher Reaktion auf die Offerte keine Erklärungsbedeutung als Annahme soll haben können. Damit ist in Erweiterung des in Art. 2 II EAG zum Ausdruck gekommenen Gedankens eine Überrumpelung des Offertenempfängers, etwa durch Zusendung unbestellter Ware mit einer Offerte, die Nicht-Zurücksendung als Annahme gewertet wissen will, verhindert worden. Aus der Formulierung „allein" („in itself") wird jedoch deutlich, dass Schweigen i. V. m. anderen Umständen durchaus Erklärungsbedeutung haben und auf Grund des Art. 18 III auch ohne Zugang einer entsprechenden Äußerung als Annahme wirken oder ausgelegt werden

---

[75] OLG Frankfurt a. M., 23.5.1995, CISG-online 185 (Übersendung einer geringeren Anzahl als der bestellten Schuhe als Gegenofferte, deren Annahme im konkreten Fall streitig blieb).
[76] S. oben Art. 14 Rn. 36 ff., zur Kenntnisverschaffungsobliegenheit oben Art. 14 Rn. 40 ff.
[77] S. oben Art. 14 Rn. 74 f. (zur Annahme); s. auch zur „battle of forms" unten Art. 19 Rn. 19 ff.
[78] *Magellan International Corp. v. Salzgitter Handel GmbH*, U. S. Dist. Ct. (N. D. Ill.), 7.12.1999, CISG-online 439 = 76 F. Supp. 2d 919 (Eröffnung eines Letter of Credit als Annahme); OLG München, 11.3.1998, CISG-online 310 = TranspR-IHR 1999, 20, 21 (Vertragsdurchführung als Annahme); ICC, 8611/1997, CISG-online 236 (Entgegennahme der Ware, der die AGB beigefügt waren, als deren Annahme); OLG Saarbrücken, 13.1.1993, CISG-online 83 (Entgegennahme der Ware als Annahme); anders Civ. 1, 16.7.1998, CISG-online 344 = D. 1998, 222 (keine Akzeptanz der in der Gegenofferte eingeführten AGB inkl. Gerichtsstandsklausel durch Vertragsdurchführung).
[79] Najvyšší súd Slovenskej republiky, 19.6.2008, CISG-online 1875 (in Rechnung enthaltenes Angebot des Verkäufers, die Fälligkeit der Kaufpreiszahlungspflicht um 180 Tage hinauszuschieben – Annahme *in casu* jedoch nicht erfolgt, weil Käufer untätig blieb; vgl. noch unten Art. 19 Rn. 8b); LG Kassel, 15.2.1996, CISG-online 190 (Angebot zur Abänderung offener Kaufpreisforderungen durch „Abfindungsvereinbarung", die vom Verkäufer durch Scheckeinreichung angenommen wurde); OLG München, 8.2.1995, CISG-online 143 (Angebot zur Änderung/Ergänzung des Liefertermins – Annahme *in casu* nicht erfolgt).
[80] *Chateau des Charmes Wines Ltd. v. Sabaté USA Inc., Sabaté S. A.*, U. S. Ct. App. (9th Cir.), 5.5.2003, CISG-online 767 = IHR 2003, 295, 296 (AGB auf Rechnungen); CA Paris, 13.12.1995, CISG-online 312 = J. C. P. éd. G, II, Nr. 22 772 (AGB auf Auftragsbestätigung, die 2 Wochen nach Vertragsschluss übersandt wurde).
[81] Najvyšší súd Slovenskej republiky, 19.6.2008, CISG-online 1875; *Honsell/Dornis*, Art. 18, Rn. 25; *Staudinger/Magnus*, Art. 18, Rn. 12; *Witz/Salger/Lorenz/Witz*, Art. 18, Rn. 9.
[82] *Bianca/Bonell/Farnsworth*, Art. 18, Anm. 2.3.; MünchKomm/*Gruber*, Art. 18, Rn. 6; *Schultz*, 35 Cornell Int'l L. J. (2001–02), 263, 273 (zur „rolling contract formation"); *Sutton*, 16 U. W. Ont. L. Rev. (1977), 113, 121.

kann.[83] Solche anderen Umstände können vor allem Bräuche, die vereinbart worden sind oder nach Art. 9 II als vereinbart gelten, sowie Gepflogenheiten, die zwischen den Parteien entstanden sind – Art. 8 III –,[84] oder auch Vorverhandlungen[85] sein.[86] Als entsprechender Handelsbrauch kommt im Einzelfall auch der Grundsatz in Betracht, dass **Schweigen auf ein kaufmännisches Bestätigungsschreiben** als Annahme gilt, wobei hier im Anwendungsbereich des CISG freilich die (strengen) Voraussetzungen des Art. 9 I, II gewahrt sein müssen.[87] (Nur) sofern die Anforderungen dieser Vorschrift erfüllt sind, mag eine Gepflogenheit der Parteien im Einzelfall auch dazu führen, dass ein CISG-Vertrag nach dem Muster einer „**rolling contract formation**" des U. S.-amerikanischen Rechts zustande kommt.[88] Natürlich können auch Rahmenvereinbarungen oder auf der Grundlage von Art. 6 Vertragsschlussvorschriften des Übereinkommens ändernde Abreden der Parteien zu einer entsprechenden Bedeutung des Schweigens führen, den Angebotsempfänger deshalb u. U. sogar zur ablehnenden Antwort verpflichten.[89]

d) Kreuzofferten. Auch eine **Kreuzofferte** kann Ausdruck der Absicht sein, einen Vertrag zustande bringen zu wollen, und deshalb als Annahme wirken.[90] Die Regeln zum Vertragsschluss sind dispositiv – Art. 6 –, so dass ein Einigwerden der Parteien auch unabhängig von dem im CISG zugrunde gelegten Ablauf der Vertragsschlusserklärungen möglich ist.[91] Da es zu inhaltlich kongruenten Kreuzofferten wohl nur kommen wird, wenn zwischen den Parteien bereits Kontakte bestanden haben, die zur Klärung der wichtigsten Punkte geführt haben, dürfte vielfach ein Einverständnis in die Abweichung vom normalen

---

[83] Vgl. OLG Köln, 22.2.1994, CISG-online 127 = EWiR 1994, 867 *(Schlechtriem)*: Schweigen sowie Absehen von der weiteren Durchführung des Vertrags, insbesondere von der Geltendmachung von Gewährleistungsansprüchen, als Annahme eines Vertragsaufgebotsangebotes – zweifelhaft; *Fogt*, IPRax 2007, 417, 418.

[84] CA Grenoble, 21.10.1999, CISG-online 574 = D. 2000, II, 441 m. Anm. *Cl. Witz*: Schweigen des Verkäufers als Annahme ausreichend, weil dieser in der Vergangenheit stets nach Eingang von Bestellungen mit der Vertragsdurchführung begonnen hatte, ohne nach außen zu reagieren; Sekretariatskommentar, Art. 16, Nr. 2, Bsp. 16A: „Wenn auf Grund einer zehnjährigen Geschäftsverbindung der Verkäufer Bestellungen des Käufers (Offerten) stets ohne Annahmeerklärung ausgeführt hat, kann sich der Käufer darauf verlassen, dass Schweigen Annahme bedeutet, sofern er keine ausdrückliche Ablehnung erhält"; ähnliches Beispiel bei *Sono*, Formation of International Contracts, S. 123 f.; *Köhler*, S. 220.

[85] Vgl. Civ. 1, 27.1.1998, CISG-online 309 = TranspR-IHR 1999, 9: Angebot des Verkäufers (hier: zur Vertragsänderung bezügl. technischer Warendetails) vom Käufer durch Schweigen angenommen, weil Käufer selbst die technischen Modifikationen verlangt und zudem später die Ware akzeptiert hatte; RB Rotterdam, 12.7.2001, CISG-online 968 = NIPR 2001, Nr. 278: Stillschweigende Annahme des vom Käufer zugesandten Lieferzeitplans durch Verkäufer denkbar, sofern während Vertragsverhandlungen die Erstellung des Lieferplans durch den Käufer verabredet hatten (in concreto streitig).

[86] Vgl. Østre Landsret, 23.4.1998, CISG-online 486 = UfR 1998, 1092 (Annahme durch Schweigen verneint, weil es an vorangegangenen Geschäftskontakten zwischen den Parteien fehlte); *Filanto, SpA. v. Chilewich International Corp.*, U. S. Dist. Ct. (S. D. N. Y.), 14.4.1992, CISG-online 45 = 789 F. Supp. 1229: Im Lichte der umfangreichen früheren Geschäfte der Parteien hätte der Offertenempfänger (= Verkäufer) der Schiedsklausel im Angebot (und damit dem Angebot) widersprechen müssen; sein Schweigen und bestimmte andere Manifestationen hätten die Absicht deutlich gemacht, dass der Verkäufer zu Angebotsbedingungen gebunden sein wollte, S. 1240; *Enderlein/Maskow/Strohbach*, Art. 18, Anm. 3.: Handelsbräuche oder Gepflogenheiten zwischen den Parteien können die ausdrückliche Ablehnung eines Angebots fordern; ähnlich *Witz/Salger/Lorenz/Witz*, Art. 18, Rn. 12; s. ferner MünchKomm/*Gruber*, Art. 18, Rn. 21 ff.; *Neumayer/Ming*, Art. 18, Anm. 2., 3.

[87] S. oben Vor Artt. 14–24 Rn. 20 f., dort auch zum kaufmännischen Bestätigungsschreiben als Beweismittel (Rn. 22).

[88] Vgl. *Schultz*, 35 Cornell Int'l L. J. (2001-02), 263, 273 f., 279, 286 f.; sehr zurückhaltend demgegenüber *Honnold/Flechtner*, Art. 19, Rn. 170.4.

[89] S. *Neumayer/Ming*, Art. 18, Anm. 3.; Sekretariatskommentar, Art. 16, Nr. 4, Bsp. 16B: Ist in einem „concession agreement" vereinbart, dass der Verkäufer eine Ablehnung von Bestellungen des Käufers innerhalb von vierzehn Tagen mitteilen müsse, dann bedeutet Schweigen über vierzehn Tage hinaus Annahme; zu solchen Vereinbarungen auf der Grundlage von Art. 6 s. *Joseph*, 3 Dick. J. Int'l L. (1984), 107, 129.

[90] *Staudinger/Magnus*, Art. 18, Rn. 4; *Honsell/Dornis*, Art. 18, Rn. 14; MünchKomm/*Gruber*, Vor Art. 14, Rn. 3. Die Frage ist aber umstritten, s. umfassend *Neumayer*, FS Riese, S. 309 ff.; *Murray*, 8 J. L. & Com. (1988), 11, 20; *Schlesinger*, Bd. 1, S. 105.

[91] S. oben Vor Artt. 14–24 Rn. 15 ff.

Ablauf des Vertragsschlusses anzunehmen sein. Das setzt allerdings voraus, dass die Vertragsschlusserklärungen tatsächlich inhaltlich übereinstimmen und bindend sein sollen.[92] Fehlt es an einem Einverständnis, den normalen Ablauf der Vertragsschlusserklärungen nach CISG zu derogieren, dann muss m. E. mindestens eine der Kreuzofferten angenommen worden sein, um einen Vertrag zustande zu bringen. Insbesondere bei zufällig, d. h. ohne vorherige Parteibeziehung inhaltsgleichen oder widerruflichen Kreuzofferten kann sich keiner der beiden Teile darauf verlassen, dass ein Vertrag zustande kommt, ohne dass er noch einmal Einverständnis zum Ausdruck bringt. Nehmen beide Teile an, so ergibt eine vernünftige Auslegung der jeweiligen Annahmeerklärung nach Art. 8 II, III, dass nur **ein** Vertrag gewollt ist, d. h. die eigene Erklärung unter dem Vorbehalt steht, dass der Vertrag nicht vorher durch eine korrespondierende Annahmeerklärung der anderen Seite zustande kommt. Leistet eine der Parteien nach Erhalt einer Kreuzofferte oder bringt sie durch anderes Verhalten zum Ausdruck, an den Vertrag gebunden zu sein, dann kann darin eine Annahme der Kreuzofferte des anderen Teils nach Art. 18 I liegen, aber auch das Einverständnis nach Art. 6, den Vertrag als bereits durch die Kreuzofferten geschlossen zu behandeln.

III. Wirksamkeit der Annahmeerklärung

1. Zeitpunkt der Wirksamkeit: Bedeutung

11 **a) Vertragsschluss.** Die Wirksamkeit der Annahmeerklärung entscheidet über den Vertragsschluss und den Zeitpunkt, zu dem der Vertrag geschlossen worden ist, Art. 23. Je nachdem, ob die Annahmeerklärung – wie regelmäßig – zugangsbedürftig ist, Art. 18 II, oder ausnahmsweise bereits mit Äußerung der Zustimmung zur Offerte wirkt, Art. 18 III, ist der Vertrag erst mit Zugang der Annahmeerklärung oder bereits mit ihrer Äußerung perfektioniert.

12 **b) Rücknehmbarkeit der Annahme.** Der Zeitpunkt des Wirksamwerdens der Annahme entscheidet aber auch über die Möglichkeit ihrer **Rücknahme**. Eine Rücknahme der Annahmeerklärung ist nach Art. 22 nur möglich, wenn sie dem Offerenten vor oder im gleichen Zeitpunkt zugeht, in dem die Annahme wirksam geworden wäre, Art. 22. Behält sich der Annehmende eine über Art. 22 hinausgehende Widerrufsmöglichkeit vor, dann fehlt regelmäßig der Wille, sich vertraglich bereits mit der Annahmeerklärung zu binden. Ein solcher Widerrufsvorbehalt kann aber auch als Annahme mit der wesentlichen Modifikation verstanden werden, dass der Annehmende sich die Möglichkeit einer Auflösung des Vertrages durch Widerruf etc. vorbehalten will; für das Zustandekommen des Vertrages gilt dann Art. 19.

2. Rechtzeitigkeit und Wirkung der zugangsbedürftigen Äußerung der Zustimmung (Annahme)

13 **a) Zugangsprinzip.** Regelmäßig gilt für die Annahme das **Zugangsprinzip:**[93] Nach Art. 18 II 1 wird die Äußerung der Zustimmung mit dem Zugang beim Offerenten – Art. 24 – wirksam.[94] Das gilt sowohl für die verbal erklärte Annahme als auch für die

---

[92] Das in der älteren französischen Lit. (*Demogue*, Traité des obligations en général, Bd. 2, Paris (1923), Nr. 583, S. 237) erörterte Beispiel, dass der Käufer zu einem höheren Preis abzuschließen anbietet als der Verkäufer in seiner Kreuzofferte, kann m. E. nicht anders beurteilt werden. Das Ergebnis, der Vertrag komme stets zum niedrigeren Preis zustande, kann nur auf eine Auslegung der Käufererklärung gestützt werden, nicht aber auf den allzu vagen Grundsatz, niedrige Preise seien generell im Interesse der Gesellschaft.
[93] Statt aller: *Herber/Czerwenka*, Art. 18, Rn. 3; *Heuzé*, Anm. 189.; *Neumayer/Ming*, Art. 18, Anm. 1., 4.; *Staudinger/Magnus*, Art. 18, Rn. 14; *Honsell/Dornis*, Art. 18, Rn. 32; *Witz/Salger/Lorenz/Witz*, Art. 18, Rn. 17.
[94] *Conservas la Costena v. Lanis San Luis & Argoindustrial Santa Adela*, Comisión para la Protección del Comercio Exterior de México, 29.4.1996, CISG-online 350 = 17 J. L. & Com. (1998), 427, 432; CA Paris, 13.12.1995, CISG-online 312 = J. C. P. éd. G, II, Nr. 22 772.

konkludent geäußerte Zustimmung, die den Offerenten erreichen muss.[95] Das Erklärungsverhalten muss von Geschäftswillen getragen sein bzw. einen solchen nach Art. 8 II zum Ausdruck bringen.[96] Freilich setzt Erklärung durch konkludentes Verhalten Zugangsfähigkeit voraus. Wo sie fehlt, z. B. bei Verbrauch der zusammen mit der Offerte übersandten Ware, kann der Vertrag nur nach Art. 18 III geschlossen worden sein. U. U. kann jedoch eine Mitteilung erfolgen, deren Zugang als Erklärungszugang wirkt.[97] Auch Annahmehandlungen, die Zugang der darin liegenden Zustimmung ermöglichen, z. B. Versendung der Ware, können von einer Mitteilung begleitet sein. Sie bewirkt, falls sie vor der durch Absendung der Ware zum Ausdruck gebrachten Zustimmung zugeht, wohl bereits Vertragsschluss.[98] Sogar die durch einen Dritten, z. B. die in den Zahlungsvorgang eingeschaltete Bank oder den Frachtführer erfolgende Mitteilung soll den Zugang der durch Einleitung des Zahlungsvorganges bzw. Versendung der Ware zum Ausdruck gebrachten Zustimmung bewirken.[99] Die **Beweislast** für den Zugang einer Annahme trifft diejenige Partei, die sich auf das Zustandekommen des Vertrages beruft.[100]

Die Annahme – verbal erklärt oder anders zum Ausdruck gebracht – muss **rechtzeitig** zugehen. Art. 18 II unterscheidet drei Fälle:

b) Rechtzeitigkeit bei Fristsetzung. Hat der Offerent eine **Frist** gesetzt, dann muss 14 die Annahmeerklärung innerhalb der gesetzten Frist zugehen,[101] sofern der Frist nicht eine andere Bedeutung zukommen soll.[102] Ist die Wirksamkeit der Annahmeerklärung von bestimmten weiteren Voraussetzungen abhängig, dann ist zunächst zu prüfen, ob es sich um nach nationalem Recht zu beurteilende Gültigkeitsvoraussetzungen handelt – Art. 4 S. 2 lit. a) – oder um CISG-interne, eventuell lückenhaft geregelte Sachfragen. Hängt die Erklärung von der Genehmigung Dritter – gesetzlicher Vertreter, übergeordneter Organe des Erklärenden oder des Vertretenen – ab, dann ist nach dem maßgeblichen nationalen Recht zu entscheiden, ob die Genehmigung zurückwirkt und deshalb Rechtzeitigkeit der Erklärung bewirkt.[103] Ausnahmsweise kann aber auch eine verspätet zugegangene Annahme wirksam sein, Art. 21 I, II.[104] Die Frist kann als Datum oder in anderer Weise gesetzt werden (z. B. „spätestens vierzehn Tage nach Eingang der Offerte", „zwei Werktage",[105] „morgen bei unserer Eröffnung"[106]); zur Fristberechnung und zum Fristbeginn s. Art. 20. Sie kann auch durch Bezugnahme auf Ereignisse, deren Datum ermittelt werden kann, erfolgen (z. B. Frankfurter Messe) oder deren genauer Termin noch ungewiss ist (z. B. Eisfreiheit eines bestimmten Hafens, Veröffentlichung einer bereits beschlossenen Aus-

---

[95] S. *Enderlein/Maskow/Strohbach*, Art. 18, Anm. 5. f.; s. auch oben Rn. 7; *Staudinger/Magnus*, Art. 18, Rn. 14: Nachricht erforderlich.

[96] S. oben Rn. 4; die von einer unbefugten Hilfsperson des Offertenempfängers vorgenommene Absendung der Ware ist keine wirksame Annahme, *Wey*, Rn. 958.

[97] Damit dürfte die Mehrzahl der Fälle erfasst werden, in denen einige Autoren bei nicht zugangsbedürftiger Annahme – Art. 18 III – eine Mitteilung des Annehmenden an den Offerenten verlangen, s. unten Rn. 23 sowie zum Einfluss der amerikanischen Auffassung, bei „offers calling for an act" bedürfe es einer Mitteilung, die aber nicht selbst Annahme sei, *Stern*, Erklärungen, Rn. 73–76. Auch *Staudinger/Magnus*, Art. 18, Rn. 14, verlangt für Annahmewirkung wohl Benachrichtigung.

[98] Vgl. *Bianca/Bonell/Farnsworth*, Art. 18, Anm. 2.7., der davon ausgeht, dass regelmäßig zum Verhalten eine Mitteilung erfolgen muss, falls die durch Verhalten zum Ausdruck gebrachte Annahme dem Offerenten nicht zugehen kann; s. aber auch Anm. 2.8. Das Absenden einer Erklärung kann freilich den Verhalten die Bedeutung nehmen, bereits Ausdruck der Zustimmung zu sein, vgl. *Dölle/Schlechtriem*, Art. 6 EAG, Rn. 44. Angesichts der Wirkung einer solchen Mitteilung, Vertragsschluss zu bewirken bzw. zeitlich früher eintreten zu lassen, sollte sie als zugangsbedürftig behandelt werden, s. *Noussias*, Zustimmungsbedürftigkeit von Mitteilungen, S. 109.

[99] *Bianca/Bonell/Farnsworth*, Art. 18, Anm. 2.7.; *Staudinger/Magnus*, Art. 18, Rn. 14.

[100] KG Freiburg, 11.10.2004, CISG-online 964 = IHR 2005, 72, 75.

[101] LG Hamburg, 23.11.2003, CISG-online 875: „Bindungsfrist"; ICC, 7844/1994, CISG-online 567.

[102] Vgl. zum BGB BGH, 16.9.1988, NJW-RR 1989, 198 f.

[103] Vgl. zum internen deutschen Recht *Jauernig*, FS Niederländer, S. 285–294.

[104] ICC, 7844/1994, CISG-online 567.

[105] OLG Frankfurt a. M., 24.3.2009, CISG-online 2165 = IHR 2010, 250, 252.

[106] LG Hamburg, 23.11.2003, CISG-online 875.

schreibung,[107] Beginn der Ernte in einem bestimmten Gebiet). Auslegungsbedürftig sind vor allem Befristungen unter Verwendung unbestimmter Zeitbegriffe (z. B. „für Prüfung erforderliche Zeit", „übliche Bedenkzeit", „Antwort sofort"). Die Auslegung hat dann in Anwendung des Art. 8 auch die Umstände und Eigenheiten des beabsichtigten Vertrages (Geschäftsumfang), die dem Adressaten verfügbaren Kommunikationsmittel und – Art. 8 III – Gepflogenheiten der Parteien usw. zu berücksichtigen.[108] So kann auch in Anwendung des CISG „Antwort sofort bei Empfang des gegenwärtigen Briefes" bei einem Empfänger, der tagsüber nicht zu Hause ist, nicht stets dahin verstanden werden, dass mit der nächsten Post geantwortet werden müsse.[109] Andererseits kann, wenn die Parteien in den Vorverhandlungen weitgehend einig waren, „umgehend" Antwort mit der nächsten Post, per Fax oder per E-Mail bedeuten.[110] „Früh" kann u. U. „bis zum Abgang der ersten Post" meinen;[111] „schnellste Mitteilung der Annahme" ist mit einer drei Tage später erfolgten telegraphischen oder elektronischen Erklärung eines Angebots über konjunkturempfindliche Ware nicht mehr rechtzeitig erfolgt.[112] Wird die Frist – wie beim Verkauf von Waren mit hochvolatilen Preisen üblich und heute auch darüber hinaus (vor allem bei Verwendung elektronischer Kommunikationsmittel) zunehmend verbreitet – unter Angabe einer präzisen Uhrzeit gesetzt („bis spätestens morgen 14.00 Uhr"), so kann beim grenzüberschreitenden Vertragsschluss auch die anwendbare Zeitzone Bedeutung gewinnen:[113] Hier ist im Zweifel auf die Zeitzone abzustellen, in welcher der Offerent niedergelassen ist, weil es im Rahmen des Art. 18 II 2 auf den Zugang beim Offerenten ankommt. **Beweislast** für fristgemäße Annahme trägt, wer Vertragsschluss behauptet, für Verspätung, wer daraus Folgen ableitet.[114]

15   c) **Rechtzeitigkeit bei angemessener Frist.** Fehlt eine – wenn auch ggf. erst durch Auslegung zu konkretisierende – Fristsetzung, dann gilt eine **„angemessene Frist"**, Art. 18 II 2. Die angemessene Frist setzt sich aus drei Teilabschnitten zusammen: Reisezeit für die Offerte, Überlegungsfrist und Rückreisezeit für die Annahmeerklärung.[115] Die Reisezeiten sind dabei durch die in Abs. 2 S. 2 HS. 2 gebotene Berücksichtigung der vom Anbietenden gewählten **Übermittlungsart** festzulegen: Bei einem Angebot per Telex, Telefax, EDI oder E-Mail[116] sind die Übermittlungszeiten entsprechend knapp anzusetzen und können sich – etwa beim elektronischen, über Internet abgewickelten Dialogverkehr oder E-Mail – so reduzieren, dass wie beim mündlichen Angebot sofort anzunehmen ist.[117] Der Rechtsprechung zufolge ist deshalb zweifelhaft, ob ein durch E-Mail übermitteltes Angebot überhaupt wirksam per Post angenommen werden kann.[118] Im Wesentlichen bestimmt sich die Angemessenheit nach dem Zeitabschnitt **„Überlegungsfrist"**, die von Umfang, Gegenstand und Eigenart des angebotenen Geschäftes abhängt, z. B. von schwankender Stabilität der Marktpreise, Beständigkeit oder Verderblichkeit des Kaufgegenstandes, von der Notwendigkeit, Informationen einzuholen, mit Vorlieferanten, Subunternehmern, Kreditgebern zu verhandeln, von dem mit einem Kauf verfolgten Zweck, der Durchführung bis zu einem bestimmten Datum verlangen kann (Weihnachtsbäume usw.). Auch

---

[107] Zu Ausschreibungen und CISG s. oben Vor Artt. 14–24 Rn. 30.
[108] KG Freiburg, 11.10.2004, CISG-online 964 = IHR 2005, 72, 74.
[109] RG, 8.2.1902, RGZ 50, 191 ff., 195.
[110] OLG Breslau, OLGRspr. 22, 148.
[111] OLG Hamburg, 20.1.1925, OLGRspr. 44, 130.
[112] KG, 7.4.1919, Recht 1920, Nr. 1140.
[113] Vgl. (zu Fristen in internationalen Schiedsverfahren) *Wegen/Wilske,* SchiedsVZ 2003, 124 ff.
[114] Vgl. *Baumgärtel/Laumen/Hepting,* Art. 18 WKR, Rn. 12–14 (auch zur Beweislast für Frist).
[115] *Brunner,* Art. 18, Rn. 3; *Honsell/Dornis,* Art. 18, Rn. 52; *Staudinger/Magnus,* Art. 18, Rn. 18; teilweise anders *Witz/Salger/Lorenz/Witz,* Art. 18, Rn. 24: Reisezeit des Angebots ist nicht einzubeziehen, da Frist erst ab Zugang der Offerte läuft.
[116] Dazu *Borges,* Verträge im elektronischen Geschäftsverkehr, S. 312 f.; *Wulf,* S. 87.
[117] *Paefgen,* JuS 1988, 592, 596 f.; teilweise a. A. *Borges,* Verträge im elektronischen Geschäftsverkehr, S. 313, der danach differenzieren will, ob die Übermittlung per E-Mail wegen der Übermittlungsgeschwindigkeit (dann Folgen für die Annahmefrist) oder aus anderen Gründen gewählt wurde (dann keine Relevanz für Fristfrage).
[118] OLG Dresden, 30.11.2010, CISG-online 2183 = IHR 2011, 142, 145.

der Prozess der Entscheidungsbildung, der bei größeren Unternehmen oder im Falle von Exportregulierungen die Konsultation einer umfangreichen Bürokratie erfordern kann, ist bei der Beurteilung der „Überlegungsfrist" zu berücksichtigen.[119] Je komplexer oder komplizierter der angebotene Vertrag ist, desto länger wird die Überlegungsfrist zu bemessen sein. Freilich kann auch für die Überlegungsfrist das für die Offerte gewählte Kommunikationsmittel Bedeutung haben.[120] Dass ein auf einer Website im WWW enthaltenes Angebot[121] nach einer Ansicht im Schrifttum im Zweifel nur während der laufenden Web-Sitzung soll angenommen werden können,[122] überzeugt allerdings nicht; für die Fristenfrage kann es hier nicht auf die Verwendung einer Website als Erklärungsmedium, sondern nur auf die Auslegung der konkreten (Angebots-)Erklärung ankommen. Auf die Beurteilung der Angemessenheit einer Frist kann auch von Einfluss sein, ob die Offerte widerruflich oder unwiderruflich ist;[123] zudem können u. U. Bräuche konkretisieren, was im grenzüberschreitenden Verkehr in bestimmten Handelszweigen als „angemessene" Annahmefrist zu gelten hat.[124]

Generalisierende Formeln lassen sich nicht aufstellen; die (wenigen) Beispiele aus der bisherigen **Rechtsprechung** sind stark von den Umständen des Einzelfalles, vor allem der betroffenen Warenart geprägt.[125] Im Ganzen wird die „angemessene Frist" nicht nennenswert von dem abweichen, was dem deutschen Juristen in Anwendung des § 147 II BGB vertraut ist.

d) Rechtzeitige Annahme einer mündlichen Offerte. Eine mündliche Offerte muss, **16** falls sie befristet ist, innerhalb der Frist angenommen werden.[126] Unterlässt der Offerent eine solche Befristung, dann muss im Zweifel nach Art. 18 II 3 „sofort" angenommen werden, sofern sich aus den Umständen nichts anderes ergibt. Solche Umstände können Verhandlungen der Parteien,[127] die Notwendigkeit für den Angebotsempfänger, Informationen oder Genehmigungen einzuholen, seine fehlende Alleinvertretungsberechtigung[128] u. ä. sein. Die fristverlängernden Umstände müssen m. E. dem Offerenten bekannt sein, denn dem Akzeptanten ist es zuzumuten, auf in seiner Person oder in seinem Geschäftsbereich gegebene Umstände hinzuweisen.[129] Im Übrigen kann eine Befristung bzw. Fristverlängerung für ein mündliches Angebot auch noch erreicht werden, nachdem es abgegeben worden ist, z. B. wenn der Angebotsempfänger darum bittet, zunächst noch einen Vorlieferanten kontaktieren zu können.[130]

---

[119] Vgl. *Schlesinger/Lorenz*, Bd. 2, S. 1525; *Enderlein/Maskow/Strohbach*, Art. 18, Anm. 9.: Prüfung, ob die auf Grund staatlicher Lenkungsmaßnahmen erforderliche Genehmigung zu erhalten ist.
[120] So *Enderlein/Maskow/Strohbach*, Art. 18, Anm. 9.
[121] Regelmäßig wird es sich bei einer Warenpräsentation im WWW allerdings nur im eine invitatio ad offerendum handeln; s. dazu oben Art. 14 Rn. 28.
[122] *Borges*, Verträge im elektronischen Geschäftsverkehr, S. 313.
[123] Vgl. *Dölle/Schlechtriem*, Art. 8 EAG, Rn. 11.
[124] Vgl. hierzu den im Jahr 1924 entschiedenen Schweizer Fall BGer, 28.1.1924, BGE 50 II 13, 17: Aufgrund einer Reihe von „Bescheinigungen" von Eiergroßhändlern wurde davon ausgegangen, dass im internationalen Eierhandel ein Offerent „auch bei dringlichem Telegrammwechsel übungsgemäß 24 Stunden an seine Offerte gebunden bleibe" (S. 18). Allerdings könnte man in diesem Fall auch Geltung eines entsprechenden Handelsbrauchs für die Befristung von Offerten im grenzüberschreitenden Eierhandel nach Art. 9 II annehmen, so dass es sich eher um eine Ausfüllung des wertungsoffenen Begriffs „angemessen" gar nicht mehr bedarf.
[125] Vgl. zum CISG LG Bielefeld, 18.1.1991, CISG-online 174: 2 Wochen bei Telefaxofferte über entschwarteten Speck noch angemessen; LG Hamburg, 21.12.2001, CISG-online 1092: 2 Monate bei Angebot über Natursteinplatten zu lang; OLG Dresden, 30.11.2010, CISG-online 2183 = IHR 2011, 142, 145: bei Offerte per E-mail allenfalls 1 Woche angemessen; zum EAG LG Bielefeld, 5.6.1987, IPRax 1988, 229 einerseits (7 Wochen bei angebotener Jeansware zu lang); andererseits OLG Koblenz, 23.12.1988, RIW 1989, 384 (6 Wochen bei Feindraht und fernschriftlichem Angebot noch angemessen).
[126] KG Freiburg, 11.10.2004, CISG-online 964 = IHR 2005, 72, 74; s. *Bianca/Bonell/Farnsworth*, Art. 18, Anm. 2.6.; *Enderlein/Maskow/Strohbach*, Art. 18, Anm. 11.
[127] *Enderlein/Maskow/Strohbach*, Art. 18, Anm. 11.; *Soergel/Lüderitz/Fenge*, Art. 18, Rn. 8; *Staudinger/Magnus*, Art. 18, Rn. 20.
[128] *MünchKomm/Gruber*, Art. 18, Rn. 17; *Witz/Salger/Lorenz/Witz*, Art. 18, Rn. 23.
[129] *Enderlein/Maskow/Strohbach*, Art. 18, Anm. 11.; *Dölle/Schlechtriem*, Art. 8 EAG, Rn. 15.
[130] S. zu solchen Fällen *Dölle/Schlechtriem*, Art. 8 EAG, Rn. 17.

„Sofort" bedeutet wie in § 147 BGB nicht nur unverzügliche Antwort, d. h. eine solche ohne schuldhaftes Zögern, sondern eine zeitlich unmittelbar an die Äußerung des Angebots anschließende Erklärung.[131]

17 e) „Mündlich", Abgrenzung zu anderen Kommunikationsmitteln. Als **mündliche Erklärung** ist zunächst das gesprochene Wort unter Anwesenden zu verstehen. Auch **telefonische Kommunikation** ist entsprechend § 147 I 2 BGB mündliche.[132] Dem Telefon stehen andere elektronische Kommunikationsmittel gleich, die gesprochene Erklärungen sofort vernehmbar übermitteln und unmittelbare Beantwortung auf gleichem Wege ermöglichen,[133] z. B. **Funkverkehr**,[134] **Videokonferenzen** und sonstige elektronische Kommunikation in Echtzeit, wie etwa in **Chat-Foren** im Internet.[135] Dagegen fallen verkörperte Erklärungen, auch wenn sie elektronisch übermittelt und erst beim Empfänger ausgedruckt werden (Telex, Telefax), nicht unter den Begriff „mündliches Angebot".[136] Auch elektronische Kommunikation per **E-Mail** kann nicht als „mündliche" behandelt werden,[137] doch wird die Wahl eines derartigen interaktiven Kommunikationsmittels regelmäßig zu einer erheblichen Verkürzung der angemessenen Frist (oben Rn. 15) führen.

Das von einem **Vertreter,** evtl. von Vertreter zu Vertreter gemachte Angebot ist ein mündliches, sofern der Erklärende bzw. beide Vertreter die erforderliche Vollmacht haben.[138] Die durch einen **Erklärungsboten** übermittelte oder einem Empfangsboten erklärte Offerte ist ebenfalls als mündliche einzuordnen, doch gehört die Erforderlichkeit der Weiterleitung an den Adressaten bzw. die zu überwindende räumliche Distanz zwischen Adressaten und Offerenten in diesem Falle zu den Umständen, die eine sofortige Annahme ausschließen und deshalb Befristung bedeuten können.

3. Rechtzeitigkeit und Wirkung der nicht zugangsbedürftigen Äußerung der Zustimmung (Annahme)

18 a) **Handlungen.** Art. 18 III lässt eine Äußerung der Zustimmung unter bestimmten Voraussetzungen[139] auch **ohne Zugang** und bereits „zum Zeitpunkt der Handlung" wirksam sein. Nach nationalem Recht zu beurteilende Wirksamkeitserfordernisse wie Geschäftsfähigkeit, ordnungsgemäße Vertretung,[140] Abwesenheit von Willensmängeln müssen wie bei den erklärungsäquivalenten, aber zugangsbedürftigen Zustimmungen durch Verhalten[141] gegeben sein. **Beispiele** für Verhaltensweisen, die Zustimmung zum Ausdruck bringen und auf Grund der besonderen Voraussetzungen nach Abs. 3 unmittelbar als Annahme wirken, sind die bereits oben in Rn. 7 ff. sowie die im Text des Abs. 3 exemplarisch genannten Fälle und dabei vor allem solche Handlungen, bei denen ein Zugang der damit zum Ausdruck gebrachten Zustimmung regelmäßig nicht für erforderlich gehalten wird, z. B. Verarbeitung der Ware oder

---

[131] *Dölle/Schlechtriem*, Art. 8 EAG, Rn. 14; dort auch zur Vorgeschichte des entsprechenden Art. 8 I 2 EAG, in dem die Wortwahl „sofort" eine bewusste Entscheidung gegen Anträge war, auch bei mündlichen Offerten eine „reasonable time" zur Überlegung zu lassen; s. *von Caemmerer*, RabelsZ 29 (1965), 101, 129; ferner *Soergel/Lüderitz/Fenge*, Art. 18, Rn. 8. A. A. *Honsell/Dornis*, Art. 18, Rn. 45.
[132] Cour de Justice Genève, 13.9.2002, CISG-online 722; MünchKomm/*Gruber*, Art. 18, Rn. 15.
[133] Cour de Justice Genève, 13.9.2002, CISG-online 722.
[134] *Schwimann/Posch*, Art. 18, Rn. 6.
[135] CISG-AC, Op. 1 *(Chr. Ramberg)*, Comment 18.4 = IHR 2003, 244, 247.
[136] Cour de Justice Genève, 13.9.2002, CISG-online 722 (zum Telefax); *Enderlein/Maskow/Strohbach*, Art. 18, Anm. 10.: Ein über Telex gegebenes Angebot zählt nicht als mündliches; *Staudinger/Magnus*, Art. 18, Rn. 21.
[137] *Brunner*, Art. 18, Rn. 3; *Staudinger/Magnus*, Art. 18, Rn. 21.
[138] Beim Vertreter des Adressaten der Offerte genügt Empfangsvollmacht, doch dürfte in der Tatsache, dass er selbst keine Annahme erklären kann, einer der Umstände zu sehen sein, aus denen sich eine angemessene Befristung des mündlichen Angebots ergibt, vgl. *Dölle/Schlechtriem*, Art. 8 EAG, Rn. 19.
[139] Dies betonend *Honnold/Flechtner*, Art. 18, Rn. 163.
[140] BGH, 18.12.1985, NJW-RR 1986, 415 f.
[141] S. oben Rn. 7 ff.

Direktleistung an einen Dritten.[142] In der Rechtsprechung ist dies etwa für das Versenden eines „reference letters" durch einen Pharmazulieferer an eine Gesundheitsbehörde (FDA) angenommen worden, in welchem die künftige Belieferung des bestellenden Arzneimittelproduzenten zugesagt wurde.[143] Markiert der Empfänger eines Angebots über geschlagenes Holz die Stämme mit seinem Zeichen, so kann das ebenfalls Annahme bedeuten.[144] Bei Einlösung eines Schecks geschieht Annahme bereits mit Einreichung, nicht erst mit der Gutschrift, der Belastungsbuchung oder der entsprechenden Benachrichtigung des Ausstellers durch die bezogene Bank.[145] Für die Auslegung eines annahmeäquivalenten Verhaltens gilt Art. 8.[146]

b) Nicht zugangsbedürftige Erklärungen? Ob mit nicht zugangsbedürftigen „Zustimmungsäußerungen" nur **annahmeäquivalente Handlungen** oder auch verbale Erklärungen gemeint sind, ist streitig.[147] Man wendet gegen letzteres ein, ein Verzicht auf den Zugang einer verbalen Annahmeerklärung würde das Verlustrisiko dem Offerenten aufbürden und bei verspätetem Zugang der Annahmeerklärung einen Vertragsschluss bei rechtzeitiger Absendung geschehen lassen, ohne dass es auf Art. 21 II ankäme. Auch der Wortlaut („Handlung") und die beiden in Abs. 3 genannten Beispiele „Absendung der Ware" oder „Zahlung des Preises", die bei Ausarbeitung des Übereinkommens mehrfach als die einzigen Fälle einer zugangslosen Annahme geregelt werden sollten, sprächen dagegen, eine **erklärte** Annahme nach Abs. 3 bereits mit Erklärung oder Absendung wirken zu lassen. M. E. hängt die Frage jedoch von den weiteren Voraussetzungen ab, die für die Wirkung eines annahmeäquivalenten Verhaltens ohne Zugang gegeben sein müssen, so dass durchaus auch Absendung einer Annahmeerklärung genügen kann.[148]

c) Rechtzeitigkeit. Für die **Rechtzeitigkeit** des annahmeäquivalenten Verhaltens ist erforderlich, dass es innerhalb der in Abs. 2 vorgeschriebenen Frist stattgefunden hat.[149] Die diesbezügliche **Beweislast** trägt der Annehmende, dessen Sphäre dieser Vorgang zuzurechnen ist.[150]

4. Voraussetzungen der Annahme ohne Zugang einer entsprechenden Äußerung

a) Ausgestaltung der Offerte. Eine **zugangslose Zustimmungsäußerung** ist möglich und wirksam, wenn der Offerent dies so angeboten hat. Das entspricht § 151 BGB. Als Beispiele solcher Vorschläge in der Offerte werden Formulierungen genannt wie „ship immediately", „rush shipment",[151] „erbitte unverzügliche Absendung".[152] Da letztlich die den Parteien durch Art. 6 eingeräumte Freiheit erlaubt, auch von den Regeln des Vertrags-

---

[142] Vgl. RG, 20.5.1930, RGZ 129, 109, 113 f. Zu den Erfüllungs-, Aneignungs- oder Gebrauchshandlungen im französischen, schweizerischen und österreichischen Recht informativ *Augner*, S. 58 f., 142 ff., 149 ff.
[143] *Geneva Pharmaceuticals Technology Corp. v. Barr Laboratories, Inc.,* U. S. Dist. Ct. (S. D. N. Y.), 10.5.2002, CISG-online 653 = 201 F. Supp. 2d 236, 282.
[144] Vgl. Com., 28.11.1956, Bull. Civ. III, no. 317.
[145] S. LG Kassel, 15.2.1996, CISG-online 190, wo der Offerent selbst „Einlösung oder Rücksendung" des Schecks vorgeschlagen hatte.
[146] Vgl. *Mattera*, 16 Pace Int'l L. Rev. (2004), 165, 184; *Stern*, Erklärungen, Rn. 80.
[147] *Wey*, Rn. 951, 952 möchte auf die annahmeäquivalenten Handlungen beschränken; Art. 18 III sei nicht auf ausdrückliche Erklärungsformen zugeschnitten; ebenso *Neumayer/Ming*, Art. 18, Anm. 6.; *Bianca/Bonell/Farnsworth*, Art. 18, Anm. 2.8.; *Enderlein/Maskow/Strohbach*, Art. 18, Anm. 12. Auf das im Wortlaut der Vorschrift verwendete Wort „Handlung" stellen offenbar auch *Enderlein/Maskow/Strohbach*, Art. 18, Anm. 12., ab („genügt ... die Vornahme der schlüssigen Handlung"). Für Gleichbehandlung dagegen *Honsell/Dornis*, Art. 18, Rn. 37; MünchKomm/*Gruber*, Art. 18, Rn. 8; wohl auch *Witz/Salger/Lorenz/Witz*, Art. 18, Rn. 10; nicht eindeutig *Staudinger/Magnus*, Art. 18, Rn. 25, 28.
[148] S. hierzu im Text Rn. 20–22.
[149] *Honnold/Flechtner*, Art. 18, Rn. 164; *Schwimann/Posch*, Art. 18, Rn. 8.
[150] *Baumgärtel/Laumen/Hepting*, Art. 18 WKR, Rn. 22; *Schwimann/Posch*, Art. 18, Rn. 8; *Staudinger/Magnus*, Art. 18, Rn. 30; a. A. MünchKomm/*Gruber*, Art. 18, Rn. 29.
[151] S. Sekretariatskommentar, Art. 16, Nr. 11 *Bianca/Bonell/Farnsworth*, Art. 18, Anm. 3.4.; *Brunner*, Art. 18, Rn. 4.
[152] *Enderlein/Maskow/Strohbach*, Art. 18, Anm. 12.; MünchKomm/*Gruber*, Art. 18, Rn. 9.

schlussverfahrens und damit vom Zugangsprinzip abzuweichen, muss es m. E. auch möglich sein, bereits in der Absendung der Annahmeerklärung eine „Handlung" i. S. d. Abs. 3 zu sehen, sofern der Offerent das so vorgeschlagen hat.[153]

21   **b) Gepflogenheiten u. ä.** Eine annahmeäquivalente Handlung kann bereits mit ihrer Vornahme wirksam sein, wenn sich entsprechende **Gepflogenheiten** zwischen den Parteien gebildet haben oder **Handelsbräuche**, die nach Art. 9 I oder II einschlägig sind, eine solche Regelung enthalten.[154] Vor allem die Gepflogenheiten zwischen den Parteien, die durch langdauernde Geschäftsbeziehungen etabliert worden sind, werden häufig einem bestimmten Verhalten des Oblaten nicht nur Erklärungsbedeutung verleihen, sondern auch einen Verzicht auf einen Zugang der so ausgedrückten Zustimmung beinhalten. Wo sogar **Rahmenvereinbarungen** zwischen den Parteien bestehen, kann einem annahmeäquivalenten Verhalten erst recht entsprechende Wirkung beigelegt worden sein.

22   **c) Wirkung.** Die Wirkung einer annahmeäquivalenten Handlung tritt, falls die Offerte, Gepflogenheiten zwischen den Parteien oder anwendbare Bräuche es so vorsehen, direkt mit der **Vornahme** ein. Eine Mitteilung an den Offerenten ist zur Wirksamkeit oder Rechtzeitigkeit der schlüssig erklärten Annahme nicht erforderlich.[155]

Soweit die Parteien ausnahmsweise, z. B. auf Grund entsprechender Rahmenvereinbarungen, **Schweigen** bzw. **Untätigkeit** als Annahme gelten lassen,[156] kommt der Vertrag grundsätzlich mit Schweigen nach Zugang der Offerte zustande, sofern nicht der Adressat widerspricht. Allerdings können die Umstände, aus denen sich die Erklärungsbedeutung des Schweigens als Annahme ergibt, anderes ergeben, z. B. Gepflogenheiten, Brauch oder Rahmenvereinbarung vorsehen, dass Nichtäußerung innerhalb einer bestimmten Frist Annahme bedeutet. Im letzteren Falle erlangt das Schweigen Erklärungsbedeutung erst mit Ablauf dieser Frist.[157]

Grundsätzlich kann annahmeäquivalentes Verhalten oder Schweigen **nicht zurückgenommen** werden, da es den Vertrag perfektioniert hat.[158] Nur wenn dem Oblaten eine Entscheidungsfrist gewährt worden und der Offerent noch in Unkenntnis des Annahmeverhaltens ist oder sich selbst Widerruf bis zum Fristablauf vorbehalten hat, kann ausnahmsweise die Rücknahme der Wirkungen des annahmeäquivalenten Verhaltens durch gegensätzliches Verhalten (z. B. Rücksendung der zunächst behaltenen Ware, Rücknahme einer Akkreditiveröffnung), durch Angebotsablehnung nach Art. 17 oder durch Rücknahmeerklärung nach Art. 22 in Betracht kommen. Auch in solchen Fällen wird aber eine Rücknahme oft am Verbot widersprüchlichen Verhaltens, das auf Art. 7 II i. V. m. Artt. 16 II lit. b), 29 II 2 zu stützen ist, scheitern, so, wenn der Angebotsempfänger durch Gebrauch übersandter Ware vor Ablauf der Angebotsfrist und in Unkenntnis des Offerenten angenommen hat und nun durch Rücksendung sein Annahmeverhalten rückgängig machen

---

[153] Wie hier *Honsell/Dornis*, Art. 18, Rn. 37; vgl. auch *Bianca/Bonell/Farnsworth*, Art. 18, Anm. 2.8., der Art. 18 III nur als spezielle Ausprägung der allgemeinen Regel in Art. 6 sieht. *Farnsworths'* Bedenken, es fehle ja noch an einer Art. 18 I, II derogierenden Einigung, kann damit ausgeräumt werden, dass das diesbezügliche Angebot des Offerenten ebenfalls zugangslos angenommen werden kann.
[154] Vgl. *Geneva Pharmaceuticals Technology Corp. v. Barr Laboratories, Inc.*, U. S. Dist. Ct. (S. D. N. Y.), 10.5.2002, CISG-online 653 = 201 F. Supp. 2d 236, 282: „industry custom" unter U. S.-amerikanischen Arzneimittelhersteller und ihren Zulieferern.
[155] S. *Bianca/Bonell/Farnsworth*, Art. 18, Anm. 2.8., 2.9.; *Joseph*, 3 Dick. J. Int'l L. (1984), 107, 131; *Honsell/Dornis*, Art. 18, Rn. 38; *Soergel/Lüderitz/Fenge*, Art. 18, Rn. 11; *Staudinger/Magnus*, Art. 18, Rn. 29; a. A. *Honnold/Flechtner*, Art. 18, Rn. 164, die davon ausgehen, dass auch im Falle des Abs. 3 der Ausdruck der Zustimmung noch übermittelt werden müsse. Ein entsprechender amerikanischer Antrag auf der Wiener Konferenz jedoch keine Unterstützung gefunden und wurde deshalb zurückgezogen, s. O. R., S. 95, 280 f. Man kann deshalb die in Wien abgelehnte Lösung nicht in den Text von Art. 18 III hineinlesen, s. hierzu noch unten Rn. 23.
[156] S. oben Rn. 9.
[157] Ausführlich zu diesen Fällen *Wey*, Rn. 977–980, 1147–1151.
[158] Vgl. *Stern*, Erklärungen, Rn. 81; *Wey*, Rn. 977, 1070; s. a. Art. 22 Rn. 3; MünchKomm/*Gruber*, Art. 18, Rn. 10; *Soergel/Lüderitz/Fenge*, Art. 18, Rn. 13, 14; *Staudinger/Magnus*, Art. 18, Rn. 28.

IV. Mitteilungsobliegenheit oder -nebenpflicht

Entgegen der Ansicht von *Honnold*[159] kommt der Vertrag durch annahmeäquivalentes **23** Verhalten unter den Voraussetzungen des Art. 18 III auch **ohne** entsprechende **Mitteilung an den Offerenten** zustande.[160] Der Offerent kann deshalb in eine vertragliche Bindung hineingeraten, ohne davon Kenntnis zu erhalten.

Fraglich könnte sein, ob der so zustande gebrachte Vertrag eine **Nebenpflicht** für den Annehmenden entstehen lässt, den Offerenten nicht im Ungewissen zu lassen, d. h. ihn zu benachrichtigen. M. E. kann eine solche Nebenpflicht zur Mitteilung nur aus einer Interpretation der Parteierklärungen im Lichte der zwischen den Beteiligten bestehenden Gepflogenheiten – Art. 8 III – oder ausnahmsweise auf Grund von Bräuchen entstehen; sie ist jedenfalls vertragliche Nebenpflicht und damit Sachfrage der Vertragsauslegung, nicht gesetzliche Pflicht, die auf Grund der Vertragsanbahnung entsteht.[161] Ihre Verletzung kann Schadenersatzpflichten auslösen; für den Inhalt des Schadenersatzanspruchs gelten die Artt. 74 ff. entsprechend. Ein Rückgriff auf nationales Recht zur Begründung – culpa in contrahendo – und zum Inhalt einer solchen Schadenersatzpflicht ist abzulehnen.[162]

Schweigt der Oblat, ohne dass Schweigen ausnahmsweise annahmeäquivalent ist, vertraut aber der Offerent fälschlich auf das Schweigen und nimmt einen Vertragsschluss an, dann hat m. E. ein Rückgriff auf nationale Rechtsbehelfe auszuscheiden: Schweigen und seine Bedeutung für einen Vertragsschluss sind eine von CISG abschließend geregelte Materie; Haftung des Schweigenden aus culpa in contrahendo in Fällen, in denen das CISG seinem schweigenden Verhalten keine Rechtswirkungen zukommen lässt, würde die Regelung des Art. 18 und die ihm zugrunde liegende Wertung teilweise korrigieren. Auch hier kann allenfalls eine unabhängig vom gescheiterten Vertrag auf Grund von Gepflogenheiten der Parteien oder Bräuchen entstandene Mitteilungspflicht in Betracht kommen, deren Verletzung nach CISG-Regeln beurteilt werden sollte.

---

[159] *Honnold/Flechtner*, Art. 18, Rn. 164; ähnlich wohl auch *Neumayer/Ming*, Art. 18, Anm. 8.
[160] Überzeugend *Herber/Czerwenka*, Art. 18, Rn. 13; ferner *Brunner*, Art. 18, Rn. 4; *Schwimann/Posch*, Art. 18, Rn. 8; *Soergel/Lüderitz/Fenge*, Art. 18, Rn. 11 (Ausnahmen möglich); *Staudinger/Magnus*, Art. 18, Rn. 29; *Witz/Salger/Lorenz/Witz*, Art. 18, Rn. 9; ausführlich zu der – in Wien abgelehnten – amerikanischen Auffassung, dass nach Art. 18 III zwar Annahme erfolgt, Perfektionierung des Vertrages aber einer Mitteilung bedarf, *Stern*, Erklärungen, Rn. 73–76; s. auch oben Rn. 13, 22 m. w. N.
[161] Vgl. zum EAG *von Caemmerer*, RabelsZ 29 (1965), 101, 125: E 1958 sah noch eine Mitteilungspflicht vor, deren Verletzung Schadensersatzfolgen auslösen konnte. Man hat diese Bestimmung jedoch gestrichen, da für derartige Nebenpflichten und ihre Verletzung der geschlossene Vertrag maßgebend sei. Eine Nebenpflicht befürworten *Enderlein/Maskow/Strohbach*, Art. 18, Anm. 16.; *MünchKomm/Gruber*, Art. 18, Rn. 11; *Rehbinder*, Vertragsschluss, S. 161; wie hier *Honsell/Dornis*, Art. 18, Rn. 37; *Staudinger/Magnus*, Art. 18, Rn. 29.
[162] Zur Anwendung von culpa in contrahendo-Grundsätzen neben dem CISG generell s. oben Vor Artt. 14–24 Rn. 1, 32.

Art. 19 [Ergänzungen, Einschränkungen und sonstige Änderungen zum Angebot]

(1) Eine Antwort auf ein Angebot, die eine Annahme darstellen soll, aber Ergänzungen, Einschränkungen oder sonstige Änderungen enthält, ist eine Ablehnung des Angebots und stellt ein Gegenangebot dar.

(2) Eine Antwort auf ein Angebot, die eine Annahme darstellen soll, aber Ergänzungen oder Abweichungen enthält, welche die Bedingungen des Angebots nicht wesentlich ändern, stellt jedoch eine Annahme dar, wenn der Anbietende das Fehlen der Übereinstimmung nicht unverzüglich mündlich beanstandet oder eine entsprechende Mitteilung absendet. Unterläßt er dies, so bilden die Bedingungen des Angebots mit den in der Annahme enthaltenen Änderungen den Vertragsinhalt.

(3) Ergänzungen oder Abweichungen, die sich insbesondere auf Preis, Bezahlung, Qualität und Menge der Ware, auf Ort und Zeit der Lieferung, auf den Umfang der Haftung der einen Partei gegenüber der anderen oder auf die Beilegung von Streitigkeiten beziehen, werden so angesehen, als änderten sie die Bedingungen des Angebots wesentlich.

Art. 19

(1) A reply to an offer which purports to be an acceptance but contains additions, limitations or other modifications is a rejection of the offer and constitutes a counter-offer.

(2) However, a reply to an offer which purports to be an acceptance but contains additional or different terms which do not materially alter the terms of the offer constitutes an acceptance, unless the offeror, without undue delay, objects orally to the discrepancy or dispatches a notice to that effect. If he does not so object, the terms of the contract are the terms of the offer with the modifications contained in the acceptance.

(3) Additional or different terms relating, among other things, to the price, payment, quality and quantity of the goods, place and time of delivery, extent of one party's liability to the other or the settlement of disputes are considered to alter the terms of the offer materially.

Art. 19

1) Une réponse qui tend à être l'acceptation d'une offre, mais qui contient des additions, les limitations ou autres modifications, est un rejet de l'offre et constitue une contre-offre.

2) Cependant, une réponse qui tend à être l'acceptation d'une offre, mais qui contient des éléments complémentaires ou différents n'altérant pas substantiellement les termes de l'offre, constitue une acceptation, à moins que l'auteur de l'offre, sans retard injustifié, n'en relève les différences verbalement ou n'adresse un avis à cet effet. S'il ne le fait pas, les termes du contrat sont ceux de l'offre, avec les modifications comprises dans l'acceptation.

3) Des éléments complémentaires ou différents relatifs notamment au prix, au paiement, à la qualité et à la quantité des marchandises, au lieu et au moment de la livraison, à l'étendue de la responsabilité d'une partie à l'égard de l'autre ou au règlement des différends, sont considérés comme altérant substantiellement les termes de l'offre.

Übersicht

	Rn.
I. Grundzüge	1
1. Vorgeschichte	1
2. Grundzüge des Art. 19 I	2
3. Grundzüge und Geschichte des Art. 19 II	3
4. Bestätigungsschreiben und kollidierende Geschäftsbedingungen in den Beratungen	4
II. Wesentliche Abweichungen	5
1. Abweichungen	5
a) Abgrenzung von der Einigkeit in der Sache	5
b) Ergänzungen zur Offerte	6
c) Erwartungen und Vorschläge des Annehmenden	7

d) Wesentliche Abweichungen nach Art. 19 III	8
aa) Erfasste Fälle	8a
bb) Art. 19 III als widerlegbare Auslegungsregel	8b
e) Wesentliche Abweichungen im Übrigen	9
2. Rechtsfolge wesentlicher Abweichungen	10
a) Ablehnung des Angebots	10
b) Gegenofferte	11
c) Annahme der Gegenofferte	12
III. Unwesentliche Abweichungen	13
1. Abweichungen	13
2. Rechtsfolgen unwesentlicher Abweichungen	14
a) Unwesentliche Ergänzungen oder Abweichungen	14
b) Widerspruch	15
c) „Unverzüglich"	16
d) Rechtzeitiger Widerspruch	18
IV. Kollidierende Standardbedingungen	19
1. Problemstellung	19
2. Lösungsansätze für die „battle of the forms"	21
a) Theorie des letzten Wortes	22
b) Restgültigkeitstheorie	23
c) Generelles Scheitern des Vertragsschlusses	24
3. Stellungnahme	25
a) Vertragsschluss trotz sich inhaltlich widersprechender Standardbedingungen	26
aa) Vorausgegangener mündlicher Vertragsschluss	27
bb) (Konkludente) Abbedingung des Art. 19 durch die Parteien	28
cc) Vertragsschluss bei Eingreifen des Art. 19	32
b) Vertragsinhalt	34

Vorläufer und **Entwürfe:** New Yorker E 1977 Art. 7, Genfer E 1977 Art. 13, New Yorker E 1978 Art. 17.

I. Grundzüge

1. Vorgeschichte

Art. 19 unterscheidet zwischen wesentlichen und unwesentlichen Divergenzen von Offerte und Annahme. Diese erstmals auf der Haager Konferenz nach dem Vorbild des schwedischen Vertragsgesetzes von 1915 eingeführte Unterscheidung[1] sollte der Gefahr vorbeugen, dass entsprechend der „mirror image rule" des Common Law geringfügige Differenzen zwischen Offerte und Annahmeerklärung zum Anlass genommen werden, einen als belastend empfundenen Vertrag als nicht zustande gekommen abzulehnen.[2]

Die Vorschrift hat sich kaum bewährt. Der entscheidende Grund für die in Anwendung des Art. 19 immer wieder auftretenden Schwierigkeiten und dadurch erforderlich werdende Gerichtsurteile ist in der Verknüpfung von endgültigem Vertragsschluss und Gestaltung des Vertragsinhalts zu sehen (vgl. oben Vor Artt. 14–24 Rn. 15): Das Fehlen einer Vorschrift, die Zustandekommen eines Vertrages trotz partiellen Dissens (vgl. §§ 154, 155 BGB) oder überhaupt ohne identifizierbare oder trotz divergierender Einzelerklärungen „Angebot" und „Annahme" ermöglicht, verursacht vor allem bei beiderseitiger Verwendung von Standardbedingungen immer wieder Probleme, deren Entscheidung durch Gerichte oft weder im Ergebnis noch in der konstruktiven Begründung voll überzeugen kann (s. unten Rn. 19 ff.) und die eine inzwischen unübersehbar gewordene Literatur veranlasst haben. Auch für neue Vertriebsformen, die zwischen den Parteien Dauerbeziehungen begründen –

---

[1] Zur Geschichte s. *von Caemmerer,* RabelsZ 29 (1965), 101, 127; *Schmidt,* 14 Am. J. Comp. L. (1965), 1, 23 ff.

[2] Vgl. *Farnsworth,* Formation of Contract, § 3.04 sub 3–15; *Vergne,* 33 Am. J. Comp. L. (1985), 233, 235 ff.; umfassend zur Entstehungsgeschichte *Perales Viscasillas,* Formación del contrato, S. 626 ff.; *van Alstine,* S. 195 ff.

etwa durch Rahmenverträge –, passt die auf einen singulären Vertrag und seinen Abschluss zugeschnittene Vorschrift nur bedingt.[3]

2. Grundzüge des Art. 19 I

2 Art. 19 I entspricht § 150 II BGB und kann als „traditionelle",[4] allgemein anerkannte[5] Regel gelten. Er ist im Verlauf der Beratungen nur sprachlich durch die Formulierung „Antwort …, die Annahme darstellen soll" verändert worden, um Annahmeerklärungen, die zusätzlich Rückfragen oder unverbindliche Vorschläge enthalten, nicht als Gegenofferten behandeln zu müssen.[6]

3. Grundzüge und Geschichte des Art. 19 II

3 Zu Art. 19 II gab es – wie schon zu Art. 7 II EAG[7] – immer wieder Vorstöße, die auf Beseitigung der Unterscheidung von wesentlichen und unwesentlichen Modifikationen als zu unsicher und schwer handhabbar abzielten,[8] und noch auf der Wiener Konferenz war es zu langen Debatten auf Grund entsprechender Anträge gekommen.[9] Bereits die Arbeitsgruppe hatte einen Kompromiss durch eine Regel – jetzt Art. 19 III – versucht, die Grenzziehung durch beispielhafte Aufzählung wesentlicher Abweichungen erleichtern sollte.[10] Diese Regel wurde jedoch auf der Wiener Konferenz dadurch verschärft, dass eine im Entwurf enthaltene mildernde, weil auf die Sicht des Angebotsempfängers abstellende Formel gestrichen wurde.[11]

4. Bestätigungsschreiben und kollidierende Geschäftsbedingungen in den Beratungen

4 Aus der Entstehungsgeschichte wird deutlich, dass mit Art. 19 auch zwei Sachfragen entschieden worden sind, die oft im Zusammenhang mit Vorschriften wie § 150 II BGB diskutiert werden: Die Arbeitsgruppe hat einen Vorschlag verworfen, **Bestätigungsschreiben mit unwesentlichen Änderungen oder Ergänzungen** vertragsmodifizierende Wirkung beizumessen, sofern der Empfänger nicht widerspricht.[12] Darin ist die Entscheidung zu sehen, dass einerseits Bestätigungsschreiben als eine vom CISG umfasste Materie gesehen und beraten worden sind, dass man aber andererseits die dem deutschen Juristen vertraute Wirkung solcher Schreiben nicht als gesetzliche Regel übernehmen wollte.[13] Auch eine

---

[3] Vgl. *Windbichler*, AcP 198 (1998), 262, 275, Fn. 57.
[4] So *Bianca/Bonell/Farnsworth*, Art. 19, Anm. 1.1.
[5] *Schlesinger*, Bd. 1, S. 125 f.; *von Mehren*, Sec. 155 ff.
[6] S. YB IX (1978), S. 42, Nr. 154; *Bianca/Bonell/Farnsworth*, Art. 19, Anm. 1.3.
[7] Dazu *von Caemmerer*, RabelsZ 29 (1965), 101, 127, Fn. 107.
[8] Vgl. YB IX (1978), S. 42, Nr. 156: „… would cause great uncertainty … lead to divergent judicial interpretations …".
[9] S. O. R., S. 284–286; *Farnsworth* bezeichnet die beiden Ansichten als „Traditionalisten" (für alleinige Geltung der Regelung des Art. 19 I = § 150 II BGB) und „Reformer" (in: *Bianca/Bonell*, Art. 19, Anm. 1.4.–1.6.); die Geschichte des Art. 19 II nennt *Farnsworth* „tumultuous". Eingehend dazu auch *Vergne*, 33 Am. J. Comp. L. (1985), 233, 235 ff.
[10] S. YB IX (1978), S. 43, Nr. 164 ff.
[11] Dazu *Bianca/Bonell/Farnsworth*, Art. 19, Anm. 1.6., der darin einen Sieg der „Traditionalisten" über die „Reformer" sieht. Ausführlich auch *Vergne*, 33 Am. J. Comp. L. (1985), 233, 235 ff. Zur Entstehung s. auch die Dokumentation bei *Kritzer*, Guide to Practical Applications, S. 178a, 178b.
[12] S. YB VIII (1977), S. 82, Nr. 105, 111 f.; YB IX (1978), S. 78, Nr. 228; S. 92, Nr. 7, 8; zu entsprechenden Versuchen, das kaufmännische Bestätigungsschreiben im Zusammenhang des Art. 7 II EAG zu regeln, s. *von Caemmerer*, RabelsZ 29 (1965), 101, 127. Angesichts der Behandlung und eindeutigen Entscheidung dieser Frage dürfte eine analoge Anwendung des Art. 19 II auf geringfügig vertragsmodifizierende Bestätigungen nicht möglich sein, so aber *Esser*, östZRVgl 1988, 167, 190 f.
[13] S. zur Vorgeschichte *Schlechtriem*, 1. und 2. Aufl., Rn. 4 sowie hier Vor Artt. 14–24 Rn. 18, Art. 18 Rn. 4.

besondere Regelung des Problems **kollidierender Geschäftsbedingungen** ist explizit unterblieben.[14]

II. Wesentliche Abweichungen

1. Abweichungen

a) **Abgrenzung von der Einigkeit in der Sache.** Abweichungen vom Angebot in der Annahmeerklärung müssen solche in der – durch Auslegung nach Art. 8 zu ermittelnden – Erklärungsbedeutung sein. Sind die Parteien in der Sache einig, dann sind sprachliche Divergenzen, wie sie sich gerade im grenzüberschreitenden Verkehr durch unvollkommene Übersetzungen oder unzureichende Beherrschung einer Fremdsprache einschleichen, aber auch als Tipp- oder Übermittlungsfehler entstehen können, keine Abweichung i. S. v. Art. 19. Trotz einer eventuellen falsa demonstratio stimmen die Vertragsschlusserklärungen in der Sache überein; es liegt materieller Konsens[15] vor und nicht etwa eine nur unwesentliche Abweichung, die nach Art. 19 II zu behandeln wäre.[16]

An einer von Art. 19 vorausgesetzten **Abweichung fehlt** es von vornherein auch dort, wo die Parteien eine regelungsbedürftige Frage vertraglich der Bestimmung durch eine der Parteien überlassen haben,[17] wie dies etwa in Bezug auf eine nach erfolgtem Vertragsschluss vorzunehmende Benennung von Verschiffungshafen, Schiff und genauem Lieferzeitpunkt überaus häufig vorkommt;[18] dasselbe gilt, wenn das Angebot dem Oblaten bestimmte Optionen präsentiert und ihm die Wahl zwischen den Vertragsvarianten überlässt.[19]

b) **Ergänzungen zur Offerte.** Art. 19 I greift, wie schon der Wortlaut ergibt, auch dann ein, wenn die Annahmeerklärung „**Ergänzungen**" enthält, also Regelungspunkte, zu denen die Offerte schweigt. Allerdings ist in solchen Fällen zunächst zu prüfen, ob nicht eine Auslegung der Offerte – insbesondere auch im Lichte der Verhandlungen zwischen den Parteien und der zwischen ihnen entstandenen Gepflogenheiten, Art. 8 III – ergibt, dass in ihr dieser Punkt bereits ebenso wie in der Annahmeerklärung vorgeschlagen worden ist, eine Divergenz also gar nicht vorliegt. Das dürfte regelmäßig der Fall sein, wenn der Annehmende Klauseln einführt, die den Regelungen des CISG entsprechen.[20] Auch Bräu-

---

[14] S. YB VIII (1977), S. 82, Nr. 105 (2b); S. 100, Nr. 12; *Enderlein/Maskow/Strohbach*, Art. 19, Anm. 10.; zu den Vorschlägen des Sekretariats und den Überlegungen der Arbeitsgruppe *Sutton*, 16 U. W. Ont. L. Rev. (1977), 113, 144–147; *Perales Viscasillas*, 10 Pace Int'l L. Rev. (1998), 97, 140 ff.; *Wey*, Rn. 1328 ff.; zur Wiener Konferenz s. O. R., S. 288 f.; *Schlechtriem*, Einheitliches UN-Kaufrecht, S. 43 f.; zur Entwicklung umfassend *van Alstine*, S. 195 ff., 207 ff.; *Neumayer*, Battle of Forms, S. 501, 513 ff.
[15] Tiefschürfend hierzu *Wey*, Rn. 580 ff., 1209 ff.; ferner *van der Velden*, Battle of Forms, S. 237; *Schmidt-Kessel*, Art. 8 Rn. 6.
[16] So aber offenbar *Bianca/Bonell/Farnsworth*, Art. 19, Anm. 1.5., der unter Verweis auf eine entsprechende Äußerung bei den Beratungen – YB IX (1978), S. 43, Nr. 159 – bei bloßen Unterschieden in der Wortwahl, grammatikalischen Änderungen oder typographischen Fehlern Abweichungen, wenn auch unwesentliche i. S. v. Abs. 2 annimmt. Wie hier *Brunner*, Art. 19, Rn. 2; *Honsell/Dornis*, Art. 19, Rn. 6; MünchKomm/*Gruber*, Art. 19, Rn. 5; *Staudinger/Magnus*, Art. 19, Rn. 9; wohl auch *Ludwig*, S. 331 f.
[17] MünchKomm/*Gruber*, Art. 19, Rn. 4.
[18] Unhaltbar daher die mexikanische Entscheidung *Kolmar Petrochemicals Americas v. Idesa Petroquímica*, Primer Tribunal Colegiado en Materia Civil del Primer Civcuito, 10.3.2005, CISG-online 1004: Die mexikanische Verkäuferin und die US-amerikanische Käuferin hatten vereinbart, dass die Verschiffung des verkauften Mono-Ethylenglykols im Januar 2003 vom Terminal der Verkäuferin in Coatzacoalcos (Mexiko) erfolgen und diese die genaueren Details mitteilen werde – nachdem die Verkäuferin vor dem Hintergrund gestiegener Marktpreise jedoch einen höheren Kaufpreis verlangt und die Käuferin daraufhin auf Lieferung geklagt hatte, verneinte das Gericht einen Vertragsschluss mit der Begründung, die Vereinbarung habe die in Art. 19 III genannten Gegenstände „Ort und Zeit der Lieferung" nicht spezifiziert; zutreffend hingegen (in einem ganz ähnlichen Fall) OGH, 6.2.1996, CISG-online 224 = ZfRVgl 1996, 248 ff.
[19] Vgl. OLG Koblenz, 1.3.2010, CISG-online 2126 = NJW-RR 2010, 1004, 1005: Angebot über Verkauf einer Asphaltmischanlage sah mehrere Vertragsvarianten vor, die sich in technischer Hinsicht unterschieden – Ablehnung einer dieser „Optionen" durch den Akzeptanten änderte nichts an der Annahme.
[20] *Honsell/Dornis*, Art. 19, Rn. 6; *Staudinger/Magnus*, Art. 19, Rn. 9.

che können zu einer Ergänzung der Offerte führen, so dass eine entsprechende „Ergänzung" durch den Annehmenden tatsächlich keine Abweichung bewirkt.[21] Enthält das Kaufangebot des Käufers keine ausdrückliche Aussage zur Übereignungspflicht des Verkäufers, dann kann sich gleichwohl im Wege der Auslegung auf Grund von Verhandlungen, Gepflogenheiten oder einer Rahmenvereinbarung, vielleicht sogar eines Brauchs i. S. v. Art. 9 ergeben, dass unter Eigentumsvorbehalt gekauft werden sollte – ein Eigentumsvorbehalt in der Annahmeerklärung des Verkäufers bewirkt deshalb keine abweichende Ergänzung.[22] Wo freilich die Offerte nicht durch Auslegung um die zusätzlichen Punkte, die in der Annahmeerklärung enthalten sind, ergänzt werden kann, bleibt es bei Art. 19. Soweit die Offerte schweigt, ist dann davon auszugehen, dass der Offerent von der ergänzenden Geltung der Vorschriften des CISG ausgeht, so dass Zusätze und Ergänzungen in der Annahmeerklärung auch mit der gesetzlichen Regelung des CISG und des Vertragsgesetzes verglichen werden müssen.[23] Enthält die Annahmeerklärung des Käufers eine Bestimmung, wonach jeder Mangel zum Rücktritt berechtigt, dann widerspricht das der in die Offerte des Verkäufers hineinzulesenden Regelung des Art. 49, die dem Käufer Aufhebung des Vertrages nur bei solchen Mängeln erlaubt, die einen wesentlichen Vertragsbruch darstellen. Eine einseitig vom Verkäufer eingeführte Bestimmung der Zinshöhe dürfte ebenfalls Modifikation sein, sofern sie nicht dem in Anwendung des Art. 78 i. V. m. über IPR berufenen Sachrecht entspricht. Wenn dagegen der Verkäufer in seiner Annahmeerklärung vorschreibt, dass der Käufer die Ware innerhalb kurzer Frist untersuchen und Mängel innerhalb angemessener Frist rügen muss, dann entspricht das der Regelung in den Artt. 38 und 39, die mangels anderer Vorschläge zu diesem Punkt als Teil der Offerte zu lesen sind; die Ergänzung ist also keine Abweichung vom Angebot.

7 **c) Erwartungen und Vorschläge des Annehmenden.** Die Formulierung des Textes („Antwort …, die eine Annahme darstellen soll") macht deutlich, dass vom Akzeptanten geäußerte **Erwartungen** oder **Vorschläge** für die weitere Entwicklung der Geschäftsbeziehungen ebenso wie eine zusätzliche, von der Annahmeerklärung unabhängige Offerte nicht als Abweichungen i. S. v. Art. 19 zu behandeln sind.[24]

Von einer geänderten Annahmeerklärung ist auch der Fall zu unterscheiden, dass eine Annahme von einer selbstständigen Offerte begleitet wird. Der vom (ersten) Offerenten angebotene Vertrag kommt zustande, während die zusätzliche Gegenofferte einer entsprechenden Annahme durch den (ersten) Offerenten bedarf. Ob eine zusätzliche Gegenofferte vorliegt, kann allerdings ein schwieriges Auslegungsproblem sein: Die Annahmeerklärung, die die Bereitschaft zu Lieferung von 200 Stück statt der in der Offerte georderten 100 Stück zum Ausdruck bringt, kann sowohl Zurückweisung und Gegenofferte als auch Annahme und zusätzliches selbstständiges Vertragsangebot sein.[25] Klärung können jedoch weitere Klauseln der Annahme oder die Umstände des Falles bewirken, z. B. wenn der Preis oder frachtfreier Versand von der Bestellung einer bestimmten Stückzahl abhängig ist.

Zu unterscheiden von Ergänzungen in der Annahme sind auch Änderungsvorschläge *nach* Vertragsschluss, etwa mit der Rechnung; für ihre Wirkung gilt nach Art. 29 I, dass sie als Offerten angenommen werden müssen.[26]

---

[21] Vgl. das Beispiel 2 bei *Bianca/Bonell/Farnsworth*, Art. 19, Anm. 2.8.: Bestimmte Schiedsklauseln seien in manchen Branchen so üblich, dass sie bereits in die Offerte hineingelesen werden könnten; *Hellner*, Standard Form Contracts, S. 340: Verweisung des Annehmenden auf Incoterms®, die auch in die – auszulegende – Offerte hineinzulesen sind; *Lookofsky*, The 1980 United Nations Convention, Anm. 124.
[22] MünchKomm/*Gruber*, Art. 19, Rn. 4.
[23] Vgl. schon BGH, 9.1.2002, CISG-online 651 = NJW 2002, 1651, 1653: „Abweichungen vom gewährleistungsrechtlichen Regelungsgefüge des CISG".
[24] S. oben Rn. 2; *Enderlein/Maskow/Strohbach*, Art. 19, Anm. 2.; *Staudinger/Magnus*, Art. 19, Rn. 8; s. auch *Bianca/Bonell/Farnsworth*, Art. 19, Anm. 2.2. zur Nutzung der Technik im Common Law, Ergänzungen als bloße Vorschläge zu verstehen, um der dort zuweilen strikt angewandten „mirror image rule" auszuweichen.
[25] Vgl. *Ludwig*, S. 323; *Staudinger/Magnus*, Art. 19, Rn. 8: durch Auslegung zu klären.
[26] Vgl. oben Art. 18 Rn. 8a m. Nachw. aus der Judikatur, Art. 29 Rn. 7 f.; *Witz/Salger/Lorenz/Witz*, Art. 19, Rn. 5.

d) **Wesentliche Abweichungen nach Art. 19 III.** Art. 19 I gilt nur für wesentliche **8**
Änderungen. Zwar lassen sich abstrakte Formeln für die **Abgrenzung wesentlicher von unwesentlichen Abweichungen** nicht aufstellen.[27] Die Aufzählung der als wesentliche Änderungen geltenden Punkte in Abs. 3 ermöglicht jedoch für die Mehrzahl der praktisch vorkommenden Vertragsklauseln eine eindeutige Grenzziehung.

aa) **Erfasste Fälle.** Auch ohne die Qualifizierung in Art. 19 III würden die dort auf- **8a**
gezählten **Gegenstände** regelmäßig als „**wesentlich**" zu bewerten sein: Eine Preisänderung[28] oder eine sonstige Änderung der Preisgestaltung etwa durch eine Gewinnbeteiligung,[29] das Verlangen von Vorauszahlung[30] oder der Zahlung durch Akkreditiv[31] (zu „Preis, Bezahlung"), Änderungen der Lieferbedingungen,[32] des Liefer- bzw. Erfüllungsorts[33] oder des Lieferzeitpunktes[34] (zu „Ort und Zeit der Lieferung"), Abweichungen bezüglich der Art der Ware[35] oder der Warenqualität,[36] eine Verringerung des Lieferumfangs[37] oder dessen Erhöhung[38] (zu „Qualität und Menge der Ware") würden ebenso wie Schiedsklauseln[39] oder Gerichtsstandsklauseln[40] (zu „Beilegung von Streitigkeiten" …)[41] als wesentliche Abweichung anzusehen sein.

---

[27] *Enderlein/Maskow/Strohbach*, Art. 19, Anm. 5.: Was wesentlich ist, hängt von den Umständen des Einzelfalles ab; *Honsell/Dornis*, Art. 19, Rn. 15 („konkrete Umstände").
[28] OGH, 9.3.2000, CISG-online 573 = IHR 2001, 39: Kilopreis ATS 40 statt ATS 28; CA Rennes, 27.5.2008, CISG-online 1746: Anhebung des Stückpreises für BH-Körbchen; *Magellan International Corp. v. Salzgitter Handel GmbH*, U. S. Dist. Ct. (N. D. Ill.), 7.12.1999, CISG-online 439 = 76 F. Supp. 2d 919: Preiserhöhungen zwischen USD 5–20/t bei Stahlbarren; HGer Zürich, 10.7.1996, CISG-online 227 = SZIER 1997, 131 f.: Preis von DM 46.651 statt DM 35.472 für 60.000 mehrfarbige Kunststoffchips, weil der Druckaufwand zunächst falsch kalkuliert worden war.
[29] BGer, 5.4.2005, CISG-online 1012 = IHR 2005, 204, 205 zur Klausel „gemeinsamer Verkauf".
[30] OLG Frankfurt a. M., 4.3.1994, CISG-online 110.
[31] OLG Frankfurt a. M., 4.3.1994, CISG-online 110.
[32] *Calzaturificio Claudia s. n. c. v. Olivieri Footwear Ltd.*, U. S. Dist. Ct. (S. D. N. Y.), 6.4.1998, CISG-online 440 zum Hinzufügen der Klausel „ex works".
[33] OLG Stuttgart, 18.4.2011, CISG-online 2226 = IHR 2011, 236, 239: Angebot der Käuferin enthielt Klausel „F. O. C.", Antwort der Verkäuferin hingegen Klausel „ex works" – wesentliche Abweichung.
[34] KG Zug, 2.12.2004, CISG-online 1194 = IHR 2006, 158, 160: Während im Angebot des Käufers Lieferung bis zur 40. KW 2002 verlangt wurde, sagte Annahme lediglich eine Teillieferung mit Abholtermin 17.10.2002 (d. h. 42. KW 2002) und Lieferung der übrigen Menge „so rasch wie möglich" zu – wesentliche Abweichung; OLG München, 8.2.1995, CISG-online 143: Bei Kaufvertrag über 11 KfZ wurde gegenüber angebotener Lieferzeit „ca. Juli, August, September, Oktober" Angabe „alle Fahrzeuge ca. Juli, August (120 Tage sind ausreichend) – unwiderruflich bis 15. August – vorgezogene Lieferung der dringenden Fahrzeuge im Juli möglich" in der Annahme als wesentliche Abweichung angesehen. Anders jedoch OLG Naumburg, 27.4.1999, CISG-online 512 = TranspR-IHR 2000, 22 f.: Gegenüber Angebot „Lieferung bis 15.3." wurde Annahme mit Angabe „April, Liefertermin bleibt vorbehalten" als *unwesentliche* Abweichung eingestuft.
[35] Hof van Beroep Gent, 8.11.2004, CISG-online 982: Verkäufer bot an Stelle des bestellten Textilstoffes „Kabul" das Gewebe „Lima" an; OLG Frankfurt a. M., 4.3.1994, CISG-online 110: Annahme eines Angebots über Spezialschrauben nannte darüber hinaus weitere Artikel, die bis dahin weder als lieferbar angeboten noch den Preisen nach bestimmt waren.
[36] OLG Frankfurt a. M., 31.3.1995, CISG-online 137: Abweichungen hinsichtlich der Glasqualität bei Bestellung von Reagenzgläsern.
[37] BGer, 5.4.2005, CISG-online 1012 = IHR 2005, 204, 205: 60t netto statt 70t Triethylen Tetramin; KG Zug, 2.12.2004, CISG-online 1194 = IHR 2006, 158, 160: Zusage von zunächst nur einer Teillieferung von 5t und erst später weiteren 10t Lebensmitteldextrose statt der bestellten 15t; OLG Frankfurt a. M., 23.5.1995, CISG-online 185: Angebot über 3240 Paar, Annahme über 2700 Paar Schuhe.
[38] OLG Frankfurt a. M., 4.3.1994, CISG-online 110: Bei Verkauf von Spezialschrauben überstieg Annahme das Angebot um 290 Teile.
[39] OLG Frankfurt a. M., 26.6.2006, CISG-online 1385 = IHR 2007, 42, 44. Aus dem Schrifttum hierzu *Bianca/Bonell/Farnsworth*, Art. 19, Anm. 2.8.; *Farnsworth*, Formation of Contract, § 3.4 sub 3–16; *Sono*, Formation of International Contracts, S. 126 f.; alle wohl beruhend auf Sekretariatskommentar, Art. 17, Nr. 13.
[40] HGer St. Gallen, 15.6.2010, CISG-online 2159 = IHR 2011, 149, 150 f.; *CSS Antenna, Inc. v. Amphenol-Tuchel Electronics GmbH*, U. S. Dist. Ct. (D. Md.), 8.2.2011, CISG-online 2177; *Hanwha Corporation v. Cedar Petrochemicals, Inc.*, U. S. Dist. Ct. (S. D. N. Y.), 18.1.2011, CISG-online 2178; *Belcher-Robinson, L. L. C. v. Linamar Corporation, et al.*, U. S. Dist. Ct. (M. D. Ala.), 31.3.2010, CISG-online 2092 (aber letztlich offen lassend); vgl. auch Civ. 1, 16.7.1998, CISG-online 344 = D. 1998, 222.
[41] S. zur Vereinbarung von Streitbeilegungsklauseln unter dem CISG bereits oben Vor Artt. 14–24 Rn. 9 ff.

8b **bb) Art. 19 III als widerlegbare Auslegungsregel.** Die Entstehungsgeschichte der Formulierung des Abs. 3[42] macht dabei deutlich, dass es für die genannten Punkte nicht notwendig auf die Umstände des Einzelfalles ankommt, sondern dass insoweit eine **Auslegungsregel** gilt.[43] Die Streichung des im New Yorker E (Art. 17 III) noch enthaltenen Halbsatzes, der die „Wesentlichkeit" der in Abs. 3 erwähnten Punkte unter bestimmten Voraussetzungen abschwächte, wie auch die Ablehnung eines in Wien gemachten Vorschlags, den Katalog in Abs. 3 durch die Worte „inter alia" zu ergänzen, was das Gewicht der aufgezählten Vertragspunkte ebenfalls relativiert hätte,[44] haben jedoch zu einer erheblichen Verschärfung dieser Auslegungsregel geführt. Gleichwohl ist damit nicht ausgeschlossen, dass auch Änderungen zu diesen Punkten in der Annahmeerklärung auf Grund der besonderen Umstände des Falles, der Parteigepflogenheiten, Vorverhandlungen oder auf Grund von Bräuchen als unwesentlich bewertet werden dürfen.[45] Abs. 3 enthält deshalb nach wohl h. M. **keine unwiderlegliche Vermutung** eines Parteiwillens, die genannten Regelungsgegenstände stets als „wesentliche" zu bewerten.[46] Die Autonomie der Parteien und die Rechtsmacht des Offerenten, seine Offerte auszustatten und Einzelpunkte, zu denen der Oblat möglicherweise andere Vorschläge unterbreitet, vorab als weniger wichtig, d. h. „unwesentlich" zu qualifizieren, sollte durch Abs. 3 jedenfalls nicht eingeschränkt werden. Auch Auslegung der Offerte nach Art. 8, Bräuche oder Parteigepflogenheiten[47] können zu einem solchen Ergebnis führen. Namentlich dem **Offerenten günstige Änderungen,**[48] z. B. ein höherer Preisrabatt, die Übernahme des Transports zum Käufer ohne Mehrkosten, die Verlängerung der vom Käufer in seiner Offerte verlangten Garantiefrist, die Einräumung einer Bestimmungsbefugnis über die Warenmenge[49] sollten erleichtert Vertragsbestandteil werden können und nicht einer Gegenannahme bedürfen.[50] Bei der Beurteilung der ausschließlichen „Günstigkeit" einer Abweichung ist freilich Sorgfalt geboten, weil bestimmten Vertragsdetails ein gleichsam zweischneidiger Effekt zukommt: So ist das Hinausschieben der Fälligkeit der Kaufpreiszahlungspflicht für den Käufer einerseits vorteilhaft, kann aber andererseits zugleich die (im CISG nicht geregelte) Verjährung hinausschieben;[51] man wird sie daher nicht zu der erwähnten Kategorie zählen können.

Trotz Erfassung durch den Katalog des Art. 19 III im **konkreten Fall** als **unwesentlich** eingestuft wurden etwa Abweichungen hinsichtlich des Preises (Erweiterung einer

---

[42] S. oben Rn. 3.
[43] OGH, 20.3.1997, CISG-online 269 = östJBl 1997, 592, 593.
[44] S. O. R., S. 287 f.
[45] Vgl. *Schlechtriem,* Einheitliches UN-Kaufrecht, S. 43, Fn. 181.
[46] BGer, 5.4.2005, CISG-online 1012 = IHR 2005, 204, 205; OGH, 20.3.1997, CISG-online 269 = östJBl 1997, 592, 593; Gerechtshof 's-Hertogenbosch, 25.2.2003, CISG-online 1834; implizit auch Civ. 1, 4.1.1995, CISG-online 138 = D. 1995, 289 m. Anm. *Witz/Wolter,* RIW 1995, 810, 812; *Bamberger/Roth/Saenger,* Art. 19, Rn. 5; *Honsell/Dornis,* Art. 19, Rn. 11; *Karollus,* S. 70; *Neumayer/Ming,* Art. 19, Anm. 3.; *Staudinger/Magnus,* Art. 19, Rn. 16; *Perales Viscasillas,* Formación del contrato, S. 660 ff.; *Piltz,* Internationales Kaufrecht, Rn. 3–99; *Soergel/Lüderitz/Fenge,* Art. 19, Rn. 3 (Beispiele); *van Alstine,* S. 200 f.; *Witz/Salger/Lorenz/Witz,* Art. 19, Rn. 9, 11; a. A. (unwiderlegliche Vermutung) hingegen *Herber/Czerwenka,* Art. 19, Rn. 11; MünchKomm/*Gruber,* Art. 19, Rn. 7; *Reinhart,* Art. 19, Rn. 6 („eo ipso"); *Ludwig,* S. 335 f.
[47] MünchKomm/*Gruber,* Art. 19, Rn. 8; *Soergel/Lüderitz/Fenge,* Art. 19, Rn. 3; anders möglicherweise *Chateau Des Charmes Wines Ltd. v. Sabate USA, Inc. et al.,* Ontario Superior Court of Justice, 28.10.2005, CISG-online 1139, Rn. 41: „I also agree that the Convention does not permit material amendments to be imposed by silence or by practice."
[48] Vgl. OGH, 20.3.1997, CISG-online 269 = östJBl 1997, 592 ff.
[49] Vgl. OGH, 20.3.1997, CISG-online 269 = östJBl 1997, 592, 593: Während die Angebotsmenge sich auf „10 000 metrische Tonnen +/– 5% nach Wahl des Schiffes" belief, lautete die Annahme auf „10 000 metrische Tonnen +/– 10% nach Wahl des Schiffes" – ob dies eine dem Offerenten günstige Änderung war, hing davon ab, welcher Partei die Wahl des Schiffes zustand.
[50] *Brunner,* Art. 19, Rn. 3; *Janssen,* wbl 2002, 453, 457; *Kramer,* FS Welser, S. 547; MünchKomm/*Gruber,* Art. 19, Rn. 8.
[51] Vgl. Najvyšší súd Slovenskej republiky, 19.6.2008, CISG-online 1875 (*in concreto* großzügigeres Zahlungsziel in Rechnung des Verkäufers genannt, d. h. in denkbarem Angebot auf Vertragsänderung gem. Art. 29 I – mangels Reaktion des Käufers wurde dieser Zahlungstermin kein Vertragsbestandteil, Art. 18 I 2).

Preisanpassungsklausel auf den Fall steigender Marktpreise),[52] der Bezahlung (Annahme des Käufers schob Zahlungstermin um 14 Tage hinaus[53]) und des Lieferzeitpunktes (Angebot „Lieferung bis 15.3.", Annahme „April, Liefertermin bleibt vorbehalten");[54] dasselbe muss für eine Änderung der Bankverbindung oder Zahlstelle (zu „Bezahlung")[55] und eine Änderung der genauen Lieferanschrift am selben Ort (zu „Ort und Zeit der Lieferung")[56] gelten. Entsprechendes wird man für Details in der Ausführung der Ware, wie etwa deren Farbgebung (zu „Qualität der Ware"), hingegen nicht generell sagen können, selbst wenn diese die allgemeine Wertschätzung der Ware nicht belasten mögen.[57] Die **Beweislast** für die Widerlegung der Vermutung des Art. 19 III trifft die Partei, die sich auf die ausnahmsweise Unwesentlichkeit einer in der Vorschrift genannten Abweichung beruft.[58]

e) **Wesentliche Abweichungen im Übrigen.** Außerhalb des – unstreitig lediglich beispielhaften[59] – Katalogs der in Art. 19 III genannten Regelungsgegenstände kommt es dagegen bei der Abgrenzung von wesentlichen/unwesentlichen Abweichungen von vornherein auf die **Umstände des Einzelfalles**, d. h. die Bedeutung einzelner Modifikationen für den Vertrag und die Parteien nach Vertragsinhalt, Auftragsvolumen, Parteibeziehungen, Wirtschaftslage usw. an.[60] Verlangen von Sicherheiten, z. B. einer **Gewährleistungsbürgschaft,** Vorschläge für die Vereinbarung einer **Vertragsstrafe, Rücktritts-, Widerrufs- oder Kündigungsvorbehalte,**[61] aber auch Abweichungen bezüglich der Verpackungs- und Versendungsart[62] sind jeweils konkret zu gewichten. Klauseln, die mündliche Nebenabreden für ungültig erklären oder mündliche Änderungen eines schriftlichen Vertrages (vgl. Art. 29 II) ausschließen, wird man als wesentliche Änderungen ansehen müssen.[63] **Rechtswahlklauseln** dürften bei einer Divergenz stets wesentliche Abweichung sein,[64] wenn man sie nicht schon im Katalog des Abs. 3 als auf die „Beilegung von Streitigkeiten" bezogen erfasst sieht.[65] Unzweifelhaft wesentlich ist ein **Ausschluss der Anwendbarkeit des UN-Kaufrechts** (Art. 6) in der Antwort des Oblaten.[66] Als wesentlich wurden zudem Abweichungen bezüglich eines **Aufrechnungsverbotes**[67] eingestuft. In der Verweisung auf **Allgemeine Geschäftsbedingungen,** insbesondere wenn sie eine pauschale Abwehrklausel enthalten, ist regelmäßig eine wesentliche Abweichung zu sehen, unabhängig davon, ob

---

[52] Civ. 1, 4.1.1995, CISG-online 138 = D. 1995, 289, Übersetzung von *C. Witz* in 16 J. L. & Com. (1997), 345 ff.; Anm. *C. Witz,* D. 1995, 290; *Witz/Wolter,* RIW 1995, 810 ff.; a. A. *Schwenzer/Mohs,* IHR 2006, 239, 244.
[53] Gerechtshof 's-Hertogenbosch, 25.2.2003, CISG-online 1834: während das Verkäuferangebot die Bezahlung des Kaufpreises für ein Springpferd (DM 90.000) bis 25. September verlangte, sah die Annahmeerklärung des Käufers als Zahlungstermin den 9. Oktober vor – unwesentliche Abweichung angenommen.
[54] OLG Naumburg, 27.4.1999, CISG-online 512 = TranspR-IHR 2000, 22 f.; ähnlich *Soergel/Lüderitz/Fenge,* Art. 19, Rn. 3.
[55] *Herber/Czerwenka,* Art. 19, Rn. 12; MünchKomm/*Gruber,* Art. 19, Rn. 8; *Staudinger/Magnus,* Art. 19, Rn. 18.
[56] *Staudinger/Magnus,* Art. 19, Rn. 18.
[57] A. A. MünchKomm/*Gruber,* Art. 19, Rn. 8. Hier wird es vielmehr maßgeblich auf die im Einzelfall betroffene Ware ankommen; vgl. etwa *Herber/Czerwenka,* Art. 19, Rn. 12 (Änderung der Farbe einer Maschine nicht wesentlich).
[58] Gerechtshof 's-Hertogenbosch, 25.2.2003, CISG-online 1834; *Baumgärtel/Laumen/Hepting,* Art. 19 WKR, Rn. 8.
[59] *Belcher-Robinson, L. L. C. v. Linamar Corporation, et al.,* U. S. Dist. Ct. (M. D. Ala.), 31.3.2010, CISG-online 2092.
[60] *Enderlein/Maskow/Strohbach,* Art. 19, Anm. 5.; *Honsell/Dornis,* Art. 19, Rn. 15.
[61] Vgl. dazu *Brunner,* Art. 19, Rn. 3: i. d. R. wesentliche Abweichung.
[62] Vgl. OLG Hamm, 22.9.1992, CISG-online 57: Ablehnung der Verpackung „in Säcken" und Anbieten „loser" Verpackungsweise bei Lieferung von Schweinespeck als wesentliche Abweichung gewertet.
[63] Ebenso *Bianca/Bonell/Farnsworth,* Art. 19, Anm. 3.1.; *Janssen,* wbl 2002, 453, 455.
[64] OLG Linz, 23.3.2005, CISG-online 1376 = IHR 2007, 123, 126; *Hanwha Corporation v. Cedar Petrochemicals, Inc.,* U. S. Dist. Ct. (S. D. N. Y.), 18.1.2011, CISG-online 2178; *Brunner,* Art. 19, Rn. 3.
[65] So Civ. 1, 16.7.1998, CISG-online 344 = D. 1998, 222; wohl auch ICC, 8611/1997, CISG-online 236.
[66] *Ferrari,* oben Art. 6 Rn. 13; *Graves,* Belgr. L. Rev. 2011, 124, 136: „undoubtedly material".
[67] OLG Linz, 23.3.2005, CISG-online 1376 = IHR 2007, 123, 126.

sie zu den in Abs. 3 aufgezählten Punkten Regelungen enthalten.[68] Andererseits können die Parteien durch Parteivereinbarung, etwa in Rahmenverträgen, die Bedeutung etwaiger Differenzen vorklären (s. auch oben Rn. 1).

Auch das **Vertragsschlussverfahren modifizierende Vorschläge** können wesentliche oder unwesentliche Abweichungen von den Bedingungen der Offerte sein: Hat der Offerent für die Annahme ein bestimmtes Kommunikationsmittel oder eine bestimmte Form[69] vorgeschrieben, für den Inhalt der Annahmeerklärung bestimmte Einzelheiten verlangt,[70] liegen ebenso Abweichungen i. S. v. Art. 19 vor wie im Verlangen des Akzeptanten, dass die Wirksamkeit seiner Annahmeerklärung von einer Gegenbestätigung abhängig sein oder dass ihm Widerruf über Art. 22 hinaus möglich bleiben soll.[71]

Eine „Antwort" auf ein Angebot, die eine Annahme darstellen soll, aber nicht von dem Oblaten abgegeben wird, sondern von einer **anderen Person** – etwa von einer Gesellschaft, die demselben Konzern angehört wie der Oblat, oder von einem Agenten in Vertretung nicht des Oblaten, sondern eines sonstigen Unternehmens[72] – stellt weder eine Annahme noch eine Ablehnung des Angebots mit Gegenangebot dar: Es handelt sich vielmehr um ein eigenständiges (separates) Angebot, weil das ursprüngliche Angebot nur vom Oblaten angenommen oder abgelehnt werden kann.[73]

2. Rechtsfolge wesentlicher Abweichungen

10 **a) Ablehnung des Angebots.** Entsprechend § 150 II BGB wird eine wesentliche Abweichung als **Ablehnung des Angebots** gesehen. Sie löst also die Rechtsfolge des Art. 17 aus, das Angebot erlischt durch die Ablehnung.[74] Gleichwohl wird das Vertragsschlussverfahren fortgesetzt, denn die als solche nicht wirksame Annahmeerklärung wirkt als Offerte (Gegenangebot).

11 **b) Gegenofferte.** Für die **Gegenofferte** gelten Artt. 14–17.[75] Sie kann also (nur) bis zum Zugang zurückgenommen werden, wobei durch Auslegung zu ermitteln ist, ob die Rücknahmeerklärung gleichzeitig als vorbehaltlose Annahme der ursprünglichen Offerte zu verstehen ist. Nach Zugang kann die Gegenofferte nach Art. 16 I widerrufen werden, sofern nicht Art. 16 II eingreift. Vor allem aber gilt für die Gegenofferte Art. 14 I. Der Bindungswille wird dabei freilich durch Art. 19 I unterstellt. Wird er vom Erklärenden ausgeschlossen, dann liegt überhaupt keine modifizierende Annahmeerklärung vor, sondern eine Ablehnung des Angebots verbunden mit dem Vorschlag, (neu) zu verhandeln.

Enthält die Gegenofferte nur einzelne Änderungen, dann würden an sich die **Mindesterfordernisse** an eine Offerte nach Art. 14 I fehlen. Auslegung nach Art. 8 sowie das mit

---

[68] Vgl. KG Zug, 11.12.2003, CISG-online 958 = IHR 2005, 119, 121; AG Kehl, 6.10.1995, CISG-online 162 = NJW-RR 1996, 565 f.; *Achilles*, Art. 19, Rn. 2; *Janssen*, wbl. 2002, 453, 455; *Kröll/Hennecke*, RIW 2001, 736, 739; teilweise anders *Honsell/Dornis*, Art. 19, Rn. 38; *Piltz*, IHR 2004, 133, 136; *Staudinger/Magnus*, Art. 19, Rn. 21; *Witz/Salger/Lorenz/Witz*, Art. 14, Rn. 11. *Hellner* erwägt sogar, Verweisung auf AGB generell als unwesentliche Modifikation zu behandeln, s. Standard Form Contracts, S. 340. S. dagegen *Schlechtriem*, Einheitliches UN-Kaufrecht, S. 44; *van der Velden*, Battle of Forms, S. 240. Zum Sonderproblem kollidierender Standardbedingungen s. oben Rn. 19 ff.
[69] MünchKomm/*Gruber*, Art. 19, Rn. 3; *Witz/Salger/Lorenz/Witz*, Art. 19, Rn. 5.
[70] Vgl. RG, 20.2.1918, RGZ 92, 232 ff., 235: Auf das Verlangen der Anerkennung der Zahlungsbedingungen des Angebots „ausdrücklich im Wortlaut" § 150 II BGB angewendet.
[71] Vgl. zu diesen Fällen *Witz/Salger/Lorenz/Witz*, Art. 19, Rn. 5; *Lagergren*, S. 68; *von Caemmerer*, RabelsZ 29 (1965), 101, 116: Bei derartigen Gegenbestätigungsklauseln oder dem Verlangen nach schriftlicher Fixierung eines mündlich angebotenen und ebenso angenommenen Vertrages ist zunächst zu prüfen, ob insoweit nicht nur eine Bitte oder ein Vorschlag geäußert wird, die Annahme selbst jedoch vorbehaltlos sein soll, s. oben Rn. 7.
[72] Vgl. oben Art. 14 Rn. 4 a. E.
[73] Die Situation liegt geringfügig anders, wenn das Angebot an einen Oblaten gerichtet war, deren „Annahme" aber durch den Oblaten *sowie* eine weitere Person erfolgt (also das Zustandekommen eines Mehrparteienvertrages in Rede steht); s. hierzu bereits oben Vor Artt. 14–24 Rn. 30a ff.
[74] OLG Linz, 23.3.2005, CISG-online 1376 = IHR 2007, 123, 126.
[75] KG Freiburg, 11.10.2004, CISG-online 964 = IHR 2005, 72, 75.

Art. 19 I verfolgte Ziel, das Vertragsschlussverfahren in Gang zu halten, ermöglichen jedoch die Folgerung, dass der Erklärende alle Bedingungen der ursprünglichen Offerte, zu denen er selbst keine abweichenden Vorschläge macht, in sein Gegenangebot aufgenommen hat.

c) **Annahme der Gegenofferte.** Die Gegenofferte bedarf ihrerseits der **Annahme**, um 12 einen Vertrag zustande zu bringen. Der Autor der ursprünglichen Offerte muss der Gegenofferte also nach Art. 18 zustimmen. Häufig wird in der Situation des Art. 19 I die Zustimmung zur Gegenofferte durch ein sonstiges Verhalten zum Ausdruck gebracht,[76] das u. U. nach Art. 18 III bereits mit Vornahme des erklärungsäquivalenten Verhaltens wirkt.[77] Reagiert der ursprüngliche Offerent nicht mehr, kommt ein Vertrag **nicht zustande**.[78]

Es ist deutlich, dass bei einer großzügigen Anwendung der Artt. 8, 18 I, III Leistungen oder Leistungsvorbereitungen des (ursprünglichen) Offerenten nach Eingang der als Gegenofferte zu verstehenden Annahmeerklärung leicht zu einer „Vertragsfalle" für den ursprünglichen Offerenten werden können. Wiederholt er freilich mit der Leistung noch einmal die Bedingungen seines Angebots, dann werden die Rollen erneut gewechselt, und Annahme der Leistung kann jetzt zum Vertrag und zur Gestaltung seines Inhalts entsprechend der Bedingungen des Offerenten führen. Die Gefahr, dass derjenige sich mit seinen Bedingungen durchsetzt, der **„das letzte Wort"** hat bzw. äußert, ist freilich vor allem bei Verwendung Allgemeiner Geschäftsbedingungen gegeben, die als Sonderproblem zu behandeln sind.[79]

III. Unwesentliche Abweichungen

1. Abweichungen

Festzustellen ist zunächst, ob überhaupt eine Abweichung vorliegt oder trotz sprachlicher 13 Divergenzen Einigkeit in der Sache besteht.[80] Sodann ist festzustellen, ob die Abweichung wesentlich ist.[81] Die Aufzählung in Abs. 3 lässt kaum Raum für unwesentliche Abweichungen, es sei denn, die Auslegungsregel wird in concreto widerlegt.[82] Die Beispiele „Sicherungsverlangen", „Vertragsstrafevereinbarung", „zusätzliche Rücktritts-, Widerrufs- oder Kündigungsrechte" dürften regelmäßig als wesentliche Abweichungen zu bewerten sein. Dagegen ist die Bitte, die Annahme vertraulich zu behandeln, wohl nicht einmal Modifikation, jedenfalls aber unwesentlich.[83] Die **Rechtsprechung** hat eine Änderung des Lieferdatums („April, Liefertermin bleibt vorbehalten" statt „Lieferung bis 15.3."),[84] die Festlegung einer Frist für „Reklamationen" von höchstens 30 Tagen ab Rechnungsdatum,[85] die Erweiterung einer Preisanpassungsklausel auf den Fall steigender Marktpreise (!),[86] das Hinausschieben des Zahlungstermins um 14 Tage,[87] die Belastung der

---

[76] S. unten Art. 18 Rn. 7 ff.
[77] S. unten Art. 18 Rn. 18 ff. sowie das Beispiel 3 bei *Bianca/Bonell/Farnsworth*, Art. 19, Anm. 2.8.
[78] *Hellner*, Standard Form Contracts, S. 341.
[79] S. unten Rn. 19 ff.
[80] S. oben Rn. 5, 6.
[81] S. oben Rn. 8–9.
[82] S. dazu oben Rn. 8b; *Murray*, 20 J. L. & Com. (2000), 1, 42; s. dagegen *Soergel/Lüderitz/Fenge*, Art. 19, Rn. 4: großzügige und vertragsfreundliche Interpretation sei angezeigt.
[83] Vgl. Legfelsöbb Biróság, 25.9.1992, CISG-online 63 = 13 J. L. & Com. (1993), 31, s. zu dieser Entscheidung auch oben Art. 14 Rn. 16.
[84] OLG Naumburg, 27.4.1999, CISG-online 512 = TranspR-IHR 2000, 22 f.
[85] LG Baden-Baden, 14.8.1991, CISG-online 24 = RIW 1992, 62 f., m. Anm. *Karollus*, RdW 1992, 169; *Neumayer*, RIW 1994, 99. Hier dürfte entscheidend gewesen sein, dass diese vom Verkäufer eingeführte Fristverlängerung für Rügen vor dem Hintergrund der damaligen Rechtsprechung für den anderen Teil (Käufer) vorteilhaft war.
[86] Civ. 1, 4.1.1995, CISG-online 138 = D. 1995, 289, dazu bereits oben Rn. 8b; a. A. *Schwenzer/Mohs*, IHR 2006, 239, 244.
[87] Gerechtshof 's-Hertogenbosch, 25.2.2003, CISG-online 1834 (Bezahlung des Restkaufpreises für ein Springpferd in Höhe von DM 90.000).

Käuferin mit Transportkosten, nachdem in deren Angebot Lieferung „frei Baustelle" vorgesehen gewesen war,[88] Abweichungen bezüglich Verschiffungsdetails (Alter des Schiffes, Verschiffungskosten) in der Annahme des Käufers, weil beide Parteien übereinstimmend die Klausel „FOB" vorgesehen hatten und daher der Transport ohnehin Sache des Käufers war[89] sowie – im Rahmen einer einvernehmlichen Vertragsaufhebung – die Bitte um das Entwerfen einer formellen Aufhebungsvereinbarung[90] als **unwesentliche** Abweichungen behandelt. Dasselbe wurde für die Ablehnung einer im Angebot genannten Vertragsvariante (betr. die technische Ausgestaltung der angebotenen Asphaltmischanlage) durch den Käufer angenommen,[91] obwohl es hier richtigerweise bereits an einer Abweichung vom Angebot fehlte.[92] Als weitere Beispiele für unwesentliche Abweichungen werden in der Literatur Verpackungs- und Versendungsart genannt,[93] doch kann auch dies im Einzelfall anders sein. So soll die Ablehnung der Verpackung „in Säcken" und das Anbieten „loser" Verpackungsweise bei der Lieferung von Schweinespeck eine wesentliche Abweichung darstellen.[94]

2. Rechtsfolgen unwesentlicher Abweichungen

14 a) **Unwesentliche Ergänzungen oder Abweichungen.** Eine Annahmeerklärung, die nur **unwesentliche Ergänzungen oder Abweichungen** vom Angebot enthält, behält die Funktion einer Annahme und führt zum Vertragsschluss, sofern der Offerent nicht widerspricht. **Beweislast** für Unwesentlichkeit trägt deshalb, wer sich auf Vertragsschluss beruft.[95] Die in der Annahme enthaltenen Änderungen und Ergänzungen werden Teil des Vertragsinhaltes, Art. 19 II 2,[96] der Annehmende setzt sich also, sofern er das letzte Wort behält, durch.[97] Ob der Vertrag erst durch Schweigen des Offerenten oder – bei ausbleibendem Widerspruch – bereits durch Zugang der Annahmeerklärung zustande kommt, ist str., aber wohl nur ein theoretisches Problem, da bei unterbliebenem Widerspruch jedenfalls als Zeitpunkt des Vertragsschlusses der Zugang der Annahmeerklärung gilt, Art. 23.[98]

15 b) **Widerspruch.** Der Offerent kann die nach Abs. 2 S. 1, 2 eintretende Rechtsfolge, dass der Vertrag mit den – wenn auch nur unwesentlich – abweichenden bzw. ergänzenden Bedingungen der anderen Seite zustande kommt, durch **Widerspruch** rückgängig machen. Er kann sich mündlich verwahren; telefonische Erklärung ist ebenso als mündliche zu bewerten wie gleichzustellende Formen unmittelbarer elektronischer Kommunikation (Funkverkehr, Videokonferenzen, Chat-Foren im Internet).[99] Alternativ kann der Anbietende den Widerspruch durch entsprechende Mitteilung vornehmen, wahlweise auch durch

---

[88] OLG Koblenz, 4.10.2002, CISG-online 716 = IHR 2003, 66, 67 (im konkreten Fall Transportkosten von DM 2.500); kritisch *Huber/Kröll*, IPRax 2003, 309, 310.
[89] CIETAC, 10.6.2002, CISG-online 1528; *in concreto* Streichung der im Verkäuferangebot enthaltenen Klausel „a ship with the age of above twenty years is not accepted" und Änderung der Klausel „carriage paid" in „carriage is paid according to charter-party".
[90] CIETAC, 1.4.1993, CISG-online 1428.
[91] OLG Koblenz, 1.3.2010, CISG-online 2126 = NJW-RR 2010, 1004, 1005.
[92] S. bereits oben Rn. 6.
[93] Vgl. *Farnsworth*, Formation of Contract, § 3.04 sub 3–16: Unwesentliche Abweichungen seien schwer vorstellbar: Vielleicht könne eine abweichende Benennung des Schiffes, auf dem die Ware auf Grund eines CIF-Vertrages versandt werden soll, oder Ergänzungen hinsichtlich der Verpackung als unwesentliche bewertet werden; *Bianca/Bonell/Farnsworth*, Art. 19, Anm. 2.8., Beispiel 4 (Benennung eines anderen Schiffes); *Honnold/Flechtner*, Art. 19, Rn. 167 (vom Verkäufer vorgeschlagene Verpackungsart „neue Säcke" keine wesentliche Abweichung von der Offerte, die „ordentliche Säcke" verlangte); s. dagegen OLG Hamm, 22.9.1992, CISG-online 57.
[94] So OLG Hamm, 22.9.1992, CISG-online 57.
[95] *Baumgärtel/Laumen/Hepting*, Art. 19 WKR, Rn. 5, 6.
[96] OLG Koblenz, 4.10.2002, CISG-online 716 = IHR 2003, 66, 67.
[97] Krit. *Kramer*, BJM 1995, 6 f.; *Neumayer*, Battle of Forms, S. 512 ff.
[98] Zu diesem Konstruktionsproblem *Honsell/Schnyder/Straub*, 1. Aufl., Art. 19, Rn. 20.
[99] S. oben Art. 18 Rn. 17; *Hahnkamper*, 25 J. L. & Com. (2005-06), 147, 149.

elektronische Benachrichtigung (E-Mail,[100] EDI),[101] sofern sich der Adressat – wie bei elektronischen Erklärungen unter dem CISG stets erforderlich – damit einverstanden erklärt hat, Erklärungen in der verwendeten Form zu erhalten.[102] Der Widerspruch muss in jedem Fall unverzüglich erfolgen.

c) „Unverzüglich". „Unverzüglich" kann, wie die englische Formulierung „without 16 undue delay" belegt, als „ohne schuldhaftes Zögern" verstanden werden,[103] so dass letztlich eine wertende Entscheidung möglich und erforderlich ist. Für den Regelfall wird im Schrifttum diesbezüglich eine Obergrenze von drei Werktagen genannt;[104] die Rechtsprechung hat einen Zeitraum von 5 Tagen bei einem per Telefax geschlossenen chinesisch-schwedischen Kaufvertrag für zu lang erachtet.[105] Sofern nach den Umständen des Einzelfalls offenkundig eine zügige Reaktion notwendig ist, so kann ein Widerspruch per E-Mail (und nicht mit normaler Post) erforderlich sein.[106] Für eine anders als mündlich zum Ausdruck gebrachte Verwahrung verdeutlicht die in Wien gefundene Fassung, dass sie lediglich absendebedürftig ist.[107] Das Risiko, dass der Widerspruch verloren geht oder verspätet ankommt, so dass der Annehmende bereits Dispositionen im Vertrauen auf einen wirksamen Vertragsschluss getroffen hat, muss den Annehmenden treffen, da er als Urheber der „Anomalie" (d. h. der Abweichung vom Angebot) dieses Risiko verursacht hat.

Aufgrund des Wortlauts von Art. 19 II 1 könnte angenommen werden, dass nur die 17 mündliche Verwahrung unverzüglich zu erfolgen hat. Der Entstehungsgeschichte ist aber zu entnehmen, dass die Worte „without undue delay" für mündliche wie anders übermittelte Erklärungen gelten sollten.[108] In der deutschen Fassung wird eine solche Auslegung möglich, indem man „entsprechend" auch auf „unverzüglich" bezieht. Sachlich wäre auch nicht zu verstehen, wenn der Offerent sich mit einer nicht-mündlichen Protesterklärung Zeit und so den Vertrag in der Schwebe lassen könnte.[109]

d) Rechtzeitiger Widerspruch. Rechtzeitiger Widerspruch („Beanstandung") führt 18 (mit Rückwirkung) zum Scheitern des Vertragsschlusses.[110] Diese Rechtsfolge ist harsch.

---

[100] Vgl. *Hanwha Corporation v. Cedar Petrochemicals, Inc.*, U.S. Dist. Ct. (S.D.N.Y.), 18.1.2011, CISG-online 2178: Widerspruch per E-mail.

[101] CISG-AC, Op. 1 *(Chr. Ramberg)*, Comment 19.1 = IHR 2003, 244, 247; *Hahnkamper*, 25 J.L. & Com. (2005-06), 147, 149.

[102] S. dazu allgemein oben Vor Artt. 14–24 Rn. 27.

[103] S. jedoch *Brunner*, Art. 19, Rn. 1; *Honsell/Dornis*, Art. 19, Rn. 28: Dem Offerenten müsse Prüfungsfrist zugestanden werden. MünchKomm/*Gruber*, Art. 19, Rn. 16 und *Staudinger/Magnus*, Art. 19, Rn. 13 formulieren (wohl wie hier) „ohne jeden vermeidbaren Aufschub"; *Piltz*, Internationales Kaufrecht, Rn. 3–105 spricht von Inanspruchnahme von nicht mehr als der erforderlichen Zeit.

[104] MünchKomm/*Gruber*, Art. 19, Rn. 16; so auch *Honsell/Schnyder/Straub*, 1. Aufl., Art. 19, Rn. 26 (grundsätzlich 1–3 Tage).

[105] CIETAC, 10.6.2002, CISG-online 1528.

[106] O. *Meyer*, Interpretation, S. 332.

[107] *Bamberger/Roth/Saenger*, Art. 19, Rn. 4; *Brunner*, Art. 19, Rn. 1; *Enderlein/Maskow/Strohbach*, Art. 19, Anm. 6.; *Herber/Czerwenka*, Art. 19, Rn. 14 (mit Hinweis auf Art. 27); *Honsell/Dornis*, Art. 19, Rn. 29; *Karollus*, S. 69; MünchKomm/*Gruber*, Art. 19, Rn. 15; *Soergel/Lüderitz/Fenge*, Art. 19, Rn. 4; *Staudinger/Magnus*, Art. 19, Rn. 12; *Stern*, Erklärungen, Rn. 108; *Witz/Salger/Lorenz/Witz*, Art. 19, Rn. 12. S. auch zu dem entsprechenden deutschen Antrag und seiner Behandlung O. R., S. 328 f.; eingehende Untersuchung dieser Frage bei *Noussias*, Zugangsbedürftigkeit von Mitteilungen, S. 119 ff. A. A. *Neumayer*, Battle of Forms, S. 519; *ders.*, RIW 1994, 99, 103; *ders.*, Erklärungen, S. 110 ff. (mit guten Gründen); *Neumayer/Ming*, Art. 19, Anm. 2.

[108] Der Entwurfstext lautete: „Unless the offeror objects to the discrepancy without undue delay". Der deutsche Änderungsantrag, der zur Unterscheidung von mündlichen und anderen Erklärungen führte, wollte lediglich die zum Haager Kaufrecht streitige Frage klären, ob andere als mündliche Erklärungen absende- oder zugangsbedürftig seien. Wie hier CIETAC, 10.6.2002, CISG-online 1528; *Honsell/Schnyder/Straub*, 1. Aufl., Art. 19, Rn. 26; *Staudinger/Magnus*, Art. 19, Rn. 23.

[109] *Bianca/Bonell/Farnsworth*, Art. 19, Anm. 3.2., geht deshalb selbstverständlich davon aus, dass sich der Offerent stets „unverzüglich" verwahren müsse.

[110] *Belcher-Robinson, L.L.C. v. Linamar Corporation, et al.*, U.S. Dist. Ct. (M.D. Ala.), 31.3.2010, CISG-online 2092: „If the offeror does make timely objections, 'the reply of the offeree is to be considered as a rejection of the offer rather than as an acceptance'" (unter Verweis auf den Sekretariatskommentar). Vgl. *Honnold/Flechtner*, Art. 19, Rn. 168, auch zu den Unterschieden zu der insoweit vertragsfreundlicheren Lösung

Ein niederländischer Antrag in Wien, im Falle des Widerspruchs dem Akzeptanten eine Zurückziehung seiner Modifikationen zu erlauben, um den Vertrag zu retten, hat keine Zustimmung gefunden.[111] Nur wenn man den Widerspruch des Offerenten als Erneuerung seiner Offerte auslegen kann, vermag ein Nachgeben der anderen Seite als (erneute) Annahme ohne Modifikationen doch noch Vertragsschluss zu bewirken. Möglich ist wohl auch, dass der Annehmende seine Ergänzungen usw. als bedingte Vorschläge einbringt, die im Falle eines Widerspruchs als fallen gelassen behandelt werden sollen.[112]

IV. Kollidierende Standardbedingungen

1. Problemstellung

19 Abweichungen in der Annahmeerklärung vom Angebot geschehen regelmäßig, ja fast immer auf Grund der Einbeziehung bzw. versuchten Einbeziehung vorformulierter Vertragsbedingungen. Vor allem die Verwendung von Allgemeinen Geschäftsbedingungen durch beide Seiten führt fast unvermeidlich zu Divergenzen zwischen Angebot und Annahme, da die jeweils verwandten Standardbedingungen kaum je übereinstimmen dürften. Regelmäßig entsteht ein Widerspruch schon durch die Einbeziehungs- und Abwehrklauseln, in denen die Geltung der eigenen Geschäftsbedingungen zum angeblich unverzichtbaren Teil der eigenen Vertragsschlusserklärung gemacht und die Berücksichtigung von Geschäftsbedingungen des anderen Teils ausdrücklich ausgeschlossen werden soll.[113] Auch wo die Geschäftsbedingungen einer Seite Punkte regeln, zu denen die Bedingungen der anderen Seite schweigen, liegt zumeist ein Widerspruch vor, da die insoweit schweigende Vertragserklärung durch die Regeln des Gesetzes zu ergänzen ist, zu denen die zum Regelungsproblem expliziten Bedingungen der anderen Seite fast immer im Widerspruch stehen.[114]

20 An einem Kollisionsfall **fehlt** es, wo und soweit beide Seiten übereinstimmend dieselben Verbandsbedingungen oder von einer dritten Stelle entwickelten standardisierten Vertragsbedingungen verwenden[115] oder wo die AGB der einen Seite ausdrücklich nur insoweit Geltung beanspruchen, wie sie nicht zu den AGB der Gegenseite im Widerspruch stehen.[116] In Einzelfällen wird man zudem auf Grund allgemeiner Übung oder zwischen den Parteien entstandener Gepflogenheiten in Anwendung des Art. 8,[117] Vertragsverhandlungen, Rahmenverträgen, eventuell auch auf Grund eines Handelsbrauchs, der nach Art. 9 Geltung beanspruchen kann, in eine Vertragsschlusserklärung einen von der gesetzlichen Regelung abweichenden Vorschlag hineinlesen können, der dann einer entsprechenden Klausel in der

---

des UCC; zur dogmatischen Konstruktion *Neumayer*, Battle of Forms, S. 518; *Honsell/Dornis*, Art. 19, Rn. 20 m. w. N.: Widerspruch als Eintritt einer auflösenden Bedingung.

[111] S. O. R., S. 96.
[112] *Schwimann/Posch*, Art. 19, Rn. 4.
[113] OLG Linz, 23.3.2005, CISG-online 1376 = IHR 2007, 123, 126; OLG Frankfurt a. M., 26.6.2006, CISG-online 1385 = IHR 2007, 42, 44.
[114] BGH, 9.1.2002, CISG-online 651 = NJW 2002, 1651, 1653; OLG Linz, 23.3.2005, CISG-online 1376 = IHR 2007, 123, 126; *Kramer*, FS Gauch, S. 504 f.; *ders.*, FS Welser, S. 553.
[115] So z. B. die Einheitsbedingungen der deutschen Textil- und Bekleidungsindustrie (OLG München, 11.3.1998, CISG-online 310 = TranspR-IHR 1999, 20, 21) oder die von der Europäischen Wirtschaftskommission der Vereinten Nationen aufgestellten E. C. E.-Lieferbedingungen, s. *Fontaine*, Recht des internationalen Warenkaufs, S. 1197 ff.; *Reithmann/Martiny/Martiny*, Rn. 766 mit Einzelnachweisen. Weitere Nachw. von Bedingungen, die regelmäßig von beiden Seiten „konfliktfrei" verwendet werden, bei *van der Velden*, Battle of Forms, S. 234.
[116] So in Gerechtshof 's-Hertogenbosch, 19.11.1996, CISG-online 323 = NIPR 1997, Nr. 123.
[117] So hat das U. S.-Bundesgericht in *Filanto, S. p. A. v. Chilewich International Corp.*, U. S. Dist. Ct. (S. D. N. Y.), 14.2.1992, CISG-online 45 = 789 F. Supp. 1229, wo Verweisungen in mehreren Verträgen auf unterschiedliche Fassungen eines Vertrages mit einem Dritten kollidierten, auf Grund von Gepflogenheiten, die zwischen den Parteien entstanden waren, eine in das Verhalten des Verkäufers hinein zu interpretierende Billigung der vom Käufer eingeführten Schiedsklausel angenommen.

Erklärung des anderen Teils entspricht, so beim einfachen Eigentumsvorbehalt oder bei der Verwendung von Incoterms®.[118]

2. Lösungsansätze für die „battle of the forms"

Bemühungen um legislative Lösungen für den Vertragsschluss unter (versuchter) Einbeziehung sich gegenseitig widersprechender Standardbedingungen sind schon alt, ohne allerdings bislang zu befriedigenden Ergebnissen geführt zu haben.[119] Das CISG enthält **keine besondere Regel** für die „battle of the forms"; entsprechende Vorschläge während der Vorarbeiten in UNCITRAL und auf der Diplomatischen Konferenz in Wien hatten keinen Erfolg.[120] Da die Sachfrage aber zweifelsfrei in den Regelungsbereich des CISG fällt und angesichts der Behandlung entsprechender Regelungsvorschläge kaum von einer Lücke ausgegangen werden kann, muss das Problem kollidierender Geschäftsbedingungen ausgehend von dem Instrumentarium des Art. 19 gelöst werden.[121] Die vorgeschlagenen Lösungen gehen allerdings – wie zum internen deutschen Recht – auseinander. Vereinfacht – und nicht immer allen Nuancen und Ausnahmen der Autoren für bestimmte Situationen gerecht werdend – lassen sich folgende Grundpositionen unterscheiden: 21

a) **Theorie des letzten Wortes.** Teilweise wird resignierend die **Theorie des letzten Wortes** vertreten, d. h. es soll sich durchsetzen, wer zuletzt unwidersprochen auf seine eigenen Bedingungen verwiesen hat.[122] Diese „last shot rule" ist auch in der Rechtsprechung angewandt worden, wobei die unterschiedlichsten Verhaltensweisen des jeweiligen Antragsgegners als konkludente Annahme der zuletzt übersandten AGB gewertet wurden.[123] Sie kann zwar für sich in Anspruch nehmen, mit dem Wortlaut des Art. 19 I 22

---

[118] Vgl. oben Rn. 6.
[119] Vgl. zu den Bemühungen um eine Reform des § 2–207 UCC zur Lösung dieser Frage *Hyland*, 97 Colum. L. Rev. (1997), 1343, 1350 ff., der resignierend schließt (S. 1360), dass es wohl keine befriedigende Lösung geben könne; *Schlechtriem*, FS Herber, S. 42 ff.; zum schließlich beschlossenen § 2–207 UCC (2003) *Flechtner*, IHR 2004, 225, 230 ff. Zu den Lösungsversuchen in Art. 2.1.22 PICC und Art. 2:209 PECL *Schlechtriem*, FS Herber, S. 40 f.
[120] S. bereits oben Rn. 4; ferner zur Verweisung auf die eigenen AGB als wesentliche oder unwesentliche Abweichung oben Rn. 9.
[121] S. BGH, 9.1.2002, CISG-online 651 = NJW 2002, 1651, 1652 f.; OLG Linz, 23.3.2005, CISG-online 1376 = IHR 2007, 123, 126; *Norfolk Southern Railway Company v. Power Source Supply, Inc.*, U. S. Dist. Ct. (W. D. Pa.), 25.7.2008, CISG-online 1776; *Gabriel*, 49 Bus. Law. (1994), 1053, 1058, 1061; *Holthausen*, RIW 1989, 513, 517 ff.; *Kramer*, FS Welser, S. 553; *Loewe*, Art. 19, S. 44; MünchKomm/*Gruber*, Art. 19, Rn. 18; *Nicholas*, 105 L. Q. R. (1989), 201, 217; *Piltz*, NJW 2003, 2056, 2060; *Schwimann/Posch*, Art. 19, Rn. 7; s. a. *Dannemann*, FS Reynolds, S. 199 ff., 205 f.: Art. 19 „mimics rather than solves the problem"; *Ventsch/Kluth*, IHR 2003, 61, 63. Gegen Anwendung des Art. 19 jedoch *Hellner*, Standard Form Contracts, S. 342 (ohne eigene Lösung); für Anwendung von Art. 7 II (allgemeine Grundsätze und subsidiär nationales Recht) *Del Duca*, 25 J. L. & Com. (2005-06), 133, 146.
[122] OLG Köln, 24.5.2006, CISG-online 1232 = IHR 2006, 147, 148 f.; *Bianca/Bonell/Farnsworth*, Art. 19, Anm. 2.5., mit dem Hinweis, dass dies in der Regel dem Verkäufer zugute komme (anders aber *ders.*, Formation of Contract, § 3.4 sub 3–16); *Blodgett*, 18 Colo. Law. (1989), 423, 426; *Draetta*, Riv. dir. int. priv. proc. 1986, 319, 326; *Enderlein/Maskow/Strohbach*, Art. 19, Anm. 10.; *Garro/Zuppi*, Compraventa internacional, S. 129 f.; *Herber/Czerwenka*, Art. 19, Rn. 18 („vom praktischen Standpunkt mag dieses Ergebnis nicht sehr hilfreich sein"); *Heuzé*, Anm. 187.; *Honsell/Dornis*, Art. 19, Rn. 40; *Janssen*, wbl 2002, 453, 456; *Karollus*, S. 71 (jedoch etwas unklar); *Kelso*, 21 Colum. J. Transnat'l L. (1983), 529, 553; *Ludwig*, S. 336 ff. („Da im Regelfall die Entgegennahme der Ware als der Akt der konkludenten Annahme anzusehen ist, wird es regelmäßig der Verkäufer sein, der – mit der Auftragsbestätigung – zuletzt auf seine Vertragsbedingungen verwiesen hat, so dass dessen Vertragsbedingungen Vertragsbestandteil werden"); MünchKommHGB/*Ferrari*, Art. 19, Rn. 15; *Murray*, 20 J. L. & Com. (2000), 1, 44 f.; *Perales Viscasillas*, Formación del contrato, 728 f.; *dies.*, 10 Pace Int'l L. Rev. (1998), 97, 117 f., 144 ff.; *Piltz*, Internationales Kaufrecht, Rn. 3–111, mit dem Hinweis darauf, dass insbesondere dann, wenn die Parteien während der Vertragsdurchführung mit dem Austausch von AGB fortfahren, ergänzend die Aussagen der Artt. 6–9 zu berücksichtigen seien; *Rudolph*, Art. 19, Rn. 11 (aber mit Variationen, Rn. 12); *Schultz*, 35 Cornell Int'l L. J. (2001-02), 263, 282; *Stadler*, AGB, S. 92 f.; *Winship*, 17 Int'l Law. (1983), 1, 12; offen gelassen in OGH, 13.9.2001, CISG-online 644 = IHR 2002, 74, 76.
[123] *Norfolk Southern Railway Company v. Power Source Supply, Inc.*, U. S. Dist. Ct. (W. D. Pa.), 25.7.2008, CISG-online 1776 („execution" des zuletzt übersandten Dokuments als Annahme); OLG Koblenz, 4.10.2002, CISG-online 716 = IHR 2003, 66, 67 (zuletzt übersandte AGB wurden Vertragsinhalt, weil keine Beanstandung i. S. von Art. 19 II erfolgte und die vom AGB-Verwender gestellte Rechnung bezahlt wurde); OLG

kompatibel zu sein, führt jedoch in ihrer praktischen Anwendung zu zufälligen und für die Parteien kaum vorhersehbaren Ergebnissen.[124]

23 **b) Restgültigkeitstheorie.** Die Vertreter der **Restgültigkeitstheorie** (oder „knock out"-Regel) wollen dagegen den Vertrag trotz kollidierender Geschäftsbedingungen zustande kommen und die Geschäftsbedingungen nur insoweit, wie sie sich widersprechen, ausfallen lassen; an ihre Stelle soll die gesetzliche Regelung (des CISG oder, sofern dieses keine Vorgaben enthält, anderer Regelkomplexe) treten.[125] Ihr sind in Übereinstimmung mit einer Grundsatzentscheidung des BGH[126] auch wesentliche Teile der Rechtsprechung gefolgt.[127] Diese Lösung, die auch in Anwendung des BGB heute wohl herrschend ist[128] und in anderen Rechtsordnungen ebenfalls bevorzugt wird,[129] wirft allerdings die Schwierigkeit auf, dass sie sich unter dem CISG – das eine Regelung des partiellen Dissens wie die §§ 154, 155 BGB nicht enthält und für inhaltlich dissentierende Erklärungen nur Art. 19 zur Verfügung stellt – nur mit erhöhtem argumentativen Aufwand konstruieren lässt.[130]

24 **c) Generelles Scheitern des Vertragsschlusses.** Vereinzelt wird schließlich auch ein generelles Scheitern des Vertragsschlusses angenommen bzw. hingenommen[131] oder ein Rückgriff auf nationales Recht für möglich gehalten.[132]

München, 11.3.1998, CISG-online 310 = TranspR-IHR 1999, 20, 21, m. Anm. *Schlechtriem*, EWiR 1998, 549 („Vertragsdurchführung" als Annahme); OLG Köln, 24.5.2006, CISG-online 1232 = IHR 2006, 147, 148 f. (in concreto offen gelassen, weil beide AGB bezüglich des streitgegenständlichen Punktes – des Gerichtsstandes – eine inhaltlich gleich lautende Regelung vorsahen).

[124] So statt vieler die Kritik bei *Kröll/Hennecke*, RIW 2001, 736, 739 f.; MünchKomm/*Gruber*, Art. 19, Rn. 24.

[125] *Audit*, Vente internationale, Anm. 71.; *Bianca/Bellelli*, S. 92 ff.; *Brunner*, Art. 4, Rn. 44; *Díez-Picazo/Cabanillas Sánchez*, Art. 19, Anm. VIII.; *Honnold/Flechtner*, Art. 19, Rn 170.4; *Keller*, FS Kritzer, S. 252; *Kühl/Hingst*, FS Herber, S. 56 f.; MünchKomm/*Gruber*, Art. 19, Rn. 24; *Niggemann*, RIW 1991, 372, 377; *Reithmann/Martiny/Martiny*, Rn. 738; *Schwenzer/Hachem/Kee*, Rn. 12.33; *Soergel/Lüderitz/Fenge*, Art. 19, Rn. 5; *Staub/Koller*, Vor § 373 HGB, Rn. 647; *Staudinger/Magnus*, Art. 19, Rn. 24; *Stoffel*, Formation du contrat, S. 75; *van der Velden*, Battle of Forms, S. 246; *Ventsch/Kluth*, IHR 2003, 61, 64 f.; *Wey*, Rn. 1343 f. (grds. „Last-Shot"-Theorie, bei Verwendung einer Abwehrklausel jedoch Restgültigkeitstheorie); *Witz/Salger/Lorenz/Witz*, Art. 19, Rn. 16. Vgl. auch *Schlechtriem*, FS Herber, S. 36–49.

[126] BGH, 9.1.2002, CISG-online 651 = NJW 2002, 1651 ff. Trotz der klärenden BGH-Entscheidung halten – wohl wegen der *obiter dicta* zur Theorie des letzten Wortes – die Frage für weiterhin offen *Piltz*, NJW 2003, 2056, 2060; *Ventsch/Kluth*, IHR 2003, 61, 64.

[127] OLG Düsseldorf, 25.7.2003, CISG-online 919; OLG Frankfurt a. M., 26.6.2006, CISG-online 1385 = IHR 2007, 42, 44; in diesem Sinne bereits zuvor Civ. 1, 16.7.1998, CISG-online 344 = D. 1998, 222 (bezgl. kollidierender Gerichtsstandsklauseln); AG Kehl, 6.10.1995, CISG-online 162 = NJW-RR 1996, 565 f. In der Sache ebenso (aber mit abzulehnender interpretativer Bezugnahme auf § 2–207 (b) UCC) *Hanwha Corporation v. Cedar Petrochemicals, Inc.*, U. S. Dist. Ct. (S. D. N. Y.), 18.1.2011, CISG-online 2178: „Here, the parties never agreed to a substantive law to displace the CISG, and their competing choices must fall away, leaving the CISG to fill the void by its own self-executing force".

[128] BGH, 20.3.1985, NJW 1985, 1838, 1839 f.; BGH, 19.6.1991, BB 1991, 1732 ff.; aus der Literatur: MünchKomm/*Busche*, § 154 BGB, Rn. 7; *Palandt/Grüneberg*, § 305, Rn. 54: „Prinzip der Kongruenzgeltung"; *Staudinger/Schlosser*, § 305, Rn. 206 ff.

[129] Vgl. für Frankreich *Will*, Conflicts, S. 99 ff.; für Österreich s. OGH, 7.6.1990, CISG-online 13 = östJBl. 1991, 120; *Tiedemann*, IPRax 1991, 424 ff. (kollidierende Rechtswahlklauseln); zum US-amerikanischen Recht *Gabriel*, 49 Bus. Law. (1994), 1053 ff.; *Petzinger*, RIW 1988, 673, 675 ff. – zu § 2–207 UCC – m. w. N. Zum amerikanischen und französischen Recht ferner *Vergne*, 33 Am. J. Comp. L. (1985), 233, 244 ff., aber auch zum insoweit immer noch traditionelleren englischen Recht S. 239 ff. Umfassend und rechtsvergleichend *von Mehren*, sec. 154–181; *ders.*, 38 Am. J. Comp. L. (1990), 265 ff.; *Kramer*, FS Gauch, S. 495 ff.; *Neumayer*, Battle of Forms, S. 503 ff.

[130] S. näher oben Rn. 25 ff.

[131] *Farnsworth*, Formation of Contract, § 3.04: „And in practice most of these transactions are carried out without incident, even though there is no contract"; *Jametti Greiner*, Vertragsabschluß, S. 52; *Neumayer/Ming*, Art. 19, Anm. 6.; wohl auch *Neumayer*, Battle of Forms, S. 521 ff.

[132] *Dessemontet*, Convention, S. 56; *Huber*, RabelsZ 43 (1979), 413, 444 f. (näher liege die Folgerung, dass bei sich kreuzenden Geschäftsbedingungen ein „offener Dissens" besteht, dass es sich also um ein im CISG nicht geregeltes „Gültigkeitsproblem" i. S. d. Art. 4 S. 2 lit. a) handelt); *Vergne*, 33 Am. J. Comp. L. (1985), 233, 257.

3. Stellungnahme

Zustimmung verdient der Lösungsansatz der sog. **Restgültigkeitstheorie,**[133] die im grenzüberschreitenden Warenkauf einen handhabbaren und vor allem sachgerechten Weg zum Umgang mit kollidierenden Standardbedingungen eröffnet. Sie hat sich auch in anderen Einheitsrechtsprojekten als mittlerweile ganz herrschend herauskristallisiert.[134] Unter dem UN-Kaufrecht hängt ihre (in Übereinstimmung mit dem Postulat des Art. 7 I anzustrebende) internationale Akzeptanz vor allem davon ab, ob die argumentative Einpassung der „knock out rule" in das Regelungssystem des CISG gelingt. Zu diesem Zweck ist es zunächst erforderlich, die unglückliche Verquickung von Vertragsschluss- und Vertragsinhaltsgestaltung, die Art. 19 zugrunde liegt (s. oben Rn. 1), aufzulösen und zwischen dem Zustandekommen des Vertrages[135] und seiner inhaltlichen Ausgestaltung[136] zu unterscheiden.[137]

25

a) Vertragsschluss trotz sich inhaltlich widersprechender Standardbedingungen. Ein Kaufvertrag kommt danach weit überwiegend auch in Konstellationen zustande, in denen Käufer und Verkäufer divergierende Standardbedingungen ausgetauscht haben. In Anknüpfung an die tatsächlichen Umstände typischer Fallgestaltungen[138] ist wie folgt zu unterscheiden:

26

aa) Vorausgegangener mündlicher Vertragsschluss. Vielfach – und dies wird häufig übersehen – ist ein Kaufvertrag zwischen den Parteien bereits mündlich abgeschlossen worden, bevor schriftliche „Bestellungen", „Bestätigungen" o. ä. erstmals übersandt werden.[139] Sofern die mündlich (regelmäßig telefonisch) ausgetauschten Erklärungen der Parteien den Voraussetzungen der Artt. 14, 18 genügen, vor allem mit aktuellem Bindungswillen[140] abgegeben wurden, ist der Kaufvertrag damit nach CISG wirksam zustande gekommen (Artt. 11, 23), ohne dass es auf eine schriftliche Bestätigung ankäme. Später ausgetauschte Standardbedingungen stellen in diesem Fall daher allenfalls einen Versuch zur einvernehmlichen Vertragsänderung dar,[141] der das Bestehen des Kaufvertrages nicht beeinflusst, sondern lediglich zu einem veränderten Vertragsinhalt führen kann (dazu sogleich Rn. 34). Hierin liegt ein entscheidender Unterschied zu manchen Rechtsordnungen, die – wie etwa der UCC in § 2–201 *(Statute of Frauds)* – die Wirksamkeit eines Kaufvertragsschlusses von einer schriftlichen Fixierung des Vertragsinhalts abhängig machen und dadurch bewirken, dass bei einem „battle of the forms" nach mündlichem Vertragsschluss zugleich die Existenz des Kaufvertrages auf dem Spiel steht.[142]

27

bb) (Konkludente) Abbedingung des Art. 19 durch die Parteien. Sofern die Standardbedingungen Bestandteil der Vertragsschlusserklärungen der Parteien sind, ist zu prüfen, ob die Geltung des (einem Vertragsschluss dem Normwortlaut nach entgegenstehenden) Art. 19 in Übereinstimmung mit Art. 6 abbedungen wurde.[143] Eine solche privatautonome

28

---

[133] S. oben Rn. 23.
[134] Art. 2.1.22 PICC; Art. 2:209 PECL; Art. II–4:209 DCFR; Art. 39 CESL-Entwurf. Dagegen enthält der AUDCG der OHADA – wie das CISG – auch nach seiner Reform im Jahre 2010 keine gesonderte Regelung zur „battle of the forms".
[135] S. sogleich Rn. 26 ff.
[136] S. Rn. 34 ff.
[137] S. a. *Perales Viscasillas*, 10 Pace Int'l L. Rev. (1998), 97, 107 ff.; *Schwenzer/Mohs*, IHR 2006, 239, 244; zur Lösung des BGH, 9.1.2002, CISG-online 651 = NJW 2002, 1651 ff. s. *Magnus*, LM Nr. 10 CISG Bl. 6; zum Ganzen *Schlechtriem*, FS Herber, S. 40.
[138] Zur Praxis s. allerdings auch *Murray*, 4 Can. Bus. L. J. (1979-80), 290–296, der als Corporate Counsel für IBM Canada darauf hinwies, dass sich das Problem kollidierender AGBs für diese Firma noch nie gestellt habe.
[139] S. den zutreffenden Hinweis in *Travelers Property Casualty Company of America et al. v. Saint-Gobain Technical Fabrics Canada Ltd.*, U. S. Dist. Ct. (D. Minn.), 31.1.2007, CISG-online 1435 = IHR 2007, 240, 243; zudem etwa Gerechtshof 's-Hertogenbosch, 19.11.1996, CISG-online 323 = NIPR 1997, Nr. 123.
[140] S. oben Art. 14 Rn. 23 ff.
[141] S. dazu noch unten Art. 29 Rn. 7 ff.
[142] Vgl. *Murray*, 20 J. L. & Com. (2000), 1, 21 ff.
[143] S. AG Kehl, 6.10.1995, CISG-online 162 = NJW-RR 1996, 565; *van Alstine*, S. 213 f.; *Kühl/Hingst*, FS Herber, S. 57; *Kramer*, FS Welser, S. 556 f.; *Murray*, 8 J. L. & Com. (1988), 11, 40 ff., 44; *Schlechtriem*, Interna-

Derogation des Art. 19 kann nach dem CISG formlos und konkludent erfolgen.[144] Bei Verwendung sich inhaltlich widersprechender Standardbedingungen durch die Vertragsparteien wird eine Abbedingung des Art. 19, soweit er einen Vertragsschluss verhindern würde, **typischerweise** anzunehmen sein, weil das Interesse der Parteien am Zustandekommen des Kaufvertrages regelmäßig ausgeprägter ist als das Interesse an einer Durchsetzung der eigenen AGB um den Preis eines Vertragsschlusses.[145]

29 Ein Vertragsschluss kommt dabei trotz sich inhaltlich widersprechender Standardbedingungen zunächst dort zustande, wo sich eine entsprechende **Gepflogenheit** zwischen den Parteien entwickelt hat (Art. 9 I), etwa weil Kaufverträge, bei deren Abschluss man schon in der Vergangenheit in entsprechender Weise verfahren war, ohne Beanstandung der Bedingungskollision durchgeführt wurden.[146]

30 Ansatzpunkt für die Feststellung eines Einigseins der Vertragsparteien über ihren Vertragsschluss ist im Übrigen die **Auslegung** ihrer (unter Bezugnahme auf ihre AGB oder Formularbedingungen abgegebenen) **Vertragsschlusserklärungen** nach Art. 8 II, III.[147] Dabei ist nicht an dem Wortlaut der Erklärungen zu haften, sondern unter Berücksichtigung aller erheblichen Umstände zu verfahren.[148] Besondere Bedeutung kommt hierbei dem **späteren** – d. h. nach Erklärungsabgabe erfolgten – **Verhalten** der Parteien zu, dessen Beachtung **Art. 8 III** vorschreibt. Die bereits ursprünglich bestehende Einigung der Vertragsparteien über den Vertragsschluss sowie darüber, dass in Art. 19 als vertragsschlusshindernd benannte Abweichungen im Falle ihrer Standardbedingungen der Vertragsbindung nicht entgegenstehen sollen, kommt dabei namentlich in der **Vertragsdurchführung** zum Ausdruck, und zwar sowohl in einer vorbehaltlosen Erbringung der wechselseitig geschuldeten Leistungen durch beide Parteien[149] als auch dadurch, dass eine Partei leistet und die andere Partei die Leistung vorbehaltlos entgegennimmt, ohne eine noch ausstehende Einigung über die kollidierenden Bedingungen zu bemängeln.[150] Dass die Standardbedingungen in ihrem Wortlaut konditional formulierte Einbeziehungs- oder Abwehrklauseln („Gültigkeit des Vertrages hängt von der Zustimmung zu unseren Klauseln ab") oder Ausschließlichkeitsvorbehalte enthalten mögen, steht der beschriebenen, zum Vertragsschluss führenden Auslegung dabei nicht entgegen.[151]

31 Daneben können aber auch **Leistungsvorbereitungen** durch beide oder eine der Parteien, die mit oder ohne Mitwirkung des Vertragspartners vorgenommen werden, nach

---

tionales UN-Kaufrecht, Rn. 92; *Schwenzer/Mohs*, IHR 2006, 239, 244; *Staudinger/Magnus*, Art. 19, Rn. 25; *Witz/Salger/Lorenz/Witz*, Art. 19, Rn. 17.

[144] Vgl. *Staudinger/Magnus*, Art. 6, Rn. 20 ff.

[145] S. *Kramer*, FS Gauch, S. 505; skeptisch hingegen *Piltz*, Internationales Kaufrecht, Rn. 3–109. Etwas anderes kommt nur in seltenen Fällen vor, und zwar vor allem dort, wo die Parteien eine längerfristige Geschäftsbeziehung planen: In diesem Fall wird über die AGB-Inhalte und deren Kollision im Einzelnen verhandelt, bevor der erste Vertragsabschluss getätigt wird (und vielfach im Ergebnis ein Rahmenvertrag abgeschlossen, der einen künftigen AGB-Austausch überflüssig macht); so etwa in *Magellan International Corp. v. Salzgitter Handel GmbH*, U. S. Dist. Ct. (N. D. Ill.), 7.12.1999, CISG-online 439 = 76 F. Supp. 2d 919, 921: „Contemplating an ongoing business relationship, Magellan and Salzgitter continued to negotiate in an effort to resolve the remaining conflicts between their respective forms…".

[146] *Kühl/Hingst*, FS Herber, S. 54; teilweise anders *Kröll/Hennecke*, RIW 2001, 736, 741. *Schwenzer/Hachem/Kee*, Rn. 12.33 wollen die Restgültigkeitstheorie hingegen als internationalen Handelsbrauch einstufen.

[147] *Achilles*, Art. 19, Rn. 5; *Hammerschmidt*, S. 103, 111 ff.; *Kröll/Hennecke*, RIW 2001, 736, 742.

[148] S. *Staudinger/Magnus*, Art. 8, Rn. 24.

[149] BGH, 9.1.2002, CISG-online 651 = NJW 2002, 1651, 1652; AG Kehl, 6.10.1995, CISG-online 162 = NJW-RR 1996, 565; *Janssen*, wbl. 2002, 453, 456 f.; MünchKomm/*Gruber*, Art. 19, Rn. 20; *Teklote*, S. 155; *Ventsch/Kluth*, IHR 2003, 61, 63; *Witz/Salger/Lorenz/Witz*, Art. 19, Rn. 16; ebenso, aber mit zweifelhafter Begründung OLG Frankfurt a. M., 26.6.2006, CISG-online 1385 = IHR 2007, 42, 44: Rechtsgedanke des § 306 BGB.

[150] MünchKomm/*Gruber*, Art. 19, Rn. 20; *Witz/Salger/Lorenz/Witz*, Art. 19, Rn. 16; wohl auch *Staudinger/Magnus*, Art. 19, Rn. 24, der allgemein „Durchführungsakte" für ausreichend hält.

[151] *Kramer*, FS Welser, S. 558; MünchKomm/*Gruber*, Art. 19, Rn. 24; *Witz/Salger/Lorenz/Witz*, Art. 19, Rn. 17.

Art. 8 III bereits zum Ausdruck bringen, dass die Parteien ihre Geschäftsbedingungen bzw. die Verweisung darauf weniger ernst als den angestrebten Vertragsschluss genommen haben, also trotz eines offenen oder versteckten Dissens über Standardbedingungen und ihre Einbeziehung gebunden sein wollen. Entscheidend sind im Ergebnis die Umstände des Einzelfalls.[152] Da entsprechende Vorgänge nach hier vertretener Ansicht bereits im Rahmen der **Interpretation der ursprünglichen Vertragsschlusserklärungen** zu berücksichtigen sind,[153] ohne dass die Verhaltensweisen selbst eine (in diesem Fall erst nachträgliche) Einigung nach Art. 6 über die Abbedingung des Art. 19 konstituieren müssten,[154] kommt es dabei auf die Einvernehmlichkeit des betreffenden Verhaltens sowie ggfs. dessen Zugang nicht zwingend an. Damit wird freilich nicht ausgeschlossen, dass die Vertragsparteien im Einzelfall tatsächlich erst während der Vertragsdurchführung konkludent die Derogation des Art. 19 vereinbaren.

cc) **Vertragsschluss bei Eingreifen des Art. 19.** Sofern hingegen keine ausreichenden 32 Anzeichen dafür feststellbar sind, dass die Parteien den Kaufvertrag im Falle einer Bedingungskollision unter Verzicht auf ihre jeweiligen Klauselwerke zustande bringen wollen, richtet sich der Vertragsschluss nach Art. 19. Entsprechende Konstellationen können auftreten, sofern zwischen den Parteien weder in der Vergangenheit Verträge trotz kollidierender Standardbedingungen durchgeführt wurden noch mit der Ausführung des konkreten Kaufvertrages begonnen wurde, bevor die „battle of the forms"-Problematik bemerkt wird – in der Praxis dürfte dies äußerst selten sein,[155] weil der Inhalt der verwendeten AGB für die Vertragsparteien typischerweise erst Bedeutung erlangt, nachdem im Verlauf der Vertragsdurchführung Schwierigkeiten aufgetreten sind.[156]

Tritt der beschriebene Ausnahmefall auf, so hängt der Vertragsschluss davon ab, ob der 33 Inhalt der unter Einschluss der kollidierenden Standardbedingungen abgegebenen Vertragsschlusserklärungen i. S. d. Art. 19 II, III wesentlich oder nur unwesentlich voneinander abweicht. Liegt eine nur unwesentliche Abweichung vor, so kommt der Vertrag trotz der Divergenz zustande, soweit die Gegenseite nicht widerspricht (Art. 19 II).[157] Eine Abwehrklausel in den AGB des Offerenten ist dabei als vorgezogener Widerspruch zu werten.[158] Für ein Eingreifen des Art. 19 II bleibt freilich kein Raum, sofern man – wie hier[159] – jede Verweisung auf AGB regelmäßig als wesentliche Abweichung einstuft. Daneben dürften allerdings auch vor dem Hintergrund des Art. 19 III im Regelfall wesentliche Abweichungen vorliegen,[160] was gemäß Art. 19 I das Scheitern des Vertragsschlusses zur Folge hat.[161]

b) **Vertragsinhalt.** Sodann ist zu prüfen, ob und inwieweit im Falle eines zustande 34 gekommenen Kaufvertrages der Vertragsinhalt durch die Geschäftsbedingungen einer oder beider Seiten inhaltlich ausgestaltet worden ist. Im **Grundsatz** werden – neben den außer-

---

[152] *Schlechtriem,* FS Herber, S. 44 f.
[153] Wie hier *Hammerschmidt,* S. 103; *Kramer,* FS Welser, S. 556 f.; wohl auch BGH, 9.1.2002, CISG-online 651 = NJW 2002, 1651, 1652. Zu sehr ähnlichen Ergebnissen gelangen Autoren, die einer nachträglichen Berufung auf die Wesentlichkeit i. S. d. Art. 19 III und damit der Einigungsbedürftigkeit das Verbot des *venire contra factum proprium* (Art. 7 I) entgegenhalten wollen, weil der Kontrahent sich zu seinem eigenen Verhalten in Widerspruch setze (so *Witz/Salger/Lorenz/Witz,* Art. 19, Rn. 17); vgl. zum gemeinsamen Kern beider Argumentationsansätze Audiencia Provincial de Navarra, 27.12.2007, CISG-online 1798; *Staudinger/Magnus,* Art. 8, Rn. 26.
[154] So hingegen *van Alstine,* S. 220 ff.; MünchKomm/*Gruber,* Art. 19, Rn. 20 (der einvernehmliche Vorbereitungs- und Mitwirkungshandlungen ausreichen lässt); strenger *Witz/Salger/Lorenz/Witz,* Art. 19, Rn. 19; unklar *Staudinger/Magnus,* Art. 19, Rn. 25.
[155] *Kramer,* FS Welser, S. 558.
[156] S. *Schlechtriem,* FS Herber, S. 45.
[157] S. oben Rn. 14 ff.; *Brunner,* Art. 4, Rn. 44; MünchKomm/*Gruber,* Art. 19, Rn. 26; MünchKommHGB/*Ferrari,* Art. 19, Rn. 15; *Staudinger/Magnus,* Art. 19, Rn. 21; *Witz/Salger/Lorenz/Witz,* Art. 19, Rn. 15.
[158] MünchKomm/*Gruber,* Art. 19, Rn. 26; *Witz/Salger/Lorenz/Witz,* Art. 19, Rn. 15.
[159] S. oben Rn. 9.
[160] S. oben Rn. 8 ff.; a. A. – stets Art. 19 II anwendend – *Lautenschlager,* 11 VJ (2007), 259, 289.
[161] MünchKomm/*Gruber,* Art. 19, Rn. 26; *Witz/Salger/Lorenz/Witz,* Art. 19, Rn. 15.

halb der AGB konsentierten Punkten (vor allem den *essentialia negotii*) – solche Bestimmungen, die in beiden Standardbedingungen inhaltlich übereinstimmen, zum Vertragsbestandteil (daher „Restgültigkeit"),[162] während im Übrigen die Regelungen des CISG sowie subsidiär des nationalen Rechts (Art. 7 II) eingreifen.[163]

35 Unter welchen Voraussetzungen von **„übereinstimmenden"** und daher trotz Kollision der Gesamtbedingungswerke geltenden Bestimmungen gesprochen werden kann, ist allerdings nicht immer einfach zu entscheiden. Geringe Schwierigkeiten bereiten einen isolierten Regelungsgegenstand betreffende Klauseln wie etwa Schieds- oder Gerichtsstandsklauseln, die zudem infolge weitgehender inhaltlicher Standardisierung auch in ihrer Ausgestaltung tatsächlich übereinstimmen mögen.[164] Gleiches gilt für Bedingungen einer Seite, die der gesetzlichen Regelung, Bräuchen oder zwischen den Parteien etablierten Gepflogenheiten entsprechen oder durch Auslegung als Erklärungsinhalt der Vertragsschlusserklärung der anderen Seite gesehen werden können. Im Allgemeinen dürfen einzelne Klauseln allerdings nicht isoliert betrachtet werden, weil vielfach ein inhaltlicher Zusammenhang mit den übrigen Bestimmungen desselben Bedingungswerkes besteht; es bedarf daher einer Gesamtwürdigung aller einschlägigen Regelungen.[165] Ohne Bedeutung ist dabei, ob die einzelne Klausel für die jeweilige Gegenpartei günstig oder ungünstig ist.[166] Für ein Übereinstimmen von Standardbedingungen wird daher im internationalen Rechtsverkehr im Ergebnis wenig Raum bleiben; etwas anderes gilt auch dort nicht, wo die Bedingungen einer Seite zu einem bestimmten Regelungsgegenstand der anderen AGB schweigen und keine Abwehrklausel enthalten, weil in diesem Fall die einseitige AGB-Regelung typischerweise von den andernfalls eingreifenden gesetzlichen Bestimmungen abweicht.[167]

36 Findet im konkreten Fall trotz der Verwendung kollidierender Standardbedingungen hingegen Art. 19 Anwendung (oben Rn. 32), so umfasst ein aufgrund lediglich unwesentlicher Abweichungen nach **Art. 19 II** zustande gekommener Vertrag die Bedingungen des Offerenten in dem Umfang, in dem diese mit den AGB des Oblaten übereinstimmen, sowie die unwesentlich davon abweichenden AGB des Oblaten.[168]

---

[162] *Brunner*, Art. 4, Rn. 44; MünchKomm/*Gruber*, Art. 19, Rn. 21; *Schwenzer/Mohs*, IHR 2006, 239, 244; *Witz/Salger/Lorenz/Witz*, Art. 19, Rn. 18.
[163] *Karollus*, S. 71; *Lookofsky*, The 1980 United Nations Convention, Anm. 125.; *Staudinger/Magnus*, Art. 19, Rn. 24; *Stoffel*, Formation du contrat, S. 75; *Witz/Salger/Lorenz/Witz*, Art. 19, Rn. 18.
[164] So etwa in OLG Köln, 24.5.2006, CISG-online 1232 = IHR 2006, 147, 148. wie hier *Schmidt-Kessel/Meyer*, IHR 2008, 177, 179.
[165] BGH, 9.1.2002, CISG-online 651 = NJW 2002, 1651, 1653; MünchKomm/*Gruber*, Art. 19, Rn. 21.
[166] BGH, 9.1.2002, CISG-online 651 = NJW 2002, 1651, 1653 (wo im konkreten Fall die Haftungsregelung in den Käufer-AGB für den Verkäufer günstiger war als die Bestimmungen seiner eigenen Bedingungen!).
[167] S. bereits oben Rn. 19; a. A. MünchKomm/*Gruber*, Art. 19, Rn. 21.
[168] MünchKommHGB/*Ferrari*, Art. 19, Rn. 15.

Art. 20 [Annahmefrist]

(1) Eine vom Anbietenden in einem Telegramm oder einem Brief gesetzte Annahmefrist beginnt mit Aufgabe des Telegramms oder mit dem im Brief angegebenen Datum oder, wenn kein Datum angegeben ist, mit dem auf dem Umschlag angegebenen Datum zu laufen. Eine vom Anbietenden telefonisch, durch Fernschreiben oder eine andere sofortige Übermittlungsart gesetzte Annahmefrist beginnt zu laufen, sobald das Angebot dem Empfänger zugeht.

(2) Gesetzliche Feiertage oder arbeitsfreie Tage, die in die Laufzeit der Annahmefrist fallen, werden bei der Fristberechnung mitgezählt. Kann jedoch die Mitteilung der Annahme am letzten Tag der Frist nicht an die Anschrift des Anbietenden zugestellt werden, weil dieser Tag am Ort der Niederlassung des Anbietenden auf einen gesetzlichen Feiertag oder arbeitsfreien Tag fällt, so verlängert sich die Frist bis zum ersten darauf folgenden Arbeitstag.

Art. 20

(1) A period of time for acceptance fixed by the offeror in a telegram or a letter begins to run from the moment the telegram is handed in for dispatch or from the date shown on the letter or, if no such date is shown, from the date shown on the envelope. A period of time for acceptance fixed by the offeror by telephone, telex or other means of instantaneous communication, begins to run from the moment that the offer reaches the offeree.

(2) Official holidays or non-business days occurring during the period for acceptance are included in calculating the period. However, if a notice of acceptance cannot be delivered at the address of the offeror on the last day of the period because that day falls on an official holiday or a non-business day at the place of business of the offeror, the period is extended until the first business day which follows.

Art. 20

1) Le délai d'acceptation fixé par l'auteur de l'offre dans un télégramme ou une lettre commence à courir au moment où le télégramme est remis pour expédition ou à la date qui apparaît sur la lettre ou, à défaut, à la date qui apparaît sur l'enveloppe. Le délai d'acceptation que l'auteur de l'offre fixe par téléphone, par télex ou par d'autres moyens de communication instantanés commence à courir au moment où l'offre parvient au destinataire.

2) Les jours fériés ou chômés qui tombent pendant que court le délai d'acceptation sont comptés dans le calcul de ce délai. Cependant, si la notification ne peut être remise à l'adresse de l'auteur de l'offre le dernier jour du délai, parce que celui-ci tombe un jour férié ou chômé au lieu d'établissement de l'auteur de l'offre, e délai est prorogé jusqu'au premier jour ouvrable suivant.

Übersicht

	Rn.
I. Fristbeginn	1
1. Frist als Zeitraum	1
2. Fristsetzung in einem Brief	2
3. Fristsetzung in telefonischer Erklärung oder mit ähnlichen unmittelbaren Kommunikationsmitteln	3
a) Unmittelbare Kommunikationsmittel	3
b) Elektronische Kommunikationsmittel	3a
4. Fristsetzung durch gesonderte Erklärung	4
II. Fristberechnung	5
1. Grundregel: Art. 20 II 1	5
2. Ausnahme: Art. 20 II 2	6
3. Anwendung auf sonstige Fristen	7

Vorläufer und **Entwürfe:** Art. 8 II EAG, New Yorker E 1977 Art. 8 II, III, Genfer E 1977 Art. 14 I, II, New Yorker E 1978 Art. 18.

I. Fristbeginn

1. Frist als Zeitraum

1 Bei einer **Annahmefrist,** die vom Offerenten nicht kalendermäßig, sondern durch Bestimmung eines Zeitraums (zehn Tage, zwei Wochen, ein Monat usw.) gesetzt wird, muss der Fristbeginn geregelt werden. Das kann durch den Offerenten geschehen („ab dem 5. 3.ᵃ, „ab Zugang dieser Offerte"); ein englischer Vorschlag in Wien, dies zur Klarstellung einzufügen, wurde als überflüssig bewertet und deshalb zurückgezogen.[1] Ein vom Offerenten gesetzter Fristbeginn kann sich auch auf Grund einer Auslegung der Offerte oder (und) der Fristsetzung ergeben.[2] Mangels Bestimmung des Fristbeginns gegenüber dem Offerenten greift die **Auslegungsregel**[3] des Art. 20 I ein. Sie gilt sowohl für eine Frist, die (nur) Widerruflichkeit ausschließen soll als auch für eine solche, nach deren Ablauf die Offerte erlischt.[4] Ist ein **Endtermin** gesetzt,[5] dann kommt es auf den Fristbeginn nicht an.[6]

2. Fristsetzung in einem Brief

2 Bei einem **Brief** beginnt die Frist mit dem im Brief angegebenen Datum, hilfsweise mit dem Datum auf dem Umschlag, also regelmäßig dem Datum des Poststempels.[7] Auf das tatsächliche Datum der Absendung kommt es nicht an.[8] Die Regelung gilt auch, wenn ein Brief nicht durch den allgemeinen (in zahlreichen Ländern staatlich organisierten) Postdienst, sondern durch einen privaten Zustelldienst übermittelt wird.[9] Bei einem **Telegramm** entscheidet dagegen das – bei der Aufgabestelle, üblicherweise auch im Telegramm festgehaltene – Aufgabedatum.

Sofern weder in dem Brief noch auf dem Umschlag ein Datum angegeben oder dieses nicht leserlich ist, ist das **Zugangsdatum** maßgeblich, weil das Fehlen jeglicher Datumsangabe dem erklärenden Offerenten zuzurechnen ist.[10] Zeigt der Briefumschlag hingegen mehrere unterschiedliche Daten, so ist nach dem Normzweck des Art. 20 auf das frühere Datum abzustellen.[11]

3. Fristsetzung in telefonischer Erklärung oder mit ähnlichen unmittelbaren Kommunikationsmitteln

3 a) **Unmittelbare Kommunikationsmittel.** Bei Erklärungsmitteln unmittelbarer Kommunikation – Art. 20 I 2 nennt Telefon und Telex als Beispiele – legt dagegen der Zugang der Offerte – Art. 24[12] – den Fristbeginn fest. Andere derartige Mittel sind etwa Telefax,[13]

---

[1] S. O. R., S. 290, Art. 18, Nr. 1–6.
[2] Vgl. *Honnold/Flechtner,* Art. 20, Rn. 171: „Fünf Tage Überlegungszeit" bedeute, dass die Frist erst mit Zugang beginnen könne, da erst ab Zugang Überlegungen zum Offerteninhalt möglich seien; MünchKomm/*Gruber,* Art. 20, Rn. 3; dazu auch *Bianca/Bonell/Farnsworth,* Art. 20, Anm. 2.1., der in diesem Fall noch Postlaufzeiten hinzurechnen will, um die volle Überlegungsfrist zu gewährleisten.
[3] *Brunner,* Art. 20, Rn. 1; *Honnold/Flechtner,* Art. 20, Rn. 171; MünchKomm/*Gruber,* Art. 20, Rn. 2; krit. im Vergleich zum UCC *Murray,* 8 J. L. & Com. (1988), 11, 20.
[4] *Bianca/Bonell/Farnsworth,* Art. 20, Anm. 3.1.
[5] Vgl. etwa LG Hamburg, 23.11.2003, CISG-online 875: in Angebot per E-Mail wurde Annahme bis „morgen bei unserer Eröffnung" verlangt.
[6] *Honsell/Dornis,* Art. 20, Rn. 3; MünchKomm/*Gruber,* Art. 20, Rn. 3; *Staudinger/Magnus,* Art. 20, Rn. 4.
[7] Zu dieser Reihenfolge s. Sekretariatskommentar, Art. 18, Nr. 3: Der Umschlag wird vom Empfänger oft weggeworfen. Geht auch der Brief verloren, so existiert zumeist beim Absender noch eine Kopie.
[8] *Enderlein/Maskow/Strohbach,* Art. 20, Anm. 2.; MünchKomm/*Gruber,* Art. 20, Rn. 5.
[9] MünchKomm/*Gruber,* Art. 20, Rn. 5; *Witz/Salger/Lorenz/Witz,* Art. 20, Rn. 6.
[10] *Bamberger/Roth/Saenger,* Art. 20, Rn. 3; *Honsell/Dornis,* Art. 20, Rn. 6; MünchKomm/*Gruber,* Art. 20, Rn. 6; *Staudinger/Magnus,* Art. 20, Rn. 8; a. A. *Witz/Salger/Lorenz/Witz,* Art. 20, Rn. 6: Absendetag entscheidend.
[11] MünchKomm/*Gruber,* Art. 20, Rn. 7; *Witz/Salger/Lorenz/Witz,* Art. 20, Rn. 6.
[12] Zum Zugang bei diesen Kommunikationsmitteln s. unten Art. 24 Rn. 16 ff.
[13] *Hahnkamper,* 25 J. L. & Com. (2005-06), 147 f.; *Honsell/Dornis,* Art. 20, Rn. 11; *Staudinger/Magnus,* Art. 20, Rn. 10.

Teletex, Bildschirmtext,[14] Minitel,[15] Funk,[16] auch Bild- und Tonübertragung in Videokonferenzen. Zu Chat-Foren im Internet s. sogleich Rn. 3a. Mündliche Erklärungen sind, soweit sie eine vom Offerenten gesetzte Frist enthalten,[17] gleich zu behandeln: Die Frist beginnt mit vernehmbarer Äußerung.[18] M. E. muss Entsprechendes auch für Erklärungen durch oder an Boten gelten: Nicht das Losschicken des Erklärungsboten, sondern seine Erklärung setzt ein für den Empfänger erkennbares Datum. Bei Empfangsboten ist wieder Zugang entscheidend.[19]

b) Elektronische Kommunikationsmittel. Elektronische Kommunikationsmittel, vom Übereinkommen nicht bedacht, sind unterschiedlich zu behandeln: E-Mails sind nicht stets „unmittelbar" i. S. v. Art. 20 I 2, enthalten andererseits aber wohl immer das genaue Absendedatum. Das rechtfertigt es, sie mit Briefen und Telegrammen gleichzusetzen, also Fristbeginn mit Absendedatum nach Art. 20 I 1 anzunehmen.[20] Auf Websites erklärte Offerten,[21] die eine Annahmefrist – z. B. „Angebot gilt für 5 Tage" – enthalten, müssen hinsichtlich des Fristbeginns nach Art. 8, insbesondere Abs. 2 und 3, ausgelegt werden.[22] Zu Lasten des Offerenten, der als Herr seiner Offerte ein Datum hätte setzen können, ist aus der Sicht eines vernünftigen Adressaten anzunehmen, dass die Frist mit der ersten Kenntnisnahme durch den (einen jeweiligen) Interessenten zu laufen beginnt.[23] Soweit dagegen elektronische Kommunikation der Parteien über Internet in Echtzeit („real time") erfolgt, etwa in sog. „chat programs", steht sie mündlicher Kommunikation gleich, ist also „unmittelbar" und fällt unter Art. 20 I 2.[24]

4. Fristsetzung durch gesonderte Erklärung

Die **Fristsetzung** kann auch **durch** eine **gesonderte,** neben oder nach der Offerte gemachte **Erklärung** erfolgen. Diese Erklärung ist zugangsbedürftig, und zwar auch dann, wenn die in ihr gesetzte Frist bereits mit dem Datum des Briefs oder des Telegramms – Art. 20 I 1 – zu laufen beginnt. Insoweit kann nichts anderes gelten, als wenn die Frist – wie üblich – in der Offerte selbst gesetzt wird.[25]

II. Fristberechnung

1. Grundregel: Art. 20 II 1

Die in Art. 20 II 1 getroffene Regelung schafft Klarheit; ein Rückgriff auf internes nationales Recht über IPR findet nicht statt. Im grenzüberschreitenden Verkehr würden Probleme entstehen, wenn **gesetzliche Feiertage** und **arbeitsfreie Tage** vom Offerenten

---

[14] MünchKomm/*Gruber*, Art. 20, Rn. 4.
[15] *Staudinger/Magnus*, Art. 20, Rn. 10.
[16] MünchKomm/*Gruber*, Art. 20, Rn. 4; *Rudolph*, Art. 20, Rn. 5; *Staudinger/Magnus*, Art. 20, Rn. 10.
[17] Vgl. oben Art. 18 Rn. 14.
[18] S. zum Zugang mündlicher Erklärungen unten Art. 24 Rn. 10 ff.
[19] S. a. *Honsell/Dornis*, Art. 20, Rn. 12; MünchKomm/*Gruber*, Art. 20, Rn. 4; *Staudinger/Magnus*, Art. 20, Rn. 11; vgl. zum Zugang bei Übermittlung von Erklärungen an Empfangsboten unten Art. 24 Rn. 8 f.
[20] Überzeugend CISG-AC, Op. 1 *(Chr. Ramberg)*, Comment 20.3, IHR 2003, 244, 247; *Honsell/Dornis*, Art. 20, Rn. 10; a. A. („unmittelbar" i. S. v. Art. 20 I 2) in Deutschland herrschend, *Bamberger/Roth/Saenger*, Art. 20, Rn. 4; *Eiselen*, 6 EDI L. Rev. (1999), 21, 30 f.; MünchKomm/*Gruber*, Art. 20, Rn. 4; *Soergel/Lüderitz/Fenge*, Art. 14, Rn. 5; *Staudinger/Magnus*, Art. 20, Rn. 10.
[21] Hierzu oben Vor Artt. 14–24 Rn. 28, Art. 14 Rn. 28.
[22] CISG-AC, Op. 1 *(Chr. Ramberg)*, Comment 20.4, IHR 2003, 244, 247.
[23] Anders möglicherweise CISG-AC, Op. 1 *(Chr. Ramberg)*, Comment 20.4, IHR 2003, 244, 248, wo größere Schutzbedürftigkeit des Offerenten wegen seiner Bindung angenommen wird; a. A. auch *Honsell/Dornis*, Art. 20, Rn. 10.
[24] CISG-AC, Op. 1 *(Chr. Ramberg)*, Comment 20.5, IHR 2003, 244, 248.
[25] Abweichend vielleicht *Bianca/Bonell/Farnsworth*, Art. 24, Anm. 1.1., der Zugangsbedürftigkeit offenbar nur für die in Art. 20 I 2 geregelte Fristsetzung erwähnt.

Art. 20 6, 7

und (oder) vom Oblaten berücksichtigt werden müssten; sie können selbst in einem Staat von Stadt zu Stadt, Region zu Region, von Bundesland zu Bundesland verschieden sein. Sie werden deshalb wie normale Tage mitgezählt. Abs. 2 ist jedoch Auslegungsregel; die Parteien können eine andere Fristberechnung vereinbart haben.

2. Ausnahme: Art. 20 II 2

6 Die in Rn. 5 berichtete ratio der Regel des Abs. 2 S. 1 trifft für den (rechtzeitigen) Zugang der Annahmeerklärung beim Offerenten nicht zu: Der Offerent kennt „seine" gesetzlichen Feiertage und arbeitsfreien Tage, nicht dagegen der Annehmende.[26] Abs. 2 S. 2 „verlängert" deshalb die Angebotsfrist bis zum nächsten Arbeitstag. Gemeint ist ein kraft Gesetzes arbeitsfreier Tag, nicht etwa ein Betriebsausflugtag oder ein Streiktag.[27] Das Recht, das am Ort der Niederlassung des Anbietenden oder (und) dort, wo die Annahme i. S. d. Art. 24 „zuzustellen" ist, gilt, entscheidet darüber, ob ein arbeitsfreier Tag gegeben ist;[28] **Beweislast** für Feiertag und Kausalität („weil") trägt, wer sich auf Rechtzeitigkeit trotz Verspätung beruft.[29] Wird eine Annahmeerklärung an einem gesetzlichen Feiertag oder arbeitsfreien Tag gleichwohl in den Organisationsbereich des Empfängers gebracht, so ist schon ihr Zugang zweifelhaft.[30] Aber auch bei Kenntnismöglichkeit des Adressaten, der vielleicht am Sonntag oder am Tag der Arbeit im Büro erreichbar wäre, ist Zugang am nächsten Tag rechtzeitig,[31] da andernfalls die durch Abs. 2 S. 2 gewährleistete Sicherheit in der Beurteilung, ob eine Frist eingehalten worden ist, durch die Notwendigkeit der Berücksichtigung von konkreten Einzelumständen gefährdet würde.

3. Anwendung auf sonstige Fristen

7 Obgleich Art. 20 II unmittelbar nur die Berechnung vom Offerenten gesetzter Annahmefristen regelt, enthält die Vorschrift allgemeine Grundsätze i. S. d Art. 7 II. Ihr Inhalt kann deshalb unter dem Übereinkommen entsprechend auf alle Fristen angewandt werden, für deren Berechnung keine ausdrückliche Regelung vorgesehen ist.[32]

---

[26] Vgl. *Enderlein/Maskow/Strohbach*, Art. 20, Anm. 5.; *Neumayer/Ming*, Art. 20, Anm. 2. Diese Überlegung schließt es m. E. aus, bei einer Fristsetzung, die auf Absendung durch den Oblaten abstellt, Abs. 2 S. 2 analog anzuwenden, falls der letzte Absendetag auf einen Feiertag oder arbeitsfreien Tag fällt; wie hier *Staudinger/Magnus*, Art. 20, Rn. 24; anders *Bianca/Bonell/Farnsworth*, Art. 20, Anm. 3.2.; *Honsell/Dornis*, Art. 20, Rn. 13 (generalisierungsfähig).
[27] A. A. *Neumayer/Ming*, Art. 20, Anm. 2., Fn. 4; (teilweise anders) *Staudinger/Magnus*, Art. 20, Rn. 19 (auch auf Grund allgemeiner Übung arbeitsfreie Tage); *Soergel/Lüderitz/Fenge*, Art. 20, Rn. 7 (auch faktisch arbeitsfreie Tage seien zu berücksichtigen); *Rudolph*, Art. 20, Rn. 6; wohl auch *Witz/Salger/Lorenz/Witz*, Art. 20, Rn. 9; wie hier *Brunner*, Art. 20, Rn. 1; *Honsell/Dornis*, Art. 20, Rn. 14; zur Rechtslage im unvereinheitlichten deutschen Recht (§ 193 BGB) *Schroeter*, JuS 2007, 29, 31.
[28] Zustellungsschwierigkeiten durch eingeschränkten Postdienst usw. können bei der Fristberechnung nicht berücksichtigt werden – so aber *Soergel/Lüderitz/Fenge*, Art. 20, Rn. 7 – es sei denn, die Parteien hätten derartiges berücksichtigt, z. B. in ihren Gepflogenheiten, Art. 9 I.
[29] *Baumgärtel/Laumen/Hepting*, Art. 20 WKR, Rn. 4.
[30] Vgl. zum Eingang an Erklärungen an gesetzlichen Feiertagen, an denen keine Möglichkeit der Kenntnisnahme besteht, unten Art. 24 Rn. 32 f.; zu den Vorschlägen auf der Haager Konferenz, die Probleme der Fristwahrung bei Erklärung an Sonn- und Feiertagen in der Zugangsregelung zu lösen, s. *von Caemmerer*, RabelsZ 29 (1965), 101, 134; *Dölle/Schlechtriem*, Art. 12 EAG, Rn. 9.
[31] *Bianca/Bonell/Farnsworth*, Art. 20, Anm. 3.5.
[32] *Herber/Czerwenka*, Art. 20, Rn. 7; *Honsell/Dornis*, Art. 20, Rn. 27; MünchKomm/*Gruber*, Art. 20, Rn. 14; MünchKommHGB/*Ferrari*, Art. 20, Rn. 12; *Staudinger/Magnus*, Art. 20, Rn. 14; *Witz/Salger/Lorenz/Witz*, Art. 20, Rn. 3.

Art. 21 [Verspätete Annahme]

(1) Eine verspätete Annahme ist dennoch als Annahme wirksam, wenn der Anbietende unverzüglich den Annehmenden in diesem Sinne mündlich unterrichtet oder eine entsprechende schriftliche Mitteilung absendet.

(2) Ergibt sich aus dem eine verspätete Annahme enthaltenden Brief oder anderen Schriftstück, daß die Mitteilung nach den Umständen, unter denen sie abgesandt worden ist, bei normaler Beförderung dem Anbietenden rechtzeitig zugegangen wäre, so ist die verspätete Annahme als Annahme wirksam, wenn der Anbietende nicht unverzüglich den Annehmenden mündlich davon unterrichtet, daß er sein Angebot als erloschen betrachtet, oder eine entsprechende schriftliche Mitteilung absendet.

Art. 21

(1) A late acceptance is nevertheless effective as an acceptance if without delay the offeror orally so informs the offeree or dispatches a notice to that effect.

(2) If a letter or other writing containing a late acceptance shows that it has been sent in such circumstances that if its transmission had been normal it would have reached the offeror in due time, the late acceptance is effective as an acceptance unless, without delay, the offeror orally informs the offeree that he considers his offer as having lapsed or dispatches a notice to that effect.

Art. 21

1) Une acceptation tardive produit néanmoins effet en tant qu'acceptation si, sans retard, l'auteur de l'offre en informe verbalement le destinataire ou lui adresse un avis à cet effet.

2) Si la lettre ou autre écrit contenant une acceptation tardive révèle qu'elle a été expédiée dans des conditions telles que, si sa transmission avait été régulière, elle serait parvenue à temps à l'auteur de l'offre, l'acceptation tardive produit effet en tant qu'acceptation à moins que, sans retard, l'auteur de l'offre n'informe verbalement le destinataire de l'offre qu'il considère que son offre avait pris fin ou qu'il ne lui adresse un avis à cet effet.

Übersicht

	Rn.
I. Grundzüge	1
II. Regelung des Abs. 1	3
1. Verspätete Annahme	3
a) Annahme nach Erlöschen der Offerte	3
b) Wesentliche und unwesentliche Verspätungen	4
c) Verspätungsgründe	5
2. Vertragsschluss trotz verspäteter Annahme	6
a) Voraussetzung: Zugang der Annahme	6
b) Billigung der verspäteten Annahme	7
c) Unverzügliche Billigung	8
d) Billigung durch schriftliche Mitteilung oder mündliche Erklärung	9
e) Zeitpunkt des Vertragsschlusses	10
f) Billigung mit Zusätzen usw	11
g) Rücknahme der Billigungserklärung	12
h) Vorzeitige Billigungserklärung	13
i) Verspätete Annahme mit Abweichungen	14
3. Dispositives Recht	15
III. Beförderungsverzögerung, Abs. 2	16
1. Rechtspolitische Zielsetzung	16
2. Gründe der Transportverzögerung	17
3. Erkennbarkeit der Transportverzögerung	18
4. „Normale Beförderung"	19
5. Verwahrung des Offerenten (Erlöschensanzeige)	20
6. Vorzeitige Verwahrung	21

IV. Einzelfragen 22
　　　　1. Art. 21 II als dispositive Regelung 22
　　　　2. Unsicherheitslage und Spekulationsmöglichkeiten 23
　　　　3. Beweislast 24

Vorläufer und **Entwürfe:** Art. 9 EAG, New Yorker E 1977 Art. 9, Genfer E 1977 Art. 15, New Yorker E 1978 Art. 19.

I. Grundzüge

1　Art. 21 geht auf Art. 9 EAG zurück und enthält die gleiche Lösung, verändert um eine geringfügige Klarstellung.[1] In den Beratungen der Arbeitsgruppe war wiederholt erwogen worden, die beiden Fälle des Abs. 1 und Abs. 2 gleich zu behandeln, da für den Offerenten schwer erkennbar sein könne, ob eine bloße Transportverzögerung gegeben sei.[2]

2　Die Vorschrift unterscheidet zwei **Verspätungsgründe**, und zwar **verspätete Absendung** der Annahme, Abs. 1, und **erkennbare Transportverzögerung**, Abs. 2. Sie ermöglicht für beide Fälle in Ausnahme von Art. 18 II 2, der an sich Unwirksamkeit einer verspäteten Annahme vorsieht, das Zustandekommen eines Vertrages durch die verspätete Annahmeerklärung. Art. 21 I regelt die in § 150 I BGB normierte Situation; Art. 21 II entspricht § 149 BGB.[3] Art. 21 I weicht jedoch von § 150 I BGB insoweit ab, als er nicht die verspätete Annahme als Gegenofferte qualifiziert, die einer – zugangsbedürftigen – Gegenannahme bedarf,[4] sondern als eine auf Grund Billigung durch den Offerenten als solche wirksame Annahme.[5] Über den **Zeitpunkt des Vertragsschlusses** entscheidet deshalb der Zugang der Annahmeerklärung, Artt. 23, 24, und nicht Zugang oder Absendung der Billigungserklärung des Offerenten.[6] Zur **Beweislast** s. unten Rn. 24.

II. Regelung des Abs. 1

1. Verspätete Annahme

3　**a) Annahme nach Erlöschen der Offerte.** Abs. 1 regelt ausdrücklich nur die **verspätete** und deshalb an sich nach Art. 18 II 2 unwirksame **Annahme**. Aber auch wo die Offerte bereits durch Fristablauf erloschen, vielleicht sogar erst nach Ablauf ihrer Geltungsfrist dem Adressaten (und jetzigem Akzeptanten) zugegangen ist, sollte die materielle Einigung der Parteien nicht an der „logischen Unmöglichkeit",[7] eine erloschene Offerte wirksam annehmen zu können, scheitern.[8] Fraglich ist nur, ob man im Falle einer bereits erloschenen Offerte die Annahme als Gegenofferte behandeln soll oder Art. 21 I anzuwen-

---

[1] Dazu unten Rn. 7.
[2] S. noch Art. 9 New Yorker E 1977 und dazu YB VIII (1977), S. 84; zur Entstehungsgeschichte ausführlich *Perales Viscasillas*, Formación del contrato, S. 595 ff.
[3] Dazu *Rehbinder*, Vertragsschluss, S. 161 f.
[4] *Bianca/Bonell/Farnsworth*, Art. 21, Anm. 1.2., nennt diese Lösung die „traditionelle" Regel; dazu auch *Schlesinger*, Bd. 1, S. 170, sowie in den einzelnen Länderberichten jeweils unter B-11 II A.
[5] *Hilger*, AcP 185 (1985), 559, 560, bezeichnet den – gleich geregelten – Vertragsschluss nach Art. 9 I EAG als dreiaktigen Vorgang, S. 585, dessen Konstruktion im Vergleich zum BGB „sinnwidrig" sei, S. 600. Zu den vergeblichen Versuchen, im EAG die Lösung des § 150 I BGB durchzusetzen, *von Caemmerer*, RabelsZ 29 (1965), 101, 129; *Dölle/Schlechtriem*, Art. 9 EAG, Rn. 2; zur Kritik am New Yorker E *Huber*, RabelsZ 43 (1979), 413, 443 f.
[6] *Enderlein/Maskow/Strohbach*, Art. 21, Anm. 3.; *Ludwig*, S. 341 f.; *Schlechtriem*, Einheitliches UN-Kaufrecht, S. 42; *Soergel/Lüderitz/Fenge*, Art. 21, Rn. 5; *Staudinger/Magnus*, Art. 21, Rn. 12; *Witz/Salger/Lorenz/Witz*, Art. 21, Rn. 4; anders wohl *Perales Viscasillas*, Formación del contrato, S. 606 ff., 608 f. (Absendung der Billigungserklärung).
[7] *Schlesinger/Lorenz*, Bd. 2, S. 1563.
[8] Vgl. *Honsell/Schnyder/Straub*, 1. Aufl., Art. 21, Rn. 7.

den ist. Zweifellos kann der Empfänger der erloschenen Offerte seine Antwort eindeutig als Gegenofferte qualifizieren. Auch Auslegung kann zu diesem Ergebnis führen, etwa wenn in der Antwort auf das bereits eingetretene Erlöschen der Offerte Bezug genommen wird. Vielfach wird freilich unsicher sein, ob die Offerte bereits vor Zugang beim Oblaten oder jedenfalls vor seiner Annahmeerklärung erloschen war, z. B. bei einer unter Verwendung unbestimmter Zeitbegriffe gesetzten oder „angemessenen" Frist.[9] Auch in diesen Fällen ist Art. 21 I anwendbar.[10] Seine Anwendung entbindet bei Absendung einer Billigungserklärung durch den Offerenten von der Klärung, ob eine „angemessene" Frist bereits verstrichen, die Offerte also an sich schon erloschen und nicht mehr annahmefähig war, oder ob ein „echter" Fall verspäteter Annahme vorliegt.[11] Ein aus anderen Gründen als Fristablauf bereits erloschenes Angebot – z. B. durch Ablehnung, Art. 17 – kann dagegen nicht mehr über Art. 21 I zur Grundlage eines Vertragsschlusses werden;[12] die Annahme muss dann ggf. als Gegenofferte behandelt bzw. geprüft werden.

b) **Wesentliche und unwesentliche Verspätungen.** Eine **Verspätung** i. S. d. Art. 21 I liegt vor, wenn die Annahme so spät erfolgt, dass sie innerhalb der Annahmefrist nicht mehr wirksam wird, z. B. die Annahmeerklärung nach Ablauf der Annahmefrist eintrifft oder die annahmeäquivalente Handlung verspätet vollzogen wird.[13] Nur für die **als solche erkennbare Beförderungsverzögerung** gilt die Sonderregel des Art. 21 II. 4

Zwischen **wesentlichen** und **unwesentlichen Verspätungen** kann **nicht unterschieden** werden:[14] Weder kann man bei unwesentlicher Verspätung Vertragsschluss annehmen, wenn der Offerent schweigt,[15] noch kann bei einer ganz erheblichen Verspätung eine „teleologische Reduktion" des dem Offerenten eingeräumten Wahlrechtes vertreten werden.[16] Es steht allein dem Offerenten zu, die Bedeutung seiner Fristsetzung zu beurteilen und den Vertragsschluss bei verspäteter Annahmeerklärung abzulehnen oder zu ermöglichen. Das Risiko, dass sich auf Grund der Verspätung die Verhältnisse geändert haben, z. B. durch fallende Preise, und die erklärte Annahme für den Annehmenden unvorteilhaft geworden ist, hat er als Folge der ihm jedenfalls in der Situation des Abs. 1 zuzurechnenden Verspätung hinzunehmen.

c) **Verspätungsgründe.** Die **Gründe,** die die **Verspätung** veranlasst haben, dürfen 5
keine Rolle spielen:[17] Zu langes Zögern des Akzeptanten, der entweder erst nach oder so kurz vor Ablauf der Annahmefrist seine Antwort absendet, dass seine Erklärung trotz normaler Beförderung den Offerenten nicht mehr rechtzeitig erreicht, oder eine als solche nicht erkennbare Beförderungsverzögerung, aber auch eine Kumulierung der Verspätungsgründe „Transportverzögerung" und „Verbrauch der Überlegungsfrist" fallen unter Abs. 1. Einer Sonderregelung bedarf lediglich die **Zugangshinderung** durch den Offerenten.[18]

---

[9] S. oben Art. 18 Rn. 14, 15.
[10] Vgl. *Enderlein/Maskow/Strohbach,* Art. 21, Anm. 1.a); *Herber/Czerwenka,* Art. 21, Rn. 2; *Neumayer/Ming,* Art. 21, Anm. 1.; *Reinhart,* Art. 21, Rn. 3 (erloschenes Angebot bleibt erhalten); *Staudinger/Magnus,* Art. 21, Rn. 8; teilweise anders *Witz/Salger/Lorenz/Witz,* Art. 21, Rn. 6 (Erklärung des Annehmenden als neue Gegenofferte).
[11] Vgl. zu dieser Schwierigkeit *Enderlein/Maskow/Strohbach,* Art. 21, Anm. 1.a).
[12] *Honsell/Dornis,* Art. 21, Rn. 2.
[13] S. *Wey,* Rn. 1155.
[14] *Herber/Czerwenka,* Art. 21, Rn. 3; *Honsell/Dornis,* Art. 21, Rn. 5; *Staudinger/Magnus,* Art. 21, Rn. 9; *Witz/Salger/Lorenz/Witz,* Art. 21, Rn. 9.
[15] Gegen eine solche Widerspruchsobliegenheit auch *Rehbinder,* Vertragsschluss, S. 162.
[16] Vgl. zu dem Risiko für den Annehmenden, dass durch eine lange Verspätung eine Veränderung der Umstände eingetreten ist und der Offerent mit seiner Wahlmöglichkeit auf Kosten des verspätet Annehmenden spekulieren kann, *Honsell/Dornis,* Art. 21, Rn. 39; *Staudinger/Magnus,* Art. 21, Rn. 19; *Honnold/Flechtner,* Art. 21, Rn. 175, die eine solche Einschränkung befürworten; zurückhaltend *Rehbinder,* Vertragsschluss, S. 162; zum Ganzen unten Rn. 23.
[17] *Brunner,* Art. 21, Rn. 2; *Herber/Czerwenka,* Art. 21, Rn. 2; *MünchKomm/Gruber,* Art. 21, Rn. 4; *Neumayer/Ming,* Art. 21, Anm. 1.
[18] S. *MünchKomm/Gruber,* Art. 21, Rn. 4; *Wey,* Rn. 1156; hierzu unten Art. 24 Rn. 41 f.

2. Vertragsschluss trotz verspäteter Annahme

6 **a) Voraussetzung: Zugang der Annahme.** Die verspätete Annahme kann den Vertrag noch zustande bringen. Voraussetzung ist jedoch, dass die Annahmeerklärung zugeht. Der Offerent kann dann die verspätete Annahme als solche wirken lassen.[19] Die Annahmeerklärung muss jedoch vom Erklärenden als solche gemeint sein: Qualifiziert der Erklärende seine Antwort als Gegenofferte – etwa weil die Verspätung bereits erheblich oder (und) die Offerte möglicherweise schon erloschen war[20] –, dann kommt der Vertrag nur zustande, wenn der Offerent die Gegenofferte fristgerecht annimmt.[21] Wird die verspätete Annahme durch Übermittlung der Vertragsleistung ausgedrückt (Art. 18 I), so muss diese den Offerenten erreichen.[22]

Auch ein **Verhalten**, das nach Art. 18 III **als Annahme** wirkt, kann **verspätet** geschehen und Grundlage eines Vertragsschlusses werden, falls der Offerent die erforderliche **Billigung** abgibt. Der Offerent kann natürlich erst reagieren, wenn er von dem annahmeäquivalenten Verhalten Kenntnis erlangt hat, also durch Ankunft der Ware, des Kaufpreises usw. oder auf Grund einer entsprechenden Mitteilung, z. B. der Belastung seines Kontos durch Scheckeinlösung oder im Lastschriftverfahren. Das Verhalten des Akzeptanten muss dabei aus Sicht des Offerenten nach Maßgabe des Art. 8 als Zustimmung zum Angebot zu verstehen sein.[23] Das Risiko für den Akzeptanten, der etwa die Ware nach Ablauf der Annahmefrist absendet, dass der Offerent nicht billigt, ist dem Akzeptanten ebenso zuzurechnen wie ein Irrtum über den Ablauf der Frist.[24]

7 **b) Billigung der verspäteten Annahme.** Zum Vertragsschluss trotz Verspätung der Annahme bedarf es einer **Verständigung** des Akzeptanten, dass der Offerent die Annahme als wirksam bewertet.[25] Sie ist **nicht** wie bei der Lösung des § 150 I BGB **zugangsbedürftige Annahmeerklärung**.[26] Zum einen unterscheiden sich Annahme und **Billigungserklärung** theoretisch im Inhalt, wenngleich insoweit in der Praxis kaum Unterschiede feststellbar sein dürften. Zum anderen hat die Billigung unverzüglich zu erfolgen, während eine Gegenannahme regelmäßig erst in angemessener Frist zu erfolgen hätte, Art. 18 II 2.[27] Vor allem aber ist die Billigungserklärung nur **absendebedürftig**.[28] Die Heilung der Annahmeverspätung durch die Billigungserklärung des Offerenten tritt also auch dann ein, wenn diese verloren geht oder ihrerseits verspätet eintrifft.[29]

---

[19] Dazu unten Rn. 7 ff.
[20] S. oben Rn. 3; ferner *Wey*, Rn. 1163, 1164: Die Selbstqualifikation als Gegenofferte muss bei Auslegung nach Art. 8 I oder II erkannt werden bzw. für einen vernünftigen Offerenten erkennbar sein.
[21] Die Antwort des Offerenten (Gegenannahme) ist – im Unterschied zur Billigungserklärung nach Art. 21 I – regelmäßig zugangsbedürftig, es sei denn, Art. 18 III ist anwendbar. Für die Frist gilt Art. 18 II 2 oder 3, s. jedoch unten Rn. 7.
[22] Zur Frage, wie lange die verspätete Annahme zurückgenommen werden kann, s. unten Rn. 10.
[23] OLG Dresden, 30.11.2010, CISG-online 2183 = IHR 2011, 142, 145.
[24] Vgl. zum EAG *von Caemmerer*, RabelsZ 29 (1965), 101, 130 Fn. 116.
[25] Vgl. OLG Dresden, 30.11.2010, CISG-online 2183 = IHR 2011, 142, 145: E-mail an Anbietenden drückte Ablehnung des Angebotsinhalts aus – keine Billigung i. S. d. Art. 21 I.
[26] S. oben Rn. 2; *Bianca/Bonell/Farnsworth*, Art. 21, Anm. 2.2.; *Karollus*, S. 75; *Piltz*, Internationales Kaufrecht, Rn. 3–119; *Reinhart*, Art. 21, Rn. 4 (einziger (?) Unterschied zu § 150 I BGB); *Stern*, Erklärungen, Rn. 96; *Witz/Salger/Lorenz/Witz*, Art. 21, Rn. 4; a. A. *Neumayer/Ming*, Art. 21, Anm. 2.
[27] Hierzu unten Rn. 8.
[28] Die zum EAG unsichere Frage ist für das CISG eindeutig entschieden worden, s. *Noussias*, Zugangsbedürftigkeit von Mitteilungen, S. 115 f.; *Rehbinder*, Vertragsschluss, S. 163.
[29] *Honsell/Dornis*, Art. 21, Rn. 12; MünchKomm/*Gruber*, Art. 21, Rn. 6; *Staudinger/Magnus*, Art. 21, Rn. 11. Ob man angesichts des Fehlens einer Art. 12 II EAG vergleichbaren Vorschrift („Mitteilungen sind mit den nach den Umständen üblichen Mitteln zu bewirken") verlangen kann, dass die Billigungserklärung jedenfalls zugangsfähig, d. h. ordnungsgemäß frankiert und hinreichend genau adressiert („properly posted") ist, könnte zweifelhaft sein. Auf der Grundlage von Art. 7 I (Wahrung des guten Glaubens in Auslegung des Übereinkommens) und Art. 7 II wird man insoweit aber wohl doch Art. 27 heranziehen dürfen, da der in der englischen Fassung „any means" zulassende Art. 24 nur für zugangsbedürftige Erklärungen – wo angesichts der Zugangsbedürftigkeit jedes Erklärungsmittel genügen mag, vgl. unten Art. 24 Rn. 16 – gilt. Im Ergebnis wie

Verspätete Annahme 8, 9 **Art. 21**

Obwohl nicht zugangsbedürftig, ist die Billigungserklärung doch Willenserklärung, so dass u. U. Geschäftsfähigkeit, Anfechtbarkeit usw. nach unvereinheitlichtem nationalen Recht zu prüfen sind.[30]

c) Unverzügliche Billigung. Die **Billigungserklärung** muss nach dem Text der deut- 8
schen Fassung **unverzüglich**, d. h. ohne schuldhaftes Zögern,[31] erfolgen. Die (authentische) englische und französische Fassung legen es nahe, hier – anders als in Art. 19 II – eine kürzere Frist maßgeblich sein zu lassen, zumal keine Notwendigkeit zeitraubender Prüfung besteht.[32] Die Rechtsprechung ist zuweilen jedoch großzügiger und hat etwa eine konkludente Billigung nach sieben Tagen ausreichen lassen, obgleich das Angebot seinerseits eine Annahme binnen zwei Werktagen gefordert hatte.[33]

Entscheidend ist der Eingang der verspäteten Annahme, nicht eine evtl. noch nicht abgelaufene Frist für die Offerte.[34] „Unverzüglich" ist jedoch disponibel – der verspätet seine Annahme Erklärende kann hinzusetzen, dass er für eine positive Rückäußerung eine Überlegungsfrist einräumt. Auslegung kann in einem solchen Fall freilich auch ergeben, dass die Antwort eine Gegenofferte sein soll.

Wird die Annahme durch annahmeäquivalentes Verhalten zum Ausdruck gebracht, dann kann, falls Art. 18 I (zugangsbedürftige Äußerung) eingreift, die Billigungserklärung natürlich erst unverzüglich nach Zugang des „Äußerungsträgers", also z. B. nach Eingang der Ware oder der Zahlung, erfolgen. Bei annahmeäquivalentem Verhalten nach Art. 18 III muss Billigung unverzüglich nach Kenntniserlangung erfolgen.[35]

d) Billigung durch schriftliche Mitteilung oder mündliche Erklärung. Die Bil- 9
ligung der verspäteten Annahme kann durch eine **„schriftliche Mitteilung"** erfolgen. Die deutsche Übersetzung von „dispatches a notice" ist zu eng. Dass eine Mitteilung durch Telegramm oder Fernschreiben gleichwertig ist, ergibt sich schon aus Art. 13. Art. 21 will aber, wie die Alternative mündlicher Unterrichtung sowie der englische und französische Text zeigen und im Übrigen auch mit Art. 11 übereinstimmt, nicht Schriftform vorschreiben, so dass auch andere Erklärungsmittel verwendet werden können.[36] Insbesondere sind Mitteilungen in elektronischer Form erfasst, vorausgesetzt – wie stets[37] – der Oblat hat sich ausdrücklich oder implizit mit elektronischer Kommunikation in der jeweiligen Form und an die jeweilige Adresse einverstanden erklärt.[38] Auch eine konkludente Billigung durch schriftliche Mitteilung ist denkbar, etwa indem der Offerent nach verspätetem Zugang der Annahme einen Lieferplan mitteilt und um die Übersendung von Pro-forma-Rechnungen bittet.[39]

---

hier *Karollus*, S. 74 f.; MünchKomm/*Gruber*, Art. 21, Rn. 6; *Soergel/Lüderitz/Fenge*, Art. 21, Rn. 3; *Wey*, Rn. 1171; *Witz/Salger/Lorenz/Witz*, Art. 21, Rn. 5.
[30] Sie ist deshalb auch nicht mit der Wissenserklärung des § 149 BGB, die nicht als rechtsgeschäftliche Erklärung verstanden wird und nicht anfechtbar sein soll (vgl. MünchKomm/*Kramer*, § 149 BGB, Rn. 4), vergleichbar.
[31] S. auch oben Art. 19 Rn. 16 f. Die deutsche Übersetzung ebnet jedoch die Unterschiede ein, heißt es doch in Art. 19 II „without undue delay", in Art. 21 I dagegen „without delay" („sans retard injustifié" v. „sans retard")! S. dazu im Text.
[32] Überzeugend *Honsell/Dornis*, Art. 21, Rn. 14; zu den sprachlichen Abweichungen von Art. 19 II in der französischen und englischen Fassung *Witz/Salger/Lorenz/Witz*, Art. 21, Rn. 5 (Redaktionsversehen). Aus der Rechtsprechung LG Hamburg, 21.12.2001, CISG-online 1092: Billigung muss „sogleich" erfolgen; vgl. auch MünchKomm/*Gruber*, Art. 21, Rn. 7: mehr als zwei Werktage ab Zugang der Annahmeerklärung sei jedenfalls in der Regel zu lang.
[33] OLG Frankfurt a. M., 24.3.2009, CISG-online 2165 = IHR 2010, 250, 252 (Art. 21 wird nicht ausdrücklich genannt).
[34] *Enderlein/Maskow/Strohbach*, Art. 21, Anm. 6.
[35] Vgl. *Wey*, Rn. 1175.
[36] *Honsell/Dornis*, Art. 21, Rn. 10; *Staudinger/Magnus*, Art. 21, Rn. 11.
[37] S. oben Vor Artt. 14–24 Rn. 27.
[38] S. CISG-AC, Op. 1 *(Chr. Ramberg)*, Comments 21.2 i. V. m. 15.1 ff., IHR 2003, 244, 248.
[39] OLG Frankfurt a. M., 24.3.2009, CISG-online 2165 = IHR 2010, 250, 252.

Die **Billigung** kann auch **mündlich** erklärt werden. Telefonische Unterrichtung oder andere elektronische Übertragung von Erklärungen in Ton (z. B. Funk) muss gleichbehandelt werden.[40] Die Wortwahl „unterrichtet" („informs", „informe") bedeutet, dass der Empfänger die Erklärung jedenfalls „aufgenommen", d. h. gehört haben muss, nicht dagegen, dass er ihren Gehalt juristisch richtig versteht. Ist die Telefonverbindung für den Offerenten unerkennbar gestört, kommt die Unterrichtung i. S. dieser Vorschrift nicht zustande.

10 **e) Zeitpunkt des Vertragsschlusses.** Der Vertrag kommt nicht erst mit der Absendung der Billigungserklärung bzw. der mündlichen Unterrichtung zustande, sondern **rückwirkend** auf den **Zugang** der verspäteten **Annahmeerklärung,** bei nicht zugangsbedürftigen annahmeäquivalenten Handlungen (Art. 18 III) zum Zeitpunkt ihrer Vornahme.[41] Das Wirksamwerden des Vertrages durch Zugang der verspäteten Annahme bedeutet aber auch, dass damit die Möglichkeit für den Annehmenden, seine Annahmeerklärung zurückzunehmen – Art. 22 –, endet.[42]

11 **f) Billigung mit Zusätzen usw.** Enthält die positive Rückäußerung des Offerenten **Zusätze, Ergänzungen** oder sonstige **Abweichungen** vom Text der vorausgegangenen Vertragsschlusserklärungen, so muss durch Auslegung geklärt werden, ob gleichwohl eine vorbehaltlose Billigung zum Ausdruck gebracht worden ist und die Abweichungen nur Vorschläge zur Vertragsänderung sind, oder ob der Offerent im Ergebnis die verspätete Annahme zurückweist und eine erneute Offerte unterbreiten will.[43] Macht der Offerent eine Billigung der verspäteten Annahme davon abhängig, dass seine Änderungen Vertragsbestandteil werden, so liegt darin eine Zurückweisung der Annahme.

12 **g) Rücknahme der Billigungserklärung.** Fraglich ist, ob die Billigungserklärung bis zum Zugang entsprechend Artt. 15 II, 22 zurückgenommen werden kann. Obwohl die Billigungserklärung nicht zugangsbedürftig ist, ist eine solche Auslegung des Art. 21 I m. E. auf der Grundlage von Art. 7 I möglich,[44] denn vor Zugang kann sich der Annehmende noch nicht in schutzwürdiger Weise auf den Vertrag eingestellt haben.[45]

13 **h) Vorzeitige Billigungserklärung.** Art. 21 I setzt voraus, dass die verspätete Annahme dem Offerenten zugegangen ist, bevor er sie billigt. M. E. hat jedoch auch eine **vor Zugang der Annahme** abgesandte bzw. mündlich erklärte **Billigung** eine die Verspätung heilende Wirkung;[46] die Möglichkeit der Rücknahme einer noch nicht zugegangenen Annahme wird dadurch nicht abgeschnitten. Haben die Parteien Schriftlichkeit der Annahme vereinbart und verständigt der Annehmende den Offerenten telefonisch von einer zu erwartenden Verspätung, dann muss der Offerent seine Billigung schon jetzt erklären können, freilich ohne damit schon einen Vertragsschluss zu bewirken. Vielfach wird man allerdings eine

---

[40] S. zu Art. 18 II 3, oben Art. 18 Rn. 17. Für jegliche elektronische Kommunikation „in real time" CISG-AC, Op. 1 (Chr. Ramberg), Opinion Art. 21(1), IHR 2003, 244, 248.
[41] S. schon oben Rn. 2 a. E.; vgl. ferner Brunner, Art. 21, Rn. 1; Enderlein/Maskow/Strohbach, Art. 21, Anm. 3.; MünchKomm/Gruber, Art. 21, Rn. 9; Soergel/Lüderitz/Fenge, Art. 21, Rn. 5; a. A. wohl Perales Viscasillas, Formación del contrato, S. 606 ff.: Absendung der Billigungserklärung.
[42] Bianca/Bonell/Farnsworth, Art. 21, Anm. 3.3., sieht darin eine zu weitgehende Bevorzugung des Offerenten, der durch seine Billigungserklärung einer nach Zugang der verspäteten Annahme eingegangenen Rücknahmeerklärung die Wirkung nehmen könne. Ohne weiteres Rücknahme bis zur Absendung der Billigungserklärung gestattend Honnold/Flechtner, Art. 21, Rn. 174 Fn. 2; Neumayer/Ming, Art. 22, Anm. 2. a. E.: Es sei „contraire à la bonne foi", wenn der Offerent eine zurückgenommene verspätete Annahme validieren könne. Nach dieser Ansicht könnte die verspätete Annahme leichter widerrufen werden als eine echte Gegenofferte.
[43] Soergel/Lüderitz/Fenge, Art. 21, Rn. 6; Schwimann/Posch, Art. 20, Rn. 2: maßgeblich seien die gleichen Maßstäbe wie nach Art. 19 II; enger Lagergren, S. 67 f.: modifizierende Billigung sei stets wirkungslos (zum EAG).
[44] MünchKomm/Gruber, Art. 21, Rn. 11; Neumayer/Ming, Art. 21, Anm. 4.; zweifelnd Honsell/Dornis, Art. 21, Rn. 17.
[45] S. zu dem grundsätzlichen Problem unten Art. 27 Rn. 14.
[46] A. A. Honsell/Dornis, Art. 21, Rn. 15.

Benachrichtigung, dass der Offerent trotz erwarteter Verspätung der Annahmeerklärung den Vertrag noch schließen wolle, als Verlängerung der Frist für die Annahme der Offerte ansehen müssen, vor allem wenn in der Mitteilung des Offerenten ein neuer Termin gesetzt wird.

i) Verspätete Annahme mit Abweichungen. Ist die Annahme nicht nur verspätet, sondern enthält sie auch Zusätze, Einschränkungen, Ergänzungen oder sonstige **Abweichungen,** dann gilt Art. 19.[47] Bei unwesentlichen Abweichungen und einer nicht nur transportverzögerten Annahme (Art. 21 II) hat aber auf jeden Fall eine Mitteilung zu erfolgen, die die Annahme als rechtzeitig gelten lässt, damit ein Vertrag geschlossen wird. 14

3. Dispositives Recht

Art. 21 I ist dispositives Recht. Aufgrund Parteivereinbarung oder (ausnahmsweise) zu beachtender Bräuche kann auch **Schweigen** als Billigung einer verspäteten Annahmeerklärung wirken. Der Annehmende kann für die erforderliche Billigung **Qualifizierungen,** z. B. eine bestimmte Form oder ein bestimmtes Erklärungsmittel, vorsehen, aber dem Offerenten die Möglichkeit der Billigung auch erleichtern. Allerdings wird man entsprechend den Regeln zur Annahmeerklärung nicht zulassen können, dass der verspätet Annehmende seiner Annahmeerklärung hinzufügt, dass ein Schweigen des Offerenten ohne weiteres (vgl. Art. 18 I 2) als Billigung gelten soll.[48] Der Annehmende kann sich auch Widerruf seiner Annahmeerklärung für die Zeit nach dem Zugang vorbehalten, z. B. wenn er dem Offerenten für die Rückäußerung eine längere Frist eingeräumt hat. Es bedarf deshalb auch keines „Missbrauchsvorbehalts", um den Annehmenden in diesem Falle gegen das Risiko verzögerter Billigung durch den Offerenten zu schützen. Soll der Widerrufsvorbehalt freilich auch noch nach Absendung der Billigungserklärung Wirkung entfalten, dann bedeutet er Auflösung des Vertrages. Eine Annahme mit einem derartigen Vorbehalt weicht vom Angebot ab und ist deshalb nach Art. 19 zu behandeln.[49] 15

III. Beförderungsverzögerung, Abs. 2

1. Rechtspolitische Zielsetzung

Art. 21 II liegt der Gedanke zugrunde, dass für den Akzeptanten durch Fehler im Beförderungssystem, auf das er keinen Einfluss hat, nicht die Chance zum Vertragsschluss entscheidend verschlechtert werden soll. Bei normaler Beförderung wäre ein Vertrag mit fristgemäßer Annahme zustande gekommen. Der Annehmende vertraut auf den Vertragsschluss und wird in diesem Vertrauen geschützt. Der Offerent, der nach Ablauf der Annahmefrist mit einer Annahmeerklärung nicht mehr rechnen muss und sich möglicherweise anderweitig gebunden oder das Interesse am Geschäft verloren hat, wird dagegen durch die Möglichkeit geschützt, sich gegen die transportverzögerte Annahmeerklärung zu verwahren und so den Vertragsschluss zu verhindern.[50] Die Vorschrift gilt nur für Annahmeerklärungen in Briefen oder anderer schriftlicher Fixierung. Elektronische Erklärungen durch E-Mail oder EDI sollten gleichstehen, vorausgesetzt, der Offerent hat sich ausdrücklich oder implizit mit dieser Art elektronischer Erklärung(en) einverstanden erklärt.[51] 16

---

[47] Ausführlich MünchKomm/*Gruber,* Art. 21, Rn. 12 ff.
[48] S. oben Art. 18 Rn. 9.
[49] Zur Möglichkeit, statt einer verspäteten Annahme eine Gegenofferte zu erklären, s. oben Rn. 6.
[50] Vgl. hierzu *Enderlein/Maskow/Strohbach,* Art. 21, Anm. 4., 5.
[51] CISG-AC, Op. 1 *(Chr. Ramberg),* Art. 21(2) Opinion Abs. 1 sowie Comment 21.3, IHR 2003, 244, 248. S. zu letztgenannter Voraussetzung bereits allgemein oben Vor Artt. 14–24 Rn. 27.

2. Gründe der Transportverzögerung

17 Transportverzögerungen können einmal durch Umstände eintreten, die singulär auf die in Frage stehende Annahmeerklärung einwirken (z. B. Irrläufer bei der Postbeförderung), aber auch durch allgemeine Beeinträchtigungen des gewählten oder in Frage kommenden Kommunikationsmittels verursacht werden, wie z. B. bei Streik von Hafenarbeitern oder Flughafenpersonal, der das Entladen von Postsäcken verhindert, Fluglotsen- oder Pilotenstreik, der den Luftpostverkehr zum Erliegen bringt, Witterungsverhältnissen, die zur Sperrung von Bahnlinien oder Flughäfen führen, zeitweiser Zusammenbruch oder Abschaltung eines zentralen Servers, über den die Kommunikation zum Offerenten läuft, usw.

Die Ratio des Art. 21 II ist nicht einschlägig, sofern die Transportverzögerung auf einem Umstand beruht, der dem Akzeptanten selbst zuzurechnen ist, wie etwa einer falschen Adressierung des Annahmeschreibens, einem Tippfehler in der Adresszeile der E-Mail oder einem Fehler des von ihm eingesetzten Boten – in diesem Fall greift die Vorschrift nicht ein, und ein Vertragsschluss kann durch bloße unterlassene Verwahrung des Offerenten nicht zustande kommen.[52]

3. Erkennbarkeit der Transportverzögerung

18 Art. 21 II setzt voraus, dass der Grund der Verspätung für den Offerenten „aus dem eine verspätete Annahme enthaltenden Brief oder anderen Schriftstück" **ersichtlich** sein muss, also z. B. durch das Absendedatum. Das gilt auch für elektronische Post, die regelmäßig ein Sendedatum erkennen lässt. Es muss aber auch ausreichen, wenn der Offerent auf andere Weise darüber informiert wird, dass die Annahmeerklärung so rechtzeitig abgesandt worden ist, dass sie normalerweise innerhalb der Annahmefrist zugegangen wäre, z. B. durch einen Anruf des Akzeptanten, der die Absendung der Annahmeerklärung mitteilt, durch ein Geständnis des säumigen Boten usw.[53] Ebenso wie zu § 149 S. 1 BGB ist nicht zu verlangen, dass sich die rechtzeitige Aufgabe aus Anhaltspunkten ergibt, auf die der Akzeptant keinen Einfluss hat (Poststempel). Denn die Rechtzeitigkeit der Absendung i. S. d. Art. 21 II bestimmt sich objektiv aus dem Brief, nicht allein aus der Datumsangabe, falls z. B. rück- oder vordatiert worden ist.

Ist die Beförderungsverspätung dagegen nicht erkennbar, dann bleibt es bei der Regelung des Art. 21 I; der Offerent braucht also nicht zu protestieren, wenn er zum Vertragsschluss nicht mehr bereit ist, und er muss seine Billigung mitteilen, wenn er der Verspätung der Annahme keine Bedeutung beimessen will.

4. „Normale Beförderung"

19 „Beförderungsverzögerung" meint, dass die Annahmeerklärung „bei normaler Beförderung" rechtzeitig zugegangen wäre. Damit wird nicht die Benutzung eines normalen Beförderungsmittels vorgeschrieben, sondern nur die Laufzeit bei Nutzung eines normalen Beförderungsmittels als Maßstab genommen: Auch wenn die Annahmeerklärung durch einen Touristen verspätet überbracht wird, muss der Offerent mit der normalen Postlaufzeit vergleichen.

5. Verwahrung des Offerenten (Erlöschensanzeige)

20 Der Offerent muss sich, wenn er den Vertragsschluss verhindern will, „unverzüglich" durch Absendung einer entsprechenden Mitteilung oder mündlich **verwahren.** Insoweit gilt das Gleiche wie zu Abs. 1: Die Mitteilung bedarf nicht der Schriftform.[54] Sie ist nur

---

[52] MünchKomm/*Gruber*, Art. 21, Rn. 17; *Staudinger/Magnus*, Art. 21, Rn. 14; *Witz/Salger/Lorenz/Witz*, Art. 21, Rn. 8.
[53] A. A. *Herber/Czerwenka*, Art. 21, Rn. 7; *Reinhart*, Art. 21, Rn. 5; wie hier wohl *Staudinger/Magnus*, Art. 21, Rn. 15 sowie Rn. 17 zu den daraus möglichen Unsicherheiten.
[54] S. oben Rn. 9.

absendebedürftig.⁵⁵ Mündliche Unterrichtung kann auch telefonisch oder durch andere elektronische Kommunikation in Echtzeit erfolgen.⁵⁶ „Mitteilung" (notice) kann trotz der zu engen deutschen Fassung („schriftlich") auch mit elektronischen Kommunikationsmitteln erfolgen.⁵⁷ Zur Wirksamkeit der Verwahrung gehört, dass der Adressat eine mündliche Erklärung „aufgenommen" hat.⁵⁸

Anders als die Billigungserklärung nach Abs. 1 hat die Verwahrung nach Abs. 2 jedoch keine vertragskonstitutive Funktion. Sie ist wie die Verwahrung nach § 149 BGB Wissenserklärung („unterrichtet").⁵⁹ Ob für ihre Abgabe Geschäftsfähigkeit erforderlich ist, ob sie bei Mängeln angefochten werden kann usw., entscheidet das vom IPR berufene unvereinheitlichte Recht.

6. Vorzeitige Verwahrung

Wird die Verwahrung gegen den Vertragsschluss abgesandt, ehe die Annahmefrist überhaupt abgelaufen ist, so ist sie entweder als Versuch eines Widerrufs der Offerte zu werten, der nur unter den in Art. 16 geregelten Voraussetzungen wirksam ist, oder sie ist ein bloßer Hinweis auf die Bedeutung der Fristsetzung. Ist dagegen die Frist bereits abgelaufen, so dass eine evtl. eingehende Annahmeerklärung zu spät kommt, dann braucht der Offerent die Antwort nicht mehr abzuwarten, sondern kann sie zurückweisen und sich somit aus dem angebahnten Geschäft lösen.⁶⁰   21

IV. Einzelfragen

1. Art. 21 II als dispositive Regelung

Auch die Regelung des Art. 21 II ist **dispositiv.** Der Annehmende kann vorsorglich für jeden Fall, also auch den der Transportverzögerung, Rückäußerung vorschreiben. Ebenso kann aber auch der Offerent die Bedeutung seiner Fristsetzung für die Offerte dahin verstärken, dass eine verspätet eintreffende Annahmeerklärung stets wirkungslos sein oder nur als Gegenofferte gelten soll.   22

2. Unsicherheitslage und Spekulationsmöglichkeiten

Bei verspäteter Annahme entsteht aus der **Wahlmöglichkeit des Offerenten** für den Akzeptanten die **Gefahr,** dass der Offerent auf Kosten des Akzeptanten **spekuliert.**⁶¹ Die Ungewissheit ist dem Akzeptanten nicht stets zurechenbar, z. B. wenn er seine Annahmeerklärung rechtzeitig abgesandt hat.⁶² Besonders riskant ist die Lage des Akzeptanten, der durch (Vor)leistung annahmeäquivalent, aber verspätet erklärt: Der Offerent kann dann sogar über die Leistung (und nicht nur über die Verpflichtung des anderen Teils) disponieren. Teilweise wird deshalb vertreten, dass bei längerdauernder (Transport)verzögerung der Offerent treuwidrig handelt, wenn er die verspätete Annahme noch als solche behandelt, oder dass die stark verspätete Annahme überhaupt unheilbar erlischt.⁶³ Andererseits soll auch   23

---

⁵⁵ S. *Honnold/Flechtner,* Art. 21, Rn. 176; MünchKomm/*Gruber,* Art. 21, Rn. 19; *Stern,* Erklärungen, Rn. 104, sowie oben Rn. 7; a. A. *Neumayer,* RIW 1994, 99, 103; *Neumayer/Ming,* Art. 21, Anm. 4.

⁵⁶ Oben Rn. 9; zur elektronischen Kommunikation „in real time" CISG-AC, Op. 1 *(Chr. Ramberg),* Opinion Art. 21(2), IHR 2003, 244, 248; zur Beweislast unten Rn. 24.

⁵⁷ CISG-AC, Op. 1 *(Chr. Ramberg),* Comment 21.6, IHR 2003, 244, 248.

⁵⁸ Oben Rn. 9.

⁵⁹ Wie hier *Honsell/Dornis,* Art. 21, Rn. 27.

⁶⁰ Vgl. § 149 S. 1 BGB: „sofern es nicht schon vorher geschehen ist"; MünchKomm/*Gruber,* Art. 21, Rn. 22; a. A. *Honsell/Dornis,* Art. 21, Rn. 29.

⁶¹ Vgl. *Brunner,* Art. 21, Rn. 3; *Bianca/Bonell/Farnsworth,* Art. 21, Anm. 3.4.; *Wey,* Rn. 1165.

⁶² Vgl. schon *Lagergren,* S. 65 f.

⁶³ S. *Bianca/Bonell/Farnsworth,* Art. 21, Anm. 3.4.; *Honnold/Flechtner,* Art. 21, Rn. 175; MünchKomm/*Gruber,* Art. 21, Rn. 10; *Rehbinder,* Vertragsschluss, S. 162, erwägt „teleologische Reduktion" des Art. 21 I;

bei unwesentlich verspäteter Annahme den Offerenten stets eine Erklärungspflicht aus Treu und Glauben treffen.[64] Der Annehmende kann sich dadurch schützen, dass er die Geltung seiner Erklärung für den Fall verspäteten Zugangs befristet.[65] M. E. ist im Fall erheblich verspäteter Annahmeerklärungen sogar von einer **immanenten Geltungsbefristung** derartiger Erklärungen auszugehen, nach deren Ablauf sie ihre Wirkung verlieren.[66] Die für die Offerte im Zweifel nach Art. 18 II 2 geltende angemessene Frist ist zwar nicht direkt zu übernehmen, doch wird Auslegung der Annahmeerklärung nach Art. 8 II eine je nach den konkreten Umständen der Parteien und des Geschäfts zu bestimmende Frist ergeben, für die die Annahme trotz Verspätung vernünftigerweise Bestand haben und dem Offerenten Vertragsschluss ermöglichen sollte.[67] Dagegen würde Annahme einer regelmäßigen Erklärungspflicht für den Offerenten den Inhalt des Art. 21 verfälschen.

Auch der Offerent kann in eine Situation der Ungewissheit geraten, wenn er den Grund der Verspätung nicht eindeutig feststellen kann.[68] Aber die Belastung durch eine derartige Ungewissheit hält sich für den Offerenten in erträglichen Grenzen, denn er kann mit einer Rückantwort die Situation stets klären; in Zweifelsfällen ist Schweigen sein eigenes Risiko.[69]

3. Beweislast

24 Die Beweislast für Vertragsschluss trotz verspäteter Annahme trägt, wer sich auf Wirksamkeit des Vertrages beruft.[70] Diese Partei hat damit die ordnungsgemäße und pünktliche („unverzügliche") Absendung der Billigung nach Abs. 1 sowie die Pünktlichkeit der Annahme bei normaler Beförderung und Beförderungsstörung sowie ihre Erkennbarkeit (Abs. 2) zu beweisen;[71] die Behauptungs- und Beweislast für die rechtzeitige Verwahrung nach Abs. 2 trägt der Offerent.[72]

Wey, Rn. 1157, 1169, will bei langer Verspätung die Annahmeerklärung als von beiden Seiten „abgeschrieben" behandeln; *Staudinger/Magnus*, Art. 21, Rn. 19.
[64] *Dilger*, RabelsZ 45 (1981), 169, 183; dagegen wohl *Achilles*, Art. 21, Rn. 4; auch *Rehbinder*, Vertragsschluss, S. 162; s. a. oben Rn. 4.
[65] *Achilles*, Art. 21, Rn. 4; *Soergel/Lüderitz/Fenge*, Art. 21, Rn. 11.
[66] So auch *Brunner*, Art. 21, Rn. 3.
[67] S. *Wey*, Rn. 1170, 1192.
[68] Vgl. *Aubrey*, 14 Int'l & Comp. L. Q. (1965), 1011, 1020: Art. 9 EAG verlange vom Offerenten intime Kenntnis des internationalen Postsystems und seiner Arbeitsweise. Ähnlich *Sutton*, 16 U. W. Ont. L. Rev. (1977), 133, 143, zu den Entwürfen.
[69] Vgl. *von Caemmerer*, RabelsZ 29 (1965), 101, 130.
[70] *Baumgärtel/Laumen/Hepting*, Art. 21 WKR, Rn. 1.
[71] Unstr., s. MünchKomm/*Gruber*, Art. 21, Rn. 25; *Staudinger/Magnus*, Art. 21, Rn. 20.
[72] Zu Abs. 2 HS 2s. *Baumgärtel/Laumen/Hepting*, Art. 21 WKR, Rn. 4: „... wenn nicht ..." kehrt Beweislast um.

Art. 22 [Rücknahme der Annahme]

Eine Annahme kann zurückgenommen werden, wenn die Rücknahmeerklärung dem Anbietenden vor oder in dem Zeitpunkt zugeht, in dem die Annahme wirksam geworden wäre.

Art. 22
An acceptance may be withdrawn if the withdrawal reaches the offeror before or at the same time as the acceptance would have become effective.

Art. 22
L'acceptation peut être rétractée si la rétractation parvient à l'auteur de l'offre avant le moment où l'acceptation aurait pris effet ou à ce moment.

Übersicht

	Rn.
I. Grundzüge	1
II. Regelungsinhalt	2
1. Wirksamkeit der Annahme	2
2. Annahmeäquivalentes Verhalten	3
3. Rücknahme als Willenserklärung	4
4. Ergänzungen	5
5. Ähnliche Erklärungen	6
6. Spekulationsproblem	7

Vorläufer und **Entwürfe:** Art. 10 EAG, New Yorker E 1977 Art. 10, Genfer E 1977 Art. 16, New Yorker E 1978 Art. 20.

I. Grundzüge

Die Vorschrift entspricht § 130 I 2 BGB und geht auf Art. 10 EAG zurück.[1] Gegenüber den Entwürfen und dem EAG ist sprachlich – wie schon in Art. 15 II – durch Verwendung des Begriffs „Rücknahme" eine klare **Unterscheidung** vom **Widerruf** erreicht worden. Die Bedeutung des Art. 22 hat man vor allem in der Ergänzung des Art. 23 gesehen.[2] Zutreffend wird die Regelung des Art. 22 als Ausdruck eines allgemeinen, auch dem Art. 15 II zugrunde liegenden Prinzips bezeichnet.[3] 1

II. Regelungsinhalt

1. Wirksamkeit der Annahme

Rücknahme kann nur bis zu oder gleichzeitig mit der Annahme erfolgen. Entscheidend ist jeweils der Zugang der Erklärung, während es auf die tatsächliche Kenntnisnahme nicht ankommt.[4] Mit Wirksamkeit der Annahme – dazu Art. 18 – ist der Vertrag geschlossen (Art. 23) und sind die Parteien gebunden. Ein actus contrarius einer Seite, der Aufhebung 2

---

[1] Zur Geschichte von Art. 10 EAG s. *von Caemmerer,* RabelsZ 29 (1965), 101, 130 f.
[2] S. schon YB IX (1978), S. 119, Art. 20; Sekretariatskommentar, Art. 20; die die Perfektionierung des Vertrages herbeiführende Wirksamkeit der Annahme ist allerdings schon in Art. 18 geregelt. *Farnsworth* bezeichnet die Vorschrift als eine der am wenigsten kontroversen Bestimmungen, s. *Bianca/Bonell/Farnsworth,* Art. 22, Anm. 1.2.
[3] *Honnold/Flechtner,* Art. 22, Rn. 177.
[4] CISG-AC, Op. 1 *(Chr. Ramberg),* Comment 22.2f, IHR 2003, 244, 249; MünchKomm/*Gruber,* Art. 22, Rn. 3.

des Vertrages bewirken könnte, müsste vorbehalten sein, sofern nicht Aufhebung wegen Leistungsstörungen kraft Gesetzes möglich ist.[5]

2. Annahmeäquivalentes Verhalten

3   Art. 22 setzt eine Situation voraus, in der die Annahmeerklärung Zeit zum Zugang braucht, also etwa bei brieflichem Vertragsschluss.[6] Bei einer Annahme nach Art. 18 III kommt Rücknahme regelmäßig nicht in Betracht,[7] es sei denn, Schweigen bewirkt Annahme erst nach Ablauf einer Annahmefrist.[8] Bei mündlicher oder telefonischer Annahme kommt Rücknahme allenfalls in Betracht, falls die Annahmeerklärung noch nicht vollständig „gemacht" worden und deshalb noch nicht zugegangen ist.[9]

3. Rücknahme als Willenserklärung

4   Rücknahme ist **Willenserklärung**; für Geschäftsfähigkeit, Willensmängel und Vertretungsmacht des Erklärenden gilt unvereinheitlichtes nationales Recht.[10] Die Rücknahme kann **mit jedem Mittel** erklärt werden; der Annehmende ist nicht darauf verwiesen, das gleiche Erklärungsmittel wie für die Annahme zu verwenden. **Zugangsbedürftigkeit** ergibt sich schon aus dem Wortlaut des Art. 22.[11] Bis zum Zugang kann die Rücknahme ihrerseits zurückgenommen werden, so dass die Annahme wieder zum Vertragsschluss führt. Ein Widerruf nach Zugang dürfte dagegen grundsätzlich ausgeschlossen sein.[12] **Beweislast** für rechtzeitigen Zugang der Rücknahmeerklärung trägt, wer sich darauf beruft, dass ein Vertrag nicht zustande gekommen ist.[13]

4. Ergänzungen

5   Vor Zugang der Annahme kann nicht nur zurückgenommen, sondern auch korrigiert, erweitert, eingeschränkt oder modifiziert werden. Zwar spricht Art. 22 nur von der Rücknahme, doch ergibt sich die **Möglichkeit nachträglicher Modifikation** einer Annahmeerklärung aus dem Grundsatz, dass Vertragsschlusserklärungen erst mit Zugang volle Wirkung entfalten und der Erklärende bis zum Wirksamwerden noch Herr seiner Erklärung bleibt.[14] Die Modifikation kann dann zu Art. 19 I oder II führen (s. Rn. 6). Der Annehmende kann aber auf diesem Wege auch noch Modifikationen in seiner Annahme, die nach Art. 19 zu beurteilen wären, zurücknehmen und so „glatt" annehmen.

5. Ähnliche Erklärungen

6   Ob eine **Rücknahme** gemeint ist, muss ggf. durch **Auslegung** geklärt werden. Eine die ursprüngliche Annahmeerklärung über- oder jedenfalls einholende Erklärung kann auch als modifizierender Zusatz zur Annahme gemeint, u. U. aber auch Rücknahme mit erneuter Annahme zu veränderten Bedingungen sein. Ob eine solche Erklärung Vertragsschluss bewirkt, hängt davon ab, ob sie innerhalb der Annahmefrist zugeht und der Offerte entspricht; bei Modifikation der Annahme durch die zweite Erklärung oder einer gleichzeitig

---

[5] Zu dieser „negativen Bedeutung" des Art. 22 s. *Bianca/Bonell/Farnsworth*, Art. 22, Anm. 2.2.
[6] S. den entsprechenden Formulierungsvorschlag des Sekretariats in YB VIII (1977), S. 102.
[7] *Brunner*, Art. 21, Rn. 2; MünchKomm/*Gruber*, Art. 20, Rn. 4; *Staudinger/Magnus*, Art. 22, Rn. 10; *Soergel/Lüderitz/Fenge*, Art. 22, Rn. 2; teilweise anders *Witz/Salger/Lorenz/Witz*, Art. 22, Rn. 1 (stellt nicht allein auf Zugang ab); s. auch oben Art. 18 Rn. 22.
[8] Hierzu oben Art. 18 Rn. 9, 22; *Wey*, Rn. 977.
[9] *Staudinger/Magnus*, Art. 22, Rn. 11; enger *Honsell/Dornis*, Art. 22, Rn. 13; *Reinhart*, Art. 22, Rn. 3; *Schwimann/Posch*, Art. 22, Rn. 2. Zum Zugang mündlicher Erklärungen s. unten Art. 24 Rn. 10 ff.
[10] S. oben Art. 15 Rn. 4.
[11] Zum Zugang s. Art. 24; zum Zugang elektronischer Rücknahmeerklärungen CISG-AC, Op. 1 (*Chr. Ramberg*), Comment 22.2, IHR 2003, 244, 249.
[12] MünchKomm/*Gruber*, Art. 20, Rn. 5.
[13] *Bamberger/Roth/Saenger*, Art. 22, Rn. 2.
[14] *Neumayer/Ming*, Art. 22, Anm. 2.

als Annahme mit Abweichungen gemeinten Zurücknahme der ersten Erklärung gilt Art. 19.[15]

6. Spekulationsproblem

Die Rücknahmemöglichkeit während der Laufzeit der Annahme, in der der Offerent nach Art. 16 I nicht mehr widerrufen kann, wird teilweise wegen möglicher Spekulationen des Annehmenden auf Kosten des gebundenen Offerenten als Belastung für den Offerenten gesehen.[16] In Rechtssystemen, denen die Möglichkeit der Bindung an die Offerte – aus der die gleiche Gefahr einer Spekulation des Adressaten auf Kosten des Offerenten entstehen kann – selbstverständlich ist, haben sich, soweit zu sehen, die befürchteten Missbräuche nicht gezeigt;[17] der Offerent kann ihnen auch durch Setzung einer knappen Frist begegnen.[18]

---

[15] Zu solchen nicht nur Rücknahme, sondern Korrektur beabsichtigenden Erklärungen des Annehmenden *Dölle/Schlechtriem*, Art. 10 EAG, Rn. 4.

[16] S. *Bianca/Bonell/Farnsworth*, Art. 22, Anm. 3.1.; *Brunner*, Art. 22, Rn. 1; *Herber/Czerwenka*, Art. 22, Rn. 2; *Honnold/Flechtner*, Art. 22, Rn. 177; *Neumayer/Ming*, Art. 22, Anm. 1.; *Staudinger/Magnus*, Art. 22, Rn. 12 (in seltenen Fällen Verstoß gegen Treu und Glauben).

[17] Überzeugend gegen das Bestehen einer korrekturbedürftigen Missbrauchsmöglichkeit *Enderlein/Maskow/Strohbach*, Art. 22, Anm. 1.; so auch MünchKomm/*Gruber*, Art. 22, Rn. 8; *Witz/Salger/Lorenz/Witz*, Art. 22 Fn. 2.

[18] Wie hier wohl *Honnold/Flechtner*, Art. 22, Rn. 177; *Honsell/Dornis*, Art. 22, Rn. 17.

Art. 23 [Zeitpunkt des Vertragsschlusses]

Ein Vertrag ist in dem Zeitpunkt geschlossen, in dem die Annahme eines Angebots nach diesem Übereinkommen wirksam wird.

Art. 23
A contract is concluded at the moment when an acceptance of an offer becomes effective in accordance with the provisions of this Convention.

Art. 23
Le contrat est conclu au moment où l'acceptation d'une offre prend effet conformément aux dispositions de la présente Convention.

Übersicht

	Rn.
I. Zeitpunkt des Vertragsschlusses	1
1. Bedeutung der Regelung	1
2. Ungeregelte Fälle	3
a) Vertragsschluss unter Bedingungen	3
b) Genehmigung	4
c) Leistungsvorbehalte	5
d) Einigwerden ohne Angebot und Annahme	6
II. Ort des Vertragsschlusses	7

Vorläufer und **Entwürfe:** New Yorker E 1977 Art. 6, Genfer E 1977 Art. 17, New Yorker E 1978 Art. 21.

I. Zeitpunkt des Vertragsschlusses

1. Bedeutung der Regelung

1 Art. 23 regelt Selbstverständliches,[1] da der Zeitpunkt des Vertragsschlusses bei „traditioneller" Vertragsschlusstechnik[2] bereits durch Art. 18 II 1 oder III festgelegt wird.[3] Der Vertrag kommt danach mit Zugang der Annahmeerklärung[4] bzw. der erklärungsäquivalenten Zustimmungsäußerung oder – ausnahmsweise – mit dem annahmeäquivalenten Verhalten nach Art. 18 III zustande.[5] Sofern ausnahmsweise Schweigen bzw. Untätigkeit als Annahme anzusehen ist,[6] ist danach der Zeitpunkt des Zugangs der Offerte entscheidend;[7] soll nach den Umständen allerdings erst die Nichtäußerung innerhalb einer bestimmten Frist Annahme bedeuten, so kommt es auf den Zeitpunkt des Fristablaufs an. Unterliegen Parteierklärungen im konkreten Fall aufgrund einer dahingehenden vertraglichen Vereinbarung oder über Artt. 12, 96 bestimmten Formanforderungen, so ist zudem erforderlich, dass diesen genügt wurde.[8]

---

[1] Art. 23 geht auf einen Vorschlag des Sekretariats zurück (YB VIII (1977), S. 81). Das EAG hatte auf eine Regelung des Zeitpunktes des Vertragsschlusses trotz vorliegender Entwürfe verzichtet, da der Begriff „Zeitpunkt des Vertragsschlusses" in verschiedenen Funktionen verwendet werde und unterschiedliche Auslegung erfordern könne (ausführlich zum EAG *von Caemmerer,* RabelsZ 29 (1965), 101, 136 ff.; *Dölle/von Caemmerer,* Art. 57 EKG, Rn. 14).

[2] S. oben Vor Artt. 14–24 Rn. 15.

[3] S. *Bianca/Bonell/Farnsworth,* Art. 23, Anm. 2.1.: „… scarcely necessary"; *Enderlein/Maskow/Strohbach,* Art. 23, Anm. 1.; *Schwimann/Posch,* Art. 23, Rn. 1: „superfluum non nocet".

[4] *Conservas la Costena v. Lanis San Luis & Argoindustrial Santa Adela,* Comisión para la Protección del Comercio Exterior de México, 29.4.1996, CISG-online 350 = 17 J. L. & Com. (1998), 427, 432; CA Paris, 22.4.1992, CISG-online 222; Fövárosi Biróság Budapest, 10.1.1992, CISG-online 43.

[5] S. oben Art. 18 Rn. 13 ff.; zum Schweigen während einer Annahmefrist oben Art. 18 Rn. 22.

[6] S. oben Art. 18 Rn. 9.

[7] S. oben Art. 22; a. A. *Brunner,* Art. 23, Rn. 1, der auf den Zeitpunkt abstellen will, zu welchem die stillschweigende Zustimmung äußerlich erkennbar ist; ebenso *Staudinger/Magnus,* Art. 23, Rn. 3.

[8] *Brunner,* Art. 23, Rn. 1; *Staudinger/Magnus,* Art. 23, Rn. 3.

Zeitpunkt des Vertragsschlusses 2–6 **Art. 23**

Auf den Zeitpunkt des Vertragsschlusses wird in Artt. 1 II, 10 lit. a), 16 I, 31 lit. b), lit. c), 35 II lit. b), III, 42 I, 55, 68, 71 I, 73 III, 74, 79 I, 100 II Bezug genommen. Wird in anderen **Rechtsvorschriften nationalen Rechts** auf den Zeitpunkt des Vertragsschlusses abgestellt – z. B. im Steuerrecht, Insolvenzrecht, Bilanzrecht, in wirtschaftslenkenden Gesetzen usw. –, muss eine Auslegung der jeweiligen Vorschrift entscheiden, ob Art. 23 als tatbestandliche Voraussetzung eingesetzt werden kann oder dieser Zeitpunkt autonom bestimmt werden muss.[9] 2

2. Ungeregelte Fälle

a) Vertragsschluss unter Bedingungen. Die Arbeitsgruppe hat einen Vorschlag verworfen, der eine Reihe von Sonderfällen regeln sollte.[10] Bei **Bedingungen** sollte Vertragswirksamkeit erst mit der aufschiebenden Bedingung eintreten, bei einer auflösenden Bedingung mit ihrem Eintritt entfallen. Die Wirkung einer Bedingung zu regeln und insoweit von Art. 23 abzuweichen ist jedoch Sache der Parteien und ihrer Regelungsautonomie nach Art. 6, so dass es einer Vorschrift nicht bedurfte;[11] s. hierzu im Einzelnen oben Art. 14 Rn. 31a ff. Die von nationalen Rechten als „Bedingung" qualifizierte Gegenleistung (wie etwa die **„consideration"** in Common Law-Rechtsordnungen[12]) und ihr Ausbleiben sind jedenfalls exklusiv vom CISG und seinen Leistungsstörungsvorschriften geregelte Materie. 3

b) Genehmigung. Hängt Wirksamkeit von der vereinbarten **Genehmigung eines Dritten** ab, dann ist es eine Frage der Auslegung des Genehmigungsvorbehaltes, ob die Genehmigung Rückwirkung haben oder erst im Zeitpunkt ihrer Erteilung wirken soll. Bei gesetzlich erforderlichen Genehmigungen, etwa durch gesetzliche Vertreter, den Vertretenen, durch Organe juristischer Personen, aber auch durch staatliche Stellen muss das jeweils anwendbare Recht den Wirkungszeitpunkt der Genehmigung bestimmen.[13] Für die Folgen der Genehmigungsverweigerung gilt ebenfalls unvereinheitlichtes nationales Recht, wie Art. 4 S. 2 lit. a) für die Folge „Ungültigkeit" verdeutlicht.[14] 4

c) Leistungsvorbehalte. Hängt der Vertragsschluss noch davon ab, dass die **Mindesterfordernisse** der Offerte – Art. 14 I 2 – durch eine Seite oder einen Dritten auf Grund eines entsprechenden Vorbehalts **bestimmt** werden,[15] muss wieder durch Auslegung des Vorbehalts festgestellt werden, ob die Parteien bereits mit Perfektionierung der Vertragsschlusserklärungen gebunden sein wollten oder erst mit Ausübung der vorbehaltenen Leistungsbestimmung;[16] mangels deutlich zum Ausdruck gebrachter Wirkung des Vorbehalts auch für den Vertragsschlusszeitpunkt wird man aber davon auszugehen haben, dass es bei Art. 23 bleibt, die **Leistungsbestimmung** also evtl. **Rückwirkung** bezüglich des Vertragsschlusses und seines Zeitpunktes hat und nicht selbst erst den Vertragsschluss bewirkt.[17] 5

d) Einigwerden ohne Angebot und Annahme. Bei Vertragsschlussverfahren, die sich nicht der traditionellen Instrumente „Angebot" und „Annahme" bedienen,[18] kann Art. 23 6

---

[9] *Honnold/Flechtner*, Art. 23, Rn. 178; MünchKomm/*Gruber*, Art. 23, Rn. 2; *Neumayer/Ming*, Art. 23, Anm. 1. a. E.; *Soergel/Lüderitz/Fenge*, Art. 23, Rn. 1; *Witz/Salger/Lorenz/Witz*, Art. 23, Rn. 3.
[10] S. YB IX (1978), S. 80 f., Nr. 268.
[11] S. ausführlich bereits oben Art. 14 Rn. 31a f. MünchKomm/*Gruber*, Art. 23, Rn. 4; *Staudinger/Magnus*, Art. 23, Rn. 4; *Witz/Salger/Lorenz/Witz*, Art. 23, Rn. 4; a. A. *Honsell/Schnyder/Straub*, 1. Aufl., Art. 23, Rn. 5: Rückgriff auf das durch IPR berufene interne Recht.
[12] S. dazu schon oben Vor Artt. 14–24 Rn. 2 sowie oben *Schmidt-Kessel*, Art. 11 Rn. 11.
[13] S. Fovárosi Biróság Budapest, 10.1.1992, CISG-online 43: dass der Erwerb U. S.-amerikanischer *Pratt & Wittney*-Flugzeugmotoren durch die ungarische Fluggesellschaft *Malev* von der Zustimmung der ungarischen und der U. S.-amerikanischen Regierung abhing, änderte (jedenfalls nach ungarischem Recht) nichts daran, dass sich der Vertragsschlusszeitpunkt nach Art. 23 bestimmte.
[14] *Staudinger/Magnus*, Art. 23, Rn. 7.
[15] S. oben Art. 14 Rn. 13 f.
[16] Vgl. für Gremienvorbehalte u. ä. *Witz/Salger/Lorenz/Witz*, Art. 23, Rn. 4.
[17] Wie hier MünchKomm/*Gruber*, Art. 23, Rn. 4.
[18] S. oben Vor Artt. 14–24 Rn. 15 ff., 23 f.

nicht helfen.[19] Werden die Parteien auf andere Weise einig, dann müssen sie notwendig auch selbst den Zeitpunkt festlegen, zu dem ihre Einigung als Vertrag bindend geworden ist. Die Feststellung des Augenblicks, in dem nach dem Willen der Parteien bindende Einigung erreicht worden ist, ergibt den Zeitpunkt des Vertragsschlusses für die Vorschriften des CISG,[20] die darauf abstellen.[21]

II. Ort des Vertragsschlusses

7   Wie schon das EAG enthält sich das CISG einer Regelung des Vertragsschlussortes.[22] Ein entsprechender Vorschlag ist in der Arbeitsgruppe gescheitert.[23] Der Abschlussort kann für die Anwendung kollisionsrechtlicher Regeln erheblich sein. M. E. liegt jedoch keine interne Lücke vor, die auf Grund Art. 7 II nach allgemeinen Grundsätzen des CISG geschlossen werden könnte.[24] Vorbehaltlich einer entsprechenden Vereinbarung durch die Parteien (und ihrer Anerkennung durch das maßgebliche nationale Recht) und eines speziellen Bedeutungsgehaltes einer auf den Ort des Vertragsschlusses abstellenden Norm oder Parteivereinbarung wird man davon ausgehen können, dass der Vertrag an dem Ort geschlossen worden ist, an dem die perfektionierende Erklärung zugeht oder die annahmeäquivalente Handlung – Art. 18 III – vorgenommen worden ist.[25] So ist im Ergebnis auch in der Rechtsprechung entschieden worden.[26]

---

[19] *Bianca/Bonell/Farnsworth*, Art. 23, Anm. 3.1.
[20] S. oben Rn. 2.
[21] Vgl. auch *Brunner*, Art. 23, Rn. 1; MünchKomm/*Gruber*, Art. 23, Rn. 3.
[22] Monomeles Protodikeio Thessaloniki, 16319/2007, CISG-online 2295: Ort des Vertragsschlusses nach Art. 192 griech. ZGB bestimmt.
[23] *Bianca/Bonell/Farnsworth*, Art. 23, Anm. 3.3.
[24] Ebenso *Bianca/Bonell/Farnsworth*, Art. 23, Anm. 3.3.: keine Frage des Übereinkommens; *Honsell/Dornis*, Art. 23, Rn. 5; *Mazzotta*, 33 Rutgers Computer & Techn. L. J. (2007), 251, 283; *Staudinger/Magnus*, Art. 23, Rn. 8; *Soergel/Lüderitz/Fenge*, Art. 23, Rn. 2; *Witz/Salger/Lorenz/Witz*, Art. 23, Rn. 5. S. auch *Kritzer*, Guide to Practical Applications, S. 189: „… provision … unnecessary".
[25] *Achilles*, Art. 21, Rn. 3; teilweise anders *Soergel/Lüderitz/Fenge*, Art. 23, Rn. 2: nach nationalem, durch IPR berufenen Recht zu bestimmen; ebenso *Honsell/Dornis*, Art. 23, Rn. 5; *Staudinger/Magnus*, Art. 23, Rn. 8; *Witz/Salger/Lorenz/Witz*, Art. 23, Rn. 6.
[26] *Roder Zelt- und Hallenkonstruktionen GmbH v. Rosedown Park Pty Ltd. and Reginald R Eustace*, FCA (SA, Adelaide), 28.4.1995, CISG-online 218 = 1995 F. C. R. (Aus.) 216 ff. (argumentativ gestützt auf Artt. 18, 24).

Art. 24 [Begriff des Zugangs]

Für die Zwecke dieses Teils des Übereinkommens „geht" ein Angebot, eine Annahmeerklärung oder sonstige Willenserklärung dem Empfänger „zu", wenn sie ihm mündlich gemacht wird oder wenn sie auf anderem Weg ihm persönlich, an seiner Niederlassung oder Postanschrift oder, wenn diese fehlen, an seinem gewöhnlichen Aufenthaltsort zugestellt wird.

Art. 24

For the purposes of this Part of the Convention, an offer, declaration of acceptance or any other indication of intention „reaches" the addressee when it is made orally to him or delivered by any other means to him personally, to his place of business or mailing address or, if he does not have a place of business or mailing address, to his habitual residence.

Art. 24

Aux fins de la présente partie de la Convention, une offre, une déclaration d'acceptation ou toute autre manifestation d'intention „parvient" à son destinataire lorsqu'elle lui est faite verbalement ou est délivrée par tout autre moyen au destinataire lui-même, à son établissement, à son adresse postale ou, s'il n'a pas d'établissement ou d'adresse postale, à sa résidence habituelle.

Übersicht

	Rn.
I. Funktion und Entstehung der Vorschrift	1
II. Geregelte Erklärungen	3
1. Zugangsbedürftige Erklärungen	3
2. Abgrenzung mündliche Erklärungen – andere Erklärungsmittel	4
a) Mündliche Erklärungen	5
b) Auf anderem Weg zugestellte Erklärungen	6
c) Einschaltung von Mittelspersonen	7
III. Zugang mündlicher Erklärungen	10
1. Zugang und Vernehmung	10
2. Fernmündliche Erklärungen	11
3. Telefonische Anrufbeantworter	13
IV. Zugang von Erklärungen „auf anderem Weg"	15
1. Erklärungsadressen	15
2. Erklärungsmittel	16
3. Zustellung	17
4. Zugang bei einzelnen Erklärungsmitteln	19
a) Brief	19
b) Telegramm	22
c) Telefax, Telex	23
d) E-Mail	24
e) Webseiten im World Wide Web	28
f) Electronic Data Interchange (EDI)	29
g) Short Message Service (SMS)	30
5. Parteiautonomie	31
6. Zugang außerhalb der Geschäftszeiten	32
7. Unverständliche Erklärungen	34
V. Fremdsprachen	36
1. Verwendung einer Fremdsprache als Zugangshindernis	36
2. Behandlung des „Sprachrisikos" im Einzelnen	37
3. Anfechtbarkeit	40
VI. Rechtsmissbrauch: Zugangsverhinderung	41
VII. Beweislast	43

Vorläufer und **Entwürfe:** Art. 12 I EAG, New Yorker E 1977 Art. 12, Genfer E 1977 Art. 7, New Yorker E 1978 Art. 22.

I. Funktion und Entstehung der Vorschrift

1 Die Vorschrift geht auf die bereits in Art. 12 I EAG formulierte Definition des Zugangsbegriffs zurück und ist in den Beratungen der Arbeitsgruppe mehrfach verändert worden, wobei nicht nur die mündliche Erklärung besondere Berücksichtigung gefunden hat, sondern auch der gewöhnliche Aufenthalt als nur subsidiäre Empfangsadresse geregelt worden ist.[1] Die Einschränkung der Erklärungsmittel in Art. 12 II EAG ist dagegen fallen gelassen worden, da man sie als Widerspruch zur Möglichkeit der Annahme „orally ... or ¼ by any other means" sah.[2]

2 Art. 24 definiert „Zugang" und ist nach Art. 7 I autonom, d. h. ohne Rückgriff auf Auslegungsgesichtspunkte des unvereinheitlichten nationalen Rechts auszulegen.[3] Er schließt jedoch nicht aus, dass als weitere Wirksamkeitsvoraussetzung des Zugangs nach nationalem Recht **Geschäftsfähigkeit des Adressaten** erforderlich sein kann; bei Maßgeblichkeit unvereinheitlichten deutschen Rechts als Personalstatut des Empfängers nach Art. 7 EGBGB ist also § 131 BGB anzuwenden.

II. Geregelte Erklärungen

1. Zugangsbedürftige Erklärungen

3 Art. 24 regelt nur die **zugangsbedürftigen Erklärungen** des Vertragsschlussteils (Teil II) des Übereinkommens. Neben der ausdrücklich genannten Offerte und Annahme (Artt. 15 I, 18 II) sind die „sonstigen Willenserklärungen": Rücknahme der Offerte (Art. 15 II), Widerruf der Offerte (Art. 16 I), Ablehnung des Angebots (Art. 17), Setzung einer Annahmefrist (Art. 20 I), Rücknahme der Annahme (Art. 22), nicht dagegen die in Art. 19 II und Art. 21 geregelten Erklärungen.[4] Art. 24 muss, da er als Ausdruck eines allgemeinen Grundsatzes zu verstehen ist, nach Art. 7 II trotz seiner Beschränkung auf Teil II des CISG auch auf die ausdrücklich als zugangsbedürftig geregelten Erklärungen im Teil III[5] – nämlich diejenigen nach Artt. 47 II, 48 IV, 63 II, 65 I, II, 79 IV – anzuwenden sein.[6] Er ist aber auch für andere, den Vertragsschlusserklärungen gleichstehende Erklärungen maßgebend, sofern die Parteien nichts anderes vereinbart haben, also z. B. auf einen vorbehaltenen Widerruf oder Rücktritt, die zur Vereinbarung einer Vertragsauflösung oder einer Vertragsänderung gewechselten Erklärungen,[7] die einer Seite oder einem Dritten vorbehaltene Leistungs- oder Preisbestimmung[8] oder eine Zahlungsaufforderung des Verkäufers nach Zurückweisung der Ware durch den Käufer.[9]

---

[1] Vgl. zur Geschichte *Bianca/Bonell/Farnsworth,* Art. 24, Anm. 1.2.
[2] S. YB VIII (1977), S. 103.
[3] Unzutreffend deshalb OLG Dresden, 10.11.2006, CISG-online 1625, wo in einer CISG-Konstellation auf Begrifflichkeiten des § 130 BGB rekurriert wurde.
[4] S. hierzu oben Art. 19 Rn. 15; s. oben Art. 21 Rn. 7, 20.
[5] Umfassend zu den Erklärungen im Einzelnen *Noussias,* Zugangsbedürftigkeit von Mitteilungen, S. 126 ff.; *Stern,* Erklärungen, Rn. 140 ff.
[6] H. A., s. *Bamberger/Roth/Saenger,* Art. 24, Rn. 1; *Bianca/Bonell/Farnsworth,* Art. 24, Anm. 3.1.; *Brunner,* Art. 24, Rn. 1; *Honnold/Flechtner,* Art. 24, Rn. 179; *Staudinger/Magnus,* Art. 24, Rn. 9; teilweise a. A. *Enderlein/Maskow/Strohbach,* Art. 24, Anm. 1.; MünchKomm/*Gruber,* Art. 24, Rn. 2 f.; *Witz/Salger/Lorenz/Witz,* Art. 24, Rn. 4 (analog); *Soergel/Lüderitz/Fenge,* Art. 24, Rn. 2; entsprechend wohl auch *Neumayer/Ming,* Art. 24, Anm. 1.
[7] S. unten Art. 29 Rn. 2, 6 ff.
[8] *Brunner,* Art. 24, Rn. 1.
[9] RB Amsterdam, 5.10.1994, CISG-online 446 = NIPR 1995, Nr. 231 (im konkreten Fall kam der auf die Zahlungsaufforderung anwendbaren Rechtsregeln deshalb Bedeutung zu, weil der Käufer vorbrachte, der Verkäufer habe seinen Kaufpreisanspruch durch dessen dauerhafte Nichtverfolgung verwirkt).

2. Abgrenzung mündliche Erklärungen – andere Erklärungsmittel

Das CISG unterscheidet – wie schon das EAG – zwischen **mündlichen** und **„auf** 4 **anderem Weg"** („by any other means", „par tout autre moyen") erfolgten Erklärungen. Art. 24 CISG setzt diese Unterscheidung bis in die Zugangsvoraussetzungen fort, ohne selbst zu definieren, was „mündlich gemachte" oder „auf anderem Weg zugestellte" Erklärungen sind.

a) Mündliche Erklärungen. Mündliche Erklärungen sind zunächst unter Anwesenden, 5 vom Erklärenden dem Adressaten gegenüber ausgesprochene Erklärungen. Auch telefonisch oder per Funk vom Erklärenden direkt an den Erklärungsempfänger mündlich übermittelte, d. h. gesprochene Erklärungen fallen unter den Begriff „mündliche Erklärungen".[10] Dasselbe muss für Erklärungen während einer Videokonferenz gelten.[11] Das auf einem Tonträger festgehaltene gesprochene und vom Empfänger mit entsprechenden Einrichtungen hörbar gemachte Wort ist dagegen keine mündliche Erklärung, denn aus der Entstehungsgeschichte wird deutlich, dass als „mündliche" Mitteilung nur die unmittelbar zu vernehmende Erklärung gesehen worden ist, deren Aufnahme vom Erklärenden jederzeit verfolgt und durch Rückfragen kontrolliert werden kann.[12] Auch dürften mündlich vom Erklärenden diktierte und dann von einem Spracherkennungssystem elektronisch in Schrift umgesetzte und übermittelte Erklärungen wie sonstige elektronische Erklärungen (sogleich Rn. 6) zu behandeln sein. Dagegen ist wohl nicht ausgeschlossen, elektronisch übermittelte und einen Dialog ähnlich wie ein mündliches Gespräch erlaubende Erklärungen (etwa in „Chat-Foren" im Internet) als „mündliche" zu behandeln.[13]

b) Auf anderem Weg zugestellte Erklärungen. Zu den „auf anderem Weg zugestell- 6 ten" Erklärungen rechnen neben brieflichen Erklärungen etwa Erklärungen per Telegramm, Telefax, Fernschreiben (Telex), Teletex, Minitel, Bildschirmtext (Btx) oder SMS.

Wie sich der Entstehungsgeschichte des Art. 24 entnehmen lässt, rechnen auch moderne elektronische Erklärungen, sofern sie nicht ein gesprochenes Wort direkt hörbar übermitteln, zu den „anderen Wegen".[14] Hierunter fallen nach dem augenblicklichen Stand der Technik u. a. Erklärungen per E-Mail, EDI, Internet, World Wide Web. Für moderne Kommunikationsmittel der genannten Spielarten ist auch für die Beurteilung des Erklärungszugangs zu fordern, dass der Adressat sich ausdrücklich oder implizit mit der Verwendung dieses elektronischen Mediums, d. h. der jeweiligen Art und dem jeweiligen Format des elektronischen Kommunikationsmittels einverstanden erklärt[15] und der Erklärende die vom Adressaten angegebene Adresse verwendet hat.

c) Einschaltung von Mittelspersonen. Bei Einschaltung von Mittelspersonen ist zu 7 unterscheiden: Die von oder gegenüber einem vertretungsberechtigten **Vertreter** ausgesprochene Erklärung ist mündliche Erklärung.[16] Auch die von einem **Erklärungsboten**

---

[10] *Honsell/Dornis*, Art. 24, Rn. 5; MünchKomm/*Gruber*, Art. 24, Rn. 4; vgl. jedoch zur Vorgeschichte des EAG und zu den Gründen, telefonische Erklärungen nicht in den Gesetzestext aufzunehmen, *von Caemmerer*, RabelsZ 29 (1965), 101, 129: Eine völlige Gleichstellung telefonischer Erklärungen hätte zu Schwierigkeiten in den Fällen geführt, in denen eine telefonische Mitteilung erst noch an den Adressaten weiterübermittelt werden muss, hierzu auch unten Rn. 20, 23.

[11] *Honsell/Dornis*, Art. 24, Rn. 5; *Staudinger/Magnus*, Art. 24, Rn. 11.

[12] *Honsell/Dornis*, Art. 24, Rn. 5; *Neumayer/Ming*, Art. 24, Anm. 3.; *Piltz*, Internationales Kaufrecht, Rn. 3–37; anders *Karollus*, S. 57; *Staudinger/Magnus*, Art. 24, Rn. 11.

[13] Vgl. oben Art. 18 Rn. 17; CISG-AC, Op. 1 *(Chr. Ramberg)*, Comment 24 i. V. m. 18.4, IHR 2003, 244, 247.

[14] S. YB VIII (1977), S. 86, Nr. 148, 150, wo „told orally" und „physically, mechanically or electronically delivered" zu unterscheiden vorgeschlagen worden war, von der Arbeitsgruppe aber zugunsten einer generalisierenden Fassung verworfen wurde, um künftige, noch zu erfindende Kommunikationsmittel einzuschließen. Wie hier *Achilles*, Art. 24, Rn. 3; *Brunner*, Art. 24, Rn. 2; *Coetzee*, 11 VJ (2007), 11, 18; *Honnold/Flechtner*, Art. 24, Rn. 179 (für Rückgriff auf allgemeine Grundsätze i. S. d. Art. 7 II); *Luig*, S. 96; *Wulf*, S. 109.

[15] S. zu dieser Grundvoraussetzung schon oben Vor Artt. 14–24 Rn. 27.

[16] *Bianca/Bonell/Farnsworth*, Art. 24, Anm. 2.2.: „… of course …"; *Enderlein/Maskow/Strohbach*, Art. 24, Anm. 6.; *Honsell/Dornis*, Art. 24, Rn. 7; *Staudinger/Magnus*, Art. 24, Rn. 23; *Wey*, Rn. 795; *Witz/Salger/*

verbal ausgerichtete Erklärung ist „mündliche" i. S. d. Art. 24. Über die Rechtsmacht dieser Mittelspersonen entscheidet freilich das über IPR berufene unvereinheitlichte nationale Recht.[17]

8 Die einem – befugten – **Empfangsboten** gegenüber **ausgesprochene** Erklärung dürfte ebenfalls als mündliche zu werten sein,[18] obwohl damit für den Geschäftsherrn des Boten ein erhebliches Risiko verbunden sein kann: Die Zugangswirkungen, insbesondere Fristlauf – Art. 20 I 2 – und Notwendigkeit sofortiger Reaktion – s. Art. 18 II 3 – können für den Adressaten nachteilige Folgen eintreten lassen unabhängig davon, wann und ob der Empfangsbote ausgerichtet oder – bei erforderlicher Weiterleitung von Telefonanrufen – weitergeleitet hat.[19] Insoweit liegt aber ein Risiko vor, das der unterbliebenen Kenntnis bei verkörperten Erklärungen[20] oder dem Nicht-Verstehen fernmündlich übermittelter Erklärungen[21] entspricht und dem Adressaten eher als dem Erklärenden, der in den Bereich des Adressaten nicht hineinsehen kann, zuzuordnen ist. U. U. ist eine solche Situation jedoch bei Art. 18 II 3 als einer der zu berücksichtigenden „Umstände" zu bewerten, der von „sofortiger" Antwort entbindet, etwa, wenn der Offerent die Offerte einem Empfangsboten erklärt, von dem er weiß, dass er nicht unmittelbar ausrichten kann.

9 Wird dagegen ein Mitarbeiter des Empfängers ohne Empfangsbotenfunktion vom Erklärenden mit der Überbringung der Erklärung betraut, also als **Erklärungsbote** eingesetzt, dann ist die von ihm überbrachte und ausgesprochene Erklärung zwar eine „mündliche" i. S. d. Art. 24, geht aber erst mit seiner Erklärung an den Adressaten zu.[22]

III. Zugang mündlicher Erklärungen

1. Zugang und Vernehmung

10 Die Formulierung „ihm mündlich gemacht" („made orally to him", „lui faite verbalement") lässt offen, ob **Vernehmung** Voraussetzung des Zugangs ist. Die Geltung der Vernehmungstheorie bei mündlichen Erklärungen ist ein international bekanntes, weithin anerkanntes Prinzip[23] und ist auch in Auslegung des EAG zugrunde gelegt worden.[24] Sie soll nach manchen auch für mündliche Erklärungen nach CISG gelten.[25] UNCITRAL hat jedoch eine Anregung, dies so zu regeln, abgelehnt, ohne dass zu ersehen ist, ob man in der Sache anders entscheiden wollte oder die Regelung für überflüssig, weil selbstverständlich, gehalten hat.[26] In der Literatur wird deshalb vertreten, dass für das CISG nicht eine „abge-

---

Lorenz/Witz, Art. 24, Rn. 8. Andernfalls könnte von oder gegenüber juristischen Personen nie mündlich erklärt werden.

[17] *Brunner*, Art. 24, Rn. 3. Vgl. BGH, 12.12.2001, NJW 2002, 1565, 1566: Nach der Verkehrsanschauung (!) zur Entgegennahme von Willenserklärungen (per Telefon!) ermächtigter Mitarbeiter (kein CISG-Fall).

[18] *Soergel/Lüderitz/Fenge*, Art. 24, Rn. 3; *Staudinger/Magnus*, Art. 24, Rn. 24; a. A. *Honsell/Dornis*, Art. 24, Rn. 8.

[19] S. den Fall BGH, 12.12.2001, NJW 2002, 1565 ff.

[20] Nach BGH, 15.3.1989, NJW-RR 1989, 757, 758, soll die einem Empfangsboten übergebene *schriftliche* Erklärung wirksam werden, wenn der Geschäftsherr die theoretische Möglichkeit der Kenntnisnahme (bei Annahme gewöhnlicher Verhältnisse) hatte. Der Empfangsbote habe die „Funktion einer personifizierten Empfangseinrichtung" des Adressaten. Andernfalls werde die Erklärung erst mit Zugang beim Geschäftsherrn wirksam, könne also vorher noch widerrufen werden. Letztere Aussage ist m. E. nur für den konkreten Fall zu rechtfertigen, in dem einem Verbraucher Widerruf des bei einem Autohändler unterschriebenen Leasingantrages ermöglicht werden sollte, der an die Leasinggesellschaft des gleichen Konzerns gerichtet war. S. auch unten Rn. 23.

[21] S. unten Rn. 11.

[22] Zum EAG s. *von Caemmerer*, RabelsZ 29 (1965), 101, 129; zum BGB RG, 17.6.1905, RGZ 61, 125, 126 f. A. A. für den Fall, dass die nicht empfangsbefugte Person dort, wo zuzustellen ist, entgegennimmt, also offenbar im Organisationsbereich des Adressaten, *Soergel/Lüderitz/Fenge*, Art. 24, Rn. 3.

[23] S. für die Annahme *Schlesinger*, Bd. 1, S. 157 f.: „... all legal systems agree ..."

[24] S. *von Caemmerer*, RabelsZ 29 (1965), 101, 135; *Dölle/Schlechtriem*, Art. 5 EAG, Rn. 5 ff.

[25] *Soergel/Lüderitz/Fenge*, Art. 24, Rn. 3.

[26] S. YB IX (1978), S. 37, Nr. 70.

sonderte Vernehmungstheorie" gelte, sondern „Zugangsprinzip und Vernehmungstheorie ... in den Zusammenhang eines integrierenden Auslegungsrechts (Art. 8 II) gestellt werden" sollen:[27] Geboten seien sorgfältiges Formulieren und Verstehen; bei unmittelbarer Verhandlungsführung sei das Vernehmen zu überprüfen und deshalb ggf. nachzufragen. Individuelle Vernehmungsstörungen beim Empfänger sollen – vorbehaltlich nationalen Gültigkeitsrechts – nicht zu Lasten des Erklärenden gehen.[28] Eine Auslegung des Begriffs im Lichte der Artt. 7 I, 8 soll dazu führen, dass der Erklärende unter Anwesenden sich hinsichtlich des aktuellen Verständnisses vergewissern müsse, unter Abwesenden sei jedenfalls Verständnis*möglichkeit* abzuklären.[29]

2. Fernmündliche Erklärungen

Die Frage, ob bei mündlichen Erklärungen Zugang erst mit **Vernehmung** durch den Adressaten geschieht, dürfte praktische Bedeutung vor allem bei **fernmündlichen Erklärungen** haben, die, wenn sie im grenzüberschreitenden Verkehr gemacht werden, durchaus von Störungen und Missverständnissen beeinträchtigt sein können.[30] Die zu diesem Punkt unklare Regelung des Art. 24 ist nach Art. 7 I autonom, d. h. ohne Rückgriff auf dogmatische Konzeptionen und Theorien der nationalen Rechtsordnungen auszulegen. Der internationale Charakter des Übereinkommens, d. h. seine Geltung gerade für grenzüberschreitende Verträge zwischen – zumeist – Partnern verschiedener Nationalität und – oft – verschiedener Muttersprache, sowie das Gebot der Wahrung des guten Glaubens im internationalen Handel haben dabei besonderes Gewicht. Diese Kriterien schließen die Zugrundelegung einer reinen Vernehmungstheorie ebenso aus wie eine Lösung, bei der die mündliche Erklärung nur dem anderen gegenüber „gemacht", d. h. ausgesprochen worden sein muss, ohne dass dessen Verständnismöglichkeit irgendeine Rolle spielte. Die Erklärung muss jedenfalls vernehmbar sein.[31] Bei Erklärungen unter Anwesenden kann vom Erklärenden erwartet werden, dass er die Aufnahme seiner Erklärung verfolgt und ggf. durch Rückfragen überprüft.[32] Er muss sich dabei m. E. auch vergewissern, dass der Adressat zuhört und verstehen kann. Bei fernmündlichen oder ähnlichen mündlichen Erklärungen unter Abwesenden kann – evtl. wiederholte – Vergewisserung dagegen nur insoweit verlangt werden, als es um das Funktionieren der Verbindung und das hinreichende Verständnis der verwendeten Sprache durch den Empfänger geht, nicht dagegen bezüglich der Aufmerksamkeit, Verständnisbereitschaft und sonstiger subjektiver Vernehmungsvoraussetzungen des Adressaten. Der Erklärende muss nur den **Empfängerhorizont einer vernünftigen Person** entsprechend Art. 8 II in Rechnung stellen.[33] Ist eine verständliche Verbindung bestätigt worden, und hat der Erklärungsempfänger sich als der vom Erklärenden verwendeten oder vorgeschlagenen Sprache mächtig dargestellt, dann ist die daraufhin ausgesprochene Erklärung zugegangen, auch wenn beim Empfänger – für den Erklärenden nicht erkennbar – Verständnisschwierigkeiten aufgetreten sind. Es ist dann Sache des Empfängers, sofort rückzufragen; ein Missverständnis ist sein – evtl. durch nationale Anfechtungsregeln für eine Gegenerklärung zu minderndes – Risiko.[34] Andererseits ist bei einer für den Erklärenden erkennbar gestörten Verbindung oder Sprachunkenntnis des Empfängers das Aussprechen der Erklärung in den Apparat nicht ausreichend, um die Erklärung zugehen zu lassen.

---

[27] *Wey*, Rn. 778, 779.
[28] *Wey*, Rn. 779; a. A. *Noussias*, Zugangsbedürftigkeit von Mitteilungen, S. 27, sub 3.4: „... angemessen, dass die Gefahr der richtigen Vernehmung der Erklärende trägt".
[29] *Honsell/Dornis*, Art. 24, Rn. 6.
[30] Vgl. unten Art. 27 Rn. 5.
[31] *Witz/Salger/Lorenz/Witz*, Art. 24, Rn. 9.
[32] Wie hier *Honsell/Dornis*, Art. 24, Rn. 6.
[33] Vgl. *Wey*, Rn. 779: Zugangsprinzip und Vernehmungstheorie integrierendes Auslegungsrecht; ebenso *Brunner*, Art. 24, Rn. 2; *Staudinger/Magnus*, Art. 24, Rn. 13; wohl auch *Honsell/Dornis*, Art. 24, Rn. 6.
[34] S. *Wey*, Rn. 776, 779.

12 Für die Äußerung einer unter den konkreten Umständen für eine vernünftige Person in der Situation des Empfängers objektiv vernehmbare Erklärung trägt der Erklärende die **Beweislast;** ob der Adressat die Voraussetzungen, die nach nationalem Recht seiner Gegenerklärung die Wirkung nehmen können, zu beweisen hat, muss das dafür maßgebliche Recht entscheiden.

3. Telefonische Anrufbeantworter

13 Schwierig ist der **Zugang** bei Aufnahme einer Erklärung durch **telefonische Anrufbeantworter** zu beurteilen: Nimmt der Offerent durch Erklärung auf ein solches Gerät um 10 Uhr seine Offerte zurück, während die schriftliche Offerte um 11 Uhr in den Briefkasten gelangt, oder widerruft er durch eine solche aufgezeichnete mündliche Erklärung rechtzeitig vor Absendung der Annahme, dann entscheidet die Bedeutung dieser Aufnahme über Wirksamkeit der bzw. Bindung an die Offerte.

14 Die Speicherung des gesprochenen Wortes beim Empfänger spricht dafür, solche Mitteilungen als Erklärungen anzusehen, die nicht erst mit Vernehmung i. S. der Ausführungen zu Rn. 10 ff., sondern bereits mit der Aufnahme zugegangen sind.[35] Das Begriffspaar „mündliche" oder „verkörperte" Erklärung und die Subsumtion unter den einen oder den anderen Begriff kann nicht befriedigen, da auch eine auf Anrufbeantworter gesprochene und vom Gerät aufgenommene Erklärung während des Speichervorgangs vom Empfänger abgehört werden kann, dann aber wie eine telefonische – mündliche – Erklärung übermittelt wird. Andererseits geschieht mit der Speicherung eine „Verkörperung". Über die Zugangswirkung und ihren Zeitpunkt sollten deshalb Sachgesichtspunkte entscheiden. Wer im geschäftlichen Verkehr einen telefonischen Anrufbeantworter einsetzt, eröffnet und betreibt damit eine Empfangseinrichtung ähnlich der eines Telex- oder Telefaxempfängers oder eines „elektronischen Briefkastens" für E-Mail. Das rechtfertigt es, Zugang bereits mit Aufnahme der zugesprochenen Erklärung anzunehmen, sofern bzw. sobald **Abhörmöglichkeit** bestand. Dies gilt insbesondere dann, wenn das Zusprechen und Speichern rechtsgeschäftlicher Erklärungen zwischen den Parteien bereits entsprechende Gepflogenheit geworden ist, so dass der Erklärende mit regelmäßigem Abfragen des Anrufbeantworters durch den Adressaten (wie mit einem regelmäßigen Leeren des Postbriefkastens) rechnen kann.[36]

IV. Zugang von Erklärungen „auf anderem Weg"

1. Erklärungsadressen

15 **Andere als mündliche Erklärungen** müssen dem Empfänger „persönlich, an seiner Niederlassung oder Postanschrift oder, wenn diese fehlen, an seinem gewöhnlichen Aufenthaltsort zugestellt" werden, um Zugang zu bewirken. Zustellungen „persönlich", an der Niederlassung oder Postanschrift haben Vorrang; nur subsidiär darf auf den gewöhnlichen Aufenthalt ausgewichen werden.[37] Bei mehreren Niederlassungen bzw. Postanschriften ist Art. 10 lit. a) direkt (Niederlassungen) bzw. entsprechend (Postanschriften) anzuwenden.[38] Wird eine postalische Mitteilung an die letzte vom Empfänger mitgeteilte Postanschrift

---

[35] So *Soergel/Lüderitz/Fenge*, Art. 24, Rn. 3 („verkörperte Erklärung"); *Neumayer/Ming*, Art. 24, Anm. 3. (Zugang mit Aufnahme).
[36] *Staudinger/Magnus*, Art. 24, Rn. 14; *Honsell/Dornis*, Art. 24, Rn. 5; a. A. *Bamberger/Roth/Saenger*, Art. 24, Rn. 2.
[37] *Honsell/Dornis*, Art. 24, Rn. 26; *Staudinger/Magnus*, Art. 24, Rn. 16; zur Entwicklung s. Art. 12 New Yorker E 1977, YB VIII (1977), S. 86, Nr. 151, wo die verschiedenen Möglichkeiten nicht gleichwertig zur Wahl gestellt worden waren, und die spätere Änderung in YB IX (1978), S. 82, Nr. 289, 294. A. A. teilweise *Wey*, Rn. 796, der jedenfalls Kenntnisnahme am gewöhnlichen Aufenthaltsort als gleichwertig sieht.
[38] Zweifelnd *Wey*, Rn. 797.

zugestellt, so ist der Zugang der Erklärung damit auch dann bewirkt, wenn sich die Adresse des Empfängers zwischenzeitlich geändert hat.[39]

2. Erklärungsmittel

Art. 24 lässt, wie die englische Fassung besser verdeutlicht, **jegliches Erklärungsmittel** 16 („by any means") und nicht nur wie Art. 27 die „nach den Umständen geeigneten Mittel" zu. Der Unterschied ist dadurch zu erklären, dass Art. 24 nur zugangsbedürftige Erklärungsmittel regelt und durch das Erfordernis des Zugangs das Empfängerrisiko einschränkt, das sonst durch eine Beschränkung der Erklärungsmittel berücksichtigt werden müsste oder – wie in Art. 27 – worden ist.

3. Zustellung

„**Zugestellt**" hat nichts mit prozessualen Zustellungen – §§ 166 ff. ZPO – zu tun, 17 wenngleich eine solche Zustellung natürlich Zugang bewirken kann.[40] Auch die verfahrensrechtlich korrekt bewirkte Übergabe durch einen Gerichtsvollzieher, Sheriff, huissier bewirkt aber Zugang nur, wenn sie den Voraussetzungen des Art. 24 entspricht: Erfolgt sie z. B. am gewöhnlichen Aufenthaltsort, obwohl der Erklärungsempfänger eine Niederlassung oder Postanschrift hat, dann ist Zugang nicht erfolgt.[41]

Mit der Formulierung „ihm persönlich ... zugestellt" ist **Übergabe** einer verkörperten 18 Erklärung **an den Adressaten** selbst gemeint. „An seiner Niederlassung oder Postanschrift" oder, hilfsweise, „an seinem gewöhnlichen Aufenthaltsort" zugestellt dürfte als **„in den Machtbereich des Empfängers gelangt"** zu verstehen sein.[42]

Fraglich ist, ob zusätzlich zum „in den Machtbereich des Empfängers Gelangen" die **Möglichkeit der Kenntnisnahme** gegeben sein muss, wie dies etwa zu § 130 I 1 BGB formelhaft vorausgesetzt wird.[43] Bei Erarbeitung des EAG ist diese Frage kontrovers gewesen, letztlich aber nicht entschieden worden.[44] Zu Art. 24 lassen zahlreiche Stellungnahmen (vor allem deutscher Autoren) den Schluss zu, dass die Möglichkeit der Kenntnisnahme vorausgesetzt wird.[45] Andere lehnen dies kategorisch ab.[46] Eine generelle Aussage zu dieser Frage lässt sich Art. 24 schon vor dem Hintergrund seiner Entstehungsgeschichte nicht entnehmen; richtigerweise ist anhand der verschiedenen Fallgestaltungen zu unterscheiden: Schwierigkeiten dürften insoweit weniger die Schulfälle an versteckter Stelle deponierter Erklärungen (dazu Rn. 21) machen als die Situation der außerhalb der Geschäftszeit oder an Feiertagen eingegangenen Erklärungen (Rn. 32 ff.) und der für den Empfänger überhaupt nicht vernehmbaren oder – insbesondere aus Gründen der verwendeten Sprache – nicht verständlichen Erklärungen (Rn. 36 ff.), die daher gesondert zu behandeln sind. Auf die

---

[39] RB Amsterdam, 5.10.1994, CISG-online 446 = NIPR 1995, Nr. 231; *Brunner*, Art. 24, Rn. 2.
[40] *Honsell/Schnyder/Straub*, 1. Aufl., Art. 24, Rn. 20. § 132 BGB und vergleichbare Vorschriften in anderen Rechtsordnungen sind jedoch m. E. nicht anwendbar. Die vereinheitlichte Regelung des Zugangs in Art. 24 würde gefährdet, wenn die ganz unterschiedlichen Möglichkeiten der Zustellung, insbesondere öffentlicher Zustellung, nach unvereinheitlichtem nationalen Recht stets Zugangswirkungen im Rahmen des CISG entfalten könnten.
[41] Allerdings steht zu befürchten, dass nationale Gerichte unter Berufung auf die Qualifikation entsprechender Vorschriften als Prozessrecht Art. 24 beiseite schieben werden.
[42] *Bianca/Bonell/Farnsworth*, Art. 24, Anm. 2.4.; *Eiselen*, 6 VJ (2002), 305, 309; *Luig*, S. 98; *Witz/Salger/Lorenz/Witz*, Art. 24, Rn. 15.
[43] Statt aller *Palandt/Ellenberger*, § 130, Rn. 5.
[44] S. *von Caemmerer*, RabelsZ 29 (1965), 101, 134; *Dölle/Schlechtriem*, Art. 12 EAG, Rn. 9; *Noussias*, Zugangsbedürftigkeit von Mitteilungen, S. 84 f.
[45] So *Luig*, S. 98; MünchKomm/*Gruber*, Art. 24, Rn. 13; *Neumayer*, RIW 1994, 99, 104; *Staudinger/Magnus*, Art. 24, Rn. 15; offenbar auch *Soergel/Lüderitz/Fenge*, Art. 24, Rn. 4, 5.
[46] *Neumayer/Ming*, Art. 24, Anm. 3. (außer im Falle des Rechtsmissbrauchs durch den Absender).

aktuelle Kenntnisnahme des Empfängers vom Inhalt der Erklärung kommt es für den Zugang nach Art. 24 jedenfalls nicht an.[47]

4. Zugang bei einzelnen Erklärungsmitteln

19 **a) Brief.** Ein Brief geht dem Empfänger im Falle der „persönlichen" Zustellung mit **Übergabe,** d. h. der Verschaffung unmittelbaren Besitzes an dem Brief, zu. Unerheblich ist, wo die Aushändigung des Briefes erfolgt; dies kann in den Geschäftsräumen des Empfängers, aber etwa auch auf einer Messe im In- oder Ausland oder im Hotel sein,[48] wohingegen eine Hinterlegung im Hotelfach nicht genügt.[49] Ebenfalls ausreichend ist der Einwurf des Briefes in einen **Briefkasten** oder ein **Postfach** des Empfängers;[50] ob Transport und Einwurf durch den allgemeinen Postdienst oder ein privates Postdienstleistungsunternehmen vorgenommen wird, spielt keine Rolle. Zugang des Briefes kann schließlich auch durch seine Übergabe an eine **autorisierte Person** erfolgen,[51] wobei trotz der Fassung des Art. 24 nicht erforderlich ist, dass diese Person den Brief im Organisationsbereich der Niederlassung oder einer Postanschrift (Außenbüro etc.) oder als befugte Person – etwa in der Wohnung als gewöhnlichem Aufenthalt des Erklärungsadressaten – entgegennimmt.[52]

20 Die Benachrichtigung von einem auf der Post lagernden **Einschreiben** oder anderen Zusendungen mit Erklärungsinhalt ist regelmäßig noch nicht „Zustellung" der Erklärung – Zugang tritt erst ein, wenn die zunächst auf der Post (oder bei einem sonstigen Zustell-, Brief- oder Paketdienst) lagernde Briefsendung dem Empfänger übergeben wird.[53] Letzteres gilt für die in Deutschland verfügbaren „Einschreiben Eigenhändig" und „Einschreiben Rückschein",[54] während das „Einschreiben Einwurf" durch Einwurf in den Briefkasten bzw. das Postfach des Empfängers „zugestellt" wird. Da der Zugang im internationalen Verkehr nur von Voraussetzungen abhängen darf, die klar und gleichmäßig sind, kommt es dabei für die Behandlung nach Art. 24 allein auf die faktische Abwicklung der jeweiligen Briefübermittlung an; die Beurteilung solcher Vorgänge nach nationalem Recht,[55] das auf postalische Eigenheiten im jeweiligen Land Rücksicht nehmen und entsprechende Kenntnis der Verkehrsteilnehmer voraussetzen kann, ist hingegen bedeutungslos. Nur wo das Postamt selbst i. S. d. Art. 24 „Postanschrift" des Adressaten ist, z. B. bei Angabe „erwarte Antwort postlagernd..." oder Angabe eines Postfachs, genügt bei Briefsendungen Abholmöglichkeit für den Zugang.

21 Wird ein Brief (oder auch ein Telegramm, dazu sogleich Rn. 22) **an ungewöhnlicher Stelle,** etwa auf der Türschwelle oder „in some other unattended place" hinterlassen, wird

---
[47] S. *Enderlein/Maskow/Strohbach,* Art. 24, Anm. 4.: „Zustellung bedeutet nicht, dass der Empfänger Kenntnis von der Erklärung genommen hat"; *Bianca/Bonell/Farnsworth,* Art. 24, Anm. 2.4.; *Borges,* Verträge im elektronischen Geschäftsverkehr, S. 319; *Brunner,* Art. 24, Rn. 2; *Eiselen,* 6 VJ (2002), 305, 311; *Staudinger/Magnus,* Art. 24, Rn. 15.
[48] Sekretariatskommentar, Art. 22, Nr. 5; *Staudinger/Magnus,* Art. 24, Rn. 16.
[49] *Piltz,* Internationales Kaufrecht, Rn. 3–41; *Staudinger/Magnus,* Art. 24, Rn. 16.
[50] *Staudinger/Magnus,* Art. 24, Rn. 16.
[51] *Bianca/Bonell/Farnsworth,* Art. 24, Anm. 2.4.; *Brunner,* Art. 24, Rn. 2; *Enderlein/Maskow/Strohbach,* Art. 24, Anm. 4.: „Die Mitteilung muss ... in seinen Empfangs- oder Verfügungsbereich gelangt sein"; *Honnold/Flechtner,* Art. 24, Rn. 179; *Wey,* Rn. 795: „Was dieser erhalten bzw. vernommen hat (auch über Boten und Erklärungsträger), gilt als zugegangen"; zum BGB teilweise anders BGH, 15.3.1989, NJW-RR 1989, 757, 758.
[52] Ebenso *Bianca/Bonell/Farnsworth,* Art. 24, Anm. 2.2.3.; *Enderlein/Maskow/Strohbach,* Art. 24, Anm. 6.; *Honnold/Flechtner,* Art. 24, Rn. 179; eine andere Auslegung würde dazu führen, dass Art. 24 die über die Autorisierung des Stellvertreters oder Boten entscheidenden nationalen Regeln modifizieren würde. Abschlüsse zwischen Vertretern auf Messen wären dann als sofort gültige nicht oder nur mündlich möglich. Das ist mit der Formulierung des Art. 24 sicher nicht gemeint.
[53] *Bamberger/Roth/Saenger,* Art. 24, Rn. 4; *Honsell/Dornis,* Art. 24, Rn. 23; ähnlich *Wey,* Rn. 804, der aber wohl auf den Zeitpunkt erstmaliger Abholmöglichkeit abstellen will; a. A. *Honsell/Schnyder/Straub,* 1. Aufl., Art. 24, Rn. 23; MünchKommHGB/*Ferrari,* Art. 24, Rn. 11; *Perales Viscasillas,* 16 J. L. & Com. (1997), 315, 325.
[54] Vgl. BGH, 26.11.1997, NJW 1998, 976, 977.
[55] Vgl. etwa § 175 ZPO.

Begriff des Zugangs

dadurch Zugang nicht bewirkt.[56] Dieses Ergebnis ist richtigerweise auf eine Interpretation des Art. 24 im Lichte des Art. 7 I zu stützen:[57] Es wäre eine gegen das Gebot der Wahrung des guten Glaubens im internationalen Handel verstoßende Auslegung der Zugangsvorschrift, wenn in solchen Fällen nicht vernehmungsfähiger Erklärungen „Zustellung" („delivery") angenommen werden könnte.[58]

b) Telegramm. Ein Telegramm geht mit Aushändigung an den Empfänger oder eine 22 von diesem autorisierte Person[59] zu. Auch ein Telegramm, das von der Empfangsstelle (Post) dem Adressaten telefonisch durchgegeben wird, ist damit zugegangen.

c) Telefax, Telex. Ein Telefax ist mit dem ordnungsgemäßen und vollständigen **Ein-** 23 **gang** der Nachricht im **Faxsystem** des Empfängers zugegangen,[60] Entsprechendes gilt für das Fernschreiben (Telex). Keine Voraussetzung für den Zugang der per Telefax bzw. Telex übermittelten Erklärung ist, dass sie tatsächlich ausgedruckt wurde;[61] es ist vielmehr ausreichend, dass die Nachricht das Empfangsgerät so erreicht hat, dass sie ausdruckbar ist.[62] Mängel des Empfangsgerätes, welche Kenntnisnahme vereiteln – etwa ein Papiermangel oder -stau im Faxgerät –, hindern den Zugang nicht,[63] ebensowenig das nachträgliche Löschen der Nachricht aufgrund eines Bedienungsfehlers.[64] Steht ein **Empfangsgerät** jedoch **nicht beim Adressaten** der Erklärung, sondern z. B. in einem Copy-Shop oder an einer Hotelrezeption, so dass ein Ausdruck noch überbracht oder abgeholt werden muss, dann ist erst mit „Zustellung" der gedruckten oder kopierten Erklärung zugegangen.[65] Befindet sich das empfangende Faxgerät zwar nicht in einer Niederlassung des Adressaten, aber doch in einem Büro, das administrative Angelegenheiten des Adressaten wahrnimmt und von dem aus dieser regelmäßig seine Geschäfte führt, so ist das Fax bereits mit Eingang in dem betreffenden Faxgerät zugegangen.[66]

d) E-Mail. Bei E-Mails ist der Zugang jedenfalls dann erfolgt, wenn die E-Mail in der 24 **Mailbox** des Empfängers **abgespeichert** ist.[67] Dies gilt dabei sowohl in denjenigen Fällen, in denen die Mailbox sich auf einem eigenen Server des Empfängers befindet,[68] als auch dann, wenn die Empfängermailbox – genauer: der dieser zugeordnete Speicherplatz – auf

---

[56] *Brunner*, Art. 24, Rn. 2, Fn. 544 („da nicht ordnungsgemäß"); *Bianca/Bonell/Farnsworth*, Art. 24, Anm. 2.4.; *Honnold/Flechtner*, Art. 24, Rn. 179; *Staudinger/Magnus*, Art. 24, Rn. 17.

[57] Für eine Berücksichtigung des Art. 7 I bei der Auslegung des Art. 24 generell *Eörsi*, 27 Am. J. Comp. L. (1979), 311, 314 f.

[58] Zum Rechtsmissbrauch s. noch unten Rn. 41.

[59] S. dazu oben Rn. 7.

[60] *Brunner*, Art. 24, Rn. 2; *Eiselen*, 6 VJ (2002), 305, 309; *Luig*, S. 99; MünchKomm/*Gruber*, Art. 24, Rn. 13.

[61] *Brunner*, Art. 24, Rn. 2; *Eiselen*, 6 VJ (2002), 305, 311; MünchKomm/*Gruber*, Art. 24, Rn. 13; a. A. MünchKommHGB/*Ferrari*, Art. 24, Rn. 11; auch *Witz/Salger/Lorenz/Witz*, Art. 24, Rn. 11: Zugang treten vor Ausdruck nur bei Telefaxübermittlung an PC oder Faxserver ein.

[62] *Staudinger/Magnus*, Art. 24, Rn. 16.

[63] MünchKomm/*Gruber*, Art. 24, Rn. 14; MünchKommHGB/*Ferrari*, Art. 24, Rn. 11.

[64] MünchKomm/*Gruber*, Art. 24, Rn. 14.

[65] MünchKommHGB/*Ferrari*, Art. 24, Rn. 11; *Neumayer/Ming*, Art. 24, Anm. 3.; a. A. *Perales Viscasillas*, 16 J. L. & Com. (1997), 315, 323.

[66] OLG Dresden, 10.11.2006, CISG-online 1625 (zu einer Bürogemeinschaft, die für eine Reihe von Unternehmen, darunter auch den in einer anderen Stadt ansässigen Adressaten tätig war).

[67] CISG-AC, Op. 1 *(Chr. Ramberg)*, Opinion Art. 24 i. V. m. Comment 15.2–5, IHR 2003, 244, 245 ff.; *Achilles*, Art. 24, Rn. 4; *Bamberger/Roth/Saenger*, Art. 24, Rn. 4; *Borges*, Verträge im elektronischen Geschäftsverkehr, S. 318; *Brunner*, Art. 24, Rn. 2; *Luig*, S. 99; MünchKomm/*Gruber*, Art. 24, Rn. 13; *Perales Viscasillas*, 16 J. L. & Com. (1997), 315, 325; *Schroeter*, UN-Kaufrecht, § 6, Rn. 330; *Staudinger/Magnus*, Art. 24, Rn. 16; *Witz/Salger/Lorenz/Witz*, Art. 24, Rn. 11; *Wulf*, S. 118. Zur erforderlichen Zustimmung des Adressaten zum Empfang elektronischer Erklärungen unter dieser Adresse s. unten Rn. 26 sowie allgemein oben Rn. 6.

[68] CISG-AC, Op. 1 *(Chr. Ramberg)*, Opinion Art. 24 i. V. m. Comment 15.2, IHR 2003, 244, 245 ff.; *Eiselen*, 6 VJ (2002), 305, 311; *Hahnkamper*, 25 J. L. & Com. (2005-06), 147, 150; *Staudinger/Magnus*, Art. 24, Rn. 16.

dem Server eines Dritten (eines Providers) angesiedelt ist.[69] Voraussetzung für den Zugang ist danach, dass der betreffende Server eingeschaltet und empfangsbereit ist,[70] die E-Mail auf dem Server eingeht, dort der Mailbox des Empfängers zugeordnet und entsprechend abrufbar gespeichert wird. **Schwierigkeiten** macht die Beurteilung des Zugangs in Konstellationen, in denen die E-Mail zwar den vom Adressaten verwendeten Server erreicht,[71] es aber nicht (oder nicht fristgerecht) zu ihrer Speicherung in der Adressatenmailbox kommt. Maßgeblich muss m. E. das von Art. 24 verfolgte Ziel sein, dem Erklärenden das Risiko der Kommunikation im Organisationsbereich des Empfängers abzunehmen.[72] Es ist daher zu unterscheiden: Eine E-Mail, welche die Schnittstelle zum Server des Empfängers passiert hat, aber aufgrund eines serverinternen Softwarefehlers o. ä. vorübergehend oder endgültig nicht in der Mailbox des Adressaten gespeichert werden kann, ist danach gleichwohl zugegangen, weil dieser Umstand zur Risikosphäre des Empfängers gehört.[73] Dasselbe muss gelten, wenn die Speicherung scheitert, weil die Mailbox überfüllt ist und deshalb keine neuen Nachrichten mehr aufnimmt.[74] Die E-Mail gilt in diesen Fällen als zu dem Zeitpunkt „zugestellt", zu dem sie bei Fehlen des betreffenden Hindernisses in der Mailbox abgespeichert worden wäre.[75] Lässt sich eine E-Mail hingegen infolge ihrer fehlerhaften Adressierung (etwa eines Tippfehlers in der Adresszeile) keiner Mailbox zuordnen oder wird sie der falschen Mailbox zugeordnet, so fehlt es i. S. des Art. 24 an einem Zugang, weil dieser Umstand allein dem Absender zuzurechnen ist.[76]

25 Dagegen kann der Zugang der E-Mail **nicht** daran scheitern, dass der Adressat die ordnungsgemäß auf dem Server eingegangene Nachricht nicht abrufen kann, weil sein eigener Computer (oder BlackBerry) defekt ist, der Server nach Empfang und Abspeicherung der E-Mail ausfällt, keine Verbindung zum Server hergestellt werden kann oder nach erfolgter Abspeicherung sonstige interne Computer- oder Netzwerkprobleme auftreten.[77] Sog. **Spam-Filter**, die u. U. eine Erklärung ganz oder teilweise (etwa nur den Anhang) herausfiltern und automatisch löschen, sollten ebenfalls dem Empfänger zuzurechnen sein.[78] Auch technische Mängel, welche die Kenntnisnahme von der E-Mail vereiteln, nachdem diese vom Server abgerufen wurde – etwa ein Defekt des Monitors oder des Druckers bzw. fehlendes oder gestautes Druckerpapier –, hindern den Zugang nicht; dasselbe muss auch für den nachträglichen Verlust einer bereits abrufbar gespeicherten E-Mail aufgrund eines „Computerabsturzes" gelten.[79] Der gelegentlich postulierten Voraussetzung, der Empfänger müsse die E-Mail jederzeit abrufen können,[80] kann also nur dann zugestimmt werden, wenn

---

[69] CISG-AC, Op. 1 *(Chr. Ramberg)*, Opinion Art. 24 i. V. m. Comment 15.2, IHR 2003, 244, 245 ff.; *Eisenen*, 6 VJ (2002), 305, 311; MünchKomm/*Gruber*, Art. 24, Rn. 13; *Wulf*, S. 118.

[70] *Brunner*, Art. 24, Rn. 2; Staudinger/*Magnus*, Art. 24, Rn. 16; *Wulf*, S. 125.

[71] Geht die E-Mail schon vorher verloren, so fehlt es jedenfalls am Zugang; zur Verwendung sog. Spam-Filter durch den Empfänger s. noch unten Rn. 25.

[72] Vgl. in diesem Sinne auch *Brunner*, Art. 24, Rn. 2; *Eiselen*, 6 EDI L. Rev. (1999), 21, 27. S. dazu noch unten Rn. 32.

[73] A. A. *Borges*, Verträge im elektronischen Geschäftsverkehr, S. 320: kein Zugang, aber Korrektur über Regelungen zur Zugangsvereitelung.

[74] A. A. MünchKomm/*Gruber*, Art. 24, Rn. 14: kein Zugang.

[75] Anders wohl CISG-AC, Op. 1 *(Chr. Ramberg)*, Opinion Art. 24, IHR 2003, 244, 249: Zugang mit Eingang im Server des Adressaten.

[76] CISG-AC, Op. 1 *(Chr. Ramberg)*, Opinion Art. 24 i. V. m. Comment 15.5, IHR 2003, 244, 245 ff. (mit Beispiel). Bei Zuordnung zu einer falschen Mailbox tritt Zugang in dem Moment ein, in dem der Empfänger die E-Mail später (etwa nach deren Weiterleitung) tatsächlich zur Kenntnis nimmt; s. unten Rn. 27.

[77] CISG-AC, Op. 1 *(Chr. Ramberg)*, Opinion Art. 24 i. V. m. Comment 15.3 ff., IHR 2003, 244, 245 ff.; *Hahnkamper*, 25 J. L. & Com. (2005-06), 147, 150; zweifelnd *Janal*, S. 96, Fn. 58.

[78] Dies gilt jedenfalls bei solchen Spam-Filtern, die durch den Empfänger selbst aktiviert werden; vgl. dazu *Wietzorek*, MMR 2007, 156, 157 f. Verhindert der Spam-Filter hingegen bereits die Abspeicherung der E-Mail auf dem Server (dazu *Heidrich*/*Tschoepe*, MMR 2004, 75, 76), so ist die Nachricht nach hier vertretener Ansicht gleichwohl zugegangen; nach a. A. scheitert der Zugang in diesem Fall, wobei allerdings möglicherweise die Grundsätze der Zugangsverweigerung greifen, s. unten Rn. 41.

[79] MünchKomm/*Gruber*, Art. 24, Rn. 14.

[80] *Achilles*, Art. 24, Rn. 4; Staudinger/*Magnus*, Art. 24, Rn. 16; wohl auch Bamberger/Roth/*Saenger*, Art. 24, Rn. 4.

man sie nicht auf die vorstehend genannten Sachfragen erstreckt, die allein der Sphäre des Empfängers zuzurechnen sind und dem Erklärungszugang daher nicht im Wege stehen dürfen.[81] Insofern gleicht die Verwendung eines externen Servers der Nutzung eines Postfaches.

Bedeutung für den Zugang von E-Mails kann schließlich das Erfordernis gewinnen, dass der Empfänger – neben der stets notwendigen, allgemeinen Zustimmung zur Kommunikation durch elektronische Erklärungen dieser Art (oben Rn. 6) – auch dem Empfang an die konkret **verwandte Adresse** zugestimmt haben muss:[82] Hier ist denkbar, dass der Zugang einer E-Mail scheitert oder zumindest verzögert wird, wenn im die Erklärung empfangenden Unternehmen – wie regelmäßig – unterschiedliche E-Mail-Adressen mit unterschiedlichen unternehmensinternen Zuständigkeiten korrelieren und die E-Mail an eine Adresse gesandt wurde, deren Verwendung für Erklärungen der betroffenen Art unter dem betroffenen Kaufvertrag nicht durch eine entsprechende Zustimmung des Empfängers gedeckt ist. In dieser Lage treten das Interesse des Empfängers an einer effektiven Organisation der passiven Kommunikation mit seinen Vertragspartnern, die insbesondere bei Notwendigkeit einer zügigen Reaktion wie nach Art. 19 II[83] entscheidend sein kann, in Widerstreit mit dem Interesse der Erklärenden, sich nicht auf ihm unbekannte interne Strukturen des Empfängers einstellen zu müssen. Der Ausgleich ist über eine Auslegung von Zustimmungserklärung und -verhalten des Empfängers nach Maßgabe des Art. 8 II, III zu suchen: Hat der Adressat eine E-Mail-Adresse gegenüber dem Erklärenden (etwa durch den E-Mail-Versand von dieser Adresse) oder der Allgemeinheit (etwa auf Briefpapier, Visitenkarten oder seiner Homepage) benannt, so hat er deren Nutzung für den Empfang jeglicher Erklärungen zugestimmt, sofern sich nicht aus gegenteiligen Absprachen (Benennung der E-Mail-Adresse des zuständigen Mitarbeiters, Mitteilung über das Ausscheiden eines bestimmten Mitarbeiters) oder Gepflogenheiten (der Abschluss der Kaufverträge wurde auf Seiten des Empfängers schon in der Vergangenheit stets durch eine andere Abteilung bearbeitet als die Vertragsabwicklung einschließlich der Entgegennahme von Mängelrügen nach Art. 39 I) etwas anderes ergibt. Ist eine E-Mail danach an eine nicht durch die Empfängerzustimmung abgedeckte Adresse gesandt worden, so geht sie dem Empfänger erst in dem Moment zu, in dem sie durch diejenige Person oder unternehmensinterne Stelle empfangen wird, die für die Entgegennahme der entsprechenden Erklärung zuständig ist.[84]

Der Zugang einer E-Mail ist schließlich spätestens bei **tatsächlicher Kenntnisnahme** des Empfängers vom Inhalt der E-Mail erfolgt.[85] Da die Beweislast für den Zugang einer Erklärung grundsätzlich derjenige trägt, der sich auf ihn beruft,[86] kann sich für den Absender einer E-Mail die Anforderung einer Eingangs- oder Lesebestätigung empfehlen, die durch das Computersystem des Empfängers bei Eingang der Nachricht auf dem Server, dem Abrufen der Nachricht von einem externen Server oder dem Öffnen der einzelnen E-Mail automatisch versandt wird.[87] Der Beweiswert einer solchen Bestätigung wird freilich vom CISG nicht geregelt und bestimmt sich daher nach dem nationalen Prozessrecht.[88]

e) **Webseiten im World Wide Web.** Erklärungen auf Websites – vor allem Warenangebote, aber auch Warengesuche – im WWW gehen mit deren Wahrnehmung durch

---

[81] CISG-AC, Op. 1 *(Chr. Ramberg)*, Opinion Art. 24 i. V. m. Comment 15.3, IHR 2003, 244, 245 ff.
[82] CISG-AC, Op. 1 *(Chr. Ramberg)*, Opinion Art. 24 i. V. m. Comment 15.5, IHR 2003, 244, 246; *Janal*, S. 96 Fn. 58; *Schwenzer/Mohs*, IHR 2006, 239, 241; *Wulf*, S. 117: „Widmung" der Mailbox.
[83] S. oben Art. 19 Rn. 16.
[84] Dies entspricht im Ergebnis der Ansicht von *Schwenzer/Mohs*, IHR 2006, 239, 241 Fn. 31, die diese argumentativ allerdings nicht auf Art. 8 stützen, sondern (unter gleichzeitiger Ablehnung der Lösung in Art. 10 II UNECIC) an Art. 2.2 ICC eTerms 2004 anknüpfen; s. zur Kritik an diesem Auslegungsansatz bereits oben Vor Artt. 14–24 Rn. 26.
[85] *Borges*, Verträge im elektronischen Geschäftsverkehr, S. 321.
[86] Unten Rn. 43.
[87] *Eiselen*, 6 VJ (2002), 305, 310; *Wulf*, S. 131.
[88] S. unten Rn. 44.

den konkreten Empfänger zu;[89] „Zustellung" und Kenntnisnahme fallen bei diesem Erklärungsmittel also zusammen. Das bloße In-das-Netz-Stellen und die Abrufbarkeit der Website durch Internetbenutzer genügen für den Zugang darauf enthaltener Erklärungen nach Art. 24 hingegen allein nicht.

Vom vorgenannten Erklärungstypus zu unterscheiden sind Erklärungen, die vom Internetbenutzer über eine ihm fremde Website abgegeben werden, etwa durch das Betätigen eines „Bestellen"-Buttons auf einer solchen Website.[90] Hier hängt der Erklärungszugang von der eingesetzten Übermittlungsart ab: Erscheint die abgegebene Erklärung unmittelbar auf dem Bildschirm des Empfängers, ohne dass zuvor eine Speicherung auf einem Server erfolgt (direkte Übermittlung), so geht sie dem Empfänger mit Passieren von dessen Schnittstelle (d. h. der Telefonbuchse des Empfängers) zu,[91] während bei Übermittlung der Erklärung an eine Mailbox des Empfängers das zur (individuellen) E-Mail Ausgeführte (oben Rn. 24 ff.) entsprechend gilt.

29 f) **Electronic Data Interchange (EDI).** Für Erklärungen per Electronic Data Interchange[92] gelten vergleichbare Grundsätze wie für Erklärungen per E-Mail (oben Rn. 24 ff.). Für die Zwecke des Art. 24 geht eine EDI-Erklärung daher in dem Moment zu, in dem die an die Adresse des Empfängers abgesandte Nachricht dessen Mailbox erreicht.[93]

30 g) **Short Message Service (SMS).** Eine Erklärung per SMS[94] (die unter dem CISG realistischerweise wohl allenfalls als Annahmeerklärung eine Rolle spielen kann) wird dem Empfänger i. S. des Art. 24 in dem Moment „zugestellt", in dem sie im Short Message Service Center (SMS C) – also demjenigen Bestandteil des Mobilfunknetzes, das die Nachricht entgegennimmt, zwischenspeichert und an den Adressaten ausliefert – zwischengespeichert wird.[95]

5. Parteiautonomie

31 Im Übrigen steht es den Parteien frei, abweichend von Art. 24 **strengere Zugangsvoraussetzungen** zu vereinbaren, aber auch **Zugangserleichterungen** – z. B. Zustellung am gewöhnlichen Aufenthaltsort als gleichwertig – vorzusehen.[96] Auch Bräuche oder Gepflogenheiten der Parteien können nach Art. 9 solche Änderungen der Zugangsvoraussetzungen bewirken.[97]

6. Zugang außerhalb der Geschäftszeiten

32 Schwierigkeiten macht die Beurteilung der Frage, wann der außerhalb der Geschäftszeiten in ein Postfach einsortierte Brief, die an einem Feiertag in einen Geschäftsbriefkasten eingeworfene Erklärung, die am Sonntag vom Faxgerät, dem Anrufbeantworter oder dem Server des Adressaten aufgenommene Mitteilung zugegangen ist. Vorgeschichte und Wortlaut, vor allem aber der Zweck der Norm, den Zugang an äußerlichen, leicht beweisbaren Tatbestandsmerkmalen festzumachen und das Risiko der Kommunikation im Organisationsbereich des Empfängers dem Erklärenden abzunehmen, sprechen für die Auslegung, in diesen Fällen die **Möglichkeit der aktuellen Kenntnisnahme** grundsätzlich **nicht** als

---

[89] *Borges*, Verträge im elektronischen Geschäftsverkehr, S. 322.
[90] S. dazu *Wulf*, S. 112 ff.
[91] *Wulf*, S. 115, so wohl auch *Staudinger/Magnus*, Art. 24, Rn. 16.
[92] Zum Begriff *Eiselen*, 6 VJ (2002), 305, 306.
[93] *Eiselen*, 6 EDI L. Rev. (1999), 21, 30: Eingang in VANS-Mailbox; *ders.*, 6 VJ (2002), 305, 309; *Wulf*, S. 117 f.; mit ausführl. technischen Details (aber ohne Behandlung des CISG) *Behling*, S. 255 ff.
[94] S. dazu *Behling*, S. 50 ff., dort auch zum Enhanced Message Service (EMS) und Multimedia Message Service (MMS).
[95] *Behling*, S. 213 f.
[96] Zur Möglichkeit parteiautonomer Regelung der Zugangsvoraussetzungen s. BGH, 7.6.1995, NJW 1995, 2217 (kein CISG-Fall).
[97] Vgl. BGH, 26.11.1997, NJW 1998, 976, 977 zum Einfluss von Treuepflichten aus Vertragsanbahnung.

Voraussetzung des Zugangs anzusehen.[98] Unterschiede in der Anwendung des Art. 24, die etwa auf nationale Feiertage und Sitten zur Geschäftszeit Bedacht zu nehmen versuchten, müssten bei einem Gesetz für grenzüberschreitende Sachverhalte bald zu Unzuträglichkeiten und Rechtsunsicherheit führen.[99] Eine für beide Teile gleichermaßen zu beachtende Verkehrsauffassung, die Voraussetzung für eine Korrektur der objektivierten Zugangsvoraussetzungen und ihrer Wirkungen wäre, wird in diesen Fällen oft gerade fehlen.[100] Auch Art. 20 II 2 bestätigt diese Wertung: Die dort geregelte Fristverlängerung ist Ausnahme für die Erklärung der Annahme[101] und verlängert nur bis zum folgenden Arbeitstag; in anderen Fällen sollen dagegen nationale Feiertage und arbeitsfreie Tage für die Fristberechnung außer Betracht bleiben. Sie sollten deshalb auch nicht generell zugangshindernd wirken.

Das schließt nicht aus, dass auf Grund der nach Art. 7 I und II vorzunehmenden 33 Auslegung und Ergänzung des Art. 24 sowie auf Grund Art. 9 I auch für diese Fälle Gepflogenheiten zwischen den Parteien oder Bräuche zu berücksichtigen sind, die Feiertagsregeln und -sitten Einfluss auf Zugang und Zugangswirkungen zukommen lassen. Auch können Feiertagssitten Zugang effektiv verhindern: Das Faxgerät oder der Anrufbeantworter werden ausgeschaltet, der Briefkasten befindet sich in einem Vorraum, der am Sonntag verschlossen ist, der zentrale Rechner ist am Sonntag außer Betrieb, usw.[102] Eine Generalisierung der so möglichen Besonderheiten verbietet sich jedoch.

7. Unverständliche Erklärungen

Die Fälle von **Erklärungsträgern,** die **für den Empfänger nicht verständliche** oder 34 **nicht vernehmbare Erklärungen** enthalten, z. B. Kassetten oder Disketten mit abzuspielenden oder auszudruckenden Erklärungen, für die der Empfänger kein Empfangsgerät besitzt, die auf einem USB-Stick, einer CD oder DVD gespeicherte Datei oder das mit einer E-Mail übersandte attachment, die der Empfänger (das Programm des Empfängers) nicht öffnen kann, müssen durch eine einschränkende Auslegung des Art. 24 im Lichte des Art. 7 I gelöst werden. Ausgangspunkt muss sein, dass bei schlechthin unverständlichen Erklärungen ein Zugangshindernis gegeben ist.[103] Im Übrigen ist zu differenzieren: Art. 24 beruht auf der vorausgesetzten Möglichkeit, die an den genannten Orten „zugestellten", d. h. in den Organisationsbereich des Empfängers gelangten Erklärungen aufzunehmen, zu vernehmen. Die innere Organisation des Empfängers, die Struktur seiner unternehmensinternen Kommunikationsvorgänge kann der Erklärende grundsätzlich nicht kennen, er kann sich nicht darauf einstellen. Sie können deshalb bei der Verteilung des Risikos der Rechtzeitigkeit oder des Verlustes von Erklärungen nicht zu seinen Lasten gehen. Ist das Fax richtig abgesandt worden, dann muss die Lesbarkeit des Ausdrucks vom Empfangsgerät Risiko des Adressaten sein;[104] ebenso ist in der Rechtsprechung zum CISG für eine E-Mail

---

[98] *Borges*, Verträge im elektronischen Geschäftsverkehr, S. 325; *Brunner*, Art. 24, Rn. 2; *Honsell/Dornis*, Art. 24, Rn. 36; *Staudinger/Magnus*, Art. 24, Rn. 18; a. A. wohl *Soergel/Lüderitz/Fenge*, Art. 24, Rn. 5; *Neumayer*, RIW 1994, 99, 104 m. w. N.
[99] Vgl. *von Caemmerer*, RabelsZ 29 (1965), 101, 134, Fn. 134 (zum EAG). Entscheidungen zu rein internen Fällen haben deshalb hier keine Bedeutung.
[100] *Wey*, Rn. 803, will jedoch danach differenzieren, ob die üblichen Geschäftszeiten des Empfängers für den Erklärenden erkennbar sind; wie hier wohl *Enderlein/Maskow/Strohbach*, Art. 24, Anm. 4. (soweit Zustellung möglich).
[101] S. hierzu oben Art. 20 Rn. 6. A. A. *Soergel/Lüderitz/Fenge*, Art. 24, Rn. 5.
[102] Mit Möglichkeit der Kenntnisnahme haben diese Fälle nichts zu tun (so aber *Soergel/Lüderitz/Fenge*, Art. 24, Rn. 5); allenfalls ist an Zugangshinderung zu denken, s. unten Rn. 41.
[103] *Borges*, Verträge im elektronischen Geschäftsverkehr, S. 323; *Honsell/Dornis*, Art. 24, Rn. 37; *Staudinger/Magnus*, Art. 24, Rn. 15.
[104] Wie hier *Ebnet*, NJW 1992, 2985, 2991: Absender trägt Gefahr der richtigen Übermittlung, wenn Zugang an einer Netzstörung oder an einem Defekt des Sendegeräts scheitert; dagegen sei Zugang zu bejahen, falls ein Defekt am Empfangsgerät Ursache der fehlerhaften Übertragung war. S. auch BGH, 19.4.1994, NJW 1994, 1881 f. zu Faxempfang; OLG Köln, 1.12.1989, CR 1990, 323, 324 f.: Mangelnde Vertrautheit mit

entschieden worden, die beim Empfänger eintraf, aber „teilweise nicht lesbar" gewesen sein soll.[105]

35   Diese Prämisse kann jedoch nur gelten und die Rechtsfolgen des Art. 24 rechtfertigen, wo und soweit **Erklärungsmittel** verwendet werden, die im jeweiligen Handelszweig oder individuell zwischen den Parteien **üblich** oder vom **Empfänger gebilligt** worden (s. oben Rn. 6 zu elektronischen Erklärungen) sind, und deren Nutzung – und damit Funktionieren und Verständlichkeit – deshalb angenommen werden kann. Die Formel zu § 130 I 1 BGB, dass der Empfänger „sich unter gewöhnlichen Verhältnissen Kenntnis vom Inhalt der Erklärung verschaffen konnte, und nach den Gepflogenheiten des Verkehrs von ihm zu erwarten war, dass er sich diese tatsächlich verschafft",[106] kann für derartige Fälle über Art. 7 I Eingang in die Auslegung des Art. 24 finden, ohne dass damit unreflektiert nationaler Rechtsüberzeugung gefolgt würde. Auch Art. 8 II bestätigt die Wertung, dass eine Erklärung jedenfalls einen für eine vernünftige Person in der Situation des Empfängers auslegungsfähigen und deshalb verständlichen Inhalt haben muss;[107] Gepflogenheiten der Parteien, ihr späteres Verhalten sowie Bräuche sind ebenfalls für die Erklärungsbedeutung erheblich, Art. 8 III, und deshalb auch für die Verständniszurechnung im Zusammenhang mit dem Zugang zu berücksichtigen. Die Erklärung auf einer CD mit einem durch und für ein bestimmtes Computerprogramm fixierten Text kann bei einem Partner, in dessen Land oder jeweiligem Handelszweig die Verwendung der entsprechenden Hardware oder Software nicht üblich ist, nicht als zugegangen bewertet werden, auch wenn der Empfänger sie schon verständnislos in der Hand hält. Gleiches gilt für elektronisch übermittelte Erklärungen;[108] bei Verwendung von Dateitypen, die durch gängige und über das Internet kostenfrei zugängliche Programme (wie etwa den Acrobat Reader) geöffnet werden können, wird man Zugang jedenfalls unter der Voraussetzung annehmen können, dass eine Person der gleichen Art in der Situation des Empfängers (Art. 8 II) sich dieses Programm unschwer beschaffen kann.

V. Fremdsprachen

1. Verwendung einer Fremdsprache als Zugangshindernis

36   Auch durch die mangelnde **sprachliche Verständlichkeit** einer rechtsgeschäftlichen Erklärung können **Zugangsprobleme** entstehen.[109] Die zum Recht des BGB vertretenen Ansichten, die die Sachfrage mit der Voraussetzung „Möglichkeit der Kenntnisnahme" lösen wollen, können auf Art. 24 hingegen nicht direkt übertragen werden, da diese Voraussetzung für das Sprachproblem gerade in Frage steht. Art. 24 enthält allerdings keine ausdrückliche Regelung des Sprachproblems beim Vertragsschluss, obwohl es sich um ein-

---

einem modernen Kommunikationssystem (Btx) und technisches Unvermögen des Empfängers, die *verzögerten* Abruf einer rechtzeitig gespeicherten Erklärung verursachen, sind Risiko des Empfängers.

[105] OLG Düsseldorf, 21.4.2004, CISG-online 915 = IHR 2005, 24, 27, wo das Gericht allerdings berechtigte Zweifel äußerte, ob die behauptete „teilweise" Unleserlichkeit bereits bei Eintreffen der E-Mail bei der Käuferin bestand oder nicht vielmehr erst durch eine Weiterleitung der ausgedruckten Datei per Telefax eingetreten sei.

[106] RG, 14.4.1920, RGZ 99, 20, 23; BGH, 13.2.1980, NJW 1980, 990 (keine CISG-Fälle).

[107] S. auch unten Rn. 36.

[108] S. oben Rn. 6, 24 ff.

[109] Für die Einordnung des Sachproblems als Frage des Erklärungszugangs allgemein *Flume*, Das Rechtsgeschäft, § 15 I 5, S. 249 f.; *Schlechtriem*, FS Weitnauer, S. 129 ff., 136 ff.; *Spellenberg*, FS Ferid, S. 475 ff.; *ders.*, IPRax 2007, 98, 101; spezifisch zum CISG OLG Hamm, 8.2.1995, CISG-online 141 = NJW-RR 1996, 1271, 1272; *Bamberger/Roth/Saenger*, Art. 24, Rn. 4; *Brunner*, Art. 24, Rn. 2; *Honsell/Dornis*, Art. 24, Rn. 38; *Luig*, S. 106; *MünchKomm/Gruber*, Art. 24, Rn. 18 f.; *MünchKommHGB/Ferrari*, Art. 24, Rn. 8; *Soergel/ Lüderitz/Fenge*, Art. 24, Rn. 6; *Staudinger/Magnus*, Art. 24, Rn. 20; *Witz/Salger/Lorenz/Witz*, Art. 24, Rn. 15. Zur Ähnlichkeit von Sprachproblemen und solchen der Lesbarkeit elektronischer Erklärungen CISG-AC, Op. 1 *(Chr. Ramberg)*, Comment 15.4, IHR 2003, 244, 246; zu mündlichen Erklärungen s. schon oben Rn. 10.

heitsrechtliche Materie i. S. v. Art. 7 II handeln dürfte. Allgemeine Grundsätze für Willenserklärungen und ihre Bedeutung, die hier heranzuziehen sind, finden sich jedoch in Art. 8:[110] Wird für die Auslegung, soweit der subjektive Erklärungswille des Erklärenden dem Adressaten nicht bekannt war, auf „eine vernünftige Person der gleichen Art wie die andere Partei unter den gleichen Umständen" abgestellt (und werden dazu nach Art. 8 III auch Gepflogenheiten und Bräuche berücksichtigt), so kann der darin zum Ausdruck kommende Grundsatz auch die Beurteilung tragen, was der Empfänger verstehen kann und deshalb als zugegangen gelten lassen muss. Die Unterschiede zu der abweichenden Auffassung, die das „Sprachrisiko" nicht als Problem des Zugangs, sondern der Tauglichkeit des Erklärungsmittels einordnen will,[111] sind damit im praktischen Ergebnis gering. Ein Rückgriff auf nationale Rechtsvorschriften zur Sprachenfrage bzw. die hierzu ergangene Rechtsprechung ist im Geltungsbereich des CISG jedenfalls ausgeschlossen.[112]

2. Behandlung des „Sprachrisikos" im Einzelnen

Die rechtliche Behandlung fremdsprachiger Erklärungen ist in der Praxis fast ausschließlich im Zusammenhang mit der **Einbeziehung von Standardbedingungen (AGB)** in Kaufverträge relevant geworden und hat in diesem Bereich zu einer umfangreichen Rechtsprechung geführt. Das dabei überwiegend praktizierte Abstellen auf eine „vernünftige Person" (Art. 8 II) erlaubt es, die dort entwickelten und oben in Art. 14 Rn. 61 ff. im Einzelnen erläuterten Lösungen in Anwendung des Art. 24 weitgehend zu übernehmen und auch auf **sonstige Erklärungsarten** anzuwenden. Jenseits der AGB-Einbeziehung hat das Sprachrisiko unter Art. 24 bislang etwa für den Zugang von Angeboten auf Vertragsänderung[113] und Abtretungsanzeigen (bei Anwendung des CISG im Rahmen des Forderungsstatuts)[114] Bedeutung erlangt.

Im Einzelnen gilt für die Zwecke des Art. 24 danach Folgendes: Was für den Erklärungsempfänger **absolut unverständlich** ist, kann nicht als zugegangene Erklärung gesehen werden.[115] Ausreichend ist unter dem CISG hingegen die Abfassung einer Erklärung in der **Verhandlungssprache,**[116] der **Vertragssprache,** die in der Sprachenfrage bezüglich während der Vertragsdurchführung erfolgten zugangsbedürftigen Mitteilungen (s. Artt. 47 II, 48 IV, 63 II, 65 I, II, 79 IV) ohne weiteres als Bezugspunkt taugt, während dies bei den Vertragsschlusserklärungen selbst Schwierigkeiten verursacht,[117] oder einer sonstigen, dem Empfänger **verständlichen** Sprache.[118] In der Praxis werden diese Grundsätze, die sämtlich an den Empfängerhorizont einer vernünftigen Person unter den gleichen Umständen (Art. 8) anknüpfen, *im Ergebnis* sehr häufig zum Zugang von Erklärungen führen, die in Englisch (als der „Sprache des Welthandels") oder anderen, in bestimmten Regionen weithin gesprochenen Sprachen (Französisch, Spanisch, Mandarin, Russisch, Deutsch) abgefasst wurden, aber eben nicht immer. Wird die verwendete Sprache hingegen nicht durch eine der oben genannten, durch ein Abstellen auf die beteiligten Vertragsparteien geprägten Fallgruppen abgedeckt, so kann der Erklärungszugang nicht mit dem Argument begründet

---

[110] So auch *Luig,* S. 106; ganz ähnlich (für analoge Anwendung des Art. 8 II) MünchKomm/*Gruber,* Art. 24, Rn. 18 f.; *Witz/Salger/Lorenz/Witz,* Art. 24, Rn. 15.

[111] So *Ladas,* S. 51 ff., 56, 62; MünchKomm/*Einsele,* § 130, Rn. 32 (beide zum BGB); zum CISG ähnlich *Lautenschlager,* 11 VJ (2007), 259, 270 ff.

[112] Zur kollisionsrechtlichen Anknüpfung *Reithmann/Martiny/Martiny,* Rn. 220.

[113] LG Kassel, 15.2.1996, CISG-online 190.

[114] OLG Hamm, 8.2.1995, CISG-online 141 = NJW-RR 1996, 1271, 1272 m. Anm. *Schlechtriem,* IPRax 1996, 184.

[115] Vgl. CA Paris, 10.9.2003, CISG-online 788: Übersendung eines kaufmännischen Bestätigungsschreibens in deutscher Sprache an französischen Käufer, das diesem nicht ausreichend verständlich war („celle-ci n'était pas suffisamment comprise"); *Honsell/Dornis,* Art. 24, Rn. 38; *Staudinger/Magnus,* Art. 24, Rn. 20.

[116] Oben Art. 14 Rn. 62; für Angebot auf Vertragsänderung ebenso LG Kassel, 15.2.1996, CISG-online 190.

[117] S. oben Art. 14 Rn. 63.

[118] Oben Art. 14 Rn. 64.

werden, die betreffende Mitteilung sei in einer **„Weltsprache"** abgefasst, und auch eine sonstige Vermutung, bestimmte Sprachen seien stets und unabhängig vom Einzelfall als verständlich zu behandeln, verbietet sich im Geltungsbereich eines Übereinkommens, das auf weltweite Geltung angelegt ist.[119] Zur Übersetzung eines ihm unverständlichen Textes durch einen Dolmetscher ist der Empfänger im Regelfall ebenso wenig verpflichtet wie zur Vornahme eines Versuches, die Erklärung mit Hilfe eines Wörterbuches selbst zu übersetzen.[120]

39 Allerdings kann der Verhaltensmaßstab einer „vernünftigen Person" i. S. des Art. 8 II bei fremdsprachigen Erklärungen, die im Rahmen der **Vertragsdurchführung** erfolgen, in Einzelfällen eine andersartige Reaktion verlangen als bei dem Empfang fremdsprachiger AGB während der Vertragsschlussphase: So soll der Empfänger nach der Rechtsprechung zur Rückfrage beim Erklärenden und zur Bitte um Übermittlung der Erklärung in einer verständlichen Sprache verpflichtet sein können, wenn er die rechtliche Relevanz der fremdsprachlichen Mitteilung etwa dadurch erkennen muss, dass diese auf zuvor erteilte Rechnungen Bezug nimmt.[121] Zugang der Erklärung ist in diesem Fall (wie auch in denjenigen Fällen, in denen der Empfänger aus eigener Initiative eine Übersetzung arrangiert) erst mit Zugang der verständlichen Klarstellung bzw. übersetzten Erklärung erfolgt.[122] Schließlich kann der Adressat einer aus Sprachgründen unverständlichen Erklärung diese gegen sich gelten lassen,[123] indem er auf das Zugangserfordernis **verzichtet.**

3. Anfechtbarkeit

40 Muss der Empfänger die auf Grund Sprachunkenntnis nicht oder missverstandene Erklärung als zugegangen gelten lassen, so kann seine daraufhin erfolgte Erklärung u. U. irrtumsbeeinflusst und deshalb nach nationalem Recht anfechtbar sein.[124]

VI. Rechtsmissbrauch: Zugangsverhinderung

41 Ein – möglicherweise vorwerfbares – Verhalten des Empfängers, das den Zugang einer Mitteilung verzögert oder verhindert, ist im CISG nicht geregelt worden. Es kann praktische Bedeutung vor allem für die rechtzeitige Annahme eines Vertragsangebots haben, aber auch für die Effektivität einer Rücknahme von Erklärungen oder eines Widerrufs der Offerte. Ob, auf Grund welcher Zurechnungskriterien und mit welchen konstruktiven Behelfen im Fall **verhinderten Zugangs** gleichwohl rechtzeitiger Zugang angenommen werden darf, ob man mit einer Fiktion des Zugangs helfen, einen Schadenersatzanspruch geben oder die Berufung auf fehlenden oder verspäteten Zugang als treuwidrig verwehren kann, ist sehr zweifelhaft.[125] Der dem deutschen Juristen vertraute Rückgriff auf Grundsätze des Rechtsmissbrauchs ist nicht ohne weiteres möglich, da man eine entsprechende Maxime

---

[119] S. oben Art. 14 Rn. 65 ff.; OLG Hamm, 8.2.1995, CISG-online 141 = NJW-RR 1996, 1271, 1272; *Lautenschlager,* 11 VJ (2007), 259, 273; MünchKomm/*Gruber,* Art. 24, Rn. 19; MünchKommHGB/*Ferrari,* Art. 24, Rn. 8; a. A. *Soergel/Lüderitz/Fenge,* Art. 24, Rn. 6.

[120] MünchKomm/*Gruber,* Art. 24, Rn. 20; wohl auch OLG Hamm, 8.2.1995, CISG-online 141 = NJW-RR 1996, 1271, 1272. Differenzierend *Lautenschlager,* 11 VJ (2007), 259, 274.

[121] OLG Hamm, 8.2.1995, CISG-online 141 = NJW-RR 1996, 1271, 1272 zu Abtretungsanzeige, die erkennbar auf vorausgegangene Rechnungen einschl. Rechnungsnummern und -beträge Bezug nahm.

[122] MünchKomm/*Gruber,* Art. 24, Rn. 20.

[123] *Reinhart,* Art. 11, Rn. 8; *Staudinger/Magnus,* Art. 24, Rn. 20.

[124] Vgl. BGH, 27.10.1994, NJW 1995, 190, 191 (Unterschrift unter missverstandenes Bürgschaftsformular); ferner oben Rn. 10 für mündliche Erklärungen; *Staudinger/Hausmann,* Art. 31 EGBGB, Rn. 102; a. A. *Luig,* S. 107.

[125] S. *Schlesinger/Lorenz,* Bd. 2, S. 1468 ff.; zum österreichischen und schweizerischen Recht *Schlesinger/Neumayer,* Bd. 1, S. 700 Fn. 5; zum deutschen Recht noch *Burghard,* AcP 195 (1995), 74, 111, *Flume,* Das Rechtsgeschäft, § 14 3e), S. 238 ff.; zum englischen Recht s. *Entores, Ltd. v. Miles Far East Corp.,* [1955] 2 All E. R. 493, 495 – dictum von *Lord Denning.*

Begriff des Zugangs

für das Verhalten der Parteien bei Abschluss und Durchführung des Vertrages gerade nicht in das Übereinkommen aufgenommen hat.[126] M. E. ist jedoch bei der Auslegung des Art. 24 und der an Zugang anknüpfenden Vorschriften anzusetzen und dabei das Auslegungsgebot aus Art. 7 I zu berücksichtigen, die Wahrung des guten Glaubens im internationalen Handel zu fördern.[127] Auch wenn man die Regelung des Art. 24 hinsichtlich dieser Fälle als lückenhaft sieht, wäre die Lücke in Anwendung des Art. 7 II durch Rückgriff auf Grundsätze, die in einer Reihe von Vorschriften zum Ausdruck kommen, mit dem gleichen Ergebnis zu schließen.

Ein arglistig verhinderter oder verzögerter Zugang kann deshalb bei einer auf Art. 7 abgestützten Auslegung des Art. 24 als in dem Zeitpunkt erfolgt gelten, in dem er ohne das verhindernde Verhalten des Erklärungsempfängers geschehen wäre.[128] Dies wird etwa bei dem Ausschalten des Empfangsgerätes (z. B. Faxgerätes) in Erwartung einer Nachricht zu gelten haben.[129] Ob dagegen die in einem trotz Benachrichtigung nicht abgeholten Brief enthaltene Mitteilung,[130] die nicht abgeholte postlagernde Erklärung, der Brief, dessen Annahme in Unkenntnis seines Inhalts verweigert worden ist,[131] ein im Copy-Shop trotz Mitteilung des Eingangs liegen gelassenes Fax, das Fernschreiben, das nicht empfangen werden konnte, weil das Gerät – z. B. am Wochenende – nicht eingeschaltet war, die E-Mail, die infolge einer überfüllten Adressatenmailbox nicht gespeichert wurde,[132] als zugegangen behandelt werden kann, hängt von den Umständen des Einzelfalles ab, vor allem dem Grad der Verantwortung des Empfängers für die Störung sowie den Gepflogenheiten, die sich zwischen Parteien entwickelt haben (können), Art. 9 I. Wurden in der Vergangenheit regelmäßig Erklärungen am Sonntag zugestellt und als rechtzeitig akzeptiert, dann kann das Abschalten eines Empfangsgeräts oder Anrufbeantworters Zugangshinderung sein. Die Entscheidung im Einzelfall muss insoweit letztlich der Bewertung des Gerichts überlassen bleiben,[133] wobei die bisherige Rechtsprechungspraxis zum CISG darauf hinweist, dass der Frage keine wesentliche praktische Bedeutung zukommt. Anzustreben ist gleichwohl, in der wissenschaftlichen Aufarbeitung des CISG entsprechende Auslegungsregeln zu Art. 24 und den einzelnen, rechtzeitigen Zugang voraussetzenden Vorschriften herauszubilden, so dass die Annahme einer nur durch Rückgriff auf nationale Rechtsregeln zu schließenden Lücke vermieden werden kann.[134] Erst wenn sich ein solcher Auslegungskanon gebildet haben sollte, wird sich vertreten lassen, dass auch Schadenersatzansprüche nach nationalem Recht wegen verhinderten Zugangs, etwa aus culpa in contrahendo, zurückzutreten haben.[135]

---

[126] Vgl. hierzu *Schlechtriem*, Einheitliches UN-Kaufrecht, S. 25. Allerdings findet sich die Regel, dass einer rechtsmissbräuchlichen Berufung auf formal ordnungsgemäße Rechtspositionen die Wirkung zu versagen ist, in verschiedenen Vorschriften, so in Artt. 16 II lit. b) und 29 II 2, so dass eine entsprechende Lückenfüllung über Art. 7 II möglich sein dürfte; dazu im Text.
[127] So *Staudinger/Magnus*, Art. 24, Rn. 25.
[128] Wie hier *Brunner*, Art. 24, Rn. 4; *Honsell/Dornis*, Art. 24, Rn. 41; *Herber/Czerwenka*, Art. 24, Rn. 5; *Neumayer/Ming*, Art. 24, Anm. 4.; *Witz/Salger/Lorenz/Witz*, Art. 24, Rn. 16; a. A. (für verhinderten Zugang) *Perales Viscasillas*, 16 J. L. & Com. (1997), 315, 332.
[129] *Borges*, Verträge im elektronischen Geschäftsverkehr, S. 324; *Honsell/Dornis*, Art. 24, Rn. 41.
[130] *Achilles*, Art. 24, Rn. 6: Zugegangen mit Ablauf der höchstzulässigen Abholfrist.
[131] RG, 13.7.1904, RGZ 58, 406 ff.; RG, 5.1.1925, RGZ 110, 34 ff.; BGH, 3.11.1976, BGHZ 67, 271, 275; s. auch *Dölle/Reinhart*, Art. 14 EKG, Rn. 23 zur Nachgebühr.
[132] S. bereits oben Rn. 24.
[133] Wie hier *Wey*, Rn. 806: Konkretisierung des Zugangsrechts gem. Art. 7 mit der gebotenen Differenzierung und Typisierung, was die Risikoverteilung bei den verschiedenen Übermittlungsträgern betrifft. Zwangszustellungen und culpa-Ansprüche seien stumpfe und deshalb subsidiäre Mittel. Vor allem müssten funktionsbezogene Auslegung und Ergänzung des Zugangs- und Wirksamkeitsbegriffes einheitsrechtlich erfolgen. Zu den Sorgfaltspflichten der Parteien auf Grund Vertragsanbahnung s. BGH, 26.11.1997, NJW 1998, 976, 977: Nur schwerste Pflichtverletzung des Empfängers könne dazu führen, Zugang als erfolgt zu sehen (kein CISG-Fall).
[134] A. A. (für Anwendung nationalen Rechts) *Borges*, Verträge im elektronischen Geschäftsverkehr, S. 324.
[135] A. A. – bereits heute gegen einen Rückgriff auf nationales Recht – *MünchKomm/Gruber*, Art. 24, Rn. 26; allgemein zum Verhältnis der Artt. 14–24 zur culpa in contrahendo-Haftung nach nationalem Recht oben Vor Artt. 14–24 Rn. 34 ff.

VII. Beweislast

43 Regeln zur **Beweislast** für den Zugang sind aus den Vorschriften des CISG zu entwickeln.[136] Beruft sich der Absender auf den Zugang, so trägt er dafür die Behauptungs- und Beweislast.[137] Der Empfänger hat dann Zugangshindernisse zu beweisen, die ihn „befreien" können.[138] Der für den Zugang Beweispflichtige hat auch den Zeitpunkt zu beweisen.[139]

44 Die **Beweiswürdigung** ist dagegen Sache des nationalen Prozessrechts.[140] Ob etwa Aufgabe zur Post oder das Sendejournal des Absenders eines Telefax jedenfalls den Beweis des ersten Anscheins für den Zugang begründen können und welches Maß an Überzeugung des Gerichts für einen Beweis erforderlich ist, muss das nationale Recht entscheiden.[141] Nach deutschem Prozessrecht beweist der Sendebericht eines Telefaxes allein noch nicht dessen vollständige Übermittlung in das Empfängergerät[142] und die Vorlage des Ein- und Auslieferungsbeleges begründet beim Einwurf-Einschreiben keinen Anscheinsbeweis für dessen Zugang,[143] während der Eingangs- bzw. Lesebestätigung bei E-Mails der Wert eines Anscheinsbeweises zukommen soll.[144]

---

[136] Vgl. *Herber/Czerwenka*, Art. 4, Rn. 8; Art. 24, Rn. 7; a. A. ICC, 6653/1993, CISG-online 71 = J. D. I. 1993, 1041, 1051 (zur Beschaffenheit der Ware).

[137] OLG Dresden, 10.11.2006, CISG-online 1625.

[138] *Baumgärtel/Laumen/Hepting*, Art. 24 WKR, Rn. 1; *Herber/Czerwenka*, Art. 24, Rn. 7; *Witz/Salger/Lorenz/Witz*, Art. 24, Rn. 17.

[139] *Baumgärtel/Laumen/Hepting*, Art. 24 WKR, Rn. 6.

[140] S. *Herber/Czerwenka*, Art. 24, Rn. 7.

[141] Zur Beweisbarkeit des Telefaxzugangs nach deutschem und englischem Recht s. *Riesenkampff*, ZVglRWiss 107 (2008), 428 ff.

[142] OLG Dresden, 10.11.2006, CISG-online 1625 (zu einem CISG-Vertrag). Ein Sendebericht des Telefaxgeräts des Absenders beweist nur, dass eine Verbindung zwischen Sender- und Empfängergerät hergestellt worden war, nicht aber geglückte Übermittlung, BGH, 7.12.1994, NJW 1995, 665, 667; umfassend zu den Beweisfragen bei Verwendung elektronischer Telekommunikationsmittel *Burghard,* AcP 195 (1995), 74, 124 ff.; *Roßnagel/Pfitzmann,* NJW 2003, 1206 ff. Aus rechtsvergleichender Perspektive *Schwenzer/Hachem/Kee,* Rn. 11.24, die die Haltung des deutschen Rechts als „extremely strict" bezeichnen.

[143] AG Kempen, 28.8.2006, NJW 2007, 1215.

[144] S. *Mankowski*, NJW 2004, 1901, 1906; MünchKomm/*Einsele*, § 130, Rn. 46; *Schwenzer/Hachem/Kee*, Rn. 11.24; *Wulf,* S. 118.

Teil III. Warenkauf

Kapitel I. Allgemeine Bestimmungen

Part III	Troisième partie
Sale of Goods	Vente de marchandises
Chapter I	Chapitre I
General provisions	Dispositions générales

Art. 25 [Wesentliche Vertragsverletzung]

Eine von einer Partei begangene Vertragsverletzung ist wesentlich, wenn sie für die andere Partei solchen Nachteil zur Folge hat, daß ihr im wesentlichen entgeht, was sie nach dem Vertrag hätte erwarten dürfen, es sei denn, daß die vertragsbrüchige Partei diese Folge nicht vorausgesehen hat und eine vernünftige Person der gleichen Art* diese Folge unter den gleichen Umständen auch nicht vorausgesehen hätte.

Art. 25

A breach of contract committed by one of the parties is fundamental if it results in such detriment to the other party as substantially to deprive him of what he is entitled to expect under the contract, un-less the party in breach did not foresee and a reasonable person of the same kind in the same circumstances would not have foreseen such a result.

Art. 25

Une contravention au contrat commise par l'une des parties est essentielle lorsqu'elle cause à l'autre partie un préjudice tel qu'elle la prive substantiellement de ce que celle-ci était en droit d'attendre du contrat, à moins que la partie en défaut n'ait pas prévu un tel résultat et qu'une personne raisonnable de même qualité placée dans la même situation ne l'aurait pas prévu non plus.

Übersicht

	Rn.
I. Grundlagen und Vorgeschichte	1
1. Rückabwicklung des Vertrages als ultima ratio	1
2. Vorgeschichte des Art. 25	3
II. Allgemeines; Funktionen des Begriffs „wesentliche Vertragsverletzung"	6
1. Voraussetzung für besonders einschneidende Rechtsbehelfe	6
2. Inhalt und Umstände des betroffenen Vertrages als vorrangiger Ansatzpunkt	8
3. Begrenzte Rolle der Nachfrist	10
4. Begriffsäquivalente außerhalb des CISG; autonome Auslegung des Art. 25	12
III. Voraussetzungen einer „wesentlichen Vertragsverletzung"	13
1. Pflichtverletzung des Schuldners	13
a) Pflichtenarten	14
aa) Vertragspflichten	15
bb) Außervertragliche Pflichten	16
cc) Schutzpflichten	17
b) Folgen eines Zurückbehaltungsrechts des Schuldners	18
c) Vorsatz des Schuldners irrelevant	19
d) Mehrere Pflichtverletzungen	20
2. Beeinträchtigung eines wesentlichen Vertragsinteresses: „Nachteil"	21
a) Bestimmung durch die Parteien entscheidend	21
b) Fallgruppen	23

---

* Schweiz: ... in gleicher Stellung.

Art. 25 1   Teil III. Kapitel I. Allgemeine Bestimmungen

        3. Definition der „Wesentlichkeit" in Allgemeinen Geschäftsbedingungen .. 25
        4. Voraussehbarkeit und/oder Kenntnis als Auslegungsumstände 26
            a) Eindeutige Benennung der Pflichtenbedeutung im Vertrag 28
            b) Erörterung der Pflichtenbedeutung während der Vertragsanbahnung .. 29
            c) Übrige Konstellationen 30
        5. Zeitpunkt der Erkennbarkeit oder Kenntnis 32
        6. Beweislast 34
            a) Vertragsverletzung 34
            b) Nachteil (d. h. Bedeutung der verletzten Pflicht) 35
            c) Vorhersehbarkeit (oder deren Fehlen) 36
    IV. Einzelfälle (1): Verletzung von Verkäuferpflichten 37
        1. Nichtleistung 37
        2. Verspätete Lieferung 38
            a) Allgemeines 38
            b) Wesentliche Vertragsverletzungen 39
            c) Keine wesentliche Vertragsverletzung 40
            d) Auswirkungen der Verwendung von Incoterms® 41
        3. Quantitätsmängel 42
        4. Sach- und Rechtsmängel der Ware 43
            a) Parteiautonome Bestimmung der Wesentlichkeit 44
            b) Berücksichtigung des Rechts des Verkäufers zur zweiten Andienung ... 47
            c) Nachfristsetzung 49
            d) Rückabwicklung als ultima ratio bei Unverwertbarkeit der Ware 50
                aa) Möglichkeit des Käufers zur Verwertung der mangelhaften Ware ... 52
                bb) Unzumutbarkeit als Grenze 54
                cc) Weitere Fälle wesentlicher Vertragsverletzungen 57
        5. Dokumente 59
            a) Begleitdokumente 60
            b) Echtes Dokumentengeschäft, Grundsatz der Dokumentenstrenge 62
    V. Einzelfälle (2): Verletzung von Käuferpflichten 66
        1. Verspätete Zahlung 66
        2. Verletzung der Abnahmepflicht 67
    VI. Einzelfälle (3): Verletzung sonstiger (Neben-)Pflichten 68

Vorläufer und **Entwürfe:** Art. 10 EKG, Genfer E 1976 Art. 9, Wiener E 1977 Art. 8, New Yorker E 1978 Art. 23.

I. Grundlagen und Vorgeschichte

1. Rückabwicklung des Vertrages als ultima ratio

1   Für die Aufhebung eines Vertrages wegen Leistungsstörungen lassen sich im Rechtsvergleich auf den ersten Blick kaum Übereinstimmungen finden: Nicht nur weichen die Rechtsordnungen in der Art und Weise, wie die Aufhebung erfolgt – durch richterliche Gestaltungsentscheidung, Parteierklärung oder ipso iure – voneinander ab, sondern vor allem auch in den Voraussetzungen, z. B. in der unterschiedlichen Bedeutung einer Verantwortung, insbesondere einer Schuld einer Partei als Aufhebungsgrund.[1] Aber es ist doch nachweisbar, dass in vielen Rechtsordnungen die Möglichkeit der Vertragsaufhebung für den von einer Leistungsstörung betroffenen Teil – anstelle einer Beschränkung auf Schadenersatzansprüche oder andere Behelfe unter Aufrechterhaltung des Vertrages – vom Gewicht der Leistungsstörung abhängt: „The most important principle" sei, dass „the default attains a certain minimum degree of seriousness".[2] Entsprechend sieht *Ghestin* als zentrales Merkmal für die Auslegung des Art. 1184 Cc die „importance de l'inexécution".[3]

---

[1] Vgl. *Treitel*, Remedies for Breach, Nr. 147 ff. und 155 ff.
[2] *Treitel*, Remedies for Breach, Nr. 161; zu Art. 25 CISG s. *Nicholas*, 105 L. Q. R. (1989), 201, 219.
[3] *Ghestin*, Les effets du contrat, Anm. 409, S. 419. Dort (Anm. 413, S. 425) auch eine Erläuterung des Art. 25, insbesondere seiner vertragserhaltenden Funktion, im Vergleich zum französischen Recht. S. zum

Moderne, am Einheitskaufrecht orientierte Gesetze wie die skandinavischen Kaufgesetze, 2
das estnische Schuldrechtsgesetz oder das niederländische Wetboek verwenden deshalb den
Zentralbegriff der wesentlichen Vertragsverletzung oder entsprechende Schlüsselbegriffe
ebenso wie Rechtsvereinheitlichungsprojekte, z. B. UNIDROIT's „Principles for International Commercial Contracts", die „Principles of European Contract Law", der Entwurf
eines „Gemeinsamen Referenzrahmens" (DCFR) der Europäischen Union oder der Vorschlag für ein „Gemeinsames Europäisches Kaufrecht" (CESL).[4] Diese Konzeption liegt seit
der Schuldrechtsreform auch dem Rücktrittsrecht des deutschen Schuldrechts zugrunde,
auch wenn § 323 I BGB vom Vorrang der Nachfristsetzung ausgeht, denn die Fälle, in
denen Nachfrist entbehrlich und deshalb sofortiger Rücktritt möglich ist, sind solche
schwerer Pflichtverletzung, also wesentlichen Vertragsbruchs (§ 323 II BGB: ernsthafte
Erfüllungsweigerung, Terminüberschreitung beim Fixgeschäft, besondere Umstände;
§ 326 V: Undurchsetzbarkeit des Erfüllungsanspruchs wegen Unmöglichkeit oder Unzumutbarkeit für den Schuldner).[5] Regelmäßig ist es bei Lösungen, die auf diesem Grundprinzip aufbauen, Sache der **Parteien**, im Vertrag selbst festzulegen, welches Gewicht
einzelne Pflichten und Pflichteninhalte für den Gläubiger und damit für den Bestand des
Vertrages haben sollen, etwa auch durch die Qualifizierung als Zusicherung, *condition* oder
warranty.[6]

2. Vorgeschichte des Art. 25

Die grundsätzliche Unterscheidung, eine Vertragsaufhebung durch rechtsgeschäftliche 3
Parteierklärung (nur) bei erheblichen Vertragsstörungen zuzulassen, bei leichteren Störungen den betroffenen Teil dagegen auf Schadenersatz zu verweisen, ist in Ansätzen schon von
Ernst Rabel gesehen worden und in den Entwürfen von 1935 und 1939/1951 nachzuweisen.[7] Als einheitliches Prinzip ist dieser Gedanke in den Entwürfen 1956 und 1963 zu finden
und in Art. 10 EKG ausformuliert worden. Die **„Wesentlichkeit" der Verletzung**,
zunächst auf die einzelne Pflicht, später dann auf den Vertrag bezogen, wurde anfänglich als
solche des hypothetischen Parteiwillens gesehen,[8] doch war die Frage einer „subjektiven"
oder „objektiven" Fassung dieser Voraussetzung einer Vertragsaufhebung schon bei den
Beratungen des EKG umstritten.[9]

Bei den Vorarbeiten zum CISG und auf der Wiener Konferenz hat man dann wieder um 4
die richtige Fassung des Grundgedankens gerungen.[10] Vor allem ging es darum, ob (allein-)
entscheidende Voraussetzung der „Wesentlichkeit" des Vertragsbruchs ein „substantial detri-

---

englischen Recht demgegenüber *Bridge,* Int'l Sale of Goods, Rn. 12.24: „This is a long way from the position in English law ...".

[4] Vgl. näher unten Rn. 12.

[5] S. hierzu *Schlechtriem,* Neues Schuldrecht, S. 71 ff., 77–79.

[6] Vgl. *Treitel,* Remedies for Breach, Nr. 167: „The basic idea behind the distinction ... reflects the principle that only a ‚substantial' breach gives rise to a right to terminate"; dadurch könnten freilich auch Vertragsverletzungen zum Aufhebungsgrund werden, die den anderen Teil wenig oder gar nicht schädigen, z. B. bei Bruch einer implied condition, dass die verkaufte Sache die im Kaufvertrag durch Beschreibung zugesagten Eigenschaften habe. Zum englischen Recht *Bridge,* Int'l Sale of Goods, Rn. 12.24: „... the test is, whether the term breached is a condition of the contract, express or implied.". S. auch BGH, 3.4.1996, CISG-online 135 = BGHZ 132, 290, 298: Zweckmäßige Möglichkeit, die für wesentlich gehaltenen Pflichten als solche im Vertrag festzuhalten.

[7] Vgl. *Rabel,* RabelsZ 9 (1935), 1, 71 f., aber auch 339, 348, abgedr. in *ders.,* Ges. Aufs., Bd. 3, S. 577, 596 f.; *von Caemmerer,* Wesentliche Vertragsverletzung, S. 35 ff. = GS Bd. 3, S. 69 ff.; *Beinert,* Wesentliche Vertragsverletzung, S. 55 ff.

[8] Dazu *von Caemmerer,* Wesentliche Vertragsverletzung, S. 39 = GS Bd. 3, S. 73: „Musste vom Satz pacta sunt servanda abgewichen werden, so sollte das auf den vermutlichen Parteiwillen gestützt werden können".

[9] Vgl. *von Caemmerer,* Wesentliche Vertragsverletzung, S. 43 ff. = GS Bd. 3, S. 77 ff.; *Bianca/Bonell/Will,* Art. 25, Anm. 1.1.1., 1.1.2.

[10] Vgl. z. B. YB I (1968–1970), S. 169, Nr. 86; YB III (1972), S. 47; YB VI (1975), S. 53, Nr. 44; S. 77, Nr. 43; S. 95, Nr. 67; YB VIII (1977), S. 127, Nr. 7. Informativ zu den diesbezüglichen Missverständnissen

ment" sein solle. Schließlich wurde entschieden, die Erheblichkeit des Vertragsbruchs nicht mehr durch das Ausmaß eines Schadens zu definieren, sondern auf die durch den Inhalt des Vertrages konkretisierten und umschriebenen **Interessen des Vertragsgläubigers** abzustellen.[11] Natürlich kann und wird häufig das Ausmaß eines dem Gläubiger aufgrund einer Pflichtverletzung drohenden Schadens die Bedeutung dieser Pflicht für den Vertrag entscheidend beeinflussen, aber dieser Schaden muss in der geltenden Fassung des Art. 25 nicht mehr notwendig substantiiert dargetan werden. Damit ist erreicht worden, dass die von einer Vertragsverletzung betroffene Vertragspartei nicht stets gezwungen werden kann, zum Nachweis ihres Nachteils ihre Bücher zu öffnen, ihre Einkaufs- oder Wiederverkaufspreise und andere schadenserhebliche Details zu offenbaren. Auch soll Aufhebung nicht selten gerade einen Schaden verhindern oder vermindern, z. B., indem sie ein günstiges Deckungsgeschäft ermöglicht oder Aufwendungen vermeidbar macht.[12] Es genügt deshalb, dass – z. B. bei einem Fixgeschäft oder durch eine vom Käufer verlangte Garantie oder Zusicherung von Eigenschaften – der Vertrag selbst eine bestimmte Pflicht oder Pflichterfüllungsmodalität als für den Vertrag essentiell festlegt.[13]

5   Auch die **„Voraussehbarkeit"** im zweiten Halbsatz war im Verlauf der Erarbeitung des Art. 25 Gegenstand von Änderungen und Änderungsvorschlägen. Die Funktion dieser Voraussetzung wurde dabei durch die verschiedenen Änderungen verschoben: Während sie zunächst noch – entsprechend Art. 10 EKG[14] – als Richtlinie für die Ermittlung der Bedeutung einzelner Vertragspflichten, also als Auslegungshilfe, gesehen wurde, setzte sich mit der Einführung des Kriteriums „substantial detriment" (zur Bestimmung der Wesentlichkeit des Vertragsbruchs) die Auffassung durch, dass es sich um eine Entlastungsmöglichkeit des vertragsbrüchigen Schuldners handele. Folgerichtig wurde auf Antrag der Philippinen[15] der Ausnahmecharakter dieser Entlastung durch die Formulierung „unless ...", „es sei denn, dass ...", zu verdeutlichen versucht: Ein substantieller Schaden, den der Schuldner weder vorausgesehen hat noch voraussehen konnte, sollte ihn nicht „belasten".

Haftung (liability) und Vertragsaufhebungsmöglichkeit wurden dabei jedoch zuweilen nicht klar unterschieden.[16] In Wien wurde dann übersehen, dass mit der Abschwächung des Kriteriums „substantial detriment" zugunsten der geltenden Bestimmung des Nachteils durch die konkreten Vertragserwartungen des Gläubigers die „Voraussehbarkeit" ihre Funktion als Entlastungsgrund bei nicht voraussehbarem Schaden verloren hatte[17] – gleichwohl blieb die auf „substantial detriment" bezogene Formel „unless ...", „es sei denn, dass ...",

---

Eörsi, 31 Am. J. Comp. L. (1983), 333, 340 f., 344; zur Geschichte umfassend *Botzenhardt*, S. 161 ff.; ferner *Bianca/Bonell/Will*, Art. 25, Anm. 1. und 2.

[11] Vgl. O. R., S. 295 ff., 300; *Lurger*, IHR 2001, 91; *Schlechtriem*, Einheitliches UN-Kaufrecht, S. 47; *Staudinger/Magnus*, Art. 25, Rn. 11; vgl. auch die Formulierung des § 323 II Nr. 2 BGB: „Leistungsinteresse des Gläubigers im Vertrag gebunden an ...".

[12] Vgl. zu diesem Argument schon die Stellungnahme der tschechoslowakischen Regierung in YB VIII (1977), S. 113, Nr. 5.

[13] Zur darin liegenden Rückkehr zu Grundgedanken des Römischen Entwurfs zum EKG s. *Eörsi*, 31 Am. J. Comp. L. (1983), 333, 340.

[14] Art. 10 EKG (Wesentliche Vertragsverletzung): „Eine Vertragsverletzung wird im Sinne dieses Gesetzes immer dann als wesentlich angesehen, wenn die *Partei*, die sie begangen hat, *im Zeitpunkt des Vertragsabschlusses gewusst hat oder hätte wissen müssen, daß eine vernünftige Person in der Lage der anderen Partei den Vertrag nicht geschlossen hätte, wenn sie die Vertragsverletzung und ihre Folgen vorausgesehen hätte*" (Hervorhebungen durch den Verf.).

[15] YB VIII (1977), S. 127, Nr. 7.

[16] Der Funktionswandel wird anschaulich vorgeführt bei *Michida*, 27 Am. J. Comp. L. (1979), 279, 282 f.: In der Fassung des E 1976 sei in einem Kaufvertrag über Weihnachtstruthähne „voraussehbar" gewesen, dass Lieferung nach den Weihnachtstagen ein wesentlicher Vertragsbruch sei, der Lieferzeitpunkt also essentiell war. Die von *Michida*, a. a. O., 284 ff. ausführlich berichtete Begründung des philippinischen Antrags lässt erkennen, dass man dann jedoch Nichtvoraussehbarkeit als „exemption from liability" verstand. So kommentiert *Ghestin*, Fusion des actions, Nr. 238, S. 224, Voraussetzung sei, dass der vertragswidrige Teil „... n'est pas en faute de ne pas l'avoir prévu (ce résultat) ...". Vgl. zu den Missverständnissen auch die Glosse von *Eörsi*, 31 Am. J. Comp. L. (1983), 333–356.

[17] S. unten Rn. 26, 27.

obwohl eigentlich überflüssig geworden, stehen; ein Umstand, der heute Schwierigkeiten im Normverständnis zur Folge hat.[18] Schließlich war in diesem Zusammenhang die Frage der Beweislast für die Voraussehbarkeit umstritten.[19]

II. Allgemeines; Funktionen des Begriffs „wesentliche Vertragsverletzung"

1. Voraussetzung für besonders einschneidende Rechtsbehelfe

Art. 25 selbst gewährt den Parteien keinen Rechtsbehelf; die darin aufstellte Definition der „wesentlichen Vertragsverletzung" fungiert vielmehr als Voraussetzung für eine Reihe besonders einschneidender Rechtsbehelfe, die in anderen Vorschriften des Übereinkommens geregelt werden.[20] „Wesentliche Vertragsverletzung" ist dabei vor allem Voraussetzung für die Aufhebung des Vertrages durch die von einer Vertragsstörung betroffene Partei, Artt. 49 I lit. a), 51 II, 64 I lit. a), 72 I, 73 I, II.[21] Sie ist ferner Voraussetzung für den Anspruch auf Ersatzlieferung, Art. 46 II, da in diesem Fall die vertragswidrige Ware oft – wie bei einer Vertragsaufhebung – (zurück)transportiert werden muss, ein Ersatzlieferungsverlangen deshalb wirtschaftlich ähnliche Konsequenzen hat wie eine Vertragsaufhebung.[22] Schließlich belässt ein wesentlicher Vertragsbruch dem Käufer alle Rechtsbehelfe trotz an sich eingetretenen Gefahrübergangs, Art. 70. Die Hauptbedeutung des Begriffs, der zutreffend als „Angelpunkt des Sanktionensystems" des CISG bezeichnet wird,[23] liegt dabei in seiner Funktion als **Vertragsaufhebungsvoraussetzung**.

6

Wie aus der systematischen Stellung des Art. 25 in den „Allgemeinen Bestimmungen" des Teil III der Konvention deutlich wird, schafft diese Vorschrift eine **einheitliche Definition** der „wesentlichen Vertragsverletzung",[24] die in allen daran anknüpfenden Übereinkommensnormen grundsätzlich inhaltsgleich zur Anwendung gelangt.[25] Ob ein bestimmter Rechtsbehelf infolge der Umstände des Einzelfalls ausscheidet, obwohl ein wesentlicher Vertragsbruch vorgefallen ist, ist keine Frage des Art. 25, sondern richtet sich nach den insoweit sachlich einschlägigen Vorschriften. Eine „rechtsfolgenorientierte" Auslegung des Art. 25, wie sie gelegentlich im Schrifttum vorgeschlagen wird,[26] ist hingegen abzulehnen.

7

2. Inhalt und Umstände des betroffenen Vertrages als vorrangiger Ansatzpunkt

Eine **Definition** der Schwelle zur Auflösung des Vertrages, d. h. **des Gewichts einer Vertragsverletzung**, muss notwendig auf das Pflichtenprogramm des jeweiligen Vertrages

8

---

[18] S. unten Rn. 26, 27, 36.
[19] S. O. R., S. 295 ff.; zum Ganzen schon *Lurger*, IHR 2001, 92 und unten Rn. 35, 36.
[20] Vgl. *Bianca/Bonell/Will*, Art. 25, Anm. 1.: „The definition [in Art. 25] purports to separate a nonfundamental and a fundamental breach of contract. The distinction is of cardinal importance for the system of remedies, because it can determine the life or death of the contract"; *Zeller*, Damages, S. 193: „... plays a crucial role within the remedial system of the CISG".
[21] In bestimmten, abschließend geregelten Fällen kann auch das Setzen einer Nachfrist über Artt. 49 I lit. b), 64 I lit. b) den Weg zur Vertragsaufhebung eröffnen; vgl. dazu noch unten Rn. 10, 11.
[22] Anschaulich *Michida*, 27 Am. J. Comp. L. (1979), 279, 281 zu den Besonderheiten im internationalen Warenverkehr: Zurückgewiesene Ware ist in nicht wenigen Ländern mangels ausreichender Kommunikations-, Transport- und Lagermöglichkeiten oft nicht umgehend zu verwerten oder zurückzusenden und deshalb der Gefahr des Verderbs ausgesetzt.
[23] *Aicher*, S. 124; *Schwimann/Posch*, Art. 25, Rn. 2.
[24] Von einer systematischen Fehlplatzierung des Art. 25 kann daher keine Rede sein; in diesem Sinne aber *Grebler*, 101 ASIL Proc. (2007), 407, 408 Fn. 5 („somewhat out of order").
[25] MünchKomm/*Gruber*, Art. 25, Rn. 8; MünchKomm/*P. Huber*, Art. 46, Rn. 30; Staudinger/*Magnus*, Art. 25, Rn. 7.
[26] *Berger/Scholl*, FS Schwenzer, S. 165; *Karollus*, ZIP 1993, 490, 496; *Honsell/Gsell*, Art. 25, Rn. 9 (im Anschluss an *Honsell/Karollus*, 1. Aufl., Art. 25, Rn. 12).

und die konkrete Vertragsverletzung bezogen sein; jede abstrakte Definition hat, sofern sie nicht als wertungsoffene, sondern als glatt subsumtionsfähige Formel (miss)verstanden wird, Kritik zu erwarten.[27] Das erklärt die wechselnden Definitionsversuche in den Entwürfen, und es überrascht nicht, dass bereits auf der Haager Konferenz und später in den UNCITRAL-Beratungen[28] immer wieder der Vorschlag gemacht worden ist, auf eine Definition dieser Auflösungsschwelle ganz zu verzichten.

9 Die schließlich angenommene und in Art. 25 niederlegte Begriffsdefinition ist vereinzelt aus Perspektive der ökonomischen Analyse des Rechts ihrer Unbestimmtheit wegen kritisiert worden; ihr wird zudem vorgeworfen, keine kosteneffiziente Auffanglösung darzustellen, die für viele Parteien passt.[29] Richtig ist das Gegenteil: Das Ziel eines **wirtschaftlich effizienten** Rechtsbehelfssystem war einer der entscheidenden Gründe dafür, dass die Verfasser des Übereinkommens die Rückabwicklung von Kaufverträgen auf Fälle „wesentlicher" Vertragsbrüche begrenzten, weil die durch eine Vertragsrückabwicklung häufig bewirkte Notwendigkeit eines Rücktransports von Waren über erhebliche Distanzen kostenträchtig und daher vielfach weniger effizient ist als ein Rückgriff auf sonstige Rechtsbehelfe.[30] Die Rolle des Art. 25 besteht in diesem Zusammenhang darin, die Präferenzen der jeweiligen Vertragsparteien – wie im Kaufvertrag festgelegt[31] oder ersatzweise anhand der Vertragsumstände ermittelbar – in das Rechtsbehelfssystem der Konvention einzuspeisen, um dadurch dessen Auffangregeln in ihrer Anwendung auf die Besonderheiten der konkreten Vertragsbeziehung abzustimmen. Die Konturen einer „wesentlichen" Vertragsverletzung sind deshalb immer so präzise oder vage wie die im Kaufvertrag ausgedrückten Parteierwartungen. Allgemeine Maßstäbe greifen im Rahmen des Art. 25 hingegen nur dann Raum, wenn die Parteien ihre Präferenzen nicht oder nicht ausreichend spezifiziert haben.

3. Begrenzte Rolle der Nachfrist

10 Neben dem Vertragsaufhebungsrecht nach wesentlicher Vertragsverletzung der anderen Partei (Artt. 49 I lit. a), 64 I lit. a)) ermöglicht das UN-Kaufrecht in bestimmten Fällen[32] auch dann eine Lösung vom Vertrag, wenn der vertragstreue Käufer (Art. 49 I lit. b)) oder Verkäufer (Art. 64 I lit. b)) der anderen Partei eine angemessene **Nachfrist** gesetzt und die geschuldete Leistung innerhalb dieser Frist nicht erfolgt ist. Es handelt sich dabei um ein **alternatives Vertragsaufhebungsrecht,** welches das Recht, bei Vorliegen einer „wesentlichen" Vertragsverletzung auf Grundlage von Art. 49 I lit. a) oder Art. 64 I lit. a) Vertragsaufhebung zu erklären, unberührt lässt. Der letztgenannte Rechtsbehelf entfällt daher weder dadurch, dass eine Nachfrist gesetzt wurde oder hätte gesetzt werden können,[33] noch ist eine (zusätzliche) Nachfristsetzung erforderlich, um nach einer erfolgten wesentlichen Vertragsverletzung i. S. d. Art. 25 Vertragsaufhebung erklären zu können.[34]

---

[27] Wie hier *Grebler,* 101 ASIL Proc. (2007), 407, 411; *Peacock,* 8 Int'l Trade & Bus. L. Ann (2003), 95, 100.
[28] Vgl. hierzu *Eörsi,* 31 Am. J. Comp. L. (1983), 333, 336.
[29] *Gillette/Scott,* 25 Int'l Rev. L. & Econ. (2005), 446, 455 u. 474; Deutlich positivere Bewertung des Art. 25 demgegenüber in *Gillette,* Transaction Costs, S. 94.
[30] *Grebler,* 101 ASIL Proc. (2007), 407, 410; *Hillman,* 1 Rev. CISG (1995), 21, 31; *U. Huber,* ZEuP 2008, 708, 727; *Singh/Leisinger,* 20 Pace Int'l L. Rev. (2008), 161, 168 f.
[31] BGH, 3.4.1996, CISG-online 135 = BGHZ 132, 290, 298 spricht von der „zweckmäßigen Möglichkeit", die „für wesentlich gehaltenen Pflichten im Vertrag ausdrücklich als solche festzuhalten".
[32] S. zu diesen sogleich im Text.
[33] Unzutreffend OLG Düsseldorf, 10.2.1994, CISG-online 115 = NJW-RR 1994, 506: im Falle einer „teilweisen Nichterfüllung" durch den Verkäufer (= Nichtlieferung) stellte das OLG fest, Art. 49 I lit. b bestimme, dass „der Käufer die Aufhebung des Vertrages nur erklären kann, wenn der Verkäufer die Ware nicht innerhalb der nach Art. 47 I gesetzten Frist liefert oder die Lieferung verweigert" – schon weil der Käufer keine Nachfrist gesetzt habe, stehe ihm kein Vertragsaufhebungsrecht zu; möglicherweise ebenso ICC, 11849/2003, CISG-online 1421 = YB Comm. Arb. 2006, 148, 156.
[34] ICC, 8786/1997, CISG-online 749; OLG Brandenburg, 18.11.2008, CISG-online 1734 = IHR 2009, 105, 111; OLG Koblenz, 21.11.2007, CISG-online 1733 = OLGR Koblenz 2008, 493, 494; unzutreffend LG Stendal, 12.10.2000, CISG-online 592 = IHR 2001, 30, 31 f.

Anders als das EKG sieht das CISG die Möglichkeit, durch Nachfristsetzung Zweifel über **11** das Gewicht einer Vertragsstörung zu beheben, dabei bewusst **nur** noch für die Fälle **Nichtlieferung** (Art. 49 I lit. b)), **Nichtzahlung** und **Nichtabnahme** (Art. 64 I lit. b)) vor.[35] Damit ist z. B. im Falle vertragswidriger Beschaffenheit der gelieferten Ware die dem Rücktritt entsprechende Vertragsaufhebung nur unter der (erschwerten) Voraussetzung möglich, dass der Sachmangel wesentlicher Vertragsbruch des Verkäufers i. S. d. Art. 25 ist. Überschreiten einer Nachfrist zur Mängelbehebung allein konstituiert dagegen unter dem CISG – anders als nach §§ 437 Nr. 2, 323 I BGB – keinen Aufhebungsgrund.[36]

4. Begriffsäquivalente außerhalb des CISG; autonome Auslegung des Art. 25

Wie bereits einleitend[37] ausgeführt, ist die Festlegung einer „Schwelle" für die Rück- **12** abwicklung gestörter Verträge allen Rechtsordnungen gemeinsam. Nationale Rechte wie auch jüngere Einheitsrechtsprojekte und Vertragsrechtsprinzipien enthalten daher jeweils funktionelle Äquivalente zur „wesentlichen Vertragsverletzung" des Art. 25. Nicht selten sind diese Rechtsfiguren – und gelegentlich auch weitere Rechtsfiguren, die einem anderen Zweck dienen – begrifflich ähnlich benannt, wie etwa die Doktrin des „fundamental breach" des englischen Rechts. Begriffsäquivalente finden sich des Weiteren naturgemäß dort, wo sich andere Rechte bewusst an Art. 25 orientiert haben,[38] wie etwa die skandinavischen Kaufgesetze,[39] das niederländische NBW, das estnische Schuldrechtsgesetz[40] oder das slowakische Handelsgesetzbuch.[41] Selbiges gilt auch für internationale oder regionale Rechtsvereinheitlichungsprojekte wie die PICC und die PECL,[42] den DCFR der Europäischen Union[43] oder den Vorschlag für ein „Gemeinsames Europäisches Kaufrecht" (CESL).[44]

In Anbetracht dieser funktionellen und begrifflichen Nähe ist daran zu erinnern, dass Art. 25 nicht in Anknüpfung an nationale Vorverständnisse konzipiert wurde, sondern ausschließlich auf Grundlage des Haager Einheitskaufrechts entstanden ist.[45] Eine **Auslegung** des einheitsrechtlichen Begriffs der „wesentlichen Vertragsverletzung" unter **Berücksichtigung begriffsähnlicher** *faux amis* aus nationalen Rechten würde aus diesem Grund eine Verletzung sowohl des Art. 25 als auch der Auslegungsmethoden des Übereinkommens (Art. 7 I) bedeuten,[46] und auch die bloße Orientierung an nationalen Rechtsinstituten ist ausnahmslos **unzulässig**.[47] M. E. muss dasselbe auch für den Rückgriff auf scheinbar parallele Regelungskonzepte („wesentliche Nichterfüllung") in internationalen Einheitsrechtstexten wie namentlich den PICC, den PECL und dem CESL-Entwurf gelten.[48]

---

[35] Der Ablauf der vergeblich gesetzten Nachfrist macht die genannten Leistungsstörungen in der Sache zum wesentlichen Vertragsbruch; anschaulich formulierten noch Art. 27 II 2, Art. 31 II 2 EKG: „Wird die Lieferung nicht innerhalb dieser Frist ... bewirkt, so stellt dies eine wesentliche Vertragsverletzung dar".
[36] S. auch unten Rn. 48 f.
[37] S. oben Rn. 1 f.
[38] Dazu bereits oben in Rn. 2.
[39] Zum Einfluss auf das Kaufrecht der skandinavischen Staaten s. *Göritz*, Wesentliche Vertragsverletzung beim Warenkauf, S. 46 ff.
[40] *Schlechtriem*, Juridica Int. 2001, 16, 20.
[41] So zu § 345 II slow. HGB Krajský súd v Košiciach, 28.5.2007, CISG-online 1950.
[42] Vgl. hierzu *Schlechtriem*, ZEuP 1993, 217, 234 ff.
[43] Vgl. (zu Art. III-3:502 DCFR) *U. Huber*, ZEuP 2008, 708, 725; *P. Huber*, FS Schwenzer, S. 821 ff.; *Troiano*, IHR 2008, 221, 247: „The similarities are striking".
[44] Art. 87 II CESL-Entwurf („wesentliche Nichterfüllung").
[45] *Honnold/Flechtner*, Art. 25, Rn. 181.1; *Zeller*, Damages, S. 198.
[46] *Bianca/Bonell/Will*, Art. 25, Anm. 2.; *Ferrari u. a./Ferrari*, Internationales Vertragsrecht, Art. 25, Rn. 3; *Honnold/Flechtner*, Art. 25, Rn. 181.1: „of course"; *Honsell/Gsell*, Art. 25, Rn. 8; *Staudinger/Magnus*, Art. 25, Rn. 10; *Zeller*, Damages, S. 195 ff.; a. A. *Musger*, S. 9.
[47] Unhaltbar deshalb der Ansatz in *Hilaturas Miel, SL v. Republic of Iraq*, U. S. Dist. Ct. (S. D. N. Y.), 20.8.2008, CISG-online 1777 = 573 F.Supp.2d 781, 799 f. (Rückgriff auf § 2–614 UCC bei Auslegung des Art. 25).
[48] Toleranter (und riskanter) *Koch*, Art. 25 CISG–PICC, S. 129 f. (zu Art. 7.3.1 PICC).

Mit Blick auf die Vorgaben des Art. 7 I unproblematisch (und im Sinne einer Kongruenz der internationalen und nationalen Begriffsverwendung wünschenswert) ist hingegen die gleichsam umgekehrte **Beachtung des Art. 25** bei der Interpretation nationalen Rechts,[49] anderer internationaler Rechtsakte und grundsätze sowie vertraglicher Klauseln. So ist in der Rechtsprechung etwa auf Art. 25 zurückgegriffen worden, um den Begriff des „material breach" in einem Schweizer unvereinheitlichtem Recht unterliegenden Vertrag auszulegen, weil die Übereinkommensvorschrift das übliche Begriffsverständnis im internationalen Handelsverkehr widerspiegele.[50] Auch Art. 87 II CESL-Entwurf dürfte in enger Anlehnung an Art. 25 CISG interpretiert werden.

III. Voraussetzungen einer „wesentlichen Vertragsverletzung"

1. Pflichtverletzung des Schuldners

13 Mittels seiner Bezugnahme auf eine „von einer Partei begangene Vertragsverletzung" setzt Art. 25 zunächst voraus, dass Verkäufer oder Käufer mindestens eine[51] ihrer Pflichten aus dem Vertrag oder dem Übereinkommen verletzt haben. Ob die Nichterfüllung dabei auf der Nichterfüllung durch einen Dritten beruht, dessen die Partei sich zur völligen oder teilweisen Vertragserfüllung bedient, oder auf einen außerhalb ihres Einflußbereichs liegenden Hinderungsgrund zurückgeht (s. **Art. 79 I, II**), macht für die Zwecke des Art. 25 keinen Unterschied.[52] Wurde die Nichterfüllung dagegen durch eine Handlung oder Unterlassung der anderen Partei verursacht, so handelt es sich – wie **Art. 80** andeutet – zwar dessen ungeachtet um eine Pflichtverletzung,[53] die jedoch regelmäßig nicht als „wesentlich" zu qualifizieren sein wird.[54] Eine Störung der Vertragserfüllung durch die andere Partei stellt allerdings ihrerseits eine Pflichtverletzung dar, sofern die störende Partei durch ihr Verhalten eine eigene Pflicht verletzt.[55]

14 a) **Pflichtenarten.** Verkäufer und Käufer im internationalen Handelsverkehr sehen sich typischerweise einer Reihe von Pflichten gegenüber, die aus den unterschiedlichsten Quellen (ausdrücklichen Vertragsklauseln und impliziten Vereinbarungen, Gepflogenheiten und Gebräuchen, den Vorschriften des UN-Kaufrechts, sonstiger internationaler Regelwerke und nationaler Rechte) fließen können. Unter diesen bezieht sich der Begriff der „Vertragsverletzung" i. S. d. Art. 25 allein auf den Vertragsparteien „nach dem Vertrag oder diesem Übereinkommen obliegende Pflichten", wie sich aus einer systematischen Auslegung der Norm unter Beachtung weiterer Übereinkommensbestimmungen erschließt, die ebenfalls den Begriff der wesentlichen Vertragsverletzung verwenden.[56] Die Rechtsfolgen der Verletzung anderer Pflichten sind demgegenüber nicht Gegenstand des Art. 25.

---

[49] Krajský súd v Košiciach, 28.5.2007, CISG-online 1950: § 345 II slow. HGB anhand von Art. 25 ausgelegt.
[50] BGer, 16.12.2009, CISG-online 2047 = IHR 2010, 258, 259 f. (das ICC-Schiedsgericht und das BGer im Aufhebungsverfahren gegen den ergangenen Schiedsspruch zogen ergänzend Art. 7.3.1 PICC heran).
[51] Zu mehrfachen Pflichtverletzungen unter Art. 25 s. noch unten Rn. 20.
[52] Vgl. ICC, 8128/1995, CISG-online 526 = J. D. I. 1996, 1024 ff.: österreichischer Verkäufer hatte sich seines ukrainischen Zulieferers bedient, um das verkaufte Düngemittel an den Schweizer Käufer zu liefern, aber der Zulieferer konnte aus technischen Gründen den Vorgaben des Kaufvertrages nicht gerecht werden – wesentlicher Vertragsbruch des Verkäufers (Art. 79 II).
[53] *Peacock*, 8 Int'l Trade & Bus. L. Ann. (2003), 95, 101; a. A. *Brunner*, Art. 25, Rn. 5; *Ferrari u. a./Ferrari*, Internationales Vertragsrecht, Art. 25, Rn. 5.
[54] S. noch unten Rn. 18.
[55] So wirkt sich eine Annahmeverweigerung durch den Käufer nicht nur auf die Erfüllung der Verkäuferpflicht zur Lieferung (Artt. 30 f.) aus und verhindert die Wesentlichkeit der Vertragsverletzung des Verkäufers (Art. 80), sondern verletzt zugleich die Pflicht des Käufers zur Annahme aus Art. 60, worin ihrerseits (potentiell) ein wesentlicher Vertragsbruch des Käufers liegen kann (s. noch unten Rn. 67).
[56] Vgl. vor allem Art. 49 I lit. a) („wenn die Nichterfüllung einer dem Verkäufer nach dem Vertrag oder diesem Übereinkommen obliegenden Pflicht eine wesentliche Vertragsverletzung darstellt") und dessen Gegenstück in Art. 64 I lit. a), aber auch die Abschnittsüberschriften zu Teil III, Kapitel II, Abschnitt III und Kapitel III, Abschnitt III des Übereinkommens („Rechtsbehelfe … wegen Vertragsverletzung durch den

aa) Vertragspflichten. Eine Vertragsverletzung i. S. d. Art. 25 liegt einerseits vor, wenn 15 der Schuldner eine vertragliche Pflicht verletzt hat, die zum **Pflichtenprogramm nach CISG** gehört (Lieferung der Ware und Dokumente zur rechten Zeit, am rechten Ort und in vertragsmäßiger Beschaffenheit, Zahlung und Abnahme), wozu auch die in Artt. 49 I lit. b), 64 I lit. b) genannten Pflichten[57] und etwa die Pflicht zur Rückgabe der Ware an den Käufer nach Vornahme einer gem. Art. 46 III geschuldeten Nachbesserung[58] zählen. Nicht erforderlich ist, dass die Pflicht im Kaufvertrag gesonderte Erwähnung gefunden hat; es genügt, dass sie sich aus den Vorschriften des Übereinkommens ergibt.

Die Vertragspflicht kann allerdings ebenso eine von den Parteien geschaffene und ausgestaltete **Pflicht** *sui generis* sein,[59] vorausgesetzt, sie ist Bestandteil eines Vertrages, der in den Anwendungsbereich des CISG fällt.[60] Beispiele sind Pflichten zur Information, zur Instruktion,[61] zur Bewahrung von Betriebsgeheimnissen, zum Schutz eines Markenrechts,[62] zu Verwendungsbeschränkungen oder Vertriebsbindungen für die Ware, etwa Reimportverbote[63] oder Exklusivitätsvereinbarungen,[64] aber auch ein im Kaufvertrag vereinbartes Wettbewerbsverbot.[65] Auch die Verletzung einer Unterlassungspflicht kann für Art. 25 ausreichen.[66] Darüber hinaus stellt auch der Verstoß gegen eine zwischen den Parteien entstandene Gepflogenheit oder gegen einen einschlägigen Handelsbrauch eine „Vertragsverletzung" i. S. d. Art. 25 dar, weil Gebräuche und Gepflogenheiten als Inhalt des Vertragsbandes zwischen den Parteien behandelt werden (Art. 9).[67]

bb) Außervertragliche Pflichten. Die Verletzung außervertraglicher Pflichten ist, selbst 16 wenn sie gravierend ist, nicht notwendig Vertragsbruch oder gar wesentliche Vertragsverletzung: Eine nach Produkthaftungsregeln „defekte", weil hinter berechtigten Sicherheitserwartungen des Publikums zurückbleibende Sache kann vertragsgemäß sein, da ihre Eigenschaften so vereinbart sein können. Auch wenn der Defekt eine Vertragswidrigkeit darstellt, muss dies nicht stets eine wesentliche Vertragsverletzung sein, und zwar selbst dann nicht, wenn der Mangel eine Körperverletzung oder Sachbeschädigung ausgelöst hat: Der Defekt eines im Vergleich zur gesamten Kaufsache geringwertigen Schwimmschalters[68] muss nicht

---

Verkäufer" bzw. „durch den Käufer") mit den sich unmittelbar anschließenden Artt. 45 I, 64 I („Erfüllt der Verkäufer [bzw. der Käufer] eine seiner Pflichten nach dem Vertrag oder diesem Übereinkommen nicht, ...").

[57] S. bereits oben Rn. 10.
[58] RB Arnhem, 29.7.2009, CISG-online 1939.
[59] OLG Brandenburg, 18.11.2008, CISG-online 1734 = IHR 2009, 105, 111. Zu Unrecht einschränkend BGer, 15.9.2000, CISG-online 770, wo vorausgesetzt wird, dass die Verletzung einer Nebenpflicht Auswirkungen auf die Erfüllung einer Hauptpflicht hat („la violation d'une obligation accessoire ne peut constituer une contravention essentielle que si elle a des répercussions sur l'exécution des obligations principales de manière telle que l'intérêt du créancier à l'exécution du contrat disparaisse").
[60] *Brunner*, Art. 25, Rn. 4; ähnlich MünchKommHGB/*Benicke*, Art. 25, Rn. 4: bei durch Parteivereinbarung begründeter Pflicht ist erforderlich, dass diese in engem Zusammenhang mit dem Güteraustausch steht. Etwas anders MünchKomm/*Gruber*, Art. 25, Rn. 10: Voraussetzung sei, die Pflicht gehöre noch zur Materie „Kaufrecht" oder sei von den Parteien einvernehmlich – eventuell konkludent – der Regelung des CISG unterstellt worden. Zur Anwendung des CISG auf Verträge, deren Pflichtenprogramm neben originär kaufrechtlichen Pflichten auch andersartige Pflichten umfasst, vgl. oben *Ferrari*, Art. 3 Rn. 12 ff., 16.
[61] Vgl. ICC, 8128/1995, CISG-online 526 = Dir. com. int. 1998, 1094 ff.: Erforderliche Instruktionen für die Herstellung von Spezialsäcken.
[62] Vgl. OLG Frankfurt a. M., 17.9.1991, CISG-online 28 = NJW 1992, 633, 635 („Marlboro"): Verpflichtung der Lieferantin, ein der Bestellerin zustehendes Markenrecht zu schützen.
[63] S. CA Grenoble, 22.2.1995, CISG-online 151 = J. D. I. 1995, 632 ff. m. Anm. *Kahn*, J. D. I. 1995, 639 ff.; *C. Witz*, D. 1995, Chron. 143; *Witz*, FS Neumayer, S. 452 f.; *Witz/Wolter*, RIW 1995, 810–811 zur Verletzung des Verbots, in ein bestimmtes Land weiterzuliefern; OLG Koblenz, 31.1.1997, CISG-online 256 = IHR 2003, 172, 174. S. zu solchen „Zusatzpflichten" auch unten Rn. 68 f.
[64] OLG Koblenz, 31.1.1997, CISG-online 256 = IHR 2003, 172, 174; HGer Aargau, 26.9.1997, CISG-online 329 = SZIER 1998, 78 ff.
[65] MünchKommHGB/*Benicke*, Art. 25, Rn. 4; a. A. MünchKomm/*Gruber*, Art. 25, Rn. 11.
[66] OLG Frankfurt a. M., 24.3.2009, CISG-online 2165 = IHR 2010, 250, 253.
[67] Trib. Forlì, 11.12.2008, CISG-online 1729; *Ferrari u. a./Ferrari*, Internationales Vertragsrecht, Art. 25, Rn. 5.
[68] Vgl. BGH, 24.11.1976, BGHZ 67, 359 ff.

notwendig einen wesentlichen Vertragsbruch darstellen, der Aufhebung des Vertrages rechtfertigt, und zwar unabhängig davon, ob er schon „weitergefressen" hat oder nicht. Entscheidend ist, ob und inwieweit die Verletzung einer außervertraglichen Pflicht zugleich die Verpflichtung des Verkäufers zur Leistung in vertragsgemäßer Beschaffenheit verletzt, und ob diese Vertragsverletzung „wesentlich" ist[69] (s. unten Rn. 68 f.).

17 **cc) Schutzpflichten.** Eine Verletzung von Schutzpflichten i. S. des § 241 II BGB ist ebenfalls (nur) dann für Art. 25 und die an die Voraussetzung „wesentlicher Vertragsbruch" anknüpfenden Vorschriften relevant, wenn und soweit sie – unabhängig von ihrem Geltungsgrund im nationalen Recht – als vertraglich vereinbart qualifiziert werden können. Dabei dürfen jedoch theoretisch-dogmatische Erklärungsversuche zu entsprechenden Rechtsfiguren im (internen) nationalen Recht, die zu einer Ausweitung unterstellter vertraglicher Abreden geführt haben, um bestimmte Vorteile der vertraglichen Haftung greifen zu lassen, nicht unbesehen übernommen werden: Pflichten zum Schutz von Sach- und Lebensgütern der jeweils anderen Partei, Informationspflichten zum gefahrlosen Umgang mit der Ware usw. können bei grenzüberschreitenden Verträgen nicht ohne weiteres als parteivereinbart unterstellt werden.

18 **b) Folgen eines Zurückbehaltungsrechts des Schuldners.** Eine Pflichtverletzung ist grundsätzlich **nicht** gegeben, wenn der Schuldner ein Recht hat, die Erfüllung der Pflicht zu verweigern: Kann der vorleistungspflichtige Verkäufer die Leistung wegen Verschlechterung der wirtschaftlichen Lage des Käufers nach Art. 71 zurückhalten, dann ist der Käufer nicht zur Auflösung des Vertrages wegen wesentlichen Vertragsbruchs des Schuldners berechtigt.[70] Entsprechendes gilt für das Aussetzungsrecht des Käufers gemäß Art. 71, das einer wesentlichen Vertragsverletzung durch den Käufer und damit einem daran anknüpfenden Vertragsaufhebungsrecht des Verkäufers (Art. 64 I lit. a)) entgegensteht.[71] Unterbleibt eine zur Pflichterfüllung erforderliche Mitwirkung des Gläubigers, dann kann die Pflichtverletzung nach Art. 80 nicht als wesentlicher Vertragsbruch bewertet werden.[72]

19 **c) Vorsatz des Schuldners irrelevant.** Im Schrifttum wird teilweise vorgeschlagen, eine vorsätzliche Pflichtverletzung **stets** als wesentlich zu qualifizieren,[73] und auch nach Art. 7.3.1 II lit. c) PICC soll berücksichtigt werden, ob eine Nichterfüllung absichtlich oder leichtfertig geschah.[74] Dem beschriebenen Ansatz ist im Anwendungsbereich des Art. 25 m. E. **nicht** zu folgen, weil dessen „wesentliche Vertragsverletzung" bewusst als objektive Schwelle konzipiert wurde;[75] da es auf die subjektive Haltung des Schuldners zur Pflichtverletzung mithin gerade nicht ankommen soll, dürfen Aspekte wie Verschulden, Fahrlässigkeit o. ä., die im Übereinkommen keine einheitsrechtliche Regelung erfahren haben, keine Rolle spielen.[76]

---

[69] Wie hier *Honsell/Gsell*, Art. 25, Rn. 11.
[70] BGH, 27.11.2007, CISG-online 1617, Rn. 32; Trib. Forlì, 11.12.2008, CISG-online 1729; *Achilles*, Art. 25, Rn. 2; *Brunner*, Art. 25, Rn. 5; *Honsell/Gsell*, Art. 25, Rn. 11; *Witz/Salger/Lorenz/Salger*, Art. 25, Rn. 5.
[71] OLG Hamm, 22.9.1992, CISG-online 57 = TranspR-IHR 1999, 24 (in concreto nicht bewiesen).
[72] Trib. Forlì, 11.12.2008, CISG-online 1729; *Brunner*, Art. 25, Rn. 5; zur Geltung des Art. 80 auch für den Rechtsbehelf der Vertragsaufhebung s. *Enderlein/Maskow/Strohbach*, Art. 80, Anm. 3.1. („kein Aufhebungsrecht"); sowie unten *Schwenzer*, Art. 80 Rn. 8.
[73] *Honsell/Karollus*, 1. Aufl., Art. 25, Rn. 23; erwogen bei Arglist von OLG Hamburg, 14.12.1994, CISG-online 216. Differenzierend *Bamberger/Roth/Saenger*, Art. 25, Rn. 8b: arglistiges Unterschieben vertragswidriger Ware erschüttert die Vertrauensgrundlage zwischen den Parteien und kann wesentliche Vertragsverletzung begründen, sofern deren Bestehen für die Vertragsbeziehung noch von Bedeutung ist, weil die vertragsbrüchige Partei z. B. noch nicht vollständig erfüllt hat.
[74] Ähnlich (zu Art. 25 CISG) *Brunner*, Art. 25, Rn. 8: Indiz für wesentliche Vertragsverletzung, wenn Vertragsbruch absichtlich oder grob fahrlässig herbeigeführt wurde. Mit Recht anders *Koch*, Art. 25 CISG–PICC, S. 130: Art. 7.3.1 PICC darf Auslegung des Art. 25 CISG nicht beeinflussen.
[75] Vgl. *Enderlein/Maskow/Strohbach*, Art. 45, Anm. 1.
[76] BGer, 15.9.2000, CISG-online 770: „L'importance de la violation n'est pas déterminante, seules l'étant les conséquences de celle-ci pour la partie lésée"; *Koch*, Art. 25 CISG–PICC, S. 130; *Magnus/Lüsing*, IHR 2007,

d) Mehrere Pflichtverletzungen. Die Schwelle einer „wesentlichen" Vertragsverlet- 20
zung muss nicht notwendigerweise durch eine einzelne Pflichtverletzung des Schuldners
verwirklicht werden. Fallen dem Schuldner unter ein und demselben Kaufvertrag mehrere
Pflichtverletzungen zur Last, so können diese **kumulativ** zur Folge haben, dass dem
Gläubiger i. S. d. Art. 25 im Wesentlichen entgeht, was er nach dem Vertrag hätte erwarten
dürfen.

2. Beeinträchtigung eines wesentlichen Vertragsinteresses: „Nachteil"

a) Bestimmung durch die Parteien entscheidend. Der von der Vertragsverletzung 21
betroffenen Partei muss ein **Nachteil** entstanden sein, den Art. 25 dadurch kennzeichnet,
„daß ihr im wesentlichen entgeht, was sie nach dem Vertrag hätte erwarten dürfen ...". Aus
der Entstehungsgeschichte[77] ergibt sich deutlich, dass damit nicht mehr – wie in den
Entwürfen – das Ausmaß eines Schadens gemeint ist, sondern die **Bedeutung des durch
den Vertrag** und seine einzelnen Pflichten **für den Gläubiger geschaffenen** und **konkretisierten Interesses.**[78] Der Vertrag lässt deshalb nicht nur die Pflichten der Parteien
entstehen, sondern bestimmt auch ihr Gewicht für den jeweiligen Gläubiger und damit das
seines „Nachteils".[79] Es ist folglich auch in erster Linie Sache der Parteien, im Vertrag selbst
deutlich zu machen, welches Gewicht den einzelnen Pflichten und den korrespondierenden
Interessen des Gläubigers zukommt.[80] Entsprechende Vertragsklauseln, die bestimmte
Pflichteninhalte explizit als „wesentlich" benennen, kommen in der jüngeren Vertragspraxis
zunehmend vor.[81]

Natürlich wird oft das Ausmaß eines möglichen Gläubigerschadens eine erhebliche Rolle 22
bei der Frage spielen, welche Bedeutung die Parteien der Erfüllung einer bestimmten Pflicht
zumessen bzw. – wenn im Nachhinein durch die Gerichte im Wege der **Vertragsauslegung (Art. 8)** zu ermitteln[82] – zugemessen haben,[83] doch ist für das Vorliegen eines
„Nachteils" i. S. d. Art. 25 eben **nicht** zwingend **erforderlich,** dass der durch die Vertragsverletzung beeinträchtigten Partei überhaupt irgendein messbarer **Schaden** entstanden ist.[84]
Eine wesentliche Vertragsverletzung kann daher bereits vorliegen, wenn ein Schaden noch
nicht eingetreten ist, sondern lediglich droht.[85]

1, 2; MünchKomm/*Gruber,* Art. 25, Rn. 13; MünchKommHGB/*Benicke,* Art. 25, Rn. 5, 30. Auch BGH, 3.4.1996, CISG-online 135 = BGHZ 132, 290, 303 bezeichnet die hier ablehnte Auffassung als „nicht unbedenklich".

[77] Oben Rn. 4.

[78] Wie hier Oberster Gerichtshof Polen, 11.5.2007, CISG-online 1790; *Ferrari/Ferrari,* Internationales Vertragsrecht, Art. 25, Rn. 9; *Lookofsky,* Understanding the CISG, § 6.8; *Peacock,* 8 Int'l Trade & Bus. L. Ann (2003), 95, 102; a. A. – auch auf den objektiv eingetretenen Schaden abstellend – MünchKommHGB/*Benicke,* Art. 25, Rn. 8.

[79] Vgl. das bei *Posch/Kandut,* S. 63, wiedergegebene Zitat von *Aicher:* Wesentlich sei ein Vertragsbruch dann, „wenn ein Risiko zu Lasten der Vertragsgegenseite verwirklicht wird, das die verletzte Vertragsbestimmung erkennbar hintanhalten sollte"; ferner *Karollus,* S. 91; *Honsell/Gsell,* Art. 25, Rn. 12; *Staudinger/Magnus,* Art. 25, Rn. 11. Mit Art. 6 – also einer vertraglichen Abweichung von Art. 25 – hat dies nichts zu tun; nicht überzeugend insoweit *Singh/Leisinger,* 20 Pace Int'l L. Rev. (2008), 161, 164.

[80] OGH, 21.6.2005, CISG-online 1047 = IHR 2005, 195, 196; BGH, 3.4.1996, CISG-online 135 = BGHZ 132, 290, 298; CISG-AC Op. 5 *(Schwenzer),* Comment 4.2, IHR 2006, 35, 38; *Peacock,* 8 Int'l Trade & Bus. L. Ann (2003), 95, 103; *Singh/Leisinger,* 20 Pace Int'l L. Rev. (2008), 161, 165.

[81] Vgl. etwa Audiencia Provincial de Madrid, 20.2.2007, CISG-online 1637 (ausführliche Klausel in spanisch-dänischem Kaufvertrag über Oliven).

[82] Oberster Gerichtshof Polen, 11.5.2007, CISG-online 1790; OLG Düsseldorf, 9.7.2010, CISG-online 2171 = IHR 2011, 116, 120.

[83] S. oben Rn. 4.

[84] BGer, 15.9.2000, CISG-online 770: „sans qu'il soit toutefois nécessaire que ce dernier [le créancier] subisse un préjudice pécuniaire"; Oberster Gerichtshof Polen, 11.5.2007, CISG-online 1790; *Ferrari u. a./ Ferrari,* Internationales Vertragsrecht, Art. 25, Rn. 8; *Neumayer/Ming,* Art. 25, Anm. 7.; *Peacock,* 8 Int'l Trade & Bus. L. Ann (2003), 95, 102; *Schwimann/Posch,* Art. 25, Rn. 9. Unklar *Grebler,* 101 ASIL Proc. (2007), 407, 409.

[85] *Staudinger/Magnus,* Art. 25, Rn. 11.

23 **b) Fallgruppen.** Kommt es den Vertragsparteien danach – wie beim Fixgeschäft – entscheidend auf den Zeitpunkt der Lieferung an, ist das vertraglich begründete Interesse, die Lieferung zu dem bestimmten Zeitpunkt zu erhalten, so wesentlich, dass unabhängig von einem konkreten Schaden des Käufers durch verspätete Lieferung Vertragsaufhebung erklärt werden kann.[86] Auch das Vorhandensein bestimmter Wareneigenschaften kann vertraglich als wesentlich definiert werden (und wird dies in der Praxis nicht selten auch[87]), sodass bei ihrem Fehlen der unmittelbare Weg zur Vertragsaufhebung eröffnet ist; bei echten Dokumentengeschäften findet sich vielfach eine vergleichbare Festlegung bezüglich der wesentlichen Bedeutung „reiner" Dokumente, wobei hier vor allem Handelsbräuche eine bedeutsame Rolle spielen.[88] Ebenso ist denkbar, dass ein Warendetail, das für den Käufer oder seinen Abnehmer von besonderer Bedeutung ist, während der Vertragsverhandlungen (Art. 8 III) als *conditio sine qua non* erwähnt wurde.[89]

24 Eine abstrakte Einteilung in Haupt- und Nebenpflichten, synallagmatische und nichtsynallagmatische Pflichten, Schutz- und Leistungspflichten ist in diesem Zusammenhang nicht erforderlich[90] und oft auch nicht hilfreich: Auch zusätzlich zu den typischen Pflichten eines (Werk-)Lieferungsvertrages vereinbarte Pflichten, z. B. zur Beachtung exklusiver Markenrechte des Bestellers, können für den Gläubiger erkennbar solche Bedeutung haben, dass ihre Verletzung als wesentlicher Vertragsbruch zu bewerten ist und Vertragsaufhebung ermöglicht.[91]

Im Übrigen sind die Konstellationen außerordentlich vielgestaltig; vgl. zur **bisherigen Rechtsprechungspraxis** im Einzelnen unten Rn. 37 ff.

3. Definition der „Wesentlichkeit" in Allgemeinen Geschäftsbedingungen

25 Fraglich ist, ob und inwieweit die „Aufwertung" einer Pflicht durch den Gläubiger in seinen vorformulierten Geschäftsbedingungen erfolgen kann, so dass damit ein wesentliches Vertragsinteresse i. S. d. Art. 25 entsteht.[92] Soweit ein Gesetzgeber bestimmte Klauseln für unzulässig erklärt, liegt eine nach nationalem Recht, also bei deutschem Vertragsstatut nach §§ 308, 309 BGB zu beurteilende **Gültigkeitsfrage** vor, Art. 4 S. 2 lit. a).[93] Eine verwendete Klausel, die generell alle Pflichten des anderen Teils zu essentiellen Vertragsbestimmungen **aufzuwerten** suchte, würde dem Verwender als Gläubiger ein weitgehendes Rücktrittsrecht verschaffen und dürfte deshalb gegen §§ 308 Nr. 3, 307 I 1, II Nr. 2 BGB verstoßen: Bei der Prüfung, ob ein „sachlich gerechtfertigter und im Vertrag angegebener Grund" vorliegt, wäre schon die Grundwertung des Einheitskaufrechts zu berücksichtigen, dass nicht jede Pflichtverletzung einen sachlich gerechtfertigten Grund zur Vertragsaufhebung darstellt, sondern nur eine Pflichtverletzung von erheblichem Gewicht für die Gläubigerinteressen.[94] Auch

---

[86] S. hierzu schon oben Rn. 4 und zu Nachweisen aus der Rechtsprechung unten Rn. 39.
[87] S. unten Rn. 44 ff.
[88] S. unten Rn. 62 ff.
[89] Trib. Busto Arsizio, 13.12.2001, CISG-online 1323 = Riv. dir. int. priv. proc. 2003, 150 ff.: Käufer einer Recyclingmaschine für Plastiksäcke hatte während der Vertragsverhandlungen wiederholt betont, dass die Maschine für einen bestimmten Sacktyp geeignet sein müsse, und hatte dem Verkäufer sogar ein Muster überlassen – Fähigkeit der Maschine zur Verarbeitung dieses Sacktyps war von wesentlicher Bedeutung. Vgl. aber OGH, 21.6.2005, CISG-online 1047 = IHR 2005, 195, 197 mit der Aussage, auf eine Vereinbarung zwischen Käufer und seinem Abnehmer könne es nicht ankommen, solange diese nicht Bestandteil des Vertrages zwischen Verkäufer und Käufer geworden sei – dies erscheint zu streng, weil der Inhalt der Absprache mit dem Abnehmer etwa während der Vertragsverhandlungen erwähnt worden sein kann, um dem Verkäufer dessen Bedeutung i. S. d. Art. 8 deutlich zu machen.
[90] Vgl. *Schwimann/Posch,* Art. 25, Rn. 12; *Witz/Salger/Lorenz/Salger,* Art. 25, Rn. 10; zu Unrecht anscheinend anders BGer, 15.9.2000, CISG-online 770.
[91] S. zur Wesentlichkeit bei der Verletzung nicht im CISG normierter Pflichten unten Rn. 68 f.
[92] Dafür *Butler,* IHR 2003, 208, 212 (mit englischsprachigem Klauselbeispiel).
[93] S. oben Vor Artt. 14–24 Rn. 3. A. A. *Peacock,* 8 Int'l Trade & Bus. L. Ann. (2003), 95, 103 (für Anwendung von Art. 7 I CISG).
[94] *Achilles,* Art. 25, Rn. 3; *Bamberger/Roth/Saenger,* Art. 25, Rn. 6; *Honsell/Gsell,* Art. 25, Rn. 25; MünchKomm/*Gruber,* Art. 25, Rn. 35; MünchKommHGB/*Benicke,* Art. 25, Rn. 39; *Witz/Salger/Lorenz/Salger,*

wird man eine solche Klausel oder auf einzelne Pflichten bezogene Standardbestimmungen, die einen solchen Effekt erreichen sollen, jedenfalls dann als überraschende Klauseln nach § 305c I BGB bewerten können, wenn nach den Umständen des Vertrages der Schuldner mit einem derartigen Gewicht der in Frage stehenden Pflichten nicht zu rechnen brauchte.[95] Unter Umständen kann bereits die Begründung einer zusätzlichen, im üblichen Leistungsprogramm grenzüberschreitender Warenkaufverträge im jeweiligen Geschäftszweig unüblichen Pflicht „überraschend" und deshalb unwirksam nach § 305c I BGB sein.

Im Übrigen müssen sich derartige Qualifizierungen von Pflichten in bzw. durch vorformulierte(n) Vertragsbedingungen des Gläubigers an § 307 BGB messen lassen.[96] Maßstab für die Abweichung von „wesentlichen Grundgedanken der gesetzlichen Regelung" ist freilich nicht das interne Recht, d. h. BGB/HGB und die daraus und in Anwendung des § 242 BGB entwickelten Wertungen, sondern das Einheitskaufrecht.[97] Dabei ist dem Einheitskaufrecht jedenfalls als Maßstab zu entnehmen, dass Auflösung des Vertrages oder Nachlieferungsverlangen, d. h. Rechtsbehelfe, die besonders im internationalen Warenverkehr kosten- und gefahrenträchtige (Rück-) Transporte und Lagerung der zurückgewiesenen Ware erfordern, nur bei schweren Leistungsstörungen gewährt werden.[98] Auch wenn das Gewicht der Leistungsstörung durch das Vertragsinteresse des Gläubigers definiert wird und damit im Rahmen der Parteiautonomie von den Vertragspartnern selbst bestimmt werden kann, dürfte eine einseitige und formelhafte Bestimmung für eine solche Aufwertung der in Frage stehenden Pflicht(en) nicht stets ausreichen. Man wird vielmehr zu prüfen haben, ob die fragliche Pflicht im jeweiligen Geschäftskreis unabhängig davon, ob sie individuell vereinbart, in vorformulierten Geschäftsbedingungen festgehalten oder auf der Grundlage von Art. 9 Vertragsinhalt geworden ist, als essentiell für den Vertrag bewertet wird.

Die vorstehend beschriebenen Grundsätze gelten entsprechend, wenn in Geschäftsbedingungen die wesentliche Vertragsverletzung – wie in der Praxis häufiger – als Grundlage für eine Vertragsaufhebung **ausgeschlossen** wird.[99]

4. Voraussehbarkeit und/oder Kenntnis als Auslegungsumstände

Selbst wenn ein Vertragsbruch wesentliche Nachteile für den Gläubiger zur Folge hat, stellt er ausweislich des Art. 25 a. E. keine wesentliche Vertragsverletzung dar, sofern der vertragsbrüchige Teil „diese Folge nicht vorausgesehen hat und eine vernünftige Person der 26

Art. 25, Rn. 17. In der Begründung anders *Peacock,* 8 Int'l Trade & Bus. L. Ann. (2003), 95, 103: Verstoß gegen guten Glauben i. S. d. Art. 7 I CISG.

[95] Zur Frage, ob § 305c I BGB funktionell als Ungültigkeitsnorm zu sehen ist, deren Anwendbarkeit nach Art. 4 S. 2 lit. a) unberührt bleibt, s. oben Vor Artt. 14–24 Rn. 5, Art. 14 Rn. 35.

[96] Vgl. BGH, 17.1.1990, BGHZ 110, 88, 97 f.: Fixklausel als überraschend i. S. v. § 3 AGBG a. F. und unangemessen i. S. v. § 9 AGBG a. F.

[97] OGH, 7.9.2000, CISG-online 642 = IHR 2001, 42, 43; OLG Linz, 23.3.2005, CISG-online 1376 = IHR 2007, 123, 127; OLG Düsseldorf, 21.4.2004, CISG-online 915 = IHR 2005, 24, 27; *Staudinger/Coester,* § 307, Rn. 238; sowie hier Vor Artt. 14–24 Rn. 3.

[98] *Botzenhardt,* S. 173.

[99] Vgl. OGH, 7.9.2000, CISG-online 642 = IHR 2001, 42, 43: „Zu den jedenfalls zu wahrenden Grundwertungen des UN-Kaufrechts zählt u. a. das Recht zur Aufhebung des Vertrages, das der vertragstreuen Partei als ultima ratio grundsätzlich erhalten bleiben muss, soweit die Gegenpartei die Ware auch nicht nach einer angemessenen verlängerten Frist liefert oder die Ware trotz einer Nacherfüllung im wesentlichen unbrauchbar bleibt. Wird auch dieses Aufhebungsrecht eingeschränkt, so muss der vertragstreuen Partei in jedem Fall ein Anspruch auf Ersatz des durch den Erfüllungsmangel entstandenen Schadens verbleiben"; AG Nordhorn, 14.6.1994, CISG-online 259: Bei italienisch-deutschem Kaufvertrag über Schuhe enthielten die AGB des italienischen Verkäufers eine Klausel, nach welcher der Käufer im Falle einer verspäteten Lieferung nur dann das Recht zur Vertragsaufhebung hatte, wenn er vorher schriftlich die Aufhebung des Vertrages angedroht hatte und die Ware nicht innerhalb von 15 Arbeitstagen ab Eingang dieses Schreibens beim Verkäufer abgesandt wurde – das Gericht erachtete die Klausel (nach ital. AGB-Recht) für wirksam, weil nach dem Klauselwortlaut nicht ausgeschlossen sei, dass die verlangte Ankündigung bereits vor Ablauf der Lieferfrist erfolgen könne; es ließ aber offen, ob dieses Ergebnis auch für Fixhandelsgeschäfte gelten würde.

gleichen Art diese Folge unter den gleichen Umständen auch nicht vorausgesehen hätte". Die Bedeutung der „Voraussehbarkeit" hat sich im Verlauf der Entstehungsgeschichte[100] geändert und ist deshalb unsicher; das unterschiedliche Verständnis der Funktion dieses Elements wird vor allem bei der Verteilung der Beweislast deutlich.[101] **Überwiegend** wird fehlende Voraussehbarkeit und Kenntnis – die sich, soviel ist sicher, im Rahmen des Art. 25 auf die Folge der Vertragsverletzung und nicht auf die Vertragsverletzung selbst oder deren Gründe bezieht[102] – als eine Art **subjektiver Entlastungsgrund** für die vertragsbrüchige Partei gesehen,[103] der Aufhebung oder Nachlieferungsverlangen sperrt. Andere Autoren erkennen in dem Tatbestandsmerkmal einen weiteren „Filter"[104] oder gar eine Art Nachteilsbegrenzung entsprechend der Voraussehbarkeitsregel für den Umfang des ersatzfähigen Schadens.[105]

27   Nach **zutreffender Auffassung** sind **Kenntnis oder Erkennbarkeit der Gläubigererwartungen** demgegenüber (lediglich) **Auslegungsumstände** für die Beurteilung des Gewichts der verletzten Pflicht und ihrer Bedeutung für den Gläubiger:[106] Ein Gläubiger ist nur dann berechtigt, „nach dem Vertrag" etwas als „wesentlich" zu erwarten, sofern sein Vertragspartner voraussah (oder eine vernünftige Person der gleichen Art unter den gleichen Umständen vorausgesehen hätte), dass durch den Vertragsschluss eine solche Erwartung begründet wurde. Was unbekannt und unvorhersehbar war, kann auch nicht berechtigterweise erwartet werden, und vermag einen Vertragsbruch daher nicht zum „wesentlichen" Vertragsbruch zu erheben.[107] Trotz der Kritik an Art. 10 EKG, der insoweit deutlicher regelte,[108] kann auf diesen Faktor für die Auslegung des Vertrages nicht verzichtet werden; Kenntnis oder Erkennbarkeit der Gläubigererwartungen sind bei der Auslegung im Übrigen auch nach Art. 8 II zu beachten.[109] Im Einzelnen sind folgende Möglichkeiten zu unterscheiden:

28   a) **Eindeutige Benennung der Pflichtenbedeutung im Vertrag.** Die Parteien können bestimmte Pflichten oder Pflichtmodalitäten im Vertrag selbst eindeutig als essentiell für den Gläubiger ausgestalten; für eine Korrektur mit Hilfe der Voraussehbarkeitsregel ist dann kein Raum. Bei eindeutigen Abmachungen, z. B. eines Fixtermins, kann der vertragsbrüchige Teil der Vertragsaufhebung nicht entgegenhalten, er habe einen Nachteil für den Gläubiger nicht vorausgesehen[110] – ganz abgesehen davon, dass es allein auf die subjektiven Erkenntnis- und Verständnismöglichkeiten bei klarem Vertragstext schon deshalb nicht

---

[100] Oben Rn. 5.
[101] Unten Rn. 36. Zum englischen Recht demgegenüber *Bridge,* Int'l Sale of Goods, Rn. 12.25: „not requiring that the party in breach foresee the requisite weight of the breach".
[102] In Int. Ct. Russian CCI, 2.11.2004, 188/2003, CISG-online 1285 wurde daher das Vorbringen des Verkäufers, er habe bei Vertragsschluss nicht vorhersehen können, dass sein Zulieferer seinen Vertrieb umorganisieren und daher nicht rechtzeitig liefern werde, zu Recht als für Art. 25 irrelevant zurückgewiesen; a. A. und unzutreffend *Butler,* IHR 2003, 208, 209.
[103] S. *Achilles,* Art. 25, Rn. 13 („Verschuldenskorrektiv"); *Bianca/Bonell/Will,* Art. 25, Anm. 2.2. et *passim; Enderlein/Maskow/Strohbach,* Art. 25, Anm. 4.1.; *Ghestin,* Fusion des actions, Nr. 238, S. 224 f.; *Heuzé,* Anm. 391; *Loewe,* Art. 25, S. 48; auch in Wien beruhten die Stellungnahmen überwiegend noch auf einem solchen Verständnis, s. O. R., S. 295 ff.; ferner oben Rn. 5.
[104] *Bianca/Bonell/Will,* Art. 25, Anm. 2.2.; MünchKommHGB/*Benicke,* Art. 25, Rn. 14; *Posch/Kandut,* S. 65; *Reinhart,* Art. 25, Rn. 7; *Schwimann/Posch,* Art. 25, Rn. 14.
[105] *Enderlein/Maskow/Strohbach,* Art. 25, Anm. 4.1. A. A. *Bridge,* Int'l Sale of Goods, Rn. 12.25.
[106] OGH, 21.6.2005, CISG-online 1047 = IHR 2005, 195, 196; *Bamberger/Roth/Saenger,* Art. 25, Rn. 9; *Brunner,* Art. 25, Rn. 5; *Honsell/Gsell,* Art. 25, Rn. 20; *Karollus,* S. 91; *Leisinger,* Fundamental Breach, S. 104 f.; wohl auch MünchKomm/*Gruber,* Art. 25, Rn. 18; *Staudinger/Magnus,* Art. 25, Rn. 15.
[107] *Bridge,* Int'l Sale of Goods, Rn. 12.25: „The justification for introducing foresight of loss at the contract date is that it defines the basis of the bargain between the parties".
[108] S. die Wiedergabe des Wortlauts von Art. 10 EKG oben in Rn. 5.
[109] Zutreffend hierzu oben *Schmidt-Kessel,* Art. 8 Rn. 39; *Witz/Salger/Lorenz/Salger,* Art. 25, Rn. 13.
[110] Wie hier Audiencia Provincial de Madrid, 20.2.2007, CISG-online 1637; CIETAC, 24.7.2007, CISG-online 2055; *Bijl,* EJCCL 2009, 19, 25; *Brunner,* Art. 25, Rn. 9; *Honsell/Gsell,* Art. 25, Rn. 19; *Peacock,* 8 Int'l Trade & Bus. L. Ann. (2003), 95, 105; *Schwenzer,* 25 J. L. & Com. (2005-06), 437; a. A. offenbar *Bianca/Bonell/Will,* Art. 25, Anm. 2.2.

ankommt, weil – und wenn – jedenfalls eine „vernünftige Person der gleichen Art" die entsprechende Vertragsbestimmung nicht missverstehen konnte.

b) Erörterung der Pflichtenbedeutung während der Vertragsanbahnung. Haben 29 die Parteien bei den Vertragsverhandlungen über die besondere Bedeutung bestimmter Pflichten und Pflichtmodalitäten gesprochen, ohne sie im Vertrag deutlicher zu qualifizieren, und kann der von einer Pflichtverletzung betroffene Gläubiger das beweisen, dann gilt das Gleiche: Ein bestimmter Lieferzeitpunkt kann entweder im Vertrag als „fix" bezeichnet werden, sich aber auch als essentiell aus dem sonstigen Inhalt des Vertrages oder – Art. 8 III – den Verhandlungen der Parteien ergeben.[111] Ein Ausstattungsdetail, vielleicht für die Abnehmer des Käufers unerlässlich, kann im Vertrag, aber auch in den Verhandlungen als conditio sine qua non, als „condition" i. S. d. englischen Rechts genannt worden sein.[112] Wesentlich wird oft die Pflicht sein, eine Transportversicherung abzuschließen.[113] Für ein bestimmtes, vom Käufer zum Export bestimmtes Gut kann eine Prüfbescheinigung, eine Ausfuhrgenehmigung etc. vom Verkäufer zu beschaffen sein und eine entsprechende Pflicht aus dem Vertrag hervorgehen.[114] Und es kann bei den Vertragsverhandlungen unmissverständlich (und beweisbar) deutlich gemacht worden sein, dass ohne diese Nebenleistungen der Käufer kein Interesse am Vertrag hatte, also ohne diese Nebenleistungspflicht den Vertrag nicht abgeschlossen hätte und deshalb bei ihrer Verletzung aufheben können will.[115] Die Information des Schuldners durch den Gläubiger, die bestimmte Pflichten entsprechend „aufwertet", kann – und wird häufig – auch in dem Hinweis auf erhebliche Schäden, die aus einer Pflichtverletzung drohen, zu sehen sein. „Entlastung" mangels Voraussehbarkeit kommt in diesen Fällen nicht in Betracht.

c) Übrige Konstellationen. Nur wenn die besondere Bedeutung einer verletzten 30 Pflicht nicht im Vertrag selbst festgeschrieben oder unstreitig in den Vertragsverhandlungen deutlich gemacht worden ist, kann es auf „Voraussehbarkeit" ankommen. Dabei geht es aber zunächst wieder um **Vertragsauslegung** nach Art. 8 II, III, denn es ist zu prüfen, ob eine vernünftige Partei der gleichen Art, d. h. im gleichen Handelszweig oder Wirtschaftssegment tätig (s. Schweizer Fassung: „... in gleicher Stellung"),[116] diese Bedeutung erkannt hätte. Für viele Pflichten ist das kein Problem: Kann der Verkäufer nicht leisten, weil er sich die Erfüllung seiner Lieferpflicht durch anderweitige Veräußerung unmöglich gemacht hat, dann muss er vernünftigerweise damit rechnen, dass die verletzte Lieferpflicht für den Käufer zentrale Bedeutung hatte.[117] Ist Saisonware versprochen worden, so ist es für einen vernünftigen Lieferanten in dieser Branche erkennbar, dass eine Verzögerung der Lieferung bis

---

[111] Vgl. ICC, 8128/1995, CISG-online 526 = Dir. com. int. 1998, 1094, 1096: Erkennbarkeit der Bedeutung des Lieferdatums auf Grund von Informationen des Abnehmers des Käufers (Drohung mit Vertragsstrafenverfall); BGer, 15.9.2000, CISG-online 770: Mitteilung an Verkäufer, dass eine Lieferverzögerung die Erfüllung der vertraglichen Verpflichtungen des Käufers gegenüber seinen Abnehmern verhindern werde; OLG Hamburg, 28.2.1997, CISG-online 261 = EWiR 1997, 791 *(Mankowski)*: Verwendung des Incoterm® CIF (s. dazu ausführlich Rn. 41); Trib. Forlì, 11.12.2008, CISG-online 1729.
[112] Hingegen sollen die Details einer Vereinbarung zwischen dem Käufer und seinem Kunden nach OGH, 21.6.2005, CISG-online 1047 = IHR 2005, 195, 197 insoweit ohne Bedeutung sein, wie diese nicht auch zwischen Verkäufer und Käufer Vertragsinhalt geworden sind – dies erscheint zu streng, weil bereits die Erwähnung von Abmachungen mit dem Endabnehmer während der Vertragsverhandlungen die daraus resultierenden Gläubigererwartungen erkennbar werden lassen kann.
[113] Vgl. *Neumayer/Ming*, Art. 25, Anm. 4.
[114] Vgl. *Enderlein/Maskow/Strohbach*, Art. 25, Anm. 3.4.: Analysezertifikate, Bedienungsanleitungen, vereinbarte Etikettierung; s. näher Rn. 60 f.
[115] Vgl. OLG Frankfurt a. M., 17.9.1991, CISG-online 28 = NJW 1992, 633, 634 („Marlboro" – Bedeutung der Exklusivität des Markenrechts für den Besteller).
[116] Vgl. *Schwimann/Posch*, Art. 25, Rn. 15: „Maßstab ist ein hypothetischer Vertragspartner, der im selben Handelszweig tätig ist, im Wesentlichen die gleiche Funktion ausübt, den gleichen sozio-ökonomischen Hintergrund und die gleiche Ausbildung hat wie der Vertragsbrüchige."
[117] Vgl. zum EKG LG Düsseldorf, 17.11.1983, in: *Schlechtriem/Magnus*, Art. 26 EKG, Nr. 6: Verkaufte PKW waren, nachdem der Käufer angeblich nicht rechtzeitig gezahlt hatte, umgehend anderweitig veräußert worden. Der Käufer hatte zu Recht aufgehoben.

zum Ende der Saison das Interesse des Käufers entscheidend beeinträchtigt.[118] Die Verwendung bestimmter Incoterms® kann ein Fixgeschäft begründen.[119] Hat der Verkäufer den Käufer damit beauftragt, seine Produkte im Käuferland zu vertreiben, so ist jeder Nachteil, der dadurch entsteht, dass die verkaufte Ware im Käuferland aus technischen Gründen gar keine Verwendung finden kann, nachgerade evident.[120] Auch das Ausmaß möglicher Verluste kann bedeuten, dass vernünftige Personen im gleichen Verkehrskreis der fraglichen Pflicht entsprechende Bedeutung beimessen. „Entlastung" mangels individueller Voraussehbarkeit kommt in solchen Fällen nicht in Betracht, da Art. 25 nicht nur fehlende Kenntnis des Schuldners, sondern **zusätzlich** auch Fehlen der objektiven Erkennbarkeit verlangt („und"). Ist auf Grund objektiver Kriterien, d. h. Erkennbarkeit der Bedeutung einer bestimmten Pflicht für Personen im gleichen Verkehrskreis, ein Interesse „essentiell" i. S. d. Art. 25, dann kann individuelle Unkenntnis oder Fehlbeurteilung nicht mehr entlasten.

31   Fehlt es an solch objektiver Erkennbarkeit, dann kommt es darauf an, ob der Schuldner die Umstände, die der fraglichen Pflicht eine besondere Bedeutung zukommen ließen (etwa drohender hoher Schaden für den Gläubiger auf Grund einer Nebenpflichtverletzung), gleichwohl kannte („vorausgesehen hat"), sei es, dass der Gläubiger rechtzeitig[121] entsprechende Hinweise gegeben hat,[122] sei es, dass der Schuldner über eigene Kenntnisse aus anderen Quellen verfügte. Dafür trägt freilich der Gläubiger die Beweislast.[123] „Entlastung" mangels Kenntnis ist dann eigentlich nur noch bei Irrtümern und Missverständnissen des Schuldners vorstellbar.

5. Zeitpunkt der Erkennbarkeit oder Kenntnis

32   Ob die Erkennbarkeit des Gläubigerinteresses für einen vernünftigen Schuldner oder die aktuelle Kenntnis in Fällen, in denen sich das Gewicht des (verletzten) Interesses nicht schon aus dem Vertrag selbst ergibt, spätestens bei Vertragsschluss gegeben sein muss oder auch noch nachträglich mit der Folge vermittelt werden kann, dass die verletzte Pflicht „aufgewertet" wird, ist in Wien trotz entsprechender Anregungen[124] nicht entschieden worden und im Schrifttum kontrovers. Ein Teil der Rechtsprechung[125] und der Autoren vertritt entsprechend der insoweit eindeutigen Fassung des Art. 10 EKG, dass der Zeitpunkt des Vertragsschlusses entscheidend sei.[126] Für die Aufhebung eines Sukzessivlieferungsvertrages

---

[118] Vgl. CA Milano, 20.3.1998, CISG-online 348 = Riv. dir. int. priv. proc. 1998, 170 ff.: Strickwaren für Jahresschlussverkauf; zu weiteren Fällen aus der Rechtsprechung s. unten Rn. 39.
[119] S. dazu näher unten Rn. 41.
[120] OGH, 21.6.2005, CISG-online 1047 = IHR 2005, 195, 197: Verkauf von Softwaremodulen von Deutschland nach Österreich, bei dem sich nach Vertragsschluss herausstellte, dass die von Seiten der Verkäuferin lieferbaren Programme in Österreich nicht verwendbar waren.
[121] S. unten Rn. 33.
[122] Vgl. OLG Frankfurt a. M., 17.9.1991, CISG-online 28 = NJW 1992, 633, 634 („Marlboro"). Zum EKG LG Dortmund, 23.9.1981, RIW 1981, 854 ff.: ausdrücklicher Hinweis des Käufers einer ratenweise zu liefernden Ware (Socken), dass die Lieferung der gesamten Warenmenge unerlässlich sei – Teillieferung rechtfertigt Vertragsaufhebung.
[123] S. unten Rn. 34 ff.
[124] S. O. R., S. 99 (Antrag A/Conf. 97/C. 1/L. 81 der Tschechoslowakei); S. 297, Nr. 20, 24. Die Frage ist auch in den Vorarbeiten behandelt worden, s. YB VIII (1977), S. 31, Nr. 90 (Entscheidung sei nicht erforderlich). S. zur Geschichte und zum Meinungsstand auch *Kritzer*, Guide to Practical Applications, S. 215 ff.
[125] OLG Hamburg, 25.1.2008, CISG-online 1681 = IHR 2008, 98, 100; OLG Düsseldorf, 24.4.1997, CISG-online 385.
[126] *Achilles*, Art. 25, Rn. 14 („grundsätzlich"); *Bertrams/Kruisinga*, S. 278; *Bridge*, Int'l Sale of Goods, Rn. 12.25; *Brunner*, Art. 25, Rn. 10; *von Caemmerer*, Wesentliche Vertragsverletzung, S. 50 = GS Bd. 3, S. 84; *Herber/Czerwenka*, Art. 25, Rn. 9 (nachträgliche Informationen über besonderes Interesse nur dann beachtlich, falls dieses Interesse durch Übernahme der vertraglichen Verpflichtung gedeckt ist – aber doch im Vertragsschlusszeitpunkt!); *Honsell/Gsell*, Art. 25, Rn. 24; *U. Huber*, RabelsZ 43 (1979), 413, 463 (zum New Yorker E 1978); *Leisinger*, Fundamental Breach, S. 112 (unter Rückgriff auf allgemeine Grundsätze i. S. d. Art. 7 II); *Lessiak*, Diskussionsbeitrag in: *Doralt* (Hrsg.), Das UNCITRAL-Kaufrecht im Vergleich zum österreichischen

in toto stellt Art. 73 III ausdrücklich auf diesen Zeitpunkt ab. Andere Stimmen wollen in Ausnahmefällen auch noch nachträglichen Informationen Bedeutung zukommen lassen.[127] Zum Teil wird schließlich nachträgliche Kenntnis des Schuldners schlechthin für erheblich gehalten.[128]

M. E. macht die oben[129] erläuterte Funktion der Voraussehbarkeit deutlich, dass es entscheidend auf den **Vertragsschluss** ankommen muss. Kenntnis oder Erkennbarkeit des Gläubigerinteresses kann für die Bedeutung einzelner Vertragspflichten und Pflichtmodalitäten die Notwendigkeit eindeutiger Vereinbarungen im Vertrag „ersetzen", d. h. eine entsprechende Auslegung ermöglichen. Das damit auch ohne eindeutige Vereinbarungen gegebene Gewicht bestimmter Pflichten für das Interesse des Gläubigers muss aber jedenfalls durch den Vertragsschluss fixiert werden. Bedeutet Kenntnis oder Erkennbarkeit ein Äquivalent für eindeutige Vereinbarungen, dann muss sie jedenfalls im Zeitpunkt des Vertragsschlusses gegeben sein.[130] Spätere Informationen können evtl. zu Vertragsergänzungen, d. h. Einvernehmen über die Aufwertung bestimmter Pflichten führen, oder auf Grund Art. 8 III („späteres Verhalten") ein Indiz im Rahmen der Beweisführung sein, dass schon bei Vertragsschluss die Bedeutung bestimmter Pflichten erkennbar oder dem Gläubiger bekannt war. Der Gläubiger kann jedoch nicht durch nachträgliche Mitteilungen, etwa, dass er mit seinen Abnehmern bei Verspätung Vertragsstrafen vereinbart habe, den Weg zur Aufhebbarkeit des Vertrages bei Vertragsverletzungen eröffnen, die ohne solche Informationen nicht wesentlich wären. 33

6. Beweislast

a) **Vertragsverletzung.** Die Verteilung der Beweislast, die allgemein als im UN-Kaufrecht geregelt eingeordnet wird,[131] verursacht im Rahmen des Art. 25[132] soweit keine besonderen Schwierigkeiten, wie das Tatbestandsmerkmal der Vertragsverletzung[133] in Rede steht: Diese muss von der Partei bewiesen werden, die sich auf die angebliche wesentliche Vertragsverletzung beruft. 34

b) **Nachteil (d. h. Bedeutung der verletzten Pflicht).** Ob eine Vertragsverletzung für die andere Partei „solchen Nachteil zur Folge hat, daß ihr im wesentlichen entgeht, was sie nach dem Vertrag hätte erwarten dürfen", hängt – wie bereits oben in Rn. 21 ff. erläutert – 35

Recht, S. 144; *Loewe*, Art. 25, S. 48; *Rudolph*, Art. 25, Rn. 7; *Schlechtriem*, Einheitliches UN-Kaufrecht, S. 49; *Schwimann/Posch*, Art. 25, Rn. 13; *Staudinger/Magnus*, Art. 25, Rn. 19; *Ziegel*, Remedial Provisions, § 9.03 (2d) sub 9–19 f. S. auch die deutliche Stellungnahme des englischen Delegierten *Feltham* auf der Wiener Konferenz, O. R., S. 302, Nr. 1: Die Parteien bestimmten mit und beim Vertragsschluss, was ihre wesentlichen Interessen seien.

[127] *Bamberger/Roth/Saenger*, Art. 25, Rn. 11 (Berücksichtigung nur nach Treu und Glauben); *Enderlein/Maskow/Strohbach*, Art. 25, Anm. 4.3.: Zweifel über die Voraussehbarkeit können durch dem Vertragsschluss nachfolgende Informationen ausgeräumt werden; ähnlich *Bianca/Bonell/Will*, Art. 25, Anm. 2.2.–2.2.5.; *MünchKomm/Gruber*, Art. 25, Rn. 43 f.; *MünchKommHGB/Benicke*, Art. 25, Rn. 16 ff. (soweit das Äquivalenzverhältnis des Vertrages nicht betroffen wird); *Posch/Kandut*, S. 66 („in spezifischen Konstellationen"); *Reinhart*, Art. 25, Rn. 9 („Sinn der Vorschrift erlaubt, … nachträgliche Informationen einzubeziehen"); *Botzenhardt*, S. 247 ff., 255 (Abwägung der beiderseitigen Interessen für Abweichung vom Grundsatz erforderlich).

[128] BGer, 15.9.2000, CISG-online 770: „le préjudice doit être prévisible pour la partie contrevenante ou pour toute personne raisonnable placée dans la même situation; il faut se placer au moment de la commission de la contravention au contrat, lequel détermine s'il existait alors un risque d'une atteinte substantielle aux mobiles et intérêts qui ont amené la partie lésée à conclure"; *Ghestin*, Fusion des actions, Nr. 238, S. 225; *Heuzé*, Anm. 391; *Honnold/Flechtner*, Art. 25, Rn. 183; *Neumayer/Ming*, Art. 25, Anm. 8.; *Neumayer*, RIW 1994, 99, 105 (der zunächst auf Zeitpunkt des Vertragsschlusses abstellt, dann aber („weitere Frage") für Voraussehbarkeit der *Folgen* auf Verletzungszeitpunkt).

[129] S. oben Rn. 26 ff.
[130] *Bridge*, Int'l Sale of Goods, Rn. 12.25.
[131] S. oben *Ferrari*, Art. 4 Rn. 48 ff.
[132] S. allgemein und erschöpfend *Antweiler*, S. 83 ff.
[133] Oben Rn. 13 ff.

von der Bedeutung ab, die die Parteien der verletzten Pflicht zugemessen haben (oder zugemessen hätten, hätten sie daran gedacht), und nicht von dem objektiv entstandenen Verlust oder Schaden. Bestehen über die Auslegung einer vertraglich vereinbarten Pflicht oder Pflichtmodalität hinsichtlich ihres Gewichts für die Interessen des Gläubigers Zweifel, hat folglich **der einen wesentlichen Vertragsbruch behauptende Teil** zu beweisen, dass die verletzte Pflicht ein entsprechendes Gewicht haben sollte.[134] Wird behauptet, dass vernünftige Personen im gleichen Geschäftskreis (Art. 8 II) ihr regelmäßig ein solches Gewicht beimessen, kann unter Umständen Beweisführung durch Zeugen oder Sachverständige, z. B. aus Industrie- und Handelskammern,[135] erforderlich werden, um darzutun, welche Erwartungen Personen im jeweiligen Verkehrskreis mit bestimmten Vereinbarungen verbinden: Ab wann die verspätete Lieferung von modischer Damenoberbekleidung deshalb wesentlicher Vertragsbruch ist, weil vernünftige Personen in diesem Geschäftszweig davon ausgehen, dass die Ware im Falle verzögerter Lieferung gegen Ende der Saison für den Käufer wertlos wird,[136] dürfte der Richter nicht stets aus eigener Sachkunde entscheiden können.

36 c) **Vorhersehbarkeit (oder deren Fehlen).** Das Fehlen der Voraussehbarkeit und konkreter Kenntnisse des Schuldners wurde als Voraussetzung einer möglichen „Entlastung" seit Einführung der Formulierung „unless ..." („es sei denn, dass ...") auf Grund eines philippinischen Antrags im E 1977[137] wohl zur **Beweislast** des vertragsbrüchigen **Schuldners** gerechnet,[138] wenngleich man in Wien einen ägyptischen Antrag, die Beweislast ausdrücklich zu ordnen, abgelehnt hat.[139] Diese Auffassung wird auch **heute noch** verschiedentlich vertreten.[140]

Es ist deutlich, dass bei diesen Vorstellungen und Erörterungen zur Beweislast noch von der Funktion der Voraussehbarkeitsregel als einer „Entlastung" für den vertragsbrüchigen Schuldner ausgegangen wurde bzw. wird, die man in Wien jedoch aufgegeben hat[141] und die daher für die Anwendung des Art. 25 **nicht** maßgeblich sein kann. Nach der hier vertretenen, **zutreffenden** Gegenansicht, die stattdessen auf die Ermittlung des besonderen Interesses der Vertragsparteien an einer bestimmten Pflicht abstellt,[142] stellt sich die Beweislast für die „Vorhersehbarkeit" eines Nachteils daher schlicht als unselbständiger **Bestandteil der Beweislast** für die **wesentliche Bedeutung der verletzten Vertragspflicht** dar, die bereits soeben in Rn. 35 behandelt wurde. Sobald dargelegt und bewiesen worden ist, dass eine vernünftige Person der gleichen Art wie der Schuldner in Übereinstimmung mit Art. 8 II, III die Bedeutung einer Pflicht erkannt hätte,[143] scheidet eine „Entlastung" des vertragsbrüchigen Schuldners folglich schon deshalb aus, weil seine individuelle Unkenntnis dafür **allein** nach Art. 25 nicht ausreicht: Unkenntnis **und** fehlende Erkennbarkeit für vernünfti-

---

[134] BGH, 3.4.1996, CISG-online 135 = BGHZ 132, 290, 299: Käufer hat zu beweisen, dass Mangel ein wesentlicher Vertragsbruch ist; ebenso SCC Institute, 5.4.2007, CISG-online 1521, Rn. 145; KG Wallis, 21.2.2005, CISG-online 1193 = IHR 2006, 155, 157; *Achilles*, Art. 25, Rn. 16; *Bamberger/Roth/Saenger*, Art. 25, Rn. 12; *Honsell/Gsell*, Art. 25, Rn. 26; *Leisinger*, Fundamental Breach, S. 109; *Staudinger/Magnus*, Art. 25, Rn. 30; *Witz/Salger/Lorenz/Salger*, Art. 25, Rn. 15.
[135] Vgl. BGH, 24.10.1979, MDR 1980, 308 (zu Art. 82 II EKG).
[136] Vgl. OLG Hamm, 8.12.1980, in: *Schlechtriem/Magnus*, Art. 26 EKG, Nr. 3; s. zu ähnlichen Fällen unten Rn. 39.
[137] S. zur Entstehungsgeschichte des Art. 25 oben Rn. 5.
[138] S. *Bianca/Bonell/Will*, Art. 25, Anm. 2.2.1.; *Michida*, 27 Am. J. Comp. L. (1979), 279, 284 ff.; *Eörsi*, 31 Am. J. Comp. L. (1983), 333, 340.
[139] Für den ägyptischen Vorschlag und die Diskussionen in der ersten Arbeitsgruppe O. R., S. 99, 295 ff., Nr. 3, 17, 21, 26, 33, 35, 41.
[140] ICC, 9187/1999, CISG-online 705; *Brunner*, Art. 25, Rn. 10; *Herber/Czerwenka*, Art. 25, Rn. 10; *Honnold/Flechtner*, Art. 25, Rn. 183; MünchKomm/*Gruber*, Art. 25, Rn. 47; wohl auch BGH, 3.4.1996, CISG-online 135 = BGHZ 132, 290, 299.
[141] S. dazu bereits oben Rn. 5.
[142] Ausführlich oben Rn. 26 ff.
[143] Insofern trifft die Beweislast diejenige Partei, die sich auf die wesentliche Vertragsverletzung beruft, was regelmäßig der Gläubiger sein wird; s. schon Rn. 35.

ge Personen der gleichen Art müssen kumuliert gegeben sein,[144] weshalb es auf die Beweislast für die individuelle Unkenntnis in dieser Konstellation nicht mehr ankommt. Werden dagegen **ungewöhnliche** Interessen des Gläubigers als Grundlage für die besondere Bedeutung einer Vertragspflicht vorgetragen, so muss die Partei, die sich auf die wesentliche Vertragsverletzung **beruft**, die Kenntnis des Schuldners von der Bedeutung dieser Interessen beweisen.

Im Ergebnis trägt die genannte Partei daher die **vollumfängliche Beweislast** für **alle Tatbestandsmerkmale** des Art. 25, und zwar einschließlich – trotz der missverständlichen Formulierung „es sei denn" – der Vorhersehbarkeit des Nachteils der vertragstreuen Partei.

IV. Einzelfälle (1): Verletzung von Verkäuferpflichten

1. Nichtleistung

Nichtleistung der verkauften Ware auf Grund objektiver oder subjektiver Unmöglichkeit, wie sie im deutschen unvereinheitlichten Kaufrecht in § 275 I BGB umschrieben ist, ist wohl stets wesentlicher Vertragsbruch,[145] etwa wenn der Verkäufer das Eigentum an der veräußerten Ware von vorneherein nicht übertragen konnte[146] oder er die Kaufgegenstände zwischenzeitlich anderweitig verkauft hat.[147] Auch ernsthafte und endgültige **Erfüllungsverweigerung** vor[148] oder bei Fälligkeit ist wesentlicher Vertragsbruch,[149] sofern dem Schuldner nicht ein Zurückbehaltungsrecht aufgrund des CISG[150] zusteht. Dasselbe gilt, wenn der Verkäufer die Lieferung von vertraglich nicht vorgesehenen Bedingungen wie etwa der vorherigen Erfüllung anderweitiger Forderungen abhängig macht.[151] Das bloße Verlangen nach Vertragsänderung, d. h. höheren Preisen, sollte aber allein noch nicht als wesentlicher Vertragsbruch gewertet werden, sofern nicht damit eine Erfüllungsverweigerung zum Ausdruck gebracht bzw. verbunden wird.[152] Auch ist Fehlleitung der Ware zum falschen Lieferort, die Einlagerung für die Empfängerin erforderlich macht, nicht notwendig wesentlicher Vertragsbruch.[153]

---

[144] S. oben Rn. 28, 30.

[145] Vgl. ICC, 9978/1999, CISG-online 708 (obiter); Schiedsgericht der serbischen Handelskammer Belgrad, 1.10.2007, CISG-online 1793.

[146] LG Freiburg, 22.8.2002, CISG-online 711 = IHR 2003, 22: verkauftes KfZ war gestohlen und wurde von der Polizei beschlagnahmt.

[147] OLG Celle, 24.5.1995, CISG-online 152 (gebrauchte Druckereimaschinen, die im Kaufvertrag mit ihren Maschinennummern bezeichnet worden waren).

[148] HGer Zürich, 22.11.2010, CISG-online 2160 = IHR 2011, 151, 152: Verkäuferin teilte bereits Monate vor dem vereinbarten Liefertermin mit, „dass die gesamte Winterkollektion 06/07 ausfalle", weil ihr chinesischer Lieferant nicht liefern könne – wesentliche Vertragsverletzung i. S. d. Art. 73 i. V. m. Art. 25.

[149] CA Grenoble, 21.10.1999, CISG-online 574 = D. 2000, II, 441: Erfüllungsverweigerung durch Bestreiten des Vertragsschlusses; OLG München, 15.9.2004, CISG-online 1013 = IHR 2005, 70: dto.; OLG Düsseldorf, 24.4.1997, CISG-online 385 (in concreto nicht bewiesen); Trib. Forlì, 11.12.2008, CISG-online 1729; s. aber OLG Düsseldorf, 10.2.1994, CISG-online 115 = NJW-RR 1994, 506: Erklärung des Verkäufers, die bestellte Ware „zur Zeit" nicht liefern zu können, ist noch keine endgültige Erfüllungsverweigerung.

[150] S. oben Rn. 18. Das Recht, Naturalerfüllung wegen Unzumutbarkeit nach § 275 II, III BGB zu verweigern, das nach Art. 28 auch eine Verurteilung zur Erfüllung durch ein deutsches Gericht ausschließen kann, ist dagegen kein Umstand, der einen wesentlichen Vertragsbruch ausschließt, sondern lässt – wie § 275 IV BGB zeigt – Rechtsbehelfe wie Vertragsaufhebung unberührt; die Nichtlieferung wegen Unzumutbarkeit der für den Verkäufer erforderlichen Leistungsanstrengungen wird regelmäßig einen wesentlichen Vertragsbruch darstellen.

[151] Schiedsgericht Hamburger freundschaftliche Arbitrage, 29.12.1998, CISG-online 638 = NJW-RR 1999, 780, 782.

[152] ICC, 20.12.1999, CISG-online 1646 = IHR 2004, 21: einseitige Herabsetzung eines Rabatts, obgleich dieser für den Zeitraum eines Jahres vereinbart gewesen war – wesentliche Vertragsverletzung; Schiedsgericht Hamburger freundschaftliche Arbitrage, 29.12.1998, CISG-online 638 = NJW-RR 1999, 780, 782: Lieferungsbereitschaft nur gegen erhöhte Gegenleistung ist wesentlicher Vertragsbruch; anders Trib. com. Poitiers, 9.12.1996, CISG-online 221.

[153] Vgl. OLG Oldenburg, 22.9.1998, CISG-online 508 = NJW-RR 2000, 1364.

2. Verspätete Lieferung

38 **a) Allgemeines.** Ist die geschuldete Leistung noch möglich und hat der Verkäufer ihre Erbringung auch nicht endgültig abgelehnt, so kommt es auf die Bedeutung des vereinbarten **Liefertermins** an. Das Vorliegen einer **wesentlichen Vertragsverletzung** hängt davon ab, ob die genaue Einhaltung des Liefertermins für den Käufer von besonderem Interesse ist, und zwar so, dass der Käufer lieber überhaupt keine Lieferung als verspätete Lieferung haben will, was für den Verkäufer bei Vertragsschluss erkennbar war;[154] nach einer Alternativformel ist erforderlich, dass „nach dem Willen der Parteien das Geschäft mit der Einhaltung der Lieferfrist stehen oder fallen" soll.[155]

39 **b) Wesentliche Vertragsverletzungen.** Dies kann sich bereits aus einer entsprechenden **Formulierung des Liefertermins** im Kaufvertrag ergeben, wie etwa bei den Bezeichnungen „fix",[156] „spätestens"[157] oder „schnellstmöglich",[158] erschließt sich jedoch häufig, ja geradezu typischerweise erst aufgrund einer Berücksichtigung der konkreten **Umstände des Vertrages** (Art. 8 II, III). Eine verspätete Lieferung stellt danach eine wesentliche Vertragsverletzung dar, wenn gegen einen vereinbarten, detaillierten Zeitplan für den Lieferfortschritt verstoßen wurde, dessen strikte Einhaltung erkennbar unerlässlich war,[159] wenn die Lieferung von Taschen „binnen 10–15 Tagen" vereinbart und die Bedeutung eines schnellen Eintreffens der Ware mehrfach betont worden war,[160] bei Saisonware[161] wie etwa Modeware aus der Frühjahrskollektion[162] oder Strickwaren für das Weihnachtsgeschäft,[163] bei einem dem Verkäufer mitgeteilten Fixtermin des Käufers gegenüber seinen Abnehmern,[164] wenn es sich um den letzten Kauf vor anstehender Geschäftsaufgabe durch die

---

[154] So die Formulierung in OLG Düsseldorf, 24.4.1997, CISG-online 385; ebenso OLG Hamm, 12.11.2001, CISG-online 1430 = OLGR Hamm 2002, 185, 188.

[155] OLG Hamm, 12.11.2001, CISG-online 1430 = OLGR Hamm 2002, 185, 188; MünchKommHGB/*Benicke*, Art. 25, Rn. 19.

[156] AG Ludwigsburg, 21.12.1990, CISG-online 17: Bestellung von Sommermode bei frz. Herstellerin mit Klausel „Livraison: 1–15/07/89 FIXE. O. N.".

[157] OLG Hamm, 12.11.2001, CISG-online 1430 = OLGR Hamm 2002, 185, 188.

[158] OLG Düsseldorf, 21.4.2004, CISG-online 915 = IHR 2005, 24, 25 f.: Verkäufer hatte Lieferung von Mobiltelefonen „schnellstmöglich" bzw. unmittelbar nach Erhalt der vereinbarten Anzahlung zugesagt, die am 29. 6. eintraf – Lieferung erst am darauf folgenden Montag, den 3. 7. stellte wesentliche Vertragsverletzung dar; zustimmend *Magnus/Lüsing*, IHR 2007, 1, 3; *Schwimann/Posch*, Art. 25, Rn. 3; kritisch *Sauthoff*, IHR 2005, 21, 23. A. A. für die Formulierung „schnellstmöglich" hingegen OLG Hamm, 12.11.2001, CISG-online 1430 = OLGR Hamm 2002, 185, 188, weil darin die ganz erhebliche Bedeutung der Einhaltung der Lieferzeit – anders als bei der Formulierung „spätestens" – nicht zum Ausdruck komme.

[159] *Diversitel Communications, Inc. v. Glacier Bay Inc.*, Ontario Superior Court of Justice, 6.10.2003, CISG-online 1436: Kauf von Isolierpanelen, welche die Käuferin zum Bau von sechs Energieversorgungsstationen benötigte, deren Abnehmer das kanadische Verteidigungsministerium war und die in der Hocharktis aufgestellt werden sollten – da dies nur während des lediglich vierwöchigen arktischen Sommers möglich war, stellte die Lieferverzögerung einen wesentlichen Vertragsbruch dar.

[160] Pretura di Parma-Fidenza, 24.11.1989, CISG-online 316 = Dir. com. int. 1995, 441: bei nach zwei Monaten noch nicht erfolgter Lieferung wesentliche Vertragsverletzung bejaht.

[161] ICC, 8786/1997, CISG-online 749; BGer, 15.9.2000, CISG-online 770 (obiter); OLG Düsseldorf, 24.4.1997, CISG-online 385 (im konkreten Fall verneint).

[162] ICC, 8786/1997, CISG-online 749: Lieferung war vertraglich für eine Woche vor Ostern vereinbart worden, damit weil die Modeware vor allem während der Osterferien abgesetzt werden sollte – Überschreitung des Liefertermins stellte wesentliche Vertragsverletzung dar.

[163] CA Milano, 20.3.1998, CISG-online 348 = Riv. dir. int. priv. proc. 1998, 170 ff.: Liefertermin 3.12.1990 – Verstreichen des Termins bedeutete wesentliche Vertragsverletzung.

[164] *Diversitel Communications, Inc. v. Glacier Bay Inc.*, Ontario Superior Court of Justice, 6.10.2003, CISG-online 1436; BGer, 15.9.2000, CISG-online 770: ägyptische Baumwolle traf so spät bei ital. Käufer ein, dass dieser sich anderweitig eindecken musste, um seine vertragliche Verpflichtungen (über die der Verkäufer informiert worden war) erfüllen zu können – wesentliche Vertragsverletzung des Verkäufers bejaht; LG Hamburg, 23.10.1995, CISG-online 395: Käufer hatte Verkäufer von bereits erfolgtem Weiterverkauf des Eisenmolybdäns in Kenntnis gesetzt und Bedeutung rechtzeitiger Lieferung betont – verspätete Abladung stellte wesentliche Vertragsverletzung dar; HGer Zürich, 25.6.2007, CISG-online 1564 = IHR 2008, 31, 32 f.: Herstellung von Druckerzeugnissen, für welche die Käuferin gegenüber ihren Abnehmern fixe Liefertermine zugesagt hatte – in concreto nicht bewiesen.

Käuferin handelte, was dem Verkäufer bekannt war,[165] wenn die verkaufte Ware starken Preisschwankungen unterliegt[166] oder aber für die Herstellung eines Produkts mit seinerseits volatilem Preis bestimmt ist, das infolge der verspäteten Lieferung nur zu einem niedrigeren Preis abgesetzt werden kann.[167] Ohne Bedeutung ist dabei, ob die betreffende Konstellation nach nationalem Recht als „Fixgeschäft" eingeordnet würde.

c) Keine wesentliche Vertragsverletzung. Keine wesentliche Vertragsverletzung stellt 40 eine verspätete Lieferung hingegen in Fällen dar, in denen lediglich Lieferung *„prima ferie non dopo"* („vor den Ferien, nicht später") vereinbart war[168] oder in denen die nach Parteigepflogenheit oder Handelsbrauch trotz festgelegten Liefertermins eine gewisse zeitliche Flexibilität üblich ist;[169] dasselbe kann trotz eines Liefertermins mit Fixcharakter unter Umständen auch dann der Fall sein, wenn der vereinbarte Termin nur ganz marginal (um 1–2 Tage) überschritten wird.[170] Wurde vertraglich kein Liefertermin bestimmt, so liegt selbst dann kein wesentlicher Vertragsbruch vor, wenn bis zur Lieferung ein nahezu doppelt so langer Zeitraum wie in der Branche üblich (14 statt üblicherweise 8 Wochen) verstreicht, der Käufer aber ständig mit der betreffenden Ware handelt und sie daher unproblematisch verwenden kann.[171] In den letztgenannten und allen sonstigen Fällen muss der Käufer, um zur Aufhebung kommen zu können, eine Nachfrist setzen (Artt. 47 I, 49 I lit. b).[172] Soweit eine wesentliche Vertragsverletzung bei Lieferverzögerung zum Teil auch dann bejaht wird, wenn weder ein Fixgeschäft vorliegt noch eine Nachfrist gesetzt wurde, der Liefertermin aber **ganz erheblich**, d. h. um einen beträchtlichen Zeitraum **überschritten** wurde,[173] ist

---

[165] OLG Karlsruhe, 20.7.2004, CISG-online 858 = IHR 2004, 246, 251.
[166] BGer, 15.9.2000, CISG-online 770: Lieferverzögerung (hier: bei ägyptischer Baumwolle) als wesentliche Vertragsverletzung bei starken („soudainement et considérablement"), nicht hingegen bei geringen Preisschwankungen („variations mineures des prix"); *Leisinger*, Fundamental Breach, S. 126 und *Takahashi*, J. Bus. L. 2003, 102, 125 ff. (beide zu *commodity sales*); a. A. OLG Hamm, 12.11.2001, CISG-online 1430 = OLGR Hamm 2002, 185, 188 für Kaufvertrag über Speichermodule zwischen Verkäufer aus Hongkong und Käufer aus Deutschland mit dem interessanten Argument, eine verspätete Lieferung könne sich für den Käufer auch als wirtschaftlich vorteilhaft erweisen, wenn nämlich der Marktpreis zwischenzeitlich gestiegen sei.
[167] *Valero Marketing & Supply Company v. Greeni Oy and Greeni Trading Oy*, U. S. Dist. Ct. (D. N. J.), 4.4.2006, CISG-online 1216: verspätete Lieferung von Naphta an Hersteller eines Petroliumprodukts, dessen Absatz statt im September erst im Oktober zu niedrigerem Marktpreis erfolgen konnte (*in concreto* Kausalität jedoch nicht bewiesen).
[168] AG Nordhorn, 14.6.1994, CISG-online 259: Klausel macht italienisch-deutschen Schuhkauf nicht zum Fixgeschäft.
[169] Vgl. *Macromex Srl. v. Globex International Inc.*, AAA, 23.10.2007, CISG-online 1645: sofern noch innerhalb dieses ‚flexiblen' Rahmens geliefert wird, liegt keine wesentliche Vertragsverletzung vor, wobei der Verkäufer die Beweislast für entsprechende Gepflogenheiten oder Bräuche trägt.
[170] So *Valero Marketing & Supply Company v. Greeni Oy and Greeni Trading Oy*, U. S. Dist. Ct. (D. N. J.), 4.4.2006, CISG-online 1216: um zwei Tage verspätete Anlieferung von Naphta, dessen geplante Verwendung dadurch im konkreten Fall nicht beeinträchtigt wurde; LG Oldenburg, 27.3.1996, CISG-online 188 für den Kauf von Kleidungsstücken (Sommerware) mit der vertraglichen Abrede, diese seien „in der Zeit von Februar/März/10. April" abzusenden – obgleich einige wenige Kleidungsstücke erst am 11. April abgesandt wurden, wurde die Wesentlichkeit der Vertragsverletzung verneint, weil der Käufer die Ware behalten und nicht zurückgewiesen hatte; AG Ludwigsburg, 21.12.1990, CISG-online 17: Absendung von Sommerbekleidung statt am 15. 7. erst am 17. 7. – keine wesentliche Vertragsverletzung, da Ware unverändert verwendbar.
[171] AppGer Turku, 18.2.1997, CISG-online 1297: deutsch-finnischer Kaufvertrag über Verpackung für Tiernahrung – wesentliche Vertragsverletzung verneint.
[172] OLG Düsseldorf, 24.4.1997, CISG-online 385; OLG Düsseldorf, 18.11.1993, CISG-online 92.
[173] BGer, 15.9.2000, CISG-online 770: „Face à un retard considérable dans l'exécution qui constitue une violation essentielle du contrat au sens de l'art. 25 CVIM, l'acheteur est fondé à mettre immédiatement fin à la vente sans avoir préalablement fixé un délai supplémentaire"; Int. Ct. Ukrainian CCI, 18.11.2004, CISG-online 1371: Überschreitung des Liefertermins um 15 Monate – wesentliche Vertragsverletzung bejaht; *Brunner*, Art. 25, Rn. 12; *Soergel/Lüderitz/Schüßler-Langeheine*, Art. 49, Rn. 5; *Witz/Salger/Lorenz/Salger*, Art. 25, Rn. 9; a. A. und zutreffend hingegen OLG Düsseldorf, 24.4.1997, CISG-online 385: keine wesentliche Bedeutung des Liefertermins, keine Art. 47 I genügende Nachfristsetzung – Vertragsaufhebung unberechtigt.

dies nicht unbedenklich, weil auf diese Weise die Anforderungen der Artt. 47 I, 49 I lit. b) (Nachfristsetzung) umgangen werden können.[174]

41   **d) Auswirkungen der Verwendung von Incoterms®.** Bei Aufnahme einer Incoterms®-Klausel in den Kaufvertrag stellt sich häufig die Frage, ob dadurch ein fixer Liefertermin vereinbart wurde, dessen Überschreitung zwangsläufig sogleich eine wesentliche Vertragsverletzung i. S. d. Art. 25 bedeutet. Die Auswirkungen von Lieferklauseln nach den Incoterms® auf CISG-Verträge wird uneinheitlich beurteilt: Während verbreitet angenommen wird, die Klausel CIF weise den betreffenden Kauf als Fixgeschäft aus, bei dem die Einhaltung der Lieferzeit eine wesentliche Vertragspflicht darstellt,[175] soll eine entsprechende Aufwertung des Lieferzeitpunkts durch die Klausel CFR nicht bewirkt werden.[176] M. E. ist zu differenzieren: Ausgangspunkt muss sein, dass es sich bei den Auswirkungen von Incoterms® im Rahmen des Art. 25 um eine Frage der **Vertragsauslegung** handelt,[177] bei welcher dem feststellbaren Willen der am konkreten Kaufvertrag beteiligten Parteien (Art. 8 I) Vorrang vor dem allgemeinen, unter Berücksichtigung der Handelsbräuche ermittelten Verständnis der Lieferklauseln (Art. 8 II, III) zukommt. Die Verwendung einer Incoterms®-Klausel, die den Kauf zu einem Abladegeschäft (CIF, FOB) und nach einem grundsätzlich zu berücksichtigenden (und ggfs. zu beweisenden[178]) Handelsbrauch damit zu einem Fixgeschäft macht,[179] stellt daher ein **Indiz** für die **wesentliche Bedeutung** der vertraglich vereinbarten Lieferzeit dar,[180] das jedoch durch andere Vertragsdetails wie etwa eine Vereinbarung, der zufolge eine Gewährleistungsbürgschaft frühestens 15 Tage nach Ablauf der Lieferfrist in Anspruch genommen werden darf, widerlegt werden kann.[181] Dementsprechend trifft denjenigen, der sich in diesen Fällen auf den üblichen Aussagegehalt der Lieferklausel stützt, nur die Beweislast für deren Vereinbarung, bei sonstigen Incoterms® hingegen auch für deren Bedeutung im Rahmen des Art. 25, während die Gegenpartei eine im konkreten Fall abweichende vertragliche Gewichtung des Lieferzeitpunktes darzulegen und zu beweisen hat.[182]

3. Quantitätsmängel

42   Bei Quantitätsdefiziten (s. Artt. 35 I, 51 II) oder ausbleibenden Raten (s. hierzu Art. 73) kommt es auf die Bedeutung der Vollständigkeit für den Käufer an, die sich aus dem Vertrag, aus der Anschauung der beteiligten Verkehrskreise oder aus besonderen Hinweisen ergeben kann.[183] Hat der Käufer die nicht im bestellten Umfang gelieferte Ware zur Erfüllung eines

---

[174] Wie hier zurückhaltend MünchKomm/*P. Huber*, Art. 49, Rn. 34. *Honsell/Gsell*, Art. 25, Rn. 35 will dadurch helfen, dass sie eine „den Vertragszweck gefährdende Terminüberschreitung" verlangt. S. noch unten Rn. 49.

[175] OLG Hamburg, 28.2.1997, CISG-online 261 = EWiR 1997, 791 *(Mankowski)*: Verkauf von Eisen-Molybdän, CIF (Incoterms® 1990); *Honsell/Gsell*, Art. 25, Rn. 32 (ebenso für Klausel „FOB"); *Huber/Mullis*, S. 226; MünchKomm/*P. Huber*, Art. 49, Rn. 34; MünchKommHGB/*Benicke*, Art. 25, Rn. 19; *Takahashi*, J. Bus. L. 2003, 102, 126; *Trommler*, S. 111.

[176] ICC, 7645/1995, CISG-online 844 = YB Comm. Arb. 2001, 130, 141: Verkauf von Rohmetall, CFR (Incoterms® 1990); a. A. *Honsell/Gsell*, Art. 25, Rn. 32.

[177] S. bereits allgemein oben Rn. 26 ff.

[178] Entscheidend ist, ob der betreffende Handelsbrauch den Anforderungen des Art. 9 genügt; s. dazu oben *Schmidt-Kessel*, Art. 9 Rn. 20.

[179] OLG Frankfurt a. M., 24.3.2009, CISG-online 2165 = IHR 2010, 250, 252; OLG Karlsruhe, 12.2.1975, RIW 1975, 225; *Baumbach/Hopt/Hopt*, § 376, Rn. 7, Incoterms® Nr. 4 Rn. 3, Nr. 6 Rn. 2; *Heymann/Emmerich/Hoffmann*, § 376, Rn. 10; MünchKomm/*P. Huber*, Art. 49, Rn. 34; MünchKommHGB/*Benicke*, Art. 25, Rn. 19; a. A. *Magnus/Lüsing*, IHR 2007, 1, 12: im Kontext des UN-Kaufrechts seien CIF- und FOB-Klauseln in Bezug auf den Fixcharakter der Lieferfrist neutral; ebenso (für CIF-Geschäfte) *Ostendorf*, IHR 2009, 100, 102.

[180] Vgl. *Schlechtriem*, 16 Pace Int'l L. Rev. (2004), 279, 284 Fn. 12; *Leisinger*, Fundamental Breach, S. 150.

[181] So etwa in ICC, 7645/1995, CISG-online 844 = YB Comm. Arb. 2001, 130, 142.

[182] Dies entspricht der üblichen Beweislastverteilung im Rahmen des Art. 25 (s. bereits oben Rn. 34 ff.) wie auch des Art. 8 I bzw. II, III (s. oben *Schmidt-Kessel*, Art. 8 Rn. 40, 61).

[183] Vgl. OLG Koblenz, 18.5.1984, in: *Schlechtriem/Magnus*, Art. 44 EKG, Nr. 6: Sind nur 20% der bestellten Menge mangelfrei geliefert, liegt wesentliche Vertragsverletzung vor; s. a. *Ziegel*, Remedial Provisions, § 9.03 (2b) sub 9–16, zu den Schwierigkeiten, zwischen 10% und 50% Minderleistung einen wesentlichen Vertrags-

Auftrages erworben, der erst mehrere Monate nach Eintreffen der Teillieferung fällig wird, so liegt keine wesentliche Vertragsverletzung vor, wenn der Käufer sich die fehlende Ware noch rechtzeitig selbst beschafft hat oder beschaffen konnte.[184]

4. Sach- und Rechtsmängel der Ware

Besondere Schwierigkeiten macht die Beurteilung von Sach- oder Rechtsmängeln. Maß- 43 geblich sind auch hier zunächst etwaige Vereinbarungen der Parteien über die Bedeutung der Sach- und Rechtsmängelfreiheit der Ware;[185] anders als nach EKG fehlt die (zusätzliche) Voraussetzung, dass zur Vertragswidrigkeit Überschreitung des Lieferzeitpunktes kommen muss.[186] In Auslegung und Anwendung des Art. 25 auf Fälle vertragswidriger Beschaffenheit, insbesondere als Voraussetzung einer Vertragsaufhebung durch den Käufer (Art. 49 I lit. a), sind im Übrigen vor allem drei Fragen auffällig geworden: Viel diskutiert wird das Verhältnis von Vertragsaufhebung wegen wesentlichen Vertragsbruchs und Nacherfüllungsrecht (Recht zur zweiten Andienung) des Verkäufers aus Art. 48.[187] Str. ist auch, ob der Käufer für die Nacherfüllung durch den Verkäufer eine Nachfrist setzen und nach deren Ablauf aufheben kann, ohne dass die Wesentlichkeit des Mangels geprüft werden müsste.[188] In der internationalen Praxis war schließlich immer wieder zu entscheiden, welche Mängel, insbesondere welcher Grad an Abweichung von der geschuldeten Beschaffenheit in denjenigen Fällen einen die Aufhebung rechtfertigenden wesentlichen Vertragsbruch darstellt, in denen die Parteien die Bedeutung dieses Umstandes nicht definiert haben.[189]

a) Parteiautonome Bestimmung der Wesentlichkeit. Im Rahmen der Beurteilung, 44 wann vertragswidrige Beschaffenheiten, insbesondere Sachmängel einen wesentlichen Vertragsbruch darstellen, ist zunächst die Bedeutung der Parteiautonomie festzuhalten:[190] Es ist vorrangig Sache der Parteien, bei Vereinbarung von Eigenschaften nach Art. 35 I deren Bedeutung „hochzustufen" und hervorzuheben, sodass deutlich ist,[191] dass mit Einhalten dieser Zusagen der Vertrag „stehen oder fallen", m. a. W. dem Käufer bei Nichteinhaltung das Recht auf Vertragsaufhebung oder Nachlieferung zustehen soll;[192] die „Zusicherung" des alten deutschen Kaufrechts hat hier weiterhin eine sinnvolle Funktion.[193]

Eine entsprechende **vertragliche Abrede über die Wesentlichkeit** ist etwa gesehen 45 worden in der Festlegung der genauen Stärke zu liefernder Aluminiumrollen,[194] der Qualität des vertragsgegenständlichen Weizenmehls[195] oder von Braugerste,[196] der genauen Sorte

---

bruch sicher zu prognostizieren. Zum Verhältnis von Minderlieferung und teilweiser Nichtlieferung und den jeweiligen „Schwellen" für wesentlichen Vertragsbruch und Aufhebung des (gesamten) Vertrages s. *Schlechtriem*, Internationales UN-Kaufrecht, Rn. 191, 192a sowie unten *Müller-Chen*, Art. 51 Rn. 2, 9 ff.

[184] LG Heidelberg, 3.7.1992, CISG-online 38: Kauf von Computerteilen.
[185] S. dazu unten Rn. 44 ff.
[186] Vgl. zu dieser Kumulierung OLG München, 9.12.1987, RIW 1988, 297, 298.
[187] S. unten Rn. 47 f.
[188] S. unten Rn. 49.
[189] S. unten Rn. 50 ff.
[190] S. bereits oben Rn. 21 f.
[191] Die Feststellung einer diesbezüglichen Einigung der Parteien obliegt regelmäßig dem Tatsachenrichter; vgl. (zur prozessualen Rechtslage in der Schweiz) BGer, 13.11.2007, CISG-online 1618.
[192] Vgl. BGH, 3.4.1996, CISG-online 135 = BGHZ 132, 290, 298: Zweckmäßige Möglichkeit, die für wesentlich gehaltenen Pflichten im Vertrag ausdrücklich als solche festzuhalten; CISG-AC, Op. 5 *(Schwenzer)*, Comment 4.2, IHR 2006, 35, 38.
[193] Wie hier *Honsell/Gsell*, Art. 25, Rn. 40.
[194] CIETAC, 30.10.1991, CISG-online 842: Abweichung der Eigenschaften der gelieferten Aluminiumrollen (0,0118 inches) von vertraglicher Vereinbarung (0,0125 inches) als wesentliche Vertragsverletzung gewertet.
[195] Gerechtshof 's-Gravenhage, 23.4.2003, CISG-online 903 = IHR 2004, 119: vereinbart war „EEC Wheatflour type Aigle du Nord with bread improver", dem gelieferten Weizenmehl war Kaliumbromat (ein krebserregender und in der gesamten EU verbotener Brotverbesserer) zugesetzt worden – wesentliche Vertragsverletzung bejaht.
[196] Schiedsgericht der Börse für landwirtschaftliche Produkte in Wien, 10.12.1997, CISG-online 351, östZRVgl 1998, 211 ff.: „Gesund, handelsüblich, mind. 90% über 2,5mm, max. 15% Feuchtigkeit, Keimfähig-

französischen, für den chinesischen Markt bestimmten Cognacs,[197] der Leistungsfähigkeit und des Stromverbrauchs von Kompressoren für Klimageräte,[198] des Herstellungsjahres eines PKWs,[199] des Vitamin-A-Gehalts der bestellten Hautpflegeprodukte, dessen zentrale Bedeutung betont worden war,[200] in der Vereinbarung, dass gekaufte Lebensmittel frei von gentechnisch veränderten Organismen sein müssen[201] oder den Anforderungen des Lebensmittelrechts im Käuferland zu entsprechen haben,[202] der genauen Beschaffenheit (insb. des Feuchtigkeitsgehalts) von Olivenkernen, die zur Verwendung in der Energieproduktion gekauft wurden,[203] der Beschreibung des Zustands der verkauften Maschine als „neuwertig",[204] der Festlegung der genauen Anforderungen an die Produktionsleistung und -qualität einer technisch komplexen Schleifmaschine[205] oder einer Abfüll- und Verpackungsanlage,[206] der Festlegung des Gewichts des gekauften Hammerkopfes einschließlich der maximal zulässigen Gewichtsabweichung,[207] der Vereinbarung von Druckpräzision und geschwindigkeit einer Druckmaschine,[208] nicht hingegen in der bloßen Beschreibung des Kaufgegenstandes (Apfelsaftkonzentrat[209]). Eine entsprechende Vereinbarung i. S. d. Art. 35 I kann auch durch stillschweigende Bezugnahme auf einen Herstellerkatalog zustande kommen, in dem etwa die Tragfähigkeit von Metallabdeckungen für Kanalisationsschächte angegeben ist.[210]

---

keit mind. 95%, Besatz max. 29%, Eiweiß Basis 11,5% max. 12%, Qualität final lt. SGS-Zertifikat" – Abweichung der gelieferten Gerste von dieser Bestimmung wäre wesentliche Vertragsverletzung gewesen (letztlich offen gelassen).

[197] Shanghai First Intermediate People's Court, 25.12.2008, CISG-online 2059: vereinbart war die Lieferung von französischem „Docher Henry Crystal Decanter 50 Years Grande Champagne Cognac X. O." mit einer Qualität „entsprechend oder besser als Louis XIII", geliefert wurde Cognac „Henry V" – wesentlicher Vertragsbruch bejaht.

[198] *Delchi Carrier SpA v. Rotorex Corp.*, U. S. Ct. App. (2nd Cir.), 6.12.1995, CISG-online 140 = 71 F. 3d 1024, 1028 f. mit dem ergänzenden Hinweis, die betreffenden Eigenschaften seien „important determinants of the product's value" – wesentliche Vertragsverletzung bejaht.

[199] Int. Ct. Russian CCI, 21.12.2004, CISG-online 1187: obgleich deutsch-russischer Kaufvertrag ausdrücklich vorsah, dass zu liefernder PKW nicht vor 1988 produziert worden sein durfte, stammte das gelieferte Fahrzeug aus dem Jahr 1981 – wesentliche Vertragsverletzung bejaht.

[200] AppGer Helsinki, 30.6.1998, CISG-online 1304 (Bestätigung der Vorinstanz): obgleich ein Vitamin-A-Gehalt von 1000–3000 IU/g vereinbart war, enthielten die gelieferten Produkte lediglich 340–750 IU/g – wesentliche Vertragsverletzung bejaht.

[201] AppGer Basel-Stadt, 22.8.2003, CISG-online 943 = IHR 2005, 117: von belgischer Verkäuferin an schweizerische Käuferin gelieferte vegetarische Schnitzel enthielten DNA von gentechnisch veränderter Soja – wesentliche Vertragsverletzung bejaht; zustimmend *Magnus,* ZEuP 2006, 96, 120.

[202] LG Ellwangen, 21.8.1995, CISG-online 279: Paprikapuder wegen überhöhter Ethylenoxidbelastung in Deutschland nicht verkäuflich – wesentliche Vertragsverletzung bejaht.

[203] Audiencia Provincial de Madrid, 20.2.2007, CISG-online 1637.

[204] KG Wallis, 21.2.2005, CISG-online 1193 = IHR 2006, 155, 156: dass gelieferte CNC-gesteuerte Strahlhaus-Maschine „komplett verrostet" und nicht funktionstüchtig war, begründete wesentliche Vertragsverletzung.

[205] CA Versailles, 29.1.1998, CISG-online 337: Produktion der Maschine lag außerhalb der vertraglich vereinbarten Parameter – nach mehrfachen erfolglosen Nachbesserungsversuchen wesentliche Vertragsverletzung bejaht.

[206] BGer, 18.5.2009, CISG-online 1900 = IHR 2010, 27, 29: vereinbart war eine Anlagenleistung von 180 Flacons/Minute, erbracht wurden lediglich 52 Flacons/Minute (29% der vereinbarten Leistung) – wesentliche Vertragsverletzung bejaht.

[207] CIETAC, Mai 2007, CISG-online 1975: vertraglich gestattet waren 2% Gewichtsabweichung, aber der gelieferte Hammerkopf wich um 10% ab – wesentliche Vertragsverletzung.

[208] CIETAC, 24.7.2007, CISG-online 2055.

[209] In OLG Stuttgart, 12.3.2001, CISG-online 841 = OLGR Stuttgart 2002, 148 ff. wurde immerhin für denkbar gehalten, dass die Lieferung mit Glukosesirup versetzter Ware schon deshalb als wesentliche Vertragsverletzung zu werten ist, weil ausdrücklich „Apfelsaftkonzentrat" bestellt gewesen war (im konkreten Fall aber verneint).

[210] So Audiencia Provincial de Barcelona, 28.4.2004, CISG-online 931: Katalog „garantierte" (*garantiza*) eine Tragfähigkeit von bis zu 40t, die gelieferten Abdeckungen trugen jedoch nur 25–35t – wesentliche Vertragsverletzung bejaht; zu stillschweigenden vertraglichen Vereinbarungen unter Art. 35 I s. unten *Schwenzer,* Art. 35 Rn. 7.

Auch die zur Bestimmung der vertragsgemäßen Beschaffenheit hilfsweise heranzuziehenden Kriterien, insbesondere der **spezielle Verwendungszweck,** der nach Art. 35 II lit. b) bestimmte Eigenschaften erfordert, und die Übereinstimmung mit **Warenmustern oder -proben** (Art. 35 II lit. c)) können Bedeutung gewinnen.[211] Dies ist namentlich beim Kauf von Investitionsgütern wie etwa Maschinen der Fall, wenn das Fehlen dieser Eigenschaften den Kaufgegenstand für die vorausgesetzte Nutzung völlig unverwendbar macht,[212] denn bei Gütern dieser Art muss der Käufer sich nicht auf eine anderweitige Verwendung nebst Schadenersatzleistung verweisen lassen: So stellt es eine wesentliche Vertragsverletzung dar, wenn die als „technische Neuerung" verkaufte Folien-Ummantelungsanlage nicht zur von den Parteien vorausgesetzten gleichzeitigen vierseitigen Ummantelung in einem Arbeitsgang geeignet ist, obgleich sie zu dreiseitigen Ummantelungen einsetzbar wäre,[213] wenn eine High-tech-Schleifmaschine, die der Käufer zur Herstellung von Einzelteilen für die Automobilherstellung erworben hat, nicht exakt gemäß vereinbarter technischer Vorgaben produziert,[214] oder wenn ein mobiles Klettergerüst für Kinder vom Käufer nicht wie geplant öffentlich aufgestellt und vermietet werden kann, weil es beim Kauf angegebenen öffentlich-rechtlichen Sicherheitsbestimmungen nicht genügt.[215] Eine wesentliche Vertragsverletzung kann aber auch in der Lieferung eines Kompressors liegen, der nicht die Spezifika eines zuvor übergebenen Musters aufweist, wenn der Käufer seine Produktion von Klimaanlagen technisch auf dieses Muster ausgerichtet hatte.[216]

Bei Produktionsmitteln oder Handelsware kann der Käufer hingegen vorrangig zu deren Weiterverkauf verpflichtet sein[217] (vgl. unten Rn. 52 ff.).

b) Berücksichtigung des Rechts des Verkäufers zur zweiten Andienung. Die 47 Sorge, dass ein Käufer bei **Mängeln,** die durch Nachbesserung oder Nachlieferung **behebbar** sind, nach Art. 49 I lit. a) aufheben und so dem Verkäufer die Möglichkeit einer zweiten Andienung nehmen könnte, hat zu der Kontroverse geführt, ob eine **Nacherfüllungsmöglichkeit** für eine angemessene Zeit den Vertragsbruch (noch) nicht wesentlich sein lässt.[218] Die Frage ist allgemeiner Natur[219] und stellt sich immer dann, wenn die Sach- oder Rechtsmangelhaftigkeit der Ware jedenfalls bei Fehlen einer Nacherfüllungsmöglichkeit so schwerwiegend wäre, dass sie einen wesentlichen Vertragsbruch darstellen würde[220] – unerheblich ist, ob diese Qualifikation im konkreten Fall auf eine

---

[211] Vgl. *Schwenzer*, 25 J. L. & Com. (2005-06), 437, 438.
[212] Zum zu beachtenden Recht des Verkäufers zur Nachbesserung s. sogleich Rn. 47.
[213] LG Heilbronn, 15.9.1997, CISG-online 562 mit dem Hinweis, „Sinn und Zweck" der Prototypentwicklung sei gerade die vierseitige Ummantelung von Werkteilen gewesen.
[214] CA Versailles, 29.1.1998, CISG-online 337: „les normes contractuellement définies étant essentielles pour le marché automobile auquel les pièces ouvrées sont destinées".
[215] Pret. Dist. Lugano, 19.4.2007, CISG-online 1724.
[216] *Delchi Carrier SpA v. Rotorex Corp.,* U. S. Ct. App. (2nd Cir.), 6.12.1995, CISG-online 140 = 71 F. 3d 1024, 1028 f.: Kompressoren brachten nach Einbau nicht die geforderte Leistung und verbrauchten zu viel Strom; mehrfache Nachbesserungsversuche waren gescheitert.
[217] Vgl. OLG Frankfurt, 18.1.1994, CISG-online 123 = NJW 1994, 1013, 1014: dass gelieferte Schuhe nicht mit einer beim Kauf vorgelegten Probe von einem Muster übereinstimmen (Art. 35 II lit. c)), reicht allein zur Annahme eines wesentlichen Vertragsbruches nicht aus.
[218] Vgl. *Achilles*, Art. 25, Rn. 4; *Enderlein/Maskow/Strohbach*, Art. 25, Anm. 3.4. („... hängt ... vom Zeitfaktor ab ... Eine nicht vertragsgemäße Lieferung (kann sich) dann zu einer wesentlichen Vertragsverletzung ausweiten, wenn der Mangel nicht beseitigt wird"); *Herber/Czerwenka*, Art. 48, Rn. 9; *Honnold/Flechtner,* Art. 25, Rn. 184; *Keller,* FS Kritzer, S. 258; ohne *Müller-Chen*, Art. 48 Rn. 14 f.; *Lurger*, IHR 2001, 98; *Musger,* S. 42; *Piltz,* Internationales Kaufrecht, Rn. 5–279; *Witz/Salger/Lorenz/Salger*, Art. 48, Rn. 2; umfassend zu diesem Problem *Botzenhardt*, S. 208 ff., der nach grammatischer, systematischer, historischer und teleologischer Interpretation (S. 208 ff.) im Wesentlichen der hier vertretenen Ansicht folgt (S. 224). Auch bei den Beratungen in UNCITRAL ist diese Ansicht mehrfach zugrunde gelegt worden, s. YB VIII (1977), S. 45, Nr. 275; S. 31, Nr. 93.
[219] OGH, 22.11.2011, CISG-online 2239 bezeichnet sie als „zentrales Problem bei Bestimmung des Begriffs der ,wesentlichen Vertragsverletzung' ".
[220] *Schlechtriem*, FS U. Huber, S. 568.

parteiautonome Betonung des betreffenden Pflichteninhalts[221] oder auf allgemeine Maßstäbe[222] zurückgeht.

In der Rechtsprechung ist nicht selten entschieden worden, dass eine behebbare Vertragswidrigkeit der gelieferten Ware jedenfalls allein keinen wesentlichen Vertragsbruch begründet, sofern die Möglichkeit einer Nacherfüllung besteht.[223] Zum gleichen Ergebnis führt die Auffassung, das Aufhebungsrecht des Käufers sei so lange suspendiert, wie Nacherfüllung möglich und ernsthaft angeboten ist und die für die Nacherfüllung erforderliche Zeit durch Überschreiten des Liefertermins nicht ihrerseits eine wesentliche Vertragsverletzung bewirkt.[224] Ein vor allem in der Formulierung abweichender, in den praktischen Resultaten jedoch ähnlicher Ansatz stellt demgegenüber auf eine Gesamtschau der Umstände des Einzelfalls ab.[225] Wieder andere Autoren wollen generell dem Aufhebungsrecht Vorrang vor einer zweiten Andienung einräumen.[226] Teilweise wird dieses rechtspolitisch kaum tragfähige Ergebnis dadurch abzuschwächen versucht, dass man den Begriff des „wesentlichen Vertragsbruchs" rechtsfolgenorientiert und damit verschieden je nach Norm, in der er als Voraussetzung verwendet wird, interpretiert.[227]

48 M. E. ist an der bereits in den Vorauflagen vertretenen Ansicht grundsätzlich festzuhalten, dass in Fällen, in denen Nachbesserung, Nachlieferung oder Beseitigung eines Mangels in einer **angemessenen,** die Nutzungserwartungen des Käufers berücksichtigenden **Frist** möglich ist[228] und vom Verkäufer erwartet werden kann, ein wesentlicher Vertragsbruch **noch nicht** geschehen ist.[229] Die Parteien müssen zunächst versuchen zu kooperieren. Ein entsprechendes Angebot des Verkäufers **allein** hindert einen wesentlichen Vertragsbruch jedoch nicht;[230] Voraussetzung ist zudem, dass die Nacherfüllung für den Käufer in zeitlicher und sachlicher Hinsicht **zumutbar** ist,[231] woran es etwa fehlen kann, wenn der Verkäufer

---

[221] S. bereits oben Rn. 44 ff.
[222] S. dazu noch unten Rn. 50 ff.
[223] OLG Köln, 14.10.2002, CISG-online 709 = IHR 2003, 15: „Selbst ein schwerwiegender Mangel stellt dann keine wesentliche Vertragsverletzung dar, wenn der Verkäufer zur Nachlieferung ohne unzumutbare Belastung des Käufers bereit ist"; OLG Koblenz, 31.1.1997, CISG-online 256 = IHR 2003, 172, 175: für Art. 25 „ist nicht nur das Gewicht des Mangels, sondern auch die Bereitschaft des Verkäufers, den Mangel ohne unzumutbare Verzögerungen und Belastungen für den Käufer zu beseitigen, von Bedeutung. Selbst ein schwerwiegender Mangel stellt dann keine *wesentliche* Vertragsverletzung im Sinne dieser Bestimmung dar, wenn der Verkäufer zur Nachlieferung ohne unzumutbare Belastung des Käufers bereit ist" – da auf ernsthafte Bereitschaft der Verkäuferin zur Nacherfüllung des Vertrages (über Acryldecken) nicht reagiert wurde, lag keine wesentliche Vertragsverletzung vor; CA Grenoble, 26.4.1995, CISG-online 154: behebbarer und inzwischen behobener Mangel an Metallelementen des verkauften Lagerhauses – wesentliche Vertragsverletzung verneint; ICC, 7754/1995, CISG-online 834: Lieferung nicht vertragsgemäßer Computerhardware, aber „the difference could be cured by way of a minor mounting adjustment and at a minimal cost" – wesentliche Vertragsverletzung verneint; HGer Zürich, 26.4.1995, CISG-online 248 = TranspR-IHR 1999, 54 (obiter); Trib. Forlì, 11.12.2008, CISG-online 1729; a. A. BGer, 15.9.2000, CISG-online 770: „En outre, il importe peu que le défaut soit objectivement réparable ou non".
[224] HGer Aargau, 5.11.2002, CISG-online 715 = IHR 2003, 178, 179; *Audit*, Vente internationale, Anm. 133.; *Bianca/Bonell/Will*, Art. 48, Anm. 2.1.1.1.1. und 3.2.2.; *Peacock*, 8 Int'l Trade & Bus. L. Ann. (2003), 95, 119.
[225] OGH, 22.11.2011, CISG-online 2239 in Anschluss an *Botzenhardt*, S. 208 ff.
[226] *Karollus*, S. 142 f.; *Neumayer*, RIW 1994, 99, 106; *Soergel/Lüderitz/Schüßler-Langeheine*, Art. 48, Rn. 4; *Staudinger/Magnus*, Art. 48, Rn. 29 f.; *Welser*, S. 124 f.
[227] *Karollus*, ZIP 1993, 490, 496 (Möglichkeit einer Mängelbehebung bei der Auslegung des wesentlichen Vertragsbruchs als Voraussetzung der Aufhebung nach Art. 49 I lit. a) mit zu berücksichtigen); dagegen bereits oben Rn. 7.
[228] *Schlechtriem*, FS U. Huber, S. 568: das Nachleistungsangebot müsse „innerhalb der gesetzten Liefertermine oder -fristen, jedenfalls aber in angemessener Frist erfüllt werden".
[229] Ebenso BGer, 18.5.2009, CISG-online 1900 = IHR 2010, 27, 28 f.; OLG Koblenz, 31.1.1997, CISG-online 256 = IHR 2003, 172, 175; eine Teilungsmöglichkeit der Nacherfüllung schadet dabei nach HGer Aargau, 5.11.2002, CISG-online 715 = IHR 2003, 178, 180 jedenfalls nicht ohne weiteres.
[230] Ein Antrag bei UNCITRAL, ein solches Angebot des Verkäufers zu berücksichtigen, fand keine Mehrheit, YB VIII (1977), S. 31 f., Nr. 93–95; ferner S. 45, Nr. 275. Man hielt diese Ergänzung für überflüssig, offenbar weil sie sich aus der Zielsetzung bereits aus der Grundregel ergebe, vgl. hierzu *Honnold/Flechtner*, Art. 25, Rn. 184; *Ziegel*, Remedial Provisions, § 9.03 (3) sub 9–23.
[231] Vgl. auch Int. Ct. Russian CCI, 25.6.2004, 120/2003, CISG-online 1437: Nachbesserung der gelieferten Produktionsanlage hätte lt. Expertengutachten bis zu 1,5 Jahre gedauert und erhebliche Kosten verursacht

gefälschte Computerchips (Prozessoren) geliefert hat, weil eine nochmalige Belieferung mit Fälschungen für die Käuferin die Gefahr einer Rufschädigung mit sich bringen würde.[232]

Erst mit **Ablauf** einer **angemessenen Frist** oder mit dem Deutlichwerden, dass (erfolgreiche) Nacherfüllung nicht zu erwarten ist, kann der anfänglich (vorübergehend noch) unwesentliche Mangel zum **wesentlichen Vertragsbruch** werden.[233] Dies ist jedenfalls dann der Fall, wenn der Verkäufer die geschuldete Nachbesserung verweigert;[234] wenn er seit 9 Monaten ergebnislos mit Nachbesserungsversuchen an der verkauften Maschine beschäftigt ist und sich zudem weigert, für die aufgelaufenen Schäden einzustehen,[235] oder dann, wenn nach versehentlicher Lieferung eines falschen gebrauchten Gabelstaplers von Belgien nach Island die Verschiffung des richtigen Geräts „in der nächsten Woche" vereinbart war, aber zwei Monate später immer noch keine Nachlieferung erfolgt ist.[236] Andererseits bedeutet Nichtbehebbarkeit eines Mangels nicht stets, dass ein wesentlicher Vertragsbruch geschehen ist.[237] Und fruchtloser Ablauf einer Nachfrist zur Nacherfüllung lässt nicht jeden Mangel zum wesentlichen Vertragsbruch werden (Rn. 49).

c) Nachfristsetzung. Das CISG weicht vom EKG dadurch ab, dass der Käufer nicht **49** durch bloße Nachfristsetzung klären kann, dass (ob) eine vertragswidrige Beschaffenheit wesentlicher Vertragsbruch ist, da Art. 49 I lit. b) **nur** den Fall der **Nichtlieferung** deckt.[238] Man sollte deshalb auch nicht eine Nachfristsetzung für den Nacherfüllungsanspruch mit dem Ziel zulassen, die Nichterfüllung des Mängelbeseitigungsanspruchs unter Art. 49 I lit. b) zu subsumieren und so doch zur Vertragsaufhebung über Setzen einer Nachfrist zur Mängelbeseitigung zu gelangen: Art. 49 I lit. b) spricht ausdrücklich von Nichterfüllung und nicht von einer innerhalb einer gesetzten Nachfrist unterbliebenen Nachbesserung usw.[239] Auch nach Ablauf einer Nachfrist bleibt folglich die **Gewichtung des Mangels** aufgegeben. Andererseits ist es nicht etwa erforderlich, bei vorliegender wesentlicher Vertragsverletzung *zusätzlich* eine Nachfrist zu setzen, um den Vertrag aufheben zu können.[240]

d) Rückabwicklung als ultima ratio bei Unverwertbarkeit der Ware. Im Übrigen **50** sind die Konstellationen, die durch die Gerichte in den Vertragsstaaten zu beurteilen waren, außerordentlich vielgestaltig. Weitgehende Einigkeit ist festzustellen, soweit es um Mängel geht, die der Verkäufer durch Nacherfüllung beheben kann (und will), ohne dass daraus für den Käufer Zeitverzögerungen, die bei Nichtlieferung selbst wesentlicher Vertragsbruch wären, und unzumutbare Belästigungen entstehen: Solche **behebbaren Mängel** sind nicht wesentliche Vertragsverletzung i. S. von Art. 25.[241] Der BGH und die meisten Kommentatoren lassen aber auch bei **unbehebbaren Mängeln** einen zwangsläufigen Schluss auf einen wesentlichen Vertragsbruch nicht zu.[242] Auch das Ausmaß der Abweichung von den als

---

– wesentliche Vertragsverletzung bejaht, ohne dass dem Verkäufer Gelegenheit zur Nachbesserung gegeben werden musste.

[232] OGH, 5.7.2001, CISG-online 652 = ZfRV 2002, 25: Verkauf gefälschter Intel Pentium II/300-Prozessoren.

[233] Überzeugend *Magnus*, FS Schlechtriem, S. 599, 605 ff.; s. unten *Müller-Chen*, Art. 48 Rn. 14 f.; s. ferner *Kritzer*, Guide to Practical Applications, S. 413, Nr. 6.

[234] S. OLG Karlsruhe, 19.12.2002, CISG-online 817 = IHR 2003, 125, 126.

[235] LG Heilbronn, 15.9.1997, CISG-online 562.

[236] RB Kortrijk, 4.6.2004, CISG-online 945.

[237] S. unten Rn. 50.

[238] S. dazu bereits oben Rn. 11. Vgl. *Leser*, Vertragsaufhebung und Rückabwicklung, S. 231; *Lurger*, IHR 2001, 98; *Staudinger/Magnus*, Art. 25, Rn. 25, Art. 49, Rn. 21; *Witz/Salger/Lorenz/Salger*, Art. 49, Rn. 4; a. A. OLG Düsseldorf, 10.2.1994, CISG-online 115 = NJW-RR 1994, 506.

[239] Gegen die Benutzung einer Nachfristsetzung zur Mängelbeseitigung, um so zur Vertragsaufhebung zu kommen, KG Zug, 14.12.2009, CISG-online 2026; *Berger/Scholl*, FS Schwenzer, S. 162; *Honnold/Flechtner*, Art. 49, Rn. 305; *Honsell/Gsell*, Art. 25, Rn. 39; *P. Huber*, FS Schwenzer, S. 817; *Schlechtriem*, FS U. Huber, S. 569.

[240] S. schon oben Rn. 10.

[241] S. bereits oben Rn. 47 f. m. Nachw.

[242] BGH, 3.4.1996, CISG-online 135 = BGHZ 132, 290, 299: auch wenn Nachbesserung – wie vorliegend – ausscheidet, bedeutet das nicht zwangsläufig und unabhängig von Art und Umfang des Mangels, dass damit

vertragsgemäß geschuldeten Eigenschaften ist nicht ausschlaggebend, so dass die Falschlieferung (aliud) auch hier keine Sonderrolle (mehr) spielt.[243]

51 Entscheidend – und m. E. zutreffend – ist nach der Rechtsprechung, der die Kommentarliteratur überwiegend folgt, dass Rückabwicklung nach Vertragsaufhebung oder Nachlieferungsbegehren möglichst vermieden werden soll, da mit zusätzlichen Kosten und Risiken für die Ware verbunden, und deshalb die Schwelle „wesentlicher Vertragsbruch" hoch anzusetzen ist; **Rückabwicklung** soll **ultima ratio** sein.[244] Deshalb soll der Käufer auf Schadenersatzansprüche und Minderung verwiesen bleiben, solange der Kaufgegenstand für ihn nicht völlig unverwertbar ist.[245]

52 **aa) Möglichkeit des Käufers zur Verwertung der mangelhaften Ware.** In der Präzisierung dieser Voraussetzung dürften die entscheidenden Differenzierungen geschehen. Wo **Weiterverkauf,** wenn auch mit Verlust, selbst zu Schleuderpreisen, **möglich** ist, sollte Rückabwicklung ausscheiden.[246] Den Mindererlös sowie etwaige Zusatzaufwendungen, die der Käufer zur Durchführung des Weiterverkaufs machen musste, kann er als Schadenersatz nach Artt. 45 I lit. b), 74 ff. liquidieren. Wurde die Ware für Zwecke der Weiterverarbeitung gekauft, so mag der Käufer sie trotz ihrer fehlenden Vertragsgemäßheit zur Herstellung anderer, weniger anspruchsvoller Produkte einsetzen können, wodurch ein wesentlicher Vertragsbruch ebenfalls ausgeschlossen wird.[247]

53 Die Rechtsprechung hat den beschriebenen Maßstab der Verwertbarkeit in jüngerer Zeit auch auf Konstellationen erstreckt, in denen die gelieferte Ware selbst nicht mangelhaft war, aber deshalb nicht verwendet werden konnte, weil der Verkäufer eine vertragliche Nebenpflicht (wie etwa zur betriebsbereiten Aufstellung gelieferter Maschinen) verletzt hatte: Kein

---

das Erfüllungsinteresse des Käufers im Wesentlichen entfällt; KG Zug, 30.8.2007, CISG-online 1722, SZIER 2008, 187. Ebenso *Honsell/Gsell,* Art. 25, Rn. 43; MünchKomm/*Gruber,* Art. 25, Rn. 23 ff.; *Staudinger/Magnus,* Art. 49, Rn. 14; *Witz/Salger/Lorenz/Salger,* Art. 25, Rn. 8.

[243] BGH, 3.4.1996, CISG-online 135 = BGHZ 132, 290, 296 ff.; OGH, 29.6.1999, CISG-online 483 = TranspR-IHR 1999, 48 ff. Ebenso OLG Düsseldorf, 9.7.2010, CISG-online 2171 = IHR 2011, 116, 120 f., wo das Gericht sodann aber – widersprüchlich – doch auf die Einordnung des gelieferten Konzentratsafts als „aliud" des geschuldeten Direktsafts abstellt.

[244] OGH, 22.11.2011, CISG-online 2239; BGer, 28.10.1998, CISG-online 413 = IHR 2000, 14; BGer, 18.5.2009, CISG-online 1900 = IHR 2010, 27, 28; BGH, 3.4.1996, CISG-online 135 = BGHZ 132, 290, 298; SCC Institute, 5.4.2007, CISG-online 1521, Rn. 145: the „concept of fundamental breach under Article 25 has been narrowly construed"; OLG Brandenburg, 18.11.2008, CISG-online 1734 = IHR 2009, 105, 111; OLG Hamburg, 25.1.2008, CISG-online 1681 = IHR 2008, 98, 100; Trib. Forlì, 11.12.2008, CISG-online 1729; *Berger/Scholl,* FS Schwenzer, S. 161; *Peacock,* 8 Int'l Trade & Bus. L. Ann. (2003), 95, 106; *Schwimann/Posch,* Art. 25, Rn. 3.

[245] So auch OLG Düsseldorf, 23.1.2004, CISG-online 918: wesentliche Vertragsverletzung bei Schlechtlieferung nur dann, „wenn die Ware aufgrund ihrer vertragswidrigen Beschaffenheit für den Käufer oder seinen Endabnehmer völlig unverwertbar ist"; OLG Hamburg, 25.1.2008, CISG-online 1681 = IHR 2008, 98, 100; ähnlich LG München I, 27.7.2002, CISG-online 654 = IHR 2003, 233, 235: keine wesentliche Vertragsverletzung, wenn Käufer *Verwendung* für die mangelhafte Ware hat; *Brunner,* Art. 25, Rn. 15; *Honsell/Gsell,* Art. 25, Rn. 43; *Huber/Mullis,* S. 231.

[246] BGer, 28.10.1998, CISG-online 413 = IHR 2000, 14: zur industriellen Fleischverarbeitung in Ägypten vorgesehenes Fleisch wäre dort trotz eines überhöhten Fettanteils sowie Blut und Nässe in den Fleischstücken zu einem tieferen Preis abzusetzen gewesen – wesentliche Vertragsverletzung verneint; CIETAC, 1.1.2000, CISG-online 1614: 71% der gelieferten, mangelhaften Andenkenmünzen waren erfolgreich (zum vollen Preis) weiterverkauft worden – wesentliche Vertragsverletzung verneint. Sehr zweifelhaft LG München I, 29.11.2005, CISG-online 1567 = RIW 2007, 146, 147: Lieferung mit erheblichen Mängeln behafteter Paprikastreifen wurde deshalb als wesentliche Vertragsverletzung gewertet, weil es der Käuferin „nicht zugemutet werden" könne, die Ware zu einem niedrigeren Preis zu verkaufen – genau dies hatte die Käuferin nach Erklärung der Vertragsaufhebung jedoch getan (!).

[247] KG Zug, 30.8.2007, CISG-online 1722, SZIER 2008, 187: Herstellerin von Mobiltelefonen hatte GMS-Module gekauft, die sich als vertragswidrig erwiesen, weil sie keine Verstellung des Lautsprechervolumens erlaubten, die von der Käuferin aber in einfachere Geräte ohne Lautstärkeregelung (mit folglich geringerem Verkaufspreis) eingebaut worden waren – wesentliche Vertragsverletzung verneint; OLG Stuttgart, 12.3.2001, CISG-online 841 = OLGR Stuttgart 2002, 148 ff.: vertragswidrig mit Glukosesirup versetztes Apfelsaftkonzentrat konnte zwar nicht zur beabsichtigten Herstellung von Apfelsaft, aber von Apfelfruchtsaftgetränk verwendet werden – wesentliche Vertragsverletzung verneint.

wesentlicher Vertragsbruch lag insoweit vor, wo es dem Käufer gelungen war, den Kaufgegenstand (Inventar für ein Eiscafé) zumindest notdürftig in Betrieb zu nehmen und für mehrere Monate zu benutzen, weil dies die Verwendbarkeit des gelieferten Inventars für den vereinbarten Zweck belegte, selbst wenn der Käufer selbst für die Aufstellung und Betriebsbereitschaft hatte sorgen müssen.[248]

bb) Unzumutbarkeit als Grenze. Eine Grenze ist dort zu ziehen, wo die Verwertung 54 der mangelhaften Ware für den Käufer unzumutbar ist.[249] Dies ist etwa der Fall, wenn der Käufer für den Weiterverkauf unzumutbare Vertriebswege suchen oder hohe Aufwendungen machen müsste, deren Erstattung als Schadensersatz durch den Verkäufer unsicher sein kann.

Verletzt die Ware bestimmte Sicherheitsstandards im Käuferland[250] – wie etwa Druck- 55 kochtöpfe, deren Benutzung wegen mangelhafter Dichtungen als gefährlich eingestuft und deren Zertifizierung durch das frz. *Laboratoire National d'Essai* daher abgelehnt wurde,[251] oder aus Deutschland nach Uganda gelieferte gebrauchte Schuhe, denen von einer ugandischen Behörde ein so schlechter und unhygienischer Zustand attestiert wurde, dass sie „für den ugandischen Markt nicht akzeptabel" seien[252] – so wird man dem Käufer nicht ohne weiteres zumuten können, sie in ein anderes Land mit geringeren Sicherheitsstandards zu exportieren. Ist die Ware wegen ihrer Sicherheitsdefizite bereits beschlagnahmt worden, dürfte zumutbare Verwertung ohnehin fast immer ausscheiden;[253] ebenso bei Gesundheitsschädlichkeit gelieferter Lebensmittel infolge der Verwendung krebserregender Zusatzstoffe[254] oder bei hochmodischer Damenoberbekleidung, die weitgehend „verschnitten" ist und infolgedessen so klein ausfällt, dass sie ihrer Größe nach nur von Kindern getragen werden könnte und daher unverkäuflich bleibt.[255] Zu berücksichtigen kann zudem sein, ob der Ruf des Käufers durch den Weiterverkauf minderwertiger Ware beeinträchtigt zu werden droht.[256]

Daneben ist von Bedeutung, ob die betreffende Ware zum Zweck der Verarbeitung oder 56 Weiterveräußerung oder aber als Investitionsgut erworben wurde:[257] In letztgenanntem Fall werden dem Käufer Bemühungen um einen Weiterverkauf seltener zumutbar sein als bei Warenarten, mit denen er im Tagesgeschäft handelt.[258] Keine Rolle spielt demgegenüber, ob die gelieferte vertragswidrige Ware vom Käufer als Produkt der vereinbarten Warenart weiterverkauft werden kann oder (weil ein „aliud" darstellend) nicht – die Zumutbarkeit des Absatzes von Konzentratsaft durch die kaufende Fruchtsafthändlerin kann also nicht mit

---

[248] OLG Hamburg, 25.1.2008, CISG-online 1681 = IHR 2008, 98, 100; vgl. auch *Achilles*, Art. 25, Rn. 9.
[249] BGer, 18.5.2009, CISG-online 1900 = IHR 2010, 27, 28; *Bridge*, Int'l Sale of Goods, Rn. 12.25: „without unreasonable efforts by the buyer". Kritisch zur maßgeblichen Anknüpfung an die Unzumutbarkeit der Verwertung hingegen *Schwimann/Posch*, Art. 25, Rn. 12.
[250] Zur Mangelhaftigkeit in diesen Fällen s. unten *Schwenzer*, Art. 35 Rn. 17.
[251] CA Paris, 4.6.2004, CISG-online 872: wesentliche Vertragsverletzung bejaht.
[252] LG Frankfurt a. M., 11.4.2005, CISG-online 1014 = IHR 2005, 162, 163: wesentliche Vertragsverletzung bejaht.
[253] Vgl. *Medical Marketing International, Inc. v. Internazionale Medico Scientifica, S. R. L.,* U.S. Dist. Ct. (E. D. La.), 17.5.1999, CISG-online 387 = IPRax 1999, 388.
[254] Vgl. Gerechtshof 's-Gravenhage, 23.4.2003, CISG-online 903 = IHR 2004, 119: Lieferung von mit krebserregendem und in der EU verbotenen Zusatzstoff versetzten Weizenmehls nach Mozambique ist wesentliche Vertragsverletzung, obgleich der betreffende Stoff in Mozambique nicht verboten war – andernfalls könnten in hoch entwickelten Ländern niedergelassene Verkäufer für den menschlichen Verzehr ungeeignete Produkte an Käufer in weniger entwickelten Ländern liefern, ohne dass dies vertraglich sanktioniert werde.
[255] OLG Köln, 14.10.2002, CISG-online 709 = IHR 2003, 15 ff. mit ausführlicher Tatsachendarstellung („... nicht mehr mit einer gewagten Designerentscheidung erklärbare Mängel ...").
[256] OLG Koblenz, 21.11.2007, CISG-online 1733 = OLGR Koblenz 2008, 493, 494: Verkauf minderwertiger Stiefel ist für ein kleines Fachgeschäft wg. drohenden Imageverlusts nicht zumutbar, „da negative Erlebnisse von Kunden regelmäßig über Mund-zu-Mund-Propaganda verbreitet werden"; LG Oldenburg, 6.7.1994, CISG-online 274 (Möbelhändler – *in concreto* offen gelassen); MünchKommHGB/*Benicke*, Art. 25, Rn. 23.
[257] S. bereits oben Rn. 46 sowie MünchKommHGB/*Benicke*, Art. 25, Rn. 22.
[258] So auch BGer, 18.5.2009, CISG-online 1900 = IHR 2010, 27, 29; *Honsell/Gsell*, Art. 25, Rn. 44.

der Begründung verneint werden, sie habe mit dem vertragsbrüchigen Verkäufer über Direktsaft kontrahiert gehabt.[259]

57 cc) **Weitere Fälle wesentlicher Vertragsverletzungen.** Im Einzelnen wird es oft eine vom Tatsachenrichter zu beurteilende Frage sein, ob dem Käufer eine Verwertung möglich und zumutbar ist. Die Rechtsprechung hat dies verneint und daher eine **wesentliche Vertragsverletzung angenommen,** wenn Wäsche beim Waschen um zwei Größen schrumpfte,[260] Schuhe Risse aufwiesen,[261] zur Verpackung von Heu bestimmte Plastikfolie weder reißfest noch abrollbar war und der Käufer aus diesem Grund zahlreiche Kunden verloren hatte[262] oder als Verpackungsmaterial erworbene Seitenfaltenbeutel einen unangenehmen Fremdgeruch aufwiesen.[263]

58 Manche Gerichte scheinen freilich zuweilen milder zu urteilen und messen der Frage der Verwertbarkeit der mangelhaften Ware auf den ersten Blick keine Bedeutung zu; gezuckerter Wein[264] und Mängel von Modelleisenbahnen[265] oder Sportkleidung[266] wurden deshalb ebenso ohne weiteres als wesentlicher Vertragsbruch gewertet wie die Tatsache, dass gelieferte, im Übrigen einwandfreie Europaletten nicht polnischen Ursprungs waren und daher bei einer Zollaußenprüfung mit bedeutendem Einfuhrzoll belegt wurden.[267] In anderen Entscheidungen wird die Verwendungs- oder Weiterverkaufsmöglichkeit zwar nicht ausdrücklich angesprochen, hat aber nach dem Sachverhalt die richterliche Bewertung wohl mit beeinflusst.[268]

5. Dokumente

59 Zur Beschaffung und Übergabe bestimmter Dokumente kann der Verkäufer aufgrund einer ausdrücklichen vertraglichen Abrede, aufgrund von Gepflogenheiten der Parteien bzw. eines Handelsbrauches (Art. 9) oder in besonderen Fällen auch nach Treu und Glauben verpflichtet sein.[269] Für die Qualifizierung diesbezüglicher Pflichtverletzungen nach Art. 25 ist zwar auch die Art der betroffenen Dokumente,[270] vorrangig aber ihre Bedeutung innerhalb des Pflichtenprogramms des konkreten Kaufvertrags maßgeblich. Im Einzelnen ist zu unterscheiden:

60 a) **Begleitdokumente.** Der Kaufvertrag kann ausdrücklich oder konkludent vorsehen, dass den Verkäufer neben seiner Hauptpflicht zur Lieferung der Ware (Artt. 31 ff.) die begleitende Pflicht trifft, bestimmte auf die Ware bezogene Dokumente zu beschaffen und an den Käufer (oder einen Dritten) zu übergeben (Art. 34). In der Praxis beziehen sich entsprechende Pflichten etwa auf die Übergabe von Waren- oder Traditionspapieren wie

---

[259] Falsch daher OLG Düsseldorf, 9.7.2010, CISG-online 2171 = IHR 2011, 116, 121 (anders hätte die Sache gelegen, wenn ein Verkauf von Konzentratsaft *in casu* als rufschädigend einzustufen gewesen wäre – hierfür waren keine Anzeichen ersichtlich).
[260] LG Landshut, 5.4.1995, CISG-online 193.
[261] OLG Frankfurt a. M., 18.1.1994, CISG-online 123 = NJW 1994, 1013, 1014.
[262] Hof van Beroep Gent, 10.5.2004, CISG-online 991.
[263] KG Glarus, 6.11.2008, CISG-online 1996 = IHR 2010, 152, 153.
[264] Civ. 1, 23.1.1996, CISG-online 159 = J. C. P. 1996, II, 2234 (Anm. *Muir Watt*); dazu auch *Witz/Wolter*, RIW 1998, 278 f.
[265] KG Schaffhausen, 27.1.2004, CISG-online 960: die gelieferten, hochpreisigen Modelle wiesen eine große Anzahl fehlerhafter Verarbeitungen auf, die das Gericht sorgfältig auflistete, ohne sie jedoch zu den Voraussetzungen des Art. 25 in Bezug zu setzen.
[266] Krajský súd v Žiline, 25.10.2007, CISG-online 1761 (ohne Begründung).
[267] LG Saarbrücken, 1.4.2004, CISG-online 1228 – zweifelhaft, weil hier dem deutschen Käufer mit einem (*in casu* auch geltend gemachten) Schadensersatzanspruch ausreichend gedient gewesen wäre.
[268] S. *Delchi Carrier SpA v. Rotorex Corp.*, U. S. Ct. App. (2nd Cir.), 6.12.1995, CISG-online 140 = 71 F. 3d 1024; ferner Civ. 1, 26.5.1999, CISG-online 487 = D. 2000, 788: Metallbleche, die auf Grund ihrer vertragswidrigen Qualität und Abmessungen für die Verwendungszwecke der Käuferin und ihrer Abnehmer absolut ungeeignet waren.
[269] Oben *Widmer Lüchinger*, Art. 30 Rn. 6; *Staudinger/Magnus*, Art. 30, Rn. 7.
[270] Vgl. CISG-AC, Op. 5 *(Schwenzer)*, Comment 4.7, IHR 2006, 35, 39.

Konnossementen, Lade- oder Lagerscheinen, des Weiteren Ursprungszeugnissen,[271] Analysezertifikaten,[272] Versicherungspolicen, Handelsrechnungen, Zollbescheinigungen, aber auch Betriebsanleitungen und Handbüchern.

Ob die Verletzung einer solchen Pflicht eine „wesentliche Vertragsverletzung" darstellt, **61** bestimmt sich nach denselben Grundsätzen, die in Bezug auf die Pflicht zur Lieferung sachmängelfreier Ware gelten (oben Rn. 50 ff.):[273] Danach kann die fehlende Übergabe dem Kaufvertrag entsprechender Begleitdokumente nach dem Vertragsinhalt von wesentlicher Bedeutung sein, wenn der Käufer dadurch in der vorgesehenen Verwendung der Ware (z. B. deren Weiterverkauf oder Einsatz im eigenen Unternehmen) beschränkt wird;[274] so etwa, wenn die Ware in Ermangelung eines Ursprungszeugnisses schon gar nicht aus dem Verkäuferland ausgeführt werden darf,[275] wenn das Fehlen von Qualitätszertifikat und Versicherungspolice dazu führt, dass die Ware am Lieferort nicht verzollt und vom Käufer entgegen genommen werden kann[276] oder der gelieferte Computer und dessen Software ohne die fehlende Benutzerdokumentation (Handbuch) nicht einsetzbar ist.[277] Dasselbe soll bei Fehlen einer Rechnung gelten, die für die Geltendmachung der Vorsteuer benötigt wird (§ 14 UStG).[278] Vereinzelt wird zudem vorausgesetzt, dass die Vertragswidrigkeit der Dokumente weder durch den Verkäufer[279] noch den Käufer selbst[280] in zumutbarer Weise behoben werden kann.

b) Echtes Dokumentengeschäft, Grundsatz der Dokumentenstrenge. Etwas anderes gilt hingegen bei echten Dokumentengeschäften *(documentary sales),*[281] die sich dadurch **62** auszeichnen, dass die Pflicht zur Übergabe bestimmter Dokumente als Hauptpflicht des Verkäufers ausgestaltet ist und insoweit gleichberechtigt neben seine Pflicht zur Lieferung der Ware (Art. 31 ff.)[282] oder gar an deren Stelle tritt.[283] Ein „echtes" Dokumentengeschäft, das nicht von Art. 2 lit. d) erfasst wird und daher dem CISG unterfallen kann,[284] liegt vielfach (aber nicht immer[285]) bei Verwendung der Lieferklausel **„CIF"**[286] und zum anderen regelmäßig dann vor, wenn die Parteien im Kaufvertrag vereinbart haben, dass die Kauf-

---

[271] Audiencia Provincial de Barcelona, 12.2.2002, CISG-online 1324.
[272] *Enderlein/Maskow/Strohbach,* Art. 25, Anm. 3.4.: Fehlen eines Analysezertifikats stellt bei Verkauf von Chemikalien wesentliche Vertragsverletzung dar.
[273] CISG-AC, Op. 5 *(Schwenzer),* Comment 4.8, IHR 2006, 35, 39.
[274] Vgl. BGH, 3.4.1996, CISG-online 135 = BGHZ 132, 290, 301 f.; *Brunner,* Art. 25, Rn. 18; *Staudinger/ Magnus,* Art. 49, Rn. 17.
[275] Audiencia Provincial de Barcelona, 12.2.2002, CISG-online 1324: wesentliche Vertragsverletzung bejaht.
[276] Int. Ct. Ukrainian CCI, 5.7.2005, CISG-online 1361: wesentliche Vertragsverletzung bejaht.
[277] OLG Nürnberg, 20.9.1995, CISG-online 267: wesentliche Vertragsverletzung bejaht.
[278] *Witz,* FS Schlechtriem, S. 294 (zu Art. 71).
[279] MünchKommHGB/*Benicke,* Art. 34, Rn. 9.
[280] BGH, 3.4.1996, CISG-online 135 = BGHZ 132, 290, 301 f.; *Brunner,* Art. 25, Rn. 18; MünchKomm/ *Gruber,* Art. 25, Rn. 29.
[281] Dass die allgemeinen Vorgaben des Art. 25 auf Dokumentengeschäfte nicht unverändert angewandt werden können, hat man schon bei Erarbeitung des CISG erkannt; vgl. Sekretariatskommentar, Art. 45, Anm. 7. Die einschlägige Begriffsverwendung im Schrifttum ist freilich nicht einheitlich; vgl. für ein besonders weites Begriffsverständnis etwa CISG-AC, Op. 5 *(Schwenzer),* Comment 4.11, IHR 2006, 35, 40, wo alle unter Einbeziehung eines Incoterm® (mit Ausnahme von EXW) abgeschlossenen Kaufverträge als „documentary sales contracts" eingeordnet werden.
[282] So *Mullis,* FS Guest, S. 147 (für CIF-Verträge): „In addition to ‚deliver' the contract goods, [the seller] must also ‚deliver' the documents"; vgl. auch *Bijl,* EJCCL 2009, 19, 27.
[283] So *Bridge,* Int'l Sale of Goods, Rn. 1.07 (für CIF-Verträge): „documents instead of goods", anders aber aaO., Rn. 9.24; *Schlechtriem,* 16 Pace Int'l L. Rev. (2004), 279, 285 f.; *Singh/Leisinger,* 20 Pace Int'l L. Rev. (2008), 161, 181. Anderes Begriffsverständnis bei *Mohs,* FS Schwenzer, S. 1297, der allein auf die Pflicht des Käufers zur Zahlung gegen Dokumente abstellt.
[284] Audiencia Provincial de Barcelona, 24.3.2009, CISG-online 2042; Sekretariatskommentar, Art. 2, Nr. 8; CISG-AC, Op. 5 *(Schwenzer),* Comment 4.12, IHR 2006, 35, 40; *Huber/Mullis,* S. 49 Fn. 169; *Mohs,* FS Schwenzer, S. 1297; *Piltz,* Internationales Kaufrecht, Rn. 2–50; *Schlechtriem,* 16 Pace Int'l L. Rev. (2004), 279, 286; *Singh/Leisinger,* 20 Pace Int'l L. Rev. (2008), 161, 182; *Zeller,* FS Kritzer, S. 633.
[285] Maßgeblich ist die Auslegung des betroffenen Vertrages (Art. 8) unter Beachtung einschlägiger Handelsbräuche (Art. 9), die ergeben kann, dass der konkrete CIF-Vertrag kein echtes Dokumentengeschäft darstellt. Entscheidend sind – wie stets – die Umstände des Einzelfalls.
[286] *Bridge,* Int'l Sale of Goods, Rn. 5.04; *Mullis,* FS Guest, S. 140.

Art. 25 63, 64 Teil III. Kapitel I. Allgemeine Bestimmungen

preiszahlungspflicht des Käufers durch Beibringung eines **Dokumentenakkreditivs** („Bankakkreditiv", „Kasse gegen Akkreditiv", „Zahlung gegen Akkreditiv" o. ä.[287]) oder im Wege des **Dokumenteninkassos** („Kasse gegen Dokumente", „cash against documents", „documents against payment", „documents against acceptance") zu erfüllen ist. Durch die betreffenden Klauseln wird bestimmt, dass der Verkäufer seinerseits darin im Einzelnen spezifizierte Dokumente zu einem bestimmten Zeitpunkt anzudienen hat (s. Art. 30).[288]

63   Es gilt dabei der **Grundsatz der Dokumentenstrenge,** der nach verbreiteter Ansicht einen internationalen Handelsbrauch darstellt und daher über Art. 9 Geltung beansprucht,[289] jedenfalls aber gemäß Art. 8 II, III bei Abschluss eines als Dokumentengeschäft ausgestalteten Kaufvertrages als vereinbart gilt:[290] Dieser Grundsatz verlangt, dass die angedienten Dokumente „rein" sind; sie müssen daher vollständig sein, den vertraglichen Anforderungen in inhaltlicher Hinsicht genauestens entsprechen und dürfen untereinander keine Widersprüche aufweisen. Hintergrund des Grundsatzes der Dokumentenstrenge ist, dass beim echten Dokumentengeschäft die Vertragsabwicklung unter Einschaltung Dritter – vor allem von Banken,[291] bei Kettengeschäften aber auch weiterer Käufer[292] – erfolgt, die häufig mangels Branchenkenntnis die Bedeutung von scheinbar geringfügigen Abweichungen nicht beurteilen können[293] und zudem typischerweise keine Kenntnis von den „Umständen" des konkreten Kaufvertrages besitzen,[294] die andernfalls über Art. 8 II, III bei der Gewichtung der Vertragswidrigkeit eine Rolle spielen könnten.[295] Beim Kettengeschäft erlauben es zudem nur „reine" Dokumente dem Käufer, seinerseits seine Verpflichtung gegenüber dem nachfolgenden Käufer in der Kette zu erfüllen. Nach dem Grundsatz der Dokumentenstrenge berechtigen daher bereits kleinste Abweichungen der Dokumente vom Vertrag den Käufer (regelmäßig vertreten durch die Bank, der die Dokumente vorgelegt werden), zu deren Zurückweisung.[296]

64   In den Kategorien des **Art. 25** gedacht, treffen die Kaufvertragsparteien mit der Vereinbarung entsprechender Klauseln eine bindende Abrede des Inhalts, dass der exakten Erfüllung der Verkäuferpflicht zur fristgemäßen Vorlage der vertraglich geforderten Dokumente **„wesentliche"** Bedeutung zukommt.[297] Da bei Anwendung des Art. 25 auf die

---

[287] Akkreditivklauseln sind häufig auch erheblich detaillierter formuliert; vgl. *Zahn/Ehrlich/Neumann,* Rn. 2/26 ff.
[288] *Bijl,* EJCCL 2009, 19, 20; *Heymann/Horn,* § 346, Rn. 116 und Anhang § 372. Bankgeschäfte, Rn. VI/92; *Zahn/Ehrlich/Neumann,* Rn. 2/33.
[289] *Bijl,* EJCCL 2009, 19, 26; *Nielsen,* WuB I H 1. – 1.97, S. 132; *Schütze,* Dokumentenakkreditiv, Rn. 16.
[290] Vgl. etwa BGH, 15.3.2004, ZIP 2004, 1047, 1049; *Koller,* WM 1990, 293; *Zahn/Ehrlich/Neumann,* Rn. 2/241 f. In Akkreditivklauseln werden dabei häufig ausdrücklich die „Einheitlichen Richtlinien und Gebräuche für Dokumentenakkreditive" (seit Juli 2007 in der Fassung „ERA 600" in Kraft) der Internationalen Handelskammer (ICC) einbezogen; zudem wird die Einbeziehung der ERA unter Kaufleuten weithin als Handelsbrauch eingestuft (so etwa BGH, 14.2.1958, WM 1958, 456, 459; MünchKommHGB/*Nielsen,* ZahlungsV, Rn. H 43 – jeweils zu § 346 HGB).
[291] In Art. 14 ERA hat die Pflicht der Banken zur Dokumentenprüfung bei Akkreditiven eine detaillierte Regelung erfahren; beim Dokumenteninkasso soll die Dokumentenstrenge hingegen in einzelnen Punkten weniger pedantisch zu handhaben sein (MünchKommHGB/*Nielsen,* ZahlungsV, Rn. I 12; vgl. auch die „Einheitlichen Richtlinien für Inkassi" (ERI 522)).
[292] Vgl. *Mullis,* Avoidance for Breach, S. 329.
[293] BGH, 10.12.1970, WM 1971, 158, 159; *Baumbach/Hopt/Hopt,* BankGesch, Rn. K/6; *Koller,* WM 1990, 293, 298; *Zahn/Ehrlich/Neumann,* Rn. 2/242.
[294] BGH, 2.7.1984, NJW 1985, 550, 551; *Bijl,* EJCCL 2009, 19; *Koller,* WM 1990, 293, 298.
[295] S. oben Rn. 22 f., 29.
[296] Nach der klassischen Formulierung von *Viscount Sumner* in *Equitable Trust Company of New York v. Dawson Partners Ltd.,* [1927] 27 Ll. L. R. 49, 52 gilt: „there is no room for documents which are almost the same or which will do as well"; OLG München, 3.7.1996, WM 1996, 2335, 2336: „geradezu pedantischer Prüfungsmaßstab"; *Bijl,* EJCCL 2009, 19, 21; *Schmitthoff,* Export Trade, Rn. 11-008. Zu CISG-Verträgen *Mohs,* FS Schwenzer, S. 1299: Zurückweisungsrecht als Handelsbrauch i. S. d. Art. 9 II.
[297] *Bijl,* EJCCL 2009, 19, 26; *Mullis,* Avoidance for Breach, S. 350 f.; MünchKomm/*P. Huber,* Art. 49, Rn. 44; *Schwenzer,* 25 J. L. & Com. (2005-06), 440 f.; *Takahashi,* J. Bus. L. 2003, 102, 129 (unwiderlegbare Vermutung). Anders für CISG-Vertrag mit Klausel „Cash against documents" aber BGH, 3.4.1996, CISG-online 135 = BGHZ 132, 290, 301 (Anwendung der oben in Rn. 33 f. für Begleitdokumente dargestellten Grundsätze); kritisch dazu *Mullis,* aaO., S. 347 f.; MünchKommHGB/*Nielsen,* ZahlungsV, Rn. I 16; *Nielsen,* WuB I H 1. – 1.97, S. 132; differenzierend MünchKomm/*P. Huber,* Art. 49, Rn. 44.

vertragliche Interessengewichtung abzustellen ist,[298] sind dem Käufer die vom Vorliegen einer wesentlichen Vertragverletzung abhängigen Rechtsbehelfe damit auch dann eröffnet, wenn ihm im konkreten Fall (etwa infolge steigender Marktpreise) kein finanzieller Schaden entstanden ist. Dem Käufer bzw. seiner Bank steht es aus diesem Grund frei, nicht vertragsgemäße Dokumente (etwa „unreine" Konnossemente) **zurückweisen**[299] oder den Kaufvertrag ohne Nachfristsetzung **aufzuheben** (Art. 49 I lit. a) i. V. m. Art. 25).[300] Eine wesentliche Vertragsverletzung liegt insoweit bereits vor, wenn der Verkäufer eine Abänderung der vertraglich vereinbarten Anforderungen an die geschuldeten Dokumente zur Voraussetzung für die seinerseitige Vertragsdurchführung macht.[301]

Ob und inwieweit bei echten Dokumentengeschäften dem vertraglich festgelegten Andienungs**zeitpunkt** wesentliche Bedeutung zukommt, seine Überschreitung also ohne weiteres eine wesentliche Vertragsverletzung i. S. d. Art. 25 darstellt oder dem Verkäufer noch eine Möglichkeit zur nachträglichen (u. U. inhaltlich nachgebesserten) Andienung zustehen soll, richtet sich vorrangig nach dem Kaufvertrag[302] und einschlägigen Handelsbräuchen.[303] Bei Kaufverträgen über Massengüter (*commodity* sales),[304] die vielfach starken Preisschwankungen unterliegen und im Wege des Kettengeschäftes „durchgehandelt", d. h. vom jeweiligen Käufer sogleich weiterveräußert werden, kommt auch der Rechtzeitigkeit der Dokumentenandienung typischerweise wesentliche Bedeutung zu.[305] Die Vertragsauslegung unter Berücksichtigung der Umstände des Einzelfalls (Art. 8 II) und allfälliger Handelsbräuche entscheidet ebenfalls über die verwandte Frage, ob eine zweite Andienung nicht zumindest dann abzuwarten ist, wenn der Verkäufer die erste, vertragswidrige Dokumentenandienung zeitlich vor dem vereinbarten Termin vorgenommen hat und dieser noch nicht verstrichen ist[306] – soweit sich aus vorrangigen Abreden nichts Gegenteiliges ergibt, sieht Art. 34 S. 2 ein solches Recht zur fristgemäßen zweiten Andienung der Dokumente vor.

65

---

[298] S. schon oben Rn. 21 ff.
[299] Dies folgt daraus, dass dem Käufer unter dem CISG nach ganz h. M. dann ein Recht zur Zurückweisung nicht vertragsgemäßer Dokumente zusteht, wenn die Voraussetzungen des Art. 25 erfüllt sind; so CISG-AC, Op. 5 *(Schwenzer)*, Comment 3.3, IHR 2006, 35, 38; *Enderlein/Maskow/Strohbach*, Art. 60, Anm. 2.1.; *Herber/Czerwenka*, Art. 53, Rn. 11; *Honsell/Schnyder/Straub*, Art. 60, Rn. 35; *Schwenzer*, 25 J. L. & Com. (2005-06), 437, 441; *Soergel/Lüderitz/Budzikiewicz*, Art. 60, Rn. 8; *Witz/Salger/Lorenz/Witz*, Art. 60, Rn. 10, 13. Soweit teilweise zusätzlich verlangt wird, dass der Käufer sein Vertragsaufhebungsrecht tatsächlich ausgeübt hat (so *Karollus*, S. 174 f.; *Piltz*, Internationales Kaufrecht, Rn. 4–172; *Staudinger/Magnus*, Art. 26, Rn. 20), überzeugt dies nicht, weil die Zurückweisung ein Minus zur Vertragsaufhebung darstellt; wie hier *Bridge*, Int'l Sale of Goods, Rn. 3.25. Nicht im Ergebnis, aber in der Begründung anders *Schlechtriem*, 16 Pace Int'l L. Rev. (2004), 279, 305: die Vereinbarung eines Dokumentengeschäfts beinhalte ein parteiautonom vereinbartes Zurückweisungsrecht; vgl. auch *dens.*, FS U. Huber, S. 570 ff.
[300] Vgl. *Singh/Leisinger*, 20 Pace Int'l L. Rev. (2008), 161, 184.
[301] *Magellan International Corp. v. Salzgitter Handel GmbH*, U. S. Dist. Ct. (N. D. Ill.), 7.12.1999, CISG-online 439 = 76 F. Supp. 2d 919, 926: Bedingungen des Letter of Credit „required ocean bills of lading to be presented as a condition precedent to Salzgitter's right to draw on the LC. But Salzgitter was permitted to substitute forwarder's Certificates of Receipt („FCR") for bills of lading as to the full order if Magellan were to be more than 20 days late in providing a vessel for shipment" – Verlangen des Verkäufers Salzgitter „to permit the unconditional substitution of FCRs for bills of lading, even for partial orders" als wesentliche Vertragsverletzung.
[302] Vgl. *Brunner*, Art. 25, Rn. 18, der die strikte Einhaltung der vertraglichen Frist zur Dokumentenvorlage nicht in jedem Fall für wesentlich erachtet.
[303] Vielfach wird hier schon deshalb ein Fixgeschäft vorliegen, weil die Parteien einen entsprechenden Incoterm® vereinbart haben; vgl. oben Rn. 41.
[304] Vgl. zu diesen instruktiv *Mohs*, FS Schwenzer, S. 1286 ff. Zur Tauglichkeit des CISG für *commodity sales* auch *Singh/Leisinger*, 20 Pace Int'l L. Rev. (2008), 161, 173 ff.
[305] CISG-AC, Op. 5 *(Schwenzer)*, Comment 4.17, IHR 2006, 35, 40; *Mullis*, Avoidance for Breach, S. 329: „time limits must be strictly complied with", um Spekulationen auf Kosten der Käufer zu verhindern; *Ostendorf*, IHR 2009, 100, 103; *Schwenzer*, 25 J. L. & Com. (2005-06), 437, 441 f.; *Zeller*, FS Kritzer, S. 632; a. A. *Bijl*, EJCCL 2009, 19, 23 f.
[306] Vgl. *Leisinger*, Fundamental Breach, S. 72; *Singh/Leisinger*, 20 Pace Int'l L. Rev. (2008), 161, 187; *Widmer Lüchinger*, unten Art. 34 Rn. 7; *Witz/Salger/Lorenz/Witz*, Art. 34, Rn. 9; CISG-AC, Op. 5 *(Schwenzer)*, Comment 4.14, IHR 2006, 35, 40.

V. Einzelfälle (2): Verletzung von Käuferpflichten

1. Verspätete Zahlung

66 Zahlungsverzögerung allein dürfte nur in Ausnahmefällen wesentliche Vertragsverletzung sein,[307] ebenso die nicht fristgemäße Eröffnung eines Akkreditivs.[308] Den Parteien steht es jedoch frei, der pünktlichen Zahlung vertraglich eine wesentliche Bedeutung zuzuschreiben, was insbesondere bei Vereinbarung einer Vertragswährung nahe liegt, die starker Entwertung ausgesetzt ist; hierzu wird es aber einer klaren Abrede bedürfen, die über die bloße Benennung der Währung hinausgeht.[309] Ein Fixcharakter der Kaufpreiszahlungspflicht wird zudem bei starken Preisschwankungen der Ware angenommen.[310] Bei ernsthafter Weigerung, überhaupt zu zahlen, wird regelmäßig wesentlicher Vertragsbruch anzunehmen sein;[311] ebenso dann, wenn der Käufer seine Zahlung von im Vertrag nicht vorgesehenen Bedingungen wie der Stellung einer Erfüllungsgarantie abhängig macht[312] oder ein Akkreditiv nicht fristgemäß eröffnet wird, obgleich die betreffende Käuferpflicht – wie vor allem bei dokumentären Zahlungsklauseln häufig[313] – nach dem Vertragsinhalt und den Umständen dazu dienen sollte, den Verkäufer vor einer weit reichenden Vorleistung (Verschiffung der Ware ohne Absicherung der Kaufpreiszahlung) und namentlich einer potentiellen „Nachverhandlung" des Kaufpreises zu schützen.[314]

Auch Konkurseröffnung dürfte – von Einzelregelungen nationaler Insolvenzrechte abgesehen – dem Verkäufer ein Recht zur Vertragsaufhebung geben.[315] Monatelange Verzögerung der Kaufpreiszahlung kann sich u. U. ebenfalls zum wesentlichen Vertragsbruch auswachsen.[316] Im Übrigen aber kann der Verkäufer bei Zahlungsverzug über Nachfristsetzung

---

[307] OLG Frankfurt a. M., 24.3.2009, CISG-online 2165 = IHR 2010, 250, 252; OLG Düsseldorf, 22.7.2004, CISG-online 916 = IHR 2005, 29, 31: Verletzung der Pflicht zur Kaufpreiszahlung ist nur im „Ausnahmefall" eine wesentliche Vertragsverletzung. S. auch den englischen Fall *Lombard North Central Plc. v. Butterworth* [1987] 2 W. L. R. 7: pünktliche Zahlung als „condition"; aus dem Schrifttum vgl. unten *Mohs*, Art. 64 Rn. 5 ff.; *Scheifele*, S. 115 ff.; zum EKG *Dölle/von Caemmerer*, Art. 62 EKG, Rn. 6: Kaufpreiszahlungspflicht mit Fixcharakter sei äußerst selten.

[308] ICC, 7585/1992, CISG-online 105 = J. D. I. 1995, 1050; LG Kassel, 21.9.1995, CISG-online 192 (zur Vorlage einer Bankbestätigung über künftige Akkreditiveröffnung). Zu Ausnahmen sogleich im Text.

[309] Vgl. *Magnus/Lüsing*, IHR 2007, 1, 4; MünchKommHGB/*Benicke*, Art. 25, Rn. 20; *Soergel/Lüderitz/Budzikiewicz*, Art. 64, Rn. 5.

[310] OLG Frankfurt a. M., 24.3.2009, CISG-online 2165 = IHR 2010, 250, 252.

[311] *Shuttle Packaging Systems, L. L. C. v. Jacob Tsonakis, INA S. A. and INA Plastics Corporation,* U. S. Dist. Ct. (W. D. Mich.), 17.12.2001, CISG-online 773: „serious non-payment" verbunden mit der Feststellung, dass vom Verkäufer vorgebrachte „complaints about performance were opportunistic and not genuine in character"; *Magnus/Lüsing*, IHR 2007, 1, 4; *Scheifele*, S. 121.

[312] Int. Ct. Russian CCI, 4.4.1998, 387/1995, CISG-online 1334: Käufer verlangte vor Zahlung vom Verkäufer eine Garantie dafür, dass dieser seine Vertragspflichten erfüllen werde – wesentliche Vertragsverletzung bejaht.

[313] S. dazu bereits oben Rn. 65; unten *Mohs*, Art. 64 Rn. 9.

[314] *Downs Investment Pty Ltd. v. Perwaja Steel SDN BHD,* Supr. Ct. of Queensland, 17.11.2000, CISG-online 587: Nichteröffnung des Akkreditivs nach Verfall des Marktpreises für Stahlschrott (vereinbarter Kaufpreis lag USD 700.000 über dem aktuellen Marktpreis) – wesentliche Vertragsverletzung bejaht; OLG Frankfurt a. M., 24.3.2009, CISG-online 2165 = IHR 2010, 250, 252: wenn Zahlung mittels Akkreditiveröffnung gegen Dokumente vorgesehen ist, muss das Akkreditiv dem Verkäufer spätestens am 1. Tag der Abladefrist zur Verfügung stehen.

[315] Vgl. *Roder Zelt- und Hallenkonstruktionen GmbH v. Rosedown Park Pty Ltd. and Reginald R Eustace,* FCA (SA, Adelaide), 28.4.1995, CISG-online 218 = 1995 F. C. R.(Aus.) 216 ff. („In my opinion the appointment of an administrator by Rosedown constituted a fundamental breach of the contract within the meaning of Article 25 which would justify Roder notifying a declaration of avoidance … the placement of the company under administration, in the circumstances of this case, resulted in such detriment to Roder as substantially to deprive it of what it was entitled to expect under the contract").

[316] *Doolim Corp. v. R Doll LLC et al.,* U. S. Dist. Ct. (S. D. N. Y.), 29.5.2009, CISG-online 1892: weniger als 20% des Gesamtkaufpreises waren bezahlt worden und ein Betrag von mehr als USD 1.000.000 stand noch aus, als Käufer angab, insolvent zu sein – wesentliche Vertragsverletzung bejaht; CIETAC, 10.5.2005, CISG-online 1022: offene Kaufpreisforderungen über USD 244.880 aus 14 Verträgen, Zahlungsrückstand von über

zur Aufhebung kommen, Art. 64 I lit. b).[317] Weitergehende Möglichkeiten erleichterter Vertragsaufhebung bei Zahlungsverzug lässt das Einheitskaufrecht nicht zu.

2. Verletzung der Abnahmepflicht

Endgültige Weigerung oder Unmöglichkeit der Abnahme bewirken regelmäßig wesentlichen Vertragsbruch.[318] Der Verkäufer muss in beiden Fällen die Möglichkeit haben, durch Aufhebung vom Vertrag loszukommen, einen Deckungsverkauf tätigen und seinen Schadensersatz auf der Grundlage von Art. 75 berechnen zu können. Ansonsten kommt es auf die Bedeutung **rechtzeitiger** Abnahme für den Verkäufer an;[319] die Rechtsprechung tendiert bislang dazu, bei Fehlen außergewöhnlicher Umstände – wie etwa der Verderblichkeit der Ware oder Besonderheiten der Lagerung bzw. Beförderung[320] – die Wesentlichkeit der Vertragsverletzung abzulehnen.[321] Ist die Lage zweifelhaft, kann Nachfristsetzung klären,[322] freilich mit den sich im Fall erfolgter Zahlung aus Art. 64 II ergebenden Einschränkungen. 67

VI. Einzelfälle (3): Verletzung sonstiger (Neben-)Pflichten

Die Bezeichnung einer sonstigen Pflicht als „Nebenpflicht" kann über die Bedeutung des korrespondierenden Gläubigerinteresses nichts aussagen.[323] Entscheidend sind der konkrete Fall und die Auslegung des Vertrages: Nebenleistungspflichten zur Stellung von Sicherheiten, zum Schutz von Markenrechten,[324] zum Verbot der Weiterlieferung in bestimmte Länder,[325] Exklusivitätsvereinbarungen,[326] Dienstleistungspflichten bei Verträgen nach Art. 3 II, Pflichten zur Einhaltung von „International Labour Standards" der ILO[327] und zur Ausstellung bestimmter Rechnungen,[328] Verkäuferpflichten zur Montage oder betriebs- 68

---

einem Jahr unter ständigem Vertrösten durch Käufer – wesentliche Vertragsverletzung bejaht; Schiedsgericht der Handelskammer Hamburg, 21.3.1996, CISG-online 187 = NJW 1996, 3229 ff.

[317] Zu den Problemen im Einzelnen s. die Kommentierung von *Mohs* zu Art. 64; ferner *Scheifele*, S. 121.

[318] Hof van Beroep Gent, 20.10.2004, CISG-online 983: Verweigerung der Annahme von Stahlspulen bereits vor Lieferung, weil Käufer der unzutreffenden Ansicht war, die Liefertermine seien nicht eingehalten – wesentliche Vertragsverletzung bejaht; Schiedsgericht der Börse für landwirtschaftliche Produkte in Wien, 10.12.1997, CISG-online 351, östZRVgl 1998, 211 ff.: erklärte Weigerung, die gekaufte Warenmenge abzurufen und abzunehmen – wesentliche Vertragsverletzung; *Magnus/Lüsing*, IHR 2007, 1, 5; unten *Mohs*, Art. 64 Rn. 6.

[319] Vgl. *Hager*, Die Rechtsbehelfe des Verkäufers, S. 207: „falls nach BGB Abnahme Hauptpflicht wäre"; *Honsell/Gsell*, Art. 25, Rn. 38; *Mohs*, Art. 64 Rn. 14: „... stellt ... nicht automatisch einen wesentlichen Vertragsbruch dar"; für den Fall einer Abnahmepflicht mit Fixcharakter s. *Herber*, Einführung, S. 37.

[320] OLG Düsseldorf, 22.7.2004, CISG-online 916 = IHR 2005, 29, 31.

[321] OLG Düsseldorf, 22.7.2004, CISG-online 916 = IHR 2005, 29, 31: Verletzung der Abnahmepflicht nur im „Ausnahmefall" wesentlich; CA Grenoble, 4.2.1999, CISG-online 443 = D. 1999, 363 (Anm. *C. Witz*): kurzfristige (einige Tage) Überschreitung des Abnahmetermins auf Grund eines Missverständnisses kein wesentlicher Vertragsbruch; s. aber OLG Hamm, 22.9.1992, CISG-online 57 = TranspR-IHR 1999, 24: Nichtabnahme von mehr als der Hälfte der gekauften Ware (116,6t von 200t eingefrorenen Schweinespecks) sei wesentliche Vertragsverletzung (dazu *Hager/Maultzsch*, 5. Aufl., Art. 64 Rn. 6: „sehr weitgehend").

[322] S. CA Grenoble, 22.2.1995, CISG-online 151 = J.D.I. 1995, 632 ff.

[323] Trib. Forlì, 11.12.2008, CISG-online 1729.

[324] OLG Frankfurt a. M., 17.9.1991, CISG-online 28 = NJW 1992, 633, 634 (wesentliche Vertragsverletzung bejaht).

[325] CA Grenoble, 22.2.1995, CISG-online 151 = J.D.I. 1995, 632 ff. (wesentliche Vertragsverletzung bejaht); dazu *Witz*, FS Neumayer, S. 425, 452.

[326] OLG Koblenz, 31.1.1997, CISG-online 256 = IHR 2003, 172, 174 (für möglich gehalten, aber offen gelassen); HGer Kanton Aargau, 26.9.1997, CISG-online 329 = SZIER 1998, 78 ff. (in concreto nicht bewiesen).

[327] *Brunner*, Art. 25, Rn. 19.

[328] Int. Ct. Ukrainian CCI, 25.11.2002, CISG-online 1267 (ohne nähere Begründung wesentliche Vertragsverletzung bejaht).

bereiten Aufstellung der Ware,[329] aus einem dem CISG unterliegenden Vergleich resultierende Pflichten zur Rücknahme mangelhafter Waren[330] können essentiell oder unwesentlich sein (s. oben Rn. 15 ff.).

69 Als wesentliche Vertragsverletzung kann auch der Verstoß gegen Pflichteninhalte zu werten sein, welche Modalitäten der bereits erörterten Hauptleistungspflichten (oben Rn. 37 ff.) betreffen und im CISG als Teil dieser Pflichten geregelt sind, wie etwa die Käuferpflicht zur Abnahme einer bestimmten Warenmenge[331] oder die Pflicht zur jährlichen Abstimmung einer Jahresmengenplanung anhand eines „Saisonschlüssels"[332] (vgl. Art. 60), Pflichten bezüglich der ordnungsgemäßen Verpackung der Ware (vgl. Art. 35 II lit. d))[333] oder des für die Lieferung zu verwendenden Transportmittels (vgl. Art. 32 II),[334] seltener wohl die unterlassene Absendung der Anzeige nach Art. 32 I oder die Nichterteilung der für den Abschluss einer Versicherung erforderlichen Auskunft (Art. 32 III).[335]

Schließlich kann ein wesentlicher Vertragsbruch auch dann vorliegen, wenn gegen eine Pflicht verstoßen wird, die erst durch die Ausübung eines Rechtsbehelfs durch die vertragstreue Partei ausgelöst wird, wie etwa die Pflicht des Verkäufers zur Rückgabe der Ware, nachdem er eine gem. Art. 46 III geschuldete Nachbesserung vorgenommen hat.[336]

---

[329] OLG Hamburg, 25.1.2008, CISG-online 1681 = IHR 2008, 98, 100: Verletzung der vertraglich übernommenen Pflicht des Verkäufers zur betriebsbereiten Aufstellung des Inventars eines Eiscafés – kein wesentlicher Vertragsbruch, weil der Käufer das Inventar selbst in Betrieb genommen hatte; *Achilles*, Art. 25, Rn. 9; MünchKomm/*Gruber*, Art. 25, Rn. 29: wesentlich, wenn Nichterfüllung dazu führt, dass Ware nicht genutzt werden kann und Montage durch Dritte nicht zumutbar ist.

[330] HGer Zürich, 24.10.2003, CISG-online 857 (wesentliche Vertragsverletzung in casu verneint); zur Anwendbarkeit des CISG auf Vergleichsvereinbarungen s. unten Art. 29 Rn. 6.

[331] OLG Brandenburg, 18.11.2008, CISG-online 1734 = IHR 2009, 105, 111: Rahmenvertrag verpflichtete die Käuferin, während eines Dreijahreszeitraums 1.200.000 hl Bier abzunehmen – Minderabnahme von 7,5% der vereinbarten Menge wurde nicht als wesentliche Vertragsverletzung angesehen (anders aber für Minderabnahme von 15,2%).

[332] OLG Brandenburg, 18.11.2008, CISG-online 1734 = IHR 2009, 105, 112 ff.: keine wesentliche Vertragsverletzung, weil fehlende Jahresmengenplanung keine Auswirkungen auf die Fähigkeit des Verkäufers hatte, seine Ware zu produzieren und an andere Käufer zu veräußern.

[333] OLG Koblenz, 10.10.2006, CISG-online 1438 = IHR 2007, 38 f.: bei Lieferung von Weinflaschen Verletzung der Pflicht zur Verwendung einer ausreichenden Verpackung, die sicherstellt, dass die Flaschen ohne Bruchschaden und in verkehrsfähigem Zustand beim Käufer ankommen – wesentliche Vertragsverletzung bejaht.

[334] Int. Ct. Ukrainian CCI, 5.7.2005, CISG-online 1361: an Stelle der vertraglich vereinbarten Versendung als Luftfracht verschickte der Verkäufer die verkauften medizinischen Geräte auf dem Seewege – wesentliche Vertragsverletzung bejaht.

[335] Vgl. MünchKomm/*Gruber*, Art. 25, Rn. 30.

[336] RB Arnhem, 29.7.2009, CISG-online 1939: Verkäufer hatte sich unberechtigt auf ein angebliches Zurückbehaltungsrecht (nach CISG) berufen – wesentliche Vertragsverletzung bejaht.

Art. 26 [Aufhebungserklärung]

Eine Erklärung, daß der Vertrag aufgehoben wird, ist nur wirksam, wenn sie der anderen Partei mitgeteilt wird.

Art. 26
A declaration of avoidance of the contract is effective only if made by notice to the other party.

Art. 26
Une déclaration de résolution du contrat n'a d'effet que si elle est faite par notification à l'autre partie.

Übersicht

	Rn.
I. Vorgeschichte	1
1. Vorläufer im EKG	1
2. Entstehungsgeschichte	2
II. Wirkungen der Vertragsaufhebung	4
1. Aufhebung der Primärpflichten; Einleitung der Rückabwicklung	4
2. Rechtsvergleich	5
III. Voraussetzungen	6
1. Bestehen des Vertragsaufhebungsrechts	6
a) Aufhebungsgründe	6
b) Rechtsfolgen bei nicht bestehendem Aufhebungsgrund	6a
2. Erklärung	7
a) Form	7
b) Inhaltliche Klarheit	8
c) Gänzlicher Wegfall der Aufhebungserklärung	10
d) Aufhebungserklärung v. Aufhebungsvereinbarung	10a
2. Einzelfragen	11
a) Übermittlungsrisiko	11
b) Bindungswirkung	12
c) Empfangsfähigkeit	13
d) Empfänger; Stellvertretung; Zession; Vertragsübernahme	14
4. Fristen	15
IV. Beweislast	17

Vorläufer und **Entwürfe:** Im EKG kein Vorläufer. CISG: Genfer E 1976 Art. 10 II; Wiener E 1977 Art. 9; New Yorker E 1978 Art. 24.

I. Vorgeschichte

1. Vorläufer im EKG

Das EKG enthielt keine eigenständige Vorschrift zur Aufhebungserklärung, sondern regelte diese jeweils im Zusammenhang mit dem spezifischen Aufhebungsgrund; es sah zudem an mehreren Stellen die ipso-facto-Aufhebung[1] vor.

---

[1] An dieser Stelle gilt mein Dank meinem Vorgänger Dr. Rainer Hornung, ohne dessen profunde Kommentierung der Artt. 26, 71–73 und 81–84, deren Grundstruktur und Gliederung im Wesentlichen beibehalten wurden, die nahtlose Übernahme nicht möglich gewesen wäre.
Hellner, Ipso facto avoidance, S. 85 ff.; kritisch dazu bereits früher *Leser,* Vertragsaufhebung und Rückabwicklung, S. 7; *Treitel,* Remedies for Breach, S. 339 u. 382.

2. Entstehungsgeschichte

2   Bei den Vorarbeiten zum CISG-Entwurf sah man das im EKG enthaltene Prinzip der automatischen Vertragsaufhebung kritisch[2] und gab hierzu eine Studie in Auftrag,[3] die im Dezember 1971 vorlag.[4] Die Arbeitsgruppe entschied sich schliesslich für das Modell der Vertragsaufhebung durch **Aufhebungserklärung** gegenüber dem vertragsbrüchigen Teil[5] und führte Gründe der Rechtssicherheit an.[6] Das Prinzip der ipso-facto-Aufhebung war damit insgesamt für das CISG verworfen.[7]

3   Der **Wortlaut** des Art. 26 war durch die Entscheidung der Arbeitsgruppe vorgeprägt[8] und wurde danach lediglich sprachlich geringfügig verändert.

II. Wirkungen der Vertragsaufhebung

1. Aufhebung der Primärpflichten; Einleitung der Rückabwicklung

4   Die Wirkungen der Vertragsaufhebungserklärung werden in Literatur und Rechtsprechung zum CISG dogmatisch uneinheitlich begründet, wobei bezeichnenderweise die nationalen Erklärungsansätze zur Wirkung der Aufhebung von Verträgen bei Leistungsstörungen relativ unkritisch herangezogen werden.[9] Unabhängig von ihrer dogmatischen Einordnung hat die Vertragsaufhebung jedenfalls die folgenden **Wirkungen:** 1) noch nicht erfüllte Primärpflichten erlöschen; 2) die Aufhebung führt zur Wiedergewinnung der Dispositionsfreiheit; 3) die Parteien sind grundsätzlich zur Rückgewähr des Empfangenen verpflichtet; 4) der vertragsbrüchige Teil schuldet regelmässig begleitenden Schadensersatz, wobei für die Schadensberechnung insbesondere auch Artt. 75, 76 gelten.

2. Rechtsvergleich

5   Das in Art. 26 gewählte Modell der eigenverantwortlichen Auflösung des Vertrages durch die Parteien ohne gerichtliche Inanspruchnahme ist international wohl vorherrschend,[10] manchen kontinental-europäischen Rechtsordnungen indes fremd.[11]

---

[2] YB I (1968–1970), S. 184 f., Nr. 92 ff.; zur Entstehungsgeschichte allgemein *Hellner*, Ipso facto avoidance, S. 85 ff.

[3] YB I (1968–1970), S. 135, Nr. 46.

[4] „Ipso facto avoidance" in the Uniform Law on the International Sale of Goods (ULIS): Report of the Secretary General, YB III (1972), S. 41–54 (mit Kommentaren Italiens, Norwegens, Spaniens, Tunesiens, Ungarns und der UdSSR).

[5] YB III (1972), S. 85, Nr. 31.

[6] YB III (1972), S. 85, Nr. 29.

[7] Vgl. *Hellner*, Ipso facto avoidance, S. 84, 88; vgl. auch OGH, 6.2.1996, CISG-online 224 = östZRVgl 1996, 248: „Eine Vertragsverletzung führt […] niemals kraft Gesetzes zur Aufhebung des Vertrages."; OLG Bamberg, 13.1.1999, CISG-online 516 = TranspR–IHR 2000, 17.

[8] YB III (1972), S. 85, Nr. 31.

[9] So wird die Wirkung der Aufhebungserklärung von den weitaus meisten deutschen Kommentatoren des UN-Kaufrechts mit der Beibehaltung des Vertrags als Rahmen bei gleichzeitiger Umsteuerung in ein Rückgewährschuldverhältnis erklärt, während andere Autoren – mit durchaus praktischen Konsequenzen – abweichende dogmatische Modelle anbieten, hierzu ausführlich unten *Fountoulakis*, Art. 81 Rn. 6 ff.

[10] Für Rechtsordnungen, die dem Erklärungsmodell folgen, vgl. etwa §§ 27, 32, 52 dänischer Sale of Goods Act; §§ 29, 39, 59 finn. und schwed. Sale of Goods Act; Art. 6:267 NBW; §§ 323 ff. BGB; Art. 8 israel. Contract Law (Remedies for Breach of Contract) 1970; für das common law, das zumindest funktional dem Erklärungsmodell folgt, vgl. *Treitel*, Law of Contract, Rn. 9–081 ff. u. 12–017 ff.; *ders.*, Remedies for Breach of Contract, S. 334 ff.; *Chen-Wishart*, Contract Law (2010), 531 f.; *Goode*, On Commercial Law, 123; *Ziegel*, Remedial Provisions, 9–12 f.; vgl. auch Art. 7.3.2(1) PICC; Art. 9.303(1) PECL; Art. III.–3.507 I DCFR; Art. 138 CESL-Entwurf. Für einen internationalen Rechtsvergleich vgl. *Schwenzer/Hachem/Kee*, GSCL, Rn. 47.178 ff. (spezifisch zum Erklärungsmodell Rn. 47.198 ff.).

[11] Vgl. Art. 1184 II frz., belg. und luxemburg. Cc, der Vertragsauflösung durch den Richter vorsieht; zur jüngeren Rsp. der frz. Cour de Cassation, die eine aussergerichtliche Aufhebung ausnahmsweise zulässt, vgl. *Fages*, ZEuP 2003, 514, 523; *Boels*, S. 61 Fn. 230; die gerichtliche Geltendmachung des Aufhebungsrechts sehen auch Art. 1453 ital. Cc und Art. 1124 span. Cc vor, wobei Letzterer die schlichte Aufhebungserklärung

III. Voraussetzungen

1. Bestehen des Vertragsaufhebungsrechts

a) Aufhebungsgründe. Art. 26 setzt voraus, dass ein Aufhebungsrecht gemäss Artt. 49, 64, 72, 73 entstanden ist. Art. 26 regelt folglich nicht, unter welchen Umständen der Vertrag aufgehoben werden darf, sondern bloss die Form und Modalitäten der Aufhebungserklärung. Des Weiteren regelt Art. 26 nur die Aufhebungserklärung, mit der ein **im CISG geregeltes Aufhebungsrecht** geltend gemacht wird; ob die Erklärung gleichzeitig den Anforderungen genügt, die beispielsweise an eine Anfechtungserklärung wegen Willensmängeln gestellt werden, richtet sich nach dem anwendbaren nationalen Recht.[12]

b) Rechtsfolgen bei nicht bestehendem Aufhebungsgrund. Erklärt eine Partei den Vertrag für aufgehoben, ohne dass die Voraussetzungen des Aufhebungsrechts erfüllt sind, so stellt dies eine Vertragsverletzung dar, die, vorbehaltlich vertraglicher Abmachungen, insbesondere zur Leistungsverweigung berechtigt (Art. 71) sowie Schadenersatzansprüche (Art. 74 ff.),[13] ein Recht zur Vertragsaufhebung (Artt. 49, 64, 72) sowie Rückerstattungsansprüche (Artt. 81 ff.) nach sich ziehen kann.[14]

6

6a

2. Erklärung

a) Form. Die Aufhebungserklärung folgt dem Grundsatz der **Formfreiheit** des Art. 11, sodass neben schriftlichen auch mündliche Erklärungen genügen.[15] Soweit der Vertrag, parteiliche Gepflogenheiten oder Handelsbräuche eine bestimmte Form vorsehen, muss diese eingehalten werden.[16] Ist Schriftlichkeit vereinbart, so ist der herkömmlichen die elektronische schriftliche Kommunikation gleichgestellt, wenn es der Empfänger nicht explizit oder implizit ausgeschlossen hat, e-mails oder sonstige elektronisch übermittelte Nachrichten zu erhalten.[17] Auch wenn mit Art. 26 die bei der ipso-facto-Aufhebung bestehende Unsicherheit überwunden werden sollte,[18] entspricht es doch den Bedürfnissen des Handelsverkehrs, dass die Aufhebungserklärung auch durch **schlüssiges Verhalten** als „sonstiges Verhalten" i. S. d. Art. 8 erfolgen kann,[19] sofern dies den inhaltlichen Anforderungen an Klarheit, Deutlichkeit und Erkennbarkeit entspricht (s. nächste Rn.).

7

---

zulässt, wenn die vertragsverletzende Partei sie akzeptiert. Für einen internationalen Rechtsvergleich vgl. *Schwenzer/Hachem/Kee*, GSCL, Rn. 47.189 ff.; rechtsvergleichend zum kontinental-europäischen Recht *Laimer*, S. 25 ff.

[12] Vgl. LG Görlitz, 27.5.2010, CISG-online 2182, Erw. II.2.

[13] Vgl. Multi-Member Court of First Instance of Athens (Griechenland), 4505/2009 (ohne Datum), CISG-online 2228, Erw. 3.3.

[14] Einzelheiten bei *Dimsey*, Consequences of Avoidance, S. 535 ff.; unten *Müller-Chen*, Art. 49 Rn. 44 ff.

[15] Sekretariatskommentar, Art. 24, Nr. 4; UNCITRAL Digest, Art. 26, Anm. 3.; vgl. auch die Entstehungsgeschichte, YB VIII (1977), S. 32, Nr. 102 f.; vgl. aus der jüngeren Rechtsprechung OLG Düsseldorf, 9.7.2010, Rn. 102 ff., CISG-online 2171 (wobei die Beweisschwierigkeiten betr. die mündliche Vertragsaufhebung paradigmatisch zum Vorschein kommen); in der Lehre ist die Formfreiheit der Aufhebungserklärung im Übrigen praktisch unbestritten, wenn auch aus Gründen der Rechtssicherheit regelmässig Schriftlichkeit empfohlen wird, vgl. *Schlechtriem*, Internationales UN-Kaufrecht, Rn. 108; *Herber/Czerwenka*, Art. 26, Rn. 3; *Bianca/Bonell/Date-Bah*, Art. 26, Anm. 3.1.; *Soergel/Lüderitz/Budzikiewicz*, Art. 26, Rn. 3; OGH, 6.2.1996, CISG-online 224 = östZRVgl 1996, 248; *Ferrari u. a./Ferrari*, Internationales Vertragsrecht, Art. 26, Rn. 3; *Piltz*, Internationales Kaufrecht, Rn. 5–308; *Kröll u. a./Björklund*, Art. 26, Rn. 3; *Honsell/Gsell*, Art. 26, Rn. 10; *Honnold/Flechtner*, Art. 27, Rn. 187.2.

[16] *Gabriel*, Contracts, S. 112; *Magnus*, 25 J. L. & Com. (2005), 423, 426.

[17] Vgl. CISG-AC, Op. 1 *(Chr. Ramberg)*, Comment 13 = IHR 2003, 244, 245; so auch *Eiselen*, 10 Wuhan University International Law Review (2008–2009), 138, 154.

[18] S. o. Rn. 2.

[19] Vgl. OLG Köln, 14.10.2002, CISG-online 709; Corte di Appello di Milano, 20.3.1998, CISG-online 348; AG Charlottenburg, 4.5.1994, CISG-online 386; ICC, 9978/1999, CISG-online 708 = 11(2) ICC Int. Ct. Arb. Bull. (2000), 117; *Schlechtriem*, Internationales UN-Kaufrecht, Rn. 108; MünchKommHGB/*Benicke*, Art. 26, Rn. 5; *Bianca/Bonell/Farnsworth*, Art. 8, Anm. 2.1.; *Witz/Salger/Lorenz/Salger*, Art. 26, Rn. 8;

8 b) Inhaltliche Klarheit. An die Klarheit, Deutlichkeit und Erkennbarkeit der Aufhebungserklärung sind **hohe Anforderungen** zu stellen.[20] Die Erklärung muss eindeutig zum Ausdruck bringen, dass der Vertrag rückabgewickelt werden soll,[21] muss aber die Worte „Vertragsaufhebung" (avoidance; résolution) nicht enthalten; ein Fax, in dem Rückzahlung des Kaufpreises verlangt wird,[22] oder ein Brief, der die Worte „the glass is full" und „enough is enough" enthält, ist für eine Vertragsaufhebung deutlich genug.[23] Entscheidend ist, dass der Wille, vom Vertrag Abstand zu nehmen, zum Ausdruck kommt, etwa durch das Deutlichmachen, dass die Rechnung wegen Vertragsverletzung der anderen Partei nicht bezahlt werde, weil die gelieferten Muster nunmehr wertlos seien,[24] durch Stornierung der Bestellung,[25] durch Kündigung einer Kauforder nach Ablauf der Lieferungsfrist,[26] durch das schriftliche Angebot, die mangelhaften Schuhe zurückzugeben,[27] oder durch die Aufforderung zur Übernahme der Kosten für die Ersatzanschaffungen[28]. Das blosse Zurücksenden der Ware ohne sonstige Kommunikation kann als Vertragsaufhebungserklärung grundsätzlich nicht genügen, da damit allein nicht klar ist, welches Recht der Käufer geltend machen will (Zurückweisung nach Art. 52 I, Nachbesserung, Ersatzlieferung, Aufhebung?).[29] Die Rückgabe der Ware muss folglich in aller Regel von einem Verhalten begleitet sein, das keine Zweifel daran lässt, dass aufgehoben und nicht etwa ein anderer Rechtsbehelf ergriffen wird. Als Aufhebung ist deshalb z. B. das Zurverfügungstellen der Ware kombiniert mit der Rückzahlung des Kaufpreises zu verstehen.[30] Nur ganz ausnahmsweise kann die blosse Rückgabe der Ware als Aufhebungserklärung ausreichen, wenn nämlich für die Warenliefe-

---

MünchKomm/*Gruber*, Art. 26, Rn. 4; *Neumayer/Ming*, Art. 26, Anm. 1.; *Piltz*, Internationales Kaufrecht, Rn. 5–308; *Enderlein*, IPRax 1991, 313, 315; *Bamberger/Roth/Saenger*, Art. 26, Rn. 3; *Staudinger/Magnus*, Art. 26, Rn. 6; *Jafarzadeh*, Termination, Part Two, 2.4.2; grundsätzlich auch *Ferrari u. a./Ferrari*, Internationales Vertragsrecht, Art. 26, Rn. 4. Gegen die Zulassung der Aufhebungserklärung durch schlüssiges Verhalten, aber ohne nähere Begründung, *Enderlein/Maskow/Strohbach*, Art. 26, Anm. 2. und Art. 8, Anm. 2.2.; *Ensthaler/Achilles*, Art. 26, Rn. 2; sehr streng auch OLG Graz, 29.7.2004, CISG-online 1627 („im Interesse der Rechtsklarheit [kommt] wohl nur eine ausdrückliche Erklärung in Betracht"); *Butler*, 27 Causes of Action 2d (2006), 597, § 9 („[a]n effective declaration of avoidance must provide prompt written notice …").

[20] ICC 9978/1999, CISG-online 708 = 11(2) ICC Int. Ct. Arb. Bull. (2000), 117 („high standard of clarity and precision"); OGH, 6.2.1996, CISG-online 224 = östZRVgl 1996, 248, 253: Es müsse „zweifelsfrei erkennbar sein, dass der Käufer an dem Vertrag nicht festhalten will"; *Bamberger/Roth/Saenger*, Art. 26, Rn. 3; MünchKomm/*Gruber*, Art. 26, Rn. 5; *Herber/Czerwenka*, Art. 49, Rn. 11; *Soergel/Lüderitz/Budzikiewicz*, Art. 26, Rn. 3; *Jacobs*, 64 U. Pitt. L. Rev. (2003), 407, 410.

[21] LG München I, 20.3.1995, CISG-online 164 = IPRax 1996, 31, 32; *Magnus*, 25 J. L. & Com. (2005), 423, 427 f.; MünchKommHGB/*Benicke*, Art. 26, Rn. 2 („eindeutig", „zweifellos"); *Ferrari u. a./Ferrari*, Internationales Vertragsrecht, Art. 26, Rn. 6 („inhaltlich derart gestaltet sein, dass sie keine Zweifel daran lässt"); *Piltz*, Internationales Kaufrecht, Rn. 5–308.

[22] ICC, 9978/1999, CISG-online 708 = 11(2) ICC Int. Ct. Arb. Bull. (2000), 117.

[23] RB Kortrijk, 4.6.2004, CISG-online 945.

[24] OLG Frankfurt a. M., 17.9.1991, CISG-online 28 = RIW 1991, 950, 951; krit. hierzu *Ferrari u. a./Ferrari*, Internationales Vertragsrecht, Art. 26, Rn. 6.

[25] Cour d'appel de Rennes, 27.5.2008, CISG-online 1746; zu streng daher CIETAC, 18.4.2008, CISG-online 2057, Erw. III.C.6. und III.E.1.: Der Käufer, der die Mangelhaftigkeit des Pulvers bereits vorgängig gerügt hatte, wies zehn Tage später den Verkäufer in einer Mail darauf hin, dass der Zoll die Rückschaffung der Ware anordne, sowie dass „we hereby notify your company about the return of the goods. Please provide the information on the original shipper … and allow the material to be returned", zudem wurde der Verkäufer angewiesen, die Zahlungsanweisung gegenüber der Korrespondenzbank zu widerrufen. Diese Erklärung dürfte, entgegen der Auffassung des Schiedsgerichts, die nach Art. 26 an die Aufhebungserklärung gestellten Voraussetzungen erfüllen.

[26] Corte di Appello di Milano, 20.3.1998, CISG-online 348.

[27] AG Charlottenburg, 4.5.1994, CISG-online 386; krit. *Ferrari u. a./Ferrari*, Internationales Vertragsrecht, Art. 26, Rn. 6.

[28] KGer Zug, 14.12.2009, CISG-online 2026, Erw. 10.1.

[29] LG Frankfurt a. M., 16.9.1991, CISG-online 26 = RIW 1991, 952 = IPRspr 1991 Nr. 41, S. 78 = Uniform L. Rev. 1991, 376; UNCITRAL Digest, Art. 26, Anm. 4.; *Kröll u. a./Björklund*, Art. 26, Rn. 9; *Butler*, Guide to the CISG, Rn. 6.05[A].

[30] Audiencia Provincial Castellón, 21.3.2006, CISG-online 1488; OLG Karlsruhe, 19.12.2002, CISG-online 817 = IHR 2003, 125; OLG Köln, 14.10.2002, CISG-online 709 = IHR 2003, 15, 17 (Sendung „sofort und total" zur Verfügung gestellt); vgl. auch RB Kortrijk, 4.6.2004, CISG-online 945.

rung ein bestimmter Verfalltag vereinbart war und die Ware zu spät geliefert wurde;[31] hier ist eine andere Deutung als die, dass mit der Rücksendung der Vertrag aufgehoben wird, ausgeschlossen. Keine ausreichende Aufhebungserklärung ist ferner die Mitteilung, in welcher der zur Vertragsaufhebung Berechtigte die Vertragsauflösung in Aussicht stellt, alternativ aber Minderung begehrt, also vom Fortgelten des Vertrages ausgeht.[32] Anderes kann nur gelten, wenn sich aus der Mitteilung objektiv (Art. 8 II) ergibt, dass es sich um abgestufte Behelfe handelt, nämlich der Vertrag einzig dann als aufgehoben gilt, wenn der Schuldner dem ersten Begehren (beispielsweise Erfüllung innerhalb der gesetzten Nachfrist; Minderung) nicht nachkommt. Allerdings ist für eine solche Leseweise eine eindeutige Formulierung zu fordern, regelmässig unter Fristsetzung für das Einlenken auf den ersten Behelf ((Nach-)Erfüllung; Minderung).[33]

Die Erklärung braucht den Aufhebungsgrund nicht zu nennen.[34] Ebenso wenig ist **9** erforderlich, dass die Partei, die den Vertrag aufheben will, die Aufhebung in einer früheren Erklärung ankündigt.[35] Die Aufhebungserklärung nach Art. 26 kann mit einer Mängelrüge[36] bzw. – wie soeben am Beispiel der Aufhebungsandrohung bei Nichterfüllung erläutert – mit einer Nachfristsetzung[37] kombiniert werden.

c) Gänzlicher Wegfall der Aufhebungserklärung. In seltenen Fällen kann vom Auf- **10** hebungsberechtigten nicht verlangt werden, dass er die Aufhebung tatsächlich erklärt, nämlich dann, wenn die andere Partei die Vertragserfüllung **ernstlich und endgültig verweigert.**[38] Rechtssicherheit, wie sie durch Art. 26 bezweckt wird,[39] muss in diesen Fällen nicht mehr geschaffen werden. Die Aufhebung ohne Erklärung ist vor allem im Hinblick auf die Schadenersatzberechnung bei (effektivem oder hypothetischem) Deckungsgeschäft relevant, da Artt. 75, 76 gemäss Wortlaut die Aufhebung des Vertrags voraussetzen.[40] Ein Deckungsgeschäft kann in den Fällen ernsthafter und endgültiger Verweigerung demnach dennoch getätigt (Art. 75) bzw. die Schadenersatzberechnung nach Art. 76

---

[31] AG Oldenburg, 24.4.1990, CISG-online 20 = IPRax 1991, 336.
[32] Vgl. AG Zweibrücken, 14.10.1992, CISG-online 46: Der klagende Käufer hatte vorprozessual den Verkäufer vor die Wahl gestellt, **entweder** die Ware zurückzunehmen **oder** 50% Preisnachlass zu gewähren. Vgl. ferner *Roder Zelt- und Hallenkonstruktionen GmbH v. Rosedown Park Pty. Ltd. and Reginald R Eustace*, FCA (Adelaide, SA), 28.4.1995, CISG-online 218 = 1995 Federal Court Reports (Australia), 216; Foreign Trade Court of Arbitration attached to the Serbian Chamber of Commerce, 15.7.2008, CISG-online 1795; Cámara Nacional de Apelaciones en lo Comercial de Buenos Aires, 24.6.2010, CISG-online 2132; LG Frankfurt a. M., 16.9.1991, CISG-online 26 = RIW 1991, 952 = IPRspr 1991 Nr. 41, S. 78 = Uniform L. Rev. 1991, 376.
[33] Ausreichend deutlich ist etwa: „Sollte ich auf dieses Schreiben keine Reaktion erhalten, gehe ich davon aus, dass Ihr an einer weiteren Zusammenarbeit kein Interesse habt.", OLG Frankfurt a. M., 6.10.2004, CISG-online 996. Abzulehnen daher die Entscheidung der ICC, 11 849/2003, CISG-online 1421, Rn. 62, die in der Nachfristsetzung mit Aufhebungsandrohung keine wirksame antizipierte Aufhebungserklärung erblicken wollte; im Sinne der zitierten ICC-Entscheidung allerdings *Kröll u. a./Björklund*, Art. 26, Rn. 6.
[34] MünchKommHGB/*Benicke*, Art. 26, Rn. 2; *Honsell/Gsell*, Art. 26, Rn. 12; a. A. *Jacobs*, 64 U. Pitt. L. Rev. (2003), 407, 409; wohl auch *Kröll u. a./Björklund*, Art. 26, Rn. 11.
[35] Sekretariatskommentar, Art. 26, Nr. 3; *Piltz*, Internationales Kaufrecht, Rn. 5–311.
[36] Vgl. BGH, 25.6.1997, CISG-online 277 = NJW 1997, 3311 = IPRax 1999, 375 = EuZW 1998, 29; Audiencia Provincial Castellón, 21.3.2006, CISG-online 1488.
[37] Int. Ct. Russian CCI, 2.11.2004, CISG-online 1285, Erw. 3.3; KG Schaffhausen, 27.1.2004, CISG-online 960, Erw. 1.f) = SZIER 2005, 120, 122; *Honsell/Gsell*, Art. 26, Rn. 17; MünchKommHGB/*Benicke*, Art. 26, Rn. 4; *Piltz*, Internationales Kaufrecht, Rn. 5–310, 5–460. Vgl. auch Art. III. – 3:507(2) DCFR, wonach eine gleichzeitig mit der Nachfristsetzung angedrohte Aufhebungserklärung nach fruchtlosem Ablauf der Frist nicht wiederholt zu werden braucht.
[38] Vgl. OLG München, 15.9.2004, CISG-online 1013, Erw. II.2.b = IHR 2005, 72 (Verlangen einer Aufhebungserklärung im Falle unzweideutiger und definitiver Leistungsverweigerung sei ‚bloße Förmelei'); OLG Graz, 29.7.2004, CISG-online 1627; OLG Hamburg, 28.2.1997, CISG-online 261 = EWiR 1997, 791 (Anm. *Mankowski*); *Staudinger/Magnus*, Art. 75, Rn. 8, Art. 76, Rn. 10; *Honsell/Gsell*, Art. 26, Rn. 14; a. A. MünchKommHGB/*Mankowski*, Art. 75, Rn. 4, Art. 76, Rn. 3; *Bamberger/Roth/Saenger*, Art. 75, Rn. 3.
[39] Dazu oben Rn. 2.
[40] Vgl. dazu etwa LG Hamburg, 26.11.2003, CISG-online 875; OLG Düsseldorf, 22.7.2004, CISG-online 916 = IHR 2005, 29; OLG München, 15.9.2004, CISG-online 1013 = IHR 2005, 72; LG München I, 6.4.2000, CISG-online 665.

vorgenommen werden.⁴¹ Davon zu trennen ist die Frage, ab wann der Vertrag als aufgehoben gilt.⁴²

10a **d) Aufhebungserklärung v. Aufhebungsvereinbarung.** Die Aufhebungserklärung gemäss Art. 26 ist eine einseitige Willenserklärung, die von der zweiseitigen, einvernehmlichen Aufhebung des Vertrags zu unterscheiden ist. Ob das eine oder das andere vorliegt, entscheidet sich nach den Regeln, die für das Zustandekommen des Aufhebungsvertrags massgeblich sind (Art. 29 I i. V. m. Artt. 8, 14 ff.). Die Unterscheidung ist nicht nur bezüglich der Voraussetzungen relevant (Art. 26 gilt nur für die einseitige Aufhebungserklärung, die einvernehmliche Aufhebung wiederum hängt vom gegenseitigen Willen der Parteien ab),⁴³ sondern auch hinsichtlich der Wirkungen der Aufhebung (insbesondere der Gefahrtragung bei der Rückabwicklung, Art. 82)⁴⁴.

2. Einzelfragen

11 a) **Übermittlungsrisiko.** Anders als für die Willenserklärungen bei Vertragsschluss, die mit Zugang wirksam werden (Zugangsprinzip; Artt. 15 I, 18 II), ist für die Aufhebungserklärung generell die Regel des **Art. 27** massgeblich.⁴⁵ Danach trägt der Empfänger das Risiko der Verspätung, des Verlusts oder der Verstümmelung der Erklärung, sobald diese abgesandt worden ist.⁴⁶ Diese Lösung folgt grundsätzlich der Absendetheorie des angloamerikanischen Rechts,⁴⁷ besagt nach dem Wortlaut des Art. 27 jedoch lediglich, dass der vertragsbrüchige Teil das **Übermittlungsrisiko** der Erklärung seines Vertragspartners tragen soll. Strittig ist, ob Art. 27 gleichzeitig die Frage beantwortet, wann die Aufhebungserklärung wirksam wird, ob die Aufhebungswirkungen also, im Sinne der dispatch-Theorie, mit Absenden⁴⁸ eintreten oder erst mit Zugang⁴⁹ der Mitteilung. Die Frage des Wirksamwerdens hat im CISG grundsätzlich praktische Bedeutung nur für die Frage, wie lange der Erklärende seine Aufhebungserklärung noch **ändern oder widerrufen**⁵⁰ kann.⁵¹ Entste-

---

⁴¹ Ausführlich *Schlechtriem*, GS Hellner, S. 229, 231; vgl. aus der Rspr. OLG München, 15.9.2004, CISG-online 1013, Erw. II.2.b = IHR 2005, 72; OLG Graz, 29.7.2004, CISG-online 1627; LG Hamburg, 26.11.2003, CISG-online 875; abw. Supreme Court Poland, 27.1.2006, CISG-online 1399.
⁴² Vgl. dazu unten *Schwenzer*, Art. 74 Rn. 44.
⁴³ Vgl. etwa OLG Köln, 19.5.2008, CISG-online 1700, II.2. = IHR 2008, 26; vgl. auch unten *Schroeter*, Art. 29 Rn. 11; *Honsell/Gsell*, Art. 26, Rn. 7.
⁴⁴ Dazu unten *Fountoulakis*, Art. 82 Rn. 28–30.
⁴⁵ *Bianca/Bonell/Date-Bah*, Art. 27, Anm. 2.1.; *Enderlein/Maskow/Strohbach*, Art. 26, Anm. 3.1.; *Schlechtriem*, Internationales UN-Kaufrecht, Rn. 109.
⁴⁶ So auch Art. 1:303 IV S. 2 PECL, der ausdrücklich vorsieht, dass bei ordnungsgemäss abgegebenen Erklärungen, die sich auf Leistungsstörungen des anderen Teils beziehen, das Übermittlungsrisiko zu Lasten des Schuldners geht. Anders als unter dem CISG (dazu sogleich) tritt die Wirksamkeit der Erklärung allerdings erst dann ein, wenn die Erklärung dem Empfänger üblicherweise zugeht.
⁴⁷ Dazu unten *Schroeter*, Art. 27 Rn. 1; *Neumayer*, FS Drobnig, S. 99 ff.
⁴⁸ So *Schlechtriem*, Internationales UN-Kaufrecht, Rn. 109; *Honnold/Flechtner*, Art. 27, Rn. 187.2; *Lookofsky*, The 1980 United Nations Convention, Rn. 138; MünchKommHGB/*Benicke*, Art. 26, Rn. 10; *Staudinger/Magnus*, Art. 26, Rn. 10; *Ferrari u. a./Ferrari*, Internationales Vertragsrecht, Art. 26, Rn. 7; *Enderlein/Maskow/Strohbach*, Art. 27, Anm. 3.1. (allerdings krit.); *Soergel/Lüderitz/Budzikiewicz*, Art. 26, Rn. 4.
⁴⁹ So noch die 4. Aufl., Rn. 12, sowie *Bamberger/Roth/Saenger*, Art. 26, Rn. 5; *Leser*, in *Schlechtriem (Hrsg.)*, Einheitliches Kaufrecht und nationales Obligationenrecht, 1987, 225, 237 f.; *Neumayer/Ming*, Art. 26, Anm. 2.; *Neumayer*, FS Drobnig, S. 105 f.; *Heuzé*, Anm. 429. Fn. 228; *Piltz*, Internationales Kaufrecht, Rn. 5–309; *Honsell/Weber*, Art. 81, Rn. 3; *Heilmann*, S. 506; *Karollus*, S. 152; *Achilles*, Art. 26, Rn. 1; *Witz/Salger/Lorenz/Salger*, Art. 26, Rn. 12.
⁵⁰ Die bei den Regeln des Vertragsschlusses getroffene Differenzierung zwischen Rücknahme (withdrawal) und Widerruf (revocation), Artt. 15 f., ist irrelevant, wenn, wie vorliegend, davon ausgegangen wird, dass die Frage des Wirksamwerdens und der Widerrufsmöglichkeit nicht zu trennen sind. Für eine Trennung der letztgenannten Punkte noch die 4. Aufl., Rn. 11.
⁵¹ Weitere Fragen, die vom Zeitpunkt der Wirksamkeit abhängen könnten, wie der Beginn der Verzinsungspflicht in Art. 84 I, hat das CISG bereits geklärt: So stellt Art. 84 I explizit auf den Zeitpunkt der Zahlung ab (dazu ausführlich Art. 84 Rn. 12); für die Unmassgeblichkeit des Zeitpunkts der Wirksamkeit der Aufhebungserklärung für allfällige Schadensersatzansprüche vgl. *Schlechtriem*, Internationales UN-Kaufrecht, Rn. 109.

hungsgeschichte und Wortlaut des Art. 27[52] sprechen jedenfalls dafür, dass die dort genannten Erklärungen **mit Absendung wirksam** werden.[53]

b) Bindungswirkung. Fraglich ist, ob die Aufhebungserklärung mit Absendung unwiderruflich wird. Nach einem Teil der – vornehmlich deutschsprachigen – Literatur[54] und Rechtsprechung[55] scheint dies die logische Schlussfolgerung aus der Annahme zu sein, dass die Aufhebungserklärung ein Gestaltungsrecht sei, das (entsprechend deutscher Dogmatik) bedingungsfeindlich und unwiderruflich sei. Tatsächlich ist das (deutsche) Dogma, eine Gestaltungserklärung könne rechtslogisch nicht ungeschehen gemacht werden, für flexible Lösungen gerade im internationalen Handelsverkehr wenig brauchbar.[56] Aus den Rechtsgedanken der Artt. 16 II b) und 29 II 2 wird man vielmehr schliessen können (Art. 7 II), dass die Aufhebungserklärung jedenfalls dann noch widerrufen werden kann, wenn der Erklärungsempfänger sich noch nicht auf die Erklärung eingestellt und keine entsprechenden Dispositionen getroffen hat.[57] Dieser Zeitpunkt wird regelmässig der Zeitpunkt des **Eintreffens der Erklärung** sein,[58] da der Widerrufende die Beweislast dafür trägt, dass sich der Empfänger auf die Erklärung noch nicht eingestellt hat, und der Nachweis späterer Kenntnisnahme bzw. des Umstandes, dass der Empfänger noch nicht auf die Erklärung vertraut hat, schwer zu erbringen sein dürfte. Der Nachweis, dass der Verkäufer auch nach Erhalt der Aufhebungserklärung noch nicht disponiert hat, dürfte jedoch beispielsweise dann gelingen, wenn zwischen Vertragsaufhebungserklärung und deren Widerruf nur wenige Stunden liegen.

c) Empfangsfähigkeit. Die Erklärung ist zur Entfaltung der Wirksamkeit nach dem Gesagten nicht zugangsbedürftig, aber sie muss „zugangsfähig" sein.[59] Es müssen – wie es Art. 27 formuliert – die „nach den Umständen geeigneten Mittel" eingesetzt werden, damit die Erklärung wirksam wird. Das Kommunikationsmittel kann grundsätzlich frei gewählt werden; der Erklärende kann sich aber auf die Wirkungen des Art. 27 nicht berufen, wenn er ein **ungeeignetes Kommunikationsmittel** gewählt hat und die Erklärung deshalb verloren gegangen bzw. verspätet oder verstümmelt angelangt ist.[60]

---

[52] Dazu unten *Schroeter*, Art. 27 Rn. 13; vgl. auch *Schlechtriem*, Internationales UN-Kaufrecht, Rn. 109.
[53] Vgl. zu den Befürwortern dieser Annahme oben Fn. 35.
[54] So noch *Leser/Hornung*, 3. Aufl., Rn. 6; *Honsell/Karollus*, Vorauflage, Art. 26, Rn. 18; MünchKommBGB/*Gruber*, Art. 26, Rn. 10; *Staudinger/Magnus*, Art. 26, Rn. 8; *Reinhart*, Art. 26, Rn. 2; *Witz/Salger/Lorenz/Salger*, Art. 26, Rn. 4.
[55] LG Berlin, 15.9.1994, CISG-online 399.
[56] S. zu den praktischen Schwierigkeiten, die sich aus der Theorie der Unwiderruflichkeit ergeben, insbes. *Schlechtriem*, Bindung an Erklärungen, S. 265 ff. Erinnert sei auch an die Klimmzüge des BGH bei der Auslegung von Rücktrittserklärungen, die Parteien in Verkennung der verunglückten – und mit dem Schuldrechtsmodernisierungsgesetz vom 26.11.2001 zu Recht abgeschafften – Alternativität von Rücktritt und Schadensersatz abgegeben hatten, ohne sich der Folge – Verlust von Schadensersatzansprüchen – bewusst zu sein. Die höchstrichterliche Rechtsprechung hat im Ergebnis zu Recht im Wege der Erklärungsauslegung das Dogma der absoluten Bindungswirkung von Gestaltungserklärungen aufgeweicht, um zu materiell gerechten Ergebnissen zu kommen.
[57] Vgl. auch *Jacobs*, 64 U. Pitt. L. Rev. (2003), 407, 426 ff.; *Schlechtriem*, Internationales UN-Kaufrecht, Rn. 109; *ders.*, Bindung an Erklärungen, S. 265 ff.; *Honnold/Flechtner*, Art. 27, Rn. 187.2; *Honsell/Gsell*, Art. 26, Rn. 19; offengelassen in OLG Hamburg, 25.1.2008, CISG-online 1681, Erw. II.1.d)aa) = IHR 2008, 98.
[58] Vgl. *Schlechtriem*, Internationales UN-Kaufrecht, Rn. 109: „Im Zweifel" sei davon auszugehen, dass sich der Empfänger mit Zugang der Erklärung auf diese eingestellt hat; MünchKommHGB/*Benicke*, Art. 26, Rn. 11: Zugang oder spätestens Kenntniserlangung; *Staudinger/Magnus*, Art. 26, Rn. 8: Zugang. Für die Vertreter des Zugangsprinzips (dazu Fn. 49) dürfte die Widerrufbarkeit der Erklärung bis zum Zeitpunkt des Zugangs selbstverständlich sein, vgl. nur *Bamberger/Roth/Saenger*, Art. 26, Rn. 5; *Neumayer/Ming*, Art. 26, Anm. 2.; *Heuzé*, Anm. 429. Fn. 228; a. A. aber *Honsell/Karollus*, Vorauflage, Art. 26, Rn. 16, Art. 27, Rn. 21: Die Möglichkeit, eine bereits wirksame Vertragsaufhebung wieder rückgängig machen zu können, sei „dogmatisch unsauber".
[59] *Schlechtriem*, Internationales UN-Kaufrecht, Rn. 110.
[60] Dazu unten *Schroeter*, Art. 27 Rn. 10 ff.

14 d) **Empfänger; Stellvertretung; Zession; Vertragsübernahme.** Die Erklärung ist **gegenüber der anderen Vertragspartei abzugeben.**[61] Mitteilungen ohne direkten Adressat, etwa Pressemeldungen, reichen nicht aus.[62] Zulänglich ist hingegen, die Aufhebung des Vertrages erstmals in der Klageschrift zu behaupten.[63] Allerdings dürfte damit die Aufhebungserklärung wegen des Erfordernisses der Aufhebungserklärung innerhalb angemessener Frist[64] regelmässig zu spät sein.[65] Da die Klageschrift jeweils der Gegenpartei zu übermitteln ist, wird die Aufhebungserklärung – via (Schieds-)Gericht – der anderen Partei mitgeteilt; dass die Erklärung allenfalls **mittelbar** erfolgt, schadet nicht. Die Fragen, ob eine wirksame Vertragsübernahme vorliegt oder eine Forderungsabtretung, bei der die entsprechenden Gestaltungsrechte, einschliesslich des Aufhebungsrechts, übergegangen sind, richten sich nach dem anwendbaren nationalen Recht. Ebenso ist für die Frage, ob sich der Absender bzw. der Empfänger auf die Vertretungsmacht des Dritten verlassen durfte, zunächst auf die über das IPR berufenen Rechtsregeln abzustellen.[66] Gleichwohl ist dabei m. E. Art. 8 II, III weiterhin massgeblich für die Frage, wie die Erklärung oder das sonstige Verhalten des Stellvertreters, mit der die andere Vertragspartei über die Befugnis zur Abgabe bzw. Entgegennahme einer Vertragsaufhebungserklärung in Kenntnis gesetzt wird, von der anderen Vertragspartei verstanden werden durfte.

4. Fristen

15 Entsprechend den tief in die Vertragsbeziehung eingreifenden Wirkungen der Aufhebungserklärung kennen die Artt. 49 II, 64 II und 73 II **angemessene Ausschlussfristen**[67] zur Abgabe der Erklärung. Dabei ist nach dem Rechtsgedanken des Art. 27 die Absendung der Aufhebungserklärung mit „nach den Umständen geeigneten Mitteln" für die Frage der Rechtzeitigkeit massgeblich.[68]

16 Anders als die Artt. 49 II, 64 II und 73 II sehen weitere Fälle der Vertragsaufhebung keine ausdrücklichen Fristen für die Ausübung des Aufhebungsrechts vor.[69] Zu Recht ging man aber in den Beratungen des Übereinkommens davon aus, dass die „angemessene Frist" in den genannten Bestimmungen die Gefahr des Missbrauchs des Aufhebungsrechts, etwa durch Spekulation bei beweglichen Marktpreisen, vielfach eindämme.[70] Tatsächlich dürften

---

[61] MünchKomm/*Gruber*, Art. 26, Rn. 3; *Staudinger/Magnus*, Art. 26, Rn. 5.
[62] *Bianca/Bonell/Date-Bah*, Art. 26, Anm. 3.3.
[63] Vgl. *Roder Zelt- und Hallenkonstruktionen GmbH v. Rosedown Park Pty Ltd et al.*, FCA (Adelaide), 28.4.1995, CISG-online 218 = 57 FCR 216; zust. *Jacobs*, 64 U. Pitt. L. Rev. (2003), 407, 414; krit. *Ziegel*, Review of the Convention on Contracts for the International Sale of Goods (CISG), (1998), 53, 60 note 23; wie hier auch Int. Ct. Russian CCI, 11.5.1997, CISG-online 1514, Erw. 3.10; OLG Linz, 23.1.2006, CISG-online 1377, Erw. 6.2; Int. Ct. Russian CCI, 27.5.2005, CISG-online 1456, Erw. 3.4; *Honsell/Gsell*, Art. 26, Rn. 6, 15; *Ferrari u. a./Ferrari*, Internationales Vertragsrecht, Art. 26, Rn. 5.
[64] Dazu hinten Rn. 15, 16.
[65] Vgl. *Gabriel*, Contracts, S. 113.
[66] Präzisierung der in der Vorauflage vertretenen Ansicht. Vgl. auch LG Frankfurt a. M., 16.9.1991, CISG-online 26 = RIW 1991, 952 = IPRspr 1991 Nr. 41, S. 78 = Uniform L. Rev. 1991, 376; *Honsell/Gsell*, Art. 26, Rn. 16; *Bianca/Bonell/Date-Bah*, Art. 26, Amn. 3.2. („normal rules of agency"); wohl auch *Herber/Czerwenka*, Art. 26, Rn. 4.
[67] Der Charakter der Ausschlussfrist ergibt sich bereits aus dem Wortlaut, siehe auch *Schlechtriem*, Internationales UN-Kaufrecht, Rn. 200 u. 241. Vgl. aus der Rechtsprechung für einen Ausschluss der Vertragsaufhebung wegen Nichteinhaltung der angemessenen Erklärungsfrist des Art. 49 II lit. b) Com., 8.11.2011, CISG-online 2310.
[68] So auch *Enderlein/Maskow/Strohbach*, Art. 26, Anm. 3.1. und Art. 27, Anm. 1.1.
[69] Keine Ausschlussfrist für die Aufhebung findet sich im Wortlaut von Artt. 49 I lit. a), 64 I lit. a), 51 II und 72 I. Vgl. demgegenüber die Fristen im EKG, Artt. 43 I, 55 I, 70 I EKG; für die automatische Auflösung vgl. die Fristen in Artt. 26 I, 30 I, 62 I EKG.
[70] YB III (1972), S. 85, Nr. 29: „[I]t was suggested that the problem of possible speculation based on price fluctuation could be dealt with directly without the use of the general concept of ipso facto avoidance."; vgl. auch *Bianca/Bonell/Date-Bah*, Art. 26, Anm. 2.3.; *Audit*, Vente internationale, Anm. 193.; zur Spekulationsgefahr bereits *Hellner*, Ipso facto avoidance, S. 92 ff., *ders.*, UN Convention, S. 93 (wobei die Gefahr der Spekulation hier als geringer angesehen wird); *Dölle/U. Huber*, Artt. 26, 27 EKG, Rn. 39–41; *Mertens/Rehbinder*, Art. 26 EKG, Rn. 9. *Honnold/Flechtner*, Art. 7, 28, 46, 77, Rn. 95, 193, 285 und 417, versuchen

Situationen, in denen sich eine Partei auf die Nichtbefristung der Aufhebungserklärung verlässt, praktisch selten sein. Wirtschaftlich zumindest hat die aufhebende Partei selbst ein Interesse an einer raschen Vertragsaufhebung mit anschliessendem Deckungsgeschäft, um ihre Schadenersatzansprüche ungekürzt geltend machen zu können und sich nicht etwa eine Verletzung ihrer Schadensminderungspflicht vorwerfen lassen zu müssen (Art. 77).[71] Um der Rechtsklarheit Willen sollte jedoch auch in den Fällen ohne ausdrücklich vorgeschriebene Aufhebungsfrist eine **angemessene Frist** für die Erklärung zu laufen beginnen, wenn die Voraussetzungen des Aufhebungsrechts für den vertragstreuen Teil erkennbar eingetreten sind.[72] Diese Lösung schafft klare Verhältnisse und hat sich auch in den PICC[73] sowie den europäischen Vereinheitlichungsprojekten durchgesetzt.[74] Zur Begründung der hier vertretenen Ansicht kann nach Art. 7 II auf die Parallele zu anderen Mitteilungs- und Anzeigepflichten der Artt. 43, 47 II, 48[75] und auch zur Rüge nach Art. 39 verwiesen werden.[76] Zudem ist auch der Grundgedanke des Art. 48 II–IV heranzuziehen, der seinerseits Ausprägung der Schadensminderungspflicht des Art. 77 ist, sodass sich die aufhebungsberechtigte Partei nach Aufforderung durch die Gegenpartei über die Aufhebung erklären muss.[77]

IV. Beweislast

Wer sich auf die Vertragsaufhebung beruft, muss beweisen, dass die Voraussetzungen für eine Vertragsaufhebung vorliegen, dass er die Aufhebung im Sinne des Art. 26 erklärt hat bzw. ausnahmsweise von einer Aufhebungserklärung abgesehen werden kann, sowie dass er die Erklärung abgesandt hat.[78]

---

unter Heranziehung aller anderen Möglichkeiten des Übereinkommens in Artt. 7, 28, 46 u. 77 hier zu einer einheitlichen, angemessenen Lösung zu gelangen.

[71] Vgl. etwa Hof van Beroep Antwerpen, 24.4.2006, CISG-online 1258, Erw. A. 5.: Kürzung der Versicherungskosten, die der Aufhebungsberechtigte als Erhaltungsmassnahme im Sinne des Art. 85 ausgegeben hatte, da der Weiterverkauf zu spät vorgenommen wurde; vgl. auch Audiencia Provincial de Valencia, 31.3.2005, CISG-online 1369: Reduktion des in Zusammenhang mit dem Deckungskauf geltend gemachten Schadens, da Vertragsaufhebung erst sechs Monate nach Tätigen des Deckungsgeschäfts erklärt wurde; ähnl. OLG Düsseldorf, 22.7.2004, CISG-online 916 = IHR 2005, 29; vgl. auch Trib. Padova, 11.1.2005, CISG-online 967 = Riv. dr. int.Priv. 2005, 791.

[72] So auch *Lookofsky*, Understanding the CISG, § 6.8; *Jan*, S. 123 ff., 215 f.; *Kröll u. a./Björklund*, Art. 26, Rn. 12; *Gabriel*, Contracts, S. 114 i. V. m. 113; *Witz/Salger/Lorenz/Salger*, Art. 26, Rn. 10; a. A. MünchKommHGB/*Benicke*, Art. 26, Rn. 8; *Staudinger/Magnus*, Art. 26, Rn. 11 f.; *Bamberger/Roth/Saenger*, Art. 26, Rn. 7; *Ferrari u. a./Ferrari*, Internationales Vertragsrecht, Art. 26, Rn. 8; *Honsell/Gsell*, Art. 26, Rn. 21; *Piltz*, Internationales Kaufrecht, 5–312, 5–462; *Tacheva*, Vertragsaufhebung, 212 f.; differenzierend MünchKomm/*Gruber*, Art. 26, Rn. 9.

[73] Vgl. Art. 7.3.2 II PICC sowie dessen Official Comment, Nr. 3, der ausdrücklich auf das ansonsten bestehende Spekulationsrisiko hinweist („the aggrieved party may easily obtain a substitute performance and may thus speculate on a rise or fall in the price ..."); vgl. dazu auch *Gabriel*, Contracts, S. 114 („What is undoubtedly implicit in the Convention is express in the Principles: the notice must be given within a reasonable time under the circumstances.").

[74] Vgl. Art. 9:303 II, III PECL; Art. 119 CESL-Entwurf; Art. III.–3:508 I DCFR. Überhaupt kritisch gegenüber den flexiblen Ausschlussfristen für die Ausübung des Aufhebungsrechts in Art. 26 sowie den entsprechenden Bestimmungen von PICC und PECL *Andersen*, Comparative analysis, S. 133, 136 f.

[75] Vgl. zum Erfordernis einer „angemessenen Frist" in Art. 48 *Schlechtriem*, Fristsetzungen, S. 332 (mit Nachweis über die Gegenauffassung).

[76] Dazu *Leser*, Vertragsaufhebung und Rückabwicklung, S. 235 f.; *Honnold/Flechtner*, Art. 7, 28, 46, 77, Rn. 95, 193, 285, 416.

[77] Vgl. auch Art. 9:303(3)(b) PECL, wonach die berechtigte Partei, sofern sie weiss bzw. wissen sollte, dass die andere Partei in vernünftiger Frist nacherfüllen will, ihrerseits innerhalb angemessener Frist mitteilen muss, dass sie die Erfüllung nicht annehmen wird; ansonsten verliert sie ihr Recht zur Vertragsaufhebung.

[78] Supreme Arbitration Court of the Russian Federation, 16.12.2009, CISG-online 2339; Audiencia Provincial de Valencia, 31.3.2005, CISG-online 1369; KG Wallis, 21.2.2005, CISG-online 1193, Erw. 4. a) aa) = IHR 2006, 155, 156 f.; OLG Düsseldorf, 22.7.2004, CISG-online 916 = IHR 2005, 29; Int. Ct. Russian CCI, 28.5.2004, CISG-online 1513, Erw. 3.4.3; MünchKomm/*Gruber*, Art. 26, Rn. 12; *Bamberger/Roth/Saenger*, Art. 26, Rn. 9; *Honsell/Gsell*, Art. 26, Rn. 24.

Art. 27 [Absendetheorie]

Soweit in diesem Teil des Übereinkommens nicht ausdrücklich etwas anderes bestimmt wird, nimmt bei einer Anzeige, Aufforderung oder sonstigen Mitteilung, die eine Partei gemäß diesem Teil mit den nach den Umständen geeigneten Mitteln macht, eine Verzögerung oder ein Irrtum bei der Übermittlung der Mitteilung oder deren Nichteintreffen dieser Partei nicht das Recht, sich auf die Mitteilung zu berufen.

Art. 27

Unless otherwise expressly provided in this Part of the Convention, if any notice, request or other communication is given or made by a party in accordance with this Part and by means appropriate in the circumstances, a delay or error in the transmission of the communication or its failure to arrive does not deprive that party of the right to rely on the communciation.

Art. 27

Sauf disposition contraire expresse de la présente partie de la Convention, si une notification, demande ou autre communication est faite par une partie au contrat conformément à la présente partie et par un moyen approprié aux circonstances, un retard ou une erreur dans la transmission de la communication ou le fait qu'elle n'est pas arrivée à destination ne prive pas cette partie au contrat du droit de s'en prévaloir.

Übersicht

	Rn.
I. Gegenstand der Vorschrift	1
II. Anwendungsbereich	4
1. Erfasste Mitteilungen	4
2. Mündliche und gleich zu behandelnde Erklärungen	5
3. Abweichende Vereinbarungen, Gepflogenheiten oder Bräuche	6
a) Vereinbarungen	6
b) Bräuche und Gepflogenheiten	6
c) Allgemeine Geschäftsbedingungen	6
III. Voraussetzungen für die Entlastung von der Transportgefahr	7
1. Nach den Umständen geeignete Mittel	7
2. Sprache	8
3. Absendung	9
IV. Rechtsfolgen	10
1. Verlust der Mitteilung	10
2. Verspätung	11
3. Irrtum bei der Übermittlung	12
4. Zeitpunkt des Wirksamwerdens	13
5. Bindung an die Erklärung	14

Vorläufer und **Entwürfe:** Genfer E 1976 Art. 10 I, III; Wiener E 1977 Art. 10; New Yorker E 1978 Art. 25.

I. Gegenstand der Vorschrift

1   Die Verfasser des Übereinkommens haben sich für andere als die Vertragsschluss bewirkenden Erklärungen grundsätzlich für die **Absendetheorie** entschieden.[1] Über die Tragweite der Vorschrift, die vor Behandlung der einzelnen Erklärungen in Teil III beschlossen worden war, ist man sich aber wohl nicht völlig klar gewesen.[2]

---

[1] OLG München, 17.11.2006, CISG-online 1395; *Kritzer,* Guide to Practical Applications, S. 220, Nr. 4: „... Art. 27 adopts a dispatch theory ..."; *Honsell/Gsell,* Art. 27, Rn. 1; *Staudinger/Magnus,* Art. 27, Rn. 7 ff.

[2] Zur Entstehungsgeschichte der Vorschrift s. *Stern,* Erklärungen, Rn. 383–407; ferner *Neumayer,* FS Drobnig, S. 100 ff., der der Ansicht ist, die Verfasser hätten die Emissionstheorie zum Ausdruck bringen wollen.

Bei Mitteilungen, die „mit den nach den Umständen geeigneten Mitteln" gemacht werden, trägt der Empfänger nach Art. 27 das Risiko eines Verlustes, einer Verzögerung oder Veränderung des Inhalts bei der Übermittlung, soweit das CISG nichts anderes vorschreibt.[3] Die Vorschrift gilt direkt nur für Teil III der Konvention, also für Mitteilungen im Zuge der Abwicklung des Kaufvertrages oder aus Anlass von Leistungsstörungen, während in Teil II (Vertragsschluss) für die einzelnen Erklärungen und Mitteilungen speziell geregelt ist, ob Zugang erforderlich ist oder Absendung genügt.[4] Soweit in Teil II nicht ausdrücklich Zugangsbedürftigkeit für eine der dort geregelten Erklärungen vorgeschrieben wird, sind die in den Begriffen „Absendung" oder „Zugang" verschlüsselten Lösungen für bestimmte Sachfragen auf der Grundlage von Art. 7 II aus den Grundsätzen, die dem Übereinkommen zugrunde liegen, zu entwickeln.[5]

Art. 27 weicht vom Zugangsprinzip, das auch § 130 I 1 BGB normiert, ab. Das **Absendeprinzip** lässt sich damit rechtfertigen, dass die in Teil III des CISG geregelten Erklärungen zumeist durch eine vom Adressaten der Erklärung verursachte Abweichung vom normalen Verlauf der Vertragsdurchführung veranlasst worden sind.[6] Dies überzeugt z. B. für die Mängelrüge, die durch vertragswidrige Leistung des Verkäufers erforderlich geworden ist.[7] Aber schon bei einer durch höhere Gewalt verursachten Leistungsstörung, die dem Gläubiger Anlass zur Vertragsaufhebung gibt, lässt sich das Transportrisiko des Empfängers der Aufhebungserklärung nicht mehr mit seiner Verantwortung für die Vertragsstörung rechtfertigen. Der Hinweis auf eine „Verantwortung" für das Übermittlungsrisiko trägt diese Lösung erst recht nicht in Fällen, in denen eine Erklärung überhaupt nicht durch den Erklärungsempfänger veranlasst worden ist, wie z. B. die (auf Grund des Vertrages mögliche) genaue Festsetzung des Liefertermins durch den Käufer, Art. 33 lit. b), eine Versendungs- oder Zuordnungsanzeige, Art. 67 II, oder eine Spezifikationsanzeige des Käufers, Art. 65.[8]

Für die Regelung des Art. 27 spricht, dass sie auf Grund ihrer Eindeutigkeit Zweifelsfragen vermeidet. Ihre Dispositivität erlaubt es im Übrigen den Parteien, für bestimmte Mitteilungen doch Zugangsbedürftigkeit vorzusehen, etwa für die Spezifikationsanzeige des Käufers.[9] Als allgemeinen Grundsatz der Konvention i. S. d. Art. 7 II wird man Art. 27 allerdings nur für Teil III der Konvention verstehen können, da dem Vertragsschlussteil (Artt. 14–24) für die dort geregelten Erklärungen grundsätzlich das Zugangsprinzip zugrunde liegt. Soweit die den Art. 27 tragenden Gedanken aber auch auf Mitteilungen zutreffen, die in Teil II geregelt sind und deren Absende- oder Zugangsbedürftigkeit offen geblieben ist, wird man den in Art. 27 normativ festgehaltenen Grundsatz auf Grund des Art. 7 II anwenden können.[10]

Art. 27 regelt nur das **Risiko** des **Verlustes,** der **Verzögerung** oder der **Veränderung** des Inhalts einer Mitteilung auf dem Übermittlungsweg. Die Qualifikation der Kommunikationsmittel – „mit den nach den Umständen geeigneten Mitteln" – ist dagegen nicht Wirksamkeitsvoraussetzung, sondern nur Voraussetzung für den Übergang des Verlustrisikos.[11] Auch die mit an sich ungeeigneten Mitteln übersandte, aber vom Empfänger richtig aufgenommene Mitteilung ist wirksam.

---

[3] S. unten Rn. 3.
[4] Den Abschlussvorschriften liegt das Zugangsprinzip zugrunde; Ausnahmen s. Art. 19 II 1, Art. 21 I 2.
[5] Vgl. unten Rn. 2, oben Art. 19 Rn. 16 und Art. 21 Rn. 20 sowie die Monographie von *Stern*.
[6] Vgl. die Stellungnahme der norwegischen Delegierten, O. R., S. 303 sub 22; *Brunner,* Art. 27, Rn. 1.
[7] S. zu § 377 IV HGB BGH, 13.5.1987, BGHZ 101, 49 ff.
[8] Vgl. zu solchen Konkretisierungserklärungen *Noussias,* Zugangsbedürftigkeit von Mitteilungen, S. 126 ff., der deshalb generell für diese Erklärungen Zugangsbedürftigkeit vorgeschlagen hat, sofern sie nicht – wie die ersatzweise Spezifikation durch den Verkäufer – wieder Reaktion auf Fehlverhalten der anderen Seite sind; dem folgend MünchKomm/*Gruber,* Art. 27, Rn. 5. S. auch *Neumayer/Ming,* Art. 27, Anm. 1., die für restriktive Auslegung plädieren: keine Geltung für vereinbarte Mitteilungen.
[9] S. unten Rn. 6.
[10] So *Enderlein/Maskow/Strohbach,* Art. 27, Anm. 4.1.; a. A. auf Grund der Entstehungsgeschichte *Reinhart,* Art. 27, Rn. 4.
[11] MünchKomm/*Gruber,* Art. 27, Rn. 3.

II. Anwendungsbereich

1. Erfasste Mitteilungen

4   Art. 27 gilt für alle Mitteilungen in Teil III („in diesem Teil") des CISG,[12] soweit nicht für einzelne Erklärungen, Anzeigen, Aufforderungen usw. in der Konvention ausdrücklich – z. B. in Artt. 47 II 1, 48 II, III i. V. m. IV, 63 II, 65 I, II, 79 IV, aber auch in Art. 29 I i. V. m. Artt. 14–24[13] – Empfangsbedürftigkeit vorgesehen[14] oder von den Parteien vereinbart worden ist.[15] Er ist also nicht auf rechtsgeschäftliche Willenserklärungen wie etwa **Vertragsaufhebungserklärungen** (Art. 26)[16] beschränkt, sondern erfasst auch **Fristsetzungen, Warnungen** (Art. 72 II) und **Anzeigen** wie Mängelrüge (Artt. 39, 43)[17] oder die Mitteilung der Absicht zum Selbsthilfeverkauf (Art. 88 I).[18] Auch von den Parteien zusätzlich **vereinbarte Mitteilungen** fallen, sofern die Vereinbarung selbst nicht etwas anderes vorsieht, unter Art. 27.[19] **Informationspflichten** dürfte der Schuldner freilich nicht schon mit der ordentlichen Absendung der Information erfüllt haben[20] – wenn „Erteilung" von Auskünften geschuldet ist, ist nach dem Inhalt der Pflicht Erfüllung nur anzunehmen, wenn die Auskunft dem Gläubiger zugegangen ist. Von vornherein **nicht** durch Art. 27 erfasst sind Mitteilungen, die als solche weder von der Konvention vorgesehen noch von den Parteien vereinbart worden sind (und denen es daher für die Zwecke des internationalen Warenkaufrechts an Rechtserheblichkeit mangelt), wie etwa anwaltliche Mahnschreiben einer der Vertragsparteien.[21]

2. Mündliche und gleich zu behandelnde Erklärungen

5   Ob Art. 27 auch für mündliche Erklärungen unter Anwesenden oder gleich zu behandelnde Erklärungen, z. B. durch **Telefon,** durch Funk oder im Rahmen einer Videokonferenz übermittelte und nicht in irgendeiner Form „verkörperte", z. B. ausgedruckte Erklärungen gilt, ist unsicher.[22] Praktische Bedeutung dürfte die Frage bei telefonischer Über-

---

[12] *Noussias,* Zugangsbedürftigkeit von Mitteilungen, S. 20 ff., unterscheidet Konkretisierungserklärungen, Mitteilungen über Vertragsstörungen und Rechtsbehelfsmitteilungen, s. die Aufzählung S. 20–22.

[13] S. unten Art. 29 Rn. 2.

[14] S. oben Art. 24 Rn. 3. Für Art. 65 a. A. *Schwimann/Posch,* Art. 27, Rn. 9; wie hier *Honsell/Gsell,* Art. 27, Rn. 4; *Mazzotta,* 33 Rutgers Computer & Tech. L.J. (2007), 251, 278; *Mohs,* oben Art. 65 Rn. 8; MünchKomm/*Gruber,* Art. 27, Rn. 4.

[15] Unten Rn. 6.

[16] OLG München, 17.11.2006, CISG-online 1395; OLG Naumburg, 27.4.1999, CISG-online 512 = TranspR-IHR 2000, 22, 23; RB Arnhem, 29.7.2009, CISG-online 1939.

[17] OGH, 24.5.2005, CISG-online 1046 = IHR 2005, 249; OGH, 30.6.1998, CISG-online 410 = östZRvgl 1998, 249; OLG Koblenz, 19.10.2006, CISG-online 1407; OLG München, 17.11.2006, CISG-online 1395; AppHof Bern, 11.2.2004, CISG-online 1191 = IHR 2006, 149, 153; RB Arnhem, 11.2.2009, CISG-online 1813.

[18] OLG Graz, 16.9.2002, CISG-online 1198 = IHR 2006, 210, 212.

[19] *Bamberger/Roth/Saenger,* Art. 27, Rn. 2; *Enderlein/Maskow/Strohbach,* Art. 27, Anm. 4.1.; *Honsell/Gsell,* Art. 27, Rn. 3; *Soergel/Lüderitz/Budzikiewicz,* Art. 27, Rn. 2; *Staudinger/Magnus,* Art. 27, Rn. 12; a. A. *Neumayer/Ming,* Art. 27, Anm. 1.

[20] Wie hier MünchKomm/*Gruber,* Art. 27, Rn. 6; anders *Enderlein/Maskow/Strohbach,* Art. 27, Anm. 3., zu Art. 32 III; *Honsell/Gsell,* Art. 27, Rn. 6 („aus Gründen der Rechtssicherheit"); MünchKommHGB/*Benicke,* Art. 27, Rn. 3 = *Staudinger/Magnus,* Art. 27, Rn. 10.

[21] Wie hier *Honsell/Gsell,* Art. 27, Rn. 3. A. A. OLG Düsseldorf, 22.7.2004, CISG-online 916 = IHR 2005, 29, 30 (Rückgriff auf Art. 27 im Rahmen der Frage, ob für anwaltliches Mahnschreiben bereits eine Geschäftsgebühr gemäß § 118 I Nr. 1 BRAGO abgerechnet werden darf).

[22] Ablehnend OGH, 15.10.1998, CISG-online 380 = östZRVgl 1999, 63: für mündliche Erklärung (Rüge) genüge Vernehmbarkeit; *Achilles,* Art. 27, Rn. 1.; *Bamberger/Roth/Saenger,* Art. 27, Rn. 4; *Schlechtriem,* Einheitliches UN-Kaufrecht, S. 50 f.; *Karollus,* S. 100; *Schwimann/Posch,* Art. 27, Rn. 12; wohl auch *Posch/Kandut,* S. 67; *Staudinger/Magnus,* Art. 27, Rn. 13; befürwortend *Herber/Czerwenka,* Art. 27, Rn. 5; *Honsell/Gsell,* Art. 27, Rn. 7; *Loewe,* Art. 27, S. 48; MünchKommHGB/*Benicke,* Art. 27, Rn. 4; für Erklärung durch Boten auch MünchKomm/*Gruber,* Art. 27, Rn. 7; *Soergel/Lüderitz/Budzikiewicz,* Art. 27, Rn. 4.

Absendetheorie   6 **Art. 27**

mittlung, etwa von Mängelrügen, haben, die auf Grund technischer Störungen vom Empfänger nur unvollständig (etwa ohne die erforderliche Substantiierung der gerügten Mängel, Art. 39 I) oder entstellt aufgenommen werden, was bei grenzüberschreitenden Ferngesprächen hin und wieder vorkommen mag. Die Formulierungen „Übermittlung der Mitteilung" und „Nichteintreffen" sprechen dafür, dass Art. 27 solche mündlichen Erklärungen unter Anwesenden oder am Telefon **nicht umfasst.** Es besteht aber auch ein sachlicher Unterschied zwischen diesen mündlichen Erklärungen und solchen, die durch Brief, Boten, Telex, Telegramm oder E-Mail übermittelt werden: Die direkte Kommunikation bei mündlichen oder fernmündlichen Erklärungen erlaubt dem Erklärenden, die Vernehmbarkeit seiner Erklärungen zu verfolgen oder doch jedenfalls durch Rückfragen zu klären, ob seine Erklärung verständlich war, während er den Transport anderer, d. h. brieflich, per Telex, Telefax, Telegramm, durch elektronische Kommunikationsmittel (außer in „Chat room"-Situationen) oder auch durch Boten übermittelter Erklärungen nicht immer zuverlässig kontrollieren oder beeinflussen kann.[23] M. E. ist deshalb für mündliche oder telefonische Erklärungen **Vernehmbarkeit** durch den Adressaten zu verlangen[24] und im Streitfalle vom Erklärenden zu beweisen. Andernfalls müsste man eine wegen Störungen unzuverlässige Telefonverbindung als „ungeeignetes Mittel" bewerten, um das „Telefonrisiko" des Empfängers zu mindern.

3. Abweichende Vereinbarungen, Gepflogenheiten oder Bräuche

a) Vereinbarungen. Die Parteien können Art. 27 generell oder für einzelne Erklärungen 6
abbedingen und Zugang, u. U. sogar noch höhere Anforderungen – z. B. Empfangsbestätigungen – vorschreiben, jedenfalls in individuell ausgehandelten **Vereinbarungen.**[25] Möglich ist auch, die „nach den Umständen geeigneten" Kommunikationsmittel (s. dazu noch Rn. 7) vertraglich zu spezifizieren und etwa zu vereinbaren, dass Mängelrügen mittels eingeschriebenen Briefs oder per Telefax erfolgen müssen.[26]

b) Bräuche und Gepflogenheiten. Von Art. 27 abweichende Zugangserfordernisse können sich aus Bräuchen ergeben, die nach Art. 9 I, II als vereinbarte oder – ausnahmsweise – normativ wirkende **Bräuche** zu beachten sind,[27] oder aus **Gepflogenheiten,** die sich zwischen den Parteien herausgebildet haben (Art. 9 I).

c) Allgemeine Geschäftsbedingungen. Vereinbarungen der Parteien, die das Transportrisiko abweichend von Art. 27 ordnen und Zugang oder erhöhte Anforderungen regeln, dürften jedoch nur dann unbedenklich sein, wenn sie individuell vereinbart worden sind. In **vorformulierten Geschäftsbedingungen** vorgesehene Zugangserfordernisse oder gar erhöhte Voraussetzungen für die Rechtzeitigkeit, z. B. das Erfordernis einer Empfangsbestätigung durch den Adressaten, dürften mit wesentlichen Grundgedanken der einschlägi-

---

[23] Vgl. für die Probleme bei grenzüberschreitenden telefonischen Rügen LG Köln, 11.7.1978, in: *Schlechtriem/Magnus,* Art. 39 EKG, Nr. 8: Eine telefonische Rüge ist nicht fristwahrend, wenn sie in ihrer allgemeinen Form dem Substantiierungsgebot nicht genügt und wegen Verständigungsschwierigkeiten ohnehin zweifelhaft ist, ob die Rüge von der Verkäuferin richtig verstanden wurde.
[24] So auch OGH, 15.10.1998, CISG-online 380 = östZRVgl 1999, 63.
[25] Vgl. *Enderlein/Maskow/Strohbach,* Art. 27, Anm. 5.: Telex mit Bestätigung durch eingeschriebenen Brief. S. a. LG Stuttgart, 13.8.1991, CISG-online 33: Rüge nur mit eingeschriebenem Brief, vereinbart in AGB (!); aaO. auch zur dadurch eintretenden Verschiebung der Beweislast: Nachweis des Zugangs trifft den Erklärenden.
[26] RB Arnhem, 11.2.2009, CISG-online 1813: AGB-Klausel verlangte, dass „every complaint regarding the amount of or damage to the delivered trees, must be reported by means of a written letter or fax…".
[27] Wären ausnahmsweise die deutschen Regeln zu den Folgen des Schweigens auf ein kaufmännisches Bestätigungsschreiben als internationaler Handelsbrauch i. S. d. Art. 9 II zu beachten (s. oben Vor Artt. 14–24 Rn. 21), dann müsste das Bestätigungsschreiben zugegangen sein. Soweit es jedoch eine in Teil III CISG geregelten Mitteilungen enthält, z. B. eine Spezifikationsanzeige, bleibt es m. E. bei der Regelung des Art. 27: Die Regeln über die Wirkung kaufmännischer Bestätigungsschreiben sollen nicht solche speziellen gesetzlichen Bestimmungen verändern.

gen gesetzlichen Regelung, d. h. des CISG, nicht in Einklang stehen und deshalb bei deutschem Recht als Vertragsstatut nach § 307 BGB, der über Art. 4 S. 2 lit. a) auch im Geltungsbereich des CISG anzuwenden ist, unwirksam sein.[28] Darüber hinaus können sie überraschende Klauseln i. S. v. § 305c I BGB oder intransparent nach § 307 I 2 BGB sein und einen Verstoß gegen § 309 Nr. 13 BGB darstellen. In AGB festgelegte Anforderungen an zu verwendende Kommunikationsmittel erscheinen demgegenüber weniger bedenklich; eine klauselmäßige Beschränkung auf eingeschriebenen Brief und Telefax (für Mängelrügen) ist in einem italienisch-niederländischen Kaufvertrag als unproblematisch angesehen worden.[29]

III. Voraussetzungen für die Entlastung von der Transportgefahr

1. Nach den Umständen geeignete Mittel

7   Art. 27 entlastet den Erklärenden nur dann von dem Risiko, dass seine Erklärung auf dem Transport verloren geht, verzögert oder verändert wird, wenn er sie mit nach den Umständen geeigneten Mitteln gemacht hat;[30] die **Beweislast** trägt der Mitteilende.[31] Gegenüber Artt. 14 EKG, 12 II EAG, wo auf „übliche Mittel" abgestellt worden war, ermöglicht Art. 27 eine größere Flexibilität für den Mitteilenden in der **Auswahl des Kommunikationsmittels.** Er kann und ggf. muss sich also bei einem Poststreik oder (und) einem Zusammenbruch des Fernmeldenetzes auch eines unüblichen, aber unter den gegebenen Umständen geeigneten reitenden, fahrenden oder laufenden **Botens** bedienen. Nationales, über IPR berufenes Recht bleibt, soweit es um Eignung eines Boten geht, außer Betracht; ein ungeeigneter Bote ist Risiko des Erklärenden.[32] Schon der Wortlaut des Art. 27 macht deutlich, dass die Eignung des Erklärungsmittels sich nach den Umständen des Einzelfalles bestimmt.[33] Danach ist etwa denkbar, dass zur Übermittlung einer Mängelrüge in der konkreten Situation nur ein Telefax, nicht aber ein Telefonanruf geeignet ist.[34] Kommunikationsmittel, die in einem Land selbstverständlich als geeignet bewertet würden, können in anderen Ländern unzuverlässig und deshalb ungeeignet sein. Die Eignung muss dabei sowohl für das Land, in dem abgesendet wird, als auch für das Empfängerland gegeben sein und kann je nach Erklärungsmittel auch für zu durchquerende Länder erforderlich werden: Wer einen im Absendeland geeigneten Übermittlungsweg, z. B. Brief, Fax, E-Mail oder Telegramm, wählt, muss deshalb auch die Verhältnisse im Lande des Adressaten bedenken, wenn er – durch Wahl eines „geeigneten" Kommunikationsmittels – die Risikoentlastung durch Absendung nach Art. 27 erreichen will.[35] Allerdings muss bei der Auswahl des geeigneten Erklärungsmittels in gewissem Maße die **Zumutbarkeit für den Absender** Berücksichtigung finden: Ist der Adressat nur postalisch erreichbar, und ist die Post im Lande des Adressaten bekanntermaßen höchst unzuverlässig und deshalb eigentlich kein geeignetes

---

[28] *Kühl/Hingst*, FS Herber, S. 60; a. A. *Achilles*, Art. 27, Rn. 1; MünchKomm/*Gruber*, Art. 27, Rn. 9; differenzierend *Honsell/Gsell*, Art. 27, Rn. 22; MünchKommHGB/*Benicke*, Art. 27, Rn. 5.
[29] RB Arnhem, 11.2.2009, CISG-online 1813.
[30] Dazu auch *Achilles*, Art. 27, Rn. 4; *Bamberger/Roth/Saenger*, Art. 27, Rn. 6; *Honsell/Gsell*, Art. 27, Rn. 8; *Soergel/Lüderitz/Budzikiewicz*, Art. 27, Rn. 5; *Staudinger/Magnus*, Art. 27, Rn. 16 f.; *Witz/Salger/Lorenz/Salger*, Art. 27, Rn. 11.
[31] OGH, 30.6.1998, CISG-online 410 = östZRVgl 1998, 249; *Baumgärtel/Laumen/Hepting*, Art. 27 WKR, Rn. 7; *Schwimann/Posch*, Art. 27, Rn. 10. Zur Beweislast für die Rechtzeitigkeit der Absendung s. unten Rn. 9.
[32] Vgl. LG Bochum, 24.1.1996, CISG-online 175 (Rüge an Verkäuferin).
[33] *Honsell/Gsell*, Art. 27, Rn. 8.
[34] So in LG Kassel, 15.2.1996, CISG-online 191 = NJW-RR 1996, 1146, 1147: Rüge deutscher Käuferin von Mamorplatten gegenüber italienischer Verkäuferin, deren Faxnummer auf den Rechnungen angegeben war; Verweis des Gerichts auf die „in gewährleistungsrechtlicher Hinsicht schwerwiegenden Auswirkungen der Mängelanzeige auf das Vertragsverhältnis".
[35] Zu elektronischen Kommunikationsmitteln *Schwenzer/Hachem/Kee*, Rn. 11.14.

Übermittlungsmittel,[36] dann kann das nicht bedeuten, dass der Erklärende sich eines zuverlässigen und deshalb geeigneten Boten bedienen *muss,* um z. B. Mängel anzuzeigen.[37] Auch kann die **Schnelligkeit** der zur Verfügung stehenden **Übermittlungswege** für ihre Eignung je nach Art der Erklärung eine Rolle spielen.[38] Unter Umständen kann bei Unzuverlässigkeit der in Betracht kommenden Übermittlungswege auch eine Doppelung einer Mitteilung erforderlich sein,[39] also zusätzlich zum Fax, dessen vollständige und lesbare Übermittlung wegen Störanfälligkeit der Leitungen oder Empfangsgeräte im Lande des Adressaten gefährdet sein kann, durch Übersendung der Faxvorlage (Brief) oder zusätzlich zum streikgefährdeten Brief durch Fax. Zur Eignung gehört auch, dass die Erklärung an den richtigen Empfänger und nicht an irgendeine mit der Vertragsabwicklung befasste Person gerichtet ist.[40] Bei Verwendung schriftübertragender **elektronischer Kommunikationsmittel** wie E-Mail usw. muss der Empfänger sich ausdrücklich oder implizit einverstanden erklärt haben, elektronische Mitteilungen dieser Art in diesem Format und unter dieser Adresse zu erhalten.[41] Angesichts des vom Adressaten zu tragenden Transportrisikos kommt dieser zusätzlichen, in Interpretation der „nach den Umständen geeigneten Mittel" nach Art. 7 I zu fordernden Voraussetzung erhebliche Bedeutung zu.

2. Sprache

Medium, d. h. Mittel für Anzeigen, Aufforderungen oder sonstige Mitteilungen ist regelmäßig die (d. h. eine) Sprache, wenngleich auch andere Erklärungsformen, etwa Zurücksenden der Ware, in Betracht kommen. Verlangt „Eignung" für die Erklärung auch die Verwendung einer bestimmten Sprache? Art. 27 will nicht die Verständlichkeit und Vernehmbarkeit von Erklärungen schlechthin regeln, sondern nur das Transportrisiko. Die verwendete Sprache wird dieses Risiko jedoch nur in Ausnahmefällen derart verändern, dass sie ein bestimmtes Kommunikationsmittel ungeeignet macht: Telegramme in einer Sprache, die den eingeschalteten Telegrammeinrichtungen (Postämtern des Empfängers oder Absenders, aber auch privaten Telegrammübermittlungsunternehmen) nicht vertraut ist, die vielleicht Buchstaben und Zeichen verwendet, die die eine oder andere der eingeschalteten Einrichtungen nicht kennt, sind in besonders hohem Maße gefährdet, entstellt oder verstümmelt zu werden, so dass in solchen Fällen ein Telegramm ungeeignet sein kann. Regelmäßig dürfte jedoch die Sprache nicht eine Frage des Transportrisikos sein, sondern eine solche der Wirksamkeit von Erklärungen überhaupt, die nicht durch Art. 27 geregelt wird.[42] Die Sprachenfrage ist vielmehr ein Ausschnitt aus dem allgemeineren, in der Konvention aber nicht generell geregelten Problem, dass Wirksamkeitsvoraussetzung für Erklärungen ist,

---

[36] *Schwimann/Posch,* Art. 27, Rn. 10 beklagt die „in einigen Staaten notorische und insgesamt wachsende Unzuverlässigkeit postalischer Dienstleistungen".
[37] Wie hier *Honsell/Gsell,* Art. 27, Rn. 8.
[38] Vgl. *Enderlein/Maskow/Strohbach,* Art. 27, Anm. 5.: „... Mittel ..., die in Schnelligkeit und Zuverlässigkeit dem Inhalt der Mitteilung entsprechen." Die Verfasser wollen darüber hinaus die Eignung auch nach der Bedeutung der Erklärung abstufen: Für die Übermittlung „einer so schwerwiegenden Entscheidung" wie der Vertragsaufhebung müsse „mit besonderer Sorgfalt vorgegangen werden"; ebenso *Honsell/Gsell,* Art. 27, Rn. 8. M. E. ist jedoch die Eignung nur im Hinblick auf die Vermeidung von Verlust, Verzögerung oder Veränderung der Erklärung zu prüfen.
[39] Vgl. *Enderlein/Maskow/Strohbach,* Art. 27, Anm. 5.: „... besondere Unsicherheiten bei der Übermittlung ..."; ebenso *Honsell/Gsell,* Art. 27, Rn. 8; MünchKomm/*Gruber,* Art. 27, Rn. 13; MünchKommHGB/*Benicke,* Art. 27, Rn. 6.
[40] Vgl. LG Kassel, 15.2.1996, CISG-online 191 = NJW-RR 1996, 1146 f.: Rüge an Makler.
[41] S. CISG-AC, Op. 1 *(Chr. Ramberg),* Opinion Art. 17, IHR 2003, 244, 246; *Coetzee,* VJ (2007), 11, 19; *Honsell/Gsell,* Art. 27, Rn. 8; allgemein zu dieser Voraussetzung unter dem CISG oben Vor Artt. 14–24 Rn. 27.
[42] Ebenso *Bamberger/Roth/Saenger,* Art. 27, Rn. 7; *Bianca/Bonell/Date-Bah,* Art. 27, Anm. 3.1.; *Honsell/Gsell,* Art. 27, Rn. 10 f.; MünchKommHGB/*Benicke,* Art. 27, Rn. 7; *Schwimann/Posch,* Art. 27, Rn. 10; *Witz/Salger/Lorenz/Salger,* Art. 27, Rn. 13; a. A. ICC, 11849/2003, CISG-online 1421 = YB Comm. Arb. 2006, 148, 165: Art. 27 „sets a general principle of effectiveness of notifications", weshalb der Adressat die Unverständlichkeit einer fremdsprachigen Erklärung (hier: italienischsprachige Nachfristsetzung gegenüber U. S.-amerikanischem Käufer) nicht geltend machen könne.

dass sie für den Adressaten oder jedenfalls eine vernünftige Person der gleichen Art verständlich sein müssen;[43] die Auslegungsregel des Art. 8 I, II setzt das voraus. Erklärungen müssen deshalb in einer für die Parteien verständlichen Sprache erfolgen.[44] Dabei können entsprechend Art. 8 III alle erheblichen Umstände, insbesondere die Vertragssprache, „... die Verhandlungen zwischen den Parteien, die zwischen ihnen entstandenen Gepflogenheiten ... und das spätere Verhalten der Parteien" erheblich sein.[45]

3. Absendung

9   Art. 27 verlangt zum Übergang des Transportrisikos auf den Empfänger Absendung der Mitteilung, formuliert das freilich undeutlich: Die Mitteilung muss jedenfalls (mit den nach den Umständen geeigneten Mitteln) „gemacht" worden sein. Funktion und Entstehungsgeschichte des Art. 27 verdeutlichen, dass der Erklärende jedenfalls alles Erforderliche getan haben muss, um die Erklärung „auf den Weg" zu bringen: Ein Brief muss nicht nur diktiert, ge- und unterschrieben, ordnungsgemäß adressiert und frankiert, sondern durch Einwurf in einen Postbriefkasten oder Abgabe bei der Post abgesandt („dispatched") worden sein. Ein Telegramm muss man aufgeben, ein Telex in das eingeschaltete Übermittlungsgerät eingeben, zur Übermittlung eines Schreibens per Telefax muss die für den telefonischen Übermittlungsvorgang erforderliche Einrichtung richtig bedient und der Sendebericht kontrolliert werden; bei Fehleranzeige ist der Vorgang zu wiederholen.[46] Eine mit elektronischer Post (E-Mail) übermittelte Mitteilung muss für den Sender erkennbar das hausinterne Netz verlassen haben[47] und das Sendeterminal dies signalisieren. Absendung verlangt deshalb, dass die Erklärung so in Lauf gesetzt wird, dass sie bei ordentlichem Funktionieren des verwendeten Kommunikationsmittels rechtzeitig und richtig angekommen wäre.

Die Erklärung ist zwar nicht zugangs*bedürftig,* muss aber zugangs*fähig* abgesandt worden sein. Für diese Absendung ist der Erklärende **beweispflichtig,** falls es auf rechtzeitige und richtige Absendung ankommt.[48] Etwas anderes kann sich aus Parteivereinbarungen ergeben, etwa, wenn für Rüge ein eingeschriebener Brief vorgesehen ist.[49]

IV. Rechtsfolgen

1. Verlust der Mitteilung

10   Eine mit den nach den Umständen geeigneten Mitteln gemachte, ordnungsgemäß und rechtzeitig abgesandte Mitteilung ist wirksam. Sie lässt m. E. die mit ihr bezweckten Rechts-

---

[43] S. auch die Dissertation von *Ladas,* der Sprache als Frage des Erklärungsmittels und seiner Eignung sieht; für die Einordnung der sprachlichen Verständlichkeit zugangsbedürftiger Erklärungen als Zugangsproblem oben Art. 24 Rn. 36.

[44] Sprachliche Missverständnisse können nach nationalem Recht Anfechtungsrechte auslösen, vgl. den Fall BGH, 27.10.1994, NJW 1995, 190: Bürgschaftsurkunde unterschrieben von einer Iranerin, die der deutschen Sprache weder in Wort noch Schrift mächtig war, in der irrigen Meinung, eine Tatsache zu bekunden (und nicht eine rechtsgeschäftliche Erklärung abzugeben): Erklärungsirrtum nach § 119 I BGB.

[45] Ähnlich *Bianca/Bonell/Date-Bah,* Art. 27, Anm. 3.2.; s. hierzu auch oben *Schmidt-Kessel,* Art. 8 Rn. 41.

[46] Vgl. OLG Naumburg, 28.6.1993, NJW 1993, 2543, 2544: Absender muss darauf achten, dass alle Seiten richtig eingelesen worden sind; *Honsell/Gsell,* Art. 27, Rn. 12.

[47] Wie hier *Honsell/Gsell,* Art. 27, Rn. 12.

[48] OGH, 30.6.1998, CISG-online 410 = östZRVgl 1998, 249; OGH, 24.5.2005, CISG-online 1046 = IHR 2005, 249; OLG Koblenz, 19.10.2006, CISG-online 1407: Beweis der Faxabsendung durch Zeugen und Auszug aus Faxchronik; OLG Naumburg, 27.4.1999, CISG-online 512 = TranspR-IHR 2000, 22, 23; RB Arnhem, 29.7.2009, CISG-online 1939; AG Freiburg, 6.7.2007, CISG-online 1596; *Achilles,* Art. 27, Rn. 6; *Bamberger/Roth/Saenger,* Art. 27, Rn. 11; *Brunner,* Art. 27, Rn. 1; *Enderlein/Maskow/Strohbach,* Art. 27, Anm. 6.; *Honsell/Karollus,* Art. 27, Rn. 24; *Soergel/Lüderitz/Budzikiewicz,* Art. 27, Rn. 10 („selbstverständlich"); *Staudinger/Magnus,* Art. 27, Rn. 26; *Witz/Salger/Lorenz/Salger,* Art. 27, Rn. 18.

[49] Vgl. LG Stuttgart, 13.8.1991, CISG-online 33 (Klausel in AGB verlangte für Verspätungsrügen zugangsbedürftigen „lettre recommandé"); zweifelnd *Brunner,* Art. 27, Rn. 5.

folgen auch dann eintreten, wenn sie beim Adressaten nicht eintrifft.[50] Das wird allerdings bestritten und behauptet, dass Art. 27 – entsprechend der Auslegung der Regelung des § 377 IV HGB durch den BGH[51] – nicht notwendig Zugang als Wirksamkeitsvoraussetzung entbehrlich sein lasse.[52] Weder Entstehungsgeschichte noch Text[53] stützen diese Auslegung.[54] Mag sie auch dem Juristen aus Rechtskreisen, die für alle Willenserklärungen vom Zugangsprinzip ausgehen, vertraut sein und deshalb als sachgerecht erscheinen – eine solche Auslegung des Art. 27 würde die erreichte Rechtseinheit erheblich gefährden.[55] Allerdings wird man eine Berufung auf Art. 27 nicht zulassen dürfen, wenn der Erklärende den Verlust selbst zu verantworten hat;[56] eine entsprechende Einschränkung des Art. 27, soweit sie nicht schon aus der Voraussetzung „Eignung des Erklärungsmittels" folgt (Rn. 7, 9), kann sich auf Art. 7 I (Wahrung des guten Glaubens bei der Übereinkommensauslegung) stützen.

2. Verspätung

Wo die Konvention für Erklärungen und Mitteilungen Fristen setzt, wie z. B. für die Mängelrüge (angemessene Frist), genügt die rechtzeitige Absendung. Rechtzeitige Absendung meint freilich, dass so abgesandt worden ist, dass bei einem normalen Verlauf der Dinge die Erklärung noch innerhalb der Frist beim Adressaten eingegangen wäre:[57] Art. 27 entlastet den Erklärenden ausdrücklich vom Risiko der Verzögerung des Transports, will aber nicht dem Erklärenden gestatten, überhaupt erst am Ende der Frist abzusenden.[58]

3. Irrtum bei der Übermittlung

Die Formulierung, dass (auch) „ein Irrtum bei der Übermittlung der Mitteilung" der erklärenden Partei nicht das Recht nimmt, sich auf die Mitteilung zu berufen, findet sich in den Vorläufern und Entwürfen zum EKG noch nicht. In Art. 39 III EKG war ebenfalls nur Verspätung oder Verlust (der Mängelrüge) geregelt.[59] Im E 1976 war jedoch bereits der Fall der ungenauen Übermittlung erwähnt worden (Art. 10 III), und im E 1977 findet sich dann der „error in transmission". Damit ist nicht der Fall gemeint, dass die Mitteilung fehlgeleitet wird, da insoweit der Fall des „Nichteintreffens" vorliegt. Die Vorgeschichte, insbesondere der Wortlaut des Art. 10 III E 1976 („inaccurately transmitted") machen deutlich, dass es um inhaltliche Entstellungen oder Veränderungen der Mitteilung geht. Wird eine telegra-

---

[50] OLG Koblenz, 19.10.2006, CISG-online 1407. Der Erklärende kann sich dabei auf die betreffende Mitteilung natürlich nur mit demjenigen Inhalt „berufen", den diese bei Absendung hatte – bringt der Käufer eine Mängelrüge auf den Weg, die den inhaltlichen Anforderungen des Art. 39 I (s. dazu unten *Schwenzer*, Art. 39 Rn. 6 ff.) von vornherein nicht genügte, so ändert Art. 27 an letzterer Tatsache nichts; vgl. *Schwimann/Posch*, Art. 25, Rn. 3.
[51] BGH, 13.5.1987, BGHZ 101, 49, 51 f.
[52] *Neumayer/Ming*, Art. 27, Anm. 2.; *Honsell/Karollus*, Art. 27, Rn. 18; für eine „teleologische Reduktion" deshalb *Stern*, Erklärungen, Rn. 454 (Zusammenfassung).
[53] „Nichteintreffen" (!); vgl. auch *Enderlein/Maskow/Strohbach*, Art. 27, Anm. 1.1.
[54] Wie hier OGH, 24.5.2005, CISG-online 1046 = IHR 2005, 249; OLG München, 17.11.2006, CISG-online 1395; *Achilles*, Art. 27, Rn. 5; *Bamberger/Roth/Saenger*, Art. 27, Rn. 9; *Bianca/Bonell/Date-Bah*, Art. 27, Anm. 2.5.; *Herber/Czerwenka*, Art. 27, Rn. 6; *Honnold/Flechtner*, Art. 27, Rn. 189; *Loewe*, Art. 27, S. 48; *Posch/Kandut*, S. 67; *Soergel/Lüderitz/Budzikiewicz*, Art. 27, Rn. 9; *Staudinger/Magnus*, Art. 27, Rn. 23; *Witz/Salger/Lorenz/Salger*, Art. 27, Rn. 17; differenzierend und teilweise abweichend *Karollus*, S. 100 f. (in der Regel Erklärungswirkung erst mit Zugang); *Neumayer/Ming*, Art. 27, Anm. 2.
[55] Vgl. *Schwenzer*, NJW 1991, 1402.
[56] Wie hier *Honsell/Gsell*, Art. 27, Rn. 15.
[57] *Brunner*, Art. 27, Rn. 2; MünchKomm/*Gruber*, Art. 27, Rn. 16.
[58] *Leser*, Vertragsaufhebung und Rückabwicklung, S. 237 f.; *Honsell/Gsell*, Art. 27, Rn. 14; *Staudinger/Magnus*, Art. 27, Rn. 16. U. U. kann die Berufung auf verspätete Absendung, falls ohnehin nicht empfangen werden konnte, jedoch rechtsmissbräuchlich sein, vgl. zur Mängelrüge nach Art. 39 EKG OLG Karlsruhe, 25.7.1986, RIW 1986, 818 ff. Dass die Berufung auf eine formale Rechtsposition missbräuchlich sein kann, ist als Grundsatz i. S. d. Art. 7 II zu sehen und z. B. auf die Artt. 16 II lit. b), 29 II 2 zu stützen; für zugangsbedürftige Erklärungen s. auch oben Art. 24 Rn. 41.
[59] Der Wortlaut der im Haag fallengelassenen Entwürfe einer allgemeineren Regel wird bei *Noussias*, Zugangsbedürftigkeit von Mitteilungen, S. 44, berichtet.

phisch übermittelte Mängelrüge so verstümmelt, dass die korrekte Substantiierung der Mängel durch den Käufer unverständlich wird oder verloren geht, dann ist gleichwohl richtig gerügt worden. Eine richtig erklärte Vertragsaufhebung führt zur Auflösung des Vertrages, auch dann, wenn sie beim Käufer entstellt und als Vertragsaufhebungserklärung nicht verständlich ankommt. Eines Rückgriffs auf nationale Anfechtungsregeln – § 120 BGB – bedarf es nicht; sie wären auch trotz Art. 4 S. 2 lit. a) ausgeschlossen, da Art. 27 diese Sachfrage exklusiv regelt.[60]

4. Zeitpunkt des Wirksamwerdens

13   Für den Zeitpunkt des Wirksamwerdens einer nur absendebedürftigen Erklärung werden drei Ansichten vertreten: Soweit in Art. 27 überhaupt nur eine Regelung des Verzögerungs- oder Verstümmelungsrisikos gesehen, also zum Wirksamwerden der Erklärung stets Zugang verlangt wird, soll (konsequent) für das Wirksamwerden auf den Zugang abzustellen sein.[61] Teilweise wird vertreten, dass es jedenfalls für den *Zeitpunkt* des Wirksamwerdens auf den Zugang bei normaler Beförderung ankommen soll, sofern nicht eine unbeachtliche Verspätung bei der Übermittlung der rechtzeitig abgesandten Erklärung geschehen ist. Das erfordert freilich bei verloren gegangenen oder verspäteten Mitteilungen die Hilfskonstruktion, dass es dann auf den Zeitpunkt nach Ablauf der regelmäßigen Beförderungszeit, also einen hypothetischen Zugangszeitpunkt, ankommen soll.[62] M. E. muss jedoch entsprechend dem Konzept der Absendetheorie und dem Verständnis der Wirkung einer nur absendebedürftigen Erklärung im angelsächsischen Recht **Wirkung bereits mit Aufgabe** (dispatch) angenommen werden.[63] Die Differenzierung von Transportrisiko, Wirksamwerden und Bindung (hierzu Rn. 14) ist für die einheitliche Handhabung eines internationalen Regelwerks, das diese Unterscheidung selbst nicht enthält, zu fein gesponnen; die praktisch wichtige Frage der Bindung (Rn. 14) kann damit auch nicht befriedigend beantwortet werden.

5. Bindung an die Erklärung

14   Im Zusammenhang mit dem Zeitpunkt des Wirksamwerdens solcher Erklärungen wird auch behandelt, ob sie bis zum Zugang zurückgezogen werden können oder mit Absendung bereits bindend werden.[64] Manche vertreten Gleichlauf von Wirksamkeit und Bindung.[65] M. E. hat die Frage des Wirksamwerdens einer nur absendebedürftigen Erklärung nicht notwendig etwas mit der Bindung des Erklärenden an seine Erklärung zu tun. Wie bei

---

[60] *Ferrari*, RabelsZ 71 (2007), 52, 70; MünchKomm/*Gruber*, Art. 27, Rn. 15; *Schlechtriem/Witz*, Convention de Vienne, Rn. 56; *Staudinger/Magnus*, Art. 27, Rn. 25. Falls jedoch der Empfänger seinerseits eine rechtsgeschäftliche Erklärung abgibt, die durch die Veränderung der Mitteilung irrtumsbehaftet ist, kann für seine Erklärung Anfechtung nach nationalem Recht in Betracht kommen.
[61] So *Stern*, Erklärungen, Rn. 454 (Zusammenfassung).
[62] So *Achilles*, Art. 27, Rn. 5; *Bamberger/Roth/Saenger*, Art. 27, Rn. 10; *Leser*, Vertragsaufhebung und Rückabwicklung, S. 237 f.; *Karollus*, S. 100; *Honsell/Karollus*, 1. Aufl., Art. 27, Rn. 18; MünchKomm/*Gruber*, Art. 27, Rn. 17; *Neumayer/Ming*, Art. 27, Anm. 2. (es wäre nicht zu begreifen, wenn rechtsgestaltende Erklärungen prinzipiell ohne Kenntnis des Adressaten Wirksamkeit erlangen könnten); *Neumayer*, FS Drobnig, S. 103 ff.; gewisse Einschränkungen für einzelne in Teil III geregelte Erklärungen halten auch *Enderlein/Maskow/Strohbach*, Art. 27, Anm. 1.1., für erwägenswert; für die Spezifikationsanzeige wird der gleiche Standpunkt vertreten z. B. von *Posch/Kandut*, S. 69. Auf den hypothetischen Zugangszeitpunkt stellt ab Art. 1:303 (4) S. 2 PECL; auf aktuellen Zugang stellt ab Art. 1.9 (2) PICC.
[63] *Brunner*, Art. 27, Rn. 1; *Honsell/Gsell*, Art. 27, Rn. 18; MünchKommHGB/*Benicke*, Art. 27, Rn. 13 ff.; *Soergel/Lüderitz/Budzikiewicz*, Art. 27, Rn. 11; *Staudinger/Magnus*, Art. 27, Rn. 24; wohl auch OGH, 30.6.1998, CISG-online 410 = östZRvgl. 1998, 249 ff.: „Rüge rechtzeitig und gehörig erhoben (abgesendet) …".
[64] Für eine Rücknahmemöglichkeit konsequent *Neumayer/Ming*, Art. 27, Anm. 4.; s. auch *Brunner*, Art. 27, Rn. 3: Widerruf bis zum Zugang der Erklärung möglich analog Artt. 15 II, 22; *Leser*, Vertragsaufhebung und Rückabwicklung, S. 237; *Stern*, Erklärungen, Rn. 455 (Zusammenfassung): „Erst mit dem Zugang der Erklärung kann sich der Empfänger schutzwürdig darauf einstellen …".
[65] *Karollus*, S. 101; *Honsell/Karollus*, 1. Aufl., Art. 27, Rn. 21.

zugangsbedürftigen Erklärungen, etwa dem Angebot, kommt nicht nur Rücknahme *bis zum* Zugang, sondern auch Widerruf *nach* Zugang in Betracht (s. Artt. 15 II, 16 I). Rücknahme- bzw. Widerrufsmöglichkeit sind deshalb für jede Erklärung gesondert zu prüfen. Da das CISG die Frage der Bindung an die in Teil III geregelten Erklärungen weitgehend offen lässt, liegt eine Lücke vor.[66] Vor einer Anwendung nationalen Rechts ist zu prüfen, ob die Lücke nicht unter Rückgriff auf im CISG festgeschriebene Grundsätze gefüllt werden kann. M. E. bringt Art. 16 II lit. b) den Grundsatz zum Ausdruck, dass ein Erklärungsadressat, der vernünftigerweise auf Unwiderruflichkeit einer Erklärung vertrauen konnte und im Vertrauen auf diese Erklärung sich auf sie eingestellt hat, gegen einen Widerruf zu schützen ist. Auch Art. 29 II 2 beruht auf dem Grundsatz, dass ein veranlasstes Vertrauen zu schützen ist und ein venire contra factum proprium ausschließen kann. Bei der Lösung des hier behandelten Problems kann dieser Grundsatz eingesetzt werden.[67] Auch dürfte bereits die Auslegung des Übereinkommens nach Art. 7 I gebieten, zur Wahrung des guten Glaubens im internationalen Handel auf die Schutzbedürftigkeit des Adressaten solcher Erklärungen abzustellen. Deshalb dürfte eine Erklärung, die der Adressat mangels Zugangs noch nicht kennt, regelmäßig zurückgenommen werden können, da eine schutzwürdige Position noch nicht entstanden sein kann.[68] Selbst eine bereits zugegangene Erklärung sollte aber, solange sich der Empfänger noch nicht darauf eingestellt hat, widerrufen oder geändert werden können. Dabei darf es m. E. auch keinen Unterschied machen, ob die fragliche Erklärung rechtsgestaltende Wirkung hat und deshalb durch Rücknahme oder Widerruf eine Rechtsgestaltung rückgängig gemacht wird.[69] Nicht nur eine Nachfristsetzung, sondern auch eine Minderung wird deshalb erst dann für den Erklärenden endgültig bindend, wenn der Empfänger sich darauf eingestellt hat. Die Beweislast dafür, dass der Erklärungsadressat sich auf die Erklärung noch nicht eingestellt hat, trägt im Bestreitensfalle der Widerrufende.[70] Als Einlassung, die Widerruf abschneidet, sollte aber eine dahingehende Erklärung des Adressaten (z. B.: „mit Minderung einverstanden") genügen.

---

[66] Wie hier *Janssen/Kiene,* General principles, S. 275 f.
[67] Zustimmend *Janssen/Kiene,* General principles, S. 276; ähnlich auch *Honsell/Gsell,* Art. 27, Rn. 20.
[68] Wer Wirksamkeit erst im (ggfs. hypothetischen) Zeitpunkt des Zugangs eintreten lassen will, hat natürlich mit der Erklärung einer Rücknahmemöglichkeit keine Probleme, vgl. *Achilles,* Art. 27, Rn. 10.
[69] Vgl. *Schlechtriem,* Bindung an Erklärungen, S. 265 ff., dort auch zu dem deutschen Dogma, eine Gestaltungserklärung könne rechtslogisch nicht ungeschehen gemacht, d. h. zurückgenommen werden; MünchKommHGB/*Benicke,* Art. 27, Rn. 17; a. A. MünchKomm/*Gruber,* Art. 27, Rn. 18.
[70] *Janssen/Kiene,* General principles, S. 276; *Krebs,* Rückabwicklung, S. 29.

Art. 28 [Erfüllungsanspruch]

Ist eine Partei nach diesem Übereinkommen berechtigt, von der anderen Partei die Erfüllung einer Verpflichtung zu verlangen, so braucht ein Gericht eine Entscheidung auf Erfüllung in Natur nur zu fällen, wenn es dies auch nach seinem eigenen Recht bei gleichartigen Kaufverträgen täte, die nicht unter dieses Übereinkommen fallen.

Art. 28

If, in accordance with the provisions of this Convention, one party is entitled to require performance of any obligation by the other party, a court is not bound to enter a judgement for specific performance unless the court would do so under its own law in respect of similar contracts of sale not governed by this Convention.

Art. 28

Si, conformément aux dispositions de la présente Convention, une partie a le droit d'exiger de l'autre l'exécution d'une obligation, un tribunal n'est tenu d'ordonner l'exécution en nature que s'il le ferait en vertu de son propre droit pour des contrats de vente semblables non régis par la présente Convention.

Übersicht

	Rn.
I. Allgemeines	1
1. Gegenstand und Zweck	1
2. Praktische Bedeutung	4
II. Voraussetzungen der Anwendung von Art. 28	5
1. Übersicht	5
2. Erfüllungsansprüche der Parteien nach dem CISG	6
3. Gericht	8
4. Eigenes Recht	9
a) Forumsrecht unter Ausschluss des IPR	9
b) Umfang der Verweisung	10
c) Anwendungsfälle	12
d) Fazit	18
5. Vergleichsmassstab des „gleichartigen Kaufvertrags"	19
6. Zusammenfassung	20
III. Rechtsfolge: Abweisung der Erfüllungsklage	21
IV. Keine Abdingbarkeit	24

Vorläufer und **Entwürfe:** EKG Art. 16 i. V. m. Art. VII des Übereinkommens zur Einführung eines EKG vom 1. Juli 1964 (BGBl. 1973 II S. 886); Genfer E 1976 Art. 12; Wiener E 1977 Art. 12; New Yorker E 1978 Art. 26.

I. Allgemeines

1. Gegenstand und Zweck

1 Art. 28 hat die Aufgabe, die bei den Beratungen zum einheitlichen Kaufrecht von Anfang an als unüberwindlich eingeschätzten Gegensätze zwischen dem kontinentaleuropäischen und dem anglo-amerikanischen Rechtskreis in der Frage des Erfüllungsanspruchs durch einen **Kompromiss** zu überbrücken.[1] Gemäss Artt. 46 I und 62 kann der Gläubiger bei Nichterfüllung einer Leistungspflicht nach dem Vorbild der kontinentaleuropäischen Rechte Erfüllung verlangen. Der Anspruch des Gläubigers auf Erfüllung in Natur erscheint diesen Rechtsordnungen als eine selbstverständliche Sache, als eine einfache Folge des Prinzips

---

[1] Vgl. zum Hintergrund der Bestimmung Sekretariatskommentar, Art. 26, Nr. 2 und O.R., S. 304 f., Nr. 43, 49, 51; ausführlich zur historischen Entwicklung: *Bianca/Bonell/Lando*, Art. 28, Anm. 1.1. ff.; vgl. auch Artt. 7.2.1 und 7.2.2 PICC; Artt. 9:101 und 9:102 PECL.

Erfüllungsanspruch 2 **Art. 28**

"pacta sunt servanda", als das "Rückgrat der Obligation".[2] Der Gläubiger soll im Fall des Vertragsbruchs des Schuldners nicht zum Deckungsgeschäft gezwungen sein. Die Gefahr, dass der Gläubiger ohne gerechtfertigtes Interesse aus Eigensinn, Schikane oder böser Absicht am Erfüllungsanspruch festhält, wird als minder schwerwiegend eingeschätzt.

Demgegenüber führt im Common Law eine Vertragsverletzung primär zum Recht, 2 Schadenersatz zu verlangen.[3] Der Erfüllungsanspruch als Rechtsbehelf in Gestalt der **specific performance**[4] (bei einer Verpflichtung zu einem positiven Tun) bzw. der **action for the price** (Kaufpreisklage) wird **nur ausnahmsweise** gewährt.[5] Die Zurückhaltung des anglo-amerikanischen Rechts bei der Anordnung der Erfüllung in natura ist einerseits historisch und vollstreckungsrechtlich begründet.[6] Andererseits kommt darin das Anliegen der Wahrung der Freiheit des Schuldners und dessen Schutz vor übermässiger wirtschaftlicher Bindung zum Ausdruck.[7] Specific performance steht sowohl dem Käufer wie dem Verkäufer zur Verfügung und wird angeordnet, wenn Geldersatz **inadäquat** ist.[8] So kann gemäss § 2–716 UCC der Gläubiger Erfüllung verlangen, wenn die Parteien dies vereinbart haben, wenn die Ware nach Ermessen des Gerichts "unique" (unersetzlich) ist oder "in other proper circumstances".[9] Eine praktisch bedeutsame Rolle spielt diese Bestimmung im Kontext des Handelskaufs insbesondere bei langfristigen Lieferverträgen ("output oder requirements contracts") oder in Situationen, in denen der Käufer sich nicht ohne weiteres anderswo Ersatz beschaffen kann, weil z. B. der Verkäufer der einzige Hersteller ist oder weil eine Mangellage besteht ("commercial uniqueness").[10] Ist hingegen ein Deckungsgeschäft möglich und zumutbar, gilt es als die ökonomisch vernünftigere, für den Schuldner schonendere Lösung, den Vertrag zu liquidieren, als seine Durchführung zu erzwingen.[11] Die

---

[2] Das geflügelte Wort geht wohl zurück auf *Rabel*, Recht des Warenkaufs, Bd. 1, S. 375; *Zweigert/Kötz*, S. 469 ff. Zur Entstehung dieser Tradition vgl. *Zimmermann*, S. 770 ff.; *Rütten*, FS Gernhuber, S. 939 ff.; *Müller-Chen*, Vertragsverletzung, S. 74 f.; zu den Besonderheiten des französischen Rechts vgl. *Treitel*, Remedies for Breach, Anm. 50.; *Viney*, S. 171 ff.; zum chinesischen Recht vgl. *Shen*, 13 Ariz. J. Int'l & Comp. L. (1996), 253, 282 ff.; rechtsvergleichend zur Entwicklung des Erfüllungsanspruchs in Civil Law und Common Law *Hachem*, FS Schwenzer, S. 647, 652 ff.
[3] *Farnsworth*, Legal Remedies, 70 Colum. L. Rev. (1970), 1145, 1156; *Yorio*, Contract Enforcement, S. 12; *Atiyah*, Law of Contract, S. 371 ff.; *Chitty* On Contracts, §§ 27-001 ff., 28-001; *Smith*, 60 Mod. L. Rev. (1997), 360, 360 f.; *Treitel*, Remedies for Breach, Anm. 63.; *Dodge*, Teaching die CISG in Contracts, 50 J. Leg. Educ. (2000), 72, 90; *McKendrick*, in: McKendrick (Hrsg.), Sale of Goods, § 10–041 ff.; vgl. auch die radikale (in ihrer allgemeinen Gültigkeit mit Vorsicht zu geniessende) Aussage von *Holmes*, S. 301: "(…) the law makes the promisor pay damages if the promised event does not come to pass. In every case it leaves him free from interference until the time for fulfilment has gone by, and therefore free to break his contract if he chooses"; zur historischen Entwicklung des Vertragsrechts im Common Law vgl. *Zimmermann*, Historische Verbindungen, S. 113 ff.
[4] Specific Performance wird nachfolgend in einem untechnischen Sinn verwendet und meint alle Rechtsbehelfe, die die Gewährung von Erfüllungszwang beinhalten; *Neufang*, S. 413.
[5] Dazu und zu weiteren Erfüllungsklagen (insb. replevin) vgl. *Neufang*, S. 74 ff.; 107 ff.
[6] *Müller-Chen*, Vertragsverletzung, S. 44 f., 78 ff.
[7] Vgl. weiterführend *Neufang*, S. 334 ff.
[8] *Zweigert/Kötz*, S. 477 ff.; zur historischen Entwicklung dieser Regeln vgl. *Rheinstein*, S. 22 ff., 38 ff., 125 ff., 139 ff.; *Neufang*, S. 35 ff.; *Müller-Chen*, Vertragsverletzung, S. 43 ff.; *Zimmermann*, S. 776 ff.; speziell zur Rechtslage nach US-amerikanischem Recht, insbesondere nach UCC, vgl. *Cerutti*, Rn. 709–713, 731–736, 771–779; *Elsing/Van Alstine*, Rn. 181, 215–226, 254–259, 267; *Chitty* On Contracts, § 28–005; §§ 359 f., 364 *Restatement* 2d Contracts; *Yorio*, 51 Ohio St. L. J. (1990), 1201, 1202 ff.; ausführlich *Dobbs*, S. 86 ff.; eingehend *Neufang*, S. 125 ff.; *Haack*, S. 42 ff.; zu sec. 52 I SGA vgl. *Piliounis*, 12 Pace Int'l L. Rev. (2000), 1, 10 ff.
[9] Weitergehend nun aber § 2–716 I UCC 2003: "(…) In a contract other than a consumer contract, specific performance may be decreed if the parties have agreed to that remedy. However, even if the parties agree to specific performance, specific performance may not be decreed if the breaching party's sole remaining contractual obligation is the payment of money".
[10] *Cerutti*, Rn. 732; *Elsing/Van Alstine*, Rn. 258; *Müller-Chen*, Vertragsverletzung, S. 81 ff.; *Catalano*, 71 Tul. L. Rev. (1997), 1807, 1824 ff.; *Verweyen/Förster/Toufar*, Handbuch, S. 128; vgl. auch *Magellan International Corporation v. Salzgitter Handels GmbH*, U. S. Dist. Ct. (N. D. Ill.), 7.12.1999, CISG-online 439.
[11] Vgl. dazu *Hager*, Rechtsbehelfe des Verkäufers, S. 26 ff.; *Honnold/Flechtner*, Art. 28, Rn. 198. Sehr pointiert *Farnsworth*, 27 Am. J. Comp. L. (1979), 247, 247 f.: Es sei ökonomisch richtig, dem Schuldner den Vertragsbruch und die Abfindung des Gläubigers mit Schadenersatz zu gestatten, wenn er sich hiervon mehr Vorteil verspreche als von der Vertragserfüllung; dies führe zu einer besseren Allokation der Ressourcen, denn der Gläubiger habe keinen Nachteil (denn er erhalte vollen Schadenersatz) und der Schuldner habe trotzdem

Kaufpreisklage des Verkäufers wird gemäss § 2–709 I UCC zugelassen, wenn der Kaufgegenstand geliefert bzw. vom Käufer akzeptiert wurde, wenn die Ware nach Gefahrübergang, z. B. auf dem Transport, untergegangen ist oder – falls die Ware noch nicht geliefert wurde – wenn dem Verkäufer ein Deckungsverkauf in angemessener Weise und zu einem angemessenen Preis nicht möglich oder nicht zuzumuten ist.[12]

3 Das Einheitskaufrecht trägt diesen Unterschieden mit Art. 28 Rechnung. Der Erfüllungsanspruch wird als **Rechtsbehelf (remedy)** zwar zugelassen, seine gerichtliche Durchsetzung ist aber beschränkt. Die Gerichte der Vertragsstaaten[13] sollen auf eine Erfüllungsklage so reagieren, wie sie das bei gleichartigen Kaufverträgen nach ihrem „eigenen Recht"[14] tun würden. Diese entstehungsgeschichtlich als Konzession an die Common Law Staaten[15] konzipierte Vorbehaltsklausel läuft allerdings dem Prinzip der Rechtsvereinheitlichung zuwider,[16] da die Gefahr besteht, dass über Art. 28 – je nach Auffassung – mehr oder weniger weitgehende nationale Beschränkungen des Erfüllungsanspruchs (specific performance) Eingang ins CISG finden.[17]

2. Praktische Bedeutung

4 Die in Art. 28 angeordnete Beschränkung der Klagbarkeit des Erfüllungsanspruchs hat nur geringe praktische Bedeutung.[18] Der Käufer hat in der Regel im internationalen Handel nur dann ein wirtschaftliches Interesse an der gerichtlichen Durchsetzung seines Lieferanspruchs,

---

einen Vorteil. Ob diese Rechnung wirklich aufgeht, erscheint allerdings zweifelhaft. Kritisch *Schwartz*, 89 Yale L. J. (1979), 271, 279 mit Fn. 28; *Kastely*, 63 Wash. L. Rev. (1988), 607, 630 ff.; *Friedmann*, 18 J. Leg. Stud. (1989), 1, 23 f.; *Fitzgerald*, 16 J. L. & Com. (2000), 291, 301.

[12] Darin kommt der Gedanke der Schadensminderungspflicht zum Vorschein; vgl. dazu *Hager*, Rechtsbehelfe des Verkäufers, S. 26 ff.; *Treitel*, Remedies for Breach, Anm. 147.; *Honnold/Flechtner*, Art. 28, Rn. 198; *Cerutti*, Rn. 771 ff.; *Elsing/Van Alstine*, Rn. 254 ff.; *Neufang*, S. 74 ff., 85 ff. Im englischen Recht ist die Lage dadurch kompliziert, dass die Kaufpreisklage grundsätzlich vom Übergang des Eigentums auf den Käufer abhängt; ausserdem wird sie in bestimmten Fällen des Fixgeschäfts gewährt. Vgl. sec. 49 I, II SGA; *Rheinstein*, S. 16 ff., 143, 222 ff.; *Rabel*, Recht des Warenkaufs, Bd. 2, S. 42 ff.; *Hager*, Rechtsbehelfe des Verkäufers, S. 13 ff.

[13] Entgegen *Honsell/Gsell*, Art. 28, Rn. 5, 14 f. ist die Anwendung von Art. 28 nicht auf Verfahren vor Common Law-Gerichten beschränkt; so schon *Honnold/Flechtner*, Art. 28, Rn. 199, 199.1; *Bianca/Bonell/Lando*, Art. 28, Anm. 2.2.; *Neumayer/Ming*, Art. 28, Anm. 4.

[14] Dazu oben Rn. 9.

[15] Diese sollten davor bewahrt werden, „[...] to alter fundamental principles of their judicial procedure." Sekretariatskommentar, Art. 28, Nr. 2; *Honsell/Gsell*, Art. 28, Rn. 5; *Enderlein/Maskow/Strohbach*, Art. 28, Anm. 1.; *Staudinger/Magnus*, Art. 28, Rn. 1; *Rudolph*, Art. 28, Rn. 1; *Achilles*, Art. 28, Rn. 1; *Honnold/Flechtner*, Art. 28, Rn. 192; *Bianca/Bonell/Lando*, Art. 28, Anm. 1.3.5.; vgl. auch *Neufang*, S. 410 ff. In der Literatur wird das von Autoren, die dem kontinentaleuropäischen Rechtskreis entstammen, häufig missverstanden und behauptet, Art. 28 solle die Gerichte des Common Law davor bewahren, eine Verurteilung zu anderen Leistungen als Geldzahlungen aussprechen zu müssen, weil ihr „innerstaatliches Verfahrensrecht das nicht zulässt" (so *Herber/Czerwenka*, Art. 28, Rn. 3, Art. 62, Rn. 7) oder weil sie „andere Exekutionsarten als solche für Geldforderungen nicht kennen" (so *Loewe*, Art. 62, S. 81). Das trifft nicht zu. Zur Zwangsvollstreckung von Urteilen, die auf specific performance lauten, vgl. *Zweigert/Kötz*, S. 481 f.; sie erfolgt vor allem mit Hilfe des Rechtsinstituts des „contempt of court". Vgl. auch *Neufang*, S. 211 ff.; *Rheinstein*, S. 125 f.; a. A. *Staudinger/Magnus*, Art. 28, Rn. 6 ff.; vgl. hinten Rn. 9 ff.

[16] Zurückhaltend allerdings *Boghossian*, S. 29, 73 f.; *Honsell/Gsell*, Art. 28, Rn. 5, 14; *Bamberger/Roth/Saenger*, Art. 28, Rn. 1; *Catalano*, 71 Tul. L. Rev. (1997), 1807, 1831 ff.; *Fitzgerald*, 16 J. L. & Com. (1997), 291, 302 ff.

[17] Vgl. unten Rn. 10 ff.

[18] Vgl. *Schlechtriem*, Einheitliches UN-Kaufrecht, S. 51; *Honnold/Flechtner*, Art. 28, Rn. 199, 286; *Bianca/Bonell/Lando*, Art. 28, Anm. 1.3.1.; *U. Huber*, Rechtsbehelfe der Parteien, S. 207; *Honsell/Gsell*, Art. 28, Rn. 6; *Bamberger/Roth/Saenger*, Art. 28, Rn. 1; *MünchKommHGB/Benicke*, Art. 28, Rn. 4. Es ist bezeichnend, dass die Rechtsprechungssammlung von *Schlechtriem/Magnus* zur früheren Bestimmung des Art. 25 EKG, die nach dem Vorbild des UCC dem Käufer den Erfüllungsanspruch versagte, wenn ein Deckungskauf üblich und möglich war, keine Entscheidungen nachweist – wohl aber zur komplementären Bestimmung des Art. 61 II EKG zur Beschränkung des Erfüllungsanspruchs des Verkäufers (*Schlechtriem/Magnus*, Art. 61 EKG, Nr. 1– 3). Die Einschätzung bei *Neumayer/Ming*, Art. 28, Anm. 2., für Kaufpreisklagen habe die Einschränkung des Art. 28 von vornherein keine praktische Bedeutung, trifft deshalb m. E. nicht zu; die Begründung, der Schadenersatzanspruch des Verkäufers wegen Nichterfüllung sei mindestens so hoch wie der Kaufpreis, trifft im Fall der Nichtabnahme der Ware durch den Käufer nicht zu.

wenn er Gewähr für eine unproblematische Vollstreckung des Urteils hat, wenn der Kaufgegenstand auf dem Markt anderweitig nicht oder nur mit unverhältnismässigem Aufwand beschaffbar ist (z. B. wegen einer Warenknappheit), wenn es sich um Nacherfüllungsansprüche handelt (Nachbesserung, Ersatzlieferung) oder wenn die zur Verfügung stehenden Alternativen (z. B. Schadenersatz in Kombination mit anderen Rechten) seine ökonomischen Verluste nicht ausgleichen.[19] Mutatis mutandis gilt dies auch für den Anspruch des Verkäufers auf Abnahme der Ware und Zahlung. In all diesen Fällen ist die Klagbarkeit des Erfüllungsanspruchs aber zumindest im Grundsatz auch nach den Rechten des Common Law gegeben,[20] so dass im wirtschaftlichen Ergebnis die Unterschiede zwischen den verschiedenen Rechtstraditionen, die zu Art. 28 geführt haben, in den Hintergrund treten.[20a]

II. Voraussetzungen der Anwendung von Art. 28

1. Übersicht

Die Anwendung von Art. 28 setzt voraus, dass „eine Partei nach dem CISG berechtigt ist, von der anderen Partei die Erfüllung einer Verpflichtung zu verlangen". Erfasst werden somit Erfüllungsansprüche der Parteien, soweit das CISG sie gewährt und nicht (ausdrücklich oder implizit) ausschliesst oder beschränkt.[21] Nur wenn der Erfüllungsanspruch nach diesem Massstab gegeben ist, kann es auf Grund von Art. 28 zu einer Abweisung der Erfüllungsklage kommen, wenn das entscheidende Gericht auf Grund seines eigenen Rechts bei gleichartigen Kaufverträgen die Klage abweisen würde.

2. Erfüllungsansprüche der Parteien nach dem CISG

Art. 28 erfasst zum einen die **Erfüllungsansprüche des Käufers:** Anspruch auf Lieferung der Ware (Art. 31), auf Übergabe der Dokumente (Art. 34) und auf Verschaffung des Eigentums (Art. 30), auf Ersatzlieferung und Nachbesserung im Fall der Lieferung nicht vertragsmässiger Ware (Art. 46)[22] und auf Erfüllung sonstiger im Kaufvertrag übernommener Leistungspflichten (wie z. B. Montage der Kaufsache, Stellung einer Bankgarantie usw.). Zum andern ist Art. 28 auch auf die **Erfüllungsansprüche des Verkäufers** anwendbar:[23] Anspruch auf Kaufpreiszahlung (Art. 53),[24] auf Abnahme (Artt. 53, 60)[25] und auf Erfüllung

---

[19] *Rudolph*, Art. 28, Rn. 10; *Honnold/Flechtner*, Art. 46, Rn. 281.1.
[20] Schon *Rabel*, RabelsZ 9 (1935), 1, 70 mit Fn. 1 = Ges. Aufs., Bd. 3, S. 522, 576 mit Fn. 32, hat darauf hingewiesen, dass die Fälle, in denen im Common Law specific performance gewährt wird, „eigentlich die Einzigen auch für den Kontinent wichtigen" seien; vgl. auch *ders.*, Recht des Warenkaufs, Bd. 1, S. 376; *Walt*, Tex. Int'l L. J. (1991), 211, 218, 232 f.; *Bridge*, Int'l Sale of Goods, Rn. 3.47.
[20a] So auch *Honnold/Flechtner*, Art. 46, Rn. 281.1.
[21] Vgl. dazu im Einzelnen Art. 46 Rn. 6 ff. und *Hager/Maultzsch*, 5. Aufl., Art. 62 Rn. 4 ff.; *Gillette/Walt*, S. 376 f.
[22] So auch *Lookofsky*, Understanding the CISG in the USA, S. 104 f.; a. A. *Honnold/Flechtner*, Art. 46, Rn. 285.1 (Art. 46 II sei lex specialis zu Art. 28).
[23] Vgl. *Hager/Maultzsch*, 5. Aufl., Art. 62 Rn. 7 ff.; Dies wird in der Literatur zum Teil mit dem Verweis auf den Wortlaut des englischen Textes bestritten: „Specific performance" beziehe sich im Sprachgebrauch des anglo-amerikanischen Rechts nur auf die Sachleistung: *Posch*, Pflichten des Käufers, S. 160; *ders.*, Pflichten des Käufers und Rechtsbehelfe des Verkäufers, S. 156 f.; *Loewe*, Art. 62, S. 81; *Herber/Czerwenka*, Art. 28, Rn. 3, Art. 62, Rn. 7; *Reinhart*, Art. 28, Rn. 4; *Soergel/Lüderitz/Budizikiewicz*, Art. 28, Rn. 1, 3. Die Begrenzung auf die Sachleistung ist schon darum zu eng, weil das CISG „specific performance" nicht als terminus technicus des Common Law verwendet, sondern darunter „Erfüllung, wie vertraglich vereinbart" im Unterschied zu „Schadenersatz wegen Nichterfüllung" versteht. Vgl. *U. Huber*, 3. Aufl., Rn. 15 mit zahlreichen Nachweisen.
[24] Vgl. Sekretariatskommentar, Art. 28, Nr. 2, 3, S. 48, Art. 58, Nr. 6; *Schlechtriem*, Einheitliches UN-Kaufrecht, S. 76; *Honnold/Flechtner*, Art. 28, Rn. 195 ff. sowie Rn. 348; *Ziegel*, Remedial Provisions, S. 9–31; *Kastely*, 63 Wash. L. Rev. (1988), 607, 634; *Karollus*, S. 178; *Honsell/Gsell*, Art. 28, Rn. 7; *Neufang*, S. 413; *Wiegand*, Pflichten des Käufers, S. 160; *Enderlein/Maskow/Strohbach*, Art. 62, Anm. 2.; *Staudinger/Magnus*, Art. 28, Rn. 14; vgl. auch unten *Hager/Maultzsch*, 5. Aufl., Art. 62 Rn. 12.
[25] Klagen auf Abnahme werden von englischen und amerikanischen Gerichten offenbar niemals zugelassen, vgl. *Hager*, Rechtsbehelfe des Verkäufers, S. 13. Nach deutschem Recht sind sie möglich (und auch in der

Art. 28 7–9

sonstiger vertraglich übernommener Pflichten (wie z. B. den Anspruch auf Stellung eines Akkreditivs).[26] **Nicht von Art. 28 erfasst** sind Rückgewähransprüche im Fall der Vertragsaufhebung (z. B. auf Rückzahlung des Kaufpreises oder auf Rückgabe der Ware (Art. 81 II); Rückgabe einer vom Käufer gestellten Bankgarantie usw.) und Schadenersatzansprüche.[27] Sie sind nicht auf „Erfüllung" des Vertrags gerichtet. Nicht unter Art. 28 fällt ferner das Recht des Gläubigers, wegen Nichterfüllung der Leistungspflicht des Schuldners die Gegenleistung einzubehalten.[28] Denn durch die Zurückhaltung der Gegenleistung sichert der Gläubiger nicht nur und nicht einmal in erster Linie seinen Anspruch auf Erfüllung in „Natur", sondern auch und sogar vorrangig seine Rechte aus einer möglichen Vertragsaufhebung und auf Schadenersatz wegen Nichterfüllung.[29]

7 Das Währungs- und Devisenrecht gehört nicht zu den im Übereinkommen geregelten Materien. **Art. 28 ist deshalb auf währungs- und devisenrechtliche Einwendungen nicht anwendbar.**[30] Sind z. B. nach dem Prozessrecht des Forumstaats Klagen in ausländischer Währung unzulässig, so ist eine trotzdem in ausländischer Währung erhobene Klage als unzulässig abzuweisen; der Kläger muss seinen Anspruch auf Inlandswährung umstellen. Fehlt eine nach dem Recht des Forumstaats erforderliche devisenrechtliche Genehmigung, so ist die Klage abzuweisen, weil der Kaufvertrag unwirksam ist; das Übereinkommen ändert hieran nichts (Art. 4 S. 2 lit. a)). Verstösst der Vertrag gegen ausländisches Devisenrecht und sind sowohl der Forumstaat als auch der Staat, der die Bestimmung erlassen hat, Vertragsstaaten des Abkommens über den Internationalen Währungsfonds,[31] so ist der Zahlungs- und Schadenersatzanspruch[32] nicht einklagbar und aus diesem Grund abzuweisen (Art. VIII Abschnitt 2 lit. b) des Abkommens).

3. Gericht

8 Art. 28 erwähnt, anders als Art. 45 III und Art. 61 III, nur die staatlichen Gerichte.[33] Es ist jedoch unbestritten, dass die Bestimmung analog auch auf **Schiedsgerichte** anzuwenden ist,[34] da kein Grund ersichtlich ist, dem vor einem Schiedsgericht beklagten Schuldner die Privilegierung durch Art. 28 zu verweigern.

4. Eigenes Recht

9 **a) Forumsrecht unter Ausschluss des IPR.** Das Gericht hat den auf das Übereinkommen gestützten Erfüllungsanspruch so zu beurteilen, wie es das „nach seinem eigenen Recht (...) täte". Massgeblich ist das **Recht des Forumstaats,** unter Ausschluss des Kollisions-

---

Praxis gelegentlich anzutreffen), aber neben der Zahlungsklage ohne eigenständige praktische Bedeutung. Nach schweizerischem Recht stellt die Abnahme entgegen dem Wortlaut von Art. 211 OR grundsätzlich nur eine Obliegenheit dar und ist deshalb nicht einklagbar, s. *Honsell,* OR BT, S. 47; *Guhl/Koller,* § 41, Rn. 124; so auch das österreichische Recht, vgl. dazu *Koziol/Welser,* Band II, S. 60; *Rummel/Aicher,* § 1062, Rn. 30.

[26] Vgl. *Achilles,* Art. 28, Rn. 2.
[27] Vgl. auch *Neumayer/Ming,* Art. 28, Anm. 3.; *Staudinger/Magnus,* Art. 28, Rn. 14–17; *Honsell/Gsell,* Art. 28, Rn. 7; *Soergel/Lüderitz/Budizikiewicz,* Art. 28, Rn. 3.
[28] Vgl. *Neufang,* S. 417 f.; zu den Rechtsgrundlagen des Leistungsverweigerungsrechts des Käufers vgl. unten Art. 45 Rn. 22.
[29] Zur Rechtslage nach US-amerikanischem Recht vgl. *Elsing/Van Alstine,* Rn. 208; *Neufang,* S. 219.
[30] *Honsell/Gsell,* Art. 28, Rn. 20; *Staub/Koller,* vor § 373 HGB, Rn. 341; *Soergel/Lüderitz/Budizikiewicz,* Art. 28, Rn. 3; *Brunner,* Art. 28, Rn. 3; a. A. *Mertens/Rehbinder,* Art. 61 EKG, Rn. 3; *Hager,* Rechtsbehelfe des Verkäufers, S. 197.
[31] In der seit 1.4.1978 geltenden Fassung: BGBl. 1978 II 13, 838; SR 0.979.1. Vgl. dazu *Soergel/Hefermehl,* § 134 BGB, Rn. 9; *Soergel/von Hoffmann,* 12. Aufl., Art. 34 EGBGB, Rn. 136 ff.
[32] *Gränicher,* S. 96 ff.; *Ebke,* S. 311.
[33] Damit sind nicht nur die Gerichte der Vertragsstaaten, sondern auch der Nichtvertragsstaaten gemeint, welche das CISG auf Grund der kollisionsrechtlichen Verweisung auf Vertragsstaatenrecht gemäss Art. 1 I lit. b) anwenden: *Honsell/Gsell,* Art. 28, Rn. 9; vgl. auch *Ferrari,* Art. 1 Rn. 69 ff.
[34] Ebenso *Enderlein/Maskow/Strohbach,* Art. 28, Anm. 4.; *Honsell/Gsell,* Art. 28, Rn. 8; *Bamberger/Roth/Saenger,* Art. 28, Rn. 6.

rechts.³⁵ Das auf den Kaufvertrag anwendbare Recht muss somit nicht ermittelt werden. Klagt z. B. der in Österreich ansässige Käufer gegen den U. S.-amerikanischen Verkäufer am schweizerischen Erfüllungsort auf Lieferung, entscheidet schweizerisches Recht über die Zulässigkeit des Erfüllungsanspruchs. Erhebt eine Partei vor einem **Schiedsgericht** Klage auf Erfüllung in Natur, so ist das „eigene Recht" des Schiedsgerichts das **materielle Recht** des Landes, dessen **lex arbitri** („loi d'arbitrage", „Schiedsverfassungsrecht") das Schiedsgericht untersteht.³⁶ Im Regelfall handelt es sich dabei entweder um das von den Parteien gewählte oder um das durch den Sitz des Schiedsgerichts bestimmte Recht. Wie bei Verfahren vor staatlichen Gerichten findet auch im Schiedsverfahren das nach den Regeln des internationalen Privatrechts ermittelte, gemäss Art. 7 I subsidiär anwendbare nationale Recht keine Beachtung.³⁷

b) Umfang der Verweisung. Es ist umstritten, in welchem Umfang nationale Schranken des Erfüllungszwangs zuzulassen sind. Die Lösung hat sich am Zweck des Art. 28 zu orientieren, der in der Privilegierung der Common Law-Gerichte wurzelt.³⁸ Dabei gilt es daran zu erinnern, dass specific performance als Rechtsbehelf („remedy") die gerichtlich zugesprochene Sanktion einer unabhängig davon festgestellten Rechts- bzw. Vertragsverletzung ist.³⁹ Dies darf nicht mit dem „Erfüllungsanspruch" des deutschen und französischen Rechtskreises gleichgesetzt werden, der sich unmittelbar aus dem Vertrag herleitet.⁴⁰ Unumstritten ist, dass die Vertragsstaaten **prozessuale** oder **vollstreckungsrechtliche Beschränkungen** des Erfüllungszwangs zur Anwendung bringen können. Denn gerade solche Überlegungen liegen den anglo-amerikanischen Vorbehalten gegen specific performance zugrunde.⁴¹ Darüber hinaus spielen aber bei der Anordnung eines „remedy" auch materiellrechtliche Erwägungen eine Rolle, was kontinentaleuropäischen Rechten, denen der Begriff des remedy fremd ist, die Anwendung von Art. 28 erschwert.⁴² Der Umfang der Verweisung des Art. 28 auf das nationale Recht kann daher nicht durch die materiellrechtliche,⁴³ prozessuale⁴⁴ oder vollstreckungsrechtliche Natur einer Vorschrift bestimmt werden.⁴⁵ Entscheidend ist vielmehr, ob der Erfüllungsanspruch im nationalen Recht verweigert wird, weil **Bedenken** gerade **gegen** den **Erfüllungszwang** (im Gegensatz zu Schadenersatz) als angemessener Rechtsbehelf (remedy) bestehen. In diesem Fall darf die Erfüllungsklage gestützt auf Art. 28 abgewiesen werden.⁴⁶ Der Erfüllungsanspruch kann

---

³⁵ *Honnold/Flechtner*, Art. 28, Rn. 195; *Enderlein/Maskow/Strohbach*, Art. 28, Anm. 5.; *Karollus*, S. 140; *Herber/Czerwenka*, Art. 28, Rn. 4 (mit allerdings missverständlichem Hinweis auf das „eigene Verfahrensrecht" des entscheidenden Gerichts); *Honsell/Gsell*, Art. 28, Rn. 11; *Neufang*, S. 414 mit Fn. 35; *Soergel/Lüderitz/Budzikiewicz*, Art. 28, Rn. 1; *Posch/Kandut*, S. 73; *Neumayer/Ming*, Art. 28, Anm. 1. Fn. 3; *Kastely*, 63 Wash. L. Rev. (1988), 607, 637 f.; *Walt*, 26 Tex. Int'l L. J. (1991), 211, 219; *Catalano*, 71 Tul. L. Rev. (1997), 1807, 1819; MünchKomm/*Gruber*, Art. 28, Rn. 8. A. A. soweit ersichtlich einzig *Grigera Naón*, UN Convention on Contracts, S. 107 f.; gegen diese abweichende Ansicht sprechen jedoch Wortlaut, Zweck und Entstehungsgeschichte: vgl. dazu *U. Huber*, 3. Aufl., Rn. 18; *Zweigert/Drobnig*, RabelsZ 29 (1965), 146, 165.
³⁶ In materiellrechtlicher Hinsicht hat ein internationales Schiedsgericht weder ein „eigenes Recht" noch eine lex fori. Es ist stattdessen von der lex arbitri zu sprechen, d. h. von dem Recht, gemäss welchem die Gültigkeit der Schiedsvereinbarung, die Schiedsfähigkeit, die Zusammensetzung des Schiedsgerichts, die Verfahrensgrundsätze, die Unterstützung durch staatliche Gerichte und die Anfechtbarkeit bestimmt werden.
³⁷ Vgl. hinten Rn. 17, 18. A. A. *Walter*, UN-Kaufrechtsübereinkommen, S. 317, 325. Wie hier *Honsell/Gsell*, Art. 28, Rn. 12.
³⁸ Vgl. oben Rn. 3; *Honsell/Gsell*, Art. 28, Rn. 15.
³⁹ *Catalano*, 71 Tul. L. Rev. (1997), 1807, 1817 f.
⁴⁰ Ausführlich *Neufang*, S. 240 ff. Zum Erfüllungsanspruch im französischen Recht, s. *Viney*, S. 171 ff.
⁴¹ *Neufang*, S. 412.
⁴² *Neufang*, S. 412.
⁴³ So z. B. insb. *U. Huber*, 3. Aufl., Rn. 17 ff.
⁴⁴ So insbesondere *Staudinger/Magnus*, Art. 28, Rn. 10 f.; *U. Huber*, Rechtsbehelfe der Parteien, S. 199, 203; Sowohl prozessuale wie materiell-rechtliche Schranken sind zu berücksichtigen gemäss *Enderlein/Maskow/Strohbach*, Art. 28, Anm. 1.5.; *Rudolph*, Art. 28, Rn. 11; *Herber/Czerverka*, Art. 28, Rn. 5; *Piltz*, Internationales Kaufrecht, § 2, Rn. 157; *Posch/Kandut*, S. 72.
⁴⁵ Diese Grenzziehung ist schon darum untauglich, weil sie von nationalen dogmatischen Überlegungen geprägt ist, die sich insbesondere im anglo-amerikanischen Recht so nicht finden. Vgl. auch *Honsell/Gsell*, Art. 28, Rn. 15.
⁴⁶ *Neufang*, S. 414.

aber auch darum nicht gegeben sein, weil bereits die Leistungspflicht als solche dahinfällt (z. B. bei Unmöglichkeit). Art. 28 ist in diesen Fällen nicht anwendbar, da das CISG Bestand und Umfang der Leistungspflicht des Schuldners selbst regelt.

11   Art. 28 ist eine **Vorbehaltsklausel,** welche dem Gericht erlaubt, unter bestimmten Voraussetzungen den an sich nach CISG gegebenen Erfüllungsanspruch zu versagen – nie aber über die durch das CISG gewährten (Nach-) Erfüllungsansprüche hinauszugehen. Versagt z. B. das CISG dem Käufer den Ersatzlieferungsanspruch nach Art. 46 II, bleibt es dabei, selbst wenn nach dem nationalen Recht die Verurteilung zur Ersatzlieferung möglich wäre.[47] Art. 28 kommt auch dann nicht zur Anwendung, wenn dem nationalen Kaufrecht ein (Nach-) Erfüllungsanspruch unbekannt ist, wie z. B. die Nachbesserung im schweizerischen Recht oder die Ersatzlieferung im Common Law.[48] Für Art. 28 bleibt schliesslich ebenso wenig Raum, wenn eine Rechtsordnung im Grundsatz dasselbe „Rechtsbehelfsystem" wie das CISG kennt, die einzelnen Rechtsbehelfe aber an andere Voraussetzungen knüpft, denn das CISG regelt diese abschliessend.[49]

12   c) **Anwendungsfälle.** Die Beschränkung des Erfüllungszwangs durch Art. 28 vor Gerichten des „Civil Law"-Systems auf Grund eigenen Rechts wird seltene **Ausnahme** bleiben: Erfüllungsansprüche des Gläubigers korrespondieren mit der entsprechenden Verpflichtung des Schuldners und sind im Grundsatz klageweise durchsetzbar. Nichtsdestotrotz finden sich auch in diesen Rechten in unterschiedlicher Ausprägung (geschriebene oder ungeschriebene) Schranken des Erfüllungsanspruchs. Führen sie nur gerade zum Ausschluss des Erfüllungszwangs, lassen aber das Einstehenmüssen des Schuldners und dessen Verpflichtung zur Leistung von Schadenersatz wegen Nichterfüllung unberührt, ist Art. 28 anwendbar.[50]

13   Ob allerdings der Schuldner für die Nichterfüllung haftet, beurteilt sich **ausschliesslich** nach dem Massstab von **Art. 79.** Entsprechende nationale Regeln sind unanwendbar.[51] Hat der Schuldner für die Vertragsverletzung nicht einzustehen, wird er von der Verpflichtung, Schadenersatz zu leisten, befreit. Da Art. 79 V den Erfüllungsanspruch nicht ausdrücklich ausschliesst, wurde verschiedentlich argumentiert, dass mit Hilfe von Art. 28 auf nationale Regeln (z. B. zur Unmöglichkeit der Leistung) zurückgegriffen werden müsse, um den Schuldner vor dem Erfüllungszwang zu bewahren.[52] Diese Ansicht ist abzulehnen, soweit diese Regeln nicht nur die gerichtliche Durchsetzung des Erfüllungsanspruchs sperren, sondern auch den Schuldner von seiner Pflicht zur Leistung befreien.[53] Lässt man es zu, dass der Schuldner sich gegenüber einem durch das Übereinkommen begründeten Erfüllungsanspruch auf Befreiungsgründe des nationalen Rechts beruft, so müssten konsequenterweise auch die Voraussetzungen, von denen die Befreiung abhängt, nach nationalem Recht beurteilt werden.[54] Das aber ist weder mit Art. 28, noch mit Art. 79, noch mit dem Grundgedanken des Übereinkommens vereinbar.

---

[47] *Neufang,* S. 416; *Shen,* 13 Ariz. J. Int'l & Comp. L. (1996), 253, 303.
[48] *Honsell/Gsell,* Art. 28, Rn. 18 m. w. N.; *Fitzgerald,* 16 J. L. & Com. (1997), 291, 298; zur Situation, dass das nationale Recht die vom CISG vorgesehene Form des Erfüllungszwangs verweigert, eine andere aber gewähren würde, vgl. *Neufang,* S. 415 ff.
[49] *Neufang,* S. 427; *Herber/Czerwenka,* Art. 79, Rn. 24.
[50] *Neufang,* S. 415; oben Rn. 4, 10.
[51] Z. B. §§ 276, 278, 280 BGB; vgl. dazu *Palandt/Heinrichs,* § 276, Rn. 30 ff., § 278, Rn. 1 ff., § 280, Rn. 2 ff., 13 f.
[52] Vgl. *Schlechtriem,* Einheitliches UN-Kaufrecht, S. 51, 97 (vgl. nun aber differenzierend zu Art. 28 i. V. m. § 275 I BGB *ders.,* Internationales UN-Kaufrecht, Rn. 118); *Honnold/Flechtner,* Art. 28, Rn. 199; *Vischer,* Gemeinsame Bestimmungen, S. 175 f.; *Enderlein/Maskow/Strohbach,* Art. 79, Anm. 13.6.; *Bianca/Bonell/Lando,* Art. 28, Anm. 2.2.; *Posch/Kandut,* S. 72; *Neumayer/Ming,* Art. 28, Anm. 4.; *Bartels/Motomura,* RabelsZ 43 (1979), 649, 663. Die Ansicht geht zurück auf einen Hinweis im Sekretariatskommentar, Art. 65, Nr. 9.
[53] *Schlechtriem,* Internationales UN-Kaufrecht, Rn. 118, der m. E. zu Recht ausführt, dass auf Grund der grundlegenden Änderungen, die § 275 BGB durch die Schuldrechtsreform erfahren hat, bei Unmöglichkeit die Verpflichtung als solche unberührt bleibt und nur die gerichtliche Durchsetzung des Erfüllungsanspruchs gesperrt wird; oben Rn. 10.
[54] Vgl. *Neumayer/Ming,* Art. 28, Anm. 4.; vgl. auch *Schlechtriem,* Internationales UN-Kaufrecht, Rn. 118.

Erfüllungsanspruch 14–16 **Art. 28**

Das Problem des Erfüllungszwangs im Fall der Befreiung des Schuldners ist vertragsautonom durch **berichtigende Auslegung** des **Art. 79 V** zu lösen.[55] Je nach Art des Leistungshindernisses, für das der Verkäufer nach dem Massstab von Art. 79 I bis III nicht einzustehen hat, ist der Erfüllungsanspruch ausgeschlossen.[56] Dies gilt jedenfalls dann, wenn die Leistungserbringung objektiv unmöglich ist[57] oder öffentlich-rechtliche Leistungsverbote[58] bestehen (z. B. Devisensperren oder Embargo). Bei anderen Leistungshindernissen besteht der Erfüllungsanspruch fort, ist aber nicht durchsetzbar.[59] Insoweit muss daher nicht auf Art. 28 zurückgegriffen werden. 14

Kann nur gerade der Schuldner nicht erfüllen, wird er im Regelfall nicht entlastet, da er beim marktbezogenen Gattungskauf das Beschaffungsrisiko trägt.[60] Ist die Überwindung des Leistungshindernisses unzumutbar, hängt die Befreiung von der Erfüllungspflicht von den Umständen des Einzelfalls ab.[61] Es ergibt sich z. B. aus Art. 46, dass ein Anspruch auf Nachbesserung ausgeschlossen ist, wenn feststeht, dass die Sache sich nicht, bzw. nur mit unverhältnismässigem Aufwand, reparieren lässt.[62] Ein Rückgriff auf Art. 28 und auf das nationale Recht erübrigt sich somit.[63] 15

Kündigt der Besteller den **Werklieferungsvertrag**[64] vor Fertigstellung der Sache, wird nach gewissen Rechten[65] der Werklohn des Unternehmers um die ersparten Aufwendungen gekürzt und der Anspruch auf Abnahme des Werkes ausgeschlossen. Der Erfüllungsanspruch des Unternehmers wird dadurch durch einen Schadenersatzanspruch wegen Nichterfüllung ersetzt. Das muss auf Grund von Art. 28 auch gelten, wenn auf den Vertrag gemäss Art. 3 I das CISG anzuwenden ist und der Unternehmer den Besteller, der die Bestellung widerrufen hat, z. B. vor einem deutschen Gericht auf Zahlung des Werklohns verklagt.[66] Es ist allerdings möglich, die Lösung direkt auf das Prinzip von Treu und Glauben (Art. 7 I) zu stützen.[67] 16

---

[55] Vgl. auch *Neufang*, S. 423–425 mit Fn. 73; *U. Huber*, 3. Aufl., Rn. 30 f.; *Soergel/Lüderitz/Budzikiewicz*, Art. 28, Rn. 2 mit Fn. 2; *Staudinger/Magnus*, Art. 28, Rn. 10 ff.; *Honsell/Gsell*, Art. 28, Rn. 13 f.; *Herber/Czerwenka*, Art. 79, Rn. 23; *Brunner*, Art. 28, Rn. 4; wohl auch *Nicholas*, Impracticability, S. 5–18 f.; differenzierend *Schwenzer*, Art. 79 Rn. 53; a. A. *Schlechtriem*, Internationales UN-Kaufrecht, Rn. 118 und Rn. 287 mit Fn. 279, der die Erfüllungsklage vor einem deutschen Gericht über Art. 28 i. V. m. § 275 I BGB sperren lassen will; s. auch *Atamer*, FS Schwenzer, 83, 93 ff.: Bei Unzumutbarkeit besteht kein Erfüllungsanspruch, was aus einer analogen Anwendung von Art. 46 III hergeleitet werden könne.
[56] Vgl. dazu die Nachweise oben Fn. 51. Differenzierend *Schwenzer*, Art. 79 Rn. 52 ff.
[57] *Müller-Chen*, Art. 46 Rn. 12; so auch viele nationale Rechtsordnungen: § 275 I BGB (*Lorenz/Riehm*, Rn. 297 ff.; *Schlechtriem*, FS Sonnenberger, S. 1 ff.; bei bloss vorübergehender Unmöglichkeit wirkt der Ausschluss für die Dauer der Unmöglichkeit; *Palandt/Heinrichs*, § 275, Rn. 10). Artt. 20, 97 I und 119 OR (*Schwenzer*, OR AT, Rn. 63.01 ff. und Rn. 61.01 ff.); § 878 f. AGBG (*Koziol/Welser*, Band II, S. 45 ff.); Artt. 1601 und 1147 frz. Cc (*Ghestin/Desché*, Anm. 691. ff.); *Yorio*, Contract Enforcement, S. 105 f., 108 f.; *Tito v. Waddell* (No. 2) [1977] Ch. D.106, 326; zum Ganzen *Caytas*, S. 435 ff.
[58] Vgl. oben Rn. 5.
[59] *Schwenzer*, Art. 79 Rn. 52 ff. Vgl. auch *U. Huber*, Rechtsbehelfe der Parteien, S. 205 ff.
[60] Vgl. Art. 46 Rn. 12 f. m. w. N.
[61] Vgl. Art. 46 Rn. 12 f. m. w. N.
[62] Vgl. Art. 46 Rn. 40; vgl. auch *Bianca/Bonell/Tallon*, Art. 79, Anm. 2.10.2.; *Honsell/Schnyder/Straub*, Art. 46, Rn. 30; *Karollus*, S. 135, 141; *Staudinger/Magnus*, Art. 46, Rn. 26.
[63] *Neufang*, S. 419.
[64] Dasselbe gilt beim Gattungskaufvertrag, bei dem der Verkäufer die Sache herzustellen und zu beschaffen hat: so *Flume*, Das Rechtsgeschäft, S. 26, 5a, S. 510. Zustimmend *Soergel/U. Huber*, 12. Aufl., § 433 BGB, Rn. 269; vgl. dazu *Hager/Maultzsch*, Art. 62 Rn. 14 m. w. N.
[65] Z. B. § 649 BGB, § 1168 Abs. 1 ABGB oder Art. 377 OR.
[66] I. E. übereinstimmend *Neufang*, S. 417 (mit der Konstruktion, dass Anspruchsgrundlage Art. 62 bleibt, dass aber auf Grund von Art. 28 der Anspruch aus Art. 62 entsprechend § 649 BGB gekürzt wird). Vgl. dazu auch das von *Honnold/Flechtner*, Art. 77, Rn. 419.3 diskutierte Beispiel 77 C. A. A. *Karollus*, S. 140. Es ist aber kaum zu verstehen, dass in einem solchen Fall zwar ein Common-Law-Gericht die Erfüllungsklage ohne weiteres unter Berufung auf Art. 28 und sein „eigenes Recht" abweisen darf (vgl. *Honnold/Flechtner*, aaO.), dass aber das deutsche Gericht an der Anwendung des § 649 BGB gehindert sein soll, der hier auf genau demselben Grundgedanken beruht und zu demselben Resultat führt wie die Regel des Common Law. Vgl. zu der Parallele zwischen § 649 BGB und der Beschränkung des Erfüllungsanspruchs des Verkäufers im Common Law auch *Treitel*, Remedies for Breach, Anm. 234.
[67] So *Hager/Maultzsch*, 5. Aufl., Art. 62 Rn. 14. Problematisch erscheinen die Vorschläge von *Schlechtriem* und *Stoll*. *Schlechtriem* (Einheitliches UN-Kaufrecht, S. 93 Fn. 408; *ders.*, Gemeinsame Bestimmungen, S. 170)

17 Bestimmungen des nationalen Rechts, welche lediglich die Durchsetzbarkeit des Erfüllungsanspruchs von besonderen formellen Voraussetzungen abhängig machen,[68] sollten auf Grund ihres engen Zusammenhangs mit anderen Normen des nationalen Rechts, an deren Stelle beim internationalen Kauf das Einheitsrecht tritt, nicht über Art. 28 angewendet werden.[69]

18 **d) Fazit.** Als Ergebnis ist festzuhalten, dass Art. 28 durch Gerichte des kontinentaleuropäischen Rechtskreises nur ausnahmsweise anzuwenden ist. Als möglicher Anwendungsbereich verbleiben nur die Fälle, in denen das eigene Recht des Gerichts Kündigungsrechte oder Befreiungsgründe vorsieht, die sich nur gerade gegen den Erfüllungszwang und nicht auch das Einstehenmüssen des Schuldners richten. Selbst in diesen Fällen wäre es möglich und vorzuziehen, die Lösung direkt aus einer einschränkenden Auslegung der Artt. 46, 62 oder dem Prinzip von Treu und Glauben (Art. 7 I) herzuleiten, statt mit Hilfe des Art. 28 auf nationales Recht zurückzugreifen.

5. Vergleichsmassstab des „gleichartigen Kaufvertrags"

19 Das Gericht braucht den Schuldner zur Erfüllung in Natur nur zu verurteilen, wenn es dies nach seinem eigenen Recht auch bei „gleichartigen Kaufverträgen" täte, die nicht unter das Übereinkommen fallen. Es hat sich somit zum Zweck des Vergleichs einen Kaufvertrag vorzustellen, dessen **Inhalt** (Leistungsgegenstand, Erfüllungsort und -zeit, sonstige Verpflichtungen) dem zu beurteilenden Fall **ähnlich** („gleichartig", „similar", „semblable") ist und dem nationalen Recht unterliegt.[70]

6. Zusammenfassung

20 Das Gericht bzw. Schiedsgericht hat in einem ersten Schritt festzustellen, ob der Gläubiger nach CISG vom Schuldner Erfüllung verlangen kann. Dabei hat es die dem CISG immanenten, geschriebenen und ungeschriebenen Grenzen zu beachten. Besteht nach diesem Massstab der Erfüllungsanspruch, muss es unter Zugrundelegung des eigenen Rechts prüfen, ob es bei einem gedachten, dem nationalen Recht unterliegenden Vertrag mit ähnlichen Rechten und Pflichten zum gleichen Ergebnis käme, d. h. die Erfüllungsklage gutheissen würde.[71] Verweigert das eigene Recht des Gerichts im konkreten Fall dem Gläubiger den Erfüllungsanspruch, weil z. B. aus vollstreckungsrechtlichen Bedenken gerade gegen den Erfüllungszwang als solchen bestehen, ist die Erfüllungsklage auf Grund von Art. 28 abzuweisen.

III. Rechtsfolge: Abweisung der Erfüllungsklage

21 Sind die Voraussetzungen von Art. 28 erfüllt, **„braucht"** ein Gericht eine Entscheidung auf Erfüllung in Natur nicht zu fällen, obwohl der (Nach-)Erfüllungsanspruch nach Artt. 46, 62 gegeben wäre. Blockiert wird m. a. W. ausschliesslich die klageweise Durchsetzung. Der (Nach-)Erfüllungsanspruch als solcher (und selbstverständlich alle anderen

---

will die Bestimmung des Art. 77 über die Schadensminderungspflicht analog anwenden, die sich aber gerade nicht auf den Erfüllungsanspruch bezieht. *Stoll* (Schadensersatzpflicht, S. 270) will eine „Lücke" im Übereinkommen annehmen, die nach Art. 7 II durch Heranziehung des international-privatrechtlich berufenen nationalen Rechts zu schliessen sei. Auf der Wiener Konferenz ist der Fall intensiv, aber ergebnislos diskutiert worden (unter dem Gesichtspunkt der Schadensminderungspflicht), vgl. O. R., S. 306 ff., Nr. 55–77; *Schlechtriem*, Einheitliches UN-Kaufrecht, S. 92 f.
[68] Z. B. die Anzeige des Gläubigers, dass er auf der Erfüllung beharrt (§ 376 I 2 HGB).
[69] Ebenso, jedoch mit anderer Begründung, *Hager*, 3. Aufl., Rn. 40; *Neufang*, S. 428.
[70] *Witz/Salger/Lorenz/Salger*, Art. 28, Rn. 13; *Honsell/Gsell*, Art. 28, Rn. 21; *Shen*, 13 Ariz. J. Int'l & Comp. L. (1996), 253, 303; *Gillette/Walt*, S. 377 f.
[71] *Honsell/Gsell*, Art. 28, Rn. 22.

Rechtsbehelfe) bleibt erhalten.[72] Will der Gläubiger in einem solchen Fall gegen den vertragsbrüchigen Schuldner vorgehen, müssen demzufolge die Voraussetzungen von Artt. 49 bzw. 64 erfüllt sein, damit der Vertrag aufgehoben bzw. Schadenersatz wegen Nichterfüllung gefordert werden kann. Der Ausschluss der Erfüllungsklage führt somit weder zu einer „Vertragsaufhebung kraft Gesetzes" noch zu einer automatischen Ersetzung des Erfüllungsanspruchs durch einen Schadenersatzanspruch wegen Nichterfüllung.[73] Ebenso verbleibt dem Verkäufer das Recht zur Nacherfüllung (Art. 48).[74]

Der Wortlaut der Vorschrift („braucht nicht"/„not bound to") räumt dem Gericht einen **22** Freiraum ein: Es kann gestützt auf Art. 28 die Erfüllungsklage abweisen, muss es aber nicht, selbst wenn es dies nach seinem eigenen Recht im konkreten Fall tun würde.[75] Dem CISG selbst lässt sich nicht entnehmen, wie dieser **Ermessensspielraum** auszufüllen ist.[76] Dies wäre auch mit der Natur dieser Bestimmung als Kollisionsnorm unvereinbar.[77] Es ist vielmehr Sache der lex fori zu entscheiden, ob Ermessens- und Beurteilungsspielräume bestehen und in welchem Umfang der erkennende Spruchkörper diese ausnutzen darf.[78] Diese Bindung des Gerichts an seine eigene Praxis ist durch eine noch auf der Wiener Konferenz vorgenommene redaktionelle Änderung des Gesetzestexts besonders hervorgehoben worden.[79] Vorgeschlagen war: „a court is not bound to enter a judgement for specific performance unless the court **could** do so under its own law". Dies wurde ersetzt durch: „unless the court **would** do so". Es genügt also nicht, dass der Richter nach seinem eigenen Recht auf Erfüllung in Natur erkennen „könnte", sondern erforderlich ist, dass er es nach eigenem Recht wirklich tun „würde".[80]

Diese Ausschöpfung des Ermessensspielraums hat sich am Zweck des Art. 28 zu **23** orientieren: Den Vertragsstaaten wird unter Preisgabe des Ziels der Rechtsvereinheitlichung die Beibehaltung **grundlegender** Rechtsprinzipien („fundamental principles") ermöglicht.[81] Unterscheiden sich daher das CISG und das eigene Recht des Gerichts nur im Detail, nicht aber in der grundsätzlichen Wertung, sollte Art. 28 nicht angewandt werden.[82]

IV. Keine Abdingbarkeit

Trotz Art. 6 ist Art. 28 gemäss h. L. unabdingbar.[83] Art. 28 beschränkt den Geltungs- **24** bereich des Übereinkommens in Bezug auf Erfüllungsansprüche und damit auch den Geltungsbereich des Art. 6. Art. 28 richtet sich an die nationalen Gerichte und betrifft nicht die der Privatautonomie zugänglichen Rechte und Pflichten der Parteien.[84] Wollen die

---

[72] *Honsell/Gsell*, Art. 28, Rn. 25.
[73] Vgl. auch *U. Huber*, Rechtsbehelfe der Parteien, S. 203; wie hier auch *Honsell/Gsell*, Art. 28, Rn. 23; *Neufang*, S. 416.
[74] *Honsell/Gsell*, Art. 28, Rn. 25.
[75] *Bianca/Bonell/Lando*, Art. 28, Anm. 2.1.; *Enderlein/Maskow/Strohbach*, Art. 28, Anm. 3.; *Reinhart*, Art. 28, Rn. 3; *Neumayer/Ming*, Art. 28, Anm. 5.; *Honsell/Gsell*, Art. 28, Rn. 24; *Honnold/Flechtner*, Art. 28, Rn. 195; ablehnend gegenüber den zu weitgehenden Vorschlägen von *Kastely*, 63 Wash. L. Rev. (1988), 607, 638 ff.; zu Recht *U. Huber*, 3. Aufl., Rn. 22; ebenso wohl auch *Posch/Kandut*, S. 70 ff.
[76] *U. Huber*, 3. Aufl., Rn. 22.
[77] Vgl. *Enderlein/Maskow/Strohbach*, Art. 28, Anm. 5.; *Rudolph*, Art. 28, Rn. 11.
[78] *U. Huber*, 3. Aufl., Rn. 22; *Staudinger/Magnus*, Art. 25, Rn. 13; *Schulz*, S. 282 f.; *Ziegler*, S. 151.
[79] O. R., S. 304, Nr. 41, auf Antrag Grossbritanniens und der USA. Vgl. dazu auch die Kritik von *Farnsworth*, 27 Am. J. Comp L. (1979), 247, 250, an Art. 26 des New Yorker E 1979.
[80] So auch *MünchKomm/Gruber*, Art. 28, Rn. 14; a. A. *Honsell/Gsell*, Art. 28, Rn. 24; *Enderlein/Maskow/Strohbach*, Art. 28, Anm. 3.; Reinhart, Art. 28, Rn. 3.
[81] *Neufang*, S. 427.
[82] *Neufang*, S. 427.
[83] Vgl. *Herber/Czerwenka*, Art. 28, Rn. 4; *Reinhart*, Art. 28, Rn. 3; *Audit*, Vente internationale, Anm. 123.; *Posch/Kandut*, S. 73; *Neumayer/Ming*, Art. 28, Anm. 6.; *Staudinger/Magnus*, Art. 28, Rn. 20; *Honsell/Gsell*, Art. 28, Rn. 25. A. A. *Bianca/Bonell/Lando*, Art. 28, Anm. 3.1.; *Kastely*, 63 Wash. L. Rev. (1988), 607, 642 f.
[84] *Schulz*, S. 283.

Parteien die Klagbarkeit der Erfüllungsansprüche vertraglich absichern (z. B. im Rahmen langfristiger Lieferverträge), können sie dies durch Wahl eines „erfüllungsfreundlichen" Gerichtsstands erreichen.[85] Treffen die Parteien eine Vereinbarung über die Erfüllung in Natur, so entscheidet allein das „eigene Recht" des urteilenden Gerichts darüber, welche Bedeutung einer solchen Vereinbarung beizulegen ist.[86]

---

[85] *Witz/Salger/Lorenz/Salger*, Art. 28, Rn. 21; zum Gerichtsstand des Erfüllungsorts vgl. *Widmer Lüchinger*, Art. 31 Rn. 87 ff.; *Müller-Chen*, Art. 45 Rn. 35.
[86] *Reinhart*, Art. 28, Rn. 3; *Audit*, Vente internationale, Anm. 123., *Honsell/Gsell*, Art. 28, Rn. 25.

Art. 29 [Vertragsänderung oder -aufhebung]

(1) Ein Vertrag kann durch bloße Vereinbarung der Parteien geändert oder aufgehoben werden.

(2) Enthält ein schriftlicher Vertrag eine Bestimmung, wonach jede Änderung oder Aufhebung durch Vereinbarung schriftlich zu erfolgen hat, so darf er nicht auf andere Weise geändert oder aufgehoben werden. Eine Partei kann jedoch aufgrund ihres Verhaltens davon ausgeschlossen sein, sich auf eine solche Bestimmung zu berufen, soweit die andere Partei sich auf dieses Verhalten verlassen hat.

Art. 29

(1) A contract may be modified or terminated by the mere agreement of the parties.

(2) A contract in writing which contains a provision requiring any modification or termination by agreement to be in writing may not be otherwise modified or terminated by agreement. However, a party may be precluded by his conduct from asserting such a provision to the extent that the other party has relied on that conduct.

Art. 29

1) Un contrat peut être modifié ou résilié par accord amiable entre les parties.

2) Un contrat écrit qui contient une disposition stipulant que toute modification ou résiliation amiable doit être faite par écrit ne peut être modifié ou résilié à l'amiable sous une autre forme. Toutefois, le comportement de l'une des parties peut l'empêcher d'invoquer une telle disposition si l'autre partie s'est fondée sur ce comportement.

Übersicht

	Rn.
I. Vertragsänderung und -aufhebung (Abs. I)	1
1. Anwendbare Bestimmungen	2
a) Vereinbarung	2
b) Formfreiheit	4
2. Erfasste Vorgänge	6
a) Änderungen und Ergänzungen	6
b) Änderungen unter Beteiligung Dritter	10
c) Aufhebung	11
II. Vereinbarte Form (Abs. II 1)	14
1. Konstitutive Wirkung von Schriftformabreden	14
2. Änderung der Formabrede	16
3. Vollständigkeitsklauseln; Bestätigungsvorbehalte; Rahmenverträge	17
4. Bedeutung von „Schriftform"	19
5. Vereinbarung	20
6. Schriftlichkeit der Schriftformabrede	21
III. Missbrauchseinwand (Abs. II 2)	23
1. Voraussetzungen	23
a) Vertrauen erzeugendes Verhalten	24
b) Durch das Verhalten der Gegenseite hervorgerufenes Vertrauen („tätiger Verlass")	27
c) Vertragliche Abdingbarkeit des Art. 29 II 2	29
2. Nationale Formvorschriften und Missbrauchseinwand	30
3. Rechtsfolge und Reichweite; Berücksichtigung von Amts wegen	31
4. Konkurrenz nationaler Rechtsbehelfe	32
IV. Beweislast	33

Vorläufer und **Entwürfe:** New Yorker E 1978 Art. 27.

I. Vertragsänderung und -aufhebung (Abs. I)

Für Juristen aus vielen Rechtsordnungen ist die aus dem Prinzip der Parteiautonomie **1** folgende Möglichkeit der Parteien, einen zwischen ihnen geschlossenen Vertrag zu ändern oder aufzuheben,[1] selbstverständlich.[2] Trotzdem war die Regelung des Art. 29 im Verlauf der Ausarbeitung des CISG und noch auf der Wiener Konferenz in Einzelheiten umstritten; sie ist stark durch amerikanische Rechtsvorstellungen beeinflusst worden.[3]

1. Anwendbare Bestimmungen

2 **a) Vereinbarung.** Für das Zustandekommen einer einen CISG-Kaufvertrag ändernden, ergänzenden oder aufhebenden Vereinbarung i. S. d. Art. 29 I gilt **Teil II des Übereinkommens**.[4] Für ein Angebot sind deshalb die Artt. 14–17, für eine entsprechende Annahme die Artt. 18–22,[5] für den Zeitpunkt der Änderung oder Aufhebung Art. 23, für den Zugang von Erklärungen Art. 24 zu beachten.[6] Die Auslegung der erforderlichen Parteierklärungen bemisst sich nach Art. 8.[7] Für nationales, über IPR berufenes Recht ist, soweit es um den äußeren Konsens bezüglich der Änderung, Ergänzung oder Aufhebung geht, kein Raum, da es sich um eine Kaufrechtsmaterie handelt, s. Art. 7 II. Die Art. 29 i. V. m. Artt. 14 ff. finden dabei auch Anwendung, sofern es um die nachträgliche Einbeziehung von Streitbeilegungsklauseln (namentlich Gerichtsstands- oder Schiedsklauseln) in dem CISG unterliegende Kaufverträge geht.[8] Ob ein kaufmännisches Bestätigungsschreiben ergänzend oder ändernd wirken kann, richtet sich nach Art. 9.[9]

3 **Nationale Gültigkeitsnormen** sind daneben nach Art. 4 S. 2 lit. a) auch im Anwendungsbereich des Art. 29 I zu beachten.[10] Soweit etwa Vertragsänderungen oder eine Aufhebung von einer Seite durch Ausnutzung wirtschaftlicher Übermacht oder rechtswidrige Drohungen durchgesetzt worden sind, haben deutsche Gerichte bei Maßgeblichkeit deutschen Rechts als Vertragstatut deshalb die §§ 138, 123 BGB als Gültigkeitsnormen zu berücksichtigen.[11]

---

[1] S. aus rechtsvergleichender Perspektive *Schwenzer/Hachem/Kee,* Rn. 14.01 ff.

[2] Vgl. zu dieser Selbstverständlichkeit für die Mitverfasser des CISG *Enderlein/Maskow/Strohbach,* Art. 29, Anm. 1.1.; auch *Kröll u. a./Björklund,* Art. 29, Rn. 2: „On its face, Art. 29 appears uncontroversial."

[3] Zur Vorgeschichte, insbesondere den Diskussionen in der Arbeitsgruppe und in Wien sowie der Behandlung der Frage, ob die Vorschrift im Abschlussteil des CISG (Teil II) oder im Teil III eingestellt werden sollte, s. *Schlechtriem* 3. Aufl., Art. 29 Rn. 1; *Geldsetzer,* S. 26 ff.

[4] Zum CISG unbestritten, vgl. OLG Köln, 22.2.1994, CISG-online 127 = RIW 1994, 972; LG Hamburg, 26.9.1990, CISG-online 21 = RIW 1990, 1015, 1018; *Achilles,* Art. 29, Rn. 1; AG Sursee, 12.9.2008, CISG-online 1728 = IHR 2009, 63, 64; *Bamberger/Roth/Saenger,* Art. 29, Rn. 2; *Brunner,* Art. 29, Rn. 1; *Enderlein/Maskow/Strohbach,* Art. 29, Anm. 1.2.; *Herber/Czerwenka,* Art. 29, Rn. 3; *Honsell/Gsell,* Art. 29, Rn. 10; *Loewe,* Art. 29, S. 50 (analog); MünchKommHGB/*Benicke,* Art. 29, Rn. 2; *Nemeczek,* IHR 2011, 49, 51; *Perales Viscasillas,* 25 J. L. & Com. (2005-06), 167, 171; *Staudinger/Magnus,* Art. 29, Rn. 10; *Witz/Salger/Lorenz/Salger,* Art. 29, Rn. 9. Teil II findet dabei auch dann Anwendung, wenn eine Partei in einem Staat niedergelassen ist, der von dem Vorbehalt des Art. 92 Gebrauch gemacht hat, denn ein solcher Vorbehalt bezieht sich (anders als ein Vorbehalt nach Art. 96, aufgrund dessen nach dem Wortlaut der Norm nicht nur Teil II, sondern auch Art. 29 in seiner Geltung eingeschränkt wird) von vornherein nicht auf Vorgänge nach Art. 29, s. *Bergsten,* FS Kritzer, S. 54 f.; *Schroeter,* FS Kritzer, S. 439 (anders insoweit noch *Schroeter* in der Voraufl.).

[5] Häufig war zu entscheiden, ob bzw. unter welchen Voraussetzungen ein Änderungsangebot konkludent angenommen worden ist, s. dazu näher unten Rn. 8 f.

[6] Art. 27 findet keine Anwendung, obgleich Parteierklärungen im Anwendungsbereich des Art. 29 I technisch als „Mitteilungen ... gemäß diesem Teil" (vgl. Art. 27) angesehen werden könnten – da das Zustandekommen von Vereinbarungen nach Art. 29 I den Bestimmungen des Teil II unterliegt, geht Art. 24 insoweit vor.

[7] BGH, 27.11.2007, CISG-online 1617 = IHR 2008, 49, 51; KG Zug, 14.12.2009, CISG-online 2026.

[8] S. oben Vor Artt. 14–24 Rn. 9; *BTC-USA Corp. v. Novacare et al.,* U. S. Dist. Ct. (D. Minn.), 16.6.2008, CISG-online 1773. Zu den anwendbaren Formvorschriften sogleich Rn. 5.

[9] Zustimmend KG Zug, 14.12.2009, CISG-online 2026. Vgl. hierzu noch unten Rn. 7 f. sowie oben Vor Artt. 14–24 Rn. 18 ff.; anders (und bedenklich) Hof van Beroep Gent, 15.5.2002, CISG-online 746.

[10] S. statt aller *Lookofsky,* 39 Am. J. Comp. L. (1991), 403, 412 f.

[11] Vgl. OLG Hamburg, 5.10.1998, CISG-online 473 = TranspR-IHR 1999, 37, 39 f.: die Zustimmung der Verkäuferin zur einvernehmlichen Kaufpreisminderung „auf Null" wurde durch arglistiges Vortäuschen der „vollständigen Unbrauchbarkeit" der gelieferten Ware erschlichen, die aber von der Käuferin tatsächlich weiterverkauft worden war (unberechtigte Kritik der Entscheidung bei *Perales Viscasillas,* 25 J. L. & Com. (2005-06), 167, 169 Fn. 9). Der Schutz einer schwächeren Vertragspartei vor solchen „opportunistischen" Vertragsänderungen, etwa der vom Verkäufer durch Androhung, im Lieferzeitpunkt nicht zu liefern, erzwungenen

b) Formfreiheit. Auch für ändernde oder aufhebende Vereinbarungen gilt **Formfrei-** 4
heit nach Art. 11.[12] Deshalb können auch schriftliche Verträge grundsätzlich – vorbehaltlich
Art. 29 II 1 oder Artt. 12, 96[13] – mündlich[14] oder gar konkludent[15] geändert werden;
Formvorschriften des nationalen Rechts[16] werden auch insoweit durch Art. 29 I i. V. m.
Art. 11 verdrängt. Praktische Bedürfnisse zu **formfreien Änderungs- und Ergänzungs-**
vereinbarungen dürften sogar die Hauptbedeutung des Art. 11 ausmachen.[17] Art. 29 I hat
dabei vor allem die Bedeutung, auch **einseitig begünstigende Änderungen**, z. B. eine
Stundung, ohne nationale Seriositätserfordernisse wie **Form**[18] oder **consideration**[19] zu
ermöglichen.[20] Die im amerikanischen Recht[21] an die Stelle der „consideration" getretene
Voraussetzung, dass eine Vertragsänderung nur gültig sei, wenn sie „in good faith" vereinbart
wurde, darf deshalb m. E. nicht unbesehen und uneingeschränkt als nationale Gültigkeitsnorm nach Art. 4 S. 2 lit. a) wieder Eingang als Kontrollinstrument finden, auch wenn als
Vertragsstatut ergänzend zum CISG amerikanisches Recht zu berücksichtigen ist.[22]

Bei Ergänzungen, u. U. auch bei Änderungen, ist jedoch darauf zu achten, ob sie noch 5
kaufrechtliche Materie regeln sollen und in den Regelungsbereich des Art. 11 fallen: Wird
ergänzend zu einem Kaufvertrag eine **Wettbewerbsbeschränkung**, eine **Schieds-** oder
Gerichtsstandsklausel vereinbart, gelten für Formfragen insoweit Art. 23 I 3 EuGVO,
Art. 23 I 3 LuganoÜ, Art. 2 II NYC oder Vorschriften des über IPR berufenen nationalen
Rechts und deshalb evtl. Formvorschriften des anwendbaren Geschäftsstatuts oder des Orts-
rechts, Art. 11 EGBGB bzw. Art. 11 Rom I–VO.[23] Soweit eine Partei in einem Vorbehalts-
staat niedergelassen ist, gelten Artt. 12, 96, weshalb das vom IPR des Forums berufene
Formstatut über Formfreiheit oder -bedürftigkeit entscheidet.[24] Abweichungen vom
Grundsatz der Formfreiheit ergeben sich zudem bei vereinbarter Form.[25]

Preiserhöhung, ist auch das rechtspolitische Motiv des im amerikanischen Recht verlangten Erfordernisses, dass
eine Vertragsänderung „in good faith" vereinbart worden sein muss, vgl. *Lookofsky*, The 1980 United Nations
Convention, Anm. 145.; ferner unten Rn. 4 sowie – umfassend – *Geldsetzer*, S. 115 ff. Wo ein Fall ökonomischer Erpressung vorliegt, der nach deutschem Recht ebenfalls die Gültigkeit des Vertrages in Frage zu
stellen nahe legt, sollte deshalb auch das „good faith"-Erfordernis als Gültigkeitsnorm beachtet werden.

[12] *Forestal Guarani S. A. v. Daros International, Inc.*, U. S. Ct. App. (3rd Cir.), 21.7.2010, CISG-online 2112;
Macromex Srl. v. Globex International Inc., AAA, 23.10.2007, CISG-online 1645; *Ferrari u. a./Ferrari*, Internationales Vertragsrecht, Art. 29, Rn. 1; *Honsell/Gsell*, Art. 29, Rn. 15; *Nemeczek*, IHR 2011, 49, 54; *Staudinger/*
Magnus, Art. 29, Rn. 9.
[13] S. dazu sogleich Rn. 5.
[14] *Raw Materials Inc. v. Manfred Forberich GmbH & Co. KG*, U. S. Dist. Ct. (N. D. Ill.), 6.7.2004, CISG-online
925.
[15] OGH, 29.6.1999, CISG-online 483 = TranspR-IHR 1999, 48, 49; *Brunner*, Art. 29, Rn. 1.
[16] Vgl. zu diesen *Schwenzer/Hachem/Kee*, Rn. 14.09 f.; *Wagner-von Papp*, 63 CLP (2010), 511, 517 ff.
[17] S. oben *Schmidt-Kessel*, Art. 11 Rn. 4.
[18] Vgl. *Wey*, Rn. 412: „causa donandi" erfolgende Erlasse.
[19] *Norfolk Southern Railway Company v. Power Source Supply, Inc.*, U. S. Dist. Ct. (W. D. Pa.), 25.7.2008, CISG-
online 1776; *Shuttle Packaging Systems, L. L. C. v. Jacob Tsonakis, INA S. A. and INA Plastics Corporation*,
U. S. Dist. Ct. (W. D. Mich.), 17.12.2001, CISG-online 773; *Bianca/Bonell/Date-Bah*, Art. 29, Anm. 2.1.;
Bridge, Int'l Sale of Goods, Rn. 12.11; *Ferrari u. a./Ferrari*, Internationales Vertragsrecht, Art. 29, Rn. 4;
Honnold/Flechtner, Art. 29, Rn. 201; *Kröll u. a./Björklund*, Art. 29, Rn. 1; *Perales Viscasillas*, 25 J. L. & Com.
(2005-06), 167, 169; *Schultz*, 35 Cornell Int'l L. J. (2001-02), 263, 278; *van Alstine*, 37 Va. J. Int'l L. (1996), 1,
16 Fn. 47. S. zu den Anforderungen an einseitig begünstigende Vertragsänderungen in Common Law-Rechtsordnungen instruktiv *Schwenzer/Hachem/Kee*, Rn. 14.02 ff.; ausführlich zu Art. 29 und der „pre-existing duty
rule" nach Common Law *Kröll u. a./Björklund*, Art. 29, Rn. 12 ff.
[20] Vgl. *Kröll u. a./Björklund*, Art. 29, Rn. 3; *Perales Viscasillas*, 25 J. L. & Com. (2005-06), 167, 170 f.
[21] S. § 2–209 UCC comment 2.
[22] *Honsell/Gsell*, Art. 29, Rn. 14; *MünchKomm/Gruber*, Art. 29, Rn. 3; a. A. *MünchKommHGB/Benicke*,
Art. 29, Rn. 2.
[23] Vgl. oben *Schmidt-Kessel*, Art. 11 Rn. 7; ferner *Wey*, Rn. 421.
[24] S. RB Rotterdam, 12.7.2001, CISG-online 968 = NIPR 2001, Nr. 278: bei niederländisch-argenti-
nischem Kaufvertrag war niederländisches Recht (und daher Artt. 11, 29) auf Formfragen anwendbar, da der
Vertragsabschluss in den Niederlanden stattgefunden hatte; vgl. aber RB Hasselt, 2.5.1995, CISG-online 371:
Schriftform des Vorbehaltsstaats (Chile) (direkt?) anwendbar; s. hier *Schmidt-Kessel*, Art. 12 Rn. 2 sowie
Schroeter, FS Kritzer, S. 443 f.
[25] S. unten Rn. 14 ff.

2. Erfasste Vorgänge

6 **a) Änderungen und Ergänzungen.** Änderungen grenzüberschreitender Warenkaufverträge sind häufig und können die unterschiedlichsten Regelungsgegenstände betreffen: „Vorschläge" zu Preisanpassungen[26] oder Änderungen der Zahlungsmodalitäten[27] wie namentlich Stundungen,[28] zu Mehr- oder Minderlieferungen,[29] zu Verschiebungen des Liefertermins[30] kommen ebenso vor wie Anträge zur Ergänzung des Vertrages um eine Pflicht des Verkäufers, vorab eine Warenprobe zu Testzwecken zu übersenden,[31] und Angebote zur einvernehmlichen Vertragsaufhebung.[32] Eine Änderung des Kaufvertrages liegt auch dort vor, wo die Vertragsparteien die Abänderung eines Akkreditivs vereinbaren, weil dadurch mittelbar auch die Zahlungsklausel im Kaufvertrag modifiziert wird.[33] Art. 29 gilt auch für **Vergleiche**, soweit sie kaufrechtliche Regelungen treffen und nicht etwa novierend an die Stelle eines Kaufvertrages ein ganz anderes Geschäft, z. B. einen Mietvertrag, setzen.[34] Da Art. 29 das Prinzip der Parteiautonomie zugrunde liegt, gilt er auch für **vertragsergänzende Vereinbarungen**, wie etwa die Ergänzung eines Kaufvertrages um eine Wettbewerbsbeschränkungsabrede.[35]

7 Vertragsänderungen stellen sich typischerweise als Reaktion auf Veränderungen in den faktischen Umständen dar, die seit dem Vertragsschluss eingetreten sind.[36] Angebote zur einvernehmlichen Umgestaltung des vereinbarten Vertragsinhalts kommen aber auch in unmittelbarem Nachgang zum Vertragsschluss vor und sind dabei nicht selten ein Versuch, beim Zustandekommen des Kaufvertrages nicht einbezogene Regelungsgegenstände durch die Übersendung inhaltlich abweichender „Auftragsbestätigungen", **„Bestätigungsschreiben"**, Rechnungen o. ä. nachträglich zum Vertragsinhalt zu machen. Die praktisch häufigsten Fälle dürften sog. **„nachgeschobene" AGB** sein,[37] aber auch Vorschläge zur nach-

---

[26] Tribunal Supremo, 28.1.2000, CISG-online 503: Vorschlag des Käufers zur Neuverhandlung des Preises.

[27] BGH, 27.11.2007, CISG-online 1617: „Erhöhung" des Kaufpreises unter gleichzeitiger Abrede, dass der Verkäufer den Differenzbetrag an Konzerntöchter der Käuferin zurückzahlt (Verschleierung des wahren Kaufpreises gegenüber Abnehmern); OLG Karlsruhe, 10.12.2003, CISG-online 911 = IHR 2004, 62, 64: Vereinbarung über auf die Gesamtrestforderung aus Kaufverträgen zahlungshalber zu erbringenden Leistungen (Scheckzahlungen) sowie über die noch bestehende Restschuld der Käuferin.

[28] Vgl. Najvyšší súd Slovenskej republiky, 19.6.2008, CISG-online 1875 (in Rechnung enthaltenes Angebot des Verkäufers (!), die Fälligkeit der Kaufpreiszahlungspflicht um 180 Tage hinauszuschieben); OLG Karlsruhe, 10.12.2003, CISG-online 911 = IHR 2004, 62, 64; OGer Basel-Land, 5.10.1999, CISG-online 492 = SZIER 2000, 115: Vereinbarung über Teilstundung aufgelaufener Kaufpreisschulden; LG Hamburg, 26.9.1990, CISG-online 21 = RIW 1990, 1015, 1018: Stundung durch Wechselbegebung.

[29] OGH, 6.2.1996, CISG-online 224 = ZfRVgl 1996, 248, 252 m. Anm. *Karollus*, RdW 1996, 203: statt ca. 700–800t nunmehr Kauf von 3.000t Flüssiggas.

[30] *Macromex Srl. v. Globex International Inc.*, AAA, 23.10.2007, CISG-online 1645; *Raw Materials Inc. v. Manfred Forberich GmbH & Co. KG*, U. S. Dist. Ct. (N. D. Ill.), 6.7.2004, CISG-online 925.

[31] Int. Ct. Russian CCI, 16.2.2004, 107/2002, CISG-online 1181.

[32] S. dazu unten Rn. 11.

[33] CIETAC, 15.4.1997, CISG-online 1162.

[34] HGer Zürich, 24.10.2003, CISG-online 857: Vergleichsvereinbarung zur Regelung von Zahlungsausständen aus Kaufverträgen; LG Kassel, 15.2.1996, CISG-online 190: Vergleichsangebot durch Übersendung eines Schecks, Annahme durch Einlösung des Schecks; *Brunner*, Art. 29, Rn. 1; *Ferrari u. a./Ferrari*, Internationales Vertragsrecht, Art. 29, Rn. 6; *Honsell/Dornis*, Vorbem 14–24, Rn. 2; *Honsell/Gsell*, Art. 29, Rn. 5; MünchKomm/*Gruber*, Art. 29, Rn. 5; MünchKommHGB/*Benicke*, Art. 29, Rn. 1; unrichtig LG Aachen, 14.5.1993, CISG-online 86 = RIW 1993, 760, 761: Ein Vergleich falle nach Art. 4 S. 1 nicht unter das CISG; anzuwenden sei das (in concreto stillschweigend gewählte) deutsche Recht. Entscheidend ist jedoch der ursprüngliche und jetzt vergleichsweise neu geregelte Vertrag. Im Übrigen wäre bei Anwendung des CISG in der Sache (Unwirksamkeit eines Vergleichs wegen Nichteintritts einer Bedingung) nicht anders zu entscheiden gewesen.

[35] *Shuttle Packaging Systems, L. L. C. v. Jacob Tsonakis, INA S. A. and INA Plastics Corporation*, U. S. Dist. Ct. (W. D. Mich.), 17.12.2001, CISG-online 773; a. A. MünchKomm/*Gruber*, Art. 29, Rn. 5. Zur Frage der Formbedürftigkeit von Vertragsergänzungen, die keine originär kaufrechtlichen Gegenstände betreffen, s. oben Rn. 5.

[36] Vgl. etwa *Norfolk Southern Railway Company v. Power Source Supply, Inc.*, U. S. Dist. Ct. (W. D. Pa.), 25.7.2008, CISG-online 1776: auf Wunsch des Käufers nachträgliche Vereinbarung einer Umrüstung der gekauften Lokomotiven durch den Verkäufer mit korrespondierender Preiserhöhung.

[37] *Chateau des Charmes Wines Ltd. v. Sabaté USA Inc.*, Sabaté S. A., U. S. Ct. App. (9th Cir.), 5.5.2003, CISG-online 767 = IHR 2003, 295, 296 (AGB auf Rechnungen); KG Zug, 11.12.2003, CISG-online 958 = IHR 2005, 119, 121 (AGB auf Rechnung bzw. Lieferschein); CA Paris, 13.12.1995, CISG-online 312 = J. C. P. éd.

Vertragsänderung oder -aufhebung   8 **Art. 29**

träglichen Anpassung von essentialia negotii wie etwa des Kaufpreises[38] kommen vor. Art. 29 I steht entsprechenden Vertragsänderungen nicht entgegen,[39] erfordert aber im konkreten Fall die Feststellung, dass die ausgetauschten Erklärungen aus der Perspektive einer „vernünftigen Person" (Art. 8 II) als auf die Änderung des vereinbarten Vertragsinhalts gerichtet aufgefasst worden wären. Hier kann häufig bereits die Qualifikation als **Änderungsangebot** (Art. 29 I i. V. m. Art. 14 I 1) **zweifelhaft** sein,[40] etwa wenn es sich bei der betreffenden Erklärung um eine anlässlich der Lieferung übersandte Rechnung mit aufgedruckten AGB,[41] eine Einzelbestellung im Rahmen eines Langzeitvertragsverhältnisses, die auf zuvor nicht einbezogene AGB verweist,[42] oder eine nach einem Vertragsschluss im Fernabsatz in Übereinstimmung mit § 312c II BGB erfolgte Informationsmitteilung in Textform[43] handelt. Gleiches gilt für ein „Bestätigungsschreiben", dem im Rahmen des Art. 29 I nur Bedeutung zukommen kann, wenn es auf die *Modifikation* des Vertrages gerichtet ist,[44] wohingegen ihm vor dem Hintergrund des deutschrechtlichen Verständnisses eines kaufmännischen Bestätigungsschreibens regelmäßig gerade ein bestätigender Aussagegehalt zukommt.[45] Schließlich kann zweifelhaft sein, ob die einseitige Nennung eines neuen Leistungstermins durch den Gläubiger eine Nachfristsetzung gem. Artt. 47 I, 63 I oder ein Angebot i. S. d. Art. 29 I auf einvernehmliche Änderung der Leistungszeit darstellen soll.[46]

Eine sorgfältige Prüfung ist aber vor allem im Rahmen der Frage notwendig, ob ein 8 Angebot auf Vertragsänderung durch die andere Vertragspartei konkludent oder durch annahmeäquivalentes Verhalten **angenommen** wurde (Art. 29 I i. V. m. Art. 18 I 1, III). Schweigen und Untätigkeit allein stellen auch hier gemäß Art. 29 I i. V. m. Art. 18 I 2 keine Annahme dar.[47] Darüber hinaus wird namentlich das Verhalten des Adressaten im Rahmen der Vertragsdurchführung durch eine vernünftige Person unter den gleichen Umständen nur ausnahmsweise als Annahme eines (regelmäßig seinerseits konkludent unterbreiteten) Vertragsänderungsangebotes aufgefasst werden können,[48] weil die handelnde Partei ja bereits Inhaberin von Rechten und Pflichten aus dem schon geschlossenen Kaufvertrag ist und es

---

G, II, Nr. 22 772 (AGB auf Auftragsbestätigung, die 2 Wochen nach Vertragsschluss übersandt wurde); OLG Düsseldorf, 23.3.2011, CISG-online 2218 (AGB auf Lieferschein); RB Kortrijk, 8.12.2004, CISG-online 1511 = IHR 2005, 114, 115 (AGB auf Rechnung).

[38] Tribunal Supremo, 28.1.2000, CISG-online 503: Vorschlag des Käufers zur Senkung („Neuverhandlung") des Kaufpreises – mangels Reaktion des Verkäufers nicht angenommen; HGer Zürich, 10.7.1996, CISG-online 227 = SZIER 1997, 131 f.: in Form einer „zweiten Auftragsbestätigung" unterbreitetes Angebot des Verkäufers zur Erhöhung des vereinbarten Kaufpreises.

[39] Oben Rn. 4.

[40] LG Aachen, 22.6.2010, CISG-online 2162 = IHR 2011, 82, 85; *Enderlein/Maskow/Strohbach*, Art. 29, Anm. 1.2.; *Schmidt-Kessel/Meyer*, IHR 2008, 177, 179.

[41] RB Kortrijk, 8.12.2004, CISG-online 1511 = IHR 2005, 114, 115: kein Angebot auf Abschluss eines Änderungsvertrages.

[42] OLG Jena, 10.11.2010, CISG-online 2216 = IHR 2011, 79, 81.

[43] *Janal*, S. 264 f.; *Schlechtriem*, Internationales UN-Kaufrecht, Rn. 42c; zur Informationspflicht nach § 312c II BGB bei CISG-Verträgen bereits oben Vor Artt. 14–24 Rn. 39.

[44] Allgemein zum Fehlen einer konstitutiven Wirkung des Schweigens auf ein kaufmännisches Bestätigungsschreiben unter dem CISG sowie der Ausnahme in den Fällen, in denen ein Handelsbrauch nach Art. 9 vorliegt, s. oben Vor Artt. 14–24 Rn. 18 ff.

[45] Vgl. BGH, 9.7.1970, BGHZ 54, 236, 239; MünchKommHGB/*K. Schmidt*, § 346, Rn. 147. Großzügiger *Kramer*, FS Welser, S. 546: kaufmännisches Bestätigungsschreiben sei nach CISG wohl als Antrag auf Vertragsänderung qualifizierbar.

[46] Vgl. *Valero Marketing & Supply Company v. Greeni Trading Oy*, U. S. Ct. App. (3rd Cir.), 19.7.2007, CISG-online 1510 = IHR 2008, 35; *Kröll u. a./Björklund*, Art. 29, Rn. 9.

[47] *Macromex Srl. v. Globex International Inc.*, AAA, 23.10.2007, CISG-online 1645: „The failure to object to a unilateral attempt to modify a contract is not an agreement to modify a contract"; Najvyšší súd Slovenskej republiky, 19.6.2008, CISG-online 1875: Schweigen des Käufers auf Vorschlag des Verkäufers, den Kaufpreiszahlungstermin um 180 Tage hinauszuschieben, ist keine Annahme (was *in concreto* bedeutete, dass die Kaufpreisforderung verjährt war; vgl. noch oben Art. 19 Rn. 8b); *Perales Viscasillas*, 25 J. L. & Com. (2005-06), 167, 172; unzutreffend Hof van Beroep Gent, 15.5.2002, CISG-online 746.

[48] OGer Bern, 19.5.2008, CISG-online 1738: „… une modification tacite ne doit pas être admise sans retenue"; *Brunner*, Art. 4, Rn. 43; *Janssen*, IHR 2004, 194, 197; *Magnus*, FS Kritzer, S. 324; *Piltz*, IHR 2007, 121 f.; s. hier auch oben Art. 18 Rn. 8a.

Art. 29 9 Teil III. Kapitel I. Allgemeine Bestimmungen

daher als fern liegend erscheint, dass sie das bestehende Äquivalenzverhältnis durch die nachträgliche Einbeziehung von (ihr regelmäßig nachteiligen) AGB der Gegenseite oder sonstiger schlechterer Konditionen soll abändern wollen.[49] Als **keine Annahme** eines Vertragsänderungsangebotes ausdrücklich wurde deshalb die widerspruchslose Entgegennahme und der Weiterverkauf gelieferter Ware,[50] die stillschweigende Annahme der Ware, vor deren Lieferung der Verkäufer vom Vertrag abweichende AGB übersandt hatte,[51] das Unterschreiben eines Lieferscheins durch Mitarbeiter des Käufers (weil dadurch gem. Art. 8 lediglich der Empfang der Ware, nicht aber das Einverständnis mit auf dem Lieferschein abgedruckten AGB bestätigt wird),[52] die Bezahlung von Rechnungen, auf denen eine Gerichtsstandsklausel aufgedruckt war (selbst wenn Rechnungen mit identischem Klauselinhalt im Laufe der Geschäftsbeziehung schon häufig verwandt worden waren)[53] sowie die Vornahme einer Teillieferung durch den Verkäufer, nachdem nur für einen Teil des Kaufpreises das vereinbarte Akkreditiv eröffnet worden war,[54] angesehen. In diesen Fällen wird dem Verhalten der Gegenpartei in der Tat regelmäßig keine Erklärungsbedeutung im Sinne einer Annahme innewohnen; entsprechende Vorgänge stellen vielmehr typischerweise nur Schritte zur Durchführung des bereits bestehenden Vertrages dar.[55] Nicht selten wird denjenigen Mitarbeitern einer Vertragspartei, die Rechnungen, Lieferscheine oder Zahlungsbelege (inklusive aufgedruckter AGB) bestimmungsgemäß entgegennehmen, zudem erkennbar die rechtliche Kompetenz fehlen, für ihren Geschäftsherrn Vertragsänderungen vorzunehmen.[56] Geringere Anforderungen an die Annahme sollen allerdings ausnahmsweise gelten, wenn Bedingungen eines Bestätigungsschreibens für den Empfänger günstiger sind als die des „bestätigten" Vertrages.[57]

9 Als nahe liegender stellt sich die Einordnung des Parteiverhaltens als in konkludenter Weise vereinbarte Vertragsänderung hingegen dort dar, wo seit dem Vertragsschluss eine **Änderung** i. S. d. Art. 8 III **„erheblicher Umstände"** (wie namentlich der Zahlungs- oder sonstigen Leistungsfähigkeit[58] einer der Vertragsparteien) stattgefunden hat.[59] In einem

---

[49] S. *Chateau Des Charmes Wines Ltd. v. Sabate USA, Inc. et al.*, Ontario Superior Court of Justice, 28.10.2005, CISG-online 1139, Rn. 29: „It is unreasonable to suggest that the plaintiff, having ordered the product (and presumably having not ordered whatever closures it would otherwise have used) would have to refuse delivery in order to avoid terms unilaterally inserted into the documents"; KG Zug, 11.12.2003, CISG-online 958 = IHR 2005, 119, 121: „Der Klägerin darf aber nicht unterstellt werden, sie habe bei Erhalt der ersten Lieferung noch eine Vereinbarung über den Erfüllungsort [...] abschließen wollen, indem sie gegen die Geltung der auf der Rückseite der Rechnung bzw. des Lieferscheins angebrachten AGB nicht remonstrierte"; OLG Jena, 10.11.2010, CISG-online 2216 = IHR 2011, 79, 81.
[50] HGer Zürich, 10.7.1996, CISG-online 227 = SZIER 1997, 131 f.
[51] CA Paris, 13.12.1995, CISG-online 312 = J. C. P. éd. G, II, Nr. 22 772.
[52] OLG Düsseldorf, 23.3.2011, CISG-online 2218.
[53] *Chateau des Charmes Wines Ltd. v. Sabaté USA Inc., Sabaté S. A.*, U. S. Ct. App. (9th Cir.), 5.5.2003, CISG-online 767 = IHR 2003, 295, 296; *Chateau Des Charmes Wines Ltd. v. Sabate USA, Inc. et al.*, Ontario Superior Court of Justice, 28.10.2005, CISG-online 1139, Rn. 29. Dem folgend (bei Auslegung kalifornischen Mietrechts) *C9 Ventures v. SVC West L. P.*, Cal. App. 4 Dist., 27.1.2012, CISG-online 2307.
[54] CIETAC, 23.5.2000, CISG-online 1461: keine Änderung des vereinbarten Lieferumfangs.
[55] *Chateau des Charmes Wines Ltd. v. Sabaté USA Inc., Sabaté S. A.*, U. S. Ct. App. (9th Cir.), 5.5.2003, CISG-online 767 = IHR 2003, 295, 296; *C9 Ventures v. SVC West L. P.*, Cal. App. 4 Dist., 27.1.2012, CISG-online 2307.
[56] In diesem Sinne *CSS Antenna, Inc. v. Amphenol-Tuchel Electronics GmbH*, U. S. Dist. Ct. (D. Md.), 8.2.2011, CISG-online 2177: Verkäuferin hatte Auftragsbestätigung einschl. AGB direkt an das *billing department* der Käuferin gesandt, „where no one with authority to enter into, modify, or otherwise accept any contracts worked" – AGB nicht wirksam in den Vertrag einbezogen.
[57] *Honsell/Gsell*, Art. 29, Rn. 10; *Kramer*, FS Welser, S. 547; ähnlich *Schmidt-Kessel/Meyer*, IHR 2008, 177, 180: wenn die Parteien nachträglich eingeführte Klauseln (wie etwa eine Skontoklausel auf einer Rechnung) beachtet haben. S. jedoch oben Art. 19 Rn. 8b.
[58] S. *Valero Marketing & Supply Company v. Greeni Trading Oy*, U. S. Ct. App. (3rd Cir.), 19.7.2007, CISG-online 1510 = IHR 2008, 35: Preissenkung und Änderung technischer Vorgaben für die Anlieferung wegen Lieferverzugs des Verkäufers; *Raw Materials Inc. v. Manfred Forberich GmbH & Co. KG*, U. S. Dist. Ct. (N. D. Ill.), 6.7.2004, CISG-online 925: Verschiebung des Liefertermins wegen Beschaffungsschwierigkeiten des Verkäufers.
[59] Vgl. KG Zug, 14.12.2009, CISG-online 2026 (zur Abgrenzung einer Vertragsänderung nach Art. 29 von einem übereinstimmenden, vom Vertragsinhalt abweichenden „späteren Verhalten" beider Parteien i. S. d. Art. 8 III).

Vertragsänderung oder -aufhebung 10 **Art. 29**

solchen Fall ist eine **Änderung des Kaufvertrages** etwa erkannt worden in einem Angebot zur Reduzierung offener Kaufpreisforderungen durch Übersendung einer „Abfindungsvereinbarung" nebst Scheck, das vom Verkäufer durch Scheckeinreichung angenommen wurde,[60] in der Annahme eines Angebots auf Teilstundung aufgelaufener Kaufpreisschulden durch stillschweigende Einlösung eines beiliegenden Schecks,[61] nicht hingegen in dem schriftlichen Vorschlag einer geänderten Lieferzeit, auf den die Adressatin nicht reagierte.[62] Die bloße „allgemeine Stimmung" während einer Besprechung reicht allerdings auch hier zur Annahme einer Vertragsänderung nicht aus, sofern nicht die konkrete Einigung der Parteien über eine bestimmte Modifikation aufgezeigt (und bewiesen) werden kann.[63] Eine Änderung des Vertragsinhalts liegt dagegen vor, wenn der Käufer die mit einer pro-forma-Rechnung übersandten AGB des Verkäufers unterschrieben bzw. mit seinen Initialien abgezeichnet hat, bevor der Verkäufer mit der Vertragsdurchführung beginnt.[64]

b) **Änderungen unter Beteiligung Dritter.** Auch die Auswechslung einer Vertragspartei **(Vertragsübernahme),** die Übertragung einzelner kaufvertraglicher Verpflichtungen auf eine dritte Partei durch den Gläubiger **(Abtretung)** oder den Schuldner **(Schuldübernahme)** und die zusätzliche Übernahme bestehender Pflichten durch einen Dritten **(Schuldbeitritt)** lassen sich begrifflich als eine Änderung des Vertrages i. S. des Art. 29 I verstehen.[65] Schon weil die h. M. sämtliche genannten Rechtsinstitute allgemein als nicht vom Anwendungsbereich des CISG umfasst einordnet,[66] erachtet eine Literaturauffassung auch die Regelung des Art. 29 als nicht auf die betreffenden Konstellationen anwendbar,[67] wohingegen die neuere Rechtsprechung Art. 29 I durchaus auf Fälle der Vertragsübernahme[68] angewandt hat. Richtigerweise erfasst Art. 29 I unmittelbar nur solche Vertragsänderungen, die allein zwischen den ursprünglichen Kaufvertragsparteien vorgenommen werden,[69] weil sich der Bestimmung weder Aussagen zu Art und Umfang der notwendigen Mitwirkung hinzutretender Dritter noch zur genauen Rechtsfolge (etwa zur kumulativen oder ausschließlichen Natur einer begründeten Verpflichtung) entnehmen lassen und bei ihrer Schaffung an dahingehende Konstellationen auch nicht gedacht wurde. Unter Einbeziehung Dritter erfolgende Änderungen des Vertragsgefüges liegen daher **außerhalb des Regelungsbereiches** der Norm und sind nach dem über das IPR[70] ermittelten nationalen Recht zu beurteilen.[71] Mittelbar kann Art. 29 i. V. m. Art. 14 ff. sodann freilich doch

---

[60] LG Kassel, 15.2.1996, CISG-online 190.
[61] OGer Basel-Land, 5.10.1999, CISG-online 492 = SZIER 2000, 115.
[62] OLG München, 8.2.1995, CISG-online 143.
[63] CA Grenoble, 29.3.1995, CISG-online 156 = J. D. I. 1995, 964 ff. m. Anm. *Kahn,* J. D. I. 1995, 969 ff. (zur angeblichen Vereinbarung eines niedrigeren Kaufpreises): „la modification d'un prix de vente ne peut pas résulter d'une ambiance générale d'une réunion."
[64] *BTC-USA Corp. v. Novacare et al.,* U. S. Dist. Ct. (D. Minn.), 16.6.2008, CISG-online 1773.
[65] Vgl. *Nemeczek,* IHR 2011, 49, 50; *Schmidt-Kessel,* RIW 1996, 60, 61.
[66] Vgl. oben *Ferrari,* Art. 4 Rn. 37 f.
[67] *Honsell/Gsell,* Art. 29, Rn. 6; *Perales Viscasillas,* 25 J. L. & Com. (2005-06), 167, 175; *Staudinger/Magnus,* Art. 29, Rn. 8.
[68] Gerechtshof Leeuwarden, 31.8.2005, CISG-online 1100: da die Übertragung des Lieferanspruches durch den Käufer eine Vertragsänderung i. S. d. Art. 29 bedeute, sei für den Übergang eine Mitteilung an den Verkäufer erforderlich, obgleich die Parteien bereits im Kaufvertrag die Übertragbarkeit des Anspruches vereinbart hatten; OLG Frankfurt a. M., 6.10.2004, CISG-online 996: die „Übertragung einer Lieferbeziehung" erfordere einen dreiseitigen Vertrag, dessen wirksamer Abschluss nach dem CISG eine Einigung aller Vertragsparteien voraussetze (wobei die konkludente Zustimmung des Lieferanten zur Übertragung des Bezugsvertrages auch in der Belieferung des neuen Händlers gesehen werden könne); ebenso (mit beachtlichen Gründen) *Nemeczek,* IHR 2011, 49, 51 ff.; *Schmidt-Kessel,* RIW 1996, 60, 61; a. A. BGH, 15.2.1995, CISG-online 149 = NJW 1995, 2101, 2102: Anwendung des unvereinheitlichten deutschen Rechts.
[69] Zur Behandlung einer bereits bestehenden Drittbegünstigung aus CISG-Kaufverträgen bei Vertragsaufhebung s. unten Rn. 12.
[70] Zur kollisionsrechtlichen Bestimmung des auf einen Schuldbeitritt anwendbaren Rechts (nach Art. 28 II, V EGBGB) BGH, 11.11.2010, NJW-RR 2011, 130.
[71] So auch BGH, 15.2.1995, CISG-online 149 = NJW 1995, 2101, 2102 (für Vertragsübernahme, aber ohne Begründung); Krajský súd v Košiciach, 22.5.2007, CISG-online 1898 (für Schuldübernahme); HGer Zürich, 10.7.1996, CISG-online 227 = SZIER 1997, 131 f. (für Schuldübernahme); LG Hamburg, 26.9.1990,

wieder Bedeutung erlangen, wenn die Regelung nämlich durch das Kollisionsrecht – bei einer von einem deutschen Gericht zu beurteilenden Abtretungskonstellation also nach Art. 14 II Rom I–VO – als Teil des Schuldstatuts der abgetretenen Forderung[72] berufen wird.[73]

11 **c) Aufhebung.** Art. 29 regelt zudem die Aufhebung des Vertrages durch Vereinbarung der Parteien, die streng von der einseitigen Vertragsaufhebung nach Artt. 49 I, 64 I zu unterscheiden ist: Während das Übereinkommen letztere Form der Vertragsauflösung von strengen Voraussetzungen (wie etwa dem Vorliegen einer „wesentlichen Vertragsverletzung" i. S. d. Art. 25) abhängig macht, müssen diese Voraussetzungen für eine Aufhebung i. S. d. Art. 29 nicht vorliegen,[74] weil es hierzu allein einer Einigung der Parteien bedarf. (Diese Unterscheidung geht aus dem englischen Übereinkommenstext, der sprachlich zwischen „avoidance" und „termination" differenziert, deutlicher hervor als aus der deutschsprachigen Übersetzung). Für die einvernehmliche Aufhebung nach Art. 29 gelten insoweit die Ausführungen oben in Rn. 2 ff. entsprechend. Ein Angebot (Art. 29 I i. V. m. Art. 14 I) auf vollständige oder teilweise Vertragsaufhebung kann daher ausdrücklich erklärt werden,[75] erfolgt aber häufig auch konkludent, wie etwa in Gestalt des Zurverfügungstellens bemängelter Ware durch den Käufer.[76] Besondere Aufmerksamkeit verlangt auch hier die Behandlung nicht ausdrücklich erklärter Annahmen entsprechender Angebote: Eine Annahme durch Schweigen oder Untätigkeit scheidet nach Art. 29 I i. V. m. Art. 18 I 2 grundsätzlich aus, und der Abschluss einer Aufhebungsvereinbarung kann und darf nur dann mit der Einordnung etwa einer durch die Verkäuferin erteilten Gutschrift,[77] einer Mitteilung der Verkäuferin, sie werde die bemängelte Ware abholen und durch eine öffentliche Prüfstelle kontrollieren lassen[78] oder gar des bloßen Schweigens der Käuferin, verbunden mit einem Absehen von der weiteren Durchführung des Vertrages (d. h. Geltendmachung von Gewährleistungsansprüchen)[79] als annahmeäquivalentes Verhalten begründet werden, sofern im konkreten Fall tatsächlich die Voraussetzungen des Art. 18 I 1, III vorliegen und eine „vernünftige Person" (Art. 8 II) dieses Verhalten als Ausdruck der Annahme eines Vertragsaufhebungsangebotes aufgefasst hätte. Vorsicht ist in diesem Zusammenhang insbesondere deshalb geboten, weil die einvernehmliche Vertragsaufhebung nach Art. 29 I auch dann keinen Fristen und sonstigen Anforderungen unterliegt, wenn sie nach einer Vertragsverletzung vorgenommen wird[80] und daher bei einer zu großzügigen Annahme konkludent getroffener Aufhebungsvereinbarungen die Gefahr droht, dass ohne entsprechenden Parteikonsens spezifische Schutzregelungen wie etwa Art. 39 I, Artt. 49 I lit. a), 64 I lit. a) i. V. m. Art. 25 und Artt. 49 II, 64 II umgangen werden.

12 Manche Rechtsordnungen beschränken in besonderer Weise die Möglichkeit der Änderung von Verträgen in Fällen, in denen **Dritte** aus diesen Verträgen **begünstigt** worden

---

CISG-online 21 = RIW 1990, 1015, 1018 (für befreiende Schuldübernahme); *Ferrari u. a./Ferrari*, Internationales Vertragsrecht, Art. 29, Rn. 6; *Perales Viscasillas*, 25 J. L. & Com. (2005-06), 167, 175.

[72] Vgl. *Reithmann/Martiny/Martiny*, Rn. 329.
[73] S. OLG Hamm, 8.2.1995, CISG-online 141 = NJW-RR 1996, 1271, 1272; anders auf Grundlage schweizerischen Kollisionsrechts HGer Zürich, 10.7.1996, CISG-online 227 = SZIER 1997, 131 f.: auch insoweit unvereinheitlichtes nationales Recht anwendbar.
[74] AG Sursee, 12.9.2008, CISG-online 1728 = IHR 2009, 63, 64 f.
[75] OLG Köln, 22.2.1994, CISG-online 127 = RIW 1994, 972, 973: Mitteilung der Verkäuferin, sie habe eine andere Firma gefunden, welche die verkaufte (mangelhafte) Ware „für sie vermarkten werde" – als Antrag auf Vertragsaufhebung gewertet; LG Ellwangen, 21.8.1995, CISG-online 279.
[76] S. OLG Düsseldorf, 12.3.1993, CISG-online 82: Angebot zum Abschluss eines Teil-Aufhebungsvertrages.
[77] OLG Düsseldorf, 12.3.1993, CISG-online 82: eingehende Tatsachenwürdigung, i. E. Annahme unter Anführung von Art. 8 I, II verneint.
[78] OLG Düsseldorf, 12.3.1993, CISG-online 82 (in concreto abgelehnt).
[79] OLG Köln, 22.2.1994, CISG-online 127 = RIW 1994, 972, 973: als Annahme gewertet – bedenklich; mit Recht kritisch zu dieser Entscheidung *Schlechtriem*, EWiR 1994, 867 f.; positiver *Reinhart*, IPRax 1995, 365, 371.
[80] *Reinhart*, IPRax 1995, 365, 371.

sind.[81] Soweit dabei – anders als im deutschen Recht – nicht zwischen der Aufhebbarkeit des Deckungsgeschäfts und der Unentziehbarkeit oder Entziehbarkeit der Drittbegünstigung unterschieden und wegen der Drittbegünstigung eine Änderung oder Aufhebung des Deckungsvertrages für ungültig gehalten wird, müsste eine solche Regel nationalen Rechts über Art. 4 S. 2 lit. a) berücksichtigt werden.[82] Ob die aus einem CISG unterliegenden Kaufvertrag entstehende Drittbegünstigung entziehbar oder unentziehbar ist, hat das CISG jedoch nicht geregelt. Die Lücke ist m. E. nach Art. 7 II unter Rückgriff auf den das CISG beherrschenden Grundsatz der Parteiautonomie zu schließen.[83] Es kommt deshalb – entsprechend § 328 II BGB – darauf an, ob die Parteien das Recht des Dritten als unentziehbar ausgestalten wollten oder nicht.[84] Eine Unentziehbarkeit der Drittbegünstigung muss aber, auch wenn nationale Rechte dies anders regeln, nicht notwendig, d. h. auch ohne entsprechende Parteivereinbarung zum Deckungsverhältnis, auf die Aufhebbarkeit des Deckungsverhältnisses durchschlagen.

Die **Folgen** einer einvernehmlichen Vertragsaufhebung regelt das CISG nicht ausdrücklich. Soweit die Parteien die Rechtsfolgen nicht im Aufhebungsvertrag bestimmen, muss die im Übereinkommen insoweit gebliebene Lücke nach Art. 7 II unter Rückgriff auf die Artt. 81 ff. geschlossen werden.[85] Allerdings bleibt den Parteien unbenommen, (z. B.) Unwirksamkeit des Vertrages ex tunc zu vereinbaren und die für Ungültigkeit von Verträgen berufenen nationalen Rückabwicklungsvorschriften zum Zuge kommen zu lassen, Art. 6.[86]

II. Vereinbarte Form (Abs. II 1)

1. Konstitutive Wirkung von Schriftformabreden

Art. 29 II 1 geht davon aus, dass vertraglichen Schriftformabreden („no oral modification clauses", im englischen Sprachgebrauch vielfach verkürzt bezeichnet als „NOM clauses"), die in der Praxis häufig verwendet werden,[87] **konstitutive** Wirkung zukommt.[88] Dies geht aus der englischsprachigen Textfassung der Norm („may not") und ihrer deutschen Übersetzung („darf nicht") nur mit beschränkter Deutlichkeit hervor, ergibt sich aber aus dem insoweit klarer gefassten französischen („ne peut être modifié…") und spanischen Wortlaut („no podrá modificarse").[89] Formlose Vereinbarungen zur Vertragsänderung, -ergänzung oder -aufhebung sind bei Eingreifen einer entsprechenden Schriftformklausel daher **unwirksam**.[90] Dies gilt unabhängig davon, ob die Schriftformklausel durch Individualabrede oder als Allgemeine Geschäftsbedingung Eingang in den Kaufvertrag gefunden hat;[91] Art. 29 II differenziert insoweit nicht.

---

[81] Vgl. zum amerikanischen Recht Restatement (2d) of Contracts, § 311(4). Zu den hiervon zu unterscheidenden Konstellationen, in denen durch eine Vertragsänderung erstmals bislang unbeteiligte Dritte in das Vertragsverhältnis einbezogen werden, s. oben Rn. 10.
[82] Zur nicht ganz eindeutigen Rechtslage in den USA s. *Geldsetzer*, S. 43 f. m. w. N. Die im Restatement festgehaltene Regel spricht m. E. eher dafür, dass nur die Drittbegünstigung unangreifbar sein soll.
[83] Wie hier MünchKomm/*Gruber*, Art. 29, Rn. 18; a. A. (für Rückgriff auf nationales Recht) Honsell/Gsell, Art. 29, Rn. 7.
[84] MünchKomm/*Gruber*, Art. 29, Rn. 18.
[85] Vgl. OGH, 29.6.1999, CISG-online 483 = TranspR-IHR 1999, 48, 49 m. Anm. *Thiele*; OLG Köln, 19.5.2008, CISG-online 1700; OLG München, 28.5.2004, CISG-online 950 = IHR 2004, 203, 209: analoge Anwendung von Art. 81 II 1; OLG Graz, 24.2.1999, CISG-online 797; AG Sursee, 12.9.2008, CISG-online 1728 = IHR 2009, 63, 64 f.; *Fountoulakis*, Vor Artt. 81–84 Rn. 7 f. m. w. N.; *Kröll u. a./Björklund*, Art. 29, Rn. 11; *Perales Viscasillas*, 25 J. L. & Com. (2005-06), 167, 175; MünchKommHGB/*Benicke*, Art. 29, Rn. 3.
[86] Hierzu *Geldsetzer*, S. 179 f.
[87] Vgl. *Wagner-von Papp*, 63 CLP (2010), 511, 520 ff. mit umfassender rechtsvergleichender Analyse.
[88] ICC, 9117/1998, CISG-online 777 = ICC Bull. 2000, 83 ff.; KG Zug, 14.12.2009, CISG-online 2026; *Brunner*, Art. 29, Rn. 2; *Honsell/Gsell*, Art. 29, Rn. 18; MünchKommHGB/*Benicke*, Art. 29, Rn. 6.
[89] *Geldsetzer*, S. 165.
[90] OLG Innsbruck, 18.12.2007, CISG-online 1735; Int. Ct. Russian CCI, 16.2.2004, CISG-online 1181; *Bamberger/Roth/Saenger*, Art. 29, Rn. 3; *Bianca/Bonell/Date-Bah*, Art. 29, Anm. 2.3.; *Breitling*, S. 57 f.; *Geldsetzer*, S. 165; MünchKommHGB/*Benicke*, Art. 29, Rn. 4.
[91] OLG Hamm, 30.11.2010, CISG-online 2217 = RdL 2011, 129; MünchKomm/*Gruber*, Art. 29, Rn. 9.

15 Theoretisch vorstellbar ist allerdings, dass die konkrete Formvereinbarung dahingehend auszulegen ist, dass die Schriftform **nur deklaratorische** Bedeutung zu Beweiszwecken besitzen soll.[92] Änderungen sind in diesem Fall ohne Einhaltung dieser Form möglich.[93] Freilich lässt sich aus Art. 29 II 1 ableiten, dass eine schriftlich abgefasste Schriftformabrede unter dem CISG **im Zweifel** konstitutive Bedeutung hat;[94] an die Grundlage einer gegenteiligen Auslegung sind daher strenge Anforderungen zu stellen. Soll einer mit konstitutiver Wirkung ausgestatteten Schriftformabrede erst nachträglich im Wege einer Vertragsänderung (Art. 29 I) lediglich deklaratorische Wirkung zuerkannt werden, so ist für die entsprechende Änderungsvereinbarung ihrerseits Schriftform erforderlich (s. sogleich Rn. 16).

2. Änderung der Formabrede

16 Art. 29 II 1 bindet bei vereinbarter Schriftform für Änderungen oder Aufhebung alle Modifikationen an die vereinbarte Form, also entgegen der Rechtsprechung zum internen deutschen Recht[95] auch Abreden über die Aufgabe der Schriftformvereinbarung.[96] Zwischen „qualifizierten" und anderen Schriftformklauseln ist grundsätzlich nicht zu unterscheiden.[97] Theoretisch bleibt nach Art. 6 möglich, dass die Parteien Art. 29 II 1 formlos abbedingen und damit doch den Weg zu formlosen Änderungen eröffnen. Jedoch widerspricht eine solche Möglichkeit dem Regelungszweck des Art. 29 II 1, den Parteien den selbstgewählten Schutz der Schriftform zu erhalten, so dass an ihre Ausdrücklichkeit und Ernsthaftigkeit strengste Anforderungen zu stellen sind.[98]

3. Vollständigkeitsklauseln; Bestätigungsvorbehalte; Rahmenverträge

17 Art. 29 II 1 muss auch für sog. **Vollständigkeitsklauseln** (merger clauses, „four corner clauses") gelten, soweit sie *nachträgliche* mündliche **Nebenabreden** oder **Ergänzungen** ausschließen wollen.[99] Auch soweit Vollständigkeitsklauseln sicherstellen sollen, dass bei oder vor Vertragsschluss keine formlosen Nebenabreden getroffen worden sind,[100] müssen sie die von den Parteien vereinbarte Wirkung haben, sofern sie nicht nach nationalen Gültigkeits-

---

[92] OLG Hamm, 30.11.2010, CISG-online 2217 = RdL 2011, 129 (obiter); *Bamberger/Roth/Saenger*, Art. 29, Rn. 3; *Brunner*, Art. 29, Rn. 2. *Breitling*, S. 52, weist darauf hin, dass die Möglichkeit deklaratorischer Klauseln von der englischen und französischen Fassung des Art. 29 II 1 gedeckt sei; die Wirkung der Klausel sei eine Sache ihrer Auslegung.
[93] Strenger *Geldsetzer*, S. 152 f.: Eine Differenzierung nach Formzwecken, insbesondere zwischen konstitutiven und deklaratorischen Formklauseln, verbiete sich im Anwendungsbereich des CISG; dagegen umfassend (rechtsvergleichend mit dem UCC) *Breitling*, S. 50, 52.
[94] OLG Hamm, 30.11.2010, CISG-online 2217 = RdL 2011, 129; *Achilles*, Art. 29, Rn. 8; MünchKomm/*Gruber*, Art. 29, Rn. 11; MünchKommHGB/*Benicke*, Art. 29, Rn. 6.
[95] Vgl. BGH, 2.6.1976, BGHZ 66, 378, 380 f.; BGH, 20.10.1994, NJW-RR 1995, 179, 180; *Teske*, S. 61 ff.; rechtsvergleichende Nachweise bei *Dölle/Reinhart*, Art. 15 EKG, Rn. 68 ff.; zum Einfluss des amerikanischen Rechts auf Art. 29 II 1s. *Geldsetzer*, S. 148 ff.
[96] *Honsell/Gsell*, Art. 29, Rn. 22; MünchKomm/*Gruber*, Art. 29, Rn. 8. Ein Antrag Italiens, der im Ergebnis auf Übernahme des deutschen Rechtszustands gerichtet war, ist auf der Wiener Konferenz der Ablehnung verfallen (A/Conf. 97/C. 1/L. 68) O. R., S. 101; dazu (A/Conf. 97/C. 1/SR. 13) O. R., S. 305, Nr. 56. S. jedoch zu Art. 29 II 2 unten Rn. 23 ff.
[97] Offen gelassen zum internen deutschen Recht in BGH, 17.4.1991, WM 1991, 1398, 1399.
[98] *Ferrari u. a./Ferrari*, Internationales Vertragsrecht, Art. 29, Rn. 10; *Honsell/Gsell*, Art. 29, Rn. 22; *Schlechtriem*, FS Kritzer, S. 424; vgl. auch *Wey*, Rn. 437: diese „probatio diabolica" bleibe möglich, sei aber Ausnahme. Anders (nur schriftliche Abbedingung) aber viele: MünchKomm/*Gruber*, Art. 29, Rn. 8; MünchKommHGB/*Benicke*, Art. 29, Rn. 4; *Perales Viscasillas*, 25 J. L. & Com. (2005-06), 167, 179; *Wagner-von Papp*, 63 CLP (2010), 511, 538 Fn. 84.
[99] People's Supreme Court, Appeal Division in Ho Chi Minh City, 5.4.1996, CISG-online 1081: vietnamesisch-singapurianischer Kaufvertrag enthielt „four corner clause" – aus diesem Grund wurde konkludente Änderung des im Vertrag vereinbarten Liefertermins durch Übersendung eines geänderten Akkreditivs für ausgeschlossen gehalten; *Achilles*, Art. 29, Rn. 3; *Brunner*, Art. 29, Rn. 2; *Honsell/Gsell*, Art. 29, Rn. 8; *Schlechtriem*, FS Kritzer, S. 422; *Schwenzer/Mohs*, IHR 2006, 239, 245; *Wey*, Rn. 435, 436; ferner oben *Schmidt-Kessel*, Art. 11 Rn. 16.
[100] So in *TeeVee Toons, Inc. & Steve Gottlieb, Inc. v. Gerhard Schubert GmbH*, U. S. Dist. Ct. (S. D. N. Y.), 23.8.2006, CISG-online 1272.

normen – Kontrolle missbräuchlicher Klauseln, AGB-Kontrolle – unzulässig sind.[101] Das Ergebnis folgt nicht nur aus einer sinngemäßen Anwendung des Art. 29 II 1,[102] sondern vor allem aus der Parteiautonomie. **Bestätigungsvorbehalte** können zunächst auf die (fehlende) Vertretungsmacht von Mitarbeitern bezogen sein und sind insoweit nach nationalem Recht zu prüfen, Art. 4 S. 2 lit. a).[103] Ein Bestätigungsvorbehalt kann aber auch als Schriftformklausel zu verstehen sein und ist dann nach Artt. 6, 29 II 1 zu beurteilen: Nicht nur hängt die Wirksamkeit des Vertrages von der durch schriftliche Bestätigung zu erfüllenden Schriftform ab, sondern auch Änderungen usw. müssen dann schriftlich bestätigt werden. Klauselkontrolle nach nationalem Recht über Art. 4 S. 2 lit. a) bleibt möglich.[104]

Art. 29 II 1 hat zudem nicht nur für den einzelnen Kaufvertrag Bedeutung, sondern auch 18 für **Rahmenvereinbarungen** zu künftigen Kaufverträgen, die so formbedürftig gemacht und gehalten werden.[105]

4. Bedeutung von „Schriftform"

Vertragliche Schriftformabreden legen in der Praxis nicht selten genau fest, welche 19 Formanforderungen allfällige Vertragsänderungen zu erfüllen haben,[106] können aber auch lediglich „Schriftform" vorschreiben. Angesichts der unterschiedlichen Bedeutung des Wortes „Schriftform" in den verschiedenen Rechtsordnungen – eigenhändige Unterschrift kann z. B. entbehrlich sein – hat für Schriftformklauseln, die von einer Seite eingeführt worden sind, Art. 13 erhebliche Bedeutung:[107] Soweit eine Partei mit dem Gebrauch dieses Wortes eine strengere Form als Art. 13 verlangen wollte, etwa, weil sie am eigenen Recht orientiert war, ist sie beweispflichtig, dass ihre Erklärung nach Art. 8 eine Abweichung von Art. 13 in den Formerfordernissen bedeuten sollte und mit diesem Inhalt von der anderen Partei akzeptiert worden ist.[108] Vereinbaren die Parteien ohne weitere Qualifikation **Schriftform,** dann genügen für Änderung oder Aufhebung wie auch für Ergänzungen **Telex, Telegramm** und **Telefax,** aber m. E. auch mit elektronischen Kommunikationsmitteln getroffene Vereinbarungen.[109] In diesem Zusammenhang wird vertreten, dass eine vertraglich vereinbarte Schriftform nach Art. 29 II 1 i. V. m. Art. 13 auch durch eine einseitig (etwa durch Telefax oder Telegramm) festgehaltene Änderungs- oder Aufhebungsvereinbarung gewahrt werde[110] – dies erscheint zweifelhaft, weil eine schriftliche „Vereinbarung" eben zwei Erklärungen voraussetzt, die folglich beide in Schriftform abgegeben werden müssen. Da Art. 13 nach Art. 6 abdingbar ist, können die Parteien aber auch strengere Formvoraussetzungen vereinbaren,[111] wobei es eine Auslegungsfrage ist, ob die

---

[101] Vgl. zum unvereinheitlichten deutschen Recht BGH, 28.1.1981, BGHZ 79, 281, 287; BGH, 26.11.1984, BGHZ 93, 29: entsprechen nur der ohnehin bestehenden Vollständigkeitsvermutung bei schriftlichen Vertragsurkunden, deshalb zulässig.
[102] So aber *Honsell/Gsell,* Art. 29, Rn. 8.
[103] *Honsell/Gsell,* Art. 29, Rn. 18; MünchKommHGB/*Benicke,* Art. 29, Rn. 8. Weitergehend *Geldsetzer,* S. 167 f., die alle Bestätigungsklauseln unter Art. 29 II fallen lassen will. Nationale Rechtsregeln zur Kontrolle solcher Bestätigungsvorbehalte wären dann jedenfalls über Art. 4 S. 2 lit. a) zu beachten, s. oben Vor Artt. 14–24 Rn. 2.
[104] S. zum deutschen Recht BGH, 2.6.1976, BGHZ 66, 378, 382 ff.
[105] *Wey,* Rn. 423: analoge Anwendung.
[106] Vgl. etwa *Graves Import Co. Ltd. et al v. Chilewich Int'l Corp.* U. S. Dist. Ct. (S. D. N. Y.), 22.9.1994, CISG-online 128: „No amendments and additions to the present contract shall be valid unless the same are in writing and signed by duly authorized representatives of both parties"; eine ganz ähnliche Klausel betraf Int. Ct. Ukrainian CCI, 25.11.2002, CISG-online 1267 (dort aber mit der zusätzlichen Bestimmung, dass auch Erklärungen per Telefax ausreichen); OLG Innsbruck, 18.12.2007, CISG-online 1735: schriftliche Bestätigung beider Vertragsparteien notwendig.
[107] OLG Innsbruck, 18.12.2007, CISG-online 1735; KG Zug, 14.12.2009, CISG-online 2026; *Schroeter,* 6 VJ (2002), 267, 269.
[108] MünchKommHGB/*Benicke,* Art. 29, Rn. 7.
[109] *Brunner,* Art. 29, Rn. 2; *Schroeter,* Art. 13 CISG-PECL, S. 293 m. w. N.; *ders.,* 6 VJ (2002), 267, 269.
[110] So OLG Innsbruck, 18.12.2007, CISG-online 1735.
[111] S. *Enderlein/Maskow/Strohbach,* Art. 29, Anm. 3.2.; *Honsell/Gsell,* Art. 29, Rn. 20; *Perales Viscasillas,* 25 J. L. & Com. (2005-06), 167, 176: Unterschrift oder Zeugen.

vereinbarte (strengere) Form auf Grund des Art. 29 II 1 auch für Modifikationen gilt;[112] nach dem Art. 29 II 1 zugrunde liegenden Gedanken, den Parteien den selbstgewählten „Formschutz" zu erhalten, wird ein solcher Parteiwille im Zweifel anzunehmen sein.[113]

5. Vereinbarung

20 Die „Bestimmung" i. S. d. Art. 29 II 1 setzt **Konsens** voraus;[114] einseitige Schriftformvorbehalte, die nicht durch Zustimmung Vertragsinhalt geworden sind, bleiben unbeachtlich.[115] Die „Bestimmung" muss, wenn auch nicht ausdrücklich, so doch deutlich sein; die Verwendung der Schriftform durch den Offerenten allein führt, falls der andere Teil das Vertragsangebot mündlich oder auch schriftlich annimmt, noch nicht zu einer Schriftformabrede i. S. d. Art. 29 II 1.[116]

6. Schriftlichkeit der Schriftformabrede

21 Die Formulierung des Art. 29 II 1 verdeutlicht, dass die **Schriftformabrede,** um die erweiterte Bindungswirkung zu haben, selbst **schriftlich** abgefasst sein muss.[117] Obgleich der Wortlaut der Vorschrift sich nur auf schriftliche Verträge bezieht, ist sie entsprechend auf mündlich abgeschlossene Kaufverträge anzuwenden, sofern jedenfalls die Schriftformabrede schriftlich getroffen wurde.[118] Eine mündliche Formabrede ist zwar möglich und wirksam, aber auch formlos aufhebbar.[119]

22 **Schriftlichkeit** der **Schriftformabrede** muss durch mindestens Art. 13 genügende Erklärungen beider Seiten bewirkt werden. Im Übrigen dürfte der durch Auslegung nach Art. 8 festzustellende Parteiwille über die Voraussetzungen der Schriftlichkeit dieser Klausel zu entscheiden haben, der aus den selbstgesetzten Anforderungen für Modifikationen, hilfsweise aus dem Umweltrecht der Parteien – bei Niederlassung in der Bundesrepublik Deutschland also aus §§ 127, 126 BGB – zu schließen ist.[120] Unterschreibt bei Verwendung vorformulierter Geschäftsbedingungen, die eine Schriftformabrede enthalten, nur der Vertragspartner des Verwenders, dann ist im Zweifel Schriftform für Änderungen usw. nicht wirksam vereinbart, vgl. § 126 II 1 BGB.

III. Missbrauchseinwand (Abs. II 2)

1. Voraussetzungen

23 Als Kompromiss zwischen Grundregel – Art. 29 II 1 – und dem Bedürfnis, doch entsprechend der deutschen Rechtsprechung mündlichen Abreden zur Änderung des Vertrages nicht jegliche Wirkung zu versagen, ist der **Missbrauchseinwand**[121] bereits im E 1978

---

[112] Weitergehend *Honnold/Flechtner*, Art. 29, Rn. 202 Fn. 5: Art. 29 II 1 gelte „a fortiori" für strengere Formabreden; MünchKommHGB/*Benicke*, Art. 29, Rn. 7; ähnlich *Wey*, Rn. 443, der in solchen Fällen mit Art. 29 II 2 (großzügig) helfen will.
[113] S. dagegen *Geldsetzer*, S. 167 f.
[114] *TeeVee Toons, Inc. & Steve Gottlieb, Inc. v. Gerhard Schubert GmbH*, U. S. Dist. Ct. (S. D. N. Y.), 23.8.2006, CISG-online 1272.
[115] KG Zug, 14.12.2009, CISG-online 2026; *Wey*, Rn. 424 f., 427.
[116] KG Zug, 14.12.2009, CISG-online 2026; *Brunner*, Art. 29, Rn. 2; MünchKommHGB/*Benicke*, Art. 29, Rn. 5; *Wey*, Rn. 425, 427.
[117] *Ferrari u. a./Ferrari*, Internationales Vertragsrecht, Art. 29, Rn. 9; *Honsell/Gsell*, Art. 29, Rn. 17; MünchKommHGB/*Benicke*, Art. 29, Rn. 5; *Staudinger/Magnus*, Art. 29, Rn. 12; zweifelnd *Kröll u. a./Björklund*, Art. 29, Rn. 19.
[118] *Honsell/Gsell*, Art. 29, Rn. 17; MünchKomm/*Gruber*, Art. 29, Rn. 7. In der Praxis dürften so gelagerte Fälle allerdings selten auftreten.
[119] *Brunner*, Art. 29, Rn. 2; *Ferrari u. a./Ferrari*, Internationales Vertragsrecht, Art. 29, Rn. 9; *Honsell/Gsell*, Art. 29, Rn. 23; MünchKomm/*Gruber*, Art. 29, Rn. 7; *Wey*, Rn. 429.
[120] S. oben *Schmidt-Kessel*, Art. 11 Rn. 16.
[121] S. *Achilles*, Art. 29, Rn. 6, 7; *Bamberger/Roth/Saenger*, Art. 29, Rn. 4; *Brunner*, Art. 29, Rn. 3; *Enderlein/Maskow/Strohbach*, Art. 29, Anm. 5.1.; *Wey*, Rn. 444; *Witz/Salger/Lorenz/Salger*, Art. 29, Rn. 16: Fall des „venire contra factum proprium".

Vertragsänderung oder -aufhebung   24, 25 **Art. 29**

vorgesehen worden. Er ist erheblich durch die Institute „waiver" und „estoppel" beeinflusst worden.¹²² Zur Begründung eines Missbrauchseinwands nach Art. 29 II 2 muss ein Vertragsänderung zugrunde legendes oder zum Ausdruck bringendes Verhalten einer Seite zu einem entsprechenden „Sich-Verlassen", also ein **Verhalten** einer Seite zu einem dadurch veranlassten **Vertrauen** der anderen Seite geführt haben.¹²³

a) **Vertrauen erzeugendes Verhalten.** Das Vertrauen darauf, dass die Schriftformabrede **24** nicht angewandt werde, muss durch das Verhalten derjenigen Vertragspartei hervorgerufen worden sein, die sich nunmehr auf die mangelnde Einhaltung der vereinbarten Form beruft und der daher der Missbrauchseinwand des Art. 29 II 2 entgegengehalten wird. Welche Anforderungen an das Vertrauen erzeugende **Verhalten** i. S. d. Art. 29 II 2 zu stellen sind, wird nicht einheitlich beurteilt. Teilweise wird davon ausgegangen, dass bereits in der formlosen Erklärung der bzw. Zustimmung zur Vertragsänderung selbst ein hinreichendes vertrauenbegründendes Verhalten liegen kann,¹²⁴ während die Gegenauffassung über eine bloße Erklärung hinausgehende vertrauensbegründende Verhaltensweisen verlangt,¹²⁵ die etwa in der Bezugnahme auf die formlose Vereinbarung in Schriftwechseln oder weiteren Verhandlungen,¹²⁶ einer widerspruchslosen Leistungserbringung¹²⁷ oder der Warenannahme in Übereinstimmung mit der Änderung¹²⁸ liegen können.

Zustimmung verdient die erstgenannte Ansicht, für die der Wortlaut des Art. 29 II 2 **25** spricht, denn nach dem in Artt. 8 I, II, 18 I 1 zum Ausdruck kommenden Sprachgebrauch des Übereinkommens werden auch Erklärungen der Parteien als Form ihres „Verhaltens" bezeichnet¹²⁹ und sollten daher auch für die Zwecke des Art. 29 II 2 ausreichen können. Das betreffende Parteiverhalten muss jedoch unabhängig davon, ob es als **Erklärung oder sonstige Handlung** hervortritt, aus Perspektive einer vernünftigen Person der gleichen Art wie die andere Partei unter den gleichen Umständen (Art. 8 II) gerade dahingehend zu verstehen sein, dass man sich nicht auf die Schriftformvereinbarung berufen werde, und damit auf die **Formwirksamkeit gerichtetes Vertrauen** erzeugen können, dessen Schutz der Missbrauchseinwand des Art. 29 II 2 dient. Ein solcher, im Streitfall zu beweisender Aussagegehalt¹³⁰ wird etwa dann vorliegen, wenn bei der mündlichen Erörterung von Vertragsmodifikationen erklärt wird, die Gegenseite „brauche sich nicht um die Schriftformklausel zu kümmern" o. ä., dagegen nicht ohne weiteres, wenn sich die Vertragspar-

---

¹²² S. *Geldsetzer*, S. 148 f.; ferner *Heuzé*, Anm. 202., zum amerikanischen und englischen Recht s. *Kritzer*, Guide to Practical Applications, S. 235; *Honnold/Flechtner*, Art. 29, Rn. 204 Fn. 8: Es gehe entsprechend § 2-209 (4) und (5) UCC um „waiver – the voluntary relinquishment of a known right"; die Vorschrift sei vergleichbar der englischen Doktrin von „promissory estoppel".

¹²³ *Enderlein/Maskow/Strohbach*, Art. 29, Anm. 6.1.; *Staudinger/Magnus*, Art. 29, Rn. 17, 18; *Wey*, Rn. 440: „tätiger Verlass"; krit. *Hillman*, 21 Cornell Int'l L. J. (1998), 449, 460; *Heuzé*, Anm. 202.: weites Beurteilungsermessen für die Richter, das die Bedeutung von Schriftformklauseln schwäche (un texte extrêmement dangereux); *Witz/Salger/Lorenz/Salger*, Art. 29, Rn. 10.

¹²⁴ OLG Hamm, 30.11.2010, CISG-online 2217 = RdL 2011, 129; *Bamberger/Roth/Saenger*, Art. 29, Rn. 4; *Bianca/Bonell/Date-Bah*, Art. 29, Anm. 2.5.; *Honnold/Flechtner*, Art. 29, Rn. 204; *Honsell/Gsell*, Art. 29, Rn. 24; *MünchKomm/Gruber*, Art. 29, Rn. 13; *Perales Viscasillas*, 25 J. L. & Com. (2005-06), 167, 178; s. a. *Wey*, Rn. 453 ff., 456: „Rechtsgeschäftsähnliche Willensäußerung" bzw. „deklaratorisch wirkende Vorstellungs- und Willensmitteilung" sei erforderlich.

¹²⁵ *Breitling*, S. 200; *Enderlein/Maskow/Strohbach*, Art. 29, Anm. 4.; *Ferrari u. a./Ferrari*, Internationales Vertragsrecht, Art. 29, Rn. 13; *Keller*, FS Kritzer, S. 251; *Reinhart*, Art. 29, Rn. 5; *Witz/Salger/Lorenz/Salger*, Art. 29, Rn. 16; wohl auch *Brunner*, Art. 29, Rn. 3; differenzierend MünchKommHGB/*Benicke*, Art. 29, Rn. 11: sofern die Initiative zur Vertragsänderung von derjenigen Partei ausgegangen sei, die sich auf Art. 29 II 2 beruft, sei erforderlich, dass die andere Partei einen über die bloße Zustimmung hinausgehenden Vertrauenstatbestand begründet hat.

¹²⁶ *Enderlein/Maskow/Strohbach*, Art. 29, Anm. 4.; *Witz/Salger/Lorenz/Salger*, Art. 29, Rn. 16.

¹²⁷ *Brunner*, Art. 29, Rn. 3; *Witz/Salger/Lorenz/Salger*, Art. 29, Rn. 16.

¹²⁸ *Brunner*, Art. 29, Rn. 3; *Enderlein/Maskow/Strohbach*, Art. 29, Anm. 4.

¹²⁹ Ohne Grund zweifelnd daher *Murray*, 8 J. L. & Com. (1988), 11, 50, der diese Auslegung aber jedenfalls durch den Willen der Übereinkommensverfasser gestützt sieht; a. A. *Keller*, FS Kritzer, S. 251: „Verhalten" sei wie „Zustimmung durch Vornahme einer Handlung" i. S. d. Art. 18 III zu verstehen. Wie hier *Honsell/Gsell*, Art. 29, Rn. 24.

¹³⁰ Zur Beweislast s. unten Rn. 33.

Art. 29 26, 27   Teil III. Kapitel I. Allgemeine Bestimmungen

teien des vertraglichen Formerfordernisses während der Änderungsverhandlungen schlicht nicht bewusst waren.[131] In letzterem Fall liegt ausreichendes Verhalten erst in der Annahme der geänderten Ware, weil dadurch ausgedrückt wird, sie entspreche den (aktuellen) vertraglichen Abmachungen.

26 Vertrauen erzeugendes Verhalten setzt dabei nach der hier vertretenen Ansicht nicht notwendig eine – abgesehen vom Schriftformerfordernis – gültige Vereinbarung voraus:[132] Hat eine Seite einem nicht vertretungsberechtigten Mitarbeiter erlaubt, vertragsmodifizierende Erklärungen abzugeben oder zu akzeptieren, so müssen m. E. nicht nationale Vorschriften zur Anscheins- oder Duldungsvollmacht bemüht werden, sondern es entscheidet die Würdigung des Verhaltens dieser Vertragspartei und seiner vertrauenerzeugenden Wirkung. Insoweit kann der Missbrauchseinwand auch in Fällen greifen, in denen nach deutschem Recht eine Vertragsänderung nicht oder nur aufwändiger konstruiert werden könnte.

27 **b) Durch das Verhalten der Gegenseite hervorgerufenes Vertrauen („tätiger Verlass").** Dass sich die andere Partei auf das Verhalten ihres Vertragspartners „verlassen", also darauf **vertraut** hat, muss sich in erkennbaren Maßnahmen auf ihrer Seite **manifestiert** haben[133] („tätiger Verlass"[134]); lediglich passives Vertrauen wird durch Art. 29 II 2 nicht geschützt.[135] Der Sekretariatskommentar nennt beispielhaft die teilweise widerspruchslose Erfüllung entsprechend einer mündlichen Änderung.[136] Im Schrifttum zu Art. 29 II 2 werden als **Beispiele** für manifestiertes Vertrauen die Aufnahme der Produktion einer verkauften Ware zu (mündlich) veränderten Spezifikationen,[137] deren Vorbereitung[138] bzw. die Erbringung von Aufwendungen hierfür,[139] die Vornahme eines Deckungsgeschäfts,[140] die Umstellung der finanziellen Planung im Vertrauen auf eine Stundungs- oder Teilzahlungsvereinbarung,[141] die Nichtlieferung zum ursprünglich vorgesehenen Liefertermin,[142] die Abwicklung des Vertrages, ein einseitiges Änderungsverlangen einer Seite, dem stattgegeben wurde und das diese Partei dann nicht gelten lassen will, gezogene Vorteile aus der Änderung, Täuschung über Formbedürftigkeit der Änderung sowie eine besonders schwerwiegende Vertrauensbetätigung, etwa in Form erheblicher Aufwendungen des Vertrauenden[143] benannt. Die Rechtsprechung hat nach mündlicher Zusage einer bestimmten Warenqualität die Ablehnung anderer Vertragsangebote sowie das Unterlassen einer ursprünglich beabsichtigten Untersuchung der Ware durch einen fachkundigen Dritten als hinreichenden tätigen Verlass des Käufers eingeordnet.[144] Ein Nachteil des Vertrauenden ist allerdings trotz dahingehender Vorschläge während der Beratungen des Art. 29 II 2[145] bewusst nicht als Voraussetzung normiert worden; er darf deshalb auch nicht stets verlangt werden.[146] Den

---

[131] A. A. *Honsell/Gsell*, Art. 29, Rn. 24.
[132] *Honnold/Flechtner*, Art. 29, Rn. 204; wohl auch wie hier *Staudinger/Magnus*, Art. 29, Rn. 18, 19; a. A. *Enderlein/Maskow/Strohbach*, Art. 29, Anm. 4.; *Honsell/Gsell*, Art. 29, Rn. 25; MünchKommHGB/*Benicke*, Art. 29, Rn. 10.
[133] OLG Hamm, 30.11.2010, CISG-online 2217 = RdL 2011, 129; *Bianca/Bonell/Date-Bah*, Art. 29, Anm. 2.6.: „an important condition"; *Honsell/Gsell*, Art. 29, Rn. 26; MünchKomm/*Gruber*, Art. 29, Rn. 14.
[134] So treffend *Wey*, Rn. 440.
[135] *Bamberger/Roth/Saenger*, Art. 29, Rn. 4; *Herber/Czerwenka*, Art. 29, Rn. 7.
[136] S. Sekretariatskommentar, Art. 27, Nr. 9, Bsp. 27 A.
[137] *Honnold/Flechtner*, Art. 29, Rn. 204; ebenso *Bamberger/Roth/Saenger*, Art. 29, Rn. 4; *Brunner*, Art. 29, Rn. 3; MünchKomm/*Gruber*, Art. 29, Rn. 14; MünchKommHGB/*Benicke*, Art. 29, Rn. 11; *Schwenzer/Mohs*, IHR 2006, 239, 246; *Staudinger/Magnus*, Art. 29, Rn. 19.
[138] *Enderlein/Maskow/Strohbach*, Art. 29, Anm. 6.1.
[139] MünchKomm/*Gruber*, Art. 29, Rn. 14 (für „erhebliche" Aufwendungen).
[140] *Bamberger/Roth/Saenger*, Art. 29, Rn. 4; *Honsell/Gsell*, Art. 29, Rn. 26.
[141] *Ferrari u. a./Ferrari*, Internationales Vertragsrecht, Art. 29, Rn. 14; *Honsell/Gsell*, Art. 29, Rn. 26.
[142] *Honnold/Flechtner*, Art. 29, Rn. 204; *Honsell/Gsell*, Art. 29, Rn. 26.
[143] *Geldsetzer*, S. 160 f. aufgrund einer Auswertung des amerikanischen Rechts.
[144] OLG Hamm, 30.11.2010, CISG-online 2217 = RdL 2011, 129 (*in casu* nicht hinreichend dargelegt).
[145] So im Vorentwurf 3A der Arbeitsgruppe, s. *Geldsetzer*, S. 164.
[146] *Honsell/Gsell*, Art. 29, Rn. 26; a. A. MünchKommHGB/*Benicke*, Art. 29, Rn. 12.

bloßen Verzicht auf u. U. befristete Rechtsbehelfe wird man hingegen kaum ausreichen lassen können.[147]

Das gefasste Vertrauen in die Geltung einer mündlichen Änderung muss unter den konkreten Umständen **vernünftig** gewesen sein, wie die Auslegung des Art. 29 II 2 im Lichte von Treu und Glauben (Art. 7 I) ergibt.[148] Es kann zudem durch eine schlichte **Mitteilung**, dass man doch am ursprünglichen Vertrag festhalte, ex nunc **zerstört** werden,[149] so dass insoweit die Wirkungen des Art. 29 II 2 hinter einer echten formlosen Vertragsänderung, die nicht einseitig widerrufbar wäre, zurückbleiben. Im Ganzen dürfte eine flexible, den Umständen des Einzelfalles gerecht werdende Handhabung den Gerichten nicht unerhebliche Bewertungsspielräume belassen.[150]

c) **Vertragliche Abdingbarkeit des Art. 29 II 2.** Fraglich ist, ob eine Schriftformklausel dadurch verstärkt werden kann, dass auch der Missbrauchseinwand, also Art. 29 II 2, ausgeschlossen wird. Ein solcher Versuch einer Verstärkung der Schriftformklausel in Allgemeinen Geschäftsbedingungen würde, falls deutsches Recht als Vertragsstatut über Gültigkeitsfragen herrscht, nach § 307 BGB unzulässig sein.[151] Nur wo eine solche Schriftformklausel unter gleich starken Parteien ausgehandelt und eindeutig vereinbart worden ist, dürfte sie eine nach Art. 6 zulässige Abweichung von Art. 29 II 2 darstellen.[152]

2. Nationale Formvorschriften und Missbrauchseinwand

Von **Formvorschriften nationaler Rechte,** die auf Grund der Artt. 96, 12 berufen sind, kann nicht abgewichen werden. (Auch) der Missbrauchseinwand wird in Art. 12 ausgeschlossen.[153] Eine in einem Vertrag mit einem Partner aus einem Vorbehaltsstaat vereinbarte Form kann jedoch nicht nur bekräftigende Bedeutung haben, sondern im Falle der Verweisung auf ein anderes Recht als das des Vorbehaltsstaates, das seinerseits von Formfreiheit ausgeht, Gültigkeitsvoraussetzung sein.[154] Abweichung und „Heilung" an sich unwirksamer Abweichung sind dann nach Art. 29 II 2 zu beurteilen.[155]

3. Rechtsfolge und Reichweite; Berücksichtigung von Amts wegen

Sind die Voraussetzungen des Art. 29 II 2 erfüllt, so wird die formunwirksame Vertragsänderung dadurch nicht wirksam;[156] der Partei, die durch ihr Verhalten bei der anderen Partei Vertrauen in die Wirksamkeit der Änderungsvereinbarung erzeugt hat, wird lediglich das Berufen auf die Schriftformklausel verwehrt. Durch das Wort „soweit" werden die Wirkungen des Missbrauchseinwands zudem auf das zum Vertrauensschutz für die andere Seite Erforderliche beschränkt:[157] Nur soweit Leistungen oder Leistungsvorbereitungen nicht mehr ohne Schaden rückgängig gemacht werden können, ist die Berufung auf die

---

[147] A. A. *Honsell/Gsell*, Art. 29, Rn. 26; MünchKomm/*Gruber*, Art. 29, Rn. 14.
[148] *Eiselen*, Modification, S. 166; *Kröll u. a./Björklund*, Art. 29, Rn. 23; ebenfalls wie hier, wenngleich in der Begründung anders *Enderlein/Maskow/Strohbach*, Art. 29, Anm. 6.1. (Analogie zu Art. 16 II lit. b)); *Honsell/Gsell*, Art. 29, Rn. 27 (allgemeiner Grundsatz nach Art. 7 II).
[149] *Honsell/Gsell*, Art. 29, Rn. 29; MünchKomm/*Gruber*, Art. 29, Rn. 14; *Schwimann/Posch*, Art. 29, Rn. 7.
[150] S. *Bianca/Bonell/Date-Bah*, Art. 29, Anm. 3.1., mit der Sorge vor Unsicherheiten; ebenso *Heuzé*, Anm. 202.; ferner zur „Verantwortlichkeitsfrage", die nach Ansicht des Autors nicht ausreichend berücksichtigt worden ist, *Wey*, Rn. 450. *Hillman*, 21 Cornell Int'l L.J. (1998), 449, 463 rät der Praxis, deshalb auf Klauseln zu verzichten, die mündliche Modifikationen ausschließen sollen.
[151] S. *Ferrari u. a./Ferrari*, Internationales Vertragsrecht, Art. 29, Rn. 15a; *Witz/Salger/Lorenz/Salger*, Art. 29, Rn. 21.
[152] Grundsätzlich gegen Abdingbarkeit *Brunner*, Art. 29, Rn. 3; *Geldsetzer*, S. 156; *Hillman*, 21 Cornell Int'l L.J. (1998), 449, 463; *Honsell/Gsell*, Art. 29, Rn. 32; *Kröll u. a./Björklund*, Art. 29, Rn. 23; MünchKomm/*Gruber*, Art. 29, Rn. 15; MünchKommHGB/*Benicke*, Art. 29, Rn. 9.
[153] *Kröll u. a./Björklund*, Art. 29, Rn. 25.
[154] Vgl. zu diesen Konstellationen oben *Schmidt-Kessel*, Art. 12 Rn. 2, 3.
[155] *Enderlein/Maskow/Strohbach*, Art. 29, Anm. 5.2.: „... durchaus erwägenswert".
[156] *Honsell/Gsell*, Art. 29, Rn. 28; MünchKommHGB/*Benicke*, Art. 29, Rn. 12; a. A. MünchKomm/*Gruber*, Art. 29, Rn. 13.
[157] MünchKomm/*Gruber*, Art. 29, Rn. 16; *Wey*, Rn. 451: Es kann Vertrags- bzw. Klauselspaltung eintreten.

Unwirksamkeit der Vertragsänderung, auf der diese Leistung oder Leistungsvorbereitung beruhen, zu versagen. Soweit allerdings auch die Gegenleistung angepasst worden ist, muss auch diese Änderung wirksam bleiben.[158] Missbrauch einer Berufung auf die Formabrede sollte **von Amts wegen zu berücksichtigen** sein.[159]

4. Konkurrenz nationaler Rechtsbehelfe

32   Das als Missbrauch nach Art. 29 II 2 zu würdigende Verhalten kann in den nationalen Rechten **andere Rechtsbehelfe** als partielle „Heilung" einer formlosen Vertragsänderung auslösen, etwa Schadenersatzansprüche aus cic, allgemeiner Vertrauenshaftung oder Delikt. Einheitskaufrecht, d. h. die Regelung des Art. 29 II 2, sollte im Interesse der Bewahrung der erreichten Rechtsvereinheitlichung Vorrang haben; Stütze ist Art. 7 I und, da die Konkurrenzfragen nicht ausdrücklich entschieden worden sind, Art. 7 II. Wo „Heilung" nach Art. 29 II 2 ausscheidet, weil es an den dafür erforderlichen Voraussetzungen fehlt, sollten deshalb Schadenersatzansprüche nach nationalem Recht, etwa gestützt auf ein verschuldetes Unterlassen genauer Aufklärung über Formerfordernisse bei den Änderungsverhandlungen, nicht möglich bleiben.[160] Nur Arglist fällt aus dem abschließenden Regelungsbereich des CISG heraus, so dass Ansprüche aus § 826 BGB – bei Maßgeblichkeit deutschen Rechts als Deliktsstatut – gegeben sein können.[161]

IV. Beweislast

33   Die behauptete Änderung, Aufhebung oder Ergänzung des Vertrages hat die Partei zu beweisen, die sich darauf beruft;[162] Mängel der Vereinbarung stehen zur Beweislast dessen, der sie geltend macht. Eine Schriftformklausel hat zu beweisen, wer Unwirksamkeit formfreier Änderungen behauptet;[163] die Voraussetzungen des Missbrauchseinwands nach Art. 29 II 2 hat zu beweisen, wer Vertrauensschutz in Anspruch nimmt.[164]

---

[158] *Wey*, Rn. 452.
[159] *Brunner*, Art. 29, Rn. 3; *Ferrari u. a./Ferrari*, Internationales Vertragsrecht, Art. 29, Rn. 15. Irreführend deshalb der Sprachgebrauch „Einrede", „Missbrauchseinrede" usw. von *Wey*, Rn. 444 ff.
[160] Wie hier *Ferrari u. a./Ferrari*, Internationales Vertragsrecht, Art. 29, Rn. 16; *Honsell/Gsell*, Art. 29, Rn. 31; *MünchKomm/Gruber*, Art. 29, Rn. 17; *Staudinger/Magnus*, Art. 29, Rn. 21; *Geldsetzer*, S. 170 f.; weitergehend, weil im Prinzip bejahend, *Wey*, Rn. 445: Culpa-Ansprüche und irrtumsrechtliche Mittel sollten jedoch nur zurückhaltend angewendet werden. S. auch oben Vor Artt. 1, 34 ff.
[161] S. oben Vor Artt. 14–24 Rn. 36.
[162] AG Sursee, 12.9.2008, CISG-online 1728 = IHR 2009, 63, 64; *MünchKommHGB/Benicke*, Art. 29, Rn. 14.
[163] *Baumgärtel/Laumen/Hepting*, Art. 29 WKR, Rn. 2.
[164] *Achilles*, Art. 29, Rn. 8; *Bamberger/Roth/Saenger*, Art. 29, Rn. 7; *Baumgärtel/Laumen/Hepting*, Art. 27 WKR, Rn. 3; *Honsell/Gsell*, Art. 29, Rn. 33; *Staudinger/Magnus*, Art. 29, Rn. 23, 24.

Kapitel II. Pflichten des Verkäufers

Chapter II
Obligations of the seller

Chapitre II
Obligations du vendeur

Art. 30 [Pflichten des Verkäufers]

Der Verkäufer ist nach Maßgabe des Vertrages und dieses Übereinkommens verpflichtet, die Ware zu liefern, die sie betreffenden Dokumente zu übergeben und das Eigentum an der Ware zu übertragen.

Art. 30
The seller must deliver the goods, hand over any documents relating to them and transfer the property in the goods, as required by the contract and this Convention.

Art. 30
Le vendeur s'oblige, dans les conditions prévues au contrat et par la présente Convention, à livrer les marchandises, à en transférer la propriété et, s'il y a lieu, à remettre les documents s'y rapportant.

Übersicht

	Rn.
I. Gegenstand und Zweck der Bestimmung	1
II. Lieferung	2
1. Begriff und Inhalt der Lieferpflicht	2
2. Incoterms®	3
3. Sachen im Besitz des Käufers	5
III. Übergabe der Dokumente	6
IV. Verschaffung des Eigentums	7
1. Übereignung	7
2. Eigentumsvorbehalt	8
V. Sonstige Pflichten des Verkäufers	9

Vorläufer und **Entwürfe:** EKG Art. 18; Genfer E 1976 Art. 14; Wiener E 1977 Art. 14; New Yorker E 1978 Art. 28.

I. Gegenstand und Zweck der Bestimmung

Art. 30 legt die hauptsächlichen Pflichten des Verkäufers fest, die in Abschnitt I des zweiten Kapitels des Übereinkommens (Artt. 31–34) konkretisiert werden.[1] Er verdeutlicht, dass für den Umfang und Inhalt dieser Pflichten in erster Linie der Inhalt des Vertrags massgeblich ist.[2] Nur soweit der Vertrag keine besonderen Bestimmungen enthält, gelten die Bestimmungen des Übereinkommens. Die entsprechende Vorschrift über die Pflichten des Käufers enthält Art. 53. 1

II. Lieferung

1. Begriff und Inhalt der Lieferpflicht

In Übereinstimmung mit der Regelung in nationalen Rechtsordnungen[3] besteht die zentrale Pflicht des Verkäufers nach dem Übereinkommen in der „Lieferung der Ware."[4] 2

---

[1] Die Übertragung des Eigentums als solche ist im Übereinkommen allerdings nicht geregelt; siehe unten Rn. 7; vgl. auch *Kröll u. a./Piltz*, Art. 30, Rn. 6.

[2] So wohl auch *Honsell/Ernst/Lauko*, Art. 30, Rn. 5. Der Vorrang der Parteivereinbarung ergibt sich bereits aus Art. 6; vgl. auch *Staudinger/Magnus*, Art. 30, Rn. 1; *Brunner*, Art. 30, Rn. 2.

[3] *Schwenzer/Hachem/Kee*, Rn. 28.02.

[4] Vgl. Commentary on the draft Convention on the International Sale of Goods, YB VII (1976), S. 103, Art. 15, Nr. 1; *Schlechtriem*, Pflichten des Verkäufers, S. 111; *Neumayer/Ming*, Art. 30, Anm. 2.

Art. 30 3, 4   Teil III. Kapitel II. Pflichten des Verkäufers

Der Ausdruck „Lieferung" zielt auf die Leistungshandlung ab, zu der der Verkäufer verpflichtet ist, um dem Käufer den Besitz an der Ware zu verschaffen. Der zu bewirkende Leistungserfolg, der Besitzerwerb des Käufers, ist dagegen nicht mit eingeschlossen.[5] Den Inhalt der Lieferpflicht und den Lieferort regelt Art. 31. Hiernach besteht die Lieferung – vorbehaltlich abweichender Vereinbarung – entweder in der Versendung der Ware an den Käufer oder darin, dass der Verkäufer die Ware für den Käufer bereitstellt, sodass dieser sie abholen kann.[6] Ergänzt wird Art. 31 durch die Vorschrift des Art. 32, die besondere Bestimmungen über die Versendungsanzeige, den Abschluss des Beförderungsvertrags und die Transportversicherung trifft. Der Zeitpunkt der Lieferung ist in Art. 33 geregelt.

2. Incoterms®

3   In der Praxis regeln die Parteien den Inhalt der Lieferpflicht und den Ort der Lieferung häufig durch **Lieferklauseln**.[7] Die Bedeutung der wichtigsten und gebräuchlichsten Lieferklauseln sind in den Incoterms® der Internationalen Handelskammer festgelegt.[8] Den Parteien steht damit ein weltweit einheitliches Instrumentarium[9] zur Verfügung, mit dessen Hilfe sie beispielsweise den Ort und den Zeitpunkt des Kosten- und Gefahrenübergangs festlegen können.[10] Hierbei handelt es sich, insoweit mit Allgemeinen Geschäftsbedingungen durchaus vergleichbar[11], lediglich um eine private Rechtsaufzeichnung, die durch die Parteien erweitert oder abgeändert werden kann.[12] Unmittelbar verbindliche Wirkung haben die Incoterms® daher nur, wenn die Parteien im Vertrag auf sie Bezug genommen haben. Fehlt eine ausdrückliche Vertragsbestimmung, so kann gemäss Art. 9 II im Zweifel angenommen werden, dass die Parteien stillschweigend auf die Incoterms® Bezug genommen haben.[13] Denn die Incoterms® sind im internationalen Handel „weithin bekannt" und sie werden „regelmäßig beachtet", und im Allgemeinen ist auch davon auszugehen, dass sie den Parteien bekannt sind oder bekannt sein müssen. Selbst wenn sich das Vorliegen der Voraussetzungen des Art. 9 II nicht feststellen lässt, hat das Gericht die Möglichkeit, die Incoterms® als Mittel der ergänzenden Vertragsauslegung heranzuziehen.[14] Weichen allerdings die allgemeinen Anschauungen im Verkäufer- und im Käuferland in einem bestimmten Punkt übereinstimmend von den Incoterms® ab, wird man diesem abweichenden Verständnis gemäss Art. 8 II im Zweifel den Vorrang einräumen.

4   Die aktualisierte Fassung der Incoterms® ist zum 1.1.2011 in Kraft getreten und baut weitgehend auf den Incoterms® 2000 auf. Gegenüber den Incoterms® 2000 hat sich die

---

[5] Dieser hängt von der Mitwirkung des Käufers ab; vgl. *Witz/Salger/Lorenz/Witz*, Art. 30, Rn. 6 unter Bezugnahme auf Art. 60.

[6] Vgl. im Einzelnen die Kommentierung zu Art. 31.

[7] Vgl. *von Bernstorff*, Incoterms® 2010, 11 ff. mit einer Übersicht über gängige standardisierte Klauseln.

[8] International Commercial Terms (Incoterms®) in der Fassung 2010. Zum Verhältnis zwischen Incoterms® und Einheitskaufrecht vgl. *Fontaine*, Recht des internationalen Warenkaufs, S. 1193 ff.

[9] Vgl. *von Bernstorff*, Incoterms® 2010, 12.

[10] *Von Bernstorff*, Incoterms® 2010, 32, mit detaillierten Hinweisen zur Wahl der geeigneten Klausel.

[11] *Von Bernstorff*, Incoterms® 2010, 19.

[12] Vgl. dazu *von Bernstorff*, Incoterms® 2010, 18, der vor den Folgen einer allfälligen Abänderung oder Erweiterung warnt.

[13] So auch KG Wallis, II. Cour Civile, 28.1.2009, CISG-online 2025; Int. Ct. Russian CCI, 13.4.2006, CISG-online 1944; *China North Chemical Industries Corp. v. Beston Chemical Corp.*, U. S. Dist. Ct. (S. D. Tex.), 7.2.2006, CISG-online 1177; *Exploration & Oil Inc. v. Empresa Estatal Petroleos de Ecuador and Saybolt Inc.*, U.S.C.A. (5th Cir.), 11.6.2003, CISG-online 730; *St. Paul Guardian Insurance Company and Travelers Insurance Company, as subrogees of Shared Imaging, Inc. v. Neuromed Medical Systems & Support GmbH et al.*, U. S. Dist. Ct. (S. D. N. Y.), 26.3.2002, CISG-online 615; vgl. auch Int. Ct. Russian CCI, 6.6.2000, CISG-online 1249 (allerdings ohne ausdrückliche Bezugnahme auf Art. 9 II); *Schwenzer/Hechem/Kee*, Rn. 29.33. *Bianca/Bonell/Bonell*, Art. 9, Anm. 3.5. schlägt vor, die Anwendbarkeit der Incoterms® im Zweifel aus Art. 9 I herzuleiten; *Bianca/Bonell/Lando*, Art. 31, Anm. 2.2. will die Anwendung auf Art. 8 III i. V. m. Art. 7 I stützen. Beides läuft im Ergebnis auf das Gleiche hinaus wie die hier vertretene Meinung. A. A. noch *Eörsi*, General Provisions, S. 24: „[…] CISG has no rules on trade terms such as Incoterms®"; ähnlich *Feltham*, 34 J. Bus. L. (1991), 413, 415 f., 425.

[14] So für internationale Kaufverträge nach deutschem Recht: OLG München, 19.12.1957, NJW 1958, 426; vgl. auch BGH, 18.6.1975, WM 1975, 917 = RIW 1975, 578. Ebenso *Brunner*, Art. 30, Rn. 11.

Anzahl der Klauseln sowie die Präsentationsform bzw. deren Unterteilung nach Transportart verändert.[15] Zudem haben die Incoterms® 2010 in terminologischer Hinsicht eine Annäherung an das CISG erfahren.[16] Den Parteien steht es offen, in ihrem Vertrag auf eine frühere Fassung der Incoterms® Bezug zu nehmen; zur Vermeidung von Unklarheiten empfiehlt es sich, die gewünschte Fassung mit Angabe der Jahreszahl zu kennzeichnen.[17]

3. Sachen im Besitz des Käufers

Befindet die verkaufte Sache sich bei Abschluss des Kaufvertrags bereits im Besitz des Käufers, so ist die Pflicht des Verkäufers zur Lieferung gegenstandslos. Die Lieferung wird hier durch die Vereinbarung im Kaufvertrag ersetzt, dass der Käufer die Sache in Zukunft als eigene besitzen soll.[18]

III. Übergabe der Dokumente

Die Frage, ob der Verkäufer zur Übergabe von Dokumenten verpflichtet ist und welche Dokumente das sind, ist durch Heranziehen des Vertrags und der nach Art. 9 massgeblichen Gebräuche zu beantworten.[19] Soweit für den Vertrag die Incoterms® maßgeblich sind,[20] ergeben sich hieraus detaillierte Bestimmungen darüber, welche Dokumente der Verkäufer dem Käufer zu verschaffen hat. In der Praxis spielen vor allem Transportdokumente (wie das Konnossement und das Frachtbriefdoppel) und Lagerpapiere (Kaiteilschein, Lieferschein, „delivery order") eine Rolle, ferner die Transportversicherungspolice und die Rechnung. Aus zoll- und aussenhandelsrechtlichen Gründen ist ausserdem vielfach die Verschaffung von Ursprungszeugnissen und Exportgenehmigungen erforderlich.[21] Hinsichtlich des Orts und der Zeit der Übergabe der Dokumente verweist Art. 34 S. 1 auf den Vertrag.

IV. Verschaffung des Eigentums

1. Übereignung

Die Übertragung des Eigentums als solche ist im Übereinkommen nicht geregelt, Art. 4 S. 2 lit. b). Tritt die Frage auf, ob der Verkäufer dem Käufer das Eigentum verschafft hat, so entscheidet daher das nach dem internationalen Privatrecht des angerufenen Gerichts maßgebliche Sachenrecht,[22] in der Regel die lex rei sitae. Verlangt das berufene Sachenrecht eine besondere, vom Kaufvertrag zu unterscheidende „Einigung" der Parteien hinsichtlich des Eigentumsübergangs, so ist der Verkäufer gemäss Art. 30 verpflichtet, eine entsprechende Erklärung abzugeben. Die erforderliche Erklärung des Verkäufers ist in der Lieferung der Sache konkludent mitenthalten. Ist der Verkäufer nach dem massgeblichen Sachenrecht nicht in der Lage, dem Käufer Eigentum zu verschaffen, etwa weil die verkaufte Sache im Eigentum eines Dritten steht, greift die Rechtsmängelhaftung nach Art. 41.[23] Daraus folgt insbesondere, dass den Käufer gemäß Art. 43 eine Rügepflicht trifft.[24]

---

[15] *Piltz,* EJCCL 2011 – 1, 2 mit einer Übersicht über die Änderungen.
[16] *Von Bernstorff,* Incoterms® 2010, 17; ebenso *Piltz,* EJCCL 2011 – 1, 2.
[17] Vgl. *von Bernstorff,* Incoterms® 2010, 13.
[18] Vgl. auch *Neumayer/Ming,* Art. 30, Anm. 2.
[19] *Honsell/Ernst/Lauko,* Art. 34, Rn. 6.
[20] Vgl. oben Rn. 3 f.
[21] Der Käufer braucht, bei Bestehen von Einfuhrkontingenten, das Dokument über die Exportgenehmigung, um die Einfuhrgenehmigung zu erhalten, vgl. *Rummel,* NJW 1988, 225, 232 f.
[22] Vgl. *Schwenzer/Hachem/Kee,* Rn. 28.09.
[23] Hierzu *Schwenzer,* Art. 41 Rn. 3.
[24] Wohl verkannt von LG Freiburg, 22.8.2002, CISG-online 711 = IHR 2003, 22 ff.; zutreffend dagegen BGH, 11.1.2006, CISG-online 1200 = IHR 2006, 82 ff. OLG Dresden, 21.3.2007, CISG-online 1626 (Rügepflicht nur für Artt. 41 und 42, nicht für Art. 30); siehe auch *Kiene,* IHR 2006, 93 ff.

2. Eigentumsvorbehalt

8   Da das Übereinkommen sich nicht mit Fragen des Eigentumsübergangs befasst, hat es auch den Eigentumsvorbehalt nicht geregelt. Die Wirksamkeit eines Eigentumsvorbehaltes richtet sich daher nach dem massgeblichen nationalen Sachen-, Konkurs- und Zwangsvollstreckungsrecht.[25] Soweit hiernach auch eine einseitige Erklärung des Verkäufers genügt, um dem Eigentumsvorbehalt Wirksamkeit zu verleihen, stellt sich die Frage, ob der Verkäufer gemäss Art. 30 dem Käufer gegenüber berechtigt ist, eine solche einseitige Erklärung abzugeben, oder ob er hierdurch eine Vertragsverletzung begeht. Im Fall des „einfachen" Eigentumsvorbehalts, der die Eigentumsübertragung nur von der Zahlung des Kaufpreises für die gelieferte Ware abhängig macht, ist eine Vertragsverletzung zu verneinen.[26] Denn nach Art. 58 I S. 2 ist der Verkäufer berechtigt, die Übergabe der Ware oder der Dokumente von der Zahlung des Kaufpreises abhängig zu machen. Erst recht muss ihm daher die Befugnis zustehen, den Eigentumsübergang von der Zahlung abhängig zu machen. Selbst dann, wenn der Verkäufer nach dem Kaufvertrag zur Vorleistung verpflichtet ist, bezieht sich die Vorleistungspflicht im Zweifel nur auf die Übergabe der Ware, nicht auf die Übereignung. Die praktische Bedeutung der Frage ist allerdings gering. Denn auch wenn man eine Vertragsverletzung bejaht, ist sie keinesfalls „wesentlich" im Sinn des Art. 25. Ein Schaden, den der Verkäufer gemäss Art. 45 I lit. b) ersetzen müsste, ist schwer vorstellbar.

V. Sonstige Pflichten des Verkäufers

9   Weitere, über Art. 30 hinausgehende Pflichten des Verkäufers können sich aus dem Vertrag, aus den für den Vertrag massgeblichen Gebräuchen (Art. 9) und aus dem Grundsatz von Treu und Glauben (als allgemeinen Grundsatz im Sinn des Art. 7 II) ergeben.[27] Auch solche Pflichten unterliegen, wenn der Vertrag insgesamt die Voraussetzungen für die Anwendung des Einheitskaufrechts erfüllt, dessen Regeln, denn es handelt sich dabei um Pflichten, die aus dem Kaufvertrag erwachsen sind (Art. 4 S. 1). Die Folgen ihrer Nichterfüllung richten sich daher nach Artt. 45 ff.[28]

---

[25] Vgl. dazu OLG Koblenz, 16.1.1992, CISG-online 47 = RIW 1992, 1019 ff. = IPRax 1994, 27 ff.; *Roder Zelt- und Hallenkonstruktionen GmbH v. Rosedown Park Pty. Ltd. and Reginald R. Eustace*, FCA (Adelaide, SA), 28.4.1995, CISG-online 218 = 1995 Federal Court Reports (Australia) 216; *Usinor Industeel v. Leeco Steel Products Inc.*, U. S. Dist. Ct. (N.D.Ill.), 28.3.2002, CISG-online 696 = 2002 WL 655 540; Foreign Trade Court of Arbitration attached to the Serbian Chamber of Commerce, 15.7.2008, CISG-online 1795.

[26] Übereinstimmend *Honsell/Ernst/Lauko*, Art. 30, Rn. 15; differenzierend *Staudinger/Magnus*, Art. 30, Rn. 12; *Soergel/Lüderitz/Budzikiewicz/Schüßler-Langeheine*, Art. 30, Rn. 7; *Achilles*, Art. 30, Rn. 4.

[27] Vgl. *MünchKomm/Gruber*, Art. 30, Rn. 7 ff.; bezüglich Treu und Glauben offen gelassen bei MünchKommHGB/*Benicke*, Art. 30, Rn. 2. Zur Streitfrage, ob der Grundsatz von Treu und Glauben aus Art. 7 I (so *U. Huber* in der 3. Auflage, Rn. 9) oder Art. 7 II abzuleiten sei, siehe *Ferrari*, Art. 7 Rn. 26; *Schlechtriem*, Internationales UN-Kaufrecht, Rn. 44, 48.

[28] Vgl. auch *Karollus*, S. 104; *Honsell/Ernst/Lauko*, Art. 30, Rn. 16; *Staudinger/Magnus*, Art. 30, Rn. 19; *Piltz*, UN-Kaufrecht, Rn. 41; MünchKommHGB/*Benicke*, Art. 30, Rn. 2; *Brunner*, Art. 30, Rn. 8. Vgl. ferner *Müller-Chen*, Art. 45 Rn. 3.

Abschnitt I. Lieferung der Ware und Übergabe der Dokumente

Section I
Delivery of the goods and handing over of documents

Section I
Livraison des marchandises et remise des documents

Art. 31 [Inhalt der Lieferpflicht und Ort der Lieferung]

Hat der Verkäufer die Ware nicht an einem anderen bestimmten Ort zu liefern, so besteht seine Lieferpflicht in folgendem:
a) Erfordert der Kaufvertrag eine Beförderung der Ware, so hat sie der Verkäufer dem ersten Beförderer zur Übermittlung an den Käufer zu übergeben;
b) bezieht sich der Vertrag in Fällen, die nicht unter Buchstabe a fallen, auf bestimmte Ware oder auf gattungsmäßig bezeichnete Ware, die aus einem bestimmten Bestand zu entnehmen ist, oder auf herzustellende oder zu erzeugende Ware und wußten die Parteien bei Vertragsabschluß, daß die Ware sich an einem bestimmten Ort befand oder dort herzustellen oder zu erzeugen war, so hat der Verkäufer die Ware dem Käufer an diesem Ort zur Verfügung zu stellen;
c) in den anderen Fällen hat der Verkäufer die Ware dem Käufer an dem Ort zur Verfügung zu stellen, an dem der Verkäufer bei Vertragsabschluß seine Niederlassung hatte.

Art. 31

If the seller is not bound to deliver the goods at any other particular place, his obligation to deliver consists:

(a) if the contract of sale involves carriage of the goods – in handing the goods over to the first carrier for transmission to the buyer;
(b) if, in cases not within the preceding subparagraph, the contract relates to specific goods, or unidentified goods to be drawn from a specific stock or to be manufactured or produced, and at the time of the conclusion of the contract the parties knew that the goods were at, or were to be manufactured or produced at, a particular place – in placing the goods at the buyer's disposal at that place;
(c) in other cases – in placing the goods at the buyer's disposal at the place where the seller had his place of business at the time of the conclusion of the contract.

Art. 31

Si le vendeur n'est pas tenu de livrer les marchandises en un autre lieu particulier, son obligation de livraison consiste:

a) lorsque le contrat de vente implique un transport des marchandises, à remettre les marchandises au premier transporteur pour transmission à l'acheteur;
b) lorsque, dans les cas non visés au précédent alinéa, le contrat porte sur un corps certain ou sur une chose de genre qui doit être prélevée sur une masse déterminée ou qui doit être fabriquée ou produite et lorsque, au moment de la conclusion du contrat, les parties savaient que les marchandises se trouvaient ou devaient être fabriquées ou produites en un lieu particulier, à mettre les marchandises à la disposition de l'acheteur en ce lieu;
c) dans les autres cas, à mettre les marchandises à la disposition de l'acheteur au lieu où le vendeur avait son établissement au moment de la conclusion du contrat.

Übersicht

	Rn.
I. Gegenstand und Funktion der Regelung	1
1. Lieferpflicht und Lieferort im Überblick	1
a) Lieferpflicht	2
b) Lieferort	5
2. Funktion der Regelung	7
a) Erfüllungsanspruch	8
b) Nachfrist	9

  c) Schadensersatz 10
  d) Lieferung und Gefahrübergang 11
  e) Gerichtsstand 12
II. Art. 31 lit. a): Lieferung durch Übergabe an den Beförderer 13
 1. Das Erfordernis der Beförderung der Ware 13
  a) Beförderung 13
  b) Erfordernis der Beförderung nach dem Kaufvertrag 17
 2. Beförderer 19
  a) Grundsatz 19
  b) Mehrheit von Beförderern 20
  c) Transport durch den Verkäufer oder seine Angestellten 21
  d) Vorlieferant 24
  e) Spediteur 25
 3. Übergabe 29
  a) Übergang des Gewahrsams auf den Beförderer 29
  b) Übergabe „zur Übermittlung an den Käufer" 30
  c) Ort der Übergabe 31
  d) Rechtsfolgen der Übergabe 32
 4. Vertragsverletzungen des Verkäufers bei der Lieferung 33
  a) Versendung nicht vertragsmässiger Ware 33
  b) Falschlieferung 34
  c) Mangelhafte Verpackung und Verladung 35
  d) Vertragswidrige Kostenbelastung des Käufers 37
  e) Versendung an den falschen Ort 39
 5. Eingriffe des Verkäufers in den Transport 41
  a) Rückbeorderung der Ware 41
  b) Anhalten der Ware 42
  c) Haftung des Verkäufers 43
 6. Teillieferung 44
III. Art. 31 lit. b), c): Lieferung durch Zur-Verfügung-Stellen der Ware 45
 1. Ausgangspunkt 45
 2. Lieferort gemäss Art. 31 lit. b) 46
  a) Die vier Fälle des Art. 31 lit. b) 46
  b) Ware auf dem Transport 47
  c) Kenntnis des Käufers bei Vertragsabschluss 48
 3. Lieferort gemäss Art. 31 lit. c) 49
 4. Zur-Verfügung-Stellen 50
  a) Bereitstellen der Ware 50
  b) Benachrichtigung des Käufers 51
  c) Verpackung 53
  d) Verladung 54
  e) Zur-Verfügung-Stellen unter Vorbehalten 55
  f) Frei zugängliche Ware 57
  g) Bei einem Dritten eingelagerte Ware 58
 5. Rechtsfolgen 61
 6. Vertragswidrige Lieferung 65
 7. Aufhebung der Bereitstellung durch den Verkäufer 67
 8. Bereitstellung am falschen Ort 68
 9. Teillieferung 69
IV. Vereinbarung eines „anderen bestimmten Orts" für die Lieferung 70
 1. Ausgangspunkt 70
 2. Incoterms® 71
  a) Mit Art. 31 übereinstimmender Lieferort 72
  b) Von Art. 31 abweichender Lieferort 73
  c) Unterlassene Mitwirkung des Käufers 75
 3. Bringschulden 76
 4. Die Haftung des Verkäufers für den Transport zum Lieferort 77
 5. Lieferung am falschen Ort 78
 6. Verkauf von Ware auf dem Transport 79
 7. Montagepflichten, Instruktionspflichten 82

V. Kosten und Genehmigungen 83
　1. Transportkosten 83
　2. Zölle und Abgaben 84
　3. Export- und Importgenehmigungen 85
VI. Gerichtsstand des Erfüllungsortes 87
　1. Allgemeines 87
　2. Rechtslage nach der EuGVO 89
　　a) Tatsächlicher Erfüllungsort der Lieferpflicht 90
　　b) Konsequenzen für Art. 31 94
　　c) Ausnahmsweiser Rückgriff auf Art. 31 nach Art. 5 Nr. 1 lit. a)
　　　 EuGVO 95
　3. Rechtslage nach dem revidierten LuganoÜ vom 30. Oktober 2007 99

Vorläufer und **Entwürfe:** EKG Artt. 19 I, II, 23; Genfer E 1976 Art. 15; Wiener E 1977 Art. 15; New Yorker E 1978 Art. 29.

I. Gegenstand und Funktion der Regelung

1. Lieferpflicht und Lieferort im Überblick

Art. 31 regelt zwei Gegenstände, die eng miteinander zusammenhängen: den Inhalt der Lieferpflicht des Verkäufers und den Ort, an dem der Verkäufer die Lieferpflicht zu erfüllen hat. Entsprechend dem Grundprinzip der Vertragsfreiheit (Art. 6) regelt die Bestimmung nur den Fall, dass der Vertrag den Ort der Lieferung nicht selbst festlegt. Bei der Bestimmung sowohl des Inhalts der Lieferpflicht als auch des Lieferorts unterscheidet Art. 31 danach, ob der Kaufvertrag eine Beförderung der Ware erfordert oder nicht, ob also nach dem Vertrag der Verkäufer für die Beförderung der Ware zum Käufer zu sorgen hat oder ob der Käufer die Ware abzuholen hat.[1]

a) Lieferpflicht. Erfordert der Vertrag eine Beförderung der Ware, so besteht die Lieferung in der Übergabe an den (ersten) Beförderer zur Übermittlung an den Käufer, Art. 31 lit. a). Die Lieferschuld aus einem Vertrag, der eine Beförderung erfordert, ist also im Zweifel „Schickschuld"; der Kauf ist, wenn er eine Beförderung erfordert, im Zweifel ein „Versendungskauf". Der Umstand, dass der Verkäufer es übernimmt, für die Beförderung der Ware zum Käufer zu sorgen, führt nicht dazu, dass der Bestimmungsort des Transports als der Erfüllungsort der Lieferpflicht anzusehen ist. Die Lieferpflicht ist im Zweifel keine „Bringschuld".[2]

Erfordert der Vertrag keine Beförderung der Ware, so besteht die Lieferung darin, dass der Verkäufer die Ware dem Käufer „zur Verfügung stellt", Art. 31 lit. b), c). Es ist Sache des Käufers, die Ware abzuholen. Die Lieferschuld aus einem Vertrag, der keine Beförderung erfordert, ist demnach „Holschuld".

Art. 31 umschreibt die Lieferung so, dass sie nur die Massnahmen umfasst, die der Verkäufer treffen muss und kann, um dem Käufer den Besitz an der Ware zu verschaffen. Unter „Lieferung" ist also nur die Leistungshandlung des Verkäufers zu verstehen, die je nach Lage des Falls in der Versendung oder in der Bereitstellung der Ware besteht. Der Leistungserfolg, der tatsächliche Besitzerwerb des Käufers (vgl. Art. 69: die „Übernahme" der Ware durch den Käufer), ist nicht mehr Bestandteil der Lieferpflicht des Verkäufers. Das Übereinkommen will damit die Lieferpflicht so bestimmen, dass der Verkäufer sie einseitig, das heisst ohne Mitwirkung des Käufers, erfüllen kann.[3]

---

[1] Dazu unten Rn. 13 ff.
[2] Vgl. Cass., 3.1.2007, CISG-online 1415; KG Zug, 11.12.2003, CISG-online 958 = IHR 2005, 119, 121 (E. 2.2.3). Anders entscheidet Art. 57 hinsichtlich der Zahlungspflicht des Käufers.
[3] Anders das frühere Einheitskaufrecht (Art. 19 EKG), vgl. hierzu die 3. Aufl., *U. Huber*, Art. 31 Rn. 1 Fn. 1 sowie die 1. Aufl., *U. Huber*, Art. 31 Rn. 14 f.

5 **b) Lieferort.** Ist eine Beförderung erforderlich, hat also der Verkäufer für den Transport der Ware zum Käufer zu sorgen, und haben die Parteien im Vertrag keinen Lieferort festgelegt, sieht das Übereinkommen keinen Grund, einen bestimmten Ort für die Versendung vorzuschreiben. Der Verkäufer soll dann die Freiheit haben, die Ware dort abzusenden, wo es ihm passt.

6 Ist keine Beförderung erforderlich, hat also der Käufer die Ware abzuholen, und enthält der Vertrag keine Bestimmung des Lieferorts, so legt dagegen Art. 31 lit. b), c) ergänzend fest, wo der Verkäufer die Ware bereitzustellen und der Käufer sie abzuholen hat. Massgeblich ist gemäss Art. 31 lit. b) in erster Linie der Ort, an dem die Ware sich befindet oder, wenn die Ware erst noch zu produzieren ist, der Produktionsort – vorausgesetzt, dieser Ort war bei Vertragsschluss beiden Parteien, vor allem also auch dem Käufer, bekannt. Anderenfalls ist Lieferort subsidiär der Ort der Niederlassung des Verkäufers, Art. 31 lit. c).[4]

2. Funktion der Regelung

7 Die Bestimmung des Inhalts der Lieferpflicht und des Lieferorts in Art. 31 bildet den Ausgangspunkt für die Regelung der Rechtsbehelfe des Käufers in Art. 45. Die wichtigsten Rechtsbehelfe sind der Anspruch auf Erfüllung gemäss Art. 45 I lit. a) i. V. m. Art. 46 I, das Recht zur Vertragsaufhebung gemäss Art. 49 I und der Anspruch auf Schadensersatz gemäss Art. 45 I lit. b).

8 **a) Erfüllungsanspruch.** Verlangt der Käufer gemäss Art. 46 I Erfüllung in Natur, also Lieferung, so bestimmt Art. 31, worauf dieser Anspruch sich richtet. Hat der Verkäufer die Lieferung i. S. d. Art. 31 bewirkt, so ist der Anspruch erfüllt, und der Verkäufer kann auf Lieferung nicht mehr in Anspruch genommen werden.

9 **b) Nachfrist.** Hat der Verkäufer die Lieferpflicht innerhalb der Frist des Art. 33 nicht erfüllt, so kann ihm der Käufer für die Lieferung Nachfrist setzen und nach erfolglosem Ablauf der Nachfrist die Vertragsaufhebung erklären, Art. 49 I lit. b) i. V. m. Art. 47. Für diesen Fall legt Art. 31 fest, auf welche Massnahme des Verkäufers die Nachfrist sich bezieht, und was der Verkäufer zu tun hat, um die Nachfrist einzuhalten und die Vertragsaufhebung abzuwenden.

10 **c) Schadensersatz.** Erfüllt der Verkäufer seine Pflicht zur Lieferung nicht, so kann der Käufer gemäss Art. 45 I lit. b) Schadensersatz nach den Artt. 74–77 verlangen. Die Schadensersatzhaftung ist im Prinzip eine vom Verschulden des Verkäufers unabhängige Garantiehaftung.[5] Umfang und Grenzen dieser Haftung ergeben sich aus Art. 31. Der Verkäufer haftet dafür, dass er die in Art. 31 beschriebenen Massnahmen richtig und rechtzeitig durchführt; hat er das getan, hat seine Haftung sich erledigt. Insbesondere kommt es für die Frage, ob der Verkäufer seine Pflicht zur Lieferung rechtzeitig erfüllt hat, auf die rechtzeitige Absendung, nicht auf die Ankunft der Ware an.[6]

11 **d) Lieferung und Gefahrübergang.** Im Allgemeinen ist es sachgerecht, dass die Gefahr dann übergeht, wenn der Verkäufer das zur Leistung Erforderliche getan hat.[7] Demgemäss gehen nach dem Übereinkommen beim Kauf, der eine Beförderung der Ware erfordert, Lieferung und Gefahrübergang grundsätzlich Hand in Hand: Ist kein besonderer Lieferort vereinbart, so erfolgt beides durch Übergabe an den ersten Beförderer, Artt. 31 lit. a), 67 I 1.[8] Wird die Lieferung dagegen schon dadurch bewirkt, dass der Verkäufer die Ware dem Käufer zur Verfügung stellt (Art. 31 lit. b), c)), geht die Gefahr unter bestimmten Voraussetzungen

---

[4] Auf die Niederlassung des Verkäufers stellt auch Art. 93 Ziff. 1 lit. b (ii) CESL ab.
[5] Vgl. *Müller-Chen*, Art. 45 Rn. 23.
[6] Vgl. HGer Zürich, 10.2.1999, CISG-online 488 = SZIER 2000, 111, 113 = IHR 2001, 44, 45. Zutreffend zur Vorläuferbestimmung des Art. 19 II EKG: LG Hamburg, 18.8.1976, RIW 1977, 424 = *Schlechtriem/Magnus*, Art. 86 EKG, Nr. 4.
[7] Zum früheren Einheitskaufrecht siehe *Hachem*, Art. 67 Rn. 1 f.
[8] Dazu *Hachem*, Art. 67 Rn. 5; so auch die Regelung gemäss Art. 145 Ziff. 2 CESL.

erst nach der Lieferung über. Befindet die zur Verfügung gestellte Ware sich noch im Gewahrsam des Verkäufers, so erscheint der sofortige Gefahrübergang als unangebracht.[9] Die Gefahr geht in diesem Fall erst über, wenn der Käufer die Ware tatsächlich übernimmt oder wenn er durch die Nichtabnahme in Annahmeverzug gerät (Art. 69 I).[10] Ist die Ware dagegen bei einem Dritten (z. B. beim Lagerhalter oder bei der Kaiverwaltung) abzuholen, geht die Gefahr mit Zur-Verfügung-Stellung, also gleichzeitig mit der Lieferung über (Art. 69 II).[11]

e) **Gerichtsstand.** Für die Praxis lag die Hauptbedeutung des Art. 31 bis anhin in Fällen, 12 in denen über die internationale und örtliche Zuständigkeit des angerufenen Gerichts gestritten wurde.[12] Von besonderer Bedeutung war in dieser Hinsicht Art. 31 lit. a). Die Bestimmung stellt klar, dass die Lieferpflicht auch dann, wenn der Verkäufer für die Beförderung der Ware zum Käufer zu sorgen hat, im Zweifel keine „Bringschuld" ist.[13] Soweit der Gerichtsstand vom Erfüllungsort abhängt (so nach Art. 5 Nr. 1 LuganoÜ, § 29 ZPO, Art. 113 IPRG), liegt deshalb der Gerichtsstand für Klagen des Käufers auf Lieferung und vor allem auch für Klagen des Käufers auf Schadensersatz wegen mangelhafter oder verspäteter Lieferung im Zweifel an der Niederlassung des Verkäufers (unten Rn. 90). Mit Inkrafttreten der EuGVO am 1. März 2002 und des revidierten Lugano Übereinkommens vom 30. Oktober 2007 ist die zuständigkeitsrechtliche Bedeutung des Erfüllungsorts nach Art. 31 jedoch stark relativiert worden, dazu unten Rn. 93 ff.

II. Art. 31 lit. a): Lieferung durch Übergabe an den Beförderer

1. Das Erfordernis der Beförderung der Ware

a) **Beförderung.** Art. 31 unterscheidet danach, ob der Vertrag eine Beförderung erfordert – dann richtet die Lieferung sich nach Art. 31 lit. a) –, oder ob das nicht der Fall ist – dann richtet die Lieferung sich nach Art. 31 lit. b), c). Unter „Beförderung" ist dabei zu verstehen ein **Transport der Ware, den der Verkäufer veranlassen muss, um dem Käufer die Übernahme der Ware zu ermöglichen.** 13

Wie sich aus Art. 31 lit. a) ergibt, ist unter Beförderung die Versendung der Ware „zur 14 Übermittlung an den Käufer" zu verstehen. **Keine Beförderung** i. S. d. Art. 31 ist also der **Transport vom Vorlieferanten an den Verkäufer.**[14] Die Lieferpflicht des Verkäufers ist in diesem Fall erst dann erfüllt, wenn der Verkäufer die Ware an den Käufer weiterversendet oder wenn er sie für den Käufer bereitstellt, je nachdem, ob im Verhältnis zwischen dem Verkäufer und dem Käufer Lieferung gemäss Art. 31 lit. a) oder gemäss Art. 31 lit. b), c) vereinbart ist.[15]

Keine Beförderung i. S. d. Art. 31 lit. a) ist auf der anderen Seite der Transport, den **der** 15 **Käufer durchführen oder veranlassen muss,** um die Ware an ihren Bestimmungsort zu bringen, nachdem er sie vom Verkäufer übernommen hat.[16] Ein solcher Transport ist auch in den Fällen des Art. 31 lit. b), c) stets erforderlich.[17] Diese Fälle sind aber nach der Ausdrucksweise des Gesetzes gerade dadurch gekennzeichnet, dass der Vertrag *keine* Beförderung der Ware erfordert. Der Abtransport der Ware durch Käufer vom Übernahmeort ist also nicht gemeint, wenn Art. 31 lit. a) davon spricht, dass der Vertrag eine Beförderung der

---

[9] Vgl. *Rabel*, Recht des Warenkaufs, Bd. 2, S. 366; *Hager*, Gefahrtragung nach UN-Kaufrecht, S. 398 f.; ders./*Maultzsch*, Art. 69 Rn. 1.
[10] Dazu *Hachem*, Art. 69 Rn. 9.
[11] Dazu *Hachem*, Art. 69 Rn. 17.
[12] Dazu unten Rn. 87 ff.
[13] Oben Rn. 2.
[14] Ebenso *Staudinger/Magnus*, Art. 31, Rn. 13; *Honsell/Ernst/Lauko*, Art. 31, Rn. 14.
[15] Die Lieferung kann auch darin bestehen, dass der Vorlieferant die Ware auf Weisung des Verkäufers direkt an den Käufer versendet („Streckengeschäft"), vgl. dazu unten Rn. 24.
[16] Zutreffend *Piltz*, Internationales Kaufrecht, Rn. 4–20; *Achilles*, Art. 31, Rn. 3; *Herber/Czerwenka*, Art. 31, Rn. 4; *Honsell/Ernst/Lauko*, Art. 31, Rn. 13; vgl. auch MünchKommHGB/*Benicke*, Art. 31, Rn. 4.
[17] Vgl. *Honnold/Fletchner*, Rn. 208: „All sales involve movement of goods".

Ware erfordert.[18] Ob der Käufer den Abtransport selbst durchführt oder durch einen selbstständigen Beförderer durchführen lässt, ist gleichgültig.[19]

16 Nicht von Art. 31 erfasst wird schliesslich der Fall, in dem **Ware auf dem Transport** – schwimmende, rollende, fliegende Ware – verkauft wird. Zwar mag man nach dem allgemeinen Sprachgebrauch auch hier sagen, dass der Kaufvertrag eine Beförderung der Ware erfordert. Aber die Lieferpflicht des Verkäufers bezieht sich hier auf einen „anderen bestimmten Ort".[20]

17 **b) Erfordernis der Beförderung nach dem Kaufvertrag.** Art. 31 lit. a) setzt voraus, dass der „Kaufvertrag" die Beförderung der Ware „erfordert" („involves carriage"). Lässt sich nicht feststellen, dass eine Beförderung erforderlich ist, und liegen auch die in Art. 31 lit. b) genannten besonderen Voraussetzungen nicht vor, so greift subsidiär Art. 31 lit. c) ein.[21] Zwar geht das Übereinkommen zu Recht davon aus, dass tatsächlich bei internationalen Kaufverträgen der Versendungskauf die Regel, der Fall der Holschuld die eher seltene Ausnahme sein wird;[22] deshalb hat es den Fall des Versendungskaufs in Art. 31 (wie auch in Art. 67) an die Spitze gestellt.[23] Diese Reihenfolge in der gesetzlichen Regelung ändert aber nichts daran, dass das Erfordernis der Beförderung stets einer besonderen Feststellung auf Grund des Kaufvertrags bedarf.[24] Das Übereinkommen selbst ordnet eine Pflicht des Verkäufers, für die Beförderung zu sorgen, nicht an.

18 In aller Regel wird sich allerdings aus einer ausdrücklichen Bestimmung im Kaufvertrag, aus den zwischen den Parteien bestehenden Gepflogenheiten (Art. 9 I) oder aus Handelsbrauch (Art. 9 II) eindeutig ergeben, ob der Verkäufer die Sache dem Käufer zuzusenden oder ob der Käufer sie beim Verkäufer zu holen hat. Lässt sich eine solche eindeutige Regelung nicht feststellen, so handelt es sich zunächst um eine Frage der ergänzenden Vertragsauslegung (Art. 8). Im Allgemeinen wird man bei einem **Distanzkauf**[25] davon ausgehen müssen, dass die Parteien sich über die Zusendung der Ware durch den Verkäufer einig sind.[26] Soll der Käufer die Ware beim Verkäufer holen, so wird man – soweit dies nicht im Einzelfall den Gepflogenheiten der Parteien oder einer allgemeinen Verkehrssitte entspricht – einen dahingehenden Hinweis im Vertrag erwarten. Die ergänzende Vertragsauslegung ergibt also, dass die Pflicht des Verkäufers zur Versendung, nicht nur in tatsächlicher, sondern auch in rechtlicher Hinsicht, im Anwendungsbereich des Einheitskaufrechts der Regelfall ist und dass die subsidiären Regeln der Art. 31 lit. b) und c) nur eingreifen, nachdem festgestellt worden ist, dass eine Versendungspflicht des Verkäufers *nicht* besteht.[27]

---

[18] Abweichend *Feltham*, 34 J. Bus. L. (1991), 413, 423; *Heuzé*, Anm. 242.; *Staudinger/Magnus*, Art. 31, Rn. 16; *Witz/Salger/Lorenz/Witz*, Art. 31, Rn. 11; *Brunner*, Art. 31, Rn. 5.

[19] Hat der Verkäufer nach dem Kaufvertrag die Ware an einen vom Käufer zu beauftragenden Beförderer zu übergeben, liegt hierin regelmässig zugleich die Vereinbarung eines „anderen bestimmten Orts" der Lieferung, welche die Anwendung des Art. 31 ausschliesst: Dazu unten Rn. 73 f.

[20] Vgl. dazu unten Rn. 79.

[21] Vgl. *Herber*, Einführung, S. 23; *Lüderitz*, Pflichten der Parteien, S. 183; *Loewe*, Art. 31, S. 52; *Garro/Zuppi*, Compraventa internacional, S. 148; *Karollus*, S. 108; *Piltz*, UN-Kaufrecht, Rn. 58; *ders.*, Internationales Kaufrecht, Rn. 4–22.

[22] Vgl. *Honnold/Flechtner*, Art. 31, Rn. 209: „a small minority of international sales"; *Enderlein/Maskow/Strohbach*, Art. 31, Anm. 3.

[23] Im Unterschied zu Art. 19 I 2 EKG.

[24] So auch *Bamberger/Roth/Saenger*, Art. 31, Rn. 5. Anders *Soergel/Lüderitz/Budzikiewicz/Schüßler-Langeheine*, Art. 31, Rn. 5; *Witz/Salger/Lorenz/Witz*, Art. 31, Rn. 11: Gesetzliche Vermutung für Versendungspflicht.

[25] Also dann, wenn Verkäufer und Käufer an verschiedenen Orten ihren Sitz haben und der Kaufvertrag nicht bei gleichzeitiger Anwesenheit beider Teile über an Ort und Stelle präsente Ware abgeschlossen wird.

[26] Ebenso wird es im deutschen Recht bei Kaufverträgen eines gewerblichen Verkäufers im Zweifel als Vertragsinhalt angesehen, dass der Verkäufer die Sache zu versenden hat, RGZ 103, 129, 130 („Handelsbrauch"); BGHZ 113, 106, 111; vgl. auch *Soergel/Huber*, § 447 BGB, Rn. 10.

[27] Wie hier auch *Honsell/Ernst/Lauko*, Art. 11, Rn. 7; *Karollus*, S. 108; *Piltz*, UN-Kaufrecht, Rn. 58; *ders.*, Internationales Kaufrecht, Rn. 4–22; ähnlich *von Hoffmann*, Passing of Risk, S. 284 f.; *Neumayer/Ming*, Art. 31, Anm. 4. Im Ergebnis ebenso *Soergel/Lüderitz/Budzikiewicz/Schüßler-Langeheine*, Art. 31, Rn. 5; Münch-KommHGB/*Benicke*, Art. 31, Rn. 38; vgl. auch LG Flensburg, 24.3.1999, CISG-online 719. Dagegen hat das

2. Beförderer

a) Grundsatz. Unter dem Beförderer, dem der Verkäufer die Ware zu übergeben hat, ist 19 jedes selbstständige Unternehmen[28] des Transportwesens zu verstehen, das den Transport zur Übermittlung an den Käufer, sei es im Ganzen, sei es zu einem Teil,[29] zu bewirken hat. In Betracht kommen etwa Frachtführer, die die Ware mit Lkw oder Binnenschiff zu transportieren haben, Eisenbahnunternehmen, die Post, Paketdienste, Verfrachter im Überseeverkehr.[30]

b) Mehrheit von Beförderern. Werden vom Verkäufer (oder vom Spediteur, der für 20 ihn den Transport organisiert) mehrere Beförderer eingesetzt, die den Transport nacheinander auf verschiedenen Teilstrecken durchzuführen haben, so genügt zur Bewirkung der Lieferung die Aushändigung an den „ersten Beförderer".[31] Es ist nicht erforderlich, dass der erste Beförderer selbst es übernimmt, für den Transport bis zum Käufer zu sorgen, und die weiteren Beförderer als Unterfrachtführer einsetzt. Unerheblich ist, ob die Transportstrecke des ersten Beförderers kurz oder lang ist. Übergibt z. B. der Verkäufer die Ware, die mit der Eisenbahn versendet werden soll, einem Rollfuhrspediteur mit dem Auftrag, sie zum Güterbahnhof zu transportieren, von dem aus dieser sie an den Käufer weiterversenden soll, so ist die Lieferpflicht mit Übergabe an den Rollfuhrspediteur erfüllt.[32] Dass abweichende Vereinbarungen im Vertrag (z. B. „frei Bahnstation" oder „FOB Flughafen") den Vorrang haben,[33] versteht sich von selbst.

c) Transport durch den Verkäufer oder seine Angestellten. Dem Verkäufer steht es, 21 wenn sich aus dem Kaufvertrag nichts Gegenteiliges ergibt, frei, den Transport der Ware zum Käufer selbst durchzuführen. Er kann sich im Kaufvertrag auch ausdrücklich verpflichten, dies zu tun. In einem solchen Fall ist er nicht „Beförderer" i. S. d. Art. 31 lit. a),[34] denn Art. 31 lit. a) setzt voraus, dass die Ware dem Beförderer „übergeben" wird, dass also der Verkäufer den Gewahrsam aufgibt. Der „Beförderer" ist notwendigerweise eine andere Person als der Verkäufer selbst. Die Lieferung wird daher in einem solchen Fall erst dadurch bewirkt, dass der Verkäufer die Ware am Bestimmungsort dem Käufer übergibt.[35] Führt der Verkäufer einen **Teil des Transports** selbst durch, wird die Lieferung erst dadurch vollzogen, dass er die Ware am Ende dieses Teiltransports dem ersten selbstständigen Beförderer übergibt.[36]

Dasselbe gilt in dem in der Praxis des Handelsverkehrs häufigeren Fall, dass der Verkäufer 22 den Transport oder einen ersten Teil des Transports durch **eigene Angestellte** durchführen lässt. Solange die Ware sich noch im Herrschafts- und Organisationsbereich des Verkäufers befindet, hat eine „Übergabe" i. S. d. Art. 31 lit. a) nicht stattgefunden. Praktisch geht es dabei um die Haftung des Verkäufers für Fehler seiner eigenen Angestellten beim Transport der Ware und vor allem bei der Aufgabe zum Post- oder Bahntransport. Art. 31 lit. a) entlastet den Verkäufer von der Haftung für den selbstständigen Beförderer, der den Transport durchführt, nicht aber von der Haftung für seinen eigenen Herrschafts- und Organisa-

---

LG Aachen, 14.5.1993, CISG-online 86 = RIW 1993, 760 in einem Fall, in dem nichts Besonderes vereinbart war, ohne weiteres das Vorliegen einer Holschuld gem. Art. 31 lit. c) angenommen.

[28] Dazu unten Rn. 22 f.
[29] Dazu unten Rn. 20.
[30] Zur Frage, ob auch der Spediteur „Beförderer" ist, wenn ihm die Ware zur Durchführung des Speditionsauftrags übergeben wird, vgl. unten Rn. 25 ff.
[31] Ebenso (zum Gefahrübergang gemäß Art. 61 I) *Honnold*, Risk of Loss, S. 10 f.
[32] Zweifelnd *Sevón*, Passing of Risk, S. 200; a. A. *von Hoffmann*, Passing of Risk, S. 286. Zur Rechtslage nach dem EKG vgl. *Dölle/Huber*, Art. 19 EKG, Rn. 82 f.
[33] Vgl. dazu unten Rn. 73 f.
[34] Vgl. LG Freiburg, 13.5.2005, CISG-online 1199; KG Wallis, 27.5.2005, CISG-online 1137; OG Zürich, 6.2.2009, CISG-online 2000; *Soergel/Lüderitz/Budzikiewicz/Schüßler-Langeheine*, Art. 31, Rn. 2; *Staudinger/Magnus*, Art. 31, Rn. 19; MünchKomm/*Gruber*, Art. 31, Rn. 16; MünchKommHGB/*Benicke*, Art. 31, Rn. 10.
[35] Vgl. dazu unten Rn. 76.
[36] Ebenso *Neumayer/Ming*, Art. 31, Anm. 7.; vgl. auch *Feltham*, 34 J. Bus. L. (1991), 413, 417.

tionsbereich.[37] „Beförderer" i. S. d. Art. 31 lit. a) ist also immer nur ein **selbstständiger Beförderer**.[38] Für den Gefahrübergang gemäss Art. 67 I gilt das Gleiche: nur die Übergabe an einen selbstständigen Beförderer lässt die Gefahr übergehen.[39]

23   **Selbstständig** ist der Beförderer, wenn er zum Verkäufer nicht in einem Anstellungsverhältnis steht und die Beförderung daher nicht auf einer innerbetrieblichen Weisung, sondern auf einem Fracht- oder Speditionsvertrag[40] beruht. Ist der Verkäufer eine juristische Person, so muss der Beförderer eine andere natürliche oder juristische Person sein, mit der der Verkäufer einen solchen Vertrag abschliessen kann. Eine unselbstständige Betriebsabteilung des Verkäufers ist niemals „Beförderer" i. S. d. Art. 31 lit. a). Dagegen ist der Beförderer auch dann „selbstständig", wenn das Unternehmen des Verkäufers und das Transportunternehmen zu demselben Konzern gehören oder staatseigene Betriebe desselben Staats sind. Sie müssen nur eigenständige Rechtspersönlichkeit haben und imstande sein, miteinander wirksame Frachtverträge abzuschliessen.[41]

24   **d) Vorlieferant.** Zulässig ist es auch, dass der Verkäufer seinen eigenen Vorlieferanten veranlasst, die Ware direkt an den Käufer zu versenden („Streckengeschäft"). Der Vorlieferant selbst ist jedoch nicht Beförderer i. S. d. Art. 31 lit. a), da die Ware sich bereits in seinem Gewahrsam befindet, es also zu der erforderlichen „Übergabe" der Ware an ihn nicht kommen kann. Die Lieferpflicht des Verkäufers ist beim Streckengeschäft erst erfüllt, wenn der Vorlieferant den Gewahrsam an der Ware durch Übergabe an einen Beförderer zur direkten Übermittlung an den Käufer aufgibt; der Vorlieferant tritt insofern als **Erfüllungsgehilfe** des Verkäufers auf.[42] Führt der Vorlieferant den Transport selbst oder durch eigene Angestellte durch, so ist es zu einer Übergabe an einen Beförderer nicht gekommen; die Lieferpflicht ist in diesem Fall erst erfüllt, wenn der Vorlieferant die Ware dem Käufer übergibt.[43]

25   **e) Spediteur.** Die Lieferung nach Art. 31 lit. a) kann auch durch Übergabe an einen Spediteur bewirkt werden, d. h. durch Übergabe an einen selbstständigen Dritten, der den Transport der Ware zu organisieren hat.[44] Das ist allerdings in der Literatur umstritten.[45] Für die Beantwortung dieser Streitfrage kann es jedenfalls nicht darauf ankommen, ob das

---

[37] Anders *Schlechtriem*, Einheitliches UN-Kaufrecht, S. 80 = Uniform Sales Law, S. 88. Er will zwar auch unselbstständige Angestellte als „Beförderer" anerkennen, den Verkäufer aber trotzdem für sie gemäß Artt. 45, 79 haften lassen. Das ist mit dem Haftungssystem des Übereinkommens nur schwer vereinbar.
[38] Allgemeine Ansicht; vgl. *Bridge*, FS Kritzer, 77, 87; *Honnold/Flechtner*, Art. 31, Rn. 208; *Bianca/Bonell/ Lando*, Art. 31, Anm. 2.4.; *Heuzé*, Anm. 245.; *Loewe*, Art. 31, S. 52; *Herber/Czerwenka*, Art. 31, Rn. 6; *Reinhart*, Art. 31, Rn. 5; *Enderlein/Maskow/Strohbach*, Art. 31, Anm. 3.; *Enderlein*, Rights and Obligations of the Seller, S. 146; *Soergel/Lüderitz/Budzikiewicz/Schüßler-Langeheine*, Art. 31, Rn. 2; *Neumayer/Ming*, Art. 31, Anm. 6.; *Staudinger/Magnus*, Art. 31, Rn. 13, 19; *Karollus*, S. 196; *Piltz*, Internationales Kaufrecht, Rn. 4–26; ders., UN-Kaufrecht, Rn. 59; *Brunner*, Art. 31, Rn. 6. Ebenso schon die h. M. zu Art. 19 EKG, vgl. OLG Frankfurt a. M., 21.9.1982, in: *Schlechtriem/Magnus*, Art. 19 EKG Nr. 8; *Mertens/Rehbinder*, Art. 19 EKG, Rn. 10; *Dölle/Huber*, Art. 19 EKG Rn. 83, 84, 87; *Soergel/Lüderitz*, Art. 19 EKG, Rn. 10, 20.
[39] Vgl. *Hachem*, Art. 67 Rn. 12 f. m. w. N.
[40] Etwa i. S. d. §§ 407, 453 HGB; Artt. 439, 440 OR; Artt. 8:20, 8:60 BW; Artt. 1678, 1737 ital. Cc.
[41] Vgl. *Hager*, Gefahrtragung nach UN-Kaufrecht, S. 392; *ders./Maultzsch*, 5. Aufl., Art. 67 Rn. 5.
[42] Ebenso *Soergel/Lüderitz/Budzikiewicz/Schüßler-Langeheine*, Art. 31, Rn. 3; MünchKommHGB/*Benicke*, Art. 31, Rn. 16. Zur Haftung des Verkäufers für fehlerhafte Versendung durch den Vorlieferanten vgl. Rn. 35.
[43] Anders scheinbar *Honsell/Ernst/Lauko*, Art. 31, Rn. 14.
[44] Vgl. zum Inhalt des Speditionsvertrages allg. *Ramberg*, S. 13 ff.; *ders.*, ULR 1998, 5 ff.; vgl. ferner die Definitionen in Art. 1737 ital. Cc; § 453 HGB; Art. 439 OR; Art. 8:60 BW. Siehe auch die Definition der „freight forwarding services" in Art. 2.1. FIATA Model Rules for Freight Forwarding Services, welche 1996 von der Weltorganisation der Spediteure angenommen wurden.
[45] Wie hier: *Hachem*, Art. 67 Rn. 15. Ebenso *Denkschrift*, S. 47; *Jayme*, IPRax 1989, 247, 248; *Schlechtriem*, Uniform Sales Law, S. 87 Fn. 348b; *Bianca/Bonell/Lando*, Art. 31, Anm. 2.4.; *Honsell/Ernst/Lauko*, Art. 25, Rn. 18; *Furtak*, Jb. It. R. 3 (1990), 127 ff.; AG Albstadt, 10.3.1989, IPRax 1989, 247 (zu Art. 19 II EKG); vgl. auch *Dölle/Huber*, Art. 19 EKG, Rn. 91. Dagegen: *Mertens/Rehbinder*, Art. 19 EKG, Rn. 9; *Staub/Koller*, Vor § 373 HGB, Rn. 662; *Soergel/Lüderitz*, Art. 19 EKG, Rn. 20; *Lüderitz*, Pflichten der Parteien, S. 183; *Sevón*, Passing of Risk, S. 199; *Loewe*, Art. 31, S. 52; *Herber/Czerwenka*, Art. 31, Rn. 6; *Piltz*, Internationales Kaufrecht, Rn. 4–26; *Erdem*, Rn. 412.

jeweils anwendbare Recht den Spediteur einem Frachtführer gleichstellt.[46] Der internationale Charakter des Übereinkommens und die Notwendigkeit, seine einheitliche Anwendung zu fördern (Art. 7 I), gebieten vielmehr eine Unterscheidung nach von den nationalen bzw. übernationalen Transportrechten losgelösten **Fallgruppen.**

Beschränkt sich die Aufgabe des Spediteurs darauf, den Transport der Ware zu organisieren, ohne dass es zur Übergabe der Ware an ihn kommt, fällt er von vorneherein als Beförderer i. S. d. Art. 31 lit. a) ausser Betracht.[47] Der Verkäufer gibt die Ware diesfalls erst aus der Hand, wenn der vom Spediteur beauftragte Frachtführer die Ware bei ihm abholt. Soweit besteht Einigkeit.

Einigkeit besteht aber auch bezüglich jener Fälle, in denen der zur Organisation des Warentransports Verpflichtete den Transport gänzlich oder auch nur teilweise selber ausführt, die Ware also etwa beim Verkäufer abholt, um anschliessend den Weitertransport zu veranlassen. Der Spediteur ist im Falle des „Abrollens" der Ware unstreitig selbst der erste Beförderer i. S. d. Art. 31 lit. a).[48] Dass die Teilstrecke, über die er das Gut selbst befördert, u. U. nur kurz ist, ist, wie schon dargelegt, unerheblich.[49]

Streitig ist mithin lediglich der Fall, in dem es zum Übergang des Gewahrsams an den Spediteur kommt, ohne dass dieser selbst den Transport oder einen Teil desselben ausführt. Transportiert der Verkäufer die Ware selbst oder durch eigene Angestellte zum Spediteur und übergibt er sie diesem mit dem Auftrag, den weiteren Transport zu veranlassen, sprechen die besseren Gründe dafür, dass die Lieferung schon durch die Übergabe der Ware vom Verkäufer an den Spediteur, und nicht erst durch die Übergabe vom Spediteur an den Frachtführer bewirkt wird.[50] Entscheidend ist, dass der Verkäufer den Gewahrsam an der Ware auf ein selbstständiges Unternehmen zum Zweck der Übermittlung an den Käufer überträgt und auf diese Weise das tut, was er zu tun hat, um die Ware zum Käufer gelangen zu lassen.

3. Übergabe

a) Übergang des Gewahrsams auf den Beförderer. Die Übergabe des Guts an den Beförderer ist vollzogen, sobald der Beförderer körperlichen Gewahrsam an der Ware zum Zweck der Beförderung erlangt.[51] Holt der Beförderer die Ware beim Verkäufer ab, genügt hierzu, dass die Ware in Anwesenheit des Beförderers (oder seines Fahrers) auf das Fahrzeug verladen wird.[52] Anders ist es, wenn der Beförderer anschliessend die Durchführung des Transports wegen vorschriftswidriger Beschaffenheit der Ware ablehnt. Wird das Fahrzeug

---

[46] So aber *Witz/Salger/Lorenz/Witz*, Art. 31, Rn. 17; *Herber/Czerwenka*, Art. 31, Rn. 6.
[47] Insoweit zutreffend *Piltz*, UN-Kaufrecht, Rn. 59; vgl. auch *Schlechtriem*, Pflichten des Verkäufers, S. 112. Diesfalls liegt nach dem Verständnis vieler Rechtsordnungen ein klassischer Speditionsvertrag vor, vgl. etwa § 453 HGB, Art. 439 OR, Art. 8:60 BW.
[48] Dass der Spediteur Beförderer ist, wenn er kraft Selbsteintritts als Frachtführer tätig wird, wird auch von denjenigen nicht bezweifelt, die ihn grundsätzlich nicht als „Beförderer" ansehen wollen, vgl. *Soergel/Lüderitz*, Art. 19 EKG, Rn. 20; *Lüderitz*, Pflichten der Parteien, S. 183; *Herber/Czerwenka*, Art. 31, Rn. 6; *Piltz*, Internationales Kaufrecht, Rn. 4–26; *Erdem*, Rn. 413. Vgl. § 458 I HGB, wonach der Spediteur hinsichtlich des ersten Teilstücks des Transports Frachtführer kraft Selbsteintritts ist; vgl. auch Art. 8:61 BW, Art. 1741 ital. Cc sowie Art. 439 OR.
[49] Vgl. oben Rn. 20.
[50] Ebenso *Honsell/Ernst/Lauko*, Art. 31, Rn. 25; *Heuzé*, Anm. 245.; *Hachem*, Art. 67 Rn. 15; *Bamberger/Roth/Saenger*, Art. 31, Rn. 6; *MünchKomm/Gruber*, Art. 31, Rn. 18; *MünchKommHGB/Benicke*, Art. 31, Rn. 12; *Brunner*, Art. 31, Rn. 6; so wohl auch *Achilles*, Art. 31, Rn. 4. Eine explizite Gleichstellung der Warenübergabe an den Spediteur („spedizioniere") und der Warenübergabe an den Frachtführer („vettore") sieht das italienische Recht in Art. 1510 II Cc vor.
[51] Vgl. auch *Heuzé*, Anm. 245.; *MünchKommHGB/Benicke*, Art. 31, Rn. 8; *MünchKomm/Gruber*, Art. 31, Rn. 19. „Übergabe zur Übermittlung an den Käufer" bedeutet also insoweit das Gleiche wie im deutschen Recht (§ 447 BGB) „Auslieferung" der Sache an den Frachtführer, vgl. dazu *Soergel/Huber*, § 447, Rn. 26; im US-amerikanischen Recht vgl. § 2–504 UCC: „[…] the seller […] must put the goods in the possession of such a carrier […]".
[52] Vgl. (zu § 447 BGB) BGHZ 113, 106, 114: Übergabe von Dieselkraftstoff, sobald er aus dem Tank des Verkäufers in das Fahrzeug des Beförderers gelangt.

in Abwesenheit des Beförderers beladen, so ist zur Übergabe noch die Übernahme des Fahrzeugs durch den Beförderer erforderlich. Das blosse Bereitstellen zur Versendung genügt nicht. Nicht ausreichend ist auch die Übergabe eines Traditionspapiers.[53]

30 **b) Übergabe „zur Übermittlung an den Käufer".** Die Ware muss dem Beförderer „zur Übermittlung an den Käufer" übergeben werden. Das setzt voraus, dass der Verkäufer mit dem Beförderer einen Frachtvertrag[54] abschliesst, auf Grund dessen der Beförderer die Ware zum Käufer zu transportieren oder transportieren zu lassen hat. Nähere Einzelheiten sind in Art. 32 geregelt.[55] Ist im Kaufvertrag vereinbart, dass der Verkäufer die Ware an einen Dritten zu versenden hat, oder hat der Käufer nachträglich den Verkäufer angewiesen, sie an einen Dritten zu versenden, so tritt der Dritte an die Stelle des Käufers.[56] Keine Übergabe „zur Übermittlung an den Käufer" liegt vor, wenn der Verkäufer dem Beförderer zunächst nur den Auftrag erteilt, die Ware einzulagern, und sich die Erteilung des Beförderungsauftrags vorbehält.[57] Hat dagegen der Beförderer den Auftrag zur Beförderung angenommen und lagert er die Ware wegen später auftretender Transportschwierigkeiten vorübergehend ein, so ändert sich hierdurch nichts daran, dass der Verkäufer seine Pflicht zur Lieferung erfüllt hat; die Transportschwierigkeiten sind in diesem Fall ein Teil des Transportrisikos, das nach Art. 67 den Käufer trifft. Erst recht ändert ein vorübergehendes Abstellen des Transportfahrzeugs durch den Beförderer während des Transports nichts daran, dass die Übergabe an den Beförderer „zur Übermittlung an den Käufer" stattgefunden hat.[58] Hat der Käufer sich im Kaufvertrag die Bestimmung, wohin und an wen die Ware zu versenden ist, vorbehalten („Destinationsvorbehalt"), so verletzt er seine Abnahmepflicht (vgl. Art. 60 lit. a)), wenn er die Bestimmung bis zum Liefertermin nicht vornimmt.[59] Scheitert die Lieferung an der unterlassenen Mitwirkung des Käufers, ist eine Haftung des Verkäufers wegen Nichterfüllung der Lieferpflicht durch Art. 80 ausgeschlossen.

31 **c) Ort der Übergabe.** Hinsichtlich des Orts der Versendung enthält das Gesetz keine Vorschriften. Schweigt auch der Vertrag hierüber, so kann der Verkäufer von jedem passenden Ort aus versenden, um seine Lieferpflicht zu erfüllen.[60] Dass er nicht einen ganz überraschenden und entlegenen Ort wählen darf, der zu erheblichen Verzögerungen des Eintreffens beim Käufer führt, ergibt sich aus Treu und Glauben (Art. 7 II)[61] und bedarf daher keiner besonderen gesetzlichen Bestimmung. Ist im Kaufvertrag ein bestimmter Ort für die Versendung vorgesehen, so ist diese Bestimmung selbstverständlich zu beachten.[62]

32 **d) Rechtsfolgen der Übergabe.** Mit der Übergabe der Ware an den Beförderer zur Übermittlung an den Käufer hat der Verkäufer im Fall des Art. 31 lit. a) die Pflicht zur Lieferung der Ware erfüllt. Wird die Ware auf dem Transport beschädigt oder zerstört, geht sie verloren, wird sie fehlgeleitet oder wird die Ablieferung an den Käufer verzögert, so kann der Käufer den Verkäufer nicht mehr gemäss Art. 45 I wegen Nichterfüllung in Anspruch nehmen. Der Beförderer ist kein Erfüllungsgehilfe des Verkäufers, für den der Verkäufer (in den Grenzen des Art. 79 II) einzustehen hätte; Fehler des Beförderers sind vielmehr Teil des in Artt. 66, 67 geregelten Transportrisikos.[63] Das gilt für alle Aufgaben, die mit einer internationalen Beförderung typischerweise verbunden sind. Soweit dagegen der Spediteur

---

[53] So auch *Achilles*, Art. 31, Rn. 5; anders *Neumayer/Ming*, Art. 31, Anm. 5.
[54] Zum Speditionsvertrag siehe oben Rn. 25 ff.
[55] Vgl. dazu Art. 32 Rn. 17 ff.
[56] Vgl. auch *Honsell/Ernst/Lauko*, Art. 31, Rn. 24.
[57] Übereinstimmend MünchKomm/*Gruber*, Art. 31, Rn. 19.
[58] Vgl. (zu § 447 BGB) BGHZ 113, 106, 114.
[59] Vgl. auch *Honsell/Ernst/Lauko*, Art. 31, Rn. 24.
[60] Ebenso *Lüderitz*, Pflichten der Parteien, S. 182 f.; *Karollus*, S. 108; *Honsell/Ernst/Lauko*, Art. 31, Rn. 18. Zur Zulässigkeit des „Streckengeschäfts" siehe oben Rn. 24.
[61] Zum Grundsatz von Treu und Glauben siehe Art. 30 Rn. 9.
[62] Vgl. dazu unten Rn. 78.
[63] Vgl. HGer Zürich, 10.2.1999, CISG-online 488 = SZIER 2000, 111, 113 = IHR 2001, 44, 45; Tribunal Cantonal de Vaud, 26.5.2000, SZIER 2002, 146, 147; vgl. auch *Neumayer/Ming*, Art. 31, Anm. 6.

oder Frachtführer, neben der eigentlichen Beförderung, eine Pflicht übernimmt, die nach dem Kaufvertrag den Verkäufer trifft, haftet der Verkäufer für Fehler des Beförderers. Das gilt insbesondere für Fehler bei der Erledigung von Zollformalitäten bei der Ausfuhr, die regelmässig Sache des Verkäufers ist, nicht dagegen für die Erledigung von Zollformalitäten bei der Einfuhr, die regelmässig zum Pflichten- und Gefahrenbereich des Käufers gehört.[64]

4. Vertragsverletzungen des Verkäufers bei der Lieferung

a) Versendung nicht vertragsmässiger Ware. Anders als nach früherem Einheitskaufrecht[65] ist es nicht mehr Begriffsmerkmal der Lieferung, dass die dem Beförderer ausgehändigte Ware „vertragsgemäß" ist. Das ändert selbstverständlich nichts an der Pflicht des Verkäufers, Ware zu liefern, die den Anforderungen des Vertrags entspricht. Dies ergibt sich bereits aus Art. 30 und wird klargestellt durch Art. 35 I.[66] Die Versendung mangelhafter Ware stellt jedoch keinen Fall der „Nichtlieferung" i. S. d. Art. 49 I lit. b) dar, der dem Käufer ohne weiteres das Recht geben würde, dem Verkäufer für die Lieferung vertragsmässiger Ware Nachfrist zu setzen und bei Fristablauf die Vertragsaufhebung zu erklären. Dem Käufer stehen vielmehr die Rechtsbehelfe zu, die das Übereinkommen speziell für den Fall der Lieferung „nicht vertragsgemässer Ware" vorsieht.[67] 33

b) Falschlieferung. Nicht vertragsgemäss ist die Ware auch dann, wenn sie hinsichtlich ihrer „Art" dem Vertrag nicht entspricht (Art. 35 I). Das Übereinkomen unterscheidet nicht zwischen „Schlechtlieferung" und „Falschlieferung".[68] Unabhängig vom objektiven Grad der Abweichung gelten deshalb auch für die Falschlieferung die speziellen Regeln über die „Lieferung nicht vertragsmässiger Ware" (Artt. 39, 46 II), nicht dagegen die Regeln über die „Nichtlieferung" (Art. 49 I lit. b)).[69] 34

c) Mangelhafte Verpackung und Verladung. Ist die Ware nur in verpacktem Zustand transportfähig, ist der Verkäufer im Rahmen seiner Lieferpflicht auch zur Verpackung verpflichtet.[70] Mangelhaft verpackte Ware ist nicht vertragsgemäss (vgl. Art. 35 II lit. d)); nimmt deshalb die Ware auf dem Transport Schaden oder ist der Käufer durch die mangelhafte Verpackung in der Verwendung der Ware behindert, haftet der Verkäufer nach Artt. 45 ff.[71] Lässt der Verkäufer die Ware im Weg des „Streckengeschäfts" durch seinen eigenen **Vorlieferanten** direkt an den Käufer versenden, so bedient er sich des Vorlieferanten zur Erfüllung seiner eigenen Lieferpflicht[72] und haftet daher für dessen Fehler bei Verpackung oder Verladung wie für eigene. 35

Übergibt der Verkäufer die Ware dem Beförderer in unverpacktem Zustand mit dem Auftrag, sie zu verpacken, so hat er seine Lieferpflicht mit der Übergabe erfüllt. Auch hier gilt die Regel, dass der Verkäufer für das Verhalten des Beförderers, nachdem dieser die Ware übernommen hat, nicht mehr haftet.[73] Entsprechendes gilt, wenn der Beförderer selbst die Verladung der Ware durchführt und sie unsachgemäss verstaut. Nicht anders sollte man 36

---

[64] Vgl. Incoterms® 2010 (dazu Art. 30 Rn. 3 f.) FCA („Frei Frachtführer"), CPT („frachtfrei") und CIP („frachtfrei versichert"), jeweils unter A 2, B 2; dazu auch unten Rn. 84.
[65] Vgl. Art. 19 I EKG; dazu *Dölle/Huber*, Art. 19 EKG, Rn. 153 ff.; zu den Gründen der Änderung vgl. 1. Aufl., *U. Huber*, Art. 31 Rn. 16.
[66] Vgl. dazu auch YB III (1972), S. 37, Nr. 48.
[67] Vgl. *Schwenzer*, Art. 35 Rn. 2.
[68] Vgl. allgemein *Schwenzer/Hachem/Kee*, Rn. 29.10. Anders dagegen das schweizerische Recht (dazu *Honsell*, OR BT, S. 129 ff.) und das österreichische Recht (dazu *Koziol/Welser*, Bd. II, S. 66 f.). Im deutschen Recht ist mit Inkrafttreten des Schuldrechtsmodernisierungsgesetzes am 1.1.2002 der früher einschlägige § 378 HGB weggefallen; der neue § 434 III BGB stellt nun ausdrücklich die Falschlieferung einem Sachmangel gleich, dazu *Hoeren/Martinek/Bohne*, Teil I, Rn. 597.
[69] So die ganz h. M.; dazu *Schwenzer*, Art. 35 Rn. 10.
[70] Vgl. auch *Neumayer/Ming*, Art. 31, Anm. 5.; *Honsell/Ernst/Lauko*, Art. 31, Rn. 22; *Staudinger/Magnus*, Art. 31, Rn. 10; MünchKommHGB/*Benicke*, Art. 31, Rn. 17.
[71] Vgl. *Schwenzer*, Art. 36 Rn. 4.
[72] Vgl. oben Rn. 24.
[73] Vgl. oben Rn. 32.

entscheiden, wenn der Beförderer auf Weisung des Verkäufers während des Transports eine Umladung oder Umverpackung vornimmt.[74]

37   **d) Vertragswidrige Kostenbelastung des Käufers.** Hat der Verkäufer nach dem Vertrag die Kosten der Versendung zu tragen, so muss er die Ware „frachtfrei" versenden. Tut er das nicht und verlangt deshalb der Beförderer vom Käufer Zahlung der Fracht gegen Aushändigung der Ware,[75] so stellt diese Art der Versendung eine Vertragsverletzung des Verkäufers dar. Zwar ist die Lieferpflicht als solche erfüllt; nicht erfüllt ist aber die Pflicht, die Ware „frei von Ansprüchen Dritter" – nämlich frei von Ansprüchen des Frachtführers – zu liefern (Art. 41).[76] Der Käufer kann also jedenfalls vom Verkäufer Schadensersatz gemäss Art. 45 I lit. b) verlangen (Ersatz der Frachtkosten). Ist die Vertragsverletzung „wesentlich" i. S. d. Art. 25, kann der Käufer die Annahme der Lieferung zurückweisen und Vertragsaufhebung gemäss Art. 49 I lit. a) erklären oder kostenfreie Ersatzlieferung analog Art. 46 II verlangen. Die Wesentlichkeit der Vertragsverletzung wird von der Höhe der Frachtkosten und vor allem davon abhängen, ob der Käufer den Kaufpreis schon bezahlt hat oder nicht, ob er also noch die einfache Möglichkeit hat, die Frachtkosten vom Kaufpreis abzusetzen.

38   Dagegen ist die **eigenmächtige Kostenbelastung** durch den Frachtführer Teil des vom Käufer zu tragenden Transportrisikos (Art. 67 I Satz 1).[77] Schliesst etwa der Frachtführer eine Transportversicherung ab, ohne dass dies im Kaufvertrag vorgesehen war und ohne dahingehende Weisung des Verkäufers oder des Käufers, und macht er dann die Ablieferung an den Käufer davon abhängig, dass dieser ihm die Versicherungsprämie erstattet, haftet der Verkäufer nicht; der Beförderer ist im Fall des Art. 31 lit. a) nicht Erfüllungsgehilfe des Verkäufers.[78]

39   **e) Versendung an den falschen Ort.** Der Verkäufer ist im Zweifel verpflichtet, dem Käufer die Ware an dessen Niederlassung zuzusenden, wenn nicht durch den Kaufvertrag oder durch eine zulässige Weisung des Käufers ein anderer Ort bestimmt ist. Adressiert der Verkäufer die Ware an den falschen Ort, so hängt die Frage, ob hierdurch die Lieferung bewirkt ist, von der tatsächlichen Entwicklung ab. Nimmt der Käufer die Ware tatsächlich ab, so ist die Lieferpflicht erfüllt, und der Käufer kann wegen etwaiger Mehrkosten Schadensersatz gemäss Art. 45 I lit. b) verlangen. Lehnt der Käufer es dagegen ab, die Ware am falschen Ort entgegenzunehmen, so ist die Lieferpflicht nicht erfüllt. Ob der Käufer zur Zurückweisung berechtigt oder aber zur Übernahme auch am falschen Ort verpflichtet ist, kann nur im Einzelfall nach Treu und Glauben (Art. 7 II) entschieden werden.[79] Unberührt bleibt, auch wenn der Käufer zur Zurückweisung berechtigt ist, die Erhaltungspflicht gemäss Art. 86 I. Unberechtigte Zurückweisung lässt einerseits die Haftung des Verkäufers entfallen (Art. 80) und führt andererseits zur Haftung des Käufers wegen Verletzung der Abnahmepflicht (Artt. 53, 60, 61 I, 64 I). Erreicht die an die falsche Adresse versendete Ware den Käufer überhaupt nicht, so hat der Verkäufer seine Lieferpflicht ebenfalls nicht erfüllt.

40   Hat dagegen der Beförderer die richtig adressierte Ware an den falschen Ort transportiert, sie vielleicht sogar an den falschen Empfänger ausgeliefert,[80] so hat der Verkäufer dennoch durch die korrekte Versendung seine Lieferpflicht erfüllt. Der Fehler des Beförderers ist Teil des vom Käufer zu tragenden Transportrisikos (Art. 67 I S. 1).[81] Der Verkäufer, der sich auf

---

[74] Anders 1. Aufl., *U. Huber,* Art. 31 Rn. 42, im Anschluss an RGZ 115, 162: Haftung des Verkäufers gemäß § 278, wenn er dem Beförderer den Auftrag erteilt, während des Transports die Plane des Güterwaggons auszuwechseln und der Beförderer versäumt, die neue Plane aufzulegen.
[75] Bei Geltung deutschen Frachtrechts: § 421 II HGB.
[76] Vgl. *Schwenzer,* Art. 41 Rn. 4.
[77] Vgl. aus der deutschen Praxis RGZ 99, 56 (zu § 447 BGB).
[78] Vgl. oben Rn. 32.
[79] Vgl. dazu auch *Hager/Maultzsch,* 5. Aufl., Art. 60 Rn. 3. Zum Grundsatz von Treu und Glauben siehe Art. 30 Rn. 9.
[80] Vgl. RGZ 62, 331: Verwechslung zweier für verschiedene Käufer bestimmter Sendungen durch den Frachtführer.
[81] Vgl. RGZ 62, 331, 333 (zu § 447 BGB); übereinstimmend MünchKommHGB/*Benicke,* Art. 31, Rn. 13.

Inhalt der Lieferpflicht und Ort der Lieferung 41–43 Art. 31

den Übergang der Transportgefahr beruft, ist nach Treu und Glauben (Art. 7 II)[82] verpflichtet, Ersatzansprüche gegen den Beförderer an den Käufer abzutreten, soweit diesem auf Grund der massgeblichen Bestimmungen des Frachtrechts keine eigenen Ersatzansprüche gegen den Beförderer zustehen.[83] Ist über den Transport oder die Transportversicherung ein Order oder Rektapapier ausgestellt (ein Konnossement, ein Ladeschein, eine Transportversicherungspolice), so kann der Käufer die betreffenden Ansprüche gegen den Beförderer oder den Versicherer geltend machen, sofern der Verkäufer seine Pflicht zur Übergabe des (indossierten) Dokuments (Art. 34 S. 1) erfüllt hat.

5. Eingriffe des Verkäufers in den Transport

a) Rückbeorderung der Ware. Häufig ist der Verkäufer auf Grund der frachtrechtlichen Vorschriften noch in der Lage, durch gegenteilige Weisung an den Beförderer die Ablieferung der Ware an den Käufer zu verhindern. Solche Eingriffe kann der Verkäufer im Interesse des Käufers vornehmen (etwa im Fall einer nachträglichen Störung der Transportverbindungen) oder im eigenen Interesse. Der Eingriff im eigenen Interesse kann rechtmässig sein (so insbesondere im Fall der Vermögensverschlechterung des Käufers, Art. 71 II) oder rechtswidrig. Ohne Rücksicht hierauf führt die Rückbeorderung der Ware, also die Rückgabe vom Beförderer an den Verkäufer dazu, dass die **bereits erfolgte Lieferung rückgängig gemacht wird,** und dass daher die **Lieferpflicht des Verkäufers wiederauflebt.**[84] Ist Grund für die Rücknahme der Ware eine Vertragsverletzung des Käufers, kann der Verkäufer der Pflicht zur erneuten Lieferung durch wirksame Erklärung der Vertragsaufhebung entgehen. Kommt es wegen zwischenzeitlicher Rückbeorderung der Ware zu Mehrkosten des Transports, so kann der Verkäufer Ersatz dieser Mehrkosten nur verlangen, wenn die Rücknahme durch eine Vertragsverletzung des Käufers oder durch einen Umstand veranlasst ist, der zu den auf den Käufer übergegangenen Transportrisiken zählt (Anspruchsgrundlage im ersten Fall: Art. 61 I lit. b), im zweiten Fall: Art. 85 in analoger Anwendung).[85] Entsprechendes gilt, wenn der Verkäufer den Beförderer veranlasst, die Ware, statt an den Käufer, an einen anderen Abnehmer auszuliefern (es sei denn, es liege ein Fall rechtmässigen Selbsthilfeverkaufs gemäss Art. 88 vor).[86] 41

b) Anhalten der Ware. Auch das Anhalten der Ware auf dem Transport auf Grund einer Weisung des Verkäufers stellt eine **Rückgängigmachung der Lieferung** insofern dar, als dem Beförderer die Ware von nun an nicht mehr „zur Übermittlung an den Käufer" überlassen ist. Die Lieferpflicht des Verkäufers lebt daher wieder auf. Die Besonderheit des Falls besteht nur darin, dass der Verkäufer die Ware nicht von neuem versenden, sondern nur den Weitertransport veranlassen muss. Wegen der Kosten gilt das zur Rückbeorderung Gesagte entsprechend.[87] 42

c) Haftung des Verkäufers. Ist der Eingriff in den Transport durch den Verkäufer nicht durch besondere Gründe (insbesondere durch objektive Transporthindernisse oder durch ein Anhalterecht gemäss Art. 71 II) gerechtfertigt, so kann er eine **Haftung des Verkäufers wegen Vertragsverletzung** begründen. Das gilt vor allem, wenn der Verkäufer dem Käufer bereits eine bindende Versendungsanzeige übermittelt hat[88] oder wenn der Eingriff 43

---

[82] Siehe Art. 30 Rn. 9.
[83] Solche eigenen Ansprüche ergeben sich z. B., wenn deutsches Frachtrecht anwendbar ist, aus § 421 I 2 HGB, bei Beförderung im internationalen Straßengütertransport aus Art. 13 I 2 CMR und, im internationalen Eisenbahnverkehr, aus Art. 28 § 4 CIM.
[84] So auch *Achilles*, Art. 31, Rn. 7; *Bamberger/Roth/Saenger*, Art. 31, Rn. 9; *Soergel/Lüderitz/Budzikiewicz/Schüßler-Langeheine*, Art. 31, Rn. 15; *Staudinger/Magnus*, Art. 31, Rn. 23.
[85] Vgl. *Soergel/Lüderitz/Budzikiewicz/Schüßler-Langeheine*, Art. 31, Rn. 15.
[86] Ebenso *Staudinger/Magnus*, Art. 31, Rn. 23; *MünchKommHGB/Benicke*, Art. 31, Rn. 13.
[87] Oben Rn. 41; vgl. auch *Soergel/Lüderitz/Budzikiewicz/Schüßler-Langeheine*, Art. 31, Rn. 15: Analoge Anwendung des Art. 87.
[88] Vgl. Art. 32 Rn. 9, 14.

zur Folge hat, dass die Ware verspätet beim Käufer eintrifft. Rechtsfolge ist unter anderem, dass die Gefahr des zufälligen Verlusts oder der zufälligen Beschädigung der Ware ab dem rechtswidrigen Eingriff des Verkäufers in den Transport wieder auf den Verkäufer zurückfällt (Art. 66, 2. HS.). Ist Grund für die Rückbeorderung oder das Anhalten der Ware eine **Vertragsverletzung des Käufers,** insbesondere die **Nichtabnahme der vom Beförderer am Bestimmungsort angebotenen Ware,** und hält der Verkäufer trotzdem an der Durchführung des Vertrags fest, so bleibt er auf Grund seiner frachtrechtlichen Verfügungsbefugnis verpflichtet, im Interesse (und auf Kosten) des Käufers für die Erhaltung der Ware zu sorgen (Art. 85). Er kann die Erhaltungspflicht insbesondere dadurch erfüllen, dass er den Beförderer anweist, die Ware einstweilen auf Lager zu nehmen (Art. 87). Erklärt der Käufer sich nachträglich noch zur Abnahme bereit, so ist der Verkäufer verpflichtet, den Frachtführer zur Auslieferung der Ware an den Käufer am Bestimmungsort anzuweisen; insoweit ist seine **Lieferpflicht** durch die zwischenzeitliche Einlagerung der Ware **wiederaufgelebt.** Er kann die Auslieferung davon abhängig machen, dass der Käufer dem Beförderer die entstandenen Mehrkosten erstattet (Art. 85 S. 2). Die Gefahr des Verlusts oder der Beschädigung der eingelagerten Ware bleibt in diesem Fall beim Käufer.[89] Denn auf ihn ist die Gefahr bereits gemäss Art. 67 I S. 1 übergegangen, und die vertragswidrige Verweigerung der Abnahme kann nicht zu einer Zurückverlagerung der Gefahr auf den Verkäufer führen.

6. Teillieferung

44   Ist eine Mehrzahl von Sachen zu liefern und versendet der Verkäufer nur einen Teil, so ist die Lieferung nicht vertragsgemäss (Art. 35 I).[90] Der Verkäufer bleibt aber gemäss Art. 37 S. 1 bis zum Ablauf der Lieferfrist berechtigt, den fehlenden Teil nachzuliefern, wenn das für den Käufer nicht mit unzumutbaren Unannehmlichkeiten verbunden ist. Beim Versendungskauf sind solche Unannehmlichkeiten für den Käufer im Allgemeinen nicht zu befürchten. Praktisch bedeutet das, dass der Verkäufer berechtigt ist, die Ware bis zum Liefertermin in mehreren Teilpartien zu versenden.[91] Hat er bis zum Ablauf der Lieferfrist den noch fehlenden Teil nicht nachgeliefert, so richten die Rechtsfolgen sich nach Art. 51.[92]

III. Art. 31 lit. b), c): Lieferung durch Zur-Verfügung-Stellen der Ware

1. Ausgangspunkt

45   Erfordert der Kaufvertrag keine Beförderung der Ware[93] und ist für die Lieferung kein anderer Ort vorgesehen,[94] so richtet der Lieferort und der Inhalt der Lieferpflicht sich in erster Linie nach Art. 31 lit. b), subsidiär nach Art. 31 lit. c). In beiden Fällen ist die Lieferschuld „Holschuld". Sie wird dadurch erfüllt, dass der Verkäufer die Ware an dem in Art. 31 lit. b) oder c) bestimmten Ort für den Käufer bereitstellt.

2. Lieferort gemäss Art. 31 lit. b)

46   **a) Die vier Fälle des Art. 31 lit. b).** Art. 31 lit. b) erfasst vier Fälle:
1. Der Kaufvertrag bezieht sich auf eine bestimmte Ware und beide Parteien wissen bei Vertragsabschluss, wo sie sich befindet (dass der Verkäufer das nicht weiss, wird wohl kaum jemals vorkommen; praktisch geht es vor allem darum, dass auch der Käufer es weiss).

---

[89] Vgl. auch *Hachem*, Art. 66 Rn. 26.
[90] Vgl. auch *Schwenzer*, Art. 35 Rn. 8.
[91] Vgl. auch *Müller-Chen*, Art. 51 Rn. 4. A. A. *Heuzé*, Anm. 246.
[92] Vgl. *Müller-Chen*, Art. 51 Rn. 5 f.
[93] Vgl. dazu oben Rn. 17 f.
[94] Vgl. dazu unten Rn. 73 f.

2. Der Kaufvertrag bezieht sich auf einen bestimmten Vorrat, z. B. ein Fuder Wein oder den Inhalt eines Öltanks oder die Ladung eines im Hafen eingetroffenen Schiffs; aus diesem Vorrat ist ein bestimmtes Quantum verkauft; beide Parteien wissen bei Vertragsabschluss, wo der Vorrat sich befindet.
3. Der Kaufvertrag bezieht sich auf Sachen, die vom Verkäufer oder einem Dritten[95] erst noch hergestellt werden sollen, und beide Parteien wissen bei Vertragsabschluss, wo die Produktionsstätte (die Fabrik oder die Werkstatt) sich befindet.
4. Der Kaufvertrag bezieht sich auf zu erzeugende Sachen, also z. b. auf Baumwolle aus der Pflanzung des Verkäufers oder eines Dritten, auf Holz aus dem Wald oder auf Kies aus der Grube, und beide Parteien wissen bei Vertragsabschluss, wo die Pflanzung, der Wald oder die Grube liegt.

Für diese Fälle bestimmt Art. 31 lit. b) in Übereinstimmung mit dem mutmasslichen Parteiwillen, dass der Käufer die Ware dort zu holen hat, wo sie nach dem Wissen beider Parteien liegt oder herzustellen oder zu erzeugen ist. Dabei regelt Art. 31 lit. b) nicht nur den allgemeinen „Ort", sondern auch die konkrete „Stelle" der Lieferung: an Ort und Stelle, wo die Ware sich befindet oder wo sie herzustellen oder zu erzeugen ist, hat der Verkäufer sie zur Verfügung zu stellen, der Käufer sie zu holen. Abweichende Vereinbarungen haben selbstverständlich Vorrang.

b) Ware auf dem Transport. Art. 31 lit. b) bezieht sich **nicht** auf den Fall, in dem die 47 Ware sich auf dem Transport befindet, in dem also rollende, schwimmende, fliegende Ware verkauft wird.[96] Hier ergibt sich aus dem Vertrag mit Sicherheit, dass der Verkäufer die Ware jedenfalls nicht dort zur Verfügung stellen, der Käufer sie nicht dort holen soll, wo sie sich zur Zeit des Vertragsabschlusses befindet. Die Parteien haben also einen von Art. 31 lit. b) abweichenden Ort, im Allgemeinen auch eine abweichende Modalität der Lieferung vereinbart. Die Anwendung des Art. 31 lit. b) wird hierdurch ausgeschlossen.[97]

c) Kenntnis des Käufers bei Vertragsabschluss. Entscheidend ist, dass die Parteien bei 48 Vertragsabschluss übereinstimmend davon ausgehen, dass die Ware sich an einem bestimmten Ort befindet. Erfährt der Käufer den Lage- oder Produktionsort erst später, so wird hierdurch ein Lieferort nicht begründet. Der Lieferort richtet sich in einem solchen Fall, wenn die Parteien nicht noch nachträglich eine Vereinbarung (nach Massgabe des Art. 29) treffen, nach Art. 31 lit. c). Erforderlich ist positive Kenntnis (die dem Käufer im Streitfall nachgewiesen werden muss); blosses „Kennen-Müssen" reicht nicht aus.[98]

3. Lieferort gemäss Art. 31 lit. c)

Erfordert der Vertrag keinen Transport der Ware, ist kein bestimmter Lieferort vereinbart 49 und liegen auch die besonderen Voraussetzungen des Art. 31 lit. b) nicht vor, so bestimmt der Lieferort sich nach Art. 31 lit. c). Lieferort und Lieferstelle ist die **Niederlassung des Verkäufers,** bei **mehreren Niederlassungen** diejenige mit der engsten Beziehung zum Vertrag (Art. 10 lit. a)), beim Fehlen einer Niederlassung der **Ort des gewöhnlichen Aufenthalts** des Verkäufers (Art. 10 lit. b)). Massgeblich ist die Niederlassung (oder der gewöhnliche Aufenthalt) **zur Zeit des Vertragsabschlusses.** Verlegt der Verkäufer seine Niederlassung

---

[95] Zu diesem Fall kritisch *Neumayer/Ming,* Art. 31, Anm. 9.
[96] Anders Sekretariatskommentar, Art. 29, Nr. 12, 17; im Anschluss hieran *Schlechtriem,* Einheitliches UN-Kaufrecht, S. 53 = Uniform Sales Law, S. 64; *Bianca/Bonell/Lando,* Art. 31, Anm. 2.6.2.; *Herber/Czerwenka,* Art. 31, Rn. 7; *Honsell/Ernst/Lauko,* Art. 31, Rn. 37; *Karollus,* S. 110; *Staudinger/Magnus,* Art. 31, Rn. 28; *Bamberger/Roth/Saenger,* Art. 31, Rn. 16; *Witz/Salger/Lorenz/Witz,* Art. 31, Rn. 23; MünchKommHGB/*Benicke,* Art. 31, Rn. 28; MünchKomm/*Gruber,* Art. 31, Rn. 12; *Brunner,* Art. 31, Rn. 10; 1. Aufl. dieses Kommentars, *U. Huber,* Art. 31 Rn 59. Zutreffend *Neumayer/Ming,* Art. 31, Anm. 13.; *Achilles,* Art. 31, Rn. 12.
[97] Näheres unten Rn. 79.
[98] Übereinstimmend MünchKommHGB/*Benicke,* Art. 31, Rn. 19; MünchKomm/*Gruber,* Art. 31, Rn. 13; *Staudinger/Magnus,* Art. 31, Rn. 26. Anders *Baumgärtel/Laumen/Prütting,* Art. 31, Rn. 6.

nachträglich oder zieht er um, so ist er zwar grundsätzlich verpflichtet, die Ware am ursprünglichen Niederlassungs- oder gewöhnlichen Aufenthaltsort zur Verfügung zu stellen. Der Käufer ist aber nach Treu und Glauben (Art. 7 II)[99] verpflichtet, sich auf den Wunsch des Verkäufers einzulassen, die Ware am neuen Niederlassungsort abzuholen, vorausgesetzt, dass dies für den Käufer nicht mit unzumutbaren Mehrbelastungen verbunden ist und dass der Verkäufer, falls Mehrkosten für den Käufer entstehen, sich bereiterklärt, sie zu erstatten.[100]

4. Zur-Verfügung-Stellen

50 **a) Bereitstellen der Ware.** Der Verkäufer stellt die Ware dem Käufer „zur Verfügung", indem er alles tut, was von seiner Seite erforderlich ist, um dem Käufer oder seinem Beauftragten das Abholen zu ermöglichen. Dazu ist vor allem erforderlich, dass er die Ware am Lieferort für den Käufer bereitstellt.[101] **Ausscheiden** der Ware aus einem grösseren Bestand oder eine besondere Kennzeichnung als für den Käufer bestimmt ist **nicht nötig**, wenn die Ausscheidung beim Eintreffen des Käufers oder seines Beauftragten ohne weiteres möglich ist.[102] Verpflichtet der Verkäufer sich, die Ware bis auf weiteres oder für eine bestimmte Zeit für den Käufer bereitzuhalten, vereinbart er also mit dem Käufer ein Besitzkonstitut, so ist die Lieferpflicht ebenfalls mit Bereitstellung erfüllt.[103] Vermietet oder verleiht der Käufer dem Verkäufer die Ware zurück, ohne sie zunächst in Besitz zu nehmen (etwa im Fall des „sale and lease back"), so ist die Lieferpflicht erfüllt, sobald das Miet- oder Leihverhältnis in Wirksamkeit tritt und die ursprünglichen Pflichten des Verkäufers aus dem Kaufvertrag ablöst.

51 **b) Benachrichtigung des Käufers.** In der Regel erfordert „Zur-Verfügung-Stellen" der Ware weiterhin, dass der Verkäufer den Käufer hiervon benachrichtigt.[104] Die richtige Übermittlung der mit geeigneten Mitteln abgesendeten Benachrichtigung fällt in das Risiko des Käufers (Art. 27); das heisst, Verlust oder Verzögerung der Nachricht auf dem Übermittlungsweg ändern nichts daran, dass der Verkäufer seine Lieferpflicht durch „Zur-Verfügung-Stellen" der Ware erfüllt hat.[105] Die Gefahr des Verlusts der Ware geht allerdings erst dann auf den Käufer über, wenn er Kenntnis von der Bereitstellung hat, also erst mit Zugang der Nachricht (Art. 69 II). Auch die Fälligkeit der Pflicht zur Kaufpreiszahlung (Art. 58 I S. 1) tritt erst mit Zugang ein.[106] Erfährt der Verkäufer, dass seine Mitteilung den Käufer nicht erreicht hat, wird er sie deshalb bereits im eigenen Interesse wiederholen wollen; nach Treu und Glauben (Art. 7 II)[107] ist er ausserdem auch dazu verpflichtet.

52 **Entbehrlich** ist die Benachrichtigung, wenn die Parteien einen festen Termin vereinbart haben, zu dem die Ware abzuholen ist, und der Verkäufer sie zu diesem Termin bereitstellt;[108] ferner dann, wenn die Ware bereits bei Vertragsabschluss abholbereit bereitsteht und der Käufer dies weiss.

---

[99] Siehe Art. 30 Rn. 9.
[100] Ebenso *Karollus*, S. 110; *Honsell/Ernst/Lauko*, Art. 31, Rn. 46; *Neumayer/Ming*, Art. 31, Anm. 13.; *Heuzé*, Anm. 243.; MünchKommHGB/*Benicke*, Art. 31, Rn. 23; MünchKomm/*Gruber*, Art. 31, Rn. 6.
[101] Vgl. OLG Hamm, 23.6.1998, CISG-online 434 = RIW 1999, 785 ff.
[102] A. A. Sekretariatskommentar, Art. 29, Nr. 16 (mit der Einschränkung „normally"); *Schlechtriem*, Einheitliches UN-Kaufrecht, S. 54 = Uniform Sales Law, S. 65; *Bianca/Bonell/Lando*, Art. 31, Anm. 2.7. Wie hier *Piltz*, Internationales Kaufrecht, Rn. 4–29; *Honsell/Ernst/Lauko*, Art. 31, Rn. 39; *Neumayer/Ming*, Art. 31, Anm. 11.; MünchKommHGB/*Benicke*, Art. 31, Rn. 24; MünchKomm/*Gruber*, Art. 31, Rn. 8.
[103] Vgl. *Neumayer/Ming*, Art. 31, Anm. 11.
[104] Sekretariatskommentar, Art. 29, Nr. 16; *Schlechtriem*, Einheitliches UN-Kaufrecht, S. 54 = Uniform Sales Law, S. 65; *Bianca/Bonell/Lando*, Art. 31, Anm. 2.7.; *Honsell/Ernst/Lauko*, Art. 31, Rn. 39; *Neumayer/Ming*, Art. 31, Anm. 12.; MünchKomm/*Gruber*, Art. 31, Rn. 8. Vgl. im US-amerikanischen Recht § 2–503 (1) UCC.
[105] Ebenso *Honsell/Ernst/Lauko*, Art. 31, Rn. 39; *Neumayer/Ming*, Art. 31, Anm. 12.; a.A. *Mohs*, unten Art. 58 Rn. 10.
[106] Insoweit sicher zutreffend *Hager/Maultzsch*, 5. Aufl., Art. 58 Rn. 4.
[107] Siehe Art. 30 Rn. 9.
[108] Ebenso *Piltz*, Internationales Kaufrecht, Rn. 4–29; *Neumayer/Ming*, Art. 31, Anm. 12.; MünchKomm/*Gruber*, Art. 31, Rn. 8.

Inhalt der Lieferpflicht und Ort der Lieferung   53–57 Art. 31

c) Verpackung. Die Ware muss dem Käufer so zur Verfügung gestellt werden, dass er sie 53
ohne weiteres abholen kann. Ist die Ware nur in verpacktem Zustand transportfähig, so muss
der Verkäufer sie verpacken.[109] Erst nachdem dies geschehen ist, hat der Verkäufer seine
Lieferpflicht erfüllt.[110]

d) Verladung. Das Beladen des Fahrzeugs oder Containers des Käufers oder seines 54
Beauftragten ist Teil der „Übernahme" der Ware, die dem Käufer im Rahmen seiner
Abnahmepflicht obliegt (Artt. 53, 60 lit. b)).[111] Ist im Einzelfall etwas anderes vereinbart
oder üblich oder den Umständen zu entnehmen,[112] ist also das Beladen des vom Käufer
geschickten Fahrzeugs oder Containers noch Sache des Verkäufers, so ist die „Zur-Verfügung-Stellung" und damit die Lieferung im Sinn des Übereinkommens gleichwohl
bewirkt, sobald die Ware verladefertig bereitsteht und der Käufer hiervon benachrichtigt ist.
Denn das Beladen des Fahrzeugs des Käufers (oder des von ihm geschickten Frachtführers)
ist bereits „Übergabe" der Ware; hierauf soll die Lieferpflicht sich nach dem Grundgedanken
des Art. 31 lit. b), c) gerade nicht erstrecken. Die Verladepflicht ist in diesem Fall eine
zusätzliche Pflicht des Verkäufers, für deren Erfüllung er gemäss Artt. 45 ff. haftet.[113]

e) Zur-Verfügung-Stellen unter Vorbehalten. Die Ware steht nicht zur Verfügung 55
des Käufers, wenn der Verkäufer seine Bereitschaft zur Übergabe von einer **aufschiebenden Bedingung** abhängig macht, die der Käufer **vor** Warenübernahme erfüllen soll. So
steht frei zugängliche Ware nicht zur Verfügung des Käufers, wenn der Verkäufer dem
Käufer das Abholen nur für den Fall gestattet, dass er zuvor den Kaufpreis bezahlt[114] oder ein
Akkreditiv stellt. Bereitstellen der Ware für sich allein genommen genügt also nicht für die
Lieferung; erforderlich ist stets das Einverständnis des Verkäufers mit der Übernahme durch
den Käufer, an dem es hier, solange der Käufer die ihm gestellte Bedingung noch nicht
erfüllt hat, noch fehlt.[115]

Anders ist es, wenn der Verkäufer das Angebot der Aushändigung der Ware an den Käufer 56
von einer Bedingung abhängig macht, die dieser **gleichzeitig** mit Übernahme der Ware
erfüllen soll, vor allem von einer **Zug-um-Zug-Zahlung des Kaufpreises** gemäss Art. 58
I, soweit der Verkäufer hierzu berechtigt ist. Diesfalls hat er seine Lieferpflicht durch die
Bereitstellung und das Angebot der Übergabe Zug um Zug gegen Zahlung erfüllt. Verknüpft der Verkäufer sein Leistungsangebot dagegen mit vertragswidrigen Bedingungen, so
kann er hierdurch die Lieferpflicht nicht erfüllen.

f) Frei zugängliche Ware. Ist die Ware frei zugänglich (Holz im Wald,[116] Silos in einem 57
verlassenen Steinbruch[117]), wird sie dem Käufer zur Verfügung gestellt, indem der Verkäufer
sich ohne weiteren Vorbehalt damit einverstanden erklärt, dass der Käufer die Ware an sich
nimmt.[118]

---

[109] Sekretariatskommentar, Art. 29, Nr. 16; *Schlechtriem*, Einheitliches UN-Kaufrecht, S. 54 = Uniform Sales Law, S. 65; *Neumayer/Ming*, Art. 31, Anm. 11.; *Staudinger/Magnus*, Art. 31, Rn. 10; *Honsell/Ernst/Lauko*, Art. 31, Rn. 40 (der allerdings missverständlich davon spricht, dass der Verkäufer die Verpackung „bereit-zustellen" habe); vgl. auch OLG Karlsruhe, 19.12.2002, CISG-online 817 = IHR 2003, 125, 126 f.; Incoterms® 2010 EXW („Ab Werk") und FCA („Frei Frachtführer") A 9.
[110] Zu den Kosten der Verpackung unten Rn. 83.
[111] OLG Karlsruhe, 19.12.2002, CISG-online 817 = IHR 2003, 125, 127.
[112] Eine Verladepflicht ordnet insbesondere das Formular FCA („Frei Frachtführer") der Incoterms® 2010 an, sofern der Lieferort beim Verkäufer liegt, vgl. A 4 II a).
[113] Ebenso *Honsell/Ernst/Lauko*, Art. 31, Rn. 40; MünchKommHGB/*Benicke*, Art. 31, Rn. 25.
[114] Vgl. auch BGHZ 93, 338, 346 (zur Frage, wann „Ablieferung" der Ware i. S. d. § 377 HGB vorliegt).
[115] Ebenso MünchKommHGB/*Benicke*, Art. 31, Rn. 26; zur Beurteilung analoger Fälle nach deutschem Recht *Tiedtke*, NJW 1988, 2578, 2580 f.
[116] Ist zum Abtransport ein „Holzabfuhrschein" erforderlich, durch den der Käufer sich der Forstbehörde gegenüber als abfuhrberechtigt legitimieren muss, so erfüllt der Verkäufer die Lieferpflicht durch Übergabe des Scheins. Vgl. dazu auch BGH, 9.7.1952, LM § 854 BGB Nr. 1 (zum Besitzerwerb des Käufers).
[117] Vgl. dazu den Fall: BGH, 30.1.1985, BGHZ 93, 338.
[118] Vgl. auch (zur Übergabe gemäß Art. 19 I EKG) *Soergel/Lüderitz*, Art. 19 EKG, Rn. 6: Die Möglichkeit illegaler Besitzergreifung genügt nicht.

Art. 31 58–60   Teil III. Kapitel II. Pflichten des Verkäufers. Abschnitt I

58   **g) Bei einem Dritten eingelagerte Ware.** Bezieht der Kaufvertrag sich auf Ware, die bei einem selbstständigen Lagerhalter eingelagert ist, und ist sie daher gemäss Art. 31 lit. b) dem Käufer am Lagerort zur Verfügung zu stellen, so erfüllt der Verkäufer seine Lieferpflicht dadurch, dass er es dem Käufer ermöglicht, sie beim Lagerhalter abzuholen. Die Zur-Verfügung-Stellung kann dadurch geschehen, dass der Verkäufer dem Käufer den Herausgabeanspruch abtritt und dem Lagerhalter die Abtretung anzeigt oder dem Käufer die an den Lagerhalter gerichtete Abtretungsanzeige aushändigt. Ist der Herausgabeanspruch in einem Wertpapier[119] oder in einem Legitimationspapier verbrieft, dessen Besitz den Käufer gegenüber dem Lagerhalter zum Empfang der Ware legitimiert,[120] so genügt es, dass der Verkäufer dem Käufer die Urkunde (ggf. mit seinem Indossament) übergibt. Der zweite, in der Praxis wohl üblichere Weg ist, dass der Verkäufer den Lagerhalter anweist, die Ware an den Käufer auszuhändigen. Diese Anweisung kann er direkt gegenüber dem Lagerhalter aussprechen, oder er kann dem Käufer eine schriftliche Anweisung an den Lagerhalter übergeben, die Ware an den Käufer auszuhändigen („delivery order", „Lieferschein").[121]

59   Zwischen diesen Möglichkeiten kann der Verkäufer wählen. Ein **Anspruch des Käufers** darauf, dass ihm der Herausgabeanspruch gegen den Lagerhalter in **wertpapiermässig verbriefter Form** übertragen wird, besteht grundsätzlich **nicht**. Der einfache, vom Lagerhalter nicht akzeptierte Lieferschein genügt also.[122] Das gilt sowohl für die in Art. 31 lit. b) geregelte Lieferung als auch für den in Art. 69 II übereinstimmend geregelten Gefahrübergang. Zu mehr, als dem Käufer die Ware zur Verfügung zu stellen oder ihre Abholung zu ermöglichen, ist der Verkäufer kraft Gesetzes nicht verpflichtet. Anders ist es nur, wenn die Pflicht zur Übergabe bestimmter qualifizierter Dokumente vereinbart ist oder sich aus Gebräuchen oder Gepflogenheiten ergibt, an die die Parteien gebunden sind (vgl. Artt. 8 III, 9 I, 9 II), so insbesondere bei Vereinbarung der Klausel „Kasse gegen Dokumente".[123]

60   Die eingelagerte Ware steht nur dann zur Verfügung des Käufers, wenn sie zu dem Zeitpunkt, zu dem der Verkäufer sie zur Verfügung stellt, im Lager tatsächlich vorhanden ist. Ist die Ware im Zeitpunkt der „Zur-Verfügung-Stellung" nicht vorhanden, so haftet der Verkäufer wegen Nichterfüllung der Lieferpflicht gemäss Artt. 45 ff., und zwar grundsätzlich auch dann, wenn die Ware schon bei Vertragsschluss nicht existierte.[124] Eine Entlastung ist nur im engen Rahmen des Art. 79 möglich.[125] Ausserdem muss der Lagerhalter zur Herausgabe bereit sein. Weigert er sich von vornherein, die Ware herauszugeben, so steht die Ware nicht „zur Verfügung" des Käufers. Gleiches gilt aber auch dann, wenn der Dritte an sich zur Herausgabe bereit ist, diese jedoch von einer vertragswidrigen (auch eigenmächtigen) Bedingung (insbesondere von der Erstattung von Kosten) abhängig macht. Der Dritte tritt insoweit als Erfüllungsgehilfe des Verkäufers auf; der Verkäufer hat die Pflicht zur Lieferung nicht erfüllt.[126]

---

[119] Z. B. einem Orderlagerschein; vgl. etwa Art. 482 OR, dazu *Meier-Hayoz/von der Crone*, § 28, Rn. 1 ff.; §§ 475c, 475f, 475g HGB. Daneben käme auch ein Lieferschein in Betracht, den der Verkäufer auf den Lagerhalter gezogen und den dieser durch Unterschrift akzeptiert hat. Zum Lieferschein vgl. *Heynen, passim; Weber*, S. 240 ff.
[120] Z. B. einem Hinterlegungsschein („Lagerempfangsschein"); vgl. *Meier-Hayoz/von der Crone*, § 28, Rn. 2.
[121] Vgl. auch *Honsell/Ernst/Lauko*, Art. 31, Rn. 41.
[122] Vgl. auch *Neumayer/Ming*, Art. 31, Anm. 11.; MünchKomm/*Gruber*, Art. 31, Rn. 11. A. A. *Hager*, Gefahrtragung nach UN-Kaufrecht, S. 400; *ders./Maultzsch*, Art. 69 Rn. 7.
[123] Nähere Einzelheiten dazu bei *Soergel/Huber*, § 433 BGB, Anhang III, Rn. 35 ff.
[124] Allfällige Ungültigkeitsvorschriften des nationalen Rechts (vgl. etwa im schweizerischen Recht Art. 20 I OR) sind in einem derartigen Fall nicht anzuwenden, vgl. *Ferrari*, Art. 4 Rn. 24 sowie *Schwenzer*, Art. 79 Rn. 12. Anders als nach dem früheren § 306 BGB führt die anfängliche Leistungsunmöglichkeit bei Vertragsschluss im *deutschen* Recht seit Inkrafttreten des Schuldrechtsmodernisierungsgesetzes am 1.1.2002 nicht mehr zur Vertragsunwirksamkeit, siehe § 311a Abs. 1 BGB.
[125] Dazu *Schwenzer*, unten Art. 79 Rn. 12; *Pichonnaz*, Rn. 1663 ff.; vgl. ferner *Zweigert/Kötz*, S. 513. Anders die 3. Aufl., *U. Huber*, Art. 31 Rn. 59 (keine Entlastung nach Art. 79 möglich); *U. Huber*, Haftung des Verkäufers, S. 16 f.; *Fischer*, Unmöglichkeit, S. 251 ff.
[126] Anders die 3. Aufl., *U. Huber*, Art. 31 Rn. 59: Lieferpflicht an sich erfüllt, jedoch Verletzung der Pflicht zur Lieferung von Ware, die frei von Rechten und Ansprüche Dritter ist (Art. 41). Wie hier (keine Lieferung) die 1. Aufl., *U. Huber*, Art. 31 Rn. 57.

5. Rechtsfolgen

Grundsätzlich hat der Verkäufer, der die Ware am Lieferort für den Käufer bereitstellt und, soweit erforderlich, die Bereitstellungsnachricht an den Käufer abgesendet hat, seine **Lieferpflicht erfüllt.** Sofern nichts anderes vereinbart ist, tritt damit **Fälligkeit des Kaufpreisanspruchs** ein (Art. 58 I S. 1). 61

Dagegen geht die **Gefahr,** solange die Sache sich noch im Gewahrsam des Verkäufers befindet, durch die Zur-Verfügung-Stellung der Ware noch nicht auf den Käufer über. Hierzu ist vielmehr erforderlich, dass der Käufer entweder die Ware übernimmt, oder dass er durch die Nichtabnahme eine Vertragsverletzung begeht (Art. 69 I).[127] Wird die Ware nach erfolgter Lieferung, aber vor Gefahrübergang **beschädigt,** haftet der Verkäufer nach Art. 36 i. V. m. Art. 35 I. Beim Gattungskauf[128] bedeutet dies insbesondere, dass der Käufer – jedenfalls wenn der Schaden sich nicht durch Reparatur beheben lässt (Art. 46 III) – Ersatzlieferung gemäss Art. 46 I, II[129] verlangen kann. Der Verkäufer trägt insoweit noch die sog. Leistungsgefahr, das heisst die Gefahr, ein zweites Mal leisten zu müssen.[130] Nicht anders zu behandeln ist der Fall, in dem die bereitgestellte Ware vor Gefahrübergang **vollkommen zerstört** wird oder auf sonstige Weise (etwa durch Diebstahl) verlorengeht.[131] Ist dagegen die Gefahr gemäss Art. 69 I auf den Käufer **übergegangen,** haftet der Verkäufer nicht mehr für die Erfüllung des Kaufvertrags.[132] Mit der Preisgefahr geht also auch die Leistungsgefahr auf den Käufer über. Der Verkäufer ist jetzt nur noch verpflichtet, zur Erhaltung der Sache „die den Umständen angemessenen Massnahmen" zu treffen (Art. 85); bei verderblichen Waren kann auch eine Pflicht zum Selbsthilfeverkauf bestehen (Art. 88 II). 62

Befindet die Ware, die dem Käufer gemäss Art. 31 lit. b) zur Verfügung zu stellen ist, sich im Gewahrsam eines **Dritten** (z. B. eines selbstständigen **Lagerhalters**),[133] so geht die Gefahr auf den Käufer über, sobald der Verkäufer dem Käufer die Ware zur Verfügung gestellt hat (Art. 69 II). Der Verkäufer, der sich auf den Gefahrübergang beruft, hat die Zur-Verfügung-Stellung zu beweisen.[134] Hat der Verkäufer die Ware jedoch schon vor Fälligkeit des Lieferanspruchs zur Verfügung gestellt, geht die Gefahr erst mit Fälligkeit oder mit vorheriger Übernahme durch den Käufer über. Die Gefahr geht trotz Zur-Verfügung-Stellung auch dann nicht über, wenn der Käufer von der Bereitstellung der Ware noch keine Kenntnis erlangt hat.[135] Ist die Gefahr für die beim Dritten zur Verfügung gestellte Ware gemäss Art. 69 II **übergegangen,** haftet der Verkäufer nur dafür (und hat daher im Streitfall zu beweisen), dass die Ware zum Zeitpunkt des Gefahrübergangs vorhanden ist,[136] dass sie sich zu diesem Zeitpunkt in einem vertragsmässigen Zustand befindet (Art. 36) und dass der Dritte zu diesem Zeitpunkt zur Herausgabe an den Käufer bereit ist.[137] Späterer Verlust der Ware (etwa Aushändigung der Ware durch den Dritten an einen Nichtberechtigten) sowie spätere Beschädigung fallen in den Risikobereich des Käufers. Da der Verkäufer nicht mehr 63

---

[127] Vgl. *Hachem,* Art. 69 Rn. 9.

[128] Beim Spezieskauf gibt es im Fall der vertragswidrigen Beschaffenheit der verkauften Sache keinen Anspruch auf Ersatzlieferung, vgl. *U. Huber* in der 3. Aufl., Art. 46 Rn. 23; teilweise a. A. *Müller-Chen,* Art. 46 Rn. 18.

[129] Zur Frage, ob die Beschränkung des Ersatzlieferungsanspruchs des Käufers auf den Fall der „wesentlichen Vertragsverletzung" auch in diesem Fall eingreift, vgl. unten Rn. 66.

[130] Für diesen Fall zustimmend auch *Karollus,* S. 193 f.

[131] Ebenso *Schlechtriem,* Pflichten des Verkäufers, S. 112 f.; *Piltz,* Internationales Kaufrecht, Rn. 4–289. A. A. *Karollus,* S. 193 f. Die Gegenansicht führt zu sachlich nicht gerechtfertigten Differenzierungen (Abgrenzung von Beschädigung und Zerstörung, Frage des Einflusses eines Verschuldens des Verkäufers und seiner Angestellten).

[132] Teilweise abweichend 1. Aufl., Rn. 74.

[133] Zum Inhalt der Lieferpflicht in diesem Fall vgl. oben Rn. 58.

[134] Vgl. OLG Hamm, 23.6.1998, CISG-online 434 = RIW 1999, 785 ff.

[135] Vgl. oben Rn. 51.

[136] Vgl. oben Rn. 60.

[137] Vgl. oben Rn. 60.

im Besitz der Ware und auch nicht mehr in der Lage ist, über die Ware zu verfügen, trifft ihn auch keine Erhaltungspflicht gemäss Art. 85. Er hat seine Pflichten aus dem Kaufvertrag vollständig erfüllt.

64 Entsprechendes gilt, wenn dem Käufer **frei zugängliche Ware** zur Verfügung gestellt ist. Auch hier geht die Gefahr gemäss Art. 69 II mit Zur-Verfügung-Stellung und Kenntnis des Käufers hiervon über, und den Verkäufer trifft keine Erhaltungspflicht gemäss Art. 85.

6. Vertragswidrige Lieferung

65 Ist die dem Käufer gemäss Art. 31 lit. b), c) zur Verfügung gestellte Ware nicht vertragsgemäss i. S. d. Art. 35,[138] so gilt im Grundsatz dasselbe wie bei der Versendung nicht vertragsgemässer Ware:[139] die Lieferung vertragswidriger Ware ist zwar Vertragsverletzung, aber keine „Nicht-Lieferung"; Art. 49 I lit. b) ist daher unanwendbar; und die Rechtsbehelfe des Käufers unterliegen den speziellen Einschränkungen des Art. 39 und des Art. 46 II, III.

66 Bemerkt der Käufer den Mangel jedoch schon *vor* dem Abtransport, ist er berechtigt, die Übernahme der nicht vertragsmässigen Ware zurückzuweisen. Beim Gattungskauf muss das auch dann gelten, wenn der Mangel nicht so schwer ist, dass er eine wesentliche Vertragsverletzung i. S. d. Art. 25 darstellt, die dem Käufer gemäss Artt. 46 II, 49 I lit. a) das Recht auf Ersatzlieferung oder Vertragsaufhebung verleiht.[140] Der Grund für die Beschränkung des Ersatzlieferungsanspruchs gemäss Art. 46 II liegt in den Umständen und Kosten des Rücktransports. Dieser Grund entfällt, solange sich die Ware noch an ihrem Ausgangsort befindet.

7. Aufhebung der Bereitstellung durch den Verkäufer

67 Hat der Verkäufer die Ware dem Käufer gemäss Art. 31 lit. b), c) ordnungsgemäss zur Verfügung gestellt, so hängt der Erfolg seiner Leistung, der Besitzerwerb des Käufers, bis zur Übernahme der Ware durch den Käufer von der fortdauernden Leistungsbereitschaft des Verkäufers ab. Der Verkäufer kann den Eintritt des Leistungserfolgs noch verhindern, indem er die bereitgestellte Ware an einen Dritten veräussert oder indem er sie vom Leistungsort entfernt oder indem er sich nachträglich weigert, die Ware an den Käufer herauszugeben.[141] Wie bei der Rückbeorderung der Ware im Fall des Versendungskaufs[142] lebt die Lieferpflicht des Verkäufers auch hier durch den actus contrarius wieder auf. Der Verkäufer ist verpflichtet, die Ware von neuem am Lieferort zur Verfügung zu stellen, und haftet hierfür von neuem gemäss Artt. 45 ff., es sei denn, er habe wegen Verletzung der Abnahmepflicht wirksam die Vertragsaufhebung erklärt (Artt. 53, 60, 64 I lit. a), b)) oder einen nach Artt. 85, 88 I, II zulässigen Selbsthilfeverkauf ausgeführt.

8. Bereitstellung am falschen Ort

68 Stellt der Verkäufer dem Käufer die Ware am falschen Ort zur Verfügung, so hat er seine Lieferpflicht nur dann erfüllt, wenn der Käufer die Ware an diesem Ort tatsächlich abnimmt. Mehrkosten sind ggf. gemäss Art. 45 I lit. b) zu ersetzen. Ob der Käufer u. U. verpflichtet sein kann, die Ware an einem anderen Ort, als in Art. 31 lit. b), c) bestimmt, abzunehmen, ist nach Treu und Glauben zu entscheiden (Art. 7 II).[143]

---

[138] Zu den Voraussetzungen der Vertragsmässigkeit siehe *Schwenzer,* Art. 35 Rn. 6 ff.; zur Falschlieferung und zur mangelhaften Verpackung siehe auch oben Rn. 34 f.
[139] Vgl. oben Rn. 33.
[140] Vgl. *Mohs,* Art. 60 Rn. 16 sowie *Müller-Chen,* Art. 46 Rn. 19.
[141] Ebenso MünchKommHGB/*Benicke,* Art. 31, Rn. 26.
[142] Vgl. oben Rn. 41.
[143] Zum Grundsatz von Treu und Glauben siehe Art. 30 Rn. 9.

9. Teillieferung

Ist eine Mehrzahl von Sachen zu liefern und stellt der Verkäufer dem Käufer nur einen **69** Teil zur Verfügung, so ist die Lieferung nicht vertragsgemäss (Art. 35 I).[144] Anders als beim Versendungskauf[145] werden die „unzumutbaren Unannehmlichkeiten", die dem Recht des Verkäufers zur Nachlieferung entgegenstehen (Artt. 37 HS. 1, 48 I HS. 1), im Fall der Holschuld im Allgemeinen anzunehmen sein: es ist dem Käufer nicht zuzumuten, sich mehrmals zum Verkäufer zu begeben oder mehrmals einen Frachtführer zum Verkäufer zu schicken, um die Ware zu übernehmen. Das Zurückweisungsrecht des Käufers ergibt sich sowohl aus einer sinngemässen Anwendung des Art. 37 als auch aus dem allgemeinen Grundsatz von Treu und Glauben (Art. 7 II);[146] übt er dieses Recht aus, ist die Lieferpflicht einstweilen nicht erfüllt. Nimmt der Käufer dagegen die Teillieferung entgegen, so richten sich seine Rechtsbehelfe nach Art. 51.[147]

IV. Vereinbarung eines „anderen bestimmten Orts" für die Lieferung

1. Ausgangspunkt

Art. 31 ist nur anwendbar, wenn der Verkäufer die Ware nach dem Kaufvertrag „nicht an **70** einen anderen bestimmten Ort zu liefern" hat. Gemeint ist ein anderer Ort als derjenige, der sich aus Art. 31 lit. a), b) oder c) ergibt. Wer einen von Art. 31 abweichenden Lieferort behauptet, hat dafür den Beweis zu erbringen.[148] Eine entsprechende Vereinbarung kann sich auch aus ergänzender Vertragsauslegung (Art. 8) ergeben. Aus der Vereinbarung ergibt sich zugleich, durch welche Handlung des Verkäufers die Lieferung zu bewirken ist.[149]

2. Incoterms®

Ist der Lieferort durch eine der in den Incoterms® geregelten Lieferklauseln bestimmt **71** und sind die Incoterms® für den Vertrag massgeblich,[150] so gilt folgendes:

a) Mit Art. 31 übereinstimmender Lieferort. In einer Reihe von Fällen führen die **72** Lieferklauseln zu demselben Lieferort und demselben Inhalt der Lieferpflicht, die sich auch aus Art. 31 ergeben. Da die Parteien diesfalls gerade keinen „anderen bestimmten Ort" vereinbart haben, bleibt Art. 31 weiterhin anwendbar; die Incoterms® haben insofern **nur ergänzende Funktion.** Das gilt namentlich für die Klauseln des Versendungskaufs „Frachtfrei" (CPT) und „Frachtfrei versichert" (CIP), die mit **Art. 31 lit. a)** übereinstimmen, und für die Klausel „Ab Werk" (EXW) (oder, je nach Lage des Falls, „ab Lager", „ab Pflanzung", „ex Tank"), die mit **Art. 31 lit. b)** übereinstimmt. Für diese Fälle enthalten die Incoterms® spezielle Regeln darüber, wie geliefert werden muss. Die Art der Lieferung deckt sich aber mit der in Art. 31 vorgesehenen: bei der Klausel „ab Werk" hat der Verkäufer dem Käufer die Ware zur Verfügung zu stellen (A 4) und den Käufer hiervon zu benachrichtigen (A 7), bei den CPT- und CIP-Klauseln hat er die Ware dem ersten Frachtführer zu übergeben (jeweils A 4). Die Klausel „frei Frachtführer" (FCA) stimmt im Prinzip mit **Art. 31 lit. c)** überein, wenn als Lieferort die Niederlassung des Verkäufers genannt ist. Der Frachtführer ist bei Verwendung dieser Klausel im Regelfall vom Käufer zu beauftragen (A 3, B 3); die Lieferschuld ist also Holschuld. Besonderheiten ergeben sich daraus, dass der Verkäufer

---

[144] Vgl. *Schwenzer,* Art. 35 Rn. 8.
[145] Vgl. oben Rn. 44.
[146] Zum Grundsatz von Treu und Glauben siehe Art. 30 Rn. 9.
[147] Vgl. *Müller-Chen,* Art. 51 Rn. 5 f.
[148] Vgl. AG Duisburg, 13.4.2000, CISG-online 659 = IHR 2001, 114, 116; *Staudinger/Magnus,* Art. 31, Rn. 34.
[149] A. A. *Kröll u. a./Piltz,* Art. 31, Rn. 20.
[150] Vgl. dazu Art. 30 Rn. 3 f.

Art. 31 73–75 Teil III. Kapitel II. Pflichten des Verkäufers. Abschnitt I

verpflichtet ist, das Beförderungsmittel des Frachtführers zu beladen, sofern der Lieferort „beim Verkäufer liegt" (vgl. Incoterms® 2010 FCA A 4 II a)).[151] Schliesst ausnahmsweise der Verkäufer selbst den Beförderungsvertrag ab (Incoterms® 2010 FCA A 3), liegt ein gewöhnlicher Versendungskauf i. S. d. **Art. 31 lit. a)** vor.[152]

73 **b) Von Art. 31 abweichender Lieferort.** Bestimmte Klauseln haben die Eigenart, dass der Verkäufer die Ware an einem Ort zu übergeben hat, der nicht mit der Niederlassung des Verkäufers oder dem Lagerort der Ware bei Vertragsabschluss identisch ist, sondern an irgendeinem Ort, der zwischen der Niederlassung des Verkäufers und der Niederlassung des Käufers liegt. Das gilt erstens bei der Klausel „frei Frachtführer" (FCA), wenn dieser Klausel eine entsprechende Ortsangabe beigefügt ist, z. B. „frei Frachtführer Flughafen X" oder „frei Bahnstation Y".[153] Es gilt ferner für die Klauseln „Frei Längsseite Schiff" (FAS),[154] „Frei an Bord" (FOB), „Kosten und Fracht" (CFR), „Kosten, Versicherung, Fracht" (CIF). Dasselbe gilt auch für die Klausel „geliefert verzollt" (DDP), wenn ein anderer Lieferort bestimmt ist als unmittelbar die Niederlassung des Käufers.

74 In allen vorgenannten Fällen stimmt der **Inhalt der Lieferpflicht** entweder mit Art. 31 lit. a) oder Art. 31 lit. b), c) überein; nur der **Lieferort** ist ein anderer. Die Lieferpflicht besteht nämlich auf Grund der Klausel und der Standardinterpretation der Incoterms® entweder darin, dass der Verkäufer die Ware am Lieferort einem **Beförderer zum Zweck des Weitertransports zu übergeben** hat, so insbesondere in den Fällen CFR, CIF, FAS und FOB[155], bei der FCA-Klausel (A 4), sowie bei Verwendung der gleichbedeutenden Klauseln „FOB Flughafen", „frei Waggon" oder „frei Bahnstation". In diesen Fällen entspricht die Lieferpflicht ihrem Inhalt nach im Wesentlichen dem **Art. 31 lit. a)**. Oder aber der Verkäufer ist verpflichtet, die Ware dem Käufer **am Lieferort** so **zur Verfügung zu stellen,** dass der Käufer (oder der von ihm beauftragte Frachtführer) imstande ist, sie von der Stelle, an der sie zu seiner Verfügung steht, abzutransportieren, so insbesondere bei den „Geliefert"-Klauseln („D-Klauseln" oder „Ankunftsklauseln") DAT, DAP und DDP.[156] Hier entspricht die Lieferung ihrem Inhalt nach dem Fall des **Art. 31 lit. b),** nur dass der Lieferort nicht der gegenwärtige Lagerort ist, sondern der Ort, an dem die Ware nach einem vom Verkäufer zunächst noch durchzuführenden Transport eintrifft. Für Einzelfragen – soweit sie nicht bereits in den Incoterms® ihre Antwort finden – kann daher auf die Ausführungen zur Lieferung gemäss Art. 31 lit. a)[157] bzw. gemäss Art. 31 lit. b), c)[158] verwiesen werden.

75 **c) Unterlassene Mitwirkung des Käufers.** Eine Besonderheit gilt in den Fällen FCA, FAS und FOB. Hier ist nämlich, wenn nicht ausnahmsweise der Verkäufer selbst den Frachtvertrag abzuschliessen hat, der Käufer verpflichtet, für den Transport zu sorgen und dem Verkäufer das Transportmittel zu benennen. Entgegen dem Grundgedanken des Art. 31[159] ist die Lieferung mithin kein von der Mitwirkung des Käufers unabhängiger Akt

---

[151] Zu den Konsequenzen für den Gefahrübergang: A 5/B 5; vgl. dazu auch oben Rn. 54. Gegenüber den Incoterms® 2000 sind die Bestimmungen zu den Pflichten nach A4 umfangreich überarbeitet worden, wobei es allerdings zu keinen wesentlichen inhaltlichen Änderungen gekommen ist; dazu *von Bernstorff,* Incoterms® 2010, 79 f.

[152] Vgl. dazu auch *von Bernstorff,* Incoterms® 2010, 78.

[153] Gleichbedeutend z. B. „franco partenza Torino", vgl. dazu BGH, 24.9.1986, BGHZ 98, 263, 272 (zu Art. 19 EKG).

[154] Die Klausel FAS (free alongside ship, Frei Längsseite Schiff) bezieht sich, zumindest ihrem Ursprung nach, auf den Fall, dass die Ware mit Binnenschiff oder Leichter an die Längsseite des vom Käufer zu benennenden Seeschiffs zu liefern und dort vom Seeschiff zu übernehmen ist. Vgl. *Haage,* S. 200. Auch an ein Binnenschiff kann „Frei Längsseite" geliefert werden.

[155] Jeweils A 4; Lieferort ist der Verschiffungshafen. Wie in den Incoterms® 2000 ist auch in den Incoterms® 2010 weiterhin von „liefern" die Rede, vgl. dazu *von Bernstorff,* Incoterms® 2010, 79 f.; zu den in den Incoterms® 2010 verwendeten Begriffen eingehend *ders.,* aaO., 40 ff.

[156] Vgl. jeweils A 4.

[157] Vgl. oben Rn. 13 ff.

[158] Vgl. oben Rn. 45 ff.

[159] Vgl. oben Rn. 4.

des Verkäufers. Scheitert die Lieferung an der unterlassenen Mitwirkung des Käufers, ist eine Haftung des Verkäufers wegen Nichterfüllung der Lieferpflicht durch Art. 80 ausgeschlossen. Der Käufer seinerseits haftet in diesem Fall wegen Nichterfüllung der Abnahmepflicht (Artt. 53, 60, 61 ff.). Hinsichtlich des Gefahrübergangs in solchen Fällen enthalten die Incoterms® (jeweils B 5) besondere Regeln, die darauf hinauslaufen, dass der Käufer ab Abnahmeverzug und Konkretisierung die Gefahr trägt. Sollten die Incoterms® nicht einschlägig sein, so wird man durch analoge Anwendung des Art. 69 I, III zur gleichen Regel kommen.

3. Bringschulden

Eine besondere Lage besteht, wenn der Verkäufer verpflichtet ist, die Ware an Ort und Stelle der Niederlassung des Käufers an diesen abzuliefern.[160] Nach den Incoterms® ist dies bei der DDP-Klausel der Fall, wenn als Bestimmungsort die Niederlassung des Käufers genannt ist. Auch die Vertragsklausel „frei Haus", so wie sie im Geschäftsverkehr üblicherweise verwendet wird, ist nicht nur eine Spesenklausel, sondern sie bedeutet, dass Lieferort die Niederlassung des Käufers ist.[161] Die Lieferpflicht des Verkäufers ist in solchen Fällen eine „Bringschuld". An sich entspräche es dem System des Übereinkommens, auch hier die Lieferpflicht des Verkäufers darin zu sehen, dass er die Ware dem Käufer an dessen Niederlassungsort „zur Verfügung stellt",[162] und in diesem Sinn ist die Frage auch in den Incoterms® geregelt (Incoterms® 2010 DDP A 5). Trifft der Verkäufer (oder der Beförderer) den Käufer am Bestimmungsort jedoch nicht an oder ist der Käufer aus irgendeinem Grund zur Übernahme nicht bereit, kann der Verkäufer die Sache nicht einfach auf der Strasse stehen lassen; vielmehr bleibt er verpflichtet, für die Erhaltung der Ware zu sorgen (Art. 85). Wird das Gut aus diesem Grund **zurücktransportiert,** so wird die Lieferung, die darin besteht, dass das Gut dem Käufer *am Lieferort* zur Verfügung gestellt wird, rückgängig gemacht. Wie auch in anderen Fällen dieser Art,[163] lebt durch die Rücknahme die Lieferpflicht des Verkäufers wieder auf.[164] Will er den Käufer am Vertrag festhalten, bleibt er verpflichtet, die Ware erneut zum Käufer zu bringen. Praktisch kann also bei Bringschulden die Lieferpflicht nur durch „Übergabe" erfüllt werden.[165] Der Käufer haftet für die unterlassene Mitwirkung gemäss Artt. 53, 60, 61 ff. und muss daher die Mehrkosten einer zweiten Lieferung ersetzen. Hält der Ver-

---

[160] Eine solche Pflicht besteht vor allem, wenn der Verkäufer verspricht, die Ware mit eigenen Transportmitteln zum Käufer zu schaffen: OLG Köln, 8.1.1997, CISG-online 217. Es kann aber auch bei Einschaltung eines selbstständigen Beförderers vereinbart werden, dass entgegen der Regel des Art. 31 lit. a) Lieferort die Niederlassung des Käufers sein soll.
[161] OLG Karlsruhe, 20.11.1992, CISG-online 54 = NJW-RR 1993, 1316, 1317; OLG Köln, 8.1.1997, CISG-online 217; OGH, 10.9.1998, CISG-online 409 = JBl 1999, 333 = RdW 1999, 210; KG Zug, 11.12.2003, CISG-online 958 = IHR 2005, 119, 121 f., E. 2.3; vgl. auch AG Duisburg, 13.4.2000, CISG-online 659 = IHR 2001, 114, 116; übereinstimmend *Soergel/Lüderitz/Budzikiewicz/Schüßler-Langeheine,* Art. 31, Rn. 13; *Rummel/Aicher,* § 1061 ABGB, Rz. 11 (zum österreichischen Recht); zurückhaltend *Piltz,* NJW 2000, 553, 557; *Brunner,* Art. 31, Rn. 3; MünchKomm/*Gruber,* Art. 31, Rn. 22. Im Fall BGH, 11.12.1996, CISG-online 225 = BGHZ 134, 201 ff. hat dagegen das OLG Schleswig als Berufungsinstanz die Klauseln „Die [...] Preise gelten frei Straßburg" und „Lieferung frei Haus [...] unverzollt" als reine Spesenklauseln interpretiert, die keine Bringschuld begründeten; der BGH (BGHZ 134, 201, 206) hat diese vor allem hinsichtlich der zweiten Klausel wohl allzu verkäuferfreundliche Auslegung nicht beanstandet. Für eine reine Spesenklausel scheint sich auch der dänische Højesteret in seinem Urt. v. 15.2.2001, CISG-online 601, auszusprechen; vgl. auch (differenzierter) OLG Köln, 16.7.2001, CISG-online 609 = IHR 2002, 66, 67; OLG Koblenz, 4.10.2002, CISG-online 716 = IHR 2003, 66 f.; OLG München, 14.1.2009, CISG-online 2011. Im Ergebnis ist diesen Entscheiden jedoch deshalb zuzustimmen, weil es lediglich um die Frage ging, ob einer solchen Klausel gerichtsstandsbegründende Wirkung zukommt; dies wird in der Regel aber gerade zu verneinen sein, dazu unten Rn. 92, 96.
[162] So auch *Honsell/Ernst/Lauko,* Art. 31, Rn. 51; *Witz/Salger/Lorenz/Witz,* Art. 31, Rn. 22; anders die 1. Aufl., *U. Huber,* Art. 31 Rn. 91.
[163] Vgl. oben Rn. 41, 67.
[164] Ebenso MünchKommHGB/*Benicke,* Art. 31, Rn. 31.
[165] A. A. *Kröll u. a./Piltz,* Art. 31, Rn. 28

käufer am Vertrag fest, so hat der Käufer gemäss Art. 69 II die Gefahr zu tragen.[166] Das gilt allerdings nicht, wenn der Verlust oder die Beschädigung der Ware darauf zurückzuführen ist, dass der Verkäufer seine Erhaltungspflicht (Art. 85) verletzt hat. Lässt er die Ware bei einem Dritten (Lagerhalter, Frachtführer, Spediteur) **einlagern,** so hat er hierdurch seine Erhaltungspflicht erfüllt (Art. 87); für Fehler des Dritten haftet er nicht.[167] Da die Einlagerung keine Erfüllungswirkung hat,[168] ist der Verkäufer auch in diesem Fall, wenn er am Vertrag festhalten will, zur erneuten Andienung der Ware am Lieferort verpflichtet.[169]

4. Die Haftung des Verkäufers für den Transport zum Lieferort

77 In aller Regel haben die vertraglichen Lieferklauseln die Folge, dass der Verkäufer die Ware zunächst zum Lieferort zu transportieren hat, um sie dort einem Beförderer zum Weitertransport zu übergeben oder dem Käufer zur Verfügung zu stellen. Der Transport zum Lieferort ist Teil der Lieferpflicht des Verkäufers. Für die ordnungsmässige und pünktliche Durchführung des Transports haftet daher der Verkäufer gemäss Artt. 45 ff., unabhängig davon, ob er den Transport mit eigenen Mitteln durchführt oder durch einen selbständigen Beförderer durchführen lässt.[170] Der Beförderer ist, soweit es um den dem Verkäufer obliegenden Transport zum Lieferort geht,[171] dessen Erfüllungsgehilfe i. S. d. Art. 79 II.[172] Die Gefahr von Beschädigung und Verlust der Ware während des Transports zum Lieferort trägt der Verkäufer;[173] gelegentlich ergibt sich allerdings aus Handelsbrauch oder besonderen Vertragsklauseln, dass schon mit Antritt des vom Verkäufer durchzuführenden Transports Konzentration der Gattungsschuld auf die abgesendete Ware eintritt, sodass die Leistungsgefahr bereits mit Versendung, die Preisgefahr dagegen erst nach Ankunft am Lieferort übergeht.[174]

5. Lieferung am falschen Ort

78 Ist ein besonderer Lieferort vertraglich bestimmt und nimmt der Verkäufer die Lieferung am falschen Ort vor,[175] ist hinsichtlich der Rechtsfolgen zu unterscheiden. Hat der Verkäufer die Ware von einem bestimmten Ort an den Käufer zu versenden und versendet er von einem anderen Ort, so hat er seine Lieferpflicht zwar erfüllt, aber in fehlerhafter Weise; der Käufer kann Ersatz eines allfälligen Schadens gemäss Art. 45 I lit. b) verlangen. Zur Zurückweisung der Ware und zur Erklärung der Vertragsaufhebung ist der Käufer nur berechtigt, wenn die Versendung vom falschen Ort als wesentliche Vertragsverletzung ein-

---

[166] Vgl. *Hachem,* Art. 69 Rn. 17 ff.; ebenso *Honsell/Ernst/Lauko,* Art. 31, Rn. 52; MünchKommHGB/*Benicke,* Art. 31, Rn. 31 i. V. m. Art. 69, Rn. 8. Anders die 3. Aufl., *U. Huber,* Art. 31 Rn. 80: Anwendung des Art. 69 I; vgl. auch *Schlechtriem,* Seller's Obligations, S. 9. Praktische Konsequenzen hat der Meinungsgegensatz nicht.

[167] Vgl. auch *Gomard/Rechnagel,* S. 237; *Neumayer/Ming,* Art. 87, Anm. 2.: Einlagerung „auf Gefahr" des Käufers. Zur Pflicht des Verkäufers zur Versicherung der eingelagerten Ware vgl. *Herber/Czerwenka,* Art. 87, Rn. 2.

[168] Vgl. *Bacher,* Art. 87 Rn. 7; *Herber/Czerwenka,* Art. 87, Rn. 5; *Neumayer/Ming,* Art. 87, Anm. 2.

[169] A. A. *Eberstein,* 2. Aufl., Art. 87 Rn. 12: Der Verkäufer dürfe den Käufer auf die hinterlegte Ware „verweisen" (offenbar in Anlehnung an § 379 I BGB).

[170] *Schlechtriem,* Seller's Obligations, S. 9 f.; *Stoll,* Schadensersatzpflicht, S. 277. Abweichend zur analogen Frage nach dem EKG *Mertens/Rehbinder,* Art. 74 EKG, Rn. 17; *Dölle/Stoll,* Art. 74 EKG, Rn. 66 m. w. N.; *Huber,* JZ 1974, 433, 436; hieran ist nicht festzuhalten.

[171] Anderes gilt dagegen in Bezug auf die Einlagerung beim Beförderer nach Maßgabe des Art. 87; siehe oben Rn. 76.

[172] *Schlechtriem,* Seller's Obligations, S. 9 f.; *Stoll,* Schadensersatzpflicht, S. 277.

[173] Vgl. auch oben Rn. 11.

[174] Zu näheren Einzelheiten vgl. *Soergel/U. Huber,* vor § 446 BGB, Rn. 8 m. w. N.

[175] Im Gegensatz zum EKG hat das CISG auf die Aufstellung besonderer Regeln für diesen Fall verzichtet. Zu den Gründen vgl. YB III (1972), S. 85 (unter Nr. 32); YB IV (1973), S. 40, Nr. 27–29; dazu auch *Honnold/Flechtner,* Art. 31, Rn. 211; *Schlechtriem,* Seller's Obligations, S. 15; *ders.,* Pflichten des Verkäufers, S. 114.

zustufen ist, Artt. 25, 49 I lit. a). Hat der Verkäufer die Ware an einen bestimmten Ort zu liefern und dort einem vom Käufer zu beauftragenden Beförderer auszuhändigen oder zur Verfügung des Käufers zu stellen, so hat der Verkäufer, der die Ware am falschen Ort anbietet, schlicht und einfach seine Lieferpflicht nicht erfüllt und haftet deswegen gemäss Artt. 45 I, 46 I, 49 I lit. a) und b). Ist der Käufer dennoch bereit, die Ware an diesem Ort zu übernehmen, wird hierdurch allerdings die Lieferpflicht erfüllt, und der Käufer kann nur Schadensersatz gemäss Art. 45 I lit. b) wegen etwaiger Mehrkosten und Verzögerungsschäden verlangen. Ob der Käufer verpflichtet ist, sich gegen Erstattung etwaiger Mehrkosten auf einen nachträglichen Wechsel des Lieferorts einzulassen, wenn die Lieferung am ursprünglich bestimmten Ort auf unvorhergesehene Schwierigkeiten stösst (Lieferung ab Kai Rotterdam statt ab Kai Hamburg, wenn in Hamburg gestreikt wird), ist nach Treu und Glauben (Art. 7 II)[176] zu entscheiden.

6. Verkauf von Ware auf dem Transport

Wird Ware auf dem Transport – schwimmende, rollende, fliegende Ware – verkauft, so liegt hierin ebenfalls eine **besondere Bestimmung** über den **Lieferort** und den **Inhalt der Lieferpflicht,** die die Anwendung des Art. 31 ausschliesst. Die Lieferung erfolgt hier also nicht nach Art. 31 lit. b) (denn der Käufer soll die Ware nicht dort übernehmen, wo sie sich bei Vertragsabschluss gerade befindet), und Lieferort ist auch nicht der Bestimmungsort des Transports (denn mit der Aushändigung der Ware durch den Beförderer an den Käufer hat der Verkäufer nichts mehr zu tun). Übereinstimmend mit dem Prinzip des Art. 31 lit. b), c) besteht die Lieferung aber auch hier darin, dass der Verkäufer dem Käufer die Ware „zur Verfügung stellt". Er erfüllt diese Pflicht, indem er den Käufer in die Lage versetzt, die Ware am Bestimmungsort zu übernehmen, das heisst durch frachtrechtliche Disposition über die reisende Ware. Ist über die Ware ein Dokument ausgestellt, das den Inhaber gegenüber dem Beförderer dazu legitimiert, die Ware in Empfang zu nehmen,[177] so erfüllt der Verkäufer seine Lieferpflicht, indem er dem Käufer das (erforderlichenfalls indossierte) Dokument übergibt.[178] Existiert kein solches Dokument, so muss er den Beförderer anweisen, die Ware an den Käufer auszuliefern.[179] Die Lieferpflicht ist erfüllt, sobald die Anweisung dem Beförderer, in dessen Gewahrsam die Ware sich gerade befindet, zugeht. Voraussetzung ist, dass der Beförderer auf Grund der Anweisung tatsächlich verpflichtet ist, die Ware am Ankunftsort dem Käufer auszuhändigen.[180] Bedient der Verkäufer sich zur Übermittlung der Anweisung eines Dritten (etwa eines Spediteurs), so wird dieser noch im Rahmen der Erfüllung der Lieferpflicht des Verkäufers tätig, ist also dessen Erfüllungsgehilfe.[181]

Nach Art. 68 geht beim Verkauf reisender Ware die **Gefahr** grundsätzlich mit **Abschluss des Kaufvertrags** auf den Käufer über. Zu diesem Zeitpunkt muss die Ware auf dem Transportmittel vorhanden und in vertragsmässigem Zustand sein. Die Beweislast trifft den Verkäufer.[182] Ist die Gefahr dagegen gemäss Art. 68 S. 2 **rückwirkend zum Beginn des Transports** auf den Käufer übergegangen,[183] haftet der Verkäufer nur dafür, dass die Ware zu Beginn des Transports vorhanden und in vertragsmässigem Zustand war, und er ist nur hierfür beweispflichtig. War die verkaufte Ware zum Zeitpunkt des Gefahrübergangs auf dem Transportmittel nicht vorhanden, haftet der Verkäufer wegen Nichterfüllung der

---

[176] Siehe Art. 30 Rn. 9.
[177] Etwa ein Konnossement oder Ladeschein oder das CTO-Dokument des kombinierten Transports; vgl. dazu *Helm,* FS Hefermehl, S. 57 ff.; *Staub/Helm,* § 444 HGB, Rn. 6 ff.; *Weber,* S. 145 ff., 170 ff.
[178] Vgl. auch *Herber/Czerwenka,* Art. 31, Rn. 7; *Honsell/Ernst/Lauko,* Art. 31, Rn. 42; *Neumayer/Ming,* Art. 31, Anm. 13.; MünchKomm/*Gruber,* Art. 31, Rn. 12.
[179] Vgl. auch *Honsell/Ernst/Lauko,* Art. 31, Rn 42; MünchKomm/*Gruber,* Art. 31, Rn. 12.
[180] Ebenso MünchKomm/*Gruber,* Art. 31, Rn. 12.
[181] Vgl. BGHZ 50, 32, 36 f. (zum Verkauf von Ware auf dem Eisenbahntransport nach deutschem Recht).
[182] Vgl. dazu *Hachem,* Art. 67 Rn. 36; Art. 68 Rn. 5.
[183] Dazu *Hachem,* Art. 68 Rn. 7.

Lieferpflicht.[184] Da es sich beim Verkauf schwimmender, rollender oder fliegender Ware nach der Natur der Sache um einen Spezieskauf handelt, ist Erfüllung in Natur nicht möglich, denn die verkaufte Ware existiert nicht. Die Haftung des Verkäufers richtet sich also von vornherein auf Schadensersatz wegen Nichterfüllung, und zwar grundsätzlich auch dann, wenn die Ware schon bei Vertragsschluss nicht existierte.[185] Eine Entlastung ist nur im Rahmen des Art. 79 möglich.[186]

81 Vereinbaren die Parteien beim Verkauf von Ware, die sich auf dem Transport befindet, dass **Lieferort** der **Bestimmungsort** sein soll (so z. B., wenn schwimmende Ware „ab Schiff" oder „ab Kai" verkauft wird), so erfolgt die Lieferung erst dadurch, dass die Ware dem Käufer am vorgesehenen Ort zur Verfügung gestellt wird. Der Verkäufer trägt daher, abweichend von Art. 68, das volle Transportrisiko, und er haftet für Fehler des Beförderers.[187] Da der Kauf reisender Ware ein Spezieskauf ist, kommt bei Verlust oder Beschädigung der Ware nur ein Schadensersatzanspruch, aber kein Anspruch auf Ersatzlieferung in Betracht.

7. Montagepflichten, Instruktionspflichten

82 Ist auf einen Liefervertrag mit Montageverpflichtung Einheitskaufrecht anzuwenden (vgl. Art. 3 II),[188] so ist **Erfüllungsort für die Montagepflicht** der Ort, an dem die Montage vorzunehmen ist. Dieser kann vom Erfüllungsort für die Lieferung abweichen. Ist insoweit nichts Besonderes vereinbart, gilt für die Lieferung Art. 31 lit. a); die Montagepflicht allein führt nicht dazu, dass die Lieferpflicht „Bringschuld" wird.[189] Der Verkäufer erfüllt also seine Lieferpflicht durch Versendung der zu montierenden Ware. Die Transportgefahr trifft den Käufer (Art. 67 I S. 1).[190] Bildet die Montagepflicht dagegen den „überwiegenden Teil" der Pflichten des Lieferanten und haben die Parteien (in Abweichung von Art. 3 II) die Geltung des CISG vertraglich vereinbart,[191] ist der Montageort als der einheitliche Erfüllungsort für Lieferung und Montage anzusehen.[192] Übernimmt der Verkäufer zusätzlich zur Montagepflicht die Pflicht, das Personal des Käufers am Aufstellungsort in den Gebrauch der Kaufsache einzuweisen **(Instruktionspflicht),** so wird auch hierfür ein besonderer Erfüllungsort am Instruktionsort begründet,[193] der mit dem Lieferort nicht zusammenfallen muss. Ist für die Instruktionspflicht kein besonderer Erfüllungsort vorgesehen (so bei schriftlichen Instruktionen), genügt der Verkäufer seiner Instruktionspflicht durch Absendung der Instruktion, gleichgültig, wo der Lieferort sich befindet.

---

[184] Vgl. den Fall des OLG Hamburg, 31.1.1910, SeuffArch 65 Nr. 160; dazu *Rabel,* RheinZ 3 (1911), 467, 479 = Ges. Aufs. Bd. 1, S. 56, 68: Verkauft waren 1000 Kisten Kartoffeln „schwimmend auf Dampfer Thekla Bohlen"; tatsächlich hatte die Thekla Bohlen keine Kartoffeln geladen. Das OLG Hamburg erklärte den Verkäufer nach deutschem Recht für schadensersatzpflichtig.

[185] Zur Unerheblichkeit allfälliger Ungültigkeitsvorschriften des nationalen Rechts siehe bereits oben Fn. 124.

[186] Vgl. die Hinweise oben in Fn. 125. Anders die 3. Aufl., *U. Huber,* Art. 31 Rn. 84.

[187] Vgl. oben Rn. 77.

[188] Vgl. dazu *Droste,* S. 162 ff.; *Ferrari,* Art. 3 Rn. 13 ff.

[189] Wie hier auch MünchKommHGB/*Benicke,* Art. 31, Rn. 29; a. A. offenbar *Brunner,* Art. 31, Rn. 4. Unzutreffend daher OLG München, 3.12.1999, CISG-online 585 = IHR 2001, 25, 26; anders scheinbar auch Cass., 19.6.2000, CISG-online 1317, wonach die zu beurteilende Montagepflicht unentbehrliche Voraussetzung für die Erfüllung der Lieferpflicht darstellte, mit der Folge, dass der Erfüllungsort der Lieferpflicht mit dem Ort zusammenfalle, an dem die Montagearbeiten durchzuführen waren („[T]ale obbligo costituisce un requisito indispensabile per l'adempimento dell'obbligazione di consegna, onde il luogo di esecuzione di tale obbligazione va considerato quello in cui le operazioni di montaggio dovevano essere compiute"). Von Bedeutung ist die Frage insbes. für die Bestimmung des zuständigkeitsbegründenden Erfüllungsortes nach Art. 5 Nr. 1 LuganoÜ, § 29 ZPO, Art. 113 IPRG (nicht dagegen nach Art. 5 Nr. 1 lit. b) 1. HS. EuGVO); zum Gerichtsstand des Erfüllungsortes siehe unten Rn. 91 ff.

[190] Geht die Ware auf dem Transport unter, ist die Erfüllung der Montagepflicht unmöglich. Ist für die Montage ein besonderes Entgelt festgesetzt, so braucht der Käufer dieses Entgelt nicht zu bezahlen (Art. 51 I analog); anderenfalls ist der Verkäufer nach Treu und Glauben (Art. 7 II; siehe Art. 30 Rn. 9) verpflichtet, sich die ersparten Montagekosten vom Kaufpreis abziehen zu lassen.

[191] Zur Zulässigkeit einer solchen Vereinbarung vgl. *Ferrari,* Art. 6 Rn. 39 ff.

[192] Vgl. auch *Soergel/U. Huber,* § 446 BGB, Rn. 6.

[193] Vgl. OLG Celle, 2.3.1984, RIW 1985, 571, 575: Gerichtsstand des Erfüllungsorts für Schadensersatzanspruch (Art. 55 EKG).

V. Kosten und Genehmigungen

1. Transportkosten

Das Übereinkommen hat keine eigenen Regeln über die Kosten der Lieferung auf- 83 gestellt.[194] Sind Lieferklauseln nach Massgabe der Incoterms® vereinbart, so ergibt die Regelung der Kostenfrage sich hieraus. Bei fehlender vertraglicher Vereinbarung ist gemäss Art. 7 II auf die allgemeinen Grundsätze des Übereinkommens zurückzugreifen; des nur hilfsweise zulässigen Rückgriffs auf nationales Recht bedarf es nicht. Auszugehen ist von dem Prinzip, dass jede Partei die Kosten ihrer eigenen Leistung zu tragen hat: also der Verkäufer die Kosten der Lieferung, der Käufer die Kosten der Übernahme.[195] Da im Fall des Versendungskaufs gemäss Art. 31 lit. a) der Verkäufer nur zur Übergabe an den Beförderer, nicht zur Durchführung des Transports verpflichtet ist, treffen die **Frachtkosten** den **Käufer**.[196] Der Verkäufer hat zwar den Frachtvertrag abzuschliessen (Art. 32 II), ist aber, wenn nichts anderes vereinbart ist („frachtfrei", „franco"),[197] berechtigt, die Ware unfrei zu versenden. Zahlt er trotzdem Fracht, darf er sie dem Käufer in Rechnung stellen. Nach dem Grundgedanken des Art. 31 ist davon auszugehen, dass der Verkäufer dem Käufer jedenfalls diejenigen Kosten in Rechnung stellen darf, die durch die **Versendung von dem in Art. 31 lit. b) oder c) bestimmten Ort** entstehen – also von demjenigen Ort, wo der Käufer, wenn der Verkäufer die Versendung nicht übernommen hätte, die Ware abholen müsste. Versendet der Verkäufer die Ware von einem dritten, entfernteren Ort und entstehen hierdurch zusätzliche Kosten, so kann er diese Mehrkosten dem Käufer, mangels besonderer Absprache, nicht in Rechnung stellen. Versendet er die Ware von einem nähergelegenen Ort und entstehen daher nur geringere Kosten, hat mangels besonderer Absprache (Vereinbarung einer „Frachtbasis") der Käufer nur die tatsächlich entstandenen Kosten zu tragen. Hat der Verkäufer **gemäss Vertrag** die Ware **von einem dritten Ort zu versenden** (wie z.B. auf Grund der Klausel FOB), so muss er die Kosten der ihm obliegenden Teilstrecke des Transports tragen, nicht aber die Kosten des weiteren Transports, wenn nichts anderes vereinbart ist (wie z.B. bei Vereinbarung der Klausel CIF).[198] Kann die Ware nur verpackt versendet werden, treffen die **Verpackungskosten** den **Verkäufer; sie gehören nicht zu den Frachtkosten.**[199] So wird die Frage auch durchgehend in den Incoterms® geregelt.[200] Entsprechendes gilt in den Fällen des Art. 31 lit. b) und c), wenn die Ware vom Käufer nur in verpacktem Zustand abtransportiert werden kann.[201] Ist der Kaufpreis nach Mass, Zahl oder Gewicht der tatsächlich gelieferten Ware zu bezahlen, oder ist es für den Transport erforderlich, dass Mass, Zahl oder Gewicht festgestellt werden, so gehört das **Messen, Zählen** und **Wägen** noch zur Lieferung, und die hierdurch entstehenden Kosten trägt ebenfalls der Verkäufer.[202] Auch dies stimmt mit der Regelung der

---

[194] Anders als das Haager Einheitskaufrecht (Art. 90 EKG) und als das deutsche Recht (§ 448 BGB).
[195] Ebenso *Staudinger/Magnus*, Art. 31, Rn. 30; *Bamberger/Roth/Saenger*, Art. 31, Rn. 20; MünchKommHGB/*Benicke*, Art. 31, Rn. 32; *Brunner*, Art. 31, Rn. 12. Auf den Zeitpunkt des Gefahrübergangs stellt das Schiedsgericht des Arb. Ct. Bulgarian CCI ab: 12.2.1998, CISG-online 436 (ab Gefahrübergang sind Kosten vom Käufer zu tragen).
[196] Ebenso *Piltz*, Internationales Kaufrecht, Rn. 4–45, 4–109; *Honsell/Ernst/Lauko*, Art. 31, Rn. 53; *Heuzé*, Anm. 245.; MünchKommHGB/*Benicke*, Art. 31, Rn. 32; *Brunner*, Art. 31, Rn. 12. Vgl. auch (zu Artt. 19 II, 90 EKG) LG Konstanz, 3 HO 3/76, in: *Schlechtriem/Magnus*, Art. 90 EKG, Nr. 1.
[197] Vgl. LG Heidelberg, 21.4.1981, in: *Schlechtriem/Magnus*, Art. 56 EKG, Nr. 4 (zu Artt. 19 II, 90 EKG).
[198] Ebenso *Piltz*, Internationales Kaufrecht, Rn. 4–45, 4–109. Vgl. auch Incoterms® 2010 FCA, FAS, FOB, jeweils unter B 6.
[199] Ebenso *Piltz*, Internationales Kaufrecht, Rn. 4–45, 4–110; *Honsell/Ernst/Lauko*, Art. 31, Rn. 53; MünchKommHGB/*Benicke*, Art. 31, Rn. 32; MünchKomm/*Gruber*, Art. 31, Rn. 24; *Soergel/Lüderitz*, Art. 90 EKG, Rn. 1.
[200] Vgl. die einschlägigen Formulare der Incoterms® 2010 (FCA, FAS, FOB, CFR, CIF, CPT, CIP), jeweils unter A 9.
[201] Vgl. insbesondere die Formulare EXW und FCA, jeweils unter A 9. Ebenso *Piltz*, Internationales Kaufrecht, Rn. 4–107; *Soergel/Lüderitz*, Art. 90 EKG, Rn. 1. Zur Verpackungspflicht vgl. oben Rn. 53.
[202] Ebenso *Piltz*, Internationales Kaufrecht, Rn. 4–110.

Incoterms® überein.²⁰³ Für Kosten einer etwa erforderlichen **Qualitätsprüfung** gilt dasselbe.²⁰⁴ Mit den Worten des sec. 29 (6) SGA 1979 lässt sich sagen: „Unless otherwise agreed, the expenses of and incidental to putting the goods into a deliverable state must be borne by the seller." Beim Verkauf **schwimmender, rollender** oder **fliegender** Ware ist, wenn nichts Abweichendes bestimmt ist (etwa durch die Klauseln FOB, frei Waggon, frei Frachtführer), der Vertrag im Zweifel so zu verstehen, dass die Kosten des laufenden Transports bis zum Zielort vom Verkäufer zu tragen sind.²⁰⁵

2. Zölle und Abgaben

84   Zölle und sonstige Ausfuhr- und Einfuhrabgaben gehören nicht zu den Transportkosten im eigentlichen Sinn. Dass der Käufer beim **Versendungskauf** gemäss Art. 31 lit. a) die Transportkosten zu tragen hat, bedeutet also nicht, dass er auch alle Zölle und Abgaben zu tragen hat. Vielmehr ist als allgemeine Auslegungsregel davon auszugehen, dass der Verkäufer die Ausfuhrabgaben, der Käufer die Einfuhrabgaben zu tragen hat.²⁰⁶ In diesem Sinne wird die Frage auch in den Incoterms® geregelt,²⁰⁷ und das dürfte einen allgemeinen Handelsbrauch widerspiegeln. Umgekehrt darf aus der Übernahme der Frachtkosten durch den Verkäufer (Verkauf „frachtfrei" oder „franco") für die Frage der Zollkosten nichts hergeleitet werden; auch hier trägt daher im Zweifel der Käufer die Importabgaben.²⁰⁸ Im Fall der **Lieferung gemäss Art. 31 lit. b) oder c)** ist die Lieferschuld „Holschuld"; hier ist im Zweifel davon auszugehen, dass der Käufer sowohl die Ausfuhrabgaben des Verkäuferstaats als auch die Einfuhrabgaben seines eigenen Staats zu tragen hat.²⁰⁹ Die Incoterms® differenzieren: bei der Klausel EXW sollen die Ausfuhrkosten vom Käufer getragen werden, bei Verwendung der Klauseln FCA, FAS und FOB vom Verkäufer.²¹⁰ Ist dagegen die Lieferschuld **Bringschuld,** so spricht dies dafür, dass der Verkäufer auch die Einfuhrabgaben zu tragen hat.²¹¹ Empfehlenswert ist gerade bei „Geliefert"-Klauseln („D-Klauseln") eine eindeutige Regelung im Vertrag.²¹²

3. Export- und Importgenehmigungen

85   Ein allgemeiner Grundsatz besagt, dass der Verkäufer die Exportlizenz, der Käufer die Importlizenz zu beschaffen hat.²¹³ Von dieser Regel gehen auch die Incoterms® aus.²¹⁴ Bei reinen Holschulden muss sich allerdings der Käufer auch um die Exportlizenz kümmern. In

---

²⁰³ Vgl. alle Formulare unter A 9.
²⁰⁴ So durchgehend die Incoterms® 2010 unter A 9.
²⁰⁵ Vgl. *Piltz,* Internationales Kaufrecht, Rn. 4–109.
²⁰⁶ Vgl. *Honnold/Flechtner,* Art. 31, Rn. 211; *Honsell/Ernst/Lauko,* Art. 31, Rn. 54; *Schlechtriem,* Seller's Obligations, S. 14 f.; MünchKommHGB/*Benicke,* Art. 31, Rn. 33; ebenso trotz abweichenden Ausgangspunkts auch *Piltz,* Internationales Kaufrecht, Rn. 4–45, 111. Abweichend *Staub/Koller,* Vor § 373 HGB, Rn. 661; *Staudinger/Magnus,* Art. 31, Rn. 30; MünchKomm/*Gruber,* Art. 31, Rn. 25.
²⁰⁷ So die Klausel CPT B 2, vgl. auch CFR und CIF B 2.
²⁰⁸ Vgl. zum deutschen Recht: RG, 11.3.1918, LZ 1918, 1208 = Recht 191 9, Nr. 908: Verkauf „Frachtfrei versichert" verpflichtet Verkäufer nicht zur Zahlung des Importzolls.
²⁰⁹ Ebenso *Honsell/Ernst/Lauko,* Art. 31, Rn. 54; MünchKommHGB/*Benicke,* Art. 31, Rn. 33.
²¹⁰ Vgl. Incoterms® 2010 EXW B 2; FCA, FAS und FOB A 2.
²¹¹ Vgl. *Honnold/Flechtner,* Art. 31, Rn. 211; *Schlechtriem,* Seller's Obligations, S. 14; MünchKommHGB/*Benicke,* Art. 31, Rn. 33.
²¹² Vgl. etwa *von Bernstorff,* Incoterms® 2010, 115 ff. (zur Klausel DDP).
²¹³ *Honnol/Flechtner,* Art. 31, Rn. 211; *Schlechtriem,* Seller's Obligations, S. 14; MünchKommHGB/*Benicke,* Art. 31, Rn. 33; *Hager/Maultzsch,* Art. 66 Rn. 4; siehe rechtsvergleichend auch *Schwenzer/Hachem/Kee,* Rn. 30.29. Abweichend *Staudinger/Magnus,* Art. 31, Rn. 30; MünchKomm/*Gruber,* Art. 31, Rn. 25; ebenso, trotz abweichenden Ausgangspunkts,*Piltz,* Internationales Kaufrecht, Rn. 4–45, 4–111. Bei Lieferort im Verkäuferstaat müsste demnach der Käufer auch die Exportlizenz, bei Lieferort im Käuferstaat der Verkäufer auch die Importlizenz besorgen (so auch *Herber/Czerwenka,* Art. 30, Rn. 9). Die Gerichte des Vereinigten Königreichs lehnen solche allgemeinen Grundsätze für die Frage der Lizenzbeschaffungspflicht ab; abzustellen sei vielmehr auf die Umstände des Einzelfalls, vgl. *A. V. Pound & Co. Ltd. v. M. W. Hardy & Co. Inc.* [1956] AC 588; *Atiyah/Adams/Macqueen,* S. 433 ff.
²¹⁴ So sämtliche Formulare Incoterms® ausser EXW einerseits, „Geliefert verzollt" (DDP) andererseits, vgl. jeweils A 2 und B 2.

diesem Sinne entscheiden auch die Incoterms® 2010 für den Fall der Klauseln EXW,[215] nicht dagegen im Fall der Klausel FCA und auch nicht bei der fas-Klausel.[216] Bei reinen Bringschulden ist anzunehmen, dass der Verkäufer auch die Importgenehmigung zu beschaffen hat; so entscheiden auch die Incoterms® 2010 für den Fall der Klausel DDP („geliefert verzollt")[217] sowie der Klauseln DAT und DAP.[218]

Diejenige Partei, die eine Export- oder Importgenehmigung zu besorgen hat, haftet für **86** ihre Beschaffung gemäss Artt. 45 I, 61 I. Die Partei, die dieses Risiko nicht übernehmen will, muss im Vertrag einen ausdrücklichen Vorbehalt anbringen. Unvorhersehbare Änderungen der Rechtslage, die nach Abschluss des Kaufvertrags eintreten, sind ein Entlastungsgrund i. S. d. Art. 79 I.

VI. Gerichtsstand des Erfüllungsortes

1. Allgemeines

Der Erfüllungsort nach Art. 31 hat nicht nur materiellrechtliche Bedeutung, sondern **87** begründet u. U. auch eine eigene gerichtliche Zuständigkeit. Sieht das einschlägige Prozessrecht für Streitigkeiten aus Vertrag einen Gerichtsstand am Erfüllungsort vor und wird der zuständigkeitsbegründende Erfüllungsort nach dem auf den Vertrag anwendbaren Recht qualifiziert,[219] folgt daraus bei Anwendbarkeit des Übereinkommens, dass sich die prozessuale Frage nach der gerichtlichen Zuständigkeit nach dessen materiellen Bestimmungen zum Erfüllungsort richtet.

Dies war denn auch die Rechtslage unter dem EuGVÜ und dem früheren LuganoÜ vom **88** 16.9.1988, deren Art. 5 Nr. 1 einen Gerichtsstand am Ort der Erfüllung der streitigen Vertragsverpflichtung begründeten. Inzwischen ist das EuGVÜ von der EuGVO abgelöst worden[220], und anstelle des LuganoÜ vom 16.9.1988 ist das revidierte LuganoÜ vom 30.10.2007 getreten.[221] In beiden Regelwerken wird die Zuständigkeit am Erfüllungsort in Art. 5 Nr. 1 neu geregelt.[222] Damit sind verschiedene Auslegungsschwierigkeiten verbunden, die indirekt die zuständigkeitsrechtliche Bedeutung des Art. 31 beeinflussen. Weiterhin zentrale Bedeutung kommt Art. 31 nach verschiedenen **nationalen Prozessrechten** (vgl. § 29 ZPO, Art. 113 IPRG) zu. Gestützt auf ein besonderes Abkommen zwischen der EG und dem Königreich Dänemark gilt die EuGVO seit dem 1.7.2007 nun weitgehend auch im Verhältnis zu **Dänemark**.[223]

---

[215] Vgl. EXW A 2, B 2: Der Käufer muss die Exportlizenz besorgen; auf Wunsch muss ihm der Verkäufer dabei „jede Hilfe" gewähren.
[216] Vgl. dort A 2, B 2.
[217] Vgl. A 2, B 2: Der Verkäufer muss die Importlizenz besorgen; auf Wunsch muss ihm der Käufer dabei „jede Hilfe" gewähren.
[218] Vgl. dort A 2, B 2.
[219] Zur umstrittenen Frage der Qualifikation des Erfüllungsortes im europäischen Zivilprozessrecht siehe Kropholler/von Hein, EUZPR, Art. 5, Rn. 21 ff.; zum Parallelproblem im deutschen Recht siehe Schack, Zivilverfahrensrecht, § 8, Rz. 299 ff.; zum schweizerischen Recht vgl. BaslerKomm/Amstutz/Vogt/Wang, Art. 113 IPRG, Rn. 13 f.
[220] Die Ablösung erfolgte per 1.3.2002.
[221] In allen Vertragsstaaten des bisherigen LuganoÜ ist das neue LuganoÜ inzwischen in Kraft getreten.
[222] Zur – zeitlich begrenzten – Sonderposition von Personen mit Wohnsitz in Luxemburg siehe Art. 63 EuGVO. Zur Rechtslage nach dem früheren LuganoÜ vom 16.9.1988 siehe ausführlich die Voraufl.; Widmer Lüchinger, Art. 31, Rn. 89 ff.
[223] Im Gegensatz zu Irland und dem Vereinigten Königreich hatte Dänemark sich ursprünglich nicht für eine Beteiligung an der EuGVO entschieden, vgl. Erwägungsgründe Nr. 20 f. der EuGVO. Gemäss Art. 2 I des am 1.7.2007 in Kraft getretenen Abkommens zwischen der Europäischen Gemeinschaft und dem Königreich Dänemark über die gerichtliche Zuständigkeit und die Anerkennung und Vollstreckung von Entscheidungen in Zivil- und Handelssachen (ABl. L 299 vom 16.11.2005, 62 ff.) findet die EuGVO nun auch im Verhältnis zu Dänemark Anwendung, allerdings nur für Gerichtsverfahren und öffentliche Urkunden, die nach Inkrafttreten des Abkommens eingeleitet bzw. aufgenommen worden sind; vgl. Art. 9 I des Abkommens. Bei Verfahren, die vor dem 1.7.2007 eingeleitet worden sind, richtet sich die direkte Zuständigkeit nach wie vor nach dem EuGVÜ; anderes gilt in bestimmtem Umfang für die Anerkennung und Vollstreckung von Urteilen, wenn die Klage vor

2. Rechtslage nach der EuGVO[224]

89 Der Erfüllungsort bei Verträgen über den Verkauf beweglicher Sachen wird in Art. 5 Nr. 1 lit. b) 1. HS. EuGVO gesondert geregelt.[225] Danach ist – **sofern nichts anderes vereinbart worden ist** – der zuständigkeitsbegründende Erfüllungsort der Verpflichtung jener Ort in einem Mitgliedstaat, an dem die Ware **nach dem Vertrag geliefert worden ist** oder **hätte geliefert werden müssen**. Die Bestimmung findet ihr Vorbild in Art. 46 des französischen Nouveau Code de Procédure Civile.[226] Aus den Materialien zur EuGVO ergibt sich, dass mit dem Hinweis auf den Lieferort der Rückgriff auf das anwendbare Recht vermieden werden soll.[227] Der gerichtsstandsbegründende Erfüllungsort ist nunmehr autonom zu bestimmen; er richtet sich nach „pragmatischen" Kriterien, d. h. nach der Vertragswirklichkeit. Dies wurde mittlerweile auch durch den EuGH bestätigt[228]. Zudem wird, anders als noch nach EuGVÜ und dem LuganoÜ vom 16.9.1988,[229] der Gerichtsstand **für alle streitigen Vertragspflichten sowohl des Verkäufers als auch des Käufers** – insbesondere also auch für die Kaufpreiszahlungspflicht des Käufers[230] – **einheitlich** am Erfüllungsort der vertragscharakteristischen Leistung, beim Verkauf beweglicher Sachen also am **tatsächlichen Erfüllungsort der Lieferpflicht** lokalisiert.[231]

90 **a) Tatsächlicher Erfüllungsort der Lieferpflicht.** Die Tragweite der neuen Regelung war lange Zeit kontrovers, wurde aber inzwischen durch den EuGH teilweise geklärt[232]. Gemäss EuGH ist der Rückgriff auf das materielle Recht zur Bestimmung des Erfüllungsortes nach Art. 5 Nr. 1 lit. b) EuGVO ausgeschlossen.[233] Der tatsächliche Erfüllungsort der

---

Inkrafttreten erhoben worden, das Urteil jedoch nach Inkrafttreten ergangen ist, siehe Art. 9 II des Abkommens. In Art. 2 II des Abkommens wird die Anwendung verschiedener Bestimmungen der EuGVO abgeändert; dies gilt jedoch nicht für die (nachfolgend allein interessierende) Bestimmung des Art. 5 Nr. 1 EuGVO.

[224] Zum revidierten LuganoÜ siehe unten Rn. 99.

[225] Auf Art. 5 Nr. 1 lit. a) ist gemäß Art. 5 Nr. 1 lit. c) EuGVO nur dann zurückzugreifen, wenn Buchstabe b) nicht anwendbar ist, siehe dazu unten Rn. 99. Dies wurde verkannt vom LG Gießen, 17.12.2002, CISG-online 766 = IHR 2003, 276 f., m. Anm. *Thiele*, EWiR 2004, 283 f.; unzutreffend auch BGH, 1.6.2005, RIW 2006, 776 ff., NJW 2005, 1518 ff., dazu unten Fn. 231 und 237; vgl. zur Struktur der Bestimmung auch *Markus*, AJP 2010, 971, 973.

[226] „Le demandeur peut saisir à son choix, outre la juridiction du lieu où demeure le défendeur: – en matière contractuelle, la juridiction du lieu de la livraison effective de la chose [...]"; dazu *Kropholler/von Hinden*, S. 401, 405 f.; *Kropholler/von Hein*, EUZPR, Art. 5, Rn. 27. Eine vergleichbare Regelung sah Art. 4.2.4.1 der von der Joint American Law Institute/UNIDROIT Working Group entwickelten Draft Rules of Transnational Civil Procedure vor („Jurisdiction may be established [...] over a person that has provided goods [...] in the forum state, or agreed to do so, when the proceeding concerns such goods [...]"). In die 2004 schliesslich verabschiedete Fassung der UNIDROIT Principles of Transnational Civil Procedure (abrufbar unter http://www.unidroit.org/english/principles/civilprocedure/ali-unidroitprinciples-e.pdf) wurde diese Bestimmung jedoch nicht aufgenommen. Eine ähnliche Bestimmung sah auch der Haager Vorentwurf für ein internationales Zuständigkeits- und Anerkennungsübereinkommen, Version Juni 2001, in Art. 6 lit. a), Alternative B, vor; dieses Projekt der Haager Konferenz wurde jedoch, da „zu ambitiös", zugunsten des Haager Übereinkommens vom 30.6.2005 über die Gerichtsstandsvereinbarungen fallen gelassen.

[227] Siehe Begründung zum Vorschlag für eine Verordnung (EG) des Rates über die gerichtliche Zuständigkeit und die Anerkennung und Vollstreckung von Entscheidungen in Zivil- und Handelssachen v. 14.7.1999, KOM (1999) 348 endg., 15.

[228] EuGH, 25.2.2010, Rs. C-381/08 (Car Trim/KeySafety Systems Srl). Vgl. In diesem Kontext auch EuGH, 11.3.2010, Rs. C-19/09, Rn. 23 (Wood Floor Solutions/Silva Trade); EuGH, 9.7.2009, Rs. C-204/08, Rn. 33 (Rehder/Air Baltic); EuGH, 3.5.2007, Rs. C-386/05, Rn. 39 (Color Drack GmbH/Lexx International Vertriebs GmbH) = IPRax 2007, 444 ff.

[229] Dazu ausführlich die Vorauflage; Widmer Lüchinger, Art. 31, Rn. 89 ff.

[230] Dazu *Mohs*, Art. 57 Rn. 23 f. Insoweit unzutreffend LG Nürnberg-Fürth, 27.2.2003, CISG-online 818 = IHR 2004, 20.

[231] Vgl. auch *Honsell/Ernst/Lauko*, Art. 31, Rn. 57; verkannt vom LG Gießen, 17.12.2002, CISG-online 766 = IHR 2003, 276 f.

[232] Siehe insbes. EuGH, 25.2.2010, Rs. C-381/08 (Car Trim/KeySafety Systems S. r. l.).

[233] EuGH, 25.2.2010, Rs. C-381/08, Rn. 53 (Car Trim/KeySafety Systems S. r. l.); hierzu ausführlich *Kropholler/von Hein*, EUZPR, Art. 5, Rn. 45 ff. mit weiteren Hinweisen. Zur früher kontrovers geführten Diskussion vgl. auch *Jegher*, FS Schnyder, S. 117, 127 f., der die Meinung vertrat, es sei durchwegs auf das Vertragsstatut zurückzugreifen. Zu Unrecht ging auch C. *Witz*, D. 2001, 3608, 3613 f. ohne weiteres davon

Lieferpflicht befindet sich dort, wo der Käufer oder der sonstige vertragliche Leistungsdestinatär den **körperlichen Gewahrsam an der Ware** erlangt hat;[234] in Ermangelung einer solchen Übergabe ist darauf abzustellen, wo diese nach dem Vertrag hätte stattfinden sollen.[235] So lässt sich denn auch der Passus in Art. 5 Nr. 1 lit. b) 1. HS. EuGVO erklären, wonach der tatsächliche Erfüllungsort sich nach dem Vertrag richtet: Der tatsächliche Erfüllungsort im Sinn der Verordnung liegt dort, wo der körperliche Gewahrsam an den Leistungsdestinatär übergeht bzw. übergehen soll; wo dieser Ort sich befindet, ergibt sich jedoch aus dem Vertrag.[236] Keinen tatsächlichen Lieferort stellt dagegen der Ort dar, an dem allfällige Dokumente i. S. d. Art. 34, etwa ein Konnossement, an den Käufer übergeben werden.[237] Zur Rechtsfolge bei fehlender vertraglicher Festlegung des Bestimmungsortes siehe Rn. 98.

Unproblematisch erscheint die vom anwendbaren Recht losgelöste Bestimmung des Erfüllungsortes zunächst in jenen Fällen, in denen die Lieferpflicht des Verkäufers sich nach dem Vertrag darauf beschränkt, die Ware an einem bestimmten Ort zuhanden des Käufers **zur Verfügung zu stellen.** An diesem Ort soll nach dem Willen der Parteien der Käufer in die Lage versetzt werden, die Ware in seinen Gewahrsam zu nehmen; hier wird tatsächlich geliefert.[238] Umgekehrt dürfte auch jener Fall keine Schwierigkeiten bereiten, in dem der Verkäufer nach dem Vertrag den **Transport der Ware zum Käufer selber,** d. h. ohne Einschaltung eines unabhängigen Transportunternehmens, **durchzuführen** hat. Diesfalls deckt sich der zuständigkeitsbegründende Erfüllungsort mit dem Bestimmungsort.

Auch die früher umstrittene Frage nach dem Erfüllungsort, wenn der Verkäufer nach dem Vertrag die **Übergabe der Ware an einen selbstständigen Beförderer** schuldet, ist inzwischen durch den EuGH geklärt worden[239]. Ist die Ware an ihren vertraglichen Bestimmungsort gelangt, liegt der zuständigkeitsbegründende **Erfüllungsort** an ebendiesem **Bestimmungsort** – und zwar unabhängig davon, ob die Lieferpflicht nach dem anwendbaren Recht eine Bring- oder Schickschuld darstellt.[240] Gleiches muss grundsätzlich

---

aus, dass der zuständigkeitsrechtliche Erfüllungsort bei Anwendbarkeit des Übereinkommens sich stets aus Art. 31 ergibt; zutreffend wies *C. Witz,* J. L. & Com. (2005-06), 325, 329 f. darauf hin, dass „[o]pinions in legal doctrine are extremely divergent […]". In der vor dem EuGH-Entscheid ergangenen Rechtsprechung zur Auslegung von Art. 5 Nr. 1 lit. b) 1. HS. EuGVO liess sich keine einheitliche Linie feststellen. Gewisse Gerichte nahmen auf Art. 31 Bezug, um den Erfüllungsort festzulegen, andere nahmen keinen Bezug auf Art. 31 und wiederum andere verwarfen ausdrücklich einen Rückgriff auf Art. 31. Vgl. dazu ausführlich die Vorauflage: *Widmer Lüchinger,* Art. 31 Rn. 94 Fn. 250.

[234] Gemäss EuGH, 25.2.2010, Rs. C-381/08, Rn. 60 (Car Trim/KeySafety Systems S. r. l.) „ist festzustellen, dass der endgültige Bestimmungsort, an dem die Waren dem Käufer körperlich übergeben wurden oder hätten übergeben werden müssen, als „Lieferort" im Sinne von Art. 5 Nr. 1 lit. b erster Gedankenstrich der Verordnung der Entstehungsgeschichte, den Zielen und der Systematik dieser Verordnung am besten entspricht." Die Normierung in lit. b) entstand unter französischem Einfluss und findet ihr Vorbild in Art. 46 NCPC. Vgl. CA Rouen, 2.5.1979, Gaz. Pal. 1980.1. Somm. 81; Com., 3.11.1988, Gaz. Pal. 1989.1. Somm. 252, obs. *Guinchard/Moussa,* Rev. trim. dr. civ. 1989, 376 ff., obs. *Normand; Cosnard,* S. 207, 215; ferner die Ausführungen von *Heuzé* zu Com., 1.3.1994, Rev. crit. dr. int. privé 1994, 673, 678 f.: „[L]e lieu de la livraison effective, au sens de l'article 46 NCPC, ne peut être que celui où l'acheteur, ou toute autre personne agissant pour son compte, est mis à même de constater les vices de la chose, c'est-à-dire où il dispose de la possibilité matérielle de prendre possession de celle-ci"; vgl. auch die Erwägungen der Vorinstanz zu Art. 5 Nr. 1 EuGVÜ in Civ. 1, 26.6.2001, CISG-online 600. Siehe für den Fall der erfüllten Lieferpflicht auch *Schack,* IPRax 1987, 215, 217 f.: Tatsächlicher Erfüllungsort am neuen Standort der Ware. Von einem ähnlichen Verständnis (noch zu Art. 5 Nr. 1 EuGVÜ) geht das OLG Köln, 16.7.2001, CISG-online 609 = IHR 2002, 66, 67 aus.

[235] Civ. 2, 18.1.2001, J. C. P. 2001, IV, 1413. Gestützt auf den Wortlaut des Art. 46 frz. NCPC verlangte die ältere Rechtsprechung demgegenüber eine tatsächlich erfolgte Lieferung, vgl. Com., 3.11.1988, Gaz. Pal. 1989.1. Somm. 252, obs. *Guinchard/Moussa.*

[236] Vgl. zu Art. 46 frz. NCPC auch *Schack,* Erfüllungsort, Rn. 247: Der tatsächliche Erfüllungsort liegt am eigentlichen *Erfolgsort* der vertragstypischen Leistung.

[237] So aber Com., 1.3.1994, Rev. crit. dr. int. privé 1994, 672 f.; ablehnend zu Recht die französische Lehre, vgl. *Heuzé,* Rev. crit. dr. int. privé 1994, 673, 678 ff.

[238] Vgl. zu Art. 46 frz. NCPC auch *Cosnard,* S. 207, 215.

[239] EuGH. 25.2.2010, Rs. C-381/08, Rn. 60 (Car Trim/KeySafety Systems S. r. l.).

[240] *Kropholler/von Hein,* EUZPR, Art. 5, Rn. 49; *Magnus,* IHR 2002, 45, 47 für den Fall, dass die Parteien keinen anderen Lieferort vereinbart haben. So (zum LuganoÜ/EuGVÜ) bereits *Valloni,* S. 293; übereinstim-

Art. 31 93   Teil III. Kapitel II. Pflichten des Verkäufers. Abschnitt I

aber auch dann gelten, wenn die Parteien (etwa mittels Bezugnahme auf eine Incoterms®-Klausel) einen **Lieferort vertraglich festgelegt** haben: Der tatsächliche Erfüllungsort der Lieferpflicht entspricht dem vertraglichen Bestimmungsort, unabhängig vom Inhalt der jeweiligen Lieferklausel.[241] Zwar begründet der tatsächliche Erfüllungsort der Lieferpflicht gemäss Art. 5 Nr. 1 lit. b) 1 HS. EuGVO nur dann einen Gerichtsstand, wenn **nichts anderes vereinbart** ist. Die Parteien können die gerichtliche Zuständigkeit also **durch eine vom tatsächlichen Lieferort abweichende Bestimmung des Erfüllungsortes** beeinflussen, ohne die Formvorschriften für Gerichtsstandsvereinbarungen nach Art. 23 EuGVO einzuhalten.[242] Eine von den Parteien vereinbarte **Lieferklausel** wird jedoch regelmässig nicht in diesem Sinne zu verstehen sein, dienen solche Klauseln doch meist nur der Regelung von Kosten- und Gefahrtragung, siehe oben Rn. 92.

93   Etwas schwieriger gestaltet sich die Rechtslage, wenn noch gar nicht geliefert worden ist, eine eigentliche Vertragswirklichkeit also gerade fehlt. Nach dem Wortlaut der EuGVO muss hier darauf abgestellt werden, wo nach dem Vertrag **tatsächlich hätte geliefert werden müssen**.[243] Auch bei vollständig ausbleibender Lieferung wird mithin der **Gerichtsstand** am vertraglichen **Bestimmungsort** begründet. Nimmt der Käufer die Ware dagegen an einem anderen als dem ursprünglichen vereinbarten Bestimmungsort tatsächlich ab, ist zu prüfen, ob dies eine Vertragsänderung darstellt, welche einen neuen Gerichtsstand begründet.[244] Auf den Bestimmungsort ist ferner auch dann abzustellen, wenn dieser erst nachträglich, etwa während des Transports, von den Parteien festgelegt wird. Dies gilt grundsätzlich auch dann, wenn der Käufer sich im Kaufvertrag die Bestimmung, wohin und an wen die Ware zu versenden ist, vorbehalten hat („Destinati-

---

mend *Hau*, IPRax 2000, 354, 358; *Kubis*, ZEuP 2001, 737, 750; *Hager/Bentele*, IPRax 2004, 73, 76; *Hackenberg*, S. 272 (die Regelung jedoch kritisierend); aus der Rechtsprechung siehe Tribunale di Reggio Emilia, 12.12.2005, RDIPP 2007, 218, 219 f. (Zuständigkeit der italienischen Gerichte nach Art. 5 Nr. 1 lit. b) EuGVO bei einem Versendungskauf i. S. d. Art. 31 lit. a) bejaht; die aus Deutschland versandte Ware wurde in Italien vom Käufer in Gewahrsam genommen); Tribunale di Rovereto, 28.8.2004 (resp. 2.9.2004), CISG-online 902 = RDIPP 2005, 162, 168 f.; Tribunale di Brescia, 28.12.2004, Int'l Lis 2005, 132, zitiert in Tribunale di Padova, 10.1.2006, CISG-online 1157 = RDIPP 2007, 147 ff.; vgl. ferner LG Trier, 8.1.2004, CISG-online 910 = IHR 2004, 115, 116 („[D]ie Fensterelemente [wurden] unstreitig nach Luxemburg geliefert. Luxemburg ist deshalb Erfüllungs- bzw. Bestimmungsort im Sinne der [Artt. 5 Nr. 1 lit. b) und 63 I EuGVO]"); OGH, 14.12.2004, CISG-online 1018; OLG Hamm, 6.12.2005, CISG-online 1221 = IHR 2006, 86 = IPRax 2006, 290, 291, m. Anm. *Jayme*; Tribunale di Verona, 22.2.2005, RDIPP 2007, 367, 369; vgl. auch den Zwischenbeschluss des OLG Köln, 30.4.2007, IHR 2007, 164, 167, der die Rechtslage im Falle eines Versendungskaufes allerdings gerade offen lässt; siehe auch OLG Köln, 21.12.2005, CISG-online 1201 = IHR 2006, 86 f. Für abweichende Auffassungen in der Gerichtspraxis siehe die Hinweise oben in Fn. 250. In Übereinstimmung mit dem – französischen – Berufungsgericht, dessen Entscheid Gegenstand des Verfahrens bildete, stellte auch der Generalanwalt *Damaso Ruiz-Carabo Colomer* in seinen Schlussanträgen v. 16.3.1999 in der Rechtssache C-440/97 (GIE Groupe Concorde/Kapitän des Schiffes „Suhadiwarno Panjan") auf den Bestimmungsort ab (Erwägung Nr. 107); so auch Generalanwalt *Lenz* in seinen Schlussanträgen v. 8.3.1994 in der Rechtssache C-288/92 (Custom Made Commercial/Stawa Metallbau), Erwägung Nr. 82. Ablehnend *Piltz*, NJW 2002, 289, 793; *Gsell*, IPRax 2002, 484, 489, 491: Rückgriff auf Art. 6.1.6 PICC bzw. Art. 7:101 PECL; Tribunale di Padova, 10.1.2006, CISG-online 1157 = RDIPP 2007, 147 ff.; kritisch hierzu *Hager/Bentele*, IPRax 2004, 73, 76. Für einen Beizug der European Principles im Rahmen des (gerade nicht auf den tatsächlichen Erfüllungsort abstellenden) Art. 5 Nr. 1 LuganoÜ/EuGVÜ bereits *Vischer/Huber/Oser*, Rn. 310.

[241] Siehe zu Art. 46 frz. NCPC CA Rouen, 2.5.1979, Gaz. Pal. 1980.1. Somm. 81; *Cosnard*, S. 207, 214 f.; *Normand*, Rev. trim. dr. civ. 1989, 376, 377; ferner insbes. *Heuzé*, Rev. crit. dr. int. privé 1994, 673, 676 ff. A. A. *Magnus*, IHR 2002, 45, 47; *Béraudo*, J. D. I. 2001, 1033, 1044.

[242] *Kropholler/von Hein*, EUZPR, Art. 5, Rn. 35. Der Erfüllungsort muss jedoch einen realen Bezug zur Vertragserfüllung haben; entsprechend den Gerichtsstandsklauseln unterliegen „abstrakte" Erfüllungsortsvereinbarungen, die lediglich darauf abzielen, einen Gerichtsstand zu begründen, den strengen Formvorschriften des Art. 23 EuGVO, siehe *Kropholler/von Hein*, EUZPR, Art. 5, Rn. 36; *Schack*, Zivilverfahrensrecht, § 8 Rz. 312; vgl. ferner OGH, 8.9.2005, IHR 2006, 122, 124; LG Trier, 8.1.2004, CISG-online 910 = IHR 2004, 115, 116 f. Entgegen BGH, 1.6.2005, RIW 2006, 776 ff., NJW 2005, 1518 ff., führt die Vereinbarung eines Erfüllungsorts nicht dazu, dass nunmehr auf Art. 5 Nr. 1 lit. a) EuGVO zurückzugreifen wäre; vgl. hierzu die berechtigte Kritik von *Mankowski*, LMK 2005, Nr. 155 248.

[243] Abweichend MünchKomm/*Gruber*, Art. 31, Rn. 32: Rückgriff auf Art. 31.

[244] Vgl. zum schweizerischen Recht auch BaslerKomm/*Amstutz/Vogt/Wang*, Art. 113 IPRG, Rn. 14.

onsvorbehalt"), es sei denn, die Ausübung dieses Rechts erscheint im Einzelfall als rechtsmissbräuchlich.[245]

b) Konsequenzen für Art. 31. Für den Rückgriff auf das auf den Vertrag anwendbare 94 Recht bleibt damit nur in den seltenen Fällen Raum, in denen 1. sich der Inhalt der Lieferpflicht dem Vertrag nicht entnehmen lässt, also unklar ist, ob der Verkäufer die Ware lediglich an einem bestimmten Ort zuhanden des Käufers zur Verfügung zu stellen oder aber an einen unabhängigen Beförderer zu übergeben hat, oder 2. in denen die Pflicht zur Übergabe an einen selbstständigen Beförderer zwar feststeht, der Vertrag jedoch zum Bestimmungsort der Ware schweigt und dieser auch nicht nachträglich festgelegt wird.[246] Damit ist aber nicht gesagt, dass der zuständigkeitsbegründende Erfüllungsort sich aus Art. 31 ergibt. Vielmehr sind Inhalt der Lieferpflicht und ggf. der Bestimmungsort mittels **ergänzender Vertragsauslegung** (Art. 8) zu bestimmen. Da nun im Anwendungsbereich des Übereinkommens der Versendungskauf die Regel bildet,[247] wird der tatsächliche Erfüllungsort regelmässig am Ort der Niederlassung des Käufers liegen, denn dorthin ist die Ware beim Versendungskauf im Zweifel zu senden.[248] Trotz Rückgriffes auf das Vertragsstatut richtet der zuständigkeitsbegründende Erfüllungsort sich auch hier nicht nach Art. 31.

c) Ausnahmsweiser Rückgriff auf Art. 31 nach Art. 5 Nr. 1 lit. a) EuGVO. Bei 95 Anwendbarkeit des Übereinkommens ist zur Bestimmung des prozessualen Erfüllungsortes nur in einer Konstellation auf Art. 31 abzustellen,[249] nämlich dann, wenn Art. 5 Nr. 1 lit. b) zu einem Gerichtsstand **ausserhalb eines Mitgliedstaates** führte. Ist etwa die Ware in Übereinstimmung mit dem Vertrag nach den USA befördert worden, soll gemäss dem Verweis in Art. 5 Nr. 1 lit. c) die allgemeine Regelung des Art. 5 Nr. 1 lit. a) EuGVO greifen.[250] Damit soll nichts anderes als die frühere Rechtsprechung des EuGH zu Art. 5 Nr. 1 EuGVÜ zum Tragen kommen.[251] Der Erfüllungsort bestimmt sich mithin nicht autonom, sondern nach dem Vertragsstatut, ggf. also nach Art. 31; zudem ist er für die jeweils streitige Vertragspflicht gesondert zu lokalisieren. Im Einzelnen:

Aus **Art. 31 lit. a)** ergibt sich zunächst einmal negativ, dass der Bestimmungsort des 96 Transports **nicht** der Lieferort ist und dass deshalb dort **kein** Gerichtsstand für Ansprüche wegen Nichterfüllung der Lieferpflicht begründet wird.[252] Da Art. 31 lit. a) keine positive Bestimmung über den Ort der Versendung enthält, sondern der Verkäufer in den Grenzen von Treu und Glauben versenden darf, von wo er will,[253] scheint es auf den ersten Blick

---

[245] Was z. B. dann der Fall sein wird, wenn der Verkäufer sich weigert, die Ware zu liefern, und der Käufer daraufhin lediglich zwecks Begründung eines für ihn günstigen Gerichtsstands den Bestimmungsort festlegt.
[246] Die Tragweite, die Art. 31 im Rahmen von Art. 5 Nr. 1 lit. b) 1. HS. EuGVO noch zukommt, ist umstritten; zu den verschiedenen Meinungen siehe die Hinweise oben in Fn. 256.
[247] Siehe oben Rn. 17 f.
[248] Siehe oben Rn. 39.
[249] Art. 5 Nr. 1 EuGVÜ gilt ausserdem auch im Verhältnis der EG-Staaten zu Dänemark, soweit Verfahren betroffen sind, die vor dem 1.7.2007 eingeleitet worden sind. Vgl. Fn. 223.
[250] Nicht zum Tragen kommt Art. 5 Nr. 1 lit. a) EuGVO dagegen, wenn die Parteien eine Erfüllungsortsvereinbarung getroffen haben. Unzutreffend BGH, 1.6.2005, RIW 2006, 776 ff., NJW 2005, 1518 ff.; vgl. hierzu *Leible*, IPRax 2006, 365 („schlicht [...] falsch"), v. a. aber die Kritik von *Mankowski*, LMK 2005, Nr. 155 248. Vgl. BGH, 22.4.2009, NJW 2009, 2606 ff.; vgl. auch *Kropholler/von Hein*, EUZPR, Art. 5 Rn. 52 ff.
[251] Begründung zum Vorschlag für eine Verordnung (EG) des Rates über die gerichtliche Zuständigkeit und die Anerkennung und Vollstreckung von Entscheidungen in Zivil- und Handelssachen v. 14.7.1999, KOM (1999) 348 endg., 15; vgl. hierzu *Kropholler/von Hinden*, S. 401, 408 f., 411; *Kropholler/von Hein*, EUZPR, Art. 5, Rn. 28 ff.; *Furrer/Schramm*, SJZ 2003, 105, 109 f.; *Junker*, RIW 2002, 569, 572; *Micklitz/Rott*, EuZW 2001, 325, 329. Aus der Rechtsprechung vgl. OLG Frankfurt a. M., 8.9.2004, RIW 2004, 864 f. (zu einem Dienstleistungsvertrag).
[252] Vgl. (zu Artt. 19, 23 EKG): BGHZ 98, 263, 272; OLG Düsseldorf, 9.7.1986, IPRax 1987, 234 = RIW 1987, 943; OLG Koblenz, 23.2.1990, RIW 1990, 316, 318 = ZIP 1991, 1098, 1101; Cass., 13.1.1978, in: *Schlechtriem/Magnus*, Art. 19 EKG, Nr. 1 sowie (zu Art. 31) BGH, 11.12.1996, CISG-online 225 = BGHZ 134, 201, 206; HR, NJB 1997, 1726, 1727; Civ. 1, 16.7.1998, CISG-online 344 = Bull. Civ. I, Nr. 252 = D. 1998 IR. 222; Civ. 1, 2.12.1997, CISG-online 294 = Bull. Civ. I, Nr. 341 = D. 1998 IR. 20.
[253] Oben Rn. 5, 31.

überhaupt keinen eigenen Gerichtsstand des Erfüllungsorts zu geben.[254] Die Lieferpflicht im Falle des Art. 31 lit. a) ist jedoch so zu verstehen, dass die eigentliche Aufgabe des Verkäufers darin besteht, den Transport der Ware zum Käufer zu veranlassen; wo er zu diesem Zweck die Ware dem Beförderer übergibt, ist demgegenüber von untergeordneter Bedeutung. Erfüllungsort für die Lieferpflicht im Sinne der prozessualen Zuständigkeitsregeln ist daher im Fall des Art. 31 lit. a) die **Niederlassung des Verkäufers**,[255] bei mehreren Niederlassungen diejenige, mit der engsten Beziehung zum Vertrag und zu seiner Erfüllung (Art. 10 lit. a)), beim Fehlen einer Niederlassung der Ort des gewöhnlichen Aufenthalts des Verkäufers (Art. 10 lit. b)).[256]

97 Da **Art. 31 lit. b)** den Erfüllungsort **gesetzlich** regelt, begründet er einen besonderen Gerichtsstand des Erfüllungsorts gemäss Art. 5 Nr. 1 lit. b) EuGVO.[257] Das ist unproblematisch, wenn der nach Art. 31 lit. b) bestimmte Lieferort mit der Niederlassung des Verkäufers zusammenfällt. Art. 31 lit. b) kann aber – z.B. beim Verkauf von Ware, die bei einem Dritten eingelagert ist – auch zu recht entlegenen Gerichtsständen führen. Ob das „sachgerecht" ist,[258] mag man bezweifeln; die Bestimmung des Erfüllungsortes nach dem auf den Vertrag anwendbaren Recht lässt aber keine andere Wahl. Dagegen begründet der Lieferort gemäss **Art. 31 lit. c)** nach dem klaren Wortlaut von Art. 5 EuGVO nur dann für Klagen des Käufers wegen Nichterfüllung der Lieferpflicht einen Gerichtsstand des Erfüllungsorts, wenn dieser nicht mit dem allgemeinen Gerichtsstand des Verkäufers (Artt. 2 I, 60 EuGVO) zusammenfällt.[259]

98 Vereinbaren die Parteien einen **von Art. 31 abweichenden besonderen Lieferort**, ohne ihn zugleich ausdrücklich zum Gerichtsstand zu erklären, so ist es eine Frage der **Vertragsauslegung**, ob sie hierdurch nur die technische Abwicklung des Vertrags oder zugleich den Gerichtsstand regeln wollten. Im Zweifel sollte man Lieferortsvereinbarungen keine zuständigkeitsbegründende Wirkung zusprechen;[260] auch die Lieferklauseln der Incoterms® sind nicht in diesem Sinn zu verstehen.[261] Ihr Zweck erschöpft sich darin, Fragen der Transportkosten, der Liefermodalitäten und der Gefahrtragung zu regeln, die mit

---

[254] So *Stoll*, Internationalprivatrechtliche Fragen, S. 5; *U. Huber*, 1. Aufl., Art. 31 Rn. 47.
[255] Hiervon geht auch die Rechtsprechung mit Selbstverständlichkeit aus, vgl. OGH, 10.9.1998, CISG-online 646 = RdW 1999, 210; BGH, 11.12.1996, CISG-online 225 = BGHZ 134, 201, 206; OLG Köln, 16.7.2001, CISG-online 609 = IHR 2002, 66, 67; ferner OLG Düsseldorf, 9.7.1986, IPRax 1987, 234 = RIW 1987, 943; OLG Koblenz, 23.2.1990, RIW 1990, 316, 318 = ZIP 1991, 1098, 1101; Cass., 13.1.1978, in: *Schlechtriem/Magnus*, Art. 19 EKG, Nr. 1, sowie BGHZ 78, 257, 260 (alle zu der insoweit mit Art. 31 lit. a) übereinstimmenden Bestimmung des Art. 19 II EKG). Wie hier auch *Bamberger/Roth/Saenger*, Art. 31, Rn. 21; so prinzipiell auch *Achilles*, Art. 31, Rn. 9; *Liguori*, Riv. dir. civ. 1999, 143, 157. Dagegen wollen *Staudinger/Magnus*, Art. 31, Rn. 24 und MünchKommHGB/*Benicke*, Art. 31, Rn. 37 auf den tatsächlichen Ort der Übergabe an den ersten Beförderer abstellen (der mit dem Ort der Niederlassung vielfach, aber nicht notwendigerweise identisch ist). In diesem Sinne anscheinend auch HR, NJB 1997, 1726, 1727; Civ. 1, 16.7.1998, CISG-online 344 = Bull. Civ. I, Nr. 252 = D. 1998 IR. 222; Tribunale di Reggio Emilia, 3.7.2000, CISG-online 771.
[256] Dies gilt auch für negative Feststellungsklagen des Verkäufers, die auf die Feststellung gerichtet sind, dass (mangelfrei) geliefert worden ist, Ansprüche des Käufers mithin nicht bestehen, vgl. BGH, 11.12.1996, CISG-online 225 = BGHZ 134, 201, 205 f.
[257] Abweichend 1. Aufl., *U. Huber*, Art. 31 Rn. 51.
[258] So *Soergel/Lüderitz*, Art. 19 EKG, Rn. 28.
[259] So auch im schweizerischen Recht, vgl. Artt. 112, 113 IPRG.
[260] So auch OGH, 10.9.1998, CISG-online 409 = RdW 1999, 210; KG Zug, 11.12.2003, CISG-online 958 = IHR 2005, 119, 121 f. (E. 2.3); Cass., 6.7.2005, RDIPP 2006, 447, 449; insoweit zutreffend auch Tribunale di Verona, 9.12.2006, CISG-online 1439 („porto franco"). Im Allgemeinen wird das von den Gerichten allerdings bedenkenlos bejaht, vor allem dann, wenn dies zur eigenen Zuständigkeit führt. Vgl. z.B. OLG Köln, 8.1.1997, CISG-online 217 (zum Fall der Bringschuld); CA d'Orléans, 29.3.2001, CISG-online 611 = IHR 2003, 146 („free destination la Bussière"); Kortrijk, 8.12.2004, IHR 2005, 114 f. (wobei das Gericht hier aufgrund der Lieferklausel „frei Haus" seine Zuständigkeit verneinte). Für diesen Fall scheint auch BGH, 11.12.1996, CISG-online 225 = BGHZ 134, 201, 206, nicht zu bezweifeln, dass ein internationaler Gerichtsstand am Sitz des Käufers begründet ist.
[261] Vgl. zu Art. 46 frz. NCPC *Heuzé*, Rev. crit. dr. int. privé 1994, 673, 678; zu § 29 dt. ZPO RGZ 111, 23, 24; *Großmann-Doerth*, Überseekauf, S. 106 ff., 181 ff.; *Liesecke*, S. 27; *Soergel/U. Huber*, § 447 BGB, Rn. 90. Abweichend *Soergel/Lüderitz*, Art. 19 EKG, Rn. 28.

Gerichtsstandsfragen zu verbinden nicht sachgemäss ist.[262] Das gilt vor allem dann, wenn die Klausel einen Lieferort festlegt, der weder mit dem Ort der Niederlassung des Verkäufers noch des Käufers identisch ist, wie z. B. die Klauseln FOB, CIF oder „geliefert Grenze".[263] Selbstverständlich ist, dass Klauseln, nach denen die Lieferpflicht in der Versendung der Ware besteht, allenfalls einen Gerichtsstand am Versendungsort begründen können, nicht aber einen Gerichtsstand am Bestimmungsort.[264] Vereinbaren die Parteien dagegen nicht eine Lieferklausel, sondern einen allgemeinen „Erfüllungsort" („Erfüllungsort ist der Sitz des Lieferanten"), so ist dies – grundsätzlich[265] – auch für den Gerichtsstand massgeblich.[266]

3. Rechtslage nach dem revidierten LuganoÜ vom 30. Oktober 2007

Nach dem revidierten LuganoÜ vom 30.10.2007, welches das LuganoÜ vom 16.9.1988 **99** abgelöst hat, ist der Erfüllungsort neu autonom und unabhängig von der konkret eingeklagten Verpflichtung zu bestimmen. Die Rechtslage deckt sich mit jener nach der EuGVO. Der Erfüllungsort gemäss Art. 5 Ziff. 1 lit. b) LuganoÜ ist demnach gleich zu bestimmen wie nach Art. 5 Nr. 1 lit. b) EuGVO.[267] Unter der Geltung des früheren LuganoÜ entsprach die Rechtslage in Bezug auf den Gerichtsstand des Erfüllungsortes jener unter Art. 5 Nr. 1 EuGVÜ.[268] Der Erfüllungsort bestimmte sich nach dem auf den streitigen Vertrag anwendbaren Recht – und damit ggf. nach Art. 31[269] – und war damit nicht für den ganzen Vertrag einheitlich, sondern für die *jeweils streitige Verpflichtung* zu lokalisieren.[270] Diese Methode führte zu mehreren möglichen Gerichtsständen pro Vertrag und damit zur Spaltung bzw. Zersplitterung von Gerichtsständen.[271]

---

[262] Übereinstimmend *Heuzé*, Rev. crit. dr. int. privé 1994, 673, 678; vgl. auch *ders.*, Rev. crit. dr. int. privé 2000, 595, 628; so nun auch OGH, 10.9.1998, CISG-online 409 = RdW 1999, 210; so im Ergebnis auch der dänische Højesteret, 15.2.2001, CISG-online 601 (siehe dazu bereits oben Fn. 159).
[263] Abweichend BGHZ 98, 263, 272: Bei Vereinbarung „franco partenza Torino" sei Turin Erfüllungsort i. S. d. Art. 5 Nr. 1 EuGVÜ. Es handelt sich aber um ein obiter dictum; denn es ging nur um die Frage, ob am Zielort des Transports in Deutschland ein Gerichtsstand des Erfüllungsortes begründet war.
[264] OGH, 10.9.1998, CISG-online 409 = JBl 1999, 333 = RdW 1999, 210; vgl. auch BGHZ 98, 263, 272; insoweit zutreffend auch CA d'Orléans, 29.3.2001, CISG-online 611 = IHR 2003, 146.
[265] Im Anwendungsbereich des LuganoÜ ist die Rechtsprechung des EuGH zu den „abstrakten" Erfüllungsortsvereinbarungen zu beachten; vgl. die Hinweise unten in Fn. 258.
[266] Vgl. OLG München, 17.10.1986, IPRax 1987, 307 = RIW 1986, 998.
[267] Der Rechtsprechung des EuGH ist bei der Anwendung dieses Übereinkommens gebührend Rechnung zu tragen vgl. Art. 1 Abs. 1 Protokoll 2 über die einheitliche Auslegung des Übereinkommens und den Ständigen Ausschuss des LugÜ; vgl. auch EuGH, 25.2.2010, Rs. C-381/08 (Car Trim/KeySafety Systems S. r. l.).
[268] Die Rechtsprechung zum LuganoÜ vom 16.9.1988 deckte sich prinzipiell mit der Praxis zum EuGVÜ, vgl. BaslerKomm/*Hofmann/Kunz*, Art. 5 LugÜ, Rn. 164 ff.
[269] EuGH, 6.10.1976, Rs. 12/76 (Tessili/Dunlop); EuGH, 28.9.1999, Rs. C-440/97 (GIE Groupe Concorde/Kapitän des Schiffes „Suhadiwarno Panjan") = RIW 1999, 951 ff.; EuGH, 29.6.1994, Rs. C-288/92 (Custom Made Commercial/Stawa Metallbau); vgl. auch EuGH, 5.10.1999, Rs. C-420/97 (Leathertex/Bodetex) = RIW 1999, 953 ff.
[270] EuGH, 6.10.1976, Rs. 14/76 (de Bloos/Bouyer); EuGH, 15.1.1987, Rs. 266/85 (Shenavai/Kreischer); EuGH, 5.10.1999, Rs. C-420/97 (Leathertex/Bodetex) = RIW 1999, 953 ff.; EuGH, 19.2.2002, Rs. C-256/00 (Besix/Kretzschmar); vgl. auch KG Zug, 11.12.2003, CISG-online 958 = IHR 2005, 119, 121 (E. 2.2). Für die Gerichtsstände nach § 29 ZPO und Art. 113 IPRG gilt dasselbe, vgl. zum deutschen Recht MünchKomm/*Patzina*, § 29 ZPO, Rn. 18; MünchKomm/*Gruber*, Art. 31, Rn. 34; zum schweizerischen Recht BaslerKomm/*Amstutz/Vogt/Wang*, Art. 113 IPRG, Rn. 7.
[271] Vgl. zum Übergangsrecht BaslerKomm/*Oetiker/Weibel*, Art. 63 LugÜ, Rn. 3 ff.; *Kropholler/von Hein*, EUZPR, Art. 66, Rn. 1, 2 ff. Zur Rechtslage nach dem früheren LuganoÜ vom 16.9.1988 vgl. ausführlich die Vorauflage: *Widmer Lüchinger*, Art. 31, Rn. 89 ff.

Art. 32 [Verpflichtungen hinsichtlich der Beförderung der Ware]

(1) Übergibt der Verkäufer nach dem Vertrag oder diesem Übereinkommen die Ware einem Beförderer und ist die Ware nicht deutlich durch daran angebrachte Kennzeichen oder durch Beförderungsdokumente oder auf andere Weise dem Vertrag zugeordnet, so hat der Verkäufer dem Käufer die Versendung anzuzeigen und dabei die Ware im einzelnen zu bezeichnen.

(2) Hat der Verkäufer für die Beförderung der Ware zu sorgen, so hat er die Verträge zu schließen, die zur Beförderung an den festgesetzten Ort mit den nach den Umständen angemessenen Beförderungsmitteln und zu den für solche Beförderungen üblichen Bedingungen erforderlich sind.

(3) Ist der Verkäufer nicht zum Abschluß einer Transportversicherung verpflichtet, so hat er dem Käufer auf dessen Verlangen alle ihm verfügbaren, zum Abschluß einer solchen Versicherung erforderlichen Auskünfte zu erteilen.

Art. 32

(1) If the seller, in accordance with the contract or this Convention, hands the goods over to a carrier and if the goods are not clearly identified to the contract by markings on the goods, by shipping documents or otherwise, the seller must give the buyer notice of the consignment specifying the goods.

(2) If the seller is bound to arrange for carriage of the goods, he must make such contracts as are necessary for carriage to the place fixed by means of transportation appropriate in the circumstances and according to the usual terms for such transportation.

(3) If the seller is not bound to effect insurance in respect of the carriage of the goods, he must, at the buyer's request, provide him with all available information necessary to enable him to effect such insurance.

Art. 32

1) Si, conformément au contrat ou à la présente Convention, le vendeur remet les marchandises à un transporteur et si les marchandises ne sont pas clairement identifiées aux fins du contrat par l'apposition d'un signe distinctif sur les marchandises, par des documents de transport ou par tout autre moyen, le vendeur doit donner à l'acheteur avis de l'expédition en désignant spécifiquement les marchandises.

2) Si le vendeur est tenu de prendre des dispositions pour le transport des marchandises, il doit conclure les contrats nécessaires pour que le transport soit effectué jusqu'au lieu prévu, par les moyens de transport appropriés aux circonstances et selon les conditions usuelles pour un tel transport.

3) Si le vendeur n'est pas tenu de souscrire lui-même une assurance de transport, il doit fournir à l'acheteur, à la demande de celui-ci, tous renseignements dont il dispose qui sont nécessaires à la conclusion de cette assurance.

Übersicht

	Rn.
I. Gegenstand und Funktion der Regelung	1
II. Versendungsanzeige (Art. 32 I)	2
1. Voraussetzungen	2
a) Lieferung durch Übergabe an den Beförderer	2
b) Keine eindeutige Zuordnung zum Vertrag	3
2. Anzeige	5
a) Inhalt	5
b) Zeitpunkt	6
c) Übermittlungsrisiko	7
3. Rechtsfolgen	8
a) Bei Beachtung der Anzeigepflicht	8
b) Bei Verletzung der Anzeigepflicht	10
4. Vertragliche Anzeigepflichten (Incoterms®)	13
III. Abschluss des Beförderungsvertrags (Art. 32 II)	15

Verpflichtungen hinsichtlich der Beförderung der Ware 1 **Art. 32**

1. Anwendungsbereich 15
2. Pflichten des Verkäufers 17
   a) Abschluss des Beförderungsvertrags 17
   b) Beförderung an den festgesetzten Ort 18
   c) Angemessenes Beförderungsmittel 19
   d) Übliche Bedingungen 20
3. Einschaltung von Dritten 21
   a) Spediteure 21
   b) Unterfrachtführer 23
   c) Vorlieferant 24
4. Transportkosten 25
5. Transportversicherung 26
6. Weisungen des Käufers 28
7. Rechtsfolgen bei Verletzung der Abschlusspflicht 30
IV. Erteilung von Auskünften zum Zweck der Transportversicherung (Art. 32 III) 31

Vorläufer und **Entwürfe:** EKG Artt. 19 III, 54 I, 54 II; Genfer E 1976 Art. 16; Wiener E 1977 Art. 16; New Yorker E 1978 Art. 30.

I. Gegenstand und Funktion der Regelung

Art. 32 erlegt dem Verkäufer, der seine Lieferpflicht durch Übergabe der Ware an einen 1 selbstständigen Beförderer erfüllt, zusätzliche Pflichten auf. Gemäss **Art. 32 I** ist der Verkäufer im eher seltenen Fall, in dem die Zuordnung der Ware zum Kaufvertrag weder aus ihrer Kennzeichnung noch aus dem Transportdokument erkennbar ist, verpflichtet, dem Käufer die Versendung der Ware anzuzeigen. Unerheblich ist dabei, ob der Beförderer vom Verkäufer oder vom Käufer beauftragt worden ist.[1] Die Regel will verhindern, dass der Verkäufer die Ware noch nachträglich, etwa nachdem sie untergegangen oder beschädigt ist, dem Vertrag zuordnet und so das Verlust- oder Schadensrisiko auf den Käufer verlagert. Ausserdem hat die Anzeigepflicht des Art. 32 I die Funktion, den Käufer über die Tatsache der Absendung zu informieren[2]. Wo ein solches Informationsbedürfnis besteht, ist es allerdings davon unabhängig, ob die Ware durch die Art der Versendung dem Vertrag eindeutig zugeordnet ist oder nicht. Deswegen sehen Verträge, Geschäftsbedingungen und handelsübliche Vertragsformulare häufig Anzeigepflichten vor, die über Art. 32 I hinausgehen.[3] Das Übereinkommen hat die Benachrichtigungspflicht nur für einen Spezialfall geregelt, in dem sie besonders naheliegt, und das Weitere den Parteien überlassen.[4] **Art. 32 II** ist eine ergänzende Regel zu Art. 31 lit. a). Ist nach dem Vertrag eine Beförderung der Ware erforderlich, hat der Verkäufer die Beförderung also zu veranlassen,[5] erfüllt er seine Lieferpflicht nach Art. 31 lit. a) im Zweifelsfall dadurch, dass er die Ware an den ersten Beförderer zur Übermittlung an den Käufer übergibt. Art. 32 II soll klarstellen, dass hierzu auch die Pflicht des Verkäufers gehört, die erforderlichen Verträge über die Beförderung abzuschliessen, und gibt einige Hinweise in Bezug auf den notwendigen Inhalt dieser Verträge. Gemäss **Art. 32 III** ist der Verkäufer schliesslich verpflichtet, dem Käufer die zum Abschluss einer Transportversicherung erforderlichen Auskünfte zu erteilen.[6]

---

[1] Vgl. auch *Witz/Salger/Lorenz/Witz*, Art. 32, Rn. 3. Die Anzeigepflicht nach Art. 32 I geht insofern über den Anwendungsbereich des Art. 31 lit. a) hinaus, da Art. 31 lit. a) nur jene Fälle erfasst, in denen der Verkäufer die Beförderung der Ware veranlasst, siehe Art. 31 Rn. 15 (str.).
[2] A. A. *Honsell/Ernst/Lauko*, Art. 32, Rn. 5; MünchKommHGB/*Benicke*, Art. 32, Rn. 3; MünchKomm/ *Gruber*, Art. 32, Rn. 4: Art. 32 I bezwecke einzig die rechtzeitige Konkretisierung der Ware.
[3] Vgl. dazu unten Rn. 13. Eine allgemeine Anzeigepflicht statuiert auch § 2–504 (c) UCC. An Art. 32 I orientiert sich dagegen eindeutig Art. 96 Ziff. 2 CESL-Entwurf.
[4] Zutreffend *Bianca/Bonell/Lando*, Art. 32, Anm. 2.1. zur Anwendbarkeit der Regeln von Art. 32 als „stop-gap rules".
[5] Vgl. oben Art. 31 Rn. 13 ff.
[6] So auch Art. 96 Ziff. 3 CESL-Entwurf.

II. Versendungsanzeige (Art. 32 I)

1. Voraussetzungen

2 **a) Lieferung durch Übergabe an den Beförderer.** Art. 32 I betrifft nur die Fälle, in denen die Lieferung der Ware nach dem Übereinkommen oder dem Vertrag dadurch bewirkt wird, dass der Verkäufer die Ware einem Beförderer zur Übermittlung an den Käufer übergibt. Das betrifft **zunächst** den in Art. 31 lit. a) geregelten Fall des einfachen Versendungskaufs, in dem der Verkäufer die Lieferpflicht durch Übergabe an den ersten Beförderer erfüllt.[7] Und es betrifft **zweitens** den Fall, in dem der Vertrag vorsieht, dass der Verkäufer die Lieferung dadurch bewirkt, dass er die Ware **an einem bestimmten Ort** dem Beförderer zu übergeben hat, so zum Beispiel, wenn die Ware auf Grund der Klauseln fca, fob, fas, cfr, cif zu versenden ist.[8] Dagegen sind Fälle, in denen der Verkäufer die Lieferpflicht gemäss Art. 31 lit. b), c) oder auf Grund besonderer Klausel durch „Zur-Verfügung-Stellen" erfüllt, durch Art. 32 I nicht erfasst.[9]

3 **b) Keine eindeutige Zuordnung zum Vertrag.** Die Anzeigepflicht setzt ferner voraus, dass die Ware nicht schon durch die Aufgabe zur Beförderung eindeutig dem Vertrag zugeordnet ist. Eine solche Zuordnung kann etwa dadurch erfolgen, dass der Verkäufer die Ware mit der Adresse des Käufers versieht, z. B. Paketversendung;[10] dadurch, dass er den Käufer im schriftlichen Frachtvertrag („Frachtbrief") als Empfänger bezeichnet, so z. B. bei Versendung mit Eisenbahn, Lkw oder Flugzeug; oder dadurch, dass er sich vom Beförderer ein Transportdokument ausstellen lässt, in dem der Käufer namentlich als Empfangsberechtigter aufgeführt ist: so beim Überseetransport ein auf den Namen des Käufers lautendes Order- oder Rektakonnossement, beim Binnenschiffstransport einen auf den Käufer ausgestellten Ladeschein, beim kombinierten Containertransport ein vom Spediteur ausgestelltes auf den Käufer lautendes cto-Dokument.[11]

4 Eine eindeutige Zuordnung der zur Beförderung an den Käufer aufgegebenen Ware zum Kaufvertrag fehlt dagegen, wenn im Frachtbrief nicht der Käufer, sondern ein Empfangsspediteur als Empfänger genannt ist, oder wenn das Transportdokument auf den Verkäufer selbst oder dessen Order ausgestellt ist. Das kommt vor allem vor, wenn der Verkäufer die Ware zusammen mit anderer gleichartiger Ware im Weg der Sammelsendung versendet.[12] Der Verkäufer bringt z. B. eine Ladung Getreide zur Verschiffung, die er in mehreren Partien an verschiedene Käufer im Bestimmungsland mit der Klausel „cif (Bestimmungshafen)" verkauft hat; er erhält von der Reederei ein auf ihn lautendes, einheitliches Konnossement,[13] das er an den Kai oder einen Lagerhalter im Bestimmungshafen weiterbegibt, der die Aufteilung (etwa durch Ausstellung von Kaiteilscheinen) vornehmen soll.[14] In solchen Fällen greift die gesetzliche Anzeigepflicht gemäss Art. 32 I ein.[15]

---

[7] Vgl. dazu oben Art. 31 Rn. 13, 17.
[8] Vgl. oben Art. 31 Rn. 73 f. Ebenso *Staudinger/Magnus*, Art. 32, Rn. 8; *Honsell/Ernst/Lauko*, Art. 32, Rn. 4; *Bamberger/Roth/Saenger*, Art. 32, Rn. 3; *Brunner*, Art. 32, Rn. 1; MünchKomm/*Gruber*, Art. 32, Rn. 3; während die Klauseln FAS, FOB, CFR und CIF auf den Schiffstransport gemünzt sind, kann die Klausel FCA für alle Transportarten verwendet werden; vgl. *von Bernstorff*, Incoterms® 2010, 33.
[9] Ebenso *Honsell/Ernst/Lauko*, Art. 32, Rn. 4; MünchKomm/*Gruber*, Art. 32, Rn. 3. Zur Anzeigepflicht im Fall der Lieferung durch Zur-Verfügung-Stellen siehe oben Art. 31 Rn. 51.
[10] Vgl. auch *Kröll u. a./Piltz*, Art. 32, Rn. 12, wonach grundsätzlich jede erdenkliche Art der Zuordnung gewährt werden kann, solange ein Dritter, der vom Vertrag Kenntnis hat, die Ware diesem zuordnen kann.
[11] Vgl. dazu Art. 31 Rn. 79.
[12] Sekretariatskommentar, Art. 30, Nr. 2.
[13] Vgl. dazu *Haage*, S. 65. Hiernach ist die in einem solchen Fall an sich mögliche Ausstellung von Teilkonnossementen „durchaus unüblich und vom Verfrachterstandpunkt aus nicht erwünscht". Der Verfrachter will und soll mit der Teilung der Ladung nichts zu tun haben.
[14] Vgl. *Haage*, S. 66.
[15] Vgl. auch *Honsell/Ernst/Lauko*, Art. 32, Rn. 5.

2. Anzeige

a) Inhalt. Besitzt der Verkäufer ein Transportdokument, das die Tatsache der Versendung 5
bekundet und die Ware bezeichnet, z. B. ein an eigene Order lautendes Konnossement, so
kann er die Anzeige vornehmen, indem er das (erforderlichenfalls indossierte) Dokument
dem Käufer zusendet.[16] Er kann die Anzeige aber auch durch einfache Mitteilung erstatten.
An bestimmte Formen ist die Anzeige nicht gebunden; sie muss nur mit den „nach den
Umständen geeigneten Mitteln" bewirkt werden (Art. 27)[17] und gemäss Art. 32 I die Ware
„im Einzelnen bezeichnen". Im Fall des Schiffstransports gehört dazu vor allem die Angabe
des Schiffsnamens. Das genügt zur Identifizierung, wenn sich auf dem Schiff keine andere
gleichartige Ware, als die für den Käufer bestimmte Ware, befindet.[18] Anderenfalls muss der
Verkäufer zusätzlich die Markierung der für den Käufer bestimmten Ware angeben, z. B. die
Sack- oder Kistennummer.[19] Bei Sammelversendung ist nur die Zahl der verladenen Einheiten oder das Gewicht anzugeben.[20]

b) Zeitpunkt. Über den Zeitpunkt der Anzeige sagt Art. 32 I nichts. Es ist aber als ein 6
allgemeiner Grundsatz i. S. d. Art. 7 II anzusehen, dass der Verkäufer die Anzeige innerhalb
angemessener Frist nach Versendung zu erstatten hat.[21]

c) Übermittlungsrisiko. Für die Erfüllung der Anzeigepflicht genügt die rechtzeitige 7
Absendung der Anzeige mit „geeigneten Mitteln". Das Risiko des Verlusts, der Verzögerung
oder der Entstellung auf dem Übermittlungsweg trägt der Käufer (Art. 27).[22]

3. Rechtsfolgen

a) Bei Beachtung der Anzeigepflicht. In den Fällen des Art. 32 I führt erst die 8
Anzeige dazu, dass die **Transportgefahr auf den Käufer übergeht,** und zwar nach dem
unmissverständlichen Wortlaut des Gesetzes mit Wirkung ex nunc (Art. 67 II).[23] Trifft die
Ware mit Transportschäden ein und lässt sich nicht feststellen, ob sie vor oder nach
Absendung der Anzeige entstanden sind, so trifft die Beweislast den Verkäufer.[24] Der
Verkäufer hat es in der Hand, die Ungewissheit zu vermeiden, indem er die Anzeige sofort
absendet.

Die Frage, ob der Verkäufer **an die Anzeige gebunden** oder im Gegenteil berechtigt ist, 9
die Anzeige zu widerrufen und durch eine andere Anzeige zu ersetzen, ist im Übereinkommen nicht ausdrücklich geregelt. Der Sache nach geht es hier darum, dass der Verkäufer,
der die Ware zur Erfüllung des Vertrags auf den Transport gebracht hat und das Transportrisiko auf den Käufer übertragen hat, die Erfüllung rückgängig machen will. Das ist für den
Käufer besonders unangenehm, wenn er im Vertrauen auf die Anzeige bereits Dispositionen

---

[16] *Herber/Czerwenka*, Art. 32, Rn. 4; *Honsell/Ernst/Lauko*, Art. 32, Rn. 10; *Neumayer/Ming*, Art. 32, Anm. 2.; *Piltz*, Internationales Kaufrecht, Rn. 4–101.
[17] Vgl. auch *Neumayer/Ming*, Art. 32, Anm. 5. Zur Anzeige mittels elektronischer Kommunikation siehe CISG-AC, Op. 1 *(Chr. Ramberg)*, Comment 32.1.
[18] *Haage*, S. 34; vgl. auch *Honsell/Ernst/Lauko*, Art. 32, Rn. 10.
[19] *Haage*, S. 33 f.
[20] *Haage*, S. 33 f.; *Piltz*, Internationales Kaufrecht, Rn. 4–101; *Staudinger/Magnus*, Art. 32, Rn. 13; *Witz/Salger/Lorenz/Witz*, Art. 32, Rn. 2; MünchKomm/*Gruber*, Art. 32, Rn. 5. Gegen Anwendbarkeit des Art. 32 I in diesem Fall *Feltham*, 34 J. Bus. L. (1991), 413, 418.
[21] Ebenso *Bianca/Bonell/Lando*, Art. 32, Anm. 2.2.2.; *Honsell/Ernst/Lauko*, Art. 32, Rn. 11; *Piltz*, Internationales Kaufrecht, Rn. 4–102; *Bamberger/Roth/Saenger*, Art. 32, Rn. 5; MünchKomm/*Gruber*, Art. 32, Rn. 6; abweichend *Staudinger/Magnus*, Art. 32, Rn. 10: ausreichend, wenn die Anzeige abgesendet wird, bis die Ware am Bestimmungsort eintrifft; *Witz/Salger/Lorenz/Witz*, Art. 32, Rn. 5: im Regelfall sei sofortige Anzeige erforderlich; vgl. auch § 2–504 (c) UCC: „[the seller must] promptly notify the buyer of the shipment".
[22] Ebenso *Honsell/Ernst/Lauko*, Art. 32, Rn. 11; *Heuzé*, Anm. 250.; *Bamberger/Roth/Saenger*, Art. 32, Rn. 5; *Witz/Salger/Lorenz/Witz*, Art. 32, Rn. 5; *Piltz*, Internationales Kaufrecht, Rn. 4–102; *Staudinger/Magnus*, Art. 32, Rn. 10; MünchKomm/*Gruber*, Art. 32, Rn. 5.
[23] Ebenso *Honsell/Ernst/Lauko*, Art. 32, Rn. 12; *Bamberger/Roth/Saenger*, Art. 32, Rn. 6; MünchKomm/*Gruber*, Art. 32, Rn. 6. Vgl. dazu *Hager*, Gefahrtragung nach UN-Kaufrecht, S. 391 ff.
[24] Vgl. *Hager/Maultzsch*, 5. Aufl., Art. 67 Rn. 11.

über die demnächst eintreffende Ware getroffen hat. Aus diesem Grund ist grundsätzlich davon auszugehen, dass der Verkäufer zu einem solchen nachträglichen Eingriff nicht berechtigt ist.[25] Anders ist es allenfalls dann, wenn der Eingriff im Interesse des Käufers liegt (der Verkäufer will einer nach Versendung eingetretenen Transportstörung ausweichen) oder wenn für den Verkäufer während des Transports ein Zurückbehaltungsrecht gemäss Art. 71 entstanden ist. Zulässig ist es, eine unzutreffende Anzeige zu berichtigen (z. B. wenn der Schiffsname oder die Waggonnummer in der Anzeige entstellt oder verwechselt worden ist).[26]

10 b) **Bei Verletzung der Anzeigepflicht.** Die wichtigste Rechtsfolge der unterlassenen Anzeige ist, dass die **Gefahr nicht übergeht,** da die abgesendete Ware dem Vertrag nicht eindeutig zugeordnet ist (Art. 67 II).[27]

11 Die Anzeige liegt aber nicht nur im Interesse des Verkäufers, sich selbst vor den Nachteilen des Aufschubs der Gefahr zu schützen, sondern sie dient auch dem Interesse des Käufers daran, über die Absendung der Ware informiert zu werden.[28] Vor allen Dingen bei Sammelsendung besteht an einer solchen Information ein besonderes Interesse des Käufers.[29] Aus diesem Grund hat das Übereinkommen in Art. 32 I eine echte Vertragspflicht zur Anzeige aufgestellt und es nicht beim Aufschub des Gefahrübergangs bewenden lassen. Erstattet der Verkäufer die Anzeige nicht innerhalb angemessener Frist,[30] so stehen deshalb dem Käufer die **Rechtsbehelfe des Art. 45 I** zu.[31] In Betracht kommt in erster Linie ein Schadensersatzanspruch gemäss Art. 45 I lit. b).[32] Der Schaden des Käufers kann insbesondere darin bestehen, dass er infolge der verspäteten Anzeige nicht in der Lage ist, rechtzeitige Vorkehrungen für die Übernahme der Ware zu treffen.[33]

12 Bei längerer Vertragsdauer, insbesondere bei Schiffstransporten, kann in der Verletzung der Anzeigepflicht eine „wesentliche Vertragsverletzung" liegen, die den Käufer gemäss Artt. 25, 49 I lit. a) zur **Vertragsaufhebung** berechtigt.[34] Der Käufer, der in einem solchen Fall nach Ablauf der Lieferfrist vom Verkäufer trotz Nachfrage weder ein Transportdokument noch eine Versendungsanzeige erhält, muss befürchten, dass der Verkäufer die Versendung überhaupt nicht vorgenommen hat; es gibt für das Schweigen des Verkäufers kaum eine andere Erklärung. Das kann für die Annahme einer wesentlichen Vertragsverletzung i. S. d. Art. 25 ausreichen.

---

[25] Ebenso *Witz/Salger/Lorenz/Witz*, Art. 32, Rn. 2; *Staudinger/Magnus*, Art. 32, Rn. 12; *MünchKomm/Gruber*, Art. 32, Rn. 8; a. A. *Honsell/Ernst/Lauko*, Art. 32, Rn. 13; *Soergel/Lüderitz/Schüßler-Langeheine*, Art. 32, Rn. 7; *Neumayer/Ming*, Art. 32, Anm. 5. Wie hier jedenfalls der Handelsbrauch des deutschen Einfuhrhandels, vgl. die Nachweise bei *Soergel/Huber*, § 433 BGB, Anhang III, Rn. 33, Fn. 55, 56.

[26] *Haage*, S. 36 ff.; vgl. auch *Honsell/Ernst/Lauko*, Art. 32, Rn. 13; *Neumayer/Ming*, Art. 32, Anm. 5.; MünchKomm/*Gruber*, Art. 32, Rn. 8.

[27] Ebenso *Staudinger/Magnus*, Art. 32, Rn. 14; *Brunner*, Art. 32, Rn. 1; *MünchKommHGB/Benicke*, Art. 32, Rn. 9. Vgl. auch oben Rn. 8.

[28] *Honnold/Flechtner*, Art. 32, Rn. 213. A. A. (Art. 32 I begründet nur eine „Obliegenheit" des Verkäufers) *Neumayer/Ming*, Art. 32, Anm. 1, 4.

[29] Vgl. dazu oben Rn. 4.

[30] Vgl. oben Rn. 6.

[31] Sekretariatskommentar, Art. 30, Nr. 3; *Schlechtriem*, Einheitliches UN-Kaufrecht, S. 55 = Uniform Sales Law, S. 65; *Honnold/Flechtner*, Art. 32, Rn. 213; *Bianca/Bonell/Lando*, Art. 32, Anm. 2.2.2.; *Loewe*, Art. 32, S. 53; *Honsell/Ernst/Lauko*, Art. 32, Rn. 14; *Staudinger/Magnus*, Art. 32, Rn. 14; *MünchKomm/Gruber*, Art. 32, Rn. 7.

[32] Vgl. *Honnold/Flechtner*, Art. 32, Rn. 213; *Bianca/Bonell/Lando*, Art. 32, Anm. 2.2.2.; *Herber/Czerwenka*, Art. 32, Rn. 5; einschränkend *Soergel/Lüderitz/Schüßler-Langeheine*, Art. 32, Rn. 6.

[33] Ebenso *Bamberger/Roth/Saenger*, Art. 32, Rn. 6.

[34] *Honnold/Flechtner*, Art. 32, Rn. 213; *Bianca/Bonell/Lando*, Art. 32, Anm. 2.2.2.; *Staudinger/Magnus*, Art. 32, Rn. 14; *MünchKommHGB/Benicke*, Art. 32, Rn. 9; vgl. auch *Herber/Czerwenka*, Art. 32, Rn. 5 sowie *Bamberger/Roth/Saenger*, Art. 32, Rn. 6 („ausnahmsweise"); *Honsell/Ernst/Lauko*, Art. 32, Rn. 14; anders *Soergel/Lüderitz/Schüßler-Langeheine*, Art. 32, Rn. 6 („kaum vorstellbar"); grundsätzlich ablehnend auch MünchKomm/*Gruber*, Art. 32, Rn. 7, mit dem Argument, Art. 32 statuiere nur eine Konkretisierungs-, nicht aber eine Informationspflicht. Ein Unterschied zwischen der durch Art. 32 I angeordneten gesetzlichen Anzeigepflicht und vertraglichen Anzeigepflichten (dazu unten Rn. 13 f.) ist in diesem Punkt nicht anzuerkennen.

4. Vertragliche Anzeigepflichten (Incoterms®)

Durch Vertrag oder Handelsbrauch wird die Pflicht zur Versendungsanzeige häufig über den durch Art. 32 I geregelten speziellen Fall hinaus erweitert. Der Verkäufer ist hiernach verpflichtet, dem Käufer unverzüglich mitzuteilen, dass er die Ware dem Beförderer übergeben hat, und zwar, über Art. 32 I hinausgehend, auch dann, wenn die Ware durch Adressierung, Frachtbrief oder Transportdokument eindeutig dem Vertrag zugeordnet ist. Vor allem die Incoterms®[35] sehen für die durch sie geregelten Typen des Versendungskaufs die Pflicht zur Versendungsanzeige vor.[36] Entsprechendes ergibt sich vielfach aus allgemeinen Geschäftsbedingungen des Einfuhrhandels.[37] Der Grund für diese Verpflichtung liegt darin, dass der Käufer, vor allem bei längeren Transportzeiten, ein Interesse daran hat, zu wissen, ob der Verkäufer seine Lieferpflicht erfüllt hat und wann mit dem Eintreffen der Ware am Bestimmungsort zu rechnen ist; auf dieser Grundlage will er seine geschäftlichen oder organisatorischen Dispositionen treffen. 13

Für die **Rechtsfolgen** vertraglich vereinbarter oder kraft Handelsbrauchs bestehender Pflichten zur Versendungsanzeige gilt folgendes: Der **Gefahrübergang** ist von der Erfüllung der vertraglichen Anzeigepflicht unabhängig, wenn die Ware bereits durch Adressierung, Frachtbrief, Transportdokument oder auf sonstige Weise dem Vertrag eindeutig zugeordnet ist (vgl. Art. 67 II). Im Übrigen gilt entsprechendes wie für die gesetzliche Anzeigepflicht des Art. 32 I.[38] 14

III. Abschluss des Beförderungsvertrags (Art. 32 II)

1. Anwendungsbereich

Art. 32 II setzt voraus, dass der Verkäufer für die Beförderung der Ware „zu sorgen" hat. Das ist ohne weiteres dann der Fall, wenn der Kaufvertrag eine Beförderung der Ware i. S. d. **Art. 31 lit. a)** „erfordert",[39] also im Falle des Versendungskaufs. Darüber hinaus hat der Verkäufer aber auch dann i. S. d. Art. 32 II für die Beförderung zu sorgen, wenn er die Versendung von einem **bestimmten Ort** aus zu veranlassen hat. Das ist vor allem der Fall bei Verwendung der Lieferklauseln CIF und CFR,[40] ausnahmsweise auch bei Verwendung der Klauseln FCA[41] und FOB.[42] Dass der Verkäufer dann nicht für die Beförderung der Ware zu sorgen hat, wenn die Abschlusspflicht nach dem Kaufvertrag den Käufer trifft, versteht sich von selbst.[43] 15

---

[35] Vgl. Art. 30 Rn. 3 f.
[36] Dazu *Kröll u. a./Piltz*, Art. 32, Rn. 30 ff.
[37] Vgl. dazu *Sieveking*, S. 217; *Haage*, S. 33 f.
[38] Oben Rn. 8 ff. Vgl. auch *Honsell/Ernst/Lauko*, Art. 32, Rn. 15. Für den Fall vertraglicher Anzeigepflichten ebenso *Neumayer/Ming*, Art. 32, Anm. 4.
[39] Vgl. Art. 31 Rn. 17 f. Ebenso *Brunner*, Art. 32, Rn. 2; *Honsell/Ernst/Lauko*, Art. 32, Rn. 17; MünchKommHGB/*Benicke*, Art. 32, Rn. 11; a. A. *Neumayer/Ming*, Art. 32, Anm. 6.: Art. 32 II sei nur anwendbar, wenn die Pflicht des Verkäufers zum Abschluss des Transportvertrags im Kaufvertrag besonders vorgesehen sei; der Anwendungsbereich des Art. 32 II sei also enger als der des Art. 31 lit. a); ähnlich MünchKomm/*Gruber*, Art. 32, Rn. 9; *Staudinger/Magnus*, Art. 32, Rn. 15 f.
[40] Vgl. dazu Art. 31 Rn. 74.
[41] Nämlich dann, wenn die Pflicht zum Abschluss des Beförderungsvertrages ausnahmsweise den Verkäufer trifft; vgl. dazu *Kröll u. a./Piltz*, Art. 32, Rn. 36.
[42] Vgl. *Herber/Czerwenka*, Art. 32, Rn. 7; *Honsell/Ernst/Lauko*, Art. 32, Rn. 17. Wird etwa mit der Klausel „FOB verschifft" verkauft, so ist, im Unterschied zum herkömmlichen FOB-Geschäft, die Lieferpflicht des Verkäufers dadurch erweitert, dass auch die Verschiffung noch Bestandteil der Lieferpflicht des Verkäufers ist, der den Seefrachtvertrag für Rechnung des Käufers abzuschliessen hat (sog. „erweitertes FOB-Geschäft"; früher auch: „uneigentliches" oder „unechtes FOB-Geschäft"), vgl. BGH, 2.10.1963, WM 1963, 1185 = LM § 346 HGB (B) Nr. 3; *Haage*, S. 165; *Liesecke*, WM 1966, 174, 175; *Digenopoulos*, S. 208 ff.
[43] Insofern ist also der Anwendungsbereich des Art. 32 II enger als der des Art. 32 I, vgl. auch *Karollus*, S. 111.

16 Ist die Lieferschuld **Bringschuld,** hat also der Verkäufer auf Grund besonderer vertraglicher Vereinbarung die Ware dem Käufer am Bestimmungsort des Transports zur Verfügung zu stellen, ist er zu mehr verpflichtet, als für den Transport zu sorgen: er muss ihn durchführen. Beispiele für solche Vereinbarungen sind die verschiedenen „Geliefert"-Klauseln („D-Klauseln") der Incoterms®[44] sowie die Vereinbarung, dass „frei Haus" zu liefern ist.[45] Bedient er sich hierzu selbstständiger Beförderer, so dient der Abschluss der Beförderungsverträge der Vorbereitung der eigenen Leistung des Verkäufers, die erst am Bestimmungsort vorgenommen wird. Kosten und Gefahr des Transports liegen beim Verkäufer, und er haftet für Fehler bei der Durchführung des Transports.[46] Der Verkäufer wahrt also nur seine eigenen Interessen, wenn er einen ordnungsmässigen Beförderungsvertrag abschliesst. Art. 32 II ist nicht anwendbar.[47]

2. Pflichten des Verkäufers

17 a) **Abschluss des Beförderungsvertrags.** Art. 32 II stellt zunächst klar, dass in den Fällen, in denen der Verkäufer für die Beförderung der Ware zu sorgen hat, der Abschluss des Beförderungsvertrags noch Teil der Lieferpflicht des Verkäufers ist.[48] Das gilt unabhängig von der Frage, wen im Verhältnis der Vertragsparteien die Transportkosten treffen. Da die Durchführung des Transports als solche in den Fällen, in denen der Verkäufer nur für den Transport „zu sorgen" hat, nicht mehr Aufgabe des Verkäufers ist, haftet der Verkäufer nur für die richtige Auswahl und die richtige Instruktion des Beförderers.

18 b) **Beförderung an den festgesetzten Ort.** Der Ort, an den die Ware zu befördern ist, ergibt sich im Allgemeinen aus dem Vertrag (z. B. „cif Hamburg"). Inwieweit der Verkäufer berechtigt oder verpflichtet ist, die Ware an einen anderen als den ursprünglich festgesetzten Ort zu versenden, wenn sich nachträglich herausstellt, dass dieser ungeeignet ist (z. B. nach Rotterdam statt nach Hamburg, wenn in Hamburg gestreikt wird), ist nach Treu und Glauben zu entscheiden.[49] Ist im Vertrag kein Ort festgesetzt, ist an die Niederlassung des Käufers zu versenden; kommen mehrere Niederlassungen in Betracht, entscheidet Art. 10 lit. a).[50]

19 c) **Angemessenes Beförderungsmittel.** Die Pflicht, „angemessene Beförderungsmittel" einzusetzen, bezieht sich auf die Art des Fahrzeugs[51] (wenn sie nicht schon im Vertrag festgelegt ist) und auf die Route. Der Verkäufer ist verpflichtet, die Ware auf der üblichen, im Zweifelsfall auf der kürzesten Route zu versenden.[52] Umladungen während des Transports sind möglichst zu vermeiden.[53] Krisen- und Streikgebieten ist nach Möglichkeit auszuweichen.

---

[44] Vgl. Art. 30 Rn. 3 f.
[45] Siehe hierzu Art. 31 Rn. 76.
[46] Vgl. Art. 31 Rn. 77.
[47] Ebenso *Honsell/Ernst/Lauko*, Art. 32, Rn. 16; *Witz/Salger/Lorenz/Witz*, Art. 32, Rn. 9; *Achilles*, Art. 32, Rn. 4; *Bamberger/Roth/Saenger*, Art. 32, Rn. 9; MünchKomm/*Gruber*, Art. 32, Rn. 3; *Brunner*, Art. 32, Rn. 3. Abweichend *Dölle/Herber*, Art. 54 EKG, Rn. 4; *Soergel/Lüderitz*, Art. 54 EKG, Rn. 2 (beide zur sachlich übereinstimmenden Vorschrift des Art. 54 I EKG; so auch noch die 1. Aufl., *U. Huber*, Art. 32 Rn. 20. Die bei *Herber*, aaO., und in der 1. Aufl., aaO., erörterte Frage der Entlastung des Verkäufers bei Transportzwischenfällen muss ohne Rückgriff auf Art. 32 II unmittelbar auf Grund des Art. 79 gelöst werden.
[48] Entsprechende Regelungen finden sich in § 2–504 (a) UCC, sec. 32 (2) SGA 1979; vgl. auch Art. 96 Ziff. 1 CESL-Entwurf.
[49] Vgl. dazu Art. 31 Rn. 78. Zum Grundsatz von Treu und Glauben siehe Art. 30 Rn. 9.
[50] Vgl. Art. 31 Rn. 39.
[51] Beispiel aus der Rechtsprechung: BezG Saane, 20.2.1997, CISG-online 426 = SZIER 1999, 195 ff.; vgl. auch Zhejiang Cixi People's Court, 18.7.2001, CISG-online 1507.
[52] *Dölle/Herber*, Art. 54 EKG, Rn. 6; *Bianca/Bonell/Lando*, Art. 32, Anm. 2.3.1.; *Piltz*, Internationales Kaufrecht, Rn. 4–98; *Honsell/Ernst/Lauko*, Art. 32, Rn. 19; *Heuzé*, Anm. 251.; *Staudinger/Magnus*, Art. 32, Rn. 17.
[53] *Bianca/Bonell/Lando*, Art. 32, Anm. 2.3.1.; *Enderlein/Maskow/Strohbach*, Art. 32, Anm. 7.; *Piltz*, Internationales Kaufrecht, Rn. 4–98; *Honsell/Ernst/Lauko*, Art. 32, Rn. 19.

d) **Übliche Bedingungen.** Die Pflicht, zu „üblichen Bedingungen" zu versenden, bezieht sich vor allem auf das **Beförderungsentgelt** und auf die **Haftung**. Bestehen, wie vielfach, feste Tarife, hat der Verkäufer allerdings keinen Entscheidungsspielraum.[54] Bei konkurrierenden Frachtangeboten ist der Verkäufer nicht unbedingt verpflichtet (wenn der Käufer die Fracht trägt) oder berechtigt (wenn er selbst die Fracht trägt), dem billigsten Angebot den Vorzug zu geben, sondern er hat auch die Zuverlässigkeit des Beförderers in Betracht zu ziehen.[55] Die Frage, inwieweit der Verkäufer berechtigt ist, sich auf Haftungsfreizeichnungen des Beförderers einzulassen, ist gegenstandslos, soweit die Haftung durch zwingendes Recht geregelt ist (so z. B. durch die CIM für den internationalen Eisenbahn- und durch die CMR für den internationalen Lkw-Transport). Soweit Vertragsfreiheit besteht, existieren regelmässig Formularbedingungen (Charterformulare der Seeschifffahrt, sog. Konnossementsbedingungen der Binnenschifffahrt). Der Verkäufer, der solche Formularbedingungen akzeptiert, schliesst zu den „üblichen" Bedingungen ab, verhält sich daher pflichtgemäss.[56] Aussergewöhnliche Haftungsfreizeichnungen (soweit sie frachtrechtlich zulässig sind) darf der Verkäufer allerdings nicht akzeptieren.[57] Auch diese Frage ist aber gegenstandslos, wenn der Verkäufer gleichzeitig für die Beförderung eine Transportversicherung abschliesst.[58]

3. Einschaltung von Dritten

a) **Spediteure.** Der Verkäufer kann den Abschluss des Beförderungsvertrags einem Spediteur überlassen, und vielfach wird das auch üblich sein. Hieraus hat man den Schluss gezogen, schon durch den Abschluss des Speditionsvertrags genüge der Verkäufer seinen Pflichten aus Art. 32 II; der Spediteur sei also beim Abschluss der eigentlichen Beförderungsverträge nicht mehr als Erfüllungsgehilfe des Verkäufers tätig.[59] Dies trifft aber jedenfalls im Regelfall, in dem der Spediteur nur die Organisation des Transports übernimmt, nicht zu.[60] Überlässt der Verkäufer die Erfüllung der Pflichten, die nach Art. 32 II ihn treffen, einem Dritten, der sich hierauf besser versteht, so muss er für den Dritten haften. Der Spediteur wird diesfalls noch im Pflichtenkreis des Verkäufers tätig.

Anders ist es in denjenigen Fällen, in denen der Verkäufer dem Spediteur die Ware zum Zweck der Durchführung des Transports übergibt und hierdurch seine Lieferpflicht gemäss Art. 31 lit. a) erfüllt. Hier genügt zur Erfüllung der Pflichten aus Art. 32 II, dass der Verkäufer bei Übergabe an den Spediteur mit diesem einen entsprechenden Vertrag abschliesst. Das ist unstreitig der Fall, wenn der Spediteur die Beförderung gänzlich oder auch nur teilweise selber ausführt.[61] Übergibt der Verkäufer dem Spediteur die Ware an dessen Lager mit dem Auftrag, für den weiteren Transport zu sorgen, so sollte man auch dies als Erfüllung der Lieferpflicht gemäss Art. 31 lit. a) anerkennen.[62] Dann muss aber auch der bei dieser Gelegenheit zwischen dem Verkäufer und dem Spediteur geschlossene Vertrag über die Beförderung der Ware zum Käufer dazu ausreichen, dass der Verkäufer seine Pflichten aus Art. 32 II erfüllt hat.

---

[54] Vgl. auch *Dölle/Herber*, Art. 54 EKG, Rn. 9.
[55] Vgl. *Haage*, S. 51, zum CIF-Geschäft. Wie hier auch *Honsell/Ernst/Lauko*, Art. 32, Rn. 19.
[56] Ebenso *Dölle/Herber*, Art. 54 EKG, Rn. 9; *Herber/Czerwenka*, Art. 32, Rn. 7; *Honsell/Ernst/Lauko*, Art. 32, Rn. 20.
[57] *Dölle/Herber*, Art. 54 EKG, Rn. 11; *Bianca/Bonell/Lando*, Art. 32, Anm. 2.3.1.; *Herber/Czerwenka*, Art. 32, Rn. 7; *Honsell/Ernst/Lauko*, Art. 32, Rn. 20; *Staudinger/Magnus*, Art. 32, Rn. 18; *Brunner*, Art. 32, Rn. 2; *MünchKomm/Gruber*, Art. 32, Rn. 12.
[58] Dazu unten Rn. 26.
[59] So *Dölle/Herber*, Art. 54 EKG, Rn. 11; *Soergel/Lüderitz*, Art. 54 EKG, Rn. 2; im Anschluss hieran auch die 1. Aufl., *U. Huber*, Art. 32 Rn. 25.
[60] Vgl. *Herber/Czerwenka*, Art. 32, Rn. 7.
[61] Vgl. Art. 31 Rn. 27.
[62] Vgl. oben Art. 31 Rn. 28; str.

23 b) Unterfrachtführer. Hat der Verkäufer mit dem Beförderer einen dem Art. 32 II entsprechenden Vertrag geschlossen, ihm die Sache übergeben, hierdurch seine Lieferpflicht gemäss Art. 31 lit. a) erfüllt und den Gefahrübergang gemäss Art. 67 I herbeigeführt, so hat er mit dem weiteren Schicksal der Sache nichts mehr zu tun. Setzt der Beförderer einen Unterfrachtführer ein, so ist der Beförderer bei Auswahl und Instruktion des Unterfrachtführers nicht mehr als Erfüllungsgehilfe des Verkäufers tätig. Fehler, die dem Beförderer hierbei unterlaufen, sind vielmehr Teil des vom Käufer zu tragenden Transportrisikos.[63]

24 c) Vorlieferant. Beauftragt der Verkäufer seinen Vorlieferanten, die Ware direkt an den Käufer zu versenden („Streckengeschäft"), so erfüllt er seine Pflicht aus Art. 32 II dadurch, dass der Vorlieferant an seiner Stelle den Beförderungsvertrag abschliesst. Für Fehler des Vorlieferanten beim Abschluss des Beförderungsvertrags haftet der Verkäufer daher gemäss Art. 45 I; der Vorlieferant ist insoweit sein Erfüllungsgehilfe.[64]

4. Transportkosten

25 Art. 32 II ordnet *nicht* an, dass der Verkäufer die Beförderungsverträge „auf eigene Kosten" zu schliessen hat. Da er für den Transport nur „zu sorgen", nicht ihn „durchzuführen" hat, bleibt es bei der allgemeinen Regel, dass die Transportkosten den Käufer treffen,[65] soweit nicht (z. B. durch die Klauseln „CIF" oder „frachtfrei") etwas anderes vereinbart ist.

5. Transportversicherung

26 Art. 32 II enthält keine spezielle Regel über die Frage, ob der Verkäufer verpflichtet ist, die Ware durch Abschluss einer Transportversicherung oder, soweit dies frachtrechtlich vorgesehen ist, durch Wertangabe im Beförderungsvertrag (z. B. durch Versendung als Wertpaket) gegen Transportrisiken zu schützen. Auch diese Frage ist daher anhand des allgemeinen Massstabs zu entscheiden, ob eine solche Versicherung oder Wertangabe zu den „üblichen" Bedingungen der Beförderung gehört.[66] Aus der Tatsache, dass der Kaufvertrag über die Versicherung schweigt, kann also nicht ohne weiteres der Schluss gezogen werden, der Verkäufer sei zur Versicherung nicht verpflichtet.[67] „Üblich" ist eine Versicherung nicht nur dann, wenn sich ein Handelsbrauch i. S. d. Art. 9 I feststellen lässt.[68] Es genügt, dass ordentliche und vorsichtige Kaufleute eine Versicherung abschließen, wenn sie Waren der vorliegenden Art versenden. Eine solche Annahme liegt vor allem bei wertvollen Waren nahe, deren Wert die bei der gewählten Transportart gesetzlich oder frachtvertraglich vorgesehenen Haftungshöchstgrenzen erheblich übersteigt. Die Kosten der Versicherung oder Wertangabe sind, soweit nichts Besonderes vereinbart ist, von derjenigen Partei zu tragen, die die Transportkosten zu tragen hat.[69] Für Inhalt und Umfang der Versicherung gilt, soweit der Kaufvertrag keine besonderen Anordnungen trifft, ebenfalls der in Art. 32 II vorgesehene Massstab des Angemessenen und Üblichen.[70]

27 In der Praxis wird die Frage vielfach durch die von den Parteien verwendete Lieferklausel positiv oder negativ geregelt. Die Incoterms®[71] gehen im praktisch allein interessierenden

---

[63] Vgl. auch Art. 31 Rn. 20, 32.
[64] Vgl. auch Art. 31 Rn. 24.
[65] Vgl. Art. 31 Rn. 83. Ebenso *Staudinger/Magnus*, Art. 32, Rn. 20.
[66] Ebenso *Karollus*, S. 111; *Piltz*, Internationales Kaufrecht, Rn. 4–104; *Witz/Salger/Lorenz/Witz*, Art. 32, Rn. 11; *Brunner*, Art. 32, Rn. 4; vgl. auch *Dölle/Herber*, Art. 54 EKG, Rn. 10; a. A. MünchKommHGB/*Benicke*, Art. 32, Rn. 13.
[67] Anders *Enderlein*, Rights and Obligations of the Seller, S. 150; *Bianca/Bonell/Lando*, Art. 32, Anm. 2.4.; *Heuzé*, Anm. 252.; *Achilles*, Art. 32, Rn. 7; *Neumayer/Ming*, Art. 32, Anm. 9.; *Honsell/Ernst/Lauko*, Art. 32, Rn. 21; *Staudinger/Magnus*, Art. 32, Rn. 22.
[68] So aber *Dölle/Herber*, Art. 54 EKG, Rn. 10; *Herber/Czerwenka*, Art. 32, Rn. 8; *Piltz*, Internationales Kaufrecht, Rn. 4–105.
[69] Ebenso *Piltz*, Internationales Kaufrecht, Rn. 4–110; *Brunner*, Art. 32, Rn. 4.
[70] Vgl. auch *Heuzé*, Anm. 252.; *Staudinger/Magnus*, Art. 32, Rn. 21.
[71] Vgl. Art. 30 Rn. 3 f.

Fall, in dem der Verkäufer den Transportvertrag abzuschliessen und der Käufer die Transportgefahr zu tragen hat, von dem Prinzip aus, dass eine Versicherungspflicht nur besteht, wenn sie in der Klausel besonders vorgesehen ist.[72]

6. Weisungen des Käufers

Art. 32 II enthält keine ausdrückliche Regel des Inhalts, dass der Verkäufer verpflichtet ist, Weisungen des Käufers hinsichtlich der Versendung zu befolgen.[73] Eine solche Pflicht ist aber auch ohnedies in den Grenzen von Treu und Glauben anzuerkennen, soweit dies für den Verkäufer nicht mit aussergewöhnlichen Kosten oder Komplikationen verbunden ist.[74] So kann der Käufer den Bestimmungsort für die Versendung zumindest dann nachträglich festlegen, wenn das nicht zu einem Wechsel der Beförderungsart oder des Bestimmungslandes führt. Er kann den Verkäufer auch anweisen, eine Transportversicherung abzuschliessen oder mit Eilfracht zu versenden. Hieraus entstehende Mehrkosten hat der Käufer zu tragen, auch dann, wenn der Verkäufer im Kaufvertrag die Transportkosten übernommen hat. Ist z. B. „frachtfrei" verkauft und bedeutet dies nach handelsüblicher Auslegung „frachtfrei unversichert", so darf sich der Verkäufer einem nachträglichen, ihm rechtzeitig zugegangenen Wunsch des Käufers, unter Transportversicherung zu versenden, nicht widersetzen; die zusätzlichen Kosten muss allerdings der Käufer tragen.[75] 28

Hält der Verkäufer eine Weisung des Käufers hinsichtlich der Beförderung für unangemessen oder für unzweckmässig und will er sie deshalb nicht befolgen, so ist er nach Treu und Glauben (Art. 7 II)[76] verpflichtet, den Käufer zu informieren. In dringenden Fällen darf er von Weisungen, die sich als unzweckmässig erweisen, auch ohne vorherige Instruktion des Käufers abweichen;[77] auch dies ist nach dem Prinzip von Treu und Glauben zu entscheiden. 29

7. Rechtsfolgen bei Verletzung der Abschlusspflicht

Verletzt der Verkäufer seine Pflichten aus Art. 32 II oder ergänzende Vertragspflichten (z. B. eine Versicherungspflicht) oder handelt er verbindlichen Weisungen des Käufers zuwider, so haftet er hierfür gemäss Art. 45 I. Führt die Vertragsverletzung des Verkäufers dazu, dass die Ware den Käufer überhaupt nicht erreicht, so liegt ein Fall der Nichterfüllung der Lieferpflicht vor.[78] Der Käufer kann daher weiterhin Erfüllung der Lieferpflicht, beim Gattungskauf auch Lieferung von Ersatzware verlangen (Art. 46 I), und er ist gemäss Art. 49 I lit. a), b) zur Vertragsaufhebung berechtigt, in der Regel aber erst nach Nachfristsetzung. Führt die vertragswidrige Versendung dazu, dass die Ware auf dem Transport beschädigt wird, so haftet der Verkäufer gemäss Art. 36 II wegen vertragswidriger Beschaffenheit der Ware, nicht anders, als wenn die Ware schon bei Gefahrübergang mangelhaft gewesen wäre.[79] Trifft die Ware unbeschädigt, aber verspätet beim Käufer ein, so kann der Käufer Ersatz des Verzögerungsschadens verlangen (Art. 45 I lit. b)); bei erheblicher Verspätung 30

---

[72] So bedeutet z. B. CFR („Kosten und Fracht") oder CPT („frachtfrei"), dass unversichert versendet werden darf, im Unterschied zu CIF („Kosten, Versicherung und Fracht") oder CIP („frachtfrei versichert"); eine Übersicht liefert *von Bernstorff*, Incoterms® 2010, 37.
[73] Anders als etwa § 447 II BGB.
[74] Vgl. auch *Honsell/Ernst/Lauko*, Art. 32, Rn. 19; *Achilles*, Art. 32, Rn. 5; *Mertens/Rehbinder*, Art. 54 EKG, Rn. 7; *Soergel/Lüderitz*, Art. 54 EKG, Rn. 3. Zu eng („nur in Ausnahmefällen") 1. Aufl., *U. Huber*, Art. 32 Rn. 26; auf ebendiese 1. Aufl. scheint sich der Verweis von *Witz/Salger/Lorenz/Witz*, Art. 32, Rn. 13, Fn. 30, zu beziehen.
[75] Vgl. *Dölle/Herber*, Art. 54 EKG, Rn. 10; *Herber/Czerwenka*, Art. 32, Rn. 8; *Honsell/Ernst/Lauko*, Art. 32, Rn. 19.
[76] Vgl. Art. 30 Rn. 9.
[77] § 447 II BGB sagt insoweit wohl nur etwas, was auch ohnedies gelten muss.
[78] Ebenso *Honsell/Ernst/Lauko*, Art. 31, Rn. 8; *MünchKomm/Gruber*, Art. 32, Rn. 13. Vgl. dazu auch Art. 31 Rn. 39: zur Versendung an den falschen Bestimmungsort.
[79] Ebenso *Honsell/Ernst/Lauko*, Art. 31, Rn. 8; *Bamberger/Roth/Saenger*, Art. 32, Rn. 11. Vgl. dazu *Schwenzer*, Art. 36 Rn. 5; vgl. auch (zu Art. 55 EKG) OLG Hamm, 29.1.1979, in: *Schlechtriem/Magnus*, Art. 55 EKG,

kann auch die Vertragsaufhebung wegen wesentlicher Vertragsverletzung (Art. 25 i. V. m. Art. 49 I lit. a)) gerechtfertigt sein.[80] Im Übrigen wird als Rechtsbehelf in erster Linie der Schadensersatzanspruch gemäss Art. 45 I lit. b) in Betracht kommen (z. B. bei fehlender oder unzulänglicher Versicherung).

IV. Erteilung von Auskünften zum Zweck der Transportversicherung (Art. 32 III)

31   Art. 32 III ist nur anwendbar, wenn der Verkäufer nicht selbst verpflichtet ist, für die Versicherung der Ware zu sorgen.[81] In diesem Fall hat er dem Käufer die für den Abschluss erforderlichen Auskünfte zu geben, wenn der Käufer dies verlangt. Die Auskünfte sind, sobald das möglich ist, unverzüglich zu erteilen. Fur Verletzung der Auskunftspflicht haftet der Verkäufer gemäss Artt. 45 ff. Dass eine wesentliche Vertragsverletzung vorliegt, die dem Käufer das Recht zur Vertragsaufhebung gibt (Artt. 25, 49 lit. I a)), ist immerhin denkbar.[82] Denn der Käufer, der die Transportgefahr trägt, muss es nicht hinnehmen, dass der Verkäufer die Ware versendet, ohne ihm Gelegenheit zur Versicherung zu geben.

Nr. 1 (betr. Transportschäden wegen mangelhafter Verpackung); OLG Celle, 2.3.1984, RIW 1985, 571, 575 = IPRax 1985, 284, 288 = *Schlechtriem/Magnus*, Art. 55 EKG, Nr. 2; *Soergel/Lüderitz*, Art. 55 EKG, Rn. 2.
[80] Vgl. auch *Honsell/Ernst/Lauko*, Art. 31, Rn. 9.
[81] Vgl. oben Rn. 26 f.
[82] So auch *Honsell/Ernst/Lauko*, Art. 32, Rn. 28; MünchKomm/*Gruber*, Art. 32, Rn. 15.

Art. 33 [Zeit der Lieferung]

Der Verkäufer hat die Ware zu liefern,
a) wenn ein Zeitpunkt im Vertrag bestimmt ist oder aufgrund des Vertrages bestimmt werden kann, zu diesem Zeitpunkt,
b) wenn ein Zeitraum im Vertrag bestimmt ist oder aufgrund des Vertrages bestimmt werden kann, jederzeit innerhalb dieses Zeitraums, sofern sich nicht aus den Umständen ergibt, daß der Käufer den Zeitpunkt zu wählen hat, oder
c) in allen anderen Fällen innerhalb einer angemessenen Frist nach Vertragsabschluß.

Art. 33

The seller must deliver the goods:
(a) if a date is fixed by or determinable from the contract, on that date;
(b) if a period of time is fixed by or determinable from the contract, at any time within that period unless circumstances indicate that the buyer is to choose a date; or
(c) in any other case, within a reasonable time after the conclusion of the contract.

Art. 33

Le vendeur doit livrer les marchandises:
a) si une date est fixée par le contrat ou déterminable par référence au contrat, à cette date;
b) si une période de temps est fixée par le contrat ou déterminable par référence au contrat, à un moment quelconque au cours de cette période, à moins qu'il ne résulte des circonstances que c'est à l'acheteur de choisir une date; ou
c) dans tous les autres cas, dans un délai raisonnable à partir de la conclusion du contrat.

Übersicht

	Rn.
I. Gegenstand und Funktion der Vorschrift	1
1. Regelungsgegenstand	1
2. Rechtsfolgen	2
3. Abnahmepflicht des Käufers	3
4. Vorleistungspflicht des Verkäufers; Einrede des nicht erfüllten Vertrags; Verschlechterungseinrede	4
5. Lieferfrist und Abnahmefrist	5
II. Vertragliche Bestimmung der Lieferzeit: Art. 33 lit. a), b)	6
1. Allgemeines	6
2. Bestimmung eines Zeitpunkts, Art. 33 lit. a)	7
3. Bestimmung eines Zeitraums, Art. 33 lit. b)	8
a) Bestimmungsrecht des Verkäufers	9
b) Bestimmungsrecht des Käufers auf Grund der „Umstände"	10
c) Vertragliches Recht des Käufers zum Abruf	11
d) Unterlassene Mitwirkung des Käufers	12
e) Fristgemässe Lieferung	13
4. Unverbindliche Lieferfrist	14
5. Beweislast	15
III. Fehlen einer vertraglichen Bestimmung der Lieferzeit: Art. 33 lit. c)	16
1. Angemessene Lieferfrist	16
2. Bestimmung des Lieferzeitpunkts	18
3. Aufschiebend bedingte oder befristete Kaufverträge	19
4. Beweislast	20

Vorläufer und **Entwürfe:** EKG Artt. 20–22; Genfer E 1976 Art. 17; Wiener E 1977 Art. 17; New Yorker E 1978 Art. 31.

I. Gegenstand und Funktion der Vorschrift

1. Regelungsgegenstand

1   Art. 33 regelt den Zeitpunkt, zu dem der Verkäufer die Lieferung i. S. d. Art. 31 vorzunehmen hat. Ist dieser Zeitpunkt im Vertrag exakt bestimmt, so ist diese Bestimmung massgeblich (Art. 33 lit. a)). Das ergibt sich schon aus dem Prinzip der Vertragsfreiheit. Art. 33 lit. b) stellt eine ergänzende Regel für den Fall auf, dass der Vertrag nicht einen genauen *Zeitpunkt* festlegt, sondern einen *Zeitraum*. Innerhalb dieses Zeitraums soll der Verkäufer das Recht haben, den genauen Lieferzeitpunkt frei zu bestimmen, sofern sich nicht aus den Umständen etwas anderes ergibt.[1] Art. 33 lit. c) enthält dagegen eine ergänzende Regel für den Fall, dass die Parteien **keine vertragliche Bestimmung** über die Lieferzeit getroffen haben. Dann hat der Verkäufer die Lieferung innerhalb einer „angemessenen Frist" zu bewirken.[2] Entsprechende Bestimmungen finden sich in Artt. 6.1.1 PICC, 7:102 PECL.

2. Rechtsfolgen

2   Die Funktion der Vorschrift des Art. 33, vor allem der subsidiär eingreifenden Regel des Art. 33c), besteht darin, festzulegen, ab wann dem Käufer, der die Ware nicht erhalten hat, die **Rechtsbehelfe der Artt. 45 ff.** zustehen. Nach unbenutztem Verstreichen der vertraglich festgesetzten Leistungszeit oder, bei Fehlen einer vertraglichen Bestimmung, der „angemessenen" Frist ist der Käufer berechtigt, auf Lieferung zu klagen (Art. 46 I), Nachfrist mit dem Ziel der Vertragsaufhebung zu setzen (Art. 49 I lit. b)) oder, wenn die Überschreitung des Liefertermins als wesentliche Vertragsverletzung i. S. d. Art. 25 zu bewerten ist, mit sofortiger Wirkung die Vertragsaufhebung zu erklären (Art. 49 I lit. a))[3] und gemäss Artt. 45 I lit. b), 74 Ersatz des **Verzugsschadens** zu verlangen. Hierfür bedarf es **keiner Mahnung.**[4] Es genügt, dass der Verkäufer trotz Eintritt des durch den Vertrag oder durch Art. 33c) festgelegten Fälligkeitstermins die Lieferung nicht bewirkt hat.

3. Abnahmepflicht des Käufers

3   Art. 33 ist ausserdem von Bedeutung für die in Artt. 53, 60 festgesetzte Abnahmepflicht des Käufers. Vor Fälligkeit der Lieferpflicht gemäss Art. 33 ist der Käufer berechtigt, die ihm angebotene Lieferung zurückzuweisen, ohne dass ihm hieraus rechtliche Nachteile erwachsen (Art. 52 I).[5] Ist für die Lieferung ein Zeitraum bestimmt, so kann allerdings innerhalb dieses Zeitraums der Verkäufer den genauen Lieferzeitpunkt bestimmen (Art. 33 lit. b)), das heisst der Käufer darf die ihm innerhalb des Lieferzeitraums angebotene Ware nicht zurückweisen.[6]

---

[1] Art. 21 EKG enthielt bereits die gleiche Regel. Vorbild ist § 13 des skandinavischen Kaufgesetzes von 1905 (deutscher Text bei *Almén*, Bd. 3, S. 3 ff.). Vgl. dazu auch *Almén*, Bd. 1, S. 146 ff.; *Rabel*, Recht des Warenkaufs, Bd. 1, S. 328.

[2] Art. 22 EKG enthielt bereits die gleiche Regel. Sie hat ihr Vorbild in sec. 29 (2) SGA 1893 (Text: *Almén*, Bd. 3, S. 114 ff.; jetzt: sec. 29 (3) SGA 1979), die allerdings nur den Versendungskauf regelt, und in § 2–309 UCC. Vgl. dazu *Rabel*, Recht des Warenkaufs, Bd. 1, S. 328. Abweichend etwa Art. 1183 I ital.Cc; Art. 6:38 BW; Art. 75 OR; § 904 ABGB; § 271 I BGB: „immediatamente", „terstond", „sogleich", „sofort"; allerdings wird die Vertrags- oder Gesetzesauslegung im Allgemeinen zu ähnlichen oder gleichen Ergebnissen führen; vgl. auch *Rabel*, aaO.; *Schlechtriem*, Seller's Obligations, S. 16; *Lando/Beale*, S. 333, Note 3 zu Art. 7:102 PECL.

[3] Für ein Anwendungsbeispiel siehe OLG Düsseldorf, 21.4.2004, CISG-online 915 = IHR 2005, 24, 25 f. (Wesentlichkeit bejaht); *Valero Marketing & Supply Company v. Green Oy & Greeni Trading Oy*, U. S. Dist. Ct. (N. J.), 4.4.2006, CISG-online 1216 (Wesentlichkeit verneint).

[4] Das ist eine Entscheidung des Einheitskaufrechts, an der bei den Beratungen, seit dem ersten Entwurf von 1935, stets festgehalten wurde, vgl. dazu *Rabel*, RabelsZ 9 (1935), 1, 59 = Ges. Aufs. Bd. 3, S. 565. Vgl. zur Entbehrlichkeit der Mahnung auch *Herber/Czerwenka*, Art. 33, Rn. 7; *Witz/Salger/Lorenz/Witz*, Art. 33, Rn. 1.

[5] Anders etwa nach § 271 II BGB; Art. 81 I OR.

4. Vorleistungspflicht des Verkäufers; Einrede des nicht erfüllten Vertrags; Verschlechterungseinrede

Aus Art. 58 folgt, dass der Verkäufer hinsichtlich der Lieferung vorleistungspflichtig ist. Hiernach kann er nicht die *Lieferung* i. S. d. Art. 31, sondern nur die *Übergabe* der Ware oder der Dokumente von der Zug-um-Zug-Begleichung des Kaufpreises durch den Käufer abhängig machen. Haben die Parteien jedoch in Abweichung von der dispositiven Regel des Art. 58 vereinbart, dass der Käufer hinsichtlich der Zahlung vorleistungspflichtig ist, so kann der Verkäufer auch dann die Lieferung verweigern, wenn der vertraglich festgesetzte Liefertermin oder die angemessene Lieferzeit (Art. 33 lit. c)) bereits verstrichen ist. Die Rechtsbehelfe wegen Nichterfüllung der Lieferpflicht (Artt. 45 ff.) stehen dem Käufer erst zu, wenn er seinerseits die Vorleistungspflicht erfüllt hat; dies ergibt sich aus Art. 80.[7] Sind die Voraussetzungen des Art. 71 I erfüllt, so etwa bei Zahlungsunfähigkeit des Käufers, ist der Verkäufer überdies berechtigt, die Erfüllung der Lieferpflicht trotz Fälligkeit „auszusetzen".[8] Hierdurch werden alle Rechtsbehelfe, die dem Käufer wegen Nichterfüllung der Lieferpflicht zustehen könnten, einstweilen aufgeschoben.[9]

5. Lieferfrist und Abnahmefrist

In allen Fällen, in denen die Lieferung darin besteht, dass der Verkäufer dem Käufer die Ware „zur Verfügung stellt" (Art. 31 lit. b), c) und analoge Lieferklauseln),[10] ist zwischen der Lieferfrist und der Frist, innerhalb derer der Käufer seine Abnahmepflicht (Artt. 53, 60) zu erfüllen hat (der „Empfangszeit"), zu unterscheiden.[11] Die Frist für die Abnahme kann erst beginnen, nachdem der Verkäufer dem Käufer die Ware zur Verfügung gestellt hat. Enthält der Vertrag keine besondere Bestimmung hinsichtlich der Empfangszeit, ist aus Art. 33 lit. c) der allgemeine Grundsatz (Art. 7 II) abzuleiten, dass jede Partei ihre Pflichten innerhalb „angemessener Frist" zu erfüllen hat.[12] Der Käufer muss infolgedessen die Ware innerhalb angemessener Frist übernehmen, nachdem sie bereitgestellt ist und er hiervon Kenntnis erlangt hat.[13]

II. Vertragliche Bestimmung der Lieferzeit: Art. 33 lit. a), b)

1. Allgemeines

Ist ein **Zeitpunkt** i. S. d. Art. 33 lit. a) bestimmt, so hat der Verkäufer genau zu diesem Zeitpunkt zu liefern. Frühere Lieferung gegen den Willen des Käufers ist nicht zulässig (Art. 52 I),[14] spätere Lieferung ist Vertragsverletzung (Art. 45 I). Ist ein **Zeitraum** i. S. d. Art. 33 lit. b) bestimmt, so hat die Lieferung frühestens bei Beginn und spätestens am Ende des Zeitraums zu erfolgen.

---

[6] Vgl. *Müller-Chen*, Art. 52 Rn. 3.
[7] Vgl. auch (zum Fall der unterlassenen Akkreditivstellung) *Herber/Czerwenka*, Art. 80, Rn. 3.
[8] Vgl. OLG Rostock, 15.9.2003, CISG-online 920.
[9] Zu Voraussetzungen und Rechtswirkungen der Verschlechterungseinrede siehe *Fountoulakis*, Art. 71 Rn. 12 ff.
[10] Vgl. Art. 31 Rn. 74.
[11] Ebenso *Herber/Czerwenka*, Art. 33, Rn. 8; *Bamberger/Roth/Saenger*, Art. 33, Rn. 2. Beides wurde nicht richtig auseinandergehalten in *Dölle/Huber*, Artt. 20–22 EKG, Rn. 11.
[12] Von einem solchen allgemeinen Grundsatz geht auch ICC, 8611/1997, 23.1.1997, CISG-online 236 aus (Lieferung von Ersatzteilen für verkaufte Ware).
[13] Vgl. *Mohs*, Art. 58 Rn. 9, Art. 60 Rn. 2 a. Vgl. auch *Herber/Czerwenka*, Art. 33, Rn. 8; *Bamberger/Roth/Saenger*, Art. 33, Rn. 2; MünchKomm/*Gruber*, Art. 33, Rn. 13. Dagegen spricht sich *Staudinger/Magnus*, Art. 33, Rn. 29 grundsätzlich für die Pflicht zur sofortigen Abnahme aus.
[14] Vgl. demgegenüber Art. 130 Ziff. 1 CESL-Entwurf, wonach „the buyer must take delivery unless the buyer has a legitimate interest in refusing to do so".

2. Bestimmung eines Zeitpunkts, Art. 33 lit. a)

7 Ein „Zeitpunkt" ist für die Lieferung bestimmt, wenn sich aus dem Vertrag ein Datum ergibt, das den Tag festlegt, an dem geliefert werden soll. Dieses Datum wird in der Regel durch den Vertrag nach dem Kalender bestimmt,[15] kann aber auch durch Bezugnahme auf ein kalendermässig unbestimmtes Ereignis festgelegt sein, wenn sich sein Eintritt objektiv feststellen lässt.[16] Ausreichend ist auch „noch heute" oder „sofort" (es sei denn, die Auslegung ergibt, dass dies nicht wörtlich zu verstehen war), ebenso „am Tag nach Abruf" oder „unmittelbar nach Eingang der Zahlung".[17] Weitere Präzisierungen (z. B. bei einem just-in-time-Vertrag: „am Tag nach Abruf spätestens bis 11 Uhr vormittags") sind selbstverständlich möglich. Wird dagegen Lieferung „alsbald" oder „so schnell wie möglich" oder etwas ähnliches versprochen, so fehlt die Bezugnahme auf ein bestimmtes Datum. Daher liegt ein besonderer Fall des Art. 33 lit. c) vor, und es ist hiernach zu entscheiden, welche Frist unter den vorliegenden Umständen „angemessen" ist.[18] Gleiches gilt, wenn der Käufer auf seinem Bestellschein den Vermerk „dringend" hinzufügt.[19] Ist vereinbart „zehn Tage nach Ostern"[20] oder „zehn Tage nach Besichtigung des Probestücks",[21] so wird man das im Zweifel nicht so zu verstehen haben, dass *genau* am zehnten Tag, sondern dass *spätestens* am zehnten Tag zu liefern ist; es ist also nicht ein „Zeitpunkt" i. S. d. Art. 33 lit. a), sondern ein „Zeitraum" i. S. d. Art. 33 lit. b) festgelegt.

3. Bestimmung eines Zeitraums, Art. 33 lit. b)

8 Ein „Zeitraum" ist für die Lieferung bestimmt, wenn im Vertrag eine Lieferzeit festgelegt ist, die zumindest mehrere Tage umfasst. Auch diese Bestimmung kann entweder anhand des Kalenders erfolgen[22] oder anhand anderer, nicht kalendermässig bestimmter Ereignisse.[23] Der Zeitraum kann sofort mit Vertragsabschluss beginnen.[24]

9 **a) Bestimmungsrecht des Verkäufers.** Innerhalb des Zeitraums kann gemäss Art. 33 lit. b) grundsätzlich der Verkäufer bestimmen, wann er liefern will: am ersten oder am letzten Tag der Lieferfrist oder irgendwann dazwischen.[25] Ist bestimmt „Lieferung innerhalb von vier Wochen" oder „spätestens am 1. Juni", so kann der Verkäufer daher sofort liefern; der Käufer kann die Lieferung nicht zurückweisen[26] und daher auch nicht verhindern, dass

---

[15] „Am 15.10.", „Mittwoch nach Ostern" oder, bei Sukzessivlieferungsverträgen, „am ersten Werktag des jeweiligen Monats."
[16] Z. B. „beim ersten offenen Wasser" oder „mit dem ersten Dampfer"; Beispiele nach *Almén*, Bd. 1, S. 137; vgl. auch *Rabel*, RabelsZ 9 (1935), 1, 59 = Ges. Aufs. Bd. 3, S. 565; *Honsell/Ernst/Lauko*, Art. 33, Rn. 4.
[17] Vgl. OLG Düsseldorf, 21.4.2004, CISG-online 915 = IHR 2005, 24, 25.
[18] Vgl. RB Kortrijk, 3.10.2001, CISG-online 757 (Lieferung „zo vlug als mogelijk", also so schnell wie möglich); *Bianca/Bonell/Lando*, Art. 33, Anm. 2.3.; *Achilles*, Art. 33, Rn. 3; MünchKommHGB/*Benicke*, Art. 33, Rn. 4; *Soergel/Lüderitz*, Artt. 20–22 EKG, Rn. 5; *Dölle/Huber*, Artt. 20–22 EKG, Rn. 13.
[19] Vgl. den Sachverhalt in CA Poitiers, 26.10.2004, CISG-online 952; vgl. dazu auch unten Rn. 16.
[20] Beispiel bei *Rabel*, RabelsZ 9 (1935), 1, 59 = Ges. Aufs. Bd. 3, S. 565 für Art. 20 EKG = Art. 33 lit. a); ebenso *Bianca/Bonell/Lando*, Art. 33, Anm. 2.2.
[21] Beispiel bei *Soergel/Lüderitz*, Artt. 20–22 EKG, Rn. 2 für Art. 20 EKG = Art. 33 lit. a).
[22] „September/Oktober", „im Lauf des Juni", „innerhalb von zehn Tagen nach Ostern" oder „nächste Woche" (zu Letzterem siehe Rechtbank van Koophandel, Kortrijk, 4.6.2004, CISG-online 945; das Gericht hielt die entsprechende Vereinbarung allerdings zu Unrecht für einen Anwendungsfall des Art. 33 lit. a)). Auch die Vereinbarung „April, Liefertermin bleibt vorbehalten" stellt einen solchen Zeitraum dar; dies hat das OLG Naumburg, 27.4.1999, CISG-online 512 = IHR 2000, 22 f. verkannt (wobei anzumerken bleibt, dass das OLG in casu – gestützt auf eine falsche Anwendung des Art. 19 – bereits das Vorliegen einer entsprechenden Vereinbarung zu Unrecht bejaht hat).
[23] „Spätestens zehn Tage nach Besichtigung des Probestücks" (vgl. *Soergel/Lüderitz*, Artt. 20–22 EKG, Rn. 2), „während der Schifffahrtszeit" oder „innerhalb sechs Wochen nach Eintritt der Schlittenbahn" (Beispiele nach *Almén*, Bd. 1, S. 137 f.); „binnen einer Woche nach Abruf."
[24] „Lieferung: bis 2. 10." oder „[…] bis Ende Juni" oder „bis zum Schluss der Schifffahrt": *Almén*, aaO.
[25] *Enderlein*, Rights and Obligations of the Seller, S. 151. Natürlich nicht später, vgl. OLG Hamm, 8.12.1980, in: *Schlechtriem/Magnus*, Art. 26 EKG, Nr. 3.
[26] Vgl. *Honnold/Flechtner*, Art. 33, Rn. 319.

der Verkäufer auf diese Weise sofort den Kaufpreis fällig stellt (vgl. Art. 58 I). Der Käufer kann sich dadurch schützen, dass er für die Lieferung nicht nur einen End-, sondern auch einen Anfangstermin vereinbart („zwischen 23. Mai und 1. Juni").[27]

b) Bestimmungsrecht des Käufers auf Grund der „Umstände". Das Bestimmungsrecht des Verkäufers besteht nur im Regelfall. Es besteht – was Art. 33 lit. b) als selbstverständlich voraussetzt – nicht, wenn im Vertrag etwas anderes vereinbart ist.[28] Und es besteht ferner nicht – wie Art. 33 lit. b) hervorhebt und klarstellt –, wenn sich „aus den Umständen" ergibt, dass das Bestimmungsrecht dem Käufer zustehen soll. Es handelt sich um einen gesetzlich besonders hervorgehobenen Fall der ergänzenden Vertragsauslegung (Art. 8). Gedacht ist hierbei vor allem an jene Fälle, in denen der Käufer für das Transportmittel zu sorgen hat,[29] wie insbesondere beim FOB-Geschäft[30] und bei den Lieferklauseln FCA und FAS. Auch die Incoterms®[31] regeln die Frage in diesem Sinn.[32] Der Käufer hat dem Verkäufer die Bereitstellung des Transportmittels mit einer angemessenen Frist anzukündigen, sodass der Verkäufer sich darauf einrichten kann (Art. 60 lit. a)).[33] Hat bei Verwendung der Klausel FCA oder FOB gleichwohl der Verkäufer es übernommen, für den Abschluss des Transportvertrags zu sorgen, so hat er im Zweifel auch den Lieferzeitpunkt festzulegen. Verfehlt ist es, in allen Fällen der Holschuld – also in allen Fällen, in denen der Verkäufer die Ware gemäss Art. 31 lit. b), c) oder an einem besonders vereinbarten Lieferort (ab Grenze, ab Schiff, ab Kai usw.) zur Verfügung zu stellen hat – dem Käufer ein Bestimmungsrecht zuzubilligen.[34] Auch die Incoterms®-Klausel EXW („ab Werk") geht davon aus, dass die Bestimmung des Liefertermins im Zweifel dem Verkäufer zusteht.[35] Im Einzelfall mag sich aus dem Vertrag oder den Umständen etwas anderes ergeben;[36] das ist aber nicht die Regel. Dass der Käufer „aus anderen Gründen (z. B. beschränkte Lagerkapazität) an einer exakten Zeitplanung für den Empfang der Ware interessiert" ist, stellt für sich genommen ebenfalls keinen Umstand dar, der ihm ein Recht zur Terminbestimmung verleiht.[37] Will der Käufer ein solches Interesse zur Geltung bringen, muss er im Kaufvertrag „Lieferung auf Abruf" vereinbaren; unterlässt er das, bleibt es beim Bestimmungsrecht des Verkäufers. Daran vermag auch die besondere Länge des vereinbarten Lieferzeitraums („Lieferung 1993–1994") nichts zu ändern.[38]

---

[27] Vgl. *Honnold/Flechtner*, Art. 33, Rn. 319. Beispiel aus der Rechtsprechung: BGer, 15.9.2000, CISG-online 770.

[28] Vgl. dazu auch unten Rn. 11.

[29] Sekretariatskommentar, Art. 31, Nr. 6; *Honsell/Ernst/Lauko*, Art. 33, Rn. 11; *Staudinger/Magnus*, Art. 33, Rn. 18; *Heuzé*, Anm. 247.; *Soergel/Lüderitz/Schüßler-Langeheine*, Art. 33, Rn. 5; *Witz/Salger/Lorenz/Witz*, Art. 33, Rn. 6; *Bamberger/Roth/Saenger*, Art. 33, Rn. 5; *MünchKommHGB/Benicke*, Art. 33, Rn. 5; *Piltz*, Internationales Kaufrecht, Rn. 4–54; *Brunner*, Art. 33, Rn. 3; *MünchKomm/Gruber*, Art. 33, Rn. 7.

[30] Vgl. ICC, 9117/1998, ICC Ct. Bull. 2000, 83, 89 = CISG-online 777; *Enderlein*, Rights and Obligations of the Seller, S. 151; *Bianca/Bonell/Lando*, Art. 33, Anm. 2.3.; *Honsell/Ernst/Lauko*, Art. 33, Rn. 11; *Herber/Czerwenka*, Art. 33, Rn. 5; *Enderlein/Maskow/Strohbach*, Art. 33, Anm. 3.; *Almén*, Bd. 1, S. 147; *Rabel*, RabelsZ 9 (1935), 1, 60 = Ges. Aufs. Bd. 3, S. 565; *ders.*, Recht des Warenkaufs, Bd. 2, S. 328; *Riese*, RabelsZ 29 (1965), 1, 35 f.; *Dölle/Huber*, Artt. 20–22 EKG, Rn. 11; *Soergel/Lüderitz*, Artt. 20–22 EKG, Rn. 3; *Lando/Beale*, S. 333, comment D (zur gleich lautenden Bestimmung des Art. 7:102 (3) PECL).

[31] Vgl. Art. 30 Rn. 3 f.

[32] Vgl. Incoterms® 2010 FCA, FAS, FOB, jeweils A 4/B 7: der Verkäufer hat „innerhalb der vereinbarten Frist" zu liefern; der Käufer hat ihm „die erforderliche Lieferzeit anzugeben".

[33] Vgl. wiederum Incoterms® 2010 FCA, FAS, FOB B 7: Benachrichtigung des Verkäufers „in angemessener Weise" und Angabe der „erforderlichen Lieferzeit".

[34] So aber *Herber/Czerwenka*, Art. 33, Rn. 5; *Enderlein/Maskow/Strohbach*, Art. 33, Anm. 3; *Achilles*, Art. 33, Rn. 4; unrichtig auch *Dölle/Huber*, Artt. 20–22 EKG, Rn. 11. Zutreffend *Staudinger/Magnus*, Art. 33, Rn. 20; *Karollus*, S. 113; *Honsell/Ernst/Lauko*, Art. 33, Rn. 11; *MünchKommHGB/Benicke*, Art. 33, Rn. 6; *Soergel/Lüderitz*, Artt. 20–22 EKG, Rn. 3.

[35] Vgl. A 4, B 7.

[36] Vgl. auch *Bianca/Bonell/Lando*, Art. 33, Anm. 2.3.: „it may also happen in some [...] cases [...]".

[37] Entgegen *Enderlein/Maskow/Strohbach*, Art. 33, Anm. 3.; ihnen folgend *Piltz*, Internationales Kaufrecht, Rn. 4–54 und wohl auch *Heuzé*, Anm. 247. (betreffend Lagerkapazität).

[38] Anders der „Dissenting Arbitrator" in ICC, 9117/1998, ICC Ct. Bull. 2000, 83, 91 = CISG-online 777.

11   **c) Vertragliches Recht des Käufers zum Abruf.** Haben die Parteien einen bestimmten Zeitraum für die Lieferung vorgesehen und vereinbart, dass innerhalb dieses Zeitraums der Verkäufer „auf Abruf" zu liefern hat, so ist Art. 33 lit. b) kraft Vorrangs der Parteiabrede ausgeschlossen. Sieht der Vertrag eine bestimmte Frist vor, innerhalb derer der Verkäufer nach Abruf zu liefern hat („Lieferung Juli/August innerhalb einer Woche nach Abruf des Käufers"), so steht innerhalb dieser zusätzlichen Frist das Bestimmungsrecht gemäss Art. 33 lit. b) wieder dem Verkäufer zu. Hat der Verkäufer nicht innerhalb einer bestimmten Frist, sondern vielmehr zu einem bestimmten **Zeitpunkt** nach Abruf des Käufers zu liefern („Lieferung am Tag nach Abruf" oder „unmittelbar nach Eingang der Zahlung des Käufers"), kommt Art. 33 lit. a) zur Anwendung.[39] Ist nichts darüber vereinbart, wann nach Abruf zu liefern ist, so muss die Lieferung nach der subsidiären Regel des Art. 33 lit. c) innerhalb „angemessener Frist" nach Abruf erfolgen. Grundsätzlich ist die Abrufvereinbarung so zu verstehen, dass der Verkäufer bei Beginn der Abrufperiode lieferbereit sein muss, also die Ware entweder auf Lager haben muss oder sie allenfalls ganz kurzfristig produzieren kann.[40] Ist überhaupt keine Lieferfrist festgesetzt („Lieferung jederzeit auf Abruf"), so ist das so zu verstehen, dass der Verkäufer ab Vertragsabschluss lieferbereit ist und die Lieferung kurzfristig nach Abruf vornehmen wird.

12   **d) Unterlassene Mitwirkung des Käufers.** Unterlässt es der Käufer, innerhalb des vertraglich festgelegten Lieferzeitraums den ihm vertraglich vorbehaltenen Abruf auszusprechen oder das von ihm zu bestellende Transportmittel zu benennen, so verletzt er hierdurch seine Abnahmepflicht (Art. 60 lit. a)).[41] Dem Verkäufer stehen deshalb die Rechte der Artt. 61 ff. zu. Der Käufer seinerseits kann dagegen nicht gegen den Verkäufer wegen Nichterfüllung der Lieferpflicht vorgehen (Art. 80).[42] Zu einer Lieferung ohne Abruf bzw. Benennung des Transportmittels ist der Verkäufer weder verpflichtet noch berechtigt.[43] Die Fälligkeit des Kaufpreisanspruchs, die an sich von der vorherigen Lieferung abhängt (Art. 58), kann der Käufer aber nicht dadurch verhindern, dass er die gebotene und geschuldete Mitwirkung bei der Lieferung unterlässt. Der Verkäufer, der am Vertrag festhalten will, kann daher nach Ablauf der Lieferfrist Klage auf Zahlung des Kaufpreises erheben. Ist dem Käufer ein unbefristetes Abrufrecht eingeräumt, ist analog Art. 33 lit. c) im Zweifel anzunehmen, dass er den Abruf innerhalb einer den Umständen nach angemessenen Frist zu erklären hat.[44] Anders ist es, wenn sich aus den Umständen ergibt, dass der Käufer das einseitige Recht haben soll, die Ware nur bei Bedarf abzurufen.

13   **e) Fristgemässe Lieferung.** Die durch den Vertrag festgesetzte Lieferfrist ist eingehalten, wenn der Verkäufer bis zum Ablauf der Frist die durch Art. 31 oder durch vertragliche Lieferklauseln[45] festgelegte Leistungshandlung vorgenommen hat. Besitzerwerb des Käufers innerhalb der Frist ist für die Rechtzeitigkeit der Leistung nicht erforderlich.[46] Im Fall des

---

[39] Siehe Rn. 7.
[40] Ebenso MünchKommHGB/*Benicke*, Art. 33, Rn. 5. A. A. *Honsell/Ernst/Lauko*, Art. 33, Rn. 12; *Soergel/Lüderitz*, Artt. 20–22 EKG, Rn. 4.
[41] Vgl. dazu *Mohs*, Art. 60 Rn. 8, sowie *Schlechtriem*, Einheitliches UN-Kaufrecht, S. 75 = Uniform Sales Law, S. 83 f.; *Honsell/Ernst/Lauko*, Art. 33, Rn. 12; *Bamberger/Roth/Saenger*, Art. 33, Rn. 5; MünchKomm/*Gruber*, Art. 33, Rn. 9; *Soergel/Lüderitz*, Artt. 20–22 EKG, Rn. 4; *Dölle/Huber*, Artt. 20–22 EKG, Rn. 11; *Huber*, RabelsZ 43 (1979), 413, 515. Abweichend *Witz/Salger/Lorenz/Witz*, Art. 33, Rn. 6: Aus dem Bestimmungsrecht des Käufers lasse sich nur selten eine Abnahmepflicht ableiten.
[42] Vgl. *Piltz*, Internationales Kaufrecht, Rn. 4–223; *Honsell/Ernst/Lauko*, Art. 33, Rn. 12. Der Sekretariatskommentar, Art. 31, Nr. 7, verweist in diesem Zusammenhang auf die Entlastungsregel des Art. 79 (damals: Art. 65). Der Hinweis ist durch die erst später erfolgte Hinzufügung des Art. 80 überholt.
[43] Ebenso *Soergel/Lüderitz*, Artt. 20–22 EKG, Rn. 4; *Soergel/Lüderitz/Schüßler-Langeheine*, Art. 33, Rn. 5; *Herber/Czerwenka*, Art. 33, Rn. 5; *Neumayer/Ming*, Art. 33, Anm. 6.; vgl. auch *Dölle/Huber*, Artt. 20–22 EKG, Rn. 11.
[44] Vgl. *Soergel/Lüderitz*, Artt. 20–22 EKG, Rn. 4; *Neumayer/Ming*, Art. 33, Anm. 7.
[45] Vgl. Art. 31 Rn. 72 ff.
[46] Vgl. Sekretariatskommentar, Art. 31, Nr. 2; *Witz/Salger/Lorenz/Witz*, Art. 33, Rn. 2; *Achilles*, Art. 33, Rn. 4; *Bamberger/Roth/Saenger*, Art. 33, Rn. 7.

Versendungskaufs (Art. 31 lit. a)) genügt es daher, dass der Verkäufer die Ware vor Ablauf der Lieferfrist dem Beförderer übergibt.[47] Im Fall der Lieferung durch „Zur-Verfügung-Stellen" (Art. 31 lit. b), c)) muss der Verkäufer die Ware bis zum Ablauf der Lieferfrist bereitstellen. Auch dies darf, wenn der Verkäufer den Liefertermin zu wählen hat, erst am letzten Tag der Lieferfrist geschehen.[48] Soweit eine Benachrichtigung des Käufers erforderlich ist,[49] muss der Verkäufer sie jedenfalls vor Ablauf der Lieferfrist und in einer Weise vornehmen, dass sie bei normalem Lauf der Dinge den Käufer vor Ablauf der Lieferfrist erreicht (das Risiko des Verlusts und der Verzögerung auf dem Übermittlungsweg trifft allerdings den Käufer, Art. 27). Nach dem Grundsatz von Treu und Glauben (Art. 7 II)[50] ist ausserdem von einem Verkäufer, der die Bereitstellung erst zum letzten möglichen Termin vornehmen will, zu verlangen, dass er die Benachrichtigung so rechtzeitig vor Ende der Lieferfrist absendet, dass der Käufer zumindest die Möglichkeit hat, die Ware noch vor Ablauf der Frist zu übernehmen.[51] Unterlässt er dies, so steht die Ware nicht rechtzeitig „zur Verfügung" des Käufers.

4. Unverbindliche Lieferfrist

Ist eine Lieferfrist vereinbart, die im Vertrag als „unverbindlich" oder „freibleibend" bezeichnet ist, so liegt der in Art. 33 lit. a), b) geregelte Fall nicht vor: die Lieferfrist ist durch den Vertrag gerade nicht verbindlich bestimmt. Infolgedessen greift subsidiär Art. 33 lit. c) ein. Das bedeutet, dass die im Vertrag genannte unverbindliche Frist sich um eine angemessene zusätzliche Frist verlängert.[52] Erst wenn auch diese zusätzliche Frist abgelaufen ist, stehen dem Käufer die Rechtsbehelfe der Artt. 45 ff. zu. Das gilt auch für den Rechtsbehelf der Nachfristsetzung gemäss Art. 49 I lit. b).[53] Der Käufer kann also nicht die unverbindliche Lieferfrist dadurch in eine verbindliche umwandeln, dass er sofort bei Ablauf eine, wenn auch angemessene, Nachfrist setzt.[54] Ist die Lieferfrist nicht ausdrücklich als „unverbindlich" bezeichnet worden, kann sich dennoch aufgrund der Vertragsauslegung ergeben, dass sie nicht verbindlich sein soll.[55]

5. Beweislast

Die Beweislast für die Vereinbarung einer bestimmten Lieferzeit trifft grundsätzlich den Käufer, der wegen Überschreitung der Lieferzeit einen Rechtsbehelf gemäss Artt. 45 ff. geltend macht.[56] Das gilt sowohl, wenn der Käufer die Vereinbarung eines bestimmten

---

[47] HGer Zürich, 10.2.1999, CISG-online 488 = SZIER 2000, 111, 113 = IHR 2001, 44, 45; ICC, 9117/1998, ICC Ct. Bull. 2000, 83, 89, 91 = CISG-online 777; OLG Hamm, 8.12.1980, in: *Schlechtriem/Magnus*, Art. 26 EKG, Nr. 3; LG Münster, 24.5.1977, in: *Schlechtriem/Magnus*, Art. 82 EKG, Nr. 6; *Soergel/Lüderitz*, Artt. 20–22, Rn. 9 (alle zu Art. 19 EKG).
[48] Vgl. BGer, 15.9.2000, CISG-online 770, Erwägung 2b), 2c) bb). Abweichend *Enderlein/Maskow/Strohbach*, Art. 33, Anm. 3.
[49] Vgl. Art. 31 Rn. 51 f.
[50] Vgl. Art. 30 Rn. 9.
[51] In der Sache übereinstimmend *Soergel/Lüderitz*, Artt. 20–22 EKG, Rn. 3; *Staudinger/Magnus*, Art. 33, Rn. 20.
[52] *Soergel/Lüderitz*, Artt. 20–22 EKG, Rn. 5; *Staudinger/Magnus*, Art. 33, Rn. 16; *Soergel/Lüderitz/Schüßler-Langeheine*, Art. 33, Rn. 9; MünchKomm/*Gruber*, Art. 33, Rn. 11. Vgl. auch (zu Art. 22 EKG) Gerechtshof Amsterdam, 8.6.1977, in: *Schlechtriem/Magnus*, Art. 22 EKG, Nr. 1: Bestellung Anfang Juli mit unverbindlicher Lieferfrist Mitte Oktober (die Verkäuferin hatte erklärt, dass „angesichts der angespannten Beschaffungslage […] nicht vor Mitte Oktober mit der Lieferung zu rechnen" sei); einmonatige Überschreitung des Liefertermins sei „angemessen".
[53] Abweichend insoweit (zu Art. 27 EKG) *Dölle/Huber*, Artt. 20–22 EKG, Rn. 5.
[54] Anders (zu Art. 27 EKG) LG Heidelberg, 30.1.1979, in: *Schlechtriem/Magnus*, Artt. 20–22 EKG, Nr. 2.
[55] Vgl. Hof van Beroep Antwerpen, 24.4.2006, CISG-online 1258: die AGB-Bestimmung, wonach „Lieferung im November/Dezember/Januar 2000 zu erwarten" sei (*„verwachte verscheping. November/december/januari 2000"*), wurde vom Gericht als unverbindliche Lieferfrist ausgelegt.
[56] Vgl. KG Wallis, 29.6.1998, CISG-online 420 = IHR 2000, 14; KG Zug, 2.12.2004, CISG-online 1194 = IHR 2006, 158 ff.; Hof van Beroep Antwerpen, 24.4.2006, CISG-online 1258.

Lieferzeitpunkts (Art. 33 lit. a)), als auch, wenn er die Vereinbarung einer bestimmten Lieferfrist (Art. 33 lit. b)) behauptet. Macht der Käufer geltend, innerhalb der – nachgewiesenen oder unstreitigen – Lieferfrist stehe das Bestimmungsrecht entgegen Art. 33 lit. b) ihm zu, trifft ebenfalls ihn die Beweislast.[57] Lässt sich die Vereinbarung einer bestimmten Lieferzeit nicht nachweisen, so greift subsidiär die Regel des Art. 33 lit. c) ein. Behauptet demgegenüber der Verkäufer, es sei eine längere Frist vereinbart worden als normalerweise angemessen erscheint, trägt er die Beweislast für diese ihm günstige Abweichung vom dispositiven Recht. Die Beweislast trägt der Verkäufer auch dann, wenn er sich darauf beruft, dass die Gefahr auf Grund der Fälligkeit der Lieferung nach Art. 69 II auf den Käufer übergegangen ist.[58]

III. Fehlen einer vertraglichen Bestimmung der Lieferzeit: Art. 33 lit. c)

1. Angemessene Lieferfrist

16   Enthält der Vertrag keine Bestimmung über die Lieferzeit,[59] so hat der Verkäufer gemäss Art. 33 lit. c) die Lieferung innerhalb einer „angemessenen Frist" nach Vertragsabschluss durchzuführen. Was angemessen ist, bestimmt sich nach den Umständen des Einzelfalls, nach dem, was unter vergleichbaren Umständen üblich ist, und letztlich nach Billigkeit.[60] In diesem Rahmen sind die Interessen beider Parteien abzuwägen; dass hierbei „in erster Linie die Verkäuferinteressen" massgeblich seien,[61] trifft nicht zu und lässt sich insbesondere auch nicht mit einem Hinweis auf Art. 33 lit. b) begründen, der lediglich eine Auslegungsregel für den Fall der Vereinbarung einer bestimmten Lieferfrist enthält. Das kann zu Fristen von ganz unterschiedlicher Dauer führen. Bei der Bestimmung der Lieferfrist dürfen zugunsten jeder Partei nur solche Umstände berücksichtigt werden, die auch der Gegenpartei bei Vertragsabschluss bekannt oder zumindest für sie erkennbar sind.[62] Auf Gründe, die zu einer ungewöhnlich langen Lieferzeit führen können, muss daher der Verkäufer den Käufer bei Vertragsabschluss hinweisen, wenn sie bei der Entscheidung über die angemessene Lieferfrist Berücksichtigung finden sollen.[63] Ergibt sich aus den dem Verkäufer erkennbaren oder vom Käufer mitgeteilten Umständen, dass der Käufer mit einer kurzfristigen Belieferung rechnet, so muss der Verkäufer den Käufer über bestehende Lieferhindernisse (etwa darüber, dass er die Ware nicht vorrätig hat) informieren; sonst bleiben sie unberücksichtigt.[64] Umgekehrt muss der Käufer den Verkäufer über Gründe – falls sie nicht offensichtlich sind – informieren, die die Lieferung als eilbedürftig erscheinen lassen,[65] sonst können sie die angemessene Lieferfrist nicht abkürzen.[66] Nachträgliche Erklärungen und

---
[57] Anders *Baumgärtel/Laumen-Hepting*, Art. 33, Rn. 4.
[58] Vgl. OLG Hamm, 23.6.1998, CISG-online 434 = IHR 2000, 7 ff.
[59] Was – entgegen OLG Naumburg, 27.4.1999, CISG-online 512 = IHR 2000, 22 f. – nicht der Fall ist, wenn hinsichtlich der Lieferzeit „April, Liefertermin bleibt vorbehalten" vereinbart ist; siehe bereits oben, Fn. 21.
[60] Für ein Anwendungsbeispiel vgl. OLG Rostock, 15.9.2003, CISG-online 920 (Verschiebung des ursprünglich vereinbarten Liefertermins für Plastikflaschen um drei Wochen angemessen, da die Verzögerung auf Änderungswünsche der Käuferin bezüglich Flaschenform zurückzuführen war und die Käuferin den damit verbundenen Mehraufwand für die Verkäuferin erkennen konnte); KG Appenzell Ausserrhoden, 10.3.2003, CISG-online 852 = IHR 2004, 254 ff. (Verkauf einer Maschine, die bei einem Dritten im Betrieb stand; der Verkäufer hatte vor Vertragsschluss im Januar 2002 erwähnt, die Maschine stehe noch bis Anfang März 2002 beim Dritten im Betrieb. Das Gericht ging davon aus, dass unter diesen Umständen eine Bereitstellung der Maschine bis Anfang April 2002 angemessen gewesen wäre).
[61] So *Soergel/Lüderitz/Schüßler-Langeheine*, Art. 33, Rn. 8 mit Hinweis auf die „Grundregel" des Art. 33 lit. b); so auch schon (mit Hinweis auf Art. 21 EKG) *Soergel/Lüderitz*, Artt. 20–22 EKG, Rn. 8.
[62] OLG Rostock, 15.9.2003, CISG-online 920; *Soergel/Lüderitz*, Artt. 20–22 EKG, Rn. 8.
[63] Vgl. auch *Honsell/Ernst/Lauko*, Art. 33, Rn. 16.
[64] *Soergel/Lüderitz*, Artt. 20–22 EKG, Rn. 8.
[65] Strenger gegenüber dem Käufer *Soergel/Lüderitz*, Artt. 20–22 EKG, Rn. 8: solche Interessen müsse er „in Vertragsklauseln formulieren und durchsetzen".

Zeit der Lieferung 17–19 **Art. 33**

Mitteilungen der Parteien sind nur zu berücksichtigen, soweit sie als „Vereinbarung der Parteien" i. S. d. Art. 29 I anzusehen sind. Dagegen kann nicht angenommen werden, dass eine unwidersprochene Mahnung des Käufers oder eine unwidersprochene Lieferankündigung des Verkäufers die Angemessenheit der Leistungszeit „indiziert".[67] Die angemessene Lieferfrist beginnt selbstverständlich erst mit Vertragsschluss zu laufen. Bezeichnet der Käufer seine Bestellung als dringend und liefert der Verkäufer die Ware erst zwei Monate später, ist deshalb für die Frage der „angemessenen Frist" wesentlich, ob der Vertrag bereits vor Lieferung zustande gekommen ist oder nicht.[68] Dies entscheidet sich nach den allgemeinen Regeln (Artt. 14 ff.).

Zu den Umständen, die – Kenntnis oder Erkennbarkeit auf beiden Seiten vorausgesetzt – für die Bestimmung der Angemessenheit von Bedeutung sind, gehört vor allem, ob der Vertrag sich auf vorrätige Ware oder aber auf Ware bezieht, die der Verkäufer herzustellen oder bei Dritten zu beschaffen hat. In letzterem Fall sind durchschnittliche Produktions- und Lieferfristen einzurechnen.[69] Ist es dem Verkäufer, der sich die Ware von dritter Seite zu beschaffen hat, gelungen, die von ihm zu beschaffende Ware nach längerer Zeit tatsächlich zu erhalten, so ist anzunehmen, dass die angemessene Lieferfrist jedenfalls von nun an erschöpft ist.[70] Bezieht der Vertrag sich auf präsente Ware, die der Verkäufer nurmehr versandfertig zu machen hat, so ist die Lieferfrist kurz zu bemessen;[71] dem Verkäufer ist nicht mehr zuzubilligen als die üblicherweise hierfür benötigte Zeit.[72] Ist dem Käufer erkennbar an einer umgehenden Belieferung gelegen (z. B. bei Bestellung eines Ersatzteils für ein Fahrzeug oder für eine Maschine), so ist die angemessene Frist entsprechend zu verkürzen. In solchen Fällen kann daher auch „sofortige" Lieferung angemessen sein.[73] 17

2. Bestimmung des Lieferzeitpunkts

Innerhalb der angemessenen Frist des Art. 33 lit. c) steht dem Verkäufer die Bestimmung des Lieferzeitpunkts frei.[74] Ist die Ware für ihn schon vor Ablauf der Frist verfügbar, die noch als „angemessen" anzusehen wäre, so darf er sofort liefern; er kann also auch sofort nach Vertragsabschluss liefern.[75] Das ist zwar in Art. 33 lit. c) nicht ausdrücklich angeordnet. Art. 33 lit. b) ist nicht unmittelbar anzuwenden, weil der Lieferzeitraum im Fall des Art. 33 lit. c) nicht „im Vertrag bestimmt" ist. Jedoch ist das Bestimmungsrecht des Verkäufers als allgemeiner Grundsatz (Art. 7 II) anzusehen. Wenn der Käufer vor einem bestimmten Termin die Lieferung nicht abnehmen und den Kaufpreis nicht bereithalten will, kann man erwarten, dass er für die Aufnahme eines entsprechenden Anfangstermins für die Lieferung im Vertrag sorgt. 18

3. Aufschiebend bedingte oder befristete Kaufverträge

Ist der Kaufvertrag durch ein künftiges Ereignis, von dem unbestimmt ist, wann, vielleicht auch, ob es überhaupt eintritt, aufschiebend befristet oder bedingt (Lieferung nach Kriegsende, nach Beendigung eines Streiks, nach Aufhebung eines Exportverbots), so kann die 19

---

[66] Vgl. auch *Honsell/Ernst/Lauko,* Art. 33, Rn. 16; *Soergel/Lüderitz,* Artt. 20–22 EKG, Rn. 8.
[67] So aber *Soergel/Lüderitz,* Artt. 20–22 EKG, Rn. 8; *Soergel/Lüderitz/Schüßler-Langeheine,* Art. 33, Rn. 8.
[68] Vgl. den Sachverhalt in CA Poitiers, 26.10.2004, CISG-online 952. Das Gericht hielt die Lieferung nicht für verspätet, allerdings ohne ausdrückliche Bezugnahme auf Art. 33 und ohne den genauen Zeitpunkt des Vertragsschlusses zu bestimmen.
[69] Vgl. RB Kortrijk, 3.10.2001, CISG-online 757 (Produktion von Seidenbändern; vereinbart war Lieferung „so schnell wie möglich"); *Soergel/Lüderitz,* Artt. 20–22 EKG, Rn. 8.
[70] LG Düsseldorf, 17.11.1983, in: *Schlechtriem/Magnus,* Art. 71 EKG, Nr. 2 (zu Art. 22 EKG); zustimmend *Soergel/Lüderitz,* Artt. 20–22 EKG, Rn. 8.
[71] *Soergel/Lüderitz,* Artt. 20–22 EKG, Rn. 8; *Piltz,* Internationales Kaufrecht, Rn. 4–56.
[72] Generell „sofortige" Lieferung zu verlangen (so *Soergel/Lüderitz,* Artt. 20–22 EKG, Rn. 8; *Piltz,* Internationales Kaufrecht, Rn. 4–56; *U. Huber,* 1. Aufl., Art. 33 Rn. 17), ist wohl zu scharf formuliert.
[73] Vgl. auch *Soergel/Lüderitz,* Artt. 20–22 EKG, Rn. 8; *Piltz,* Internationales Kaufrecht, Rn. 4–56.
[74] So auch *Honsell/Ernst/Lauko,* Art. 33, Rn. 16; *MünchKomm/Gruber,* Art. 33, Rn. 12.
[75] Zutreffend *Reinhart,* Art. 33, Rn. 4; a. A. *Piltz,* Internationales Kaufrecht, Rn. 4–56.

Lieferpflicht frühestens mit dem Eintritt dieses Ereignisses fällig werden. Je nach dem Inhalt des Vertrags hat der Verkäufer jetzt in der für diesen Fall bestimmten Frist („14 Tage nach Ende des Streiks") oder innerhalb einer von nun an berechneten „angemessenen" Frist zu liefern. Dagegen lässt sich aus Art. 33 lit. c) nicht im Umkehrschluss die Regel entnehmen, dass der Verkäufer an das bedingte Leistungsversprechen nicht mehr gebunden ist, wenn das Leistungshindernis nicht innerhalb angemessener Frist behoben wird.[76] Eine Entlastung des Verkäufers kommt lediglich nach Massgabe des Art. 79 in Betracht.[77]

4. Beweislast

20 Art. 33 lit. c) ist immer anzuwenden, wenn nicht unstreitig oder nachgewiesen ist, dass für die Lieferung ein bestimmter Zeitpunkt oder Zeitraum vereinbart ist.[78] Macht der Käufer Rechtsbehelfe wegen Überschreitung der angemessenen Lieferfrist geltend, so hat er diejenigen Tatsachen zu beweisen, auf die er die Bestimmung der angemessenen Lieferfrist stützt.[79]

---

[76] So aber *Bianca/Bonell/Lando*, Art. 33, Anm. 2.4.; wie hier *Neumayer/Ming*, Art. 33, Anm. 8.; *Staudinger/Magnus*, Art. 33, Rn. 14.
[77] Vgl. dazu *Stoll/Gruber*, 4. Aufl., Art. 79 Rn. 30 ff.
[78] Vgl. oben Rn. 15.
[79] Nicht eindeutig insoweit *Baumgärtel/Laumen-Hepting*, Art. 33, Rn. 5.

Art. 34 [Übergabe von Dokumenten]

Hat der Verkäufer Dokumente zu übergeben, die sich auf die Ware beziehen, so hat er sie zu dem Zeitpunkt, an dem Ort und in der Form zu übergeben, die im Vertrag vorgesehen sind. Hat der Verkäufer die Dokumente bereits vorher übergeben, so kann er bis zu dem für die Übergabe vorgesehenen Zeitpunkt jede Vertragswidrigkeit der Dokumente beheben, wenn die Ausübung dieses Rechts dem Käufer nicht unzumutbare Unannehmlichkeiten oder unverhältnismäßige Kosten verursacht. Der Käufer behält jedoch das Recht, Schadenersatz nach diesem Übereinkommen zu verlangen.

Art. 34

If the seller is bound to hand over documents relating to the goods, he must hand them over at the time and place and in the form required by the contract. If the seller has handed over documents before that time, he may, up to that time, cure any lack of conformity in the documents, if the exercise of this right does not cause the buyer unreasonable inconvenience or unreasonable expense. However, the buyer retains any right to claim damages as provided for in this Convention.

Art. 34

Si le vendeur est tenu de remettre les documents se rapportant aux marchandises, il doit s'acquitter de cette obligation au moment, au lieu et dans la forme prévus au contrat. En cas de remise anticipée, le vendeur conserve, jusqu'au moment prévu pour la remise, le droit de réparer tout défaut de conformité des documents, à condition que l'exercice de ce droit ne cause à l'acheteur ni inconvénients ni frais déraisonnables. Toutefois, l'acheteur conserve le droit de demander des dommages-intérêts conformément à la présente Convention.

Übersicht

	Rn.
I. Zeit, Ort und Form der Übergabe von Dokumenten (Art. 34 S. 1)	1
1. Die Verweisung auf den Kaufvertrag	1
2. Ergänzende Vertragsauslegung	2
a) Zeitpunkt der Übergabe	2
b) Übergabeort	3
c) Form der Übergabe	4
3. Rechtsfolgen der Nichterfüllung der Übergabepflicht	5
4. Beweislast	5a
II. Recht zur zweiten Andienung (Art. 34 S. 2, 3)	6
1. Allgemeines	6
2. Einzelfragen	8
a) Vertragswidrigkeit der Dokumente	8
b) Übergabe der vertragswidrigen Dokumente	9
c) Behebung der Vertragswidrigkeit	10
d) Unzumutbare Unannehmlichkeiten und unverhältnismässige Kosten	11
e) Schadensersatz (Satz 3)	12
f) Beweislast	12a
III. Gerichtsstand	13

Vorläufer und **Entwürfe:** EKG Artt. 50, 51; Genfer E 1976 Art. 18; Wiener E 1977 Art. 18; New Yorker E 1978 Art. 32.

I. Zeit, Ort und Form der Übergabe von Dokumenten (Art. 34 S. 1)

1. Die Verweisung auf den Kaufvertrag

Ist der Verkäufer nach dem Kaufvertrag verpflichtet, Dokumente zu übergeben,[1] so wird hierdurch eine Pflicht des Verkäufers begründet, die in der Regel selbstständig neben der

---

[1] Vgl. dazu Art. 30 Rn. 6. Zur nachträglichen Abänderung der vertraglichen Vereinbarung mittels konkludenten Verhaltens siehe Hof van Beroep Antwerpen, 24.4.2006, CISG-online 1258.

Pflicht des Verkäufers zur Lieferung der Ware steht.[2] Artt. 31 und 33, die Form, Ort und Zeit der Lieferung regeln, sind daher nicht anwendbar.[3] Das Übereinkommen hat darauf verzichtet, in Analogie hierzu eigene Bestimmungen im Hinblick auf die Dokumentenübergabe aufzustellen, und es bei einem Hinweis auf den Vertrag bewenden lassen.[4] Der Hinweis dient nur der systematischen Vollständigkeit; in der Sache sagt er nur etwas, was sich auch ohnedies von selbst verstünde.[5] Eine genaue Abgrenzung dessen, was Art. 34 S. 1 unter „Dokumenten" versteht, „die sich auf die Ware beziehen", ist angesichts des nur deklaratorischen Charakters der Bestimmung nicht erforderlich.[6] Zu nennen sind etwa:[7] Wertpapiere des Güterverkehrs (z. B. das Konnossement, der Lagerschein); Dokumente des Güterverkehrs ohne Wertpapiercharakter (wie z. B. das Frachtbriefdoppel, der Lieferschein oder Kaiteilschein); öffentlich-rechtliche Bescheinigungen, die der Käufer für die Einfuhr benötigt (z. B. Ursprungszeugnisse);[8] die Versicherungspolice;[9] die Rechnung.[10] Trifft der Vertrag keine ausdrückliche Regelung über Zeit, Ort und Form der Übergabe derartiger Dokumente, so ist auf die ergänzende Vertragsauslegung (Art. 8), auf die massgeblichen Gebräuche (Art. 9) und notfalls auf die allgemeinen Grundsätze des Übereinkommens (Art. 7 II) zurückzugreifen.

1a Nach diesen Grundsätzen ist auch zu bestimmen, ob der Verkäufer **elektronische Dokumente** verwenden kann.[11] Die Möglichkeit, Dokumente auf elektronischem Wege zu übertragen, wird in allen Klauseln der Incoterms® 2010 jeweils in der Regel A1 und B1 erwähnt. Vorausgesetzt wird entweder, dass sich die Parteien auf die elektronische Datenkommunikation geeinigt haben, oder dass dieser Übermittlungsweg einem allgemeinen Handelsbrauch entspricht.[12]

2. Ergänzende Vertragsauslegung

2 **a) Zeitpunkt der Übergabe.** Die im internationalen Handel üblichen Vertragsformulare und Vertragsklauseln enthalten häufig besondere Regeln hinsichtlich der Übergabezeit. Ist der Käufer verpflichtet, dem Verkäufer ein Dokumentenakkreditiv zu stellen, so ergibt sich aus der Laufzeit des Akkreditivs mittelbar auch die Frist, innerhalb derer der Verkäufer die Dokumente zu übergeben hat.[13] Ist der Verkäufer nach dem Kaufvertrag verpflichtet, die Lieferung dadurch zu bewirken, dass er die Ware dem Käufer innerhalb einer bestimmten Frist an einem bestimmten Ort zur Verfügung stellt, und benötigt der Käufer das Doku-

---

[2] Ausnahme: Verkauf schwimmender Ware und ähnliche Fälle; hier erfüllt der Verkäufer durch Übergabe des Dokuments zugleich seine Lieferpflicht. Vgl. Art. 31 Rn. 79.

[3] A. A. *Kröll u. a./Piltz*, Art. 34, Rn. 5.

[4] Übereinstimmend bereits Art. 50 EKG.

[5] Vgl. *Honnold/Flechtner*, Art. 34, Rn. 219: „This sentence merely states that the seller must perform the contract"; *Honsell/Ernst/Lauko*, Art. 34, Rn. 7.

[6] Vgl. auch *Dölle/Herber*, Art. 50 EKG, Rn. 4.

[7] Vgl. auch Sekretariatskommentar, Art. 32, Nr. 2; *Schlechtriem*, Seller's Obligations, S. 16 f.; *Herber/Czerwenka*, Art. 34, Rn. 3; *Reinhart*, Art. 34, Rn. 2; *Enderlein/Maskow/Strohbach*, Art. 34, Anm. 2.; *Honsell/Ernst/Lauko*, Art. 34, Rn. 4; *Staudinger/Magnus*, Art. 34, Rn. 7; *Piltz*, Internationales Kaufrecht, Rn. 4–76 ff.; MünchKomm/*Gruber*, Art. 34, Rn. 3; *Brunner*, Art. 34, Rn. 1.

[8] Vgl. Sekretariatskommentar, Art. 32, Nr. 2; *Dölle/Herber*, Art. 50 EKG, Rn. 5; *Soergel/Lüderitz*, Art. 50 EKG, Rn. 2; *Herber/Czerwenka*, Art. 34, Rn. 2.

[9] Vgl. Sekretariatskommentar, Art. 32, Nr. 2; Int. Ct. Ukrainian CCI, 5.7.2005, CISG-online 1361.

[10] So insbesondere im Fall der Klausel „Kasse gegen Dokumente" und bei Vereinbarung eines Dokumentenakkreditivs. Ob man auch *Gebrauchsanweisungen* und *technische Dokumentationen* (Pläne, Bauanleitungen etc.) unter Art. 34 subsumiert (so *Enderlein/Maskow/Strohbach*, Art. 34, Anm. 2.; *Loewe*, Art. 34, S. 54 f.; *Reinhart*, Art. 34, Rn. 2) oder ob man diese vielmehr als Teil der Ware betrachtet (so *Piltz*, Internationales Kaufrecht, Rn. 4–75; *Staudinger/Magnus*, Art. 34, Rn. 7; *Honsell/Ernst/Lauko*, Art. 34, Rn. 4; *Soergel/Lüderitz/Schüßler-Langeheine*, Art. 34, Rn. 3; *Achilles*, Art. 34, Rn. 1; *Bamberger/Roth/Saenger*, Art. 34, Rn. 3; MünchKomm/*Gruber*, Art. 34, Rn. 3; MünchKommHGB/*Benicke*, Art. 34, Rn. 3), ist letztlich unerheblich, denn das Recht des Verkäufers zur zweiten Andienung und die Untersuchungs- und Rügepflicht des Käufers greifen in beiden Fällen; unterschiedlich sind nur die Rechtsgrundlagen. Zur analogen Anwendung der Artt. 38 f. bei vertragswidrigen Dokumenten siehe unten Rn. 5.

[11] *Staudinger/Magnus*, Art. 34, Rn. 8; *Magnus*, Draft Digest, S. 328; vgl. auch *Brunner*, Art. 34, Rn. 2.

[12] Vgl. dazu *von Bernstorff*, Incoterms® 2010, 38 und 67.

[13] Vgl. auch *Honsell/Ernst/Lauko*, Art. 34, Rn. 8.

ment, um die Ware zu übernehmen, so muss der Verkäufer, auch wenn nichts Besonderes hierüber bestimmt ist, dem Käufer das Dokument so rechtzeitig übergeben, dass er die Ware noch innerhalb der Lieferfrist übernehmen kann. Beim Versendungskauf sind Dokumente, die der Käufer zum Empfang der Ware benötigt (wie Konnossement oder Ladeschein), nach Absendung der Ware so zu übergeben, dass der Käufer sie spätestens bei Eintreffen der Ware in der Hand hat.[14] Mangels besonderer Anhaltspunkte kann man es als allgemeinen Grundsatz des Übereinkommens (Art. 7 II) ansehen, dass der Verkäufer die Dokumente innerhalb „angemessener Frist" zu übergeben hat (Art. 33 lit. c)).[15]

b) Übergabeort. Ist nichts Besonderes vereinbart, so folgt der Übergabeort häufig aus der im Vertrag vereinbarten Modalität der Kaufpreiszahlung. Hat der Käufer ein **Dokumentenakkreditiv** zu stellen, so folgt hieraus, dass der Verkäufer die Dokumente am Ort der Niederlassung der Akkreditivbank oder der von ihr benannten Zahlstelle (d. h. ihrer Korrespondenzbank im Land des Verkäufers) zu übergeben hat.[16] Ist Zahlung **Kasse gegen Dokumente** vereinbart, so ist dies im Zweifel so zu verstehen, dass der Verkäufer dem Käufer die Dokumente an dessen Niederlassung zur Einlösung zu präsentieren hat.[17] Hat der Käufer eine Bank als Zahlstelle benannt, so ist Übergabeort für die Dokumente die Niederlassung der Bank. Bedient der Verkäufer sich in diesen Fällen für die Übermittlung der Dokumente und die Einziehung des Kaufpreises seinerseits der Hilfe von Banken (**„Dokumenteninkasso"**), so sind die Inkassobanken hinsichtlich der Übergabe der Dokumente seine Erfüllungsgehilfen (Art. 79 II). Die Gefahr der Übermittlung der Dokumente an den Übergabeort trifft den Verkäufer. Aber auch ohne besonderen Anhaltspunkt im Vertrag ist die Verpflichtung des Verkäufers, dem Käufer bestimmte Dokumente zu übergeben, im Zweifel so zu verstehen, dass der Verkäufer verpflichtet ist, die Dokumente auf **eigene Kosten und eigene Gefahr** dem Käufer zuzusenden, dass er also auf dem Übermittlungsweg verlorengegangene Dokumente wiederzubeschaffen und für Verzögerungen auf dem Übermittlungsweg einzustehen hat. Denn die Pflicht, dem Käufer Dokumente zu „übergeben", ist erst erfüllt, wenn der Käufer oder sein Beauftragter tatsächlich Besitz an den Dokumenten erlangt hat.[18] Eine analoge Anwendung der Artt. 31 lit. a), 67 ist insoweit nicht angebracht. Hat allerdings der Käufer die Ware gemäss Art. 31 lit. b), c) beim Verkäufer abzuholen, kann der Verkäufer ihm (oder seinem Beauftragten) bei dieser Gelegenheit die Dokumente übergeben, die zum Abtransport der Ware ins Bestimmungsland erforderlich sind (wie z. B. das Ursprungszeugnis oder die Rechnung).[19]

c) Form der Übergabe. Handelt es sich bei dem zu übergebenden Dokument um ein **Orderpapier**, so ist der Verkäufer verpflichtet, das Dokument dem Käufer in indossierter Form zu übergeben.[20] Bei Wertpapieren richtet sich die einzuhaltende Übergabeform im Einzelnen nach dem jeweils anwendbaren Wertpapierrecht. Ob überhaupt eine Pflicht des Verkäufers besteht, dem Käufer ein Dokument in Form eines umlauffähigen („negotiablen") Wertpapiers zu verschaffen, ist auf Grund des Vertrags und der Handelsbräuche zu entscheiden.[21] Eine allgemeine Regel in dieser Hinsicht lässt sich nicht aufstellen.[22]

---

[14] So auch *Bianca/Bonell/Lando*, Art. 34, Anm. 2.2.; vgl. auch *Enderlein/Maskow/Strohbach*, Art. 34, Anm. 3.; *Honsell/Ernst/Lauko*, Art. 34, Rn. 8; *Staudinger/Magnus*, Art. 34, Rn. 8; *Brunner*, Art. 34, Rn. 3.
[15] Ebenso *Neumayer/Ming*, Art. 34, Anm. 4.; *Honsell/Ernst/Lauko*, Art. 34, Rn. 8; *Brunner*, Art. 34, Rn. 3; MünchKomm/*Gruber*, Art. 34, Rn. 5; *Kröll u. a./Piltz*, Art. 34, Rn. 20, der darauf hinweist, dass die deutsche Übersetzung („Zeitpunkt") insofern zu eng sei.
[16] Ebenso *Neumayer/Ming*, Art. 34, Anm. 4. Vgl. dazu auch *Mohs*, Art. 57 Rn. 10.
[17] Vgl. dazu auch *Mohs*, Art. 57 Rn. 10; ebenso *Honsell/Ernst/Lauko*, Art. 34, Rn. 9.
[18] Ebenso *Honsell/Ernst/Lauko*, Art. 34, Rn. 9; *Achilles*, Art. 34, Rn. 3; MünchKommHGB/*Benicke*, Art. 34, Rn. 4; *Brunner*, Art. 34, Rn. 4. Vgl. auch *Soergel/Lüderitz/Schüßler-Langeheine*, Art. 34, Rn. 2: im Zweifel Übergabe am Käufersitz. Abweichend die 1. Aufl., *U. Huber*, Art. 34 Rn. 16; *Staudinger/Magnus*, Art. 34, Rn. 8; *Witz/Salger/Lorenz/Witz*, Art. 34, Rn. 6; MünchKomm/*Gruber*, Art. 34, Rn. 6.
[19] Vgl. auch *Honsell/Ernst/Lauko*, Art. 34, Rn. 9.
[20] Vgl. auch *Honsell/Ernst/Lauko*, Art. 34, Rn. 9.
[21] Vgl. dazu auch Incoterms® 2010 CFR und CIF A 8.
[22] Vgl. auch Art. 31 Rn. 59 zur Frage, ob der Käufer einen Anspruch darauf hat, dass ihm der Herausgabeanspruch gegen den Lagerhalter in wertpapiermässig verbriefter Form übertragen werde.

3. Rechtsfolgen der Nichterfüllung der Übergabepflicht

5 Erfüllt der Verkäufer seine Pflicht nicht, die vertraglich vorgeschriebenen Dokumente zur vorgesehenen Zeit, am vorgesehenen Ort und in der vorgesehenen Form zu übergeben, so bestimmen die Rechtsfolgen sich nach Artt. 45 ff. Das Recht, wegen der Nichtbeschaffung der vertragsmässigen Dokumente die **Vertragsaufhebung** zu erklären, steht dem Käufer nur zu, wenn die Voraussetzungen einer „wesentlichen Vertragsverletzung" gegeben sind (Art. 49 I lit. a) i. V. m. Art. 25).[23] Ein Recht, die Vertragsaufhebung ausserdem auch auf erfolglose Nachfristsetzung zu stützen, ist im Übereinkommen nicht vorgesehen,[24] kann sich aber in bestimmten Fällen aus einer analogen Anwendung des Art. 49 I lit. b) ergeben.[25] Übergibt der Verkäufer **vertragswidrige Dokumente,** so hat der Käufer – wenn das Recht des Verkäufers zur zweiten Andienung nach Artt. 34 S. 2, 48 nicht leerlaufen soll – die Dokumente **analog Artt. 38, 39 innerhalb einer angemessenen Frist zu untersuchen und rügen.**[26] In der Handelspraxis wird der Verkäufer, wenn Zahlung „Kasse gegen Dokumente" oder durch Dokumentenakkreditiv vereinbart ist, über die Vertragswidrigkeit der Dokumente regelmässig dadurch unterrichtet, dass der Käufer oder dessen Bank die Aufnahme und Bezahlung der Dokumente verweigert.[27] Ob die Aufnahme und Bezahlung eines vertragswidrigen Dokuments durch den Käufer als konkludentes Einverständnis des Käufers zu interpretieren ist, ist Frage des Einzelfalls.

4. Beweislast

5a Für das Bestehen einer Pflicht zur Übergabe von (bestimmten) Dokumenten ist der Käufer beweispflichtig.[28] Dagegen trägt der Verkäufer die Beweislast dafür, dass er dieser Pflicht auch nachgekommen ist.[29]

II. Recht zur zweiten Andienung (Art. 34 S. 2, 3)

1. Allgemeines

6 Art. 34 S. 2 will klarstellen, dass der Käufer, dem der Verkäufer vertragswidrige Dokumente andient, jedenfalls innerhalb der vertraglich vorgesehenen Frist für die Übergabe ein Recht zur „zweiten Andienung" hat. Hierdurch soll vor allem verhindert werden, dass der Käufer die in dem Angebot der vertragswidrigen Dokumente liegende Vertragsverletzung

---

[23] Für ein Anwendungsbeispiel vgl. Int. Ct. Ukrainian CCI, 5.7.2005, CISG-online 1361; hier hatte das Fehlen bestimmter Dokumente die Zollabfertigung bei der Einfuhr verunmöglicht. Allerdings stützte das Gericht das Vertragsaufhebungsrecht des Käufers noch auf zahlreiche weitere wesentliche Vertragsverletzungen des Verkäufers ab. Vgl. ferner BGH, 3.4.1996 (Kobaltsulfat), CISG-online 135 = BGHZ 132, 290, m. Anm. *Schlechtriem,* EWiR 1996, 597, wo der Verkäufer ein unzutreffendes Ursprungszeugnis übergeben hatte; der BGH verneinte die Wesentlichkeit der Vertragsverletzung mit der Begründung, dass sich die Käuferin ohne weiteres selber ein zutreffendes Zeugnis hätte beschaffen können.
[24] Anders das frühere Einheitskaufrecht, vgl. Art. 51 i. V. m. Art. 27 EKG.
[25] Vgl. dazu unten *Müller-Chen,* Art. 49 Rn. 18; a. A. MünchKomm/*Gruber,* Art. 34, Rn. 7.
[26] Ebenso *Schwenzer,* Art. 38 Rn. 7 m. w. N.; *Honnold/Flechtner,* Art. 34, Rn. 256; *Enderlein/Maskow/Strohbach,* Art. 39, Anm. 2; *Herber/Czerwenka,* Art. 34, Rn. 7; *Staudinger/Magnus,* Art. 34, Rn. 9, 18; *Soergel/Lüderitz/Schüßler-Langeheine,* Art. 34, Rn. 4; MünchKommHGB/*Benicke,* Art. 34, Rn. 9; *Brunner,* Art. 34, Rn. 5; anders *Honsell/Ernst/Lauko,* Art. 34, Rn. 14; *Bamberger/Roth/Saenger,* Art. 34, Rn. 5; *Witz/Salger/Lorenz/Witz,* Art. 34, Rn. 10; MünchKomm/*Gruber,* Art. 34, Rn. 7; anders auch die 3. Aufl., *U. Huber,* Art. 34 Rn. 5, wonach die verspätete Berufung auf die Vertragswidrigkeit aber immerhin im Einzelfall gegen Treu und Glauben verstossen könne; so auch *Achilles,* Art. 34, Rn. 7. Nach früherem Einheitskaufrecht ergab die Rügepflicht sich mittelbar durch die Verweisung des Art. 51 EKG auf Art. 49 EKG.
[27] Zur Frage des Zurückweisungsrechts des Käufers bei fehlender Wesentlichkeit der Vertragsverletzung siehe *Bridge,* International Sale of Goods, Rn. 3.24.
[28] Vgl. KG St. Gallen, 12.8.1997, CISG-online 330.
[29] Vgl. Int. Ct. Ukrainian CCI, 5.7.2005, CISG-online 1361; ebenso MünchKomm/*Gruber,* Art. 34, Rn. 11. Dagegen ist der Käufer dafür beweispflichtig, dass die übergebenen Dokumente fehlerhaft waren; vgl. unten Rn. 12a.

sofort zum Anlass nimmt, gemäss Artt. 49 I lit. a), 25 die Vertragsaufhebung wegen „wesentlicher Vertragsverletzung" zu erklären.[30] Dagegen soll das Recht des Käufers unberührt bleiben, gemäss Art. 45 I lit. b) Ersatz des durch die vertragswidrige Andienung entstandenen Schadens zu verlangen; dies wird durch Satz 3 klargestellt. Die Regelung hat ihr Vorbild in Art. 37, der ein entsprechendes Recht zur zweiten Andienung im Fall der Lieferung vertragswidriger Ware vorsieht.[31] Das Recht besteht nur bis zu dem Termin, zu dem die Dokumente nach dem Vertrag spätestens übergeben werden müssen.[32] Von da an kann der Verkäufer ein Recht zur zweiten Andienung nur noch auf die Bestimmung des Art. 48 stützen;[33] im Übrigen gelten die allgemeinen Bestimmungen über die Nichterfüllung von Vertragspflichten (Artt. 45 ff.).[34]

Unanwendbar ist die Regelung des Art. 34 S. 2, 3 – wie sich nach Art. 6 von selbst 7 versteht –, wenn etwas Abweichendes vereinbart ist. In manchen Geschäftszweigen, in denen es um Waren mit schwankendem Preis und daher um besondere spekulative Risiken geht, besteht der Handelsbrauch, dass der Verkäufer zur zweiten Andienung *nicht* berechtigt ist.[35] Solche Handelsbräuche sind nur unter den Voraussetzungen des Art. 9 massgeblich. Die allgemeine Einstellung des Übereinkommens ist eine andere.[36]

2. Einzelfragen

a) Vertragswidrigkeit der Dokumente. Der Verkäufer hat nach Art. 34 S. 2 grund- 8 sätzlich das Recht, „jede" Vertragswidrigkeit der von ihm übergebenen Dokumente zu beheben. Worin sie ihren Grund hat, ist gleichgültig. Beispiele sind: die Nichtübereinstimmung der Rechnung mit dem Vertragspreis;[37] die Übergabe eines Reedereikonnossements statt des geschuldeten Bordkonnossements; eines Rektakonnossements statt eines Orderkonnossements; eines Konnossements, aus dem sich ergibt, dass die Ware an Deck statt unter Deck verladen ist; eines „unreinen" Konnossements, aus dem hervorgeht, dass die an Bord genommene Ware oder ihre Verpackung beschädigt ist; eines Konnossements, aus dem sich ergibt, dass die Ware später als im Vertrag vorgesehen oder an einen anderen als dem vertraglich vorgeschriebenen Ort verschifft ist. Nicht vertragsgemäss ist die Transportversicherungspolice, wenn sie nicht den im Kaufvertrag vereinbarten Versicherungsbedingungen entspricht. Nicht vertragsgemäss sind Dokumente auch dann, wenn sie unvollständig sind, wenn also z. B. das Ursprungszeugnis oder die Konsulatsfaktura fehlt.[38]

b) Übergabe der vertragswidrigen Dokumente. Art. 34 S. 2 setzt voraus, dass der 9 Verkäufer die Dokumente „bereits vorher übergeben hat" (nämlich vor dem Termin, zu dem er sie spätestens hätte übergeben müssen).[39] Erfasst ist aber auch der Fall, dass er die Dokumente nur angeboten hat und dass der Käufer (oder die von ihm mit der Aufnahme der Dokumente und der Zahlung des Kaufpreises beauftragte Bank) die Dokumente wegen

---

[30] Vgl. auch *Neumayer/Ming,* Art. 34, Anm. 7.
[31] Sie ist erst auf der Wiener Konferenz auf Antrag Kanadas in das Übereinkommen eingefügt worden, als Ergänzung und Gegenstück zu Art. 37. Vgl. dazu *Schlechtriem,* Einheitliches UN-Kaufrecht, S. 55 f. = Uniform Sales Law, S. 66; O. R., S. 106, Art. 35, Nr. 2 ff. und S. 309 f. Zum entsprechenden Nachbesserungsrecht nach Art. 51 EKG i. V. m. Art. 44 EKG vgl. 1. Aufl., *U. Huber,* Art. 34 Rn. 8.
[32] Vgl. dazu oben Rn. 2.
[33] Vgl. *Herber/Czerwenka,* Art. 34, Rn. 6; *Enderlein/Maskow/Strohbach,* Art. 34, Anm. 5.; *Piltz,* Internationales Kaufrecht, Rn. 4–80; MünchKommHGB/*Benicke,* Art. 34, Rn. 5.
[34] Oben Rn. 5.
[35] Vgl. *Haage,* S. 93 ff.; kritisch und differenzierend *Großmann-Doerth,* Andienung, S. 103 ff.
[36] Vgl. auch *Honsell/Ernst/Lauko,* Art. 34, Rn. 20.
[37] Vgl. Comisión para la Protección del Comercio Exterior de México, 29.4.1996, CISG-online 350 = 17 J. L. & Com. (1998), 427.
[38] Vgl. *Honsell/Ernst/Lauko,* Art. 34, Rn. 13; *Soergel/Lüderitz/Schüßler-Langeheine,* Art. 34, Rn. 6; *Staudinger/Magnus,* Art. 34, Rn. 12.
[39] Vgl. oben Rn. 2.

ihrer vertragswidrigen Beschaffenheit **zurückgewiesen** hat.[40] Auch und gerade in diesem Fall steht dem Verkäufer das Recht zu, die Vertragswidrigkeit der Dokumente bis zum vertraglichen Übergabetermin durch „zweite Andienung" zu beheben.

10 **c) Behebung der Vertragswidrigkeit.** Der Verkäufer behebt die Vertragswidrigkeit, indem er fehlende Dokumente nachreicht oder indem er fehlerhafte Dokumente durch fehlerfreie ersetzt. Ist z. B. das Konnossement „unrein", weil es Hinweise auf Schäden der Ware oder auf Verpackungsmängel enthält, kann der Verkäufer ein neues Konnossement über andere Ware andienen, das keine solche Beanstandungen enthält. Weist das Konnossement ein verspätetes Abladedatum auf, kann der Verkäufer noch nachträglich Ware, die rechtzeitig abgeladen ist, als „schwimmende" Ware einkaufen und dem Käufer das über sie ausgestellte Konnossement andienen. Enthält die Transportversicherungspolice nicht vertragsmässige Versicherungsbedingungen, so mag der Verkäufer, falls das noch möglich ist, eine neue Versicherung abschliessen und dem Käufer die neue Police vorlegen. Solche Dokumente dürfen bis zum Ablauf der Übergabefrist vom Käufer nicht zurückgewiesen werden. Werden sie dagegen verspätet angeboten, greift Art. 48 ein.[41] Dass der Verkäufer den Fehler auch dadurch beheben kann, dass er das vertragswidrige Dokument „korrigiert" („berichtigt"),[42] kann man sich praktisch nur schwer vorstellen. Entweder ist er selbst der Aussteller; dann kann er ohne weiteres das fehlerhafte durch ein fehlerfreies Dokument ersetzen. Oder das Dokument ist durch einen Dritten ausgestellt; dann kommt eine „Korrektur" durch den Verkäufer nicht in Betracht.

11 **d) Unzumutbare Unannehmlichkeiten und unverhältnismässige Kosten.** Das Recht des Verkäufers zur Auswechselung oder Ergänzung der vertragswidrigen Dokumente steht unter dem Vorbehalt, dass seine Ausübung dem Käufer nicht „unzumutbare Unannehmlichkeiten" oder „unverhältnismäßige Kosten" verursacht. Der Vorbehalt ist übernommen der Bestimmung des Art. 37 S. 1, nach deren Vorbild Art. 34 S. 2 formuliert ist.[43] Im Fall des Art. 37, in dem es um die Behebung von Sachmängeln geht, hat der Vorbehalt seinen guten Sinn. Im Fall des Art. 34 wird er wohl keine praktische Bedeutung erlangen.[44] Man kann sich kaum vorstellen, dass eine zweite Andienung von Dokumenten Unannehmlichkeiten oder Kosten verursachen kann, die unzumutbar und unverhältnismässig sind.

12 **e) Schadensersatz (Satz 3).** Entsteht dem Käufer durch die erste, vertragswidrige Andienung der Dokumente ein Schaden, der sich durch die zweite, vertragsmässige Andienung der Dokumente nicht mehr beseitigen lässt, so „behält" der Käufer nach Satz 3 das Recht, Ersatz dieses Schadens zu verlangen. Grundlage des Schadensersatzanspruchs ist Art. 45 I lit. b), denn die Übergabe vertragswidriger Dokumente ist Vertragsverletzung. Art. 34 S. 3 stellt klar (ebenso wie die Parallelbestimmung des Art. 37 S. 2), dass der Käufer, indem er die nachgereichten vertragsmässigen Dokumente akzeptiert, auf diesen Schadensersatzanspruch nicht verzichtet. In Betracht kommen z. B. Kosten der Prüfung und Zurücksendung der vertragswidrigen Dokumente.[45] Denkbar ist auch, dass der Verkäufer dem Käufer die Versendung der Ware bereits angekündigt hat und dass der Käufer im Hinblick auf das bevorstehende Eintreffen der Ware Dispositionen getroffen hat, die er nach Erhalt des vertragswidrigen Dokuments wieder rückgängig gemacht hat.[46] Die hiermit verbunde-

---

[40] Ebenso *Neumayer/Ming*, Art. 34, Anm. 6.; *Honsell/Ernst/Lauko*, Art. 34, Rn. 15; MünchKommHGB/*Benicke*, Art. 34, Rn. 5. Vgl. auch die entsprechende Bestimmung des § 2–508 (1) UCC: „Where any tender or delivery by the seller is **rejected** because non-conforming and the time for performance has not yet expired, [...]" (Hervorhebung durch die Verfasserin).
[41] Oben Rn. 6.
[42] So *Honsell/Ernst/Lauko*, Art. 34, Rn. 15; *Staudinger/Magnus*, Art. 34, Rn. 13.
[43] Vgl. oben Fn. 30.
[44] Vgl. auch *Herber/Czerwenka*, Art. 34, Rn. 6; *Soergel/Lüderitz/Schüßler-Langeheine*, Art. 34, Rn. 6; *Neumayer/Ming*, Art. 34, Anm. 6.; *Honsell/Ernst/Lauko*, Art. 34, Rn. 17; *Staudinger/Magnus*, Art. 34, Rn. 15; MünchKommHGB/*Benicke*, Art. 34, Rn. 6; MünchKomm/*Gruber*, Art. 34, Rn. 8; *Brunner*, Art. 34, Rn. 6.
[45] Vgl. *Karollus*, S. 114; *Honsell/Ernst/Lauko*, Art. 34, Rn. 19; *Neumayer/Ming*, Art. 34, Anm. 7.
[46] Vgl. *Karollus*, S. 114; *Honsell/Ernst/Lauko*, Art. 34, Rn. 19.

nen Kosten muss der Verkäufer ersetzen, auch wenn er den eigentlichen Fehler durch Übersendung eines zweiten, vertragsmässigen Konnossements noch beheben kann.

f) Beweislast. Die Fehlerhaftigkeit der Dokumente hat der Käufer zu beweisen; dagegen ist der Verkäufer dafür beweispflichtig, dass die geschuldeten Dokumente vollständig übergeben wurden.[47] Der Verkäufer trägt auch die Beweislast dafür, dass er eine bestehende Vertragswidrigkeit rechtzeitig behoben hat. Beruft sich der Käufer darauf, dass die zweite Andienung „unzumutbare Unannehmlichkeiten" oder „unverhältnismässige Kosten" verursacht hätte, ist er hierfür beweispflichtig.[48]

III. Gerichtsstand

Soweit die Verpflichtung zur Übergabe der Dokumente „Bringschuld" ist, insbesondere aber im Fall der Vereinbarung der Klausel „Kasse gegen Dokumente" mit Angabe einer Bank im Käuferland als Zahlstelle,[49] kann dies für den Verkäufer Konsequenzen hinsichtlich des **Gerichtsstands** haben. Erfüllungsort ist hier die Niederlassung der vom Käufer als Zahlstelle benannten Bank. Soweit für das dortige Gericht der Gerichtsstand des Erfüllungsorts die internationale und örtliche Zuständigkeit begründet (etwa nach § 29 ZPO, Art. 113 IPRG), kann daher der Käufer den Verkäufer, ausser an dessen (Wohn-)Sitz als dem allgemeinen Gerichtsstand, auch am Sitz der Zahlstelle als dem Gerichtsstand des Erfüllungsorts verklagen. Die Zuständigkeit des Gerichts beschränkt sich allerdings auf Klagen, die darauf gestützt sind, dass gerade die Pflicht zur rechtzeitigen und vollständigen Übergabe vertragsmässiger Dokumente verletzt ist.[50] Für Klagen, die auf andere Vertragsverletzungen gestützt sind, z. B. auf Mängel der gelieferten Sache, ist das Gericht des Übergabeorts der Dokumente nicht zuständig. Grundsätzlich[51] keinen eigenständigen Gerichtsstand des Übergabeorts gibt es dagegen nach der **EuGVO** und dem revidierten **LuganoÜ** vom 30. Oktober 2007. Denn nach Art. 5 Nr. 1 EuGVO/rev. LuganoÜ ist das Gericht am tatsächlichen Erfüllungsort der *Lieferpflicht* zur Beurteilung *aller* Vertragsverletzungen, einschliesslich solcher betreffend Dokumentenübergabe, zuständig.[52]

---

[47] Oben Rn. 5a.
[48] Ebenso MünchKomm/*Gruber,* Art. 34, Rn. 11.
[49] Oben Rn. 3.
[50] Vgl. hierzu U. Huber in der 3. Aufl., Art. 45 Rn. 66.
[51] Eine Ausnahme greift dann, wenn der tatsächliche Erfüllungsort der Lieferpflicht nicht in einem Mitgliedstaat, also z. B. in den USA liegt; diesfalls kommt es, wie schon nach Art. 5 Nr. 1 EuGVÜ, auf den Erfüllungsort der *jeweils streitigen Verpflichtung* an, siehe oben Art. 31 Rn. 99, 89.
[52] Vgl. oben Art. 31 Rn. 93.

Abschnitt II. Vertragsmäßigkeit der Ware sowie Rechte oder Ansprüche Dritter

Art. 35 [Vertragsmäßigkeit der Ware]

(1) **Der Verkäufer hat Ware zu liefern, die in Menge, Qualität und Art sowie hinsichtlich Verpackung oder Behältnis den Anforderungen des Vertrages entspricht.**

(2) **Haben die Parteien nichts anderes vereinbart, so entspricht die Ware dem Vertrag nur,**
a) wenn sie sich für die Zwecke eignet, für die Ware der gleichen Art gewöhnlich gebraucht wird;
b) wenn sie sich für einen bestimmten Zweck eignet, der dem Verkäufer bei Vertragsabschluß ausdrücklich oder auf andere Weise zur Kenntnis gebracht wurde, sofern sich nicht aus den Umständen ergibt, daß der Käufer auf die Sachkenntnis und das Urteilsvermögen des Verkäufers nicht vertraute oder vernünftigerweise nicht vertrauen konnte;
c) wenn sie die Eigenschaften einer Ware besitzt, die der Verkäufer dem Käufer als Probe oder Muster vorgelegt hat;
d) wenn sie in der für Ware dieser Art üblichen Weise oder, falls es eine solche Weise nicht gibt, in einer für die Erhaltung und den Schutz der Ware angemessenen Weise verpackt ist.

(3) **Der Verkäufer haftet nach Absatz 2 Buchstaben a bis d nicht für eine Vertragswidrigkeit der Ware, wenn der Käufer bei Vertragsabschluß diese Vertragswidrigkeit kannte oder darüber nicht in Unkenntnis sein konnte.**

Art. 35

(1) The seller must deliver goods which are of the quantity, quality and description required by the contract and which are contained or packaged in the manner required by the contract.

(2) Except where the parties have agreed otherwise, the goods do not conform with the contract unless they:
(a) are fit for the purposes for which goods of the same description would ordinarily be used;
(b) are fit for any particular purpose expressly or impliedly made known to the seller at the time of the conclusion of the contract, except where the circumstances show that the buyer did not rely, or that it was unreasonable for him to rely, on the seller's skill and judgement;
(c) possess the qualities of goods which the seller has held out to the buyer as a sample or model;
(d) are contained or packaged in the manner usual for such goods or, where there is no such manner, in a manner adequate to preserve and protect the goods.

(3) The seller is not liable under subparagraphs (a) to (d) of the preceding paragraph for any lack of conformity of the goods if at the time of the conclusion of the contract the buyer knew or could not have been unaware of such lack of conformity.

Art. 35

1) Le vendeur doit livrer des marchandises dont la quantité, la qualité et le type répondent à ceux qui sont prévus au contrat et dont l'emballage ou le conditionnement correspond à celui qui est prévu au contrat.

2) A moins que les parties n'en soient convenues autrement, les marchandises ne sont conformes au contrat que si:
a) elles sont propres aux usages auxquels serviraient habituellement des marchandises du même type;
b) elles sont propres à tout usage spécial qui a été porté expressément ou tacitement à la connaissance du vendeur au moment de la conclusion du contrat, sauf s'il résulte des circonstances que l'acheteur ne s'en est pas remis à la compétence ou à l'appréciation du vendeur ou qu'il n'était pas raisonnable de sa part de le faire;
c) elles possèdent les qualités d'une marchandise que le vendeur a présentée à l'acheteur comme échantillon ou modèle;
d) elles sont emballées ou conditionnées selon le mode habituel pour les marchandises du même type ou, à défaut de mode habituel, d'une manière propre à les conserver et à les protéger.

3) Le vendeur n'est pas responsable, au regard des alinéas a) à d) du paragraphe précédent, d'un défaut de conformité que l'acheteur connaissait ou ne pouvait ignorer au moment de la conclusion du contrat.

Übersicht

	Rn.
I. Vorgeschichte	1
II. Allgemeines	4
1. Vergleich zur Sachmängelhaftung nach nationalen Rechtsordnungen	4
2. Vertragsmässigkeit und Rechtsmängel	5
III. Voraussetzungen der Vertragsmässigkeit	6
1. Vertragliche Leistungsbeschreibung – Abs. 1	6
a) Quantitätsabweichungen	8
b) Qualitätsabweichungen	9
c) Artabweichungen	10
d) Verpackung oder Behältnis	11
2. Subsidiäre Bestimmung der Vertragsmässigkeit – Abs. 2	12
a) Eignung für gewöhnlichen Gebrauchszweck – Abs. 2 a)	13
b) Eignung für bestimmten Gebrauchszweck – Abs. 2 b)	18
c) Kauf nach Probe oder Muster – Abs. 2 c)	24
d) Übliche oder angemessene Verpackung – Abs. 2 d)	28
3. Unerhebliche Abweichungen	32
4. Gemischte Verträge	32a
5. Auf den Käufer zurückzuführende Vertragswidrigkeit	33
IV. Haftungsausschluss	34
1. Kenntnis des Käufers – Abs. 3	34
2. Unterlassene Anzeige	40
3. Freizeichnung	41
V. Rechtsbehelfe	43
1. Nach CISG	43
2. Nach nationalem Recht	44
a) Irrtumsanfechtung	45
b) Fahrlässige Falschangaben	47
c) Arglist oder Betrug	48
VI. Beweisfragen	49
1. Allgemeines, Regelungsbereich	49
2. Beweisgegenstand	50
3. Beweislast	51
a) Vertragswidrigkeit gemäss Abs. 1	52
b) Vertragswidrigkeit gemäss Abs. 2	53
c) Ausschluss der Haftung gemäss Abs. 3	54
4. Beweismass	55

Vorläufer und **Entwürfe:** Artt. 33, 36 EKG, Genfer E 1976 Art. 19, Wiener E 1977 Art. 19, New Yorker E 1978 Art. 33.

I. Vorgeschichte

Art. 35 umschreibt die **Vertragsmässigkeit der Ware** unter Ausschluss der Rechts- **1** mängel und Belastung mit gewerblichen Schutzrechten Dritter, die in Artt. 41, 42 geregelt sind. In der Sache entspricht Art. 35 weitgehend Art. 33 EKG. Die Vorschrift ist jedoch wesentlich einfacher und präziser gefasst als ihr Vorläufer. Die Grundregel, dass die Ware den vertraglichen Vereinbarungen entsprechen muss, steht nunmehr am Anfang; in Art. 33 I f) EKG erschien sie als subsidiäre Auffangregel.

Unterschiede zwischen Art. 35 und Art. 33 EKG bestehen einmal im Hinblick auf die **2** **dogmatische Einordnung** der Vertragswidrigkeit. Während nach Art. 33 EKG fehlende Vertragsmässigkeit der Ware automatisch eine gleichzeitige Verletzung der Lieferpflicht bedeutete, bleibt nach CISG bei Vertragswidrigkeit die Lieferung unberührt, der Käufer hat jedoch die Rechtsbehelfe nach Artt. 45 ff.[1] Ein weiterer Unterschied besteht darin, dass

---

[1] Vgl. Sekretariatskommentar, Art. 33, Nr. 2, 3.

Art. 33 II EKG, der **unerhebliche Abweichungen** für irrelevant erklärte, weggefallen ist.² Man sah für eine solche Vorschrift keine Berechtigung, wenn Vertragsaufhebung nur bei wesentlicher Vertragsverletzung möglich ist.³ Ein australischer Antrag, eine dem Art. 33 II EKG entsprechende Bestimmung wieder aufzunehmen, wurde auf der diplomatischen Konferenz abgelehnt.⁴ Zurückgezogen wurde ein von der kanadischen Delegation auf der Konferenz eingebrachter Vorschlag, wonach die Anforderungen an die normale und besondere Geeignetheit der Ware nur auf professionelle Verkäufer anwendbar sein und die Massstäbe der normalen Eignung der Ware präziser gefasst werden sollten.⁵

3   Art. 35 III lehnt sich an Art. 36 EKG an. Dort war jedoch der Kauf nach Probe und Muster von der Ausschlussregelung nicht erfasst.

II. Allgemeines

1. Vergleich zur Sachmängelhaftung nach nationalen Rechtsordnungen⁶

4   Art. 35 geht von einem **einheitlichen Begriff** der Vertragswidrigkeit aus. Darunter fallen nicht nur **Qualitätsabweichungen,** sondern auch **Quantitätsabweichungen,** die Lieferung eines **aliud** und **Verpackungsfehler.** Damit unterscheidet sich das CISG entscheidend von den meisten nationalen Regelungen zur Sachgewährleistung, die auf oftmals subtilen Differenzierungen aufbauen. Grundsätzlich⁷ keine Bedeutung kommt der aus dem Schweizer Recht bekannten Unterscheidung zwischen einfacher Sacheigenschaft und Zusicherung,⁸ sowie der auch noch im österreichischen Recht relevanten Unterscheidung zwischen peius und aliud bzw. genehmigungsfähigem und nicht genehmigungsfähigem aliud zu.⁹ Auch die französische Unterscheidung zwischen vice caché und vice apparent¹⁰ hat keinen Eingang in das CISG gefunden.¹¹ Schliesslich differenziert Art. 35 auch nicht wie etwa das englische Recht zwischen conditions und warranties¹² oder wie das US-amerikanische Recht zwischen express und implied warranties.¹³ Bei der Auslegung des Begriffs der Vertragsmässigkeit muss dies im Auge behalten werden (Art. 7 I), da sonst die Gefahr besteht, dass jeder Richter Art. 35 i. S. der Einordnung der Gewährleistung im eigenen nationalen Recht begreift und Auslegungsdivergenzen die Rechtsvereinheitlichung in Frage stellen.¹⁴ Die skandinavischen Kaufgesetze sowie später die EG-Verbrauchskaufsrichtlinie, der OHADA AUDCG¹⁵ und nun auch das CESL¹⁶ haben demgegenüber den einheitlichen Begriff der Vertragswidrigkeit aus Art. 35 übernommen.¹⁷ Deutschland, die

---

² Vgl. YB IV (1973), S. 64, Nr. 43.
³ Vgl. YB IV (1973), S. 44, Nr. 61 Fn. 8.
⁴ Vgl. O. R., S. 104, Nr. 6, S. 308 f., Nr. 29 ff.
⁵ Vgl. O. R., S. 103, 315, Nr. 45.
⁶ Vgl. dazu ausführlich *Schwenzer/Hachem/Kee,* Rn. 31.26 ff.
⁷ Vgl. aber unten Art. 36 Rn. 7 ff.
⁸ Vgl. Art. 197 OR, dazu BGer, 22.12.2000, CISG-online 628.
⁹ Vgl. dazu unten Rn. 10.
¹⁰ Vgl. Artt. 1641, 1642 Cc.
¹¹ Ausdrücklich so Trib. com. Montargis, 6.10.2000, CISG-online 577.
¹² Vgl. sec. 14, 15, 15A SGA; allerdings ist der Begriff der wesentlichen Vertragsverletzung dem Bruch einer condition nicht unähnlich, vgl. *Nickel/Saenger,* JZ 1991, 1050, 1051 und allgemein *Benjamin,* Rn. 10–029.
¹³ Vgl. §§ 2–313 ff. UCC; verschiedene amerikanische Autoren glauben allerdings, in Art. 35 I die express warranties, in Art. 35 II die implied warranties des UCC wiederzufinden, vgl. *Hyland,* Conformity of Goods, S. 308 ff., 312; vgl. auch *DiMatteo/Dhooge/Greene/Maurer/Pagnattaro,* International Sales Law, S. 107 ff.
¹⁴ Vgl. *Hyland,* Conformity of Goods, S. 327; *Murray,* Primer, S. 892.
¹⁵ Vgl. Art. 255 AUDCG; allerdings enthält Art. 259 AUDCG die aus dem französischen Recht übernommene Unterscheidung zwischen vice caché und vice apparent, was zu nicht unerheblichen inneren Widersprüchen führt, dazu auch *Schwenzer/Hachem/Kee,* Rn. 31.39, 31.41; *Schroeter,* Recht in Afrika 2001, 163, 167 f.
¹⁶ Vgl. Artt. 99, 100 CESL-Entwurf.
¹⁷ Vgl. Norwegen: § 17 KaufG 1988; Schweden: § 17 KaufG 1990; Finnland: § 17 KaufG 1991; vgl. dazu *Henschel,* FS Kritzer, S. 177, 187 ff.

Niederlande sowie einige osteuropäische und zentralasiatische Staaten sehen in der Sache weitgehend entsprechende Regelungen vor.[18]

2. Vertragsmässigkeit und Rechtsmängel

Wie in allen nationalen Rechtsordnungen sowie im EKG behält das CISG die Differenzierung zwischen Vertragsmässigkeit im Hinblick auf Sachmängel einerseits und Einstehenmüssen für Rechtsmängel andererseits (Art. 41) bei. Die **Abgrenzung zwischen Sach- und Rechtsmangel** ist zwar im Hinblick auf allfällige Rechtsbehelfe nur von geringer Relevanz;[19] sie erlangt aber vor allem Bedeutung im Hinblick auf den Haftungsausschluss bei Kenntnis des Käufers. Nach Art. 35 III schadet dem Käufer bereits das Nicht-in-Unkenntnis-Sein-Können, während die Rechtsmängelhaftung nur bei Einwilligung des Käufers ausgeschlossen ist.[20] Auch ist die Ausschlussfrist von zwei Jahren – Art. 39 II – nur auf Sachmängel, nicht jedoch auf Rechtsmängel anwendbar. Wenngleich im Einzelfall die Abgrenzung nicht immer leicht sein mag, so wird man doch generalisierend davon ausgehen dürfen, dass die Haftung für Vertragsmässigkeit immer dort eingreift, wo es um **konkrete Eigenschaften** der Ware oder der Verpackung geht; Rechtsmängel werden hingegen zumeist ihre Grundlage in der **Vorgeschichte** der Ware oder einem Verhalten des Verkäufers haben.[21] Unproblematisch ist die Abgrenzung zwischen Art. 35 und der Haftung wegen Belastung mit Schutzrechten (Art. 42), da dort Anknüpfungspunkt das von einem Dritten behauptete Schutzrecht ist.

III. Voraussetzungen der Vertragsmässigkeit

1. Vertragliche Leistungsbeschreibung – Abs. 1

Nach Abs. 1 sind zunächst die vertraglichen Vereinbarungen zu berücksichtigen. Primär kommt es also auf die im konkreten Vertrag durch quantitative und qualitative Daten und Beschreibungen festgelegten Eigenschaften an.[22] Art. 35 I geht also von einem **subjektiven Fehlerbegriff**[23] aus, wie er von der h. M. zum deutschen Recht angenommen[24] und auch in anderen Rechtsordnungen vertreten wird.[25]

Die vertragliche Festlegung ist anhand von Art. 8 zu bestimmen.[26] Sie kann **ausdrücklich** aber auch **stillschweigend** erfolgen.[27] Eine stillschweigende Vereinbarung dürfte vor allem bei Bezugnahme auf bestimmte Standards vorliegen (z. B. DIN-Normen).[28] Dasselbe

---

[18] Deutschland: § 434 BGB; Niederlande: Art. 7:17 BW; Georgien: Art. 488 ZGB; Litauen: Art. 6.333 ZGB; Tschechien: Art. 412 HGB; Turkmenistan: Art. 512 ZGB. Vgl. zu Osteuropa und Zentralasien auch *Lapiashvili*, S. 202.
[19] Vgl. aber Artt. 46 II und III, 50; vgl. dazu auch Art. 41 Rn. 20.
[20] Vgl. unten Art. 41 Rn. 19 f.
[21] Zur Abgrenzung bei öffentlich-rechtlichen Belastungen vgl. auch unten Art. 41 Rn. 5 ff.; *Heilmann*, S. 143.
[22] Vgl. *Schlechtriem*, Internationales UN-Kaufrecht, Rn. 133; *Staudinger/Magnus*, Art. 35, Rn. 10, 13; *Herber/Czerwenka*, Art. 35, Rn. 3; *Reinhart*, Art. 35, Rn. 2; *Karollus*, S. 116; *Enderlein/Maskow/Strohbach*, Art. 35, Anm. 1.; *Welser*, S. 108; *Heuzé*, Anm. 289.
[23] Vgl. demgegenüber Art. 2 II d) EG-RL zu bestimmten Aspekten des Verbrauchsgüterkaufs und der Garantien für Verbrauchsgüter v. 25.5.1999, ABlEG Nr. L 171/12 v. 7.7.1999; zum Entwurf vgl. *Schlechtriem*, JZ 1997, 441, 444 f.
[24] Vgl. *Hoeren/Martinek/Malzer*, § 434, Rn. 8; *Schlechtriem*, SchuldR BT, Rn. 33. Für das CISG folgen dem *Flesch*, S. 132; *Karollus*, S. 116; *Ben Abderrahmane*, Dr. prat. com. int. 1989, 551, 553; *Hutter*, S. 30; *Heilmann*, S. 166; *Reinhart*, Art. 35, Rn. 2; *Herber/Czerwenka*, Art. 35, Rn. 3; *Honsell*, SJZ 1992, 345, 350 mit zahlreichen Beispielen.
[25] Vgl. *Hyland*, Conformity of Goods, S. 319; vgl. für das französische Recht: *Ben Abderrahmane*, Dr. prat. com. int. 1989, 551, 553; für die Schweiz: vgl. *Honsell*, OR BT, S. 74; für Österreich: vgl. *Koziol/Welser*, S. 253 („konkreter Fehlerbegriff"); weitergehend rechtsvergleichend *Schwenzer/Hachem/Kee*, Rn. 31.46 ff.
[26] Vgl. BGer, 22.12.2000, CISG-online 628; P. *Huber/Mullis/Mullis*, S. 131. Zur Begründung der Anwendbarkeit von Art. 8 vgl. oben *Schmidt-Kessel*, Art. 8 Rn. 3.
[27] Vgl. *Staudinger/Magnus*, Art. 35, Rn. 13; *Herber/Czerwenka*, Art. 35, Rn. 3; *Enderlein/Maskow/Strohbach*, Art. 35, Anm. 1.; *Reinhart*, Art. 35, Rn. 2; *Ferrari u. a./Ferrari*, Internationales Vertragsrecht, Art. 35, Rn. 6; *Koch*, IHR 2009, 233, 235; a. A. *Posch*, Pflichten des Käufers, S. 151; *Hyland*, Conformity of Goods, S. 308.
[28] Vgl. für das deutsche Recht *Schlechtriem*, SchuldR BT, Rn. 38.

gilt für bestimmte Herstellungspraktiken bei Bezugnahme auf internationale Vereinbarungen (UN Global Compact,[29] Atlanta Agreement[30] etc.). Die vertragliche Festlegung nach Abs. 1 kann individuell ausgehandelt sein, sie kann sich aber auch aus **AGB** sowohl des Verkäufers als auch des Käufers ergeben. Auch die **Werbung** des Verkäufers, in der er z. B. auf bestimmte Eigenschaften der Ware hinweist,[31] oder vom Käufer bereitgestellte Muster[32] können zur Bestimmung der Vertragsmässigkeit nach Abs. 1 herangezogen werden. Schliesslich können sich Beschaffenheitsvereinbarungen auch aus Angaben des Verkäufers, die auf Grund von Informationspflichten gemacht wurden, ergeben.[33] **Gebräuche** und **Gepflogenheiten** sind nach Art. 9 zu berücksichtigen.[34]

8   **a) Quantitätsabweichungen.** Der Verkäufer hat Waren zu liefern, deren Menge den Anforderungen des Vertrages entspricht. Dabei sind allerdings handelsübliche Abweichungen, wie sie in verschiedenen Branchen gelten,[35] nicht als Vertragswidrigkeit anzusehen.[36] Jede Quantitätsabweichung, d. h. sowohl eine **Zuviel-** als auch eine **Zuwenig-Lieferung**, stellt eine Vertragswidrigkeit i. S. des Abs. 1 dar[37] und muss deshalb vom Käufer nach Art. 39 gerügt werden.[38] Dies gilt auch, wenn sich die Quantitätsabweichung bereits aus den Dokumenten ergibt.[39] Auch in diesem Fall liegt eine Vertragswidrigkeit und nicht partielle Nichtlieferung und ggf. Teilverzug vor.[40] Allenfalls kann sich der Verkäufer hier wegen Art. 40 (Kenntnis der Vertragswidrigkeit) nicht auf ein Unterlassen der Rüge durch den Käufer berufen. Im Einzelfall mag die Abgrenzung von Quantitäts- und Qualitätsabweichung schwierig sein.[41] Aufgrund der Gleichsetzung in Art. 35 ist diese Abgrenzung indes nicht erforderlich.

9   **b) Qualitätsabweichungen.** Unter Qualität sind neben der physischen Beschaffenheit[42] alle tatsächlichen und rechtlichen Verhältnisse zu verstehen, die die Beziehung der Sache zur Umwelt betreffen.[43] Ob sie wegen ihrer Art und Dauer die **Brauchbarkeit** oder den

---

[29] http://www.unglobalcompact.org/AboutTheGC/TheTenPrinciples/index.html.
[30] http://www.imacpak.org/atlanta.htm.
[31] Ähnlich *Bianca/Bonell/Bianca*, Art. 35, Anm. 2.3.; vgl. auch Art. 2 II d) EG-RL zu bestimmten Aspekten des Verbrauchsgüterkaufs und der Garantien für Verbrauchsgüter v. 25.5.1999, ABlEG Nr. L 171/12 v. 7.7.1999.
[32] LG Aschaffenburg, 20.4.2006, CISG-online 1446 = IHR 2007, 109, 112, wobei unklar bleibt, ob sich das Gericht letztlich auf Art. 35 I oder Art. 35 II stützt.
[33] Vgl. *Schlechtriem*, Internationales UN-Kaufrecht, Rn. 42c; *Wilhelmsson*, S. 255 unter 1.; für den Kunsthandel *Mosimann/Müller-Chen*, FS Schwenzer, S. 1303, 1315.
[34] Vgl. Polimeles Protodikio Athinon, 2009, CISG-online 2228; *Kröll u. a./Kröll*, Art. 35, Rn. 54.
[35] Vgl. etwa *Hutter*, S. 31, wonach die deutschen Einheitsbedingungen im Getreidehandel eine fünfprozentige Mengentoleranz zulassen. Die GAFTA 100 lassen eine zweiprozentige Abweichung zu, vgl. dazu *Winsor*, 14 VJ (2010), 83, 93. Allgemein zu internationalen Standardbedingungen *Fontaine*, Recht des internationalen Warenkaufs, S. 1193.
[36] So *Stumpf*, 1. Aufl., Art. 35 Rn. 18; *Staudinger/Magnus*, Art. 35, Rn. 11; *Soergel/Lüderitz/Schüßler-Langeheine*, Art. 35, Rn. 7; *Heuzé*, Anm. 289. *Reinhart*, Art. 35, Rn. 3, begründet dies mit Hinweis auf Artikel 9; vgl. dazu ICC, 9083/1999, CISG-online 706 = 11:2 ICC Int. Ct. Arb. Bull. (2000), 78.
[37] *P. Huber/Mullis/Mullis*, S. 131.
[38] Vgl. BGer, 7.7.2004, CISG-online 848, E. 2.1; LG Landshut, 5.4.1995, CISG-online 193; *Schlechtriem*, Internationales UN-Kaufrecht, Rn. 134, 192a; *Staudinger/Magnus*, Art. 35, Rn. 15; auch *Heilmann*, S. 171 f. Zu den Folgen der Rügeversäumung bei Quantitätsabweichung vgl. unten Art. 39 Rn. 30. A. A. zu Unrecht Civ. 1, 4.1.1995, CISG-online 138 = RIW 1995, 811 = UNILEX unter Hinweis auf Art. 86.
[39] Vgl. OLG Rostock, 25.9.2002, CISG-online 672 = IHR 2003, 19, 20.
[40] A. A. *Enderlein/Maskow/Strohbach*, Art. 35, Anm. 3.; *Witz/Salger/Lorenz/Salger*, Art. 35, Rn. 6. Wie hier dagegen *Piltz*, Internationales Kaufrecht, Rn. 5–33; *Herber/Czerwenka*, Art. 35, Rn. 2; *Reinhart*, Art. 35, Rn. 2; *Audit*, Vente internationale, Anm. 99.; *Niggemann*, Pflichten des Verkäufers, S. 83; *Aue*, Mängelgewährleistung im UN-Kaufrecht, S. 71; MünchKomm/*Gruber*, Art. 35, Rn. 7; *Henschel*, Conformity of Goods, S. 155.
[41] Vgl. *Henschel*, Conformity of Goods, S. 154 f.
[42] Vgl. Civ. 1, 23.1.1996, CISG-online 159 = D. 1996, 334, m. Anm. *Witz* = J. C. P. 1996, II, 2234, und m. Anm. *Muir Watt*: gezuckerter Wein; LG Aachen, 3.4.1990, CISG-online 12 = RIW 1990, 491: Lieferung von Schuhen mit fünf Nieten an der Spitze statt gänzlich ohne Nieten; LG Landshut, 5.4.1995, CISG-online 193: übermässiges Einlaufen von Kleidungsstücken; weitere Beispiele bei *Henschel*, Conformity of Goods, S. 156 ff.
[43] *P. Huber/Mullis/Mullis*, S. 132. Vgl. auch *Schwenzer*, Physical Features, S. 103 ff.

Vertragsmäßigkeit der Ware   10   **Art. 35**

Wert der Sache beeinflussen, ist im Rahmen der Vertragsmässigkeit nach Abs. 1 nicht relevant.[44] Diese Frage stellt sich erst, wenn es etwa bei Vertragsaufhebung um die Wesentlichkeit des Vertragsbruches oder im Rahmen des Schadenersatzes um den vom Käufer erlittenen Schaden geht. Jede Qualitätsabweichung – gleichgültig, ob es sich im Vergleich zu den Bestimmungen des Vertrages um **mindere** oder um **bessere Qualität** handelt – stellt eine Vertragswidrigkeit dar[45] und muss vom Käufer nach Art. 39 gerügt werden.[46] Zu den Qualitätsmerkmalen gehört auch die vereinbarte Herkunft der Ware.[47] Dasselbe gilt für die Einhaltung bestimmter Standards bei der Herstellung, insbesondere von Good Manufacturing Practices,[48] grundlegenden ethischen Prinzipien[49] oder religiösen Produktionsvorgaben.[50] Im Einzelfall können auch fehlende Dokumente eine Qualitätsabweichung darstellen.[51] Auch im Hinblick auf die Qualität sind jedoch handelsübliche Abweichungen, wie sie in verschiedenen Branchen gelten, nicht als vertragswidrig anzusehen.[52]

c) Artabweichungen. Nach CISG stellt auch jede Artabweichung – mag sie auch noch   10
so krass sein – eine Vertragswidrigkeit i. S. des Art. 35 dar.[53] Die vor allem in Österreich und

---

[44] Vgl. auch *Piltz*, Internationales Kaufrecht, Rn. 5–31. A. A. *Stumpf*, 1. Aufl., Art. 35 Rn. 19. Zur Frage der unerheblichen Abweichungen vgl. unten Rn. 33.

[45] Vgl. auch *P. Huber/Mullis/Mullis*, S. 132; *Ferrari u. a./Ferrari*, Internationales Vertragsrecht, Art. 35, Rn. 8.

[46] Zu den Rechtsfolgen bei Unterlassung der Rüge im Falle von Lieferung von Ware besserer Qualität vgl. unten Art. 39 Rn. 30.

[47] Vgl. BGH, 3.4.1996 (Kobaltsulfat), CISG-online 135 = BGHZ 132, 290, m. Anm. *Schlechtriem*, EWiR 1996, 597; OLG Zweibrücken, 2.2.2004, CISG-online 877, E. II. 6; *Schwenzer*, Physical Features, S. 103, 106; *P. Huber/Mullis/Mullis*, S. 132; *Witz/Salger/Lorenz/Salger*, Art. 35, Rn. 8.

[48] Diese sind z. B. in den Verordnungen der EU für Produktgruppen, die mit der CE-Kennzeichnung versehen sein müssen, enthalten: vgl. etwa Elektrische Betriebsmittel (72/23/EWG); Einfache Druckbehälter (87/404/EWG); Spielzeug (88/378/EWG); Bauprodukte (89/106/EWG); Persönliche Schutzausrüstungen (89/686/EWG); Gasverbrauchseinrichtungen (90/396/EWG); Warmwasserheizkessel (92/42/EWG); Explosivstoffe für zivile Zwecke (93/15/EWG); Geräte und Schutzsysteme zur bestimmungsgemässen Verwendung in explosionsgefährdeten Bereichen (94/9/EG); Sportboote (2003/44/EG, in Abänderung von 94/25/EG); Aufzüge (95/16/EG); Druckgeräte (97/23/EG); Maschinen (98/37/EG); In-vitro-Diagnostika (98/79/EG); Funkanlagen und Telekommunikationsendeinrichtungen (99/5/EG); Seilbahnen für den Personenverkehr (2000/9/EG); Messgeräte (2004/22/EG); Elektro- und Elektronikprodukte (2004/108/EG, ersetzte 89/336/EWG); Maschinen (2006/42/EG, früher 98/37/EG); Elektrische Betriebsmittel (2006/95/EG, früher 73/23/EG, geändert durch 93/68/EWG); Pyrotechnische Gegenstände (2007/23/EG); Aktive implantierbare medizinische Geräte (2007/47/EG, früher 90/385/EWG); Medizinprodukte (2007/47/EG, früher 93/42/EWG); Nichtselbsttätige Waagen (2009/23/EG, früher 90/384/EWG); Spielzeug (2009/48/EG); Einfache Druckbehälter (2009/105/EG); Ökodesign-Richtlinie (2009/125/EG). Für die USA vgl. sec. 520 FD&C Act. Rechtsvergleichend *Schwenzer/Hachem/Kee*, Rn. 31.79 ff.

[49] Vgl. *Schwenzer/Leisinger*, GS Hellner, S. 249, 263 ff.; *Schlechtriem*, (2007) 19 Pace Int'l L. Rev. 89, 100 erkennt ebenfalls an, dass Produktionsstandards, die sich auf ethische Werte beziehen, als Teil der Qualitätsanforderungen vereinbart werden können, lehnt es aber ab, diese als objektive Standards anzusehen, S. 101, 102. Rechtsvergleichend *Schwenzer/Hachem/Kee*, Rn. 31.86 ff.

[50] Vgl. *Schwenzer*, Physical Features, S. 103, 105.

[51] Das Fehlen eines Zertifikats nach der EWG-VO Nr. 2092/91 vom 24.6.1991 über den ökologischen Landbau, ABlEG. 1991 L 198, S. 1, ersetzt durch Verordnung (EG) Nr. 834/2007 des Rates vom 28.6.2007 über die ökologische/biologische Produktion und die Kennzeichnung von ökologischen/biologischen Erzeugnissen und zur Aufhebung der Verordnung (EWG) Nr. 2092/91, das die Ware als ‚bio' ausweist, wurde als Sachmangel gesehen, vgl. OLG München, 13.11.2002, CISG-online 786 = NJW-RR 2003, 849, m. Anm. *Hohloch*, JuS 2003, 1134 f. Vgl. auch Serbian Chamber of Commerce, 23.1.2008, CISG-online 1946 (Herkunftszertifikat, das den Käufer von der Zollpflicht im Importstaat befreit hätte); *Schwenzer*, Physical Features, S. 103, 103 f.; *Mosimann/Müller-Chen*, FS Schwenzer, S. 1303, 1312 (Echtheitszertifikat bei Kunstwerken). Wohl anders *Saidov*, Documentary Performance, S. 49, 59.

[52] Vgl. *Kircher*, S. 163.

[53] So die ganz h. M., vgl. BGH, 3.4.1996 (Kobaltsulfat), CISG-online 135 = BGHZ 132, 290, 296: offengelassen allerdings für krasses aliud; OLG Düsseldorf, 21.4.2004, CISG-online 914: Der Käufer muss dem Verkäufer auch ein offensichtliches aliud zur Kenntnis bringen; HG St. Gallen, 11.2.2003, CISG-online 900; Sø-og Handelsretten, 31.1.2002, CISG-online 679 (andere Art von Makrelen); OGH, 29.6.1999, CISG-online 483 (Plattenrohlinge statt zugeschnittener und gebohrter Platten); unten *Müller-Chen*, Art. 45 Rn. 7; *Schlechtriem*, Internationales UN-Kaufrecht, Rn. 134; *Piltz*, Internationales Kaufrecht, Rn. 5–30; *Herber/Czerwenka*, Art. 35, Rn. 2; *Audit*, Vente internationale, Anm. 98.; *Karollus*, S. 105; *Aue*, Mängelgewährleistung im UN-

der Schweiz relevante Abgrenzung zwischen peius und aliud[54] hat für das CISG keine Bedeutung.[55] Ist Zucker verkauft und wird Salz geliefert, so liegt eine Vertragswidrigkeit vor, die der Käufer nach Art. 39 rügen muss. Zwar nimmt Art. 35 im Gegensatz zu Art. 33 I b) EKG[56] auf den Fall der Falschlieferung nicht mehr ausdrücklich Bezug, eine Herausnahme der Falschlieferung aus der Regelung der Vertragswidrigkeit war damit jedoch nicht beabsichtigt.[57] Einzelne Autoren[58] namentlich des deutschen Rechtskreises berufen sich für ihre gegenteilige Auffassung nun freilich auf den Sekretariatskommentar, wonach die Lieferung von Kartoffeln statt Mais keine Erfüllung der Lieferpflicht i. S. des Art. 30 sein soll.[59] Die Entstehungsgeschichte trägt diese Aussage des Sekretariatskommentars jedoch nicht.[60] Auch in der Sache ist es gerechtfertigt, jede aliud-Lieferung als Vertragswidrigkeit und nicht als Nicht-Lieferung zu behandeln.[61] Bei **krasser aliud-Lieferung** wird sich der Verkäufer oft wegen Art. 40 (Kenntnis) nicht auf ein Unterlassen der Rüge berufen können;[62] ist er jedoch ausnahmsweise gutgläubig, so erscheint er auch als schutzwürdig; gerade offensichtliche Falschlieferungen kann der Käufer ohne weiteres erkennen und deshalb rügen.

11 **d) Verpackung oder Behältnis.** Soweit die Parteien Vereinbarungen über Verpackung oder Behältnisse, d. h. insbesondere Container, getroffen haben, gehört auch die Übereinstimmung insoweit zur Vertragsmässigkeit der Ware.[63] Dies unterscheidet das CISG von manchen nationalen Rechtsordnungen, die Verpackungsfehler nicht der Sachgewährleistung zuordnen, sondern als Nebenpflichtverletzung beispielsweise nach den Grundsätzen der positiven Forderungsverletzung sanktionieren.[64] Auch konkludente Vereinbarungen über Verpackung oder Behältnis sind denkbar; freilich genügt dazu nicht bereits, dass vorangegangene Lieferungen in gleicher Art und Weise – aber beförderungsunsicher – verpackt waren.[65]

Kaufrecht, S. 70; *U. Huber*, Haftung des Verkäufers, S. 11; *Ryffel*, S. 17; *Mouly*, D. 1991, Chron. 77, Rn. 4; *P. Widmer*, Droits et obligations du vendeur, S. 95; *Soergel/Lüderitz/Schüßler-Langeheine*, Art. 35, Rn. 5; *Niggemann*, Pflichten des Verkäufers, S. 86; *Hutter*, S. 35 ff.; *U. Huber*, RabelsZ 43 (1979), 413, 483 f.; *ders.*, öStJBl 1989, 273, 278; *Enderlein/Maskow/Strohbach*, Art. 35, Anm. 5.; *Doralt/Binder*, UNCITRAL-Kaufrecht im Vergleich zum österreichischen Recht, S. 146; *Janssen*, S. 76 ff.; *Kruisinga*, Non-conformity, S. 38–42; *Brunner*, Art. 35, Rn. 3; MünchKommHGB/*Benicke*, Art 35, Rn. 4; *Ferrari u. a./Ferrari*, Internationales Vertragsrecht, Art. 35, Rn. 9; auch *Lüderitz*, in: *Schlechtriem* (Hrsg.), Einheitliches Kaufrecht und nationales Obligationenrecht, S. 185; *Bianca/Bonell/Bianca*, Art. 35, Anm. 2.4. A. A. *Neumayer*, RIW 1994, 99, 105; *Neumayer/Ming*, Art. 35, Anm. 3.; *Enderlein/Maskow/Strohbach*, Art. 35, Anm. 3.; *Witz/Salger/Lorenz/Salger*, Art. 35, Rn. 6.

[54] Für Österreich vgl. *Kramer*, FS Honsell, S. 256–258 m. Nachw.; für die Schweiz vgl. *Honsell*, OR BT, S. 118 ff. Vgl. demgegenüber nunmehr für Deutschland: § 434 III BGB.

[55] Vgl. auch *P. Huber/Mullis/Mullis*, S. 132 f.; *Piltz*, Internationales Kaufrecht, Rn. 5–30.

[56] Vgl. dazu BGH, 2.6.1982, NJW 1982, 2730 (Lieferung gefälschter Ware statt der vereinbarten Originalware).

[57] Vgl. *Schlechtriem*, Einheitliches UN-Kaufrecht, S. 57.

[58] Vgl. *Doralt/Neumayer*, UNCITRAL-Kaufrecht im Vergleich zum österreichischen Recht, S. 136; *Bydlinski*, Allgemeines Vertragsrecht, S. 137; *Loewe*, Art. 31, S. 52; vgl. auch österreichische Regierungsvorlage zum UN-Kaufrecht, S. 57.

[59] Sekretariatskommentar, Art. 29, Nr. 3.

[60] Vgl. *Kromer*, S. 273 f. Ebenso *Piltz*, Internationales Kaufrecht, Rn. 4–34; *Schlechtriem*, Uniform Sales Law, S. 67; *ders.*, Einheitliches UN-Kaufrecht, S. 57, jeweils mit Belegen aus der Entstehungsgeschichte.

[61] Vgl. *Karollus*, S. 105 f.; *Heilmann*, S. 170 f., 339; *U. Huber*, öStJBl 1989, 273, 278; *Niggemann*, Pflichten des Verkäufers, S. 86; *Resch*, ÖJZ 1992, 470, 472; *Kircher*, S. 51; MünchKomm/*Gruber*, Art. 35, Rn. 4; *Kröll u. a./Kröll*, Art. 35, Rn. 33. A. A. OLG Düsseldorf, 10.2.1994, CISG-online 115 = NJW-RR 1994, 506 (Lieferung von Stoff in nicht bestellter Farbe als Nichtlieferung).

[62] Vgl. OLG Zweibrücken, 2.2.2004, CISG-online 877, E. II. 6.

[63] Vgl. Compromex Schiedsverfahren, 29.4.1996, CISG-online 350; *Heilmann*, S. 175.

[64] Vgl. Deutschland: *Lorenz/Riehm*, Rn. 475; *Schlechtriem*, SchuldR BT, Rn. 54; nach neuem deutschen Recht stehen dem Käufer die allgemeinen Rechtsbehelfe zu, *ders.*, aaO, Rn. 108; Schweiz: *Honsell*, OR BT, S. 44; Österreich: *Koziol/Welser*, S. 146; Frankreich: *Sonnenberger*, Rn. VI 41, 57 sowie *Niggemann*, Pflichten des Verkäufers, S. 83; vgl. aber § 2–314 (2) (e) UCC, wo die Verpackung ausdrücklich im Rahmen der warranty of merchantability erwähnt wird.

[65] OLG Saarbrücken, 17.1.2007, CISG-online 1642 = IHR 2008, 55, 58 m. Anm. *Bach*, IPRax 2009, 299, 301, 302.

2. Subsidiäre Bestimmung der Vertragsmässigkeit – Abs. 2

Haben die Parteien in ihrem Vertrag keine oder keine ausreichend detaillierte Leistungsbeschreibung nach Abs. 1 getroffen, so greift hilfsweise[66] Abs. 2 ein, der eine Reihe **objektiver Kriterien**[67] zur Bestimmung der Vertragsmässigkeit aufstellt. Dabei kommt dem **Zweck**, dem die Ware zugeführt werden soll, besondere Bedeutung zu.[68] Es handelt sich dabei in der Sache um Vermutungen für das, was vernünftige Parteien als vertragsgemässe Beschaffenheit vereinbart hätten, wenn sie an die Notwendigkeit entsprechender Abreden gedacht hätten.[69] Umstritten ist die daraus resultierende dogmatische Einordnung des Art. 35 II. Insbesondere U. S.-amerikanische Gerichte[70] und Autoren[71] verstehen die Pflichten des Art. 35 II in Anlehnung an ihr nationales Recht[72] im Sinne von implied warranties, die grundsätzlich neben den Pflichten des Art. 35 I gelten.[73] Wollten die Parteien davon abweichen, sei eine zumindest konkludente Abbedingung des Art. 35 II erforderlich.[74] Einigen kontinentaleuropäischen Gerichten[75] zufolge greift Art. 35 II hingegen schon nicht ein, wenn überhaupt eine Vereinbarung zur Qualität der Ware gemäss Art. 35 I getroffen wurde. Im rechten Licht betrachtet liegen diese Auffassungen im Ergebnis dicht beieinander. Eine Beschaffenheitsvereinbarung wird jedenfalls insoweit als **konkludenter Ausschluss** der Haftung nach Art. 35 II zu verstehen sein, als zwischen beiden ein Widerspruch besteht.[76] Richtig ist indes, dass ein Käufer erwarten darf, dass die gelieferte Ware in Bezug auf nicht vereinbarte Eigenschaften für den gewöhnlichen Gebrauchszweck geeignet ist.[77] Die Pflichten des Art. 35 II werden durch eine Eigenschaftsvereinbarung nur in Bezug auf die vereinbarte Eigenschaft ausgeschlossen; im Übrigen **bestehen sie fort** und gelten neben Art. 35 I.[78] Gleiches gilt für das Verhältnis der einzelnen Pflichten des Art. 35 II: Soweit widerspruchsfrei gelten sie nebeneinander.[79] Im Falle eines Widerspruchs ist für jede in Frage stehende Eigenschaft gesondert eine **Hierarchie** der Pflichten der lit. a) bis d) zu bestimmen. Ausschlaggebend ist für diese Hierarchie in erster Line der Wille der Parteien, Art. 8, sowie allfällige Handelsbräuche, Art. 9. Führen diese zu keinem eindeutigen Ergebnis, so sind die übrigen Umstände des Einzelfalls zu würdigen. In der Regel dürfte lit. c) vorrangig zu lit. b)[80] gelten, der wiederum lit. a) vorgeht[81], neben dem praktisch widerspruchsfrei lit. d) steht.

---

[66] Vgl. demgegenüber Artt. 99, 100 CESL-Entwurf, die subjektive und objektive Kriterien kumulieren.
[67] Vgl. OGH, 27.2.2003, CISG-online 794; Tribunale di Forlì, 11.12.2008, CISG-online 1729 = 1788; *Staudinger/Magnus*, Art. 35, Rn. 17; *Ferrari u. a./Ferrari*, Internationales Vertragsrecht, Art. 35, Rn. 11. Vgl. aber Polimeles Protodikio Athenon, 2009, CISG-online 2228 (Art. 35 II lit. a) und d) objektive, lit. b) und c) subjektive Kriterien).
[68] Vgl. hierzu *Schlechtriem*, Pflichten des Verkäufers, S. 116 f. mit zahlreichen, instruktiven Beispielen.
[69] Vgl. *Schlechtriem*, 50 Jahre BGH, S. 407, 429.
[70] *Norfolk Southern Railway Company v. Power Source Supply, Inc.*, U. S. Dist. Ct. (W. D. Pa.), 25.7.2008, CiSG-online 1776; vgl. auch CIETAC Award, 18.4.2008, CISG-online 2057; Dänisches ad hoc Tribunal, 10.11.2000, CISG-online 2154; *Cortem SpA v. Controlmatic Pty. Ltd.*, Federal Court of Australia, 13.8.2010, CISG-online 2128; *Fryer Holdings v. Liaoning MEC Group*, Supreme Court of New South Wales, 30.1.2012, CISG-online 2325. Ebenfalls in diese Richtung *R. J. & A. M. Smallmon v. Transport Sales Limited and Grant Alan Miller*, High Court New Zealand, 30.7.2010, CISG-online 2113, Rn. 79.
[71] *Flechtner*, FS Bergsten, S. 571, 579 ff. In eine ähnliche Richtung auch *Winsor*, 14 VJ (2010), 83, 94 („implied CISG obligations"). Vgl. auch *Kröll u. a./Kröll*, Art. 35, Rn. 62 („implied obligations").
[72] Vgl. § 2–317 UCC.
[73] So auch ausdrücklich Art. 99 II CESL-Entwurf („überdies"), sowie Art. 100 lit. f) CESL-Entwurf („und").
[74] Vgl. *Flechtner*, FS Bergsten, S. 571, 580.
[75] Vgl. Oberster Gerichtshof Tschechien, 29.3.2006, CISG-online 1747.
[76] So auch *Flechtner*, FS Bergsten, S. 571, 580 f., der davon jedoch bei Irrtümern des Käufers bzgl. des Widerspruchs ausnahmsweise abweichen möchte. Dies ist abzulehnen. Der Inhalt des Vertrags ist nach objektiviertem Verständnis zu bestimmen, vgl. oben *Schmidt-Kessel*, Art. 8 Rn. 10.
[77] So auch mit Blick auf nicht von Art. 35 II b) erfasste Eigenschaften *Koch*, IHR 2009, 233, 235.
[78] Vgl. auch *Kröll u. a./Kröll*, Art. 35, Rn. 65.
[79] *Staudinger/Magnus*, Art. 35, Rn. 10; *Kröll u. a./Kröll*, Art. 35, Rn. 61.
[80] Vgl. unten Rn. 25.
[81] Vgl. *Schlechtriem*, IPRax 2001, 161, 163; *Honnold/Flechtner*, Art. 35, Rn. 231; *Kröll u. a./Kröll*, Art. 35, Rn. 61; *P. Huber/Mullis/Mullis*, S. 134; *Koch*, IHR 2009, 233, 235; *ders.*, IHR 2011, 129, 129.

Art. 35 13, 14   Teil III. Kapitel II. Pflichten des Verkäufers. Abschnitt II

13   **a) Eignung für gewöhnlichen Gebrauchszweck – Abs. 2 a).** Mangels anderweitiger Vereinbarung muss die Ware zum gewöhnlichen Gebrauch geeignet sein. Dies entspricht der Regelung in vielen nationalen Rechtsordnungen.[82] Deckt die Ware nicht alle üblichen, sondern nur einzelne Gebrauchszwecke ab, so hat der Verkäufer den Käufer hierüber zu informieren.[83] Andererseits haftet der Verkäufer nicht dafür, dass die Ware auch für zwar gelegentlich vorkommende, aber eben nicht übliche Verwendungszwecke geeignet ist.[84] Ein Einstehenmüssen hierfür kommt nur nach den einschränkenden Voraussetzungen des Abs. 2 b) in Betracht.

14   Primär muss die Ware für die **kaufmännische Verwendung** geeignet sein. Hierzu gehört zunächst die **Wiederverkäuflichkeit** der Ware.[85] Für die Wiederverkäuflichkeit der Ware spricht eine amtliche Zertifizierung.[86] Im europäischen Handel müssen bestimmte Produktgruppen[87] mit der **CE-Kennzeichnung** versehen sein. Darüber hinaus ist insbesondere Art. 2 II d) RL zu bestimmten Aspekten des Verbrauchsgüterkaufs und der Garantien für Verbrauchsgüter[88] zu beachten, wonach **Verbrauchsgüter** eine Qualität und Leistungen aufweisen müssen, die bei Gütern der gleichen Art üblich sind und die der Verbraucher vernünftigerweise erwarten konnte, wenn die Beschaffenheit des Gutes und gegebenenfalls die insbesondere in der Werbung oder bei Etikettierung gemachten öffentlichen Äusserungen des Verkäufers, des Herstellers oder dessen Vertreters über die konkreten Eigenschaften des Gutes in Betracht gezogen werden. Indirekt findet damit eine Objektivierung des Fehlerbegriffs auch im CISG statt, auch wenn der Regress des dem Verbraucher haftenden Verkäufers gegenüber seinem Lieferanten von der RL dem anwendbaren Recht, d. h. u. U. dem CISG, überlassen bleibt.[89] Über die Geeignetheit für andere gewöhnliche Nutzung ist nach objektiver Verkehrsanschauung zu entscheiden. So müssen etwa Konfektionskleidungsstücke den angegebenen Konfektionsgrössen entsprechen und dürfen kei-

---

[82] Vgl. Deutschland: § 434 I BGB; Schweiz: Art. 197 I OR; Österreich: § 922 ABGB; Frankreich: Art. 1641 Cc; England: sec. 14 (2B) (a) SGA; USA: § 2–314 (2) UCC.

[83] Vgl. BGH, 26.9.2012, CISG-online 2348; Sekretariatskommentar, Art. 33, Nr. 5; *Staudinger/Magnus*, Art. 35, Rn. 20; *Benedick*, Informationspflichten, Rn. 278; *Piltz*, Internationales Kaufrecht, Rn. 5–45; *Heilmann*, S. 186.

[84] Vgl. BGH, 26.9.2012, CISG-online 2348; *Piltz*, Internationales Kaufrecht, Rn. 5–45; *Enderlein/Maskow/Strohbach*, Art. 35, Anm. 8.; *Hutter*, S. 41. Bedenklich KG Glarus, 6.11.2008, CISG-online 1996: Ohne Angaben zur beabsichtigten Verwendung bestellte Seidenfaltbeutel müssen zur Verpackung von Lebensmitteln geeignet sein.

[85] Vgl. BGH, 2.3.2005, CISG-online 999 = NJW-RR 2005, 1218 ff. (belgisches Schweinefleisch), m. Anm. *Schlechtriem*, JZ 2005, 846 ff.; *International Housewares Ltd. v. SEB SA*, High Court (Auckland, New Zealand), 31.3.2003, CISG-online 833, Rn. 56 ff., 59. Tribunale di Forlì, 11.12.2008, CISG-online 1729 = 1788; KG Glarus, 6.11.2008, CISG-online 1996; *Winsor*, 14 VJ (2010), 83, 94; *Audit*, Vente internationale, Anm. 98.; *Honnold/Flechtner*, Art. 35, Rn. 225; *Lookofsky*, Understanding the CISG, S. 79; *Neumayer/Ming*, Art. 35, Anm. 6.; *Piltz*, Internationales Kaufrecht, Rn. 5–46; *Soergel/Lüderitz/Schüßler-Langeheine*, Art. 35, Rn. 11; *Witz/Salger/Lorenz/Salger*, Art. 35, Rn. 9; *Bianca/Bonell/Bianca*, Art. 35, Anm. 2.5.1.; *Aue*, Mängelgewährleistung im UN-Kaufrecht, S. 74; *Enderlein/Maskow/Strohbach*, Art. 35, Anm. 8.; *Hutter*, S. 40; *Janssen*, S. 80.

[86] CA Rouen, 19.12.2006, CISG-online 1933.

[87] Elektrische Betriebsmittel (72/23/EWG); Einfache Druckbehälter (87/404/EWG); Spielzeug (88/378/EWG); Bauprodukte (89/106/EWG); Persönliche Schutzausrüstungen (89/686/EWG); Gasverbrauchseinrichtungen (90/396/EWG); Warmwasserheizkessel (92/42/EWG); Explosivstoffe für zivile Zwecke (93/15/EWG); Geräte und Schutzsysteme zur bestimmungsgemässen Verwendung in explosionsgefährdeten Bereichen (94/9/EG); Sportboote (2003/44/EG, in Abänderung von 94/25/EG); Aufzüge (95/16/EG); Druckgeräte (97/23/EG); Maschinen (98/37/EG); In-vitro-Diagnostika (98/79/EG); Funkanlagen und Telekommunikationsendeinrichtungen (99/5/EG); Seilbahnen für den Personenverkehr (2000/9/EG); Messgeräte (2004/22/EG); Elektro- und Elektronikprodukte (2004/108/EG, ersetzte 89/336/EWG); Maschinen (2006/42/EG, früher 98/37/EG); Elektrische Betriebsmittel (2006/95/EG, früher 73/23/EG, geändert durch 93/68/EWG); Pyrotechnische Gegenstände (2007/23/EG); Aktive implantierbare medizinische Geräte (2007/47/EG, früher 90/385/EWG); Medizinprodukte (2007/47/EG, früher 93/42/EWG); Nichtselbsttätige Waagen (2009/23/EG, früher 90/384/EWG); Spielzeug (2009/48/EG); Einfache Druckbehälter (2009/105/EG); Ökodesign-Richtlinie (2009/125/EG).

[88] RL 1999/44/EG v. 25.5.1999, ABlEG Nr. L 171/12 v. 7.7.1999; zum Vergleich zwischen CISG und RL vgl. *Grundmann*, AcP 202 (2002), 40 ff.

[89] Vgl. Art. 4 RL.

Vertragsmäßigkeit der Ware 15 **Art. 35**

ne Schnittfehler oder Passformmängel aufweisen.[90] Nahrung muss für den Verzehr geeignet,[91] Backformen aus Keramik müssen hitzeresistent sein.[92] Auch optische Abweichungen können die berechtigte Gebrauchserwartung des Käufers beeinträchtigen.[93] Je nach Art des Produktes muss es mit technischen Instruktionen, einer **Betriebs- oder Gebrauchsanleitung** geliefert werden,[94] sowie die nach der Produktsicherheits-Richtlinie[95] erforderlichen Warnhinweise aufweisen. Auch eine fehlerhafte Montageanleitung[96] kann Vertragswidrigkeit begründen. Verderbliche Ware muss entsprechend den jeweiligen Gebräuchen für eine angemessene Zeit über die Lieferung hinaus **haltbar** sein.[97] Aber auch dauerhafte Ware (Maschinen, Konsumgüter etc.) muss für eine gewisse Zeit zum gewöhnlichen Gebrauch geeignet bleiben.[98] In zunehmendem Masse ist die Wiederverkäuflichkeit von der Einhaltung bestimmter Herstellungsstandards und -praktiken abhängig.[99] Auch der **Verdacht**, dass Ware mangelhaft sein könnte,[100] kann die Wiederverkäuflichkeit beeinträchtigen und deshalb zu einer Haftung nach Abs. 2 a) führen. Eine andere Frage ist, ob der Verkäufer insofern allenfalls von der Schadenersatzhaftung nach Art. 79 I befreit ist.

In der Literatur umstritten ist die Frage, ob zur Eignung zum gewöhnlichen Gebrauch 15 auch gehört, dass Gattungsware von **durchschnittlicher Qualität (average quality)** ist.[101] Viele nationale Rechtsordnungen enthalten eine ausdrückliche Regelung, wonach Gattungsware grundsätzlich von mittlerer Art und Güte sein muss.[102] Ein bei der Wiener Konferenz eingebrachter kanadischer Antrag, dies auch in Art. 35 ausdrücklich aufzunehmen, wurde allerdings nach Abstimmung mit den Vertretern aus anderen Common Law Staaten zurückgenommen.[103] Hintergrund für diesen Antrag war, dass der Begriff der

---

[90] Vgl. zu Art. 33 I d) EKG: OLG Karlsruhe, 14.4.1978, RIW 1978, 544; OLG Hamm, 17.9.1981, in: *Schlechtriem/Magnus*, Art. 40 EKG, Nr. 4; OLG Hamm, 14.4.1983, in: *Schlechtriem/Magnus*, Art. 33 EKG, Nr. 13.
[91] Vgl. BGH, 2.3.2005, CISG-online 999 = NJW-RR 2005, 1218 ff. (belgisches Schweinefleisch), m. Anm. *Schlechtriem*, JZ 2005, 846 ff.
[92] Com., 17.12.1996, CISG-online 220 = D. 1997, 337, m. Anm. *Witz*.
[93] Zu Art. 33 EKG vgl. OLG Celle, 2.9.1986, IPRax 1987, 313.
[94] Vgl. BGH, 4.12.1996, CISG-online 260 = NJW-RR 1997, 690 (Handbuch für Computer); *Piltz*, Internationales Kaufrecht, Rn. 5–46; *Kröll u. a./Kröll*, Art. 35, Rn. 102.
[95] Art. 5 RL 2001/95/EG v. 3.12.2001.
[96] Vgl. auch Art. 2 V Verbrauchsgüterkauf-RL; § 434 II 2 BGB.
[97] Vgl. *Kröll u. a./Kröll*, Art. 35, Rn. 101; *Ferrari u. a./Ferrari*, Internationales Vertragsrecht, Art. 35, Rn. 16. Da bislang allgemeine Standards hinsichtlich von Haltbarkeits- und Verwendungsdauer fehlen, empfehlen *Enderlein/Maskow/Strohbach*, Art. 35, Anm. 8.; *Schlechtriem*, Pflichten des Verkäufers, S. 119, in derartigen Fällen eine ausdrückliche Vereinbarung in den Vertrag aufzunehmen; die Vertragsgemässheit der Ware beurteilt sich dann nach Absatz 1. Zum Problem der Haltbarkeitsgarantie generell vgl. Art. 36 Rn. 9 ff.
[98] Vgl. LG München I, 27.2.2002, CISG-online 654 = IHR 2003, 233, 234 (Motoren für Globen müssen sich für mehrjährigen Betrieb eignen). Vgl. auch sec. 14 (2B) (e) SGA. Vgl. auch *Ferrari u. a./Ferrari*, Internationales Vertragsrecht, Art. 35, Rn. 16; *Kröll u. a./Kröll*, Art. 35, Rn. 101 (hochwertige Maschinen: mehrere Jahre).
[99] Vgl. nur Good Manufacturing Practices in Verordnungen über bestimmte Produktgruppen, dazu *Schwenzer*, Physical Features, S. 103, 104.
[100] Vgl. BGH, 2.3.2005, CISG-online 999, m. krit. Anm. *Schlechtriem*, JZ 2005, 846, krit. auch *Nakamura*, 15 VJ (2011), 53, 57 ff.; *Kröll u. a./Kröll*, Art. 35, Rn. 99.
[101] Bejahend *Brunner*, Art. 35, Rn. 8 (wenn die Umstände nicht auf eine vernünftige Qualität hindeuten); *Herber/Czerwenka*, Art. 35, Rn. 4; *Piltz*, Internationales Kaufrecht, Rn. 5–46: „wird grundsätzlich ausreichend sein, solange nicht der übliche Verwendungszweck gefährdet ist"; ähnlich *Staudinger/Magnus*, Art. 35, Rn. 19; *Ferrari u. a./Ferrari*, Internationales Vertragsrecht, Art. 35, Rn. 15; *Achilles*, Art. 35, Rn. 6; *Aue*, Mängelgewährleistung im UN-Kaufrecht, S. 74 f.; *Heilmann*, S. 201; *Otto*, MDR 1992, 533, 534; zum EKG vgl. OLG Hamm, 29.4.1982, IPRax 1983, 231; OLG Koblenz, 18.5.1984, in: *Schlechtriem/Magnus*, Art. 44 EKG, Nr. 6; offengelassen von: *Bianca/Bonell/Bianca*, Art. 35, Anm. 3.1.; *Audit*, Vente internationale, Anm. 98.; verneinend *Enderlein/Maskow/Strohbach*, Art. 35, Anm. 8.; *Heuzé*, Anm. 293.; *Soergel/Lüderitz/Schüßler-Langeheine*, Art. 35, Rn. 10; für eine unabhängige Interpretation *Lookofsky*, Understanding the CISG, S. 80 f.; Netherlands Arbitration Institute, 15.10.2002, CISG-online 780, Rn. 103 ff.; vgl. auch Audiencia Provincial de Barcelona, 24.3.2009 (Weiterverkäuflichkeit als „Prime quality product" nicht geschuldet); kritisch bezüglich des Konzepts der durchschnittlichen Qualität *Krätzschmar*, Öffentlichrechtliche Beschaffenheitsvorgaben, S. 130 f.
[102] Deutschland: § 243 I BGB, § 360 HGB; Schweiz: Art. 71 II OR; Frankreich: Art. 1246 Cc; USA: § 2–314 (2) (b) UCC.
[103] Vgl. oben Rn. 2; dazu Netherlands Arbitration Institute, 15.10.2002, CISG-online 780, Rn. 111 ff.

Handelbarkeit (merchantability) vor allem in der Rechtsprechung der englischen Gerichte[104] mit erheblichen Auslegungsunsicherheiten verbunden war und eine Klarstellung deshalb erwünscht sei.[105] I. E. wird wohl mit Auslegungsdivergenzen zu rechnen sein. Während kontinentaleuropäische, aber auch US-amerikanische Richter Abs. 2 a) ohne weiteres so verstehen werden, dass nur Ware durchschnittlicher Qualität als vertragsmässig gelten kann,[106] kann die Gefahr nicht von der Hand gewiesen werden, dass ein englischer Richter auch Ware von unterdurchschnittlicher Qualität noch als vertragsmässig ansieht, soweit sie nur weiterverkauft werden kann.[107] Inzwischen wurde allerdings durch den SSGA 1994[108] der Begriff der merchantability durch jenen der satisfactory quality ersetzt, der auf die vernünftigen Käufererwartungen abstellt. Dies könnte zu einer Annäherung der Standpunkte führen.[109] Auch ein jüngerer Schiedsspruch[110] hat unter Verwerfung der beiden bisher vertretenen Ansichten **angemessene Qualität (reasonable quality)** als nach Abs. 2 a) geschuldet angesehen, die sich nach den berechtigten Erwartungen des Käufers richtet. Damit nähert man sich allerdings bereits Abs. 2 b).

16   Fraglich mag auch sein, wessen Massstab – derjenige des **Verkäufer-** oder der des **Käuferstaates** – zur Bestimmung der für den gewöhnlichen Gebrauch erforderlichen Eigenschaften heranzuziehen ist. Während teilweise insoweit auf den Verkäuferstaat abgestellt wird,[111] erachten andere Autoren die Standards im Verwendungsstaat für entscheidend.[112] Letztlich ist jedoch auch die Frage der Standards ein Problem der Auslegung des Vertrages.[113] Primär geht es darum, ob ein besonderer Verwendungszweck i. S. d. Abs. 2 b) vorliegt.[114] Ist subsidiär auf den gewöhnlichen Gebrauch abzustellen, so wird man von folgenden Prämissen ausgehen können: Wo **internationale Handelsbräuche** im Hinblick auf bestimmte Sacheigenschaften oder Herstellungsstandards bestehen, müssen diese als Minimalqualität prästiert werden.[115] Auch ein sowohl im Verkäufer- als auch im Käuferstaat geltender Standard – wenn beispielsweise beide Vertragsparteien ihren Sitz in EU-Staaten haben – ist grundsätzlich einzuhalten, es sei denn, für den nach dem Vertrag in Aussicht genommenen Verwendungsstaat gelten geringere Anforderungen und es ist den Umständen – etwa der Preisgestaltung – zu entnehmen, dass die Parteien nur diese geringeren Standards im Auge hatten. Im Übrigen verbietet sich jede generelle Regel, und es ist auf die **Umstände des Einzelfalles** abzustellen.[116] Wenn die Standards im Käuferstaat höher sind als jene im Verkäuferstaat, ist es Sache des Käufers, den Verkäufer hierauf hinzuweisen. Umgekehrt wird nicht immer Vertragswidrigkeit angenommen werden können, wenn die Ware zwar den Standards im Verkäuferstaat nicht gerecht wird, der gewöhnliche Gebrauch

---

[104] Vgl. dazu *Benjamin*, Rn. 11–032 ff.
[105] Vgl. O. R., S. 308, Nr. 30.
[106] Vgl. LG Berlin, 15.9.1994, CISG-online 399.
[107] Vgl. *Cehave N. V. v. Bremer Handelsgesellschaft m. b. H. (The Hansa Nord)*, [1976] Q. B. 44.
[108] Sec. 14 (2) SSGA (in der Fassung von 1994).
[109] Vgl. *Atiyah/Adams*, S. 153 ff.; *Fryer Holdings v. Liaoning MEC Group*, Supreme Court of New South Wales, 30.1.2012, CISG-online 2325. Vgl. auch Art. 5.6 PICC.
[110] Netherlands Arbitration Institute, 15.10.2002, CISG-online 780, Rn. 71, 108, unter Bezugnahme auf *Bernstein/Lookofsky*, 1. Aufl., S. 59 f.; vgl. auch *Beijing Light Automobile Co., Ltd. v. Connell Limited Partnership*, SCC International, 5.6.1998, CISG-online 379, unter 6.3 a); *Lookofsky*, Understanding the CISG, S. 80 f.; *Kröll u. a./Kröll*, Art. 35, Rn. 79. Für den Kunsthandel: *Mosimann/Müller-Chen*, FS Schwenzer, S. 1303, 1316. Ähnlich auch *Honnold/Flechtner*, Art. 35, Rn. 225 (auf die Erwartungen der Parteien betreffend der Eignung der Ware für die gewöhnliche Verwendung abstellend).
[111] Vgl. OLG Hamm, 30.11.2010, CISG-online 2217; *Koch*, IHR 2009, 233, 236; *Bianca/Bonell/Bianca*, Art. 35, Anm. 2.5.1.; *Enderlein/Maskow/Strohbach*, Art. 35, Anm. 8.; *Neumayer/Ming*, Art. 35, Anm. 7.; *Piltz*, Internationales Kaufrecht, Rn. 5–48; *Aue*, Mängelgewährleistung im UN-Kaufrecht, S. 75.
[112] Vgl. *Schlechtriem*, Seller's Obligations, § 6.03, S. 6–21; in diese Richtung tendieren wohl auch *Staudinger/Magnus*, Art. 35, Rn. 21; *Otto*, MDR 1992, 533, 534; *Conrad*, S. 28 ff.
[113] So vor allem *Honnold/Flechtner*, Art. 35, Rn. 225.
[114] Vgl. *Schlechtriem*, IPRax 2001, 161, 163; *P. Huber/Mullis/Mullis*, S. 137; *Koch*, IHR 2011, 129, 129 f.
[115] Vgl. OGH, 27.2.2003, CISG-online 794 = IHR 2004, 25, 28 = IPRax 2004, 350, 352, m. Anm. *P. Huber*, IPRax 2004, 358, 359; *Krätzschmar*, Öffentlichrechtliche Beschaffenheitsvorgaben, S. 199.
[116] Zustimmend *Audit*, Vente internationale, Anm. 98.; *Heilmann*, S. 185; *Koch*, IHR 2009, 233, 236.

Vertragsmäßigkeit der Ware 17 Art. 35

im Käufer- oder Verwendungsstaat aber nicht beeinträchtigt wird,[117] es sei denn, der Käufer habe gerade erkennbaren Wert auf die im Verkäuferstaat übliche Produktqualität gelegt, was sich in aller Regel in der Höhe des Kaufpreises widerspiegeln wird.

Besonderes gilt für die Einhaltung von sog. **öffentlich-rechtlichen Vorgaben,**[118] d. h. 17 vor allem nationalen öffentlich-rechtlichen Bestimmungen zum Schutze von Verbrauchern, Arbeitnehmern oder Umwelt, z. B. für Normen zur Produktsicherheit, aber auch für die Herkunft der Ware wegen Exportfähigkeit in bestimmte Länder.[119] Soweit solche Normen Sacheigenschaften voraussetzen, die nicht als solche bereits auf Grund Handelsbrauchs zum gewöhnlichen Gebrauch der Ware erforderlich sind oder nicht – wie zum Teil innerhalb der EU[120] – sowohl im Verkäufer- als auch im Käuferstaat gelten,[121] wollen verschiedene Gerichte[122] und Autoren[123] grundsätzlich auf die Situation im Verkäuferstaat abstellen,[124] da vom Verkäufer nicht erwartet werden könne, dass er die besonderen Vorschriften im Käufer- oder Verwendungsstaat kennt. Auch allein daraus, dass der Käufer dem Verkäufer das Bestimmungsland mitgeteilt hat, könne noch nicht abgeleitet werden, dass der Verkäufer verpflichtet sein soll, die dort geltenden öffentlich-rechtlichen Bestimmungen einzuhalten.[125] Es sei vielmehr Sache des Käufers, sich um die besonderen öffentlich-rechtlichen Normen im Verwendungsstaat zu kümmern und sie – sei es nach Abs. 1 oder nach Abs. 2 b) – zum Gegenstand des Vertrages zu machen. Ohne ausdrücklichen Hinweis des Käufers auf spezielle öffentlich-rechtliche Vorschriften könne man eine Verpflichtung des Verkäufers zur Einhaltung dieser Vorschriften allenfalls annehmen, wenn der Verkäufer z. B. auf Grund bereits vorher bestehender Geschäftsbeziehung mit dem Käufer[126] oder weil er regelmässig

---

[117] Vgl. *Piltz*, Internationales Kaufrecht, Rn. 5–50.
[118] Ähnliche Wirkungen können auch allgemeine gesellschaftliche Überzeugungen haben, vgl. Münch-Komm/*Gruber*, Art. 35, Rn. 19. Zu öffentlichrechtlichen Standards und Vertragsgemässheit der Ware nach CISG vgl. *Krätzschmar*, Öffentlichrechtliche Beschaffenheitsvorgaben, *passim*.
[119] Vgl. BGH, 3.4.1996, CISG-online 135 = BGHZ 132, 290, 300.
[120] Vgl. grundlegend BGH, 2.3.2005, CISG-online 999 = NJW-RR 2005, 1218 ff. (belgisches Schweinefleisch), m. Anm. *Schlechtriem*, JZ 2005, 846 ff. Vgl. zur Anwendung der europäischen Norm HD 1000 auf Haken in Stahlgerüsten OGH, 19.4.2007, CISG-online 1495; vgl. auch EU-RL 2001/95/EG über die allgemeine Produktsicherheit v. 3.12.2001, ABlEG Nr. L 11/4 v. 15.1.2002; EU-RL 2006/42/EG über Maschinen v. 17.5.2006, ABlEG Nr. L 157/24 v. 9.6.2006 (früher 98/37/EG v. 22.6.1998, ABlEG Nr. L 207 v. 23.7.1998).
[121] Vgl. RB Rotterdam, 15.10.2008, CISG-online 1899, E. 7.6; RB Zwolle, 9.12.2009, CISG-online 2069; *Ferrari u. a./Ferrari*, Internationales Vertragsrecht, Art. 35, Rn. 14. Kritisch gegenüber der Annahme, dass die Ware den Anforderungen des Käuferstaates oder des Verwendungsstaates entsprechen muss, wenn diese mit den Anforderungen des Verkäuferstaates übereinstimmen: *Krätzschmar*, Öffentlichrechtliche Beschaffenheitsvorgaben, S. 160 ff.
[122] Vgl. BGH, 8.3.1995, CISG-online 144 = BGHZ 129, 75, 81 (Muschel-Fall), m. Anm. *Schlechtriem*, IPRax 1996, 12–16 und m. Anm. *Daun*, NJW 1996, 29–30, zur vorinstanzlichen Entscheidung des OLG Frankfurt a. M., 20.4.1994, CISG-online 125, kritisch *Magnus*, ZEuP 1995, 202, 210, demzufolge die Vertragswidrigkeit in der Lieferung gesundheitsgefährdender Ware zu sehen sei; BGH, 2.3.2005, CISG-online 999 = NJW-RR 2005, 1218, m. krit. Anm. *Nakamura*, 15 VJ (2011), 53, 57 ff.; OGH, 13.4.2000, CISG-online 576 = IHR 2001, 117, 120 = IPRax 2001, 149, 152, m. krit. Anm. *Schlechtriem*, IPRax 2001, 161, 162 f.; vgl. dazu auch Anm. *Klindt*, IHR 2001, 103 ff. (zu den EG-maschinenrechtlichen Aspekten); OGH, 27.2.2003, CISG-online 794 = IHR 2004, 25, 28; m. zust. Anm. *P. Huber*, IPRax 2004, 358, 359; OGH, 25.1.2006, CISG-online 1223 (Schweineleber); zuletzt bestätigt durch OGH, 19.4.2007, CISG-online 1495; *R. J. & A. M. Smallmon v. Transport Sales Limited and Grant Alan Miller*, CA New Zealand, 22.7.2011, CISG-online 2215, Rn. 58 ff.; vgl. auch die bestätigte Vorinstanz, High Court New Zealand, 30.7.2010, CISG-online 2113, Rn. 80 ff.
[123] *Enderlein/Maskow/Strohbach*, Art. 35, Anm. 8.; *Bianca/Bonell/Bianca*, Art. 35, Anm. 3.2.; *Audit*, Vente internationale, Anm. 98.; *Herber/Czerwenka*, Art. 35, Rn. 5; *Achilles*, Art. 35, Rn. 6; *Piltz*, Internationales Kaufrecht, Rn. 5–43, 5–48; *ders.*, Export- und Importgeschäfte, § 12, Rn. 165; *Kröll u. a./Kröll*, Art. 35, Rn. 88; *Ferrari u. a./Ferrari*, Internationales Vertragsrecht, Art. 35, Rn. 14; *Heuzé*, Anm. 290.; *Kruisinga*, Nonconformity, S. 43–52; wohl auch *Hutter*, S. 46 f.
[124] Anders ohne nähere Begründung CIETAC Award, 18.4.2008, CISG-online 2057: Importanforderungen im Käuferstaat nach Art. 35 II a) massgeblich.
[125] RB Rotterdam, 15.10.2008, CISG-online 1899, E. 7.6.
[126] Hat freilich der Käufer jahrelang die Ware akzeptiert, obwohl diese den öffentlich-rechtlichen Bestimmungen nicht entsprach, so kann er dies dem Verkäufer nicht vorhalten, vgl. Gerechtshof Arnhem, 27.4.1999, UNILEX, zit. nach *Dokter/Kruisinga*, IHR 2003, 105, 109. Die Einhaltung gewisser öffentlichrechtlicher

Art. 35 17a Teil III. Kapitel II. Pflichten des Verkäufers. Abschnitt II

in das betreffende Land exportiert,[127] seine Produkte dort bewirbt[128] oder dort eine eigene Zweigniederlassung betreibt,[129] Kenntnis dieser Vorschriften besitzt.[130] Auch hier ist die Beurteilung allerdings im Wesentlichen eine Frage des Einzelfalls.[131] Ein zweitinstanzliches niederländisches Gericht liess nicht einmal den Hinweis des Käufers, dass deutsche Behörden „strenge Regeln" anwenden, genügen.[132]

17a Gegen diese Rechtsprechung wendet sich insbesondere *Schlechtriem*[133] mit überzeugenden Argumenten.[134] Wurde dem Verkäufer das Verwendungsland zur Kenntnis gebracht (Abs. 2 b)), so hat der Verkäufer nicht nur die für die faktische Verwendung in diesem Land erforderlichen Eigenschaften zu prästieren, sondern auch die jeweiligen öffentlich-rechtlichen Vorgaben einzuhalten. Von einem weltweit agierenden Unternehmen wird man Kenntnis der entsprechenden Bestimmungen erwarten dürfen. Handelt es sich um besondere öffentlich-rechtliche Vorgaben im Verwendungsland, die der Verkäufer weder kannte noch kennen konnte, so wird es regelmässig daran fehlen, dass der Käufer „auf die Sachkenntnis und das Urteilsvermögen des Verkäufers" vertraut hat oder vernünftigerweise vertrauen durfte.[135] Nur in seltenen Fällen, in denen der Käufer über das Verwendungsland weder ausdrückliche noch konkludente Angaben gemacht hat, ist bezüglich der für die vertragsgemässe Beschaffenheit erforderlichen Eigenschaften auf den gewöhnlichen Gebrauch der Ware abzustellen. Dafür mag man dann an die Verwendungsbedingungen einschliesslich der öffentlich-rechtlichen Vorgaben im Verkäuferland abstellen.[136] Mit der Anknüpfung an Abs. 2 b) löst sich auch die Frage nach der **zeitlichen Relevanz** öffentlich-rechtlicher Vorgaben. Grundsätzlich hat der Verkäufer Konformität mit im Zeitpunkt des Vertragsschlusses[137] bestehenden Vorschriften zu prästieren, nicht jedoch mit später erlassenen und ggf. erst im Zeitpunkt des Gefahrübergangs relevanten Bestimmungen.

Vorschriften kann auch eine Gepflogenheit zwischen den Parteien gemäss Art. 9 I darstellen, vgl. *Krätzschmar*, Öffentlichrechtliche Beschaffenheitsvorgaben, S. 118 f.

[127] *Soergel/Lüderitz/Schüßler-Langeheine*, Art 35, Rn. 13; *Kröll u. a./Kröll*, Art. 35, Rn. 96; *Ferrari u. a./Ferrari*, Internationales Vertragsrecht, Art. 35, Rn. 14.

[128] Dazu *R. J. & A. M. Smallmon v. Transport Sales Limited and Grant Alan Miller*, CA New Zealand, 22.7.2011, CISG-online 2215, Rn. 58 ff. (in casu letztlich abgelehnt, da schon in der Werbung zum Ausdruck kam [„landed in"], dass der Verkäufer nicht für etwaige Anforderungen im Käuferstaat einstehen wollte); vgl. auch die bestätigte Vorinstanz, High Court New Zealand, 30.7.2010, CISG-online 2113, Rn. 80 ff.; *Staudinger/Magnus*, Art. 35, Rn. 22; *Kröll u. a./Kröll*, Art. 35, Rn. 96.

[129] Vgl. *Kröll u. a./Kröll*, Art. 35, Rn. 96.

[130] Beispiele aufführend, aber i. E. ablehnend: BGH, 8.3.1995, CISG-online 144 = BGHZ 129, 75, 84 (Muschel-Fall); i. E. bejahend: *Medical Marketing International Inc. v. Internazionale Medico Scientifica, S. R. L.*, U. S. Dist. Ct. (E. D. La.), 17.5.1999, CISG-online 387 = 1999 WL 311 945; CA Grenoble, 13.9.1995, CISG-online 157 = J. C. P. 1996, IV, 712, zu Unrecht kritisiert von *Ferrari*, RabelsZ 68 (2004), 473, 477; LG Ellwangen, 21.8.1995, CISG-online 279; RB Rotterdam, 15.10.2008, CISG-online 1899, E. 7.6.; *Staudinger/Magnus*, Art. 35, Rn. 34; *Witz/Salger/Lorenz/Salger*, Art. 35, Rn. 10; *Bianca/Bonell/Bianca*, Art. 35, Anm. 3.2.; *Neumayer/Ming*, Art. 35, Anm. 7.; *Audit*, Vente internationale, Anm. 98.; *Heilmann*, S. 185; *Otto*, MDR 1992, 533, 534.

[131] *P. Huber/Mullis/Mullis*, S. 137. Für die Vertragspraxis empfehlen *Detzer/Thamm*, BB 1992, 2369, 2371 und *Piltz*, Internationales Kaufrecht, Rn. 5–44 eine ausdrückliche vertragliche Regelung.

[132] Vgl. Gerechtshof Arnhem, 27.4.1999, CISG-online 741, zit. nach *Dokter/Kruisinga*, IHR 2003, 105, 109.

[133] Vgl. *Schlechtriem*, IPRax 1996, 12 ff.; *ders.*, 50 Jahre BGH, 407, 431 ff.; *ders.*, IPRax 2001, 161, 162 f.; ihm folgend *Lurger*, IHR 2001, 91, 101 unter Verdeutlichung anhand der Parallelproblematik des Art. 42; *Koch*, IHR 2009, 233, 235 f.; *ders.*, IHR 2011, 129, 129 f.; *Kröll u. a./Kröll*, Art. 35, Rn. 120 f.; a. A. MünchKomm/*Gruber*, Art. 35, Rn. 23; *Kruisinga*, Non-conformity, S. 52. Vgl. auch Federal Court of Australia *Cortem ApA v. Controlmatic Pty. Ltd.*, 13.8.2010, CISG-online 2128: Nichtzertifizierung durch eine Behörde im Käuferstaat als Beeinträchtigung des kommunizierten Zwecks des die Zertifizierung voraussetzenden gewerblichen Vertriebs im Käuferstaat und damit als Mangel nach Art. 35 II b) gedeutet.

[134] Vgl. hingegen *Benedick*, Informationspflichten, Rn. 340, demzufolge die Ansichten der Gerichte und Schlechtriems einen gemeinsamen Kern haben: Beide fordern, dass öffentlichrechtliche Vorschriften des Verwendungsstaats eingehalten werden müssen, sofern die Umstände des konkreten Falls zeigen, dass der Verkäufer diese kannte oder hätte kennen müssen.

[135] Vgl. *Schlechtriem*, IPRax 2001, 161, 163.

[136] Vgl. *Schlechtriem*, IPRax 2001, 161, 163.

[137] Vgl. dazu unten Rn. 22.

b) Eignung für bestimmten Gebrauchszweck – Abs. 2 b).

Für die Eignung der Ware für einen vom gewöhnlichen Gebrauch abweichenden besonderen Zweck hat der Verkäufer nach Abs. 2 b) nur einzustehen, wenn dieser Zweck dem Verkäufer ausdrücklich oder implizit bekannt gemacht wurde, der Käufer auf die Sachkunde des Verkäufers vertraute und dieses Vertrauen vernünftig war. Die Vorschrift ist sec. 14 (3) englischer SGA 1979 und § 2–315 U. S.-amerikanischer UCC nachgebildet. Führt der Käufer die Ware einer Verwendung zu, für die sie nach den vertraglichen Vereinbarungen nicht bestimmt ist, haftet der Verkäufer nicht.[138]

Ein **besonderer Gebrauchszweck** liegt z. B. vor, wenn der Käufer von Maschinen diese unter aussergewöhnlichen klimatischen Bedingungen einsetzen will.[139] Auch öffentlich-rechtliche Vorschriften im Verwendungsstaat können einen solchen besonderen Verwendungszweck darstellen.[140] Ein besonderer Gebrauchszweck kann auch vorliegen, wenn der Käufer auf einem Markt tätig ist, der besonderen Wert auf fairen Handel und Einhaltung ethischer Prinzipien legt.[141]

Erforderlich ist zunächst, dass der besondere Gebrauchszweck dem Verkäufer **zur Kenntnis gebracht** wurde. Anders als noch in Art. 33 I e) EKG und in den nationalen Kaufrechten vieler kontinentaler Rechtsordnungen[142] ist nicht Voraussetzung, dass der spezielle Verwendungszweck **vertraglich vereinbart** wurde. Ein von der Bundesrepublik Deutschland auf der diplomatischen Konferenz eingebrachter Antrag, einen besonderen Verwendungszweck nur anzuerkennen, wenn er zum Gegenstand des Vertrages gemacht wurde, fand keine Unterstützung.[143] Dies würde die Haftung des Verkäufers für die Eignung zu einem besonderen Gebrauchszweck in ungerechtfertigter Weise einengen.[144] Zur Kenntnis gebracht ist damit weniger als vertraglich vereinbart.[145] Wird dem Verkäufer der Verwendungsstaat zur Kenntnis gebracht, so hat er für die Eignung der Ware im Hinblick auf sowohl faktische Verwendungsbedingungen (z. B. Klimabedingungen, kulturelle, religiöse oder weltanschauliche Traditionen und Überzeugungen) als auch öffentlich-rechtliche Vorgaben einzustehen.[146]

Keine Probleme entstehen, wenn der besondere Gebrauchszweck dem Verkäufer **ausdrücklich** zur Kenntnis gebracht wurde. Will der Verkäufer die daraus entspringende Einstandspflicht vermeiden, so muss er widersprechen.[147] Es reicht jedoch auch eine **konkludente Bekanntgabe** des besonderen Verwendungszwecks aus.[148] Problematisch erscheint insoweit der Fall, dass der Verkäufer den besonderen Verwendungszweck nicht erkannte, ihn aber vernünftigerweise hätte erkennen können. Nach dem Sekretariatskommentar scheint es insoweit auf die aktuelle Kenntnis des Verkäufers anzukommen.[149] Nach

---

[138] Dies gilt selbst dann, wenn die Ware auch für den in Aussicht genommenen Verwendungszweck nicht geeignet war, vgl. BGH, 24.3.1999, CISG-online 396 = BGHZ 141, 129, 136 f. = JZ 1999, 791 ff. (Rebwachs), m. Anm. *Schlechtriem*, JZ 1999, 794–797.

[139] Vgl. das Bsp. von *Schlechtriem*, Seller's Obligations, § 6.03, S. 6–21; *ders.*, JZ 1999, 794, 795.

[140] Vgl. oben Rn. 17, 18; vgl. auch *Herber/Czerwenka*, Art. 35, Rn. 5.

[141] Vgl. *Schwenzer/Leisinger*, GS Hellner, S. 249, 267; eher skeptisch *Schlechtriem*, (2007) 19 Pace Int'l L. Rev. 89, 97 f.

[142] Vgl. Deutschland: § 434 I Nr. 1 BGB; Schweiz: Art. 197 I OR; Österreich: § 922 I 2 ABGB; Frankreich: Art. 1641 Cc.

[143] Vgl. O. R., S. 316, Nr. 57 ff.

[144] Vgl. auch YB VIII (1977), S. 37, Nr. 173.

[145] Vgl. *Staudinger/Magnus*, Art. 35, Rn. 26 ff.; *Soergel/Lüderitz/Schüßler-Langeheine*, Art. 35, Rn. 12; *Enderlein/Maskow/Strohbach*, Art. 35, Anm. 11.; *U. Huber*, RabelsZ 43 (1979), 413, 480 f.; *P. Huber/Mullis/Mullis*, S. 138; *Heilmann*, S. 179 f.; zweifelnd *Welser*, S. 109. Die Formulierungen, wann eine Inkenntnissetzung vorliegt, variieren bei den einzelnen Autoren: *Niggemann*, Pflichten des Verkäufers, S. 84 hält einen „konkludenten Hinweis" für erforderlich, *Aue*, Mängelgewährleistung im UN-Kaufrecht, S. 75 f. die ausdrückliche oder stillschweigende Mitteilung. *Karollus*, S. 117 verlangt schließlich eine „hinreichend deutliche Bekanntgabe" der speziellen, vom Käufer intendierten Verwendung der Kaufsache.

[146] Vgl. *Schlechtriem*, IPRax 2001, 161, 162; vgl. auch *Kröll u. a./Kröll*, Art. 35, Rn. 120.

[147] Vgl. *Lüderitz*, Pflichten der Parteien, S. 186; *Enderlein/Maskow/Strohbach*, Art. 35, Anm. 9.

[148] Vgl. LG München I, 27.2.2002, CISG-online 654 = IHR 2003, 233, 234; so auch *P. Huber/Mullis/Mullis*, S. 138; *Ferrari u. a./Ferrari*, Internationales Vertragsrecht, Art. 35, Rn. 19.

[149] Vgl. O. R., Art. 33, Nr. 8; vgl. auch *Reinhart*, Art. 35, Rn. 6; tendenziell auch *Hyland*, Conformity of Goods, S. 321.

U. S.-amerikanischem Recht genügt jedoch schon, dass der Verkäufer Grund hatte, den Verwendungszweck zu erkennen.[150] Auch der Wortlaut des Abs. 2 b) – der auf den Akt der Bekanntgabe abstellt – spricht dafür, dass es ausreichend sein muss, dass ein vernünftiger Verkäufer aus den Umständen den besonderen Gebrauchszweck **erkennen konnte.**[151] Darüber hinaus erscheint eine solche Auslegung auch aus Beweisgründen geboten, da aktuelle Kenntnis nur schwer bewiesen werden könnte. Um sicher zu gehen, ist dem Käufer zu raten, auf besondere Gebrauchszwecke bei Vertragsschluss ausdrücklich aufmerksam zu machen.

22 Der besondere Gebrauchszweck muss dem Verkäufer im **Zeitpunkt des Vertragsschlusses** zur Kenntnis gebracht werden. Eine spätere Bekanntgabe ist nicht ausreichend.[152]

23 Voraussetzung ist weiter, dass der **Käufer** auf die Sachkenntnis und das Urteilsvermögen des Verkäufers **vertraut hat.** Dieses Vertrauen wird regelmässig vorliegen, wenn der Verkäufer Spezialist oder Experte für die Herstellung oder Beschaffung von Waren für den vom Käufer beabsichtigten besonderen Verwendungszweck ist[153] oder sich gegenüber dem Käufer jedenfalls als solcher ausgibt. **Eigene Sachkunde** des Käufers lässt das Vertrauen noch nicht entfallen.[154] Anderes mag gelten, wenn der Käufer selbst über grössere Sachkunde als der Verkäufer verfügt.[155] Das **Vertrauen** kann jedoch **entfallen,** wenn der Käufer an der Auswahl der Ware teilnimmt, die Ware vor dem Kauf untersucht, auf den Herstellungsprozess Einfluss nimmt, genaue Spezifikationen erteilt oder auf eine bestimmte Marke besteht.[156] Es liegt dann ein Konflikt vor zwischen nach Abs. 1 vereinbarten Eigenschaften und Eigenschaften, die für den besonderen Verwendungszweck nach Abs. 2 b) erforderlich sind.[157] Erkennt der Verkäufer, dass die so vom Käufer ausgewählte Ware nicht zu dem in Aussicht genommenen Zweck geeignet ist, trifft ihn allerdings eine aus Treu und Glauben abzuleitende Informationspflicht.[158] Besteht der Käufer gleichwohl auf dieser Ware, kommt eine Einstandspflicht des Verkäufers nach Abs. 2 b) nicht in Betracht. Das **Vertrauen** des Käufers in die Sachkunde des Verkäufers ist darüber hinaus **nicht gerechtfertigt,** wenn der Verkäufer z. B. nicht Hersteller der Ware, sondern einfacher Zwischenhändler ist[159] und dem Käufer

---

[150] Vgl. *Hyland,* Conformity of Goods, S. 320.
[151] Vgl. auch *P. Huber/Mullis/Mullis,* S. 138; *Staudinger/Magnus,* Art. 35, Rn. 28; *Karollus,* S. 117; *Enderlein/Maskow/Strohbach,* Art. 35, Anm. 11.; MünchKomm/*Gruber,* Art. 35, Rn. 11; *Benedick,* Informationspflichten, Rn. 297; *Kröll u. a./Kröll,* Art. 35, Rn. 111; a. A. *Heilmann,* S. 180.
[152] Vgl. *Staudinger/Magnus,* Art. 35, Rn. 30; *Enderlein/Maskow/Strohbach,* Art. 35, Anm. 10.; *Aue,* Mängelgewährleistung im UN-Kaufrecht, S. 75 f.; *Hutter,* S. 44; *Heilmann,* S. 180.
[153] Vgl. *Schlechtriem,* Einheitliches UN-Kaufrecht, S. 67; *Heilmann,* S. 181; weitergehend *Staudinger/Magnus,* Art. 35, Rn. 31, demzufolge der Käufer im Zweifel auf die Sachkenntnis und das Urteilsvermögen des Verkäufers vertrauen darf.
[154] Wie hier: *Krätzschmar,* Öffentlichrechtliche Beschaffenheitsvorgaben, S. 58; a. A. LG Coburg, 12.12.2006, CISG-online 1447 = IHR 2007, 117 (kein Vertrauen, wenn der Käufer die Verwendbarkeit der Ware genauso gut beurteilen kann wie der Verkäufer); *U. Huber,* RabelsZ 43 (1979), 413, 481; *Honsell,* SJZ 1992, 345, 351; *Stumpf,* 1. Aufl., Art. 35 Rn. 24. Für Wegfall des Vertrauens bei gleicher Sachkunde *Honsell/Magnus,* Art. 35, Rn. 22; *Ferrari u. a./Ferrari,* Internationales Vertragsrecht, Art. 35, Rn. 20; ähnlich *Staudinger/Magnus,* Art. 35, Rn. 32 und *Benedick,* Informationspflichten, Rn. 305, die jedoch beide für die Vermutung plädieren, dass der Käufer auf die Sachkunde des Verkäufers vertrauen konnte, wenn nicht geklärt werden kann, wer die grössere Sachkunde besitzt.
[155] Vgl. *Lüderitz,* Pflichten der Parteien, S. 186; ähnlich *Hyland,* Conformity of Goods, S. 321; *Benedick,* Informationspflichten, Rn. 303; *Piltz,* Internationales Kaufrecht, Rn. 5–42: grundsätzlich kein Vertrauen; a. A. *Krätzschmar,* Öffentlichrechtliche Beschaffenheitsvorgaben, S. 58: sogar bei grösserer Sachkenntnis auf Seiten des Käufers ist Vertrauen möglich.
[156] Vgl. *Staudinger/Magnus,* Art. 35, Rn. 33; *Hyland,* Conformity of Goods, S. 321; *Heilmann,* S. 182; *Aue,* Mängelgewährleistung im UN-Kaufrecht, S. 76; *Benedick,* Informationspflichten, Rn. 308; *Enderlein/Maskow/Strohbach,* Art. 35, Anm. 13.; *Ferrari u. a./Ferrari,* Internationales Vertragsrecht, Art. 35, Rn. 20; *Hutter,* S. 44 f.; *Piltz,* Internationales Kaufrecht, Rn. 5–42.
[157] Vgl. *Schlechtriem,* Einheitliches UN-Kaufrecht, S. 57, Fn. 253.
[158] Vgl. Sekretariatskommentar, Art. 33, Nr. 9; *Neumayer/Ming,* Art. 35, Anm. 9.; *Niggemann,* Pflichten des Verkäufers, S. 855; *Otto,* MDR 1992, 533, 534; zweifelnd, ob Warnpflicht auch gegenüber sachkundigem Käufer besteht, *Karollus,* S. 118 Fn. 49.
[159] Gegen die Differenzierung zwischen Hersteller und Zwischenhändler: *Ferrari u. a./Ferrari,* Internationales Vertragsrecht, Art. 35, Rn. 20.

z. B. durch Empfehlung oder Vermittlung von Experten auf dem fraglichen Gebiet[160] zu verstehen gibt, dass er über keine Spezialkenntnisse verfügt,[161] oder wenn das erforderliche Urteilsvermögen in der jeweiligen Handelsbranche unüblich ist.[162] Vernünftigerweise vertrauen kann der Käufer nur auf das, was für den konkreten Verkäufer mit dessen erkennbaren Fähigkeiten erreichbar ist.[163] Am Vertrauen des Käufers kann es auch im Falle spezieller, abseitiger oder singulärer öffentlich-rechtlicher Vorgaben im Verwendungsland fehlen.[164]

c) **Kauf nach Probe oder Muster – Abs. 2 c).** Wie in den meisten nationalen Kaufrechten[165] hat der Verkäufer nach CISG auch dafür einzustehen, dass die Ware die Eigenschaften von vorgelegten Proben oder Mustern besitzt. Es genügt die Vorlage durch den Verkäufer; eine konkludente Vereinbarung ist nicht erforderlich.[166] Die als Probe oder Muster vorgelegte Ware ist damit Massstab für den Vertragsinhalt.[167] Während eine **Probe** der Gesamtheit der zu liefernden Waren entnommen wird, wird ein **Muster** dem Käufer zur Untersuchung angeboten, wenn die Ware selbst nicht zur Hand ist. Ein Muster mag alle, viele oder auch nur einzelne Eigenschaften – wie z. B. die Farbe – der Ware präsentieren.[168] Im Falle einer Probe hat der Verkäufer dafür einzustehen, dass die Ware alle Eigenschaften der Probe besitzt. Bei einem Muster ist durch Auslegung des Vertrages zu ermitteln, welche Eigenschaften der Ware durch das Muster verdeutlicht und deshalb Vertragsinhalt werden sollten.[169]

Schwierigkeiten können entstehen bei Abweichungen zwischen **Probe oder Muster** einerseits und **vertraglicher Beschreibung** der Ware nach Abs. 1 andererseits.[170] Soweit die vertragliche Beschreibung nicht im Widerspruch zu den Eigenschaften der Probe oder des Musters steht, wird man davon ausgehen können, dass die Ware sowohl die vertraglich vereinbarten als auch die Eigenschaften der Probe oder des Musters aufweisen muss.[171] Bei einem Widerspruch zwischen vertraglicher Vereinbarung und Probe ist im Einzelfall durch Auslegung des Vertrages zu ermitteln, welchen Eigenschaften nach dem gemeinsamen Parteiwillen der Vorrang zukommen sollte.[172] Auch sind Friktionen mit Abs. 2 a) **(Eignung für den gewöhnlichen Gebrauch)** denkbar: Sind sowohl Probe als auch Lieferung nicht zum gewöhnlichen Gebrauch geeignet, so kann der Verkäufer sich nicht darauf berufen, dass die Lieferung der Probe entspreche.[173] Weitere Abgrenzungsprobleme können sich zwischen Abs. 2 b) **(Eignung für einen bestimmten Zweck)** und Abs. 2 c) ergeben,

---

[160] *R. J. & A. M. Smallmon v. Transport Sales Limited and Grant Alan Miller*, High Court New Zealand, 30.7.2010, CISG-online 2113, Rn. 99, bestätigt durch CA New Zealand, 22.7.2011, CISG-online 2215.
[161] So auch *Ferrari u. a./Ferrari*, Internationales Vertragsrecht, Art. 35, Rn. 20.
[162] Vgl. *Staudinger/Magnus*, Art. 35, Rn. 33; *Enderlein/Maskow/Strohbach*, Art. 35, Anm. 14.; *Bianca/Bonell/Bianca*, Art. 35, Anm. 2.5.3.
[163] *Schmidt-Kessel*, FS Schwenzer, 1513, 1521.
[164] Vgl. *Schlechtriem*, IPRax 2001, 161, 163.
[165] Vgl. Deutschland: § 454 I BGB; Schweiz: Art. 222 OR; Österreich: Art. 8 Nr. 17 4. EVHGB; Frankreich: Art. 1588 Cc; Großbritannien: sec. 15 SGA; USA: § 2–313 (1) (c) UCC (express warranty).
[166] Vgl. MünchKommHGB/*Benicke*, Art. 35, Rn. 14; Vgl. auch LG Berlin, 15.9.1994, CISG-online 399; *Herber/Czerwenka*, Art. 35, Rn. 6; *Ferrari*, RabelsZ 68 (2004), 473, 477; a. A. LG Hamburg, 31.1.2001, CISG-online 876; *Staudinger/Magnus*, Art. 35, Rn. 36.
[167] Vgl. LG München I, 27.2.2002, CISG-online 654 = IHR 2003, 233, 235.
[168] Vgl. in Anlehnung an das US-amerikanische Recht *Hyland*, Conformity of Goods, S. 324.
[169] Ähnlich *Audit*, Vente internationale, Anm. 98.; *Bianca/Bonell/Bianca*, Art. 35, Anm. 2.6.2.11.
[170] Vgl. hierzu ausführlich *Staudinger/Magnus*, Art. 35, Rn. 37 ff.; *Hutter*, S. 50; *Benedick*, Informationspflichten, Rn. 309 ff.; *Neumayer/Ming*, Art. 35, Anm. 10.: Vorrang der vertraglichen Leistungsbeschreibung; zu dem vergleichbaren Problem im Rahmen des Art. 33 EKG *Mertens/Rehbinder*, Art. 33 EKG, Rn. 13.
[171] So auch *Staudinger/Magnus*, Art. 35, Rn. 39; *Achilles*, Art. 35, Rn. 11; *Heilmann*, S. 186 f.; aus der Rechtsprechung vgl. *Delchi Carrier, S. p. A. v. Rotorex Corp.*, U. S. Ct. App. (2nd Cir.), 6.12.1995, CISG-online 140 = 10 F. 3d. 1024.
[172] Zustimmung *Staudinger/Magnus*, Art. 35, Rn. 39; *Heilmann*, S. 186; *Benedick*, Informationspflichten, Rn. 312. Vgl. auch OGH, 11.3.1999, CISG-online 524. Für einen grundsätzlichen Vorrang von Art. 35 I: *Ferrari u. a./Ferrari*, Internationales Vertragsrecht, Art. 35, Rn. 22; *Kröll u. a./Kröll*, Art. 35, Rn. 133 (mit Ausnahme eines auf Handelsbrauch basierenden Erfordernisses).
[173] Vgl. OGH, 27.2.2003, CISG-online 794 = IHR 2004, 25, 28 = IPRax 2004, 350, 353, m. Anm. *P. Huber*, IPRax 2004, 358 f.; a. *A. Benedick*, Informationspflichten, Rn. 314, im Falle offensichtlicher Eigenschaften der Probe. Differenzierend: *P. Huber/Mullis/Mullis*, S. 140.

wenn die der Probe oder dem Muster entsprechende Ware sich nicht für den vom Käufer in Aussicht genommenen Zweck eignet. Ausgehend vom Sinn und Zweck einer Probe oder eines Musters, die dem Käufer eine Untersuchung, probeweise Verarbeitung etc. ermöglichen sollen, ist hier im Regelfall[174] ein Vorrang der nach Abs. 2 c) massgeblichen Eigenschaften anzunehmen, da insoweit auch kein Vertrauen in die Fähigkeiten und Sachkunde des Verkäufers auf Seiten des Käufers vorliegt. Wo freilich im Einzelfall der Verkäufer die Eignung der Ware zu einem bestimmten Zweck bejaht, ohne dass der Käufer dies anhand der Probe oder des Musters überprüfen kann, muss Abs. 2 b) vorgehen.

26 Der Verkäufer haftet nach Abs. 2 c) nicht, wenn die Probe oder das Muster nur **unverbindlich zur Ansicht** vorgelegt wurde.[175] Zwar wurde eine dahingehende ausdrückliche Regelung – wie sie noch Art. 33 I c) EKG vorsah – nicht in das CISG aufgenommen. Der Wortlaut „als Probe oder Muster vorgelegt" spricht jedoch dafür, unverbindliche Vorlagen nicht unter Abs. 2 c) fallen zu lassen.

27 Abs. 2 c) greift nur ein, wenn der Verkäufer die Probe oder das Muster vorgelegt hat, nicht jedoch bei der Vorlage einer Probe oder eines Musters durch den Käufer (sog. **Bestellprobe**). In diesem Fall können jedoch die Eigenschaften der Probe oder des Musters als nach Abs. 1 konkludent vereinbarte Eigenschaften angesehen werden.[176] Ebenfalls nicht unter Abs. 2 c) zu subsumieren ist der Fall, dass der Käufer zunächst eine kleinere Menge zur Probe und dann im Rahmen eines zweiten Vertrages eine grössere Menge „wie gehabt" oder „entsprechender Qualität" bestellt.[177] Auch hier wird jedoch eine konkludente Eigenschaftsvereinbarung nach Abs. 1 anzunehmen sein.

28 **d) Übliche oder angemessene Verpackung – Abs. 2 d).** Nach Abs. 2 d) gehört zur Vertragsmässigkeit der Ware auch deren Verpackung. Im EKG fehlte eine derartige Bestimmung.[178] Auch in den meisten kontinentalen Rechten werden Fehler der Verpackung nicht zur Sachgewährleistung gerechnet,[179] wohingegen im US-amerikanischen Recht ausdrücklich die Pflicht zur Verpackung mit zur implied warranty of merchantability gehört.[180]

29 Die Ware muss grundsätzlich in der für sie üblichen Art verpackt sein. Dazu können auch Behältnisse, insbesondere also Container, gehören.[181] Die **Üblichkeit** ist zunächst nach den in der Branche geltenden Bräuchen zu bestimmen,[182] wohingegen Versuche, die Standards im Land der Niederlassung einer der Parteien, z.B. des Verkäufers, als massgebend anzusehen,[183] wenig angebracht erscheinen. Massgeblich ist hingegen der Zweck der Verpackung, nämlich der angemessene Schutz der Ware auf dem Transport.[184] Zur Üblichkeit der Verpackung können auch Kennzeichnungen und Aufschriften – insbesondere im Hinblick

---

[174] Vgl. auch *Benedick*, Informationspflichten, Rn. 324; *Ferrari u.a./Ferrari*, Internationales Vertragsrecht, Art. 35, Rn. 22; *Kröll u.a./Kröll*, Art. 35, Rn. 135. Für generellen Vorrang sprechen sich *Bianca/Bonell/Bianca*, Art. 35, Anm. 2.6.1. aus.

[175] Vgl. *Schlechtriem*, Pflichten des Verkäufers, S. 117; *ders.*, Internationales UN-Kaufrecht, Rn. 141; *Staudinger/Magnus*, Art. 35, Rn. 36; *Achilles*, Art. 35, Rn. 10.

[176] Dies war der Fall in LG Aschaffenburg, 20.4.2006, CISG-online 1446 = IHR 2007, 109, 112; vgl. *Schlechtriem*, Internationales UN-Kaufrecht, Rn. 141; *Staudinger/Magnus*, Art. 35, Rn. 40; *Kröll u.a./Kröll*, Art. 35, Rn. 136; ähnlich *Karollus*, S. 118; *Hyland*, Conformity of Goods, S. 323 Fn. 105.

[177] Vgl. *Heilmann*, S. 188; zum EKG *Mertens/Rehbinder*, Art. 33 EKG, Rn. 15.

[178] Mangelhafte Verpackung wurde deshalb nicht unter Art. 33 I f) EKG subsumiert, vgl. RB Alkmaar, 2.5.1985, in: *Schlechtriem/Magnus*, Art. 33 EKG, Nr. 19.

[179] Vgl. die Nachweise oben Rn. 11.

[180] Vgl. § 2–314 (2) (e) UCC.

[181] Vgl. *Herber/Czerwenka*, Art. 35, Rn. 7; *Ferrari u.a./Ferrari*, Internationales Vertragsrecht, Art. 35, Rn. 23.

[182] Vgl. *P. Huber/Mullis/Mullis*, S. 141; *Hutter*, S. 51.

[183] So aber OLG Zweibrücken, 17.1.2007, CISG-online 1642 = IHR 2008, 55, 58 unter Bezugnahme auf die Rechtsprechung zu öffentlich-rechtlichen Vorschriften; s. dazu oben Rn. 17 f. Hilfsweise wollen auch *Bianca/Bonell/Bianca*, Art. 35, Anm. 2.7.1., auf den Ort der Niederlassung des Verkäufers abstellen; ähnlich *Audit*, Vente internationale, Anm. 100.; *Heilmann*, S. 189; *Ferrari u.a./Ferrari*, Internationales Vertragsrecht, Art. 35, Rn. 23.

[184] Vgl. OLG Zweibrücken, 17.1.2007, CISG-online 1642 = IHR 2008, 55, 58; *Staudinger/Magnus*, Art. 35, Rn. 42; *Ferrari u.a./Ferrari*, Internationales Vertragsrecht, Art. 35, Rn. 24.

auf die erforderliche Handhabung durch Transportpersonen – gehören, obgleich dies in Abs. 2 d) im Gegensatz etwa zu § 2–314 (2) (e) UCC nicht ausdrücklich erwähnt ist. Dasselbe gilt für Angabe von Inhaltsstoffen und Verfalldaten.[185]

Die Pflicht zur Verpackung gilt unabhängig davon, ob die Ware zu **versenden** oder dem Käufer lediglich zur **Abholung** zur Verfügung zu stellen ist.[186] Im zuletzt genannten Fall mag es sich allerdings aus den Vereinbarungen der Parteien ergeben oder auf Grund Handelsbrauchs üblich sein, dass der Käufer selbst die zum Transport erforderlichen Behältnisse stellt, so dass für den Verkäufer die entsprechende Verpackungspflicht entfällt.[187] 30

Fehlt es an Gebräuchen, anhand derer sich die Üblichkeit der Verpackung bestimmen lässt, so ist eine **angemessene Verpackung** geschuldet. Dies gilt namentlich für neue oder speziell für den Käufer hergestellte Ware. Im Rahmen der Angemessenheit der Verpackung sind die Warenart, die Dauer und Art des Transportes, die klimatischen Verhältnisse etc. zu berücksichtigen. Auch im Hinblick auf eine dem Verkäufer bei Vertragsschluss bekannte Um- oder Weiterleitung der Ware muss die Verpackung hinreichenden Schutz bieten.[188] Wird während des Transports der Ware die Verpackung beschädigt, ohne dass die Ware selbst Schaden erleidet, haftet der Verkäufer nicht, sofern die Verpackung ausschliesslich den Schutz der Ware während des Transports sicherstellen sollte.[189] Etwas anderes gilt, wenn die Verpackung **Bestandteil der Ware** ist, beispielsweise die Originalverpackung bei Markenware oder die Dauerverpackung, die zum Weiterverkauf bestimmt ist, wie etwa Flaschen oder Säcke.[190] Wird die Ware selbst auf Grund mangelhafter Verpackung auf dem Transport beschädigt, so hat der Verkäufer einzustehen, auch wenn das eigentliche Schadensereignis selbst erst nach Gefahrübergang eingetreten ist.[191] 31

3. Unerhebliche Abweichungen[192]

Der Verkäufer hat grundsätzlich auch für unerhebliche Abweichungen einzustehen.[193] Die Vorschrift des Art. 33 II EKG, nach der unerhebliche Abweichungen nicht zu berücksichtigen waren, ist bewusst fallengelassen worden.[194] Unerhebliche Abweichungen werden allerdings kaum eine **wesentliche Vertragsverletzung** darstellen, so dass eine Ersatzlieferung (Art. 46 II) oder Vertragsaufhebung (Art. 49 I) nicht in Betracht kommt, es sei denn, ein objektiv als unerheblich zu bezeichnender Mangel hat für den Käufer entscheidende Bedeutung.[195] Im Rahmen der Minderung (Art. 50) ist Voraussetzung, dass die unerhebliche Abweichung den Wert der Sache negativ beeinflusst; will der Käufer Schadenersatz (Art. 74), muss er nachweisen, dass ihm auf Grund der unerheblichen Abweichung ein Schaden entstanden ist. Verlangt der Käufer Nachbesserung (Art. 46 III) bei unerheblichen 32

---

[185] Vgl. CA Grenoble, 13.9.1995, CISG-online 157 = J. C. P. 1996, IV, 712.
[186] So auch *Bamberger/Roth/Saenger*, Art. 35, Rn. 10; *Staudinger/Magnus*, Art. 35, Rn. 42.
[187] Vgl. *Staudinger/Magnus*, Art. 35, Rn. 42 f.; *Audit*, Vente internationale, Anm. 100.; enger wohl *Bianca/Bonell/Bianca*, Art. 35, Anm. 2.7.1.: nur bei eindeutiger Vertragsabrede entfalle Pflicht zur Verpackung; ebenso *Enderlein/Maskow/Strohbach*, Art. 35, Anm. 17.
[188] Vgl. *Bianca/Bonell/Bianca*, Art. 35, Anm. 2.7.1.; *Neumayer/Ming*, Art. 35, Anm. 11.; *Enderlein/Maskow/Strohbach*, Art. 35, Anm. 17.
[189] Vgl. *Staudinger/Magnus*, Art. 35, Rn. 44; *Piltz*, Internationales Kaufrecht, Rn. 5–36; *Neumayer/Ming*, Art. 35, Anm. 11.; *Kröll u. a./Kröll*, Art. 35, Rn. 144.
[190] Vgl. *Herber/Czerwenka*, Art. 35, Rn. 7; *Audit*, Vente internationale, Anm. 100.
[191] Vgl. auch *P. Huber/Mullis/Mullis*, S. 141; vgl. dazu Art. 36 Rn. 4.
[192] Rechtsvergleichend *Schwenzer/Hachem/Kee*, Rn. 31.150 ff.
[193] Vgl. HG Zürich, 30.11.1998, CISG-online 415 = SZIER 1999, 188; *Staudinger/Magnus*, Art. 35, Rn. 11; *Kircher*, S. 51; *Piltz*, Internationales Kaufrecht, Rn. 5–32; *Ferrari u. a./Ferrari*, Internationales Vertragsrecht, Art. 35, Rn. 3; a. A. *Neumayer/Ming*, Art. 35, Anm. 2.; *Heilmann*, S. 202 ff.; Schiedsspruch des SCC Institute, 5.4.2007, CISG-online 1521, Rn. 144.
[194] Vgl. oben Rn. 1 und im Detail *Hutter*, S. 52 f.; dies bedauernd *Schlechtriem*, Seller's Obligations, § 6.03, S. 6–22 ff.
[195] Vgl. AppGer Basel-Stadt, 22.8.2003, CISG-online 943 = IHR 2005, 117 (Produkte aus gentechnisch veränderten Sojabohnen).

Mängeln, ist besonders sorgfältig zu prüfen, ob diese dem Verkäufer im Hinblick auf die gesamten Umstände zumutbar ist oder nicht.[196]

4. Gemischte Verträge

32a In gemischten Verträgen, die nach Art. 3 II dem CISG unterliegen, wird häufig unklar sein, ob fehlende Vertragsmässigkeit auf die Sache selbst oder auf fehlerhafte Erfüllung dienstvertraglicher Elemente zurückzuführen ist. Entsprechend dem in Art. 3 niedergelegten Grundsatz der einheitlichen Behandlung des Vertrages sollte auch insoweit an Art. 35 angeknüpft werden. Dies hat zur Folge, dass auf jeden Fall gerügt (Artt. 38, 39) und ein einheitlicher Haftungsmassstab[197] angewandt werden muss.

5. Auf den Käufer zurückzuführende Vertragswidrigkeit

33 Nicht ausdrücklich geregelt ist der Fall, dass die Vertragswidrigkeit der Ware auf den Käufer selbst zurückzuführen ist, wie wenn beispielsweise Fehler der vom Käufer gelieferten Grundstoffe zur Vertragswidrigkeit der vom Verkäufer herzustellenden Ware führen. Im Rahmen der UNCITRAL-Sitzung 1977[198] hatte man erwogen, eine Vorschrift aufzunehmen, wonach der Verkäufer in einem solchen Fall für die Vertragswidrigkeit nicht einzustehen hat, falls er den Fehler des vom Käufer gestellten Materials nicht kannte oder erkennen konnte oder falls der Käufer nach einer Warnung durch den Verkäufer auf der Verwendung bestand. Trotz Unterstützung in der Sache wurde der Vorschlag nicht angenommen; zum Teil hielt man die Lösung ohnehin für selbstverständlich. Das Nichteinstehen des Verkäufers, der den Fehler des vom Käufer gelieferten Materials nicht kannte, ergibt sich zwanglos aus **Art. 80**. Wo der Verkäufer freilich den Fehler des Materials erkennt, ist er nach Treu und Glauben verpflichtet, den Käufer hierüber zu informieren. Insoweit ist der Fall der Situation der Schutzrechtsbelastung auf Grund Befolgens technischer Anweisungen des Käufers vergleichbar.[199]

IV. Haftungsausschluss

1. Kenntnis des Käufers – Abs. 3[200]

34 Gemäss Abs. 3 hat der Verkäufer für eine Vertragswidrigkeit nach Abs. 2 nicht einzustehen, die der Käufer bei Vertragsschluss kannte oder über die er nicht in Unkenntnis sein konnte.[201] Die Kenntnis des Käufers muss sich auf den konkreten Mangel beziehen, der die Grundlage des geltend gemachten Anspruchs ist; Kenntnis eines anderen Mangels der Ware schliesst die Haftung nicht aus.[202] Nicht-in-Unkenntnis-Sein-Können ist dabei mehr als grobe Fahrlässigkeit.[203] Ausgeschlossen ist die Haftung lediglich für gleichsam **ins Auge**

---

[196] Vgl. auch unten *Müller-Chen*, Art. 46 Rn. 40.
[197] A. A. *Schmidt-Kessel*, FS Schwenzer, S. 1513, 1524 f.
[198] Vgl. YB VIII (1977), S. 38, Nr. 180 ff.
[199] Vgl. dazu unten Art. 42 Rn. 20 ff.
[200] Rechtsvergleichend *Schwenzer/Hachem/Kee*, Rn. 31.156 ff.
[201] Zur Regelung in nationalen Rechtsordnungen vgl. Deutschland: § 442 I BGB; Schweiz: Art. 200 OR; Österreich: § 928 ABGB; Frankreich: Art. 1642 Cc (keine Haftung für vices apparents); USA: § 2–316 (3) (b) UCC.
[202] *Castel Electronics Pty. Ltd. v. Toshiba Singapore Pte. Ltd.*, Federal Court of Australia, 20.4.2011, CISG-online 2219.
[203] Wie hier P. *Huber/Mullis/Mullis*, S. 142; *Neumayer/Ming*, Art. 35, Anm. 13.; *U. Huber*, RabelsZ 43 (1979), 413, 479; *Loewe*, Art. 35, S. 56; *Aue*, Mängelgewährleistung im UN-Kaufrecht, S. 85; *Welser*, S. 109; *Hyland*, Conformity of Goods, S. 325; ähnlich *Honnold/Flechtner*, Art. 35, Rn. 229 („facts that are before the eyes of one who can see"). Im Sinne grober Fahrlässigkeit interpretieren die Bestimmung: *Stumpf*, 1. Aufl., Art. 35 Rn. 32; *Staudinger/Magnus*, Art. 35, Rn. 47; *Schlechtriem*, Internationales UN-Kaufrecht, Rn. 143; *Herber/Czerwenka*, Art. 35, Rn. 10; *Karollus*, S. 119; *Reinhart*, Art. 35, Rn. 9; *Achilles*, Art. 35, Rn. 16; *Bamberger/Roth/Saenger*, Art. 35, Rn. 11; *Ferrari u. a./Ferrari*, Internationales Vertragsrecht, Art. 35, Rn. 29; wohl auch *Bianca/Bonell/Bianca*, Art. 35, Anm. 2.8.1.; *Honsell*, SJZ 1992, 345, 351; *Heilmann*, S. 208 f.; unklar *Audit*, Vente interna-

springende Vertragswidrigkeiten. Insoweit stellt die Formulierung eine Beweiserleichterung für anders nur schwer zu beweisende Kenntnis dar.[204] Welche Vertragswidrigkeiten dem Käufer solchermassen ins Auge springen mussten, ist nicht rein objektiv zu bestimmen, vielmehr muss auch die Position des Käufers berücksichtigt werden.[205] In der Praxis relevant wird der Haftungsausschluss nach Abs. 3 vor allem beim Verkauf einer Speziessache, wie insbesondere bei gebrauchten Maschinen.[206]

Vor Vertragsschluss trifft den Käufer jedoch **keine Pflicht,** die Ware **zu untersuchen.**[207] 35 Fraglich mag sein, ob der Käufer, wenn er vom Verkäufer **zur Untersuchung aufgefordert** wurde, diese unterlassen und sich später auf Vertragswidrigkeit berufen kann, oder ob er dann seine Rechte nach Abs. 3 verliert.[208] Viel wird insoweit von den Umständen des Einzelfalles, wie etwa der Art der Ware, der jeweiligen Sachkunde beider Parteien, der Zumutbarkeit einer Untersuchung für den Käufer etc. abhängen. Jedenfalls wenn der Verkäufer mit der Aufforderung zur Untersuchung den Hinweis auf mögliche Mängel der Ware verbindet, verliert der Käufer seine Rechte nach Abs. 3 für bei einer solchen Untersuchung ins Auge springende Fehler, auch wenn er sie nicht vornimmt.[209] Im Übrigen kann sich der Verkäufer im Regelfall nicht schon dadurch der Verantwortung für Vertragswidrigkeiten entziehen, dass er dem Käufer die Untersuchung anbietet.[210]

Trotz Kenntnis des Käufers von der Vertragswidrigkeit bei Vertragsschluss hat der Ver- 36 käufer aber einzustehen, wenn der Käufer auf einwandfreier Qualität bestand;[211] insoweit kann vom Verkäufer eine **Beseitigung des Mangels** erwartet werden.[212]

Im Gegensatz zu § 442 I BGB und entsprechenden Regelungen in anderen Rechtsord- 37 nungen[213] ist in Abs. 3 der Fall nicht ausdrücklich geregelt, dass der Verkäufer eine **Garantie** für die Beschaffenheit übernommen, eine **Eigenschaft zugesichert** oder einen Mangel **arglistig verschwiegen** hat. Bei Zusicherung liegt freilich ohnehin eine vertragliche Beschaffenheitsvereinbarung nach Abs. 1 vor, so dass Abs. 3 nicht eingreift.[214] Bei Arglist des Verkäufers darf aus dem Grundgedanken des Art. 40, wonach der Verkäufer sich nicht auf ein Verhalten des Käufers berufen kann, wenn ihn selbst ein grösserer Vorwurf trifft, in Verbindung mit Art. 7 I gefolgert werden, dass der Verkäufer auch dann einzustehen hat, wenn der Käufer über den Mangel nicht in Unkenntnis sein konnte. Der bloss grob fahrlässig unwissende Käufer erscheint schutzwürdiger als der arglistig handelnde Verkäufer.[215]

---

tionale, Anm. 101.; *Ebenroth,* östJBl 1986, 681, 689; *Hutter,* S. 67, der die Abgrenzung im Einzelfall den Gerichten überlassen will. Nur geringe praktische Relevanz sieht *Kröll u. a./Kröll,* Art. 35, Rn. 159 f.

[204] Vgl. *Honnold/Flechtner,* Art. 35, Rn. 229.
[205] Vgl. *Herber/Czerwenka,* Art. 35, Rn. 10; *Heuzé,* Anm. 296.; wohl auch *Ghestin,* Obligations du vendeur, S. 100 ff.
[206] Vgl. *Honnold/Flechtner,* Art. 35, Rn. 229; KG Wallis, 28.10.1997, CISG-online 328, E. 4) b).
[207] So die ganz h. M., vgl. *Schlechtriem,* Internationales UN-Kaufrecht, Rn. 143; *P. Huber/Mullis/Mullis,* S. 143; *Staudinger/Magnus,* Art. 35, Rn. 48; *Honnold/Flechtner,* Art. 35, Rn. 229; *Hyland,* Conformity of Goods, S. 325; *Ryffel,* S. 20; *Piltz,* Internationales Kaufrecht, Rn. 5–52; *Aue,* Mängelgewährleistung im UN-Kaufrecht, S. 83; *Heilmann,* S. 209; *Enderlein/Maskow/Strohbach,* Art. 35, Anm. 20.; teilweise a. A.: *Audit,* Vente internationale, Anm. 101.; *Heuzé,* Anm. 291.: Untersuchungsobliegenheit jedenfalls bei Stückschulden, ausnahmsweise auch bei Gattungssachen; *Garro/Zuppi,* Compraventa internacional, S. 159. Im nationalen französischen Recht wird eine Untersuchungspflicht angenommen, vgl. *Ghestin/Desché,* Traité des contrats, Anm. 729, 733.
[208] Vgl. *Honnold/Flechtner,* Art. 35, Rn. 229; KG Wallis, 28.10.1997, CISG-online 328, E. 4) b). Für eine detaillierte Betrachtung dieses Problems, vgl. *Hyland,* Conformity of Goods, S. 325 f.; *Aue,* Mängelgewährleistung im UN-Kaufrecht, S. 85; *Staudinger/Magnus,* Art. 35, Rn. 48.
[209] Ebenso *Ryffel,* S. 20.
[210] KG Wallis, 28.10.1997, CISG-online 328; *Henschel,* (2004) 1 Nordic J. Com. L. 1, 11; *P. Huber/Mullis/Mullis,* S. 143; *Piltz,* Internationales Kaufrecht, Rn. 5–52; *Ferrari u. a./Ferrari,* Internationales Vertragsrecht, Art. 35, Rn. 29.
[211] *Piltz,* Internationales Kaufrecht, Rn. 5–53.
[212] Vgl. Sekretariatskommentar, Art. 33, Nr. 14.
[213] Vgl. Deutschland: § 442 I BGB; Schweiz: Art. 200 II OR; Österreich: § 928 ABGB. Ebenso im französischen Recht, vgl. den Hinweis bei *Niggemann,* Pflichten des Verkäufers, S. 85, Fn. 27.
[214] Vgl. unten Rn. 38; i. E. zustimmend *Heuzé,* Anm. 296.
[215] Vgl. OLG Köln, 21.5.1996, CISG-online 254; *Staudinger/Magnus,* Art. 35, Rn. 52; *Achilles,* Art. 35, Rn. 16; *Karollus,* S. 119; *Welser,* S. 110; *Heilmann,* S. 211; *Kröll u. a./Kröll,* Art. 35, Rn. 162.

38   Abs. 3 bezieht sich nur auf die Fälle der **Vertragswidrigkeit nach Abs. 2,** nicht jedoch auch auf die vertragliche **Leistungsbeschreibung nach Abs. 1.**[216] Auch eine analoge Anwendung ist insoweit nicht möglich.[217] Dies ergibt sich nicht allein aus dem klaren Wortlaut des Abs. 3 und seiner Entstehungsgeschichte,[218] sondern ist darüber hinaus auch von der Sache her geboten. Bei Quantitätsabweichung oder aliud-Lieferung ist Kenntnis des Käufers schon gar nicht denkbar. Aber auch wenn der Käufer eine Qualitätsabweichung bei Vertragsschluss kennt, verbietet sich eine pauschalierende Betrachtung, wie sie Abs. 3 vornimmt. Hier muss im Einzelfall durch Auslegung ermittelt werden, welche Warenbeschaffenheit nun wirklich i. S. des Abs. 1 vereinbart wurde.[219] Es mag sein, dass die Qualität, wie der Käufer sie kannte, zum Vertragsinhalt wurde. Möglich ist jedoch auch, dass der Verkäufer die der Leistungsbeschreibung entsprechenden Eigenschaften noch bis zur Lieferung herstellen soll, bzw. ihr Fehlen nach Lieferung zu beheben hat. Dies gilt insbesondere, wenn der Käufer von der Qualitätsabweichung keine positive Kenntnis hat, sondern darüber lediglich nicht in Unkenntnis sein konnte. Ist dem Käufer jedoch von vornherein bekannt, dass die Ware bis zur Lieferung nicht mit der Vereinbarung nach Abs. 1 in Einklang zu bringen ist, stellt ein Beharren auf deren Einhaltung ein venire contra factum proprium dar.[220]

39   Keine praktische Bedeutung erlangt Abs. 3 im Rahmen des Abs. 2 c), d. h. wo sich die Eigenschaften der Ware nach einer vorgelegten **Probe** oder einem **Muster** bestimmen. Die Ware ist schon nach Abs. 2 vertragsgemäss, wenn sie der Probe oder dem Muster entspricht, auch wenn der Käufer bei einer allfälligen Untersuchung der Probe oder des Musters Mängel erkannt hat oder darüber nicht in Unkenntnis sein konnte.[221]

2. Unterlassene Anzeige

40   Der Verkäufer hat für eine Vertragswidrigkeit nicht einzustehen, wenn der Käufer die erforderliche Anzeige nach Art. 39 unterlässt, es sei denn, es läge ein Ausnahmetatbestand nach **Artt. 40, 44** vor.

3. Freizeichnung

41   Nach Art. 6 ist es den Parteien unbenommen, die Bestimmung des Art. 35 **insgesamt** oder **einzelne ihrer Teile** vertraglich abzubedingen.[222] Einzelne US-amerikanische Autoren[223] vertreten nun allerdings die Auffassung, der Verkäufer könne sich nur von der

---

[216] Vgl. Sekretariatskommentar, Art. 33, Nr. 14; *P. Huber/Mullis/Mullis*, S. 142; *Aue*, Mängelgewährleistung im UN-Kaufrecht, S. 80 f.; *Karollus*, S. 119; *Ebenroth*, östJBl 1986, 681, 689; *Loewe*, Art. 35, S. 56; *Bianca/Bonell/Bianca*, Art. 35, Anm. 2.9.2.; *Soergel/Lüderitz/Schüßler-Langeheine*, Art. 35, Rn. 8; *Kröll u. a./Kröll*, Art. 35, Rn. 153; *Audit*, Vente internationale, Anm. 101. Fn. 3; *Schlechtriem*, Pflichten des Verkäufers, S. 118; *Hutter*, S. 65; *Flesch*, S. 133; *Heilmann*, S. 206.

[217] A. A. *Stumpf*, 1. Aufl., Art. 35 Rn. 32; *Herber/Czerwenka*, Art. 35, Rn. 11; *Enderlein/Maskow/Strohbach*, Art. 35, Anm. 19.; *Reinhart*, Art. 35, Rn. 10; wohl auch *Neumayer/Ming*, Art. 35, Anm. 14. Ebenfalls kritisch gegenüber einer auf Abs. 2 beschränkten Anwendung *Niggemann*, Pflichten des Verkäufers, S. 85; differenzierend *Staudinger/Magnus*, Art. 35, Rn. 49 ff.; offengelassen von *Hyland*, Conformity of Goods, S. 327; *Piltz*, Internationales Kaufrecht, Rn. 5–54, plädiert gegen eine automatische Ausweitung des Art. 35 III zugrundeliegenden Prinzips, hält es aber für möglich ähnliche Prinzipien zur Anwendung zu bringen, wenn der Käufer weiss oder hätte wissen müssen, dass die Ware nicht vertragsgemäss sein wird.

[218] Ein Antrag Norwegens, auch Abs. 1 in den Anwendungsbereich des Abs. 3 einzubeziehen, wurde auf der diplomatischen Konferenz abgelehnt, vgl. O. R., S. 426 f., Nr. 5 ff.

[219] Vgl. *Karollus*, S. 119; vgl. auch *P. Huber/Mullis/Mullis*, S. 142.

[220] Vgl. *Bamberger/Roth/Saenger*, Art. 35, Rn. 12; *Achilles*, Art. 35, Rn. 17; *Kircher*, S. 55; vgl. auch *Kröll u. a./Kröll*, Art. 35, Rn. 154.

[221] Vgl. LG München I, 27.2.2002, CISG-online 654 = IHR 2003, 233, 235.

[222] Vgl. OLG Dresden, 27.5.2010, CISG-online 2182 unter II. 3. C. a) = IHR 2011, 185, 188. Vgl. auch die Formulierungsbeispiele bei *Piltz*, Lieferverträge, S. 378 ff., 421 ff.; *Woltjer*, Limitations of Liability, S. 219 ff.

[223] Vgl. *Murray*, Primer, S. 893; *Hancock*, Convention on Contracts, S. 106–121; *Hyland*, Conformity of Goods, S. 316; *Honnold/Flechtner*, Art. 35, Rn. 230, stellt klar, dass die Frage der Freizeichnung in Bezug auf Art. 35 I irrelevant ist, da die Pflichten, die sich aus diesem Absatz ergeben, ausschliesslich auf der Vereinbarung der Parteien beruhen.

Vertragsmässigkeit nach Abs. 2 freizeichnen, nicht jedoch von jener nach Abs. 1, da nur in Abs. 2 auf eine abweichende Vereinbarung der Parteien Bezug genommen werde. Indes kann der Einleitungssatz des Abs. 2 nicht i. S. der generellen Zulässigkeit von Freizeichnungsklauseln interpretiert werden, vielmehr wird hiermit lediglich auf Abs. 1 Bezug genommen. Ein Haftungsausschluss ist deshalb grundsätzlich auch bei vertraglicher Leistungsbeschreibung möglich.[224]

Während sich die **Einbeziehung** von Freizeichnungsklauseln nach Artt. 14 ff. und ihre **Auslegung** nach Art. 8 bestimmt, ist die **Inhaltskontrolle** eine Frage der Gültigkeit, die nach Art. 4 a) nicht dem CISG unterliegt, sondern nach dem über IPR anwendbaren nationalen Recht zu bestimmen ist.[225] Der Massstab, der dabei an Freizeichnungsklauseln angelegt wird, differiert im internationalen Vergleich nicht unerheblich.[226] Soweit es sich nicht um Verbrauchergeschäfte handelt, schafft auch die EG-RL über missbräuchliche Klauseln in Verbraucherverträgen[227] keine Rechtsvereinheitlichung. Als kleinster gemeinsamer Nenner kann jedoch für alle Rechtsordnungen davon ausgegangen werden, dass dem Käufer bei fehlender Vertragsgemässheit der Ware ein Minimalrechtsschutz (minimum adequate remedy) verbleiben muss,[228] so dass jedenfalls der gänzliche Ausschluss der Haftung als unwirksam zu betrachten ist. Des Weiteren ist anerkannt, dass sich niemand von eigenem arglistigem Verhalten freizeichnen kann.[229] Jedenfalls nach deutschem Verständnis ist Arglist schon anzunehmen, wenn der Verkäufer unrichtige Aussagen ohne ausreichende Erkenntnisgrundlage „ins Blaue hinein" tätigt und mit der Unwahrheit seiner Aussagen zumindest rechnet.[230] In diesem Zusammenhang relevant sind auch Informationspflichten des Verkäufers, deren zumindest bedingt vorsätzliche Nichterfüllung ein arglistiges Verschweigen darstellt.[231] Ebenfalls ausgeschlossen ist eine Freizeichnung, wenn der Verkäufer sich für das Vorhandensein bestimmter Eigenschaften durch eine Garantie, Zusicherung, express warranty oder dgl. stark gemacht hat.[232] Unterliegt der Vertrag subsidiär **deutschem Recht,** so ist nach § 307 II Nr. 1 BGB entscheidend, ob die Freizeichnungsklausel mit „wesentlichen Grundgedanken der gesetzlichen Regelung" nicht zu vereinbaren ist, oder ob sie wesentliche Pflichten des Verkäufers so einschränkt, dass „die Erreichung des Vertragszwecks" gefährdet ist (§ 307 II Nr. 2 BGB). Prüfungsmassstab ist insoweit das CISG.[233] Bei der Frage, ob der Verkäufer generell[234] seine Einstandspflicht für Vertragswidrigkeit der Ware abbedingen kann, ist zunächst auf die **Wesentlichkeit** der in Frage stehenden Vertragsverletzung abzustellen. Wo immer eine wesentliche Vertragsverletzung i. S. des Art. 25 anzunehmen ist,[235] liegt die Vermutung nahe, dass auch i. S. von § 307 II

---

[224] *Kröll u. a./Kröll,* Art. 35, Rn. 164.
[225] *Norfolk Southern Railway Company v. Power Source Supply, Inc.,* U. S. Dist. Ct. (W. D. Pa.), 25.7.2008, CISG-online 1776. Vgl. auch oben *Ferrari,* Art. 4 Rn. 20; *Honnold/Flechtner,* Art. 35, Rn. 230.
[226] Einen Überblick gibt *von Westphalen,* Handbuch des Kaufvertragsrechts, bei den jeweiligen nationalen Rechtsordnungen; vgl. auch *Kötz,* Europäisches Vertragsrecht I, S. 224 ff. Zur Rechtslage in den USA vgl. *Stone,* UCC in a Nutshell, S. 54 ff.; für Frankreich: vgl. *Niggemann,* RIW 1991, 372, 375; für Österreich: vgl. *Karollus,* S. 118 f.; für England: vgl. *Schmidt-Kessel,* Standards, S. 465 ff.; *Benjamin,* Rn. 14–015 ff.; *Atiyah/Adams,* S. 188 ff.
[227] RL 93/13/EWG v. 5.4.1993, ABlEG Nr. L 95/29 v. 21.4.1993; vgl. dazu *Bunte,* FS Locher, S. 325 ff.; *Brandner/Ulmer,* BB 1991, 701–709.
[228] Vgl. *Lookofsky,* Understanding the CISG, S. 167.
[229] OLG Dresden, 27.5.2010, CISG-online 2182 unter II. 3. C. a) = IHR 2011, 185, 188.
[230] OLG Dresden, 27.5.2010, CISG-online 2182 = IHR 2011, 185, 189.
[231] Am Beispiel des Autokaufs: OLG Dresden, 27.5.2010, CISG-online 2182 = IHR 2011, 185, 188 ff.
[232] Vgl. für Deutschland: § 444 BGB (allerdings wird auch die Auffassung vertreten, dass § 444 BGB nicht anzuwenden sei, da es sich insoweit nicht um eine Gültigkeitsvorschrift handele, vgl. *Schlechtriem,* Internationales UN-Kaufrecht, Rn. 147; *Piltz,* IHR 2002, 2, 4 f.); für die Schweiz: Art. 199 OR (Arglist), Zusicherung: vgl. *Schwenzer,* OR AT, Rn. 45.09; für die USA: § 2–316 UCC; für Frankreich: CA Versailles, 11.7.1985, Juris Data 042 231.
[233] Vgl. *von Westphalen,* AGB und einheitliches Kaufgesetz, S. 68; *Teklote,* S. 180 ff.; zum EKG vgl. *Schlechtriem,* Haager Einheitliches Kaufrecht, S. 257 f.; *Hausmann,* WM 1980, 726, 735.
[234] Zum Ausschluss einzelner Rechtsbehelfe vgl. *U. Huber,* 1. Aufl., Art. 45 Rn. 67 f., 72 ff.
[235] Für Einzelheiten vgl. oben *Schroeter,* Art. 25 Rn. 43 ff.

Nr. 2 BGB eine unangemessene Benachteiligung vorliegt.[236] Umgekehrt bestehen bei unwesentlichen Abweichungen von der Vertragsmässigkeit an der Wirksamkeit einer Freizeichnungsklausel grundsätzlich keine Bedenken. Darüber hinaus kann auch die aus dem internen deutschen Recht bekannte Regel, dass eine Freizeichnung für den Fall **grober Fahrlässigkeit** nicht zulässig ist,[237] im Rahmen des CISG bei Freizeichnung von Vertragswidrigkeit angewandt werden.

V. Rechtsbehelfe

1. Nach CISG[238]

43   Bei jeglicher Vertragswidrigkeit nach Art. 35 hat der Käufer grundsätzlich einen Anspruch auf Erfüllung. Bei Quantitätsabweichungen kann er daher zunächst Lieferung des fehlenden Teils verlangen (Artt. 51 I, 46 I). Bei anderen Formen fehlender Vertragsmässigkeit (Qualitätsabweichung, aliud-Lieferung) besteht der Erfüllungsanspruch in Form einer Ersatzlieferung nur, soweit die Vertragswidrigkeit eine wesentliche Vertragsverletzung darstellt (Art. 46 II). Nachbesserung kann bei Zumutbarkeit verlangt werden (Art. 46 III). **Vertragsaufhebung** wegen fehlender Vertragsmässigkeit kommt nur in Betracht, soweit eine wesentliche Vertragsverletzung vorliegt, Art. 49 I a).[239] Im Übrigen hat der Käufer bei jeder Art der Vertragswidrigkeit nach Art. 35, d. h. auch bei Minderlieferung,[240] das Recht auf **Minderung** nach Art. 50 und auf **Schadenersatz** nach Art. 74. Zur einredeweisen Geltendmachung der Vertragswidrigkeit gegenüber einer Inanspruchnahme auf Zahlung des Kaufpreises vgl. unten *Mohs*, Art. 58 Rn. 25 ff.

2. Nach nationalem Recht[241]

44   Das EKG enthielt in Art. 34 die ausdrückliche Bestimmung, dass in den Fällen einer Vertragswidrigkeit alle dem Käufer nach nationalem Recht zustehenden Rechtsbehelfe neben solchen des EKG ausgeschlossen sein sollten. Diese Bestimmung wurde zwar nicht in das CISG übernommen,[242] gleichwohl darf aus dieser Tatsache nicht geschlossen werden, dass der Käufer nun uneingeschränkt auf nationale Rechtsbehelfe zurückgreifen könnte.[243] Für die nach nationalem Recht denkbaren Rechtsbehelfe gilt im Einzelnen folgendes:

45   a) **Irrtumsanfechtung.**[244] In der Literatur war zunächst umstritten, ob neben den Rechtsbehelfen nach CISG wegen Vertragswidrigkeit eine Anfechtung wegen Irrtums über Sacheigenschaften nach dem über IPR anwendbaren nationalen Recht zulässig ist.[245] Dabei wurde oft die im jeweiligen nationalen Recht vertretene Lösung zur Konkurrenz zwischen Irrtumsanfechtung und Gewährleistung auf das Einheitsrecht übertragen.[246] Die h. M. in **Deutschland** geht deshalb – entsprechend der Situation im internen Recht –

---

[236] Vgl. auch *U. Huber*, 1. Aufl., Art. 45 Rn. 67; zum Umkehrschluss vgl. *Frense*, S. 145 f.
[237] Vgl. § 309 Nr. 7 b) BGB; für den kaufmännischen Verkehr vgl. MünchKomm/*Basedow*, § 309 Nr. 7, Rn. 31 ff.
[238] Für Einzelheiten vgl. unten *Müller-Chen*, Art. 46 Rn. 20 ff.; Art. 49 Rn. 7 ff.; Art. 50 Rn. 2 f.; *Heilmann*, S. 392 ff.
[239] Ausführlich hierzu oben *Schroeter*, Art. 25 Rn. 43 ff.
[240] Vgl. *Bergsten*, 27 Am. J. Comp. L. (1979), 255, 258.
[241] Nach Art. 57 CESL-Entwurf können verschiedene Rechtsbehelfe unabhängig voneinander geltend gemacht werden.
[242] Zur Diskussion vgl. YB IX (1978), S. 66.
[243] Grundsätzlich zum Konkurrenzproblem unten *Müller-Chen*, Art. 45 Rn. 30 ff.
[244] Rechtsvergleichend *Schwenzer/Hachem/Kee*, Rn. 49.15 ff.
[245] Vgl. *Flesch*, S. 129 ff.
[246] Ausdrücklich in diesem Sinne *Neumayer*, Anfechtung wegen Eigenschaftsirrtums, S. 1267, 1275 f.; rechtsvergleichend zu dieser Problematik *Kramer*, Irrtum beim Vertragsschluss, S. 148 ff., Rn. 130 ff.

von der Exklusivität der Rechtsbehelfe nach CISG aus.[247] Dagegen wurde immer wieder von der **österreichischen** Literatur – da dort schon im internen Recht Irrtumsanfechtung neben Gewährleistungsrecht geltend gemacht werden kann – eine Konkurrenz beider Rechtsbehelfe gefordert.[248] Im nationalen **Schweizer Recht** wird zwar ebenfalls Irrtumsanfechtung neben Gewährleistung zugelassen, für das CISG wird jedoch mehrheitlich eine andere Auffassung vertreten.[249] Dasselbe gilt für **Frankreich,** wo eine einheitsfreundliche Lösung bevorzugt wird, so dass die Irrtumsanfechtung ausgeschlossen, bzw. nur unter identischen Voraussetzungen wie im CISG möglich sein soll.[250] Auch in **England** und den **USA,** wo im internen Recht von einer Konkurrenz der Rechtsbehelfe auszugehen ist, überwiegt die Auffassung von der Exklusivität der Rechtsbehelfe des CISG.[251]

Inzwischen hat sich auch in den Ländern, in denen zunächst das Verhältnis zwischen Irrtumsanfechtung nach nationalem Recht und Gewährleistung nach CISG unsicher war, in der höchstrichterlichen Rechtsprechung die Auffassung durchgesetzt, dass das CISG im Bereich der Vertragswidrigkeit der Ware eine **abschliessende Regelung** enthält und für Rechtsbehelfe wegen Irrtums nach nationalem Recht deshalb kein Raum mehr ist.[252] Allein diese Auffassung erscheint auch als sachgerecht, da sonst das Abkommen in einem Zentralbereich ausgehöhlt werden könnte.[253]

b) Fahrlässige Falschangaben. Auch für nationale Rechtsbehelfe, die sich auf fahrlässige Falschangaben des Verkäufers anlässlich des Vertragsschlusses stützen, seien sie auf **culpa in contrahendo** oder auf **Delikt** gegründet, kann neben Art. 35 kein Raum sein.[254] Dies gilt insbesondere auch für Ansprüche wegen negligent misrepresentation nach angloamerikanischem Recht.[255]

---

[247] Vgl. LG Aachen, 14.5.1993, CISG-online 86 = RIW 1993, 760; *Schlechtriem,* AJP 1992, 339, 352; *ders.,* 21 Cornell Int'l L. J. (1988), 467, 474; *ders.,* Internationales UN-Kaufrecht, Rn. 261; *Schmid,* Lückenfüllung und Normenkonkurrenz, S. 185; *P. Huber,* ZEuP 1994, 585, 597 ff.; *ders.,* FS Hadding, 105, 115 ff.; *Reinhart,* Art. 45, Rn. 10; *Herber/Czerwenka,* Art. 4, Rn. 22; *Karollus,* JuS 1993, 381; *Siehr,* FS Schwenzer, S. 1593, 1597 f., 1603; *Heilmann,* S. 146. Dieselbe Ansicht wird auch zum neuen deutschen Kaufrecht vertreten, vgl. *P. Huber,* FS Hadding, 105, 115 ff.

[248] Vgl. *Bydlinsky,* Allgemeines Vertragsrecht, S. 86; *Lessiak,* östJBl 1989, 487–496; *Karollus,* östJBl 1993, 22, 31 Fn. 49; *Ebenroth,* östJBl 1986, 681, 688; a. A. *Loewe,* Art. 45, S. 66; eine vermittelnde Lösung – Irrtumsanfechtung unter den Voraussetzungen des CISG – schlägt *Karollus,* S. 41 f. vor.

[249] Vgl. *Benedick,* Informationspflichten, Rn. 717 ff.; *Honsell,* plädoyer 1990/2, 38, 39; *Schwenzer,* recht 1991, 113, 115; *Wiegand,* S. 139; a. A. *Stoffel,* Droit applicable, S. 37 f.; *Neumayer,* RIW 1994, 99, 102; *Neumayer/Ming,* Art. 39, Anm. 4.

[250] Vgl. Civ. 1, 14.5.1996, J. C. P. 1997, I, 4009, m. Anm. *Radé; Boulanger,* J. C. P. 1996, I, 1585–1590; *Audit,* Vente internationale, Anm. 121.; *Heuzé,* Anm. 282.: völliger Ausschluss nationaler Rechtsbehelfe; *Niggemann,* RIW 1991, 372, 374.

[251] Vgl. *Honnold/Flechtner,* Art. 35, Rn. 240.

[252] Vgl. für Frankreich: Civ. 1, 14.5.1996, J. C. P. 1997, I, 4009, m. Anm. *Radé; Boulanger,* J. C. P. 1996, I, 1585–1590; für Österreich: OGH, 13.4.2000, CISG-online 576 = IPRax 2001, 149, 150, m. Anm. *Schlechtriem,* IPRax 2001, 161 f.

[253] Vgl. *Niggemann,* R. D. A. I. 1994, 397 – 412; *Kröll u. a./Kröll,* Art. 35, Rn. 204; umfassend *P. Huber,* Irrtumsanfechtung, S. 275 ff., der insbesondere auf den ultima ratio Rechtsbehelf der Vertragsaufhebung verweist; *ders.,* IPRax 2004, 358, 360; *Schwenzer,* (2007) 101 ASIL Proc. 416, 421; *dies./Hachem,* (2009) 57 Am. J. Comp. L. 457, 471; vgl. auch Art. 3.7 PICC.

[254] Vgl. Polimeles Protodikio Athinon, 2009, CISG-online 2228 (Delikt); OLG Koblenz, 24.2.2011, CISG-online 2301 (Delikt und culpa in contrahendo); *Schlechtriem,* Internationales UN-Kaufrecht, Rn. 42, s. auch unten *Müller-Chen,* Art. 45 Rn. 32; a. A. Polimeles Protodikio Athinon, 2009, CISG-online 2228 (culpa in contrahendo); *Magnus,* ZEuP 2010, 881, 893 (Delikt). Einzelnes zu Ansprüchen aus cic bei *U. Huber,* 3. Aufl., Art. 45 Rn. 56; aus Delikt *ders.,* 3. Aufl., Art. 45 Rn. 58 ff.

[255] *Schwenzer,* (2007) 101 ASIL Proc 416, 421; *dies./Hachem,* (2009) 57 Am. J. Comp. L., 457, 471; wie hier betreffend innocent misrepresentation vgl. *Honnold/Flechtner,* Art. 35, Rn. 240. A. A. *Lookofsky,* 13 Duke J. Comp. & Int'l L. (2003), 263, 283; *Miami Valley Paper, LLC v. Lebbing Eng'g GmbH,* U. S. Dist. Ct. (S. D. Ohio), 10.10.2006, CISG-online 1362; *Sky Cast, Inc. v. Global Direct Distribution, LLC,* U. S. Dist. Ct. (E. D. Kent), 18.3.2008, CISG-online 1652 = IHR 2009, 24, 27; *Electrocraft Arkansas, Inc. v. Super Electric Motors, Ltd. et al.,* U. S. Dist. Ct. (E. D. Ark.), 23.12.2009, CISG-online 2045.

48 **c) Arglist oder Betrug.**[256] Nicht ausgeschlossen sind dagegen Rechtsbehelfe, die dem Käufer nach nationalem Recht bei Arglist oder Betrug des Verkäufers zustehen.[257] Hier beruhen die Ansprüche des Käufers auf besonderen Umständen, die über eine blosse Vertragswidrigkeit der Ware hinausgehen.

VI. Beweisfragen

1. Allgemeines, Regelungsbereich

49 Weder die **Beweislast** noch das **Beweismass** sind im CISG ausdrücklich geregelt.[258] Dennoch können dem Übereinkommen gemäss Art. 7 II Regeln entnommen werden, die ein Zurückfallen auf das Prozessrecht des Forums für diese Fragen ausschliessen. Dem Prozessrecht verbleibt, die **Art und Weise der Beweisführung**, insbesondere die zulässigen Beweismittel, zu bestimmen.[259]

2. Beweisgegenstand

50 Im Zusammenhang mit Art. 35 ist der Beweisgegenstand das Vorliegen einer Vertragswidrigkeit im Zeitpunkt des Gefahrübergangs (Artt. 36, 67–69). Das Vorliegen einer Vertragswidrigkeit setzt voraus, dass sowohl die **Anforderungen des Vertrags** als auch deren **Nichteinhaltung** bewiesen werden können.[260] Um die Anforderungen des Vertrags zu beweisen, muss die beweisbelastete Partei entweder die vertragliche Leistungsbeschreibung gemäss Abs. 1 oder das Eingreifen einer der Vermutungen des Abs. 2 beweisen.

3. Beweislast

51 Die Verteilung der Beweislast ergibt sich aus dem Regel-Ausnahme-Prinzip[261] und dem Prinzip der Beweisnähe.[262]

52 **a) Vertragswidrigkeit gemäss Abs. 1.** Grundsätzlich hat der **Käufer** vom Zeitpunkt der physischen Übernahme der Ware an (Art. 60 lit. b) deren Vertragswidrigkeit im Zeitpunkt des Gefahrübergangs zu beweisen.[263] Die vor allem im deutschen Schrifttum ver-

---

[256] Rechtsvergleichend *Schwenzer/Hachem/Kee*, Rn. 49.25 ff.
[257] Vgl. *Schlechtriem*, Internationales UN-Kaufrecht, Rn. 261 (im Zusammenhang mit Art. 71); *Honnold/Flechtner*, Art. 4, Rn. 65; *P. Huber*, ZEuP 1994, 585, 601; *Reinhart*, Art. 35, Rn. 11; *Heilmann*, S. 145 f.; *Schwenzer*, (2007) 101 ASIL Proc. 416, 421; *dies./Hachem*, (2009) 57 Am. J. Comp. L. 457, 471; Einzelheiten bei *U. Huber*, 3. Aufl., Art. 45 Rn. 55.
[258] Für Einzelheiten zur Beweislast vgl. oben *Ferrari*, Art. 4 Rn. 48 ff.; *Schlechtriem/Schwenzer/Schwenzer/Hachem*, CISG Commentary, Art. 4, Rn. 25. Ein Antrag, eine Bestimmung zur Beweislast bei Vertragswidrigkeit aufzunehmen, wurde im Rahmen von UNCITRAL abgelehnt, vgl. YB VIII (1977), S. 37, Nr. 177 f. Zum Beweismass vgl. oben *Ferrari*, Art. 4 Rn. 53; *Schlechtriem/Schwenzer/Schwenzer/Hachem*, CISG Commentary, Art. 4, Rn. 26; vgl. auch *Schmitz-Werke GmbH & Co. v. Rockland Industries, Inc.*, U. S. Ct. App. (4th Cir.), 21.6.2002, CISG-online 625; Cámara Nacional de Apelaciones en lo Comercial, 24.4.2000, CISG-online 699.
[259] Vgl. unten Art. 74 Rn. 66.
[260] Vgl. Schiedsspruch des SCC Institute, 5.4.2007, CISG-online 1521, Rn. 117 ff., 137 ff.
[261] Vgl. OGH, 12.9.2006, CISG-online 1364; BGer, 13.11.2003, CISG-online 840, E. 5.3 = BGE 130 III 258, 264, m. zust. Anm. *Mohs*, IHR 2004, 219; BGH, 9.1.2002, CISG-online 651 = NJW 2002, 1651, 1653; OLG Koblenz, 22.4.2010, CISG-online 2290; oben *Ferrari*, Art. 4 Rn. 50 f.; unten *Müller-Chen*, Art. 45 Rn. 9; *Schlechtriem/Schwenzer/Schwenzer/Hachem*, CISG Commentary, Art. 4, Rn. 25; *Schlechtriem*, Internationales UN-Kaufrecht, Rn. 50; *Veneziano*, R. D. A. I. 1997, 39, 47 f.; *Hutter*, S. 54; *Kröll*, 15 VJ (2011), 33, 41; a. A. ICC, 6653/1993, CISG-online 71 = J. D. I. 1993, 1041, 1051.
[262] Zum Prinzip der Beweisnähe BGer, 7.7.2004, CISG-online 848, E. 3.3; BGer, 13.11.2003, CISG-online 840, E. 5.3 = BGE 130 III 258, 264 f., m. zust. Anm. *Mohs*, IHR 2004, 219, 220. Vgl. auch unten *Müller-Chen*, Art. 45 Rn. 9; *Kröll*, 15 VJ (2011), 33, 41.
[263] Vgl. BGer, 16.7.2012, CISG-online 2371, E. 8.1 = BGE 138 III, 601 ff.; BGer, 7.7.2004, CISG-online 848, E. 3.3; BGer, 13.11.2003, CISG-online 840, E. 5.3 = BGE 130 III 258, 265, m. zust. Anm. *Mohs*, IHR 2004, 219, m. abl. Anm. *Stalder*, AJP 2004, 1472, 1475 ff.; *Chicago Prime Packers, Inc. v. Northam Food Trading Co.*, U. S. Ct. App. (7th Cir.), 23.5.2005, CISG-online 1026; Hof van Beroep Gent, 28.1.2004, CISG-online 830; Netherlands Arbitration Institute, 15.10.2002, CISG-online 780, Rn. 64 ff.; OLG Innsbruck, 1.7.1994,

tretene Gegenauffassung, wonach grundsätzlich der Verkäufer die Vertragsmässigkeit der Ware zu beweisen hat, findet keine Grundlage im CISG und versucht nationale Vorverständnisse ins Einheitskaufrecht zu übertragen.[264] Der Käufer ist jedoch in Ausnahmefällen von seiner grundsätzlich bestehenden Beweisbelastung im Sinne einer einheitsrechtlichen **Beweislastumkehr** zu befreien. Weist der Käufer die Ware zurück oder rügt er sofort bei Empfang der Ware,[265] so hat der Verkäufer die Vertragsmässigkeit der Ware bei Gefahrübergang zu beweisen.[266] Abzulehnen ist hingegen die weitergehende Auffassung, dass in allen Fällen, in denen der Käufer in angemessener Frist i. S. d. Art. 39 rügt, dem Verkäufer die Beweislast auferlegt werden sollte.[267] Ansonsten würde der Käufer die Beweislast nur noch in Fällen tragen, in denen er sich wegen Präklusion nach Art. 39 ohnehin nicht mehr auf die Vertragswidrigkeit berufen könnte und deshalb die Frage nach der Beweislast letztlich irrelevant ist.[268] Durch Abkoppelung der Beweislastverteilung von der Rügeobliegenheit wird zudem bewirkt, dass längere Fristen bei Art. 39 nicht zu einer im internationalen Warenverkehr unerträglich langen Beweisbelastung des Verkäufers führen.[269] Ausnahmsweise trägt der Verkäufer die Beweislast indes dann, wenn er – bevor der Käufer gerügt hat – die Ware untersuchen und eine mögliche Vertragswidrigkeit erkennen konnte, da in einem solchen Fall das Prinzip der Beweisnähe aufgrund der grösseren Sachkenntnis des Verkäufers von seiner Ware nicht trägt.[270] Nicht zu einer Umkehr der Beweislast führt hingegen selbst akute Beweisnot jedenfalls dann, wenn auch die andere Partei von ihr betroffen wäre.[271]

CISG-online 107; Audiencia Provincial Valencia, 7.6.2003, CISG-online 948; vgl. auch BGH, 9.1.2002, CISG-online 651 = NJW 2002, 1651, 1653; vgl. auch Cour de Cassation, 24.9.2003, CISG-online 791; LG München I, 18.5.2009, CISG-online 1998; Polimeles Protodikio Athinon, 2009, CISG-online 2228; unten *Müller-Chen*, Art. 45 Rn. 10; *Kröll*, 15 VJ (2011), 33, 46; *Audit*, Vente internationale, Anm. 102.; *Bianca/Bonell/Bianca*, Art. 36, Anm. 3.1.; *Brunner*, Art. 35, Rn. 24; *Enderlein/Maskow/Strohbach*, Art. 36, Anm. 2.; *Kruisinga*, Non-conformity, S. 168 ff.; *T. M. Müller*, Beweislast, S. 84; *Welser*, S. 110; einschränkend *Karollus*, S. 121; *Piltz*, Internationales Kaufrecht, Rn. 5–23; *Staudinger/Magnus*, Art. 35, Rn. 55, Art. 36, Rn. 25, demzufolge der Käufer nur die Vertragswidrigkeit im Zeitpunkt der Besitzübernahme beweisen muss; vgl. auch *Ferrari*, RabelsZ 64 (2004), 473, 479 (ohne jegliche Differenzierung).

[264] So vor allem *Mohs*, IHR 2004, 219, 220.

[265] Auch Rügen innerhalb kurzer Untersuchungsfrist i. S. d. Art. 58 Abs. 3 genügen, vgl. *Brunner*, Art. 35, Rn. 24; *Mohs*, IHR 2004, 219, 220; MünchKommHGB/*Benicke*, Art. 36, Rn. 8; *Kröll u. a./Kröll*, Art. 35, Rn. 181; gegen diese Konstruktion, aber über die Annahme eines Anscheinsbeweises zum gleichen Ergebnis kommend, *Kröll*, 15 VJ (2011), 33, 47, 49.

[266] Vgl. BGer, 7.7.2004, CISG-online 848, E. 3.3; BGH, 9.1.2002, CISG-online 651 = NJW 2002, 1651; BGH, 8.3.1995, CISG-online 144 = BGHZ 129, 75, 81 (Muschel-Fall); CA Mons, 8.3.2001, CISG-online 605; OLG Innsbruck, 1.7.1994, CISG-online 107; CA Grenoble, 15.5.1996, CISG-online 219 = D. 1997, Somm. 221, m. Anm. *Witz;* OLG Frankfurt a. M., 13.6.1991, CISG-online 23 = RIW 1991, 591; *Ferrari*, Art. 4 Rn. 52; MünchKommHGB/*Benicke*, Art. 36, Rn. 10; *Herber/Czerwenka*, Art. 35, Rn. 9; *Piltz*, Internationales Kaufrecht, Rn. 5–23; *Staub/Koller*, Vor § 373 HGB, Rn. 670; a. A. *Kruisinga*, Non-conformity, S. 174; *Aue*, Mängelgewährleistung im UN-Kaufrecht, S. 113. Im Ergebnis genauso *Kröll*, 15 VJ (2011), 33, 47.

[267] Die noch in der 4. Auflage dieses Werkes vertretene Auffassung, wonach der Verkäufer die Beweislast trägt, falls der Käufer rechtzeitig i. S. d. Artikel 39 gerügt hat, ist aufgegeben. Wie hier *Brunner*, Art. 35, Rn. 25; *Kröll*, 15 VJ (2011), 33, 48. Vgl. aber die vorige Auffassung befürwortend BGer, 7.7.2004, CISG-online 848, E. 3.1 (wo sich das Bundesgericht nicht nachvollziehbarerweise auf die vorige Auffassung beruft, ungeachtet seiner eigenen Entscheidung vom 13.11.2003, CISG-online 840, E. 5.3 = BGE 130 III 258); OGer Luzern, 12.5.2003, CISG-online 846 = SZIER 2004, 103, 104 f.; OGer Zug, 24.3.1998, CISG-online 897, E. 3 d) aa); HG Zürich, 30.11.1998, CISG-online 415 = SZIER 1999, 185, 188; Polimeles Protodikio Athinon, 2009, CISG-online 2228; MünchKomm/*Gruber*, Art 35, Rn. 45; *Antweiler*, S. 169; *Henninger*, S. 222; *Baumgärtel/Laumen/Hepting*, Art. 35 WKR, Rn. 1, Art. 36 WKR, Rn. 11 f.; *Achilles*, Art. 35, Rn. 19; *Stalder*, AJP 2002, 1472, 1478 ff. (differenzierend: für versteckte Mängel trage der Käufer die Beweislast). Wie hier *Piltz*, Internationales Kaufrecht, Rn. 5–24.

[268] Vgl. vor allem *Mohs*, IHR 2004, 219, 220.

[269] Vgl. *Mohs*, IHR 2004, 219, 220; *Benicke*, FS Giessen, S. 373, 390 ff.

[270] Vgl. *Mohs*, IHR 2004, 219, 221; anders aber BGer, 13.11.2003, CISG-online 840, E. 5.4 = BGE 130 III 258, 266.

[271] LG München I, 18.5.2009, CISG-online 1998 in Bezug auf im Blumenhandel übliche mündliche Vertragsschlüsse.

53 **b) Vertragswidrigkeit gemäss Abs. 2.** Ein **bestimmter Gebrauchszweck** muss vom Käufer bewiesen werden, indem er zeigt, dass dem Verkäufer der besondere Zweck **bei Vertragsschluss zur Kenntnis gebracht** wurde.[272] Der Verkäufer kann sich verteidigen, indem er beweist, dass der Käufer auf die Sachkenntnis und das Urteilsvermögen des Verkäufers nicht vertraute oder vernünftigerweise nicht vertrauen konnte.[273] Das Vorliegen eines **Kaufs nach Probe oder Muster** hat der Käufer zu beweisen.[274]

54 **c) Ausschluss der Haftung gemäss Abs. 3.** Beruft sich der Verkäufer auf die **Kenntnis des Käufers von der Vertragswidrigkeit** gemäss Abs. 3, so muss er beweisen, dass der Käufer bei Vertragsschluss eine Vertragswidrigkeit nach Abs. 2 kannte oder darüber nicht in Unkenntnis sein konnte.[275]

4. Beweismass

55 Für das Beweismass wurde herkömmlicher Weise auf das nationale Prozessrecht des Forums abgestellt;[276] aufgrund des engen Regelungszusammenhangs ist hingegen ein einheitlicher Standard zu definieren.[277] Hierzu bietet sich der **Standard der *reasonableness*** an: Die beweisbelastete Partei muss das Gericht oder Schiedsgericht überzeugen, dass eine Vertragswidrigkeit mit einem **vernünftigen Grad an Sicherheit** vorliegt.[278] Im Einzelfall bedeutet dies, dass in Fällen, in denen herkömmlich auf das Beweisrecht des Forums zurückgegriffen wurde, nunmehr ein einheitsrechtlicher Massstab gilt. Das gilt insbesondere für den **Anscheinsbeweis;**[279] in solchen Fällen ist eben gerade der Beweis mit einem vernünftigen Grad an Sicherheit erbracht. Vom Empfänger quittierte Transportdokumente bieten ein vernünftiges Mass an Sicherheit, dass die im Dokument bezeichneten Tatsachen auch tatsächlich vorliegen.[280] Auch kann der Verkäufer an einer früheren Aussage festgehalten werden, durch die er eine Vertragswidrigkeit anerkannt hat.[281]

---

[272] Vgl. OLG Schleswig, 22.8.2002, CISG-online 710; *P. Huber/Mullis/Mullis*, S. 139; *Kröll*, 15 VJ (2011), 33, 46. Zu den Anforderungen hieran vgl. oben Rn. 20 ff.
[273] Vgl. *Honnold/Flechtner*, Art. 35, Rn. 226; *P. Huber/Mullis/Mullis*, S. 139; *Hyland*, Conformity of Goods, S. 322; *T. M. Müller*, Beweislast, S. 66; *Aue*, Mängelgewährleistung im UN-Kaufrecht, S. 76; *Hutter*, S. 44; *Kröll*, 15 VJ (2011), 33, 46.
[274] Ebenso *T. M. Müller*, Beweislast, S. 65; *Hutter*, S. 49.
[275] Vgl. *Audit*, Vente internationale, Anm. 101.; *Aue*, Mängelgewährleistung im UN-Kaufrecht, S. 81.
[276] Vgl. KG Nidwalden, 23.5.2005, CISG-online 1086, E. 3.1 = IHR 2005, 253, 254; OLG Koblenz, 22.4.2010, CISG-online 2290.
[277] In diese Richtung auch *Kröll*, 15 VJ (2011), 33, 50. Für Einzelheiten vgl. unten Art. 74 Rn. 65.
[278] Vgl. unten Art. 74 Rn. 65.
[279] Zum Anscheinsbeweis nach dem Prozessrecht des Forums vgl. MünchKommHGB/*Benicke*, Art. 36, Rn. 8 ff.; *Herber/Czerwenka*, Art. 35, Rn. 9; *Bianca/Bonell/Bianca*, Art. 36, Anm. 3.1.; *Audit*, Vente internationale, Anm. 102.
[280] Vgl. für den Fall einer Zuwenig-Lieferung LG Tübingen, 18.6.2003, CISG-online 784 = IHR 2003, 236 sowie BGer, 7.7.2004, CISG-online 848, E. 4. Vgl. dazu auch *Saidov*, Documentary Performance, S. 49, 84.
[281] Vgl. BGH, 9.1.2002, CISG-online 651 = NJW 2002, 1651, m. Anm. *Perales Viscasillas*, 6 VJ (2002), 217, 227 f.

Art. 36 [Maßgeblicher Zeitpunkt für die Vertragsmäßigkeit]

(1) Der Verkäufer haftet nach dem Vertrag und diesem Übereinkommen für eine Vertragswidrigkeit, die im Zeitpunkt des Übergangs der Gefahr auf den Käufer besteht, auch wenn die Vertragswidrigkeit erst nach diesem Zeitpunkt offenbar wird.

(2) Der Verkäufer haftet auch für eine Vertragswidrigkeit, die nach dem in Absatz 1 angegebenen Zeitpunkt eintritt und auf die Verletzung einer seiner Pflichten zurückzuführen ist, einschließlich der Verletzung einer Garantie dafür, daß die Ware für eine bestimmte Zeit für den üblichen Zweck oder für einen bestimmten Zweck geeignet bleiben oder besondere Eigenschaften oder Merkmale behalten wird.

Art. 36

(1) The seller is liable in accordance with the contract and this Convention for any lack of conformity which exists at the time when the risk passes to the buyer, even though the lack of conformity becomes apparent only after that time.

(2) The seller is also liable for any lack of conformity which occurs after the time indicated in the preceding paragraph and which is due to a breach of any of his obligations, including a breach of any guarantee that for a period of time the goods will remain fit for their ordinary purpose or for some particular purpose or will retain specified qualities or characteristics.

Art. 36

1) Le vendeur est responsable, conformément au contrat et à la présente Convention, de tout défaut de conformité qui existe au moment du transfert des risques à l'acheteur, meme si ce défaut n'apparaît qu'ultérieurement.

2) Le vendeur est également responsable de tout défaut de conformité qui survient après le moment indiqué au paragraphe précédent et qui est imputable à l'inexécution de l'une quelconque de ses obligations, y compris à un manquement à une garantie que, pendant une certaine période, les marchandises resteront propres à leur usage normal ou à un usage spécial ou conserveront des qualités ou caractéristiques spécifiées.

Übersicht

	Rn.
I. Vorgeschichte	1
II. Allgemeines	2
III. Vertragswidrigkeit bei Gefahrübergang – Abs. 1	3
IV. Später eintretende Vertragswidrigkeit – Abs. 2	5
1. Pflichtverletzung des Verkäufers	5
2. Garantie	7
V. Beweislast	12
1. Im Allgemeinen	12
2. Haltbarkeitsgarantie	13

Vorläufer und **Entwürfe**: Art. 35 EKG, Genfer E 1976 Art. 20, Wiener E 1977 Art. 20, New Yorker E 1978 Art. 34.

I. Vorgeschichte

Art. 36 regelt den **massgeblichen Zeitpunkt** für die Beurteilung der Vertragsmässigkeit 1 der Ware. Die Vorschrift hat ihren Vorläufer in Art. 35 EKG. Unterschiede bestehen vor allem im Bereich des Abs. 2, der die Verantwortung des Verkäufers auch auf bestimmte, nach Gefahrübergang eingetretene Vertragswidrigkeiten ausdehnt. Zum einen ist die ausdrückliche Erwähnung des Einstehenmüssens des Verkäufers für Handlungen seiner **Hilfspersonen** entfallen.[1] Zum anderen hat der Verkäufer nach CISG für eine nach Gefahrüber-

---

[1] Vgl. hierzu unten Rn. 6.

gang eingetretene Vertragswidrigkeit nunmehr auch einzustehen, wenn hierdurch eine **Garantie** verletzt wurde.² Diese Bestimmung war auf der diplomatischen Konferenz höchst umstritten.³ Nach Art. 34 New Yorker Entwurf 1978 sollte der Verkäufer insoweit nur einstehen müssen, wenn er eine „express guarantee" für eine „specific period" gegeben hatte. Auf der Konferenz stellte Pakistan den Antrag, neben ausdrücklichen auch stillschweigende Garantiezusagen zu berücksichtigen und hierfür einen „angemessenen" Zeitraum der Gewährleistung vorzusehen.⁴ Dieser Antrag wurde zwar abgelehnt;⁵ angenommen wurde jedoch ein weiterer Antrag, das Wort „ausdrücklich" zu streichen,⁶ so dass nunmehr auch stillschweigende Garantien vom Wortlaut der Vorschrift miterfasst werden.⁷ Die Zeitbestimmung wurde der Möglichkeit stillschweigender Garantien angepasst und dementsprechend der Ausdruck „specific period" durch „a period of time" ersetzt.⁸

II. Allgemeines

2   Die Regelung in Abs. 1, wonach für die Frage der Vertragsmässigkeit der Ware der **Zeitpunkt des Gefahrübergangs** massgebend ist, entspricht der Lösung in den meisten nationalen Kaufrechten.⁹ **Haltbarkeitsgarantien,** die nach Abs. 2 die Rechtsbehelfe des Käufers wegen Vertragswidrigkeit auslösen, werden auf nationaler Ebene hingegen unterschiedlich behandelt.¹⁰

III. Vertragswidrigkeit bei Gefahrübergang – Abs. 1

3   Massgeblich für die Frage der Vertragsmässigkeit i. S. des Art. 35 ist der **Zeitpunkt des Gefahrübergangs.**¹¹ Dieser richtet sich nach den Absprachen der Parteien, Handelsbräuchen – namentlich in Form von sog. Handelsklauseln – oder Gepflogenheiten, bzw. hilfsweise nach Artt. 67–69. Entscheidend ist dabei der **„abstrakte"** Zeitpunkt des Gefahrübergangs, die Sonderregeln der Artt. 66, 70 bleiben ausser Betracht.¹² Liegt im Zeitpunkt des Gefahrübergangs Vertragsmässigkeit vor, so stehen dem Käufer grundsätzlich keine Rechte zu, wenn sich die Ware auf Grund äusserer Einwirkungen nach diesem Zeitpunkt verschlechtert und damit nicht mehr den Bestimmungen des Vertrages entspricht.¹³ Für öffentlich-rechtliche Vorgaben im Käuferstaat vgl. oben Art. 35 Rn. 17.

4   Der Verkäufer haftet auch für eine Vertragswidrigkeit, die im Zeitpunkt des Gefahrübergangs zwar noch nicht erkennbar, deren Ursache jedoch bereits bei Gefahrübergang ange-

---

² Zur Entstehungsgeschichte vgl. YB IV (1973), S. 44 f., Nr. 65 ff.; S. 65, Nr. 46 ff.; zusammenfassend *Aue,* Mängelgewährleistung im UN-Kaufrecht, S. 89 ff.
³ Vgl. O. R., S. 312 ff., Nr. 1 ff.
⁴ Vgl. O. R., S. 105, Nr. 3 par. (2) (ii).
⁵ Vgl. O. R., S. 314, Nr. 29.
⁶ Vgl. O. R., S. 115, Nr. 31.
⁷ Vgl. hierzu im Einzelnen unten Rn. 8.
⁸ Zu den Konsequenzen dieser Änderung vgl. unten Rn. 9.
⁹ Vgl. Deutschland: § 434 I 1 BGB; Schweiz: vgl. *Honsell,* OR BT, S. 77; Österreich: vgl. *Koziol/Welser,* S. 260; Frankreich: vgl. *Ghestin/Desché,* Traité des contrats, Anm. 735. m. w. N.; USA: vgl. *Honnold/Flechtner,* Art. 36, Rn. 242; Grossbritannien: vgl. *Benjamin,* Rn. 6-001; siehe weiter rechtsvergleichend *Schwenzer/Hachem/Kee,* Rn. 31.165 ff.
¹⁰ Vgl. zum deutschen Recht: § 443 BGB; im österreichischen Recht existiert – ausser nunmehr § 9b Konsumentenschutzgesetz – keine Entsprechung, vgl. *Welser,* S. 110; für das Schweizer Recht: vgl. *Honsell,* OR BT, S. 84; für Frankreich: vgl. *Ghestin/Desché,* Traité des contrats, Anm. 982. ff.; allgemein *Schwenzer/Hachem/Kee,* Rn. 31.172.
¹¹ Vgl. hierzu *Heilmann,* S. 220 ff.
¹² Vgl. *Staudinger/Magnus,* Art. 36, Rn. 8; *Ferrari u. a./Ferrari,* Internationales Vertragsrecht, Art. 36, Rn. 3; *Karollus,* S. 120.
¹³ Vgl. RB Arnhem, 17.7.1997, CISG-online 548 (nach Gefahrübergang änderte sich die Meinung im Kunsthandel über Zuschreibung des Bildes an einen alten Meister); krit. *Ferrari,* RabelsZ 68 (2004), 473, 480.

legt war, d. h. für **versteckte Mängel**.[14] Hierzu zählt beispielsweise die Lieferung von Stoffen, die beim ersten Waschen über die Üblichkeit hinaus einlaufen, oder deren Farben sich nicht als licht- oder waschecht herausstellen, oder von Lebensmitteln, die infolge unzureichenden Gefrierens einem verfrühten Zersetzungsprozess unterliegen.[15] Ebenfalls hierher gehört die Lieferung einer Ware, die aufgrund **mangelhafter Verpackung** auf dem Transport Schaden nimmt. Die Vertragswidrigkeit i. S. des Art. 35 liegt bei mangelhafter Verpackung bereits im Zeitpunkt des Gefahrübergangs vor, auch wenn die Auswirkungen auf die Ware erst später eintreten.[16]

IV. Später eintretende Vertragswidrigkeit – Abs. 2

1. Pflichtverletzung des Verkäufers

Für eine nach Gefahrübergang eintretende Vertragswidrigkeit hat der Verkäufer einzustehen, wenn er diese durch eine Pflichtverletzung verursacht hat. Die Pflichtverletzung mag **vor** dem Zeitpunkt des **Gefahrübergangs** liegen, wie beispielsweise Auswahl einer unzuverlässigen Transportperson, Wahl eines falschen Versendungsweges oder fehlerhafte Gebrauchsinstruktionen.[17] Aber auch **nach Gefahrübergang** begangene Pflichtverletzungen können die Einstandspflicht nach Abs. 2 begründen.[18] Zu denken ist etwa an Fälle, in denen der Verkäufer die Ware nach Gefahrübergang bei Rücknahme der Container beschädigt oder bei einem insgesamt dem CISG unterliegenden Kaufvertrag mit Montageverpflichtung Teile beschädigt werden, bezüglich derer die Gefahr bereits auf den Käufer übergegangen ist.[19] Die Einbeziehung solcher, nach Gefahrübergang begangener Pflichtverletzungen in den Anwendungsbereich des Art. 36 II erscheint schon im Hinblick auf Art. 7 I geboten, da sonst für solche Pflichtverletzungen subsidiär anwendbares nationales Delikts- oder Vertragsrecht eingreifen würde.[20]

Die Pflichtverletzung des Verkäufers kann sowohl in einem **positiven Tun** als auch in einem **Unterlassen** bestehen. Ein **Verschulden** ist nicht erforderlich. Soweit jedoch ein

---

[14] Vgl. grundlegend BGH, 2.3.2005, CISG-online 999 = NJW-RR 2005, 1218 ff. (belgisches Schweinefleisch), m. Anm. *Schlechtriem*, JZ 2005, 846 ff.; kritisch *Krätzschmar*, Öffentlichrechtliche Beschaffenheitsvorgaben, S. 168 ff.; aus der Literatur vgl. *Schlechtriem*, Internationales UN-Kaufrecht, Rn. 145; *P. Huber/Mullis/Mullis*, S. 144; *Staudinger/Magnus*, Art. 36, Rn. 9; *Herber/Czerwenka*, Art. 36, Rn. 2; *Neumayer/Ming*, Art. 36, Anm. 2.; *Hutter*, S. 58; *Soergel/Lüderitz/Schüßler-Langeheine*, Art. 36, Rn. 4; *Kröll u. a./Kröll*, Art. 36, Rn. 8; *Audit*, Vente internationale, Anm. 102.; *Heuzé*, Anm. 299.; *Aue*, Mängelgewährleistung im UN-Kaufrecht, S. 99; *Heilmann*, S. 221.

[15] Vgl. *Piltz*, Internationales Kaufrecht, Rn. 5–22. Vgl. BGH, 2.3.2005, CISG-online 999 = NJW-RR 2005, 1218 ff. (belgisches Schweinefleisch).

[16] Wie hier MünchKomm/*Gruber*, Art. 36, Rn. 7; *Staudinger/Magnus*, Art. 36, Rn. 11; *Herber/Czerwenka*, Art. 36, Rn. 3; *Honnold/Flechtner*, Art. 36, Rn. 242; *Soergel/Lüderitz/Schüßler-Langeheine*, Art. 36, Rn. 5; *Kröll u. a./Kröll*, Art. 36, Rn. 9; *Ferrari u. a./Ferrari*, Internationales Vertragsrecht, Art. 36, Rn. 4. Von vielen Autoren wird dieser Fall allerdings unter Abs. 2 subsumiert, vgl. *Audit*, Vente internationale, Anm. 103.; *Karollus*, S. 120; *Reinhart*, Art. 36, Rn. 3; *Neumayer/Ming*, Art. 36, Anm. 5.; *Hutter*, S. 59; *Aue*, Mängelgewährleistung im UN-Kaufrecht, S. 117 Fn. 88; *Enderlein/Maskow/Strohbach*, Art. 36, Anm. 5.; *Welser*, S. 110; wohl auch *Ryffel*, S. 18.

[17] Soweit man den Fall fehlerhafter Verpackung mit anschliessender Beschädigung der Ware nicht bereits unter Abs. 1 subsumiert – vgl. oben Rn. 4 –, fällt er jedenfalls unter den Fall der Pflichtverletzung nach Abs. 2.

[18] Vgl. OLG Frankfurt a. M., 29.1.2004, CISG-online 822 (Käufer unterliess es, den nach Gefahrübergang aufgekommenen Verdacht, das Fleisch sei kontaminiert, durch Übersendung einer Unbedenklichkeitsbescheinigung zu widerlegen. Dabei stützte sich das Gericht auf Art. 36 I.); ebenso *P. Huber/Mullis/Mullis*, S. 145; *Staudinger/Magnus*, Art. 36, Rn. 11; *Enderlein/Maskow/Strohbach*, Art. 36, Anm. 5.; MünchKomm/*Gruber*, Art. 36, Rn. 11; a. A. *Piltz*, Internationales Kaufrecht, Rn. 5–25; *Karollus*, S. 120; *Aue*, Mängelgewährleistung im UN-Kaufrecht, S. 117; wohl auch *Welser*, S. 110.

[19] Vgl. auch *Achilles*, Art. 36, Rn. 4; zustimmend auch MünchKomm/*Gruber*, Art. 36, Rn. 10.

[20] So ausdrücklich *Karollus*, S. 120; vgl. auch *Bamberger/Roth/Saenger*, Art. 36, Rn. 4: Haftung nach Art. 36 II, wenn Pflichtverletzung in zeitlichem Zusammenhang mit Vertragsverletzung; weitergehend MünchKomm/*Gruber*, Art. 36, Rn. 12; vgl. dagegen *Staudinger/Magnus*, Art. 36, Rn. 11: subsidiär anwendbares Deliktsrecht nach endgültiger Vertragsdurchführung.

Entlastungsgrund nach Art. 79 vorliegt, bleibt die Pflichtverletzung auch im Rahmen des Art. 36 II unberücksichtigt.[21] Über Art. 79 ist auch die – in Art. 35 II EKG noch ausdrücklich geregelte – Frage des Einstehenmüssens des Verkäufers für **Hilfspersonen**[22] zu lösen.[23]

2. Garantie

7 Nach Abs. 2 haftet der Verkäufer auch für eine nach Gefahrübergang eintretende Vertragswidrigkeit, die auf die Verletzung einer Garantie dafür, dass die Ware für eine bestimmte Zeit für den üblichen Zweck oder für einen bestimmten Zweck geeignet bleibt oder besondere Eigenschaften oder Merkmale behalten wird, zurückzuführen ist. Es geht insoweit um sog. **Haltbarkeitsgarantien**.[24] Fraglich ist, welcher **Anwendungsbereich** der Bestimmung zukommt. Schon nach Art. 35 hat der Verkäufer dafür einzustehen, dass die Ware für eine gewisse Zeit zum gewöhnlichen oder einem bestimmten Gebrauch geeignet bleibt.[25] Zeigt sich nach Gefahrübergang, dass die Ware einer vom Verkäufer gegebenen Haltbarkeitszusage nicht entspricht, so wird es sich regelmäßig um Fehler handeln, die im Keim bereits zum Zeitpunkt des Gefahrübergangs angelegt waren, so dass der Verkäufer hierfür nach Art. 35 in Verbindung mit Art. 36 I einzustehen hat. Art. 36 II kommt insoweit lediglich die Funktion einer **Beweiserleichterung** zugunsten des Käufers zu.[26] Darüber hinausgehend wird man aus einer vom Verkäufer abgegebenen Haltbarkeitsgarantie auch nach CISG grundsätzlich nicht den Schluss ziehen dürfen, dass der Verkäufer auch für Mängel einzustehen habe, die nicht aus seiner Risikosphäre stammen, sondern etwa auf **unsachgemässen Gebrauch** oder **Bedienungsfehler** des Käufers, nicht dem gewöhnlichen oder beabsichtigten Gebrauch entsprechende Einwirkungen Dritter oder höhere Gewalt zurückzuführen sind.[27] Zwar ist es grundsätzlich denkbar, dass der Verkäufer die Haltbarkeit seiner Ware auch im Hinblick auf nicht sachgemässen Gebrauch garantieren will;[28] solche Garantiezusagen sind jedoch höchst ungewöhnlich und dürfen nur angenommen werden, falls sich ausnahmsweise ein entsprechender Wille aus der Garantiezusage eindeutig ergibt.[29]

8 Die Garantiezusage kann ausdrücklich aber auch stillschweigend erfolgen.[30] Um **ausdrückliche Garantien** handelt es sich bei den Herstellergarantien, in denen der Verkäufer typischerweise die Funktionsfähigkeit der Ware für eine bestimmte Zeit (z. B. 2 Jahre, 10 000 km oder 5 000 Betriebsstunden) verspricht. Um Auslegungszweifel zu vermeiden, sollte die Garantie präzise Angaben darüber enthalten, für welche Eigenschaften und Qualitätsmerkmale der Verkäufer einstehen will.[31] Die Garantieübernahme kann jedoch

---

[21] Vgl. *Staudinger/Magnus*, Art. 36, Rn. 12; *Herber/Czerwenka*, Art. 36, Rn. 3; *Kröll u. a./Kröll*, Art. 36, Rn. 12; *Hutter*, S. 59.
[22] Vgl. ausführlich hierzu unten Art. 79 Rn. 20, 33 ff.
[23] So auch *Staudinger/Magnus*, Art. 36, Rn. 13; *Witz/Salger/Lorenz/Salger*, Art. 36, Rn. 7; *Karollus*, S. 120; *Soergel/Lüderitz/Schüßler-Langeheine*, Art. 36, Rn. 6; *Kröll u. a./Kröll*, Art. 36, Rn. 11; a. A. *Stumpf*, 1. Aufl., Art. 36 Rn. 7: Rückgriff auf nationales Recht.
[24] Zu ihrer Behandlung im deutschen Recht vgl. *Schlechtriem*, SchuldR BT, Rn. 86–88.
[25] Vgl. *Neumayer/Ming*, Art. 36, Anm. 3.; *Lookofsky*, Understanding the CISG, S. 84; vgl. auch oben Art. 35 Rn. 14.
[26] Vgl. *Schlechtriem*, Seller's Obligations, § 6.03, S. 6–26; *ders.*, Internationales UN-Kaufrecht, Rn. 146; i. E. auch *Staudinger/Magnus*, Art. 36, Rn. 16; *Honnold/Flechtner*, Art. 36, Rn. 243; *Aue*, Mängelgewährleistung im UN-Kaufrecht, S. 144; *Kruisinga*, Non-conformity, S. 36; vgl. auch schon YB IV (1973), S. 45, Nr. 67.
[27] Vgl. *Schlechtriem*, Seller's Obligations, § 6.03, S. 6–26; *ders.*, Internationales UN-Kaufrecht, Rn. 146; *Honnold/Flechtner*, Art 36, Rn. 243; *Bianca/Bonell/Bianca*, Art. 36, Anm. 2.4.; *Audit*, Vente internationale, Anm. 103.; *Aue*, Mängelgewährleistung im UN-Kaufrecht, S. 136; *Bollée*, Theory of Risks, S. 282; unklar *Kruisinga*, Non-conformity, S. 36.
[28] *Heuzé*, Anm. 301. sieht hierin das eigentliche Anwendungsfeld der Bestimmung; vgl. auch *Piltz*, Internationales Kaufrecht, Rn. 5–26.
[29] So auch *Schlechtriem*, Internationales UN-Kaufrecht, Rn. 146; *Heuzé*, Anm. 301.
[30] Vgl. zur Entstehungsgeschichte oben Rn. 1.
[31] Vgl. *Aue*, Mängelgewährleistung im UN-Kaufrecht, S. 119 ff. mit Einzelbeispielen.

Maßgeblicher Zeitpunkt für die Vertragsmäßigkeit 9–11 **Art. 36**

auch **stillschweigend** erfolgen.[32] Derartige stillschweigende Haltbarkeitsgarantien mögen sich aus der Natur der Ware – wie z. B. bei Lebensmitteln und Arzneimitteln – oder aufgrund Handelsbrauchs ergeben, sie können aber auch im Einzelfall aus Werbeaussagen des Verkäufers abgeleitet werden.[33] Wann die Garantie übernommen wurde – bei oder nach Vertragsschluss oder gar nach Gefahrübergang – ist irrelevant.[34]

Im Falle einer ausdrücklichen oder stillschweigenden Haltbarkeitsgarantie hat der Verkäufer für „**eine bestimmte Zeit**" (engl.: „a period of time", frz.: „une certaine période", span.: „determinado período") für die Vertragsmässigkeit einzustehen. Wo eine ausdrückliche Garantie vorliegt, wird auch die Zeitspanne für die Eignung der Ware explizit festgelegt sein. Problematisch ist die Bestimmung der Haltbarkeitsdauer im Falle einer **stillschweigenden Garantie**. Die deutsche Fassung lässt darauf schliessen, dass die Zeitdauer vertraglich fixiert sein muss.[35] Einer solchen Auslegung steht indessen die Fassung in den Originalsprachen entgegen, die sämtlich von einer „gewissen", d. h. gerade unbestimmten Zeitdauer sprechen.[36] Man wird deshalb von einer **den Umständen entsprechenden vernünftigen Haltbarkeitsdauer** ausgehen müssen,[37] auch wenn sich der Antrag, die Gebrauchstauglichkeit für eine „reasonable period as the case may be" anzuordnen, auf der diplomatischen Konferenz nicht durchsetzen konnte.[38] Die Unterschiede in den praktischen Ergebnissen dürften freilich ohnehin gering sein.[39] Folgt man der Auffassung, wonach die Zeitdauer vertraglich bestimmt wird, so muss der Richter im Falle einer stillschweigenden Garantie über Art. 8 II auch berücksichtigen, was vernünftige Parteien unter den gegebenen Umständen vereinbart hätten.[40] Geht man umgekehrt von einer vom Richter zu bestimmenden vernünftigen Haltbarkeitsdauer aus, gebührt auch hier etwa vorhandenen Parteiabreden nach Art. 6 der Vorrang. 9

Die eigentliche Frage – die vom CISG weder gelöst wurde noch gelöst werden konnte – ist jedoch, was die unter den Umständen **zu erwartende Haltbarkeitsdauer** einer Ware ist. Über den Einzelfall hinausgehende Kriterien lassen sich insoweit nur begrenzt entwickeln.[41] **Verderbliche Ware,** die zum Weiterverkauf bestimmt ist, muss eine angemessene Zeit über den Zeitpunkt hinaus, in dem nach den branchenüblichen Umständen mit einem Erwerb durch den Letztabnehmer zu rechnen ist, haltbar sein. **Andere Waren** dürfen nicht weit vor Ablauf ihrer nach den Umständen zu erwartenden Lebensdauer die Gebrauchstauglichkeit verlieren. 10

Auch bei einer ausdrücklich gegebenen Haltbarkeitsgarantie kann der Verkäufer seine **Haftung ausschliessen** bzw. **begrenzen.**[42] So kann er insbesondere die Haltbarkeit der 11

---

[32] Vgl. hierzu die eingehende Diskussion auf der diplomatischen Konferenz O.R., S. 312 ff., Nr. 1 ff. Bejahend: *Staudinger/Magnus*, Art. 36, Rn. 19; *Schlechtriem*, Einheitliches UN-Kaufrecht, S. 58; *Piltz*, Internationales Kaufrecht, Rn 5–26; *Hutter*, S. 61; *Audit*, Vente internationale, Anm. 103.; *Loewe*, Art. 36, S. 57; *Aue*, Mängelgewährleistung im UN-Kaufrecht, S. 131 f.; *Ferrari u. a./Ferrari*, Internationales Vertragsrecht, Art. 36, Rn. 6. A. A. wohl *Enderlein/Maskow/Strohbach*, Art. 36, Anm. 6.: dass eine Garantie auch stillschweigend abgegeben werden könne, sei „kaum vorstellbar"; ebenfalls ablehnend *Soergel/Lüderitz/Schüßler-Langeheine*, Art. 36, Rn. 7. Auch *Niggemann*, Pflichten des Verkäufers, S. 88 will unter Abs. 2 nur konkrete Garantiezusagen fassen; im Übrigen solle es bei Art. 35 II a) bzw. b) sein Bewenden haben.
[33] Zurückhaltend *Achilles*, Art. 36, Rn. 5.
[34] Vgl. *Staudinger/Magnus*, Art. 36, Rn. 20; *Achilles*, Art. 36, Rn. 5; MünchKomm/*Gruber*, Art. 36, Rn. 21.
[35] So insbes. *Schlechtriem*, Einheitliches UN-Kaufrecht, S. 58; *ders.*, Seller's Obligations, § 6.03, S. 6–26.
[36] „Bestimmte Zeit" müsste auf Englisch „specific period of time", auf Französisch „une période certaine" und auf Spanisch „un período determinado" heissen; vgl. auch *Staudinger/Magnus*, Art. 36, Rn. 17: deutsche Übersetzung sei falsch.
[37] Wie hier *Staudinger/Magnus*, Art. 36, Rn. 17; *Aue*, Mängelgewährleistung im UN-Kaufrecht, S. 140 f.; *Bianca/Bonell/Bianca*, Art. 36, Anm. 3.2.; MünchKomm/*Gruber*, Art. 36, Rn. 23; *Piltz*, Internationales Kaufrecht, Rn. 5–26.
[38] Vgl. oben Rn. 1.
[39] Vgl. *Schlechtriem*, Internationales UN-Kaufrecht, Rn. 147.
[40] *Kröll u. a./Kröll*, Art. 36, Rn. 20.
[41] Ausführlich hierzu *Aue*, Mängelgewährleistung im UN-Kaufrecht, S. 142 ff. mit Beispielen aus der englischen Rechtsprechung; vgl. auch *Atiyah/Adams*, S. 154 f.
[42] Vgl. dazu *Aue*, Mängelgewährleistung im UN-Kaufrecht, S. 136 f.; *Enderlein/Maskow/Strohbach*, Art. 36, Anm. 9., führen beispielsweise die Möglichkeit an, dass der Verkäufer Verschleissteile von der Garantie ausnimmt.

Ware nur i. S. der Freiheit von Fehlern in Konstruktion und Herstellung oder beispielsweise nur für den Fall, dass der Käufer die Ware regelmässig fachgerecht warten lässt, garantieren. Die Annahme einer stillschweigenden Garantie muss schliesslich in jedem Fall scheitern, wenn der Verkäufer seine Einstandspflicht für Vertragswidrigkeiten nach Art. 35 wirksam abbedungen hat.[43]

V. Beweislast

1. Im Allgemeinen

12   Vgl. hierzu oben Art. 35 Rn. 50 ff.

2. Haltbarkeitsgarantie

13   Muss der Käufer nach rügeloser Entgegennahme der Ware beweisen, dass allfällige Mängel bereits im Zeitpunkt des Gefahrübergangs vorhanden waren – wobei ihm allerdings Beweiserleichterungen zugute kommen –,[44] so **kehrt sich die Beweislast** im Falle einer **Haltbarkeitsgarantie um**.[45] Beweist der Käufer das Auftreten eines Mangels innerhalb der Garantiefrist, so ist es nunmehr am Verkäufer darzutun, dass der Mangel auf eine nicht in seine Risikosphäre fallende Ursache – wie z. B. unsachgemässes Käuferverhalten, Einwirkung durch Dritte oder höhere Gewalt etc. – zurückzuführen ist.[46]

---

[43] Vgl. dazu oben Art. 35 Rn. 42, 43.
[44] Anders *Soergel/Lüderitz/Schüßler-Langeheine*, Art. 36, Rn. 9, die dem Käufer nur die Beweislast für das Vorliegen einer bei Annahme gegenwärtigen Vertragswidrigkeit aufbürden wollen; der Verkäufer müsse hingegen beweisen, dass die Ware bei Gefahrübergang vertragsmässig war.
[45] Vgl. OLG Innsbruck, 1.7.1994, CISG-online 107; *Aue*, Mängelgewährleistung im UN-Kaufrecht, S. 144; *Karollus*, S. 121; *Niggemann*, Pflichten des Verkäufers, S. 87; MünchKomm/*Gruber*, Art. 36, Rn. 27; *Kröll u. a./Kröll*, Art. 36, Rn. 25; wohl auch *Schlechtriem*, Seller's Obligations, § 6.03, S. 6–26; *ders.*, Pflichten des Verkäufers, S. 119; *Audit*, Vente internationale, Anm. 103.; *Enderlein/Maskow/Strohbach*, Art. 36, Anm. 9.; *Achilles*, Art. 36, Rn. 6.
[46] Vgl. *Staudinger/Magnus*, Art. 36, Rn. 27; *Kröll u. a./Kröll*, Art. 36, Rn. 25; *Antweiler*, S. 173.

Art. 37 [Nacherfüllung bei vorzeitiger Lieferung]

Bei vorzeitiger Lieferung der Ware behält der Verkäufer bis zu dem für die Lieferung festgesetzten Zeitpunkt das Recht, fehlende Teile nachzuliefern, eine fehlende Menge auszugleichen, für nicht vertragsgemäße Ware Ersatz zu liefern oder die Vertragswidrigkeit der gelieferten Ware zu beheben, wenn die Ausübung dieses Rechts dem Käufer nicht unzumutbare Unannehmlichkeiten oder unverhältnismäßige Kosten verursacht. Der Käufer behält jedoch das Recht, Schadenersatz nach diesem Übereinkommen zu verlangen.

Art. 37

If the seller has delivered goods before the date for delivery, he may, up to that date, deliver any missing part or make up any deficiency in the quantity of the goods delivered, or deliver goods in replacement of any non-conforming goods delivered or remedy any lack of conformity in the goods delivered, provided that the exercise of this right does not cause the buyer unreasonable inconvenience or unreasonable expense. However, the buyer retains any right to claim damages as provided for in this Convention.

Art. 37

En cas de livraison anticipée, le vendeur a le droit, jusqu'à la date prévue pour la livraison, soit de livrer une partie ou une quantité manquante, ou des marchandises nouvelles en remplacement des marchandises non conformes au contrat, soit de réparer tout défaut de conformité des marchandises, à condition que l'exercice de ce droit ne cause à l'acheteur ni inconvénients ni frais déraisonnables. Toutefois, l'acheteur conserve le droit de demander des dommages-intérêts conformément à la présente Convention.

Übersicht

	Rn.
I. Vorgeschichte	1
II. Allgemeines	2
III. Vorzeitige Lieferung	4
IV. Recht zur Mängelbeseitigung	6
1. Anwendungsbereich	6
2. Arten der Mängelbeseitigung	7
a) Nachlieferung	8
b) Ersatzlieferung	9
c) Nachbesserung	10
3. Unvollständige Mängelbeseitigung	11
4. Grenzen	12
V. Rechtsfolgen	15
1. Ausschluss der Rechtsbehelfe nach Artt. 45 ff.	15
2. Schadenersatz	16
3. Weigerung des Käufers	17
VI. Beweislast	18

Vorläufer und **Entwürfe:** Art. 37 EKG, Genfer E 1976 Art. 21, Wiener E 1977 Art. 21, New Yorker E 1978 Art. 35.

I. Vorgeschichte

Die Vorschrift entspricht im Wesentlichen Art. 37 EKG. Neu ist jedoch S. 2, wonach ein **1** Schadenersatzanspruch des Käufers auch bei erfolgter Mängelbeseitigung unberührt bleibt.[1] Ein auf der Diplomatischen Konferenz von der kanadischen Delegation eingebrachter Antrag, die Regelung auf den Fall nicht vertragsgemässer Dokumente zu erstrecken, führte aus systematischen Gründen zu einer entsprechenden Ergänzung des Art. 34.[2]

---

[1] Vgl. dazu YB III (1972), S. 63, Nr. 44; S. 87, Nr. 69.
[2] Vgl. oben *Widmer Lüchinger*, Art. 34 Rn. 8.

II. Allgemeines

2 Art. 37 gibt dem Verkäufer bei vorzeitiger vertragswidriger Lieferung ein **Mängelbeseitigungsrecht**. Das US-amerikanische Recht kennt in sec. 2–508 UCC eine entsprechende ausdrückliche gesetzliche Regelung.[3] Doch auch in den kontinental-europäischen Rechtsordnungen, denen – auf dem römischen Recht fussend – ein „Recht zur zweiten Andienung" des Verkäufers nach dem vertraglichen Lieferzeitpunkt grundsätzlich unbekannt ist,[4] kann der Verkäufer bei vorzeitiger Lieferung Mängel beseitigen. Im Übrigen wird ein Mängelbeseitigungsrecht regelmässig in AGB vorgesehen.

3 Das Mängelbeseitigungsrecht des Verkäufers nach Art. 37 erscheint als Selbstverständlichkeit,[5] denn bis zum Lieferzeitpunkt kann eine wesentliche Vertragsverletzung nur in Form des antizipierten Vertragsbruchs nach Art. 72 I angenommen werden. Das Schwergewicht der Regelung des Art. 37 liegt deshalb nicht darin, dass er ein Mängelbeseitigungsrecht bei vorzeitiger Lieferung überhaupt vorsieht, sondern in der Bestimmung seiner **Grenzen** (Unzumutbarkeit, Schadenersatz).[6]

III. Vorzeitige Lieferung

4 Das uneingeschränkte Mängelbeseitigungsrecht nach Art. 37 steht dem Verkäufer nur bei **vorzeitiger Lieferung** zu. Soweit die Lieferung nicht vorzeitig erfolgt ist, kommt allenfalls das – eingeschränkte – Mängelbeseitigungsrecht nach Art. 48 in Betracht. Eine vorzeitige Lieferung braucht der Käufer nach Art. 52 I allerdings erst gar nicht abzunehmen.

5 **Vorzeitige Lieferung** liegt sicher vor, wenn vor einem für die Lieferung festgesetzten **Zeitpunkt** (einem bestimmten Tag oder dem Anfangstermin einer bestimmten Frist) geliefert wird. Dasselbe gilt bei einer Klausel „Lieferung: auf Abruf des Käufers", solange dieser die Ware noch nicht abgerufen hat. Fraglich ist, ob auch eine Lieferung, die nach dem Anfangstermin, aber noch vor Ablauf eines **Lieferzeitraums** (vgl. Art. 33 b)), oder innerhalb einer **Frist** (vgl. Art. 33 c)) erfolgt, noch als vorzeitig i. S. des Art. 37 gelten kann, oder ob der Verkäufer insoweit das Recht zur Mängelbeseitigung nur im Rahmen des Art. 48 besitzt. Der Wortlaut allein erlaubt – vor allem auch unter Berücksichtigung der englischen und französischen Fassung – keine eindeutige Aussage.[7] Auch die Materialien geben zu dieser Frage keine Auskunft. Sinn und Zweck des Art. 37 sowie die dem CISG insgesamt zugrunde liegenden Wertungen gebieten jedoch, dem Verkäufer das uneingeschränkte Mängelbeseitigungsrecht nach Art. 37 bis zum spätesten zulässigen Liefertermin zu gewähren.[8] Das CISG geht vom Prinzip aus, dass der Vertrag wo irgend möglich aufrecht erhalten werden soll; das Recht zur Vertragsaufhebung wird dementsprechend auf Fälle wesentlicher Vertragsverletzung beschränkt. Wendet man auf vertragswidrige Lieferung während eines Lieferzeitraumes nicht Art. 37, sondern bereits Art. 48 an, so besteht die Gefahr, dass dem Verkäufer bei wesentlicher Vertragsverletzung kein Recht auf Beseitigung der Vertragswidrigkeit zugestanden wird.[9] Richtigerweise liegt jedoch solange (noch) kein

---

[3] Vgl. hierzu *Bridge*, FS Schwenzer, S. 221, 222 ff.
[4] Vgl. unten *Müller-Chen*, Art. 48 Rn. 1.
[5] Vgl. *Schlechtriem*, Seller's Obligations, § 6.03, S. 6–28; *P. Widmer*, Droits et obligations du vendeur, S. 99; *Bridge*, FS Schwenzer, S. 221, 229 („evident redundancy of Article 37").
[6] Vgl. *Schlechtriem*, Seller's Obligations, § 6.03, S. 6–28; *Loewe*, Art. 37, S. 57.
[7] A. A. *Herber/Czerwenka*, Art. 37, Rn. 3.
[8] So die h. M., vgl. *Staudinger/Magnus*, Art. 37, Rn. 9 f.; MünchKomm/*Gruber*, Art. 37, Rn. 5; *Honnold/Flechtner*, Art. 37, Rn. 245; *U. Huber*, östJBl 1989, 273, 281; *Enderlein/Maskow/Strohbach*, Art. 37, Anm. 1.; *Karollus*, S. 122; *Heuzé*, Anm. 302.; *Gutknecht*, S. 45; *Ferrari u. a./Ferrari*, Internationales Vertragsrecht, Art. 37, Rn. 5; i. E. so auch *Witz/Salger/Lorenz/Salger*, Art. 37, Rn. 6; zum EKG vgl. *Mertens/Rehbinder*, Art. 37 EKG, Rn. 2. A. A. *Herber/Czerwenka*, Art. 37, Rn. 3 unter Berufung darauf, dass der Käufer in diesem Fall die Lieferung nicht zurückweisen könne, ihm deshalb Nachbesserung nur in den Grenzen des Art. 48 zumutbar sei.
[9] Zum Streitstand vgl. die Nachweise oben bei *Schroeter*, Art. 25 Rn. 47 f.

wesentlicher Vertragsbruch vor, als dem Verkäufer Nachbesserung, Nachlieferung oder Beseitigung in angemessener Frist möglich ist,[10] so dass der Streit, ob Art. 37 oder Art. 48 greift, im Ergebnis nicht praktisch wird. Vielmehr steht dem Verkäufer grundsätzlich in beiden Fällen das Recht zur Mängelbeseitigung zu.

IV. Recht zur Mängelbeseitigung

1. Anwendungsbereich

Das Mängelbeseitigungsrecht des Verkäufers besteht bei **sämtlichen Vertragswidrigkeiten** i. S. des Art. 35. Im Gegensatz zu Art. 48 ist es auch irrelevant, ob die Vertragswidrigkeit einen wesentlichen Vertragsbruch darstellt oder nicht. Art. 34 enthält für den Fall der vorzeitigen Übergabe von **Dokumenten** ein entsprechendes Mängelbeseitigungsrecht für vertragswidrige Dokumente. Bei Lieferung höherwertiger Ware kann der Verkäufer diesen Mangel bis zur vereinbarten Lieferzeit beheben.[11] Im CISG nicht geregelt ist die Frage, ob dem Verkäufer bei vorzeitiger Lieferung auch ein Mängelbeseitigungsrecht in Bezug auf Rechte oder Ansprüche Dritter, d. h. bei **Rechtsmängeln** oder **Belastung mit Schutzrechten Dritter** (Artt. 41, 42), zusteht. Offenbar wurde diese Problematik bei den Beratungen übersehen.[12] Es ist indes kein Grund ersichtlich, das Mängelbeseitigungsrecht insoweit anders als im Falle der Vertragswidrigkeit oder bei Mängeln der Dokumente zu behandeln. Denn es erscheint weder angemessen, den Verkäufer hier lediglich auf das eingeschränkte Nacherfüllungsrecht nach Art. 48 zu beschränken, noch für diese Frage subsidiär auf nationales Recht zurückzugreifen. Die allgemeinen Prinzipien des CISG (Art. 7 II), die im Rahmen der Rechtsbehelfe deutlich werden,[13] gebieten es vielmehr, Art. 37 im Rahmen der Artt. 41, 42 entsprechend anzuwenden.[14] 6

2. Arten der Mängelbeseitigung

Art. 37 sieht drei Formen des Mängelbeseitigungsrechtes vor: Nachlieferung von Teilen oder bei zu geringer Menge, Ersatzlieferung und Nachbesserung. Welche Art der Mängelbeseitigung der Verkäufer wählt, steht – in den Grenzen der Zumutbarkeit für den Käufer[15] – in seinem **Ermessen**.[16] Einer **Aufforderung** des Verkäufers an den Käufer zur Erklärung der Annahmebereitschaft mit Fristsetzung, wie sie das Nacherfüllungsrecht nach Art. 48 II 1 voraussetzt, bedarf es im Rahmen des Art. 37 nicht. 7

a) **Nachlieferung.** Fehlende Teile einer grösseren Einheit oder eine fehlende Menge bei Quantitätsabweichung kann der Verkäufer nachliefern.[17] Auch dieses an sich selbstverständ- 8

---

[10] CISG-AC, Op. 5 *(Schwenzer)*, Opinion 3 und Comment 4.4; oben *Schroeter*, Art. 25 Rn. 48.
[11] Vgl. oben Art. 35 Rn. 9; unten Art. 39 Rn. 30; Art. 40 Rn. 5; *Müller-Chen*, Art. 52 Rn. 11; kritisch *Keller*, Right to Cure, CISG Pace unter (f).
[12] Der Sekretariatskommentar – Art. 39, Nr. 8 – erwähnt Art. 37 zwar unter den Bestimmungen, die auf die Vertragswidrigkeit der Ware beschränkt und auf die Rechtsmängelhaftung deshalb nicht anwendbar sein sollen, eine Diskussion dieser Frage hat aber weder bei UNCITRAL noch auf der Diplomatischen Konferenz stattgefunden.
[13] Vgl. auch unten Art. 41 Rn. 23 f.; Art. 42 Rn. 27 f.
[14] Vgl. *Staudinger/Magnus*, Art. 37, Rn. 13; MünchKomm/*Gruber*, Art. 37, Rn. 10; MünchKommHGB/*Benicke*, Art. 37, Rn. 5; *Brunner*, Art. 37, Rn. 6; *Honnold/Flechtner*, Art. 37, Rn. 245.1; *Soergel/Lüderitz/Schüßler-Langeheine*, Art. 37, Rn. 4; *Kröll u. a./Kröll*, Art. 37, Rn. 9; *Ferrari u. a./Ferrari*, Internationales Vertragsrecht, Art. 37, Rn. 7; i. E. ebenso, jedoch ohne Begründung *Herber/Czerwenka*, Art. 37, Rn. 6; *Piltz*, Internationales Kaufrecht, Rn. 4–58; *Enderlein/Maskow/Strohbach*, Art. 37, Anm. 4.; *Enderlein*, Rights and Obligations of the Seller, S. 164 f.
[15] Vgl. dazu unten Rn. 12 ff.
[16] Ebenso *Staudinger/Magnus*, Art. 37, Rn. 12; *Herber/Czerwenka*, Art. 37, Rn. 4; *Heilmann*, S. 382; a. A. MünchKommHGB/*Benicke*, Art. 37, Rn. 7 (grdsl. am wenigsten belastende Massnahme, es sei denn Vorteile für den Verkäufer überwiegen die Nachteile für den Käufer „ganz erheblich"). Im Einzelfall mögen auch andere als in Art. 37 S. 1 genannte Mängelbeseitigungsmassnahmen in Betracht kommen, vgl. *Bamberger/Roth/Saenger*, Art. 37, Rn. 3; *Soergel/Lüderitz/Schüßler-Langeheine*, Art. 37, Rn. 6.
[17] Vgl. ICC, 9083/1999, CISG-online 706 = 11:2 ICC Int. Ct. Arb. Bull. (2000), 78 (der Vertrag sah mehrere Teillieferungen innerhalb eines Gesamtzeitraums vor).

liche Nachlieferungsrecht steht unter dem Vorbehalt der Zumutbarkeit für den Käufer.[18] Im CISG fehlt freilich eine Bestimmung, wie sie in vielen nationalen Rechtsordnungen vorgesehen ist,[19] wonach der Käufer zur Annahme einer **Teillieferung** nicht verpflichtet ist.[20] Die Nachlieferung wird deshalb nur im Ausnahmefall dem Käufer nicht zumutbar sein.[21]

9   b) **Ersatzlieferung.** Anstelle nicht vertragsmässiger Ware (Sachmängel, Rechtsmängel, aliud-Lieferung) kann der Verkäufer Ersatz liefern. Die Ersatzlieferung hat grundsätzlich **Zug-um-Zug** gegen Rückgabe der bereits gelieferten Ware zu erfolgen.[22] Anders als im Rahmen des Art. 46 II,[23] wo es um das Recht des Käufers und nicht wie hier um das Recht des Verkäufers auf Ersatzlieferung geht, wird man dem Käufer, der den Kaufpreis, ohne dass er vorleistungspflichtig war, bereits bezahlt hat, ein **Zurückbehaltungsrecht** an der gelieferten Ware zugestehen müssen.

10   c) **Nachbesserung.** Sach- und Rechtsmängel können vom Verkäufer auch nachgebessert werden. Bei Sachmängeln steht es dem Verkäufer – in den Grenzen der Zumutbarkeit für den Käufer – frei, ob er die Reparatur auf seine Kosten **selbst** oder **durch einen Dritten** beim Käufer oder nach Rücknahme in seiner Werkstatt oder durch einen Dritten – etwa den Hersteller – durchführt. In letzterem Falle läuft der Käufer, der den Kaufpreis bereits bezahlt hat, ein ähnliches wirtschaftliches Risiko wie bei der Ersatzlieferung.[24] Es ist ihm deshalb auch insoweit ein **Zurückbehaltungsrecht** zuzugestehen, das der Verkäufer jedoch durch Sicherheitsleistung abwenden kann.[25]

3. Unvollständige Mängelbeseitigung

11   Unternimmt der Verkäufer einen Mängelbeseitigungsversuch, der jedoch fehlschlägt – z. B. auch die als Ersatz gelieferte Ware ist fehlerhaft, trotz Reparatur funktioniert die gelieferte Maschine nicht befriedigend, trotz Nachlieferung verbleibt eine Fehlmenge –, so fragt sich, ob dem Verkäufer **weitere Mängelbeseitigungsversuche** zustehen. Der Wortlaut des Art. 37 beschränkt den Verkäufer nicht auf einen Versuch. Bis zum vertraglich vorgesehenen Lieferzeitpunkt kann der Verkäufer deshalb auch mehrere Mängelbeseitigungsversuche unternehmen.[26] Allerdings dürfte mit jedem Versuch die Schwelle der Zumutbarkeit für den Käufer sinken.

4. Grenzen

12   Das Mängelbeseitigungsrecht des Verkäufers besteht nicht, wenn seine Ausübung dem Käufer **unzumutbare Unannehmlichkeiten** oder **unverhältnismässige Kosten** verursacht.

13   Nicht jede **Unannehmlichkeit** schliesst das Mängelbeseitigungsrecht des Verkäufers aus, sondern nur eine **unzumutbare.** Was eine unzumutbare Unannehmlichkeit darstellt, ist weitgehend eine Frage des Einzelfalls. Unzumutbar dürfte beispielsweise eine längere Zeit in Anspruch nehmende Reparatur der gelieferten Maschine sein, wenn der Käufer diese bereits in eine Fertigungsstrasse eingebaut hat; hier käme nur unverzügliche Ersatzlieferung

---

[18] Vgl. dazu unten Rn. 13.
[19] Vgl. Deutschland: § 266 BGB; Schweiz: Art. 69 I OR; Frankreich: Art. 1244 Cc; Österreich: § 1415 ABGB.
[20] Vgl. unten *Müller-Chen,* Art. 51 Rn. 4.
[21] Vgl. *Staudinger/Magnus,* Art. 37, Rn. 23.
[22] Vgl. *Herber/Czerwenka,* Art. 37, Rn. 7.
[23] Vgl. dazu unten *Müller-Chen,* Art. 46 Rn. 34.
[24] Vgl. oben Rn. 9.
[25] Vgl. *Herber/Czerwenka,* Art. 37, Rn. 7. Zu Recht weist allerdings *Staudinger/Magnus,* Art. 37, Rn. 17, darauf hin, dass dieses Zurückbehaltungsrecht nutzlos ist, wenn die Ware nicht am Käufersitz nachgebessert oder repariert werden kann.
[26] Vgl. *Honnold/Flechtner,* Art. 37, Rn. 247; vgl. aber *Staudinger/Magnus,* Art. 37, Rn. 16: grundsätzlich unzumutbar; in diesem Sinne auch *Soergel/Lüderitz/Schüßler-Langeheine,* Art. 37, Rn. 7.

in Betracht.[27] Unzumutbar wäre weiterhin das Angebot einer Nachlieferung, wenn der Verkäufer nicht bereit ist, die Transportkosten zu übernehmen. Schliesslich kann Unzumutbarkeit vorliegen, wenn der Verkäufer den Käufer mit der Mängelbeseitigung „überfällt", ohne ihn über seine diesbezügliche Absicht in Kenntnis zu setzen.[28] Mehrere erfolglose Reparaturversuche mögen ebenfalls Unzumutbarkeit begründen.

Kosten, die dem Käufer aus der Mängelbeseitigung erwachsen, kann der Käufer an sich im Wege des Schadenersatzes vom Verkäufer ersetzt verlangen.[29] Die ausdrückliche Erwähnung der unverhältnismässigen Kosten als Ausschlussgrund lässt sich demnach dahin verstehen, dass dem Käufer kein unverhältnismässiges Kostenrisiko zuzumuten ist.[30] Insbesondere muss der Käufer nicht mit erheblichen Beträgen in Vorlage gehen oder dem Verkäufer die bereits bezahlte Ware ohne Sicherheiten überlassen.[31] Bietet der Verkäufer dem Käufer hierfür sofortige Erstattung oder Sicherheitsleistung an, bleibt sein Mängelbeseitigungsrecht unberührt.[32] Auf **spätere Kostenrückerstattung** braucht sich der Käufer wegen des darin liegenden wirtschaftlichen Risikos jedoch nicht einzulassen, falls die Kosten einen nennenswerten Betrag übersteigen.[33] Ausschlaggebend kann dabei die Leistungsfähigkeit des Käufers sein, im Grundsatz jedoch nicht das Verhältnis des Betrags zum Vertragsvolumen.[34] Das Mängelbeseitigungsrecht des Verkäufers besteht dann nicht.

V. Rechtsfolgen

1. Ausschluss der Rechtsbehelfe nach Artt. 45 ff.

Solange dem Verkäufer das Recht zur Mängelbeseitigung zusteht, kann der Käufer seine Rechte nach Artt. 45 ff. nicht geltend machen. Diese stehen ihm erst mit Ablauf der Lieferfrist zu. Ist in der vorzeitigen vertragswidrigen Lieferung allerdings ein **antizipierter Vertragsbruch** zu sehen, wie z. B. wenn die Vertragswidrigkeit weder durch Ersatzlieferung noch durch Nachbesserung behoben werden kann, kann der Käufer nach Art. 72 vorgehen.[35]

2. Schadenersatz

Nach S. 2 behält der Käufer das Recht auf Schadenersatz nach Artt. 74 ff. In Betracht kommen insoweit Schäden, die auch durch die spätere vertragsgemässe Erfüllung nicht beseitigt werden können.[36] Hierzu gehören zunächst alle **Aufwendungen,** die dem Käufer **im Zusammenhang mit der Mängelbeseitigung** durch den Verkäufer entstanden sind,[37] wie beispielsweise vom Käufer verauslagte Kosten zum Rücktransport der Ware, Nutzungsausfall bezüglich anderer Sachen als der gelieferten Ware selbst während der Reparaturzeit[38]

---

[27] Vgl. *Honnold/Flechtner,* Art. 37, Rn. 245; *Enderlein/Maskow/Strohbach,* Art. 37, Anm. 6.; *Neumayer/Ming,* Art. 37, Anm. 4.
[28] Ebenso *Staudinger/Magnus,* Art. 37, Rn. 16; *Enderlein/Maskow/Strohbach,* Art. 37, Anm. 6.; vgl. auch *Keller,* Right to Cure, i) mit Hinweis auf Art. 7.1.4 I a) PICC und § 2–508 UCC.
[29] Vgl. unten Rn. 16.
[30] Vgl. MünchKomm/*Gruber,* Art. 37, Rn. 15; *Staudinger/Magnus,* Art. 37, Rn. 17.
[31] Vgl. MünchKomm/*Gruber,* Art. 37, Rn. 15; *Staudinger/Magnus,* Art. 37, Rn. 17.
[32] Vgl. *Kröll u. a./Kröll,* Art. 37, Rn. 16.
[33] Vgl. *Herber/Czerwenka,* Art. 37, Rn. 9; *Bianca/Bonell/Bianca,* Art. 37, Anm. 2.5.; *Enderlein/Maskow/Strohbach,* Art. 34, Rn. 8.
[34] A. A. *Staudinger/Magnus,* Art. 37, Rn. 17; *Ferrari u. a./Ferrari,* Internationales Vertragsrecht, Art. 37, Rn. 12.
[35] Vgl. *Staudinger/Magnus,* Art. 37, Rn. 20; MünchKomm/*Gruber,* Art. 37, Rn. 16; *Brunner,* Art. 37, Rn. 7; *Gutknecht,* S. 52.
[36] Vgl. *Bridge,* FS Schwenzer, S. 221, 228.
[37] Vgl. YB III (1972), S. 87, Nr. 69: „any inconvenience or expense". Vgl. Auch *Kröll u. a./Kröll,* Art. 37, Rn. 24.
[38] Bsp.: Eine Fertigungsstrasse, in die die gelieferte Maschine eingebaut wurde, muss während der Reparatur stillgelegt werden.

etc. Auch **Schäden,** die die zunächst vertragswidrig gelieferte Ware an anderem Eigentum des Käufers verursacht hat – z. B. die Maschine produziert Holzverschnitt –, sind zu ersetzen.[39] Schäden, die daraus entstehen, dass auch eine allfällige Ersatzlieferung nicht vertragsgemäss ist, fallen jedoch – jedenfalls soweit die Vertragswidrigkeit zum letzten Lieferzeitpunkt noch andauert – nicht unter Art. 37 S. 2, sondern sind nach Artt. 45 ff., 74 ff. zu beurteilen.[40] Zur Ersatzfähigkeit von Aufwendungen, die der Käufer allein in Zusammenhang mit der vorzeitigen Annahme getätigt hat, vgl. unten Art. 52 Rn. 4.

3. Weigerung des Käufers

17 Nicht ausdrücklich geregelt ist die Frage, welche Konsequenzen es hat, wenn der Käufer die Mängelbeseitigung durch den Verkäufer zu Unrecht verweigert. Aus dem Rechtsgedanken des Art. 80 muss jedoch gefolgert werden, dass der Käufer in diesem Fall die **Rechte aus der Vertragswidrigkeit verliert,** falls er dem Verkäufer die Mängelbeseitigung nicht doch noch ermöglicht.[41] Dies gilt allerdings nicht für den Nacherfüllungsanspruch bei Fehlen einzelner Teile oder Quantitätsabweichungen, auch wenn der Käufer die Annahme der Nachlieferung zunächst verweigert hat.[42]

VI. Beweislast

18 Entsprechend allgemeinen Prinzipien trifft den Verkäufer die Beweislast für die Voraussetzungen des Nacherfüllungsrechtes.[43] Hingegen hat der Käufer die Tatsachen, die zu Unzumutbarkeit der Mängelbeseitigung führen, zu beweisen.[44]

---

[39] Vgl. *Staudinger/Magnus,* Art. 37, Rn. 25; MünchKomm/*Gruber,* Art. 37, Rn. 19; MünchKommHGB/ *Benicke,* Art. 37, Rn. 11; *Brunner,* Art. 37, Rn. 8; *Karollus,* S. 122.

[40] Vgl. *Schlechtriem,* Seller's Obligations, § 6.03, S. 6–28; unklar *Honnold/Flechtner,* Art. 37, Rn. 247; *Ferrari u. a./Ferrari,* Internationales Vertragsrecht, Art. 37, Rn. 15; a. A. offenbar *Reinhart,* Art. 37, Rn. 3.

[41] Vgl. *Bianca/Bonell/Bianca,* Art. 37, Anm. 3.2.; *Herber/Czerwenka,* Art. 37, Rn. 8; *Enderlein/Maskow/Strohbach,* Art. 37, Anm. 2. a. E.; *Neumayer/Ming,* Art. 37, Anm. 4.; *Soergel/Lüderitz/Schüßler-Langeheine,* Art. 37, Rn. 8; *Heuzé,* Anm. 297.; zum EKG vgl. *Mertens/Rehbinder,* Art. 37 EKG, Rn. 3; *Dölle/Stumpf,* Art. 37 EKG, Rn. 6; vgl. jedoch *Piltz,* Internationales Kaufrecht, Rn. 5–27: ungerechtfertigte Zurückweisung durch den Käufer stellt einen Vertragsbruch dar.

[42] Vgl. *Staudinger/Magnus,* Art. 37, Rn. 22; *Herber/Czerwenka,* Art. 37, Rn. 8.

[43] Vgl. *Staudinger/Magnus,* Art. 37, Rn. 26; *Bamberger/Roth/Saenger,* Art. 37, Rn. 7; MünchKomm/*Gruber,* Art. 37, Rn. 20; MünchKommHGB/*Benicke,* Art. 37, Rn. 12.

[44] Vgl. *Staudinger/Magnus,* Art. 37, Rn. 26; *Bamberger/Roth/Saenger,* Art. 37, Rn. 7; *Kröll u. a./Kröll,* Art. 37, Rn. 25.

Art. 38 [Untersuchung der Ware]

(1) Der Käufer hat die Ware innerhalb einer so kurzen Frist zu untersuchen oder untersuchen zu lassen, wie es die Umstände erlauben.

(2) Erfordert der Vertrag eine Beförderung der Ware, so kann die Untersuchung bis nach dem Eintreffen der Ware am Bestimmungsort aufgeschoben werden.

(3) Wird die Ware vom Käufer umgeleitet oder von ihm weiterversandt, ohne daß er ausreichend Gelegenheit hatte, sie zu untersuchen, und kannte der Verkäufer bei Vertragsabschluß die Möglichkeit einer solchen Umleitung oder Weiterversendung oder mußte er sie kennen, so kann die Untersuchung bis nach dem Eintreffen der Ware an ihrem neuen Bestimmungsort aufgeschoben werden.

Art. 38

(1) The buyer must examine the goods, or cause them to be examined, within as short a period as is practicable in the circumstances.

(2) If the contract involves carriage of the goods, examination may be deferred until after the goods have arrived at their destination.

(3) If the goods are redirected in transit or redispatched by the buyer without a reasonable opportunity for examination by him and at the time of the conclusion of the contract the seller knew or ought to have known of the possibility of such redirection or redispatch, examination may be deferred until after the goods have arrived at the new destination.

Art. 38

1) L'acheteur doit examiner les marchandises ou les faire examiner dans un délai aussi bref que possible eu égard aux circonstances.

2) Si le contrat implique un transport des marchandises, l'examen peut être différé jusqu'à leur arrivée à destination.

3) Si les marchandises sont déroutées ou réexpédiées par l'acheteur sans que celui-ci ait eu raisonnablement la possibilité de les examiner et si, au moment de la conclusion du contrat, le vendeur connaissait ou aurait du connaître la possibilité de ce déroutage ou de cette réexpédition, l'examen peut être différé jusqu'à l'arrivée des marchandises à leur nouvelle destination.

Übersicht

	Rn.
I. Vorgeschichte	1
II. Allgemeines	3
1. Zweck und Rechtsnatur	3
2. Rechtsvergleichung	6
3. Anwendungsbereich	7
III. Art und Weise der Untersuchung	10
1. Untersuchung durch Käufer oder Dritte	10
2. Parteivereinbarungen und Gebräuche	11
3. Art und Weise der Untersuchung in Ermangelung von Parteivereinbarungen und Gebräuchen	12
a) Recht des Untersuchungsorts	12
b) Allgemeine Prinzipien	13
c) Fallgruppen	14
IV. Frist zur Untersuchung	15
1. Bemessung der Frist	15
2. Fristbeginn	19
a) Im Allgemeinen	19
b) Vorzeitige Lieferung; verspätete Lieferung; Teillieferungen	20
c) Versendungskauf – Abs. 2	21
d) Umleitung oder Weiterversendung – Abs. 3	23
V. Kosten der Untersuchung	27
VI. Abdingbarkeit	28

Vorläufer und **Entwürfe:** Art. 38 EKG, Genfer E 1976 Art. 22, Wiener E 1977 Art. 22, New Yorker E 1978 Art. 36.

I. Vorgeschichte

1 Art. 38 regelt den **Zeitpunkt der Untersuchung** und hat seinen Vorläufer in Art. 38 EKG. Wesentliche Unterschiede bestehen insoweit, als nach Art. 38 I EKG die Ware **„innerhalb kurzer Frist"** zu untersuchen war,[1] während das CISG nunmehr lediglich die Einhaltung „einer so kurzen Frist [...] wie es die Umstände erlauben" verlangt. Ein darüber hinausgehender Antrag Kanadas, in Abs. 1 stattdessen eine „angemessene Frist" vorzusehen, fand zwar die Unterstützung verschiedener Delegationen, konnte sich aber schliesslich nicht durchsetzen, weil man Probleme vor allem beim Kauf von verderblichen Waren befürchtete.[2] Änderungen ergeben sich auch insoweit, als Abs. 3 im Gegensatz zu Art. 38 III EKG einen Aufschub der Untersuchung bei **Weiterversendung** der Ware auch dann zulässt, wenn die Ware umgeladen wird. Man wollte dadurch dem Fall Rechnung tragen, dass die Ware in Containern befördert wird und es unangemessen wäre, diese vor Ankunft am letzten Bestimmungsort zu öffnen.[3] Schliesslich ist die Regelung des Art. 38 IV EKG, wonach sich die **Form der Untersuchung** mangels anderer Vereinbarungen der Parteien nach dem Recht oder den Gebräuchen des Ortes richtet, an dem die Untersuchung vorzunehmen ist, weggefallen. Der Ort, an dem die Untersuchung stattfinde, könne vom Zufall abhängen und u. U. von den Parteien im Zeitpunkt des Vertragsschlusses nicht vorhersehbar sein, ausserdem könne jeglicher Bezug zu den Parteien fehlen.[4] Auch sei nicht klar, ob Art. 38 IV EKG auf internationale Gebräuche i. S. d. Art. 9 oder auf lediglich lokale Gebräuche abstelle. Schliesslich müsse eine Parteivereinbarung zwingenden gesetzlichen Bestimmungen am Recht des Untersuchungsortes weichen.[5]

2 Die Änderungen gegenüber dem EKG wie auch der neu aufgenommene Art. 44[6] lassen die eindeutige Tendenz erkennen, die Untersuchungs- und Rügepflicht nicht nur flexibler, sondern insgesamt auch **käuferfreundlicher** als im EKG zu gestalten. Damit wurde einem gerade von Seiten der Entwicklungsländer vorgebrachten Anliegen entsprochen.[7] Dies muss bei der Auslegung der Artt. 38, 39 berücksichtigt werden, so dass insoweit auch nicht einfach an die – oft vom deutschen § 377 HGB inspirierte – strenge Rechtsprechung zum EKG angeknüpft werden kann.[8]

II. Allgemeines

1. Zweck und Rechtsnatur

3 Art. 38 regelt als einleitende Bestimmung die Pflicht des Käufers zur Untersuchung der Ware innerhalb eines bestimmten Zeitraumes. Damit nicht zu verwechseln ist das Recht des Käufers, nach Art. 58 III die Ware vor Zahlung des Kaufpreises zu untersuchen.[9] Die Untersuchungspflicht ist **Grundlage für die Rügepflicht** nach Art. 39. Der Zeitpunkt, in

---

[1] Vgl. aber Art. 11 EKG, wonach die „kurze Frist" ebenfalls unter Berücksichtigung der Umstände zu bestimmen war.
[2] Vgl. O. R., S. 310 ff., Nr. 75 ff.
[3] Vgl. YB III (1972), S. 87, Nr. 71.
[4] Vgl. YB IV (1973), S. 47, Nr. 83.
[5] Vgl. YB IV (1973), S. 66, Nr. 57 f.
[6] Zur Entstehungsgeschichte vgl. unten Art. 44 Rn. 2 ff.
[7] Vgl. *Schlechtriem*, Pflichten des Verkäufers, S. 125; *Staudinger/Magnus*, Art. 38, Rn. 6; *Loewe*, Art. 38, S. 58.
[8] Vgl. für Deutschland: § 377 HGB. Wie hier OGer Bern, 11.2.2004, CISG-online 1191, E. 4.; *Soergel/Lüderitz/Schüßler-Langeheine*, Art. 38, Rn. 3; *Resch*, ÖJZ 1992, 470, 471; *Janssen*, S. 129 ff.; *Ben Abderrahmane*, Dr. prat. com. int. 1989, 551, 555; *MünchKomm/Gruber*, Art. 38, Rn. 6; a. A. vor allem deutschsprachige Autoren, vgl. z. B. *Stumpf*, 1. Aufl., Art. 38 Rn. 5; *Herber/Czerwenka*, Art. 38, Rn. 7; *Detzer/Thamm*, BB 1992, 2369, 2375; *Karollus*, S. 126 (grundsätzlich sehr kurze Frist); *Tannò*, S. 270 f.; *Recknagel*, S. 106 f.; wohl auch *Reinhart*, Art. 38, Rn. 2; *Loewe*, Art. 38, S. 58; *Asam*, RIW 1989, 942, 944; OLG Oldenburg, 5.12.2000, CISG-online 618.
[9] Vgl. dazu *Mohs*, Art. 58 Rn. 33 ff.

dem der Käufer die Ware nach Art. 38 untersucht haben muss, entspricht in Art. 39 dem Zeitpunkt, in dem der Käufer eine Vertragswidrigkeit hätte feststellen müssen und ab dem die „angemessene Frist" zur Mängelrüge zu laufen beginnt.[10] Bedeutung hat der Zeitpunkt der ordnungsgemässen Untersuchung auch im Rahmen des Art. 49 II b) i), denn danach muss der Käufer die Aufhebung des Vertrages innerhalb einer angemessenen Frist, nachdem er die Vertragsverletzung kennen musste, erklären.

Die Untersuchungs- und Rügepflicht soll vor allem den Verkäufer in die Lage versetzen, **4** durch Nachlieferung, Ersatzlieferung oder Nachbesserung die Vertragswidrigkeit u. U. zu beheben oder einen **Schaden** des Käufers **zu verringern.** Zum anderen soll der Verkäufer durch die Rüge die Möglichkeit erhalten, sich auf allfällige **Verhandlungen** oder Streitigkeiten mit dem Käufer über die Vertragswidrigkeit der Ware einzustellen und sich darauf **vorzubereiten,** indem er beispielsweise das notwendige Beweismaterial sichert. Ausserdem muss der Verkäufer u. U. einen **Rückgriff** auf einen Zulieferer vorbereiten. Schliesslich soll dem Verkäufer auch zu einem bestimmten Zeitpunkt Gewissheit darüber verschafft werden, welche Rechnungsposten er in seine Bücher einstellen kann.

Die Untersuchungspflicht ist keine Rechtspflicht, sondern lediglich eine **Obliegenheit**.[11] **5** Ihre Verletzung zieht deshalb keinen Schadenersatzanspruch nach sich, sondern führt dazu, dass der Käufer seiner Rügepflicht nicht nachkommen kann und deshalb u. U. die aus der Vertragswidrigkeit der Ware herrührenden Rechtsbehelfe verliert. Sollte ausnahmsweise eine ordnungsgemässe Rüge auch ohne angemessene Untersuchung vorliegen, so ist dies zum Erhalt der Rechtsbehelfe ausreichend; die unzureichende Untersuchung bleibt dann ausser Betracht.[12] Erst recht bleibt das Unterlassen der Untersuchung ohne Folgen, wenn die Vertragswidrigkeit bei einer ordnungsgemässen Untersuchung ohnehin nicht hätte erkannt werden können.[13]

2. Rechtsvergleichung[14]

Eine ebenfalls ausdrücklich angeordnete Untersuchungspflicht des Käufers kennen na- **6** mentlich die Rechtsordnungen des **deutschen Rechtskreises,**[15] wobei diese im deutschen und österreichischen Recht freilich auf den beidseitigen Handelskauf beschränkt ist. Während das deutsche Recht eine „unverzügliche" Untersuchung verlangen, lässt das österreichische und das schweizerische Recht eine „nach dem üblichen Geschäftsgange tunlich[e]" Untersuchung genügen. Der CESL-Entwurf verlangt eine Untersuchung „innerhalb einer so kurzen Frist (...), wie es die Umstände erlauben", wobei diese Frist maximal 14 Tage betragen darf. Im **angloamerikanischen Recht**[16] wird allein Mängelrüge innerhalb einer

---

[10] Vgl. CISG-AC, Op. 2 *(Bergsten),* Comment 4.1 = IHR 2004, 163, 165; *Ferrari,* RabelsZ 68 (2004), 473, 480.

[11] Vgl. *Staudinger/Magnus,* Art. 38, Rn. 12; *Herber/Czerwenka,* Art. 38, Rn. 2; *Bianca/Bonell/Bianca,* Art. 38, Anm. 2.1.; *Enderlein/Maskow/Strohbach,* Art. 38, Anm. 1.; *Honnold/Flechtner,* Art. 38, Rn. 249; *P. Huber/Mullis/Mullis,* S. 149; *Neumayer/Ming,* Art. 39, Anm. 2.; *Karollus,* S. 124; *Piltz,* Internationales Kaufrecht, Rn. 5–97; *Soergel/Lüderitz/Schüßler-Langeheine,* Art. 38, Rn. 1; *Heilmann,* S. 289 f.; *Staub/Koller,* Vor § 373 HGB, Rn. 673; vgl. auch *Schlechtriem,* Einheitliches UN-Kaufrecht, S. 61 Fn. 271 a. E., der darauf hinweist, dass die dogmatische Frage, ob Obliegenheit oder Rechtspflicht vorliegt, anlässlich der Vorarbeiten nicht vertieft worden sei.

[12] Vgl. *Staudinger/Magnus,* Art. 38, Rn. 13; für das deutsche Recht vgl. *Baumbach/Hopt,* § 377 HGB, Rn. 3 A; dies trifft umso mehr für das neue österreichische UGB zu, vgl. *Krejci/Schauer,* § 377 UGB, Rn. 5, hatte aber schon unter dem alten österreichischen HGB Geltung, vgl. *Straube/Kramer,* §§ 377, 378 HGB, Rn. 31. Der Ansatz von *Andersen,* FS Schwenzer, S. 33, 40, eine nicht ordnungsgemässe Untersuchung könne ein Faktor bei der Entscheidung über die Anwendung der Rechtsfolge des Art. 39 sein, vermischt die zwar verknüpften aber dennoch getrennten Tatbestände der Artt. 38 und 39 in unzulässiger Weise und ist deshalb abzulehnen.

[13] Zum EKG vgl. BGH, 2.6.1982, NJW 1982, 2730, 2731; a. A. *Mertens/Rehbinder,* Art. 38/39 EKG, Rn. 11. Zum Beginn der Rügefrist in solchen Fällen, vgl. unten Art. 39 Rn. 20.

[14] Für Einzelheiten vgl. auch unten Rn. 16; CISG-AC, Op. 2 *(Bergsten),* Comment 2 = IHR 2004, 163, 164; *Schwenzer/Hachem/Kee,* Rn. 34.29.

[15] Vgl. Deutschland: § 377 HGB; Österreich: §§ 377, 378 UGB; Schweiz: Art. 201 OR. Vgl. auch Art. 121 CESL-Entwurf.

[16] Vgl. USA: § 2–607 (3) (a) UCC; England: sec. 35 (4) SGA.

Art. 38 7–9   Teil III. Kapitel II. Pflichten des Verkäufers. Abschnitt II

„reasonable time" verlangt, was jedoch ebenfalls eine entsprechende Untersuchung voraussetzt. Nur inzident kennt schliesslich auch das **französische Recht** eine Untersuchungspflicht des Käufers, da dieser seine Rechte innerhalb von zwei Jahren nach der Entdeckung des Mangels gerichtlich geltend machen muss.[17]

3. Anwendungsbereich

7   Art. 38 gilt für **alle Vertragswidrigkeiten** i. S. des Art. 35, d. h. auch für Quantitätsabweichungen und Lieferung eines aliud; dies gilt selbst dann, wenn die gelieferte Ware vom vertraglich Vereinbarten in krassester Weise abweicht.[18] Für **Rechtsmängel** und die **Belastung mit Schutzrechten Dritter** wird in Art. 43 zwar eine Rüge-, jedoch keine Untersuchungspflicht normiert.[19] Für vertragswidrige **Dokumente**[20] fehlt es sowohl an einer ausdrücklich geregelten Untersuchungs- als auch an einer Rügepflicht. Artt. 38, 39 müssen jedoch insoweit entsprechend angewandt werden, da sonst das Nacherfüllungsrecht des Verkäufers faktisch leerlaufen würde.[21]

8   Die Untersuchungs- und Rügepflicht trifft – im Gegensatz zum deutschen und österreichischen Recht – nicht nur den **kaufmännischen Käufer,** sondern gilt auch für Kaufverträge mit **Verbrauchern,** wenngleich diese unter dem CISG die Ausnahme sein werden – vgl. Art. 2 a). Der jeweiligen Stellung des Käufers im Wirtschaftsverkehr ist jedoch im Rahmen der Anforderungen an die ordnungsgemässe Untersuchung und Rüge Rechnung zu tragen.[22]

9   Artt. 38, 39 gelten nicht nur für die ursprüngliche Lieferung der Ware, sondern ebenso für allfällige **Nach- und Ersatzlieferungen sowie für Nachbesserungen.**[23] Bei einem **Sukzessivlieferungsvertrag** – vgl. Art. 73 – ist jede Einzellieferung vom Käufer zu untersuchen und ggf. zu rügen. Unterlässt der Käufer Untersuchung und Rüge bezüglich einer Teillieferung, so verliert er dadurch nicht mögliche Rechtsbehelfe wegen späterer nicht vertragsgemässer Lieferungen.[24] Auch verliert er nicht das Recht, Vertragsaufhebung nach Art. 73 II hinsichtlich der noch nicht gelieferten weiteren Teilmengen zu begehren.[25] Bei einem **Kauf nach Probe oder Muster** muss die Hauptlieferung auch dann untersucht

---

[17] Vgl. den neu gefassten Art. 1648 Cc. Entsprechend dem bisherigen französischen Recht aber noch Art. 1648 belgischer Cc, der von „bref délai" spricht. Das italienische Recht – Art. 1495 I Cc – sieht eine achttägige Rügefrist ab Entdeckung des Mangels vor, ohne dass eine Untersuchungsobliegenheit normiert ist. Ebenso verfährt das niederländische Recht, das in Art. 7:23.1 BW eine Rüge in angemessener Zeit nach Entdeckung verlangt.

[18] Vgl. *Staudinger/Magnus,* Art. 39, Rn. 9; *Honnold/Flechtner,* Artt. 39, 40, 44, Rn. 256.1; *Karollus,* S. 125 f.; *Resch,* ÖJZ 1992, 470, 472; *Herber/Czerwenka,* Art. 38, Rn. 6; *Schlechtriem,* Internationales UN-Kaufrecht, Rn. 153; *ders.,* Pflichten des Verkäufers, S. 125; *Enderlein/Maskow/Strohbach,* Art. 38, Anm. 1.; *Welser,* S. 111; *Ebenroth,* östJBl 1986, 681, 689; a. A. *Bydlinski,* Allgemeines Vertragsrecht, S. 137; *Neumayer/Ming,* Art. 39, Anm. 1.; *Doralt/Neumayer,* UNCITRAL-Kaufrecht, S. 136. Vgl. demgegenüber im österreichischen Recht die Unterscheidung zwischen genehmigungsfähigem und genehmigungsfähigem aliud; dazu *Straube/Kramer,* §§ 377, 378 HGB, Rn. 62 ff. In der Schweiz soll jede aliud-Lieferung Nichterfüllung sein, die dann auch nicht gerügt werden muss, vgl. BGer, 5.12.1995, BGE 121 III 453, 455 ff.; kritisch hierzu *Schwenzer,* OR AT, Rn. 8.07. Str. ist die Anwendbarkeit des Art. 38 bei höherwertiger Ware, vgl. Art. 39, Rn. 30; dagegen MünchKomm/*Gruber,* Art. 38, Rn. 10 f.

[19] Vgl. unten Art. 43 Rn. 4.

[20] Für den Fall, dass Dokumente als Sachmangel eingeordnet werden vgl. OLG München, 13.11.2002, CISG-online 786 = NJW-RR 2003, 849, m. Anm. *Hohloch,* JuS 2003, 1134 f. Vgl. auch Art. 39 Rn. 9 Fn. 28b.

[21] Vgl. oben *Widmer Lüchinger,* Art. 34 Rn. 5; *Herber/Czerwenka,* Art. 34, Rn. 7; *Honnold/Flechtner,* Artt. 39, 40, 44, Rn. 256; *P. Huber/Mullis/Mullis,* S. 148 f.; *Witz/Salger/Lorenz/Salger,* Art. 38, Rn. 10; *Vogel,* S. 42 ff.; *Ferrari u. a./Ferrari,* Internationales Vertragsrecht, Art. 38, Rn. 6; *Enderlein/Maskow/Strohbach,* Art. 38, Anm. 2.; a. A. MünchKomm/*Gruber,* Art. 38, Rn. 13; wohl auch *Kröll u. a./Kröll,* Art. 38, Rn. 30.

[22] Vgl. unten Rn. 18; Art. 39 Rn. 7.

[23] Vgl. LG Oldenburg, 9.11.1994, CISG-online 114 = NJW-RR 1995, 438; Hof van Beroep Ghent, 14.11.2008, CISG-online 1908 (analoge Anwendung); MünchKomm/*Gruber,* Art. 38, Rn. 14.

[24] Vgl. Schiedsgericht der Börse für landwirtschaftliche Produkte in Wien, 10.12.1997, CISG-online 351 = ZfRVgl 1998, 211, 215.

[25] Vgl. *Staudinger/Magnus,* Art. 38, Rn. 24.

werden, wenn Probe oder Muster mangelfrei waren. Wurde jedoch vereinbart, dass die **Ausfallprobe** die ganze Ware vertreten soll, so muss nur diese untersucht werden.

III. Art und Weise der Untersuchung

1. Untersuchung durch Käufer oder Dritte

Die Untersuchung kann durch den **Käufer selbst,** seine Leute oder durch **dritte** 10
Personen (Abnehmer der Ware,[26] Sachverständige) erfolgen.[27] Auch eine **gemeinsame Untersuchung** durch Käufer und Verkäufer ist denkbar und in manchen Branchen üblich. Dies gilt insbesondere bei komplexeren Verträgen, wie z. B. Anlagenverträgen. Häufig vereinbaren die Parteien auch die Zuständigkeit einer **neutralen Prüfstelle.**[28] Am Untersuchungsort mögen auch **staatliche Stellen** für die Untersuchung zuständig sein.[29] Eine nicht sachgerechte Untersuchung durch Dritte muss sich der Käufer grundsätzlich **zurechnen** lassen.[30] Dies kann freilich nicht gelten, wenn die Parteien übereinstimmend einen neutralen Dritten ins Auge gefasst haben[31] oder wenn gar der Verkäufer auf Untersuchung durch einen bestimmten Dritten bestanden hat. Eine Zurechnung kommt grundsätzlich auch nicht bei nicht ordnungsgemässer Untersuchung seitens staatlicher Stellen in Betracht; jedenfalls müsste insoweit eine vernünftige Entschuldigung des Käufers i. S. des Art. 44 angenommen werden.[32]

2. Parteivereinbarungen und Gebräuche

Primär massgebend für die Art und Weise der Untersuchung sind die **Vereinbarungen** 11
der Parteien – Art. 6.[33] Beispielsweise können die Parteien etwa die Zahl der zu entnehmenden Stichproben oder bestimmte chemische Analysen vorsehen. Vor allem beim Kauf von Maschinen ist es üblich und zu empfehlen, die Untersuchungsmodalitäten (Art und Dauer von Probeläufen etc.) vertraglich im Einzelnen festzulegen.[34] Fehlen konkrete Parteivereinbarungen, so kann sich die erforderliche Art und Weise der Untersuchung vor allem auch aus **Handelsbräuchen** und **Gepflogenheiten** ergeben.[35]

3. Art und Weise der Untersuchung in Ermangelung von Parteivereinbarungen und Gebräuchen

a) Recht des Untersuchungsorts. Für die Art und Weise der Untersuchung verweist 12
Art. 38 im Gegensatz zu Art. 38 IV EKG nicht mehr subsidiär auf das Recht des Unter-

---

[26] Vgl. OLG Koblenz, 18.11.1999, CISG-online 570; OLG Düsseldorf, 23.1.2004, CISG-online 918; OLG Stuttgart, 12.3.2001, CISG-online 841; *Kuoppala*, Examination, 3.2.1.; MünchKomm/*Gruber,* Art. 38, Rn. 17.
[27] Vgl. LG Aschaffenburg, 20.4.2006, CISG-online 1446 = IHR 2007, 109, 112; *P. Huber/Mullis/Mullis,* S. 150.
[28] Vgl. *Enderlein/Maskow/Strohbach,* Art. 38, Anm. 1.; *Kuoppala,* Examination, 3.2.1.; Einzelheiten bei *Staub/Brüggemann,* § 377 HGB, Rn. 99.
[29] Vgl. *Tannò,* S. 272. Allerdings ist zu berücksichtigen, dass die früheren zollamtlichen Wareneinfuhruntersuchungen an der Grenze mit der Schaffung des EU-Binnenmarktes für Produkte aus EU-Mitgliedsstaaten entfallen sind.
[30] Vgl. OLG Düsseldorf, 23.1.2004, CISG-online 918; OLG Stuttgart, 12.3.2001, CISG-online 841; *Staudinger/Magnus,* Art. 38, Rn. 15; *Bianca/Bonell/Bianca,* Art. 38, Anm. 2.2.; *Heuzé,* Anm. 301.
[31] ICC, 9187/1999, CISG-online 705 = 11:2 ICC Int. Ct. Arb. Bull. (2000), 94; *Ferrari u. a./Ferrari,* Internationales Vertragsrecht, Art. 38, Rn. 8; a. A. *P. Huber/Mullis/Mullis,* S. 150.
[32] Zustimmend wohl ICC, 9187/1999, CISG-online 705 = 11:2 ICC Int. Ct. Arb. Bull. (2000), 94.
[33] Vgl. die Praxishinweise bei *Rudolph,* Art. 38, Rn. 9.
[34] Vgl. *Reinhart,* Art. 38, Rn. 2; *Herber/Czerwenka,* Art. 38, Rn. 4; *Schlechtriem,* Einheitliches UN-Kaufrecht, S. 62; *Enderlein/Maskow/Strohbach,* Art. 38, Anm. 1.; *Tannò,* S. 266 f., 272.
[35] *Kröll u. a./Kröll,* Art. 38, Rn. 24 ff.; vgl. zum Kunsthandel *Mosimann/Müller-Chen,* FS Schwenzer, S. 1303, 1321.

suchungsorts.³⁶ Auch **internationalprivatrechtliche Regelungen,** die das Recht des Untersuchungsorts als massgeblich bestimmen,³⁷ können im Rahmen des CISG nicht angewandt werden.³⁸ Vielmehr sind die Einzelheiten aus dem CISG selbst zu entwickeln. Dies schliesst freilich nicht aus, dass im Einzelfall auf Grund Parteivereinbarung oder internationalen Handelsbrauchs dann doch an das massgebliche Ortsrecht anzuknüpfen ist.³⁹

13 **b) Allgemeine Prinzipien.** Mangels Parteivereinbarung oder Handelsbrauchs muss der Käufer die Ware entsprechend ihrer Art, ihrer Menge, ihrer Verpackung und unter Berücksichtigung aller weiteren Umstände in angemessener Weise untersuchen. Grundsätzlich ist hierbei ein **objektiver Massstab** zugrunde zu legen. Dies schliesst jedoch die Berücksichtigung **subjektiver Faktoren,** die dem Verkäufer bekannt sind oder bekannt sein müssen⁴⁰ – wie beispielsweise mangelnde Fachkunde des Käufers, Fehlen einer für die sachgemässe Untersuchung erforderlichen Infrastruktur am Untersuchungsort etc. –, nicht aus. Dasselbe gilt für die Tatsache, dass nach unvereinheitlichtem Recht am Käufersitz Untersuchung und Rüge nicht erforderlich sind.⁴¹ Die Untersuchung muss unter Berücksichtigung sämtlicher Umstände **geeignet sein, erkennbare Mängel zu offenbaren.**⁴² Bei entsprechender Sachkunde hat der Käufer eine fachmännische, gründliche Untersuchung vorzunehmen.⁴³ Dies gilt umso mehr, wenn er bereits durch Mängel anlässlich vorangegangener Lieferungen vorgewarnt ist.⁴⁴ Bei Gefahr eventuell hoher Mangelfolgeschäden muss die Untersuchung gründlicher als im Normalfall ausfallen.⁴⁵ Im Einzelfall mag auch die Hinzuziehung eines Fachmannes erforderlich sein; allerdings dürfen die Anforderungen gerade in diesem Punkt nicht überspannt werden.⁴⁶ Die Untersuchung braucht sich ohne entsprechende Hinweise nicht auf verbotene Manipulationen der Ware zu erstrecken, wie z. B. Wasserzusatz bei Wein.⁴⁷ Kosten und Aufwand der Untersuchung müssen in einem vernünftigen Verhältnis zu dem zu erwartenden Ergebnis der Untersuchung stehen.⁴⁸

---

³⁶ Zur Vorgeschichte vgl. Rn. 1.
³⁷ Vgl. Deutschland: Art. 32 II EGBGB; Schweiz: Art. 125 IPRG; Art. 4 Haager Übereinkommen betreffend das auf internationale Kaufverträge über bewegliche Sachen anzuwendende Recht v. 15.6.1955; Art. 13 Haager Übereinkommen betreffend das auf internationale Kaufverträge über bewegliche Sachen anzuwendende Recht v. 22.12.1986 (noch nicht in Kraft getreten).
³⁸ Vgl. *Staudinger/Magnus,* Art. 38, Rn. 19; *Herber/Czerwenka,* Art. 38, Rn. 3; a. A. wohl Cámara Nacional de Apelaciones en lo Comercial de Buenos Aires, 31.5.2007, CISG-online 1517.
³⁹ Vgl. *Schlechtriem,* Internationales UN-Kaufrecht, Rn. 151 m. Bsp.; *Staudinger/Magnus,* Art. 38, Rn. 19; *Enderlein/Maskow/Strohbach,* Art. 38, Anm. 1.; ähnlich auch *Tannò,* S. 275. *Neumayer/Ming,* Art. 38, Anm. 2., wollen subsidiär allerdings immer an das Recht des Untersuchungsorts anknüpfen.
⁴⁰ Vgl. *Kröll u. a./Kröll,* Art. 38, Rn. 48.
⁴¹ A. A. OGH, 27.8.1999, CISG-online 485 = IHR 2001, 80; MünchKomm/*Gruber,* Art. 38, Rn. 23.
⁴² Ebenso *Staudinger/Magnus,* Art. 38, Rn. 28; *Herber/Czerwenka,* Art. 38, Rn. 5; *Heuzé,* Anm. 301.; *Neumayer/Ming,* Art. 38, Anm. 2.; *Heilmann,* S. 291.
⁴³ Vgl. OLG München, 11.3.1998, CISG-online 310, m. Anm. *Schlechtriem,* EWiR 1998, 549 f.; gegen zu strenge Anforderungen v. a. *Lookofsky,* Understanding the CISG, S. 87 f.; *Kuoppala,* Examination, 3.3.1.
⁴⁴ Vgl. LG Stuttgart, 31.8.1989, CISG-online 11 = RIW 1989, 984, m. Anm. *Asam,* RIW 1989, 942, m. Anm. *Reinhart,* IPRax 1990, 289–292; krit. hierzu *Staudinger/Magnus,* Art. 38, Rn. 33; a. A. auch *Ferrari u. a./Ferrari,* Internationales Vertragsrecht, Art. 38, Rn. 10.
⁴⁵ Vgl. LG Aschaffenburg, 20.4.2006, CISG-online 1446 = IHR 2007, 109, 112; vgl. auch *Kuoppala,* Examination, 3.3.1.
⁴⁶ Vgl. *Staudinger/Magnus,* Art. 38, Rn. 4, 31; *Herber/Czerwenka,* Art. 38, Rn. 5; LG Paderborn, 25.6.1996, CISG-online 262 (keine chemische Analyse von PVC erforderlich); LG Trier, 12.10.1995, CISG-online 160 = NJW-RR 1996, 564 (keine chemische Analyse von Wein erforderlich); ähnlich auch österreichische Recht, vgl. *Straube/Kramer,* §§ 377, 378 HGB, Rn. 35; gilt auch für § 377 UGB, vgl. Erläuterungen zur Regierungsvorlage, § 377 sub b., 1058 BlgNR 22. GP, 61: Keine materielle Änderung der Rechtslage angestrebt. Eine chemische Analyse halten hingegen für erforderlich, wenn eine besondere Zusammensetzung erforderlich ist: *Kröll u. a./Kröll,* Art. 38, Rn. 36, 57; *Ferrari u. a./Ferrari,* Internationales Vertragsrecht, Art. 38, Rn. 11.
⁴⁷ Vgl. LG Trier, 12.10.1995, CISG-online 160 = NJW-RR 1996, 564, 565; *Bamberger/Roth/Saenger,* Art. 38, Rn. 4; *Staudinger/Magnus,* Art. 38, Rn. 32; *Kröll u. a./Kröll,* Art. 38, Rn. 36, 56.
⁴⁸ Vgl. OLG Dresden, 8.11.2007, CISG-online 1624 (kein vernünftiges Verhältnis bei Einbau von Schachtabdeckungen in den Strassenbelag und aufwändigem Testverfahren zur Simulation der Belastungen des

c) Fallgruppen. Bei Lieferung grösserer Mengen muss der Käufer nicht die gesamte 14
Ware untersuchen, sondern kann sich auf repräsentative **Stichproben** beschränken.[49]
Soweit mit der Untersuchung ein **Eingriff in die Substanz** verbunden ist, muss der
Käufer die Ware jedenfalls durch Besehen, Messen, Riechen, Betasten[50] etc. untersuchen.
Darüber hinaus sind auch hier Stichproben – etwa Öffnen von Konserven, Auftauen
gefrorener Ware[51] – erforderlich, selbst wenn die untersuchte Ware dabei unbrauchbar
wird.[52] Die Zahl der Stichproben ist hier allerdings auf wenige Promille der Gesamtmenge
herabzusetzen.[53] Dasselbe gilt für **originalverpackte Ware,** die durch Öffnen der Verpackung unverkäuflich wird. Fällt schon bei oberflächlicher Untersuchung der untypische
Zustand der Ware auf, sind Stichproben unerlässlich.[54] Ware, die zur **Weiterverarbeitung**
bestimmt ist, ist probeweise zu verarbeiten.[55] Ebenso muss Ware stichprobenweise in
denjenigen Zustand gebracht werden, der zur Vertragserfüllung nötig ist, z. B. muss sie
montiert und zusammengefügt werden.[56] Bei Stoffen gehört dazu auch die Prüfung des
Einlaufverhaltens durch Anfertigung von Wasch- und Bügelproben von allen Sorten und
Farben, die Überprüfung der Farbechtheit jedenfalls mit einfachen Mitteln[57] sowie das
probeweise Färben.[58] Bekleidungsstücke müssen jedoch weder im Hinblick auf ihr Einlaufverhalten stichprobenartig gewaschen werden,[59] noch kann vom Käufer erwartet werden
Mängel zu entdecken, die erst beim ersten Tragen erkennbar werden.[60] Kommt ein
regulärer Arbeitseinsatz einer Maschine derzeit nicht in Betracht, ist ein Test- oder Probelauf durchzuführen.[61] Bei **komplizierten technischen Gütern,** wie beispielsweise Maschinen, Apparaten oder Fahrzeugen genügt es hingegen, wenn der Käufer ihre Funktions-

---

üblichen Strassenverkehrs); OLG Köln, 12.1.2007, CISG-online 1581 = IHR 2007, 200, 205; *Kröll u. a./Kröll,*
Art. 38, Rn. 35.

[49] Vgl. *Bianca/Bonell/Bianca,* Art. 38, Anm. 2.3.; *Audit,* Vente internationale, Anm. 105.; *Heilmann,*
S. 292 f.; *DiMatteo/Dhooge/Greene/Maurer/Pagnattaro,* 34 Nw. J. Int'l L. & Bus. (2004), 299, 362; *Kruisinga,*
Non-conformity, S. 68; *P. Huber/Mullis/Mullis,* S. 151; vgl. OLG Köln, 31.8.2006, CISG-online 1406 = IHR
2007, 71; OLG Saarbrücken, 13.1.1993, CISG-online 83; HGer Zürich, 30.11.1998, CISG-online 415 =
SZIER 1999, 186; zum EKG vgl. OLG Hamburg, 3.3.1982, RIW 1982, 435; offenbar nicht beachtet von
Regional Court Zilina, 25.10.2007, CISG-online 1761 („[...] 500 bis 700 [...] Kleidungsstücke wurden
geliefert. In Anbetracht dieser Menge wäre es unbillig von [Käufer] zu erwarten, dass er alle Güter zum
Zeitpunkt ihres Eintreffens zu untersuchen hat'). Im deutschen und schweizerischen Recht geht die Rechtsprechung davon aus, dass der Käufer einige Prozent der Gesamtwaren als Proben zu ziehen hat, vgl. *Tannò,*
S. 56, 187. Entsprechendes gilt nach österreichischem Recht, vgl. *Straube/Kramer,* §§ 377, 378 HGB, Rn. 36.
[50] Vgl. OLG München, 11.3.1998, CISG-online 310 (Cashmere-Ware).
[51] Vgl. RB Roermond, 19.12.1991, CISG-online 29; Sø og Handelsretten, 31.1.2002, CISG-online
679. Trib Vigevano, 12.7.2000, CISG-online 493; *Chicago Prime Packers, Inc. v. Northam Food Trading Co.,*
U. S. Dist. Ct. (N. D. Ill.), 21.5.2004, CISG-online 851 = IHR 2004, 156, 161, m. Anm. *Teiling,* Uniform
L. Rev. (2004), 431–435, wo die Umstände allerdings darauf hindeuten, dass die War nicht hätte aufgetaut
werden müssen, um die Mängel erkennen zu können.
[52] Vgl. OLG Köln, 12.1.2007, CISG-online 1581 = IHR 2007, 200, 205; *Schlechtriem,* Internationales UN-Kaufrecht, Rn. 151; *Staudinger/Magnus,* Art. 38, Rn. 30.
[53] Vgl. OGer Zug, 24.3.1998, CISG-online 897, E. 3) d) ee). Für das deutsche und schweizerische Recht
vgl. *Tannò,* S. 56, 187; für das österreichische Recht vgl. *Straube/Kramer,* §§ 377, 378 HGB, Rn. 36.
[54] Vgl. LG Aschaffenburg, 20.4.2006, CISG-online 1446 = IHR 2007, 109, 112; zum EKG vgl. OLG
Hamburg, 3.3.1982, RIW 1982, 435; zum deutschen Recht vgl. BGH, 16.9.1987, BGHZ 101, 337 (Weinkorken).
[55] Vgl. OLG Karlsruhe, 25.6.1997, CISG-online 263, m. Anm. *Schlechtriem,* EWiR 1997, 785 f. und
m. Anm. *Witz,* D. 1998, Somm. 310 f.; Trib. Vigevano, 12.7.2000, CISG-online 493; vgl. auch *P. Huber/
Mullis/Mullis,* S. 151; so im Grundsatz auch *Staudinger/Magnus,* Art. 38, Rn. 31.
[56] OLG Dresden, 8.11.2007, CISG-online 1624 (Schachtabdeckungen, bestehend aus Abdeckung und
Rahmenkonstruktion).
[57] *Magnus,* TranspR-IHR 1999, 29, 30; vgl. AG Kehl, 6.10.1995, CISG-online 162 = RIW 1996, 957 f.
[58] Vgl. LG Berlin, 21.3.2003, CISG-online 785 = IHR 2003, 228, 229; LG Berlin, 25.5.1999, CISG-online
1311; KG Schaffhausen, 27.1.2004, CISG-online 960; *Kröll u. a./Kröll,* Art. 38, Rn. 55, 59; *Ferrari u. a./
Ferrari,* Internationales Vertragsrecht, Art. 38, Rn. 13.
[59] Vgl. LG Landshut, 5.4.1995, CISG-online 193; MünchKommHGB/*Benicke,* Art. 38, Rn. 5.
[60] Regional Court Zilina, 25.10.2007, CISG-online 1761 (Fitnessbekleidung).
[61] Vgl. OLG Oldenburg, 5.12.2000, CISG-online 618; OLG Koblenz, 11.9.1998, CISG-online 505; RB
Roermond, 19.12.1991, CISG-online 29, zit. nach *Dokter/Kruisinga,* IHR 2003, 105, 110.

tüchtigkeit überprüft.[62] Hingegen besteht keine Verpflichtung des Käufers, ein Gerät auf die elektrische Betriebssicherheit hin zu überprüfen.[63] Bei **zur Fertigung anderer Güter bestimmter Maschinen** ist stichprobenweise Fertigung unter ähnlichen Bedingungen wie bei Serienproduktion erforderlich.[64] Besonderheiten gelten bei **verderblicher Ware;** das dort bestehende Bedürfnis einer besonders raschen Rüge führt als solches schon zum Ausschluss zeitaufwändiger Prüfmethoden. Wenn die Ware allerdings zum menschlichen Verzehr bestimmt ist, ist grössere Sorgfalt erforderlich.[65] In der Regel sind hier einfache Untersuchungen – Besicht, Riechen, Aufschneiden einzelner Früchte etc. – ausreichend. Im Hinblick auf Quantitätsabweichungen muss gezählt bzw. gewogen werden.[66] Kunstwerke sind jedenfalls bei konkreten Verdachtsmomenten, darüber hinaus aber auch generell bei hohen Kaufpreisen auf ihre Echtheit hin zu überprüfen.[67]

IV. Frist zur Untersuchung

1. Bemessung der Frist[68]

15 Das CISG verlangt nicht Untersuchung innerhalb „kurzer Frist", sondern innerhalb „so kurzer Frist [...] wie es die Umstände erlauben". Angesichts der grossen Vielfalt von Gütern, die Gegenstand eines internationalen Kaufvertrages sein können, hat das CISG zu Recht eine solchermassen **flexible Frist** und nicht etwa eine Bestimmung nach Tagen, Wochen oder Monaten gewählt.[69] Bei der Bestimmung der Fristdauer sind die **Umstände des Einzelfalls**[70] und die angemessenen Möglichkeiten der Parteien heranzuziehen. Zu diesen Umständen gehört beispielsweise der Ort, an dem sich die Ware im Zeitpunkt der Lieferung befindet, und die Art und Weise der Verpackung der Ware. Besondere Bedeutung kommt jedoch der Art der Ware zu.[71]

16 Wirklich rasches Handeln ist bei **verderblicher Ware** geboten.[72] Allgemeine Geschäftsbedingungen und Handelsbräuche sehen hier oft Fristen von einigen Stunden bis zu wenigen Tagen vor.[73] Dasselbe gilt, wenn aus anderen Gründen eine Veränderung der Ware

---

[62] Vgl. *Enderlein/Maskow/Strohbach*, Art. 38, Anm. 1.: bei komplexen Waren braucht der Käufer weder eine vollständige Untersuchung jedes einzelnen Stückes der Lieferung noch jedes einzelnen Teiles vorzunehmen.

[63] Vgl. LG München I, 27.2.2002, CISG-online 654 = IHR 2003, 233, 235.

[64] Zum deutschen Recht vgl. BGH, 16.3.1977, NJW 1977, 1150; OLG Köln, 14.7.1986, BB 1988, 20.

[65] Audiencia Provincial de Pontevedra, 19.12.2007, CISG-online 1688 (gefrorene Meeresfrüchte); *Kröll u. a./Kröll*, Art. 38, Rn. 38.

[66] LG Landshut, 5.4.1995, CISG-online 193; *Magnus*, TranspR-IHR 1999, 29, 31.

[67] Vgl. *Mosimann/Müller-Chen*, FS Schwenzer, S. 1303, 1321, soweit dort auch das Alter eines Kunstwerk als alleiniger Auslöser für die Pflicht zur Überprüfung der Echtheit als ausreichend angesehen wird, erscheint dies als zu weitgehend.

[68] Rechtsvergleichend *Schwenzer/Hachem/Kee*, Rn. 34.40 ff.

[69] Vgl. *Ferrari*, RabelsZ 68 (2004), 472, 483; *Kuoppala*, Examination, 3.4.1. Mit diesem Ausgangspunkt nicht zu vereinbaren ist die Auffassung von *Piltz*, Internationales Kaufrecht, Rn. 5–77, der als Mittelwert von fünf Arbeitstagen ausgehen will; ähnlich auch *Asam*, RIW 1989, 944; *Neumayer/Ming*, Art. 38, Anm. 3.: „außergewöhnlich kurze Frist". Dasselbe gilt für die vom OGH in ständiger Rspr. – vgl. nur OGH, 15.10.1998, CISG-online 380 = JBl 1999, 318 ff. – vertretene Gesamtuntersuchungs- und -rügefrist von 14 Tagen. Eine starre Maximalfrist von 14 Tagen enthält hingegen Art. 121 I CESL-Entwurf, krit. dazu *Schmidt-Kessel/Wiese*, Europäisches Kaufrecht, S. 409 f.

[70] Vgl. CISG-AC, Op. 2 *(Bergsten)*, passim = IHR (2004), 163; *P. Huber/Mullis/Mullis*, S. 154. Gerechtshof 's-Hertogenbosch, 9.3.2010, CISG-online 2341 hat beispielsweise die vertragliche Klausel „Good quality accepted in Holland and Germany" zum Anlass genommen, eine Untersuchung erst bei Eintreffen der Ware bei den Kunden des Käufers in den Niederlanden und Deutschland ausreichen zu lassen.

[71] Vgl. OGH, 14.1.2002, CISG-online 643; OLG Linz, 1.6.2005, CISG-online 1088.

[72] Vgl. *P. Huber/Mullis/Mullis*, S. 154.

[73] Vgl. AG Riedlingen, 21.10.1994, CISG-online 358 (Schinken: 3 Tage); *Tannò*, S. 192 f.; *Chicago Prime Packers, Inc. v. Northam Food Trading Co.*, U. S. Dist. Ct. (N. D. Ill.), 21.5.2004, CISG-online 851 = IHR 2004, 156, 161 (sogar gefrorenes Fleisch, das mehr als drei Monate haltbar ist), m. Anm. *Teiling*, Uniform L. Rev. (2004), 431–435; OGer Zug, 24.3.1998, CISG-online 897 (gefrorenes Fleisch verderblich, nicht beständig);

zu besorgen ist, oder bei Saisonware.[74] Wird die Ware z. B. mit anderer gleichartiger Ware vermischt, hat die Untersuchung vor der Vermischung stattzufinden.[75] Anders ist die Situation bei **dauerhaften Gütern**.[76] Die Rechtsprechung zum EKG,[77] die in Anlehnung an die Rechtsprechung zu § 377 HGB auch hier oft schon eine Rüge nach elf bis vierzehn Tagen als verspätet ansah, kann zur Bestimmung der Dauer der Untersuchungsfrist nicht mehr herangezogen werden.[78] Zum einen hat man ausweislich der Materialien nur im Hinblick auf verderbliche Ware davon abgesehen, die „kurze Frist" in eine „vernünftige (reasonable) Frist" abzuändern.[79] Zum anderen zeigt die Rechtsvergleichung, dass sich in den meisten ausländischen Rechtsordnungen[80] die Rechtsprechung bei Beurteilung der Untersuchungs- und Rügefrist wesentlich käuferfreundlicher zeigt, als dies namentlich in Deutschland, Österreich und der Schweiz der Fall ist. In Frankreich etwa war es keine Seltenheit, dass auch eine Klageerhebung zwischen zwei und drei Jahren nach Lieferung der Ware als innerhalb des „bref délai" liegend beurteilt wurde.[81] Auch die „reasonable time" im Rahmen der § 2–607 (3) (a) UCC wird von amerikanischen Gerichten grosszügig ausgelegt.[82]

Unter Berücksichtigung dieser Gesichtspunkte wird man bei Waren, bei denen durch Zeitablauf weder ein Verderb noch eine Veränderung ihrer Qualität zu besorgen ist, von folgenden Prinzipien ausgehen können: eine **sofortige Untersuchung** kann man auch bei dauerhaften Gütern im Hinblick auf **Anzahl** und **Gattungszugehörigkeit** – soweit diese ohne weiteres feststellbar ist – erwarten.[83] Dasselbe gilt im Hinblick auf Mängel, die durch blossen Besicht der Ware festgestellt werden können.[84] Sofortige **genauere Unter-**

Tannò, S. 192 f.; zum amerikanischen Recht vgl. etwa *A. C. Carpenter, Inc. v. Boyer Potato Chips*, U. S. Dept. Agric., 2.12.1969, 7 UCC Rep. Serv. 493.

[74] Vgl. OGH, 14.1.2002, CISG-online 643; AG Kehl, 6.10.1995, CISG-online 162 = NJW-RR 1996, 565; *P. Huber/Mullis/Mullis*, S. 154.

[75] Vgl. AG Kehl, 6.10.1995, CISG-online 162 = NJW-RR 1996, 565; OGH, 14.1.2002, CISG-online 643; OLG Köln, 21.8.1997, CISG-online 290, m. Anm. *C. Witz*, D. 1998, Somm. 311 f.; *P. Huber/Mullis/Mullis*, S. 154 f.; *Piltz*, Internationales Kaufrecht, Rn. 5–77.

[76] Missverständlich Hof van Beroep Antwerpen, 22.1.2007, CISG-online 1586: für Strassenreinigungsfahrzeuge, die „*ex usine Saumur*" zu liefern waren, nahm das Gericht an, die Untersuchung habe zu dem Zeitpunkt zu erfolgen, in dem der Verkäufer die Fahrzeuge am Fabrik dem Käufer zu dessen Verfügung stellt.

[77] Vgl. nur OLG Düsseldorf, 14.12.1988, IPRax 1990, 178, mit kritischer Anm. *Lüderitz*, IPRax 1990, 162 (Untersuchungsfrist für Lautsprecherboxen: drei bis vier Tage inkl. Wochenende: zu lang); OLG Köln, 24.10.1984, RIW 1985, 404 (Untersuchungsfrist für Schmutzmatten: elf Tage inkl. zwei Wochenenden und Weihnachten: zu lang); LG Siegen, 29.1.1986, in: *Schlechtriem/Magnus*, Art. 39 EKG, Nr. 50 (Untersuchungs- und Rügefrist für Pfähle: sieben bis acht Tage); OLG Koblenz, 3.3.1989, RIW 1989, 310 (Untersuchung und Rüge von Marmorplatten: fünf Tage inkl. Wochenende: zu lang).

[78] Zu eng deshalb LG Stuttgart, 31.8.1989, CISG-online 11 = IPRax 1990, 317; OLG Düsseldorf, 10.2.1994, CISG-online 116 = RIW 1995, 53 (Textilien: wenige Tage); wie hier *Staudinger/Magnus*, Art. 38, Rn. 50: mindestens eine Woche oder fünf Arbeitstage; LG Lübeck, 30.12.2010, CISG-online 2292 (ein bis zwei Wochen); a. A. *Herber/Czerwenka*, Art. 38, Rn. 7, die von einer regelmässigen Untersuchungsfrist von nicht länger als einer Woche ausgehen und für eine Fortgeltung der Auffassungen zum EKG eintreten. Die Fortgeltung der Rechtsprechung zum EKG wird weiterhin bejaht von *Witz/Salger/Lorenz/Salger*, Art. 38, Rn. 3; *Tannò*, S. 270 ff.; *Recknagel*, S. 106 f.; *Asam*, RIW 1989, 944; *Piltz*, Internationales Kaufrecht, Rn. 5–77 (drei bis vier Werktage). Wie hier jedoch LG Frankfurt a. M., 11.4.2005, CISG-online 1014 = IHR 2005, 161, 162; *MünchKomm/Gruber*, Art. 38, Rn. 58.

[79] Vgl. *O. R.*, S. 311, Nr. 84.

[80] Vgl. zum niederländischen Recht *Janssen*, S. 134 f., unter Bezugnahme auf Art. 7:23 BW; grosszügiger sind auch internationale Handelsbräuche, vgl. ICC, 5713/1989, CISG-online 3 = YB Comm. Arb. 1990, 70, 73.

[81] Vgl. die Nachweise bei *Ghestin/Desché*, Traité des contrats, Anm. 737.; bei Anm. 740. Nachweise zu weiteren Rechtsordnungen des französischen Rechtskreises.

[82] Vgl. die Nachweise bei *White/Summers*, § 11-10, S. 417 ff.

[83] Vgl. LG Landshut, 5.4.1995, CISG-online 193; vgl. auch *Ferrari u. a./Ferrari*, Internationales Vertragsrecht, Art. 38, Rn. 17.

[84] Vgl. OLG Koblenz, 18.11.1999, CISG-online 570: eine Woche für Fehler, die durch blosses Aufrollen der Ware erkennbar; LG Darmstadt, 29.5.2001, CISG-online 686: zehn Tage bei Möbeln; LG München I, 16.11.2000, CISG-online 667: zehn Tage bei Gaststätten-Einrichtung; OLG Schleswig, 22.8.2002, CISG-online 710 = IHR 2003, 20, 22: drei bis vier Tage bei lebendem Vieh; KG St. Gallen, 11.2.2003, CISG-online 900, E. II. 2. b): wenige Arbeitstage bei Musik-CDs; ähnlich *P. Huber/Mullis/Mullis*, S. 155.

Art. 38 18–20 Teil III. Kapitel II. Pflichten des Verkäufers. Abschnitt II

suchungen insbesondere im Hinblick auf Qualitätsabweichungen sind jedoch nicht zumutbar, wenn andere Geschäfte den Käufer in Anspruch nehmen.[85] Dies gilt auch dann, wenn Fehler erst bei einer Weiterverarbeitung der Ware festgestellt werden können.[86] Bei **komplizierten technischen Anlagen** und Maschinen, mit denen der Käufer nicht vertraut ist und deren Mängel erst nach Probeläufen festgestellt werden können, wird man die Frist so grosszügig bemessen müssen, dass es dem Käufer möglich ist, sich darüber schlüssig zu werden, inwieweit Funktionsstörungen auf Mängel der Anlage oder auf Bedienungsfehler zurückzuführen sind.[87] Dies mögen u. U. Wochen oder im Einzelfall selbst Monate sein.[88] Dasselbe gilt bei **Zulieferteilen** oder **Grundstoffen,** die der Käufer weiterverarbeitet.

18   Bei der Bestimmung der Untersuchungsfrist sind schliesslich auch die dem Verkäufer bekannte **Stellung des Käufers** im Wirtschaftsleben (Wiederverkäufer, Endverbraucher, Familienbetrieb),[89] seine betrieblichen und persönlichen Verhältnisse,[90] die Gesamtumstände und die Infrastruktur am Untersuchungsort (Verfügbarkeit technischer Einrichtungen[91] oder Sachverständiger[92], Generalstreik bzw. Streik im Unternehmen des Käufers)[93] sowie kulturelle Verschiedenheiten[94] zu berücksichtigen. Ausser Betracht bleiben lediglich **rein subjektive Faktoren,** mit denen der Verkäufer nicht zu rechnen braucht, wie z. B. Krankheit des Käufers.[95] Sie können aber bei Art. 44 eine Rolle spielen.[96]

2. Fristbeginn

19   **a) Im Allgemeinen.** Die Frist zur Untersuchung der Ware beginnt grundsätzlich mit der **Lieferung** zu laufen, d. h. beim Platz- und Fernkauf mit Aushändigung der Ware an den Käufer.[97] Dies gilt auch dann, wenn ein Lieferzeitraum vereinbart ist und der Verkäufer nach dem Anfangs- aber vor dem Endtermin leistet.[98] Fehlt bei technischen Geräten eine zur Inbetriebnahme erforderliche **Bedienungsanleitung** oder steht eine vom Verkäufer vertraglich übernommene **Einweisung** des Käufers noch aus, so dass eine sachgerechte Untersuchung durch den Käufer noch gar nicht vorgenommen werden kann, so kann freilich auch die Untersuchungsfrist nicht zu laufen beginnen.[99]

20   **b) Vorzeitige Lieferung; verspätete Lieferung; Teillieferungen.** Bei vorzeitiger Lieferung, d. h. vor dem vereinbarten Lieferzeitpunkt oder dem Beginn eines Lieferzeitraums, kann auch vom Käufer, der die Ware angenommen hat, nicht erwartet werden,

---

[85] Vgl. *Soergel/Lüderitz/Schüßler-Langeheine,* Art. 38, Rn. 4; *Heuzé,* Anm. 300.
[86] Vgl. Bsp. 38A bei *Honnold/Flechtner,* Art. 38, Rn. 252; *Staudinger/Magnus,* Art. 38, Rn. 43; a. A. OLG Karlsruhe, 25.6.1997, CISG-online 263 = RIW 1998, 235: drei bis vier Tage.
[87] Vgl. BGH, 3.11.1999, CISG-online 475, m. krit. Anm. *Schlechtriem,* EWiR 2000, 125, 126; *ders.,* 50 Jahre BGH, S. 407, 439 f.; abl. *Taschner,* TranspR-IHR 2000, 3, 4.
[88] Vgl. auch LG Düsseldorf, 23.6.1994, CISG-online 179: vier Monate bei Einbau von Motoren in Pressen allerdings zu lang; *Heilmann,* S. 296; a. A. *Tannò,* S. 271.
[89] Vgl. Sekretariatskommentar, Art. 36, Nr. 3; *Staudinger/Magnus,* Art. 38, Rn. 11; *P. Huber/Mullis/Mullis,* S. 155.
[90] Vgl. OGH, 14.1.2002, CISG-online 643.
[91] Vgl. LG Hamburg, 6.9.2004, CISG-online 1085.
[92] *P. Huber/Mullis/Mullis,* S. 155.
[93] Vgl. *Staudinger/Magnus,* Art. 38, Rn. 44 ff.; *Herber/Czerwenka,* Art. 38, Rn. 7; *Enderlein/Maskow/Strohbach,* Art. 38, Anm. 2.3.; *Audit,* Vente internationale, Anm. 105.; *Heilmann,* S. 296.
[94] Vgl. *Soergel/Lüderitz/Schüßler-Langeheine,* Art. 38, Rn. 4; *Andersen,* 9 VJ (2005), 17, 41; a. A. MünchKommHGB/*Benicke,* Art. 38, Rn. 7.
[95] Vgl. *Staudinger/Magnus,* Art. 38, Rn. 49; *Bianca/Bonell/Bianca,* Art. 38, Anm. 2.5.; *Herber/Czerwenka,* Art. 38, Rn. 7; *Enderlein/Maskow/Strohbach,* Art. 38, Anm. 2.; *Tannò,* S. 273.
[96] Vgl. *Staudinger/Magnus,* Art. 38, Rn. 49.
[97] Im Falle verderblicher Ware kann dies zur Verpflichtung führen, die Ware bereits vor Transport zur Niederlassung des Käufers zu untersuchen, vgl. RB Breda, 16.1.2009, CISG-online 1789 (Wassermelonen).
[98] Vgl. *Staudinger/Magnus,* Art. 38, Rn. 36; *Herber/Czerwenka,* Art. 38, Rn. 8; *Karollus,* S. 125, 126; *Tannò,* S. 267; a. A. *Stumpf,* 1. Aufl., Art. 38 Rn. 5; wie hier zum EKG *Mertens/Rehbinder,* Art. 38/39 EKG, Rn. 14.
[99] Vgl. auch *Kuoppala,* Examination, 3.4.1. Zum deutschen Recht vgl. OLG Hamm, 22.10.1990, CR 1991, 335.

dass er die Ware vor dem vereinbarten Liefertermin untersucht.[100] Jedenfalls müsste der vereinbarte Lieferzeitpunkt bei der Bestimmung der Untersuchungsfrist mit einfliessen.[101] Verspätete Lieferung entbindet den Käufer zwar grundsätzlich nicht von seiner Untersuchungspflicht,[102] es muss jedoch im Einzelfall geprüft werden, ob sich der Käufer leicht auf die Verspätung einstellen konnte.[103] Bei Teillieferungen kommt es auf den Zeitpunkt der jeweiligen Teillieferung an, es sei denn, es handelt sich um eine Einheit, deren Vertragsmässigkeit erst nach Eintreffen der letzten Teillieferung festgestellt werden kann.[104]

c) Versendungskauf – Abs. 2. Ist nach dem Vertrag eine Beförderung der Ware vorgesehen, so beginnt nach Abs. 2 die Frist für die Untersuchung der Ware erst mit deren Eintreffen am Bestimmungsort zu laufen. Hierunter fällt vor allem der Regelfall im internationalen Handel, nämlich der **Versendungskauf,** aber auch beim Verkauf **reisender Ware** erlangt diese Bestimmung Bedeutung.[105] Eine Beförderung ist insbesondere erforderlich, wenn etwa **Incoterms®-Klauseln** der Gruppe F (z. B. FOB), C (z. B. CIF) und D (z. B. DAT) verwendet werden.[106] Art. 38 II trägt der Tatsache Rechnung, dass beim Versendungskauf eine Untersuchung im Zeitpunkt der Lieferung, d. h. mit Übergabe der Ware an den ersten Beförderer, meist nicht möglich, dem Käufer aber jedenfalls nicht zumutbar ist. Die Vorschrift gilt unabhängig davon, welche der Parteien den **Beförderungsvertrag** abgeschlossen hat.[107] Ist der Beförderer – wie regelmässig – nach dem Transportvertrag verpflichtet, die übernommenen Waren im Hinblick auf ihre äussere Beschaffenheit hin zu überprüfen,[108] so handelt er insoweit nicht als Vertreter des Käufers. Ergibt sich aus den Transportpapieren, dass die Ware bei Übergabe an die Transportperson nicht in äusserlich gutem Zustand war, so hat der Käufer mit Erhalt der Transportpapiere hiervon Kenntnis, so dass damit die Rügefrist – hinsichtlich dieser Mängel – nach Art. 39 zu laufen beginnt.[109] Auf den Beginn der Frist zur Untersuchung durch den Käufer hat dies im Übrigen jedoch keinen Einfluss. 21

Bestimmungsort ist der Ort, an den die Ware nach dem Vertrag versandt werden soll. Beim Vertrag „CIF" oder „FOB" z. B. ist dies der Bestimmungshafen; bei sonstigen Kaufverträgen ist Bestimmungsort regelmässig die Niederlassung des Käufers, bei Direktversand an einen Abnehmer des Käufers dessen Niederlassung.[110] 22

d) Umleitung oder Weiterversendung – Abs. 3. Bei Umleitung oder Weiterversendung der Ware beginnt die Frist zur Untersuchung u. U. erst mit Eintreffen der Ware am neuen Bestimmungsort zu laufen. Eine **Umleitung** liegt vor, wenn die Ware auf dem Transport vor dem Erreichen des ursprünglich in Aussicht genommenen Bestimmungsortes an einen anderen Bestimmungsort umdirigiert wird. Unerheblich ist, wer die Umleitung 23

---

[100] Vgl. *Staudinger/Magnus*, Art. 38, Rn. 37; *Herber/Czerwenka*, Art. 38, Rn. 8; *Neumayer/Ming*, Art. 38, Anm. 5.; *Heilmann*, S. 294; *Kuoppala*, Examination, 3.4.1.; *Enderlein/Maskow/Strohbach*, Art. 38, Anm. 2., die allerdings eine Einschränkung machen für den Fall, dass der Käufer der vorzeitigen Lieferung zugestimmt hat; a. A. *Resch*, ÖJZ 1992, 470, 477; *Ferrari u. a./Ferrari*, Internationales Vertragsrecht, Art. 38, Rn. 4, 19; MünchKommHGB/*Benicke*, Art. 38, Rn. 8.
[101] Vgl. *Schlechtriem*, Einheitliches UN-Kaufrecht, S. 59 Fn. 263; ähnlich *Achilles*, Art. 38, Rn. 8; *Ferrari u. a./Ferrari*, Internationales Vertragsrecht, Art. 38, Rn. 4.
[102] Vgl. *Staudinger/Magnus*, Art. 38, Rn. 21.
[103] Vgl. OGH, 14.1.2002, CISG-online 643 = IHR 2002, 76, 79; so auch *Staudinger/Magnus*, Art. 38, Rn. 37.
[104] Vgl. MünchKomm/*Gruber*, Art. 38, Rn. 39; *Vogel*, S. 54.
[105] Vgl. *Karollus*, S. 125.
[106] Vgl. *Staudinger/Magnus*, Art. 38, Rn. 52.
[107] Vgl. *Staudinger/Magnus*, Art. 38, Rn. 52; *Herber/Czerwenka*, Art. 38, Rn. 9; *Bianca/Bonell/Bianca*, Art. 38, Anm. 2.6.; *Kuoppala*, Examination, 3.4.2.
[108] Vgl. dazu *Herber/Czerwenka*, Art. 38, Rn. 9.
[109] A. A. *Staudinger/Magnus*, Art. 38, Rn. 54; *Ferrari u. a./Ferrari*, Internationales Vertragsrecht, Art. 38, Rn. 21.
[110] Vgl. etwa Gerechtshof 's-Hertogenbosch, 9.3.2010, CISG-online 2341 zur Klausel „Good quality accepted in Holland and Germany".

anordnet, sei es der Käufer oder etwa bei einem Direktversand ein Abnehmer des Käufers.[111] Eine **Weiterversendung** liegt vor, wenn der Käufer oder beim Direktversand ein Abnehmer des Käufers die Ware nach Empfangnahme am Bestimmungsort weiterversendet. Ob dabei eine **Umladung** erfolgt oder nicht, ist im Gegensatz zu Art. 38 III EKG ohne Belang. Weiterversendung wird vor allem beim Erwerb von Ware durch einen Zwischenhändler erfolgen; denkbar ist jedoch auch, dass der Käufer selbst die Ware an einem anderen Ort als dem ursprünglichen Bestimmungsort benötigt.[112] Unerheblich ist auch hier, wer die Weiterversendung veranlasst. Der **blosse Weiterverkauf** ohne zusätzlichen Transport – wie er gerade im Einzelhandel anzutreffen ist, wo der Käufer die Ware zunächst auf das eigene Lager nimmt – fällt nicht unter Abs. 3.[113] Die Tatsache des Weiterverkaufs, ohne dass der Käufer ausreichend Gelegenheit zur Untersuchung der Ware hatte, ist jedoch im Rahmen des Abs. 1 sowohl im Hinblick auf die Form der Untersuchung als auch vor allem im Hinblick auf die Dauer der Frist zu berücksichtigen.

24 Voraussetzung für einen Aufschub des Beginns der Untersuchungsfrist ist, dass der **Verkäufer** die Möglichkeit der Umleitung oder der Weiterversendung bei Vertragsschluss **kannte oder kennen musste.** Hiervon wird regelmässig auszugehen sein, wenn der Käufer **Zwischenhändler** ist.[114] In anderen Fällen ist es ratsam, dass der Käufer den Verkäufer bei Vertragsschluss ausdrücklich auf die Möglichkeit der Umleitung oder Weiterversendung aufmerksam macht, wenngleich sich die Weiterversendungsabsicht des Käufers im Einzelfall auch aus den Umständen ergeben mag.[115] Einer Zustimmung des Verkäufers zur Umleitung oder Weiterversendung bedarf es nicht.[116]

25 Umleitung und Weiterversendung führen jedoch nur dann zu einem Aufschub des Beginns der Untersuchungsfrist, wenn der Käufer vorher **keine ausreichende Gelegenheit** hatte, die Ware **zu untersuchen.** Ob dies der Fall ist, hängt einmal davon ab, wie lange sich die Ware vor der Weiterversendung beim Käufer befindet.[117] Von besonderer Bedeutung ist aber vor allem die **Art und Weise der Verpackung.** Soweit für eine Untersuchung der Ware Behältnisse oder Verpackungen geöffnet werden müssten, die für den Schutz der Ware auf dem Weitertransport erforderlich sind, oder Container zeit- und kostenaufwändig umgepackt werden müssten, ist die Untersuchung vor Weiterversendung nicht zumutbar.[118] Gleiches gilt, wenn zur Untersuchung eine **Marke** entfernt werden müsste, die die Echtheit der Ware bestätigt.[119] In diesen Fällen

---

[111] Umleitung auf Grund gerichtlicher Beschlagnahme fällt mangels Voraussehbarkeit bei Vertragsschluss nicht unter Abs. 3, sondern mag zu einer Verlängerung der Frist nach Abs. 1 führen, vgl. *Bianca/Bonell/Bianca*, Art. 38, Anm. 3.2.; a. A. *Herber/Czerwenka*, Art. 38, Rn. 12; *Staudinger/Magnus*, Art. 38, Rn. 57.

[112] Vgl. Sekretariatskommentar, Art. 36, Nr. 6.

[113] Vgl. auch MünchKomm/*Gruber*, Art. 38, Rn. 46; *P. Huber*, IPRax 2004, 358, 360; *Bianca/Bonell/Bianca*, Art. 38, Anm. 3.1.; *Enderlein/Maskow/Strohbach*, Art. 38, Anm. 7.; *Heilmann*, S. 301; für eine Analogie jedoch *Staudinger/Magnus*, Art. 38, Rn. 59; *Herber/Czerwenka*, Art. 38, Rn. 12; OLG Saarbrücken, 13.1.1993, CISG-online 83.

[114] Vgl. *Staudinger/Magnus*, Art. 38, Rn. 62; *Bianca/Bonell/Bianca*, Art. 38, Anm. 2.9.2.; *P. Huber/Mullis/Mullis*, S. 154; *Enderlein/Maskow/Strohbach*, Art. 38, Anm. 8.; *Herber/Czerwenka*, Art. 38, Rn. 14; *Reinhart*, Art. 38, Rn. 3; *Audit*, Vente internationale, Anm. 106.

[115] *Herber/Czerwenka*, Art. 38, Rn. 14 nennen als Bsp. das Verlangen des Käufers, die auf dem Landweg zu ihm zu befördernde Ware seefest zu verpacken. Dies sollte auch bei Auseinanderfallen von Zwischenhafen und Käufersitz grundsätzlich angenommen werden, vgl. *Kuoppala*, Examination, 3.4.3.; a. A. LG Frankfurt a. M., 11.4.2005, CISG-online 1014 = IHR 2005, 163, m. krit. Anm. *Flechtner*, 26 B. U. Int'l L. J., 19 ff. und *Honnold/Flechtner*, Art. 38, Rn. 252.

[116] Vgl. *Staudinger/Magnus*, Art. 38, Rn. 63.

[117] Bei einfacher Montage und Belastungstests wurden zehn Wochen als genügend Zeit für die Untersuchung erachtet, sodass sich der Käufer nicht auf Art. 38 III stützen konnte, OLG Dresden, 8.11.2007, CISG-online 1624. Vgl. auch LG Lübeck, 30.12.2010, CISG-online 2292: ausreichend Gelegenheit bei Lagerung und allmählicher Weiterversendung.

[118] Vgl. *Staudinger/Magnus*, Art. 38, Rn. 60; *Bianca/Bonell/Bianca*, Art. 38, Anm. 2.8.; *Achilles*, Art. 38, Rn. 14; *Enderlein/Maskow/Strohbach*, Art. 38, Anm. 9.; *Schlechtriem*, Einheitliches UN-Kaufrecht, S. 59; *Heuzé*, Anm. 300.; *Heilmann*, S. 300; enger wohl *Herber/Czerwenka*, Art. 38, Rn. 13; OLG Saarbrücken, 13.1.1993, CISG-online 83.

[119] Vgl. *Bianca/Bonell/Bianca*, Art. 38, Anm. 2.8.

ist eine Untersuchung dem Käufer unzumutbar, selbst wenn sie zeitlich möglich wäre.[120]

Liegen die Voraussetzungen des Abs. 3 vor, so beginnt die Untersuchungsfrist mit **Eintreffen der Ware am neuen Bestimmungsort** zu laufen. Untersuchungs- und rügepflichtig bleibt freilich insoweit der Käufer selbst. Überlässt er die Untersuchung seinem Abnehmer, so muss er sich dessen Handeln und Unterlassen zurechnen lassen.[121] 26

V. Kosten der Untersuchung

Die Kosten der Untersuchung hat mangels anderweitiger Parteivereinbarung oder Gebräuche grundsätzlich der **Käufer** zu tragen.[122] Wird der Vertrag aufgehoben oder fallen Untersuchungskosten ein zweites Mal z. B. in Folge Ersatzlieferung an, so kann der Käufer die (ersten) Untersuchungskosten im Wege des Schadenersatzes ersetzt verlangen.[123] 27

VI. Abdingbarkeit

Art. 38 kann von den Parteien **abbedungen** werden; Untersuchung und Frist können jedoch auch **näher konkretisiert** werden – Art. 6.[124] 28

Vor allem bei **just-in-time-Geschäften** ist es üblich, dass der Käufer sich praktisch von jeder Untersuchungs- und Rügeobliegenheit freizeichnet und die Verantwortung durch sog. Qualitätssicherungsvereinbarungen auf den Verkäufer überträgt.[125] Die Wirksamkeit solcher Vereinbarungen richtet sich nach nationalem Recht (Art. 4 a)). Ist auf den Vertrag subsidiär deutsches Recht anwendbar, so ist im Rahmen des § 307 BGB zu prüfen, ob durch eine solche Regelung von wesentlichen Grundgedanken des CISG abgewichen wird. Für rein inländische Sachverhalte, wo Prüfungsmassstab § 377 HGB ist, sollen unangemessen lange Rügefristen – und dementsprechend erst recht ein gänzlicher Ausschluss der Untersuchungs- und Rügepflicht – an § 307 II Nr. 1 BGB scheitern.[126] Für das EKG wurde sogar eine noch restriktivere Beurteilung der Verlängerung von Untersuchungs- und Rügefrist vertreten.[127] Diese Sichtweise kann in Fällen, in denen das CISG Prüfungsmassstab ist, nicht aufrecht erhalten werden.[128] Denn im Gegensatz zu den Rechtsordnungen des deutschen Rechtskreises wird die Untersuchungs- und Rügepflicht des Käufers im CISG nicht strikt geregelt, wie sich aus einer Gesamtschau der Artt. 38, 39 und 44 ergibt. Sowohl eine 29

---

[120] Vgl. auch *Bamberger/Roth/Saenger*, Art. 38, Rn. 25; *Kruisinga*, Non-conformity, S. 75; a. A. *Stumpf*, 1. Aufl., Art. 38 Rn. 9; *Herber/Czerwenka*, Art. 38, Rn. 13: in diesen Fällen soll der Käufer mindestens oberflächlich und stichprobenweise untersuchen müssen; LG Frankfurt a. M., 11.4.2005, CISG-online 1014 = IHR 2005, 163: Aufbrechen von Zollsiegel unter Anfall von Zollgebühren im Zwischenhafen zumutbar.
[121] Vgl. *Enderlein/Maskow/Strohbach*, Art. 38, Anm. 3.; *Neumayer/Ming*, Art. 38, Anm. 8.
[122] Vgl. *Staudinger/Magnus*, Art. 38, Rn. 27; *Bamberger/Roth/Saenger*, Art. 38, Rn. 12; *Hutter*, S. 78; *Heilmann*, S. 302.
[123] Vgl. unten Art. 74 Rn. 27; *Müller-Chen*, Art. 48 Rn. 21. Weitergehend noch *Stoll/Gruber*, 4. Aufl., Art. 74 Rn. 19; *Staudinger/Magnus*, Art. 38, Rn. 27.
[124] Praxishinweise bei Rudolph, Art. 38, Rn. 9; zu streng hingegen *DiMatteo/Dhooge/Greene/Maurer/Pagnattaro*, 34 Nw. J. Int'l L. & Bus. (2004), 299, 362 ff. (der U. S.-amerikanischen Ansicht folgend, Abbedingung sei nur ausdrücklich möglich).
[125] Vgl. *Staudinger/Magnus*, Art. 38, Rn. 16; *Kröll u. a./Kröll*, Art. 38, Rn. 20; *Martinek*, FS Jahr, S. 305 ff.; umfassend *Steinmann*, passim; *Ensthaler*, NJW 1994, 817 ff. Vertragsmuster bei *von Westphalen*, in: Münchener Vertragshandbuch III/2, S. 578 ff.
[126] Vgl. BGH, 22.5.1985, ZIP 1985, 1204, 1206 f.; BGH, 10.10.1991, BGHZ 115, 324, 326 f.; *von Westphalen*, ZIP 1984, 529, 531; *Steinmann*, S. 47 ff., differenzierend allerdings bei der Verlängerung der Frist: S. 121 ff.; *Schmidt*, NJW 1991, 144, 150 – ebenfalls differenzierend bei der bloss zeitlichen Erstreckung; a. A. *Martinek*, FS Jahr, S. 337; *Ulmer/Brandner/Hensen*, Anh. zu §§ 9–11, Rn. 299, 300.
[127] Vgl. *von Westphalen*, AGB und einheitliches Kaufgesetz, S. 71 f.
[128] A. A. *Piltz*, Internationales Kaufrecht, Rn. 5–76.

Verlängerung der Fristen als auch ein **gänzlicher Ausschluss** der Untersuchungs- und Rügepflicht sind deshalb möglich.[129]

30 Auch im Interesse des Verkäufers können bestimmte **Untersuchungs- und Rügefristen festgelegt** werden.[130] Hier stellt sich ebenfalls bei subsidiärer Geltung deutschen Rechts im Rahmen des § 307 II Nr. 1 BGB die Frage der Vereinbarkeit mit grundlegenden Wertungen des CISG.[131] Soweit dem Käufer im Rahmen der vertraglichen Frist faktisch Gelegenheit bleibt, die Ware zu untersuchen, bestehen an der Wirksamkeit einer solchen Vereinbarung keine Zweifel. Anders müsste etwa der Fall beurteilt werden, wenn entgegen der Wertung von Abs. 2, 3 dem Käufer eine Untersuchung innerhalb einer Frist aufgebürdet wird, in der er mangels Zugriff auf die Ware zu einer Untersuchung noch gar nicht in der Lage ist.

31 Schliesslich sind vertragliche Vereinbarungen vor allem möglich im Hinblick auf die **Untersuchungsmodalitäten**.[132] Auch eine vertragliche Festlegung des **Untersuchungsorts** in Abweichung von Abs. 2, 3 ist zulässig,[133] jedoch sollte eine solche wegen der einschneidenden Konsequenzen für den Käufer nur angenommen werden, wenn die Einigkeit der Parteien über die Abänderung hinreichend deutlich manifestiert ist.[134]

---

[129] Vgl. aus französischer Sicht *Ben Abderrahmane*, Dr. prat. com. int. 1989, 551, 555. Zustimmend für das unvereinheitlichte deutsche Recht wohl *Martinek*, FS Jahr, S. 337 f.
[130] Vgl. dazu *Herber*, Möglichkeiten der Vertragsgestaltung, S. 229 f.
[131] Zur Beurteilung anhand des internen deutschen Rechts vgl. MünchKomm/*Wurmnest*, § 307, Rn. 89.
[132] Vgl. dazu näher oben Rn. 11.
[133] Vgl. OLG Düsseldorf, 8.1.1993, CISG-online 76 = RIW 1993, 325, m. Anm. *Magnus*, IPRax 1993, 390–392; *Staudinger/Magnus*, Art. 38, Rn. 17, 34, 53.
[134] Vgl. *Magnus*, IPRax 1993, 390, 392; zu streng hingegen *DiMatteo/Dhooge/Greene/Maurer/Pagnattaro*, 34 Nw. J. Int'l L. & Bus. (2004), 299, 362 f.

Art. 39 [Mängelrüge]

(1) Der Käufer verliert das Recht, sich auf eine Vertragswidrigkeit der Ware zu berufen, wenn er sie dem Verkäufer nicht innerhalb einer angemessenen Frist nach dem Zeitpunkt, in dem er sie festgestellt hat oder hätte feststellen müssen, anzeigt und dabei die Art der Vertragswidrigkeit genau bezeichnet.

(2) Der Käufer verliert in jedem Fall das Recht, sich auf die Vertragswidrigkeit der Ware zu berufen, wenn er sie nicht spätestens innerhalb von zwei Jahren, nachdem ihm die Ware tatsächlich übergeben worden ist, dem Verkäufer anzeigt, es sei denn, daß diese Frist mit einer vertraglichen Garantiefrist unvereinbar ist.

Art. 39

(1) The buyer loses the right to rely on a lack of conformity of the goods if he does not give notice to the seller specifying the nature of the lack of conformity within a reasonable time after he has discovered it or ought to have discovered it.

(2) In any event, the buyer loses the right to rely on a lack of conformity of the goods if he does not give the seller notice thereof at the latest within a period of two years from the date on which the goods were actually handed over to the buyer, unless this time-limit is inconsistent with a contractual period of guarantee.

Art. 39

1) L'acheteur est déchu du droit de se prévaloir d'un défaut de conformité s'il ne le dénonce pas au vendeur, en précisant la nature de ce défaut, dans un délai raisonnable à partir du moment où il l'a constaté ou aurait dû le constater.

2) Dans tous les cas, l'acheteur est déchu du droit de se prévaloir d'un défaut de conformité, s'il ne le dénonce pas au plus tard dans un délai de deux ans à compter de la date à laquelle les marchandises lui ont été effectivement remises, à moins que ce délai ne soit incompatible avec la durée d'une garantie contractuelle.

Übersicht

	Rn.
I. Vorgeschichte	1
II. Allgemeines	3
1. Zweck und Rechtsnatur	3
2. Rechtsvergleichung	4
3. Anwendungsbereich	5
III. Anzeige	6
1. Inhaltliche Anforderungen	6
2. Form und Übermittlungsrisiko	11
3. Adressat	14
IV. Rügefrist – Abs. 1	15
1. Angemessene Frist	15
2. Fristbeginn	19
V. Ausschlussfrist – Abs. 2	22
1. Zweijahresfrist	22
2. Garantiefrist	26
3. Verjährung	28
VI. Rechtsfolgen unterlassener oder nicht gehöriger Anzeige	30
1. Ausschluss der Rechtsbehelfe	30
2. Ausnahmen	31
a) Art. 40	31
b) Art. 44	32
c) Verzicht des Verkäufers	33
d) Verwirkung	33a
e) Anderweitige Kenntniserlangung	33c
f) Keine Nachteile für Verkäufer	33d
VII. Abdingbarkeit	34
1. Im Allgemeinen	34
2. Garantieerklärungen	36
VIII. Beweislast	37

Art. 39 1–4   Teil III. Kapitel II. Pflichten des Verkäufers. Abschnitt II

Vorläufer und **Entwürfe:** Art. 39 EKG, Genfer E 1976 Art. 23, Wiener E 1977 Art. 23, New Yorker E 1978 Art. 37.

I. Vorgeschichte

1   Art. 39 hat seinen Vorläufer in Art. 39 EKG. Der Grundgedanke der Rügepflicht des Käufers wurde im CISG aufrechterhalten, in Einzelheiten ergeben sich allerdings wichtige Unterschiede zum EKG. Schon im Rahmen der Beratungen von UNCITRAL wurde die „kurze Frist" des EKG, innerhalb derer der Käufer die Vertragswidrigkeit der Ware zu rügen hatte, ersetzt durch eine **„angemessene Frist".**[1] Dies ist bedeutend käuferfreundlicher[2] und muss sich in der Praxis niederschlagen. Die Regelung des Art. 39 I 2 EKG ist entfallen, da sie als überflüssig erachtet wurde.[3] Verzichtet wurde auch auf die in Art. 39 II EKG enthaltene Bestimmung, wonach der Käufer mit der Anzeige der Vertragswidrigkeit den Verkäufer **aufzufordern** hatte, die Ware zu untersuchen oder untersuchen zu lassen, da dies den Gepflogenheiten im internationalen Handel nicht entspreche.[4] Änderungen ergeben sich schliesslich daraus, dass die in Art. 39 III EKG enthaltene Bestimmung nunmehr von der allgemeinen Regel des Art. 27 erfasst wird.

2   Die **Folgen der Rügepflichtverletzung** des Käufers sowie die in Abs. 2 enthaltene **zweijährige Ausschlussfrist** waren auf der Diplomatischen Konferenz einer der Hauptstreitpunkte des gesamten Abkommens.[5] Ein Antrag Ghanas, Art. 39 I ganz zu streichen, bzw. jedenfalls auf die Folgen des Rechtsverlustes bei unterlassener Rüge zu verzichten, konnte sich zwar nicht durchsetzen; als Kompromiss verständigte man sich jedoch auf Art. 44, der im Falle entschuldigter Rügeversäumnis dem Käufer das Recht auf Minderung und Schadenersatz – ausser für entgangenen Gewinn – belässt.

II. Allgemeines

1. Zweck und Rechtsnatur

3   Vgl. hierzu oben Art. 38 Rn. 3 ff.

2. Rechtsvergleichung[6]

4   Eine **ausdrückliche Rügepflicht** des Käufers kennen traditionell das deutsche,[7] österreichische[8] und schweizerische Recht,[9] wobei diese im deutschen und österreichischen Recht auf den Handelskauf beschränkt ist, bei dem in letzterem beide Parteien Unternehmer sein müssen.[10] Eine Rügepflicht kennen viele ibero-amerikanische,[11] arabische, sowie auf dem CISG aufbauende Rechtsordnungen.[12] Auch der US-amerikanische UCC sieht eine Rü-

---

[1] Vgl. dazu YB III (1972), S. 87, Nr. 74 ff.; YB IV (1973), S. 48, Nr. 85.
[2] Vgl. *Staudinger/Magnus*, Art. 39, Rn. 5; *Schlechtriem*, Einheitliches UN-Kaufrecht, S. 60 f.; *Welser*, S. 111; *Resch*, ÖJZ 1992, 476; Einzelheiten bei Rn. 15 ff.
[3] Vgl. YB VII (1976), S. 110 f.
[4] Vgl. YB III (1972), S. 87, Nr. 79; die Auslegung dieser Bestimmung war zudem im EKG höchst umstritten, vgl. die Nachw. bei BGH, 25.9.1991, IPRax 1993, 242.
[5] Vgl. O. R., S. 320 ff., Nr. 32 ff., S. 345 ff., Nr. 1 ff.
[6] Vgl. hierzu auch *Schwenzer*, (2007) 19 Pace Int'l L. Rev. 103,104 f.; dies., (2005) 7 EJLR 353, 354, 355; *Schwenzer/Hachem/Kee*, Rn. 34.03, 34.61 ff.
[7] Vgl. § 377 HGB.
[8] Vgl. §§ 377, 378 UGB.
[9] Vgl. Art. 201 OR.
[10] Seit 2007 das neue österreichische UGB in Kraft getreten ist, ist die Anwendung der §§ 377, 378 UGB nicht mehr auf Geschäftsleute beschränkt; sie finden vielmehr Anwendung auf alle Arten von unternehmensbezogenen Warenkaufverträgen, Werkverträgen über herzustellende bewegliche Sachen und Tauschverträgen über bewegliche Sachen, vgl. *Krejci/Schauer*, § 377 UGB, Rn. 3.
[11] Vgl. *E. Muñoz*, S. 323 ff.
[12] Vgl. *Schwenzer/Hachem/Kee*, Rn. 34.3.

gepflicht vor;[13] im englischen Recht hingegen braucht der Käufer nur zu rügen, wenn er Vertragsaufhebung geltend machen will.[14] Im französischen Recht und vielen dem französischen Recht nahe stehenden Rechtsordnungen fehlt eine Rügepflicht; einzige Voraussetzung ist, dass der Käufer Sachmängel rechtzeitig – in Frankreich nach zwei Jahren, in den dem französischen Recht nahestehenden Rechtsordnungen innerhalb eines „bref délai" – gerichtlich geltend macht.[15] Die **Frist,** innerhalb derer gerügt werden muss, wird recht unterschiedlich bemessen. Während die meisten Rechtsordnungen des deutschen Rechtskreises unverzügliche,[16] bzw. sofortige[17] Anzeige verlangen, genügt im angloamerikanischen[18] und niederländischen Recht[19] die Einhaltung einer „reasonable time", bzw. einer gebührenden Frist ab Entdeckung bzw. ab Entdeckbarkeit des Mangels.[20] Dasselbe gilt jetzt auch für das österreichische Recht.[21] Einige Rechtsordnungen kennen jedoch auch eine zeitlich genau bestimmte Rügefrist, die in der Regel zwischen 7 und 15 Tagen liegt.[22]

3. Anwendungsbereich

Nach Art. 39 I muss **jede Vertragswidrigkeit,**[23] die der Käufer bei ordnungsgemässer 5 Untersuchung festgestellt hat oder hätte feststellen können, sowie jede später erkannte Vertragswidrigkeit gerügt werden. Unerheblich ist der Entstehungsgrund der Vertragswidrigkeit.[24] Vgl. im Übrigen zum Anwendungsbereich oben Art. 38 Rn. 7 ff.

III. Anzeige

1. Inhaltliche Anforderungen

Die Rüge muss den Beanstandungswillen erkennen lassen[25] sowie die Art der Vertrags- 6 widrigkeit **genau bezeichnen.** Mit diesem Erfordernis soll der Verkäufer in die Lage

---

[13] Vgl. § 2–607 (3) (a) UCC.
[14] Vgl. sec. 35 (1) SGA.
[15] Vgl. Frankreich: Art. 1648 Cc; Belgien: Art. 1648 Cc; aus dem französischen Rechtskreis kennen eine Rügepflicht: Italien: Art. 1495 I Cc; Niederlande: Art. 7:23.1 BW; Portugal: Art. 471 Cc; Mexico: Art. 383 Cc; in Spanien ist die Rechtslage unsicher, vgl. *Martí*, in: *von Westphalen*, Handbuch des Kaufvertragsrechts, S. 1017 ff.
[16] Deutschland: § 377 HGB.
[17] Schweiz: Art. 201 OR. Vgl. auch Dänemark: § 52 (1) SGA; Polen: Art. 563 Kodeks cywilny.
[18] England: sec. 35 (1) SGA; USA: § 2–607 (3) (a) UCC.
[19] Art. 7:23.1 BW.
[20] Vgl. auch Art. 122 CESL-Entwurf. Zum chinesischen Recht vgl. *Su*, S. 190 ff. Vgl. auch *Kuoppala*, Examination, 5.2.3. für Finnland: 3 Jahre nach Lieferung eingegangene Rüge rechtzeitig.
[21] § 377 I UGB wurde mit dem ausdrücklichen Ziel der Angleichung an die Rügepflicht des CISG geändert und verlangt nun ebenfalls eine Rüge binnen angemessener Frist ab dem Zeitpunkt, in dem der Käufer den Mangel entdeckt hat oder hätte entdecken müssen, vgl. Erläuterungen zur Regierungsvorlage, § 377, sub c., BlgNR 22. GP, 61.
[22] Fünf Tage: Mexico: Art. 383 Código de Comercio; sieben Tage: Argentinien: Art. 472 Código de Comercio; Chile: Art. 159 Código de Comercio; Costa Rica: Art. 450 II Código de Comercio; Ecuador: Art. 192 II Código de Comercio; Spanien: Art. 336 II Código de Comercio; Libanon: Art. 446 OR; Marrokko: Art. 553 OR; Mexiko: Art. 383 Código de Comercio; El Salvador: Art. 1019 II Código de Comercio; Tunesien: Art. 652 OR; Uruguay: Art. 546 Código de Comercio; acht Tage: Italien: 1495 Cc; Portugal: Art. 471 Código de Comercio; 15 Tage: Vereinigte Arabische Emirate: Art. 111 I HGB; Bahrain: Art. 111 I HGB; Ägypten: Art. 101 II HGB; Guatemala: Art. 705 Código de Comercio; Qatar: Art. 112 HGB; vgl. aber auch Moldawien: Art. 20 Kaufgesetz (ein Tag für offenkundige, drei Tage für versteckte Mängel); OHADA: Art. 258 AUDCG (ein Monat).
[23] Für aliud vgl. OLG Celle, 10.3.2004, CISG-online 824 = IHR 2004, 106; OLG Düsseldorf, 21.4.2004, CISG-online 914. Auch offene Zuvielleferungen, bei denen die Mengenabweichung durch Dokumente, insbesondere die Rechnung offen zutage tritt, vgl. OLG Rostock, 25.9.2002, CISG-online 672 = IHR 2003, 19, 20. Zur jedenfalls analogen Anwendung im Fall einer fehlerhaften Rechnung vgl. AG Geldern, 17.8.2011, CISG-online 2302.
[24] Vgl. BGer, 13.11.2003, CISG-online 840 = BGE 130 III 258, 262; *Ramos Muñoz*, Communication of Defects, V) 2) A).
[25] Vgl. OLG Karlsruhe, 8.2.2006, CISG-online 1328, E. II) 1) d) = IHR 2006, 106, 107; vgl. auch OLG Hamburg, 25.1.2008, CISG-online 1681 = IHR 2008, 98, 100: Die Aussage, es fehle an der „vertragsgetreue

Art. 39 7   Teil III. Kapitel II. Pflichten des Verkäufers. Abschnitt II

versetzt werden, sich ein Bild über die Vertragswidrigkeit zu machen und die erforderlichen Schritte zu ergreifen,[26] wie beispielsweise einen Vertreter zur Untersuchung der Ware zum Käufer zu schicken,[27] notwendiges Beweismaterial für allfällige Auseinandersetzungen über die Vertragsmässigkeit zu sichern, Ersatz-, Nachlieferung oder Nachbesserung in die Wege zu leiten oder Rückgriff bei einem Zulieferanten zu nehmen. Die **Anforderungen an die Spezifizierung** der Vertragswidrigkeit dürfen jedoch nicht überspannt werden.[28] Schon die Originaltexte der Vorschrift (specifying, en précisant, especificando) lassen eine grosszügigere Interpretation zu, als dies nach der deutschen Übersetzung „genau bezeichnet" geboten erscheint. Vor allem aber zeigt die Rechtsvergleichung, dass das Erfordernis der Substantiierung wiederum allein den Rechtsordnungen des deutschen Rechtskreises eigen,[29] in anderen Rechtsordnungen jedoch nicht, jedenfalls nicht in so schneidiger Ausprägung bekannt ist.[30] Auch was die Genauigkeit der Anzeige betrifft, kann deshalb nicht unbesehen auf die Rechtsprechung zu § 377 HGB und die weitgehend darauf aufbauende Rechtsprechung zu Art. 39 EKG[31] zurückgegriffen werden.[32] Daher musste die ursprüngliche deutsche Rechtsprechung[33] zu dieser Frage als zu eng angesehen werden.[34] Inzwischen legt der BGH einen weniger strengen Massstab an.[35]

7   Bei der Frage, welche Anforderungen an die Substantiierungspflicht des Käufers zu stellen sind, ist von einem **gemischt objektiv-subjektiven Massstab** auszugehen,[36] der die Stellung des Käufers und des Verkäufers[37] im Wirtschaftsverkehr, allfällige kulturelle Unterschiede, vor allem aber auch die Art der Ware berücksichtigt. Von einem Fachmann kann u. U. eine genauere Bezeichnung der Vertragswidrigkeit der Ware erwartet werden als von

---

[n] betriebsbereite[n] Aufstellung der Maschinen für die Eisproduktion und den Eiscafébetrieb" kann nicht als Rüge der sachlichen Beschaffenheit der Ware verstanden werden, sondern lediglich als Mahnung, die Maschinen aufzustellen.

[26] Vgl. OGH, 31.8.2010, CISG-online, 2236; OLG Hamm, 2.4.2009, CISG-online 1978; LG Stuttgart, 15.8.2009, CISG-online 2019; Appelationsgericht Szeged, 5.12.2008, CISG-online 1938.

[27] Wenn die Waren jedoch bereits von einem Vertreter des Verkäufers zusammen mit dem Käufer überprüft wurden, kann sich der Verkäufer nicht mehr auf die fehlende Bestimmtheit der Rüge berufen, siehe *Mohs*, IHR 2004, 219, m. krit. Analyse von BGer, 13.11.2003, CISG-online-840 = IHR 2004, 215 (Rüge nicht hinreichend bestimmt).

[28] Vgl. *Staudinger/Magnus*, Art. 39, Rn. 24; *P. Huber/Mullis/Mullis*, S. 158; *Resch*, ÖJZ 1992, 470, 475; *Kröll u. a./Kröll*, Art. 39, Rn. 35; *Heilmann*, S. 306; *Ferrari*, RabelsZ 68 (2004), 473, 488. Vgl. auch OGH, 14.1.2002, CISG-online 643; OGH, 31.8.2010, CISG-online 2236; BGH, 4.12.1996, CISG-online 260 = LM CISG Nr. 3a; HGer Zürich, 21.9.1998, CISG-online 416; OGer Zug, 24.3.1998, CISG-online 897. Kritisch zur europäischen Rspr. U. S. Bankr. D. Or., *In re: Siskiyou Evergreens, Inc.*, 29.3.2004, CISG-online 1174.

[29] Deutschland: vgl. *Staub/Brüggemann*, § 377 HGB, Rn. 134 ff.; Österreich: vgl. *Straube/Kramer*, §§ 377, 378 HGB, Rn. 42; Schweiz: vgl. *Tannò*, S. 82 f. Für strengere Wertung von Art. 201 OR im Vergleich zum CISG, BGer, 28.5.2002, CISG-online 676, E. 2.1.2.; zust. *Rüetschi*, recht 2003, 115, 119 ff. Rechtsvergleichend *Schwenzer/Hachem/Kee*, Rn. 34.52 ff.

[30] Vgl. nur Official Comment Nr. 4 zu § 2–607 UCC.

[31] Vgl. die Nachw. bei *Stumpf*, 1. Aufl., Art. 39 Rn. 13 Fn. 43.

[32] So auch *Staudinger/Magnus*, Art. 39, Rn. 5; *MünchKomm/Gruber*, Art. 39, Rn. 8; *MünchKommHGB/Benicke*, Art. 39, Rn. 6. Zur Gegenauffassung *Reinhart*, Art. 39, Rn. 6; *Herber/Czerwenka*, Art. 39, Rn. 7; hingegen wahrscheinlich wie hier *Staudinger/Magnus*, Art. 39, Rn. 5; *ders.*, ZEuP 1993, 79, 88.

[33] Vgl. BGH, 4.12.1996, CISG-online 260 = NJW-RR 1997, 690, 691, m. krit. Anm. *Schlechtriem/Schmidt-Kessel*, EWiR 1997, 653, 654, hingegen zustimmend *Magnus*, TranspR-IHR 2000, 29, 31; OLG Düsseldorf, 10.2.1994, CISG-online 115 = NJW-RR 1994, 506; OLG Frankfurt a. M., 13.6.1991, CISG-online 23 = RIW 1991, 592; OLG Frankfurt a. M., 18.1.1994, CISG-online 123 = NJW 1994, 1013, 1014; OLG Saarbrücken, 13.1.1993, CISG-online 83; OLG Saarbrücken, 3.6.1998, CISG-online 354 = NJW-RR 1999, 780; unhaltbar auch LG München I, 8.2.1995, CISG-online 203: Mitteilung des Problems noch keine Mängelrüge; LG Marburg, 12.12.1995, CISG-online 148 = NJW-RR 1996, 760; vgl. dagegen HR, 20.2.1998, CISG-online 313 = NJB 1998, 566.

[34] So vor allem ausländische Autoren, vgl. *Lookofsky*, Understanding the CISG, S. 88 f.; *C. Witz*, Les premières applications, S. 91; *P. Huber/Mullis/Mullis*, S. 158; vgl. auch *Su*, S. 59.

[35] BGH, 3.11.1999, CISG-online 475.

[36] Vgl. *Audit*, Vente internationale, Anm. 108.; *Kritzer*, ICM-Guide, S. 309.

[37] Vgl. OLG Schleswig, 22.8.2002, CISG-online 710 = IHR 2003, 20, 22 (Verkäufer als Viehhändler musste Anzeige als Rüge zu geringen Gewichts verstehen).

Mängelrüge   8, 9 **Art. 39**

einem Fachunkundigen.³⁸ Ganz **allgemein gehaltene Beanstandungen** („nicht in Ordnung",³⁹ „mangelhafte Beschaffenheit bzw. Falschlieferung",⁴⁰ „mindere und schlechte Qualität",⁴¹ „zweite Wahl",⁴² „schlechte Verarbeitung",⁴³ „Maschine musste repariert werden",⁴⁴ „es [gebe] eine Reklamation")⁴⁵ oder allgemeine **Äusserungen der Unzufriedenheit** („nicht unseren Vorstellungen/Vorgaben entsprechend")⁴⁶ reichen auch nach CISG grundsätzlich nicht aus.⁴⁷ Ebenso kann die blosse Bestellung neuer Ware selbst dann nicht als Rüge in Bezug auf Mängel der gelieferten Ware verstanden werden, wenn der Käufer auf entstandene Schäden hinweist.⁴⁸ Freilich darf man im Zeitalter elektronischer Kommunikation vom Verkäufer erwarten, dass er bei unsubstantiierter Rüge beim Käufer **rückfragt;**⁴⁹ dem Käufer muss also grds. eine sofortige Ergänzung seiner Anzeige gestattet werden.⁵⁰ Unterlässt der Verkäufer eine allfällige Rückfrage trotz Zumutbarkeit, kann er sich nicht auf mangelnde Substantiierung berufen.

Im Einzelnen wird man vom Käufer verlangen können, dass er zunächst angibt, ob und in   8
welchem Umfang er **Minder-**⁵¹ oder **Zuviellieferung** geltend macht, welche **Qualitätsabweichungen** er rügt und inwieweit die gelieferte Ware ein **aliud**⁵² gegenüber dem vertraglich Vereinbarten darstellt.⁵³ Soweit eine Untersuchung der Ware stattgefunden hat, hat der Käufer die wesentlichen Ergebnisse dieser Untersuchung mitzuteilen.⁵⁴ Vor allem bei Maschinen und technischen Geräten kann vom Käufer allerdings nur eine **Darlegung der Symptome,** nicht jedoch eine Angabe der diesen zugrundeliegenden Ursachen gefordert werden.⁵⁵ Hat ein Vertreter des Verkäufers der Untersuchung beigewohnt, sind die Anforderungen an die Spezifizierung herabzusetzen.⁵⁶

Fraglich ist, ob zur Substantiierung der Mängelanzeige auch gehört, dass der Käufer   9
angibt, **in welchem Umfang** die gelieferte Ware von der Vertragswidrigkeit betroffen ist.⁵⁷

---

³⁸ So auch OGer Zug, 19.12.2006, CISG-online 1427; MünchKommHGB/*Benicke*, Art. 39, Rn. 2.
³⁹ Zum EKG vgl. OLG Hamm, 17.9.1981, in: *Schlechtriem/Magnus*, Art. 39 EKG, Nr. 22.
⁴⁰ Vgl. HGer Zürich, 21.9.1998, CISG-online 416 = SZIER 1999, 198; zum EKG vgl. LG Lahn-Giessen, 16.6.1978, in: *Schlechtriem/Magnus*, Art. 39 EKG, Nr. 6.
⁴¹ Vgl. LG Hannover, 1.12.1993, CISG-online 244.
⁴² Vgl. OLG Oldenburg, 28.4.2000, CISG-online 683.
⁴³ Vgl. LG München I, 3.7.1989, CISG-online 4 = IPRax 1990, 316, vgl. dazu Anm. *Reinhart*, IPRax 1990, 289.
⁴⁴ Vgl. OLG Köln, 8.1.1997, CISG-online 217.
⁴⁵ Vgl. LG Saarbrücken, 2.7.2002, CISG-online 713 = IHR 2003, 27.
⁴⁶ Vgl. OLG München, 9.7.1997, CISG-online 282; zum EKG vgl. LG Heidelberg, 21.4.1981, in: *Schlechtriem/Magnus*, Art. 39 EKG, Nr. 21.
⁴⁷ Allgemeine Ansicht, vgl. *Staudinger/Magnus*, Art. 39, Rn. 21; *Reinhart*, Art. 39, Rn. 6; *Karollus*, S. 126; *Herber/Czerwenka*, Art. 39, Rn. 7; *Piltz*, Internationales Kaufrecht, 5–93; *Soergel/Lüderitz/Schüßler-Langeheine*, Art. 39, Rn. 8; *Hutter*, S. 80 f.; *Heilmann*, S. 308. Vgl. aber KG Wallis, 21.2.2005, CISG-online 1193: Mitteilung, dass Maschine nicht funktioniert, ausreichend.
⁴⁸ OLG Saarbrücken, 17.1.2007, CISG-online 1642, *IHR* 2008, 55, 59.
⁴⁹ Vgl. *Honnold/Flechtner*, Artt. 39, 40, 44, Rn. 256; *Brunner*, Art. 39, Rn. 5; *Lookofsky*, Understanding the CISG, S. 89; *Flechtner*, Draft Digest, S. 381; *Gerny*, S. 199, *Ramos Muñoz*, Communication of Defects, V) 2) A); MünchKomm/*Gruber*, Art. 39, Rn. 16. Problematisch insoweit BGer, 13.11.2003, CISG-online 840 = BGE 130 III 258, 262, m. krit. Anm. *Mohs, IHR* 2004, 219; OLG Düsseldorf, 23.1.2004, CISG-online 918.
⁵⁰ *Lookofsky*, Understanding the CISG, S. 89 den Schwerpunkt auf Artt. 7 II, 21 II setzend. Auch ohne Rückfrage des Verkäufers darf der Käufer seine Rüge innert angemessener Frist substantiieren, vgl. OGer Zug, 24.3.1998, CISG-online 897, E. 3. b) cc).
⁵¹ Vgl. OLG Koblenz, 31.1.1997, CISG-online 256.
⁵² Zum EKG vgl. KG Berlin, 5.7.1983, in: *Schlechtriem/Magnus*, Art. 39 EKG, Nr. 37.
⁵³ Vgl. *Piltz*, Internationales Kaufrecht, Rn. 5–93.
⁵⁴ Ebenso OGH, 31.8.2010, CISG-online 2236; *Herber/Czerwenka*, Art. 39, Rn. 6; *Enderlein/Maskow/Strohbach*, Art. 39, Anm. 5.
⁵⁵ Vgl. BGH, 3.11.1999, CISG-online 475, zust. *Schlechtriem*, 50 Jahre BGH, S. 407, 437; OLG Hamm, 2.4.2009, CISG-online 1978; ebenso CISG-AC, Op. 2 *(Bergsten)*, Comment 5.14; abl. *Taschner*, TranspR-IHR 2000, 3, 4, da in casu bereits Sachverständigengutachten vorlag.
⁵⁶ Vgl. *Mohs, IHR* 2004, 219; *Kröll u. a./Kröll*, Art. 39, Rn. 38; problematisch insoweit BGer, 13.11.2003, CISG-online 840 = BGE 130 III 258, 262.
⁵⁷ Generell bejahend: *Staudinger/Magnus*, Art. 39, Rn. 25; *Piltz*, Internationales Kaufrecht, Rn. 5–95; *Herber/Czerwenka*, Art. 39, Rn. 7; abl.: *Ramberg*, International Transactions, S. 133.

Schwenzer

Ausgehend von Sinn und Zweck der Rügepflicht kann man diese Frage für **Mengenabweichungen** ohne weiteres bejahen, da insbesondere nur eine genaue Angabe der Zuweniglieferung den Verkäufer in die Lage versetzt, eine entsprechende Nachlieferung vorzubereiten. Bei **anderen Vertragswidrigkeiten** wird viel von den Umständen des Einzelfalles abhängen, ob eine genaue Quantifizierung der von der Vertragswidrigkeit betroffenen Warenmenge verlangt werden kann. Ist für die Bezifferung ein erheblicher Arbeitsaufwand erforderlich, so überschreitet dies die Grenze des dem Käufer Zumutbaren.[58] Bei schnell **verderblicher Ware**[59] ist eher eine genaue Quantifizierung zu fordern, als bei dauerhafter Ware, wo sich der Verkäufer auf die Rüge hin ohne weiteres selbst ein Bild vom Umfang der Vertragswidrigkeit verschaffen kann. Soweit möglich und dem Käufer zumutbar, ist jedoch auch hier eine ungefähre Angabe des Ausmasses der Abweichung zu verlangen.[60]

10   Weist die Ware **verschiedene Mängel** auf (z. B. Quantitäts- und Qualitätsfehler), so müssen diese einzeln bezeichnet werden.[61] Bei mehreren vertragswidrigen **Teillieferungen** ist jede Teillieferung gesondert zu rügen.[62] Dies gilt freilich nicht, soweit ein Konstruktionsfehler geltend gemacht wird, der jeder (Teil-)Lieferung anhaftet.[63]

2. Form und Übermittlungsrisiko

11   Die Rüge ist grundsätzlich **formlos** möglich, Artt. 11, 7 II.[64] Nach Art. 27 trägt der Verkäufer das **Übermittlungsrisiko** für die Mängelanzeige,[65] d. h. die Rechte des Käufers bleiben mit Absendung, also auch dann gewahrt, wenn die Anzeige nicht,[66] verspätet[67] oder mit anderem Inhalt beim Verkäufer eintrifft. Dies setzt freilich voraus, dass die Anzeige mit den nach den Umständen geeigneten Mitteln erfolgen muss.[68] Unproblematisch ist sicher die im internationalen Handel übliche Benutzung von **Telefax**[69] oder **E-Mail**.[70] Der reguläre Postweg dürfte nur bei kurzen, postalisch gut erschlossenen Regionen angemessen sein.[71] Zu heutiger Zeit muss u. U. – soweit ohne weiteres verfügbar – auf ein schnelleres Medium zurückgegriffen werden.[72] **Mündliche** oder **telefonische Rüge** ist ausreichend,[73] wenn-

---

[58] Zum EKG vgl. OLG Celle, 2.9.1986, IPRax 1987, 313.
[59] Vgl. LG München I, 20.3.1995, CISG-online 164 = RIW 1996, 688, m. Anm. *Kindler*, IPRax 1996, 16–22.
[60] Zum EKG vgl. OLG Koblenz, 28.3.1991, RIW 1991, 592; OLG Koblenz, 3.3.1989, RIW 1989, 310; vgl. aber OLG Bamberg, 23.2.1979, RIW 1979, 566: Der Hinweis auf die Beschädigung etwa der Hälfte der Sendung reiche nicht aus.
[61] Vgl. BGer, 13.11.2003, CISG-online 840 = BGE 130 III 258, 262; OGer Zug 24.3.1998, CISG-online 897, E. 3. b) cc) (dies kann mittels separater Rügen innert angemessener Frist erfolgen); OLG Celle, 10.3.2004, 106, 107; *Staudinger/Magnus*, Art. 39, Rn. 22; *Karollus*, S. 126; *Piltz*, Internationales Kaufrecht, Rn. 5–93; *Heilmann*, S. 307 f.; MünchKommHGB/*Benicke*, Art. 39, Rn. 3; *Freiburg*, IHR 2005, 56, 62.
[62] Vgl. *Staudinger/Magnus*, Art. 39, Rn. 22; *DiMatteo/Dhooge/Greene/Maurer/Pagnattaro*, 34 Nw. J. Int'l L. & Bus. (2004), 299, 368.
[63] Vgl. LG München I, 27.2.2002, CISG-online 654 = IHR 2003, 233, 235.
[64] So auch oben *Schmidt-Kessel*, Art. 11 Rn. 10; *P. Huber/Mullis/Mullis*, S. 156, 157; OGH, 15.10.1998, CISG-online 380.
[65] Vgl. oben *Schroeter*, Art. 27 Rn. 1, 4; *Staudinger/Magnus*, Art. 39, Rn. 53; *Ramos Muñoz*, Communication of Defects, V) 2) B); OGH, 24.5.2005, CISG-online 1046 = IHR 2005, 249; OGH, 30.6.1998, CISG-online 410; OLG Koblenz, 19.10.2006, CISG-online 1407.
[66] Tribunale di Forlì, 26.9.2009, CISG-online 2336; OLG Naumburg, 27.4.1999, CISG-online 512.
[67] Unzutreffend daher LG Trier, 28.6.2001, CISG-online 673, m. abl. Anm. *P. Huber/Kröll*, IPRax 2003, 309, 313. A. A. *Kröll u. a./Kröll*, Art. 39, Rn. 53. Wie hier *Ferrari u. a./Ferrari*, Internationales Vertragsrecht, Art. 39, Rn. 18.
[68] Vgl. Audiencia Provincial de Barcelona, 24.3.2009, CISG-online 2042; Einzelheiten oben bei *Schroeter*, Art. 27 Rn. 7.
[69] Vgl. etwa LG Düsseldorf, 25.8.1994, CISG-online 451.
[70] *Ferrari u. a./Ferrari*, Internationales Vertragsrecht, Art. 39, Rn. 18; *Magnus*, TranspR-IHR 1999, 29, 31; *Janssen*, S. 159, vgl. CISG-AC, Op. 1 *(Ramberg)*, Comment 39.1. = IHR 2003, 244, 250.
[71] Vgl. *Herber/Czerwenka*, Art. 39, Rn. 12; *Henzé*, Anm. 304.
[72] Vgl. MünchKommHGB/*Benicke*, Art. 39, Rn. 11; MünchKomm/*Gruber*, Art. 39, Rn. 22.
[73] Vgl. *Staudinger/Magnus*, Art. 39, Rn. 51; MünchKomm/*Gruber*, Art. 39, Rn. 22; *Ramos Muñoz*, Communication of Defects, V) 2) B); OGH, 15.10.1998, CISG-online 380: für Empfänger vernehmbar und verständlich; OLG Karlsruhe, 6.3.2003, CISG-online 812 = IHR 2003, 226, 227.

gleich dem Käufer aus Beweisgründen anzuraten ist, eine mündlich oder telefonisch vorgebrachte Rüge schriftlich zu bestätigen.[74] Zum Sprachproblem vgl. oben Art. 27 Rn. 10.

Es steht den Parteien allerdings frei, für die Rüge eine bestimmte **Form zu vereinbaren.** Ist lediglich Schriftform vorgesehen, so ist nach Art. 13 die Übermittlung durch Telegramm oder Telex, heute vor allem durch E-Mail und Telefax, ausreichend.[75]

Mit der Rüge muss der Käufer weder – wie nach Art. 39 II EKG – die **Aufforderung** an den Verkäufer verbinden, die Ware zu untersuchen, noch ist er verpflichtet, bereits in diesem Zeitpunkt anzugeben, welche **Rechtsbehelfe** er geltend zu machen gedenkt.[76] Da jedoch sowohl der Anspruch auf Ersatzlieferung und Nachbesserung (Art. 46 II, III) als auch die Vertragsaufhebung (Art. 49 II b) i)) grundsätzlich davon abhängen, dass der Käufer innerhalb angemessener Frist nach Rüge, bzw. nach Kenntnis oder Erkennbarkeit der Vertragsverletzung ein entsprechendes Verlangen dem Verkäufer mitteilt, empfiehlt es sich, mit der Mängelrüge bereits die Ansprüche, die der Käufer geltend machen will, mitzuteilen.[77]

3. Adressat

Adressat der Anzeige ist der **Verkäufer.**[78] Welche Personen berechtigt sind, mit Wirkung für den Verkäufer Mängelrügen entgegenzunehmen, ist im CISG nicht geregelt.[79] Diese Frage bestimmt sich vielmehr nach dem jeweiligen über IPR anwendbaren nationalen Recht.[80] Überwiegend wird dabei die **Vertretungsmacht** selbstständig, d. h. nicht entsprechend dem Vertragsstatut angeknüpft. Demgemäss gilt bei der rechtsgeschäftlichen Vertretung grundsätzlich das Recht des Wirkungslandes,[81] bei Anscheinsvollmacht und Ermächtigung eines Empfangsboten für die Entgegennahme einer Erklärung das Recht des Landes, in dem der Rechtsschein entstanden ist.[82] Soweit **deutsches materielles Recht** zur Anwendung gelangt, sind zur Entgegennahme der Mängelrüge etwa der **Handelsvertreter** (§ 91 II HGB) oder der **Reisende** (§ 55 IV HGB) befugt,[83] nicht jedoch der **Fahrer** des Verkäufers, der Spediteur oder dessen Fahrer.[84] Werden diese Personen vom Käufer als **(Erklärungs-)Boten** zur Überbringung der Mängelanzeige an den Verkäufer eingesetzt, so muss nach Art. 27 geprüft werden, ob es sich insoweit noch um ein nach den Umständen geeignetes Kommunikationsmittel handelt. Im Regelfall dürfte diese Frage zu verneinen

---

[74] Vgl. Hof van Beroep Gent, 28.1.2004, CISG-online 830; MünchKomm/*Gruber,* Art. 39, Rn. 22; Honnold/Flechtner, Artt. 39, 40, 44, Rn. 257.2; *Ramos Muñoz,* Communication of Defects, V) 2) B). Zur Beweislast vgl. unten Rn. 40 f.
[75] Vgl. oben *Schmidt-Kessel,* Art. 13 Rn. 6 f.
[76] Vgl. auch *Staudinger/Magnus,* Art. 39, Rn. 26; *Brunner,* Art. 39, Rn. 10; *Ramberg,* International Transactions, S. 133.
[77] Vgl. *Brunner,* Art. 39, Rn. 10; *Enderlein/Maskow/Strohbach,* Art. 39, Anm. 5.; *Audit,* Vente internationale, Anm. 108.; a. A. – ohne Begründung – *Tannò,* S. 279.
[78] Vgl. Audiencia Provincial de Barcelona, 24.3.2009, CISG-online 2042; LG Bielefeld, 15.8.2003, CISG-online 906 (Rüge gegenüber Hersteller grds. nicht ausreichend); vgl. aber HR, 4.2.2005, CISG-online 1003.
[79] Vgl. oben *Ferrari,* Art. 4 Rn. 34; *Schlechriem/Schwenzer/Schwenzer/Hachem,* CISG Commentary, Art. 4, Rn. 34; *Kröll u. a./Kröll,* Art. 39, Rn. 49. Die Convention on Agency in the International Sale of Goods v. 17.2.1983, die als Parallelabkommen zum CISG gedacht ist, ist noch nicht in Kraft getreten; vgl. dazu *Enderlein/Maskow/Strohbach,* Teil C, S. 347 ff.; *Hanisch,* in: FS Giger, S. 251 ff.; *Stöcker,* WM 1983, 778–785; *Mouly,* Rev. int. dr. comp. 1983, 829–839.
[80] Das Haager Abkommen über das auf Vermittlungsgeschäfte und auf die Stellvertretung anwendbare Recht v. 14.3.1978 – abgedruckt in RabelsZ 43 (1979), 176–189 – ist inzwischen für Argentinien, Frankreich, die Niederlande und Portugal in Kraft getreten.
[81] Zum deutschen IPR vgl. *Kegel/Schurig,* S. 619 ff.; *Kropholler,* S. 299 ff.; *Stoll,* Internationalprivatrechtliche Fragen, S. 495–518; Schweiz: vgl. Art. 126 II, III IPRG; Österreich: vgl. § 49 IPR-Gesetz sowie *Schwind,* Rn. 461 ff.; Frankreich: vgl. *Batiffol/Lagarde,* Droit international privé, Rn. 581; nach Art. 11 I des Haager Abkommens, ist auf das Recht der Niederlassung des Vertreters abzustellen; Art. 11 II macht hiervon wesentliche Ausnahmen zugunsten des Rechts des Handlungsortes.
[82] Vgl. OLG Karlsruhe, 25.7.1986, IPRax 1987, 237, 239; MünchKomm/*Gruber,* Art. 39, Rn. 19; *Stoll,* Internationalprivatrechtliche Fragen, S. 499.
[83] Vgl. auch MünchKomm/*Gruber,* Art. 39, Rn. 20.
[84] MünchKomm/*Gruber,* Art. 39, Rn. 20; *Brunner,* Art. 39, Rn. 11.

sein,[85] so dass der Käufer das Risiko trägt, wenn die so auf den Weg gebrachte Mängelanzeige den Verkäufer nicht oder nicht rechtzeitig erreicht.

IV. Rügefrist – Abs. 1

1. Angemessene Frist

15   Nach Abs. 1 hat die Anzeige der Vertragswidrigkeit innerhalb angemessener Frist, nachdem der Käufer die Vertragswidrigkeit festgestellt hat oder hätte feststellen müssen, zu erfolgen. Es sind also im Regelfall **zwei Fristen** zu beachten, nämlich einerseits die Untersuchungsfrist[86] und andererseits die Rügefrist. Diese Fristen sind nicht zu einer Pauschalfrist zusammen zu rechnen.[87] Gegenüber der Vorschrift des Art. 39 I EKG, die Anzeige innerhalb „kurzer Frist" verlangte, ist die Rügefrist im CISG wesentlich flexibler. Sie kann weder mit der kurzen Frist des EKG noch mit dem Begriff „unverzüglich" – wie ihn das deutsche und das bis 2006 geltende österreichische Recht in § 377 I HGB verwenden – gleichgesetzt werden.[88] Auf die Rechtsprechung zu Art. 39 EKG kann deshalb nur sehr begrenzt zurückgegriffen werden.[89]

16   Die **„angemessene Frist"** ist anhand der **Umstände des Einzelfalls** zu bestimmen,[90] wozu auch Handelsbräuche und Gepflogenheiten zwischen den Parteien gehören.[91] Des Weiteren kommt es zunächst auf die Art der Ware,[92] d. h. insb. darauf an, ob es sich um **verderbliche** oder **dauerhafte** Ware handelt.[93] Bei ersterer muss die Rüge oft innerhalb Stunden oder jedenfalls innerhalb weniger Tage erfolgen,[94] bei letzterer ist die Frist gross-

---

[85] Vgl. LG Kassel, 15.2.1996, CISG-online 191 = NJW-RR 1996, 1146, 1147 (Handelsmakler); LG Bielefeld, 15.8.2003, CISG-online 906 (Hersteller); *Staudinger/Magnus*, Art. 39, Rn. 53.

[86] Vgl. dazu oben Art. 38 Rn. 15 ff.

[87] So *Schlechtriem*, 50 Jahre BGH, S. 407, 439 f.; *ders.*, Internationales UN-Kaufrecht, Rn. 154; MünchKomm/*Gruber*, Art. 39, Rn. 25; *C.Witz*, 11 : 2 ICC Int. Ct. Arb. Bull. (2000), 15, 17; CISG-AC, Op. 2 (*Bergsten*), Comment 5.9 = IHR 2004, 163, 167; *P. Huber/Mullis/Mullis*, S.159; *Andersen*, FS Schwenzer, S. 33, 36 f. A. A. *Kramer*, FS Koppensteiner, S. 617, 624: Rügegesamtfrist auf Basis zweier Fristkomponenten; *Achilles*, Art. 39, Rn. 9; *Kröll u. a./Kröll*, Art. 39, Rn. 59; OGH, 15.10.1998, CISG-online 380; OLG Koblenz, 18.11.1999, CISG-online 570 = IHR 2001, 109, 110; so scheinbar auch BGH, 3.11.1999, CISG-online 475, m. abl. Anm. *Schlechtriem*, EWiR 2000, 125. Inkorrekt: OLG Hamburg, 25.1.2008, CISG-online 1681 = IHR 2008, 98, 99 f., das eine kombinierte Frist für Untersuchung und Rüge von zwei Wochen bis einem Monat ab Lieferung annimmt und sich dabei fälschlicherweise auf BGH, 8.3.1995, CISG-online 144 = BGHZ 129, 75 = NJW 1995, 2099, 2101 sowie auf dieses Werk beruft.

[88] A. A. freilich viele der deutschsprachigen Autoren, vgl. *Herber/Czerwenka*, Art. 39, Rn. 9; *Detzer/Thamm*, BB 1992, 2369, 2375 („zu vermuten, dass die Frist etwas laxer ausgelegt wird als die Anzeigefrist des HGB"); *Ryffel*, S. 21; *Enderlein/Maskow/Strohbach*, Art. 39, Anm. 3.; *Reinhart*, Art. 39, Rn. 5; *Neumayer/Ming*, Art. 39, Anm. 3.; *Heilmann*, S. 323 („kaum Unterschiede"); *Grunewald*, Kaufrecht, S. 270; so auch RB Hasselt, 21.1.1997, CISG-online 360; wie hier: *Karollus*, S. 126; *Resch*, ÖJZ 1992, 470, 476; *Magnus*, IPRax 1993, 390, 392; *ders.*, ZEuP 1993, 79, 88; vgl. auch *Hutter*, S. 82 f.

[89] So wohl auch *Staudinger/Magnus*, Art. 39, Rn. 35 ff.; *Soergel/Lüderitz/Schüßler-Langeheine*, Art. 39, Rn. 3; *Ferrari u. a./Ferrari*, Internationales Vertragsrecht, Art. 39, Rn. 1; ebenso *Magnus*, IPRax 1993, 390, 391, der aber auch eine sieben Tage nach der Untersuchung erfolgte Rüge als verspätet ansieht.

[90] Ausführlich *Andersen*, FS Schwenzer, S. 33 ff.

[91] LG München I, 18.5.2009, CISG-online 1998 (Blumenhandel); Int. Ct. Hungarian CCI, 5.12.1995, CISG-online 163 = NJW-RR 1996, 1145; OLG Saarbrücken, 3.6.1998, CISG-online 354 = NJW-RR 1999, 780 (int. Blumenhandel: ein Tag); OGH, 21.3.2000, CISG-online 641 („„Tegernseer Gebräuche" im Holzhandel: 14 Kalendertage); Trib. Forlì. 9 .12. 2008, CISG-online 1788; *P. Huber/Mullis/Mullis*, S. 159.

[92] Vgl. OGH, 31.8.2010, CISG-online 2236; Audiencia Provincial de Barcelona, 24.3.2009, CISG-online 2042; District Court of Komarno, 24.2.2009, CISG-online 1992.

[93] Vgl. LG München I, 18.5.2009, CISG-online 1998.

[94] Vgl. OGH, 30.6.1998, CISG-online 410 (sechs bzw. zwölf Stunden nach COFREUROP im Obsthandel); OLG Düsseldorf, 8.1.1993, CISG-online 76 = RIW 1993, 325 (Einlegegurken: sieben Tage verspätet); OLG Schleswig, 22.8.2002, CISG-online 710 = IHR 2003, 20, 22 (lebende Schafe: bei Auslieferung, spätestens Folgetag); LG München I, 18.5.2009, CISG-online 1998 (Blumen: möglichst schnelle Rüge, Stunden bis wenige Tage); Gerechtshof 's-Hertogenbosch, 9.3.2010, CISG-online 2341 (Kartoffeln: drei bis max. sechs Tage); RB Breda, 16.1.2009, CISG-online 1789 (Wassermelonen: „[Käufer] hätte entweder sofort oder zumindest wenige Tage nach Lieferung rügen müssen"); RB Zupthen, 27.2.2008, CISG-online 1692 (Zitrusfrüchte: vier Tage

zügiger zu bemessen. Raschere Rüge ist geboten bei **Saisonwaren**,[95] oder wenn eine schnelle Untersuchung der Ware durch einen unparteiischen Sachverständigen erforderlich ist.[96] Vor allem ist bei der Bemessung der Frist auch zu berücksichtigen, auf welche **Rechtsbehelfe** sich der Käufer beruft.[97] Will er die Sache behalten und lediglich Schadenersatz oder Minderung geltend machen, kann die Frist länger bemessen werden, als wenn er die Ware zurückweisen will.[98] Hier muss durch rasche Rüge nicht nur dem Verkäufer die Möglichkeit zur vertragsgemäßen Nacherfüllung gegeben werden, der Verkäufer muss auch Vorsorge für einen allfälligen Rücktransport der Ware treffen können. Für eine längere Frist kann es sprechen, wenn der Vorwurf einer **vorsätzlichen Vertragsverletzung** durch den Verkäufer im Raum steht[99] oder wenn der Käufer noch Zeit benötigt, um von seinen Abnehmern erhobene **Beanstandungen** im Einzelnen zu **prüfen.**[100] Zu berücksichtigen ist auch die Zeit, die der Käufer zur **Abklärung von Rechtsverfolgungsmöglichkeiten im Ausland** benötigt[101] und die Tatsache, dass der Zwischenhändler auf Reaktionen seines Endabnehmers warten muss.[102]

Wie nun die Frist bei **dauerhaften Gütern** im Normalfall, d. h. ohne dass besondere **17** Umstände für eine Verkürzung oder Verlängerung sprechen, zu bemessen ist, ist nach wie vor umstritten.[103] Deutsche Autoren tendierten anfänglich zu recht kurzen Fristen.[104] Auch die ersten deutschen und schweizerischen Entscheidungen zum CISG wiesen in diese Richtung.[105] Zustimmung hat eine solche Fristbemessung in Ländern gefunden, deren nationales Recht ebenfalls kurze Rügefristen vorsieht.[106] In mehreren Entscheidungen hat

---

verspätet); AG Riedlingen, 21.10.1994, CISG-online 358 (Schinken: 20 Tage verspätet); vgl. auch *Staudinger/ Magnus*, Art. 39, Rn. 43; *C. Witz*, L'interprétation, S. 297; *Lurger*, IHR 2005, 177, 184; *Brunner*, Art. 39, Rn. 13.

[95] Vgl. LG München II, 20.2.2002, CISG-online 712 = IHR 2003, 24, 25; Vestre Landsret, 10.11.1999, CISG-online 704 (Weihnachtsbäume: 2 Tage angemessen).

[96] So auch *C. Witz*, L'interprétation, S. 297; *Ramos Muñoz*, Communication of Defects, V) 3) B).

[97] Vgl. YB III (1972), S. 87, Nr. 76; OGH, 31.8.2010, CISG-online 2236; *Staudinger/Magnus*, Art. 39, Rn. 48; *Bianca/Bonell/Sono*, Art. 39, Anm. 2.4.; *Audit*, Vente internationale, Anm. 107.; mit Einschränkungen *Honnold/Flechtner*, Art. 39, 40, 44, Rn 257; ablehnend gegenüber dieser Differenzierung *Witz/Salger/Lorenz/ Salger*, Art. 39, Rn. 6; *Enderlein/Maskow/Strohbach*, Art. 39, Anm. 3.

[98] Vgl. *C. Witz*, L'interprétation, S. 297; *Ramos Muñoz*, Communication of Defects, V) 3) B); *Kröll u. a./ Kröll*, Art. 39, Rn. 89.

[99] Vgl. zum EKG BGH, 2.6.1982, NJW 1982, 2730 (Lieferung vorsätzlich gefälschter Ware).

[100] Zu eng dagegen OLG Düsseldorf, 23.1.2004, CISG-online 918.

[101] Vgl. *Resch*, ÖJZ 1992, 470, 476.

[102] Vgl. LG Berlin, 13.9.2006, CISG-online 1620 = IHR 2008, 168, m. krit. Anm. *Bach*, IPRax 2009, 299, 301 f.

[103] Ausführlich *Andersen*, Reasonable Time, III); dies., FS Schwenzer, S. 33 ff.; *Schwenzer*, (2007) 19 Pace Int'l L. Rev. 103, 109 ff.; dies., (2007) 101 ASIL Proc. 416, 417 ff.; dies., (2005) 7 EJLR 353, 357 ff. Für ausschliessliche Berücksichtigung der Umstände des Einzelfalls: *Lookofsky*, Understanding the CISG, S. 86 f.; *Ramos Muñoz*, Communication of Defects, V) 2) B).

[104] Vgl. *Witz/Salger/Lorenz/Salger*, Art. 39, Rn. 6; *Herber/Czerwenka*, Art. 39, Rn. 9; *Asam*, RIW 1989, 944: 5 Tage; *Reinhart*, Art. 39, Rn. 5: nur wenige Tage. Vgl. auch Regional Court Nitra, 3.11.2008, CISG-online 1954: acht Tage.

[105] Vgl. LG Stuttgart, 31.8.1989, CISG-online 11 = RIW 1989, 984 (Schuhe: 16 Tage verspätet), m. Anm. *Reinhart*, RIW 1989, 942 ff., m. Anm. *Reinhart*, IPRax 1990, 292; LG Aachen, 3.4.1990, CISG-online 12 = RIW 1990, 491 (Schuhe: Tag nach der Lieferung nicht verspätet); OLG Düsseldorf, 8.1.1993, CISG-online 76 = RIW 1993, 325 (Einlegegurken: sieben Tage verspätet), m. Anm. *Magnus*, IPRax 1993, 390 ff.; OLG Saarbrücken, 13.1.1993, CISG-online 83 (Türen: zweieinhalb Monate verspätet); OLG Düsseldorf, 12.3.1993, CISG-online 82 (Webfehler: 25 Tage verspätet); OLG Düsseldorf, 10.2.1994, CISG-online 116 = RIW 1995, 53, 55 (Textilien: zwei Monate verspätet); OLG Oldenburg, 28.4.2000, CISG-online 683 (Möbel: 14 Tage); LG Tübingen, 18.6.2003, CISG-online 784 = IHR 2003, 236 (Computer: neun Tage als verspätet); HGer Zürich, 21.9.1995, CISG-online 246 = SZIER 1996, 51, 52 (Floatarium: 24 Tage verspätet); HGer Zürich, 30.11.1998, CISG-online 415 = SZIER 1999, 186 (Lammfelljacken: mehr als 14 Tage verspätet). Aus neuerer Zeit: KG Schaffhausen, 27.1.2004, CISG-online 960, E. 1) c) (Modellbahn: eine Woche); KG Appenzell Ausserrhoden, 9.3.2006, CISG-online 1375 (Fitnessgeräte: eine Woche).

[106] So vor allem in der Schweiz, vgl. die umfangreichen Nachweise bei *Tannò*, S. 90 ff.; Italien: Art. 1495 I Cc; vgl. Trib. Cuneo, 31.1.1996, CISG-online 268 (Sportbekleidung: 23 Tage verspätet), m. krit. Anm. *Spiegel, D.* 1997, Somm. 222.

Art. 39 17
Teil III. Kapitel II. Pflichten des Verkäufers. Abschnitt II

sich namentlich der österreichische OGH inzwischen für eine Rügegesamtfrist (Untersuchungs- und Rügefrist) von insgesamt 14 Tagen ausgesprochen.[107] Wo jedoch auf Grund langjähriger Tradition im nationalen Recht auch eine Rüge erst **mehrere Monate** nach Entdeckung des Mangels als noch innerhalb „angemessener Frist" erhoben gilt – wie dies namentlich im US-amerikanischen Recht der Fall ist –,[108] schlägt diese Sichtweise auch auf die Auslegung des CISG durch.[109] Dasselbe gilt für Frankreich, wo die Gerichte bis zur Neufassung des Art. 1648 Cc im Rahmen des „bref délai" oft Fristen von zwei bis drei Jahren für die Klageerhebung anerkannten.[110] Dementsprechend wurde die deutsche Literatur und Rechtsprechung von ausländischen Autoren durchwegs kritisch aufgenommen.[111] Will man allzu grossen Auslegungsdivergenzen vorbeugen, erscheint eine Annäherung der Standpunkte unabdingbar. Als grobem Mittelwert sollte man deshalb wenigstens von **ca. einem Monat** ausgehen.[112] Inzwischen scheint sich auch die Rechtsprechung in Deutschland und der Schweiz bei diesem Mittelwert einzupendeln.[113] Der deutsche

---

[107] Vgl. OGH, 15.10.1998, CISG-online 380, m. zust. Anm. *Karollus,* JBl. 1999, 321; OGH, 27.8.1999, CISG-online 485; OGH, 14.1.2002, CISG-online 643; OGH, 31.8.2010, CISG-online 2236; OGH, 2.4.2009, CISG-online 1889. Unter dem neuen § 377 UGB, der eine Rüge in „angemessener Frist" fordert, ist diese Durchschnittsfrist von 14 Tagen, die bereits unter dem CISG angewandt wurde, auch im nationalen Recht anzuwenden. Ebenfalls für eine 14-tägige Frist: *Staudinger/Magnus,* Art. 39, Rn. 49; *ders.,* TranspR-IHR 1999, 29, 33; *Kramer,* FS Koppensteiner, S. 617, 628.

[108] Vgl. die umfassenden Nachw. zur amerikanischen Rechtsprechung bei *White/Summers,* § 11-10, S. 418 ff. Zur englischen Rechtsprechung zu sec. 35 SGA vgl. *Benjamin,* Rn. 12–055.

[109] Vgl. *Sky Cast, Inc v. Global Direct Distribution, LLC,* U. S. Dist. Ct. (E. D. Ky.), 18.3.2008, CISG-online 1652; elf Monate fristgemäss, m. krit. Anm. *Bach,* IPRax 2009, 299, 301 f.; *TeeVee Tons, Inc. & Steve Gottlieb, Inc. v. Gerhard Schubert GmbH,* U. S. Dist. Ct. (S. D. N. Y.), 23.8.2006, CISG-online 1272: ca. zwei Monate wurden ohne nähere Begründung als angemessen erachtet; *Shuttle Packaging Systems, L. L. C. v. Jacob Tsonakis, INA S. A. and INA Plastics Corporation,* U. S. Dist. Ct. (W. D. Mich.), 17.12.2001, CISG-online 773 = 2001 U. S. Dist. LEXIS 21 630: Bei komplizierten Maschinen kann Rüge nicht innerhalb weniger Wochen erwartet werden; Aus der chinesischen Schiedsgerichtsbarkeit vgl. CIETAC, 3.6.2003, CISG-online 1451: zur bereits vergangenen Zeit „it is only nine months".

[110] Vgl. *Ghestin,* R. D. A. I. 1988, 13 ff.; *Ghestin/Desché,* Traité des contrats, Anm. 737. Vgl. auch *Audit,* Vente internationale, Anm. 107., der ausdrücklich auf Art. 1648 Cc verweist.

[111] Vgl. *C. Witz,* Les premières applications, S. 90 f.; *ders.,* 11 : 2 ICC Int. Ct. Arb. Bull. (2000), 15, 20; *Lookofsky,* Understanding the CISG, S. 86 f.; *Flechtner,* Draft Digest, S. 379; *Flechtner,* FS Schwenzer, S. 493, 503 (eine zu strikte Handhabung widerspricht dem Gebot des guten Glaubens); *Schneider, D.* 2002, Somm. 314.

[112] Ausführlich hierzu *Schwenzer,* 19 Pace Int'l L. Rev. (2007), 103, 111 ff.; *dies.,* 7 EJLR (2005), 353, 358 ff. Vgl. auch CA Grenoble, 13.9.1995, CISG-online 157 = J. C. P. 1996, IV, 712; so auch MünchKomm/*Gruber,* Art. 39, Rn. 34; *Kröll u. a./Kröll,* Art. 39, Rn. 86; *T. M. Müller,* Beweislast. S. 108; *Schwenzer/Hachem,* 57 Am. J. Comp. L. (2009), 457, 469; *Schwenzer* (2010) 10 ASIL Proc. (2007), 416, 418; *Su,* S. 56; *Werro,* Sem. jud. 2002, 289, 301; *C. Witz,* L'interprétation, S. 298; *ders.,* 11:2 ICC Int. Ct. Arb. Bull. (2000), 15, 20; *Gerny,* S. 205; *Janssen,* S. 165. *Brunner,* Art. 39, Rn. 13; MünchKommHGB*Benicke,* Art. 39, Rn. 9. *Andersen,* FS Schwenzer, S. 33, 46 betont die Flexibilität und Relativität dieses Massstabs. Ähnlich auch *Piltz,* Internationales Kaufrecht, Rn. 5–67, der als grobe Richtlinie einen Monat für komplexe und zwei Wochen für einfache Fälle vorschlägt. Siehe aber *Kruisinga,* Non-conformity, S. 81 ff., 88 (15 Tage); gegen alle Vermutungen bzgl. einer angemessenen Frist: *Honnold/Flechtner,* Art. 39, 40, 44, Rn. 257.1; *Flechtner,* 26 B. U. Int'l L. J. (2008), 17, 18; *Ferrari u. a./Ferrari,* Internationales Vertragsrecht, Art. 39, Rn. 25; Tribunale di Forlì, 26.9.2007, CISG-online 2336.

[113] Vgl. BGH, 30.6.2004, CISG-online 847 = IHR 2004, 201 (mehr als zwei Monate unangemessen); ansatzweise schon BGH, 8.3.1995, CISG-online 144 = BGHZ 129, 75 = NJW 1995, 2099, 2101 (Muschel-Fall), m. Anm. *Schlechtriem,* IPRax 1996, 12–16; OLG Stuttgart, 21.8.1995, CISG-online 150 = RIW 1995, 943, 944, m. Anm. *Kronke,* IPRax 1996, 139–140; OLG Köln, 21.8.1997, CISG-online 290, m. Anm. *C. Witz, D.* 1998, Somm. 311 f.; OLG München, 11.3.1998, CISG-online 310, m. Anm. *Schlechtriem,* EWiR 1998, 549 f.; LG Saarbrücken, 2.7.2002, CISG-online 713 = IHR 2003, 27; LG Hamburg, 6.9.2004, CISG-online 1085; LG Darmstadt, 29.5.2001, CISG-online 686 = IHR 2001, 160, 161; AG Augsburg, 29.1.1996, CISG-online 172; BGer, 13.11.2003, CISG-online 840 = BGE 130 III 258; OGer Appenzell Ausserrhoden, 18.8.2008, CISG-online 1838, E. 2.4.2 (ein Monat „üblich"); OGer Luzern, 12.5.2003, CISG-online 846 = ZBJV 2004, 704; OGer Luzern, 8.1.1997, CISG-online 228 = SZIER 1997, 132, 133; OLG Hamm, 2.4.2009, CISG-online 1978; LG Münster, 29.8.2008, CISG-online 2167; LG Stuttgart, 15.10.2009, CISG-online 2019; KG Glarus, 6.11.2008, CISG-online 1996; HGer St. Gallen, 11.2.2003, CISG-online 960 (mehr als drei Monate unangemessen); offen gelassen von OLG Oldenburg, 5.12.2000, CISG-online 618; zu gewissen Konzessionen bereit nunmehr auch *Piltz,* Export- und Importgeschäfte, § 12, Rn. 169; zu diesem Ergebnis gelangt nach ausführlichem Fallstudium auch *Andersen,* Reasonable Time, III. 1. 3. 3. 2. Eine Ana-

Mängelrüge 18, 19 **Art. 39**

BGH[114] hat sich inzwischen gar für eine regelmässige einmonatige Rügefrist ausgesprochen.[115] Der französische Kassationshof[116] legt die Fristbemessung in das Ermessen des Tatrichters, hat dabei jedoch ebenfalls die Monatsfrist als ermessensfehlerfrei akzeptiert. Teilweise wird auch von kontinentaleuropäischen Gerichten ein Monat als Mittelwert anerkannt,[117] teilweise jedoch auch noch weit über die Monatsfrist hinausgegangen.[118]

Zur Fristwahrung genügt die rechtzeitige **Absendung der Anzeige,** sofern sie mit dem 18 nach den Umständen geeigneten Kommunikationsmittel erfolgt – Art. 27.[119]

2. Fristbeginn

Die Rügefrist beginnt mit dem Zeitpunkt zu laufen, in dem der Käufer die **Vertrags-** 19 **widrigkeit festgestellt hat oder hätte feststellen müssen.**[120] Hat der Käufer aktuelle Kenntnis von der Vertragswidrigkeit, so läuft die Frist für die Anzeige unabhängig davon, ob die Frist für die Untersuchung bereits abgelaufen ist.[121] So muss der Käufer beispielsweise eine bereits bei Aushändigung der Ware festgestellte Quantitätsabweichung rügen, auch wenn die Untersuchung der Ware auf Qualitätsabweichung noch nicht abgeschlossen ist oder zu sein braucht.

---

lyse der jüngeren deutschen Rechtsprechung von *ders.,* FS Schwenzer, S. 33, 38 ff. gelangt entsprechend zum Ergebnis: „the ‚Noble Month' emerges as the clear leader in setting a benchmark for reasonable time". Anders noch OLG Koblenz, 18.11.1999, CISG-online 570 = IHR 2001, 109, 111, m. zust. Anm. *Thiele;* OLG Düsseldorf, 23.1.2004, CISG-online 918: vier Wochen im Fall von Stahlblech unangemessen (unter falscher Bestimmung des Beginns der Frist, die unter den gegebenen Umständen mit Lieferung begonnen hätte); OLG Hamburg, 25.1.2008, CISG-online 1681 = IHR 2008, 98, 99 f., das fälschlicherweise eine kombinierte Frist für Untersuchung und Rüge von zwei Wochen bis einem Monat ab Lieferung annimmt und sich dabei fälschlicherweise auf BGH, 8.3.1995, CISG-online 144 = BGHZ 129, 75 = NJW 1995, 2099, 2101 sowie auf dieses Werk beruft; LG Frankfurt a.M., 11.4.2005, CISG-online 1014 = IHR 2005, 163 (drei Wochen unangemessen); m. krit. Anm. *Flechtner,* 26 B.U. Int'l L.J. (2008), 19 ff.; zu dieser Entscheidung ebenfalls kritisch *Schwenzer,* 19 Pace Int'l L. Rev. (2007), 103, 114, 115.
[114] Vgl. BGH, 3.11.1999, CISG-online 475 (Mahlgarnitur); zust. *Bamberger/Roth/Saenger,* Art. 39, Rn. 8; krit. hierzu *Schlechtriem,* 50 Jahre BGH, S. 407, 438.
[115] Kritisch hierzu *Andersen,* FS Schwenzer, S. 33, 47 f. („ravenous appetite for predictability and doctrine").
[116] Vgl. Civ. 1, 26.5.1999, CISG-online 487 (Walzbleche), m. krit. Anm. *C. Witz,* D. 2000, 788; implizit Civ. 1, 4.10.2005, CISG-online 1097 = J.C.P. 2005, IV, 3342; *C. Witz,* L'interprétation, S. 299 f.
[117] Vgl. Monomeles Protodikio Athinon, 2009, CISG-online 2294. In diese Richtung auch Appelationsgericht Szeged, 5.12.2008, CISG-online 1938 (zwei Monate nicht angemessen); Foreign Trade Court of Arbitration attached to the Serbian Chamber of Commerce, 21.2.2005, CISG-online 2038 (drei Monate nicht angemessen).
[118] Vgl. CA Colmar, 24.10.2000, CISG-online 578 (Klebefolie: ca. sechs Wochen), D. 2002, Somm. 393, m. Anm. *C. Witz,* drei Monate wurden indessen als zu lang betrachtet, vgl. CA Paris, 6.11.2001, CISG-online 677 = D. 2002, 2795, m. Anm. *C. Witz;* CA Aix-en-Provence, 1.7.2005, CISG-online 1096 (über zwei Monate); CA Versailles, 29.1.1998, CISG-online 337 (sechs/elf Monate); Regional Court Zilina, 25.10.2007, CISG-online 1761 (Fitnesskleidung: fast drei Monate); Hof van Beroep, Gent, 4.10.2004, CISG-online 985 (neun Monate); RB Veurne, 15.1.2003, CISG-online 1056 (fast drei Monate); Trib. Rimini, 26.11.2002, CISG-online 737 (sechs Monate); Audiencia Provincial de La Coruña, 21.6.2002, CISG-online 1049 (2,5 Monate); RB Hasselt, 6.3.2002, CISG-online 623 (zwei Monate); Sø og Handelsretten, 31.1.2002, CISG-online 868 (sieben Monate); Gerechtshof Arnhem, 27.4.1999, CISG-online 741 (zwei Jahre). Hinweise darauf, dass das CISG als liberaler wahrgenommen wird als nationale Bestimmungen finden sich in ICC, 1.10.1995, CISG-online 1275, wo Art. 39 zur Auslegung des französischen Art. 1648 Cc (in der aktuellen Fassung) herangezogen und so eine längere Rügefrist unter dem Konzept des bref délai erreicht wurde.
[119] Näheres hierzu oben bei *Schroeter,* Art. 27 Rn. 13.
[120] Nicht überzeugend ist die Regelung in Art. 122 I UAbs. 2 CESL-Entwurf, nach dem die Frist am spätesten der möglichen Anknüpfungszeitpunkte beginnt, was bei wörtlichem Verständnis dazu führt, dass die Frist nicht mit Kennenmüssen des Mangels sondern erst mit später eintretender tatsächlicher Kenntnis zu laufen beginnt, vgl. *Schmidt-Kessel/Wiese,* Europäisches Kaufrecht, S. 412. Darüber hinaus führt auch das fixe Ende der Untersuchungsfrist nach 14 Tagen (Art. 121 I CESL-Entwurf) und das daran geknüpfte Kennenmüssen des Mangels zu nicht sachgerechten Fristläufen.
[121] Vgl. *Piltz,* Internationales Kaufrecht, Rn. 5–70; *Heilmann,* S. 313; *Kröll u.a./Kröll,* Art. 39, Rn. 65. Fraglich ist, ob dem Verkäufer noch ein weiterer Zeitraum für die Abklärung der Ursachen zuzugestehen ist; dagegen MünchKomm/*Gruber,* Art. 39, Rn. 25.

20 Für die Frage, wann der Käufer eine Vertragswidrigkeit hätte feststellen müssen, kommt es auf die **Art des Mangels** an. Hätte der Mangel auf Grund einer **sachgemässen Untersuchung**[122] aufgedeckt werden können, so beginnt die Rügefrist mit dem Ende der Untersuchungsfrist.[123] Beide Fristen werden also hintereinander geschaltet. Hat der Käufer die erforderliche Untersuchung der Ware über Gebühr verzögert, so kann er dies durch eine besonders rasche Anzeige wieder ausgleichen.[124] Vertragswidrigkeiten, die bei einer ordnungsgemässen Untersuchung **nicht erkennbar** sind, muss der Käufer innerhalb einer angemessenen Frist anzeigen, nachdem er sie tatsächlich festgestellt hat oder hätte feststellen müssen.[125] Hieraus kann jedoch nicht eine Pflicht des Käufers zur **fortlaufenden Untersuchung** der Ware abgeleitet werden.[126] So kann vom Käufer beispielsweise nicht erwartet werden, dass er eine sachgemäss untersuchte Maschine auch alsbald in Betrieb nimmt, um Vertragswidrigkeiten rechtzeitig zu erkennen. Es geht vielmehr nur darum, dass später auftretende, ins Auge springende Mängel ebenfalls der Anzeigepflicht unterstellt werden. Zeigen sich Mängelsymptome, lebt die Untersuchungspflicht wieder auf.[127]

21 Bei **vorzeitiger Lieferung**, d. h. vor dem vereinbarten Lieferzeitpunkt oder vor dem Beginn eines Lieferzeitraumes, beginnt die Rügefrist[128] nicht vor dem massgeblichen Liefertermin zu laufen, auch wenn der Käufer eine Vertragswidrigkeit bereits vor diesem Zeitpunkt tatsächlich festgestellt hat.[129]

V. Ausschlussfrist – Abs. 2

1. Zweijahresfrist

22 Neben der relativen Rügefrist nach Abs. 1 enthält Abs. 2 eine zweijährige **Ausschlussfrist** für die Erhebung der Mängelanzeige.[130] Die Mängelanzeige muss also spätestens so rechtzeitig abgesandt werden, dass sie bei ordentlichem Funktionieren des verwendeten Kommunikationsmittels innerhalb der Zweijahresfrist beim Verkäufer ankommen kann – Art. 27. Die Ausschlussfrist greift immer dann ein, wenn eine Vertragswidrigkeit auf Grund sachgemässer Untersuchung nicht erkennbar war und der Käufer sie auch zu einem späteren Zeitpunkt **nicht festgestellt hat oder hätte feststellen müssen**.[131] Darüber hinaus findet sie in den Fällen Anwendung, in denen der Käufer eine **vernünftige Entschuldigung**

---

[122] Vgl. dazu oben Art. 38 Rn. 10 ff.
[123] Vgl. dazu oben Art. 38 Rn. 15 ff.
[124] Vgl. BGH, 3.11.1999, CISG-online 475; *Staudinger/Magnus*, Art. 39, Rn. 30; *P. Huber/Mullis/Mullis*, S. 160; *Piltz*, Internationales Kaufrecht, Rn. 5–76; *Heilmann*, S. 302; folglich inkorrekt: LG Frankfurt a. M., 11.4.2005, CISG-online 1014 = IHR 2005, 163 m. krit. Anm. *Flechtner*, 26 B. U. Int'l L. J. (2008), 19 ff.; krit. *Schlechtriem*, 50 Jahre BGH, S. 407, 439.
[125] Vgl. BGH, 3.11.1999, CISG-online 475 (Mahlgarnitur): offen gelassen, ob Kenntnis oder Erkennbarkeit entscheidend.
[126] Vgl. *Staudinger/Magnus*, Art. 39, Rn. 32; *Reinhart*, Art. 39, Rn. 4; *Heilmann*, S. 324 f.; *Flechtner*, Draft Digest, S. 389; *Honnold/Flechtner*, Art. 38, Rn. 252.1; nun auch *Piltz*, Internationales Kaufrecht, Rn. 5–84, der ausdrücklich eine Verpflichtung zur fortlaufenden Untersuchung verneint, aber trotzdem von einer „abgeschwächten (…) Obliegenheit zur weiteren Beobachtung der Ware" ausgeht.
[127] Vgl. *Schlechtriem*, 50 Jahre BGH, S. 407, 440; *Flechtner*, Draft Digest, S. 389; CISG-AC, Op. 2 *(Bergsten)*, Comment 3 = IHR 2004, 163, 164.
[128] Zur Untersuchungsfrist bei vorzeitiger Lieferung vgl. oben Art. 38 Rn. 20.
[129] Vgl. *Staudinger/Magnus*, Art. 39, Rn. 33; *Kröll u. a./Kröll*, Art. 39, Rn. 73; wohl auch *Tannò*, S. 277; a. A. *Reinhart*, Art. 39, Rn. 3; *Resch*, ÖJZ 1992, 470, 477; *Soergel/Lüderitz/Schüßler-Langeheine*, Art. 39, Rn. 5; *Ferrari u. a./Ferrari*, Internationales Vertragsrecht, Art. 39, Rn. 22.; *Piltz*, Internationales Kaufrecht, Rn. 5–72 erachtet allein die tatsächliche Möglichkeit, den Mangel zu entdecken als relevant. Für das EKG vgl. BGH, 25.3.1992, NJW-RR 1992, 886 (Beginn der Rügefrist schon vor Beendigung der Montage einer Maschine durch den Verkäufer).
[130] Ausführlich hierzu *Leisinger*, IHR 2006, 76 ff. Vgl. auch *Hayward/Perlen*, 15 VJ (2011), 119, 135 (déchéance). Vgl. weiter Art. 122 II CESL-Entwurf.
[131] Vgl. auch OGH, 19.5.1999, CISG-online 484; OGH, 19.12.2007, CISG-online 1628 = IHR 2008, 106, 108, m. Anm. *P. Huber*, IPRax 2009, 89; CA Rouen, 19.12.2006, CISG-online 1933.

Mängelrüge 23–25a **Art. 39**

dafür hat, dass er die nach Abs. 1 erforderliche Anzeige unterlassen hat (Art. 44).[132] Nach Ablauf der Zweijahresfrist kann der Käufer daher auch die Rechtsbehelfe, die er nach Art. 44 behält, nicht mehr geltend machen. War der **Verkäufer** allerdings **bösgläubig** i. S. des Art. 40, so kommt auch die zweijährige Ausschlussfrist nicht zum Tragen. Die Ausschlussfrist des Abs. 2 war auf der Diplomatischen Konferenz **höchst umstritten**.[133] Sie wurde auch von vielen Vertretern der Industrienationen als willkürlich und z. B. in Bezug auf Maschinen als unangemessen angesehen.[134] Letztlich ist sie Teil des Gesamtkompromisses zur Regelung der Rügepflicht, der auch Art. 44 erfasst. Sie dient dazu, dem Verkäufer Sicherheit zu verschaffen, dass er nach einem bestimmten Zeitpunkt nicht mehr mit Reklamationen zu rechnen braucht und das Geschäft endgültig zur Seite legen kann.

Die Frist nach Abs. 2 ist eine **absolute Ausschlussfrist**, d. h. eine Hemmung oder Unterbrechung kommt nicht in Betracht,[135] und sie ist von Amts wegen zu beachten.[136] 23

Die Zweijahresfrist **beginnt** erst **mit tatsächlicher Übergabe** der Ware an den Käufer zu laufen, unabhängig davon, ob schon zu einem früheren Zeitpunkt die Gefahr übergegangen ist oder der Käufer eventuell durch Übergabe der Dokumente bereits Eigentümer der Ware geworden ist.[137] Unter tatsächlicher Übergabe ist die **physische Aushändigung** der Ware an den Käufer zu verstehen.[138] Bei Direktlieferung an einen Abnehmer des Käufers – sei es mit oder ohne Umleitung der Ware i. S. des Art. 38 III – kommt es auf die Aushändigung der Ware an den Abnehmer an.[139] Dies gilt jedoch nicht im Falle einer Weiterversendung an einen Abnehmer, denn hier ist eine Aushändigung der Ware an den Käufer bereits erfolgt, auch wenn ihm nach Art. 38 III zu diesem Zeitpunkt noch keine Untersuchung zugemutet wird.[140] Wurde die Ware zerstört, konfisziert oder zurückgewiesen, ist der Zeitpunkt der hypothetischen Übergabe entscheidend.[141] 24

Abs. 2 sagt nichts darüber aus, wie das **Ende der Zweijahresfrist** exakt zu bestimmen ist. Auch aus dem Gesamtzusammenhang des CISG lässt sich hierfür keine Lösung entwickeln. Es muss deshalb insoweit auf das über IPR anwendbare nationale Recht zurückgegriffen werden.[142] Ist deutsches Recht Vertragsstatut, so gilt § 188 II BGB. 25

In einer Entscheidung der Cour de cassation aus dem Jahr 2008[143] wurde die Frage aufgeworfen, ob die Ausschlussfrist des Art. 39 II im Widerspruch zum Recht auf ein faires 25a

---

[132] OLG Linz, 24.9.2007, CISG-online 1583 = IHR 2008, 28, 30; bestätigt durch OGH, 19.12.2007, CISG-online 1628 = IHR 2008, 106, 108, m. Anm. *P. Huber*, IPRax 2009, 89.
[133] Vgl. O. R., S. 347 ff., Nr. 29 ff.
[134] Vgl. auch *Heuzé*, Anm. 306.; *Ghestin*, R. D. A. I. 1988, 16; *Ben Abderrahmane*, Dr. prat. com. int. 1989, 551, 563; *Niggemann*, Pflichten des Verkäufers, S. 91.
[135] Vgl. Com., 13.2.2007, CISG-online 1562; CA Rouen, 19.12.2006, CISG-online 1933; *Schlechtriem*, Internationales UN-Kaufrecht, Rn. 160; *ders.*, FS Jayme, S. 1353, 1356, betreffend § 479 II BGB; *Staudinger/Magnus*, Art. 39, Rn. 63; *Heuzé*, Anm. 306.; *Audit*, Vente internationale, Anm. 107.; *Enderlein/Maskow/Strohbach*, Art. 39, Anm. 6.; *Neumayer/Ming*, Art. 39, Anm. 6.; *Piltz*, Internationales Kaufrecht, Rn. 5–86; *Reinhart*, Art. 39, Rn. 8; *Tannò*, S. 286.
[136] Vgl. OLG Linz, 24.9.2007, CISG-online 1583 = IHR 2008, 28, 30; bestätigt durch OGH, 19.12.2007, CISG-online 1628 = IHR 2008, 106, 108, m. Anm. *P. Huber*, IPRax 2009, 89; vgl. auch *Leisinger*, IHR 2006, 76, 80 f.; *Staudinger/Magnus*, Art. 39, Rn. 63.
[137] Vgl. OLG Linz, 24.9.2007, CISG-online 1583 = IHR 2008, 28, 30; O. R., S. 349, Nr. 62 f.; *Staudinger/Magnus*, Art. 39, Rn. 64; MünchKommHGB/*Benicke*, Art. 39, Rn. 15; *Brunner*, Art. 39, Rn. 16; *Bianca/Bonell/Sono*, Art. 39, Anm. 2.7.; *Heuzé*, Anm. 306.; *Audit*, Vente internationale, Anm. 107.; *Enderlein/Maskow/Strohbach*, Art. 39, Anm. 7.; *Leisinger*, IHR 2006, 76, 78.
[138] Vgl. OLG Linz, 24.9.2007, CISG-online 1583 = IHR 2008, 28, 30; vgl. auch *Ramos Muñoz*, Communication of Defects, V) 3) C).
[139] Vgl. *Schlechtriem*, Einheitliches UN-Kaufrecht, S. 62; *Heuzé*, Anm. 306.; *Enderlein/Maskow/Strohbach*, Art. 39, Anm. 7.
[140] Vgl. *Bianca/Bonell/Sono*, Art. 39, Anm. 2.7.; *Audit*, Vente internationale, Anm. 107.; *Enderlein/Maskow/Strohbach*, Art. 39, Anm. 7.
[141] Vgl. *Leisinger*, IHR 2006, 76, 78 ff.; vgl. auch MünchKomm/*Gruber*, Art. 39, Rn. 39.
[142] Vgl. *Heuzé*, Anm. 306.; *Leisinger*, IHR 2006, 76, 80.
[143] Vgl. Com., 16.9.2008, CISG-online 1851. Die Cour de cassation hatte diese Frage nicht zu beantworten, da die entsprechende Argumentation erst in letzter Instanz vorgebracht wurde und die Revision deshalb insoweit unzulässig war.

Verfahren nach Art. 6 EMRK steht. Ein solcher Widerspruch ist zu verneinen, da das Recht auf Zugang zu einem Gericht nicht uneingeschränkt gilt, sondern schon nach seinem Wesen eine staatliche Reglementierung erfordert.[144] Der legitime Zweck der Ausschlussfrist des Art. 39 II liegt darin, dem Verkäufer Rechtssicherheit zu verschaffen. Die Regelung ist auch verhältnismässig, da sie nicht übermässig kurz, dispositiv[145] sowie durch Art. 40 bei fehlender Schutzwürdigkeit des Verkäufers eingeschränkt ist und so die Rechte des Käufers hinreichend wahrt.[146]

2. Garantiefrist

26 Die zweijährige Ausschlussfrist greift nicht ein, wenn sie **mit einer vertraglichen Garantiefrist**[147] **nicht zu vereinbaren** ist.[148] Im Rahmen einer Garantie kann die Frist des Abs. 2 **verlängert,** aber auch **verkürzt** werden.[149] Im Wege der Auslegung der vertraglichen Vereinbarung muss geklärt werden, ob die Garantiefrist mit der in Abs. 2 bestimmten Ausschlussfrist zu vereinbaren ist oder nicht.[150] Bestimmt etwa der Vertrag, dass der Verkäufer für eine Vertragswidrigkeit nur einzustehen hat, wenn der Käufer diese innerhalb von 90 Tagen nach Lieferung gerügt hat, so ist darin eine Verkürzung der Ausschlussfrist zu sehen. Eine Garantie des Verkäufers, die verkaufte Maschine werde ein Jahr lang einen bestimmten Verbrauch nicht überschreiten, ist als solche aber noch nicht unvereinbar mit der Ausschlussfrist nach Abs. 2, so dass der Käufer auch Mängel geltend machen kann, die sich nach Ablauf der einjährigen Garantiefrist aber noch innerhalb der Zweijahresfrist zeigen.[151] Sieht der Vertrag eine **über zwei Jahre hinausgehende Garantiefrist** vor, so dürfte diese im Rahmen ihres Regelungsbereichs in der Regel freilich mit der Ausschlussfrist nach Abs. 2 unvereinbar sein.[152]

27 Eine andere Frage ist es, ob auch bei einer vertraglichen Garantie eine **Anzeige der Vertragswidrigkeit innerhalb angemessener Frist** nach Kenntnis oder Kennenmüssen zu erfolgen hat, oder ob der Käufer bis zum Ende der Garantiefrist zuwarten darf. Soweit die Parteien nichts anderes vereinbart haben, ist insoweit ohne weiteres von der Anwendbarkeit des Abs. 1 auszugehen.[153] Ebenfalls durch Auslegung ist zu ermitteln, ob bei **Mängeln, die gegen Ende der vertraglichen Garantiefrist auftreten,** entsprechend Abs. 2 die Anzeige jedenfalls so rechtzeitig erfolgen muss, dass sie den Verkäufer unter normalen Umständen noch vor Ablauf der Garantiefrist erreicht, oder ob dem Käufer bei Auftreten des Mangels eine angemessene Frist zur Anzeige zur Verfügung steht, selbst wenn diese über das Ende der Garantiefrist hinausreicht. Soweit der Verkäufer bestimmte Eigenschaften der Ware oder ihre Eignung zum normalen oder zu einem bestimmten Gebrauch für einen gewissen Zeitraum garantiert und im Hinblick auf die Anzeige keine

---

[144] Vgl. EGMR, 22.10.1996, Sammlung 1996-IV, Rn. 50.
[145] Vgl. unten Rn. 34 ff.
[146] Ebenso der Rapporteur *Potocki,* Rapport zu Com., 16.9.2008, abrufbar unter CISG-france.org; *C. Witz/Hlawon,* IHR 2011, S. 93, 99.
[147] Beispiele und Fallgruppen bei *Brunner,* Art. 39, Rn. 22. Eine Klausel, wonach Schiedsklage innerhalb von 30 Tagen nach Nichteinigung erhoben werden muss, stellt keine Garantiefrist i. S. d. Art. 39 II dar, vgl. ICC, 7565/1994, CISG-online 566; a. A. offenbar ICC, 7660/1994 CISG-online 129.
[148] Eine ähnliche Bestimmung – allerdings bezogen auf die Verjährung von Gewährleistungsansprüchen – findet sich in § 2–725 (2) UCC.
[149] Vgl. *Staudinger/Magnus,* Art. 39, Rn. 68; *Schlechtriem,* Internationales UN-Kaufrecht, Rn. 160; *Heuzé,* Anm. 308.; *Reinhart,* Art. 39, Rn. 9; *Enderlein/Maskow/Strohbach,* Art. 39, Anm. 8.; nur von Verlängerung sprechen *Honnold/Flechtner,* Artt. 39, 40, 44, Rn. 258.
[150] Vgl. CA Paris, 7.10.2009, CISG-online 2034; *Piltz,* NJW 2011, 2261, 2265; Sekretariatskommentar, Art. 37, Nr. 7 mit Beispielen; vgl. auch *P. Huber/Mullis/Mullis,* S. 162.
[151] Vgl. Sekretariatskommentar, Art. 37, Nr. 7, Bsp. 37 C; *Bianca/Bonell/Sono,* Art. 39, Anm. 3.3.; *Aue,* Mängelgewährleistung im UN-Kaufrecht, S. 122; a. A. *Staudinger/Magnus,* Art. 39, Rn. 69.
[152] Vgl. auch *Leisinger,* IHR 2006, 76, 80; *P. Huber/Mullis/Mullis,* S. 162.
[153] Vgl. *Staudinger/Magnus,* Art. 39, Rn. 70; *Herber/Czerwenka,* Art. 39, Rn. 19; *Enderlein/Maskow/Strohbach,* Art. 39, Anm. 8.; wohl auch *Bianca/Bonell/Sono,* Art. 39, Anm. 3.3.; YB IV (1973), S. 48, Nr. 87.

näheren Bestimmungen getroffen wurden, spricht viel für eine Auslegung in letzterem Sinne.[154]

3. Verjährung

Die Ausschlussfrist nach Abs. 2 darf nicht mit der Verjährung der Gewährleistungsansprüche verwechselt werden,[155] die bestimmt, innerhalb welcher Frist der Käufer bestehende Ansprüche gerichtlich geltend machen muss. Die Fragen der Verjährung sind im CISG nicht geregelt. Insoweit gilt das **UN-Übereinkommen über die Verjährung beim internationalen Warenkauf** vom 14.6.1974,[156] falls die Parteien ihre Niederlassungen in Vertragsstaaten dieses Übereinkommens haben oder das IPR auf das Recht eines Vertragsstaates verweist (Art. 3 I VerjÜbk). In den übrigen Fällen gilt das nach dem **IPR als Vertragsstatut** berufene unvereinheitlichte nationale Recht.[157] 28

Soweit das VerjÜbk zur Anwendung kommt, ergeben sich keine **Friktionen** mit Art. 39 II. Denn nach Art. 8 VerjÜbk beträgt die Verjährungsfrist vier Jahre; sie beginnt nach Art. 10 II VerjÜbk ebenfalls mit tatsächlicher Übergabe der Ware an den Käufer zu laufen. Probleme entstehen jedoch, wenn das als Vertragsstatut berufene nationale Recht für Gewährleistungsansprüche eine kürzere Frist als Art. 39 II vorsieht. In Deutschland[158] und in anderen EU-Staaten[159] hat sich das Problem mit der Heraufsetzung der früheren kurzen Verjährungsfristen auf 2 Jahre weitgehend erledigt. Der Konflikt zwischen Art. 39 II und nationalem Recht bestand bis 1.1.2013 in der Schweiz,[160] wo Art. 210 I OR a. F. eine einjährige Verjährungsfrist festlegte; seit 1.1.2013 gilt auch in der Schweiz eine zweijährige Verjährungsfrist. Zu dem vormaligen Konflikt wurde teilweise von der Literatur die Auffassung vertreten, dass auf sämtliche Vertragswidrigkeiten nach Art. 35 nicht die kürzere nationale Verjährungsvorschrift für Gewährleistungsansprüche, sondern die zehnjährige **Verjährungsfrist für allgemeine vertragliche Ansprüche** (Art. 127 OR) zur Anwendung kommen müsse.[161] Indes ist diese allgemeine Verjährungsfrist für den internationalen 29

---

[154] Vgl. *Bianca/Bonell/Sono*, Art. 39, Anm. 3.3.; *Enderlein/Maskow/Strohbach*, Art. 39, Anm. 8.; *Brunner*, Art. 39, Rn. 26.

[155] Com., 3.2.2009, CISG-online 1843 gegen die Vorinstanz CA Amiens, 27.9.2007, CISG-online 1934 (fälschlich Verjährungsfrist); *Hayward/Perlen*, 15 VJ (2011), 119, 135; *P. Huber/Mullis/Mullis*, S. 162. Fälschlich von „prescription" spricht Oberster Gerichtshof Israel, 17.3.2009, CISG-online 1980. Ebenfalls inkorrekt *Sky Cast, Inc. v. Global Direct Distribution, LLC*, U. S. Dist. Ct. (E. D. Ky.), 18.3.2008, CISG-online 1652, m. krit. Anm. *Bach*, IPRax 2009, 299, 301, 303.

[156] I. d. F. des Protokolls v. 11.4.1980; vgl. die Kommentierung von *Müller-Chen* unten.

[157] Vgl. RB Rotterdam, 2.6.2010, CISG-online 2340; zustimmend *Piltz* NJW 2011, 2261, 2265; ebenso *C. Witz/Hlawon*, IHR 2011, 93, 101. Die Verjährung von Gewährleistungsansprüchen ist in den nationalen Rechten sehr unterschiedlich geregelt. Deutschland: § 438 I Nr. 3, II BGB (zwei Jahre ab Ablieferung), vgl. aber für Regressansprüche des Zwischenhändlers § 479 BGB; Schweiz: Art. 210 I OR (ein Jahr ab Ablieferung); Österreich: § 933 I ABGB (zwei Jahre ab Ablieferung); Frankreich: Art. 1648 (zwei Jahre ab Entdeckung); Belgien: Art. 1648 Cc (bref délai ab Kenntnis); Italien: Art. 1495 III Cc (ein Jahr ab Übergabe); Spanien: Art. 1490 Cc (sechs Monate ab Übergabe); Niederlande: Art. 3:310 BW (Schadensersatz: fünf Jahre ab Entdeckung des Schadens); England: sec. 5 Limitation Act 1980 (sechs Jahre ab Übergabe); USA: § 2–725 UCC (vier Jahre ab Übergabe), vgl. auch UCC-Draft v. 2.8.2002, wonach unter bestimmten Voraussetzungen eine 5-Jahresfrist gilt. China: für internationale Warenkaufverträge vgl. Art. 129 Vertragsgesetz der PRC (vier Jahre ab dem Zeitpunkt, an welchem die Partei von der Rechtsverletzung Kenntnis hat oder Kenntnis haben müsste). Umfassende rechtsvergleichende Nachweise bei *Schwenzer/Hachem/Kee*, Rn. 51.23 ff. Zu den Problemen bezüglich Qualifikation, Dauer und Abdingbarkeit insgesamt *Schwenzer/Manner*, 23 Arb. Int'l (2007), 293 ff.

[158] Vgl. § 477 BGB a. F. und § 438 I Nr. 3 BGB n. F. § 479 BGB ist nun auf den Regress des Zwischenhändlers anwendbar, vgl. dazu *Magnus*, RIW 2002, 577, 583; *Schlechtriem*, FS Jayme, S. 1353, 1356.

[159] Vgl. insb. Frankreich: § 1648 I Cc enthält seit 2005 eine Zweijahresfrist anstelle der früheren bref délai.

[160] Das gleiche Problem existiert in Spanien (Art. 1490 Cc), Italien (Art. 1495 III Cc) und den meisten lateinamerikanischen Staaten. Dort findet sich jedoch bisher diesbzgl. keine eingehende Diskussion. Vgl. zu den Verjährungsfristen *E. Muñoz*, S. 523 f.

[161] Vgl. *Ryffel*, S. 23; *Honsell*, plädoyer 1990, 44; wohl auch *Bucher*, Neuerungen, S. 48 f.; *Spiro*, Befristung und Verjährung, S. 200, 203. Diese Ansicht wurde auch zum früheren französischen Recht vertreten: Com., 17.12.1996, CISG-online 220 = D. 1997, 337, m. Anm. *C. Witz*; *Heuzé*, Anm. 307. (Anwendung des Art. 189bis Ccom: 10 Jahre).

Warenhandel zu lang.[162] Das schweizerische Bundesgericht hat kürzlich – noch zur alten Verjährungsfrist – die Anwendung der einjährigen Verjährungsfrist des Art. 210 I OR verneint, dabei aber ausdrücklich offengelassen, ob die Zwei- oder die Zehnjahresfrist anwendbar ist.[163] Ein Untergericht hat die kurze Verjährungsfrist bis zum Ablauf der in Art. 39 II normierten Ausschlussfrist **ausgedehnt**.[164] Diese Lösung wird von einer wachsenden Anzahl Autoren unterstützt.[165] Auch diese Lösung hat den Nachteil, dass bei spät auftretenden Mängeln eine vernünftige Zeitspanne zwischen letzter Rügemöglichkeit und Verjährung fehlt.[166] Immerhin wohnt ihr eine gewisse Vereinheitlichungstendenz inne, denn auch bei Anwendung z. B. deutschen Verjährungsrechts gelangt man nun zu diesem Ergebnis.[167] Andere Gerichte knüpfen an die frühere deutsche Lösung an und lassen die kurze Verjährungsfrist mit erfolgter Rüge zu laufen beginnen.[168] Da die Lösung dieses Problems nach wie vor unsicher scheint, empfiehlt sich eine vertragliche Vereinbarung der Verjährung in Anpassung an Art. 39 II.[169]

VI. Rechtsfolgen unterlassener oder nicht gehöriger Anzeige

1. Ausschluss der Rechtsbehelfe

30   Nach Abs. 1 verliert der Käufer das Recht, sich auf eine Vertragswidrigkeit der Ware zu berufen, wenn er diese nicht oder nicht gehörig rügt, d. h. die Ware gilt als **genehmigt**. Der Käufer verliert daher sämtliche Rechtsbehelfe, die ihm nach Art. 45 zustehen würden. Auch Rechtsbehelfe, die dem Käufer nach nationalem Deliktsrecht oder Irrtumsrecht zustehen könnten, bleiben ausgeschlossen.[170] Bei **Minderlieferung,**[171] Lieferung von **Ware minderer Qualität** oder eines **geringerwertigen aliud** muss der Käufer deshalb den vereinbarten Kaufpreis bezahlen, ohne dass ihm irgendwelche Einreden zuständen oder er mit Gegenansprüchen aufrechnen könnte.[172] Liefert der Verkäufer eine **grössere** als die vertraglich vereinbarte **Menge** und unterbleibt die Rüge, so muss der Käufer nach Art. 52 II 2 einen entsprechend höheren Kaufpreis bezahlen.[173] Fraglich ist, ob eine Kaufpreis-

---

[162] Vgl. insbesondere *Will*, FS Lorenz, S. 623, 636 m. w. N.
[163] BGer, 18.5.2009, CISG-online 1900, E 10.3., m. Anm. *Th. Koller*, Jusletter 20.7.2009.
[164] Vgl. Cour de justice de Genève, 10.10.1997, CISG-online 295 = D. 1998, Somm. 316, m. krit. Anm. *C. Witz*; krit. *Will*, FS Lorenz, S. 623, 638 ff.; ICC, 3.11.1999, zit. bei *Will*, aaO., 625.
[165] Vgl. *Benedick*, Informationspflichten, Rn. 635 ff.; *Girsberger*, 25 J. L. & Com. (2005), 241, 250; *Th. Koller*, recht 2003, 41, 53; *Tannò*, S. 288; de lege lata auch *Hachem/Mohs*, AJP 2009, 1541, 1548; kritisch *Will*, FS Lorenz, S. 623, 638 ff.; unklar oder für ein Tätigwerden des Gesetzgebers, *Th. Widmer*, Droits et obligations du vendeur, S. 102; *Chaudet*, S. 124; *Krapp*, ZSR 1984, 289, 315 ff.; *Honsell*, OR BT, S. 151.
[166] Vgl. *Hachem/Mohs*, AJP 2009, 1541, 1548; *Will*, FS Lorenz, S. 623, 640.
[167] Zu Art. 3 VertragsG in der revidierten Fassung vgl. *Schroeter*, Art. 3 VertragsG Rn. 4.
[168] Vgl. Polimeles Protodikio Athinon, 2009, CISG-online 2228; HGer Bern, 30.10.2001, CISG-online 956, m. krit. Anm. *Th. Koller*, recht 2003, 41, 48; HGer Bern, 17.1.2002, CISG-online 725; zust. *Janssen*, IPRax 2003, 369, 371. De lege ferenda auch *Hachem/Mohs*, AJP 2009, 1541, 1548. Diesen Fall missversteht *P. Huber/Mullis/Mullis*, S. 163, nach dem die kürzere nationale Verjährungsfrist Vorrang haben sollte und der Käufer deshalb die Klagemöglichkeit schon vor Ablauf der Zweijahresfrist verlieren kann.
[169] Für die Schweiz vgl. *Schwenzer*, recht 1991, 113, 118. Zur Problematik im Rahmen von Schiedsverfahren vgl. *Schwenzer/Manner*, 23 Arb. Int'l (2007), 293, 300 f. Vgl. auch *Schlechtriem*, FS Jayme, S. 1353, 1356.
[170] Vgl. *Herber/Czerwenka*, Art. 39, Rn. 14; *Herber*, FS Schlechtriem, S. 207, 218; *Herber*, IHR 2001, 187, 189; *Schneider*, S. 246 f.; ebenso MünchKomm/*Gruber*, Art. 39, Rn. 48; *Schwenzer*, 101 ASIL Proc. 416, 421 (2007); a. A. oben *Ferrari*, Art. 5 Rn. 11 f.; *Ferrari u. a./Ferrari*, Internationales Vertragsrecht, Art. 39, Rn. 31; Staudinger/*Magnus*, Art. 39, Rn. 62 und Art. 5, Rn. 11 ff., 14; *Witz/Salger/Lorenz/Salger*, Art. 39, Rn. 2.; *Lookofsky*, Understanding the CISG, S. 78, möchte die Entscheidung dem Ermessen der entsprechenden Richter und Schiedsrichter überlassen.
[171] Vgl. Staudinger/*Magnus*, Art. 39, Rn. 59; MünchKomm/*Gruber*, Art. 39, Rn. 48.
[172] Vgl. OLG Düsseldorf, 8.1.1993, CISG-online 76 = RIW 1993, 325; OLG Koblenz, 31.1.1997, CISG-online 256; Staudinger/*Magnus*, Artt. 39, Rn. 59; *Herber/Czerwenka*, Art. 39, Rn. 15; *Enderlein/Maskow/Strohbach*, Art. 39, Anm. 1.; *Honnold/Flechtner*, Art. 39, 40, 44, Rn. 259; für Minderlieferung a. A. *Stumpf*, 1. Aufl., Artt. 39 Rn. 11.
[173] Einzelheiten unten bei *Müller-Chen*, Art. 52 Rn. 10; vgl. OLG Rostock, 25.9.2002, CISG-online 672 = IHR 2003, 19, 20; dagegen inkorrekt Civ. 1., 4.1.1995, CISG-online 138 = RIW 1995, 811.

erhöhung auch bei **Lieferung von höherwertiger Ware** (bessere Qualität, höherwertiges aliud) in Betracht kommt.[174] In der Sache erscheint eine Analogie zu Art. 52 II insoweit geboten, da sonst auf ausserkaufrechtliche Rechtsbehelfe des Verkäufers nach unvereinheitlichtem nationalen Recht zurückgegriffen werden müsste[175] und damit u. U. Wertungswidersprüche zum CISG auftreten könnten. Bei Lieferung höherwertiger Ware wird freilich oft Art. 40 eingreifen, so dass sich der Verkäufer schon deshalb auf eine Rügeversäumnis nicht berufen kann und es beim ursprünglichen Kaufpreis verbleibt. Versäumt der Käufer beim **Sukzessivlieferungsvertrag** die Rüge bezüglich einer Teillieferung, so verliert er die Rechte nur im Hinblick auf diese, nicht aber auch das Recht, Vertragsaufhebung nach Art. 73 II hinsichtlich der noch nicht gelieferten weiteren Teilmengen zu begehren.[176]

2. Ausnahmen

a) **Art. 40.** Die Rechtsfolgen unterlassener Rüge treten nicht ein, wenn die Vertragswidrigkeit auf Tatsachen beruht, die der Verkäufer kannte oder über die er nicht in Unkenntnis sein konnte und die er dem Käufer nicht offenbart hat.[177] Die Ausschlussfrist des Art. 39 II greift in diesem Fall nicht ein. **31**

b) **Art. 44.** Hat der Käufer für das Unterlassen der Rüge eine vernünftige Entschuldigung,[178] so verbleibt ihm jedenfalls das Recht auf Minderung und auf Schadenersatz unter Ausnahme des Schadenersatzes für entgangenen Gewinn. Auch diese Rechtsbehelfe unterliegen freilich der zweijährigen Ausschlussfrist nach Art. 39 II. **32**

c) **Verzicht des Verkäufers.** Der Verkäufer kann auf den Einwand, die Anzeige der Vertragswidrigkeit sei nicht rechtzeitig oder nicht gehörig erfolgt, verzichten, was insbesondere **konkludent**, auch schon vor Lieferung,[179] möglich ist.[180] Ein solcher Verzicht kann weitergehend als nach internem deutschen Recht[181] immer dann angenommen werden, wenn der Verkäufer **vorbehaltlos** die Vertragswidrigkeit anerkennt, die Ware zurücknimmt,[182] sich zur Nachbesserung oder Ersatzlieferung bereit erklärt[183] oder sich vorbehaltlos auf die sachliche Prüfung der gerügten Mängel einlässt.[184] In der blossen Aufnahme von **Verhandlungen** über die gerügten Mängel ist noch kein Verzicht zu sehen.[185] Dasselbe gilt für die Zusage einer Nachbesserung bei gleichzeitigem Verlangen vollständiger Zahlung[186] sowie Geltendmachung des Verspätungseinwandes erstmals vor Gericht.[187] Ein Verzicht ist **33**

---

[174] Bejahend: unten *Müller-Chen*, Art. 52 Rn. 11; *Herber/Czerwenka*, Art. 39, Rn. 15; *Staudinger/Magnus*, Art. 39, Rn. 60; *Karollus*, S. 77; *Resch*, ÖJZ 1992, 470, 474; MünchKomm/*Gruber*, Art. 38, Rn. 16 f.; *Kröll u. a./Kröll*, Art. 39, Rn. 101; verneinend: *Piltz*, Internationales Kaufrecht, Rn. 7–97.
[175] So ausdrücklich unten *Müller-Chen*, Art. 52 Rn. 11.
[176] Vgl. Schiedsgericht der Börse für landwirtschaftliche Produkte – Wien, 10.12.1997, CISG-online 351; *Staudinger/Magnus*, Art. 39, Rn. 59.
[177] Einzelheiten unten bei Art. 40 Rn. 4 ff.
[178] Einzelheiten unten bei Art. 44 Rn. 4 ff.
[179] Vgl. OGH, 15.10.1998, CISG-online 380.
[180] Vgl. ausführlich hierzu *Schlechtriem*, 50 Jahre BGH, S. 407, 434 f.; *Herber/Czerwenka*, Art. 39, Rn. 17; MünchKomm/*Gruber*, Art. 39, Rn. 52; vgl. auch *P. Huber/Mullis/Mullis*, S. 167 f.; zum internen deutschen Recht vgl. *Staub/Brüggemann*, § 377 HGB, Rn. 172; zum österreichischen Recht vgl. *Straube/Kramer*, §§ 377 f. HGB, Rn. 28 ff.
[181] Wonach „eindeutige Umstände" erforderlich sind: BGH, 29.3.1978, NJW 1978, 2394, 2395; BGH, 19.6.1991, NJW 1991, 2633, 2634; *Koller/Roth/Morck/Roth*, § 377, Rn. 33.
[182] Vgl. OGH, 5.7.2001, CISG-online 652 = ZfRVgl 2002, 25.
[183] Vgl. Trib Forlì, 9.12.2008, CISG-online 1788.
[184] So auch BGH, 25.6.1997, CISG-online 277 = NJW 1997, 3311, 3312; BGH, 25.11.1998, CISG-online 353 = NJW 1999, 1261, m. Anm. *Schlechtriem/Schmidt-Kessel*, EWiR 1999, 257 f.; *Heilmann*, S. 330.
[185] Vgl. BGH, 25.11.1998, CISG-online 353; OLG Oldenburg, 5.12.2000, CISG-online 618.
[186] Zum EKG vgl. LG Heidelberg, 21.4.1981, in: *Schlechtriem/Magnus*, Art. 39 EKG, Nr. 21.
[187] Vgl. MünchKomm/*Gruber*, Art. 39, Rn. 46; OLG Oldenburg, 5.12.2000, CISG-online 618 = IHR 2001, 112.

nicht von Amts wegen zu berücksichtigen, sondern muss vor Gericht geltend gemacht werden.[188]

33a **d) Verwirkung.** Fraglich ist, ob über Artt. 40, 44 hinausgehend auch eine Verwirkung der Einrede der verspäteten Anzeige der Vertragswidrigkeit denkbar ist.[189] Zwar liegt unzweifelhaft auch dem CISG der allgemeine Grundsatz des Verbots des **venire contra factum proprium**[190] zugrunde. Will man jedoch den in den Artt. 38 ff. vorgenommenen Interessenausgleich nicht beiseiteschieben, ist die Annahme eines Verzichts auf Fälle zu beschränken, in denen der Verkäufer im Käufer das berechtigte Vertrauen erweckte, er werde sich nicht auf Rügeversäumung berufen, und der Käufer deshalb die Vornahme anderer Schritte unterlassen hat.

33b Art. 39 liegt grundsätzlich das **Alles-oder-Nichts-Prinzip** zugrunde. Eine flexiblere Handhabung wird indes den Interessen beider Parteien oft besser gerecht. Sinnvoller kann es deshalb sein, die Anforderungen an die Rüge einerseits drastisch herabzusetzen, andererseits den Käufer für einen möglichen Schaden des Verkäufers, den dieser aufgrund der Rügepflichtverletzung erlitten hat, einstehen zu lassen. Eine solche Vertragsgestaltung ist den Parteien anzuraten (vgl. auch unten Art. 74 Rn. 13).

33c **e) Anderweitige Kenntniserlangung.** Die Rechtsfolgen unterlassener Rüge treten dann nicht ein, wenn der Verkäufer im Zeitpunkt des Ablaufs der Rügefrist auf andere Weise – z. B. durch Anzeige durch Dritte – Kenntnis von der Vertragswidrigkeit erlangt hat.[191]

33d **f) Keine Nachteile für Verkäufer.** Fraglich ist, ob sich der Verkäufer auch dann auf unterlassene Rüge berufen kann, wenn ihm daraus keinerlei Nachteile entstanden sind. Während namentlich US-amerikanische Autoren[192] und Gerichte[193] diese Frage verneinen, dürfte diese Auffassung Gerichten im deutschen Rechtskreis aufgrund ihres Vorverständnisses nur schwer nahe zu bringen sein.

VII. Abdingbarkeit

1. Im Allgemeinen

34 Art. 39 ist dispositiver Natur. Die Parteien können deshalb die Pflicht zur Anzeige der Vertragswidrigkeit ganz **abbedingen,**[194] Einzelheiten der Rüge, z. B. Form und Inhalt,[195] **näher festlegen**[196] oder die **Frist verkürzen** oder **verlängern.**[197] Auch eine Modifizie-

---

[188] Vgl. OGH, 2.4.2009, CISG-online 1889.
[189] So Int. Schiedsgericht der Bundeskammer der gewerblichen Wirtschaft in Wien, 15.6.1994, CISG-online 121 = 691 = RIW 1995, 590, m. krit. Anm. *Schlechtriem*. Vgl. auch *Ferrari u. a./Ferrari*, Internationales Vertragsrecht, Art. 39, Rn. 7.
[190] Vgl. oben *Ferrari*, Art. 7 Rn. 50.
[191] Vgl. MünchKomm/*Gruber*, Art. 39, Rn. 47; *Staudinger/Magnus*, Art. 39, Rn. 55.; *Benedick*, Informationspflichten, Rn. 1200 ff. erachtet den Verkäufer sogar als verpflichtet, den Käufer zu informieren, wenn er nach Lieferung Mängel feststellt, die eine Gefahr für den Käufer oder andere darstellen könnten.
[192] So vor allem *Flechtner*, Draft Digest, S. 387 f.; *ders.*, 26 B. U. Int'l L. J. (2008), 18 ff.; *Honnold/Flechtner*, Artt. 39, 40, 44, Rn 257.1; vgl. auch § 2–607 (3) (a) UCC-Draft v. 2.8.2002, wonach „failure to give timely notice bars the buyer from a remedy only to the extent that the seller is prejudiced by the failure".
[193] Vgl. U. S. Bankr. D. Or., In re: *Siskiyou Evergreens, Inc.*, 29.3.2004, CISG-online 1174: Als versteckte Mängel an Weihnachtsbäumen entdeckt wurden, war die Weihnachtssaison praktisch vorbei. Eine Nacherfüllung sei deshalb mangels Nutzen für den Käufer nicht mehr möglich gewesen. Vgl. dazu auch *Andersen*, FS Schwenzer, S. 33, 45 („does-it-actually-make-a-difference-approach"). Die innere Logik dieser Entscheidung erscheint bedenklich, da sie die den Verkäufer schützende Rüge als nutzlos und damit entbehrlich einstuft, weil der Käufer kein Interesse an einer Nacherfüllung hat.
[194] Vgl. *Andersen*, Reasonable Time, III.1.3.1. A. A. *DiMatteo/Dhooge/Greene/Maurer/Pagnattaro*, 34 Nw. Int'l L. & Bus. (2004), 229, 366, die starke Einschränkungen vorschlagen.
[195] Vgl. ICC, 7731/1994, ICC Ct. Bull. (1995), 73 (Beifügung eines Gutachtens).
[196] Vgl. OGH, 30.6.1998, CISG-online 410 (6 bzw. 12 Stunden nach COFREUROP im Obsthandel).
[197] Vgl. OGH, 19.12.2007, CISG-online 1628 = IHR 2008, 106, 108, m. Anm. *P. Huber*, IPRax 2009, 89; RB Arnhem, 11.2.2009, CISG-online 1813; AppGer Tessin, 8.6.1999, CISG-online 497; vgl. auch die Praxishinweise bei *Rudolph*, Art. 39, Rn. 23 ff.

rung der Rechtsfolgen bei unterlassener Rüge ist denkbar. Die Wirksamkeit solcher Vereinbarungen bestimmt sich nach nationalem Recht (Art. 4 a)).

Ist **deutsches Recht** Vertragsstatut, so sind im Rahmen des § 307 BGB die grundlegenden Wertungen des CISG zu beachten. Einer **Verkürzung der Rügefrist** nach Abs. 1 dürften kaum Bedenken entgegenstehen,[198] sofern sie den Käufer namentlich bei verdeckten Mängeln nicht der generellen Möglichkeit, diese geltend zu machen, beraubt. Die Wirksamkeit einer **Verkürzung der Ausschlussfrist** nach Abs. 2 wird vor allem von der Art der Ware und des Mangels sowie den entsprechenden Handelsbräuchen abhängen.[199] Zur Wirksamkeit des **Ausschlusses der Rügepflicht** und der **Verlängerung der Rügefrist** vgl. oben Art. 38 Rn. 29.   35

2. Garantieerklärungen

Vgl. hierzu oben Rn. 26.   36

VIII. Beweislast

Der **Käufer** trägt die Beweislast für die **ordnungsgemässe Absendung** der Anzeige.[200] Da Art. 27 neben dem Verlustrisiko zugleich das Beweisrisiko abdeckt, braucht der Käufer den Zugang der Anzeige nicht zu beweisen.[201] Bei Anzeige mittels Telefax muss die Vorlage des Schriftstücks und des Sendeberichts ausreichen. Rüge per E-Mail kann durch Ausdruck der gesendeten E-Mail bewiesen werden.[202] Bei **schriftlicher Mängelrüge** wird der Beweis der Absendung in der Regel durch Vorlage eines Annahmebelegs der Post erbracht.[203] Bei **telefonischer Anzeige** muss der Käufer jedenfalls genaue Angaben zum Datum und zum Namen des Gesprächspartners machen können.[204]   37

Ist streitig, ob die Anzeige noch rechtzeitig innerhalb der **zweijährigen Ausschlussfrist** nach Abs. 2 erfolgt ist, so trägt der Käufer auch hierfür die Beweislast, denn regelmässig wird nur er in der Lage sein, den genauen Termin der Aushändigung der Ware nachzuweisen.[205]   38

---

[198] Vgl. OLG München, 11.3.1998, CISG-online 310 (14-Tage-Frist gemäss Einheitsbedingungen der Deutschen Textilindustrie), m. Anm. *Schlechtriem*, EWiR 1998, 549 f.; LG Baden-Baden, 14.8.1991, CISG-online 24 = RIW 1992, 62 (30 Tage-Frist bei Fliesen); OLG Saarbrücken, 13.1.1993, CISG-online 83.

[199] Vgl. *Herber/Czerwenka*, Art. 39, Rn. 19; *Detzer/Thamm*, BB 1992, 2369, 2376 empfehlen dem Verkäufer ausdrücklich, die Garantiefrist vertraglich zu verkürzen; für Unzulässigkeit einer solchen Klausel hingegen *Teklote*, S. 217.

[200] OGH, 24.5.2005, CISG-online 2005, 249; Gerechtshof Arnhem, 18.7.2006, CISG-online 1266; LG München I, 18.5.2009, CISG-online 1998; LG Stuttgart, 15.10.2009, CISG-online 2019; Audiencia Provincial de Barcelona, 24.3.2009, CISG-online 2042; Polimeles Protodikio Athinon, 2009, CISG-online 2228; *Ramos Muñoz*, Communication of Defects, V) 6); zahlreiche weitere Nachweise bei MünchKomm/*Gruber*, Art. 39, Rn. 55. Ausführlich zur Beweislast *Antweiler*, S. 128 ff.; *T. M. Müller*, Beweislast, S. 104 ff.

[201] Anders offenbar LG Darmstadt, 29.5.2001, CISG-online 686 = IHR 2001, 160, 161, m. abl. Anm. *Piltz*, IHR 2001, 162 f.

[202] So auch *Kröll u. a./Kröll*, Art. 39, Rn. 126.

[203] Zum EKG vgl. LG Osnabrück, 19.2.1982, in: *Schlechtriem/Magnus*, Art. 59 EKG, Nr. 11.

[204] Vgl. OLG Frankfurt a. M., 23.5.1995, CISG-online 185; OLG Koblenz, 18.11.1999, CISG-online 570 = IHR 2001, 109, 111; LG Kassel, 22.6.1995, CISG-online 370; LG Marburg, 12.12.1995, CISG-online 148 = NJW-RR 1996, 760; Hof van Beroep Gent, 28.1.2004, CISG-online 830; *Staudinger/Magnus*, Art. 39, Rn. 72; *T. M. Müller*, Beweislast, S. 105; krit. *Karollus*, 1 Rev. CISG (1995), 51, 71.

[205] Vgl. *Heuzé*, Anm. 306.; a. A. *Antweiler*, S. 135; diff. *T. M. Müller*, Beweislast, S. 111 f.

Art. 40 [Bösgläubigkeit des Verkäufers]

Der Verkäufer kann sich auf die Artikel 38 und 39 nicht berufen, wenn die Vertragswidrigkeit auf Tatsachen beruht, die er kannte oder über die er nicht in Unkenntnis sein konnte und die er dem Käufer nicht offenbart hat.

Art. 40
The seller is not entitled to rely on the provisions of articles 38 and 39 if the lack of conformity relates to facts of which he knew or could not have been unaware and which he did not disclose to the buyer.

Art. 40
Le vendeur ne peut pas se prévaloir des dispositions des articles 38 et 39 lorsque le défaut de conformité porte sur des faits qu'il connaissait ou ne pouvait ignorer et qu'il n'a pas révélés à l'acheteur.

Übersicht

	Rn.
I. Vorgeschichte	1
II. Allgemeines	2
III. Voraussetzungen	4
1. Kenntnis oder nicht in Unkenntnis sein können	4
2. Keine Offenbarung	7
3. Zeitpunkt	8
IV. Rechtsfolgen	9
1. Nach CISG	9
2. Nach nationalem Recht	10
V. Abdingbarkeit	11
VI. Beweislast	12

Vorläufer und **Entwürfe:** Art. 40 EKG, Genfer E 1976 Art. 24, Wiener E 1977 Art. 24, New Yorker E 1978 Art. 38.

I. Vorgeschichte

1   Art. 40 wurde praktisch wörtlich aus dem EKG – Art. 40 – übernommen und gab im Rahmen der Abkommensentstehung keinen Anlass zu Diskussionen.[1]

II. Allgemeines

2   Die nicht rechtzeitige oder nicht gehörige Anzeige bleibt **ohne Konsequenzen,** wenn der Verkäufer die Tatsachen, auf denen die Vertragswidrigkeit beruht, kannte oder darüber nicht in Unkenntnis sein konnte. Auch hier zeigt sich das CISG wesentlich **käuferfreundlicher** als namentlich die Rechtsordnungen des deutschen Rechtskreises, die eine Ausnahme vom Verlust der Rechtsbehelfe bei Rügeversäumnis nur im Falle der Arglist des Verkäufers kennen.[2] Die meisten nationalen Regelungen verlangen hingegen lediglich grobe Fahrlässigkeit.[3]

---

[1] Vgl. YB IV (1973), S. 49, Nr. 92.
[2] Vgl. Deutschland: § 377 V HGB; Schweiz: Art. 203 OR; jetzt käuferfreundlicher: Österreich: § 377 V UGB, der eine Ausnahme für den Fall enthält, dass der Verkäufer die Vertragswidrigkeit entweder willentlich oder in grob fahrlässiger Art und Weise verursacht oder verbirgt, vgl. Krejci/Schauer UGB § 377, Rn. 17 ff.
[3] Vgl. *Schwenzer/Hachem/Kee,* Rn. 34.87.

Art. 40 stellt eine Konkretisierung des allgemeinen Grundsatzes von Treu und Glauben 2a dar[4] und bringt zum Ausdruck, dass ein Verkäufer, der den Mangel jedenfalls hätte entdecken müssen, keine Rüge benötigt und so des Schutzes durch Art. 39 ausnahmsweise nicht bedarf.[5]

Art. 43 II enthält für **Rechtsmängel** und **Belastung mit Schutzrechten** eine Art. 40 3 entsprechende Regelung, wobei dort freilich allein auf positive Kenntnis des Verkäufers abgestellt wird.

III. Voraussetzungen

1. Kenntnis oder nicht in Unkenntnis sein können

Nicht in Unkenntnis sein können ist mehr als **grobe Fahrlässigkeit**.[6] Es muss sich 4 vielmehr um ins Auge springende Vertragswidrigkeiten handeln.[7] Insoweit stellt die Formulierung eine Beweiserleichterung für anders nur schwer zu beweisende Kenntnis dar.[8] Teilweise wird sogar ein noch strengerer Massstab angelegt.[9]

Über welche Vertragswidrigkeiten der Verkäufer solchermassen **nicht in Unkenntnis** 5 **sein konnte**, hängt vor allem von seiner Stellung im Wirtschaftsverkehr und der Art der Ware und der Vertragswidrigkeit ab.[10] Eine generelle **Untersuchungspflicht** für jeden Verkäufer kann nicht angenommen werden.[11] Auch kann nicht bei jedem gewerblichen Verkäufer Bösgläubigkeit unterstellt werden.[12] Bei **Quantitätsabweichung** und **aliud-Lieferung** wird man oft davon ausgehen können, dass der Verkäufer hierüber nicht in

---

[4] Vgl. Oberster Gerichtshof Israel, 17.3.2009, CISG-online 1980, Rn. 27; Hof van Beroep Antwerpen, 27.6.2001, CISG-online 2342; *Kröll u. a./Kröll*, Art. 40, Rn. 4; vgl. auch *Staudinger/Magnus*, Art. 40, Rn. 1 („unbillig und mit den Grundsätzen redlichen Geschäftsverkehrs nicht vereinbar").

[5] Vgl. Oberster Gerichtshof Israel, 17.3.2009, CISG-online 1980, Rn. 27, 31; OGH, 14.2.2012, CISG-online 2308; *Honnold/Flechtner*, Artt. 39, 40, 44, Rn. 260.

[6] Vgl. oben Art. 35 Rn. 35; so auch *Beijing Light Automobile Co., Ltd. v. Connell Limited Partnership*, SCC Institute, 5.6.1998, CISG-online 379 = SZIER 1999, 204 f.; OLG Zweibrücken, 2.2.2004, CISG-online 877, E. II. 6; *Andersen*, 9 VJ (2005), 17, 25 ff.; *Garro*, 25 J. L. & Com. (2005), 253, 257 f.; *Honnold/Flechtner*, Art. 35, Rn. 229; *Heilmann*, S. 340 f.; i. S. grober Fahrlässigkeit wird die Bestimmung interpretiert von *Schlechtriem*, Internationales UN-Kaufrecht, Rn. 156; *Staudinger/Magnus*, Art. 40, Rn. 5; MünchKommHGB/*Benicke*, Art. 40, Rn. 2; *Brunner*, Art. 40, Rn. 2; *Herber/Czerwenka*, Art. 40, Rn. 2; *Welser*, S. 113; *Soergel/Lüderitz/Schüßler-Langeheine*, Art. 40, Rn. 3; *Kröll u. a./Kröll*, Art. 40, Rn. 13; *Neumayer/Ming*, Art. 40, Anm. 2. (annäherungsweise bewusste Fahrlässigkeit); *Loewe*, Art. 40, S. 61; *Karollus*, S. 128; *Hutter*, S. 95; *Resch*, ÖJZ 1992, 470, 478; BGH, 30.6.2004, CISG-online 847 = NJW 2004, 3181; OLG Celle, 10.3.2004, CISG-online 824 = IHR 2004, 106, 107; OLG Düsseldorf, 23.1.2004, CISG-online 918; OLG Hamm, 2.4.2009, CISG-online 1978, Rn. 77; *P. Huber/Mullis/Mullis*, S. 165: einfache Fahrlässigkeit reicht nicht aus. *Enderlein/Maskow/Strohbach*, Art. 40, Anm. 3. und wohl auch *P. Widmer*, Droits et obligations du vendeur, S. 102 halten sogar eine Auslegung i. S. einfacher Fahrlässigkeit für möglich.

[7] Vgl. OLG Zweibrücken, 2.2.2004, CISG-online 877, E. II. 6; LG Trier, 12.10.1995, CISG-online 160 = NJW-RR 1996, 564, 565 (mit Wasser versetzter Wein). In der Sache handelte es sich auch in den Fällen, in denen von der Rechtsprechung zu Art. 40 EKG „nicht in Unkenntnis sein können" angenommen wurde, immer um augenfällige Fehler, vgl. OLG Hamm, 6.7.1981, in: *Schlechtriem/Magnus*, Art. 40 EKG, Nr. 3; OLG Hamm, 17.9.1981, in: *Schlechtriem/Magnus*, Art. 40 EKG, Nr. 4; OLG Hamm, 19.12.1983, in: *Schlechtriem/Magnus*, Art. 40 EKG, Nr. 7; OLG Koblenz, 18.5.1984, in: *Schlechtriem/Magnus*, Art. 44 EKG, Nr. 6.

[8] Zur Beweislast vgl. unten Rn. 12.

[9] Vgl. CA Rouen, 19.12.2006, CISG-online 1933: Art. 40 verlange eine „*dissimulation*", in die gleiche Richtung auch Com., 16.9.2008, CISG-online 1821 = 1851.

[10] Vgl. *Audit*, Vente internationale, Anm. 112.; *Heuzé*, Anm. 310.; *Ramos Muñoz*, Communication of Defects, VII) 2) B). Vgl. auch OLG Hamm, 2.4.2009, CISG-online 1978, Rn. 78 (Autohändler zu Sichtprüfung verpflichtet).

[11] Vgl. OLG Oldenburg, 28.4.2000, CISG-online 683 (verpackte Ware).

[12] Dies in Abweichung vom internen französischen Recht, vgl. *Audit*, Vente internationale, Anm. 112.; *Heuzé*, Anm. 310.; *Mouly*, D. 1991, Chron. 77, 78; *Ghestin/Desché*, Traité des contrats, Anm. 1056., 1058.; *Niggemann*, RIW 1991, 372, 375. Ausführlich zur vermuteten Bösgläubigkeit des vendeur professionnel *Ghestin/Desché*, Traité des contrats, Anm. 852. ff. Zuweilen verfallen französische Gerichte nun allerdings ins andere Extrem und übersehen Art. 40, vgl. CA Paris, 6.11.2001, CISG-online 677 = D. 2002, 2795, m. krit. Anm. *C. Witz*.

Unkenntnis sein konnte,[13] es sei denn, es hat lediglich eine leicht fahrlässige Verwechslung stattgefunden.[14] Hat sich freilich ein **Zwischenhändler** bei original verpackter Ware auf Angaben des Herstellers verlassen, kann ihm Kennenmüssen nicht unterstellt werden. Bei **Qualitätsabweichungen** kommt es vor allem darauf an, ob der Verkäufer selbst Hersteller der Ware oder blosser Zwischenhändler ist.[15] Der **Hersteller** kann über Fehler, die bei oberflächlicher Kontrolle oder einer Serienprobe ohne weiteres erkennbar sind, nicht in Unkenntnis sein.[16] Kenntnis ist auch zu unterstellen bei Mängeln, die bei bereits verkauften Produkten zu Tage getreten sind und über die in der Fachpresse berichtet wurde, oder – allgemeiner gesprochen – die dem Hersteller auf Grund seiner Produktbeobachtungspflicht bekannt sein müssten.[17] Allerdings ist bei Herstellern, die eine grössere Anzahl von Produkten in grösseren Mengen herstellen und vermarkten, für eine Anwendung von Art. 40 erforderlich, dass die bekannten früheren Mängel gerade bei dem in casu mangelhaften Produkt aufgetreten sind.[18] Beim **Zwischenhändler** wird jedoch Bösgläubigkeit in Bezug auf verdeckte Mängel nur äusserst selten angenommen werden können.[19] Im Fall der Lieferung höherwertiger Güter wird sich der Verkäufer aufgrund von Art. 40 meist nicht darauf berufen können, dass der Käufer nicht ordnungsgemäss gerügt hat.[20] Eine amtliche Zertifizierung spricht in Bezug auf das Fehlen von zertifizierten Eigenschaften gegen ein Kennenmüssen des Verkäufers.[21]

6   Das Wissen von **Hilfspersonen** – eigenes Personal und Erfüllungsgehilfen im engeren Sinne[22] – ist dem Verkäufer zuzurechnen,[23] sowie auch das von blossen Zulieferern. Dies gilt indes nicht für neutrale Prüfer, von denen die Untersuchung für beide Parteien durchgeführt wird.[24]

2. Keine Offenbarung

7   Art. 40 setzt weiter voraus, dass der Verkäufer dem Käufer die Vertragswidrigkeit nicht offenbart hat. Diese Bestimmung ist missverständlich.[25] Eine **allgemeine Offenbarungspflicht** des Verkäufers kann hieraus nicht abgeleitet werden.[26] Hat der Verkäufer dem Käufer Mängel bereits anlässlich des Vertragsschlusses mitgeteilt, so fehlt es bereits an den

---

[13] Vgl. *Heuzé*, Anm. 310.; für aliud auch *Staudinger/Magnus*, Art. 40, Rn. 6; *Piltz*, Internationales Kaufrecht, Rn. 5–102; *Kröll u. a./Kröll*, Art. 40, Rn. 15.
[14] Vgl. *Ziegler*, S. 101. Zur Lieferung höherwertiger Ware vgl. auch oben Art. 35 Rn. 9; Art. 39 Rn. 30; unten *Müller-Chen*, Art. 52 Rn. 11.
[15] Vgl. *Heuzé*, Anm. 310. Vgl. auch OGH, 27.2.2003, CISG-online 794 = IHR 2004, 25 ff. (Fisch nicht entsprechend Handelsbrauch als letzter Fangquote); Civ. 1, 4.10.2005, CISG-online 1097 = J. C. P. 2005, éd. G, IV, 3342 (Verkäufer verweigert Vorlage von Testberichten).
[16] Vgl. *Beijing Light Automobile Co., Ltd. v. Connell Limited Partnership*, SCC Institute, 5.6.1998, CISG-online 379 = SZIER 1999, 204, 205; *Staudinger/Magnus*, Art. 40, Rn. 5.
[17] Vgl. Shanghai First Intermediate People's Court, 25.12.2008, CISG-online 2059 (andere Cognacsorte), zustimmend hierzu *Piltz*, NJW 2011, 2261, 2265; *Otto*, MDR 1992, 533, 535.
[18] Vgl. Oberster Gerichtshof Israel, 17.3.2009, CISG-online 1980, Rn. 45 f.; vgl. auch *Kröll u. a./Kröll*, Art. 40, Rn. 9.
[19] Vgl. *Kröll u. a./Kröll*, Art. 40, Rn. 18.
[20] Vgl. oben Art. 35 Rn. 9; Art. 39 Rn. 30; unten *Müller-Chen*, Art. 52 Rn. 11.
[21] Vgl. CA Rouen, 19.12.2006, CISG-online 1933; bestätigt durch Com. 1, 16.9.2008, CISG-online 1821 – 1851; zustimmend *Piltz*, NJW 2011, 2261, 2265.
[22] Vgl. dazu unten Art. 79 Rn. 34 ff.
[23] Vgl. ICC, 9187/1999, CISG-online 705 = 11:2 ICC Int. Ct. Arb. Bull. (2000), 94: analog Art. 79 II; so auch *Witz/Salger/Lorenz/Salger*, Art. 40, Rn. 4; *Staudinger/Magnus*, Art. 40, Rn. 9; *Herber/Czerwenka*, Art. 40, Rn. 5; *Reinhart*, Art. 40, Rn. 2; *Enderlein/Maskow/Strohbach*, Art. 40, Anm. 2.; *Karollus*, S. 128; *Resch*, ÖJZ 1992, 470, 478; zum EKG vgl. OLG Hamm, 19.12.1983, in: *Schlechtriem/Magnus*, Art. 40 EKG, Nr. 7; OLG Koblenz, 18.5.1984, in: *Schlechtriem/Magnus*, Art. 44 EKG, Nr. 6.
[24] ICC, 9187/1999, CISG-online 705 = 11:2 ICC Int. Ct. Arb. Bull. (2000), 94.
[25] Vgl. *Herber/Czerwenka*, Art. 40, Rn. 3; *Heuzé*, Anm. 310.
[26] Vgl. *Staudinger/Magnus*, Art. 40, Rn. 10; *Herber/Czerwenka*, Art. 40, Rn. 3; *Bamberger/Roth/Saenger*, Art. 40, Rn. 4; *Ebenroth*, östJBl 1986, 681, 690; a. A. *Enderlein/Maskow/Strohbach*, Art. 40, Anm. 1.; *Benedick*, Informationspflichten, Rn. 170 f.; *Heilmann*, S. 340; *Janssen*, S. 189; wohl auch *P. Widmer*, Droits et obligations du vendeur, S. 102; *Chaudet*, S. 125; *Ghestin/Desché*, Traité des contrats, Anm. 1055.; *Kröll u. a./Kröll*, Art. 40,

Haftungsvoraussetzungen nach Art. 35, sei es weil die vertraglichen Anforderungen zumindest konkludent den Eigenschaften der Ware angepasst wurden oder weil sich der Käufer gemäss Art. 35 III nicht auf den Mangel berufen kann.[27] Bei einer Offenbarung nach Vertragsschluss liegt zwar Vertragswidrigkeit vor; der Käufer wird die Ware dann im Regelfall zurückweisen oder billigen. Nichts spricht hier jedoch für die Notwendigkeit einer Mängelanzeige, wo der Käufer doch gerade vom Verkäufer die Kenntnis von der Vertragswidrigkeit erlangt hat.[28] In der Sache kann es sich deshalb nur um Fälle handeln, in denen der Verkäufer dem Käufer die **Gefahr eines Mangels** offenbart.[29] Hier macht es Sinn, vom Käufer eine Anzeige zu verlangen, wenn sich der Mangel als tatsächlich existent herausstellt.

3. Zeitpunkt

Art. 40 sagt nichts über den Zeitpunkt, in dem die Kenntnis oder das Nicht-in-Unkenntnis-Sein-Können des Verkäufers vorliegen muss. Von Sinn und Zweck der Rügepflicht ausgehend,[30] kann dies nicht der Zeitpunkt der Aushändigung der Ware sein.[31] Abzustellen ist vielmehr auf den normalen **Zeitpunkt des Ablaufs der Anzeigefrist** für den Käufer,[32] wenngleich auch die Fälle, in denen der Verkäufer nach Aushändigung der Ware von der Vertragswidrigkeit in anderer Weise als durch Anzeige des Käufers erfährt, selten sein dürften.[33]

IV. Rechtsfolgen

1. Nach CISG

Nach Art. 40 verliert der Verkäufer das Recht, sich auf eine Verletzung der Untersuchungs- und Rügepflicht durch den Käufer zu berufen. Auch die **Ausschlussfrist** des Art. 39 II greift in diesem Fall nicht ein.[34] Haben die Parteien **vertragliche Vereinbarungen** über die Untersuchungs- und Rügepflicht getroffen, so kann sich der Verkäufer auch auf diese zu seinen Gunsten nicht berufen.[35]

Rn. 25 („de facto"); unklar *Reinhart,* Art. 40, Rn. 2; anders offenbar auch ICC, 9083/1999, CISG-online 706 = 11:2 ICC Int. Ct. Arb. Bull. (2000), 78.
[27] Vgl. zu letzterem: *P. Huber/Mullis/Mullis,* S. 165.
[28] So auch *Ramos Muñoz,* Communication of Defects, VII) 6) A); *Honnold/Flechtner,* Artt. 39, 40, 44, Rn. 260. Anders OLG Rostock, 25.9.2002, CISG-online 672: Offene Zuviellieferungen, die in Dokumenten zutage treten, müssen gerügt werden; OLG Düsseldorf, 23.1.2004, CISG-online 918: Falsche Abmessungen der Stahlbleche auf Rechnungen.
[29] So auch *Herber/Czerwenka,* Art. 40, Rn. 3; *Heuzé,* Anm. 310.; *Honnold/Flechtner,* Artt. 39, 40, 44, Rn. 260; vgl. auch *Staudinger/Magnus,* Art. 40, Rn. 10.
[30] Vgl. dazu oben Art. 38 Rn. 3.
[31] So aber *Staudinger/Magnus,* Art. 40, Rn. 8; *Stumpf,* 1. Aufl., Art. 40 Rn. 6; *Herber/Czerwenka,* Art. 40, Rn. 4; *Enderlein/Maskow/Strohbach,* Art. 40, Anm. 2.; *Reinhart,* Art. 40, Rn. 2; *Witz/Salger/Lorenz/Salger,* Art. 40, Rn. 5; *Bamberger/Roth/Saenger,* Art. 40, Rn. 3; *Resch,* ÖJZ 1992, 470, 478; *Heilmann,* S. 339 f.; *Janssen,* S. 191.
[32] Wie hier MünchKomm/*Gruber,* Art. 40, Rn. 8; MünchKommHGB/*Benicke,* Art. 40, Rn. 5; *Kröll u. a./Kröll,* Art. 40, Rn. 23; *Brunner,* Art. 40, Rn. 2; *Ramos Muñoz,* Communication of Defects, VII) 3); *Honnold/Flechtner,* Artt. 39, 40, 44, Rn. 260; *Soergel/Lüderitz/Schüßler-Langeheine,* Art. 40, Rn. 2; *Neumayer/Ming,* Art. 40, Anm. 3.; *Antweiler,* S. 138; *Karollus,* S. 128; *Hutter,* S. 95; unklar *Garro,* 25 J. L. & Com. (2005), 253, 255.
[33] Zu denken ist an einen der gesamten Warengattung anhaftenden Konstruktionsfehler, der von anderen Abnehmern des Verkäufers gerügt wird, oder an Rügen von Abnehmern des Käufers, die direkt an den Verkäufer gerichtet werden.
[34] Vgl. *Staudinger/Magnus,* Art. 40, Rn. 11; MünchKomm/*Gruber,* Art. 40, Rn. 11; *Piltz,* Internationales Kaufrecht, Rn. 5–105; *Brunner,* Art. 40, Rn. 1.
[35] Vgl. *Staudinger/Magnus,* Art. 40, Rn. 12; *Ghestin,* Obligations du vendeur, S. 102; *Brunner,* Art. 40, Rn. 1.

2. Nach nationalem Recht

10 Neben den Rechtsbehelfen wegen Vertragswidrigkeit nach CISG kann sich der Käufer bei Kenntnis des Verkäufers von der Vertragswidrigkeit auf konkurrierende nationale Rechtsbehelfe – vor allem aus Delikt – wegen **Betrugs** stützen.[36] Weiterhin kann eine Anfechtung nach dem anwendbaren nationalen Recht wegen arglistiger Täuschung in Betracht kommen.[37] Die kurzen Verjährungsvorschriften für Gewährleistungsansprüche in manchen nationalen Rechtsordnungen[38] greifen jedenfalls bei Arglist des Verkäufers nicht ein;[39] ist deutsches Recht Vertragsstatut, so gilt dies nach Art. 3 VertragsG auch dann, wenn der Verkäufer über die Vertragswidrigkeit nicht in Unkenntnis sein konnte.

V. Abdingbarkeit

11 Zwar ist auch Art. 40 nach Art. 6 grundsätzlich abdingbar.[40] Jedoch gilt in den nationalen Rechtsordnungen übereinstimmend der Grundsatz, dass sich niemand von den Folgen eigenen **arglistigen Handelns** oder auch von **grober Fahrlässigkeit** freizeichnen kann,[41] so dass ein vertraglicher Ausschluss von Art. 40 im Ergebnis nicht in Betracht kommen dürfte.[42]

VI. Beweislast

12 Kenntnis oder nicht in Unkenntnis sein Können des Verkäufers hat grundsätzlich der **Käufer** zu beweisen.[43] Kann der Käufer aber beweisen, dass die Vertragswidrigkeit ihre Ursache im Verantwortungsbereich des Verkäufers hat, muss sich – unter dem Gesichtspunkt der Beweisnähe – der Verkäufer entlasten.[44] Beruft sich der Verkäufer darauf, dass er dem Käufer das Risiko einer Vertragswidrigkeit offenbart habe, so trägt er hierfür die Beweislast.[45]

---

[36] Vgl. *Herber*, 2. Aufl., Art. 4, Rn. 23.
[37] Vgl. *Brunner*, Art. 40, Rn. 1.
[38] Vgl. hierzu die Nachweise oben in Art. 39 Rn. 28, 29.
[39] Vgl. Deutschland: § 438 III BGB; Schweiz: Art. 210 III OR; Österreich: § 933 I ABGB.
[40] Wie hier *Andersen*, 9 VJ (2005), 17, 20 f.; *Garro*, 25 J. L. & Com. (2005), 253, 258. Anders aber offenbar *Beijing Light Automobile Co., Ltd. v. Connell Limited Partnership*, SCC Institute, 5.6.1998, CISG-online 379.
[41] Deutschland: vgl. §§ 276 III, 309 Nr. 7 b), 444 BGB; Schweiz: Artt. 100, 199 OR; Österreich: § 6 I Nr. 9 KSchG; Frankreich: Art. 1643 Cc; England: vgl. *Benjamin*, Rn. 13–081 f.; USA· vgl. *Schwenzer*, Freizeichnung, S. 69; vgl. auch rechtsvergleichend *Eörsi*, 23 Am. J. Comp. L. (1975), 215, 217.
[42] So das Schiedsgericht in seiner hilfsweisen Argumentation in *Beijing Light Automobile Co, Ltd. v. Connell Limited Partnership*, SCC Institute, 5.6.1998, CISG-online 379; ebenso *Brunner*, Art. 40, Rn. 1.
[43] Vgl. BGH, 30.6.2004, CISG-online 847 = IHR 2004, 201, 202 (Paprikapulver), m. Anm. *T. M. Müller*, IHR 2005, 16 ff.; OGH, 14.2.2012, CISG-online 2308; LG Flensburg, 19.1.2001, CISG-online 619; LG Lübeck, 30.12.2010, CISG-online 2292; LG Stendal, 12.10.2000, CISG-online 592; RB Roermond, 19.12.1991, CISG-online 29; *Antweiler*, S. 137; *Audit*, Vente internationale, Anm. 112.; *Heuzé*, Anm. 310.; *Kröll u. a./Kröll*, Art. 40, Rn. 28; *P. Huber/Mullis/Mullis*, S. 164; a. A. *Staudinger/Magnus*, Art. 40, Rn. 13; *Herber/Czerwenka*, Art. 40, Rn. 7.
[44] Vgl. BGH, 30.6.2004, CISG-online 847 = IHR 2004, 201, 202 (Paprikapulver), m. Anm. *T. M. Müller*, IHR 2005, 16 ff.; vgl. auch *T. M. Müller*, Beweislast, S. 112 ff.; *Garro*, 25 J. L. & Com. (2005), 253; *Andersen*, 9 VJ (2005), 17, 29 ff.
[45] Vgl. LG Landshut, 5.4.1995, CISG-online 193; *Kröll u. a./Kröll*, Art. 40, Rn. 31; *Heuzé*, Anm. 310.

Art. 41 [Rechtsmängel]

Der Verkäufer hat Ware zu liefern, die frei von Rechten oder Ansprüchen Dritter ist, es sei denn, daß der Käufer eingewilligt hat, die mit einem solchen Recht oder Anspruch behaftete Ware zu nehmen.* Beruhen jedoch solche Rechte oder Ansprüche auf gewerblichem oder anderem geistigen Eigentum, so regelt Artikel 42 die Verpflichtung des Verkäufers.

Art. 41

The seller must deliver goods which are free from any right or claim of a third party, unless the buyer agreed to take the goods subject to that right or claim. However, if such right or claim is based on industrial property or other intellectual property, the seller's obligation is governed by article 42.

Art. 41

Le vendeur doit livrer les marchandises libres de tout droit ou prétention d'un tiers, à moins que l'acheteur n'accepte de prendre les marchandises dans ces conditions. Toutefois, si ce droit ou cette prétention est fondé sur la propriété industrielle ou autre propriété intellectuelle, l'obligation du vendeur est régie par l'article 42.

Übersicht

	Rn.
I. Vorgeschichte	1
II. Eigentumsübertragung und gutgläubiger bzw lastenfreier Erwerb	2
III. Voraussetzungen der Rechtsmängelhaftung	3
1. Rechte Dritter	3
a) Verkauf einer fremden Sache	3
b) Belastungen mit dinglichen oder obligatorischen Rechten Dritter	4
c) Öffentlich-rechtliche Belastungen	5
d) Rechte auf Grund geistigen Eigentums	8
2. Ansprüche Dritter	9
3. Rechte oder Ansprüche Dritter auf Grund Verhaltens des Käufers	13
4. Eigene Rechte oder Ansprüche des Verkäufers	14
5. Massgeblicher Zeitpunkt	15
6. Räumlicher Anwendungsbereich	16a
IV. Ausschluss der Rechtsmängelhaftung	17
1. Einwilligung des Käufers	17
2. Unterlassene Anzeige	19
3. Freizeichnungsklauseln	19a
V. Rechtsbehelfe	20
1. Nach CISG	20
2. Nach nationalem Recht	22
VI. Beweislast	25

Vorläufer und **Entwürfe:** Art. 52 EKG, Genfer E 1976 Art. 25, Wiener E 1977 Art. 25 I, New Yorker E 1978 Art. 39 I.

I. Vorgeschichte

Die Regelung der allgemeinen Rechtsmängelhaftung in Art. 41 S. 1 entspricht vom **1** Grundsatz her Art. 52 EKG; sie ist jedoch redaktionell wesentlich klarer gefasst als jene des EKG,[1] die unter der Überschrift „Übertragung des Eigentums" stand und vom Wortlaut her primär die Anzeigepflicht des Käufers bei Rechtsmängeln betraf. Die entscheidende Neue-

---

* Österreich, Schweiz: belastete Ware anzunehmen.
[1] Vgl. YB IV (1974), S. 73, Nr. 104.

Art. 41 2, 3   Teil III. Kapitel II. Pflichten des Verkäufers. Abschnitt II

rung gegenüber dem EKG liegt darin, dass Art. 41 S. 2 ausdrücklich die Haftung des Verkäufers für Rechte oder Ansprüche Dritter, die auf gewerblichem oder anderem geistigen Eigentum beruhen, aus der allgemeinen Rechtsmängelhaftung herausnimmt und der Sonderregelung des Art. 42 unterwirft. Der Sache nach haftet der Verkäufer für die Freiheit von gewerblichen Schutzrechten nur unter sehr viel engeren Voraussetzungen als für sonstige Rechtsmängel.[2]

II. Eigentumsübertragung und gutgläubiger bzw. lastenfreier Erwerb

2   **Übertragung des Eigentums** und möglicher **gutgläubiger** oder **lastenfreier Erwerb** sind im CISG nicht geregelt, Art. 4 S. 2 b).[3] Hierüber entscheidet das nach dem internationalen Privatrecht des angerufenen Gerichts massgebliche Sachrecht, in der Regel die **lex rei sitae**. Zwar wird teilweise in neuerer Zeit auch im internationalen Sachenrecht eine beschränkte Rechtswahl für zulässig gehalten[4] bzw. die Eigentumsübertragung dem Vertragsstatut[5] unterworfen. Dies gilt jedoch grundsätzlich nur inter partes, Rechte Dritter bleiben davon unberührt;[6] insoweit verbleibt es bei der lex rei sitae.

III. Voraussetzungen der Rechtsmängelhaftung

1. Rechte Dritter

3   **a) Verkauf einer fremden Sache.** Die Verpflichtung des Verkäufers, Waren frei von Rechten Dritter zu liefern, entspricht der Regelung in den meisten nationalen Rechtsordnungen.[7] Art. 41 S. 1 greift zunächst ein, wenn der Verkäufer gar nicht in der Lage ist, dem Käufer Eigentum zu verschaffen, d. h. insbesondere beim **Verkauf einer fremden Sache,** wenn die nach anwendbarem nationalen Recht erforderlichen Voraussetzungen für einen gutgläubigen Erwerb nicht gegeben sind. Soweit **gutgläubiger Erwerb** seitens des Käufers eintritt, ist die Ware damit zwar frei von Rechten Dritter; eine Haftung des Verkäufers nach Art. 41 S. 1 kann gleichwohl in Betracht kommen,[8] wenn der Dritte aus seinem (früheren) Recht Ansprüche gegen den Käufer geltend macht.[9]

---

[2] Vgl. im Einzelnen zur Vorgeschichte unten Art. 42 Rn. 1 f.
[3] Zu diesbezüglichen Vereinheitlichungsbestrebungen vgl. Explanatory Report on Draft Uniform Law on the Protection of Bona Fide Purchaser of Corporal Movables (UNIDROIT 1968).
[4] Vgl. Schweiz: Art. 104 I IPRG; zur Diskussion in Deutschland vgl. *Staudinger/Stoll,* Int. SachenR, Rn. 216 ff.; MünchKomm/*Kreuzer,* nach Art. 38, Anh. I, Rn. 66 ff.
[5] Vgl. etwa die Auffassungen mancher französischer Autoren: *Gaudemet-Tallon,* Anm. zu Civ. 1, 8.7.1969, J. C. P. 1970, éd. G, II, 16 182, will es primär beim gewählten Recht belassen und nur hilfsweise auf die Situs-Regel zurückgreifen. *Mayer,* J. C. P. 1981, éd. E, II, 13 481 Rn. 14, spricht sich indessen für die auf den Schutz von Interessen Dritter begrenzte Anwendung der lex rei sitae aus, die praktisch nur als eine das gewählte Sachstatut korrigierende loi de police zum Zuge käme.
[6] Vgl. Schweiz: Art. 104 II IPRG; vgl. auch Art. 12 e) Haager Übereinkommen betreffend das auf internationale Kaufverträge über bewegliche Sachen anzuwendende Recht v. 22.12.1986 sowie Art. 2 Nr. 4 Haager Übereinkommen über das auf den Eigentumserwerb bei internationalen Käufen beweglicher Sachen anzuwendende Recht v. 15.4.1958, wo der Eigentumsvorbehalt ebenfalls nur inter partes dem Vertragsstatut unterstellt wird.
[7] Vgl. Deutschland: §§ 433 I 2, 435 BGB; Grossbritannien: sec. 12 SGA; USA § 2–312 (1) UCC; Schweiz: Artt. 192–196 OR; Frankreich: Artt. 1625 ff. Cc; Österreich: § 923 ABGB; rechtsvergleichend *Schwenzer/Hachem/Kee,* Rn. 32.01 m. w. N.
[8] Vgl. *U. Huber,* 1. Aufl., Art. 30 Rn. 15; *Karollus,* S. 123; *Wolff,* S. 68; a. A. *Neumayer/Ming,* Art. 41, Anm. 4.
[9] Vgl. dazu unten Rn. 12.

b) Belastungen mit dinglichen oder obligatorischen Rechten Dritter. Rechte 4 Dritter, für die der Verkäufer einzustehen hat, können **dinglicher** oder **obligatorischer** Natur sein; die Einzelheiten ergeben sich jeweils aus der lex rei sitae. Entscheidend ist, dass der Dritte auf Grund seines Rechtes auf die Sache einwirken oder den Käufer in sonstiger Weise in der Benutzung, Verwertung oder Verfügung beschränken kann.[10] Praktisch bedeutsam werden dabei vor allem **Sicherungsrechte** von Waren- und Geldkreditgläubigern des Verkäufers.[11] In Betracht kommen aber auch dingliche Besitzrechte, wie z. B. **Niessbrauch** oder **lease,** und obligatorische Rechte Dritter, die gegen den Käufer wirken.[12] **Sicherungsrechte,** wie sie sich namentlich zu Gunsten von **Lagerhaltern, Frachtführern** etc. finden – gleichgültig, ob nach der jeweiligen nationalen Rechtsordnung mit dinglicher oder nur obligatorischer Wirkung ausgestattet – werden zwar oft bereits Lieferung verhindern und damit nach Art. 30 zu beurteilen sein;[13] wo jedoch Lieferung erfolgt ist und das Sicherungsrecht fortbesteht, lösen sie die Rechtsmängelhaftung aus.[14] Bei Verträgen über herzustellende Waren kommen weiterhin Werkunternehmer- oder Bauhandwerkerpfandrechte[15] in Betracht, soweit diese Rechte nach dem jeweiligen nationalen Recht in Bezug auf in den Anwendungsbereich des CISG fallende Waren[16] entstehen.[17] Auch **Anfechtungsrechte** nach nationalem **Konkursrecht** oder dergleichen[18] sowie nationale Rechtsregeln zur **Vermögensübernahme,** die wie § 1409 ABGB zwar zunächst nur eine Haftung des Käufers statuieren, letztendlich aber dem Dritten Zugriff auf die Sache ermöglichen,[19] stellen einen Rechtsmangel i. S. d. Art. 41 S. 1 dar. **Schuldrechtliche Bindungen,** die nur den Verkäufer persönlich treffen, wie z. B. ein zeitlich früherer Verkauf an einen Dritten, begründen zwar – soweit noch keine Eigentumsübertragung stattgefunden hat – kein Recht des Dritten an der Sache,[20] sie können jedoch dann zur Haftung nach Art. 41 S. 1 führen, wenn der Dritte daraus einen **Anspruch** gegen den Käufer ableitet.[21]

---

[10] Vgl. *Schlechtriem,* Internationales UN-Kaufrecht, Rn. 165; *Staudinger/Magnus,* Art. 41, Rn. 7, 10; *P. Huber/Mullis/Mullis,* S. 170; *Reinhart,* Art. 41, Rn. 3; *Herber/Czerwenka,* Art. 41, Rn. 3; *Enderlein/Maskow/Strohbach,* Art. 41, Anm. 2.; *Loewe,* Art. 41, S. 62; *Ghestin/Desché,* Traité des contrats, Anm. 1047; *Schlechtriem,* Pflichten des Verkäufers, S. 120; *Piltz,* Internationales Kaufrecht, Rn. 5–120; *Neumayer/Ming,* Art. 41, Anm. 3; *Kröll u. a./Kröll,* Art. 41, Rn. 12.

[11] Das Recht der Mobiliarsicherheiten differiert in den nationalen Rechtsordnungen so erheblich, dass hier auf Erwähnung einzelner Sicherungsrechte verzichtet werden musste. Vgl. für weiterführende Hinweise zum deutschen Recht *Reinicke/Tiedtke;* zum Schweizer Recht *Wiegand;* zum österreichischen Recht *Hadding/Schneider,* Teil VI; zum US-amerikanischen Recht *White/Summers,* Chapter 21–25, S. 709–919 (Hinweis: seit 1.7.2001 gilt eine erheblich veränderte Fassung der Art. 9 UCC); zum französischen Recht *von Westphalen,* Handbuch des Kaufrechts, S. 417–479; zum belgischen Recht *Hadding/Schneider,* Teil III; zum englischen Recht *Hadding/Schneider,* Teil IV; zum spanischen Recht *Hadding/Schneider,* Teil VII; zum griechischen Recht *Hadding/Schneider,* Teil VIII; zum polnischen Recht *Hadding/Schneider,* Teil XI; zum Einfluss des EG-Rechts *Wilmowsky* sowie *Kieninger;* zu Konventionen und weiteren Vereinheitlichungsbestrebungen s. Unidroit Convention on International Interests in Mobile Equipment mit Protocol on Matters Specific to Aircraft Equipment sowie die Preliminary draft Protocols on Matters specific to Railway Rolling Stock bzw. Space Assets, vgl. http://www.unidroit.org; vgl. auch *Kreuzer,* Mobiliarsicherheiten; *ders.,* FS Schlechtriem; *Drobnig,* FS Schlechtriem; *Rott.*

[12] Vgl. OGH, 6.2.1996, CISG-online 224 = ZfRVgl. 1996, 248, 253; *Staudinger/Magnus,* Art. 41, Rn. 11; *Bamberger/Roth/Saenger,* Art. 41, Rn. 3; a. A. *Bucher,* Neuerungen, S. 30.

[13] Zum Verhältnis zwischen Art. 41 und Art. 30 vgl. *Kiene,* IHR 2006, 93, 96.

[14] Vgl. *Metzger,* RabelsZ 73 (2009), 842, 846.

[15] Vgl. OGer Aargau, 3.3.2002, CISG-online 2013, Rn. 5.3.3. (an Bauteilen eines Fertigbauhauses).

[16] Vgl. oben *Ferrari,* Art. 3 Rn. 4 ff.

[17] Dies kann beispielsweise bei einem Auseinanderfallen der durch Art. 3 getroffenen und der jeweiligen nationalen Abgrenzung der Anwendungsbereiche der kauf- und werkvertraglichen Regelungen vorkommen. Vgl. zu dieser Abgrenzung rechtsvergleichend *Schwenzer/Hachem/Kee,* Rn. 8.30 ff.

[18] *Kröll u. a./Kröll,* Art. 41, Rn. 14. Zur entsprechenden Ansicht im deutschen Recht vgl. *Soergel/U. Huber,* § 434 BGB, Rn. 44; *Grunewald,* S. 45; *Erman/Grunewald,* § 434 BGB, Rn. 3; einschränkend *Staudinger/Köhler,* § 434 BGB, Rn. 12.

[19] Vgl. für § 1409 ABGB (Vermögensübernahme) *Karollus,* S. 123.

[20] Vgl. für § 434 BGB a. F. *Soergel/U. Huber,* § 434 BGB, Rn. 45.

[21] Vgl. unten Rn. 9 ff.

5   c) **Öffentlich-rechtliche Belastungen.** Nicht pauschal kann die Frage beantwortet werden, ob öffentlich-rechtliche Belastungen einen Rechtsmangel i. S. d. Art. 41 S. 1 darstellen oder ob sie eventuell als Sachmangel i. S. d. Art. 35 zu beurteilen sind. Unter Art. 52 EKG wurden öffentlich-rechtliche Belastungen meist lapidar entweder der Rechtsmängelhaftung zugeordnet,[22] oder die Anwendbarkeit des Art. 52 EKG wurde verneint.[23] Auch im Rahmen des CISG bleibt namentlich die **Abgrenzung zwischen Rechts- und Sachmangel** von Bedeutung, da einmal die Haftung wegen Rechtsmangels nur bei Einwilligung des Käufers,[24] jene wegen Sachmangels nach Art. 35 III jedoch bereits bei grobfahrlässiger Unkenntnis ausgeschlossen ist, zum anderen die in Art. 39 II vorgesehene Ausschlussfrist von zwei Jahren nur für Sachmängel, nicht aber für Rechtsmängel gilt. Auch ist die Verjährung in vielen nationalen Rechtsordnungen für Sach- und Rechtsmängel unterschiedlich geregelt.[25]

6   Aus der Entstehungsgeschichte des Art. 41 lassen sich nur wenige Anhaltspunkte für die Zuordnung öffentlich-rechtlicher Beschränkungen gewinnen. Auf der dritten Sitzung von UNCITRAL wurden zwar Anträge, in die Vorschrift zur Rechtsmängelhaftung ausdrücklich auch Beschränkungen durch staatliche Stellen aufzunehmen, abgelehnt,[26] da diese Fragen als zu komplex beurteilt wurden. Hieraus wird man nun freilich nicht den Schluss ziehen dürfen, dass öffentlich-rechtliche Belastungen generell keinen Rechtsmangel darstellen können.[27] Es gilt vielmehr zu differenzieren anhand des Grundes, auf den die jeweilige staatliche Massnahme zurückgeht. Allgemeine, auf wirtschaftslenkenden Massnahmen basierende **Export-** und **Importverbote** hat die jeweils betroffene Partei zu tragen.[28] Bei Exportverboten wird in der Regel die Lieferpflicht des Verkäufers verletzt sein (Art. 30), Importverbote können die Pflicht des Käufers zur Abnahme der Ware (Art. 53) berühren.[29] Fraglich kann dann jeweils nur sein, ob die betroffene Partei diesen Hinderungsgrund bei Vertragsschluss in Betracht zu ziehen oder ihn oder seine Folgen zu vermeiden oder zu überwinden hatte (Art. 79 I).[30] Öffentlich-rechtliche Beschränkungen, die in Zusammenhang mit **Eigenschaften der Ware** stehen, wie z. B. fehlende Übereinstimmung mit nationalen Normen zum Schutze von Verbrauchern, Arbeitnehmern oder Umwelt, stellen keinen Rechtsmangel dar, können aber Sachmängelhaftung nach Art. 35 auslösen.[31]

7   Einen Rechtsmangel können jedoch die Belastung mit **Steuern** und **Zöllen**[32] und daraus entspringende öffentlich-rechtliche Massnahmen darstellen, sofern diese Kosten nach dem

---

[22] Vgl. *Riese*, RabelsZ 22 (1957), 16, 74; *U. Huber*, RabelsZ 43 (1979), 413, 501; *Stötter*, Art. 52 EKG, Anm. 5 b); für das CISG noch *Welser*, S. 114.
[23] Vgl. *Dölle/Neumayer*, Art. 52 EKG, Rn. 7; *Staub/Koller*, Vor § 373 HGB, Art. 52 EKG, Rn. 442; differenzierend *Mertens/Rehbinder*, Art. 52 EKG, Rn. 5: Rechtsmangel bei Belastung mit Abgaben und Steuern; *Soergel/Lüderitz*, Art. 52 EKG, Rn. 2: Sachmangel bei staatlichen Exportverboten; *Herber/Czerwenka*, Art. 41, Rn. 4: Sachmangel bei eingeschränkter Nutzbarkeit etwa auf Grund von Sicherheitsanforderungen.
[24] Vgl. hierzu unten Rn. 19.
[25] Vgl. oben Art. 39 Rn. 28; unten Art. 43 Rn. 7.
[26] Vgl. YB III (1972), S. 68, Nr. 76; S. 90, Nr. 130.
[27] Anders *Hutter*, S. 45 f.; *Neumayer/Ming*, Art. 41, Anm. 6., ohne Begründung.
[28] So auch *Bamberger/Roth/Saenger*, Art. 41, Rn. 4; *Detzer/Thamm*, BB 1992, 2369, 2372. Vgl. auch zum deutschen Recht *Hager*, Gefahrtragung, S. 251 f.
[29] Zustimmend *Metzger*, RabelsZ 73 (2009), 842, 846.
[30] Einzelheiten hierzu unten bei Art. 79 Rn. 17.
[31] Vgl. hierzu ausführlich oben Art. 35 Rn. 17 f., 20, 23; vgl. auch Sekretariatskommentar, Art. 39, Nr. 5; *P. Huber/Mullis/Mullis*, S. 171. Vgl. auch *Kröll u. a./Kröll*, Art. 41, Rn. 25.
[32] Vgl. Int. Ct. Russian CCI, 21.1.1997, CISG-online 1246; *Schlechtriem*, Pflichten des Verkäufers, S. 120; *Witz/Salger/Lorenz/Salger*, Art. 41, Rn. 9; *Brunner*, Art. 41, Rn. 2; MünchKommHGB/*Benicke*, Art. 41, Rn. 4; *Kröll u. a./Kröll*, Art. 41, Rn. 27; für eine jedenfalls analoge Anwendung von Art. 41 auch *Metzger*, RabelsZ 73 (2009), 842, 846. A. A. *Staudinger/Magnus*, Art. 41, Rn. 14; *Soergel/Lüderitz/Schüßler-Langeheine*, Art. 41, Rn. 5; MünchKomm/*Gruber*, Art. 41, Rn. 14 (anders aber für Beschlagnahme, Rn. 15). Vgl. auch Serbian Chamber of Commerce, 23.1.2008, CISG-online 1946, wo der Verkäufer gewisse Zertifikate nicht lieferte und der Käufer deshalb nicht von der Zollpflicht befreit wurde. Richtigerweise hat das Schiedsgericht hier keinen Rechtsmangel nach Art. 41, sondern einen Sachmangel nach Art. 35 I angenommen, da der Mangel in dem Fehlen der Dokumente lag und die Zollpflicht lediglich Folge dessen war.

Vertrag vom Verkäufer zu tragen sind. Rechtsmängelhaftung kann auch eingreifen, wenn die Ware in Zusammenhang mit dem Recht eines Dritten beschlagnahmt wird,[33] wie z. B. **Beschlagnahme gestohlener Ware.**[34] Wo die behördliche Massnahme allerdings an ein Schutzrecht eines Dritten auf Grund **geistigen Eigentums** anknüpft, z. B. Weigerung der Zollbehörden, Ware herauszugeben, die das Schutzrecht eines Dritten verletzt,[35] richtet sich die Verkäuferhaftung nicht nach Art. 41 S. 1, sondern nach Art. 42.

Die Frage, ob öffentlich-rechtliche Belastungen einen Rechtsmangel oder einen Sachmangel begründen, stellt sich ebenfalls in Bezug auf Massnahmen, die – gestützt auf internationale Abkommen[36] oder Europarecht[37] – getroffen wurden, um Kulturgüter zurückzuführen, die illegal aus ihrem Herkunftsstaat entwendet wurden. Das Recht des Käufers, die Ware zu besitzen und zu benützen, ist dabei stets eingeschränkt, unabhängig davon, ob die Rückführung auf die genannten Regelungen oder auf Rechte privater Dritter gestützt wird. Demnach ist die (mögliche) Rückführung kultureller Güter in ihren Herkunftsstaat in beiden Fällen als Rechtsmangel gem. Art. 41 zu werten.[38] Dies gilt selbst dann, wenn für die Rückführung eine Entschädigung gezahlt wird.[39] 7a

d) Rechte auf Grund geistigen Eigentums. Rechte Dritter, die auf gewerblichem oder anderem geistigen Eigentum beruhen, stellen keinen Rechtsmangel i. S. d. Art. 41 S. 1 dar (Art. 41 S. 2). Für sie gilt ausschliesslich Art. 42.[40] 8

2. Ansprüche Dritter

Wie schon nach Art. 52 I EKG obliegt dem Verkäufer auch nach Art. 41 S. 1 die Pflicht, nicht nur Ware frei von Rechten Dritter, sondern auch frei von Ansprüchen Dritter zu liefern.[41] Auf das **Bestehen eines Rechts** des Dritten kommt es hier nicht an.[42] Das Einheitsrecht weicht damit von der Regelung in vielen nationalen Rechtsordnungen, die die Rechtsmängelhaftung vom Bestand des Drittrechts abhängig ma- 9

---

[33] Praktische Bedeutung hat die Einordnung dieses Falles als Rechtsmangel, wenn das Recht des Dritten in Wahrheit nicht (mehr) besteht und der Dritte selbst gegen den Käufer keine unmittelbaren Ansprüche geltend macht.

[34] Vgl. grundlegend BGH, 11.1.2006, CISG-online 1200 = IHR 2006, 82 ff.; *Metzger*, RabelsZ 73 (2009), 842, 846; vgl. auch *American Container Corp. v. Hanley Trucking Corp*, N. J. Super. Ct., 31.7.1970, 268 A 2d 313, 7 UCC Rep. Serv. 1301: Beschlagnahme gestohlener Waren; *Ricklefs v. Clemens*, Supr. Ct. Kann., 25.1.1975, 531 P 2d 94, 16 UCC Rep. Serv. 322: Ein FBI-Agent setzte den Käufer darüber in Kenntnis, dass die Waren möglicherweise gestohlen seien und der Käufer sich durch die Benutzung der Waren strafbar machen könnte. Vgl. weiterhin MünchKomm/*Gruber*, Art. 41, Rn. 15; *Kiene*, IHR 2006, 93; unklar MünchKommHGB/*Benicke*, Art. 41, Rn. 4; *Brunner*, Art. 41, Rn. 2; verneinend wohl Staudinger/*Magnus*, Art. 41, Rn. 13.

[35] Vgl. *Niblett, Ltd. v. Confectioners Materials Co., Ltd.*, [1921] 3 K. B. 387 (C. A.). Nach §§ 146 MarkenG, 111b UrhG, 142a PatG, 25a GebrMG, 40a SortSchG (i. d. F. des PrPG v. 7.3.1990, BGBl. I 422) ist eine Grenzbeschlagnahme durch die Zollbehörden möglich, vgl. *Braun*, S. 234. Vgl. auch Artt. 5 ff. EG-VO Nr. 1383/2003 des Rates v. 22.7.2003 über das Vorgehen der Zollbehörden gegen Waren, die im Verdacht stehen, bestimmte Rechte geistigen Eigentums zu verletzen, und die Massnahmen gegenüber Waren, die erkanntermassen derartige Rechte verletzen (ABlEG Nr. L 196v. 2.8.2003, S. 7–14); diese VO ist zum 1.7.2004 an die Stelle der EG-VO Nr. 3295/94 getreten.

[36] Die UNESCO Convention on the Means of Prohibiting and Preventing the Illicit Import, Export and Transfer of Ownership of Cultural Property 1970, in Kraft getreten am 24.4.1972, wurde von 117 Staaten ratifiziert. Das UNIDROIT-Übereinkommen über gestohlene oder rechtswidrig ausgeführte Kulturgüter, in Kraft getreten am 1.7.1998, wurde von 29 Staaten ratifiziert.

[37] Richtlinie 93/7/EWG des Rates vom 15. März 1993 über die Rückgabe von unrechtmäßig aus dem Hoheitsgebiet eines Mitgliedstaats verbrachten Kulturgütern, ABlEG. 1993 L 74, S. 74–79.

[38] Zur Abgrenzung zwischen Rechts- und Sachmängeln in Bezug auf Kulturgüter, vgl. *Schönenberger*, BJM 2009, 173 ff.; *Siehr*, FS Schwenzer, S. 1593, 1599 f.

[39] Vgl. *Siehr*, FS Schwenzer, S. 1593, 1599 f.

[40] Vgl. im Einzelnen zur Abgrenzung unten Art. 42 Rn. 4 f.

[41] Zur erneuten Diskussion bei UNCITRAL, ob auch Ansprüche Dritter Rechtsmängelhaftung auslösen sollen, vgl. YB III (1972), S. 68, Nr. 73.

[42] Vgl. Staudinger/*Magnus*, Art. 41, Rn. 15; *Karollus*, S. 123; *Loewe*, Art. 41, S. 61; *Piltz*, Internationales Kaufrecht, Rn. 5–121; *Ryffel*, S. 24; *Heuzé*, Anm. 312.; a. A. *Bucher*, Neuerungen, S. 30 f.

Art. 41 10   Teil III. Kapitel II. Pflichten des Verkäufers. Abschnitt II

chen,⁴³ bewusst ab. Dem Käufer soll nicht zugemutet werden, sich mit dem Dritten auseinandersetzen zu müssen.⁴⁴ Ansprüche Dritter richten sich nach nationalem Recht, häufig dem des Verkäuferstaates. Sie werden sich regelmässig aus der Vorgeschichte der Ware oder einem Vorverhalten des Verkäufers ergeben. Dem Verkäufer kann deshalb bei einem internationalen Warenkauf grundsätzlich eher zugemutet werden, die erforderlichen Schritte zur Klärung der Sach- und Rechtslage zu unternehmen, als dem Käufer.⁴⁵

10   Auch **unbegründete Ansprüche Dritter** lösen die Rechtsmängelhaftung nach Art. 41 S. 1 aus. Wie schon zum EKG so wird auch zum CISG die Auffassung vertreten, dass jedoch offensichtlich aus der Luft gegriffene Rechtsbehauptungen ausgeschlossen sein sollen.⁴⁶ Wo freilich die Grenze verlaufen soll zu derart „**frivolen**" **Ansprüchen,** bleibt unklar. Nach heute herrschender Ansicht⁴⁷ kann es jedoch darauf nicht ankommen: ob der geltend gemachte Anspruch aus der Luft gegriffen ist, kann der Käufer in der Regel nicht beurteilen. Auch hier ist es zunächst Sache des Verkäufers, den Anspruch abzuwehren. In einem solchen Fall wird er hierzu ohne weiteres und ohne grössere Verzögerung in der Lage sein, so dass häufig keine wesentliche Vertragsverletzung seitens des Verkäufers vorliegt, die den Käufer zur Vertragsaufhebung berechtigt.⁴⁸ Sollte sich jedoch aus der vertraglichen Vereinbarung ergeben, dass der Käufer besonderen Wert auf die Einhaltung des Lieferzeitpunktes legt, so kann die Annahme einer wesentlichen Vertragsverletzung gerechtfertigt sein.⁴⁹ Soweit dem Käufer aus dem „frivolen" Vorgehen eines Dritten Kosten entstehen, hat ihm der Verkäufer diese im Wege des Schadenersatzes grundsätzlich zu ersetzen.⁵⁰ Ausnahmsweise mag das Verhalten des Dritten einen Hinderungsgrund i. S. d. Art. 79 I darstellen, so dass der Verkäufer insoweit befreit ist.⁵¹ Liegt hingegen ein Fall des kollusiven Zusammenwirkens zwischen Käufer und Drittem vor, kann sich der Käufer schon wegen Art. 80 nicht auf die Ansprüche des Dritten berufen.⁵²

---

⁴³ Vgl. rechtsvergleichend *Schwenzer/Hachem/Kee*, Rn. 32.31 ff.; für das deutsche Recht *Schlechtriem*, SchuldR BT, Rn. 46; für das Schweizer Recht *Keller/Siehr*, S. 52; für das französische Recht *Mazeaud/de Juglart*, Nr. 958; für das österreichische Recht *Ehrenzweig/Mayrhofer*, § 67 II (S. 430). Im angloamerikanischen Recht scheint die Rechtslage diesbezüglich allerdings unklar zu sein, vgl. zu sec. 12 SGA *Benjamin*, Rn. 4–025: Verkäufer hafte nicht für „wrongful act" eines Dritten; zu § 2–312 UCC vgl. *White/Summers*, § 9–12, S. 535 ff.
⁴⁴ Sehr treffend drückt dies *Honnold/Flechtner*, Art. 41, Rn. 266 aus: „[...] protect the normal expectation of a buyer that he is not purchasing a lawsuit".
⁴⁵ Vgl. *Schlechtriem*, SchuldR BT, Rn. 46: Verkäufer sei „näher dran".
⁴⁶ Vgl. *Schlechtriem*, Seller's Obligations, § 6.03, S. 6–32; *ders.*, Internationales UN-Kaufrecht, Rn. 165; *Herber/Czerwenka*, Art. 41, Rn. 6: „gewisse Ernsthaftigkeit"; *Soergel/Lüderitz/Schüßler-Langeheine*, Art. 41, Rn. 7; *Heilmann*, S. 660; *Niggemann*, Pflichten des Verkäufers, S. 92: „ernsthafte und substantiierte Anspruchsstellung"; *Neumayer/Ming*, Art. 41, Anm. 3.; *Zhang*, S. 77; *Prager*, S. 72: nur „schlüssige" Ansprüche sollen Rechtsmängelhaftung auslösen. Jetzt auch ausdrücklich Art. 102 I CESL-Entwurf.
⁴⁷ Vgl. *Honnold/Flechtner*, Art. 41, Rn. 266; *P. Huber/Mullis/Mullis*, S. 172 *Brunner*, Art. 41, Rn. 2; *Staudinger/Magnus*, Art. 41, Rn. 17; *Bamberger/Roth/Saenger*, Art. 41, Rn. 10; *MünchKommHGB/Benicke*, Art. 41, Rn. 7 f.; *MünchKomm/Gruber*, Art. 41, Rn. 8; *Witz/Salger/Lorenz/Salger*, Art. 41, Rn. 7; *Kröll u. a./Kröll*, Art. 41, Rn. 19; *Langenecker*, S. 69; vgl. auch Sekretariatskommentar, Art. 39, Nr. 4: Zwar hafte der Verkäufer nicht immer bei „frivolen" Ansprüchen. Er müsse jedoch dem Käufer beweisen, dass der Anspruch „frivol" sei, andernfalls habe er entsprechende Schritte zu unternehmen, um den Anspruch abzuwehren. A. A. *Achilles*, Art. 41, Rn. 3; *ders.*, FS Schwenzer, S. 1, 7 f. (Rechtsmangel erst bei einem „liquiden Erkenntnisquellen nicht auszuschliessende[m] Risiko einer erfolgreichen Inanspruchnahme"); unklar *Soergel/Lüderitz/Schüßler-Langeheine*, Art. 41, Rn. 7; ausdrücklich offengelassen von BGH, 11.1.2006, CISG-online 1200, Rn. 19 = NJW 2006, 1343, 1344.
⁴⁸ So auch *Lookofsky*, Understanding the CISG, S. 92, Fn. 179.
⁴⁹ *Schwenzer/Tebel*, Produktpiraterie, 1, 4.
⁵⁰ Vgl. *Schwenzer/Tebel*, Produktpiraterie, 1, 4; *Honnold/Flechtner*, Art. 41, Rn. 266; *Lookofsky*, Understanding the CISG, S. 92 Fn. 179; *Enderlein/Maskow/Strohbach*, Art. 41, Anm. 4.; *Audit*, Vente internationale, Anm. 114.; *Heuzé*, Anm. 312.; *Reinhart*, Art. 41, Rn. 2; *Schlechtriem*, Pflichten des Verkäufers, S. 120; *ders.*, Internationales UN-Kaufrecht, Rn. 165.
⁵¹ *Schwenzer/Tebel*, Produktpiraterie, 1, 4.
⁵² *Schwenzer/Tebel*, Produktpiraterie, 1, 4. Vgl. auch *Achilles*, FS Schwenzer, S. 1, 6. Auf diesen Fall stellt auch *Schlechtriem*, Seller's Obligations, § 6.03, S. 6–32 vornehmlich ab.

Es ist ausreichend, dass sich der Dritte des Anspruchs in irgendeiner Weise berühmt. Einer **11** besonderen **Form der Geltendmachung** des Anspruchs gegenüber dem Käufer bedarf es nicht,[53] insbesondere ist keine Klageerhebung[54] durch den Dritten gegenüber dem Käufer erforderlich.[55]

Gutgläubiger oder **lastenfreier Erwerb** durch den Käufer lässt die Rechtsmängelhaftung des Verkäufers unberührt,[56] wenn der Dritte Ansprüche wegen seines angeblich noch **12** bestehenden Rechtes geltend macht. Es ist gerade Zweck der weiten Fassung des Art. 41 S. 1, dem Käufer das Risiko unter Umständen jahrelanger Ungewissheit und Prozessführung darüber, ob er gutgläubig oder lastenfrei Eigentum erworben hat, abzunehmen.

3. Rechte oder Ansprüche Dritter auf Grund Verhaltens des Käufers

Art. 41 S. 1 geht davon aus, dass der Verkäufer für Rechte oder Ansprüche Dritter einstehen **13** muss, die in Umständen vor der Lieferung wurzeln, mithin zu seiner Risikosphäre zu rechnen sind. Soweit Rechte oder Ansprüche Dritter auf ein eigenes **Verhalten des Käufers** zurückzuführen sind, kommt die Rechtsmängelhaftung nicht in Frage,[57] vgl. auch Art. 80.

4. Eigene Rechte oder Ansprüche des Verkäufers

Vom Wortlaut her erfasst Art. 41 S. 1 nur die Belastung mit Rechten oder Ansprüchen **14** Dritter, nicht jedoch mit eigenen Rechten des Verkäufers. Gleichwohl dürfte kein Zweifel daran bestehen, dass Art. 41 S. 1 auch hierauf Anwendung findet.[58] In praxi wird es sich insoweit meist um **Sicherungsrechte** wegen noch ausstehender Kaufpreiszahlung handeln. Soweit sich der Verkäufer vertragswidrig das Eigentum vorbehalten hat, beurteilt sich dies nach Art. 30,[59] bei vertragswidrigem Vorbehalt eines Sicherungsrechtes kommt hingegen grundsätzlich Art. 41 S. 1 zur Anwendung. Allerdings wird hier in der Regel jedenfalls keine wesentliche Vertragsverletzung vorliegen, da das Sicherungsrecht grundsätzlich mit vollständiger Kaufpreiszahlung durch den Käufer erlischt.[60] Auch **gesetzliche Sicherungsrechte** des Verkäufers, die in ausländischen Rechtsordnungen oft an die Stelle des Eigentumsvorbehalts treten, können die Einstandspflicht nach Art. 41 S. 1 auslösen,[61] da das CISG, sofern nichts anderes – u. U. auch stillschweigend – vereinbart ist, von einer unbedingten Übereignungspflicht ausgeht.

5. Massgeblicher Zeitpunkt

Zum EKG wurde die Auffassung vertreten, dass es für die Frage, ob die Sache frei von **15** Rechten oder Ansprüchen Dritter ist, auf den **Zeitpunkt der Lieferung** ankomme.[62]

---

[53] A. A. *Achilles*, FS Schwenzer, S. 1, 6, der eine Dokumentierung der Bereitschaft zur Geltendmachung des Anspruchs durch Inanspruchnahme des Käufers durch den Dritten verlangt.
[54] Anders als beispielsweise im internen französischen Recht, vgl. dazu *Mazeaud/de Juglart*, Nr. 961, jedoch wird in Bezug auf das CISG auch in Frankreich der hier vertretenen Auffassung gefolgt, s. *Audit*, Vente internationale, Anm. 114. Für das EKG vgl. schon *Dölle/Neumayer*, Art. 52 EKG, Rn. 9.
[55] Insoweit zustimmend *Achilles*, FS Schwenzer, S. 1, 5.
[56] Vgl. *U. Huber*, 1. Aufl., Art. 30 Rn. 15; a. A. *Neumayer/Ming*, Art. 41, Anm. 4.; zum EKG *Dölle/Neumayer*, Art. 52 EKG, Rn. 10; *Graveson/Cohn/Graveson*, Uniform Laws on International Sales Act, Art. 52 EKG; wie hier jedoch auch zum EKG *Mertens/Rehbinder*, Art. 52 EKG, Rn. 8.
[57] *Achilles*, FS Schwenzer, S. 1, 6.
[58] Vgl. MünchKomm/*Gruber*, Art. 41, Rn. 13; *Honsell/Magnus*, Art. 41, Rn. 5; *Zhang*, S. 79; *Heilmann*, 660; zum EKG *Mertens/Rehbinder*, Art. 52 EKG, Rn. 9; zum deutschen Recht vgl. *Soergel/P. Huber*, § 434 BGB, Rn. 34; *Erman/Grunewald*, § 434 BGB, Rn. 4; siehe hierzu auch *Schwenzer/Hachem/Kee*, Rn. 32.24.
[59] Zur Zulässigkeit des Eigentumsvorbehalts vgl. oben *Widmer Lüchinger*, Art. 30 Rn. 8. Vgl. Art. 4 EG-RL 2000/35/EG des Europäischen Parlaments und des Rates vom 29.6.2000 zur Bekämpfung von Zahlungsverzug im Handelsverkehr, ABlEG L 200v. 8.8.2000, S. 35–38, dazu *Schmidt-Kessel*, NJW 2001, 97, 101 f.
[60] Vgl. zur entsprechenden Wertung bei vertragswidrigem Eigentumsvorbehalt oben *Widmer Lüchinger*, Art. 30 Rn. 8.
[61] A. A. *Lüderitz*, Pflichten der Parteien, S. 187.
[62] Vgl. *Dölle/Neumayer*, Art. 52 EKG, Rn. 8 unter Hinweis auf die Entstehungsgeschichte.

Auch die Formulierung des Art. 41 S. 1 „hat Ware zu liefern" legt zunächst die Massgeblichkeit des Lieferzeitpunktes nahe.[63] Beim Versendungskauf[64] sowie generell dort, wo die Rechtsmängelhaftung an die blosse Geltendmachung des Anspruchs durch einen Dritten anknüpft, kann dies freilich zu unter Umständen untragbaren Ergebnissen führen. Beim **Versendungskauf** erfolgt Lieferung grundsätzlich durch Übergabe der Ware an den ersten Beförderer. Wird die Ware auf dem Transport zugunsten von Gläubigern des Verkäufers im Verkäuferstaat beschlagnahmt oder gepfändet, so können die Rechte des Käufers aber schlechterdings nicht davon abhängen, ob der Verkäufer „ab Lager"[65] oder „geliefert Grenze"[66] zu liefern hat. Ähnliche Probleme treten im Hinblick auf das in der Praxis bedeutsame Pfand- oder Sicherungsrecht des Frachtführers auf, wenn der Verkäufer im Kaufvertrag die Kosten des Transports vom Liefer- zum Bestimmungsort übernommen hat[67] und die Frachtkosten abredewidrig nicht bezahlt. Das Sicherungsrecht des Frachtführers entsteht hier praktisch gleichzeitig mit Lieferung. Zu untragbaren Ergebnissen führt die Anknüpfung an den Zeitpunkt der Lieferung, wo es um die Geltendmachung von **Ansprüchen** durch Dritte geht. Derartige Ansprüche werden gegen den Käufer regelmässig erst nach Lieferung erhoben. Auf die Lieferung abzustellen, hiesse indirekt dann doch nur begründete Ansprüche Dritter anzuerkennen, bzw. den Käufer bei unbegründeten Ansprüchen Dritter im Verhältnis zum Verkäufer oft schutzlos zu lassen.[68] Gleichwohl liegt im Begriff der Lieferung ein zutreffender Kern, der auch für die Bestimmung des für die Rechtsmängelhaftung massgeblichen Zeitpunktes fruchtbar gemacht werden kann. Lieferung markiert – grob gesprochen – die Grenze zwischen den jeweiligen Verantwortungsbereichen des Verkäufers und des Käufers. Der Sache nach sollte deshalb darauf abgestellt werden, ob die **Umstände,** auf die der Rechtsmangel zurückzuführen ist, **vor oder nach Lieferung** liegen. Auch bei Ansprüchen Dritter ist deshalb entscheidend, ob diese ihr angebliches Recht aus Umständen vor Lieferung ableiten.[69]

16 Der **Zeitpunkt des Vertragsschlusses** spielt für die allgemeine Rechtsmängelhaftung keine Rolle.[70] Auch für erst nach Vertragsschluss begründete Rechte Dritter hat der Verkäufer einzustehen. Andererseits kann er bei Vertragsschluss bestehende Rechte ohne weiteres bis zur Lieferung ablösen.

6. Räumlicher Anwendungsbereich

16a Im Gegensatz zu Art. 42 I[71] enthält Art. 41 **keine territoriale Beschränkung.** Der Käufer darf davon ausgehen, dass die weitere Verfügung in seinem Bereich liegt und nicht weiter beschränkt ist. Es ist Sache des Verkäufers, z.B. auf Lieferbeschränkungen seiner eigenen Lieferanten, durch die die freie Verfügbarkeit über die Ware in bestimmten Ländern begrenzt wird, hinzuweisen.[72]

---

[63] Vgl. *Enderlein,* Rights and Obligations of the Seller, S. 179; *Reinhart,* Art. 41, Rn. 4; *Herber/Czerwenka,* Art. 41, Rn. 8; *Enderlein/Maskow/Strohbach,* Art. 41, Anm. 1.; *Wolff,* S. 65; *Piltz,* Internationales Kaufrecht, Rn. 5–122; *Achilles,* FS Schwenzer, S. 1, 6; zweifelnd hingegen *Honnold/Flechtner,* Art. 41, Rn. 266 Fn. 6.
[64] Einzelheiten oben bei *Widmer Lüchinger,* Art. 31 Rn. 13 ff.
[65] Vgl. dazu oben *Widmer Lüchinger,* Art. 31 Rn. 72.
[66] Vgl. dazu oben *Widmer Lüchinger,* Art. 31 Rn. 73 f.
[67] Durch Klauseln wie CIF, C & F, frachtfrei, vgl. dazu oben *Widmer Lüchinger,* Art. 31 Rn. 83.
[68] So offenbar *Enderlein,* Rights and Obligations of the Seller, S. 179.
[69] So auch *Bamberger/Roth/Saenger,* Art. 41, Rn. 7; *MünchKomm/Gruber,* Art. 41, Rn. 6; *MünchKommHGB/Benicke,* Art. 41, Rn. 11; *Brunner,* Art. 41, Rn. 4; *Kröll u.a./Kröll,* Art. 41, Rn. 29; ähnlich *Staudinger/Magnus,* Art. 41, Rn. 19.
[70] Vgl. nur *Lookofsky,* Understanding the CISG, S. 92.
[71] Vgl. unten Art. 42 Rn. 9 ff.
[72] Vgl. OGH, 6.2.1996, CISG-online 224 = ZfRVgl. 1996, 248, 253.

IV. Ausschluss der Rechtsmängelhaftung

1. Einwilligung des Käufers

Im Gegensatz zur Sachmängelhaftung, die bereits bei Kenntnis und grobfahrlässiger **17** Unkenntnis des Käufers von der Vertragswidrigkeit ausgeschlossen ist (Art. 35 III)[73] und einigen nationalen Rechtsordnungen, wo jedenfalls Kenntnis des Käufers den Verkäufer befreit,[74] entfällt die Verantwortlichkeit des Verkäufers nach Art. 41 S. 1 nur, wenn der Käufer eingewilligt hat, mit einem Recht oder Anspruch behaftete Ware zu nehmen.[75] **Einwilligung** bedeutet dabei **mehr als blosse Kenntnis;**[76] sie kann andererseits aber auch stillschweigend erklärt werden.[77]

Einwilligung des Käufers kann bereits im Zeitpunkt des Vertragsschlusses vorliegen, so **18** etwa wenn bei eingelagerter Ware der Käufer die noch ausstehenden Lagerkosten tragen soll. Hier wird regelmässig eine entsprechende Anrechnung auf den Kaufpreis erfolgen, so dass von einer Einwilligung in die Belastung der Ware mit dem Pfand- oder Sicherungsrecht des Lagerhalters auszugehen ist. Nicht ausreichen kann hingegen die blosse Kenntnis des Käufers, dass Frachtführer und Lagerhalter im Allgemeinen ein Pfand- oder sonstiges Sicherungsrecht an der Ware besitzen[78] oder dass der Verkäufer mit Bankkredit arbeitet. Der Käufer darf hier darauf vertrauen, dass der Verkäufer die Sicherungsrechte ordnungsgemäss ablöst. Weitere Indizien können jedoch zu einer Einwilligung führen.[79] Dementsprechend wird man, wenn der Verkäufer dem Käufer mitteilt, dass ein Dritter ein Sicherungsrecht an der Ware besitzt, und ihn anweist, den Kaufpreis deshalb direkt an den Gläubiger zu leisten, Einwilligung bei **vorbehaltloser Annahme** der Ware bejahen können.[80] Einseitige Erklärungen des Verkäufers vermögen indes keinen Haftungsausschluss zu begründen.[81]

2. Unterlassene Anzeige

Der Käufer verliert seine Ansprüche wegen Rechtsmängeln im Falle unterlassener Anzeige (Art. 43 I), sofern nicht die Ausnahmetatbestände der Artt. 43 II, 44 vorliegen. **19**

---

[73] Art. 104 CESL-Entwurf sieht hingegen in B2B-Verträgen auch in Bezug auf die Rechtsmängelhaftung (vgl. Art. 99 II CESL-Entwurf) einen Haftungsausschluss nicht nur bei Kenntnis, sondern auch bei grober Fahrlässigkeit vor. In B2C-Verträgen ist jedoch keine entsprechende Ausnahme vorgesehen und die Rechtsmängelhaftung hat hier überdies zwingenden Charakter (Art. 102 V CESL-Entwurf), so dass auch eine konkludente Abbedingung bei Einwilligung des Käufers ausscheidet.
[74] Rechtsvergleichend *Schwenzer/Hachem/Kee*, Rn. 32.40 f.; für England vgl. *Benjamin*, Rn. 4–027; für Deutschland vgl. § 442 BGB; für die Schweiz vgl. Art. 192 II OR.
[75] So jetzt auch § 435 S. 1 BGB, demzufolge die Verkäuferhaftung entfällt, wenn der Käufer die Rechte Dritter „übernommen" hat, vgl. *Schlechtriem*, SchuldR BT, Rn. 44. Für Frankreich vgl. Cass., 9.3.1937, D. H. 1937, 253; für Österreich vgl. §§ 928 und – über CISG hinausgehend (*Loewe*, Art. 41, S. 62) – § 929 ABGB.
[76] Vgl. auch *Lookofsky*, Understanding the CISG, S. 92; wie hier *Honnold/Flechtner*, Art. 41, Rn. 266.1.
[77] Vgl. *Schlechtriem*, Internationales UN-Kaufrecht, Rn. 163; *P. Huber/Mullis/Mullis*, S. 173; *Staudinger/Magnus*, Art. 41, Rn. 22; MünchKomm/*Gruber*, Art. 41, Rn. 19; MünchKommHGB/*Benicke*, Art. 41, Rn. 12; *Brunner*, Art. 41, Rn. 5; *Metzger*, RabelsZ 73 (2009), 842, 847.
[78] Vgl. *Schlechtriem*, Seller's Obligations, § 6.03, S. 6–31; *Kröll u. a./Kröll*, Art. 41, Rn. 33.
[79] Vgl. *Staudinger/Magnus*, Art. 41, Rn. 22; MünchKomm/*Gruber*, Art. 41, Rn. 20; *Metzger*, RabelsZ 73 (2009), 842, 846.
[80] Vgl. *Schlechtriem*, Seller's Obligations, § 6.03, S. 6–31; *Staudinger/Magnus*, Art. 41, Rn. 22; zu weit hingegen *Enderlein/Maskow/Strohbach*, Art. 41, Anm. 3., wonach Einwilligung generell bei vorbehaltloser Annahme trotz „definitiver" Kenntnis vorliege. Vgl. aber MünchKomm/*Gruber*, Art. 41, Rn. 20.
[81] Vgl. MünchKomm/*Gruber*, Art. 41, Rn. 20.

3. Freizeichnungsklauseln

19a Nach Art. 6 ist es den Parteien unbenommen, die Bestimmung des Art. 41 **insgesamt** oder **einzelne ihrer Teile** abzudingen.[82] Die Gültigkeit solcher Abreden unterliegt nach Art. 4 a) dem nach IPR anwendbaren nationalen Recht.[83] Ist **deutsches Recht** subsidiäres Vertragsstatut, so ist im Rahmen des § 307 BGB zu prüfen, ob die Freizeichnung mit den wesentlichen Grundgedanken des CISG zu vereinbaren ist. Wie beim Ausschluss der Haftung wegen Vertragswidrigkeit der Ware nach Art. 35[84] muss eine unangemessene Benachteiligung i. S. des § 307 II Nr. 2 BGB jedenfalls dann angenommen werden, wenn sich der Rechtsmangel als **wesentliche Vertragverletzung**[85] darstellt oder der Verkäufer **grob fahrlässig** gehandelt hat.

V. Rechtsbehelfe

1. Nach CISG

20 Im Gegensatz zu Art. 52 EKG regelt Art. 41 die Rechtsbehelfe des Käufers bei Rechtsmängeln nicht mehr gesondert, sie ergeben sich vielmehr aus Art. 45 und den dort genannten weiteren Vorschriften. Unsicher ist freilich, ob die Bestimmungen, die ausdrücklich daran anknüpfen, dass die Ware nicht vertragsgemäss ist (Artt. 46 II und III, 50), auch auf die Rechtsmängelhaftung nach Art. 41 S. 1 anzuwenden oder auf die Sachmängelhaftung zu beschränken sind.[86] Nach dem Sekretariatskommentar[87] scheint es eindeutig, dass diese Vorschriften nur die Sachmängelhaftung betreffen. Systematik und Wortlaut unterstützen diese Auffassung. Zum einen differenziert die Überschrift des zweiten Abschnitts ausdrücklich zwischen „Vertragsgemässheit der Ware" und „Rechten oder Ansprüchen Dritter", d. h. nach herkömmlichem Verständnis zwischen Sach- und Rechtsmängelhaftung; zum anderen knüpfen Art. 46 II und III nur an die Anzeige nach Art. 39 und nicht an jene nach Art. 43 an.[88]

21 Im Einzelnen kommen folgende Rechtsbehelfe des Käufers in Betracht: Nach Art. 46 I kann der Käufer bei einem Rechtsmangel zunächst **Erfüllung** verlangen, was vor allem durch Abhilfe in Form der **Ablösung der Drittbelastung** möglich ist. Auch die verbindliche Erklärung des Dritten, den Käufer nicht in Anspruch zu nehmen, wird als ausreichend anzusehen sein.[89] Bei **Gattungsware** besteht ein Anspruch auf **Nachlieferung** rechtsmängelfreier Ware.[90] **Vertragsaufhebung** kann der Käufer nur verlangen, wenn sich der Rechtsmangel als wesentliche Vertragsverletzung darstellt, Art. 49 I a). Nicht jeder Rechtsmangel ist indessen per se eine wesentliche Vertragsverletzung.[91] Eine **wesentliche**

---

[82] Vgl. OLG Dresden, 21.3.2007, CISG-online 1626 (Verkauf eines Autos „ohne Gewährleistung" wurde als Ausschluss von Art. 41 verstanden; allerdings wurde die Eigentumsverschaffungspflicht aus Art. 30 als nicht vom Gewährleistungsausschluss erfasst gesehen); m. krit. Anm. von *Bach*, IPRax 2009, 299, 301, 303.

[83] Zum Ausschluss der Rechtsgewährleistung in den nationalen Kaufrechten vgl. Deutschland: §§ 444, 309 Nr. 7 b) und Nr. 8 b) BGB; Schweiz: Art. 192 II OR; Österreich: § 929 AGBG; Frankreich: Art. 1627 Cc, vgl. dazu *Ghestin/Desché*, Traité des contrats, Anm. 832. ff.; Italien: Art. 1487 Cc; England: vgl. *Benjamin*, Rn. 4–017; USA: § 2–312 (2) UCC; zum US-amerikanischen Recht vgl. *Honnold/Flechtner*, Art. 41, Rn. 266.1.

[84] Vgl. oben Art. 35 Rn. 42.

[85] Vgl. unten Rn. 21.

[86] Vgl. *Schlechtriem*, Internationales UN-Kaufrecht, Rn. 184; *Staudinger/Magnus*, Art. 41, Rn. 23; *Bianca/Bonell/Will*, Art. 46, Anm. 3.1., Art. 50, Anm. 3.4.; *Honnold/Flechtner*, Art. 41, Rn. 280; *Metzger*, RabelsZ 73 (2009), 842, 847; Einzelheiten unten bei *Müller-Chen*, Art. 46 Rn. 22; Art. 50 Rn. 2.

[87] Sekretariatskommentar, Art. 39, Nr. 7, 8.

[88] Nach *Mohs*, IHR 2002, 59, 64 sind diese Vorschriften zwar auch auf Belastungen mit Schutzrechten nach Art. 42, aber nicht auf allgemeine Rechtsmängel nach Art. 41 anzuwenden.

[89] Vgl. auch MünchKomm/*Gruber*, Art. 41, Rn. 21.

[90] Fraglich kann nur sein, ob hierfür die Grenzen des Art. 46 II und III gelten, so: *Herber/Czerwenka*, Art. 41, Rn. 10; vgl. oben Rn. 20.

[91] Vgl. die Diskussion bei UNCITRAL, YB III (1972), S. 90, Nr. 132 ff. Für Einzelheiten vgl. oben *Schroeter*, Art. 25 Rn. 43 ff.

Vertragsverletzung wird vorliegen, wenn der Dritte auf Grund seines Rechtes sofortige Herausgabe verlangen oder die vertragsgemässe Nutzung durch den Käufer unterbinden kann, ohne dass eine Ablösung des Drittrechts möglich oder dem Käufer zumutbar ist.[92] Anders ist der Fall zu beurteilen, wenn eine unmittelbare Beeinträchtigung für den Käufer nicht zu besorgen und eine Ablösung des Drittrechts innerhalb angemessener Zeit möglich ist.[93] Die vereinfachte Vertragsaufhebung qua Nachfristsetzung nach Art. 49 I b) ist bei einem Rechtsmangel nicht möglich, da insoweit keine Nichtlieferung vorliegt.[94] In jedem Fall kann der Käufer **Schadenersatz** nach Art. 74 verlangen, wozu insbesondere die Kosten einer möglichen **Rechtsverteidigung,** selbstverständlich inklusive Anwaltskosten, gegenüber dem Dritten gehören. Relevant wird dies vor allem in jenen Rechtsordnungen, wo auch im Falle des Obsiegens prozessrechtlich keine Kostenerstattung erfolgt.[95] Ob der Käufer, der die Sache behält, auch den Weg der **Minderung** – Art. 50 – beschreiten kann, ist unsicher;[96] die Frage verliert indes angesichts des Schadenersatzanspruchs des Käufers und der Tatsache, dass bei Rechtsmängeln nur selten eine Befreiung nach Art. 79 vorliegen dürfte,[97] viel von ihrer praktischen Bedeutung.[98] Zur einredeweisen Geltendmachung des Rechtsmangels gegenüber einer Inanspruchnahme auf Zahlung des Kaufpreises vgl. unten Art. 58 Rn. 28, 29. Zum Recht des Verkäufers auf Mängelbeseitigung bei vorzeitiger Lieferung vgl. oben Art. 37 Rn. 6.

2. Nach nationalem Recht

Art. 53 EKG enthielt die ausdrückliche Bestimmung, dass dem Käufer andere Rechts- **22** behelfe als die nach EKG wegen Rechtsmängeln nicht zustehen. Ziel dieser Vorschrift war insbesondere, dem Käufer die nach französischem Recht mögliche (Art. 1599 Cc)[99] Berufung auf die **Vertragsnichtigkeit** bei Verkauf einer fremden Sache abzuschneiden.[100] Art. 53 EKG ist ersatzlos weggefallen; man glaubte, seine Aussage sei selbstverständlich, schon Art. 7 I verbiete dem Richter einen vorschnellen Rückgriff auf nationales Recht.[101] Indes sind Zweifel daran anzumelden, ob ohne ausdrückliche Klarstellung nun nicht doch ein französischer Richter unter Berufung auf Art. 4 S. 2 a) dem gutgläubigen Käufer die Geltendmachung der Vertragsnichtigkeit nach Art. 1599 Cc gestatten wird.[102]

Ähnliche Zweifel ergeben sich bei Rechtsmängeln für die **Irrtumsanfechtung** oder **23** Ansprüche aus **culpa in contrahendo** oder **Delikt** wegen **fahrlässiger Falschangaben** nach nationalem Recht.[103] Der Sache nach kann es freilich nicht fraglich sein, dass derartige Rechtsbehelfe nach nationalem Recht neben der Rechtsmängelhaftung nach CISG nicht in

---

[92] So auch *Kröll u. a./Kröll,* Art. 41, Rn. 43.
[93] Ähnlich *Staudinger/Magnus,* Art. 41, Rn. 24; MünchKomm/*Gruber,* Art. 41, Rn. 24; *Wolff,* S. 165; *Piltz,* Internationales Kaufrecht, Rn. 5–286; *Honnold/Flechtner,* Art. 41, Rn. 266: Differenzierung nach zeitlichem Aufwand und sonstigen Unannehmlichkeiten, die die Ablösung bereitet.
[94] Vgl. unten *Müller-Chen,* Art. 49 Rn. 15; *Metzger,* RabelsZ 73 (2009), 842, 850.
[95] So vor allem die American-Rule in den USA. Vgl. *Herber/Czerwenka,* Art. 41, Rn. 6.
[96] Vgl. oben Rn. 23; bejahend *Staudinger/Magnus,* Art. 41, Rn. 26; *Neumayer,* RIW 1994, 99, 106; *Herber/Czerwenka,* Art. 41, Rn. 10; *Brunner,* Art. 50, Rn. 3; verneinend unten *Müller-Chen,* Art. 50 Rn. 2; *Mohs,* IHR 2002, 59, 64; *Honnold/Flechtner,* Art. 41, Rn. 313.1; *Schlechtriem,* Internationales UN-Kaufrecht, Rn. 202; MünchKomm/*Gruber,* Art. 41, Rn. 43; *Bamberger/Roth/Saenger,* Art. 50, Rn. 2; *Karollus,* S. 158; *Piltz,* Internationales Kaufrecht, Rn. 5–345; *Metzger,* RabelsZ 73 (2009), 842, 848 f.
[97] Vgl. unten Art. 79 Rn. 28; *Stoll/Gruber,* 4. Aufl., Art. 79 Rn. 39 f.; *Metzger,* RabelsZ 73 (2009), 842, 849. Gegen die Anwendung von Art. 79 im Rahmen des Art. 41 aber MünchKommHGB/*Benicke,* Art. 41, Rn. 9.
[98] Vgl. *Honnold/Flechtner,* Art. 41, Rn. 313.
[99] Einzelheiten hierzu bei *Mazeaud/de Juglart,* Nr. 818 ff.
[100] Vgl. *Mertens/Rehbinder,* Art. 53 EKG, Rn. 2; *Dölle/Neumayer,* Art. 53 EKG, Rn. 2.
[101] Vgl. *Schlechtriem,* Seller's Obligations, § 6.03, S. 6–31; YB IV (1973), S. 44, Nr. 62 ff. (zum Wegfall des für die Sachmängelhaftung entsprechenden Art. 34 EKG); S. 73, Nr. 146.
[102] So auch *von Caemmerer,* Vertragspflichten und Vertragsgültigkeit, S. 39; vgl. *Schlechtriem,* Internationales UN-Kaufrecht, Rn. 166.
[103] Vgl. *von Caemmerer,* Vertragspflichten und Vertragsgültigkeit, S. 39.

Betracht kommen, da sonst in einem Kernbereich der Verkäuferhaftung das Abkommen unterlaufen würde.[104]

24 Nicht ausgeschlossen sind jedoch Rechtsbehelfe, die dem Käufer nach nationalem Recht bei **Arglist** oder **Betrug** des Verkäufers zustehen.[105] Hier beruhen die Ansprüche des Käufers auf besonderen Umständen, die über die Belastung der Ware mit einem Rechtsmangel hinausgehen und nicht mehr in den Regelungsbereich des CISG fallen.

VI. Beweislast[106]

25 Der Käufer hat zu beweisen, dass ein Dritter ein Recht an der Sache behauptet sowie einen eventuell eingetretenen Schaden. Der Verkäufer trägt die Beweislast, wenn er sich auf Einwilligung des Käufers beruft.[107]

---

[104] Vgl. *Neumayer/Ming*, Art. 41, Anm. 7.; *Langenecker*, S. 282; zweifelnd aber *Lookofsky*, Understanding the CISG, S. 25 ff.; vgl. auch ausführlich oben Art. 35 Rn. 45 ff.

[105] Vgl. *Schlechtriem*, 21 Cornell Int'l L.J. (1988), 467, 474; *Staudinger/Magnus*, Art. 41, Rn. 27; MünchKomm/*Gruber*, Art. 41, Rn. 25; *Audit*, Vente internationale, Anm. 121.; *Karollus*, S. 41; *Heilmann*, S. 157. Zum Parallelproblem bei der Sachmängelhaftung vgl. oben Art. 35 Rn. 49.

[106] Die Beweislastverteilung ergibt sich inzident aus dem Regel-Ausnahme-Prinzip des CISG, vgl. oben Art. 35 Rn. 52; *Ferrari*, Art. 4 Rn. 25; i. E. ebenso unten *Müller-Chen*, Art. 45 Rn. 9, 10; Schlechtriem/Schwenzer/*Schwenzer/Hachem*, CISG Commentary, Art. 4, Rn. 25.

[107] Vgl. *Zhang*, S. 83; *Kröll u. a./Kröll*, Art. 41, Rn. 46.

Art. 42 [Belastung mit Schutzrechten Dritter]

(1) Der Verkäufer hat Ware zu liefern, die frei von Rechten oder Ansprüchen Dritter ist, die auf gewerblichem oder anderem geistigen Eigentum beruhen und die der Verkäufer bei Vertragsabschluß kannte oder über die er nicht in Unkenntnis sein konnte, vorausgesetzt, das Recht oder der Anspruch beruht auf gewerblichem oder anderem geistigen Eigentum

a) nach dem Recht des Staates, in dem die Ware weiterverkauft oder in dem sie in anderer Weise verwendet wird,* wenn die Parteien bei Vertragsabschluß in Betracht gezogen haben, daß die Ware dort weiterverkauft oder verwendet werden wird, oder
b) in jedem anderen Falle nach dem Recht des Staates, in dem der Käufer seine Niederlassung hat.

(2) Die Verpflichtung des Verkäufers nach Absatz 1 erstreckt sich nicht auf Fälle,
a) in denen der Käufer im Zeitpunkt des Vertragsabschlusses das Recht oder den Anspruch kannte oder darüber nicht in Unkenntnis sein konnte, oder
b) in denen das Recht oder der Anspruch sich daraus ergibt, daß der Verkäufer sich nach technischen Zeichnungen, Entwürfen, Formeln oder sonstigen Angaben gerichtet hat, die der Käufer zur Verfügung gestellt hat.

Art. 42

(1) The seller must deliver goods which are free from any right or claim of a third party based on industrial property or other intellectual property, of which at the time of the conclusion of the contract the seller knew or could not have been unaware, provided that the right or claim is based on industrial property or other intellectual property:
(a) under the law of the State where the goods will be resold or otherwise used, if it was contemplated by the parties at the time of the conclusion of the contract that the goods would be resold or otherwise used in that State; or
(b) in any other case, under the law of the State where the buyer has his place of business.

(2) The obligation of the seller under the preceding paragraph does not extend to cases where:
(a) at the time of the conclusion of the contract the buyer knew or could not have been unaware of the right or claim; or
(b) the right or claim results from the seller's compliance with technical drawings, designs, formulae or other such specifications furnished by the buyer.

Art. 42

1) Le vendeur doit livrer les marchandises libres de tout droit ou prétention d'un tiers fondé sur la propriété industrielle ou autre propriété intellectuelle, qu'il connaissait ou ne pouvait ignorer au moment de la conclusion du contrat, à condition que ce droit ou cette prétention soit fondé sur la propriété industrielle ou autre propriété intellectuelle:
a) en vertu de la loi de l'Etat où les marchandises doivent être revendues ou utilisées, si les parties ont envisagé au moment de la conclusion du contrat que les marchandises seraient revendues ou utilisées dans cet Etat; ou
b) dans tous les autres cas, en vertu de la loi de l'Etat où l'acheteur a son établissement.

2) Dans les cas suivants, le vendeur n'est pas tenu de l'obligation prévue au paragraphe précédent:
a) au moment de la conclusion du contrat, l'acheteur connaissait ou ne pouvait ignorer l'existence du droit ou de la prétention; ou
b) le droit ou la prétention résulte de ce que le vendeur s'est conformé aux plans techniques, dessins, formules ou autres spécifications analogues fournis par l'acheteur.

Übersicht

	Rn.
I. Vorgeschichte	1
II. Bestehen von Schutzrechten	3
III. Haftungsvoraussetzungen	4
1. Rechte Dritter auf Grund geistigen Eigentums	4
a) Geistiges Eigentum	4
b) Persönlichkeits-, Namensrechte u. ä.	5

---

* Schweiz: oder verwendet werden soll.

Art. 42 1, 2   Teil III. Kap. II. Pflichten des Verkäufers. Abschn. II

      2. Ansprüche Dritter 6
      3. Eigene Rechte des Verkäufers 7
      4. Massgeblicher Zeitpunkt 8
      5. Territoriale Begrenzung 9
         a) Verwendungsstaat 10
         b) Käuferstaat 12
         c) Verkäuferstaat 13
         d) Transitstaat 13a
      6. Kenntnis oder vorwerfbare Unkenntnis des Verkäufers 14
   IV. Haftungsausschluss 16
      1. Kenntnis oder vorwerfbare Unkenntnis des Käufers, Abs. 2 lit. a) 16
      2. Befolgen technischer Anweisungen etc., Abs. 2 lit. b) 19
         a) Freiwerden des Verkäufers 19
         b) Rechtsbehelfe des Verkäufers 22
      3. Unterlassene Anzeige 24
      4. Freizeichnungsklauseln 24a
   V. Rechtsbehelfe 25
      1. Nach CISG 25
      2. Nach nationalem Recht 27
  VI. Beweislast 29

Vorläufer und **Entwürfe:** Genfer E 1976 Art. 7 II; Wiener E 1977 Art. 26 I u. II; New Yorker E 1978 Art. 40 I u. II.

I. Vorgeschichte

1   Im Rahmen des Art. 52 EKG war die Frage, ob und in welchem Umfang der Verkäufer auch für die Freiheit von Schutzrechten einzustehen hat, nicht ausdrücklich geregelt. Vor allem deutsche Autoren vertraten die Ansicht, namentlich die Belastung mit einem gewerblichen Schutzrecht stelle einen Rechtsmangel i. S. d. Art. 52 EKG dar.[1] In einem dictum hat sich auch das OLG Düsseldorf in diesem Sinne ausgesprochen.[2] Auch in den meisten nationalen Rechtsordnungen wird die Haftung des Verkäufers für die Freiheit von Schutzrechten der allgemeinen Rechtsmängelhaftung zugeordnet.[3] Im nationalen Kontext erscheint eine solche strikte Einstandspflicht wegen der räumlichen Überschaubarkeit sachgerecht; im internationalen Kontext kann jedoch angesichts der Territorialität der Schutzrechte eine Pflicht des Verkäufers, weltweit Schutzrechtsfreiheit zu garantieren, nicht befriedigen.[4]

2   UNCITRAL nahm sich erst in einem relativ späten Stadium der Frage der Schutzrechte an. Zunächst erwog man, die gesamte Materie wegen ihrer Komplexität ganz aus dem Abkommen auszugrenzen, Genfer E 1976 Art. 7 II. In ihren Stellungnahmen votierten jedoch die meisten Regierungen für eine ausdrückliche Regelung der Haftung für Schutz-

---

[1] Vgl. *Soergel/Lüderitz,* Art. 52 EKG, Rn. 2; *Mertens/Rehbinder,* Art. 52 EKG, Rn. 5; *U. Huber,* RabelsZ 43 (1979), 413, 502; vgl. auch schon *Riese,* RabelsZ 22 (1957), 16, 74; zweifelnd dagegen *Honnold/Flechtner,* Art. 42, Rn. 268; zur geschichtlichen Entwicklung vgl. *Prager,* S. 62 ff.

[2] OLG Düsseldorf, 20.1.1983, in: *Schlechtriem/Magnus,* Art. 76 EKG, Nr. 4.

[3] Rechtsvergleichend *Schwenzer/Hachem/Kee,* Rn. 33.14 f. Zum deutschen Recht vgl. *Schlechtriem,* SchuldR BT, Rn. 45, zu § 434 BGB a. F. vgl. BGH, 31.1.1990, BGHZ 110, 197 (Aufbügelmotive, deren Vertrieb vom darauf Abgebildeten untersagt wurde); OLG Hamm, 7.2.1992, NJW-RR 1992, 1201 (Aufdruck für Kinderkleidung, der Urheberrecht eines Dritten verletzte); zum österreichischen Recht vgl. OGH, 3.11.1981, SZ 54/152; zum englischen Recht vgl. *Benjamin,* Rn. 4–024 (sec. 12 II (b) SGA); vgl. aber zum Schweizer Recht BGer, 14.2.1956, BGE 82 II 238 (rechtlicher Mangel i. S. d. Art. 197 I OR und damit Gleichstellung mit Sachmangel); in § 2–312 III UCC wird die Belastung mit gewerblichen Schutzrechten ausdrücklich den sonstigen Rechtsmängeln gleichgestellt, vgl. dazu *White/Summers,* § 9–12, S. 534 f. Im internen französischen Recht kann eine mit Rechten Dritter belastete Sache (in casu gefälschte Kleider) nicht Gegenstand eines Kaufvertrages im Sinne der Artt. 1128, 1598 Cc sein, Rechtsfolge ist die Nichtigkeit, vgl. Com., 24.9.2003, D. 2003, 2683. Das CESL regelt die Materie als Spezialfall der Rechtsmängelhaftung, Art. 102 II-IV CESL-Entwurf.

[4] Vgl. Sekretariatskommentar, Art. 40, Nr. 4.

rechtsbelastungen.[5] Eine Sonderarbeitsgruppe bei der zehnten Sitzung von UNCITRAL[6] erarbeitete dann einen Entwurf, mit dem die jetzige Fassung des Art. 42 im Wesentlichen übereinstimmt. Ziel war es, die Verkäuferhaftung für Freiheit von Schutzrechten in voraussehbaren Grenzen zu halten.[7] Dies wurde einerseits erreicht durch eine territoriale Beschränkung auf bestimmte Rechtsordnungen und andererseits durch Einführung eines Verschuldenselementes im Zeitpunkt des Vertragsschlusses.

II. Bestehen von Schutzrechten

Das CISG regelt ausschliesslich das Verhältnis zwischen Verkäufer und Käufer. Ob Rechte Dritter aus gewerblichem oder anderem geistigen Eigentum an der Sache bestehen, welche Rechtsbehelfe daraus gegen den Käufer abgeleitet werden können und ob gutgläubiger lastenfreier Erwerb möglich ist, bestimmt sich nach dem durch das auf Grund internationalen Privatrechts des angerufenen Gerichts berufenen nationalen Recht, in der Regel jenem des **Schutzlandes**.[8] Die Besonderheit der Schutzrechte liegt dabei in ihrer **territorialen Beschränkung,** womit sie sich wesentlich von Sachenrechten unterscheiden.[9] Eine weitere Besonderheit liegt in der herausragenden Bedeutung von auf diesen Gebieten geschaffenen **internationalen Abkommen,**[10] die zumeist sogenannte Inländerbehandlung und einen einheitlichen Grundschutz sicherstellen wollen.

III. Haftungsvoraussetzungen

1. Rechte Dritter auf Grund geistigen Eigentums

a) Geistiges Eigentum. Im Immaterialgüterrecht stellt „geistiges Eigentum" den Oberbegriff dar, der sowohl **Urheberrecht** als auch **gewerbliches Eigentum** umfasst. Die ausdrückliche Erwähnung des gewerblichen Eigentums neben dem geistigen Eigentum hat – wie auch der Wortlaut der Vorschrift erkennen lässt – nur klarstellende Funktion.[11] Was im Einzelnen zum geistigen Eigentum zu rechnen ist, kann den auf breitem internationalen Konsens basierenden internationalen Konventionen entnommen werden. So umschreibt das Übereinkommen zur Errichtung der Weltorganisation für geistiges Eigentum von 1967[12] im Wesentlichen in Übereinstimmung mit anderen internationalen Konventionen den Begriff als „alle Rechte, die sich aus der **geistigen Tätigkeit auf gewerblichem, wissenschaftlichem, literarischem oder künstlerischem Gebiet** ergeben". Beispielhaft werden genannt „die Rechte betreffend die Werke der Literatur, Kunst und Wissenschaft; die Leistungen der ausübenden Künstler, die Tonträger und Funksendungen; die Erfindungen auf allen Gebieten der menschlichen Tätigkeit; die wissenschaftlichen Entdeckungen; die gewerblichen Muster und Modelle; die Fabrik-, Handels- und Dienstleistungsmarken sowie die Handelsnamen und Geschäftsbezeichnungen; den Schutz gegen unlauteren Wettbewerb". Diese weite Fassung des Begriffs „geistiges Eigentum" sollte auch dem CISG zugrunde gelegt werden, will man nicht die von Art. 42 intendierte Begrenzung der Verkäuferhaftung unterlaufen. Anzuknüpfen ist an

---

[5] Vgl. YB VIII (1977), S. 110, Nr. 6; S. 115, Nr. 5, 9; S. 116, Nr. 10; S. 121, Nr. 18; S. 130, Nr. 3.
[6] Vgl. YB VIII (1977), S. 40f., Nr. 211 ff.
[7] Vgl. YB VIII (1977), S. 40, Nr. 215.
[8] Vgl. *Ulmer,* Die Immaterialgüterrechte im internationalen Privatrecht; *ders.,* RabelsZ 41 (1977), 479–512; *Neuhaus/Drobnig/von Hoffmann/Martiny,* RabelsZ 40 (1976), 189–232; *Sandrock,* S. 380 ff.
[9] Zu grenzüberschreitenden Unterlassungsgeboten von Patentverletzungen mit Wirkung im europäischen Ausland vgl. *D. Stauder,* IPRax 1998, 317 ff.
[10] Eine Übersicht der internationalen Abkommen (sowie nationaler Gesetzgebung) auf dem Gebiet des gewerblichen Rechtsschutzes ermöglicht WIPO Lex, online verfügbar, vgl. www.wipo.int/wipolex/en/.
[11] Vgl. Sekretariatskommentar, Art. 40, Nr. 1 Fn. 1.
[12] BGBl. 1970 II 295 ff., Art. 2 viii).

Art. 42 4   Teil III. Kap. II. Pflichten des Verkäufers. Abschn. II

den **materiellen Begriff** des geistigen Eigentums; auf Merkmale wie Registrierbarkeit oder Erfindungshöhe kann es ebenso wenig ankommen wie auf die rechtstechnische Einordnung und Ausgestaltung im jeweiligen Schutzland. Insbesondere ist nicht entscheidend, ob die Schutzrechtsordnung das jeweilige Recht einem speziellen Regelwerk für Immaterialgüterrechte unterstellt oder Schutz über die Regeln des **unlauteren Wettbewerbs,** das allgemeine **Delikts-** oder **Bereicherungsrecht** gewährt.[13] Auf europäischer Ebene kann an den Anwendungsbereich von Rechtsakten[14] zum Schutz des geistigen Eigentums angeknüpft werden. Aus deutscher Sicht kommt vor allem der Belastung mit **Patent-, Marken-, Geschmacks-** und **Gebrauchsmusterrechten** sowie mit **Urheberrechten** Dritter zentrale praktische Bedeutung zu.[15] Dabei wird der Verkäufer nicht nur einzustehen haben, wenn die Ware selbst mit dem Schutzrecht eines Dritten belastet ist, sondern auch, wenn z. B. die als solches nicht patentierte Maschine dazu bestimmt ist, nach einem **Verfahren** zu arbeiten, das für Dritte patentiert ist, oder Waren herzustellen, die ihrerseits dem gewerblichen Schutzrecht eines Dritten unterliegen.[16] Entscheidend

---

[13] Vgl. *Kröll u. a./Kröll*, Art. 42, Rn. 13. So müssen etwa zum geistigen Eigentum auch gezählt werden: im deutschen Recht Ansprüche aus ergänzendem wettbewerbsrechtlichen Leistungsschutz, vgl. dazu *Köhler/ Bornkamm/Köhler*, § 4 UWG, Rn. 9.1 ff.; im US-amerikanischen Recht Ansprüche wegen passing off, vgl. dazu *Prosser*, S. 1015 ff.; Ansprüche wegen unbefugter Verwendung von Know-how, das in den USA als „property right" angesehen wird, vgl. dazu *Dessemontet*, S. 324 ff., 356 ff., nach deutschem Recht gemäss § 17 UWG, bzw. § 823 BGB geschützt wird, *Stumpf*, S. 30 ff.; vgl. dazu auch *Metzger*, RabelsZ 73 (2009), 842, 863; *Shinn*, 2 Minn. J. Global Trade (1993), 115, 122; die Ansicht von *Enderlein*, Rights and Obligations of the Seller, S. 182, in Staaten, in denen kein eigenständiges Immaterialgüterrecht existiere, und die auch nicht an internationalen Konventionen beteiligt seien, bestehe keine Gefahr, dass Dritte Schutzrechte geltend machen, greift m. E. viel zu kurz. Wie hier *Witz/Salger/Lorenz/Salger*, Art. 42, Rn. 4.

[14] RL 87/54/EWG des Rates v. 16.12.1986 über den Rechtsschutz der Topographien von Halbleitererzeugnissen, ABlEG L 24 v. 27.1.1987, S. 36; Erste RL 89/104/EWG des Rates v. 21.12.1988 zur Angleichung der Rechtsvorschriften der Mitgliedstaaten über die Marken, ABlEG L 40 v. 11.2.1989, S. 1; VO (EWG) Nr. 1576/89 des Rates v. 29.5.1989 zur Festlegung der allgemeinen Regeln für die Begriffsbestimmung, Bezeichnung und Aufmachung von Spirituosen, ABlEG L 160 v. 12.6.1989, S. 1; VO (EWG) Nr. 1014/90 der Kommission v. 24.4.1990 mit Durchführungsbestimmungen für Begriffsbestimmung, Bezeichnung und Aufmachung von Spirituosen, ABlEG L 105 v. 25.4.1990, S. 9; RL 91/250/EWG des Rates v. 14.5.1991 über den Rechtsschutz von Computerprogrammen, ABlEG L 122 v. 17.5.1991, S. 42; RL 92/100/EWG des Rates v. 19.11.1992 zum Vermietrecht und Verleihrecht sowie zu bestimmten dem Urheberrecht verwandten Schutzrechten im Bereich des geistigen Eigentums, ABlEG L 346 v. 27.11.1992, S. 61; RL 93/83/EWG des Rates vom 7. 11 1993 zur Koordinierung bestimmter urheber- und leistungsschutzrechtlicher Vorschriften betreffend Satellitenrundfunk und Kabelweiterverbreitung, ABlEG L 248 v. 6.10.1993, S. 15; RL 93/98/EWG des Rates v. 29.10.1993 zur Harmonisierung der Schutzdauer des Urheberrechts und bestimmter verwandter Schutzrechte, ABlEG L 290 v. 24.11.1993, S. 9; RL 96/9/EG des Europäischen Parlaments und des Rates v. 11.3.1996 über den rechtlichen Schutz von Datenbanken, ABlEG L 77 v. 27.3.1996, S. 20; RL 98/71/EG des Europäischen Parlaments und des Rates v. 13.10.1998 über den rechtlichen Schutz von Mustern und Modellen, ABlEG L 289 v. 28.10.1998, S. 28; RL 98/44/EG des Europäischen Parlaments und des Rates v. 6.7.1998 über den rechtlichen Schutz biotechnologischer Erfindungen, ABlEG L 213 v. 30.7.1998, S. 13; EG-VO Nr. 1493/1999 des Rates v. 17.5.1999 über die gemeinsame Marktorganisation für Wein, ABlEG L 179 v. 14.7.1999, S. 1; RL 2001/29/EG des Europäischen Parlaments und des Rates v. 22.5.2001 zur Harmonisierung bestimmter Aspekte des Urheberrechts und der verwandten Schutzrechte in der Informationsgesellschaft, ABlEG L 167 v. 22.6.2001, S. 10; RL 2001/ 84/EG des Europäischen Parlaments und des Rates v. 27.9.2001 über das Folgerecht des Urhebers des Originals eines Kunstwerks, ABlEG L 272 v. 13.10.2001, S. 32; VO (EWG) Nr. 1768/92 des Rates v. 18.6.1992 über die Schaffung eines ergänzenden Schutzzertifikats für Arzneimittel, ABlEG L 182 v. 2.7.1992, S. 1; EG VO Nr. 1610/96 des Europäischen Parlaments und des Rates v. 23.7.1996 über die Schaffung eines ergänzenden Schutzzertifikats für Pflanzenschutzmittel, ABlEG L 198 v. 8.8.1996, S. 30; EG-VO Nr. 510/2006 des Rates v. 20.3.2006 zum Schutz von geographischen Angaben und Ursprungsbezeichnungen für Agrarerzeugnisse und Lebensmittel; EG-VO Nr. 40/94 des Rates v. 29.12.1993 über die Gemeinschaftsmarke, ABlEG L 11 v. 14.1.1994, S. 1, geändert durch EG-VO Nr. 422/2004 des Rates v. 19.2.2004; EG-VO Nr. 2100/94 des Rates v. 27.7.1994 über den gemeinschaftlichen Sortenschutz, ABlEG L 227 v. 1.9.1994, S. 1, geändert durch EG-VO Nr. 873/2004 des Rates v. 29.4.2004; EG-VO Nr. 6/2002 des Rates v. 12.12.2001 über das Gemeinschaftsgeschmacksmuster, ABlEG L 3 v. 5.1.2002, S. 1; Übereinkommen über die Erteilung europäischer Patente (Europäisches Patentübereinkommen) v. 5.10.1973.

[15] Vgl. darüber hinaus auch die Rechte nach dem SortSchG v. 11.12.1985, BGBl. I 2170 ff.; nach dem Halbleiterschutzgesetz v. 22.10.1987, BGBl. I 2294 ff.

[16] OGH, 12.9.2006, CISG-online 1364; *Schlechtriem*, Internationales UN-Kaufrecht, Rn. 171; *Wolff*, S. 74; *Vida*, RTD com. 1994, 21, 26; *Bacher*, FS Schwenzer, S. 115, 117; a. A. *Prager*, S. 148.

muss sein, ob das Schutzrecht des Dritten geeignet ist, die vertragsgemässe Verwendung der Ware zu beeinträchtigen.[17] Verbleibt dem Käufer eine nicht schutzrechtsverletzende, andere sinnvolle Verwendungsmöglichkeit, so mag es allenfalls an der Wesentlichkeit der Vertragsverletzung fehlen.[18]

b) Persönlichkeits-, Namensrechte u. ä. Vom Begriff des geistigen Eigentums nicht erfasst sind **Persönlichkeitsrechte** und **Namensrechte** Dritter,[19] soweit es sich nicht um Handelsnamen handelt, sowie beispielsweise **Verbietungsrechte**, die dem Eigentümer einer ohne seine Einwilligung photographierten Sache gegen die Verwertung der Photographie zustehen mögen.[20] Unter CISG stellt sich die Frage, ob man diese Fälle der allgemeinen Rechtsmängelhaftung nach Art. 41 S. 1 zuordnet und damit den Verkäufer strikt und weltweit für die Freiheit von derartigen Schutzrechten einstehen lassen will, oder ob man Art. 42 direkt oder jedenfalls entsprechend auf diese Drittbelastungen anwendet und damit dem Verkäufer nur ein umgrenztes Einstehenmüssen auferlegt. M. E. spricht viel für letzteren Weg. Oft wird schon eine klare Abgrenzung von geistigem Eigentum und Persönlichkeits- oder Namensrecht schwierig sein.[21] Vor allem handelt es sich im Unterschied zu den klar unter Art. 41 S. 1 fallenden dinglichen und obligatorischen Rechten Dritter bei Persönlichkeitsrechten etc. nicht um Rechte an einer konkreten Sache, sie betreffen vielmehr eine Vielzahl gleichartiger, oftmals eine gesamte Gattung von Waren. Funktional sind diese Rechte dem geistigen Eigentum ähnlich. Hinzu tritt die Vergleichbarkeit der Interessenlage. Die Haftung des Verkäufers ist nach Art. 42 vor allem deshalb eingegrenzt, weil die Schutzrechte von Staat zu Staat variieren können. Kaum anders ist es aber beispielsweise bei Persönlichkeitsverletzungen. Nicht selten trennt hier ein schmaler, von Land zu Land verschieden verlaufender Grat die Gefilde von Recht und Unrecht.[22] So mag es vorkommen, dass etwa der Namensträger den Vertrieb der Ware im Käuferstaat hinzunehmen hat, in einem anderen Staat jedoch unterbinden kann. Dies aber rückt Persönlichkeitsrecht, Namensrecht wie auch Verbietungsrecht aus Eigentum in die Nähe zu den Rechten aus geistigem Eigentum, so dass jedenfalls eine entsprechende Anwendung des Art. 42 gerechtfertigt scheint.[23]

2. Ansprüche Dritter

Wie im Rahmen des Art. 41 genügt auch hier, dass ein Dritter Ansprüche gegen den Käufer geltend macht, auf das **Bestehen eines Schutzrechtes** kommt es nicht an.[24]

---

[17] Neben der ausdrücklichen Vereinbarung ist insoweit auf die Wertungen des Art. 35 II zurückzugreifen, vgl. *Bacher*, FS Schwenzer, S. 115, 119.

[18] Zustimmend *Achilles*, FS Schwenzer, S. 1, 14; *Bacher*, FS Schwenzer, S. 115, 120.

[19] Vgl. die Entscheidung BGH, 26.6.1981, BGHZ 81, 75 (Carrera): auf Eingriffskondiktion gestützte angemessene Lizenzgebühr bei Eingriff in Persönlichkeits- und Namensrecht; BGH, 8.6.1989, NJW 1990, 1986 (Emil Nolde): Anspruch auf Beseitigung einer gefälschten Signatur auf einer Bildfälschung; BGH, 31.1.1990, BGHZ 110, 197: Unterlassungsanspruch aus § 12 BGB ist ein Rechtsmangel; BGH, 1.12.1999, NJW 2000, 2195 (Marlene Dietrich): Schadensersatzforderung des Erben wegen unbefugter Verwendung des Bildnisses und Namens der Verstorbenen.

[20] Vgl. BGH, 20.9.1974, NJW 1975, 778 (Schloss Tegel).

[21] Vgl. nur BGH, 26.6.1981, BGHZ 81, 75. Erinnert sei darüber hinaus auch daran, dass die Immaterialgüterrechte oft aus dem Persönlichkeitsrecht abgeleitet wurden, vgl. nur *Troller*, S. 87 ff.

[22] Vgl. *Heldrich*, S. 374, der deshalb für das internationale Privatrecht in diesem Bereich eindeutige Anknüpfungsmomente fordert.

[23] So auch *Schlechtriem*, Internationales UN-Kaufrecht, Rn. 171; MünchKomm/*Gruber*, Art. 42, Rn. 7; MünchKommHGB/*Benicke*, Art. 42, Rn. 3; *Brunner*, Art. 42, Rn. 3; *Witz/Salger/Lorenz/Salger*, Art. 42, Rn. 4; *Metzger*, RabelsZ 73 (2009), 842, 863 f.; *P. Huber/Mullis/Mullis*, S. 174 hält dies für die herrschende Meinung; *Staudinger/Magnus*, Art. 42, Rn. 12 (direkt anwendbar); *Bamberger/Roth/Saenger*, Art. 42, Rn. 5 (direkt anwendbar); *Kröll u. a./Kröll*, Art. 42, Rn. 13 (covered by Art. 42); *Soergel/Lüderitz/Schüßler-Langeheine*, Art. 42, Rn. 2; a. A. *Langenecker*, S. 88; *Schwerha*, 16 Mich. J. Int'l L. (1995), 441, 460 (unter Berufung auf den UCC); *Rauda/Etier*, 4 VJ (2000), 30, 35. Ausführlich Kremer, Persönlichkeitsrecht, S. 160 ff.

[24] Vgl. BGer, 17.4.2012, CISG-online 2346, E.2.3; OGH, 12.9.2006, CISG-online 1364; *Honnold/Flechtner*, Art. 42, Rn. 270; *Lookofsky*, Understanding the CISG, S. 93; MünchKomm/*Gruber*, Art. 42, Rn. 9; MünchKommHGB/*Benicke*, Art. 42, Rn. 4; *Schwenzer/Tebel*, Produktpiraterie, 1, 3 f.; *Staudinger/Magnus*, Art. 42,

Art. 42 7, 8

Praktisch bedeutsam werden dürfte dies z. B. beim Verkauf einer Ware unter einer Marke, die der geschützten ähnlich ist, von der der Verkäufer zwar meint, dass keine Verwechslungsgefahr bestünde, der Inhaber des ähnlichen Zeichens aber Ansprüche geltend macht. Vergleichbare Situationen sind auch bei Geschmacksmustern oder Urheberrechten vorstellbar. Soweit die übrigen Haftungsvoraussetzungen vorliegen, ist es dann Sache des Verkäufers, Schutzrechtsansprüche Dritter gegen den Käufer abzuwehren. **Unbegründete Ansprüche** werden hier jedoch faktisch eher selten zu einer Haftung des Verkäufers führen, weil es insoweit oft an der nach Abs. 1 erforderlichen Kenntnis des Verkäufers im Zeitpunkt des Vertragsschlusses mangeln dürfte. Wo freilich der Verkäufer schon bei Vertragsschluss weiss, dass sich z. B. ein Dritter im Verwendungsstaat eines die Ware betreffenden Patentes berühmt, mag er den Käufer hiervon in Kenntnis setzen, so dass seine Haftung nach Abs. 2 lit. a) entfällt; andernfalls hat er auch den unbegründeten Schutzrechtsanspruch abzuwehren.[25] Basiert der unbegründete Anspruch auf einem existenten und dem Verkäufer bekannten Schutzrecht, so haftet er; im Einzelfall kann eine Befreiung nach Art. 79 I in Betracht kommen. Auch sog. **Berechtigungsanfragen,** die lediglich einen Informationsaustausch im Vorfeld der eigentlichen Anspruchsgeltendmachung darstellen, können so gestellt werden, dass der Eindruck entsteht, der Dritte gehe bereits fest von einer Schutzrechtsverletzung aus. Dadurch kann der Käufer bereits ernstlich in seiner freien Verfügung über die Ware beeinträchtigt werden, so dass funktional eine Anspruchsgeltendmachung im Sinne des Art. 42 vorliegt.[26]

3. Eigene Rechte des Verkäufers

7   Auch **eigene Rechte oder Ansprüche des Verkäufers** fallen unter Art. 42.[27] Für den Käufer spielt es keine Rolle, ob er in der Verwendung der Ware auf Grund von Schutzrechten Dritter oder solchen des Verkäufers selbst behindert wird. Häufig wird allerdings mit der Lieferung eine sog. Schutzrechtserschöpfung eintreten, so dass der Käufer mangels anderweitiger Absprachen die Ware im Rahmen der allgemeinen Grenzen verwenden kann.[28]

4. Massgeblicher Zeitpunkt

8   Wie bei Art. 41 so kommt es auch für die Schutzrechtsfreiheit grundsätzlich auf den **Zeitpunkt der Lieferung** an.[29] Soweit Lieferung im Verkäuferstaat erfolgt, ist freilich nicht auf das Bestehen des Schutzrechtes dort, sondern im Verwendungsstaat abzustellen. Macht der Dritte Ansprüche aus einem (angeblichen) Schutzrecht geltend, muss wiederum ausreichen, dass er das Bestehen eines Schutzrechts im Zeitpunkt der Lieferung behauptet.[30] Auf den Zeitpunkt des **Vertragsschlusses** kommt es nur für die Kenntnis und die Bestimmung des Verwendungsstaates an.[31] Ein bei Vertragsschluss bestehendes Schutzrecht löst als solches noch keine Haftung aus, denn der Verkäufer kann dieses bis zur Lieferung

---

Rn. 13; *Soergel/Lüderitz/Schüßler-Langeheine,* Art. 42, Rn. 5; *Wolff,* S. 73; *Piltz,* Internationales Kaufrecht, Rn. 5–127; a. A. *Bucher,* Neuerungen, S. 30 f.; vgl. auch *Schwerha,* 16 Mich. J. Int'l L. (1995), 441, 457: „claims should be made in good faith". Auch Art. 102 II CESL-Entwurf schliesst eine Haftung für offensichtlich unbegründete Ansprüche aus Schutzrechten aus.
[25] Vgl. oben Art. 41 Rn. 10 ff. Vgl. auch *Schwenzer/Tebel,* Produktpiraterie, 1, 4; *Rauda/Etier,* 4 VJ (2000), 30, 39; *Metzger,*RabelsZ 73 (2009), 842, 847.
[26] Vgl. *Achilles,* FS Schwenzer, S. 1, 10.
[27] Vgl. im Übrigen oben Art. 41 Rn. 14. A. A. offenbar *Schwerha,* 16 Mich. J. Int'l L. (1995), 441, 458.
[28] Vgl. MünchKomm/*Gruber,* Art. 42, Rn. 9.
[29] Vgl. *Staudinger/Magnus,* Art. 42, Rn. 25; *Herber/Czerwenka,* Art. 42, Rn. 4; *Piltz,* Internationales Kaufrecht, Rn. 5–126; *Heilmann,* S. 664; *Vida,* RTD com. 1994, 21, 26; *Kröll u. a./Kröll,* Art. 42, Rn. 23; a. A. offenbar *Shinn,* 2 Minn. J. Global Trade (1993), 115, 127 (time of contracting).
[30] Vgl. oben Art. 41 Rn. 15.
[31] Vgl. dazu unten Rn. 10 ff. und 14 f.

ablösen, indem er etwa vom Berechtigten eine Lizenz erwirbt oder infolge eines Nichtigkeits- bzw. Nichtbenutzungsverfahrens die Wirkungen des Schutzrechts ausräumt.

5. Territoriale Begrenzung

Eine wesentliche Begrenzung der Verkäuferhaftung ergibt sich daraus, dass der Verkäufer für Schutzrechtsfreiheit nur in **bestimmten Staaten** einzustehen hat. **9**

a) Verwendungsstaat. De Verkäufer haftet zunächst dafür, dass die Ware nach dem Recht des Staates,[32] in dem sie weiterverkauft oder verwendet werden soll, schutzrechtsfrei ist, sofern die Parteien diesen Verwendungsstaat bei Vertragsschluss in Betracht gezogen haben, Abs. 1 lit. a). Dies rückt die Haftung für Schutzrechtsfreiheit in die Nähe der Sachmängelhaftung,[33] denn auch nach Art. 35 II lit. b) hat der Verkäufer für die Eignung der Ware zu einem bestimmten Zweck nur zu haften, wenn ihm dieser Zweck bei Vertragsschluss zur Kenntnis gebracht wurde. Abs. 1 lit. a) berücksichtigt die legitimen Verwendungsinteressen des Käufers; er soll weder in der Weiterveräusserung noch in sonstiger Verwendung der Ware durch Schutzrechte Dritter beeinträchtigt werden. Hierzu gehört auch, dass der Käufer vor eventuellen Regressansprüchen seiner eigenen Abnehmer geschützt wird. **Weiterverkauf** und **sonstige Verwendung** sind deshalb nicht alternativ zu verstehen, sie können vielmehr **kumulativ** zur Anwendung kommen, wenn der Käufer beispielsweise deutlich macht, er wolle die Ware im Staat A verkaufen, von seinem Abnehmer solle sie jedoch zur Verwendung in Staat B verbracht werden.[34] Auch **mehrere Verwendungsstaaten** können gleichzeitig in Betracht kommen.[35] Will oder kann der Verkäufer für Schutzrechtsfreiheit nicht in verschiedenen Staaten einstehen, mag er sich entsprechend freizeichnen. **10**

Schutzrechtsfreiheit im Verwendungsstaat ist nur zu prästieren, wenn die Parteien Verwendung in diesem Staat bei Vertragsschluss **in Betracht gezogen** haben.[36] Dabei wird man keine ausdrückliche Abrede über den Verwendungsstaat voraussetzen können. Es muss vielmehr als ausreichend angesehen werden, wenn der Verkäufer aus den Umständen den Verwendungsstaat erkennen kann, wie wenn beispielsweise der Käufer bei Vertragsschluss Versendung in einen anderen als den Käuferstaat verlangt oder der Verkäufer weiss, dass der Käufer in diesem Markt tätig ist.[37] Um Auslegungszweifeln zu begegnen, ist dem Käufer allerdings eine deutliche Klarstellung des Verwendungsstaates zu empfehlen.[38] Eine spätere Änderung des Bestimmungsortes bleibt unberücksichtigt, selbst wenn der Verkäufer hiervon positive Kenntnis erlangt. **11**

b) Käuferstaat. Subsidiär, d. h. nur wenn kein besonderer Verwendungsstaat bei Vertragsschluss in Betracht gezogen wurde, hat der Verkäufer für Schutzrechtsfreiheit im Käuferstaat einzustehen, Abs. 1 lit. b). Für die Bestimmung des **Käuferstaates** ist auf Art. 10 zurückzugreifen, wobei massgeblich der Sitz des Käufers im Zeitpunkt des Vertrags- **12**

---

[32] Streitig ist, ob es sich insoweit um eine Sachnormverweisung (so *Staudinger/Magnus*, Art. 42, Rn. 15; *Neumayer/Ming*, Art. 42, Rn. 1; *Loewe*, S. 63) oder um eine Kollisionsnormverweisung handelt (so MünchKomm/*Gruber*, Art. 42, Rn. 12; wohl auch MünchKommHGB/*Benicke*, Art. 42, Rn. 4).
[33] Die Parallele hebt vor allem *Schlechtriem*, Seller's Obligations, § 6-03, S. 6–33 hervor; vgl. auch *Mohs*, IHR 2002, 59, 63.
[34] Vgl. auch *Metzger*, RabelsZ 73 (2009), 842, 858.
[35] Vgl. OGH, 12.9.2006, CISG-online 1364; *Schlechtriem*, Internationales UN-Kaufrecht, Rn. 173; *Staudinger/Magnus*, Art. 42, Rn. 19; *U. Huber*, RabelsZ 43 (1979), 413, 502; *Vida*, RTD com. 1994, 21, 27; *Langenecker*, S. 152 ff.; *Rauda/Etier*, 4 VJ (2000), 30, 53; *Janal*, FS Kritzer, S. 203, 220; *Kröll u. a./Kröll*, Art. 42, Rn. 17; a. A. offenbar *Enderlein*, Rights and Obligations of the Seller, S. 181; *Shinn*, 2 Minn. J. Global Trade (1993), 115, 128 ff.
[36] Ohne ersichtlichen Grund strenger: Art. 102 II lit. a) CESL-Entwurf: „entsprechend dem Vertrag".
[37] Vgl. OGH, 12.9.2006, CISG-online 1364; *Kröll u. a./Kröll*, Art. 42, Rn. 16; tendenziell strenger *Metzger*, RabelsZ 73 (2009), 842, 858: Indizien für eine tatsächliche Verwendung im jeweiligen Staat erforderlich.
[38] Vgl. *Staudinger/Magnus*, Art. 42, Rn. 17; gem. *Benedick*, Informationspflichten, Rn. 338 gehen Zweifel zulasten des Käufers.

Art. 42 13, 13a Teil III. Kap. II. Pflichten des Verkäufers. Abschn. II

schlusses sein muss. Eine Sitzverlegung nach Vertragsschluss vermag die Haftung des Verkäufers nicht zu verändern oder zu erweitern. Abs. 1 lit. b) kommt **alternativ** zu und **nicht kumulativ** neben Abs. 1 lit. a) zur Anwendung.[39] Abs. 1 lit. b) umschreibt gewissermassen, freilich nur sofern die Parteien nichts anderes vereinbart haben, in Bezug auf Schutzrechte das Erfordernis der Eignung der Ware zum gewöhnlichen Gebrauch; auch insoweit liegt eine unbestreitbare Parallele zur Sachmängelhaftung nach Art. 35 II lit. a) vor.

13   c) **Verkäuferstaat.** Belastung der Ware mit einem Schutzrecht im Verkäuferstaat löst als solche nicht die Haftung nach Art. 42 aus,[40] es sei denn, dies wäre gleichzeitig der Verwendungsstaat. Wegen des territorialen Geltungsbereichs der Schutzrechte ist der Käufer nicht an der Situation im Verkäuferstaat, sondern nur in seinem eigenen Land oder im Land der Bestimmung der Ware interessiert.[41] Anders ist es freilich, wenn die Belastung im Verkäuferstaat gleichzeitig zu einer Belastung in einem der in Abs. 1 lit. a) oder b) genannten Staaten führt, etwa weil dort auf Grund der Regeln des internationalen Privatrechts oder auf Grund von internationalen Abkommen wie beispielsweise Art. 64 I EPÜ oder Art. 4 I MMA[42] das ausländische Schutzrecht anerkannt wird. Geht der Schutzrechtsinhaber im Verkäuferstaat noch vor Lieferung unmittelbar gegen den Verkäufer vor, kann dies dessen Haftung wegen Verletzung der Lieferpflicht (Art. 30) begründen.

13a d) **Transitstaat.**[43] Auch durch Zollmassnahmen wie Beschlagnahme, Zerstörung oder Anhalten der Ware im Transitstaat aufgrund von dort existierenden Schutzrechten kann es zu einer Beeinträchtigung der Nutzbarkeit der Ware für den Käufer kommen. Erfolgen diese Zollmassnahmen vor Lieferung (beispielsweise bei Vereinbarung einer D-Klausel), so kommt eine Verletzung der Lieferpflicht in Betracht. Ist jedoch Lieferung bereits erfolgt (beispielsweise aufgrund der Vereinbarung einer FOB-Klausel), ist zu unterscheiden: Unproblematisch ist der Fall, in dem eine Zollmassnahme erfolgt, weil ein Inverkehrbringen im Transitstaat, z. B. durch Ver- oder Bearbeitung, Komplettierung oder Umverpackung,[44] droht. In diesem Fall ist der Transitstaat Verwendungsstaat und die Haftung des Verkäufers richtet sich nach den oben (Rn. 10) geschilderten Kriterien. Eine Haftung nach Art. 42 trifft den Verkäufer weiterhin, falls die Beschlagnahme in einem Transitstaat erfolgt, in dem ein Schutzniveau herrscht, das demjenigen im Verwendungsstaat entspricht.[45] Hier kann der zufällige Ort der Beschlagnahme die Haftung des Verkäufers nicht beeinflussen. Gleiches gilt auch in Fällen, in denen unabhängig vom Bestehen eines Schutzrechts im Transitstaat dort eine Beschlagnahme erfolgt, weil ein Schutzrecht im Verwendungsstaat verletzt ist. Fraglich ist indes, ob der Verkäufer auch haftet, wenn die Beschlagnahme erfolgt, obwohl weder im Verkäuferstaat noch im Verwendungsstaat, sondern allein im Transitstaat eine Schutzrechtsverletzung gegeben ist. Während der EuGH[46] jüngst derartige Massnahmen nur dann für mit Unionsrecht vereinbar gehalten hat, wenn die Waren dazu bestimmt sind, in der Union in Verkehr gebracht zu werden und der Transitstaat demnach im Sinne von Art. 42 Verwendungsstaat ist, haben insbesondere niederländische und belgische Gerichte Zollmass-

---

[39] Vgl. zur Diskussion YB VIII (1977), S. 41, Nr. 219.
[40] Vgl. *Neumayer/Ming*, Art. 42, Anm. 1. Anders noch in den ersten Vorschlägen zur Begrenzung der Schutzrechtshaftung, vgl. YB VII (1976), S. 111, Art. 25; YB VIII (1977), S. 115, Nr. 5, 9; S. 121, Nr 18
[41] Vgl. *Schlechtriem*, Internationales UN-Kaufrecht, Rn. 174; *Enderlein*, ZfRVgl. 1988, 10, 18.
[42] Vgl. *Honnold/Flechtner*, Art. 42, Rn. 267.
[43] Vgl. hierzu auch *Vida*, RTD com. 1994, 21, 27 f.
[44] Ebenso *Vida*, RTD com. 1994, 21, 28. Vgl. auch *Kröll u. a./Kröll*, Art. 42, Rn. 22.
[45] Vgl. in Bezug auf die EU Art. 4 ff. EG-VO Nr. 1383/2003 des Rates v. 22.7.2003 über das Vorgehen der Zollbehörden gegen Waren, die im Verdacht stehen, bestimmte Rechte geistigen Eigentums zu verletzen, und die Massnahmen gegenüber Waren, die erkanntermassen derartige Rechte verletzen (ABlEG L 196 v. 2.8.2003, S. 7–14); diese VO ist zum 1.7.2004 an die Stelle der EG-VO Nr. 3295/94 getreten; vgl. dazu die Durchführungsvorschriften der EG-VO Nr. 1891/2004 der Kommission v. 21.10.2004 (ABlEG L 328 v. 30. 10 2004); siehe ferner EuGH, 6.4.2000, Rs. C-383/98 und EuGH, 7.1.2004, Rs. C-60/02 (EG-VO auch anwendbar, wenn Waren auf dem Transitweg zwischen zwei Drittstaaten in einem Mitgliedstaat angehalten werden).
[46] Vgl. auch Art. 9 IV PVÜ; Art. 51 TRIPS.

nahmen in solchen Fällen allein gestützt auf die Verletzung des Schutzrechts im Transitstaat zugelassen.[47] In derartigen Fällen haftet der Verkäufer allenfalls entsprechend Art. 42, falls er im Zeitpunkt des Vertragsschlusses Kenntnis nicht nur des in Aussicht gestellten Transitstaats und dem dortigen Bestehen des Schutzrechts sondern auch von der Gefahr dortiger Zollmassnahmen hat – so beispielsweise wenn die Praxis der Zollbehörden im Transitstaat dem Verkäufer aufgrund eigener Erfahrung oder sogar branchenweit bekannt ist. Gerade im letzten Fall wird die Haftung jedoch häufig gem. Art. 42 II lit. a) ausgeschlossen sein, da der Käufer die entsprechende Praxis ebenfalls kannte oder nicht darüber in Unkenntnis sein konnte. Grundsätzlich kann sich der Verkäufer demnach von einer Haftung befreien, indem er die ihm zur Verfügung stehenden Informationen zu allfälligen Schutzrechtskollisionen und zu erwartenden Zollmassnahmen im ihm bekannten Transitstaat vor Vertragsschluss an den Käufer weitergibt.

6. Kenntnis oder vorwerfbare Unkenntnis des Verkäufers

Zusätzlich eingeschränkt ist die Einstandspflicht des Verkäufers für die Freiheit von **14** Schutzrechten dadurch, dass er nur für solche Rechte oder Ansprüche haftet, die er bei Vertragsschluss kannte oder über die er nicht in Unkenntnis sein konnte. Während der Fall der **Kenntnis** in praxi kaum Schwierigkeiten bereiten wird,[48] ist fraglich, wie das Merkmal „**nicht in Unkenntnis sein konnte**" auszulegen ist. Nach dem Sekretariatskommentar soll vorwerfbare Unkenntnis vorliegen, wenn das betreffende Schutzrecht im Bestimmungsstaat publiziert ist.[49] Dies legt eine **Erkundigungspflicht** jedenfalls hinsichtlich **registrierter Schutzrechte** nahe.[50] Im Ergebnis erscheint eine solche Auslegung auch sachgerecht, da häufig nur der Verkäufer Kenntnis über einzelne Bestandteile der Ware besitzen wird und dementsprechend mögliche Schutzrechtsverletzungen vorhersehen kann,[51] sei es, dass er selbst Hersteller ist oder als Zwischenhändler die Informationen vom Hersteller beschaffen kann. Für eine Erkundigungspflicht des Verkäufers spricht weiterhin, dass dieser zur Vermeidung einer eigenen immaterialgüterrechtlichen Haftung ohnehin gehalten ist, eine Schutzrechtsrecherche durchzuführen; wenn die Erkundigung immaterialgüterrechtlich zumutbar ist, muss sie dies erst recht im Verhältnis zum Vertragspartner sein.[52] Weiterhin

---

[47] Gestützt wurde dies auf eine sogenannte „Herkunftsfiktion", nach der sich die Rechtmässigkeit der Zollmassnahmen so beurteilt, als wäre die Ware im Transitstaat hergestellt worden.
[48] Die in Bezug auf Frankreich in der 1. Aufl. geäusserte Befürchtung, dass französische Gerichte entsprechend der zu Artt. 1643, 1645 Cc bestehenden Tradition auch in Anwendung des CISG beim gewerblichen Verkäufer stets Kenntnis unterstellen könnten, ist nicht eingetreten; im Rahmen des CISG gilt die Vermutung nicht, vgl. *Ghestin/Desché*, Traité des contrats, Anm. 1057.; *Audit*, Vente internationale, Anm. 112.; *Mouly, D.* 1991. Chron. 77, Rn. 4.
[49] Sekretariatskommentar, Art. 40, Nr. 6. *Bacher*, FS Schwenzer, S. 115, 124 bezeichnet diese Annahme als „reine Fiktion", die jedoch „grundsätzlich sachgerecht" sei.
[50] In diesem Sinne auch *Schlechtriem*, Einheitliches UN-Kaufrecht, S. 65; *Staudinger/Magnus*, Art. 42, Rn. 22; *Herber/Czerwenka*, Art. 42, Rn. 5; *Vida*, RTD com. 1994, 21, 28; jetzt auch *Honnold/Flechtner*, Art. 42, Rn. 270.1; ähnlich auch *Reinhart*, Art. 42, Rn. 4; *Enderlein/Maskow/Strohbach*, Art. 42, Anm. 4.; *Neumayer/Ming*, Art. 42, Anm. 1. (publizierte Schutzrechte); *Niggemann*, Pflichten des Verkäufers, S. 93; *Audit*, Vente internationale, Anm. 117.; *Piltz*, Internationales Kaufrecht, Rn. 5–132; ausführlich und differenzierend *Rauda/Etier*, 4 VJ (2000), 30, 45 ff.; ähnlich auch *Heuzé*, Anm. 316., der jedoch zusätzlich noch danach differenzieren will, ob das Lieferangebot vom Käufer oder vom Verkäufer ausgegangen ist; die entsprechende Partei treffe die Pflicht, Erkundigungen einzuziehen; differenzierend auch *Langenecker*, S. 191 ff.; dagegen *Prager*, S. 167 ff., *Wolff*, S. 75; *Honnold/Flechtner*, Art. 42, Rn. 270, 229; zu eng wohl auch *U. Huber*, RabelsZ 43 (1979), 413, 503, der meint, der Verkäufer hafte nur bei arglistigem Verschweigen; von grob fahrlässiger Unkenntnis sprechen: *Herber*, Einführung, S. 27; *ders.*, Denkschrift, S. 50 hält grobfahrlässige Unkenntnis für erforderlich; ähnlich wohl auch *Shinn*, 2 Minn. J. Global Trade (1993), 115, 126 f.; wohl auch *P. Huber/Mullis/Mullis*, S. 176 (für eine Pflicht des Verkäufers nicht die Augen vor offensichtlichen Tatsachen zu verschliessen oder grob fahrlässig zu sein). A. A. *Janal*, FS Kritzer, S. 203, 213 ff. *Benedick*, Informationspflichten, Rn. 394 ff. befürwortet eine allgemeine Nachforschungspflicht. Für Zuweisung der Erkundigungspflicht zu Verkäufer oder Käufer (Art. 42 II lit. a)) nach ökonomischen Gesichtspunkten und damit unabhängig davon, ob das Schutzrecht registriert ist, *Metzger*, RabelsZ 73 (2009), 842, 853 f.; 861.
[51] Anders *Janal*, FS Kritzer, S. 203, 211.
[52] Vgl. *Metzger*, RabelsZ 73 (2009), 842, 856 f.

beeinflusst die Beantwortung der Schutzrechtsfrage unmittelbar den Wert der Ware[53] und ist damit der Sphäre des Verkäufers zuzuordnen. Zudem wäre bei Verneinung einer Erkundigungspflicht die Bedeutung der Schutzrechtshaftung derartig abgeschwächt, dass sie kaum eine praktische Bedeutung hätte. Nicht ausgeschlossen ist freilich, dass die Parteien vereinbaren, der Käufer solle sich um etwaige registrierte Schutzrechte im Verwendungsstaat kümmern. Eine solche **Vereinbarung** entbindet den Verkäufer von der Pflicht, Erkundigungen einzuziehen; Unkenntnis ist ihm dann nicht mehr vorwerfbar. Bei **nicht registrierten Schutzrechten** wie Ausstattung oder Know-how wird man dem Verkäufer eine Erkundigungspflicht allerdings kaum zumuten können.[54]

15 Massgeblicher Zeitpunkt für Kenntnis oder vorwerfbare Unkenntnis ist der **Vertragsschluss.** Später erlangte Kenntnis begründet keine Einstandspflicht des Verkäufers nach Art. 42 I.[55] Für den Verkäufer kann sich freilich hier die Pflicht ergeben, den Käufer über das nachträglich bekanntgewordene Schutzrecht zu **informieren,** damit dieser die Ware eventuell in einen schutzrechtsfreien Staat umleiten oder sich rechtzeitig um Einräumung einer Lizenz bemühen kann.[56] Eine Verletzung dieser aus Treu und Glauben fliessenden Nebenpflicht kann den Verkäufer schadenersatzpflichtig machen.[57]

IV. Haftungsausschluss

1. Kenntnis oder vorwerfbare Unkenntnis des Käufers, Abs. 2 lit. a)

16 Der Verkäufer haftet nicht nach Abs. 1, wenn der **Käufer** das Recht oder den Anspruch des Dritten bei Vertragsschluss **kannte** oder darüber **nicht in Unkenntnis sein konnte.**[58] Auch damit steht Art. 42 der Sachmängelhaftung, die in Art. 35 III einen entsprechenden Haftungsausschluss enthält, näher als der allgemeinen Rechtsmängelhaftung nach Art. 41 S. 1, die nur bei Einwilligung des Käufers ausgeschlossen ist.[59]

17 Im Normalfall trifft den Käufer **keine Erkundigungspflicht,**[60] da ihm Einzelheiten der Ware oder ihrer Fertigung oft gar nicht bekannt sein werden. Problematisch erscheint auch die französische Rechtsprechung, die allzu schnell Kenntnis des gewerblichen Käufers unterstellt.[61] Anders kann der Fall zu beurteilen sein, wenn es der Käufer übernommen hat, sich um etwaige Schutzrechte im Verwendungsstaat zu kümmern. Spiegelbildlich zur Einstandspflicht des Verkäufers[62] wird in einem solchen Fall vorwerfbare Unkenntnis jedenfalls in Bezug auf **publizierte Schutzrechte** anzunehmen sein. Vorwerfbare Unkenntnis wird man schliesslich auch z. B. in Bezug auf international bekannte oder notorische Marken sowie auf Erfindungen usw., für die geworben wird, annehmen können.[63] Weiterhin erscheint es

---

[53] Vgl. *Bacher,* FS Schwenzer, S. 115, 125.
[54] Ähnlich *Staudinger/Magnus,* Art. 42, Rn. 22; *Herber/Czerwenka,* Art. 42, Rn. 5; *Piltz,* Internationales Kaufrecht, Rn. 5–132; a. A. *Kröll u. a./Kröll,* Art. 42, Rn. 17 (für Verkäufer, die gleichzeitig Hersteller sind).
[55] So auch *Staudinger/Magnus,* Art. 42, Rn. 23; *Herber/Czerwenka,* Art. 42, Rn. 4; *Reinhart,* Art. 42, Rn. 3.
[56] Vgl. *Vida,* RTD com. 1994, 21, 28; *Achilles,* FS Schwenzer, S. 1, 16; einschränkend *Benedick,* Informationspflichten, Rn. 1145 ff.; a. A. offenbar *Shinn,* 2 Minn. J. Global Trade (1993), 115, 126.
[57] Vgl. *Benedick,* Informationspflichten, Rn. 576 ff., 1205 ff.; *Achilles,* FS Schwenzer, S. 1, 17.
[58] Ähnlich Art. 102 III CESL-Entwurf für B2B-Verträge. Für B2C Verträge fordert Art. 102 IV CESL-Entwurf jedoch positive Kenntnis des Käufers.
[59] Vgl. *Mohs,* IHR 2002, 59, 62; *Su,* IPRax 1997, 284, 287; *Rauda/Etier,* 4 VJ (2000), 30, 50 f.
[60] Vgl. auch *Staudinger/Magnus,* Art. 42, Rn. 26; *Enderlein,* Rights and Obligations of the Seller, S. 182; *Herber/Czerwenka,* Art. 42, Rn. 6; *Enderlein/Maskow/Strohbach,* Art. 42, Anm. 9.; *Witz/Salger/Lorenz/Salger,* Art. 42, Rn. 8; *Kröll u. a./Kröll,* Art. 42, Rn. 38; *Piltz,* Internationales Kaufrecht, Rn. 5–134; *Vida,* RTD com. 1994, 21, 30; a. A. offenbar *Shinn,* 2 Minn. J. Global Trade (1993), 115, 125. Gegen eine allgemeine Regel und für Einzelfallbetrachtung: *Benedick,* Informationspflichten, Rn. 404 ff.
[61] Vgl. Civ. 1, 19.3.2002, CISG-online 662, m. Anm. *C. Witz,* D. 2003, Somm. 2361, 2366 f.; CA Colmar, 13.11.2002, CISG-online 792; TGI Versailles, 23.11.2004, CISG-online 953; krit. *T. M. Müller,* Beweislast, S. 122 f.; *Kröll u. a./Kröll,* Art. 42, Rn. 38; mit ökonomischer Argumentation zustimmend *Metzger,* RabelsZ 73 (2009), 842, 862.
[62] Vgl. oben Rn. 14.
[63] Ebenso *Vida,* RTD com. 1994, 21, 30 f.; *Bamberger/Roth/Saenger,* Art. 42, Rn. 12; vgl. auch *Langenecker,* S. 212 (alle notorisch bekannten Schutzrechte); *Kröll u. a./Kröll,* Art. 42, Rn. 39; weitergehend wohl Civ. 1,

zumutbar, einem Käufer, der vertieftes Fachwissen über den Kaufgegenstand hat, eine Erkundigungspflicht aufzuerlegen, beispielsweise weil er selbst Hersteller von vergleichbaren Gegenständen ist.[64] Auch das Vorhaben des Käufers, eine universell einsetzbare Ware auf eine spezielle Art zu verwenden, kann zu einer Erkundigungspflicht des Käufers führen.[65]

Wie für die Begründung der Verkäuferhaftung kommt es auch hier auf den Zeitpunkt des **Vertragsschlusses** an. Später erlangte Kenntnis des Käufers führt nicht zum Haftungsausschluss nach Abs. 2 lit. a), kann aber die Frist zur Anzeige nach Art. 43 I in Gang setzen. 18

2. Befolgen technischer Anweisungen etc., Abs. 2 lit. b)

a) Freiwerden des Verkäufers. Die Haftung des Verkäufers nach Abs. 1 ist ferner ausgeschlossen, wenn sich das Recht oder der Anspruch des Dritten daraus ergibt, dass der Verkäufer sich nach **technischen Zeichnungen, Entwürfen, Formeln** oder **sonstigen Angaben** – wie beispielsweise die Marke, unter der die Ware geliefert werden soll[66] – gerichtet hat, die der Käufer zur Verfügung gestellt hat. In diesem Fall fehlt es an einem Verschulden des Verkäufers, der Schutzrechtsverstoss geht vielmehr auf das eigene Verhalten des Käufers zurück, so dass er auch das daraus resultierende Risiko tragen muss (vgl. auch Art. 80). 19

Für den Haftungsausschluss nach Abs. 2 lit. b) wird man freilich eine gewisse **Genauigkeit** der Angaben voraussetzen müssen, wie sich schon aus der beispielhaften Aufzählung von technischen Zeichnungen, Entwürfen und Formeln und der insoweit eindeutigen englischen und französischen Fassung[67] ergibt. Allgemeine Angaben und Wünsche des Käufers, die dem Verkäufer einen eigenen Entscheidungsspielraum belassen, insbesondere schutzrechtsfreie Herstellung als Alternative offen halten, können den Verkäufer nicht von seiner Einstandspflicht entbinden,[68] die ja ohnehin nur bei Kenntnis bzw. vorwerfbarer Unkenntnis eingreift. Nicht erforderlich ist hingegen **Kenntnis des Käufers**, dass ein Befolgen seiner Angaben zu einem Schutzrechtsverstoss führt.[69] 20

Erkennt der Verkäufer jedoch den Verstoss gegen das Schutzrecht eines Dritten, ist er nach Treu und Glauben verpflichtet, den Käufer hierüber zu **informieren**.[70] Unterlässt er diese Mitteilung, so wird er sich – vorausgesetzt, Kenntnis vom Schutzrecht lag bereits im Zeitpunkt des Vertragsschlusses vor – nicht auf Haftungsbefreiung nach Abs. 2 lit. b) berufen können. Wo er später Kenntnis erlangt und Mitteilung an den Käufer unterlässt, kann dies zur Haftung auf **Schadenersatz** wegen Nebenpflichtverletzung führen.[71] Besteht freilich der Käufer nach Mitteilung durch den Verkäufer darauf, dass der Verkäufer seinen Anweisungen Folge leistet, entfällt die Haftung des Verkäufers. 21

b) Rechtsbehelfe des Verkäufers. In Abs. 2 lit. b) nicht geregelt ist die Frage, welche Rechtsbehelfe dem Verkäufer gegenüber dem Käufer zustehen, wenn dessen Anweisungen zu einer Schutzrechtsverletzung führen bzw. eine solche abzusehen ist.[72] Dabei interessiert vor allem auch eine mögliche Schutzrechtsbelastung im **Verkäuferstaat**. Die Lösung der 22

19.3.2002, CISG-online 662, m. Anm. *C. Witz,* D. 2003, Somm. 2361, 2366 f.; *Rauda/Etier,* 4 VJ (2000), 30, 57.
[64] Vgl. *Bacher,* FS Schwenzer, S. 115, 125 f.; i. E. gleich *Metzger,* RabelsZ 73 (2009), 842, 861.
[65] Vgl. *Bacher,* FS Schwenzer, S. 115, 120, 126, der in dieser Situation zusätzlich mit der Wertung des Art. 42 II lit. b) argumentiert, S. 120, 127.
[66] Über Verpackung, Ausstattung, Marken in dieser Beziehung vgl. *Herber/Czerwenka,* Art. 42, Rn. 7.
[67] „Other *„such* specifications", „autres spécifications *analogues*".
[68] Ähnlich auch *Schlechtriem,* Seller's Obligations, § 6.03, S. 6–34; *Staudinger/Magnus,* Art. 42, Rn. 29; *Prager,* S. 177; *Wolff,* S. 78; differenzierend *Langenecker,* S. 233 ff.
[69] Vgl. *Staudinger/Magnus,* Art. 42, Rn. 29.
[70] Vgl. *Staudinger/Magnus,* Art. 42, Rn. 31; *Enderlein,* Rights and Obligations of the Seller, S. 183; *Audit,* Vente internationale, Anm. 117.; *Reinhart,* Art. 42, Rn. 6; *Enderlein/Maskow/Strohbach,* Art. 42, Anm. 10.; *Vida,* RTD com. 1994, 21, 31; einschränkend *Benedick,* Informationspflichten, Rn. 1095 ff.
[71] Vgl. *Achilles,* FS Schwenzer, S. 1, 17; *Benedick,* Informationspflichten, Rn. 1205 ff.
[72] Anders § 2–312 III UCC, wonach der Käufer, der technische Anweisungen liefert, die zu einer Schutzrechtsverletzung führen, den Verkäufer von der Haftung im Verhältnis zum Schutzrechtsinhaber freizustellen bzw. ihn hierfür zu entschädigen hat.

Art. 42 23–25 Teil III. Kap. II. Pflichten des Verkäufers. Abschn. II

Frage der Rechtsbehelfe des Verkäufers bei Schutzrechtsbelastung im Verkäuferstaat kann ohne weiteres den Vorschriften des CISG (Artt. 61–65) selbst entnommen werden;[73] ein Rückgriff auf nationales Recht kommt nicht in Betracht (Art. 7 II).

23 Die Pflicht des Käufers, technische Pläne oder dergleichen zur Verfügung zu stellen, stellt eine vertragliche **Nebenpflicht** dar.[74] Gleichzeitig erwächst dem Käufer gegenüber dem Verkäufer die Schutzpflicht, die Anweisungen so zu fassen, dass ihm deren Befolgung nicht zum Nachteil gereicht. Erkennt der Verkäufer die bei Befolgen der Anweisungen drohende Schutzrechtsverletzung, kann er zunächst vom Käufer **Erfüllung** verlangen, Art. 62, und ihm eine Nachfrist zur Erteilung anderer Anweisungen oder ggf. der Erlangung einer Lizenz setzen, Art. 63 I. Ist eine schutzrechtsfreie Gestaltung nicht möglich, oder besteht der Käufer auf Befolgung der zu einer Schutzrechtsverletzung führenden Anweisungen, liegt eine wesentliche Vertragsverletzung seitens des Käufers vor, die den Verkäufer zur **Aufhebung des Vertrages** berechtigt, Art. 64 I lit. a). Denn dem Verkäufer kann nicht zugemutet werden, bei Befolgen der Anweisungen des Käufers sehenden Auges das Schutzrecht eines Dritten zu verletzen und sich damit womöglich selbst diesem gegenüber schadenersatzpflichtig zu machen. Wo die Befolgung der Anweisungen des Käufers zu einer Schutzrechtsverletzung geführt hat, haftet der Käufer dem Verkäufer wegen Nebenpflichtverletzung auf **Schadenersatz**, Art. 74, wobei der dem Verkäufer erwachsende Haftpflichtschaden immer als voraussehbare Folge i. S. d. Art. 74 S. 2 anzusehen ist. Erkannte der Verkäufer freilich die mögliche Schutzrechtsverletzung, kommt Herabsetzung des Schadenersatzanspruchs nach Art. 77 S. 2 in Betracht.

3. Unterlassene Anzeige

24 Der Käufer verliert seine Ansprüche wegen Belastung mit einem Schutzrecht im Falle unterlassener Anzeige (Art. 43 I), sofern nicht die Ausnahmetatbestände der Artt. 43 II, 44 vorliegen.

4. Freizeichnungsklauseln

24a Nach Art. 6 ist es den Parteien unbenommen, die Bestimmung des Art. 42 **insgesamt** oder **einzelne ihrer Teile** abzubedingen. Die Gültigkeit solcher Abreden unterliegt nach Art. 4 lit. a) dem über IPR anwendbaren nationalen Recht.[75] In den nationalen Rechtsordnungen gilt jedoch übereinstimmend der Grundsatz, dass sich niemand von den Folgen eigenen **arglistigen Handelns** oder auch von **grober Fahrlässigkeit** freizeichnen kann.[76] Da die Haftung nach Art. 42 ohnehin nur eingreift, wenn der Verkäufer das Schutzrecht kannte oder darüber nicht in Unkenntnis sein konnte, dürfte danach ein vertraglicher Ausschluss der Haftung nicht in Betracht kommen.

V. Rechtsbehelfe

1. Nach CISG

25 Die Rechtsbehelfe bei Belastung mit Schutzrechten entsprechen im Prinzip jenen bei allgemeinen Rechtsmängeln.[77] Wiederum stellt sich jedoch die Frage, ob die Vorschriften, die ausdrücklich an die Vertragsgemässheit der Ware anknüpfen (Artt. 46 II und III, 50), auf die Haftung nach Art. 42 I anzuwenden sind. Sprechen auch hier Wortlaut, Systematik und

---

[73] So auch *Langenecker*, S. 242.
[74] Vgl. hierzu allgemein unten *Mohs*, Art. 53 Rn. 1.
[75] Zum Ausschluss der Rechtsgewährleistung in den nationalen Kaufrechten vgl. oben Art. 41 Rn. 19a.
[76] Deutschland: §§ 276 III, 444 BGB; Schweiz: Artt. 100, 199 OR; Österreich: § 6 I Nr. 9 KSchG; Frankreich: Artt. 1643 Cc; England: vgl. *Benjamin*, Rn. 13–081, 13–082; USA: vgl. *Schwenzer*, Freizeichnung, S. 69; vgl. auch rechtsvergleichend *Eörsi*, 23 Am. J. Comp. L. (1975), 215, 217.
[77] Vgl. im Einzelnen oben Art. 41 Rn. 21.

Entstehungsgeschichte gegen eine Anwendung auf die Schutzrechtshaftung,[78] so mögen doch Zweifel an dieser Auffassung deshalb entstehen, weil die Schutzrechtshaftung sowohl von der Interessenlage als auch von ihrer konkreten Ausgestaltung in Art. 42 her der Sachmängelhaftung näher steht als der allgemeinen Rechtsmängelhaftung nach Art. 41.[79] Praktisch bedeutsam wird das Problem vor allem für die Frage, ob der Käufer Erfüllung in Form der **Ersatzlieferung bei Gattungsware** – wie beispielsweise Lieferung unter anderer Marke, die kein Schutzrecht verletzt, oder Lieferung neutraler Ware – oder der **Nachbesserung** – wie beispielsweise durch Ersatz der patentverletzenden durch schutzrechtsfreie Bestandteile oder durch Vereinbarung mit dem Schutzrechtsinhaber – generell (Art. 46 I) oder nur in den Grenzen des Art. 46 II und III verlangen kann. Die Interessenlage zwischen den Parteien spricht jedenfalls für Anwendung des Art. 46 II. Ersatzlieferung stellt für den Verkäufer bei einem internationalen Kaufvertrag immer eine erhebliche Belastung dar. Andererseits mag es im Einzelfall durchaus vorkommen, dass die Belastung mit einem Schutzrecht – wohl anders als bei einem allgemeinen Rechtsmangel – die Verwendungsinteressen des Käufers gar nicht beeinträchtigt, so wenn die Ware zwar im Käuferstaat mit einem Schutzrecht belastet, in jenem Staat, in dem sie der Käufer aber tatsächlich verwendet, jedoch schutzrechtsfrei ist. Ein Abstellen auf die Wesentlichkeit der Vertragsverletzung würde insoweit einen angemessenen Interessenausgleich zwischen den Parteien bewirken. Deshalb mehren sich in der Literatur die Stimmen, die in Bezug auf die Rechtsbehelfe für einen Gleichlauf von Sachmängel- und Schutzrechtsmängelhaftung plädieren.[80]

26 Gleichwohl sind die aus Wortlaut, Systematik und Entstehungsgeschichte abzuleitenden Argumente nicht gering zu schätzen. Es ist zu erwarten, dass international betrachtet dieser tendenziell formalen Auslegung der Vorzug gegeben wird. Trotz der geäusserten sachlichen Bedenken sollte man deshalb um der einheitlichen Auslegung und Rechtssicherheit willen (Art. 7 I) jedenfalls Art. 46 II und III nicht auf die Schutzrechtshaftung nach Art. 42 I anwenden.[81]

2. Nach nationalem Recht

27 Wie bei Art. 41[82] stellt sich auch hier das Problem, ob nach dem Wegfall des Art. 53 EKG noch hinreichend sichergestellt ist, dass ein Rückgriff auf nationale Rechtsbehelfe wegen eines sich auf ein Schutzrecht beziehenden **Irrtums** oder wegen **fahrlässiger Falschangaben** ausgeschlossen ist. Sachlich können hieran keine Zweifel bestehen. Nationale Rechtsbehelfe dürfen vor allem nicht dazu führen, dass die von Art. 42 bezweckte Beschränkung der Verkäuferhaftung letztlich unterlaufen wird.

28 Nicht ausgeschlossen werden freilich auch hier die dem Käufer bei **Arglist** oder **Betrug** des Verkäufers zustehenden nationalen Rechtsbehelfe.[83]

VI. Beweislast[84]

29 Der Käufer hat das Schutzrecht bzw. die Beanspruchung eines solchen durch einen Dritten zu beweisen sowie Kenntnis bzw. vorwerfbare Unkenntnis des Verkäufers im Zeit-

---

[78] Vgl. oben Art. 41 Rn. 20; vgl. auch Sekretariatskommentar, Art. 40, Nr. 12.
[79] Vgl. *Schlechtriem*, Seller's Obligations, § 6.03, S. 635; *Honnold/Flechtner*, Art. 42, Rn. 270; *Mohs*, IHR 2002, 59, 63.
[80] So vor allem *Mohs*, IHR 2002, 59, 63 f. Vgl. OGH, 12.9.2006, CISG-online 1364 bezüglich Zurückbehaltungsrecht.
[81] Vgl. auch unten *Müller-Chen*, Art. 46 Rn. 22; zur Anwendung des Art. 50 vgl. unten *Müller-Chen*, Art. 50 Rn. 2. A. A. *Mohs*, IHR 2002, 59, 63; *Janal*, FS Kritzer, S. 203, 211 f.
[82] Vgl. oben Art. 41 Rn. 23.
[83] Vgl. oben Art. 41 Rn. 24.
[84] Die Beweislastverteilung richtet sich nach dem Regel-Ausnahme-Prinzip, vgl. oben Art. 35 Rn. 52; *Schlechtriem/Schwenzer/Schwenzer/Hachem*, CISG Commentary, Art. 4, Rn. 25; i. E. gleich unten *Müller-Chen*, Art. 45 Rn. 9, 10.

punkt des Vertragsschlusses.[85] Ebenfalls vom Käufer zu beweisen ist, dass sich das Schutzrecht bzw. dessen Beanspruchung gerade auf die Kaufsache bezieht.[86] Eine Beweislastumkehr erscheint hingegen angezeigt, wenn der Käufer nicht über das zur Beurteilung der möglichen Verletzung des Schutzrechts nötige Fachwissen verfügt, weil z. B. nur der Verkäufer von gewissen Herstellungsinformationen Kenntnis hat.[87] Im Falle des Abs. 1 lit. a) obliegt dem Käufer ferner der Nachweis, dass die Parteien einen bestimmten Verwendungsstaat in Betracht gezogen haben. Den Verkäufer trifft die Beweislast, wenn er sich auf Kenntnis bzw. vorwerfbare Unkenntnis des Käufers, Abs. 2 lit. a), oder darauf beruft, dass der Schutzrechtsverstoss auf Anweisungen des Käufers zurückzuführen ist, Abs. 2 lit. b).[88]

---

[85] Vgl. BGer, 17.4.2012, CISG-online 2346, E.2.3; OGH, 12.9.2006, CISG-online 1364, zust. *Janal*, FS Kritzer, S. 203, 211; RB Zwolle, 1.3.1995, CISG-online 372; *Schwenzer/Tebel*, Produktpiraterie, 1, 4 f.; *Zhang*, S. 93. Ausführlich insbesondere zur Beweislast bezüglich der Erkennbarkeit *Antweiler*, S. 190 ff.
[86] BGer, 17.4.2012, CISG-online 2346, E.2.3, zust. *Schwenzer/Tebel*, Produktpiraterie, 1, 5.
[87] Vgl. *Janal*, FS Kritzer, S. 203, 211 f.
[88] *Kröll u. a./Kröll*, Art. 42, Rn. 57.

Art. 43 [Rügepflicht]

(1) Der Käufer kann sich auf Artikel 41 oder 42 nicht berufen, wenn er dem Verkäufer das Recht oder den Anspruch des Dritten nicht innerhalb einer angemessenen Frist nach dem Zeitpunkt, in dem er davon Kenntnis erlangt hat oder hätte erlangen müssen,* anzeigt und dabei genau bezeichnet, welcher Art das Recht oder der Anspruch des Dritten ist.

(2) Der Verkäufer kann sich nicht auf Absatz 1 berufen, wenn er das Recht oder den Anspruch des Dritten und seine Art kannte.

Art. 43

(1) The buyer loses the right to rely on the provisions of article 41 or article 42 if he does not give notice to the seller specifying the nature of the right or claim of the third party within a reasonable time after he has become aware or ought to have become aware of the right or claim.

(2) The seller is not entitled to rely on the provisions of the preceding paragraph if he knew of the right or claim of the third party and the nature of it.

Art. 43

1) L'acheteur perd le droit de se prévaloir des dispositions des articles 41 et 42 s'il ne dénonce pas au vendeur le droit ou la prétention du tiers, en précisant la nature de ce droit ou de cette prétention, dans un délai raisonnable à partir dû moment où il en a eu connaissance ou aurait dû en avoir connaissance.

2) Le vendeur ne peut pas se prévaloir des dispositions du paragraphe précédent s'il connaissait le droit ou la prétention du tiers et sa nature.

Übersicht

	Rn.
I. Vorgeschichte	1
II. Ausschluss der Einstandspflicht, Abs. 1	2
1. Anzeigepflicht	2
2. Frist	3
3. Form, Übermittlungsrisiko und Adressat	5
4. Fehlen einer Ausschlussfrist	6
5. Rechtsfolgen unterlassener Anzeige	8
III. Ausnahme, Abs. 2	9
IV. Beweislast	12

Vorläufer und **Entwürfe**: Art. 52 EKG, Wiener E 1977 Artt. 25 II, 26 III, New Yorker E 1978 Artt. 39 II, 40 III.

I. Vorgeschichte

Die Rügepflicht des Käufers bei Rechtsmängeln, die den meisten nationalen Rechtsordnungen fremd ist, war der Sache nach bereits in Art. 52 EKG enthalten. Im Genfer Entwurf fehlte zunächst eine entsprechende Vorschrift. Im Wiener und New Yorker Entwurf wurde die Rügepflicht jeweils gesondert bei den Vorschriften zur allgemeinen Rechtsmängelhaftung und zur Schutzrechtshaftung geregelt; auf der Wiener Konferenz wurden die beiden Einzelbestimmungen zu Abs. 1 verschmolzen. Die Ausnahme des Abs. 2 entspricht sachlich der Regelung in Art. 52 I EKG; sie war in den Vorentwürfen zunächst nicht enthalten und wurde erst auf Grund eines Vorschlags der Bundesrepublik auf der Wiener Konferenz eingefügt.[1]

1

---

* Schweiz: von dem an er davon Kenntnis hatte oder haben musste.
[1] O.R., S. 110, Art. 40, Nr. 3, 5; S. 350, Art. 40 bis, Nr. 77 ff.; S. 351, Art. 40 bis, Nr. 1 ff.

II. Ausschluss der Einstandspflicht, Abs. 1

1. Anzeigepflicht

2   Der Käufer kann sich auf allgemeine Rechtsmängel oder Schutzrechtsbelastung nicht berufen, wenn er dem Verkäufer das Recht oder den Anspruch des Dritten nicht anzeigt. Dasselbe gilt für Rechtsmängel, für die der Verkäufer eine über Artt. 41, 42 hinausgehende Einstandspflicht übernommen hat.[2] Dies entspricht im Wesentlichen der Regelung des Art. 39 I bei Sachmängeln. Ähnlich wie in Art. 39 I, wo der Käufer die Art der Vertragswidrigkeit genau zu bezeichnen hat, ist eine allgemeine Anzeige, dass die Ware mit dem Recht eines Dritten belastet ist, nicht ausreichend.[3] Der Käufer muss vielmehr die **Art des Rechts oder des Anspruchs** des Dritten genau bezeichnen. Die Anforderungen an die Genauigkeit der Anzeige müssen dabei aus dem Zweck, den die Anzeigepflicht verfolgt, hergeleitet werden. Durch die Anzeige soll der Verkäufer in die Lage gesetzt werden, das Recht oder den Anspruch des Dritten abzuwehren.[4] Die Anzeige wird deshalb zunächst die Person des Dritten und die Art des geltend gemachten Drittrechtes umfassen müssen. Darüber hinaus muss der Käufer den Verkäufer auch über die bereits vom Dritten unternommenen Schritte unterrichten.[5] Wie bei Art. 39 I ist es jedoch auch hier dem Verkäufer bei unspezifischer Anzeige zumutbar, beim Käufer rückzufragen.[6] Die Mängelanzeige ist auch erforderlich, wenn der Dritte sein Recht noch nicht geltend gemacht hat.[7] Im Unterschied zu Art. 52 I EKG muss der Käufer allerdings nicht mehr das Verlangen nach Abhilfe oder Ersatzlieferung unmittelbar mit der Rechtsmängelanzeige verbinden.[8]

2. Frist

3   Wie nach Art. 39 I[9] muss auch hier die Anzeige nicht sofort, sondern innerhalb einer **angemessenen Frist** erfolgen. Ausschlaggebend für die Bemessung der Frist müssen die Umstände des Einzelfalles sein. Zu berücksichtigen ist dabei die Zeit, die der Käufer benötigt, um sich von der Rechtslage ein ungefähres Bild zu machen,[10] was oft nicht ohne die Einholung von Rechtsrat möglich sein wird.[11] Andererseits werden auch die **Art des Rechtsmangels** und die von Seiten des Dritten bereits **unternommenen Schritte** zu

---

[2] Vgl. MünchKomm/*Gruber*, Art. 43, Rn. 4; *Staudinger/Magnus*, Art. 43, Rn. 11; *Soergel/Lüderitz/Schüßler-Langeheine*, Art. 43, Rn. 5; *Bianca/Bonell/Sono*, Art. 43, Rn. 5.

[3] BGH, 11.1.2006, CISG-online 1200, Rn. 21 = IHR 2006, 82, 84 (Mitteilung polizeilicher Beschlagnahme wegen Diebstahlsverdachts nicht ausreichend) m. Anm. *Schroeter*, EWiR 2006, 427 f.

[4] Vgl. *Staudinger/Magnus*, Art. 43, Rn. 12; *Enderlein*, Rights and Obligations of the Seller, S. 184; *Audit*, Vente internationale, Anm. 115.

[5] Vgl. BGH, 11.1.2006, CISG-online 1200, Rn. 21 = IHR 2006, 82, 84, m. Anm. *Schroeter*, EWiR 2006, 427 f.; *Enderlein/Maskow/Strohbach*, Art. 43, Anm. 4.; *Ferrari u. a./Ferrari*, Internationales Vertragsrecht, Art. 43, Rn. 5; ähnlich *Herber/Czerwenka*, Art. 43, Rn. 2; *Reinhart*, Art. 42, Rn. 2; *Karollus*, S. 127; *Heuzé*, Anm. 313.; *Piltz*, Internationales Kaufrecht, Rn. 5–151: Unterschiedliche, nach und nach auftretende Rechtsmängel sind jedes Mal erneut zu rügen.

[6] Vgl. MünchKommHGB/*Benicke*, Art. 43, Rn. 3; ähnlich *J. Ramberg*, International Transactions, S. 134.

[7] Vgl. MünchKomm/*Gruber*, Art. 43, Rn. 4; *Staudinger Magnus*, Art. 43, Rn. 16.

[8] Vgl. *Staudinger/Magnus*, Art. 43, Rn. 13; vgl. im Übrigen auch Art. 39 Rn. 6 ff.

[9] Vgl. Art. 39 Rn. 15 ff.; *Piltz*, Internationales Kaufrecht, Rn. 5–139 weist darauf hin, dass trotz gleichen Wortlauts die konkrete Fixierung der Frist nach Art. 43 nicht mit derjenigen nach Art. 39 identisch sein müsse; wohl anders *Honnold/Flechtner*, Art 43, Rn. 271, der es für vernünftig hält, sich bei der Interpretation des Artikel 43 von der Interpretation des Artikel 39 I leiten zu lassen.

[10] Vgl. BGH, 11.1.2006, CISG-online 1200, Rn. 12 = IHR 2006, 82, 83, m. Anm. *Schroeter*, EWiR 2006, 427 f.; *Staudinger/Magnus*, Art. 43, Rn. 20; *Enderlein*, Rights and Obligations of the Seller, S. 184; *Enderlein/Maskow/Strohbach*, Art. 43, Anm. 2.; *Reinhart*, Art. 43, Rn. 2; *Soergel/Lüderitz/Schüßler-Langeheine*, Art. 43, Rn. 3; *Neumayer/Ming*, Art. 43.

[11] A. A. *Herber/Czerwenka*, Art. 43, Rn. 3: In aller Regel wird es dem Käufer nicht gestattet sein, die Rüge bis zur Einholung eines Rechtsgutachtens hinauszuschieben; *Witz/Salger/Lorenz/Salger*, Art. 43, Rn. 5; *Ferrari u. a./Ferrari*, Internationales Vertragsrecht, Art. 43, Rn. 11. In casu nicht für erforderlich gehalten in BGH, 11.1.2006, CISG-online 1200, Rn. 13 = IHR 2006, 82, 83, m. Anm. *Schroeter*, EWiR 2006, 427 f.

berücksichtigen sein.[12] Entzieht der Dritte aufgrund seines Rechtes dem Käufer den Besitz an der Ware, ist schnelleres Handeln geboten, als wenn der Dritte etwa nur eine angemessene Lizenzgebühr für sich in Anspruch nimmt.[13] Erkennt der Käufer, dass bei längerem Zuwarten für den Verkäufer die Gefahr besteht, seine eventuellen Rechte gegenüber dem Dritten nicht mehr durchsetzen zu können, ist rasche Anzeige erforderlich. Den im Rahmen von Art. 39 I vertretenen groben Mittelwert von einem Monat[14] wird man auch im Rahmen von Art. 43 heranziehen können.[15]

Die **Frist** zur Anzeige **beginnt** mit dem Zeitpunkt, in dem der Käufer von dem Recht oder Anspruch des Dritten Kenntnis erlangt hat oder hätte erlangen müssen. Eine Erkundigungspflicht obliegt dem Käufer insoweit nicht.[16] **Fahrlässige Unkenntnis** kann hier nur bedeuten, dass sich der Käufer nicht sorglos über konkrete Anhaltspunkte, die für ein Recht oder einen Anspruch eines Dritten sprechen, hinwegsetzen darf,[17] so beispielsweise, wenn er durch eine Werbekampagne von einem neuen Produkt oder einer Markenware Kenntnis erlangt. Die Frist beginnt jedoch frühestens mit Lieferung.[18] Eine Vorverlegung des Beginns auch nur in Ausnahmefällen verwischt die Grenzen der Risikosphären von Verkäufer und Käufer.[19]

3. Form, Übermittlungsrisiko und Adressat

Vgl. dazu die Ausführungen zur Mängelrüge nach Art. 39.[20]

4. Fehlen einer Ausschlussfrist

Im Gegensatz zu Art. 39 II, der – auch bei nicht erkennbaren Sachmängeln – eine Ausschlussfrist von zwei Jahren vorsieht, fehlt eine derartige absolute zeitliche Grenze in Art. 43. Ein auf der Wiener Konferenz eingebrachter Antrag der ehemaligen DDR, auch für die Rechtsmängelhaftung eine zweijährige Ausschlussfrist einzuführen, wurde nicht angenommen.[21] Rechtsmängel i. S. d. Artt. 41, 42 werden häufig erst viel später erkennbar als Sachmängel.[22] Vor allem bei Schutzrechten wird der Dritte oft erst nach einiger Zeit von der Schutzrechtsverletzung Kenntnis erlangen und gegen den Käufer vorgehen. Die bei Schutzrechtsbelastung ohnedies nur eng begrenzte Verkäuferhaftung würde praktisch bedeutungslos, würde man sie zusätzlich auf Rechte oder Ansprüche beschränken, die innerhalb einer Zweijahresfrist geltend gemacht werden.

---

[12] Vgl. auch BGH, 11.1.2006, CISG-online 1200, Rn. 12 = IHR 2006, 82, 83, m. Anm. *Schroeter*, EWiR 2006, 427 f.; *Staudinger/Magnus*, Art. 43, Rn. 20; *Bamberger/Roth/Saenger*, Art. 43, Rn. 5. Differenzierend MünchKomm/*Gruber*, Art. 43, Rn. 12.
[13] Vgl. *Staudinger/Magnus*, Art. 43, Rn. 21; *Vida*, RTD com. 1994, 21, 32.
[14] Vgl. oben Art. 39 Rn. 17.
[15] Vgl. MünchKomm/*Gruber*, Art. 43, Rn. 15; *Kröll u. a./Kröll*, Art. 43, Rn. 20. Der BGH, 11.1.2006, CISG-online 1200, Rn. 12 = IHR 2006, 82, 83 hielt jedenfalls zwei Monate für zu lang, ohne jedoch klarzustellen, was eine angemessene Frist ist; daher zu Recht kritisch *Schroeter*, EWiR 2006, 427, 428 der empfiehlt, sich an der durchschnittlichen Frist von einem Monat zu orientieren, die sich im Rahmen des Art. 39 I etabliert hat.
[16] Vgl. *Enderlein/Maskow/Strohbach*, Art. 43, Anm. 3.; MünchKomm/*Gruber*, Art. 43, Rn. 9; MünchKommHGB/*Benicke*, Art. 43, Rn. 4; *Herber/Czerwenka*, Art. 43, Rn. 3; *Langenecker*, S. 247 f.; jetzt auch *Piltz*, Internationales Kaufrecht, Rn. 5–145; wohl ebenso *Karollus*, S. 126.
[17] Vgl. *Herber/Czerwenka*, Art. 43, Rn. 3; *Staudinger/Magnus*, Art. 43, Rn. 18; MünchKommHGB/*Benicke*, Art. 43, Rn. 4; MünchKomm/*Gruber*, Art. 43, Rn. 9; so ebenfalls P. *Huber/Mullis/Mullis*, S. 177.
[18] So auch *Staudinger/Magnus*, Art. 43, Rn. 15; *Achilles*, FS Schwenzer, S. 1, 12; a. A. MünchKomm/*Gruber*, Art. 43, Rn. 10; MünchKommHGB/*Benicke*, Art. 43, Rn. 5.
[19] Vgl. *Achilles*, FS Schwenzer, S. 1, 12: allenfalls Hinweispflicht aus der allgemeinen vertraglichen Treuepflicht, deren Verletzung in Schadenersatz, nicht jedoch in Rechtsverlust nach Art. 43 resultieren kann.
[20] Vgl. oben Art. 39 Rn. 11–14. Vgl. zu Fragen der elektronischen Kommunikation CISG-AC, Op. 1 (Chr. *Ramberg*), Comment 43.1. = IHR 2003, 244, 250.
[21] O.R., S. 110, Art. 40, Nr. 3; zur Diskussion im First Committee vgl. O.R., S. 327 f., Nr. 80 ff. Eine Analogie zu Art. 39 II befürwortet dennoch *Schwerha*, 16 Mich. J. Int'l L. (1995), 441, 479.
[22] *Heuzé*, Anm. 313. weist zu Recht darauf hin, dass eine Ausschlussfrist zur Folge hätte, dass das Risiko verspätet gestellter Ansprüche von dritter Seite allein dem Käufer auferlegt würde.

7 Hiervon unberührt bleibt freilich die Frage, in welchem Zeitpunkt Ansprüche wegen Rechtsmängeln verjähren. Die **Verjährung** ist im CISG nicht geregelt, sie bestimmt sich grundsätzlich[23] nach dem durch das internationale Privatrecht des angerufenen Gerichts massgeblichen Recht, in der Regel nach dem Vertragsstatut.[24] Ist deutsches Recht Vertragsstatut, so gilt die 30-jährige Verjährungsfrist des § 438 I Nr. 1 lit. a) BGB, wenn der Mangel in einem zum Besitz berechtigenden dinglichen Recht eines Dritten besteht, im Übrigen nach § 438 I Nr. 3 BGB eine zweijährige Frist.[25] Im Hinblick auf die 30-jährige Verjährungsfrist[26] ist deutschen Verkäufern dringend anzuraten, vertraglich eine Abkürzung der Verjährung für Rechtsmängel zu vereinbaren.

5. Rechtsfolgen unterlassener Anzeige

8 Versäumt der Käufer die nach Abs. 1 gebotene Rechtsmängelanzeige, so kann er sich – vorbehaltlich der Ausnahmen in Abs. 2 und Art. 44 – auf einen Rechtsmangel nach Artt. 41, 42 nicht berufen. Anders als nach Art. 52 IV EKG, wo Rügeversäumung vom Wortlaut der Vorschrift her lediglich zum Verlust des Vertragsaufhebungsanspruchs führte, der Ausschluss anderer Rechtsbehelfe hingegen unsicher war,[27] lässt Abs. 1 **sämtliche Rechtsbehelfe** des Käufers wegen Rechtsmängeln entfallen.[28] Rechtsmängelhaftung und Sachmängelhaftung werden insoweit gleich behandelt.

III. Ausnahme, Abs. 2

9 Der Käufer behält seine Rechte wegen Verletzung der Pflichten aus Artt. 41, 42 trotz unterlassener Anzeige, wenn der Verkäufer das Recht oder den Anspruch des Dritten und seine Art kannte. Die Vorschrift geht auf einen Vorschlag der deutschen Delegation bei der Wiener Konferenz zurück[29] und ähnelt Art. 40 bei der Sachmängelhaftung, lässt im Gegensatz zu diesem jedoch nur **positive Kenntnis,** nicht bereits vorwerfbare Unkenntnis des Verkäufers ausreichen.[30] Bei nur vorwerfbarer Unkenntnis bleibt dem Verkäufer die Möglichkeit, sich darauf zu berufen, dass der Käufer nicht ordnungsgemäss gerügt hat.

10 Blosse Kenntnis vom Recht oder Anspruch des Dritten reicht nicht aus, auch die **Art des Rechts** oder **des Anspruchs** muss dem Verkäufer bekannt sein. Hingegen kann positive Kenntnis von den Schritten, die der Dritte bereits gegen den Käufer unternommen hat, nicht verlangt werden.[31]

11 Abs. 2 sagt nichts über den **Zeitpunkt** aus, wann diese Kenntnis auf Seiten des Verkäufers vorliegen muss. Auf den Zeitpunkt des Vertragsschlusses kann es freilich nicht ankommen, denn die Art des Rechts oder Anspruchs des Dritten wird hier nur selten bereits bekannt

---

[23] Vgl. dazu oben Art. 39 Rn. 28, 29.
[24] Einzelheiten bei *Schroeter*, Art. 3 VertragsG Rn. 2.
[25] Vgl. *Schroeter*, Art. 3 VertragsG Rn. 5 f.
[26] Ausländische Rechtsordnungen sehen demgegenüber meist eine kürzere Verjährungsfrist vor, vgl. etwa USA: § 2–725 I UCC: 4 Jahre; Schweiz: Art. 127 OR: 10 Jahre (für allgemeine Rechtsmängel), Art. 210 OR: 1 Jahr (für die unter Art. 197 I OR fallende Schutzrechtsbelastung); England: sec. 5 Limitation Act 1980 i. d. F. 1986: 6 Jahre; Österreich: § 933 Abs. 1 ABGB: 2 Jahre ab Kenntnis des Rechtsmangels und ohne Rücksicht auf die Kenntnis in 30 Jahren seit Vertragsschluss, § 1478 ABGB; Frankreich: Art. 189bis Ccom: 10 Jahre.
[27] Vgl. *Dölle/Neumayer*, Art. 52 EKG, Rn. 22; *Mertens/Rehbinder*, Art. 52 EKG, Rn. 12; *Soergel/Lüderitz*, Art. 52 EKG, Rn. 7; *Stötter*, Art. 52 EKG, Anm. 8.
[28] Unklar insoweit *Enderlein*, Rights and Obligations of the Seller, S. 184.
[29] Zur Diskussion vgl. O. R., S. 350, Art. 40bis, Nr. 77 ff.; S. 351, Art. 40 bis, Nr. 1 ff.
[30] Zur Zurechnung des Wissens von Hilfspersonen und anderen Dritten, die der Verkäufer in seinem Risikobereich bei der Vertragserfüllung einsetzt, vgl. Art. 40 Rn. 6.
[31] Vgl. *Staudinger/Magnus*, Art. 43, Rn. 31; *Bamberger/Roth/Saenger*, Art. 43, Rn. 8; *Enderlein*, Rights and Obligations of the Seller, S. 185; nicht eindeutig äussern sich *Bianca/Bonell/Sono*, Art. 43, Anm. 2.3.; *Schlechtriem*, Seller's Obligations, § 6.03, S. 6–35. Die abweichende Auffassung in der 3. Aufl. ist aufgegeben.

sein.³² Gleiches gilt für den Zeitpunkt der Lieferung.³³ Zu berücksichtigen ist vielmehr, dass sich Abs. 2 als Ausnahme zu Abs. 1 darstellt. Die Anzeige soll den Verkäufer in die Lage versetzen, das Recht oder den Anspruch des Dritten abzuwehren. Entscheidend ist deshalb der Zeitpunkt, in dem die **Anzeige** des Käufers dem Verkäufer **hätte zugehen müssen**.³⁴ Hat der Verkäufer in diesem Zeitpunkt Kenntnis von der Art des Rechts oder Anspruchs des Dritten, bedarf es keiner Anzeige mehr.

IV. Beweislast

Der Käufer trägt die Beweislast, dass er die Anzeige innerhalb angemessener Frist abgesandt hat. Bei Rügeversäumung hat er die Voraussetzungen des Abs. 2, d. h. die Kenntnis des Verkäufers zu beweisen.³⁵

---

³² A. A. *Schwerha*, 16 Mich. J. Int'l L. (1995), 457, 469.
³³ A. A. *Ferrari u. a./Ferrari*, Internationales Vertragsrecht, Art. 43, Rn. 15; wie hier jetzt auch *Piltz*, Internationales Kaufrecht, Rn. 5–156.
³⁴ So auch *Schlechtriem*, Internationales UN-Kaufrecht, Rn. 169; *Staudinger/Magnus*, Art. 43, Rn. 32; MünchKommHGB/*Benicke*, Art. 43, Rn. 9; MünchKomm/*Gruber*, Art. 43, Rn. 19; *Honnold/Flechtner*, Art. 43, Rn. 271; *Witz/Salger/Lorenz/Salger*, Art. 43, Rn. 9; *Langenecker*, S. 253; *Vida*, RTD com. 1994, 21, 33. Vgl. zum Parallelproblem im Rahmen der Sachmängelhaftung Art. 40 Rn. 8.
³⁵ Vgl. ausführlich dazu *T. M. Müller*, Beweislast, S. 124 f.; MünchKomm/*Gruber*, Art. 43, Rn. 23; *Witz/Salger/Lorenz/Salger*, Art. 43, Rn. 10; *Soergel/Lüderitz/Schüßler-Langeheine*, Art. 43, Rn. 9; *Kröll u. a./Kröll*, Art. 43, Rn. 28; *Ferrari u. a./Ferrari*, Internationales Vertragsrecht, Art. 43, Rn. 16; a. A. *Staudinger/Magnus*, Art. 43, Rn. 36.

Art. 44 [Entschuldigung für unterlassene Anzeige]

Ungeachtet des Artikels 39 Absatz 1 und des Artikels 43 Absatz 1 kann der Käufer den Preis nach Artikel 50 herabsetzen oder Schadenersatz, außer für entgangenen Gewinn, verlangen, wenn er eine vernünftige Entschuldigung dafür hat, daß er die erforderliche Anzeige unterlassen hat.

Art. 44

Notwithstanding the provisions of paragraph (1) of article 39 and paragraph (1) of article 43, the buyer may reduce the price in accordance with article 50 or claim damages, except for loss of profit, if he has a reasonable excuse for his failure to give the required notice.

Art. 44

Nonobstant les dispositions du paragraphe 1 de l'article 39 et du paragraphe 1 de l'article 43, l'acheteur peut réduire le prix conformément à l'article 50 ou demander des dommages-intérêts, sauf pour le gain manqué, s'il a une excuse raisonnable pour n'avoir pas procédé à la dénonciation requise.

Übersicht

	Rn.
I. Gegenstand und Zweck der Regelung	1
II. Vernünftige Entschuldigung	4
1. „Entschuldigung" im Sinn der Billigkeit	4
2. Entschuldigung wegen unterlassener Untersuchung und wegen unterlassener Rüge	5a
3. Einzelfälle	6
III. Rechtsfolgen	10
1. Schadenersatzanspruch	10
a) Umfang des zu ersetzenden Schadens	10
b) Verletzung der Schadensminderungspflicht durch unterlassene Untersuchung	11
2. Minderung	14
3. Recht des Verkäufers zur Mängelbeseitigung	15
4. Schadenersatzanspruch des Verkäufers wegen Versäumung der Rügefrist	16
5. Verjährung	17
6. Abweichende Vereinbarungen und Gebräuche	18
VI. Beweislast	19

Vorläufer und Entwürfe fehlen.

I. Gegenstand und Zweck der Regelung

1   Grundsätzlich schliessen **Art. 39 I** und **Art. 43 I** alle Rechte des Käufers wegen vertragswidriger Beschaffenheit der Ware oder wegen Rechtsmangels bzw. Schutzrechtsbelastung aus, wenn er den Mangel nicht innerhalb der dort vorgesehenen „angemessenen Frist" gerügt hat. Nach Art. 44 gilt das aber nicht für das Recht auf Minderung (Art. 50) und, mit Ausnahme des entgangenen Gewinns, für den Anspruch auf Schadenersatz (Art. 45 I lit. b)), vorausgesetzt, der Käufer kann für die Versäumung der Rügefrist eine „vernünftige Entschuldigung" anführen. Unbedingt ausgeschlossen, auch im Fall der „Entschuldigung", sind dagegen infolge der Versäumung der Rügefrist die Ansprüche auf Ersatzlieferung und Nachbesserung (Art. 46 II, III), das Recht zur Vertragsaufhebung (Art. 49 I) und der Anspruch auf Schadenersatz (Art. 45 I lit. b)) insoweit, als er auf Ersatz von entgangenem Gewinn gerichtet ist. Die durch Art. 44 eingeführte Abmilderung der Folgen der Rügeversäumung erfasst nur den Fall, dass die durch Art. 39 I und Art. 43 I gesetzten Fristen vom

Käufer versäumt werden. Nicht genannt ist die Frist des **Art. 39 II**. Die Folgen einer Versäumung der dort festgesetzten zweijährigen Ausschlussfrist für die Rüge fehlender Vertragsmässigkeit der Ware bleiben also unberührt.[1] Der Käufer verliert in diesem Fall alle Rechtsbehelfe; auf eine „vernünftige Entschuldigung" kann er sich nicht berufen.

Art. 44 ist im Haager Kaufrecht und in den nationalen Kaufrechten **ohne Vorbild**. Die 2 Bestimmung ist erst auf der Wiener Konferenz von 1980 in das Übereinkommen eingeführt worden. Namentlich bei den Delegationen von Entwicklungsländern war die Befürchtung entstanden, die Rügepflicht des Art. 39 könne sich als eine Falle für den Käufer erweisen; vor allem für Käufer aus Entwicklungsländern, die beispielsweise Maschinen und sonstiges technisches Gerät erwerben und mangels Sachkunde den Mangel nicht entdecken oder nicht genau bezeichnen können, oder die mit dem Erfordernis sofortiger Untersuchung und alsbaldiger Rüge nach ihrem Heimatrecht und ihren heimischen Gepflogenheiten nicht vertraut sind.[2] Diese Befürchtungen sind sicherlich berechtigt. Hinzuzufügen ist, dass auch das englische Recht und viele seiner Tochterrechtsordnungen keine eigentliche Untersuchungs- und Anzeigeobliegenheit und vor allem keinen völligen Rechtsverlust bei ihrer Verletzung kennen. – Letzteres gilt auch für viele Osteuropäische und Zentralasiatische Rechtsordnungen.[3] Auf der Wiener Konferenz führte der Widerstand der Sprecher von Entwicklungsländern gegen das Institut der Rügepflicht und seine Verteidigung durch Sprecher der anderen Staaten zu einer schwierigen Kontroverse,[4] die schliesslich durch den Kompromiss des Art. 44 beigelegt wurde.[5]

Art. 44 muss vor dem Hintergrund der Artt. 38, 39 gesehen werden. In erster Linie 3 sollte ein Gericht Unbilligkeiten dadurch vermeiden, dass es bei der Bestimmung der angemessenen Frist auf die Art des Betriebs des Käufers und die Umstände des Einzelfalls Rücksicht nimmt.[6] Wird die Frist des Art. 39 vom Gericht „vernünftig" bemessen, so wird für eine zusätzliche „Entschuldigung" des Schuldners weniger Anlass bestehen als wenn man an der früheren Praxis der deutschen Gerichte, Rügefristen eher knapp zu bemessen, festhält.

II. Vernünftige Entschuldigung

1. „Entschuldigung" im Sinn der Billigkeit

Bei der Auslegung des Begriffs der „vernünftigen Entschuldigung" („reasonable excuse") 4 darf man sich nicht von dogmatischen Vorstellungen des eigenen Rechts leiten lassen. Auf **„Verschulden"** im technischen Sinn kann es im Zusammenhang des Art. 44 von vornherein **nicht ankommen**.[7] Das gilt auch, wenn man den Verschuldensbegriff, was im vorliegenden Zusammenhang an sich naheliegt, „subjektiv", auf die Person des Käufers bezogen, auffasst.[8] Das ist in den Fällen der Rügeversäumnis, wie man sie in der Praxis

---

[1] Vgl. O. R., S. 345 f., Nr. 7, 9; *Denkschrift*, S. 50 f.; *Honnold/Flechtner*, Artt. 39, 40, 44, Rn. 258; *Bianca/Bonell/Sono*, Art. 44, Anm. 1.; *P. Huber/Mullis/Mullis*, S. 166; *Karollus*, S. 129; *Staudinger/Magnus*, Art. 44, Rn. 7; *Magnus*, TranspR-IHR 1999, 29, 34; *Flechtner*, Draft Digest, Art. 44; *Leisinger*, IHR 2006, 76, 77; OLG Linz, 24.9.2007, CISG-online 1583, IHR 2008, 28, 30. Übersehen von OLG Zweibrücken, 2.2.2004, CISG-online 877, das trotz Ablauf der Zwei-Jahres-Frist die Voraussetzungen des Art. 44 prüft.
[2] Vgl. dazu *Date-Bah*, Problems of Unification, S. 47 ff.
[3] Vgl. *Benjamin*, Rn. 12–081; vgl. auch *Staudinger/Magnus*, Art. 44, Rn. 3. Rechtsvergleichend *Schwenzer/Hachem/Kee*, Rn. 34.5 ff.
[4] Gegen die Rügepflicht: Kenia, Pakistan, China, Nigeria, Mexiko, Singapur, Libyen (O. R., S. 321 f., Nr. 42, 46, 47, 48, 50, 51, 59) sowie Grossbritannien (O. R., S. 321 f., Nr. 49); dafür: Niederlande, Korea, Schweiz, Schweden, Bulgarien, Dänemark, Österreich, Australien, Japan, Bundesrepublik Deutschland, Belgien, Spanien (O. R., S. 321 f., Nr. 43, 44, 45, 52, 53, 55, 58, 60, 61, 62, 66, 68).
[5] Zu weiteren Einzelheiten der Entstehungsgeschichte vgl. *U. Huber*, 1. Aufl., Rn. 4 ff.
[6] Vgl. dazu oben Art. 39 Rn. 15–17.
[7] Vgl. OLG Saarbrücken, 17.1.2007, CISG-online 1642 = IHR 2008, 55, 59.
[8] So *Herber/Czerwenka*, Art. 44, Rn. 2.

beobachtet, nicht das Problem. „Entschuldigung" kann also nicht im Sinn von „fehlender Fahrlässigkeit" verstanden werden.[9]

5 Bei der „Entschuldigung" i. S. d. Art. 44 geht es primär um eine Entscheidung nach **Billigkeit**.[10] Entschuldigt ist ein Verhalten des Schuldners, das zwar an sich nicht vorschriftsmässig und korrekt ist, das aber nach den Umständen des Einzelfalls billigerweise ein gewisses Verständnis und eine gewisse Nachsicht verdient.[11] Bei der Würdigung dieser Umstände sind die **schützenswerten Interessen** beider Parteien zu berücksichtigen.[12] Auf Seite des **Verkäufers** spielt vor allem das Interesse an alsbaldiger Beweissicherung eine Rolle.[13] Dieses Interesse besteht unabhängig von der Frage, welche Partei im Streitfall die Beweislast für den Mangel zu tragen hat.[14] Oft stehen auch mögliche Regressansprüche des Verkäufers gegen den Zulieferer auf dem Spiel. Dem weiteren Interesse des Verkäufers, das darin besteht, möglichst schnell über die nicht vertragsmässige, aber darum meist nicht völlig wertlose Ware disponieren zu können, trägt Art. 44 schon dadurch Rechnung, dass der Käufer, der sich auf eine „vernünftige Entschuldigung" beruft, keine Rechtsbehelfe ausüben kann, die zu einer Rückgabe der Ware führen (wie Vertragsaufhebung oder Verlangen von Ersatzlieferung). Sind dem Verkäufer keinerlei Nachteile aufgrund unterlassener oder verspäteter Rüge entstanden, ist eher eine Entschuldigung anzunehmen.[15] Auf der Seite des **Käufers** geht es vor allem um das Interesse, nicht durch ein verhältnismässig geringfügiges Versehen sämtliche Mängelansprüche zu verlieren. Weitere zu berücksichtigende Kriterien sind die Schwere des Vertragsbruchs, die Folgen eines Verlusts aller aus der Vertragsverletzung resultierenden Rechte[16] sowie die Bemühungen der vertragstreuen Partei, der Rügeobliegenheit nachzukommen.[17]

2. Entschuldigung wegen unterlassener Untersuchung und wegen unterlassener Rüge

5a Art. 44 differenziert nicht danach, aus welchem Grund der Käufer die rechtzeitige Anzeige gem. Art. 39 I unterlassen hat. Die verspätete Anzeige kann ihren Grund entweder darin haben, dass der Käufer die Ware nicht hinreichend untersucht hat, oder darin, dass er den Mangel bei der gebotenen Untersuchung zwar erkannt, es aber versäumt hat, die Anzeige rechtzeitig abzusenden oder den Mangel hinreichend zu substantiieren. In der Praxis ist der erste Fall der wichtigere. Gerade auch in diesem Fall kommt eine „Entschuldigung" gem. Art. 44 in Betracht.[18] Keinesfalls darf man aus der Nichterwähnung des Art. 38 in Art. 44 den Schluss ziehen, eine nicht hinreichende Untersuchung könne niemals i. S. d. Art. 44 „entschuldigt" sein. Hat der Käufer einen Entschuldigungsgrund dafür, dass

---

[9] A. A. *Herber/Czerwenka*, Art. 44, Rn. 2; MünchKomm/*Gruber*, Art. 44, Rn. 6 ff.; *Schlechtriem*, Internationales UN-Kaufrecht, Rn. 158; wohl auch OGH, 17.4.2002, CISG-online 1020.

[10] So auch *Resch*, ÖJZ 1992, 470, 479; *P. Huber/Mullis/Mullis*, S. 167; *Reinhart*, Art. 44, Rn. 4; *Staudinger/Magnus*, Art. 44, Rn. 10; OLG München, 8.2.1995, CISG-online 142. Den Charakter als Ausnahmevorschrift betonen: BGH, 11.1.2006, CISG-online 1200, Rn. 15 = IHR 2006, 82, 83; Saarländisches OLG, 17.1.2007, CISG-online 1642 = IHR 2008, 55, 59; OGH, 17.4.2002, CISG-online 1020; *Staudinger/Magnus*, Art. 44, Rn. 11; *Brunner*, Art. 44, Rn. 4; dagegen *Cañellas*, 25 J. L. & Com. (2005), 261, 265.

[11] Ebenso OLG München, 8.2.1995, CISG-online 142.

[12] So auch BGH, 11.1.2006, CISG-online 1200, Rn. 15 = IHR 2006, 82, 83.

[13] Vgl. O. R., S. 321, Nr. 53 (*Hjerner*/Schweden: „the main purpose of the rule was in fact to secure evidence in case of dispute"); S. 322, Nr. 62 (*Herber*/Deutschland: „the provisions […] were crucial because one of the main difficulties in cases of nonconformity was to secure proof").

[14] Das wäre in den Fällen, um die es hier geht, der Käufer, vgl. oben Art. 35 Rn. 49.

[15] Vgl. OLG Saarbrücken, 17.1.2007, CISG-online 1642 = IHR 2008, 55, 59; *Flechtner*, Draft Digest, S. 388; *ders.*, 26 B. U. Int'l L. J. (2008), 24, 25 will dies bereits bei Art. 39 I berücksichtigen.

[16] Vgl. *P. Huber/Mullis/Mullis*, S. 167.

[17] Vgl. OLG Saarbrücken, 17.1.2007, CISG-online 1642 = IHR 2008, 55, 59.

[18] *Honnold/Flechtner*, Artt. 39, 40, 44, Rn. 261; *Staudinger/Magnus*, Art. 44, Rn. 5; MünchKomm/*Gruber*, Art. 44, Rn. 4; *Ramos Muñoz*, Communication of Defects, VI) 2); jetzt auch *Piltz*, Internationales Kaufrecht, Rn. 5–106. A. A. OLG Karlsruhe, 25.6.1997, CISG-online 263 = BB 1998, 393 ff. = RIW 1998, 235 ff. (mit unzutreffender Berufung auf *U. Huber*, 2. Aufl., Rn. 1, 4; *Andersen*, 9 VJ (2005), 17, 39; wohl auch *Schlechtriem*, Internationales UN-Kaufrecht, Rn. 158.

er die Untersuchung nicht korrekt durchgeführt hat, dann hat er auch einen Entschuldigungsgrund dafür, dass er den Mangel der Ware nicht rechtzeitig angezeigt hat, und der Tatbestand des Art. 44 ist erfüllt.

3. Einzelfälle

Bei der Entscheidung der Frage der „vernünftigen Entschuldigung" spielt zunächst das **Gewicht des Pflichtverstosses des Käufers** eine wesentliche Rolle. Nachsicht ist nur zu gewähren, wenn es um einen minder schweren Verstoss geht.[19] Ein minder schwerer Verstoss ist z. B. dann anzunehmen, wenn es sich um einen Mangel handelt, mit dem normalerweise nicht gerechnet wird und auf den hin der Käufer daher die Ware nicht untersucht hat; oder wenn der Käufer zwar gerügt hat, aber bei der Rüge den Fehler nicht hinreichend spezifiziert hat;[20] oder wenn die angemessene Zeit nur geringfügig überschritten ist. Allerdings genügt der Umstand der Geringfügigkeit des Pflichtverstosses allein noch nicht, um die Anwendung von Art. 44 zu rechtfertigen.[21]

Auch die **Art des Unternehmens** des Käufers spielt eine Rolle. Versehen von Käufern, die ein Einzelhandelsgeschäft, ein Handwerk, die Landwirtschaft oder einen freien Beruf betreiben, wiegen leichter als Versehen von Grosskaufleuten, deren Geschäft auf rasche und pünktliche Abwicklung eingerichtet sein muss.[22] Vor allem ist auch auf den **Sitz des Käufers,** die dortigen Gepflogenheiten und die Vertrautheit mit Rügeerfordernissen Rücksicht zu nehmen.[23] Allerdings wird der Käufer nicht entschuldigt, wenn er glaubt, auf Grund Falschlieferung sei der Vertrag aufgehoben.[24] Zu berücksichtigen sind schliesslich rein **subjektive Faktoren,** die im Rahmen der Artt. 38, 39 ausser Betracht bleiben,[25] wie z. B. Krankheit, betriebliche Organisationsschwierigkeiten[26] oder auch Übermittlung der Rüge an den falschen (vorherigen) Vertreter des Verkäufers.[27] Eine vernünftige Entschuldigung mag sich im Einzelfall auch daraus ergeben, dass der Verkäufer deutlich zum Ausdruck gebracht hat, an einer (rechtzeitigen) Rüge nicht interessiert zu sein, soweit darin im Einzelfall nicht sogar ein Verzicht auf die Rüge zu sehen ist.[28]

Auch die **Art der Ware** und die **Art des Mangels** kann eine Rolle spielen. Geht es um Waren, die natürlichem Verderb ausgesetzt sind, wie z. B. Nahrungsmittel, so hat der Verkäufer ein besonderes Interesse an alsbaldiger Beweissicherung. Darüber muss sich auch der Käufer im Klaren sein. Hier kann man sich nur schwer vorstellen, dass eine verspätete Rüge entschuldigt ist. Geht es dagegen um unveränderliche Waren und um Mängel, bei denen, wenn sie festgestellt werden, zugleich feststeht, dass sie bereits zurzeit der Lieferung vorhanden waren (z. B. um Konstruktions- oder Fabrikationsfehler) oder um Fälle, in denen

---

[19] Vgl. auch ICC, 9187/1999, CISG-online 705 = 11:2 ICC Int. Ct. Arb. Bull. (2000), 94; *Brunner*, Art. 44, Rn. 3.

[20] Ähnlich OLG Saarbrücken, 17.1.2007, CISG-online 1642, IHR 2008, 55, 60: Die Güter wurden in einem Unfall während des Transports beschädigt, worauf der Käufer den Verkäufer zunächst lediglich über diese Tatsache informierte und erst mehr als zwei Monate später, als ein Sachverständigengutachten vorlag, Schadenersatz aufgrund unzulänglicher Verpackung verlangte. Das Gericht befand, dass dem Käufer nicht hätte zugemutet werden können, seine Ansprüche früher geltend zu machen, weil eine solche Klage ‚ins Blaue hinein' nicht hinreichend substantiiert gewesen wäre.

[21] Vgl. OGH, 15.10.1998, CISG-online 380 = östJBl. 1999, 318 m. Anm. *Karollus; Staudinger/Magnus,* Art. 44, Rn. 11.

[22] Ebenso OLG München, 8.2.1995, CISG-online 142. Im Ergebnis wurde die Entschuldigung mit Rücksicht auf den Zuschnitt des Betriebs des Käufers verneint. Vgl. auch MünchKommHGB/*Benicke*, Art. 44, Rn. 6.

[23] Vgl. oben Rn. 2; vgl. auch *Soergel/Lüderitz/Schüßler-Langeheine,* Art. 44, Rn. 3; *Staudinger/Magnus,* Art. 44, Rn. 14.

[24] Vgl. Sø og Handelsretten, 31.1.2002, CISG-online 679.

[25] Vgl. nur oben Art. 38 Rn. 18.

[26] Zu streng OLG Koblenz, 11.9.1998, CISG-online 505 = OLGR Koblenz, 1999, 49 ff.; krit. hierzu *Andersen,* 9 VJ (2005), 17, 41.

[27] Vgl. zu diesem Fall *U. Huber,* 3. Aufl., Art. 44 Rn. 8; vgl. auch *Staudinger/Magnus,* Art. 44, Rn. 13.

[28] Vgl. OGH, 15.10.1998, CISG-online 380; vgl. auch oben Art. 39 Rn. 33.

die Mängel umgehend festgestellt und von einem Experten untersucht werden,[29] so fällt das Interesse des Verkäufers an schneller Unterrichtung weniger schwer ins Gewicht – jedenfalls, soweit es um die dem Käufer in Art. 44 allein vorbehaltenen Rechte auf Minderung des Kaufpreises oder Schadenersatz geht. Hier ist deshalb eine grosszügigere Beurteilung angebracht. Dies gilt freilich nicht in Fällen, in denen der Verkäufer seinerseits durch Zeitablauf Regressansprüche gegen Zulieferer verliert.[30]

9   Nach den dem Art. 44 zugrundeliegenden Intentionen sollte insbesondere auch **mangelnde Erfahrung des Käufers** einen Entschuldigungsgrund bilden.[31] Der Käufer eines Computers oder einer Maschine mag z. B. Funktionsmängel zunächst darauf zurückführen, dass Anlauf- und Bedienungsschwierigkeiten vorliegen. Erst nach mehreren Monaten erkennt er, dass der Fehler am Gerät liegt. Gewiss sollte man in einem solchen Fall Abhilfe zunächst im Bereich der Untersuchungsfrist (Art. 38) schaffen und dem Käufer eine angemessene Erprobungszeit zubilligen.[32] Darüber hinaus sollte man aber dem Käufer auch eine „vernünftige Entschuldigung" i. S. d. Art. 44 in solchen Fällen nicht versagen. Auch in Fällen, in denen der Käufer aufgrund der Komplexität der Anlage den Mangel nicht hinreichend spezifiziert, kann Art. 44 zum Zuge kommen.[33]

III. Rechtsfolgen

1. Schadenersatzanspruch

10   **a) Umfang des zu ersetzenden Schadens.** Nach Art. 44 behält der Käufer, der die Rügefrist des Art. 39 I oder des Art. 43 I versäumt hat, im Fall einer „vernünftigen Entschuldigung" den Schadenersatzanspruch gemäss Art. 45 I lit. b); die Bestimmung schränkt den sich aus Art. 74 ergebenden Umfang allerdings ein, indem Ersatz des entgangenen Gewinns ausgenommen wird. Ersatzfähig ist also in erster Linie der **Minderwert** der Sache als solcher, das heisst die Differenz zwischen dem tatsächlichen Wert der nicht vertragsmässigen oder mit einem Rechtsmangel behafteten Sache und dem Kaufpreis. Ist die Sache vollkommen wertlos, ist dieser Minderwert gleich dem Kaufpreis. Hat der Käufer die Sache für 100 gekauft, ist sie infolge des Mangels vollkommen wertlos und hätte er die mangelfreie Sache für 150 weiterverkaufen können, beschränkt sich der Schadenersatz trotzdem auf 100, weil entgangener Gewinn nicht zu ersetzen ist. Ersatzfähig sind ferner **Mangelfolgeschäden,** die der Käufer bei Verwendung der nicht vertragsmässigen Sache erlitten hat, also z. B. Kosten einer fehlgeschlagenen Verarbeitung, vergebens aufgewendete Baukosten bei Lieferung von fehlerhaftem Baumaterial,[34] vergebens aufgewendete Transportkosten, oder Schäden, die die gelieferte Sache infolge ihrer vertragswidrigen Beschaffenheit anderen Sachen des Käufers zufügt. Dass es sich bei den zu ersetzenden Mangelfolgeschäden stets um „voraussehbare" Schäden handeln muss, ergibt sich aus Art. 74 S. 2.

11   **b) Verletzung der Schadensminderungspflicht durch unterlassene Untersuchung.** Fraglich ist, inwieweit der Verkäufer in solchen Fällen dem Schadenersatzanspruch des Käufers entgegenhalten kann, der Käufer habe durch das Unterlassen rechtzeitiger Untersuchung und Rüge seine Schadensminderungspflicht gemäss Art. 77 S. 1 verletzt, mit der Folge, dass der Schadenersatz gemäss Art. 77 S. 2 herabzusetzen sei. Hierbei ist zu unterscheiden, ob der Käufer Ausgleich des Minderwerts oder Ersatz von Mangelfolgeschäden verlangt.

---

[29] Vgl. OLG Saarbrücken, 17.1.2007, CISG-online 1642 = IHR 2008, 55, 60.
[30] Vgl. *Soergel/Lüderitz/Schüßler-Langeheine*, Art. 44, Rn. 3.
[31] Vgl. oben Rn. 2.
[32] Vgl. dazu oben Art. 38 Rn. 15 ff., 17.
[33] Vgl. *Ramos Muñoz*, Communication of Defects, VI) 2).
[34] Vgl. dazu den deutschen Fall BGH, 30.4.1975, WM 1975, 562 = NJW 1975, 2011.

Verlangt der Käufer **Ausgleich des Minderwerts,** so ist denkbar, dass der Schaden 12
geringer ausgefallen wäre, wenn der Käufer den Mangel rechtzeitig erkannt und gerügt
hätte. Entdeckt z. B. der Käufer einen Mangel, den er bei gehöriger Untersuchung (Art. 38)
spätestens am 31.7. hätte erkennen müssen, erst am 31.8., hat er hierfür eine „vernünftige
Entschuldigung" i. S. d. Art. 44 und verkauft er nunmehr die mangelhafte Ware Anfang
September unter Einstandspreis, so kann er doch nur Ersatz desjenigen Schadens verlangen,
der auch bei rechtzeitiger Untersuchung der Ware entstanden wäre. Wäre also bei einem
Verkauf Anfang August ein günstigerer Preis zu erzielen gewesen, so kann der Käufer
Schadenersatz nur in Höhe der Differenz dieses günstigeren Preises zum Kaufpreis verlangen. Der weitere Schaden, der durch die Verzögerung des Verkaufs entstanden ist, geht
gemäss Art. 77 zu seinen Lasten. Die „vernünftige Entschuldigung" i. S. d. Art. 44 ändert
hieran nichts.[35]

Erleidet der Käufer dagegen bei Verwendung der Ware einen **Mangelfolgeschaden,** so 13
kann der Verkäufer dem Käufer, der gemäss Art. 44 trotz Versäumung der Rügefrist
Schadenersatz verlangen kann, nicht unter Berufung auf Art. 77 entgegenhalten, der Schaden wäre bei rechtzeitiger Untersuchung (Art. 38) nicht eingetreten, weil der Käufer, hätte
er die Ware rechtzeitig untersucht, den Mangel entdeckt und die Ware nicht verwendet
hätte.[36] Es ist Sache des Verkäufers, dafür zu sorgen, dass die Ware nicht infolge verdeckter
Mängel zu Schäden beim Käufer führt, und die erforderlichen Kontrollen durchzuführen.
Es ist nicht der Sinn des Art. 38, ihm die Möglichkeit zu geben, diese Sorgfalts- und
Kontrollpflichten auf den Käufer abzuwälzen. Art. 38 bestimmt nur die Grundlage und
Grenze der Rügepflicht und dient, wie diese, nur dem Interesse des Verkäufers an schneller
Information.[37] Dagegen kann bei der Entstehung von Mangelfolgeschäden ein mitwirkendes Verschulden des Käufers, das nach Art. 77 zu berücksichtigen ist, selbstverständlich darin
liegen, dass er die Ware verwendet hat, obwohl ihm hierbei ihre fehlerhafte Beschaffenheit
hätte auffallen müssen. Mit Art. 38 hat das nichts zu tun. Nicht die Verletzung der Untersuchungspflicht, wohl aber das sorgfaltswidrige Verhalten bei der Verwendung der mangelhaften Ware kann zu einer Herabsetzung des Schadenersatzes, also zu einer Schadensteilung gemäss Art. 77 führen.[38] Soweit Art. 77 zur Anwendung gelangt, ist aber auch
Art. 79 zu beachten.[39]

2. Minderung

Nach Art. 44 behält der Käufer, im Fall einer „vernünftigen Entschuldigung" ausserdem 14
das Recht zur Minderung (Art. 50). Eine Berufung des Verkäufers auf Art. 77 ist demgegenüber nicht möglich.[40] Denn gemäss Art. 50 kommt es für die Berechnung der Minderung auf das Verhältnis des Werts der mangelhaften Ware zum Wert der mangelfreien
Ware im Zeitpunkt der Lieferung an. Der Betrag, den der Verkäufer hiernach zu erhalten
hat, kann sich durch eine Verzögerung der Mängelanzeige nicht erhöhen. Art. 44 erhält
dem Käufer das Minderungsrecht allerdings nur, wenn es nach den allgemeinen Regeln
begründet ist, grundsätzlich also nur bei Sachmängeln.[41]

---

[35] So auch *Staudinger/Magnus,* Art. 44, Rn. 18.
[36] Wie hier *Honsell/Magnus,* Art. 44, Rn. 15; *Staudinger/Magnus,* Art. 44, Rn. 23. Abweichend wohl *Schlechtriem,* Internationales UN-Kaufrecht, Rn. 158: die „Entschuldigung" des Art. 44 beziehe sich nur auf die versäumte Rüge und unzureichende Substantiierung.
[37] Es gilt das Gleiche wie für die „Untersuchungspflicht" nach deutschem Recht (§ 377 HGB), vgl. dazu
K. *Schmidt,* Handelsrecht, § 28 III 3.
[38] Zustimmend *Honsell/Magnus,* Art. 44, Rn. 17; *Staudinger/Magnus,* Art. 44, Rn. 19, 20.
[39] Vgl. *Herber/Czerwenka,* Art. 44, Rn. 4; *Staudinger/Magnus,* Art. 44, Rn. 19.
[40] Vgl. auch *Honsell/Magnus,* Art. 44, Rn. 16; a. A. *Bianca/Bonell/Sono,* Art. 44, Rn. 2.5.
[41] Vgl. unten *Müller-Chen,* Art. 50 Rn. 2; Einzelheiten bei *Mohs,* IHR 2002, 59, 61; a. A. *Staudinger/Magnus,*
Art. 44, Rn. 17.

3. Recht des Verkäufers zur Mängelbeseitigung

15 Auch im Fall einer verspäteten Mängelanzeige, die gemäss Art. 44 „entschuldigt" ist, behält der Verkäufer das Recht, den Mangel durch Ersatzlieferung oder Nachbesserung zu beheben (Art. 48). Hierdurch kann er die Minderung und (soweit nicht schon vorher ein Mangelfolgeschaden beim Käufer eingetreten ist) auch den Schadenersatzanspruch des Käufers abwenden. In der Literatur wird die Frage erörtert, ob der Verkäufer, der gemäss Art. 44 auf Schadenersatz oder Minderung in Anspruch genommen wird, einwenden kann, bei rechtzeitiger Rüge wäre er zur Ersatzlieferung bereit und imstande gewesen; nur infolge des Zeitablaufs sei die Ersatzlieferung nicht mehr möglich (etwa weil Ware der verkauften Art inzwischen nicht mehr am Markt oder nicht mehr im Produktionsprogramm des Verkäufers ist). Als mögliche Grundlage für den Einwand wird Art. 80 genannt.[42] Hiernach sind Ansprüche wegen Vertragsverletzung ausgeschlossen, wenn die Vertragsverletzung durch ein Verhalten des Gläubigers verursacht ist. Die Bestimmung trifft auf den vorliegenden Fall aber nicht zu: die Verletzung der Verkäuferpflicht liegt schon in der Lieferung der vertragswidrigen Ware und ist nicht dadurch „verursacht", dass der Käufer später die Rügefrist nicht eingehalten hat. Der Verkäufer, der zur Ersatzlieferung nicht mehr imstande ist, kann sein Recht zur Mängelbeseitigung aus Art. 48 nicht mehr ausüben und muss es deshalb hinnehmen, dass der Käufer, gestützt auf Art. 44, Schadenersatz oder Minderung verlangt.[43]

4. Schadenersatzanspruch des Verkäufers wegen Versäumung der Rügefrist

16 In der Literatur wird weiter erwogen, ob dem Verkäufer, der vom Käufer trotz Versäumung der Rügefrist gemäss Art. 44 auf Schadenersatz oder Minderung in Anspruch genommen wird, wegen der Fristversäumung ein eigener Schadenersatzanspruch gegen den Käufer zustehen kann, mit dem er gegen den Anspruch des Käufers aufrechnen kann.[44] Dabei geht es um den Fall, dass der Verkäufer sich darauf beruft, bei rechtzeitiger Mängelanzeige hätte er seinerseits gegen seinen eigenen Vorlieferanten Sachmängelansprüche geltend machen können, die er infolge der verspäteten Mängelanzeige verloren habe. Auch das ist abzulehnen. Es geht um die Frage, ob der Käufer dem Verkäufer gegenüber zur Untersuchung der Ware und zur Mängelanzeige „verpflichtet" ist. Das ist nicht der Fall.[45] Die sogenannte „Untersuchungspflicht" (Art. 38) hat nur vorbereitenden Charakter und legt nur den Beginn der Anzeigefrist und den Umfang der Mängel fest, die innerhalb der Frist des Art. 39 I anzuzeigen sind. Art. 39 I bestimmt nicht, dass der Käufer zur Anzeige von Mängeln verpflichtet ist, sondern ordnet nur an, dass er seine Rechte verliert, wenn er die Anzeige unterlässt. Diese nachteilige Rechtsfolge schränkt Art. 44 ein. Allerdings würde der Zweck der Entschuldigung wiederum unterlaufen, gewährte man dem Verkäufer einen Schadenersatzanspruch bei Versäumung der Rügepflicht, obwohl die Voraussetzungen von Art. 44 erfüllt sind. Auch die Bestimmung des Art. 77 kann dem Verkäufer im geschilderten Fall nichts nützen.[46] Verlangt der Käufer Minderung, ist Art. 77 von vornherein unanwendbar.[47] Verlangt er Schadenersatz, so scheitert die Berufung auf Art. 77 daran, dass der dort geregelte Fall hier nicht vorliegt: es geht nicht darum, dass der Schaden des Käufers sich durch die Verzögerung erhöht hat, sondern darum, dass dem Verkäufer ein eigener Schaden entstanden ist. Diesen Schaden hat er sich indessen selbst zuzuschreiben. Er hätte sich gegen

---

[42] *Schlechtriem*, Einheitliches UN-Kaufrecht, S. 61 = Uniform Sales Law, S. 71.
[43] So auch MünchKomm/*Gruber*, Art. 44, Rn. 23; *Honnold/Flechtner*, Artt. 39, 40, 44, Rn. 261.
[44] In diesem Sinn *Bianca/Bonell/Sono*, Art. 44, Anm. 3.1.; *Resch*, ÖJZ 1992, 470, 479; vgl. auch *Schlechtriem*, Einheitliches UN-Kaufrecht, S. 61 (es „könnte" auch an eigene Schadenersatzansprüche des Verkäufers gedacht werden).
[45] A. A. *Bianca/Bonell/Sono*, Art. 44, Anm. 3.1.; *Resch*, ÖJZ 1992, 470, 479.
[46] *Heuzé*, Anm. 305. Fn. 117. A. A. *Herber/Czerwenka*, Art. 34, Rn. 4.
[47] Wie hier *Staudinger/Magnus*, Art. 44, Rn. 21; MünchKomm/*Gruber*, Art. 44, Rn. 22; MünchKommHGB/*Benicke*, Art. 44, Rn. 9. Schon auf der Wiener Konferenz wurde der Zusatz ausdrücklich abgelehnt, der Verkäufer könne seinen Schaden, der ihm aus unterbliebener Anzeige erwächst, den Ansprüchen des Käufers entgegensetzen, vgl. O. R., S. 108, Nr. 7, 9.

den Verlust der Sachmängelansprüche gegenüber seinem Vorlieferanten schützen können, indem er selbst die Ware untersuchte. Versäumt er dies oder verlässt er sich auf die Untersuchung durch den Käufer, hat er die nachteiligen Folgen selbst zu tragen.

5. Verjährung

Die Verjährung der durch Art. 44 vorbehaltenen Rechte richtet sich nach den allgemeinen Bestimmungen, soweit deutsches Recht anwendbar ist, nach § 438 BGB.[48] **17**

6. Abweichende Vereinbarungen und Gebräuche

Wird im Vertrag eine bestimmte Rügefrist festgesetzt, so kann allein hieraus nicht gefolgert werden, dass Art. 44 nicht zur Anwendung gelangt. Im Zweifel soll die Festlegung einer Rügefrist nur die in Artt. 38, 39 vorgesehenen Fristen konkretisieren. Auch wenn Handelsbräuche strikte Rügefristen vorsehen, ist Art. 44 nicht generell ausgeschlossen.[49] **18**

VI. Beweislast

Die **Beweislast** für die Tatsachen, aus denen sich die Entschuldigung ergibt, trifft den Käufer.[50] **19**

---

[48] Vgl. dazu unten *Schroeter*, Art. 3 VertragsG Rn. 4.
[49] Vgl. *Staudinger/Magnus*, Art. 44, Rn. 9; *Soergel/Lüderitz/Schüßler-Langeheine*, Art. 44, Rn. 8; a. A. *U. Huber*, 3. Aufl., Rn. 18; *Bianca/Bonell/Sono*, Art. 44, Anm. 3.3.; *Kuoppala*, Examination, 4.7.1.; *Kruisinga*, Nonconformity, S. 117 ff., 122 empfiehlt, die Anwendung von Art. 44 explizit auszuschliessen.
[50] A. A. *U. Huber*, 3. Aufl., Rn. 18.

Abschnitt III. Rechtsbehelfe* des Käufers wegen Vertragsverletzung durch den Verkäufer

Section III
Remedies for breach of contract by the seller

Section III
Moyens dont dispose l'acheteur en cas de contravention au contrat par le vendeur

Art. 45 [Rechtsbehelfe des Käufers; keine zusätzliche Frist]

(1) Erfüllt der Verkäufer eine seiner Pflichten nach dem Vertrag oder diesem Übereinkommen nicht, so kann der Käufer

a) die in Artikel 46 bis 52 vorgesehenen Rechte ausüben;
b) Schadenersatz nach Artikel 74 bis 77 verlangen.

(2) Der Käufer verliert das Recht, Schadenersatz zu verlangen, nicht dadurch, dass er andere Rechtsbehelfe** ausübt.

(3) Übt der Käufer einen Rechtsbehelf*** wegen Vertragsverletzung aus, so darf ein Gericht oder Schiedsgericht dem Verkäufer keine zusätzliche Frist gewähren.

Art. 45

(1) If the seller fails to perform any of his obligations under the contract or this Convention, the buyer may:

(a) exercise the rights provided in articles 46 to 52;
(b) claim damages as provided in articles 74 to 77.

(2) The buyer is not deprived of any right he may have to claim damages by exercising his right to other remedies.

(3) No period of grace may be granted to the seller by a court or arbitral tribunal when the buyer resorts to a remedy for breach of contract.

Art. 45

1) Si le vendeur n'a pas exécuté l'une quelconque des obligations résultant pour lui du contrat de vente ou de la présente Convention, l'acheteur est fondé à:

a) exercer les droits prévus aux articles 46 à 52;
b) demander les dommages-intérêts prévus aux articles 74 à 77.

2) L'acheteur ne perd pas le droit de demander des dommages-intérêts lorsqu'il exerce son droit de recourir à un autre moyen.

3) Aucun délai de grâce ne peut être accordé au vendeur par un juge ou par un arbitre lorsque l'acheteur se prévaut d'un des moyens dont il dispose en cas de contravention au contrat.

Übersicht

	Rn.
I. Gegenstand und Funktion der Vorschrift	1
II. Nichterfüllung einer Verkäuferpflicht (Abs. 1)	2
1. Nichterfüllung einer Vertragspflicht als Grundtatbestand der Verkäuferhaftung	2
a) Pflichten des Verkäufers	3
b) Nichterfüllung	5
2. Unabhängigkeit des Tatbestands der Nichterfüllung vom Verschulden und von sonstigen vom Verkäufer zu vertretenden Umständen	8
3. Beweislast	9
III. Rechtsbehelfe der Artt. 46–52 (Abs. 1 lit. a)	11
1. Erfüllungsanspruch, Vertragsaufhebung, Minderung	11
2. Wahlrecht, Wechsel des Rechtsbehelfs (ius variandi)	12
a) Wahlrecht	12

---

* Schweiz: Rechte
** Schweiz: Rechte
*** Schweiz: ein Recht

	b) Wechsel des Rechtsbehelfs (ius variandi)	13
	aa) Erfüllungsanspruch	14
	bb) Vertragsaufhebung	16
	cc) Minderung	17
	c) Zwang zur Entscheidung zwischen den Rechtsbehelfen	21
3.	Leistungsverweigerungsrecht	22
IV.	Schadenersatz (Abs. 1 lit. b), Abs. 2)	23
1.	Garantiehaftung des Verkäufers (Abs. 1 lit. b))	23
2.	Verbindung des Schadenersatzanspruchs mit anderen Rechtsbehelfen (Abs. 2)	25
	a) Verbindung mit dem Erfüllungsanspruch	26
	b) Verbindung mit der Vertragsaufhebung	27
	c) Verbindung mit der Minderung	28
V.	Unzulässigkeit einer Gnadenfrist (Abs. 3)	29
VI.	Konkurrierende Rechtsbehelfe des nationalen Rechts	30
VII.	Verjährung	33
VIII.	Zuständigkeitsbegründender Erfüllungsort	34
IX.	Freizeichnung	36

Vorläufer und **Entwürfe:** EKG Artt. 24, 41, 51, 52, 55; Genfer E 1976 Art. 26; Wiener E 1977 Art. 27; New Yorker E 1978 Art. 41.

I. Gegenstand und Funktion der Vorschrift

Art. 45 I enthält eine zusammenfassende Regelung der Rechtsbehelfe des Käufers für alle Fälle, in denen der Verkäufer irgendeine seiner vertraglichen Pflichten nicht erfüllt. Die spiegelbildliche Regelung der Rechtsbehelfe des Verkäufers für die Fälle, in denen der Käufer eine seiner Pflichten nicht erfüllt, findet sich in Art. 61. Die rechtliche Bedeutung der beiden Unterabsätze des Art. 45 I ist unterschiedlich. **Abs. 1 lit. a)** enthält nur einen **deklaratorischen**, allerdings nicht ganz vollständigen[1] Hinweis auf die verschiedenen, in Artt. 46–52 im Einzelnen geregelten Rechtsbehelfe des Erfüllungsanspruchs, der Vertragsaufhebung und der Minderung.[2] **Abs. 1 lit. b)** hat dagegen eine selbstständige Funktion: Er bildet die **Anspruchsgrundlage** für den Schadenersatzanspruch des Käufers in allen Fällen der Vertragsverletzung des Verkäufers.[3] Die Artt. 74–77, auf die hier verwiesen wird, regeln nur Inhalt und Umfang des Schadenersatzanspruchs, nicht seine Voraussetzungen.[4] Art. 45 II stellt klar, dass die in Abs. 1 lit. a) geregelten Rechtsbehelfe und der in Abs. 1 lit. b) geregelte Schadenersatzanspruch vom Käufer nebeneinander geltend gemacht werden können.[5] Art. 45 III enthält einen gegenüber dem romanischen Recht klarstellenden Hinweis.

---

[1] Es fehlt insbesondere der Verweis auf die Artt. 71–73, 78, 80, 86–88.
[2] Vgl. Sekretariatskommentar, Art. 41, Nr. 1: „an index to the remedies available to the buyer"; rechtsvergleichende Synopse des Leistungsstörungsrechts bei *Göttig*, ZfRVgl 2006, 138, 151 f.; überblicksartige Darstellung des Rechtsbehelfssystems bei *P. Huber*, RabelsZ 71 (2007), 13, 15 ff.; vergleichender Überblick über das Rechtsbehelfsystem des DCFR bei *P. Huber*, FS Schwenzer, S. 807, 819 ff.
[3] BGH, 24.3.1999, CISG-online 396; Sekretariatskommentar, aaO.: „the source for the buyer's right to claim damages". So auch *Herber/Czerwenka*, Art. 45, Rn. 5; *Soergel/Lüderitz/Schüßler-Langeheine*, Art. 45, Rn. 1; *Staudinger/Magnus*, Art. 45, Rn. 3; *Zeller*, Damages, S. 65; „Daher ist in Art. 45 Abs. 1 CISG eine Rechtsfolgenverweisung, mithin eine echte Anspruchsgrundlage zu sehen." (*Jungmeyer*, S. 80); „It must be remembered that Article 45 (not Article 79) is the source of the buyer's right to damages." (*Lookofsky*, S. 127 f.).
[4] Vgl. auch *Honnold/Flechtner*, Art. 45, Rn. 276; *Bianca/Bonell/Will*, Art. 45, Anm. 2.1.1.; *Enderlein/Maskow/Strohbach*, Art. 45, Anm. 5.; *Neumayer/Ming*, Art. 45, Anm. 1.
[5] *Zeller*, Damages, S. 62; Art. 7.4.1 PICC.

II. Nichterfüllung einer Verkäuferpflicht (Abs. 1)

1. Nichterfüllung einer Vertragspflicht als Grundtatbestand der Verkäuferhaftung

2   Alle in Art. 45 I geregelten Rechtsbehelfe des Käufers setzen einzig voraus, dass der Verkäufer **irgendeine** seiner durch den Vertrag oder das Kaufrechtsübereinkommen begründeten Pflichten („any of his obligations", „l'une quelconque des obligations") nicht erfüllt.[6]

3   a) **Pflichten des Verkäufers.** Als Pflichten des Verkäufers i. S. d. Art. 45 I kommen unabhängig davon, ob es sich um Haupt- oder Nebenpflichten handelt, insbesondere in Betracht: Die Pflicht zur Lieferung der Ware (Artt. 30, 31), in vertragsmässigem Zustand (Artt. 30, 35); die Pflicht zur Verschaffung des Eigentums (Art. 30), frei von Rechten und Ansprüchen Dritter (Artt. 41 f.); die Pflicht zur Verschaffung der durch Vertrag oder Handelsbrauch bestimmten Dokumente (Artt. 30, 34); sonstige im Vertrag vorgesehene Pflichten (wie z. B. die Pflicht, eine Bankgarantie zu stellen oder die verkaufte Maschine oder das verkaufte Gerät beim Käufer zu montieren). Auch **Unterlassungspflichten** können Grundlage einer Haftung nach Art. 45 I sein. Soweit in ergänzender Auslegung des Vertrags oder des Übereinkommens davon auszugehen ist, dass den Verkäufer **Schutz-, Aufklärungs-** oder **Warnpflichten** treffen, fällt auch ihre Verletzung unter Art. 45 I (so z. B. die Pflicht, darauf hinzuweisen, dass das verkaufte Unkrautbekämpfungsmittel mit anderen Mitteln unvereinbar ist). Auch die Pflicht des Verkäufers zur Erhaltung der Ware bei Annahmeverzug des Käufers (Art. 85) und die Pflicht zum Selbsthilfeverkauf (Art. 88 II) fallen unter Art. 45 I.

4   Von den Pflichten des Verkäufers i. S. d. Art. 45 I zu unterscheiden sind blosse **Obliegenheiten,** deren Erfüllung nach dem Übereinkommen nur die Voraussetzung für die Ausübung eigener Rechte der betroffenen Partei ist. Verletzt der Verkäufer z. B. seine „Pflicht" zur Schadensminderung gemäss Art. 77 S. 1, so ist die Rechtsfolge gemäss Art. 77 S. 2 ausschliesslich die Herabsetzung des Schadenersatzes und nicht eine Haftung gemäss Art. 45 I.[7]

5   b) **Nichterfüllung.** Das Tatbestandsmerkmal der Nichterfüllung einer Pflicht bei Fälligkeit[8] ist in einem denkbar weiten Sinn zu verstehen. Was „Nichterfüllung" bzw. der synonyme Begriff „Vertragsverletzung"[9] bedeutet, ergibt sich immer aus dem Inhalt der Pflicht, um die es geht. Die Pflicht zur Lieferung ist z. B. nicht erfüllt, wenn der Verkäufer die in Artt. 31 ff. oder im Vertrag beschriebenen Massnahmen bis zur Fälligkeit (Art. 33) nicht durchgeführt hat. Die Ursache der Nichterfüllung, d. h. ob der Verkäufer nicht liefern kann oder will, qualitativ oder quantitativ mangelhaft etc. erfüllt, ist im Gegensatz zu gewissen nationalen Rechten gleichgültig.[10] Massgeblich ist hinsichtlich der dem Käufer

---

[6] So auch § 235 Restatement 2d Contracts: „When performance of a duty under a contract is due any nonperformance is a breach"; HGer Zürich, 10.2.1999, CISG-online 488; OLG München, 5.3.2008, CISG-online 1686 = IHR 2008, 253–255: Nichterfüllung einer Vertragsvoraussetzung als einheitlicher Störungstatbestand; nicht richtig daher ICC, 9978/1997, CISG-online 708 („Art. 45 (1) CISG […] only entitled the buyer to damages for breach of primary obligations by the seller"); rechtsvergleichend zum Common Frame of Reference vgl. *Magnus,* ZEuP 2007, 260, 262 ff.; *Zoll,* ZEuP 2007, 229, 231 ff.

[7] Vgl. auch *Schwenzer,* Art. 74 Rn. 13.

[8] Vor Fälligkeit stehen dem Käufer unter Vorbehalt von Art. 52 keine Rechtsbehelfe zu, es sei denn, es läge ein antizipierter Vertragsbruch vor (Art. 72); zur besonderen Situation der künftig drohenden Vertragsverletzungen beim Sukzessivlieferungsvertrag s. Art. 73.

[9] *Von Caemmerer,* SJZ 1981, 257, 264 = GS Bd. 3, S. 100; *Bianca/Bonell/Will,* Art. 45, Anm. 2.1.2.

[10] Vgl. etwa zum schweiz. Recht: Artt. 97 I, 102 ff., 119 OR, dazu *Schwenzer,* OR AT, Rn. 60.02; *Gauch/Schluep/Schmid/Rey,* Rn. 2602 ff.; zum deutschen Recht: vgl. § 280 BGB, der nunmehr vom einheitlichen Begriff der Pflichtverletzung ausgeht, vgl. *Lorenz/Riehm,* Rn. 465; zum österreichischen Recht: §§ 918–922, 1447 ABGB, vgl. *Koziol/Welser/Kletečka,* Band II, S. 45 ff.; Die ibero-amerik. (*E. Muñoz,* S. 381), osteuropäischen und zentralasiatischen (*Lapiashvili,* S. 261) Rechtsordnungen differenzieren die Rechtsbehelfe nach den

offen stehenden Rechtsbehelfe hingegen, ob die Nichterfüllung wesentlich ist oder nicht.[11] Ungeachtet der Tatsache, dass jede Pflichtverletzung eine Nichterfüllung darstellt und im Grundsatz unabhängig von der Art der Vertragsverletzung die in den Artt. 45 I bzw. 61 I enummerierten Rechtsbehelfe auslöst, können die verschiedenen Arten der Leistungsstörungen im Rechtsbehelfesystem jedoch nicht gänzlich ignoriert werden.[12]

So kann im Fall der **„Nichtlieferung"** (Nichterfüllung der Lieferpflicht) der Käufer die **6** Vertragsaufhebung nicht nur erklären, wenn die Überschreitung des Liefertermins eine wesentliche Vertragsverletzung ist (Art. 49 I lit. a)), sondern auch dann, wenn er dem Verkäufer für die Lieferung erfolglos Nachfrist gesetzt hat (Art. 49 I lit. b)). In allen anderen Fällen der Nichterfüllung von Verkäuferpflichten (insbesondere im Fall der Lieferung nicht vertragsmässiger Ware) hängt dagegen das Recht zur Vertragsaufhebung ausschliesslich davon ab, ob die Vertragsverletzung i. S. d. Art. 25 „wesentlich" ist. Der Käufer kann nicht eine unwesentliche Vertragsverletzung zur wesentlichen Vertragsverletzung „wandlen", indem er dem Verkäufer für die Erfüllung der Pflicht eine Nachfrist setzt.

Im Fall der **Lieferung nicht vertragsmässiger Ware** ist der Erfüllungsanspruch be- **7** schränkt: Der Käufer kann Ersatzlieferung nur verlangen, wenn die Vertragswidrigkeit eine wesentliche Vertragsverletzung darstellt (Art. 46 II). Im Fall der Nichtlieferung gibt es keine vergleichbare Beschränkung des Erfüllungsanspruchs (Art. 46 I). Auch aus diesem Grund (und nicht nur im Hinblick auf die Rügepflicht des Art. 39) macht es z. B. einen praktischen Unterschied, wie die „Falschlieferung" (also die Lieferung einer anderen als der verkauften Sache und, beim Gattungskauf, die Lieferung einer Sache anderer Art) einzuordnen ist: Als „Nichtlieferung" oder als „Lieferung nicht vertragsmässiger Ware". Richtig ist es, die Falschlieferung als Lieferung nicht vertragsmässiger Ware anzusehen.[13] Schliesslich kann der Käufer nur im Falle der Lieferung nicht vertragsmässiger Ware den Kaufpreis mindern (Art. 50).

2. Unabhängigkeit des Tatbestands der Nichterfüllung vom Verschulden und von sonstigen vom Verkäufer zu vertretenden Umständen

Der Tatbestand der „Nichterfüllung" setzt nicht voraus, dass der Verkäufer die Nicht- **8** erfüllung verschuldet oder aus sonstigen Gründen zu vertreten hat.[14] Nichterfüllung liegt daher auch vor, wenn der Verkäufer gemäss Art. 79 entlastet wird. Dies hat zur Konsequenz, dass dem Käufer die Rechtsbehelfe der Artt. 46–52, insbesondere die Vertragsaufhebung, erhalten bleiben. Ausgeschlossen wird einzig die Schadenersatzpflicht und – je nach Ursache der Nichterfüllung – der Erfüllungsanspruch (Art. 79 V).[15] Etwas anderes gilt, wenn der Verkäufer entlastet wird, weil die Nichterfüllung durch eine **Handlung oder Unterlassung des Käufers** verursacht ist (Art. 80).[16] Ausgeschlossen sind in diesem Fall nicht nur Schadenersatzansprüche des Käufers gemäss Art. 45 I lit. b), sondern auch alle Rechtsbehelfe des Käufers gemäss Art. 45 I lit. a).[17] Dem Verkäufer seinerseits bleibt es unbenommen, gegen den Käufer die Rechtsbehelfe gemäss Art. 61 auszuüben.[18] Im Ergebnis enthält also Art. 80 eine Einschränkung des Haftungstatbestands des Art. 45 I.

Ursachen der Pflichtverletzung; zu den afrikanischen Rechten (Sub-Sahara Länder) s. *Penda Matipé*, S. 366 ff.; rechtsvergleichender Überblick über die verschiedenen Ansätze bei *Schwenzer/Hachem/Kee*, Rn. 41.1 f.

[11] *Staudinger/Magnus*, Art. 45, Rn. 10; vgl. sogleich zur Ausnahme von diesem Grundsatz.
[12] S. auch *Schwenzer/Hachem/Kee*, Rn. 41.38.
[13] Vgl. dazu *Widmer Lüchinger*, Art. 31 Rn. 34; *Schwenzer*, Art. 35 Rn. 10.
[14] Vgl. *Honnold/Flechtner*, Art. 45, Rn. 276; *Bianca/Bonell/Will*, Art. 45, Anm. 2.1.2.; *Neumayer/Ming*, Art. 45, Anm. 1.; *Staudinger/Magnus*, Art. 45, Rn. 1, 11, 18; *MünchKommHGB/Benicke*, Art. 46, Rn. 2; *Atamer*, FS Hopt, S. 3, 6.
[15] *Müller-Chen*, Art. 28 Rn. 13 ff., Art. 46 Rn. 9 f.; *Schwenzer*, Art. 79 Rn. 53.
[16] Vgl. *Schwenzer*, Art. 80 Rn. 8, 9.
[17] Vgl. *Schwenzer*, Art. 80 Rn. 8, 9.
[18] Vgl. *Schwenzer*, Art. 80 Rn. 10.

3. Beweislast

9 Die Beweislast für die die Nichterfüllung begründenden Tatsachen ist im Übereinkommen nicht explizit geregelt, gehört aber zu den i. S. v. Art. 7 II vom Übereinkommen erfassten Gegenstände.[19] Die konkrete Verteilung hat sich am allgemeinen, international weit verbreiteten Grundsatz zu orientieren, dass jede Partei für die tatsächlichen Voraussetzungen der Vorschrift, auf die sie ihren Anspruch stützt, beweispflichtig ist.[20] Wer sich auf eine Ausnahmebestimmung beruft (z. B. Art. 79 im Verhältnis zu Art. 45 I lit. b)), hat nachzuweisen, dass die entsprechenden Voraussetzungen erfüllt sind.[21] Tatsachen aus einem Bereich, der einer Partei deutlich besser bekannt sind als der anderen, sind von der Partei nachzuweisen, welche die Herrschaft über diesen Bereich hat (Beweisnähe).[22] Da sich die Frage der Beweislast für eine Vertragsverletzung praktisch im Zusammenhang mit den Rechtsbehelfen des Käufers stellt, von denen einzig die Schadenersatzpflicht ihre Grundlage in Art. 45 I hat, ist nachfolgend nur dieser Tatbestand zu erörtern.[23]

10 Die Schadenersatzpflicht des Verkäufers setzt gemäss Art. 45 I das Vorliegen eines Schadens und die Nichterfüllung einer Pflicht voraus. Das CISG geht von der Regel aus, dass der Verkäufer für die Vertragsverletzung einzustehen hat, es sei denn, es liege ein Entlastungsgrund im Sinne von Art. 79 vor. Aus dem Regel-Ausnahme-Prinzip folgt, dass bei einer Schadenersatzklage des Käufers dieser im Grundsatz die Beweislast für die Tatsachen trägt, aus denen sich der Schaden und die Vertragswidrigkeit der Lieferung ergeben.[24] Der Verkäufer hat demgegenüber das Vorliegen eines Entlastungsgrundes nachzuweisen.[25] Hat jedoch der Käufer die Vertragswidrigkeit der Ware bei Empfang sofort gerügt oder die Ware zurückgewiesen,[26] trägt der Verkäufer die Beweislast dafür, dass die Ware **bei Gefahrübergang vertragsgemäss** war.[27] Für Einzelheiten der Beweislastverteilung wird auf die Kommentierung der entsprechenden Pflichten des Verkäufers verwiesen.[28]

---

[19] *Stalder*, AJP 2004, 1472, 1473; *Ferrari*, Art. 4 Rn. 48 ff., Art. 7 Rn. 56; *Brunner*, Art. 7, Rn. 56; *Witz/Salger/Lorenz*, Art. 7, Rn. 31; *Honsell/Siehr*, Art. 4, Rn. 14; *Bamberger/Roth/Saenger*, Art. 4, Rn. 11; *Mohs*, AJP 2011, 425, 426. Die allgemeine Ansicht bei den Vorberatungen des Übereinkommens war die, dass es nicht Sache des Einheitskaufrechts sei, Fragen des „Beweis- und Verfahrensrechts" („matters of evidence or procedure") zu regeln. Vgl. Report of Committee of the Whole I relating to the draft Convention on the International Sale of Goods, YB VIII (1977), S. 37, Nr. 177 f. Allerdings hat das Übereinkommen sich in Art. 79 an diese Selbstbeschränkung nicht gehalten.

[20] Vgl. *Ferrari*, Art. 4 Rn. 48 ff.; *Staudinger/Magnus*, Art. 7, Rn. 57; rechtsvergleichend *E. Muñoz*, S. 143 f. (ibero-amerik. Rechtsordnungen); *Penda Matipé*, S. 99 f. (sub-sahara-afrikanische Rechte); *Hafez*, S. 99 f. (arabische Rechtsordnungen); *Lapiashvili*, S. 88 (osteuropäische und zentralasiatische Staaten); *S. J. Yang*, S. 81 f. chines. Recht).

[21] *Magnus*, RabelsZ 59 (1995), 469, 490.

[22] BGer, 13.11.2004, CISG-online 840 = BGE 130 III 258, 265, m. zust. Anm. *Mohs*, IHR 2004, 215 ff.

[23] Vgl. zum Erfüllungsanspruch *Müller-Chen*, Art. 46 Rn. 16, 31, 40; zur Vertragsaufhebung *Müller-Chen*, Art. 49 Rn. 13; zur Minderung *Müller-Chen*, Art. 50 Rn. 15.

[24] Die in der 4. Aufl. vertretene Meinung (Käufer muss Nichterfüllung der Pflicht nur behaupten, nicht beweisen) wird aufgegeben; *Schwenzer*, Art. 35 Rn. 52; BGer, 13.11.2003, CISG-online 840, E. 5.3 = BGE 130 III 258, 265, m. zust. Anm. *Mohs*, IHR 2004, 219; BGer, 13.11.2007, CISG-online 1618; ablehnend hingegen *Stalder*, AJP 2004, 1472, 1476 ff. (Beweisbelastung des Käufers im Grundsatz erst ab dem Zeitpunkt des Ablaufs der Rügefrist nach Art. 39 I); *Chicago Prime Packers, Inc. v. Northam Food Trading Co.*, U. S. Ct. App. (7th Cir.), 23.5.2005, CISG-online 1026; Hof van Beroep, Gent, 28.1.2004, CISG-online 830; Netherlands Arbitration Institute, 15.10.2002, CISG-online 780, Rn. 64 ff.; *Kruisinga*, Non-conformity, S. 157 ff.; *Zeller*, Damages, S. 82 f.; rechtsvergleichend s. auch *T. M. Müller*, Beweislast, S. 70 ff.

[25] Vgl. *Schwenzer*, Art. 79 Rn. 59.

[26] Zu den Ausnahmen aufgrund fehlender Beweisnähe vgl. *Schwenzer*, Art. 35 Rn. 52.

[27] Vgl. *Schwenzer*, Art. 35 Rn. 52; KG Zug, 14.12.2009, CISG-online 2026; OLG Karlsruhe, 8.2.2006, CISG-online 1328 = IHR 2006, 106, m. Anm. *C. Witz*, D. 2007, Panorama, 530, 538; *Enstahler/Achilles*, GK-HGB, nach § 382, Art. 45, Rn. 13; BGer, 7.7.2004, CISG-online 848, E. 3.3; BGH, 9.1.2002, CISG-online 651 = NJW 2002, 1651; BGH, 8.3.1995, CISG-online 144 = BGHZ 129, 75, 81 (Muschel-Fall); CA Mons, 8.3.2001, CISG-online 605; OLG Innsbruck, 1.7.1994, CISG-online 107; CA Grenoble, 15.5.1996, CISG-online 219 = D. 1997, Somm. 221, m. Anm. *C. Witz*; OLG Frankfurt a. M., 13.6.1991, CISG-online 23 = RIW 1991, 591.

[28] Zum Inhalt der Lieferpflicht und Ort der Lieferung vgl. *Widmer Lüchinger*, Art. 31 Rn. 61, 70, 82; zur Zeit der Lieferung vgl. *Widmer Lüchinger*, Art. 33 Rn. 15; zur Vertragsmässigkeit der Ware vgl. *Schwenzer*,

III. Rechtsbehelfe der Artt. 46–52 (Abs. 1 lit. a))

1. Erfüllungsanspruch, Vertragsaufhebung, Minderung

Die Artt. 46–52, auf die Art. 45 I lit. a) verweist, verleihen dem Käufer im Fall der 11 Nichterfüllung der Verkäuferpflichten drei Rechtsbehelfe: den Anspruch auf (Nach-)Erfüllung (Art. 46, unter dem Vorbehalt des Art. 28), das Recht zur Vertragsaufhebung (Art. 49) und das Recht zur Minderung (Art. 50). Die übrigen in Art. 45 I lit. a) genannten Bestimmungen haben nur ergänzenden Charakter. So regelt Art. 47 die Nachfristsetzung für den Erfüllungsanspruch und Art. 48 das Recht des Verkäufers zur Behebung von Mängeln. Für den Fall der teilweisen Nichterfüllung enthält Art. 51 eine ergänzende Bestimmung. Bei der vorzeitigen Lieferung und der Zuviellieferung kommt die Regelung des Art. 52 zur Anwendung. Nicht in jedem Fall stehen allerdings dem Käufer alle drei Rechtsbehelfe nebeneinander zur Auswahl.

2. Wahlrecht, Wechsel des Rechtsbehelfs (ius variandi)

a) Wahlrecht. Soweit die Voraussetzungen der drei Rechtsbehelfe des Erfüllungs- 12 anspruchs (Art. 46), der Vertragsaufhebung (Art. 49) und der Minderung (Art. 50) nebeneinander bestehen, kann der Käufer zwischen ihnen wählen. Ist z. B. die gelieferte Sache nicht vertragsgemäss und stellt die Vertragswidrigkeit eine wesentliche Vertragsverletzung dar (es sind z. B. die für die Autofabrik des Käufers gelieferten Bleche rostig und für Fabrikationszwecke ungeeignet), so hat der Käufer die Wahl: Er kann Lieferung einwandfreier Ware verlangen (Art. 46 II), er kann die Vertragsaufhebung (Art. 49 I lit. a)) erklären oder Minderung verlangen (Art. 50; etwa weil er es vorzieht, die Bleche als Schrott zu verkaufen und die Differenz zwischen dem Kaufpreis und dem Nettoerlös vom Kaufpreis abzuziehen). Diese Wahl *muss* er auch treffen. Eine Kombination der drei Rechtsbehelfe ist nicht möglich, weil ihre Rechtsfolgen miteinander unvereinbar sind. Entscheidet der Käufer sich für Ersatzlieferung, bleibt der Verkäufer zur Lieferung, der Käufer zur Zahlung verpflichtet. Entscheidet er sich für Vertragsaufhebung, so entfällt die Pflicht des Verkäufers zur Lieferung und die Pflicht des Käufers zur Zahlung (Art. 81 I 1). Entscheidet er sich für Minderung, so entfällt die Pflicht des Verkäufers zur Ersatzlieferung, der Käufer bleibt zur Zahlung des reduzierten Kaufpreises verpflichtet und behält die gelieferte Sache (während er sowohl im Fall der Ersatzlieferung als auch im Fall der Vertragsaufhebung zur Rückgabe verpflichtet ist, Artt. 81 II, 82 I).[29]

b) Wechsel des Rechtsbehelfs (ius variandi). Da die drei Rechtsbehelfe einander 13 ausschliessen, stellt sich die Frage, ob der Käufer an den einmal gewählten Rechtsbehelf gebunden ist oder ob er zu einem andern wechseln kann (ius variandi). Wird dies bejaht, muss entschieden werden, innerhalb welcher Frist dies möglich sein soll. Diese Frage ist für die verschiedenen Rechtsbehelfe unterschiedlich zu beantworten.

aa) Erfüllungsanspruch. Verlangt der Käufer gemäss Art. 46 (Nach-)Erfüllung, so ist er 14 hieran **nicht gebunden.** Dies gilt im Grundsatz sowohl für den Fall der Nichterfüllung der Lieferpflicht[30] wie auch der Lieferung nicht vertragsgemässer Ware.[31] Eine zeitlich begrenzte Bindung tritt nur ein, wenn der Käufer dem Verkäufer für die Erfüllung eine **Nachfrist**

Art. 35 Rn. 49 ff.; zur Haltbarkeitsgarantie vgl. *Schwenzer*, Art. 36 Rn. 13; zur Mängelrüge vgl. *Schwenzer*, Art. 39 Rn. 37 f.; zur Kenntnis der Vertragswidrigkeit vgl. *Schwenzer*, Art. 40 Rn. 12; zum Rechtsmangel und Schutzrechte Dritter vgl. *Schwenzer*, Art. 41 Rn. 25 und Art. 42 Rn. 29; zur Rügepflicht vgl. *Schwenzer*, Art. 43 Rn. 12.

[29] Die Rückgabepflicht im Fall der Ersatzlieferung wird im Übereinkommen nicht ausdrücklich und direkt angeordnet, aber in Art. 82 I als selbstverständlich vorausgesetzt, vgl. dazu Art. 46 Rn. 34.
[30] Vgl. im Einzelnen Art. 46 Rn. 6.
[31] Vgl. Art. 46 Rn. 17 ff., 39 ff.

setzt (Art. 47 II 1). In diesem Fall kann er vor Ablauf der Nachfrist oder Zugang einer Ablehnungserklärung des Verkäufers keinen anderen Rechtsbehelf wegen Vertragsverletzung ausüben. Nach Ablauf der Nachfrist (oder vorherigem Zugang einer Ablehnungserklärung) gewinnt der Käufer seine Entscheidungsfreiheit wieder zurück.

15 Ausnahmsweise kann der Wechsel vom zunächst geltend gemachten Erfüllungsanspruch zu einem andern Rechtsbehelf **rechtsmissbräuchlich** sein.[32] Das gilt z. B. dann, wenn der Käufer im Falle einer wesentlichen Vertragsverletzung zunächst auf Lieferung besteht und dann den Rechtsbehelf kurzfristig wechselt, obwohl der Verkäufer in der Zwischenzeit die Lieferung bewirkt hat. Erfolgt die Lieferung, bevor der Käufer die Vertragsaufhebung gemäss Art. 49 I erklärt hat, ist das Recht des Käufers zur Vertragsaufhebung gemäss Art. 7 I (Treu und Glauben) ausgeschlossen.[33]

16 **bb) Vertragsaufhebung.** Erklärt der Käufer gemäss Art. 49 I **berechtigterweise**[34] die Vertragsaufhebung, so beurteilt sich die Frage, ob und in welchem Zeitpunkt er daran gebunden ist, nach den allgemeinen zum CISG entwickelten Grundsätzen zur Bindung an eine bzw. zum Widerruf einer Erklärung.[35] Entscheidend ist danach, ob der Verkäufer ein **schutzwürdiges Interesse** an der Unwiderruflichkeit der Erklärung der Vertragsaufhebung hat, weil er vernünftigerweise darauf vertrauen durfte und sich auf die veränderte Rechtslage eingestellt und entsprechend disponiert hat.[36] Kennt der Verkäufer die Vertragsaufhebung mangels Zugang nicht oder weist er die Erklärung zurück und bringt dadurch zum Ausdruck, dass er die Vertragsdurchführung wünscht, benötigt und verdient er keinen Vertrauens- und Dispositionsschutz.[37] Bestreitet z. B. der Verkäufer die vom Käufer geltend gemachte Vertragswidrigkeit der Ware und die darauf gestützte Vertragsaufhebung, kann der Käufer die Ware verwerten und den Ausgleich des Minderwertes auf dem Weg des Schadenersatzes oder der Minderung verlangen. Eine Berufung des Verkäufers auf die Unwiderruflichkeit der Vertragsaufhebung käme einem „Venire contra factum proprium" gleich. Stimmt der Verkäufer der Vertragsaufhebung ausdrücklich oder durch entsprechende Handlungen konkludent zu, tritt die Unwiderruflichkeit der Erklärung ein und ein Widerruf der Vertragsaufhebung durch den Käufer ist nicht mehr möglich.[38] Von diesen Kriterien hängt es demzufolge ab, ob der Käufer zu den anderen Rechtsbehelfen der Erfüllung und Minderung wechseln kann.[39] Nur wenn im soeben dargestellten Sinn beim Verkäufer schutzwürdiges Vertrauen in die Erklärung der Vertragsaufhebung entstanden ist, ist der Käufer gebunden. Ihn trifft auch die Beweislast dafür, dass der Verkäufer sich nicht auf die Vertragsaufhebung eingestellt hat.

---

[32] Es liegt noch kein rechtsmissbräuchliches Verhalten des Käufers vor, wenn er mit der Erklärung der Vertragsaufhebung lange zuwartet und so u. U. auf Kosten des Verkäufers spekuliert.
[33] Vgl. auch *Honnold/Flechtner*, Art. 47, Rn. 291: „A party may not refuse performance that he has invited"; *Piltz*, Internationales Kaufrecht, § 5, Rn. 211 (weitergehend als hier: Der Käufer sei in jedem Fall für eine angemessene Frist an sein Erfüllungsbegehren gebunden). Da sich die einschlägigen Fälle durch Rückgriff auf Treu und Glauben lösen lassen, hielt die Wiener Konferenz eine besondere Regelung der Frage für überflüssig, vgl. Art. 47 Rn. 14.
[34] Zu den Folgen einer unberechtigten Vertragsaufhebung vgl. *Müller-Chen*, Art. 49 Rn. 44: „Der Käufer ist insoweit gebunden, als ihn der Verkäufer „beim Wort nehmen" kann (aber nicht muss).
[35] Vgl. *Schroeter*, Art. 16 Rn. 8 f.; Art. 27 Rn. 14.
[36] Vgl. *Schlechtriem*, Bindung an Erklärungen, S. 272 f.
[37] *Schroeter*, Art. 27 Rn. 14; *Fountoulakis*, Art. 26 Rn. 12; HGer Zürich, 25.10.2007, CISG-online 1564 = SZIER 2008, 180, 181.
[38] Dies steht unter dem selbstverständlichen Vorbehalt einer anderslautenden einverständlichen Regelung der Parteien (z. B. Neuabschluss).
[39] Im deutschen Recht tritt die Bindung nunmehr direkt mit der Erklärung des Käufers ein, vgl. *Lorenz/Riehm*, Rn. 522 (Erklärung der Vertragsaufhebung), 528 (Minderungserklärung), 543 (Geltendmachung von Schadenersatz statt Leistung gemäss § 281 IV). Im schweiz. Recht tritt die Bindung ebenfalls mit der Erklärung ein, vgl. BGer, 15.1.1997, BGE 123 III 16, 22 (Unwiderruflichkeit der Wahlerklärung beim Verzug nach Art. 107 OR); BGer, 19.8.2002 (hat sich der Käufer eines Werkes für Nachbesserung entschieden, kann er nicht mehr zur Vertragsaufhebung wechseln, es sei denn die Nachbesserung bzw. Ersatzlieferung wäre unmöglich). Zum österreichischen Recht vgl. *Koziol/Welser/Kletečka*, Band II, S. 45 ff.

cc) **Minderung.** Mit der in der Literatur herrschenden Meinung[40] ist das Minderungsrecht des Käufers als ein **einseitig auszuübendes Recht** anzusehen.[41] Von der Rechtsnatur der Minderung ist die Frage der Bindung des Käufers an die einmal ausgeübte Minderung zu trennen, wodurch der Meinungsstreit zur dogmatischen Einordnung der Minderung an praktischer Relevanz verliert.[42]

Von der Interessenlage des Verkäufers her gibt es keinen Grund, die Frage des Wechsels von der Minderung zu einem anderen Rechtsbehelf anders zu beurteilen als bei der Vertragsaufhebung.[43] Danach tritt eine Bindung des Käufers grundsätzlich erst ab Zugang ein, da der Verkäufer vorher nicht gegen eine Rücknahme geschützt werden muss.[44] Bei **Kenntnis** bzw. Kennenmüssen des Verkäufers ist die Minderungserklärung unwiderruflich, wenn der Verkäufer sich schutzwürdig auf die Minderung eingestellt hat, indem er z. B. sein Einverständnis erklärt oder Dispositionen getroffen hat. Falls der Verkäufer sich nicht vernehmen liess, ist zu vermuten, dass er sich auf die Minderung eingestellt hat und es ist am Käufer, diese Vermutung zu widerlegen.[45]

Die Problematik des Wechsels von der Minderung zur Erfüllung bzw. Vertragsaufhebung wird allerdings aus praktischen Gründen entschärft. Denn der Käufer muss die Entscheidung für die Minderung alsbald revidieren, wenn er auf den Erfüllungsanspruch bzw. die Vertragsaufhebung zurückgreifen will, da die entsprechenden Erklärungen innerhalb einer **angemessenen Frist** seit Mängelrüge bzw. Kenntnis der Vertragswidrigkeit der Ware abgegeben werden müssen (Artt. 46 II, III bzw. 49 II lit. b) i)). Hat der Käufer die Frist sowohl für den Erfüllungsanspruch als auch für die Vertragsaufhebung verstreichen lassen, kann er dem Verkäufer für die Erfüllung keine wirksame Nachfrist gemäss Art. 47 I mehr setzen. Eine „Pflicht" des Verkäufers zur Ersatzlieferung oder Nachbesserung besteht nicht mehr. Damit entfällt aber auch die Möglichkeit, das Recht zur Vertragsaufhebung mit Hilfe einer Nachfristsetzung gemäss Art. 49 II lit. b) ii) wiederherzustellen. Nach Ablauf der Frist bleibt dem Käufer nur noch die Möglichkeit, statt der Minderung Schadenersatz gemäss Art. 45 I lit. b) zu verlangen oder die Minderung anders, als ursprünglich verlangt, zu berechnen. Dagegen bestehen keine Bedenken. Auch wenn der Käufer sofort Schadenersatz verlangt, ist er an die erste dem Verkäufer vorgelegte Berechnung nicht gebunden. Dafür, dass das im Fall der Minderung anders sein soll, besteht kein Grund.

Hat der Käufer wegen eines von ihm entdeckten Mangels der Sache Minderung verlangt und zeigt sich nachträglich ein **zweiter, neuartiger Mangel,** so kann der Käufer, soweit die Rügefrist (Art. 39) nicht verstrichen ist, wegen dieses zweiten Mangels alle Rechte gemäss Art. 45 I lit. a) wieder in Anspruch nehmen. Hieran wird er auch dadurch nicht gehindert, dass er sich wegen des zuerst entdeckten Mangels mit dem Verkäufer auf Minderung geeinigt hat. Denn auf diesen zweiten Mangel hat sich die Einigung der Parteien nicht bezogen.

c) **Zwang zur Entscheidung zwischen den Rechtsbehelfen.** Wartet der Käufer mit der Wahl des Rechtsbehelfs zu, ohne sich zu entscheiden, läuft er Gefahr, wegen Fristversäumnis einen Rechtsbehelf zu verlieren. Insofern besteht ein Zwang zur Entscheidung. Dies gilt im Falle der Lieferung nicht vertragsgemässer Ware für den Ersatzlieferungs- und

---

[40] Vgl. mit überzeugender Begründung *Hirner*, S. 276 ff.; *Schlechtriem*, Einheitliches UN-Kaufrecht, S. 70; *Herber/Czerwenka*, Art. 50, Rn. 4, sowie Art. 3, Rn. 8; *Soergel/Lüderitz/Schüßler-Langeheine*, Art. 50, Rn. 6; *Staudinger/Magnus*, Art. 50, Rn. 31; *Neumayer/Ming*, Art. 50, Anm. 1.; *Karollus*, S. 157; *Piltz*, Internationales Kaufrecht, Rn. 5–350; Rn. 530; *Welser*, S. 117; *Venturi*, Rn. 285, 881 f., 894; i. E. übereinstimmend auch *Honsell/Schnyder/Straub*, Art. 50, Rn. 31; ebenso *U. Huber*, 1. Aufl., Art. 50, Rn. 11; vgl. auch *U. Huber*, RabelsZ 43 (1979), 413, 492; a. A. soweit ersichtlich einzig *U. Huber*, 3. Aufl., Art. 50, Rn. 30 f.
[41] AG Sursee, 12.9.2008, CISG-online 1728 = SZIER 2011, 560 f.; der terminus technicus des „Gestaltungsrechts" ist auf Grund seiner Nähe zu dogmatischen Konzepten des nationalen Rechts zu vermeiden, vgl. auch *Hirner*, S. 280.
[42] Wodurch i. E. die hier vertretene Ansicht sich wieder der 3. Aufl. nähert, vgl. *U. Huber*, 3. Aufl., Rn. 32.
[43] Vgl. vorne Rn. 16.
[44] Vgl. dazu und zum Folgenden *Hirner*, S. 286 ff.; *Schlechtriem*, Bindung an Erklärungen, S. 272 f.
[45] *Hirner*, S. 290 f.

Nachbesserungsanspruch sowie den Rechtsbehelf der Vertragsaufhebung.[46] Bei der schlichten Nichterfüllung der Lieferpflicht kann der Käufer jedoch mit seiner Entscheidung zwischen dem Erfüllungsanspruch und der Vertragsaufhebung zuwarten, selbst wenn er dem Verkäufer gemäss Art. 47 eine Nachfrist zur Erfüllung gesetzt hat.[47] Erst wenn die Lieferung tatsächlich, aber verspätet erfolgt ist, muss diese Erklärung in angemessener Frist erfolgen (Art. 49 II lit. a)).

3. Leistungsverweigerungsrecht

22   Das CISG enthält keine Norm, welche einer Partei ein allgemeines Leistungsverweigerungsrecht bei einer Vertragsverletzung der Gegenseite einräumt.[48] Ein solches Zurückbehaltungsrecht wird jedoch in einzelnen Vorschriften vorgesehen (insbes. Artt. 58 I 2, II, 71, 85 S. 2, 86 I 2),[49] aus denen ein **allgemeines Zurückbehaltungsrecht** bei der Nichterfüllung aller Pflichten deduziert werden kann, die von einigem Gewicht sind.[50] So kann der Käufer z. B. im Falle der Nichtlieferung die Zahlung des Kaufpreises verweigern, da gemäss Art. 58 der Kaufpreis erst fällig wird, wenn die Ware dem Käufer zur Verfügung gestellt ist. Ist der Käufer vorleistungspflichtig und verweigert der Verkäufer die Erfüllung der Lieferpflicht schon im Voraus, kann der Käufer, statt gemäss Art. 72 die Vertragsaufhebung zu erklären, den Verkäufer am Vertrag festhalten, aber die Zahlung des Kaufpreises gemäss Art. 71 I lit. b) einstweilen verweigern.[51] Ist die gelieferte Ware nicht vertragsgemäss und verlangt der Käufer gemäss Art. 46 II, III Ersatzlieferung oder Nachbesserung, so muss der Käufer die mangelhafte Ware im Grundsatz (entgegen der perfect tender rule des Common Law) die Ware entgegennehmen.[52] Er wird sich aber im Regelfall hinsichtlich der Kaufpreiszahlung auf den Einwand der fehlenden Fälligkeit berufen können; denn die Fälligkeit nach Art. 58 hängt davon ab, dass die dem Käufer zur Verfügung gestellte Ware vertragsgemäss ist; anderenfalls hätte das Untersuchungsrecht des Art. 58 III keinen Sinn.[53]

IV. Schadenersatz (Abs. 1 lit. b), Abs. 2)

1. Garantiehaftung des Verkäufers (Abs. 1 lit. b))

23   Der Schadenersatzanspruch gemäss Art. 45 I lit. b) beruht auf dem Prinzip, dass den Verkäufer im Hinblick auf die Erfüllung der vertraglich übernommenen Pflichten kraft Gesetzes eine generelle Garantiehaftung trifft.[54] Die Haftung ist daher von einem **Ver-**

---

[46] Vgl. Artt. 46 II, III, 49 II lit. b).
[47] Vgl. Art. 49 Rn. 27.
[48] Anders etwa Art. 9:201 PECL oder Art. 7.1.3 PICC.
[49] Vgl. *W. Witz*, FS Schlechtriem, S. 293 ff.
[50] OGH, 8.11.2005, CISG-online 1156; *Hager/Maultzsch*, 5. Aufl. Art. 58 Rn. 13 m. w. N.; *Schlechtriem*, Symposium Vischer, S. 47; *Brunner*, Art. 45, Rn. 4; *Schwenzer/Hachem/Kee*, Rn. 42.7; a. A. *Honsell/Schnyder/Straub*, Art. 45, Rn. 55 ff.; rechtsvergleichend s. *Schwenzer/Hachem/Kee*, Rn. 42.3 ff.; *Nyer*, 18 Pace Int'l L. Rev. (2006), 29, 36 ff., 72 ff.; das allgemeine Zurückbehaltungsrecht ist international weit verbreitet, s. *Penda Matipé*, S. 371 ff. (sub-sahara-afrikanische Rechte); *Hafez*, S. 299 ff. (arabische Rechtsordnungen); *Lapiashvili*, S. 264 ff. (osteurop. Rechtsordnungen); *S. J. Yang*, S. 294 ff.; *E. Muñoz*, S. 389 ff. (ibero-amerik. Rechtsordnungen); Leistungsverweigerungsrechte sehen auch vor: Art. 7.1.3 UNIDROIT Principles; Art. 9:201 PECL; Art. III.–3:401 DCFR; Art. 282 UAGCL.
[51] Für weitere Fälle vgl. *Fountoulakis*, Art. 71 Rn. 12 ff.; *Honsell*, Art. 49, Rn. 25 mit Hinweis auf BGH, 27.11.2007, CISG-online 1617.
[52] *Schlechtriem*, Symposium Vischer, S. 47; CISG-AC, Op. 5 *(Schwenzer)*, Art. 49 Opinion 8 und Comment 4.18 ff.
[53] Für weitere Fälle vgl. *Hager/Maultzsch*, 5. Aufl. Art. 58 Rn. 3 ff.
[54] *Honnold/Flechtner*, Art. 45, Rn. 276; *Staudinger/Magnus*, Art. 45, Rn. 18; *Schlechtriem*, Internationales UN-Kaufrecht, Rn. 201; *Jungmeyer*, S. 80; *Stoll*, Schadensersatzpflicht, S. 270 ff. („objektive Haftung"); *Karollus*, S. 206 („Garantiehaftung"); BGer, 17.12.2009, CISG-online 2022; zum engl. Recht vgl. *McKendrick*, in: *McKendrick* (Hrsg.), Sale of Goods, § 10–012; Arb. Ct. Russian CCI, 24.1.2000, CISG Pace; vgl. auch *Schwenzer*, Art. 79 Rn. 1; im deutschen Recht setzt die Haftung des Verkäufers Verschulden voraus, das allerdings vermutet wird. Durch Übernahme einer Garantie oder des Beschaffungsrisikos (z. B. Gattungs-

schulden oder von besonderen **vertraglichen Garantiezusagen** („Zusicherungen") **unabhängig**.[55] Die Haftung beruht also nicht auf einer vom Verkäufer übernommenen, neben dem vertraglichen Leistungsversprechen stehenden zusätzlichen Garantieerklärung des Verkäufers, sondern allein auf der Nichterfüllung der im Vertrag übernommenen Pflicht. Der Verkäufer ist daher sowohl für den Schaden, der durch die Nichteinhaltung der Lieferpflicht, als auch für den Schaden, der durch die vertragswidrige Beschaffenheit der Ware entsteht, dem Käufer ohne weiteres ersatzpflichtig. Die Vertragsverletzung muss **nicht wesentlich** sein.[56] Die Schadenersatzpflicht besteht nur dem Käufer gegenüber; ein Anspruch Dritter, etwa der Abnehmer des Käufers, an die dieser die Ware weiterverkauft hat, wird durch das Einheitskaufrecht nicht begründet.[57]

Voraussetzung des Schadenersatzanspruchs für einen Sachmangel ist unter Vorbehalt von Art. 40, dass die Nichterfüllung der Verkäuferpflicht durch den Käufer rechtzeitig gerügt wurde (Art. 39).[58] 23a

Die Schadenersatzpflicht entfällt in den Fällen eines unvorhersehbaren und nicht zu überwindenden, objektiven Leistungshindernisses i. S. d. Art. 79 und gemäss Art. 80 ferner dann, wenn die Nichterfüllung durch ein Verhalten des Käufers verusacht wurde.[59] Einzelheiten der Schadensberechnung sind in den Artt. 74–77 geregelt; die Pflicht zur Verzinsung ergibt sich aus Art. 78.[60] 24

2. Verbindung des Schadenersatzanspruchs mit anderen Rechtsbehelfen (Abs. 2)

Gemäss Art. 45 II hat der Käufer das Recht, den Schadenersatzanspruch mit den ihm nach Artt. 45 I lit. a), 46–52 zustehenden Rechtsbehelfen zu kombinieren. Dies hat für den Käufer den praktischen Vorteil, dass er Schadenersatz verlangen kann, selbst wenn ihm die Ausübung anderer Rechtsbehelfe verwehrt ist. Der Umfang des Schadenersatzanspruchs ist, je nachdem mit welchem Rechtsbehelf er verbunden wird, verschieden. Generell gilt, dass die Kumulation nicht zu einer Überentschädigung des Käufers führen darf. Der Schadenersatzanspruch umfasst daher nur den Nachteil, der durch den gewählten anderen Rechtsbehelf nicht kompensiert wird.[61] 25

a) **Verbindung mit dem Erfüllungsanspruch.** Neben der **Erfüllung** bzw. der Ersatzlieferung und Nachbesserung gemäss Art. 46 kann der Käufer nur noch Ersatz der Verspätungs-, Begleit- und Folgeschäden verlangen,[62] da sein unmittelbares Erfüllungsinteresse bereits durch den Erfüllungsanspruch befriedigt wird. Ist z. B. die gelieferte Sache fehlerhaft, ist auch der hierdurch begründete Minderwert der Sache ersatzfähig. Dies gilt nur, soweit der Mangel nicht durch Ersatzlieferung oder Nachbesserung beseitigt wird. Soweit dem Käufer durch die erste fehlerhafte Lieferung und die anschliessende Ersatzlieferung oder Nachbesserung Mehrkosten entstanden sind, die bei sofortiger fehlerfreier Lieferung nicht entstanden wären, sind diese Mehrkosten gemäss Art. 45 I lit. b) vom Verkäufer zu ersetzen.[63] 26

---

schuld) können die Parteien eine verschuldensunabhängige Haftung vereinbaren, vgl. dazu *Lorenz/Riehm*, Rn. 173 ff., 525, 530, 545.
[55] Grundlegend BGH, 24.3.1999, CISG-online 396 = RIW 1999, 617 ff. (zur Haftung des Händlers für die von seinem Vorlieferanten fehlerhaft hergestellte Ware). Vgl. auch OGH, 6.2.1996, CISG-online 224 = ZfRVgl 1996, 248 ff.; *Zeller*, Damages, S. 63 f.
[56] *Schwenzer*, Art. 74 Rn. 11 f.; LG München I, 18.5.2009, CISG-online 1998 = IHR 2010, 150, 151: Ein Vertragsbruch konnte nicht nachgewiesen werden; missverständlich OLG Köln, 8.1.1997, CISG-online 217.
[57] Vgl. *Schwenzer*, Art. 74 Rn. 15.
[58] *Honsell/Schnyder/Straub*, Art. 45, Rn. 73.
[59] *Schwenzer*, Art. 80 Rn. 3 ff.
[60] Vgl. dazu *Bacher*, Art. 78 Rn. 5 f., 10, 14 ff.
[61] Vgl. auch *Herber/Czerwenka*, Art. 45, Rn. 6; *Piltz*, Internationales Kaufrecht, Rn. 5–366; *Karollus*, S. 93.
[62] Vgl. BGH, 24.3.1999, CISG-online 396 = RIW 1999, 617 ff.; OGH, 6.2.1996, CISG-online 224 = ZfRVgl 1996, 248 ff.
[63] Zutreffend LG Oldenburg, 9.11.1994, CISG-online 114 = NJW-RR 1995, 438 = RIW 1996, 65 f.

27 **b) Verbindung mit der Vertragsaufhebung.** Erklärt der Käufer die **Vertragsaufhebung,** kann er vollen Schadenersatz wegen Nichterfüllung hinsichtlich aller eingetretenen Vermögenseinbussen (z. B. Kosten der Demontage einer vertragswidrigen Sache oder des Deckungsverkaufs, Ersatz für Verzögerungs-, Begleit- und Folgeschäden) verlangen.[64] Die Rückerstattung des allenfalls bezahlten Kaufpreises erfolgt gemäss Art. 81 II. Allerdings kann der Käufer nicht alleine über Art. 45 I lit. b) die **Rückzahlung bzw. Verweigerung der Bezahlung des Kaufpreises** erreichen, wenn die Voraussetzungen der Vertragsaufhebung gemäss Art. 49 nicht erfüllt sind.[65] Denn sonst könnte er im wirtschaftlichen Ergebnis die Wirkungen der Vertragsaufhebung unter Ausserachtlassung der Beschränkung des Art. 49, insbesondere der rechtzeitigen Erklärung der Vertragsaufhebung (Art. 49 II), erzielen.[66] Liegen diese Voraussetzungen nicht vor, ist der Käufer verpflichtet, dem Verkäufer den Kaufpreis zu belassen bzw. (unter Umständen gegen Aufrechnung mit seinem Schadenersatzanspruch)[67] zu bezahlen.

28 **c) Verbindung mit der Minderung.** Die Verbindung des Schadenersatzanspruchs mit der Minderung ist ebenfalls zulässig.[68] Allerdings verringert der Betrag, der dem Verkäufer als Minderung in Rechnung gestellt wird, den zu ersetzenden Gesamtschaden.[69] Für den Käufer, der die Kaufsache behalten und wegen ihres Fehlers Schadenersatz verlangen will, liegt es deshalb näher, von vornherein seinen gesamten Schaden gemäss Art. 74 zu berechnen und von einer gesonderten Berechnung der Minderung abzusehen.

V. Unzulässigkeit einer Gnadenfrist (Abs. 3)

29 Abs. 3 stellt klar, dass die richterliche Gewährung einer Gnadenfrist für die Vertragserfüllung, während derer die Rechtsbehelfe des Käufers, vor allem das Recht zur Vertragsaufhebung, einstweilen ruhen, im Anwendungsbereich des Einheitskaufrechts **nicht in Betracht** kommt. Anlass für die Klarstellung ist vor allem die dahingehende Regelung des französischen Rechts (Art. 1184 III Cc).[70] Solche Regeln passen nicht zu internationalen Kaufverträgen.[71] Auch in Frankreich scheint es so zu sein, dass bei Handelskäufen die Bestimmung des Art. 1184 III Cc weitgehend durch eine vertragliche „clause expresse de résolution" ersetzt wird.[72] Es ist aber gerade ein Hauptzweck des einheitlichen Kaufrechts, die Vertragspartner davon zu entlasten, in internationalen Kaufverträgen auf solche Besonderheiten des jeweiligen nationalen Rechts der Gegenpartei Rücksicht nehmen zu müssen. Ausgeschlossen ist durch Abs. 3 auch die Anwendung des Art. 1244 II Cc.[73] Hiernach hat

---

[64] Zu Umfang und Grenzen des Schadenersatzes vgl. Artt. 74–77; LG München I, 6.4.2000, CISG-online 665.

[65] Vgl. auch *Honsell*, Art. 45, Rn. 83 mit Hinweis auf OLG Stuttgart, 31.3.2008, CISG-online 1658.

[66] So auch *Staudinger/Magnus*, Art. 44, Rn. 22; unrichtig insoweit LG Trier, 12.10.1995, CISG-online 160 = NJW-RR 1996, 564, 565. Allerdings waren hier die Voraussetzungen einer Vertragsaufhebung wegen wesentlicher Vertragsverletzung gem. Art. 49 I lit. a) zweifellos gegeben (der gelieferte Wein war zu 9% mit Wasser „gepanscht").

[67] Einschränkend *Schlechtriem*, Internationales UN-Kaufrecht, Rn. 42e; vgl. OLG Hamm, 9.6.1995, CISG-online 146 = NJW-RR 1996, 179, 180 = IPRax 1996, 269, 270; *Honsell/Siehr*, Art. 4, Rn. 24; *Ferrari*, Art. 4 Rn. 39; *Fountoulakis*, Art. 48 Rn. 21 f.

[68] Vgl. Trib. com. Namur, 15.1.2002, CISG-online 759; HGer Zürich, 10.2.1999, CISG-online 488.

[69] Vgl. auch *Piltz*, Internationales Kaufrecht, 5–369.

[70] Nach Art. 1184 Cc erfolgt die Vertragsaufhebung durch Gestaltungsurteil. Dabei kann der Richter dem Schuldner zunächst eine Frist nach Massgabe der Umstände („un délai selon les circonstances", sog. délai de grâce) einräumen; vgl. *Starck/Roland/Boyer*, S. 553 ff., Nr. 1596 ff., 1600; die frz. Praxis leitet aus Art. 1184 Cc auch das Recht des Richters ab, die Vertragsaufhebung überhaupt abzulehnen, vgl. *Treitel*, Remedies for Breach, Anm. 243., 247. f., 252. Richterliche Gnadenfristen kennen auch die Rechte von Louisiana und Québec sowie einige lateinamerikanische Rechtsordnungen (vgl. *Garro/Zuppi*, Compraventa internacional, S. 181).

[71] Vgl. Sekretariatskommentar, Artt. 41, Nr. 6, 43, Nr. 7.

[72] Vgl. dazu *Treitel*, Remedies for Breach, Anm. 244.; *Ghestin/Desché*, Traité des Contrats, Anm. 699.

[73] *Neumayer/Ming*, Art. 45, Anm. 3.

Rechtsbehelfe des Käufers; keine zusätzliche Frist 30–32 **Art. 45**

der Richter das Recht, für vertragliche Zahlungspflichten aller Art, also auch für Schadenersatzpflichten, einen Zahlungsaufschub zu gewähren. Dieses Recht kann vertraglich nicht abbedungen werden.[74] Ohne Abs. 3 bestünde gerade hier die Gefahr, dass ein Richter, dessen eigenes Recht eine Gnadenfrist für den Schuldner vorsieht, die entsprechende Regel nicht dem im Einheitskaufrecht geregelten Bereich des materiellen Kaufrechts zuordnet, sondern dem Verfahrens- und Vollstreckungsrecht, und deshalb nach der lex fori verfährt. Dem wird durch Abs. 3 vorgebeugt. Art. 45 III gilt, wie ausdrücklich klargestellt ist, auch für **Schiedsgerichte,** die das Einheitskaufrecht anzuwenden haben.

VI. Konkurrierende Rechtsbehelfe des nationalen Rechts

Die Frage, ob der Käufer bei Vertragsverletzung des Verkäufers neben den Ansprüchen 30 aus Art. 45 I oder an ihrer Stelle weitere Ansprüche geltend machen kann, die er aus dem nach internationalem Privatrecht subsidiär oder ergänzend anwendbaren nationalen Recht herleitet, hat praktische Bedeutung fast ausschliesslich im Fall der **Lieferung nicht vertragsmässiger Ware.** Hier sind die Rechtsbehelfe des Einheitskaufrechts an die Rügefristen des Art. 39 gebunden. Ausserdem beschränkt Art. 74 S. 2 den Schadenersatz auf den „voraussehbaren" Schaden, während dem jeweils in Betracht kommenden nationalen Recht eine solche Beschränkung vielfach unbekannt ist, oder sie hat eine andere Bedeutung.[75] Das nationale Recht mag selbst in einem Fall, in dem die gelieferte Sache nach Artt. 35, 36 vertragsgemäss ist, dem enttäuschten Käufer irgendwelche Rechtsbehelfe (z. B. Irrtumsanfechtung, culpa in contrahendo) gewähren. Der Käufer, der die Rüge- oder Verjährungsfrist versäumt hat oder mehr ersetzt haben will als den „voraussehbaren" Schaden, oder der es versäumt hat, bei den Vertragsverhandlungen auf einen speziellen Verwendungszweck der Sache hinzuweisen, hat deshalb ein Interesse daran, auf Rechtsbehelfe des nationalen Rechts zurückzugreifen, die weiter gehen als diejenigen des einheitlichen Kaufrechts.

Im Vordergrund steht neben der Berufung auf einen **Willensmangel** die Frage, ob der 31 Käufer, der durch die vertragswidrige Beschaffenheit der Ware geschädigt wird, auf **nationales Deliktsrecht** zurückgreifen kann.[76] Die Konkurrenzfrage stellt sich allerdings von vornherein nur bei Sach- oder reinen Vermögensschäden: Die Haftung des Verkäufers für Personenschäden liegt ausserhalb des Anwendungsbereichs des CISG (Art. 5) und ist somit nach dem durch die einschlägigen Kollisionsnormen berufenen nationalen Recht zu beurteilen.[77]

Generell gilt, dass von der **Exklusivität des Einheitsrechts** auszugehen ist.[78] Dieses hat 32 in den Artt. 35 ff. bzw. 74 eine Bewertung der Parteiinteressen mit Blick auf den Schutz des Verkäufers vor übermässiger Inanspruchnahme vorgenommen. Die ausgewogene Beurteilung soll nicht – je nach anwendbarem Recht auch noch in unterschiedlichem Umfang – durch nationales Recht ausgehebelt werden.[79] Ein konkurrierender Rechtsbehelf des Käufers, der auf nationales Recht gestützt wird, ist nur unter drei Voraussetzungen zuzulassen: Der Grund, auf den der Rechtsbehelf gestützt ist, darf nicht in den Regelungsbereich des Einheitskaufrechts fallen;[80] der Rechtsbehelf darf nicht zu Regelungszielen des Einheits-

---

[74] J. C. Civ. Artt. 1235–1248 Cc Fasc. 3 Nr. 32 *(Issa-Sayegh).*
[75] Vgl. *Honsell,* OR BT, S. 141 f.
[76] Vgl. ausführlich *U. Huber,* 3. Aufl., Rn. 59 ff.
[77] Vgl. *Ferrari,* Art. 5 Rn. 3 ff.; zum Verhältnis von CISG zur deliktischen Haftung im Speziellen s. *Herber,* FS Schlechtriem, S. 207 ff.
[78] So auch *Brunner,* Art. 45, Rn. 18; *Ensthaler/Achilles,* GK-HGB, nach § 382, Art. 45, Rn. 1; Münch-Komm/*P. Huber,* Art. 45, Rn. 18; MünchKommHGB/*Benicke,* Art. 45, Rn. 3.
[79] Vgl. *U. Huber,* 3. Aufl., Rn. 47; MünchKomm/*P. Huber,* Art. 45, Rn. 18 ff.
[80] Für Bestimmungen des nationalen Vertrags- oder Sachmängelrechts (wie z. B. Wandelung, Minderung, positive Vertragsverletzung, Vertrag mit Schutzwirkung für Dritte, culpa in contrahendo usw.) bleibt deshalb kein Raum; vgl. *U. Huber,* 3. Aufl., Rn. 50; *Ferrari,* Art. 4 Rn. 46.

kaufrechts im Widerspruch stehen;[81] und das nationale Recht selbst muss die konkurrierende Geltendmachung des Rechtsbehelfs zulassen.[82] Für weitere Einzelheiten und rechtsvergleichende Hinweise wird auf die Kommentierung zu Art. 35 (Konkurrenz der Rechtsbehelfe bei Vertragswidrigkeit der Ware) und Art. 4 (Konkurrenz nationaler deliktischer Ansprüche bei Sachschäden) verwiesen.[83]

VII. Verjährung

33   Die Verjährung ist im Übereinkommen nicht geregelt.[84] Sie unterliegt dem nach internationalem Privatrecht anzuwendenden nationalen Recht oder dem Verjährungsübereinkommen.[85]

VIII. Zuständigkeitsbegründender Erfüllungsort

34   Das CISG regelt in Art. 31 den Erfüllungsort der Lieferpflicht,[86] enthält aber nichts zur Frage, wo Schadenersatzansprüche zu erfüllen sind. Die Bestimmung des Erfüllungsortes ist von Bedeutung, weil viele Prozessordnungen einen Gerichtsstand am Erfüllungsort begründen.[87] Im praktisch bedeutsamen Anwendungsbereich der EuGVO[88] muss beachtet werden, dass Art. 5 I lit. b) den Erfüllungsort prozessrechtlich **autonom** bestimmt: Massgebend ist danach für alle Verpflichtungen aus einem Kaufvertrag, d. h. auch für die auf Geld gerichteten Leistungen, der Ort in einem Mitgliedstaat, an dem die Ware nach dem Vertrag geliefert worden ist oder hätte geliefert werden müssen. Damit wird am tatsächlichen bzw. vereinbarten **Lieferort** ein **Schwerpunktsgerichtsstand** für sämtliche Streitigkeiten aus dem Kaufvertrag begründet.[89]

35   Diese Lösung sollte m. E. auch für die Bestimmung des zuständigkeitsbegründenden Erfüllungsortes im Anwendungsbereich des CISG fruchtbar gemacht werden. Demgemäss können alle auf die Nichterfüllung des Vertrags gestützten Rechtsbehelfe des Käufers (neben dem allgemeinen Wohnsitzgerichtsstand des Verkäufers) am **Lieferort als Erfüllungsort** erhoben werden.[90] Solange die Ware noch nicht geliefert wurde, ist der Ort massgeblich, wo sie nach dem Vertrag hätte geliefert werden müssen. Fehlt es an einer solchen Regelung,

---

[81] Vgl. *U. Huber*, 3. Aufl., Rn. 51.
[82] Vgl. *U. Huber*, 3. Aufl., Rn. 52; z. B. kennt das französische Recht grundsätzlich keine Anspruchskonkurrenz (Prinzip des non-cumul), vgl. *Ghestin/Desché*, Traité des Contrats, Anm. 873.; *Niggemann*, RIW, 372, 377. Das schweizerische Bundesgericht lässt hingegen regelmässig die Irrtumsanfechtung neben den Rechtsbehelfen der Sachmängelgewährleistung zu, s. dazu *Schwenzer*, OR AT, Rn. 39.39 ff.; BGE 114 II 134 m. w. N. (Irrtumsanfechtung wird aber durch Art. 71 ausgeschlossen, soweit nicht arglistige Täuschung vorliegt, vgl. *Reinhart*, Zurückbehaltungsrecht, S. 378; *Herber/Czerwenka*, vor Art. 71, Rn. 2).
[83] Vgl. *Schwenzer*, Art. 35 Rn. 44 ff.; *Ferrari*, Art. 4 Rn. 24 f. und Art. 5 Rn. 11 ff.
[84] Vgl. demgegenüber *Williams*, 10 VJ (2006), 229, 244 ff., der dafür plädiert, die Verjährung über Art. 7 II in den Regelungsbereich des CISG einzubeziehen.
[85] Vgl. *Ferrari*, Art. 4 Rn. 35 f.; vgl. die Kommentierung von *Müller-Chen* (unten ab S. 1227); zur Verjährung der Ansprüche aus Vertragswidrigkeit der Ware vgl. *Schwenzer*, Art. 39 Rn. 28 f.; *Schroeter*, Art. 3 VertragsG Rn. 3 ff.
[86] Vgl. Kommentierung *Widmer Lüchinger*, zu Art. 31.
[87] Art. 29 deutsche ZPO; Art. 113 I schweiz. IPRG; Artt. 46, 1425 II NCPC; Art. 88 JN; Art. 5 Ziff. 1 LuganoÜ; Art. 5 I lit. b) EuGVO; Art. 20 CPC; Art. 395 (a) CCP California. Vgl. auch *Schack*, Zivilverfahrensrecht, Rn. 269 ff.
[88] Gleiches gilt für das am 1. Januar 2011 in Kraft getretene revidierte LuganoÜ.
[89] Vgl. dazu *Kropholler*, EUZPR, Art. 5, Rn. 29 ff.; *Magnus*, IHR 2002, 45, 47; *Schoibl*, östJBl 2003, 149, 156 f.
[90] So auch *Ensthaler/Achilles*, GK-HGB, nach § 382, Art. 45, Rn. 12; a. A. OLG Düsseldorf, 2.7.1993, CISG-online 74; *Hager/Maultzsch*, 5. Aufl. Art. 57 Rn. 25, die für Schadenersatz- bzw. Rückzahlungsansprüche in Analogie zum Anspruch auf Kaufpreiszahlung (Art. 57 I) einen Verkäufergerichtsstand begründen wollen.

ist auf Art. 31 zurückzugreifen. Dies wird in vielen Fällen zu einem Gerichtsstand am Sitz bzw. an der Niederlassung des Verkäufers führen, da beim praktisch wichtigen Versendungskauf der Absendeort Lieferort ist. Nach erfolgter Lieferung ist der tatsächliche Auslieferungsort massgeblich, wenn der Käufer die Ware dort (als vertragsgemäss) angenommen hat.[91] Wird an einen anderen Ort geliefert als vereinbart und akzeptiert der Käufer dies nicht, bleibt es bei der Zuständigkeit am ursprünglich vereinbarten Lieferort.[92] Muss die Leistung in mehreren Staaten erbracht werden oder treffen den Verkäufer mehrere an verschiedenen Orten zu erfüllende Pflichten, kann am jeweiligen Ort nur wegen des dort zu erbringenden Teils der Leistung geklagt werden.[93]

IX. Freizeichnung

Alle Rechtsbehelfe, die dem Käufer nach Art. 45 zustehen, sind **dispositives Recht** und können durch Parteivereinbarung abbedungen werden (Art. 6). Das ist unproblematisch, soweit es durch individuelle Vereinbarung geschieht. Die Frage der Zulässigkeit von Klauseln in **Allgemeinen Geschäftsbedingungen** ("Lieferbedingungen"),[94] durch der Verkäufer sich von den Haftungsfolgen des Art. 45 freizeichnet, betrifft die „Gültigkeit" des Vertrags und ist im Einheitskaufrecht nicht geregelt (Art. 4 S. 2 lit. a)).[95] Anwendbar ist das nach international-privatrechtlichen Grundsätzen zu bestimmende Vertragsstatut.[96] Massgeblich ist also dasjenige nationale Recht,[97] das nach den anwendbaren Kollisionsregeln auch dann anzuwenden wäre, wenn der Vertrag nicht dem einheitlichen Kaufrecht unterläge.[98] In den allermeisten Rechten ist das von den Parteien gewählte Recht anzuwenden.[99] Fehlt eine derartige Rechtswahl, ist in der Regel das Sachrecht des Verkäuferstaates anwendbar.[100] 36

Bei der Inhaltskontrolle der AGB nach nationalem Recht gilt es zu beachten, dass **Kontrollmassstab** z. B. gemäss § 307 BGB das **Einheitskaufrecht,** nicht das nationale 37

---

[91] *Magnus,* IHR 2002, 45, 47 f.
[92] *Kropholler,* EUZPR, Art. 5, Rn. 40 ff.
[93] So auch *U. Huber,* 3. Aufl., Rn. 66; zu den mit einer solchen „Mosaiklösung" verbundenen Problemen vgl. *Kropholler,* EUZPR, Art. 5, Rn. 50; vgl. auch EuGH, 19.2.2002, Rs. C-256/00, *Besix SA v. WABAG* (entscheidend ist die besonders enge Verbindung des Erfüllungsortes mit dem Gericht); dazu *Magnus,* IHR 2002, 45, 49.
[94] Die nachfolgenden Ausführungen sind mutatis mutandis auch auf haftungsverschärfende Klauseln in allgemeinen Einkaufsbedingungen anwendbar.
[95] Vgl. auch *Ferrari,* Art. 4 Rn. 20; *Schwenzer,* Art. 79 Rn. 51; *Schlechtriem,* JZ 1988, 1037, 1040; *Frense,* S. 47 ff. m. w. N.; rechtsvergleichend zur Inhaltskontrolle *Schultheiß,* S. 52 ff.
[96] Die Frage, ob die AGB Vertragsbestandteil geworden sind, richtet sich nach den Regeln des CISG: vgl. *Ferrari,* Art. 4 Rn. 21; *Schroeter,* Vor Artt. 14–24 Rn. 4; BGH, 31.10.2001, CISG-online 617.
[97] Ist deutsches Recht auf Grund Rechtswahl oder objektiver Anknüpfung Vertragsstatut, sind die §§ 305b–310 BGB einschlägig; im österreichischen Recht s. §§ 864a, 879 III ABGB; im schweiz. Recht ist der anwendbaren Regeln nicht kodifiziert, vgl. *Schwenzer,* OR AT, Rn. 44.04; im ital. Recht, s. Artt. 1341, 1342 und 1470 Cc; nach US-amerikanischem Recht sind die §§ 2–302, 2–316, 2–718, 2–719 (2) UCC einschlägig, vgl. dazu *Gillette/Walt,* S. 385 ff. (Voraussetzung ist, dass dem Gläubiger „at least minimum adequate remedies" verbleiben); *Scoles/Hay/Borchers/Symeonides,* § 2 mit Fn. 5, § 18.8–18.12; *Munz,* S. 27 ff. Im französischen Recht können beim contrat d'adhésion die Haftung für Vorsatz (dol) und grobe Fahrlässigkeit (faute lourde) weder ausgeschlossen noch beschränkt werden; vgl. *Müller/Otto,* S. 134 ff. ausführlich *Neumayer,* S. 255 ff., 281 ff.
[98] Vgl. *Ferrari,* Art. 4 Rn. 20; *Bianca/Bonell/Bonell,* Art. 7, Anm. 2.3.3.3.; *Frense,* S. 49 ff.; *Ryffel,* S. 113. Abzulehnen ist die Ansicht von *Stoll,* Internationalprivatrechtliche Fragen, S. 502 ff., der diese sog. „Restfragen" selbstständig anknüpfen will nach der „engsten Verbindung" der jeweils zu beurteilenden Einzelfrage und für die Massgeblichkeit des Rechts der zu schützenden Partei plädiert.
[99] Art. 27 EGBGB; Art. 116 schweiz. IPRG; § 187 Restatement 2d Conflict of Laws; § 1–105 (1) UCC, weitergehend § 1–301 (2) UCC Draft 2001; Art. 3 EuIPRÜ; Art. 12 III NCPC (das französische Recht lässt die freie Rechtswahl ebenfalls zu, jedoch mit der Einschränkung, dass das ausländische Recht nur zugunsten der lex fori abgewählt werden kann und dass der Richter grundsätzlich nicht an die Rechtswahl gebunden ist, vgl. dazu *Koerner,* S. 88 ff.).
[100] Art. 28 EGBGB; Art. 118 schweiz. IPRG i. V. m. Art. 3 HJPRÜ; § 188 Restatement 2d Conflict of Laws; Art. 4 EuIPRÜ.

Recht ist.[101] Inwieweit danach die einzelnen Rechtsbehelfe des Einheitskaufrechts abdingbar sind, ist im Zusammenhang der jeweiligen Einzelbestimmung zu erörtern.[102] Generell gilt, dass es unzulässig ist, die Ansprüche des Käufers wegen der Nichterfüllung einer Verkäuferpflicht insgesamt auszuschliessen. Dem Käufer muss m. a. W. ein minimaler adäquater Schutz gegen Vertragsverletzungen des Verkäufers verbleiben.[103]

---

[101] *Von Westphalen*, AGB und Einheitliches Kaufgesetz, S. 67; *Hausmann*, WM 1980, 726, 735; *Frense*, S. 47 m. w. N.; vgl. auch *Ferrari*, Art. 4 Rn. 20; *Schwenzer*, Art. 35 Rn. 42.

[102] Dazu eingehend *Frense*, S. 102 ff.; vgl. Art. 46 Rn. 48; Art. 48 Rn. 31; Art. 49 Rn. 49 f.; Art. 50 Rn. 19.

[103] S. rechtsvergleichend *Schwenzer/Hachem/Kee*, Rn. 41.62 mit Verweis auf Official Comment 1 zu § 2–719 UCC.

Art. 46 [Recht des Käufers auf Erfüllung oder Nacherfüllung]

(1) Der Käufer kann vom Verkäufer Erfüllung seiner Pflichten verlangen, es sei denn, daß der Käufer einen Rechtsbehelf* ausgeübt hat, der mit diesem Verlangen unvereinbar ist.

(2) Ist die Ware nicht vertragsgemäß, so kann der Käufer Ersatzlieferung nur verlangen, wenn die Vertragswidrigkeit eine wesentliche Vertragsverletzung darstellt und die Ersatzlieferung entweder zusammen mit einer Anzeige nach Artikel 39 oder innerhalb einer angemessenen Frist danach verlangt wird.

(3) Ist die Ware nicht vertragsgemäß, so kann der Käufer den Verkäufer auffordern, die Vertragswidrigkeit durch Nachbesserung** zu beheben, es sei denn, daß dies unter Berücksichtigung aller Umstände unzumutbar ist. Nachbesserung muß entweder zusammen mit einer Anzeige nach Artikel 39 oder innerhalb einer angemessenen Frist danach verlangt werden.

Art. 46

(1) The buyer may require performance by the seller of his obligations unless the buyer has resorted to a remedy which is inconsistent with this requirement.

(2) If the goods do not conform with the contract, the buyer may require delivery of substitute goods only if the lack of conformity constitutes a fundamental breach of contract and a request for substitute goods is made either in conjunction with notice given under article 39 or within a reasonable time thereafter.

(3) If the goods do not conform with the contract, the buyer may require the seller to remedy the lack of conformity by repair, unless this is unreasonable having regard to all the circumstances. A request for repair must be made either in conjunction with notice given under article 39 or within a reasonable time thereafter.

Art. 46

1) L'acheteur peut exiger du vendeur l'exécution de ses obligations, à moins qu'il ne se soit prévalu d'un moyen incompatible avec cette exigence.

2) Si les marchandises ne sont pas conformes au contrat, l'acheteur ne peut exiger du vendeur la livraison de marchandises de remplacement que si le défaut de conformité constitue une contravention essentielle au contrat et si cette livraison est demandée au moment de la dénonciation du défaut de conformité faite conformément à l'article 39 ou dans un délai raisonnable à compter de cette dénonciation.

3) Si les marchandises ne sont pas conformes au contrat, l'acheteur peut exiger du vendeur qu'il répare le défaut de conformité, à moins que cela ne soit déraisonnable compte tenu de toutes les circonstances. La réparation doit être demandée au moment de la dénonciation du défaut de conformité faite conformément à l'article 39 ou dans un délai raisonnable à compter de cette dénonciation.

Übersicht

	Rn.
I. Gegenstand und Grundgedanke der Regelung	1
1. Vorrang des Erfüllungsanspruchs	1
2. Ersatzlieferung und Nachbesserung	3
II. Allgemeiner Erfüllungsanspruch (Abs. 1)	6
1. Voraussetzungen und Inhalt	6
2. Grenzen	7
a) Ausübung eines mit dem Erfüllungsanspruch unvereinbaren Rechtsbehelfs	7
b) Einschränkung der Durchsetzbarkeit durch Art. 28	8
c) Leistungshindernisse	9
aa) Befreiung nach Artt. 79, 80	9
bb) Unmöglichkeit, Unzumutbarkeit	12

---

* Schweiz: ein Recht.
** Österreich: Verbesserung.

d) Schadensminderungspflicht	14
e) Deckungskauf	15
3. Beweislast	16
III. Anspruch auf Ersatzlieferung (Abs. 2)	17
1. Anwendungsbereich	17
2. Begriff der Ersatzlieferung	19
3. Vertragswidrige Beschaffenheit der verkauften Sache	20
4. Wesentliche Vertragsverletzung	23
a) Objektives Gewicht des Mangels	24
b) Keine Beseitigung des Mangels	26
aa) Durch Nachbesserung	26
bb) Bei nicht nachbesserungsfähigen Mängeln	28
cc) Ausnahmen	30
c) Beweislast	31
d) Zusammenfassung	32
5. Abwicklung der Ersatzlieferung	33
a) Frist für die Geltendmachung des Ersatzlieferungsanspruchs und Ort	33
b) Rückgabe der vertragswidrigen Sache	34
c) Wahl des Verkäufers zwischen Ersatzlieferung und Nachbesserung	35
6. Rechtsfolgen	36
IV. Anspruch auf Nachbesserung (Abs. 3)	39
1. Voraussetzungen	39
a) Allgemeines	39
b) Zumutbarkeit	40
c) Frist	43
2. Inhalt	44
a) Allgemeines	44
b) Ort, Zeit, Kosten	45
3. Rechtsfolgen der Nichterfüllung des Nachbesserungsanspruchs	46
V. Abweichende Vereinbarungen	48

Vorläufer und **Entwürfe:** EKG Artt. 24 I lit. a), 25, 26 I, 27 I, 30 I, 31 I, 41 I lit. a), 42 I, 51, 52 I, 55 II; Genfer E 1976 Art. 27; Wiener E 1977 Art. 28; New Yorker E 1978 Art. 42.

I. Gegenstand und Grundgedanke der Regelung

1. Vorrang des Erfüllungsanspruchs

1   Art. 46 gewährt dem Käufer den Rechtsbehelf der Erfüllung (Abs. 1), der Ersatzlieferung (Abs. 2) und der Nachbesserung (Abs. 3), falls der Verkäufer eine seiner Pflichten nicht erfüllt. In dieser Bestimmung kommt im Zusammenspiel mit Artt. 48, 49 das Prinzip des **Vorrangs des Erfüllungsanspruchs** zum Ausdruck.[1] Der Käufer kann Vertragsaufhebung kombiniert mit Schadenersatz verlangen, wenn die Vertragsverletzung wesentlich ist oder wenn er dem Verkäufer Nachfrist gesetzt (Art. 49) bzw. wenn der Verkäufer den Mangel nicht durch Nacherfüllung (Art. 48) behoben hat. Der Vorrang des Erfüllungsanspruchs bedeutet allerdings nicht, dass der Käufer zuerst (Nach-) Erfüllung wählen muss. Er kann sich auch für einen anderen Rechtsbehelf (z. B. Schadenersatz) entscheiden, soweit dessen Voraussetzungen gegeben sind.[2]

---

[1] So auch *Schulz*, S. 230 f.; *Staudinger/Magnus*, Art. 46, Rn. 4; *Achilles*, Art. 46, Rn. 1; *Vahle*, ZVerglRW 1999, 54, 55 f.; *Lookofsky*, Understanding the CISG in the USA, S. 99 f.; *Verweyen*, S. 65; *Sivesand*, Buyer's Remedies, S. 121 ff.; abweichend soweit ersichtlich nur *Soergel/Lüderitz/Schüßler-Langeheine*, Art. 46, Rn. 1; unzutreffend Schiedsgericht der Handelskammer Zürich, 31.5.1996, CISG-online 1291 (CISG gewährt keinen Erfüllungsanspruch). Der Vorrang des Erfüllungsanspruchs gilt auch in den Ländern des mittleren Ostens und den arabischen Ländern; vgl. *Hafez*, S. 204; noch deutlicher betont den Vorrang das CESL, welches dem Verkäufer das Recht gibt, jeden Mangel an den gelieferten Gütern nachzubessern, solange er seine Absicht dem Käufer ohne Verzögerung anzeigt, vgl. *Kruisinga*, ERPL 2011, 918.

[2] *Schwenzer/Hachem/Kee*, Rn. 43.59.

Die Regelung des Erfüllungsanspruchs stellt eine Mischung verschiedener Rechtstraditionen dar.[3] Aus den kontinentaleuropäischen Rechten stammt das Prinzip des Vorrangs des Erfüllungsanspruchs, aus dem Common Law die Konstruktion des Erfüllungsanspruch als Rechtsbehelf.[4]

2. Ersatzlieferung und Nachbesserung

Die Absätze 2 und 3 enthalten inhaltliche Klarstellungen und Einschränkungen des Erfüllungsanspruchs für den Fall der Lieferung nicht vertragsmässiger Ware.[5]

Der Anspruch des Käufers auf **Ersatzlieferung,** und damit die Rückgabe der vertragswidrigen Ware ist für den Verkäufer im internationalen Handel belastend.[6] Er muss entweder auf eigene Kosten für den Rücktransport der vertragswidrigen Ware sorgen oder die Ware am ausländischen, unter Umständen schwer zugänglichen und ihm fremden Bestimmungsort verwerten.[7] Dabei besteht die Gefahr, dass die Ware durch Zeitablauf oder Lagerschäden einen zusätzlichen Wertverlust erleidet. Bei minder schwerwiegenden Mängeln kann es dem Käufer aber zugemutet werden, entweder die Ware selbst zu verwerten und die damit verbundenen Kosten und Nachteile dem Verkäufer als Schadenersatz in Rechnung zu stellen oder die Ware trotz des Mangels zu behalten und Ausgleich des Minderwerts zu verlangen. Deshalb ist das Recht des Käufers zur Rückgabe vertragswidriger Ware auf schwerwiegende Fälle, die eine wesentliche Vertragsverletzung darstellen, beschränkt.

Im Gegensatz zur Ersatzlieferung setzt der Anspruch auf **Nachbesserung** nicht voraus, dass die Vertragswidrigkeit der Ware eine wesentliche Vertragsverletzung darstellt, sondern nur, dass die Erfüllung dem Verkäufer zuzumuten ist. Auch der Nachbesserungsanspruch muss, wie der Anspruch auf Ersatzlieferung, in angemessener Frist ab Mängelrüge geltend gemacht werden. Damit wird verhindert, dass der Käufer den Verkäufer beliebig lange über die Wahl des Rechtsbehelfs im Ungewissen lässt.

II. Allgemeiner Erfüllungsanspruch (Abs. 1)

1. Voraussetzungen und Inhalt

Der allgemeine Erfüllungsanspruch gemäss Art. 46 I setzt voraus, dass der Verkäufer irgendeine seiner **Pflichten nicht erfüllt** (Art. 46 I i. V. m. Art. 45 I 1 lit. a)).[8] Darunter fallen vor allem die Nichterfüllung der Lieferpflicht innerhalb der vorgeschriebenen Zeit (Artt. 30, 31, 33), der Pflicht zur Verschaffung der durch Vertrag oder Handelsbrauch vorgeschriebenen Dokumente[9] (Art. 30, 34) und der Pflicht zur Verschaffung des unbelasteten Eigentums (Artt. 41 f.)[10] oder sonstiger vertraglich übernommener Pflichten (z. B. Montage). Der Inhalt des Erfüllungsanspruchs richtet sich nach der verletzten Pflicht.

---

[3] Vgl. Art. 28 Rn. 1 ff.

[4] Der Erfüllungsanspruch des Gläubigers ist nicht wie z. B. im deutschen Rechtskreis identisch mit der Leistungspflicht des Schuldners, vgl. Art. 28 Rn. 6, 10; *Atamer,* FS Hopt, 3.9 ff.; rechtsvergleichender Überblick bei *S. J. Yang,* S. 304; *Schwenzer/Hachem/Kee,* Rn. 43.10 (Civil Law Rechtsordnungen) bzw. Rn. 43.24 ff. (Common Law).

[5] Vgl. rechtsvergleichend *Sivesand,* Buyer's Remedies, S. 29 ff.; *Schwenzer/Hachem/Kee,* Rn. 43.17 ff. und 43.38 ff.; zum Anspruch auf Nacherfüllung in asiatischen Rechtsordnungen s. *S. J. Yang,* S. 305 f.; zur Rechtslage in den ibero-amerik. Rechtsordnungen s. *E. Muñoz,* S. 403 ff.

[6] Sekretariatskommentar, Art. 42, Nr. 12.

[7] Dieser Ort verfügt möglicherweise auch nicht über die Infrastruktur der grossen Handelsplätze oder es besteht beispielsweise wegen nationaler Handelsverbote kein Markt, vgl. *Michida,* 27 Am. J. Comp. L. (1979), 279, 280 f.

[8] Vgl. dazu im Einzelnen Art. 45 Rn. 2 ff.; *Gillette/Walt,* S. 375.

[9] Das Fehlen von notwendigen Dokumenten wird in den arabischen Ländern bzw. mittleren Osten als „Nichtleistung" der gesamten Ware betrachtet, vgl. *Hafez,* S. 354.

[10] Vgl. *Schwenzer,* Art. 41 Rn. 21. Beim Gattungskauf können Rechtsmängel u. U. auch durch Ersatzlieferung behoben werden, vgl. dazu unten Rn. 22.

Die Erfüllungsansprüche im Falle der Lieferung vertragswidriger Ware (mit Ausnahme von Rechtsmängeln) richten sich nach den Absätzen 2 und 3.[11]

2. Grenzen

7 **a) Ausübung eines mit dem Erfüllungsanspruch unvereinbaren Rechtsbehelfs.** Der Erfüllungsanspruch gemäss Art. 46 I–III ist ausgeschlossen, wenn der Käufer einen Rechtsbehelf ausgeübt hat, der hiermit unvereinbar ist. Dies trifft zu für die wirksame Geltendmachung der Vertragsaufhebung,[12] der Minderung und des Schadenersatzes wegen Nichterfüllung, da diese Rechtsbehelfe den Anspruch auf eine Leistungserbringung in natura ausschliessen.[13] Der Käufer ist an seine Erklärung unter Beachtung der Grundsätze von Artt. 26, 27 gebunden.[14] Hat der Käufer einen der Rechtsbehelfe zu Unrecht erklärt, ist er hieran gebunden, wenn der Verkäufer sich ausdrücklich oder konkludent einverstanden erklärt.[15] Widersetzt sich der Verkäufer der ungerechtfertigten Vertragsaufhebung, besteht der Vertrag fort;[16] ungerechtfertigt erklärte Minderungs- oder Schadenersatzbegehren sind wirkungslos.[17]

8 **b) Einschränkung der Durchsetzbarkeit durch Art. 28.** Der Erfüllungsanspruch nach Art. 46 ist nicht durchsetzbar, wenn das berufene Gericht nach seinem eigenen Recht eine Entscheidung auf Erfüllung in Natur bei gleichartigen Kaufverträgen nicht fällen würde (Art. 28).[18]

9 **c) Leistungshindernisse. aa) Befreiung nach Artt. 79, 80.** Beruht die Nichterfüllung auf einem Hinderungsgrund, für den der Verkäufer gemäss Art. 79 I–III nicht einzustehen hat, so ist der Erfüllungsanspruch in gewissen Fällen ausgeschlossen.[19] Der Ausschluss ergibt sich aus dem Sinn der Vorschrift: Es wäre in sich widersprüchlich, dem Käufer einen Erfüllungsanspruch zu gewähren in einem Fall, in dem die Erfüllung auf ein Hindernis stösst, zu dessen Überwindung der Verkäufer gemäss Art. 79 I–III nicht verpflichtet ist.[20]

10 Dies gilt für dauernde Leistungshindernisse, für vorübergehende für die Dauer des Bestehens des Hinderungsgrundes (Art. 79 III).[21] Befreiungsgründe im Sinne von Art. 79 I, die zum Ausschluss des Erfüllungsanspruchs führen, sind etwa die Unmöglichkeit und eine unzumutbare Leistungserschwerung.[22]

11 Da die Erfüllungsansprüche gemäss Art. 46 unteilbar sind und somit sinnvollerweise nur ganzheitlich ausgeübt werden können, entfällt der Anspruch des Käufers auf Erfüllung (bzw.

---

[11] Vgl. unten Rn. 17 ff., 39 ff.
[12] Tribunale di Forlì, 16.2.2009, CISG-online 1780. Der Ausschluss des Erfüllungsanspruchs ergibt sich bereits aus Art. 81 I 1; vgl. zur Gestaltungswirkung der Vertragsaufhebung auch Art. 45 Rn. 16.
[13] *Honsell/Schnyder/Straub*, Art. 46, Rn. 23 ff.; *Staudinger/Magnus*, Art. 46, Rn. 19; *Karollus*, S. 135; *Bianca/Bonell/Will*, Art. 46, Anm. 2.1.1.1.; *Enderlein/Maskow/Strohbach*, Art. 46, Anm. 2.; *Brunner*, Art. 46, Rn. 5; MünchKommHGB/*Benicke*, Art. 46, Rn. 4; *Catalano*, 71 Tul. L. Rev. (1997), 1807, 1810.
[14] Vgl. im Einzelnen Art. 45 Rn. 16 ff.; *Staudinger/Magnus*, Art. 46, Rn. 19; abweichend zur Minderung und zum Schadenersatzanspruch *U. Huber*, 3. Aufl., Rn. 10 (wie hier aber *U. Huber*, 1. Aufl., Rn. 31 f.).
[15] Vgl. Art. 49 Rn. 45; *Staudinger/Magnus*, Art. 46, Rn. 21.
[16] Vgl. Art. 49 Rn. 47 f.; *Staudinger/Magnus*, Art. 46, Rn. 22.
[17] *Staudinger/Magnus*, Art. 46, Rn. 23.
[18] Vgl. dazu Art. 28 Rn. 5 ff.
[19] Vgl. sogleich Rn. 10 ff.; *Staudinger/Magnus*, Art. 79, Rn. 58, 59; *Tacheva*, S. 65 f.; *Flambouras*, 13 Pace Int'l L. Rev. (2001), 261, 275 f.; differenzierend *Trachsel*, S. 381: Erfüllungsanspruch erlischt nur bei objektiver Unmöglichkeit, bei subjektiver Unmöglichkeit nur soweit der Schuldner überobligationenmässige Anstrengungen auf sich nehmen müsste. Zur Gegenmeinung *Honsell/Schnyder/Straub*, Art. 46, Rn. 28; *Vahle*, ZVerglRW 1999, 54, 59 ff.; *Catalano*, 71 Tul. L. Rev. (1997), 1807, 1812.
[20] Vgl. oben Art. 28 Rn. 14; differenzierend *Schwenzer*, Art. 79 Rn. 52 f.; so auch Art. 8:101 II PECL.
[21] *Schwenzer*, Art. 79 Rn. 54; übersteigen vorübergehende Hindernisse eine auf Grund des konkreten Vertrags und dem Grundsatz von Treu und Glauben im internationalen Handel individuell festzulegende Zumutbarkeit, tritt ebenfalls eine dauernde Befreiung ein.
[22] So der Sache nach unter Berufung auf Art. 7.2.2 PICC *Gabriel*, Sale of Goods, S. 149 f.; *Brunner*, Art. 46, Rn. 7; vgl. rechtsvergleichend *Müller-Chen*, Vertragsverletzung, S. 118 ff.; restriktiver *Schwenzer*, Art. 79 Rn. 30.

Ersatzlieferung oder Nachbesserung), wenn dieser die überwiegende Verantwortung an der Vertragsverletzung (Nichtlieferung, Vertragswidrigkeit der Ware) trägt (Art. 80).[23]

bb) Unmöglichkeit, Unzumutbarkeit. Steht fest, dass die vertragsgemässe Leistung für jedermann **unmöglich** ist, entfällt der Erfüllungsanspruch ohne Rücksicht darauf, ob der Verkäufer sich hinsichtlich der Ursache, die die Unmöglichkeit herbeigeführt hat, gemäss Art. 79 entlasten kann oder nicht.[24] Dies gilt für dauernde Unmöglichkeit (im Falle des Speziekaufes wird die Kaufsache zerstört; beim Gattungskauf ist die ganze Gattung für den vertraglich vorausgesetzten Zweck untauglich) wie auch für vorübergehende Unmöglichkeit während der Dauer des Hindernisses (die Kaufsache wurde gestohlen).[25] Kann nur der Verkäufer nicht erfüllen (subjektive Unmöglichkeit), wird er nur in Ausnahmefällen entlastet, da er im Fall des marktbezogenen Gattungskaufes, der im internationalen Handel die Regel ist, das Beschaffungsrisiko trägt.[26]

Beruft der Verkäufer im Fall eines Leistungshindernisses, das er i. S. d. Art. 79 zu vertreten hat, sich darauf, die Überwindung des Hindernisses sei für ihn **unzumutbar**, hängt die Befreiung von der Erfüllungspflicht von den Umständen des Einzelfalls ab. Das materielle und immaterielle Interesse des Käufers an der Erfüllung in Natur ist unter Berücksichtigung des konkreten Vertrags (insbes. auch des Kaufpreises) und des Grundsatzes von Treu und Glauben im internationalen Handel gegen den nicht vorhersehbaren Erfüllungsaufwand des Verkäufers abzuwägen. Dabei sind auch die zur behaupteten Unzumutbarkeit führenden Gründe einzubeziehen. Wird so ein grobes Missverhältnis zwischen den Käuferinteressen und dem Aufwand des Verkäufers festgestellt, erlischt der Erfüllungsanspruch des Käufers.[27]

d) Schadensminderungspflicht. Es wird gelegentlich angenommen, dass die Schadensminderungspflicht (Art. 77) den Käufer dazu zwingen kann, bei Erfüllungsverweigerung des Verkäufers den Vertrag aufzuheben und einen Deckungskauf zu tätigen, wenn ein weiteres Festhalten am Erfüllungsanspruch den Schaden ansteigen lassen könnte.[28] Entsprechende Anträge, den Erfüllungsanspruch durch die Schadensminderungspflicht einzuschränken, wurden jedoch auf der Wiener Konferenz abgelehnt.[29] Es bleibt damit insofern beim –

---

[23] Vgl. im Einzelnen *Trachsel*, S. 409; *Schwenzer*, Art. 80 Rn. 8 f.
[24] So i. E. wohl auch *Atamer*, FS Schwenzer, 83, 86 mit der Begründung, dass die Geltendmachung einer unmöglichen Leistung die Ausübung eines Rechts ist, das gemäss Art. 46 I mit dem Erfüllungsanspruch unvereinbar ist.
[25] Vgl. auch Art. 28 Rn. 15; *Honsell/Schnyder/Straub*, Art. 46, Rn. 30; *Staudinger/Magnus*, Art. 46, Rn. 26; *E. Muñoz*, S. 400.
[26] Das sog. Unvermögen führt dann zum Ausschluss der Leistungspflicht, wenn die Ware am Markt nicht mehr erhältlich ist und bei Vertragsschluss damit nicht gerechnet werden musste. Handelt es sich hingegen um eine Speziessache (vgl. hinten Rn. 18) oder um eine persönliche Leistungspflicht (z. B. bei Werklieferungsverträgen), dürfte der Erfüllungsanspruch regelmässig dahinfallen, vgl. *Honsell/Schnyder/Straub*, Art. 46, Rn. 31; *Achilles*, Art. 46, Rn. 3; *Staudinger/Magnus*, Art. 46, Rn. 27; *Schulz*, S. 283; *Trachsel*, S. 377; i. E. gleich mit anderer Begründung (nicht durchsetzbar) *Schwenzer*, Art. 79 Rn. 54; die nationalen Regeln zum Leistungsstörungsrecht bieten kein einheitliches Bild: Im deutschen Rechtskreis werden objektive und subjektive Unmöglichkeit mehrheitlich gleichbehandelt (vgl. zum deutschen Recht § 311a I i. V. m. 275 BGB, s. dazu *Palandt/Heinrichs*, § 275, Rn. 23 ff. und *Lorenz/Riehm*, Rn. 176; zum schweiz. Recht vgl. Art. 119 OR, s. dazu *Schwenzer*, OR AT, Rn. 64.08 ff.; zum österreichischen Recht vgl. § 1447 ABGB, s. *Koziol/Welser/Kletečka*, Band II, S. 45 ff.). Im frz. Recht führt das Unvermögen in der Regel nicht zum Ausschluss des Erfüllungsanspruchs, es besteht jedoch das richterliche Auflösungsrecht in Art. 1184 III Cc.
[27] Vgl. rechtsvergleichend *Müller-Chen*, Vertragsverletzungen, S. 375 ff.; zum deutschen Recht § 275 II, III BGB (dazu *Palandt/Heinrichs*, § 275, Rn. 26 ff.); zum schweiz. Recht s. *Schwenzer*, OR AT, Rn. 63.06; zum österreichischen Recht s. *Koziol/Welser/Kletečka*, Band II, S. 48 ff. Im frz. Recht befreit die übermässige Leistungserschwerung den Schuldner grundsätzlich nicht von seiner Leistungspflicht; die handelsrechtliche Praxis behilft sich mit hardship- bzw. force majeure-Klauseln (vgl. *Müller-Chen*, Vertragsverletzung, S. 255 ff. m. w. N.; *Caytas*, S. 280, 299 f.); i. E. ähnlich, wenn auch mit anderer Begründung (Rechtsmissbrauch) *U. Huber*, 3. Aufl., Rn. 18; *Staudinger/Magnus*, Art. 46, Rn. 27 a. E.; i. E. wohl auch *Honsell/Schnyder/Straub*, Art. 46, Rn. 31; s. auch *Atamer*, FS Schwenzer, 83, 93 ff.: Bei Unzumutbarkeit besteht kein Erfüllungsanspruch, wobei in einer analogen Anwendung von Art. 46 III hergeleitet werden könne.
[28] *Honnold/Flechtner*, Art. 77, Rn. 419.3.
[29] Nachweise bei *Hager/Maultzsch*, 5. Aufl. Art. 62 Rn. 14.

allenfalls durch den guten Glauben (Art. 7 I) im internationalen Handel begrenzten – Recht des Käufers am Erfüllungsanspruch festzuhalten, solange er sich einen Vorteil davon verspricht.³⁰

15 **e) Deckungskauf.** Ein Anspruch auf Erfüllung entfiel im Haager Kaufrecht, wenn bei Verzug des Verkäufers ein Deckungskauf üblich und zumutbar war. Der Vertrag galt als von Gesetzes wegen aufgehoben („ipso facto avoidance").³¹ Das CISG kennt keine entsprechende Bestimmung; eine Pflicht zum Abschluss eines Deckungskaufs und damit eine Beschränkung des Erfüllungsanspruchs des Käufers existiert nicht.³²

3. Beweislast

16 Ausgehend vom Grundsatz, dass der Verkäufer zur vorgeschriebenen Zeit vertragsmässige Ware zu liefern hat, trägt er die Beweislast dafür, dass er geliefert hat und dass die Ware bei Gefahrübergang vertragsgemäss war.³³ Die Beweislast kehrt sich im Grundsatz um, wenn der Käufer die Ware rügelos als Erfüllung angenommen hat.³⁴ Die Beweislast für nicht zu vertretende Leistungshindernisse trifft gemäss Art. 79 den Verkäufer, und zwar sowohl was den Hinderungsgrund, als auch was seine Gründe betrifft. Die Beweislast für Unmöglichkeit und Unzumutbarkeit trifft ebenfalls den Verkäufer.³⁵

III. Anspruch auf Ersatzlieferung (Abs. 2)

1. Anwendungsbereich

17 Abs. 2 schränkt den Erfüllungsanspruch für den Fall der Lieferung vertragswidriger Ware ein. Will der Käufer Ersatzlieferung, müssen die Voraussetzungen des Abs. 1 (keine Ausübung eines mit dem Erfüllungsanspruch unvereinbaren Rechtsbehelfs, keine Leistungshindernisse, Durchsetzbarkeit nach Art. 28) und zusätzlich des Abs. 2 (wesentliche Vertragsverletzung, grundsätzlich Rüge nach Art. 39 und rechtzeitige Geltendmachung) erfüllt sein.

18 Der Ersatzlieferungsanspruch ist auf den **Gattungskauf** zugeschnitten. In diesem Fall ist der Verkäufer jedoch dann nicht zur Lieferung von Ware einer anderen Gattung verpflichtet, wenn die gesamte Gattung untergegangen ist. Dies gilt selbst dann, wenn die andere Gattung für den vertraglichen Zweck geeignet sein mag.³⁶ Entsprechendes gilt beim **Spezieskauf,** bei dem sich die Lieferpflicht auf die gelieferte Sache (der Gebrauchtwagen, eine bestimmte Ladung Schuhe) beschränkt. Der Käufer hat hingegen bei der Lieferung einer mangelhaften Speziessache dann einen Anspruch auf Ersatzlieferung, wenn es sich um eine Sache handelt, die einer vertretbaren Sache wirtschaftlich entspricht und das Leistungsinteresse des Käufers zufriedenstellt.³⁷ Ein Ersatzlieferungsanspruch besteht ferner dann,

---

[30] So auch *U. Huber*, 3. Aufl., Art. 28, Rn. 8; *Hager/Maultzsch*, 5. Aufl. Art. 62 Rn. 14; differenzierend *Schwenzer*, Art. 77 Rn. 10; *Schulz*, S. 265 f.; *Gillette/Walt*, S. 376; *Catalano*, 71 Tul.L.Rev. (1997), 1807, 1811 f.; z. T. a. A. *Lookofsky*, Understanding the CISG in the USA, S. 103 (Erfüllungsanspruch des Käufers wird durch Schadensminderungspflicht beschränkt).
[31] *U. Huber*, 3. Aufl., Art. 28, Rn. 7.
[32] *Bianca/Bonell/Will*, Art. 46, Anm. 1.1.2.; MünchKommHGB/*Benicke*, Art. 46, Rn. 8.
[33] Vgl. Art. 45 Rn. 8 f.; *Schwenzer*, Art. 35 Rn. 52; *Herber/Czerwenka*, Art. 36, Rn. 5; *Ensthaler/Achilles*, GK-HGB, nach § 382, Art. 46, Rn. 10; a. A. *Bianca/Bonell/Bianca*, Art. 36, Anm. 3.1.; *Honsell/Schnyder/ Straub*, Art. 46, Rn. 49; *T. M. Müller*, Beweislast, S. 137 f.
[34] Vgl. Art. 45 Rn. 9; *Schwenzer*, Art. 35 Rn. 52 m. w. N.; i. E. ähnlich *Staudinger/Magnus*, Art. 46, Rn. 68, Art. 35, Rn. 56; *Soergel/Lüderitz/Schüßler-Langeheine*, Art. 46, Rn. 16; zur Beweislast bei Rechtsmängeln s. *Schwenzer*, Art. 41 Rn. 25.
[35] So auch *Staudinger/Magnus*, Art. 46, Rn. 70; *Baumgärtel/Laumen/Hepting*, Art. 46, Rn. 20; *Honsell/Schnyder/Straub*, Art. 46, Rn. 50; *Achilles*, Art. 46, Rn. 10; *Soergel/Lüderitz/Schüßler-Langeheine*, Art. 46, Rn. 16.
[36] Vgl. vorne Rn. 12 (Fall der Unmöglichkeit); *Schulz*, S. 237 f.
[37] So im deutschen Recht, vgl. LG Ellwangen, 13.12.2002, NJW 2003, 517, 517; *Palandt/Weidenkaff*, § 439, Rn. 15; *von Hoffmann*, Gewährleistungsansprüche, S. 295; so wohl auch *Staudinger/Magnus*, Art. 46, Rn. 34; a. A. *Grunewald*, Kaufrecht, § 9 II, Rn. 113 (Ersatzlieferung bei einer Stückschuld nur mit einer Sache mit denselben Eigenschaften); *Reinhart*, Art. 46, Rn. 5; *Soergel/Lüderitz/Schüßler-Langeheine*, Art. 46, Rn. 6; *Neu-*

wenn der Verkäufer **eine andere Sache** (aliud) geliefert hat, als verkauft war:[38] Der Verkäufer hat die richtige Sache zu liefern.

2. Begriff der Ersatzlieferung

„Ersatzlieferung" („delivery of substitute goods", „livraison de marchandises de remplacement") setzt voraus, dass es bereits zu einer Lieferung vertragswidriger Ware gekommen ist, die zu einem Abtransport der Ware von der Niederlassung des Verkäufers oder von dem in Art. 31 lit. b) genannten Ort geführt hat. Um eine „Ersatzlieferung" handelt es sich nicht, wenn der Käufer die Ware bereits vor der Lieferung wegen ihrer vertragswidrigen Beschaffenheit zurückweist und vom Verkäufer die Lieferung anderer, fehlerfreier Ware verlangt oder wenn der Verkäufer die Ware gemäss Art. 31 lit. b) oder lit. c) zur Verfügung stellt und der Käufer die Übernahme der ihm angebotenen Ware wegen ihrer vertragswidrigen Beschaffenheit ablehnt.[39] Da in diesem Fall die Ware nicht versandt wurde, sind dem Verkäufer noch keine Transportkosten entstanden, womit kein Grund besteht, den Anspruch des Käufers auf Lieferung vertragsmässiger Ware den einschränkenden Voraussetzungen des Art. 46 II zu unterwerfen. Anspruchsgrundlage ist somit Art. 46 I.

3. Vertragswidrige Beschaffenheit der verkauften Sache

Abs. 2 setzt voraus, dass die gelieferte Ware gemäss der Definition von Art. 35 nicht vertragsgemäss ist („do not conform with the contract"), d. h. nach Art, Menge, Qualität oder Verpackung nicht dem Vertrag bzw. dem Übereinkommen entspricht.[40] Insbesondere werden die **„Schlechtlieferung"** und **„Falschlieferung"** gleichbehandelt, so dass selbst bei krassen Abweichungen der Anspruch auf Ersatzlieferung an die besonderen Voraussetzungen des Abs. 2, insbesondere die Wesentlichkeit der Vertragsverletzung, gebunden ist.[41] Voraussetzung des Ersatzlieferungsanspruchs ist unter Vorbehalt von Art. 40, dass die Vertragswidrigkeit der gelieferten Ware rechtzeitig, innerhalb der Fristen des Art. 39 **gerügt** worden ist.

Quantitäts- und Rechtsmängel fallen aus unterschiedlichen Gründen nicht unter Art. 46 II. Der Fall der **Zuweniglieferung** wird zwar an sich durch die Artt. 35 I, 46 II erfasst: Ware, die „in Menge" den Anforderungen des Vertrags nicht entspricht, ist nicht vertragsgemäss. Aber die Regel des Art. 46 II wird für diesen Fall durch die Sondervorschrift des Art. 51 verdrängt. Hiernach gelten „für den Teil, der fehlt", die Artikel 46–50. Hinsichtlich des fehlenden Teils liegt aber einfache Nichterfüllung i. S. d. Art. 46 I vor, nicht Vertragswidrigkeit i. S. d. Art. 46 II. Da dieser Teil gerade noch nicht geliefert wurde, tritt auch das Problem des Rücktransports, das die ratio legis des Art. 46 II bildet, nicht auf. Infolgedessen kann der Käufer Lieferung des fehlenden Teils nach Art. 46 I verlangen, ohne an die einschränkenden Voraussetzungen des Art. 46 II gebunden zu sein.[42] Zu beachten hat der Käufer nur die Rügefrist des Art. 39 (vorbehaltlich des Falls des Art. 40). Ob bei ganz geringfügigen Fehlmengen der Anspruch auf Nachlieferung rechtsmissbräuchlich sein kann und daher am Grundsatz von Treu und Glauben (Art. 7 I) scheitert, ist Frage des Einzelfalls. Der Fall der **Zuviellieferung** ist in Art. 52 II besonders geregelt.

---

mayer/Ming, Art. 46, Anm. 6.; *Karollus*, S. 137; *Welser*, S. 117; *Piltz*, Internationales Kaufrecht, Rn. 5–191; MünchKommHGB/*Benicke*, Art. 46, Rn. 13; MünchKomm/*P. Huber*, Art. 46, Rn. 38.
[38] *Karollus*, S. 137; *Staudinger/Magnus*, Art. 46, Rn. 14, 34; *Brunner*, Art. 46, Rn. 12; *Schulz*, S. 238; *Niemann*, S. 202 f.
[39] Vgl. dazu auch *Widmer Lüchinger*, Art. 31 Rn. 65 f.; *Hager/Maultzsch*, 5. Aufl. Art. 60 Rn. 3; a. A. *Honold/Flechtner*, Art. 46, Rn. 383.
[40] Vgl. im Einzelnen *Schwenzer*, Art. 35 Rn. 6 ff.; zu den Rechtsmängeln s. Rn. 22.
[41] Vgl. *Schwenzer*, Art. 35 Rn. 10 m. w. N. Ebenso *Bianca/Bonell/Will*, Art. 46, Anm. 2.1.1.1.; *Enderlein/Maskow/Strohbach*, Art. 46, Anm. 3.; *Honsell/Schnyder/Straub*, Art. 46, Rn. 18; *Staudinger/Magnus*, Art. 46, Rn. 14, 35, 39. Vgl. auch *Schlechtriem*, Seller's Obligations, S. 6–19; *U. Huber*, RabelsZ 43 (1979), 413, 483 f.
[42] *Piltz*, Internationales Kaufrecht, Rn. 5–180 f., 5–190; *Karollus*, S. 136; *Staudinger/Magnus*, Art. 46, Rn. 10; *Herber/Czerwenka*, Art. 46, Rn. 2; a. A. *Honsell/Schnyder/Straub*, Art. 46, Rn. 19.

Art. 46 22–24   Teil III. Kapitel II. Pflichten des Verkäufers. Abschnitt III

22   Die Fälle des **Rechtsmangels** (Artt. 41, 42) werden durch Art. 46 II **nicht erfasst**.[43] Der Begriff der „Vertragsmässigkeit der Ware" ist ein terminus technicus, der nur die Fälle des Art. 35 erfasst und die Fälle der „Rechte und Ansprüche Dritter" (Artt. 41, 42) ausschliesst (vgl. die Überschrift vor Art. 35). Dass Art. 46 II den Begriff „nicht vertragsgemäss" in diesem technischen Sinn versteht, wird auch dadurch bestätigt, dass die hier vorgesehene Fristbestimmung nur an die Rügefrist des Art. 39, nicht an die des Art. 43 anknüpft. Auf den Erfüllungsanspruch des Käufers bei Rechtsmängeln ist somit mit den bereits beschriebenen Konsequenzen[44] nur Art. 46 I anzuwenden. Dieser richtet sich auf Abwehr der Drittrechte oder, falls dies nicht zum Ziel führt, auf Lieferung rechtsmängelfreier Ware aus derselben Gattung.[45]

4. Wesentliche Vertragsverletzung

23   Der Anspruch auf Ersatzlieferung setzt gemäss Art. 46 II voraus, dass die Vertragswidrigkeit der gelieferten Ware eine wesentliche Vertragsverletzung i. S. d. Art. 25 darstellt. Liegt diese nicht vor, bleiben dem Käufer nur die Rechtsbehelfe des Nachbesserungsanspruchs (Art. 46 III), des Schadenersatzanspruchs (Art. 45 I lit. b)) und der Minderung (Art. 50). Wesentlich ist die Vertragswidrigkeit dann, wenn sie objektiv ein gewisses Gewicht erreicht und vom Verkäufer nachträglich nicht beseitigt wird.[46]

24   **a) Objektives Gewicht des Mangels.** Der Mangel muss, um eine „wesentliche Vertragsverletzung" darzustellen, objektiv ins Gewicht fallen. Die Abweichung muss so gravierend sein, dass es dem Käufer nicht zuzumuten ist, die Ware trotz des Mangels zu behalten und sich mit Schadenersatz wegen des Minderwerts oder Minderung zufriedenzugeben. Es muss ihm „im Wesentlichen das entgehen, was er nach dem Vertrag hätte erwarten dürfen" (Art. 25).[47] Es kommt also darauf an, „ob eine anderweitige Verarbeitung oder der Absatz der Ware im gewöhnlichen Geschäftsverkehr, wenn auch etwa mit einem Preisabschlag, ohne unverhältnismässigen Aufwand möglich und zumutbar ist".[48] Im konkreten Fall werden hierfür vor allem der **Verwendungszweck der Ware,** das Ausmass der Qualitätsabweichung,[49] im Kaufvertrag vereinbarte spezielle Eigenschaften der Kaufsache oder der ausdrückliche Hinweis des Käufers auf bestimmte Zwecke (Art. 35 II lit. b)) von Bedeutung sein.[50] Es lässt sich aber keine starre Regel aufstellen: Selbst bei krasser Falschlieferung beim Gattungskauf, bei fehlender Probe- oder Muster-

---

[43] Vgl. auch *Schwenzer,* Art. 41 Rn. 20, Art. 42 Rn. 25 f.; Sekretariatskommentar, Art. 39, Nr. 7, 8; *Karollus,* S. 136; *Piltz,* Internationales Kaufrecht, Rn. 5–182; *Schlechtriem,* Internationales UN-Kaufrecht, Rn. 184; *Staudinger/Magnus,* Art. 46, Rn. 15, 17; *Honsell/Schnyder/Straub,* Art. 46, Rn. 18a, 55; *Schulz,* S. 236; so wohl auch *Schlechtriem/P. Butler,* Rn. 184; a. A. *Bianca/Bonell/Will,* Art. 46, Anm. 3.1.; *Enderlein/Maskow/Strohbach,* Art. 46, Anm. 3.; *Herber/Czerwenka,* Art. 46, Rn. 6; *Audit,* Vente internationale, Anm. 128.; *Neumayer/Ming,* Art. 46, Anm. 8.; *von Hoffmann,* Gewährleistungsansprüche, S. 294; *Vahle,* ZVerglRW 1999, 54, 57 f.
[44] Vgl. vorne Rn. 17, 20 f.
[45] *Karollus,* S. 136; *U. Huber,* RabelsZ 43 (1979), 413, 503. Zur Rechtslage beim Spezieskauf, vgl. vorne Rn. 18; *Bianca/Bonell/Will,* Art. 46, Anm. 3.1.
[46] Vgl. *Schroeter,* Art. 25 Rn. 26; *Troiano,* IHR 2008, 221, 229.
[47] Vgl. OLG Frankfurt a. M., 18.1.1994, CISG-online 123 = NJW 1994, 1013, 1014 = RIW 1994, 240, 241 (zur Vertragsaufhebung); dazu *Kappus,* NJW 1994, 984, 984; sowie (krit.) *Koch,* RIW 1995, 98, 99 f.
[48] BGH, 3.4.1996, CISG-online 135 = BGHZ 132, 290, 298 (mit Anm. *Schlechtriem,* EWiR 1996, 597). Südafrikanisches Kobaltsulfat ist trotz falscher Herkunftsangabe (Großbritannien) weiterverkäuflich. Eine wesentliche Vertragsverletzung nur dann anzunehmen, wenn „der Mangel nicht behebbar und die Sache anderweitig praktisch überhaupt nicht verwendbar ist" (so *Schlechtriem,* Internationales UN-Kaufrecht, Rn. 186), geht dagegen zu weit; die ausgewogenere Formel des BGH verdient demgegenüber den Vorzug. Auch sie bedarf gegebenenfalls der Anpassung an besondere Umstände des Einzelfalls.
[49] Im deutschen Importhandel mit Früchten, Konserven, Gewürzen u. dgl. gilt kraft Allgemeiner Geschäftsbedingungen die Regel, dass der Käufer ausschliesslich Vergütung des Minderwerts (d. h. Erstattung der Differenz zwischen dem Wert vertragsmässiger Ware und dem tatsächlichen Wert der vertragswidrigen Ware am Tag der Mängelanzeige) verlangen kann, wenn der Minderwert 10% nicht übersteigt, vgl. *Sieveking,* S. 106, 115 f.
[50] *Schroeter,* Art. 25 Rn. 23 ff.

übereinstimmung⁵¹ oder beim Bruch einer Zusicherung liegt nicht stets und automatisch eine wesentliche Vertragsverletzung vor.⁵² Auch in diesen Fällen muss die Zumutbarkeit der Verwertung durch den Käufer geprüft werden.⁵³ Diese dürfte umso eher zu verneinen sein, je gravierender die Qualitätsabweichung ist. So wird insbesondere die aliud-Lieferung beim Spezieskauf regelmässig für den Käufer unbrauchbar sein und damit das notwendige Gewicht erreichen (das verkaufte Bild ist eine Fälschung, der Verkäufer liefert eine andere als die vom Käufer ausgesuchte Holzplatte).⁵⁴

Ist die Ware noch marktgängig und lässt sich für den Käufer ein angemessener Preis **25** abschätzen, kann es einem **Grosshändler** je nach Lage des Einzelfalls zugemutet werden, die Ware trotz Vertragswidrigkeit weiterzuverkaufen, oder, wenn es ihm ohne Schwierigkeiten möglich ist, den Mangel selbst zu beheben.⁵⁵ So wird z. B. der Grossist Pullover mit kleineren Webfehlern als zweite Qualität weiterverkaufen und dem Verkäufer die Differenz zur vertraglich vereinbarten Qualität in Rechnung stellen können. Einem **Einzelhändler** kann hingegen wohl nicht zugemutet werden, minderwertige Ware an seine Kunden weiterzuverkaufen, selbst dann nicht, wenn die Gebrauchstauglichkeit als solche nicht beeinträchtigt wird. So kann z. B. im Modegeschäft bereits eine unbedeutende Farbabweichung der bestellten Kollektion von gravierendem Gewicht sein.⁵⁶ Veräusserung ausserhalb des gewöhnlichen Geschäftsverkehrs ist dem Einzelhändler niemals zuzumuten.⁵⁷ Ist die Ware zur **Weiterverarbeitung** durch den Käufer oder zum **Gebrauch** oder **Verbrauch** im Rahmen seiner Berufs- und Geschäftstätigkeit bestimmt, ist es ihm grundsätzlich nicht zuzumuten, die Ware trotz ihrer vertragswidrigen Beschaffenheit selbst zu verwenden. Die Vertragswidrigkeit der Sache weist daher in diesen Fällen regelmässig das erforderliche Gewicht auf.⁵⁸

b) Keine Beseitigung des Mangels. aa) Durch Nachbesserung. Das objektive Ge- **26** wicht des Mangels ist immer notwendig,⁵⁹ nicht aber ausreichend, um eine wesentliche Vertragsverletzung zu begründen.⁶⁰ Vor allem bei Fahrzeugen, Maschinen, Anlagen und

---

⁵¹ OLG Frankfurt a. M., 18.1.1994, CISG-online 123 = NJW 1994, 1013, 1014 = RIW 1994, 240, 241 (zur Vertragsaufhebung).
⁵² *Schroeter*, Art. 25 Rn. 23; *Enderlein/Maskow/Strohbach*, Art. 25, Anm. 3.4.
⁵³ *U. Huber*, 3. Aufl., Rn. 39 mit Fn. 89; krit. dazu *A. Butler*, IHR 2003, 208, 211 f.
⁵⁴ *Karollus*, S. 137 mit Fn. 13; Ausnahmen sind denkbar, vgl. *U. Huber*, 3. Aufl., Rn. 40: Es wird eine bestimmte Partie Zucker ab Lager gekauft, ohne dass der Käufer diese besichtigt oder ausgesucht hat.
⁵⁵ Bsp.: Verkauf von Obstkonserven aus Korea nach Hamburg; falsche Angabe der Fruchteinwaage auf dem Etikett; Möglichkeit, den Mangel mit geringen Kosten (2 Pfennig pro Dose) durch Überetikettierung zu beheben. Der Fall wurde auf Grund Allgemeiner Geschäftsbedingungen entschieden vom Schiedsgericht des Warenvereins der Hamburger Börse, 27.11.1979, in: *Straatmann/Ulmer*, HSG Bd. 3 E 6b Nr. 78. Nach den Geschäftsbedingungen ist Wandelung nur bei schwerwiegenden Mängeln möglich (ähnlich wie nach Art. 49 I lit. a)), vgl. dazu *Sieveking*, S. 106 ff. Einen solchen schwerwiegenden Mangel hat das Schiedsgericht wegen der Reparaturmöglichkeit verneint. Vgl. auch das Bsp. von *Schlechtriem*, Pflichten des Verkäufers, S. 129: Die gelieferten Schalbretter sind wenige Zentimeter länger als im Kaufvertrag angegeben und können vom Käufer ohne Schwierigkeiten passend zurechtgesägt werden.
⁵⁶ Faltiges statt glattes Aussehen der gelieferten Schuhe sollte m. E. ausreichen; *Kappus*, NJW 1994, 984, 984. Der Weiterverkauf minderwertiger Ware kann auch dann unzumutbar sein, wenn eine starke Bindung zu einer qualitätsbewussten Kundschaft besteht, so dass langfristig mit Imageschäden zu rechnen ist.
⁵⁷ Vgl. auch *Kappus*, NJW 1994, 984, 984.
⁵⁸ Ausnahmen sind denkbar, wenn ein dem Käufer leicht zugänglicher Markt existiert, auf dem der Käufer die Ware ohne grössere Schwierigkeiten zu einem gut abschätzbaren Preis verwerten kann; vgl. als Bsp. den Sachverhalt der Entscheidung BGH, 29.1.1968, BGHZ 49, 356, 357. Offenbar war hier dem Käufer – den Fordwerken Köln – der Weiterverkauf der aus Italien importierten, unterwegs infolge eines Schiffslecks verrosteten Bleche ohne Schwierigkeit möglich. Ausnahmsweise kann daher entgegen BGH, 3.4.1996, CISG-online 135 = BGHZ 132, 290, 298 dem Käufer auch eine Verwertung „im aussergewöhnlichen Geschäftsverkehr" zugemutet werden.
⁵⁹ BGH, 3.4.1996, CISG-online 135 = BGHZ 132, 290, 299: Der Käufer kann aus Verweigerung, Verzögerung oder Fehlschlag der Nachbesserung keinen Anspruch auf Ersatzlieferung ableiten, wenn der Mangel objektiv nicht von hinreichendem Gewicht ist (vgl. auch *U. Huber*, 3. Aufl., Rn. 48); daran ändert sich auch durch Nachfristsetzung durch den Käufer nichts.
⁶⁰ *Schroeter*, Art. 25 Rn. 30.

technischen Geräten ist es häufig möglich, Defekte, welche die Brauchbarkeit gravierend beeinträchtigen, nachträglich durch Nachbesserung gemäss Art. 46 III zu beseitigen (z. B. durch Auswechslung von defekten Einzelteilen).[61] Wird der Mangel innerhalb angemessener Frist **nicht vollständig** beseitigt,[62] **weigert** der Verkäufer sich, die Nachbesserung vorzunehmen oder bleibt er einfach **untätig**, liegt eine wesentliche Vertragsverletzung vor.[63] Der Käufer kann nunmehr Auswechslung der Sache im Ganzen (Ersatzlieferung) verlangen.[64] Bietet der Verkäufer rechtzeitig Nachbesserung an und **weist der Käufer das Angebot** ohne zureichenden Grund **zurück**, so verhindert er die Vertragserfüllung durch sein eigenes Verhalten. Solange er an der Zurückweisung festhält, kann er daher gegen den Verkäufer keine Ansprüche wegen der unterlassenen Nachbesserung geltend machen (Art. 80).

27   Die angemessene **Dauer der Frist,** innerhalb welcher der Verkäufer zur Abwendung des Ersatzlieferungsanspruchs des Käufers nachzubessern hat, lässt sich am besten mit Blick auf Art. 48 I konkretisieren. Nach diesem Massstab kann der Verkäufer nachbessern, wenn dies für den Käufer keine „unzumutbare Verzögerung" nach sich zieht bzw. keine „unzumutbaren Unannehmlichkeiten" verursacht, was z. B. bei mehreren Nachbesserungsversuchen der Fall sein kann.[65] Der fruchtlose Ablauf einer nach Art. 47 gesetzten Nachfrist stellt ein starkes Indiz für das Vorliegen einer unzumutbaren Verzögerung und damit einer wesentlichen Vertragsverletzung dar.[66]

28   bb) **Bei nicht nachbesserungsfähigen Mängeln.** Ist der Mangel objektiv von erheblichem Gewicht und lässt er sich durch Nachbesserung (Reparatur, Auswechslung schadhafter Einzelteile) nicht beheben, wohl aber durch Ersatzlieferung, bereitet das Erfordernis der „wesentlichen Vertragsverletzung" eine gewisse Schwierigkeit. Es scheint paradox zu sein,[67] dass der Ersatzlieferungsanspruch des Käufers eine wesentliche Vertragsverletzung voraussetzt, die Wesentlichkeit aber erst gegeben ist, wenn der Mangel vom Verkäufer nicht gemäss Art. 48 durch Ersatzlieferung behoben wird.[68]

29   Der scheinbare Widerspruch löst sich aber auf, wenn bedacht wird, dass das Einheitskaufrecht den **Erfüllungsanspruch** als „**Rechtsbehelf**" („remedy") für den Fall der Ver-

---

[61] Vgl. dazu unten Rn. 44; vgl. auch das Bsp. von *U. Huber*, 3. Aufl., Rn. 42: Ist ein Element der elektronischen Wegfahrsperre eines Autos defekt, liegt zwar ein gravierender Mangel vor, wenn deswegen der Wagen nicht gestartet werden kann. Der Anspruch des Käufers auf ein neues Auto gemäss Art. 46 II ist aber unsinnig, da das Element in der Regel ohne Probleme ersetzt werden kann; so i. E. auch LG München I, 27.2.2002, CISG-online 654.

[62] Verbleibt als Folge der Nachbesserung ein lediglich minimaler (Schönheits-) Fehler, ist es eine nach Treu und Glauben (Art. 7 I) zu entscheidende Frage, ob das Beharren des Käufers auf Ersatzlieferung oder Vertragsaufhebung rechtsmissbräuchlich ist.

[63] Vgl. *Schroeter*, Art. 25 Rn. 27; *Rudolph*, Art. 46, Rn. 20; *Honnold/Flechtner*, Art. 25, Rn. 184; *Ziegel*, Remedial Provisions, S. 9–23; *Enderlein/Maskow/Strohbach*, Art. 25, Anm. 3.4.; *Herber/Czerwenka*, Art. 25, Rn. 7, Art. 46, Rn. 6; *Staudinger/Magnus*, Art. 46, Rn. 40; *Audit*, Vente internationale, Anm. 133.; *Heuzé*, Anm. 419.; *Piltz*, Internationales Kaufrecht, Rn. 5–194, 5–279 f.; *Aicher*, S. 136 ff.; *Karollus*, ZIP 1993, 490, 496; *Diedrich*, RIW 1995, 11, 13. Auch in den Beratungen der Wiener Konferenz von 1980 ist hierauf immer wieder hingewiesen worden, vgl. O. R., S. 341 ff., Nr. 39, 44, 48; Standardbeispiel war der Verkauf einer Maschine, die nicht arbeitet, wobei der der Defekt sich aber durch Auswechslung eines Einzelteils beheben lässt. Im gleichen Sinn, wenn auch etwas vage, äussert sich der Sekretariatskommentar, Art. 45, Nr. 6 („However, in some cases the fact that the seller is able and willing to remedy the non-conformity of the goods without inconvenience to the buyer may mean that there would be no fundamental breach unless the seller failed to remedy the non-conformity within an appropriate period of time"). I. E. übereinstimmend, trotz abweichendem Ausgangspunkts, *Bianca/Bonell/Will*, Art. 48, Anm. 3.2.2. a. E. – A. A. sind *Soergel/Lüderitz/Schüßler-Langeheine*, Art. 46, Rn. 5 (es sei „grundsätzlich unerheblich, ob die gelieferte Ware reparierbar ist"); *Holthausen*, RIW 1990, 101, 104, 106. Vgl. dazu auch Art. 48 Rn. 5, 15 ff.

[64] Oder wahlweise Vertragsaufhebung gemäss Art. 49 I lit. a).

[65] Vgl. dazu im Einzelnen Art. 48 Rn. 9 ff.; s. auch Art. 111 II CESL (30-tägige Frist für den Verkäufer, um Sache zu reparieren oder Ersatz zu liefern).

[66] Der Käufer muss keine Nachfrist setzen, um zum Ersatzlieferungsanspruch zu gelangen; es kann aus praktischen Gründen empfehlenswert sein.

[67] *Karollus*, ZIP 1993, 490, 493; *Schulz*, S. 248; *Witz/Salger/Lorenz/Salger*, Art 46, Rn. 10.

[68] Vgl. Art. 48 Rn. 15.

tragsverletzung konzipiert hat.[69] Der Rechtsbehelf soll dem Käufer nicht schon bei einfacher, sondern erst bei wesentlicher Vertragsverletzung zustehen. Nach Art. 48 soll der Verkäufer auf Mängelrüge des Käufers zunächst die Chance haben, die Vertragswidrigkeit der gelieferten Sache – sei es durch Nachbesserung, sei es durch Ersatzlieferung – zu beheben. Nimmt er diese Chance wahr, liefert er also freiwillig und ohne unangemessene Verzögerung vertragsmässige Ware, so braucht der Käufer keinen Rechtsbehelf: Der Vertrag ist erfüllt, der Ersatzlieferungsanspruch ist gegenstandslos. Auch im Fall des Art. 46 II ist daher der Tatbestand der wesentlichen Vertragsverletzung im Regelfall erst erfüllt und eine Klage auf Ersatzlieferung erst begründet, wenn der Verkäufer es versäumt hat, den zwar nicht durch Nachbesserung, aber durch Ersatzlieferung behebbaren Mangel in **angemessener Frist** bzw. innerhalb der vom Käufer gesetzten **Nachfrist** zu beseitigen.[70]

cc) **Ausnahmen.** Zum Grundsatz, dass eine Vertragsverletzung nur dann wesentlich ist, wenn der objektiv gravierende Mangel nachträglich nicht beseitigt wird, gibt es Ausnahmen. Der mit der Beseitigung verbundene Zeitverlust kann dem Käufer bei **Fixgeschäften**[71] und bei sonstigen, strikt zeitgebundenen Lieferungen nicht zugemutet werden. Das objektive Gewicht des Fehlers und die Überschreitung des Liefertermins reichen aus, um die Annahme einer wesentlichen Vertragsverletzung und den Anspruch des Käufers auf Ersatzlieferung (oder Vertragsaufhebung) zu begründen. Des Weiteren kann dem Käufer die Nachbesserung nicht zugemutet werden, wenn die **Vertrauensgrundlage** des Vertrags, z. B. durch betrügerisches Verhalten des Verkäufers,[72] **zerstört** ist.[73]

30

c) **Beweislast.** Die Substanziierungs- und Beweislast für die Tatsachen, aus denen sich das Vorliegen einer wesentlichen Vertragsverletzung ergibt (insbesondere die Unzumutbarkeit bzw. fehlende Möglichkeit der Verwertung der Ware), trifft den Käufer, der die Ersatzlieferung verlangt.[74]

31

d) **Zusammenfassung.** Der Anspruch des Käufers auf Ersatzlieferung setzt eine wesentliche Vertragsverletzung voraus. Diese ist gegeben, wenn der Mangel objektiv gravierend und vom Verkäufer nicht durch Nachbesserung oder Ersatzlieferung beseitigt wird. Der Käufer hat m. a. W. dem Verkäufer eine angemessene Frist einzuräumen, innerhalb derer dieser gemäss Art. 46 III nachbessern bzw. gemäss Art. 48 sein Recht auf Nacherfüllung (Nachbesserung oder Ersatzlieferung) ausüben kann. Erst wenn diese Frist ergebnislos verstrichen ist oder der Verkäufer die Nacherfüllung verweigert, kann der Käufer Ersatzlieferung nach Art. 46 II beanspruchen oder Vertragsaufhebung nach Art. 49 erklären. Ausnahmsweise hat der Käufer ein sofortiges Ersatzlieferungs- bzw. Vertragsaufhebungsrecht, wenn der Mangel gravierend ist und ihm der mit der Beseitigung verbundene Zeitverlust nicht zugemutet werden kann (z. B. bei Fixgeschäften).

32

---

[69] Vgl. Art. 28 Rn. 6, 10 sowie vorne Rn. 2.
[70] So auch *Schulz*, S. 248 f.; vgl. auch die Nachweise bei Rn. 26 mit Fn. 59; a. A. MünchKomm/*P. Huber*, Art. 46, Rn. 32, s. auch Rn. 29 ff.; *Karollus*, ZIP 1993, 490, 495 f.; der den Begriff der wesentlichen Vertragsverletzung in Art. 46 II und 49 I lit. a) unterschiedlich interpretieren will.
[71] Vgl. *Schroeter*, Art. 25 Rn. 18. Selbstverständlich gilt dies nur, wenn der Mangel ein hinreichendes „objektives Gewicht" hat, das die Vertragsaufhebung oder das Verlangen des Käufers nach Ersatzlieferung rechtfertigt. Mängel mit untergeordnetem Gewicht rechtfertigen die Vertragsaufhebung oder das Verlangen nach Ersatzlieferung auch dann nicht, wenn sie sich durch Nachbesserung nicht beheben lassen. Es ist also nicht so, dass eine wesentliche Vertragsverletzung immer schon dann angenommen werden darf, wenn eine Nachbesserung nicht möglich ist; zutreffend BGH, 3.4.1996, CISG-online 135 = BGHZ 132, 290, 299.
[72] Z. B. durch bewusste Lieferung billiger Imitationen. Auch in einem solchen Fall muss aber geprüft werden, ob der Mangel objektiv von hinreichendem Gewicht ist; BGH, 3.4.1996, CISG-online 135 = BGHZ 132, 290, 303 liess offen, ob arglistiges Unterschieben vertragswidriger Ware stets eine wesentliche Vertragsverletzung darstellt. Dies ist m. E. zu bejahen, denn dem Käufer sollte bei arglistigem Verhalten des Verkäufers neben der Ersatzlieferung durch Annahme der Wesentlichkeit ohne weiteres die Möglichkeit der Vertragsaufhebung offen stehen. Ausserdem wird i. d. R. Arglist des Verkäufers die Vertrauensgrundlage des Vertrages zerstören.
[73] *Karollus*, ZIP 1993, 490, 497.
[74] Vgl. dazu auch *Schroeter*, Art. 25 Rn. 16; OLG Frankfurt a. M., 18.1.1994, CISG-online 123 = NJW 1994, 1013, 1014 = RIW 1994, 240, 241; *T. M. Müller*, Beweislast, S. 129.

5. Abwicklung der Ersatzlieferung

33 a) Frist für die Geltendmachung des Ersatzlieferungsanspruchs und Ort. Der Anspruch auf Ersatzlieferung hängt nach Art. 46 II weiter davon ab, dass der Käufer ihn spätestens innerhalb einer **angemessenen** Frist nach Anzeige des Mangels geltend macht.[75] Versäumt der Käufer die Frist sowohl für den Ersatzlieferungsanspruch als auch für die Vertragsaufhebung (Art. 49 II lit. b) i)), reduzieren sich seine Rechte auf Schadenersatz und Minderung. Der Begriff der „angemessenen" Frist ist grundsätzlich nach dem Massstab von Art. 39[76] anhand der Umstände des Einzelfalls abzuschätzen. Bei der Bewertung der Angemessenheit ist auch die vom Käufer in Anspruch genommene Rügefrist nach Art. 39 einzubeziehen.[77] Zur Wahrung der Frist genügt Absendung der Erklärung mit geeigneten Mitteln (Art. 27); das Risiko der Verzögerung und des Verlusts auf dem Übermittlungsweg trifft den Verkäufer. Erübrigt sich eine Mängelrüge (z. B. gemäss Art. 40), beginnt der Fristenlauf mit Entdeckung des Mangels.[78] Verlangt der Käufer zunächst Nachbesserung (Art. 46 III) oder bietet der Verkäufer auf die Mängelrüge hin zunächst Nachbesserung an und schlägt die Nachbesserung fehl, so ist dies bei der Dauer der „angemessenen" Frist mit zu berücksichtigen; der Käufer muss also den Erfüllungsanspruch innerhalb angemessener Frist geltend machen, nachdem der Fehlschlag der Nachbesserung feststeht. Da der Verkäufer durch die Mängelrüge über die Tatsache und die Art des Mangels bereits unterrichtet ist, besteht kein Grund, bei der Bestimmung der Frist allzu kleinlich zu verfahren und etwa eine „unverzügliche" Entscheidung des Käufers zu verlangen.[79] Art. 46 II will, in Verbindung mit der Parallelbestimmung des Art. 49 II lit. b) i), nur verhindern, dass der Käufer, der den Mangel bereits gerügt hat, die Entscheidung über den Rechtsbehelf unangemessen verzögert. Die Erklärung muss **eindeutig** zu erkennen geben, dass der Käufer Ersatzlieferung verlangt. Die **Beweislast** für die rechtzeitige Absendung einer eindeutigen Erklärung trifft den Käufer. Die Ersatzlieferung hat an den Ort zu erfolgen, an dem sich die Kaufsache bei Entdeckung des Mangels befindet.[80]

34 b) Rückgabe der vertragswidrigen Sache. Der Käufer kann Ersatzlieferung nur verlangen, wenn er imstande ist, die ursprünglich gelieferte, vertragswidrige Ware zurückzugeben (Art. 82 I). Das gilt nicht, wenn einer der drei Ausnahmefälle des Art. 82 II lit. a)–c) vorliegt; nach Treu und Glauben (Art. 7 I) ferner dann nicht, wenn die zuerst gelieferte Ware völlig wertlos ist. Die Rückgabepflicht als solche ist nicht ausdrücklich angeordnet, aber in Art. 82 als selbstverständlich vorausgesetzt.[81] Die Pflicht zur Rückgabe entsteht sofort, sobald der Käufer den Anspruch auf Ersatzlieferung geltend macht. Ein Recht des Käufers, die Rückgabe der zuerst gelieferten Ware Zug um Zug von der Ersatzlieferung abhängig zu machen, ist nicht vorgesehen[82] und steht dem Käufer im Grundsatz nicht zu, wie sich im Gegenschluss aus Art. 81 II 2 ergibt.[83] Der Verkäufer kann ein schutzwürdiges Interesse daran haben, über die beim Käufer liegende fehlerhafte Ware sofort disponieren zu

---

[75] Die Anzeige des Mangels nach Art. 39 hat ebenfalls innerhalb angemessener Frist nach Kenntnis bzw. Kennen-Müssen des Mangels, jedenfalls spätestens 2 Jahre nach der Lieferung, zu erfolgen.

[76] *Staudinger/Magnus*, Art. 46, Rn. 43; zurückhaltend *Achilles*, Art. 46, Rn. 5; *Schwenzer*, Art. 39 Rn. 16 f.

[77] *Soergel/Lüderitz/Schüßler-Langeheine*, Art. 46, Rn. 10.

[78] *Staudinger/Magnus*, Art. 46, Rn. 45; *Honsell/Schnyder/Straub*, Art. 46, Rn. 66; *Achilles*, Art. 46, Rn. 5; a. A. *Herber/Czerwenka*, Art. 46, Rn. 8; *Schulz*, S. 260 (Zeitpunkt, in dem die Mängelrüge hätte erhoben werden müssen).

[79] Vgl. eingehend *Achilles*, Art. 46, Rn. 5; *Schulz*, S. 258 ff.

[80] *Grunewald*, Kaufrecht, § 9 II, Rn. 117 f.; a. A. MünchKomm/*P. Huber*, Art. 46, Rn. 41.

[81] Vgl. *Fountoulakis*, Vor Artt. 81–84 Rn. 5; *Schlechtriem*, Einheitliches UN-Kaufrecht, S. 102 mit Fn. 447; *U. Huber*, RabelsZ 43 (1979), 413, 493.

[82] Ein dahingehender Antrag Norwegens wurde auf der Wiener Konferenz abgelehnt, vgl. O. R., S. 136, Art. 66, Nr. 3 II, 5, S. 387 f., Nr. 67 ff.

[83] Ebenso *Schlechtriem*, Einheitliches UN-Kaufrecht, S. 102; *Honsell/Schnyder/Straub*, Art. 46, Rn. 62; *Leser*, Vertragsaufhebung und Rückabwicklung, S. 242 Fn. 81; *Staudinger/Magnus*, Art. 46, Rn. 49; *Vischer*, Gemeinsame Bestimmungen, S. 182; *Achilles*, Art. 46, Rn. 6. A. A. *Herber/Czerwenka*, Art. 46, Rn. 7; *Karollus*, S. 138.

können, noch ehe die Ersatzlieferung beim Käufer eintrifft. Erfolgte die nicht vertragsgemässe Lieferung Zug-um-Zug gegen Bezahlung des Kaufpreises, sollte dem Käufer das Recht zugestanden werden, den Kaufpreis zurückzufordern und Zug-um-Zug Zahlung bei Erhalt der Ersatzlieferung zu verlangen.[84] Die Zug-um-Zug-Abwicklung bei Distanzkäufen führt oft zu erheblichen Schwierigkeiten, wenn nicht Ware gegen Geld, sondern Ware gegen Ware ausgetauscht werden soll.[85] Die Organisation und die Kosten des Rücktransports sind Sache des Verkäufers.

c) Wahl des Verkäufers zwischen Ersatzlieferung und Nachbesserung. Lässt ein Mangel sich sowohl durch Nachbesserung als auch durch Ersatzlieferung beheben und verlangt der Käufer Ersatzlieferung, so kann der Verkäufer den Anspruch innerhalb der Frist und unter den Bedingungen des Art. 48 I durch Nachbesserung abwehren.[86] Das folgt sowohl daraus, dass im Regelfall einstweilen noch keine „wesentliche Vertragsverletzung" vorliegt,[87] als auch daraus, dass im Rahmen des Nacherfüllungsrechts des Art. 48 die Wahl des Mittels dem Verkäufer zusteht.[88] Nimmt allerdings der Verkäufer die Nachbesserung nicht innerhalb der Frist des Art. 48 vor, so kann er den Anspruch des Käufers auf Ersatzlieferung nicht mehr dadurch abwenden, dass er nachträglich doch noch Nachbesserung anbietet. 35

6. Rechtsfolgen

Sind die Voraussetzungen erfüllt, hat der Käufer Anspruch auf **Austausch der nicht vertragsgemässen gegen vertragsgemässe Ware.** Die Kosten des Transports der Ersatzware und der Aufbewahrung der mangelhaften Ware (Artt. 86, 87) sind vom Verkäufer zu tragen.[89] Darüber hinaus hat er alle anderen Nachteile zu ersetzen, die dem Käufer durch die Fehlerhaftigkeit der ersten Lieferung entstanden sind, soweit sie durch die Ersatzlieferung nicht behoben werden können (z. B. Verzögerungsschäden oder Begleitschäden gemäss Art. 45 I lit. b)). 36

Ist die Ersatzlieferung ihrerseits nicht vertragsgemäss, entstehen für den Käufer die Rechtsbehelfe aus den Artt. 45 ff. von neuem. Er kann somit bei Vorliegen der entsprechenden Voraussetzungen (insbes. der Mängelrüge) erneut Ersatzlieferung oder Nachbesserung verlangen. Hat der neue Fehler ein hinreichendes, objektives Gewicht, wird die sofortige Vertragsaufhebung ohne weiteres gerechtfertigt sein, weil die Vertrauensgrundlage des Vertrags erschüttert ist.[90] 37

Verweigert der Verkäufer die Ersatzlieferung oder lässt er die ihm vom Käufer gemäss Art. 47 gesetzte Nachfrist verstreichen, kann der Käufer den Vertrag gestützt auf Art. 49 I lit. a) i. V. m. Art. 49 II lit. b) ii) aufheben.[91] Der Käufer kann dann den Mangel auch selbst beheben oder durch Dritte beseitigen lassen und dem Verkäufer die Kosten gemäss Art. 45 I lit. b) in Rechnung stellen. 38

---

[84] *Brunner,* Art. 46, Rn. 16.
[85] Vgl. dazu *Honnold,* Documentary history; O. R., S. 388, Nr. 72.
[86] Ebenso *Karollus,* S. 138; i. E. auch *Audit,* Vente internationale, Anm. 133. (unter Berufung auf das Prinzip des Art. 77); *Neumayer/Ming,* Art. 46, Anm. 4.; *Schulz,* S. 244 ff. Anders *Welser,* S. 119; *Honsell/Schnyder/Straub,* Art. 46, Rn. 78: Wahlrecht des Käufers; Art. 111 I CESL lässt hingegen bei Konsumentenverträgen dem Käufer die Wahl zwischen Reparatur und Ersatzlieferung.
[87] Dazu vorne Rn. 26 ff.
[88] *Karollus,* S. 138; vgl. auch Art. 48 Rn. 18.
[89] Zur Beteiligung des Käufers an den Kosten der Ersatzlieferung für den Fall, dass er die Nichterfüllung mitzuverantworten hat, vgl. *Trachsel,* S. 74 ff.
[90] Vgl. vorne Rn. 30.
[91] Vgl. dazu Art. 49 Rn. 39 f.; zum praktisch wohl selten relevanten Fall, dass der Käufer zunächst Ersatzlieferung fordert und sich später entschliesst, die Ware zu behalten und Minderung zu verlangen vgl. *U. Huber,* 3. Aufl., Art. 45, Rn. 26 (Wechsel gegen den Willen des Verkäufers nur möglich, wenn der Verkäufer Ersatzlieferung nicht innerhalb angemessener Frist bewirkt).

IV. Anspruch auf Nachbesserung (Abs. 3)

1. Voraussetzungen

39 **a) Allgemeines.** Der Anspruch[92] auf Nachbesserung ist, wie der Anspruch auf Ersatzlieferung, eine besondere Ausprägung des allgemeinen Erfüllungsanspruchs (Art. 46 I), an dessen Anwendungsvoraussetzungen er geknüpft ist.[93] Er setzt zusätzlich voraus, dass die gelieferte Sache mangelhaft ist (Art. 35)[94] und dass der Mangel rechtzeitig gerügt ist (Artt. 39, 50). Er kommt beim Gattungs- wie beim Spezieskauf in Betracht. An die einschränkende Voraussetzung einer wesentlichen Vertragsverletzung ist der Nachbesserungsanspruch nicht gebunden.

40 **b) Zumutbarkeit.** Der Verkäufer ist nur dann zur Nachbesserung verpflichtet, wenn dies unter Berücksichtigung aller Umstände **für ihn** zumutbar ist.[95] Dies bedeutet, dass zwischen den Interessen des Käufers an der Nachbesserung und dem Aufwand des Verkäufers abzuwägen ist.[96] Besteht ein objektives Missverhältnis, ist die Nachbesserung unzumutbar,[97] was insbesondere der Fall ist, wenn die Nachbesserung für den Verkäufer unverhältnismässig kostspielig ist:[98] Die Kosten der Reparatur sind unverhältnismässig höher als die Kosten der Ersatzbeschaffung oder der Reparaturaufwand (z. B. der Aufwand zur Beseitigung eines Schönheitsfehlers) steht in keinem vernünftigen Verhältnis zu dem Vorteil, den der Käufer durch die Beseitigung des Fehlers erlangt.[99] Das Verhältnis der Nachbesserungskosten zum Kaufpreis spielt allerdings keine Rolle.[100] Abgestellt wird allein auf das Verhältnis zwischen Nachbesserung und Ersatzlieferung.[101] Unzumutbarkeit kann auch auf tatsächlichen Gegebenheiten beruhen. Dies ist z. B. der Fall, wenn die Beseitigung des Fehlers an sich einfach ist und dem Käufer leichter fällt als dem – räumlich möglicherweise weit entfernten[102] – Verkäufer.[103] Verfügt der Verkäufer als **Zwischen- oder Einzelhändler** nicht über die technischen, handwerklichen oder sonstigen Fähigkeiten zur Nachbesserung und kann er auch nicht ohne weiteres einen Dritten (z. B. Vertragswerkstatt) einschalten, ist die Nachbesserung unzumutbar.[104] Hat allerdings der Käufer, wie z. B. beim Kauf komplizierter technischer Geräte, ein besonderes Interesse daran, dass gerade der Verkäufer als Fachmann den Fehler beseitigt, so kann der Verkäufer u. U. zu erheblichen Aufwendungen und

---

[92] Der Käufer hat einen Anspruch trotz der insoweit missverständlichen „kann"-Formulierung des deutschen Wortlauts, vgl. die eindeutige engl. und frz. Fassung („require"/„exiger"); *Staudinger/Magnus*, Art. 46, Rn. 55.
[93] Vgl. oben Rn. 6 ff.
[94] Für die Beseitigung von Rechtsmängeln gilt Art. 46 I, nicht Art. 46 III; vgl. oben Rn. 6, 20, 22; a. A. *Neumayer/Ming*, Art. 46, Anm. 8.
[95] *Staudinger/Magnus*, Art. 46, Rn. 60; *Herber/Czerwenka*, Art. 46, Rn. 10; *Schulz*, S. 299; *Achilles*, Art. 46, Rn. 7; Nicht so im CESL, wo die Nachbesserung grundsätzlich immer zulässig ist, so lange sie ohne ungerechtfertigte Verzögerung angezeigt wird, *Kruisinga*, ERPL 2011, 918.
[96] O. R., S. 336, Nr. 35, 37.
[97] *Staudinger/Magnus*, Art. 46, Rn. 60 f.; *Schulz*, S. 299; *Honsell/Schnyder/Straub*, Art. 46, Rn. 94 ff.
[98] *Schlechtriem*, Einheitliches UN-Kaufrecht, S. 67; *Enderlein/Maskow/Strohbach*, Art. 46, Anm. 8.; *Bianca/Bonell/Will*, Art. 46, Anm. 2.2.2.2.; *Herber/Czerwenka*, Art. 46, Rn. 10; *Staudinger/Magnus*, Art. 46, Rn. 61; *Schulz*, S. 300.
[99] *Honsell/Schnyder/Straub*, Art. 46, Rn. 97.
[100] A. A. *von Hoffmann*, Gewährleistungsansprüche, S. 297 f.; dagegen zutreffend KG Schaffhausen, 27.12.2004, CISG-online 960; *Piltz*, Internationales Kaufrecht, Rn. 5–188, wie hier auch *Honsell/Schnyder/Straub*, Art. 46, Rn. 97; *Schulz*, S. 300; *Witz/Salger/Lorenz/Salger*, Art. 46, Rn. 8; vgl. zu § 439 III BGB OLG Braunschweig, 4.2.2003, NJW 2003, 1053 f.
[101] Es kann die in deutschen Recht geltende Faustregel übernommen werden, dass die Kosten der Nachbesserung die Kosten der Ersatzlieferung um nicht mehr als 20% übersteigen dürfen, bei besonderem Affektionsinteresse nicht mehr als 30%; vgl. dazu LG Ellwangen, 13.12.2002, NJW 2003, 517 f.; OLG Braunschweig, 4.2.2003, NJW 2003, 1053 f.
[102] Zu diesem Gesichtspunkt *Honnold/Flechtner*, Art. 46, Rn. 284.
[103] Vgl. dazu die Bsp. oben Rn. 26.
[104] *Schulz*, S. 300; *Witz/Salger/Lorenz/Salger*, Art. 46, Rn. 8; *Soergel/Lüderitz/Schüßler-Langeheine*, Art. 46, Rn. 9; *Staudinger/Magnus*, Art. 46, Rn. 62.

Anstrengungen verpflichtet sein.[105] Im Allgemeinen wird die Zumutbarkeit allerdings wenig Probleme bereiten. Denn Sachen, bei denen eine Nachbesserung vorzugsweise in Betracht kommt, wie Fahrzeuge, Maschinen oder hochwertige technische Geräte, haben im Allgemeinen auch dann, wenn sie fehlerfrei sind, im Lauf der Zeit einen Reparaturbedarf, den der Verkäufer, gleichviel ob er Hersteller oder Zwischenhändler ist, in irgendeiner Weise sicherstellen muss. Der hierfür bereitgestellten, organisatorischen Mittel kann er sich auch im Fall der Nachbesserung bedienen.[106] Den Verkäufer trifft die **Beweislast** für die Tatsachen, aus denen er die Unzumutbarkeit der Nachbesserung herleitet, denn die Nachbesserungspflicht ist die Regel, Unzumutbarkeit die Ausnahme.[107]

Der Fall, dass die Nachbesserung zwar für den Verkäufer zumutbar, aber **für den Käufer** 41 **unzumutbar** ist, ist im Rahmen des Art. 46 III unproblematisch. Der Käufer wird in einem solchen Fall einfach davon Abstand nehmen, den Anspruch auf Nachbesserung geltend zu machen. Gemäss Art. 48 I S. 1 hat der Verkäufer in einem solchen Fall kein Recht, dem Käufer die Nachbesserung gegen dessen Willen aufzudrängen.

Scheidet Nachbesserung wegen Unzumutbarkeit für den Verkäufer (Art. 46 III) oder für 42 den Käufer (Art. 48 I S. 1) aus, stehen dem Käufer die Rechtsbehelfe des Ersatzlieferungsanspruchs (Art. 46 II) und der Vertragsaufhebung (Art. 49 I lit. a)) zur Verfügung, wenn der Mangel **objektiv erheblich** ist.[108] Der Verkäufer kann die Vertragsaufhebung durch das Angebot prompter Ersatzlieferung abwenden.[109] Bei Mängeln von untergeordnetem Gewicht hat es bei den Rechten auf Schadenersatz (Art. 45 I lit. b)) und Minderung (Art. 50) sein Bewenden.

c) Frist. Der Anspruch auf Nachbesserung unterliegt den gleichen zeitlichen Beschrän- 43 kungen wie der Anspruch auf Ersatzlieferung.[110] Der Käufer muss spätestens innerhalb **angemessener** Frist nach der Mängelrüge eine eindeutige Erklärung abgeben, dass er Nachbesserung verlangt;[111] Absendung genügt (Art. 27); die Beweislast liegt beim Käufer.

2. Inhalt

a) Allgemeines. Die Art und Weise der Nachbesserung ergibt sich aus dem in Frage 44 stehenden Mangel, wobei die **Wahl** der Mittel **dem Verkäufer** zusteht. Im Gegensatz zur Ersatzlieferung gemäss Art. 46 II wird nicht die Sache als solche ausgetauscht. Denkbar ist die Ausbesserung des Mangels, indem z. B. ein defektes Ventil richtig eingestellt wird, bei einer zusammengesetzten Sache Ersatzteile geliefert und eingebaut werden[112] oder ursprünglich fehlende Komponenten nachträglich eingebaut werden. Der Verkäufer kann grundsätzlich auch durch Ersatzlieferung, d. h. Lieferung eines fehlerfreien Exemplars, nachbessern.[113] Ist hingegen bei einer teilbaren Lieferung ein Teil mangelhaft, richtet sich der Anspruch des Käufers nach Art. 46 I i. V. m. Art. 51 I.[114]

---

[105] Darauf ist bei den Beratungen zutreffend hingewiesen worden, vgl. O. R., S. 336, Nr. 35, 37; vgl. auch *Bianca/Bonell/Will*, Art. 46, Anm. 2.2.2.2.
[106] Vgl. dazu den Hinweis O. R., S. 335, Nr. 20.
[107] *T. M. Müller*, Beweislast, S. 130.
[108] Vgl. dazu vorne Rn. 29 f.
[109] Vgl. vorne Rn. 29.
[110] Vgl. vorne Rn. 33.
[111] Bei der Prüfung der Angemessenheit der Frist sind die zwischen den Parteien und den Versicherungen geführten Verhandlungen über die Folgen der fehlerhaften Lieferung zu berücksichtigen, im konkreten Fall verstrichen deswegen 2 Jahre zwischen der Mängelrüge und dem Nachbesserungsbegehren, was vom Gericht als angemessene Frist angesehen wurde, CA Colmar, 24.10.2000, CISG-online 578.
[112] Die Lieferung von Ersatzteilen ist somit Nachbesserung und nicht Ersatzlieferung und als solche nur von der Zumutbarkeit abhängig; *Enderlein/Maskow/Strohbach*, Art. 46, Anm. 7.; *Herber/Czerwenka*, Art. 46, Rn. 9; *Reinhart*, Art. 46, Rn. 8; *Piltz*, Internationales Kaufrecht, Rn. 5–186; *Schlechtriem*, IPRax 1996, 256; *Staudinger/Magnus*, Art. 46, Rn. 54. Vgl. auch O. R., S. 336 f.
[113] *Honsell/Schnyder/Straub*, Art. 46, Rn. 108; *Neumayer/Ming*, Art. 46, Anm. 5.; *Staudinger/Magnus*, Art. 46, Rn. 61; *Herber/Czerwenka*, Art. 46, Rn. 10; *Brunner*, Art. 46, Rn. 21; a. A. *Witz/Salger/Lorenz*, Art. 46, Rn. 11.
[114] Vgl. vorne Rn. 21.

45 **b) Ort, Zeit, Kosten.** Mangels abweichender Vereinbarungen der Parteien[115] hat der Verkäufer die Sache am **Ort** zu reparieren, wo sie sich gemäss dem Vertrag befindet, also am Bestimmungsort.[116] Muss die Sache zum Zweck der Reparatur in eine Werkstatt des Verkäufers geschafft werden, so ist es vorbehaltlich Treu und Glauben (Art. 7 I) und der Verkehrssitte (Art. 9 II) Sache des Verkäufers, hierfür zu sorgen. Der Verkäufer hat die Nachbesserung **innerhalb angemessener Frist** (vgl. Art. 33 lit. c)) bzw. innerhalb der vom Käufer gesetzten Nachfrist vorzunehmen. **Kosten** und **Gefahr** der Nachbesserung sind vom Verkäufer zu tragen.[117] Desgleichen hat er dem Käufer wie im Falle der Ersatzlieferung[118] alle **Schäden** zu ersetzen, die diesem durch den Mangel oder anlässlich der Nachbesserung entstehen (Art. 45 I lit. b)).

3. Rechtsfolgen der Nichterfüllung des Nachbesserungsanspruchs

46 Schlägt die Nachbesserung fehl, nimmt der Verkäufer diese gemäss Art. 46 III oder Art. 48 nicht innerhalb angemessener Frist vor oder ist ihm dies nicht zumutbar,[119] kann der Käufer den **Mangel selbst beheben** oder durch Dritte beheben lassen und dem Verkäufer die Kosten als Schadenersatz (Art. 45 I lit. b)) in Rechnung stellen.[120] Allerdings darf der Käufer dabei keinen unvernünftigen Aufwand treiben (Art. 77). Obwohl im CISG nicht besonders vorgesehen, hat m. E. der Verkäufer die Kosten der Ersatzvornahme zu bevorschussen.[121]

47 Ist der vom Verkäufer nicht behobene Mangel gewichtig, kann der Käufer **Ersatzlieferung** gemäss Art. 46 II[122] verlangen oder **Vertragsaufhebung** nach Art. 49 I lit. a) erklären (und Schadenersatz wegen Nichterfüllung gem. Art. 45 I lit. b) verlangen).[123] Ist dagegen der Mangel minder gewichtig, bleiben dem Käufer nur die Rechtsbehelfe des **Schadenersatzanspruchs** (Art. 45 I lit. b)) und der **Minderung** (Art. 50); er kann auch sein Nachbesserungsrecht weiterverfolgen.[124] Keiner dieser Rechtsbehelfe hängt von einer erneuten Mängelrüge ab, da der Mangel bereits gerügt wurde und der Verkäufer untätig blieb. Schlägt hingegen die Nachbesserung fehl, muss der Käufer den Mangel rügen, bevor er erneut Rechtsbehelfe in Anspruch nehmen kann.[125]

---

[115] AG Cloppenburg, 14.4.1993, CISG-online 85.
[116] Ebenso *Honsell/Schnyder/Straub*, Art. 46, Rn. 104; *Ferrari u. a./Saenger*, Internationales Vertragsrecht, Art. 46, Rn. 15; *Brunner*, Art. 46, Rn. 21; a. A. *Staudinger/Magnus*, Art. 46, Rn. 66; MünchKomm/*P. Huber*, Art. 46, Rn. 59; *Kröll u. a./P. Huber*, Art. 46, Rn. 52; MünchKommHGB/*Benicke*, Art. 46, Rn. 25; *Grunewald*, Kaufrecht, § 9 II, Rn. 108 (Sache ist immer am Ort zu ersetzen, wo sie sich befindet, auch wenn dies nicht der vertragliche Bestimmungsort ist). A. A. *Witz/Salger/Lorenz/Salger*, Art. 46, Rn. 11; CA Paris, 4.3.1998, CISG-online 533 (Sache ist am Erfüllungsort der ursprünglichen Lieferung zu reparieren); a. A. BGH, 13.4.2011, BGHZ 189, 196, 206 ff. (fehlen vertragliche Vereinbarungen, ist für die Bestimmung des Ortes, wo die Sache zu reparieren ist, auf die Umstände abzustellen, insbes. auf die konkrete Natur des Schuldverhältnisses. Hilft auch dies nicht weiter, ist Erfüllungsort der Ort, an dem der Verkäufer zum Zeitpunkt des Vertragsschlusses seine Niederlassung hatte).
[117] Vgl. oben Rn. 36; OLG Hamm, 9.6.1995, CISG-online 146 = NJW-RR 1996, 179, 180 = IPRax 1996, 269, 270 (mit Anm. *Schlechtriem*, S. 256).
[118] Vgl. oben Rn. 36.
[119] *Schlechtriem*, IPRax 1996, 256.
[120] Vgl. OLG Hamm, 9.6.1995, CISG-online 146 = NJW-RR 1996, 179, 180 = IPRax 1996, 269, 270 (mit zustimmender Anm. *Schlechtriem*, S. 256); *Honsell/Schnyder/Straub*, Art. 46, Rn. 109; *Brunner*, Art. 46, Rn. 22; rechtsvergleichend *Schwenzer/Hachem/Kee*, Rn. 43.69 ff.; vgl. zur Möglichkeit der Aufrechnung gegen die Kaufpreisforderung OLG Hamm aaO. und *Müller-Chen*, Art. 45 Rn. 27.
[121] A. A. *Brunner*, Art. 46, Rn. 22.
[122] Vgl. vorne Rn. 17 ff.
[123] Vgl. zu den Einzelheiten Art. 49 Rn. 7 ff.
[124] *U. Huber*, 3. Aufl., Rn. 67.
[125] Vgl. vorne Rn. 37 zur Ersatzlieferung; offengelassen von LG Oldenburg, 9.11.1994, CISG-online 114 = NJW-RR 1995, 438.

V. Abweichende Vereinbarungen

Abweichende Vereinbarungen sind zulässig (Art. 6), auch wenn sie in **Allgemeinen** 48 **Geschäftsbedingungen** getroffen werden. Die Inhaltskontrolle richtet sich nach nationalem Recht.[126] Als zulässig und mit den Grundwertungen des CISG vereinbar gelten Vertragsklauseln in **allgemeinen Lieferbedingungen,** durch die der Verkäufer den Erfüllungsanspruch des Käufers (Art. 46 I) für Fälle der höheren Gewalt, der Betriebsunterbrechung und ähnliche Fälle ausschliesst.[127] Zulässig ist auch der Ausschluss des Anspruchs auf Ersatzlieferung (Art. 46 II) oder auf Nachbesserung (Art. 46 III),[128] wenn dem Käufer in einem solchen Fall das Recht verbleibt, bei wesentlicher Vertragsverletzung die Vertragsaufhebung zu erklären.[129] Auf der anderen Seite kann in **allgemeinen Einkaufsbedingungen** der Erfüllungsanspruch des Käufers erweitert werden, insbesondere in dem Sinn, dass der Käufer sich für den Fall der Lieferung vertragswidriger Ware einen Anspruch auf Ersatzlieferung ausbedingt, der nicht von den einschränkenden Voraussetzungen des Art. 46 II abhängt.

---

[126] *Piltz,* UN-Kaufrecht, Rn. 47 ff.; für einen Überblick über die nationalen Rechtsordnungen vgl. *Piltz,* aaO.
[127] *Frense,* S. 139 mit Fn. 17.
[128] So auch *Frense,* S. 137 ff., 139.
[129] Vgl. dazu OGH, 7.9.2000, CISG-online 642 = IHR 2001, 42, 43; dem Sinn nach auch *Gillette/Walt,* S. 389 ff.; Art. 49 Rn. 36 f.

Art. 47 [Nachfrist]

(1) **Der Käufer kann dem Verkäufer eine angemessene Nachfrist zur Erfüllung seiner Pflichten setzen.**

(2) **Der Käufer kann vor Ablauf dieser Frist keinen Rechtsbehelf* wegen Vertragsverletzung ausüben, ausser wenn er vom Verkäufer die Anzeige erhalten hat, dass dieser seine Pflichten nicht innerhalb der so gesetzten Frist erfüllen wird. Der Käufer behält jedoch das Recht, Schadensersatz wegen verspäteter Erfüllung zu verlangen.**

Art. 47

(1) The buyer may fix an additional period of time of reasonable length for performance by the seller of his obligations.

(2) Unless the buyer has received notice from the seller that he will not perform within the period so fixed, the buyer may not, during that period, resort to any remedy for breach of contract. However, the buyer is not deprived thereby of any right he may have to claim damages for delay in performance.

Art. 47

(1) L'acheteur peut impartir au vendeur un délai supplémentaire de durée raisonnable pour l'exécution de ses obligations.

(2) A moins qu'il n'ait reçu du vendeur une notification l'informant que celui-ci n'exécuterait pas ses obligations dans le délai ainsi imparti, l'acheteur ne peut, avant l'expiration de ce délai, se prévaloir d'aucun des moyens dont il dispose en cas de contravention au contrat. Toutefois, l'acheteur ne perd pas, de ce fait, le droit de demander des dommages-intérêts pour retard dans l'exécution.

Übersicht

	Rn.
I. Funktionen der Nachfristsetzung	1
II. Nachfristsetzung (Abs. 1)	4
1. Fristbestimmung und Aufforderung zur Leistung	4
a) Fristbestimmung	4
b) Aufforderung zur Leistung	5
2. Angemessene Frist	6
a) Massgeblichkeit der Umstände des Einzelfalls	6
b) Wirkungen einer zu kurz bemessenen Nachfrist	7
c) Zu lang bemessene Nachfrist	10
3. Formalien der Nachfristsetzung	11
a) Zeitpunkt	11
b) Form und Übermittlungsrisiko	12
4. Beweislast	13
III. Bindung des Käufers (Abs. 2)	14
1. Keine Ausübung von Rechtsbehelfen vor Ablauf der Frist	14
2. Ablauf und Wahrung der Frist	16
3. Erfüllungsverweigerung	17
4. Recht auf Schadensersatz	18
a) Verzögerungsschaden	18
b) Sonstige Schäden	19
c) Vertragsstrafen	20
5. Bindung des Käufers bei unbefristeter Mahnung	21

Vorläufer und **Entwürfe:** EKG –; Genfer E 1976 Art. 28; Wiener E 1977 Art. 29; New Yorker E 1978 Art. 43.

---

* Schweiz: kein Recht.

I. Funktionen der Nachfristsetzung

Der Käufer kann dem Verkäufer für die Erfüllung **jeder beliebigen Pflicht,** unabhängig 1
davon, ob es sich um eine Haupt- oder Nebenpflicht handelt,[1] eine oder mehrere Nachfristen setzen.[2] Diese Möglichkeit bestünde auch ohne besondere gesetzliche Ermächtigung. Das Einheitskaufrecht knüpft aber an die Nachfristsetzung verschiedene Rechtswirkungen, die auf der Bestimmung des Art. 47 I aufbauen. Praktische Relevanz erlangt diese vornehmlich in Verbindung mit Art. 49: Hat der Verkäufer die Ware nicht bis zu dem gemäss Art. 33 vorgesehenen Zeitpunkt geliefert, eröffnet sich dem Käufer durch Setzung einer Nachfrist die Möglichkeit, sich nach fruchtlosem Ablauf der Frist vom Vertrag zu lösen (Art. 49 I lit. b)).[3] Auf die Frage, ob der **Lieferverzug** eine wesentliche Vertragsverletzung ist (Art. 49 I lit. a) i. V. m. Art. 25), kommt es dann nicht an.[4] In **allen anderen Fällen** von Pflichtverletzungen des Verkäufers, insbesondere bei der Lieferung vertragswidriger Ware, hängt das Recht des Käufers zur Vertragsaufhebung nur davon ab, ob die Vertragsverletzung als solche **„wesentlich"** i. S. d. Art. 25 ist. Die Setzung einer **Nachfrist** ändert daran nichts. Bedeutung erlangt diese jedoch im Fall, dass die Lieferung mangelhafter Ware eine wesentliche Vertragsverletzung darstellt und der Käufer sich zunächst dafür entscheidet, auf Vertragserfüllung (durch Ersatzlieferung oder Nachbesserung) zu bestehen.[5] Dies wird vielfach dazu führen, dass die Frist des Art. 49 II lit. b) i) zur Erklärung der Vertragsaufhebung verstreicht. Will der Käufer nun den **Rechtsbehelf wechseln,** so kann er das zunächst verlorene **Recht zur Vertragsaufhebung zurückgewinnen,** indem er dem Verkäufer für die Ersatzlieferung oder Nachbesserung Nachfrist setzt.[6]

Sonstige Rechtsbehelfe des Käufers (ausser der Vertragsaufhebung), also insbesondere der 2
Erfüllungsanspruch (Art. 46), die Minderung (Art. 50) und grundsätzlich auch der Schadenersatzanspruch (Art. 45 I lit. b)), soweit er nicht seinerseits die Vertragsaufhebung voraussetzt, hängen niemals von der förmlichen Voraussetzung einer Nachfrist ab. Es sind nur, aber immerhin die entsprechenden Voraussetzungen des jeweiligen Rechtsbehelfs zu erfüllen.

Zugunsten des Verkäufers begründet die vom Käufer gesetzte Nachfrist gemäss Art. 47 3
II eine **Bindungswirkung.**[7] Der Verkäufer darf sich auf die Nachfrist verlassen. Ehe sie abgelaufen ist, kann der Käufer keine weiteren Rechtsbehelfe geltend machen. Der rechtfertigende Grund für die Bindung liegt im Verbot des „venire contra factum proprium". Die Regel des Art. 47 II hätte sich deshalb wohl auch ohne ausdrückliche Bestimmung aus dem Grundsatz von Treu und Glauben ableiten lassen; sie besagt eigentlich nur etwas Selbstverständliches.[8] Die Bindungswirkung von Art. 47 hindert die Parteien nicht, sich

---

[1] So auch *Duncan, Jr.,* B. Y. U. L. Rev. (2000), 1363, 1383.
[2] Die Möglichkeit der Nachfristsetzung setzt damit das Bestehen eines Erfüllungsanspruchs nach Art. 46 voraus; die Durchsetzbarkeit desselben gemäss Art. 28 ist dagegen irrelevant, vgl. *Neumayer/Ming,* Art. 47, Anm. 1.; *Staudinger/Magnus,* Art. 47, Rn. 11; *Honsell/Schnyder/Straub,* Art. 47, Rn. 12; vgl. auch *Audit,* Vente internationale, Anm. 126.; die Nachfrist in Art. 47 geht zurück auf die Nachfrist in § 326 I BGB a. F. und die „mise en demeure" des frz. Rechts, s. dazu *van Vuuren,* 15 Ariz. J. Int'l & Comp. L. (1998), 583, 613; *Duncan, Jr.,* B. Y. U. L. Rev. (2000), 1363, 1383; zum Vergleich mit dem Common Law, insbes. dem UCC, vgl. *Frisch,* 74 Tul. L. Rev. (1999–2000), 495, 553 ff.; *Piliounis,* 12 Pace Int'l L. Rev. (2000), 1, 22 f.; *Kimbel,* 18 J. L. & Com. (1999), 301, 305 f.; rechtsvergleichender Überblick bei *Schwenzer/Hachem/Kee,* Rn. 47.49 ff.
[3] Vgl. zur Nachfristsetzung in diesen Fällen Art. 49 Rn. 15 ff.; OLG München, 1.7.2002, CISG-online 656; HGer Aargau, 10.3.2010, CISG-online 2176 = SZIER 2011, 551 ff.
[4] Der Käufer kann aber, wenn er das will, auch in diesen Fällen eine Nachfrist setzen, unrichtig daher Gerechtshof Leeuwarden, 31.8.2005, CISG-online 1100 (keine Nachfristsetzung möglich, wenn der Lieferverzug eine wesentliche Vertragsverletzung ist).
[5] Gemäss *Will* kann ein wiederholtes Nichtnachkommen der Nachbesserungspflicht eine wesentliche Vertragsverletzung darstellen und somit zur Vertragsaufhebung nach Art. 49 I lit. a), niemals aber nach Art. 49 I lit. b) berechtigen (*Bianca/Bonell/Will,* Art. 47, Anm. 2.2.1.).
[6] Vgl. dazu Art. 49 Rn. 36 ff.
[7] „Selbstbindung des Gläubigers": *Friehe,* IHR 2010, 230, 232 ff.
[8] *Honnold/Flechtner,* Art. 47, Rn. 291: „A basic principle that might have gone without saying: A party may not refuse performance that he has invited". Vgl. auch *Enderlein/Maskow/Strohbach,* Art. 47, Anm. 5.

auf eine Vertragsänderung gemäss Art. 29 zu verständigen, selbst wenn im geänderten Vertrag dem Käufer zusätzliche Rechte für den Fall der Vertragsverletzung eingeräumt werden.[9]

II. Nachfristsetzung (Abs. 1)

1. Fristbestimmung und Aufforderung zur Leistung

4   a) **Fristbestimmung.** Die Nachfristsetzung muss, um ihre Wirkung zu entfalten,[10] eine Aufforderung zur Leistung mit Setzung eines **bestimmten Termins** enthalten, z. B. „bis zum 31. 10." oder „innerhalb von zwei Wochen". Eine Mahnung ohne Terminbestimmung reicht nicht aus. Das gilt auch für dringende Mahnungen, z. B. die Aufforderung, die Lieferung „alsbald", „so schnell wie möglich" oder „sofort" zu bewirken.[11]

5   b) **Aufforderung zur Leistung.** Die Nachfristsetzung muss ausserdem eine bestimmte Aufforderung zur Leistung enthalten.[12] Der Käufer ist hingegen nicht verpflichtet, die Fristsetzung mit der Androhung zu verbinden, nach Ablauf der Frist die Annahme der Leistung als Erfüllung abzulehnen oder den Vertrag aufzuheben.[13] Ausreichend ist z. B. „Für die Lieferung setzen wir Ihnen Frist bis zum 31. 10." oder auch „Wir fordern Sie auf, die Lieferung bis zum 31. 10. durchzuführen". Das Wort „Nachfrist" („additional period of time", „délai supplémentaire") braucht nicht verwendet zu werden, obwohl das aus Gründen der Klarheit zweckmässig ist.[14] Allzu höfliche Umschreibungen (wie z. B.: „Hoffen sehr, dass die Ware bis zum 1. Juli eintrifft"), genügen nicht und sind deshalb zu vermeiden.[15] Aus derartigen Formulierungen lässt sich eher ein **Lieferaufschub** oder eine Stundung ableiten mit der Folge, dass der Käufer einerseits keinen Schadenersatz wegen Verzug verlangen und anderseits vor Ablauf der gesetzten Frist den Vertrag nicht aufheben kann, selbst wenn es sich um eine wesentliche Vertragsverletzung handeln würde. Bittet der Verkäufer selbst um einen Aufschub und bewilligt der Käufer ihn mit dem Zusatz, die Einhaltung der Frist sei für ihn, eigener Verpflichtungen wegen, „sehr wichtig" und bei Nichteinhaltung sei er gezwungen, sich auf Kosten des Verkäufers „anderweitig einzudecken", so reicht das als Nachfristsetzung aus.[16]

---

[9] *Valero Marketing & Supply Company v. Greeni Trading Oy*, U. S. Ct. App. (3rd Cir.), 19.7.2007, CISG-online 1510.
[10] Bindung des Käufers nach Art. 47 II: *Soergel/Lüderitz/Schüßler-Langeheine*, Art. 47, Rn. 1. Zur Frage, ob der Käufer aus anderen Gründen (Treu und Glauben) an ein Erfüllungsverlangen gebunden ist, das er geltend macht, ohne es mit einer Nachfrist zu verbinden, vgl. Art. 45 Rn. 14 f.; Vertragsaufhebung gemäss Art. 49 I lit. b): *Honnold/Flechtner*, Art. 47, Rn. 289.
[11] Vgl. Sekretariatskommentar, Art. 43, Nr. 7; *Honnold/Flechtner*, Art. 47, Rn. 289; *Bianca/Bonell/Will*, Art. 47, Anm. 2.1.3.1.; *Herber/Czerwenka*, Art. 47, Rn. 3; *Neumayer/Ming*, Art. 47, Anm. 1.; *Karollus*, S. 139; *Honsell/Schnyder/Straub*, Art. 47, Rn. 20; *Staudinger/Magnus*, Art. 47, Rn. 17.
[12] Hof Arnheim, 7.10.2008, CISG-online 1749; *Audit*, Vente internationale, Anm. 126. Es gilt Ähnliches wie im deutschen Recht für die Mahnung i. S. d. § 286 I BGB, vgl. *Lorenz/Riehm*, Rn. 262; *Palandt/Heinrichs*, § 286, Rn. 16 ff., § 281, Rn. 9; Art. 102 I OR, vgl. dazu *Schwenzer*, OR AT, Rn. 65.08; Artt. 1139, 1146 frz. Cc, vgl. dazu *Ghestin/Desché*, Traité des Contrats, Anm. 672.
[13] *Reinhart*, Art. 47, Rn. 2; *Herber/Czerwenka*, Art. 47, Rn. 3; *Soergel/Lüderitz/Schüßler-Langeheine*, Art. 47, Rn. 4; *Neumayer/Ming*, Art. 47, Anm. 1.; *Honsell/Schnyder/Straub*, Art. 47, Rn. 19; *Staudinger/Magnus*, Art. 47, Rn. 18; *Piltz*, Internationales Kaufrecht, Rn. 5–265; anders *Enderlein/Maskow/Strohbach*, Art. 47, Anm. 4.; *Garro/Zuppi*, Compraventa internacional, S. 180 f.; *Audit*, Vente internationale, Anm. 130. So nun auch § 323 I BGB, der keine Ablehnungsandrohung mehr verlangt.
[14] So auch *Staudinger/Magnus*, Art. 47, Rn. 18; *Witz/Salger/Lorenz/Salger*, Art. 47, Rn. 4.
[15] *Honnold/Flechtner*, Art. 47, Rn. 289; vgl. auch *Bianca/Bonell/Will*, Art. 47, Anm. 2.1.3.1.; *Herber/Czerwenka*, Art. 47, Rn. 3. Das OLG Nürnberg erachtete die Formulierung „Wir ersuchen Sie um Erledigung bis 25.2.93" als ausreichend, während die Vorinstanz dies verneinte, 20.9.1995, CISG-online 267, Vorinstanz: LG Nürnberg-Fürth, 26.7.1994, CISG-online 266.
[16] OLG Hamburg, 28.2.1997, CISG-online 261.

2. Angemessene Frist

a) Massgeblichkeit der Umstände des Einzelfalls. Die Nachfrist muss „angemessen"[17] sein. Ob die Nachfrist angemessen ist, kann nicht generell, sondern nur unter Berücksichtigung des Einzelfalles entschieden werden. Dabei sind zu berücksichtigen: Die **Länge** der vertraglichen **Lieferzeit** (kurzfristige Geschäfte rechtfertigen kurze, langfristige erfordern längere Nachfristen); das dem Verkäufer bei Vertragsabschluss erkennbare **Interesse** an **rascher Lieferung;**[18] **Umfang** und **Art** der Leistung des Verkäufers (für die Lieferung komplizierter Anlagen und Maschinen, die der Verkäufer herzustellen hat, ist eine längere Nachfrist angemessen als für die Lieferung marktgängiger Ware durch den Grosshändler); die **Ursache** der Nichterfüllung[19] (ist der Verkäufer von einer Brandkatastrophe oder einem Streik betroffen, so ist dem Käufer, wenn die Lieferung für ihn nicht besonders eilbedürftig ist, ein gewisses Abwarten eher zuzumuten). Schliesslich müssen auch die **Übermittlungsdauer** für die Erklärung der Nachfristsetzung[20] und die **Umstände der Lieferung** an sich für die Bemessung der Nachfrist herangezogen werden. So muss die Nachfrist länger sein, wenn beispielsweise die Ware zu verschiffen und der Verkäufer zur Organisation der Fracht auf den Fahrplan der Schiffe bzw. auf freie Ladekapazitäten angewiesen ist.[21] In kritischen Fällen gibt das bei Vertragsabschluss erkennbare Interesse des Käufers den Ausschlag. Ein Interesse des Käufers an besonders schneller Lieferung, das für den Verkäufer bei Abschluss des Kaufvertrags nicht erkennbar war, ist nicht zu berücksichtigen; in diesem Punkt kann für die Vertragsaufhebung kraft Nachfristsetzung (Art. 49 I lit. b)) nichts anderes gelten als für die Vertragsaufhebung kraft wesentlicher Vertragsverletzung (Art. 49 I lit. a) i. V. m. Art. 25[22]). Der Verkäufer muss ausserdem durch die Nachfrist eine realistische Möglichkeit zur Nachbesserung oder Ersatzlieferung haben.[23] Allerdings ist die Nachfrist eine zur ursprünglichen Lieferfrist zusätzlich gewährte Frist. Der Verkäufer hat damit kein Recht darauf, dass die Frist so bemessen wird, als würde der Vertrag erst jetzt abgeschlossen. Daher ist es nicht der Sinn der Nachfrist, dem Verkäufer, wenn die Lieferung eine längere Vorbereitungszeit erfordert, die Möglichkeit zu geben, die Lieferung innerhalb der Nachfrist auch dann durchzuführen, wenn er bei Beginn der Nachfrist noch nicht einmal mit den Vorbereitungen begonnen hat.[24]

---

[17] KG Zug, 14.12.2009, CISG-online 2026; ZivG Basel-Stadt, 8.11.2006, CISG-online 1731 = SZIER 2011 540 ff. (15tägige Frist für die Verbesserung einer Anlage ist hinreichend, da „die Beklagte schon zwei Monate lang im WErk der Klägerin versucht hatte, die Anlageauf den vertragsgemässen Stand zu bringen"). Ausführlich zur Angemessenheit der Nachfrist: *Rudolph*, Art. 47, Rn. 6; *Enderlein/Maskow/Strohbach*, Art. 47, Anm. 2. Gemäss Art. 115 II CESL (Vertragsverletzung wegen Verzug) gilt die dem Verkäufer im Rahmen eines Verbraucherkaufvertrages zur Erfüllung gesetzte Nachfrist dann als angemessen, wenn der Verkäufer ihr nicht unverzüglich widerspricht.

[18] Für die Bemessung einer angemessenen Frist ist vorrangig auf den Parteiwillen im konkreten Vertragsverhältnis abzustellen, unabhängig davon, ob Lieferfristüberschreitungen von 2–4 Wochen im internationalen Handel üblich sind, OLG Naumburg, 27.4.1999, CISG-online 512; das Interesse an rascher Lieferung kann sich z. B. daraus ergeben, dass der Käufer die Ware weiterverkauft hat oder mit den zu liefernden Maschinen zeitgebundene Arbeiten zu bewirken hat; vgl. etwa das Bsp. bei *Kimbel*, 18 J. L. & Com. (1999), 301, 310 ff.; vgl. auch BGer, 15.9.2000, CISG-online 770.

[19] Vgl. auch *Soergel/Lüderitz*, 11. Aufl., Art. 27 EKG, Rn. 3.

[20] *Staudinger/Magnus*, Art. 47, Rn. 19.

[21] OLG Celle, 24.5.1995, CISG-online 152: 11 Tage Nachfrist sind möglicherweise zu kurz, 7 Wochen hingegen sind mehr als angemessen.

[22] Vgl. dazu *Schroeter*, Art. 25 Rn. 18.

[23] *Soergel/Lüderitz/Schüßler-Langeheine*, Art. 47, Rn. 3; *Honsell*, SJZ 1992, 345, 352 f.; vgl. CA Versailles, 29.1.1998, CISG-online 337: Die Komplexität der Reparatur hochtechnologischer Maschinen muss bei der Bemessung der Nachfrist berücksichtigt werden.

[24] Vgl. auch *Honsell/Schnyder/Straub*, Art. 47, Rn. 23. Im deutschen Recht wurde zu § 326 BGB a. F. genauso entschieden, RG, 24.11.1916, RGZ 89, 123, 125 und seither ständige Rspr., vgl. *Soergel/Wiedemann*, 12. Aufl., § 326 BGB, Rn. 37 mit Fn. 77 m. w. N. Abweichend *Audit*, Vente internationale, Anm. 130. („[...] suffisant pour permettre au vendeur de s'exécuter").

7 **b) Wirkungen einer zu kurz bemessenen Nachfrist.** Ist die vom Käufer gesetzte Nachfrist, z. B. wegen Wahl einer zeitraubenden Übermittlungsform, zu kurz, so ist hinsichtlich der Wirkungen zu unterscheiden.

8 Die zu kurze Frist setzt eine angemessene Nachfrist in Gang, an die der Käufer gemäss Art. 47 II 1 gebunden ist.[25]

9 Dagegen kann der Käufer durch den Ablauf einer zu kurz bemessenen Nachfrist nicht das Recht erwerben, gemäss **Art. 49 I lit. b)** die **Vertragsaufhebung** zu erklären. Erklärt er in einem solchen Fall unmittelbar nach Ablauf der Nachfrist die Vertragsaufhebung, so ist diese Erklärung nur wirksam, wenn infolge der Verzögerung der Lieferung der Tatbestand einer wesentlichen Vertragsverletzung ohnehin schon erfüllt ist.[26] Ist das nicht der Fall, so begeht der Käufer durch die vorschnelle Erklärung der Vertragsaufhebung seinerseits eine Vertragsverletzung, die es dem Verkäufer erlaubt, nach Art. 72 I, III vorzugehen.[27] Anders ist die Rechtslage, wenn der Käufer nach Ablauf der zu kurz bemessenen Nachfrist die Vertragsaufhebung nicht sofort erklärt, sondern noch eine weitere Zeit abwartet. Ist die Nachfrist und die durch das weitere Abwarten zusätzlich gewährte Frist insgesamt als „angemessene Frist" i. S. d. Art. 47 I zu bewerten, so muss dem Käufer nunmehr das Recht zustehen, die Vertragsaufhebung gemäss Art. 49 I lit. b) zu erklären.[28] Für die Anwendung des Art. 49 I lit. b) gilt somit die Regel, dass eine **zu kurz bemessene Nachfrist eine „angemessene" Nachfrist in Lauf setzt,** nach deren Ablauf der Käufer zur Vertragsaufhebung berechtigt ist.[29] Für den Käufer, der eine sehr knappe Nachfrist gesetzt hat, von der nicht sicher ist, ob sie im Streitfall als „angemessen" anerkannt wird, kann es sich daher empfehlen, mit der Erklärung der Vertragsaufhebung nach Ablauf der Nachfrist noch zu warten, bis die „angemessene Frist" mit Sicherheit abgelaufen ist.

10 **c) Zu lang bemessene Nachfrist.** Setzt der Käufer eine Nachfrist, die länger ist als erforderlich, so ist er gleichwohl während der Dauer der Nachfrist gemäss Art. 47 II gebunden.[30] Eine Vertragsaufhebung ist erst nach Ablauf der Nachfrist möglich.

3. Formalien der Nachfristsetzung

11 **a) Zeitpunkt.** Der Käufer kann eine Nachfrist für die Lieferung mit der Wirkung des Art. 49 I lit. b) erst gültig setzen, wenn der (vertragliche) **Liefertermin** (bzw. die Frist gemäss Art. 33 lit. c))[31] **verstrichen** ist.[32] Das ergibt sich einerseits aus dem Wesen der

---

[25] Ebenso: *Herber/Czerwenka*, Art. 47, Rn. 4; *Karollus*, S. 139; *Staudinger/Magnus*, Art. 47, Rn. 20; vgl. auch OLG Naumburg, 27.4.1999, CISG-online 512; *Friehe*, IHR 2010, 230 ff.; anders *U. Huber*, 3. Aufl., Rn. 11; *Soergel/Lüderitz/Schüßler-Langeheine*, Art. 47, Rn. 7 (Bindungswirkung beschränkt auf die vom Käufer gesetzte Frist); noch anders *Honsell/Schnyder/Straub*, Art. 47, Rn. 24 (eine zu kurze Frist hat gar keine Wirkung).
[26] Die Vertragsaufhebung richtet sich in dem Fall nach Art. 49 I lit. a) und nicht nach I lit. b).
[27] Vgl. auch *Piltz*, Internationales Kaufrecht, 1. Aufl., § 5, Rn. 266.
[28] Vgl. OLG Celle, 24.5.1995, CISG-online 152; LG Ellwangen, 21.8.1995, CISG-online 279.
[29] So auch Art. 8:106 III PECL; *Herber/Czerwenka*, Art. 47, Rn. 4; *Karollus*, S. 139; *Piltz*, Internationales Kaufrecht, Rn. 5–266 f.; *Staudinger/Magnus*, Art. 47, Rn. 20; MünchKommHGB/*Benicke*, Art. 47, Rn. 7; MünchKomm/*P. Huber*, Art. 47, Rn. 13. *Friehe*, IHR 2010, 230, 235: *Friehe* scheint zu sagen, dass eine neue Frist gesetzt werden muss und nicht automatisch in Gang gesetzt wird. Anders *Honsell/Schnyder/Straub*, Art. 47, Rn. 24; anders auch BGer, 24.9.1990, BGE 116 II 436, 440 zum schweiz. Recht: Ist die Nachfrist objektiv zu kurz, muss der Verkäufer widersprechen und eine Verlängerung verlangen, ansonsten sie als genehmigt gilt. Erfolgt der Widerspruch und verspricht der Verkäufer innerhalb angemessener Frist zu erfüllen, setzt die zu kurze Frist den Lauf einer angemessenen Frist in Gang. Das CISG eröffnet dem erfüllungsbereiten Verkäufer im Übrigen auch die Möglichkeit, eine Gegenfrist gemäss Art. 48 II, III zu setzen, wenn ihm die Frist zu kurz erscheint, vgl. dazu *Honsell*, SJZ 1992, 345, 353; *Müller-Chen*, Art. 48 Rn. 22 ff.
[30] *Soergel/Lüderitz/Schüßler-Langeheine*, Art. 47, Rn. 3; a. A. *Honsell/Schnyder/Straub*, Art. 47, Rn. 25.
[31] Vgl. dazu auch *Widmer Lüchinger*, Art. 33 Rn. 14.
[32] Ebenso *Kimbel*, 18 J. L. & Com. (1999), 301, 326 ff.; *Herber/Czerwenka*, Art. 47, Rn. 5; *Honsell/Schnyder/Straub*, Art. 47, Rn. 14; *Piltz*, Internationales Kaufrecht, Rn. 5–266 (Frist kann vorzeitig gesetzt werden, fängt aber erst mit dem Liefertermin an zu laufen); a. A. MünchKommHGB/*Benicke*, Art. 47, Rn. 5; *Bridge*, Int'l Sale of Goods, Rn. 12.28; bei Lieferung auf Abruf kann die Nachfristsetzung mit dem Abruf der Leistung verbunden werden, *Honsell/Schnyder/Straub*, Art. 47, Rn. 14a mit Verweis auf OLG München, 19.10.2006, CISG-online 1394.

Nachfrist als einer „zusätzlichen" Frist („additional period of time", „délai supplémentaire") und anderseits aus Art. 45 I 1, wonach dem Käufer die Rechte gemäss Artt. 46–52 erst zustehen, wenn der Verkäufer eine seiner Pflichten, z. B. Lieferung bei Fälligkeit, nicht erfüllt. Die vorzeitige Nachfrist setzt auch keine „angemessene" Frist (vom Ablauf der Lieferfrist an gerechnet) in Gang. Selbstverständlich muss dagegen der Käufer, der vorzeitig Nachfrist gesetzt hat, gemäss Art. 47 II mindestens den Ablauf dieser Frist abwarten, ehe er weitere Schritte ergreifen kann.

b) Form und Übermittlungsrisiko. Die Nachfristsetzung ist an **keine Form** gebunden.[33] Sie kann auch mündlich erfolgen, was allerdings aus Beweisgründen nicht ratsam ist. Das Übermittlungsrisiko für die Mitteilung trägt unter den Voraussetzungen von Art. 27 der Verkäufer;[34] die Wirkungen der Nachfrist setzen daher **keinen Zugang** beim Verkäufer voraus.[35] Dies gilt nicht für die Bindung des Käufers gemäss Art. 47 II, da der Vertrauenstatbestand, den Art. 47 II schützen will, vor Zugang nicht entstanden ist.[36]   12

4. Beweislast

Der **Käufer,** der sich auf die Nachfristsetzung beruft, um eine von ihm erklärte Vertragsaufhebung zu rechtfertigen (Art. 49 I lit. b), Art. 49 II lit. b) ii)), muss im Streitfall gemäss Art. 27 nur die **Absendung** mit **geeigneten Mitteln,** nicht den Zugang beweisen.[37] Der **Verkäufer,** der sich auf die Bindungswirkung des Art. 47 II beruft, muss im Streitfall beweisen, dass ihm eine **Nachfristerklärung** des Käufers **zugegangen** ist, an die der Käufer sich nicht gehalten hat.[38]   13

III. Bindung des Käufers (Abs. 2)

1. Keine Ausübung von Rechtsbehelfen vor Ablauf der Frist

Nach Abs. 2 S. 1 kann der Käufer, der dem Verkäufer für die Erfüllung Nachfrist gesetzt hat, vor Ablauf der Nachfrist „keinen Rechtsbehelf wegen Vertragsverletzung" ausüben. Ausgeschlossen sind also die Rechtsbehelfe, die in Art. 45 I genannt sind. Das Recht, die **Vertragsaufhebung** zu erklären und **Schadenersatz wegen Nichterfüllung** zu verlangen, ist während der Nachfrist auch dann suspendiert, wenn die Vertragsverletzung wesentlich ist. Ist die gelieferte Ware mangelhaft und setzt der Käufer Nachfrist für Ersatzlieferung oder Nachbesserung, so ist während der Nachfrist nicht nur das Recht zur Vertragsaufhebung, sondern auch das Recht zur **Minderung** (Art. 50) ausgeschlossen. Der Käufer, der Nachfrist für eine Nachbesserung setzt, darf nicht vor Fristablauf **den Mangel selbst beseitigen** und dem Verkäufer die **Kosten als Schadenersatz** gemäss Art. 45 I lit. b) in Rechnung stellen, sondern er muss die Kosten der voreiligen Selbsthilfe selbst tragen. Ebenso ist, solange die Nachfrist für die Nachbesserung läuft, der Anspruch auf **Ersatzlieferung** suspendiert, auch wenn er an sich nach Art. 46 II   14

---

[33] *Enderlein/Maskow/Strohbach,* Art. 47, Anm. 4.; *Piltz,* Internationales Kaufrecht, Rn. 5–265; *Staudinger/Magnus,* Art. 47, Rn. 15; vgl. auch O. R., S. 338, Nr. 70, 72.
[34] Vgl. *Schroeter,* Art. 27 Rn. 4; sowie *Enderlein/Maskow/Strohbach,* Art. 47, Anm. 4.; *Herber/Czerwenka,* Art. 47, Rn. 3; *Soergel/Lüderitz/Schüßler-Langeheine,* Art. 47, Rn. 4; *Neumayer/Ming,* Art. 47, Anm. 1.; *Karollus,* S. 139; *Piltz,* Internationales Kaufrecht, Rn. 5–265; *Staudinger/Magnus,* Art. 47, Rn. 15; *Kimbel,* 18 J. L. & Com. (1999), 301, 312 ff.
[35] Diese Konsequenz hat auf der Wiener Konferenz zu einer ausgedehnten Diskussion und zum Vorschlag geführt, eine abweichende Sonderregel einzuführen. Vgl. den britischen Antrag, O. R., S. 113, Art. 43, Nr. 3 II und den Diskussionsbericht, O. R., S. 337 f., Nr. 61–74, S. 339 ff., Nr. 1–32. Der Vorschlag verfiel der Ablehnung, vgl. O. R., S. 340, Nr. 17 f., 31 f.; a. A. (Wirksamkeit erst mit Zugang) *Bianca/Bonell/Will,* Anm. 2.1.3.1.; *Fagan,* J. Small & Emerg. Bus. L. (1998), 317, 343.
[36] Ebenso *Staudinger/Magnus,* Art. 47, Rn. 15; teilweise abweichend *Karollus,* S. 139, der neben dem tatsächlichen auch den hypothetischen Zugang erfassen will.
[37] *Baumgärtel/Laumen/Hepting,* Art. 47, Rn. 2; vgl. auch *Piltz,* Internationales Kaufrecht, Rn. 5–91, 5–265.
[38] So auch *Baumgärtel/Laumen/Hepting,* Art. 47, Rn. 2.

begründet wäre.[39] Auch der Rechtsbehelf des **Erfüllungsanspruchs** selbst ist, solange für die Erfüllung Nachfrist gesetzt ist, suspendiert.[40] Eine vor Fristablauf erhobene Klage auf Erfüllung wäre, solange die Nachfrist nicht abgelaufen ist, als zurzeit unbegründet abzuweisen, nicht anders, als eine vor Fälligkeit erhobene Erfüllungsklage.

15 Eine besondere Lage besteht, wenn der Verkäufer vor Ablauf der Nachfrist eine **erneute Vertragsverletzung** begeht, die die sofortige Vertragsaufhebung rechtfertigt. Der Käufer setzt dem Verkäufer z. B. Nachfrist für die Lieferung oder für eine Ersatzlieferung, und die vor Ablauf der Frist gelieferte Ware weist einen erheblichen Mangel auf, der als „wesentliche Vertragsverletzung" anzusehen ist. In einem solchen Fall muss der Käufer, wie sich von selbst versteht, nicht den Ablauf der restlichen Nachfrist abwarten, ehe er die Vertragsaufhebung erklären darf.[41]

2. Ablauf und Wahrung der Frist

16 Die Frist läuft an dem Tag ab, der sich aus der Erklärung des Käufers ergibt. Spätestens an diesem Tag muss der Verkäufer die Leistung erbracht haben, sonst gewinnt der Käufer die Freiheit des Handelns zurück. Was zu geschehen hat, um die Frist zu wahren, ergibt sich aus dem Inhalt der Pflicht, deren Erfüllung der Käufer verlangt. Hat der Käufer Nachfrist für die Lieferung gesetzt, muss der Verkäufer die Ware bis zum Fristablauf entweder absenden oder am Erfüllungsort zur Verfügung des Käufers stellen; massgebend ist Art. 31. Verlangt der Käufer unter Nachfristsetzung Nachbesserung, muss die Reparatur bis zum Fristablauf abgeschlossen sein und die reparierte Ware am Erfüllungsort zur Verfügung des Käufers stehen.

3. Erfüllungsverweigerung

17 Die Bindung des Käufers endet schon **vor Ablauf der Nachfrist,** sobald ihm eine Mitteilung des Verkäufers zugeht, durch die dieser erklärt, dass er die Pflicht nicht innerhalb der Frist erfüllen werde (Abs. 2 S. 1 a. E.).[42] Gleichgültig ist, ob der Verkäufer erklärt, dass er zur Erfüllung überhaupt nicht bereit oder imstande sei, oder dass er nur innerhalb der Frist nicht in der Lage sei, die Leistung zu bewirken.[43] Nennt der Verkäufer eine längere Frist, innerhalb derer er zur Erfüllung imstande oder bereit sei, so gilt für diese Gegenfrist Art. 48 II, III.[44] Eine Erfüllungsverweigerung wird erst mit Zugang beim Käufer wirksam und kann vor diesem Zeitpunkt demzufolge widerrufen werden.[45]

4. Recht auf Schadenersatz

18 a) **Verzögerungsschaden.** Abs. 2 S. 2 stellt klar, dass der Anspruch des Käufers auf Ersatz des Verzögerungsschadens gemäss Art. 45 I lit. b) durch die Suspensivwirkung der

---

[39] *Enderlein/Maskow/Strohbach*, Art. 47, Anm. 5. Selbstverständlich tritt die Bindung nur ein, wenn der Käufer tatsächlich Nachfrist gesetzt hat. Unrichtig daher OLG Düsseldorf, 10.2.1994, CISG-online 115 = NJW-RR 1994, 506. Art. 47 II ordnet nicht an, dass der Käufer zunächst Nachfrist setzen muss, ehe er irgendeinen Rechtsbehelf geltend machen kann; vgl. auch *Honsell/Schnyder/Straub*, Art. 47, Rn. 4.
[40] Ebenso *Hager/Maultzsch*, 5. Aufl. Art. 63 Rn. 4; *Valero Marketing & Supply Company v. Greeni Trading Oy*, U. S. Ct. App. (3rd Cir.), 19.7.2007, CISG-online 1510.
[41] Vgl. *Leser*, Vertragsaufhebung und Rückabwicklung, S. 236 mit Fn. 51; *Enderlein/Maskow/Strohbach*, Art. 47, Anm. 5.; *Neumayer/Ming*, Art. 47, Anm. 2. mit Fn. 8; a. A. MünchKommHGB/*Benicke*, Art. 47, Rn. 10.
[42] Es reicht, wenn die Mitteilung auf elektronischem Weg erfolgt, CISG-AC, Op. 1 *(Chr. Ramberg)*, Comment 47.1.
[43] Vgl. OLG Düsseldorf, 10.2.1994, CISG-online 115: Die Erklärung „zurzeit nicht liefern zu können" stellt noch keine Erfüllungsverweigerung dar, da es an der Endgültigkeit fehlt. Macht der Verkäufer jedoch die Erfüllung von der Begleichung einer Forderung aus einer früheren Lieferung abhängig, liegt eine Erfüllungsverweigerung vor, vgl. dazu Schiedsgericht der Handelskammer Hamburg, 21.3.1996, CISG-online 187.
[44] Vgl. Art. 48 Rn. 22 ff.
[45] Vgl. Art. 49 Rn. 41, 46.

Nachfrist gemäss Satz 1 nicht beseitigt wird. Damit ist zugleich klargestellt, dass die Nachfristsetzung im Zweifel nicht den Charakter eines Stundungsangebots hat.

b) Sonstige Schäden. Ist dem Käufer schon vor Nachfristsetzung ein Schaden entstanden, der durch die nachträgliche Erfüllung nicht mehr ausgeglichen werden kann, so verliert er diesen Anspruch nicht dadurch, dass er dem Verkäufer für die Erfüllung Nachfrist setzt.[46] 19

c) Vertragsstrafen. Nicht geregelt ist die Frage, ob der Käufer für die Zeit, während derer die Nachfrist läuft, die Zahlung einer Vertragsstrafe verlangen kann, die er sich für den Fall verspäteter Erfüllung hat versprechen lassen. Da aber Abs. 2 S. 2 von dem Grundgedanken ausgeht, dass die Nachfristsetzung im Zweifel gerade **nicht** als Stundungsangebot zu verstehen ist, muss folgerichtig auch der Anspruch auf Vertragsstrafe bestehen bleiben.[47] 20

5. Bindung des Käufers bei unbefristeter Mahnung

Zur Frage, ob der Käufer auch dann, wenn er wegen der Erfüllung mahnt, ohne Nachfrist zu setzen, für eine gewisse Zeit an den Rechtsbehelf des Erfüllungsanspruchs gebunden ist, vgl. *Müller-Chen,* Art. 45 Rn. 14 f.[48] 21

---

[46] Vgl. *Herber/Czerwenka,* Art. 47, Rn. 8.
[47] Vgl. auch *Bejcek/Fritzsche,* Vertragsstrafe, WiRO 1994, 111, 114; *Honsell/Schnyder/Straub,* Art. 47, Rn. 29; *Staudinger/Magnus,* Art. 47, Rn. 23; MünchKomm/P. *Huber,* Art. 47, Rn. 25.
[48] In den Beratungen war ohne Erfolg angeregt worden, eine ausdrückliche Regelung dieses Inhalts zu treffen. Vgl. O. R., S. 112, Art. 42, Nr. 3 X (Antrag Japans). Der Antrag wurde zurückgezogen, da die allgemeine Ansicht dahin ging, die Regeln der Artt. 48 II und 7 I (Prinzip von Treu und Glauben) trügen dem Fall hinreichend Rechnung.

Art. 48 [Recht des Verkäufers zur Nacherfüllung]

(1) Vorbehaltlich des Artikels 49 kann der Verkäufer einen Mangel in der Erfüllung seiner Pflichten auch nach dem Liefertermin auf eigene Kosten beheben, wenn dies keine unzumutbare Verzögerung nach sich zieht und dem Käufer weder unzumutbare Unannehmlichkeiten noch Ungewißheit über die Erstattung seiner Auslagen durch den Verkäufer verursacht. Der Käufer behält jedoch das Recht, Schadensersatz nach diesem Übereinkommen zu verlangen.

(2) Fordert der Verkäufer den Käufer auf, ihm mitzuteilen, ob er die Erfüllung annehmen will, und entspricht der Käufer der Aufforderung nicht innerhalb einer angemessenen Frist, so kann der Verkäufer innerhalb der in seiner Aufforderung angegebenen Frist erfüllen. Der Käufer kann vor Ablauf dieser Frist keinen Rechtsbehelf ausüben, der mit der Erfüllung durch den Verkäufer unvereinbar ist.

(3) Zeigt der Verkäufer dem Käufer an, daß er innerhalb einer bestimmten Frist erfüllen wird, so wird vermutet, daß die Anzeige eine Aufforderung an den Käufer nach Absatz 2 enthält, seine Entscheidung mitzuteilen.

(4) Eine Aufforderung oder Anzeige des Verkäufers nach Absatz 2 oder 3 ist nur wirksam, wenn der Käufer sie erhalten hat.

Art. 48

(1) Subject to article 49, the seller may, even after the date for delivery, remedy at his own expense any failure to perform his obligations, if he can do so without unreasonable delay and without causing the buyer unreasonable inconvenience or uncerainty of reimbursement by the seller of expenses advanced by the buyer. However, the buyer retains any right to claim damages as provided for in this Convention.

(2) If the seller requests the buyer to make known whether he will accept performance and the buyer does not comply with the request within a reasonable time, the seller may perform within the time indicated in his request. The buyer may not, during that period of time, resort to any remedy which is inconsistent with performance by the seller.

(3) A notice by the seller that he will perform within a specified period of time is assumed to include a request, under the preceding paragraph, that the buyer make known his decision.

(4) A request or notice by the seller under paragraph (2) or (3) of this article is not effective unless received by the buyer.

Art. 48

1) Sous réserve de l'article 49, le vendeur peut, même après la date de la livraison, réparer à ses frais tout manquement à ses obligations, à condition que cela n'entraîne pas un retard déraisonnable et ne cause à l'acheteur ni inconvénients déraisonnables ni incertitude quant au remboursement par le vendeur des frais faits par l'acheteur. Toutefois, l'acheteur conserve le droit de demander des dommages-intérêts conformément à la présente Convention.

2) Si le vendeur demande à l'acheteur de lui faire savoir s'il accepte l'exécution et si l'acheteur ne lui répond pas dans un délai raisonnable, le vendeur peut exécuter ses obligations dans le délai qu'il a indiqué dans sa demande. L'acheteur ne peut, avant l'expiration de ce délai, se prévaloir d'un moyen incompatible avec l'exécution par le vendeur de ses obligations.

3) Lorsque le vendeur notifie à l'acheteur son intention d'exécuter ses obligations dans un délai déterminé, il est présumé demander à l'acheteur de lui faire connaître sa décision conformément au paragraphe précédent.

4) Une demande ou une notification faite par le vendeur en vertu des paragraphes 2 ou 3 du présent article n'a d'effet que si elle est reçue par l'acheteur.

Übersicht

	Rn.
I. Gegenstand und Grundgedanke der Regelung	1
II. Recht zur Behebung des Mangels in der Erfüllung (Abs. 1 S. 1)	3
1. Mangel in der Erfüllung	3

2. Behebung des Mangels 5
   a) Allgemeines 5
   b) Modalitäten 6
3. Kosten 8
4. Zumutbarkeit 9
   a) Allgemeines 9
   b) Kriterien 10
   c) Beweislast 13
5. Vorbehalt der Vertragsaufhebung 14
   a) Zweck des Vorbehalts 14
   b) Wesentlichkeit der Vertragsverletzung 15
   c) Aufhebungslage entscheidet über Vorrang 17
6. Verhältnis zu anderen Rechtsbehelfen 18
   a) Vertragsaufhebung 18
   b) Minderung 19
   c) Ersatzlieferung/Nachbesserung 20
   d) Schadenersatz 21
7. Rechtsfolgen 22
III. Recht zur Behebung des Mangels auf Grund unwidersprochener Anzeige der Erfüllungsbereitschaft (Abs. 2–4) 24
1. Aufforderung zur Erklärung der Annahmebereitschaft mit Fristsetzung (Abs. 2) 24
   a) Zweck 24
   b) Voraussetzungen 25
   c) Rechtsfolgen 27
2. Anzeige der Erfüllungsbereitschaft mit Fristsetzung ohne Aufforderung zur Erklärung (Abs. 3) 28
3. Zugangserfordernis (Abs. 4) 29
4. Kreuzende Erklärungen des Verkäufers 30
IV. Abweichende Vereinbarungen 31

Vorläufer und **Entwürfe:** EKG Artt. 43, 44 I; Genfer E 1976 Art. 29; Wiener E 1977 Art. 30; New Yorker E 1978 Art. 44.

I. Gegenstand und Grundgedanke der Regelung

Art. 48 I stellt den Grundsatz auf, dass der Verkäufer vorbehaltlich Art. 49[1] im Allgemeinen auch noch **nach Verstreichen des Liefertermins** berechtigt ist, den **Vertrag zu erfüllen** („right to cure", „Recht zur zweiten Andienung") und dadurch die **Vertragsverletzung zu beheben**.[2] Das praktische Hauptgewicht der Bestimmung liegt im Fall der **Lieferung vertragswidriger Ware**. Zwar hat der Verkäufer auch im Fall der Überschreitung des Liefertermins ein Nacherfüllungsrecht in Gestalt der Lieferung der Ware.[3] Da jedoch Nichtlieferung nur in besonders schwerwiegenden Ausnahmefällen schon als solche die Vertragsaufhebung rechtfertigt, folgt die Pflicht des Käufers, die verspätet gelieferte Ware abzunehmen, schon aus Artt. 53, 60.

1

---

[1] Vgl. dazu unten Rn. 14 ff.
[2] Das Recht des Verkäufers, den Sachmangel auch noch nach dem Liefertermin zu beheben, ist einerseits der Praxis der allgemeinen Geschäfts- und Lieferungsbedingungen wohlvertraut; andererseits kennen auch manche nationale Rechte das Nacherfüllungsrecht, vgl. *Treitel*, Remedies for Breach, Anm. 276.; im deutschen Kaufrecht stehen dem Käufer die Rechtsbehelfe des Rücktritts, der Minderung und des Schadenersatzes wegen Nichterfüllung erst nach fruchtlosem Verstreichen einer (vom Käufer gesetzten) Nachfrist zur Verfügung, vgl. dazu §§ 281 I, 323 I, 441 BGB; § 36 I Köpl; rechtsvergleichend *Sivesand*, Buyer's Remedies, S. 106 ff.; *Woschnagg*, RIW 1992, 117, 119; § 2–508 UCC (vgl. dazu *Fagan*, J. Small & Emerg. Bus. L. (1998), 317, 349 ff.; *Schneider*, 7 Ariz. J. Int'l & Comp. L. (1989), 69, 98 ff.; *Gillette/Walt*, S. 224 ff.; *Bridge*, FS Schwenzer, S. 221, 222 ff.; Art. 8:104 PECL; 7.1.4 PICC.
[3] *Schneider*, 7 Ariz. J. Int'l & Comp. L. (1989), 69, 86.

2 Die Regel des Art. 48 I ist für den Verkäufer mit gewissen **Unsicherheiten** belastet. Ausser im unproblematischen Fall, in dem der Käufer von sich aus zugleich mit der Mängelrüge Nachbesserung oder Ersatzlieferung verlangt, weiss der Verkäufer zunächst nicht, ob der Käufer zur Annahme der nachträglichen Erfüllung bereit ist, ob er den Vertrag aufheben will, oder sich darauf beruft, dass die Beseitigung des Mangels für ihn i. S. d. Art. 48 I „unzumutbar" sei. Art. 48 II bis IV hat daher Regeln aufgestellt, die es dem Verkäufer erleichtern sollen, diese Ungewissheit zu beseitigen. Der Grundgedanke ist, dass der Käufer einem **Angebot des Verkäufers,** den Mangel innerhalb einer bestimmten Frist zu beseitigen, **unverzüglich widersprechen** muss, wenn er es zurückweisen will, und dass daher Schweigen auf ein solches Angebot als Zustimmung gilt. Reden muss und kann der Käufer aber nur, wenn ihm das Angebot des Verkäufers zugegangen ist: deshalb weist Abs. 4 das Risiko, dass das Angebot unterwegs verloren geht, dem Verkäufer zu.

II. Recht zur Behebung des Mangels in der Erfüllung (Abs. 1 S. 1)

1. Mangel in der Erfüllung

3 Der in Abs. 1 vorausgesetzte Mangel in der Erfüllung ist bei **jeder Art** der Vertragsverletzung gegeben. Er umfasst die Lieferung vertragswidriger oder rechtsmangelbelasteter Ware, die verspätete Lieferung,[4] die Übergabe vertragswidriger Dokumente, die teilweise Lieferung gemäss Art. 51 oder die Verletzung sonstiger vereinbarter Pflichten (Stellung einer Bankgarantie, Montage etc.).[5]

4 Das Recht des Verkäufers zur Nacherfüllung besteht gemäss Art. 48 erst nach Ablauf des Liefertermins. Vor diesem Zeitpunkt regeln Artt. 34, 37 die Behebung des Mangels.[6] Hat der Verkäufer bis zu einem bestimmten Termin eine **Bankgarantie** für rechtzeitige und mangelfreie Lieferung zu stellen, und versäumt er diesen Termin, oder entspricht die Bankgarantie inhaltlich nicht den Bestimmungen des Kaufvertrags, tritt für die Ausübung des Nacherfüllungsrechts an die Stelle des Liefertermins derjenige Termin, an dem die betreffende Pflicht zu erfüllen war. Dasselbe gilt z. B. für den Fall, dass die zugesagte **Montage** nicht frist- oder fachgerecht durchgeführt wird, oder dass der für die Übergabe von **Dokumenten** festgesetzte Termin verstrichen ist und diese unvollständig oder fehlerhaft sind. In all diesen Fällen richtet sich das Nacherfüllungsrecht nach Art. 48 (und nicht nach Artt. 34, 37), wenn der Montage- oder Übergabetermin verstrichen ist.

2. Behebung des Mangels

5 a) **Allgemeines.** In welcher Form der Verkäufer den Mangel zu beheben hat, ergibt sich aus dem Inhalt der verletzten Pflicht: So können z. B. fehlende Teile oder Fehlmengen nachgeliefert, für mangelhafte Ware kann beim Gattungskauf Ersatz geliefert, oder der Mangel kann durch Reparatur behoben werden (vgl. auch Art. 37). Eine fehlerhafte Bankgarantie kann gegen eine neue Garantie ausgetauscht werden, Montagefehler sind durch Nachbesserung zu beheben, fehlerhafte Dokumente können durch fehlerfreie ersetzt werden, etc. Vorausgesetzt ist immer, dass der Mangel sich seiner Natur nach beheben lässt. Ist dies unmöglich,[7] ist das Recht des Verkäufers zur Mängelbeseitigung gegenstandslos. Beim Spezieskauf ist der Verkäufer berechtigt, einen nicht behebbaren Mangel der verkauften

---

[4] Vgl. dazu hinten die Einschränkung in Rn. 9 ff.; *Staudinger/Magnus,* Art. 48, Rn. 9.

[5] *Herber/Czerwenka,* Art. 48, Rn. 2; *Soergel/Lüderitz/Schüßler-Langeheine,* Art. 48, Rn. 2.

[6] Art. 37 setzt weder eine unzumutbare Verzögerung voraus, noch enthält er einen Vorbehalt zugunsten von Art. 49, vgl. *Widmer Lüchinger,* Art. 34 Rn. 6 und *Schwenzer,* Art. 37 Rn. 6; *Treitel,* Remedies for Breach, Anm. 276.; § 2–508 (1) UCC: Vgl. dazu *Traynor v. Walters,* U. S. Dist. Ct. (M. D. Pa.), 15.5.1972, 10 UCC Rep. 967; *Allied Semi-Conductors international Limited v. Pulsar Components International, Inc.,* U. S. Dist. Ct. (E. D. N. Y.), 17.12.1993, 842 F. Supp. 653; *Schneider,* 7 Ariz. J. Int'l & Comp. L. (1989), 69, 75 ff.; zum schwedischen Kaufrecht s. *Woschnagg,* RIW 1992, 117, 119 f.

[7] Vgl. zur Unmöglichkeit Art. 46 Rn. 12.

Sache durch Lieferung einer fehlerfreien Sache zu beheben, wenn es sich um eine Sache handelt, die einer vertretbaren Sache wirtschaftlich entspricht und das Leistungsinteresse des Käufers zufriedenstellt.[8]

b) Modalitäten. Entscheidend ist, dass der Mangel vollständig behoben wird. Wie der Verkäufer diesen Erfolg erreicht, ist seine Sache.[9] Lässt sich also ein Sachmangel sowohl durch Ersatzlieferung als auch durch Nachbesserung beseitigen, hat der Verkäufer unter der Voraussetzung der Zumutbarkeit[10] für den Käufer ein **Wahlrecht**. Es ist ihm auch gestattet, wiederum unter dem Vorbehalt der Zumutbarkeit, **mehrere Nacherfüllungsversuche** zu unternehmen, die auch unterschiedlicher Art sein dürfen (z. B. zunächst Nachbesserung, dann Ersatzlieferung).[11] 6

Der **Ort für die nachträgliche Erfüllung** ist derselbe, wie der Ort für die Erfüllung der ursprünglichen Pflicht. Eine Besonderheit, die in der Natur der Sache liegt, gilt dann, wenn ein Mangel der gelieferten Sache durch Nachbesserung behoben werden soll. Grundsätzlich muss eine solche Nachbesserung dort vorgenommen werden, wo die Sache sich dem Vertrag gemäss befindet, also regelmässig beim Käufer. Ist das nicht möglich oder mit unangemessenem Aufwand verbunden, so kann der Verkäufer die Nachbesserung aber auch auf eigene Kosten bei sich selbst oder an einem dritten Ort (z. B. einer Vertragswerkstatt) durchführen lassen.[12] 7

3. Kosten

Der Verkäufer hat den Mangel der Erfüllung „auf eigene Kosten" zu beheben. Das heisst zweierlei. Erstens darf der Verkäufer zusätzliche Aufwendungen, die ihm selbst durch die nachträgliche Erfüllung entstehen, dem Käufer nicht in Rechnung stellen, und er darf die Mängelbeseitigung nicht davon abhängig machen, dass der Käufer sich bereit erklärt, solche Kosten zu übernehmen. Zweitens muss der Verkäufer dem Käufer solche Kosten erstatten, die diesem z. B. durch die Rücksendung der Ware oder durch die Beseitigung des Mangels entstehen,[13] z. B. durch eine zeitweilige Betriebsunterbrechung, die zum Zweck der Reparatur erforderlich ist, oder die Kosten für ein Ersatzgerät.[14] Musste der Käufer erhebliche Kosten bevorschussen, ist das Nacherfüllungsrecht des Verkäufers von der Leistung einer Sicherheit für diese Kosten abhängig zu machen.[15] Das gilt unabhängig davon, ob (wie meist in solchen Fällen) für den Käufer zugleich die Voraussetzungen eines Schadenersatzanspruchs (Artt. 45 I lit. b), 48 I 2, 74 S. 2, 79) gegeben sind. 8

4. Zumutbarkeit

a) Allgemeines. Der Verkäufer darf gemäss Art. 48 I nur nachbessern, wenn dies für den Käufer nicht unzumutbar ist in zeitlicher Hinsicht („unzumutbare Verzögerung"), bei der Durchführung („unzumutbare Unannehmlichkeiten") und bei der Kostentragung („Ungewissheit über die Erstattung seiner Auslagen").[16] Ob die Zumutbarkeitsschwelle überschrit- 9

---

[8] Vgl. Art. 46 Rn. 18; a. A. *U. Huber*, 3. Aufl., Rn. 8.
[9] *Herber/Czerwenka*, Art. 48, Rn. 2; *Karollus*, S. 138; *Audit*, Vente internationale, Anm. 133.; *Bianca/Bonell/ Will*, Art. 48, Anm. 3.1.1., 3.1.2.; vgl. auch *Müller-Chen*, Art. 46 Rn. 35, 44; *Staudinger/Magnus*, Art. 48, Rn. 11; *Honsell/Schnyder/Straub*, Art. 48, Rn. 10. Auf der Wiener Konferenz hatten die USA beantragt, in Art. 48 I einen Zusatz aufzunehmen, der das Wahlrecht klarstellen sollte, vgl. O. R., S. 114 f., Art. 44, Nr. 3 V, S. 352, Nr. 31–34. Der Antrag wurde mit 10:10 Stimmen abgelehnt. Das Wahlrecht des Verkäufers versteht sich aber auch ohnedies von selbst.
[10] Vgl. dazu hinten Rn. 9 ff.
[11] *Herber/Czerwenka*, Art. 48, Rn. 2; *Honsell/Schnyder/Straub*, Art. 48, Rn. 12.
[12] Ausnahmen können durch die Verkehrssitte oder Treu und Glauben begründet sein, vgl. dazu *Müller-Chen*, Art. 46 Rn. 45; *Achilles*, Art. 48 Rn. 3.
[13] Vgl. rechtsvergleichend *Giuliano*, 18 Fla. J. Int'l L. (2006), 331, 345 ff. OLG Hamm, 9.6.1995, CISG-online 146 = NJW-RR 1996, 179, 180 = IPRax 1996, 269, 270; so nunmehr auch § 2–508 UCC 2003.
[14] Vgl. auch *Honsell/Schnyder/Straub*, Art. 48, Rn. 27.
[15] *U. Huber*, 3. Aufl., Rn. 15; *Brunner*, Art. 48, Rn. 6.
[16] Das Nachbesserungsrecht des Käufers setzt jedoch keine Zustimmung des Käufers voraus, unrichtig daher ICC, 7531/1994, CISG-online 565; s. auch *Gillette/Walt*, S. 233.

Art. 48 10–13   Teil III. Kapitel II. Pflichten des Verkäufers. Abschnitt III

ten ist, kann nicht allgemein, sondern nur auf Grund der Umstände des Einzelfalls entschieden werden.[17] Festhalten lässt sich jedenfalls, dass Unzumutbarkeit nicht erst dann eintritt, wenn alle mit der Nachbesserung verbundenen Umstände zu einer wesentlichen Vertragsverletzung führen würden.[18] Der englische und französische Wortlaut, der von „Unangemessenheit" („unreasonable"/„déraisonnable") spricht, zeigt, dass die Belastungen für den Käufer nicht geradezu unerträglich sein müssen, solange sie nur nicht bloss geringfügig sind.[19] Massgeblich ist die **objektivierte Käuferperspektive** und nicht die Einschätzungen des Verkäufers.[20]

10   b) **Kriterien.** Der Verkäufer muss die Erfüllung **ohne unzumutbare Verzögerung** bewirken, d. h. innerhalb einer „angemessenen" Frist nach dem Massstab, wie ihn Art. 47 auch für die Nachfrist verwendet.[21] Beabsichtigt der Verkäufer nachzubessern, kann ihn der Käufer durch Ansetzung einer im konkreten Fall angemessenen Frist in Zugzwang bringen. Denn behebt der Verkäufer den Mangel nicht innerhalb dieser Zeit, wird dem Käufer der Nachweis der Unzumutbarkeit leichter gelingen.

11   Des Weiteren darf die Nacherfüllung dem Käufer **keine „unzumutbaren Unannehmlichkeiten"** („unreasonable inconvenience"/„inconvénients déraisonnables") verursachen (so auch Art. 37). Derartige gravierende Belastungen können z. B. sein: Betriebsunterbrechungen oder -störungen beim Käufer auf Grund von Reparaturen,[22] drohende Schadenersatzklagen von Abnehmern des Käufers[23] oder offensichtlich nicht fachmännisches Vorgehen des Verkäufers, welches zu mehreren Nacherfüllungsversuchen führt.[24] Ob Letztere zumutbar sind, hängt auch von der vom Verkäufer in Anspruch genommenen Frist ab.

12   Schliesslich setzt das Recht des Verkäufers zur nachträglichen Erfüllung voraus, dass für den Käufer **keine „Ungewissheit über die Erstattung seiner Auslagen durch den Verkäufer"** entsteht.[25] Da der Verkäufer die Kosten der Ersatzlieferung oder Nachbesserung ohnehin selbst zu tragen hat, können dem Käufer „Auslagen" allerdings nur in Ausnahmefällen entstehen. Zu denken ist etwa an die Kosten einer vom Käufer zu veranlassenden Rücksendung der Ware, einer aus sonstigen Gründen erforderlichen Mitwirkung bei der Mängelbeseitigung,[26] an die Kosten einer Betriebsunterbrechung,[27] oder an den Fall, in dem der Verkäufer die Nacherfüllung nur gegen Kostenerstattung anbietet.[28] Bestehen begründete Zweifel an der Bereitschaft oder Fähigkeit des Verkäufers, die Kosten zu erstatten, und handelt es sich um einigermassen ins Gewicht fallende Beträge, so ist der Verkäufer zur nachträglichen Erfüllung nur gegen Sicherheitsleistung bzw. Zusicherung der Kostenübernahme berechtigt.[29]

13   c) **Beweislast.** Die Beweislast für die Unzumutbarkeit der Nachbesserung trifft den Käufer, der das Angebot der nachträglichen Erfüllung zurückweisen will.[30] Denn das Recht

---

[17] *Bianca/Bonell/Will*, Art. 48, Anm. 2.1.1.1.2.
[18] So auch *Staudinger/Magnus*, Art. 48, Rn. 14; *Soergel/Lüderitz/Schüßler-Langeheine*, Art. 48, Rn. 7; a. A. *Enderlein/Maskow/Strohbach*, Art. 48, Anm. 5.
[19] So zu Recht *Honsell/Schnyder/Straub*, Art. 48, Rn. 21.
[20] *Staudinger/Magnus*, Art. 48, Rn. 14; *Honsell/Schnyder/Straub*, Art. 48, Rn. 20.
[21] Vgl. Art. 47 Rn. 6; *Soergel/Lüderitz/Schüßler-Langeheine*, Art. 48, Rn. 7; *Friehe*, IHR 2011, 16, 37.
[22] Vgl. *Soergel/Lüderitz/Schüßler-Langeheine*, Art. 48, Rn. 5; *Honsell/Schnyder/Straub*, Art. 48, Rn. 25.
[23] *Soergel/Lüderitz/Schüßler-Langeheine*, Art. 48, Rn. 7; AG München, 23.6.1995, CISG-online 368.
[24] A. A. *U. Huber*, 3. Aufl., Rn. 14; wie hier: *Audit, Vente internationale*, Anm. 132.; *Achilles*, Art. 48, Rn. 4; *Honsell/Schnyder/Straub*, Art. 48, Rn. 25; *MünchKommHGB/Benicke*, Art. 48, Rn. 6.
[25] Entgegen *U. Huber*, 3. Aufl., Rn. 15 muss m. E. die Ungewissheit nicht unzumutbar sein, vgl. insbes. den frz. Wortlaut; s. auch *T. & S. Brass & Bronze Works, Inc. v. Pic-Air, Inc.*, U. S. Ct. App. (4th Cir.), 12.5.1986, 1 UCC Rep. Serv. 2d 433.
[26] Vgl. *Audit, Vente internationale*, Anm. 132.
[27] Vgl. vorne Rn. 11.
[28] Auch dieser Fall der Erfüllungsverweigerung (s. Art. 47 Rn. 17) führt zur Unzumutbarkeit für den Käufer.
[29] Vgl. auch *Herber/Czerwenka*, Art. 48, Rn. 3; *Honsell/Schnyder/Straub*, Art. 48, Rn. 26; *Staudinger/Magnus*, Art. 48, Rn. 16.
[30] Ebenso *Baumgärtel/Laumen/Hepting*, Art. 48, Rn. 4 ff. mit eingehender Begründung; *Achilles*, Art. 48, Rn. 10.

des Verkäufers zur nachträglichen Erfüllung ist die Regel, Unzumutbarkeit die Ausnahme, die derjenige beweisen muss, der sich darauf beruft.[31] Der Verkäufer ist beweispflichtig für die Tauglichkeit der beabsichtigten Nacherfüllung.[32]

5. Vorbehalt der Vertragsaufhebung

a) Zweck des Vorbehalts. Gemäss Art. 48 I steht dem Verkäufer das Recht zur nach- **14** träglichen Erfüllung nur „vorbehaltlich des Art. 49" zu. Damit wird dem Recht des Käufers zur **Vertragsaufhebung der Vorrang** vor dem Nacherfüllungsrecht des Verkäufers eingeräumt. Liegt somit eine wesentliche Vertragsverletzung nach Art. 49 I lit. a) vor oder ist die vom Käufer gesetzte Nachfrist gemäss Art. 49 I lit. b) fruchtlos verstrichen, kann der Verkäufer nicht unter Berufung auf Art. 48 I eine zusätzliche Frist zur Nacherfüllung beanspruchen. Darüber besteht soweit ersichtlich ein weitreichender internationaler Konsens.[33] Von Anfang an umstritten war jedoch, in welchem Umfang das Vertragsaufhebungsrecht das Recht zur Nacherfüllung verdrängen soll.[34] Es wurde insbesondere befürchtet, dass das Recht des Verkäufers zur Mängelbeseitigung obsolet werde, wenn das objektive Gewicht des Mangels bereits eine wesentliche Vertragsverletzung konstituiere, die zum Recht des Käufers führe, den Vertrag aufzuheben.[35] Im Kern geht es um die Frage, ob die Behebbarkeit des Mangels innerhalb einer angemessenen Frist die Wesentlichkeit der Vertragsverletzung ausschliesst bzw. suspendiert.[36]

b) Wesentlichkeit der Vertragsverletzung. Für die Wesentlichkeit der Vertragsverlet- **15** zung kommt es nicht alleine auf das **objektive Gewicht des Mangels** im Zeitpunkt der Lieferung an.[37] Entscheidend ist vielmehr eine Abwägung sämtlicher Gesichtspunkte des Einzelfalls, wozu auch die Fähigkeit und Bereitschaft des Verkäufers gehört, den Mangel vollständig ohne unzumutbare Verzögerung und unzumutbare Belastung des Käufers durch die dem Einzelfall angemessene Art der Nacherfüllung zu beheben.[38] Dem Käufer entgeht diesfalls nicht im Wesentlichen, „was er nach dem Vertrag hätte erwarten dürfen", womit keine wesentliche Vertragsverletzung gemäss Art. 25 vorliegt.[39] Das Recht des Käufers zur Vertragsaufhebung gemäss Art. 49 I lit. a) ist somit erst dann begründet, wenn der Verkäufer von seinem **Nacherfüllungsrecht** durch Ersatzlieferung oder Nachbesserung innerhalb angemessener Frist nach der Mängelanzeige **keinen Gebrauch** gemacht hat oder der Mangel unter den Voraussetzungen des Art. 48 I **nicht behoben wird** bzw. nicht behoben

---

[31] I. E. ebenso *Staudinger/Magnus*, Art. 48, Rn. 46; *Bamberger/Roth/Saenger*, Art. 48, Rn. 17; *Baumgärtel/Laumen/Hepting*, Art. 48, Rn. 4 ff.

[32] *Achilles*, Art. 48, Rn. 10; a. A. *Honsell/Schnyder/Straub*, Art. 48, Rn. 64.

[33] Vgl. *Schroeter*, Art. 25, Rn. 26 f.; grundlegend *Schlechtriem*, Einheitliches UN-Kaufrecht, S. 69; *Bridge*, Int'l Sale of Goods, Rn. 12.39; *Honnold/Flechtner*, Art. 25, Rn. 184, 296; *Ziegel*, Remedial Provisions, S. 9–23; *Enderlein/Maskow/Strohbach*, Art. 25, Anm. 3.4.; *Herber/Czerwenka*, Art. 48, Rn. 9; *Audit*, Vente internationale, Anm. 133.; *Heuzé*, Anm. 422.; *Piltz*, Internationales Kaufrecht, Rn. 4–63 f.; sowie – besonders eingehend – *Aicher*, S. 137 ff. und *Karollus*, ZIP 1993, 490 ff. I. E. wohl ebenso *Honsell/Schnyder/Straub*, Art. 48, Rn. 32. Aus der Rspr. vgl. OLG Koblenz, 31.1.1997, CISG-online 256. A. A., soweit ersichtlich, einzig *Bianca/Bonell/Will*, Art. 48, Anm. 1.3., 2.1.1.1.1., 3.2.2.

[34] Zum Meinungsstand vgl. *Magnus*, Aufhebungsrecht, S. 601 ff.

[35] Zur Entstehungsgeschichte vgl. ausführlich *U. Huber*, 1. Aufl., Rn. 5–9; *U. Huber*, 3. Aufl., Rn. 18; *Petrikic*, S. 80 ff.; *Honnold/Flechtner*, Art. 48, Rn. 296; *Schlechtriem*, Einheitliches UN-Kaufrecht, S. 69; *Magnus*, FS Schechtriem, S. 606 f.; O. R., S. 114 f., Art. 44, Nr. 3 I, III, IV und Nr. 6; S. 343, Nr. 66; S. 341 ff., Nr. 38, 39, 42–44, 48, 51, 52, 53, 56.

[36] Vgl. *Schroeter*, Art. 25 Rn. 26 f.

[37] So *Witz/Salger/Lorenz/Salger*, Art. 48, Rn. 2; *Petrikic*, S. 95 f.; *Honsell/Schnyder/Straub*, Art. 48, Rn. 32 f.; i. E. auch *Staudinger/Magnus*, Art. 48, Rn. 29 ff.; *Gutknecht*, S. 64; a. A. mit zum Teil unterschiedlicher Begründung: *Achilles*, Art. 48, Rn. 5; *Soergel/Lüderitz/Schüßler-Langeheine*, Art. 46, Rn. 3; *Welser*, S. 125; *von Hoffmann*, Gewährleistungsansprüche, S. 299; *Holthausen*, RIW 1990, 101, 104, 106; *Reinhart*, Art. 48, Rn. 4; *Neumayer/Ming*, Art. 48, Anm. 4., Art. 49, Anm. 4.; im Ausgangspunkt auch *Bianca/Bonell/Will*, Art. 48, Anm. 3.2.1.f.; *Bamberger/Roth/Saenger*, Art. 48, Rn. 5.

[38] Vgl. OLG Koblenz, 31.1.1997, CISG-online 256; *Petrikic*, S. 95 f.; i. E. wohl auch übereinstimmend *Schroeter*, Art. 25 Rn. 26 und *Honnold/Flechtner*, Art. 25, 48, Rn. 184, 296.

[39] So i. E. wohl auch *Gillette/Walt*, S. 234.

werden kann.⁴⁰ Eine Ausnahme gilt nur, wenn der Mangel objektiv schwerwiegend und die sofortige Vertragsaufhebung durch ein besonderes Interesse des Käufers gerechtfertigt ist. Ein solches Interesse liegt vor allem bei Fixgeschäften und ähnlichen Fällen vor, in denen die verspätete Erfüllung für den Käufer ohne Interesse ist.⁴¹ Auch wenn durch die mangelhafte Leistung die Vertrauensgrundlage des Vertrags erschüttert ist (z. B. betrügerisches Verhalten des Verkäufers,⁴² offensichtliche Unfähigkeit⁴³), darf ein derartiges Interesse angenommen werden. Die Setzung einer Nachfrist für die Beseitigung des Mangels ist keine förmliche Voraussetzung der Vertragsaufhebung, kann sich aber aus praktischen Gründen für den Käufer empfehlen.⁴⁴

16 Schliesslich ist darauf hinzuweisen, dass die dargestellten dogmatischen Schwierigkeiten im Verhältnis zwischen dem Nacherfüllungsrecht des Verkäufers und dem Aufhebungsrecht des Käufers vor allem dann auftreten, wenn die Parteien nur ungenügend miteinander kommunizieren und kooperieren.⁴⁵ Die Frage des Vorrangs stellt sich insbesondere dann nicht, wenn der Verkäufer auf die Mängelrüge des Käufers hin gemäss Art. 48 II, III (Nach-)Erfüllung anbietet.⁴⁶ Dadurch wird der Käufer gezwungen, sich darüber zu äussern, ob er die Nacherfüllung annehmen oder den Vertrag aufheben will, womit die Unsicherheit beseitigt wird.⁴⁷

17 c) **Aufhebungslage entscheidet über Vorrang.** In der Literatur besteht Uneinigkeit darüber, ob das Nacherfüllungsrecht des Verkäufers bereits durch das Vorliegen einer wesentlichen Vertragsverletzung oder erst mit der berechtigten Erklärung der Vertragsaufhebung verdrängt wird.⁴⁸ Entscheidend ist m. E. der Zeitpunkt, in dem der Käufer das Recht zur Vertragsaufhebung gemäss Art. 49 I erlangt hat.⁴⁹ Die **Reihenfolge** der Erklärungen der Parteien ist somit **unerheblich**.⁵⁰ Besteht ein Nacherfüllungsrecht des Verkäufers, kann der Käufer es ihm nicht dadurch aus der Hand schlagen, dass er mit der Mängelrüge sofort die Erklärung der Vertragsaufhebung verbindet.⁵¹ Besteht umgekehrt ein Recht des Käufers zur

---

⁴⁰ *Staudinger/Magnus*, Art. 48, Rn. 30 f.; *Petrikic*, S. 94 f.; *Niemann*, S. 195 f.; HGer Aargau, 5.11.2002, CISG-online 715 = SZIER 2003, 103 ff., dazu *Fountoulakis*, IHR 2003, 160, 168; *Schlechtriem*, 18 Pace Int'l L. Rev. (2006), 83, 89 f.; *ders.*, FS U. Huber, S. 563, 568 f.; CISG-AC, Op. 5 *(Schwenzer)*, Art. 49 Opinion 3 und Comment 4.4.; *Brunner*, Art. 48, Rn. 8 f.; *Lookofsky*, Understanding the CISG in the USA, S. 111; MünchKommHGB/*Benicke*, Art. 48, Rn. 10; MünchKomm/*P. Huber*, Art. 48, Rn. 10; *Verweyen/Förster/Toufar*, Handbuch, S. 117 f., 125 f.
⁴¹ Vgl. *Schlechtriem*, Einheitliches UN-Kaufrecht, S. 69; *Staudinger/Magnus*, Art. 48, Rn. 30 f.; *Gutknecht*, S. 64 f.; *Honsell/Schnyder/Straub*, Art. 48, Rn. 32 f.; *Petrikic*, S. 93; HGer Zürich, 26.6.2007, CISG-online 1564 = SZIER 2008, 180 f.
⁴² Vgl. *Karollus*, ZIP 1993, 490, 497; *Petrikic*, S. 93; *Müller-Chen*, Art. 46 Rn. 30.
⁴³ Vgl. *Karollus*, ZIP 1993, 490, 497.
⁴⁴ Vgl. vorne Rn. 10; *Karollus*, ZIP 1993, 490, 496.
⁴⁵ *Honnold/Flechtner*, Art. 48, Rn. 296; *Magnus*, FS Schlechtriem, S. 608 ff.
⁴⁶ Im Normalfall wird der Verkäufer alles daran setzen, die aufgetretenen Mängel zu beseitigen, wenn ihm an einer Aufrechterhaltung der geschäftlichen Beziehung gelegen ist.
⁴⁷ *Müller-Chen/Pair*, FS Bergsten, S. 674; für den Fall, dass der Verkäufer nicht mit einer Erfüllungsanzeige reagiert, schlägt *Magnus*, FS Schlechtriem, S. 609 f. vor, dass fingiert wird, die Mängelanzeige des Käufers enthalte bei gravierenden, aber leicht behebbaren Mängeln die Aufforderung an den Verkäufer, die Mängel in angemessener Frist zu beheben; erfüllt der Verkäufer in ordnungsgemässer Weise, scheidet die Vertragsaufhebung aus (ebenso *Staudinger/Magnus*, Art. 48, Rn. 30a).
⁴⁸ Für die Massgeblichkeit der wesentlichen Vertragsverletzung sind: *Staudinger/Magnus*, Art. 48, Rn. 22; *Gutknecht*, S. 67; *Piltz*, Internationales Kaufrecht, § 4, Rn. 65; für Massgeblichkeit der Aufhebungserklärung sprechen sich aus: *Honnold/Flechtner*, Art. 48, Rn. 296; *Honsell/Schnyder/Straub*, Art. 48, Rn. 35; *Enderlein/Maskow/Strohbach*, Art. 48, Anm. 1.; *Witz/Salger/Lorenz/Salger*, Art. 48, Rn. 2; *Bamberger/Roth/Saenger*, Art. 48, Rn. 5.
⁴⁹ So auch *U. Huber*, 3. Aufl., Rn. 17; *Brunner*, Art. 48, Rn. 7.
⁵⁰ So auch MünchKomm/*P. Huber*, Art. 48, Rn. 10.
⁵¹ So auch *Lookofsky*, S. 121; *Dejesus v. Cat Auto Tech. Corp.*, N. Y. Ct. Cl., 23.5.1994, 23 UCC Rep. 2d 755 zu § 2–508 (2) UCC: Der Käufer stellte einen Tag nach Lieferung von 10 000 Geschenkgutscheinen gewisse Mängel fest und liess daraufhin sofort die Überweisung des Kaufpreises stornieren, ohne den Verkäufer zu informieren. Das Gericht entschied, dass der Käufer dadurch das grundsätzlich bestehende Nachbesserungsrecht des Verkäufers vereitelt hatte, und verurteilte ihn zur Kaufpreiszahlung. Vgl. auch LG Regensburg, 17.12.1998, CISG-online 514: Der Käufer hatte es versäumt, dem Verkäufer notwendige Informationen

Vertragsaufhebung, so kann der Verkäufer dieses Recht nicht dadurch durchkreuzen, dass er die Beseitigung des Mangels anbietet, noch ehe der Käufer die Vertragsaufhebung erklärt hat.[52] Würde auf den Zeitpunkt der Aufhebungserklärung des Käufers abgestellt, wäre Art. 48 II sinnlos. Es gäbe dann keinen Grund, warum der Verkäufer den Käufer auffordern sollte, ihm mitzuteilen, ob er die Erfüllung annehmen will, wenn sein Nacherfüllungsrecht das Aufhebungsrecht bis zur Erklärung der Aufhebung ohnehin verdrängt.[53]

6. Verhältnis zu anderen Rechtsbehelfen

a) Vertragsaufhebung. Das Recht zur Vertragsaufhebung wird durch ein Nachbesserungsrecht des Verkäufers, wie soeben dargelegt, nicht ausgeschlossen. Indirekt ergibt ein Ausschluss sich nur daraus, dass im Regelfall, solange die Voraussetzungen des Art. 48 I vorliegen, die Voraussetzungen einer wesentlichen Vertragsverletzung (Artt. 25, 49 I lit. a)) nicht vorliegen.[54]

b) Minderung. Solange das Recht zur Mängelbeseitigung besteht, ist eine Minderung des Kaufpreises nicht möglich. Das wird in Art. 50 S. 2 ausdrücklich klargestellt.

c) Ersatzlieferung/Nachbesserung. Verlangt der Käufer Ersatzlieferung gemäss Art. 46 II und bietet der Verkäufer Nachbesserung gestützt auf Art. 48 I an, stellt sich die Frage, welches Recht vorgeht. Da dem Verkäufer die Wahl zusteht, wie er den Mangel beseitigen will,[55] setzt er sich mit der Nachbesserung durch.[56] Dies folgt auch daraus, dass bei Nachbesserungsfähigkeit des Mangels i. d. R. keine wesentliche Vertragsverletzung vorliegt und somit kein Anspruch auf Ersatzlieferung gegeben ist.[57] Der Verkäufer setzt sich auch im umgekehrten Fall durch, wenn er Ersatz liefern, der Käufer aber die Sache bloss repariert haben möchte.[58]

d) Schadenersatz. Art. 48 I 2 behält dem Käufer das Recht vor, Schadenersatz nach Art. 45 I lit. b) zu verlangen. Es handelt sich dabei um solche Schäden, die dem Käufer durch die ursprüngliche Vertragsverletzung entstanden sind und die durch die nachträgliche Erfüllung nicht mehr beseitigt werden können, also um Verzögerungs- und Begleitschäden (z. B. um Kosten der Abnahme, der Untersuchung[59] oder der Demontage der zuerst gelieferten unbrauchbaren Sache). Selbstverständlich entfällt der Schadenersatzanspruch, soweit der Verkäufer den Schaden durch die nachträgliche Erfüllung behoben hat.[60] Repariert z. B. der Verkäufer die gelieferte mangelhafte Sache vollständig, so kann der Käufer keinen Schadenersatz wegen Minderwerts verlangen. Solange das Recht zur Mängelbeseitigung besteht, ist der Käufer nicht berechtigt, den Mangel selbst zu beseitigen und die

---

mitzuteilen, um die dieser geboten hatte, um die Nachbesserung ordnungsgemäss durchzuführen zu können. Das Gericht kam zum Schluss, dass der Käufer das Nacherfüllungsrecht des Verkäufers ausgehebelt hatte, und hiess die Kaufpreisklage gut. A. A. *Honsell/Schnyder/Straub*, Art. 48, Rn. 36.
[52] A. A. *Honsell/Schnyder/Straub*, Art. 48, Rn. 35.
[53] *Staudinger/Magnus*, Art. 48, Rn. 23; *Gutknecht*, S. 67.
[54] Vgl. vorne Rn. 3 ff.
[55] Vgl. vorne Rn. 6.
[56] Es versteht sich auf Grund des Grundsatzes von Treu und Glauben (Art. 7 I) von selbst, dass der Verkäufer bei seiner Wahl auf die Interessen und Bedürfnisse des Käufers Rücksicht zu nehmen hat; a. A. *Bridge*, FS Schwenzer, S. 221, 231 ff.
[57] Vgl. vorne Rn. 15; *Müller-Chen*, Art. 46 Rn. 23 ff.; *Karollus*, S. 138; *Audit*, Vente internationale, Anm. 133.; *Bianca/Bonell/Will*, Art. 48, Anm. 3.1.2.; *Neumayer/Ming*, Art. 46, Anm. 4.; a. A. (Wahlrecht des Käufers): *Staudinger/Magnus*, Art. 48, Rn. 32; *Welser*, S. 119; *Soergel/Lüderitz/Schüßler-Langeheine*, Art. 48, Rn. 6; *Petrikic*, S. 96 f.; differenziert *Honsell/Schnyder/Straub*, Art. 48, Rn. 58–61.
[58] So auch *Bianca/Bonell/Will*, Art. 48, Anm. 3.1.2.
[59] Vgl. *Schwenzer*, Art. 38 Rn. 27; dies., Art. 74 Rn. 27. Diese Kosten wären zwar bei vertragsmässiger Beschaffenheit der Ware ebenfalls entstanden. In diesem Fall hätte aber der Käufer die Möglichkeit gehabt, sie durch gewinnbringende Verwendung der Ware wieder wettzumachen („Rentabilitätsvermutung").
[60] Vgl. Sekretariatskommentar, Art. 44, Nr. 9 Fn. 1: „The original damage claim will, of course, be modified by the cure".

Kosten dem Verkäufer als Schadenersatz gemäss Art. 45 I lit. b) oder gestützt auf eine Anspruchsgrundlage des nationalen, unvereinheitlichten Rechts in Rechnung zu stellen. Denn hierdurch hindert er den Verkäufer daran, den Vertrag noch nachträglich selbst zu erfüllen; er kann daher aus der Nichterfüllung keine Rechte herleiten (Art. 80).[61] Dies gilt unter dem Vorbehalt der Schadensminderungspflicht (Art. 77) dann nicht, wenn der Verkäufer den Mangel bestreitet oder dessen Beseitigung aus anderen Gründen verweigert.[62]

7. Rechtsfolgen

22 Führt die Nacherfüllung des Verkäufers zum Erfolg, ist die Vertragsverletzung behoben und alle Rechte des Käufers erlöschen unter Vorbehalt des Schadenersatzanspruchs nach Art. 48 I 2.

23 Wird die Vertragsverletzung nicht beseitigt, weil die Nacherfüllung mit unzumutbarer Verzögerung oder mit unzumutbaren Unannehmlichkeiten verbunden ist oder scheitert diese aus anderen Gründen, erlangt der Käufer dadurch alle bisher suspendierten Rechtsbehelfe des Art. 45 I zurück. Ob er berechtigt ist, den Vertrag aufzuheben und im Falle der verspäteten Lieferung die Annahme zu verweigern und den Kaufpreis nicht zu bezahlen, hängt davon ab, ob die Voraussetzungen des Art. 49 vorliegen. Im Fall der Lieferung nicht vertragsmässiger Ware ist jetzt nur noch das objektive Gewicht des Mangels für die Beurteilung der Vertragsaufhebung entscheidend.[63] Mängel von nur untergeordnetem Gewicht werden auch nicht dadurch zur „wesentlichen Vertragsverletzung", dass der Verkäufer die an sich mögliche Nachbesserung unterlässt; der Käufer kann soweit möglich den Mangel selbst beheben und für die Kosten Schadenersatz verlangen, oder er kann für den Minderwert der Sache Minderung und Schadenersatz fordern.[64]

III. Recht zur Behebung des Mangels auf Grund unwidersprochener Anzeige der Erfüllungsbereitschaft (Abs. 2–4)

1. Aufforderung zur Erklärung der Annahmebereitschaft mit Fristsetzung (Abs. 2)

24 **a) Zweck.** Der Verkäufer, der den Liefertermin nicht eingehalten oder wegen vertragswidriger Ware eine Mängelanzeige erhalten hat, befindet sich in der Ungewissheit, ob der Käufer die nachträgliche Lieferung noch entgegennimmt bzw. die Mängelbeseitigung zulässt, oder ob er die Vertragsaufhebung wegen wesentlicher Vertragsverletzung erklärt. Art. 48 II gibt dem Verkäufer die Möglichkeit, die Lage zu klären, um ihn vor vergeblichen Nacherfüllungsversuchen zu schützen. Zu diesem Zweck wird auch vom Käufer eine gewisse Kooperation und Bereitschaft zur Kommunikation erwartet.[65] Das Nacherfüllungsrecht gemäss Art. 48 II besteht auch dann, wenn der Verkäufer gemäss Art. 48 I dazu nicht berechtigt ist.[66]

25 **b) Voraussetzungen.** Abs. 2 setzt voraus, dass der Verkäufer den Käufer **auffordert,** ihm zu erklären, ob er bereit ist, die nachträgliche Erfüllung – Lieferung, Nachbesserung,

---

[61] Vgl. dazu auch *Schwenzer,* Art. 80 Rn. 8 ff.
[62] Weitergehend *Honnold/Flechtner,* Art. 48, Rn. 296.1, die dem Käufer die Möglichkeit der Ersatzvornahme ganz generell einräumen.
[63] Vgl. dazu Art. 46 Rn. 26 ff.
[64] Der Käufer ist jedoch nicht verpflichtet, dem Verkäufer eine Nachfrist zu setzen, bevor er den Mangel anderweitig behebt und die Kosten dem Verkäufer in Rechnung stellt. Die Nachfrist ist keine förmliche Voraussetzung für den Schadenersatzanspruch, AG München, 23.6.1995, CISG-online 368.
[65] So auch *Petrikic,* S. 98 f.; *Honnold/Flechtner,* Art. 48, Rn. 297; a. A. *Honsell/Schnyder/Straub,* Art. 48, Rn. 39.
[66] *Staudinger/Magnus,* Art. 48, Rn. 37, 41; *Bianca/Bonell/Will,* Art. 48, Anm. 2.2.; *Honnold/Flechtner,* Art. 48, Rn. 297 f.; *Enderlein/Maskow/Strohbach,* Art. 48, Anm. 10.; *Karollus,* S. 145; *Soergel/Lüderitz/Schüßler-Langeheine,* Art. 48, Rn. 9; *Petrikic,* S. 98 f.; a. A. *Honsell/Schnyder/Straub,* Art. 48, Rn. 39.

Ersatzlieferung – anzunehmen, und dass er eine **bestimmte Frist oder einen bestimmten Termin nennt,** innerhalb derer er nacherfüllen wird.[67] Die Fristbestimmung ist erforderlich, um dem Käufer noch vor Fristablauf eine Entscheidung über Annahme oder Ablehnung zu ermöglichen und um im Fall des Schweigens die Dauer der Bindung des Käufers festzulegen. Ob die Frist „angemessen" ist oder nicht, ist gleichgültig;[68] entscheidend ist nur, dass überhaupt eine Frist genannt wird. Erscheint dem Käufer die Frist als zu lang, kann er das Angebot ablehnen. Auf der anderen Seite darf die Frist nicht so kurz sein, dass dem Käufer bis zum Eintritt des Termins eine Antwort nicht möglich ist; in diesem Fall kann eine Bindung des Käufers gemäss Art. 48 II nicht eintreten.

Die Bindung des Käufers an das Angebot des Verkäufers tritt ein, wenn der Käufer das 26 Angebot **nicht innerhalb „angemessener Frist" beantwortet.** Da die Sache für den Verkäufer, der seinerseits die von ihm gesetzte Frist einhalten muss, eilbedürftig ist, wird es „angemessen" sein, dass der Käufer sich unter Berücksichtigung der Umstände des Einzelfalls (Art und Umfang der Vertragsverletzung, Art der Nacherfüllung und die vom Käufer für die Nacherfüllung zu treffenden Vorkehrungen, Länge der vom Verkäufer gesetzten Frist etc.) ohne Verzögerung äussert.[69] Zur Fristwahrung genügt die Absendung einer entsprechenden Erklärung; das Risiko der Verzögerung oder des Verlusts auf dem Übermittlungsweg trifft gemäss Art. 27 den Verkäufer.[70] Die **Beweislast** für den Widerspruch und seine rechtzeitige Absendung trifft den Käufer.[71]

c) **Rechtsfolgen.** Nimmt der Käufer das Angebot der nachträglichen Erfüllung an, so ist 27 er hieran schon nach allgemeinen Rechtsgrundsätzen gebunden. Lehnt er das Angebot innerhalb angemessener Frist ab, kann er unter Vorbehalt von Art. 48 I die ihm nach Art. 45 I zustehenden Rechtsbehelfe ausüben.[72] Widerspricht der Käufer nicht rechtzeitig oder schweigt er, ist der Verkäufer innerhalb der von ihm genannten Frist zur nachträglichen Erfüllung berechtigt, auch wenn die Voraussetzungen eines Nacherfüllungsrechts nach Art. 48 I nicht gegeben sein sollten (Abs. 2 S. 1). Der Käufer ist innerhalb der Frist nicht berechtigt, irgendeinen Rechtsbehelf auszuüben, der mit der Erfüllung unvereinbar ist (Abs. 2 S. 2: Vertragsaufhebung, Minderung, Mängelbeseitigung auf Kosten des Verkäufers).[73] Unberührt bleibt das Recht auf Ersatz solcher Schäden, die sich durch die nachträgliche Erfüllung nicht mehr beseitigen lassen, also auf Ersatz von Verzögerungs- und Begleitschäden. Versäumt der Verkäufer die selbstgesetzte Frist, gewinnt der Käufer die Freiheit des Handelns zurück und kann alle ihm nach Art. 45 I zustehenden Rechtsbehelfe wieder ausüben.

2. Anzeige der Erfüllungsbereitschaft mit Fristsetzung ohne Aufforderung zur Erklärung (Abs. 3)

Der Verkäufer muss den Käufer nicht explizit auffordern, ihm mitzuteilen, ob er die 28 Erfüllung annehmen will. Es wird gemäss Art. 48 III unwiderlegbar angenommen („vermutet", „assumed", „présumé"), dass die Anzeige der Erfüllungsbereitschaft mit Fristanset-

---

[67] Bsp.: „Bitte um Mitteilung innerhalb von Tagen, ob Ersatzlieferung angenommen wird." oder „Ware wird am 10. Mai versandt, falls bis 9. Mai keine gegenteilige Anweisung bei uns eingeht".
[68] Zustimmend *Staudinger/Magnus*, Art. 48, Rn. 39; *Achilles*, Art. 48, Rn. 7; dem Käufer muss zur Erklärung der Annahme auch keine Frist gesetzt werden, vgl. *Gutknecht*, S. 343 Fn. 2180; *Honsell/Schnyder/Straub*, Art. 48, Rn. 42; a. A. *Friehe*, IHR 2011, 16, 37: „Die Selbstbindung des Gläubigers tritt nur ein, wenn er eine Nachfrist von angemessener Dauer gesetzt hat."
[69] Ebenso *Piltz*, Internationales Kaufrecht, Rn. 5–236; *Staudinger/Magnus*, Art. 48, Rn. 42; *Bamberger/Roth/Saenger*, Art. 48, Rn. 11; *Honsell/Schnyder/Straub*, Art. 48, Rn. 42, 47 (der Käufer soll „einige Tage" Zeit haben); *Petrikic*, S. 99; *Bianca/Bonell/Will*, Art. 48, Anm. 2.2.2.; für eine „sehr kurze" Frist bzw. „unverzügliche" Reaktion plädieren *Enderlein/Maskow/Strohbach*, Art. 48, Anm. 11.; *U. Huber*, 3. Aufl., Rn. 33; *Achilles*, Art. 48, Rn. 9; HGer Aargau, 5.11.2002, CISG-online 715.
[70] Vgl. Sekretariatskommentar, Art. 44, Nr. 15.
[71] Ebenso *Baumgärtel/Laumen/Hepting*, Art. 48, Rn. 21; *Achilles*, Art. 48, Rn. 10.
[72] So auch *Neumayer/Ming*, Art. 48, Anm. 8.; zu Einzelheiten vgl. *Müller-Chen*, Art. 49 Rn. 41 f.
[73] Nicht anders als im Fall des Abs. 1, dazu vorne Rn. 18 ff.

zung diese Aufforderung enthält.[74] Die Rechtsfolgen sind dieselben, als hätte der Verkäufer den Käufer ausdrücklich aufgefordert, sich zu äussern.[75]

3. Zugangserfordernis (Abs. 4)

29   Die Aufforderung (Abs. 2) oder das Angebot (Abs. 3) sind nur wirksam, d. h. Schweigen des Käufers gilt nur als Zustimmung, wenn sie dem Käufer zugegangen sind. Diese Klarstellung war mit Rücksicht auf Art. 27 erforderlich. Die Widerspruchsfrist beginnt daher mit dem Zugang. Wird der Sinn des Angebots auf dem Übermittlungsweg entstellt, so ist der Käufer nur an den Text gebunden, der ihm zugegangen ist. Die **Beweislast** für das Angebot und für seinen Zugang trifft den Verkäufer.[76]

4. Kreuzende Erklärungen des Verkäufers

30   Hat der Käufer zu Recht die **Vertragsaufhebung** erklärt (Art. 49 I), bevor ihm das Angebot des Verkäufers zugegangen ist, so ist das Nacherfüllungsrecht untergegangen und der Vertrag aufgelöst. Hat der Käufer dem Verkäufer eine **Nachfrist** für die Erfüllung gesetzt und bietet der Verkäufer, dem die Nachfrist zu kurz ist, Erfüllung innerhalb einer längeren Frist an, so sind Art. 48 II und III anwendbar. Widerspricht also der Käufer der vom Verkäufer angebotenen Gegenfrist nicht ohne Verzögerung, so gilt sein Schweigen als Zustimmung. Dies gilt nach Treu und Glauben auch dann, wenn der Käufer die Nachfristsetzung bereits mit der **bedingten Erklärung der Vertragsaufhebung** für den Fall verbunden hat, dass die Nachfrist ungenutzt verstreicht.[77]

IV. Abweichende Vereinbarungen

31   Abweichende Vereinbarungen sind **zulässig** (Art. 6). Dies gilt auch dann, wenn sie in allgemeinen Geschäftsbedingungen enthalten sind, soweit sie mit den grundsätzlichen Wertungen des CISG nicht in Widerspruch stehen. Erweiterungen des Nacherfüllungsrechts in allgemeinen Lieferbedingungen sind zulässig. Ein Ausschluss, der den Käufer bei Vertragsverletzung des Verkäufers, insbesondere im Fall mangelhafter Lieferung, sofort zur Vertragsaufhebung berechtigt, ist hingegen aufgrund der dem CISG zugrunde liegenden Präferenz für die Aufrechterhaltung des Vertrags problematisch.[78]

---

[74] Ebenso *Baumgärtel/Laumen/Hepting*, Art. 48, Rn. 18; *Honsell/Schnyder/Straub*, Art. 48, Rn. 43; *Karollus*, S. 144; *Soergel/Lüderitz/Schüßler-Langeheine*, Art. 48, Rn. 10; i. E. übereinstimmend (unwiderlegbare Vermutung) *Herber/Czerwenka*, Art. 48, Rn. 4; *Petrikic*, S. 100; i. E. wohl auch *Witz/Salger/Lorenz/Salger*, Art. 48, Rn. 6; a. A. *Achilles*, Art. 47, Rn. 7; *Ensthaler/Achilles*, GK-HGB, nach § 382, Art. 48, Rn. 7 (blosse Auslegungsregel).
[75] Vgl. vorne Rn. 26.
[76] Ebenso *Baumgärtel/Laumen/Hepting*, Art. 48, Rn. 17–19; *Achilles*, Art. 48, Rn. 10.
[77] Vgl. dazu Art. 49 Rn. 41.
[78] So auch *Ensthaler/Achilles*, GK-HGB, nach § 382; a. A. *Witz/Salger/Lorenz/Salger*, Art. 48, Rn. 8.

Art. 49 [Vertragsaufhebung]

(1) Der Käufer kann die Aufhebung des Vertrages erklären,

a) wenn die Nichterfüllung einer dem Verkäufer nach dem Vertrag oder diesem Übereinkommen obliegenden Pflicht eine wesentliche Vertragsverletzung darstellt oder
b) wenn im Falle der Nichtlieferung der Verkäufer die Ware nicht innerhalb der vom Käufer nach Artikel 47 Absatz 1 gesetzten Nachfrist liefert oder wenn er erklärt, daß er nicht innerhalb der so gesetzten Frist liefern wird.

(2) Hat der Verkäufer die Ware geliefert, so verliert jedoch der Käufer sein Recht, die Aufhebung des Vertrages zu erklären, wenn er

a) im Falle der verspäteten Lieferung die Aufhebung nicht innerhalb einer angemessenen Frist erklärt, nachdem er erfahren hat, daß die Lieferung erfolgt ist, oder
b) im Falle einer anderen Vertragsverletzung als verspäteter Lieferung die Aufhebung nicht innerhalb einer angemessenen Frist erklärt,
 i) nachdem er die Vertragsverletzung kannte oder kennen mußte,
 ii) nachdem eine vom Käufer nach Artikel 47 Absatz 1 gesetzte Nachfrist abgelaufen ist oder nachdem der Verkäufer erklärt hat, daß er seine Pflichten nicht innerhalb der Nachfrist erfüllen wird, oder
 iii) nachdem eine vom Verkäufer nach Artikel 48 Absatz 2 gesetzte Frist abgelaufen ist oder nachdem der Käufer erklärt hat, daß er die Erfüllung nicht annehmen wird.

Art. 49

(1) The buyer may declare the contract avoided:
(a) if the failure by the seller to perform any of his obligations under the contract or this Convention amounts to a fundamental breach of contract; or
(b) in case of non-delivery, if the seller does not deliver the goods within the additional period of time fixed by the buyer in accordance with paragraph (1) of article 47 or declares that he will not deliver within the period so fixed.

(2) However, in cases where the seller has delivered the goods, the buyer loses the right to declare the contract avoided unless he does so:
(a) in respect of late delivery, within a reasonable time after he has become aware that delivery has been made;
(b) in respect of any breach other than late delivery, within a reasonable time:
 (i) after he knew or ought to have known of the breach;
 (ii) after the expiration of any additional period of time fixed by the buyer in accordance with paragraph (1) of article 47, or after the seller has declared that he will not perform his obligations within such an additional period; or
 (iii) after the expiration of any additional period of time indicated by the seller in accordance with paragraph (2) of article 48, or after the buyer has declared that he will not accept performance.

Art. 49

1) L'acheteur peut déclarer le contrat résolu:
a) si l'inexécution par le vendeur de l'une quelconque des obligations résultant pour lui du contrat ou de la présente Convention constitue une contravention essentielle au contrat; ou
b) en cas de défaut de livraison, si le vendeur ne livre pas les marchandises dans le délai supplémentaire imparti par l'acheteur conformément au paragraphe 1 de l'article 47 ou s'il déclare qu'il ne les livrera pas dans le délai ainsi imparti.

2) Cependant, lorsque le vendeur a livré les marchandises, l'acheteur est déchu du droit de déclarer le contrat résolu s'il ne l'a pas fait:
a) en cas de livraison tardive, dans un délai raisonnable à partir du moment où il a su que la livraison avait été effectuée;
b) en cas de contravention autre que la livraison tardive, dans un délai raisonnable:
 i) à partir du moment où il a eu connaissance ou aurait du avoir connaissance de cette contravention;
 ii) après l'expiration de tout délai supplémentaire imparti par l'acheteur conformément au paragraphe 1 de l'article 47 ou après que le vendeur a déclaré qu'il n'exécuterait pas ses obligations dans ce délai supplémentaire; ou
 iii) après l'expiration de tout délai supplémentaire indiqué par le vendeur conformément au paragraphe 2 de l'article 48 ou après que l'acheteur a déclaré qu'il n'accepterait pas l'exécution.

Art. 49

Übersicht

	Rn.
I. Gegenstand und Grundgedanke der Vorschrift	1
1. Abs. 1	1
2. Abs. 2	3
II. Voraussetzungen der Vertragsaufhebung (1): Wesentliche Vertragsverletzung (Art. 49 I lit. a))	4
1. Allgemeines	4
2. Nichterfüllung der Lieferpflicht	5
a) Verzug	5
b) Nichtleistung	6
3. Lieferung vertragswidriger Ware	7
4. Rechtsmängel	10
5. Vertragswidrige Dokumente	11
6. Sonstige Vertragsverletzungen	12
7. Beweislast	13
8. Vertragliche Regelung	14
III. Voraussetzungen der Vertragsaufhebung (2): Nachfristsetzung für die Lieferung (Art. 49 I lit. b))	15
1. Nichtlieferung	15
a) Grundsatz	15
b) Ausnahmen	17
c) Vertragswidrige bzw. fehlende Dokumente	18
2. Nichterfüllung der Lieferpflicht innerhalb der Nachfrist	20
IV. Erklärung der Vertragsaufhebung	23
1. Erfordernis einer Erklärung	23
2. Form, Inhalt und Adressat der Erklärung	24
3. Teilweise Vertragsaufhebung	26
V. Erklärungsfrist (1): Nichteinhaltung des Liefertermins (Abs. 2 lit. a))	27
1. Vor Lieferung: Keine Befristung der Aufhebungserklärung	27
2. Nach Lieferung: Erklärung der Vertragsaufhebung innerhalb angemessener Frist	28
VI. Erklärungsfrist (2): Sonstige Vertragsverletzungen (Abs. 2 lit. b))	30
1. Grundsatz	30
2. Erklärung innerhalb angemessener Frist	31
a) Allgemeines	31
b) Angemessene Frist	32
c) Folgen des Fristversäumnisses	33
3. Fristbeginn	34
a) Kenntnis und Kennen-Müssen (Abs. 2 lit. b) i))	34
b) Ablauf einer vom Käufer gesetzten Nachfrist und Erfüllungsverweigerung (Abs. 2 lit. b) ii))	36
aa) Grundgedanke	36
bb) Voraussetzungen	37
cc) Rechtsfolgen	39
c) Ablauf der Erklärungsfrist nach Art. 48 II und Ablehnung der Erfüllung (Abs. 2 lit. b) iii))	41
VII. Rechtsfolgen	43
1. Berechtigte Vertragsaufhebung	43
2. Unberechtigte Vertragsaufhebung	44
a) Einverständnis des Verkäufers mit der Vertragsaufhebung	45
b) Vertragsaufhebung durch den Verkäufer wegen Erfüllungsverweigerung des Käufers	46
c) Aufrechterhaltung des Vertrags durch den Verkäufer	47
VIII. Abweichende Vereinbarungen	49

Vorläufer und **Entwürfe**: EKG Artt. 25–28, 30–32, 43, 44, 51, 52, 55; Genfer E 1976 Art. 30; Wiener E 1977 Art. 31; New Yorker E 1978 Art. 45.

I. Gegenstand und Grundgedanke der Vorschrift

1. Abs. 1

Art. 49 I legt fest, unter welchen Voraussetzungen dem Käufer im Fall einer Vertragsverletzung des Verkäufers der Rechtsbehelf der Vertragsaufhebung zusteht. Das Gegenstück für den Fall einer Vertragsverletzung des Käufers bildet Art. 64 I. Die Vertragsaufhebung hat zur Folge, dass die beiderseitigen Leistungspflichten erlöschen (Art. 81 I) und dass bereits erbrachte Leistungen zurückzugewähren sind (Art. 81 II). Ist der Käufer zur Rückgabe der gelieferten Ware nicht imstande, verliert er unter den Voraussetzungen von Art. 82 das Vertragsaufhebungsrecht.

In Abweichung von vielen nationalen Rechtsordnungen[1] begründet nur eine wesentliche Vertragsverletzung das Recht zur Vertragsaufhebung. Die Vertragsaufhebung soll – vor allem dann, wenn die Lieferung bereits erfolgt ist – für den Gläubiger die **„ultima ratio"** darstellen,[2] die dann eingreift, wenn die sonstigen Rechtsbehelfe – Erfüllungsanspruch, Schadenersatzanspruch, Minderung – nicht ausreichen. Ist der Mangel der Sache nur von untergeordneter Bedeutung, kann der Käufer das Recht zur Vertragsaufhebung auch nicht dadurch erwerben, dass er dem Verkäufer für seine Beseitigung eine Nachfrist setzt.[3] Die Nichterfüllung der Lieferpflicht trotz Nachfristsetzung erschien den Verfassern der Konvention dagegen in jedem Fall als eine gewichtige Vertragsverletzung, die die Vertragsaufhebung rechtfertigt, ohne dass die Wesentlichkeit noch besonders nachgewiesen werden müsste.

2. Abs. 2

Gemäss Art. 49 II verliert der Käufer das Recht zur Vertragsaufhebung unabhängig von der Frage der Wesentlichkeit in bestimmten Fällen, wenn er nicht innerhalb angemessener Frist die Aufhebung erklärt. Durch diese in ihrer Ausgestaltung sehr differenzierte (und komplizierte) Befristung soll das Schicksal des Vertrags und die gegenseitigen Leistungspflichten der Parteien geklärt und verhindert werden, dass der Käufer die Vertragsaufhebung in spekulativer Absicht verzögert, nachdem die Ware geliefert wurde.[4] Die Vertragsaufhebung und damit die Rückabwicklung des Vertrags sollen nicht unangemessen verzögert werden.

---

[1] Rechtsvergleichender Überblick bei *Schwenzer/Fountoulakis*, International Sales Law, S. 369 ff.; *Schwenzer/Hachem/Kee*, Rn. 47.26 ff.; *Sivesand*, Buyer's Remedies, S. 68 ff.; gewisse Rechtsordnungen osteuropäischer, zentralasiatischer (dazu *Lapiashvili*, S. 316) und asiatischer Staaten (s. zu letzteren *S. J. Yang*, S. 361 f.) kennen eine wesentliche Vertragsverletzung als Voraussetzung der Vertragsaufhebung, s. *Schwenzer/Hachem/Kee*, Rn. 47.81; andere Rechtsordnungen verlangen eine gewisse Schwere der Nichterfüllung bzw. dass der Mangel nicht behoben wird oder werden kann (z. B. § 932 IV ABGB), dazu im Allgemeinen *Schwenzer/Hachem/Kee*, Rn. 47.83 ff.; zur Rechtslage in den arabischen bzw. ibero-amerik. Staaten s. *Hafez*, S. 350 ff. bzw. *E. Muñoz*, S. 475 ff.; vgl. auch § 323 BGB; Art. 205 OR; §§ 918, 920 ABGB; Art. 1644 Cc; sec. 11 (3) SGA; § 2–601 UCC (perfect tender rule vor „acceptance" der Ware); § 241 i. V. m. § 237 Restatement 2d Contracts; dem CISG angenähert ist sec. 15A SGA, dazu *McKendrick*, § 10–005; *Bridge*, Int'l Sale of Goods, Rn. 12.26; *Schwenzer/Hachem/Kee*, Rn. 41.42 und 47.2; vgl. auch Art. 6:265 BW; § 2–608 (1) UCC („substantial impairment" nach „acceptance" der Ware); Art. 7.3.1 (2) PICC („material" breach), dazu *van Vuuren*, 15 Ariz. J. Int'l & Comp. L. (1998), 583, 620 ff.; Artt. 9:301 i. V. m. 8:103/106 PECL („fundamental non-performance"); rechtsvergleichend *K. Schmidt*, Vertragsaufhebung, S. 23 ff.

[2] Vgl. auch Tribunale di Forlì, 11.12.2008, CISG-online 1788: Keine Vertragsaufhebung unter Art. 49 (1) (lit. a), da andere Rechtsbehelfe zur Verfügung stehen; BGH, 3.4.1996, CISG-online 135 = BGHZ 132, 290, 298: Vertragsaufhebung als letzte Möglichkeit für den Gläubiger; *Staudinger/Magnus*, Art. 49, Rn. 4; *Magnus*, 25 J. L. & Com. (2005), 423, 424; so auch Art. 3 VI der EG-Verbrauchsgüterkaufrichtlinie; dies kann auch als Ausdruck des Verhältnismässigkeitsgrundsatzes verstanden werden, vgl. *Lando*, 13 Pace Int'l L. Rev. (2001), 339, 361 ff.; *Torsello*, 9 VJ 2005, 253, 263 f.

[3] Vgl. Art. 45 Rn. 6; *Schlechtriem*, Einheitliches UN-Kaufrecht, S. 69 f.; *Heuzé*, Anm. 427.; MünchKomm/*P. Huber*, Art. 49, Rn. 6.

[4] *U. Huber*, RabelsZ 43 (1979), 413, 417 f. m. w. N.

II. Voraussetzungen der Vertragsaufhebung (1): Wesentliche Vertragsverletzung (Art. 49 I lit. a))

1. Allgemeines

4 Die Aufhebung des Vertrags gemäss Art. 49 I lit. a) setzt voraus, dass erstens der Verkäufer eine seiner Pflichten nicht erfüllt hat und dass zweitens diese „Nichterfüllung" eine „wesentliche Vertragsverletzung" darstellt.[5] **Unerheblich** ist, ob der Verkäufer das Leistungshindernis i. S. d. Art. 79 **zu vertreten hat** (vgl. Art. 79 V). Der Tatbestand der Nichterfüllung ist bei Art. 45 erläutert.[6] Der Begriff der „wesentlichen Vertragsverletzung" ist in Art. 25 näher umschrieben. Auf die Kommentierung hierzu wird verwiesen; im Folgenden soll nur eine Übersicht über die wichtigsten Einzelfälle gegeben werden.[7]

2. Nichterfüllung der Lieferpflicht

5 a) **Verzug.** Ist die Lieferung an sich noch möglich, stellt die blosse Nichteinhaltung des Liefertermins in der Regel keine wesentliche Vertragsverletzung dar.[8] Ein Aufhebungsrecht entsteht nur nach fruchtlosem Ablauf einer angemessenen Nachfrist (Art. 49 I lit. b)).[9] Wesentlichkeit liegt aber vor, wenn sich aus dem Vertrag (beim Fixgeschäft oder just-in-time Geschäft)[10] oder den Umständen (z. B. Verkauf von Saisonware)[11] ergibt, dass der Käufer an der Einhaltung des Liefertermins ein besonderes Interesse hat.[12] Allerdings kann auch in sonstigen Fällen die Überschreitung des Liefertermins bei **längerer Dauer** oder in Kombination mit anderen Vertragsverletzungen in eine wesentliche Vertragsverletzung umschlagen.[13] Dies kann z. B. geschehen, wenn der Verkäufer dem Käufer mehr-

---

[5] Vgl. rechtsvergleichend und zur Entstehungsgeschichte *Schwenzer*, 36 Vict. U. Well. L. Rev. (2005/4), 795, 795 ff.; *Schwenzer/Hachem/Kee*, Rn. 47.119 und 47.130 ff.

[6] Vgl. Art. 45 Rn. 2 ff.

[7] CISG-AC, Op. 5 *(Schwenzer)*, Art. 49 Opinion 1 f. und Comment 4.1 ff.

[8] *Valero Marketing & Supply Company v. Green Oy and Greeni Trading Oy*, U. S. Dist. Ct. (N. J.), 4.4.2006, CISG-online 1216, dazu: *Spaic*, http://cisgw3.law.pace.edu/cisg/biblio/spaic.pdf, besucht am 12.12.2012; ebenso American Arbitration Association, 23.10.2007, CISG-online 1645; OGH, 22.11.2011, CISG-online 2239 = IHR 2012, 114 ff.

[9] Vgl. dazu Art. 47 Rn. 6 ff.

[10] HGer Zürich, 25.6.2007, CISG-online 1564 = SZIER 2008, 180 f. Zur CIF-Klausel vgl. OLG Hamburg, 28.2.1997, CISG-online 261: Wesentlichkeit bejaht; *K. Schmidt*, Vertragsaufhebung, S. 91.

[11] Vgl. *Schroeter*, Art. 25 Rn. 18 m. w. N.; übersehen vom AG Oldenburg, 24.4.1990, CISG-online 20 = IPRax 1991, 336; mit krit. Anm. *Enderlein*, IPRax 1991, 313. Vgl. dazu CA Milano, 20.3.1998, CISG-online 348 = Riv. dir. int. priv. proc. 1998, 170 ff.: Die nicht rechtzeitige Lieferung von Strickwaren für den Jahresschlussverkauf ist wesentliche Vertragsverletzung; unter diesen Voraussetzungen ist der Liefertermin (3.12.1990) als Fixtermin anzusehen; ebenso HGer Zürich, 25.6.2007, CISG-online 1564. Die blosse Tatsache, dass die Ware einen Börsen- oder Marktpreis hat, führt bei Verzug nicht zur Annahme einer wesentlichen Vertragsverletzung, vgl. *U. Huber*, 3. Aufl., Rn. 5 mit Fn. 15; *Neumayer/Ming*, Art. 49, Anm. 3.

[12] OLG Düsseldorf, 21.4.2004, CISG-online 915 = IHR 2005, 24 ff. Die Lieferung von Auto-Mobiltelefonen wurde „schnellstmöglich" bzw. „unmittelbar nach Eingang der Zahlung" zugesichert. Die Zahlung erfolgte am 29.6.2000 die Lieferung blieb daraufhin aus, so dass die Käuferin zu Recht am 5.7.2000 die Vertragsaufhebung gestützt auf Art. 49 I lit. a) erklärte; vgl. dazu auch *Sauthoff*, IHR 2005, 21 ff.; rechtsvergleichende Hinweise zur Wesentlichkeit des Liefertermins bei *Schwenzer/Hachem/Kee*, Rn. 47.125 ff.

[13] Ein Grenzfall wohl Int. Ct. Ukrainian CCI, 5.7.2005, CISG-online 1361, der eine wesentliche Vertragsverletzung annahm, obwohl der Liefertermin um nur 12 Tage überschritten wurde. Der Verkäufer änderte aber zudem einseitig die Art des Transports (Seetransport statt Lufttracht) und übergab die Transportdokumente (Versicherungspolice und Qualitätszertifikat) nicht rechtzeitig, so dass die Zollabfertigung und die Abnahme der Ware gemäss der Vertragsbedingungen nicht durchgeführt werden konnte; vgl. auch OLG Graz, 28.9.2000, CISG-online 798 (Lieferverzug kombiniert mit Verletzung der vertraglich vereinbarten Weiterentwicklungspflicht ermöglicht dem Käufer die Vertragsaufhebung nach Art. 49 I lit. a)); Int. Ct. Ukrainian CCI, 18.11.2004, CISG-online 1371 (Lieferverzug von 15 Monaten ist eine wesentliche Vertragsverletzung gemäss Art. 49 I lit. a)); *Soergel/Lüderitz/Schüßler-Langeheine*, Art. 49, Rn. 2, 5; *Neumayer/Ming*, Art. 49, Anm. 3.; LG Halle, 27.3.1998, CISG-online 521; *K. Schmidt*, Vertragsaufhebung, S. 92 f.; übersehen vom AG Oldenburg, 24.4.1990, CISG-online 20 = IPRax 1991, 336; vgl. auch – zum Haager Kaufrecht – OLG Oldenburg,

fach verspricht, zu einem späteren Termin zu liefern und ihn so unangemessen lange hinhält.[14]

b) Nichtleistung. Eine wesentliche Vertragsverletzung liegt vor, wenn die Lieferung objektiv oder subjektiv, anfänglich oder nachträglich, unmöglich[15] ist oder wenn der Verkäufer vor oder nach Verstreichen des Liefertermins ernsthaft und endgültig erklärt,[16] die Lieferung nicht mehr zu den vertraglich vereinbarten Bedingungen erbringen zu können oder zu wollen.[17] Eine derartige **Erfüllungsverweigerung** kann z. B. vorliegen, wenn der Verkäufer sich zu Unrecht auf ein Leistungsverweigerungsrecht, die Unwirksamkeit des Vertrags oder auf das Vorliegen von höherer Gewalt beruft[18] oder wenn er versucht, eine ungerechtfertigte Preiserhöhung durchzusetzen.[19] Ist der Käufer unsicher, ob der Verkäufer die Leistung noch wird erbringen können oder wollen (z. B. bei vorübergehender Unmöglichkeit), sollte er ihm zur Sicherheit eine Nachfrist setzen.[20]

3. Lieferung vertragswidriger Ware

Will der Käufer den Vertrag bei der Lieferung nicht vertragsgemässer Ware (Art. 35) aufheben,[21] hat er vorbehaltlich Art. 40 den Mangel zu rügen (Art. 39). Ausserdem muss er grundsätzlich imstande sein, die Ware im Wesentlichen unversehrt zurückgeben (Art. 82). Nicht jeder Mangel stellt eine wesentliche Vertragsverletzung dar. Eine solche liegt im Grundsatz dann vor, wenn der Mangel objektiv gravierend ist und durch den Verkäufer nicht beseitigt wird (Artt. 37, 46, 48).[22] Trotz Nichtbehebbarkeit des Mangels kann umgekehrt eine unwesentliche Vertragsverletzung vorliegen, wenn der Käufer durch

---

27.4.1982, in: *Schlechtriem/Magnus*, Art. 26 EKG, Nr. 5: Die mehrmonatige Verspätung der Lieferung von Schuhen vom Hersteller an den Einzelhändler stellt keine wesentliche Vertragsverletzung dar. Durch Nachfristsetzung hätte der Käufer innerhalb viel kürzerer Frist vom Vertrag loskommen können, wenn die Lieferung nicht innerhalb der Nachfrist erfolgt wäre.

[14] Vgl. OLG Hamburg, 28.2.1997, CISG-online 261.
[15] So auch *Schroeter*, Art. 25 Rn. 17; a. A. hinsichtlich der subjektiven Unmöglichkeit: *U. Huber*, 3. Aufl., Rn. 7; *Ferrari*, Art. 4 Rn. 24.
[16] OLG München, 15.9.2004, CISG-online 1013 = IPRax 2005, 448 ff. (Erklärung der Verkäuferin, sie habe sich nicht zur Lieferung bestimmter Möbelleder verpflichtet, stellt eine Erfüllungsverweigerung und eine wesentliche Vertragsverletzung dar); vgl. OLG Düsseldorf, 10.2.1994, CISG-online 115 = NJW-RR 1994, 506: Erklärung, „zurzeit" nicht liefern zu können, reicht nicht aus.
[17] OLG Karlsruhe, 19.12.2002, CISG-online 817, UNILEX = IHR 2003, 125; *Soergel/Lüderitz/Schüßler-Langeheine*, Art. 49, Rn. 3; *Piltz*, Internationales Kaufrecht, Rn. 5–255, 5–287; *Staudinger/Magnus*, Art. 49, Rn. 13.
[18] *Fountoulakis*, Art. 72 Rn. 35; vgl. auch Schiedsgericht der Handelskammer Hamburg, 21.3.1996, CISG-online 187 = RIW 1996, 766 ff. = NJW 1996, 3229: Die Erfüllungsverweigerung kann auch darin liegen, dass der Verkäufer die Lieferung unberechtigterweise von der Bezahlung von Gegenforderungen abhängig macht, nachdem er bereits Vorkasse für die Ausführung der Lieferung erhalten hat.
[19] *Herber/Czerwenka*, Art. 72, Rn. 3; i. E. wohl auch *Schroeter*, Art. 25 Rn. 17.
[20] Vgl. *Piltz*, Internationales Kaufrecht, Rn. 5–259, 5–287.
[21] Zum Begriff der Vertragswidrigkeit vgl. *Schwenzer*, Art. 35 Rn. 6 ff.; auch Falschlieferung fällt unter die „nicht vertragsgemässe" Ware, vgl. *Schwenzer*, Art. 35 Rn. 10; *Müller-Chen*, Art. 46 Rn. 20.
[22] Vgl. zur Auslegung der Wesentlichkeit im Einzelnen die Erläuterungen bei *Schroeter*, Art. 25 Rn. 7 ff.; *Müller-Chen*, Art. 46 Rn. 24 ff., Art. 48 Rn. 14 f.; *Staudinger/Magnus*, Art. 49 Rn. 14 f.; i. E. wohl ähnlich *Honsell/Schnyder/Straub*, Art. 49, Rn. 23; *Kazimierska*, CISG Review (1999–2000), 79, 81, 107; KG Wallis, 21.2.2005, CISG-online 1193 = IHR 2006, 155 ff. (Kauf einer „neuwertigen" CNC-Strahlhaus Maschine mit Drehtisch; geliefert wurde eine verrostete, generell funktionsuntüchtige Maschine, die ein Jahr im Freien der Witterung ausgesetzt war, obwohl der Käufer dem Verkäufer Gebühren für eine Lagerhalle bezahlte); CA Grenoble, 26.4.1995, CISG-online 154: Keine wesentliche Vertragsverletzung liegt vor, wenn die im Ganzen vertragsmässige Kaufsache durch Auswechslung schadhafter Einzelteile repariert werden kann; OLG Koblenz, 31.1.1997, CISG-online 256: Angebot durch Ersatzlieferung schliesst Wesentlichkeit aus; OGH, 7.9.2000, CISG-online 642 = IHR 2001, 42, 43; LG München I, 27.7.2002, CISG-online 654, krit. dazu *A. Butler*, IHR 2003, 208, 210 ff.; a. A. *Neumayer/Ming*, Art. 49, Anm. 4.; Cour d'Appel Rennes, 27.5.2008, CISG-online 1746: Erwiesene Nonkonformität der Ware, Verweigerung der Nachlieferung möglich und vom Käufer angeboten; *Miami Valley Paper, LLC v. Lebbing Engineering & Consulting GmbH*, U. S. Dist. Ct. (S.D. Ohio), 26.3.2009, CISG-online 1880; BGer, 18.5.2009, CISG-online 1900: Verpackungsmaschine deren Output deutlich unter der vereinbarten Leistung blieb; KG Jura, 26.7.2007, CISG-online 1723 =

den Schadenersatzanspruch, die Minderung oder durch zumutbare Verwertung der Ware im Wesentlichen das erhält, was er nach dem Vertrag hätte erwarten dürfen.[23] Anderseits liegt nie eine wesentliche Vertragsverletzung vor, wenn der Mangel nicht objektiv schwerwiegend ist; daran ändert auch die fruchtlose Setzung einer Nachfrist zur Mängelbeseitigung nichts.[24]

8   Der Käufer kann erst dann die Vertragsaufhebung erklären, wenn der gravierende Mangel nicht innerhalb angemessener Frist durch Nachbesserung oder Ersatzlieferung beseitigt wurde,[25] es sei denn, dass der gravierende Mangel seiner Natur nach nicht behebbar ist (das im Rahmen eines Spezieskaufes gelieferte Bild ist eine Fälschung). Die Vertragsaufhebung wegen Lieferung vertragswidriger Ware setzt keine Nachfrist voraus.[26] Weigert sich der Käufer grundlos, die Nacherfüllung anzunehmen, verliert er sein Aufhebungsrecht (Art. 80).[27]

9   Den mit der Beseitigung verbundenen Zeitverlust muss sich der Käufer in bestimmten Fällen nicht gefallen lassen.[28] Bei schwerwiegenden Mängeln ist er trotz Behebbarkeit zur sofortigen Vertragsaufhebung berechtigt, wenn ein Fixgeschäft (oder ein ähnlicher Fall) vorliegt, wenn die Vertrauensgrundlage, z. B. durch betrügerisches Verhalten des Verkäufers zerstört ist, wenn die Beseitigung für den Käufer unzumutbar ist (Art. 48 I) oder wenn der Verkäufer die Mängelbeseitigung ernsthaft und endgültig verweigert.[29]

4. Rechtsmängel

10   Zur wesentlichen Vertragsverletzung bei Rechtsmängeln ist auf die Kommentierung zu Artt. 41, 42 zu verweisen.[30] Diese begründen in der Regel jedenfalls dann eine wesentliche Vertragsverletzung, wenn sie nicht innerhalb angemessener Frist vom Verkäufer beseitigt werden.

5. Vertragswidrige Dokumente

11   Ist der Verkäufer zur Übergabe von Dokumenten verpflichtet und sind die Dokumente in irgendeiner Hinsicht vertragswidrig, ist die Vertragsaufhebung nach ähnlichen Grundsätzen wie bei der Lieferung vertragswidriger Ware zu entscheiden.[31] Werden die Dokumente – wenn auch fehlerbehaftet – übergeben, sind sie „geliefert" und eine Anwendung von Art. 49 I lit. b) scheidet im Grundsatz aus.[32] Es ist bei der Beurteilung der Wesentlichkeit nach der Art des Dokuments zu differenzieren. Liefert der Verkäufer Dokumente nicht, die

---

SZIER 2008, 192 f.; OGer Zug, 19.12.2006, CISG-online 1727 und 1565 = SZIER 2008, 182, 183; *Piltz*, NJW 2009, 2258, 2263; KG Wallis, 27.4.2007, CISG-online 1721 = SZIER 2008, 184, 186 f.

[23] *Schroeter*, Art. 25 Rn. 29; BGH, 3.4.1996, CISG-online 135 = BGHZ 132, 290, 299; BGer, 28.10.1998, CISG-online 413 = SZIER 1999, 179, 180.

[24] Ein Bsp. für einen objektiv schweren Mangel ist etwa die fehlende Originaleigenschaft eines Werkes der bildenden Kunst, *Mosimann/Müller-Chen*, FS Schwenzer, S. 1322; missverständlich *Neumayer/Ming*, Art. 49, Anm. 3.; BGer, 18.5.2009, CISG-online 1900.

[25] *Karollus*, ZIP 1993, 490, 496; vgl. auch *Müller-Chen*, Art. 46 Rn. 26 f., Art. 48 Rn. 14 f.; vgl. HGer Aargau, 5.11.2002, CISG-online 715.

[26] Unrichtig daher OLG Düsseldorf, 10.2.1994, CISG-online 115 = NJW-RR 1994, 506 f.

[27] Vgl. auch Art. 46 Rn. 26.

[28] Zum Ganzen vgl. Art. 46 Rn. 27, Art. 48 Rn. 9 ff.; *Karollus*, ZIP 1993, 490, 496 f.

[29] Gemäss *Karollus*, ZIP 1993, 490, 496 könne der Käufer dem Verkäufer eine kurze Frist zur Äusserung setzen, Nichtbeantwortung innerhalb dieser Frist sei wesentliche Vertragsverletzung; ähnlich *Honnold/Flechtner*, Art. 48, Rn. 296. Die Passivität des Verkäufers alleine ist jedoch nicht der Erfüllungsverweigerung gleichzustellen.

[30] *Schwenzer*, Art. 41 Rn. 20, Art. 42 Rn. 25; zum Fall, dass der vom Dritten geltend gemachte Anspruch offensichtlich unbegründet ist, Art. 41 Rn. 10.

[31] Vgl. auch *Widmer Lüchinger*, Art. 34 Rn. 5; *Schwenzer*, 36 Vict. U. Well. L. Rev. (2005/4), 795, 803; CISG-AC, Op. 5 (*Schwenzer*), Art. 49 Opinion 5 und Comment 4.8 ff.; rechtsvergleichender Überblick bei *Schwenzer/Hachem/Kee*, Rn. 47.166.

[32] BGH, 3.4.1996, CISG-online 135 = BGHZ 132, 290, 301; zur Ausnahme beim echten Dokumentenkauf vgl. hinten Rn. 19; *Brunner*, Art. 49, Rn. 6.

zur Verfügung über die Ware berechtigen (Wertpapiere wie z. B. Konnossemente, Lade- oder Lagerscheine u. dgl.) oder sind diese inhaltlich nicht vertragsgerecht, liegt ein objektiv schwerwiegender Mangel vor.[33] Dasselbe gilt für Dokumente, die bei der Kaufpreiszahlung im Verfahren „Kasse gegen Dokumente" oder auf Grund eines Dokumentenakkreditivs zu einer vertragsmässigen Andienung erforderlich sind.[34] Bei anderen Dokumenten (z. B. Versicherungspolice, Analysenzertifikat, Zoll- und Ursprungsbescheinigung u. dgl.) hängt das Gewicht des Mangels davon ab, ob der Käufer in der Verwendung der Ware eingeschränkt ist oder ob er sich die Dokumente leicht selbst beschaffen kann.[35] Vorbehaltlich spezieller Fälle (Fixgeschäfte u. Ä.)[36] setzt die Wesentlichkeit ferner voraus, dass der Verkäufer den Mangel nicht gemäss Art. 34 S. 2, Art. 46 II, III oder 48 I innerhalb angemessener Frist beseitigt. Ergibt sich aus dem an sich vertragskonformen Dokument, dass die Ware nicht vertragsgemäss ist, hängt es von der Beschaffenheitsabweichung der Ware ab, ob eine Vertragsaufhebung gerechtfertigt ist.[37]

6. Sonstige Vertragsverletzungen

Auch im Fall der Nichterfüllung sonstiger Pflichten des Verkäufers (etwa der Pflicht, eine **12 Bankgarantie** für rechtzeitige und fehlerfreie Erfüllung zu stellen, einer zusätzlich zur Lieferpflicht übernommenen **Montagepflicht** oder einer **Ausschliesslichkeitsabrede**)[38] hängt die Frage, ob eine wesentliche Vertragsverletzung vorliegt, in der Regel vom objektiven Gewicht der Vertragsverletzung und von der Behebbarkeit des Mangels innerhalb angemessener Frist ab.[39] Im Fall einer vom Verkäufer zusätzlich zur Lieferpflicht übernommenen Montagepflicht[40] wird man z. B. ein hinreichendes objektives Gewicht der fehlerhaften Montage dann verneinen, wenn es für den Käufer ohne unverhältnismässigen Aufwand möglich und zumutbar ist, den Montagefehler selbst zu beheben oder durch einen geeigneten Dritten beheben zu lassen. Dagegen wird man die Wesentlichkeit bejahen, wenn hierzu spezielle technische Fähigkeiten und Kenntnisse des Verkäufers erforderlich sind und dieser die Behebung unzumutbar verzögert. Art. 49 I lit. b) ist auf die Montagepflicht nicht anwendbar, denn die Montagepflicht und die Lieferpflicht stehen als selbstständige Pflichten nebeneinander. Nur für die Verletzung der Lieferpflicht gilt aber die Nachfristregel des Art. 49 I lit. b). Im Übrigen führt Art. 49 I lit. a) über die Auslegung der Wesentlichkeit zu differenzierten, dem Einzelfall angemessenen Lösungen. Auch der Verstoss gegen **Unterlassungspflichten** (z. B. gegen eine vom Verkäufer übernommene Ausschliesslichkeitsbindung) kann eine wesentliche Vertragsverletzung darstellen und die Vertragsaufhebung rechtfertigen;[41] das liegt insbesondere bei wiederholten Verstössen nahe, aber auch ein einmaliger Verstoss kann ausreichen.[42]

---

[33] Audiencia Provincial de Barcelona, 12.2.2002, CISG-online 1324, UNILEX.
[34] Es spielt dabei keine Rolle, ob die Ware trotz dieser fehlenden oder fehlerhaften Dokumente geliefert worden ist, *Freiburg*, S. 156; s. auch *Mohs*, FS Schwenzer, S. 1285, 1298 ff.
[35] *Staudinger/Magnus*, Art. 49, Rn. 17; BGH, 3.4.1996, CISG-online 135 = BGHZ 132, 290, 301.
[36] Vgl. vorne Rn. 9.
[37] BGH, 3.4.1996, CISG-online 135 = BGHZ 132, 290, 301 ff.; zur Ausnahme vgl. vorne Rn. 7 ff.
[38] HGer Aargau, 26.9.1997, CISG-online 329: Die Beweislast für das Bestehen einer solchen Abrede trägt der Verkäufer, der sich darauf beruft.
[39] Vgl. auch *Piltz*, Internationales Kaufrecht, Rn. 5–292; HGer Aargau, 26.9.1997, CISG-online 329.
[40] Soweit diese überhaupt dem CISG untersteht, vgl. *Widmer Lüchinger*, Art. 31 Rn. 82; vgl. auch *Ferrari*, Art. 3 Rn. 4 ff. (zum Werklieferungsvertrag).
[41] Vgl. auch *Piltz*, Internationales Kaufrecht, Rn. 5–292; OLG Koblenz, 31.1.1997, CISG-online 256.
[42] Zu einem derartigen Fall vgl. OLG Frankfurt a. M., 17.9.1991, CISG-online 28 = RIW 1991, 950, 952 = NJW 1992, 633: Die Verkäuferin bietet Schuhe einer bestimmten Marke auf einer Fachmesse an, obwohl sie sich zuvor im Kaufvertrag verpflichtet hatte, Schuhe dieser Marke nur an die Käuferin zu liefern: Wesentlichkeit der Vertragsverletzung gegeben.

7. Beweislast

13 Behauptet der Käufer, zur Vertragsaufhebung berechtigt zu sein, trifft ihn die Substantiierungs- und Beweislast für die Umstände, aus denen sich ihr Charakter als „wesentliche Vertragsverletzung" ergibt.[43]

8. Vertragliche Regelung

14 Die vorstehenden Erläuterungen haben gezeigt, dass es oft zweifelhaft ist, ob eine Vertragsverletzung wesentlich ist. Der Käufer ist damit mit dem Risiko belastet, dass ein Gericht eine Pflichtverletzung als bloss unwesentlich einstuft. Die von ihm erklärte Vertragsaufhebung ist diesfalls zu Unrecht erfolgt und wird somit selbst zur wesentlichen Vertragsverletzung. Es ist daher ratsam, vertraglich eindeutig festzulegen, welche Pflichten so bedeutend sind, dass ihre Verletzung als wesentliche Vertragsverletzung zu betrachten ist. Ferner ist es auch sinnvoll, den fruchtlosen Ablauf der Nachfrist in jedem Fall, d. h. nicht nur für die Nichtlieferung, mit dem Recht auf Vertragsaufhebung zu verknüpfen.[44]

III. Voraussetzungen der Vertragsaufhebung (2): Nachfristsetzung für die Lieferung (Art. 49 I lit. b))

1. Nichtlieferung

15 a) **Grundsatz.** Liefert der Verkäufer die Ware nicht bis zu dem in Art. 33 vorgesehenen Zeitpunkt, kann der Käufer gemäss Art. 49 I lit. b) i. V. m. Art. 47 I eine angemessene Nachfrist setzen und nach fruchtlosem Ablauf den Vertrag aufheben. Er wird für den Fall der Nichtlieferung vom Nachweis einer wesentlichen Vertragsverletzung entbunden. Dasselbe gilt gemäss Art. 49 I lit. b) HS. 2 für den Fall, dass der Verkäufer vor Ablauf der ihm nach Art. 47 gesetzten Nachfrist die Erfüllung innerhalb der Frist oder gänzlich verweigert.[45] Die Möglichkeit der Vertragsaufhebung durch Nachfristsetzung steht dem Käufer nur zur Verfügung, wenn die Lieferung vollständig oder teilweise (Art. 51)[46] ausbleibt, nicht aber wenn die gelieferte Ware im Sinne der Artt. 35, 41, 42 vertragswidrig ist;[47] in diesen Fällen ist unter Vorbehalt der sogleich darzustellenden Ausnahmen[48] allein Art. 49 I lit. a) anwendbar.[49]

16 Aus Art. 49 I lit. b) und Art. 64 I lit. b) wird deutlich, dass die Nachfristsetzung nur im Fall der drei vertraglichen Kernpflichten Lieferung, Zahlung und Abnahme bei Ablauf der Nachfrist zum Recht auf Vertragsaufhebung führen soll. In allen anderen Fällen kommt es

---

[43] Vgl. dazu Art. 45 Rn. 9 f.; *Schroeter*, Art. 25 Rn. 16; OLG Frankfurt a. M., 18.1.1994, CISG-online 123 = RIW 1994, 240, 241; *T. M. Müller*, Beweislast, S. 135; MünchKomm/*P. Huber*, Art. 49, Rn. 86; weist der Käufer die Ware (bei Lieferung) zurück, trägt der Verkäufer die Beweislast für die ordnungsgemässe Erfüllung und die Vertragsmässigkeit der Ware, *Honsell/Schnyder/Straub*, Art. 49, Rn. 126 mit Hinweis auf BGer, 13.11.2007, CISG-online 1618.

[44] So auch *Staudinger/Magnus*, Art. 49, Rn. 20; *Soergel/Lüderitz/Schüßler-Langeheine*, Art. 49, Rn. 11; *Freiburg*, S. 154 m. w. N.

[45] Verweigert der Verkäufer die Erfüllung, bevor der Käufer Nachfrist gesetzt hat, ist diese entbehrlich, vgl. vorne Rn. 6; die Beweislast für die Erfüllungsverweigerung trägt der Käufer, vgl. *Baumgärtel/Laumen/Hepting*, Art. 49, Rn. 7.

[46] Vgl. Art. 51 Rn. 5 f.

[47] Vgl. *Schwenzer*, Art. 35 Rn. 6 ff. Unrichtig OLG Düsseldorf, 10.2.1992, CISG-online 115 = NJW-RR 1994, 506; unklar Juzgado de primera instancia e instrucción de Tudela, 29.3.2005, CISG-online 1016, krit. dazu *Schlechtriem/Perales Viscasillas, passim*; vgl. auch *Staudinger/Magnus*, Art. 49, Rn. 21. Auch die Falschlieferung ist nicht vertragsgemässe Lieferung, vgl. *Schwenzer*, Art. 35 Rn. 10; BGH, 3.4.1996, CISG-online 135 = BGHZ 132, 290, 297; OLG Stuttgart, 12.3.2001, CISG-online 841; zur parallelen Rechtslage beim Ersatzlieferungsanspruch vgl. Art. 46 Rn. 19.

[48] Vgl. Rn. 17, 19.

[49] *Widmer Lüchinger*, Art. 31 Rn. 33; BGH, 3.4.1996, CISG-online 135 = BGHZ 132, 290, 301; OLG Frankfurt a. M., 18.1.1994, CISG-online 123 = NJW 1994, 1013 = RIW 1994, 240.

Vertragsaufhebung 17, 18 **Art. 49**

nur[50] auf die Wesentlichkeit der Vertragspflicht und ihrer Verletzung im Einzelfall an. Minder schwerwiegende Vertragsverletzungen werden durch Nachfristsetzung nicht zum Aufhebungsgrund. Gleichwohl kann es sich für den Käufer auch bei der Lieferung vertragswidriger Ware empfehlen, dem Verkäufer für die Nacherfüllung Nachfrist zu setzen. Er erwirbt zwar dadurch bei erfolglosem Ablauf kein Vertragsaufhebungsrecht; bei der Beurteilung der Wesentlichkeit der Vertragsverletzung kann aber der Umstand berücksichtigt werden, dass der Verkäufer eine Pflicht, welche dem Käufer wichtig ist, trotz Aufforderung zur Leistung und Nachfristsetzung nicht erfüllt hat.[51]

b) Ausnahmen. Ausnahmsweise verschafft auch die vertragswidrige Beschaffenheit der 17 Ware dem Käufer das Recht zur Vertragsaufhebung gemäss Art. 49 I lit. b). Wird der Mangel im Falle des Versendungskaufs oder einer Holschuld bereits vor Abtransport der Ware entdeckt und weist der Käufer die Ware deshalb zurück,[52] liegt nach der ratio legis ein Fall der „Nichtlieferung" vor.[53] Da dem Verkäufer diesfalls durch die Vertragsaufhebung keine zusätzlichen Kosten entstehen und ihm die Verwertung der Ware leicht möglich ist, besteht kein Grund, die Vertragsaufhebung vom Erfordernis der Wesentlichkeit abhängig zu machen. Der Käufer kann deshalb dem Verkäufer für die Lieferung vertragsmässiger Ware eine Nachfrist setzen[54] und nach Ablauf der Nachfrist die Vertragsaufhebung gemäss Art. 49 I lit. b) erklären. Daneben kommt auch eine sofortige Vertragsaufhebung nach Art. 49 I lit. a) ohne Nachfristsetzung in Betracht, wenn die hierfür erforderlichen Voraussetzungen vorliegen (z. B. schwerwiegender Mangel und besondere Bedeutung des Liefertermins, Unmöglichkeit der Lieferung vertragsgemässer Ware oder Erfüllungsverweigerung des Verkäufers).[55]

c) Vertragswidrige bzw. fehlende Dokumente. Übergibt der Verkäufer dem Käufer 18 beim Verkauf eingelagerter Ware oder von Ware auf dem Transport nicht rechtzeitig Dokumente, die dieser zur Verfügung über die Ware benötigt (z. B. Konnossement, Lagerschein, CTO-Dokumente u. dgl.), liegt ein Fall der Nichtlieferung vor.[56] Kein Fall der „Nichtlieferung" liegt bei anderen Dokumenten (z. B. Versicherungspolicen, Ursprungsbescheinigungen) vor, die nicht zur Verfügung über die Ware berechtigen. Eine Vertragsaufhebung z. B. wegen einer nicht übergebenen oder inhaltlich nicht vertragsgerechten Versicherungspolice, richtet sich somit immer nach Art. 49 I lit. a).[57] Ist der Verkäufer nach dem Vertrag und den Gebräuchen und Gepflogenheiten (Art. 9) verpflichtet, den Transport der Ware zu veranlassen und die auf den Weg gebrachte Ware dem Käufer bis zu einem bestimmten Termin durch Übergabe der vom Beförderer über den Transport ausgestellter Dokumente (Konnossement, Ladeschein, CTO-Dokument, Frachtbriefdoppel u. Ä.) „anzudienen",[58] besteht die „Lieferung" i. S. d. Art. 31 lit. a) in der Übergabe an den Beförderer.[59] Die Pflicht zur „Andienung" ist hier eine von der Lieferpflicht unterschiedene,

---

[50] Die Nachfrist ist keine förmliche Voraussetzung der Vertragsaufhebung im Falle von Art. 49 I lit. a), unrichtig daher OLG Düsseldorf, 10.2.1992, CISG-online 115 = NJW-RR 1994, 506, sowie LG Stendal, 12.10.2000, CISG-online 592.
[51] Piltz, Internationales Kaufrecht, § 5, Rn. 294.
[52] Auch bei nicht wesentlichen Fehlern, dies ist allerdings umstritten, vgl. Hager/Maultzsch, Art. 60 Rn. 3 m. w. N.
[53] Vgl. auch Widmer Lüchinger, Art. 31 Rn. 66 und Müller-Chen, Art. 46 Rn. 19.
[54] Anspruchsgrundlage ist in diesem Fall Art. 46 I, nicht Art. 46 II, vgl. vorne Müller-Chen, Art. 46 Rn. 19; a. A. Honold/Flechtner, Art. 49, Rn. 304.
[55] Vgl. vorne Rn. 5, 6; vgl. auch Pretura di Parma-Fidenza, 24.11.1989, CISG-online 316: Das Gericht erachtete die Wesentlichkeit als gegeben und somit eine förmliche Nachfrist nach Art. 47 entbehrlich, da der Verkäufer nach mehrmaliger Zusicherung der Lieferung schliesslich nur einen Drittel der Ware lieferte, nachdem der Käufer nach insgesamt 2 Monaten die Vertragsaufhebung erklärt hatte.
[56] Vgl. Rn. 11 und 19; Honsell/Ernst/Lanko, Art. 34, Rn. 14; Brunner, Art. 49, Rn. 11; MünchKommHGB/Benicke, Art. 49, Rn. 8; vgl. auch Honsell/Schnyder/Straub, Art. 49, Rn. 100; Staudinger/Magnus, Art. 49, Rn. 17, 22; vgl. auch Widmer Lüchinger, Art. 31 Rn. 74; anders wohl Herber/Czerwenka, Art. 49, Rn. 9; Honsell/Schnyder/Straub, Art. 49, Rn. 27.
[57] Vgl. dazu vorne Rn. 11; Honsell/Schnyder/Straub, Art. 49, Rn. 27.
[58] Vgl. dazu Soergel/U. Huber, § 433 BGB, Anhang III, Rn. 31.
[59] Vgl. dazu Widmer Lüchinger, Art. 31 Rn. 79; so auch Herber/Czerwenka, Art. 49, Rn. 9.

besondere Pflicht des Verkäufers, weshalb Art. 49 I lit. b) analog anzuwenden ist. Dies gilt unabhängig davon, ob der Käufer das Dokument benötigt, um die Ware am Bestimmungsort in Empfang zu nehmen[60] (wie das Konnossement, der Ladeschein und das übliche CTO-Dokument[61]) oder nicht (z. B. Frachtbriefdoppel und ähnliche Dokumente).[62]

19 Beim **Dokumentenkauf im eigentlichen Sinn,** bei dem die Ware in Gestalt der sie vertretenden Dokumente (z. B. Konnossement) anzudienen ist und die Kaufpreiszahlung im Verfahren „Kasse gegen Dokumente" oder auf Grund eines „Dokumentenakkreditivs" durch die Bank des Käufers erfolgt, gilt gemäss Handelsbrauch (Art. 9) der Grundsatz der Dokumentenstrenge.[63] Der Käufer und vor allem auch die von ihm eingeschaltete Bank sind berechtigt, Dokumente, die nicht vertragsgerecht sind oder aus denen sich die vertragswidrige Beschaffenheit der Ware oder der Verpackung ergibt (sog. „unreines Konnossement") zurückzuweisen, Nachfrist zu setzen und nach erfolglosem Ablauf den Vertrag aufzuheben (Art. 49 I lit. b). Wird dagegen das Dokument vom Käufer oder von der von ihm beauftragten Bank entgegengenommen, so ist es geliefert mit der Konsequenz, dass die Folgen sich nur nach Art. 49 I lit. a) richten, während eine Anwendung des Art. 49 I lit. b) von nun an ausscheidet.[64]

2. Nichterfüllung der Lieferpflicht innerhalb der Nachfrist

20 Der Käufer erwirbt das Recht zur Vertragsaufhebung, wenn der Verkäufer die Ware nicht innerhalb der vom Käufer gesetzten Nachfrist liefert.[65] Der Verkäufer muss also bis zum letzten Tag der Frist diejenigen Handlungen vornehmen, die nach Art. 31 oder nach den besonderen Bestimmungen des Vertrags die „Lieferung" darstellen.[66] Die **Beweislast** für die Erfüllung der Lieferpflicht innerhalb der Nachfrist trifft den Verkäufer.[67] Die Nachfrist ist nicht gewahrt, wenn der Verkäufer innerhalb der Frist zwar Lieferung anbietet, das Angebot aber von Gegenleistungen abhängig macht, auf die er keinen Anspruch hat (z. B. Lieferung gegen Vorkasse).[68]

21 Erklärt der Verkäufer, dem eine Nachfrist gesetzt ist, seine Erfüllungsbereitschaft für einen nach Ablauf der Nachfrist liegenden Termin, bevor der Käufer die Vertragsaufhebung erklärt hat, so muss der Käufer, wenn er hiermit nicht einverstanden ist, unverzüglich widersprechen. Sonst verlängert die Frist sich gemäss Art. 48 II, III bis zum Ablauf des vom Verkäufer genannten Termins.[69] Dies gilt auch, wenn der Käufer schon bei Nachfristsetzung vorsorglich erklärt hat, dass er die Leistung des Verkäufers nach Ablauf der Nachfrist nicht mehr annehmen werde. Denn der Verkäufer kann davon ausgehen, dass der Käufer einem vernünftigen Gegenvorschlag widerspricht, wenn er mit diesem nicht einverstanden ist.[70]

---

[60] Vgl. *Schlechtriem,* Einheitliches UN-Kaufrecht, S. 69; *Honsell/Ernst/Lanko,* Art. 34, Rn. 14; *Honsell/Schnyder/Straub,* Art. 49, Rn. 100; *Staudinger/Magnus,* Art. 49, Rn. 17, 22; *Loewe,* Art. 49, S. 72; *Niggemann,* Pflichten des Verkäufers, S. 104 und *Piltz,* Internationales Kaufrecht, Rn. 4–81, 5–263 (halten hier den Tatbestand der „Nichtlieferung" für gegeben und wenden daher Art. 49 I lit. b) direkt und nicht nur analog an); a. A. *Herber/Czerwenka,* Art. 49, Rn. 9.

[61] Vgl. dazu *Widmer Lüchinger,* Art. 31 Rn. 79. Das gilt nur, wenn das CTO-Dokument in „negotiabler" Form ausgestellt ist; anderenfalls ist es, ähnlich dem Frachtbriefdoppel, nur „Sperrpapier"(vgl. *Weber,* S. 179).

[62] Vgl. dazu *Weber,* S. 61 ff., 83 (Frachtbriefdoppel des Eisenbahnverkehrs), 96 (Absenderausfertigung des CMR-Frachtbriefs im internationalen Lkw-Verkehr).

[63] CISG-AC, Op. 5 *(Schwenzer),* Art. 49 Opinion 6 und Comment 4.11 ff.

[64] Vgl. BGH, 3.4.1996, CISG-online 135 = BGHZ 132, 290, 301.

[65] *Friehe,* IHR 2010, 230, 231 ff.; *Troiano,* IHR 2008, 221, 231; KG Zug, 14.12.2009, CISG-online 2026; Zur Bestimmung, Angemessenheit und Formalitäten der Nachfrist vgl. die Erläuterungen zu Art. 47 Rn. 4–13.

[66] Vgl. auch *Müller-Chen,* Art. 47 Rn. 16.

[67] *Baumgärtel/Laumen/Hepting,* Art. 49, Rn. 7; *T. M. Müller,* Beweislast, S. 134.

[68] BGer, 20.12.2006, CISG-online 1426 = SZIER 2008, 174, 175; OLG Celle, 24.5.1995, CISG-online 152; s. auch *Müller-Chen,* Art. 47 Rn. 17, Art. 48 Rn. 12.

[69] Vgl. *Müller-Chen,* Art. 47 Rn. 17, Art. 48 Rn. 30; *Piltz,* Internationales Kaufrecht, Rn. 5–237.

[70] Vgl. *Müller-Chen,* Art. 48 Rn. 30.

Hat der Käufer die Aufhebungserklärung schon vorsorglich mit der Nachfristsetzung 22
verbunden, ist der Vertrag mit erfolglosem Verstreichen der Nachfrist automatisch aufgehoben.[71] Von diesem besonderen Fall abgesehen, hat aber der Käufer auch nach Ablauf der Nachfrist die Wahl, am Erfüllungsanspruch festzuhalten oder die Vertragsaufhebung zu erklären. Der Käufer kann deshalb auch mehrere Nachfristen nacheinander setzen oder die laufende Nachfrist verlängern; sein Vertragsaufhebungsrecht ist dann wiederum suspendiert.[72] Setzt der Käufer eine erneute Nachfrist, nachdem er die Vertragsaufhebung bereits erklärt hat, so liegt hierin ein befristetes (und daher für ihn gemäss Art. 16 II lit. a) bindendes) Angebot auf Neuabschluss des Vertrags, welches vom Verkäufer z. B. durch fristgerechte Lieferung angenommen werden kann.[73]

IV. Erklärung der Vertragsaufhebung

1. Erfordernis einer Erklärung

Die Vertragsaufhebung bedarf stets einer Erklärung des Käufers (vgl. Art. 26).[74] Die 23
Vertragsverletzung führt, auch wenn sie wesentlich und eindeutig ist (z. B. bei objektiver Unmöglichkeit), niemals kraft Gesetzes („ipso facto", „de plein droit") zur Vertragsaufhebung.[75] Ebenso führt im Fall der Nachfristsetzung der Ablauf der Nachfrist als solcher im Regelfall nicht zur Vertragsaufhebung.[76] Allerdings hat der Käufer die Möglichkeit, die Nachfristsetzung mit einer bedingten Erklärung der Vertragsaufhebung zu verbinden (antizipierte Vertragsaufhebung).[77] Erklärt der Käufer z. B. mit der Nachfristsetzung, dass er „nach fruchtlosem Verstreichen der Nachfrist die Leistungen des Verkäufers ablehne", ist der Vertrag nach erfolglosem Ablauf der Frist aufgehoben.[78]

2. Form, Inhalt und Adressat der Erklärung

Die Erklärung ist an **keine bestimmte Form** gebunden; sie kann daher auch mündlich 24
und, bei hinreichend eindeutigem Verhalten, auch **konkludent** erfolgen.[79] Sie hat in einer

---

[71] Vgl. dazu hinten Rn. 23.
[72] Vgl. *Garro/Zuppi*, Compraventa internacional, S. 178; *Piltz*, Internationales Kaufrecht, Rn. 5–239, 5–267; vgl. auch *Müller-Chen*, Art. 47 Rn. 1. A. A. *Honsell/Schnyder/Straub*, Art. 49, Rn. 87.
[73] Ein einseitiger Widerruf der Vertragsaufhebung ist nicht möglich; der Vertrag kann nur durch Neuabschluss wiederhergestellt werden.
[74] So auch die Rechtslage in den asiatischen Staaten, dazu *S. J. Yang*, S. 370 f.
[75] *Freiburg*, S. 304; OGH, 6.2.1996, CISG-online 224 = ZVerglRW 1996, 248 ff.; KG Zug, 14.12.2009, CISG-online 2026; *Bridge*, Int'l Sale of Goods, Rn. 12.24; anders noch das Haager Einheitskaufrecht und nationale Rechtsordnungen wie z. B. § 275 I i. V. m. § 326 I BGB; Art. 119 I OR; § 1147 ABGB; so auch bei Nichtlieferung am vereinbarten Liefertermin in gewissen arabischen Rechtsordnungen, s. *Hafez*, S. 352; ex lege Aufhebung des Vertrags in den osteuropäischen und zentralasiatischen Ländern, dazu *Lapiashvili*, S. 323; sowie in gewissen ibero-amerik. Rechten, dazu *E. Muñoz*, S. 486 ff.; im frz. Recht tritt die Vertragsaufhebung im Regelfall des Art. 1184 Cc erst auf Grund richterlichen Urteils ein, vgl. *Malaurie/Aynès*, Les obligations, Rn. 481; zu den Ausnahmen, vgl. *Müller-Chen*, Vertragsverletzung, S. 293 f., so auch die Rechtslage unter dem UAGCL (Art. 281) und in den meisten ibero-amerik. Rechtsordnungen, s. *E. Muñoz*, S. 281; im anglo-amerik. Recht tritt diese Wirkung in den Fällen der „frustration of contracts" bzw. „impracticability" ein, vgl. *Chitty*, Chitty On Contracts, General Principles, §§ 23–053, 24-001; *Farnsworth*, Farnsworth On Contracts, S. 664 ff.
[76] Vgl. vorne Rn. 20.
[77] Int. Ct. Russian CCI, 2.11.2004, CISG-online 1285; *Honsell/Schnyder/Straub*, Art. 49, Rn. 37; *Achilles*, Art. 49, Rn. 5; *Herber/Czerwenka*, Art. 49, Rn. 11; *Soergel/Lüderitz/Schüßler-Langeheine*, Art. 47, Rn. 4, 9; *Staudinger/Magnus*, Art. 49, Rn. 26; so ausdrücklich Art. 115 III CESL.
[78] OGH, 28.4.2000, CISG-online 581; es ist Auslegungssache, ob der Käufer sich bereits bindend festlegt oder die Aufhebung bloss androht, vgl. dazu BGH, 28.3.1979, BGHZ 74, 193, 204 (zum deutschen Recht) (Androhung von Schadensersatz wegen „Nichterfüllung" wurde als bedingte Erklärung der Vertragsaufhebung angesehen).
[79] BGer, 15.9.2000, CISG-online 770; KG Zug, 30.8.2007, CISG-online 1722 = SZIER 2008, 187, 190; OLG Graz, 28.9.2000, CISG-online 798; *Fountoulakis*, Art. 26 Rn. 8; *Soergel/Lüderitz/Schüßler-Langeheine*, Art. 49, Rn. 12; *Staudinger/Magnus*, Art. 49, Rn. 25; *Freiburg*, S. 309; a. A. *Enderlein/Maskow/Strohbach*,

den Parteien verständlichen Sprache zu erfolgen.[80] Die Formulierung („Aufhebung", „Rücktritt", „Wandelung", „Annullierung" des Auftrags, „Stornierung") ist gleichgültig, solange nur eindeutig aus der Erklärung hervorgeht, dass der Käufer zur Erfüllung des Vertrags wegen der Vertragsverletzung nicht mehr bereit ist.[81] Die schlichte Zurückweisung der Ware als verspätet[82] oder die Rückforderung des gezahlten Kaufpreises[83] können unter Berücksichtigung der Umstände des Einzelfalles ausreichen.[84] Schickt der Käufer die gelieferte Ware mit Mängelrüge zurück oder erklärt er, „die Ware stehe zur Verfügung des Verkäufers", darf eine Vertragsaufhebung nur angenommen werden, wenn Ersatzlieferung fehlerfreier Ware nicht möglich oder offensichtlich ist, dass der Käufer an Ersatzlieferung nicht interessiert ist.[85] Die Erklärung, „entweder die Ware zurückzunehmen oder 50% Preisnachlass zu gewähren", reicht nicht aus, da nicht klar wird, ob der Käufer den Vertrag aufheben oder mindern will.[86]

25 Ausreichend für die Aufhebung, insbesondere für die Wahrung der Fristen des Art. 49 II, ist die **Absendung** der Anzeige.[87] Das Risiko des Verlusts, der Verzögerung oder der Entstellung auf dem Übermittlungsweg trägt der Verkäufer (Art. 27). **Adressat** der Aufhebungserklärung ist der Verkäufer. Welche Personen berechtigt sind, mit Wirkung für den Verkäufer diese Erklärung entgegenzunehmen, ist im CISG nicht geregelt, sondern beurteilt sich nach dem jeweils anwendbaren nationalen Recht.[88] Die **Beweislast** für die Absendung oder die mündliche Abgabe der Erklärung und für ihren Inhalt trifft den Käufer.

3. Teilweise Vertragsaufhebung

26 Die Vertragsaufhebung ist bei Teilbarkeit der Leistung gemäss Art. 51 I auf einen Teil des Vertrags beschränkt.[89] Dieses Recht steht dem Käufer bei einheitlichen, aus mehreren Teilen zusammengesetzten Sachen nicht zu.[90] Gemäss Art. 51 I ist das teilweise Aufhebungsrecht gegeben, wenn der Verkäufer nur einen Teil der Ware liefert oder nur ein Teil der gelieferten Ware mangelhaft ist. Obwohl nicht ausdrücklich vorgesehen, ist die Teilaufhebung unter Vorbehalt des Rechtsmissbrauchs auch bei an sich zulässiger Gesamtaufhebung des Vertrags möglich.[91]

Art. 26, Anm. 1.2.; *Herber/Czerwenka*, Art. 26, Rn. 3; *Reinhart*, Art. 26, Rn 2; *Piltz*, Internationales Kaufrecht, Rn. 5–308; *Karollus*, S. 151; *Conrad*, S. 76f.

[80] Z. B. in der Vertragssprache, vgl. dazu auch *Schroeter*, Art. 27 Rn. 8.

[81] RB Kortrijk, 4.6.2004, CISG-online 945 (Verkäufer teilte dem Käufer mit, dass „the glass is full"/ „enough is enough" und forderte den Kaufpreis und die Transportkosten zurück und verlangte, dass der Vertragsgegenstand abgeholt wurde); HGer Zürich, 25.6.2007, CISG-online 1564 = SZIER 2008, 180 f. = IHR 2008, 31, 33; OGH, 6.2.1996, CISG-online 224; LG Frankfurt a. M., 16.9.1991, CISG-online 26 = RIW 1991, 922, 953; OLG Frankfurt a. M., 17.9.1991, CISG-online 28 = RIW 1991, 950, 951: Erklärung des Käufers, die beim Verkäufer bestellte Schuhkollektion bei einem anderen Hersteller fertigen zu lassen und die Zusammenarbeit sofort zu beenden, gilt auch als Vertragsaufhebung hinsichtlich einer vereinbarten Musterlieferung; strenger wohl *Honsell/Schnyder/Straub*, Art. 49, Rn. 34.

[82] Insoweit zutreffend AG Oldenburg, 24.4.1990, CISG-online 20 = IPRax 1991, 336, 338.

[83] Int. Ct. Russian CCI, 25.6.2003, CISG-online 978 (Rückforderung des Kaufpreises verbunden mit Aufforderung, die zurückgewiesene Ware zu entsorgen); OLG Celle, 24.5.1995, CISG-online 152.

[84] BGer, 15.9.2000, CISG-online 880; *Achilles*, Art. 49, Rn. 6.

[85] Zutreffend daher LG München I, 20.3.1995, CISG-online 164 = IPRax 1996, 31, 32: Ersatzlieferung kam nach den Umständen nicht in Betracht; „Zur-Verfügung-Stellen" reichte daher als Aufhebungserklärung aus. Auch BGH, 25.6.1995, CISG-online 277 = NJW 1997, 3311 = RIW 1997, 1037 lässt „Zur-Verfügung-Stellen" ohne weiteres ausreichen; keine ausreichende Vertragsaufhebungserklärung erfolgte m. E. in (dem unter schweiz. Recht entschiedenen) BGer, 28.5.2002, CISG-online 676 *("wir stellen Ihnen daher das Holz wieder zur Verfügung. Es liegt auf der Sägerei D. Gerne erwarten wir Ihre Stellungnahme");* das BGer hat m. E. zu Unrecht zu dieser Frage nichts ausgeführt, sondern sich auf die Frage der rechtzeitigen Mängelrüge beschränkt (und diese bejaht); vgl. dazu *Girsberger*, FS Richli, S. 226 ff.

[86] AG Zweibrücken, 14.10.1992, CISG-online 46: a. A. *U. Huber*, 3. Aufl., Rn. 29.

[87] So auch *Honsell/Schnyder/Straub*, Art. 49, Rn. 108 mit Hinweis auf HGer Zürich, 25.06.2007, CISG-online 1564.

[88] Vgl. im Einzelnen *Schwenzer*, Art. 39 Rn. 14.

[89] *Herber/Czerwenka*, Art. 49, Rn. 12; *Staudinger/Magnus*, Art. 49, Rn. 27; *Achilles*, Art. 49, Rn. 9.

[90] Vgl. Art. 51 Rn. 2.

[91] *Honsell/Schnyder/Straub*, Art 49, Rn. 94; BGH, 2.6.1982, NJW 1982, 2730, 2732 (zum deutschen Recht).

V. Erklärungsfrist (1): Nichteinhaltung des Liefertermins (Abs. 2 lit. a))

1. Vor Lieferung: Keine Befristung der Aufhebungserklärung

Ist der Liefertermin verstrichen und die Lieferung noch nicht vollständig erfolgt, so kann der Käufer, wie sich aus Art. 49 II lit. a) und lit. b) im Gegenschluss ergibt, **beliebig lange warten,** ehe er sein Recht zur Vertragsaufhebung ausübt.[92] Das gilt unabhängig davon, ob er sein Recht zur Vertragsaufhebung auf Art. 49 I lit. a) oder auf Art. 49 I lit. b) stützt. Die Lieferung hat durch den Verkäufer oder durch einen ihm zuzurechnenden Dritten, z. B. ein Betriebshändler, zu erfolgen,[93] andernfalls dem Käufer die Vertragsaufhebungserklärung ohne zeitliche Beschränkung erhalten bleibt.[94] Der Käufer, der auf eine Lieferverweigerung des Verkäufers über längere Zeit nicht reagiert, verwirkt möglicherweise nach Treu und Glauben noch vor Ablauf der Verjährung etwaige Schadenersatzansprüche; das Recht zur Vertragsaufhebung behält er in jedem Fall.[95] Er ist auch nicht zur Vornahme eines Deckungskaufs verpflichtet, selbst wenn sein Zuwarten mit der Vertragsaufhebung den vom Verkäufer zu ersetzenden Schaden erhöht.[96] Es ist am Verkäufer, durch rasche Lieferung den Schaden von sich abzuwenden. Will der Verkäufer Klarheit erhalten, ob der Käufer bereit ist, die Erfüllung anzunehmen, kann er ihm gemäss Art. 48 II und III seine Lieferbereitschaft unter Nennung einer Frist anzeigen.[97] Der Käufer wird so gezwungen, innerhalb angemessener Frist die Leistung abzulehnen, d. h. den Vertrag aufzuheben, weil er sonst die Lieferung annehmen muss, wenn sie fristgerecht erfolgt.[98] Der Verkäufer kann den Käufer nicht zum Deckungskauf und damit mittelbar zur Vertragsaufhebung zwingen, indem er die Lieferung ernsthaft und endgültig verweigert,[99] denn sonst könnte er sich von seiner Lieferpflicht „loskaufen". Eine Verletzung der Schadensminderungspflicht durch den Käufer liegt hingegen dann vor, wenn er z. B. bei feststehender Unmöglichkeit der Leistung nur darum am Vertrag festhält, um bei steigenden Preisen den Schadenersatz in die Höhe zu treiben.

---

[92] Ebenso Herber/Czerwenka, Art. 49, Rn. 14; Honsell/Schnyder/Straub, Art. 49, Rn. 39; Neumayer/Ming, Art. 49, Anm. 7.; Staudinger/Magnus, Art. 49, Rn. 30; Piltz, Internationales Kaufrecht, Rn. 5–312; Karollus, S. 146; Schlechtriem, Internationales UN-Kaufrecht, Rn. 200; a. A. Fountoulakis, Art. 26 Rn. 16; vgl. auch U. Huber, RabelsZ 43 (1979), 413, 475; unrichtig BGH, 15.2.1995, CISG-online 149 = IPRax 1996, 195, 196 mit krit. Anm. Enderlein, IPRax 1996, 182, 182 f. Die Setzung einer Nachfrist gemäss Art. 47 I unterliegt bei Nichtlieferung keiner zeitlichen Schranke, unrichtig daher BGer, 15.9.2000, CISG-online 770.

[93] Schlechtriem, EWiR 1995, 451, 452; dies war wohl nicht der Fall in BGH, 15.2.1995, CISG-online 149: Der Käufer einer Maschine bezog diese nicht vom Verkäufer, sondern direkt vom Hersteller, nachdem der Hersteller die Zusammenarbeit mit dem Verkäufer, seinem Vertragshändler, kündigte. Der BGH verweigerte dem Käufer fälschlicherweise ein Vertragsaufhebungsrecht, obwohl feststand, dass der Verkäufer nicht mehr würde liefern können und das Vertragsaufhebungsrecht wohl im Zeitpunkt der Lieferung durch den Hersteller bereits bestand. Aus diesem Grund war auch keine Berufung des Verkäufers auf Art. 80 möglich; vgl. ausführlich U. Huber, 3. Aufl., Rn. 40a.

[94] Dasselbe gilt auch, wenn der Käufer vor Erklärung der Vertragsaufhebung einen Deckungskauf getätigt hat und von Dritten beliefert wurde.

[95] Vgl. dazu den vom Obersten Gerichtshof Israels zum Haager Kaufrecht entschiedenen Fall v. 10.10.1982, in: Schlechtriem/Magnus, Art. 84 EKG, Nr. 1a).

[96] Bei der Erarbeitung des CISG wurde insbesondere der Vorschlag verworfen, den Erfüllungsanspruch (nach dem Vorbild des Art. 25 EKG) überhaupt auszuschliessen, wenn ein Deckungskauf zu angemessenen Bedingungen möglich ist (vgl. dazu O. R., S. 78, Art. 42, Nr. 3, S. 111, Art. 42, Nr. 3 II, S. 113, Art. 42, Nr. 6, S. 331 f.; vgl. dazu auch Honnold/Flechtner, Art. 46, Rn. 286; ebenso abgelehnt wurde auch ein Vorschlag, den Erfüllungsanspruch (nach dem Vorbild des Art. 26 EKG) nur innerhalb einer „angemessenen Frist" nach Ablauf der Lieferfrist zu gewähren (vgl. dazu O. R., S. 78, Art. 42, Nr. 4, S. 112, Art. 42, Nr. 3 IX, S. 113, Art. 42, Nr. 10, S. 334 f.), und schliesslich scheiterte auch der Versuch, die Pflicht zum Deckungsgeschäft in Art. 77 zu verankern (vgl. dazu Stoll/Gruber, 4. Aufl., Art. 77, Rn. 2); a. A. Schlechtriem, FS Georgiades, S. 383 (Schadenminderungspflicht *kann* zur Folge haben, dass Käufer zum frühest möglichen Zeitpunkt Deckungskauf tätigen muss, z. B. in einem steigenden Markt); vgl. auch OLG Hamm, 22.9.1992, CISG-online 57, UNILEX = TranspR-IHR 1999, 24; OLG Celle, 2.9.1998, CISG-online 506; OGH, 28.4.2000, CISG-online 581 = IHR 2001, 208 ff.; ZfRVgl 2000, 188 f.

[97] Vgl. Art. 48 Rn. 25.

[98] Vgl. Art. 48 Rn. 26 f.; Staudinger/Magnus, Art. 49, Rn. 30.

[99] Differenzierend Schwenzer, Art. 77 Rn 10.

2. Nach Lieferung: Erklärung der Vertragsaufhebung innerhalb angemessener Frist

28 Liefert der Verkäufer nach Verstreichen des Liefertermins die Ware, obwohl die Terminüberschreitung bereits den Tatbestand einer wesentlichen Vertragsverletzung begründet (z. B. weil ein Fixgeschäft vorliegt) oder obwohl eine vom Käufer gemäss Art. 47 gesetzte Nachfrist bereits abgelaufen ist, und hat der Käufer die Vertragsaufhebung noch nicht erklärt,[100] muss die Vertragsaufhebung nunmehr gemäss Art. 49 II lit. a) **innerhalb angemessener Frist** erklärt werden. Die Frist **beginnt,** sobald der Käufer von der Tatsache der Lieferung **Kenntnis** erlangt,[101] also sobald er z. B. eine Versendungsanzeige erhält oder sobald die Transportdokumente bei ihm eintreffen, natürlich auch, sobald die Ware selbst bei ihm eintrifft. Die **Beweislast** hierfür trifft den Verkäufer.[102] Die Frist wird durch **Absendung der Erklärung der Vertragsaufhebung** gewahrt (Art. 27); die **Darlegungs-** und **Beweislast** hierfür trifft den Käufer.[103] Steht nach dem Beweisergebnis oder dem unstreitigen Tatbestand das Fristversäumnis fest, hat das Gericht es als Ausschlussgrund der Vertragsaufhebung von Amts wegen zu beachten.

29 Welche Frist **angemessen** ist, hängt nicht nur von den Umständen des jeweiligen Einzelfalls ab, sondern auch vom Zweck der jeweiligen Vorschrift des Übereinkommens, die für eine Handlung oder Erklärung eine angemessene Frist anordnet.[104] Im vorliegenden Zusammenhang besteht ein erhebliches Interesse des Verkäufers daran, von der Zurückweisung der Lieferung durch den Käufer unterrichtet zu werden, weil er anschliessend die Ware anderweitig zu verwerten hat. Insbesondere bei Ware mit schwankendem Marktpreis besteht überdies die Gefahr für den Verkäufer, dass der Käufer auf seine Kosten spekuliert und die Ware bei fallendem Preis zurückweist (und den Kaufpreis zurückfordert oder verweigert), bei steigendem Preis behält (und den Gewinn realisiert).[105] Auf der anderen Seite hat der Käufer, wenn er die Ware erhält, kein schutzwürdiges Interesse an längerer Überlegungsfrist. Die angemessene Frist i. S. d. Art. 49 II lit. a) ist deshalb eher knapp zu bemessen.[106] Beachtet werden müssen auch die Art der Ware, die Verwendungs- und Absatzmöglichkeiten, die Verderblichkeit oder Saisongebundenheit der Ware etc.[107] Versäumt der Käufer die Frist, verliert er das Recht, wegen der verspäteten Lieferung die Vertragsaufhebung zu erklären,

---

[100] Wurde die Vertragsaufhebung vor der Lieferung erklärt, ist und bleibt der Vertrag aufgehoben und die trotzdem erfolgte Lieferung ist als konkretes Angebot zum Neuabschluss anzusehen.

[101] Vgl. auch *Schlechtriem*, Internationales UN-Kaufrecht, Rn. 200; *Staudinger/Magnus*, Art. 49, Rn. 35; *Achilles*, Art. 49, Rn. 8; RB Arnheim, 29.7.2009, CISG-online 1939: Käufer hat Recht zur Vertragsaufhebung verloren, da er sich nicht innerhalb angemessener Frist über die verspätete Lieferung beschwert hat. Dass dem Käufer konkrete Umstände bekannt werden, dass „mit der Auslieferung begonnen wurde" (so *Honsell/Schnyder/Straub*, Art. 49, Rn. 42), reicht nicht aus; *Achilles*, Art. 49, Rn. 8; für die Gleichsetzung des Begriffs „erfahren hat" mit „Kenntnis" in Art. 49 II lit. b) i) spricht auch, dass in anderen offiziellen Fassungen des Übereinkommens (z. B. der spanische und russische Text) dasselbe Wort verwendet wird, vgl. *Bianca/Bonell/Will*, Art. 49, Anm. 2.2.1.1. Darüber hinaus wurde ein Antrag der österreichischen Delegation auf der Konferenz verworfen, Art. 49 II a) dahingehend zu ergänzen, dass die Frist auch dann zu laufen beginnt, wenn der Käufer „von der Lieferung hätte erfahren müssen", vgl. O. R., S. 357, Nr. 9–14.

[102] Ebenso *Baumgärtel/Laumen/Hepting*, Art. 49, Rn. 9; MünchKomm/*P. Huber*, Art. 49, Rn. 86.

[103] Ebenso *Baumgärtel/Laumen/Hepting*, Art. 49, Rn. 12, 14.

[104] Verfehlt deshalb *Kappus*, RIW 1992, 528, 532, der generell unter einer „angemessenen Frist" eine ein- bis zweimonatige Frist verstehen will.

[105] Spekulationen mit der abstrakten Schadensberechnung werden dagegen in diesem Fall durch Art. 76 I 2 verhindert.

[106] Die von *Brunner*, Art. 49, Rn. 12 vorgeschlagenen maximal 6–7 Wochen (bei dauerhaften Waren) bzw. 7–9 Wochen (bei offenen Mängeln) sind daher m. E. zu lang.

[107] Übereinstimmend *Schlechtriem*, Internationales UN-Kaufrecht, Rn. 200 („vom Käufer kann im Regelfall verlangt werden, sich schnell zu entscheiden"); *Soergel/Lüderitz/Schüßler-Langeheine*, Art. 49, Rn. 15 („die angemessene Frist ist hier eher kurz"); *Enderlein/Maskow/Strohbach*, Art. 49, Anm. 7. (mehr oder weniger identisch mit „unverzüglich"). Vgl. auch *Honsell/Schnyder/Straub*, Art. 49, Rn. 43 (2–3 Tage); *Achilles*, Art. 49, Rn. 8. Vgl. auch AG Ludwigsburg, 21.12.1990, CISG-online 17: Vertragsaufhebung nach 6 Wochen ist deutlich zu spät; auch gemäss CA Turku, 12.4.2002, CISG-online 660 soll die Frist zur Vertragsaufhebung sehr kurz sein; eine längere Frist würde zwingende Umstände („pressing circumstances") voraussetzen, wie beispielsweise eine trotz Reparatur andauernde, schwerwiegende Funktionsstörung einer Maschine.

und muss den Kaufpreis, abzüglich eines etwaigen Verzögerungsschadens (Art. 45 I lit. b)), bezahlen. Er behält jedoch das Recht, wegen anderer Vertragsverletzungen (etwa wegen eines erst später entdeckten verborgenen Mangels der Ware) die Vertragsaufhebung zu erklären.[108]

VI. Erklärungsfrist (2): Sonstige Vertragsverletzungen (Abs. 2 lit. b))

1. Grundsatz

Die Bestimmung des Abs. 2 lit. b) erfasst alle anderen Vertragsverletzungen, ausser der schlichten Nichterfüllung der Lieferpflicht zum vorgeschriebenen Termin. Insbesondere bezieht sie sich auf die **Lieferung nicht vertragsmässiger Ware,** die Pflicht, dem Verkäufer das Eigentum zu verschaffen, frei von Rechten und Ansprüchen Dritter,[109] die Pflicht zur Übergabe vertragsmässiger Dokumente[110] und sonstige Vertragspflichten (z. B. Montagepflichten, die Pflicht zur Einhaltung von Ausschliesslichkeitsbindungen usw.). Auch die Erklärungsfristen des Art. 49 II lit. b) setzen in jedem Fall voraus, dass die **Lieferung als solche** (sei es auch in vertragswidriger Weise) **bereits erfolgt** und dass die Vertragsverletzung wesentlich ist (Art. 49 II lit. a) i. V. m. Art. 25).[111] Der Mangel muss ferner gemäss Artt. 39, 43 I gerügt werden,[112] es sei denn, es liege Bösgläubigkeit des Verkäufers vor (Artt. 40, 43 II). Die Vertragsaufhebung muss innerhalb angemessener Frist gemäss Art. 49 II lit. b) i)–iii) erklärt werden. Die Frist ist mit rechtzeitiger Absendung der Erklärung gewahrt (Art. 27).[113]

2. Erklärung innerhalb angemessener Frist

a) Allgemeines. Die Frage, welche Frist „angemessen" ist, beurteilt sich nach den Umständen des einzelnen Falls und dem Zweck der Vorschrift des Art. 49 II lit. b). Die Angemessenheit gemäss Art. 49 II lit. b)[114] ist grosszügiger zu bemessen als bei Art. 49 II lit. a), da zusätzliche Faktoren zu berücksichtigen sind.[115] In die Beurteilung einzubeziehen sind u. a. die Dauer der Rügefrist in Art. 39 I, die Bestimmungen des Vertrags, die Art der Ware und des Mangels sowie das Verhalten des Verkäufers nach erfolgter Mängelanzeige.[116]

b) Angemessene Frist. Im Falle der Lieferung vertragswidriger Ware steht dem Käufer zunächst eine angemessene Frist zur Rüge des Mangels zur Verfügung.[117] Ist die Rüge gemäss Artt. 40, 43 II entbehrlich, muss die Frist des Art. 49 II lit. b) aber gleichwohl eingehalten werden.[118] Die „angemessene" Frist nach Art. 49 II lit. b) ist aber nicht identisch mit der Rügefrist nach Art. 39 I. Der Käufer muss somit die Vertragsaufhebung

---

[108] Vgl. auch *Staudinger/Magnus,* Art. 49, Rn. 36.
[109] Insoweit zutreffend BGH, 15.2.1995, CISG-online 149 = NJW 1995, 2101, 2102 = RIW 1995, 505, 506.
[110] Soweit die Nichterfüllung der Übergabepflicht nicht dem Fall der „Nichtlieferung", sei es direkt, sei es im Weg der Analogie, gleichzustellen ist, vgl. dazu vorne Rn. 11.
[111] Vgl. vorne Rn. 7 ff.
[112] Die gilt auch für vertragswidrige Dokumente, vgl. *Schwenzer,* Art. 38 Rn. 7; a. A. *U. Huber,* 3. Aufl., Art. 34 Rn. 5.
[113] Zur Darlegungs- und Beweislast vgl. vorne Rn. 28.
[114] S. eingehend *Honsell/Schnyder/Straub,* Art. 49, Rn. 46 ff.
[115] Vgl. *Piltz,* Internationales Kaufrecht, Rn. 5–313; *Soergel/Lüderitz/Schüßler-Langeheine,* Art. 49, Rn. 14; *Herber/Czerwenka,* Art. 49, Rn. 13.
[116] Vgl. zu § 2–608 (2) UCC *White/Summers,* S. 318 ff.; s. auch OLG Stuttgart, 31.3.2008, CISG-online 1658 = IHR 2008, 102 = IPrax 2009, 299, 303: Umstände des Einzelfalls, besondere Umstände können zur Verlängerung der Frist führen; BGer, 18.5.2009, CISG-online 1900 = IHR 2010, 27, 30; Pretore del Distretto di Lugano, 19.4.2007, CISG-online 1724 = SZIER 2008, 193 f.: 6 Tage genügen bei Kinderspielplatzeinrichtung.
[117] Vgl. zu Art. 39 I *Schwenzer,* Art. 39 Rn. 15 ff.; BGH, 8.3.1995, CISG-online 144 = BGHZ 129, 75, 85.
[118] Vgl. *Honnold/Flechtner,* Art. 49, Rn. 308.1; *Staudinger/Magnus,* Art. 49, Rn. 39; a. A. *Bianca/Bonell/Will,* Art. 49, Anm. 2.2.2.2.

nicht zusammen mit der Mängelrüge erklären.[119] Es ist ihm eine zusätzliche Frist zur Abklärung der Nacherfüllungs- und Absatzmöglichkeiten zu gewähren,[120] ansonsten er die Vertragsaufhebung erklären müsste, bevor er gemäss Art. 46 II Ersatzlieferung verlangen könnte.[121] Ist die Ware verderblich,[122] handelt es sich um Saisonprodukte[123] oder ist die Kaufsache starken Preisschwankungen unterworfen,[124] muss vom Käufer eine rasche Entscheidung erwartet werden können. Er hat sich deshalb innerhalb kurzer Zeit nach Ablauf der Rügefrist für oder gegen die Vertragsaufhebung zu entscheiden.[125] Hat der Verkäufer aber auf Rüge des Käufers hin eine Untersuchung eingeleitet oder unternimmt er einen Versuch, den Mangel zu beseitigen, beginnt die angemessene Frist erst nach Beendigung der Prüfung bzw. Fehlschlagen der Nachbesserung zu laufen.[126]

33   c) **Folgen des Fristversäumnisses.** Versäumt der Käufer die angemessene Frist, verliert er das Recht zur Vertragsaufhebung. Es bleiben ihm die Rechte auf Minderung (Art. 50)[127] und auf Schadenersatz (Art. 45 I lit. b))[128] erhalten, die nicht fristgebunden sind. Diese können immerhin einen gewissen Ausgleich für den Verlust des Rechts zur Vertragsaufhebung bzw. einen Schutz vor der Kaufpreisklage bieten. Die Ansprüche auf Ersatzlieferung und Nachbesserung werden hingegen auf Grund der Parallelität der Fristen des Art. 49 II lit. b) i) und des Art. 46 II, III regelmässig verwirkt sein.

3. Fristbeginn

34   a) **Kenntnis und Kennen-Müssen (Abs. 2 lit. b) i)).** Die Frist beginnt gemäss Art. 49 II lit. b) i) zu laufen, wenn der Käufer die Vertragsverletzung kennt oder kennen muss. Zur **Kenntnis** gehört, dass der Käufer Tatsache, Umfang und Tragweite der Vertragsverletzung

---

[119] *Honsell/Schnyder/Straub*, Art. 49, Rn. 77; *Achilles*, Art. 49, Rn. 11; *Piltz*, Internationales Kaufrecht, Rn. 5–314; *Soergel/Lüderitz/Schüßler-Langeheine*, Art. 49, Rn. 16; *Staudinger/Magnus*, Art. 49, Rn. 38 f.; *Witz/Salger/Lorenz/Salger*, Art. 49, Rn. 7; a. A. *Bianca/Bonell/Will*, Art. 49, Anm. 2.2.2.1.; LG Oldenburg, 8.3.1995, CISG-online 114 = NJW-RR 1995, 438; OLG Köln, 22.2.1994, CISG-online 127 = RIW 1994, 972, 973.
[120] Trib. Busto Arsizio, 13.12.2001, CISG-online 1323; OLG Stuttgart, 31.3.2008, CISG-online 1658 = IHR 2008, 102, 164.
[121] Die Fristen gemäss Art. 49 II lit. b) und Art. 46 II entsprechen sich daher im Grundsatz, so auch *Honsell/Schnyder/Straub*, Art. 49, Rn. 81.
[122] *In re East Coast Brokers & Packers, Inc.*, Bankr. M. D. Fla., 12.10.1990, 14 UCC 2d 46 l: Vertragsaufhebung beim Verkauf von Tomaten musste innerhalb von 24 Stunden erfolgen.
[123] Im Falle von Weihnachtsbäumen, für die nur ein zeitlich begrenzter Markt besteht, ist u. U. eine Woche schon zu lange, VLK, 10.11.1999, CISG-online 704.
[124] *Audit*, Vente internationale, Anm. 136.
[125] Zu lang: Viereinhalb Monate bei Lieferung von Koks, OLG München, 2.3.1994, CISG-online 108 = RIW 1994, 595, 596; 4 Monate bei Lieferung von Schweinespeck, LG München I, 20.3.1995, CISG-online 164 = IPRax 1996, 31, 32. Ferner OLG Koblenz, 31.1.1997, CISG-online 256 (knapp 2 Monate nach Kenntnis vom Verstoss gegen eine Alleinvertriebsabrede zu spät); CA Paris, 14.6.2001, CISG-online 693 (der Käufer hätte nicht das Ergebnis einer Expertise über die Ursache der Mängel abwarten sollen, da die Mängel offensichtlich waren); Hof's-Gravenhage, 23.4.2003, CISG-online 903 = IHR 2004, 119 f. (Lieferung von Weizenmehl mit krebserregendem, kaliumbromathaltigem Brotverbesserer: Kenntnis der Vertragswidrigkeit am 20. November bzw. „im Dezember", Erklärung der Vertragsaufhebung am 7. Januar erfolgte angesichts der schwierigen tatsächlichen und rechtlichen Fragen und der Feiertage innerhalb angemessener Frist gemäss Art. 49 I 2 lit. b)); grosszügig LG Freiburg, 22.8.2002, CISG-online 711 = IHR 2003, 22 ff. (Verkauf eines Gebrauchtwagens, der später beschlagnahmt wurde, weil er als gestohlen gemeldet war. Der Käufer erklärte erst drei Monate später die Aufhebung des Vertrags. Das Gericht erachtete diese Frist unter Berücksichtigung aller Umstände als angemessen, da der Käufer sich über die Beschlagnahme zugrundeliegenden Tatsachen zu vergewissern und die hierfür notwendigen Unterlagen zu beschaffen hatte); OLG Hamburg, 26.11.1999, CISG-online 515: Erklärung der Vertragsaufhebung 3 Wochen nach der Mängelrüge ist bei vertragswidrigen Jeans noch angemessen, nachdem dem Käufer angesichts der Menge und der Art der Vertragswidrigkeit mehrere Monate Zeit eingeräumt werden musste, um die Ware zu prüfen und zu rügen.
[126] *Achilles*, Art. 49, Rn. 17; *Leser*, Vertragsaufhebung und Rückabwicklung, S. 234; *Herber/Czerwenka*, Art. 49, Rn. 13; *Enderlein/Maskow/Strohbach*, Art. 49, Anm. 7.; *Piltz*, Internationales Kaufrecht, Rn. 5–313; *Staudinger/Magnus*, Art. 49, Rn. 42; ZivG Basel-Stadt, 8.11.2006, CISG-online 1731 = SZIER 2011, 540 ff.
[127] Vgl. Art. 50 Rn. 16.
[128] Vgl. zur Schadensberechnung Art. 45 Rn. 25.

kennt. Erst dann kann er beurteilen, ob eine wesentliche Vertragsverletzung vorliegt, die eine Aufhebung des Vertrags gemäss Art. 49 I lit. a) rechtfertigt. „**Kennen-Müssen**" bedeutet, dass die Unkenntnis des Käufers auf einem pflichtwidrigen, fahrlässigen Verhalten beruht. Der Käufer „darf sich nicht sorglos über konkrete Anhaltspunkte (...) hinwegsetzen",[129] die auf eine wesentliche Vertragsverletzung des Verkäufers hinweisen. Im Fall der **Lieferung nicht vertragsmässiger Ware** trifft den Käufer die Untersuchungspflicht des Art. 38. Fahrlässige Unkenntnis ist hier hinsichtlich solcher Mängel gegeben, die der Käufer zwar nicht gekannt hat, aber bei einer dem **Art. 38 entsprechenden Untersuchung hätte erkennen müssen**, und zwar ab dem Zeitpunkt, zu dem die Untersuchung gemäss Art. 38 hätte vorgenommen werden müssen.[130] Im Fall von **wiederholten Vertragsverletzungen** (z. B. mehrfachen Verstössen gegen eine Ausschliesslichkeitsbindung) begründet jede Vertragsverletzung eine neue Frist. Die **Beweislast** für die Kenntnis und das „Kennen-Müssen" trifft den Verkäufer, der sich auf die Versäumung der Aufhebungsfrist durch den Käufer beruft.[131]

Verlangt der Käufer innerhalb angemessener Frist gemäss Art. 46 II, III Ersatzlieferung **35** oder Nachbesserung, stellt sich die Frage nach dem Schicksal des Vertragsaufhebungsrechts, wenn jene Ansprüche aus irgendwelchen Gründen scheitern. Art. 49 II lit. b) i) scheint nahezulegen, dass die Vertragsaufhebung verwirkt ist, weil die angemessene Frist zur Geltendmachung der Vertragsaufhebung zwischenzeitlich verstrichen ist. In der Sache selbst kann es aber nicht zweifelhaft sein, dass der Käufer durch ein solch rechtzeitiges Bestehen auf vertragsmässiger Erfüllung das Recht zur späteren Vertragsaufhebung nicht verliert, wenn der Erfüllungsanspruch sich nicht durchsetzen lässt.[132] Denn bevor nicht klar ist, ob der objektiv gewichtige Mangel durch den Verkäufer beseitigt wird, fehlt es an der Voraussetzung der Wesentlichkeit, welche Art. 49 II lit. b) i) zugrundeliegt; ein Recht zur Vertragsaufhebung gemäss Art. 49 I lit. a) ist somit gar (noch) nicht gegeben. Dies bedeutet, dass die angemessene Frist in diesem Fall erst zu laufen beginnt, wenn die Mängelbeseitigung durch Nachbesserung oder Ersatzlieferung aus irgendwelchen Gründen scheitert, da erst dann eine „wesentliche Vertragsverletzung" i. S. v. Art. 49 II lit. b) i) i. V. m. Art. 49 I lit. a) vorliegt.[133]

b) Ablauf einer vom Käufer gesetzten Nachfrist und Erfüllungsverweigerung (Abs. 2 lit. b) ii)). aa) Grundgedanke. Art. 49 II lit. b) ii) eröffnet dem Käufer eine in **36** der Praxis wohl wenig genutzte zusätzliche Möglichkeit der Vertragsaufhebung für den Fall, dass die Frist des Art. 49 II lit. b) i) verstrichen ist.[134] Der Käufer, der den Verkäufer im Fall der wesentlichen Vertragsverletzung mit Nachsicht behandelt und ihm eine zusätzliche Frist für die Erfüllung einräumt, soll auf Grund seines Entgegenkommens keinen Nachteil erleiden.[135]

---

[129] So zutreffend *Schwenzer*, Art. 43 Rn. 4, zum übereinstimmenden Begriff des „Kenntnis-Erlangen-Müssens" in Art. 43 I.
[130] *Audit*, Vente internationale, Anm. 136.; *Honsell/Schnyder/Straub*, Art. 49, Rn. 55; *Staudinger/Magnus*, Art. 49, Rn. 37. Das gilt allerdings dann nicht, wenn der Mangel dem Verkäufer bekannt ist, denn in diesem Fall ist Art. 38 gem. Art. 40 nicht anwendbar; vgl. *Staudinger/Magnus*, Art. 49, Rn. 39. Die Frist gemäss Art. 49 II lit. b) i) wird aber durch Art. 40 nicht berührt, sie beginnt diesfalls mit Kenntnis des Käufers vom Mangel.
[131] Ebenso *Baumgärtel/Laumen/Hepting*, Art. 49, Rn. 15.
[132] *Soergel/Lüderitz/Schüßler-Langeheine*, Art. 49, Rn. 19; *Enderlein/Maskow/Strobach*, Art. 49, Anm. 10.; *Karollus*, S. 148; *Piltz*, Internationales Kaufrecht, Rn. 5–313; *Witz/Salger/Lorenz/Salger*, Art. 49, Rn. 8; so nunmehr auch *Staudinger/Magnus*, 49, Rn. 42; a. A. *Honsell/Schnyder/Straub*, Art. 49, Rn. 86; *Achilles*, Art. 49, Rn. 12.
[133] *Ziegler*, S. 186; so auch schon eine der frühesten Diskussionsgrundlagen zum CISG (Art. 44, Alternative B, III YB, S. 81 f.); BGer, 18.5.2009, CISG-online 1900.
[134] A. A. *Bianca/Bonell/Will*, Art. 49, Anm. 2.2.1.2. a. E.: Art. 49 II lit. b) ii) sei „überflüssig" („redundant"); ähnlich auch *Audit*, Vente internationale, Anm. 136.; *Honsell/Schnyder/Straub*, Art. 49, Rn. 58.
[135] A. A. *Enderlein/Maskow/Strohbach*, Art. 49, Anm. 10. f.; *Piltz*, Internationales Kaufrecht, Rn. 5–316; *Witz/Salger/Lorenz/Salger*, Art. 49, Rn. 8; *Soergel/Lüderitz/Schüßler-Langeheine*, Art. 49, Rn. 16; a. A. die in der Vorauflage vertretene Meinung, wonach der Käufer sich der Frist von Art. 49 II lit. b) ii) auch bedienen

37 **bb) Voraussetzungen.** Art. 49 II lit. b) ii) setzt die Berechtigung zur Vertragsaufhebung nach Art. 49 I lit. a), das Bestehen eines Anspruchs auf Erfüllung gemäss Art. 46 und die ordnungsgemässe Setzung einer Nachfrist nach Art. 47 voraus.[136] Im Falle der Lieferung vertragswidriger Ware muss der Käufer den Anspruch auf Ersatzlieferung oder Nachbesserung spätestens innerhalb angemessener Frist nach der Mängelrüge geltend machen. Verhält er sich in diesem Zeitraum passiv und verlangt weder Erfüllung noch Vertragsaufhebung, verliert er diese Rechte endgültig (Art. 46 II, III bzw. Art. 49 II lit. b) i)). In einem solchen Fall kann er das verlorene Vertragaufhebungsrecht auch nicht mehr gemäss Art. 49 II lit. b) ii) dadurch zurückgewinnen, dass er dem Verkäufer für die Mängelbeseitigung Nachfrist setzt. Denn der Verkäufer ist zur Mängelbeseitigung nicht mehr verpflichtet.[137]

38 Verlangt der Käufer aber Ersatzlieferung oder Nachbesserung innerhalb angemessener Frist, kann er dem Verkäufer im Rahmen der für den Vertrag geltenden Verjährungsregeln[138] Nachfrist setzen, wann er will, ohne dass er das Aufhebungsrecht verliert. Diese Möglichkeit hat er auch dann, wenn der Verkäufer die Erfüllung ernsthaft und endgültig verweigert, denn dem Käufer muss es unbenommen bleiben, auch in diesem Fall noch einmal Nachfrist für die Ersatzlieferung oder Nachbesserung zu setzen.[139] Diese Lösung steht auch im Einklang mit dem allgemeinen Prinzip des CISG, die Aufrechterhaltung des Vertrags zu begünstigen.

39 **cc) Rechtsfolgen.** Die Nachfristsetzung hat im Fall des Art. 49 II lit. b) ii) die Rechtsfolge, dass der Käufer die Vertragsaufhebung innerhalb angemessener Frist erklären kann, wenn der Verkäufer die Erfüllung nicht innerhalb der Nachfrist bewirkt. Die Frist beginnt mit Ablauf der vom Käufer gesetzten Nachfrist, bei vorheriger Erklärung der Erfüllungsverweigerung durch den Verkäufer mit Zugang dieser Erklärung.[140] Bis dahin ist der Käufer an den Erfüllungsanspruch gebunden. Am einfachsten wahrt der Käufer die Frist dadurch, dass er schon die Nachfristsetzung mit der bedingten Erklärung der Vertragsaufhebung für den Fall verbindet, dass die Nachfrist ungenutzt bleibt.[141] Beruft der Verkäufer sich darauf, der Käufer habe sein Recht zur Vertragsaufhebung gemäss Art. 49 II lit. b) ii) verloren, so trifft ihn die **Beweislast** für die Nachfristsetzung durch den Käufer.[142] Dagegen muss der Käufer beweisen, dass er die Aufhebungserklärung rechtzeitig nach Ablauf der Nachfrist abgesandt hat.[143]

40 Der Käufer ist allerdings nach Ablauf der Nachfrist auch berechtigt, statt die Vertragsaufhebung zu erklären, am Vertrag festzuhalten.[144] Er kann auch **mehrere Nachfristen** nacheinander setzen.[145] Die zweite Nachfrist führt wie die Erste zur erneuten Bindung des Käufers an die Frist bis zum Ablauf der Frist oder bis zur (u. U. wiederholten) Erklärung der Erfüllungsverweigerung (Art. 47 II); danach besteht ein erneutes Recht zur Vertragsaufhebung gemäss Art. 49 II lit. b) ii). Nach dem Grundgedanken des Art. 49 II, dass der Käufer die Vertragsaufhebung nicht unangemessen verzögern darf, muss er die zweite Nachfristsetzung innerhalb einer angemessenen Frist aussprechen, nachdem die erste Nachfrist abgelaufen ist. Somit muss der Käufer sich im Ergebnis innerhalb angemessener Frist nach Ablauf der ersten Nachfrist entscheiden, ob er Erfüllung oder Aufhebung des Vertrages verlangen will.

---

kann, wenn er die Frist von Art. 49 II lit. b) i) aus Unachtsamkeit oder Unkenntnis hat verstreichen lassen, wird hiermit aufgegeben; so auch *Staudinger/Magnus*, Art. 49, Rn. 42; *Honsell/Schnyder/Straub*, Art. 49, Rn. 85; *Achilles*, Art. 49, Rn. 12; *Honold/Flechtner*, Art. 49, Rn. 308.

[136] Vgl. im Einzelnen Art. 46 Rn. 6ff. und Art. 47 Rn. 4f.
[137] Minderung und Schadenersatzansprüche bleiben jedoch unberührt.
[138] Vgl. dazu die Bem. zu Art. 3 VertragsG.
[139] Anders *Piltz*, Internationales Kaufrecht, Rn. 5–316.
[140] Vgl. auch *Honsell/Schnyder/Straub*, Art. 49, Rn. 62.
[141] Vgl. vorne Rn. 22 f.; KG Schaffhausen, 27.1.2004, CISG-online 960 = SZIER 2005, 120 ff.
[142] *Baumgärtel/Laumen/Hepting*, Art. 49, Rn. 16.
[143] *Baumgärtel/Laumen/Hepting*, Art. 49, Rn. 14, auch vorne Rn. 28.
[144] Vgl. vorne Rn. 22.
[145] Vgl. vorne Rn. 22; a. A. *Honold/Flechtner*, Art. 49, Rn. 308.

c) Ablauf der Erklärungsfrist nach Art. 48 II und Ablehnung der Erfüllung 41
(Abs. 2 lit. b) iii)). Für den Fall, dass nicht der Käufer Nachfrist zur Erfüllung setzt, sondern der Verkäufer nach Art. 48 II, III Erfüllung innerhalb einer bestimmten Frist anbietet, bevor der Käufer den Vertrag aufhebt, enthält Abs. 2 lit. b) iii) eine zum vorhergehenden Absatz spiegelbildliche Regelung. Erklärt der Käufer sich mit diesem Angebot ausdrücklich oder durch Stillschweigen (Unterlassen alsbaldigen Widerspruchs) einverstanden, so ist das Recht des Käufers, gemäss Art. 49 I lit. a) die Vertragsaufhebung zu erklären, während der vom Verkäufer in seinem Angebot genannten Frist suspendiert (Art. 48 II). Es tritt aber wieder in Kraft, wenn der Verkäufer den Mangel innerhalb der Frist nicht behebt. Das gilt auch dann, wenn die ursprüngliche Frist des Art. 49 II lit. b) i) zurzeit, als der Verkäufer sein Angebot abgegeben hat, bereits verstrichen war.[146] Das ist einleuchtend: Die vom Verkäufer selbst für die Erfüllung gesetzte Nachfrist kann keine schwächere Wirkung haben als eine vom Käufer gesetzte Nachfrist.

Der Käufer muss die Vertragsaufhebung innerhalb **angemessener Frist** nach Ablauf der 42 vom Verkäufer genannten Erfüllungsfrist oder nach Ablehnung der Nacherfüllung[147] erklären.[148] Diese Ablehnungserklärung wird regelmässig, zumindest konkludent, die Aufhebung des Vertrags beinhalten, welche im Grundsatz eine wesentliche Vertragsverletzung voraussetzt.[149] **Versäumt** der Käufer die Frist, so kann er sein Aufhebungsrecht nicht mehr auf Art. 49 II lit. b) iii) stützen. Er kann es aber, sofern die Voraussetzungen des Art. 49 II lit. b) ii) (insbesondere: ein weiterbestehender Erfüllungsanspruch) vorliegen, zurückgewinnen, indem er seinerseits nochmals Nachfrist für die Erfüllung setzt;[150] dies gilt natürlich dann nicht, wenn er die Nacherfüllung des Verkäufers abgelehnt hat.[151]

VII. Rechtsfolgen

1. Berechtigte Vertragsaufhebung

Die Rechtsfolgen einer berechtigten Aufhebung des Vertrags durch den Käufer ergeben 43 sich aus Art. 81. Der Käufer ist an die Erklärung ab Zugang der Erklärung beim Verkäufer gebunden.[152] Eine Wiederherstellung des ursprünglichen Vertrags ist nur durch Neuabschluss möglich.

2. Unberechtigte Vertragsaufhebung

Erklärt der Käufer die Vertragsaufhebung, ohne hierzu nach Art. 49 berechtigt zu sein, so 44 richten sich die weiteren Rechtsfolgen nach dem Verhalten des Verkäufers.

a) Einverständnis des Verkäufers mit der Vertragsaufhebung. Der Verkäufer kann 45 sich mit der vom Käufer zu Unrecht erklärten Vertragsaufhebung ausdrücklich oder konkludent (z.B. durch Rücknahme der Ware) einverstanden erklären. In diesem Fall ist der Vertrag einverständlich aufgehoben. Beide Parteien sind gebunden.[153] Die Rechtsfolgen der

---

[146] A. A. *Bianca/Bonell/Will,* Art. 49, Anm. 2.2.1.2.; ähnlich auch *Audit,* Vente internationale, Anm. 136.; *Honsell/Schnyder/Straub,* Art. 49, Rn. 58.
[147] Vgl. dazu Art. 48 Rn. 25 ff.
[148] Zur Dauer der Frist vgl. vorne Rn. 31 f.; zur Beweislast Rn. 39. Beruft der Verkäufer sich darauf, dass der Käufer sein Recht zur Vertragsaufhebung verloren hat, trägt er die Beweislast für die Ablehnung seines Erfüllungsangebots, vgl. *Baumgärtel/Laumen/Hepting,* Art. 49, Rn. 19.
[149] *Soergel/Lüderitz/Schüßler-Langeheine,* Art. 49, Rn. 18; *Enderlein/Maskow/Strohbach,* Art. 49, Anm. 14.; *Freiburg,* S. 318.
[150] A. A. *Honold/Flechtner,* Art. 49, Rn. 308.
[151] Ein solches Verhalten würde ein „venire contra factum proprium" darstellen und wäre mit Treu und Glauben unvereinbar (Art. 7 I).
[152] Vgl. Art. 45 Rn. 16.
[153] Vgl. auch BGH, 8.7.1987, WM 1987, 1254 = ZIP 1987, 1125 = IPRax 1988, 169 mit Anm. *U. Huber,* IPRax 1988, 147: Keine Berufung des Verkäufers auf Verjährung der Sachmängelansprüche gemäss Art. 49 EKG, wenn er sich mit der vom Käufer erklärten Vertragsaufhebung einverstanden erklärt hat.

einverständlichen Aufhebung richten sich nach Art. 81. Die Einverständniserklärung des Verkäufers steht unter dem selbstverständlichen Vorbehalt der Bereitschaft und Fähigkeit des Käufers zur Rückgabe der gelieferten Ware. Kann der Käufer die Ware nicht unversehrt zurückgeben und wusste der Verkäufer dies nicht, ist er an sein Einverständnis zur Vertragsaufhebung nicht gebunden.

46 **b) Vertragsaufhebung durch den Verkäufer wegen Erfüllungsverweigerung des Käufers.** In der Vertragsaufhebung durch den Käufer ist stets die Erklärung mitenthalten, dass der Käufer nicht bereit ist, noch offene Leistungspflichten aus dem Vertrag zu erfüllen, insbesondere den Kaufpreis zu zahlen. Ist die Erklärung der Vertragsaufhebung unberechtigt, so verwirklicht der Käufer, der den Vertrag seinerseits noch nicht erfüllt hat, stets den Tatbestand der Erfüllungsverweigerung.[154] Der Verkäufer, der nicht bereit ist, sich mit dem Käufer gütlich zu einigen, kann daher die unberechtigte Aufhebungserklärung in allen Fällen, in denen wesentliche Käuferpflichten noch offen stehen, zum Anlass nehmen, seinerseits die Vertragsaufhebung gemäss Art. 64 I oder Art. 72 zu erklären und Schadenersatz gemäss Art. 61 I lit. b) zu verlangen. Nimmt der Käufer, *bevor* der Verkäufer die Vertragsaufhebung erklärt hat, die Erfüllungsverweigerung zurück, erklärt er sich also vorbehaltlos zur Erfüllung bereit, so kann der Verkäufer die Vertragsaufhebung nicht mehr auf den Tatbestand der Erfüllungsverweigerung stützen; die Vertragsverletzung ist insoweit beseitigt.[155]

47 **c) Aufrechterhaltung des Vertrags durch den Verkäufer.** Der Verkäufer kann schliesslich gegenüber einer unberechtigten Aufhebungserklärung des Käufers auch einfach am Vertrag festhalten. Einer besonderen Erklärung des Verkäufers (etwa der Zurückweisung der Aufhebungserklärung) bedarf es hierzu nicht. Solange der Verkäufer sich weder mit der Aufhebungserklärung des Käufers einverstanden erklärt, noch seinerseits die Vertragsaufhebung erklärt, besteht der Vertrag von alleine fort.

48 Das Festhalten am Vertrag ist für den Verkäufer allerdings mit einem Problem verbunden, wenn der Käufer die unberechtigte Vertragsaufhebung zu einem Zeitpunkt erklärt, zu dem weder die Ware geliefert, noch der Kaufpreis bezahlt ist. Zwar kann der Käufer durch seine unberechtigte Erfüllungsverweigerung den Verkäufer nicht zwingen, gemäss Art. 72 seinerseits die Vertragsaufhebung zu erklären. Andererseits ist es dem Verkäufer nicht zuzumuten, in dieser Lage die Lieferung durchzuführen, obwohl er, auf Grund der rechtswidrigen Aufhebungserklärung des Käufers, mit Sicherheit damit rechnen muss, dass der Käufer die Abnahme ablehnen und vor allem den Kaufpreis nicht bezahlen wird. In dieser Lage muss der Verkäufer die Möglichkeit haben, vom Käufer Zahlung des Kaufpreises zu verlangen, ohne vorher die Lieferung durchzuführen. Dies gilt auch dann, wenn der Kaufpreis erst fällig wird, nachdem der Verkäufer die Lieferung vorgenommen hat. Der Käufer hat die einstweilige Nichterfüllung der Lieferpflicht durch den Verkäufer selbst veranlasst, indem er unberechtigt die Erfüllung verweigert hat; es ist ihm deshalb verwehrt, hierauf den Einwand der mangelnden Fälligkeit der Kaufpreisforderung zu stützen (vgl. Art. 80). Neben dem Recht der Vertragsaufhebung steht dem Verkäufer daher auch das schwächere Recht zu, die Erfüllung der Lieferpflicht einstweilen aufzuschieben, um den Käufer zu veranlassen, seine unberechtigte Erfüllungsverweigerung zurückzunehmen. Nimmt er sie zurück, ist der Vertrag wie vorgesehen abzuwickeln.

VIII. Abweichende Vereinbarungen

49 Abweichende Vereinbarungen sind zulässig (Art. 6). Es verstösst aber gegen den wesentlichen Grundgedanken der gesetzlichen Regelung und den Vertragszweck, wenn in **allgemeinen Lieferbedingungen des Verkäufers** das Recht des Käufers ausgeschlossen

---

[154] Vgl. auch *Frisch*, 74 Tul. L. Rev. (1999–2000), 495, 554.
[155] So auch *Fountoulakis*, Art. 72 Rn. 36; *Stoll*, RabelsZ 52 (1988), 617, 633 f.; so auch das deutsche Recht, vgl. BGH, 5.7.1990, BB 1990, 1662; *Wertenbruch*, AcP 193 (1993), 191, 197 f.; *Emmerich*, § 18 IV 2a.

wird, im Fall der **Nichterfüllung der Lieferpflicht** Nachfrist zu setzen und nach Fristablauf die Vertragsaufhebung zu erklären (Art. 49 I lit. b)), da damit der Verkäufer den Käufer trotz Verstreichens des Liefertermins auf unabsehbare Zeit am Vertrag festhalten könnte. Der Verkäufer kann sich formularmässig auch nicht das Recht ausbedingen, den Käufer im Fall der Lieferung vertragswidriger Ware auch dann am Vertrag festzuhalten, wenn der Fehler objektiv erheblich ist und die Beseitigung des Fehlers nicht innerhalb angemessener Frist erfolgt oder fehlschlägt.[156] Dagegen stimmt es mit Artt. 49 I lit. a), 50 überein, formularmässig eine Vertragsklausel zu vereinbaren, durch die der Käufer bei **Sachmängeln von geringerer Bedeutung** auf den Rechtsbehelf der Minderung beschränkt wird. In diesem Rahmen ist es auch zulässig, durch die Klausel zu präzisieren, wann ein solcher „unwesentlicher" Mangel vorliegt (z. B. bis zu einem Minderwert von 10 Prozent). Derartige Abgrenzungsklauseln sind nur dann unzulässig, wenn sie gegen den Grundgedanken des Art. 25 in eklatanter Weise verstossen.

Unzulässig ist eine Klausel in **allgemeinen Einkaufsbedingungen,** durch die der Käufer sich das Recht ausbedingt, im Fall der nicht rechtzeitigen Lieferung auch dann, wenn die Voraussetzungen einer wesentlichen Vertragsverletzung i. S. d. Art. 25 nicht vorliegen, ohne Nachfristsetzung die Vertragsaufhebung zu erklären. Denn der Käufer kann nicht dem individuell vereinbarten Liefertermin durch Formularklausel einseitig Fixcharakter beilegen.[157] Problematisch sind auch Klauseln, durch die im Fall der Lieferung vertragswidriger Ware das Recht des Verkäufers zur Nacherfüllung entgegen Art. 48 ausgeschlossen wird.[158]

---

[156] Vgl. *Frense,* S. 112 ff., 119 f.; *Schwenzer,* Art. 35 Rn. 42; anders OGH, 7.9.2000, CISG-online 642; *Honsell/Schnyder/Straub,* Art. 45, Rn. 63 ff.; *Verweyen/Förster/Toufar,* Handbuch, S. 205.
[157] Vgl. BGH, 17.1.1990, BGHZ 110, 88, 97; *Schroeter,* Art. 25 Rn. 10.
[158] Vgl. dazu Art. 48 Rn. 31.

Art. 50 [Minderung]

Ist die Ware nicht vertragsgemäß, so kann der Käufer unabhängig davon, ob der Kaufpreis bereits gezahlt worden ist oder nicht, den Preis in dem Verhältnis herabsetzen, in dem der Wert, den die tatsächlich gelieferte Ware im Zeitpunkt der Lieferung hatte, zu dem Wert steht, den vertragsgemäße Ware zu diesem Zeitpunkt gehabt hätte. Behebt jedoch der Verkäufer nach Artikel 37 oder 48 einen Mangel in der Erfüllung seiner Pflichten oder weigert sich der Käufer, Erfüllung durch den Verkäufer nach den genannten Artikeln anzunehmen, so kann der Käufer den Preis nicht herabsetzen.

Art. 50

If the goods do not conform with the contract and whether or not the price has already been paid, the buyer may reduce the price in the same proportion as the value that the goods actually delivered had at the time of the delivery bears to the value that conforming goods would have had at that time. However, if the seller remedies any failure to perform his obligations in accordance with article 37 or article 48 or if the buyer refuses to accept performance by the seller in accordance with those articles, the buyer may not reduce the price.

Art. 50

En cas de défaut de conformité des marchandises au contrat, que le prix ait été ou non déjà payé, l'acheteur peut réduire le prix proportionnellement à la différence entre la valeur que les marchandises effectivement livrées avaient au moment de la livraison et la valeur que des marchandises conformes auraient eue à ce moment. Cependant, si le vendeur répare tout manquement à ses obligations conformément à l'article 37 ou l'article 48 ou si l'acheteur refuse d'accepter l'exécution par le vendeur conformément à ces articles, l'acheteur ne peut réduire le prix.

Übersicht

	Rn.
I. Gegenstand und Grundgedanke der Vorschrift	1
II. Voraussetzungen	2
1. Nicht vertragsmässige Ware	2
2. Rüge	3
3. Erklärung der Minderung	4
4. Vorrang der Nacherfüllung	7
III. Berechnung	8
1. Proportionale Berechnung	8
2. Massgeblicher Zeitpunkt und Ort	9
a) Zeitpunkt	9
b) Ort	12
3. Wertlose Ware	13
4. Unabhängigkeit vom Schaden des Käufers	14
5. Beweislast	15
IV. Rechtsfolgen	16
1. Allgemeines	16
2. Verhältnis zu anderen Rechtsbehelfen	17
V. Abweichende Vereinbarungen	19

Vorläufer und **Entwürfe:** EKG Art. 46; Genfer E 1976 Art. 31; Wiener E 1977 Art. 32; New Yorker E 1978 Art. 46.

I. Gegenstand und Grundgedanke der Vorschrift

1   Die in Art. 50 geregelte Minderung ist ein Rechtsinstitut der kontinentaleuropäischen Rechtsordnungen.[1] Dem Common Law ist es fremd; an seine Stelle tritt dort der Schaden-

---

[1] Die Minderung wurzelt in der actio quanti minoris des römischen Rechts, vgl. *Jörs/Kunkel/Honsell*, S. 316 f.; *Rabel*, Recht des Warenkaufs, Bd. 2, S. 232 ff.; *Zimmermann*, S. 322 ff.; vgl. § 441 BGB; Art. 205 OR; im Gegensatz zu den Principles of European Contract Law (Art. 9:401) und Art. III.–3:601 DCFR kennen die UNIDROIT Principles keine Minderungsbestimmung; vgl. rechtsvergleichend *Sivesand*, Buyer's Remedies, S. 59 ff.; *Bridge*, Int'l Sale of Goods, Rn. 12.51 ff.; *Schwenzer/Hachem/Kee*, Rn. 48.1 ff.

Minderung 2 **Art. 50**

ersatzanspruch.[2] Der **Grundgedanke** der Minderung besteht darin, dass der Käufer die vom Verkäufer gelieferte, nicht vertragsmässige Sache behalten kann und dass **der Kaufvertrag an die veränderte Lage angepasst** wird: Der Preis wird so herabgesetzt, als ob von vornherein die nicht vertragsmässige, weniger wertvolle Ware, wie sie der Verkäufer tatsächlich geliefert hat, Vertragsgegenstand gewesen wäre. Die Minderung ist somit weder Schadenersatz noch partielle Vertragsaufhebung, sondern Vertragsanpassung.[3] Der Vertrag bleibt bestehen, weshalb die Minderung gemäss Art. 50 S. 2 bei Nacherfüllung durch den Verkäufer ausgeschlossen ist.[4] Die praktische Bedeutung der Minderung wird allerdings durch den verschuldensunabhängigen Schadenersatzanspruch eingeschränkt.[5]

II. Voraussetzungen

1. Nicht vertragsmässige Ware

Art. 50 setzt voraus, dass die Ware nicht „vertragsgemäss" ist.[6] Der Begriff der nicht 2 vertragsgemässen Ware ist in Übereinstimmung mit Art. 46 II, III und der Entstehungsgeschichte[7] dahingehend auszulegen, dass er **Rechtsmängel** nach Artt. 41 f. **nicht** erfasst.[8] Es besteht auch kein praktisches Bedürfnis für ein Minderungsrecht bei Rechtsmängeln, da der Käufer durch den Schadenersatzanspruch nach Art. 45 I lit. b) genügend geschützt wird und eine Entlastung nach Art. 79 selten vorliegen wird.[9] Erfasst ist der Fall der Lieferung mangelhafter Ware als auch der Fall der Falschlieferung. Der Fall des Quantitätsmangels, der an sich durch Art. 35 I ebenfalls gedeckt wird, ist in den Artt. 51 I, 52 besonders geregelt;

---

[2] Vgl. *Bergsten/Miller*, 27 Am. J. Comp. L. (1979), 255, 272 ff.; *Piliounis*, 12 Pace Int'l L. Rev. (2000), 1, 37 ff.; *Honnold/Flechtner*, Art. 50, Rn. 313; *Schwenzer/Hachem/Kee*, Rn. 48.4; Sekretariatskommentar, Art. 46, Nr. 3; vgl. auch O. R., S. 358, Nr. 39 (*Feltham/Grossbritannien*). Gemäss § 2–714 (2) UCC wird der Schadenersatz bei vertragswidriger Ware, die vom Käufer angenommen wurde, durch das Verhältnis zwischen Minderwert und hypothetischem Wert berechnet; vgl. dazu *Interag Company Ltd. v. Stafford Phase Corporation*, U. S. Dist. Ct. (S. D. N. Y.), 22.5.1990, CISG-online 18 (§ 2–714 (2) UCC entspricht funktionell Art. 50 CISG).

[3] Vgl. auch *Schlechtriem*, Internationales UN-Kaufrecht, Rn. 203; mit ausführlicher Begründung *Hirner*, S. 191 ff.; allerdings kann mit dem Schadenersatzanspruch in der Praxis ein ähnliches Ergebnis erzielt werden (vgl. z. B. § 2–714 (2) UCC), vgl. Sekretariatskommentar, Art. 46, Nr. 4, 11 („a similar effect to a partial avoidance of the contract"); a. A. *Bergsten/Miller*, 27 Am. J. Comp. L. (1979), 255, 275 („reduction of price [¼] is justified if it is seen as a partial avoidance of contract"); *Lookofsky*, Understanding the CISG in the USA, S. 115 („partial avoidance"); *Audit*, Vente internationale, Anm. 138.; *Karollus*, S. 157; *Staudinger/Magnus*, Art. 50, Rn. 1; *Schwenzer/Hachem/Kee*, Rn. 48.1 und 48.20; anders *Heuzé*, Anm. 459. („mi-chemin entre les dommages intérêts et la résolution").

[4] *Achilles*, Art. 50, Rn. 1; vgl. hinten Rn. 17.

[5] Vgl. hinten Rn. 18.

[6] Rechtsvergleichend s. *Schwenzer/Hachem/Kee*, Rn. 48.6 ff.

[7] Versuche, den Anwendungsbereich auf Rechtsmängel auszudehnen, scheiterten bei den Beratungen: Vgl. dazu O. R., S. 118, Art. 46, Nr. 3 a. E. (Antrag Norwegen); O. R., S. 360 f., Nr. 68–76 (der Antrag wurde zurückgezogen).

[8] So auch *Schwenzer*, Art. 41 Rn. 20, zurückhaltend bei der Belastung der Ware mit Schutzrechten Dritter: Art. 42 Rn. 25 f.; *Schlechtriem*, Einheitliches UN-Kaufrecht, S. 56 Fn. 248, S. 70; *ders.*, Internationales UN-Kaufrecht, Rn. 202; *Enderlein/Maskow/Strohbach*, Art. 50, Anm. 1.; *Grunewald*, § 9 II, Rn. 120; *Honnold/Flechtner*, Art. 50, Rn. 313.1; *Honsell/Schnyder/Straub*, Art. 50, Rn. 11; *Kritzer*, Guide to Practical Applications, S. 374; *Karollus*, S. 158; *Piltz*, Internationales Kaufrecht, Rn. 5–345; *Garro/Zuppi*, Compraventa internacional, S. 190 (im Widerspruch zu S. 171) MünchKomm/*P. Huber*, Art. 50, Rn. 8; a. A. *Brunner*, Art. 50, Rn. 3; *Verweyen*, S. 192; *Tacheva*, S. 190; *Welser*, Die Vertragsverletzung des Verkäufers, S. 122 f.; *Loewe*, Art. 50, Rn. 72; *Reinhart*, Art. 50, Rn. 2; *Herber/Czerwenka*, Art. 50, Rn. 3; *Neumayer/Ming*, Art. 50, Anm. 2.; vgl. auch *Neumayer*, RIW 1994, 99, 106; *Niggemann*, Pflichten des Verkäufers, S. 106; *Staudinger/Magnus*, Art. 50, Rn. 9, 10; abwägend *Bianca/Bonell/Will*, Art. 50, Anm. 3.4. Im Gegensatz zum CISG unterstellt das deutsche Schuldrecht die Rechtsmängel nunmehr dem allgemeinen Leistungsstörungsrecht, mit der Folge, dass Minderung auch bei Rechtsmängeln möglich ist (§ 433 I 2 BGB), vgl. dazu *Lorenz/Riehm*, Rn. 465, 569, 570.

[9] So auch *Schwenzer*, Art. 41 Rn. 21; *Bamberger/Roth/Saenger*, Art. 50, Rn. 2; *Hirner*, S. 211, 274; *Verweyen*, Internationaler Warenkauf, S. 192. An diesem Befund vermag auch Art. 44 nichts zu ändern, der, was das Verhältnis zwischen den Rechtsmängeln und der Minderung angeht, einschränkend auszulegen ist: So auch *Honnold/Flechtner*, Art. 50, Rn. 313.1; *Hirner*, S. 202; differenzierend *Mohs*, IHR 2002, 59, 64 ff.

diese Regelungen haben vor Art. 50 Vorrang.[10] Da die Haftung des Verkäufers gemäss Art. 36 davon abhängt, dass die Ware zurzeit des Gefahrübergangs mangelhaft ist, kommt eine Minderung grundsätzlich erst nach Gefahrübergang in Betracht. Steht allerdings ausnahmsweise schon vor Gefahrübergang fest, dass die verkaufte Sache einen Fehler aufweist, den der Verkäufer nicht beheben kann oder will, kann der Käufer auch schon vorher Minderung geltend machen.[11] **Objektive Vertragswidrigkeit** der Ware genügt; es ist unerheblich, ob der Verkäufer den Sachmangel nach dem Massstab von Art. 79 zu vertreten hat.[12] Unerheblich ist auch, ob der Mangel i. S. d. Art. 25 „wesentlich" oder absolut geringfügig ist.[13] Letzterer Fall erledigt sich dadurch, dass hier dem Käufer der Nachweis des Minderwerts nicht möglich sein wird.

2. Rüge

3   Das Recht zur Minderung setzt voraus, dass der Mangel unter Vorbehalt von Artt. 40, 44 rechtzeitig gerügt wurde (Art. 39).[14] Die Rüge muss die Vertragswidrigkeit substanziiert begründen.

3. Erklärung der Minderung

4   Die Minderung ist ein einseitiges Recht des Käufers, welches er durch **formfreie Erklärung** ausübt.[15] Diese muss unzweideutig erkennen lassen, dass der Käufer mindern will;[16] ein bestimmter Betrag muss nicht, wird aber wohl im Regelfall genannt werden.[17] Die Zahlung des verminderten Kaufpreises verbunden mit einer ordnungsgemässen Rüge ist wohl keine zweifelsfreie Erklärung der Minderung, da daraus nur ein vorläufiges Zurückbehalten eines Teils des Kaufpreises ersichtlich wird, nicht aber die endgültige Wahl des Rechtsbehelfs.[18] Umgekehrt kann die Bezahlung des vollen Kaufpreises nicht als Verzicht auf die Geltendmachung des Minderungsrechtes gewertet werden, da dieser Rechtsbehelf

---

[10] Vgl. Art. 51 Rn. 6; so auch *S. V. Braun, Inc. v. Alitalia-Linee Aeree Italiana, SpA,* U.S. Dist. Ct. (S.D.N.Y.), 6.4.1994, CISG-online 112 = No. 91 CIV. 8484 (LBS), 1994 WL 121 680; dazu *Sondahl,* 7 VJ (2003), 255, 271; a. A. *Honsell/Schnyder/Straub,* Art. 50, Rn. 10 und Art. 51, Rn. 34; *Staudinger/Magnus,* Art. 50, Rn. 8; *Gabriel,* Sale of Goods, S. 159; *Bergsten/Miller,* 27 Am. J. Comp. L. (1979), 255, 265 ff. (1979).

[11] So auch *Staudinger/Magnus,* Art. 50, Rn. 12; *Soergel/Lüderitz/Schüßler-Langeheine,* Art. 50, Rn. 3.

[12] Vgl. *Schwenzer,* Art. 79 Rn. 55; Progress Report of the Working Group, Annex II, YB VII (1976), S. 16, Art. 31, Nr. 2–4.

[13] *Herber/Czerwenka,* Art. 50, Rn. 3; *Soergel/Lüderitz/Schüßler-Langeheine,* Art. 50, Rn. 2; *Rudolph,* Art. 50, Rn. 6.

[14] LG Darmstadt, 29.5.2001, CISG-online 686; LG Stendal, 12.10.2000, CISG-online 592.

[15] So mittlerweile auch § 441 BGB; *Staudinger/Magnus,* Art. 50, Rn. 15; *Ziegler,* S. 253; *Enderlein/Maskow/Strohbach,* Art. 50, Anm. 2.; *Audit,* Vente internationale, Anm. 138.; *Soergel/Lüderitz/Schüßler-Langeheine,* Art. 50, Rn. 5; *van der Mersch/Phillippe,* S. 710; *Gabriel,* Sale of Goods, S. 161; a. A. *U. Huber,* 3. Aufl., Rn. 17; der bei *Honnold/Flechtner,* Art. 50, Rn. 313.2 Fn. 17 und bei *U. Huber,* 3. Aufl., Rn. 17 Fn. 35 zur Begründung der abweichenden Meinung enthaltene Verweis auf die Entstehungsgeschichte geht fehl. Wie aus O.R., S. 359 f., Nr. 56–62 hervorgeht, diente der Antrag Grossbritanniens, die Formulierung „the buyer may declare the price to be reduced" zu streichen, nur dem Zweck der Verdeutlichung, dass die Minderung ein einseitiges Recht des Käufers ist, „may" schien zu schwach. Es bestand Einigkeit „[…] about the unilateral right of the buyer to declare the price to be reduced […]" (Nr. 61).

[16] OLG München, 2.3.1994, CISG-online 108 = RIW 1994, 595, 596 (Unzweideutigkeit der Erklärung i. c. verneint), vgl. dazu *Shin,* 25 J. L. & Com. (2005), 349, 350 f.; gemäss Hof van Beroep Antwerpen, 4.11.1998, CISG-online 1310, kann der Antrag eines Gläubigers zur Abweisung der Kaufpreisklage des Verkäufers als Minderungsbegehren interpretiert werden, wenn der Gläubiger sonst keine Rechtsbehelfe geltend macht, s. dazu *Piltz,* NJW 2003, 2056, 2062.

[17] *Piltz,* NJW 2009, 2258, 2264. Eine Bezifferung des Minderbetrags wird je nach den anwendbaren Prozessregeln spätestens bei der klageweisen Durchsetzung der Minderung notwendig werden, vgl. dazu Cour de Justice Genève, 15.11.2002, CISG-online 853 (Minderungsbegehren abgewiesen, da in der Klage kein Minderungsbetrag genannt wurde).

[18] FCA, 24.10.2008, CISG-online 1782. Es ist daher dem Käufer zu empfehlen, entweder die Zahlung des verminderten Kaufpreises mit der Minderungserklärung zu verbinden oder die Minderung später geltend zu machen, vgl. *Hirner,* S. 295 f.; missverständlich *Soergel/Lüderitz/Schüßler-Langeheine,* Art. 50, Rn. 6 („Minderung wird erklärt durch Herabsetzung des Preises.").

gemäss Art. 50 S. 1 dem Käufer **unabhängig** davon zusteht, „ob der **Kaufpreis bereits bezahlt** ist oder nicht".[19]

Der Käufer ist an seine Minderungserklärung **gebunden,** wenn der Verkäufer vernünfti- 5 gerweise auf die Unwiderruflichkeit der Erklärung vertrauen konnte und sich auf sie eingestellt hat.[20] Kennt der Verkäufer die Minderungserklärung mangels Zugang noch nicht oder hat er sich trotz Zugangs noch nicht auf sie eingestellt, kann der Käufer daher die Minderungserklärung zurücknehmen und – unter den jeweiligen Voraussetzungen – einen anderen Rechtsbehelf wählen.[21]

Art. 50 sieht für die Ausübung des Minderungsrechts **keine Frist** vor. Rechtzeitige Rüge 6 vorausgesetzt, wird das Minderungsrecht nur durch die nationalen Verjährungsfristen begrenzt.[22]

4. Vorrang der Nacherfüllung

Soweit der Verkäufer nach Art. 37 oder Art. 48 berechtigt ist, den Mangel durch nach- 7 trägliche Erfüllung (Ersatzlieferung oder Nachbesserung) zu beheben, hat dieses Recht, wie Art. 50 S. 2 ausdrücklich klarstellt, vor dem Recht des Käufers auf Minderung den **Vorrang.**[23] Der Verkäufer kann auch dann noch nacherfüllen, wenn der Käufer die Minderung sofort erklärt hat, z. B. schon in Verbindung mit der Mängelrüge, ohne dem Verkäufer zunächst die Möglichkeit der Mängelbeseitigung zu geben.[24] Das Minderungsrecht ist diesfalls durch das Nachbesserungsangebot auflösend bedingt.[25] Minderung kann auch nicht verlangt werden, solange eine vom Käufer gemäss Art. 47 dem Verkäufer zur Nacherfüllung gesetzte Frist läuft. Der Käufer verliert das Minderungsrecht, wenn die Parteien sich auf eine bestimmte Art der Mängelbeseitigung verständigt haben und der Käufer die Absprache nicht einhält[26] oder wenn der Käufer das rechtzeitige Angebot des Verkäufers, den Mangel zu beseitigen, zurückweist.

III. Berechnung

1. Proportionale Berechnung

Der herabgesetzte Kaufpreis soll sich zum vertraglichen Kaufpreis so verhalten, wie der 8 Wert der gelieferten Ware im Zeitpunkt der Lieferung zum hypothetischen Wert der vertragsmässigen Ware in diesem Zeitpunkt. Für die Ermittlung des herabgesetzten Kaufpreises gilt also die Formel:[27]

---

[19] Vgl. dazu *Honsell/Schnyder/Straub,* Art. 50, Rn. 19; *Bergsten/Miller,* 27 Am. J. Comp. L. (1979), 255, 270 ff.

[20] Art. 45 Rn. 18; *Schroeter,* Art. 27 Rn. 14; anders *U. Huber,* 3. Aufl., Art. 45, Rn. 30–32 und Art. 50, Rn. 17, der eine bindende Wirkung der einmal geltend gemachten Minderung verneint.

[21] *Achilles,* Art. 50, Rn. 5; *Herber/Czerwenka,* Art. 50, Rn. 4; a. A. *Grunewald,* Kaufrecht, § 9 II, Rn. 135; MünchKomm/*P. Huber,* Art. 50, Rn. 29.

[22] OGH, 23.5.2005, CISG-online 1041; Cour de Justice Genève, 15.11.2002; CISG-online 853. Eine Übersicht dieser Bestimmungen findet sich bei *Müller-Chen,* Art. 9 VerjÜbk, Rn. 1 Fn. 1.

[23] Die Frage war bei den Beratungen umstritten. Art. 46 EKG hatte sie nicht ausdrücklich geregelt, was zu Auslegungsdifferenzen geführt hatte (für Vorrang des Mängelbeseitigungsrechts gem. Art. 44 I EKG: *Dölle/Stumpf,* Art. 46 EKG, Rn. 2 m. w. N.; dagegen *Mertens/Rehbinder,* Art. 46 EKG, Rn. 3; *Soergel/Lüderitz,* 11. Aufl., Art. 46 EKG, Rn. 3). Der Genfer E 1976 (Art. 29 I) hatte sich gegen den Vorrang des Mängelbeseitigungsrechts entschieden, vgl. dazu YB IV (1973), S. 92. Das wurde auf der UNCITRAL-Konferenz von 1977 auf Antrag Finnlands und der Bundesrepublik geändert, vgl. YB VIII (1977), S. 44 f., Nr. 272, S. 154 f., Art. 29, Nr. 1, Art. 31, Nr. 1.

[24] Vgl. im Übrigen *Schwenzer,* Art. 37 Rn. 5; *Müller-Chen,* Art. 48 Rn. 17.

[25] Sekretariatskommentar, Art. 46, Nr. 14; *Soergel/Lüderitz/Schüßler-Langeheine,* Art. 50, Rn. 9; vgl. auch *U. Huber,* RabelsZ 43 (1979), 413, 490. *Honsell/Schnyder/Straub,* Art. 50, Rn. 22. *U. Huber,* 3. Aufl., Rn. 6 spricht von Unwirksamkeit der vorzeitigen Minderungserklärung.

[26] AG Cloppenburg, 14.4.1993, CISG-online 85.

[27] Andere Berechnungsmethoden sind unzulässig, *Hirner,* S. 311; *Staudinger/Magnus,* Art. 50, Rn. 20; vgl. auch HGer Zürich, 10.2.1999, CISG-online 488.

$$\frac{\text{herabgesetzter Kaufpreis}}{\text{Vertragspreis}} = \frac{\text{Wert der gelieferten Ware}}{\text{hypothetischer Wert der mangelfreien Ware}}$$

$$\text{oder herabgesetzter Kaufpreis} = \frac{\text{Wert der gelieferten Ware} \times \text{Vertragspreis}}{\text{hypothetischer Wert der mangelfreien Ware}}$$

Durch diese proportionale („relative") Berechnungsmethode wird das **Äquivalenzverhältnis** von Leistung und Gegenleistung, so wie die Parteien es sich bei Vertragsabschluss vorgestellt haben, der veränderten Sachlage **angepasst**.[28] Der geminderte Kaufpreis besteht damit nicht einfach in der absoluten Wertdifferenz zwischen der mangelfreien und der mangelhaften Sache,[29] etwa im geschätzten[30] Minderwert oder im erforderlichen Reparaturaufwand (sog. „lineare" oder „absolute" Berechnungsmethode).[31] Ist allerdings mangels anderweitiger Anhaltspunkte davon auszugehen, dass der Kaufpreis dem wirklichen Wert der Ware entsprach und dass sich dieser Wert bis zur Lieferung nicht veränderte, entspricht der geminderte Kaufpreis dem geschätzten Wert der mangelhaften Ware.[32]

2. Massgeblicher Zeitpunkt und Ort

9 **a) Zeitpunkt.** Gemäss Art. 50 S. 1 ist für die Berechnung der Minderung einerseits der Wert zu ermitteln, den die tatsächlich gelieferte Ware im Zeitpunkt der Lieferung hatte und anderseits der Wert, den die vertragsgemässe Ware zu diesem Zeitpunkt gehabt hätte. Massgeblicher Zeitpunkt für die Bestimmung des Wertes der mangelhaften *und* der vertragsgemässen Ware ist somit derjenige der **tatsächlichen Lieferung.**[33] Unter dem Begriff der Lieferung wird überwiegend die (einseitige) Erfüllung der Lieferpflicht des Verkäufers gemäss Art. 31 verstanden.[34] Die Lieferung ist erfolgt, wenn der Verkäufer die nach Vertrag bzw. nach Art. 31 erforderlichen Handlungen vorgenommen hat. Für die Berechnung der Minderung ist folglich beim **Platzkauf** der Zeitpunkt massgebend, in dem der Verkäufer dem Käufer die Ware zur Verfügung stellt (Art. 31 lit. b), lit. c)); beim **Fernkauf** ist es der Zeitpunkt der Übergabe der Ware an den Käufer. Beim **Versendungskauf** wäre nach dieser Argumentation der entscheidende Zeitpunkt eigentlich die Übergabe der Ware an den (ersten) Beförderer (Art. 31 lit. a)). Da aber diesfalls (sowie beim Verkauf reisender Ware) der Kaufgegenstand seinen wirtschaftlichen Wert vom Bestimmungsort bezieht, wird nach h. L. auf den Wert der Ware bei Eintreffen am Bestimmungsort abgestellt.[35]

---

[28] *Staudinger/Magnus*, Art. 50, Rn. 20; gem. *Bock*, FS Schwenzer, S. 175, 188, kann auf Grundlage von Art. 50 unter Umständen der Verkäufer verpflichtet werden, den Ersparnisgewinn herauszugeben, wenn der von ihm gesparte Aufwand einen Einfluss auf den Kaufpreis hatte, selbst wenn kein finanzieller Mindertwert entsteht.
[29] Unzutreffend deshalb BBl. 1989 I, 745, 801; vgl. dazu *Venturi*, Rn. 1334 ff.
[30] Bei der Ermittlung des Minderwertes von Granitplatten, deren Wert sich vor allem aus der Färbung und Musterung des Gesteins ergibt, ist ein Durchschnittswert der Gesteinsart anhand Farbmustern und Katalogen zu erheben. Ein Hinweis auf eine bestimmte Grösse eines Abzugs auf Grund eines Gutachtens reicht für sich allein nicht aus, OLG Graz, 9.11.1995, CISG-online 308; LG Stuttgart, 29.10.2009, CISG-online 20717: Minderungsbetrag von 10% bei erheblicher Wertminderung des gelieferten Rasens.
[31] Zu den Berechnungsmethoden vgl. *Rabel*, Recht des Warenkaufs, Bd. 2, S. 232 f.; *Audit*, Vente internationale, Anm. 139.; *Schlechtriem*, Internationales UN-Kaufrecht, Rn. 203; *Venturi*, Rn. 964, 1323 ff., 1338 ff.
[32] Vgl. *Audit*, Vente internationale, Anm. 139.; LG München I, 27.2.2002, CISG-online 654.
[33] So auch Art. 9:401 I PECL; vgl. auch OLG Graz, 9.11.1995, CISG-online 308, anders das deutsche und das österreichische Recht, die beide auf den Zeitpunkt des Vertragsabschlusses abstellen (§ 441 III BGB und § 932 ABGB, vgl. dazu *Rummel/Reischauer*, § 932, Rn. 8); im schweiz. Recht ist der Zeitpunkt des Gefahrübergangs massgebend (Art. 205 OR); vgl. ausführlich *Hirner*, S. 366 ff. zu den unterschiedlichen Bewertungszeitpunkten und den praktischen Unterschieden.
[34] *U. Huber*, 3. Aufl., Rn. 10; *Honsell/Schnyder/Straub*, Art. 50, Rn. 39; *Ziegler*, S. 255; *Herber/Czerwenka*, Art. 50, Rn. 7; *Neumayer/Ming*, Art. 50, Anm. 1.; a. A. *Hirner*, S. 383 ff.
[35] So auch *von Hoffmann*, Gewährleistungsansprüche, S. 301; *Piltz*, Internationales Kaufrecht, Rn. 5–355; *Staudinger/Magnus*, Art. 50, Rn. 22; *Ziegler*, S. 255; *Hirner*, S. 380 ff.; a. A. *Honsell/Schnyder/Straub*, Art. 50, Rn. 39.

Diese von der herrschenden Lehre vertretene Auslegung des Lieferzeitpunkts macht **10** indessen nicht nur beim Versendungskauf eine Korrektur notwendig. Darüber hinaus sind zwei weitere Ausnahmen zu machen. Diese hängen damit zusammen, dass der Zeitpunkt der Berechnung der Minderung einerseits und der **Gefahrübergang** andererseits beim Platz- und Versendungskauf sowie beim Verkauf reisender Ware auseinanderfallen. Beim Platzkauf tritt der Gefahrübergang gemäss Art. 69 I erst dann ein, wenn der Käufer die Ware tatsächlich übernimmt; die Lieferpflicht ist aber gemäss Art. 31 lit. c) bereits mit dem Zurverfügungstellen der Ware beim Verkäufer erfüllt.[36] Dies hat zur Konsequenz, dass der Käufer bei Mängeln, welche nach dem Bereitstellen der Ware, aber noch vor der tatsächlichen Übernahme der Ware entstehen, zwar theoretisch mindern kann, aber, da die Ware im entscheidenden Berechnungszeitpunkt mängelfrei war, keine Herabsetzung des Kaufpreises verlangen kann.[37] Beim Versendungskauf und beim Verkauf reisender Ware liegt der umgekehrte Fall vor: Die Gefahr geht bereits durch Übergabe der Ware an den ersten Beförderer auf den Käufer über (Art. 67 I) bzw. (bei reisender Ware) im Zeitpunkt des Vertragsschlusses (Art. 68 I). Für die Berechnung der Minderung wird aber auf das Eintreffen der Ware am Bestimmungsort abgestellt. Es ist unbestritten, dass Verschlechterungen der gelieferten Ware, die in der Zeit zwischen Gefahrübergang und Berechnungszeitpunkt eingetreten sind und für die der Verkäufer auch nicht nach Art. 66 HS. 2 einzustehen hat, bei der Feststellung des tatsächlichen Werts der gelieferten Ware nicht berücksichtigt werden dürfen.

Es fragt sich, ob angesichts dieser weitreichenden, praktisch relevanten Ausnahmen die **11** Regel aufrechterhalten werden soll, dass der Zeitpunkt der Lieferung in Art. 50 und somit der Berechnungszeitpunkt für die Minderung mit der Erfüllung der Lieferpflicht gemäss Art. 31 gleichzusetzen ist.[38] Sachgerechter erscheint eine Auslegung des Lieferbegriffs, mit der die verschiedenen Liefermodalitäten nach einem einheitlichen Massstab gelöst werden können. Dazu ist mit der neueren Literatur der Begriff der Lieferung von Art. 31 zu lösen und nicht nur die Handlung des Verkäufers (**Angebot** bzw. **Übergabe der Ware**) sondern auch das Verhalten des Käufers (**Übernahme der Ware**) einzubeziehen.[39] Beim Platzkauf wird so das Problem beseitigt, dass der Gefahrübergang nach dem Berechnungszeitpunkt liegt. Beim Versendungskauf und beim Verkauf reisender Ware erübrigt sich die bei der h. L. notwendige Korrektur. Allerdings ist nicht auf das Eintreffen der Ware am Bestimmungsort abzustellen, sondern auf den Zeitpunkt, an dem die Ware dort zur Verfügung des Käufers steht.[40] Die hier vertretene Auslegung des Lieferbegriffs ist auch wirtschaftlich sinnvoll, da sich der wirtschaftliche Wert der Ware in der Regel nach dem Wert in dem Zeitpunkt bemisst, in dem der Käufer die Ware übernimmt und über sie verfügen kann; dies entspricht im Regelfall auch dem Zeitpunkt, in dem er den Kaufpreis zahlen muss (Art. 58).[41] Darüber hinaus stimmt dieser Zeitpunkt auch mit dem für die Schadenersatzberechnung massgeblichen Zeitpunkt überein.[42] Zusammengefasst ist somit für die Berechnung der Minderung immer auf den Zeitpunkt abzustellen, in dem der Käufer die Ware übernommen hat bzw. übernehmen musste.[43]

---

[36] Darauf weist zu Recht hin *Hirner*, S. 378 f., 384 f.
[37] Zum Lösungsansatz vgl. sogleich Rn. 11.
[38] Dazu und zum Folgenden mit überzeugender Begründung *Hirner*, S. 385 ff.
[39] *Hirner*, S. 386; so schon *Wilhelm*, S. 28.
[40] Das blosse Eintreffen der Ware am Bestimmungsort kann nicht massgeblich sein, da die Feststellung der Vertragswidrigkeit, welche den Rechtsbehelf der Minderung auslöst, Untersuchung und Rüge voraussetzt. Diese darf beim Versendungskauf gem. Art. 38 II am Bestimmungsort vorgenommen werden; untersucht werden kann aber die Ware erst, wenn sie dem Käufer zur Verfügung steht.
[41] *Hirner*, S. 386 f.
[42] *Hirner*, S. 387.
[43] So auch der funktional äquivalente § 2–714 (2) UCC. Sollte der Gefahrübergang vor dem Bewertungszeitpunkt liegen, darf bei der Herabsetzung des Kaufpreises eine erst nach Gefahrübergang eingetretene Vertragswidrigkeit, für die der Verkäufer nicht einzustehen hat, nicht wertmindernd berücksichtigt werden, vgl. vorne Rn. 10 und *Hirner*, S. 391.

12 b) Ort. Nicht nur der Zeitpunkt, sondern auch die Verhältnisse am Ort, an dem die Wertbestimmung der Ware erfolgt, können einen Einfluss auf die Schätzung des Minderwertes haben. Art. 50 legt diesen Ort nicht fest. Wegen des engen Zusammenhangs zwischen Bewertungszeitpunkt und -ort ist nach h. L. auch für den Bewertungsort auf den Lieferort gemäss Art. 31 abzustellen. Die oben (Rn. 9 f.) dargestellte Auslegung des Zeitpunkts der Lieferung führt im Ergebnis dazu, dass beim **Versendungskauf** und beim **Verkauf reisender Ware** in Abweichung von Art. 31 lit. a) die Verhältnisse am **Bestimmungsort** massgeblich sind,[44] in allen **anderen Fällen** der **Lieferort** gemäss Art. 31 lit. b), lit. c), d. h. beim Platzkauf der Ort, an dem der Verkäufer die Ware dem Käufer zur Verfügung stellt und beim Fernkauf der Bestimmungsort.[45] Der Ort der Niederlassung des Käufers ist grundsätzlich nicht massgeblich.[46] In der Sache ist der herrschenden Meinung zuzustimmen; allerdings erscheint es aus Gründen der Kohärenz sinnvoll, auch für den Bewertungsort generell auf den Ort der **tatsächlichen Übernahme** durch den Käufer abzustellen.[47] Eine Ausnahme von diesem Grundsatz kann gemacht werden, wenn der vertraglichen Preisgestaltung erkennbar die Wertverhältnisse an einem anderen Ort zugrundegelegt wurden.[48]

3. Wertlose Ware

13 Steht fest, dass die gelieferte Ware vollkommen wertlos ist,[49] so führt die Minderung zu einer Herabsetzung des Kaufpreises auf Null.[50] Normalerweise wird der Käufer in einem solchen Fall die Vertragsaufhebung erklären. Die Minderung ist ihm aber nützlich, wenn die Vertragsaufhebung aus irgendwelchen Gründen nicht möglich ist, z. B. weil er eine Frist nach Art. 49 II lit. b) versäumt hat.

---

[44] *Schlechtriem*, Einheitliches UN-Kaufrecht, S. 70 Fn. 311; *Enderlein/Maskow/Strohbach*, Art. 50, Anm. 4.; *Reinhart*, Art. 50, Rn. 4; *Herber/Czerwenka*, Art. 50, Rn. 7; *Neumayer/Ming*, Art. 50, Anm. 1.; *Audit*, Vente internationale, Anm. 139; *Karollus*, S. 157; *Piltz*, Internationales Kaufrecht, Rn. 5–355; *Staudinger/Magnus*, Art. 50, Rn. 22; *Loewe*, Art. 50, S. 73; grundsätzlich auch *Bianca/Bonell/Will*, Art. 50, Anm. 3.3.; *Venturi*, Rn. 1318.

[45] *Schlechtriem*, Einheitliches UN-Kaufrecht, S. 70 Fn. 311; *Enderlein/Maskow/Strohbach*, Art. 50, Anm. 4.; *Herber/Czerwenka*, Art. 50, Rn. 7; *Karollus*, S. 157; *Piltz*, Internationales Kaufrecht, Rn. 5–355; *Staudinger/Magnus*, Art. 50, Rn. 22; a. A. *von Hoffmann*, Gewährleistungsansprüche, S. 301 (Verkehrswert im Käuferland massgeblich); *Honsell/Schnyder/Straub*, Art. 50, Rn. 47 (massgeblich ist im Fall der Holschuld der Ort sein, an den der Käufer die Ware verbringt): zu Recht krit. dazu *Hirner*, S. 394 f.

[46] Dafür aber *von Hoffmann*, Gewährleistungsansprüche, S. 301; *Reinhart*, Art. 50, Rn. 4; subsidiär auch *Bianca/Bonell/Will*, Art. 50, Anm. 3.3.; *Loewe*, Art. 50, S. 73. Auch auf der Wiener Konferenz war vorgeschlagen worden, allgemein den Ort der Niederlassung des Käufers für massgeblich zu erklären (Antrag Argentinien/Spanien/Portugal, O. R., S. 118, Art. 46, Nr. 3 III). Der Vorschlag ist zu Recht abgelehnt worden (O. R., S. 358 f., Nr. 42–54), nicht nur, weil es nicht Aufgabe des Gesetzes ist, solche Detailfragen zu regeln (O. R., S. 359, Nr. 49), sondern auch, weil bei dem Vorschlag offenbar übersehen worden war, dass der Niederlassungsort des Käufers weder mit dem Lieferort, noch mit dem Bestimmungsort der Ware identisch sein muss (O. R., S. 359, Nr. 48).

[47] So auch der funktional äquivalente § 2–714 (2) UCC. Wie *Hirner*, S. 394 zu Recht ausführt, besteht zur h. L. i. E. kein sachlicher Unterschied: Der Ort, an dem der Käufer die Ware übernimmt, ist sowohl mit dem Bestimmungsort beim Versendungskauf und beim Verkauf reisender Ware als auch mit dem Ort des Zurverfügungstellens bzw. der Übergabe bei der Hol- und Bringschuld identisch.

[48] *Hirner*, S. 395 ff. (Bsp: Bestimmte Mercedes-Limousinen waren zu einer gewissen Zeit in Deutschland schwer absetzbar, in Hongkong aber sehr teuer. Kauft ein Händler aus Hongkong einen solchen Wagen ab Werk in Deutschland unter Zugrundelegung der Werte in Hongkong und transportiert er ihn selbst nach Hongkong, muss für die Berechnung der Minderung auf den dortigen Wert abgestellt werden); vgl. auch *Schlechtriem*, Pflichten des Verkäufers, S. 117.

[49] Die Wertlosigkeit kann sich auch daraus ergeben, dass die Ware am massgeblichen Bewertungsort nicht handelsfähig ist und der Transport zum nächstgelegenen Verwertungsort höher als der dort erzielte Preis ist.

[50] Ebenso OGH, 23.5.2005, CISG-online 1041 = IHR 2005, 165 ff. = ÖJZ 2005, 761 f.; BGH, 2.3.2005, CISG-online 999 = RIW 2005, 547 ff. = IHR 2005, 158 ff. = JZ 2005, 844 ff. = NJW-RR 2005, 1218 ff.; OLG Koblenz, 10.10.2006, CISG-online 1438; *Piltz*, Internationales Kaufrecht, Rn. 5–357; *Staudinger/Magnus*, Art. 50, Rn. 23; *Hirner*, S. 332; *Brunner*, Art. 50, Rn. 11; *MünchKomm/P. Huber*, Art. 50, Rn. 24; a. A. *Rabel*, Recht des Warenkaufs, Bd. 2, S. 235; *Honsell/Schnyder/Straub*, Art. 50, Rn. 46.

4. Unabhängigkeit vom Schaden des Käufers

Die Minderung setzt nicht voraus, dass dem Käufer infolge des Minderwerts tatsächlich ein Schaden entstanden ist.[51] Ebensowenig sind Vorteile, die der Käufer aus der Sache tatsächlich gezogen hat (z. B. durch Weiterveräusserung oder Vermietung), auf den vom Verkäufer zu erstattenden Betrag anzurechnen[52]. Massgeblich ist allein das abstrakte Verhältnis des Werts der gelieferten Ware zum hypothetischen Wert der fehlerfreien Ware. 14

5. Beweislast

Die Beweislast für beide Werte, den der gelieferten und den der mangelfreien Ware, trifft den Käufer, da er es ist, der die Minderung geltend macht.[53] Soweit es sich nicht um Ware handelt, für die ein laufender Börsen- und Marktpreis besteht, ist prima facie davon auszugehen, dass der Vertragspreis mit dem Wert der mangelfreien Ware zum Zeitpunkt der Lieferung übereinstimmt.[54] In diesem Fall kann der Minderwert vom Gericht frei geschätzt werden.[55] 15

IV. Rechtsfolgen

1. Allgemeines

Hat der Käufer den Kaufpreis noch nicht bezahlt, übt er sein Minderungsrecht durch entsprechende **Kürzung** des Kaufpreises oder als Einrede gegen die Kaufpreisklage[56] aus; wenn er den Kaufpreis bereits bezahlt hat durch **Rückforderung** des zu viel bezahlten Betrages. Grundlage des Rückzahlungsanspruchs ist Art. 50 selbst, was durch den Zusatz, dass Minderung auch nach Zahlung des Kaufpreises möglich ist, noch einmal klargestellt wird.[57] Der zurückzuzahlende Betrag ist gemäss Art. 78 ab Empfang des zu viel bezahlten Kaufpreises durch den Verkäufer zu **verzinsen**.[58] Verzögerung der Rückzahlung durch den Verkäufer ist Nichterfüllung einer nach dem Übereinkommen bestehenden Pflicht, durch die der Verkäufer gemäss Art. 45 I lit. b) **schadenersatzpflichtig** wird. Zwar ist der gemäss Art. 78 zu zahlende Zins auf den Schaden anzurechnen. Der Schaden, der dem Käufer durch die Vorenthaltung des zurückgeforderten Betrags entsteht, kann aber höher sein als der gemäss Art. 78 zu zahlende Zins. 16

---

[51] Vgl. auch *Staudinger/Magnus*, Art. 50, Rn. 4; *Brunner*, Art. 50, Rn. 9.
[52] Den Käufer trifft daher auch keine Schadensminderungspflicht nach Art. 77. Die Konzeption der Minderung entspricht eben gerade nicht derjenigen des Schadenersatzes.
[53] *Baumgärtel/Laumen/Hepting*, Art. 50, Rn. 4; LG Flensburg, 24.3.1999, CISG-online 719: Das Risiko der Beweislosigkeit in Bezug auf die Vertragswidrigkeit der Ware im Zeitpunkt des Gefahrübergangs trägt der Käufer, nachdem dieser es unterlassen hatte, die Mängel zu rügen. Laut MünchKommHGB/*Benicke*, Art. 50, Rn. 10 soll der Käufer die Beweislast für den hypothetischen Wert der mangelfreien Ware tragen, wenn er geltend macht, dass der hypothetische Wert der mangelfreien Ware höher als der Kaufpreis sei, er also relativ billig gekauft habe. Hat er relativ teuer gekauft, so soll der Verkäufer den hypothetischen Wert beweisen.
[54] Ebenso *Staudinger/Magnus*, Art. 50, Rn. 34; *Baumgärtel/Laumen/Hepting*, Art. 50, Rn. 5.
[55] *Baumgärtel/Laumen/Hepting*, Art. 50, Rn. 5. Manche nationale Rechtsordnungen räumen dem Gericht explizit Schätzungsbefugnisse ein, da die Ermittlung des Minderwertes in der Praxis oft mit Schwierigkeiten verbunden ist, vgl. z. B. Art. 441 III 2 BGB, § 287 deutsche ZPO, § 273 I österreichische ZPO, OLG Graz, 9.11.1995, CISG-online 308. Solche Beweiserleichterungsvorschriften sind als prozessuale Normen zu qualifizieren und damit auch anwendbar, wenn der Vertrag dem CISG unterliegt, vgl. *Schlechtriem*, Internationales Kaufrecht, Rn. 203.
[56] HGer Aargau, 11.6.1999, CISG-online 494.
[57] Vgl. auch *Staudinger/Magnus*, Art. 50, Rn. 26; *Venturi*, Rn. 1382.
[58] So auch *Bacher*, Art. 78 Rn. 13; *Piltz*, Internationales Kaufrecht, Rn. 5–359; *Venturi*, Rn. 1389, 1391; MünchKommHGB/*Benicke*, Art. 50, Rn. 13; i. E. auch *Staudinger/Magnus*, Art. 50, Rn. 26 und *Karollus*, S. 157 (beide gestützt auf Art. 84 I); a. A. *Honsell/Schnyder/Straub*, Art. 50, Rn. 52 (Verzinsung erst „ab Abgabe einer rechtzeitigen Minderungserklärung" durch den Käufer). Die in Art. 78 nicht geregelte Zinshöhe ist nach herrschender und zutreffender Ansicht internationalprivatrechtlich zu ermitteln, und zwar nach dem Vertragsstatut (vgl. dazu die Nachweise von *Bacher*, Art. 78 Fn. 25, 35, 36). Massgeblich ist also im Zweifel der gesetzliche Zinssatz im Verkäuferstaat.

2. Verhältnis zu anderen Rechtsbehelfen

17 Der Käufer, der Minderung verlangt, kann nicht zugleich Beseitigung des Mangels durch Ersatzlieferung oder Nachbesserung verlangen.[59] Er kann die Rechtsbehelfe zwar wechseln, aber **nicht kombinieren**. Der Käufer, der die Vertragsaufhebung erklärt, verliert die Möglichkeit der Minderung. Sobald der Käufer an die Minderung gebunden ist, sind der Anspruch auf Mängelbeseitigung und das Recht zur Vertragsaufhebung ausgeschlossen.[60]

18 Der Käufer ist berechtigt, die Minderung mit einem **Schadenersatzanspruch** aus Art. 45 I lit. b) zu kombinieren (Art. 45 II).[61] Der Käufer kann also den Anspruch auf Erstattung des Minderwerts auf Art. 50 stützen und weitere Schäden – Folgeschäden, Kosten eines Sachverständigengutachtens[62] usw. – nach Art. 45 I lit. b) geltend machen.[63] Die Minderung hat neben dem Schadenersatzanspruch im Wesentlichen aber nur in zwei Fällen eine selbstständige Bedeutung.[64] Zum einen ist dies dann gegeben, wenn der Schadenersatzanspruch wegen Entlastung des Verkäufers gemäss Art. 79 entfällt.[65] Zum anderen erhält der Käufer einen höheren Ausgleich über die Minderung, wenn die Preise zwischen Vertragsschluss und Lieferung gefallen sind: Der vom Käufer bezahlte Kaufpreis beträgt z. B. 100. Bei Lieferung sind die Preise für die Vertragsware um 50% gefallen. Es stellt sich heraus, dass die gelieferte Ware wegen eines Sachmangels nur 80 wert ist. Der Minderwert beträgt diesfalls 20, der Schaden des Käufers hingegen bloss 10.[66] Praktisch bedeutet das, dass der Käufer, soweit es speziell um den Minderwert geht, wählen kann, welche Berechnungsart ihm günstiger und bequemer erscheint: die Berechnung nach Artt. 45 I lit. b), 74 oder nach Art. 50.[67] Nur darf er nicht für denselben Nachteil doppelten Ausgleich verlangen.

V. Abweichende Vereinbarungen

19 Das Recht des Käufers zur Minderung kann vertraglich **ausgeschlossen** werden. Gegen einen formularmässigen Ausschluss bestehen keine Bedenken. Im Fall einer wesentlichen Vertragsverletzung ist der Verkäufer durch das Recht zur Vertragsaufhebung ausreichend geschützt, das formularmässig nicht abbedungen werden kann.[68] Im Fall von untergeordneten Sachmängeln wird der Käufer durch den Schadenersatzanspruch des Art. 45 I lit. b) ausreichend geschützt; dies bedeutet aber auch, dass es nicht zulässig ist, sowohl den Schadenersatzanspruch als auch die Minderung auszuschliessen.[69]

---

[59] Vgl. *Müller-Chen*, Art. 46 Rn. 7.
[60] Zur Problematik der Vertragsaufhebung bei Entdeckung weiterer Mängel nach erfolgter Minderungserklärung, vgl. *Müller-Chen*, Art. 45 Rn. 20.
[61] Sekretariatskommentar, Art. 46, Nr. 13; vgl. auch *Venturi*, Rn. 1699 ff.; *Herber/Czerwenka*, Art. 50, Rn. 9; *Soergel/Lüderitz/Schüßler-Langeheine*, Art. 50, Rn. 13; *Hirner*, S. 377; *Piliounis*, 12 Pace Int'l L. Rev. (2000), 1, 33 ff.; a. A. *Heuzé*, Anm. 460. Fn. 401; *Gabriel*, Sale of Goods, S. 159.
[62] *Herber/Czerwenka*, Art. 50, Rn. 9.
[63] Stützt der Käufer seinen Anspruch auf Erstattung des Minderwertes auf Art. 50 und macht er gleichzeitig Schadenersatz gem. Art. 45 I lit. b) geltend, verringert sich der zu ersetzende Schaden um den Betrag, der dem Käufer auf Grund der Minderung vergütet wird, vgl. Art. 45 Rn. 28; *Audit*, Vente internationale, Anm. 140. Fn. 1; *Piltz*, Internationales Kaufrecht, Rn. 5–361; *Staudinger/Magnus*, Art. 50, Rn. 30.
[64] Dazu kommt noch der Fall, dass der Käufer Mühe hat, seinen Schaden nachzuweisen, vgl. *U. Huber*, 3. Aufl., Rn. 3; *Piltz*, Internationales Kaufrecht, Rn. 5–333; dazu und zum Folgenden *Brunner*, Art. 50, Rn. 2.
[65] *Honnold/Flechtner*, Art. 50, Rn. 312; *Piltz*, Internationales Kaufrecht, Rn. 5–333; *Audit*, Vente internationale, Anm. 140.; *Verweyen/Förster/Toufar*, Handbuch, S. 136.
[66] Vgl. ausführlich *Honnold/Flechtner*, Art. 50, Rn. 312; *Venturi*, Rn. 1694; *Audit*, Vente internationale, Anm. 139.; *Verweyen/Förster/Toufar*, Handbuch, S. 135 f.; *Kritzer*, Guide to Practical Applications, S. 344, 377; *Heuzé*, Anm. 460. Fn. 400; *Gillette/Walt*, S. 362 ff.
[67] Vgl. auch *Honnold/Flechtner*, Art. 50, Rn. 312.
[68] Vgl. *Frense*, S. 136 f.; *Hirner*, S. 272.
[69] *Hirner*, S. 272 ff.; a. A. *U. Huber*, 3. Aufl., Rn. 20; *Frense*, S. 92 f., 125 f., 135 (bei nicht wesentlicher Vertragswidrigkeit der Ware kann sowohl Minderung wie Schadenersatz ausgeschlossen werden).

Art. 51 [Teilweise Nichterfüllung]

(1) Liefert der Verkäufer nur einen Teil der Ware oder ist nur ein Teil der gelieferten Ware vertragsgemäß, so gelten für den Teil, der fehlt oder der nicht vertragsgemäß ist, die Artikel 46–50.

(2) Der Käufer kann nur dann die Aufhebung des gesamten Vertrages erklären, wenn die unvollständige oder nicht vertragsgemäße Lieferung eine wesentliche Vertragsverletzung darstellt.

Art. 51

(1) If the seller delivers only a part of the goods or if only a part of the goods delivered is in conformity with the contract, articles 46 to 50 apply in respect of the part which is missing or which does not conform.

(2) The buyer may declare the contract avoided in its entirety only if the failure to make delivery completely or in conformity with the contract amounts to a fundamental breach of the contract.

Art. 51

1) Si le vendeur ne livre qu'une partie des marchandises ou si une partie seulement des marchandises livrées est conforme au contrat, les articles 46 à 50 s'appliquent en ce qui concerne la partie manquante ou non conforme.

2) L'acheteur ne peut déclarer le contrat résolu dans sa totalité que si l'inexécution partielle ou le défaut de conformité constitue une contravention essentielle au contrat.

Übersicht

	Rn.
I. Gegenstand und Anwendungsbereich der Regelung	1
1. Regelungsgegenstand	1
2. Teilbarkeit der Lieferung	2
3. Sukzessivlieferungsverträge	3
4. Zurückweisung der Teillieferung	4
II. Abs. 1: Rechtsbehelfe bei teilweiser Nichterfüllung	5
1. Teilweise Lieferung (Quantitätsmängel)	5
2. Teilweise mangelhafte Lieferung	7
3. Rügepflicht	8
III. Abs. 2: Aufhebung des gesamten Vertrags	9

Vorläufer und **Entwürfe:** EKG Art. 45; Genfer E 1976 Art. 32; Wiener E 1977 Art. 33; New Yorker E 1978 Art. 47.

I. Gegenstand und Anwendungsbereich der Regelung

1. Regelungsgegenstand

Art. 51 enthält ergänzende und klarstellende Regeln für den Fall, dass der Verkäufer nur **1** einen Teil der verkauften Ware liefert oder dass die gelieferte Ware teilweise nicht vertragsgemäss ist.[1] Viererlei wird klargestellt: Erstens, dass die Rechtsbehelfe sich grundsätzlich auf den fehlenden Teil beschränken;[2] zweitens, dass auch eine teilweise Aufhebung des Vertrags

---

[1] Gemäss *Staudinger/Magnus*, Art. 51, Rn. 20, soll Art. 51 analog auch auf andere Fälle übertragen werden, in denen bloss eine von mehreren Vertragspflichten verletzt wird (z. B. eine Exklusivlieferverpflichtung). Daran besteht m. E. kein praktisches Interesse; die Artt. 45 ff. sind direkt anwendbar, so auch *Soergel/Lüderitz/Schüßler-Langeheine*, Art. 51, Rn. 3.

[2] Das ist für den Regelfall auch die Lösung des deutschen Rechts, vgl. §§ 281 I 2, 323 V BGB; vgl. dazu *Heiderhoff/Skamel*, JZ 2006, 383, 383 ff. Abweichend insbesondere § 2–601 UCC („[…] if the goods or the tender of delivery fail in any respect to conform to the contract, the buyer may a) reject the whole; or b) accept the whole; or c) accept any commercial unit or units and reject the rest"); dazu *Gabriel*, Sale of Goods, S. 164; ebenso sec. 30 I SGA.

in Betracht kommt;[3] drittens, dass der Vertrag im ganzen nur dann aufgehoben werden kann, wenn die teilweise Nichterfüllung eine wesentliche Vertragsverletzung im Hinblick auf den Vertrag im Ganzen darstellt[4] und viertens, dass der Käufer Anspruch auf Schadenersatz gemäss Art. 45 I lit. b) für jeden durch die teilweise Nichterfüllung veranlassten Schaden hat.[5]

2. Teilbarkeit der Lieferung

2 Art. 51 setzt voraus, dass die Lieferung teilbar ist. Es müssen also in einem einheitlichen Kaufvertrag mehrere getrennte Sachen verkauft sein. Eine teilbare Lieferung liegt vor, wenn die Lieferung auch an mehrere verschiedene Abnehmer möglich wäre, weil die Sachen physisch und wirtschaftlich eigenständig sind.[6] Trotz Selbstständigkeit kann die Teilbarkeit fehlen, wenn die einzelnen Sachen funktionell zusammengehören und so nach Verkehrsauffassung eine Sachgesamtheit bilden.[7] Es spielt keine Rolle, ob die einzelnen Sachen gleichartig sind, d. h. nur nach Mengen- oder Grösseneinheiten differenzierbar (z. B. 100 Ballen Baumwolle) oder ungleichartig (Computer mit Software und Benutzerhandbuch). **Unanwendbar** ist Art. 51 dagegen, wenn eine aus **verschiedenen Bestandteilen zusammengesetzte einheitliche Sache** verkauft wird und einzelne Komponenten fehlen oder mangelhaft sind.[8] Ist z. B. ein Auto verkauft und fehlt entgegen der Beschreibung im Kaufvertrag im gelieferten Fahrzeug die elektronische Wegfahrsperre oder ist der Motor defekt, handelt es sich um gewöhnliche Sachmängel der gelieferten Sache im Ganzen. Artt. 46–50 sind unmittelbar anzuwenden. Eine teilweise Aufhebung des Vertrags kommt nicht in Betracht.[9] Auswechslung defekter Einzelteile ist Nachbesserung i. S. d. Artt. 46 III, 48. Unanwendbar ist Art. 51 ferner, wenn die **gelieferte Sache als solche einen Quantitätsmangel** aufweist. Verkauft sind z. B. Weihnachtsstollen zu 1500g, die gelieferten Stollen wiegen aber nur 1350g, oder verkauft ist eine bestimmte Schiffsladung Kohle mit Gewichtsangabe, der tatsächliche Bestand bleibt hinter der Angabe im Vertrag zurück. Auch dies ist ein gewöhnlicher Sachmangel i. S. d. Art. 35 I, der sich auf die verkaufte Sachgesamtheit im Ganzen bezieht.[10]

3. Sukzessivlieferungsverträge

3 Für Sukzessivlieferungsverträge gilt die **Sonderregelung des Art. 73**. Ein Sukzessivlieferungsvertrag im Sinn dieser Vorschrift setzt voraus, dass schon im Kaufvertrag eine Mehrzahl von Lieferungen vorgesehen ist, für die im Vertrag verschiedene, zeitlich aufeinander folgende Liefertermine oder Lieferfristen bestimmt sind. Werden im Fall des Sukzessivlieferungsvertrags einzelne Teillieferungen nicht rechtzeitig erbracht oder sind sie mangelhaft, so ist für die Frage, welche Auswirkungen dies für den Vertrag insgesamt hat, ausschliesslich Art. 73 massgeblich.[11] Art. 51 ist beim Sukzessivlieferungsvertrag nur ergänzend anwendbar,

---

[3] Vgl. dazu Sekretariatskommentar, Art. 47, Nr. 2: „This rule was necessary because in some legal systems a party cannot avoid only a part of the contract". Im deutschen Recht wird diese Möglichkeit allerdings in § 326 I 1 HS. 2 BGB als selbstverständlich vorausgesetzt. Rechtsvergleichende Hinweise bei *Schwenzer/Hachem/Kee*, Rn. 47.155 ff.
[4] Im deutschen Recht führt § 281 i. V. m. § 323 V 1 BGB praktisch zum gleichen Resultat.
[5] *Brunner*, Art. 51, Rn. 4; OLG Düsseldorf, 10.2.1994, CISG-online 115 = NJW-RR 1994, 506 f.; RIW 1994, 1050 f.
[6] Vgl. *Staudinger/Magnus*, Art. 51, Rn. 4; *Soergel/Lüderitz/Schüßler-Langeheine*, Art. 51, Rn. 2; OGH, 31.8.2010, CISG-online 2236 = IHR 2011, 85, 87.
[7] *Achilles*, Art. 51, Rn. 1.
[8] Vgl. auch *Bianca/Bonell/Will*, Art. 51, Anm. 2.1.1.; *Herber/Czerwenka*, Art. 51, Rn. 3; *Honsell/Schnyder/Straub*, Art. 51, Rn. 10; *Staudinger/Magnus*, Art. 51, Rn. 4; *Audit*, Vente internationale, Anm. 135.; *Karollus*, S. 159.
[9] Vgl. Art. 49 Rn. 26.
[10] *Staudinger/Magnus*, Art. 51, Rn. 5.
[11] Ebenso *Honsell/Schnyder/Straub*, Art. 51, Rn. 25; *Staudinger/Magnus*, Art. 51, Rn. 6; MünchKomm/ *P. Huber*, Art. 51, Rn. 5; MünchKommHGB/*Benicke*, Art. 51, Rn. 3.

wenn eine der sukzessiv geschuldeten Teillieferungen, für sich genommen, unvollständig oder teilweise mangelhaft ist. Rechtsbehelfe des Käufers beschränken sich dann gem. Art. 73 I grundsätzlich auf diese Teillieferung und hier nach Art. 51 I grundsätzlich auf den fehlenden oder fehlerhaften Teil. Will der Käufer wegen der unvollständigen oder teilweise mangelhaften Teillieferung die Vertragsaufhebung bezüglich der ganzen Teillieferung erklären, so kann er dies nur unter den Voraussetzungen des insoweit sinngemäss anzuwendenden Art. 51 II. Will er weitergehend die Vertragsaufhebung auf künftige oder sogar auf frühere Teillieferungen erstrecken, so ist dies nur unter den Voraussetzungen des Art. 73 II und III möglich.

4. Zurückweisung der Teillieferung

Aus der Regel des Art. 51 I, die die Rechtsbehelfe des Käufers grundsätzlich auf den fehlenden Teil der Lieferung beschränkt, folgt inzident, dass der Käufer zur Zurückweisung von Teillieferungen nicht berechtigt ist; er muss den vertragsgemäss gelieferten Teil der Ware bezahlen.[12] Etwas anderes gilt nur dann, wenn die Teillieferung eine wesentliche Verletzung des ganzen Vertrags darstellt.[13] Es ist anhand der erkennbaren Bedeutung der Vollständigkeit der Lieferung für den Käufer zu beurteilen, ob das Ausbleiben eines Teils der Lieferung eine wesentliche Verletzung des Gesamtvertrages ist.[14] Diesfalls treten die Rechtsfolgen von Abs. 2 ein;[15] der Käufer kann dann die Teillieferung zurückweisen.[16] Der Käufer, der die Übernahme der ihm angebotenen Teillieferung mit Hinweis auf die Unvollständigkeit ablehnt, verletzt im Grundsatz seine Abnahmepflicht (vgl. Artt. 53, 62).[17]

II. Abs. 1: Rechtsbehelfe bei teilweiser Nichterfüllung

1. Teilweise Lieferung (Quantitätsmängel)

Liefert der Verkäufer weniger als vertraglich vereinbart (Zuwenig-Lieferung), kann der Käufer gem. Artt. 51 I, 46 I zunächst Lieferung des fehlenden Teils verlangen. Hat der Verkäufer durch vertragliche Abrede („„Circa-Klausel") oder Handelsbrauch (Art. 9 I) das Recht, von der vereinbarten Menge oder dem Gewicht abzuweichen, liegt keine Vertragswidrigkeit vor, wenn die tatsächlich erfolgte Lieferung im Toleranzbereich liegt.[18] Art. 51 findet keine Anwendung; der Käufer muss aber lediglich einen reduzierten Kaufpreis bezahlen.

Quantitätsabweichung ist eine Vertragswidrigkeit nach Art. 35.[19] Dabei liegt hinsichtlich des „Teils, der fehlt" allerdings eine einfache Nichtlieferung gemäss Art. 46 I vor. Ersatzlieferung und Nachbesserung (Art. 46 II, III) machen diesbezüglich keinen Sinn, da keine Ware geliefert wurde, wofür entweder „Ersatz" geleistet oder die repariert werden könn-

---

[12] OGH, 21.6.2005, CISG-online 1047 = IHR 2005, 195 ff. = ZfRVgl 2005, 230 ff.
[13] OGH, 31.8.2010 = OJZ 2011, 175, 176; Der Verkäufer liefert z. B. am letzten Tag der Nachfrist einen Teil der Ware, die für sich genommen für den Käufer unbrauchbar ist; ebenso MünchKomm/*P. Huber*, Art. 52, Rn. 16.
[14] *Verweyen/Förster/Toufar*, Handbuch, S. 145.
[15] Vgl. hinten Rn. 9 ff.
[16] Ebenso *Honsell/Schnyder/Straub*, Art. 51, Rn. 40 f.; *Staudinger/Magnus*, Art. 51, Rn. 11; ähnlich Art. 6.1.3 UNIDROIT Principles: „The obligee may reject an offer to perform in part at the time performance is due (...), unless the obligee has no legitimate interest in so doing"; anders etwa § 266 BGB; Art. 69 I OR; § 1415 ABGB; Art. 1244 frz. Cc; sec. 31 SGA; im Übrigen *Rabel*, Recht des Warenkaufs, Bd. 1, S. 410; vgl. auch *Garro/Zuppi*, Compraventa internacional, S. 184.
[17] Sollte ausnahmsweise für den Käufer die Abnahme der Teillieferung aus besonderen Gründen unzumutbar sein, ist eine Korrektur auf Grund des Prinzips von Treu und Glauben möglich (Art. 7 I); vgl. dazu auch *Widmer Lüchinger*, Art. 31 Rn. 44, 69.
[18] Die Abweichung kann vertraglich fixiert sein (z. B. 3%) oder sich aus Handelsusanzen ergeben; vgl. *Schwenzer*, Art. 35 Rn. 8; *Bamberger/Roth/Saenger*, Art. 51, Rn. 4; vgl. *Müller-Chen*, Art. 46 Rn. 21 zu den geringfügigen Fehlmengen.
[19] Vgl. *Schwenzer*, Art. 35 Rn. 4, 8; vgl. dazu auch OGH, 20.3.1997, CISG-online 269 = ZfRVgl 1997, 204.

te.²⁰ Dem Käufer steht es unbenommen, Nachfrist zu setzen (Art. 47) und bei erfolglosem Ablauf der Nachfrist gemäss Art. 49 I lit. b) ii) (i. V. m. Art. 51 I) Vertragsaufhebung hinsichtlich des fehlenden Teils zu erklären. Stellt die bloss teilweise Lieferung als solche eine wesentliche Vertragsverletzung dar, setzt die Vertragsaufhebung keine Nachfristsetzung voraus (Artt. 49 I lit. a), 25 i. V. m. Art. 51 I). Die Folge der teilweisen Aufhebung des Kaufvertrags ist, dass der Kaufpreis im Verhältnis des Anteils der gelieferten Ware zur gesamten Liefermenge gekürzt wird. Unter den Voraussetzungen des Art. 48 bleibt der Verkäufer berechtigt, den fehlenden Teil nachzuliefern.²¹ Dieses Recht des Verkäufers zur Nacherfüllung hat Vorrang vor der Minderung des Kaufpreises durch den Käufer.²² Da die Minderung jedoch im Falle der partiellen Lieferung zum gleichen Ergebnis wie die Vertragsaufhebung hinsichtlich des fehlenden Teils führt, besteht kein praktisches Interesse an Art. 50.²³ In beiden Fällen kann (und muss) der Käufer den gelieferten Teil behalten, darf aber den Kaufpreis anteilsmässig kürzen.

2. Teilweise mangelhafte Lieferung

7   Ist die gelieferte Ware zum Teil mangelfrei, zum Teil mangelhaft, so kann der Käufer hinsichtlich des mangelhaften Teils die Rechte aus Artt. 46 ff. ausüben.²⁴ Sind z. B. 100 Ballen Baumwolle verkauft und geliefert und 10 Ballen mangelhaft,²⁵ so kann der Käufer, wenn es sich hinsichtlich dieser 10 Ballen um eine wesentliche Vertragsverletzung handelt, nach entsprechender Rüge (Art. 39) Ersatzlieferung von 10 Ballen verlangen (Art. 46 II) oder im Hinblick auf die fehlerhaften 10 Ballen die Vertragsaufhebung erklären und demgemäss den Kaufpreis um ein Zehntel kürzen (Art. 49 I lit. a) i. V. m. Art. 51 I).²⁶ Er kann auch die gesamte Lieferung behalten und hinsichtlich der mangelhaften zehn Ballen Ausgleich des Minderwerts im Weg des Schadenersatzes (Art. 45 I lit. b)) oder der Minderung (Art. 50) verlangen.²⁷ In jedem der drei Fälle (Ersatzlieferung, teilweise Vertragsaufhebung, Minderung) behält der Verkäufer den ungekürzten Kaufpreisanspruch für die fehlerfreien 90 Ballen in Höhe von 90 Prozent des Gesamtkaufpreises.

3. Rügepflicht

8   Will der Käufer aus Art. 51 Rechte ableiten, hat er die Zuwenig-Lieferung nach Art. 39 zu rügen: Die Teillieferung ist nicht vertragsgemässe Lieferung nach Art. 35.²⁸ Unterlässt er die Rüge, verliert er die Rechtsbehelfe nach Art. 51 und hat den vereinbarten Kaufpreis zu bezahlen,²⁹ es sei denn, es liege ein Fall von Art. 40 vor³⁰ oder es handle sich um einen offenkundigen Fall einer Teillieferung.³¹

---

²⁰ Vgl. Art. 46 Rn. 17; gl. M. *Honsell/Schnyder/Straub*, Art. 51, Rn. 26–36; wie hier *Staudinger/Magnus*, Art. 51, Rn. 12.
²¹ KG Zug, 14.12.2009, CISG-online 2026: Partielle Aufhebung des Vertrages, wenn Ware nicht innert Nachfrist geliefert wird. Vgl. auch Art. 48 Rn. 3, 15.
²² Art. 50 Rn. 7.
²³ So i. E. auch *U. Huber*, 3. Aufl., Rn. 4 Fn. 9; *Schwenzer*, Art. 35 Rn. 43; mit anderer Begründung *Honsell/Schnyder/Straub*, Art. 51, Rn. 40; *Hirner*, S. 136; a. A. *Staudinger/Magnus*, Art. 51, Rn. 14; vgl. auch KG Glarus, 6.11.2008, CISG-online 1996 = SZIER 2011, 563 ff.
²⁴ Bsp.: BGH, 25.6.1997, CISG-online 277 = NJW 1997, 3311 ff. = RIW 1997, 1037 ff.
²⁵ Bsp. nach *Honnold/Flechtner*, Art. 51, Rn. 315.
²⁶ Vgl. auch *Heuzé*, Anm. 418.
²⁷ *Honnold/Flechtner*, Art. 51, Rn. 316.
²⁸ Vgl. vorne Rn. 6; *Schwenzer*, Art. 35 Rn. 4, 8; *Müller-Chen*, Art. 46 Rn. 21; *Staudinger/Magnus*, Art. 51, Rn. 12.
²⁹ Vorbehalten bleibt der Fall, dass der Verkäufer nur für den tatsächlich gelieferten Teil Rechnung stellt, vgl. *U. Huber*, 3. Aufl., Rn. 10.
³⁰ *Schwenzer*, Art. 40 Rn. 4 ff.; es liegt kein Fall von Art. 40 vor, wenn der Verkäufer 100 Einheiten verspricht, aber nur 80 liefert und auch nur 80 in Rechnung stellt, da die Nichtlieferung offenbar wurde; der Käufer muss demgemäss diesfalls rügen.
³¹ Obwohl 100 Säcke Zucker geliefert werden sollen, liefert der Verkäufer nur 60 und erklärt „Rest folgt später".

III. Abs. 2: Aufhebung des gesamten Vertrags

Zur Aufhebung des gesamten Vertrags ist der Käufer nur berechtigt, wenn die unvollständige oder teilweise nicht vertragsmässige Lieferung eine wesentliche Vertragsverletzung nicht nur im Hinblick auf diesen Teil, sondern auch im Hinblick auf den Vertrag im Ganzen („a fundamental breach of **the** contract") darstellt.[32] Damit kann der Vertrag gemäss Art. 51 II nicht aufgehoben werden, wenn der Käufer seine Berechtigung zur Vertragsaufhebung lediglich auf Art. 49 I lit. b), d. h. auf den fruchtlosen Ablauf einer bei Nichtleistung einer Teilleistung gesetzten Nachfrist, stützen kann.[33]

Ein Fall nach Abs. 2 kann vor allem dann eintreten, wenn **verschiedenartige Sachen** als zusammengehörig verkauft sind und der Käufer an der Teillieferung bzw. am fehlerfreien Teil der Lieferung ohne den fehlerhaften Teil kein Interesse hat, weil die vertragsgemäss gelieferten Teile nicht selbstständig dem Vertragszweck gemäss verwendbar oder absetzbar sind.[34] Werden z. B. im Rahmen eines kompletten, individuell für den Käufer produzierten Raumprogrammes aufeinander abgestimmte Möbel verkauft und ist ein Teil davon (z. B. die Stühle) wegen eines Fabrikationsfehlers für den Käufer unbrauchbar und schlägt eine vom Verkäufer angebotene Nachbesserung fehl, kann der Käufer gemäss Art. 49 I lit. a) i. V. m. Art. 51 II die Aufhebung des ganzen Vertrags erklären, wenn er für die restlichen Möbel keine Verwendung hat.

Beim Verkauf von **gleichartigen Sachen** wird dieser Fall nicht so leicht eintreten. Sind von 100 Ballen Baumwolle bloss 70 geliefert oder 50 Ballen mangelhaft, so wird das in der Regel nicht dazu führen, dass der Käufer mit den gelieferten 70 oder den fehlerfreien 50 Ballen nichts anfangen kann. Ausnahmen sind aber denkbar, so z. B., wenn Schuhe an einen Einzelhändler verkauft sind, die gelieferten Schuhe zu 80% mangelhaft sind und der mangelfreie Rest für den Käufer „aus Gründen einer ordnungsgemässen Präsentation oder auch wegen des geregelten Abverkaufs uninteressant" ist;[35] oder wenn die fehlerhaften und die fehlerfreien Stücke sich nur mit Schwierigkeiten oder praktisch überhaupt nicht unterscheiden und sortieren lassen. Hier ist der Käufer zur Aufhebung des ganzen Vertrags berechtigt.

---

[32] *Honnold/Flechtner*, Art. 51, Rn. 317; LG Heidelberg, 3.7.1992, CISG-online 38.
[33] *Honnold/Flechtner*, Art. 51, Rn. 317; *Kimbel*, 18 J. L. & Com. (1991), 301, 325 f.
[34] *Staudinger/Magnus*, Art. 51, Rn. 18.
[35] Vgl. zu Art. 45 EKG OLG Koblenz v. 18.5.1984, in: *Schlechtriem/Magnus*, Art. 44 EKG, Rn. 6.

Art. 52 [Vorzeitige Lieferung und Zuviellieferung]

(1) Liefert der Verkäufer die Ware vor dem festgesetzten Zeitpunkt, so steht es dem Käufer frei, sie abzunehmen oder die Abnahme zu verweigern.

(2) Liefert der Verkäufer eine größere als die vereinbarte Menge, so kann der Käufer die zuviel gelieferte Menge abnehmen oder ihre Abnahme verweigern. Nimmt der Käufer die zuviel gelieferte Menge ganz oder teilweise ab, so hat er sie entsprechend dem vertraglichen Preis zu bezahlen.

Art. 52

(1) If the seller delivers the goods before the date fixed, the buyer may take delivery or refuse to take delivery.

(2) If the seller delivers a quantity of goods greater than that provided for in the contract, the buyer may take delivery or refuse to take delivery of the excess quantity. If the buyer takes delivery of all or part of the excess quantity, he must pay for it at the contract rate.

Art. 52

1) Si le vendeur livre les marchandises avant la date fixée, l'acheteur a la faculté d'en prendre livraison ou de refuser d'en prendre livraison.

2) Si le vendeur livre une quantité supérieure à celle prévue au contrat, l'acheteur peut accepter ou refuser de prendre livraison de la quantité excédentaire. Si l'acheteur accepte d'en prendre livraison en tout ou en partie, il doit la payer au tarif du contrat.

Übersicht

	Rn.
I. Vorzeitige Lieferung (Abs. 1)	1
1. Grundsatz	1
2. Zurückweisungsrecht	3
3. Folgen der Annahme	4
II. Zuviellieferung (Abs. 2)	6
1. Lieferung einer grösseren Menge	6
2. Zurückweisung	7
a) Voraussetzung	7
b) Folgen	9
3. Annahme	10
4. Lieferung höherwertiger Ware	11

Vorläufer und **Entwürfe**: EKG Artt. 29, 47; Genfer E 1976 Art. 33; Wiener E 1977 Art. 34; New Yorker E 1978 Art. 48.

I. Vorzeitige Lieferung (Abs. 1)

1. Grundsatz

1 Art. 52 I bestimmt, dass der Verkäufer, wenn nichts anderes vereinbart ist und sich auch aus Handelsbrauch (Art. 9) nichts anderes ergibt, **zur vorzeitigen Lieferung nicht berechtigt** ist.[1] Voraussetzung ist, dass für die Lieferung im Vertrag ein bestimmter **Zeitpunkt** festgesetzt ist: ein bestimmter Tag oder eine bestimmte Frist mit Anfangstermin.[2] Ist also z. B. vereinbart „Lieferung: im Lauf des Juni", so darf der Verkäufer nicht schon im Mai liefern; ist festgesetzt „Lieferung: auf Abruf des Käufers", darf er nicht liefern, bevor der Käufer die Ware abgerufen hat. Der Grund liegt darin, dass der Käufer nicht auf die vorzeitige Lieferung eingestellt ist und nicht mit den dadurch verbundenen Kosten und Umständlichkeiten (z. B. der Lagerung) belastet werden soll.[3]

---

[1] So dem Grundsatz nach auch Art. 6.1.5 I PICC; Art. 7:103 I PECL; anders § 271 II BGB; Art. 81 I OR.
[2] *Bamberger/Roth/Saenger*, Art. 52, Rn. 2; *Staudinger/Magnus*, Art. 52, Rn. 7.
[3] Sekretariatskommentar, Art. 48, Nr. 2.

Art. 52 I ist unanwendbar, wenn kein bestimmter Liefertermin festgesetzt ist, die Lieferzeit sich also nach Art. 33 lit. c) richtet. In einem solchen Fall darf der Verkäufer sofort liefern,[4] ebenso, wenn nur ein Termin festgesetzt ist, zu dem der Verkäufer spätestens liefern muss (vereinbart ist z. B. „Lieferung: innerhalb zwei Wochen").[5]

2. Zurückweisungsrecht

Liefert der Verkäufer vorzeitig, so kann der Käufer gemäss Art. 52 I die Abnahme verweigern, d. h. die Lieferung zurückweisen.[6] Die Folge ist, dass der Verkäufer verpflichtet bleibt, die Lieferung zur vorgesehenen Zeit erneut zu bewirken.[7] Das Zurückweisungsrecht, das für den Verkäufer u. U. sehr belastend sein kann, darf allerdings nicht schikanös ausgeübt werden; es steht unter dem Vorbehalt von Treu und Glauben (Art. 7 I).[8] Hiervon abgesehen, braucht der Käufer aber für die Zurückweisung keine Gründe anzugeben.[9] Im Übrigen steht das Zurückweisungsrecht unter dem **Vorbehalt des Art. 86**, d. h. der Käufer ist unter den dort genannten Voraussetzungen verpflichtet, für die Erhaltung der Ware zu sorgen.[10] Dadurch entstehende angemessene Kosten hat allerdings der Verkäufer zu tragen (Artt. 86 I 2, II 1, 87). Aus Art. 52 I kann der Käufer kein Vertragsaufhebungsrecht ableiten;[11] in speziellen Konstellationen (z. B. bei just-in-time Verträgen) kann sich ein Aufhebungsrecht aus Art. 72 I ergeben.[12]

3. Folgen der Annahme

Es steht dem Käufer frei, die vorzeitige Lieferung anzunehmen. Entstehen ihm hierdurch zusätzliche Kosten (z. B. Lagerkosten), die bei termingerechter Lieferung nicht angefallen wären, kann er vom Verkäufer **Schadenersatz** gemäss Art. 45 I lit. b) verlangen.[13] Die vorzeitige Lieferung ist Vertragsverletzung, nicht anders als die verspätete.[14] Durch die Annahme der vorzeitigen Lieferung darf die Stellung des Käufers nicht verschlechtert werden, weshalb er nicht zur vorzeitigen **Untersuchung** und **Rüge** verpflichtet ist.[15] Ist der **Kaufpreis** gemäss Vertrag mit Lieferung der Ware geschuldet, soll

---

[4] *Widmer Lüchinger*, Art. 33 Rn. 18; *Staudinger/Magnus*, Art. 52, Rn. 7; *Achilles*, Art. 52, Rn. 2.
[5] Vgl. *Honnold/Flechtner*, Art. 52, Rn. 319; *Widmer Lüchinger*, Art. 33 Rn. 8 f.
[6] *Schlechtriem*, 18 Pace Int'l L. Rev. (2006), 83, 91 ff.
[7] Sekretariatskommentar, Art. 48, Nr. 5; *Herber/Czerwenka*, Art. 52, Rn. 2; *Staudinger/Magnus*, Art. 52, Rn. 10; *Piltz*, Internationales Kaufrecht, Rn. 4–57.
[8] So ausdrücklich Art. 7:103 I PECL („A party may decline a tender of performance made before it is due except where acceptance of the tender would not unreasonably prejudice its interests"); Sekretariatskommentar, Art. 48, Nr. 3 Fn. 1; *Bianca/Bonell/Will*, Art. 52, Anm. 2.1.3.; *Herber/Czerwenka*, Art. 52, Rn. 3; *Neumayer/Ming*, Art. 52, Anm. 1.; *Staudinger/Magnus*, Art. 52, Rn. 11; *Karollus*, S. 173; krit. *Heuzé*, Anm. 248. Fn. 34. Im Übrigen kann in Fällen, in denen die vorzeitige Lieferung für den Käufer keine besondere Belastung darstellt, schon die Vertragsauslegung ergeben, dass der Verkäufer zur vorzeitigen Lieferung berechtigt sein soll, zutreffend *Soergel/Lüderitz*, 11. Aufl., Art. 29 EKG, Rn. 5.
[9] Sekretariatskommentar, Art. 48, Nr. 3; *Herber/Czerwenka*, Art. 52, Rn. 3; *Bianca/Bonell/Will*, Art. 52, Anm. 2.1.3.; *Enderlein/Maskow/Strohbach*, Art. 52, Anm. 2.; *Staudinger/Magnus*, Art. 52, Rn. 10; *Rudolph*, Art. 52, Rn. 4.
[10] Sekretariatskommentar, Art. 48, Nr. 4; *Herber/Czerwenka*, Art. 52, Rn. 2; *Enderlein/Maskow/Strohbach*, Art. 52, Anm. 2.
[11] *Honnold/Flechtner*, Art. 52, Rn. 319.
[12] Art. 52 I regelt die Folgen der vorzeitigen Lieferung abschliessend; für ein auf Art. 49 I lit. a) gestütztes Aufhebungsrecht bleibt (schon wegen mangelnder Wesentlichkeit) kein Raum; so auch *Staudinger/Magnus*, Art. 52, Rn. 13; a. A. *Honsell/Schnyder/Straub*, Art. 52, Rn. 30.
[13] Sekretariatskommentar, Art. 48, Nr. 6; *Bianca/Bonell/Will*, Art. 52, Anm. 2.1.5.; *Herber/Czerwenka*, Art. 52, Rn. 3, 4; *Soergel/Lüderitz/Schüßler-Langeheine*, Art. 52, Rn. 3; *Enderlein/Maskow/Strohbach*, Art. 52, Anm. 2., 5.; *Staudinger/Magnus*, Art. 52, Rn. 15; *Honsell/Schnyder/Straub*, Art. 52, Rn. 28; *Karollus*, S. 173; a. A. *Reinhart*, Art. 52, Rn. 2.
[14] *Herber/Czerwenka*, Art. 52, Rn. 4; *Piltz*, Internationales Kaufrecht, Rn. 4–57, 4–170; a. A. *Reinhart*, Art. 52, Rn. 2; *Witz/Salger/Lorenz*, Art. 52, Rn. 3.
[15] *Herber/Czerwenka*, Art. 52, Rn. 4; *Staudinger/Magnus*, Art. 52, Rn. 14; *Piltz*, Internationales Kaufrecht, Rn. 5–68, 5–78; *Schlechtriem*, Einheitliches UN-Kaufrecht, S. 71; *Soergel/Lüderitz/Schüßler-Langeheine*, Art. 52,

nach überwiegender Ansicht in der Literatur die Zahlung auch bei vorzeitiger Lieferung sofort erfolgen müssen.[16] Dies ist m. E. zu verneinen, da die vorzeitige Bereitstellung des Kaufpreises dem Käufer nicht zuzumuten und ihm u. U. auch gar nicht möglich ist (es müssen z. B. noch Akkreditive gestellt werden). Zudem kann der Verkäufer nicht aus einer Vertragsverletzung das Recht auf frühere Zahlung erwerben, das ihm bei vertragsgemässer Leistung nicht zustünde.[17]

5 Der Schadenersatzanspruch entfällt und die vorzeitige Untersuchungs-, Rüge- und Kaufpreiszahlungspflicht besteht jedoch, wenn die Abnahme der vorzeitig gelieferten Ware als **konkludentes Einverständnis** mit einer entsprechenden Abänderung des Vertrages anzusehen ist. Art. 52 I hat das Erfordernis eines ausdrücklichen Vorbehalts fallen lassen. Stillschweigende Entgegennahme der Ware kann nicht ohne weiteres als Genehmigung des Käufers angesehen werden;[18] sie kann ihren Grund auch darin haben, dass der Käufer nur seiner Aufbewahrungspflicht nach Art. 86 nachkommen und dem Verkäufer die mit der Zurückweisung verbundenen Kosten und Unannehmlichkeiten ersparen will.[19] Die Feststellung einer stillschweigenden Abänderung des Vertrags kann daher nur anhand der Umstände des Einzelfalls getroffen werden.[20] Insgesamt ist deshalb dem Käufer zu empfehlen, sich seine Rechte bei oder unverzüglich nach Abnahme ausdrücklich vorzubehalten, wenn er aus der Vorzeitigkeit der Lieferung irgendwelche Rechte oder Einwendungen herleiten will.[21]

II. Zuviellieferung (Abs. 2)

1. Lieferung einer grösseren Menge

6 Liefert der Verkäufer eine grössere Quantität als vertraglich vereinbart, verletzt er den Vertrag (Art. 35 I);[22] ausgenommen sind Fälle, in denen sich die Liefermenge innerhalb der vereinbarten **Circa-Toleranz** bewegt.[23] Ein Quantitätsmangel liegt vor, wenn die Gesamtmenge über das vertragliche Mass hinausgeht; die Ware ist z. B. grösser, schwerer oder sie wird in höherer Stückzahl geliefert.[24] Im Hinblick auf das im Grundsatz auf die zu viel

---

Rn. 3; a. A. *Reinhart*, Art. 52, Rn. 2; *Bamberger/Roth/Saenger*, Art. 52, Rn. 4; *Witz/Salger/Lorenz/Salger*, Art. 52, Rn. 3; *Schwenzer*, Art. 38 Rn. 20 und Art. 39 Rn. 21 (hinsichtlich der Rügepflicht); differenzierend *Honsell/Schnyder/Straub*, Art. 52, Rn. 21–23.

[16] *U. Huber*, 3. Aufl., Rn. 1; Sekretariatskommentar, Art. 48, Nr. 2; *Bianca/Bonell/Will*, Art. 52, Anm. 2.1.2.; *Bamberger/Roth/Saenger*, Art. 52, Rn. 4; *Reinhart*, Art. 52, Rn. 2; *Piltz*, Internationales Kaufrecht, Rn. 4–169; *Honsell/Schnyder/Straub*, Art. 52, Rn. 24; nach *Karollus*, S. 171, soll dem Käufer bei einer unvorhergesehenen Lieferung eine angemessene Frist eingeräumt werden, um die Zahlung zu veranlassen; *Herber/Czerwenka*, Art. 52, Rn. 4 stellen auf das Zustandekommen einer Vertragsänderung ab, ebenso *Enderlein/Maskow/Strobach*, Art. 52, Anm. 2.

[17] So auch *Staudinger/Magnus*, Art. 52, Rn. 14; *Achilles*, Art. 52, Rn. 3.

[18] *Bianca/Bonell/Will*, Art. 52, Anm. 2.1.5.; *Herber/Czerwenka*, Art. 52, Rn. 4; *Soergel/Lüderitz/Schüßler-Langeheine*, Art. 52, Rn. 3; *Staudinger/Magnus*, Art. 52, Rn. 9, 14; *Honsell/Schnyder/Straub*, Art. 52, Rn. 26; *Karollus*, S. 173 f.; *Piltz*, Internationales Kaufrecht, Rn. 4–57, 4–170; a. A. *Neumayer/Ming*, Art. 52, Anm. 1.; *Reinhart*, Art. 52, Rn. 2.

[19] Vgl. auch *Karollus*, S. 174; *Piltz*, Internationales Kaufrecht, Rn. 4–57.

[20] Sekretariatskommentar, Art. 48, Nr. 6; *Herber/Czerwenka*, Art. 52, Rn. 4; *Honsell/Schnyder/Straub*, Art. 52, Rn. 26.

[21] Vgl. auch *Enderlein/Maskow/Strohbach*, Art. 52, Anm. 2.

[22] Vgl. *Schwenzer*, Art. 35 Rn. 8.

[23] Vgl. dazu oben Art. 51 Rn. 5; *Honnold/Flechtner*, Art. 52, Rn. 320; *Bamberger/Roth/Saenger*, Art. 52, Rn. 5.

[24] Werden der Ware nicht vertragsgemässe Beimengungen zugefügt oder ist das höhere Gewicht auf ein anderes als das vertraglich vereinbarte Material zurückzuführen, liegt keine Zuviellieferung, sondern ein Qualitätsmangel vor: *Staudinger/Magnus*, Art. 52, Rn. 18.

gelieferte Menge beschränkte Zurückweisungsrecht muss sich die Übermenge auf das vertraglich vereinbarte Mass reduzieren lassen.[25]

2. Zurückweisung

a) **Voraussetzung.** Will der Käufer von seinem Zurückweisungsrecht gemäss Art. 52 II 1 Gebrauch machen, hat er die Zuviellieferung gemäss Art. 39 innerhalb angemessener Frist nach Feststellung der Vertragswidrigkeit zu **rügen**.[26] Die Genehmigungsfiktion auf Grund der unterlassenen Rüge tritt nicht ein, wenn der Verkäufer die Tatsache der Zuviellieferung kannte bzw. wenn er darüber nicht in Unkenntnis sein konnte (Art. 40).[27] Damit kann der Verkäufer in einem Markt mit sinkenden Preisen den Käufer nicht durch heimliche Lieferung grösserer Quantitäten zur Abnahme und Bezahlung der Übermenge zwingen.[28] Wird dagegen die Zuviellieferung in den Warendokumenten, dem Lieferschein oder in der innerhalb der Anzeigefrist zugegangenen Rechnung ausgewiesen, ist sie dem Käufer „offenbart" worden. In diesen Fällen ist eine Rüge erforderlich, ansonsten der Käufer gemäss Art. 52 II 2 auch für die zu viel gelieferte Menge, entsprechend dem im Kaufvertrag festgesetzten Preis bezahlen muss.[29] Auf der anderen Seite enthält eine rechtzeitige Rüge stets eine „Verweigerung der Abnahme" im Sinn des Art. 52 II 1. Nicht erforderlich ist, dass der Käufer schon die rein körperliche Übernahme verweigert.[30] Im Hinblick auf seine Pflicht zur Inbesitznahme gemäss Art. 86 II ist dies u. U. auch nicht möglich. Soweit keine Toleranzen vereinbart oder handelsüblich sind, darf der Käufer unter Beachtung von Art. 86 II[31] auch geringfügige Zuviellieferungen rügen und ihre Bezahlung verweigern.[32]

Grundsätzlich beschränkt sich das Recht zur Zurückweisung auf den zu viel gelieferten 8 Teil.[33] Unter Umständen ist dem Käufer aber die **teilweise Zurückweisung** aus technischen Gründen **nicht möglich.** Sind z. B. 100 Zuckersäcke mit der Klausel CIF verkauft und dient der Verkäufer ein Konnossement an, das über 120 Säcke lautet, kann der Käufer das Konnossement nur entweder im Ganzen annehmen oder zurückweisen. Der Käufer kann daher in diesem Fall sein Recht, die überschiessende Menge zurückzuweisen, nur wahrnehmen, indem er das Konnossement, also die ganze Lieferung, zurückweist.[34] Dassel-

---

[25] Sind z. B. 100 Ziegelsteine mit einer Kantenlänge von 20 cm geschuldet und werden stattdessen 100 Stück mit einer Länge von 23 cm geliefert, liegt ein Sachmangel nach Art. 35 vor, der die Rechtsbehelfe der Artt. 45 I lit. b), 46–50 auslöst; so auch *Honsell/Schnyder/Straub*, Art. 52, Rn. 41; MünchKomm/*P. Huber*, Art. 52, Rn. 14; a. A. *Staudinger/Magnus*, Art. 52, Rn. 17, der das Wahlrecht des Käufers gemäss Art. 52 II auch auf diesen Fall ausdehnen will, um ein Ausweichen auf nationale ausserkaufrechtliche Rechtsbehelfe (z. B. Irrtum) zu vermeiden.

[26] Vgl. auch *Staudinger/Magnus*, Art. 52, Rn. 21 m. w. N.

[27] Kenntnis oder Kennenmüssen des Verkäufers kann bei grösseren Mengenabweichungen regelmässig angenommen werden; vgl. *Staudinger/Magnus*, Art. 52, Rn. 21.

[28] *Soergel/Lüderitz/Schüßler-Langeheine*, Art. 47, Rn. 4; *Neumayer/Ming*, Art. 52, Anm. 2.

[29] *Schwenzer*, Art. 39 Rn. 30; *Bianca/Bonell/Will*, Art. 52, Anm. 2.2.1.; *Herber/Czerwenka*, Art. 52, Rn. 5; *Soergel/Lüderitz/Schüßler-Langeheine*, Art. 52, Rn. 8; *Enderlein/Maskow/Strohbach*, Art. 52, Anm. 4.; *Karollus*, S. 77; *Piltz*, Internationales Kaufrecht, Rn. 4–171, 5–33, 5–97; *Bamberger/Roth/Saenger*, Art. 52, Rn. 6; vgl. auch OLG Rostock, 25.9.2002, CISG-online 672.

[30] *Soergel/Lüderitz/Schüßler-Langeheine*, Art. 52, Rn. 5; *Karollus*, S. 77; *Rudolph*, Art. 52, Rn. 11; MünchKomm/*P. Huber*, Art. 52, Rn. 17.

[31] Vgl. *U. Huber*, 3. Aufl., Rn. 7.

[32] So auch sec. 30 II SGA; i. E. ebenso *Herber/Czerwenka*, Art. 52, Rn. 7; *Neumayer/Ming*, Art. 52, Anm. 2.; *Honsell/Schnyder/Straub*, Art. 52, Rn. 43; a. A. *Honnold/Flechtner*, Art. 52, Rn. 320; *Staudinger/Magnus*, Art. 52, Rn. 23 (Abnahme, aber keine Zahlungspflicht); *Enderlein/Maskow/Strohbach*, Art. 52, Anm. 3.; *Karollus*, S. 174 und *Rudolph*, Art. 52, Rn. 9 wollen das Zurückweisungsrecht durch den Grundsatz von Treu und Glauben beschränken, was i. E. dazu führen kann, dass geringfügige Zuviellieferungen angenommen werden müssen.

[33] Anders sec. 30 (2) SGA und § 2–601 (a) UCC, welche dem Käufer erlauben, die Lieferung als Ganzes zurückzuweisen; Sekretariatskommentar, Art. 48, Nr. 8; *Bianca/Bonell/Will*, Art. 52, Anm. 2.2.1.; *Enderlein/Maskow/Strohbach*, Art. 52, Anm. 4.; *Staudinger/Magnus*, Art. 51, Rn. 22; *Karollus*, S. 174.

[34] Vgl. Sekretariatskommentar, Art. 48, Nr. 9; *Piltz*, Internationales Kaufrecht, Rn. 5–270; *Staudinger/Magnus*, Art. 52, Rn. 22; sec. 30 (2) (A) SGA räumt dem Käufer das Recht ein, bei Übermenge die ganze Lieferung zurückzuweisen, es sei denn, es liege eine bloss geringfügige Überschneidung vor, so dass die

be gilt – selbst bei geringfügigen Übermengen – bei Verwendung der Klausel „Kasse gegen Dokumente". Da es lediglich um ein Zurückweisungsrecht und nicht um eine Aufhebung des Vertrags geht, muss die Zuviellieferung auch keine **„wesentliche Vertragsverletzung"** darstellen.[35]

9 b) **Folgen.** Weist der Käufer die zu viel gelieferte Menge zurück, so ist er gemäss Art. 86 unter den dort näher bestimmten Voraussetzungen verpflichtet, einstweilen die notwendigen **Erhaltungsmassnahmen** zu treffen. Der Verkäufer ist gemäss Artt. 86 I 2, 87 zur Kostenerstattung verpflichtet. Darüber hinaus hat der Käufer, soweit ihm ein durch Artt. 86, 87 nicht gedeckter Schaden entsteht, Anspruch auf Schadenersatz gemäß Art. 45 I lit. b) i. V. m. Artt. 74, 77.[36] Bei Verzögerung der Rücknahme oder der Zahlung der Erhaltungskosten ist der Käufer gemäss Art. 88 zum **Selbsthilfeverkauf** berechtigt. Eine Zurücksendung der Ware auf Kosten des Verkäufers kommt allenfalls dann in Betracht, wenn ein Selbsthilfeverkauf „in geeigneter Weise" nicht möglich ist; die Kosten hat der Verkäufer gemäss Art. 45 I lit. b) zu ersetzen, soweit Art. 77 nicht entgegensteht.[37] Dagegen führt die Zuviellieferung als solche **nicht zu einem Recht auf Vertragsaufhebung,** da dem Käufer nicht „im Wesentlichen entgeht, was er nach dem Vertrag hätte erwarten dürfen" (Artt. 25, 49 I lit. a)).[38] Nur wenn der Käufer zur ungetrennten Zurückweisung der Gesamtlieferung berechtigt ist[39] und die Lieferung der vertraglich geschuldeten Menge nicht innerhalb angemessener Frist erfolgt, kann eine wesentliche Vertragsverletzung vorliegen.[40]

3. Annahme

10 Zur Annahme wird der Käufer sich insbesondere dann entschliessen, wenn der Marktpreis der Ware gestiegen ist. Nimmt der Käufer die Zuviellieferung an, sei es durch ausdrückliche Erklärung, sei es durch Versäumung der Rügefrist, erhöht sich der Kaufpreis proportional im Verhältnis der gelieferten zur ursprünglich vereinbarten Menge.[41] Kostenerstattungsansprüche und Schadensersatzansprüche kommen nicht in Betracht.[42] Die Annahme führt nach Art. 52 II S. 2 zur Änderung des Kaufvertrags; die Vertragsverletzung ist rückwirkend behoben.[43] Bei teilweiser Annahme der Zuviellieferung gilt Entsprechendes für den Teil, den der Käufer angenommen hat.

Zurückweisung des Ganzen treuwidrig wäre; vgl. auch nachfolgende Autoren, die allerdings das Zurückweisungsrecht hinsichtlich der ganzen Lieferung von einer wesentlichen Vertragsverletzung abhängig machen: *Schlechtriem,* Einheitliches UN-Kaufrecht, S. 71; *Honnold/Flechtner,* Art. 52, Rn. 320; *Bianca/Bonell/Will,* Art. 52, Anm. 2.2.1.; *Herber/Czerwenka,* Art. 52, Rn. 7; *Enderlein/Maskow/Strohbach,* Art. 52, Anm. 4.; *Karollus,* S. 174.
[35] Zutreffend *Soergel/Lüderitz/Schüßler-Langeheine,* Art. 52, Rn. 7; *Karollus,* S. 174; *Piltz,* Internationales Kaufrecht, Rn. 5–270; *Staudinger/Magnus,* Art. 52, Rn. 22; i. E. ebenso *Honsell/Schnyder/Straub,* Art. 52, Rn. 56. Die Gegenansicht geht zurück auf den Sekretariatskommentar, Art. 48, Nr. 9.
[36] Sekretariatskommentar, Art. 48, Nr. 8; *Herber/Czerwenka,* Art. 52, Rn. 6; *Reinhart,* Art. 52, Rn. 4; *Soergel/Lüderitz/Schüßler-Langeheine,* Art. 52, Rn. 3; *Enderlein/Maskow/Strohbach,* Art. 52, Anm. 5.; *Staudinger/Magnus,* Art. 52, Rn. 26.
[37] Abweichend *Honsell/Schnyder/Straub,* Art. 52, Rn. 65, die dem Käufer einen „Anspruch auf „Beseitigung der Übermenge" gemäss Art. 46 III einräumen wollen.
[38] So auch *Soergel/Lüderitz/Schüßler-Langeheine,* Art. 47, Rn. 2. Abweichend *Honsell/Schnyder/Straub,* Art. 52, Rn. 66.
[39] Vgl. oben Rn. 8.
[40] Vgl. auch *Staudinger/Magnus,* Art. 52, Rn. 22; *Bianca/Bonell/Will,* Art. 52, Anm. 2.2.1.; *Enderlein/Maskow/Strohbach,* Art. 52, Anm. 4.
[41] Vgl. OLG Rostock, 25.9.2002, CISG-online 672.
[42] So auch *Staudinger/Magnus,* Art. 52, Rn. 26; *Schlechtriem,* Einheitliches UN-Kaufrecht, Rn. 208.
[43] Vgl. Ontario Superior Court of Justice, 31.8.1999, CISG-online 433: Bei Annahme und korrekter Bezahlung der Zuviellieferung kann nicht mehr wegen Vertragswidrigkeit geklagt werden.

4. Lieferung höherwertiger Ware

Auch die Lieferung von Ware, die höherwertig ist als die vertraglich geschuldete Ware, stellt eine zu rügende Vertragswidrigkeit dar.[44] Umstritten ist, ob der Käufer bei unterlassener Rüge in Analogie zu Art. 52 II S. 2 verpflichtet sein soll, den **höheren Kaufpreis** zu bezahlen.[45] Vorausgesetzt, der Verkäufer befindet sich in einem Irrtum hinsichtlich der gelieferten (höherwertigen) Ware, ist eine **analoge Anwendung** von Art. 52 II S. 2 sachlich **geboten,** da sonst der Verkäufer auf Rechtsbehelfe des unvereinheitlichten nationalen Rechts zurückgreifen müsste, was u. U. zu Wertungswidersprüchen zum CISG führen kann.[46] Liegt ein Fall von Art. 40 vor, muss der Käufer auch bei Rügeversäumnis nicht mehr bezahlen als vertraglich vereinbart wurde.

11

---

[44] *Schwenzer,* Art. 35 Rn. 9.
[45] Bejahend *Schwenzer,* Art. 39 Rn. 30; *Herber/Czerwenka,* Art. 39, Rn. 15; *Staudinger/Magnus,* Art. 52, Rn. 29; i. E. auch *Honsell/Schnyder/Straub,* Art. 52, Rn. 42; z. T. anders *U. Huber,* 3. Aufl., Art. 52, Rn. 11; *Achilles,* Art. 52, Rn. 8; *Karollus,* S. 78; *Piltz,* Internationales Kaufrecht, Rn. 4–134; differenzierend *Soergel/Lüderitz/Schüßler-Langeheine,* Art. 52, Rn. 9. Laut MünchKomm/*P. Huber,* Art. 52, Rn. 26 und MünchKommHGB/*Benicke,* Art. 52, Rn. 20 ist Art. 52 II nicht auf höherwertige Ware anwendbar.
[46] So auch *Brunner,* Art. 52, Rn. 9; *Benedick,* Informationspflichten, Kap. 4, Rn. 744.

Kapitel III. Pflichten des Käufers

Chapter III.
Obligations of the buyer

Chapitre III.
Obligations de l'acheteur

Art. 53 [Zahlung des Kaufpreises; Abnahme der Ware]

Der Käufer ist nach Maßgabe des Vertrages und dieses Übereinkommens verpflichtet, den Kaufpreis zu zahlen und die Ware abzunehmen.*

Art. 53
The buyer must pay the price for the goods and take delivery of them as required by the contract and this Convention.

Art. 53
L'acheteur s'oblige, dans les conditions prévues au contrat et par la présente Convention, à payer le prix et à prendre livraison des marchandises.

Übersicht**

	Rn.
I. Regelungsgegenstand	1
II. Die Pflicht des Käufers zur Zahlung des Kaufpreises	2
1. Bestimmung des Kaufpreises	2
2. Währung	4
a) Vertragliche Währung	4
b) Die Währung als vom CISG geregelter, aber nicht ausdrücklich entschiedener Gegenstand	5
c) Das Recht des Käufers zur Zahlung in der am Zahlungsort geltenden Währung	8
d) Das Recht des Verkäufers, Zahlung in der Währung des Zahlungsortes zu verlangen	9
3. Zahlungsmittel	10
a) Offene Rechnung/Barzahlung/Überweisung	10
b) Annahme eines Wechsels	13
c) Dokumentarinkasso	15
d) Dokumentenakkreditive	17
4. Zahlungsort	19
5. Zahlungszeit	20
6. Fälligkeitszinsen	21
7. Zahlungskosten	22
8. Teilzahlungen	23
9. Anrechnung von Zahlungen	24
10. Kaufpreisklage	25
11. Devisenkontrolle	26
12. Verjährungsfristen	27
13. Tauschhandel	28
14. Abtretung und Abtretbarkeit	29
15. Zahlungen durch Dritte	30
16. Die Verpflichtung des Käufers zur Stellung von Sicherheiten	31
a) Zahlungsgarantien	32
b) Bankgarantien in Akkreditivform	33

---

* Schweiz, Österreich: anzunehmen.

** Anm. d. Autors: Mein Dank gilt meinem Vorgänger, Herrn Professor em. Dr. Günter Hager, ehem. Direktor des Instituts für Ausländisches und Internationales Privatrecht, Abt. I, an der Albert-Ludwigs-Universität Freiburg i. Brsg., ohne dessen Bearbeitung der Vorauflagen die vorliegende Kommentierung nicht möglich gewesen wäre. Trotz Beibehaltung des grundlegenden Aufbaus seiner Kommentierung habe ich eine umfassende Neubearbeitung vorgenommen und vertrete in einzelnen Streitfragen eine andere Auffassung als die Vorauflage.

III. Die Verpflichtung des Käufers zur Abnahme der Ware 34
   1. Lieferung von Teilen der für die Herstellung oder Erzeugung der Ware
      notwendigen Stoffe 35
   2. Spezifizierung der Ware 37
   3. Incoterms 2010 ® 38
   4. Kooperations- und Informationspflichten 39
IV. Andere Pflichten des Käufers 40
V. Die Rechtsbehelfe des Verkäufers bei Vertragsbruch durch den Käufer 41
VI. Beweislast 42

Vorläufer und **Entwürfe:** Art. 56 EKG; Genfer E 1976 Art. 34; Wiener E 1977 Art. 35; New Yorker E 1978 Art. 49.

I. Regelungsgegenstand

Art. 53 schreibt die zwei **charakteristischen Pflichten** des Käufers fest: Er ist verpflichtet, den Kaufpreis zu zahlen und die Ware abzunehmen. Das Pendant in Kapitel II über die Pflichten des Verkäufers ist Art. 30, wonach der Verkäufer verpflichtet ist, die Ware zu liefern, die sie betreffenden Dokumente zu übergeben und das Eigentum an der Ware zu übertragen. Zusammengenommen beschreiben diese beiden Artikel die charakteristischen Vertragspflichten, die sich aus einem dem CISG unterstehenden Kaufvertrag ergeben.[1] Abschnitt I, Art. 54–59, enthält detailliertere Beschreibungen der Pflicht zur Zahlung des Kaufpreises. Nähere Ausführungen zur Pflicht zur Abnahme der Ware finden sich in Abschnitt II, Art. 60. Im Einzelfall können der konkrete Kaufvertrag oder das CISG **weitere Pflichten** des Käufers vorsehen.[2] Im Unterschied zu einigen nationalen Rechtsordnungen unterscheidet das CISG nicht zwischen **Haupt- und Nebenpflichten;**[3] vielmehr unterstehen alle Pflichten demselben **einheitlichen Rechtsbehelfssystem.**[4] Insbesondere ist im CISG die Pflicht des Käufers zur Abnahme der Ware von gleicher Natur wie seine Pflicht zur Zahlung des Kaufpreises, so dass der Verkäufer (unter den Voraussetzungen des Art. 28) einen Anspruch auf Erfüllung hat.[5] Die Pflichten des Käufers sind zu unterscheiden von seinen blossen **Obliegenheiten.** Obliegenheiten sind vom Käufer in seinem eigenen Interesse zu erfüllen, und der Verkäufer hat bei deren Nichterfüllung keinen Anspruch auf Schadenersatz.[6] Die Verletzung von Obliegenheiten führt zu Rechtsnachteilen, wobei die konkreten Rechtsnachteile von der verletzten Obliegenheit abhängen. Zum Beispiel verliert der Käufer bei Verletzung seiner Obliegenheit zur Rüge von Vertragswidrigkeiten der Ware nach Art. 39 das Recht, sich auf diese Vertragswidrigkeiten zu berufen.[7] Verletzt der Käufer seine Obliegenheit zur Schadensminderung nach Art. 77, kann der Verkäufer Herabsetzung des Schadenersatzes in der Höhe des Betrags verlangen, um den der Schaden hätte verringert werden können.[8]

---

[1] *Honnold/Flechtner,* Art. 53, Rn. 322; *Kröll u. a./P. Butler/Harindranath,* Art. 53, Rn. 1.
[2] Vgl. unten Rn. 34–40.
[3] *Bianca/Bonell/Maskow,* Art. 53, Anm. 2.2.; *Bamberger/Roth/Saenger,* Art. 53, Rn. 2; *Honsell/Schnyder/Straub,* Art. 53, Rn. 7.
[4] Vgl. unten Rn. 41.
[5] *Staudinger/Magnus,* Art. 60, Rn. 1; MünchKomm/*P. Huber,* Art. 53, Rn. 2; vgl. *Honsell/Schnyder/Straub,* Art. 53, Rn. 4; *Ferrari u. a./Mankowski,* Internationales Vertragsrecht, Art. 53, Rn. 4.
[6] Vgl. *Ferrari u. a./Mankowski,* Internationales Vertragsrecht, Art. 53, Rn. 11.
[7] Vgl. dazu ausführlich oben *Schwenzer,* Art. 38 Rn. 1 ff.; Art. 39 Rn. 1 ff.
[8] Unten *Schwenzer,* Art. 77 Rn. 1 ff.

II. Die Pflicht des Käufers zur Zahlung des Kaufpreises

1. Bestimmung des Kaufpreises

2   In den meisten Fällen werden die Vertragsparteien den **Kaufpreis bestimmt** oder eine **Methode zur Berechnung des Kaufpreises** festlegt haben.[9] Wenn der Kaufpreis im Vertrag allerdings weder ausdrücklich noch stillschweigend festsetzt und seine Festsetzung auch nicht anderweitig ermöglicht wurde, erlaubt Art. 55 den Rückgriff auf den Marktpreis.[10] Zusätzlich enthält Art. 56 eine Auslegungsregel für den Fall, dass der Kaufpreis nach dem Gewicht der Ware festgesetzt wurde.[11] Üblicherweise deckt der Preis **sämtliche Leistungen** des Verkäufers ab;[12] insoweit kann sich der Preis aus verschiedenen Elementen zusammensetzen und z. B. die Transportkosten beinhalten.[13]

3   Das CISG kennt kein Prinzip des *iustum pretium* (angemessener Preis). Nur in besonderen Fällen der **Leistungserschwerung,** wenn also aussergewöhnliche und wesentliche Veränderungen in den ökonomischen Umständen eingetreten sind, kann eine Befreiung des Käufers von seiner Pflicht zur Zahlung des vereinbarten Kaufpreises nach Art. 79 in Betracht kommen.[14]

2. Währung

4   a) **Vertragliche Währung.** Normalerweise vereinbaren die Vertragsparteien eine bestimmte Währung, wenn sie den Kaufpreis festsetzen. Eine solche **vertragliche Regelung** der Parteien gilt gemäss Art. 6 vorrangig.[15] Haben die Vertragsparteien eine Währung hingegen nicht ausdrücklich vereinbart, so können gemäss Art. 9 die Gebräuche, mit denen sie sich einverstanden erklärt haben, oder die Gepflogenheiten, die zwischen ihnen entstanden sind, sowie ein etwaiger internationaler Handelsbrauch berücksichtigt werden, um festzustellen, ob die Parteien sich stillschweigend auf eine Währung geeinigt haben.[16] Zum Beispiel kann der US-Dollar heutzutage als die im internationalen Rohwarenhandel massgebende Währung angesehen werden, insbesondere nachdem die führenden, öffentlichen Notierungen von Preisen an Rohstoffbörsen auch ausserhalb der USA, insbesondere an der LME (London Metal Exchange), in US-Dollar angegeben werden.[17] Wenn der Kaufpreis als absolute Zahl ohne Angabe einer Währung ausgedrückt wurde, wird es in der Praxis unter

---

[9] Vgl. oben *Schroeter*, Art. 14 Rn. 8 f.; *Kröll u. a./P. Butler/Harindranath*, Art. 53, Rn. 6.
[10] Vgl. unten Art. 55 Rn. 1 ff.
[11] Vgl. unten Art. 56 Rn. 1 ff.
[12] *Ferrari u. a./Mankowski*, Internationales Vertragsrecht, Art. 53, Rn. 6; *Honsell/Schnyder/Straub*, Art. 54, Rn. 10.
[13] OLG Saarbrücken, 12.5.2010, CISG-online 2155, B. II.1.
[14] Vgl. unten Art. 62 Rn. 17; *Schwenzer*, Art. 79 Rn. 30, 54; *dies.*, 40 Vic. U. Well. L. Rev. (2009), 709, 713. Vgl. Artt. 6.2.1 ff. PICC, die vom belgischen Kassationsgericht in einem CISG-Fall angewendet wurden, vgl. Cour de Cassation, 19.6.2009, CISG-online 1963. A. A. BGH, 27.11.2007, CISG-online 1617 = IHR 2008, 49, 53, m. Anm. *Schroeter*, EWiR 2008, 303 ff.: Währungsschwankungen im Staat des Wiederverkaufs (Russland) geben dem Käufer/Weiterverkäufer nicht das Recht, den Kaufvertrag aufzuheben, weil Art. 79 nicht auf den Kaufpreisanspruch des Verkäufers/Herstellers Anwendung findet.
[15] OLG Frankfurt a. M., 18.1.1994, CISC-online 123 = CLOUT Nr. 79, englische Übersetzung m. Anm. *E. Diederichsen*, 14 J. L. & Com. (1995), 177, 201 ff.; KG Berlin, 24.1.1994, CISG-online 130 = RIW 194, 683; KG Wallis, 27.4.2007, CISG-online 1721; KG Wallis, 27.10.2006, CISG-online 1563; KG Wallis, 23.5.2006, CISG-online 1532; BezG St. Gallen, 3.7.1997, CISG-online 336; *Bianca/Bonell/Maskow*, Art. 54, Anm. 3.1.; *Magnus*, RabelsZ 53 (1989), 116, 127 ff.; *Neumayer/Ming*, Art. 54, Anm. 4.; *Bamberger/Roth/Saenger*, Art. 54, Rn. 3; *Eckert/Maifeld/Matthiessen*, Rn. 1285; *Ferrari u. a./Mankowski*, Internationales Vertragsrecht, Art. 53, Rn. 4; *Kröll u. a./P. Butler/Harindranath*, Art. 54, Rn. 7. A. A. Cámara Nacional de Apelaciones en lo Comercial de Buenos Aires, 31.5.2007, CISG-online 1517, dem zufolge nationales Recht auf eine Parteivereinbarung über die Währung anwendbar sei.
[16] *Magnus*, RabelsZ 53 (1989), 116, 128; *Bamberger/Roth/Saenger*, Art. 54, Rn. 3; *Kröll u. a./P. Butler/Harindranath*, Art. 54, Rn. 7.
[17] Für den Rohölhandel vgl. *Honsell/Schnyder/Straub*, Art. 54, Rn. 26.

Umständen möglich sein, die von den Parteien gewollte Währung durch den Warenwert zu bestimmen.

b) Die Währung als vom CISG geregelter, aber nicht ausdrücklich entschiedener 5
Gegenstand. Wenn keine ausdrückliche oder stillschweigende Einigung der Vertragsparteien über die Währung vorliegt, stellt sich die Frage, ob das CISG die anwendbare Währung regelt und, falls ja, wie diese zu bestimmen ist. Obwohl das Übereinkommen keine ausdrückliche Regelung der anwendbaren Währung enthält, sollte nicht vorschnell auf das nationale Recht zurückgegriffen,[18] sondern eine **einheitliche Regelung** gefunden werden.[19] Die Währung eines Geldanspruchs im internationalen Handel ist ein Regelungsgegenstand des CISG, weil die Frage der Währung untrennbar mit dem Kaufpreisanspruch verbunden ist. Gemäss Art. 7 II ist die anwendbare Währung nach den allgemeinen Grundsätzen zu entscheiden, die dem CISG zu Grunde liegen. Haben die Parteien vereinbart, dass der Kaufpreis an einem bestimmten Ort zu zahlen ist, so bestimmt der **Zahlungsort** nach dem allgemeinen Grundsatz der Parteiautonomie (Art. 6) auch die Währung. Haben die Parteien hingegen keinen bestimmten Zahlungsort vereinbart, so kann Art. 57 I als allgemeiner Grundsatz des Übereinkommens herangezogen werden. Demnach ist diejenige Währung anwendbar, die an dem **Übergabeort** gilt, an welchem die Übergabe der Ware oder der Dokumente stattfindet, wenn Zahlung gegen Übergabe der Ware oder von Dokumenten zu erfolgen hat (Art. 57 I lit. b)). In allen anderen Fällen ist die Währung anzuwenden, die am **Ort der Niederlassung des Verkäufers** gilt (Art. 57 I lit. a)).[20] Einer Gegenansicht zufolge, die grundsätzlich auch für eine einheitsrechtliche Lösung eintritt, soll nicht auf den Zahlungsort, sondern in allen Fällen direkt auf den Ort der Niederlassung des Verkäufers abgestellt werden.[21] Obwohl diese Gegenansicht zum gleichen Ergebnis wie die hier vertretene Ansicht führt, wenn der Zahlungsort nach Art. 57 I lit. a) zu bestimmen ist, ist sie abzulehnen, weil sie weder eine etwaige Parteivereinbarung bezüglich des Zahlungsorts noch die Bedeutung des Ortes, an dem die Ware oder die Dokumente zu übergeben sind, berücksichtigt. So macht es wenig Sinn, die Währung am Ort der Niederlassung des Verkäufers zur Anwendung zu bringen, wenn die Zahlung auf ein Bankkonto des Verkäufers bei einer Bank, die ihren Sitz nicht in dem Staat seiner Niederlassung hat, oder gegen Vorlage von Dokumenten durch eine bestätigende Bank im Rahmen eines Dokumentenakkreditivs zu erfolgen hat. In solchen Fällen sollte die Währung am Zahlungsort Anwendung finden.[22]

Einer anderen Gegenansicht zufolge kann überhaupt keine einheitsrechtliche Lösung auf 6 die Frage gefunden werden, welche Währung Anwendung findet, wenn die Parteien sich nicht auf eine Währung geeinigt haben. Vielmehr muss dieser Gegenansicht zufolge gemäss Art. 7 II das (unvereinheitlichte) Recht zur Anwendung gebracht werden, das nach den Regeln des **Internationalen Privatrechts** anzuwenden ist.[23] Die anwendbaren Regeln des

---

[18] Wie z. B. § 361 HGB, der auf die Währung am Erfüllungsort des Vertrags verweist.
[19] Fovárosi Birósag Budapest, 24.3.1992, CISG-online 61 = IPRax 1993, 263; KG Berlin, 24.1.1994, CISG-online 130 = RIW 1994, 683; *Magnus*, RabelsZ 53 (1989), 116, 129, 130.
[20] KG Berlin, 24.1.1994, CISG-online 130 = RIW 1994, 683; *Šarčević*, Draft Digest, 382, 484; *Gabriel*, 25 J. L. & Com. (2005-06), 273, 275; MünchKommHGB/*Benicke*, Art. 54, Rn. 7; *Audit*, Rd. 147, 150; *Brunner*, Art. 54, Rn. 14; *Karollus*, S. 167; *Piltz*, Internationales Kaufrecht, Rn. 4–127; *Wiegand*, Pflichten des Käufers, S. 143, 152; OLG Koblenz, 17.9.1993, CISG-online 91 = RIW 1993, 934, 936. Eine inhaltsgleiche Lösung sieht Art. 6.1.10 PICC vor.
[21] Fovárosi Birósag Budapest, 24.3.1992, CISG-online 61 = IPRax 1993, 263; KG Berlin, 24.1.1994, CISG-online 130 = RIW 1994, 683; *Staudinger/Magnus*, Art. 53, Rn. 22; *Brunner*, Art. 54, Rn. 13 ff.; MünchKomm/*P. Huber*, Art. 53, Rn. 19; *Reithmann/Martiny/Martiny*, Rn. 743; *Rudolph*, Art. 54, Rn. 8; *Magnus*, RabelsZ 53 (1989), 116, 129 ff.; *Ferrari u. a./Mankowski*, Internationales Vertragsrecht, Art. 54, Rn. 22; *Kröll u. a./P. Butler/Harindranath*, Art. 54, Rn. 9.
[22] A. A. MünchKomm/*P. Huber*, Art. 53, Rn. 19, der die Bedeutung des Ortes, an dem die Ware oder die Dokumente übergeben werden sollen, negiert und argumentiert, dass die Parteien diesen Ort oft nur aus praktischen Gründen wählen, der für die anwendbare Währung keine Bedeutung erlangen sollten.
[23] KG Wallis, 28.1.2009, CISG-online 2025, E. 4. b) bb); KG Wallis, 27.4.2007, CISG-online 1721; KG Wallis, 23.5.2006, CISG-online 1532; KG Wallis, 27.10.2006, CISG-online 1563; KG Wallis, 27.5.2005,

Internationalen Privatrechts werden auf die Währungsfrage oft dasjenige Recht anwenden, das auf den Kaufvertrag als Ganzes Anwendung findet *(lex contractus)*.[24] In der Literatur wurde dagegen die Ansicht vertreten, dass im Rahmen des anwendbaren Internationalen Privatrechts eine **besondere Kollisionsnorm** gefunden werden müsse, welche die anwendbare Währung am Ort der Zahlung anknüpft.[25] Eine solche kollisionsrechtliche Lösung ist übertrieben umständlich und missachtet allgemeine Prinzipien des CISG in seinem Regelungsbereich der Kaufpreiszahlung. Vor allem aber wird eine solche kollisionsrechtliche Lösung oft zu den gleichen Ergebnissen gelangen wie die einheitsrechtliche Lösung, die den von den Vertragsparteien vereinbarten oder durch Art. 57 bestimmbaren Zahlungsort für massgebend erklärt.

7   Auf jeden Fall abzulehnen ist die Ansicht, dass ein Kaufpreis ohne ausdrückliche oder stillschweigende Bestimmung einer Währung das **Zustandekommen eines Vertrages** verhindern könne, weil ein entsprechendes Angebot nicht bestimmt genug sei.[26] Die anwendbare Währung kann vielmehr nach der hier vertretenen Ansicht bestimmt werden.[27]

8   **c) Das Recht des Käufers zur Zahlung in der am Zahlungsort geltenden Währung.** Die meisten nationalen Rechtsordnungen[28] sowie die PICC[29] sehen vor, dass der Kaufpreis auch in der Währung, die am **Zahlungsort rechtliches Zahlungsmittel** ist, gezahlt werden kann, obwohl der Kaufpreis in einer anderen Währung ausgedrückt ist. Nur wenn die Parteien ausdrücklich vereinbart haben, dass die Zahlung nur in der vertraglich vereinbarten Währung möglich sein soll (sog. **Effektivklausel**), verpflichten diese nationalen Rechtsordnungen sowie die PICC den Schuldner dazu, in der vertraglich vereinbarten Währung zu zahlen.[30] Das CISG kennt eine solche Regel nicht. Auch kann ein solches **Umwandlungsrecht des Schuldners** nicht auf allgemeine Prinzipien des CISG gestützt werden, weil es das wichtige Prinzip der Parteiautonomie nach Art. 6 verletzen würde.[31] Ein weiterer Grund, der gegen ein Umwandlungsrecht des Käufers, das ihn berechtigen würde, statt in der vertraglich vereinbarten Währung in Landeswährung zu zahlen, ergibt sich aus dem Zweck der entsprechenden nationalen Regelungen; sie schützen die Möglichkeit der Zahlung in ihren entsprechenden Landeswährungen.[32] Ein solcher Schutzzweck, der im nationalen Recht durchaus legitim ist, kann in einer internationalen Handelsrechtskonvention, die geltendes Recht in vielen unterschiedlichen Handelsnationen geworden ist, keine Bedeutung erlangen. Auch die Ansicht, dass sich Umwandlungsrechte des Käufers, in der Landeswährung am Ort der Zahlung zu bezahlen, aus dem gemäss Art. 7 II nach den

---

CISG-online 1137; KG Wallis, 19.8.2003, CISG-online 895; KG Wallis, 30.6.1998, CISG-online 419; *Hager/Maultzsch*, 5. Aufl., Art. 54 Rn. 9; *Bianca/Bonell/Maskow*, Art. 54, Anm. 3.1.; *Herber/Czerwenka*, Art. 53, Rn. 5; *Neumayer/Ming*, Art. 54, Anm. 4.; *Bamberger/Roth/Saenger*, Art. 54, Rn. 4.

[24] Für Deutschland vgl. MünchKommBGB/*Spellenberg*, Art. 12 Rom I-VO, Rn. 181; *Palandt/Thorn*, (IPR) Rom I 12, Rn. 6; *Ferrari u. a./Ferrari*, Art. 12 Rom I-VO, Rn. 36. Ohne Rechtswahl führt dies gemäss Art. 4 I lit. a) Rom I-VO zur Anwendung des Verkäuferrechts. Findet deutsches internes Recht als Verkäuferrecht Anwendung, so verweist § 361 HGB wiederum auf die Währung, die am Erfüllungsort der Zahlungspflicht gilt. Zu dem Ganzen (unter Geltung des EGBGB) vgl. *Hager/Maultzsch*, 5. Aufl., Art. 54 Rn. 9a.

[25] *Hager/Maultzsch*, 5. Aufl., Art. 54 Rn. 9a. Vgl. für die Schweiz: Art. 147 III IPRG.

[26] A. A. *Honsell/Schnyder/Straub*, Art. 54, Rn. 26.

[27] S. oben Rn. 5.

[28] Deutschland: § 244 I BGB; Schweiz: Art. 84 II OR; Italien: Art. 1278 Cc; England: *Barclays Int. Ltd. v. Levin Bros* [1977] QB 270, 277, s. auch *Mann*, Rn. 7.37; USA: § 2–511 II UCC.

[29] Art. 6.1.9 I PICC.

[30] Gemäss Art. 6.1.9 I lit. a) PICC ist der Schuldner auch dann verpflichtet, in der vertraglich vereinbarten Währung zu zahlen, wenn die Währung, die am Ort der Zahlung gilt, nicht frei umtauschbar ist.

[31] OGH, 22.10.2001, CISG-online 614; *Staudinger/Magnus*, Art. 53, Rn. 28; *Bianca/Bonell/Maskow*, Art. 54, Anm. 3.1.; *Honsell/Schnyder/Straub*, Art. 54, Rn. 28; *Piltz*, Internationales Kaufrecht, Rn. 4–126; *Witz/Salger/Lorenz/Witz*, Art. 53, Rn. 6; *Bamberger/Roth/Saenger*, Art. 54, Rn. 5; *Ferrari u. a./Mankowski*, Internationales Vertragsrecht, Art. 54, Rn. 24; *Magnus*, RabelsZ 53 (1989), 116, 122. A. A. *Soergel/Lüderitz/Budzikiewicz*, Art. 53, Rn. 3; *Herber/Czerwenka*, Art. 53, Rn. 6.

[32] Vgl. OGH, 22.10.2001, CISG-online 614.

Regeln des **Internationalen Privatrechts** anwendbaren nationalen Recht ergeben könnten, ist abzulehnen.[33]

d) Das Recht des Verkäufers, Zahlung in der Währung des Zahlungsortes zu verlangen. Anders als manche nationalen Rechtsordnungen[34] kennt das CISG kein **Recht des Verkäufers,** Zahlung in der Währung des Zahlungsortes zu verlangen.[35] Nur wenn es dem Käufer **unmöglich** ist, seine Zahlungspflicht in der Währung zu erfüllen, in welcher der Kaufpreis ausgedrückt ist, kann der Verkäufer Zahlung in der Währung des Zahlungsortes verlangen.[36] Gleiches gilt, wenn das **Prozessrecht des Forums** den Verkäufer verpflichtet, seine Klage in Landeswährung auszudrücken.[37] Andererseits muss die nach dem anwendbaren Prozessrecht bestehende Möglichkeit des Verkäufers, seine Klage in Landeswährung auszudrücken, im Falle eines CISG-Vertrags ausgeschlossen bleiben.[38] Das Recht des Verkäufers, den Käufer bei Unmöglichkeit bzw. zwingendem Prozessrecht zur Zahlung in der Währung des Zahlungsortes anzuhalten, resultiert aus Art. 79 V i. V. m. Art. 7 I, weil die Unmöglichkeit der Zahlung in der vertraglich vereinbarten Währung den Käufer nicht von seiner Pflicht zur Zahlung des Kaufpreises befreit. Der Verkäufer ist allerdings verpflichtet, eine **angemessene Ersatzwährung** zu wählen. Mit anderen Worten darf die verlangte Währung dem Käufer keine unangemessenen Nachteile aufbürden.[39] Je nach Fallkonstellation kann die Ersatzwährung eine der folgenden Währungen sein: die Währung am Ort der Niederlassung des Käufers, die Währung am Ort der Niederlassung des Verkäufers oder die Währung am Ort, an dem die Übergabe der Ware oder von Dokumenten gegen Zahlung zu erfolgen hat. Wenn der Käufer in einer anderen als der vertraglich vereinbarten Währung zu zahlen hat, richtet sich der zu zahlende Betrag nach dem Wechselkurs im Zeitpunkt der Fälligkeit und nicht nach dem Wechselkurs im Zeitpunkt der Zahlung.[40] Jedweder Währungsschaden, der sich aus dem Umstand ergibt, dass der Wechselkurs im Zeitpunkt der Zahlung benutzt wurde, kann als Schadensposten unter Art. 74

---

[33] Vgl. BezG St. Gallen, 3.7.1997, CISG-online 336, das die Frage offengelassen hat, ob das CISG Vorrang vor nationalen Regelungen zur Währungsfrage hat. A. A. HGer Aargau, 25.1.2005, CISG-online 1091 = IHR 2006, 34, 35, das die Anwendung von Art. 84 II OR ausschloss, weil diese Vorschrift nur dem Käufer ein Umwandlungsrecht gäbe, nicht aber dem Verkäufer; OLG Koblenz, 17.9.1993, CISG-online 91 = RIW 1993, 934, das die Anwendung von § 244 BGB verneinte, weil die Zahlung in französischen Francs nicht in Deutschland, sondern in Frankreich zu erfolgen hatte; *Herber/Czerwenka*, Art. 53, Rn. 6.

[34] USA: § 2–511 (2) UCC; Italien: Art. 1277 Cc.

[35] *Hager/Maultzsch*, 5. Aufl., Art. 54 Rn. 11; *Staudinger/Magnus*, Art. 53, Rn. 30; *Achilles*, Art. 53, Rn. 1; *Brunner*, Art. 54, Rn. 15; MünchKommHGB/*Benicke*, Art. 54, Rn. 9; *Piltz*, Internationales Kaufrecht, Rn. 4–125; *Witz/Salger/Lorenz/Witz*, Art. 53, Rn. 7; *Bamberger/Roth/Saenger*, Art. 54, Rn. 6; *Ferrari u. a./Mankowski*, Internationales Vertragsrecht, Art. 54, Rn. 23; *Magnus*, RabelsZ 53 (1989), 116, 132. Für Rechtsprechung zum EKG vgl. *Hager/Maultzsch*, 5. Aufl., Art. 54 Rn. 11.

[36] Vgl. Art. 6.1.9 II PICC; zum CISG vgl. *Hager/Maultzsch*, 5. Aufl., Art. 54 Rn. 11; *Staudinger/Magnus*, Art. 53, Rn. 29; MünchKomm/*P. Huber*, Art. 53, Rn. 21; *Piltz*, Internationales Kaufrecht, Rn. 4–125; *Witz/Salger/Lorenz/Witz*, Art. 53, Rn. 7; *Ferrari u. a./Mankowski*, Internationales Vertragsrecht, Art. 54, Rn. 23; *Kröll u. a./P. Butler/Harindranath*, Art. 54, Rn. 14; *Magnus*, RabelsZ 53 (1989), 116, 133.

[37] Vgl. Art. 67 I Ziff. 3 SchKG (Schweizer Schuldbetreibungs- und Konkursgesetz), wonach der Gläubiger seinen Anspruch in Schweizer Währung auszudrücken hat. Dies gilt freilich nicht im ordentlichen Zivilprozess, vgl. KG Wallis, 30.6.1998, CISG-online 419: Ein in Schweizer Franken ausgedrücktes Rechtsbegehren auf Kaufpreiszahlung wurde in Anwendung italienischen Rechts in italienische Lire umgerechnet. Vgl. KG Wallis, 27.10.2006, CISG-online 1563: das Gericht erließ ein Abwesenheitsurteil unter der fälschlichen Annahme, dass die in Schweizer Franken ausgedrückte Klage des Verkäufers eine Vertragsänderung darstelle, weil der Käufer dies nicht bestritten hatte. Vgl. oben *Müller-Chen*, Art. 28 Rn. 7, dem zufolge Art. 28 keine Anwendung auf Einwendungen basierend auf ausländischem Wechsel- und Währungsrecht findet, da dieser Regelungsbereich ausserhalb des CISG liege.

[38] Eine andere Ansicht vertrat das zweitinstanzliche Gericht in der vom OGH, 10.11.1994, CISG-online 117, berichteten Sache, der zufolge der deutsche Verkäufer seine Kaufpreisklage in österreichischen Schilling gegenüber dem österreichischen Käufer einreichen konnte, obwohl der Kaufpreis in deutscher Mark ausgedrückt war.

[39] Vgl. *Ferrari u. a./Mankowski*, Internationales Vertragsrecht, Art. 54, Rn. 23.

[40] Art. 6.1.9 III PICC verweisen auch auf den Wechselkurs im Zeitpunkt der Fälligkeit. A. A. *Dölle/von Caemmerer*, Art. 57 EKG, Rn. 23, dem zufolge der Zeitpunkt der Zahlung unter Geltung des EKG massgebend war.

ersetzt verlangt werden. Selbst wenn der Vertrag eine Effektivklausel vorsieht, der zufolge ausschliesslich Zahlung in der Vertragswährung den Käufer von seiner Zahlungspflicht befreit, hat der Verkäufer das soeben beschriebene Wahlrecht.[41]

3. Zahlungsmittel

10 **a) Offene Rechnung/Barzahlung/Überweisung.** Normalerweise vereinbaren die Parteien in ihrem Vertrag, welches **Zahlungsmittel** der Käufer zu benutzen hat; eine **Parteivereinbarung** gilt gemäss Art. 6 vorrangig. Eine bloss einmalige Abweichung vom vertraglich vereinbarten Zahlungsmittel für eine Zahlungstranche beinhaltet nicht notwendigerweise eine Vertragsänderung mit Blick auf zukünftige Tranchen.[42] Das CISG enthält keine ausdrückliche **Auffangregelung** für den Fall, dass sich die Parteien eines internationalen Warenkaufvertrags über das Zahlungsmittel nicht ausdrücklich einigen und auch keine stillschweigende Einigung nach Art. 8 oder 9 angenommen werden kann. In einem solchen Fall muss der Käufer grundsätzlich bar zahlen. Im internationalen Warenhandel beinhaltet **Barzahlung** grundsätzlich auch die **Zahlung durch Überweisung,** die in der Praxis häufig als telegraphischer Transfer („T/T") bezeichnet wird.[43] Eine Überweisung wird unter praktischen Gesichtspunkten nur dann möglich sein, wenn der Verkäufer eine **Bankverbindung** angegeben oder zumindest den Umstand, dass er eine Bankverbindung zu einer bestimmten Bank unterhält, bekanntgemacht hat.[44] Hat der Verkäufer ein **bestimmtes Bankkonto** angegeben, so kann oft eine Einigung der Parteien dahingehend angenommen werden, dass die Zahlung nur per Überweisung möglich sein soll.

11 **Telegrafischer Transfer („T/T")** ist immer noch der im internationalen Handel benutzte Begriff, um eine **internationale Überweisung** zu bezeichnen, obwohl heutzutage die computerbasierte Interbank-Telekommunikation den Telegrafen des 19. Jahrhunderts längst abgelöst hat, der seit Mitte der 1970er Jahre nicht mehr benutzt wird. Auf internationaler Ebene wurde der Versuch unternommen, das Recht der internationalen Überweisungen zu vereinheitlichen, was zu dem **UNCITRAL Modellgesetz über internationale Überweisungen** von 1992 führte.[45] Auf diesem Modellgesetz basierend wurde die **Verordnung 97/5/EC des Europäischen Parlaments und des Rates vom 27. Januar 2007 über grenzüberschreitende Überweisungen** erlassen.[46] Ausserhalb des Anwendungsbereichs dieser Verordnung muss das auf die Bankbeziehungen, die zur Abwicklung einer internationalen Überweisung notwendig sind, anzuwendende Recht nach den anwendbaren Regelungen des **Internationalen Privatrechts** bestimmt werden.

12 Das CISG hingegen ist nur mit der **Erfüllungswirkung** einer Überweisung auf die Zahlungspflicht des Käufers befasst. Eine angemessene Lösung dieser schwierigen Frage steht im Zentrum der Auseinandersetzungen in den verschiedenen Rechtsordnungen, welche unterschiedliche Antworten dazu hervorgebracht haben.[47] Für das CISG muss die Lösung dieser Frage aus Art. 57 entwickelt werden. Haben die Parteien als Zahlungsmittel

---

[41] Vgl. Art. 6.1.9 II PICC.
[42] CIETAC, 9.9.2002, CISG-online 1555: das Schiedsgericht verneinte die Behauptung des Käufers, dass seine einmalige Überweisung und die Annahme der Überweisung durch den Verkäufer eine Vertragsänderung durch Handeln darstelle und hielt ihn dafür haftbar, dass er das im ursprünglichen Vertrag vorgesehene Dokumentenakkreditiv für die nächsten Lieferungen nicht stellte; vgl. ICC, 11849/2003, CISG-online 1321, Rn. 31 ff.
[43] *Hager/Maultzsch*, 5. Aufl., Art. 57 Rn. 9; *Staudinger/Magnus*, Art. 53, Rn. 8; MünchKomm/*P. Huber*, Art. 53, Rn. 13; *Honsell/Schnyder/Straub*, Art. 54, Rn. 13; *Witz/Salger/Lorenz/Witz*, Art. 53, Rn. 8; *Bamberger/Roth/Saenger*, Art. 54, Rn. 7; *Eckert/Maifeld/Matthiessen*, Rn. 1285; *Kröll u. a./P. Butler/Harindranath*, Art. 53, Rn. 10.
[44] Vgl. Art. 6.1.8 I PICC.
[45] Siehe www.uncitral.org.
[46] AblEG 1997 Nr. L 043, Rn. 25.
[47] Vgl. Anm. 2. zu Art. 6.1.8 II PICC, der wie folgt lautet: „*In case of payment by a transfer the obligation of the obligor is discharged when the transfer to the obligee's financial institution becomes effective.*"

die Überweisung auf ein Konto bei der Bank des Verkäufers vereinbart, so ist die **Gutschrift auf dem Konto des Verkäufers** bei seiner Bank massgebend.[48] Wenn die Zahlung an eine Bank erfolgt, bei der der Verkäufer erklärtermassen ein Bankkonto unterhält, so ist die Zahlungspflicht des Käufers nur dann erfüllt, wenn der Verkäufer die **Gutschrift** auf seinem Konto **angezeigt** erhält. Mit anderen Worten kommt es auf die Umstände des Einzelfalls an, wann die Zahlungspflicht erfüllt ist. Im Allgemeinen kann gesagt werden, dass der Verkäufer über einen dem Kaufpreis entsprechenden Geldwert **unwiderruflich verfügen** können muss.[49]

b) Annahme eines Wechsels. Seit dem 12. Jahrhundert besteht ein enger Zusammenhang zwischen dem internationalen Warenhandel und den **gezogenen Wechseln** und **Eigenwechseln**.[50] Wegen ihrer früher grossen Bedeutung waren diese Zahlungsinstrumente Gegenstand früher Vereinheitlichungsbestrebungen, die in den **Genfer Konventionen über gezogene Wechsel und Eigenwechsel** mündeten.[51] Allerdings wurden die Genfer Konventionen von den meisten Staaten des Common Law nicht ratifiziert (ausser von Australien); stattdessen wurde ein System auf Grundlage des UK Bills of Exchange Act 1832 und des United States Uniform Negotiable Instruments Act 1896 geschaffen. Wegen einiger wesentlichen Unterschiede zwischen den Genfer Konventionen und den Systemen des Common Law wurde 1987 von **UNCITRAL** die **Konvention der Vereinigten Staaten über internationale gezogene Wechsel und internationale Eigenwechsel** verabschiedet. Diese Konvention ist allerdings nie in Kraft getreten.[52]

Obwohl die Bedeutung internationaler gezogener Wechsel und internationaler Eigenwechsel als Zahlungsinstrumente im internationalen Warenhandel stark nachgelassen hat, müssen die Wirkungen der Benutzung eines solchen Zahlungsinstruments auf einen CISG-Vertrag erläutert werden. In einem CISG-Vertrag ist Zahlung durch Scheck, gezogenen Wechsel oder Eigenwechsel nur dann möglich, wenn die Parteien sich vorgängig darauf verständigt haben oder die Vertragsauslegung nach Art. 8 oder 9 eine entsprechende stillschweigende **Einigung** ergibt.[53] Eine andere Lösung ist in Art. 6.1.7 I PICC vorgesehen, wonach Zahlung in jeder Form, die am Zahlungsort üblich ist, vorgenommen werden kann. Allerdings kann eine der PICC entsprechende Lösung auch unter Geltung des CISG gefunden werden. Nach dieser Interpretation kann die Zurückweisung eines Schecks durch den Verkäufer in besonderen Umständen einen Vertragsbruch darstellen, da der Verkäufer seine **Mitwirkungspflicht** verletzt, wenn der Scheck am Zahlungsort zahlbar ist und dem Verkäufer keinerlei Kosten oder sonstige Unannehmlichkeiten aufbürdet.[54] In jedem Fall wird der Käufer von seiner Zahlungspflicht nur dann befreit, wenn der Scheck oder eine andere Anweisung auch **eingelöst** wird.[55] Vereinbaren die Parteien nach Vertragsschluss, dass der Käufer dem Verkäufer einen gezogenen Wechsel anstelle von Bargeld im Fälligkeitszeitpunkt geben kann, so stellt diese Vereinbarung eine **Vertragsänderung** im Sinne von Art. 29 mit dem Inhalt dar, dass der Verkäufer den vertraglichen Fälligkeitszeitpunkt bis zur Fälligkeit des gezogenen Wechsels aufschiebt und keine Zinspflicht für die Zwischenzeit entsteht (Stundung).[56]

---

[48] OLG München, 9.7.1997, CISG-online 282.
[49] *Hager/Maultzsch*, 5. Aufl., Art. 57 Rn. 9; MünchKomm/*P. Huber*, Art. 53, Rn. 13; vgl. *Honsell/Schnyder/Straub*, Art. 54, Rn. 13; *Witz/Salger/Lorenz/Witz*, Art. 53, Rn. 8; *Kröll u.a./P. Butler/Harindranath*, Art. 53, Rn. 10.
[50] *Van Houtte*, International Trade, Rn. 9.27.
[51] Die Genfer Konventionen von 1930 hatten folgende Regelungsgegenstände: 1. Einheitsrecht für Wechsel und Eigenwechsel, 2. Internationales Privatrecht und 3. Stempelrecht.
[52] Im Zeitpunkt der Niederschrift waren nur fünf Staaten der Konvention beigetreten, vgl. www.uncitral.org.
[53] *Staudinger/Magnus*, Art. 53, Rn. 8; *Brunner*, Art. 54, Rn. 3; MünchKomm/*P. Huber*, Art. 53, Rn. 13; *Kröll u.a./P. Butler/Harindranath*, Art. 53, Rn. 10.
[54] *Witz/Salger/Lorenz/Witz*, Art. 53, Rn. 8.
[55] Vgl. Art. 6.1.7 PICC; § 2–511 (3) UCC.
[56] LG Hamburg, 26.9.1990, CISG-online 21 = RIW 1990, 1015, 1018; *Staudinger/Magnus*, Art. 53, Rn. 8; MünchKomm/*P. Huber*, Art. 53, Rn. 13; *Witz/Salger/Lorenz/Witz*, Art. 53, Rn. 8.

15 **c) Dokumentarinkasso.** Bei einem Dokumentarinkasso zieht eine Bank, üblicherweise eine Bank im Staat des Käufers, als Mittelsperson zwischen dem Verkäufer und dem Käufer den Kaufpreis beim Käufer ein, entweder in bar oder durch Akzeptierung eines gezogenen Wechsels (Tratte).[57] Die Bank muss dazu dem Käufer im Auftrag des Verkäufers sämtliche (vereinbarten) Dokumente vorlegen, die regelmässig die Versendung der gekauften Ware belegen.

16 Ein solches Dokumentarinkasso wird in internationalen Warenkaufverträgen häufig durch die Verwendung einer **Standardzahlungsklausel,** wie **D/A** oder **D/P,** vereinbart. Der Inhalt solcher Standardzahlungsklauseln ergibt sich aus internationalem Handelsbrauch, den die Parteien stillschweigend zum Inhalt ihres Kaufvertrags gemäss Art. 9 II gemacht haben. Bezüglich der Standardklauseln D/A und D/P hat die IHK **einheitliche Richtlinien für Inkassi (ERI 522)** veröffentlicht. Obwohl diese Richtlinien vor allem auf die Rechtsbeziehungen zwischen den Banken auf Seiten des Verkäufers und auf Seiten des Käufers ausgerichtet sind, kann Art. 7 ERI 522 benutzt werden, um den Inhalt der Standardklauseln D/A und D/P bei Verwendung in einem internationalen Warenkauf gemäss Art. 9 II kraft seiner Eigenschaft als internationaler Handelsbrauch zu definieren. **D/P** bedeutet „**Dokumente gegen Zahlung**" und führt dazu, dass der Käufer eine Barzahlung gegen Vorlage der Dokumente, wie z. B. Rechnungen, Transportdokumente oder Traditionspapiere, vorzunehmen hat. **D/A** bedeutet „**Dokumente gegen Akzept**" und führt dazu, dass der Käufer eine Tratte (gezogenen Wechsel) gegen Vorlage von Dokumenten akzeptiert.[58] **CAD** bedeutet „**Cash Against Documents**" und hat dieselbe Bedeutung wie D/P.[59] Im Hinblick auf die anwendbare Währung[60] setzen Artt. 17 und 18 ERI 522 voraus, dass die vorlegende Bank die Dokumente nur gegen Zahlung in der Währung des Zahlungslandes oder in einer anderen Währung freigibt, wenn die gewählte Währung in Übereinstimmung mit den Instruktionen im Dokumenteninkasso sofort verfügbar ist. Die ERI wollen auf diese Weise gewährleisten, dass die Zahlung in der Währung der Vertragsdokumente auch in Übereinstimmung mit den anwendbaren Landesgesetzen durchgeführt werden kann, da diese möglicherweise Wechselbeschränkungen kennen.

17 **d) Dokumentenakkreditive.** Die beste Möglichkeit, die Zahlung des Kaufpreises sicherzustellen, bietet das Dokumentenakkreditiv. Bei einem Dokumentenakkreditiv handelt es sich üblicherweise um eine unwiderrufliche Verpflichtung einer Bank, dem Verkäufer den Kaufpreis gegen Vorlage von Dokumenten auszuzahlen, die den erfolgten Versand der Ware beweisen. Beim Dokumentenakkreditiv werden vier Haupttypen nach ihrer Zahlungsmodalität unterschieden. Ein Dokumentenakkreditiv muss gemäss Art. 6 ERA 600 angeben, ob es durch Sichtbezahlung, hinausgeschobene Zahlung, Akzeptleistung oder Negoziierung benutzbar ist. Bei einem **Sichtakkreditiv** erhält der Verkäufer die Zahlung Zug-um-Zug gegen die Vorlage von Dokumenten. Beim **Akzeptakkreditiv** erhält der Verkäufer statt Zahlung ein Wechselakzept, das die eröffnende Bank, die bestätigende Bank oder eine Drittbank verpflichtet, bei Fälligkeit des Wechsels zu zahlen. Beim **Akkreditiv mit aufgeschobener Zahlung** verpflichtet sich eine Bank zur Zahlung am Fälligkeitstag, ohne dass ein Wechselakzept begeben wird. **Negoziierungsakkreditive** sehen eine Negoziierung der Tratten oder Dokumente durch irgendeine Bank oder eine ausdrücklich nominierte Bank vor, die dem Begünstigten (Verkäufer) den Kaufpreis unter Abzug eines Diskonts auszahlt, möglicherweise bevor sie einen Rückzahlungsanspruch gegen die eröffnende Bank hat.

18 Die Zahlung durch Dokumentenakkreditiv findet üblicherweise Eingang in einen internationalen Warenkaufvertrag durch Benutzung einer **Standardzahlungsklausel „L/C"**

---

[57] Vgl. *van Houtte,* International Trade, Rn. 9.3.3.
[58] Zu gezogenen Wechseln vgl. oben Rn. 13–14.
[59] BGH, 25.10.1984, NJW 1985, 555; OLG Dresden, 9.7.1998, CISG-online 559 = IHR 2001, 18; *Staudinger/Magnus,* Art. 53, Rn. 17; MünchKomm/*P. Huber,* Art. 53, Rn. 15.
[60] Zur Währung im Allgemeinen s. oben Rn. 4 ff.

oder **„Letter of Credit"** oder (in deutschsprachigen Verträgen) **„per Akkreditiv".** Solche Zahlungsklauseln finden sich häufig im internationalen Handel, weil sie einen der sichersten Wege zur Durchführung einer internationalen Zahlung darstellen. Die von der IHK veröffentlichten **ERA 600** können zur Interpretation einer Akkreditivklausel in einem CISG-Vertrag herangezogen werden, sofern sie durch ausdrückliche Verweisung oder stillschweigend als internationaler Handelsbrauch einbezogen wurden.[61] Abgesehen von dieser Unterstützungsfunktion bei Interpretationsfragen werden die ERA 600 üblicherweise durch ausdrücklichen Verweis auf dem Akkreditivdokument einbezogen. Die **Pflicht des Käufers zur Stellung eines bestätigten Dokumentenakkreditivs** ist nur dann erfüllt, wenn und sobald dem Verkäufer ein **eigenständiger Anspruch gegen die eröffnende Bank** zusteht.[62] Allerdings bedeutet diese Erfüllung nicht sogleich die Erfüllung der Verpflichtung zur Zahlung des Kaufpreises.[63] Im Gegenteil: Sollte die eröffnende Bank es versäumen, dem Verkäufer oder seiner Bank den fälligen Geldanspruch zu überweisen, so hat der Verkäufer nach wie vor seinen Anspruch auf Kaufpreiszahlung gegen den Käufer, den er gemäss Art. 62 als Kaufpreisklage geltend machen kann (freilich unter den Voraussetzungen von Art. 28).[64] Dies gilt selbst dann, wenn das Bankkonto des Käufers von der eröffnenden Bank belastet wurde. Da es sich bei der eröffnenden Bank um „seine Bank" handelt, muss der Käufer die Gefahr tragen, zweimal zu zahlen.[65]

4. Zahlungsort

Art. 57 regelt Einzelheiten des Zahlungsorts.[66]

5. Zahlungszeit

Art. 58 regelt Einzelheiten der Fälligkeit.[67]

6. Fälligkeitszinsen

Die Fälligkeit des Kaufpreisanspruchs bestimmt sich nach Art. 58. Wenn der Käufer bei Fälligkeit nicht zahlt, hat der Verkäufer für diesen Betrag **Anspruch auf Zinsen, Art. 78**, oder möglicherweise einen Anspruch auf Ersatz seines Zinsschadens.[68] Die Parteien können einvernehmlich die Fälligkeit aufschieben, zum Beispiel durch Annahme eines gezogenen Wechsels anstelle einer Barzahlung.[69]

7. Zahlungskosten

Die Parteien können sich gemäss Art. 6 ausdrücklich oder stillschweigend über die **Verteilung der Zahlungskosten** einigen. Haben sie nichts Gegenteiliges vereinbart, so findet **Art. 57** auf die Verteilung der Zahlungskosten Anwendung, weil den Zahlungsort bestimmt und damit zugleich regelt, dass der Käufer sicherstellen muss, dass das Geld in Höhe

---

[61] *Schwenzer*, 36 Vict. U. Well. L. Rev. (2005), 795, 804.
[62] OGH, 6.2.1996, CISG-online 224.
[63] CIETAC, 28.1.1999, CISG-online 1206.
[64] Vgl. Cámara Nacional de Apelaciones en lo Comercial de Buenos Aires, 7.10.2010, CISG-online 2156 = UNILEX; CIETAC, 28.1.1999, CISG-online 1206, mit Bezug auf eine eröffnende Bank kurz vor ihrer Insolvenz.
[65] CIETAC, 28.1.1999, CISG-online 1206.
[66] S. unten Art. 57 Rn. 1 ff.
[67] S. unten Art. 58 Rn. 1 ff.
[68] Zu Zinsen vgl. unten *Bacher*, Art. 78 Rn. 8; OLG Koblenz, 19.10.2006, CISG-online 1407 = CLOUT Nr. 723; KG Nidwalden, 23.5.2005, CISG-online 1086. A. A. LG Flensburg, 24.3.1999, CISG-online 719 = IHR 2001, 202, 203, das fälschlicherweise deutsches internes Recht auf diese Frage anwandte. Zum Schadenersatz vgl. unten *Bacher*, Art. 78 Rn. 44; *Schwenzer*, Art. 74 Rn. 25 f.
[69] LG Hamburg, 26.9.1990, CISG-online 21 = RIW 1990, 1015, 1018; *Bacher*, Art. 78, Rn. 8; *Staudinger/Magnus*, Art. 53, Rn. 8, der richtigerweise herausstellt, dass ein Sichtakkreditiv keine vertragliche Stundung beinhaltet.

des Kaufpreises an diesem Ort ankommt und dem Verkäufer zur Verfügung steht. Da der Käufer im Zweifelsfall den Kaufpreis am Ort der Niederlassung des Verkäufers zu zahlen hat (Art. 57 I lit. a)),[70] trägt der **Käufer grundsätzlich** auch die **Zahlungskosten**. Diese Kosten beinhalten sämtliche für die Benutzung des vertraglichen Zahlungsmittels an die Banken zu zahlenden **Kommissionen** oder **Gebühren**. Das heisst der Käufer trägt sämtliche aus der Übermittlung des Bargeldes[71] oder jeder anderen notwendigen Transaktion entstehenden Kosten, um das Geld in Höhe des Kaufpreises an den Zahlungsort zu bringen.[72] Zum Beispiel muss der Käufer die Kosten für die Übersendung eines Checks[73] tragen, sowie die Kosten, die dem Verkäufer dadurch entstanden sind, dass er versucht hat, einen ungedeckten Check einzulösen.[74] Im Falle eines Dokumentarinkassos trägt der Verkäufer die Kosten des Inkassos. Im Falle eines Dokumentenakkreditivs trägt der Käufer die Kosten für die Stellung des Akkreditivs. Sollten die Parteien sich nicht ausdrücklich über die Zahlungskosten geeinigt haben, so wird sich die Verteilung der Kosten oft aus den Anweisungen an die jeweiligen Banken ergeben, die selbstverständlich nicht die Vereinbarung zwischen dem Verkäufer und dem Käufer inhaltlich abändern können, aber jedenfalls doch gemäss Art. 8 I und III als Beweismittel für die Feststellung des Willens der anweisenden Partei herangezogen werden können. Für den Fall, dass der Verkäufer seine Niederlassung zwischen dem Zeitpunkt des Vertragsschlusses und dem Zeitpunkt der Zahlung wechselt, muss der Verkäufer gemäss Art. 57 II jede daraus folgende Erhöhung der Kosten tragen.[75]

8. Teilzahlungen

23   Wenn die Parteien nichts anderes vereinbart haben, muss der Käufer den Kaufpreis **auf ein Mal** und **im Ganzen** zahlen.[76] Zahlt der Käufer den Kaufpreis nicht im Ganzen, sondern nur zum Teil, so stellt seine teilweise Erfüllung einen Vertragsbruch dar.[77] In der Literatur ist die Ansicht herrschend, dass ein solcher Vertragsbruch dem Verkäufer das **Recht zur Zurückweisung der Teilzahlung** gibt.[78] Dieser herrschenden Auffassung ist nicht zu folgen. Zum einen wurde an der Wiener Konferenz ein Vorschlag zur Aufnahme einer besonderen Bestimmung zum Recht des Verkäufers, Teilzahlungen zurückzuweisen, abgelehnt.[79] Zum anderen widerspricht ein solches Zurückweisungsrecht dem Rechtsbehelfssystem der Art. 61 ff.[80] Ein Zurückweisungsrecht von Teilzahlungen ist nämlich nur dann verfügbar, wenn die **Teilzahlung** einen **wesentlichen Vertragsbruch** im Sinne des Art. 25 darstellt. Ein wesentlicher Vertragsbruch wird aber nur in ganz besonderen Fällen gegeben sein, z. B. wenn der Käufer Teilzahlungen vornimmt, die dem Verkäufer unzumutbare Unannehmlichkeiten bereiten. Solange aber kein wesentlicher Vertragsbruch gegeben ist, hat der Verkäufer eine Teilzahlung anzunehmen. Etwaige Zusatzkosten, die durch die Teilzahlung entstehen, kann der Verkäufer als Schadenersatz nach Art. 74 erstattet verlangen. Darüber hinaus kann der Verkäufer berechtigt sein, seine eigene Leistung, also die Lieferung der Ware oder der Dokumente, solange zurückzuhalten, bis er vom Käufer vollständig bezahlt wurde. Wenn der Käufer den Kaufpreis nicht bis zum Fälligkeitszeitpunkt vollständig

---

[70] Vgl. unten Art. 57 Rn. 1.
[71] OLG München, 9.7.1997, CISG-online 282.
[72] OLG München, 9.7.1997, CISG-online 282; *Hager/Maultzsch*, 5. Aufl., Art. 57 Rn. 9.
[73] LG Duisburg, 17.4.1996, CISG-online 186 = RIW 1996, 774.
[74] OLG München, 9.7.1997, CISG-online 282.
[75] Vgl. unten Art. 57 Rn. 17–19, 33.
[76] Vgl. *Staudinger/Magnus*, Art. 53, Rn. 7; MünchKomm/*P. Huber*, Art. 53, Rn. 12; *Kröll u. a./P. Butler/Harindranath*, Art. 53, Rn. 10.
[77] Vgl. *Honsell/Schnyder/Straub*, Art. 54, Rn. 18.
[78] *Hager/Maultzsch*, 5. Aufl., Art. 59 Rn. 3; *Bianca/Bonell/Maskow*, Art. 59, Anm. 2.3.; *Ferrari u. a./Mankowski*, Internationales Vertragsrecht, Art. 54, Rn. 32; *Herber/Czerwenka*, Art. 58, Rn. 11; MünchKommBGB/*P. Huber*, Art. 58, Rn. 29; *Staudinger/Magnus*, Art. 58, Rn. 32; *Witz/Salger/Lorenz/Witz*, Artt. 58–59, Rn. 16.
[79] O. R., S. 370, Nr. 51–64. So auch *Honsell/Schnyder/Straub*, Art. 54, Rn. 18.
[80] So auch *Honsell/Schnyder/Straub*, Art. 54, Rn. 19; Art. 61, Rn. 52 f.

gezahlt hat, ist der Verkäufer berechtigt, die Rechtsbehelfe nach Artt. 61 ff. auszuüben. Vor allem ist der Verkäufer berechtigt, dem Käufer gemäss Art. 63 eine angemessene Nachfrist zur Erfüllung seiner Zahlungsverpflichtung zu setzen, nach deren fruchtlosen Ablauf er gemäss Art. 64 I lit. b) berechtigt ist, den Vertrag aufzuheben.

9. Anrechnung von Zahlungen

Wenn der Käufer mehr als eine zahlbare Schuld beim Verkäufer offenstehen hat, wird er 24 üblicherweise im Zeitpunkt der Zahlung festlegen, auf welche Schuld die Zahlung angerechnet werden soll. Eine solche **Tilgungsbestimmung** ist vom Regelungsbereich des CISG erfasst und muss nach Art. 8 und 9 ausgelegt werden, soweit die verschiedenen Schulden aus dem gleichen CISG-Vertrag stammen. Hingegen ist das CISG auf die Frage der Anrechnung von Zahlungen nicht anwendbar, wenn der Käufer keine Tilgungsbestimmung getroffen hat oder wenn die Schulden aus verschiedenen Verträgen stammen. Für diese Fragen ist vielmehr auf das **subsidiär anwendbare nationale Recht** zu rekurrieren.[81] Die Anrechnung von Zahlungen wird in der Praxis besonders relevant im Zusammenhang mit dem Zinslauf und dem Verjährungslauf, insbesondere wenn der Käufer den in Rechnung gestellten Betrag nicht zahlt und die bereits offenen Schulden unterschiedliche Fälligkeitszeitpunkte haben.

10. Kaufpreisklage

Unter Geltung des CISG kann der Verkäufer vom Käufer selbst dann die Kaufpreiszah- 25 lung verlangen, wenn die Ware noch nicht geliefert wurde.[82] Freilich ist gemäss Art. 28 ein staatliches Gericht oder ein Schiedsgericht nicht verpflichtet, ein Urteil oder einen Schiedsspruch auf **Leistung in Natur** *(specific performance)* auszusprechen, solange das staatliche Gericht oder das Schiedsgericht dies nicht in Anwendung seines eigenen Rechts auch für vergleichbare Kaufverträge, die nicht dem Übereinkommen unterstehen, aussprechen würde.[83] Obwohl gemäss herrschender Auffassung nicht direkt auf den Kaufpreisanspruch anwendbar, kann die Obliegenheit zur **Schadensminderung** nach Art. 77 dazu führen, dass ein Kaufpreisanspruch in besonderen Umständen nicht gegeben ist, wenn es nämlich für den Käufer unzumutbar wäre, an den Vertrag gebunden zu bleiben.[84]

11. Devisenkontrolle

Gesetze und sonstige Vorschriften zur Devisenkontrolle können verschiedene Auswirkun- 26 gen auf die Zahlungsverpflichtungen aus einem CISG-Vertrag haben. Zunächst können solche Gesetze und Vorschriften die **Unwirksamkeit** des Kaufvertrags in seiner Gesamtheit anordnen. Gemäss **Art. 4 lit. a)** müssen internationale bzw. nationale Gesetze und Vorschriften, denen zufolge der Kaufvertrag unwirksam ist, berücksichtigt werden.[85] Statt die Unwirksamkeit des ganzen Vertrags anzuordnen, können Gesetze und Vorschriften zur Devisenkontrolle den Verkäufer auch daran hindern, den Kaufpreis vom Käufer zu verlangen bzw. den Kaufpreisanspruch gegenüber dem Käufer durchzusetzen.

12. Verjährungsfristen

Das CISG enthält keine Vorschriften über die Verjährung von Ansprüchen aus CISG- 27 Verträgen. Soweit die Parteien ihre Niederlassungen in verschiedenen Vertragsstaaten der **Verjährungskonvention vom 14. Juni 1994** haben oder die anwendbaren Kollisions-

---

[81] Gerechtshof 's-Hertogenbosch, 2.1.2007, CISG-online 1434 = CLOUT Nr. 828. Vgl. Art. 6.1.12 PICC.
[82] Vgl. unten Art. 62 Rn. 1 ff.
[83] Vgl. oben *Müller-Chen*, Art. 28 Rn. 1 ff., 8–9.
[84] Vgl. unten Art. 62 Rn. 16; *Schwenzer*, Art. 77 Rn. 4, 5; *Schwenzer/Manner*, FS Kritzer, S. 470, 483 ff.
[85] *Staudinger/Magnus*, Art. 53, Rn. 31; *Herber/Czerwenka*, Art. 53, Rn. 8; *Honsell/Schnyder/Straub*, Art. 54, Rn. 29; *Piltz*, Internationales Kaufrecht, Rn. 4–128; *Witz/Salger/Lorenz/Witz*, Art. 53, Rn. 7.

normen zur Anwendung des Rechts eines Vertragsstaats dieser Konvention führen, sieht Art. 8 der Verjährungskonvention eine Verjährungsfrist von 4 Jahren vor.[86] In allen anderen Fällen bestimmt das anwendbare **Internationale Privatrecht** das in der Sache anwendbare nationale Verjährungsrecht. Da die Verjährungskonvention nur von 20 Staaten ratifiziert wurde, wird oft der kollisionsrechtliche Weg zur Bestimmung der anwendbaren Verjährungsfrist unumgänglich sein, falls nicht ein staatliches Gericht, wahrscheinlicher aber ein Schiedsgericht, die **PICC** zur Anwendung bringt, um zu einer in der Sache angemessenen Lösung zu gelangen.[87]

13. Tauschhandel

28   Nach den Vorstellungen des CISG sieht ein Kaufvertrag den **Austausch von Ware gegen Geld** vor. Aus ganz unterschiedlichen Gründen, z. B. Knappheit starker Devisen, Knappheit an Krediten oder wegen ausländischer Devisenkontrollen, besteht der internationale Handel, insbesondere der Handel mit Entwicklungsländern, nicht immer aus einem Austausch von Ware gegen Geld, sondern kann auch die Form eines **Tauschs verschiedener Waren** annehmen.[88] In einem **Gegenkauf** *(counterpurchase)* verkauft ein Exporteur Ware an einen Importeur und schliesst gleichzeitig einen anderen Vertrag ab, in dem er sich verpflichtet, vom Importeur andere Waren zu kaufen.[89] In einem **Produktabnahmevertrag** *(buy-back transaction)* verpflichtet sich der ursprüngliche Käufer, seine Produkte, die er mit den Maschinen oder anderen unter dem ersten Vertrag gelieferten Waren hergestellt hat, an den ursprünglichen Verkäufer zu liefern.[90] In einem **Barter-Geschäft** werden Waren gegen andere Waren in einem einheitlichen Vertrag ausgetauscht, wobei der wirtschaftliche Wert der ausgetauschten Waren festgelegt oder nicht festgelegt werden kann.[91] Daneben existieren weitere Formen des Tauschhandels, z. B. der Off-set Vertrag,[92] der allerdings für das CISG nicht relevant wird. Während der **Gegenkauf** und der **Produktabnahmevertrag** als zwei selbstständige Kaufverträge verstanden werden können,[93] die bei Vorliegen der sonstigen Anwendungsvoraussetzungen dem CISG unterstehen, ist die **Anwendung des CISG auf Barter-Geschäfte** höchst umstritten.[94] Der Hauptgrund dafür ist, dass Barter-Geschäfte üblicherweise nicht in Form von zwei eigenständigen Kaufverträgen, sondern als ein einziger Tauschvertrag strukturiert werden. Nichtsdestotrotz können nach der hier vertretenen Auffassung die wirtschaftlichen Barter-Geschäfte rechtlich als zwei unabhängige Kaufverträge aufgefasst werden, die durch Parteivereinbarung dergestalt miteinander verbunden sind, dass ihre jeweiligen Zahlungsverpflichtungen, so wie sie durch den wirtschaftlichen Wert der ausgetauschten Waren bestimmt sind, miteinander aufgerechnet werden. Selbst wenn nationales Recht über das anwendbare Kollisionsrecht auf Barter-Geschäfte anzuwenden wäre, würde im Ergebnis zumeist Kaufrecht anwendbar sein, weil viele nationale Rechtsordnungen für Tauschverträge wiederum auf das Kaufrecht verweisen.[95]

---

[86] Siehe unten den Volltext der Verjährungskonvention und die dazugehörige Kommentierung von *Müller-Chen*.
[87] Vgl. *Schwenzer/Manner*, 23 Arb. Int'l (2007), 293 ff.; *Hayward*, 26 J. Int'l Arb. (2009), 405 ff.
[88] Vgl. UNCITRAL Legal Guide on International Countertrade Transactions von 1992.
[89] *Van Houtte*, International Trade, para. 9.40; UNCITRAL Legal Guide on International Countertrade Transactions, Kapitel I, Rn. 15.
[90] *Van Houtte*, International Trade, Rn. 9.41; UNCITRAL Legal Guide on International Countertrade Transactions, Kapitel I, Rn. 16.
[91] Barter-Geschäfte ohne Festlegung des wirtschaftlichen Werts der ausgetauschten Waren sind heutzutage nur noch selten im internationalen Handel anzutreffen. Vgl. *Van Houtte*, International Trade, Rn. 9.39.
[92] UNCITRAL Legal Guide on International Countertrade Transactions, Kapitel I, Rn. 17.
[93] *Staudinger/Magnus*, Art. 1, Rn. 30; *Ferrari*, 15 J. L. & Com. (1995), 1, 53; *Piltz*, Internationales Kaufrecht, Rn. 2–24.
[94] Vgl. *Schlechtriem/Schwenzer/Schwenzer/Hachem*, CISG Commentary, Art. 1, Rn. 11, die für die Anwendbarkeit des CISG auf Barter-Geschäfte eintreten.
[95] Belgien: Art. 1707 Cc; Dänemark: Art. 2 II Kaufrechtsgesetz; Deutschland: § 480 BGB; Estland: Art. 254 OR; Finnland: Art. 1 II Kaufrechtsgesetz; Frankreich: Art. 1707 Cc; Griechenland: Art. 573 Cc; Italien: Art. 1555 Cc; Lettland: Art. 2092 Cc; Litauen: Art. 6:432 Cc; Niederlande: Art. 7:50 Cc; Norwegen: Art. 1 II

Ein solcher Verweis auf das Kaufrecht müsste sogar als Verweis auf das CISG verstanden werden, wenn sich ein solcher Verweis im nationalen Recht eines Vertragsstaats des Übereinkommens findet, weil der materiell-rechtliche Zweig von Art. 6 ins Einheitskaufrecht führt. Um solche Zirkelschlussanwendungen und die Anwendung von nationalem Kaufrecht auf internationale Barter-Geschäfte überhaupt zu vermeiden, sollte das CISG einheitlich und eigenständig auf Barter-Geschäfte angewendet werden. Wenn also das CISG auf diese Formen des Tauschhandels angewendet werden kann, stellt sich die Frage, ob Artt. 53 ff., die die Verpflichtung des Käufers zur Zahlung des Kaufpreises betreffen, auf Tauschverträge angewendet werden können. Solange der wirtschaftliche Wert der ausgetauschten Waren vereinbart wurde oder nach Art. 55 bestimmt werden kann, können die Vorschriften des CISG über die Kaufpreiszahlungspflicht des Käufers auf Barter-Geschäfte angewendet werden. Als weiteres Problem taucht die Frage auf, welches Recht auf die Aufrechnung Anwendung findet, wenn die zwei Zahlungsverpflichtungen aus unterschiedlichen Verträgen, die aber beide dem CISG unterstehen, resultieren. Während die Möglichkeit der Aufrechnung nach CISG bestimmt werden kann, entscheidet nationales Recht über die Ausübung und Wirkung der Aufrechnung.[96]

14. Abtretung und Abtretbarkeit

Die Abtretung von Kaufpreisforderungen ist wichtig zur Finanzierung des internationalen Warenhandels. Das CISG selbst behandelt die Frage der Abtretung von Kaufpreisforderungen nicht.[97] Dennoch ist die Frage der **Abtretbarkeit** von Kaufpreisforderungen teilweise vom CISG mitgeregelt. **Gesetzliche Beschränkungen** der Abtretbarkeit von Kaufpreisforderungen werden vom CISG nach Art. 4 lit. a) als Gültigkeitsfrage beachtet. **Vertragliche Beschränkungen** der Abtretbarkeit von Kaufpreisforderungen, sogenannte *pacta de non cedendo*, unterstehen dem CISG. Folglich findet das CISG auf die Frage Anwendung, ob die Parteien eine vertragliche Beschränkung der Abtretbarkeit der Kaufpreisforderung in ihren CISG-Vertrag aufgenommen haben. Ausserdem findet das CISG Anwendung auf die Interpretation der Bedeutung einer solchen Klausel, welche die Abtretbarkeit der Kaufpreisforderung beschränkt. Hingegen findet nationales Recht auf die Frage Anwendung, ob eine solche vertragliche Beschränkung der Abtretbarkeit der Kaufpreisforderung gültig ist.[98] In Frankreich wirken vertragliche Abtretungsbeschränkungen zum Beispiel nur zwischen den unmittelbaren Vertragsparteien *(inter partes)*, hingegen nicht gegenüber Drittparteien.[99]

15. Zahlungen durch Dritte

Das CISG behandelt unmittelbar nur Zweiparteiensituationen, in denen der Verkäufer seine Ware gegen Zahlung durch den Käufer liefert. In der Praxis wird die Zahlung freilich nicht in allen Fällen durch den Käufer selbst ausgeführt werden, sondern kann auch durch eine Drittpartei, z. B. eine mit dem Käufer in derselben Konzerngruppe verbundene Partei,

---

Kaufrechtsgesetz; Österreich: § 1045 ABGB; Polen: Art. 604 Cc; Schweden: Art. 1 II Kaufrechtsgesetz; Schweiz: Art. 273 OR; Slowenien: Art. 529 OR; Slowakei: Art. 611 Cc; Spanien: Artt. 1446, 1541 Cc; Tschechische Republik: Art. 611 Cc; Ungarn: Art. 378 Cc. Vgl. *Hondius/Heutger/Jeloschek/Sivesand/Wiewiorowska*, S. 126 ff.

[96] Vgl. unten Art. 61 Rn. 19. Schweiz: Verrechnung.
[97] Vgl. oben *Ferrari*, Art. 4 Rn. 38; LG Bielefeld, 9.11.2010, CISG-online 2204/2293 = BeckRS 2011, 08294, E. 2. b): das auf die Abtretung anwendbare Recht bestimmt sich nach dem IPR der lex fori.
[98] Für Deutschland vgl. § 354a HGB.
[99] Cass. Com., 21.11.2000, D. 2001, 123, m. Anm. *Avena-Robardet; Rosch*, RIW 2001, 604, 608 ff. Noch weitergehend Art. 6 I UNIDROIT Übereinkommen über Internationales Factoring vom 28.5.1988 sowie US-amerikanisches Recht und der Entwurf eines UNCITRAL Übereinkommens über Forderungsabtretungen zu Finanzierungszwecken, denen zufolge Abtretungen grundsätzlich voll wirksam sind und nicht einmal *inter partes* wirken, vgl. § 9–318 (4) UCC (revidiert § 9–406 (d) (1) UCC Entwurf vom 30.7.1998); Art. 11 I Entwurf des Übereinkommens über Forderungsabtretung zu Finanzierungszwecken, UN doc a/cn.9/489, S. 29 ff. Dazu umfassend *Müller-Chen*, FS Schlechtriem, S. 903 ff.

vorgenommen werden.[100] Selbstverständlich können die Parteien eines Kaufvertrages eine **besondere Klausel** in ihren Vertrag aufnehmen, der zufolge **Drittzahlungen** zulässig sind.[101] Wenn der Vertrag aber eine solche Klausel nicht vorsieht, lässt das CISG Drittzahlungen nur dann zu, wenn die Zahlung gemäss Vertrag vorgenommen wird, also vollständig, zur richtigen Zeit und am richtigen Ort.[102] Wenn der vertragliche Zahlungsmechanismus den Verkäufer zur Teilnahme am Zahlungsprozess verpflichtet, z. B. durch Zustellung eines Entwurfs des zu benutzenden Dokumentenakkreditivs an den Käufer, kann der Verkäufer nicht auf Grundlage des CISG verpflichtet werden, eine solches Arrangement mit einer Drittpartei durchzuführen, da kein vertragliches Verhältnis zwischen dem Verkäufer und der Drittpartei besteht.

16. Die Verpflichtung des Käufers zur Stellung von Sicherheiten

31   Solange die Parteien eines internationalen Warenkaufvertrags noch keine etablierte Geschäftsbeziehung miteinander haben, wird der Verkäufer den Käufer oft zur Stellung von Sicherheiten für den Fall der Nichtzahlung des Kaufpreises anhalten. Abgesehen von der Sicherung, die durch die Stellung eines Dokumentenakkreditivs gewährt wird,[103] kann der Käufer angehalten sein, weitere Sicherheiten zu stellen, z. B. eine Bankgarantie oder eine Bankengarantie in Form eines Akkreditivs *(standby letter of credit)*.

32   a) **Zahlungsgarantien.** Eine Zahlungsgarantie wird von einer Bank gegeben, indem diese sich verpflichtet, die Zahlungsverpflichtung des Käufers als ihre eigene, vom zugrunde liegenden Kausalgeschäft (Kaufvertrag) unabhängige, rechtliche Verpflichtung zu erfüllen. Das CISG findet nur auf Fragen Anwendung, die eine solche Bankgarantie für das Rechtsverhältnis zwischen dem Käufer und dem Verkäufer aufwirft. Das Rechtsverhältnis zwischen dem Verkäufer als Begünstigten und der Bank als Garantiegeber untersteht hingegen nicht dem CISG, sondern dem anwendbaren nationalem Recht bzw. anderem anwendbaren Einheitsrecht. Insofern sind die **einheitlichen Richtlinien der Internationalen Handelskammer für Garantien auf ersten Abruf** von grosser praktischer Bedeutung.[104]

33   b) **Bankgarantien in Akkreditivform** *(standby letter of credit)*. Eine Bankgarantie in Akkreditivform ist materiell ein der Bankgarantie ähnliches Instrument, das formell in Akkreditivform gestellt wird. Diese besonderen Bankgarantien stammen aus den Vereinigten Staaten, wo die Gesetzgebung US-Banken ursprünglich untersagte, Garantieverpflichtungen zugunsten von Drittparteien einzugehen. Obwohl die Internationale Handelskammer die **ISP98 (International Standby Practices)** eingeführt hat, werden die meisten Bankgarantien in Akkreditvform unter Geltung der **UCP600** gestellt.

III. Die Verpflichtung des Käufers zur Abnahme der Ware

34   Art. 60 beschreibt die Pflicht des Käufers zur Abnahme dahingehend, dass der Käufer alle Handlungen vorzunehmen hat, die vernünftigerweise von ihm erwartet werden können, damit dem Verkäufer die Lieferung ermöglicht wird, und dass er die Ware zu übernehmen hat.[105] Was damit im Einzelnen gemeint ist, hängt von den ausdrücklich oder stillschweigend

---

[100] Vgl. Hof van Beroep Gent, 31.1.2002, CISG-online 1349 = UNILEX: Tochtergesellschaft des Käufers zahlte an Schwestergesellschaft des Verkäufers.
[101] Vgl. CIETAC, 24.2.2005, CISG-online 1825 (zweiter Schweinefleisch-Fall).
[102] Int. Ct. Russian CCI, 22.1.1996, CISG-online 1830. A. A. Hof van Beroep Gent, 31.1.2002, CISG-online 1349 = UNILEX: Die Zahlung an eine Schwestergesellschaft der Verkäuferin befreite den Käufer nach belgischem Recht von seiner Verpflichtung zur Zahlung des Kaufpreises.
[103] Vgl. oben Rn. 17 f.
[104] ICC Uniform Rules for Demand Guarantees (URDG), ICC Publication No. 458.
[105] Vgl. unten Art. 60 Rn. 1 ff.

vereinbarten Vertragsbedingungen ab, die sich aus der Verwendung einer **Incoterms®** Klausel, dem späteren Verhalten der Vertragsparteien sowie dem derogativen Gesetzesrecht des CISG ergeben können.

1. Lieferung von Teilen der für die Herstellung oder Erzeugung der Ware notwendigen Stoffe

Gemäss Art. 3 I stehen Verträge über die Lieferung herzustellender oder zu erzeugender 35 Ware den Kaufverträgen gleich, es sei denn, dass der Besteller einen wesentlichen Teil der für die Herstellung oder Erzeugung notwendigen Stoffe selbst zur Verfügung zu stellen hat.[106] Mit anderen Worten findet das CISG auf Verträge Anwendung, in denen der Käufer es unternimmt, nicht wesentliche Teile der für die Herstellung oder Erzeugung notwendigen **Stoffe** zu liefern.[107] Die Verpflichtung des Käufers, nicht wesentliche Teile der für die Herstellung oder Erzeugung notwendigen Stoffe bereitzustellen, kann sich nur aus einer ausdrücklichen oder stillschweigenden Vereinbarung ergeben.

Je nach den Umständen des Einzelfalls kann der Käufer verpflichtet sein, den Verkäufer 36 mit **Plänen** oder **Know-How** zu beliefern; eine solche Verpflichtung kann wiederum nur durch Parteivereinbarung entstehen.[108]

2. Spezifizierung der Ware

Bei Vertragsschluss können die Parteien Einzelheiten der zu liefernden Ware zur späteren 37 Spezifizierung offen lassen. Solche Verträge mit Selbstspezifikationsrecht sind unter Geltung des CISG wirksame Kaufverträge, wenn die Vertragsparteien einen bestimmten Mechanismus zur Spezifizierung der Ware vorgesehen oder das Spezifikationsrecht einer der Vertragsparteien oder einer dritten Partei überlassen haben. Insbesondere in den Fällen, in denen der Käufer ein Abrufrecht bezüglich der zu liefernden Ware hat, wird es oft der Käufer sein, der zudem das Recht hat, die zu liefernde Ware nach seinen Bedürfnissen und Wünschen zu spezifizieren. In einer solchen Situation wird der Vertrag meist ausdrücklich oder stillschweigend einen Mechanismus vorsehen, wie der Käufer sein Spezifikationsrecht auszuüben hat. Art. 65 ist eine Spezialvorschrift für Verträge, in denen der Käufer die Form, die Masse oder andere Merkmale der Ware näher zu bestimmen hat und diese Spezifizierung gar nicht bzw. nicht termingerecht vornimmt.[109]

3. Incoterms 2010®

Im internationalen Handel beziehen die Parteien zumeist das Regelwerk Incoterms 38 2010®, das zurzeit in seiner Fassung von 2010 vorliegt,[110] durch Verwendung einer Handelsklausel in den Lieferbedingungen unter ausdrücklicher Bezugnahme auf die Incoterms® in ihren Vertrag ein. Selbst ohne ausdrücklichen Verweis auf die Incoterms®, können diese zur Auslegung der Lieferbedingungen als internationaler Handelsbrauch gemäss Art. 9 II, sofern ein solcher im betroffenen Geschäftszweig besteht,[111] oder zumindest als Auslegungs-

---

[106] Vgl. *Schlechtriem/Schwenzer/Schwenzer/Hachem*, CISG Commentary, Art. 3, Rn. 1 ff.
[107] Vgl. *Schlechtriem/Schwenzer/Schwenzer/Hachem*, CISG Commentary, Art. 3, Rn. 4 ff., insbesondere zur Bedeutung des Begriffs wesentlicher Teil.
[108] Vgl. *Schlechtriem/Schwenzer/Schwenzer/Hachem*, CISG Commentary, Art. 3, Rn. 8, denen zufolge Pläne, Design, Know-How, Lizenzen, usw. nicht unter Art. 3 I fallen.
[109] Vgl. unten Art. 65 Rn. 1 ff.
[110] Vgl. Appendix V für den Volltext der Incoterms 2010.
[111] CA Genova, 24.3.1995, CISG-online 315; *Elastar Sacifi a v. Bettcher Industries, Inc.*, Juzgado Nacional de Primera Instancia en lo Comercial No. 7, 20.5.1991, CISG-online 461; *St. Paul Guardian Insurance Co. and Travelers Insurance Co. v. Neuromed Medical Systems & Support GmbH*, U. S. Dist. Ct. (S. D. N. Y.), 26.3.2002, CISG-online 615 = 2002 U. S. Dist. LEXIS 5096 = IHR 2005, 256; *BP International Ltd. v. Empresa Estatal Petroleos de Ecuador et al*, U. S. Ct. App. (5th Cir.), 11.6.2003, CISG-online 730 = 332 F. 3d 333 = 2003 U. S. App. LEXIS 12013; vgl. *Schwenzer*, 36 Vict. U. Well. L. Rev. (2005), 795, 803.

material gemäss Art. 8 III herangezogen werden.[112] Sämtliche Incoterms® enthalten die **Käuferpflichten** in ihren **Regeln B1 bis B10**. Abhängig von der gewählten Handelsklausel kann der Käufer verpflichtet sein, **Lizenzen, behördliche Genehmigungen,** oder **Zollformalitäten** für die Einfuhr der Waren beizubringen. Darüber hinaus kann der Käufer verpflichtet sein, den **Transportvertrag** oder die **Transportversicherung** abzuschliessen. Zusätzlich verteilen die Incoterms® die Kosten zwischen Verkäufer und Käufer und verpflichten den Käufer, dem Verkäufer gewisse **Informationen mitzuteilen,** wie z. B. bei FOB den Namen des Schiffs, den Ladeplatz und die erforderliche Lieferzeit. Aus der Vereinbarung der Incoterms® ergeben sich auch **Kooperationspflichten** des Käufers, wie z. B. die Pflicht des Käufers, den vom Verkäufer erbrachten Liefernachweis sowie gegebenenfalls die Transportdokumente anzunehmen. An dieser Stelle können nicht alle den Käufer betreffenden Pflichten aus der Vereinbarung eines Incoterms® dargestellt werden.[113]

4. Kooperations- und Informationspflichten

39   Internationale Warenkaufverträge, insbesondere Sukzessivlieferungsverträge, sehen oft ein ausgeklügeltes System vor, wie die Parteien miteinander zu kommunizieren haben. Wenn ein Vertrag ein solches Kommunikationssystem nicht vorsieht und die Parteien auch noch nicht entsprechende Gepflogenheiten entwickelt haben, kann sich für den Käufer eine **generelle Kooperationspflicht** mit dem Verkäufer aus Art. 60 lit. a) i. V. m. Art. 7 I ergeben.[114] Diese allgemeine Kooperationspflicht beinhaltet auch eine **allgemeine Informationspflicht,** den Verkäufer auf sämtliche Umstände hinzuweisen, die für die Ausführung des Vertrages relevant sind.[115] Wenn gleich es im Allgemeinen leicht fällt, eine solche allgemeine Kooperationspflicht anzunehmen, so ist ihre Anwendung und Begrenzung im Einzelfall stark von den Besonderheiten des Einzelfalls abhängig und kann in der Praxis erhebliche Schwierigkeiten aufwerfen.[116]

IV. Andere Pflichten des Käufers

40   Je nach den besonderen Umständen im Einzelfall kann der Käufer neben den charakteristischen Pflichten zur Zahlung des Kaufpreises und zur Abnahme der Ware noch **weitere Verpflichtungen** zu erfüllen haben. Solche weiteren Pflichten können darin bestehen, dass der Käufer sich verpflichtet, nicht direkt von den Lieferanten des Verkäufers Ware zu beziehen,[117] die Ware nicht in gewisse Länder zu liefern[118] oder den Vertrag geheim zu halten. Solche Verpflichtungen können nur aufgrund ausdrücklicher oder stillschweigender Parteivereinbarung und unter Rückgriff auf Art. 8 oder 9 entstehen.

V. Die Rechtsbehelfe des Verkäufers für Vertragsbruch durch den Käufer

41   Das CISG sanktioniert sämtliche Pflichten des Käufers mit einem **einheitlichen System an Rechtsbehelfen,** die dem Verkäufer im Falle eines Vertragsbruchs durch den Käufer zur

---

[112] Vgl. oben *Schmidt-Kessel*, Art. 9 Rn. 26.
[113] Für Detailfragen zu den Incoterms® vgl. *Ramberg*, ICC Guide to Incoterms.
[114] Vgl. oben *Ferrari*, Art. 7 Rn. 54; *Staudinger/Magnus*, Art. 60, Rn. 9, der die Kooperationspflicht direkt auf Art. 60 lit. a) abstützt; *Honsell/Schnyder/Straub*, Art. 53, Rn. 14; vgl. *Witz/Salger/Lorenz/Witz*, Art. 53, Rn. 16. Vgl. Art. 5.1.3 PICC.
[115] Vgl. oben *Ferrari*, Art. 7 Rn. 54 m. w. N.; *Staudinger/Magnus*, Art. 7, Rn. 48; *Witz/Salger/Lorenz/Witz*, Art. 7, Rn. 15; *Honnold/Flechtner*, Art. 7, Rn. 100; *Mather*, 20 J. L. & Com. (2001), 155, 157; BGH, 31.10.2001, CISG-online 617 = BGHZ 149, 113, 118 = NJW 2002, 370.
[116] Vgl. unten Art. 60 Rn. 9.
[117] Vgl. KG Zug, 16.10.1997, CISG-online 335.
[118] Vgl. KG St. Gallen, 13.5.2008, CISG-online 1768.

Verfügung stehen. Der Verkäufer kann vom Käufer verlangen, dass der Käufer seine vertraglichen **Pflichten erfüllt** (Art. 61 I lit. a) i. V. m. Art. 62) oder **Schadenersatz** leistet (Art. 61 I lit. b) i. V. m. Art. 74 ff.). Wenn die Vertragsverletzung des Käufers einen **wesentlichen Vertragsbruch** darstellt, kann der Verkäufer den Kaufvertrag gemäss Art. 61 I lit. a) i. V. m. Art. 64 I lit. a) **aufheben**. Wenn der Käufer den Kaufpreis nicht zahlt oder die Ware nicht abnimmt, kann der Verkäufer ihm gemäss Art. 63 eine **angemessene Nachfrist zur Erfüllung** setzen, nach deren fruchtlosen Ablauf der Verkäufer den Vertrag selbst dann aufheben kann, wenn die Pflichtverletzung an sich keinen wesentlichen Vertragsbruch darstellt (Art. 61 I lit. a) i. V. m. Art. 64 I lit. b)). Hat der Käufer die Form, die Masse oder andere Merkmale der Ware nicht in Übereinstimmung mit dem Vertrag spezifiziert, so kann der Verkäufer gemäss Art. 61 I lit. a) i. V. m. Art. 65 die **Spezifizierung selbst vornehmen**. Das CISG unterstellt sämtliche Pflichten des Käufers diesem einheitlichen System an Rechtsbehelfen. Blosse **Obliegenheiten** des Käufers, wie z. B. Art. 38 und 39 sowie Art. 77, lösen diese Rechtsbehelfe hingegen nicht aus.[119] Von diesen blossen Obliegenheiten abgesehen unterscheidet das CISG nicht weitergehend zwischen den einzelnen Pflichten des Käufers, d. h. es ist grundsätzlich irrelevant, ob der Käufer seine Pflicht zur Zahlung des Kaufpreises, seine Pflicht zur Abnahme der Ware oder eine seiner sonstigen Pflichten verletzt hat.[120] Die teilweise in der Literatur geäusserte Ansicht, dass die verletzte Pflicht für die Frage von Bedeutung ist, ob ein wesentlicher Vertragsbruch vorliegt, ist abzulehnen.[121] Die Natur der Verpflichtung ist irrelevant im Zusammenhang mit der Feststellung der Bedeutung ihrer ordentlichen Erfüllung für den Verkäufer.[122] Nur für die Frage, ob Nachfristsetzung den Weg zur Vertragsaufhebung eröffnet, ist es relevant, ob die verletzte Pflicht des Käufers als Teil seiner Pflicht zur Zahlung des Kaufpreises oder zur Abnahme der Ware angesehen werden kann. Gemäss Art. 64 I lit. b) führt die erfolglose Nachfristsetzung nämlich nur dann zum Recht zur Vertragsaufhebung, wenn der Käufer seine Pflicht zur Zahlung des Kaufpreises oder zur Abnahme der Ware verletzt hat.[123] Hinsichtlich aller anderen Pflichten des Käufers kann Vertragsaufhebung nur bei wesentlichem Vertragsbruch erklärt werden.

VI. Beweislast

Obwohl das CISG Fragen der **Beweislast nicht ausdrücklich regelt**,[124] kann die Beweislast nach dem **Regel-Ausnahme-Prinzip** sowie dem **Prinzip der Beweisnähe** verteilt werden.[125] Dem zufolge hat der Verkäufer zu beweisen, dass der Käufer verpflichtet ist, den Kaufpreis zu zahlen; dazu gehört die genaue Höhe des Kaufpreises sowie die Feststellung der Fälligkeit.[126] Wenn der Käufer geltend macht, dass ein vereinbarter **Zahlungsskonto** in der Rechnung des Verkäufers nicht berücksichtigt wurde, so liegt die Beweislast insofern beim Verkäufer, da er die genaue Höhe seiner Kaufpreisforderung beweisen muss.[127] Anders ist zu entscheiden, wenn der Kaufpreis an sich feststeht und der

---

[119] Vgl. oben Rn. 1; *Pilz,* Internationales Kaufrecht, Rn. 5–378.
[120] Vgl. oben Rn. 1.
[121] Diese Ansicht wird vertreten von *Enderlein/Maskow/Strohbach,* Art. 53, Anm. 4.1.; *Bianca/Bonell/Maskow,* Art. 53, Anm. 2.2. Vgl. *Kröll u. a./P. Butler/Harindranath,* Art. 53, Rn. 3, die betonen, dass der Unterschied zwischen den Ansichten im praktischen Ergebnis marginal sei.
[122] Vgl. oben *Schroeter,* Art. 25 Rn. 24; *Hager/Maultzsch,* 5. Aufl., Art. 53 Rn. 4.
[123] Vgl. unten Art. 64 Rn. 19 ff.
[124] Vgl. oben *Schwenzer,* Art. 35 Rn. 49 ff. und unten Art. 74 Rn. 64; *Schlechtriem/Schwenzer/Schwenzer/Hachem,* CISG Commentary, Art. 4, Rn. 25, Art. 7, Rn. 35; oben *Ferrari,* Art. 7 Rn. 56.
[125] Vgl. oben *Schwenzer,* Art. 35 Rn. 51; *Schlechtriem/Schwenzer/Schwenzer/Hachem,* CISG Commentary, Art. 4, Rn. 25.
[126] Vgl. OLG Saarbrücken, 12.5.2010, CISG-online 2155, B. II. 2. a) bb) (1); *Staudinger/Magnus,* Art. 53, Rn. 83.
[127] LG Kassel, 15.2.1996, CISG-online 191 = NJW-RR 1996, 1146 ff. Vgl. auch OLG Saarbrücken, 12.5.2010, CISG-online 2155, B. II. 2. a) bb) (1) bezüglich eines vom Umfang der Bestellung abhängigen Mengenrabatts (obiter).

Käufer die Vereinbarung eines Rabatts oder Skontos behauptet; ein solcher **Teilerlass** ist vom Käufer zu beweisen.[128] Wenn der Käufer der Inanspruchnahme entgegensetzt, dass er den Kaufpreis bereits bezahlt habe, so liegt die Beweislast dafür beim Käufer, der zeigen muss, dass er bereits in Übereinstimmung mit dem Vertrag und dem Übereinkommen gezahlt hat.[129] Um diesen Beweis zu erbringen, kann der Käufer eine Bestätigung vorlegen, die den Eingang der Zahlung beim Verkäufer belegt. Der Verkäufer ist nach der allgemeinen Kooperationspflicht unter dem CISG angehalten, dem Käufer eine solche **Zahlungsbestätigung** auszustellen.[130] Wenn der Käufer Ansprüche wegen Sachmängeln einwendet, trägt grundsätzlich der Käufer für das Vorliegen einer **Vertragswidrigkeit** die Beweislast.[131] Wenn der Verkäufer behauptet, der Käufer habe die **Ware noch nicht abgenommen,** so liegt die Beweislast dafür beim Verkäufer.[132] Beruft sich der Verkäufer auf eine **andere Pflicht** des Käufers, so muss der Verkäufer beweisen, dass eine solche Verpflichtung nach dem Vertrag oder dem Übereinkommen besteht, und dass der Käufer diese tatsächlich verletzt hat.

---

[128] OLG Saarbrücken, 12.5.2010, CISG-online 2155, B. II. 2. a) bb) (1).
[129] OLG München, 9.7.1997, CISG-online 282; KG Nidwalden, 23.5.2005, CISG-online 1086 = IHR 2005, 253, 255, m. zust. Anm. *Fountoulakis,* IHR 2005, 244, 245; *A v. B,* Juzgado Sexto de Primera Instancia del Partido de Tijuana (Estado de Baja California), 14.7.2000, CISG-online 571 = IHR 2001, 38; *Staudinger/ Magnus,* Art. 53, Rn. 38; *Murray,* Draft Digest, S. 440, 449; *Gabriel,* 25 J. L. & Com. (2005-06), 273, 278; *Kröll u. a. / P. Butler / Harindranath,* Art. 53, Rn. 16.
[130] *Witz,* FS Schlechtriem, S. 291, 295; *Fountoulakis,* IHR 2005, 244, 246.
[131] Vgl. oben *Schwenzer,* Art. 35 Rn. 53, mit Ausnahmen zu dieser Grundregel.
[132] *Staudinger/Magnus,* Art. 53, Rn. 38; *Baumgärtel/Laumen/Hepting,* Art. 53, Rn. 2.

Abschnitt I. Zahlung des Kaufpreises
Section I.
Payment of the price

Section I.
Paiement du prix

Art. 54 [Kaufpreiszahlung]

Zur Pflicht des Käufers, den Kaufpreis zu zahlen, gehört es auch, die Maßnahmen zu treffen und die Förmlichkeiten* zu erfüllen, die der Vertrag oder Rechtsvorschriften erfordern,** damit Zahlung geleistet werden kann.

Art. 54
The buyer's obligation to pay the price includes taking such steps and complying with such formalities as may be required under the contract or any laws and regulations to enable payment to be made.

Art. 54
L'obligation qu'a l'acheteur de payer le prix comprend celle de prendre les mesures et d'accomplir les formalités destinées à permettre le paiement du prix qui sont prévues par le contrat ou par les lois et les règlements.

Übersicht

	Rn.
I. Regelungsgegenstand	1
II. Die Einhaltung behördlicher Förmlichkeiten	2
1. Gesetze und Vorschriften zur Devisenkontrolle	2
2. Direkte Anwendung der Gesetze und Vorschriften zur Devisenkontrolle	3
III. Die Einhaltung von Bankformalitäten	5
IV. Die Rechtsbehelfe des Verkäufers	8

Vorläufer und **Entwürfe:** Art. 69 EKG; Genfer E 1976 Art. 36; Wiener E 1977 Art. 36; New Yorker E 1978 Art. 51.

I. Regelungsgegenstand

Art. 54 stellt klar, dass zur Kaufpreiszahlungspflicht des Käufers auch die **Erfüllung aller** **Massnahmen** und **sonstigen Förmlichkeiten** gehört, die der Vertrag oder eine Rechtsvorschrift erfordern, damit Zahlung geleistet werden kann. Diese Vorschrift wird relevant mit Blick auf behördliche Förmlichkeiten einerseits sowie Bankvorschriften andererseits.

II. Die Einhaltung behördlicher Förmlichkeiten

1. Gesetze und Vorschriften zur Devisenkontrolle

Art. 54 verpflichtet den Käufer zur Einhaltung aller Förmlichkeiten, die ein Gesetz oder 2 eine Vorschrift aufstellt, um die Zahlung des Kaufpreises zu bewirken. Damit sind vor allem **öffentlich-rechtliche Vorgaben** gemeint, wie z. B. die Verpflichtung des Käufers zur Einhaltung von Vorschriften zur **Devisenkontrolle,** z. B. durch das Erfordernis einer behördlichen Genehmigung für eine internationale Überweisung oder für die Beschaffung ausländischer Devisen.[1]

---

*Schweiz: Formalitäten.
**Schweiz: die nach Vertrag oder Gesetz erforderlich sind.
[1] Vgl. Int. Ct. Russian CCI, 17.10.1995, CISG-online 207; *DiMatteo/Dhooge/Greene/Maurer/Pagnattaro*, 34 Nw. J. Int'l L. & Bus. (2004), 299, 372.

2. Direkte Anwendung der Gesetze und Vorschriften zur Devisenkontrolle

3 Da das CISG nicht von den anwendbaren nationalen Rechtsvorschriften, sondern ganz allgemein von Rechtsvorschriften spricht, die es einzuhalten gilt, damit Zahlung geleistet werden kann, bedarf es **keiner kollisionsrechtlichen Analyse,** welche Rechtsvorschriften im Einzelfall anwendbar sind. Vielmehr muss der Käufer **sämtliche Rechtsvorschriften** beachten, die möglicherweise Auswirkung auf die Durchführung der Zahlung haben können.[2] Die Gegenansicht, der zufolge Art. 54 nur die Einhaltung der nach den Regeln des Internationalen Privatrechts anwendbaren Rechtsvorschriften erfordert, ist abzulehnen.[3]

4 In der Praxis wird der **Käufer** üblicherweise verpflichtet sein, die **devisenrechtlichen Bestimmungen im Staat seiner Niederlassung** zu beachten. Daneben ist der Käufer aber auch verpflichtet, die **Rechtsvorschriften aller anderen Staaten** zu beachten, die Auswirkungen auf die Ausführung seiner Zahlung haben können. Dies beinhaltet vor allem Rechtsvorschriften, die **im Staat der Niederlassung des Verkäufers** gelten. Freilich ist der Verkäufer hinsichtlich devisenrechtlicher Bestimmungen des Staates seiner Niederlassung verpflichtet, mit dem Käufer zu kooperieren und ihn über die anwendbaren Rechtsvorschriften **zu informieren.**[4] Diese Informationspflicht ergibt sich aus der allgemeinen Kooperations- und Informationspflicht.[5]

III. Die Einhaltung von Bankformalitäten

5 Art. 54 verpflichtet den Käufer, sämtliche vertraglichen Förmlichkeiten einzuhalten, um Zahlung bewirken zu können. Der Sekretariatskommentar nennt als Beispiele für solche vertraglichen Förmlichkeiten die **Stellung eines Dokumentenakkreditivs** oder einer **Banksicherheit.**[6] Auch das EKG enthielt in seinem Art. 69 Beispiele von vertraglichen Förmlichkeiten, die der Käufer einzuhalten hatte, um Zahlung bewirken zu können: Annahme eines gezogenen Wechsels oder Stellung eines Dokumentenakkreditivs oder einer Bankgarantie.[7] Während der Ausarbeitung des CISG wurde aber entschieden, diese Beispiele zu streichen, um klar zu stellen, dass solche Förmlichkeiten **nur durch Vereinbarung der Parteien** und nicht durch das derogative Recht des Übereinkommens Vertragsinhalt werden können.[8] In diesem Sinne hat **Art. 54 nur klarstellende Bedeutung,** da der Käufer zur Einhaltung nur solcher Förmlichkeiten verpflichtet ist, zu deren Einhaltung er sich selbst vertraglich verpflichtet hat.

6 Jedenfalls besteht im CISG **kein Qualifikationsproblem** bezüglich der vom Käufer einzuhaltenden Förmlichkeiten, wie z. B. der Stellung eines Dokumentenakkreditivs, da das CISG die Pflicht zur Zahlung des Kaufpreises nach Art. 53 genau denselben Rechtsbehelfen unterstellt wie die Pflicht zur Einhaltung aller Förmlichkeiten gemäss Art. 54.[9] Mit anderen Worten ist die Pflicht zur Einhaltung sämtlicher Förmlichkeiten, die der Vertrag oder

---

[2] *Dölle/von Caemmerer,* Art. 69 EKG, Rn. 3; *Hager/Maultzsch,* 5. Aufl., Art. 54 Rn. 4; *Staudinger/Magnus,* Art. 54, Rn. 5; *Witz/Salger/Lorenz/Witz,* Art. 54, Rn. 4; *Brunner,* Art. 54, Rn. 17; *Bamberger/Roth/Saenger,* Art. 54, Rn. 2.

[3] A. A. *Kröll u. a./P. Butler/Harindranath,* Art. 54, Rn. 2 – unklar aber Rn. 5. Diese Gegenansicht war unter Art. 69 EKG noch herrschend, wenngleich sie auch zu dieser Zeit bereits eindrucksvoll zurückgewiesen wurde, vgl. *Dölle/von Caemmerer,* Art. 69 EKG, Rn. 3.

[4] *Bianca/Bonell/Maskow,* Art. 54, Anm. 2.7.; *Staudinger/Magnus,* Art. 54, Rn. 5; *Witz/Salger/Lorenz/Witz,* Art. 54, Rn. 6; MünchKomm/*P. Huber,* Art. 54, Rn. 3; *Benedict,* Informationspflichten, Rn. 1130.

[5] Vgl. oben Art. 53, Rn. 39.

[6] Sekretariatskommentar, Art. 50, Nr. 2. Zum Dokumentenakkreditiv vgl. ICC, 7197/1992, CISG-online 36; OGH, 6.2.1996, CISG-online 224; BezG Saane, 20.2.1997, CISG-online 426. Zur Bankgarantie vgl. CCI Ct. Arb., 17.11.1995, CISG-online 250.

[7] *Dölle/von Caemmerer,* Art. 69 EKG, Rn. 1 ff.

[8] YB VIII (1977), S. 318 ff.; *Staudinger/Magnus,* Art. 54, Rn. 2.

[9] Vgl. unten Rn. 8; oben Art. 53, Rn. 41; unten Art. 61, Rn. 4.

Rechtsvorschriften erfordern, damit Zahlung geleistet werden kann, wie z. B. Stellung eines Dokumentenakkreditivs, **Teil der Pflicht des Käufers zur Zahlung des Kaufpreises**.[10]

Wenn die Parteien die Gültigkeit eines **Dokumentakkreditivs** oder einer **Bankgarantie** zeitlich nicht beschränkt haben, muss das Zahlungsinstrument für eine angemessene Zeit gültig sein, wobei sich die Angemessenheit nach den Umständen des Einzelfalls richtet, insbesondere nach dem Risiko, das durch das Dokumentenakkreditiv oder die Bankgarantie abgedeckt werden sollte. Wenn sich die Parteien im Wege einer Vertragsänderung geeinigt haben, dass der Käufer eine Bankgarantie erneuert, so erfüllt er seine Pflicht nicht durch Vorlage einer Bankgarantie, die das ursprüngliche Gültigkeitsdatum ausweist und dieses bereits abgelaufen ist.[11] Im Falle eines Dokumentenakkreditivs ist der Käufer grundsätzlich verpflichtet, dem Verkäufer ein Dokumentenakkreditiv auszustellen, das sowohl die gesamte Lieferzeit als auch die gesamte Zahlungszeit abdeckt. Keine zur Zahlung erforderliche Förmlichkeit i. S. v. Art. 54, sondern eine blosse Willensbekundung, stellt die Bestätigung einer Bank dar, dass sie in der Zukunft ein Dokumentenakkreditiv gegen Vorlage eines Inspektionsberichts für jede Einzellieferung stellen wird.[12] Diese Einordnung hat zur Folge, dass bei Nichtvorlage der Bankbestätigung allein ein antizipierter Vertragsbruch in Frage kommt. 7

IV. Die Rechtsbehelfe des Verkäufers

Das CISG unterscheidet für die Rechtsbehelfe des Verkäufers nicht zwischen der Pflicht zur Zahlung des Kaufpreises und den mit der Zahlung verbundenen, anderen Pflichten gemäss Art. 54.[13] Da dieselben Rechtsbehelfe unabhängig davon eingreifen, ob die verletzte Pflicht die Kaufpreiszahlungspflicht oder eine mit dieser verbundenen, anderen Pflicht gemäss Art. 54 ist, wird die Unterscheidung zwischen solchen anderen Pflichten und der Kaufpreiszahlungspflicht in der Praxis nicht relevant. Insbesondere stellt die Nichterfüllung einer mit der Zahlung verbundenen, anderen Pflicht i. S. v. Art. 54 einen **eigenständigen Vertragsbruch** und nicht nur einen antizipierten Vertragsbruch hinsichtlich der Kaufpreiszahlungspflicht dar.[14] Der Verkäufer kann also jeden der ihm gemäss Art. 61 zustehenden **Rechtsbehelfe wegen Vertragsbruchs** ausüben. Darüber hinaus kann der Verkäufer die Lieferung der Ware gemäss Art. 71 I lit. b) zurückhalten, wenn das Verhalten des Käufers bei der Vorbereitung der Erfüllung oder bei der Erfüllung des Vertrags Anlass zur Annahme gibt, dass der Käufer einen wesentlichen Teil seiner Pflichten nicht erfüllen wird.[15] Für den Fall, dass der Vertragsbruch des Käufers in der Verletzung einer ausländischen Devisenkontrollbestimmung liegt, mag der Käufer im Einzelfall von seiner Haftung nach Art. 79 befreit sein, wenn es ihm gelingt zu zeigen, dass die Nichterfüllung auf einem ausserhalb seines Einflussbereichs liegenden Hinderungsgrund beruhte und dass von ihm vernünftigerweise nicht erwartet werden konnte, den Hinderungsgrund bei Vertragsschluss in Betracht zu 8

---

[10] ICC, 11849/2003, CISG-online 1421, Rn. 17; ICC, 7585/1992, CISG-online 105 = JDI 1995, 1015 ff.; *Downs Investments Pty Ltd. v. Perwaja Steel SDN BHD*, Supreme Court of Queensland, 17.11.2000, CISG-online 587 = 2000 QSC 421, Rn. 63; OGH, 6.2.1996, CISG-online 224 = östZRVgl 1996, 248.

[11] CCI Ct. Arb., 17.11.1995, CISG-online 250, mit Bezug auf Art. 7 I und Art. 8 III.

[12] LG Kassel, 21.9.1995, CISG-online 192 (obiter), dieses Ergebnis ablehnend *Kröll u. a./P. Butler/Harindranath*, Art. 54, Rn. 3.

[13] Anders noch Art. 70 EKG; dazu *Dölle/von Caemmerer*, Art. 70 EKG, Rn. 1 ff.

[14] OGH, 6.2.1996, CISG-online 224 = östZRVgl 1996, 248 = RdW 1996, 203, m. Anm. *Karollus*, RdW 1996, 197; *Staudinger/Magnus*, Art. 54, Rn. 7; Sekretariatskommentar, Art. 50, Nr. 5; *Hager/Maultzsch*, 5. Aufl., Art. 54 Rn. 7; *Hellner*, Standard Form Contracts, S. 335, 352 ff.; *Honnold/Flechtner*, Art. 54, Rn. 323; MünchKommHGB/*Benicke*, Art. 54, Rn. 5 ff.; *Witz/Salger/Lorenz/Witz*, Art. 54, Rn. 5; *Bamberger/Roth/Saenger*, Art. 54, Rn. 2; *Eckert/Maifeld/Matthiessen*, Rn. 1285; *Honsell/Schnyder/Straub*, Art. 54, Rn. 36. A. A. CCI Ct. Arb., 17.11.1995, CISG-online 250, fälschlicherweise Art. 73 II anwendend; *DiMatteo/Dhooge/Greene/Maurer/Pagnattaro*, 34 Nw. J. Int'l L. & Bus. (2004), 299, 372; *Gabriel*, 25 J. L. & Com. (2005-06), 273, 274, denen zufolge der Verkäufer wählen kann, ob er sich auf einen gegenwärtigen oder einen antizipierten Vertragsbruch berufen möchte.

[15] CCI Ct. Arb., 17.11.1995, CISG-online 250. Vgl. *Honnold/Flechtner*, Art. 54, Rn. 323.

ziehen oder den Hinderungsgrund oder seine Folgen zu vermeiden oder zu überwinden.[16] Liegt der Hinderungsgrund darin, dass nicht genügend frei wechselbare Devisen auf dem Bankkonto des Käufers zur Verfügung stehen, so kann der Käufer sich nicht auf Art. 79 berufen.[17] Der Käufer kann im Einzelfall auch nach Art. 80 von seiner Haftung befreit sein, wenn der Verkäufer es unterlassen hat, ihm notwendige Informationen für die Stellung eines Dokumentenakkreditivs zukommen zu lassen, z. B. den Name des Herkunftshafens.[18] Bereits die Nichterfüllung einer die spätere Zahlung betreffenden Vorbereitungshandlung, wie z. B. die Stellung eines benutzbaren Dokumentenakkreditivs, kann einen **wesentlichen Vertragsbruch** darstellen.[19]

IV. Beweislast

9   Der **Verkäufer** trägt die Beweislast dafür, dass der Käufer verpflichtet war, eine die Zahlung betreffende Vorbereitungshandlung i. S. v. Art. 54 vorzunehmen, und dass er dieser Pflicht nicht nachgekommen ist.[20]

---

[16] Vgl. unten *Schwenzer*, Art. 79 Rn. 17. Der Streit darüber, ob eine Pflicht zur Einholung einer behördlichen Genehmigung als eine *obligation de résultat* oder eine *obligation de moyens* zu qualifizieren ist, bleibt in der Praxis unerheblich, vgl. *Murray,* Draft Digest, S. 440, 442.

[17] Arb. Ct. Russian CCI, 17.10.1995, CISG-online 207 = CLOUT Nr. 142.

[18] OGH, 6.2.1996, CISG-online 224 = CLOUT Nr. 176; *Kröll u. a./P. Butler/Harindranath,* Art. 54, Rn. 3.

[19] *Helen Kaminski Pty. Ltd. v. Marketing Australian Products Inc.,* U. S. Dist. Ct. (S. D. N. Y.), 23.7.1997, CISG-online 297 = CLOUT Nr. 187 = 1997 LEXIS 10603 (obiter); *Kröll u. a./P. Butler/Harindranath,* Art. 54, Rn. 1; *Osuna-González,* 25 J. L. & Com. (2005-06), 299, 302. Für eine ausführliche Analyse vgl. Art. 64 Rn. 9 f.

[20] Anders *Staudinger/Magnus,* Art. 54, Rn. 11, dem zufolge der Käufer die ordentliche Erfüllung seiner mit der Zahlung verbundenen Vorbereitungspflichten beweisen müsse.

Art. 55 [Bestimmung des Preises]

Ist ein Vertrag gültig geschlossen worden, ohne daß er den Kaufpreis ausdrücklich oder stillschweigend festsetzt oder dessen Festsetzung ermöglicht, so wird mangels gegenteiliger Anhaltspunkte vermutet, daß die Parteien sich stillschweigend auf den Kaufpreis bezogen haben, der bei Vertragsabschluß allgemein für derartige Ware berechnet wurde, die in dem betreffenden Geschäftszweig unter vergleichbaren Umständen verkauft wurde.

Art. 55

Where a contract has been validly concluded but does not expressly or implicitly fix or make provision for determining the price, the parties are considered, in the absence of any indication to the contrary, to have impliedly made reference to the price generally charged at the time of the conclusion of the contract for such goods sold under comparable circumstances in the trade concerned.

Art. 55

Si la vente est valablement conclue sans que le prix des marchandises vendues ait été fixé dans le contrat expressément ou implicitement ou par une disposition permettant de le déterminer, les parties sont réputées, sauf indications contraires, s'être tacitement référées au prix habituellement pratiqué au moment de la conclusion du contrat, dans la branche commerciale considérée, pour les mêmes marchandises vendues dans des circonstances comparables.

Übersicht

	Rn.
I. Regelungsgegenstand	1
1. Rechtsvergleichender Hintergrund	1
2. Entstehungsgeschichte	2
3. Heutiger Anwendungsbereich	3
II. Verträge mit offenem Preis	4
1. Kaufpreis bei Vertragsschluss nicht bestimmt oder bestimmbar	4
a) Verträge mit bewusst offengelassenem Preis	5
b) Erfüllung eines Vertrags mit offenem Preis	6
c) Nicht durch Angebot und Annahme zustande gekommener Vertrag	7
d) Festsetzung des Preises durch eine der Parteien, durch die Parteien zusammen oder durch eine Drittpartei	8
e) Vorbehalt betreffend Teil II des Übereinkommens	9
f) Art. 55 bei der Auslegung stillschweigender Preisabreden	10
2. Gültigkeit	11
a) Kein Rückgriff auf nationale Bestimmtheitsanforderungen	11
b) Einseitige Bestimmungsrechte	12
3. Ausschluss einseitiger Bestimmungsrechte nach nationalem Recht	13
III. Preisfestsetzung	14
1. Kaufpreis, der allgemein für derartige Ware in dem betreffenden Geschäftszweig unter vergleichbaren Umständen verlangt wird	14
2. Marktpreis	15
3. Der allgemeine Preis im Zeitpunkt des Vertragsschlusses	16
4. Angemessener Preis	17
IV. Beweislast	18

Vorläufer und **Entwürfe:** Art. 57 EKG; Genfer E 1976 Art. 36; Wiener E 1977 Art. 37; New Yorker E 1978 Art. 51.

I. Regelungsgegenstand

1. Rechtsvergleichender Hintergrund

1   Die sich im Zusammenhang mit Art. 55 stellenden Probleme haben eine lange Geschichte in den verschiedenen nationalen Rechtsordnungen. Ob ein Kaufvertrag ohne ausdrückliche oder stillschweigende Vereinbarung eines Preises wirksam geschlossen werden kann, ist eine sehr umstrittene Frage und die nationalen Antworten darauf fallen sehr unterschiedlich aus. Das traditionelle Konzept eines *pretium certum*, das seine Wurzeln im mittelalterlichen gemeinen Recht Europas hat, hatte starken Einfluss auf einige Rechtssysteme Europas, namentlich Frankreich, wo Art. 1583 Cc eine Einigung über den Preis für den wirksamen Abschluss eines Kaufvertrages voraussetzt.[1] Diese Voraussetzung wurde von vielen Rechtssystemen übernommen, die sich am französischen Recht orientiert bzw. dieses rezipiert haben, namentlich das spanische[2] und das mexikanische Recht.[3] Aber auch das österreichische Recht verlangt zumindest, dass der Preis nicht unbestimmt geblieben ist.[4] Andere kontinentale Rechtssysteme, namentlich das deutsche Recht, geben dem **Verkäufer** hingegen **das Recht zur Kaufpreisbestimmung**.[5] Die Rechtssysteme des Common Law, namentlich das englische und das US-amerikanische Recht, aber auch einige Rechtsordnungen des Civil Law, namentlich das Schweizer Recht, verfolgen einen flexibleren Ansatz und nehmen einen **angemessenen Preis** bzw. den **Marktpreis** als stillschweigend vereinbart an.[6] Die Rechtsvergleichung zeigt, dass der flexiblere Ansatz, dem zufolge Kaufverträge mit offenem Preis als gültig angesehen und ein angemessener Preis bzw. ein Marktpreis zum Inhalt des Vertrages erhoben werden, sich durchzusetzen scheint und im Vergleich zum traditionellen Model den moderneren und besseren Ansatz darstellt. Selbst in Frankreich hat die Cour de Cassation das Prinzip des *pretium certum* mittlerweile faktisch abgeschafft,[7] und auch der russische Gesetzgeber hat entschieden, offene Preise in Kaufverträgen zu akzeptieren.[8]

2. Entstehungsgeschichte

2   Als das Übereinkommen verfasst wurde, war die Frage, ob ein Kaufvertrag auch ohne ausdrückliche oder stillschweigende Einigung über den Preis als wirksam geschlossen angesehen werden kann, noch sehr umstritten. Die früheren sozialistischen Staaten des Rats für gegenseitige Wirtschaftshilfe Osteuropas und Asiens (Comecon), unterstützt von Frankreich, bestanden auf die strikte Voraussetzung eines *pretium certum*. Allerdings sah bereits das Vorgängerübereinkommen in Art. 57 EKG vor, dass der Käufer den Preis zu zahlen hatte, den der Verkäufer im Zeitpunkt des Vertragsschlusses für ähnliche Waren üblicherweise verlangte, wenn der Vertrag keinen Preis vorsah und die Preisbestimmung auch nicht anderweitig ermöglichte. Dieser Ansatz wurde während der Ausarbeitung des CISG in zweierlei Hinsicht kritisiert.[9] Zunächst wurde das Problem unbestimmter Preise als Gültigkeitsfrage aufgefasst, die als solche außerhalb des Anwendungsbereiches des CISG liege.

---

[1] Vgl. auch Art. 1591 Cc: '*Le prix de la vente doit être déterminé et désigné par les parties*'.
[2] Spanien: Artt. 1449, 1450 Cc. Freilich ist anzumerken, dass sich das interne spanische Recht hin zur Anerkennung von Kaufverträgen mit offenem Preis entwickelt, vgl. Audiencia Provincial de Barcelona, 27.11.2003, CISG-online 1102 = CLOUT Nr. 556.
[3] Art. 2248 Cc, vgl. *Gabuardi*, Open Price Terms, CISG Pace, unter VI.
[4] § 1054 ABGB.
[5] §§ 315, 316 BGB, vgl. auch § 5 der skandinavischen Kaufrechte.
[6] Vgl. Art. 212 I OR; sec. 8 (2) SGA 1979; §§ 2–204 (3), 2–305 (1) UCC. Vgl. die ausgiebige Studie von *Witz*, Der unbestimmte Kaufpreis.
[7] Civ. 1, 4.1.1995, CISG-online 138, m. Anm. *Witz*, 16 J. L. & Com. (1997), 345.
[8] Art. 485 I, 424 III Cc, vgl. *De Ly*, Draft Digest, S. 468, 479.
[9] *Hager/Maultzsch*, 5. Aufl., Art. 55 Rn. 3.

Zudem wurde die Regel, dass der Preis, den der Verkäufer üblicherweise für ähnliche Ware verlangt, als kaum pragmatisch und inhaltlich unangemessen angesehen, insbesondere weil der Käufer so keinen Schutz gegen überzogene Preise habe. Gleichwohl sahen sowohl der Genfer Entwurf als auch der Wiener Entwurf eine Art. 57 EKG entsprechende Vorschrift vor. Dafür setzte Art. 37 des Wiener Entwurfs voraus, dass ein Vertrag wirksam geschlossen worden war, und dieser Wortlaut wurde als Verweis auf nationales Recht verstanden, wodurch den Rechtsordnungen, die zu dieser Zeit noch einen bestimmten Preis als Gültigkeitsvoraussetzung verlangten, insofern Vorrang eingeräumt werden sollte.[10] Der New Yorker Entwurf übernahm Art. 37 des Wiener Entwurfs als Art. 51 und bestimmte in den Regeln über den Vertragsschluss gleichzeitig, dass ein Angebot nur dann bestimmt genug ist, wenn es den Preis ausdrücklich oder stillschweigend festsetzt oder dessen Festsetzung ermöglicht (Art. 12 des New Yorker Entwurfs).[11] Der augenscheinliche Widerspruch zwischen Art. 12 und Art. 51 des New Yorker Entwurfs war dann Gegenstand einer intensiven Debatte auf der Wiener Konferenz, konnte aber nicht gelöst werden.[12] Schliesslich wurde eine Ad hoc-Arbeitsgruppe eingesetzt, die den Entwurfstext in die heutige Fassung des Übereinkommens mit dem Ziel umschrieb, Art. 14 gegenüber Art. 55 Vorrang einzuräumen.[13]

3. Heutiger Anwendungsbereich

Die gegenläufigen Ansichten zu Verträgen mit offenem Preis sind auch heute noch sichtbar durch den augenscheinlichen **Widerspruch zwischen Art. 14 und Art. 55**. Während Art. 14 I voraussetzt, dass ein Angebot den Preis ausdrücklich oder stillschweigend festsetzt oder dessen Festsetzung ermöglicht, sieht Art. 55 einen Mechanismus zur Preisbestimmung vor, wenn ein Vertrag gültig geschlossen worden ist, ohne dass er den Kaufpreis ausdrücklich oder stillschweigend festsetzt oder dessen Festsetzung ermöglicht. Auch heutzutage besteht noch ein breites Angebot an unterschiedlichen Ansichten, wie dieser Anwendungskonflikt zwischen den beiden Vorschriften zu lösen sei.[14] Auf beiden Seiten des Meinungsspektrums werden klare Positionen bezogen. Auf der einen Seite wird die Ansicht vertreten, dass Art. 14 gegenüber Art. 55 Vorrang geniesse.[15] Auf der anderen Seite wird die Ansicht vertreten, dass grundsätzlich Art. 55 Vorrang gegenüber Art. 14 habe.[16] Zwischen diesen beiden Polen wird eine Vielzahl unterschiedlicher Ansichten vertreten, und es erscheint fast unmöglich, diese unterschiedlichen Ansichten in einer generalisierenden Art und Weise adäquat zu beschreiben. In der Praxis freilich wird die Entscheidung zwischen den Ansichten nicht auf Grund ihrer dogmatischen Schärfe, sondern **von Fall zu Fall** auf Grund einer **Interessensbewertung** vorgenommen.[17]

II. Verträge mit offenem Preis

1. Kaufpreis bei Vertragsschluss nicht bestimmt oder bestimmbar

Art. 55 kommt nur dann zur Anwendung, wenn der Vertrag den Kaufpreis weder ausdrücklich noch stillschweigend festsetzt und dessen spätere Festsetzung auch nicht er-

---

[10] Vgl. YB III (1977), S. 49, Nr. 340.
[11] Art. 12 des New Yorker Entwurfs.
[12] O. R., S. 363–366, Nr. 21–62.
[13] O. R., S. 366, Nr. 59–62, S. 392, Nr. 44–62 (insb. Nr. 45, 46); vgl. auch O. R., S. 367, Nr. 1, 4.
[14] Vgl. oben *Schroeter*, Art. 14 Rn. 19 m. w. N.
[15] *Farnsworth*, Formation of Contract, § 3.04; *Ghestin*, RDAI 1988, S. 5–6; *Heuzé,* Anm. 169. ff., 173. ff.
[16] *Corbisier*, 1988 Rev. int. dr. com. 777, 828 ff.; *Fortier*, J.D.I. 1990, 381, 390; *Honnold/Flechtner*, Art. 14, Rn. 137.6; *Gabuardi*, Open Price Terms, CISG Pace, unter III; *Joseph*, (1984) 3 Dick. J. Int'l L. 107, 122; *Karollus*, S. 62; *Kritzer*, ICM-Guide, S. 189 ff.; *Loewe*, Art. 55, S. 76.
[17] Vgl. auch oben *Schroeter*, Art. 14 Rn. 19; auch *Ferrari u. a./Mankowski*, Internationales Vertragsrecht, Art. 55, Rn. 9.

möglicht.[18] Zwischen den Parteien entstandene Gepflogenheiten können die Festsetzung des Preises ermöglichen.[19] Schliesslich kann Art. 55 als Orientierungshilfe für die Festsetzung eines von den Parteien unbestimmt belassenen Preises benutzt werden.[20]

5 **a) Verträge mit bewusst offengelassenem Preis.** Das CISG sieht Verträge mit offenem Preis als wirksam geschlossen an, wenn die Parteien bei Vertragsschluss einen gemeinsamen Bindungswillen hatten. In einem solchen Fall führt die Parteivereinbarung gemäss Art. 6 zu einer **Derogation von Art. 14.**[21] Dabei müssen drei Situationen unterschieden werden. Wenn die Umstände des Einzelfalls keinerlei Hinweise auf eine Einigung über den Preis enthalten, können die Parteien trotzdem einen gültigen Vertrag wirksam abgeschlossen haben.[22] Hingegen besteht kein wirksam geschlossener Vertrag, wenn die Parteien solange nicht vertraglich gebunden sein wollten, bis sie eine Einigung über den Preis erreicht haben.[23] Schwierig zu behandeln sind Situationen, in denen die Einigung der Parteien über den Preis zu einem späteren Zeitpunkt erfolgen sollte, die Parteien aber schlussendlich keine Einigung erreichen konnten. Anders als der US-amerikanische UCC[24] verweist das CISG in einem solchen Fall nicht auf den Marktpreis. Vielmehr scheint das allgemeine Prinzip der Parteiautonomie (Art. 6) den Verkäufer daran zu hindern, einen solchen Vorvertrag *(agreement to agree)* durchzusetzen. Allerdings ist nach der hier vertretenen Auffassung auch die Einbeziehung eines solchen Vorvertrages in den Anwendungsbereich des CISG angezeigt, um zu verhindern, dass zunächst eine Klage nach nationalem Recht nötig wäre, um die Gegenpartei zur Einigung auf einen Preis zu verpflichten, um im Anschluss daran eine Kaufpreisklage nach CISG zu erheben. Vielmehr sollte der Verkäufer das Recht haben, vom Käufer direkt die Zahlung des Marktpreises verlangen zu können.[25]

6 **b) Erfüllung eines Vertrags mit offenem Preis.** Ein offensichtliches Beispiel eines gültigen Vertrags mit offenem Preis liegt vor, wenn die Parteien den Vertrag (teilweise) erfüllt haben, obwohl der Preis offengeblieben war.[26] Die **(teilweise) Vertragserfüllung** erlaubt die Festsetzung des Preises gemäss Art. 55 selbst dann, wenn die Parteien ursprünglich eine Einigung über den Preis zu einem späteren Zeitpunkt erreichen wollten.[27] Selbst wenn die Parteien unterschiedliche Preisvorstellungen in ihren Vertragsschlusserklärungen miteinander ausgetauscht haben, führt die Vertragserfüllung zu einem gültigen Vertrag und zur Festsetzung des Preises nach Art. 55. In einem solchen Fall haben die Parteien stillschweigend Art. 19 derogiert, und zwar unabhängig davon, ob die sich widersprechenden Preise in allgemeinen Geschäftsbedingungen oder direkt in den Vertragsschlusserklärungen enthalten waren.[28]

---

[18] Vgl. oben *Schroeter*, Art. 14 Rn. 8, 12–15; *Kröll u. a./P. Butler/Harindranath*, Art. 55, Rn. 3; *Ferrari u. a./Mankowski*, Internationales Vertragsrecht, Art. 55, Rn. 3; *Mistelis*, 25 J.L. & Com. (2005-06), 285, 288; *Honsell/Schnyder/Straub*, Art. 55, Rn. 12.

[19] Municipal Court Budapest, 24.3.1992, CISG-online 61 = CLOUT Nr. 52, m. Anm. *Vida*, IPRax 1993, 263; oben *Schroeter*, Art. 14 Rn. 9; *Honsell/Schnyder/Straub*, Art. 55, Rn. 12.

[20] Vgl. unten Rn. 10.

[21] *Bamberger/Roth/Saenger*, Art. 55, Rn. 2.

[22] KG Wallis, 27.4.2007, CISG-online 1721 = SZIER 2008, 184 ff.; BezG St. Gallen, 3.7.1997, CISG-online 336.

[23] Int. Ct. Russian CCI, 3.3.1995, CISG-online 204 = CLOUT Nr. 139, zustimmend *Mistelis*, 25 J.L. & Com. (2005-06), 285, 289; *Murray*, Draft Digest, S. 440, 445; *Gabriel*, 25 J.L. & Com. (2005-06), 273, 275; *Ferrari u. a./Mankowski*, Internationales Vertragsrecht, Art. 55, Rn. 7.

[24] § 2–305 (1) (b) UCC.

[25] LG Neubrandenburg, 3.8.2005, CISG-online 1190 = IHR 2006, 26, 30 (obiter); *Schlechtriem/P. Butler*, UN Law, Rn. 24b; *Bridge*, Int'l Sale of Goods: Es wäre pedantisch zwischen einem Kaufvertrag (Contract *of* Sale) und einem Vorvertrag über den Abschluss eines Kaufvertrages (Contracts *for* Sale) zu unterscheiden. Es sollte auf jeden Fall ein Widerspruch zwischen dem CISG und dem auf den Vorvertrag anwendbaren Recht vermieden werden. A. A. Int. Ct. Russian CCI, 3.3.1995, CISG-online 204; *Staudinger/Magnus*, Art. 55, Rn. 8; *Honsell/Schnyder/Straub*, Art. 55, Rn. 12.

[26] BezG St. Gallen, 3.7.1997, CISG-online 336 = SZIER 1998, 84; *Bucher*, FS Piotet, S. 371, 398 ff.; *Kramer*, FS Welser, S. 539, 544 ff.; oben *Schroeter*, Art. 14 Rn. 21.

[27] Vgl. oben Rn. 5.

[28] Zu kollidierenden AGB vgl. oben *Schroeter*, Art. 19 Rn. 30 f.

Bestimmung des Preises   7–10 **Art. 55**

c) Nicht durch Angebot und Annahme zustande gekommener Vertrag. Die 7
Voraussetzung eines bestimmten oder bestimmbaren Preises in Art. 14 betrifft dem Wortlaut
nach nur die Bestimmtheit des Angebots. Vor diesem Hintergrund wird die Ansicht vertreten, dass Art. 14 mit seiner Bestimmtheitsanforderung nur dann zur Anwendung gelange,
wenn der Vertrag auf herkömmliche Art und Weise durch Angebot und Annahme geschlossen wurde.[29] Obwohl Artt. 14–24 bzw. die hinter ihnen stehenden allgemeinen Prinzipien
grundsätzlich auch auf Verträge, die anders als durch Angebot und Annahme zu Stande
gekommen sind, Anwendung finden und die Minimalvoraussetzungen an den Inhalt eines
Vertrages beschreiben,[30] ist der beschriebenen Auffassung zuzustimmen, weil davon ausgegangen werden kann, dass die Parteien **Art. 14** mit seiner Bestimmtheitsanforderung
gemäss Art. 6 **stillschweigend derogiert** haben.[31]

d) Festsetzung des Preises durch eine der Parteien, durch die Parteien zusam- 8
men oder durch eine Drittpartei. Sieht der Vertrag vor, dass eine der Parteien, beide
Parteien zusammen oder eine Drittpartei den Kaufpreis festsetzen kann, so stellt sich die
Frage, ob Art. 55 angewendet werden kann, wenn die berechtigte Partei, die Parteien oder
die Drittpartei es versäumen, das **Bestimmungsrecht** auszuüben. Haben die Vertragsparteien ein Festsetzungsrecht zu Gunsten einer **Drittpartei** vereinbart und übt die
bezeichnete Drittpartei dieses Recht nicht aus, so sind die Parteien auf Grund ihrer
allgemeinen Kooperationspflicht (Art. 7) verpflichtet, eine neue Drittpartei zu bezeichnen.[32] Sieht der Vertrag hingegen vor, dass **beide Vertragsparteien einvernehmlich** den
Kaufpreis festsetzen und können die Parteien keine Einigung über den Preis erreichen, so
findet Art. 55 Anwendung.[33] Wenn zur Festsetzung des Kaufpreises nur eine der Vertragsparteien berechtigt und ein solches **einseitiges Bestimmungsrecht** nach dem anwendbaren nationalen Recht gültig ist,[34] so führt die Nichtausübung des Bestimmungsrechts zur
Anwendung von Art. 55. Der Grund für diese Lösung liegt darin, dass die Nichtausübung
des Bestimmungsrechts durch die bezeichnete Partei nicht zu einer Besserstellung dieser
Partei führen soll, sondern es der anderen Partei ermöglicht werden muss, den Vertrag zu
erfüllen.

e) Vorbehalt betreffend Teil II des Übereinkommens. Art. 14 findet keine Anwen- 9
dung, wenn Teil II des Übereinkommens nicht anwendbar ist, weil das Recht eines Vertragsstaates anwendbar ist, der einen Vorbehalt betreffend Teil II des Übereinkommens nach
Art. 92 eingelegt hat.[35] In einem solchen Fall findet nationales Recht auf den Vertragsschluss Anwendung. Ist nach nationalem Recht ein Vertrag trotz offenem Preis gültig
zustande gekommen, so kann freilich Art. 55 Anwendung finden.[36]

f) Art. 55 bei der Auslegung stillschweigender Preisabreden. In der Praxis wird 10
man oft stillschweigende Preisabreden vorfinden, die den Kaufpreis in einem konkreten Fall
bestimmbar machen. Solche stillschweigenden Preisabreden können das Ergebnis einer
Vertragsauslegung nach Art. 8 bzw. Art. 9 sein.[37] Für die Vertragsauslegung kann Art. 55

---

[29] *Honnold/Flechtner,* Art. 14, Rn. 137.5, 137.8; *Honnold,* Open-Price Contract, S. 915, 923 ff.; *Brunner,* Art. 14, Rn. 11; *Bucher,* FS Piotet, S. 371, 390 ff.; *Lookofsky,* The 1980 United Nations Convention, Anm. 102.; *Stoffel,* Formation du contrat, S. 63 ff.; *Staudinger/Magnus,* Art. 55, Rn. 5.
[30] Vgl. oben *Schroeter,* Vor Artt. 14–24 Rn. 24.
[31] Vgl. *Schroeter,* Art. 14 Rn. 21.
[32] *Bridge,* Int'l Sale of Goods, Rn. 12.09.
[33] Vgl. oben Rn. 5; *Schroeter,* Art. 14 Rn. 13.
[34] S. Art. 4 lit. a).
[35] *Honnold,* Open-Price Contract, S. 915, 929; *Staudinger/Magnus,* Art. 55, Rn. 5; *Enderlein/Maskow/Strohbach,* Art. 55, Anm. 2.; *Herber/Czerwenka,* Art. 55, Rn. 5; *Plantard,* Droits et obligations de l'acheteur, S. 113; *Soergel/Lüderitz/Budzikiewicz,* Art. 55, Rn. 4–5.
[36] Vgl. oben *Schroeter,* Art. 14 Rn. 20; *Hager/Maultzsch,* 5. Aufl., Art. 55 Rn. 6; *Bamberger/Roth/Saenger,* Art. 55, Rn. 2; *MünchKomm/P. Huber,* Art. 55, Rn. 9.
[37] Vgl. BezG St. Gallen, 3.7.1997, CISG-online 336 = CLOUT Nr. 215 = SZIER 1998, 84 ff.; vgl. Sekretariatskommentar, Art. 12, Nr. 16; *Piltz,* Internationales Kaufrecht, Rn. 3–26; *Sono,* Formation of International Contracts, S. 120; *Winship,* 17 Int'l Law. (1983), 5 ff.

nutzbar werden, in dem der nach Art. 55 bestimmte **Marktpreis als stillschweigende Parteiabrede** in Frage kommt.[38] Z.B. kann angenommen werden, dass ein Käufer, der Ersatzteile bestellt, dem Marktpreis für solche Ersatzteile im Zeitpunkt des Vertragsschlusses stillschweigend zugestimmt hat.[39]

2. Gültigkeit

11 a) **Kein Rückgriff auf nationale Bestimmtheitsanforderungen.** Die Formulierung „gültig geschlossen" in Art. 55 verweist auf Art. 14, wodurch ein Rückgriff auf nationale Anforderungen an die Bestimmtheit, wie z. B. das Erfordernis eines *pretium certum,* ausgeschlossen ist. Die Entstehungsgeschichte von Art. 55 zeigt, dass die einleitenden Worte „ist ein Vertrag gültig geschlossen worden" ursprünglich als Verweis auf nationales Recht gemeint waren, um die Anwendung nationaler Bestimmtheitsanforderungen, wie z. B. das Erfordernis eines *pretium certum,* sicher zu stellen.[40] Dieser Ansicht kann heutzutage nicht mehr gefolgt werden. Vielmehr verweisen diese einleitenden Worte auf Art. 14 und nicht auf das subsidiär anwendbare nationale Recht. Da bereits Art. 14 den Käufer vor übermässigen Preisen schützt, in dem ein bestimmter oder bestimmbarer Kaufpreis gefordert wird, ist ein Rückgriff auf nationale Bestimmtheitsanforderungen nicht mehr erforderlich. Daher sind **nationale Bestimmtheitsanforderungen durch Art. 14 ausgeschlossen.**[41] Das CISG schliesst sämtliche Gültigkeitsvorschriften des nationalen Rechts aus, die an einen offen gebliebenen Preis anknüpfen, so z. B. auch die Anfechtung des Vertrags wegen Irrtums.

12 b) **Einseitige Bestimmungsrechte.** Nationale Gültigkeitsvorschriften können gemäss Art. 4 S. 2 lit. a) Vertragsklauseln angreifbar machen, die ein **einseitiges Bestimmungsrecht** vorsehen, in der Praxis meistens zu Gunsten des Verkäufers.[42] Gleiches gilt für Vertragsklauseln, die als Kaufpreis den Marktpreis am Tag der Lieferung vorsehen.[43]

3. Ausschluss einseitiger Bestimmungsrechte nach nationalem Recht

13 Sobald das CISG auf einen Vertrag Anwendung findet, sind einseitige Bestimmungsrechte nach nationalem Recht, in der Praxis meistens zu Gunsten des Verkäufers, ausgeschlossen.[44]

---

[38] OGH, 10.11.1994, CISG-online 117 = CLOUT Nr. 106 = IPRax 1996, 137 ff.: Der Kaufpreis war gemäss Art. 14 bestimmbar, weil Chinchilla-Felle mittlerer bis besserer Qualität zu einem Preis im Bereich von DM 35 bis 60 pro Fell verkauft worden waren. Die Vorinstanz hatte noch Art. 55 herangezogen, um festzustellen, dass DM 50 pro Fell angemessen seien, da der Marktpreis DM 60 pro Fell betrage. LG Neubrandenburg, 3.8.2005, CISG-online 1190 = IHR 2006, 26, 30: Die Preisklausel „*Price: To be fixed during the season*" führte zur Anwendung von Art. 55 und einem bestimmbaren Preis; oben *Schroeter,* Art. 14 Rn. 20; *Hager/Maultzsch,* 5. Aufl., Art. 55 Rn. 7; *Sono,* Formation of International Contracts, S. 120; *Doralt/Šarčević,* UNCITRAL Kaufrecht, S. 77; *Bamberger/Roth/Saenger,* Art. 55, Rn. 2; zurückhaltend *Ferrari u. a./Mankowski,* Internationales Vertragsrecht, Art. 55, Rn. 4.

[39] Vgl. oben *Schroeter,* Art. 14 Rn. 20.

[40] *Hager/Maultzsch,* 5. Aufl., Art. 55 Rn. 5.

[41] Vgl. ICC, 7819/1999, ICC Ct. Bull. 2001, 56, 57; *Hager/Maultzsch,* 5. Aufl., Art. 55 Rn. 5.

[42] Vgl. oben *Schroeter,* Art. 14 Rn. 14 m. w. N. zum deutschen und zum schweizerischen Recht. Vgl. Ass. plén., 1.12.1995, D. 1996, 13, m. Anm. *Krenz,* RIW 1997, 201 ff.: Vorverträge bzw. Rahmenverträge, die dem Verkäufer ein Preisbestimmungsrecht geben, sind nach französischem Recht nicht mehr ungültig; anders aber noch *De Ly,* Draft Digest, S. 468, 481, dem zufolge Kaufverträge, die einer Partei das alleinige Preisbestimmungsrecht geben, nach französischem Recht nach wie vor ungültig sind.

[43] Vgl. oben *Schroeter,* Art. 14 Rn. 15.

[44] Vgl. BGH, 27.6.1990, NJW 1990, 3077, 3079 (zu Art. 57 EKG).

III. Preisfestsetzung

1. Kaufpreis, der allgemein für derartige Ware in dem betreffenden Geschäftszweig unter vergleichbaren Umständen verlangt wird

Während das EKG noch den Preis vorsah, den der Verkäufer für seine Ware üblicherweise verlangt,[45] verweisen die nationalen Rechtsordnungen, die Kaufverträge mit unbestimmtem Preis als gültig ansehen, entweder auf einen angemessenen Preis, wie z. B. das englische oder das US-amerikanische Recht,[46] oder auf einen Durchschnittsmarktpreis, wie er im Zeitpunkt und am Ort der Erfüllung bestand, wie z. B. das Schweizer Recht.[47] Hingegen verweist Art. 55 auf den Kaufpreis, der bei Vertragsschluss allgemein für derartige Ware berechnet wurde, die in dem betreffenden Geschäftszweig unter vergleichbaren Umständen verkauft wurde.[48] Der Wortlaut beschreibt also einen **objektiven Standard** für die Festsetzung des Marktpreises.[49] Der Zweck dieses objektiven Standards ist der **Schutz des Käufers vor der einseitigen Festsetzung übermässiger Preise** durch den Verkäufer. Freilich kann dieser Schutz im Einzelfall fehl gehen, wenn z. B. der Verkäufer bereit war, seine Ware unterhalb des Marktpreises zu verkaufen.[50] 14

2. Marktpreis

Die Festsetzung des Preises durch Bezugnahme auf den Kaufpreis, der bei Vertragsschluss allgemein für derartige Ware berechnet wurde, die in dem betreffenden Geschäftszweig unter vergleichbaren Umständen verkauft wurde, wird nur dann relativ leicht möglich sein, wenn ein **Marktpreis** oder eine **Börsennotierung** vorliegt.[51] Zur Bestimmung des anwendbaren Marktpreises kann Art. 76 II herangezogen werden.[52] Aus Art. 76 II folgt, dass der Marktpreis massgebend ist, der an dem **Ort** gilt, an dem die **Lieferung der Ware** hätte erfolgen sollen.[53] Besteht am Lieferort kein Marktpreis, so kann auf den Marktpreis an einem **angemessenen Ersatzort** zurückgegriffen werden, wobei die Unterschiede in den Kosten der Beförderung der Ware zu berücksichtigen sind. In einer Lieferkette ist der relevante Markt der **Verkaufsmarkt des Verkäufers,** nicht etwa der Einkaufsmarkt des Käufers.[54] **Prämien und Abzüge** auf Marktpreise für die gehandelte Ware müssen berücksichtigt werden.[55] Wenn kein Marktpreis am Lieferort oder an einem angemessenen Ersatzort besteht, wird die Festlegung des gemäss Art. 55 zu bestimmenden Preises sehr schwierig.[56] Die Bestimmung des allgemeinen Preises für gleichwertige Ware kann dann nur durch Verweis auf **allgemeine Listenpreise** versucht werden.[57] Darüber Beweis zu führen wird in der Praxis nur sehr schwer oder gar nicht möglich sein, vor allem wenn es sich bei der Ware 15

---

[45] Vgl. Art. 57 EKG.
[46] § 2–305 (1) UCC; sec. 8 (2) SGA 1979.
[47] Art. 212 I OR.
[48] Vgl. BezG St. Gallen, 3.7.1997, CISG-online 336 = SZIER 1998, 84.
[49] *Hager/Maultzsch,* 5. Aufl., Art. 55 Rn. 8; *Staudinger/Magnus,* Art. 55, Rn. 9.
[50] KG Wallis, 27.4.2007, CISG-online 1721 = SZIER 2008, 184 ff.; *Sevòn,* Obligations of the Buyer, S. 219; *Hager/Maultzsch,* 5. Aufl., Art. 55 Rn. 8.
[51] *Staudinger/Magnus,* Art. 55, Rn. 9; *Kröll u. a./P. Butler/Harindranath,* Art. 55, Rn. 7; *Ferrari u. a./Mankowski,* Internationales Vertragsrecht, Art. 55, Rn. 11.
[52] Vgl. unten *Schwenzer,* Art. 76 Rn. 4; *Honnold/Flechtner,* Art. 55, Rn. 325.4.
[53] Vgl. *Ferrari u. a./Mankowski,* Internationales Vertragsrecht, Art. 55, Rn. 18. Anders LG Neubrandenburg, 3.8.2005, CISG-online 1190 = IHR 2006, 26, 30: Marktpreis am Ort der Niederlassung des Verkäufers; KG Wallis, 27.4.2007, CISG-online 1721 = SZIER 2008, 184 ff.: Marktpreis der Niederlassung des Verkäufers; *Honsell/Schnyder/Straub,* Art. 55, Rn. 18: Referenzmarkt für gleichartige Geschäfte.
[54] LG Neubrandenburg, 3.8.2005, CISG-online 1190 = IHR 2006, 26, 30.
[55] ICC, 8324/1995, CISG-online 596 = J. D. I. 1996, 1019 ff.; *Witz/Salger/Lorenz/Witz,* Art. 55, Rn. 3.
[56] *Heuzé,* Anm. 358.
[57] OLG Rostock, 10.10.2001, CISG-online 671 = IHR 2003, 17; KG Wallis, 27.4.2007, CISG-online 1721 = SZIER 2008, 184 ff.; *Hager/Maultzsch,* 5. Aufl., Art. 55 Rn. 8.

um herzustellende oder zu erzeugende Güter handelt.[58] Die in Art. 55 verwendete Formulierung „unter vergleichbaren Umständen" bedeutet, dass der Vergleichspreis auch unter **vergleichbaren Liefer- und Zahlungsbedingungen** berechnet werden muss. Insbesondere die für die Preisbasis wesentliche Handelsklausel (Incoterms®), z. B. FOB oder CIF, sowie anwendbare Prämien und Abzüge, wie z. B. Rabatte, müssen berücksichtigt werden.[59] Sofern Unterschiede in den vertraglichen Bedingungen für den Vertragspreis und den Vergleichspreis bestehen, muss deren wirtschaftlicher Wert ausgeglichen werden.[60]

3. Der allgemeine Preis im Zeitpunkt des Vertragsschlusses

16   Wenn ein allgemeiner Preis im Einzelfall bestimmbar ist, so muss auf den **Zeitpunkt des Vertragsschlusses** und nicht auf den Zeitpunkt der Lieferung[61] abgestellt werden.[62] Diese Regelung verhindert, dass der Verkäufer von einem Preisanstieg und der Käufer von einem Preisverfall profitieren.[63]

4. Angemessener Preis

17   Wenn kein allgemeiner Preis nach den Massstäben des Art. 55 festgelegt werden kann, kommt die herrschende Auffassung zu der unbefriedigenden Lösung, dass ein Vertrag gar nicht geschlossen wurde.[64] Der Rückgriff auf nationale Vorschriften, die möglicherweise eine alternative Festlegung des unbestimmten Preises vorsehen, z. B. durch ein Bestimmungsrecht des Verkäufers,[65] ist ausgeschlossen.[66] Ein solcher Rückgriff auf nationales Recht würde nämlich die Vorschriften des CISG umgehen. Um aber die unbefriedigende Lösung, dass ein Kaufvertrag gar nicht zustande kommt, zu vermeiden, muss ein einheitlicher Massstab auf der Grundlage der dem CISG eigenen Prinzipien entwickelt werden. Als ein solches Prinzip kann der Standard der **Angemessenheit** angewendet werden. Der gleiche Ansatz wird in den PICC verfolgt, die ausdrücklich bestimmen, dass ein angemessener Preis gilt, wenn der allgemeine Preis für gleichwertige Ware, die in dem betreffenden Geschäftszweig unter vergleichbaren Umständen verkauft wurde, nicht festgestellt werden kann.[67] Ein solcher angemessener Preis wird zu meist ein **Durchschnittspreis** sein.[68]

---

[58] *Hager/Maultzsch,* 5. Aufl., Art. 55 Rn. 8.
[59] Vgl. CIETAC, 25.5.2005, CISG-online 1685; LG Neubrandenburg, 3.8.2005, CISG-online 1190 = IHR 2006, 26, 30: Menge ist ein Preisfaktor; *Enderlein/Maskow/Strohbach,* Art. 55, Anm. 10.; *Heuzé,* Anm. 358.; *Hager/Maultzsch,* 5. Aufl., Art. 55 Rn. 8; *Kröll u. a./P. Butler/Harindranath,* Art. 55, Rn. 7; *Honsell/Schnyder/Straub,* Art. 55, Rn. 17.
[60] Vgl. CIETAC, 25.5.2005, CISG-online 1685; unten *Schwenzer,* Art. 76 Rn. 4.
[61] Anders § 2–305 (1) UCC: angemessener Preis im Zeitpunkt der Lieferung.
[62] *Hager/Maultzsch,* 5. Aufl., Art. 55 Rn. 9; *Staudinger/Magnus,* Art. 55, Rn. 10; *Kröll u. a./P. Butler/Harindranath,* Art. 55, Rn. 7; *Ferrari u. a./Mankowski,* Internationales Vertragsrecht, Art. 55, Rn. 14; *Mistelis,* 25 J. L. & Com. (2005-06), 285, 294.
[63] *Hager/Maultzsch,* 5. Aufl., Art. 55 Rn. 9; *Staudinger/Magnus,* Art. 55, Rn. 10; *MünchKommHGB/Benicke,* Art. 55, Rn. 10; *Enderlein/Maskow/Strohbach,* Art. 55, Anm. 7.; Sekretariatskommentar, Art. 51, Nr. 3; *Mistelis,* 25 J. L. & Com. (2005-06), 285, 294; *Honsell/Schnyder/Straub,* Art. 55, Rn. 19.
[64] BGH, 27.6.1990, NJW 1990, 3077 (zu Art. 57 EKG); *Pratt & Whitney v. Malev Hungarian Airlines,* Legfelsóbb Birósag, 25.9.1992, CISG-online 63 = 13 J. L. & Com. (1993), 31, m. Anm. *Amato,* 13 J. L. & Com. (1993), 1 ff.; *Bamberger/Roth/Saenger,* Art. 55, Rn. 3; *Witz/Salger/Lorenz/Witz,* Art. 55, Rn. 11; oben *Schroeter,* Art. 14 Rn. 22; *Kröll u. a./P. Butler/Harindranath,* Art. 55, Rn. 8; *Ferrari u. a./Mankowski,* Internationales Vertragsrecht, Art. 55, Rn. 21, dem zufolge zunächst versucht werden sollte, ein Käuferteilmarkt zu identifizieren; *Honsell/Schnyder/Straub,* Art. 55, Rn. 23, denen zufolge zunächst auf nationales Recht zu rekurrieren ist; *Vogenauer/Kleinheisterkamp/Kleinheisterkamp,* Art. 5.1.7, Rn. 5.
[65] Vgl. § 316 BGB.
[66] Vgl. oben Rn. 13; *Hager/Maultzsch,* 5. Aufl., Art. 55 Rn. 22. A. A. *Honsell/Schnyder/Straub,* Art. 55, Rn. 23; *Kramer,* FS Welser, S. 545 ff., dem zufolge eine einheitliche Lösung auf Basis von Art. 7 II Vorzug zu geben sei, wobei er allerdings eine Lösung über nationales Recht subsidiär zulassen will; ähnlich *Kröll u. a./P. Butler/Harindranath,* Art. 55, Rn. 8; anders *Ebenroth,* östJBl 1986, 681, 685; *Jametti Greiner,* Vertragsabschluß, S. 49; *Audit,* Vente internationale, Anm. 63.; *Heuzé,* Anm. 169. ff., 173. ff.
[67] Art. 5.1.7 PICC, Kommentar 1: Diese Vorschrift orientiert sich an Art. 55 CISG und wurde angepasst, um den Bedürfnissen von internationalen Verträgen entgegenzukommen, die sich auf einzigartige oder

IV. Beweislast

Die **sich auf Art. 55 berufende Partei** hat die Voraussetzungen des Art. 55 zu beweisen.[69] Dies wird in den meisten Fällen der Verkäufer sein, der gegen den Käufer eine Kaufpreisklage anstrengt, um Zahlung zu erhalten. Da aber die Preisfestsetzung in engem Zusammenhang mit der Frage des Vertragsschlusses steht, kann auch der Käufer sich auf Art. 55 beziehen, um den Vertragsschluss zu behaupten und zu beweisen und so seine Klage auf Lieferung der Ware oder Schadenersatz zu substantiieren. In der Literatur wird die Auffassung vertreten, dass die Preisfestlegung nach Art. 55 in die *ex officio* Befugnisse eines staatlichen Gerichts oder eines Schiedsgerichts falle.[70] Nach dieser Auffassung kann das staatliche Gericht oder das Schiedsgericht die Parteien zur Mitwirkung an der Erforschung des Sachverhalts verpflichten.[71] Diese Ansicht ist aber abzulehnen, weil sie ohne Grund von den allgemeinen Beweislastregeln abweicht.[72]

---

jedenfalls besondere Gegenstände beziehen; vgl. *Vogenauer/Kleinheisterkamp*, Art. 5.1.7, Rn. 4. Vgl. auch Art. 6:104 PECL.

[68] Vgl. OLG Celle, 2.9.1998, CISG-online 506; unten *Schwenzer*, Art. 76 Rn. 4; MünchKomm/*P. Huber*, Art. 76, Rn. 3; *Staudinger/Magnus*, Art. 76, Rn. 13; *Witz/Salger/Lorenz/Witz*, Art. 76, Rn. 3, 9; *Achilles*, Art. 76, Rn. 3. Kritisch *Vogenauer/Kleinheisterkamp*, Art. 5.1.7, Rn. 9.

[69] *Staudinger/Magnus*, Art. 55, Rn. 11; *Witz/Salger/Lorenz/Witz*, Art. 55, Rn. 5; *Kröll u. a./P. Butler/Harindranath*, Art. 55, Rn. 9; *Ferrari u. a./Mankowski*, Internationales Vertragsrecht, Art. 55, Rn. 22.

[70] *Staudinger/Magnus*, Art. 55, Rn. 11.

[71] *Staudinger/Magnus*, Art. 55, Rn. 11.

[72] Vgl. *Hager/Maultzsch*, 5. Aufl., Art. 55 Rn. 8; MünchKommHGB/*Benicke*, Art. 55, Rn. 12; *Ferrari u. a./Mankowski*, Internationales Vertragsrecht, Art. 55, Rn. 22.

Art. 56 [Kaufpreis nach Gewicht]

Ist der Kaufpreis nach dem Gewicht der Ware festgesetzt, so bestimmt er sich im Zweifel nach dem Nettogewicht.

Art. 56
If the price is fixed according to the weight of the goods, in case of doubt it is to be determined by the net weight.

Art. 56
Si le prix est fixé d'après le poids des marchandises, c'est le poids net qui, en cas de doute, détermine ce prix.

Übersicht

	Rn.
I. Regelungsbereich	1
II. Preisfestlegung nach Gewicht	2
III. Beweislast	5

Vorläufer und **Entwürfe:** Art. 58 EKG; Genfer E 1976 Art. 37; Wiener E 1977 Art. 38; New Yorker E 1978 Art. 52.

I. Regelungsbereich

1   Art. 56 behandelt Verträge, in denen der Kaufpreis nach dem Gewicht der Ware festgesetzt wurde. Für den Fall einer solchen Preisvereinbarung bestimmt Art. 56, dass sich der Preis im Zweifel nach dem **Nettogewicht** bestimmt. Es handelt sich also um eine **Auslegungsregel,** die nur dann eingreift, wenn die Parteien weder ausdrücklich noch stillschweigend eine andere Regelung getroffen haben (Art. 6 und Art. 8) und auch nicht an abweichende Gebräuche oder Gepflogenheiten gebunden sind (Art. 9).[1] Eine ähnliche Auslegungsregel kennen auch einige nationale Rechtsordnungen; auch war eine solche bereits im EKG enthalten.[2]

II. Preisfestlegung nach Gewicht

2   Art. 56 findet nur dann Anwendung, wenn der Vertrag den **Kaufpreis nach dem Gewicht der Ware** festsetzt. Dabei kann es sich um einen **Pauschalpreis** für das **Gesamtgewicht** der zu liefernden Ware handeln.[3] Hingegen ist Art. 56 nicht anzuwenden, wenn der **Preis pro Einheit** festgesetzt wurde, selbst wenn das Gewicht der Einheiten zum Zwecke der Spezifizierung angegeben wurde.[4]

3   Als Auslegungsregel findet Art. 56 nur dann Anwendung, wenn die Parteien weder ausdrücklich noch stillschweigend etwas anderes vereinbart haben (Art. 6 und Art. 8) und auch nicht an abweichende Gebräuche oder Gepflogenheiten gebunden sind (Art. 9). Bei Vereinbarung der Klausel „**brutto für netto**", wird der Preis durch das Gesamtgewicht von Ware und Verpackung bestimmt.[5] Wenn der Vertrag keine abweichende Regelung

---

[1] Sekretariatskommentar, Art. 52, Nr. 1; *Honnold/Flechtner*, Art. 56, Rn. 328; *Kröll u. a./P. Butler/Harindranath*, Art. 56, Rn. 2; *Honsell/Schnyder/Straub*, Art. 56, Rn. 4.
[2] Vgl. Art. 58 EKG; Deutschland: § 380 I HGB; Russland: Art. 485 II Cc; Schweiz: Art. 212 II OR.
[3] *Staudinger/Magnus*, Art. 56, Rn. 4; *Honsell/Schnyder/Straub*, Art. 56, Rn. 6; MünchKommHGB/*Benicke*, Art. 56, Rn. 1; MünchKomm/*P. Huber*, Art. 56, Rn. 2.
[4] *Staudinger/Magnus*, Art. 56, Rn. 5; *Enderlein/Maskow/Strohbach*, Art. 56, Anm. 2.; MünchKommHGB/ *Benicke*, Art. 56, Rn. 1; MünchKomm/*P. Huber*, Art. 56, Rn. 2; *Kröll u. a./P. Butler/Harindranath*, Art. 56, Rn. 3.
[5] *Staudinger/Magnus*, Art. 56, Rn. 6; *Bianca/Bonell/Maskow*, Art. 56, Anm. 2.6.; *Hager/Maultzsch*, 5. Aufl., Art. 56 Rn. 2; *Bamberger/Roth/Saenger*, Art. 56, Rn. 1.

enthält, bedeutet **Nettogewicht** das Gesamtgewicht abzüglich des Gewichts der Verpackung.[6]

In der Literatur ist umstritten, ob das Nettogewicht am **Lieferort** gemäss Art. 31[7] oder an dem **Ort, an dem die Gefahr** auf den Käufer gemäss Artt. 67–69 **übergeht,**[8] zu bestimmen ist. In der Praxis werden diese zwei Ansichten oft zum gleichen Ergebnis führen, insbesondere bei **Beförderung der Ware,** weil sowohl Art. 31 als auch Art. 67 auf den Ort verweisen, an dem die Ware an den ersten Beförderer zur Übermittlung an den Käufer übergeben wird.[9] In allen anderen Fällen ist Art. 31 massgebend, weil das Nettogewicht an dem Ort bestimmt werden muss, an dem der Verkäufer die Ware an den Käufer liefert. Bei Verträgen, die eine Beförderung von losem Schüttgut erfordern, wird das Nettogewicht regelmässig durch das Konnossement oder ein ähnliches Dokument ausgewiesen. Wenn Ware verkauft wird, die sich bereits **auf dem Transport** befindet, ist der **Destinationshafen** (ex ship oder ex quay) massgebend, weil weder durch Abstellen auf den Zeitpunkt des Vertragsschlusses gemäss Art. 68, noch durch Abstellen auf den Zeitpunkt der Übergabe der Transportdokumente an den Käufer oder der Instruktion des Beförderers durch den Verkäufer, die Ware an den Käufer auszuliefern,[10] eine angemessene Lösung des Problems erreicht werden kann. Alle anderen Fälle, also wenn die Ware dem Käufer an der **Niederlassung des Verkäufers** oder an einem **anderen bestimmten Ort** zur Verfügung gestellt wird (Art. 31 lit. b) und lit. c)), werfen keine Probleme auf; das Nettogewicht kann an diesem Ort festgestellt werden.

III. Beweislast

Diejenige Partei, die sich zur Preisbestimmung nach dem Gewicht der Ware auf eine ausdrückliche oder stillschweigende Parteivereinbarung oder Gebräuche bzw. Gepflogenheiten bezieht, muss das Vorliegen einer solchen Preisbestimmung beweisen.[11] Ansonsten gilt gemäss Art. 56 das Nettogewicht als vereinbart. Diejenige Partei, die sich auf Art. 56 stützt, muss das Nettogewicht am richtigen Bestimmungsort nachweisen.

---

[6] *Hager/Maultzsch,* 5. Aufl., Art. 56 Rn. 2; *Staudinger/Magnus,* Art. 56, Rn. 3; Sekretariatskommentar, Art. 52, Nr. 1; *Bianca/Bonell/Maskow,* Art. 56, Anm. 2.2.; *Kröll u. a./P. Butler/Harindranath,* Art. 56, Rn. 4.
[7] *Staudinger/Magnus,* Art. 56, Rn. 3; *Enderlein/Maskow/Strohbach,* Art. 56, Anm. 4.; *Herber/Czerwenka,* Art. 56, Rn. 2; *Reinhard,* Art. 56, Rn. 2; *Witz/Salger/Lorenz/Witz,* Art. 56, Rn. 2.
[8] *Hager/Maultzsch,* 5. Aufl., Art. 56 Rn. 2; *Šarčević,* Draft Digest, S. 482, 485; *Bamberger/Roth/Saenger,* Art. 56, Rn. 1; *Soergel/Lüderitz/Budzikiewicz,* Art. 56, Rn. 3; *Kröll u. a./P. Butler/Harindranath,* Art. 56, Rn. 4; *Honsell/Schnyder/Straub,* Art. 56, Rn. 8.
[9] Vgl. Art. 31 lit. a), Art. 67 I. Vgl. *Staudinger/Magnus,* Art. 56, Rn. 3; MünchKomm/*P. Huber,* Art. 56, Rn. 3.
[10] Vgl. oben *Widmer Lüchinger,* Art. 31 Rn. 79 ff.
[11] *Staudinger/Magnus,* Art. 56, Rn. 7; *Baumgärtel/Laumen/Hepting,* Art. 56, Rn. 1.

Art. 57 [Zahlungsort]

(1) Ist der Käufer nicht verpflichtet, den Kaufpreis an einem anderen bestimmten Ort zu zahlen, so hat er ihn dem Verkäufer wie folgt zu zahlen:
a) am Ort der Niederlassung des Verkäufers oder,
b) wenn die Zahlung gegen Übergabe der Ware oder von Dokumenten zu leisten ist, an dem Ort, an dem die Übergabe stattfindet.

(2) Der Verkäufer hat alle mit der Zahlung zusammenhängenden Mehrkosten zu tragen, die durch einen Wechsel seiner Niederlassung nach Vertragsabschluß entstehen.

Art. 57

(1) If the buyer is not bound to pay the price at any other particular place, he must pay it to the seller:
(a) at the seller's place of business; or
(b) if the payment is to be made against the handing over of the goods or of documents, at the place where the handing over takes place.

(2) The seller must bear any increase in the expenses incidental to payment which is caused by a change in his place of business subsequent to the conclusion of the contract.

Art. 57

1) Si l'acheteur n'est pas tenu de payer le prix en un autre lieu particulier, il doit payer le vendeur:
a) à l'établissement de celui-ci; ou
b) si le paiement doit être fait contre la remise des marchandises ou des documents, au lieu de cette remise.

2) Le vendeur doit supporter toute augmentation des frais accessoires au paiement qui résultent de son changement d'établissement après la conclusion du contrat.

Übersicht

	Rn.
I. Regelungsgegenstand	1
II. Vertraglich vereinbarter Zahlungsort	5
III. Zahlung gegen Übergabe der Ware oder der Dokumente, Art. 57 I lit. b)	9
1. Anwendungsbereich – Zug-um-Zug-Erfüllung	9
2. Zahlung gegen Dokumente, Art. 58 I	10
3. Verträge, die eine Beförderung der Ware erfordern oder Ware betreffen, die sich auf dem Transport befindet, wenn der Käufer sie mit der Massgabe versendet hat, dass die Ware oder die Dokumente dem Käufer nur gegen Zahlung des Kaufpreises zu übergeben sind, Art. 58 II	12
4. Verträge über Ware, die bei einer Drittpartei lagert	13
IV. Zahlung am Ort der Niederlassung des Verkäufers, Art. 57 I lit. a)	14
1. Anwendungsbereich – Vorleistungspflicht einer der Parteien	14
2. Offene Rechnung	15
3. Verträge, welche die Beförderung der Ware erfordern oder Ware betreffen, die sich auf dem Transport oder in einem Lagerhaus bei einer Drittpartei befindet, wenn der Verkäufer sie nicht mit der Massgabe versendet hat, dass die Ware oder die Dokumente dem Käufer nur gegen Zahlung zu übergeben sind	16
4. Wechsel der Niederlassung durch den Verkäufer, Art. 57 II	17
V. Erfüllung von Zahlungspflichten – Risiko des Verlusts und der Verzögerung	20
VI. Abtretung des Anspruchs auf Kaufpreiszahlung – Auswirkungen auf den Zahlungsort	21
VII. Internationale Zuständigkeit am Zahlungsort	23
1. Brüsseler Übereinkommen/Lugano-Übereinkommen/Nationale Zuständigkeitsregeln	23
2. EUGVO und revidiertes Lugano-Übereinkommen	25
VIII. Zahlungsort für andere Zahlungen als die Kaufpreispreiszahlung	29
1. Schadenersatz und Vertragsstrafen	29
2. Rückzahlung des Kaufpreises	31
3. Zinsen	32
IX. Beweislast	33

Zahlungsort   1–4   **Art. 57**

Vorläufer und **Entwürfe:** Art. 59 EKG; Genfer E 1976 Art. 38; Wiener E 1977 Art. 39; New Yorker E 1978 Art. 53.

I. Regelungsgegenstand

Art. 57 bestimmt den **Zahlungsort** in einem dreistufigen Vorgang. Zunächst können die 1
Vertragsparteien den Zahlungsort ausdrücklich (Art. 57 I i. V. m. Art. 6) oder stillschweigend (Art. 57 I i. V. m. Art. 8 bzw. Art. 9) bestimmt haben. Haben die Parteien den Zahlungsort weder ausdrücklich noch stillschweigend vereinbart, so hat der Käufer gemäss Art. 57 I lit. b) den Kaufpreis an dem Ort zu zahlen, an dem die Übergabe der Ware oder der Dokumente gegen Zahlung stattfindet. Liegt schliesslich weder eine Parteivereinbarung über den Zahlungsort noch eine Zahlung gegen Übergabe der Ware oder der Dokumente vor, so hat der Käufer gemäss Art. 57 I lit. a) den Kaufpreis am Ort der Niederlassung des Verkäufers zu zahlen. Aus diesem Stufenaufbau folgt, dass Art. 57 I lit. a) eine allgemeine Regel für die Bestimmung des Zahlungsorts nach CISG aufstellt, der zufolge Zahlungspflichten nur dann erfüllt sind, wenn das Geld am Ort der Niederlassung des Gläubigers diesem zur Verfügung steht.

Das in **Art. 57 I lit. a)** enthaltene **allgemeine Prinzip,** dem zufolge der Käufer den 2
Kaufpreis **am Ort der Niederlassung des Verkäufers** zu zahlen hat, kennen auch einige nationale Rechtsordnungen Europas, wie z. B. das Schweizer Recht,[1] das englische Recht, das irische Recht, das schottische Recht, das niederländische Recht,[2] das skandinavische Recht, das italienische Recht,[3] das portugiesische Recht,[4] das polnische Recht, das griechische Recht,[5] sowie das türkische Recht[6] und das US-amerikanische Recht.[7] Auch stimmt das Prinzip mit der allgemeinen Vertragspraxis im internationalen Handel überein.[8] Im Gegensatz dazu wird der Zahlungsort im deutschen Recht[9] und anderen Rechtsordnungen, so z. B. im französischen Recht,[10] im belgischen Recht, im luxemburgischen Recht und im österreichischen Recht[11] durch den Ort der Niederlassung des Schuldners bestimmt.[12]

Durch Festlegung des Zahlungsorts ist Art. 57 zusammen mit Art. 58, der die Zahlungs- 3
zeit regelt, eine der wichtigsten Vorschriften des CISG, welche die Pflicht des Käufers zur Zahlung des Kaufpreises regeln. In materiell-rechtlicher Hinsicht regelt Art. 57 die Frage, wann der Käufer von seiner Pflicht zur Zahlung des Kaufpreises durch Erfüllung **befreit** ist. Dabei regelt er zugleich die Frage, wer das **Risiko des Verlusts** und **der Verzögerung** der Zahlung trägt.

Das CISG regelt Fragen des (internationalen) Zivilprozessrechts grundsätzlich nicht. 4
Nichtsdestotrotz kann das CISG durch Festlegung des Erfüllungsorts der Verpflichtung des Käufers zur Zahlung des Kaufpreises nebenbei auch prozessrechtliche Aspekte beeinflussen, wie z. B. die Frage der **internationalen Zuständigkeit.**[13]

---

[1] Schweiz: Art. 74 II Ziff. 1 OR.
[2] Niederlande: Art. 1429 BWB.
[3] Italien: Art. 1182 Cc.
[4] Portugal: Art. 454 Cc.
[5] Griechenland: Art. 321 Cc.
[6] Türkei: Art. 74 OR.
[7] USA: § 2–310 (a) UCC.
[8] *Honnold/Flechtner*, Art. 57, Rn. 331.
[9] Deutschland: §§ 269, 270 BGB.
[10] Frankreich: Art. 1247 Cc.
[11] Österreich: § 905 II ABGB.
[12] Für einen Überblick der nationalen Rechtsordnungen Europas vgl. *Lando/Beale,* Part I and II, Art. 7:101 PECL, Nr. 1, S. 331.
[13] Vgl. unten Rn. 23 ff.

II. Vertraglich vereinbarter Zahlungsort

5   Art. 57 bestätigt ausdrücklich das allgemeine Prinzip der Privatautonomie (Art. 6). Der Verkäufer und der Käufer können in ihrem Vertrag den Zahlungsort zunächst **ausdrücklich vereinbaren**. Eine Parteivereinbarung über den Zahlungsort ist z. B. dann gegeben, wenn der Vertrag ein **Konto bezeichnet,** das der Verkäufer bei einer Bank unterhält. Oft wird die Bank des Verkäufers ihren Sitz nicht in dem Staat haben, in dem der Verkäufer seine Niederlassung hat. In einem solchen Fall ist für die Bestimmung des Zahlungsortes die Niederlassung der Bank und nicht die Niederlassung des Verkäufers massgebend. Eine Parteivereinbarung über den Zahlungsort kann auch in der Vereinbarung eines **Abbuchungsauftragsverfahrens** gesehen werden; in diesem Fall ist der Zahlungsort der Ort der Niederlassung der Bank des Käufers.[14]

6   Auch ohne ausdrückliche Vereinbarung der Parteien wird sich der Zahlungsort oft aus einer **stillschweigenden Vereinbarung** der Parteien ergeben. Wenn z. B. der Verkäufer seine **Bankverbindung** in einer Vertragsschlusserklärung oder einer Rechnung angibt, wird man nach der hier vertretenen Auffassung von einer stillschweigenden Zustimmung des Käufers zu diesem Zahlungsort auszugehen haben, wenigstens im Wege der Vertragsänderung nach Art. 29, wenn der Käufer seine Bank instruiert, Geld auf dieses Konto zu überweisen. Eine Gegenansicht qualifiziert den Hinweis des Verkäufers auf seine Bankverbindung nicht als stillschweigende Vereinbarung des Zahlungsortes, sondern nur als vertragliche Befugnis zu Gunsten des Käufers, auf dieses Konto mit Erfüllungswirkung zahlen zu können.[15] Verweist der Verkäufer auf seine Bankverbindung zum ersten Mal in der Rechnung, die vom Käufer unbezahlt bleibt, so besteht jedenfalls keine vertragliche Vereinbarung über den Zahlungsort, mit der Folge, dass Art. 57 I lit. a) Anwendung findet.[16]

7   In der Praxis wird durch die Benutzung von **Zahlungsklauseln** zumeist auch der Zahlungsort stillschweigend festgelegt. Die Zahlungsklauseln „net cash", „cash against invoice" oder „cash before delivery" bzw. „Vorkasse" (CBD) legen fest, dass die Zahlung am Ort der Niederlassung des Verkäufers zu erfolgen hat,[17] weil sie keine Zug-um-Zug-Erfüllung, sondern die Vorleistung einer der Parteien vorsehen.[18] Die Zahlungsklauseln „documents against payment" (D/P) bzw. „Kasse gegen Dokumente" oder „cash on delivery" (COD) bzw. (auf deutsch) Nachnahme entsprechen der Regelung in Art. 57 I lit. b) und legen fest, dass Zahlungsort der Ort ist, an dem die Übergabe der Dokumente bzw. der Ware stattfindet.[19] Eine etwaige **Stundung** der Zahlung ändert nicht den Zahlungsort.[20]

---

[14] LG Trier, 7.12.2000, CISG-online 595 = IHR 2001, 35 (betreffend internationale Zuständigkeit); *Ferrari u. a./Mankowski*, Internationales Vertragsrecht, Art. 57, Rn. 3.

[15] ZGer Basel-Stadt, 3.12.1997, CISG-online 346 = CLOUT Nr. 221 = TranspR-IHR 1999, 11 = SZIER 1999, 190; vgl. Gerechtshof 's-Hertogenbosch, 5.2.1997, CISG-online 542 = NIPR 1997, Nr. 245; MünchKommHGB/*Benicke*, Art. 57, Rn. 4; *Piltz,* NJB 2000, 557; *Staudinger/Magnus,* Art. 57, Rn. 8; *Brunner,* Art. 57, Rn. 5; *Honsell/Schnyder/Straub,* Art. 57, Rn. 6; *Ferrari u. a./Mankowski*, Internationales Vertragsrecht, Art. 57, Rn. 7.

[16] ZGer Basel-Stadt, 3.12.1997, CISG-online 346 = CLOUT Nr. 221 = TranspR-IHR 1999, 11 = SZIER 1999, 190; *Ferrari u. a./Mankowski*, Internationales Vertragsrecht, Art. 57, Rn. 4.

[17] RB 's-Hertogenbosch, 6.5.1999, NIPR 1994, Nr. 464 (offene Rechnung); *Staudinger/Magnus*, Art. 57, Rn. 7; *Achilles*, Art. 57, Rn. 3; *Bamberger/Roth/Saenger*, Art. 57, Rn. 2; *Brunner*, Art. 57, Rn. 3; MünchKomm/*P. Huber*, Art. 57, Rn. 4; MünchKommHGB/*Benicke*, Art. 57, Rn. 3; *Soergel/Lüderitz/Budzikiewicz*, Art. 57, Rn. 3; *Witz/Salger/Lorenz/Witz*, Art. 57, Rn. 7; *Honsell/Schnyder/Straub*, Art. 57, Rn. 7.

[18] *Staudinger/Magnus*, Art. 57, Rn. 7.

[19] LG Nürnberg-Fürth, 27.2.2003, CISG-online 818 = IHR 2004, 20; *Staudinger/Magnus*, Art. 57, Rn. 7; *Brunner*, Art. 57, Rn. 4; *Herber/Czerwenka*, Art. 57, Rn. 8; *Honsell/Schnyder/Straub*, Art. 57, Rn. 7 für D/P. A. A. *Piltz*, Internationales Kaufrecht, Rn. 4–137: COD bestimmt nur die Zahlungszeit; *Bamberger/Roth/Saenger*, Art. 57, Rn. 1: COD bedeutet, dass der Ort der Niederlassung des Verkäufers zugleich der Zahlungsort sei; *Ferrari u. a./Mankowski*, Internationales Vertragsrecht, Art. 57, Rn. 5: COD bestimmt Zahlungsort an der Niederlassung des Käufers.

[20] LG Freiburg, 26.4.2002, CISG-online 690 = IHR 2002, 72; *Staudinger/Magnus*, Art. 57, Rn. 7; *Ferrari u. a./Mankowski*, Internationales Vertragsrecht, Art. 57, Rn. 5.

Wenn die Parteien sich auf Zahlung durch **Dokumentenakkreditiv** geeinigt haben, kann der Kaufvertrag angeben, ob das Dokumentenakkreditiv bei der eröffnenden Bank, die ihren Sitz meist im Land des Käufers haben wird, oder bei der bestätigenden Bank, die ihren Sitz oft im Land des Verkäufers haben wird, benutzbar ist. Wenn eine solche Bestimmung Eingang in den Kaufvertrag gefunden hat, stellt sie eine ausdrückliche Vereinbarung des Zahlungsortes dar.[21] Sollte der Kaufpreis schliesslich nicht wie vorgesehen im Wege des Dokumentenakkreditivs beglichen werden, so stellt sich die Frage, ob für den Kaufpreisanspruch des Verkäufers auch der durch das Akkreditiv bestimmte Zahlungsort oder die allgemeine Regel des Art. 57, also Zahlung am Ort der Niederlassung des Verkäufers, gilt.[22] Nach hier vertretener Auffassung ist danach zu unterscheiden, ob der Verkäufer den Käufer auf Zahlung gemäss den vertraglichen Bestimmungen, im Falle eines Dokumentenakkreditivs also gegen Übergabe der Dokumente, in Anspruch nimmt; dann ist der in der Akkreditivklausel vorgesehene Übergabeort auch Zahlungsort. Wenn aber der Verkäufer den Vertrag aufhebt und Schadenersatz geltend macht, ist die Akkreditivklausel nicht mehr anwendbar und der Käufer gemäss Art. 57 I lit. a) verpflichtet, Schadenersatz am Ort der Niederlassung des Verkäufers zu leisten.[23] Die Annahme eines gezogenen Wechsels (wenn dies im Vertrag nicht vorgesehen war)[24] oder das Recht des Käufers, durch Bankcheck zu zahlen,[25] modifiziert den Zahlungsort nicht. Die Benutzung eines **Incoterms®** beeinträchtigt den vertraglichen Zahlungsort nicht, weil Regel B1 zu allen Incoterms® keine eigenständige Regelung vorsieht, sondern lediglich daran erinnert, dass der Käufer den Kaufpreis entsprechend den kaufvertraglichen Bedingungen zu zahlen hat. Allerdings können die Incoterms® durch Festlegung des Lieferortes indirekt Einfluss auf die Bestimmung des Zahlungsortes haben, wenn der Zahlungsort gemäss Art. 57 I lit. b) zu bestimmen ist.[26]

Haben die Parteien den Zahlungsort weder ausdrücklich noch stillschweigend vereinbart, **8** so kann der Zahlungsort gemäss Art. 9 nach **Gebräuchen** bzw. **Gepflogenheiten** der Parteien bestimmbar sein.[27] Hat z. B. der Verkäufer in einer langfristigen Geschäftsbeziehung stets die Kosten der Zahlung getragen, so kann in Übereinstimmung mit dieser bisherigen Handhabung davon ausgegangen werden, dass der Ort der Niederlassung des Käufers der Zahlungsort ist.[28] Ist dem Verkäufer hingegen die direkte Abbuchung auf dem Konto des Käufers gestattet, so bestimmt der Ort der Niederlassung der Bank des Käufers den Zahlungsort.[29]

---

[21] Vgl. OLG Düsseldorf, 24.7.2007, CISG-online 1531, Rn. 83; zweifelnd OLG München, 9.7.1997, CISG-online 281 = BB 1997, 2295, wobei die Frage offen gelassen wurde, ob ein Dokumentenakkreditiv den Zahlungsort unberührt lasse oder den Zahlungsort als den Ort festschreibe, an dem das Dokumentenakkreditiv benutzbar ist. Vgl. *Bianca/Bonell/Maskow*, Art. 57, Anm. 2.8.; *Brunner*, Art. 57, Rn. 4; *Enderlein/Maskow/ Strohbach*, Art. 57, Anm. 8.3.; *Herber/Czerwenka*, Art. 57, Rn. 8; *Honsell/Schnyder/Straub*, Art. 47, Rn. 7; MünchKommHGB/*Benicke,* Art. 57, Rn. 4; *Staudinger/Magnus,* Art. 57, Rn. 8. A. A. *Piltz,* Internationales Kaufrecht, Rn. 4–137.
[22] Für die Ansicht, dass das Dokumentenakkreditiv den Zahlungsort unberührt lässt: OLG München, 9.7.1997, CISG-online 281 = BB 1997, 2295; *Piltz,* NJB 2000, 557; *Staudinger/Magnus,* Art. 57, Rn. 8; *Ferrari u. a./Mankowski*, Internationales Vertragsrecht, Art. 57, Rn. 6.
[23] Für den Zahlungsort bei Schadenersatz vgl. unten Rn. 29.
[24] Zum EKG vgl. Cass., Riv. dir. int. priv. proc. 1983, 338; *Staudinger/Magnus,* Art. 57, Rn. 8.
[25] OLG München, 9.7.1997, CISG-online 282.
[26] *Brunner,* Art. 57, Rn. 8.
[27] LG Bielefeld, 24.11.1998, CISG-online 697 = CLOUT Nr. 363 = IHR 2001, 199 ff.
[28] LG Bielefeld, 24.11.1998, CISG-online 697 = CLOUT Nr. 363 = IHR 2001, 199, 200d; *Ferrari u. a./ Mankowski*, Internationales Vertragsrecht, Art. 57, Rn. 4.
[29] LG Trier, 7.12.2000, CISG-online = IHR 2001, 35.

III. Zahlung gegen Übergabe der Ware oder der Dokumente, Art. 57 I lit. b)

1. Anwendungsbereich – Zug-um-Zug-Erfüllung

9   Art. 57 I lit. b) kommt nur dann zur Anwendung, wenn die Parteien einen Zahlungsort weder ausdrücklich noch stillschweigend vereinbart haben. Darüber hinaus muss für die Anwendbarkeit von Art. 57 I lit. b) die **Zahlung gegen Übergabe der Ware oder von Dokumenten** zu leisten sein. In einem solchen Fall muss der Käufer dem Verkäufer den Kaufpreis an dem Ort zahlen, an dem die Übergabe der Ware oder der Dokumente stattfindet. Ob Zahlung gegen Übergabe der Ware oder von Dokumenten zu erfolgen hat, ist eine Frage der Vertragsauslegung. Haben die Parteien nichts vereinbart, so richtet sich die Frage nach Art. 58.[30] Wenn die Parteien nichts anderes vereinbart haben, so hat der Käufer gemäss Art. 58 I den Preis zu zahlen, sobald ihm der Verkäufer die Ware oder die Dokumente, die zur Verfügung über die Ware berechtigen, zur Verfügung gestellt hat. Mit anderen Worten erhebt Art. 58 I die **Zug-um-Zug-Erfüllung** zu einem **allgemeinen Prinzip,** dem zufolge der Käufer den Kaufpreis Zug um Zug gegen die Lieferung der Ware oder der Dokumente zu zahlen hat.[31] Andererseits findet Art. 57 I lit. b) keine Anwendung, wenn eine der Parteien vorleistungspflichtig ist. Wenn z. B. ein Vertrag für die Lieferung und Installation von Maschinen die Zahlung des Kaufpreises in verschiedenen Tranchen vorsieht, z. B. je 30% bei Bestellung, bei Beginn der Installation und bei Beendigung der Installation sowie 10% bei Inbetriebnahme, kann nicht von einer Zug-um-Zug-Erfüllung gesprochen werden, weder bezüglich des Gesamtpreises noch bezüglich der einzelnen Tranchen, obwohl das Zahlungsregime das Kreditrisiko des Verkäufers abzusichern versucht; folglich muss Art. 57 I lit. a) angewendet werden.[32] Wenn Zahlung nach Vorlage eines Konnossements zu erfolgen hat, findet Art. 57 I lit. a) Anwendung, weil keine Zug-um-Zug-Erfüllung vereinbart wurde.[33]

2. Zahlung gegen Dokumente, Art. 58 I

10   Wenn Zahlung gegen Dokumente vereinbart wurde, ist der Zahlungsort der Ort, an dem die Übergabe der Dokumente stattfindet, welcher sich wiederum nach der ausdrücklichen oder stillschweigenden Parteivereinbarung richtet (Art. 6 i. V. m. Art. 34).[34] Wenn „**cash against documents**" (CAD) oder „**cash against delivery**" vereinbart wurde, so muss der Verkäufer die Dokumente grundsätzlich am Ort der Niederlassung des Käufers andienen.[35] Freilich können die Parteien aber auch vereinbaren, dass die Dokumente bei einer durch den Käufer zu bestimmenden Bank anzudienen sind, womit der Ort der Niederlassung der Bank zugleich Zahlungsort wäre.[36] Haben die Parteien ein **Dokumenteninkasso** vereinbart, welches die Handhabung der Dokumente durch eine Einreicherbank bzw. möglicherweise weitere Inkassobanken vorsieht, bis sie schlussendlich dem Bezogenen/ Käufer durch die vorlegende Bank angedient werden, so ist der Ort der Niederlassung des Käufers zugleich Zahlungsort.[37] Enthält der Kaufvertrag eine **Akkreditivklausel,** so wird

---

[30] Vgl. unten Art. 58 Rn. 5 ff.
[31] Vgl. unten Art. 58 Rn. 1.
[32] BGer, 18.1.1996, CISG-online 214 = BGE 122 III 43, 46 ff., m. Anm. *Schwenzer,* AJP 1996, 1051 f.; C. *Witz,* D. 1997, 224 f.; *Ferrari u. a./Mankowski,* Internationales Vertragsrecht, Art. 57, Rn. 19.
[33] ZGer Basel-Stadt, 3.12.1997, CISG-online 346 = CLOUT Nr. 221 = TranspR-IHR 1999, 11 = SZIER 1999, 190.
[34] Vgl. oben *Widmer Lüchinger,* Art. 34 Rn. 3; *Hager/Maultzsch,* 5. Aufl., Art. 57 Rn. 22.
[35] LG Nürnberg-Fürth, 27.2.2003, CISG-online 818 = IHR 2004, 20 („Cash against delivery"); *Hager/ Maultzsch,* 5. Aufl., Art. 57 Rn. 22; oben *Widmer Lüchinger,* Art. 34 Rn. 3; *Bianca/Bonell/Maskow,* Art. 57, Anm. 2.6.; *Kröll u. a./P. Butler/Harindranath,* Art. 57, Rn. 25.
[36] Vgl. oben *Widmer Lüchinger,* Art. 34 Rn. 3.
[37] *Hager/Maultzsch,* 5. Aufl., Art. 57 Rn. 23.

Zahlungsort 11–13 **Art. 57**

die Frage, ob das Dokumentenakkreditiv bei der eröffnenden Bank, üblicherweise im Land des Käufers, oder bei der bestätigenden Bank, üblicherweise im Land des Verkäufers, benutzbar ist, vom Wortlaut und der Interpretation der Akkreditivklausel abhängen.

Das CISG bestimmt nicht, auf **welche Dokumente** sich Art. 57 I lit. b) bezieht, wenn **11** dort von Zahlung gegen Übergabe von Dokumenten gesprochen wird. Da Art. 57 I lit. b) mit Art. 58 I im Zusammenhang steht, sollte der Begriff der Dokumente in beiden Artikeln einheitlich ausgelegt werden.[38] Mit Dokumenten in diesem Sinne sind daher alle operativen Handelspapiere gemeint, die der Kaufvertrag in seiner Liefer- und Zahlungsklausel als vorlegungspflichtig bezeichnet.[39] Bezeichnet der Kaufvertrag ausnahmsweise nicht die vorlegungspflichtigen Dokumente, so kommt es auch bei Art. 57 I lit. b) auf die Dokumente an, die zur Verfügung über die Ware berechtigen.

3. Verträge, die eine Beförderung der Ware erfordern oder Ware betreffen, die sich auf dem Transport befindet, wenn der Käufer sie mit der Massgabe versendet hat, dass die Ware oder die Dokumente dem Käufer nur gegen Zahlung des Kaufpreises zu übergeben sind, Art. 58 II

Wenn der Vertrag die Beförderung der Ware erfordert, wird der Verkäufer üblicherweise **12** in Vorleistung treten, da er bereits mit Übergabe der Ware an den ersten Beförderer zur Übermittlung an den Käufer liefert (Art. 31 lit. a)), wohingegen der Käufer den Kaufpreis erst dann zahlen muss, wenn sich die Ware oder die vertraglich vereinbarten Dokumente in seiner Verfügungsgewalt befinden, Art. 58 I. Freilich sieht **Art. 58 II** vor, dass der Verkäufer die Ware mit der **Massgabe** versenden kann, dass die **Ware** oder die **Dokumente,** die zur Verfügung darüber berechtigen, dem Käufer **nur gegen Zahlung des Kaufpreises** zu übergeben sind. Hat der Verkäufer die Ware mit dieser Massgabe versandt, so finden Lieferung und Zahlung Zug um Zug statt, so dass Art. 57 I lit. b) Anwendung findet.[40] Eine solche Massgabe muss der Verkäufer mit dem Beförderer vereinbaren, wenn die Beförderung Sache des Verkäufers ist, wie z. B. bei Verwendung einer C-Klausel der Incoterms®.[41] Wird Ware verkauft, die sich bereits auf dem Transport befindet, so kann die hier vertretene Lösung auch auf diese Fallgruppe angewendet werden.[42]

4. Verträge über Ware, die bei einer Drittpartei lagert

Art. 57 I lit. b) findet auch auf Kaufverträge Anwendung, die Ware betreffen, die sich bei **13** einem Lagerhalter in einem **Lagerhaus** befindet und der Lagerhalter die Ware nur gegen Zahlung des Kaufpreises herauszugeben hat.[43] Eine solche Abwicklung kann sich aus einer entsprechenden Vereinbarung des Verkäufers und des Käufers oder einer entsprechenden Instruktion des Verkäufers an den Lagerhalter ergeben. Das Instruktionsrecht des Verkäufers ergibt sich aus dem allgemeinen Prinzip, das hinter **Art. 58 II** steht. Besteht hingegen eine solche Vereinbarung zwischen den Parteien nicht und macht der Verkäufer auch nicht von seinem Instruktionsrecht nach Art. 58 II Gebrauch, so fällt der Verkauf von Ware, die bei einer Drittpartei lagert, in den Anwendungsbereich des Art. 57 I lit. a), weil die Zahlung dann nicht Zug um Zug gegen Lieferung erfolgt.[44]

---

[38] Vgl. unten Art. 58 Rn. 16; *Hager/Maultzsch*, 5. Aufl., Art. 57 Rn. 23; *Kröll u. a./P. Butler/Harindranath*, Art. 57, Rn. 26.
[39] Vgl. unten Art. 58 Rn. 16. A. A. *Ferrari u. a./Mankowski*, Internationales Vertragsrecht, Art. 57, Rn. 20: nur die zur Verfügung über die Ware berechtigenden Traditionspapiere.
[40] Vgl. *Kröll u. a./P. Butler/Harindranath*, Art. 57, Rn. 23. A. A. BGHZ 74, 136, 142 ff. zum EKG; zur Anwendung dieser Ansicht auch auf das CISG vgl. *Koch,* RIW 1996, 379, 381.
[41] Vgl. *Hager/Maultzsch*, 5. Aufl., Art. 58 Rn. 7, die auch auf die Situation verweisen, dass der Käufer die Beförderung zu organisieren hat. Dieser Hinweis läuft meines Erachtens fehl, da ein Vertrag, demgemäss der Käufer die Beförderung zu organisieren hat, nicht als Vertrag im Sinne von Art. 31 lit. a), der eine Beförderung der Ware erfordert, qualifiziert werden kann. So auch oben *Widmer Lüchinger*, Art. 31 Rn. 15.
[42] *Hager/Maultzsch*, 5. Aufl., Art. 57 Rn. 21.
[43] *Hager/Maultzsch*, 5. Aufl., Art. 57 Rn. 14; *Kröll u. a./P. Butler/Harindranath*, Art. 57, Rn. 21.
[44] *Hager/Maultzsch*, 5. Aufl., Art. 57 Rn. 14.

IV. Zahlung am Ort der Niederlassung des Verkäufers, Art. 57 I lit. a)

1. Anwendungsbereich – Vorleistungspflicht einer der Parteien

14 Art. 57 I lit. a) findet nur dann Anwendung, wenn die Parteien keine Vereinbarung über den Zahlungsort getroffen haben und der Vertrag auch keine Zug-um-Zug-Erfüllung vorsieht. Anders ausgedrückt findet Art. 57 I lit. a) nur dann Anwendung, wenn eine Partei verpflichtet ist, in **Vorleistung** zu treten.[45] Wenn z. B. der Verkäufer die Ware zu verschiffen und der Käufer den Kaufpreis erst 85 Tage nach Verschiffung zu zahlen hat, muss der Verkäufer in Vorleistung treten, was zur Folge hat, dass der Käufer gemäss Art. 57 I lit. a) den Kaufpreis am Ort der Niederlassung des Verkäufers zu zahlen hat.[46]

2. Offene Rechnung

15 Wenn die Parteien ihr Geschäft auf Basis **offener Rechnungen** abwickeln, was üblicherweise vor allem dann der Fall sein wird, wenn sich die Parteien bereits kennen und einander vertrauen, also zumeist in einer langfristigen Geschäftsbeziehung zu einander stehen, ist es der Verkäufer, der mit Lieferung der Ware in Vorleistung tritt und erst zu einem späteren Zeitpunkt nach Rechnungsstellung vom Käufer Zahlung erhält. Oft wird die Rechnung die Ware begleiten und den Käufer auffordern, den Rechnungsbetrag innerhalb eines bestimmten Zeitraums zu begleichen.[47] Auch die **Zahlungsklauseln** „net cash" oder „net cash after receipt of the goods" führen im Ergebnis zur Zahlungsabwicklung über offene Rechnungen.[48]

3. Verträge, welche die Beförderung der Ware erfordern oder Ware betreffen, die sich auf dem Transport oder in einem Lagerhaus bei einer Drittpartei befindet, wenn der Verkäufer sie nicht mit der Massgabe versendet hat, dass die Ware oder die Dokumente dem Käufer nur gegen Zahlung zu übergeben sind

16 Art. 57 I lit. a) findet auf Verträge Anwendung, welche die Beförderung der Ware erfordern, wenn der Verkäufer von seinem Instruktionsrecht nach Art. 58 II keinen Gebrauch gemacht hat, die Ware also nicht mit der Massgabe versendet hat, dass die Ware oder die Dokumente dem Käufer nur gegen Zahlung des Kaufpreises zu übergeben sind.[49] In einem solchen Fall ist der Verkäufer verpflichtet, mit der **Lieferung der Ware** in **Vorleistung** zu treten.[50] Das Gleiche gilt für den Verkauf von Ware, die sich **auf dem Transport** befindet.[51] Wenn sich die Ware in einem **Lagerhaus** bei einer Drittpartei befindet und die Parteien nicht vereinbart haben, dass die Ware oder die Dokumente nur gegen Zahlung herausgegeben werden, so erfüllt der Verkäufer seine Lieferpflicht vor Empfang der Zahlung.[52]

4. Wechsel der Niederlassung durch den Verkäufer, Art. 57 II

17 Wo der Verkäufer seine **Niederlassung** hat, bestimmt sich **autonom** nach Art. 10.[53] Für die Zwecke der Zahlung kommt es auf die Niederlassung des Verkäufers **im Zeitpunkt**

---

[45] LG Krefeld, 20.9.2006, CISG-online 1459 = IHR 2007, 161, 162; *Honsell/Schnyder/Straub*, Art. 57, Rn. 16; *Ferrari u. a./Mankowski*, Internationales Vertragsrecht, Art. 57, Rn. 9.
[46] LG Krefeld, 20.9.2006, CISG-online 1459 = IHR 2007, 161, 162; vgl. LG Freiburg, 26.4.2002, CISG-online 690 = IHR 2002, 72, 73.
[47] Vgl. OGH, 10.11.1994, CISG-online 117 = IPRax 1996, 137, 139.
[48] *Hager/Maultzsch*, 5. Aufl., Art. 57 Rn. 3; *Soergel/Lüderitz/Budzikiewicz*, Art. 57, Rn. 3; *Ferrari u. a./* Mankowski, Internationales Vertragsrecht, Art. 57, Rn. 8.
[49] LG Krefeld, 20.9.2006, CISG-online 1459 = IHR 2007, 161, 162.
[50] Vgl. unten Art. 58 Rn. 12.
[51] Vgl. unten Art. 58 Rn. 13.
[52] Vgl. unten Art. 58 Rn. 14.
[53] *Schwenzer/Hachem*, CISG Commentary, Art. 10, Rn. 2.

der **Zahlung** an.[54] Wechselt der Verkäufer seine Niederlassung zwischen Vertragsschluss und Zahlung, muss der Käufer den Kaufpreis an der neuen Niederlassung zahlen.[55] Die Verpflichtung des Käufers zur Zahlung des Kaufpreises an der Niederlassung des Verkäufers im Zeitpunkt der Zahlung folgt mittelbar aus Art. 57 II.[56] Freilich besteht diese Verpflichtung nur dann, wenn der Verkäufer den Käufer über den Wechsel seiner Niederlassung zeitgerecht informiert hat.[57] Diese **Informationspflicht** ergibt sich aus Art. 7 II als Teil der allgemeinen Kooperations- und Informationspflicht.[58] Unterlässt es der Verkäufer, den Käufer über den Wechsel seiner Niederlassung zu informieren, so muss er die Zahlung des Käufers an dem Ort seiner ursprünglichen Niederlassung akzeptieren, was sich aus Art. 80 ergibt.[59] Der Verkäufer kann sich auch dann nicht auf seine neue Niederlassung berufen, wenn die Anzeige des Niederlassungswechsels beim Käufer nicht angekommen ist, da der **Verkäufer** entgegen der allgemeinen Regel des Art. 27 das **Risiko der Verzögerung** bzw. **des Nichteintreffens** trägt. Diese Risikoverteilung ergibt sich aus der Überlegung, dass der Wechsel der Niederlassung alleine in der Sphäre des Verkäufers und ausserhalb des Einflussbereichs des Käufers liegt.[60] Sollte das Geld, dass der Käufer am ursprünglichen Ort der Niederlassung des Verkäufers gezahlt hat, ihm später rückerstattet werden, so lebt die Pflicht zur Kaufpreiszahlung wieder auf, freilich ohne dass der Käufer wegen zu spät erfolgter Zahlung haftbar gemacht werden könnte; das Verspätungsrisiko trägt vielmehr der Verkäufer.[61]

Hat der Verkäufer seine Niederlassung gemäss Art. 57 gewechselt, so ist der Käufer nicht nur verpflichtet, am neuen Ort zu zahlen, sondern auch alle **der Zahlung vorausgehenden Pflichten** zu erfüllen, um rechtzeitige Zahlung an diesem Ort zu bewirken. So kann der Käufer z. B. verpflichtet sein, **neue devisenrechtliche Vorschriften** zu beachten.[62] Je nach Einzelfall kann der Käufer auch verpflichtet sein, **früher als ursprünglich anvisiert** zu zahlen, um den rechtzeitigen Eingang der Zahlung beim Verkäufer an seiner neuen Niederlassung zu gewährleisten.[63] Der Käufer trägt die Gefahr des Nichteintreffens des Geldes, selbst wenn sich das Risiko durch den Niederlassungswechsel des Verkäufers erhöht haben sollte.[64]

Der Verkäufer trägt gemäss Art. 57 II alle mit der Zahlung zusammenhängenden **Mehrkosten,** die durch den Wechsel seiner Niederlassung nach Vertragsschluss entstehen. Dies beinhaltet auch entgangene Zinsen oder Währungsschäden, sofern sie eine Folge des Wechsels der Niederlassung durch den Verkäufer sind.[65]

---

[54] *Hager/Maultzsch,* 5. Aufl., Art. 57 Rn. 6; *Piltz,* Internationales Kaufrecht, Rn. 4–142; MünchKomm/ *P. Huber,* Art. 57, Rn. 19.
[55] *Hager/Maultzsch,* 5. Aufl., Art. 57 Rn. 6.
[56] *Hager/Maultzsch,* 5. Aufl., Art. 57 Rn. 6; *Honsell/Schnyder/Straub,* Art. 57, Rn. 21.
[57] *Piltz,* Internationales Kaufrecht, Rn. 4–142; MünchKomm/*P. Huber,* Art. 57, Rn. 21; *Honsell/Schnyder/ Straub,* Art. 57, Rn. 22.
[58] Vgl. oben Art. 53 Rn. 39. Vgl. Art. 6.1.6 II PICC, Anm. 3.
[59] *Hager/Maultzsch,* 5. Aufl., Art. 57 Rn. 6; *Brunner,* Art. 57, Rn. 10; MünchKomm/*P. Huber,* Art. 57, Rn. 21.
[60] *Bianca/Bonell/Maskow,* Art. 57, Anm. 2.2.; *Herber/Czerwenka,* Art. 57, Rn. 11; *Hager/Maultzsch,* 5. Aufl., Art. 57 Rn. 6; MünchKomm/*P. Huber,* Art. 57, Rn. 21; *Honsell/Schnyder/Straub,* Art. 57, Rn. 22; *Kröll u. a./ P. Butler/Harindranath,* Art. 57, Rn. 15.
[61] *Hager/Maultzsch,* 5. Aufl., Art. 57 Rn. 6; *Karollus,* S. 168, Anm. 14.
[62] *Hager/Maultzsch,* 5. Aufl., Art. 57 Rn. 7; *Kröll u. a./P. Butler/Harindranath,* Art. 57, Rn. 14.
[63] *Hager/Maultzsch,* 5. Aufl., Art. 57 Rn. 7.
[64] *Bamberger/Roth/Saenger,* Art. 57, Rn. 2; *Karollus,* S. 168; *Reinhart,* Art. 57, Rn. 7; MünchKomm/*P. Huber,* Art. 57, Rn. 22; *Kröll u. a./P. Butler/Harindranath,* Art. 57, Rn. 14. A. A. *Herber/Czerwenka,* Art. 57, Rn. 9; *Loewe,* Art. 57, S. 77; MünchKommHGB/*Benicke,* Art. 57, Rn. 12; *Witz/Salger/Lorenz/Witz,* Art. 57, Rn. 14; *Honsell/Schnyder/Straub,* Art. 57, Rn. 23.
[65] *Bianca/Bonell/Maskow,* Art. 57, Anm. 2.9.; *Hager/Maultzsch,* 5. Aufl., Art. 57 Rn. 7; *Ferrari u. a./Mankowski,* Internationales Vertragsrecht, Art. 57, Rn. 10; für Zinsen vgl. *Honsell/Schnyder/Straub,* Art. 57, Rn. 19.

V. Erfüllung von Zahlungspflichten – Risiko des Verlusts und der Verzögerung

20 Der Käufer trägt das Risiko, dass seine Zahlung **vollständig** und **zeitgerecht** am Zahlungsort **ankommt**. Er trägt das Risiko des Nichteintreffens und der Verzögerung.[66] Dazu hat er die Zahlung vorzunehmen sowie sämtliche Massnahmen zu treffen und Formalitäten zu erfüllen, die nach Vertrag oder Gesetz erforderlich sind, damit Zahlung geleistet werden kann (Art. 54). Wenn der Käufer eine Drittpartei in die Ausführung der Zahlung einbezieht, trägt er gemäss Art. 79 II die Verantwortung für etwaiges Fehlverhalten dieser Drittpartei.[67] Eine Haftungsbefreiung ist nur unter den begrenzten Möglichkeiten des Art. 79 und des Art. 80 denkbar.[68] Insbesondere befreit Art. 79 den Käufer nicht vom Risiko, über genügend ausländische Devisen zu verfügen.[69]

VI. Abtretung des Anspruchs auf Kaufpreiszahlung – Auswirkungen auf den Zahlungsort

21 In der Praxis wird der Verkäufer seinen Anspruch auf Kaufpreiszahlung oft an eine Drittpartei abtreten, um sein Geschäft zu finanzieren, z. B. an seinen Lieferanten oder einen Finanzdienstleister.[70] Wenn eine gültige **Abtretung der Kaufpreisforderung** nach dem anwendbaren Recht vorliegt, stellt sich die Frage, wo die abgetretene Forderung zu erfüllen ist. Keine Probleme treten auf, wenn der Zahlungsort von den Parteien im Kaufvertrag bestimmt wurde oder sich aus Art. 57 I lit. b) ergibt, wenn also Zahlung an dem Ort zu erfolgen hat, an dem die Übergabe der Ware oder der Dokumenten stattfindet. Nur in den Fällen, in denen die Niederlassung des Verkäufers den Zahlungsort gemäss **Art. 57 I lit. a)** bestimmt, stellt sich das Problem, ob der Käufer den Kaufpreis **am Ort der Niederlassung des Zedenten/Verkäufers** oder **des Zessionars** zahlen muss. Eine Auffassung geht dahin, Art. 57 II als allgemeines Prinzip gemäss Art. 7 II aufzufassen, mit der Folge, dass der Käufer den Kaufpreis am Ort der Niederlassung des Zessionars zu zahlen hat.[71] Eine Gegenansicht will nationales Recht nach Massgabe des anwendbaren Internationalen Privatrechts zur Anwendung bringen, um zu entscheiden, ob der Käufer an den Zedenten mit Erfüllungswirkung zahlen kann, was – stark verallgemeinert – üblicherweise bis zur Anzeige der Abtretung möglich ist.[72] Obwohl die einheitsrechtliche Ansicht korrekterweise davon aus-

---

[66] *Bianca/Bonell/Maskow*, Art. 57, Anm. 2.5.; *Hager/Maultzsch*, 5. Aufl., Art. 57 Rn. 4; *Enderlein/Maskow/Strohbach*, Art. 57, Anm. 1.2.; *Herber/Czerwenka*, Art. 57, Rn. 3; *MünchKommHGB/Benicke*, Art. 57, Rn. 9; *Staudinger/Magnus*, Art. 57, Rn. 19; *Kröll u. a./P. Butler/Harindranath*, Art. 57, Rn. 13; *Ferrari u. a./Mankowski*, Internationales Vertragsrecht, Art. 57, Rn. 21.

[67] AG Alsfeld, 12.5.1995, CISG-online 170 = NJW-RR 1996, 120 ff.: Der Käufer zahlte an eine Person, die sich selbst als Agent des Verkäufers ausgegeben hatte, in Wahrheit aber das Geld für ihre eigenen Zwecke missbrauchte; unten *Schwenzer*, Art. 79 Rn. 25.

[68] *Staudinger/Magnus*, Art. 57, Rn. 19.

[69] Int. Ct. Russian CCI, 17.10.1995, CISG-online 207 = CLOUT Nr. 142; unten *Schwenzer*, Art. 79 Rn. 25.

[70] Zur Abtretung und Abtretbarkeit vgl. oben Art. 53 Rn. 29.

[71] OLG Celle, 11.11.1998, CISG-online 507 = IPRax 1999, 456, m. krit. Anm. *Gebauer*, IPRax 1999, 432 ff., der zwar der Anwendbarkeit des CISG zustimmt, aber die Anwendung von Art. 57 II und das Ergebnis ablehnt, das am Ort der Niederlassung des Zessionars zu zahlen ist. Die Frage wurde ausdrücklich offen gelassen von BGH, 7.11.2001, CISG-online 682; *Hager/Maultzsch*, 5. Aufl., Art. 57 Rn. 8; *Staudinger/Magnus*, Art. 57, Rn. 18; *Ferrari u. a./Mankowski*, Internationales Vertragsrecht, Art. 57, Rn. 17; unklar *Brunner*, Art. 57, Rn. 11, dem zufolge der Ort der Niederlassung des Zessionars erst nach Anzeige der Abtretung an den Käufer massgebend sein soll.

[72] *C. Witz*, Draft Digest, S. 424, 433 ff.; *Lehner*, Geldschulden, S. 75; *MünchKomm/P. Huber*, Art. 57, Rn. 3; *Witz/Salger/Lorenz/Witz*, Art. 57, Rn. 15; *Piltz*, Internationales Kaufrecht, Rn. 4–142. A. A. *Bianca/Bonell/Maskow*, Art. 57, Anm. 3.1.; *Herber/Czerwenka*, Art. 57, Rn. 10; *Honsell/Schnyder/Straub*, Art. 57, Rn. 24.

Zahlungsort 22, 23 **Art. 57**

geht, dass ohne Wechsel des Zahlungsortes an den Ort der Niederlassung des Zessionars die Zahlung praktisch nicht möglich sein wird, ist es dennoch unangemessen, die Risiken und Kosten des Zahlungsortwechsels dem Käufer in Anwendung von Art. 57 II aufzubürden.[73] Daher wird hier die Auffassung vertreten, dass die Erfüllungswirkung einer Zahlung auf einen abgetretenen Kaufpreisanspruch aus einem CISG-Vertrag nach dem **auf die Abtretung anwendbaren nationalen Recht** zu bestimmen ist.

Ferner ist darauf hinzuweisen, dass die Abtretung und die damit einhergehende Änderung 22 des Zahlungsortes auch **prozessrechtliche Folgen** haben können, wenn sich die internationale Zuständigkeit nach dem Erfüllungsort bestimmt.[74]

VII. Internationale Zuständigkeit am Zahlungsort

1. Brüsseler Übereinkommen/Lugano-Übereinkommen/Nationale Zuständigkeitsregeln

Das CISG ist ein Übereinkommen, das materiell-rechtliche Fragen des Vertragsschlusses 23 und des Kaufrechts regelt und **prozessuale Fragen grundsätzlich nicht** zum Gegenstand hat. Allerdings kann das CISG **prozessuale Wirkungen** zeitigen, wenn das anwendbare Prozessrecht des Forums für seine Gerichte eine **internationale Zuständigkeit am Erfüllungsort** vorsieht. Vorschriften, welche die Gerichte des Staates, in dem der Erfüllungsort liegt, für international zuständig erklären, finden sich in vielen nationalen Prozessordnungen[75] sowie in internationalen Instrumenten, wie z. B. Art. 5 I des Brüsseler Übereinkommens, das freilich durch eine Brüsseler Verordnung (auch im Verhältnis zu Dänemark) ersetzt wurde,[76] sowie Art. 5 I des Lugano Übereinkommens, das im Verhältnis zu den EFTA-Staaten gilt.[77] Für die Vorschriften dieser internationalen Instrumente gilt, dass der Erfüllungsort nicht für alle Pflichten aus einem Vertrag einheitlich durch die charakteristische Leistung des Vertrages bestimmt wird, was im Falle eines Kaufvertrages die Pflicht des Verkäufers zur Lieferung der Ware wäre,[78] sondern durch die **im Streit liegende Pflicht,** welche auch die Pflicht des Käufers zur Zahlung des Kaufpreises sein kann.[79] Wenn die im Streit liegende Pflicht die Pflicht des Käufers zur Zahlung des Kaufpreises ist, so **qualifizieren** die Vorschriften dieser internationalen Instrumente den **Erfüllungsort** *lege causae,*[80] d. h. in Anwendung des auf den Vertrag im Ganzen anwendbaren Rechts *(lex contractus).*[81] Wenn also die im Streit liegende Pflicht die Pflicht des Käufers zur Kaufpreiszahlung und das CISG das auf den Vertrag anwendbare

---

[73] Vgl. *Honsell/Schnyder/Straub,* Art. 57, Rn. 23.
[74] OLG Celle, 11.11.1998, CISG-online 507 = IPRax 1999, 456, m. Anm. *Gebauer,* IPRax 1999, 432, 434 ff.; *Staudinger/Magnus,* Art. 57, Rn. 18; *Brunner,* Art. 57, Rn. 11; *Ferrari u. a./Mankowski,* Internationales Vertragsrecht, Art. 57, Rn. 16.
[75] Deutschland: § 29 ZPO; Schweiz: Art. 113 IPRG; Frankreich: Art. 46 CCP; Belgien: Art. 635 Code Judiciare; Portugal: Art. 65 CCP; Spanien: Art. 22 Ley Orgánica del Poder Judicial; Türkei: Art. 40 des türkischen IPR-Gesetzes von 2007 i. V. m. Art. 10 der neuen türkischen ZPO von 2011.
[76] Vgl. unten Rn. 25 ff. Am 1. Juli 2007 schlossen die Europäische Gemeinschaft und das Königreich Dänemark ein Übereinkommen über die Zuständigkeit sowie die Anerkennung und Vollstreckbarkeit von Urteilen in Zivil- und Handelssachen, dem gemäss die Brüsseler Verordnung auch im Verhältnis zu Dänemark Anwendung findet, OJ L 299, S. 62.
[77] Das Lugano-Übereinkommen ist seinerseits revidiert worden, um den Entwicklungen des Brüsseler Übereinkommens und der Brüsseler Verordnung Rechnung zu tragen, vgl. unten Rn. 27.
[78] Anders mit Bezug auf mehrere Ansprüche auf Grund verschiedener Verpflichtungen: Cass., 19.6.2000, CISG-online 1317 = CLOUT Nr. 647, englische Übersetzung bei CISG Pace.
[79] EuGH, 6.10.1976, Rs. 14/76 *(De Bloos/Bouyer),* Slg. 1497 betr. Brüsseler Übereinkommen; BGer, 18.1.1996, CISG-online 214 = BGE 122 III 43 betr. Lugano-Übereinkommen; *Schack,* Zivilverfahrensrecht, Rn. 265 ff.
[80] EuGH, 6.10.1976, Rs. 12/76 *(Industrie Tessili Italiana Como/Dunlop AG),* Slg. 1473 = NJW 1977, 491, m. Anm. *Geimer;* zuletzt bestätigt in EuGH, 28.9.1999, Rs. C-440/97 *(GIE Groupe Concorde/The Master of the vessel Suhadiwarno Panjan),* Slg. 1999, I-6307; BGH, 4.4.1979, BGHZ 74, 136 ff.
[81] *Schack,* Zivilverfahrensrecht, Rn. 269 ff.

Recht ist, so kann sich eine internationale Zuständigkeit an dem **nach Art. 57 zu bestimmenden Erfüllungsort (Zahlungsort)** ergeben.[82] Haben die Parteien den Zahlungsort vertraglich nicht bestimmt,[83] so wird dies im Zweifel der Ort der Niederlassung des Verkäufers sein.[84] Folglich wird der Verkäufer berechtigt sein, seine sich aus einem CISG-Vertrag ergebende Kaufpreisklage vor den staatlichen Gerichten am Ort seiner Niederlassung einzuleiten.[85]

24 Das Ergebnis eines **sog. Verkäufer- bzw. Gläubigergerichtsstands** ist seit Beginn dieser Rechtsprechung stark kritisiert worden. Um dieses unerwünschte Ergebnis zu vermeiden, ist vorgeschlagen worden, dass der **Erfüllungsort autonom nach dem anwendbaren Prozessrecht** des Forums und ohne Rückgriff auf das auf den Vertrag anwendbare Recht zu bestimmen sei.[86] Diese Ansicht trägt dem Problem Rechnung, dass der Zweck der materiell-rechtlichen Vorschriften des CISG zum Zahlungsort ein völlig anderer ist als derjenige der Prozessrechte, welche die Gerichte am Erfüllungsort für international zuständig erklären.[87] Insbesondere Art. 57 II würde besorgniserregende Ergebnisse verursachen, wenn nach einem **Wechsel der Niederlassung** durch den Verkäufer die internationale Zuständigkeit am Ort seiner neuen Niederlassung anerkannt würde, welche in einem anderen Staat liegen kann.[88] Ein weiteres unerwünschtes Ergebnis würde produziert, wenn im Falle der **Abtretung der Kaufpreisforderung** die Gerichte am Ort der Niederlassung des Zessionars international zuständig wären, weil der Käufer dort den Kaufpreis zu zahlen hat.[89] Bereits anlässlich der Wiener Konferenz hatte die Bundesrepublik Deutschland den Vorschlag gemacht, eine Vorschrift aufzunehmen, die klarstellen sollte, dass den Gerichten am Erfüllungsort keine Zuständigkeit kraft dieses Übereinkommens zukommen sollte.[90] Dieser Vorschlag wurde damals allerdings mit dem Argument verworfen, dass die Konferenz keine Mandat habe, über prozessuale Fragen, wie die internationale Zuständigkeit, zu verhandeln.[91]

---

[82] Zu Art. 57 I lit. a) vgl. BGH, 4.12.1996, CISG-online 260 = NJW-RR 1997, 690; BGH, 26.3.1992, CISG-online 67 = EuZw 1992, 514 (obiter); OLG München, 9.7.1997, CISG-online 282; Cass. Civ. 1er, 26.6.2001, CISG-online 695 = D. 2001, 2593; CA Paris, 10.11.1993, CISG-online 80 = JCP 1994, II, 22314, m. Anm. *Audit;* CA Grenoble, 16.6.1993, CISG-online 90, m. Anm. *Callaghan,* 14 J.L. & Com. (1995), 183 ff.; BGer, 18.1.1996, CISG-online 214 = BGE 122 III 43, m. krit. Anm. *Schwenzer,* AJP 1996, 1050 ff.; Cass., 9.6.1995, CISG-online 314 (obiter); Sø og Handelsretten, 1. 7. 1992, CISG-online 459 = UfR 1992, A, 920; Østre Landsret, 22.1.1996, CISG-online 362 = UfR 1996, 616; Hof van Beroep Gent, 15.5.2002, CISG-online 746; RB Kortrijk, 27.6.1997, CISG-online 529; Gerechtshof Amsterdam, 20.11.1997, CISG-online 553; Gerechtshof 's-Hertogenbosch, 5.2.1997, CISG-online 542; Gerechtshof 's-Hertogenbosch, 26.10.1994, CISG-online 318; Audiencia Provincial de Navarra, 23.7.1999, CISG-online 1342. Zu Art. 59 I EKG vgl. EuGH, 29.6.1994, Rs. C-288/92 *(Custom Made Commercial Ltd./Stawa Metallbau GmbH),* CLOUT Nr. 298 = Slg. 1994, I-2913, 2949 ff. = IPRax 1995, 31, m. abl. Anm. *Jayme,* IPRax 1995, 13, m. Anm. *Koch,* RIW 1996, 379; das Urteil des EuGH beruhte auf einer Vorlage durch den BGH, 26.3.1992, CISG-online 67 = EuZW 1992, 514. Gleiches gilt für § 29 ZPO i. V. m. Art. 57 I lit. a) vgl. BGH, 4.12.1996, CISG-online 260, NJW-RR 1997, 690.

[83] Vgl. BGH, 25.2.2004, CISG-online 1051 betr. Art. 57 I lit. b).

[84] Vgl. oben Rn. 1, 14 ff.

[85] EuGH, 29.6.1994, CISG-online 272 = RIW 1994, 676; BGH, 11.12.1996, CISG-online 225 = NJW 1997, 870; BGer, 18.1.1996, CISG-online 214 = BGE 122 III 343 = Rev. crit. dr. int. privé 1999, 122, m. Anm. *Ancel/Muir Watt;* Gerechtshof Amsterdam, 20.11.1997, CISG-online 553 = NIPR 1998, Nr. 220; vgl. *Magnus,* IHR 2000, 45 ff.

[86] *Schack,* Zivilverfahrensrecht, Rn. 271 ff.; *ders.,* IPRax 1986, 82, 84; *ders.,* ZIP 1995, 661; *Schwenzer,* IPRax 1989, 274. Vgl. *De Cristofaro,* Rev. dr. unif. 2000, 43 ff.

[87] *Hager/Maultzsch,* 5. Aufl., Art. 57 Rn. 11.

[88] *Hager/Maultzsch,* 5. Aufl., Art. 57 Rn. 11. A. A. OLG München, 9.7.1997, CISG-online 282 (obiter).

[89] Vgl. oben Rn. 21 f.; *Schack,* Zivilverfahrensrecht, Rn. 272. A. A. OLG Celle, 11.11.1998, CISG-online 507 = IPRax 1999, 456, 458, m. krit. Anm. *Bauer,* IPRax 1999, 432 ff.: das Gericht verneinte seine Zuständigkeit betr. eines zur Aufrechnung gestellten Kaufpreisanspruchs des Zessionars. Die Frage wurde offengelassen vom BGH, 7.11.2001, CISG-online 682 = IHR 2002, 31, 34.

[90] O. R., S. 122, Nr. 3; zur Diskussion des Vorschlags vgl. O. R., S. 368, 369, Art. 53, Nr. 27–35.

[91] O. R., S. 122, Nr. 5; O. R., S. 369, Nr. 30, 31, 33.

2. EUGVO und revidiertes Lugano-Übereinkommen

Für alle Staaten der europäischen Gemeinschaft versucht die EUGVO[92] die prozessrechtlichen Probleme im Zusammenhang mit dem Erfüllungsort zu lösen, in dem **Art. 5 I lit. b) EUGVO** eine **autonome Bestimmung** des **Erfüllungsorts für Kaufverträge** vorsieht. Haben die Parteien nichts anderes vereinbart, so soll der Erfüllungsort der im Streit liegenden Pflicht an dem Ort in einem EG-Mitgliedstaat liegen, an dem nach dem Vertrag die Ware geliefert wurde oder zu liefern war. Nach dieser Vorschrift wird also nicht auf die im Streit liegende Pflicht, sondern auf den Vertrag im Ganzen abgestellt. Handelt es sich bei der im Streit liegenden Pflicht um die Pflicht zur Zahlung des Kaufpreises, so sind nicht die Gerichte am Zahlungsort international zuständig, sondern die Gerichte am **Erfüllungsort der charakteristischen Leistung** des Kaufvertrags, also der Pflicht des Verkäufers zur **Lieferung der Ware**.[93] Folglich muss der Verkäufer seine Kaufpreisklage – sofern nichts anderes vereinbart worden ist – an dem Ort einleiten, an dem er seine Pflicht zur Lieferung der Ware **faktisch erfüllt** hat bzw. hätte erfüllen sollen.[94] Die Entstehungsgeschichte der EUGVO belegt, dass der Ort, an dem die Ware geliefert wurde bzw. hätte geliefert werden sollen, sich nicht nach dem auf den Vertrag anwendbaren Recht, sondern **autonom** bestimmt.[95] Die Begrifflichkeiten der EUGVO sind durch die Rechtsprechung der Gerichte der Mitgliedstaaten und des Europäischen Gerichtshofs noch nicht vollständig geklärt. Der herrschenden Meinung zufolge verweist die „faktische" Lieferung der Ware auf den Ort, an dem der Käufer **die Ware physisch übernimmt**.[96] Bestehen nach dieser Definition mehr als ein Lieferort, so sind die Gerichte des Ortes, zu dem die engste Verbindung besteht, für alle Ansprüche zuständig.[97] **Vertragliche Erfüllungsortsvereinbarungen,** die ausschliesslich dazu dienen, eine Zuständigkeit der Gerichte am vertraglichen Lieferort zu begründen, bleiben nach Art. 5 I lit. b) EUGVO unberücksichtigt, es sei denn, sie stellten eine Gerichtsstandvereinbarung dar, die den anwendbaren Schriftlichkeitsvoraussetzungen genügt.[98] Erfordert der Kaufvertrag die **Beförderung der Ware,** so wird der Ort der physischen Übernahme nach

---

[92] Verordnung (EG) Nr. 44/2001 des Rates über die gerichtliche Zuständigkeit und die Anerkennung und Vollstreckung von Entscheidungen in Zivil- und Handelssachen vom 22.10.2000, AblEG Nr. L 12v. 2001, S. 1. Im Verhältnis zu Dänemark vgl. oben Rn. 23.

[93] EuGH, 25.2.2010, Rs. C-381/08 *(Car Trim GmbH/KeySafety Systems Srl)*, NJW 2010, 1059; EuGH, 3.5.2007, Rs. C-386/05 *(Color Drack GmbH/Lexx International Vertriebs GmbH)*, Slg. 2007, I-3699; BGH, 23.6.2010, CISG-online 2129; OGH, 14.12.2004, CISG-online 1018; Cass., 14.6.2007, CISG-online 1702 = IHR 2009, 74, 75 ff.; Schack, Zivilverfahrensrecht, Rn. 273a; *Kannowski,* IHR 2008, 2, 5; oben *Widmer Lüchinger,* Art. 31 Rn. 89, die auf Art. 46 des französischen Nouveau code de procédure civile als Regelungsmodell für den neuen Art. 5 EUGVO verweist. Sie verweist auch auf den Entwurf des American Law Institute (UNIDROIT Working Group on Transnational Civil Procedure) sowie auf den Entwurf der Haager Konvention über internationale Zuständigkeit und Anerkennung und Vollstreckung.

[94] Vgl. oben *Widmer Lüchinger,* Art. 31 Rn. 90. Übersehen von LG Giessen, 17.12.2002, CISG-online 766 = IHR 2003, 276 ff.; LG Nürnberg-Fürth, 27.2.2003, CISG-online 818 = IHR 2004, 20.

[95] EuGH, 25.2.2010, Rs. C-381/08 *(Car Trim GmbH/KeySafety Systems Srl)*, NJW 2010, 1059, 1061; EuGH, 3.5.2007, Rs. C-386/05 *(Color Drack GmbH/Lexx International Vertriebs GmbH)*, Slg. 2007, I-3699; BGH, 23.6.2010, CISG-online 2129; LG Neubrandenburg, 3.8.2005, CISG-online 1190 = IHR 2006, 26 ff.; OGH, 3.4.2008, CISG-online 1680 = IHR 2008, 188; OGH, 14.12.2004, CISG-online 1018; oben *Widmer Lüchinger,* Art. 31 Rn. 89. Unklar *Scottish & Newcastle International Ltd. v. Othon Ghalanos Ltd.* [2008] UKHL 11 = IHR 2009, 76 ff.

[96] OGH, 14.12.2004, CISG-online 1018; OLG Köln, 21.12.2005, CISG-online 1201 = IHR 2006, 86; Trib. Padova, 10.1.2006, CISG-online 1157 = CLOUT Nr. 652: Lieferung erfolgte in einem Fall herzustellender Ware (Art. 3 I) an dem Ort, an dem die Ware installiert wurde; vgl. oben *Widmer Lüchinger,* Art. 31 Rn. 90. m. w. N.; *Kannowski,* IHR 2008, 2, 5 ff.

[97] EuGH, 3.5.2007, Rs. C-386/05 *(Color Drack GmbH/Lexx International Vertriebs GmbH)*, Slg. 2007, I-3699.

[98] OGH, 8.9.2005, CISG-online 1901: die AGB des Verkäufers enthielten eine Vorschrift, der zufolge die Produktions-, Aufbewahrungs- und Versendungsräumlichkeiten des Verkäufers als Erfüllungsort galten; das Gericht urteilte, dass eine solche „abstrakte" Erfüllungsortsvereinbarung nicht den Schriftlichkeitsvoraussetzungen von Art. 23 EUGVO genügte; OLG Köln, 21.12.2005, CISG-online 1201 = IHR 2006, 86, 87.

der hier vertretenen Auffassung der **Bestimmungsort** sein, und zwar unabhängig davon, welche Partei den Transport organisiert und zahlt.[99] Einer Gegenansicht zufolge soll in diesem Fall hingegen Art. 31 lit. a) angewendet werden, so dass die Gerichte des Ortes international zuständig wären, an dem die Ware dem ersten Beförderer zur Übermittlung an den Käufer übergeben wird.[100] Wenn die Lieferung noch gar nicht erfolgt ist, bereitet die Bestimmung des Ortes der faktischen Übergabe grosse Schwierigkeiten. Diese Bestimmung kann nur nach dem Vertrag erfolgen, wobei neben ausdrücklichen auch stillschweigende Erfüllungsortsvereinbarungen (wie z. B. INCOTERMS®) zu berücksichtigen sind.[101] Fehlen Vertragsbestimmungen wird aber in diesem Zusammenhang letztlich wiederum Art. 31 herangezogen werden müssen.[102]

26 Wenngleich die prozessrechtliche Auswirkungen von Art. 57 auf den internationalen Gerichtsstand am Erfüllungsort durch die EUGVO nicht vollständig ausgeschlossen wurden, so konnten sie jedenfalls signifikant begrenzt werden.[103] Art. 57 bleibt aber nach wie vor relevant für die Bestimmung der internationalen Zuständigkeit, wenn Art. 5 I lit. b) EUGVO auf einen **Ort ausserhalb der europäischen Gemeinschaft** verweist.[104] Wenn z. B. die Ware in die USA geliefert wurde oder geliefert werden sollte, läge die nach Art. 5 I lit. b) EUGVO autonom zu bestimmende internationale Zuständigkeit in den USA. Weil die USA kein Mitglied der europäischen Gemeinschaft sind, würde gemäss Art. 5 I lit. c) EUGVO die Regelung des Art. 5 I lit. a) EUGVO Anwendung finden. Demnach würden die Gerichte am Ort der Erfüllung der im Streit liegenden Verpflichtung international zuständig sein, wobei der Erfüllungsort wiederum nach der herkömmlichen Rechtsprechung zu Art. 57 zu bestimmen wäre.[105]

27 Das **revidierte Lugano-Übereinkommen** enthält wortgleiche Bestimmungen wie die EUGVO und führt zu den gleichen Interpretationsschwierigkeiten.[106]

28 Vor dem Hintergrund der beschriebenen Schwierigkeiten im Zusammenhang mit der internationalen Zuständigkeit staatlicher Gerichte am Erfüllungsort sind die Parteien eines

---

[99] EuGH, 25.2.2010, Rs. C-381/08 *(Car Trim GmbH/KeySafety Systems Srl)*, NJW 2010, 1059, 1061, m. krit. Anm. *Piltz;* BGH, 23.6.2010, CISG-online 2129: „Ort, an dem die mit dem Kaufvertrag erstrebte Übertragung der Sachen vom Verkäufer an den Käufer durch deren Ankunft an ihrem endgültigen Bestimmungsort vollständig abgeschlossen ist und der Käufer die tatsächliche Verfügungsgewalt über die Waren erlangt hat oder hätte erlangen müssen"; die Klausel „Resa: Franco Partenza" wurde als reine Kostentragungsklausel verstanden und blieb ohne Auswirkung auf den Erfüllungsort; vgl. bereits den Vorlagebeschluss BGH, 9.7.2008, CISG-online 1717; OGH, 14.12.2004, CISG-online 1018; OLG Hamm, 6.12.2005, CISG-online 1221 = IHR 2006, 84, 86; OLG Köln, 21.12.2005, CISG-online 1201 = IHR 2006, 86; OLG Köln, 30.4.2007, IHR 2007, 164, 166; *Hager/Bentele*, IPRax 2004, 72; oben *Widmer Lüchinger*, Art. 31 Rn. 92 f. m. w. N.

[100] Cass., 27.9.2006, CISG-online 1393 = ZEuP 2008, 165 ff.; Cass., 14.6.2007, CISG-online 1702 = IHR 2009, 74, 75 ff.; OLG Oldenburg, 20.12.2007, CISG-online 1644 = IHR 2008, 112, 118; *Piltz*, NJW 2007, 1801 ff.; *Mankowski*, IHR 2009, 45, 55 ff., der klarstellt, dass Art. 31 nicht zur Anwendung kommt, sondern nur zur Auslegung von Art. 5 I lit. a) EUGVO herangezogen wird. Zur gleichen Ansicht bei FOB-Verträgen nach englischem Recht vgl. *Scottish & Newcastle International Ltd. v. Othon Ghalanos Ltd.* [2008] UKHL 11 = IHR 2009, 76 ff.

[101] Vgl. EuGH, 9.6.2011, Rs. C-87/10 *(Electrosteel Europe SA/Edil Centro SpA)*, NJW 2011, 3018 f.

[102] LG Bamberg, 23.10.2006, CISG-online 1400 = IHR 2007, 113, 117; LG Neubrandenburg, 3.8.2005, CISG-online 1190 = IHR 2006, 26, 28; Trib. Padova, 10.1.2006, CISG-online 1157 = CLOUT Nr. 652 (obiter); oben *Widmer Lüchinger*, Art. 31 Rn. 93 f., die sich gegen eine Anwendung von Art. 31 und für die Geltung des Ortes der Niederlassung des Käufers ausspricht; *Markus*, Vertragserfüllungsort, S. 188 ff.

[103] Art. 57 I lit. a) findet auch dann keine Anwendung, wenn der Vertrag vor Inkrafttreten der EUGVO geschlossen wurde, die EUGVO aber Anwendung findet, weil die Klage erst nach Inkrafttreten eingeleitet wurde, vgl. OLG Köln, 21.12.2005, CISG-online 1201, IHR 2006, 86 ff.

[104] Vgl. *De Ly*, Draft Digest, S. 468, 473 ff.; *Bamberger/Roth/Saenger*, Art. 57, Rn. 5; *Ferrari u .a./Mankowski*, Internationales Vertragsrecht, Art. 57, Rn. 29.

[105] Trib. Padova, 10.1.2006, CISG-online 1157 = CLOUT Nr. 652; oben *Widmer Lüchinger*, Art. 31 Rn. 95 ff.; *Kannowski*, IHR 2008, 2, 6 ff.; *Kropholler/von Hinden*, S. 401, 408-9, 411; *Kropholler*, EUZPR, Art. 5, Rn. 24 ff.; *Furrer/Schramm*, SJZ 2003, 105, 109, 110; *Junker*, RIW 2002, 569, 572; *Micklitz/Rott*, EuZW 2001, 325, 329; *Ferrari u. a./Mankowski*, Internationales Vertragsrecht, Art. 57, Rn. 29.

[106] Vgl. oben Rn. 25 ff.

internationalen Kaufvertrags am besten beraten, eine **Schieds- oder Gerichtsstandvereinbarung** in ihren Vertrag aufzunehmen.[107]

VIII. Zahlungsort für andere Zahlungen als die Kaufpreispreiszahlung

1. Schadenersatz und Vertragsstrafen

Art. 57 regelt ausdrücklich nur den Zahlungsort der Kaufpreisforderung. Hingegen enthält das CISG keine allgemeine Regel für andere Zahlungen, wie z. B. Schadenersatz in Geld. Diese interne Lücke des Übereinkommens kann aber durch Rückgriff auf allgemeine Prinzipien des CISG geschlossen werden.[108] Österreichische und deutsche Gerichte haben angenommen, dass eine **Schadenersatzpflicht** an dem Ort zu erfüllen ist, an dem die verletzte Pflicht zu erfüllen gewesen wäre.[109] Nur wenn Zahlung am Ort der Niederlassung des Verkäufers zu leisten gewesen wäre (Art. 57 I lit. a)), würde diese Ansicht zu einem angemessenen Ergebnis führen.[110] In allen anderen Fällen würde diese Ansicht zu unangemessenen Ergebnissen führen, weil der Schadenersatzanspruch am Ort der Übergabe der Ware oder der Dokumenten (Art. 57 I lit. b)) oder an dem für die Kaufpreiszahlung vereinbarten Zahlungsort zu erfüllen wäre. Um diese unangemessenen Ergebnisse zu vermeiden, muss **Art. 57 I lit. a)** direkt als **allgemeines Prinzip** des CISG angewendet werden, mit der Folge, dass Schadenersatz in Geld am **Ort der Niederlassung des Gläubigers** zu zahlen ist.[111] Sämtliche Schadenersatzansprüche des Verkäufers für jedwedes Fehlverhalten des Käufers sind am einheitlichen Zahlungsort der Niederlassung des Verkäufers zu zahlen. Aus materiell-rechtlicher Sicht ist dies ein angemessenes Ergebnis. Nur aus prozessrechtlicher Sicht kann dieses Ergebnis fragwürdig sein, was aber wiederum durch das anwendbare Prozessrecht und nicht durch das CISG zu lösen ist.[112]

Vertragsstrafen und **Schadenspauschalen** sind gemäss dem allgemeinen Prinzip des Art. 57 I lit. a) am Ort der Niederlassung des Gläubigers zu zahlen.[113] Das Gleiche gilt für vertragliche Ansprüche des Käufers auf **Zahlung einer Prämie**, die ihm der Verkäufer versprochen hatte.[114]

---

[107] Vgl. *DiMatteo/Dhooge/Greene/Maurer/Pagnattaro*, 34 Nw. J. Int'l L. & Bus. (2004), 299, 373 ff. = CISG Pace; *Šarčević*, Draft Digest, S. 482, 486.

[108] OLG Düsseldorf, 2.7.1993, CISG-online 74 = RIW 1993, 845, m. zust. Anm. *Schlechtriem*, EWiR 1993, 1075; *Hager/Maultzsch*, 5. Aufl., Art. 57 Rn. 25.

[109] OGH, 29.3.2004, CISG-online 926; OLG Braunschweig, 28.10.1999, CISG-online 510 = TranspR-IHR 2000, 4, 5; LG Aachen, 14.5.1993, CISG-online 86 = RIW 1993, 760. Die Rspr. scheint sich an der Rspr. des EuGH zur internationalen Zuständigkeit zu orientieren (EuGH, 6.10.1976, Rs. 14/76 *(de Bloos/Bouyer)*, Slg. 1497).

[110] Vgl. OGH, 29.3.2004, CISG-online 926; *Hager/Maultzsch*, 5. Aufl., Art. 57 Rn. 25.

[111] OLG Braunschweig, 28.10.1999, CISG-online 510 = CLOUT Nr. 361 = TranspR-IHR, 2000, 4; OLG Düsseldorf, 2.7.1993, CISG-online 74 = RIW 1993, 845, 846; m. insoweit zust. Anm. *Schlechtriem*, EWiR 1993, 1075; implizierend BGH, 26.3.1992, CISG-online 67 = EuZW 1992, 514; vgl. die alternative Begründung des OGH, 29.3.2004, CISG-online 926. Wie hier *Rudolph*, Art. 57, Rn. 6; *Wichard*, RabelsZ 60 (1996), 269, 298, 299, mit Bezug auf Artt 6.1.6 I lit. a) PICC; *C. Witz*, Draft Digest, S. 424, 431 ff., 433; *Honsell/Schnyder/Straub*, Art. 57, Rn. 32; *Kröll u. a./P. Butler/Harindranath*, Art. 57, Rn. 28; *Ferrari u. a./Mankowski*, Internationales Vertragsrecht, Art. 57, Rn. 23. Für die Anwendung von Art. 57 auf Schadenersatzansprüche vgl. *Herber/Czerwenka*, Art. 57, Rn. 14; *Achilles*, Art. 57, Rn. 1; *Bamberger/Roth/Saenger*, Art. 57, Rn. 6; *Witz/Salger/Lorenz/Witz*, Art. 57, Rn. 4; *Soergel/Lüderitz/Budzikiewicz*, Art. 57, Rn. 8. A. A. *Hackenberg*, S. 151 ff.

[112] Vgl. *Hager/Maultzsch*, 5. Aufl., Art. 57 Rn. 25; *Ferrari u. a./Mankowski*, Internationales Vertragsrecht, Art. 57, Rn. 23.

[113] Vgl. *Staudinger/Magnus*, Art. 57, Rn. 24; *Enderlein/Maskow/Strohbach*, Art. 57, Anm. 2.; *Honsell/Schnyder/Straub*, Art. 57, Rn. 32; *Ferrari u. a./Mankowski*, Internationales Vertragsrecht, Art. 57, Rn. 25.

[114] OGH, 18.12.2002, CISG-online 1279.

2. Rückzahlung des Kaufpreises

31 Das allgemeine Prinzip des CISG, dem zufolge jede Zahlungspflicht am Ort der Niederlassung des Gläubigers zu erfüllen ist, muss auch auf Ansprüche auf **Rückzahlung des Kaufpreises** angewendet werden.[115] Folglich ist der Verkäufer verpflichtet, den Kaufpreis am **Ort der Niederlassung des Käufers** zurückzuzahlen.[116] Ein Anspruch auf Rückzahlung des Kaufpreises kann sich in folgenden Konstellationen ergeben: Zunächst kann der Verkäufer nach Art. 81 II zur Rückzahlung des Kaufpreises verpflichtet sein, wenn die Parteien zur Rückabwicklung des Vertrages nach **Aufhebung des Vertrags** durch die vertragstreue Partei[117] oder im Einvernehmen beider Parteien[118] verpflichtet sind. Die teilweise Rückzahlung des Kaufpreises kann auch notwendig werden, wenn der Käufer den Kaufpreis bereits gezahlt hatte, dann aber den Kaufpreis in Anwendung von Art. 50 wegen vertragswidriger Ware **mindert**.[119] Es können aber auch **Vorauszahlungen** des Käufers auf Basis vorläufiger Rechnungen vorliegen, die vom Verkäufer teilweise zurückzuzahlen sind, wenn die endgültigen Rechnungen einen geringeren Kaufpreis als die vorläufigen Rechnungen ausweisen. Diese Zurückzahlungspflicht hat ihre Grundlage nicht im nationalen Bereicherungsrecht, sondern entsteht aus Vertrag und wird folglich vom CISG erfasst. Folglich hat der Verkäufer den Überschuss am Ort der Niederlassung des Käufers zurück zu zahlen. Das Gleiche gilt, wenn der Käufer den Verkäufer **überzahlt** hat und Rückzahlung des Überschusses verlangt.[120]

3. Zinsen

32 Zinsen nach Art. 78 sind am gleichen Ort wie die zu Grunde liegende Zahlungspflicht zu begleichen.[121] Zinsen auf den Kaufpreis sind folglich in Übereinstimmung mit Art. 57 zu zahlen.

---

[115] CA Grenoble, 23.10.1996, CISG-online 305 = CLOUT Nr. 205, m. Anm. *Sinay-Cytermann*, Rev. crit. dr. int. privé 1997, 762 = TranspR-IHR 1999, 8; LG Giessen, 17.12.2002, CISG-online 766 = IHR 2003, 276 ff.; MünchKomm/*P. Huber*, Art. 57, Rn. 11; *Schlechtriem*, IPRax 1981, 113 ff.; *Bamberger/Roth/Saenger*, Art. 57, Rn. 6. A. A. OGH, 10.3.1998, CISG-online 356 = östZRVgl 1998, 161 = D. Somm. 1999, 357, m. Anm. *Niessen*; OLG Wien, 1.6.2004, CISG-online 954; CA Paris, 14.1.1998, CISG-online 347, 1010 = D. Somm. 1998, 288, m. Anm. *Audit*: Rückgriff auf das subsidiär anwendbare nationale Recht; *Herber/Czerwenka*, Art. 57, Rn. 14; *C. Witz*, Draft Digest, S. 424, 427 f., 430, der vorschlägt, dass unter Berücksichtigung von Treu und Glauben die Rückzahlung im Falle eines Vertragsbruchs seitens des Käufers am Ort der Niederlassung des Verkäufers und im Falle eines Vertragsbruchs seitens des Verkäufers am Ort der Niederlassung des Käufers erfolgen solle.

[116] Vgl. unten *Fountoulakis*, Art. 81 Rn. 24; CISG-AC Op. 9 (*Bridge*), Comment 3.15, so dass der Käufer ein Bankkonto seiner Wahl benennen kann, wenn Zahlung durch Überweisung erfolgt war; *Staudinger/Magnus*, Art. 57, Rn. 23; *Honsell/Schnyder/Straub*, Art. 57, Rn. 32; *Kröll u. a./P. Butler/Harindranath*, Art. 57, Rn. 29. Vgl. vorhergehende Fussnote für weitere Nachweise.

[117] Vgl. unten *Fountoulakis*, Art. 81 Rn. 3 f.

[118] Vgl. unten *Fountoulakis*, Art. 81 Rn. 15. A. A. OGH, 10.3.1998, CISG-online 356 = ÖstZRVgl 1998, 161 = D. Somm. 1999, 357, m. Anm. *Niessen*: das Gericht verneinte die Anwendbarkeit von Art. 57 auf einen Anspruch auf teilweise Rückzahlung des Kaufpreises nach einvernehmlicher Aufhebung des CISG-Vertrags, fälschlicherweise annehmend, dass dieser Anspruch seine Grundlage in nationalem Bereicherungsrecht habe.

[119] *Staudinger/Magnus*, Art. 57, Rn. 23; *Ferrari u. a./Mankowski*, Internationales Vertragsrecht, Art. 57, Rn. 25.

[120] Für einen Fall, in dem ein solcher Sachverhalt nach dem anwendbaren nationalen Bereicherungsrecht beurteilt wurde: CA Grenoble, 23.10.1996, CISG-online 305 = CLOUT Nr. 205; *Staudinger/Magnus*, Art. 57, Rn. 23. A. A. *C. Witz*, Draft Digest, S. 424, 431, der zwei Situationen unterscheidet: hat der Verkäufer die Überzahlung veranlasst, so soll Rückzahlung am Ort der Niederlassung des Käufers erfolgen. Hat hingegen der Käufer die Überzahlung selbst zu vertreten, so soll Rückzahlung am Ort der Niederlassung des Verkäufers erfolgen.

[121] *Staudinger/Magnus*, Art. 57, Rn. 24; *Ferrari u. a./Mankowski*, Internationales Vertragsrecht, Art. 57, Rn. 25. A. A. *Enderlein/Maskow/Strohbach*, Art. 57, Anm. 2.; *Honsell/Schnyder/Straub*, Art. 57, Rn. 32.

IX. Beweislast

Art. 57 I lit. a) enthält das allgemeine Prinzip des Übereinkommens, dass der Kaufpreis **33** grundsätzlich am Ort der Niederlassung des Verkäufers und jedwede andere Geldsumme am Ort der Niederlassung des Gläubigers zu bezahlen ist. Diejenige Partei, die eine vertragliche Vereinbarung über den Zahlungsort oder über den Ort, an dem Zahlung gegen Übergabe der Ware oder von Dokumenten gemäss Art. 57 I lit. b) zu erfolgen hat, behauptet, trägt die Beweislast für die entsprechenden Fakten.[122] Der Verkäufer muss den Wechsel seiner Niederlassung im Sinne von Art. 57 II beweisen. Wenn der Käufer behauptet, dass ihm zusätzliche Kosten durch den Niederlassungswechsel des Verkäufers entstanden sind, so muss der Käufer diese Kosten beweisen.[123]

---

[122] Undeutlich *Staudinger/Magnus*, Art. 57, Rn. 25, dem zufolge auch die Partei, die sich auf Art. 57 I lit. a) beruft, beweispflichtig sein kann; *Kröll u. a./P. Butler/Harindranath*, Art. 57, Rn. 30.
[123] *Achilles*, Art. 57, Rn. 6; *Baumgärtel/Laumen/Hepting*, Art. 57, Rn. 7; *Staudinger/Magnus*, Art. 57, Rn. 25; *Kröll u. a./P. Butler/Harindranath*, Art. 57, Rn. 30; *Ferrari u. a./Mankowski*, Internationales Vertragsrecht, Art. 57, Rn. 30.

Art. 58 [Zahlungszeit; Zahlung als Bedingung der Übergabe; Untersuchung vor Zahlung]

(1) Ist der Käufer nicht verpflichtet, den Kaufpreis zu einer bestimmten Zeit zu zahlen, so hat er den Preis zu zahlen, sobald ihm der Verkäufer entweder die Ware oder die Dokumente, die zur Verfügung darüber berechtigen, nach dem Vertrag und diesem Übereinkommen zur Verfügung gestellt hat. Der Verkäufer kann die Übergabe der Ware oder der Dokumente von der Zahlung abhängig machen.

(2) Erfordert der Vertrag eine Beförderung der Ware, so kann der Verkäufer sie mit der Maßgabe versenden, daß die Ware oder die Dokumente, die zur Verfügung darüber berechtigen, dem Käufer nur gegen Zahlung des Kaufpreises zu übergeben sind.

(3) Der Käufer ist nicht verpflichtet, den Kaufpreis zu zahlen, bevor er Gelegenheit gehabt hat, die Ware zu untersuchen, es sei denn, die von den Parteien vereinbarten Lieferungs- oder Zahlungsmodalitäten bieten hierzu keine Gelegenheit.

Art. 58

(1) If the buyer is not bound to pay the price at any other specific time, he must pay it when the seller places either the goods or documents controlling their disposition at the buyer's disposal in accordance with the contract and this Convention. The seller may make such payment a condition for handing over the goods or documents.

(2) If the contract involves carriage of the goods, the seller may dispatch the goods on terms whereby the goods, or documents controlling their disposition, will not be handed over to the buyer except against payment of the price.

(3) The buyer is not bound to pay the price until he has had an opportunity to examine the goods, unless the procedures for delivery or payment agreed upon by the parties are inconsistent with his having such an opportunity.

Art. 58

1) Si l'acheteur n'est pas tenu de payer le prix à un autre moment déterminé, il doit le payer lorsque, conformément au contrat et à la présente Convention, le vendeur met à sa disposition soit les marchandises soit des documents représentatifs des marchandises. Le vendeur peut faire du paiement une condition de la remise des marchandises ou des documents.

2) Si le contrat implique un transport des marchandises, le vendeur peut en faire l'expédition souscondition que celles-ci ou les documents représentatifs ne seront remis à l'acheteur que contre paiement du prix.

3) L'acheteur n'est pas tenu de payer le prix avant d'avoir eu la possibilité d'examiner les marchandises, à moins que les modalités de livraison ou de paiement dont sont convenues les parties ne lui en laissent pas la possibilité.

Übersicht

	Rn.
I. Regelungsgegenstand	1
II. Vertraglich vereinbarte Zahlungszeit	5
III. Zahlung Zug um Zug gegen Ware oder Dokumente, Art. 58 I	7
1. Lieferung durch Zur-Verfügung-Stellen der Ware am Ort der Niederlassung des Verkäufers oder am Ort der Lagerung bzw. der Produktion	8
2. Lieferung durch Zur-Verfügung-Stellen der Ware am Ort der Niederlassung des Käufers oder an jedem anderen vereinbarten Ort	11
3. Verträge, die eine Beförderung der Ware erfordern	12
4. Verträge über Ware, die sich auf dem Transport befindet	13
5. Verträge über Ware, die sich in einem Lagerhaus eines Dritten befindet	14
6. Zahlung gegen Dokumente	15
IV. Verträge über zu befördernde Ware, die mit der Massgabe des Verkäufers versendet wird, dass sie oder die sie vertretenden Dokumente nur gegen Zahlung übergeben werden, Art. 58 II	17
V. Rechtsfolgen bei Nichtbeachtung der Zahlungszeit	18
1. Die Rechtsbehelfe des Verkäufers wegen verspäteter Zahlung	18
2. Das Recht des Verkäufers zur Zurückweisung einer vorzeitigen Zahlung	19
3. Zinsen	21

VI. Zurückbehaltungsrechte 23
    1. Das Zurückbehaltungsrecht des Verkäufers gemäss Art. 58 I und II 23
    2. Das Zurückbehaltungsrecht des Käufers gemäss Art. 58 I 25
    3. Art. 71 und das allgemeine Zurückbehaltungsrecht 26
VII. Das Untersuchungsrecht des Käufers vor Zahlung gemäss Art. 58 III 33
VIII. Beweislast 37

Vorläufer und **Entwürfe:** Artt. 60, 71, 72 EKG; Genfer E 1976 Art. 39; Wiener E 1977 Art. 40; New Yorker E 1978 Art. 54.

I. Regelungsgegenstand

Art. 58 regelt zwei Aspekte: Zunächst begründet Art. 58 das allgemeine Prinzip des 1
Übereinkommens, dass Zahlung und Übergabe der Ware oder von zur Verfügung über die Ware berechtigenden Dokumenten in einem **synallagmatischen Verhältnis** zueinander stehen, die Zahlung des Kaufpreises also nur **Zug um Zug** gegen Übergabe der Ware oder der Dokumente geschuldet ist.[1] Neben diesem allgemeinen Prinzip bestimmt Art. 58 den **Zeitpunkt, in dem der Kaufpreis fällig wird,** also zu zahlen ist.[2]

Daneben beschreiben Art. 58 I 2 und Art. 58 II **Zurückbehaltungsrechte des Ver-** 2
käufers. Gemäss Art. 58 III hat der Käufer das Recht, die **Ware vor Zahlung kurz zu untersuchen.**

Der Inhalt von Art. 58 entspricht weitestgehend seinen Vorgängervorschriften im **EKG,** 3
wobei dort das Prinzip der Zug-um-Zug-Erfüllung und die Zahlungszeit getrennt in zwei Artikeln geregelt waren.[3] Die Arbeitsgruppe beendete das System des EKG, dem ein zentraler Lieferbegriff zugrunde lag, knüpfte für die Zahlung stattdessen an den Zeitpunkt an, zu dem die Ware dem Käufer zur Verfügung gestellt wird,[4] und verband die zwei Vorschriften des EKG in einer einzelnen Vorschrift.[5] Darüber hinaus wurde Art. 72 I EKG abgeschafft, dem zufolge der Verkäufer das Recht hatte, die Lieferung der Ware bis Erhalt der Zahlung aufzuschieben, weil ein solches Recht mit der Kaufrechtspraxis in zahlreichen Ländern nicht vereinbar war.[6]

Für die Bestimmung der **Zahlungszeit** bzw. der Fälligkeit sieht Art. 58 ein **dreistufiges** 4
Vorgehen vor: Zunächst ist es Sache der Parteien, die Zahlungszeit zu vereinbaren, Art. 58 I i. V. m. Art. 6. Sollten die Parteien eine Zahlungszeit nicht vereinbart haben, so muss der Käufer den Preis zahlen, sobald ihm der Verkäufer entweder die Ware oder die Dokumente, die zur Verfügung darüber berechtigen, zur Verfügung gestellt hat, Art. 58 I. Diese Regel beinhaltet das allgemeine Prinzip des Übereinkommens, dass Ware bzw. die sie vertretenden Dokumente Zug um Zug gegen Zahlung des Preises auszutauschen sind. Da sich der Austausch von Ware bzw. Dokumenten gegen Zahlung des Preises schwieriger gestaltet, wenn der Vertrag die Beförderung der Ware erfordert, sieht Art. 58 II das einseitige Recht des Verkäufers vor, die Ware mit der Massgabe zu versenden, dass die Ware oder die Dokumente, die zur Verfügung darüber berechtigen, dem Käufer nur gegen Zahlung des

---

[1] KG Wallis, 27.4.2007, CISG-online 1721 = SZIER 2008, 184 ff.: „La CVIM consacre la règle du ‚trait pour trait'"; *Honnold/Flechtner,* Art. 58, Rn. 339.2; *Staudinger/Magnus,* Art. 58, Rn. 3; MünchKomm/*P. Huber,* Art. 58, Rn. 1; *Hager/Maultzsch,* 5. Aufl., Art. 58 Rn. 1 ff.; MünchKomm HGB/*Benicke,* Art. 58, Rn. 1; *Herber/Czerwenka,* Art. 58, Rn. 2; *Brunner,* Art. 58, Rn. 1; *Ferrari u. a./Mankowski,* Internationales Vertragsrecht, Art. 58, Rn. 1. A. A. *Honsell/Schnyder/Straub,* Art. 58, Rn. 58; *Piltz,* Internationales Kaufrecht, Rn. 4–152.
[2] *Staudinger/Magnus,* Art. 58, Rn. 1; *Bamberger/Roth/Saenger,* Art. 58, Rn. 1; *Ferrari u. a./Mankowski,* Internationales Vertragsrecht, Art. 58, Rn. 1.
[3] Vgl. Artt. 60, 71, 72 EKG.
[4] YB III (1972), S. 31, Nr. 1–63 (insbes. Nr. 37–40), S. 83, Nr. 15–21; die Abkehr von einem zentralen Lieferbegriff wirkte sich vor allem bei der Regelung des Gefahrübergangs aus, siehe unten *Hachem,* Art. 67 Rn. 1 ff.
[5] YB V (1974), S. 31, 32, Nr. 22–35; zum Bericht des Generalsekretärs s. YB V (1974), S. 81–83, Nr. 4–21.
[6] *Dölle/U. Huber,* Art. 72 EKG, Rn. 27, 28; YB V (1974), S. 32, Nr. 32.

Art. 58 5

Kaufpreises zu übergeben sind. Schliesslich sieht Art. 58 III das Recht des Käufers vor, die Ware zu untersuchen, bevor er den Kaufpreis zahlt, es sei denn, die von den Parteien vereinbarten Lieferungs- oder Zahlungsmodalitäten bieten hierzu keine Gelegenheit.

II. Vertraglich vereinbarte Zahlungszeit

5   Zumeist werden die Parteien eines internationalen Kaufvertrags die Zahlungszeit **ausdrücklich,** wenigstens aber **stillschweigend,** in ihrem Vertrag regeln. Eine solche **Parteivereinbarung** geniesst absoluten Vorrang, Art. 6.[7] Die Eingangsworte zu Art. 58 I, dass diese Vorschrift nur dann gilt, wenn „der Käufer nicht verpflichtet [ist], den Kaufpreis zu einer bestimmten Zeit zu zahlen", bestätigen diesen selbstverständlichen Vorrang nur.[8] Die Bestimmung der Zahlungszeit kann durch Benennung eines **bestimmten Zeitpunkts** oder durch Festlegung einer **Zahlungsfrist,** innerhalb welcher Zahlung zu leisten ist, festgelegt werden.[9] Die Zahlungszeit muss nicht zwingend bestimmt sein, es reicht, dass sie **bestimmbar** ist.[10] Jede Vertragsklausel, die für die Zahlungszeit relevant ist, muss gemäss Art. 8 und Art. 9 ausgelegt werden.[11] Zum Beispiel kann die Vertragsinterpretation ergeben, dass eine **Rechnung** für die Fälligkeit des Kaufpreises erforderlich ist.[12] Auch kann die Zahlung auf die **Vornahme einer bestimmten Handlung** durch eine der Parteien bedingt worden sein,[13] zum Beispiel Anzeige der Lieferbereitschaft (notice of readiness)[14], Lieferung,[15] Erhalt der Rechnung,[16] Inbetriebnahme einer Maschine, Benutzung von Material einer Lieferung,[17] Annahme des Käufers von saisonalen Kaufbestätigungen,[18] oder auf die Vornahme einer Handlung durch eine Drittpartei, z. B. Zahlung durch einen Abnehmer.[19] Oft wird sich die Zahlungszeit aus der Benutzung einer üblichen **Zahlungsklausel** ergeben.[20] Zum Beispiel muss die Klausel „cash against documents" oder eine Akkreditivklausel dahingehend verstanden werden, dass als Zahlungszeit der Zeitpunkt vereinbart wurde, in dem vertragsgemässe Dokumente der bezeichneten Bank vorgelegt werden.[21] Klauseln wie „60 Tage nach Erhalt der Lieferung", „zwei Wochen nach Lieferung" oder „bar vor Lieferung" sind

---

[7] OLG München, 19.10.2006, CISG-online 1394 = IHR 2007, 30, 33.
[8] O. R., S. 369.
[9] *Witz/Salger/Lorenz/Witz,* Artt. 58–59, Rn. 3.
[10] *Witz/Salger/Lorenz/Witz,* Artt. 58–59, Rn. 3.
[11] CIETAC, 23.4.1995, CISG-online 1031: Das Schiedsgericht sah die Behauptung des Käufers, dass im Wollhandel ein Handelsbrauch bestehe, dem zufolge ein Dokumentenakkreditiv spätestens 15 Tage vor Verschiffung gestellt werden müsse, als unbewiesen an. Es verlangte, dass das Dokumentenakkreditiv eine angemessene Zeit vor Verschiffung gestellt werden müsse, so dass der Verkäufer genügend Zeit zur Organisation des Transports hat, was es im konkreten Fall bei zwölf Tagen vor Verschiffung bejahte.
[12] OLG München, 3.4.2006, CISG-online 1218.
[13] *Witz/Salger/Lorenz/Witz,* Artt. 58–59, Rn. 3.
[14] OLG München, 19.10.2006, CISG-online 1394 = IHR 2007, 30, 32.
[15] *Doolim Corp. v. R Doll, LLC,* U. S. Dist. Ct. (S. D. N. Y.), 29.5.2009, CISG-online 1892: Zahlung 15 Tage nach Erhalt der Ware.
[16] OLG Braunschweig, 28.10.1999, CISG-online 510 = CLOUT Nr. 361 = TranspR-IHR 2000, 4 ff.; HGer St. Gallen, 29.4.2004, CISG-online 962 = SZIER 2005, 115, 121; HGer Aargau, 26.9.1997, CISG-online 329.
[17] *Treibacher Industrie, A. G. v. TDY Industries, Inc.,* U. S. Dist. Ct. (N. D. Ala.), 27.4.2005, CISG-online 1178: Das Gericht entschied, dass trotz Benutzung des im Hartmetallmarkt der Vereinigten Staaten üblichen Begriffs der Lieferung eines „consignment", der bedeutet, dass die Zahlungsverpflichtung für das Material erst dann entsteht, wenn das Material dem „consignment store" (Lager beim Kunden) entnommen wurde, die Parteien im vorliegenden Fall davon abweichend vereinbart hatten, dass das Material nach Lieferung nicht zurückgegeben werden konnte, sondern benutzt und bezahlt werden musste, Zahlung also nur bis zur Entnahme des Materials aus dem „consignment store" (Lager beim Kunden) gestundet war.
[18] ICC, 11849/2003, CISG-online 1421, Rn. 36 ff.
[19] Vgl. CIETAC, 21.2.2005, CISG-online 1706: Der Vertrag sah vor, dass der Käufer dem Verkäufer den Kaufpreis sieben Tage nach Erhalt des entsprechenden Kaufpreises von seinen Abnehmern zu zahlen hatte.
[20] *Staudinger/Magnus,* Art. 58, Rn. 8; *Herber/Czerwenka,* Art. 58, Rn. 10.
[21] Zum deutschen internen Recht vgl. BGH, 5.3.1997, RIW 1997, 958 = NJW 1997, 1775 ff.; *Witz/Salger/Lorenz/Witz,* Artt. 58–59, Rn. 3.

bestimmt genug.²² Klauseln wie „Zahlung gegen Rechnung", „Zahlung gegen Erhalt der Rechnung" oder „14 Tage netto" stellen vertragliche Vereinbarungen der Zahlungszeit dar, weil die Fälligkeit der Zahlung nicht von der Lieferung der Ware, sondern von der Lieferung einer Rechnung abhängig gemacht wird.²³ Wenn der Eintritt der Bedingung von einer Handlung der anderen Partei abhängt, kann trotz Nichtvornahme der Handlung durch die andere Partei, um so den Bedingungseintritt zu vermeiden, dennoch Fälligkeit eintreten.²⁴ Wenngleich die **Incoterms®** die Zahlungszeit nicht direkt bestimmen, kann die Benutzung eines Incoterms® indirekt Auswirkungen auf die Zahlungszeit haben.²⁵ Zum Beispiel kann die Vertragsinterpretation ergeben, dass die Parteien mit Festsetzung des Lieferzeitpunkts durch die Incoterms®-Klausel gleichzeitig auch die Fälligkeit bestimmen wollten.²⁶ Allerdings beinhalten Incoterms® ohne Zahlungsklausel eine solche Bedeutung nicht.²⁷ Ist die Zahlungszeit im Vertrag weder ausdrücklich noch stillschweigend vereinbart worden und wird die Ware von einer Rechnung begleitet, der zufolge der Kaufpreis zu einem bestimmten Zeitpunkt nach dem Zeitpunkt der Lieferung zahlbar ist, so kann der Verkäufer nicht sofortige Zahlung verlangen, da ein solches Verhalten widersprüchlich wäre und ein Verstoss gegen das allgemeine Verbot eines *venire contra factum proprium* bedeuten würde.²⁸ Nationales Recht kann Gültigkeitsvoraussetzungen i. S. v. Art. 4 an die Vereinbarung von Zahlungszielen stellen, wie z. B. in Art. 3 V der Zahlungsverzugsrichtlinie vorgesehen.²⁹

Nicht nur vom Fälligkeitszeitpunkt, sondern auch von allen anderen Regelungen des Art. 58, wie z. B. der Zug-um-Zug-Erfüllung, der Zurückbehaltungsrechte des Verkäufers oder dem Untersuchungsrecht des Käufers vor Zahlung, können die Parteien durch Übereinkunft **abweichen** oder ihre Anwendung ganz **ausschliessen,** Art. 6.³⁰ So hat z. B. das Schweizerische Bundesgericht festgestellt, dass Lieferung und Zahlung nicht in einem Zug-um-Zug-Verhältnis standen, weil der Vertrag eine mehrphasige Installationspflicht mit entsprechenden Teilzahlungen für die einzelnen Phasen der Inbetriebnahme vorsah.³¹ Aber auch wenn der Verkäufer dem Käufer einen Kredit auf die Ware einräumt, kann die Übergabe der Ware oder der Dokumente den Käufer nicht zur Zahlung verpflichten; vielmehr wurde der Kaufpreis auf ein unbestimmtes Datum gestundet.³² Auch die Vereinbarung, einen gezogenen Wechsel zu negoziieren, beinhaltet die Stundung des Kaufpreises.³³

III. Zahlung Zug um Zug gegen Ware oder Dokumente, Art. 58 I

Gemäss Art. 58 I S. 1 wird der Kaufpreis fällig, wenn der Verkäufer die Ware oder die Dokumente, die zur Verfügung darüber berechtigen, dem Käufer **zur Verfügung gestellt** hat. Was genau unter Zur-Verfügung-Stellen an den Käufer gemeint ist, hängt von den jeweiligen **Lieferbedingungen** des Vertrags ab, welche die Parteien entweder ausdrücklich

---

[22] *Witz/Salger/Lorenz/Witz,* Artt. 58–59, Rn. 3.
[23] KGer Zug, 2.12.2004, CISG-online 1194 = *IHR* 2006, 158, 160: Die Klausel „14 Tage netto" bedeutet, dass Zahlung 14 Tage nach Erhalt der Rechnung erfolgen muss.
[24] *Witz/Salger/Lorenz/Witz,* Artt. 58–59, Rn. 3.
[25] *Staudinger/Magnus,* Art. 58, Rn. 8; MünchKomm/*P. Huber,* Art. 58, Rn. 20; *Ferrari u. a./Mankowski,* Internationales Vertragsrecht, Art. 58, Rn. 6.
[26] Vgl. Serbische Handelskammer, 28.1.2009, CISG-online 1856: Der Zeitraum 45 Tage nach Lieferung begann in Übereinstimmung mit der Handelsklausel CIP Tirana mit der Übergabe der Ware an den Beförderer.
[27] Vgl. unten Rn. 12.
[28] Trib. Padova, 31.3.2004, CISG-online 823 = IHR 2005, 33.
[29] Vertragliche Zahlungsziele über 60 Tage können, soweit sie für den Gläubiger grob nachteilig sind, dazu führen, dass sie nicht durchsetzbar sind oder Schadenersatz auslösen, vgl. Art. 3 V i. V. m. Art. 7 I Richtlinie 2011/7/EU des Europäischen Parlaments und des Rates vom 16. Februar 2011 zur Bekämpfung von Zahlungsverzug im Geschäftsverkehr, AblEG Nr. L 48/1 ff., 23.2.2011.
[30] *Hager/Maultzsch,* 5. Aufl., Art. 58 Rn. 2.
[31] BGer, 18.1.1996, CISG-online 214 = BGE 122 III 43, 47 ff.
[32] OLG München, 21.1.1998, CISG-online 536 = IHR 2001, 197, 198.
[33] LG Hamburg, 26.9.1990, CISG-online 21 = EuZW 1991, 188, 191.

oder stillschweigend (z. B. durch Benutzung eines Incoterms®) festgelegt haben oder sich aus Art. 31 ergeben.

1. Lieferung durch Zur-Verfügung-Stellen der Ware am Ort der Niederlassung des Verkäufers oder am Ort der Lagerung bzw. der Produktion

8   Ohne anderweitige Parteivereinbarung muss der Käufer den Kaufpreis bezahlen, wenn der Verkäufer ihm die Ware zur Verfügung gestellt hat.[34] Betrifft ein Vertrag bestimmte Güter oder unbestimmte Güter, die aus einem bestimmten **Lager** stammen oder die **herzustellen** oder **zu erzeugen** sind, und wussten die Parteien bei Vertragsschluss, dass die Ware sich an einem **bestimmten Ort** befindet oder an einem bestimmten Ort herzustellen oder zu erzeugen war, so erfüllt der Verkäufer seine Lieferpflicht, indem er dem Käufer die Ware an diesem Ort zur Verfügung stellt, Art. 31 lit. b). Ähnliche Pflichten ergeben sich für den Verkäufer aus der Handelsklausel **EXW** (Incoterms® 2010), wonach der Verkäufer die Ware dem Käufer an dem benannten Lieferort zur Verfügung zu stellen hat, und zwar ohne Verladung auf das abholende Beförderungsmittel.[35] Weder das CISG noch die Incoterms® definieren, was **Zur-Verfügung-Stellen** an den Käufer bedeutet. Eine autonome Auslegung des CISG führt zu den Grundvoraussetzungen, dass die **Ware einem Vertrag zugewiesen** werden kann[36] und dass der Verkäufer dem Käufer **anzeigt,** dass die Ware zur Abholung bereitsteht.[37] Die Anzeigepflicht des Verkäufers ist auch in der Handelsklausel EXW vorgesehen; gemäss Regel A7 muss der Verkäufer den Käufer in angemessener Weise benachrichtigen, an welchem Ort und zu welcher Zeit ihm die Ware zur Verfügung gestellt wird. Die Grundvoraussetzungen der Zuordnung und der Anzeige stellen klar, dass es nicht darauf ankommen kann, ob der Käufer die Ware schon in einem **physischen Sinne übernommen** hat.[38] In der Einleitung zu den Incoterms® 2000 stellt die IHK ausdrücklich fest, dass der Begriff des Zur-Verfügung-Stellen die gleiche Bedeutung haben soll wie der Begriff der Übernahme der Ware nach CISG.[39] Dieser Hinweis ist missverständlich und darf nicht dahingehend missverstanden werden, dass physische Übernahme der Ware durch den Käufer Voraussetzung des Zur-Verfügung-Stellen sei. Vielmehr sollte sich der Hinweis auf das CISG auf den Begriff des Zur-Verfügung-Stellen beziehen. Folglich setzen die Incoterms® genauso wie das CISG die Zuordnung zum Vertrag und die Anzeige an den Käufer voraus.[40] Zur-Verfügung-Stellen kann darüber hinaus auch die **Prüfung,** die **Verpackung**[41] sowie die **Kennzeichnung** gemäss Regel A9 der Handelsklausel EXW (Incoterms® 2010) beinhalten. **Beladung** hingegen ist weder nach CISG noch nach der Handelsklausel EXW Incoterms® 2010 erforderlich.[42]

9   Nach Erhalt der Anzeige des Verkäufers ist der Käufer verpflichtet, die Ware innerhalb einer **angemessenen kurzen Frist** abzunehmen.[43] Diese kurze Reaktionszeit gilt un-

---

[34] Als Beispiel für eine anderweitige Parteivereinbarung vgl. OLG Braunschweig, 28.10.1999, CISG-online 510 = CLOUT Nr. 361 = TranspR-IHR 2000, 4: Der Käufer war nach dem Vertrag verpflichtet, den Kaufpreis vorauszuzahlen (Verschiffung war abhängig von Zahlung der Rechnung) und konnte deshalb nicht den Verkäufer anhalten, ihm die Ware vor Zahlung zur Verfügung zu stellen.
[35] Incoterms 2010, EXW, A 4.
[36] Vgl. oben *Widmer Lüchinger,* Art. 31 Rn. 50: Ausscheiden der Ware oder besondere Kennzeichnung nicht nötig.
[37] Sekretariatskommentar, Art. 29, Nr. 16, Art. 81, Nr. 7; oben *Widmer Lüchinger,* Art. 31 Rn. 51; *Kröll u. a./P. Butler/Harindranath,* Art. 58, Rn. 20; *Ferrari u. a./Mankowski,* Internationales Vertragsrecht, Art. 58, Rn. 10.
[38] *Hager/Maultzsch,* 5. Aufl., Art. 58 Rn. 3; *Staudinger/Magnus,* Art. 58, Rn. 9; *Honsell/Schnyder/Straub,* Art. 58, Rn. 21.
[39] Incoterms® 2000, ICC Publication No. 560, Introduction, S. 6.
[40] *Bredow/Seiffert,* Incoterms® 2000, Erläuterungen EXW, Rn. 15.
[41] Vgl. oben *Widmer Lüchinger,* Art. 31 Rn. 53.
[42] Vgl. oben *Widmer Lüchinger,* Art. 31 Rn. 54; Incoterms® 2010, EXW, Regel A 4.
[43] *Hager/Maultzsch,* 5. Aufl., Art. 58 Rn. 4, die von einer angemessen Zeit sprechen; *Staudinger/Magnus,* Art. 58, Rn. 11; *Bianca/Bonell/Maskow,* Art. 58, Anm. 2.4.; *Brunner,* Art. 58, Rn. 1, dem zufolge diese Zeitspanne nur einem Käufer zugutekommt, der nicht von einer Anlieferung in diesem Zeitpunkt hätte ausgehen

abhängig vom Recht des Käufers, die Ware nach Art. 58 III kurz zu untersuchen. Der Käufer ist also verpflichtet, die kurze Frist zur Abnahme der Ware auch dann einzuhalten, wenn er die Ware nach Art. 58 III untersuchen will; in diesem Fall muss er beantragen, dass die kurze Untersuchung innerhalb der Abnahmefrist stattfindet.

Die **Anzeige der Lieferbereitschaft** durch den Verkäufer wird **wirksam,** wenn sie dem **10** Käufer **zugeht.**[44] Art. 27, dem zufolge jede Anzeige nach Teil III des Übereinkommens auf Risiko des Empfängers reist, findet keine Anwendung.[45] Dies ist gerechtfertigt, weil die hier besprochene Anzeige im Übereinkommen nicht ausdrücklich vorgesehen ist[46] und Art. 27 keine passende Risikoverteilung für solche Fälle vorsieht, in denen – wie hier – eine Anzeige Pflichten des Erklärungsempfängers begründet.[47]

2. Lieferung durch Zur-Verfügung-Stellen der Ware am Ort der Niederlassung des Käufers oder an jedem anderen vereinbarten Ort

Wenn der Verkäufer verpflichtet ist, die Ware dem Käufer an dem Ort seiner Nieder- **11** lassung oder an jedem anderen bestimmten Ort zur Verfügung zu stellen (Art. 31 i. V. m. Art. 6), so muss der Verkäufer die Ware an diesem Ort zur Verfügung stellen und dem Käufer dies im Falle der Lieferung an einem anderen Ort als der Niederlassung des Käufers anzeigen.[48] Das Gleiche gilt für sämtliche Handelsklauseln der **Klassen F und D der Incoterms®**. Bei Vereinbarung der Handelsklauseln DAP oder DDP (Incoterms® 2010) muss der Verkäufer die Ware dem Käufer entladebereit auf dem ankommenden Beförderungsmittel am benannten Bestimmungsort zur Verfügung stellen.[49] Auch hat der Verkäufer den Käufer über alles Nötige zu benachrichtigen, damit dieser die üblicherweise notwendigen Massnahmen zur Übernahme der Ware treffen kann.[50] Für das Risiko der (rechtzeitigen) Übermittlung solcher Anzeigen gilt das Gleiche wie beim Zur-Verfügung-Stellen an den Käufer am Ort der Lagerung oder der Produktion.[51] Abhängig davon, ob der Käufer sein Recht zur kurzen Untersuchung der Ware gemäss Art. 58 III ausübt, wird der Kaufpreis fällig, wenn der Verkäufer dem Käufer die Ware zur Verfügung stellt und, im Falle der Lieferung an einem anderen Ort als der Niederlassung des Käufers, ihm dies anzeigt. Wenn der Verkäufer das Inkasso des Kaufpreises nicht vorbereitet hat, indem er entweder ein Dokumentarinkasso mit dem Käufer vereinbart oder den Beförderer der Ware zur Entgegennahme der Zahlung berechtigt hat, kommt dem Käufer eine angemessene Zeit zur Ausführung der Zahlung zu (Art. 57 I lit. a)).[52]

3. Verträge, die eine Beförderung der Ware erfordern

Erfordert ein Kaufvertrag die Beförderung der Ware, so liefert der Verkäufer gemäss **12** Art. 31 lit. a), wenn er die Ware dem ersten Beförderer zur Übermittlung an den Käufer übergeben hat. Übt der Verkäufer sein Recht nach Art. 58 II, die Ware mit der Massgabe zu versenden, dass die Ware oder die Dokumente, die zur Verfügung darüber berechtigen, dem

---

müssen; *Enderlein/Maskow/Strohbach,* Art. 58, Anm. 5.2.; *U. Huber,* RabelsZ 43 (1979), 413, 515; *Piltz,* Internationales Kaufrecht, Rn. 4–155.
[44] *Hager/Maultzsch,* 5. Aufl., Art. 58 Rn. 4.
[45] *Hager/Maultzsch,* 5. Aufl., Art. 58 Rn. 4; *Kröll u. a./P. Butler/Harindranath,* Art. 58, Rn. 20; *Ferrari u. a./ Mankowski,* Internationales Vertragsrecht, Art. 58, Rn. 10.
[46] *Hager/Maultzsch,* 5. Aufl., Art. 58 Rn. 4.
[47] *Hager/Maultzsch,* 5. Aufl., Art. 58 Rn. 4; *Noussias,* Zugangsbedürftigkeit von Mitteilungen, S. 126 ff.; *Kröll u. a./P. Butler/Harindranath,* Art. 58, Rn. 20; *Ferrari u. a./Mankowski,* Internationales Vertragsrecht, Art. 58, Rn. 10.
[48] OLG Düsseldorf, 28.5.2004, CISG-online 850 = IHR 2004, 203; *Hager/Maultzsch,* 5. Aufl., Art. 58 Rn. 5; *Kröll u. a./P. Butler/Harindranath,* Art. 58, Rn. 21 beschränken die Anzeigepflicht auf die Fälle der zeitlich nicht gebundenen Lieferung an einem dritten Ort.
[49] DAP/DDP Incoterms® 2010, Regel A 4.
[50] DAP/DDP Incoterms® 2010, Regel A 7.
[51] Vgl. oben Rn. 10.
[52] *Hager/Maultzsch,* 5. Aufl., Art. 58 Rn. 5.

Käufer nur gegen Zahlung des Kaufpreises übergeben werden, nicht aus,[53] so ist der Käufer gemäss Art. 58 I erst dann zur Zahlung des Kaufpreises verpflichtet, wenn ihm die Ware zur Verfügung gestellt wurde. Zur Verfügung gestellt wird dem Käufer die Ware nicht an dem Ort, an dem der Verkäufer die Ware dem ersten Beförderer zur Übermittlung an den Käufer übergibt, sondern am **Ankunftsort,** wo der Käufer die Ware vom Beförderer übernimmt.[54] Der Verkäufer muss den Käufer von der Ankunft der Ware **unterrichten.**[55] Abhängig vom vereinbarten Zahlungsmittel steht dem Käufer sodann eine angemessen lange Frist zur Zahlung am Ort der Niederlassung des Verkäufers zu.[56] Wenn die Ware während des Transports untergeht oder beschädigt wird, muss der Käufer gemäss Art. 67 i. V. m. Art. 66 trotzdem den Kaufpreis zahlen. Diese Pflicht wird fällig ab dem Zeitpunkt der erwarteten Ankunft der Ware am Empfangsort.[57] Gleiches gilt für Handelsklauseln der C-Klasse (Incoterms® 2010), bei deren Geltung der Verkäufer die Beförderung der Ware organisieren muss.[58] Freilich wird in der Praxis ein Vertrag, der die Beförderung der Ware erfordert, zumeist auf der Basis einer **dokumentären Zahlungsklausel** abgewickelt.[59]

4. Verträge über Ware, die sich auf dem Transport befindet

13 Für Verträge über Ware, die sich auf dem Transport befindet, gelten die gleichen Regeln wie für Verträge, welche die Beförderung der Ware erfordern.[60] Folglich wird der Kaufpreis fällig, wenn dem Käufer die Ware am **Empfangsort** zur Verfügung gestellt wurde.[61] In der Praxis werden Verträge über Ware, die sich auf dem Transport befindet, zumeist auf der Basis einer **dokumentären Zahlungsklausel** abgewickelt.[62]

5. Verträge über Ware, die sich in einem Lagerhaus eines Dritten befindet

14 Verträge über Ware, die sich in einem Lagerhaus einer Drittpartei befindet, folgen grundsätzlich den gleichen Regeln wie Verträge über Ware, die dem Käufer am Ort der Lagerung (in diesem Fall ein Lagerhaus des Verkäufers) oder der Produktion zur Verfügung gestellt werden.[63] Der einzige Unterschied besteht darin, dass die **Drittpartei als Lagerhalter** dem Käufer die Ware zur Verfügung stellen muss. In der Literatur ist umstritten, ob es erforderlich ist, dass der Lagerhalter das Recht des Käufers auf Besitz der Ware anerkennt,[64] oder ob es genügt, dass der Verkäufer dem Käufer einen Lagerschein aushändigt oder die Drittpartei als Lagerhalter anweist, die Ware dem Käufer auszuhändigen.[65] Gemäss Art. 58 II kann der Verkäufer dabei die Drittpartei instruieren, dem Käufer die Ware nur gegen Empfang der Zahlung auszuhändigen.[66] Freilich werden in den meisten

---

[53] Vgl. unten Rn. 17.
[54] Vgl. *U. Huber*, RabelsZ 43 (1979), 413, 514; *Karollus*, S. 169; *Soergel/Lüderitz/Budzikiewicz*, Art. 58, Rn. 3; *Neumayer/Ming*, Art. 58, Anm. 3b.; *Piltz*, Internationales Kaufrecht, Rn. 4–155; *Staudinger/Magnus*, Art. 58, Rn. 15; *Honsell/Schnyder/Straub*, Art. 58, Rn. 27; *Kröll u. a./P. Butler/Harindranath*, Art. 58, Rn. 23.
[55] Vgl. CIF Incoterms® 2010, Regel A 7.
[56] Vgl. oben Art. 57 Rn. 16; *Hager/Maultzsch*, 5. Aufl., Art. 58 Rn. 7; *Kröll u. a./P. Butler/Harindranath*, Art. 58, Rn. 23.
[57] *Staudinger/Magnus*, Art. 58, Rn. 15; *Hager/Maultzsch*, 5. Aufl., Art. 58 Rn. 7; MünchKomm/*P. Huber*, Art. 58, Rn. 18.
[58] Vgl. CFR, CIF, CPT, CIP Incoterms® 2010.
[59] Vgl. unten Rn. 15–16.
[60] Vgl. oben Rn. 12. *Honsell/Schnyder/Straub*, Art. 58, Rn. 28; *Kröll u. a./P. Butler/Harindranath*, Art. 58, Rn. 24; *Ferrari u. a./Mankowski*, Internationales Vertragsrecht, Art. 58, Rn. 18.
[61] Vgl. *Hager/Maultzsch*, 5. Aufl., Art. 58 Rn. 8.
[62] Vgl. unten Rn. 15–16. *Honsell/Schnyder/Straub*, Art. 58, Rn. 28; *Kröll u. a./P. Butler/Harindranath*, Art. 58, Rn. 24.
[63] Vgl. oben Rn. 8 ff.
[64] *Hager/Maultzsch*, 5. Aufl., Art. 58 Rn. 6; *Honsell/Schnyder/Straub*, Art. 58, Rn. 25.
[65] *Staudinger/Magnus*, Art. 58, Rn. 12; *Ferrari u. a./Mankowski*, Internationales Vertragsrecht, Art. 58, Rn. 12; vgl. auch *Widmer Lüchinger*, Art. 31 Rn. 58 ff.
[66] Diese Vorschrift gilt analog; so auch *Kröll u. a./P. Butler/Harindranath*, Art. 58, Rn. 22; *Ferrari u. a./Mankowski*, Internationales Vertragsrecht, Art. 58, Rn. 12.

Fällen bestimmte **Zahlungsklauseln,** wie zum Beispiel „cash against warehouse receipt" (Kasse gegen Lagerschein) oder „cash against documents" (Kasse gegen Dokumente), vereinbart sein, aus denen wiederum eine stillschweigende Vereinbarung der Zahlungszeit folgt.[67]

6. Zahlung gegen Dokumente

Sieht ein Vertrag Zahlung gegen Dokumente vor, so werden die Einzelheiten der Dokumentenvorlage, also die Frage, welche Dokumente unter Einbezug welcher Banken an welchem Ort vorzulegen sind, üblicherweise im Vertrag detailliert geregelt sein. In solchen Fällen wird der Kaufpreis nur dann fällig, wenn **vertragsgemässe Dokumente** vorgelegt werden.[68] Soweit darin tatsächlich ein Konflikt mit dem engen Wortlaut von Art. 58, dem zufolge nur Dokumente vorzulegen sind, die zur Verfügung über die Ware berechtigen, zu sehen ist, muss von einer Derogation von Art. 58 ausgegangen werden. Der Vertrag kann dabei ausdrücklich oder stillschweigend, in der Praxis oft durch Verweis auf die Incoterms®, diejenigen Dokumente bezeichnen, die der Verkäufer vorlegen muss. Abhängig von der gewählten Liefermodalität und den dazu benötigten Transport- und Lagerverhältnissen, wird der Verkäufer zumeist verpflichtet sein, traditionelle Warenpapiere, wie z. B. ein Konnossement (bill of lading) oder einen Lagerschein (warehouse receipts), vorzulegen.[69] Viele Incoterms® verpflichten den Verkäufer, das übliche Transportdokument vorzulegen.[70] Dabei stellen die traditionellen Warenpapiere die wichtigsten Dokumente dar, weil sie zur Verfügung über die Ware berechtigen und somit als „Ersatz für die Ware" dienen. Der Vertrag oder die insofern relevante Zahlungsklausel kann den Verkäufer darüber hinaus verpflichten, weitere Dokumente, wie z. B. Rechnungen, multimodale oder kombinierte Transportdokumente, Versicherungsdokumente oder Herkunfts-, Qualitäts- oder Zollbescheinigungen vorzulegen.[71] Der Grund für die Einbeziehung sämtlicher Dokumente, die der Vertrag erfordert, liegt darin, dass eine dokumentäre Transaktion den Verkäufer verpflichtet, vertragsgemässe Dokumente vorzulegen (Dokumentenstrenge). Jede Vertragswidrigkeit kann verhindern, dass der Kaufpreis fällig wird.[72] Dokumente werden dem Käufer üblicherweise dadurch zur Verfügung gestellt, dass sie einer Bank des Käufers (z. B. im Falle der Zahlungsklausel „cash against documents") oder einer bestätigenden Bank im Land des Verkäufers (z. B. im Falle einer Akkreditivklausel) vorgelegt werden. Dokumentäre Zahlungsklauseln beinhalten üblicherweise eine **Derogation von Art. 58 III,** mit der Folge, dass der Käufer vor Zahlung kein Recht auf kurze Untersuchung der Ware hat.[73]

Wenn der Vertrag eine Zahlung gegen Dokumente vorsieht, ohne allerdings eine detaillierte Regelung der Dokumentenvorlage zu enthalten, so bestimmt Art. 58, dass die Fälligkeit des Kaufpreisanspruchs nur dann eintritt, wenn dem Käufer Dokumente zur Verfügung gestellt wurden, die zur Verfügung über die Ware berechtigen. **Welche Dokumente** der Verkäufer genau vorzulegen hat, lässt sich Art. 58 hingegen nicht entnehmen.[74] Indem Art. 58 auf Dokumente verweist, die zur Verfügung über die Ware berechtigen, weist er einen engeren Wortlaut auf als Art. 57, der schlicht von Dokumenten spricht. Der Wortlaut von Art. 58 ist insofern auch enger als der von Art. 34, der von Dokumenten

---

[67] Vgl. oben Rn. 5; *Honsell/Schnyder/Straub,* Art. 58, Rn. 25; *Kröll u. a./P. Butler/Harindranath,* Art. 58, Rn. 22; *Ferrari u. a./Mankowski,* Internationales Vertragsrecht, Art. 58, Rn. 12.
[68] *Hager/Maultzsch,* 5. Aufl., Art. 58 Rn. 9; *Staudinger/Magnus,* Art. 58, Rn. 14.
[69] *Murray,* Draft Digest, S. 440, 452; *Hager/Maultzsch,* 5. Aufl., Art. 58 Rn. 10.
[70] Vgl. Regel A8 der entsprechenden Handelsklauseln; vgl. *Schwenzer,* (2005) Vict. U. Well. L. Rev. 37, 795, 802 ff.
[71] KGer St. Gallen, 12.8.1997, CISG-online 330 = CLOUT Nr. 216: Zollpapiere sind nicht erforderlich, wenn dem Käufer die Ware an einem bestimmten Ort im Land des Verkäufers zur Verfügung gestellt wurde. A. A. *Murray,* Draft Digest, S. 440, 452, der sich gegen die Einbeziehung von Zolldokumenten sowie von Herkunfts- und Qualitätsbescheinigungen wehrt.
[72] Vgl. CIETAC, 24.2.2005, CISG-online 1824 (Schweinefleisch-Fall).
[73] *Staudinger/Magnus,* Art. 58, Rn. 14.
[74] *Hager/Maultzsch,* 5. Aufl., Art. 58 Rn. 10; *Honsell/Schnyder/Straub,* Art. 58, Rn. 34.

spricht, die sich auf die Ware beziehen.[75] Der engere Wortlaut von Art. 58 hat zum Ziel, die Fälligkeit des Kaufpreises durch Vorlage bloss nebensächlicher Dokumente zu verhindern. Ohne Lieferung von **Warenpapieren** oder **Sperrpapieren,** die den Käufer unter Ausschluss des Verkäufers zur Verfügung über die Ware berechtigen, aber unabhängig davon, ob sie schuldrechtlich oder sachenrechtlich wirken, wird der Kaufpreis nicht fällig.[76] Zu den Waren- und Sperrpapieren zählen die **echten Traditionspapiere,** wie z. B. **Konnossement** oder **Orderlagerschein,** sowie Papiere, die ein **Auslieferungsversprechen des Gewahrsamsinhabers** enthalten, wie z. B. Verpflichtungsscheine, akzeptierte Anweisungen, Konnossementteilschein, Kaiteilschein, delivery warrant, Frachtbriefdoppel bei der Eisenbahnbeförderung, CMR Frachtbrief bei der internationalen Strassenbeförderung und das Luftfrachtbriefdritt, nicht dagegen ein Lieferschein, Qualitätszeugnisse, Rechnungen oder Empfangsbestätigungen.[77] Auch eine Versicherungspolice reicht nicht aus.[78] Enthält der Vertrag keine dokumentäre Zahlungsklausel, so berechtigt Art. 58 den Verkäufer nicht, bereits aufgrund einer Dokumentenvorlage Zahlung zu verlangen; vielmehr kommt es in einem solchen Fall auf das Zur-Verfügung-Stellen der Ware an.

IV. Verträge über zu befördernde Ware, die mit der Massgabe des Verkäufers versendet wird, dass sie oder die sie vertretenden Dokumente nur gegen Zahlung übergeben werden, Art. 58 II

17   Erfordert ein Vertrag die Beförderung der Ware, so erfüllt der Verkäufer seine Lieferpflicht gemäss Art. 31 lit. a), wenn er die Ware dem ersten Beförderer zur Übermittlung an den Käufer übergibt. Durch Vornahme dieser Handlung wird der Käufer freilich noch nicht in die Position versetzt, über die Ware zu verfügen. Der Käufer übernimmt die Ware vielmehr erst am **Empfangsort,** d. h. dort, wo der Beförderer die Ware an den Käufer aushändigt. Dabei wird der Kaufpreis bereits mit Erhalt der Anzeige der Erfüllungsbereitschaft durch den Verkäufer fällig, Art. 58 I.[79] Allerdings kann der Verkäufer gemäss Art. 58 II die Ware mit der Massgabe versenden, dass sie oder die zu ihrer Verfügung berechtigenden Dokumente dem Käufer nur gegen Zahlung des Kaufpreises ausgehändigt werden. Nichtsdestotrotz hat der Käufer nach Art. 58 III das Recht, die Ware vor Zahlung kurz zu untersuchen.

V. Rechtsfolgen bei Nichtbeachtung der Zahlungszeit

1. Die Rechtsbehelfe des Verkäufers wegen verspäteter Zahlung

18   Durch Festlegung der Zahlungszeit stellt Art. 58 zusammen mit Art. 57 bezüglich des Zahlungsortes eine der wichtigsten Regelungen der Pflicht des Käufers zur Zahlung des Kaufpreises dar. Wenn der Käufer den Kaufpreis bei Fälligkeit nicht zahlt, ist der Verkäufer berechtigt, die Rechtsbehelfe gemäss Artt. 61 ff. auszuüben. Zunächst kann der Verkäufer den Käufer gemäss Art. 61 I lit. a) i. V. m. Art. 62 verpflichten, den Kaufpreis zu zahlen. Die Geltendmachung des **Erfüllungsanspruchs** wird nur dann Sinn machen, wenn der Verkäufer den Kaufvertrag grundsätzlich aufrecht erhalten will und weiterhin willens und in der Lage ist, die Ware gemäss Vertrag zu liefern. Zweitens kann der Verkäufer gemäss Art. 61 I

---

[75] Vgl. oben Art. 57 Rn. 11; *Widmer Lüchinger,* Art. 34 Rn. 1; *Ferrari u. a./Mankowski,* Internationales Vertragsrecht, Art. 58, Rn. 22.
[76] BGH, 3.4.1996, CISG-online 135 = CLOUT Nr. 171: Herkunftszertifikate und Qualitätsbescheinigungen reichen nicht, um die Zahlung fällig werden zu lassen; *Gabriel,* (2005-06) 25 J. L. & Com. 273, 280 ff.; *Ferrari u. a./Mankowski,* Internationales Vertragsrecht, Art. 58, Rn. 19 ff.: nur Traditions- und Sperrpapiere („Dokumente statt der Ware"). Anders *Kröll u. a./P. Butler/Harindranath,* Art. 58, Rn. 27: sämtliche Dokumente, die der Verkäufer zur Erfüllung seiner Lieferpflicht benutzen kann.
[77] *Hager/Maultzsch,* 5. Aufl., Art. 58 Rn. 10.
[78] So auch *Staudinger/Magnus,* Art. 58, Rn. 21. A. A. *Hager/Maultzsch,* 5. Aufl., Art. 58 Rn. 10.
[79] Vgl. oben Rn. 12.

lit. b) i. V. m. Art. 74 **Schadenersatz** für den durch die verspätete Zahlung entstandenen Schaden verlangen. Drittens kann der Verkäufer dem Käufer gemäss Art. 61 I lit. a) i. V. m. Art. 63 I eine angemessene **Nachfrist zur Erfüllung** seiner Pflicht zur Zahlung des Kaufpreises setzen. Zahlt der Käufer auch innerhalb der angemessenen Nachfrist den Kaufpreis nicht, so kann der Verkäufer gemäss Art. 61 I lit. a) i. V. m. Art. 64 I lit. b) den Vertrag aufheben. Nur in besonderen Ausnahmefällen wird der Verkäufer unmittelbar zur **Vertragsaufhebung** berechtigt sein, wenn der Käufer nicht zeitgerecht zahlt. Das Recht zur Vertragsaufhebung setzt nämlich einen wesentlichen Vertragsbruch i. S. v. Art. 25 voraus und ein solcher wesentlicher Vertragsbruch wird im Falle einer Nichtzahlung nur dann gegeben sein, wenn der Käufer die Erfüllung des Vertrags endgültig verweigert oder die Zahlungszeit von besonderer Bedeutung war.[80] In einem solchen Fall wird der Verkäufer gemäss Art. 61 I lit. a) i. V. m. Art. 64 I lit. a) berechtigt sein, unmittelbar den Vertrag aufzuheben.

2. Das Recht des Verkäufers zur Zurückweisung einer vorzeitigen Zahlung

Wenn der Käufer den Kaufpreis zahlt, bevor Fälligkeit im Sinne von Art. 58 eingetreten ist, stellt sich die Frage, ob der Verkäufer eine solche **vorzeitige Zahlung zurückweisen** kann. Die herrschende Meinung in der Literatur vertritt ein solches allgemeines Zurückweisungsrecht des Verkäufers bei vorzeitigen Zahlungen.[81] Als Begründung wird auf eine analoge Anwendung von Art. 52 I verwiesen, dem zufolge der Käufer das Recht hat, die Abnahme der Ware zu verweigern, wenn der Verkäufer die Ware vor dem festgesetzten Zeitpunkt liefert.

Nach hier vertretener Ansicht kann der herrschenden Meinung nicht gefolgt werden. Art. 52 I kann nicht im Wege der Analogie angewendet werden, weil eine **bewusste Lücke** innerhalb des Übereinkommens besteht.[82] Der Vorschlag, eine Art. 52 I entsprechende Regel einzuführen, der zufolge der Verkäufer vorzeitige Zahlungen hätte zurückweisen können, wurde an der Wiener Konferenz ausdrücklich abgelehnt.[83] Ohne eine solche Regel aber finden die **allgemeinen Rechtsbehelfe** des Verkäufers Anwendung. Gemäss Art. 61 I lit. a) i. V. m. Art. 64 I lit. a) und Art. 25 kann der Verkäufer die Zahlung des Kaufpreises vor Fälligkeit aber nur dann zurückweisen, wenn die **vorzeitige Zahlung** einen **wesentlichen Vertragsbruch** darstellt. Ein wesentlicher Vertragsbruch wird aber nur ganz selten vorliegen, z. B. wenn vorhersehbar war, dass die vorzeitige Zahlung dem Käufer unzumutbare Unannehmlichkeiten verursachen würde. In der Regel wird freilich kein wesentlicher Vertragsbruch vorliegen, was zur Folge hat, dass der Verkäufer die Zahlung annehmen muss und etwaige Nachteile als **Schadenersatz** geltend machen muss. Im Wege des Schadenersatzes kann der Verkäufer etwaige **Währungsverluste** ersetzt verlangen. Die „Annahme" der vorzeitigen Zahlung stellt insoweit keinen Verzicht auf die Geltendmachung von Schadenersatz dar.[84] Der praktische Unterschied zwischen der herrschenden Auffassung und der hier vertretenen Auffassung liegt in der Verteilung der **Beweislast** für einen Schadenersatzanspruch auf Ersatz von durch vorzeitige Zahlung entstandene Währungsverluste. Der herrschenden Auffassung zur Folge kann der Verkäufer eine vorzeitige Zahlung zurückweisen und so die Entstehung eines Währungsverlusts vermeiden. Nach der hier vertretenen Auffassung muss der Verkäufer die vorzeitige Zahlung grundsätzlich annehmen (es sei denn, es läge ausnahmsweise ein wesentlicher Vertragsbruch vor); erst dann kann der Käufer Ersatz seines Währungsverlustes verlangen. Im Rahmen des Schadenersatzprozesses muss der Ver-

---

[80] Vgl. unten Art. 64 Rn. 6 ff.
[81] *Hager/Maultzsch*, 5. Aufl., Art. 59 Rn. 3; *Staudinger/Magnus*, Art. 59, Rn. 31; *Bamberger/Roth/Saenger*, Art. 58, Rn. 8; *Bianca/Bonell/Maskow*, Art. 58, Anm. 2.4.; *Enderlein/Maskow/Strohbach*, Art. 58, Anm. 1.2.; *Herber/Czerwenka*, Art. 58, Rn. 12; *Loewe*, Art. 58, S. 79; MünchKomm/*P. Huber*, Art. 58, Rn. 28; *Reinhard*, Art. 58, Rn. 7; *Witz/Salger/Lorenz/Witz*, Artt. 58–59, Rn. 16; *Kröll u. a./P. Butler/Harindranath*, Art. 58, Rn. 33; *Ferrari u. a./Mankowski*, Internationales Vertragsrecht, Art. 59, Rn. 10.
[82] So auch *Honsell/Schnyder/Straub*, Art. 58, Rn. 86.
[83] O. R., S. 123, 370 ff.
[84] A. A. *Kröll u. a./P. Butler/Harindranath*, Art. 58, Rn. 33.

käufer sodann die Fakten bezüglich seines Währungsverlustes behaupten und beweisen. Daneben besteht ein weiterer Unterschied zwischen den zwei Ansichten in der Verteilung der Beweislast: Nach der hier vertretenen Auffassung kann der Verkäufer vorzeitige Zahlungen nur dann zurückweisen, wenn er einen wesentlichen Vertragsbruch geltend machen kann. Nach der herrschenden Auffassung (sowie gemäss PICC und einigen nationalen Rechtsordnungen) kann der Verkäufer hingegen vorzeitige Zahlungen zurückweisen, es sei denn, er habe kein legitimes Interesse an der Ausübung seines Zurückweisungsrechts.[85] Bezüglich vorzeitiger Zahlungen wird der Verkäufer üblicherweise aber gerade kein legitimes Interesse an der Zurückweisung haben.[86]

3. Zinsen

21 Zahlt der Käufer einen fälligen Kaufpreis nicht, so kann der Verkäufer nach Art. 78 **Fälligkeitszinsen** verlangen.[87] Anders als nach manchen nationalen Rechtsordnungen bedarf es zur Geltendmachung von Fälligkeitszinsen nach Art. 59 weder einer Aufforderung zur Zahlung noch der Einhaltung sonstiger Förmlichkeiten seitens des Verkäufers.[88] Das CISG setzt die Zinshöhe nicht autonom fest; nach herrschender Meinung muss daher insoweit nationales Recht nach dem anwendbaren Kollisionsrecht angewendet werden.[89]

22 In der europäischen Gemeinschaft hat die **Richtlinie zur Bekämpfung von Zahlungsverzug im Geschäftsverkehr,** die nunmehr in einer Neufassung vorliegt,[90] das Recht der Mitgliedstaaten bezüglich der Zeit, zu welcher Zahlungen im Geschäftsverkehr fällig werden, angeglichen.[91] Gemäss Art. 3 der Richtlinie fallen Zinsen automatisch, d. h. ohne besondere Aufforderung, mit Ablauf des vertraglich vereinbarten Zeitpunkts an.[92] Haben die Parteien keinen Zahlungszeitpunkt vereinbart, so fallen Zinsen 30 Tage nach Erhalt der Rechnung oder einer äquivalenten Zahlungsaufforderung durch den Gläubiger an.[93] Erhält der Schuldner die Rechnung oder eine äquivalente Zahlungsaufforderung vor der Ware, so fallen Zinsen 30 Tage nach Erhalt der Ware an.[94] Im Anwendungsbereich des CISG hat Art. 78 freilich Vorrang vor jeder nationalen Regelung, auch wenn diese auf die Zahlungsverzugsrichtlinie zurückzuführen ist.[95] Dieser Vorrang ergibt sich daraus, dass nationale Umsetzungen von EG-Richtlinien keine völkerrechtlichen Übereinkünfte i. S. v. Art. 90 sind.[96]

VI. Zurückbehaltungsrechte

1. Das Zurückbehaltungsrecht des Verkäufers gemäss Art. 58 I und II

23 Das Prinzip der **Zug-um-Zug-Erfüllung** wird begrenzt durch die **Zurückbehaltungsrechte des Verkäufers.** Gemäss Art. 58 I 2 kann der Verkäufer die Übergabe der

---

[85] Vgl. Art. 6.1.5 I PICC.
[86] Vgl. *Brunner,* Art. 58, Rn. 13.
[87] Vgl. oben Art. 53 Rn. 21. Anders: Dist. Ct. Dolny Kubin (Slowakische Republik), 21.1.2008, CISG-online 1762: das Gericht wendete fälschlicherweise nationales Recht auf die Zinsfrage an und sprach Zinsen vom Zeitpunkt des Vertragsschlusses zu.
[88] Vgl. oben Art. 59 Rn. 1 ff.
[89] Vgl. unten *Bacher,* Art. 78 Rn. 26 ff.
[90] Richtlinie 2011/7/EU des Europäischen Parlaments und des Rates vom 16. Februar 2011 zur Bekämpfung von Zahlungsverzug im Geschäftsverkehr, ABlEG Nr. L 48/1 ff., 23.2.2011.
[91] Siehe auch die Vorgängerrichtlinie 2000/35/EU des Europäischen Parlaments und des Rates vom 29. Juni 2000 zur Bekämpfung von Zahlungsverzug im Geschäftsverkehr, ABlEG Nr. L 200/35, 8. August 2000.
[92] Art. 3 III lit. a) der Zahlungsverzugsrichtlinie.
[93] Art. 3 III lit. b) (i) der Zahlungsverzugsrichtlinie.
[94] Art. 3 III lit. b) (iii) der Zahlungsverzugsrichtlinie.
[95] *Schlechtriem,* Internationales Kaufrecht, Rn. 319; *Schlechtriem/P. Butler,* UN Law, Rn. 319; *Ferrari,* IHR 2003, 153, 159. A. A. *Faust,* RabelsZ 68 (2004), 511, 514, der auf Art. 6 II der Richtlinie abstellt.
[96] *Schlechtriem,* Internationales Kaufrecht, Rn. 345a; *Schlechtriem/P. Butler,* UN Law, Rn. 235a; *Kröll u. a./P. Butler/Harindranath,* Art. 58, Rn. 3.

Ware oder der Dokumente von der Zahlung abhängig machen, wenn Lieferung am Ort der Niederlassung des Verkäufers, am Ort der Niederlassung des Käufers oder an einem sonstigen bestimmten Ort stattfindet.[97] Befindet sich die Ware hingegen in einem Lagerhaus bei einer Drittpartei, so kann der Verkäufer die Übergabe der Ware oder der Dokumente praktisch nicht von der Zahlung abhängig machen; Art. 58 I 2 gilt für diesen Fall nicht.[98]

Gemäss Art. 58 II kann der Verkäufer die Ware mit der Massgabe versenden, dass die Ware oder die Dokumente dem Käufer nur gegen Zahlung des Kaufpreises zu übergeben sind. Diese Bestimmung gilt sowohl für Verträge, die eine Beförderung der Ware erfordern, als auch für Verträge über Ware, die sich auf dem Transport befindet.[99] Art. 58 II gilt darüber hinaus auch in den Fällen, in denen sich die Ware in einem Lagerhaus bei einer Drittpartei befindet; der Verkäufer kann den Lagerhalter anweisen, die Ware nur gegen Zahlung des Kaufpreises herauszugeben.[100] 24

2. Das Zurückbehaltungsrecht des Käufers gemäss Art. 58 I

Das **Zurückbehaltungsrecht des Käufers** folgt aus Art. 58 I 1, dem zufolge der Kaufpreis nur dann fällig wird, wenn die Ware oder die Dokumente, die zur Verfügung darüber berechtigen, dem Käufer zur Verfügung gestellt wurden.[101] Mit anderen Worten hat der Käufer das Recht den Kaufpreis so lange zurückzubehalten, bis der Verkäufer ihm die Ware oder die Dokumente zur Verfügung gestellt, ihn darüber informiert und ihm eine kurze Untersuchung der Ware gemäss Art. 58 III gestattet hat.[102] 25

3. Art. 71 und das allgemeine Zurückbehaltungsrecht

Weitere Zurückbehaltungsrechte können sich aus Art. 71 ergeben, wonach eine Partei die Erfüllung ihrer Pflichten aussetzen kann, wenn sich nach Vertragsabschluss herausstellt, dass die andere Partei einen wesentlichen Teil ihrer Pflichten nicht erfüllen wird, und zwar a) wegen eines schwerwiegenden Mangels ihrer Fähigkeit, den Vertrag zu erfüllen, oder ihrer Kreditwürdigkeit oder b) wegen ihres Verhaltens bei der Vorbereitung der Erfüllung oder bei der Erfüllung des Vertrags.[103] Art. 71 II stellt ein besonderes Zurückbehaltungsrecht für den Verkäufer zur Verfügung, der die Ware bereits abgesandt hat, bevor sich die oben beschriebenen Gründe herausgestellt haben: In einem solchen Fall kann der Verkäufer die Übergabe der Ware an den Käufer anhalten, selbst wenn der Käufer ein Dokument besitzt, das ihn berechtigt, über die Ware zu verfügen. 26

Da die Zurückbehaltungsrechte nach Art. 58 auf die charakteristischen Leistungen der Parteien, also Lieferung der Ware und Zahlung des Kaufpreises, beschränkt sind, und Art. 71 auf Umstände beschränkt ist, die sich nach Vertragsschluss herausstellen, und Zurückbehaltungsrechte nur vor Fälligkeit ausgeübt werden können,[104] haben Rechtsprechung und Literatur ein **allgemeines Zurückbehaltungsrecht** gemäss Art. 7 II entwickelt, indem sie sich auf die allgemeinen Prinzipien des CISG gestützt haben, die sich aus Art. 58, 71, 80, 81 II 2, 85 S. 2, 86 I 2 ergeben.[105] Die Anerkennung eines allgemeinen Zurückbehaltungsrechts 27

---

[97] *Hager/Maultzsch,* 5. Aufl., Art. 58 Rn. 13.
[98] *Hager/Maultzsch,* 5. Aufl., Art. 58 Rn. 13.
[99] *Hager/Maultzsch,* 5. Aufl., Art. 58 Rn. 13; *Kröll u. a./P. Butler/Harindranath,* Art. 58, Rn. 31.
[100] *Hager/Maultzsch,* 5. Aufl., Art. 58 Rn. 13; *Kröll u. a./P. Butler/Harindranath,* Art. 58, Rn. 31.
[101] *Hager/Maultzsch,* 5. Aufl., Art. 58 Rn. 13; *Kröll u. a./P. Butler/Harindranath,* Art. 58, Rn. 30.
[102] LG Stendal, 12.10.2000, CISG-online 592 = IHR 2001, 30: das Gericht vermischte fälschlicherweise Art. 58 III und Art. 38; *Staudinger/Magnus,* Art. 58, Rn. 22; *Kern,* ZEuP 2000, 839.
[103] Vgl. unten *Fountoulakis,* Art. 71 Rn. 1 ff.
[104] Vgl. unten *Fountoulakis,* Art. 71 Rn. 12 ff.
[105] OGH, 8.11.2005, CISG-online 1156 = IHR 2006, 87, m. zust. Anm. *Cl. Witz,* D. 2007, 530, 540; Schiedsgericht der Handelskammer Zürich, 31.5.1996, CISG-online 1291 = (1998) XXIII YB. Comm. Arb. 128, 144; Audiencia Provincial de Navarra, Spain, 27.3.2000, CISG-online 575 = CLOUT Nr. 397; RB Arnhem, 29.7.2009, CISG-online 1939; CISG-AC, Op. 5 *Schwenzer,* Rule 8 („If the non-conformity does not amount to a

Art. 58 28–30   Teil III. Kapitel III. Pflichten des Käufers

findet weitere Unterstützung in Art. 7.1.3 PICC.[106] Freilich sind der Anwendungsbereich und die Grenzen des allgemeinen Zurückbehaltungsrechts noch nicht vollständig herausgearbeitet worden. Folgende **Fallgruppen** müssen insofern unterschieden werden.

28   Der österreichische Oberste Gerichtshof hat ein allgemeines Zurückbehaltungsrecht zugunsten des Käufers im Falle der **Lieferung von vertragswidriger Ware** anerkannt.[107] Das Hauptargument, ein allgemeines Zurückbehaltungsrecht in diesem Fall anzuerkennen, sah das Gericht darin, dass ansonsten das Untersuchungsrecht des Käufers nach Art. 58 III leerlaufen würde.[108] Eine derart weitgehende Anwendung des allgemeinen Zurückbehaltungsrechts muss zurückgewiesen werden, weil sie die Voraussetzung eines wesentlichen Vertragsbruchs nach Art. 25 bzw. die Voraussetzung einer zukünftigen Verletzung eines wesentlichen Teils der Pflichten nach Art. 71 umgeht und die Bedeutung des Untersuchungsrechts nach Art. 58 III überbewertet.[109] Nach der hier vertretenen Auffassung kann ein allgemeines Zurückbehaltungsrecht nur im Falle **offensichtlicher Vertragswidrigkeiten**, d. h. Vertragswidrigkeiten, die der Käufer während der Übernahme der Ware und der kurzen Untersuchung nach Art. 58 III feststellt, geltend gemacht werden, um den Kaufpreis zurückzuhalten.[110] Wenn die Vertragswidrigkeit einen wesentlichen Vertragsbruch oder zumindest einen wesentlichen Teil der Pflicht zur Lieferung vertragsmässiger Ware betrifft, kann der gesamte Kaufpreis zurückbehalten werden. Stellt die Vertragswidrigkeit hingegen keinen wesentlichen Vertragsbruch dar, so kann der Käufer den Kaufpreis nur teilweise zurückbehalten, und zwar in dem Umfang, in dem er den Kaufpreis nach Art. 50 mindern könnte.[111]

29   Dem Käufer kann ein allgemeines Zurückbehaltungsrecht auch in Fällen zustehen, in denen der Verkäufer nicht seine Pflicht zur Lieferung der Ware oder der Dokumente, sondern eine **andere Pflicht** verletzt hat. Zum Beispiel hat ein Schweizer Gericht festgestellt, dass der Verkäufer den Käufer nicht zur Kaufpreiszahlung verpflichten kann, wenn der Verkäufer selbst es unterlassen hat, dem Käufer den Ort der Lieferung anzuzeigen, obwohl der Verkäufer 14 Tage vor Lieferung dazu vertraglich verpflichtet war.[112] Weigert sich der Verkäufer im Voraus, dem Käufer eine Bestätigung über die vorzunehmende Zahlung auszustellen, so kann der Käufer seine Zahlung zurückhalten.[113] Ein Schiedsgericht verweigerte dem Käufer ein Zurückbehaltungsrecht bezüglich der Stellung eines Dokumentenakkreditivs, weil die Pflicht des Käufers nur von der Vorlage einer Preisliste durch den Verkäufer abhängig war und der Verkäufer nicht nur eine, sondern zwei Preislisten vorgelegt hatte, wenngleich diese unannehmbare Preisvorstellungen enthielten.[114]

30   Der Verkäufer kann sich auf ein allgemeines Zurückbehaltungsrecht berufen, wenn der Käufer einen **wesentlichen Vertragsbruch** bezüglich einer **anderen Pflicht** als seiner Pflicht zur Kaufpreiszahlung und zur Abnahme der Ware begeht, z. B. der Pflicht, die

---

fundamental breach, the buyer still has a right to withhold payment and to refuse to take delivery if reasonable under the circumstances"), Comment 4.d), Rn. 4.18 ff.; *Schwenzer/Hachem*, Art. 4, Rn. 20 und Art. 7, Rn. 40; *Schlechtriem*, (2004) 16 Pace Int'l L. Rev., 279, 289 ff.; *ders.*, Internationales Kaufrecht, Rn. 42d; *ders.*, Auslegung, S. 47, 62 ff.; *ders.*, Symposium Vischer 2005, S. 62 ff.; *ders.*, FS U. Huber 2006, S. 570; *Kern*, ZEuP 2000, 837, 850; *ders.*, Leistungsverweigerungsrechte im UN-Kaufrecht, S. 73 ff.; *Schlechtriem/P. Butler*, UN Law, Rn. 206; unten *Fountoulakis*, Art. 71 Rn. 9 ff.; *dies.*, IHR 2005, 244, 247; oben *Müller-Chen*, Art. 45 Rn. 22; *Nyer*, (2006) 18 Pace Int'l L. Rev., 29, 79; *W. Witz*, FS Schlechtriem, S. 291, 295; *Hartmann*, IHR 2006, 181, 184; *Witz/Salger/Lorenz/Witz*, Art. 7, Rn. 28; *Staudinger/Magnus*, Art. 58, Rn. 23. A. A. *Honsell/Schnyder/Straub*, Art. 58, Rn. 64 ff.

[106] Vgl. *Hartmann*, IHR 2006, 181, 185.
[107] OGH, 8.11.2005, CISG-online 1156 = IHR 2006, 87, 90 ff.
[108] OGH, 8.11.2005, CISG-online 1156 = IHR 2006, 87, 91; oben *Müller-Chen*, Art. 45 Rn. 22.
[109] Vgl. *Shuttle Packaging Systems, LLC v. Jacob Tsonakis, INA SA and INA Plastics Corp.*, U. S. Dist. Ct. (W. D. Mich.), 17.12.2001, CISG-online 773; so auch *Honsell/Schnyder/Straub*, Art. 58, Rn. 66c.
[110] A. A. *Honsell/Schnyder/Straub*, Art. 58, Rn. 66c: Beschränkung des Zurückbehaltungsrechts auf wesentliche Vertragswidrigkeiten.
[111] *Schlechtriem*, Internationales Kaufrecht, Rn. 206; *Schlechtriem*, (2004) 16 Pace Int'l L. Rev., 279, 303; *Schlechtriem/P. Butler*, UN Law, Rn. 206.
[112] KGer Appenzell Ausserhoden, 10.3.2003, CISG-online 852 = IHR 2004, 254, 256.
[113] *Fountoulakis*, IHR 2005, 244, 247 ff.
[114] Vgl. ICC, 11849/2003, CISG-online 1421, Rn. 36 ff.

Herkunft der Ware geheim zu halten.[115] Liegt ein nicht wesentlicher Vertragsbruch bezüglich einer anderen Pflicht als der Pflicht zur Zahlung des Kaufpreises und der Abnahme der Ware vor, so ist in der Literatur vorgeschlagen worden, dass der Verkäufer seine Pflicht zur Lieferung der Ware teilweise zurückbehalten kann, und zwar im Umfang der Höhe seines Schadenersatzanspruches gegen den Käufer, was freilich voraussetzt, dass seine Leistung teilbar ist.[116] Ob der Verkäufer in einem solchen Fall darüber hinaus berechtigt ist, einen **Selbsthilfeverkauf** nach Art. 88 auszuüben, ist noch unentschieden.[117] Nach hier vertretener Ansicht sollte der Verkäufer nicht zum Selbsthilfeverkauf berechtigt sein, da sonst die Schwelle des wesentlichen Vertragsbruchs als Voraussetzung für einen Deckungsverkauf faktisch umgangen werden würde.[118]

Weitergehende **Zurückbehaltungsrechte nach nationalem Recht** sind ausgeschlossen, sofern es um Leistungen aus demselben Vertrag geht.[119] Andererseits können Zurückbehaltungsrechte nach nationalem Recht ausgeübt werden, wenn sie sich aus der Erfüllung eines anderen Vertrages ergeben und zwar unabhängig davon, ob auf diesen anderen Vertrag auch das CISG Anwendung findet.[120] Auch können Zurückbehaltungsrechte nach nationalem Recht geltend gemacht werden, wenn ihr Zweck nicht in der Durchsetzung der Erfüllung des Vertrages, sondern in der Befriedigung des Gläubigers liegt.[121] Auch findet gemäss Art. 4 lit. a) nationales Recht auf möglicherweise bestehende Vorzugsrechte Anwendung, die sich aus sachenrechtlichen oder vertraglichen Sicherungsrechten ergeben. 31

Jedes Zurückbehaltungsrecht, das sich aus dem Übereinkommen ergibt, muss durch die berechtigte Partei durch **Erklärung** gegenüber der anderen Partei ausgeübt werden und findet keinesfalls ipso facto Berücksichtigung.[122] Insofern kann **Art. 71 III als allgemeines Prinzip** des Übereinkommens auch auf Zurückbehaltungsrechte, die sich aus einer anderen Vorschrift des CISG ergeben, sowie auf das allgemeine Zurückbehaltungsrecht angewendet werden. 32

VII. Das Untersuchungsrecht des Käufers vor Zahlung gemäss Art. 58 III

Gemäss Art. 58 III hat der Käufer das Recht, die Ware zu untersuchen, bevor er den Kaufpreis zahlt. Dieses Recht des Käufers beinhaltet naturgemäss nur eine **kurze** und **oberflächliche Untersuchung** der Ware,[123] die sich meist auf die Feststellung der gelieferten **Quantität** beschränken wird. Eine weitergehende Untersuchung der **Qualität** der Ware wird in diesem Zusammenhang nicht möglich sein. Insofern ist es wichtig, das Untersuchungsrecht nach Art. 58 III nicht mit der Obliegenheit des Käufers nach Art. 38 zu verwechseln, wonach der Käufer die Ware auf mögliche Vertragswidrigkeiten hin zu untersuchen hat.[124] Nur im Falle **offensichtlicher Vertragswidrigkeiten,** die in der Praxis zumeist im Falle von Zuviel- oder Zuwenig-Lieferungen gegeben sein werden, wird durch 33

---

[115] *Schlechtriem/P. Butler,* UN Law, Rn. 251; *Schlechtriem,* Internationales Kaufrecht, Rn. 251; vgl. *Bamberger/Roth/Saenger,* Art. 58, Rn. 6; *Ferrari u. a./Mankowski,* Internationales Vertragsrecht, Art. 58, Rn. 27.

[116] *Schlechtriem/P. Butler,* UN Law, Rn. 251.

[117] Vgl. *Hartmann,* IHR 2006, 181, 189 ff.; *Schlechtriem,* (2004) 16 Pace Int'l L. Rev., 279, 301; *Schwenzer/Hachem,* CISG Commentary, Art. 7, Rn. 41.

[118] Anders: *Hartmann,* IHR 2006, 181, 190.

[119] Vgl. OLG Köln, 19.5.2008, CISG-online 1700; *W. Witz,* FS Schlechtriem, S. 291, 295.

[120] *W. Witz,* FS Schlechtriem, S. 291, 295 ff. Vgl. Shanghai No 1 Intermediate People's Court, 29.6.2005, CISG-online 1656: Das Gericht verneinte ein Zurückbehaltungsrecht des Käufers wegen Nichterfüllung des Verkäufers gegenüber einer Kaufpreisklage des Verkäufers aus einem separaten und unabhängigem Vertrag. A. A. RB Arnhem, 29.7.2009, CISG-online 1939.

[121] *W. Witz,* FS Schlechtriem, S. 291, 296; *Hartmann,* IHR 2006, 181, 190.

[122] Vgl. zu Art. 71 LG Stendal, 12.10.2000, CISG-online 592 = IHR 2001, 30; *W. Witz,* FS Schlechtriem, S. 291, 302; *Schlechtriem,* (2004) 16 Pace Int'l L. Rev., 279, 300 ff.; *Schlechtriem/Schwenzer/Schwenzer/Hachem,* CISG Commentary, Art. 4, Rn. 20.

[123] Vgl. *Honsell/Schnyder/Straub,* Art. 58, Rn. 72; *Kröll u. a./P. Butler/Harindranath,* Art. 58, Rn. 5; *Ferrari u. a./Mankowski,* Internationales Vertragsrecht, Art. 58, Rn. 29.

[124] Vgl. oben *Schwenzer,* Art. 38 Rn. 3; *Honnold/Flechtner,* Art. 58, Rn. 339.1; *Piltz,* Internationales Kaufrecht, Rn. 4–158; *Bamberger/Roth/Saenger,* Art. 58, Rn. 6; *Honsell/Schnyder/Straub,* Art. 58, Rn. 70; *Kröll u. a./P. Butler/Harindranath,* Art. 58, Rn. 5. Anders: LG Stendal, 12.10.2000, CISG-online 592 = IHR 2001,

Art. 58 34, 35

das Untersuchungsrecht des Käufers nach Art. 58 III der Beginn der angemessenen Frist nach Art. 39 bestimmt.[125] Die **Kosten** der Untersuchung nach Art. 58 III trägt der Käufer.[126]

34   Das CISG bestimmt nicht, an welchem **Ort** die Untersuchung gemäss Art. 58 III durchgeführt werden kann. In der Literatur ist vorgeschlagen worden, dass diese Untersuchung am **Lieferort** nach Art. 31 zu erfolgen habe.[127] Soweit die Ware am Ort der Niederlassung des Verkäufers, am Ort der Niederlassung des Käufers oder an jedem anderen bestimmten Ort, wie z. B. der Ort der Herstellung, der Erzeugung oder der Lagerung, zu liefern ist (Art. 31 lit. b), lit. c), Art. 6) entstehen keine Probleme, da die Ware an diesen Orten leicht vor Zahlung untersucht werden kann.[128] Als weiterer Grund für diese Ansicht kann angefügt werden, dass in diesen Fällen der Lieferort mit dem Zahlungsort nach Art. 58 I, Art. 57 I lit. b) identisch ist. Anders liegen die Dinge im Falle eines Vertrages, der die **Beförderung der Ware** erfordert, da der Lieferort (Art. 31 lit. a)) und der Zahlungsort (Art. 58 I i. V. m. Art. 57 I lit. a)) verschiedene Orte sein werden, soweit der Verkäufer von seinem Recht nach Art. 58 II keinen Gebrauch macht. In diesem Fall ist die Untersuchung am **Empfangsort** der Ware vorzunehmen.[129] Diese Ansicht wird durch Art. 38 II gestützt, dem zufolge die Untersuchung nach Art. 38 bis nach dem Eintreffen der Ware am Bestimmungsort aufgeschoben werden kann, soweit der Vertrag eine Beförderung der Ware erfordert. Selbst wenn der Verkäufer die Ware mit der Massgabe versendet hat, dass die Ware oder die Dokumente dem Verkäufer nur gegen Zahlung des Kaufpreises übergeben werden (Art. 58 II), kann der Käufer sein Recht gemäss Art. 58 III auf Untersuchung der Ware vor Zahlung ausüben.[130] Sieht ein Vertrag, der die Beförderung der Ware erfordert, Zahlung gegen offene Rechnung vor oder hat der Verkäufer auf sein Recht nach Art. 58 II verzichtet, entstehen keine weiteren Probleme hinsichtlich des Rechts des Käufers, die Ware vor Zahlung zu untersuchen.[131] Die Überlegungen zu Verträgen, welche die Beförderung der Ware erfordern, gelten gleichermassen für Verträge über Ware, die sich bereits auf dem Transport befindet.[132]

35   Das Untersuchungsrecht des Käufers nach Art. 58 III kann **durch Parteivereinbarung ausgeschlossen** werden, Art. 6. Art. 58 III stellt dies selbst klar, indem Fälle vorbehalten bleiben, in welchen die von den Parteien vereinbarten Lieferungs- oder Zahlungsmodalitäten zur Untersuchung keine Gelegenheit bieten. Das praktisch wichtigste Beispiel einer solchen **Zahlungsklausel** ist „cash against documents".[133] „Cash against documents" bedeutet, dass der Käufer gegen Vorlage der vertraglich vereinbarten Dokumente zahlen muss, ohne Möglichkeit, die Ware zuvor zu untersuchen. Dabei spielt es keine Rolle, ob sich im Zeitpunkt der Vorlage der Dokumente die Ware noch auf dem Transport befindet oder bereits angekommen ist.[134] Andere Zahlungsklauseln, die das Untersuchungsrecht des Käufers vor Zahlung ausschliessen, sind „cash against letter of credit" oder „documents against draft".[135]

30: Das Gericht vermischte fälschlicherweise Art. 58 III mit Art. 38 und entschied, dass zwei Monate eine angemessene Zeit darstelle; *Šarčević*, Draft Digest, S. 482, 488.

[125] Vgl. oben *Schwenzer*, Art. 39 Rn. 19.
[126] *Hager/Maultzsch*, 5. Aufl., Art. 58 Rn. 11; MünchKomm/*P. Huber*, Art. 58, Rn. 5; *Staudinger/Magnus*, Art. 58, Rn. 27; *Achilles*, Art. 58, Rn. 7; *Honsell/Schnyder/Straub*, Art. 58, Rn. 77; *Ferrari u. a./Mankowski*, Internationales Vertragsrecht, Art. 58, Rn. 34.
[127] *Staudinger/Magnus*, Art. 58, Rn. 24; *Kröll u. a./P. Butler/Harindranath*, Art. 58, Rn. 6; vgl. *Ferrari u. a./Mankowski*, Internationales Vertragsrecht, Art. 58, Rn. 31.
[128] *Hager/Maultzsch*, 5. Aufl., Art. 58 Rn. 11.
[129] Sekretariatskommentar, Art. 54, Nr. 6.
[130] *Staudinger/Magnus*, Art. 58, Rn. 29; Sekretariatskommentar, Art. 54, Nr. 9, Beispiel 54b; *Hager/Maultzsch*, 5. Aufl., Art. 58 Rn. 11.
[131] Vgl. *Hager/Maultzsch*, 5. Aufl., Art. 58 Rn. 11.
[132] Vgl. *Hager/Maultzsch*, 5. Aufl., Art. 58 Rn. 11.
[133] Sekretariatskommentar, Art. 54, Nr. 7, 9, Beispiel 54a; *Honsell/Schnyder/Straub*, Art. 58, Rn. 80; *Kröll u. a./P. Butler/Harindranath*, Art. 58, Rn. 8; *Ferrari u. a./Mankowski*, Internationales Vertragsrecht, Art. 58, Rn. 35.
[134] *Hager/Maultzsch*, 5. Aufl., Art. 58 Rn. 12.
[135] *Staudinger/Magnus*, Art. 58, Rn. 28; *Achilles*, Art. 58, Rn. 8; *Audit*, Vente internationale, Anm. 145.; *Bianca/Bonell/Maskow*, Art. 58, Anm. 2.9.; *Brunner*, Art. 58, Rn. 11; *Enderlein/Maskow/Strohbach*, Art. 58, Anm. 10.; *Herber/Czerwenka*, Art. 58, Rn. 8, 10; *Karollus*, S. 170; *Witz/Salger/Lorenz/Witz*, Art. 58, Rn. 15.

Gleiches gilt für die Zahlungsklauseln „cash against delivery note"[136] oder „cash on delivery".[137] Hingegen schliesst die Klausel „payment against handing over the goods on their arrival" das Untersuchungsrecht des Käufers vor Zahlung nicht aus.[138] Probleme können entstehen, wenn die Parteien die Zahlungsklauseln „cash against invoice" oder „cash upon receipt of invoice" vereinbart haben. Wenn die Rechnung mit der Ware reist, kann der Käufer die Ware nach Art. 58 III untersuchen.[139] Kommt die Rechnung hingegen vor der Ware beim Käufer an, so muss dieser den Kaufpreis zahlen, ohne die Lieferung der Ware abwarten zu können.[140]

Um das Risiko des Erhalts vertragswidriger Ware zu minimieren, kann der Käufer eine **36** **Inspektion vor Verladung** der Ware auf das Transportmittel organisieren.[141] Haben die Parteien ein **Dokumentenakkreditiv** vereinbart, so ist der Verkäufer üblicherweise verpflichtet, eine Qualitätsbescheinigung einer unabhängigen Inspektionsagentur vorzulegen.[142]

VIII. Beweislast

Der Verkäufer muss die **Zahlungszeit,** also die Fälligkeit des Kaufpreises beweisen.[143] Um **37** die Fälligkeit des Kaufpreises zu beweisen, muss der Verkäufer je nach den Umständen des Einzelfalls nachweisen, dass er dem Käufer die Ware oder die Dokumente zur Verfügung gestellt hat oder dass er die Lieferung bis zur Zahlung durch den Käufer zurückbehält.[144] Der Beweis, dass die Ware oder die Dokumente dem Käufer zur Verfügung gestellt wurden, umfasst auch den Umstand, dass der Verkäufer dem Käufer dies angezeigt hat. Im Falle eines Vertrages, der die Beförderung der Ware erfordert, muss der Verkäufer beweisen, dass die Ware an ihrem Bestimmungsort angekommen ist. Je nach Fallgestaltung mag dies beinhalten, dass der Verkäufer dem Käufer die Ankunft der Ware am Bestimmungsort angezeigt hat.

Der Käufer trägt die Beweislast für den Umstand, dass er die **Zahlung** zur richtigen Zeit **38** und am richtigen Ort **bewirkt** hat.[145]

Macht eine der Parteien ein **Zurückbehaltungsrecht** geltend, so trägt diejenige Partei, **39** die sich auf das Zurückbehaltungsrecht beruft, die Beweislast für die Umstände, die ein solches Zurückbehaltungsrecht begründen.[146]

---

[136] *Liesecke,* WM 1978, Beilage Nr. 3, S. 11; *Hager/Maultzsch,* 5. Aufl., Art. 58 Rn. 12.
[137] *Liesecke,* WM 1978, Beilage Nr. 3, S. 8; *Hager/Maultzsch,* 5. Aufl., Art. 58 Rn. 12.
[138] Sekretariatskommentar, Art. 54, Nr. 9, Beispiel 54c.
[139] *Hager/Maultzsch,* 5. Aufl. Art. 58 Rn. 12.
[140] KGer Zug, 2.12.2004, CISG-online 1194 = IHR 2006, 158; *Hager/Maultzsch,* 5. Aufl., Art. 58 Rn. 12; *Herber/Czerwenka,* Art. 58, Rn. 10; *Honsell/Schnyder/Straub,* Art. 58, Rn. 80. A. A. *Staudinger/Magnus,* Art. 58, Rn. 28; *Enderlein/Maskow/Strohbach,* Art. 58, Anm. 10.; *Lieseke,* WM 1978, Beilage 3, S. 8.
[141] *Honnold/Flechtner,* Art. 58, Rn. 338.
[142] *Honnold/Flechtner,* Art. 58, Rn. 338; *Goldstajin,* (1965) 14 Am. J. Comp. L., 338; *Hager/Maultzsch,* 5. Aufl., Art. 58 Rn. 12; *Soergel/Lüderitz/Budzikiewicz,* Art. 58, Rn. 7; *Kröll u. a./P. Butler/Harindranath,* Art. 58, Rn. 6.
[143] *A v. B,* Juzgado Sexto de Primera Instancia del Partido de Tijuana (Estado de Baja California), 14.7.2000, CISG-online 571 = IHR 2001, 38; *Baumgärtel/Laumen/Hepting,* Art. 58, Rn. 2; *Staudinger/Magnus,* Art. 58, Rn. 33; *Honsell/Schnyder/Straub,* Art. 58, Rn. 90; *Kröll u. a./P. Butler/Harindranath,* Art. 58, Rn. 35; *Ferrari u. a./Mankowski,* Internationales Vertragsrecht, Art. 58, Rn. 37.
[144] Vgl. OLG Karlsruhe, 20.11.1992, CISG-online 54 = CLOUT Nr. 317 = NJW-RR 1993, 1316: das Gericht entschied, dass der vom Käufer nicht unterschriebene, aber abgestempelte Lieferschein des Verkäufers nach § 416 ZPO keinen genügenden Beweis für die erfolge Lieferung/Abladung erbringt – ein abzulehnendes Ergebnis.
[145] *A v. B,* Juzgado Sexto de Primera Instancia del Partido de Tijuana (Estado de Baja California), 14.7.2000, CISG-online 571 = IHR 2001, 38; *Baumgärtel/Laumen/Hepting,* Art. 58, Rn. 2; *Staudinger/Magnus,* Art. 58, Rn. 33; *Honsell/Schnyder/Straub,* Art. 58, Rn. 90; *Kröll u. a./P. Butler/Harindranath,* Art. 58, Rn. 35; *Ferrari u. a./Mankowski,* Internationales Vertragsrecht, Art. 58, Rn. 37.
[146] *Staudinger/Magnus,* Art. 58, Rn. 33; *Achilles,* Art. 58, Rn. 9; *Honsell/Schnyder/Straub,* Art. 58, Rn. 90; *Ferrari u. a./Mankowski,* Internationales Vertragsrecht, Art. 58, Rn. 37.

Art. 59 [Zahlung ohne Aufforderung]

Der Käufer hat den Kaufpreis zu dem Zeitpunkt, der in dem Vertrag festgesetzt oder nach dem Vertrag und diesem Übereinkommen bestimmbar ist, zu zahlen, ohne daß es einer Aufforderung oder der Einhaltung von Förmlichkeiten* seitens des Verkäufers bedarf.

Art. 59

The buyer must pay the price on the date fixed by or determinable from the contract and this Convention without the need for any request or compliance with any formality on the part of the seller.

Art. 59

L'acheteur doit payer le prix à la date fixée au contrat ou résultant du contrat et de la présente Convention, sans qu'il soit besoin d'aucune demande ou autre formalité de la part du vendeur.

Übersicht

	Rn.
I. Regelungsgegenstand	1
II. Ausschluss des Erfordernisses einer Aufforderung zur Zahlung oder sonstiger Förmlichkeiten	2
III. Rechnung	4
IV. Anwendung von Art. 59 auf sonstige Zahlungen, die nicht den Kaufpreis betreffen	6

Vorläufer und **Entwürfe:** Art. 60 EKG; Genfer E 1976 Art. 40; Wiener E 1977 Art. 41; New Yorker E 1978 Art. 55.

I. Regelungsgegenstand

1   Gemäss Art. 59 muss der Käufer den Kaufpreis zu dem Zeitpunkt zahlen, der im Vertrag festgesetzt oder nach dem Vertrag[1] und diesem Übereinkommen (Art. 58)[2] bestimmbar ist, **ohne** dass es eine **Aufforderung** oder der **Einhaltung von Förmlichkeiten** seitens des Käufers bedarf. Diese Vorschrift schliesst den Rückgriff auf nationale Erfordernisse einer Zahlungsaufforderung aus,[3] wie z. B. die französische *mise en demeure*[4] oder die deutsche bzw. schweizerische Mahnung[5]. Folglich wird der Kaufpreis nach dem CISG automatisch an dem im Vertrag bestimmten oder bestimmbaren Tag bzw. dem nach Art. 58 zu bestimmenden Tag fällig.[6] Art. 59 gilt auch bezüglich der vom Käufer nach Art. 54 vorzunehmenden Massnahmen bzw. Förmlichkeiten, um Zahlung zu leisten, wie z. B. die Stellung eines Dokumentenakkreditivs.[7]

---

* Schweiz: Formalitäten.
[1] Vgl. oben Art. 58 Rn. 5.
[2] Vgl. oben Art. 58 Rn. 4, 8 ff.
[3] Art. 2080 Mexican Federal Cc; see *Hardwoods California, LLP v. Kyriakidez Garcia,* Juzgado Sexto de Primera Instancia del Partido de Tijuana, Baja California, 30.8.2005, CISG-online 1158; *Hardwoods California, LLP v. Kyriakidez Garcia,* Tribunal Superior de Justicia del Estado de Baja California, 24.3.2006, CISG-online 1392, m. Anm. *Osuna González,* Tijuana CISG Judgment; vgl. *Honsell/Schnyder/Straub,* Art. 59, Rn. 3.
[4] Vgl. Art. 1139 Cc.
[5] Deutschland: § 286 BGB; Schweiz: Art. 102 OR; siehe aber Art. 213 II OR, dem zufolge eine Mahnung dann nicht erforderlich ist, wenn ein entsprechender Handelsbrauch besteht. Vgl. Cour de Justice de Genève, 19.9.2003, CISG-online 854; HGer Aargau, 26.9.1997, CISG-online 329.
[6] KG Wallis, 20.12.1994, CISG-online 302 = CLOUT Nr. 197; LG Stendal, 12.10.2000, CISG-online 592 = IHR 2001, 30 ff.
[7] CIETAC, 15.9.2005, CISG-online 1714.

II. Ausschluss des Erfordernisses einer Aufforderung zur Zahlung oder sonstiger Förmlichkeiten

Der **Fälligkeitszeitpunkt** des Kaufpreises bestimmt sich nach dem Vertrag bzw. Art. 58.[8] Wenn der Kaufpreis fällig ist und der Käufer nicht zahlt, fallen gemäss Art. 78 **Zinsen** auf den Kaufpreis ab Fälligkeit an.[9] Darüber hinaus kann der Verkäufer **Schadenersatz** nach Art. 61 I lit. b) i. V. m. Art. 74 verlangen, wenn ihm ein Verlust entstanden ist,[10] z. B. ein **Währungsverlust** oder ein **Zinsschaden** durch höhere Zinsraten als ihm gemäss Art. 78 zustehen. Nur in sehr seltenen Fällen wird der Verkäufer gemäss Art. 64 I lit. a) berechtigt sein, den Vertrag wegen wesentlichen Vertragsbruchs unmittelbar aufzuheben.[11] Daher wird der Verkäufer den Weg über Art. 63 wählen und dem Käufer eine angemessene Nachfrist zur Erfüllung ansetzen. Diese Fristsetzung nach Art. 63 ist keine Voraussetzung für die Fälligkeit, sondern eröffnet dem Verkäufer die Möglichkeit herauszufinden, ob der Käufer den Vertrag erfüllen wird.[12] Wenn der Käufer den Kaufpreis innerhalb der angemessenen Nachfrist nicht zahlt oder auf andere Weise klarstellt, dass er den Vertrag nicht erfüllen wird, ist der Verkäufer gemäss Art. 64 I lit. b) berechtigt, den Vertrag aufzuheben, selbst wenn an sich kein wesentlicher Vertragsbruch vorliegt.[13]

Der verkäuferfreundlichen Vorschrift des Art. 59 wird durch Art. 58 I etwas entgegengewirkt, in dem unter besonderen Umständen der Verkäufer verpflichtet ist, dem Käufer anzuzeigen, dass die Ware zur Abholung bereit steht.[14] Auch das Recht des Käufers, die Ware nach Art. 58 III vor Zahlung kurz zu untersuchen, wirkt dem automatischen Anfall von Zinsen entgegen. Allerdings besteht darüber hinaus kein Raum für die Anwendung eines allgemeinen Prinzips des guten Glaubens, wonach der Verkäufer Erkundigungen beim Käufer über die Gründe seiner Nichtzahlung einzuholen hat und dem Käufer dazu eine weitere Frist nach Fälligkeit zu gewähren wäre.[15]

III. Rechnung

Die Anwendung von Art. 59 setzt voraus, dass der Kaufpreis bestimmt oder bestimmbar ist. Sollte der Vertrag den Kaufpreis nicht bestimmen, sondern der **Verkäufer zur Preisbestimmung berechtigt** sein, so wird der Käufer zur Zahlung des Kaufpreises nur nach Erhalt einer **Rechnung** verpflichtet sein.[16] Zinsen fallen in einem solchen Fall erst dann an, wenn Zahlung nicht innerhalb einer angemessenen Zeit nach Erhalt der Rechnung erfolgt ist.[17]

In der Praxis wird der Verkäufer dem Käufer so gut wie immer eine **Rechnung** stellen.[18] Um im Einzelfall festzustellen, ob der Verkäufer verpflichtet ist, dem Käufer eine Rechnung

---

[8] Vgl. oben Art. 58 Rn. 4 ff.
[9] Vgl. unten *Bacher*, Art. 78 Rn. 7 f.; *Honsell/Schnyder/Straub*, Art. 59, Rn. 5.
[10] Vgl. OLG Düsseldorf, 22.6.2004, CISG-online 916 = IHR 2005, 29.
[11] Vgl. unten Art. 64 Rn. 6 ff.
[12] Trib. Padova, 31.3.2004, CISG-online 823 = IHR 2005, 33: Der Verkäufer war berechtigt, die unverzügliche Zahlung ohne vorherige Setzung einer Nachfrist zu verlangen, obwohl die Lieferung bereits sechs Monate zurück lag.
[13] Vgl. unten Art. 64 Rn. 19 ff.
[14] Vgl. oben Art. 58 Rn. 8 ff.
[15] A. A. Trib. Padova, 25.2.2004, CISG-online 819 = IHR 2005, 31.
[16] OLG München, 9.7.1997, CISG-online 282: die Zahlungspflicht wurde spätestens fällig, als die Rechnungen im Zivilprozess vorgelegt wurden.
[17] *Achilles*, Art. 59, Rn. 2; *Bianca/Bonell/Maskow*, Art. 59, Anm. 3.1.; *Brunner*, Art. 59, Rn. 2; *Enderlein/Maskow/Strohbach*, Art. 59, Anm. 4.1.; *Herber/Czerwenka*, Art. 59, Rn. 3; *Karollus*, S. 170; MünchKommHGB/*Benicke*, Art. 59, Rn. 1. Das CISG hat Vorrang vor nationalen Vorschriften, selbst wenn solche auf der Zahlungsverzugsrichtlinie der EG, wie z. B. § 286 III BGB beruhen, wonach Fälligkeit 30 Tage nach Erhalt der Rechnung eintritt. Allerdings können die Parteien eine solche Regelung vereinbaren, vgl. Int. Ct. Russian CCI, 13.2.2006, CISG-online 1623.
[18] *Piltz*, Internationales Kaufrecht, Rn. 4–148.

zu stellen, kommt es auf die vertragliche Vereinbarung und allenfalls bindende internationale Handelsgebräuche an. Verweist der Vertrag auf eine Handelsklausel der **Incoterms®**, so ist der Verkäufer gemäss Regel A1 in jedem Fall verpflichtet, eine Rechnung zu stellen.[19] Aber selbst ohne ausdrückliche Verweisung auf die Incoterms® in einem Vertrag, ist der Verkäufer verpflichtet, dem Käufer eine Rechnung zu stellen, und zwar nach dem **allgemeinen Prinzip der Kooperation,** wenn der Käufer die Rechnung benötigt, um die Ware abzunehmen, z. B. um Zollformalitäten zu erledigen oder sich mit den Steuerbehörden des Importlandes auseinander zu setzen.[20] Schliesslich kann das Erfordernis der Rechnungsstellung in den meisten Industriezweigen als allgemeiner **internationaler Handelsbrauch** nach Art. 9 II aufgefasst werden und andernfalls zumindest gemäss Art. 8 III Eingang in den Vertrag finden. Freilich kann der Kaufpreis nach Art. 59 unabhängig von der Vorlage einer Rechnung fällig werden, selbst wenn der Verkäufer zur Vorlage einer Rechnung verpflichtet war.[21]

IV. Anwendung von Art. 59 auf sonstige Zahlungen, die nicht den Kaufpreis betreffen

6   Dem **Wortlaut** nach findet Art. 59 nur auf die Pflicht des Käufers zur Zahlung des Kaufpreises Anwendung. Dennoch kann Art. 59 ein **allgemeines Prinzip des Übereinkommens** entnommen werden, nämlich dass **nationale Förmlichkeiten,** wie die französische *mise en demeur,* welche eine förmliche Aufforderung für jedwede Zahlung erfordert, im Anwendungsbereich des CISG **ausgeschlossen** sind, weil deren Anwendung mit den wesentlichen Pflichten und Rechtsbehelfen der Parteien gemäss CISG unvereinbar wäre.[22]

7   Als ein weiteres, zweites Prinzip kann Art. 59 entnommen werden, dass die **Haftung für fällige Geldbeträge** immer voraussetzt, dass an einem bestimmten oder bestimmbaren Tag nicht gezahlt wurde.[23]

8   Diese zwei allgemeinen Prinzipien des Art. 59 gelten auch für **sonstige Zahlungspflichten,** die nicht den Kaufpreis betreffen, wie z. B. die Pflicht zur **Rückzahlung des Kaufpreises** in Folge einer Vertragsaufhebung gemäss Art. 81 II[24] sowie die darauf gemäss Art. 84 I geschuldeten Zinsen, die **Zinspflicht** gemäss Art. 78 im Allgemeinen, die Pflicht zur Rückzahlung der Differenz zwischen dem vereinbarten und dem nach Art. 50 **geminderten Kaufpreis** sowie die Pflicht zur Rückzahlung von **Überzahlungen**[25] oder zur Zahlung einer **Vertragsstrafe**[26]. Grundsätzlich findet Art. 59 auch auf **Schadenersatzansprüche** und Ansprüche auf **Erstattung von Aufwendungen** Anwendung, wenn der Schuldner Kenntnis von der genauen Höhe des Schadens oder der Aufwendung hat.[27]

---

[19] Vgl. *Ferrari u. a./Mankowski,* Internationales Vertragsrecht, Art. 59, Rn. 4.
[20] Vgl. OLG Köln, 3.4.2006, CISG-online 1218; vgl. *Honsell/Schnyder/Straub,* Art. 59, Rn. 13; *Kröll u. a./ P. Butler/Harindranath,* Art. 59, Rn. 4.
[21] *Piltz,* Internationales Kaufrecht, Rn. 4–148; *Witz/Salger/Lorenz/Witz,* Artt. 58–59, Rn. 4.
[22] *Honnold/Flechtner,* Art. 59, Rn. 340; *Honsell/Schnyder/Straub,* Art. 59, Rn. 13 f.; *Kröll u. a./P. Butler/Harindranath,* Art. 59, Rn. 1; *Ferrari u. a./Mankowski,* Internationales Vertragsrecht, Art. 59, Rn. 11.
[23] *Honnold/Flechtner,* Art. 59, Rn. 340.
[24] *Murray,* Draft Digest, S. 440, 454.
[25] Vgl. *Murray,* Draft Digest, S. 440, 454: „*compensation payments*".
[26] OLG Hamburg, 25.1.2008, CISG-online 1681 = IHR 2008, 98, 102.
[27] *Staudinger/Magnus,* Art. 59, Rn. 10; *Ferrari u. a./Mankowski,* Internationales Vertragsrecht, Art. 59, Rn. 11.

Abschnitt II. Abnahme

Section II.
Taking delivery

Section II.
Prise de livraison

Art. 60 [Begriff der Abnahme]

Die Pflicht des Käufers zur Abnahme* besteht darin,

a) alle Handlungen vorzunehmen, die vernünftigerweise von ihm erwartet werden können, damit dem Verkäufer die Lieferung ermöglicht wird, und
b) die Ware zu übernehmen.

Art. 60

The buyer's obligation to take delivery consists:
(a) in doing all the acts which could reasonably be expected of him in order to enable the seller to make delivery; and
(b) in taking over the goods.

Art. 60

L'obligation de l'acheteur de prendre livraison consiste:
a) à accomplir tout acte qu'on peut raisonnablement attendre de lui pour permettre au vendeur d'effectuer la livraison; et
b) à retirer les marchandises.

Übersicht

	Rn.
I. Regelungsgegenstand	1
II. Die Pflicht des Käufers zur Abnahme der Ware	2
1. Übernahme der Ware und/oder der Dokumente	2
2. Mitwirkungshandlungen zur Ermöglichung der Lieferung durch den Verkäufer	7
3. Zurückbehaltungsrechte	11
(a) Vorzeitige Lieferung, Art. 52 I	12
(b) Zuviel-Lieferung, Art. 52 II	13
(c) Verspätete Lieferung	14
(d) Vertragswidrige Ware	15
(e) Vertragswidrige Dokumente	18
III. Andere Pflichten des Käufers	19
IV. Beweislast	20

Vorläufer und **Entwürfe:** Art. 65 EKG; Genfer E 1976 Art. 41; Wiener E 1977 Art. 42; New Yorker E 1978 Art. 56.

I. Regelungsgegenstand

Abschnitt II des Teils III über die Pflichten des Käufers enthält nur eine Vorschrift, nämlich **1** Art. 60, welche die Pflicht des Käufers zur **Abnahme der Ware** genauer umschreibt. Art. 60 muss im Zusammenhang mit Art. 53 gelesen werden, aus dem sich die Pflicht des Käufers zur Abnahme der Ware ergibt. Gemäss Art. 60 besteht die Pflicht des Käufers zur Abnahme darin, (a) alle Handlungen vorzunehmen, die vernünftigerweise von ihm erwartet werden können, damit dem Verkäufer die Lieferung ermöglicht wird, und (b) die Ware zu übernehmen.

---

* Schweiz, Österreich: Annahme.

II. Die Pflicht des Käufers zur Abnahme der Ware

1. Übernahme der Ware und/oder der Dokumente

2   Die Ware zu übernehmen heisst, dass der Käufer die Ware **körperlich entgegennehmen muss**.[1] Mit anderen Worten ist die Übernahme eine rein **tatsächliche Handlung** und beinhaltet **kein rechtliches Konzept,** wie z. B. die Abnahme oder die Billigung als vertragskonform, wie sie in einigen nationalen Rechtsordnungen vorgesehen ist.[2] Vielmehr kann der Käufer seine Ansprüche wegen Vertragswidrigkeit nach Übernahme der Ware geltend machen, solange er die Vertragswidrigkeit innerhalb einer angemessenen Frist gemäss Art. 39 rügt.

3   Der **Ort** und die **Zeit** der Übernahme der Ware sind nicht unbedingt identisch mit dem Ort und der Zeit der Lieferung, die sich aus Art. 31 und Art. 33 ergeben, oder dem Ort und der Zeit der Zahlung, die sich aus Art. 57 und Art. 58 ergeben.[3] Freilich wird die Übernahme der Ware oft an dem Ort vorzunehmen sein, an dem der Verkäufer die Ware gem. Art. 31 liefert. Wenn die Ware am Ort der Niederlassung des Käufers oder des Verkäufers oder an einem anderen bestimmten Ort geliefert wird, muss die Ware an diesem Ort abgenommen werden, sobald die Ware dem Käufer zur Verfügung gestellt wurde. Erfordert der Vertrag die Beförderung der Ware oder betrifft der Vertrag Ware, die sich auf dem Transport befindet, so muss die Ware nicht an dem Ort abgenommen werden, an dem der Käufer die Ware dem ersten Beförderer zur Übermittlung an den Käufer übergibt (Art. 31 lit. a)), sondern am Bestimmungsort.[4] Befindet sich die verkaufte Ware in einem Lagerhaus einer Drittpartei und wird der Kaufvertrag nicht durch Übergabe von Dokumenten abgewickelt, die den Käufer an der Ware berechtigen, so erfordert die Abnahme der Ware keine faktische Handlung des Käufers, da der Verkäufer seine Lieferpflicht durch Instruktion der Drittpartei erfüllen kann, die Ware nunmehr für den Käufer aufzubewahren und ihm die Ware auf Verlangen hin auszuhändigen.[5]

4   Für die Frage, wann der Käufer die Ware oder die Dokumente abzunehmen hat, gilt Art. 58 I. Folglich hat der Käufer die Ware oder die Dokumente zu übernehmen, wenn sie ihm zur Verfügung gestellt werden. Freilich ist dem Käufer eine kurze Frist zur Übernahme der Ware oder der Dokumente zu gewähren, nachdem er die Anzeige des Verkäufers erhalten hat, dass die Ware bzw. die Dokumente ihm nunmehr zur Verfügung stehen.[6]

5   In der Praxis wird die Abnahmepflicht oft im Vertrag genau beschrieben, z. B. durch Benutzung einer **Handelsklausel.** Wichtig ist vor allem die Frage, welche Partei die Ware

---

[1] Vgl. BGH, 8.3.1995, CISG-online 144, sub II. 1. b) aa); OLG Karlsruhe, 8.2.2006, CISG-online 1328, sub II. 1. a); LG Aachen, 14.5.1993, CISG-online 86 = RIW 1993, 760; BGer, 13.11.2003, CISG-online 840 = BGE 130 III 258, 265, E. 5.3; *Hager/Maultzsch,* 5. Aufl., Art. 60 Rn. 2a; *Staudinger/Magnus,* Art. 60, Rn. 5; MünchKomm/*P. Huber,* Art. 60, Rn. 2; *Bamberger/Roth/Saenger,* Art. 60, Rn. 2; *Bianca/Bonell/Maskow,* Art. 60, Anm. 2.5., 2.6.1.; *Brunner,* Art. 60, Rn. 2; *Herber/Czerwenka,* Art. 60, Rn. 6; *Piltz,* Internationales Kaufrecht, Rn. 4–166; *Ferrari u. a./Mankowski,* Internationales Vertragsrecht, Art. 60, Rn. 2; *Honsell/Schnyder/Straub,* Art. 60, Rn. 6; *Kröll u. a./P. Butler/Harindranath,* Art. 60, Rn. 2.

[2] Z. B. Billigung nach deutschem Werkvertragsrecht, vgl. § 640 BGB. Vgl. KG Schaffhausen, 27.1.2004, CISG-online 960, E. 3. c); *Ferrari u. a./Mankowski,* Internationales Vertragsrecht, Art. 60, Rn. 3; *Honsell/Schnyder/Straub,* Art. 60, Rn. 3, 15.

[3] Vgl. *Honsell/Schnyder/Straub,* Art. 60, Rn. 16.

[4] *Hager/Maultzsch,* 5. Aufl., Art. 60 Rn. 2a; MünchKomm/*P. Huber,* Art. 60, Rn. 2; *Audit,* Vente internationale, Anm. 143.; *Brunner,* Art. 60, Rn. 2; *Witz/Salger/Lorenz/Witz,* Art. 60, Rn. 7; *Honsell/Schnyder/Straub,* Art. 60, Rn. 17a; ähnlich *Staudinger/Magnus,* Art. 60, Rn. 5; *Heuzé,* Anm. 334.

[5] *Hager/Maultzsch,* 5. Aufl., Art. 60 Rn. 2a; *Staudinger/Magnus,* Art. 60, Rn. 5; *Piltz,* Internationales Kaufrecht, Rn. 4–166; zu konstruiert *Honsell/Schnyder/Straub,* Art. 60, Rn. 19a.

[6] Vgl. oben Art. 58 Rn. 8; YB VIII (1977), S. 50; vgl. auch *Hager/Maultzsch,* 5. Aufl., Art. 60 Rn. 2a; *Staudinger/Magnus,* Art. 60, Rn. 7; MünchKomm/*P. Huber,* Art. 60, Rn. 2; *Achilles,* Art. 60, Rn. 1; *Brunner,* Art. 60, Rn. 2; *Herber/Czerwenka,* Art. 60, Rn. 5; *Witz/Salger/Lorenz/Witz,* Art. 60, Rn. 8; vgl. auch *Honnold/Flechtner,* Art. 60, Rn. 341.1. Anders *Piltz,* Internationales Kaufrecht, Rn. 4–167 (keine zusätzliche Abnahmefrist bei Abnahme am Lieferort, allerdings bei Verträgen, die die Beförderung der Ware erfordern); *Reinhart,* Art. 60, Rn. 5; *Honsell/Schnyder/Straub,* Art. 60, Rn. 21 ff.: angemessene Frist zur Abnahme nur bei fehlender Vereinbarung über den Lieferzeitpunkt.

zu verladen bzw. abzuladen hat. Regel A4 aller **Incoterms**® beschreibt die Pflicht zur Verladung bzw. Abladung genauer. Z. B. ist der Verkäufer bei Vereinbarung der Handelsklausel EXW nicht verpflichtet, die Ware auf das abholende Beförderungsmittel zu verladen; bei FOB muss der Verkäufer die Ware an Bord des Schiffes entsprechend dem Hafenbrauch liefern; Gleiches gilt für CIF; bei DDP muss der Verkäufer die Ware auf dem ankommenden Beförderungsmittel entladebereit zur Verfügung stellen.

Wenngleich Art. 60 explizit nur von der Abnahme der Ware spricht, ist der Käufer **6** selbstverständlich auch verpflichtet, die vom Verkäufer vorgelegten **Dokumente** aufzunehmen.[7] Der Begriff „Dokumente" umfasst in dem hier benutzten Sinne sämtliche vertraglich erforderlichen Dokumente, die sich auf die Ware beziehen (Art. 34), ohne Beschränkung auf besondere Typen von Dokumenten. Wenn **nicht konforme Dokumente** vorgelegt werden, hat der Käufer das Recht, die Abnahme der Dokumente zurückzuhalten, also die Dokumente **zurückzuweisen**.[8]

2. Mitwirkungshandlungen zur Ermöglichung der Lieferung durch den Verkäufer

Die Pflicht des Käufers zur Abnahme der Ware beinhaltet auch die Vornahme sämtlicher **7** **Mitwirkungshandlungen,** die vernünftigerweise von ihm erwartet werden können, um dem Verkäufer die **Lieferung zu ermöglichen.** Diese Mitwirkungspflichten müssen von den sonstigen, sich aus dem Vertrag oder dem Übereinkommen ergebenden Pflichten des Käufers unterschieden werden.[9] Diese Unterscheidung ist notwendig, da Art. 64 I lit. b) dem Verkäufer das Recht zur Vertragsaufhebung gibt, wenn der Käufer nicht innerhalb der vom Verkäufer gesetzten Nachfrist seine Pflicht zur Abnahme der Ware erfüllt, oder wenn er erklärt, dass er dies nicht innerhalb der so gesetzten Frist tun wird. Mit anderen Worten entscheidet die Qualifikation einer Pflicht als Mitwirkungspflicht i. S. v. Art. 60 lit. a) darüber, ob der Verkäufer neben der Vertragsaufhebung wegen wesentlichen Vertragsbruchs die Möglichkeit hat, über **Nachfristsetzung** zum Vertragsaufhebungsrecht zu gelangen.[10] Qualifiziert eine Pflicht nicht als Mitwirkungspflicht, so ist der Verkäufer zur Vertragsaufhebung nur dann berechtigt, wenn die Pflichtverletzung des Käufers einen wesentlichen Vertragsbruch darstellt.

Die Mitwirkungspflichten des Käufers bei der Lieferung werden im Vertrag oft ausdrücklich **8** oder stillschweigend geregelt sein.[11] Z. B. kann ein Vertrag den Käufer verpflichten, die Ware vor Verschiffung zu untersuchen.[12] Auch die **Incoterms**® sehen eine Anzahl von zusätzlichen Pflichten des Käufers vor, die dem Verkäufer die Lieferung ermöglichen sollen. Haben die Parteien FOB Incoterms® 2010 vereinbart, so hat der Käufer dem Verkäufer in angemessener Weise den Namen des Schiffs, die Ladestelle und, falls erforderlich, die gewählte Lieferzeit anzugeben.[13] Andere Beispiele sind sogenannte **Bezugsverträge,** bei denen der Käufer verpflichtet oder berechtigt ist, die Lieferung der Ware abzurufen. Je nach Fallgestaltung kann die Säumnis des Käufers, die Ware in Übereinstimmung mit den ver-

---

[7] *Hager/Maultzsch*, 5. Aufl., Art. 60 Rn. 2b; *Staudinger/Magnus*, Art. 60, Rn. 6; MünchKomm/*P. Huber*, Art. 60, Rn. 3; *Achilles*, Art. 60, Rn. 1; *Bamberger/Roth/Saenger*, Art. 60, Rn. 2; *Bianca/Bonell/Maskow*, Art. 60, Anm. 2.6.2.; *Brunner*, Art. 60, Rn. 2; *Herber/Czerwenka*, Art. 60, Rn. 7; *Piltz*, Internationales Kaufrecht, Rn. 4–161, 4–166; *Witz/Salger/Lorenz/Witz*, Art. 60, Rn. 13; *Ferrari u. a./Mankowski*, Internationales Vertragsrecht, Art. 60, Rn. 6; *Honsell/Schnyder/Straub*, Art. 60, Rn. 31; *Kröll u. a./P. Butler/Harindranath*, Art. 60, Rn. 3.

[8] Vgl. unten Rn. 15; vgl. auch *Witz/Salger/Lorenz/Witz*, Art. 60, Rn. 13.

[9] Vgl. oben Art. 53 Rn. 41; für Beispiele solcher Pflichten vgl. oben Art. 53 Rn. 31 ff.; *Honnold/Flechtner*, Art. 60, Rn. 342.

[10] *Honnold/Flechtner*, Art. 60, Rn. 342.

[11] *Hager/Maultzsch*, 5. Aufl., Art. 60 Rn. 2.

[12] CIETAC, 29.9.2000, CISG-online 1592.

[13] Incoterms® 2010, FOB, Regel B7, vgl. CIETAC, 22.3.2001, CISG-online 1442. Die Pflicht des Käufers zur Beschaffung von Einfuhrformalitäten in einem CPT-Vertrag dient nicht der Ermöglichung der Lieferung seitens des Verkäufers, weil dieser bereits mit Übergabe an den Beförderer liefert, vgl. Int. Ct. Russian CCI, 24.1.2002, CISG-online 887.

traglichen Bestimmungen abzurufen, eine Verletzung seiner Pflicht zur Abnahme der Ware bedeuten.[14] Hat der Käufer nach dem Vertrag die Form, die Masse oder andere Merkmale der Ware näher zu bestimmen, so ist er gemäss Art. 65 verpflichtet, diese Spezifizierung zu dem vereinbarten Zeitpunkt oder innerhalb einer angemessenen Frist nach Eingang einer Aufforderung durch den Verkäufer vorzunehmen. Die **Spezifikationspflicht** ist Teil der Pflicht zur Abnahme der Ware.[15] Fordert der Vertrag vom Käufer, dass er dem Verkäufer **Pläne oder andere Daten** liefern muss, die für die Herstellung der Ware erforderlich sind, so stellen solche Mitwirkungspflichten einen Teil der Pflicht zur Abnahme der Ware dar.[16] Nicht geschuldet sind hingegen ungewöhnliche Akte, wie die Übernahme einer Verpflichtung, die Ware nicht weiter zu exportieren.[17]

9   Selbst ohne ausdrückliche oder stillschweigende Vereinbarung im Vertrag ist der Käufer verpflichtet, **den Verkäufer über besondere Umstände im Land des Käufers zu informieren;** dies ergibt sich aus der allgemeinen Kooperations- und Informationspflicht.[18] Ein US-Gericht hat einen Käufer verpflichtet, dem Verkäufer zum Import notwendige Dokumente zu liefern.[19] Auch können die Incoterms® als Auslegungshilfe bei der Bestimmung der Pflichten des Käufers herangezogen werden, selbst wenn diese im Vertrag nicht gewählt wurden.[20] So kann der Käufer verpflichtet sein, Zollformalitäten zu erfüllen.[21] Wenn Lieferung am Ort der Niederlassung des Käufers zu erfolgen hat, so ist der Käufer verpflichtet, alles Notwendige zu unternehmen, um seine Anlagen für die Abnahme der Ware bereit zu haben.[22] Die Pflicht des Käufers, dem Verkäufer die Lieferung zu ermöglichen, beinhaltet als negative Verpflichtung, dass der Käufer nichts unternehmen darf, was die Erfüllungshandlungen des Verkäufers erschweren könnte.[23]

10 Der **Erfüllungsort** und die **Erfüllungszeit** der Mitwirkungspflichten des Käufers bei der Lieferung hängen stark von den Umständen des Einzelfalls ab.[24] Kann durch Vertragsauslegung kein genauer Zeitpunkt für die Vornahme einer Mitwirkungspflicht be-

---

[14] Anders OLG Brandenburg, 18.11.2008, CISG-online 1734 = IHR 2009, 105, 111. Vgl. *Bianca/Bonell/Maskow*, Art. 60, Anm. 2.4.3., die einen Vertragsbruch verneinen, wenn der Verkäufer die Ware am Ende einer vereinbarten Frist trotz Säumnis des Käufers liefern kann; ähnlich *Honsell/Schnyder/Straub*, Art. 60, Rn. 30 f.

[15] *Hager/Maultzsch*, 5. Aufl., Art. 60 Rn. 2; *Staudinger/Magnus*, Art. 60, Rn. 14; *ders.*, Art. 65, Rn. 6; *Bamberger/Roth/Saenger*, Art. 60, Rn. 3; *Enderlein/Maskow/Strohbach*, Art. 60, Anm. 6.2.; MünchKomm/*P. Huber*, Art. 60, Rn. 7; *Reinhart*, Art. 60, Rn. 2; *Witz/Salger/Lorenz/Witz*, Art. 60, Rn. 4. A. A. *Bianca/Bonell/Knapp*, Art. 65, Anm. 2.6., 3.2.; *Enderlein/Maskow/Strohbach*, Art. 65, Rn. 5; *Herber/Czerwenka*, Art. 65, Rn. 7; *Honsell/Schnyder/Straub*, Art. 65, Rn. 30e; *Kröll u. a./P. Butler/Harindranath*, Art. 60, Rn. 7.

[16] *Geneva Pharmaceuticals Technology Corp v. Barr Laboratories, Inc.*, U. S. Dist. Ct. (S. D. N. Y.), 10.5.2002, CISG-online 653 = 201 F. Supp. 2d 236; vgl. CIETAC, 30.9.2000, CISG-online 1592; *Hager/Maultzsch*, 5. Aufl., Art. 60 Rn. 2; *Kritzer*, ICM-Guide, S. 479; *Kröll u. a./P. Butler/Harindranath*, Art. 60, Rn. 7; offengelassen bei *Witz/Salger/Lorenz/Witz*, Art. 60, Rn. 4. Vgl. *Staudinger/Magnus*, Art. 60, Rn. 10, der richtigerweise darauf hinweist, dass sich eine solche Pflicht nur aus dem Vertrag ergeben kann. A. A. MünchKomm/*P. Huber*, Art. 60, Rn. 7; *Honsell/Schnyder/Straub*, Art. 60, Rn. 30c; *Enderlein/Maskow/Strohbach*, Art. 60, Anm. 6.2.

[17] Vgl. OGH, 6.2.1996, CISG-online 224; *Hager/Maultzsch*, 5. Aufl., Art. 60 Rn. 2; *Honsell/Schnyder/Straub*, Art. 60, Rn. 28; *Kröll u. a./P. Butler/Harindranath*, Art. 60, Rn. 7. A. A. *Ferrari u. a./Mankowski*, Internationales Vertragsrecht, Art. 60, Rn. 12.

[18] So auch *Kröll u. a./P. Butler/Harindranath*, Art. 60, Rn. 6.

[19] *Geneva Pharmaceuticals Technology Corp v. Barr Laboratories, Inc.*, U. S. Dist. Ct. (S. D. N. Y.), 10.5.2002, CISG-online 653 = 201 F. Supp. 2d 236, 284, m. zust. Anm. *Murray*, Draft Digest, S. 454; *Staudinger/Magnus*, Art. 60, Rn. 10; MünchKomm/*P. Huber*, Art. 60, Rn. 6.

[20] *Geneva Pharmaceuticals Technology Corp v. Barr Laboratories, Inc.*, U. S. Dist. Ct. (S. D. N. Y.), 10.5.2002, CISG-online 653 = 201 F 2d 236, 284, m. zust. Anm. *Murray*, Draft Digest, S. 454; *Staudinger/Magnus*, Art. 60, Rn. 10; MünchKomm/*P. Huber*, Art. 60, Rn. 5; *Achilles*, Art. 60, Rn. 2; *Brunner*, Art. 60, Rn. 3; *Benedick*, Informationspflichten, Rn. 1184.

[21] *Hager/Maultzsch*, 5. Aufl., Art. 60 Rn. 2; *Kröll u. a./P. Butler/Harindranath*, Art. 60, Rn. 6.

[22] *Hager/Maultzsch*, 5. Aufl., Art. 60 Rn. 2; *Staudinger/Magnus*, Art. 60, Rn. 11; MünchKomm/*P. Huber*, Art. 60, Rn. 6; *Enderlein/Maskow/Strohbach*, Art. 60, Anm. 6.1.; *Herber/Czerwenka*, Art. 60, Rn. 9; *Honsell/Schnyder/Straub*, Art. 60, Rn. 29; *Witz/Salger/Lorenz/Witz*, Art. 60, Rn. 4; *Ferrari u. a./Mankowski*, Internationales Vertragsrecht, Art. 60, Rn. 13; *Kröll u. a./P. Butler/Harindranath*, Art. 60, Rn. 6.

[23] *Witz/Salger/Lorenz/Witz*, Art. 60, Rn. 3; YB VIII (1977), S. 50.

[24] *Witz/Salger/Lorenz/Witz*, Art. 60, Rn. 9.

Begriff der Abnahme 11–15 **Art. 60**

stimmt werden, so kann Art. 65 I als allgemeinem Prinzip des Übereinkommens entnommen werden, dass der Käufer seine Mitwirkungshandlung **innerhalb einer angemessenen Frist nach Eingang einer Aufforderung** durch den Verkäufer vorzunehmen hat.[25]

3. Zurückbehaltungsrechte

In unterschiedlichen Fallkonstellationen hat der Käufer das Recht, seine Mitwirkung bei 11
der Lieferung zurückzubehalten.

(a) **Vorzeitige Lieferung, Art. 52 I.** Gemäss Art. 52 I kann der Käufer die Abnahme 12
der Ware verweigern, wenn der Verkäufer die Ware vor dem festgesetzten Zeitpunkt
liefert.[26] Dieses Verweigerungsrecht gilt auch für sämtliche vorgängigen Mitwirkungshandlungen des Käufers, die für die Lieferung erforderlich sind.

(b) **Zuviel-Lieferung, Art. 52 II.** Gemäss Art. 52 II kann der Käufer die Abnahme der 13
zu viel gelieferten Menge verweigern, wenn der Verkäufer eine grössere als die vereinbarte
Menge geliefert hat.[27] Dieses Verweigerungsrecht gilt auch für sämtliche vorgängigen Mitwirkungspflichten des Käufers, die zur Lieferung erforderlich sind.

(c) **Verspätete Lieferung.** Der Käufer muss eine verspätete Lieferung abnehmen, es sei 14
denn, dass er gemäss Art. 49 I, II lit. a) **zur Vertragsaufhebung berechtigt** ist.[28] Da der
Verkäufer schlussendlich geliefert hat, kann der Käufer den Vertrag nur dann aufheben,
wenn die Verspätung der Lieferung selbst einen wesentlichen Vertragsbruch gemäss Art. 49
I lit. a) darstellt[29] oder die Lieferung nach Ablauf der angemessenen Nachfrist i. S. v. Art. 49
I lit. b) erfolgt ist.[30] Der Käufer verliert gemäss Art. 49 II lit. a) das Recht, die Aufhebung
des Vertrags zu erklären, wenn er die Aufhebung nicht innerhalb einer angemessenen Frist
erklärt, nachdem er erfahren hat, dass die Lieferung schlussendlich erfolgt ist.[31]

(d) **Vertragswidrige Ware.** Grundsätzlich kann der Käufer die Lieferung vertragswid- 15
riger Ware nur dann zurückweisen, wenn die Vertragswidrigkeit einen **wesentlichen Vertragsbruch** i. S. v. Art. 25 darstellt.[32] Im Falle eines wesentlichen Vertragsbruches kann der
Käufer nämlich nicht gezwungen werden, zuerst Lieferung anzunehmen, um dann Ersatzlieferung nach Art. 46 II zu verlangen oder den Vertrag nach Art. 49 I lit. a) aufzuheben. Ist
die Wesentlichkeit der Vertragswidrigkeit im Zeitpunkt der Lieferung erkennbar, kann der
Käufer vielmehr die Annahme der Lieferung zurückweisen. In der Praxis wird der Käufer
freilich die Lieferung oft annehmen müssen, da er die Wesentlichkeit der Vertragswidrigkeit
bei Lieferung nur schwer wird erkennen können, da es dazu meist einer genaueren Untersuchung bedarf.

---

[25] *Witz/Salger/Lorenz/Witz,* Art. 60, Rn. 9.
[26] Vgl. oben *Müller-Chen,* Art. 52 Rn. 3; *Honsell/Schnyder/Straub,* Art. 60, Rn. 34. Liefert der Verkäufer innerhalb des vereinbarten Liefermonats, aber bevor der Käufer wie vertraglich vereinbart ein Dokumentenakkreditiv stellt, so kann der Käufer die Lieferung nicht als vorzeitig zurückweisen, vgl. CIETAC, 5.5.2005, CISG-online 1685.
[27] Vgl. oben *Müller-Chen,* Art. 52 Rn. 7 ff.; *Honsell/Schnyder/Straub,* Art. 60, Rn. 34.
[28] *Hager/Maultzsch,* 5. Aufl., Art. 60 Rn. 3. Vgl. auch *Staudinger/Magnus,* Art. 60, Rn. 20; MünchKomm/ *P. Huber,* Art. 60, Rn. 9; *Achilles,* Art. 60, Rn. 3; *Bianca/Bonell/Maskow,* Art. 53, Anm. 3.2.1. ff.; *Brunner,* Art. 60, Rn. 4; *Enderlein/Maskow/Strohbach,* Art. 60, Anm. 2.1.; *Herber/Czerwenka,* Art. 53, Rn. 11; *Honsell/ Schnyder/Straub,* Art. 60, Rn. 35 ff.; *Murray,* Draft Digest, S. 455; *Piltz,* Internationales Kaufrecht, Rn. 4–172; *Soergel/Lüderitz/Budzikiewicz,* Art. 60, Rn. 8; Witz/Salger/Lorenz/Witz, Art. 60, Rn. 10. A. A. *Reinhart,* Art. 60, Rn. 7.
[29] Vgl. oben *Müller-Chen,* Art. 49 Rn. 5.
[30] Vgl. oben *Müller-Chen,* Art. 49 Rn. 20.
[31] Vgl. oben *Müller-Chen,* Art. 49 Rn. 28.
[32] Vgl. OLG Frankfurt a. M., 18.1.1994, CISG-online 123 = CLOUT Nr. 79; *Gabriel,* 25 J. L. & Com. (2005-06), 273, 283; *Kröll u. a./P. Butler/Harindranath,* Art. 60, Rn. 8. Zum Recht des Käufers, den Kaufpreis zurückzubehalten, vgl. oben Art. 58 Rn. 28.

16 Ob der Käufer berechtigt ist, **vertragswidrige Ware** auch dann zurückzuweisen, wenn **kein wesentlicher Vertragsbruch** vorliegt, ist eine offene Frage.[33] Einer Ansicht nach kann ein solches Zurückweisungsrecht dem Käufer nicht gewährt werden, weil es das System der Rechtsbehelfe des CISG aushebeln würde.[34] Im Falle vertragswidriger Ware, die keinen wesentlichen Vertragsbruch darstellt, stellt das Übereinkommen folgende Rechtsbehelfe dem Käufer zur Verfügung: Er kann gemäss Art. 46 III vom Verkäufer verlangen, dass die Vertragswidrigkeit durch Nachbesserung behoben wird; er kann den Kaufpreis gemäss Art. 50 mindern oder Schadenersatz nach Artt. 74 ff. fordern. Einer anderen in der Literatur vertretenen Ansicht nach kann dem Käufer auch im Falle eines nicht wesentlichen Vertragsbruchs ein allgemeines Zurückbehaltungsrecht auf der Basis von Art. 7 und unter Berücksichtigung des Rechts des Verkäufers auf zweite Andienung nach Art. 48 gewährt werden.[35] Dieser Ansicht nach kommt es entscheidend darauf an, wo die Ware zu liefern war. Wurde die Ware am Ort der Niederlassung des Verkäufers oder an einem anderen bestimmten Ort, wie z. B. einem Lagerplatz, geliefert, so sollte der Käufer zur Zurückweisung der Ware berechtigt sein.[36] Sieht der Vertrag hingegen die Beförderung der Ware vor oder wurde die Ware dem Käufer an dem Ort seiner Niederlassung oder einem anderen bestimmten Ort in seinem Land zur Verfügung gestellt, so soll der Käufer nicht zur Zurückweisung der Ware berechtigt sein.[37] Dieser Ansicht liegt die Überlegung zugrunde, dass dem Verkäufer in diesen Fällen nicht die Last der Umleitung bzw. der sonstigen Verfügung über die Ware aufgebürdet werden sollte. Diese Last soll dem Verkäufer nur dann aufgebürdet werden, wenn ein wesentlicher Vertragsbruch vorliegt.

17 Unter besonderen Umständen hat der Käufer gemäss Art. 86 II die Pflicht, die Ware am Bestimmungsort **vorläufig** und auf Rechnung des Verkäufers **in Besitz zu nehmen.** Diese Pflicht trifft den Käufer nur dann, wenn ihm die zugesandte Ware am Bestimmungsort zur Verfügung gestellt worden ist und er ein Zurückweisungsrecht ausgeübt hat. Weiter setzt Art. 86 II voraus, dass dem Käufer die vorläufige Inbesitznahme ohne Zahlung des Kaufpreises und ohne unzumutbare Unannehmlichkeiten oder unverhältnismässige Kosten möglich ist. Diese Pflicht greift nicht, wenn der Verkäufer oder eine von ihm autorisierte Person am Bestimmungsort zugegen ist und die Ware in Besitz nehmen kann. In der Praxis wird Art. 86 II wenig Bedeutung zukommen.

18 **(e) Vertragswidrige Dokumente.** Im Falle einer **dokumentären Zahlungsklausel** stellt das Erfordernis einer Lieferung **konformer Dokumente** einen internationalen Handelsbrauch dar, was zur Folge hat, dass **jede Vertragswidrigkeit** einer Dokumentenvorlage den Käufer berechtigt, die Abnahme der Dokumente zu verweigern.[38] In der Praxis finden dokumentäre Kaufgeschäfte oft auf der Basis von **CIF/CFR Incoterms®** statt; in diesen Fällen ergibt sich das Zurückweisungsrecht unmittelbar aus der Regel B8.[39] Sollte Zahlung durch **Dokumentenakkreditiv** erfolgen, so kann das Zurückweisungsrecht nicht konformer Dokumente auch auf die UCP600 gestützt werden.[40] Die in der Literatur sonst ver-

---

[33] Ablehnend MünchKomm/*P. Huber,* Art. 60, Rn. 9.
[34] *Staudinger/Magnus,* Art. 60, Rn. 21.
[35] Vgl. *Hartmann,* IHR 2006, 181, 187 ff.
[36] *Hager/Maultzsch,* 5. Aufl., Art. 60 Rn. 3; *Audit,* Vente internationale, Anm. 145.; *Neumayer/Ming,* Art. 60, Anm. 5.; *Wiegand,* Pflichten des Käufers, S. 143, 148, 149; *Hartmann,* IHR 2006, 181, 188.
[37] *Hartmann,* IHR 2006, 181, 188.
[38] *Schlechtriem,* 16 Pace Int'l L. Rev. (2004), 279, 304 ff.; *Mohs,* FS Schwenzer, S. 1285, 1299 f. Vgl. *St. Paul Guardian Insurance Co. and Travelers Insurance v. Neuromed Medical Systems & Support GmbH et al.,* U. S. Dist. Ct. (S. D. N. Y.), 26.3.2002, CISG-online 615, wo das Gericht entschied, dass die Incoterms® als Handelsbrauch zur Auslegung der Handelsklausel CIF herangezogen werden können, auch wenn die Parteien nicht ausdrücklich auf die Incoterms® Bezug genommen haben; für CFR vgl. *BP Oil International, Ltd., et al. v. Empresa Estatal Petroleos de Ecuador, et al.,* U. S. Ct. App. (5th Cir.), 11.6.2003, CISG-online 730; ICC, 8790/2000, CISG-online 1172 = YB. Comm. Arb. XXIX, 13 ff., Rn. 15; Hanseatisches OLG, 28.2.1997, CISG-online 261.
[39] *Schlechtriem,* 16 Pace Int'l L. Rev. (2004), 279, 305; *Witz/Salger/Lorenz/Witz,* Art. 60, Rn. 13; *Mohs,* FS Schwenzer, S. 1285, 1299 f.
[40] *Schlechtriem,* 16 Pace Int'l L. Rev. (2004), 279, 305 ff.; *Witz/Salger/Lorenz/Witz,* Art. 60, Rn. 13; *Mohs,* FS Schwenzer, S. 1285, 1299 f.

tretene Auffassung impliziert bei einem dokumentären Kaufgeschäft die Wesentlichkeit der Vorlage konformer Dokumente und geht davon aus, dass bei Vorlage nicht konformer Dokumente stets und sofort ein wesentlicher Vertragsbruch vorläge.[41] Zwar führt diese Auffassung zum gleichen Ergebnis eines sofortigen Zurückweisungsrechts des Käufers bezüglich nicht konformer Dokumente, nivelliert aber die nach der hier vertretenen Auffassung gewünschte Unterscheidung zwischen einem sofortigen Zurückweisungsrecht und einem nur bei wesentlichem Vertragsbruch gegebenen Aufhebungsrecht.[42] Ein **sofortiges Recht zur Aufhebung des Vertrags bzw. der betroffenen Teillieferung** steht dem Käufer entgegen der in der Literatur vertretenen Auffassung nur in besonderen Situationen zu, wie z. B. *string trade*-**Situationen,** in denen der Käufer kein Interesse an der physischen Warenlieferung hat.[43]

III. Andere Pflichten des Käufers

Für sonstige Pflichten des Käufers, die nicht die Abnahme der Ware oder Mitwirkungspflichten bei der Lieferung betreffen, kann Art. 60 in Verbindung mit Art. 53 als **Rechtsgrundlage für die Entwicklung sonstiger Pflichten** herangezogen werden.[44] 19

IV. Beweislast

Der **Verkäufer** als die Partei, die sich auf eine Pflicht des Käufers beruft, hat den Bestand und den Inhalt der Pflicht des Käufers zur Abnahme der Ware oder die konkrete Mitwirkungshandlung des Käufers bei der Lieferung in den besonderen Umständen des Einzelfalls zu beweisen.[45] Auch muss der Verkäufer beweisen, dass der Käufer eine solche Pflicht verletzt hat.[46] 20

---

[41] Sekretariatskommentar, Art. 45, Rn. 7; *Schwenzer*, 36 Vict. U. Well. L. Rev. (2005/4), 795, 807; *Schwenzer/Hachem*, 57 American Journal of Comparative Law (2009) 457, 475 ff.; *Ramberg*, FS Kritzer, S. 394, 400; *Mullis*, FS Guest, S. 137, Text zu Fn. 151–155; *Zeller*, FS Kritzer, S. 627, 631; *Bijl*, 1 European Journal of Commerical Contract Law (2009), 19, 22.
[42] *Mohs*, FS Schwenzer, S. 1285, 1299 f.
[43] *Mohs*, FS Schwenzer, S. 1285, 1299 f.
[44] Vgl. oben Art. 53 Rn. 40; ähnlich *Bianca/Bonell/Maskow*, Art. 60, Anm. 2.2.
[45] *Staudinger/Magnus*, Art. 60, Rn. 22; *Honsell/Schnyder/Straub*, Art. 60, Rn. 38; *Kröll u. a./P. Butler/Harindranath*, Art. 60, Rn. 9.
[46] Vgl. *Staudinger/Magnus*, Art. 60, Rn. 22; *Achilles*, Art. 60, Rn. 4; *Baumgärtel/Laumen/Hepting*, Art. 60, Rn. 1 ff.; *Jung*, S. 167. A. A. *Ferrari u. a./Mankowski*, Internationales Vertragsrecht, Art. 60, Rn. 15; *Honsell/Schnyder/Straub*, Art. 60, Rn. 38; *Kröll u. a./P. Butler/Harindranath*, Art. 60, Rn. 9.

Abschnitt III. Rechtsbehelfe des Verkäufers wegen Vertragsverletzung durch den Käufer

Section III.
Remedies for breach of contract by the buyer

Section III.
Moyens dont dispose le vendeur en cas de contravention au contrat par l'acheteur

Art. 61 [Rechtsbehelfe* des Verkäufers; keine zusätzliche Frist]

(1) Erfüllt der Käufer eine seiner Pflichten nach dem Vertrag oder diesem Übereinkommen nicht, so kann der Verkäufer

a) die in Artikel 62 bis 65 vorgesehenen Rechte ausüben;
b) Schadenersatz nach Artikel 74 bis 77 verlangen.

(2) Der Verkäufer verliert das Recht, Schadenersatz zu verlangen, nicht dadurch, daß er andere Rechtsbehelfe ausübt.

(3) Übt der Verkäufer einen Rechtsbehelf wegen Vertragsverletzung aus, so darf ein Gericht oder Schiedsgericht dem Käufer keine zusätzliche Frist gewähren.

Art. 61

(1) If the buyer fails to perform any of his obligations under the contract or this Convention, the seller may:

(a) exercise the rights provided in articles 62 to 65;
(b) claim damages as provided in articles 74 to 77.

(2) The seller is not deprived of any right he may have to claim damages by exercising his right to other remedies.

(3) No period of grace may be granted to the buyer by a court or arbitral tribunal when the seller resorts to a remedy for breach of contract.

Art. 61

1) Si l'acheteur n'a pas exécuté l'une quelconque des obligations résultant pour lui du contrat de vente ou de la présente Convention, le vendeur est fondé à:

a) exercer les droits prévus aux articles 62 à 65;
b) demander les dommages-intérêts prévus aux articles 74 à 77.

2) Le vendeur ne perd pas le droit de demander des dommages-intérêts lorsqu'il exerce son droit de recourir à un autre moyen.

3) Aucun délai de grâce ne peut être accordé à l'acheteur par un juge ou par un arbitre lorsque le vendeur se prévaut d'un des moyens dont il dispose en cas de contravention au contrat.

Übersicht

	Rn.
I. Regelungsgegenstand	1
II. Pflichtverletzung durch den Käufer	4
III. Die Rechtsbehelfe des Verkäufers	6
1. Erfüllung, Nachfrist, Vertragsaufhebung, Spezifizierung durch den Verkäufer, Artt. 61 I lit. a), 62–65	6
2. Schadenersatz, Art. 61 I lit. b) i. V. m. Artt. 74–77	7
3. Zurückbehaltungsrechte	8
4. Vertragsstrafen	9
5. Antizipierter Vertragsbruch, Art. 72	10
6. Sukzessivlieferungsverträge, Art. 73	11
IV. Schadenersatz und konkurrierende Rechtsbehelfe, Art. 61 II	12
V. Haftungsbefreiungen, Artt. 79, 80	14
VI. Vertragliche Haftungsbefreiungen	16
VII. Keine Gnadenfrist, Art. 61 III	18
VIII. Das Recht des Käufers zur Aufrechnung	19
IX. Konkurrierende Rechtsbehelfe nach nationalem Recht	20
X. Verjährung	21

---

* Schweiz: Rechte.

Vorläufer und **Entwürfe:** Artt. 61–64, 66–68, 70 EKG; Genfer E 1976 Art. 42; Wiener E 1977 Art. 43; New Yorker E 1978 Art. 57.

I. Regelungsgegenstand

Abschnitt III (Artt. 61–65) beinhaltet die **Rechtsbehelfe des Verkäufers** wegen Vertragsverletzung durch den Käufer und folgt so dem gleichen Aufbau wie Abschnitt III des vorhergehenden Kapitels (Artt. 45–52) über die Rechtsbehelfe des Käufers wegen Vertragsverletzung durch den Verkäufer. Die Rechtsbehelfe des Verkäufers in Abschnitt III werden ergänzt durch die gemeinsamen Bestimmungen über die Pflichten des Verkäufers und des Käufers in Kapitel V, insbesondere durch die Vorschriften über Schadenersatz, antizipierten Vertragsbruch, Wirkungen der Vertragsaufhebung und Erhaltung der Ware. Art. 61 kommt vor allem die Funktion zu, sämtliche Rechtsbehelfe des Verkäufers zusammenzufassen. 1

Art. 61 II betrifft **konkurrierende Rechtsbehelfe**, spezifisch das Recht des Verkäufers, Schadenersatz neben anderen Rechtsbehelfen geltend zu machen. 2

Art. 61 III stellt klar, dass ein Gericht oder Schiedsgericht dem Käufer **keine zusätzliche Gnadenfrist** gewähren darf, wenn der Vertrag, aus dem der Verkäufer seine Rechte ableitet, dem CISG untersteht, wenngleich das Gericht oder Schiedsgericht nach dem subsidiär geltenden nationalen Recht dazu berechtigt wäre. 3

II. Pflichtverletzung durch den Käufer

Die Einleitungsworte in Art. 61 „*[e]rfüllt der Käufer eine seiner Pflichten nach dem Vertrag oder diesem Übereinkommen nicht*" haben – frei nach *Honnold* – juristischen Biss.[1] Diese Worte beschreiben nämlich das **einheitliche Vertragsbruchskonzept** des CISG.[2] Der Typ oder die Natur der verletzten Pflicht spielt im CISG keine Rolle. Nur die Bedeutung, die die Parteien der Erfüllung einer vertraglichen Pflicht zugemessen haben, ist relevant für die Beurteilung, ob der Verkäufer gemäss Art. 64 I lit. a) i. V. m. Art. 25 den Vertrag wegen wesentlichen Vertragsbruchs des Käufers aufheben kann. Mit anderen Worten spielt es grundsätzlich keine Rolle, ob der Käufer den Kaufpreis nicht gezahlt hat; die Ware nicht abgenommen hat; Massnahmen nicht getroffen oder Förmlichkeiten nicht erfüllt hat, die der Vertrag oder Rechtsvorschriften erfordern, damit Zahlung geleistet werden kann; Handlungen nicht vorgenommen hat, die vernünftigerweise von ihm erwartet werden konnten, um dem Verkäufer die Lieferung zu ermöglichen; oder eine andere Pflicht verletzt hat, die ihm der Vertrag oder das Übereinkommen auferlegen. Nur im Zusammenhang mit Art. 64 I lit. b) wird eine Abgrenzung nötig, da diese Vorschrift das Recht des Verkäufers zur Vertragsaufhebung auch ohne wesentlichen Vertragsbruch des Käufers durch fruchtlosen Ablauf einer angemessenen Nachfrist auf die Fälle beschränkt, in denen der Käufer seine Pflicht zur Zahlung des Kaufpreises oder zur Abnahme der Ware nicht erfüllt. Die Verletzung blosser Obliegenheiten, wie sie z. B. in Artt. 38, 39 und 77 vorgesehen sind, fällt von vornherein nicht in den Anwendungsbereich von Art. 61.[3] 4

Anders als etliche nationale Rechtsordnungen liegt dem CISG **kein Verschuldensprinzip** zu Grunde.[4] Die Frage, ob ein Vertragsbruch vorliegt, ist nach rein objektiven Kriterien zu beantworten und nicht durch Bezugnahme auf subjektive Vorstellungen des Schuldners, 5

---

[1] *Honnold/Flechtner*, Art. 45, Rn. 276, sprechen von „legal bite" in Bezug auf die Rechtsbehelfe des Käufers wegen Vertragsbruchs des Verkäufers.
[2] Rechtsvergleichend zum einheitlichen Vertragsbruchskonzept gegenüber Leistungsstörungsrechten, die nach der Art der Störung unterscheiden, vgl. *Schwenzer/Hachem/Kee*, Rn. 41.01 ff. Zum CISG vgl. *Honsell/ Schnyder/Straub*, Art. 61, Rn. 21.
[3] Vgl. oben Art. 53 Rn. 1, 41; *Piltz*, Internationales Kaufrecht, Rn. 5–378.
[4] Rechtsvergleichend zum Verschuldensprinzip und der Vorhersehbarkeitsregel vgl. *Schwenzer/Hachem/Kee*, Rn. 44.59 ff. Zum CISG wie hier Sekretariatskommentar, Art. 57, Nr. 3; *Honnold/Flechtner*, Art. 61, Rn. 344; *Honsell/Schnyder/Straub*, Art. 61, Rn. 11; *Kröll u. a./Bell*, Art. 61, Rn. 3; *Ferrari u. a./Mankowski*, Internationales Vertragsrecht, Art. 61, Rn. 5; *Bartolotti*, (2005) 25 J. L. & Com., 335.

wie z. B. eine fahrlässige Handlungsweise. Ausnahmsweise kann der Käufer jedoch von seiner Haftung befreit sein, z. B. nach Art. 79, wenn die Nichterfüllung auf einem ausserhalb seines Einflussbereichs liegenden Hinderungsgrund beruhte,[5] wobei Art. 79 sich vornehmlich auf den Schadenersatzanspruch des Käufers bezieht, oder nach Art. 80, der wiederum auf sämtliche Rechtsbehelfe des Verkäufers Anwendung findet, wenn die Nichterfüllung durch eine Handlung oder Unterlassung des Verkäufers verursacht worden war.[6]

III. Die Rechtsbehelfe des Verkäufers

1. Erfüllung, Nachfrist, Vertragsaufhebung, Spezifizierung durch den Verkäufer, Artt. 61 I lit. a), 62–65

6   Art. 61 I lit. a) enthält eine **Zusammenfassung der Rechtsbehelfe** des Verkäufers, wie sie in Artt. 62–65 vorgesehen sind. Art. 62 berechtigt den Verkäufer, vom Käufer zu verlangen, dass er eine Pflicht erfüllt, wobei die Pflicht zur Zahlung des Kaufpreises in der Praxis am häufigsten mit Erfüllung durchgesetzt werden wird. Jede Pflicht, auch die Pflicht zur Zahlung des Preises, kann gemäss Art. 28 gerichtlich auf Erfüllung durchgesetzt werden, soweit das befasste Gericht eine Entscheidung auf Erfüllung in Natur nach dem anwendbaren Prozessrecht fällen kann. Gemäss Art. 63 kann der Verkäufer dem Käufer eine angemessene Nachfrist zur Erfüllung seiner Pflichten ansetzen, was der Verkäufer üblicherweise zur Klarstellung benutzen wird, ob der Käufer den Vertrag noch erfüllen wird. Art. 64 beschreibt die Vertragsaufhebung durch den Verkäufer wegen Vertragsbruchs des Käufers. Gemäss Art. 65 hat der Verkäufer das Recht, die Ware selbst zu spezifizieren, wenn der Käufer eine Spezifizierung nicht oder nicht fristgerecht vornimmt.

2. Schadenersatz, Art. 61 I lit. b) i. V. m. Artt. 74–77

7   Art. 61 I lit. b) hat anders als Art. 61 I lit. a) nicht nur eine zusammenfassende Funktion, sondern stellt die **Anspruchsgrundlage** für einen **Schadenersatzanspruch** wegen Pflichtverletzung seitens des Käufers dar.[7] Artt. 74–77 regeln hingegen den Umfang und den Inhalt sowie die Höhe des Schadenersatzes.

3. Zurückbehaltungsrechte

8   Neben den in Art. 61 ausdrücklich genannten Rechtsbehelfen stehen dem Verkäufer Zurückbehaltungsrechte in verschiedenen Situationen zu. Gemäss Art. 58 I 2 kann der Verkäufer die Übergabe der Ware oder der Dokumente von der Zahlung abhängig machen. Gemäss Art. 58 II kann der Verkäufer im Falle des Versendungskaufes die Ware mit der Massgabe versenden, dass die Ware oder die Dokumente, die zur Verfügung über die Ware berechtigen, dem Käufer nur gegen Zahlung des Kaufpreises übergeben werden. Art. 71 schliesslich berechtigt den Verkäufer zur Aussetzung der Erfüllung seiner Pflichten, wenn sich nach Vertragsschluss herausstellt, dass der Käufer einen wesentlichen Teil seiner Pflichten nicht erfüllen wird. Ob dem Verkäufer in besonderen Situationen darüber hinaus ein **allgemeines Zurückbehaltungsrecht** zur Verfügung steht, stellt eine ungeklärte Sachfrage dar.[8]

---

[5] S. Art. 79 V; vgl. unten *Schwenzer*, Art. 79 Rn. 49 ff.; *Witz/Salger/Lorenz/Witz*, Art. 61, Rn. 7.
[6] Vgl. unten *Schwenzer*, Art. 80 Rn. 1 ff.
[7] Vgl. OLG Karlsruhe, 8.2.2006, CISG-online 1328; OLG Düsseldorf, 11.7.1996, CISG-online 201; CA Colmar, 12.6.2001, CISG-online 694; Sekretariatskommentar, Art. 57, Nr. 1; *Honnold/Flechtner*, Art. 61, Rn. 344; *Honsell/Schnyder/Straub*, Art. 61, Rn. 4; *Kröll u. a./Bell*, Art. 61, Rn. 4; *Ferrari u. a./Mankowski*, Internationales Vertragsrecht, Art. 61, Rn. 1, 8; *Bartolotti*, (2005) 25 J. L. & Com., 335.
[8] Vgl. oben Art. 58 Rn. 27 ff.

4. Vertragsstrafen

Sieht der Vertrag eine Konventionalstrafe für den Fall einer Pflichtverletzung durch den 9
Käufer vor, so ist diese Konventionalstrafe nach Art. 6 grundsätzlich durchsetzbar, vorausgesetzt dass sie nach dem subsidiär anwendbaren nationalen Recht gültig ist, Art. 4 lit. a).[9]
Ob die vertragstreue Partei neben der Vertragsstrafe auch noch Schadenersatz oder Zinsen beanspruchen kann, ist durch Auslegung der Vereinbarung über die Vertragsstrafe nach Art. 8 und 9 zu entscheiden. Dabei ist massgebend, ob die Vertragsstrafe die Folgen der Pflichtverletzung abschliessend regeln sollte;[10] diesbezügliche nationale Auslegungsregeln (bzw. nationales derogatives Recht) sind nicht anzuwenden.[11]

5. Antizipierter Vertragsbruch, Art. 72

Art. 72 kann je nach Fallgestaltung ein Rechtsbehelf des Verkäufers oder des Käufers sein, 10
wenn ein antizipierter Vertragsbruch der Gegenseite vorliegt. Ist es offensichtlich, dass der Käufer einen wesentlichen Vertragsbruch begehen wird, so kann der Verkäufer gemäss Art. 72 I die Aufhebung des Vertrags schon vor dem für die Vertragserfüllung festgesetzten Zeitpunkt erklären. Dies kann der Käufer verhindern, indem er dem Verkäufer gemäss Art. 72 II für die Erfüllung seiner Pflichten ausreichende Gewähr gibt.[12]

6. Sukzessivlieferungsverträge, Art. 73

Art. 73 sieht besondere Rechtsbehelfe im Falle eines Sukzessivlieferungsvertrags vor. 11
Grundsätzlich berechtigt gemäss Art. 73 I eine wesentliche Vertragsverletzung in Bezug auf eine Teillieferung nur zur Vertragsaufhebung in Bezug auf diese Teillieferung. Nur wenn der Verkäufer durch die Pflichtverletzung des Käufers bezüglich der einen Teillieferung triftigen Grund zu der Annahme hat, dass eine wesentliche Vertragsverletzung in Bezug auf künftige Teillieferungen zu erwarten ist, so kann der Verkäufer gemäss Art. 73 II die Aufhebung des Vertrags auch für die zukünftigen Teillieferungen erklären.

IV. Schadenersatz und konkurrierende Rechtsbehelfe, Art. 61 II

Art. 61 II regelt das Verhältnis der einzelnen Rechtsbehelfe zueinander und bestimmt, 12
dass der Verkäufer durch Ausübung anderer Rechtsbehelfe nicht das Recht verliert, Schadenersatz zu verlangen. Nur wenige Probleme ergeben sich im Verhältnis der Rechtsbehelfe nach Art. 61 I lit. a) untereinander, weil der Käufer entweder beim Vertrag stehen bleibt und Zahlung des Kaufpreises verlangt oder vom Vertrag Abstand nimmt und ihn daher für aufgehoben erklärt. Art. 63 wiederum lässt den Vertrag als solchen zunächst unberührt. Die Nachfristsetzung gemäss Art. 63 eröffnet dem Verkäufer nur die Möglichkeit, den Willen und die Möglichkeiten des Käufers, den Vertrag zu erfüllen, herauszufinden und so die Vertragssituation klarzustellen. So kann der Verkäufer zunächst am Vertrag festhalten und dem Käufer eine angemessene Nachfrist zur Erfüllung ansetzen, um nach fruchtlosem Fristablauf den Vertrag aufzuheben. Vor diesem Hintergrund beschreibt Art. 61 II nur das Verhältnis zwischen Schadenersatz und den anderen Rechtsbehelfen nach Art. 61 I lit. a).[13]

---

[9] *Mohs/Zeller*, (2006) 21 Mealey's Int'l Arb. Rep., 1 ff.; *Hachem*, (2009) 13 VJ 200, 205, der vorschlägt, dass sich die Gültigkeit einer Vertragsstrafe nach nationalem Recht an einem internationalen Standard orientieren sollte. Nationale Formvorschriften sollten gemäss Artikel 11 unbeachtlich bleiben; a. A. Dist. Ct. Nitra, 29.6.2006, CISG-online 1757. Rechtsvergleichend zur Gültigkeit von Vertragsstrafen vgl. *Schwenzer/Hachem/Kee*, Rn. 44.267 ff.; *Hachem*, Agreed Sums, *et passim*.
[10] ICC, 7585/1992, 1.1.1992, CISG-online 105 = J. D. I. 1995, 1015 ff.; *Mohs/Zeller*, (2006) 21 Mealey's Int'l Arb. Rep., 1, 2.
[11] A. A. Int. Ct. Russian CCI, 13.1.2006, CISG-online 1622. Rechtsvergleichend zu solchen nationalen Auslegungsregeln vgl. *Schwenzer/Hachem/Kee*, Rn. 44.287 ff.; *Hachem*, Agreed Sums, S. 161 ff.
[12] Vgl. unten *Fountoulakis*, Art. 72 Rn. 1 ff.
[13] Zum Verhältnis von Schadenersatz zu Vertragsstrafen, vgl. oben Rn. 9.

13 Gemäss Art. 61 II kann Schadenersatz neben den anderen Rechtsbehelfen verlangt werden, d. h. der Verkäufer kann entweder Kaufpreiszahlung und Erfüllung des Vertrags sowie Schadensersatz verlangen oder den Vertrag aufheben und Schadensersatz verlangen. Selbstredend ist der Verkäufer nicht berechtigt, im Wege des Schadensersatzes Verluste ersetzt zu verlangen, die bereits durch die Ausübung eines anderen Rechtsbehelfs abgedeckt werden. Mit anderen Worten darf der Verkäufer nicht doppelt entschädigt werden.[14] Daraus ergeben sich folgende Möglichkeiten: Entscheidet sich der Verkäufer am Vertrag festzuhalten und Kaufpreiszahlung sowie Vertragserfüllung zu verlangen, so kann er im Wege des Schadenersatzes nur die Folgen der Erfüllungsverzögerung ersetzt erhalten, nicht aber Schadenersatz wegen Nichterfüllung oder statt der Leistung.[15] Entschliesst sich hingegen der Verkäufer den Vertrag aufzuheben, so kann er im Wege des Schadenersatzes sein Erfüllungsinteresse ersetzt verlangen, dessen genaue Höhe vor allem davon abhängen wird, ob der Verkäufer die Ware bereits geliefert hat. Hat der Verkäufer die Ware noch nicht geliefert, so kann er einen Deckungsverkauf vornehmen und gemäss Art. 75 den Unterschied zwischen dem im Vertrag vereinbarten Preis und dem Preis des Deckungsverkaufs als Schadenersatz verlangen. Hat die Ware einen Marktpreis, so kann der Verkäufer gemäss Art. 76 den Unterschied zwischen dem im Vertrag vereinbarten Preis und dem Marktpreis zur Zeit der Aufhebung als Schadenersatz verlangen. Weder Art. 75 noch Art. 76 beschränken das Recht des Verkäufers, Schadenersatz nach Art. 74 zu verlangen.[16] Allerdings muss die Schwelle eines wesentlichen Vertragsbruchs erreicht sein, wenn der Verkäufer im Wege des Schadenersatzes versucht, sein Erfüllungsinteresse ersetzt zu erhalten. Hat der Verkäufer die Ware bereits geliefert, so kann er die Rückgabe der Ware gemäss Art. 81 II sowie Schadenersatz für allfällige Begleitschäden verlangen. Andererseits kann der Verkäufer die Ware auch dem Käufer überlassen und sein Erfüllungsinteresse als Schadenersatz verlangen[17] bzw., sofern der Käufer bereits bezahlt hatte, die Differenz zwischen seinem Erfüllungsinteresse und dem bereits gezahlten Kaufpreis.

V. Haftungsbefreiungen, Artt. 79, 80

14 Der Käufer ist gemäss Art. 79 von seiner Haftung befreit, wenn die Nichterfüllung auf einem ausserhalb seines Einflussbereichs liegenden Hinderungsgrund beruhte. Diese Vorschrift gilt gemäss Art. 79 V nur für Schadenersatzansprüche.[18]

15 Gemäss Art. 80 kann sich der Verkäufer nicht auf die Pflichtverletzung des Käufers berufen, soweit diese Nichterfüllung durch seine Handlung oder Unterlassung verursacht wurde. Diese Vorschrift gilt für sämtliche Rechtsbehelfe des Verkäufers. Sie ist von grosser praktischer Bedeutung und hängt eng mit dem Zug-um-Zug-Prinzip des CISG zusammen. Oft sieht ein Vertrag den genauen Ablauf der Zug-um-Zug zu erfolgenden Warenleistung gegen Zahlung vor. In einem solchen Fall kann eine Handlung des Verkäufers nötig sein, um dem Käufer seine nächste Handlung zu ermöglichen. Z. B. kann der Verkäufer verpflichtet sein, dem Käufer den Entwurf eines Dokumentenakkreditivs zukommen zu lassen, damit der Käufer das Dokumentenakkreditiv stellen kann. Unterlässt es der Verkäufer nun,

---

[14] *Honsell/Schnyder/Straub*, Art. 61, Rn. 70.

[15] Vgl. OLG Karlsruhe, 8.2.2006, CISG-online 1328 = IHR 2006, 106 ff.: Schadenersatz für Lagerkosten wegen verspäteter Abnahme zuzüglich zum Kaufpreis; OLG Düsseldorf, 11.7.1996, CISG-online 201 = RIW 1996, 958, 960: Schadenersatz für aussenprozessuale Anwaltskosten, z. B. anwaltliche Mahnung; LG München I, 18.5.2009, CISG-online 1998; a. A. LG Hannover, 1.12.1993, CISG-online 244: kein Schadenersatz für Mahnspesen, da es einer Mahnung gemäss Art. 59 nicht bedarf.

[16] Vgl. unten *Schwenzer*, Art. 74 Rn. 22, Art. 75 Rn. 5 und Art. 76 Rn. 3.

[17] Vgl. OLG Karlsruhe, 14.2.2008, CISG-online 1649: Art. 84 II lit. b) sei analog anwendbar, so dass der den Vertrag aufhebende Verkäufer den Nettoerlös des Käufers aus Weiterverkauf der Ware herausverlangen könne.

[18] BGH, 27.11.2007, CISG-online 1617 = CLOUT Nr. 721 = IHR 2008, 49, 53, m. Anm. *Schroeter*, EWiR 2008, 303 ff.: offengelassen, ob der Verfall des Rubelkurses den Käufer entlasten konnte, weil Art. 79 jedenfalls nicht auf den Erfüllungsanspruch des Verkäufers auf Kaufpreiszahlung Anwendung findet.

dem Käufer ein solches Dokument zukommen zu lassen, kann sich der Käufer auf Art. 80 berufen, um die Nichtstellung eines für den Verkäufer akzeptierbaren Dokumentenakkreditivs zu entschuldigen.

VI. Vertragliche Haftungsbefreiungen

Sämtliche Rechtsbehelfe des Verkäufers können gemäss Art. 6 durch Parteivereinbarung **16** abbedungen werden. Probleme entstehen vor allem, wenn sich Haftungsbefreiungen in den AGB des Käufers befinden. Die Frage der Einbeziehung von AGB sowie ihre Interpretation betreffen in diesem Übereinkommen geregelte Gegenstände und können nach den allgemeinen Grundsätzen des CISG entschieden werden. Freilich entscheidet sich die Gültigkeit von Haftungsbefreiungen in AGB nach dem subsidiär anwendbaren nationalen Recht, Art. 4 lit. a). Lässt das anwendbare nationale Recht die Inhaltskontrolle von AGB zu, so können die Regelungen des CISG als Vergleichsmassstab zur Beurteilung der Frage der Angemessenheit der AGB-Regelungen herangezogen werden.[19]

Vor dem Hintergrund der Regelungen des CISG muss es dem Verkäufer in jedem Fall **17** möglich sein, den Vertrag wegen wesentlichen Vertragsbruchs des Käufers aufzuheben.[20] Gemessen am Massstab des CISG sind Haftungsbefreiungen grundsätzlich zulässig, ausser für Vorsatz und Betrug.[21]

VII. Keine Gnadenfrist, Art. 61 III

Art. 61 III verbietet einem Gericht oder Schiedsgericht, dem Käufer eine zusätzliche Frist **18** zu gewähren, wenn der Verkäufer einen Rechtsbehelf wegen Vertragsverletzung ausübt. Diese Vorschrift dient vor allem der **Vermeidung von gerichtlich angeordneten Gnadenfristen,** wie sie vor allem in Ländern Europas, des Mittleren Ostens und Südamerikas bekannt sind, die in der französischen Rechtstradition stehen.[22] Solche Gnadenfristen sind im internationalen Handel nicht akzeptierbar, weil sie die Parteien eines internationalen Warenkaufvertrags dem breiten Ermessen eines Gerichts oder Schiedsgerichts und damit unvorhersehbaren Ergebnissen aussetzen würden.[23] Hingegen schneidet Art. 61 III einem Schiedsgericht nicht die Möglichkeit ab, eine Gnadenfrist zu erlauben, wenn die Parteien das Schiedsgericht ermächtigt haben, *ex aequo et bono* zu entscheiden.[24] Auch andere auf einen CISG-Vertrag zusätzlich anwendbare Rechtsvorschriften, die sich aus nationalem Verfahrens-, Vollstreckungs- oder Insolvenzrecht ergeben und auf deren Grundlage dem Schuldner eine zusätzliche Gnadenfrist zur Zahlung einzuräumen ist, sind nicht nach Art. 61 III ausgeschlossen, sondern können angewendet werden.[25]

---

[19] *Ferrari u. a./Mankowski,* Internationales Vertragsrecht, Art. 61, Rn. 15.
[20] *Staudinger/Magnus,* Art. 61, Rn. 40-1; *Honsell/Schnyder/Straub,* Art. 61, Rn. 57; *Ferrari u. a./Mankowski,* Internationales Vertragsrecht, Art. 61, Rn. 16.
[21] *Staudinger/Magnus,* Art. 61, Rn. 40-1; oben *Schwenzer,* Art. 35 Rn. 41 f., mit Bezug auf die Haftung des Verkäufers für vertragswidrige Ware; *Honsell/Schnyder/Straub,* Art. 61, Rn. 57, die auch einen Haftungsausschluss für grobe Fahrlässigkeit ablehnen; so auch *Ferrari u. a./Mankowski,* Internationales Vertragsrecht, Art. 61, Rn. 16.
[22] Frankreich: Art. 1184 III Cc. Rechtsvergleichend dazu *Schwenzer/Hachem/Kee,* Rn. 47.58 ff.
[23] Wie hier *Kröll u. a./Bell,* Art. 61, Rn. 8.
[24] MünchKomm/*P. Huber,* Art. 61, Rn. 9; *Hager/Maultzsch,* 5. Aufl., Art. 61 Rn. 5; *Staudinger/Magnus,* Art. 61, Rn. 32; *Ferrari u. a./Mankowski,* Internationales Vertragsrecht, Art. 61, Rn. 13.
[25] *Helen Kaminski Pty. Ltd. v. Marketing Australian Products, Inc.,* U. S. Dist. Ct. (S. D. N. Y.), 23.7.1997, CISG-online 297 = CLOUT Nr. 187 = 1997 U. S. Dist. Lexis 10603 *(obiter); Hager/Maultzsch,* 5. Aufl., Art. 61 Rn. 5; *Staudinger/Magnus,* Art. 61, Rn. 35; *Witz/Salger/Lorenz/Witz,* Art. 61, Rn. 8; MünchKomm/*P. Huber,* Art. 61, Rn. 9; *Soergel/Lüderitz/Budzikiewicz,* Art. 61, Rn. 8; *Herber/Czerwenka,* Art. 45, Rn. 10; *Honsell/Schnyder/Straub,* Art. 61, Rn. 81; *Ferrari u. a./Mankowski,* Internationales Vertragsrecht, Art. 61, Rn. 14; a. A. *Schmidt-Kessel,* FS Schlechtriem, S. 255, 273 ff.

VIII. Das Recht des Käufers zur Aufrechnung

19 Je nach Fallkonstellation kann der Käufer gegen die Inanspruchnahme durch den Verkäufer eigene Geldansprüche geltend machen. Stark vereinfacht hat der Käufer dabei zwei Möglichkeiten: Zum einen kann er eine Widerklage erheben, also eine eigene Klage für seinen Anspruch vor dem mit der Klage des Verkäufers befassten Gericht oder Schiedsgericht, soweit es das Prozessrecht des Gerichts oder Schiedsgerichts zulässt. Zum anderen kann der Käufer seinen Anspruch gegen den Anspruch des Verkäufers aufrechnen, was zur Folge hat, dass nur ein Geldanspruch auf die Differenz zwischen den beiden Beträgen übrig bleibt und von der Partei, die den höheren Anspruch geltend macht, eingeklagt werden kann. Das CISG selbst enthält keine Regeln zur Aufrechnung. Dennoch ist in Rechtsprechung und Literatur die Ansicht vertreten worden, dass das CISG die **Aufrechnung** insoweit regele, als sich zwei Geldansprüche gegenüberstehen, die ihre Grundlage im gleichen Vertrag haben und dieser Vertrag dem CISG untersteht.[26] Richtigerweise kann aber nur die Frage der **Aufrechenbarkeit** nach CISG beurteilt werden, also die Frage, ob die von den Parteien geltend gemachten Forderungen aufrechenbar sind. Wie hingegen die Aufrechnung auszuüben ist, also ob Aufrechnung automatisch,[27] durch Parteierklärung oder durch Urteil eines Gerichts[28] oder Schiedsgerichts[29] eintritt, und wann die miteinander aufgerechneten Ansprüche als erfüllt anzusehen sind, kann nicht nach CISG beurteilt werden und muss daher dem subsidiär anwendbaren nationalen Recht entnommen werden.[30] Zur Aufrechenbarkeit gehören auch Vertragsbestimmungen über das Recht zur Aufrechnung, sodass vertragliche Bestimmungen zur Aufrechnung nach Artt. 8, 9, 14 ff. zu beurteilen sind.[31] In diesem Zusammenhang spielen **Zahlungsklauseln** eine bedeutende Rolle, weil manchen Zahlungsklauseln ein **stillschweigendes Aufrechnungsverbot** zu entnehmen ist. Nettozahlungsklauseln, z. B. „net 40 days"[32], oder Barzahlungsklauseln, z. B. „cash against documents" (CAD)[33] oder „cash on delivery" (COD),[34] schliessen das Recht des Käufers auf Aufrechnung aus und verpflichten ihn erst zu zahlen und später zu streiten. Daneben müssen auch gesetzliche Verbote von vertraglichen Aufrechnungsbeschränkungen als Gültigkeitsfragen berücksichtigt werden, Art. 4 lit. a).[35] Im Falle eines vorsätzlichen Vertragsbruchs durch den Verkäufer kann dieser sich nicht auf eine vertragliche Aufrechnungsbeschränkung gegenüber dem Schadenersatzanspruch des Käufers beru-

---

[26] OLG Hamburg, 26.11.1999, CISG-online 515 = IHR 2001, 19 ff.; OLG München, 9.7.1997, CISG-online 282; AG Duisburg, 13.4.2000, CISG-online 659 = IHR 2001, 114, 115; unten *Fountoulakis*, Art. 81 Rn. 21; *Schlechtriem/Schwenzer/Schwenzer/Hachem*, CISG Commentary, Art. 4, Rn. 28 (die sogar dafür eintreten, dass Ansprüche aus verschieden, dem CISG unterstehenden Verträgen gegeneinander aufgerechnet werden können, sofern sie sich aus dem gleichen Vertragsverhältnis ergeben); *Staudinger/Magnus*, Art. 4, Rn. 47. Offengelassen in BGer, 20.12.2006, CISG-online 1426 = IHR 2007, 127, 128; OLG Karlsruhe, 20.7.2004, CISG-online 858 = IHR 2004, 246, 251; a. A. oben *Ferrari*, Art. 4 Rn. 39; *Schlechtriem/P. Butler*, UN Law, Rn. 42e.

[27] Vgl. Frankreich: Art. 1290 Cc (*ipso iure compensatur*), in einem CISG-Fall angewendet von OLG Koblenz, 17.9.1993, CISG-online 91 = RIW 1993, 934 ff. Vgl. Italien: Art. 1243 I Cc.

[28] Vgl. Italien Art. 1243 II Cc, in einem CISG-Fall angewendet von OLG Köln, 19.5.2008, CISG-online 1700.

[29] A. A. *Staudinger/Magnus*, Art. 4, Rn. 47, dem zufolge die Aufrechnung ausdrücklich oder stillschweigend erklärt werden muss.

[30] *Schlechtriem/P. Butler*, UN Law, Rn. 42e; a. A. unten *Fountoulakis*, Art. 81 Rn. 21, die die Ansicht vertritt, dass sich dem CISG Prinzipien entnehmen lassen, denen zufolge die Aufrechnung erklärt werden muss, die Erfüllungswirkung im Zeitpunkt der Absendung der Aufrechnungserklärung eintritt und die gegeneinander aufgerechneten Ansprüche dem Grunde und der Höhe nach bestimmt sein müssen; zustimmend *Schlechtriem/ Schwenzer/Schwenzer/Hachem*, CISG Commentary, Art. 4, Rn. 28.

[31] Vgl. oben *Schmidt-Kessel*, Art. 8 Rn. 5; *Schlechtriem/P. Butler*, UN Law, Rn. 42e; a. A. OLG München, 28.1.1998, CISG-online 339 = RIW 1998, 559ff = IHR 2001, 23 ff. (ohne Begründung).

[32] OLG Hamburg, 5.10.1998, CISG-online 473 = TranspR-IHR 1999, 37 ff.; *Staudinger/Magnus*, Art. 53, Rn. 14.

[33] *Staudinger/Magnus*, Art. 4, Rn. 47; *ders.*, Art. 53, Rn. 11.

[34] *Staudinger/Magnus*, Art. 53, Rn. 13.

[35] Vgl. § 309 Nr. 3 BGB, wonach vertragliche Aufrechnungsverbote in AGB unzulässig sind.

fen.[36] Schliesslich können die Parteien gemäss Art. 6 in ihren Vertrag eine ausdrückliche Regelung aufnehmen, also ein Aufrechnungsrecht vorsehen oder ein nach nationalem Recht bestehendes Aufrechnungsrecht ausschliessen. Auch zwischen den Parteien entstandene Gepflogenheiten und etwaige Handelsgebräuche können nach Art. 9 Beachtung erlangen. Sämtliche Fragen der Aufrechnung und Aufrechenbarkeit unterstehen dem subsidiär anwendbaren nationalen Recht, wenn einer der beiden Ansprüche nicht dem CISG untersteht oder die Ansprüche aus zwei verschiedenen Verträgen resultieren, selbst wenn beide Verträge dem CISG unterstehen. Gleiches gilt, wenn einer der Ansprüche seine Grundlage in einer ausserhalb des Übereinkommens geregelten Materie hat.[37] Ein Schiedsgericht kann auf die PICC rekurrieren, die ausdrückliche Regelungen zur Aufrechnung beinhalten.[38]

IX. Konkurrierende Rechtsbehelfe nach nationalem Recht

Die in Artt. 61 ff. vorgesehenen Rechtsbehelfe des Verkäufers schliessen etwaige **konkurrierende Rechtsbehelfe** nach nationalem Recht aus.[39] Der Rückgriff auf nationale Rechtsvorschriften bezüglich der gleichen Sachverhalte, die den Rechtsbehelf nach CISG auslösen, ist ausgeschlossen.[40]

X. Verjährung

Das CISG enthält keine Regelung der **Verjährung** der sich aus den Rechtsbehelfen des Verkäufers ergebenen Ansprüche.[41]

---

[36] Offengelassen in OLG Hamburg, 5.10.1998, CISG-online 473 = TranspR-IHR 1999, 37 ff.
[37] OGH, 22.10.2001, CISG-online 614; OLG Düsseldorf, 22.6.2004, CISG-online 916 = IHR 2005, 29.
[38] Art. 8.1–8.5 PICC.
[39] *Staudinger/Magnus*, Art. 61, Rn. 36.
[40] LG Aachen, 14.5.1993, CISG-online 86 = RIW 1993, 760; Botschaft des Schweizer Bundesrats, S. 808; *Brunner*, Art. 61, Rn. 18; MünchKommHGB/*Benicke*, Art. 61, Rn. 3.
[41] Zu Verjährungsfragen vgl. oben Art. 53 Rn. 27.

Art. 62 [Zahlung des Kaufpreises; Abnahme der Ware]

Der Verkäufer kann vom Käufer verlangen, daß er den Kaufpreis zahlt, die Ware abnimmt* sowie seine sonstigen Pflichten erfüllt, es sei denn, daß der Verkäufer einen Rechtsbehelf** ausgeübt hat, der mit diesem Verlangen unvereinbar ist.

Art. 62
The seller may require the buyer to pay the price, take delivery or perform his other obligations, unless the seller has resorted to a remedy which is inconsistent with this requirement.

Art. 62
Le vendeur peut exiger de l'acheteur le paiement du prix, la prise de livraison des marchandises ou l'exécution des autres obligations de l'acheteur, à moins qu'il ne se soit prévalu d'un moyen incompatible avec ces exigences.

Übersicht

	Rn.
I. Regelungsgegenstand	1
1. Rechtsvergleichender Hintergrund	2
2. Geschichte des Übereinkommens	6
II. Das Recht des Verkäufers, vom Käufer Erfüllung des Vertrages zu verlangen	9
1. Kaufpreisanspruch	10
2. Klage auf Abnahme der Ware oder Erfüllung sonstiger Pflichten	11
III. Beschränkungen des Erfüllungsanspruchs des Verkäufers	12
1. Widersprüchliche Rechtsbehelfe	12
2. Erfüllung in Natur, Art. 28	13
a) Kaufpreisklage	14
b) Klage auf Abnahme der Ware oder Erfüllung einer sonstigen Pflicht	15
3. Schadensminderungspflicht, Art. 77	16
4. Haftungsbefreiung, Artt. 79 und 80	17
5. Selbsthilfeverkauf, Art. 88	18
IV. Konkurrierende Rechtsbehelfe	19
V. Beweislast	20

Vorläufer und **Entwürfe:** Artt. 61 I, 70 II EKG; Genfer E 1976 Art. 43; Wiener E 1977 Art. 44; New Yorker E 1978 Art. 58.

I. Regelungsgegenstand

1   Gemäss Art. 62 kann der Verkäufer vom Käufer verlangen, dass er den Kaufpreis zahlt, die Ware annimmt sowie seine sonstigen Pflichten erfüllt. Art. 62 spiegelt die Pflichten des Käufers gemäss Art. 53 auf der Rechtsbehelfsseite wider. Dieser Systematik liegt die während der Ausarbeitung des Übereinkommens getroffene Entscheidung zu Grunde, zunächst sämtliche Pflichten des Käufers aufzustellen und dann die dem Verkäufer im Falle eines Vertragsbruchs durch den Käufer zustehenden Rechtsbehelfe zu behandeln. Das rechtliche Konzept, dem Gläubiger ein Recht zu geben, vom Schuldner Erfüllung der versprochenen Leistung zu verlangen, folgt aus dem allgemein anerkannten Prinzip *pacta sunt servanda*,[1] das allen Rechtssystemen der Welt bekannt ist. Die Idee hingegen, die Parteien zur Erfüllung ihrer jeweiligen Versprechen zu zwingen, wird in den Rechtsordnungen des Civil Law bedeutend strenger befolgt als in den Rechtssystemen des Common Law, welche die zwangsweise Erfüllung nur unter gewissen Voraussetzungen und Beschrän-

---

* Schweiz, Österreich: annimmt.
** Schweiz: ein Recht.
[1] Dazu *Hachem*, FS Schwenzer, S. 647, 652 ff.

kungen kennen.² Diese doch deutlichen Unterschiede auf der konzeptionellen Ebene führen in der Praxis jedoch zumeist nicht zu unterschiedlichen Ergebnissen in einem konkreten Fall.³ Im Grossen und Ganzen kann gesagt werden, dass das CISG davon Abstand genommen hat, den Ansatz des Common Law zu übernehmen, welcher sich noch im EKG wiederfand,⁴ sondern stärker dem Ansatz des Civil Law folgt.⁵

1. Rechtsvergleichender Hintergrund

Im **englischen Recht** steht der Anspruch des Verkäufers auf Zahlung von Schadenersatz wegen Nichtabnahme im Vordergrund, wenn der Käufer versäumt oder ablehnt, die Ware anzunehmen und für sie zu zahlen, sec. 50 (1) SGA 1979.⁶ Nur in ganz besonderen Fällen wird es dem Verkäufer möglich sein, mittels Kaufpreisklage vorzugehen. So ist die Kaufpreisklage z. B. dann zulässig, wenn der Kaufpreis auf einen bestimmten Tag fällig gestellt ist, der von der Lieferung unabhängig ist (sec. 49 (2) SGA 1979), oder wenn das Eigentum der Ware bereits auf den Käufer übergegangen ist (sec. 49 (1) SGA 1979). Da das Eigentum bereits vor Übernahme der Ware auf den Käufer übergehen kann, besteht zwischen dem Kaufpreisanspruch und dem Anspruch auf Schadenersatz wegen Nichtabnahme Anspruchskonkurrenz,⁷ ein Zusammenhang der nur historisch erklärt werden kann.⁸ **2**

In den **USA** hat der UCC diese historischen Überlappungen beseitigt und die Rechtsbehelfe des Verkäufers von der Frage der Eigentumsübertragung getrennt. Dies führte freilich zu noch strengeren Beschränkungen des Anspruchs auf Kaufpreiszahlung. Gemäss § 2–709 UCC kann der Verkäufer den Kaufpreis beanspruchen, wenn der Käufer die Ware angenommen hat oder die vertragsgemässe Ware nach Gefahrübergang auf den Käufer verloren gegangen ist oder beschädigt wurde. In allen anderen Fällen kann der Verkäufer nur Schadenersatz wegen Nichtabnahme oder Annahmeverweigerung verlangen, § 2–708 UCC. Nur wenn es dem Verkäufer unmöglich sein sollte, die Ware im Wege eines Deckungsverkaufs zu einem angemessenen Preis abzusetzen, kann er subsidiär berechtigt sein, den Käufer auf Kaufpreiszahlung in Anspruch zu nehmen. Hinter dieser Regelung stehen Überlegungen der ökonomischen Effizienz, da der Verkäufer durch Verweis auf Schadenersatz dazu angehalten ist, die Ware im Wege eines Deckungsverkaufs an einen anderen Abnehmer zu bringen und nicht den Käufer zur Abnahme der Ware anzuhalten.⁹ **3**

Im Gegensatz zum englischen und US-amerikanischen Recht sehen **sämtliche kontinentalen Rechtsordnungen** vor, dass der Verkäufer als Gläubiger die Erfüllung der Pflicht zur Zahlung des Kaufpreises verlangen kann.¹⁰ **4**

In der **Praxis** werden die beschriebenen unterschiedlichen Ausgangspunkte in den Rechtsordnungen des Common Law und des Civil Law freilich zu wenig unterschiedlichen Ergebnissen im konkreten Einzelfall führen. Der Hauptunterschied zwischen den verschiedenen Rechtsordnungen liegt in der Berechnung des Schadenersatzes. Wenn es dem Verkäufer gestattet ist, beim Vertrag stehen zu bleiben und vom Käufer Erfüllung zu verlangen, wie es die meisten Rechtsordnungen des Civil Law zulassen, so liegt die Entscheidung darüber, ob und wann er den Vertrag aufhebt, ausschliesslich bei ihm. Folglich kann der Verkäufer nach seinem Ermessen den Zeitpunkt für die Berechnung des Schadenersatzes bestimmen und dadurch auf gewisse Marktentwicklungen spekulieren, um sich auf Kosten **5**

---

² Rechtsvergleichend dazu *Schwenzer/Hachem/Kee*, Rn. 43.10 ff.
³ Vgl. *Kröll u. a./Bell*, Art. 62, Rn. 5.
⁴ Art. 61 II EKG.
⁵ Vgl. *Kröll u. a./Bell*, Art. 62, Rn. 3.
⁶ *Chitty*, Chitty on Contracts, Vol. II, Rn. 43–399; *Schwenzer/Hachem/Kee*, Rn. 43.31; *Dölle/von Caemmerer*, Art. 61, Rn. 6.
⁷ *Chitty*, Chitty on Contracts, Vol. II, Rn. 43–390.
⁸ *Dölle/von Caemmerer*, Art. 61, Rn. 6; *Rabel*, Recht des Warenkaufs, Bd. 2, S. 41 ff.
⁹ *Dölle/von Caemmerer*, Art. 61, Rn. 7, 8; vgl. *Hager*, Rechtsbehelfe des Verkäufers, S. 26 ff.; *Honnold/Flechtner*, Art. 62, Rn. 346.
¹⁰ Vgl. *Schwenzer/Hachem/Kee*, Rn. 43.11 ff.; vgl. Art 9:101 PECL, Anm. 1.

des Käufers einen Vorteil zu verschaffen. Ein solches Vorgehen ist in den Rechtsordnungen des Common Law ausgeschlossen, weil der Verkäufer verpflichtet ist, den Vertrag aufzuheben und einen Deckungsverkauf vorzunehmen, um den Schaden zu minimieren. Freilich wird in der Geschäftswelt ein umsichtig handelnder Verkäufer von sich aus versuchen, seine Risiken und Kosten durch rechtzeitigen Deckungsverkauf zu minimieren und daher freiwillig dem Ansatz der Rechtsordnungen des Common Law folgen.

2. Geschichte des Übereinkommens

6   Die Möglichkeit der vertragstreuen Partei, den relevanten Tag für die Berechnung des Schadens durch Festhalten am Vertrag zu bestimmen und so auf Kosten der vertragsbrüchigen Partei zu spekulieren, war der Hauptgrund, warum im **EKG** das Konzept der sogenannten *ipso facto*-**Vertragsaufhebung** galt.[11] Unter Geltung des EKG konnte der Verkäufer den Käufer nicht verpflichten, den Kaufpreis zu zahlen, wenn es ihm selbst möglich war, die Ware in einem Deckungsgeschäft abzusetzen; in einem solchen Fall war der Vertrag als aufgehoben anzusehen *(ipso facto)*.[12] Stellte die Nichtzahlung des Kaufpreises einen wesentlichen Vertragsbruch dar, so konnte der Verkäufer Erfüllung während angemessener Nachfrist verlangen, nach deren nutzlosen Ablauf der Vertrag als aufgehoben galt *(ipso facto)*.[13]

7   Während der **Ausarbeitung des CISG** war die *ipso facto*-Vertragsaufhebung des EKG Gegenstand detaillierter Beratschlagung.[14] Schlussendlich wurde die *ipso facto*-Vertragsaufhebung abgeschafft, weil das Konzept mit zu vielen Unsicherheiten verbunden war und sich im Ergebnis zu Ungunsten des Verkäufers, der die Ware bereits geliefert hatte, auswirken konnte.[15]

8   Vor diesem Hintergrund hat das CISG die folgende Systematik. Grundsätzlich kann der Käufer verpflichtet werden, den Kaufpreis zu zahlen, und zwar unabhängig davon, ob Lieferung bereits stattgefunden hat. Im Falle eines wesentlichen Vertragsbruchs oder des nutzlosen Ablaufs einer angemessenen Nachfrist zur Erfüllung durch den Käufer, kann der Verkäufer den Vertrag aufheben. Das Problem möglicher Spekulationsversuche bezüglich des eingetretenen Schadens wird durch die richtige Anwendung der Schadenersatzvorschriften zu lösen sein.[16] Schliesslich nimmt Art. 28 dem Kaufpreisanspruch seine Durchsetzungskraft, indem das Prozessrecht des zuständigen Gerichts für die Frage als massgebend erklärt wird, ob ein Gericht eine Entscheidung auf Erfüllung in Natur fällen kann. Nur wenn das Gericht auch nach seinem eigenen Recht bei gleichartigen Kaufverträgen, die nicht dem CISG unterstehen, eine Verurteilung in Natur aussprechen würde, muss es dazu auch im Falle eines dem Übereinkommen unterstehenden Vertrags kommen.[17]

II. Das Recht des Verkäufers, vom Käufer Erfüllung des Vertrages zu verlangen

9   Art. 62 gibt dem Verkäufer das Recht, den Käufer zur Erfüllung des Vertrags zu verpflichten, was die Erfüllung **sämtlicher Pflichten** des Käufers einschliesst, also die Pflicht zur Kaufpreiszahlung, zur Abnahme der Ware sowie sämtliche seiner sonstigen Pflichten. Selbst für **unwesentliche Pflichtverletzungen** kann der Verkäufer sein Recht auf Erfül-

---

[11] *Hager/Maultzsch*, 5. Aufl., Art. 62 Rn. 2; vgl. *Dölle/von Caemmerer*, Art. 61, Rn. 11, 15.
[12] Art. 61 II EKG; *Hager/Maultzsch*, 5. Aufl., Art. 62 Rn. 2; vgl. auch *Bianca/Bonell/Knapp*, Art. 62, Anm. 1.4.
[13] Art. 62 I 2 EKG; *Hager/Maultzsch*, 5. Aufl., Art. 62 Rn. 2.
[14] Vgl. den Spezialbericht des Generalsekretärs sowie die Kommentare, YB III (1972), S. 41–54, sowie den Bericht der Arbeitsgruppe, YB III (1972), S. 85, 86, Nr. 28–47; vgl. auch *Hager/Maultzsch*, 5. Aufl., Art. 62 Rn. 3; *Staudinger/Magnus*, Art. 62, Rn. 4; *Hellner*, Ipso facto avoidance, S. 45 ff.
[15] *Hager/Maultzsch*, 5. Aufl., Art. 62 Rn. 3; vgl. auch *Bamberger/Roth/Saenger*, Art. 62, Rn. 1; *Bianca/Bonell/Knapp*, Art. 62, Anm. 1.3.
[16] Vgl. unten Art. 64 Rn. 37; *Schwenzer*, Art. 76 Rn. 10.
[17] Vgl. unten Rn. 14.

lung ausüben.[18] In einem solchen Fall findet das Recht des Verkäufers auf Erfüllung seine Begrenzung erst durch das Prinzip des Verbots des **Rechtsmissbrauchs,** das ein allgemeines Prinzip des Übereinkommens gemäss Art. 7 I darstellt. Erfüllung kann auch von **Unterlassungspflichten,** also der Pflicht, gewisse Tätigkeiten nicht vorzunehmen, sowie von **Schutzpflichten** verlangt werden.[19] In der Praxis wird der Erfüllungsanspruch in solchen Fällen besonders für die Geltendmachung einstweiligen Rechtsschutzes vor dem zuständigen Gericht relevant.[20]

1. Kaufpreisanspruch

Von vornehmlicher praktischer Bedeutung ist der Kaufpreisanspruch des Verkäufers. Für die Inanspruchnahme auf Kaufpreiszahlung muss der Kaufpreis bestimmt oder bestimmbar und fällig sein. Wird der Kaufpreis erst durch Übergabe der Ware oder der Dokumente an den Käufer fällig, so kann der Verkäufer die Zahlung des Kaufpreises nur gegen Lieferung verlangen.[21]

2. Klage auf Abnahme der Ware oder Erfüllung sonstiger Pflichten

Gemäss Art. 62 kann der Verkäufer vom Käufer verlangen, dass dieser die Ware abnimmt und/oder seine sonstigen Pflichten aus dem Vertrag oder diesem Übereinkommen erfüllt. Dieses Recht ist unabhängig vom Anspruch auf Zahlung des Kaufpreises, was in einem Verfahren betreffend einstweiligen Rechtsschutz Bedeutung erlangen kann. Auch kann diese Unabhängigkeit praktisch werden, wenn die Ware im Land des Käufers auf Rechnung des Verkäufers gelagert werden muss. Freilich werden solche Fälle in der Praxis von beschränkter Bedeutung bleiben, weil der Verkäufer, der beim Vertrag stehen bleiben will, obwohl der Käufer die Abnahme der Ware verweigert, üblicherweise einen Selbsthilfeverkauf nach Art. 88 durchführen wird.[22]

III. Beschränkungen des Erfüllungsanspruchs des Verkäufers

1. Widersprüchliche Rechtsbehelfe

Gemäss Art. 62 verliert der Verkäufer seinen Anspruch auf Erfüllung des Kaufvertrages, wenn er ein Recht ausgeübt hat, das mit diesem Verlangen unvereinbar ist. Eine solche unvereinbare Rechtsausübung stellt die **erklärte Vertragsaufhebung** dar.[23] Selbstredend kann der Verkäufer nicht den Vertrag aufheben und gleichzeitig seine Erfüllung verlangen. Ein anderer unvereinbarer Rechtsbehelf ist der Anspruch des Verkäufers auf **Ersatz seines Erfüllungsinteresses** (Schadenersatz wegen Nichterfüllung oder Schadensersatz statt der Leistung),[24] da dieser je nach Ansicht eine Vertragsaufhebung voraussetzt oder impliziert, zumindest aber einen wesentlichen Vertragsbruch voraussetzt. Jedenfalls kann der Verkäufer nicht das Erfüllungsinteresse als Schadensersatz verlangen und zur gleichen Zeit vom Käufer

---

[18] *Hager/Maultzsch,* 5. Aufl., Art. 62 Rn. 4; vgl. *Staudinger/Magnus,* Art. 62, Rn. 6; vgl. auch MünchKomm/ *P. Huber,* Art. 62, Rn. 2; *Bianca/Bonell/Knapp,* Art. 62, Anm. 2.1.; *Honsell/Schnyder/Straub,* Art. 62, Rn. 10.
[19] *Staudinger/Magnus,* Art. 62, Rn. 9; vgl. auch MünchKomm/*P. Huber,* Art. 62, Rn. 2; *Achilles,* Art. 62, Rn. 2; *Brunner,* Art. 62, Rn. 1; *Ferrari u. a./Mankowski,* Internationales Vertragsrecht, Art. 62, Rn. 7.
[20] *Staudinger/Magnus,* Art. 62, Rn. 9; *Ferrari u. a./Mankowski,* Internationales Vertragsrecht, Art. 62, Rn. 7.
[21] *Staudinger/Magnus,* Art. 62, Rn. 8; *Herber/Czerwenka,* Art. 62, Rn. 3; vgl. *Ferrari u. a./Mankowski,* Internationales Vertragsrecht, Art. 62, Rn. 5.
[22] *Hager/Maultzsch,* 5. Aufl., Art. 62 Rn. 4; vgl. auch MünchKomm/*P. Huber,* Art. 62, Rn. 1. Das EKG kannte keinen Erfüllungsanspruch bezüglich anderer Pflichten als der Pflicht zur Zahlung des Kaufpreises, weil ein solcher Anspruch als unpraktisch angesehen worden war, vgl. *Dölle/von Caemmerer,* Art. 66, Rn. 4.
[23] Vgl. *Honsell/Schnyder/Straub,* Art. 62, Rn. 16; *Kröll u. a./Bell,* Art. 62, Rn. 8; *Ferrari u. a./Mankowski,* Internationales Vertragsrecht, Art. 62, Rn. 12.
[24] Vgl. *Honsell/Schnyder/Straub,* Art. 62, Rn. 16; *Ferrari u. a./Mankowski,* Internationales Vertragsrecht, Art. 62, Rn. 14.

die Erfüllung des Vertrages verlangen.[25] Ohne praktische Bedeutung ist die Diskussion, ob der Verkäufer vom Käufer Erfüllung des Vertrags verlangen und ihm zur gleichen Zeit eine angemessene Nachfrist zur Erfüllung gemäss Art. 63 ansetzen kann, weil beide Rechtsbehelfe auf Erfüllung des Vertrages zielen. Freilich kann der Verkäufer während des Laufs einer von ihm gesetzten angemessenen Nachfrist zur Erfüllung nicht **Klage auf Erfüllung** einreichen.[26] Eine solche Vorgehensweise würde dem Käufer die Möglichkeit nehmen, während des Laufs der Nachfrist freiwillig zu erfüllen. Auch kann der Verkäufer den Käufer nicht dazu anhalten, die Form, die Masse oder andere Merkmale der Ware näher zu spezifizieren, weil Art. 65 den Verkäufer autorisiert, die **Spezifizierung** selbst vorzunehmen.[27] Ein **Selbsthilfeverkauf** nach Art. 88 ist unvereinbar mit dem Verlangen nach Abnahme der Ware.[28] Freilich kann der Verkäufer durchaus einen Selbsthilfeverkauf vornehmen und zur gleichen Zeit den Käufer zur Zahlung des Kaufpreises anhalten.[29] In einem solchen Fall wird der durch den Selbsthilfeverkauf erzielte Kaufpreis vom Anspruch des Verkäufers auf Kaufpreiszahlung abgezogen.[30] Dieser Abzug stützt sich auf das in Art. 88 III enthaltene Prinzip.

2. Erfüllung in Natur, Art. 28

13   Gemäss Art. 28 braucht ein Gericht eine **Entscheidung auf Erfüllung in Natur** nur dann zu fällen, wenn es dies auch nach seinem eigenen Recht bei gleichartigen Kaufverträgen täte, die nicht unter dieses Übereinkommen fallen.[31] Diese Vorschrift ist Folge des zwischen den Delegierten der Common Law- und Civil Law-Staaten erreichten Kompromisses, dass unter dem CISG ein Schuldner vom Gläubiger zur Erfüllung seiner Pflichten angehalten werden kann. Art. 28 hat die Funktion eines Ventils für nationale Traditionen und Vorverständnisse, denen zufolge Gerichte und Vollzugsbehörden in manchen Vertragsstaaten, insbesondere solchen des Common Law, nicht in der Lage sind, Entscheidungen auf Erfüllung in Natur zu fällen und zu vollziehen. Die Unterschiede zwischen dem Common Law und dem Civil Law wurden bei Ausarbeitung des Übereinkommens als zu grundsätzlich angesehen, als dass eine Vereinheitlichung möglich gewesen wäre. Um diese Probleme bei der Urteilsfindung und der Urteilsvollstreckung zu umgehen, wurde Art. 28 implementiert. Diese Bestimmung verweist nicht nur auf das anwendbare Prozessrecht mit seinen spezifischen Voraussetzungen und Vorgehensweisen,[32] sondern anerkennt auch nationale Vorschriften materiell-rechtlicher Natur, die Ansprüche bzw. Klagen auf Erfüllung in Natur beschränken.[33] Art. 28 hat primäre Bedeutung für die Erfüllungsansprüche des

---

[25] *Hager/Maultzsch*, 5. Aufl., Art. 62 Rn. 5; MünchKomm/*P. Huber*, Art. 62, Rn. 4; *Staudinger/Magnus*, Art. 62, Rn. 13; vgl. auch *Bamberger/Roth/Saenger*, Art. 62, Rn. 5; *Bianca/Bonell/Knapp*, Art. 62, Anm. 3.5.; *Brunner*, Art. 62, Rn. 4; *Achilles*, Art. 62, Rn. 3; *Kröll u. a./Bell*, Art. 62, Rn. 9.

[26] Vgl. *Ferrari u. a./Mankowski*, Internationales Vertragsrecht, Art. 62, Rn. 13.

[27] *Hager/Maultzsch*, 5. Aufl., Art. 65 Rn. 8; *Karollus*, S. 184; *Herber/Czerwenka*, Art. 65, Rn. 7; *Loewe*, Art. 65, S. 83; *Neumayer/Ming*, Art. 65, Anm. 2.; vgl. auch *Bianca/Bonell/Knapp*, Art. 62, Anm. 3.5., dem zufolge der Verkäufer keine Erfüllung mehr vom Käufer verlangen kann, nachdem die Selbstspezifikation des Verkäufers gemäss Art. 65 II verbindlich wurde. A. A. *Honsell/Schnyder/Straub*, Art. 65, Rn. 54; *Soergel/Lüderitz/Budzikiewicz*, Art. 65, Rn. 8; vgl. auch *Ferrari u. a./Mankowski*, Internationales Vertragsrecht, Art. 62, Rn. 7.

[28] Vgl. *Ferrari u. a./Mankowski*, Internationales Vertragsrecht, Art. 62, Rn. 16.

[29] *Hager/Maultzsch*, 5. Aufl., Art. 62 Rn. 5; vgl. auch *Staudinger/Magnus*, Art. 62, Rn. 15; *Bamberger/Roth/Saenger*, Art. 62, Rn. 5; *Achilles*, Art. 62, Rn. 3.

[30] *Hager/Maultzsch*, 5. Aufl., Art. 62 Rn. 5; MünchKomm/*P. Huber*, Art. 62, Rn. 4; *Staudinger/Magnus*, Art. 62, Rn. 15; Vgl. *Ferrari u. a./Mankowski*, Internationales Vertragsrecht, Art. 62, Rn. 16; vgl. auch *Bamberger/Roth/Saenger*, Art. 62, Rn. 5.

[31] Vgl. oben *Müller-Chen*, Art. 28 Rn. 1 ff. Das EKG enthielt eine vergleichbare Vorschrift in Art. 16, vgl. *Dölle/Reinhart*, Art. 16, Rn. 1 ff.

[32] *Loewe*, Art. 62, S. 81.

[33] Dies folgt aus dem Umstand, dass an der Wiener Konferenz das Wort „could" durch das Wort „would" ersetzt wurde, vgl. O. R., S. 304 f., Nr. 41-2; S. 100, Nr. 2–5. Kritisch *Kastely*, (1988) 3 Wash. L. Rev., 607, 625 ff.

Käufers im Falle eines Vertragsbruchs durch den Verkäufer, gilt aber auch für die Erfüllungsansprüche des Verkäufers im Falle eines Vertragsbruchs durch den Käufer.[34]

a) **Kaufpreisklage.** Art. 28 findet auf die **Kaufpreisklage** des Verkäufers Anwendung.[35] **14** Diese Ansicht wird durch den **Wortlaut** von Art. 28 gestützt. Dieser enthält keinerlei Beschränkungen und spricht sehr weitgehend davon, dass die eine Partei berechtigt ist, von der anderen Partei die Erfüllung einer Verpflichtung zu verlangen.[36] Bisherige Zweifel an dieser Auslegung waren rein nationalen Vorverständnissen geschuldet, da die Rechtsordnungen des Common Law die Kaufpreisklage nicht dem Institut der *specific performance* zuordnen, sondern darunter nur solche Urteile verstehen, die traditioneller Weise durch Equity-Gerichte ausgesprochen und durch unterschiedliche Pönalen, einschliesslich des Freiheitsentzugs wegen *contempt of court*,[37] vollzogen wurden. Dies betraf ausschliesslich die Pflicht des Verkäufers zur Lieferung der Ware. Auch das französische Vorverständnis der *l'exécution en nature* betraf nur die Pflichten des Verkäufers. Diese Zweifel können heutzutage als überkommen angesehen werden. Nationale Vorverständnisse können gerade nicht für die Auslegung eines internationalen Übereinkommens herangezogen werden.[38] Die Ansicht, dass Art. 28 auch auf die Kaufpreisklage Anwendung findet, wird darüber hinaus durch die **Entstehungsgeschichte** des Übereinkommens gestützt. Während anfänglich die nationalen Beschränkungen eines Anspruchs auf Erfüllung in Natur auf sämtliche Rechtsbehelfe des Verkäufers Anwendung finden sollten,[39] wurden diese Beschränkungen nach Kritik auf die Fälle der Nichtabnahme der Ware bzw. der Nichterfüllung der sonstigen Pflichten des Käufers begrenzt.[40] Diese Unterscheidung zwischen der Kaufpreisklage und anderer Klagen des Verkäufers wurde hingegen fallen gelassen, als die Beschränkung der Rechtsbehelfe des Verkäufers im Falle eines Vertragsbruchs durch den Käufer mit den Rechtsbehelfen des Käufers zu einer allgemeinen Regel verschmolzen wurde.[41] Dementsprechend sieht auch der Sekretariatskommentar vor, dass Art. 28 auf die Kaufpreisklage Anwendung findet.[42] Schlussendlich spricht auch die **Systematik** des CISG für die Ansicht, dass Art. 28 auch auf die Kaufpreisklage Anwendung findet, weil Art. 28 im ersten Kapitel des dritten Teils über die allgemeinen Bestimmungen zu finden ist, das eben gerade für die Rechte und Pflichten sowohl des Verkäufers als auch des Käufers gelten soll.[43]

b) **Klage auf Abnahme der Ware oder Erfüllung einer sonstigen Pflicht.** Art. 28 **15** gilt auch für die Klage des Verkäufers auf Abnahme der Ware oder Erfüllung jeder sonstigen Pflicht des Käufers.[44] Keine Zweifel wurden gegen diese Auslegung geäussert, weil der Wortlaut, die Systematik und die Entstehungsgeschichte (insofern anders als bei der Kaufpreisklage) diese Ansicht stützen.[45]

---

[34] Über die entsprechende, richtige Auslegung von Art. 16 EKG bestand Unsicherheit, vgl. *Hager*, Rechtsbehelfe des Verkäufers, S. 194 ff.; *Dölle/von Caemmerer*, Art. 61, Rn. 19 ff.; vgl. auch *Hager/Maultzsch*, 5. Aufl., Art. 62 Rn. 7, 12; MünchKomm/*P. Huber*, Art. 62, Rn. 6.
[35] *Honnold/Flechtner*, Art. 62, Rn. 348; *Schlechtriem/P. Butler*, UN Law, Rn. 236; *Kastely*, (1988) 3 Wash. L. Rev., 607, 635; Report of the ABA, House of Delegates, (1984) 18 Int'l Law, 39, 48; oben *Müller-Chen*, Art. 28 Rn. 6; *Bamberger/Roth/Saenger*, Art. 62, Rn. 6; *Honsell/Schnyder/Straub*, Art. 62, Rn. 14; MünchKommBGB/*P. Huber*, Art. 62, Rn. 5; *Staudinger/Magnus*, Art. 62, Rn. 12; *Soergel/Lüderitz/Budzikiewicz*, Art. 62, Rn. 1; *Witz/Salger/Lorenz/Witz*, Art. 62, Rn. 3; *Scheifele*, S. 101 ff.; *Kröll u. a./Bell*, Art. 62, Rn. 11; kritisch, aber im Ergebnis ebenso auch *Ferrari u. a./Mankowski*, Internationales Vertragsrecht, Art. 62, Rn. 10 f.
[36] *Hager/Maultzsch*, 5. Aufl., Art. 62 Rn. 9.
[37] *Honnold/Flechtner*, Art. 62, Rn. 348.
[38] *Honnold/Flechtner*, Art. 62, Rn. 348; *Kröll u. a./Bell*, Art. 62, Rn. 11.
[39] YB V (1974), S. 33, Nr. 40, Art. 71.
[40] YB V (1974), S. 34, Nr. 50.
[41] YB VI (1975), S. 79, Art. 16; S. 81, Art. 41 sowie Art. 72; S. 101, Nr. 122; S. 105, Nr. 163.
[42] Sekretariatskommentar, Art. 26, Nr. 3; Art. 58, Nr. 6.
[43] *Hager/Maultzsch*, 5. Aufl., Art. 62 Rn. 11.
[44] Vgl. oben Rn. 9 ff.; *Staudinger/Magnus*, Art. 62, Rn. 12; *Honsell/Schnyder/Straub*, Art. 62, Rn. 13; *Ferrari u. a./Mankowski*, Internationales Vertragsrecht, Art. 62, Rn. 9.
[45] *Hager/Maultzsch*, 5. Aufl., Art. 62 Rn. 13.

3. Schadensminderungspflicht, Art. 77

16 Die herrschende Ansicht in der Literatur will Art. 77, wonach diejenige Partei, die sich auf eine Vertragsverletzung beruft, alle den Umständen nach angemessenen Massnahmen zur Verringerung des aus der Vertragsverletzung folgenden Verlusts zu treffen hat, nur auf **Schadenersatzansprüche** anwenden.[46] Während der Vorarbeiten zum CISG machte die US-Delegation mehrere Versuche, ausdrücklich auch die Kaufpreisklage der Schadensminderungspflicht zu unterstellen.[47] Diese Versuche blieben schlussendlich erfolglos.[48] Probleme entstehen vor allem im Bezug auf **Verträge über herzustellende oder zu erzeugende Ware,** die gemäss Art. 3 I dem CISG unterstehen, wenn der Käufer die Nichterfüllung des Vertrages erklärt, bevor oder kurz nachdem der Verkäufer mit der Herstellung oder der Erzeugung der Ware begonnen hat.[49] Anders als viele **nationale Rechtsordnungen**[50] kennt das CISG kein besonderes Recht des Käufers zur Vertragsaufhebung in einem solchen Falle. Setzt der Verkäufer die Herstellung der Ware in Kenntnis der Abstandnahmeerklärung des Käufers fort und versucht diesen durch Kaufpreisklage zur Erfüllung des Vertrages zu zwingen, so findet Art. 28 Anwendung und führt zum Ausschluss der Kaufpreisklage in denjenigen Rechtsordnungen, in denen ein Gericht in einer solchen Situation nicht auf Erfüllung in Natur erkennen würde, ginge es um einen gleichartigen Kaufvertrag, der nicht dem CISG unterstünde.[51] Versucht der Verkäufer hingegen den unbezahlten Kaufpreis als Verlust im Wege des Schadenersatzes ersetzt zu verlangen, so findet Art. 77 Anwendung und führt zur Herabsetzung des Schadenersatzes in der Höhe des Betrages, um den der Verlust hätte verringert werden können, wenn der Verkäufer die Herstellung eingestellt und die gegebenenfalls bereits hergestellte Ware im Wege des Deckungsverkaufs verkauft hätte.[52] Kennt das nationale Recht des Forums keinen besonderen Rechtsbehelf des Käufers, mit dem er die Vertragsaufhebung in einer solchen Situation herbeiführen kann, so ist in der Literatur eine **einheitsrechtliche Lösung** im Rahmen des CISG vorgeschlagen worden, wobei zwei unterschiedliche Ansätze unterschieden werden können. Zum einen könnte die **Schadensminderungspflicht gemäss Art. 77 auf die Kaufpreisklage** angewendet werden, obwohl die Entstehungsgeschichte, die systematische Einordnung von Art. 77 im Abschnitt über Schadenersatz sowie der Wortlaut von Satz 2 gegen diese Lösung sprechen.[53] Eine Gegenansicht will dem gegenüber eine einheitsrechtliche Lösung auf Grundlage von allgemeinen Prinzipien gemäss. Art. 7 II entwickeln, die wiederum zu zwei unterschiedlichen Lösungen führt. Zum einen kann das allgemeine **Verwirkungsprinzip** auf die Kaufpreisklage des Verkäufers angewendet werden.[54] Zum anderen könnte der Käufer einen **Gegenanspruch auf Schadenersatz** einklagen oder zur **Aufrechnung** bringen, da der Verkäufer seine allgemeine Kooperationspflicht, wie sie aus Art. 7 II entwickelt werden kann, verletzt hat.[55]

---

[46] Sekretariatskommentar, Art. 73, Rn. 3; unten *Schwenzer,* Art. 77 Rn. 4 f.; *Schlechtriem/P. Butler,* UN Law, Rn. 236; *Staudinger/Magnus,* Art. 77, Rn. 6; *Witz/Salger/Lorenz/Witz,* Art. 77, Rn. 3; MünchKomm/*Mankowski,* Art. 77, Rn. 4; vgl. *Honsell/Schnyder/Straub,* Art. 62, Rn. 19.
[47] YB III (1977), S. 132, 136 Nr. 12 ff.; S. 61, Nr. 502 ff.; O. R., S. 133, Nr. 3; S. 396 ff., Nr. 55–78; vgl. *Honnold/Flechtner,* Art. 77, Rn. 419.3.
[48] O. R., S. 398, Nr. 78; vgl. *Honnold/Flechtner,* Art. 77, Rn. 419.3.
[49] Vgl. CIETAC, 29.9.2000, CISG-online 1592; unten *Schwenzer,* Art. 77 Rn. 5.
[50] Vgl. Art. 9:101 II PECL; USA: § 2–709 (1) UCC; Grossbritannien: sec. 49 (1) (2) SGA; Deutschland: § 649 BGB; Frankreich: Art. 1794 Cc; Italien: Art. 1671 Cc; Österreich: § 1168 I lit. a) ABGB; Schweiz: Art. 377 OR.
[51] *Hager/Maultzsch,* 5. Aufl., Art. 62 Rn. 14; *Schlechtriem/P. Butler,* UN Law, Rn. 236; *Schlechtriem,* Internationales Kaufrecht, Rn. 236.
[52] *Hager/Maultzsch,* 5. Aufl., Art. 62 Rn. 14; *Schlechtriem/P. Butler,* UN Law, Rn. 236.
[53] *Schwenzer/Manner,* FS Kritzer, S. 470, 483, 485; MünchKomm/*P. Huber,* Art. 77, Rn. 3; *Staudinger/Magnus,* Art. 77, Rn. 6; MünchKommHGB/*Mankowski,* Art. 77, Rn. 5.
[54] *Schlechtriem/P. Butler,* UN Law, Rn. 236.
[55] *Schlechtriem/P. Butler,* UN Law, Rn. 236.

4. Haftungsbefreiung, Artt. 79 und 80

Art. 80 findet auf den Kaufpreisanspruch des Verkäufers ohne Einschränkung Anwendung. Dagegen findet Art. 79 nur auf den Schadenersatzanspruch des Verkäufers Anwendung, Art. 79 V.[56] Wenn gleich für die Rechtsbehelfe des Käufers argumentiert wird, dass Art. 79 entgegen seines Abs. 5 auch auf Erfüllungsansprüche angewendet werden kann, ist für die hier in Frage stehenden Rechtsbehelfe des Verkäufers, insbesondere den Kaufpreisanspruch, festzuhalten, dass ein Anwendungsfall von Art. 79 praktisch ausgeschlossen ist, solange das Risiko, über ausreichend ausländische Währung zu verfügen, dem Käufer zugewiesen wird.[57] Nur wenn die Leistungserschwerung unzumutbar ist und einen Fall von *hardship* darstellt,[58] kann der Käufer ausnahmsweise nach Art. 79 von seiner Haftung befreit sein.[59] 17

5. Selbsthilfeverkauf, Art. 88

Der Verkäufer ist berechtigt, einen Selbsthilfeverkauf durchzuführen, wenn der Käufer die Inbesitznahme oder die Kaufpreiszahlung ungebührlich hinauszögert und der Verkäufer zur Erhaltung der Ware nach Art. 85 i. V. m. Art. 88 I verpflichtet ist. Ist die Ware einer raschen Verschlechterung ausgesetzt oder würde ihre Erhaltung unverhältnismässige Kosten verursachen, so ist der Verkäufer gemäss Art. 88 II verpflichtet, sich in angemessener Weise um einen Selbsthilfeverkauf zu bemühen. Ein solcher Selbsthilfeverkauf ist grundsätzlich unabhängig vom Anspruch auf Zahlung des Kaufpreises. Dies ergibt sich bereits aus Art. 88 III, wonach der Überschuss aus dem Selbsthilfeverkauf, also die Summe, die nach Abzug der Kosten der Erhaltung und des Verkaufs übrig bleibt, dem Käufer zusteht.[60] Nach Ausführung eines Selbsthilfeverkaufs steht dem Verkäufer nur die Differenz zwischen dem Vertragspreis und dem Ertrag aus dem Selbsthilfeverkauf zu.[61] Mit anderen Worten beschränkt die Verpflichtung zum Selbsthilfeverkauf den Anspruch des Verkäufers auf Kaufpreiszahlung.[62] Freilich wird der Käufer von seiner Pflicht zur Übernahme der Ware befreit, wenn der Verkäufer einen Selbsthilfeverkauf durchführt.[63] 18

IV. Konkurrierende Rechtsbehelfe

Der Anspruch des Verkäufers auf Kaufpreiszahlung wird durch den Anspruch auf Zinsen gemäss Art. 78 und den Anspruch auf Ersatz jedes weiteren Verlusts nach Art. 61 I lit. b) i. V. m. Art. 74 ergänzt. Andere, unvereinbare Rechtsbehelfe[64] können hingegen nur dann ausgeübt werden, wenn sich der Verkäufer für einen Wechsel seiner Rechtsbehelfe entscheidet.[65] Der Verkäufer kann einen Wechsel seiner Rechtsbehelfe jederzeit vornehmen, wobei er nur die anwendbaren Verjährungsfristen berücksichtigen muss.[66] 19

---

[56] Vgl. oben Art. 61 Rn. 14; unten *Schwenzer*, Art. 79 Rn. 52 ff.; BGH, 27.11.2007, CISG-online 1617 = IHR 2008, 49, 53, m. Anm. *Schroeter*, EWiR 2008, 303 ff.: Währungsschwankungen im Staat des Wiederverkaufs (Russland) geben dem Käufer/Weiterverkäufer nicht das Recht, den Kaufvertrag aufzuheben, weil Art. 79 nicht auf den Kaufpreisanspruch des Verkäufers/Herstellers Anwendung findet.
[57] *Hager/Maultzsch*, 5. Aufl., Art. 62 Rn. 16; so auch *Ferrari u. a./Mankowski*, Internationales Vertragsrecht, Art. 62, Rn. 17.
[58] Vgl. Art. 6.2.2 PICC.
[59] Vgl. oben Art. 53 Rn. 3; unten *Schwenzer*, Art. 79 Rn. 54. Vgl. Art. 6.2.3 PICC.
[60] *Hager/Maultzsch*, 5. Aufl., Art. 62 Rn. 15.
[61] Vgl. *Honsell/Schnyder/Straub*, Art. 62, Rn. 36.
[62] *Honnold/Flechtner*, Art. 28, Rn. 193; *Hager/Maultzsch*, 5. Aufl., Art. 62 Rn. 15.
[63] Vgl. *Piltz*, Internationales Kaufrecht, Rn. 5–382.
[64] Vgl. oben Art. 61 Rn. 12 f.
[65] *Staudinger/Magnus*, Art. 62, Rn. 21; *Achilles*, Art. 62, Rn. 3; *Bianca/Bonell/Knapp*, Art. 62, Anm. 3.2.; *Enderlein/Maskow/Strohbach*, Art. 62, Anm. 3.2.; *Herber/Czerwenka*, Art. 62, Rn. 8; MünchKomm/*P. Huber*, Art. 62, Rn. 11; MünchKommHGB/*Benicke*, Art. 62, Rn. 6.
[66] *Piltz*, Internationales Kaufrecht, Rn. 5–480. Zur Verjährung vgl. oben Art. 53 Rn. 27.

Setzt der Verkäufer dem Käufer eine angemessene Nachfrist zur Erfüllung des Vertrags, so bindet sich der Verkäufer für den Lauf dieser angemessenen Nachfrist an die Erfüllung des Vertrags.[67] Das allgemeine Verwirkungskonzept gemäss Art. 7 II hält den Verkäufer davon ab, von Vertragserfüllung auf Vertragsaufhebung zu wechseln, wenn der Käufer bereits Schritte zur Erfüllung seiner Pflichten und damit zur Erfüllung des Vertrags vorgenommen hat.[68]

V. Beweislast

20 Zur Beweislast siehe oben Art. 53 Rn. 42.

---

[67] *Staudinger/Magnus*, Art. 62, Rn. 21.
[68] *Staudinger/Magnus*, Art. 62, Rn. 21.

Art. 63 [Nachfrist]

(1) Der Verkäufer kann dem Käufer eine angemessene Nachfrist zur Erfüllung seiner Pflichten setzen.

(2) Der Verkäufer kann vor Ablauf dieser Frist keinen Rechtsbehelf* wegen Vertragsverletzung ausüben, außer wenn er vom Käufer die Anzeige erhalten hat, daß dieser seine Pflichten nicht innerhalb der so gesetzten Frist erfüllen wird. Der Verkäufer verliert dadurch jedoch nicht das Recht, Schadenersatz wegen verspäteter Erfüllung zu verlangen.

Art. 63

(1) The seller may fix an additional period of time of reasonable length for performance by the buyer of his obligations.

(2) Unless the seller has received notice from the buyer that he will not perform within the period so fixed, the seller may not, during that period, resort to any remedy for breach of contract. However, the seller is not deprived thereby of any right he may have to claim damages for delay in performance.

Art. 63

1) Le vendeur peut impartir à l'acheteur un délai supplémentaire de durée raisonnable pour l'exécution de ses obligations.

2) A moins qu'il n'ait reçu de l'acheteur une notification l'informant que celui-ci n'exécuterait pas ses obligations dans le délai ainsi imparti, le vendeur ne peut, avant l'expiration de ce délai, se prévaloir d'aucun des moyens dont il dispose en cas de contravention au contrat. Toutefois, le vendeur ne perd pas, de ce fait, le droit de demander des dommages-intérêts pour retard dans l'exécution.

Übersicht

	Rn.
I. Regelungsgegenstand	1
II. Voraussetzungen der Nachfristsetzung gemäss Art. 63	4
1. Anwendungsbereich	4
2. Zeitliche Anforderungen an die Nachfristsetzung	5
III. Erklärung der Nachfrist nach Art. 63 I	6
1. Inhaltliche Anforderungen	6
a) Kalendermässig bestimmte oder bestimmbare Nachfrist	7
b) Angemessenheit der Nachfrist	8
2. Übermittlungsrisiko, Art. 27	10
IV. Bindungswirkung der Nachfristsetzung, Art. 63 II	11
1. Vorläufig präkludierte Rechtsbehelfe während des Laufs der gesetzten Nachfrist	12
2. Nach fruchtlosem Ablauf der Nachfrist stehen sämtliche Rechtsbehelfe zur Verfügung	14
3. Das Recht des Verkäufers auf Schadenersatz	15
V. Beweislast	16

Vorläufer und **Entwürfe:** Artt. 62 II, 66 II EKG; Genfer E 1976 Art. 44; Wiener E 1977 Art. 45; New Yorker E 1978 Art. 59.

I. Regelungsgegenstand

Nach dem Konzept des CISG ist der vorrangige Rechtsbehelf des Verkäufers bei Vertragsbruch durch den Käufer sein Recht, vom Käufer gemäss Art. 62 die Erfüllung seiner Pflichten zu verlangen. In der Praxis freilich steht das Recht des Verkäufers auf Schadenersatz im 1

---

* Schweiz: kein Recht.

Art. 63 2, 3

Vordergrund und kann vom Verkäufer gemäss Art. 61 I lit. b) i. V. m. Art. 74 ff. bei Verletzung irgendeiner Pflicht durch den Käufer verlangt werden. Um das Erfüllungsinteresse im Wege des Schadenersatzes ersetzt zu verlangen, muss der Verkäufer freilich berechtigt sein, den Vertrag aufzuheben. Einige Autoren vertreten sogar die Ansicht, dass der Verkäufer den Vertrag tatsächlich für aufgehoben erklärt haben muss, bevor er Schadenersatz wegen Nichterfüllung bzw. statt der Leistung verlangen kann.[1] Jedenfalls muss der Verkäufer berechtigt sein, den Vertrag aufzuheben, was wiederum gemäss Art. 61 I lit. a) i. V. m. Art. 25 einen wesentlichen Vertragsbruch des Käufers voraussetzt. In der Praxis wird es für den vertragstreuen Verkäufer oft schwierig festzustellen sein, ob ein wesentlicher Vertragsbruch vorliegt.[2] An dieser Stelle erlangt Art. 63 seine Bedeutung. Art. 63 gibt dem Verkäufer die Möglichkeit aufzuklären, ob der Käufer beabsichtigt und in der Lage ist, den Vertrag zu erfüllen. Dazu kann der Verkäufer dem Käufer eine **angemessene Nachfrist** ansetzen. Art. 63 ist in seinem Anwendungsbereich nicht auf besondere Pflichten des Käufers beschränkt. Vielmehr kann der Verkäufer dem Käufer bezüglich jeder seiner Pflichten eine angemessene Nachfrist setzen. Dennoch kommt Art. 63 eine besondere Bedeutung in Bezug auf die Pflicht des Käufers zur Zahlung des Kaufpreises und zur Abnahme der Ware zu. Hat nämlich der Verkäufer dem Käufer eine angemessene Nachfrist zur Zahlung des Kaufpreises oder zur Übernahme der Ware angesetzt, welche abgelaufen ist, ohne dass der Käufer seine Pflicht erfüllt hat, so ist der Verkäufer gemäss Art. 61 I lit. a) i. V. m. Art. 64 I lit. b) zur Vertragsaufhebung berechtigt, und zwar unabhängig davon, ob ein wesentlicher Vertragsbruch vorliegt. Durch Nachfristsetzung zum Recht auf Vertragsaufhebung zu gelangen hat für den Verkäufer den Vorteil, dass er sich selbst nicht der Gefahr aussetzt, durch unberechtigte Ausübung der Vertragsaufhebung, weil tatsächlich kein wesentlicher Vertragsbruch vorlag, selbst einen Vertragsbruch zu begehen, der dann meist selbst einen wesentlichen Vertragsbruch (Erfüllungsverweigerung) darstellt.[3] Erfüllt der Käufer hingegen eine seiner anderen Pflichten (ausser seiner Pflicht zur Zahlung des Kaufpreises und zur Abnahme der Ware) nicht innerhalb der ihm vom Verkäufer gesetzten Nachfrist, so ist der Verkäufer dadurch nicht zur Vertragsaufhebung berechtigt. Für alle diese anderen Pflichten muss stets ein wesentlicher Vertragsbruch vorliegen, damit der Verkäufer zur Vertragsaufhebung berechtigt ist.

2   Neben dieser Hauptwirkung hat die Nachfristsetzung freilich auch noch weitere rechtliche Wirkungen. Gemäss Art. 63 II ist der Verkäufer **vorübergehend präkludiert,** einen anderen Rechtsbehelf wegen Vertragsverletzung auszuüben, mit Ausnahme des Rechts, Schadenersatz wegen verspäteter Erfüllung zu verlangen. Des Weiteren verliert der Verkäufer sein Recht zur Vertragsaufhebung nicht, obwohl der Käufer den Kaufpreis bereits gezahlt hat, wenn er im Falle einer anderen Vertragsverletzung als verspäteter Erfüllung durch den Käufer die Aufhebung nicht innerhalb einer angemessenen Zeit erklärt, nachdem der Verkäufer die Vertragsverletzung kannte oder kennen musste. Vielmehr verliert der Verkäufer sein Recht zur Vertragsaufhebung erst, nachdem eine von ihm gesetzte Nachfrist gemäss Art. 63 I abgelaufen ist oder nachdem der Käufer erklärt hat, dass er seine Pflichten nicht innerhalb der Nachfrist erfüllen wird, Art. 64 II lit. b) ii).[4] Mit anderen Worten verlängert sich durch die Nachfristsetzung die Zeit, innerhalb derer der Verkäufer Vertragsaufhebung wegen einer anderen Vertragsverletzung als verspäteter Erfüllung durch den Käufer erklären kann.

3   Art. 63 I ist ein Recht des Verkäufers, das er nach seinem **Ermessen** ausüben kann. Der Verkäufer ist nicht verpflichtet, eine Nachfrist zu setzen.[5] Auch ist das Setzen einer Nachfrist

---

[1] A. A. zu recht unten *Schwenzer,* Art. 74 Rn. 22 m. w. N., Art. 75 Rn. 5 und Art. 76 Rn. 3.
[2] Sekretariatskommentar, Art. 59, Nr. 6.
[3] CA Grenoble, 4.2.1999, CISG-online 443; RB Arnhem, 1.3.2006, CISG-online 1475; *Hager/Maultzsch,* 5. Aufl., Art. 63 Rn. 2; *Staudinger/Magnus,* Art. 63, Rn. 2.
[4] *Hager/Maultzsch,* 5. Aufl., Art. 63 Rn. 2; *Enderlein/Maskow/Strohbach,* Art. 63, Anm. 2.1.
[5] Vgl. Trib. Padova, 31.3.2004, CISG-online 823 = IHR 2005, 33; Sekretariatskommentar, Art. 59, Nr. 8; *Honsell/Schnyder/Straub,* Art. 63, Rn. 5; *Kröll u. a./Bell,* Art. 63, Rn. 3; *Ferrari u. a./Mankowski,* Internationales Vertragsrecht, Art. 63, Rn. 2.

keine Voraussetzung für die Vertragsaufhebung, wenn ein wesentlicher Vertragsbruch vorliegt. In einem solchen Fall kann der Käufer vom Verkäufer nicht verlangen, dass ihm eine angemessene Nachfrist zur Erfüllung angesetzt wird.[6]

II. Voraussetzungen der Nachfristsetzung gemäss Art. 63

1. Anwendungsbereich

Art. 63 I findet auf **sämtliche Pflichten des Käufers** Anwendung, die ihre Grundlage 4 im Kaufvertrag haben.[7] Ob der Verkäufer tatsächlich ein Recht hat, vom Käufer die Erfüllung seiner Pflichten zu verlangen, ergibt sich aus Art. 62. Daher darf der Verkäufer im Zeitpunkt der Nachfristsetzung nicht bereits einen mit der Nachfristsetzung **unvereinbaren Rechtsbehelf** ausgeübt haben.[8] Dabei ist es freilich irrelevant, ob Art. 28 das Recht des Verkäufers ausschliesst, vom Käufer die Erfüllung des Vertrags zu verlangen, weil Art. 28 nur an Gerichte bzw. Schiedsgerichte, aber nicht an die Parteien selbst adressiert ist, und somit nicht die Rechte und Rechtsbehelfe der Parteien nach CISG direkt beeinflusst.[9] Art. 63 I gilt **nicht für sekundäre Pflichten** des Käufers, die erst nach Vertragsbruch entstehen, wie z. B. Schadenersatzpflichten oder Rückabwicklungspflichten.[10] Freilich kann der Verkäufer auch in diesen Fällen dem Käufer eine Frist ansetzen und ihn zur Zahlung von Schadenersatz oder zur Rückgabe der Ware auffordern, um z. B. den Weg zur Einleitung einer Klage vor einem zuständigen Gericht oder Schiedsgericht zu ebnen. In diesen Fällen greift allerdings nicht Art. 63 ein, so dass der Verkäufer auch nicht nach Art. 63 II vorläufig präkludiert wird, seine anderen Rechtsbehelfe auszuüben.[11]

2. Zeitliche Anforderungen an die Nachfristsetzung

Nachfristsetzung gemäss Art. 63 I kann **grundsätzlich erst nach Fälligkeit** der nicht 5 erfüllten Pflicht des Käufers erfolgen.[12] Wenn z. B. die Ware von einer Rechnung begleitet wird, der zufolge die Zahlung des Kaufpreises aufgeschoben wird und erst an einem bestimmten Tag nach Lieferung der Ware zu erfolgen hat, kann in der Rechnungsstellung nicht die Ansetzung einer Nachfrist gesehen werden, sondern die Festlegung der ursprünglichen Erfüllungszeit, technisch gesprochen ein Angebot zur Vertragsänderung.[13] In einem solchen Fall kann der Verkäufer während des Laufs der in der Rechnung gesetzten Frist den Kaufpreis nicht verlangen, weil sonst widersprüchliches Verhalten vorläge, was nach dem Prinzip des *venire contra factum proprium* unzulässig ist.[14] Erst nach dem Fälligkeitsdatum ist der Verkäufer berechtigt, dem Käufer für die Erfüllung eine

---

[6] Vgl. Sekretariatskommentar, Art. 59, Nr. 8; *Staudinger/Magnus*, Art. 63, Rn. 8; *Bianca/Bonell/Knapp*, Art. 63, Anm. 2.7.; *Honsell/Schnyder/Straub*, Art. 63, Rn. 5; *Kröll u. a./Bell*, Art. 63, Rn. 3.
[7] *Staudinger/Magnus*, Art. 63, Rn. 5; *Achilles*, Art. 63, Rn. 2; *Audit*, S. 148; *Bianca/Bonell/Knapp*, Art. 63, Anm. 3.1.; *Herber/Czerwenka*, Art. 63, Rn. 2; *Honsell/Schnyder/Straub*, Art. 63, Rn. 8; MünchKommHGB/*Benicke*, Art. 63, Rn. 2; *Piltz*, Internationales Kaufrecht, Rn. 5–394; *Hager/Maultzsch*, 5. Aufl., Art. 63 Rn. 2; *Enderlein/Maskow/Strohbach*, Art. 63, Anm. 2.1.; *Kröll u. a./Bell*, Art. 63, Rn. 5.
[8] Vgl. oben Art. 62 Rn. 12.
[9] *Staudinger/Magnus*, Art. 63, Rn. 6; MünchKommHGB/*Benicke*, Art. 63, Rn. 2; *Piltz*, Internationales Kaufrecht, Rn. 5–394; MünchKomm/*P. Huber*, Art. 63, Rn. 6.
[10] *Staudinger/Magnus*, Art. 63, Rn. 9; *Honsell/Schnyder/Straub*, Art. 63, Rn. 9; *Ferrari u. a./Mankowski*, Internationales Vertragsrecht, Art. 63, Rn. 8. A. A. *Herber/Czerwenka*, Art. 47, Rn. 9.
[11] *Staudinger/Magnus*, Art. 63, Rn. 9.
[12] OLG Brandenburg, 18.11.2008, CISG-online 1734 = IHR 2009, 105, 111 ff.; Trib. Padova, 31.3.2004, CISG-online 823 = IHR 2005, 33; *Hager/Maultzsch*, 5. Aufl., Art. 63 Rn. 3a; *Staudinger/Magnus*, Art. 63, Rn. 10; *Achilles*, Art. 63, Rn. 3; *Bianca/Bonell/Knapp*, Art. 63, Anm. 2.4.; *Honsell/Schnyder/Straub*, Art. 63, Rn. 10, 15; *Ferrari u. a./Mankowski*, Internationales Vertragsrecht, Art. 63, Rn. 5. A. A. *Enderlein/Maskow/Strohbach*, Art. 63, Anm. 2.3.
[13] Trib. Padova, 31.3.2004, CISG-online 823 = IHR 2005, 33. Vgl. Art. 29.
[14] Trib. Padova, 31.3.2004, CISG-online 823 = IHR 2005, 33.

Nachfrist anzusetzen. diese Auslegung folgt vor allem aus dem Begriff der „angemessenen Nachfrist".[15] Der Verkäufer kann allerdings die Nachfristsetzung mit einer anderen Korrespondenz verbinden, von der die Fälligkeit des Kaufpreises abhängt.[16] In einer deutschen Entscheidung hatten die Parteien eines Autokaufvertrags vereinbart, dass der Kaufpreis erst dann fällig werde, wenn der Verkäufer den Käufer über seine Erfüllungsbereitschaft und die Karosserienummer informiert habe.[17] Das Gericht stellte fest, dass es reiner Formalismus sei, vom Verkäufer zwei separate Erklärungen zu verlangen und liess die Frage offen, ob eine Nachfrist sogar bereits vor Fälligkeit gesetzt werden könne. Der Käufer werde in einem solchen Falle nicht seiner Rechte beraubt.[18] Diese Entscheidung stützt die Ansicht, dass der Verkäufer bereits vor Fälligkeit eine angemessene Nachfrist zur Erfüllung durch den Käufer ansetzen kann, wenn die Nachfrist so bemessen ist, dass sie den Fälligkeitszeitpunkt um eine angemessene Frist überschreitet.[19]

III. Erklärung der Nachfrist nach Art. 63 I

1. Inhaltliche Anforderungen

6   Die Nachfristsetzung braucht **nicht schriftlich** zu erfolgen oder nachgewiesen werden und unterliegt auch sonst keinen Formvorschriften, was sich aus dem allgemeinen Prinzip der Formfreiheit gemäss Art. 11 i. V. m. Art. 7 II ergibt.[20] Allerdings bestehen gewisse Anforderungen in inhaltlicher Hinsicht.

7   **a) Kalendermässig bestimmte oder bestimmbare Nachfrist.** Die Nachfrist muss kalendermässig bestimmt oder bestimmbar sein. Z. B. wäre das Setzen eines genauen Datums oder die Formulierung „x Tage nach Erhalt dieser Erklärung" für die Zwecke dieser Vorschrift bestimmt genug.[21] Auch die Festsetzung eines Zeitraums ist genügend bestimmt; der Käufer hat bis zum letzten Tag des angegebenen Zeitraums zu leisten.[22] Andererseits sind ungenaue Bezeichnungen wie „prompte", „unverzügliche" oder „sofortige" Zahlung unzureichend.[23] Aus der Erklärung des Verkäufers muss sich ergeben, dass er den Käufer zur Erfüllung seiner Pflichten anhält.[24] Andererseits muss die Erklärung des Verkäufers nicht benennen, welchen Rechtsbehelf er auszuüben gedenkt, insbesondere muss der Verkäufer nicht ankündigen, dass er den Vertrag aufheben oder ein rechtliches Verfahren gegen den Käufer anstrengen wird.[25]

---

[15] *Hager/Maultzsch*, 5. Aufl., Art. 63 Rn. 3a; *Herber/Czerwenka*, Art. 57, Rn. 5; *Bamberger/Roth/Saenger*, Art. 63, Rn. 4. A. A. *Enderlein/Maskow/Strohbach*, Art. 63, Anm. 2.3.; *Witz/Salger/Lorenz/Witz*, Art. 63, Rn. 8, dem zufolge die Nachfrist bereits vor Fälligkeit gesetzt werden kann, wenn diese Frist das Fälligkeitsdatum um eine angemessene Frist überschreitet.
[16] Vgl. *Honsell/Schnyder/Straub*, Art. 63, Rn. 15; *Ferrari u. a./Mankowski*, Internationales Vertragsrecht, Art. 63, Rn. 5.
[17] OLG München, 19.10.2006, CISG-online 1394 = IHR 2007, 30. Vgl. Art. 58 Rn. 5.
[18] OLG München, 19.10.2006, CISG-online 1394 = IHR 2007, 30.
[19] *Witz/Salger/Lorenz/Witz*, Art. 63, Rn. 8; *Enderlein/Maskow/Strohbach*, Art. 63, Anm. 2.3. A. A. OLG Brandenburg, 18.11.2008, CISG-online 1734, S. 37.
[20] Vgl. oben *Schmidt-Kessel*, Art. 11 Rn. 9; *Enderlein/Maskow/Strohbach*, Art. 11, Anm. 1.3.; *Wey*, Rn. 404; *Bamberger/Roth/Saenger*, Art. 11, Rn. 4; *Staudinger/Magnus*, Art. 11, Rn. 7; *Ferrari*, Draft Digest, S. 206, 207.
[21] *Hager/Maultzsch*, 5. Aufl., Art. 63 Rn. 3; *Staudinger/Magnus*, Art. 63, Rn. 12; *Witz/Salger/Lorenz/Witz*, Art. 63, Rn. 7; *Ferrari u. a./Mankowski*, Internationales Vertragsrecht, Art. 63, Rn. 12; vgl. auch *Kröll u. a./Bell*, Art. 63, Rn. 6.
[22] *Witz/Salger/Lorenz/Witz*, Art. 63, Rn. 7.
[23] Sekretariatskommentar, Art. 53, Nr. 7; *Hager/Maultzsch*, 5. Aufl., Art. 63 Rn. 3; *Staudinger/Magnus*, Art. 63, Rn. 13; *Bamberger/Roth/Saenger*, Art. 63, Rn. 4; *Bianca/Bonell/Knapp*, Art. 63, Anm. 2.9.; *Brunner*, Art. 63, Rn. 3; *Reinhart*, Art. 63, Rn. 3.
[24] OLG München, 19.10.2006, CISG-online 1394 = IHR 2007, 30, 33; *Hager/Maultzsch*, 5. Aufl., Art. 63 Rn. 3; *Staudinger/Magnus*, Art. 63, Rn. 12; *Witz/Salger/Lorenz/Witz*, Art. 63, Rn. 7; Sekretariatskommentar, Art. 59, Nr. 7. A. A. ICC, 1.1.1992, 7585/1992, CISG-online 105: das 3-monatige Zuwarten des Verkäufers vor Vertragsaufhebung wurde offenbar als angemessene Nachfrist gewertet.
[25] OLG München, 19.10.2006, CISG-online 1394 = IHR 2007, 30, 33; *Hager/Maultzsch*, 5. Aufl., Art. 63 Rn. 3; *Witz/Salger/Lorenz/Witz*, Art. 63, Rn. 7; *Herber/Czerwenka*, Art. 47, Rn. 2; *Enderlein/Maskow/Strohbach*, Art. 63, Anm. 2.4.

b) Angemessenheit der Nachfrist. Wenn der Verkäufer dem Käufer eine Nachfrist zur 8
Erfüllung des Vertrages ansetzt, muss diese Frist angemessen sein. Vor allem muss es dem
Käufer in tatsächlicher Hinsicht möglich sein, die betroffene Pflicht innerhalb der gesetzten
Nachfrist zu erfüllen.[26] Des Weiteren bemisst sich die Angemessenheit der Nachfrist nach
sämtlichen Umständen des Einzelfalls,[27] worunter auch Handelsbräuche und zwischen den
Parteien entstandene Gepflogenheiten fallen. Der Verkäufer muss auch allfällige Hindernisse berücksichtigen, die der Erfüllung durch den Käufer im Wege stehen und von denen
er Kenntnis hat oder über die er nicht in Unkenntnis sein kann.[28] In der Praxis wird eine
Nachfrist zur Zahlung grundsätzlich kürzer bemessen sein als eine Nachfrist zur Abnahme
der Ware.[29] Ein Schiedsgericht hat eine Nachfrist von sieben Tagen zur Zahlung des
Kaufpreises als angemessen betrachtet,[30] während ein deutsches Gericht sieben Tage als
unangemessen kurz ansah[31].[32] Eine Nachfrist von zehn Tagen zur Zahlung wurde in einem
Fall als angemessen angesehen, in dem der Fälligkeitszeitpunkt bereits mehrere Monate
zurücklag.[33] Je grösser das Interesse des Verkäufers an rechtzeitiger Zahlung oder rechtzeitiger Abnahme der Ware ist, desto kürzer kann er die Nachfrist bemessen.[34] Z. B. kann
in einem fallenden Markt das Interesse des Verkäufers an schneller Vertragsaufhebung und
Durchführung eines angemessenen Deckungsverkaufs das Interesse des Käufers an genügender Reaktionszeit aufwiegen.[35] Gleiches gilt in Fällen, in denen der Verkäufer zusätzlichen
Lagerraum benötigt und solcher Lagerraum entweder gar nicht oder nur zu übersetzten
Preisen erhältlich ist.[36]

Die rechtliche Konsequenz einer zu kurz bemessenen Nachfrist ist, dass anstelle der 9
gesetzten Nachfrist eine **Frist von angemessener Länge** läuft.[37] Hingegen beginnt eine
Nachfrist nicht zu laufen, wenn der Verkäufer eine Nachfrist nur antäuscht, ohne dem
Käufer wirklich eine zweite Erfüllungschance einräumen zu wollen, oder angibt, dass er
selbst seinen Pflichten aus dem Vertrag nicht nachkommen wird.[38] Gleiches gilt, wenn der
Verkäufer plötzlich eine sehr kurze Nachfrist zur Erfüllung ansetzt, nachdem er sich über
längere Zeit hinweg über die Nichterfüllung eines unwesentlichen Teils der Pflichten des
Käufers nicht beschwert hatte.[39]

---

[26] LG Kassel, 21.9.1995, CISG-online 192; *Ferrari u. a./Mankowski,* Internationales Vertragsrecht, Art. 63, Rn. 14.
[27] TGI Strasbourg, 22.12.2006, CISG-online 1629: sieben Tage waren zur Aussonderung und Abnahme von 110 Lastwagenladungen unangemessen kurz, da es unmöglich war, die Ware in einer solch kurzen Frist abzunehmen. Vgl. *Ferrari u. a./Mankowski,* Internationales Vertragsrecht, Art. 63, Rn. 14 ff.
[28] *Hager/Maultzsch,* 5. Aufl., Art. 63 Rn. 3; *Enderlein/Maskow/Strohbach,* Art. 60, Anm. 3.; *Soergel/Lüderitz/Budzikiewicz,* Art. 60, Rn. 5.
[29] *Hager/Maultzsch,* 5. Aufl., Art. 63 Rn. 3; *Staudinger/Magnus,* Art. 63, Rn. 15.
[30] Int. Ct. Ukrainian CCI, 19.9.2005, CISG-online 1287 (obiter); vgl. auch ICC, 11849/2003, CISG-online 1421, Rn. 52 ff.: 20 Tage zur Stellung eines Dokumentenakkreditivs – angemessen; OLG München, 19.10.2006, CISG-online 1394 = IHR 2007, 30, 33: neun Tage zur Zahlung – angemessen.
[31] OLG Karlsruhe, 14.2.2008, CISG-online 1649 = IHR 2008, 53, 55.
[32] Vgl. Serbische Handelskammer, 15.7.2008, CISG-online 1795: vier Monate – angemessen.
[33] HGer St. Gallen, 3.12.2002, CISG-online 727 = IHR 2003, 181 = SZIER 2003, 104; CA Milano, 11.12.1998, CISG-online 430.
[34] *Hager/Maultzsch,* 5. Aufl., Art. 63 Rn. 3.
[35] *Hager/Maultzsch,* 5. Aufl., Art. 63 Rn. 3; *Enderlein/Maskow/Strohbach,* Art. 63, Anm. 3.; *Kröll u. a./Bell,* Art. 63, Rn. 7.
[36] *Hager/Maultzsch,* 5. Aufl., Art. 63 Rn. 3; *Enderlein/Maskow/Strohbach,* Art. 63, Anm. 3.; *Soergel/Lüderitz/Budzikiewicz,* Art. 60, Rn. 4.
[37] OLG Karlsruhe, 14.2.2008, CISG-online 1649 = IHR 2008, 53, 55: zwei Wochen anstatt sieben Tagen; *Hager/Maultzsch,* 5. Aufl., Art. 63 Rn. 3; *Staudinger/Magnus,* Art. 63, Rn. 16; *Bamberger/Roth/Saenger,* Art. 63, Rn. 4; *Brunner,* Art. 63, Rn. 4; *Kröll u. a./Bell,* Art. 63, Rn. 9; *Ferrari u. a./Mankowski,* Internationales Vertragsrecht, Art. 63, Rn. 17. A. A. *Honsell/Schnyder/Straub,* Art. 63, Rn. 20d, denen zufolge eine unangemessene Frist keine angemessene Frist in Gang setzen kann; MünchKomm/*P. Huber,* Art. 63, Rn. 10, der wie folgt differenziert: der Verkäufer darf erst nach Ablauf einer angemessenen Frist den Vertrag aufheben, wohingegen der Käufer zum Zwecke der Erfüllung nur auf die gesetzte, unangemessene Frist vertrauen darf.
[38] LG Kassel, 21.9.1995, CISG-online 192, unter (unrichtiger) Berufung auf § 242 BGB.
[39] LG Kassel, 21.9.1995, CISG-online 192.

2. Übermittlungsrisiko, Art. 27

10 Gemäss Art. 27 muss eine nach den Umständen mit geeigneten Mitteln gesetzte Nachfrist dem Käufer nicht zugehen, damit sich der Verkäufer auf die Mitteilung berufen kann.[40] Allerdings kann die Mitteilung zurückgenommen werden, solange die Mitteilung dem Käufer nicht zugegangen ist, wenn die Rücknahmeerklärung dem Käufer vor oder gleichzeitig mit der Nachfrist zugeht, was sich aus dem allgemeinen Prinzip des Art. 15 II i. V. m. Art. 7 II ergibt.[41]

IV. Bindungswirkung der Nachfristsetzung, Art. 63 II

11 Gemäss Art. 63 II kann der Verkäufer vor Ablauf der Nachfrist keinen Rechtsbehelf wegen Vertragsverletzung ausüben, ausser wenn er vom Käufer die Anzeige erhalten hat, dass dieser seine Pflichten nicht innerhalb der so gesetzten Frist erfüllen wird. Der Zweck dieser Vorschrift liegt im Schutz des Käufers während des Laufs der gesetzten Nachfrist.[42]

1. Vorläufig präkludierte Rechtsbehelfe während des Laufs der gesetzten Nachfrist

12 Art. 63 II präkludiert **sämtliche Rechtsbehelfe** des Verkäufers wegen Vertragsbruchs des Käufers, ausser seinem Recht, Schadenersatz wegen verspäteter Erfüllung zu verlangen. Folglich kann der Verkäufer den Vertrag nicht aufheben, selbst dann nicht, wenn die Nichterfüllung einen wesentlichen Vertragsbruch darstellt.[43] Auch kann der Verkäufer keine Erfüllungsklage nach Art. 62 einleiten.[44] Auch das Recht auf Selbsthilfeverkauf nach Art. 88 I ist präkludiert; nur der Selbsthilfeverkauf nach Art. 88 II bleibt möglich.[45] Der Grund für den Ausschluss des Selbsthilfeverkaufs nach Art. 88 I liegt darin, dass der Käufer bereits Schritte eingeleitet haben kann, um die Abnahme der Ware vorzubereiten, und dass eine ungebührliche Hinauszögerung der Inbesitznahme der Ware oder der Zahlung des Kaufpreises während des Laufs der Nachfrist nicht denkbar ist.[46] Der Verkäufer darf auch nicht das Spezifikationsrecht nach Art. 65 während des Laufs der Nachfrist ausüben.[47]

13 Das Setzen einer Nachfrist zur Erfüllung beinhaltet nicht die Aufschiebung der Zahlungszeit.[48] Daher bleibt der Verkäufer berechtigt, **Schadenersatz wegen verspäteter Erfüllung** zu verlangen.[49] Dieser Schadenersatzanspruch schützt den Verkäufer vor Währungsverlusten, Zinsverlusten und führt zum Ersatz von Aufwendungen im Zusammenhang mit

---

[40] *Hager/Maultzsch*, 5. Aufl., Art. 63 Rn. 3; *Achilles*, Art. 63, Rn. 5; *Enderlein/Maskow/Strohbach*, Art. 63, Anm. 2.2.; *Honsell/Schnyder/Straub*, Art. 63, Rn. 17; *Soergel/Lüderitz/Budzikiewicz*, Art. 60, Rn. 5. A. A. Botschaft des Schweizer Bundesrats, S. 809; *Bianca/Bonell/Knapp*, Art. 63, Anm. 2.2.; *Ferrari u. a./Mankowski*, Internationales Vertragsrecht, Art. 63, Rn. 11.

[41] *Staudinger/Magnus*, Art. 63, Rn. 11; *Achilles*, Art. 63, Rn. 5; *Ferrari u. a./Mankowski*, Internationales Vertragsrecht, Art. 63, Rn. 11.

[42] *Hager/Maultzsch*, 5. Aufl., Art. 63 Rn. 4.

[43] *Hager/Maultzsch*, 5. Aufl., Art. 63 Rn. 4; *Staudinger/Magnus*, Art. 63, Rn. 17; MünchKomm/*P. Huber*, Art. 63, Rn. 13; *Brunner*, Art. 63, Rn. 5; *Ferrari u. a./Mankowski*, Internationales Vertragsrecht, Art. 63, Rn. 19.

[44] Vgl. oben Art. 62 Rn. 12; *Hager/Maultzsch*, 5. Aufl., Art. 63 Rn. 4; *Staudinger/Magnus*, Art. 63, Rn. 17; *Ferrari u. a./Mankowski*, Internationales Vertragsrecht, Art. 63, Rn. 19.

[45] *Hager/Maultzsch*, 5. Aufl., Art. 63 Rn. 4; *Staudinger/Magnus*, Art. 63, Rn. 17; MünchKomm/*P. Huber*, Art. 63, Rn. 13; *Ferrari u. a./Mankowski*, Internationales Vertragsrecht, Art. 63, Rn. 19.

[46] *Hager/Maultzsch*, 5. Aufl., Art. 63 Rn. 4; *Enderlein/Maskow/Strohbach*, Art. 63, Anm. 5.; *Soergel/Lüderitz/Budzikiewicz*, Art. 60, Rn. 7; *Staudinger/Magnus*, Art. 63, Rn. 17; MünchKomm/*P. Huber*, Art. 63, Rn. 13; *Brunner*, Art. 63, Rn. 5.

[47] *Hager/Maultzsch*, 5. Aufl., Art. 63 Rn. 4; *Enderlein/Maskow/Strohbach*, Art. 63, Anm. 5.; *Soergel/Lüderitz/Budzikiewicz*, Art. 60, Rn. 7; *Ferrari u. a./Mankowski*, Internationales Vertragsrecht, Art. 63, Rn. 19.

[48] *Staudinger/Magnus*, Art. 63, Rn. 19; *Brunner*, Art. 63, Rn. 5.

[49] Vgl. unten Rn. 15; *Hager/Maultzsch*, 5. Aufl., Art. 63 Rn. 6; *Brunner*, Art. 63, Rn. 5.

der Erhaltung und der Aufbewahrung der Ware.[50] Der Anspruch des Verkäufers nach Art. 85 bzw. Art. 87 auf **Ersatz angemessener Aufwendungen,** die im Zusammenhang mit dem Erhalt und der Aufbewahrung der Ware entstanden sind, bleibt ihm erhalten.[51] Der Anspruch des Verkäufers auf **Zinsen** nach Art. 78 wird durch das Setzen einer Nachfrist nicht beeinflusst.[52] All diese Rechtsbehelfe sind vergleichbar mit einem Schadenersatzanspruch wegen verzögerter Erfüllung und aus diesem Grunde durch das Setzen einer Nachfrist zur Erfüllung nicht präkludiert.[53] Gleiches muss für **Vertragsstrafen für verzögerte Erfüllung** gelten.[54] Der Lauf einer Nachfrist präkludiert den Verkäufer nicht, den Vertrag wegen eines anderen Vertragsbruchs aufzuheben, der während des Laufs der Nachfrist eintritt, z. B., wenn der Verkäufer eine Nachfrist zur Kaufpreiszahlung gesetzt hat und während dieser Nachfrist der Käufer die Abnahme der Ware verweigert.[55]

2. Nach fruchtlosem Ablauf der Nachfrist stehen sämtliche Rechtsbehelfe zur Verfügung

Sobald die Nachfrist abgelaufen ist oder der Verkäufer vom Käufer informiert wurde, dass der Käufer innerhalb der Nachfrist nicht erfüllen wird, ist die vorläufige Präklusion der anderen Rechtsbehelfe des Verkäufers aufgehoben. Aus dem Wortlaut „Anzeige erhalten hat" folgt, dass die Anzeige des Käufers, dass dieser seine Pflichten nicht innerhalb der gesetzten Nachfrist erfüllen wird, entgegen Art. 27 dem Verkäufer zugegangen sein muss.[56] Auch muss diese Anzeige mit Ernsthaftigkeit zum Ausdruck bringen, dass der Käufer den Vertrag während der Nachfrist nicht erfüllen wird.[57]

3. Das Recht des Verkäufers auf Schadenersatz

Gemäss Art. 63 II 2 verliert der Verkäufer nicht das Recht, Schadenersatz wegen verspäteter Erfüllung zu verlangen, obwohl gemäss Art. 63 II 1 sämtliche anderen Rechtsbehelfe wegen Vertragsverletzung vorläufig präkludiert sind.[58] Das Recht auf Schadenersatz verliert der Verkäufer weder durch das Setzen einer Nachfrist noch durch die Erfüllung des Käufers während der laufenden Nachfrist.[59] Aus dieser Vorschrift kann ein allgemeines Prinzip des Übereinkommens abgeleitet werden, nämlich, dass der Verkäufer berechtigt ist, jeden anderen Verlust im Wege des Schadenersatzes ersetzt zu verlangen, der nicht durch Nachbesserung während der Nachfrist beseitigt wird.[60]

---

[50] *Hager/Maultzsch*, 5. Aufl., Art. 63 Rn. 6.
[51] *Hager/Maultzsch*, 5. Aufl., Art. 63 Rn. 6; MünchKomm/*P. Huber*, Art. 63, Rn. 16; *Brunner*, Art. 63, Rn. 5; *Ferrari u. a./Mankowski*, Internationales Vertragsrecht, Art. 63, Rn. 23.
[52] *Hager/Maultzsch*, 5. Aufl., Art. 63 Rn. 6; MünchKomm/*P. Huber*, Art. 63, Rn. 16; *Ferrari u. a./Mankowski*, Internationales Vertragsrecht, Art. 63 Rn. 23.
[53] *Hager/Maultzsch*, 5. Aufl., Art. 63 Rn. 6; *Enderlein/Maskow/Strohbach*, Art. 63, Anm. 5.; MünchKomm/*P. Huber*, Art. 63, Rn. 16; MünchKommHGB/*Benicke*, Art. 63, Rn. 5.
[54] *Hager/Maultzsch*, 5. Aufl., Art. 63 Rn. 6; *Enderlein/Maskow/Strohbach*, Art. 63, Anm. 5.; *Staudinger/Magnus*, Art. 63, Rn. 17; MünchKomm/*P. Huber*, Art. 63, Rn. 16; *Ferrari u. a./Mankowski*, Internationales Vertragsrecht, Art. 63, Rn. 24.
[55] *Hager/Maultzsch*, 5. Aufl., Art. 63 Rn. 6a; MünchKomm/*P. Huber*, Art. 63, Rn. 13; *Staudinger/Magnus*, Art. 63, Rn. 20; vgl. *Ferrari u. a./Mankowski*, Internationales Vertragsrecht, Art. 63, Rn. 21.
[56] *Hager/Maultzsch*, 5. Aufl., Art. 63 Rn. 5; *Staudinger/Magnus*, Art. 63, Rn. 20; *Enderlein/Maskow/Strohbach*, Art. 63, Anm. 6.; MünchKommHGB/*Benicke*, Art. 63, Rn. 6; *Ferrari u. a./Mankowski*, Internationales Vertragsrecht, Art. 63, Rn. 20.
[57] HGer St. Gallen, 3.12.2002, CISG-online 727 = IHR 2003, 181 = SZIER 2003, 104; *Achilles*, Art. 63, Rn. 7; *Staudinger/Magnus*, Art. 63, Rn. 20.
[58] Vgl. oben Rn. 13.
[59] *Staudinger/Magnus*, Art. 63, Rn. 23.
[60] *Hager/Maultzsch*, 5. Aufl., Art. 63 Rn. 6; *Staudinger/Magnus*, Art. 63, Rn. 23; *Herber/Czerwenka*, Art. 63, Rn. 5.

V. Beweislast

16 Aus den allgemeinen Prinzipien über die Verteilung der Beweislast folgt, dass die Partei, die sich auf Art. 63 beruft, die Beweislast für die entsprechenden Fakten trägt. Wenn sich der Verkäufer auf die Nichterfüllung trotz Nachfristsetzung zur Begründung seiner Vertragsaufhebung beruft, so trägt der Verkäufer die Beweislast.[61] Beruft sich hingegen der Käufer auf Art. 63 II, um sich vor Inanspruchnahme durch den Verkäufer wegen vorläufiger Präklusion zu schützen, so trägt die Beweislast der Käufer.[62]

17 Beruft sich der Verkäufer auf eine von ihm erklärte Nachfrist zur Erfüllung durch den Käufer, so muss er nur die Absendung dieser Erklärung mit den nach den Umständen geeigneten Mitteln nachweisen, nicht aber den Zugang dieser Erklärung beim Käufer (Art. 27).[63] Bezieht sich hingegen der Käufer auf eine Nachfristansetzung durch den Verkäufer, um so die vorläufige Präklusion nach Art. 63 II zu behaupten, so muss er den Zugang der Erklärung des Verkäufers nachweisen.[64] Hat der Käufer dem Verkäufer gegenüber erklärt, dass er den Vertrag während der Nachfrist nicht erfüllen wird, so trägt der Verkäufer die Beweislast für diese Erklärung, weil sie sich zu seinem Vorteil auswirkt, indem die vorläufige Präklusion seiner anderen Rechtsbehelfe aufgehoben wird.[65]

---

[61] Vgl. *Ferrari u. a./Mankowski*, Internationales Vertragsrecht, Art. 63, Rn. 25.

[62] *Staudinger/Magnus*, Art. 63, Rn. 24; *Achilles*, Art. 63, Rn. 9; *Ferrari u. a./Mankowski*, Internationales Vertragsrecht, Art. 63, Rn. 26.

[63] Vgl. *Ferrari u. a./Mankowski*, Internationales Vertragsrecht, Art. 63, Rn. 25.

[64] Vgl. oben *Müller-Chen*, Art. 47 Rn. 13, bezüglich der vergleichbaren Vorschrift in Art. 47 betreffend die Rechtsbehelfe des Käufers wegen Vertragsbruchs des Verkäufers.

[65] *Staudinger/Magnus*, Art. 63, Rn. 24; *Ferrari u. a./Mankowski*, Internationales Vertragsrecht, Art. 63, Rn. 26. A. A. *Honsell/Schnyder/Straub*, Art. 63, Rn. 34.

Art. 64 [Vertragsaufhebung]

(1) Der Verkäufer kann die Aufhebung des Vertrages erklären,
a) wenn die Nichterfüllung einer dem Käufer nach dem Vertrag oder diesem Übereinkommen obliegenden Pflicht eine wesentliche Vertragsverletzung darstellt oder
b) wenn der Käufer nicht innerhalb der vom Verkäufer nach Artikel 63 Absatz 1 gesetzten Nachfrist seine Pflicht zur Zahlung des Kaufpreises oder zur Abnahme* der Ware erfüllt oder wenn er erklärt, daß er dies nicht innerhalb der so gesetzten Frist tun wird.

(2) Hat der Käufer den Kaufpreis gezahlt, so verliert jedoch der Verkäufer sein Recht, die Aufhebung des Vertrages zu erklären, wenn er
a) im Falle verspäteter Erfullung durch den Käufer die Aufhebung nicht erklärt, bevor er erfahren hat, daß erfüllt worden ist, oder
b) im Falle einer anderen Vertragsverletzung als verspäteter Erfüllung durch den Käufer die Aufhebung nicht innerhalb einer angemessenen Zeit erklärt,
  i) nachdem der Verkäufer die Vertragsverletzung kannte oder kennen mußte oder
  ii) nachdem eine vom Verkäufer nach Artikel 63 Absatz 1 gesetzte Nachfrist abgelaufen ist oder nachdem der Käufer erklärt hat, daß er seine Pflichten nicht innerhalb der Nachfrist erfüllen wird.

Art. 64

(1) The seller may declare the contract avoided:

(a) if the failure by the buyer to perform any of his obligations under the contract or this Convention amounts to a fundamental breach of contract; or
(b) if the buyer does not, within the additional period of time fixed by the seller in accordance with paragraph (1) of article 63, perform his obligation to pay the price or take delivery of the goods, or if he declares that he will not do so within the period so fixed;

(2) However, in cases where the buyer has paid the price, the seller loses the right to declare the contract avoided unless he does so:

(a) in respect of late performance by the buyer, before the seller has become aware that performance has been rendered; or
(b) in respect of any breach other than late performance by the buyer, within a reasonable time:
  (i) after the seller knew or ought to have known of the breach; or
  (ii) after the expiration of any additional period of time fixed by the seller in accordance with paragraph (1) of article 63, or after the buyer has declared that he will not perform his obligations within such an additional period.

Art. 64

1) Le vendeur peut déclarer le contrat résolu:

a) si l'inexécution par l'acheteur de l'une quelconque des obligations résultant pour lui du contrat ou de la présente Convention constitue une contravention essentielle au contrat; ou
b) si l'acheteur n'exécute pas son obligation de payer le prix ou ne prend pas livraison des marchandises dans le délai supplémentaire imparti par le vendeur conformément au paragraphe 1 de l'article 63 ou s'il déclare qu'il ne le fera pas dans le délai ainsi imparti.

2) Cependant, lorsque l'acheteur a payé le prix, le vendeur est déchu du droit de déclarer le contrat résolu s'il ne l'a pas fait:

a) en cas d'exécution tardive par l'acheteur, avant d'avoir su qu'il y avait eu exécution; ou
b) en cas de contravention par l'acheteur autre que l'exécution tardive, dans un délai raisonnable:
  i) à partir du moment où le vendeur a eu connaissance ou aurait dû avoir connaissance de cette contravention; ou
  ii) après l'expiration de tout délai supplémentaire imparti par le vendeur conformément au paragraphe 1 de l'article 63 ou après que l'acheteur a déclaré qu'il n'exécuterait pas ses obligations dans ce délai supplémentaire.

---

* Schweiz, Österreich: Annahme.

Übersicht

	Rn.
I. Regelungsgegenstand	1
II. Voraussetzungen der Vertragsaufhebung durch den Verkäufer, Art. 64 I	5
1. Wesentlicher Vertragsbruch des Käufers, Art. 64 I lit. a)	5
a) Nichtzahlung	6
b) Nichtabnahme der Ware	13
c) Nichterfüllung einer anderen Pflicht	17
2. Ablauf einer angemessenen Nachfrist zur Zahlung oder Abnahme der Ware, Art. 64 I lit. b)	19
III. Zeitliche Grenzen des Vertragsaufhebungsrechts des Verkäufers nach erfolgter Zahlung, Art. 64 II	22
1. Verspätete Erfüllung, Art. 64 II lit. a)	26
2. Andauernder Vertragsbruch, Art. 64 II lit. b)	29
3. Präklusion des Vertragsaufhebungsrechts	31
IV. Mitteilung der Vertragsaufhebungserklärung, Art. 26	32
V. Wirkungen der Vertragsaufhebung	33
1. Erlöschen der Leistungspflichten, Artt. 81–84	33
2. Schadenersatz, Artt. 74–77	34
3. Verhältnis der Vertragsaufhebung zum Erfüllungsanspruch	35
VI. Beweislast	38

Vorläufer und **Entwürfe:** Artt. 62, 66, 70 I lit. a) EKG; Genfer E 1976 Art. 45; Wiener E 1977 Art. 46; New Yorker E 1978 Art. 60.

I. Regelungsgegenstand

1   Art. 64 regelt die **Vertragsaufhebung als Rechtsbehelf des Verkäufers** wegen Vertragsbruchs durch den Käufer. Sein Pendant in Abschnitt III des vorhergehenden Kapitels über die Rechtsbehelfe des Käufers wegen Vertragsbruchs durch den Verkäufer ist Art. 49, der im Wesentlichen ähnliche Regeln festschreibt.[1] Art. 64 beschreibt die **Voraussetzungen** für eine Vertragsaufhebung durch den Verkäufer und sieht zudem gewisse **zeitliche Beschränkungen** für die Ausübung dieses Rechts vor, während die Wirkungen der Vertragsaufhebung für den Verkäufer und den Käufer gemeinsam in den Artt. 81–84 geregelt sind. Zudem müssen die Regelungen über den Schadenersatz, insbesondere Art. 75 und Art. 76, herangezogen werden, um die Parteiinteressen im Falle der Vertragsaufhebung vollständig abzuwickeln. Das CISG kennt keine automatische (*ipso-facto-*) Vertragsaufhebung, sondern verlangt gemäss Art. 26, dass der Verkäufer die Erklärung, dass er den Vertrag aufhebt, dem Käufer mitteilt.[2]

2   Unabhängig davon, welche konkrete Pflicht der Käufer verletzt hat,[3] kann der Verkäufer gemäss Art. 64 I lit. a) den Vertrag aufheben, wenn die Pflichtverletzung einen **wesentlichen Vertragsbruch** darstellt. Ein weiterer Grund für die Vertragsaufhebung ist gemäss Art. 64 I lit. b) gegeben, wenn der Käufer seine Pflicht zur Zahlung des Kaufpreises oder zur Übernahme der Ware verletzt hat und nicht innerhalb einer vom Verkäufer gesetzten **Nachfrist** erfüllt. Dies stellt die wesentliche rechtliche Konsequenz des Rechts des Verkäufers zur Nachfristsetzung nach Art. 63 I dar.[4] Im Falle der Verletzung einer anderen Pflicht als der Pflicht zur Zahlung des Kaufpreises oder zur Übernahme der Ware hat der Verkäufer kein Recht zur Vertragsaufhebung wegen fruchtlosen Ablaufs einer von ihm gesetzten Nachfrist. In einem solchen Fall muss vielmehr von vornherein ein wesentlicher Vertragsbruch vorliegen, damit der Verkäufer ein Recht zur Vertragsaufhebung hat.[5]

---

[1] Vgl. oben *Müller-Chen*, Art. 49 Rn. 1 ff.
[2] Vgl. oben *Fountoulakis*, Art. 26 Rn. 1 ff.
[3] BGH, 3.4.1996, CISG-online 135 = NJW 1996, 2364 = BGHZ 132, 290, 298; OLG Brandenburg, 18.11.2008, CISG-online 1734 = IHR 2009, 105, 111.
[4] Vgl. oben Art 63, Rn. 1.
[5] Zur Möglichkeit der vertraglichen Anpassung dieser Regelung vgl. unten Rn. 21.

Art. 64 II sieht gewisse **zeitliche Beschränkungen** für die Ausübung der Vertragsaufhe- 3
bung durch den Verkäufer vor. Diese zeitlichen Beschränkungen kommen nur dann zur
Anwendung, wenn der Käufer den Kaufpreis bereits bezahlt hat. Im Falle verspäteter
Erfüllung durch den Käufer muss der Verkäufer gemäss Art. 64 II lit. a) sein Recht zur
Vertragsaufhebung ausüben, bevor er erfährt, dass erfüllt worden ist.[6] Im Falle einer anderen
Vertragsverletzung als verspäteter Erfüllung durch den Käufer muss der Verkäufer die Vertragsaufhebung innerhalb einer angemessenen Zeit erklären, nachdem er von der Vertragsverletzung Kenntnis erlangt hat oder hätte erlangen können, nachdem eine von ihm nach
Art. 63 I gesetzte Nachfrist abgelaufen ist oder nachdem der Käufer erklärt hat, dass er seine
Pflichten nicht innerhalb der Nachfrist erfüllen wird.

Innerhalb des Rechtsbehelfssystems, das dem Verkäufer wegen Vertragsverletzung des 4
Käufers zusteht, stellt die Vertragsaufhebung das **letzte Mittel (ultima ratio)** dar, was sich
bereits aus dem Erfordernis eines wesentlichen Vertragsbruchs ergibt.[7] Das CISG bevorzugt
in diesem Sinne das Festhalten am Vertrag und den Ausgleich von Vertragsverletzungen
durch Schadenersatz. Den Hintergrund für die nur beschränkten Möglichkeiten zur Vertragsaufhebung stellen die Gegebenheiten des internationalen Handels dar, da die Vertragsaufhebung durch die mit ihrer Abwicklung verbundenen, zusätzlichen Transport- und Versicherungskosten durch (Rück-)Transport der Ware und Rückzahlung des Kaufpreises oft
ein unerwünschtes Ereignis mit unnötigen Kosten für die involvierten Parteien und die
Wirtschaft im allgemeinen darstellt. Diese Überlegungen greifen freilich nicht, wenn der
Verkäufer die Möglichkeit hat, die Ware durch Deckungsverkauf abzusetzen oder nach
Art. 76 vorzugehen. Geht der Verkäufer im Wege des Schadenersatzes vor, so trägt er den
besonderen Gegebenheiten des internationalen Handels Rechnung und sollte daran nicht
durch zu hohe Hürden, wie das Erfordernis einer vorgängigen, ausdrücklich erklärten
Vertragsaufhebung, gehindert werden.[8]

II. Voraussetzungen der Vertragsaufhebung durch den Verkäufer, Art. 64 I

1. Wesentlicher Vertragsbruch des Käufers, Art. 64 I lit. a)

Der Verkäufer kann den Vertrag gemäss Art. 64 I lit. a) wegen jeder Pflichtverletzung des 5
Käufers aufheben, die einen **wesentlichen Vertragsbruch** darstellt. Art. 25 beschreibt
einheitlich für Pflichtverletzungen sowohl des Verkäufers als auch des Käufers, wann sie
einen wesentlichen Vertragsbruch darstellen. Auf Vertragsverletzungen des Käufers angewendet, setzt Art. 25 voraus, dass dem Verkäufer ein solcher Nachteil entstanden ist, dass
ihm im Wesentlichen entgeht, was er nach dem Vertrag hätte erwarten dürfen. Der Wortlaut
von Art. 25 verweist dabei nicht auf den rein wirtschaftlichen Schaden, der dem Verkäufer
entstanden ist, sondern auf die Bedeutung der verletzten Pflicht für den Verkäufer innerhalb
des vertraglichen Pflichtenprogramms des Käufers. Der Verkäufer ist zur Vertragsaufhebung
berechtigt, wenn ein Vergleich zwischen dem vom Käufer Versprochenen und den tatsächlichen Gegebenheiten den Schluss nahelegt, dass der Verkäufer sein Interesse an der Vertragserfüllung verloren hat.[9] Die Bestimmung, ob ein wesentlicher Vertragsbruch vorliegt,

---

[6] In dieser Hinsicht weicht Art. 64 von seinem Pendant Art. 49 II lit. a) ab, der nämlich für den Fall von verspäteten Lieferung durch den Verkäufer vorsieht, dass der Käufer sein Recht zur Vertragsaufhebung innerhalb einer angemessenen Frist erklären muss, nachdem er erfahren hat, dass die Lieferung erfolgt ist.
[7] BGH, 3.4.1996, CISG-online 135 = NJW 1996, 2364 = BGHZ 132, 290, 298; OLG Brandenburg, 18.11.2008, CISG-online 1734 = IHR 2009, 105, 111; *Farnsworth*, Rights and Obligations, S. 84 ff.; *Honnold/Flechtner*, Art. 49, Rn. 304; *von Caemmerer*, FS Coing, Bd. 2, S. 50; oben *Müller-Chen*, Art. 49, Rn. 2, bezüglich Vertragsaufhebung durch den Käufer wegen Vertragsbruch des Verkäufers; *Staudinger/Magnus*, Art. 64, Rn. 4; *Bamberger/Roth/Saenger*, Art. 64, Rn. 1; *Achilles*, Art. 64, Rn. 1; *Honsell/Schnyder/Straub*, Art. 64, Rn. 2; *Ferrari u. a./Mankowski*, Internationales Vertragsrecht, Art. 64, Rn. 1.
[8] Vgl. oben Art. 61, Rn. 13 m. w. N.
[9] Vgl. oben *Schroeter*, Art. 25 Rn. 21 ff.; *Hager/Maultzsch*, 5. Aufl., Art. 64 Rn. 4; *Bamberger/Roth/Saenger*, Art. 64, Rn. 3.

hängt dabei nicht von der Art der verletzten Pflicht[10] oder von dem Umstand ab, ob der Käufer die Ware bereits übernommen hat.[11] Das Konzept des wesentlichen Vertragsbruchs ist flexibel, z. B. können mehrere nicht wesentliche Pflichtverletzungen des Käufers zusammen einen wesentlichen Vertragsbruch ergeben[12] oder ein ursprünglich nicht wesentlicher Vertragsbruch kann durch Zeitablauf zu einem wesentlichen Vertragsbruch werden. Letztlich kann die Entscheidung, ob ein wesentlicher Vertragsbruch vorliegt, nur im konkreten Einzelfall unter Berücksichtigung aller Umstände getroffen werden.[13] Trotzdem können einige allgemeine Aussagen getroffen werden.

6   **a) Nichtzahlung.** Wenn der Käufer den Kaufpreis letztlich nicht zahlt, stellt seine **Nichtzahlung** einen wesentlichen Vertragsbruch dar.[14] Allerdings wird es in der Praxis oft schwierig festzustellen sein, ob der Käufer den Kaufpreis nicht zahlen wird, sodass von einer endgültigen Nichtzahlung in der Praxis nur dann ausgegangen werden kann, wenn der Käufer dem Verkäufer gegenüber erklärt, dass er den Vertrag nicht erfüllen wird.[15] Erklärt der Käufer vor Fälligkeit, dass er den Kaufpreis nicht bezahlen wird, so kann der Verkäufer den Vertrag gemäss Art. 72 I wegen antizipierten Vertragsbruchs aufheben.

7   Bezahlt der Käufer den Kaufpreis bei Fälligkeit nicht, so stellt die **verzögerte Zahlung** alleine noch keinen wesentlichen Vertragsbruch dar, auf dessen Grundlage der Verkäufer den Kaufvertrag aufheben könnte.[16] Gleiches gilt für die verzögerte Zahlung von fälligen Zinsen.[17] Dahinter steht die Überlegung, dass im Allgemeinen das Interesse des Verkäufers an rechtzeitiger Zahlung nicht von so grosser Bedeutung ist, dass der Verkäufer bei blossem Überschreiten des Fälligkeitszeitpunktes sofort den Vertrag aufheben könnte. Im Allgemeinen wird das Interesse des Verkäufers an rechtzeitiger Zahlung durch die Pflicht des Käufers zur Zahlung von Fälligkeitszinsen gemäss Art. 78 abgedeckt. Weil die blosse Überschreitung des Fälligkeitszeitpunktes im Allgemeinen keinen wesentlichen Vertragsbruch darstellt, wird der Verkäufer dem Käufer eine Nachfrist gemäss Art. 63 I zur Zahlung des Kaufpreises ansetzen, nach deren fruchtlosem Ablauf der Verkäufer berechtigt ist, den Vertrag gemäss Art. 64 I lit. b) aufzuheben, und zwar unabhängig davon, ob die Verzögerung bei der Zahlung einen wesentlichen Vertragsbruch darstellte.[18] Allerdings kann der Verkäufer in Ausnahmefällen auch zur Vertragsaufhebung wegen wesentlichen Vertragsbruchs ohne Setzung einer Nachfrist berechtigt sein, wenn der Käufer über eine unangemessen lange Zeit eine Verzögerungstaktik

---

[10] BGH, 3.4.1996, CISG-online 135 = NJW 1996, 2364 = BGHZ 132, 290, 298; OLG Brandenburg, 18.11.2008, CISG-online 1734 = IHR 2009, 105, 111.
[11] Vergleiche aber die begrenzten Rechtsbehelfe des Verkäufers nach Art. 2 UCC, wenn der vertragsbrüchige Käufer die Ware angenommen hat, vgl. *Flechtner*, J. L. & Com. (1988), 53 ff.
[12] Vgl. oben *Schroeter*, Art. 25 Rn. 20.
[13] BGH, 3.4.1996, CISG-online 135 = NJW 1996, 2364 = BGHZ 132, 290, 298; OLG Brandenburg, 18.11.2008, CISG-online 1734 = IHR 2009, 105, 111.
[14] *Shuttle Packaging Systems, LLC v. Jacob Tsonakis, INA SA and INA Plastics Corp.*, U. S. Dist. Ct. (W. D. Mich.), 17.12.2001, CISG-online 773, m. zust. Anm. *Bridge*, 25 J. L. & Com. (2005-06), 405, 409.
[15] OLG Braunschweig, 28.10.1999, CISG-online 510 = CLOUT Nr. 361 = TranspR-IHR 2000, 4, 5; OLG Düsseldorf, 14.1.1994, CISG-online 119 = CLOUT Nr. 130; KG Zug, 12.12.2002, CISG-online 720; KG Wallis, 2.12.2002, CISG-online 733; Int. Ct. Russian CCI, 5.10.1998, CISG-online 1831 = CLOUT Nr. 468; *Hager/Maultzsch*, 5. Aufl., Art. 64 Rn. 5; oben *Schroeter*, Art. 25 Rn. 66; *Soergel/Lüderitz/Budzikiewicz*, Art. 64, Rn. 5; *Achilles*, Art. 64, Rn. 3; *Piltz*, Internationales Kaufrecht, Rn. 5–426; *Honsell/Schnyder/Straub*, Art. 64, Rn. 20a; *Ferrari u. a./Mankowski*, Internationales Vertragsrecht, Art. 64, Rn. 10; *Sevón*, Obligations of the Buyer, S. 224; *Wiegand*, Pflichten des Käufers, S. 161.
[16] ICC, 7585/1992, CISG-online 105 = J. D. I. 1995, 1015; OLG Düsseldorf, 22.7.2004, CISG-online 916 = IHR 2005, 29; oben *Schroeter*, Art. 25 Rn. 66; *Bamberger/Roth/Saenger*, Art. 64, Rn. 3; *Ferrari*, IHR 2005, 1, 8; *Piltz*, Internationales Kaufrecht, Rn. 5–441; *Soergel/Lüderitz/Budzikiewicz*, Art. 64, Rn. 3; *Honsell/Schnyder/Straub*, Art. 64, Rn. 20c; *Ferrari u. a./Mankowski*, Internationales Vertragsrecht, Art. 64, Rn. 7. Die rechtsvergleichende Untersuchung von *Clausson*, 6 N. Y. L. Sch. J. Int'l & Comp. L. (1984), 93 ff. bestätigt dieses Ergebnis für das englische, US-amerikanische und schwedische Recht.
[17] *Roder Zelt- und Hallenkonstruktionen v. Rosedown Park Pty. Ltd. and Reginald R. Eustace*, Fed. Ct. Aust. (Adelaide, S. A.), 28.4.1995, CISG-online 218 = [1995] FCR 216.
[18] Vgl. CIETAC, 28.2.2005, CISG-online 1580: in den mehrfachen Versuchen des Verkäufers, den Käufer zur Stellung eines Dokumentenakkreditivs zu bewegen, sahen die Schiedsrichter keine Nachfristsetzung i. S. v. Art. 63.

betreibt, um den Verkäufer an den Verhandlungstisch zu binden, oder wenn der Käufer einen signifikanten Geldbetrag über eine unangemessen lange Zeit zurückhält.[19]

Die verzögerte Zahlung kann allerdings auch dann einen wesentlichen Vertragsbruch **8** darstellen, wenn die **Zahlungszeit,** also der Fälligkeitszeitpunkt, für den Verkäufer **von wesentlicher Bedeutung** war *(time of the essence).*[20] Ob der Fälligkeitszeitpunkt wesentlich war, ist eine Frage der Vertragsauslegung nach Art. 8 und Art. 9. Wenn z. B. Zahlung gegen Lieferung der Ware oder von Dokumenten zu erfolgen hat oder die Ware leicht verderblich ist, wird die Zahlungszeit wesentlich sein.[21] Auch kann die Zahlungszeit wesentlich sein, wenn die Vertragswährung starken Fluktuationen in den Währungsmärkten ausgesetzt ist, insbesondere wenn der Kaufpreis in der Währung des Staats zu begleichen ist, in dem der Käufer seinen Sitz hat.[22] Auch wenn die Ware selbst starken Preisfluktuationen in volatilen Märkten ausgesetzt ist, wird rechtzeitige Zahlung oft wesentlich sein.[23] In der Praxis wird der Verkäufer im Falle von starken Preisfluktuationen in volatilen Märkten üblicherweise in ein Deckungsverkaufsgeschäft eintreten, um die Ware vor fallenden Preisen oder fallender Währung zu schützen und so seiner Obliegenheit zur Schadensminderung nach Art. 77 nachkommen. Die sofortige Verfügung über die Ware durch den Verkäufer wird auch im Interesse des Käufers sein, der ansonsten für jedweden Verlust im Wege des Schadenersatzes haften würde (für die Differenz zwischen dem Vertragspreis und dem durch das Deckungsgeschäft erzielten Preis).[24] In diesem Zusammenhang spielt das Recht des Verkäufers zur Vertragsaufhebung eine inzidente Rolle, in dem die Vertragsaufhebung eine Voraussetzung zur Berechnung des Schadenersatzes nach Artt. 75 und 76 darstellt, jedenfalls nach der Ansicht, die an einer wortgetreuen Auslegung festhält.[25]

Vereinbaren die Parteien Zahlung durch **Dokumentenakkreditiv,** so werden sie oft **9** einen genauen Zeitpunkt in ihren Vertrag aufnehmen, zu dem der Käufer ein für den Verkäufer akzeptables Dokumentenakkreditiv gestellt haben muss.[26] Stellt der Käufer das Dokumentenakkreditiv nicht rechtzeitig, so ist der Verkäufer berechtigt, die Erfüllung seiner Pflichten zu suspendieren, z. B. seine Pflicht zur Lieferung der Ware oder von Dokumenten[27] oder seine Pflicht, den Käufer über das Schiff zu informieren.[28] Allerdings kann der Verkäufer den Vertrag nicht sofort aufheben.[29] Der Grund dafür liegt im Sicherungszweck

---

[19] Vgl. *Doolim Corp. v. R. Doll, LLC,* U. S. Dist. Ct. (S. D. N. Y.), 29.5.2009, CISG-online 1892: der Käufer zahlte nach zweimonatiger Verspätung nur einen kleinen Teil (weniger als 20%) des ausstehenden Kaufpreises; OLG Brandenburg, 18.11.2008, CISG-online 1734 = IHR 2009, 105, 111 (obiter); vgl. Gerechtshof van Beroep Antwerpen, 22.1.2007, CISG-online 1585: die unterlassene Beibringung eines Dokumentenakkreditivs, die Nichtzahlung des Kaufpreises und die Nichtabnahme der Ware begründeten einen wesentlichen Vertragsbruch des Käufers, der den Verkäufer auch ohne Nachfristsetzung berechtigte, einen Deckungsverkauf vorzunehmen und seinen Schadenersatz nach Art. 75 zu berechnen; CIETAC, 25.5.2005, CISG-online 1685.

[20] *Hager/Maultzsch,* 5. Aufl., Art. 64 Rn. 5; *Piltz,* Internationales Kaufrecht, Rn. 5–441; *Staudinger/Magnus,* Art. 64, Rn. 11; *Bamberger/Roth/Saenger,* Art. 64, Rn. 3; *Enderlein/Maskow/Strohbach,* Art. 64, Anm. 3.; *Herber/Czerwenka,* Art. 64, Rn. 3; *Honsell/Schnyder/Straub,* Art. 64, Rn. 20b; *Ferrari u. a./Mankowski,* Internationales Vertragsrecht, Art. 64, Rn. 9.

[21] *Murray,* Draft Digest, S. 440, 462.

[22] *Schlechtriem,* Uniform Sales Law, S. 84; *Murray,* Draft Digest, S. 440, 462.

[23] *Staudinger/Magnus,* Art. 64, Rn. 12; Botschaft des Schweizer Bundesrats, S. 809; *Herber/Czerwenka,* Art. 64, Rn. 3; *Scheifele,* S. 119; *Soergel/Lüderitz/Budzikiewicz,* Art. 64, Rn. 4.

[24] *Hager/Maultzsch,* 5. Aufl., Art. 64 Rn. 5.

[25] Vgl. oben Rn. 4; Art. 61, Rn. 13 m. w. N.

[26] Vgl. CIETAC, 25.5.2005, CISG-online 1685; CIETAC, 15.9.2005, CISG-online 1714: ein Monat vor Verschiffung.

[27] Vgl. LG Kassel, 21.9.1995, CISG-online 192.

[28] Vgl. CIETAC, 15.9.2005, CISG-online 1714: da der Käufer bis ein Monat vor Verschiffung kein Dokumentenakkreditiv stellte, war der Verkäufer nicht verpflichtet, seinen vertraglichen Pflichten nachzukommen und den Käufer 15 Tage vor Verschiffung über das Schiff zu informieren.

[29] CIETAC, 23.4.1995, CISG-online 1031; vgl. LG Kassel, 21.9.1995, CISG-online 192: Wenn der Käufer dem Verkäufer eine Bankbestätigung nicht beibringt, in der die Bank erklären sollte, dass sie dem Verkäufer nach jeder Inspektion ein der inspizierten Quantität entsprechendes Akkreditiv errichtet, liegt kein wesentlicher Vertragsbruch vor, da diese Bankbestätigung nur „in höchst unvollkommener Weise" das übliche Beschaffungsrisiko des Verkäufers sichern sollte; *Clausson,* 106 N. Y. L. Sch. J. Int'l & Comp. L. (1984-86), 93,

des Dokumentenakkreditivs, der üblicherweise darin besteht, die Erfüllungshandlung des Verkäufers zu sichern. Wenn der Verkäufer aber mit der Lieferung der Ware noch nicht begonnen hat, so hat er noch kein offenes Risiko, dem mit dem Recht zur sofortigen Vertragsaufhebung begegnet werden müsste. Anders zu entscheiden sind Fälle, in denen die Stellung eines Dokumentenakkreditivs mit der Pflicht des Verkäufers zur Ladung der Ware verknüpft ist, weil in einem solchen Falle die rechtzeitige Stellung des Dokumentenakkreditivs wesentlich ist und der Verkäufer daher zur sofortigen Vertragsaufhebung berechtigt sein muss.[30] Auch kann die rechtzeitige Stellung eines Dokumentenakkreditivs für den Verkäufer wesentlich sein, wenn z. B. ein bereits gestelltes Dokumentenakkreditiv während der Erfüllungshandlung des Verkäufers abläuft, weil z. B. die Herstellung der Ware durch ein von keiner Seite zu vertretenen Umstand verzögert wurde. Auch liegt ein wesentlicher Vertragsbruch vor, wenn aus dem Umstand, dass der Käufer das Dokumentenakkreditiv nicht rechtzeitig geöffnet hat, folgt, dass er den Kaufpreis letztendlich nicht zahlen wird.[31] Selbstverständlich können die Parteien in ihrem Vertrag auch vereinbaren (Art. 6), dass der Verkäufer ein sofortiges Vertragsaufhebungsrecht hat, sobald der Käufer das Dokumentenakkreditiv nicht rechtzeitig stellt.

10 Eine Verletzung der Zahlungspflicht liegt bereits dann vor, wenn der Käufer es unterlässt, die nach dem Vertrag oder dem anwendbaren Recht erforderlichen Massnahmen zu treffen oder Förmlichkeiten zu erfüllen, damit Zahlung geleistet werden kann (Art. 54). Bereits die Verletzung einer solchen vorgelagerten Pflicht kann einen wesentlichen Vertragsbruch darstellen. Dies müsste selbstredend für die Stellung eines Dokumentenakkreditivs gelten, wenn die Stellung eines Dokumentenakkreditivs nicht bereits als Teil der Pflicht des Käufers zur Zahlung des Kaufpreises nach Art. 53 (so nach der hier vertretenen Auffassung), sondern als ein die Zahlung vorbereitender Schritt nach Art. 54 zu qualifizieren wäre.[32] Bereits durch **Nichtvornahme eines die Zahlung vorbereitenden Schritts** kann der Käufer einen wesentlichen Vertragsbruch begehen.[33] Allein schon die Unterlassung, dem Verkäufer eine Bankbestätigung zukommen zu lassen, in der die Bank erklärt, dass sie später ein Dokumentenakkreditiv zu Gunsten des Verkäufers stellen wird, kann bereits einen wesentlichen Vertragsbruch darstellen, wenn die Zahlungszeit selbst wesentlich war.[34] Ein weiteres Beispiel stellt der Fall dar, in dem der Käufer sich vertraglich verpflichtet hatte, eine Bankgarantie beizubringen, die den Verkäufer vor dem Zahlungsausfall des Käufers schützen sollte. Stellt der Käufer dem Verkäufer eine solche Bankgarantie nicht, so ist der Verkäufer zunächst berechtigt, die Erfüllung seiner Pflichten auszusetzen. War in einem solchen Fall die Zahlungszeit für den Verkäufer wesentlich, so kann er darüber hinaus auch zur Vertragsaufhebung wegen wesentlichen Vertragsbruchs durch den Käufer berechtigt sein. In den Fällen, in denen die rechtzeitige Stellung eines Dokumentenakkreditivs oder die rechtzeitige Beibringung einer Bankgarantie in sich selbst noch nicht als wesentlicher Vertragsbruch

---

106; *Staudinger/Magnus,* Art. 64, Rn. 14; *Bamberger/Roth/Saenger,* Art. 64, Rn. 3; *Enderlein/Maskow/Strohbach,* Art. 64, Anm. 3.; *Piltz,* NJW 2003, 2063; *ders.,* NJW 2005, 2126, 2130.

[30] *Downs Investments Pty. Ltd. v. Perwaja Steel SDN BHD,* Sup. Ct. QLD, 17.11.2000, CISG-online 587 = 2000 QSC 421, Rn. 62 ff.: Die fehlende Beibringung eines Dokumentenakkreditivs stellte einen wesentlichen Vertragsbruch dar, weil das nominierte Schiff ladebereit im Hafen lag und zudem der Markt für Stahlschrott zwischen Vertragsschluss und dem Verschiffungsmonat signifikant gefallen war; das Urteil wurde bestätigt durch Supreme Court of Queensland – Court of Appeal, 12.10.2001, CISG-online 955 = [2001] 1 QCA 433, Rn. 30 f., m. zust. Anm. *Bridge,* (2005-06) 25 J. L. & Com. 405, 409; *Helen Kaminski Pty. Ltd. v. Marketing Australian Products, Inc.,* U. S. Dist. Ct. (S. D. N. Y.), 23.7.1997, CISG-online 297 = CLOUT Nr. 187 = 1997 WL 414137 (obiter); *Hager/Maultzsch,* 5. Aufl., Art. 64 Rn. 5.

[31] *Downs Investments Pty. Ltd. v. Perwaja Steel SDN BHD,* Sup. Ct. QLD, 17.11.2000, CISG-online 587 = 2000 QSC 421, Rn. 75, bestätigt durch Supreme Court of Queensland – Court of Appeal, 12.10.2001, CISG-online 955 = [2001] 1 QCA 433, Rn. 30.; ICC, 10274/1999, CISG-online 1159 = (2004) 29 YB Comm. Arb. 89, 102; *Hager/Maultzsch,* 5. Aufl., Art. 64 Rn. 5.

[32] Vgl. oben Art. 54, Rn. 5 ff.

[33] *Staudinger/Magnus,* Art. 54, Rn. 15.

[34] A. A. LG Kassel, 21.9.1995, CISG-online 192: Art. 71 würde den Käufer in einem solchen Fall genügend schützen; *Ferrari,* IHR 2005, 1, 8 ff.

angesehen werden kann, muss der Verkäufer dem Käufer zunächst eine angemessene Nachfrist zur Stellung des Dokumentenakkreditivs oder zur Beibringung der Bankgarantie setzen, nach deren fruchtlosen Ablauf er gemäss Art. 64 I lit. b) berechtigt ist, den Vertrag aufzuheben, ohne einen wesentlichen Vertragsbruch des Käufers nachzuweisen.[35] Auch in Situationen, in denen der Käufer ein Dokumentenakkreditiv zwar gestellt hat, aber die Bedingungen des Akkreditivs, wie z. B. die Gültigkeit oder der Lieferzeitpunkt, vertraglich modifiziert werden müssen, kann der Verkäufer den Vertrag gemäss Art. 64 I lit. b) aufheben, wenn der Käufer das Dokumentenakkreditiv nicht innerhalb einer vom Verkäufer gesetzten, angemessenen Nachfrist abändert.[36]

Wird die Zahlung des Käufers durch eine **amtliche Handlung eines Staates** unmöglich, z. B. durch ein amtliches Verbot einer ausländischen Devise, so kann der Verkäufer berechtigt sein, den Vertrag aufzuheben, um die Situation zu klären,[37] selbst wenn der Käufer von seiner Zahlungspflicht nach Art. 79 befreit sein sollte.

Ein wesentlicher Vertragsbruch liegt auch vor, wenn der **Käufer insolvent** wird.[38] In der Praxis wird es für den Verkäufer oft zu spät sein, den Vertrag noch aufzuheben, wenn er von den finanziellen Schwierigkeiten des Käufers erst durch die Eröffnung des Insolvenzverfahrens Kenntnis erhält. Um einer solchen Situation vorzubeugen, kann in internationalen Warenkaufverträgen eine Klausel aufgenommen werden, der zufolge der Vertrag automatisch beendet wird, wenn eine der Parteien ein Insolvenzgesuch stellt oder gegen eine Partei ein Insolvenzbegehren gestellt wird.[39] Das CISG anerkennt die Wirkung solcher Klauseln nach Art. 6, wobei das anwendbare nationale Insolvenzrecht gewisse Beschränkungen solcher Klauseln vorsehen kann, die dann als Gültigkeitsnorm Geltung nach Art. 4 S. 2 lit. a) beanspruchen.

b) Nichtabnahme der Ware. Nimmt der Käufer dem Verkäufer die Ware endgültig nicht ab, so begeht er einen wesentlichen Vertragsbruch. Ausser in Fällen, in denen der Käufer **die Ware oder die Dokumente zurückweist oder zurückgibt,**[40] wird es in der Praxis freilich schwierig sein festzustellen, ob der Käufer noch erfüllen wird. Eine **endgültige Nichtabnahme** kann meist nur dann angenommen werden, wenn der Käufer eine **entsprechende Erklärung** abgegeben hat.[41] Wenn ein Langzeitvertrag, den die Parteien für eine mehrere Jahre dauernde Zeitperiode abgeschlossen haben, die Lieferung einer bestimmten Warenmenge pro Jahr vorsieht und der Käufer zu wenig Ware in einem Jahr abnimmt, muss die Frage, ob die Abnahme einer zu geringen Menge einen wesentlichen Vertragsbruch darstellt im Verhältnis zur Warenmenge unter dem Gesamtvertrag und nicht im Verhältnis zur Warenmenge pro Jahr beantwortet werden.[42] Die Abnahme von zu wenig Ware pro Jahr kann den Verkäufer allenfalls zur Vertragsaufhebung nach Art. 73 II in Bezug auf zukünftige Teillieferungen berechtigen.[43] Die Abnahme einer zu geringen Jahresmenge

---

[35] CIETAC, 15.9.2005, CISG-online 1714; BezG Saane, 20.2.1997, CISG-online 426; *Staudinger/Magnus*, Art. 64, Rn. 15; *Honnold/Flechtner*, Art. 64, Rn. 354.
[36] Vgl. CIETAC, 23.4.1995, CISG-online 1031.
[37] Sekretariatskommentar, Art. 63, Nr. 2; *Staudinger/Magnus*, Art. 64, Rn. 16; *Ferrari u. a./Mankowski*, Internationales Vertragsrecht, Art. 64, Rn. 11. A. A. *Piltz*, Internationales Kaufrecht, Rn. 5–429, 5–444.
[38] *Roder Zelt- und Hallenkonstruktionen v. Rosedown Park Pty. Ltd. and Reginald R. Eustace*, Fed. Ct. Aust. (Adelaide, SA), 28.4.1995, CISG-online 218 = [1995] FCR 216; oben *Schroeter*, Art. 25 Rn. 66.
[39] Vgl. BGH, 30.10.2008, IHR 2009, 128 betreffend § 41 der Einheitlichen Bedingungen des deutschen Kornhandels.
[40] AG Hamburg-Altona, 14.12.2000, CISG-online 692 = IPRax 2001, 582 ff.
[41] Hof van Beroep Gent, 20.10.2004, CISG-online 983: Abnahmeverweigerung vor dem Lieferzeitpunkt, weil der Käufer fälschlicherweise davon ausging, dass das Material zu spät geliefert werden würde; OLG Hamm, 22.9.1992, CISG-online 57: Abnahmeverweigerung von mehr als der Hälfte der Ware, weil der Käufer fälschlicherweise behauptete, dass der Verkäufer den Speck nicht verzollungsfähig in einem hygienerechtlich einwandfreien Zustand versandt habe; *Hager/Maultzsch*, 5. Aufl., Art. 64 Rn. 6; *Magnus/Lüsing*, IHR 2007, 1, 5; *Soergel/Lüderitz/Budzikiewicz*, Art. 64, Rn. 12; *Ferrari u. a./Mankowski*, Internationales Vertragsrecht, Art. 64, Rn. 12.
[42] OLG Brandenburg, 18.11.2008, CISG-online 1734 = IHR 2009, 105, 110 ff.
[43] OLG Brandenburg, 18.11.2008, CISG-online 1734 = IHR 2009, 105, 113 ff.

mag ihre Grundlage in der mangelnden Verfügbarkeit von Schiffen oder Ware kurz vor Jahresende haben.[44]

14 Versäumt der Käufer die Annahme der Ware bei Fälligkeit, so stellt die blosse **Verzögerung der Abnahme** nicht automatisch einen wesentlichen Vertragsbruch dar.[45] Ein wesentlicher Vertragsbruch wird nur dann gegeben sein, wenn der Verkäufer ein besonderes Interesse an rechtzeitiger Abnahme der Ware durch den Käufer hat.[46] Ein solches besonderes Interesse wird beispielsweise dann gegeben sein, wenn schnell verderbliche Ware geliefert wurde.[47] Auch wird ein solches besonderes Interesse gegeben sein, wenn der Verkäufer seine Lagerräume schnell wieder für neue Ware benötigt oder die von ihm gestellten Beförderungsmittel abgeladen werden müssen.[48] Gleiches gilt für die Lieferung von Schüttgut (*bulk commodities*), wenn die Infrastruktur des Verkäufers sofortige Beladung oder Abladung durch den Käufer oder seinen Beförderer erfordert.[49]

15 Im Falle eines **dokumentären Kaufvertrags** wird die Weigerung des Käufers, konforme Dokumente aufzunehmen, nicht automatisch einen wesentlichen Vertragsbruch darstellen, so dass der Verkäufer zur Vertragsaufhebung nur durch Setzung einer Nachfrist gelangen kann.[50] Wenn allerdings die Aufnahme der Dokumente einen wesentlichen Teil der Zug-um-Zug-Erfüllung des Vertrages darstellt oder die Lieferung des Verkäufers beeinträchtigt, kann ein wesentlicher Vertragsbruch vorliegen, der den Verkäufer zur sofortigen Vertragsaufhebung berechtigt.

16 Im Falle eines sogenannten **Abrufvertrags**, in dem sich der Käufer zum Abruf der jeweiligen Teillieferungen verpflichtet hat oder durch den der Käufer zur Spezifikation der Ware nach Art. 65 angehalten ist, führt der Nichtabruf oder die Nichtspezifikation des Käufers nicht automatisch zu einem wesentlichen Vertragsbruch. Der Verkäufer muss dem Käufer zunächst eine Nachfrist zur Erfüllung seiner Pflichten ansetzen.[51] Im Falle von Art. 65 hat der Verkäufer freilich den besonderen Rechtsbehelf der Selbstspezifikation.

17 **c) Nichterfüllung einer anderen Pflicht.** Andere Pflichten des Käufers, also Pflichten, die nicht Teil seiner Pflicht zur Zahlung des Kaufpreises, einschließlich sämtlicher Vorbereitungsschritte nach Art. 54, oder seiner Pflicht zur Abnahme der Ware, einschließlich aller Schritte, die erforderlich sind, um dem Verkäufer die Lieferung zu ermöglichen, folgen ähnlichen Regeln. Wenn der Käufer eine andere Pflicht endgültig nicht erfüllt und die Erfüllung dieser Pflicht für den Verkäufer wesentlich war, so kann die Pflichtverletzung des Käufers einen wesentlichen Vertragsbruch darstellen. Z. B. kann ein wesentlicher Vertragsbruch gegeben sein, wenn der Käufer ein vertragliches Re-Importverbot ständig und in beträchtlichem Umfang missachtet.[52] Andererseits liegt noch kein wesentlicher Vertragsbruch vor, wenn es der Käufer unterlässt, mit dem Verkäufer einen Lieferplan für das nächste Jahr auszuarbeiten, der Verkäufer aber auf der Grundlage eines achtwöchigen Ausblicks des Käufers tatsächlich liefern kann.[53] Da es auch bezüglich solcher anderen Pflichten schwierig

---

[44] OLG Brandenburg, 18.11.2008, CISG-online 1734 = IHR 2009, 105, 113 ff.: der Verkäufer war Hersteller von Bier und das Gericht stellte fest, dass er nicht im Voraus produzieren müsse.

[45] TGI Strasbourg, 22.12.2006, CISG-online 1629: ein Monat Verspätung nicht wesentlich; CA Grenoble, 4.2.1999, CISG-online 434; vgl. *Ferrari u. a./Mankowski*, Internationales Vertragsrecht, Art. 64, Rn. 12; *Ferrari*, IHR 2005, 1, 8.

[46] *Hager/Maultzsch*, 5. Aufl., Art. 64 Rn. 6; *Ferrari u. a./Mankowski*, Internationales Vertragsrecht, Art. 64, Rn. 12; *Ferrari*, IHR 2005, 1, 8; *Soergel/Lüderitz/Budzikiewicz*, Art. 64, Rn. 7.

[47] OLG Düsseldorf, 22.7.2004, CISG-online 919 = IHR 2005, 29, 31.

[48] *Hager/Maultzsch*, 5. Aufl., Art. 64 Rn. 6; *Soergel/Lüderitz/Budzikiewicz*, Art. 64, Rn. 7; *Staudinger/Magnus*, Art. 64, Rn. 17.

[49] *Hager/Maultzsch*, 5. Aufl., Art. 64 Rn. 6.

[50] *Staudinger/Magnus*, Art. 64, Rn. 18. Die Differenzierung nach der Art der Dokumente bei *Honsell/Schnyder/Straub*, Art. 64, Rn. 21 ist unangebracht.

[51] Vgl. *Staudinger/Magnus*, Art. 64, Rn. 19.

[52] CA Grenoble, 22.2.1995, CISG-online 151 = J. D. I. 1995, 632, m. Anm. *Witz/Wolter*, RIW 1995, 811: Ein US-amerikanischer Käufer hatte französische Jeans nach Europa reimportiert und insofern seine Vertragspflichten verletzt; *Staudinger/Magnus*, Art. 64, Rn. 20; *Honsell/Schnyder/Straub*, Art. 64, Rn. 22.

[53] OLG Brandenburg, 18.11.2008, CISG-online 1734 = IHR 2009, 105, 112.

zu bestimmen sein wird, ob der Käufer seinen Pflichten endgültig nicht nachkommt, wird in der Praxis ein wesentlicher Vertragsbruch nur dann angenommen werden können, wenn der Käufer dem Verkäufer gegenüber erklärt, dass er seinen Pflichten nicht nachkommen wird.

Kommt der Käufer seinen anderen Pflichten nur vorübergehend nicht nach, so stellt die **verzögerte Pflichterfüllung** regelmässig keinen wesentlichen Vertragsbruch dar. Nur wenn die Erfüllungszeit dieser Pflicht für den Verkäufer wesentlich war, kann bereits die Verzögerung einen wesentlichen Vertragsbruch darstellen. Wenn z. B. der Käufer dem Verkäufer gewisse Informationen schuldet, die zur Herstellung der Ware erforderlich sind, und die Produktionskapazität des Verkäufers bereits entsprechend der erwarteten Lieferzeit dieser Informationen organisiert ist, kann ein wesentlicher Vertragsbruch gegeben sein.[54] Der Umstand, dass die anderen Pflichten des Käufers keine für einen Kaufvertrag charakteristischen Leistungen darstellen und manchmal als Nebenpflichten bezeichnet werden, ist für die Feststellung eines wesentlichen Vertragsbruchs irrelevant.[55] Stellt die Verletzung einer anderen Pflicht durch den Käufer keinen wesentlichen Vertragsbruch dar, so ist der Verkäufer nicht zur Vertragsaufhebung berechtigt.[56] Wenngleich der Verkäufer dem Käufer eine Nachfrist zur Erfüllung ansetzen kann, so führt die Nichterfüllung des Käufers innerhalb der angesetzten Nachfrist dennoch nicht dazu, dass der Verkäufer den Vertrag aufheben kann, sondern hat nur die rechtlichen Konsequenzen gemäss Art. 63 II.[57] Mit anderen Worten läuft der Verkäufer ein gewisses Risiko, wenn er die Vertragsaufhebung auf Grundlage eines wesentlichen Vertragsbruchs erklärt, der auf die Verletzung einer anderen Pflicht des Käufers beruht, da ein Gericht oder Schiedsgericht im Streitfall zur Auffassung gelangen kann, dass tatsächlich kein wesentlicher Vertragsbruch vorlag.[58]

2. Ablauf einer angemessenen Nachfrist zur Zahlung oder Abnahme der Ware, Art. 64 I lit. b)

In der Praxis wird es oft schwierig sein festzustellen, ob eine Pflichtverletzung des Käufers einen wesentlichen Vertragsbruch darstellt. Das Risiko des Verkäufers besteht darin, dass in einem späteren Streitfall, das mit der Sache befasste Schiedsgericht oder staatliche Gericht seiner Einschätzung nicht folgt, sondern entscheidet, dass kein wesentlicher Vertragsbruch des Käufers vorlag. Dann aber stellt die ungerechtfertigte Vertragsaufhebung durch den Verkäufer selbst einen wesentlichen Vertragsbruch dar. Daher ist es für den Verkäufer am sichersten, dem Käufer vorgängig eine **angemessene Nachfrist zur Erfüllung gemäss Art. 63 I** zu setzen. Freilich besteht dieser Weg zur Vertragsaufhebung aber nur dann, wenn der Käufer seine Pflicht **zur Zahlung des Kaufpreises** oder **zur Abnahme der Ware oder von Dokumenten** verletzt hat. Nur in diesen Fällen kann der Verkäufer den Vertrag gemäss Art. 64 I lit. b) aufheben, ohne einen wesentlichen Vertragsbruch nachzuweisen, wenn der Käufer nicht innerhalb der ihm angesetzten Nachfrist erfüllt. Gleiches gilt, wenn der Käufer erklärt, dass er nicht innerhalb der gesetzten Nachfrist zahlen oder die Ware bzw. die Dokumente abnehmen wird. Die Erklärung des Käufers, dass er während der Nachfrist nicht erfüllen wird, muss dem Verkäufer zugehen, um wirksam zu werden.[59]

Der zu Art. 64 I lit. b) beschriebene Mechanismus findet nur dann Anwendung, wenn der Käufer seine Pflicht zur Zahlung des Kaufpreises oder zur Abnahme der Ware verletzt hat; nicht hingegen, wenn der Käufer eine andere Pflicht verletzt hat. Daher ist es von herausragender praktischer Bedeutung, ob eine **Nebenpflicht des Käufers** als Teil seiner Pflicht

---

[54] *Hager/Maultzsch*, 5. Aufl., Art. 64 Rn. 7; *Enderlein/Maskow/Strohbach*, Art. 64, Anm. 3.
[55] *Hager/Maultzsch*, 5. Aufl., Art. 64 Rn. 7.
[56] *Schlechtriem/P. Butler*, UN Law, Rn. 244; *Staudinger/Magnus*, Art. 64, Rn. 20.
[57] *Schlechtriem/P. Butler*, UN Law, Rn. 244.
[58] CA Grenoble, 4.2.1999, CISG-online 443 = CLOUT Nr. 243 = TranspR-IHR 1999, 43; *Staudinger/ Magnus*, Art. 64, Rn. 21; *Enderlein/Maskow/Strohbach*, Art. 64, Anm. 2.3.; *von Hoffmann*, Einheitliches Kaufrecht und Nationales Obligationenrecht, S. 300; MünchKommHGB/*Benicke*, Art. 64, Rn. 3.
[59] *Ferrari u. a./Mankowski*, Internationales Vertragsrecht, Art. 64, Rn. 21.

zur Zahlung des Kaufpreises oder zur Abnahme der Ware qualifiziert werden kann. Vorbereitungsschritte, die ergriffen werden müssen, um die Zahlung zu ermöglichen, wie z. B. die Stellung eines Dokumentenakkreditivs, sind Teil der Pflicht des Käufers zur Zahlung des Kaufpreises und fallen daher in den Anwendungsbereich des Art. 64 I lit. b).[60] Die Pflicht des Käufers zur Abnahme umfasst nicht nur seine Pflicht, die Ware und/oder die Dokumente physisch zu übernehmen, sondern besteht gemäss Art. 60 lit. a) auch darin, alle Handlungen vorzunehmen, die vernünftigerweise von ihm erwartet werden können, damit dem Verkäufer die Lieferung ermöglicht wird. Gleiches gilt für die Pflicht des Käufers zum Abruf der Ware oder zur Spezifizierung der Ware.[61] Alle anderen Pflichten des Käufers, die nicht Teil seiner Pflicht zur Zahlung des Kaufpreises oder zur Abnahme darstellen, wie z. B. die Pflicht des Käufers, die Ware in bestimmten Ländern zu vertreiben und zu bewerben, können nicht zu einem Aufhebungsrecht des Verkäufers gemäss Art. 64 I lit. b) führen. Zwar kann der Verkäufer dem Käufer auch in diesen Fällen eine Nachfrist zur Erfüllung ansetzen, die Nichterfüllung des Käufers innerhalb dieser Nachfrist führt aber nicht zu einem Vertragsaufhebungsrecht nach Art. 64 I lit. b). Die Nachfrist in solchen Fällen hat nur die Rechtsfolge des Art. 63 II. Allerdings kann die dauerhafte Nichterfüllung des Käufers, die sich über den Zeitraum der Nachfrist erstreckt, für sich selbst einen wesentlichen Vertragsbruch im Sinne des Art. 25 darstellen und dem Verkäufer ein Recht zur Vertragsaufhebung nach Art. 64 I lit. a) geben.[62] Da eine solche Analyse im Ergebnis zu einer Umgehung des Art. 64 I lit. b) führt, sollte vorsichtig erwogen werden, ob der Ablauf einer Nachfrist tatsächlich dazu führt, dass der ursprünglich nicht wesentliche Vertragsbruch nun mehr wesentlich geworden ist.

21 Für die **Vertragsredaktion** bedeutet dies, dass Verkäufer versuchen sollten, in ihren Verträgen die Möglichkeit der Vertragsaufhebung durch fruchtlosen Ablauf einer gesetzten Nachfrist auch für die sonstigen, anderen Pflichten des Käufers zu vereinbaren. Art. 64 I lit. b) kann selbstverständlich gemäss Art. 6 durch Parteivereinbarung derogiert werden, wobei man nicht vorschnell von einer stillschweigenden Derogation ausgehen sollte, sobald die Parteien weitere Aufhebungsrechte in ihrem Vertrag vorsehen.[63] Neuere Einheitsrechtsprojekte, wie z. B. Art. 7.1.5 PICC und Art. 8:106 PECL, geben der vertragstreuen Partei immer das Recht zur Vertragsaufhebung, wenn die vertragsbrüchige Partei nicht innerhalb einer angemessenen Nachfrist ihre Pflicht erfüllt.[64]

III. Zeitliche Grenzen des Vertragsaufhebungsrechts des Verkäufers nach erfolgter Zahlung, Art. 64 II

22 Art. 64 II begrenzt das Recht des Verkäufers, den Vertrag aufzuheben, in zeitlicher Hinsicht. Die **allgemeine Anwendungsvoraussetzung** für Art. 64 II ist, dass der Käufer den **Kaufpreis vollumfänglich bezahlt** hat.[65] Solange der Kaufpreis noch nicht voll-

---

[60] ICC, 11849/2003, CISG-online 1421, Rn. 18 bezüglich der Stellung eines Dokumentenakkreditivs; HGer St. Gallen, 3.12.2002, CISG-online 727; BezG Saane, 20.2.1997, CISG-online 426; *Hager/Maultzsch*, 5. Aufl., Art. 64 Rn. 8; *Staudinger/Magnus*, Art. 64, Rn. 23; Sekretariatskommentar, Art. 60, Nr. 7.

[61] *Hager/Maultzsch*, 5. Aufl., Art. 64 Rn. 8; *Staudinger/Magnus*, Art. 64, Rn. 24. A. A. OLG Brandenburg, 18.11.2008, CISG-online 1734 = IHR 2009, 105, 111; vgl. *Honsell/Schnyder/Straub*, Art. 60, Rn. 30 ff., zustimmend bezüglich Abruf (Art. 60, Rn. 30 f.), ablehnend bezüglich Spezifikation (Art. 60, Rn. 30e).

[62] Vgl. *Kritzers* Analyse des ICC-Schiedsspruchs, 7585/1992, 1.1.1992, CISG-online 105 auf CISG Pace; *Hager/Maultzsch*, 5. Aufl., Art. 64 Rn. 8; CA Grenoble, 22.2.1995, CISG-online 151 = J. D. I. 1995, 632; MünchKomm/*P. Huber*, Art. 64 Rn. 10; *Staudinger/Magnus*, Art. 64, Rn. 22, der auf den Fall verweist, dass der Käufer die vereinbarten Absatzbemühungen schliesslich ganz einstellt.

[63] ICC, 11849/2003, CISG-online 1421, Rn. 21 ff.: das Schiedsgericht verwarf die Behauptung des Käufers, dass die Vertragsklauseln, die zusätzliche Vertragsaufhebungsrechte für den Fall des Nichterreichens gewisser Verkaufszahlen und für den Fall der Insolvenz vorsahen, Art. 64 I lit. b) ausschliessen würden; zust. *Honsell/Schnyder/Straub*, Art. 64, Rn. 97.

[64] Vgl. *Liu*, Additional Period, passim.

[65] Vgl. *Schlechtriem*, Rn. 246; *Honsell/Schnyder/Straub*, Art. 64, Rn. 28; *Staudinger/Magnus*, Art. 64, Rn. 39; *Ferrari u. a./Mankowski*, Internationales Vertragsrecht, Art. 64, Rn. 38.

ständig bezahlt wurde, untersteht das Vertragsaufhebungsrecht des Verkäufers keinen zeitlichen Grenzen.[66] Nur das allgemeine Prinzip der Verwirkung kann das Vertragsaufhebungsrecht des Verkäufers begrenzen.[67] Hat die Zahlung in mehreren Teilzahlungen zu erfolgen, so müssen sämtliche Teilzahlungen erfolgt sein.[68] Die Zahlung am falschen Ort oder in der falschen Währung löst nicht die Fristen des Art. 64 II aus.[69] Die Bestimmung des Zeitpunktes, in dem der Verkäufer sein Vertragsaufhebungsrecht verliert, hängt davon ab, ob es sich um einen Fall **verspäteter Erfüllung** (Art. 64 II lit. a)) oder um einen Fall einer **anderen Vertragsverletzung** als verspäteter Erfüllung (Art. 64 II lit. b)) handelt.

Die **Abgrenzung der Anwendungsbereiche von Art. 64 II lit. a) und Art. 64 II lit. b)** hat in der Theorie zu einigen Schwierigkeiten geführt, die sich aber offenbar noch nie in der Praxis gestellt haben.[70] Entscheidendes Abgrenzungskriterium ist dabei der Begriff „*late performance*" (verspätete Erfüllung). Unter **verspäteter Erfüllung** in diesem Zusammenhang sind alle Fälle zu verstehen, in denen der Käufer schlussendlich den Vertrag erfüllt hat, seine Erfüllung aber verspätet war.[71] Solange hingegen die Vertragsverletzung andauert, solange also der Käufer seinen vertraglichen Verpflichtungen nicht nachgekommen ist, liegt ein Fall einer anderen Vertragsverletzung als verspäteter Erfüllung durch den Käufer vor, so dass Art. 64 II lit. b) Anwendung findet.[72] Diese Unterscheidung kann von praktischer Wichtigkeit sein, wenn der Käufer den Kaufpreis bereits bezahlt hat, die Lieferung aber noch nicht abgenommen hat. Nach der hier vertretenen Ansicht fällt dieser Fall unter Art. 64 II lit. b) mit der Folge, dass das Vertragsaufhebungsrecht des Verkäufers erst verwirkt, nachdem er von der Vertragsverletzung erfahren hat oder nachdem eine von ihm gesetzte Nachfrist abgelaufen ist.[73]

Einer in der Literatur geäusserten Gegenansicht zufolge, soll hingegen Art. 64 II lit. a) nur dann Anwendung finden, wenn der Käufer nicht zahlt oder nicht abnimmt.[74] Das Hauptproblem dieser Ansicht liegt darin, dass in Fällen, in denen der Käufer den Kaufpreis zwar gezahlt, die Lieferung aber nicht abgenommen hat, keine zeitliche Begrenzung gelten würde, solange er die Lieferung nicht abnimmt. Dieser Fall würde unter Art. 64 II lit. a) fallen, dem zufolge das Recht zur Vertragsaufhebung verwirkt ist, wenn der Vertragsbruch später geheilt wird. Diese Ansicht ignoriert darüber hinaus den Wortlaut des Art. 64 II, der von verspäteter Erfüllung spricht; solange aber die Nichterfüllung andauert, würde man üblicherweise nicht von verspäteter Erfüllung sprechen.[75]

Einer anderen Gegenansicht in der Literatur zufolge soll Art. 64 II lit. a) nur dann zur Anwendung gelangen, wenn der Käufer eine seiner sonstigen Pflichten nicht rechtzeitig

---

[66] Vgl. Sekretariatskommentar, Art. 60, Nr. 8; *Honnold/Flechtner*, Art. 64, Rn. 356.1; *Kröll u. a./Bell*, Art. 64, Rn. 11; *Honsell/Schnyder/Straub*, Art. 64, Rn. 26. Anders OLG Karlsruhe, 14.2.2008, CISG-online 1649 = IHR 2008, 53, 55 unter irrtümlicher Anwendung von Art. 64 II lit. b) ii).

[67] OLG München, 19.10.2006, CISG-online 1394 = IHR 2007, 30, 33: der Verkäufer hatte sein Recht zur Vertragsaufhebung nicht dadurch verwirkt, dass er sechs Monate wartete, nachdem er dem Käufer eine Nachfrist zur Erfüllung gesetzt hatte.

[68] Sekretariatskommentar, Art. 60, Nr. 12; *Hager/Maultzsch*, 5. Aufl., Art. 64 Rn. 11; MünchKomm/*P. Huber*, Art. 64, Rn. 19; *Ferrari u. a./Mankowski*, Internationales Vertragsrecht, Art. 64, Rn. 38.

[69] *Staudinger/Magnus*, Art. 64, Rn. 39; *Bianca/Bonnell/Knapp*, Art. 64, Anm. 3.7.; MünchKommHGB/*Benicke*, Art. 64, Rn. 19; *Piltz*, Internationales Kaufrecht, Rn. 5–412; *Ferrari u. a./Mankowski*, Internationales Vertragsrecht, Art. 64, Rn. 39.

[70] Vgl. *Bridge*, 25 J. L. & Com. (2005-06), 405, 410; *Staudinger/Magnus*, Art. 64, Rn. 40; *Honsell/Schnyder/Straub*, Art. 64, Rn. 25.

[71] MünchKomm/*P. Huber*, Art. 64, Rn. 20 ff.; *Staudinger/Magnus*, Art. 64, Rn. 41 ff.; *Soergel/Lüderitz/Budzikiewicz*, Art. 64, Rn. 15; *Kröll u. a./Bell*, Art. 64, Rn. 15; *Honsell/Schnyder/Straub*, Art. 64, Rn. 31; *Ferrari u. a./Mankowski*, Internationales Vertragsrecht, Art. 64, Rn. 46; vgl. oben *Müller-Chen*, Art. 49 Rn. 28, bezüglich Art. 49 II lit. a).

[72] *Hager/Maultzsch*, 5. Aufl., Art. 64 Rn. 14; *Honsell/Schnyder/Straub*, Art. 64, Rn. 31; *Ferrari u. a./Mankowski*, Internationales Vertragsrecht, Art. 64, Rn. 46.

[73] *Hellner*, UN Convention, S. 97; *Sevón*, Obligations of the buyer, S. 234.

[74] *Karollus*, S. 180 ff.; MünchKommHGB/*Benicke*, Art. 64, Rn. 16.

[75] *Hager/Maultzsch*, 5. Aufl., Art. 64 Rn. 13.

erfüllt.⁷⁶ Diese Ansicht ist zurückzuweisen, weil sie zu unangemessenen Ergebnissen führt. Der Anwendungsbereich von Art. 64 II lit. b) würde unangemessen beschnitten, wollte man diese Vorschrift nur auf die sonstigen Pflichten des Käufers anwenden, also diejenigen Pflichten, die nicht die Zahlung des Kaufpreises oder die Abnahme betreffen. Da in den Fällen der Verletzung sonstiger Pflichten ein wesentlicher Vertragsbruch von vornherein schwer denkbar ist, würde Art. 64 II lit. b) faktisch leerlaufen, da überhaupt kein Vertragsaufhebungsrecht in diesen Fällen entstünde, das seine zeitliche Begrenzung in dieser Vorschrift finden könnte.

1. Verspätete Erfüllung, Art. 64 II lit. a)

26 Gemäss Art. 64 II lit. a) verliert der Verkäufer sein Recht, die Aufhebung des Vertrags zu erklären, wenn er die Aufhebung im Falle einer verspäteten Erfüllung durch den Käufer nicht erklärt, bevor er erfahren hat, dass erfüllt worden ist. Wie oben besprochen muss der **Begriff der verspäteten Erfüllung** dahingehend verstanden werden, dass der Käufer seine vertragliche Pflicht schlussendlich erfüllt hat, wenngleich verspätet.⁷⁷ Besteht der wesentliche Vertragsbruch in der Nichtzahlung des Kaufpreises bei Fälligkeit oder hatte der Verkäufer das Vertragsaufhebungsrecht, weil der Käufer den Kaufpreis auch nicht während der ihm vom Verkäufer gesetzten Nachfrist gezahlt hat, so verliert der Verkäufer sein Vertragsaufhebungsrecht in dem Zeitpunkt, in dem er von der Zahlung des Käufers Kenntnis erhält.⁷⁸ Gleiches gilt für Fälle verspäteter Erfüllung der Käuferpflicht zur Abnahme oder zur Erfüllung seiner sonstigen Pflichten. Der Verkäufer erfährt spätestens dann von der Erfüllung des Käufers, wenn ihm eine entsprechende Erklärung zugeht.⁷⁹ Ohne eine solche Erklärung seitens des Käufers wird es in der Praxis schwierig sein, die Kenntnis des Verkäufers vom Umstand der Erfüllung nachzuweisen. Dabei ist ein angemessener Massstab anzulegen, wobei die Kenntnis des Verkäufers von der Erfüllung dann angenommen werden kann, wenn eine neutrale Drittperson darüber nicht in Unkenntnis sein konnte. Für die Frage, wann der Verkäufer sein Vertragsaufhebungsrecht ausübt, muss das Absenden der Aufhebungserklärung massgebend sein.⁸⁰

27 Nach **Ansicht des Sekretariatskommentars** kann die Erfüllung des Käufers nach Ablauf der durch den Verkäufer gesetzten Nachfrist nicht als verspätete Erfüllung im Sinne von Art. 64 II lit. a) verstanden werden, vielmehr falle diese Fallgruppe unter Art. 64 II lit. b) ii). Diese Ansicht muss zurückgewiesen werden, weil sie den Wortlaut von Art. 64 II lit. a) ignoriert und zu unangemessenen Ergebnissen führt.⁸¹ Selbst wenn der Käufer erst nach Ablauf einer Nachfrist zahlt, erhält der Verkäufer schlussendlich seinen vertraglichen Gegenwert. Daher ist es gerechtfertigt, das Recht des Verkäufers zur Vertragsaufhebung verwirken zu lassen, wenn er von der Erfüllung Kenntnis erhält. Ausserdem würde die im Sekretariatskommentar vertretene Ansicht zu praktischen Schwierigkeiten für den Verkäufer führen. Solange die Zahlung durch den Käufer noch aussteht ist, würde das Recht des Verkäufers zur Vertragsaufhebung keinerlei zeitlichen Grenzen unterstehen. Zahlt der Käufer dann lange Zeit nach Ablauf einer durch den Verkäufer gesetzten Nachfrist, hätte der Verkäufer sein Vertragsaufhebungsrecht bereits verwirkt, weil er es nicht innerhalb einer angemessenen Frist nach Ablauf der Nachfrist ausgeübt hat.⁸²

28 Schwierig gestaltet sich die Rechtsanwendung, wenn der Käufer **mehrere Vertragsbrüche** begangen hat, z. B. wenn er den Kaufpreis nicht gezahlt und auch die Ware nicht

---

⁷⁶ *Enderlein/Maskow/Strohbach*, Art. 64, Anm. 7.10.; *Herber/Czerwenka*, Art. 64, Rn. 9, 10; *Scheifele*, S. 122, 156.
⁷⁷ Vgl. oben Rn. 23.
⁷⁸ Vgl. ICC, 11849/2003, CISG-online 1421, Rn. 64 ff.; *Schlechtriem*, Rn. 247, mit Beispiel.
⁷⁹ *Hager/Maultzsch*, 5. Aufl., Art. 64 Rn. 17; *Staudinger/Magnus*, Art. 64, Rn. 44; *Honsell/Schnyder/Straub*, Art. 64, Rn. 35; *Ferrari u. a./Mankowski*, Internationales Vertragsrecht, Art. 64, Rn. 47.
⁸⁰ Vgl. *Schlechtriem*, Rn. 247, mit Beispiel.
⁸¹ So auch *Kröll u. a./Bell*, Art. 64, Rn. 18.
⁸² *Hager/Maultzsch*, 5. Aufl., Art. 64 Rn. 15.

abgenommen hat. Stellt die nicht rechtzeitige Zahlung durch den Käufer einen wesentlichen Vertragsbruch dar, der den Verkäufer zur Vertragsaufhebung berechtigt, so führt die spätere Zahlung durch den Käufer zur Anwendung von Art. 64 II lit. a) und der Verkäufer verliert sein Vertragsaufhebungsrecht. Die Gegenansicht versteht unter verspäteter Erfüllung im Sinne von Art. 64 II lit. a) nicht nur die verletzte Pflicht, die den Verkäufer zur Vertragsaufhebung berechtigt, sondern die Erfüllung des gesamten Vertrags. Diese Ansicht führt zu dem unangemessenen Ergebnis, dass das Recht des Verkäufers, den Vertrag aufzuheben, schlussendlich auf einem Vertragsbruch beruhen würde, der in sich selbst den Verkäufer nicht zur Vertragsaufhebung berechtigen würde.[83] Die Entstehungsgeschichte ist in dieser Hinsicht unklar, weil zwei Vorschläge zur Änderung der Vorschrift, die eine Klarstellung dieser Auslegungsfrage gebracht hätten, aus redaktionellen Gründen zurückgewiesen wurden.[84] Wenn aber die Nichtabnahme der Ware alleine den Verkäufer zur Vertragsaufhebung berechtigt, so ist der Verkäufer berechtigt, den Vertrag unter Berücksichtigung der zeitlichen Grenzen des Art. 64 II lit. b) aufzuheben, und zwar unabhängig von der verspäteten Erfüllung der Kaufpreiszahlungspflicht durch den Käufer.[85]

2. Andauernder Vertragsbruch, Art. 64 II lit. b)

Art. 64 II lit. b) beschreibt die zeitlichen Grenzen des Vertragsaufhebungsrechts des Verkäufers, das auf einer **anderen Vertragsverletzung als verspäteter Erfüllung** durch den Käufer beruht. Diese Vorschrift findet auf Fälle Anwendung, in denen die Pflicht des Käufers zur Abnahme der Ware oder zur Erfüllung einer sonstigen Pflicht nach wie vor nicht erfüllt wurde. Steht hingegen die Zahlung nach wie vor selbst aus, so findet Art. 64 II überhaupt keine Anwendung und das Vertragsaufhebungsrecht des Verkäufers ist zeitlich nicht begrenzt.

Beruht das Vertragsaufhebungsrecht auf **Nichtabnahme** oder einer **sonstigen Nichterfüllung,** so muss der Verkäufer den Vertrag innerhalb einer angemessenen Zeit aufheben. Welcher Zeitraum unter einer angemessenen Zeit zu verstehen ist, hängt von den besonderen Umständen des Einzelfalls ab. Der Zeitraum muss mindestens so lange bemessen sein, dass eine angemessen handelnde Drittpartei genügend Zeit für die Entscheidungsfindung und die Abgabe der Erklärung hätte.[86] Das CISG nennt zwei unterschiedliche Zeitpunkte, in denen die angemessene Frist zu laufen beginnt. Entweder beginnt die Frist in dem Zeitpunkt zu laufen, in dem der Verkäufer von der Vertragsverletzung Kenntnis erhält (Art. 64 II lit. b) i)) oder in dem Zeitpunkt, in dem eine vom Verkäufer gemäss Art. 63 I gesetzte Nachfrist abläuft oder der Käufer erklärt hat, dass er seine Pflichten nicht innerhalb der Nachfrist erfüllen wird (Art. 64 II lit. b) ii)). Der Wortlaut von Art. 64 II lit. b) i), der auf Vertragsverletzungen verweist, die der Verkäufer „kennen musste", verlangt konkrete Hinweise auf einen existierenden Vertragsbruch.[87] Vertragsverletzung in diesem Zusammenhang kann nur einen wesentlichen Vertragsbruch meinen, weil andernfalls der Verkäufer gar nicht zur Vertragsaufhebung berechtigt wäre. Hätte nämlich der Verkäufer eine Nachfrist zur Erfüllung gesetzt, würde Art. 64 II lit. b) ii) Anwendung

---

[83] *Achilles,* Art. 64, Rn. 8; *Bianca/Bonnell/Knapp,* Art. 64, Anm. 3.15.; *Scheifele,* S. 124 ff.; *Soergel/Lüderitz/Budzikiewicz,* Art. 64, Rn. 15.
[84] Vgl. für die Vorschläge O. R., S. 125, Nr. 7; S. 170 (Norwegen); für die Ablehnung, O. R., S. 412, 413, Nr. 47 ff.; S. 212, Nr. 48 ff. Ein norwegischer Abgeordneter wies auf das Auslegungsproblem hin, vgl. O. R., S. 371, Nr. 65; vgl. YB VIII (1977), S. 123, Nr. 33 ff.
[85] *Hager/Maultzsch,* 5. Aufl., Art. 64 Rn. 18.
[86] Vgl. *Honsell/Schnyder/Straub,* Art. 64, Rn. 39; *Ferrari u. a./Mankowski,* Internationales Vertragsrecht, Art. 64, Rn. 51. A. A. *Witz/Salger/Lorenz/Witz,* Art. 64, Rn. 21, dem zufolge darauf abzustellen sei, wann ein vernünftiger Dritter in der Position des Käufers aus der Nichtausübung der Vertragsaufhebung davon ausgehen dürfe, dass der Vertrag erfüllt werde.
[87] *Hager/Maultzsch,* 5. Aufl., Art. 64 Rn. 20; *Achilles,* Art. 64, Rn. 9; *Staudinger/Magnus,* Art. 64, Rn. 47; *Ferrari u. a./Mankowski,* Internationales Vertragsrecht, Art. 64, Rn. 49. Vgl. *Honsell/Schnyder/Straub,* Art. 64, Rn. 44.

finden, selbst wenn die Nichterfüllung selbst bereits einen wesentlichen Vertragsbruch darstellen würde.[88] Dies folgt aus Art. 63 II und ist für den Verkäufer vorteilhaft, da der Beginn der angemessenen Zeit, innerhalb derer der Verkäufer sein Vertragsaufhebungsrecht erklären muss, bis zum Ablauf der Nachfrist aufgeschoben wird.[89] War hingegen das Recht zur Vertragsaufhebung wegen wesentlichen Vertragsbruchs bereits nach Art. 64 II lit. b) i) im Zeitpunkt der Nachfristsetzung durch den Verkäufer verwirkt, so lebt es nach Ablauf der Nachfrist nicht wieder auf.[90]

3. Präklusion des Vertragsaufhebungsrechts

31 Beachtet der Verkäufer die zeitlichen Grenzen des Art. 64 II nicht, so verliert er sein Recht, den Vertrag aufzuheben. Ähnlich wie bei Art. 49 bezüglich der Rechtsbehelfe des Käufers wegen Vertragsbruchs durch den Verkäufer schliessen die zeitlichen Grenzen des Art. 64 II das **Vertragsaufhebungsrecht** des Verkäufers **endgültig** aus (**Ausschlussfrist**).[91] Eine Gegenansicht, der zufolge das Vertragsaufhebungsrecht des Verkäufers durch Nichteinhalten der zeitlichen Grenzen des Art. 64 II nur suspendiert werde und wieder aufleben könne, wenn der Verkäufer zwischenzeitlich wieder Erfüllung der ausstehenden Leistung fordern würde, muss zurückgewiesen werden, weil sie mit dem Wortlaut des Artikel 64 II nicht vereinbar ist und dem Zweck des Artikel 64 II zuwiderläuft.[92] Die zeitlichen Grenzen des Art. 64 II haben jedoch keine Auswirkung auf die **anderen Rechtsbehelfe** des Verkäufers.[93]

IV. Mitteilung der Vertragsaufhebungserklärung, Art. 26

32 Der Verkäufer muss sein Vertragsaufhebungsrecht ausüben, in dem er gemäss Art. 26 dem Verkäufer eine **Erklärung** mitteilt, dass er den Vertrag aufhebe. Gemäss Art. 27 genügt die **Absendung**, d. h. eine Verzögerung oder ein Irrtum bei der Übermittlung dieser Mitteilung oder deren Nichteintreffen nimmt dem Verkäufer nicht das Recht, sich auf sie zu berufen.[94] Aus diesen Grundsätzen folgt, dass das CISG **keine automatische Vertragsaufhebung** kennt.[95] Die Vertragsaufhebungserklärung braucht gemäss Art. 11 i. V. m. Art. 7 II **nicht schriftlich** zu erfolgen oder nachgewiesen zu werden und unterliegt auch sonst keinen Formvorschriften. Jedenfalls muss die Sprache, der Wortlaut sowie der Inhalt der Erklärung dem Käufer verständlich sein und unmissverständlich zum Ausdruck bringen, dass der Verkäufer den Vertrag aufhebt und sich nicht länger an den Vertrag gebunden fühlt.[96] Die **blosse Androhung** der Vertragsaufhebung genügt nicht.[97] Die Erklärung der Vertrags-

---

[88] *Hager/Maultzsch*, 5. Aufl., Art. 64 Rn. 20; MünchKommHGB/*Benicke*, Art. 64, Rn. 23.
[89] *Hager/Maultzsch*, 5. Aufl., Art. 64 Rn. 20; *Bamberger/Roth/Saenger*, Art. 63, Rn. 2; ders., Art. 64, Rn. 10; Enderlein/Maskow/Strohbach, Art. 63, Anm. 2.1.
[90] *Hager/Maultzsch*, 5. Aufl., Art. 64 Rn. 20; MünchKommHGB/*Benicke*, Art. 64, Rn. 24. A. A. *Bamberger/Roth/Saenger*, Art. 63, Rn. 2; ders., Art. 64, Rn. 10; MünchKomm/*P. Huber*, Art. 64, Rn. 29; *Ferrari u. a./Mankowski*, Internationales Vertragsrecht, Art. 64, Rn. 55; oben *Müller-Chen*, Art. 49 Rn. 36 bezüglich Art. 49.
[91] *Staudinger/Magnus*, Art. 64, Rn. 50; *Achilles*, Art. 64, Rn. 13; *Honsell/Schnyder/Straub*, Art. 64, Rn. 62; *Leser*, Vertragsaufhebung und Rückabwicklung, S. 234; *Ferrari u. a./Mankowski*, Internationales Vertragsrecht, Art. 64, Rn. 57.
[92] *Staudinger/Magnus*, Art. 64, Rn. 50; *Ferrari u. a./Mankowski*, Internationales Vertragsrecht, Art. 64, Rn. 57. A. A. *Karollus*, S. 181; *Piltz*, Internationales Kaufrecht, Rn. 5–463, 5–466.
[93] Vgl. *Staudinger/Magnus*, Art. 64, Rn. 51.
[94] Zweifelnd *Ferrari u. a./Mankowski*, Internationales Vertragsrecht, Art. 64, Rn. 31.
[95] *Staudinger/Magnus*, Art. 64, Rn. 27. Dies in ausdrücklicher Abweichung von der Vorgängerkonvention EKG.
[96] OGH, 28.4.2000, CISG-online 581 = IHR 2001, 206 ff.; *Hager/Maultzsch*, 5. Aufl., Art. 64 Rn. 9; *Staudinger/Magnus*, Art. 64, Rn. 29.
[97] ICC, 11849/2003, CISG-online 1421, Rn. 61 f.; OLG München, 2.3.1994, CISG-online 108 = CLOUT Nr. 83; vgl. auch OLG Graz, 29.7.2004, CISG-online 1627, E. 2; *Honsell/Schnyder/Straub*, Art. 64, Rn. 78a.

aufhebung kann **auch stillschweigend** erfolgen.⁹⁸ So können die Klageeinleitung⁹⁹ oder die Geltendmachung eines Schadenersatzanspruches wegen Nichterfüllung (statt der Leistung) eine Vertragsaufhebungserklärung beinhalten.¹⁰⁰ Dies ist vor allem für die **Schadenersatzberechnung nach Art. 75 und Art. 76** von Bedeutung, da diese Vorschriften ihrem Wortlaut nach verlangen, dass der Vertrag aufgehoben ist. Nur dann kann der Verkäufer seinen Schaden als Differenz zwischen dem Vertragspreis und dem Preis des Deckungsverkaufs bzw. dem Marktpreis zur Zeit der Aufhebung ersetzt verlangen. In letzter Konsequenz führt die Zulassung stillschweigender Vertragsaufhebungserklärungen dazu, dass in diesen Fällen nur noch die **Schwelle der Vertragsaufhebung** erreicht sein, also ein wesentlicher Vertragsbruch des Käufers oder eine Nichterfüllung trotz Nachfristsetzung vorliegen muss, damit der Verkäufer einen Deckungsverkauf vornehmen und seinen Schaden nach Art. 75 oder seinen Schaden nach der Marktpreisregel nach Art. 76 berechnen kann.¹⁰¹ Da die Vertragsaufhebung das Rechtsverhältnis zwischen den Parteien in ein Rückabwicklungsverhältnis überführt, darf die Vertragsaufhebung nicht von dem Eintritt einer **Bedingung** abhängig gemacht werden, es sei denn, diese Bedingung würde nur an das Verhalten des Käufers anknüpfen. So kann der Verkäufer gleichzeitig mit dem Ansetzen einer Nachfrist für die Erfüllung durch den Käufer die Vertragsaufhebung unter der Bedingung erklären, dass nach fruchtlosem Ablauf der Nachfrist der Vertrag als aufgehoben gilt.¹⁰² Auch kann der Verkäufer die Vertragsaufhebung als subsidiäre Position in einem Schriftsatz an das Gericht oder das Schiedsgericht für den Fall erklären, dass das Gericht oder das Schiedsgericht seiner ersten Argumentationslinie nicht folgt.¹⁰³ Die Erklärung der Vertragsaufhebung kann nicht zurückgenommen werden, nachdem dem Käufer die Mitteilung zugegangen ist und er im Vertrauen darauf Dispositionen vorgenommen hat, Artt. 15 II, 22 i. V. m. Art. 7 II.¹⁰⁴ Betrifft der wesentliche Vertragsbruch des Käufers bzw. seine Nichterfüllung nur Teile des Vertrags, so kann der Verkäufer seine Vertragsaufhebungserklärung auf die betroffenen Vertragsteile beschränken.¹⁰⁵ Im Falle eines Sukzessivlieferungsvertrags gilt Art. 73.

V. Wirkungen der Vertragsaufhebung

1. Erlöschen der Leistungspflichten, Artt. 81–84

Die Wirkungen der Vertragsaufhebung sind in den Artt. 81–84 einheitlich geregelt, also **33** unabhängig davon, ob die Vertragsaufhebung durch den Verkäufer oder den Käufer erklärt wurde. Aus Sicht des Verkäufers hat die Vertragsaufhebung vor allem zur Folge, dass er von

---

⁹⁸ *Hager/Maultzsch*, 5. Aufl., Art. 64 Rn. 9; *Staudinger/Magnus*, Art. 64, Rn. 29. A. A. *Enderlein/Maskow/Strohbach*, Art. 64, Anm. 2.1.; *Herber/Czerwenka*, Art. 64, Rn. 7; *Piltz*, Internationales Kaufrecht, Rn. 5–458; *Kazimierska*, CISG Review 79 (1999–2000), 114.
⁹⁹ OGH, 28.4.2000, CISG-online 581 = IHR 2001, 206 ff.; LG Kassel, 21.9.1995, CISG-online 192; *Staudinger/Magnus*, Art. 64, Rn. 28; *Ferrari u. a./Mankowski*, Internationales Vertragsrecht, Art. 64, Rn. 28.
¹⁰⁰ HGer St Gallen, 3.12.2002, CISG-online 727 = SZIER 2003, 107 = IHR 2003, 181 ff.; Schiedsgericht der Hamburger freundliche Arbitrage, 29.12.1998, CISG-online 638 = NJW-RR 1999, 780; *Staudinger/Magnus*, Art. 64, Rn. 29; *Hager/Maultzsch*, 5. Aufl., Art. 64 Rn. 9. Anders OLG Düsseldorf, 22.6.2004, CISG-online 916 = IHR 2005, 29: der Verkäufer habe keine Umstände vorgetragen, aus denen sich eine auch nur stillschweigende Vertragsaufhebung ergeben könne.
¹⁰¹ In diesem Sinne ist die Entscheidung OLG Graz, 24.1.2002, CISG-online 801 zu verstehen.
¹⁰² Vgl. HGer St. Gallen, 3.12.2002, CISG-online 727 = SZIER 2003, 107 = IHR 2003, 181 ff.; vgl. auch (sehr weitgehend, aber im Rahmen von Art. 75 vertretbar) OLG Graz, 24.1.2002, CISG-online 801, S. 5, 11, für die Formulierung, dass ohne Zahlung bis zu einem bestimmten Datum die Erfüllung abgelehnt und Schadenersatz wegen Nichterfüllung verlangt würde; das Gericht sprach Schadenersatz nach Art. 75 zu; vgl. auch OLG Graz, 29.7.2004, CISG-online 1627, E. 2 (obiter). Vgl. *Staudinger/Magnus*, Art. 64, Rn. 31; *Achilles*, Art. 64, Rn. 5; *Piltz*, Internationales Kaufrecht, Rn. 5–460; *Honsell/Schnyder/Straub*, Art. 64, Rn. 78a; *Ferrari u. a./Mankowski*, Internationales Vertragsrecht, Art. 64, Rn. 30.
¹⁰³ Vgl. BGH, 27.11.2007, CISG-online 1617, Rn. 22 = IHR 2008, 49, 52.
¹⁰⁴ Vgl. *Staudinger/Magnus*, Art. 64, Rn. 28; *Achilles*, Art. 64, Rn. 5; *Bianca/Bonnell/Knapp*, Art. 64, Anm. 2.7.; anders *Piltz*, Internationales Kaufrecht, Rn. 5–460 (mit Zugang unwiderruflich).
¹⁰⁵ *Staudinger/Magnus*, Art. 64, Rn. 32, der Art. 51 analog anwenden will; *Herber/Czerwenka*, Art. 64, Rn. 8.

seinen **Pflichten zur Lieferung der Ware, zur Übergabe der Dokumente und zur Übertragung des Eigentums an der Ware befreit** wird. Soweit der Verkäufer die Ware oder die Dokumente bereits geliefert hat, kann er gemäss Art. 81 II die **Rückgabe des Geleisteten** verlangen. War Eigentum an der Ware bereits vom Verkäufer auf den Käufer nach dem anwendbaren Recht (Art. 4 lit. b)) übergegangen, so hat der Verkäufer einen vertraglichen Anspruch auf **Rückübertragung des Eigentums** an der Ware nach CISG. Auch schuldet der Käufer gemäss Art. 84 II dem Verkäufer den **Gegenwert aller Vorteile,** die er aus der Ware gezogen hat. Hat der Käufer die Ware bereits weiterverkauft, so beinhaltet der Gegenwert aller Vorteile gemäss Art. 84 II lit. b) analog auch den Nettogewinn aus dem Weiterverkauf.[106] Im Gegenzug muss der Verkäufer gemäss Art. 81 II 1 i. V. m. Art. 84 I den Kaufpreis zuzüglich Zinsen vom Tag der Zahlung des Kaufpreises an zurückzahlen. Art. 82 und Art. 83 betreffen Situationen, in denen der Käufer sein Recht auf Vertragsaufhebung verliert; diese Artikel gelten nicht für den Fall, dass der Verkäufer den Vertrag aufhebt.[107] Auch kann aus Art. 82 II lit. c) kein allgemeines Prinzip des CISG abgeleitet werden, dem zufolge ein Käufer, der die Ware gutgläubig und im normalen Geschäftsverkehr weiterverkauft hat, dadurch privilegiert würde, dass der Verkäufer in einem solchen Fall den Vertrag nicht aufheben könne.[108]

2. Schadenersatz, Artt. 74–77

34 Gemäss Art. 61 II verliert der Verkäufer das Recht, Schadenersatz zu verlangen, nicht dadurch, dass er den Vertrag aufhebt. Erklärt der Verkäufer den Vertrag als aufgehoben und verlangt Schadenersatz, so kann er das **vollständige Erfüllungsinteresse** ersetzt verlangen. Der Umfang seines Erfüllungsinteresses hängt dabei davon ab, ob der Verkäufer die Ware bereits geliefert hat. Hat der Verkäufer die Ware noch nicht geliefert, so kann er grundsätzlich einen Deckungsverkauf nach Art. 75 vornehmen oder seinen Schaden nach Art. 76 berechnen und die Differenz zwischen dem Vertragspreis und dem Marktpreis zur Zeit der Aufhebung ersetzt verlangen. Zusatzkosten können vom Verkäufer nach Art. 74 ersetzt verlangt werden. Hat der Verkäufer die Ware bereits geliefert und verlangt er diese nach Art. 81 II heraus, so beschränkt sich sein Schadenersatzanspruch auf Zusatz- und Nebenkosten. Andererseits kann der Verkäufer die Ware auch dem Käufer überlassen und sein vollständiges Erfüllungsinteresse geltend machen, soweit der Käufer den Kaufpreis noch nicht gezahlt hat. Hat der Käufer den Kaufpreis hingegen bereits bezahlt, so kann der Verkäufer nur die Differenz zwischen dem vom Käufer gezahlten Kaufpreis und seinem Erfüllungsinteresse geltend machen.[109]

3. Verhältnis der Vertragsaufhebung zum Erfüllungsanspruch

35 Das Verhältnis zwischen Vertragsaufhebung und Erfüllungsanspruch ist theoretisch einfach: Der Verkäufer kann nicht beide Rechtsbehelfe zugleich ausüben. Entweder bleibt der Verkäufer beim Vertrag und verlangt vom Käufer die Erfüllung seiner vertraglichen Pflichten oder er zieht sich vom Vertrag zurück und erklärt den Vertrag als aufgehoben. In der Praxis stellen sich aber oft schwierige Probleme, nämlich ob der Verkäufer **zwischen den Rechtsbehelfen wechseln** kann und ab welchem Zeitpunkt der Verkäufer von einer etwaigen Wechselmöglichkeit ausgeschlossen ist. Grundsätzlich kann der Verkäufer als vertragstreue Partei wählen, welchen seiner Rechtsbehelfe er wegen der Vertragsverletzung des Käufers ausüben möchte. Im Normalfall wird der Verkäufer zunächst versuchen, den Käufer zur Erfüllung des Vertrages anzuhalten, und erst dann zur Vertragsaufhebung übergehen, wenn der Käufer seine Pflichten weiterhin nicht erfüllt. Das Recht des Verkäufers, zur Vertrags-

---

[106] OLG Karlsruhe, 14.2.2008, CISG-online 1649 = IHR 2008, 53, 55.
[107] OLG Karlsruhe, 14.2.2008, CISG-online 1649 = IHR 2008, 53, 54.
[108] OLG Karlsruhe, 14.2.2008, CISG-online 1649 = IHR 2008, 53, 54 ff.
[109] Vgl. oben Art. 61 Rn. 13.

aufhebung zu wechseln, ist gesperrt, solange eine von ihm dem Käufer gemäss Art. 63 gesetzte Nachfrist läuft, weil die Vertragsaufhebung ein mit der Nachfrist unvereinbarer Rechtsbehelf im Sinne von Art. 63 II ist. Nach Ablauf der Nachfrist kann der Verkäufer freilich den Vertrag als aufgehoben erklären. Der Verkäufer muss die zeitlichen Grenzen des Art. 64 II lit. b) ii) berücksichtigen, innerhalb derer er die Vertragsaufhebung erklären muss. Bei besonderen Umständen, z. B. fallenden Preisen in volatilen Märkten, kann der Verkäufer verpflichtet sein, den Vertrag sofort aufzuheben anstatt zuerst Erfüllung vom Käufer zu verlangen. Diese Verpflichtung kann sich entweder aus seiner Schadensminderungspflicht nach Art. 77 oder aus dem allgemeinen Verwirkungsprinzip ergeben.[110]

Die Fälle, in denen ein Verkäufer, der den Vertrag bereits als aufgehoben erklärt hat, zum Erfüllungsanspruch zurückwechseln möchte, sind eher selten. In der deutschsprachigen Literatur zum CISG wird dem Verkäufer ein solches Recht, nach Erklärung der Vertragsaufhebung zurück zur Vertragserfüllung zu wechseln, übereinstimmend abgesprochen, weil die Vertragsaufhebung als die **Ausübung eines Gestaltungsrechts** angesehen wird, mit der rechtlichen Konsequenz, dass das ursprüngliche Vertragsverhältnis in ein Rückabwicklungsverhältnis überführt wird. Der Zweck dieser Ansicht ist der **Schutz des Käufers,** dem Sicherheit bezüglich des weiteren Ablaufs gegeben werden soll. Nach hier vertretener Auffassung müssen verschiedene Situationen unterschieden werden. Zunächst kann der Verkäufer seine Vertragsaufhebungserklärung solange zurücknehmen, bis sie dem Käufer zugegangen ist. Selbst nach Zugang der Vertragsaufhebungserklärung ist der Käufer solange nicht schutzbedürftig, so lange er noch nicht mit der Erfüllung seiner Rückabwicklungspflichten begonnen hat, insbesondere mit dem Rücktransport der Ware an den Verkäufer. Daher muss es dem Verkäufer möglich sein, solange zur Vertragserfüllung zurückzukehren, solange der Käufer noch nicht im Vertrauen auf die Vertragsaufhebungserklärung gehandelt hat. Dieser Ansatz entspricht dem anglo-amerikanischen Konzept des *estoppel*. Sobald der Verkäufer hingegen begonnen hat, seine Rückabwicklungspflichten zu erfüllen, ist der Verkäufer an seine Entscheidung, den Vertrag aufzuheben, gebunden.

Solange der Verkäufer auf beide Rechtsbehelfe zurückgreifen und zwischen Vertragserfüllung und Vertragsaufhebung wählen kann, besteht für den Verkäufer die Möglichkeit, über die **Entwicklung des Marktpreises** für die verkaufte Ware zulasten des Käufers **zu spekulieren.** Dies liegt vor allem daran, dass der Verkäufer seinen Schadenersatz als Differenz zwischen dem Markt- und dem Vertragspreis gemäss Art. 76 berechnen kann und Art. 76 auf den Zeitpunkt der Vertragsaufhebung als für die Berechnung dieser Differenz massgebenden Zeitpunkt hinweist. Art. 76 I 2, wonach der Marktpreis zur Zeit der Übernahme der Ware und nicht der Marktpreis zur Zeit der Aufhebung gilt, wenn die Partei, die Schadenersatz verlangt, den Vertrag aufgehoben hat, nachdem sie die Ware übernommen hat, schützt nicht den Käufer vor möglichen Spekulationen des Verkäufers, sondern nur den Verkäufer vor Spekulationen des Käufers.[111] Dies liegt daran, dass der Käufer die einzige Partei ist, die die Ware nach dem Vertragsprogramm übernimmt.[112] Auch Art. 88 II, dem zufolge die Partei, der nach Art. 85 oder Art. 86 die Erhaltung der Ware obliegt, sich in angemessener Weise um ihren Verkauf zu bemühen hat, wenn die Ware einer raschen Verschlechterung ausgesetzt ist oder ihre Erhaltung unverhältnismässige Kosten verursacht, schützt nicht den Käufer vor Spekulationen des Verkäufers. Dies vor allem deshalb, weil Verschlechterung nicht fallende Preise umfasst.[113] Dieses Verständnis wird durch die Entstehungsgeschichte des Übereinkommens gestützt, da eine vorherige Version, die noch von

---

[110] Vgl. oben Art. 62 Rn. 16.
[111] So auch *Ferrari u. a./Mankowski,* Internationales Vertragsrecht, Art. 64, Rn. 24.
[112] *Hager/Maultzsch,* 5. Aufl., Art. 64 Rn. 25; O. R., S. 222, Nr. 38–50. A. A. *Honnold/Flechtner,* Art. 76, Rn. 412, die mögliche Anwendungsfälle von Art. 76 I 2 für den Fall einer durch den Verkäufer erklärten Vertragsaufhebung diskutieren.
[113] Vgl. OLG Braunschweig, 28.10.1999, CISG-online 510 = CLOUT Nr. 361, E. 3. a): ein nach den Weihnachtsfeiertagen zu erwartender Preisrückgang bei Wildfleisch keine Verschlechterung i. d. S.; *Hager/Maultzsch,* 5. Aufl., Art. 64 Rn. 26; auch *Ferrari u. a./Mankowski,* Internationales Vertragsrecht, Art. 64, Rn. 24.

„*loss or rapid deterioration*"[114] (Verlust oder rasche Verschlechterung) sprach und unter *loss* (Verlust) auch fallende Preise verstand,[115] in die jetzige Version überführt und dabei die Fallgruppe des Verlusts ausdrücklich fallen gelassen wurde.[116] Die einzige Möglichkeit, den Käufer zu schützen, besteht darin, Art. 77 auf den Erfüllungsanspruch des Verkäufers anzuwenden und den Verkäufer so anzuhalten, den Vertrag aufgrund seiner **Obliegenheit zur Schadensminderung** zu einem möglichst frühen Zeitpunkt aufzuheben, wenn die Marktpreise augenfällig fallen.[117] Ansonsten kann der Käufer nur dadurch geschützt werden, dass die Ausübung des Erfüllungsanspruchs in Extremfällen Art. 7 I verletzt.[118] Auch internationale Handelsgebräuche (Art. 9) können den Verkäufer zur sofortigen Vertragsaufhebung und zum Abschluss eines Deckungsverkaufs verpflichten.[119] Schliesslich findet Art. 77 spätestens dann Anwendung und verpflichtet den Verkäufer zum Abschluss eines Deckungsverkaufs, wenn das Recht des Verkäufers, den Käufer zur Vertragserfüllung zu zwingen, nach nationalem Recht ausgeschlossen ist, das wiederum gemäss Art. 28 auf diese Frage Anwendung findet.[120]

VI. Beweislast

38   Der **Verkäufer** trägt die Beweislast für den **Bestand** und den **Inhalt der Pflicht des Käufers,** die verletzt worden ist und die Grundlage der Vertragsaufhebung bildet. Im Falle von Art. 64 I lit. a) muss der Verkäufer darüber hinaus beweisen, dass der Käufer einen **wesentlichen Vertragsbruch** begangen hat. In den Fällen des Art. 64 I lit. b) muss der Verkäufer beweisen, dass der Käufer einen Vertragsbruch begangen hat, und dass er dem Käufer eine **angemessene Nachfrist** zur Erfüllung angesetzt hat, der Käufer aber innerhalb dieser Nachfrist nicht erfüllt bzw. erklärt hat, dass er innerhalb dieser Frist nicht erfüllen wird.[121] Des Weiteren muss der Verkäufer beweisen, dass er dem Käufer durch Erklärung mitgeteilt hat, dass er den Vertrag aufhebe, und dass seine **Vertragsaufhebungserklärung** zumindest abgegeben wurde.[122]

39   Der **Käufer** trägt die Beweislast für sämtliche Umstände, die für die Anwendung einer **zeitlichen Begrenzung des Vertragsaufhebungsrechts** des Verkäufers nach Art. 64 II nötig sind. Im Falle von Art. 64 II lit. a) muss der Käufer zeigen, dass er den Vertrag erfüllt und dem Verkäufer die Erfüllung angezeigt hat. Im Falle von Art. 64 II lit. b) muss der Käufer beweisen, dass der Verkäufer den Vertrag nicht innerhalb einer angemessenen Zeit aufgehoben hat, nachdem er von der Vertragsverletzung erfahren hat, nachdem eine vom Verkäufer nach Art. 63 I gesetzte Nachfrist abgelaufen ist oder nachdem der Käufer erklärt hat, dass er seine Pflicht nicht innerhalb der Nachfrist erfüllen wird.

40   Der **Käufer** trägt die Beweislast dafür, dass er mit der Vertragserfüllung begonnen hat, um den Verkäufer von einem Wechsel von Vertragserfüllung zu Vertragsaufhebung abzuhalten. Versucht der Verkäufer seine Vertragsaufhebung zurückzunehmen und zur Vertragserfüllung zurückzukehren, muss der Käufer beweisen, dass er bereits mit der Erfüllung seiner Rückabwicklungspflichten begonnen hat, wodurch dem Verkäufer dieser Wechsel der Rechtsbehelfe nicht möglich wäre. Der Käufer trägt die Beweislast dafür, dass der Verkäufer durch seine Obliegenheit zur Schadensminderung angehalten war, einen Deckungsverkauf vorzunehmen, bevor er den Vertrag als aufgehoben erklärt hat.

---

[114] Art. 77 II des New Yorker Entwurfs.
[115] Sekretariatskommentar, Art. 77, Nr. 6.
[116] O. R., S. 227, 228, Nr. 39–53.
[117] *Schlechtriem*, 18 Israel L. Rev. (1983), 309, 322; unten *Schwenzer*, Art. 77 Rn. 10; ähnlich *Ferrari u. a. / Mankowski*, Internationales Vertragsrecht, Art. 64, Rn. 25 .
[118] *Hager/Maultzsch*, 5. Aufl., Art. 64 Rn. 27.
[119] Schiedsgericht des Vereins der am Kaffeehandel beteiligten Firmen, 9.11.1973/17.12.1973, HSG J 5A, Nr. 43.
[120] Vgl. oben Art. 62 Rn. 16.
[121] Vgl. *Staudinger/Magnus*, Art. 64, Rn. 52; *Achilles*, Art. 64, Rn. 15; *Bamberger/Roth/Saenger*, Art. 64, Rn. 11; *Baumgärtel/Laumen/Hepting*, Art. 64, Rn. 1.
[122] Vgl. Art. 26 und Art. 27.

Art. 65 [Spezifizierung durch den Verkäufer]

(1) Hat der Käufer nach dem Vertrag die Form, die Maße oder andere Merkmale der Ware näher zu bestimmen* und nimmt er diese Spezifizierung nicht zu dem vereinbarten Zeitpunkt oder innerhalb einer angemessenen Frist nach Eingang einer Aufforderung durch den Verkäufer vor, so kann der Verkäufer unbeschadet aller ihm zustehenden sonstigen Rechte die Spezifizierung nach den Bedürfnissen des Käufers, soweit ihm diese bekannt sind, selbst vornehmen.

(2) Nimmt der Verkäufer die Spezifizierung selbst vor, so hat er dem Käufer deren Einzelheiten mitzuteilen und ihm eine angemessene Frist zu setzen, innerhalb deren der Käufer eine abweichende Spezifizierung vornehmen kann. Macht der Käufer nach Eingang einer solchen Mitteilung von dieser Möglichkeit innerhalb der so gesetzten Frist keinen Gebrauch, so ist die vom Verkäufer vorgenommene Spezifizierung verbindlich.

Art. 65

(1) If under the contract the buyer is to specify the form, measurement or other features of the goods and he fails to make such specification either on the date agreed upon or within a reasonable time after receipt of a request from the seller, the seller may, without prejudice to any other rights he may have, make the specification himself in accordance with the requirements of the buyer that may be known to him.

(2) If the seller makes the specification himself, he must inform the buyer of the details thereof and must fix a reasonable time within which the buyer may make a different specification. If, after receipt of such a communication, the buyer fails to do so within the time so fixed, the specification made by the seller is binding.

Art. 65

1) Si le contrat prévoit que l'acheteur doit spécifier la forme, la mesure ou d'autres caractéristiques des marchandises et si l'acheteur n'effectue pas cette spécification à la date convenue ou dans un délai raisonnable à compter de la réception d'une demande du vendeur, celui-ci peut, sans préjudice de tous autres droits qu'il peut avoir, effectuer lui-même cette spécification d'après les besoins de l'acheteur dont il peut avoir connaissance.

2) Si le vendeur effectue lui-même la spécification, il doit en faire connaître les modalités à l'acheteur et lui impartir un délai raisonnable pour une spécification différente. Si, après réception de la communication du vendeur, l'acheteur n'utilise pas cette possibilité dans le délai ainsi imparti, la spécification effectuée par le vendeur est définitive.

Übersicht

	Rn.
I. Regelungsgegenstand	1
II. Voraussetzungen des Selbstspezifikationsrechts des Verkäufers	4
1. Vertrag verlangt Spezifizierung der Ware durch den Käufer	4
2. Die Nichtausübung der Spezifizierung durch den Käufer	5
a) Vereinbarter Zeitpunkt	6
b) Die Aufforderung des Verkäufers an den Käufer, eine Spezifizierung vorzunehmen	7
III. Selbstvornahme der Spezifikation durch den Verkäufer	9
1. Die Mitteilung der Selbstspezifikation durch den Verkäufer	9
a) Bedürfnisse des Käufers, die dem Verkäufer bekannt sind	10
b) Information des Käufers über die Selbstspezifikation und ihre Einzelheiten	11
c) Angemessene Frist für den Käufer zur Vornahme einer abweichenden Spezifizierung	12
d) Rechtliche Konsequenzen	14
2. Die abweichende Spezifizierung des Käufers	15
3. Verbleibende Risiken für den Verkäufer	16

---

* Schweiz: zu spezifizieren.

IV. Mögliche Beschränkungen des Selbstspezifikationsrechts des Verkäufers	18
1. Anwendbarkeit von Art. 28	18
2. Anwendbarkeit von Art. 77	19
V. Die allgemeinen Rechtsbehelfe des Verkäufers	20
VI. Das allgemeine Prinzip hinter Art. 65 und mögliche Anwendungsfälle	24
VII. Beweislast	25

Vorläufer und **Entwürfe:** Art. 67 EKG; Genfer E 1976 Art. 46; Wiener E 1977 Art. 47; New Yorker E 1978 Art. 61.

I. Regelungsgegenstand

1   Art. 65 beschreibt einen besonderen Rechtsbehelf des Verkäufers, der nur dann zur Anwendung kommt, wenn der Käufer nach dem Vertrag die Ware zu einem späteren Zeitpunkt spezifizieren muss, er diese Spezifizierung aber tatsächlich nicht vornimmt. Die Bedeutung des Art. 65 liegt zunächst darin, dass **trotz mangelnder Bestimmtheit des Kaufgegenstandes ein wirksamer Vertrag** vorliegt, wenn einer Vertragspartei vertraglich das Recht gegeben wurde, die zu liefernde Ware zu spezifizieren. Ein solcher Vertrag erfüllt die Anforderungen des Art. 14 an einen genügend bestimmten Vertrag, der die Ware bezeichnet.[1] In der Praxis räumt das **Selbstspezifikationsrecht** nach Art. 65 dem Verkäufer die Möglichkeit ein, vom Käufer **Vertragserfüllung** zu verlangen, also Zahlung und Abnahme der vom Verkäufer spezifizierten Ware. Auch ermöglicht das Selbstspezifikationsrecht nach Art. 65 dem Verkäufer, seinen **Schadenersatzanspruch** gegen den Käufer wegen dessen Vertragsverletzung zu berechnen.[2] Da die Verpflichtung des Käufers, die Form, die Masse oder andere Merkmale der Ware näher zu bestimmen, Teil seiner vertraglichen Pflicht zur Abnahme gemäss Art. 60 lit. a) darstellt, ist der Verkäufer aber auch berechtigt, **jeden anderen Rechtsbehelf** nach Art. 61 auszuüben.[3]

2   Art. 65 behandelt einen besonderen Fall eines vertraglichen Rechts einer der Parteien zur einseitigen Bestimmung des Inhalts eines abgeschlossenen Vertrags. Seine **Entstehungsgeschichte** kann über Art. 67 EKG bis hin zu § 375 HGB zurückverfolgt werden.[4] Ein solches Spezifikationsrecht ist auch anderen Ländern bekannt, wie z. B. Finnland, den Niederlanden, Norwegen, Polen, Slowenien, Schweden, Österreich, Tschechien und der Slowakei.[5] Historisch betrachtet waren solche Selbstspezifikationsrechte den Rechtsordnungen des Common Law unbekannt,[6] da die Nichtvornahme einer Spezifikation als Nichtabnahme gewertet wurde, die wiederum mit Schadenersatz beschwert war. Hingegen kennt der US-amerikanische UCC einen solchen besonderen Rechtsbehelf, in dem § 2–311 (3) (b) UCC der vertragstreuen Partei das Recht gibt, den Vertrag in angemessener Weise zu erfüllen, wenn eine Spezifizierung die Leistung der vertragstreuen Partei wesentlich beeinträchtigt und nicht innerhalb angemessener Zeit vorgenommen wurde. Auch **andere einheitsrechtliche Instrumente** sehen ähnliche Lösungen vor, so z. B. Art. 3:002 des europäischen einheitlichen Referenzrahmens,[7] der eine wortgleiche Übernahme von Art. 65 darstellt. Die PECL enthalten keine besondere Vorschrift zum Selbstspezifikationsrecht und behandeln solche Fallkonstellationen unter der allgemeinen Vorschrift des Art. 7:105 über

---

[1] Vgl. CIETAC, 23.4.1997, CISG-online 1151; LG Aachen, 19.4.1996, CISG-online 165 (obiter); Sekretariatskommentar, Art. 61, Nr. 4; oben *Schroeter*, Art. 14 Rn. 3; *Hager/Maultzsch*, 5. Aufl., Art. 65 Rn. 2; *Bamberger/Roth/Saenger*, Art. 65, Rn. 1; *Honsell/Schnyder/Straub*, Art. 65, Rn. 2.
[2] *Hager/Maultzsch*, 5. Aufl., Art. 65 Rn. 2; *Honnold/Flechtner*, Art. 65, Rn. 357; *Honsell/Schnyder/Straub*, Art. 65, Rn. 4.
[3] Vgl. unten Rn. 20 ff.; *Hager/Maultzsch*, 5. Aufl., Art. 65 Rn. 8; *Schlechtriem/P. Butler*, UN Law, Rn. 252; *Schlechtriem*, Internationales UN-Kaufrecht, Rn. 252.
[4] *Hager/Maultzsch*, 5. Aufl., Art. 65 Rn. 1; *Dölle/von Caemmerer*, Art. 67 EKG, Rn. 1.
[5] *Hondius/Heutger/Jeloschek/Sivesand/Wiewiorowska*, Principles of European Law: Sales, Art. 3:002, Anm. 1.
[6] *Dölle/von Caemmerer*, Art. 77 EKG, Rn. 5.
[7] *Hondius/Heutger/Jeloschek/Sivesand/Wiewiorowska*, Principles of European Law: Sales, Art. 3:001.

alternative Leistungen.[8] Die PICC geben der vertragstreuen Partei kein Selbstspezifikationsrecht, sondern lösen das Problem dahingehend, dass der Schuldner einen angemessenen oder vernünftigen Vertragsgegenstand liefern muss, eine dem US-amerikanischen UCC entsprechende Lösung.[9]

Warenkaufverträge, welche die nähere Bestimmung der Ware zunächst offen lassen, finden 3 sich in der Praxis vor allem im Rohwarenhandel, im Handel mit Halbfertigprodukten, Metallen, Papier, Holz und Textilien.[10]

II. Voraussetzungen des Selbstspezifikationsrechts des Verkäufers

1. Vertrag verlangt Spezifizierung der Ware durch den Käufer

Art. 65 verlangt zunächst, dass der Vertrag den **Käufer verpflichtet,** die Form, die Masse 4 oder andere Merkmale der Ware näher zu bestimmen. Freilich kann Art. 65 auch dann angewendet werden, wenn der Vertrag den Käufer zur Spezifizierung nicht verpflichtet, aber **berechtigt,** sofern die Spezifizierung für die Erfüllung des Verkäufers Voraussetzung ist.[11] Darüber hinaus kann Art. 65 auch dann angewendet werden, wenn der Vertrag den Käufer zur einseitigen Spezifizierung weder verpflichtet noch berechtigt, sondern die Spezifizierung **beiden Parteien** durch nachträgliche Vereinbarung auferlegt und die Parteien sich später nicht einigen können.[12] Wenn ein Vertrag andererseits die Form, die Masse oder andere Merkmale der Ware selbst bestimmt und dem Käufer nur ein Recht zur Änderung dieser Bestimmungen einräumt, so kann Art. 65 nicht angewendet werden, wenn der Käufer sein **Optionsrecht** nicht ausübt; vielmehr gelten die ursprünglichen Bestimmungen des Vertrags.[13] Bei einem **Wahlrecht** zwischen verschiedenen Spezifizierungen kann hingegen wiederum Art. 65 angewendet werden.[14]

2. Die Nichtausübung der Spezifizierung durch den Käufer

Die zweite Voraussetzung von Art. 65 ist, dass der Käufer die Spezifizierung nicht zu dem 5 vereinbarten Zeitpunkt oder nicht innerhalb einer angemessenen Frist nach Eingang einer Aufforderung des Verkäufers vornimmt.

a) Vereinbarter Zeitpunkt. Die Parteien können **in ihrem Vertrag** einen Zeitpunkt 6 vereinbaren, zu dem der Käufer die Form, die Masse oder andere Merkmale der Ware zu bestimmen hat. In einem solchen Fall steht dem Verkäufer das Selbstspezifikationsrecht nach Art. 65 sofort nach Ablauf dieses vereinbarten Zeitpunkts zu, ohne dass es einer Aufforderung oder einer anderen Formalität bedürfte. Die Härte dieser Regelung wird durch Art. 65 II abgefangen, wonach der Käufer die Möglichkeit hat, eine abweichende Spezifizierung nach Eingang der Mitteilung des Verkäufers von den Einzelheiten der Spezifizierung durch den Verkäufer vorzunehmen.

b) Die Aufforderung des Verkäufers an den Käufer, eine Spezifizierung vor- 7 **zunehmen.** Haben die Parteien im Vertrag keinen Zeitpunkt vorgesehen, zu dem der Käufer die Spezifizierung vornehmen muss, so hat der Verkäufer den Käufer **aufzufordern,**

---

[8] *Charters,* Specifications and the Contractual Relationship, S. 456, 458 ff.
[9] Vgl. Artt. 2.1.14, 4.8, 5.1.6 PECL.
[10] Vgl. *Dölle/von Caemmerer,* Art. 67 EKG, Rn. 2.
[11] *Hager/Maultzsch,* 5. Aufl., Art. 65 Rn. 4a; *Achilles,* Art. 65, Rn. 1; *Bamberger/Roth/Saenger,* Art. 65, Rn. 2; *Witz/Salger/Lorenz/Witz,* Art. 65, Rn. 2. A. A. *Herber/Czerwenka,* Art. 65, Rn. 7; *Honsell/Schnyder/Straub,* Art. 65, Rn. 11; *Ferrari u. a./Mankowski,* Internationales Vertragsrecht, Art. 65, Rn. 8.
[12] Vgl. CIETAC, 23.4.1997, CISG-online 1151.
[13] *Hager/Maultzsch,* 5. Aufl., Art. 65 Rn. 4a; *Enderlein/Maskow/Strohbach,* Art. 65, Anm. 2.; *Kröll u. a./Bell,* Art. 65, Rn. 3; *Honsell/Schnyder/Straub,* Art. 65, Rn. 11; *Ferrari u. a./Mankowski,* Internationales Vertragsrecht, Art. 65, Rn. 8.
[14] *Honsell/Schnyder/Straub,* Art. 65, Rn. 13.

die Spezifizierung vorzunehmen. Der Verkäufer kann dem Käufer zur Vornahme der Spezifizierung eine **angemessene Frist** setzen, er ist dazu aber **nicht verpflichtet**. Wenn der Verkäufer den Käufer zur Spezifizierung auffordert, ohne ihm eine angemessene Frist zu setzen, beginnt gemäss Art. 65 eine angemessene Zeit **automatisch** zu laufen.[15] Dies ergibt sich daraus, dass das CISG zwischen der Aufforderung des Verkäufers, eine Spezifizierung nach Art. 65 vorzunehmen, und dem Recht des Verkäufers, dem Käufer gemäss Art. 63 eine angemessene Nachfrist zur Erfüllung zu setzen, unterscheidet.[16] Der nutzlose Ablauf einer angemessenen Frist nach Art. 65 führt nicht zur Anwendung von Art. 64 I lit. b) und berechtigt den Verkäufer nicht zur Vertragsaufhebung, sollte der Käufer die Spezifizierung innerhalb der angemessenen Frist nicht vornehmen. Um zur Vertragsaufhebung berechtigt zu sein, muss der Verkäufer vielmehr eine angemessene Nachfrist zur Erfüllung nach Art. 63 setzen.

8 Die Aufforderung des Verkäufers an den Käufer, die Spezifizierung vorzunehmen, muss dem Käufer **zugehen**, um wirksam zu werden. Dies folgt aus dem Wortlaut („nach Eingang") und ist eine ausdrückliche Abweichung von Art. 27.[17] Wenn der Käufer der Aufforderung Folge leistet und die Spezifizierung innerhalb einer angemessenen Zeit vornimmt, so bindet diese Spezifizierung beide Parteien und bestimmt den vertraglichen Standard für die Vertragsmässigkeit der Ware nach Art. 35.[18] Das Risiko des Verlusts oder der Verzögerung der Spezifizierung durch den Käufer bestimmt sich nach Art. 27.[19] Der Käufer wird an seine Spezifizierung gebunden, sobald der Verkäufer die Mitteilung der Spezifizierung erhalten und im Vertrauen darauf gehandelt hat. In Übereinstimmung mit allgemeinen Prinzipien des Übereinkommens betreffend die Wirksamkeit von Erklärungen nach Art. 7 II kann der Käufer seine Spezifizierung zurücknehmen, solange der Verkäufer sie noch nicht erhalten hat, und widerrufen, solange der Verkäufer noch nicht im Vertrauen darauf Dispositionen getroffen hat.[20] Nimmt der Käufer keine Spezifizierung innerhalb einer angemessenen Frist nach Art. 65 vor, so ist der Verkäufer gemäss Art. 65 I berechtigt, die Spezifizierung selbst vorzunehmen. Dennoch muss eine verspätete Spezifizierung des Käufers als Reaktion unter Art. 65 II angesehen werden, also als eine **abweichende Spezifizierung** des Käufers, welche der Spezifizierung des Verkäufers vorgeht.[21]

III. Selbstvornahme der Spezifikation durch den Verkäufer

1. Die Mitteilung der Selbstspezifikation durch den Verkäufer

9 Der Verkäufer muss sein **Selbstspezifikationsrecht** durch **Mitteilung** an den Käufer ausüben. An eine solche Mitteilung sind drei Anforderungen zu stellen: Die Selbstspezifikation muss sich nach den Bedürfnissen des Käufers richten, soweit diese dem Verkäufer bekannt sind, der Verkäufer muss den Käufer über die Einzelheiten der Selbstspezifikation unterrichten und der Verkäufer muss dem Käufer eine angemessene Frist setzen, innerhalb derer der Käufer eine abweichende Spezifizierung vornehmen kann.[22]

10 **a) Bedürfnisse des Käufers, die dem Verkäufer bekannt sind.** Die erste Anforderung an die Selbstspezifikation des Verkäufers ist, dass sie sich nach den **Bedürfnissen des**

---

[15] A. A. *Dölle/von Caemmerer*, Art. 67 EKG, Rn. 12, bezgl. Art. 67 EKG.
[16] Sekretariatskommentar, Art. 61, Nr. 7 Fn. 2; *Hager/Maultzsch*, 5. Aufl., Art. 65 Rn. 5; *Bamberger/Roth/Saenger*, Art. 65, Rn. 3; *Herber/Czerwenka*, Art. 65, Rn. 4; *Honsell/Schnyder/Straub*, Art. 65, Rn. 21.
[17] *Honsell/Schnyder/Straub*, Art. 65, Rn. 22; *Ferrari u. a./Mankowski*, Internationales Vertragsrecht, Art. 65, Rn. 11.
[18] Vgl. oben *Schwenzer*, Art. 35 Rn. 6 ff.
[19] *Hager/Maultzsch*, 5. Aufl., Art. 65 Rn. 5.
[20] Vgl. oben *Schroeter*, Art. 27 Rn. 14; *Hager/Maultzsch*, 5. Aufl., Art. 65 Rn. 5.
[21] *Hager/Maultzsch*, 5. Aufl., Art. 65 Rn. 5; *Lohs/Nolting*, ZVerglRW 1998, 4, 23.
[22] Sekretariatskommentar, Art. 60, Nr. 8; LG Aachen, 9.4.1996, CISG-online 165.

Käufers zu richten hat, die der Verkäufer kennen konnte.[23] In dieser Hinsicht sind sämtliche Umstände des Einzelfalls zu berücksichtigen, einschliesslich der Verhandlungen, der zwischen den Parteien entstandenen Gepflogenheiten sowie allfällige Handelsbräuche. Wenn z. B. die Qualität eines Rohstoffes zu spezifizieren war, muss der Verkäufer Aussagen des Käufers berücksichtigen, die zwar selbst keine Spezifizierung darstellten, aus denen aber hervorgeht, dass bestimmte Qualitäten von vornherein ausgeschlossen sein sollten, weil sie z. B. zu viel Prozent eines bestimmten chemischen Elements beinhalteten und vom Käufer daher nicht verarbeitet werden konnten. Nimmt der Käufer seine Spezifizierung zu spät, also nach dem vereinbarten Termin oder nach Ablauf einer angemessenen Frist gemäss Art. 65 I vor, so kann seine **verspätete Spezifizierung** immer noch als Umstand herangezogen werden, von dem der Verkäufer Kenntnis hatte.[24]

b) Information des Käufers über die Selbstspezifikation und ihre Einzelheiten. 11
Die zweite Anforderung an die Mitteilung des Verkäufers ist, dass der Verkäufer dem Käufer **die Spezifizierung und deren Einzelheiten** mitzuteilen hat. Die blosse Mitteilung, dass der Verkäufer eine Selbstspezifikation vorgenommen hat, ist unzureichend. Der Grund dafür liegt darin, dass die Spezifizierung den vertraglichen Standard der Vertragsmässigkeit der Ware festlegt, den der Käufer vor Lieferung kennen muss.

c) Angemessene Frist für den Käufer zur Vornahme einer abweichenden Spezi- 12
fizierung. Abweichend von den Anforderungen an die erste Aufforderung des Verkäufers nach Art. 65 I **muss** der Verkäufer dem Käufer eine **angemessene Frist** zur Vornahme einer abweichenden Spezifizierung nach Art. 65 II setzen. Die Angemessenheit der Frist kann nur unter Berücksichtigung sämtlicher Umstände des Einzelfalles beurteilt werden. Jedenfalls muss die Frist genügend Zeit für den Käufer beinhalten, damit er eine Entscheidung treffen und dem Verkäufer die abweichende Spezifizierung mitteilen kann. Andererseits kann die Frist so kurz bemessen sein, dass sie vom Käufer eine zügige Reaktion erfordert.

Die Gegenansicht, nach der auch gemäss Art. 65 II eine angemessene Frist **automatisch** 13
zu laufen beginnt, wenn der Verkäufer keine Frist ansetzt, ist zurückzuweisen.[25] Hat der Verkäufer hingegen eine Nachfrist angesetzt, diese aber **zu kurz bemessen,** so beginnt eine **angemessene Frist** zu laufen.[26]

d) Rechtliche Konsequenzen. Erfüllt die Mitteilung des Verkäufers eine der drei 14
genannten Anforderungen an seine Selbstspezifikation nicht, so ist der Käufer an eine solche Selbstspezifikation des Verkäufers **nicht gebunden.**[27] Freilich wird man vom Käufer in Anwendung der **allgemeinen Kooperationspflicht** verlangen können, dass dieser auf eine Selbstspezifikation des Verkäufers reagiert und eine seines Erachtens ungültige Spezifikation zurückweist, insbesondere wenn sie inhaltlich nicht seinen Bedürfnissen entspricht.[28] Hat der Verkäufer eine Selbstspezifikation in Übereinstimmung mit den drei Anforderungen vorgenommen, kommt aber seine Mitteilung beim Käufer nicht an, so ist die Selbstspezifikation unwirksam, weil Art. 65 II den Zugang der Mitteilung beim Käufer voraus-

---

[23] Der deutsche Text muss vor dem Hintergrund der Originaltexte (z. B. engl.: *„requirements of the buyer that may be known to him")* korrigiert und weiter ausgelegt werden, vgl. *Hager/Maultzsch,* 5. Aufl., Art. 65 Rn. 6; *Honsell/Schnyder/Straub,* Art. 65, Rn. 27; *Ferrari u. a./Mankowski,* Internationales Vertragsrecht, Art. 65, Rn. 3.

[24] Zieht der Verkäufer die verspätete Spezifizierung des Käufers nicht in Betracht, kann diese als Reaktion des Käufers gemäss Art. 65 II berücksichtigt werden.

[25] *Hager/Maultzsch,* 5. Aufl., Art. 65 Rn. 6; MünchKommHGB/*Benicke,* Art. 65, Rn. 8; *Honsell/Schnyder/ Straub,* Art. 65, Rn. 33. A. A. *Staudinger/Magnus,* Art. 65, Rn. 15; *Ferrari u. a./Mankowski,* Internationales Vertragsrecht, Art. 65, Rn. 24.

[26] Ähnlich wie bei der durch den Verkäufer gesetzten angemessene Nachfrist zur Erfüllung nach Art. 63, vgl. oben Art. 63 Rn. 9; *Ferrari u. a./Mankowski,* Internationales Vertragsrecht, Art. 65, Rn. 24. A. A. *Honsell/ Schnyder/Straub,* Art. 65, Rn. 33.

[27] LG Aachen, 19.4.1996, CISG-online 165; *Hager/Maultzsch,* 5. Aufl., Art. 65 Rn. 6; *Staudinger/Magnus,* Art. 65, Rn. 17.

[28] *Hager/Maultzsch,* 5. Aufl., Art. 65 Rn. 6; *Ferrari u. a./Mankowski,* Internationales Vertragsrecht, Art. 65, Rn. 19. A. A. *Soergel/Lüderitz/Budzikiewicz,* Art. 65, Rn. 7; *Honsell/Schnyder/Straub,* Art. 65, Rn. 43.

setzt.[29] Die Mitteilung des Verkäufers reist in Abweichung von Art. 27 auf das Risiko des Verkäufers.[30] Dies ergibt sich daraus, dass eine solche Spezifikation ihrer Rechtsnatur nach als eine den Vertragsschluss betreffende Mitteilung anzusehen ist.[31] Hat der Verkäufer die Selbstspezifikation in Übereinstimmung mit den drei Anforderungen vorgenommen und ist seine Mitteilung dem Käufer zugegangen, so bindet die Selbstspezifikation beide Parteien und beschreibt den **Vertragsinhalt** in Bezug auf die **Vertragsmässigkeit der Ware,** es sei denn, der Käufer nimmt eine abweichende Spezifizierung nach Art. 65 II vor.

2. Die abweichende Spezifizierung des Käufers

15   Versäumt es der Käufer, auf eine wirksame Selbstspezifikation des Verkäufers zu reagieren, so wird die **Selbstspezifikation** des Verkäufers für beide Parteien **bindend.** Dieselbe Konsequenz tritt ein, wenn der Käufer die Selbstspezifikation des Verkäufers zwar zurückweist, es aber unterlässt, eine abweichende Spezifizierung vorzunehmen.[32] Dies ergibt sich aus dem Umstand, dass Art. 65 II vom Käufer verlangt, dass dieser eine **abweichende Spezifikation** vornimmt. Nimmt der Käufer aber eine abweichende Spezifizierung vor, so bindet diese beide Parteien und bestimmt den Vertragsinhalt in Bezug auf die Vertragsmässigkeit der Ware. Verlust und Verzögerung des Zugangs der abweichenden Spezifizierung des Käufers sind Risiken, die der Verkäufer in Übereinstimmung mit Art. 27 trägt.[33] Diese Risikoverteilung verletzt zwar das Prinzip, dass Mitteilungen, die Pflichten für den Empfänger begründen, erst wirksam werden, wenn sie dem Empfänger zugegangen sind, entspricht aber dem klaren Wortlaut von Art. 27, der Entstehungsgeschichte des Übereinkommens[34] und dem Zweck von Art. 65, der darin besteht, die Möglichkeiten des Verkäufers zur Selbstspezifikation möglichst zu beschränken.[35]

3. Verbleibende Risiken für den Verkäufer

16   Das Verfahren der Selbstspezifikation ist für den Verkäufer nicht ohne Risiken.[36] Geht eine vom Verkäufer abgesandte Spezifizierungsmitteilung beim Käufer nicht ein oder ist sie aus einem anderen Grund unverbindlich oder erhält der Verkäufer eine vom Käufer nach Aufforderung ordnungsgemäss abgesandte und damit verbindliche, abweichende Spezifizierung nicht, so kann es passieren, dass der Verkäufer **entsprechend seiner nichtverbindlichen Selbstspezifikation liefert oder produziert.** Dem Käufer stehen in einem solchen Fall sämtliche Rechtsbehelfe wegen Vertragswidrigkeit der Ware zu. Unter besonderen Umständen wird es dem Verkäufer möglich sein, Art. 79 oder Art. 80 einzuwenden und so von seiner Haftung befreit zu werden.[37]

17   Lehnt der Käufer jede Spezifikation ab und weist er auch die vom Verkäufer vorgenommene Spezifikation zurück, so stellt sich die Frage, ob der Verkäufer die Ware entsprechend seiner Spezifikation herstellen darf oder ob in einem solchen Vorgehen ein Verstoss gegen die **Schadensminderungspflicht** gemäss Art. 77 zu sehen ist.[38] Nach hier vertretener Auffassung kann Art. 77 auf den Kaufpreiszahlungsanspruch des Verkäufers oder seinen

---

[29] *Hager/Maultzsch,* 5. Aufl., Art. 65 Rn. 6.
[30] Sekretariatskommentar, Art. 61, Nr. 10; *Hager/Maultzsch,* 5. Aufl., Art. 65 Rn. 6; *Honsell/Schnyder/Straub,* Art. 65, Rn. 29.
[31] Vgl. oben *Schroeter,* Art. 24 Rn. 3.
[32] *Hager/Maultzsch,* 5. Aufl., Art. 65 Rn. 7; MünchKommHGB/*Benicke,* Art. 65, Rn. 9; *Staudinger/Magnus,* Art. 65, Rn. 16.
[33] *Hager/Maultzsch,* 5. Aufl., Art. 65 Rn. 7; *Karollus,* S. 183. A. A. *Herber/Czerwenka,* Art. 65, Rn. 6; *Lichtsteiner,* Convention, S. 257; MünchKomm/*P. Huber,* Art. 65, Rn. 10; *Noussias,* Zugangsbedürftigkeit von Mitteilungen, S. 127 ff.; *Staudinger/Magnus,* Art. 65, Rn. 7; *Honsell/Schnyder/Straub,* Art. 65, Rn. 39; *Ferrari u. a./Mankowski,* Internationales Vertragsrecht, Art. 65, Rn. 26.
[34] *Noussias,* Zugangsbedürftigkeit von Mitteilungen, S. 128 Fn. 6.
[35] *Hager/Maultzsch,* 5. Aufl., Art. 65 Rn. 7.
[36] So auch *Kröll u. a./Bell,* Art. 65, Rn. 9 ff.
[37] *Hager/Maultzsch,* 5. Aufl., Art. 65 Rn. 7a; *Enderlein/Maskow/Strohbach,* Art. 65, Anm. 11.2.
[38] Vgl. oben Art. 62 Rn. 16.

Anspruch auf Abnahme Anwendung finden.[39] In der Praxis wird der Verkäufer zur Vermeidung von Streitigkeiten freilich den Vertrag aufheben und Schadenersatz verlangen.

IV. Mögliche Beschränkungen des Selbstspezifikationsrechts des Verkäufers

1. Anwendbarkeit von Art. 28

Das Recht des Verkäufers auf Selbstspezifikation hat im Ergebnis ähnliche rechtliche Konsequenzen wie ein Erfüllungsanspruch auf Leistung in Natur. Dennoch findet Art. 28 **keine Anwendung** auf Art. 65.[40] Art. 65 gibt nämlich dem Verkäufer die Möglichkeit der Selbstvollstreckung, ohne dass er ein Gericht oder Schiedsgericht einschalten müsste, um zu einer Entscheidung auf Erfüllung in Natur zu gelangen.[41] Während der Ausarbeitung des EKG wurde ein besonderer Vorbehalt nationalen Rechts auch unter Zustimmung der Repräsentanten von Common Law Staaten zurückgewiesen.[42]

2. Anwendbarkeit von Art. 77

Durch sein Recht auf Selbstspezifikation kann der Verkäufer den Vertragsinhalt einseitig bestimmen. Es stellt sich die Frage, ob die **Schadensminderungspflicht** gemäss Art. 77 auf Art. 65 Anwendung findet. Nach hier vertretener Auffassung findet Art. 77 Anwendung, so dass der Verkäufer zur Schadensminderung und somit zum Produktions- oder Lieferstopp verpflichtet ist, wenn der Käufer endgültig und uneingeschränkt erklärt hat, dass er die Ware nicht abnehmen wird.[43] Auch stellt sich die Frage, ob der Verkäufer seine Schadensminderungspflicht verletzt, wenn er eine Selbstspezifikation der Ware unterlässt, obwohl er gemäss Art. 65 dazu berechtigt wäre. Nach hier vertretener Auffassung findet Art. 77 auch in einem solchen Fall Anwendung, da es unsinnig wäre, den Käufer zur Spezifizierung der Ware anzuhalten.[44] Die Gegenauffassung, der zufolge der Verkäufer den Käufer zur Spezifizierung anhalten kann, ist abzulehnen.[45]

V. Die allgemeinen Rechtsbehelfe des Verkäufers

Die Nichtvornahme einer Spezifizierung durch den Käufer stellt einen Vertragsbruch dar. Folglich ist der Verkäufer berechtigt, seine **allgemeinen Rechtsbehelfe** gemäss Art. 61 auszuüben. Folglich kann der Verkäufer den Käufer zur Spezifizierung gemäss Art. 62 anhalten.[46] Um die Sachlage zu klären, kann der Verkäufer dem Käufer eine angemessene Nachfrist zur Vornahme seiner Spezifizierung gemäss Art. 63 I ansetzen.

Nimmt der Käufer die Spezifizierung innerhalb der angemessen Nachfrist nicht vor, so kann der Verkäufer den **Vertrag** gemäss Art. 64 I lit. b) **aufheben,** weil die Pflicht zur Spezifizierung der Ware Teil der Pflicht des Käufers zur Abnahme der Ware ist.[47] Gemäss

---
[39] A. A. *Hager/Maultzsch,* 5. Aufl., Art. 65 Rn. 7a. Wie hier *Heuzé,* Anm. 331.
[40] *Scheiffele,* S. 147; *Dölle/von Caemmerer,* Art. 67 EKG, Rn. 7; *Hager,* Rechtsbehelfe des Verkäufers, S. 197 ff.
[41] *Hager/Maultzsch,* 5. Aufl., Art. 65 Rn. 3.
[42] Donaldson-Report, S. 51; *Dölle/von Caemmerer,* Art. 67 EKG, Rn. 7.
[43] Vgl. oben Rn. 17; Art. 62 Rn. 16; vgl. *Honnold/Flechtner,* Art. 65, Rn. 357. A. A. *Hager/Maultzsch,* 5. Aufl., Art. 65 Rn. 4, Art. 62 Rn. 14.
[44] *Herber/Czerwenka,* Art. 65, Rn. 7. A. A. *Honsell/Schnyder/Straub,* Art. 65, Rn. 56.
[45] A. A. *Hager/Maultzsch,* 5. Aufl., Art. 65 Rn. 4; *Achilles,* Art. 65, Rn. 1; *Witz/Salger/Lorenz/Witz,* Art. 65, Rn. 2.
[46] Freilich kann der Verkäufer nicht auf Erfüllung in Natur klagen, vgl. unten Rn. 23.
[47] Vgl. oben Art. 60 Rn. 8; *Hager/Maultzsch,* 5. Aufl., Art. 65 Rn. 8; MünchKomm/*P. Huber,* Art. 65, Rn. 11; *Witz/Salger/Lorenz/Witz,* Art. 65, Rn. 13; *Kröll u. a./Bell,* Art. 65, Rn. 10. A. A. *Bianca/Bonell/Knapp,* Art. 65, Anm. 2.6.; *Enderlein/Maskow/Strohbach,* Art. 65, Anm. 5.; *Herber/Czerwenka,* Art. 65, Rn. 7; *Honsell/Schnyder/Straub,* Art. 65, Rn. 55b.

Art. 63 II kann der Verkäufer vor Ablauf der Nachfrist den Vertrag nicht aufheben.[48] Das Gleiche gilt, wenn der Verkäufer den Käufer zur Spezifizierung nach Art. 65 I auffordert, wodurch eine angemessene Frist für den Käufer zur Vornahme der Spezifizierung zu laufen beginnt, oder wenn der Verkäufer eine Selbstspezifikation gemäss Art. 65 II vornimmt, die zugleich eine Ansetzung einer angemessenen Frist enthalten muss, innerhalb derer der Käufer eine abweichende Spezifizierung vornehmen kann.[49] Stellt die Nichtvornahme der Spezifizierung durch den Käufer einen wesentlichen Vertragsbruch dar, so hat der Verkäufer das Recht, den Vertrag gemäss Art. 64 I lit. a) sofort aufzuheben.[50]

22 Zusätzlich kann der Verkäufer **Schadenersatz** wegen verspäteter Erfüllung gemäss Art. 61 I lit. b) i. V. m. Art. 74 verlangen. Dieser Schadensersatzanspruch kann neben der Erfüllung geltend gemacht werden. Hat der Verkäufer den Vertrag aufgehoben, so kann er Schadenersatz wegen Nichterfüllung (statt der Leistung) verlangen.

23 Der Verkäufer kann den Käufer **nicht** auf **Erfüllung in Natur** verklagen, um ihn zur Vornahme einer Spezifizierung zu zwingen, weil einer solchen Klage Art. 65 im Wege steht, und zwar unabhängig vom Vorbehalt des Art. 28.[51]

VI. Das allgemeine Prinzip hinter Art. 65 und mögliche Anwendungsfälle

24 Art. 65 regelt ausdrücklich nur die Folgen einer unterbliebenen Spezifizierung der Form, der Masse oder anderer Merkmale der Ware. In der Literatur wird jedoch erwogen, ob Art. 65 ein **allgemeines Prinzip** des Übereinkommens gemäss Art. 7 II entnommen werden kann, dem zufolge die vertragstreue Partei anstelle der vertragsbrüchigen Partei handeln kann, wenn die Kooperation der vertragsbrüchigen Partei Voraussetzung für die Erfüllung durch die vertragstreue Partei ist. Beispielsweise wurde erwogen, ob der Verkäufer anstelle des Käufers das **Transportschiff nominieren** darf, wenn der Käufer dazu vertraglich verpflichtet ist, die Nominierung aber unterlässt.[52] Auch wurde vorgeschlagen, dass der Verkäufer zur Vornahme bestimmter **Inspektionen** anstelle des Käufers berechtigt sein soll, wenn der Käufer zur Vornahme von Inspektionen vertraglich verpflichtet ist, es aber unterlässt, diese innerhalb der bestimmten Zeit vorzunehmen.[53] Mögliche andere Anwendungsfälle könnten gegeben sein, wenn der Käufer es unterlässt, die **Lieferzeit** oder die **Menge** der zu liefernden Ware zu bestimmen.[54] Die Anerkennung eines solchen allgemeinen Prinzips und seine Anwendung auf die vorgeschlagenen Fallgruppen **ist zurückzuweisen**, da Art. 65 eine sehr spezifische Situation beschreibt und nicht unbesehen auf andere Situationen übertragen werden kann.[55] Ein solches allgemeines Prinzip würde nämlich die allgemeinen Rechtsbehelfe des Verkäufers unterlaufen. Auch ist die Lösung der beschriebenen Fallgruppen durch ein solches allgemeines Prinzip **unnötig**, da die Nichtvornahme der angesprochenen Bestimmungen durch den Käufer als Verletzung seiner Pflicht zur Abnahme der Ware qualifiziert werden kann, die den Verkäufer nach fruchtlosem Ablauf einer angemessenen Nachfrist berechtigt, den Vertrag gemäss Art. 64 I lit. b)

---

[48] So auch *Ferrari u. a./Mankowski*, Internationales Vertragsrecht, Art. 65, Rn. 29.
[49] *Hager/Maultzsch*, 5. Aufl., Art. 65 Rn. 8; *Herber/Czerwenka*, Art. 65, Rn. 7; *Soergel/Lüderitz/Budzikiewicz*, Art. 65, Rn. 8.
[50] Nach *Kröll u. a./Bell*, Art. 65, Rn. 12, 16 liegt stets ein wesentlicher Vertragsbruch vor, da der Verkäufer gehindert ist, die Ware zu liefern.
[51] *Hager/Maultzsch*, 5. Aufl., Art. 65 Rn. 8; *Karollus*, S. 184; *Herber/Czerwenka*, Art. 65, Rn. 7; *Loewe*, Art. 65, S. 83; *Neumayer/Ming*, Art. 65, Anm. 2. A. A. *Honsell/Schnyder/Straub*, Art. 65, Rn. 54; *Soergel/Lüderitz/Budzikiewicz*, Art. 65, Rn. 8.
[52] Sekretariatskommentar, Art. 62, Nr. 9; *Kritzer*, ICM-Guide, Rn. 91:132.
[53] *Kritzer*, ICM-Guide, Rn. 91:132.
[54] *Heuzé*, Anm. 332.
[55] *Schlechtriem/P. Butler*, UN Law, Rn. 254a; *Schlechtriem*, Internationales UN-Kaufrecht, Rn. 254; MünchKommHGB/*Benicke*, Art. 65, Rn. 4; *Honsell/Schnyder/Straub*, Art. 65, Rn. 15 a f.; *Ferrari u. a./Mankowski*, Internationales Vertragsrecht, Art. 65, Rn. 31. A. A. Sekretariatskommentar, Art. 62, Nr. 9; *Hager/Maultzsch*, 5. Aufl., Art. 65 Rn. 7b; *Kritzer*, ICM-Guide, Rn. 91:132.

aufzuheben.[56] Die Gegenansicht basiert offensichtlich auf dem US-amerikanischen Konzept, das in § 2–311 UCC Niederschlag gefunden hat, und wonach die vertragstreue Partei den Vertrag in angemessener Weise erfüllen darf, wenn die Kooperation der Gegenpartei für die Erfüllung der vertragstreuen Partei notwendige Voraussetzung ist, aber nicht zeitgemäss erfolgt. Solche nationalen Vorverständnisse sollten bei der Auslegung des Übereinkommens keine Berücksichtigung finden.

VII. Beweislast

Der **Verkäufer** trägt die Beweislast dafür, dass die Voraussetzungen für seine Selbstspezifikation vorlagen, also dass der Vertrag eine Spezifizierung durch den Käufer vorsah und dass der Käufer diese Spezifizierung nicht zu dem vereinbarten Zeitpunkt oder innerhalb einer angemessenen Frist nach Aufforderung durch den Verkäufer vorgenommen hat. Im letzteren Fall muss der Verkäufer zeigen, dass seine Aufforderung dem Käufer zugegangen ist. Auch trägt der Verkäufer die Beweislast dafür, dass (a) seine Selbstspezifikation dem Käufer zugegangen ist, dass sie (b) den Bedürfnissen des Käufers, soweit ihm diese bekannt waren, entsprach, dass sie (c) detailliert genug war und dass (d) dem Käufer genügend Zeit blieb, eine abweichende Spezifizierung vorzunehmen. Unabhängig davon, dass der Verkäufer diesbezüglich die Beweislast trägt, muss der **Käufer** behaupten, dass die Aufforderung des Verkäufers, eine unterbliebene Spezifizierung vorzunehmen, eine der drei Voraussetzungen ((b) bis (d)), nicht erfüllt hat. 25

Der **Käufer** trägt die Beweislast dafür, dass der Verkäufer gemäss Art. 77 zur Selbstspezifikation verpflichtet war oder dass die Nichtvornahme einer Selbstspezifikation eine Verletzung der Schadensminderungspflicht nach Art. 77 darstellte. Bezüglich seiner abweichenden Spezifizierung muss der Käufer lediglich zeigen, dass er seine Mitteilung rechtzeitig abgegeben hat. 26

---

[56] *Hager/Maultzsch*, 5. Aufl., Art. 65 Rn. 7b.

Kapitel IV. Übergang der Gefahr

Chapter IV.
Passing of risk

Chapitre IV.
Transfert des risques

Vorbemerkungen zu Artt. 66–70 CISG*

Übersicht

	Rn.
I. Allgemeines	1
II. Rechtsvergleichung	4
1. Periculum est emptoris	5
2. Res perit domino	8
3. Übergabe der Ware	11
III. Die Grundzüge der Gefahrtragung nach CISG	15
1. Ausgangspunkt	15
2. Individualisierung	19
3. Rudimentär bzw. nicht ausdrückliche geregelte Fragen	20
IV. CISG und Incoterms®	23

I. Allgemeines

1   Vom Zeitpunkt ihrer Entstehung an ist Ware verschiedenen Gefahren ausgesetzt.[1] Neben den Grundfällen des physischen Untergangs und der Beschädigung[2] kommen hier vor allem auch staatliche Eingriffe in Betracht, beispielsweise Beschlagnahmungen aber auch Export- und Importverbote. Der Verlust durch Diebstahl oder die Beschädigung durch Vandalismus rechnet ebenfalls hierher. Materialisiert sich eine solche Gefahr, sind die Auswirkungen des die Ware beeinträchtigenden Ereignisses auf die Vertragsbeziehung zwischen Verkäufer und Käufer zu klären. Dies ist die Aufgabe der jeweils zur Anwendung gelangenden Regelungen über die Gefahrtragung. Im Anwendungsbereich des CISG sind dies Artt. 66–70. In der Praxis wird im Regelfall gegen die erwähnten Gefahren ein Versicherungsschutz bestehen,[3] soweit dieser angeboten wird.[4] Der Konflikt zwischen Käufer und Verkäufer wird damit entschärft. Die Auseinandersetzung mit der Versicherung bleibt allerdings ebenso bestehen,

---

* In der Vorauflage wurde der Bereich der Gefahrtragung bearbeitet von Prof. em. Dr. Günter Hager, ehem. Direktor des Instituts für Ausländisches und Internationales Privatrecht, Abt. I, an der Albert-Ludwigs-Universität Freiburg i. Brsg. und Prof. Dr. Felix Maultzsch, LL.M., Goethe-Universität Frankfurt a. M. Beiden Herren bin ich zu grossem Dank für ihre Bearbeitungen verpflichtet, welche mir die Weiterführung sehr erleichtert haben. In vielen wichtigen Punkten halte ich die von meinen Vorgängern vertretenen Auffassungen nach wie vor für richtig, in manchen Punkten schien mir aber eine Neupositionierung angezeigt.

[1] In der Literatur werden zahlreiche Beispiele für Beeinträchtigungen genannt, vgl. statt vieler *Brunner*, Art. 66, Rn. 11. Ob diese Ereignisse Einfluss auf die Gefahrtragung haben, hängt freilich vom Gefahrbegriff des jeweils anwendbaren Rechts ab. Zum Gefahrbegriff des CISG vgl. unten Art. 66 Rn. 4 ff.

[2] Neben Art. 66 CISG beschränken sich auch die Incoterms® 2010 auf die ausdrückliche Nennung dieser beiden Fälle.

[3] *Hager/Maultzsch*, 5. Aufl., Art. 66 Rn. 2; *Honnold/Flechtner*, Art. 66, Rn. 361; *Witz/Salger/Lorenz/Witz*, vor Artt. 66–70, Rn. 3; MünchKomm/*P. Huber*, Art. 66, Rn. 4; MünchKommHGB/*Benicke*, Art. 66, Rn. 2; *Honsell/Schönle/Th. Koller*, Vorbem. 66–70, Rn. 3.

[4] Für Ausnahmen vgl. *Hager/Maultzsch*, 5. Aufl., Art. 66 Rn. 2 mit Verweis auf die kasuistische Aufzählung in Lloyds-Marine-Policy-Institute-Clauses B und C.

wie diejenige mit dem Frachtführer.[5] Die Gefahrtragungsregeln weisen insofern auch die Auseinandersetzungslast zu.[6]

Aus den obigen Beispielen wird deutlich, dass die Regeln über die Gefahrtragung ausschliesslich auf Situationen reagieren wollen, in denen sich die jeweilige Gefahr zufällig verwirklicht hat. Art. 66 bringt diesen allgemein anerkannten Grundsatz[7] deutlich zum Ausdruck, wenn er die Kaufpreisklage des Verkäufers trotz Untergangs oder Beschädigung der Ware nach Gefahrübergang nur schützt, wenn weder ein Handeln noch ein Unterlassen des Verkäufers für den Untergang bzw. die Beschädigung der Ware ursächlich gewesen sind.[8]

Die Regeln der Gefahrtragung erfassen nicht ökonomische Risiken.[9] Gelingt es dem Käufer also nicht, die Ware aufgrund eines veränderten Marktumfeldes abzusetzen, so ist die Marktschwankung gleichwohl keine Verschlechterung oder Beschädigung der Ware im Sinne der Regeln über die Gefahrtragung.[10] Gleiches gilt für Währungsschwankungen.[11] Aufgrund der vergleichsweise restriktiven Verwendung des Begriffs „Gefahr" in der deutschen Rechtssprache, jedenfalls im Bereich des Privatrechts, ist dieser Grundsatz dem deutschsprachigen Juristen selbstverständlich. Demgegenüber wird im Englischen für den Bereich der Gefahrtragung der auch in wirtschaftlichen Zusammenhängen verwendete Begriff „risk" gebraucht.[12] Insbesondere im Rahmen der Ausarbeitung von Verträgen in englischer Sprache ist dem deutschsprachigen Juristen deshalb besondere Sorgfalt hinsichtlich der verwendeten Begrifflichkeiten anzuraten, um Missverständnisse über die vertraglichen Risikozuweisungen zu vermeiden.

II. Rechtsvergleichung

Das Problem der Gefahrtragung wurde und wird noch heute unterschiedlich gelöst, freilich immer unter dem *caveat*, dass die Parteien keine Regelung im Vertrag aufgestellt haben.[13]

1. Periculum est emptoris

Das römische Recht war dem Grundsatz *periculum est emptoris* gefolgt, wonach die Gefahr bei Vertragsschluss auf den Käufer übergeht.[14] Gleichzeitig knüpfte das römische Recht den Eigentumsübergang an die *traditio*.[15] Orientiert am Stückkauf unter Anwesenden bereitet dieser Ansatz in den vorranging in den Blick genommenen Szenarien kaum einmal Probleme, als Vertragsschluss, Vertragserfüllung und Eigentumsübergang zeitlich zusammenfallen.

---

[5] *Witz/Salger/Lorenz/Witz*, vor Artt. 66–70, Rn. 3 ff.; MünchKomm/*P. Huber*, Art. 66, Rn. 4; MünchKommHGB/*Benicke*, Art. 66, Rn. 2; *Honsell/Schönle/Th. Koller*, Vorbem. 66–70, Rn. 3.

[6] *Hager/Maultzsch*, 5. Aufl., Art. 66 Rn. 2; *Witz/Salger/Lorenz/Witz*, vor Artt. 66–70, Rn. 3; MünchKomm/*P. Huber*, Art. 66, Rn. 4; MünchKommHGB/*Benicke*, Art. 66, Rn. 2; *Honsell/Schönle/Th. Koller*, Vorbem. 66–70, Rn. 3.

[7] *Schwenzer/Hachem/Kee*, Rn. 38.02: Grundsatz so selbstverständlich, dass regelmässig auf eine ausdrückliche gesetzliche Regelung verzichtet wird. Vgl. aber in den USA die Überschrift zu § 2–509 UCC: „Risk of Loss in the Absence of Breach".

[8] Vgl. dazu unten Art. 66 Rn. 16 ff.

[9] Zur Frage der Tragung aussergewöhnlich hoher Transportkosten vgl. unten Art. 66 Rn. 12 ff.

[10] *Kröll u. a./Erauw*, Art. 66, Rn. 40.

[11] *Kröll u. a./Erauw*, Art. 66, Rn. 40.

[12] Vgl. England: sec. 20 SGA; Hongkong: sec. 22 SGO; Indien: sec. 26 SGA; Irland: sec. 20 SGA; Neuseeland: sec. 22 SGA; Singapur: sec. 20 SGA; USA: § 2–509 UCC. Für weitere Nachweise vgl. *Schwenzer/Hachem/Kee*, Rn. 38.08. Siehe auch *Bridge*, FS Kritzer, S. 77: „As a broad concept, risk underpins the entire structure of commercial law and commercial dealings." Nicht zu Unrecht grenzt deshalb *Kröll u. a./Erauw*, Art. 66, Rn. 40 ff. ausdrücklich „economic risk", „risk of insolvency" und „contractual risk" vom Anwendungsbereich der Artt. 66–70 ab.

[13] Zum Verhältnis des CISG zu den Incoterms® vgl. unten Rn. 23.

[14] *Kaser/Knütel*, § 41, Rn. 21.

[15] *Kaser/Knütel*, § 24, Rn. 11.

6 Grosse Probleme bereitet dieser Ansatz, wenn zwischen Vertragsschluss und Vertragserfüllung ein Zeitfenster liegt, während dessen die Ware in Besitz und Eigentum des Verkäufers verbleibt und dieser durch den bereits erfolgten Gefahrübergang keinen wirtschaftlichen Anreiz mehr hat, bei der Verwahrung der Sache besondere Sorgfalt walten zu lassen. Geht die Ware dann unter, so wird der Käufer stets den Gefahrübergang mit der Behauptung bestreiten, der Verkäufer habe sich sorgfaltswidrig verhalten. Der römischrechtliche Ansatz ist insoweit nicht praktikabel und ist in seiner Reinform heute nur noch von geringer Bedeutung.

7 Eine prominente Ausnahme bildet das in Rechtswahlklauseln äusserst populäre Schweizer Recht.[16] Art. 185 I OR sieht für den Spezieskauf den Gefahrübergang bei Vertragsschluss vor, „sofern nicht besondere Verhältnisse oder Verabredungen eine Ausnahme begründen". Das für den Eigentumsübergang zuständige Zivilgesetzbuch knüpft, wie das römische Recht, die Eigentumsübertragung an die *traditio*.[17] Der seit langem von allen Seiten kritisierte Art. 185 I OR ist von der Rechtsprechung allerdings praktisch abgeschafft worden.[18] Das im Gesetzeswortlaut niedergelegte Regel-Ausnahme-Verhältnis wurde durch eine extrem weite Auslegung der besonderen Verhältnisse und Verabredungen letztlich umgekehrt,[19] so dass die Gefahr praktisch erst mit Übergabe der Ware an den Käufer bzw. bei Schickschuld an den Beförderer übergeht.

2. Res perit domino

8 Im Anschluss an die Arbeiten von Hugo Grotius im 17. Jahrhundert begannen Rechtsordnungen, den Gefahrübergang vom Vertragsschluss abzulösen und an den Eigentumsübergang zu knüpfen.[20] Es ist deshalb der Eigentümer, dem die Sache verloren geht *(res perit domino)*. Im Ergebnis ist dieser Grundsatz nach wie vor der weltweit vorherrschende. Seine klarste Ausprägung findet sich im französischen Rechtskreis im engeren Sinne,[21] sowie in einigen ostasiatischen, dem Civil Law zuzurechnenden, Staaten[22]. Darüber hinaus vermuten die rein am Parteiwillen orientierten, Englisch geprägten Rechtsordnungen des Common Law in allen Teilen der Welt, dass dieser beim Spezieskauf auf Gefahr- und Eigentumsübergang im Zeitpunkt des Vertragsschlusses gerichtet sei.[23] Auf einheitsrechtlicher Ebene folgt das einheitliche Kaufrecht der OHADA Staaten dem französischen Beispiel.[24]

9 Die überwiegende Zahl der Rechtsordnungen gelangt auf Umwegen zur Geltung von *res perit domino*. Er ergibt sich dann aus dem Zusammenspiel derjenigen Vorschriften, die den Gefahrübergang bei Vertragsschluss anordnen, mit denjenigen Vorschriften, die den Eigentumsübergang mit dem Vertragsschluss bzw. – bei Gattungsware – mit der Individualisierung verknüpfen. Dies gilt namentlich für die überwiegende Zahl der ibero-amerikanischen[25] und arabischen[26] Rechtsordnungen.

10 Unabhängig von der jeweiligen Ausgestaltung von *res perit domino* ist doch festzustellen, dass sich im praktischen Ergebnis kaum Abweichungen von *periculum est emptoris* ergeben. Dies gilt insbesondere auch für das erhebliche Streitpotential, dass beide Grundsätze in sich bergen.

---

[16] Eine weitere Ausnahme ist das traditionell noch sehr stark im römischen Recht verankerte südafrikanische Recht, vgl. *Zimmermann*, S. 281.
[17] Vgl. Schweiz: Art. 714 I ZGB.
[18] Vgl. die ausführliche Stellungnahme in BGer, 18.4.1958, BGE 84 II 158. Kritik auch bei *Schwenzer*, OR AT, Rn. 34.06; BaslerKomm/*A. Koller*, Art. 185 OR, Rn. 35 ff., 46; *Honsell*, OR BT, S. 55 ff.
[19] Grundlegend insoweit BGer, 18.4.1958, BGE 84 II 158.
[20] Vgl. *Hager*, Gefahrtragung, S. 40.
[21] Frankreich: Art. 1138 CC; Belgien: Art. 1138 CC; Luxemburg: Art. 1138 CC.
[22] Nachweise bei *Schwenzer/Hachem/Kee*, Rn. 38.37.
[23] Nachweise bei *Schwenzer/Hachem/Kee*, Rn. 38.38.
[24] Art. 277 AUDCG.
[25] Nachweise bei *Schwenzer/Hachem/Kee*, Rn. 38.36.
[26] Nachweise bei *Schwenzer/Hachem/Kee*, Rn. 38.36.

3. Übergabe der Ware

Im Vordringen ist mittlerweile der Ansatz, den Gefahrübergang an die Übergabe der Ware **11** zu knüpfen. Während die Wurzeln dieser Lösung ebenfalls bis in das 17. Jahrhundert zurück reichen, folgt ihre heutige Ausgestaltung aus Entwicklungen beginnend mit dem 19. Jahrhundert. Frühere Vertreter der Übergabe-Lösung folgten dem Grundsatz *res perit domino*, knüpften den Eigentumsübergang allerdings nicht an den Vertragsschluss, sondern an die römisch-rechtliche *traditio*.[27] Damit hätte aber beim Distanzkauf – entgegen aller Gewohnheiten – das Transportrisiko grundsätzlich beim Verkäufer gelegen,[28] so dass für diese Fälle Sonderregelungen geschaffen werden mussten[29].

Für den Bereich des kaufmännischen Verkehrs vollzogen demgegenüber insbesondere **12** zahlreiche Ibero-Amerikanische Rechtsordnungen mit Beginn des 19. Jahrhunderts einen weiter reichenden Wechsel. Während der dort über das gesamte 19. Jahrhundert andauernden Kodifikationswelle auf dem Gebiet des Handelsrechts wurde der im Übrigen zum Zuge kommende Grundsatz *res perit domino* aufgegeben, und für den Handelskauf der Gefahrübergang an die Gewahrsamsaufgabe durch den Verkäufer geknüpft.[30]

Weitergehend löste dann insbesondere das deutsche BGB den Gefahrübergang für alle **13** Kaufverträge aus dem Eigentumsübergang heraus – ohne ihn allerdings wieder an den Vertragsschluss zu koppeln.[31] Der US-amerikanische UCC ist diesem Beispiel gefolgt.[32] Im Mittelpunkt steht seither die Aufgabe des Gewahrsams durch den Verkäufer im Wege der Übergabe der Ware an den Käufer selbst oder den Beförderer. Notabene setzt dieses Verständnis des Gefahrübergangs weder einen damit einhergehenden Eigentumsübergang voraus, noch, dass damit auch die Erfüllung der Lieferpflicht eintritt, wenngleich Letzteres in der Praxis regelmässig der Fall sein wird.[33] Entsprechend dem regelmäßigen, praktischen Ergebnis der Zeitgleichheit von Gefahrübergang und Erfüllung der Lieferpflicht hatten nordische Rechtsordnungen deshalb schon früh den Gefahrübergang mit der Lieferung verbunden, was dann auch für das EKG übernommen, für das CISG aber abgelehnt wurde.[34] In der Sache besteht aber trotz dieser Nuancierungen kein Unterschied in der modernen Ausgestaltung des Übergabe-Ansatzes.[35]

Diesem Übergabe-Ansatz sind im ausgehenden 20. Jahrhundert insbesondere die Reformstaaten **14** Osteuropas[36] sowie moderne, dem Civil Law zuzurechnende, zentral- und ostasiatische Rechtsordnungen[37] gefolgt. Wenngleich also *res perit domino* nach wie vor in der Mehrzahl der Rechtsordnungen den Ausgangspunkt bildet, so steht doch insbesondere vor dem Hintergrund der einheitsrechtlichen Entwicklung zu erwarten, dass dieser seine Vormachtstellung verlieren wird.

III. Die Grundzüge der Gefahrtragung nach CISG

1. Ausgangspunkt

Das CISG regelt die Gefahrtragung in seinen Artt. 66–70. Unsicherheiten bestehen **15** hinsichtlich der Reichweite des in Art. 66 niedergelegten Gefahrbegriffs.[38] Umstritten ist

---

[27] Vgl. dazu mit Nachweisen *Schwenzer/Hachem/Kee*, Rn. 38.41.
[28] *Hager*, Gefahrtragung, S. 42.
[29] Nachweise bei *Schwenzer/Hachem/Kee*, Rn. 38.41.
[30] *E. Muñoz*, S. 358.
[31] §§ 446, 447 BGB; *Hager*, Gefahrtragung, S. 54 ff.
[32] Vgl. USA: § 2–509 UCC.
[33] Dies gilt auch für USA: § 2–509 UCC, obwohl diese Vorschrift von „delivery" spricht. Die Vorschrift wird so verstanden, dass es nur um die Aufgabe der physischen Kontrolle über die Ware durch den Verkäufer ankommt, vgl. *Hager*, Gefahrtragung, S. 62.
[34] *Hager/Maultzsch*, 5. Aufl., Art. 67 Rn. 1.
[35] So schon für den Übergang von EKG zum CISG *Hager/Maultzsch*, 5. Aufl., Art. 67 Rn. 1.
[36] Nachweise bei *Schwenzer/Hachem/Kee*, Rn. 38.43.
[37] Nachweise bei *Schwenzer/Hachem/Kee*, Rn. 38.43.
[38] Vgl. dazu unten Art. 66 Rn. 4 ff.

insbesondere die Einordnung hoheitlicher Eingriffe.[39] Die Regelungen kommen in Rückabwicklungsverhältnissen nicht zur Anwendung, sondern treten hinter Artt. 81 ff. zurück.[40]

16 Im Ausgangspunkt folgt das CISG dem Übergabe-Ansatz[41] und ist insoweit für den deutschen Juristen gewohntes Terrain. Sonderregelungen enthält die Konvention allerdings für den Fall des Verkaufs reisender Ware.[42] Im Einzelnen knüpft das CISG also grundsätzlich weder an den Vertragsschluss, noch an den Eigentumsübergang[43] an. Auch spielt die Verteilung der Transport- und Versicherungskosten keine Rolle.[44]

17 Im Gegensatz zu der an den nordischen Rechtsordnungen orientierten Rechtslage unter dem EKG kommt der Lieferung nach dem Willen der Konventionsverfasser unter dem CISG ebenfalls keine Bedeutung für den Gefahrübergang zu.[45] Befürchtet wurde eine Überfrachtung des Lieferbegriffs.[46] Dieses Bedenken hat allerdings weniger sachlichen als vielmehr regelungstechnischen Niederschlag gefunden.[47] In der Sache hat sich keine Änderung ergeben und wird der Gefahrübergang in den meisten Fällen mit der Lieferung einhergehen.[48]

18 Die Anknüpfung an die Gewahrsamsaufgabe durch den Verkäufer ist sachgerecht. Der Grundsatz *periculum est emptoris* ist gerade für den im internationalen Warenhandel typischen Distanzkauf nicht praktikabel. Die Anknüpfung an den Eigentumsübergang gemäss dem Grundsatz *res perit domino* hätte zu ganz erheblicher Rechtsunsicherheit geführt. Das CISG schliesst in Art. 4 S. 2 lit. b) Fragen des Eigentumsübergangs wegen der grossen Unterschiede auf nationaler Ebene von seinem Anwendungsbereich gerade aus, so dass eine Anknüpfung daran wenig sachgerecht gewesen wäre.[49] Daraus folgt aber nicht, dass nationale Vorschriften, die mit dem Eigentumsübergang auch den Übergang der Gefahr anordnen, unberührt bleiben. Die Gefahrtragungsvorschriften der Konvention regeln diesen Bereich abschliessend und verdrängen deshalb nationales Recht.[50]

2. Individualisierung

19 Das CISG verlangt schliesslich für den Gefahrübergang die hinreichende Individualisierung der Ware. Diesem „generellen Prinzip"[51] wird zwar nur an zwei Stellen Ausdruck verliehen,[52] jedoch besteht kein Zweifel, dass es sich dabei um eine allgemeine Voraussetzung handelt.[53] Je nach den Umständen des Falles können dazu verschiedene Massnahmen notwendig sein. Sicher geht der Verkäufer, wenn er die Ware mit Etiketten versieht,

---

[39] Vgl. dazu unten Art. 66 Rn. 6 ff.
[40] *Honnold/Flechtner*, Intro to Arts 66–70, Rn. 359.1; *MünchKomm/P. Huber*, Art. 66, Rn. 4.
[41] Vgl. Artt. 67, 69.
[42] Vgl. Art. 68.
[43] *St. Paul Guardian Insurance Company and Travelers Insurance Company v. Neuromed Medical Systems & Support GmbH, et al.*, U. S. Dist. Ct. (S. D. N. Y.), 26.3.2002, CISG-online 615; OLG Schleswig, 29.10.2002, CISG-online 717; *Schlechtriem/Schwenzer/Hager/Schmidt-Kessel*, CISG Commentary, Art. 66, Rn. 3; *Staudinger/Magnus*, Vorbem. zu Art. 66 ff., Rn. 2; *Honnold/Flechtner*, Art. 66, Rn. 361.
[44] Audiencia Provincial de Córdoba, 31.10.1997, CISG-online 502; Cámara Nacional de Apelaciones en lo Comercial, 31.10.1995, CISG-online 299; *Schlechtriem/Schwenzer/Hager/Schmidt-Kessel*, CISG Commentary, Art. 66, Rn. 3.
[45] Vgl. *Hager/Maultzsch*, 5. Aufl., Art. 67 Rn. 1; *Schlechtriem/Schwenzer/Hager/Schmidt-Kessel*, CISG Commentary, Art. 67, Rn. 1; *Staudinger/Magnus*, Vorbem. zu Art. 66 ff., Rn. 5.
[46] Vgl. *Hager/Maultzsch*, 5. Aufl., Art. 67 Rn. 1; *Schlechtriem/Schwenzer/Hager/Schmidt-Kessel*, CISG Commentary, Art. 67, Rn. 1; *Staudinger/Magnus*, Vorbem. zu Art. 66 ff., Rn. 6.
[47] Sachliche Konsequenz dieses Grundentscheids ist allerdings, dass Art. 67 II CISG anders als noch das EKG gegen einen rückwirkenden Gefahrübergang durch nachträgliche Individualisierung der Ware entscheidet, *Hager/Maultzsch*, 5. Aufl., Art. 67 Rn. 9 f. Vgl. unten Art. 67 Rn. 35.
[48] Vgl. *Hager/Maultzsch*, 5. Aufl., Art. 67 Rn. 1; *Bridge*, FS Kritzer, S. 105.
[49] *Brunner*, Art. 66, Rn. 2.
[50] *Kröll u. a./Erauw*, Art. 66, Rn. 5.
[51] *Piltz*, Internationales Kaufrecht, § 4, Rn. 275.
[52] Artt. 67 II, 69 III.
[53] Vgl. unten bei Art. 67 Rn. 29 f.

die den Käufer als Empfänger ausweisen. Entsprechende Frachtpapiere und Packlisten werden in der Regel die Zuordnung der Ware zum Vertrag erlauben. Diese Fragen, insbesondere dann wenn Sammelladungen betroffen sind, stellen sich in erster Linie im Zusammenhang mit dem Versendungskauf und dem Verkauf reisender Ware und werden entsprechend dort behandelt.[54]

3. Rudimentär bzw. nicht ausdrückliche geregelte Fragen

Deutschsprachige Autoren insbesondere legen Wert auf die Feststellung, dass die Konvention zwar nur die Preisgefahr ausdrücklich regelt, aber auch Aufschluss über die Sach-/Leistungs- oder Sachleistungsgefahr gibt.[55] Die Konvention koppelt den Gefahrübergang, anders als ihre Vorgängerin, anders als die Incoterms® 2010 und eben anders als manche nationalen Rechtsordnungen, gerade nicht an die Lieferung der Ware, sondern an die Gewahrsamsaufgabe. Gleichzeitig haftet der Verkäufer nach Art. 36 I auch nur bis zu diesem Zeitpunkt für Mängel, die in diesem Zeitpunkt bestehen oder – Art. 36 II – in diesem Zeitpunkt bereits angelegt sind. Selbstverständlich reicht die Beschaffungspflicht des Verkäufers nicht über den Zeitpunkt hinaus, in dem er Mängelfreiheit zu gewährleisten hat.[56] Es erstaunt allerdings nicht, dass diese Frage, nicht zuletzt weil die in Rede stehende Differenzierung vielen Rechtsordnungen unbekannt ist,[57] in der Praxis noch nie eine Rolle gespielt hat. 20

Nur rudimentäre Regelungen hält das CISG für die Konstellation des Zusammentreffens einer Pflichtverletzung des Verkäufers mit zufälligem Untergang bzw. zufälliger Beschädigung der Ware bereit. Einen Teilbereich regelt der – im Übrigen aber weiter gehende[58] – letzte Halbsatz von Art. 66. Immerhin stehen dem Käufer gemäss Art. 70 im Falle der wesentlichen Vertragsverletzung des Käufers die dafür vorgesehenen Rechtsbehelfe zur Verfügung, wenn die Ware zufällig untergegangen oder beschädigt worden ist.[59] Art. 70 verhindert damit, dass der Verkäufer durch Zufall vor den Folgen einer von ihm begangenen wesentlichen Vertragsverletzung geschützt wird.[60] 21

Keine Regelungen enthält die Konvention über die Verteilung von Nutzungen und Lasten. Gemeinhin wird davon ausgegangen, auch für diese Frage auf den Zeitpunkt des Gefahrübergangs abzustellen.[61] 22

IV. CISG und Incoterms®

In der Praxis sind die Gefahrtragungsregeln des CISG aufgrund des gängigen Gebrauchs von Trade Terms, insbesondere der Incoterms®, nur von beschränkter Bedeutung.[62] Dabei dürften die Incoterms® trotz ihrer Popularität nicht schon für sich genommen ein Handelsbrauch nach Art. 9 II sein, zumal dann weitergehend zu klären wäre, welche Klausel für welche Art von Verträgen (Warengattung? Geographische Anknüpfung?) üblich ist. Allerdings darf im Anwendungsbereich des CISG gestützt auf Art. 9 II ein generischer Verweis auf „Incoterms" bzw. die Verwendung eines dreibuchstabigen Term als Verweis auf die Incoterms® verstanden werden.[63] Heranzuziehen ist dann die zum Zeitpunkt des Vertrags- 23

---

[54] Vgl. dazu unten Art. 67 Rn. 31 ff., Art. 68 Rn. 22 ff.
[55] *Staudinger/Magnus*, Vorbem. zu Art. 66 ff., Rn. 9.
[56] *Hager/Maultzsch*, 5. Aufl., Art. 67 Rn. 10; MünchKomm/*P. Huber*, Art. 66, Rn. 1, 15.
[57] *Hager/Maultzsch*, 5. Aufl., Art. 67 Rn. 10.
[58] Vgl. dazu unten Art. 66 Rn. 16 ff.
[59] Vgl. dazu unten Art. 70 Rn. 1 ff.
[60] Vgl. dazu auch unten Art. 70 Rn. 2.
[61] *Staudinger/Magnus*, Vorbem. zu Art. 66 ff., Rn. 10.
[62] *Staudinger/Magnus*, Vorbem. zu Art. 66 ff., Rn. 8; MünchKomm/*P. Huber*, Art. 66, Rn. 4; *Brunner*, Art. 66, Rn. 9. Vgl. zum Verhältnis der beiden Regelwerke *Mohs*, FS Schwenzer, S. 1293 ff.
[63] *China North Chemical Industries Corp. v. Beston Chemical Corp.*, U. S. Dist. Ct. (S. D. T.), 7.2.2006, CISG-online 1177; *Piltz*, FS Herber, S. 22.

schlusses gültige Version. Denkbar wäre auch eine Auslegung zugunsten der jeweils gültigen Fassung der Incoterms®, beachtet würde dann aber nicht, dass die jeweilige neue Fassung – wie im Falle der Incoterms® 2010 – relevante Zeitpunkte verschoben haben kann oder verschiedene Terms nicht mehr existieren bzw. neue eingeführt wurden. In jedem Fall sollte gerade bei fein austarierten Klauseln wie den Incoterms® vermieden werden, die im Zeitpunkt des Vertragsschlusses vorgenommene Risikoverteilung zu verfälschen.

24   Die in der Literatur bisweilen anzutreffende Behauptung, das CISG passe nicht zu den Incoterms®,[64] ist natürlich aufgrund des hohen Übereinstimmungsgrades[65] beider Regelwerke nicht richtig. Sie geht auch an der Sache vorbei, als es zwischen beiden Regelwerken nie zum Konflikt kommt. Mit der Verwendung solcher Klauseln nehmen die Parteien im Sinne von Art. 6 einen Ausschluss bzw. eine Modifizierung der Konvention vor.[66] Soweit die verwendete Klausel die jeweilige Sachfrage regelt, treten die damit befassten Regelungen des CISG, und solche, die das Ergebnis der Klauselwahl konterkarieren würden, zurück. Die Verwendung eines Trade Terms führt auch nicht zum gänzlichen Ausschluss des betroffenen Regelungsbereichs der Konvention. Die Reichweite des jeweiligen Terms und sein daraus folgender Vorrang gegenüber den Regelungen des CISG muss letztlich über die Auslegungsregeln der Artt. 8, 9 ermittelt werden. Dies gilt insbesondere für die Frage, ob eine Vertragsklausel (lediglich) die Kostenverteilung oder auch den Gefahrübergang regelt.[67] Art. 101 EKG hatte dies sogar noch ausdrücklich festgehalten mit der Formulierung, dass es für die Bestimmung der Gefahrtragung nicht notwendig auf die vertragliche Kostenverteilung ankommt.

---

[64] So insbes. *Bridge*, FS Kritzer, S. 105; weitere Nachweise bei *Staudinger/Magnus*, Vorbem. zu Art. 66 ff., Rn. 8.
[65] *Staudinger/Magnus*, Vorbem. zu Art. 66 ff., Rn. 7; *Brunner*, Art. 66, Rn. 9, die freilich mit Recht darauf hinweisen, dass die Konvention den Detaillierungsgrad der Incoterms® weder erreichen konnte noch wollte.
[66] *Staudinger/Magnus*, Vorbem. zu Art. 66 ff., Rn. 8; *Ramberg*, FS Kritzer, S. 400. Der Verweis auf die Incoterms® führt freilich nicht zu einem gesamthaften Ausschluss der Konvention, OGH 22.10.2001, CISG-online 614; oben *Ferrari*, Art. 6 Rn. 29; *Schlechtriem/Schwenzer/Schwenzer/Hachem*, CISG Commentary, Art. 6, Rn. 26; *Mohs*, FS Schwenzer, S. 1293.
[67] *Staudinger/Magnus*, Vorbem. zu Art. 66 ff., Rn. 7; *Brunner*, Art. 66, Rn. 9.

Art. 66 [Wirkung des Gefahrübergangs]

Untergang oder Beschädigung der Ware nach Übergang der Gefahr auf den Käufer befreit diesen nicht von der Pflicht, den Kaufpreis zu zahlen, es sei denn, daß der Untergang oder die Beschädigung auf eine Handlung oder Unterlassung des Verkäufers zurückzuführen ist.

Art. 66

Loss of or damage to the goods after the risk has passed to the buyer does not discharge him from his obligation to pay the price, unless the loss or damage is due to an act or omission of the seller.

Art. 66

La perte ou la détérioration des marchandises survenue après le transfert des risques à l'acheteur ne libère pas celui-ci de son obligation de payer le prix, à moins que ces événements ne soient dus à un fait du vendeur.

Übersicht

	Rn.
I. Vorgeschichte	1
II. Regelungsgegenstand	2
III. Gefahrbegriff	4
1. Ausgangspunkt	4
2. Hoheitliche Eingriffe	6
3. Veränderungen des Transports	12
IV. Gefahrtragung und Haftung	16
1. Reichweite von Art. 66 *in fine*	17
2. Massstab für das Verkäuferverhalten	22
3. Rechtmässiges Verkäuferverhalten	26
V. Gefahrtragung und Kaufpreisklage	27
1. Grundsatz	27
2. Begrenzung der Kaufpreisklage	29
VI. Beweislast	35

I. Vorgeschichte

Art. 66 entspricht, von wenigen sprachlichen Änderungen abgesehen, Art. 96 EKG.[1]   **1**

II. Regelungsgegenstand

Die Vorschrift ist keine im eigentlichen Sinne operative Norm. Vielmehr bringt Art. 66 **2** das dem CISG zugrunde liegende Verständnis der Gefahrtragung zum Ausdruck.[2] Das Gefahrtragungskonzept der Konvention entspricht dabei dem weltweit allgemein anerkannten.[3] Die Grundpfeiler des Gefahrbegriffs sind der Untergang der Ware bzw. ihre Beschädigung und die Unabhängigkeit dieser Beeinträchtigungen von einem Verhalten des Verkäufers, also das Erfordernis der Zufälligkeit.

Art. 66 regelt demgegenüber nicht den Zeitpunkt des Gefahrübergangs. Dieser richtet **3** sich nach den Artt. 67–69.

---

[1] *Hager/Maultzsch*, 5. Aufl., Art. 66 Rn. 1; *Schlechtriem/Schwenzer/Hager/Schmidt-Kessel*, CISG Commentary, Art. 66, Rn. 2; *Staudinger/Magnus*, Art. 66, Rn. 2 ff., alle mit Nachweisen zu den Veränderungen während der Beratungen.

[2] *Schlechtriem/Schwenzer/Hager/Schmidt-Kessel*, CISG Commentary, Art. 66, Rn. 1.

[3] *Staudinger/Magnus*, Art. 66, Rn. 5.

III. Gefahrbegriff

1. Ausgangspunkt

4 Die Konventionsverfasser haben dem Gefahrbegriff selbst keine besondere Aufmerksamkeit gewidmet.[4] Die Beschränkung auf die ausdrückliche Nennung des Untergangs bzw. der Beschädigung der Ware ist so auch weltweit regelmässig in den nationalen Rechtsordnungen anzutreffen.[5] Auch die Incoterms® begnügen sich in den jeweiligen A5-Klauseln mit der Erwähnung dieser beiden Fallgruppen. Die am 1.1.2011 in Kraft getretene Version 2010 hat insoweit ebenfalls keine Neuerung gebracht.

5 Gleichwohl herrscht in der Literatur Einigkeit darüber, dass Art. 66 keineswegs abschliessend ist. So gehört der Verlust durch Diebstahl sicher auch zum Gefahrbegriff der Konvention.[6] Gleiches gilt für die Notentladung oder Fehlgriffe des Transporteurs, darunter etwa die Auslieferung an den falschen Empfänger.[7] Auch der Gewichtsschwund wird erfasst.[8] Die weiteren oft genannten Beispiele, Vandalismus, Unfall und ähnliche Beeinträchtigungen,[9] dürften von der Beschädigung bzw. dem Untergang der Ware in den allermeisten Fällen erfasst sein. Keinen Einfluss auf den Gefahrbegriff und damit die Reichweite der Artt. 66–70 hat die Versicherbarkeit des Risikos.[10] Der Anwendungsbereich der Konvention richtet sich nicht nach der Risikobereitschaft der Versicherungswirtschaft.

2. Hoheitliche Eingriffe

6 Seit langem umstritten ist, ob die Gefahrtragungsnormen des CISG auch hoheitliche Eingriffe erfassen. Die wohl ältere Ansicht, der auch noch die Vorauflage dieses Werks gefolgt ist, schliesst hoheitliche Eingriffe grundsätzlich vom Anwendungsbereich der Gefahrtragungsnormen der Konvention aus.[11] Zur Begründung wird im Wesentlichen vorgetragen, gegen hoheitliche Eingriffe bestünde kein Versicherungsschutz.[12] Weiterhin könne der Betroffene auch gegen hoheitliche Eingriffe vorgehen.[13] Zudem richteten sich Beschlagnahmungen typisch gegen den Eigentümer und sollten deshalb diesen treffen.[14] Eine Ausnahme von diesem Grundsatz sei nur im Falle der Beschlagnahmung der Ware durch einen feindlichen Staat im Kriegsfall zu machen.[15] Diese Situation komme dem Untergang der Ware gleich und zudem sei dieses Risiko auch versicherbar.[16]

---

[4] *Hager/Maultzsch*, 5. Aufl., Art. 66 Rn. 3; *Schlechtriem/Schwenzer/Hager/Schmidt-Kessel*, CISG Commentary, Art. 66, Rn. 4.

[5] *Schwenzer/Hachem/Kee*, Rn. 38.03.

[6] *Hager/Maultzsch*, 5. Aufl., Art. 66, Rn. 3; *Schlechtriem/Schwenzer/Hager/Schmidt-Kessel*, CISG Commentary, Art. 66, Rn. 4; *Staudinger/Magnus*, Art. 66, Rn. 6; MünchKomm/*P. Huber*, Art. 66, Rn. 6; *Brunner*, Art. 66, Rn. 11.

[7] OLG Oldenburg, 22.9.1998, CISG-online 508 = NJW-RR 2000, 1634; *Hager/Maultzsch*, 5. Aufl., Art. 66, Rn. 3; *Schlechtriem/Schwenzer/Hager/Schmidt-Kessel*, CISG Commentary, Art. 66, Rn. 4; Honsell/Schönle/*Th. Koller*, Art. 66, Rn. 17.

[8] *Hager/Maultzsch*, 5. Aufl., Art. 66, Rn. 3; *Schlechtriem/Schwenzer/Hager/Schmidt-Kessel*, CISG Commentary, Art. 66, Rn. 4; MünchKomm/*P. Huber*, Art. 66, Rn. 7. Ist dieser allerdings auf unsachgemässe Verpackung durch den Verkäufer zurückzuführen, liegt ein den Gefahrübergang hindernder „act or omission of the seller" vor.

[9] Vgl. die vielen Bsp. bei *Brunner*, Art. 66, Rn. 11; *Ferrari u. a./Mankowski*, Internationales Vertragsrecht, Art. 66, Rn. 2.

[10] A. A. Bamberger/Roth/*Saenger*, Art. 66, Rn. 2.

[11] *Hager/Maultzsch*, 5. Aufl., Art. 66 Rn. 4; MünchKommHGB/*Benicke*, Art. 66, Rn. 4; Bamberger/Roth/*Saenger*, Art. 66, Rn. 2.

[12] *Hager/Maultzsch*, 5. Aufl., Art. 66 Rn. 4.

[13] *Hager/Maultzsch*, 5. Aufl., Art. 66 Rn. 4.

[14] *Hager/Maultzsch*, 5. Aufl., Art. 66 Rn. 4.

[15] *Hager/Maultzsch*, 5. Aufl., Art. 66 Rn. 4.

[16] *Hager/Maultzsch*, 5. Aufl., Art. 66 Rn. 4 mit Verweis auf die Institute War Clause (Air Cargo).

Die vorzugswürdige neuere, und mittlerweile herrschende, Auffassung betrachtet hoheitliche Eingriffe demgegenüber als gefahrtragungsrelevante Ereignisse.[17] Mit Recht wird darauf hingewiesen, dass das fehlende Angebot eines Versicherungsschutzes kein relevantes Kriterium sein kann.[18] Im Gegenteil erscheint es sachgerechter, ein – für beide Seiten – nicht versicherbares Risiko derjenigen Partei aufzubürden, die nach vertraglicher Vereinbarung, oder sonst nach den subsidiären Regelungen des CISG, die Gefahr für Untergang und Beschädigung der Ware trägt. Das wohl in diesem wertenden Zusammenhang zu verstehende Argument der Gegenauffassung, Beschlagnahmen richteten sich regelmässig gegen den Eigentümer, weshalb diesen auch die Folgen zu treffen hätten,[19] überzeugt nicht. Bereits die Prämisse ist fragwürdig. Wird Ware während des Transports in einem Transitland beschlagnahmt, weil sie dort geistiges Eigentum verletzt, so ist diese Beschlagnahme sicher nicht gegen den Eigentümer als solchen, sondern gegen die Existenz der Ware gerichtet, die dann regelmässig auch vernichtet wird. Die Anknüpfung an das Eigentum ist auch deshalb nicht sachgerecht, weil das CISG Fragen des Eigentumsübergangs nach Art. 4 S. 2 lit. b) von seinem Anwendungsbereich ausschliesst. Die nationalen Rechtsordnungen unterscheiden sich ganz erheblich in den Mechanismen der Eigentumsübertragung. Damit würde für die Gefahrtragung eine nicht zu rechtfertigende Rechtsunsicherheit geschaffen. Diese würde dann noch vergrössert, wenn über das jeweils anwendbare Kollisionsrecht das Recht eines Transitstaates, als dem (zufälligen) Belegenheitsort der Ware, heranzuziehen wäre. 7

Hoheitliche Eingriffe generell mit den Gefahrtragungsregeln des CISG zu erfassen hat darüber hinaus den praktischen Vorteil, die gerade bei Wegnahme der Ware auftretende Frage zu vermeiden, ob diese hoheitlicher Natur – und damit eine Beschlagnahmung – oder schlichter Diebstahl ist. Den Fall der Seepiraterie wird man regelmässig nicht als hoheitlichen Eingriff, sondern als Diebstahl einzustufen haben, wenngleich sie faktisch von den lokalen Autoritäten gesteuert sein mag. Nach allgemeiner Ansicht träfen die Folgen deshalb die gefahrbelastete Partei. Ob das auch gilt, wenn nach einem Staatsstreich die neuen Machthaber einen solchen Eingriff vornehmen, ist dann schon weniger einfach zu beantworten; von der Situation in „failing states" mit regionalen Autoritäten ganz zu schweigen.[20] Im Anschluss daran müsste die Qualifikation von Eingriffen als hoheitlich oder nicht von Fragen der Legitimität der jeweiligen Institution abhängig gemacht werden. Das wiederum führt zur weiteren Frage, inwieweit die Anerkennung durch (wie viele?) andere Staaten notwendig ist, um das Handeln einer Institution als „hoheitlich" einordnen zu können. Das CISG sollte sich solcher Fragen enthalten und der faktisch simple Vorgang „Wegnahme der Ware" nicht mit komplizierten politischen Dimensionen befrachtet werden. 8

Die praktischen Auswirkungen des Streits dürften letztlich oft weniger drastisch ausfallen, als es die Verschiedenheit der Positionen zunächst vermuten lässt. War der hoheitliche Eingriff vorhersehbar, so wird der Verkäufer, wenn er für die Organisation des Transports zuständig war, sich nicht auf den Gefahrübergang berufen können. Er muss sich dann einen „act or omission"[21] nach Art. 66 *in fine* entgegen halten lassen, der den Gefahrübergang unbeachtlich werden lässt. Dies wird zum Beispiel sicher der Fall sein, wenn bei unmittel- 9

---

[17] Int. Ct. Hungarian CCI, 10.12.1996, CISG-online 774; *Schlechtriem/Schwenzer/Hager/Schmidt-Kessel*, CISG Commentary, Art. 66, Rn. 5; *Witz/Salger/Lorenz/Witz*, Art. 66, Rn. 4; *Staudinger/Magnus*, Art. 66, Rn. 6; MünchKomm/*P. Huber*, Art. 66, Rn. 7; *Brunner*, Art. 66, Rn. 12; *Ferrari u. a./Mankowski*, Internationales Vertragsrecht, Art. 66, Rn. 8; *Kröll u. a./Erauw*, Art. 66, Rn. 34; wohl auch *Honsell/Schönle/Th. Koller*, Art. 66, Rn. 19; *Bridge*, FS Kritzer, S. 78 f.

[18] Int. Ct. Hungarian CCI, 10.12.1996, CISG-online 774; *Schlechtriem/Schwenzer/Hager/Schmidt-Kessel*, CISG Commentary, Art. 66, Rn. 5; *Staudinger/Magnus*, Art. 66, Rn. 6; *Honsell/Schönle/Th. Koller*, Art. 66, Rn. 19.

[19] So noch *Hager/Maultzsch*, 5. Aufl., Art. 66 Rn. 4.

[20] Gelangt man in diesen Konstellationen zu einem hoheitlichen Handeln, so vermag dessen Ausschluss von den Gefahrtragungsregeln mit dem Argument, der Betroffene könne gegen den Eingriff vorgehen, sicher nicht zu überzeugen.

[21] Ob der unsorgfältig organisierte Transport dann eine Handlung oder die Unterlassung eines sorgfältig organisierten Transports ist, braucht wohl nicht entschieden zu werden.

barer Kriegsgefahr ein Transportweg durch das betroffene Gebiet gewählt wird.[22] Gleiches gilt, wenn der Verkäufer mit einer auf der Verletzung geistigen Eigentums beruhenden Beschlagnahmung im Transitstaat zu rechnen hatte, etwa weil er die dortige rechtliche Situation aus früheren Geschäften kannte.[23] In beiden Szenarien fehlt es an der geschuldeten angemessenen Organisation des Transports.

10 Generell existierende **Export- und/oder Importbeschränkungen** bzw. Genehmigungserfordernisse berühren, recht besehen, nicht den Regelungsbereich der Gefahrtragungsnormen, sondern betreffen in erster Linie den Pflichtenkreis der Parteien.[24] Im Kern geht es darum, welche der Parteien für die Beschaffung der erforderlichen Lizenzen zuständig ist. Enthält der Vertrag keine Regelung,[25] so ist die Beschaffung der Exportlizenz Teil der Lieferpflicht des Verkäufers, die Beschaffung der Importlizenz Teil der Abnahmepflicht des Käufers im Sinne des Art. 60 lit. a).[26] Wird die Lizenz versagt, so führt dies zu einer Pflichtverletzung der für die Beschaffung der jeweiligen Lizenz zuständigen Partei. In Betracht kommt dann allenfalls eine Entlastung von der Schadenersatzpflicht nach Art. 79.[27] Dies gilt im Falle des Verkäufers auch dann, wenn zum Zeitpunkt der Lizenzverweigerung der Zeitpunkt des Gefahrübergangs schon überschritten ist, etwa weil die Ware im Land des Verkäufers vor Abschluss des Genehmigungsverfahrens an den ersten Beförderer (Art. 67 I) übergeben wurde. Da die Konvention kein Verschulden voraussetzt, liegt auch in dieser Konstellation eine den Gefahrübergang unbeachtlich machende „omission of the seller" nach Art. 66 *in fine* vor, namentlich die unterlassene Besorgung der Exportlizenz.

11 Unvorhersehbar in Kraft gesetzte **Aus- und Einfuhrverbote,** etwa im Rahmen von Handelsembargos, fallen, vor dem Hintergrund des oben (Rn. 6 ff.) zu hoheitlichen Eingriffen Gesagten, in den Anwendungsbereich der Gefahrtragungsregeln des CISG. Vor dem Zeitpunkt des Gefahrübergangs treffen die Folgen deshalb den Verkäufer, der sich gegebenenfalls auf Grundlage von Art. 79 entlasten, aber eben auch das Hindernis zu überwinden suchen muss, beispielsweise durch (legale) Bemühungen um eine Ausnahmegenehmigung.[28]

3. Veränderungen des Transports

12 Die Gefahrtragungsregeln des CISG erfassen grundsätzlich nicht ökonomische Risiken.[29] Ein in diesen Bereich hineinspielendes Problem entsteht aber, wenn nach Gefahrübergang eine Umleitung des Transports notwendig wird und dadurch zusätzliche Kosten entstehen, die in solchen Situation sehr schnell signifikante Grössenordnungen erreichen.

13 Das Problem lässt sich zunächst auf die – freilich oft vorkommenden – Fälle eingrenzen, in denen der Verkäufer für die Organisation des Transports zuständig ist, Lieferung und Gefahrübergang aber bereits vor dem eigentlichen Transport erfolgen. Bei Verwendung der Incoterms® 2010 betrifft dies die C-Terms, bei denen der Verkäufer gemäss der jeweiligen A3-Klausel den Transport organisieren muss, Lieferung und Gefahrübergang gemäss der jeweiligen A4- und A5-Klauseln aber bereits entweder bei Übergabe an den Beförderer (CPT, CIP) oder an Bord des Schiffes (CFR, CIF) erfolgen. Bei Verwendung der F-Terms entsteht das Problem nur, wenn der Verkäufer – Parteivereinbarung oder Handelsüblichkeit

---

[22] Vgl. *Honsell/Schönle/Th. Koller,* Art. 66, Rn. 19.
[23] Zum möglichen Szenario der Haftung des Verkäufers nach Art. 42 für die Verletzung geistigen Eigentums im Transitstaat vgl. oben *Schwenzer,* Art. 42 Rn. 13 a.
[24] Vorausgesetzt natürlich, dass ein Vertrag über von solchen Beschränkungen oder gar Verboten erfassten Waren oder Vertragsparteien nach dem anwendbaren nationalen Recht – Art. 4 S. 2 lit. a) – gültig ist.
[25] Eine einseitige Auferlegung dieser Pflicht sehen auch die Incoterms® 2010 nur ausnahmsweise vor, namentlich bei Verwendung von DDP.
[26] *Hager/Maultzsch,* 5. Aufl., Art 66 Rn. 4; oben *Widmer Lüchinger,* Art. 31 Rn. 85; *Schlechtriem/Schwenzer/Hager/Schmidt-Kessel,* CISG Commentary, Art. 66, Rn. 6. Auch die Incoterms® 2010 sehen diese Pflichtenaufteilung in allen Terms, mit Ausnahme von EXW und DDP, vor.
[27] Zu den unterschiedlichen Auffassungen, ob Lizenzversagungen ein „impediment beyond his control" ist, vgl. unten *Schwenzer,* Art. 79 Rn. 17.
[28] *Schlechtriem/Schwenzer/Hager/Schmidt-Kessel,* CISG Commentary, Art. 66, Rn. 6.
[29] Vgl. oben Vor Artt. 66–70 Rn. 3.

folgend – in Abweichung vom Ausgangspunkt der jeweiligen A3-Klausel den Transport organisiert. In diesen Fällen erfolgen Lieferung und Gefahrübergang nach Verladung auf das Transportmittel (FCA, Klausel A3(a)) bzw. Schiff des Beförderers (FOB), oder wenn die Ware zur Verladung auf das Transportmittel (FCA, Klausel A3(b)) bzw. längsseits des Schiffes bereitgestellt wird (FAS). Finden die Vorschriften des CISG Anwendung, so kann das Problem bei Einschlägigkeit der Grundnormen in Artt. 31 I, 67 I und einer Verpflichtung des Verkäufers zur Organisation des Transports nach Art. 32 II entstehen.

In der Sache geht es letztlich darum, wer die Kosten dafür zu tragen hat, dass die Ware trotz **14** eines Hindernisses auf dem in Aussicht genommenen Transportweg überhaupt bzw. rechtzeitig eintrifft. Nach Art. 31 schuldet der Verkäufer nicht den tatsächlichen Besitzerwerb durch den Käufer.[30] Die nach Art. 79 I dem Verkäufer obliegende Pflicht, Hindernisse zu überwinden, findet deshalb ihr zeitliches Ende grundsätzlich mit der Lieferung im Sinne der in Rn. 13 beschriebenen Fälle.[31] Fraglich wäre also allenfalls, ob die Verwendung eines Incoterm® oder einer anderen vertraglichen Abrede, welche dem Verkäufer die Organisation des Transports auferlegt, dazu führt, dass der Verkäufer letztlich auch die erfolgreiche Durchführung des von ihm selbst gewählten Transports gewährleistet. Er müsste dann nach den so auf Grundlage von Art. 6 erweiterten Artt. 31 I, 79 I beim Transport entstehende Hindernisse auf eigene Kosten überwinden. Für diese Lösung spräche, dass der Verkäufer selbst eine Risikobewertung bei der Wahl der Transportroute vornimmt und es dann stossend erscheinen könnte, dem Käufer die Konsequenzen dieser Entscheidung des Verkäufers aufzubürden. Allerdings ist zu bedenken, dass der Käufer sich gegen dieses Risiko absichern kann, indem er, gegebenenfalls im Austausch gegen einen höheren Kaufpreis, Liefer- und Gefahrübergangszeitpunkt nach hinten verlagert, etwa wenn es ihm gelingt, die Verwendung eines Incoterm® aus der D-Gruppe durchzusetzen. Die Orientierung an den Gefahrtragungsregeln für die Allozierung zusätzlicher Kosten ist deshalb sachgerecht[32] und wird dementsprechend auch für die C-Terms in den Incoterms® 2010 vertreten.[33] Sie trägt auch dem von den Parteien gewählten Verhältnis von Preis und Risikoverteilung am besten Rechnung. Soweit es um Verzögerungen geht, kann dann auch der Käufer durch Ergreifen oder Unterlassen entsprechender Massnahmen entscheiden, wie viel ihm das rechtzeitige Eintreffen der Ware wert ist.

Im Übrigen ist zu beachten, dass der Verkäufer in den zuvor genannten Konstellationen **15** (oben Rn. 13) einen angemessenen Transport zu den üblichen Bedingungen schuldet.[34] An dieser Angemessenheit wird es insbesondere fehlen, wenn der Verkäufer, sehenden Auges, eine Transportroute wählt, bei der mit Hindernissen zu rechnen ist. In diesen Fällen liegt eine Pflichtverletzung des Verkäufers vor, so dass nach Art. 66 *in fine* die Gefahr ohnehin nicht auf den Käufer übergeht.

IV. Gefahrtragung und Haftung

Mit seinem letzen Halbsatz bringt Art. 66 das Zufälligkeitserfordernis zum Ausdruck. **16** Genauer gesagt, die Beeinträchtigung der Ware darf nicht dem Verkäufer zugerechnet werden können. Auch Art. 36 enthält diesen Grundsatz. Dieser koppelt den für die Mangelfreiheit relevanten Zeitpunkt grundsätzlich an den Gefahrübergang (Art. 36 I). Diese Grundregel greift aber nicht, wenn der erst später auftretende Mangel auf eine vorherige Pflichtverletzung des Verkäufers zurückzuführen ist (Art. 36 II).

---

[30] Vgl. oben *Widmer Lüchinger*, Art. 31 Rn. 4.
[31] Nicht zuletzt deshalb taugt Art. 79 nicht als Grundlage für die Ermittlung des nach Art. 66 *in fine* an das Verhalten des Verkäufers anzulegenden Massstabs, vgl. unten Rn. 23.
[32] *Hager/Maultzsch*, 5. Aufl., Art 66 Rn. 3; *Schlechtriem/Schwenzer/Hager/Schmidt-Kessel*, CISG Commentary, Art. 66, Rn. 3; MünchKomm/*P. Huber*, Art. 66, Rn. 6; *Brunner*, Art. 66, Rn. 11. Für diese Auffassung zu den C-Terms in den Incoterms® 2010 *Ramberg*, Guide to Incoterms, S. 77.
[33] *Ramberg*, Guide to Incoterms, S. 77. Für frühere Entscheide zum CIF-Geschäft vgl. *Hager/Maultzsch*, 5. Aufl., Art 66 Rn. 3.
[34] Für das CISG oben *Widmer Lüchinger*, Art 32 Rn. 15 ff.; Brunner, Art. 66, Rn. 11. Für die Incoterms® vgl. die jeweilige A3-Klausel zu den C-Terms.

1. Reichweite von Art. 66 in fine

17 Anders als Art. 36 II stellt Art. 66 *in fine* nicht auf einen „breach of obligations", sondern auf einen „act or omission of the seller" ab. Das Verständnis dieses letzten Halbsatzes war deshalb in der Lehre lange umstritten. Die in Art. 66 verwendete Formulierung ist zweifellos, und nach dem expliziten Willen der Konventionsverfasser,[35] erheblich weiter als die in Art. 36 II verwendete. Versuchen, den letzten Halbsatz in Art. 66 auf die Reichweite von Art. 36 II zu begrenzen,[36] stehen deshalb mit dem Wortlaut sowie der Entstehungsgeschichte unüberwindbare Hindernisse entgegen.[37]

18 Mittlerweile scheint sich ein, vorzugswürdiges, weiteres Verständnis von Art. 66 *in fine* durchgesetzt zu haben.[38] Konkret bringt die dort gewählte Formulierung nach dieser Auffassung die – bis zur endgültigen Durchführung des Vertrags andauernde[39] – Pflicht des Verkäufers zum Ausdruck, das Vertragsziel nicht zu gefährden.[40] Die über Art. 36 II hinausgehende Formulierung stellt klar, dass die jeweilige Qualifikation einer solchen Pflicht auf nationaler Ebene keine Rolle spielt und es ebenfalls gleichgültig ist, ob nach nationalem Verständnis der jeweilige „act or omission of the seller" dem Vertragsrecht oder dem Haftpflichtrecht zuzuordnen wäre.[41] Art. 66 vermeidet gerade die Unterschiede auf nationaler Ebene hinsichtlich vertrags- und haftpflichtrechtlicher Qualifikationen.

19 Nicht ganz zu Unrecht wird von vielen Stimmen die geringe Bedeutung des Disputs in der Praxis betont.[42] Bisweilen werden hierbei aber doch arg vereinfachende Betrachtungen vorgenommen. Behauptet wird, die Fälle, die von der weiteren Formulierung des Art. 66, nicht aber von der engeren des Art. 36 II erfasst seien, liessen sich „durch die Bank weg"[43] als Verletzung vertraglicher Nebenpflichten qualifizieren.[44] Genannt werden die Situationen, in denen die Ware beschädigt wird, weil der Verkäufer sein right of stoppage in transitu ausübt, er sie wegen eines Mangelverdachts untersuchen lässt oder nach der Abladung im Zielhafen bei der Rücknahme der Container ein Missgeschick passiert.[45]

20 In Erinnerung zu rufen ist, dass die Vorstellung hierarchisch organisierter, vertraglicher Haupt- und Nebenpflichten nicht ohne weiteres über den deutschsprachigen Raum hinaus verallgemeinert werden darf. Auch dem CISG ist ausweislich des Art. 3 diese Hierarchie unbekannt. Im Bereich der, nach dem Verständnis des deutschen Rechtskreises, leistungsbezogenen Nebenpflichten ist diese häufig anzutreffende, bedenkenlose Ausweitung falsch (Art. 7 I), aber wenigstens noch unschädlich, da Art. 3 unzweifelhaft von weiteren, nicht

---

[35] *Hager/Maultzsch*, 5. Aufl., Art. 66 Rn. 7; *Schlechtriem/Schwenzer/Hager/Schmidt-Kessel*, CISG Commentary, Art. 66, Rn. 9.
[36] So noch *Enderlein/Maskow/Strohbach*, Art. 66, Anm. 3.; *Herber/Czerwenka*, Art. 66, Rn. 5.
[37] *Witz/Salger/Lorenz/Witz*, Art. 66, Rn. 8; *Ferrari u. a./Mankowski*, Internationales Vertragsrecht, Art. 66, Rn. 18.
[38] *Hager/Maultzsch*, 5. Aufl., Art. 66 Rn. 7; *Schlechtriem/Schwenzer/Hager/Schmidt-Kessel*, CISG Commentary, Art. 66, Rn. 8; *Staudinger/Magnus*, Art. 66, Rn. 13 ff.; MünchKomm/*P. Huber*, Art. 66, Rn. 12.
[39] *Staudinger/Magnus*, Art. 66, Rn. 15.
[40] MünchKomm/*P. Huber*, Art. 66, Rn. 12 f.; *Ferrari u. a./Mankowski*, Internationales Vertragsrecht, Art. 66, Rn. 20; *Honsell/Schönle/Th. Koller*, Art. 66, Rn. 12.
[41] *Hager/Maultzsch*, 5. Aufl., Art. 66 Rn. 7; *Schlechtriem/Schwenzer/Hager/Schmidt-Kessel*, CISG Commentary, Art. 66, Rn. 9; *Honnold/Flechtner*, Art. 66, Rn. 362, alle mit Verweisen auf die Entstehungsgeschichte. I. S. eines einheitlichen Verständnisses der Konvention empfiehlt es sich in diesem Zusammenhang auf die Verwendung des deutschrechtlich konnotierten Begriffs der „nachvertraglichen Pflicht" zu verzichten.
[42] *Hager/Maultzsch*, 5. Aufl., Art. 66 Rn. 6; *Schlechtriem/Schwenzer/Hager/Schmidt-Kessel*, CISG Commentary, Art. 66, Rn. 8; MünchKomm/*P. Huber*, Art. 66, Rn. 12; *Ferrari u. a./Mankowski*, Internationales Vertragsrecht, Art 66, Rn. 16.
[43] So die Formulierung bei *Ferrari u. a./Mankowski*, Internationales Vertragsrecht, Art. 66, Rn. 16.
[44] *Ferrari u. a./Mankowski*, Internationales Vertragsrecht, Art. 66, Rn. 16. Solche Verallgemeinerungen finden sich auch in OLG Koblenz, 14.12.2006, CISG-online 1408 = IHR 2007, 36; OLG Schleswig, 22.8.2002, CISG-online 710 = IHR 2003, 20. Demgegenüber mit Recht vorsichtig und differenzierend *Hager/Maultzsch*, 5. Aufl., Art. 66 Rn. 7; *Schlechtriem/Schwenzer/Hager/Schmidt-Kessel*, CISG Commentary, Art. 66, Rn. 10.
[45] Vgl. für diese Bsp. *Hager/Maultzsch*, 5. Aufl., Art. 66 Rn. 7; *Schlechtriem/Schwenzer/Hager/Schmidt-Kessel*, CISG Commentary, Art. 66, Rn. 9; *Witz/Salger/Lorenz/Witz*, Art. 66, Rn. 8; MünchKomm/*P. Huber*, Art. 66, Rn. 12.

kaufvertragstypischen Pflichten des Verkäufers ausgeht. Anders liegt es mit dem, was der deutschsprachige Jurist unter Schutzpflichten versteht. Diese generell als vom Vertrag, und damit von der anwendbaren *lex causae*, mit umfasst zu sehen, ist ein Verständnis, dessen Übertragung auf das CISG dann mit Art. 7 I endgültig unvereinbar ist. Die im letzten Halbsatz von Art. 66 gewählte Formulierung trägt dem in sachgerechter Weise Rechnung und schützt die Konvention insoweit vor der Übertragung nationaler Vorverständnisse.

Keine Frage der Gefahrtragung, sondern der Vertragswidrigkeit und des dafür relevanten Zeitpunktes ist der in der Praxis sicher am häufigsten auftretende Fall des durch mangelhafte Verpackung eingetretenen Schadens, so dass es auf Art. 66 *in fine* gerade nicht ankommt.[46] Gleiches gilt selbstverständlich für das der Konvention gänzlich fremde, rein deutsche, und auch dort wohl endgültig überflüssige, Konzept des Weiterfressermangels, der immer eine einfache Mangelhaftigkeit war, ist und bleibt.[47] Zum Zuge kommen in diesen Fällen die üblichen Rechtsbehelfe des Käufers wegen einer Pflichtverletzung des Verkäufers nach Artt. 45 ff. Auch kommt Art. 70 nicht zur Anwendung, der die von der wesentlichen Vertragsverletzung des Verkäufers unabhängige, zufällige Beeinträchtigung der Ware in den Blick nimmt.[48]

2. Massstab für das Verkäuferverhalten

Nicht abschliessend geklärt ist allerdings, welcher Massstab an das Verhalten des Verkäufers anzulegen ist, wenn sich die Frage stellt, ob der Gefahrübergang wegen „act or omission of the seller" unbeachtlich ist. Verschiedentlich wird von einem Verstoss gegen objektiv gebotene Verhaltensweisen gesprochen.[49] Der Hinweis darauf, es könne sich nur um Ereignisse handeln, die nicht schon nach den Wertungen des Art. 79 ausserhalb des Einflussbereichs des Verkäufers liegen,[50] ist in jedem Fall zutreffend. Zweifelhaft ist allerdings, ob sich daraus aber auch der Massstab für die Anstrengungen entnehmen lässt, die der Verkäufer zu unternehmen hat, um das Vertragsziel nicht zu gefährden.[51]

Dagegen spricht zunächst, dass die – letztlich ja dann doch stattfindende – Ausdehnung von Art. 79 über den Zeitpunkt der Leistungserbringung hinaus effektiv die Wertungen des Gefahrübergangs gefährdet und nicht zum System der Leistungszeit des CISG passt. Eine allfällige Abschwächung der Anforderungen im Rahmen der Übertragung der Wertungen aus Art. 79 auf den Bereich der Gefahrtragung könnte darüber hinaus zu gefährlichen Rückschlüssen und Parallelwertungen auf den originären Anwendungsbereich dieser Vorschrift führen, wo die Anforderungen mit Recht ausserordentlich hoch sind.

Die Konvention scheint demgegenüber eher vom Massstab der „reasonableness" auszugehen. Besonders deutlich wird dies bei der Organisation des Transports durch den Verkäufer. Nach der (subsidiären) Ausgangslage des CISG geht die Gefahr beim Versendungskauf mit der Übergabe an den ersten Beförderer über (Art. 67 I). Ist der Verkäufer im Sinne des Art. 32 II für die Organisation des Transports zuständig, so schuldet er nach dieser Vorschrift im Lichte der „circumstances" Transportverträge, die „necessary" sind, die Verwendung von „appropriate" Transportmitteln vorsehen und in Übereinstimmung mit den „usual terms for

---

[46] *Schlechtriem/Schwenzer/Hager/Schmidt-Kessel*, CISG Commentary, Art. 66, Rn. 11 mit zutreffendem Hinweis darauf, dass dies von OLG Koblenz, 14.12.2006, CISG-online 1408 = IHR 2007, 36 übersehen worden ist. Das Gericht hat hier offensichtlich die deutsche Konzeption von der adäquaten Verpackung als hierarchisch untergeordnete Nebenleistungspflicht trotz Art. 35 II lit. d) auf das CISG übertragen. I. S. dieser Entscheidung aber offenbar auch *Honsell/Schönle/Th. Koller*, Art. 66, Rn. 13. Schlecht gewählt ist deshalb auch das von *Honnold/Flechtner*, Art. 66, Rn. 362 verwendete Bsp. des zu alten Reissacks, der deshalb auf dem Transport reisst.

[47] Rechtspolitisch mag die vor der Schuldrechtsreform ergangene Rspr. aus Gründen des Käuferschutzes ihre Berechtigung gehabt haben; in der Nähe des CISG hat sie – wie mit Recht von OLG Jena, 26.5.1998, CISG-online 513 = TranspR-IHR 2000, 25 schon vor nunmehr fast 15 Jahren festgestellt – nichts zu suchen.

[48] *Schlechtriem/Schwenzer/Hager/Schmidt-Kessel*, CISG Commentary, Art. 66, Rn. 11. Vgl. unten Art. 70 Rn. 5 ff.

[49] *Honsell/Schönle/Th. Koller*, Art. 66, Rn. 12.

[50] *Schlechtriem/Schwenzer/Hager/Schmidt-Kessel*, CISG Commentary, Art. 66, Rn. 10.

[51] So aber *Schlechtriem/Schwenzer/Hager/Schmidt-Kessel*, CISG Commentary, Art. 66, Rn. 10: Zwar keine direkte Anwendung von Art. 79 aber doch Anlehnung an die darin zum Ausdruck gebrachten Wertungen. Ebenso MünchKomm/*P. Huber*, Art. 66, Rn. 13.

such transportation" stehen. Diese Anforderungen lassen sich als ein allgemeines Angemessenheitserfordernis lesen. Sachgerecht erscheint in diesem Zusammenhang auch die Orientierung an den Artt. 85–88, die durchwegs an den Massstab der „reasonableness" anknüpfen.

25 Vorzugswürdig erscheint es deshalb, auch an die übrigen „acts or omissions of the seller", die ebenfalls den Zeitraum nach dem Gefahrübergang betreffen, den Massstab der Angemessenheit anzulegen. In vielen Fällen wird es sich dabei um Handlungen bzw. Unterlassungen handeln, die auch das Kriterium des rechtmässigen Verkäuferverhaltens erfüllen.

3. Rechtmässiges Verkäuferverhalten

26 Rechtmässiges Verhalten des Verkäufers hindert den Gefahrübergang freilich nicht. Übt er also sein right of stoppage in transitu aus und geht die Ware dann zufällig unter bzw. wird sie zufällig beschädigt, so liegt darin kein „act or omission of the seller" im Sinne von Art. 66 *in fine*, der den Gefahrübergang unbeachtlich werden liesse.[52] Dies gilt auch, wenn der Verkäufer die bereits versandte Ware aufgrund eines Mangelverdachts untersuchen lässt und die Ware dabei zu Schaden kommt.[53]

V. Gefahrtragung und Kaufpreisklage

1. Grundsatz

27 Nach der grundsätzlichen Konzeption der Gefahrtragung, und so auch in Art. 66 zum Ausdruck gebracht, behält der Verkäufer nach Gefahrübergang den Anspruch auf die Zahlung des Kaufpreises, obwohl die Ware danach untergegangen oder beschädigt worden ist.

28 Liegt ein Fall des Art. 66 *in fine* vor, so ist der Gefahrübergang unbeachtlich und die Artt. 45 ff. gelangen zugunsten des Käufers zur Anwendung.[54]

2. Begrenzung der Kaufpreisklage

29 Zu beachten ist allerdings, dass der Kaufpreisanspruch des Verkäufers dem Vorbehalt des Art. 28 unterliegt.[55] Würde das befasste Gericht also nach eigenem Recht den Anspruch nicht gewähren, ist es auch nicht verpflichtet das im Anwendungsbereich der Konvention zu tun. In der Praxis wird sich diese Frage kaum einmal stellen. Die Vorbehalte der Rechtsordnungen des Common Law gegenüber dem Erfüllungsanspruch fokussieren vornehmlich die Sachleistung.[56] Der Zahlungsanspruch scheitert regelmässig nicht an diesem Punkt.

30 Der Zahlungsanspruch kann allerdings auf nationaler Ebene in bestimmten Konstellationen aus anderen Gründen scheitern. Ein Beispiel dafür findet sich in den U.S.-amerikanischen Bundesstaaten. Dort versagen die jeweiligen in bundesstaatliches Recht umgesetzten §§ 2–510 (3), 2–709 (1a, 1b) des UCC dem Verkäufer marktgängiger Ware den Zahlungsanspruch, wenn er nach der käuferseitigen Verletzung der Abnahmepflicht die Ware noch unangemessen lange verwahrt und die Sache dann untergeht oder beschädigt wird. Die Frage, ob solche Regelungen nach Art. 28 auf den Zahlungsanspruch nach CISG durchschlagen können, ist nicht leicht zu beantworten.

31 Zunächst lassen sich die in der vorigen Rn. (30) zitierten Vorschriften des UCC teilweise dem Bereich der Gefahrtragung zuordnen.[57] Dafür spricht insbesondere der Wortlaut von

---

[52] *Hager/Maultzsch*, 5. Aufl., Art. 66 Rn. 7; *Staudinger/Magnus*, Art. 66, Rn. 16; MünchKomm/*P. Huber*, Art. 66, Rn. 13; *Brunner*, Art. 66, Rn. 15.
[53] *Hager/Maultzsch*, 5. Aufl., Art. 66 Rn. 6; *Schlechtriem/Schwenzer/Hager/Schmidt-Kessel*, CISG Commentary, Art. 66, Rn. 6; MünchKomm/*P. Huber*, Art. 66, Rn. 13. Dagegen MünchKommHGB/*Benicke*, Art. 66, Rn. 9.
[54] *Hager/Maultzsch*, 5. Aufl., Art. 66 Rn. 5; MünchKomm/*P. Huber*, Art. 66, Rn. 14; *Honsell/Schönle/Th. Koller*, Art. 66, Rn. 4; *Brunner*, Art. 66, Rn. 14.
[55] Dazu näher und überzeugend oben *Mohs*, Art. 62 Rn. 14. Auch schon *Hager/Maultzsch*, 5. Aufl., Art. 66 Rn. 7a; Art. 62, Rn. 12; *Schlechtriem/Schwenzer/Hager/Schmidt-Kessel*, CISG Commentary, Art. 66, Rn. 12.
[56] Vgl. dazu *Schwenzer/Hachem/Kee*, Rn. 43.24 ff.
[57] So *Schlechtriem/Schwenzer/Hager/Schmidt-Kessel*, CISG Commentary, Art. 66, Rn. 12.

§ 2–510 (3) UCC, wonach der Verkäufer den vor Gefahrübergang leistungsverweigernden Käufer für eine „commercially reasonable time" so behandeln darf, als trüge dieser die Gefahr. In diesem Fall ist tatsächlich von einer Kollision mit Art. 66 auszugehen, so dass die nationale – in diesem Fall bundesstaatliche – Regelung verdrängt wird.[58] Dies gilt, soweit der UCC bei Leistungsverweigerung des Käufers vor Gefahrübergang diesen nur fingiert,[59] während nach zutreffender vorherrschender Ansicht zum CISG – trotz Fehlens einer entsprechenden Regelung – bei Leistungsverzug des Käufers dieser auch die Gefahr zu tragen hat.[60]

Eine andere, und davon zu unterscheidende Frage ist es, ob das zeitliche Ende der Gefahrübergangsfiktion in § 2–510 (3) UCC nach einer „commercially reasonable time" über Art. 28 dem Zahlungsanspruch des Verkäufers entgegen steht. Bei funktionaler Betrachtung handelt es sich dabei um eine speziell geregelte zeitliche Begrenzung des Zahlungsanspruches.[61] Die Konvention erfasst aber – von den Rügefristen in Artt. 39, 43 zu unterscheidende – zeitliche Anspruchsbegrenzungen gerade nicht.[62] Dass diese zeitliche Begrenzung in der Form des Endes der Gefahrübergangsfiktion auftritt, erscheint als reine Rechtstechnik. Vermieden wird damit spekulatives Verhalten des Verkäufers, der ohne Anreiz zur sorgfältigen Erhaltung der Ware die Entwicklung des Marktpreises abwartet und als Mindesterlös den Zahlungsanspruch gegen den Käufer in der Hand behält. 32

Ein Konflikt ergibt sich deshalb in diesem Zusammenhang eher mit den Artt. 85–88 als mit den Regelungen über die Gefahrtragung. Nach Art. 85 I ist der Verkäufer zum Selbsthilfeverkauf berechtigt („may") und dazu gemäss Art. 85 II („must") nur verpflichtet, wenn die Ware „rapid deterioration" ausgesetzt ist. Dem Verkäufer über Art. 28 nach § 2–510 (3) UCC den Zahlungsanspruch nach einer „commercially reasonable time" aus der Hand zu schlagen, weil er im Anschluss an den Gefahrübergang bei Leistungsverzug des Käufers die Ware nicht schnell genug veräussert hat, würde dem Verkäufer damit entgegen Art. 85 I indirekt die Pflicht auferlegen, zum Selbsthilfeverkauf zu greifen. 33

Allgemein gesprochen kann deshalb eine auf nationaler Ebene existierende zeitliche Begrenzung des Zahlungsanspruchs, welche an den Selbsthilfeverkauf der Ware durch den Verkäufer anknüpft, nicht über Art. 28 dem Verkäufer entgegen gehalten werden. Diese Verdrängungswirkung des CISG sollte gelten, auch wenn nicht von der Hand zu weisen ist, dass die diskutierte Regelung des UCC aus dem oben (Rn. 31) genannten Gesichtspunkt heraus auch als besonderer Ausdruck der zeitlichen Anspruchsbegrenzung durch „estoppel" verstanden werden kann, die wiederum von der Konvention, auch funktional, nicht erfasst und deshalb nicht verdrängt wäre. 34

VI. Beweislast

Wie auch sonst hat das Vorliegen der Voraussetzungen des Gefahrübergangs zu beweisen, wer sich darauf beruft, dies wird für Art. 66 HS. 1 der Verkäufer sein.[63] Die Formulierung des zweiten Halbsatzes weist die Beweislast für die Unbeachtlichkeit des Gefahrübergangs eindeutig dem Käufer zu.[64] 35

---

[58] So *Schlechtriem/Schwenzer/Hager/Schmidt-Kessel*, CISG Commentary, Art. 66, Rn. 12.
[59] Der Verkäufer ist ausweislich des Wortlauts von § 2–510 (3) UCC eben nur berechtigt, den Käufer so zu behandeln, als sei die Gefahr übergegangen. Am Ende der „commercially reasonable time" springt also technisch die Gefahr nicht zurück auf den Verkäufer, er darf schlicht den Käufer nicht mehr so behandeln, als sei die Gefahr jemals übergegangen.
[60] Vgl. dazu unten Art. 69 Rn. 9 ff.
[61] Ob dabei der Anspruch selbst erlischt oder einfach nicht mehr durchsetzbar ist, spielt für das CISG keine Rolle.
[62] Vgl. oben *Schwenzer*, Art. 39 Rn. 28.
[63] *Staudinger/Magnus*, Art. 66, Rn. 20; MünchKommHGB/*Benicke*, Art. 66, Rn. 11; *Ferrari u. a./Mankowski*, Internationales Vertragsrecht, Art. 66, Rn. 32.
[64] Int. Ct. Hungarian CCI, 10.12.1996, CISG-online 774; Cámara Nacional de Apelaciones en lo Comercial, 31.10.1995, CISG-online 299; *Ferrari u. a./Mankowski*, Internationales Vertragsrecht, Art. 66, Rn. 32.

Art. 67 [Gefahrübergang bei Beförderung der Ware]

(1) Erfordert der Kaufvertrag eine Beförderung der Ware und ist der Verkäufer nicht verpflichtet, sie an einem bestimmten Ort zu übergeben, so geht die Gefahr auf den Käufer über, sobald die Ware gemäß dem Kaufvertrag dem ersten Beförderer zur Übermittlung an den Käufer übergeben wird. Hat der Verkäufer dem Beförderer die Ware an einem bestimmten Ort zu übergeben, so geht die Gefahr erst auf den Käufer über, wenn die Ware dem Beförderer an diesem Ort übergeben wird. Ist der Verkäufer befugt, die Dokumente, die zur Verfügung über die Ware berechtigen, zurückzubehalten, so hat dies keinen Einfluß auf den Übergang der Gefahr.

(2) Die Gefahr geht jedoch erst auf den Käufer über, wenn die Ware eindeutig dem Vertrag zugeordnet ist, sei es durch an der Ware angebrachte Kennzeichen, durch Beförderungsdokumente, durch eine Anzeige an den Käufer oder auf andere Weise.

Art. 67

(1) If the contract of sale involves carriage of the goods and the seller is not bound to hand them over at a particular place, the risk passes to the buyer when the goods are handed over to the first carrier for transmission to the buyer in accordance with the contract of sale. If the seller is bound to hand the goods over to a carrier at a particular place, the risk does not pass to the buyer until the goods are handed over to the carrier at that place. The fact that the seller is authorized to retain documents controlling the disposition of the goods does not affect the passage of the risk.

(2) Nevertheless, the risk does not pass to the buyer until the goods are clearly identified to the contract, whether by markings on the goods, by shipping documents, by notice given to the buyer or otherwise.

Art. 67

1) Lorsque le contrat de vente implique un transport des marchandises et que le vendeur n'est pas tenu de les remettre en un lieu déterminé, les risques sont transférés à l'acheteur à partir de la remise des marchandises au premier transporteur pour transmission à l'acheteur conformément au contrat de vente. Lorsque le vendeur est tenu de remettre les marchandises à un transporteur en un lieu déterminé, les risques ne sont pas transférés à l'acheteur tant que les marchandises n'ont pas été remises au transporteur en ce lieu. Le fait que le vendeur soit autorisé à conserver les documents représentatifs des marchandises n'affecte pas le transfert des risques.

2) Cependant, les risques ne sont pas transférés à l'acheteur tant que les marchandises n'ont pas été clairement identifiées aux fins du contrat, que ce soit par l'apposition d'un signe distinctif sur les marchandises, par des documents de transport, par un avis donné à l'acheteur ou par tout autre moyen.

Übersicht

	Rn.
I. Vorgeschichte	1
II. Regelungsgegenstand	4
III. Grundregel (Art. 67 I 1)	8
1. Erforderlichkeit der Beförderung	9
2. Beförderer	12
3. Übergabe	17
IV. Versand ab einem bestimmten Ort (Art. 67 I 2)	22
V. Zurückbehaltung der Dokumente (Art. 67 I 3)	27
VI. Individualisierung der Ware (Art. 67 II)	29
1. Allgemeines	29
2. Sammelladungen (bulk cargo)	31
3. Keine Rückwirkung	35
VII. Beweisfragen	36

I. Vorgeschichte

Art. 67 I hat keinen direkten Vorläufer im EKG.[1] Hingegen enthielt Art. 19 III EKG eine Art. 67 II im Wesentlichen entsprechende Regelung.[2] Die heutige Fassung von Art. 67 CISG geht auf Art. 65 des Wiener Entwurfs zurück,[3] der auf der Wiener Abschlusskonferenz nur noch geringfügig geändert wurde.[4] **1**

Das EKG hatte den Gefahrübergang noch mit der Lieferung vertragsgemässer Ware verknüpft.[5] Dieser Ansatz wurde jedoch schon während den Vorarbeiten zum CISG aufgegeben.[6] Besonderen Anstoss dazu hatte das komplizierte System des EKG in Fällen der Lieferung mangelhafter Ware gegeben.[7] In diesen Situationen hatte es den Gefahrübergang gerade wieder von der Lieferung entkoppeln müssen (Art. 99 II EKG).[8] **2**

Gleichwohl sind die sachlichen Unterschiede von nachrangiger Bedeutung.[9] Sie schlagen sich letztlich nur darin nieder, dass die Individualisierung nach Vertragsschluss nicht zu einem rückwirkenden Gefahrübergang führt.[10] Praktische Relevanz kann dieser Veränderung aber in den oft vorkommenden Konstellationen des Verkaufs reisender Ware (Art. 68) zukommen. Freilich wird in diesen Situationen aber die Grundregel des Art. 68 S. 1 praktisch in den meisten Fällen von dem eigentlich als Ausnahmevorschrift konzipierten Art. 68 S. 2 überlagert.[11] Die im Wegfall des rückwirkenden Gefahrübergangs bei nachträglicher Individualisierung angelegte Gefahr der Streitförderung durch Gefahrsplittung dürfte sich deshalb regelmässig nicht materialisieren. **3**

II. Regelungsgegenstand

Art. 67 regelt den **Zeitpunkt des Gefahrübergangs beim Distanzkauf.** Regelmässig dürfte die Vorschrift aber von den Parteien durch Verwendung eines Incoterm®, z. B. CIF oder FOB, nach Artt. 6, 9 verdrängt sein. Ihre praktische Relevanz ist deshalb begrenzt.[12] **4**

Die Grundregel des Abs. 1 S. 1 entspricht dem weltweit gängigen Ansatz, dem Käufer das Untergangs- bzw. Beschädigungsrisiko für den gesamten Transport aufzubürden.[13] Der Verkäufer gibt mit der Übergabe an den ersten Beförderer den Gewahrsam an der Sache auf und es ist bei allfälligen Schäden oft dem Käufer einfacher, diese zunächst festzustellen und sich dann mit dem Beförderer auseinanderzusetzen.[14] Dies wird insbesondere dann der Fall **5**

---

[1] *Staudinger/Magnus*, Art. 67, Rn. 5; *Ferrari u. a./Mankowski*, Internationales Vertragsrecht, Art. 67, Rn. 2.
[2] *Staudinger/Magnus*, Art. 67, Rn. 5.
[3] *Staudinger/Magnus*, Art. 67, Rn. 6.
[4] *Staudinger/Magnus*, Art. 67, Rn. 7. Insbesondere wurde Art. 67 II erweitert, vgl. zu dieser Vorschrift unten Rn. 29 ff.
[5] *Hager/Maultzsch*, 5. Aufl., Art. 67 Rn. 1; *Schlechtriem/Schwenzer/Hager/Schmidt-Kessel*, CISG Commentary, Art. 67, Rn. 1; *Staudinger/Magnus*, Art. 67, Rn. 5.
[6] *Hager/Maultzsch*, 5. Aufl., Art. 67 Rn. 1; *Schlechtriem/Schwenzer/Hager/Schmidt-Kessel*, CISG Commentary, Art. 67, Rn. 1; *Staudinger/Magnus*, Art. 67, Rn. 5.
[7] *Hager/Maultzsch*, 5. Aufl., Art. 67 Rn. 1; *Schlechtriem/Schwenzer/Hager/Schmidt-Kessel*, CISG Commentary, Art. 67, Rn. 1; *Staudinger/Magnus*, Art. 67, Rn. 5.
[8] *Hager/Maultzsch*, 5. Aufl., Art. 67 Rn. 1; *Schlechtriem/Schwenzer/Hager/Schmidt-Kessel*, CISG Commentary, Art. 67, Rn. 1.
[9] *Hager/Maultzsch*, 5. Aufl., Art. 67 Rn. 1; *Schlechtriem/Schwenzer/Hager/Schmidt-Kessel*, CISG Commentary, Art. 67, Rn. 1; *Mohs*, FS Schwenzer, S. 1293.
[10] *Hager/Maultzsch*, 5. Aufl., Art. 67 Rn. 1; *Schlechtriem/Schwenzer/Hager/Schmidt-Kessel*, CISG Commentary, Art. 67, Rn. 1.
[11] *Mohs*, FS Schwenzer, S. 1295; vgl. dazu auch unten Art. 68 Rn. 7.
[12] *Hager/Maultzsch*, 5. Aufl., Art. 67 Rn. 2; *Staudinger/Magnus*, Art. 67, Rn. 3; *MünchKomm/P. Huber*, Art. 67, Rn. 3; MünchKommHGB/*Benicke*, Art. 67, Rn. 1.
[13] *Hager/Maultzsch*, 5. Aufl., Art. 67 Rn. 3; *Schwenzer/Hachem/Kee*, Rn. 38.40 ff.; *Hager*, Gefahrtragung, S. 81 Fn. 38.
[14] *Hager/Maultzsch*, 5. Aufl., Art. 67 Rn. 3; *MünchKomm/P. Huber*, Art. 67, Rn. 1; *Honnold/Flechtner*, Art. 67, Rn. 367; MünchKommHGB/*Benicke*, Art. 67, Rn. 2.

sein, wenn der Käufer die Kosten des Transports zu tragen hat und den Lohn des Beförderers zurückbehalten und gegebenenfalls mit einem Schadenersatzanspruch verrechnen kann.

6   Die in Art. 67 I 2[15] als Sonderfall geregelte Konstellation des vereinbarten „particular place" entspricht dem in der Praxis häufigen Fall, dass die Parteien einen Incoterm® mit Ortsangabe verwenden, z. B. „CIF Hamburg".[16] Art. 67 I 3 stellt klar, dass die Zurückbehaltung der Dokumente den Gefahrübergang nicht hindert. Ihren praktischen Anwendungsbereich hat die Vorschrift, wenn der Verkäufer die Kaufpreiszahlung sichern will.

7   Schliesslich verlangt Art. 67 II die hinreichende Individualisierung der Ware. Im Zusammenspiel mit Art. 69 III ergibt sich daraus ein für die Konvention allgemeines Prinzip (Art. 7 II), dass der Gefahrübergang in allen Fällen nur bei hinreichender Individualisierung der Ware, die freilich eine Sammelladung nicht ausschliesst, erfolgen kann.[17]

III. Grundregel (Art. 67 I 1)

8   Art. 67 I enthält in S. 1 drei Voraussetzungen. Namentlich muss die Beförderung der Ware erforderlich, der Transporteur ein „Beförderer" und die „Übergabe" an ihn erfolgt sein. Selbstverständlich gelten diese Voraussetzungen entsprechend für S. 2.

1. Erforderlichkeit der Beförderung

9   Die Erforderlichkeit der Beförderung nach dem Kaufvertrag im Sinne des Art. 67 I ergibt sich nicht schon aus dem einfachen Sachverhalt, dass die verkaufte Ware von der Niederlassung des Verkäufers zur Niederlassung des Käufers transportiert werden muss. Hat also nach dem Vertrag der Käufer die Ware beim Verkäufer abzuholen oder der Verkäufer dem Käufer die Ware zu bringen, so handelt es sich jeweils nicht um einen Versendungskauf, für den Art. 67 gilt, sondern es liegt dann ein Fall des Art. 69 vor.[18] Art. 67 I erfasst deshalb die Fälle, in denen der Verkäufer seine Lieferpflicht erfüllt, indem er die Ware an den Beförderer übergibt.[19] Für das Erforderlichkeitskriterium ist deshalb Rückgriff auf Art. 31 lit. a) zu nehmen.[20]

10 Für die Frage, ob die Beförderung erforderlich ist, stellt Art. 67 I nach seinem klaren Wortlaut in erster Linie auf den Vertrag ab. In Betracht zu ziehen sind deshalb Kostentragungsregeln und Organisationspflichten für den Transport selbst und gegebenenfalls den Versicherungsschutz.[21] Nicht vergessen werden darf dabei allerdings, dass vertragliche Regelungen solcher Art aber den Gefahrübergang weder herbeiführen noch verhindern.[22]

11 Die Grenzziehung zwischen reinen Kostentragungs- und Gefahrtragungsregeln kann erhebliche Schwierigkeiten bereiten. Das gilt bislang insbesondere für die Klauseln „frei Haus" und „frei Bestimmungsort".[23] Die Formulierung „[d]er Preis beträgt frei Haus B.

---

[15] Die Vorschrift war im EKG noch nicht enthalten und geht auf einen Vorschlag der deutschen Bundesregierung zurück, YB VIII (1977), S. 118, Nr. 31, S. 162, Art. 65, Nr. 1, S. 63, Nr. 535 – 537; *Hager/Maultzsch*, 5. Aufl., Art. 67 Rn. 2 Fn. 3.
[16] Dazu näher unten Rn. 22 ff.
[17] Vgl. oben vor Artt. 66–70 Rn. 19.
[18] *Hager/Maultzsch*, 5. Aufl., Art. 67 Rn. 3; *Staudinger/Magnus*, Art. 67, Rn. 10; MünchKomm/*P. Huber*, Art. 67, Rn. 5; *Herber/Czerwenka*, Art. 67, Rn. 3.
[19] *Hager/Maultzsch*, 5. Aufl., Art. 67 Rn. 3; *Staudinger/Magnus*, Art. 67, Rn. 9; MünchKomm/*P. Huber*, Art. 67, Rn. 5; *Brunner*, Art. 67, Rn. 2.
[20] Vgl. dazu oben näher *Widmer Lüchinger*, Art. 31 Rn. 13 ff. So auch *Staudinger/Magnus*, Art. 67, Rn. 9; MünchKomm/*P. Huber*, Art. 67, Rn. 5; *Honnold/Flechtner*, Art. 67, Rn. 364.
[21] *Staudinger/Magnus*, Art. 67, Rn. 9; MünchKommHGB/*Benicke*, Art. 67, Rn. 2.
[22] Audiencia Provincial de Córdoba, 31.10.1997, CISG-online 502; Cámara Nacional de Apelaciones en lo Comercial, 31.10.1995, CISG-online 299; *Schlechtriem/Schwenzer/Hager/Schmidt-Kessel*, CISG Commentary, Art. 66, Rn. 3; *Staudinger/Magnus*, Art. 67, Rn. 9; MünchKomm/*P. Huber*, Art. 67, Rn. 7; MünchKommHGB/*Benicke*, Art. 67, Rn. 2; *Honsell/Schönle/Th. Koller*, Art. 67, Rn. 16.
[23] Vgl. dazu auch MünchKomm/*P. Huber*, Art. 67, Rn. 6.

unverzollt, unversteuert" wurde als reine Kostentragungsregel eingestuft.[24] Insoweit bliebe es dann beim Gefahrübergang mit der Übergabe der Ware an den ersten Beförderer.[25] Anders bewertet wurde die Klausel „frei Haus, verzollt, unversteuert" in einem Fall, in dem der Verkäufer auch die Transportversicherung abgeschlossen und die Ware an den Käufer regelmässig nicht nur durch Spediteure, sondern auch durch eigene Leute geliefert hatte.[26] Hier nahm das Gericht das Vorliegen einer Bestimmung über den Erfüllungsort und die Gefahrtragung an. Art. 67 I war deshalb nach Auffassung des Gerichts nicht einschlägig. Letztlich können solche Klauseln aber auch so verstanden werden, dass zwar nicht der Lieferort, doch aber der Ort des Gefahrübergangs verschoben wurde. Damit bliebe es zwar bei der Erforderlichkeit der Versendung und fiele der Vertrag in den Anwendungsbereich von Art. 67 I, doch hätten die Parteien im Wege des Art. 6 eine von Art. 67 I abweichende Regelung des Gefahrübergangs getroffen, die dann Vorrang hätte.[27] Im Ergebnis wird es in diesen Konstellationen – wie dies auch die Gerichte bislang gehandhabt haben – um eine Berücksichtigung aller Umstände des jeweiligen Falles gehen und sich eine allein auf die Formulierung „frei Haus" und „frei Bestimmungsort" abstellende „hard and fast rule" nicht entwickeln lassen.[28]

2. Beförderer

Der Begriff des Beförderers in Art. 67 I entspricht dem in Art. 31 lit. a).[29] Zentral für die 12 Frage, ob es sich bei dem gewählten Transporteur um einen „Beförderer" im Sinne des Art. 67 I handelt, ist, ob der Transporteur selbständig/unabhängig ist.[30] Auch die Incoterms® 2010 gehen, wie schon die vorherige Version,[31] von diesem Verständnis aus.[32]

Insbesondere **eigene Leute des Verkäufers** sind nach einhelliger Auffassung **keine** 13 **„Beförderer"** für die Zwecke des Art. 67 I.[33] Nach verbreiteter Auffassung soll es gleichwohl nicht zu einem Gefahrrückfall kommen, wenn eigene Leute des Verkäufers zu einem späteren Zeitpunkt in der Transportkette als Beförderer auftreten.[34] Dieser Ansatz eröffnet freilich gefährliche Umgehungsmöglichkeiten. So könnte der Verkäufer einen unabhängigen lokalen Transporteur für einige hundert Meter verwenden, um den Gefahrübergang herbeizuführen, den eigentlichen Transport aber mit eigenen Leuten durchführen und sich damit den Gewahrsam an der Sache erhalten. Verneint man einen Gefahrrückfall in diesen Fällen, so muss gleichwohl Art. 66 *in fine* anwendbar bleiben, um den Käufer zu schützen und den Verkäufer trotz mangelndem wirtschaftlichen Interesses an der Ankunft der Ware zur hinreichenden Sorgfalt anzuhalten.

Abgrenzungsprobleme können entstehen, wenn das **Transportunternehmen eine** 14 **Tochter des Verkäuferunternehmens** ist. Anhaltspunkte für die Unabhängigkeit des

---

[24] BGH, 11.12.1996, CISG-online 225 = BGHZ 134, 201, 206 = NJW 1997, 870, 871 unter ausdrücklicher Bestätigung des vorinstanzlichen Urteils.
[25] MünchKomm/*P. Huber*, Art. 67, Rn. 6.
[26] OLG Karlsruhe, 20.11.1992, CISG-online 54 = NJW-RR 1993, 1316, 1317.
[27] Dies in Betracht ziehend OLG Köln, 16.7.2001, CISG-online 609; OLG Koblenz, 4.10.2002, CISG-online 716 = IHR 2003, 66. Vgl. auch MünchKomm/*P. Huber*, Art. 67, Rn. 6.
[28] Besonders deutlich OLG Köln, 16.7.2001, CISG-online 609 = IHR 2002, 66, wo die Ähnlichkeit des Sachverhalts mit OLG Karlsruhe, 20.11.1992, CISG-online 54 = NJW-RR 1993, 1316 festgestellt, der Fall aber aufgrund der Umstände anders entschieden wurde.
[29] AG Duisburg, 13.4.2000, CISG-online 659 = IHR 2001, 114; *Staudinger/Magnus*, Art. 67, Rn. 11; MünchKomm/*P. Huber*, Art. 67, Rn. 10; *Ferrari u. a./Mankowski*, Internationales Vertragsrecht, Art. 67, Rn. 7; MünchKommHGB/*Benicke*, Art. 67, Rn. 4; *Brunner*, Art. 67, Rn. 3.
[30] Oben *Widmer Lüchinger*, Art. 31, Rn. 19 ff.; *Hager/Maultzsch*, 5. Aufl., Art. 67 Rn. 5; *Staudinger/Magnus*, Art. 67, Rn. 11; MünchKomm/*P. Huber*, Art. 67, Rn. 10; *Honnold/Flechtner*, Art. 67, Rn. 369.1; *Herber/Czerwenka*, Art. 67, Rn. 4.
[31] *Ramberg*, Guide to Incoterms 2000, S. 77.
[32] MünchKomm/*P. Huber*, Art. 67, Rn. 10.
[33] Statt aller *Hager/Maultzsch*, 5. Aufl., Art. 67 Rn. 5; *Staudinger/Magnus*, Art. 67, Rn. 11.
[34] *Staudinger/Magnus*, Art. 67, Rn. 14; *Ferrari u. a./Mankowski*, Internationales Vertragsrecht, Art. 67, Rn. 14.

Transporteurs können sich in diesen Fällen zunächst aus dem anwendbaren Gesellschaftsstatut ergeben.[35] Keine Einigkeit besteht darüber, ob das Bestehen eigenständiger Ansprüche aus dem Beförderungsvertrag von Relevanz für die Unabhängigkeit des Transporteurs ist.[36] Eine pauschale Antwort lässt sich nicht geben, da verbund- bzw. konzerninterne Buchungs-, Abrechnungs- und Abtretungsmechanismen den Sachverhalt in die eine oder andere Richtung kippen lassen können.[37] Im Kern geht es, anknüpfend an die Gefahrtragungskonzeption des CISG, um die Aufgabe des Gewahrsams an der Ware durch den Verkäufer. „Beförderer" kann ein Transporteur deshalb nur sein, wenn die Ware mit Übergabe dem faktischen Einflussbereich des Verkäufers entzogen ist. Kann der Verkäufer – ausserhalb eines allfälligen Stoppungsrechts – faktische Herrschaft über die Ware ausüben, etwa durch Weisungsrechte, die sich aus der personellen Identität der Organe des Verkäuferunternehmens mit den Organe des Transportunternehmens ergeben, so handelt es sich bei dem Transporteur nicht um einen „Beförderer". Eine Splittung des Transportrisikos findet statt, wenn der Verkäufer einen Teil des Transports selbst bewerkstelligt, etwa zwischen Werk und Hafen, und erst dann die Ware an einen unabhängigen Beförderer übergibt.[38] Die Frage, ob der Schaden schon auf dem ersten Abschnitt entstanden ist, kann dann erhebliche Probleme bereiten.

15 Ob die Übergabe der Ware an einen **Spediteur** für den Gefahrübergang ausreicht, ist umstritten. Einigkeit besteht immerhin insoweit, als der Gefahrübergang durch Übergabe der Ware an den Spediteur erfolgen soll, wenn dieser selbst als Frachtführer tätig wird, die Spedition also zu Fixgebühren übernimmt.[39] Im Übrigen soll die Frage nach überwiegender Auffassung differenziert zu beantworten sein, d. h., der Spediteur soll nur dann als „Beförderer" gelten, wenn er ein Selbsteintrittsrecht ausübt, nicht aber, wenn er den Transport nur organisiert.[40] Nach der vorzugswürdigen Gegenauffassung spielen solche Differenzierungen indes keine Rolle und sind auch unpraktikabel.[41] Der Zeitpunkt der Ausübung des Selbsteintrittsrechts dürfte kaum mit letzter Sicherheit, oder jedenfalls nicht ohne ganz erheblichen Aufwand, zu bestimmen sein.[42] Zudem sollten die zufälligen Interna des Spediteurs, also vor allem die Organisations- und Entscheidungsabläufe, nicht auf den Übergang der Gefahr einwirken können.[43]

16 Die Konvention stellt nach dem klaren Wortlaut für den Gefahrübergang auf den **ersten Beförderer** ab.[44] Bei einem multimodalen Transport trägt der Käufer deshalb die Gefahr von Beginn des Transports an. Diese Regelung passt auf den modernen Containerverkehr und vermeidet die Schwierigkeit, feststellen zu müssen, auf welchem Transportabschnitt Schäden eingetreten sind.[45] Es kommt damit insbesondere auch nicht auf den Anteil des

---

[35] *Hager/Maultzsch*, 5. Aufl., Art. 67 Rn. 5; *Staudinger/Magnus*, Art. 67, Rn. 13. Dagegen MünchKomm/*P. Huber*, Art. 67, Rn. 10.

[36] Diesem Gesichtspunkt Priorität zumessend MünchKomm/*P. Huber*, Art. 67, Rn. 10. Für Berücksichtigung in Zweifelsfällen *Staudinger/Magnus*, Art. 67, Rn. 13. Gänzlich dagegen *Ferrari u. a./Mankowski*, Internationales Vertragsrecht, Art. 67, Rn. 8.

[37] Aus diesem Grund hält *Ferrari u. a./Mankowski*, Internationales Vertragsrecht, Art. 67, Rn. 8 das Kriterium der selbständigen Ansprüche aus dem Beförderungsvertrag insgesamt für untauglich.

[38] *Hager/Maultzsch*, 5. Aufl., Art. 67 Rn. 5.

[39] *Hager/Maultzsch*, 5. Aufl., Art. 67 Rn. 5; *Staudinger/Magnus*, Art. 67, Rn. 11; *Witz/Salger/Lorenz/Witz*, Art. 67, Rn. 6; MünchKomm/*P. Huber*, Art. 67, Rn. 10; *Herber/Czerwenka*, Art. 67, Rn. 4; *Honsell/Schönle/Th. Koller*, Art. 67, Rn. 21; *Enderlein/Maskow/Strohbach*, Art. 67, Anm. 3.1.

[40] *Staudinger/Magnus*, Art. 67, Rn. 11; *Witz/Salger/Lorenz/Witz*, Art. 67, Rn. 6; *Ferrari u. a./Mankowski*, Internationales Vertragsrecht, Art. 67, Rn. 5 f.; *Herber/Czerwenka*, Art. 67, Rn. 4; *Honsell/Schönle/Th. Koller*, Art. 67, Rn. 21; *Enderlein/Maskow/Strohbach*, Art. 67, Anm. 3.1.

[41] Oben *Widmer Lüchinger*, Art. 31 Rn. 28; *Hager/Maultzsch*, 5. Aufl., Art. 67 Rn. 5; MünchKomm/*P. Huber*, Art. 67, Rn. 10; *Bamberger/Roth/Saenger*, Art. 67, Rn. 2.

[42] *Hager/Maultzsch*, 5. Aufl., Art. 67 Rn. 5.

[43] *Hager/Maultzsch*, 5. Aufl., Art. 67 Rn. 5; MünchKomm/*P. Huber*, Art. 67, Rn. 10.

[44] Notabene besteht hier ein Unterschied zu Art. 68 S. 2 bei dem es auf den ersten Beförderer ankommt, der die Dokumente ausgestellt hat, welche den Beförderungsvertrag enthalten. Zur Situation, wenn der Beförderungsvertrag ohne Dokumente abgeschlossen wird, vgl. unten Art. 68 Rn. 13.

[45] *Hager/Maultzsch*, 5. Aufl., Art. 67 Rn. 5; *Staudinger/Magnus*, Art. 67, Rn. 17.

ersten Beförderers am Gesamttransport, bzw. darauf an, ob er grenzüberschreitend transportiert. Beauftragt also der Verkäufer ein lokales Unternehmen mit dem Transport der Ware vom Werk des Verkäufers zum nahe gelegenen Bahnhof, Hafen oder Flugplatz, so geht die Gefahr mit Übergabe der Ware an dieses Unternehmen über.[46]

3. Übergabe

Art. 67 I 1 (gilt aber selbstverständlich auch für S. 2) verlangt darüber hinaus die Übergabe der Ware. Im Sinne der Gefahrtragungskonzeption des CISG erfordert dies die Aufgabe des Gewahrsams an der Ware durch den Verkäufer, also die **Aufgabe der faktischen Obhut.** Es reicht allerdings nicht, dass der Verkäufer die Ware bloss zur Verfügung stellt, ohne dass der Beförderer sie in seine Obhut nimmt.[47] **17**

Mit der Formulierung, die Übergabe habe „in accordance with the contract of sale" zu erfolgen, ist **nicht gemeint,** dass die Ware von **vertragsgemässer Beschaffenheit** im Sinne des Art. 35 sein muss.[48] Der Gefahrübergang hängt nicht von der Mangelfreiheit der Ware ab. Das Verhältnis von Gefahrtragung und der Lieferung mangelhafter Ware wird in den Artt. 66 II, 70 behandelt, nicht in Art. 67 I. Die gewählte Formulierung stellt lediglich klar, dass die Beförderung vertraglich geschuldet sein muss, es sich mithin um einen Versendungskauf handelt.[49] Keinen Einfluss auf den Gefahrübergang hat es deshalb, wenn der Verkäufer ein Zurückbehaltungsrecht nach Art. 58 II oder Art. 71 II ausübt.[50] Anders liegt es, wenn der Verkäufer die Versandanweisung widerruft. Dann wird der Gefahrübergang rückwirkend aufgehoben.[51] **18**

Anders als die Incoterms® 2010 differenziert der Wortlaut der Konvention nicht nach den verschiedenen Transportarten, sondern verwendet schlicht den Begriff der Übergabe. Wann der Beförderer die Ware in seiner Obhut hat, hängt deshalb zunächst von den Umständen des Einzelfalles ab. Allerdings können die Incoterms® 2010 – soweit sie auf den Versendungskauf passen[52] und nicht ohnehin einer der Terms vereinbart wurde – Orientierung bieten. **19**

Für den Versendungskauf über den Seeweg indizieren die Veränderungen der Incoterms® 2000 zu den Incoterms® 2010 eine Tendenz, den Verkäufer beim Versendungskauf mit dem Verladerisiko zu belasten. Die dabei bedeutendsten Terms CIF und FOB, aber auch CFR, lassen nach ihren jeweiligen A4, A5 Klauseln die Gefahr jetzt nicht mehr schon übergehen, wenn die Waren erstmals die Schiffsreling überqueren, sondern erst mit „placing them on board the vessel". Eine Ausnahme bildet freilich FAS, bei dem entsprechend seines Namens nach wie vor die Zurverfügungstellung längsseits des Schiffes genügt. Zumindest für den **Seetransport** lässt sich aber für das CISG die Vermutung aufstellen, dass die „Übergabe" im Sinne des Art. 67 I mit der **Verladung** – nicht aber erst der Verstauung[53] – auf das Schiff abgeschlossen ist.[54] **20**

---

[46] *Staudinger/Magnus,* Art. 67, Rn. 12; MünchKommHGB/*Benicke,* Art. 67, Rn. 7; *Ferrari u. a./Mankowski,* Internationales Vertragsrecht, Art. 67, Rn. 6.
[47] *Hager/Maultzsch,* 5. Aufl., Art. 67 Rn. 3a; MünchKomm/*P. Huber,* Art. 67, Rn. 9.
[48] *Hager/Maultzsch,* 5. Aufl., Art. 67 Rn. 5a; *Staudinger/Magnus,* Art. 67, Rn. 18; MünchKomm/*P. Huber,* Art. 67, Rn. 13; MünchKommHGB/*Benicke,* Art. 67, Rn. 6.
[49] *Staudinger/Magnus,* Art. 67, Rn. 18; *Honnold/Flechtner,* Art. 67, Rn. 369.3; MünchKommHGB/*Benicke,* Art. 67, Rn. 6.
[50] *Hager/Maultzsch,* 5. Aufl., Art. 67 Rn. 5a.
[51] *Hager/Maultzsch,* 5. Aufl., Art. 67 Rn. 5a.
[52] Ausgeschlossen sind damit die E- und D-Terms.
[53] *China North Chemical Industries Corp. v. Boston Chemical Corp.,* U. S. Dist. Ct. (S. D. T), 7.2.2006, CISG-online 1177: Verstauen nicht Pflicht des Verkäufers.
[54] LG Bamberg, 23.10.2006, CISG-online 1400 = IHR 2007, 113; *Staudinger/Magnus,* Art. 67, Rn. 15; *Witz/Salger/Lorenz/Witz,* Art. 67, Rn. 13; *Enderlein/Maskow/Strohbach,* Art. 67, Anm. 5. Anders noch *Hager/Maultzsch,* 5. Aufl., Art. 67 Rn. 3a: Übergabe erfolgt bei Zurverfügungstellung längsseits des Schiffes, wenn der Verfrachter die Ware in seine Obhut nimmt. So auch MünchKomm/*P. Huber,* Art. 67, Rn. 13; *Ferrari u. a./Mankowski,* Internationales Vertragsrecht, Art. 67, Rn. 12; *Herber/Czerwenka,* Art. 67, Rn. 5.

21 Unabhängig von der Transportart sieht FCA nach dem Grundfall der Klausel A3 lit. a) vor, dass Lieferung und Gefahrübergang erfolgen, wenn die Verladung der Ware auf das Transportmittel des Beförderers abgeschlossen ist.[55] Demgegenüber verlangen CPT und CIP lediglich das „handing over" der Ware. Blickt man auf die – auf die Bringschuld zugeschnittene – D-Gruppe, so ergibt sich dort für den Verkäufer die Pflicht, die Ware zur Verfügung zu stellen. DAP und DDP stellen klar, dass die Ware nur „ready for unloading" sein muss, das Abladerisiko also den Käufer trifft. Im Zusammenspiel mit den Unterschieden im Wortlaut von Art. 69 I („placed at his disposal") und Art. 67 I („handed over") ergibt sich daraus, dass im Bereich des Versendungskaufs mehr verlangt ist, als die blosse Zurverfügungstellung der Ware.[56] Deshalb sollte beim Versendungskauf auch ausserhalb des Seetransports die Gefahr im Zweifel erst mit **Abschluss des Verladevorgangs** auf den Käufer übergehen.[57]

IV. Versand ab einem bestimmten Ort (Art. 67 I 2)

22 Haben die Parteien vereinbart, dass die Ware an einem bestimmten Ort, also etwa einem Bahnhof, Flug- oder Seehafen, an den Beförderer übergeben werden soll, so geht die Gefahr auch erst mit der dortigen Übergabe an den Beförderer über. Die Regelung ist für den Verkäufer insbesondere dann riskant, wenn die Ware in versiegelten Containern transportiert wird.[58] Es wird sich im Nachhinein kaum feststellen lassen, ob ein Schaden noch auf dem Weg zum Absendeort, oder erst nach der dort erfolgten Übergabe eingetreten ist. Art. 67 I 2 splittet insoweit also die Gefahrtragung.[59] Über allfällige Streitigkeiten dürften dann letztlich die Regeln der Beweislast entscheiden.[60]

23 Art. 67 I 2 ist nicht anwendbar, wenn der bestimmte Ort mit der Niederlassung des Verkäufers bzw. der Niederlassung des Käufers identisch ist. Es liegt dann eine Hol- bzw. Bringschuld vor und der Gefahrübergang richtet sich nach Art. 69.[61] Gleiches gilt, wenn die Ware an dem bestimmten Ort dem Käufer selbst zu übergeben ist.[62]

24 Art. 67 I 2 ist hingegen nicht deshalb ausgeschlossen, weil der Absendeort nicht eindeutig ist, die Parteien also etwa „„Abzuladen deutsche Nordseeküste" vereinbart haben.[63] In diesen Fällen ist zunächst auf die Auslegungsregeln der Artt. 8, 9 zurückzugreifen.[64] Führt dies zu keinem Ergebnis, so ist die vertragliche Formulierung aber doch so zu verstehen, dass der Verkäufer ein Bestimmungsrecht haben soll und deshalb der von ihm dann gewählte Absendeort der bestimmte Ort im Sinne des Art. 67 I 2 ist.[65] Der Verkäufer trägt dann die Gefahr bis zur Übergabe an dem von ihm gewählten Ort.

25 In der Praxis liegt die von Art. 67 I 2 in den Blick genommene Konstellation vor allem bei Verwendung eines Incoterms® vor, etwa „„CIF Rotterdam".[66] Freilich ergibt sich dann

---

[55] FCA A3 lit. b) belastet den Käufer mit dem Verladerisiko, wenn der Lieferort nicht der Ort des Verkäufers ist. Der Verkäufer hat die Ware dann auf seinem Transportmittel dem Beförderer abladebereit zur Verfügung zu stellen.

[56] So hinsichtlich der Wortlautunterschiede zwischen Art. 67 und Art. 69 *Staudinger/Magnus*, Art. 67, Rn. 15.

[57] *Staudinger/Magnus*, Art. 67, Rn. 15; *Witz/Salger/Lorenz/Witz*, Art. 67, Rn. 13; *Enderlein/Maskow/Strohbach*, Art. 67, Anm. 5.

[58] *Staudinger/Magnus*, Art. 67, Rn. 20.

[59] *Hager/Maultzsch*, 5. Aufl., Art. 67 Rn. 11; *Staudinger/Magnus*, Art. 67, Rn. 20.

[60] *Hager/Maultzsch*, 5. Aufl., Art. 67 Rn. 11; *Staudinger/Magnus*, Art. 67, Rn. 20.

[61] *Hager/Maultzsch*, 5. Aufl., Art. 67 Rn. 7; *Schlechtriem/Schwenzer/Hager/Schmidt-Kessel*, CISG Commentary, Art. 67, Rn. 2; *Staudinger/Magnus*, Art. 67, Rn. 19; MünchKomm/*P. Huber*, Art. 67, Rn. 14; *Brunner*, Art. 67, Rn. 5.

[62] *Staudinger/Magnus*, Art. 67, Rn. 22.

[63] Beispiel bei *Hager/Maultzsch*, 5. Aufl., Art. 67 Rn. 6.

[64] *Witz/Salger/Lorenz/Witz*, Art. 67, Rn. 10.

[65] *Hager/Maultzsch*, 5. Aufl., Art. 67 Rn. 6; *Staudinger/Magnus*, Art. 67, Rn. 19; MünchKomm/*P. Huber*, Art. 67, Rn. 14; *Herber/Czerwenka*, Art. 67, Rn. 7. Im Ergebnis wohl auch *Witz/Salger/Lorenz/Witz*, Art. 67, Rn. 10, der allerdings das Wahlrecht des Verkäufers mit Art. 67 I 1 verbindet.

[66] *Hager/Maultzsch*, 5. Aufl., Art. 67 Rn. 6; *Staudinger/Magnus*, Art. 67, Rn. 21; MünchKomm/*P. Huber*, Art. 67, Rn. 14.

der Zeitpunkt des Gefahrübergangs wegen Art. 6 aus dem verwendeten Term selbst und eine Anwendung von Art. 67 I 2 findet nicht statt.[67]

Unerheblich ist, ob es sich bei dem Beförderer am Absendeort um den ersten Beförderer handelt. Hat also der in Freiburg i. Br. niedergelassene Verkäufer die Ware im Hamburger Hafen an den Beförderer zu übergeben, so kommt es für den Gefahrübergang nicht darauf an, ob er für den Transport von seiner Niederlassung zum Hafen eigene Leute oder einen selbständigen/unabhängigen Transporteur einsetzt.[68]

V. Zurückbehaltung der Dokumente (Art. 67 I 3)

Gemäss Art. 67 I 3 hat die Zurückbehaltung der zur Verfügung über die Ware berechtigenden Dokumente keinen Einfluss auf den Gefahrübergang, hindert diesen also nicht. Dies gilt unabhängig davon, ob der Verkäufer die Dokumente berechtigt oder unberechtigt zurückbehält. Vor dem Hintergrund, dass die Konvention den Gefahrübergang gerade nicht mit der Eigentumsübertragung verknüpft,[69] ist dies nur konsequent. Die Vorschrift hat deshalb lediglich klarstellende Funktion. Sie gilt nach einhelliger Auffassung aber nicht nur für solche Dokumente, welche zur Disposition über die Ware berechtigen, sondern *a fortiori* auch für andere, grundsätzlich mit weniger Befugnissen ausgestattete Dokumente. Verwiesen wird üblicherweise auf das Beispiel des Beförderungsvertrags, der im modernen dokumentenlosen Verkehr zur Disposition über die Ware berechtigen kann.[70]

Macht der Verkäufer von der in den Dokumenten enthaltenen Dispositionsbefugnis Gebrauch, so kommt es zu einem Gefahrrückfall, wenn die Ware schliesslich nicht mehr an den Käufer übermittelt werden soll.[71] Verkauft also der Verkäufer die dann reisende Ware nochmals und leitet er die Ware an den neuen Käufer um, so trifft ihn gemäss Art. 68 die Gefahr bis zum Vertragsschluss mit dem zweiten Käufer. Anders liegt es hingegen, wenn der Verkäufer von seinen Zurückbehaltungsrechten nach Art. 58 II bzw. 71 II Gebrauch macht.[72] Ist dieses Vorgehen gerechtfertigt, so ist die Ausübung der Dispositionsbefugnis durch den Verkäufer letztlich dem Käufer zuzurechnen und ist es deshalb gerechtfertigt, ihn mit dem Untergangs- bzw. Schadensrisiko zu belasten.

VI. Individualisierung der Ware (Art. 67 II)

1. Allgemeines

Bereits das Konzept der Gefahrtragung verlangt die hinreichende Individualisierung der Ware, damit die Gefahr übergehen kann. Diesem allgemeinen Prinzip verleiht das CISG Ausdruck in Art. 67 II und Art. 69 III.[73] Welche Massnahmen nach der erstgenannten Vorschrift für die hinreichende Individualisierung der (Gattungs-)Ware geeignet sein sollten, war auf der Wiener Konferenz nicht unumstritten. Anträge, die Gefahr erst übergehen zu lassen, wenn dem Käufer alle zur Versicherung der Ware notwendigen Informationen zur Verfügung gestellt wurden, fanden keine Mehrheit.[74] Gegenteilig zu dieser angestrebten

---

[67] *Hager/Maultzsch*, 5. Aufl., Art. 67 Rn. 6; *Staudinger/Magnus*, Art. 67, Rn. 21; MünchKomm/*P. Huber*, Art. 67, Rn. 14. A. A. *Bridge*, FS Kritzer, S. 87 f.
[68] *Hager/Maultzsch*, 5. Aufl., Art. 67 Rn. 7; *Staudinger/Magnus*, Art. 67, Rn. 19; MünchKomm/*P. Huber*, Art. 67, Rn. 14; *Honnold/Flechtner*, Art. 67, Rn. 369.2; MünchKommHBG/*Benicke*, Art. 67, Rn. 11; *Honsell/Schönle/Th. Koller*, Art. 67 Rn. 9; *Brunner*, Art. 67, Rn. 5.
[69] Vgl. dazu oben vor Artt. 66–70 Rn. 16.
[70] *Hager/Maultzsch*, 5. Aufl., Art. 67 Rn. 6; MünchKomm/*P. Huber*, Art. 67, Rn. 16.
[71] *Staudinger/Magnus*, Art. 67, Rn. 24; *Ferrari u. a./Mankowski*, Internationales Vertragsrecht, Art. 67, Rn. 30; *Honsell/Schönle/Th. Koller*, Art. 67, Rn. 34; *Brunner*, Art. 67, Rn. 7.
[72] Vgl. auch schon oben Rn 18.
[73] Vgl. dazu schon oben vor Artt. 66–70 Rn. 19.
[74] *Staudinger/Magnus*, Art. 67, Rn. 7; *Ferrari u. a./Mankowski*, Internationales Vertragsrecht, Art. 67, Rn. 2.

Verengung der Vorschrift wurde ein Antrag der USA angenommen, die Vorschrift über die Adressierung der Ware oder die Versandanzeige hinaus zu flexibilisieren und alle Formen der Identifikation ausreichen zu lassen.[75] Niederschlag hat dies in der Formulierung „or otherwise" gefunden. Die (nicht abschliessenden) Beispiele sind „markings on the goods", „shipping documents" und „notice given to the buyer".

30 Keine Probleme entstehen, wenn die Ware an den Käufer adressiert ist, wie dies oft beim Überlandtransport der Fall sein wird.[76] Kann die Ware durch ihre Bezeichnung in den Beförderungsdokumenten dem Vertrag zugeordnet werden, so ist dies ebenfalls für die geforderte Individualisierung ausreichend.[77] Wählt der Verkäufer die Notifizierung des Käufers durch Zusendung der Verladeanzeige, so trägt der Käufer das Übermittlungsrisiko (Art. 27), es kommt also auf den Versand der Anzeige, nicht deren Zugang an.[78]

2. Sammelladungen (bulk cargo)

31 Erhebliche Probleme bereitet die Individualisierung bei Sammelladungen, wie sie insbesondere beim Überseehandel vorkommt. Dabei wird es im Zeitpunkt der Verschiffung oft an einer eindeutigen Zuordnung der Ware zu einem bestimmten Vertrag fehlen. Dies gilt erst recht, wenn Füll- und Schüttgüter in Tanks, Silos oder dem Speicherraum von Schiffen transportiert werden.[79]

32 Praktisch wird das Problem in Konstellationen, in denen die Ware nur teilweise untergangen oder beschädigt worden ist. Ist dem Verkäufer die Lieferung aus einer Sammelladung nach Vertrag (ggf. durch Auslegung nach Artt. 8, 9) gestattet und wird dem Käufer die Verladung einer Sammelladung angezeigt, so ergibt sich daraus zunächst, dass sich die Schuld des Verkäufers auf diese Sammelladung beschränkt.[80]

33 Soweit vertreten wird, es bedürfe bei Sammelladungen, insbesondere Füll- und Schüttgütern, ohnehin keiner Anzeige,[81] kann dem nicht gefolgt werden, denn dies steht in offensichtlichem Widerspruch zum Wortlaut der Konvention.[82] Zu weitgehend erscheint auch die Auffassung, die Berechtigung des Verkäufers aus einer Sammelladung zu leisten, führe über Artt. 6, 8, 9 schon zur Abbedingung des Individualisierungserfordernisses.[83]

34 Abzulehnen ist aber auch die wohl überwiegende Auffassung, die Verladeanzeige bei Sammelladungen sei notwendig aber auch ausreichend, um die vollständige Individualisierung der Ware für die einzelnen Kaufverträge herbeizuführen.[84] Das aus dieser Auffassung folgende Konstrukt, die Käufer bildeten eine Gefahrengemeinschaft und hätten deshalb bei teilweisem Verlust bzw. teilweiser Beschädigung der Ware den Schaden anteilig zu tragen,[85] liesse sich allenfalls vertreten, wenn alle beteiligten Käufer bewusst eine Gefahrengemein-

---

[75] *Staudinger/Magnus*, Art. 67, Rn. 7.
[76] *Hager/Maultzsch*, 5. Aufl., Art. 67 Rn. 9; *Staudinger/Magnus*, Art. 67, Rn. 27.
[77] AG Duisburg, 13.4.2000, CISG-online 659 = IHR 2001, 114; *Staudinger/Magnus*, Art. 67, Rn. 27.
[78] *Hager/Maultzsch*, 5. Aufl., Art. 67 Rn. 10; *Staudinger/Magnus*, Art. 67, Rn. 27; *Witz/Salger/Lorenz/Witz*, Art. 67, Rn. 17; MünchKomm/*P. Huber*, Art. 67, Rn. 17; *Herber/Czerwenka*, Art. 67, Rn. 6; *Honsell/Schönle/Th. Koller*, Art. 67, Rn. 29; *Brunner*, Art. 67, Rn. 8.
[79] *Witz/Salger/Lorenz/Witz*, Art. 67, Rn. 16.
[80] *Hager/Maultzsch*, 5. Aufl., Art. 67 Rn. 10a; *Schlechtriem/Schwenzer/Hager/Schmidt-Kessel*, CISG Commentary, Art. 67, Rn. 15.
[81] So *Enderlein/Maskow/Strohbach*, Art. 67, Anm. 13.2. In diese Richtung auch *Piltz*, Internationales Kaufrecht, § 4, Rn. 277: Konkretisierung, wenn Ware durchgängig gleichwertig beschädigt wird.
[82] So auch *Witz/Salger/Lorenz/Witz*, Art. 67, Rn. 16.
[83] So aber *Witz/Salger/Lorenz/Witz*, Art. 67, Rn. 16. Ablehnend auch *Honnold/Flechtner*, Art. 67, Rn. 371; *Honsell/Schönle/Th. Koller*, Art. 67, Rn. 30; *Bamberger/Roth/Saenger*, Art. 67, Rn. 5.
[84] So auch *Bamberger/Roth/Saenger*, Art. 67, Rn. 5. Für die h. M. *Hager/Maultzsch*, 5. Aufl., Art. 67 Rn. 10a; *Schlechtriem/Schwenzer/Hager/Schmidt-Kessel*, CISG Commentary, Art. 67, Rn. 15; *Staudinger/Magnus*, Art. 67, Rn. 31; MünchKomm/*P. Huber*, Art. 67, Rn. 18; *Herber/Czerwenka*, Art. 67, Rn. 10; *Brunner*, Art. 67, Rn. 8.
[85] So *Hager/Maultzsch*, 5. Aufl., Art. 67 Rn. 10a; *Schlechtriem/Schwenzer/Hager/Schmidt-Kessel*, CISG Commentary, Art. 67, Rn. 15; *Staudinger/Magnus*, Art. 67, Rn. 31; MünchKomm/*P. Huber*, Art. 67, Rn. 18; *Ferrari u. a./Mankowski*, Internationales Vertragsrecht, Art. 67, Rn. 38; *Enderlein/Maskow/Strohbach*, Art. 67, Anm. 13.2.; *Brunner*, Art. 67, Rn. 8.

schaft bilden würden.⁸⁶ Ist dies nicht der Fall, so ist nicht einzusehen, wieso sich der einzelne Käufer die Entscheidung des Verkäufers gefallen lassen muss, alle Käufer anteilig zu bedienen, wenn der einzelne Kaufvertrag aus dem unbeeinträchtigt gebliebenen Teil der Sammelladung (jedenfalls soweit als möglich) hätte erfüllt werden können. Jeder Käufer hat einen vertraglichen Anspruch darauf, mit unbeeinträchtigter Ware in dem Umfang beliefert zu werden, in dem diese noch vorhanden ist *(pacta sunt servanda!)*. Er ist vom teilweisen Untergang bzw. der teilweisen Beschädigung nur in dem Umfang betroffen, als der verbliebene unbeeinträchtigte Teil der Sammelladung die vertraglich geschuldete Menge nicht abzudecken vermag. Eine *pro-rata* Verteilung des Risikos hiesse, dass die einzelnen vom Verkäufer abgeschlossenen Kaufverträge sich wechselseitig begrenzten. Mit dem Grundsatz der Relativität der Schuldverhältnisse ist das nicht zu vereinbaren. Letztlich wird damit auch gegen das Verbot des Vertrages zu Lasten Dritter verstossen, denn der Verkäufer erfüllt dann – wenn auch nur teilweise – haftungsbefreiend den einen Vertrag zu Lasten des anderen. Nicht vergessen werden darf, dass es die ökonomische Entscheidung des Verkäufers war, einen bulk komplett – und eben nicht mit einer Rückstellung – an verschiedene Käufer zu verkaufen und damit die Chance auf den Gewinn aus der maximalen Anzahl an möglichen Transaktionen zu erhalten. Es erscheint daher nicht ungerechtfertigt, ihn auch das Verlustrisiko tragen zu lassen. Er kann den Umfang seiner Haftung dann dadurch beeinflussen, wie er die verbliebene unbeeinträchtigte Ware zuteilt.

3. Keine Rückwirkung

Nach dem eindeutigen Wortlaut des Art. 67 II wirkt die Individualisierung der Ware nur **35** *ex nunc* („the risk does not pass to the buyer until"). Das ist misslich, denn so führt Art. 67 II zu einer Splittung der Gefahr.⁸⁷ Dieser Ansatz ist eine Folge der Entkoppelung der Gefahrtragung von der Lieferung.⁸⁸ Die Frage der Rückwirkung des Gefahrübergangs hat insbesondere auch im Zusammenhang mit dem Verkauf reisender Ware (Art. 68) Anlass zu heftigem Streit im Rahmen der Wiener Konferenz gegeben.⁸⁹

VII. Beweisfragen

Entsprechend eines allgemeinen Grundsatzes (Art. 7 II) hat die Partei, die aus einer Norm **36** für sie günstige Rechtsfolgen herzuleiten sucht, das Vorliegen ihrer Tatbestandsvoraussetzungen zu beweisen.⁹⁰ In der Regel wird deshalb der Verkäufer zu beweisen haben, dass die Voraussetzungen des Art. 67 I 1 vorgelegen haben und die Ware gemäss Art. 67 II hinreichend individualisiert war.⁹¹ Ist die Ware zwischen Niederlassung des Verkäufers und einem Verladeort untergegangen oder beschädigt worden, so hat der Käufer zu beweisen, dass es sich bei dem Verladeort um einen bestimmten Absendeort nach Art. 67 I 2 handelt und der Verkäufer bis dorthin deshalb gefahrbelastet war.⁹²

---

⁸⁶ Zutreffend *Honsell/Schönle/Th. Koller*, Art. 67, Rn. 30. Ablehnend auch *Bamberger/Roth/Saenger*, Art. 67, Rn. 5.
⁸⁷ *Hager/Maultzsch*, 5. Aufl., Art. 67 Rn. 11; *Schlechtriem/Schwenzer/Hager/Schmidt-Kessel*, CISG Commentary, Art. 67, Rn. 16.
⁸⁸ *Hager/Maultzsch*, 5. Aufl., Art. 67 Rn. 10.
⁸⁹ Vgl. dazu unten Art. 68 Rn. 3.
⁹⁰ Vgl. oben *Ferrari*, Art. 4 Rn. 48 ff.; *Staudinger/Magnus*, Art. 7, Rn. 57.
⁹¹ *Staudinger/Magnus*, Art. 67, Rn. 33.
⁹² MünchKomm/*P. Huber*, Art. 67, Rn. 21.

Art. 68 [Gefahrübergang bei Verkauf der Ware, die sich auf dem Transport befindet]

Wird Ware, die sich auf dem Transport befindet, verkauft, so geht die Gefahr im Zeitpunkt des Vertragsabschlusses auf den Käufer über. Die Gefahr wird jedoch bereits im Zeitpunkt der Übergabe der Ware an den Beförderer, der die Dokumente über den Beförderungsvertrag ausgestellt hat, von dem Käufer übernommen, falls die Umstände diesen Schluß nahelegen. Wenn dagegen der Verkäufer bei Abschluß des Kaufvertrages wußte oder wissen mußte, daß die Ware untergegangen oder beschädigt war, und er dies dem Käufer nicht offenbart hat, geht der Untergang oder die Beschädigung zu Lasten des Verkäufers.

Art. 68

The risk in respect of goods sold in transit passes to the buyer from the time of the conclusion of the contract. However, if the circumstances so indicate, the risk is assumed by the buyer from the time the goods were handed over to the carrier who issued the documents embodying the contract of carriage. Nevertheless, if at the time of the conclusion of the contract of sale the seller knew or ought to have known that the goods had been lost or damaged and did not disclose this to the buyer, the loss or damage is at the risk of the seller.

Art. 68

En ce qui concerne les marchandises vendues en cours de transport, les risques sont transférés à l'acheteur à partir du moment où le contrat est conclu. Toutefois, si les circonstances l'impliquent, les risques sont à la charge de l'acheteur à compter du moment où les marchandises ont été remises au transporteur qui a émis les documents constatant le contrat de transport. Néanmoins, si, au moment de la conclusion du contrat de vente, le vendeur avait connaissance ou aurait dû avoir connaissance du fait que les marchandises avaient péri ou avaient été détériorées et qu'il n'en a pas informé l'acheteur, la perte ou la détérioration est à la charge du vendeur.

Übersicht

	Rn.
I. Vorgeschichte	1
II. Regelungsgegenstand	4
III. Grundregel (Art. 68 S. 1)	5
IV. Ausnahme (Art. 68 S. 2)	7
1. Ausgangspunkt	7
2. Besondere Umstände	8
3. Beförderer	12
V. Bösgläubigkeit des Verkäufers (Art. 68 S. 3)	14
1. Anwendungsbereich	15
2. Reichweite	17
3. Massstab der Bösgläubigkeit	21
VI. Sammelladungen	22
VII. Beweisfragen	25

I. Vorgeschichte

1 Wird reisende Ware verkauft, so ist es regelmässig mit grossen Schwierigkeiten verbunden und oft unmöglich, den genauen Ort des Schadenseintritts festzustellen.[1] Bereits das EKG war deshalb der – schon aus Gründen der Praktikabilität überzeugenden – Idee des rückwirkenden Gefahrübergangs beim Kauf reisender Ware gefolgt. In diesem Sinne hatte Art. 99 I EKG für den Kauf schwimmender Ware die Gefahrtragung des Käufers auf den

---

[1] *Hager/Maultzsch,* 5. Aufl., Art. 68 Rn. 1; *Schlechtriem/Schwenzer/Hager/Schmidt-Kessel,* CISG Commentary, Art. 68, Rn. 2; MünchKomm/*P. Huber,* Art. 68, Rn. 2; *Sekretariatskommentar,* Art. 80, Nr. 1.

Zeitpunkt der Übergabe an den ersten Beförderer zurück verlagert. Gemäss Art. 99 II EKG galt diese Regelung dann nicht, wenn der Verkäufer den Verlust kannte oder hätte kennen müssen.

Die Regelung des EKG wurde ihrem Grundgedanken nach über das gesamte Vorent- 2 wurfsstadium aufrechterhalten.[2] Allerdings wurde ihr Anwendungsbereich über den Wassertransport hinaus auf alle Transportarten ausgedehnt.[3] Ausserdem wurde für die Übergabe nicht mehr schlicht an den Beförderer angeknüpft, sondern an denjenigen Beförderer, der die Dokumente über den Frachtvertrag ausgestellt hatte.[4]

Auf der Wiener Konferenz kam es dann zu ganz erheblichem Widerstand, vorgetragen 3 vor allem von den importorientierten Entwicklungsländern. Diesen erschien unter anderem stossend, dass sich der Käufer nicht rückwirkend gegen den Untergang der Ware versichern könne.[5] Zwar wurde verschiedentlich auf die praktischen Vorzüge der Regelung hingewiesen,[6] allerdings brauchte es schliesslich einen von Pakistan unmittelbar vor Ende der Konferenz eingebrachten Vorschlag, um zur Kompromisslösung des jetzigen Art. 68 zu gelangen.[7]

II. Regelungsgegenstand

Art. 68 verteilt das Risiko des vorvertraglichen Untergangs reisender Ware. Zahlreiche 4 nationale Rechtsordnungen aller Rechtsfamilien ordnen nach wie vor, zumindest beim Spezieskauf, die Ungültigkeit des Vertrages im Falle anfänglich objektiver Unmöglichkeit an.[8] Allerdings sperrt das CISG mit Art. 68 die Anwendung dieser Vorschriften.[9] Zwar sind Gültigkeitsfragen gemäss Art. 4 S. 2 lit. a) vom Anwendungsbereich der Konvention ausgeschlossen, allerdings gilt dieser Ausschluss nach dem klaren Wortlaut von Art. 4 S. 1 nur „except as expressly otherwise provided in this Convention". Art. 68 ist ein solcher ausdrücklich geregelter Fall, in dem das CISG eine Gültigkeitsaussage trifft.[10] Daraus darf aber nicht der Schluss gezogen werden, nationale Ungültigkeitsvorschriften gelangten ausserhalb des Anwendungsbereichs von Art. 68 zur Anwendung.[11] Vielmehr ist der Vorschrift im Zusammenspiel mit Art. 79 ein der Konvention im Sinne von Art. 7 II zugrunde liegendes Prinzip zu entnehmen, dass Unmöglichkeit der Leistung nicht zur Unwirksamkeit des Vertrages führt.

---

[2] Art. 65 II Genfer E.; Art. 66 Wiener E.; Art. 80 New Yorker E.; *Hager/Maultzsch*, 5. Aufl., Art. 68 Rn. 1; *Schlechtriem/Schwenzer/Hager/Schmidt-Kessel*, CISG Commentary, Art. 68, Rn. 1; *Staudinger/Magnus*, Art. 68, Rn. 3.

[3] *Hager/Maultzsch*, 5. Aufl., Art. 68 Rn. 1; *Schlechtriem/Schwenzer/Hager/Schmidt-Kessel*, CISG Commentary, Art. 68, Rn. 1; *Staudinger/Magnus*, Art. 68, Rn. 3.

[4] *Staudinger/Magnus*, Art. 68, Rn. 3.

[5] O. R., S. 403, 404, Nr. 2, 10, S. 213, Nr. 70; *Hager/Maultzsch*, 5. Aufl., Art. 68 Rn. 1; *Schlechtriem/Schwenzer/Hager/Schmidt-Kessel*, CISG Commentary, Art. 68, Rn. 1; *Staudinger/Magnus*, Art. 68, Rn. 4; MünchKomm/*P. Huber*, Art. 68, Rn. 2.

[6] O. R., S. 403, 404, Nr. 5–7, S. 213, Nr. 74, S. 215 ff., Nr. 4, 7, 10–15; *Hager/Maultzsch*, 5. Aufl., Art. 68 Rn. 1; *Schlechtriem/Schwenzer/Hager/Schmidt-Kessel*, CISG Commentary, Art. 68, Rn. 1.

[7] O. R., S. 217, Nr. 29, S. 221, Nr. 27; *Hager/Maultzsch*, 5. Aufl., Art. 68 Rn. 1; *Schlechtriem/Schwenzer/Hager/Schmidt-Kessel*, CISG Commentary, Art. 68, Rn. 1; *Staudinger/Magnus*, Art. 68, Rn. 4; *Witz/Salger/Lorenz/Witz*, Art. 68, Rn. 1; *Schlechtriem*, From Hague to Vienna, S. 130 ff. Zur Entstehungsgeschichte auch *Ferrari u. a./Mankowski*, Internationales Vertragsrecht, Art. 68, Rn. 2 ff.

[8] *Schwenzer/Hachem/Kee*, Rn. 45-27, 47–183 mit Nachweisen.

[9] Unten *Ferrari*, Art. 79 Rn. 2; *Hager/Maultzsch*, 5. Aufl., Art. 68 Rn. 2; *Schlechtriem/Schwenzer/Hager/Schmidt-Kessel*, CISG Commentary, Art. 68, Rn. 2; *Staudinger/Magnus*, Art. 68, Rn. 22; *Witz/Salger/Lorenz/Witz*, Art. 68, Rn. 3; MünchKomm/*P. Huber*, Art. 68, Rn. 4; *Honsell/Schönle/Th. Koller*, Art. 68, Rn. 3; *Brunner*, Art. 68, Rn. 2; *Schlechtriem*, Einheitliches UN-Kaufrecht, S. 22. Für die Diskussion auf der Wiener Konferenz vgl. O. R., S. 406, Nr. 38–41.

[10] Oben *Ferrari*, Art. 4 Rn. 24; *Schlechtriem/Schwenzer/Schwenzer/Hachem*, CISG Commentary, Art. 4, Rn. 33; *Witz/Salger/Lorenz/Witz*, Art. 68, Rn. 3; *Brunner*, Art. 4, Rn. 9.

[11] *Honsell/Schönle/Th. Koller*, Art. 68, Rn. 19.

III. Grundregel (Art. 68 S. 1)

5   Gemäss der in Art. 68 S. 1 enthaltenen Grundregel trägt der Käufer reisender Ware die Gefahr ab dem Zeitpunkt des Vertragsschlusses. Die Konvention verlangt ausdrücklich, dass die Ware „in transit" verkauft wird.[12] Nach allgemeiner Ansicht reicht dafür die bereits erfolgte Übergabe der Ware an den selbständigen Beförderer aus.[13] Ihre Verladung bzw. der Beginn des Transports im engeren Sinne werden nicht vorausgesetzt.[14] Auch auf die Art des Transports kommt es, anders als noch nach dem EKG, gerade nicht an. Gehen die Parteien irrtümlich vom Verkauf reisender Ware aus, so geht die Gefahr erst mit der tatsächlichen Übergabe an den Beförderer über.[15]

6   Art. 68 S. 1 führt zu einer Teilung der Gefahrtragung zwischen Verkäufer und Käufer, wobei ersterer die Gefahr vor und bis Vertragsschluss und letzterer die Gefahr ab diesem Zeitpunkt trägt.[16] In vielen Fällen wird nicht geklärt werden können, ob die Ware zum Zeitpunkt des Vertragsschlusses schon untergegangen war. Entschieden werden diese Fälle letztlich durch die Verteilung der Beweislast.[17] Mit Recht ist deshalb auf die streitfördernde Wirkung dieser Vorschrift hingewiesen worden.[18]

IV. Ausnahme (Art. 68 S. 2)

1. Ausgangspunkt

7   In Ausnahme zur Rückwirkung der Gefahrtragung auf den Zeitpunkt des Vertragsschlusses kann nach Art. 68 S. 2, bei entsprechendem Sachverhalt, der Gefahrübergang auch schon auf den Zeitpunkt zurück verlagert werden, in dem die Übergabe der Ware an den Beförderer erfolgte, der die Dokumente über den Beförderungsvertrag ausgestellt hat. Diese Vorschrift geht also weiter als die Grundregel und kommt der ursprünglich im Anschluss an das EKG intendierten, später umstrittenen, Fassung am nächsten. S. 2 beseitigt eine Reihe schwieriger Sachverhaltsfragen und bringt damit erhebliche praktische Vorteile. Insbesondere wird die zufallsbehaftete Frage, ob der Vertrag zum Zeitpunkt des Untergangs der Ware schon geschlossen war, obsolet.

2. Besondere Umstände

8   Die Ausnahmeregelung des Art. 68 S. 2 greift nur „if the circumstances so indicate" und damit unter einer äusserst vagen Voraussetzung.[19] Vor dem Hintergrund der Entstehungsgeschichte kommt exportorientierten Rechtsordnungen ein weites Verständnis dieser Regel entgegen, während importorientierte Rechtsordnungen eine enge, streng am Ausnahme-

---

[12] Damit wird eingelagerte Ware nicht von Art. 68 erfasst, *Ferrari u. a./Mankowski*, Internationales Vertragsrecht, Art. 68, Rn. 5.

[13] *Hager/Maultzsch*, 5. Aufl., Art. 68 Rn. 2; *Staudinger/Magnus*, Art. 68, Rn. 6. Zum Erfordernis der Selbständigkeit des Beförderers vgl. oben Art. 67 Rn. 12 ff.

[14] *Hager/Maultzsch*, 5. Aufl., Art. 68 Rn. 2; *Staudinger/Magnus*, Art. 68, Rn. 6.

[15] Staudinger/Magnus, Art. 68, Rn. 8; MünchKomm/*P. Huber*, Art. 68, Rn. 4. Auch in dieser Konstellation kommt es nach dem oben Rn. 4 Gesagten nicht zu einem Wiederaufleben nationaler Ungültigkeitsvorschriften, sollte die Ware vor der Übergabe untergehen. Der Vertrag ist gültig und der Verkäufer muss sich eben nach Art. 79 von der Schadensersatzhaftung zu befreien suchen.

[16] *Hager/Maultzsch*, 5. Aufl., Art. 68 Rn. 3.

[17] *Hager/Maultzsch*, 5. Aufl., Art. 68 Rn. 4; *Schlechtriem/Schwenzer/Hager/Schmidt-Kessel*, CISG Commentary, Art. 68, Rn. 3; *Ferrari u. a./Mankowski*, Internationales Vertragsrecht, Art. 68, Rn. 10. Vgl. dazu unten Rn. 25.

[18] *Hager/Maultzsch*, 5. Aufl., Art. 68 Rn. 4; *Schlechtriem/Schwenzer/Hager/Schmidt-Kessel*, CISG Commentary, Art. 68, Rn. 3.

[19] *Hager/Maultzsch*, 5. Aufl., Art. 68 Rn. 4; *Schlechtriem/Schwenzer/Hager/Schmidt-Kessel*, CISG Commentary, Art. 68, Rn. 4; *Staudinger/Magnus*, Art. 68, Rn. 11.

charakter der Vorschrift ausgerichtete Handhabung bevorzugen dürften. Hier besteht die Gefahr einer – nach Art. 7 I gerade zu vermeidenden – uneinheitlichen Auslegung und Anwendung der Konvention.

Einigkeit besteht insoweit, dass die geforderten „circumstances" vorliegen, wenn ein auf den Zeitpunkt der Übergabe der Ware an den Beförderer zurückwirkender Versicherungsschutz besteht.[20] Dies gilt auch, wenn dieser erst durch Abtretung dem Käufer zugute kommt.[21] Den im Rahmen der Wiener Konferenz von den Entwicklungsländern vorgetragenen Bedenken des mangelnden Versicherungsschutzes ist dann Rechnung getragen. Damit greift Art. 68 S. 2 insbesondere bei CIF-Geschäften,[22] die einen signifikanten Teil der Fälle abdecken. Auch in diesen Konstellationen findet eine Rückverlagerung allerdings nur statt, soweit von der Versicherung erfasste Risiken betroffen sind. Ist etwa das Schiff bei Vertragsschluss bereits länger als geplant auf See und haben die transportierten Früchte deshalb bereits einen Reifegrad erreicht, der sie für die geplanten industriellen Reifungsprozesse untauglich macht, so kommt es nur dann zu einer Rückverlagerung des Gefahrübergangs auf den Zeitpunkt der Übergabe, wenn der Käufer sich für diesen Vorgang an die Versicherung halten kann. Andernfalls würde die Rückverlagerung des Gefahrübergangs dazu führen, dass im Sinne von Art. 36 I zum relevanten Zeitpunkt kein Mangel vorgelegen hätte oder angelegt gewesen wäre. Auch Art. 36 II griffe nicht ein, so dass der Käufer in diesen Situationen schutzlos bliebe. In den Fällen, in denen der Käufer noch rückwirkend Versicherungsschutz nehmen kann,[23] kommt die Vorschrift zu Anwendung. Beispielsweise mag der Käufer bei Abschluss des Versicherungsvertrages noch keine Kenntnis von deren Untergang gehabt haben.[24] Dies gilt allerdings nicht für den ebenfalls sehr gebräuchlichen Term FOB.[25]

Abzulehnen ist die Auffassung, S. 2 könne nur Anwendung finden, wenn zum Versicherungsschutz für den gesamten Transportweg kumulativ Schwierigkeiten in der Feststellung des Schadenseintrittszeitpunktes hinzutreten.[26] Ein solches Erfordernis ergibt sich weder aus dem Wortlaut, noch ist diese Anhebung der Hürde vor dem Hintergrund der Entstehungsgeschichte geboten. Auch aus praktischer Sicht ist es wenig wünschenswert, den Anwendungsbereich von S. 2, der gerade die sich aus S. 1 ergebenden praktischen Schwierigkeiten beseitigt, unnötig zurückzuschneiden. Gänzlich ohne Abstützung in Wortlaut, Entstehungsgeschichte und Zweck ist die Auffassung, S. 2 werde immer gesperrt, wenn Sicherheit über den Zeitpunkt des Schadenseintritts besteht.[27]

Zu weit in die andere Richtung geht der – freilich praktikable – Vorschlag, bei jeder Unsicherheit über den Zeitpunkt des Schadenseintritts den Käufer mit der Gefahr ab Übergabe der Ware an den Beförderer zu belasten.[28] Gerechtfertigt erscheint es demgegenüber, dem Verkäufer das Transportrisiko zu übertragen, sofern kein Versicherungsschutz besteht, also von einem Fernkauf auszugehen.[29] Dafür spricht, dass es im Ermessen des Verkäufers

---

[20] O. R., S. 215, Nr. 3; *Hager/Maultzsch*, 5. Aufl., Art. 68 Rn. 4; *Schlechtriem/Schwenzer/Hager/Schmidt-Kessel*, CISG Commentary, Art. 68, Rn. 5; *Staudinger/Magnus*, Art. 68, Rn. 4; *Honnold/Flechtner*, Art. 68, Rn. 372.2; *Witz/Salger/Lorenz/Witz*, Art. 68, Rn. 7; MünchKomm/*P. Huber*, Art. 68, Rn. 8; MünchKommHGB/*Benicke*, Art. 68, Rn. 7; *Ferrari u. a./Mankowski*, Internationales Vertragsrecht, Art. 68, Rn. 14; *Brunner*, Art. 68, Rn. 3; *Herber/Czerwenka*, Art. 68, Rn. 3; *Enderlein/Maskow/Strohbach*, Art. 68, Anm. 3.; *Schlechtriem*, Einheitliches UN-Kaufrecht, S. 82. Dagegen *Honsell/Schönle/Th. Koller*, Art. 68, Rn. 15 f. (lediglich zu berücksichtigen).
[21] *Staudinger/Magnus*, Art. 68, Rn. 11; *Ferrari u. a./Mankowski*, Internationales Vertragsrecht, Art. 68, Rn. 14; *Brunner*, Art. 68, Rn. 3.
[22] *Hager/Maultzsch*, 5. Aufl., Art. 68 Rn. 4; *Schlechtriem/Schwenzer/Hager/Schmidt-Kessel*, CISG Commentary, Art. 68, Rn. 5; *Herber/Czerwenka*, Art. 68, Rn. 3; *Bridge*, FS Kritzer, S. 95 f.
[23] Institute Cargo Clauses A, B und C Clause 11.2; Deutschland § 2 I VVG.
[24] *Hager/Maultzsch*, 5. Aufl., Art. 68 Rn. 4; *Schlechtriem/Schwenzer/Hager/Schmidt-Kessel*, CISG Commentary, Art. 68, Rn. 5.
[25] *Hager/Maultzsch*, 5. Aufl., Art. 68 Rn. 4; *Herber/Czerwenka*, Art. 68, Rn. 3; *Bridge*, FS Kritzer, S. 95 f.
[26] So aber *Honsell/Schönle/Th. Koller*, Art. 68, Rn. 16.
[27] So aber *Honsell/Schönle/Th. Koller*, Art. 68, Rn. 16.
[28] So aber *Heuzé*, Anm. 378.
[29] *Hager/Maultzsch*, 5. Aufl., Art. 68 Rn. 4; *Schlechtriem/Schwenzer/Hager/Schmidt-Kessel*, CISG Commentary, Art. 68, Rn. 4.

liegt, vor Übergabe der Ware zum Transport für Versicherungsschutz zu sorgen. Zudem besteht zu diesem Zeitpunkt noch keine Sicherheit, dass er die dann reisende Ware wird verkaufen können. Insofern zeigt der Verkäufer also durchaus seine Bereitschaft, das Untergangsrisiko für die Dauer des Transports zu übernehmen.

3. Beförderer

12 Im Unterschied zu Art. 99 I EKG spricht Art. 68 S. 2 nicht generisch von der Übergabe an den „carrier", sondern spezifisch von der Übergabe der Ware an den „carrier who issued the documents embodying the contract of carriage". Vorausgesetzt wird damit nach dem klaren Wortlaut – anders als in Art. 58 I, II – nicht, dass die ausgestellten Dokumente auch zur Verfügung über die Ware berechtigen.[30] Entscheidend ist allein ihre Beweiskraft für die Existenz des Frachtvertrags. Praktisch wird beides oft im Konnossement (Bill of Lading) zusammentreffen. Sind mehrere Beförderer hintereinander geschaltet, etwa beim multimodalen Transport, so ist auf den ersten Beförderer abzustellen, der die geforderten Dokumente ausgestellt hat.[31] Stellen mehrere Beförderer entsprechende Dokumente aus, so kommt es auch dabei auf den ersten davon an.[32]

13 Unsicherheit besteht darüber, ob die Anwendung von Art. 68 S. 2 auch dann in Betracht kommt, wenn der Frachtvertrag ohne Dokumente abgeschlossen wurde. So wird es vor allem dann liegen, wenn der Frachtvertrag im Wege der elektronischen Kommunikationssysteme (EDI) geschlossen wird, die kein weiteres menschliches Zutun mehr erfordern. Nach einer Auffassung soll Art. 68 S. 2 in diesen Fällen wenigstens analog Anwendung finden.[33] Nach der vorzugswürdigen Gegenauffassung bleibt die Vorschrift in diesen Fällen unanwendbar.[34] Der rückwirkende Gefahrübergang erlegt es dem Käufer auf, bei der Versicherung Regress zu nehmen. Die den Frachtvertrag dokumentierenden Papiere helfen, die Berechtigung des Regressverlangens zu beweisen. Es ist nicht einzusehen, wieso die Stellung des Käufers gegenüber der Versicherung verschlechtert werden soll, wenn der Verkäufer einen Vertragsschlussmechanismus wählt, der zu einer lückenhaften Dokumentation führt. Festzuhalten ist auch, dass die Verfasser des CISG von der weiteren Formulierung des EKG, das lediglich von „carrier" gesprochen hatte, abgewichen sind. Für eine entsprechende Anwendung von Art. 68 S. 2 bleibt deshalb kein Raum.

V. Bösgläubigkeit des Verkäufers (Art. 68 S. 3)

14 Eine ganze Reihe von Unsicherheiten besteht im Zusammenhang mit Art. 68 S. 3, wonach der Verkäufer die Gefahr des Untergangs bzw. der Beschädigung der Ware trägt, wenn er diesen bzw. diese, bei Vertragsschluss kannte oder kennen musste.

---

[30] *Hager/Maultzsch*, 5. Aufl., Art. 68 Rn. 4a; *Schlechtriem/Schwenzer/Hager/Schmidt-Kessel*, CISG Commentary, Art. 68, Rn. 6; *Staudinger/Magnus*, Art. 68, Rn. 12; MüncherKomm/*P. Huber*, Art. 68, Rn. 9; MünchKommHGB/*Benicke*, Art. 68, Rn. 7; *Bianca/Bonell/Nicholas*, Art. 68, Anm. 2.2.; *Herber/Czerwenka*, Art. 68, Rn. 4; *Enderlein/Maskow/Strohbach*, Art. 68, Anm. 4. Missverständlich *Honsell/Schönle/Th. Koller*, Art. 68, Rn. 10, der „in erster Linie" Traditionswertpapiere umfasst sieht, andere Dokumente, die den Frachtvertrag beweisen, seien „auch" erfasst.

[31] *Hager/Maultzsch*, 5. Aufl., Art. 68 Rn. 4; *Schlechtriem/Schwenzer/Hager/Schmidt-Kessel*, CISG Commentary, Art. 68, Rn. 6; *Enderlein/Maskow/Strohbach*, Art. 68, Anm. 4.

[32] *Staudinger/Magnus*, Art. 68, Rn. 12; MünchKommHGB/*Benicke*, Art. 68, Rn. 7.

[33] *Staudinger/Magnus*, Art. 68, Rn. 13; *Witz/Salger/Lorenz/Witz*, Art. 68, Rn. 9 (nur bei Abschluss des Vertrags mittels elektronischer Datenübermittlung, fehlen Dokumente sonst, keine Anwendung von Art. 68 S. 2); MünchKomm/*P. Huber*, Art. 68, Rn. 9; MünchKommHGB/*Benicke*, Art. 68, Rn. 8; *Ferrari u. a./Mankowski*, Internationales Vertragsrecht, Art. 68, Rn. 18; *Honsell/Schönle/Th. Koller*, Art. 68, Rn. 11.

[34] *Hager/Maultzsch*, 5. Aufl., Art. 68 Rn. 4; *Schlechtriem/Schwenzer/Hager/Schmidt-Kessel*, CISG Commentary, Art. 68, Rn. 6; *Herber/Czerwenka*, Art. 68, Rn. 6.

1. Anwendungsbereich

Der Anwendungsbereich von Art. 68 S. 3 wird nach wie vor nicht vollständig einheitlich beurteilt, genauer gesagt, ob die Vorschrift sowohl für S. 1 und S. 2 gilt oder sich auf S. 2 beschränkt. Ihre praktische Spitze erlangt die Frage in Fällen, in denen die Ware bereits bei Vertragsschluss beschädigt – und damit vertragswidrig – war, der Verkäufer dies wusste oder wissen musste, und die Ware im Anschluss durch Zufall untergegangen ist.[35] Gilt S. 3 auch für S. 1, so bleibt der Verkäufer in diesem Fall gefahrbelastet; ist S. 3 aber auf S. 2 begrenzt, so geht die Gefahr gleichwohl auf den Käufer über.[36]

Der Wortlaut gibt keinen entscheidenden Hinweis. Durchgesetzt hat sich mittlerweile die Begrenzung von S. 3 auf S. 2.[37] Dafür spricht zunächst die systematische Positionierung der Vorschrift,[38] genauer gesagt die Tatsache, dass sie nicht als eigener Absatz ausgestaltet wurde. Darüber hinaus ist die Frage, ob die Ware bei Vertragsschluss beschädigt und deshalb mangelhaft war, keine Frage der Gefahrtragung.[39] Dass Art. 36 den für die Mangelfreiheit der Ware relevanten Zeitpunkt an den Gefahrübergang knüpft und dieser wegen Art. 68 S. 1 mit dem Vertragsschluss zusammenfällt, ändert daran nichts. Die noch im EKG vorgenommene Verknüpfung von Gefahrübergang und Lieferung mangelfreier Ware wurde aufgegeben.[40] Es handelt sich um einen einfachen Fall der Sachgewährleistung nach Art. 35.[41] Verdeutlicht wird dies auch durch Art. 70, der gerade nur für den Fall der wesentlichen Vertragsverletzung dem Käufer die dafür vorgesehenen Rechtsbehelfe erhält. Ist der Verkäufer bösgläubig hinsichtlich der Beschädigung der Ware, so ist dies im Rahmen der Artt. 40, 43 zu berücksichtigen.[42]

2. Reichweite

Probleme bereitet sodann die Frage, in welchem Umfang der bösgläubige Verkäufer gefahrbelastet bleibt. Gedacht ist dabei an die Konstellation, in welcher der Verkäufer bei Vertragsschluss weiss, dass die Ware bereits verdorben ist, aber nicht wissen musste, dass sie auch schon durch Zufall untergegangen ist.[43] So mag der Verkäufer also bereits über den nachteiligen Kontakt des verschifften Weizens mit Wasser informiert gewesen sein, aber von der Notentladung in der Nacht vor dem Vertragsschluss noch keine Meldung erhalten haben.

In der Literatur wird zur Lösung des Problems der Entstehungsgeschichte der Vorschrift besondere Beachtung geschenkt.[44] In Abkehr vom EKG hatte der Genfer Entwurf dem Verkäufer noch das gesamte Risiko zugewiesen: „**the risk of loss** sold in transit does not pass to the buyer".[45] Diese Regel wurde dann in den Entwürfen von Wien und New York zurückgeschnitten: „if the seller knew or ought to have known, that the goods had been lost

---

[35] *Hager/Maultzsch*, 5. Aufl., Art. 68 Rn. 5.
[36] *Hager/Maultzsch*, 5. Aufl., Art. 68 Rn. 5.
[37] So *Hager/Maultzsch*, 5. Aufl., Art. 68 Rn. 5; *Staudinger/Magnus*, Art. 68, Rn. 16; *Witz/Salger/Lorenz/Witz*, Art. 68, Rn. 11 („logischerweise"); *Honnold/Flechtner*, Art. 68, Rn. 372.2; MünchKomm/*P. Huber*, Art. 68, Rn. 10; MünchKommHGB/*Benicke*, Art. 68, Rn. 9; *Bamberger/Roth/Saenger*, Art. 68, Rn. 4; *Herber/Czerwenka*, Art. 68, Rn. 7; *Enderlein/Maskow/Strohbach*, Art. 68, Anm. 5.1. Differenzierend *Honsell/Schönle/Th. Koller*, Art. 68, Rn. 23 ff. Dagegen in neuerer Zeit nur noch *Piltz*, Internationales Kaufrecht, Rn. 4–284.
[38] *Hager/Maultzsch*, 5. Aufl., Art. 68 Rn. 5; *Ferrari u. a./Mankowski*, Internationales Vertragsrecht, Art. 68, Rn. 21.
[39] *Hager/Maultzsch*, 5. Aufl., Art. 68 Rn. 5; *Staudinger/Magnus*, Art. 68, Rn. 17.
[40] *Staudinger/Magnus*, Art. 68, Rn. 17.
[41] *Hager/Maultzsch*, 5. Aufl., Art. 68 Rn. 5; *Staudinger/Magnus*, Art. 68, Rn. 17.
[42] *Staudinger/Magnus*, Art. 68, Rn. 17.
[43] Beispiel bei *Hager/Maultzsch*, 5. Aufl., Art. 68 Rn. 5a.
[44] Insbesondere *Hager/Maultzsch*, 5. Aufl., Art. 68 Rn. 5a; *Schlechtriem/Schwenzer/Hager/Schmidt-Kessel*, CISG Commentary, Art. 68, Rn. 8.
[45] Art. 65 II Genfer E; YB V (1974), S. 92, Nr. 81, S. 48, Nr. 223; *Hager/Maultzsch*, 5. Aufl., Art. 68 Rn. 5a; *Schlechtriem/Schwenzer/Hager/Schmidt-Kessel*, CISG Commentary, Art. 68, Rn. 8.

or damaged ... such loss or damage is at the risk of the seller".[46] Während der Wiener Konferenz wurde der Text dann erneut geändert und spricht heute von „**the** loss or damage" bzw. „**la** perte ou **la** détérioration".

19 Überwiegend wird aus der Entstehungsgeschichte,[47] insbesondere aus den Veränderungen zwischen Genfer Entwurf und der Fassung in den Entwürfen von Wien und New York, die letztlich auch Gegenstand der Beratungen der Wiener Konferenz war, geschlossen, dass der Verkäufer nur bezüglich derjenigen Beschädigungen gefahrbelastet bleibt, hinsichtlich derer er bösgläubig war.[48] Eingeräumt wird allerdings, dass diese Form des Gefahrtragungssplittings streitfördernd wirkt und damit praktische Nachteile hat.[49]

20 Demgegenüber vertritt die Gegenauffassung eine Alles-oder-Nichts-Lösung, wonach dem bösgläubigen Verkäufer das volle Risiko auferlegt wird.[50] Dieser Ansatz vermeidet zwar die praktischen Schwierigkeiten, die sich aus dem Ansatz der herrschenden Meinung ergeben, geht letztlich aber zu weit. So erscheint es unverhältnismässig und mit dem Zweck von Art. 68 nicht vereinbar, die Bösgläubigkeit des Verkäufers hinsichtlich jeder noch so kleinen Beeinträchtigung der Ware zum Anlass zu nehmen, den Verkäufer das volle weitere Beschädigungs- bzw. Untergangsrisiko tragen zu lassen. Die jeweilige Vertragswidrigkeit hätte den Käufer womöglich nicht einmal zur Neulieferung oder Vertragsaufhebung berechtigt. Sollte die Ware dann tatsächlich nach Vertragsschluss noch untergehen, so käme der Käufer aber im wirtschaftlichen Ergebnis über die Regeln der Gefahrtragung doch noch in den Genuss dieser Rechtsbehelfe, unabhängig von der Schwere der Pflichtverletzung des Verkäufers. Umgekehrt macht aber Art. 70 die „Rettung" des (gutgläubigen) Verkäufers durch die Gefahrtragungsregeln vor den Folgen seiner Vertragsverletzung gerade von der Schwere dieser Pflichtverletzung abhängig. Der Ansatz der herrschenden Ansicht berücksichtigt den besonderen Umstand der Bösgläubigkeit des Verkäufers angemessen, indem dessen Haftung in dem Umfang fortbesteht, in dem sie auch fortbestanden hätte, wäre der Ware im weiteren Verlauf nichts mehr zugestossen.

3. Massstab der Bösgläubigkeit

21 Umstritten ist schliesslich der Massstab für die Bösgläubigkeit des Verkäufers. Nach einer Auffassung soll diese nur bei grober Fahrlässigkeit gegeben sein.[51] Nach der zutreffenden herrschenden Ansicht reicht indessen einfache Fahrlässigkeit aus.[52] Die Konvention bedient sich der Wendung „ought to have known" auch an anderer Stelle (z. B. Artt. 38 III, 39 I) und nimmt in diesen Fällen unstreitig Bezug auf einfache Fahrlässigkeit.[53] Soweit grobe Fahrlässigkeit verlangt wird, verwendet das CISG die Formulierung „could not have been unaware" (z. B. Artt. 8, 35 III, 40, 42).[54]

---

[46] *Hager/Maultzsch*, 5. Aufl., Art. 68 Rn. 5a; *Schlechtriem/Schwenzer/Hager/Schmidt-Kessel*, CISG Commentary, Art. 68, Rn. 8.
[47] Vgl. auch Sekretariatskommentar, Art. 80, Nr. 2.
[48] *Hager/Maultzsch*, 5. Aufl., Art. 68 Rn. 5a; *Schlechtriem/Schwenzer/Hager/Schmidt-Kessel*, CISG Commentary, Art. 68, Rn. 8; *Staudinger/Magnus*, Art. 68, Rn. 20; *Witz/Salger/Lorenz/Witz*, Art. 68, Rn. 12; MünchKomm/*P. Huber*, Art. 68, Rn. 19; *Herber/Czerwenka*, Art. 68, Rn. 7; *Enderlein/Maskow/Strohbach*, Art. 68, Anm. 5.2.; *Schlechtriem*, Internationales UN-Kaufrecht, Rn. 231.
[49] *Hager/Maultzsch*, 5. Aufl., Art. 68 Rn. 5a; *Schlechtriem/Schwenzer/Hager/Schmidt-Kessel*, CISG Commentary, Art. 68, Rn. 8.
[50] *Honnold/Flechtner*, Art. 68, Rn. 372.2; *Bianca/Bonell/Nicholas*, Art. 68, Anm. 2.3.; MünchKommHGB/*Benicke*, Art. 68, Rn. 10.
[51] MünchKommHGB/*Benicke*, Art. 68, Rn. 9; *Herber/Czerwenka*, Art. 68, Rn. 9; *Karollus*, S. 199.
[52] *Staudinger/Magnus*, Art. 68, Rn. 21; MünchKomm/*P. Huber*, Art. 68, Rn. 10; *Ferrari u. a./Mankowski*, Internationales Vertragsrecht, Art. 68, Rn. 20; *Honsell/Schönle/Th. Koller*, Art. 68, Rn. 20; *Brunner*, Art. 68, Rn. 7.
[53] *Staudinger/Magnus*, Art. 68, Rn. 21.
[54] *Staudinger/Magnus*, Art. 68, Rn. 21.

VI. Sammelladungen

Obwohl am Spezieskauf orientiert, findet Art. 68 auch auf Sammelladungen („bulks") Anwendung.[55] Voraussetzung ist allerdings, dass der Verkäufer nach Vertrag oder Handelsbrauch berechtigt ist, dem Käufer die Ware in dieser Form anzudienen. Ist dies nicht der Fall, so geht die Gefahr erst mit der Individualisierung der Ware über. Dieses Erfordernis ist zwar nur in Art. 67 II ausdrücklich niedergelegt, dem Konzept der Gefahrtragung aber inhärent und deshalb auch ohne weiteres in Art. 68 enthalten. 22

Ist die Andienung in Form der Sammelladung hingegen gestattet, so geht die Gefahr mit Vertragsschluss auf die jeweiligen Käufer über. Geht die Ware teilweise unter bzw. wird sie teilweise beschädigt, so liegt es beim Verkäufer zu entscheiden, welchem Käufer er den Restbestand bzw. den unbeschädigten Teil der Ware überlässt. Er haftet dann den übrigen Käufern in dem Umfang, in dem der Restbestand bzw. der unbeschädigte Teil der Ware deren Bestellmenge noch abgedeckt hätte. 23

Eine anteilsmässige Verteilung des Verlusts bzw. der Beschädigung findet nicht von Gesetzes wegen statt.[56] Entscheidend ist, inwieweit die Ware im Verhältnis zum individuellen Käufer noch hätte geliefert werden können. Dies gebietet schon der Grundsatz der Relativität der Schuldverhältnisse. Darüber hinaus folgt aus dem Prinzip *pacta sunt servanda*, dass jeder Käufer zunächst einen Anspruch darauf hat, soweit die Ware noch vorhanden bzw. unbeschädigt ist, diese auch entsprechend dem Kaufvertrag zu erhalten. Jeder Käufer trägt das Verlust- bzw. Beschädigungsrisiko nur insoweit, als die Bestellmenge selbst bei maximaler Zuteilung des Restbestandes bzw. der unbeschädigten Ware nicht erreicht wird. 24

VII. Beweisfragen

Regelmässig wird sich der Verkäufer darauf berufen, der Gefahrübergang sei bereits erfolgt. Folglich trägt er dafür auch die Beweislast.[57] Dieser hat auch das Vorliegen der Voraussetzungen für den rückwirkenden Gefahrübergang nach Art. 68 S. 2 zu beweisen.[58] Hingegen obliegt es dem Käufer, eine allfällige Bösgläubigkeit des Verkäufers im Sinne des Art. 68 S. 3 nachzuweisen.[59] 25

---

[55] *Hager/Maultzsch*, 5. Aufl., Art. 68 Rn. 6; *Schlechtriem/Schwenzer/Hager/Schmidt-Kessel*, CISG Commentary, Art. 68, Rn. 10; *Staudinger/Magnus*, Art. 68, Rn. 23; *Ferrari u. a./Mankowski*, Internationales Vertragsrecht, Art. 68, Rn. 25.

[56] So auch *Honsell/Schönle/Th. Koller*, Art. 68, Rn. 7. Anders noch *Hager/Maultzsch*, 5. Aufl., Art. 68 Rn. 6. A. A. auch *Schlechtriem/Schwenzer/Hager/Schmidt-Kessel*, CISG Commentary, Art. 68, Rn. 10; *Ferrari u. a./Mankowski*, Internationales Vertragsrecht, Art. 68, Rn. 26.

[57] *Staudinger/Magnus*, Art. 68, Rn. 24; MünchKomm/*P. Huber*, Art. 68, Rn. 12.

[58] *Staudinger/Magnus*, Art. 68, Rn. 24; MünchKomm/*P. Huber*, Art. 68, Rn. 12.

[59] *Staudinger/Magnus*, Art. 68, Rn. 26; MünchKomm/*P. Huber*, Art. 68, Rn. 12.

Art. 69 [Gefahrübergang in anderen Fällen]

(1) In den durch Artikel 67 und 68 nicht geregelten Fällen geht die Gefahr auf den Käufer über, sobald er die Ware übernimmt oder, wenn er sie nicht rechtzeitig übernimmt, in dem Zeitpunkt, in dem ihm die Ware zur Verfügung gestellt wird und er durch Nichtabnahme* eine Vertragsverletzung begeht.

(2) Hat jedoch der Käufer die Ware an einem anderen Ort als einer Niederlassung des Verkäufers zu übernehmen, so geht die Gefahr über, sobald die Lieferung fällig ist und der Käufer Kenntnis davon hat, daß ihm die Ware an diesem Ort zur Verfügung steht.

(3) Betrifft der Vertrag Ware, die noch nicht individualisiert ist,** so gilt sie erst dann als dem Käufer zur Verfügung gestellt, wenn sie eindeutig dem Vertrag zugeordnet worden ist.

Art. 69

(1) In cases not within articles 67 and 68, the risk passes to the buyer when he takes over the goods or, if he does not do so in due time, from the time when the goods are placed at his disposal and he commits a breach of contract by failing to take delivery.

(2) However, if the buyer is bound to take over the goods at a place other than a place of business of the seller, the risk passes when delivery is due and the buyer is aware of the fact that the goods are placed at his disposal at that place.

(3) If the contract relates to goods not then identified, the goods are considered not to be placed at the disposal of the buyer until they are clearly identified to the contract.

Art. 69

1) Dans les cas non visés par les articles 67 et 68, les risques sont transférés à l'acheteur lorsqu'il retire les marchandiises ou, s'il ne le fait pas en temps voulu, à partir du moment où les marchandises sont mises à sa disposition et où il commet une contravention au contrat en n'en prenant pas livraison.

2) Cependant, si l'acheteur est tenu de retirer les marchandises en un lieu autre qu'un établissement du vendeur, les risques sont transférés lorsque la livraison est due et que l'acheteur sait que les marchandises sont mises à sa disposition en ce lieu.

3) Si la vente porte sur des marchandises non encore individualisées, les marchandises ne sont réputées avoir été mises à la disposition de l'acheteur que lorsqu'elles ont été clairement identifiées aux fins du contrat.

Übersicht

	Rn.
I. Vorgeschichte	1
II. Regelungsgegenstand	4
III. Platzkauf (Art. 69 I)	5
1. Übernahme der Ware am Ort des Verkäufers (Art. 69 I Alt. 1)	5
2. Gefahrübergang bei Abnahmeverzug (Art. 69 I Alt. 2)	9
a) Abnahmeverzug	10
b) Zurverfügungstellung	11
c) Entlastung; sonstige Pflichtverletzungen des Käufers	14
IV. Sonstiger Ort als Lieferort (Art. 69 II)	17
1. Zurverfügungstellung	20
2. Kenntnis des Käufers	21
V. Individualisierung (Art. 69 III)	24
VI. Beweisfragen	25

---

* Schweiz, Österreich: Nichtannahme.
** Österreich: die ihm noch nicht zugeordnet ist.

I. Vorgeschichte

Der Sache nach war Art. 69 bereits in Artt. 97 I, 98 EKG enthalten. Allerdings hatte das EKG den Gefahrübergang noch an die ordnungsgemässe Lieferung geknüpft.[1] Die Konvention hat den Gefahrübergang von der Lieferung entkoppelt und stellt auf die tatsächliche Gewahrsamsaufgabe durch den Verkäufer und Gewahrsamsübernahme durch den Käufer bzw. den Beförderer ab.[2] Dies geschah vor allem aus praktischen Gesichtspunkten. Der Gewahrsamsinhaber ist regelmässig am besten in der Lage, die Ware vor Beeinträchtigungen zu schützen oder doch zumindest für Versicherungsschutz zu sorgen.[3] Dementsprechend knüpft Art. 69 I an die Übernahme der Ware an.[4] 1

Art. 69 II hat keinen direkten Vorläufer im EKG, sondern wurde auf norwegischen Vorschlag hin aufgenommen.[5] In den Blick genommen wurde dabei insbesondere der Verkauf eingelagerter Ware.[6] Auch dabei geht es mit dem Erfordernis der Zurverfügungstellung letztlich um den Gewahrsam an der Sache. 2

Keine Mehrheit fand ein Antrag der deutschen Delegation, die Gefahr immer auf den Käufer übergehen zu lassen, wenn dieser durch eine Pflichtverletzung den sonst vorgesehenen Gefahrübergang verhindert.[7] Art. 69 I Alt. 2 ordnet diese Rechtsfolge ausdrücklich nur für den Fall des Abnahmeverzugs des Käufers an. Festzuhalten ist allerdings, dass die Ablehnung des deutschen Antrags deshalb erfolgte, weil man die beantragte ausdrückliche Festschreibung für überflüssig hielt.[8] 3

II. Regelungsgegenstand

Art. 69 fängt ausweislich seines Wortlauts als subsidiärer Grundtatbestand alle Fälle auf,[9] die nicht schon in den Anwendungsbereich von Artt. 67, 68 fallen, also weder als Versendungskauf noch als Kauf reisender Ware zu qualifizieren sind. Dabei geht es in Art. 69 I zunächst um den Platzkauf.[10] Der Fernkauf, bei dem der Verkäufer die Ware am Ort des Käufers abzuliefern hat, fällt nicht unter Art. 69 I, sondern ist in Art. 69 II geregelt.[11] Schliesslich verlangt Art. 69 III die hinreichende Individualisierung der Ware. Zusammen mit Art. 67 II enthält die Vorschrift ein allgemeines Prinzip im Sinne des Art. 7 II, dass der Gefahrübergang nur bei hinreichender Konkretisierung der Ware erfolgen kann.[12] 4

---

[1] *Hager/Maultzsch*, 5. Aufl., Art. 69 Rn. 1, Art. 67, Rn. 1; *Schlechtriem/Schwenzer/Hager/Schmidt-Kessel*, CISG Commentary, Art. 69, Rn. 1, Art. 67, Rn. 1; *Staudinger/Magnus*, Art. 69, Rn. 4.

[2] *Hager/Maultzsch*, 5. Aufl., Art. 69 Rn. 1; *Schlechtriem/Schwenzer/Hager/Schmidt-Kessel*, CISG Commentary, Art. 69, Rn. 1.

[3] *Hager/Maultzsch*, 5. Aufl., Art. 69 Rn. 1; *Schlechtriem/Schwenzer/Hager/Schmidt-Kessel*, CISG Commentary, Art. 69, Rn. 1.

[4] *Hager/Maultzsch*, 5. Aufl., Art. 69 Rn. 1; *Schlechtriem/Schwenzer/Hager/Schmidt-Kessel*, CISG Commentary, Art. 69, Rn. 1.

[5] *Hager/Maultzsch*, 5. Aufl., Art. 69 Rn. 1; *Schlechtriem/Schwenzer/Hager/Schmidt-Kessel*, CISG Commentary, Art. 69, Rn. 1; *Staudinger/Magnus*, Art. 69, Rn. 5.

[6] YB VIII (1977), S. 125, 126, Nr. 56, 59, S. 163, Art. 66, Nr. 5, S. 64, Nr. 550–552; *Hager/Maultzsch*, 5. Aufl., Art. 69 Rn. 1; *Schlechtriem/Schwenzer/Hager/Schmidt-Kessel*, CISG Commentary, Art. 69, Rn. 1; *Staudinger/Magnus*, Art. 69, Rn. 5.

[7] O. R., S. 406; *Hager/Maultzsch*, 5. Aufl., Art. 69 Rn. 1; *Schlechtriem/Schwenzer/Hager/Schmidt-Kessel*, CISG Commentary, Art. 69, Rn. 1.

[8] O. R., S. 407; *Staudinger/Magnus*, Art. 69, Rn. 6.

[9] *MünchKomm/P. Huber*, Art. 69, Rn. 3: „Auffangregel"; *Staudinger/Magnus*, Art. 69, Rn. 7.

[10] AG Duisburg, 13.4.2000, CISG-online 659; *Hager/Maultzsch*, 5. Aufl., Art. 69 Rn. 2; *Schlechtriem/Schwenzer/Hager/Schmidt-Kessel*, CISG Commentary, Art. 69, Rn. 2; *Staudinger/Magnus*, Art. 69, Rn. 7; *Witz/Salger/Lorenz/Witz*, Art. 69, Rn. 5; *MünchKomm/P. Huber*, Art. 69, Rn. 1; *Honnold/Flechtner*, Art. 69, Rn. 373; *MünchKommHGB/Benicke*, Art. 69, Rn. 2.

[11] A. A. *Enderlein/Maskow/Strohbach*, Art. 69, Anm. 1.

[12] Vgl. auch oben vor Artt. 66–70 Rn. 19; *MünchKomm/P. Huber*, Art. 69, Rn. 14, Art. 67, Rn. 19.

III. Platzkauf (Art. 69 I)

1. Übernahme der Ware am Ort des Verkäufers (Art. 69 I Alt. 1)

5   Der in Art. 69 I Alt. 1 geregelte Grundfall geht von der Übernahme des Gewahrsams an der Sache durch den Käufer am Ort des Verkäufers aus.[13] Die Vorschrift korrespondiert so mit Art. 31 lit. c) und entspricht weitgehend dem Regelungsgehalt der Incoterm® Klausel 2010 EXW.[14] Art. 69 I nennt zwar den Ort des Verkäufers nicht ausdrücklich, doch ergibt sich dies jedenfalls *e contrario* aus dem Wortlaut von Abs. 2.[15] Der Übergabe der Ware an den Käufer steht die Übergabe an eigene Leute des Käufers bzw. an einen von ihm beauftragten Transporteur gleich.[16] Die nach Abs. 3 geforderte Individualisierung der Ware dürfte in diesen Fällen keine Probleme bereiten.[17]

6   Wer das Verladerisiko zu tragen hat, ist bislang nicht abschliessend geklärt. Im Zweifel wird man dieses aber dem Käufer aufzuerlegen haben.[18] Dafür spricht zunächst der Wortlaut von Art. 69 I („takes over/placed at his disposal"), der weniger verlangt als Art. 67 I („handed over").[19] Weiterhin verlangt auch Incoterm® 2010 EXW in Klausel A4 für die Lieferung und den in den Incoterms® 2010 damit verknüpften Gefahrübergang nicht, dass der Verkäufer die Ware auf das Transportmittel des Käufers bzw. des von ihm beauftragten Transporteurs verlädt.[20]

7   Aus den unterschiedlichen Formulierungen in Art. 69 I Alt. 1 („takes over") und Alt. 2 („placed at his disposal") ergibt sich auch, dass nach Abs. 1 Alt. 1 die reine Zurverfügungstellung der Ware nicht für den Gefahrübergang ausreicht, sondern der Käufer, dessen eigene Leute oder ein von ihm beauftragter Transporteur die Ware übernehmen muss.[21] Diese Voraussetzung ist mit dem Beginn des Verladevorgangs, während dem der Käufer schon gefahrbelastet ist,[22] erfüllt.[23]

8   Das generische Abstellen auf die Übernahme der Ware durch den Käufer in Art. 69 I Alt. 1 zeigt auch, dass bei vorzeitiger Lieferung die Gefahr gleichwohl übergeht, wenn der Käufer, eigene Leute oder ein beauftragter Transporteur sie übernimmt.[24] Ist der Käufer zur Zurückweisung berechtigt und macht davon Gebrauch, so geht die Gefahr nicht auf ihn über, obwohl er die Ware übernimmt, denn gemäss Art. 86 ist der Käufer zur Erhaltung der Ware verpflichtet.[25]

---

[13] *Hager/Maultzsch*, 5. Aufl., Art. 69 Rn. 2; *Schlechtriem/Schwenzer/Hager/Schmidt-Kessel*, CISG Commentary, Art. 69, Rn. 2; *Staudinger/Magnus*, Art. 69, Rn. 9; MünchKomm/*P. Huber*, Art. 69, Rn. 3; *Honnold/Flechtner*, Art. 69, Rn. 373; *Ferrari u. a./Mankowski*, Internationales Vertragsrecht, Art. 69, Rn. 5; *Herber/Czerwenka*, Art. 69, Rn. 2.

[14] *Hager/Maultzsch*, 5. Aufl., Art. 69 Rn. 2; *Schlechtriem/Schwenzer/Hager/Schmidt-Kessel*, CISG Commentary, Art. 69, Rn. 2; *Staudinger/Magnus*, Art. 69, Rn. 9; MünchKomm/*P. Huber*, Art. 69, Rn. 3; *Honnold/Flechtner*, Art. 69, Rn. 373; *Ferrari u. a./Mankowski*, Internationales Vertragsrecht, Art. 69, Rn. 5; *Herber/Czerwenka*, Art. 69, Rn. 2. Mit Recht weist *Mohs*, FS Schwenzer, S. 1285, 1295 darauf hin, dass aber bei EXW die Zurverfügungstellung der Ware ausreicht.

[15] *Hager/Maultzsch*, 5. Aufl., Art. 69 Rn. 2; *Schlechtriem/Schwenzer/Hager/Schmidt-Kessel*, CISG Commentary, Art. 69, Rn. 2.

[16] *Staudinger/Magnus*, Art. 69, Rn. 9; *Witz/Salger/Lorenz/Witz*, Art. 69, Rn. 5 f.; MünchKomm/*P. Huber*, Art. 69, Rn. 3; *Herber/Czerwenka*, Art. 69, Rn. 2; MünchKommHGB/*Benicke*, Art. 69, Rn. 2.

[17] MünchKomm/*P. Huber*, Art. 69, Rn. 4.

[18] So auch MünchKomm/*P. Huber*, Art. 69, Rn. 4.

[19] Vgl. zu diesem Problem auch schon oben Art. 67 Rn. 17 ff.

[20] Darauf abstellend auch MünchKomm/*P. Huber*, Art. 69, Rn. 4.

[21] *Hager/Maultzsch*, 5. Aufl., Art. 69 Rn. 3; *Schlechtriem/Schwenzer/Hager/Schmidt-Kessel*, CISG Commentary, Art. 69, Rn. 3.

[22] Vgl. oben Rn. 6.

[23] *Witz/Salger/Lorenz/Witz*, Art. 69, Rn. 6; MünchKomm/*P. Huber*, Art. 69, Rn. 4; *Ferrari u. a./Mankowski*, Internationales Vertragsrecht, Art. 69, Rn. 4.

[24] *Staudinger/Magnus*, Art. 69, Rn. 10.

[25] *Staudinger/Magnus*, Art. 69, Rn. 10.

2. Gefahrübergang bei Abnahmeverzug (Art. 69 I Alt. 2)

Der Käufer kann durch Abnahmeverzug den Gefahrübergang nicht verhindern und damit **9** unbegrenzt den Verkäufer mit dem Untergangs- bzw. Beschädigungsrisiko belasten. Dies stellt Art. 69 I Alt. 2 klar, indem die Gefahr auf den Käufer übergeht, wenn der Käufer die Ware nicht rechtzeitig übernimmt, obgleich sie ihm zur Verfügung gestellt wurde.

a) Abnahmeverzug. Der Abnahmeverzug des Käufers tritt nach dem klaren Wortlaut **10** der Konvention mit Verstreichen des Fälligkeitszeitpunktes für die Übernahme ein („if he does not do so in due time"). Mahnung und Fristsetzung, wie sie zahlreiche nationale Rechtsordnungen zur Begründung des Verzugs vorsehen[26] und die dort auch notwendig sind, um den sich im Verzug befindlichen Schuldner der Abnahmepflicht bzw. den Gläubiger der Lieferpflicht mit der Gefahr zu belasten,[27] existieren in der Konvention nicht, dürfen nicht in sie hinein gelesen werden und auch ein Rückgriff auf nationales Recht ist ausgeschlossen. Die Konvention bedient sich des Nachfrist-Konzepts nur, wenn der Abnahmeverzug keine wesentliche Vertragsverletzung darstellt und der Verkäufer den Vertrag aufheben will (Art. 64). Umgekehrt kann der Verkäufer den Gefahrübergang selbstverständlich nicht herbeiführen, indem er vor Fälligkeit der Abnahme die Ware individualisiert, zur Übernahme bereit macht und den Käufer hierüber in Kenntnis setzt.

b) Zurverfügungstellung. Neben dem Abnahmeverzug ist die Zurverfügungstellung **11** der Ware durch den Verkäufer zentrales Element des Gefahrübergangs nach Art. 69 I Alt. 2 („placed at his disposal"). Damit wird vor allem die hinreichende Individualisierung der Ware gemäss Art. 69 III verlangt.[28] Bei Füll- und Schüttgütern, die in Tanks oder Silos aufbewahrt und dann typisch direkt in Transportfahrzeuge geleitet werden, ist dafür aber keine Umlagerung in separate Behältnisse notwendig. Hier reicht es aus, dass die geschuldete Menge vorhanden und die Übernahme möglich ist.[29]

Ob die Zurverfügungstellung nach Art. 69 I Alt. 2 auch der **Notifizierung des Käufers** **12** durch den Verkäufer bedarf, ist umstritten. Einigkeit besteht nur insoweit, dass unabhängig davon, ob es die Anzeige braucht, eine versandte Anzeige entgegen Art. 27 jedenfalls auf Risiko des Verkäufers reist.[30] Die h. M. lehnt das Notifizierungserfordernis ab.[31] Einschränkend verlangen manche Stimmen aber die Notifizierung in Fällen, in denen die Übernahme durch den Käufer sonst nicht möglich wäre.[32] In der Tat ergibt sich aus dem Wortlaut **keine Pflicht zur Anzeige**. Auch Art. 69 II nennt die Zurverfügungstellung und die Kenntnis des Käufers als zwei verschiedene Tatbestandsmerkmale.[33] Vertretbar erscheint allenfalls, auf das Gebot des Art. 7 I Bezug zu nehmen, wonach Vorschriften unter Wahrung des guten Glaubens im internationalen Handel auszulegen sind und im Anschluss daran Art. 69 I Alt. 2 eine Auslegung solcher Art angedeihen zu lassen, dass der Verkäufer zur Notifizierung verpflichtet ist. Allerdings ist diese Konstruktion brüchig und es bleiben Zweifel bestehen,

---

[26] *Schwenzer/Hachem/Kee*, Rn. 47.41 ff.
[27] Vgl. *Schwenzer/Hachem/Kee*, Rn. 38.68.
[28] Anders aber *Ferrari u. a./Mankowski*, Internationales Vertragsrecht, Art. 69, Rn. 12: Nicht zwingend erforderlich, denn Kollision mit Fallkonstellationen möglich, in denen Individualisierung ohne Mitwirkung des Käufers nicht oder kaum möglich ist. Vgl. demgegenüber Art. 69 III: „[G]oods are considered not to be placed at the disposal of the buyer until they are clearly identified to the contract.". Zur Individualisierung nach Art. 69 III vgl. unten Rn. 24 und für Art. 67 II oben Art. 67 Rn. 29 ff.
[29] *Hager/Maultzsch*, 5. Aufl., Art. 69 Rn. 3; *Schlechtriem/Schwenzer/Hager/Schmidt-Kessel*, CISG Commentary, Art. 69, Rn. 3; *Staudinger/Magnus*, Art. 69, Rn. 13; *Witz/Salger/Lorenz/Witz*, Art. 69, Rn. 15; MünchKomm/P. *Huber*, Art. 69, Rn. 15; MünchKommHGB/*Benicke*, Art. 69, Rn. 12; *Ferrari u. a./Mankowski*, Internationales Vertragsrecht, Art. 69, Rn. 31.
[30] Statt aller *Staudinger/Magnus*, Art. 69, Rn.14.
[31] *Staudinger/Magnus*, Art. 69, Rn. 14; *Honnold/Flechtner*, Art. 69, Rn. 374. Anders aber *Hager/Maultzsch*, 5. Aufl., Art. 69 Rn. 4; *Schlechtriem/Schwenzer/Hager/Schmidt-Kessel*, CISG Commentary, Art. 69, Rn. 4, beide unter Berufung auf Sekretariatskommentar, Art. 29, Nr. 16, Art. 81, Nr. 7.
[32] *Staudinger/Magnus*, Art. 69, Rn. 14; MünchKomm/P. *Huber*, Art. 69, Rn. 4; *Enderlein/Maskow/Strohbach*, Art. 69, Anm. 4.3.
[33] *Ferrari u. a./Mankowski*, Internationales Vertragsrecht, Art. 69, Rn. 13.

ob eine solche Auslegung international anschlussfähig wäre, wie dies eben auch von Art. 7 I gefordert wird. In der Sache geht es m. E. ohnehin um die Frage der Individualisierung nach Art. 69 III, die eine Notifizierung nach den Umständen des Falles erfordern kann, weshalb das Problem dort besser aufgehoben ist. Für das Erfordernis „placed at his disposal" gemäss Art. 69 I Alt. 2 besteht jedenfalls keine Anzeigepflicht. Der für den Gefahrübergang beweisbelastete Verkäufer hat freilich immer ein praktisches Interesse daran, den Käufer zu notifizieren.

13 Probleme entstehen, wenn bei Füll- und Schüttgütern die in einem Silo oder Tank gelagerte Ware an mehrere Käufer mit Holschuld verkauft worden ist, von denen sich aber z. B. nur einer im Abnahmeverzug befindet und deshalb gemäss dem in der vorigen Rn. 12 beschriebenen Mechanismus nach Art. 69 I Alt. 2 gefahrbelastet ist. Geht die Ware teilweise unter, so stellt sich, wie sonst auch bei Sammelladungen (Art. 67 II), das Problem, dass letztlich nicht gesagt werden kann, wessen Ware genau untergegangen ist. Der schon grundsätzlich bei Sammelladungen abzulehnende Ansatz der h. M., das Risiko standardmässig *pro-rata* zu verteilen,[34] versagt in der hier beschriebenen Konstellation vollends. Selbst die h. M. dürfte ihn auch nur zur Anwendung bringen, wenn sich alle Käufer im Abnahmeverzug befänden, was oft nicht der Fall sein dürfte.[35] Eine darüber hinausgehende pauschale Anwendung des *pro-rata*-Ansatzes würde bedeuten, die nicht vertragsbrüchigen Käufer bereits mit dem Risiko für den Teil zu belasten, den sie deshalb nicht bekommen, weil der vertragsbrüchige Käufer noch anteilig bedient wird. Damit würde aber faktisch der Gefahrübergang für diesen Teil stattfinden, noch bevor die Voraussetzungen dafür vorgelegen haben. Nicht zu rechtfertigen ist darüber hinaus, dass der vertragsbrüchige Käufer so gestellt wird wie die Käufer, die sich nicht im Verzug befinden. M. E. sollte der Verkäufer deshalb zuerst die Käufer bedienen, die noch nicht in Verzug geraten sind. Es gelten dafür, wenn nicht alle Käufer voll bedient werden können, die zur Sammelladung gemachten Ausführungen (oben Art. 67 Rn. 31 ff.). Bleibt ein Teil der Ware übrig,[36] so kommt dieser dem in Verzug geratenen Käufer zu. In diesem Sinne wird im Ausschlussverfahren bestimmt, für welchen Teil der Ware der vertragsbrüchige Käufer schon die Gefahr getragen hat.

14 **c) Entlastung; sonstige Pflichtverletzungen des Käufers.** Nach einhelliger Auffassung hindert eine erfolgreiche Berufung des in Verzug geratenen Käufers auf Art. 79 nicht den Gefahrübergang, da diese Vorschrift nur von allfälligen Schadenersatzansprüchen des Verkäufers befreit (Art. 79 V).[37]

15 Umstritten ist hingegen, ob auch **andere Pflichtverletzungen des Käufers** den Gefahrübergang nach Art. 69 I Alt. 2 bewirken können. Gehen wird es in den meisten Fällen darum, dass der Käufer das Akkreditiv nicht eröffnet oder anderweitig seiner Zahlungspflicht nicht nachkommt und der Verkäufer deshalb die Ware zurückbehält. In anderen Situationen mag der Käufer das Transportschiff nicht benannt oder bestätigt haben, so dass der Verkäufer die Ware be- und erhalten (Artt. 85, 88 II) muss. Nach ganz überwiegender und zutreffender Auffassung greift in diesen Situationen Art. 69 I Alt. 2 zumindest analog oder wird als allgemeines Prinzip (Art. 7 II) verstanden.[38] Richtig ist zwar, dass ein deutscher Antrag, eine entsprechende Regelung in die Konvention aufzunehmen, abgelehnt wurde, allerdings ging

---

[34] Vgl. dazu oben Art. 67 Rn. 31 ff.
[35] Insbesondere wird man sicher nicht eine Gefahrgemeinschaft rechtfertigen können, wenn ein oder mehrere Käufer vertragsbrüchig und deshalb gefahrbelastet ist bzw. sind, während die anderen Käufer sich dies gerade nicht entgegen halten lassen müssen.
[36] Zu dem oben in Art. 67 Rn. 31 ff. dargestellten Streit kommt es dann natürlich nicht unter den anderen, nicht in Verzug geratenen Verkäufern, da in dieser Konstellation alle vollständig bedient werden konnten.
[37] *Hager/Maultzsch*, 5. Aufl., Art. 69 Rn. 4; *Schlechtriem/Schwenzer/Hager/Schmidt-Kessel*, CISG Commentary, Art. 69, Rn. 4; *Staudinger/Magnus*, Art. 69, Rn. 15; *Witz/Salger/Lorenz/Witz*, Art. 69, Rn. 7; MünchKomm/*P. Huber*, Art. 69, Rn. 6; *Honsell/Schönle/Th. Koller*, Art. 69, Rn. 12; *Brunner*, Art. 69, Rn. 3.
[38] *Hager/Maultzsch*, 5. Aufl., Art. 69 Rn. 4; *Schlechtriem/Schwenzer/Hager/Schmidt-Kessel*, CISG Commentary, Art. 69, Rn. 4; *Staudinger/Magnus*, Art. 69, Rn. 17; MünchKomm/*P. Huber*, Art. 69, Rn. 6. A. A. MünchKommHGB/*Benicke*, Art. 69, Rn. 4.

man seinerzeit davon aus, dass dies schlicht überflüssig sei.[39] Der Gefahrübergang erhält dadurch auch keinen Sanktionscharakter,[40] sondern schützt, ganz im Sinne seiner originären Funktion, den Verkäufer davor, vom Käufer unilateral mit der Gefahr weiter belastet zu werden.[41] Die unterlassene Benennung bzw. Bestätigung des Schiffes kann freilich auch als originärer Teil der Übernahmeverpflichtung qualifiziert werden,[42] so dass für sie Art. 69 I Alt. 2 direkt gilt. Der Ansatz der h. M. kann auch als Spiegelbild zu Art. 66 *in fine* verstanden werden,[43] wo der Gefahrübergang gerade dadurch unbeachtlich wird, dass der Verkäufer das Erreichen des Vertragsziels beeinträchtigt.[44]

Keine Pflichtverletzung des Käufers liegt natürlich vor, wenn er die Ware auf Grund ihrer Mangelhaftigkeit gleich zurückweist.[45] In diesen Konstellationen wird der Käufer dies oft auch dadurch zum Ausdruck bringen, dass er die Benennung bzw. Bestätigung des Schiffes verweigert. **16**

IV. Sonstiger Ort als Lieferort (Art. 69 II)

Hat der Käufer die Ware an einem anderen Ort als dem Sitz des Verkäufers zu übernehmen, so erfolgt der Gefahrübergang an diesem Ort, wenn die Ware dort zur Verfügung steht und der Käufer davon Kenntnis hat. Auch hier ist nach Abs. 3 die hinreichende Individualisierung gefordert. Gleichsam gilt auch für Abs. 2 die Subsidiarität der Vorschrift zu Artt. 67, 68. Hat der Verkäufer mehrere Niederlassungen, so greift Abs. 2 nur in den Fällen, in denen der Käufer die Ware an keiner von ihnen abzunehmen hat.[46] **17**

Die Vorschrift ist auf den Verkauf eingelagerter oder sonst verwahrter Ware zugeschnitten, erfasst aber auch die Bringschuld und den Fernkauf.[47] Unter den Incoterms® entsprechen ihr deshalb insbesondere die D-Terms.[48] Soweit die Verwendung der Klausel „frei Haus" oder „frei Bestimmungsort" nach den Umständen des Einzelfalles nicht als reine Organisations- und Kostentragungs-, sondern auch als Gefahrtragungsregel zu verstehen ist,[49] deckt sie sich mit Art. 69 II.[50] Die EXW-Konstellation, in welcher der Käufer eine Holschuld hat, ist von Art. 69 II erfasst, wenn das Werk nicht gleichzeitig eine Niederlassung des Verkäufers ist. In Betracht kommen hier vor allem Fälle, in denen der Käufer die Ware am Werk des – vom Verkäufer verschiedenen – Herstellers zu übernehmen hat.[51] Der Zeitpunkt des Gefahrübergangs ist in diesen Fällen an die Fälligkeit der Lieferung (Art. 33) geknüpft. Darüber hinaus muss der Verkäufer die Ware am anderen Ort dem Käufer zur Verfügung stellen und letzterer davon Kenntnis haben. **18**

Abweichend von seinem Ausgangspunkt, den Gefahrübergang mit dem Gewahrsamsübergang zu verknüpfen, verlagert Art. 69 II den Zeitpunkt des Gefahrübergangs vor den **19**

---

[39] *Hager/Maultzsch*, 5. Aufl., Art. 69 Rn. 9; *Schlechtriem/Schwenzer/Hager/Schmidt-Kessel*, CISG Commentary, Art. 69, Rn. 9.
[40] So aber noch *Enderlein/Maskow/Strohbach*, Art. 69, Anm. 5.1.
[41] *Hager/Maultzsch*, 5. Aufl., Art. 69 Rn. 4; *Schlechtriem/Schwenzer/Hager/Schmidt-Kessel*, CISG Commentary, Art. 69, Rn. 9.
[42] Zu den Details der Abnahmepflicht vgl. oben *Mohs*, Art. 60 Rn. 2 ff.
[43] Vgl. *Hager/Maultzsch*, 5. Aufl., Art. 69 Rn. 9; *Schlechtriem/Schwenzer/Hager/Schmidt-Kessel*, CISG Commentary, Art. 69, Rn. 9.
[44] Vgl. zur Bedeutung von Art. 66 *in fine* oben Art. 66 Rn. 16 ff.
[45] *Honsell/Schönle/Th. Koller*, Art. 69, Rn. 12.
[46] *Staudinger/Magnus*, Art. 69, Rn. 19.
[47] *Hager/Maultzsch*, 5. Aufl., Art. 69 Rn. 4; *Schlechtriem/Schwenzer/Hager/Schmidt-Kessel*, CISG Commentary, Art. 69, Rn. 4; *Staudinger/Magnus*, Art. 69, Rn. 18.
[48] *Mohs*, FS Schwenzer, S. 1285, 1295 f.
[49] So in OLG Karlsruhe, 20.11.1922, CISG-online 54 = NJW-RR 1993, 1316. Vgl. dazu oben Art. 67 Rn. 11.
[50] *Hager/Maultzsch*, 5. Aufl., Art. 69 Rn. 6; *Schlechtriem/Schwenzer/Hager/Schmidt-Kessel*, CISG Commentary, Art. 69, Rn. 6.
[51] *Hager/Maultzsch*, 5. Aufl., Art. 69 Rn. 6; *Schlechtriem/Schwenzer/Hager/Schmidt-Kessel*, CISG Commentary, Art. 69, Rn. 6.

Zeitpunkt der Übernahme. Damit wird dem Umstand Rechnung getragen, dass die Ware den Herrschaftsbereich des Verkäufers verlässt und häufig nicht versichert ist.[52] Bisweilen wird, gestützt auf Art. 7 II, vertreten, der Gefahrübergang erfolge aber gleichwohl erst, wenn der Käufer die Gelegenheit hatte, die bei dem Dritten lagernde Ware zu versichern.[53] Für diese Auffassung findet sich indes im Wortlaut der Vorschrift keine Stütze. Darüber hinaus entsteht eine Unsicherheit über den genauen Zeitpunkt des Gefahrübergangs. Auch die Frage, wie lange der Verkäufer gefahrbelastet bleibt, um dem Käufer die Gelegenheit zu geben, Versicherungsschutz zu organisieren, dürfte sich streitfördernd auswirken. Schliesslich steht dem auch der Zweck der Vorschrift, den Verkäufer zu schützen, im Widerspruch zu diesem Ansatz.[54]

1. Zurverfügungstellung

20   Das Erfordernis der Zurverfügungstellung ist inhaltsgleich zum dem in Art. 69 I Alt. 2 aufgestellten.[55] Beim Fernkauf hat der Verkäufer die Ware dem Käufer an dessen Sitz bzw. an dem vereinbarten dritten Ort anzubieten.[56] Allfällige Montageverpflichtungen müssen erfüllt, das heisst Vorgänge solcher Art abgeschlossen sein.[57] Beim Verkauf eingelagerter Ware ist diese dem Käufer im Sinne von Art. 69 II zur Verfügung gestellt, wenn der Käufer die Herausgabe der Ware verlangen kann. Dies ist in verschiedenen Konstellationen der Fall. So mag der Käufer im Besitz eines Wertpapieres sein, das den Herausgabeanspruch gegen den Lagerhalter verbrieft. Indes ist dies nicht erforderlich. Ausreichend, dann aber auch notwendig, ist, dass der Lagerhalter die Anweisung des Verkäufers zur Auslieferung oder sonst das Besitzrecht des Käufers anerkennt.[58] Die Übergabe eines Lieferscheins an den Käufer mit der darin enthaltenen Anweisung an den Lagerhalter reicht für sich genommen deshalb nicht aus.[59] Die Ware lagert also weiterhin auf Gefahr des Verkäufers.[60]

2. Kenntnis des Käufers

21   Gemäss Art. 69 II geht die Gefahr erst über, „when the buyer is aware of the fact that the goods are placed at his disposal at that place". Der Wortlaut „aware" setzt nach einhelliger Auffassung positive Kenntnis des Käufers hinsichtlich der erfolgten Zurverfügungstellung voraus.[61] Nicht ausreichend sind deshalb fahrlässige oder grob fahrlässige Unkenntnis.[62] Daraus ergibt sich aber nicht etwa ein rechtliches Anzeigeerfordernis. Vorbehaltlich entsprechender Mitteilungen an den Käufer durch Dritte, wird eine Notifizierung des Käufers

---

[52] *Hager/Maultzsch*, 5. Aufl., Art. 69 Rn. 6; *Schlechtriem/Schwenzer/Hager/Schmidt-Kessel*, CISG Commentary, Art. 69, Rn. 6.
[53] *Bridge*, FS Kritzer, S. 101.
[54] Darauf abstellend *Hager/Maultzsch*, 5. Aufl., Art. 69 Rn. 6; *Schlechtriem/Schwenzer/Hager/Schmidt-Kessel*, CISG Commentary, Art. 69, Rn. 6.
[55] *Hager/Maultzsch*, 5. Aufl., Art. 69 Rn. 6; *Schlechtriem/Schwenzer/Hager/Schmidt-Kessel*, CISG Commentary, Art. 69, Rn. 6; *Ferrari u. a./Mankowski*, Internationales Vertragsrecht, Art. 69, Rn. 22. Zur geforderten Individualisierung vgl. unten Rn. 24.
[56] *Hager/Maultzsch*, 5. Aufl., Art. 69 Rn. 7; *Schlechtriem/Schwenzer/Hager/Schmidt-Kessel*, CISG Commentary, Art. 69, Rn. 7; *Ferrari u. a./Mankowski*, Internationales Vertragsrecht, Art. 69, Rn. 23. Zur geforderten Individualisierung vgl. unten Rn. 24.
[57] *Staudinger/Magnus*, Art. 69, Rn. 22; *Ferrari u. a./Mankowski*, Internationales Vertragsrecht, Art. 69, Rn. 23.
[58] *Hager/Maultzsch*, 5. Aufl., Art. 69 Rn. 7; *Schlechtriem/Schwenzer/Hager/Schmidt-Kessel*, CISG Commentary, Art. 69, Rn. 7; *Staudinger/Magnus*, Art. 69, Rn. 22; MünchKomm/*P. Huber*, Art. 69, Rn. 12; *Ferrari u. a./Mankowski*, Internationales Vertragsrecht, Art. 69, Rn. 24; *Herber/Czerwenka*, Art. 69, Rn. 7.
[59] *Hager/Maultzsch*, 5. Aufl., Art. 69 Rn. 7; *Schlechtriem/Schwenzer/Hager/Schmidt-Kessel*, CISG Commentary, Art. 69, Rn. 7.
[60] *Hager/Maultzsch*, 5. Aufl., Art. 69 Rn. 7; *Schlechtriem/Schwenzer/Hager/Schmidt-Kessel*, CISG Commentary, Art. 69, Rn. 7.
[61] Statt aller *Staudinger/Magnus*, Art. 69, Rn. 23; MünchKomm/*P. Huber*, Art. 69, Rn. 13.
[62] Statt aller *Staudinger/Magnus*, Art. 69, Rn. 23; MünchKomm/*P. Huber*, Art. 69, Rn. 13.

aber regelmässig notwendig sein, um ihn über die erfolgte Zurverfügungstellung in Kenntnis zu setzen. Diese Anzeige reist abweichend von Art. 27 auf Gefahr des Verkäufers.[63]

Das Erfordernis der positiven Kenntnis des Käufers von der Zurverfügungstellung der Ware durch den Verkäufer darf aber nicht dem Käufer als Vehikel dafür dienen, den Gefahrübergang zu Lasten des Verkäufers aufzuschieben.[64] Insbesondere vor dem Hintergrund, dass der Verkäufer die Beweislast für die positive Kenntnis des Käufers trägt, darf diese Voraussetzung nicht vollständig subjektiviert werden.[65] Es muss deshalb ausreichen, wenn der Verkäufer die Anzeige so in den Machtbereich des Käufers gebracht hat, dass unter normalen Umständen mit Kenntnisnahme und daraus folgend mit positiver Kenntnis gerechnet werden durfte.[66] 22

Indes dürfte die Voraussetzung positiver Kenntnis in der Praxis selten Probleme bereiten. Im Falle des Verkaufs eingelagerter oder sonst verwahrter Ware wird der Käufer zwangsläufig Kenntnis von der Zurverfügungstellung erhalten, da diese erst mit dem Erhalt eines den Herausgabeanspruch gegen den Lagerhalter enthaltenden Wertpapiers bzw. das sonstige Anerkenntnis des Besitzrechts durch den Lagerhalter eintritt.[67] Bei Bringschulden sowie dem Fernkauf muss der Verkäufer die Ware andienen, so dass auch hier der Käufer zwangsläufig Kenntnis erhält. Für den wohl selteneren Fall, dass die Holschuld unter Art. 69 II fällt, kann sich das Problem der positiven Kenntnis allerdings stellen, da die Ware hier nur so bereit gestellt werden muss, dass der Käufer die Ware ohne weiteres übernehmen kann. 23

V. Individualisierung (Art. 69 III)

Art. 69 III verlangt für den Gefahrübergang die hinreichende Individualisierung. Im Zusammenspiel mit Art. 67 II ergibt sich daraus das allgemeine Prinzip (Art. 7 II), dass der Gefahrübergang die Individualisierung voraussetzt. Art. 69 III nimmt die (nicht abschliessenden) Beispiele des Art. 67 II nicht noch einmal auf, ist aber gleich zu verstehen. Für weitere Details, insbesondere auch zur Problematik von Sammelladungen, die im Anwendungsbereich von Art. 69 freilich Vorratsschulden sind, kann deshalb auf die obigen Ausführungen verwiesen werden.[68] 24

VI. Beweisfragen

Entsprechend einem allgemeinen Prinzip der Konvention (Art. 7 II) muss die Partei, die Vorteile aus einer Bestimmung herleitet, das Vorliegen der tatbestandsmässigen Voraussetzungen nachweisen. Im Rahmen des Art. 69 I Alt. 2 trifft deshalb den Verkäufer die Beweislast für die Zurverfügungstellung der Ware, den Abnahmeverzug des Käufers sowie dessen Kenntnis von der Zurverfügungstellung.[69] 25

---

[63] *Hager/Maultzsch*, 5. Aufl., Art. 69 Rn. 4; *Schlechtriem/Schwenzer/Hager/Schmidt-Kessel*, CISG Commentary, Art. 69, Rn. 4; *Staudinger/Magnus*, Art. 69, Rn. 23; MünchKomm/*P. Huber*, Art. 69, Rn. 13.
[64] *Ferrari u. a./Mankowski*, Internationales Vertragsrecht, Art. 69, Rn. 25.
[65] *Ferrari u. a./Mankowski*, Internationales Vertragsrecht, Art. 69, Rn. 25.
[66] *Staudinger/Magnus*, Art. 69, Rn. 23; *Ferrari u. a./Mankowski*, Internationales Vertragsrecht, Art. 69, Rn. 25.
[67] Vgl. oben Rn. 20.
[68] Art. 67 Rn. 31 ff.
[69] *Staudinger/Magnus*, Art. 69, Rn. 25.

Art. 70 [Wesentliche Vertragsverletzung und Gefahrübergang]

Hat der Verkäufer eine wesentliche Vertragsverletzung begangen, so berühren die Artikel 67, 68 und 69 nicht die dem Käufer wegen einer solchen Verletzung zustehenden Rechtsbehelfe.*

Art. 70

If the seller has committed a fundamental breach of contract, articles 67, 68 and 69 do not impair the remedies available to the buyer on account of the breach.

Art. 70

Si le vendeur a commis une contravention essentielle au contrat, les dispositions des articles 67, 68 et 69 ne portent pas atteinte aux moyens dont l'acheteur dispose en raison de cette contravention.

Übersicht

	Rn.
I. Vorgeschichte	1
II. Regelungsgegenstand	2
III. Anwendungsbereich	5
1. Wesentliche Vertragsverletzung	5
2. Nicht wesentliche Vertragsverletzungen	8
3. Gefahrrückfall	10

I. Vorgeschichte

1   Das EKG hatte noch den Gefahrübergang an den Zeitpunkt der Lieferung mangelfreier Ware geknüpft.[1] In Art. 97 II EKG war allerdings ausdrücklich vorgesehen, dass auch bei Lieferung vertragswidriger Ware die Gefahr auf den Käufer übergehen sollte, solange dieser weder sein Rücktritts- noch Ersatzlieferungsrecht ausgeübt hatte. Dieser Bruch des EKG mit seinem System der Verbindung von Lieferung und Gefahrübergang und die daraus folgenden Komplikationen veranlasste schliesslich auch die Verfasser des CISG den Gefahrübergang von der Lieferung der Ware zu entkoppeln.[2] In der Sache weicht Art. 70 in seiner heutigen Fassung nicht von seinem Vorläufer im EKG ab.[3]

II. Regelungsgegenstand

2   Art. 70 regelt das Verhältnis zwischen dem Gefahrübergang und den Rechtsbehelfen des Käufers wegen einer wesentlichen Vertragsverletzung des Käufers.[4] Die für Art. 70 gewählte Formulierung ist jedoch gefährlich und kann leicht zu Missverständnissen führen.[5] Es wird

---

* Schweiz: Rechte.
[1] *Hager/Maultzsch*, 5. Aufl., Art. 70 Rn. 1; *Schlechtriem/Schwenzer/Hager/Schmidt-Kessel*, CISG Commentary, Art. 70, Rn. 1; Staudinger/Magnus, Art. 70, Rn. 3.
[2] *Hager/Maultzsch*, 5. Aufl., Art. 70 Rn. 1; *Schlechtriem/Schwenzer/Hager/Schmidt-Kessel*, CISG Commentary, Art. 70, Rn. 1; Witz/Salger/Lorenz/Witz, Art. 70, Rn. 1.
[3] *Hager/Maultzsch*, 5. Aufl., Art. 70 Rn. 1; *Schlechtriem/Schwenzer/Hager/Schmidt-Kessel*, CISG Commentary, Art. 70, Rn. 1. Weiter zur Entstehungsgeschichte Ferrari u. a./Mankowski, Internationales Vertragsrecht, Art. 70, Rn. 2 f.
[4] *Hager/Maultzsch*, 5. Aufl., Art. 70 Rn. 2; *Schlechtriem/Schwenzer/Hager/Schmidt-Kessel*, CISG Commentary, Art. 70, Rn. 1; Staudinger/Magnus, Art. 70, Rn. 3; Ferrari u. a./Mankowski, Internationales Vertragsrecht, Art. 70, Rn. 1; Honsell/Schönle/Th. Koller, Art. 70, Rn. 2.
[5] *Staudinger/Magnus*, Art. 70, Rn. 5: „nicht sehr klar gefasst". In diesem Sinne auch MünchKomm/P. Huber, Art. 70, Rn. 1; Bianca/Bonell/Nicholas, Art. 70, Anm. 2.1.; Herber/Czerwenka, Art. 70, Rn. 2; Honsell/Schönle/Th. Koller, Art. 70, Rn. 1.

gerade **nicht** der Fall erfasst, in dem die wesentliche Vertragsverletzung des Verkäufers zum Untergang der Ware geführt hat.[6] In dieser Konstellation liegt ausweislich Art. 66 *in fine* schon überhaupt keine Frage der Gefahrtragung vor,[7] sondern es ist dies ein regulärer Fall der Sachmangelgewährleistung. **Erfasst** wird die Konstellation in der die wesentliche Vertragsverletzung und der spätere Untergang der Ware in keinem Zusammenhang stehen.[8] War also Weizen bei der Verschiffung mangelhaft verpackt, nimmt auf See Feuchtigkeit auf und verdirbt, so behält der Käufer seine Rechtsbehelfe wegen dieser (sicher) wesentlichen Vertragsverletzung, obwohl das Schiff später in Seenot gerät und die Ware notentladen wird. Art. 70 verhindert also, dass der Verkäufer durch den Zufall des Warenuntergangs vor den Folgen seiner wesentlichen Vertragsverletzung „gerettet" wird und sogar noch den Kaufpreisanspruch in der Hand hat.

Indes hindert Art. 70 den Gefahrübergang nicht grundsätzlich. Ein amerikanischer Antrag 3 auf der Wiener Konferenz, die Gefahr bei wesentlicher Vertragsverletzung erst mit der Berechtigung des Käufers zur Ersatzlieferung oder Vertragsaufhebung übergehen zu lassen, wurde abgelehnt.[9] Vielmehr geht die Gefahr nach den Artt. 67–69 auf den Käufer über, springt aber mit *ex tunc* Wirkung auf den Verkäufer zurück, wenn der Käufer seine Rechtsbehelfe, wie von Art. 70 vorgesehen, wegen wesentlicher Vertragsverletzung ausübt.[10]

Die Vorschrift ist darüber hinaus im Zusammenhang mit den Regeln über die Rückabwick- 4 lung, insbesondere Art. 82, zu lesen.[11] Es erscheint zunächst selbstverständlich, dass der Käufer bereits vor Gefahrübergang entstandene Rechte nicht verliert, wenn die Regeln der Gefahrtragung ihm erst zu einem späteren Zeitpunkt Verlustrisiken zuweisen.[12] Allerdings wäre der Käufer bei Untergang der Ware dann wegen Art. 82 I daran gehindert, die Vertragsaufhebung zu erklären bzw. Ersatzlieferung zu verlangen, schliesslich gelänge es ihm dann nicht, die Sache wieder zurückzugeben. Art. 70 stellt deshalb klar, dass in Ausnahme zu Art. 82 I und Bestätigung zu Art. 82 II lit. a) der Käufer diese beiden – gerade an die wesentliche Vertragsverletzung anknüpfenden – Rechtsbehelfe trotz Unmöglichkeit der Rückgabe ausüben kann.[13]

III. Anwendungsbereich

1. Wesentliche Vertragsverletzung

Nach seinem klaren Wortlaut lässt Art. 70 die Rechtsbehelfe des Käufers bei wesentlicher 5 Vertragsverletzung nicht entfallen. Dies sind freilich alle sich aus Artt. 45 ff. ergebenden Rechtsbehelfe, also Nacherfüllung in Form der Ersatzlieferung (Art. 46 II) oder Nachbesserung (Art. 46 III), Vertragsaufhebung (Art. 49 I lit. a)) oder Preisminderung (Art. 50) sowie Schadenersatzansprüche (Artt. 45 I lit. b), 74 ff.).[14]

---

[6] *Hager/Maultzsch*, 5. Aufl., Art. 70 Rn. 2; *Schlechtriem/Schwenzer/Hager/Schmidt-Kessel*, CISG Commentary, Art. 70, Rn. 2; MünchKomm/*P. Huber*, Art. 70, Rn. 2.
[7] *Hager/Maultzsch*, 5. Aufl., Art. 70 Rn. 2; *Schlechtriem/Schwenzer/Hager/Schmidt-Kessel*, CISG Commentary, Art. 70, Rn. 2; MünchKomm/*P. Huber*, Art. 70, Rn. 2.
[8] MünchKomm/*P. Huber*, Art. 70, Rn. 2.
[9] *Staudinger/Magnus*, Art. 70, Rn. 4.
[10] *Hager/Maultzsch*, 5. Aufl., Art. 70 Rn. 2a; *Schlechtriem/Schwenzer/Hager/Schmidt-Kessel*, CISG Commentary, Art. 70, Rn. 4; *Staudinger/Magnus*, Art. 70, Rn. 13; *Witz/Salger/Lorenz/Witz*, Art. 70, Rn. 1, 6; MünchKomm/*P. Huber*, Art. 70, Rn. 8; *Bianca/Bonell/Nicholas*, Art. 70, Anm. 2.3.; *Ferrari u. a./Mankowski*, Internationales Vertragsrecht, Art. 70, Rn. 5; *Honsell/Schönle/Th. Koller*, Art. 70, Rn. 18.
[11] *Hager/Maultzsch*, 5. Aufl., Art. 70 Rn. 4; *Schlechtriem/Schwenzer/Hager/Schmidt-Kessel*, CISG Commentary, Art. 70, Rn. 4; *Staudinger/Magnus*, Art. 70, Rn. 1; *Witz/Salger/Lorenz/Witz*, Art. 70, Rn. 1; MünchKomm/*P. Huber*, Art. 70, Rn. 3; *Brunner*, Art. 70, Rn. 1.
[12] *Staudinger/Magnus*, Art. 70, Rn. 5.
[13] *Hager/Maultzsch*, 5. Aufl., Art. 70 Rn. 2a; *Schlechtriem/Schwenzer/Hager/Schmidt-Kessel*, CISG Commentary, Art. 70, Rn. 4; *Staudinger/Magnus*, Art. 70, Rn. 5; *Witz/Salger/Lorenz/Witz*, Art. 70, Rn. 1; MünchKomm/*P. Huber*, Art. 70, Rn. 3; *Brunner*, Art. 70, Rn. 1.
[14] *Hager/Maultzsch*, 5. Aufl., Art. 70 Rn. 2a; *Schlechtriem/Schwenzer/Hager/Schmidt-Kessel*, CISG Commentary, Art. 70, Rn. 4; *Staudinger/Magnus*, Art. 70, Rn. 11; MünchKomm/*P. Huber*, Art. 70, Rn. 5; *Ferrari u. a./Mankowski*, Internationales Vertragsrecht, Art. 70, Rn. 10.

6 Gedacht haben dürften die Konventionsverfasser vorranging an die Ersatzlieferung und die Vertragsaufhebung.[15] Zunächst setzen diese beiden Rechtsbehelfe gerade die wesentliche Vertragsverletzung für ihre Verfügbarkeit voraus.[16] Weiterhin passen diese Rechtsbehelfe auch am besten zur Interessenlage des Käufers. Kommt es zu einem Fall, in dem Art. 70 relevant wird, also dem zur wesentlichen Vertragsverletzung hinzutretenden, zufälligen Untergang der Ware bzw. ihrer Beschädigung, so wird die rein auf die bestehende Vertragsverletzung bezogene Nachbesserung dem Käufer nicht von Nutzen sein.[17] Gleiches gilt für die Preisminderung, bei deren Berechnung schliesslich nur auf den durch die Vertragsverletzung verminderten Wert der Ware abzustellen wäre, nicht auf den durch die allfällige Beschädigung weiter verminderten Wert.[18] Aus diesem Grund wird auch der Schadenersatz dem Käufer nicht weiterhelfen.[19] Zudem bliebe in allen diesen Fällen der Käufer letztlich auch gefahrbelastet.[20] Der Käufer wird deshalb entweder den Vertrag aufzuheben suchen oder Ersatzlieferung verlangen.

7 Dem Fall der wesentlichen Vertragsverletzung ohne weiteres gleichzustellen ist – trotz des redaktionell ungenauen Wortlauts[21] – die Konstellation, in welcher der Käufer zwar nicht über Art. 49 I lit. a) aber doch über Art. 49 I lit. b) zur Vertragsaufhebung gelangt.[22] Es geht dabei um die Situation, in welcher der ohnehin verspätete Verkäufer noch nach Ablauf der ihm vom Käufer gemäss Artt. 49 I lit. b), 47 gesetzten Frist liefert und die Ware dann untergeht, bzw. beschädigt wird. Zu diesem Zeitpunkt ist der Käufer dann ebenso zur Vertragsaufhebung berechtigt, wie er dies auch gewesen wäre, hätte von Beginn an eine wesentliche Vertragsverletzung vorgelegen. Es ist dann nicht zu rechtfertigen, den doppelt verspäteten Verkäufer besser zu stellen, indem er trotz fruchtlosen Ablaufs der Nachfrist den Kaufpreiszahlungsanspruch behalten soll.[23]

2. Nicht wesentliche Vertragsverletzungen

8 Art. 70 sagt nichts zum Verhältnis der Gefahrtragung zu bereits bei Gefahrübergang vorliegenden, nicht wesentlichen Pflichtverletzungen des Verkäufers. Der Wortlaut der Vorschrift mit der darin enthaltenen Erwähnung der wesentlichen Vertragsverletzung darf aber nicht dahingehend missverstanden werden, dass im Falle einer nicht wesentlichen Vertragsverletzung die dadurch ausgelösten Rechtsbehelfe gewissermassen mit der Ware untergehen bzw. Schaden erleiden. Der Käufer bleibt in dieser Konstellation gefahrbelastet, kann aber die ihm wegen der Vertragsverletzung zustehenden Rechtsbehelfe ausüben.[24] Dazu zählen dann freilich nicht die Ersatzlieferung bzw. die Vertragsaufhebung.[25]

---

[15] *Hager/Maultzsch*, 5. Aufl., Art. 70 Rn. 2a; *Schlechtriem/Schwenzer/Hager/Schmidt-Kessel*, CISG Commentary, Art. 70, Rn. 4; *Ferrari u.a./Mankowski*, Internationales Vertragsrecht, Art. 70, Rn. 14.

[16] *Hager/Maultzsch*, 5. Aufl., Art. 70 Rn. 2a; *Schlechtriem/Schwenzer/Hager/Schmidt-Kessel*, CISG Commentary, Art. 70, Rn. 4.

[17] *Hager/Maultzsch*, 5. Aufl., Art. 70 Rn. 2a; *Schlechtriem/Schwenzer/Hager/Schmidt-Kessel*, CISG Commentary, Art. 70, Rn. 4.

[18] *Hager/Maultzsch*, 5. Aufl., Art. 70 Rn. 2a; *Schlechtriem/Schwenzer/Hager/Schmidt-Kessel*, CISG Commentary, Art. 70, Rn. 4; *Brunner*, Art. 70, Rn. 4.

[19] *Hager/Maultzsch*, 5. Aufl., Art. 70 Rn. 2a; *Schlechtriem/Schwenzer/Hager/Schmidt-Kessel*, CISG Commentary, Art. 70, Rn. 4; *Brunner*, Art. 70, Rn. 4.

[20] *Hager/Maultzsch*, 5. Aufl., Art. 70 Rn. 2a; *Schlechtriem/Schwenzer/Hager/Schmidt-Kessel*, CISG Commentary, Art. 70, Rn. 4; *Staudinger/Magnus*, Art. 70, Rn. 15; *Honsell/Schönle/Th. Koller*, Art. 70, Rn. 18; *Brunner*, Art. 70, Rn. 4.

[21] So schon *Hager/Maultzsch*, 5. Aufl., Art. 70 Rn. 3; *Schlechtriem/Schwenzer/Hager/Schmidt-Kessel*, CISG Commentary, Art. 70, Rn. 5.

[22] *Hager/Maultzsch*, 5. Aufl., Art. 70 Rn. 3; *Schlechtriem/Schwenzer/Hager/Schmidt-Kessel*, CISG Commentary, Art. 70, Rn. 5; *Staudinger/Magnus*, Art. 70, Rn. 14; *Honsell/Schönle/Th. Koller*, Art. 70, Rn. 1; *Brunner*, Art. 70, Rn. 4.

[23] MünchKomm/*P. Huber*, Art. 70, Rn. 12; *Ferrari u.a./Mankowski*, Internationales Vertragsrecht, Art. 70, Rn. 16.

[24] *Hager/Maultzsch*, 5. Aufl., Art. 70 Rn. 5a; *Schlechtriem/Schwenzer/Hager/Schmidt-Kessel*, CISG Commentary, Art. 70, Rn. 6; *Staudinger/Magnus*, Art. 70, Rn. 6; MünchKomm/*P. Huber*, Art. 70, Rn. 11; MünchKommHGB/*Benicke*, Art. 70, Rn. 8; *Honsell/Schönle/Th. Koller*, Art. 70, Rn. 13.

[25] *Hager/Maultzsch*, 5. Aufl., Art. 70 Rn. 5a; *Schlechtriem/Schwenzer/Hager/Schmidt-Kessel*, CISG Commentary, Art. 70, Rn. 6.

In den in Betracht kommenden Fällen ist deshalb dem Käufer bei weiterer zufälliger **9** Beschädigung der Ware mit der Nachbesserung regelmässig nicht gedient.[26] Im Wege der Preisminderung kann der Käufer wenigstens die Zahlung insoweit reduzieren, als die Ware ohnehin im Wert vermindert gewesen wäre.[27] Zu diesem Ergebnis gelangt der Käufer auch im Wege des Schadenersatzes, wenn er den vollen Kaufpreis bereits bezahlt hat.

3. Gefahrrückfall

Der Gefahrrückfall wird nach Wortlaut und Konzeption des Art. 70 durch die Geltend- **10** machung derjenigen Rechtsbehelfe ausgelöst, die dem Käufer bei wesentlicher Vertragsverletzung zustehen. Dies bedeutet, dass bei Lieferung einer vertragswidrigen Ware, deren Mangelhaftigkeit die Voraussetzungen des Art. 25 erfüllt, der Käufer mit dem Ersatzlieferungsverlangen bzw. der Aufhebungserklärung die Gefahr auf den Verkäufer wälzt.[28] Damit trägt der Verkäufer dann das Untergangs- bzw. Beschädigungsrisiko für die Ware, obwohl diese sich noch im Herrschaftsbereich des Käufers befindet.[29] Geht die Ware unter und kann dann nicht mehr geklärt werden, ob die Ware tatsächlich mangelhaft war, so wird sich der Fall letztlich an den Beweislastregeln entscheiden.[30] Bis zur Übernahme durch den Käufer nach Art. 60 lit. b) trifft dies den Verkäufer, danach den Käufer.[31]

Die Gefahr fällt auch dann auf den Verkäufer zurück, wenn bei Lieferung vertragswidriger **11** Ware – die Erfüllung der Anforderungen von Art. 25 vorausgesetzt – der an sich zur Ersatzlieferung bzw. Vertragsaufhebung berechtigte Käufer zunächst Nachbesserung verlangt und die Ware dann während der gesetzten Frist aber vor Behebung des Mangels untergeht.[32] Im Ergebnis ist damit die Nachbesserung im Sinne von Art. 47 II gescheitert und dem Käufer der Weg zu seinen anderen Rechtsbehelfen eröffnet.[33] Aus dem Nachbesserungsverlangen des Käufers auf dessen Verzicht auf Ersatzlieferung bzw. Vertragsaufhebung zu schliessen, würde bedeuten, den Käufer dafür zu bestrafen, sich zunächst mit dem Nachbesserungsverlangen begnügt zu haben.[34] Sowohl die Ersatzlieferung, als auch die Vertragsaufhebung, bringen die Notwendigkeit der Rücksendung der gelieferten Ware bzw. die vollständige Rückabwicklung mit sich. Gerade deshalb werden hohe Anforderungen gestellt, damit diese Rechtsbehelfe überhaupt verfügbar sind. Der Käufer, der diesen Aufwand zunächst zu vermeiden sucht, sollte deshalb darunter nicht zu leiden haben.

In Fällen der Zuviellieferung bzw. bei vorzeitiger Lieferung kommt es jeweils darauf an, **12** ob der Käufer die Ware abnimmt.[35] Tut er dies, so gilt die vorzeitige Lieferung als Erfüllung und die Gefahr geht auf den Käufer über.[36] Dieser Ansatz passt nicht ohne weiteres auf den Versendungskauf, bei dem der Käufer gegen die vorzeitige Lieferung nichts ausrichten kann,

---

[26] *Hager/Maultzsch*, 5. Aufl., Art. 70 Rn. 5a; *Schlechtriem/Schwenzer/Hager/Schmidt-Kessel*, CISG Commentary, Art. 70, Rn. 6.
[27] *Hager/Maultzsch*, 5. Aufl., Art. 70 Rn. 5a; *Schlechtriem/Schwenzer/Hager/Schmidt-Kessel*, CISG Commentary, Art. 70, Rn. 6; *Ferrari u. a./Mankowski*, Internationales Vertragsrecht, Art. 70, Rn. 15.
[28] *Hager/Maultzsch*, 5. Aufl., Art. 70 Rn. 2a; *Schlechtriem/Schwenzer/Hager/Schmidt-Kessel*, CISG Commentary, Art. 70, Rn. 7; *Ferrari u. a./Mankowski*, Internationales Vertragsrecht, Art. 70, Rn. 15.
[29] *Hager/Maultzsch*, 5. Aufl., Art. 70 Rn. 6; *Schlechtriem/Schwenzer/Hager/Schmidt-Kessel*, CISG Commentary, Art. 70, Rn. 7.
[30] *Hager/Maultzsch*, 5. Aufl., Art. 70 Rn. 6; *Schlechtriem/Schwenzer/Hager/Schmidt-Kessel*, CISG Commentary, Art. 70, Rn. 7.
[31] Oben *Schwenzer*, Art. 35 Rn. 52; *Hager/Maultzsch*, 5. Aufl., Art. 70 Rn. 6.
[32] *Hager/Maultzsch*, 5. Aufl., Art. 70 Rn. 7; *Schlechtriem/Schwenzer/Hager/Schmidt-Kessel*, CISG Commentary, Art. 70, Rn. 8; *Honsell/Schönle/Th. Koller*, Art. 70, Rn. 19.
[33] *Hager/Maultzsch*, 5. Aufl., Art. 70 Rn. 7; *Schlechtriem/Schwenzer/Hager/Schmidt-Kessel*, CISG Commentary, Art. 70, Rn. 8.
[34] *Hager/Maultzsch*, 5. Aufl., Art. 70 Rn. 7; *Schlechtriem/Schwenzer/Hager/Schmidt-Kessel*, CISG Commentary, Art. 70, Rn. 8.
[35] *Hager/Maultzsch*, 5. Aufl., Art. 70 Rn. 9; *Schlechtriem/Schwenzer/Hager/Schmidt-Kessel*, CISG Commentary, Art. 70, Rn. 10; *Staudinger/Magnus*, Art. 70, Rn. 16; *Ferrari u. a./Mankowski*, Internationales Vertragsrecht, Art. 70, Rn. 20; *Honsell/Schönle/Th. Koller*, Art. 70, Rn. 21.
[36] *Hager/Maultzsch*, 5. Aufl., Art. 70 Rn. 9; *Schlechtriem/Schwenzer/Hager/Schmidt-Kessel*, CISG Commentary, Art. 70, Rn. 10; *Staudinger/Magnus*, Art. 70, Rn. 16; *Honsell/Schönle/Th. Koller*, Art. 70, Rn. 21.

da die Lieferung durch Übergabe an den Beförderer erfolgt.[37] Der Käufer muss dann die ihm vom Beförderer angebotene Ware zurückweisen, will er den Gefahrübergang vermeiden.[38] Der Verkäufer muss dann die Ware zu dem Zeitpunkt erneut anbieten, zu dem sie bei korrekter Versendung angekommen wäre.[39] Bietet der Verkäufer beim Abladegeschäft Dokumente über zu früh abgeladene Ware an, kann der Käufer die Dokumente zurückweisen.[40] Die Nachholung kann dann nur erfolgen, indem der Verkäufer Dokumente über korrekt abgeladene Ware anbietet.[41] Analog gelten diese Grundsätze auch für die Lieferung an den falschen Ort.[42]

13 Versendet der Verkäufer die Ware zu spät und handelt es sich dabei um eine wesentliche Vertragsverletzung bzw. läuft eine Nachfrist ab, so reist sie letztlich auf seine Gefahr, denn der Käufer kann dann Ersatzlieferung verlangen bzw. den Vertrag aufheben.[43] Anders liegt es, wenn der Käufer die Lieferung annimmt.[44]

---

[37] *Hager/Maultzsch*, 5. Aufl., Art. 70 Rn. 9; *Schlechtriem/Schwenzer/Hager/Schmidt-Kessel*, CISG Commentary, Art. 70, Rn. 10.

[38] *Hager/Maultzsch*, 5. Aufl., Art. 70 Rn. 9; *Schlechtriem/Schwenzer/Hager/Schmidt-Kessel*, CISG Commentary, Art. 70, Rn. 10; *Honsell/Schönle/Th. Koller*, Art. 70, Rn. 21.

[39] *Hager/Maultzsch*, Voraufl., Art. 70 Rn. 9; *Schlechtriem/Schwenzer/Hager/Schmidt-Kessel*, CISG Commentary, Art. 70, Rn. 10.

[40] *Hager/Maultzsch*, 5. Aufl., Art. 70 Rn. 9; *Schlechtriem/Schwenzer/Hager/Schmidt-Kessel*, CISG Commentary, Art. 70, Rn. 10.

[41] *Hager/Maultzsch*, 5. Aufl., Art. 70 Rn. 9; *Schlechtriem/Schwenzer/Hager/Schmidt-Kessel*, CISG Commentary, Art. 70, Rn. 10.

[42] *Hager/Maultzsch*, 5. Aufl., Art. 70 Rn. 9; *Schlechtriem/Schwenzer/Hager/Schmidt-Kessel*, CISG Commentary, Art. 70, Rn. 10.

[43] *Hager/Maultzsch*, 5. Aufl., Art. 70 Rn. 8; *Schlechtriem/Schwenzer/Hager/Schmidt-Kessel*, CISG Commentary, Art. 70, Rn. 9; *Honsell/Schönle/Th. Koller*, Art. 70, Rn. 5.

[44] *Hager/Maultzsch*, 5. Aufl., Art. 70 Rn. 8; *Schlechtriem/Schwenzer/Hager/Schmidt-Kessel*, CISG Commentary, Art. 70, Rn. 9.

Kapitel V. Gemeinsame Bestimmungen über die Pflichten
des Verkäufers und des Käufers

Chapter V.
Provisions common to the obligations of
the seller and of the buyer

Chapitre V.
Dispositions communes aux obligations
du vendeur et de l'acheteur

Abschnitt I. Vorweggenommene Vertragsverletzung und Verträge
über aufeinander folgende Lieferungen

Section I.
Anticipatory breach and instalment contracts

Section I
Contravention anticipée et contrats à livraisons successives

Art. 71 [Verschlechterungseinrede]

(1) Eine Partei kann die Erfüllung ihrer Pflichten aussetzen, wenn sich nach Vertragsabschluß herausstellt, daß die andere Partei einen wesentlichen Teil ihrer Pflichten nicht erfüllen wird

a) wegen eines schwerwiegenden Mangels ihrer Fähigkeit, den Vertrag zu erfüllen, oder ihrer Kreditwürdigkeit* oder

b) wegen ihres Verhaltens bei der Vorbereitung der Erfüllung oder bei der Erfüllung des Vertrages.

(2) Hat der Verkäufer die Ware bereits abgesandt, bevor sich die in Absatz 1 bezeichneten Gründe herausstellen, so kann er sich der Übergabe der Ware an den Käufer widersetzen, selbst wenn der Käufer ein Dokument hat, das ihn berechtigt, die Ware zu erlangen. Der vorliegende Absatz betrifft nur die Rechte auf die Ware im Verhältnis zwischen Käufer und Verkäufer.

(3) Setzt eine Partei vor oder nach der Absendung der Ware die Erfüllung aus, so hat sie dies der anderen Partei sofort anzuzeigen; sie hat die Erfüllung fortzusetzen, wenn die andere Partei für die Erfüllung ihrer Pflichten ausreichende Gewähr gibt.**

Art. 71

(1) A party may suspend the performance of his obligations if, after the conclusion of the contract, it becomes apparent that the other party will not perform a substantial part of his obligations as a result of:

(a) a serious deficiency in his ability to perform or in his creditworthiness; or

(b) his conduct in preparing to perform or in performing the contract.

(2) If the seller has already dispatched the goods before the grounds described in the preceding paragraph become evident, he may prevent the handing over of the goods to the buyer even though the buyer holds a document which entitles him to obtain them.

Art. 71

1) Une partie peut différer l'exécution de ses obligations lorsqu'il apparaît, après la conclusion du contrat, que l'autre partie n'exécutera pas une partie essentielle de ses obligations du fait:

a) d'une grave insuffisance dans la capacité d'exécution de cette partie ou sa solvabilité; ou

b) de la manière dont elle s'apprête à exécuter ou exécute le contrat.

2) Si le vendeur a déjà expédié les marchandises lorsque se révèlent les raisons prévues au paragraphe précédent, il peut s'opposer à ce que les marchandises soient remises à l'acheteur, même si celui-ci détient un document lui permettant de les obtenir. Le présent paragraphe ne con

---

* Schweiz: Zahlungsfähigkeit.
** Schweiz: Sicherheit bietet.

Art. 71

The present paragraph relates only to the rights in the goods as between the buyer and the seller.

(3) A party suspending performance, whether before or after dispatch of the goods, must immediately give notice of the suspension to the other party and must continue with performance if the other party provides adequate assurance of his performance.

cerne que les droits respectifs du vendeur et de l'acheteur sur les marchandises.

3) La partie qui diffère l'exécution, avant ou après l'expédition des marchandises, doit adresser immédiatement une notification à cet effet à l'autre partie, et elle doit procéder à l'exécution si l'autre partie donne des assurances suffisantes de la bonne exécution de ses obligations.

Übersicht

	Rn.
I. Vorgeschichte	1
II. Aufgaben und Anwendungsbereich	2
1. Kontext	2
2. Normzweck	3
3. Anwendungsbereich	5
a) Zug-um-Zug- und Vorleistungsvereinbarungen	5
b) Sukzessivlieferungsverträge	7
c) Bei Sekundäransprüchen	8
d) Zurückbehaltungsrecht nach Fälligkeit der Leistung	9
e) Zurückbehaltungsrecht bei nicht-synallagmatischen Leistungen	9a
4. Umfang der zurückgehaltenen Leistung	9c
5. Wirkung	10
6. Abdingbarkeit	11
III. Drohende künftige Verletzung eines wesentlichen Teils der Vertragspflichten und Prognose	12
1. Tatbestandsvoraussetzungen	12
2. Im Einzelnen	13
a) Drohende Pflichtverletzung	13
b) Gründe für die Gefährdung	15
aa) Lit. a)	15
bb) Lit. b)	17
c) Herausstellen nach Vertragsschluss	19
d) Prognose	22
IV. Aussetzungsrecht	25
1. Ausübung	25
2. Zeitliche Grenzen	26
3. Informationspflicht (Anzeige)	27
a) Frist	27
b) Form	28
4. Wirkungen	29
a) Bei erfolgter Anzeige	29
b) Bei unterlassener Anzeige	30
5. Konkurrenzverhältnis zu nationalen Zurückbehaltungsrechten	31
V. Anhalterecht	32
1. Normzweck	32
2. Geltung nur für Verkäufer	33
3. Voraussetzungen	34
4. Wirkungen	37
5. Schuldrechtliche Natur	38
6. Erlöschen des Rechts	40
VI. Wegfall der Rechtsbehelfe	41
1. Erlöschensgründe	41
a) Übersicht	41
b) Insbesondere: Stellung von Sicherheiten	43
aa) Allgemeines	43
bb) Schwebezustand	47

cc) Wirkung der Sicherheitsleistung 48
dd) Rechtsfolgen bei Nichtstellen von Sicherheiten 49
2. Wiederaufnahme des vertraglichen Zeitplans 50
VII. Schadensersatzansprüche 51
1. Schadensersatzansprüche des Gläubigers 51
2. Schadensersatzansprüche des Schuldners 52
VIII. Beweislast 53

Vorläufer und **Entwürfe:** Art. 73 EKG; Genfer E 1976 Art. 47; Wiener E 1977 Art. 48; New Yorker E 1978 Art. 62.

I. Vorgeschichte

Zurückbehaltungsrecht und Anhalterecht[1] bei drohenden Vertragsverletzungen waren seit 1935 in allen Entwürfen zum internationalen Kaufrecht enthalten[2] und fanden schliesslich Niederschlag in Art. 73 EKG, dem Art. 71 weitgehend folgt. Art. 73 EKG war aber tatbestandlich enger und gewährte ein Zurückbehaltungsrecht nur bei Verschlechterung der wirtschaftlichen Lage des Schuldners. Neu sind gegenüber Art. 73 EKG die **Pflicht zur Information** der Gegenseite über die Ausübung des Zurückbehaltungs- und Anhalterechts (Abs. 3 HS. 1) und die Möglichkeit des Schuldners, **Sicherheiten** zu stellen (Abs. 3 HS. 2).[3] Versuche, bei Nichtbeibringung von Sicherheiten ein Vertragsaufhebungsrecht zu gewähren, führten nicht zum Erfolg;[4] ebenso wurde ein Art. 71 II entsprechendes Anhalterecht für Zahlungen wegen der Kollision mit allgemeinen Regeln des Zahlungsverkehrs abgelehnt.[5] 1

II. Aufgaben und Anwendungsbereich

1. Kontext

Art. 71 muss in Zusammenhang mit Artt. 72 und 73 gelesen werden. Die drei Bestimmungen finden – mit gewissen Ausnahmen –[6] auf Käufer und Verkäufer gleichermassen Anwendung[7] und regeln die Rechtslage bei **Störungen im Vorfeld der (vollständigen) Vertragserfüllung,** sei es, dass eine Pflichtverletzung seitens einer Partei zu befürchten ist (Art. 71), sei es durch antizipierte wesentliche Vertragsverletzung (Art. 72) oder durch Störungen bei der Abwicklung eines Sukzessivlieferungsvertrags (Art. 73). Dadurch tritt neben die eigentliche Vertragsverletzung die weitere Dimension der Gefährdung der Erfüllung mit den spezifischen Problemen der Prognose und der Erfassung einer Störung in ihrer Tragweite für die künftige Erfüllung. Sie führt zu vorläufigen Rechtsbehelfen in Art. 71 und zu vorzeitigen Behelfen in Artt. 72 und 73, also vor Fälligkeit oder endgültiger Erfüllung. 2

2. Normzweck

Art. 71 erlaubt es dem Gläubiger, bei drohender Verletzung eines wesentlichen Teils der Pflichten durch den Schuldner die eigene Leistung zurückzuhalten. Er schützt damit den 3

---

[1] Zur Terminologie der beiden Behelfe vgl. bereits *Rabel,* Recht des Warenkaufs, Bd. 1, S. 135: „Einrede der Unsicherheit" und den römisch-rechtlichen Begriff der „exceptio non adimpleti contractus". Für einen rechtsvergleichenden Überblick vgl. *Schwenzer/Hachem/Kee,* Kap. 42.
[2] EKG: E 1935 Artt. 88–90, E 1939 Artt. 73–75, E 1956 Artt. 82–84, E 1963 Artt. 82–84.
[3] Siehe schon YB V (1974), S. 37, Nr. 92.
[4] YB V (1974), S. 37, Nr. 92 und Kritik dazu bereits in YB V (1974), S. 38, Nr. 97. Vgl. auch *Bianca/Bonell/Bennett,* Art. 71, Anm. 1.12.
[5] YB VIII (1977), S. 54, Nr. 412 ff.; *Bianca/Bonell/Bennett,* Art. 71, Anm. 1.12.
[6] Vgl. Art. 71 II, 73 III.
[7] Vgl. schon im Jahre 1936 *Rabel,* Recht des Warenkaufs, Bd. 1, S. 135 ff. hinsichtlich der Unsicherheitseinrede. Genauso alle Entwürfe zum einheitlichen Kaufrecht (oben Fn. 2).

Gläubiger davor, sich **sehenden Auges** dem Risiko aussetzen zu müssen, keine Gegenleistung für die seinerseits erbrachte Leistung zu erhalten. Gleichzeitig fördert Art. 71 den Dialog und die Kooperation unter den Parteien und mag so dazu dienen, den Vertrag aufrechtzuerhalten und dessen Durchführung zu begünstigen.[8] Schliesslich kann Art. 71 auch als Druckmittel dienen, um den Schuldner zur Erfüllung anzuhalten;[9] allerdings wird das Leistungsverweigerungsrecht in den Fällen „höherer Gewalt" (Art. 71 I lit. a)) als Druckmittel häufig versagen.

4   Bis vor kurzem wurde jeweils festgehalten, dass in Art. 71 der **Grundsatz des gegenseitigen Leistungsaustausches**[10] zum Zuge komme. Entsprechend erstrecke sich das Zurückbehaltungsrecht des Art. 71 I nach einem Teil der Literatur[11] und Rechtsprechung[12] nur auf synallagmatische Pflichten. In jüngerer Zeit wird die Frage differenzierter betrachtet (vgl. Rn. 9a ff.).

3. Anwendungsbereich

5   a) **Zug-um-Zug- und Vorleistungsvereinbarungen.** Anders als das Aussetzungsrecht unter den PICC[13] und den PECL[14] findet Art. 71 nicht nur Anwendung, wenn die Leistungen Zug um Zug zu erfüllen sind oder der Schuldner vorleistungspflichtig ist, sondern auch dann, wenn den Gläubiger eine **Vorleistungspflicht** trifft.[15] Gerade im letztgenannten Fall ist Art. 71 von Interesse:[16] Dem vorleistungspflichtigen Gläubiger, der sich nicht auf den Zug-um-Zug-Grundsatz (Art. 58 I S. 2) berufen kann, wird dadurch dennoch ermöglicht, mit der eigenen Leistung zuzuwarten.[17] Aber auch in den Fällen, in denen das **Zug-um-Zug**-Prinzip greift, kann Art. 71 von hoher praktischer Bedeutung sein, wenn nämlich der vertragstreue Teil erhebliche Vorleistungen erbringen muss, die angesichts einer drohenden Nichterfüllung durch den anderen Teil leer laufen könnten.[18]

---

[8] *Conference Center Ltd v. TRC – The Research Corp. of New England*, 455 A2d 857, 863 f. (1983), zit. in *Carter*, Suspending Contract Performance, S. 522; vgl. ferner *Saidov*, Unif. dr. Rev. 2006, 795, 817; *Nyer*, 18 Pace Int'l L. Rev. (2006), 29, 36 ff.; *Karton*, 58 Int'l & Comp. L. Q. (2009), 863, 865 („The distinct characteristic of suspension of performance is that it paralyses the contract but does not kill it."); HGer Aargau, 10.3.2010, Erw. 7.2.2.5., CISG-online 2176.

[9] Vgl. *Carter,* Suspending Contract Performance, S. 492.

[10] Vgl. *Rabel,* Recht des Warenkaufs, Bd. 1, S. 128 ff. für den Zusammenhang zwischen Synallagma, exceptio non adimpleti contractus und der Zug-um-Zug-Leistung.

[11] Vgl. *Staudinger/Magnus*, Art. 71, Rn. 5; MünchKommHGB/*Mankowski*, Art. 71, Rn. 2; *Brunner*, Art. 71, Rn. 5; *Honsell/Brunner/Hurni*, Art. 71, Rn. 2; vgl. auch *Saidov*, Unif. dr. Rev. 2006, 795, 818 f. (für Artt. 7.3.3 f. PICC) sowie Art. III.–3:401 DCFR („reciprocal obligation").

[12] Vgl. OGH, 8.11.2005, CISG-online 1156, Erw. 2 = IHR 2006, 87; OLG Frankfurt a. M., 6.10.2004, CISG-online 996, Erw. 2; LG Darmstadt, 29.5.2001, CISG-online 686; OLG Karlsruhe, 20.7.2004, CISG-online 858, Erw. II.B)2.b)bb) = IHR 2004, 246, 249; ebenso OLG Dresden, 27.12.1999, CISG-online 511 = TranspR-IHR 2000, 20; OLG Düsseldorf, 24.4.1997, CISG-online 385; ICC, 8611/1997, 23.1.1997, CISG-online 236 (Kein Anwendungsfall des Art. 71 liege vor, wenn eine der zwei in laufenden Geschäftsbeziehungen stehenden Parteien sich weigere, zukünftig Verträge zu schliessen; auch eine Informationspflicht bestehe insoweit nicht.); vgl. zur Voraussetzung eines Synallagmas auch *Strub,* 38 Int'l & Comp. L. Q. (1989), 475, 494 („no right to use suspension to coerce the other party into performing minor obligations").

[13] Art. 7.1.3 PICC: „(1) Where the parties are to perform simultaneously, either party may withhold performance until the other party tenders its performance. (2) Where the parties are to perform consecutively, **the party that is to perform later** may withhold its performance until the first party has performed." (Hervorhebung hinzugefügt); vgl. dazu *Vogenauer/Kleinheisterkamp/Schelhaas,* Art. 7.1.3 PICC, Rn. 23 ff.

[14] Art. 9:201 II PECL („A party who is to perform **simultaneously with or after the other party** may withhold performance") (Hervorhebung hinzugefügt).

[15] Dies ist auch die in Artt. 113 I, II, 133 I, II CESL-Entwurf sowie in Art. III.–3:401 I, II DCFR gewählte Lösung.

[16] So auch *Staudinger/Magnus,* Art. 71, Rn. 16, 30.

[17] Nach chines. Recht ist das Zurückbehaltungsrecht gar auf die vorleistungspflichtige Partei beschränkt, Art. 68 chines. UCL, dazu *Y. Yang,* 18 China Law & Practice (2004), 23 vor Fn. 23; *Pattison/Herron,* 40 Am. Bus. L. J. (2003), 459, 471.

[18] Vgl. Sekretariatskommentar, Art. 62, Nr. 8; *Honnold/Flechtner,* Art. 71, Rn. 389; *Schlechtriem,* Gemeinsame Bestimmungen, S. 154; ders., Internationales UN-Kaufrecht, Rn. 264; *Strub,* 38 Int'l & Comp. L. Q.

Die einzelnen Gefährdungstatbestände sind so weit gefasst, dass **praktisch alle Störungs-** 6
gründe abgedeckt sind. Das Zurückbehaltungsrecht des Verkäufers wird in Abs. 2 um das
Recht erweitert, die verkaufte Ware, die sich bereits auf dem Weg zum Käufer befindet,
anzuhalten und die Aushändigung an den Käufer zu verhindern (Anhalterecht, right of
stoppage in transitu).[19]

b) Sukzessivlieferungsverträge. Anwendung findet Art. 71 auch auf Sukzessivliefe- 7
rungsverträge, Art. 73.[20] Sind die Voraussetzungen beider Vorschriften erfüllt, so hat die
vertragstreue Partei die Wahl, ob sie nach Art. 71 ihre Leistung aussetzt oder nach Art. 73 II
den Vertrag aufhebt.[21]

c) Bei Sekundäransprüchen. Art. 71 gilt auch bei Sekundäransprüchen, insbesondere 8
Schadenersatzansprüchen, die anstelle der im Synallagma stehenden Primärleistung treten.[22]
Für die Möglichkeit, die eigene Leistung auch bei nicht im Austauschverhältnis stehenden
Pflichten zurückzuhalten, siehe Rn. 9a.

d) Zurückbehaltungsrecht nach Fälligkeit der Leistung. Art. 71 beschränkt das 9
Aussetzungs- bzw. Anhalterecht auf die Fälle *vor* Fälligkeit; er gewährt kein Leistungsverweigerungsrecht nach diesem Zeitpunkt. Streng genommen muss der vertragstreue Teil, der
mangelhafte Lieferung erhält, seine Gegenleistung voll erbringen und bleibt auf die Rechtsbehelfe der Artt. 45, 61 verwiesen.[23] Art. 71 kann also, bildlich gesprochen, bloss als
Schwert, aber nicht als Schild eingesetzt werden: Der Gläubiger wird durch sein Aussetzungsrecht die Durchführung des Vertrags verhindern können, hat aber keine Möglichkeit,
bei bereits erhaltener, mangelhafter Leistung die eigene Gegenleistung zu verweigern.[24] Ab
Fälligkeit der eigenen Leistung bleibt es für den Gläubiger, anders als beispielsweise unter
§ 2–609 UCC, bei „a promise plus the right to win a law suit"[25]. Diesem unökonomischen
Vorgehen hat man in jüngerer Zeit so zu begegnen versucht, dass Rspr.[26] und Literatur[27] aus

---

(1989), 475, 495; wohl auch *Bianca/Bonell/Bennett*, Art. 71, Anm. 1.1.; *Enderlein/Maskow/Strohbach*, Art. 71, Anm. 1.

[19] Vgl. zur Herkunft aus dem anglo-amerikanischen Recht *Fischer*, Die Unsicherheitseinrede, S. 62 ff.; *Treitel*, Remedies for Breach, S. 245 ff., Nr. 188 ff. sowie aus dem skandinavischen Kaufrecht *Almén*, Bd. I, S. 588, und dazu *U. Huber*, FS Weber, S. 253 ff.

[20] Vgl. Chamber of National and International Arbitration of Milan, 28.9.2001, Erw. G. 5.2., CISG-online 1582.

[21] *Gabriel*, Contracts, S. 214; UNCITRAL Digest, Art. 71, Anm. 3.

[22] Krit. MünchKomm/*P. Huber*, Art. 71, Rn. 4; a. A. wohl OLG Dresden, 27.12.1999, CISG-online 511 = TranspR-IHR 2000, 20, 22; OLG Düsseldorf, 24.4.1997, CISG-online 385.

[23] *Schlechtriem*, 16 Pace Int'l L. Rev. (2004), 279, 301 f.; *ders.*, Symposium Vischer, S. 47, 65 f.; *Nyer*, 18 Pace Int'l L. Rev. (2006), 29, 72.

[24] Vgl. demgegenüber Art. 68 chines. PRC Contract Law, das ein Leistungsverweigerungsrecht erst ab Fälligkeit der Leistung der vertragsuntreuen Partei gewährt, dazu *Y. Yang*, 18 China Law & Practice (2004), 23 vor Fn. 23; ähnlich dem chines. ist das frz. Recht, vgl. Com., 20.2.2007, CISG-online 1492.

[25] Der Official Comment zu § 2–609 UCC betont, dass § 2–609 UCC gerade die Situation, dass der Gläubiger zuerst leisten und hinterher Rechtsbehelfe geltend machen muss, vermeidet; vgl. auch *McMahon*, 39 UCC L. J. 4 Art. 3 (2007), a. E. des Textes; *Rowley*, 69 U. Cin. L. Rev. (2001), 565, 636. Ein Zurückbehaltungsrecht nach Fälligkeit sehen auch bestimmte Rechte Lateinamerikas vor, etwa das argentinische Recht, vgl. für einen Überblick *Schwenzer/E. Muñoz/E. Muñoz*, Sec Comp, Artt. 71–73, Rn. 7 sowie *E. Muñoz*, Modern Law, Kap. 48; weitere rechtsvergleichende Hinweise bei *Schwenzer/Hachem/Kee*, Rn. 42.07 ff.

[26] OGH, 8.11.2005, CISG-online 1156, Erw. 2 = IHR 2006, 87, 90 f. (zust. *C. Witz*, D. 2007, 530, 540); Schiedsgericht der Handelskammer Zürich, 31.5.1996, CISG-online 1291 = YB. Comm. Arb. 128 (1998); Audiencia Provincial de Navarra (Spanien), 27.3.2000, CISG-online 575 = CLOUT Nr. 797.

[27] *Schlechtriem*, 16 Pace Int'l L. Rev. (2004), 279, 289 ff.; *ders.*, Internationales UN-Kaufrecht, Rn. 42 d: „allgemeine[r] und zur Regelbildung nach Art. 7 II geeignete[r] Grundsatz"; *ders.*, Symposium Vischer, S. 47, 62 ff.; *W. Witz*, FS Schlechtriem, S. 291, 295; *Bridge*, 59 Int'l & Comp. L. Q. (2010), 911, 938; *Kern*, ZEuP 2000, 837, 850; *Hartmann*, IHR 2006, 181, 184 f.; *Fountoulakis*, IHR 2005, 244, 247; *Nyer*, 18 Pace Int'l L. Rev. (2006), 29, 79; *Schlechtriem/Schwenzer/Mohs*, CISG Commentary, Art. 58, Rn. 27 ff.; *Schlechtriem/Schwenzer/Hachem*, CISG Commentary, Art. 4, Rn. 20; *Witz/Salger/Lorenz/Witz*, Art. 7, Rn. 28; *Honsell/Brunner/Hurni*, Art. 71, Rn. 8, 18 a. E.; a. A. UNCITRAL Digest, Art. 71, Anm. 1.; *Ferrari u. a./Saenger*, Internationales Vertragsrecht, Art. 71, Rn. 5; *Bamberger/Roth/Saenger*, Art. 71, Rn. 5.

Art. 71 – in Kombination mit Artt. 58 I 2, 81 II 2, 85 S. 2, 86 I 2 – ein **allgemeines Zurückbehaltungsrecht** abgeleitet haben, das auch dann ausgeübt werden kann, wenn die Leistung fällig und bereits erbracht worden ist, allerdings in wesentlichen Teilen mangelhaft. So kann der Käufer den Kaufpreis zurückhalten, wenn bei den gelieferten Maschinen zahlreiche Mängel auftauchen[28] oder die bereits gelieferten Wasserboiler Betriebsstörungen aufweisen,[29] ebenso wie der Verkäufer den nachgebesserten Minibus solange zurückbehalten darf, wie der Käufer den Kaufpreis für den andern, bereits gelieferten Minibus nicht zahlt[30]. Kerngedanke dieses allgemeinen Zurückbehaltungsrechts ist, dass der Gläubiger seine Leistung nicht sehenden Auges aus der Hand geben muss, mit dem Risiko, darauf keine zufrieden stellende Gegenleistung zu erhalten.

9a e) **Zurückbehaltungsrecht bei nicht-synallagmatischen Leistungen.** Die lange Zeit vorherrschende und teilweise immer noch vertretene Ansicht, dass das Zurückbehaltungsrecht lediglich bei synallagmatischen Leistungen ausgeübt werden kann, die also in Entstehung, Fortbestand und Durchsetzbarkeit voneinander abhängig sind,[31] ist zu relativieren. Dies erfordert bereits der Wortlaut von Art. 71 I, der von einem „wesentlichen Teil" unerfüllter Pflichten spricht (a substantial part of obligations, une partie essentielle des obligations); denn ob ein wesentlicher oder bloss ein unwesentlicher Teil der Pflichten bedroht ist, entscheidet sich danach, was der Gläubiger – für den Schuldner erkennbar – aus dem Vertrag erwartete.[32] Damit kommt es unter Art. 71 nicht darauf an, ob die zurückgehaltene Leistung zu der bedrohten in einem Gegenseitigkeits- und Abhängigkeitsverhältnis steht, sondern massgeblich ist die Wesentlichkeit der bedrohten Leistung für den Gläubiger. Es kann daher sein, dass Pflichten, die nicht in einem wechselseitigen Bezug zu bestimmten Pflichten des Gläubigers gehören, wie das Stellen von Sicherheiten, Geheimhaltungspflichten, Informations-, Kommunikations-, Auskunfts- und Bestätigungspflichten, für den Gläubiger von erkennbar wesentlicher Bedeutung sind. Die Voraussetzung des „wesentlichen Teils" der Pflichten in Art. 71 ist damit zweifellos erfüllt, ohne dass die bedrohte Leistung das kaufvertragliche Synallagma betrifft.[33]

9b Nicht aus dem Wortlaut von Art. 71, wohl aber aus den der Bestimmung zugrundeliegenden Gedanken der Zug-um-Zug-Leistung, der aussergerichtlichen Vertragsdurchsetzung und dem allgemeinen Grundsatz der Angemessenheit *(reasonability)* dürfte ferner ein Leistungsverweigerungsrecht auch in den Fällen zu bejahen sein, in denen die bedrohte Leistung des Wesentlichkeitserfordernis von Art. 71 I nicht erreicht, der Gläubiger aber trotzdem, zum Beispiel aus Beweisgründen, auf Erfüllung durch den Schuldner angewiesen ist.[34] So sollte etwa dem Gläubiger das Recht zustehen, einen Teil des Kaufpreises solange zurückzuhalten, bis der Verkäufer zum Ausstellen einer Empfangsbestätigung bereit ist.[35] Den Gläubiger zur Zahlung anzuhalten und ihn anschliessend auf den (beweistechnisch hoffnungslosen und wegen Art. 28 unsicheren) Prozessweg zu verweisen, wider-

---

[28] Vgl. OGH, 8.11.2005, CISG-online 1156 = IHR 2006, 87; dem Grundsatz nach auch LG Stuttgart, 11.11.2009, CISG-online 2018 (Zurückbehaltungsrecht allerdings in casu verneint); vgl. ferner *Schlechtriem*, Symposium Vischer, S. 47, 66 ff. zur Möglichkeit, den Kaufpreis bei vertragswidriger Ware oder unreinen Dokumenten einzubehalten; a. A. freilich Int. Ct. Russian CCI, 24.5.2004, CISG-online 1210, Erw. 3.4.1.: Kaufpreis dürfe bei mangelhafter Lieferung nicht zurückbehalten werden.
[29] Audiencia Provincial de Navarra (Spanien), 27.3.2000, CISG-online 575 = CLOUT Nr. 397.
[30] RB Arnhem, 29.7.2009, CISG-online 1939.
[31] Vgl. oben Rn. 4.
[32] Vgl. unten Rn. 14.
[33] Vgl. CIETAC, 27.12.2002, CISG-online 2205, B.4 („the adoption of the packages developed by the seller would expose the new expertise of the seller to the attention of its competitors, Therefore, the seller was entitled to refuse the delivery of the equipment"); vgl. auch LG Dresden, 29.5.2009, CISG-online 2174, Erw. II.3.a); *Kröll u. a./Saidov*, Art. 71, Rn. 29; *MünchKomm/P. Huber*, Art. 71, Rn. 4; wohl auch *Honsell/Brunner/Hurni*, Art. 71, Rn. 12.
[34] Vgl. bereits *Schlechtriem/Schwenzer/Mohs*, CISG Commentary, Art. 58, Rn. 29; wie hier wohl auch *Hartmann*, IHR 2006, 181, 186; a. A. *Honsell/Brunner/Hurni*, Art. 71, Rn. 9 a. E., 18.
[35] Vgl. *Fountoulakis*, IHR 2005, 244, 247 f.; für weitere Bsp. vgl. *Kern*, ZEuP 2000, 837 ff.; *Hartmann*, IHR 2006, 181 ff.

spräche nicht nur dem Gedanken von informeller Vertragsdurchsetzung und Zug-um-Zug-Leistung, sondern auch dem dem CISG zugrundeliegenden Grundsatz der Abwendung unnötiger (Transaktions-)Kosten und der Vermeidung von Unwirtschaftlichkeit.[36]

4. Umfang der zurückgehaltenen Leistung

Das CISG schweigt sich darüber aus, wieviel von der eigenen Leistung zurückbehalten werden darf. Aus den Grundsätzen der Teilbarkeit der Leistung (Artt. 51, 73) sowie aus dem Zug-um-Zug-Prinzip (Artt. 58 I 2, 81 II 2, 85 S. 2, 86 I 2, dazu oben Rn. 9) lässt sich allerdings der allgemeine Rechtsgedanken ableiten, dass die zurückbehaltene Leistung umfangmässig der Leistung, die nicht erfüllt zu werden droht, entsprechen soll. Dies lässt sich zusätzlich auf die dem Übereinkommen zugrundeliegenden Prinzipien der Angemessenheit *(reasonableness)* und Verhältnismässigkeit *(proportionality)*[37] stützen, die nicht mehr gewahrt wären, wenn der Gläubiger jeweils seine ganze Leistung aussetzen dürfte. Bei Teillieferungen sollte demnach jeweils nur der dieser Teillieferung entsprechende Teil der eigenen Leistung zurückbehalten werden.[38] Auch in den anderen Konstellationen, insbesondere bei drohender Nichterfüllung nicht-synallagmatischer Pflichten, sollte sich der Umfang der zurückbehaltenen Leistung nach der wahrscheinlich ausbleibenden Leistung des Schuldners richten. Dabei braucht es sich nicht um eine rechnerische Entsprechung von gefährdeter und zurückbehaltener Leistung zu handeln; entscheidend ist, dass der Umfang der ausgesetzten eigenen Leistung erforderlich ist, um den Schuldner zur (richtigen) Erfüllung anzuhalten, ohne dass die Grundsätze der Angemessenheit und Verhältnismässigkeit verletzt werden.[39]

9c

5. Wirkung

Durch das Aussetzungs- und Anhalterecht wird die Fälligkeit der eigenen Leistung hinausgeschoben. Es tritt ein **Schwebezustand** ein, der in das Vertragsprogramm eingreift, aber nicht ohne weitere Gründe zu einem Aufhebungsrecht führt.[40] Es bleibt vielmehr möglich, zum ursprünglichen Vertragsprogramm zurückzukehren, sei es durch Wegfall der Gefährdung, sei es durch deren Neutralisierung in Form der Stellung von Sicherheiten nach Abs. 3 HS. 2. Der eigenverantwortlichen Gestaltung des Vertrages durch die Parteien entspricht eine **Mitteilungspflicht** über Zurückhalten oder Anhalten der Leistung nach Abs. 3 HS. 1.

10

6. Abdingbarkeit

Art. 71 ist **dispositiver Natur** und darf nicht dazu missbraucht werden, eine vereinbarte strikte Vorleistungspflicht nachträglich abzuändern.[41] So bleibt etwa der Käufer bei Vereinbarung eines unwiderruflichen Dokumentenakkreditivs[42] zur Vorleistung verpflichtet, wenn die Ware zwar voraussichtlich fehlerhaft sein wird, aber die notwendigen Dokumente

11

---

[36] Zu den letztgenannten allgemeinen Rechtsgedanken vgl. *Schlechtriem/Schwenzer/Schwenzer/Hachem*, CISG Commentary, Art. 7, Rn. 35. Zur zunehmenden Bedeutungslosigkeit des Erfordernisses synallagmatischer Pflichten im Rahmen eines – gestützt auf CISG, PICC und PECL entwickelten – allgemeinen Rechtsprinzips des Zurückbehaltendürfens vertraglicher Leistungen in der internationalen Schiedsgerichtsbarkeit vgl. *Karton*, 58 Int'l & Comp. L. Q. (2009), 863, 884 ff.
[37] Zum Grundsatz der Angemessenheit im CISG vgl. *Kröll u. a./Perales Viscasillas*, Art. 7, Rn. 26; zum Grundsatz der Verhältnismässigkeit vgl. *Lando*, 53 AJCL (2005) 379, 397 ff.; *ders.*, 13 Pace Int'l L. Rev. (2001), 339, 360 ff.
[38] Vgl. Chamber of National and International Arbitration of Milan, 28.9.2001, Erw. G. 5.2., CISG-online 1582: Zurückbehalten werden darf nur der sich auf die dritte, ausgebliebene Teillieferung beziehende Kaufpreis.
[39] Vgl. *Schlechtriem*, 16 Pace Int'l L. Rev. (2004), 279, 289 ff.; *Carter*, Suspending Contract Performance, S. 511 ff.; *Nyer*, 18 Pace Int'l L. Rev. (2006), 29, 42 ff.; ähnl. *Kröll u. a./Saidov*, Art. 71, Rn. 31 ff.
[40] Mehrfache Ansätze, in den Beratungen eine Steigerung des Zurückbehaltungsrechts zum Aufhebungsrecht vorzusehen (s. nur YB V (1974), S. 37, Nr. 92), waren nicht erfolgreich. Bei gegebenen Voraussetzungen kann aber der Vertrag gem. Art. 72 vor Fälligkeit aufgehoben werden, vgl. hinten Rn. 49.
[41] *Staudinger/Magnus*, Art. 71, Rn. 17.
[42] Vgl. die ERA 600, Artt. 4, 15.

vorgelegt werden. Andernfalls würde die vereinbarte strikte Vorleistungspflicht des Käufers ausgehebelt.[43]

III. Drohende künftige Verletzung eines wesentlichen Teils der Vertragspflichten und Prognose

1. Tatbestandsvoraussetzungen

12 Der Gläubiger darf seine Leistung nach Art. 71 I unter den folgenden Voraussetzungen aussetzen: Es muss sich 1) nach Vertragsschluss herausstellen, dass 2) aus den in Abs. 1 lit. a) und b) genannten Gründen der Schuldner 3) mit hoher Wahrscheinlichkeit 4) einen wesentlichen Teil seiner Pflichten 5) nicht erfüllen wird. Hingegen stellt das Anzeigeerfordernis in Art. 71 III keine Tatbestandsvoraussetzung dar.[44]

2. Im Einzelnen

13 **a) Drohende Pflichtverletzung.** Voraussetzung sowohl für das Aussetzungs- wie für das Anhalterecht ist, dass die Verletzung eines wesentlichen Teils der Pflichten durch den Vertragspartner droht. Die Verletzung eines wesentlichen Teils der Pflichten, die gemäss Art. 71 I drohen muss, ist dabei nicht gleichzusetzen mit einer wesentlichen Vertragsverletzung im Sinne von Art. 25; die Anforderungen unter Art. 71 I sind geringer.[45] Dies entspricht auch der Vorläufigkeit des Behelfs, da ansonsten Art. 72, der die Vertragsaufhebung bei antizipierter wesentlicher Vertragsverletzung erlaubt, neben Art. 71 überflüssig wäre. Immerhin bedarf es der Gefährdung eines **wesentlichen Teils der Pflichten.**

14 Welche Anforderungen an die Grösse „wesentlicher Teil" im Einzelnen zu stellen sind, kann nur aus der Gesamtbetrachtung des Vertrages folgen.[46] Masstab für die Wesentlichkeit ist die **für den Schuldner erkennbare Leistungserwartung** des Gläubigers.[47] Sie entscheidet auch darüber, wie weit eine besondere Bedeutung einzelner Pflichten für den vertragstreuen Teil berücksichtigt werden kann, wie z.B. Geheimhaltungs-,[48] Informations- und Sorgfaltspflichten, oder die Rechtzeitigkeit[49] oder der richtige Ort der Pflichterfüllung. Der Erkennbarkeit eines solchen gesteigerten Interesses im Vertrag kommt wesentliches Gewicht zu. Insgesamt ist bei der Abwägung im Auge zu behalten, dass der Rechtsbehelf auf einer möglichst ausgeglichenen Balance zwischen den Rechten beider Parteien beruht.[50] Verschulden gehört entsprechend den Grundprinzipien des Übereinkommens nicht zu den Voraussetzungen.[51] Eine Entlastung, wie sie für den Bereich des Schadensersatzes im Rahmen von Art. 79 möglich ist, wirkt nicht für das Zurückbehal-

---

[43] OLG Köln, 8.1.1997, CISG-online 217; *Bamberger/Roth/Saenger*, Art. 71, Rn. 1; *Staudinger/Magnus*, Art. 71, Rn. 17; MünchKomm/*P. Huber*, Art. 71, Rn. 36; *Heuzé*, Anm. 407.

[44] Vgl. unten Rn. 30.

[45] *Schlechtriem*, Internationales UN-Kaufrecht, Rn. 263; *Staudinger/Magnus*, Art. 71, Rn. 15; *Honsell/Brunner/Hurni*, Art. 71, Rn. 22; *Bamberger/Roth/Saenger*, Art. 71, Rn. 2; MünchKomm/*P. Huber*, Art. 71, Rn. 4; *Bianca/Bonell/Bennett*, Art. 71, Anm. 2.4.; *Neumayer/Ming*, Art. 71, Anm. 4.; *Kröll u.a./Saidov*, Art. 71, Rn. 4; *Ferrari u.a./Saenger*, Internationales Vertragsrecht, Art. 71, Rn. 1; *Brunner*, Art. 71, Rn. 6, 12; *Achilles*, Art. 71, Rn. 2; in der Rspr. LG Berlin, 15.9.1994, CISG-online 399. Vgl. auch unten *Fountoulakis*, Art. 72 Rn. 13.

[46] So auch *Heuzé*, Anm. 354.; *Soergel/Lüderitz/Dettmeier*, Art. 71, Rn. 9.

[47] MünchKommHGB/*Mankowski*, Art. 71, Rn. 6; *Kröll u.a./Saidov*, Art. 71, Rn. 5.

[48] CIETAC, 27.12.2002, CISG-online 2205.

[49] OLG Karlsruhe, 20.7.2004, CISG-online 858, Erw. II.B)2.b)bb) = IHR 2004, 246, 249; KG Appenzell AR, 10.3.2003, CISG-online 852, Erw. 2.b) = IHR 2006, 254.

[50] So bereits oben Rn. 3. Skeptisch gegenüber der Funktionsfähigkeit des Behelfs allgemein *Vilus*, Provisions, S. 239, 241 f., aber doch auch den Kompromisscharakter betonend, S. 245 f.

[51] *Schlechtriem/Witz*, Convention de Vienne, Rn. 335; *Staudinger/Magnus*, Art. 71, Rn. 13; *Herber/Czerwenka*, Art. 71, Rn. 7; *Neumayer/Ming*, Art. 71, Anm. 5.; *Reinhart*, Art. 71, Rn. 4; *Jan*, S. 170; *Achilles*, Art. 71, Rn. 4; *Bamberger/Roth/Saenger*, Art. 71, Rn. 2.

tungsrecht (Art. 79 V). Bei der Beurteilung der Pflichtverletzung ist ferner Art. 80 zu beachten; die Aussetzung ist demgemäss nicht statthaft, wenn der Gläubiger für die zu befürchtende Pflichtverletzung des Schuldners verantwortlich ist.[52]

b) Gründe für die Gefährdung. aa) Lit. a). Das Übereinkommen umschreibt einzelne 15 Gründe für die Gefährdung der Leistungspflichten. Die Gründe sind dabei so umfassend berücksichtigt, dass wohl alle Ursachen einer zukünftigen Störung abgedeckt sind. Dabei erfasst Art. 71 I lit. a) mit dem schwerwiegenden Mangel der Fähigkeit, den Vertrag zu erfüllen, die **generellen Leistungshindernisse,** zu denen man Streik, Verlust von Produktionsanlagen durch Brand oder Naturereignis, aber auch allgemein wirkende rechtliche Hindernisse zählen kann.[53] Allgemeine Informationen über die Rahmenbedingungen von Märkten oder über Marktentwicklungen, die die Erfüllung gefährden könnten, etwa weil das Eindecken auf dem Markt erheblich teurer würde, reichen dagegen nicht aus.[54]

Der mangelnden Fähigkeit zur Vertragserfüllung steht ein schwerwiegender Mangel der 16 **Zahlungsfähigkeit** gleich,[55] der zwar in erster Linie auf den Käufer zugeschnitten ist, aber auch für den Verkäufer bei Beschaffung der zu liefernden Ware oder bei der Erfüllungsvorbereitung allgemein Anwendung findet.[56] Ein solcher schwerwiegender Mangel der Zahlungsfähigkeit ergibt sich etwa bei Insolvenz und gleichstehenden Formen oder bei Zahlungseinstellung.[57] Wie weit einzelne Wechselproteste oder der Verzug mit der Zahlung einzelner oder mehrerer anderer Verpflichtungen als Aussetzungsgrund ausreichen, ist wiederum nur durch Gesamtwürdigung der Umstände und unter Einbeziehung von Art. 80 zu beurteilen.[58] Eine allgemein schleppende Zahlungsweise genügt nicht,[59] wohl aber, wenn die Schuldnerin mit den Zahlungen im Rahmen derselben Geschäftsverbindung regelmässig in Verzug war.[60]

---

[52] Vgl. etwa LG München I, 6.4.2000, CISG-online 665: „Die Klägerin war nicht berechtigt, die Lieferung der Konsolmöbel auszusetzen (Art. 71 CISG) [...] Die Beklagte hatte zwar den Scheck für die ihr gelieferten Polstermöbel sperren lassen. Hierzu war sie jedoch berechtigt (Art. 71 I lit. b)), da die Klägerin die Möbel in einer nicht vertragsgemässen Materialkombination geliefert und damit ihre Verpflichtung zur Lieferung vertragsgemässer Ware nicht erfüllt hatte (Art. 35 I)."; vgl. ferner *Vanwijk-Alexandre*, RDAI 2001, 353, 361; *P. Huber/Mullis/P. Huber*, S. 341.
[53] In der Literatur werden beispielhaft Kriegsausbruch, Ausfuhrverbot, Streik, Grossfeuer genannt, vgl. Sekretariatskommentar, Art. 62, Nr. 4; *Staudinger/Magnus*, Art. 71, Rn. 24; *Honsell/Brunner/Hurni*, Art. 71, Rn. 21; *Bianca/Bonell/Bennett*, Art. 71, Anm. 2.6.; *Herber/Czerwenka*, Art. 71, Rn. 7; MünchKomm/*P. Huber*, Art. 71, Rn. 8; *Piltz*, Internationales Kaufrecht, Rn. 4–204; *Neumayer/Ming*, Art. 71, Anm. 5.; *Karollus*, S. 87; *Schlechtriem*, JZ 1988, 1037, 1046; *ders.*, IPRax 1990, 277, 282. Die Beispielsfälle in der Rspr. sind weit weniger spektakulär: Kann etwa der Verkäufer schlechterdings nicht mehr liefern, weil die Ware bei ihm nicht mehr vorhanden ist, so berechtigt dies den Käufer zur Aussetzung der Kaufpreiszahlung gem. Art. 71 I, OLG Hamm, 23.6.1998, CISG-online 434 = RIW 1999, 786 = TranspR-IHR 2000, 7.
[54] MünchKommHGB/*Mankowski*, Art. 71, Rn. 12.
[55] Zu diesem klassischen Fall vgl. *Rabel*, Recht des Warenkaufs, Bd. 1, S. 135.
[56] *Schlechtriem/Witz*, Convention de Vienne, Rn. 335.
[57] *Enderlein/Maskow/Strohbach*, Art. 71, Anm. 4.; *Heuzé*, Anm. 355; MünchKommHGB/*Mankowski*, Art. 71, Rn. 14 f.; *Bamberger/Roth/Saenger*, Art. 71, Rn. 3; vgl. RB Hasselt, 1.3.1995, CISG-online 373: Ein wesentlicher Zahlungsverzug von 7 Monaten berechtigt den Verkäufer zur Aussetzung der Restlieferung, weil er unvernünftigerweise auch von zukünftigen Zahlungsschwierigkeiten ausgehen darf; vgl. auch OLG Frankfurt a. M., 6.10.2004, CISG-online 996; vgl. demgegenüber LG München I, 6.4.2000, CISG-online 665: Wenn der Käufer den Scheck für gelieferte Möbel nur deshalb sperren lässt, weil die benutzten Materialien nicht vertragskonform waren, liegt darin keine Zahlungseinstellung, die den Verkäufer zur Aussetzung gem. Art. 71 I berechtigen würde.
[58] Sekretariatskommentar, Art. 62, Nr. 6; *Bianca/Bonell/Bennett*, Art. 71, Anm. 2.6.; vgl. Supr. Ct. BC, 21.8.2003, CISG-online 1017 = 2003 BCS C 1298, Rn. 79: Aussetzungsrecht gegeben, solange der Käufer das vereinbarte Akkreditiv nicht eröffnet; vgl. auch Int. Ct. Belarusian CCI, 5.10.1995, CISG-online 861, übersetzt und besprochen bei *Seliazniova*, 24 J. L. & Com. (2004), 111, 120 ff.: Nichtzahlung eines Grossteils der Raten durch den vorleistungspflichtigen Käufer berechtigt den Verkäufer, die restlichen Lieferungen zurückzuhalten.
[59] So auch in der Rechtsprechung OGH, 12.2.1998, CISG-online 349 = östJBl 1999, 54, 56 = östZRVgl 1999, 65, 68; a. A. *Piltz*, Internationales Kaufrecht, 4–204; *Witz/Salger/Lorenz/Lorenz*, Art. 71, Rn. 12.
[60] Vgl. Com., 20.2.2007, CISG-online 1492 („de manière habituelle en retard"); *Doolim Corp. v. R Doll, L. L. C. et al.*, US Federal Dist. Ct. (N. Y.), 29.5.2009, Rn. 40, CISG-online 1892.

17 **bb) Lit. b).** Neben diesen generellen Gefährdungsgründen regelt Art. 71 I lit. b) **vertragsbezogene Hindernisse,** die sich aus den Verhältnissen des Schuldners bei Vorbereitung der Erfüllung oder bei der Erfüllung selbst ergeben. Auch hier gilt die Voraussetzung, dass dadurch die Gefahr der Nichterfüllung eines wesentlichen Teils der Pflichten drohen muss. Dabei kommt dem Zeitmoment besondere Bedeutung zu, z. B. in Form der Nichtbeschaffung oder der nicht rechtzeitigen Beschaffung von Roh- und Hilfsstoffen, Lizenzen, Exportgenehmigungen und Ähnlichem. Aber auch die Benutzung nicht zugelassener oder nicht tauglicher Rohstoffe und Bestandteile, der Einsatz ungeeigneter Transporteinrichtungen, mangelnde Verpackung, fehlende Instruktionen oder ein Betrugsversuch bei der Vorbereitung oder bei Erfüllungshandlungen zählen hierher.[61] Die unberechtigte Erfüllungsweigerung berechtigt den Gläubiger immer zur Aussetzung der Kaufpreiszahlung gemäss Art. 71 I lit. b).[62]

18 Die Abgrenzung zwischen Art. 71 I lit. a) und lit. b) kann **nicht immer haarscharf** vorgenommen werden,[63] was aber unschädlich ist, da die Rechtsfolge dieselbe ist. Entscheidend ist, ob auf Grund der unterlassenen oder nicht korrekt vorgenommenen Vorbereitungshandlungen künftige Störungen bei der Vertragsabwicklung zu befürchten sind.[64] Blosse Gerüchte, dass der Schuldner nicht erfüllen wird, reichen als Gefährdungsgrund i. S. v. Art. 71 I lit. b) nicht aus, ebenso wenig der Umstand, dass der Schuldner in Verträgen mit anderen Partnern nicht korrekt erfüllte.[65] Auch reicht verspätete Lieferung nicht, wenn sie keine weiteren Konsequenzen nach sich zieht und deshalb nicht als Indiz für weitere Vertragsverletzungen dienen kann.[66]

19 **c) Herausstellen nach Vertragsschluss.** Die drohende Pflichtverletzung muss sich **nach Vertragsschluss herausstellen.** Die Störungsgründe können aber durchaus bereits vor Vertragsschluss vorgelegen haben; entscheidend ist, dass sie erst nachher bekannt werden.[67]

20 Der Vorgang des „Sichherausstellens" ist trotz des subjektiven Elements der Kenntnisnahme **objektiv** zu beurteilen.[68] Allgemein verbreitete Kenntnisse und Informationen in den beteiligten Handelskreisen muss sich die vertragstreue Partei als bekannt zurechnen lassen.[69] Dabei ist derjenige Massstab an Informations- und Erkundigungspflichten anzulegen, der der Beurteilung durch die vernünftige Person, Art. 8 II, entspricht. Es wird

---

[61] Vgl. Sekretariatskommentar, Art. 62, Nr. 6; *Bianca/Bonell/Bennett*, Art. 71, Anm. 2.6.

[62] Zur Möglichkeit, in einem solchen Fall auch den Vertrag aufzuheben, vgl. LG Berlin, 15.9.1994, CISG-online 399.

[63] Vgl. etwa OLG Rostock, 15.9.2003, CISG-online 920, Erw. II.3.: Die Verkäuferin durfte die weitere Lieferung von Gewürzketchup-Flaschen einstellen, da die Käuferin im Zusammenhang mit früheren Lieferungen ihre Zahlungspflicht verletzt hatte. Das OLG wie auch die Vorinstanz stützten das Aussetzungsrecht der Verkäuferin ohne nähere Begründung auf AR. 71 I lit. b) KG Appenzell AR, 10.3.2003, CISG-online 852, Erw. 2.b). = IHR 2006, 254: Unklar, ob die zu befürchtende nicht rechtzeitige Zahlung des Kaufpreises auf Art. 71 I lit. a) oder lit. b) gestützt wird.

[64] *Bamberger/Roth/Saenger*, Art. 71, Rn. 4.

[65] *Y. Yang*, 18 China Law & Practice (2004), 23, 27.

[66] Gerechtshof Leeuwarden, 31.8.2005, CISG-online 1100, Erw. 2.6.4.1.: Der Käufer darf die fällige Teilzahlung nicht zurückhalten mit der Begründung, der Verkäufer hätte den vorangehenden Schritt in der Vertragserfüllung mit beträchtlicher Verspätung ausgeführt, sofern dem Käufer dadurch kein Schaden entstanden ist.

[67] *Bianca/Bonell/Bennett*, Art. 71, Anm. 1.9.; *Herber/Czerwenka*, Art. 71, Rn. 3; *Heuzé*, Anm. 405.; *Kröll u. a./Saidov*, Art. 71, Rn. 16; *Piltz*, Internationales Kaufrecht, Rn. 4–205; *Fischer*, Die Unsicherheitseinrede, S. 210; *Reinhart*, Zurückbehaltungsrecht, S. 380; *Schlechtriem*, Gemeinsame Bestimmungen, S. 152 ff.; *Achilles*, Art. 71, Rn. 7; *Tunc*, Actes, S. 382 f. Zur Entstehungsgeschichte vgl. *Schlechtriem*, Einheitliches UN-Kaufrecht, S. 84 ff.; *Bianca/Bonell/Bennett*, Art. 71, Anm. 1.9. Für einen rechtsvergleichenden Überblick *Schwenzer/Hachem/Kee*, Rn. 42.45.

[68] MünchKomm/*P. Huber*, Art. 71, Rn. 10; *Enderlein/Maskow/Strohbach*, Art. 71, Anm. 2.; *Fischer*, Die Unsicherheitseinrede, S. 210 f.; *Schlechtriem*, Uniform Sales Law, S. 94.

[69] *Bianca/Bonell/Bennett*, Art. 71, Anm. 3.2. f.; *Schlechtriem*, Einheitliches UN-Kaufrecht, S. 86 f.; *Achilles*, Art. 71, Rn. 7: Umstände, die für einen objektiven Beobachter offen zu Tage gelegen hätten.

entsprechend vorausgesetzt, dass beide Parteien im Vorfeld des Vertrags genügend Auskünfte über den Vertragspartner eingeholt haben, um sich zu vergewissern, dass dieser faktisch und wirtschaftlich in der Lage ist, den Vertrag zu erfüllen. Allerdings ist hierbei zu berücksichtigen, dass das Einholen von entsprechender Information im Fernhandel teuer und schwierig sein kann. Eine allzu gründliche Recherche darf von den Vertragspartnern nicht erwartet werden.[70] War die drohende Pflichtverletzung vor Vertragsschluss bereits objektiv erkennbar, entfällt das Aussetzungsrecht.

Die nachträgliche Berücksichtigung der vor oder bei Vertragsschluss bereits vorhandenen 21 Störungsgründe i. S. d. Art. 71 I stellt ihrem Gehalt nach die Regelung eines Tatbestands dar, der sonst durch Vorschriften über die Irrtumsanfechtung und sonstige Willensmängel oder über die Geschäftsgrundlage erfasst wird.[71] Diesbezüglich verbietet sich ein Rückgriff auf nationales Recht, da das **Übereinkommen insoweit eine eigene Regelung** enthält, Art. 7 II.[72] Nicht ausgeschlossen ist jedoch die Anfechtung wegen arglistiger Täuschung, da das Übereinkommen diesen Tatbestand mit seiner deliktsähnlichen Komponente nicht abdeckt.[73]

d) Prognose. Da die Nichterfüllung der Pflichten in der Zukunft liegt, der Rechtsbehelf 22 aber jetzt geltend gemacht werden soll, bedarf es einer Prognose, ob die gegenwärtigen Umstände den Eintritt der künftigen Störungen erwarten lassen. Hierfür darf man keine mit an Sicherheit grenzende Wahrscheinlichkeit fordern, wohl aber eine **beträchtliche Wahrscheinlichkeit**. Erforderlich ist sie, um zu vermeiden, dass sich der Gläubiger gestützt auf vorschnelle Behauptungen missbräuchlich auf Art. 71 beruft.[74] Ob die künftige Pflichtverletzung wahrscheinlich ist, ist aus Sicht des objektiven und vernünftigen Betrachters in den Schuhen des Gläubigers zu beurteilen (Art. 8 II), der auch über die Kenntnisse der beteiligten Handelskreise verfügt.[75] Unerheblich sind danach bloss subjektive Befürchtungen eines überängstlichen oder übervorsichtigen Gläubigers.[76] Vielmehr müssen darlegungs- und beweisfähige Tatsachen eine genügende Prognosebasis bilden.[77] Dass der Schuldner in der Folge möglicherweise dennoch leistet, falsifiziert die Prognose, die der Gläubiger ja ex ante treffen muss, im Nachhinein nicht.

Ob die Voraussetzungen der beträchtlichen Wahrscheinlichkeit der Pflichtverletzung 22a erfüllt sind, ergibt sich in aller Regel aus einer Gesamtbetrachtung. Die **Kasuistik** ist recht reichhaltig. Die Wahrscheinlichkeit einer Pflichtverletzung wurde bejaht, wenn der Käufer die Leistung der vereinbarten Anzahlung,[78] die Eröffnung oder Verlängerung eines Ak-

---

[70] So auch *von Ziegler*, 25 J. L. & Comm. (2005), 353, 363; *Kröll u. a./Saidov*, Art. 71, Rn. 17.
[71] *Rabel*, Recht des Warenkaufs, Bd. 1, S. 136; *Fischer*, Die Unsicherheitseinrede, S. 210 Fn. 46; *Schlechtriem*, Einheitliches UN-Kaufrecht, S. 85; *ders.*, Gemeinsame Bestimmungen, S. 153.
[72] *Staudinger/Magnus*, Art. 71, Rn. 41 und 42; *Soergel/Lüderitz/Dettmeier*, Art. 71, Rn. 23; *Herber/Czerwenka*, Art. 71, Rn. 16; *Reinhart*, Art. 71, Rn. 10; *Schlechtriem*, Internationales UN-Kaufrecht, Rn. 261; *Ferrari*, RabelsZ 71 (2007), 52, 69.
[73] Vgl. *Schlechtriem*, Internationales UN-Kaufrecht, Rn. 261; *Staudinger/Magnus*, Art. 71, Rn. 44; MünchKomm/*P. Huber*, Art. 71, Rn. 27.
[74] MünchKommHGB/*Mankowski*, Art. 71, Rn. 8.
[75] Vgl. aus der Rspr. OGH, 12.2.1998, CISG-online 349 = östJBl 1999, 54, 56 = östZRVgl 1999, 65, 68: „hohe Wahrscheinlichkeit". S. ferner in der Literatur *Schlechtriem*, Internationales UN-Kaufrecht, Rn. 262; *Staudinger/Magnus*, Art. 71, Rn. 18 und 19 („hohe Wahrscheinlichkeit"); MünchKommHGB/*Mankowski*, Art. 71, Rn. 8 („hohe, überwiegende Wahrscheinlichkeit"); *Honsell/Brunner/Hurni*, Art. 71, Rn. 19 („hohe, jedoch nicht sehr hohe oder gar an Sicherheit grenzende Wahrscheinlichkeit"); *Honnold/Flechtner*, Art. 71, Rn. 388 a. E. („substantial probability of non-performance"); *Ensthaler/Achilles*, GK-HGB, Art. 71, Rn. 3 („aus den Umständen zu schliessende überwiegende Wahrscheinlichkeit"); vgl. auch *Bianca/Bonell/Bennett*, Art. 71, Anm. 3.3.; *Enderlein/Maskow/Strohbach*, Art. 71, Anm. 2.; *Herber/Czerwenka*, Art. 71, Rn. 4; *Reinhart*, Art. 71, Rn. 10; *Jan*, S. 211; *Piltz*, Internationales Kaufrecht, Rn. 4–205; *Reinhart*, Zurückbehaltungsrecht, S. 380 f.; *Ziegel*, Remedial Provisions, S. 9–34; *Strub*, 38 Int'l & Comp. L. Q. (1989), 475, 494 („high degree of probability").
[76] So ausdrücklich *Staudinger/Magnus*, Art. 71, Rn. 19.
[77] MünchKommHGB/*Mankowski*, Art. 71, Rn. 9.
[78] Vgl. CIETAC, 1.1.1989, CISG-online 1230.

kreditivs⁷⁹ oder das Beibringen einer Bankgarantie verweigerte⁸⁰. Eine Pflichtverletzung durch den Verkäufer wurde als wahrscheinlich angesehen, wenn er die Mangelhaftigkeit bereits gelieferter Ware abstreitet,⁸¹ sich weigert, Belege dafür beizubringen, dass die Ware frei von Rechtsmängeln ist,⁸² oder die Ware, die sich in einem Warenlager befand, gestohlen worden ist und der Verkäufer sie nicht wiederauffindet.⁸³ Nimmt der Käufer oder Verkäufer einseitige Vertragsmodifizierungen vor, so kann, muss aber nicht unbedingt, darin die Wahrscheinlichkeit einer künftigen Pflichtverletzung gesehen werden. So war das Schiedsgericht in einem Fall, bei dem der Käufer statt der vereinbarten Beibringung einer Bankgarantie ein Akkreditiv eröffnete, woraufhin wegen fehlerhafter Warenbeschreibung die Ware nicht verladen wurde, dass es wahrscheinlich sei, dass auch künftige Pflichten verletzt würden.⁸⁴

23 Der Massstab des Herausstellens (become apparent; il apparaît) unterscheidet sich von dem für die Prognose des antizipierten Vertragsbruches in Art. 72, wo die künftige Begehung einer wesentlichen Vertragsverletzung „offensichtlich" werden muss (if [...] it is clear that; [s'il] est manifeste qu[e]). „Herausstellen" ist auch nicht dasselbe wie der „triftige Grund", der Art. 73 II zu Grunde gelegt wird (good grounds; de sérieuses raisons). Das Übereinkommen versucht also bereits rein sprachlich, die einzelnen **Wahrscheinlichkeitsgrade in Artt. 71 I, 72 I, 73 II abzustufen,** wobei für Art. 71 I die geringsten Anforderungen an die Prognose gestellt werden. Dies ergibt sich schon dadurch, dass das Suspendierungsrecht in Art. 71 im Unterschied zu Artt. 72, 73 ein lediglich vorläufiger Rechtsbehelf ist.⁸⁵

24 Diese Wertung ergibt sich auch bei der Lektüre der strukturell vergleichbaren Regelungen der neueren **Einheitsrechtsprojekte:** Art. 7.3.4 S. 1 PICC erlaubt es dem Gläubiger „who **reasonably believes** that there will be a fundamental non-performance", vom Schuldner eine angemessene Sicherheit zu fordern und seine eigene Erfüllung zurückzuhalten. Im Rahmen des antizipierten Vertragsbruchs fordert Art. 7.3.3 PICC hingegen, dass „**it is clear** that there will be a fundamental non-performance". Es wird sichtbar auf einen höheren Wahrscheinlichkeitsgrad abgestellt. Eine praktisch identische Differenzierung findet sich in den PECL in Artt. 8:105 I resp. 9:201 II.⁸⁶

IV. Aussetzungsrecht

1. Ausübung

25 Liegen sämtliche Voraussetzungen vor, so gewährt Abs. 1 dem Gläubiger das Recht, die eigene Leistung zurückzubehalten. Die **Zurückhaltung** der eigenen Leistung umfasst alle die Erfüllung hinausschiebenden Handlungen und Unterlassungen, soweit dadurch nicht die Erfüllung endgültig unmöglich gemacht wird. Letzteres ergibt sich aus der **Vorläufigkeit** des Rechtsbehelfs.

---

⁷⁹ Vgl. Supr. Ct. BC, 21.8.2003, CISG-online 1017 = 2003 BCS C 1298, Rn. 76 ff.; CIETAC, 18.12.1996, CISG-online 2281.
⁸⁰ Arb. Ct. Hungarian CCI, 17.11.1995, CISG-online 250.
⁸¹ LG Berlin, 15.9.1944, CISG-online 399.
⁸² Federal Arbitration Court for the Western Siberia Circuit, 6.8.2002, CISG-online 2282. Berlin, 15.9.1994, CISG-online 399.
⁸³ OLG Hamm, 23.6.1998, CISG-online 434 = RIW 1999, 786 = TranspR-IHR 2000, 7.
⁸⁴ Tribunal of International Commercial Arbitration at the Russian Federation Chamber of Commerce and Industry, 22.1.1998, CISG-online 2283.
⁸⁵ *Flechtner,* 8 J. L. & Com. (1988), 53, 94 f.; *Bianca/Bonell/Bennett,* Art. 71, Anm. 3.2. f.; *Enderlein/Maskow/ Strohbach,* Art. 71, Anm. 2.; *Jan,* S. 211 f.; *Achilles,* Art. 71, Rn. 3; *Bamberger/Roth/Saenger,* Art. 71, Rn. 4; *Ferrari u. a./Saenger,* Internationales Vertragsrecht, Art. 71, Rn. 4; *Witz/Salger/Lorenz/Lorenz,* Art. 71, Rn. 8; *Kröll u. a./Saidov,* Art. 71, Rn. 20 a. E. ; vgl. ausführlich bei Art. 73 Rn. 21.
⁸⁶ Vgl. die ausdrückliche Abgrenzung der beiden Wahrscheinlichkeitsgrade in Art. 9:201 PECL, Comment 3.

2. Zeitliche Grenzen

Die Leistung kann **jederzeit zwischen Vertragsschluss und Fälligkeit** der Leistung 26 des Schuldners zurückgehalten werden. Der vertragstreue Teil braucht das Zurückbehaltungsrecht nicht unmittelbar, nachdem sich die drohende Vertragsverletzung herausgestellt hat, auszuüben. Allerdings dürfte die Schadensminderungspflicht des Art. 77 in der Regel eine rasche Ausübung des Zurückbehaltungsrechts diktieren.[87]

3. Informationspflicht (Anzeige)

a) Frist. Die Ausübung des Zurückbehaltungsrechts hat der vertragstreue Teil dem 27 Vertragspartner „sofort" (immediately, immédiatement) anzuzeigen, Art. 71 III. Das entspricht dem Netz an Informations- und Rücksichtspflichten, die das Abkommen als Grundlage für die eigenverantwortliche Gestaltung und Durchführung des Vertrages durch die Parteien geknüpft hat.[88] Sofortige Anzeige erfordert Information des Partners **ohne jede vermeidbare Verzögerung,** sobald der Gläubiger seine Pflichten nicht mehr fristgemäss erfüllt.[89] Sie kann auch vor Aussetzen bzw. Anhalten der eigenen Leistung erfolgen.

b) Form. Für die angemessene Form und das Transportrisiko der Anzeige gilt Art. 27; 28 die rechtzeitige Absendung der Anzeige genügt.[90] Eine bestimmte Form ist nicht einzuhalten. Indes ersetzt nicht schon die blosse Nichtzahlung eines Kaufpreisteils die für die Ausübung des Aussetzungsrechts erforderliche Anzeige.[91] Vielmehr ist eine **Substantiierung** erforderlich: Die Mitteilungspflicht soll dem Schuldner die Möglichkeit geben, durch hinreichende Sicherungsleistung Gewähr für die seinerseitige Erfüllung zu bieten und so den Verdacht einer zukünftigen Vertragsverletzung auszuräumen.[92] Deshalb muss der Gläubiger angeben, auf welchen Sachverhalt er die Geltendmachung seines Aussetzungs- bzw. Anhalterechts stützt,[93] sowie begründen, inwiefern dieser Anlass zu berechtigten Zweifeln an der Erfüllung durch den Schuldner gibt.[94]

4. Wirkungen

a) Bei erfolgter Anzeige. Solange die Gründe für die Gefährdung und damit das 29 Zurückbehaltungsrecht bestehen, befindet sich der Vertrag in einem **Schwebezustand.**[95] Zur Beendigung des Schwebezustands siehe unten Rn. 47 ff.

b) Bei unterlassener Anzeige. Die Folgen des Unterbleibens der Anzeige sind bisher 30 noch wenig geklärt. Die Materialien geben dazu keine Anhaltspunkte. In der Literatur wird überwiegend angenommen, dass die Verletzung der Informationspflicht (nur) zu **Schadens-**

---

[87] Weniger streng bzgl. der durch Art. 77 vorgegebenen Schadensminderungspflicht die Voraufl. sowie etwa *Honsell/Brunner/Hurni*, Art. 71, Rn. 26. Wie hier *Schlechtriem/Schwenzer/Fountoulakis*, CISG Commentary, Art. 71, Rn. 30.
[88] *Leser*, Vertragsaufhebung und Rückabwicklung, S. 225, 234. Zur Bedeutung der Anzeige auch *Strub*, 38 Int'l & Comp. L. Q. (1989), 475, 489 ff.; *Audit*, Vente Internationale, Anm. 163.
[89] Vgl. LG Stendal, 12.10.2000, CISG-online 592 = IHR 2001, 30, 34 (Anzeige nach Ablauf von 3 Jahren zu spät); Hof van Beroep Gent, 26.4.2000, CISG-online 1316 (Anzeige mehrere Monate nach Geltendmachung des Zurückbehaltungsrechts zu spät); LG Darmstadt, 29.5.2001, CISG-online 686 (Anzeige nach 13 Tagen zu spät).
[90] Vgl. im Einzelnen *Schroeter*, Art. 27 Rn. 13.
[91] *Bamberger/Roth/Saenger*, Art. 71, Rn. 6; LG Stendal, 12.10.2000, CISG-online 592 = IHR 2001, 30, 34.
[92] Zur Sicherheitenstellung vgl. unten Rn. 43 ff.
[93] Supr. Ct. BC, 21.8.2003, CISG-online 1017 = 2003 BCS C 1298, Rn. 78; BG, 20.12.2006, CISG-online 1426 = IHR 2007, 127 = SZIER 2008, 173 = ZEuP 2008, 318, 333 (Anm. *Magnus*); MünchKommHGB/*Mankowski*, Art. 71, Rn. 27; *Staudinger/Magnus*, Art. 71, Rn. 45; weitaus weniger streng *Honsell/Brunner/Hurni*, Art. 71, Rn. 26 (‚bloß rudimentäre Begründung' verlangt, und auch dies nur, wenn der Schuldner diese benötigt).
[94] LG Stuttgart, 11.11.2009, CISG-online 2018.
[95] *Enderlein/Maskow/Strohbach*, Art. 71, Anm. 1.; *Jan*, S. 173; *Karollus*, S. 88; *Piltz*, Internationales Kaufrecht, Rn. 4–208.

ersatz führe.⁹⁶ Diese Auffassung ist flexibler als die Ansicht, die in der – allerdings vornehmlich erstinstanzlichen – Rechtsprechung noch vorzuherrschen scheint und auch in den DCFR⁹⁷ übernommen wurde und wonach die Informationspflicht kategorisch zur Wirksamkeitsvoraussetzung für das Zurückbehaltungsrecht erhoben wird.⁹⁸ Die Schadensersatzlösung wird insbesondere den Bedürfnissen des grenzüberschreitenden Warenverkehrs gerecht.⁹⁹ Es ist insbesondere nicht recht einzusehen, warum die nicht (rechtzeitig) erfolgte Information automatisch dazu führen soll, dass sich die an sich vertragstreue Partei nun selbst im Vertragsbruch wegen Nichterfüllung befinden soll. Damit würde, gerade vor dem Hintergrund der vergleichsweise streng gefassten Voraussetzungen für die Anwendung des Aussetzungsrechts, wohl mit Kanonen auf Spatzen geschossen. Vielmehr trägt es dem in Art. 77 verankerten Grundgedanken der Schadensminderungspflicht ausreichend Rechnung, wenn die vertragstreue Partei im Einzelfall die finanziellen Folgen dafür zu tragen hat, dass sie den anderen Teil nicht rechtzeitig über die Zurückhaltung informiert und dieser deshalb bereits Dispositionen getroffen hat. Die Frage des Vertragsbruchs durch den Zurückhaltenden sollte folglich nur dann gestellt werden, wenn das Aussetzungsrecht **materiell unberechtigt** geltend gemacht wird.

5. Konkurrenzverhältnis zu nationalen Zurückbehaltungsrechten

31 Durch die lückenlose Regelung des Art. 71 werden sämtliche **Rechtsbehelfe des anwendbaren nationalen Rechts ausgeschlossen,** die sich auf die nach Vertragsschluss zu Tage tretende fehlende Erfüllungsfähigkeit des Schuldners beziehen, sodass der Gläubiger insbesondere keine umfassenderen Zurückhaltungsrechte nach nationalem Recht geltend machen kann.¹⁰⁰

V. Anhalterecht

1. Normzweck

32 Vom Zeitpunkt der Absendung der Ware bis zur deren Aushändigung an den Käufer darf der Verkäufer die Aushändigung an den Käufer verhindern. Voraussetzung für dieses Anhalterecht in Art. 71 II ist, dass in der Zwischenzeit eine durch den Käufer drohende Vertragsverschlechterung zu Tage tritt. Bedeutung hat das Anhalterecht in den Fällen, in denen sich die Verschlechterung der Erfüllungsmöglichkeit durch den Käufer erst nach Versendung der Ware herausstellt, da in den übrigen Fällen der Verkäufer bereits die

---

⁹⁶ MünchKommHGB/*Mankowski*, Art. 71, Rn. 28; MünchKomm/*P. Huber*, Art. 71, Rn. 19; *Lookofsky*, Understanding the CISG, § 6.26, S. 149; *Honsell/Brunner/Hurni*, Art. 71, Rn. 27; Staudinger/*Magnus*, Art. 71, Rn. 47; *Herber/Czerwenka*, Art. 71, Rn. 12; *Bianca/Bonell/Bennett*, Art. 71, Anm. 2.5.; *Soergel/Lüderitz/Dettmeier*, Art. 71, Rn. 18; *Neumayer/Ming*, Art. 71, Anm. 10.; *Schlechtriem*, Internationales UN-Kaufrecht, Rn. 229; *P. Huber/Mullis/P. Huber*, S. 343; *Jan*, S. 172 f.; *Brunner*, Art. 71, Rn. 20; *Piltz*, Internationales Kaufrecht, Rn. 4–215; *Witz/Salger/Lorenz/Lorenz*, Art. 71, Rn. 22. Netherlands Arbitration Institute, 15.10.2002, CISG-online 780, knüpft an die Verletzung der Anzeigepflicht ebenfalls lediglich Schadensersatzfolgen. Vgl. demgegenüber die konstitutive Wirkung der Anzeigepflicht in Art. 72 II, unten Art. 72 Rn. 19 f. Rechtsvergleichend *Schwenzer/Hachem/Kee*, Rn. 42.27 ff., die bzgl. der Anzeigepflicht im CISG allerdings von einer Wirksamkeitsvoraussetzung auszugehen scheinen.
⁹⁷ Vgl. Art. III.–3:401 III DCFR.
⁹⁸ ICC, 11 849/2003, CISG-online 1421, Rn. 46 f.; Int. Ct. Russian CCI, 27.7.1999, CISG-online 779; LG Stendal, 12.10.2000, CISG-online 592 = IHR 2001, 30; LG Darmstadt, 29.5.2001, CISG-online 686; AG Frankfurt a. M., 31.1.1991, CISG-online 34 = IPRax 1991, 345; aus der Literatur vgl. *Heuzé*, Anm. 406; *Kröll u. a./Saidov*, Art. 71, Rn. 39; *Bamberger/Roth/Saenger*, Art. 71, Rn. 6; *Ferrari u. a./Saenger*, Internationales Vertragsrecht, Art. 71, Rn. 6; *Achilles*, Art. 71, Rn. 11.
⁹⁹ Das amerikanische Recht z. B. kennt keine Informationspflicht des Aussetzenden. Es wäre nicht sinnvoll, durch die Erhebung der Informationspflicht zur konstitutiven Voraussetzung des Aussetzungsrechts eine unüberbrückbare Differenz zum praktisch wichtigen amerikanischen Handelsrecht zu schaffen.
¹⁰⁰ OGH, 12.2.1998, CISG-online 349 = östJBl 1999, 54, 55; Staudinger/*Magnus*, Art. 71, Rn. 40; *Herber/Czerwenka*, Art. 71, Rn. 16; *Achilles*, Art. 71, Rn. 1.

Versendung als solche unterlassen kann (Art. 71 I).[101] Das Anhalterecht stellt die **„Suspendierung der Erfüllung nach Erfüllung"**[102] dar: Es annulliert die Wirkungen der Erfüllung seitens des Verkäufers und behandelt die Rechtslage so, als ob der Verkäufer noch nicht geleistet hätte. Von der „Suspendierung der Erfüllung" kann indes nur bei den – wenn auch überwiegenden – Fällen gesprochen werden, in denen Abgabe an den ersten Beförderer Erfüllung bewirkt, Art. 31 lit. a). Die Vorschrift, die weitgehend mit Art. 73 II EKG übereinstimmt, geht auf vergleichbare Regelungen des englischen, amerikanischen und skandinavischen Rechts zurück.[103] Im deutschen Recht gibt es keine vergleichbare Regelung.[104]

2. Geltung nur für Verkäufer

Art. 71 II gilt nur für den Verkäufer. Ein Anhalterecht des Käufers für **Zahlungen** wurde in den Beratungen zwar erörtert, wegen der Unvereinbarkeit mit den Regelungen über den internationalen Zahlungsverkehr aber nicht eingeführt.[105]

3. Voraussetzungen

Für das Anhalterecht als Fortsetzung des Zurückbehaltungsrechts gelten dieselben Voraussetzungen.[106] Insoweit kann auf III. und IV. verwiesen werden.

Das Anhalterecht ermöglicht dem Verkäufer den Zugriff auf die **auf dem Transport befindliche Ware.** Demzufolge muss diese abgesandt, aber dem Käufer noch nicht ausgehändigt, d. h. von diesem noch nicht körperlich entgegengenommen worden sein.[107] Das Anhalterecht besteht auch dann, wenn die Ware auf Veranlassung des Verkäufers von dessen Lieferanten direkt an den Käufer abgesandt wurde oder aber auf Weisung des Käufers der Versand an dessen Abnehmer erfolgt.[108] Ebenso besteht das Anhalterecht beim **Platzkauf,** solange der Käufer nicht selbst oder durch eigene Leute abholt.[109] Unbeachtlich ist, ob dem Käufer schon das Eigentum übertragen wurde oder ob er Inhaber von Herausgabeansprüchen geworden ist, etwa wegen Übergabe frachtrechtlicher Traditionspapiere (Abs. 2 S. 1).[110]

Die Nichteinhaltung der Informationspflicht des Abs. 3 ist auch hier nicht Wirksamkeitsvoraussetzung des geltend gemachten Rechts, kann aber ggf. zu Schadensersatzansprüchen des Vertragsgegners führen (oben Rn. 30).

---

[101] *Schlechtriem,* Internationales UN-Kaufrecht, Rn. 265.
[102] *Von Ziegler,* 25 J. L. & Comm. (2005), 353, 366.
[103] Vgl. sec. 44–46 SGA, dazu *Chitty,* Chitty On Contracts, Vol. II, Rn. 43–357 ff.; §§ 2–609, 2–705 UCC sowie § 39 schwedisches Kaufgesetz. Dazu auch *Dölle/U. Huber,* Art. 73 EKG, Rn. 26; *Fischer,* Die Unsicherheitseinrede, S. 62 ff.; *Honnold/Flechtner,* Art. 71, Rn. 390 Fn. 25; *Hellner,* UN Convention, S. 84.
[104] *Dölle/U. Huber,* Art. 73 EKG, Rn. 29; *Vanwijk-Alexandre,* R. D. A. I. 2001, 353, 355 f.
[105] YB VIII (1977), S. 54, Nr. 412 ff.; *Bianca/Bonell/Bennett,* Art. 71, Anm. 1.12.; *Kröll u. a./Saidov,* Art. 71, Rn. 44. Nach einem Teil der Lehre solle aber auch der Käufer die Auszahlung des Kaufpreises anhalten können, wenn ganz eindeutig ist, dass der Verkäufer keine auch nur annähernd adäquate Gegenleistung erbringen wird, vgl. *Staudinger/Magnus,* Art. 71, Rn. 53; *Bamberger/Roth/Saenger,* Art. 71, Rn. 8; *Ferrari u. a./Saenger,* Internationales Vertragsrecht, Art. 71, Rn. 8; *Brunner,* Art. 71, Rn. 5. Dies ist m. E. aufgrund der Entstehungsgeschichte abzulehnen. Es bleibt folglich bei einem Aussetzungsrecht des Käufers nach Abs. 1 bzw. gestützt auf ein allgemeines Zurückbehaltungsrecht (vgl. zum Ganzen oben Rn. 6, 9).
[106] *Schlechtriem,* Internationales UN-Kaufrecht, Rn. 265.
[107] *Enderlein/Maskow/Strohbach,* Art. 71, Anm. 6.; *MünchKomm/P. Huber,* Art. 71, Rn. 30; *Herber/Czerwenka,* Art. 71, Rn. 13; *Jan,* S. 175; *Schlechtriem,* Einheitliches UN-Kaufrecht, S. 87.
[108] Vgl. schon zum EKG *Dölle/U. Huber,* Art. 73 EKG, Rn. 34; *Mertens/Rehbinder,* Art. 73 EKG, Rn. 10.
[109] *Dölle/U. Huber,* Art. 73 EKG, Rn. 35.
[110] *Enderlein/Maskow/Strohbach,* Art. 71, Anm. 6.; *Schlechtriem,* Internationales UN-Kaufrecht, Rn. 265. Anders ist die Lösung im UCC, gem. dessen § 2–705 (2) (d) das Anhalterecht ausgeschlossen ist, wenn der Käufer bereits ein „negotiable document of title covering the goods" erhalten hat.

Art. 71 37–40   Teil III. Kapitel V. Pflichten des Verkäufers und des Käufers. Abschnitt I

4. Wirkungen

37   Während der Ausübung des Anhalterechts entfällt die Vorleistungspflicht ebenso wie beim Zurückbehaltungsrecht.[111] Der Vertrag befindet sich im **Schwebezustand**. Die Veränderung der Leistungszeit stellt keine Vertragsverletzung dar, sondern ist rechtmässig.[112] Der Käufer ist gegenüber dem Verkäufer verpflichtet, das Anhalten der Ware zu dulden. Er kann das Anhalterecht aber unterwandern, wenn er die Ware gestützt auf die Transportdokumente vom Dritten herausverlangt. Damit begeht er freilich eine weitere Vertragsverletzung und macht sich nach Art. 61 I lit. b) schadensersatzpflichtig.[113] Wirtschaftlich ist dem Verkäufer ein solcher Schadensersatzanspruch allerdings ein schwacher Trost, wenn die bevorstehende Vertragsverletzung des Käufers gerade in dessen Zahlungsschwierigkeiten gründet.[114] Angesagt ist in diesen Fällen das Ergreifen prozessualer Mittel, vgl. dazu Rn. 39.

5. Schuldrechtliche Natur

38   Das Anhalterecht besteht nur im Verhältnis **zwischen Verkäufer und Käufer**, wie sich aus Abs. 2 S. 2 ergibt.[115] Es gilt nicht im Verhältnis des Verkäufers zu Dritten, insbesondere Frachtführern, Spediteuren, Lagerhaltern und Abnehmern des Käufers.[116] Insofern ist auch unbeachtlich, durch wen beim Versendungskauf der Frachtvertrag geschlossen wurde, wenn die Ware nur vom Verkäufer dem Transportunternehmer übergeben wurde. Ob das Anhalterecht von Dritten (Frachtführer, Lagerhalter etc.) zu beachten ist, richtet sich nach dem auf den jeweiligen Vertrag anwendbaren Recht.[117] Soweit der Verkäufer den Frachtvertrag geschlossen hat, kann ihm ein vertragliches Weisungsrecht aus diesem Vertrag zustehen, das die Durchsetzung des Anhalterechts ermöglicht. Dies ist bei der Mehrheit der Incotermklauseln 2010 der Fall;[118] hier kann der Verkäufer dem Frachtführer nach Massgabe des Frachtvertrags die Weisung erteilen, die Ware nicht an den Käufer auszuhändigen oder den Transport abzubrechen.

39   Wirklich durchsetzen kann der Verkäufer sein Anhalterecht aber nur, wenn er dem Käufer durch **einstweilige Verfügung** untersagen lässt, die Ware in Besitz zu nehmen. Die Zulässigkeit und prozessualen Voraussetzungen vorläufigen Rechtsschutzes richten sich nach der lex fori des angerufenen Gerichts bzw. nach dem anwendbaren Schiedsrecht; in materieller Hinsicht müssen die Voraussetzungen von Art. 71 vorliegen.[119]

6. Erlöschen des Rechts

40   Das Anhalterecht endet aus denselben Gründen wie das Aussetzungsrecht.[120] Ausserdem erlischt es, wenn die Ware an den Käufer oder an einen Vertreter, Besitzmittler oder sonst zum Empfang Ermächtigten ausgehändigt worden ist.[121] Dazu zählt der Beförderer nur dann, wenn er anzeigt, dass er die Ware anstelle des Käufers und nicht bloss zum Zwecke

---

[111] *Enderlein/Maskow/Strohbach*, Art. 71, Anm. 1.; *Bamberger/Roth/Saenger*, Art. 71, Rn. 8.
[112] *Honnold/Flechtner*, Art. 71, Rn. 393; *Enderlein/Maskow/Strohbach*, Art. 71, Anm. 1.; Netherlands Arbitration Institute, 15.10.2002, CISG-online 780.
[113] *Schlechtriem*, Internationales UN-Kaufrecht, Rn. 265; *Staudinger/Magnus*, Art. 71, Rn. 54; *Ferrari u. a./Saenger*, Internationales Vertragsrecht, Art. 71, Rn. 9; *Bamberger/Roth/Saenger*, Art. 71, Rn. 9; *P. Huber/Mullis/P. Huber*, S. 344.
[114] MünchKommHGB/*Mankowski*, Art. 71, Rn. 39.
[115] *Bamberger/Roth/Saenger*, Art. 71, Rn. 9; *Piltz*, Internationales Kaufrecht, Rn. 4–213; *Ferrari u. a./Saenger*, Internationales Vertragsrecht, Art. 71, Rn. 9; *Achilles*, Art. 71, Rn. 10; *Soergel/Lüderitz/Dettmeier*, Art. 71, Rn. 12.
[116] MünchKommHGB/*Mankowski*, Art. 71, Rn. 37.
[117] Sekretariatskommentar, Art. 62, Nr. 12; *Schlechtriem*, Internationales UN-Kaufrecht, Rn. 265; *Staudinger/Magnus*, Art. 71, Rn. 54a; MünchKomm/*P. Huber*, Art. 71, Rn. 33.
[118] Namentlich bei sämtlichen D-Klauseln.
[119] Vgl. auch MünchKommHGB/*Mankowski*, Art. 71, Rn. 39.
[120] Dazu sogleich Rn. 41 ff.
[121] MünchKommHGB/*Mankowski*, Art. 71, Rn. 40.

des Transports in Empfang nimmt, oder aber ein Weitertransport **nach** Aushändigung an den Käufer ausgeführt wird.

VI. Wegfall der Rechtsbehelfe

1. Erlöschensgründe

a) Übersicht. Das Aussetzungs- bzw. Anhalterecht erlischt, wenn kein Aussetzungs- 41
grund im Sinne von Art. 71 I a), b) mehr vorliegt, d. h. wenn der Streik oder das sonstige Hindernis, das an der Erfüllungsfähigkeit des Schuldners berechtigte Zweifel aufkommen liess, aufgehoben wird. Es erlischt ebenfalls, wenn der Schuldner ausreichende Sicherheiten stellt (vgl. nächste Rn.) oder wenn der Vertrag rechtmässig aufgehoben worden ist, sei es, weil ein antizipierter wesentlicher Vertragsbruch vorliegt (Artt. 72, 73 II), sei es wegen Nichterfüllung nach Fälligkeit (Artt. 49 I b), 64 I a)).[122] Für die Frage, ob das Leistungsverweigerungsrecht bei Leistung durch den Schuldner erlischt, ist in zeitlicher und qualitativer Hinsicht zu differenzieren: Leistet der Schuldner bei Fälligkeit und zwar vertragsgemäss, kann sich der Gläubiger nicht mehr auf Art. 71 berufen und muss seinerseits erfüllen. Leistet der Schuldner bei Fälligkeit, allerdings mangelhaft, so ist, in der Annahme eines allgemeinen, auch nach Fälligkeit bestehenden Leistungsverweigerungsrechts,[123] der Gläubiger weiterhin zum Zurückhalten der eigenen Leistung berechtigt. Die Leistung des Schuldners *vor* Fälligkeit führt zum Erlöschen des Aussetzungsrechts in dem Fall, dass der Gläubiger diese annimmt. Wird die Abnahme der vor Fälligkeit angebotenen Leistung verweigert (vgl. Art. 52 I), erlischt das Aussetzungsrecht nach Art. 71 dann, wenn in der vorzeitigen Leistung eine angemessene Gewähr für die ordnungsgemässe Leistung erblickt werden kann.[124] Dies mag der Fall sein, wenn das Aussetzungsrecht des Käufers im Zweifel gründete, ob der Verkäufer über genügend Produktionsmittel oder die richtigem Anlagen verfügt; hier vermag eine verfrühte Leistung als Beleg dafür dienen, dass der vom Käufer gehegte Verdacht unbegründet ist, und führt so zum Erlöschen des Aussetzungsrechts.[125]

Es ist zu bedauern, dass die insoweit erheblich präzisere und strengere Regelung des 42
amerikanischen Handelsrechts, die zu einer **Auflösung des Schwebezustandes** nach spätestens 30 Tagen führt, keinen Eingang in das Einheitsrecht gefunden hat.[126] Unter dem Übereinkommen besteht so die Gefahr, dass der Schwebezustand perpetuiert wird und damit faktisch einer Vertragsaufhebung gleichkommt.[127]

b) Insbesondere: Stellung von Sicherheiten. aa) Allgemeines. Das Aussetzungs- 43
bzw. Anhalterecht fällt weg, wenn und sobald von Seiten des Schuldners ausreichende Sicherheit bereitgestellt wird. Mit dieser Möglichkeit[128] ist dem Schuldner ein Instrument zur Abwendung des lähmenden Schwebezustandes an die Hand gegeben. Allerdings hat der

---

[122] Vgl. etwa OLG Karlsruhe, 20.7.2004, CISG-online 858, Erw. II.B)2.b)bb)) = IHR 2004, 246, 249; KG Appenzell AR, 10.3.2003, CISG-online 852, Erw. 2.b) = IHR 2006, 254.
[123] Vgl. oben Rn. 9.
[124] Vgl. *Kröll u. a./Saidov*, Art. 71, Rn. 57.
[125] Vgl. Supr. Ct. BC, 21.8.2003, CISG-online 1017 = 2003 BCS C 1298, Rn. 79 ff.: Eröffnet der Käufer letztlich das Akkreditiv, entfällt das Aussetzungsrecht des Verkäufers.
[126] Vgl. § 2–609 (4) UCC, wo ausdrücklich festgehalten ist, dass es eine Vertragsaufsage („repudiation") durch den Schuldner darstelle, wenn er nicht in einer vernünftigen Frist von maximal 30 Tagen ausreichende Gewähr für seine Leistungsfähigkeit biete.
[127] Vgl. auch *Rowley*, 69 U. Cin. L. Rev. (2001), 565, 634, der deshalb erwägt, den in Art. 71 genannten „wesentlichen Teil [der] Pflichten" der in Art. 72 geforderten „wesentlichen Vertragsverletzung" gleichzusetzen.
[128] Zur Entstehungsgeschichte *Bianca/Bonell/Bennett*, Art. 71, Anm. 1.12. Für einen rechtsvergleichend-historischen Überblick zu der durchaus uneinheitlichen Lage in den verschiedenen Rechtsordnungen vgl. *Rabel*, Recht des Warenkaufs, Bd. 1, S. 235, 260 sowie jüngst *Schwenzer/Hachem/Kee*, Rn. 42.38 ff.

Gläubiger – anders als unter § 2–609 UCC[129] – **keinen Anspruch** auf Stellung einer Sicherheit;[130] es bleibt im CISG bei einem reinen Abwendungsrecht des Schuldners.

44 **Sicherheit** (assurance, assurances) ist nach der Entstehungsgeschichte[131] nicht auf Kreditsicherheiten im engen Sinne begrenzt, wie sie (Grund-)Pfandrechte und sonstige Sicherungsrechte wie Sicherungsübereignung, Sicherungszession und Bürgschaft darstellen. Es sind auch andere Mittel und Formen denkbar, die für die andere Partei die Befürchtung einer Vertragsverletzung ausräumen, wie z. B. Bankgarantien oder Stillhaltezusagen und Vorrangeinräumungen Dritter.[132]

45 Die vom Schuldner gestellte Sicherheit muss nach dem Wortlaut des Gesetzes **ausreichend** sein, um die Erfüllungspflicht wieder erstarken zu lassen. Ob die Sicherheit den erforderlichen Umfang aufweist, bestimmt sich mit Blick auf Art. 71 III 2. HS nach der Leistung, die der Schuldner zu erbringen hat, nicht aber nach weiteren, eventuell erfolgenden Schäden. Die gestellten Sicherheiten müssen demnach ihrem Umfang nach die geschuldete Leistung wertmässig abdecken, nicht aber mögliche weitere Schadenersatzansprüche des Gläubigers.[133] Für weitere Schäden ist nicht Art. 71 III 2. HS einschlägig, der nur auf die Gewähr der konkreten Vertragspflicht abstellt, sondern es gelten die allgemeinen Regeln der Vertragsstörung. Art und notwendiger Umfang der Sicherheit sind unter Berücksichtigung der gefährdeten Leistung, der spezifischen drohenden Gefahr und des Vertragsrahmens zu beurteilen. Irrelevant ist, ob der Gläubiger die Sicherheit subjektiv als genügend erachtet; es gilt auch hier der **objektive Massstab** der vernünftigen Person (Art. 8 II, III).[134] Massgeblich ist, ob die Sicherheit die vom Schuldner zu erbringende Leistung in wirtschaftlicher Hinsicht abdeckt, so dass der Gläubiger im Sicherungsfall wertmässig soviel erhält wie er es bei ordentlicher Erfüllung durch den Schuldner täte. Es wird indes genügen müssen, wenn die vom Schuldner gestellte Sicherheit indiziert, dass die Leistung im Wesentlichen wie versprochen erbracht werden wird;[135] eine unwesentliche Abweichung, etwa eine kurze Verzögerung bei Verträgen, in denen das exakte Einhalten von Fristen nicht entscheidend ist, darf deshalb nicht als ungenügende Sicherheit angesehen werden; Erfüllungsfehler des Schuldners sind dann aber über Art. 74 zu kompensieren.[136]

46 Die Sicherheit wird in der Regel **tatsächlich** gestellt werden müssen; die blosse Ankündigung, etwa eine Absichtserklärung oder verbale Zusage, reicht grundsätzlich

---

[129] § 2–609 (1) (2) UCC: „When reasonable grounds for insecurity arise with respect to the performance of either party the other may in writing demand adequate assurance of due performance and until he receives such assurance may if commercially reasonable suspend any performance for which he has not already received the agreed return."
[130] MünchKommHGB/*Mankowski*, Art. 71, Rn. 29; MünchKomm/*P. Huber*, Art. 71, Rn. 20; *Staudinger/Magnus*, Art. 71, Rn. 48.
[131] Sekretariatskommentar, Art. 62, Nr. 13.
[132] *Herber/Czerwenka/Eckardt*, Art. 71, Rn. 14; *Neumayer/Ming*, Art. 71, Anm. 11.; *Karollus*, S. 88; *Achilles*, Art. 71, Rn. 10 sowie *Enstaler/Achilles*, GK-HGB, Art. 71, Rn. 12: Das Versprechen einer Konventionalstrafe bei entsprechender Bonität oder eine Einstandserklärung Dritter sind ausreichende Sicherheiten.
[133] Wie hier MünchKomm/*P. Huber*, Art. 71, Rn. 21; *Bianca/Bonell/Bennett*, Art. 71, Anm. 3.4.; *Enstaler/Achilles*, GK-HGB, Art. 71, Rn. 12; *Bamberger/Roth/Saenger*, Art. 71, Rn. 6; a. A. hingegen Sekretariatskommentar, Art. 62, Nr. 13 ff.; *Staudinger/Magnus*, Art. 71, Rn. 49; *Soergel/Lüderitz/Dettmeier*, Art. 71, Rn. 19; *Honnold/Flechtner*, Art. 71, Rn. 392; MünchKommHGB/*Mankowski*, Art. 71, Rn. 31; *von Ziegler*, 25 J. L. & Com. (2005), 353, 370; *Piltz*, Internationales Kaufrecht, Rn. 4–216; *Honsell/Brunner/Hurni*, Art. 71, Rn. 30, nach denen die Sicherstellung auch sämtliche Folgeschäden, die infolge der Nichterfüllung entstehen könnten, abdecken muss.
[134] Vgl. *Bianca/Bonell/Bennett*, Art. 71, Anm. 3.3.
[135] Nach der Rspr. kann eine ausreichende Gewähr i. S. d. Art. 71 III S. 2 auch darin liegen, dass sich die Parteien wegen nicht vollständiger Vertragskonformität der Ware auf eine Herabsetzung des Kaufpreises einigen, LG München I, 6.4.2000, CISG-online 665. Ebenso reicht es aus, wenn der Verkäufer eine Verbesserung des Qualitätsstandards seines Produkts nachweist, Netherlands Arbitration Institute, 15.10.2002, CISG-online 780.
[136] So auch *Strub*, 28 Int'l & Comp. L. Q. (1989), 457, 495; *Azeredo da Silveira*, 2 Nordic J. Com. L. (2005), 15; *Bridge*, 59 Int'l & Comp. L. Q. (2010), 911, 938; *Honnold/Flechtner*, Art. 71, Rn. 392; *Kröll u. a./Saidov*, Art. 71, Rn. 52.

Verschlechterungseinrede   47–49 **Art. 71**

nicht.[137] Anderes mag aber gelten, wenn das makellose Renommee des Schuldners oder dessen bisherige einwandfreie Erfüllung früherer Verträge zeigen, dass er seine Versprechen stets gehalten hat und deshalb die schlichte Abgabe eines Erfüllungsversprechens ausnahmsweise „Gewähr für die Erfüllung der Pflichten" darzustellen vermag, Art. 71 III S. 2.[138] War die Erfüllung des Vertrag deshalb unsicher, weil der Schuldner dessen Ungültigkeit behauptete, widerruft er diese Behauptungen aber nachträglich, dann mag darin ebenfalls eine ausreichende Sicherheit im Sinne von Art. 71 III liegen.[139]

bb) Schwebezustand. Der Gläubiger begeht, solange er auf eine Sicherheitsleistung des 47 Schuldners wartet, keine Vertragsverletzung, wenn er seine Erfüllungshandlungen **aussetzt** und dadurch von den im Vertrag vorgesehenen Fristen und Terminen abweicht.[140] Die im Vertragsprogramm vorgesehenen Fristen werden für diese Phase der Unsicherheit gehemmt (vgl. Rn. 50).

cc) Wirkung der Sicherheitsleistung. Bietet der Schuldner ausreichende Gewähr für 48 die Erfüllung seiner Pflichten, so leben die Leistungspflichten des Gläubigers wieder auf. Er muss ihnen grundsätzlich wie im Vertrag vorgesehen nachkommen.

dd) Rechtsfolgen bei Nichtstellen von Sicherheiten. Das Übereinkommen regelt 49 die Rechtsfolgen bei Nichtstellen von Sicherheiten nicht, im Unterschied zu PICC und PECL[141] sowie gewissen nationalen Rechtsordnungen[142]. Es sieht auch keine Frist vor, innerhalb welcher der Schuldner sein Abwendungsrecht auszuüben hat.[143] Nähme man Art. 71 III wörtlich, so bliebe es dabei, dass für den Gläubiger solange ein **Aussetzungsrecht** bestünde, wie der Schuldner keine Sicherheit stellte, ohne dass sich gleichzeitig ein Recht zur Vertragsaufhebung ergäbe. Richtigerweise ist aber die Aufhebung des Vertrags bei ausgebliebener Sicherheitsleistung selbstredend möglich, wenn die Parteien Entsprechendes vertraglich vereinbart haben. Aufgehoben werden darf der Vertrag auch, wenn gleichzeitig die Voraussetzungen von Art. 72 I, II erfüllt sind und der Gläubiger bloss vorsichtshalber zunächst den provisorischen Rechtsbehelf des Art. 71 ausgeübt hat. Fraglich bleibt, ob das blosse Nichtstellen von Sicherheiten zur Aufhebung des Vertrags berechtigt. In der Lehre wird diesbezüglich mehrheitlich betont, das Nichtstellen von Sicherheiten sei ein Indiz für eine definitive Erfüllungsverweigerung im Sinne von Art. 72 III; aus Art. 71 III allein resultiere kein Aufhebungsrecht.[144] Richtig daran ist, dass die

---

[137] MünchKommHGB/*Mankowski*, Art. 71, Rn. 32; *Staudinger/Magnus*, Art. 71, Rn. 50; MünchKomm/ *P. Huber*, Art. 71, Rn. 21. Dem Schuldner ist natürlich unbenommen, sich auf ein blosses Versprechen des Schuldners, von seiner Bank ein Akkreditiv zu verlangen, zu verlassen und seinerseits mit der Erfüllung des Vertrags fortzufahren, vgl. *Doolim Corp. v. R Doll, L.L.C. et al.*, U.S. Federal Dist Ct (N.Y.), 29.5.2009, CISG-online 1892, Rn. 40.
[138] So auch *Saidov*, Unif. dr. Rev. 2006, 795, 815; ähnl. *Bianca/Bonell/Bennett*, Art. 71, Anm. 3.4.; *Audit*, Vente Internationale, Anm. 163.; *Strub*, 38 Int'l & Comp. L.Q. (1989), 475, 495; strenger *Honsell/Brunner/ Hurni*, Art. 71, Rn. 30 a. E.
[139] Vgl. *Carter*, Suspending Contract Performance, S. 515, m. w. N.
[140] *Bianca/Bonell/Bennett*, Art. 71, Anm. 2.1.; *Soergel/Lüderitz/Dettmeier*, Art. 71, Rn. 16; *Enderlein/Maskow/ Strohbach*, Art. 71, Anm. 1.; *Reinhart*, Zurückbehaltungsrecht, S. 379; *Vanwijk-Alexandre*, R. D. A. I. 2001, 353, 367. Hinsichtlich der Auswirkung auf den Gefahrübergang vgl. Art. 69.
[141] Unter Art. 7.3.4 PICC und Art. 8:105 PECL darf der Gläubiger, wenn der Schuldner nicht innerhalb angemessener Frist Sicherheiten stellt, den Vertrag aufheben. Offenbar nicht geregelt ist die Frage im DCFR und im CESL-Entwurf.
[142] Vgl. § 2–609 (4) UCC („failure to provide within a reasonable time [...] such assurance [...] is a repudiation of the contract"); ferner erlauben unter anderem das österreichische sowie das chines. Recht die Vertragsaufhebung nach fruchtlosem Ablauf einer Frist, vgl. *Schwenzer/Hachem/Kee*, Rn. 42.48.
[143] MünchKommHGB/*Mankowski*, Art. 71, Rn. 30; *Staudinger/Magnus*, Art. 71, Rn. 50. Anders unter § 2–609 (4) UCC: 30-tägige Frist; Art. 7.3.4 PICC: „reasonable time".
[144] *Schlechtriem*, Gemeinsame Bestimmungen, S. 156 Fn. 15; *Vanwijk-Alexandre*, R. D. A. I. 2001, 353, 361; *von Ziegler*, 25 J. L. & Comm. (2005), 353, 371; *Strub*, 38 Int'l & Comp. L.Q. (1989), 475, 484; *Ziegel*, Remedial Provisions, S. 9–13; *Bianca/Bonell/Bennett*, Art. 71, Anm. 3.7.; *Kröll u. a./Saidov*, Art. 71, Rn. 55; MünchKommHGB/*Mankowski*, Art. 71, Rn. 34; *Ferrari u. a./Saenger*, Internationales Vertragsrecht, Art. 71, Rn. 7; *Bamberger/Roth/Saenger*, Art. 71, Rn. 7; *Honsell/Brunner/Hurni*, Art. 71, Rn. 32; *Brunner*, Art. 71,

Frage, ob das Nichtstellen von Sicherheiten den Gläubiger zur Vertragsaufhebung berechtigt, in Anwendung von Art. 72 zu beantworten ist.[145] Diesbezüglich allerdings erscheint die Auffassung, das Nichtleisten von Sicherheiten sei lediglich ein Hinweis auf eine Erfüllungsverweigerung im Sinne von Art. 72 III, zu eng. Vielmehr dürfte, unter Umkehrung der gewöhnlichen Beweislastregel, bei Ausbleiben einer ausreichenden Sicherheit und mangels weiterer Hinweise regelmässig auf eine Erfüllungsverweigerung zu schliessen sein.[146] Damit muss der Gläubiger, ausser dem Ausbleiben der ausreichenden Gewähr, keine weiteren Nachweise erbringen; vielmehr ist es Aufgabe des Schuldners, gegebenenfalls nachzuweisen, dass das Nichtstellen von Sicherheiten nicht die Verweigerung der Erfüllung bedeutete, sondern anderen Sinngehalt hatte. Angesichts dessen, dass der Nachweis weiterer Umstände ausser demjenigen, dass die Sicherheit ausblieb, für beide Parteien eine zusätzliche Schwierigkeit bedeutet, erscheint es angebracht, diese Bürde dem Schuldner aufzuerlegen, in dessen Risikosphäre die Unsicherheit hinsichtlich der Vertragserfüllung fällt. Die Vermutungslösung im Rahmen von Art. 71 III i. V. m. Art. 72 III wird nicht nur der wirtschaftlichen Realität handelsrechtlicher Verträge gerecht, in der zügig klare Verhältnisse zu schaffen sind (zu denken ist etwa an das kommentarlose Ausbleiben von Sicherheiten im Rahmen von Kettenverträgen, sog. „string contracts"), sondern sie entspricht auch der dogmatischen Struktur des CISG. So stellt die ausdrückliche Erklärung des Schuldners, dass er keine Sicherheiten leisten werde, ohne Weiteres eine Erfüllungsverweigerung nach Art. 72 III dar; bei blosser Nichtleistung von Sicherheiten erklärt der Schuldner aber durch schlüssiges Verhalten dasselbe. Da das CISG nicht zwischen ausdrücklichen und stillschweigenden Erklärungen differenziert, sondern diese als Kommunikation gleichen Wertgehalts betrachtet (vgl. Art. 8), ist eine derartige Differenzierung auch im Rahmen von Art. 72 III nicht angebracht.[147] Damit ist auch die Frage, ob der Gläubiger die Vertragsaufhebung gemäss Art. 72 II anzeigen muss,[148] zu verneinen: Da das Nichtstellen von Sicherheiten im Zweifel als Erfüllungsverweigerung nach Art. 72 III anzusehen ist, untersteht die entsprechende Vertragsaufhebung nicht dem Mitteilungserfordernis des Art. 72 II.[149]

2. Wiederaufnahme des vertraglichen Zeitplans

50 Ist aufgrund der zwischenzeitlichen Ausübung des Aussetzungs- oder Anhalterechts der ursprüngliche Terminplan nicht mehr einzuhalten, so wird die Erfüllungsfrist für die Leistung des Gläubigers als während der wirksamen Ausübung des Aussetzungs- bzw. Anhalterechts **gehemmt** angesehen; die entsprechende Zeit wird also von der Gesamtfrist subtrahiert und der Leistungstermin um diese Zeit hinausgeschoben.[150]

Rn. 25; *Achilles,* Art. 71, Rn. 14; *Staudinger/Magnus,* Art. 71, Rn. 52; *Schlechtriem/Witz,* Convention de Vienne, Rn. 351.
  [145] So auch MünchKomm/*P. Huber,* Art. 71, Rn. 23; *Witz/Salger/Lorenz/Lorenz,* Art. 71, Rn. 24.
  [146] So auch *Carter,* Suspending Contract Performance, S. 517; *Flechtner,* Pittsburgh Symposium 92, Rn. 190; *Nicholas,* 105 L.Q.R. (1989), 201, 234; *Reinhart,* Zurückbehaltungsrecht, S. 382; *Karollus,* S. 89; ähnl. *Honnold/Flechtner,* Art. 71, Rn. 394, 396 a. E. („This solution is important to the sensible operation of Article 71"); vgl. bereits *Schlechtriem/Schwenzer/Fountoulakis,* CISG Commentary, Art. 71, Rn. 53.
  [147] *Schlechtriem,* Internationales UN-Kaufrecht, Rn. 273; *Schlechtriem/Schwenzer/Fountoulakis,* CISG Commentary, Art. 7,1 Rn. 53
  [148] Vgl. *Honnold/Flechtner,* Art. 72, Rn. 398 a. E.; MünchKomm/*P. Huber,* Art. 71, Rn. 23.
  [149] Vgl. Wortlaut in Art. 72 III, dazu *Fountoulakis,* Art. 72 Rn. 33.
  [150] MünchKommHGB/*Mankowski,* Art. 71, Rn. 33; a. A. *Staudinger/Magnus,* Art. 71, Rn. 51; *Brunner,* Art. 71, 24: Verlängerung des Erfüllungstermins um eine angemessene Frist; differenzierend MünchKomm/*P. Huber,* Art. 71, Rn. 22.

VII. Schadensersatzansprüche

1. Schadensersatzansprüche des Gläubigers

Dem Gläubiger kann durch das Zurückhalten seiner Leistungen ein Schaden entstehen, **51** etwa indem die Ausübung des Aussetzungs- oder Anhaltungsrechts mit Kosten verbunden ist, oder weil die Wiederaufnahme der zwischenzeitlich gestoppten Produktion oder die Eindeckung mit Rohstoffen nur zu höheren Kosten erfolgen kann, etc. Für diesen Schaden wird er in entsprechender Anwendung von Artt. 45 I lit. b), 61 I lit. b) vom Schuldner Ersatz verlangen können.[151] Andernfalls wäre die Ausübung des in Art. 71 vorgesehenen Rechts für den Gläubiger mit beträchtlichen Risiken verbunden.

2. Schadensersatzansprüche des Schuldners

Hält der Gläubiger seine Leistungen zurück, ohne dass die Voraussetzungen des Art. 71 **52** gegeben sind, so begeht er seinerseits eine Vertragsverletzung in Form der Erfüllungsverweigerung, für die er nach Artt. 45 I lit. b), 61 I lit. b) einstehen muss.[152] Schadensersatzpflichtig wird der Gläubiger auch bei unterlassener Anzeige nach Art. 71 III. Er kann sich in beiden Fällen bei gegebenen Voraussetzungen nach Art. 79 entlasten.

VIII. Beweislast

Der Gläubiger, der sich auf das Aussetzungs- bzw. Anhalterecht beruft, muss beweisen, **53** dass deren Voraussetzungen vorliegen.[153] Dass eine ausreichende Sicherheit gestellt worden ist, hat hingegen der Schuldner zu beweisen.[154]

---

[151] Zwar sind die Vorschriften nicht direkt anwendbar, da vor dem Fälligkeitstermin noch keine Verletzung der Leistungspflicht des Schuldners vorliegt; doch erfordert die Wertung des Art. 71 die Anwendung dieser Bestimmungen als Ausdruck eines allgemeinen Rechtsgedankens, vgl. etwa MünchKomm/*P. Huber*, Art. 71, Rn. 16; *Kröll u. a./Saidov*, Art. 71, Rn. 60.

[152] Vgl. LG Dresden, 29.5.2009, CISG-online 2174, Erw. II.3.; Audiencia Provincial de Cantabria, 5.2.2004, CISG-online 837; OLG Köln, 8.1.1997, CISG-online 217; ICC, 8611/1997, CISG-online 236; UNCITRAL Digest, Art. 71, Anm. 1.; *Vanwijk-Alexandre*, R. D. A. I. 2001, 353, 361; *Achilles*, Art. 71, Rn. 8; *Witz/Salger/Lorenz/Lorenz*, Art. 71, Rn. 20; MünchKomm/*P. Huber*, Art. 71, Rn. 28; *Brunner*, Art. 71, Rn. 3.

[153] *Bamberger/Roth/Saenger*, Art. 71, Rn. 10; *Staudinger/Magnus*, Art. 71, Rn. 56; *Baumgärtel/Laumen/Prütting/Hepting/Müller*, Art. 71, Rn. 1; vgl. auch Int. Ct. Ukrainian CCI, No. 48/2005, CISG-online 1372, Erw. 4.; BGer, 17.7.2007, CISG-online 1515, Erw. 5.3 = IHR 2007, 206 (ausführlich zum Sachverhalt die Vorinstanz, KassGer Zürich, 2.4.2007, CISG-online 1526, Erw. 2.4); LG Stuttgart, 11.11.2009, CISG-online 2018.

[154] *Staudinger/Magnus*, Art. 71, Rn. 57; *Baumgärtel/Laumen/Prütting/Hepting/Müller*, Art. 71, Rn. 9; *Kröll u. a./Saidov*, Art. 71, Rn. 56.

Art. 72 [Antizipierter Vertragsbruch]

(1) Ist schon vor dem für die Vertragserfüllung festgesetzten Zeitpunkt offensichtlich, daß eine Partei eine wesentliche Vertragsverletzung begehen wird, so kann die andere Partei die Aufhebung des Vertrages erklären.

(2) Wenn es die Zeit erlaubt und es nach den Umständen vernünftig ist, hat die Partei, welche die Aufhebung des Vertrages erklären will, dies der anderen Partei anzuzeigen, um ihr zu ermöglichen, für die Erfüllung ihrer Pflichten ausreichende Gewähr zu geben.*

(3) Absatz 2 ist nicht anzuwenden, wenn die andere Partei erklärt hat, daß sie ihre Pflichten nicht erfüllen wird.

Art. 72

(1) If prior to the date for performance of the contract it is clear that one of the parties will commit a fundamental breach of contract, the other party may declare the contract avoided.

(2) If time allows, the party intending to declare the contract avoided must give reasonable notice to the other party in order to permit him to provide adequate assurance of his performance.

(3) The requirements of the preceding paragraph do not apply if the other party has declared that he will not perform his obligations.

Art. 72

1) Si, avant la date de l'exécution du contrat, il est manifeste qu'une partie commettra une contravention essentielle au contrat, l'autre partie peut déclarer celui-ci résolu.

2) Si elle dispose du temps nécessaire, la partie qui a l'intention de déclarer le contrat résolu doit le notifier à l'autre partie dans des conditions raisonnables pour lui permettre de donner des assurances suffisantes de la bonne exécution de ses obligations.

3) Les dispositions du paragraphe précédent ne s'appliquent pas si l'autre partie a déclaré qu'elle n'exécuterait pas ses obligations.

Übersicht

	Rn.
I. Vorgeschichte	1
1. EKG	1
2. CISG	2
II. Aufgaben und Anwendungsbereich	4
1. Präventiver Schutz	4
2. Rechtsvergleich	6
3. Differenzierung zwischen objektiven und im Verhalten des Schuldners liegenden Gründen	9
4. Abgrenzung zu anderen Behelfen	10
III. Aufhebungsrecht bei künftiger wesentlicher Vertragsverletzung, Art. 72 I	11
1. Aufhebungsvoraussetzungen	11
2. Künftige wesentliche Vertragsverletzung	12
3. Prognose	14
IV. Anzeigepflicht, Art. 72 II	17
1. Ratio	17
2. Konstitutive Wirkung	19
3. Form und Frist der Anzeige	21
4. Substantiierungspflicht	22
5. Zumutbarkeit der Anzeige	23
6. Fristsetzung für Sicherheitsleistung	26
7. Kombination der Anzeigen nach Artt. 72 II bzw. 71 III	28
8. Stellung von Sicherheiten	29
a) Ausreichende Sicherheit	29

---

* Schweiz: Sicherheit zu bieten.

b) Wirkungen	30
c) Ausbleiben von bzw. Stellen nicht ausreichender Sicherheiten	31
d) Formen und Fristen	32
V. Vorzeitige Erfüllungsweigerung, Art. 72 III (ohne Anzeigepflicht)	33
1. Erfüllungsverweigerung (ungerechtfertigte antizipierte Vertragsaufhebung)	33
a) Ratio	33
b) Umfang	34
c) Erklärung der Erfüllungsverweigerung	35
d) Widerrufbarkeit	36
VI. Aufhebungsrecht und Aufhebungserklärung	37
1. Art. 26	37
2. Fristen	38
3. Wirkungen	40
VII. Schadensersatz	41
VIII. Beweislast	42

Vorläufer und **Entwürfe:** Art. 76 EKG; Genfer E 1976 Art. 49; Wiener E 1977 Art. 49; New Yorker E 1978 Art. 63.

I. Vorgeschichte

1. EKG

Der antizipierte Vertragsbruch beschäftigte auf rechtsvergleichender Ebene bereits im Jahre 1929 *Ernst Rabel*,[1] der in seinen Vorschlägen zur Vereinheitlichung der Regeln zur vorzeitigen Erfüllungsweigerung ursprünglich allein auf die Kundgabe des Willens einer Partei zur künftigen wesentlichen Vertragsverletzung abstellte.[2] Art. 76 EKG kannte dann bereits das objektive Kriterium der Offensichtlichkeit der zukünftigen Vertragsverletzung.[3] **1**

2. CISG

Art. 72 I hat Art. 76 EKG bei nur geringfügigen Änderungen im Wortlaut übernommen. Amerikanische Versuche, auf der Basis früherer Entwürfe zum EKG[4] das Verhalten der Parteien und ihre Negierung der Vertragsbindung[5] entsprechend der anglo-amerikanischen Konzeption des anticipatory breach[6] in den Mittelpunkt der Regelung zu stellen und dagegen die objektiv leistungsstörenden Umstände an den Rand zu rücken,[7] scheiterten. **2**

Erst kurz vor der Beschlussfassung über den endgültigen Text der Konvention wurde der heutige Wortlaut des **Art. 72 II und III**[8] auf der Basis eines ägyptischen Kompromissvorschlages zu den Artt. 62 und 63 New Yorker E 1978 formuliert,[9] wobei man **3**

---

[1] *Rabel*, Ges. Aufs. Bd. 3, S. 425, 426; zur Entwicklung im anglo-amerikanischen und französischen Recht vgl. auch *Strub*, 38 Int'l & Comp. L. Q. (1989), 475, 479–487; *Rowley*, 69 U. Cin. L. Rev. (2001), 565–639; *Schwenzer/Hachem/Kee*, Rn. 47.137 ff.; für das deutsche und anglo-amerikanische Recht *Stoll*, RabelsZ 52 (1988), 617, 618 f. sowie *Leser*, Erfüllungsweigerung, S. 643 ff.

[2] So Art. 87 zu E 1963 des EKG. Vgl. zur Vorgeschichte von Art. 76 EKG *Dölle/Leser*, Art. 76 EKG, Rn. 2–5.

[3] Vgl. Fn. 2.

[4] YB V (1974), S. 68, Nr. 6 f.: „when [...] either party so conducts himself as to disclose an intention to commit a fundamental breach of contract."

[5] S. die Argumente in YB V (1974), S. 41, Nr. 130.

[6] *Bianca/Bonell/Bennett*, Art. 72, Anm. 1.4.; *Treitel*, Remedies for Breach, S. 379 ff., Nr. 279.

[7] YB V (1974), S. 41, Nr. 131.

[8] Vgl. O. R., S. 422, Nr. 23.

[9] *Schlechtriem*, Einheitliches UN-Kaufrecht, S. 88 f.; *Bianca/Bonell/Bennett*, Art. 72, Anm. 1.7.; *Strub*, 38 Int'l & Comp. L. Q. (1989), 475, 491 f. Zur Diskussion vgl. O. R., S. 420 ff., Nr. 1 ff.

den Entwicklungsländern durch die Abwendungsbefugnis mit Sicherheiten entgegenkam,[10] sich andererseits aber nicht darauf einliess, die wichtige Ausnahmeformulierung „if time allows" zu Beginn von Abs. 2 zu streichen.[11] So entstand ein hinsichtlich seiner Konsequenzen wohl nicht vollständig überblickter Kompromiss.[12]

II. Aufgaben und Anwendungsbereich

1. Präventiver Schutz

4   Art. 72 betrifft ebenso wie Artt. 71 und 73 II, III Störungen im Vorfeld der (vollständigen) Vertragserfüllung. Ist bereits vor Fälligkeit offensichtlich, dass die andere Partei eine wesentliche Vertragsverletzung begehen wird, muss die vertragstreue Partei den Eintritt der Vertragsverletzung nicht abwarten, sondern darf bereits vor Fälligkeit die Vertragsaufhebung erklären.[13] Für Vertragsverletzungen, die mit Fälligkeit auftreten, richtet sich das Recht zur Vertragsaufhebung nach Artt. 49, 64 CISG. Die Möglichkeit der vorzeitigen Vertragsaufhebung trägt zum einen dem **Effizienzgedanken** Rechnung, indem sie bereits frühzeitig eine Reaktion auf drohende Leistungshindernisse zulässt; sie sorgt zum anderen für eine ausgeglichene **Wahrung der Interessen beider Parteien:** Der Gläubiger soll seine Dispositionsfreiheit rasch zurückgewinnen,[14] jedoch nicht ohne dass der Schuldner die Chance hat, seine Leistungsbereitschaft unter Beweis zu stellen.

5   Das Aufhebungsrecht stellt eine **Wahlmöglichkeit** dar und entspricht damit der allgemeinen Struktur des CISG. Es gehört in den Rahmen der selbstverantwortlichen Gestaltung des Vertrages durch die Parteien. Zu der Frage, wie weit hierbei den Interessen auch der vertragsgefährdenden Partei Rechnung zu tragen ist, vgl. unten Rn. 17 ff.[15]

2. Rechtsvergleich

6   Die Wurzeln des Art. 72 stammen aus dem anglo-amerikanischen Recht. Sie haben dort als **anticipatory breach,**[16] als Sonderform des allgemeinen breach of contract,[17] ihre frühe Ausprägung gefunden. *Ernst Rabel* hat sie als wertvolle Ergänzung der allgemeinen Regeln des Vertragsbruchs von daher übernehmen können.[18]

7   Das französische Recht gewährt für den Fall, dass der Schuldner bei Fälligkeit nicht erfüllt, lediglich ein Zurückbehaltungsrecht. Es sieht jedoch kein Recht zur Vertragsaufhebung bei vorweggenommener Vertragsverletzung vor,[19] ebenso wenig wie das Schweizer

---

[10] O. R., S. 431, Nr. 96; *Schlechtriem,* Einheitliches UN-Kaufrecht, S. 88 f.; *Strub,* 38 Int'l & Comp. L. Q. (1989), 475, 493.

[11] O. R., S. 431, Nr. 96.

[12] *Schlechtriem,* Einheitliches UN-Kaufrecht, S. 88 f. Näher dazu unten Rn. 23 f.

[13] So ausdrücklich BGH, 15.2.1995, CISG-online 149 = NJW 1995, 2101, 2102; vgl. in der Literatur *Bamberger/Roth/Saenger,* Art. 72, Rn. 2; *Achilles,* Art. 72, Rn. 1; MünchKommHGB/*Mankowski,* Art. 72, Rn. 3; MünchKomm/*P. Huber,* Art. 72, Rn. 3.

[14] *Leser,* Lösung vom Vertrag, S. 374 f.; *ders.,* Vertragsaufhebung im Einheitlichen Kaufgesetz, S. 6; *Strub,* 38 Int'l & Comp. L. Q. (1989), 475, 480: „to avoid having to carry an accounting loss for an excessive amount of time"; vgl. auch *Carter/Phang/Phang,* 15 J. Cont. L. (1999), 100, 107 ff. (allgemein zu Effizienzaspekten bei vorzeitigem Vertragsbruch).

[15] Kritisch zur angeblich verunsichernden Wirkung des Behelfs *Kahn,* Rev. int. dr. comp. (1981), 951, 983; *Plantard,* J. D. I. (1988), 311, 358; *Strub,* 38 Int'l & Comp. L. Q. (1989), 475, 493 ff.

[16] *Chesire/Fifoot/Furmston,* S. 682 f.; *Treitel,* Remedies for Breach, S. 379 ff., Nr. 279; *Chitty* On Contracts, Vol. I, Rn. 24-021 ff. Dazu auch *Stoll,* RabelsZ 52 (1988), 617, 620 ff.; *Leser,* Erfüllungsweigerung, S. 651 f. mit Beispielen. Vgl. zum amerikanischen Recht § 2–610 UCC, dessen Legaldefinition der „anticipatory repudiation" unter (2) laut Autorenkommentar auf § 250 Restatement of the Law 2d, Contracts 2d, 1981, zurückgeht; *Corbin,* §§ 959–989 (S. 851–969); *Williston,* Band 11, § 1337 (S. 185–189); *Strub,* 38 Int'l & Comp. L. Q. (1989), 475, 478–484.

[17] *Treitel,* Remedies for Breach, S. 379 ff., Nr. 279.

[18] *Rabel,* Recht des Warenkaufs, Bd. 1, § 34 II 3, S. 273 f.

[19] Vgl. Artt. 1612 f., 1653 Cc.

Recht[20] oder das Vertragsrecht der iberoamerikanischen Länder[21]. Auch das deutsche Recht kannte lange Zeit keine ausdrückliche Regelung des antizipierten Vertragsbruchs, fand aber über den Umweg der positiven Vertragsverletzung[22] zu befriedigenden praktischen Lösungen.[23] Seit dem Schuldrechtsmodernisierungsgesetz vom 26.11.2001 trifft § 323 IV BGB für den antizipierten Vertragsbruch die offenkundig an Art. 72 orientierte Regelung, dass bereits vor Fälligkeit vom Vertrag zurückgetreten werden kann, wenn offensichtlich ist, dass die Rücktrittsvoraussetzungen eintreten werden.[24]

Artt. 9:304, 8:105 PECL sowie Artt. 7.3.3 f. PICC weisen Ähnlichkeiten zu Art. 72 auf, weichen aber insofern davon ab, als sie nicht zwischen der Erfüllungsverweigerung (Art. 72 III) und sonstigem künftigem wesentlichen Vertragsbruch (Art. 72 I) unterscheiden. Auch sehen Artt. 7.3.4 PICC, 8:105 PECL keine Anzeigepflicht des Gläubigers vor, die Art. 72 II entsprechen würde; der Gläubiger darf vom Schuldner ausreichende Sicherstellung verlangen, ist dazu jedoch nicht verpflichtet, sondern kann den Vertrag auch direkt aufheben.[25] Art. 8:105 PECL verlangt explizit, dass der Gläubiger, der keine ausreichende Sicherheit erhalten hat, die Vertragsaufhebung „without delay" erklärt; die Parallelbestimmungen von CISG und PICC enthalten keine vergleichbare ausdrückliche Frist.[26] Der CESL-Entwurf[27] und der DCFR[28] unterscheiden bloss terminologisch, jedoch nicht inhaltlich zwischen der ‚Erklärung' und ‚anderweitigen' Gründen für eine offensichtliche künftige Nichterfüllung; eine Anzeigepflicht besteht nicht, ebenso wenig wie die Pflicht, dem Schuldner die Möglichkeit des Beibringens von Sicherheiten einzuräumen.[29]

3. Differenzierung zwischen objektiven und im Verhalten des Schuldners liegenden Gründen

Es ist zwischen der endgültigen Erfüllungsverweigerung (Vertragsaufsage) einerseits **(Art. 72 III)** und der sonstigen künftigen wesentlichen Vertragsverletzung **(Art. 72 I)** zu unterscheiden.[30] Die endgültige Erfüllungsverweigerung in Art. 72 III folgt insofern eigenen Regeln, als sie keiner Anzeige nach Art. 72 II bedarf.

4. Abgrenzung zu anderen Behelfen

Art. 71 beruht auf ähnlicher Grundlage, nämlich der sich abzeichnenden künftigen Vertragsverletzung, setzt aber keine wesentliche Vertragsverletzung i. S. d. Art. 25 voraus. Entsprechend gewährt er nur die vorläufigen Behelfe des Zurückbehaltungs- und Anhalterechts.[31] Art. 72 greift dann, wenn sich die Situation derart verschärft, dass bei Fälligkeit mit einer wesentlichen Vertragsverletzung zu rechnen ist.[32] Die beiden Vorschriften können auch gleichzeitig angewandt werden; dies wird sich in der Regel sogar empfehlen. Es

---

[20] Der einzige Rechtsbehelf vor Fälligkeit ist die Leistungsverweigerungseinrede in Art. 82 OR; für den antizipierten Vertragsbruch muss ansonsten grunds. über die Regeln des Schuldnerverzugs vorgegangen werden, vgl. im Einzelnen *Schwenzer*, OR AT, Rn. 66.19.
[21] Vgl. dazu *Schwenzer/E. Muñoz/E. Muñoz*, Sec Comp Arts. 71–73, Rn. 12.
[22] *Stoll*, RabelsZ 52 (1988), 617, 619: „Verlegenheitskategorie der positiven Vertragsverletzung".
[23] Vgl. *Leser*, Erfüllungsweigerung, S. 651 f.
[24] Für einen weitergehenden internationalen Rechtsvergleich vgl. *Schwenzer/Hachem/Kee*, Rn. 47.136 ff.
[25] Für eine Gegenüberstellung von Art. 72 und Artt. 7.3.3 f. PICC, Artt. 9:304, 8:105 PECL vgl. *Eiselen*, Anticipatory breach, S. 207 ff., 461 ff.; *Liu*, Suspension, sub. 2.3, 2.4.; *Saidov*, Unif. dr. Rev. 2006, 795 ff. (zu Artt. 7.3.3 f. PICC).
[26] Vgl. aber zur Sinnhaftigkeit, in Art. 72 eine angemessene Ausschlussfrist hineinzulesen, unten Rn. 38.
[27] Vgl. Artt. 116, 136 CESL-Entwurf.
[28] Vgl. Art. III.–3:504 DCFR.
[29] Wie die PICC und die PECL sieht Art. III.–3:505 DCFR das Recht des Gläubigers vor, Sicherheiten zu verlangen, wobei der Gläubiger, anders als nach Art. 72 II CISG, dazu nicht verpflichtet ist. Bei Nichtstellen innerhalb angemessener Zeit besteht, wie nach PICC und PCL, das Recht zur Vertragsaufhebung.
[30] Vgl. Sekretariatskommentar, Art. 72, Anm. 2.; *Witz/Salger/Lorenz/Lorenz*, Art. 72, Rn. 2.
[31] Vgl. auch ICC, 8786/1997, CISG-online 749 = ICC Ct. Bull. 2000, 70 ff.; *Gabriel*, Contracts, S. 217.
[32] Zu den unterschiedlichen Prognosemassstäben vgl. *Fountoulakis*, Art. 71, Rn. 23, hinten Rn. 14 ff. und unten Art. 73 Rn. 21.

Art. 72 11–12a Teil III. Kapitel V. Pflichten des Verkäufers und des Käufers. Abschnitt I

müssen dann allerdings die Voraussetzungen beider Tatbestände erfüllt sein, was vor allem für die Anzeigepflichten relevant ist, die jeweils unterschiedliche Zwecke verfolgen.[33] Zur Abgrenzung von Artt. 72 und 73 II siehe bei Art. 73 Rn. 28.

III. Aufhebungsrecht bei künftiger wesentlicher Vertragsverletzung, Art. 72 I

1. Aufhebungsvoraussetzungen

11 Eine wirksame Vertragsaufsage unter Art. 72 I setzt Folgendes voraus: Es muss 1) vor Fälligkeit offensichtlich sein, dass 2) die andere Partei eine wesentliche Vertragsverletzung begehen wird. Die vertragstreue Partei muss dann, 3) sofern zeitlich zumutbar, 4) dem Schuldner in angemessener Weise anzeigen, dass sie den Vertrag aufheben will. 5) Stellt der Schuldner daraufhin keine ausreichende Sicherheit, darf die vertragstreue Partei 6) die Vertragsaufhebung erklären.

2. Künftige wesentliche Vertragsverletzung

12 Die antizipierte wesentliche Vertragsverletzung ist die Grundvoraussetzung von Art. 72; sie ist insofern antizipiert, als die Leistung des Schuldners noch nicht fällig ist. Es müssen Umstände vorliegen, die die künftige Vertragsverletzung bereits jetzt erwarten lassen. Für die Wesentlichkeit der Vertragsverletzung gilt der **Massstab von Art. 25**.[34] Die künftige Vertragsverletzung muss so gewichtig sein, dass dem Gläubiger – für den Schuldner erkennbar – im Wesentlichen entgehen wird, was er nach dem Vertrag hätte erwarten dürfen. Es muss also eine Vertragsverletzung drohen, die, bei ihrem Eintritt nach Artt. 49 bzw. 64 zur Vertragsaufhebung berechtigen würde. Die zu diesen Vorschriften entwickelten Fallgruppen[35] sind auch für Art. 72 I heranzuziehen.

12a Die **Rechtsprechung** hat eine künftige wesentliche Vertragsverletzung des Verkäufers insbesondere bejaht bei Zusendung von nichtvertragsgemässen Plänen, die auf seine Unfähigkeit schliessen liessen, vertragskonforme Ware zu produzieren und zu liefern;[36] bei Lieferung mangelhafter Ware in der Vergangenheit, die die Wesentlichkeitsschwelle von Art. 25 erreichte und die, insbesondere weil der Verkäufer die Bezugsquelle seitdem nicht geändert hatte, darauf schliessen liess, dass auch künftige Lieferungen wesentlich mangelhaft sein würden.[37] Auf Seiten des Käufers wurde eine künftige wesentliche Vertragsverletzung bejaht bei Nichtbezahlen früherer Lieferungen,[38] bei Nichteröffnen eines Akkreditivs trotz anderslautender Vereinbarung und wiederholter Mahnung seitens des Verkäufers[39] und bei Ignorieren wiederholter Aufforderungen des Verkäufers, fehlerhafte Angaben im Akkreditiv zu ergänzen bzw. zu korrigieren.

---

[33] Dazu Rn. 17 ff.
[34] *Downs Investments Pty Ltd v. Perjawa Steel SDN BHD*, Supreme Court of Queensland, 17.11.2000, CISG-online 587=859, Rn. 62; *Magellan International v. Salzgitter Handel*, U. S. Dist. Ct. (N. D. Ill.), 7.12.1999, CISG-online 439; *Bianca/Bonell/Bennett*, Art. 25, Anm. 2.2.; *Enderlein/Maskow/Strohbach*, Art. 25, Anm. 2.; *Staudinger/Magnus*, Art. 72, Rn. 6; MünchKommHGB/*Mankowski*, Art. 72, Rn. 3; MünchKomm/*P. Huber*, Art. 72, Rn. 2; *Witz/Salger/Lorenz/Lorenz*, Art. 72, Rn. 9; *Kröll u. a./Saidov*, Art. 72, Rn. 2. Eine grundlegende Vertragsstörung wird auch in den nationalen Rechtsordnungen, die die Vertragsaufhebung bei antizipiertem Vertragsbruch kennen, vorausgesetzt, vgl. *Schwenzer/Hachem/Kee*, Rn. 47.143.
[35] Vgl. oben *Müller-Chen*, Art. 49 Rn. 4 ff.; *Mohs*, Art. 64 Rn. 5 ff.
[36] Tribunal of International Commercial Arbitration at the Russian Federation Chamber of Commerce and Industry, 25.4.1995, CISG-online 206=367.
[37] Vgl. Netherlands Arbitration Institute, 15.10.2002, CISG-online 740; vgl. Auch AppGer Helsinki, 30.6.1998, CISG-online 1304 (allerdings in Anwendung von Art. 73 II).
[38] OLG Düsseldorf, 14.1.1994, CISG-online 119.
[39] *Downs Investments Pty Ltd v. Perjawa Steel SDN BHD*, Supreme Court of Queensland, 17.11.2000, CISG-online 587 = 859, Rn. 62; vgl. auch LG Kassel, 21.9.1995, CISG-online 192, wo die künftige wesentliche Vertragsverletzung in casu verneint wurde.

Anders als Art. 71 I zählt Art. 72 I die Gründe für die künftige Vertragsverletzung nicht **13** auf. Man wird hier die in Art. 71 I lit. a) und I lit. b) erwähnten Gründe bei Art. 72 I als **Orientierungshilfe** heranziehen dürfen, da sie die Störungsfälle wohl umfassend abdecken.[40] Jedoch ist zu berücksichtigen, dass theoretisch Konstellationen möglich bleiben, in denen die künftige Verletzung „eines wesentlichen Teils der Pflichten" (Art. 71 I) keine künftige wesentliche Vertragsverletzung i. S. v. Artt. 72 I, 25 darstellt.[41] Zu denken ist etwa daran, dass der Schuldner einem vereinbarten Verbot zuwiderzuhandeln droht, vertrauliches Material zu kopieren, und dies zwar den Gläubiger noch nicht dessen berauben würde, was er unter dem Vertrag erwarten dürfte, das Unterlassen der Reproduktion aber doch klarer und berechtigter Bestandteil der Vertragsvereinbarung war.[42] Sowohl unter Art. 71 I lit. a) und I lit. b) als auch unter Art. 72 I fallen hingegen Fälle wie der Verlust von Produktionsstätten (Krieg, Brand), Einschränkungen des Zahlungsverkehrs (Devisenbestimmungen), fehlende Patente, das Verbot oder der Ausfall von Rohstoffen, Streik, Insolvenz des Schuldners[43] und ähnliche Umstände.[44] Auf ein Vertretenmüssen kommt es nicht an.[45]

3. Prognose

Ob sich der Gläubiger nach Art. 72 I vorzeitig vom Vertrag lösen kann, hängt davon ab, **14** wie wahrscheinlich die erwartete Störung zur Zeit der Fälligkeit eintreten oder andauern wird. Die Formulierung in Art. 72 I, **„Offensichtlichsein"** („clear", „manifeste"), umfasst nicht nur die Kenntnis oder Kenntniserlangung der für die Störung erheblichen Umstände, sondern stellt zugleich an den Grad der Wahrscheinlichkeit des Eintretens hohe Anforderungen.[46]

Eine genaue Festlegung des Grades der Wahrscheinlichkeit ist mit dem auslegungsbedürf- **15** tigen Begriff des „Offensichtlichseins" aber nicht erreicht. Auch wenn man keine mit an Sicherheit grenzende Wahrscheinlichkeit fordern darf, ist doch eine **sehr hohe nahe liegende Wahrscheinlichkeit** gemeint, die allgemein einleuchtet.[47] Betrachtet man die

---

[40] So auch *Staudinger/Magnus*, Art. 72, Rn. 11; MünchKomm/*P. Huber*, Art. 72, Rn. 2.

[41] Dies gilt insbesondere vor dem Hintergrund, dass ein ägyptischer Vorschlag, das Aussetzungsrecht in Art. 71 I von einer „künftigen wesentlichen Vertragsverletzung" abhängig zu machen, abgelehnt wurde, dazu *Schlechtriem*, Uniform Sales Law, S. 93; für die hier hervorgehobene Unterscheidung auch *Strub*, 38 Int'l & Comp. L. Q. (1989), 475, 494; *Schlechtriem*, Internationales UN-Kaufrecht, Rn. 263.

[42] Vgl. den Sachverhalt in Arbitration Institute of the Stockholm Chamber of Commerce, 5.4.2007, CISG-online 1521. Vgl. für weitere mögliche Fälle *Schlechtriem*, Internationales UN-Kaufrecht, Rn. 263.

[43] Vgl. *Roder Zelt- und Hallenkonstruktionen GmbH v. Rosedown Park Pty Ltd and Reginald R Eustace*, FCA (Adelaide, SA), 28.4.1995, CISG-online 218 = 1995 Federal Court Reports (Australia), 216 (wo die drohende Insolvenz des Schuldners jedoch fälschlicherweise nicht als Fall von Art. 72(1), sondern von Art. 25 behandelt wurde, dazu krit. *Lubbe*, RabelsZ 68 (2004), 444, 463 f.); *Zeller*, CISG in Austriaslasia, S. 293, 314.

[44] Dazu oben *Fountoulakis*, Art. 71 Rn. 15. Vgl. auch die im Sekretariatskommentar, Art. 72, Anm. 2., sowie bei *Audit*, Vente Internationale, Anm. 165.; *Achilles*, Art. 72, Rn. 2, und *Neumayer/Ming*, Art. 72, Anm. 2., genannten Beispiele.

[45] Die Vorschrift des Art. 79 ist alleine in Hinsicht auf Schadensersatz von Bedeutung, wie aus Abs. 5 ausdrücklich hervorgeht. Vgl. auch *Hellner*, UN Convention, S. 81.

[46] Vgl. *Bianca/Bonell/Bennett*, Art. 72, Anm. 2.2.; *Plantard*, J. D. I. (1988), 311, 357; *Nicholas*, L. Q. R. (1989), 201, 233; *Fountoulakis*, ERA Forum (2011) 12:7, 17; *P. Huber/Mullis/P. Huber*, S. 345 („very high probability"). Siehe zur Stufung des Grades der Wahrscheinlichkeit insgesamt Art. 73 Rn. 21.

[47] *Bianca/Bonell/Bennett*, Art. 72, Anm. 2.2.; *Soergel/Lüderitz/Dettmeier*, Art. 72, Rn. 6; *Schlechtriem*, Internationales UN-Kaufrecht, Rn. 270 („mit einem hohen Grad an Wahrscheinlichkeit zu erwarten"); *Kröll u. a./Saidov*, Art. 72, Rn. 7; *Honsell/Brunner/Hurni*, Art. 72, Rn. 4. Ebenso in der Rechtsprechung LG Berlin, 30.9.1992, CISG-online 70 (eine an Sicherheit grenzende Wahrscheinlichkeit sei nicht erforderlich); LG Krefeld, 28.4.1993, CISG-online 101 (bestätigt durch OLG Düsseldorf, 14.1.1994, CISG-online 119). Strenger *Staudinger/Magnus*, Art. 72, Rn. 9 („nahezu sicher") sowie *Heuzé*, Anm. 430., nach dem es notwendig ist „que la commission de la contravention apparaisse d'ores et déjà comme inéluctible"; *Achilles*, Art. 72, Rn. 2, sowie MünchKomm/*P. Huber*, Art. 72, Rn. 7: „Die Vertragsverletzung [muss] für einen objektiven Beobachter klar auf der Hand liegen"; *Bamberger/Roth/Saenger*, Art. 72, Rn. 4 („besonders hohe Anforderungen"); *Gabriel*, Contracts. S. 216 („very high probability"); *Lookofsky*, Understanding the CISG, § 6.11, S. 124 („very high degree of probability"); MünchKommHGB/*Mankowski*, Art. 72, Rn. 5 („nahezu sicher"); *Verweyen/Foerster/Toufar*, S. 216 („überwiegend wahrscheinlich, aber nicht gewiss"). Vgl. auch § 2–610 (2) UCC zur „anticipatory repudiation" in der – allerdings bisher nicht umgesetzten – Fassung von 2003: „Repudiation includes

verwandten Formulierungen für die Prognose in Artt. 71 I und 73 II, liegen die Anforderungen für die Wahrscheinlichkeit hier am höchsten.[48] Die anzulegenden objektiven Massstäbe entsprechen denen der vernünftigen Person.[49]

16 Der Wortlaut von Art. 72 I verlangt im Unterschied zu Art. 71 I nicht ausdrücklich, dass sich die künftige Vertragsverletzung erst nach Vertragsschluss herausstellt. Allerdings muss in den Fällen, in denen bereits vor Vertragsschluss offensichtlich war, dass der Schuldner eine wesentliche Vertragsverletzung begehen würde, das Aufhebungsrecht nach Art. 72 I versagt werden.[50] Dies ergibt sich aus den Artt. 80, 77 zugrundeliegenden Rechtsgedanken, wonach die vertragstreue Partei insoweit nicht zu schützen ist, als sie für die Vertragsstörung mitverantwortlich ist. Insofern ist unter Art. 72 I die **vertragliche Risikenverteilung** massgeblich: Wer einen Vertrag bewusst spekulativ abschliesst, kann ihn nicht vorzeitig aufheben, wenn sich nach Vertragsschluss genau die in Kauf genommenen Risiken realisieren.[51]

IV. Anzeigepflicht, Art. 72 II

1. Ratio

17 Auch wenn eine offensichtliche künftige wesentliche Vertragsverletzung droht, kann der Vertrag nicht sogleich aufgehoben werden; vielmehr ist der Schuldner grundsätzlich davon zu unterrichten, dass von dem Aufhebungsrecht Gebrauch gemacht werden soll. Dadurch soll der Schuldner die Möglichkeit haben, Zweifel an seiner Vertragstreue durch das Stellen ausreichender Sicherheiten auszuräumen.[52] Art. 72 II ist somit ein Instrument „**forcierter Kommunikation**", dient der Schaffung von Klarheit und verhindert, dass sich der Gläubiger voreilig vom Vertrag löst. Vermag der Schuldner Gewähr zu leisten, wird dadurch das Aufhebungsrecht für den vertragstreuen Teil entbehrlich.

18 Aus dem Normzweck von Art. 72 II ergibt sich, dass die **Anzeigepflicht nur für die Fälle des Art. 72 I,** nicht jedoch für die Erfüllungsverweigerung nach Art. 72 III gilt: Dem Schuldner, der erklärt, er werde nicht erfüllen, fehlt der Wille zur Durchführung des Vertrags, weshalb ihm auch keine Chance eingeräumt zu werden braucht, die Vertragsaufhebung doch noch zu verhindern.[53]

2. Konstitutive Wirkung

19 Anders als die Anzeige nach Art. 71 III ist die Anzeige gemäss Art. 72 II **Voraussetzung** für die wirksame Aufhebung des Vertrags.[54] Bleibt sie aus, obwohl sie unter den konkreten

---

language that a reasonable person would interpret to mean that the other party will not or cannot make a performance still due under the contract or voluntary, affirmative conduct that would appear to a reasonable person to make a future performance by the other party impossible."

[48] *Witz/Salger/Lorenz/Lorenz,* Art. 72, Rn. 7; *Staudinger/Magnus,* Art. 72, Rn. 9; *Soergel/Lüderitz/Dettmeier,* Art. 72, Rn. 6; *Ferrari u. a./Saenger,* Internationales Vertragsrecht, Art. 72, Rn. 4; *Audit,* Vente internationale, Anm. 165.; *Reinhart,* Art. 72, Rn. 2; *Enderlein/Maskow/Strohbach,* Art. 71, Anm. 2. und Art. 72, Anm. 1.; *Bamberger/Roth/Saenger,* Art. 72, Rn. 4. Vgl. dazu Art. 73 Rn. 21. Eine Differenzierung hinsichtlich Artt. 71 und 72 verneinen dagegen *Herber/Czerwenka,* Art. 72, Rn. 2.

[49] Grundgedanke des Art. 8 II. Vgl. etwa *van der Velden,* Main Items, S. 59, und auch Art. 71 Rn. 22.

[50] Vgl. MünchKomm/*P. Huber,* Art. 72, Rn. 4.

[51] Vgl. MünchKommHGB/*Mankowski,* Art. 72, Rn. 6, der zur Lösung solcher risikobehafteter Geschäfte ein vertraglich vereinbartes Lösungsrecht vorschlägt.

[52] Ähnl. *Strub,* 38 Int'l & Comp. L. Q. (1989), 475, 498; *Saidov,* Unif. dr. Rev. 2006, 795, 813. Über YB V (1974), S. 41, Nr. 133, hinaus finden sich in den Beratungen (vgl. etwa O. R., S. 420 ff.) keine weiteren Einzelheiten zur Sicherheitsleistung.

[53] *Schlechtriem,* Internationales UN-Kaufrecht, Rn. 273.

[54] So auch *Neumayer/Ming,* Art. 72, Anm. 6.; *Reinhart,* Art. 72, Rn. 3; *Bamberger/Roth/Saenger,* Art. 72, Rn. 6; *Ensthaler/Achilles,* GK-HGB, Art. 72, Rn. 6; *Ferrari u. a./Saenger,* Internationales Vertragsrecht, Art. 72, Rn. 6; *Schlechtriem/Witz,* Convention de Vienne, Rn. 353; unklar ist insoweit der Sekretariatskommentar,

Gegebenheiten zeitlich zumutbar gewesen wäre,[55] ist eine wegen Art. 72 I erklärte Vertragsaufhebung unwirksam, das heisst der Vertrag besteht, sofern die andere Partei daran festhält, fort.[56] Dem Schuldner steht es allerdings frei, sich mit der zu Unrecht erklärten Vertragsaufhebung einverstanden zu erklären; in diesem Falle liegt eine einverständliche Vertragsaufhebung vor.

Der Gegenmeinung,[57] die bei Unterlassen der Anzeige nur Schadensersatzansprüche zusprechen und die Theorie von der Unwirksamkeit der Aufhebung deutscher Dogmatik zuschreiben will,[58] ist entgegenzuhalten, dass das Übereinkommen immer von der Unwirksamkeit der Aufhebung ausgeht, wenn die Voraussetzungen dafür nicht gegeben sind.[59] Die hier vertretene Auffassung entspricht also durchaus „**konventionsautonomer Auslegung**" (Art. 7 I). Die einzige entscheidende Frage in diesem Zusammenhang ist, ob in Art. 72 II eine Aufhebungsvoraussetzung zu erblicken ist, deren Nichtvorliegen das Aufhebungsrecht entfallen lässt, oder aber eine blosse Formalität, deren Missachtung lediglich Schadensersatzansprüche ausgelöst[60] – und diese Frage ist im erstgenannten Sinne zu entscheiden: Es widerspräche dem Zweck von Art. 72 II, nämlich dem Schuldner die Chance zur Aufrechterhaltung des Vertrags zu gewähren, wenn die Aufhebung trotz unterbliebener Anzeige wirksam wäre, obwohl dem Schuldner damit genau diese Chance genommen würde. So würde gleichzeitig der Mechanismus ausgehebelt, der in der Literatur als innovativste und wirtschaftlich sinnvollste Entwicklung des Vertragsrechts des 20. Jahrhunderts[61] bezeichnet worden ist, nämlich das Vermeiden einer Vertragsaufhebung durch Kooperation und vorläufiges Zufriedenstellen des Vertragspartners. Die hier vertretene Auffassung entspricht nicht zuletzt auch dem allgemeinen Grundsatz des „favor validitatis", der von der möglichst weitgehenden Aufrechterhaltung des Vertrags ausgeht.[62]

3. Form und Frist der Anzeige

Hinsichtlich der Form gilt für die Anzeige – wie bei Art. 71 III – Art. 27.[63] Eine Frist für die Anzeige nach Art. 72 II ist im CISG nicht vorgesehen. Dies wäre beim antizipierten Vertragsbruch auch sinnwidrig, da es der vertragstreuen Partei stets unbenommen bleiben muss, die Fälligkeit der vom anderen Teil zu erbringenden Leistung abzuwarten und erst dann gegebenenfalls die normalen Behelfe des Übereinkommens geltend zu machen. Es besteht mit anderen Worten **grundsätzlich keine Pflicht zur vorzeitigen Vertragsaufhebung**,[64] doch reduziert sich ein allfälliger Schadensersatzanspruch des Gläubigers,

---

Art. 72, Anm. 2.: zwar sei die Vertragsaufhebung bei Nichtvorliegen der Voraussetzungen „void", doch bezieht sich das wohl nicht konkret auf das Unterlassen der Anzeige.

[55] Dazu Rn. 23 f.
[56] Vgl. auch unten Rn. 40.
[57] *Enderlein/Maskow/Strohbach*, Art. 72, Anm. 6. und 7.; *Soergel/Lüderitz/Dettmeier*, Art. 72, Rn. 14; *Witz/Salger/Lorenz/Lorenz*, Art. 72, Rn. 18; *Staudinger/Magnus*, Art. 72, Rn. 28; *MünchKomm/P. Huber*, Art. 72, Rn. 6, 16; *Honsell/Brunner/Hurni*, Art. 71, Rn. 9; wohl auch CIETAC, 31.12.1996, CISG-online 1524, Erw. 5; *Herber/Czerwenka*, Art. 72, Rn. 4 f.; *Piltz*, Internationales Kaufrecht, Rn. 5–424, 5–461; *Verweyen/Foerster/Toufar*, S. 216.
[58] So insbesondere *Witz/Salger/Lorenz/Lorenz*, Art. 72, Rn. 18.
[59] Vgl. oben *Müller-Chen*, Art. 49 Rn. 44 ff.
[60] Die Anzeigepflicht des Art. 71 III stellt eine solche Formalität dar, vgl. dazu oben *Fountoulakis*, Art. 71 Rn. 30.
[61] *Robertson*, 38 Drake Law Review (1988-89) 305, 353.
[62] Vgl. auch *Saidov*, Unif. dr. Rev. 2006, 795, 810 f.
[63] Es handelt sich um eine dort ausdrücklich genannte Anzeige. Siehe auch *Enderlein/Maskow/Strohbach*, Art. 27, Anm. 7.; *Neumayer/Ming*, Art. 72, Anm. 6.; *Bamberger/Roth/Saenger*, Art. 72, Rn. 6; *MünchKomm/P. Huber*, Art. 72, Rn. 15; *Noussias*, Zugangsbedürftigkeit von Mitteilungen, S. 146.
[64] *Bridge*, 25 J. L. & Com. (2005-06), 405, 416 f.; *MünchKomm/P. Huber*, Art. 72, Rn. 8; *Achilles*, Rn. 3; *Staudinger/Magnus*, Art. 72, Rn. 16; *MünchKomm/Mankowski*, Art. 72, Rn. 10; *Soergel/Lüderitz/Dettmeier*, Art. 72, Rn. 9; vgl. auch § 2–610 UCC, der der vertragstreuen Partei alle Optionen offenhält (Vorgehen wegen Vertragsbruchs, Zurückhalten der eigenen Leistung, Abwarten der Erfüllung).

wenn er zur Schadensminderung erforderliche Schritte unterlässt.[65] Allerdings wird in **Artt. 77, 80** der allgemeine Rechtsgedanke geäussert, dass der vertragstreuen Partei, die sehenden Auges eine Vertragsverletzung nicht verhindert bzw. deren Folgen nicht einzudämmen versucht, die ihr eigentlich zustehenden **Rechtsbehelfe beschnitten werden oder wegfallen** können. Daraus kann sich im Rahmen von Art. 72 II die Pflicht des Gläubigers ergeben, die Situation durch das Setzen einer Anzeige möglichst rasch zu klären. Dies wird insbesondere der Fall sein bei Waren mit volatilen Marktpreisen sowie in Situationen, in denen es bis zur Fälligkeit der schuldnerischen Leistung noch lange hin ist.[66]

4. Substantiierungspflicht

22   Da die Anzeige dem Schuldner die Möglichkeit einräumen soll, ausreichende Sicherheiten zu stellen, muss sie den **Anlass der Aufhebung** und die **Ursache** der befürchteten wesentlichen Vertragsverletzung in hinreichender Deutlichkeit nennen.[67] Auf die Möglichkeit, dass der Schuldner die Vertragsaufhebung durch die Stellung von Sicherheiten abwenden kann, muss der Gläubiger in der Anzeige allerdings nicht hinweisen; „der Gläubiger ist eben bei gleich informierten Unternehmen nicht cheapest information provider".[68]

5. Zumutbarkeit der Anzeige

23   Die deutsche Fassung verlangt eine Anzeige nur, „wenn es die Zeit erlaubt und es nach den Umständen vernünftig ist". Es handelt sich hierbei um eine missglückte Übersetzung der Originalfassungen, die im Englischen von „**if time allows,** the party intending to declare the contract avoided must give reasonable notice" und im Französischen von „**si elle dispose du temps nécessaire,** la partie qui a l'intention de déclarer le contrat résolu doit le notifier à l'autre partie dans des conditions raisonnables" sprechen. In der deutschsprachigen Literatur wird auf Grundlage der deutschen Übersetzung darum gefochten, ob kumulativ ein Mangel an Zeit und sonstige Umstände, die eine Anzeige als unvernünftig erscheinen lassen, bestehen müssen, damit die Anzeigepflicht entfällt,[69] oder ob es einzig auf das Zeitelement ankommt,[70] also ein Mangel an Zeit allein von der Anzeigepflicht entbindet. Der Meinungsstreit wird allerdings auf falscher Grundlage ausgetragen, da es für die Auslegung des Übereinkommens einzig auf die verbindlichen Fassungen ankommt[71] – und diese sind hinreichend deutlich: Die Anzeige steht einzig unter dem Vorbehalt, dass die zeitlichen Umstände eine solche zulassen. Das Attribut „reasonable", im Deutschen mit „vernünftig" übersetzt, bezieht sich demgegenüber auf die Anzeige selbst. Diese muss „reasonable" sein, und das kann nur dahingehend verstanden werden, dass sie ihren Zweck erfüllen muss, nämlich es dem Schuldner „zu ermöglichen, für die Erfüllung [seiner] Pflichten ausreichende Gewähr zu geben" (Art. 72 II). Die Anzeige hat dementsprechend genügend substantiiert zu sein und, falls sie für das Stellen von Sicherheiten eine Frist setzt, eine solche von angemessener Dauer vorzusehen (zu beiden Erfordernissen s. Rn. 22 bzw. 26). Ihren Zweck erfüllen kann eine Anzeige aber auch dann nicht, wenn die Anzeige als Warnung zwecklos erscheint, weil Abhilfe oder Sicherheitsstellung nicht (rechtzeitig) erwartet werden kön-

---

[65] Vgl. auch § 2–610 (a) UCC: Die Erfüllung soll nur für eine „commercially reasonable time" abgewartet werden. Eine Nichtbeachtung dieses Erfordernisses führt nach Autorenkommentar (1) dazu, dass dadurch entstandene vermeidbare Schäden nicht ersetzt werden.
[66] Vgl. *Schwenzer,* Art. 77 Rn. 3; wie hier bereits die englische Fassung in der dritten Auflage, Schlechtriem/Schwenzer/Fountoulakis, CISG Commentary, Art. 72, Rn. 20; anders noch die Vorauflage.
[67] *Staudinger/Magnus,* Art. 72, Rn. 24; *Bamberger/Roth/Saenger,* Art. 72, Rn. 5; *Ferrari u. a./Saenger,* Internationales Vertragsrecht, Art. 72, Rn. 5; MünchKommHGB/*Mankowski,* Art. 72, Rn. 14; *Honsell/Brunner/Hurni,* Art. 72, Rn. 8.
[68] MünchKommHGB/*Mankowski,* Art. 72, Rn. 14.
[69] So die 4. Auflage („Art. 72 II [knüpft] die Anzeigepflicht an zwei zusätzliche Voraussetzungen.").
[70] *Staudinger/Magnus,* Art. 72, Rn. 21; *Honsell/Schnyder/Straub* (Vorauflage), Art. 72, Rn. 45; MünchKommHGB/*Mankowski,* Art. 72, Rn. 15.
[71] Vgl. oben *Ferrari,* Art. 7 Rn. 31.

nen, etwa bei besonders kurzen Lieferfristen oder sehr rapiden Preisveränderungen. Zwecklos ist eine Anzeige ferner, wenn Sicherheiten den drohenden Vertragsbruch nicht ausgleichen können, wenn durch Zeitablauf eine Leistung ihren Charakter verändert (Saisongeschäft) oder anderweitige sofortige Deckung unumgänglich erscheint.[72]

Angesichts der Vielzahl der Gründe, die eine Anzeige abgesehen vom Zeitmoment als „unreasonable" erscheinen lassen können, ist der oben geschilderte Gegensatz in der Literatur zu recht als „unnötig zugespitzt"[73] bezeichnet worden, denn beide Ansichten berücksichtigen über das Zeitelement hinaus noch weitere Kriterien, unterscheiden sich also im Ergebnis kaum voneinander. Um jedoch das Anzeigeerfordernis nicht auszuhebeln, ist ein **strenger Beurteilungsmassstab** anzulegen. Da der Gläubiger praktisch immer irgendeinen Grund dafür anzugeben vermögen wird, weshalb er die Anzeige in concreto unterliess,[74] besteht ein hohes Missbrauchspotential, das einzig dadurch kontrolliert werden kann, dass bei der Beurteilung (Art. 8 II) das Schwergewicht auf das Zeitelement gelegt wird („if time allows") und für die Behauptung des Gläubigers, eine Anzeige wäre zwecklos („unreasonable") gewesen, eine stringente Substantiierung verlangt wird. 24

Ist eine Anzeige **unzumutbar,** sei es, weil die Zeit dafür nicht ausreicht, sei es, weil die Anzeige zwecklos wäre, so kann der vertragstreue Teil den Vertrag ohne Verzögerung aufheben. 25

6. Fristsetzung für Sicherheitsleistung

Die Anzeige wird meist eine Frist enthalten, innerhalb welcher der Schuldner Sicherheit leisten soll.[75] Das ergibt sich grundsätzlich bereits aus dem Erfordernis der „reasonable notice",[76] da die „reasonability" der Anzeige primär an der Angemessenheit der in der Anzeige enthaltenen Frist zu messen ist.[77] Aber selbst wenn keine ausdrückliche Frist gesetzt wird, ist dem Schuldner eine **angemessene Frist** zur Stellung von Sicherheiten zuzugestehen, während der das Aufhebungsrecht des Gläubigers suspendiert ist. Bei der Bemessung dieser Frist ist auf die jeweiligen Umstände, den Abstand zum eigentlichen Erfüllungstermin und die Art der Störung Rücksicht zu nehmen.[78] Die 30-tägige Frist des § 2–609(4) UCC könnte insofern eine Orientierungshilfe für die entsprechende Handhabung unter Art. 72 II bieten.[79] 26

Nicht geregelt ist der Fall, dass die Anzeige des Gläubigers nach den Umständen nicht vernünftig („unreasonable") ist, indem sie etwa eine zu knappe Frist gewährt, nicht genügend substantiiert ist oder auf andere Weise ihren Zweck nicht erfüllt. Dem Gläubiger wird grundsätzlich die Möglichkeit einzuräumen sein, seine Anzeige zu vervollständigen bzw. zu verbessern, so dass sie dem Angemessenheitserfordernis entspricht; dies setzt eine **entsprechende Beanstandung des Schuldners** voraus. Wehrt sich der Schuldner nicht rechtzeitig gegen die „unreasonable notice", d. h. sobald deren Unangemessenheit erkennbar war 27

---

[72] Vgl. auch *Strub*, 38 Int'l & Comp. L. Q. (1989), 475, 500; *Honnold/Flechtner*, Art. 72, Rn. 398; *Bridge*, 25 J. L. & Com. (2005-06), 405, 416 f.; *Azeredo da Silveira*, 2 Nordic Journal of Commercial Law (2005), 30; *Neumayer/Ming*, Art. 72, Anm. 5.; *Schlechtriem*, Internationales UN-Kaufrecht, Rn. 274; *Bamberger/Roth/Saenger*, Art. 72, Rn. 9; *Achilles*, Art. 72, Rn. 4; nun auch MünchKomm/*P. Huber*, Art. 72, Rn. 13; *Honsell/Brunner/Hurni*, Art. 72, Rn. 10; nur auf das Zeitmoment abstellend *Vanwijk-Alexandre*, R. D. A. I. 2001, 353, 369 f.

[73] *Schlechtriem*, Internationales UN-Kaufrecht, Rn. 274; dem zustimmend *Bamberger/Roth/Saenger*, Art. 72, Rn. 10; *Ferrari u. a./Saenger*, Internationales Vertragsrecht, Art. 72, Rn. 10.

[74] So auch *Strub*, 38 Int'l & Comp. L. Q. (1989), 475, 499; *Heuzé*, Anm. 406.; krit. auch *Schmidt*, Vertragsaufhebung, S. 197 („ganz erhebliche[r] Zuwachs an Rechtsunsicherheit").

[75] Vgl. zur Fristsetzung auch die Vorauflage („Beschleunigung des Procederes") sowie MünchKommHGB/*Mankowski*, Art. 72, Rn. 14 („schafft Formaltatbestände").

[76] Die 4. Auflage, Rn. 19, stützte das Ansetzen einer Frist auf Artt. 49 I lit. b), 64 I lit. b), 48 II analog.

[77] Oben Rn. 23.

[78] MünchKomm/*P. Huber*, Art. 72, Rn. 17.

[79] So auch *Strub*, 38 Int'l & Comp. L. Q. (1989), 475, 598.

(Art. 8 II), so bleibt ihm die spätere Berufung auf Unwirksamkeit der Vertragsaufhebung wegen mangelhafter Anzeige verwehrt.

7. Kombination der Anzeigen nach Artt. 72 II bzw. 71 III

28   Manifestiert sich eine künftige wesentliche Vertragsverletzung, so kann gerade der vorleistungspflichtige Gläubiger daran interessiert sein, sowohl Mitteilung i. S. v. Art. 72 II zu geben als auch seine Leistung einstweilen zurückzuhalten. Er wird dann **mit ein und derselben Mitteilung** sowohl den Anforderungen von Art. 72 II als auch denjenigen von Art. 71 III entsprechen können, wenn er darin einerseits informiert, dass er sein Aussetzungsrecht ausüben wird (Art. 71 III), und andererseits, dass er sein Aufhebungsrecht auszuüben gedenkt (Art. 72 II).[80] Stellt der Schuldner daraufhin ausreichende Sicherheit, muss der Gläubiger seinerseits sein Pflichtenprogramm wieder aufnehmen und darf den Vertrag nicht aufheben.[81]

8. Stellung von Sicherheiten

29   **a) Ausreichende Sicherheit.** Erforderlich ist die Stellung von ausreichenden Sicherheiten. Es gelten die zu Art. 71 III gemachten Ausführungen[82] bezüglich Art und Umfang der zu stellenden Sicherheit. Letztere kann insbesondere auch in anderen als banküblichen Sicherheiten bestehen; zu denken ist vielmehr an einen weiteren Kreis von Massnahmen, der im Verhältnis zu der drohenden wesentlichen Vertragsverletzung den vertragstreuen Teil angemessen absichert (wie Lieferzusagen Dritter, Bürgschaften, Nachweise von Bezugsmöglichkeiten etc.).[83] Die blosse Rücknahme einer als implizite Vertragsaufsage zu wertenden Aussage dürfte dagegen keine ausreichende Gewähr bieten.

30   **b) Wirkungen.** Ist die gestellte Sicherheit nach objektivem Massstab (Art. 8 II) ausreichend, so dass der Gläubiger sie akzeptieren muss, entfällt sein Aufhebungsrecht.[84] Solange die Anzeige überhaupt nicht abgegeben ist, kann das **Aufhebungsrecht** nicht ausgeübt werden. Es ist zeitlich **blockiert,** weil die Anzeige anders als bei Art. 71 III zu den konstitutiven Voraussetzungen des Behelfs gehört.[85] Die Anzeige kann, solange die künftige Vertragsverletzung offensichtlich droht, noch nachgeholt werden und führt dann zum Sicherungsverfahren. Verweigert die Partei, die den Vertrag zu verletzen droht, die Stellung einer ausreichenden Sicherheit oder reagiert sie auf die Anzeige nicht innerhalb angemessener Zeit, kann das Aufhebungsrecht ohne weitere Verzögerung ausgeübt werden.[86]

31   **c) Ausbleiben von bzw. Stellen nicht ausreichender Sicherheiten.** Stellt der Schuldner innerhalb der ihm gewährten Frist keine Sicherheit, so kann er die Vertragsaufhebung durch den Gläubiger nicht abwenden.[87] **Unklar** bleiben die Fälle, in denen zwar Sicherheit angeboten wird, diese aber nicht ausreichend ist (auch hier gilt der Massstab des Art. 8 II), oder wenn zwar ausreichende Sicherheit angeboten wird, ihre tatsächliche Verschaffung aber nicht in angemessener Zeit erfolgt. Anders als im Falle des schlichten Nichtleistens einer Sicherheit wird der Schuldner in den letztgenannten Situationen zumindest tätig, und es mag Fälle geben, in denen das rigorose Ignorieren der Bemühungen des

---

[80] Dies erfordert eine Substantiierung der Anzeige wie vorne Rn. 22 erörtert.
[81] Vgl. auch *Bianca/Bonell/Bennett,* Art. 72, Anm. 3.2.
[82] Vgl. oben *Fountoulakis,* Art. 71 Rn. 44 ff.
[83] Dazu *Enderlein/Maskow/Strohbach,* Art. 72, Anm. 8.; vgl. auch oben *Fountoulakis,* Art. 71 Rn. 44 ff.
[84] *Reinhart,* Art. 72, Rn. 3.
[85] Vgl. vorne Rn. 19 f., sowie oben *Fountoulakis,* Art. 71 Rn. 30.
[86] Im Verweigerungsfall liegt eine Parallele zu Art. 72 III nahe, die das Verfahren der Anzeige und Sicherheitsstellung entbehrlich macht.
[87] Ganz h. M., vgl. statt Vieler Sekretariatskommentar, Art. 72, Anm. 2.; *Bianca/Bonell/Bennett,* Art. 72, Anm. 2.3.; *Kröll u. a./Saidov,* Art. 72, Rn. 25.

Schuldners unangemessen wäre. Es scheint hier angebracht, in Anlehnung an Art. 48 dem Schuldner die Möglichkeit einzuräumen, nachträglich noch ausreichende Sicherheit zu stellen, allerdings unter den engen Voraussetzungen, dass dies dem Gläubiger in zeitlicher Hinsicht noch zumutbar ist und ihm auch sonst keine unzumutbaren Unannehmlichkeiten oder Ungewissheiten verursacht (vgl. Art. 48 I).

d) Formen und Fristen. Der Schuldner muss, wenn er die Vertragsaufhebung durch den Gläubiger abwenden will, die Sicherheit innerhalb angemessener Frist stellen.[88] Für die Erklärung des Schuldners gilt das **Zugangsprinzip** und nicht etwa Art. 27. Nach Art. 27 reisen Erklärungen auf Risiko des Empfängers, beruhen also auf dem Gedanken, dass der Empfänger die vertragsverletzende Partei ist.[89] Auf den Fall des Art. 72 II passt Art. 27 nicht, da es hier der Schuldner ist, der die Erklärung (dass er Sicherheit stellt) abgibt. Es gilt folglich das Zugangsprinzip, d. h. die Erklärung des Schuldners wird erst mit Zugang wirksam. Dies liegt auf einer Linie mit den im CISG vorgesehenen Ausnahmeregelungen in Artt. 47 II, 63 II.[90] Darüber hinaus dürften – abgesehen von der Anzeige selbst – Erklärungen auch der vertragstreuen Partei im Zusammenhang mit der Einigung über die Bestellung der Sicherheit den Regeln des ergänzenden Vertragsschlusses zuzurechnen sein, sodass auch insoweit das Zugangsprinzip gilt.[91] 32

V. Vorzeitige Erfüllungsweigerung, Art. 72 III (ohne Anzeigepflicht)

1. Erfüllungsverweigerung (ungerechtfertigte antizipierte Vertragsaufhebung)

a) Ratio. Erklärt der Schuldner bereits vor Fälligkeit, dass er seine Pflichten nicht erfüllen wird, entfällt die Anzeigepflicht des Gläubigers. Art. 72 III fusst ganz auf der historisch gesehen älteren Grundlage des **anticipatory breach** im anglo-amerikanischen Recht. Der Schuldner, der ernstlich, ausdrücklich und unzweideutig seine Vertragspflicht verneint oder leugnet, verstösst in zentraler Weise gegen den Vertrag.[92] Durch die Erfüllungsweigerung wird dem Vertrag die Basis entzogen; die Vertragsverletzung begegnet hier in ihrer reinsten Form. 33

b) Umfang. Die Erfüllungsverweigerung muss Pflichten berühren, deren Verletzung wesentlich i. S. v. Art. 25 ist. Dies ergibt sich aus der Wertung in Art. 72 I.[93] 34

c) Erklärung der Erfüllungsverweigerung. Jede schriftliche Mitteilung, auch in elektronischer Form, wie auch jede mündliche Äusserung, dass die Erfüllung nicht erfolgen werde, stellt eine Erklärung im Sinne von Art. 72 III dar.[94] Dieser sind Erklärungen gleich- 35

---

[88] Es ist zu erinnern, dass der Schuldner unter Art. 72 – anders als nach § 2-609 (4) UCC in der Fassung von 2003 – zur Sicherheitsleistung nicht verpflichtet ist. Er kann sich auch für das Nichtstun entscheiden, allerdings mit entsprechenden Konsequenzen (dazu Rn. 31).
[89] Vgl. dazu oben *Schroeter*, Art. 27 Rn. 1; *Schlechtriem*, Internationales UN-Kaufrecht, Rn. 109.
[90] Vgl. zu diesen Vorschriften *Noussias*, Zugangsbedürftigkeit von Mitteilungen, S. 142, 148 ff.; zum Zusammenhang mit Art. 72 s. S. 147.
[91] Hierbei handelt es sich nicht um Mitteilungen über Vertragsstörungen. Die Verhandlungen über das einverständliche Zustandekommen der Stellung von Sicherheiten sind eher mit der Situation des Vertragsschlusses vergleichbar. Diesbezüglich gilt daher das Zugangsprinzip, vgl. Artt. 15 I, 18 II; dazu auch *Noussias*, Zugangsbedürftigkeit von Mitteilungen, S. 90 ff.
[92] *Leser*, Erfüllungsweigerung, S. 651; *Stoll*, RabelsZ 52 (1988), 617, 622; *Schlechtriem*, Internationales UN-Kaufrecht, Rn. 273; OLG Düsseldorf, 22.7.2004, CISG-online 916, Erw. 4.
[93] Vgl. auch § 2-610 UCC für den Fall der antizipierten Erfüllungsverweigerung („anticipatory repudiation") („the loss [must] **substantially impair** the value of the contract to the other"); so auch Art. 94 chines. UCL („The parties may terminate the contract if: (i) before the time of performance, the other party expressly stated or indicated by its conduct that it will not perform its **„main obligations"**) (Hervorhebungen hinzugefügt); vgl. auch Art. III.–3:504 DCFR („fundamental non-performance"), Artt. 116, 136 CESL-Entwurf („wenn die Nichterfüllung die Beendigung des Vertrags rechtfertigen würde") Auch Art. 7.3.3 PICC und Art. 9:304 PECL verlangen „fundamental non-performance", allerdings ohne zwischen Erfüllungsverweigerung und sonstigem antizipierten Vertragsbruch zu differenzieren.
[94] Handelskammer Zürich, 31.5.1996, CISG-online 1291 = YB Comm. Arb. 1998, 128 ff.; CIETAC, 30.1.1996, CISG-online 1120; *Honnold/Flechtner*, Art. 72, Rn. 396; *Kröll u. a./Saidov*, Art. 72, Rn. 28.

gestellt, aus denen die Erfüllungsverweigerung **bloss indirekt** hervorgeht, etwa indem der Verkäufer mitteilt, er könne weder rechtzeitig liefern noch ein Datum nennen, an dem Lieferung erfolgen würde.[95] **In der Praxis** taucht die Vertragsaufsage allerdings meist noch verbrämter auf: durch unzutreffende Behauptungen, etwa eines Rücktrittsrechts oder eines Vertragsabschlussmangels, durch unberechtigtes Verlangen von Preiserhöhungen, durch die Behauptung eines Rechts auf Fristverlängerung oder andere Modifikationen des bestehenden Vertrages.[96] All dies ist als Erfüllungsverweigerung zu werten, sofern daraus deutlich hervorgeht, dass der Schuldner seine Leistung nicht erbringen wird.[97] In der Rechtsprechung ist als ernsthafte und endgültige Erfüllungsverweigerung befunden worden die Weigerung des Käufers, für frühere Lieferungen zu zahlen[98] oder ein Akkreditiv zu eröffnen,[99] das willkürliche Aussetzen der Lieferung durch den Verkäufer[100] oder das Abhängigmachen der Erfüllung von nicht vereinbarten Zusatzbedingungen oder Nachforderungen.[101] Allerdings könnten etwa die letztgenannten Zusatzbedingungen auf einem Irrtum des anderen beruhen, auf einer Fehlinterpretation des Vertrags oder einem anderen Missverständnis.[102] Es wird hier – wie bei jeder anderen Erklärung des Schuldners – darauf ankommen, ob die Erklärung objektiv (Art. 8 II) tatsächlich als Erfüllungsverweigerung verstanden werden durfte. Das gilt sowohl für die **Deutlichkeit und Ernstlichkeit** der Erfüllungsweigerung, für die das Element der Offensichtlichkeit aus Art. 72 I herangezogen werden kann, wie auch für die Wesentlichkeit der betroffenen Vertragspflichten i. S. v. Art. 25.

35a   Auch das **Nichtstellen von Sicherheiten** im Rahmen von Art. 72 II, aber auch Art. 71 III kann eine hinreichend deutliche und definitive, implizite Erfüllungsverweigerung gemäss Art. 72 III darstellen.[103]

36   **d) Widerrufbarkeit.** Der Schuldner kann seine Vertragsaufsage **widerrufen,** solange sich der Gläubiger noch nicht auf die Vertragsbeendigung eingestellt hat.[104] In dieser (kurzen)

---

[95] CIETAC, 29.3.1996, CISG-online 2279 = 2289. Vgl. auch *Bridge,* 59 Int'l & Comp. L. Q. (2010), 911, 927.
[96] *Leser,* Erfüllungsweigerung, S. 643 f.; *Honnold/Flechtner,* Art. 72, Rn. 396; *Vanwijk-Alexandre,* R. D. A. I. 2001, 353, 362 f.; *Neumayer/Ming,* Art. 72, Anm. 9.; *Witz/Salger/Lorenz/Lorenz,* Art. 72, Rn. 8.
[97] So auch Sekretariatskommentar, Art. 72, Anm. 2. („words or actions of the party which constitute a repudiation of the contract"); *Bridge,* 25 J. Law & Comm. (2005-06), 405, 415 („by words or conduct"); *Honnold/Flechtner,* Rn. 396; im Ergebnis auch *Kröll u. a./Saidov,* Art. 72, Rn. 6, 27; insofern hat der Meinungsstreit in der Literatur, ob die Erklärung der Erfüllungsweigerung ausdrücklich erfolgen muss (so etwa *Staudinger/Magnus,* Art. 72, Rn. 27 m. w. N.) oder ob auch eine konkludente Erfüllungsweigerung ausreichend ist (so *Honsell/Brunner/Hurni,* Art. 72, Rn. 11, und *Bamberger/Roth/Saenger,* Art. 72, Rn. 11), keine praktischen Auswirkungen, da es beiden Ansichten (auch dann) eine Erfüllungsweigerung i. S. d. Art. 72 III darstellt, wenn der Schuldner die Erfüllung von nicht vereinbarten Zusatzbedingungen oder Nachforderungen abhängig macht (*Staudinger/Magnus* und *Honsell/Brunner/Hurni,* jeweils aaO.); wie hier auch MünchKomm/*P. Huber,* Art. 72, Rn. 14. Sehr streng in der Rechtsprechung OLG Düsseldorf, 24.4.1997, CISG-online 385: Unkooperatives Verhalten des einen Teils berechtige den anderen Teil nur dann zur Vertragsaufhebung gem. Art. 72, wenn es „den sicheren Schluss" zulasse, dass „die restliche Erfüllung des Vertrages ernsthaft und endgültig verweigert" werde.
[98] OLG Düsseldorf, 14.1.1994, CISG-online 119 = IHR 2005, 29 (so bereits die Vorinstanz in LG Krefeld, 28.4.1993, CISG-online 101); LG Berlin, 30.9.1992, CISG online 70.
[99] *Downs Investments Pty Ltd v. Perjawa Steel SDN BHD,* Supreme Court of Queensland, 17.11.2000, CISG-online 587 = 859, Rn. 67.
[100] Schiedsgericht der Handelskammer Zürich, 31.5.1996, CISG-online 1291 = YB Comm. Arb. 1998, 128 ff., Rn. 168.
[101] *Magellan International v. Salzgitter Handel,* U. S. Dist. Ct. (N. D. Ill.), 7.12.1999, CISG-online 439.
[102] Vgl. etwa die Ansicht in der anglo-amerikanischen Literatur, dass in der irrtümlichen Annahme des Schuldners, Zusatzforderungen stellen zu dürfen, keine Erfüllungsweigerung zu erblicken sei, so etwa *Chesire/Fifoot/Furmstone,* S. 683 f.; *Chen-Wishart,* Contract Law (2010), 515, m. Nachw. zur Rsp.; so vorsichtig auch *Azeredo da Silveira,* 2 Nordic Journal of Commercial Law, 27; vgl. auch *Kröll u. a./Saidov,* Art. 72, Rn. 12 ff., mit dem Vorschlag, die Klausel im Vertrag, die Anlass zu dem Missverständnissen gibt, dem Gericht im Rahmen eines *construction summons* zur Auslegung vorzulegen, der gleichzeitig aber auch die Grenzen dieses Vorgehens bei zeitlicher Dringlichkeit anerkennt bzw. die Tatsache, dass ein solches Vorlageverfahren ausserhalb des common laws selten möglich sein wird.
[103] Vgl. oben *Fountoulakis,* Art. 71 Rn. 49, sowie vorne Art. 72 Rn. 31.
[104] Vgl. zum Ganzen oben *Fountoulakis,* Art. 26 Rn. 12. Vgl. auch *Leser,* Erfüllungsweigerung, S. 652 f.; nun auch *Kröll u. a./Saidov,* Art. 72, Rn. 30. Dies ist auch die ausdrückliche Lösung des § 2–611 (1) UCC.

Zeit kann also der Schuldner sich eines Besseren besinnen und seine Leistungsbereitschaft kundtun; der Gläubiger muss die angebotene Leistung annehmen (sofern sie fällig ist) und die eigene Gegenleistung liefern. Schadenersatzansprüche des Gläubigers bleiben vorbehalten.

VI. Aufhebungsrecht und Aufhebungserklärung

1. Art. 26

Liegt ein Fall von Art. 72 I vor und hat der Schuldner keine ausreichende Sicherheit geleistet, oder verweigert der Schuldner die Vertragserfüllung (Art. 72 III), so darf der Gläubiger den Vertrag aufheben. Es muss sich dabei um eine Aufhebungserklärung nach Art. 26 handeln, die **von der Anzeige gemäss Art. 72 II zu unterscheiden** ist.[105] 37

2. Fristen

Eine Frist für die Aufhebungserklärung ist nicht vorgesehen. Solange der Gläubiger den Vertrag nicht aufhebt, bleibt dieser weiterhin bestehen.[106] Hier gilt freilich das zu Art. 26 Ausgeführte:[107] Wenn die Voraussetzungen des Aufhebungsrechts für den vertragstreuen Teil erkennbar eingetreten sind, sollte eine angemessene Frist für die Erklärung zu laufen beginnen, um den Schwebezustand nicht unbeschränkt andauern zu lassen. Die Perpetuierung des Schwebezustands könnte Spekulationen der vertragstreuen auf Kosten der vertragsbrüchigen Partei hervorrufen.[108] Die Gefahr solcher Spekulationen könnte auch nicht allein im Schadensersatz und seiner Berechnung aufgefangen werden.[109] Darüber hinaus kann auch der im Vertragsbruch befindliche Partner ein schutzwürdiges Interesse an der Beendigung des Schwebezustandes haben.[110] Es sollte daher für die Ausübung des Aufhebungsrechts eine **angemessene Frist** angenommen werden,[111] wie dies bereits für das EKG vertreten wurde.[112] Nach Ablauf der Frist ist die Vertragsaufhebung für die Zeit vor Fälligkeit blockiert und erst wieder als normaler Behelf nach Fälligkeit auszuüben. 38

Denkbar ist schliesslich auch, dass der Schuldner den Schwebezustand durch **Aufforderung** an den Gläubiger, sich in angemessener Frist zu erklären, auflöst.[113] In jedem Fall endet das Aufhebungsrecht bei Erfüllung des Vertrags durch den Schuldner.[114] 39

---

[105] ICC, 8574/1996, 1.9.1996, CISG-online 1293; *Downs Investments Pty Ltd v. Perjawa Steel SDN BHD*, Supreme Court of Queensland, 17.11.2000, CISG-online 587 = 859, Rn. 80; *Kröll u. a./Saidov*, Art. 72, Rn. 19.

[106] Eine ipso-facto-Aufhebung, wonach der Gläubiger ohne entsprechende Erklärung nicht mehr an den Vertrag gebunden wäre, lässt sich mit Art. 26 nicht vereinbaren, vgl. ICC, 8574/1996, 1.9.1996, CISG-online 1293; *Leser*, Lösung vom Vertrag, S. 374; so aber *Stoll*, RabelsZ 52 (1988), 617, 629.

[107] Vgl. oben *Fountoulakis*, Art. 26 Rn. 16.

[108] Vgl. *Schlechtriem*, Internationales UN-Kaufrecht, Rn. 275.

[109] So aber *Stoll*, RabelsZ 52 (1988), 617, 633; *Witz/Salger/Lorenz/Lorenz*, Art. 72, Rn. 19, was dann im Einzelfall zu sehr schwierigen Abgrenzungen führt, zumal die Pflicht zur Schadensminderung in Art. 77 durch den Zusammenhang mit Art. 80 modifiziert werden kann.

[110] Vgl. dazu *Stoll*, RabelsZ 52 (1988), 617, 638.

[111] *Schlechtriem*, Internationales UN-Kaufrecht, Rn. 275; ders., GS Hellner, S. 229, 233; *Jan*, S. 123 ff.; vgl. auch *Achilles*, Art. 72, Rn. 3: Das allgemeine Verbot rechtsmissbräuchlichen Verhaltens könne im Einzelfall dem Aufhebungsrecht nach Art. 72 eine Grenze setzen. A. A. *Stoll*, RabelsZ 52 (1988), 617, 632 f.; *Bamberger/Roth/Saenger*, Art. 72, Rn. 12; MünchKommHGB/*Mankowski*, Art. 72, Rn. 10; MünchKomm/*P. Huber*, Art. 72, Rn. 8; *Witz/Salger/Lorenz/Lorenz*, Art. 72, Rn. 19; *Enderlein/Maskow/Strohbach*, Art. 72, Anm. 4.; *Soergel/Lüderitz/Dettmeier*, Art. 72, Rn. 9; *Piltz*, Internationales Kaufrecht, Rn. 5–461.

[112] Vgl. *Dölle/Leser*, Art. 76 EKG, Rn. 29–31; *Hager*, Rechtsbehelfe des Verkäufers, S. 222 f.

[113] Siehe dazu schon *Dölle/Leser*, Art. 76 EKG, Rn. 32.

[114] *Witz/Salger/Lorenz/Lorenz*, Art. 72, Rn. 19.

3. Wirkungen

40 Mit der Vertragsaufhebung entfallen die künftigen Pflichten aus dem Vertrag. Eine Rückabwicklung i. S. d. Artt. 81 ff. ergibt sich nur in den Ausnahmefällen, in denen bereits Vorleistungen erbracht wurden, wie Anzahlungen, Zurverfügungstellung von Plänen, Lizenzen etc.[115] Zur Bindungswirkung der Aufhebungserklärung vgl. oben Art. 26.[116] Hat der Gläubiger die Vertragsaufhebung wegen antizipierten Vertragsbruchs **zu Unrecht** erklärt, hat er selbst eine – allenfalls auch bloss antizipierte, u. U. sogar wesentliche – Vertragsverletzung begangen, die dem Schuldner den Weg zu allen im CISG vorgesehenen Rechtsbehelfen (insbesondere dem Schadensersatzanspruch aus Artt. 74 ff.) ebnet.[117]

VII. Schadensersatz

41 Der Gläubiger kann zusätzlich zu seinem Aufhebungsrecht auch Schadensersatz verlangen, sofern ihm durch den antizipierten Vertragsbruch des Schuldners ein Schaden entstanden ist.[118] Für die Berechnungsmethode gelten, sofern der Vertrag aufgehoben worden ist, insbesondere auch Artt. 75, 76.[119] Das Tätigen eines Deckungsgeschäfts wird im Sinne einer Schadensminderung häufig angezeigt sein, Art. 77.[120] Aber auch bei nicht aufgehobenem Vertrag kann die in Art. 75 vorgesehene Schadensberechnungsmethode – im Rahmen von Art. 74 – angewandt werden.[121]

VIII. Beweislast

42 Die Beweislast für das tatsächliche Vorliegen der Voraussetzungen des Aufhebungsrechts trägt nach allgemeinen Grundsätzen der Gläubiger, während der Schuldner wiederum nachzuweisen hat, dass er ausreichende Gewähr für die Erfüllung seiner Pflichten gegeben hat.[122]

---

[115] Vgl. Art. 73 Rn. 27.
[116] Art. 26 Rn. 12.
[117] Vgl. *Staudinger/Magnus*, Art. 72, Rn. 19; *Enderlein/Maskow/Strohbach*, Art. 81, Anm. 1.; Bianca/Bonell/Bennett, Art. 72, Anm. 2.3.; *Honsell/Brunner/Hurni*, Art. 72, Rn. 14; MünchKomm/P. Huber, Art. 72, Rn. 11.
[118] *Schlechtriem*, Internationales UN-Kaufrecht, Rn. 275a. In Art. 77 EKG war für die vorzeitige Vertragsverletzung wie für das Zurückbehaltungsrecht noch ausdrücklich die Schadensersatzpflicht geregelt. Das CISG hat dies nicht übernommen (bereits durch Beschluss der Arbeitsgruppe 1974 abgelehnt, vgl. YB V (1974), S. 42, Nr. 137), da in allen Fällen der Vertragsverletzung Schadensersatz entsprechend dem allgemeinen Prinzip des Übereinkommens geschuldet wird und eine explizite Erwähnung, dass das Vertragsaufhebungsrecht nach Art. 72 von einem Schadensersatzanspruch begleitet sein könne, für überflüssig erachtet wurde.
[119] Vgl. *Schlechtriem*, GS Hellner, S. 229, 231; *Honnold/Flechtner*, Art. 72, Rn. 397; *Kröll u. a./Saidov*, Art. 72, Rn. 34.
[120] *Vgl. Bianca/Bonell/Bennett*, Anm. 2.4.; *Schlechtriem*, GS Hellner, S. 229, 230; *ders.*, FS Georgiades, S. 383, 394 f., 397, m. w. N.
[121] *Schlechtriem*, FS Georgiades, S. 383, 386. Zu Einzelheiten vgl. *Schwenzer*, Art. 74 Rn. 22.
[122] Vgl. *Baumgärtel/Laumen/Prütting/Hepting/Müller*, Art. 72, Rn. 1; *Staudinger/Magnus*, Art. 71, Rn. 30; Bamberger/Roth/Saenger, Art. 71, Rn. 13; MünchKomm/P. Huber, Art. 72, Rn. 18; Achilles, Art. 72, Rn. 7; *Jung*, S. 232; aus der Rspr. etwa OLG Düsseldorf, 22.7.2004, CISG-online 916.

Art. 73 [Sukzessivlieferungsvertrag; Aufhebung]

(1) Sieht ein Vertrag aufeinander folgende Lieferungen von Ware vor und begeht eine Partei durch Nichterfüllung einer eine Teillieferung betreffenden Pflicht eine wesentliche Vertragsverletzung in bezug auf diese Teillieferung, so kann die andere Partei die Aufhebung des Vertrages in bezug auf diese Teillieferung erklären.

(2) Gibt die Nichterfüllung einer eine Teillieferung betreffenden Pflicht durch eine der Parteien der anderen Partei triftigen Grund zu der Annahme, daß eine wesentliche Vertragsverletzung in bezug auf künftige Teillieferungen zu erwarten ist, so kann die andere Partei innerhalb angemessener Frist die Aufhebung des Vertrages für die Zukunft erklären.

(3) Ein Käufer, der den Vertrag in bezug auf eine Lieferung als aufgehoben erklärt, kann gleichzeitig die Aufhebung des Vertrages in bezug auf bereits erhaltene Lieferungen oder in bezug auf künftige Lieferungen erklären, wenn diese Lieferungen wegen des zwischen ihnen bestehenden Zusammenhangs nicht mehr für den Zweck verwendet werden können, den die Parteien im Zeitpunkt des Vertragsabschlusses in Betracht gezogen haben.

Art. 73

(1) In the case of a contract for delivery of goods by instalments, if the failure of one party to perform any of his obligations in respect of any instalment constitutes a fundamental breach of contract with respect to that instalment, the other party may declare the contract avoided with respect to that instalment.

(2) If one party's failure to perform any of his obligations in respect of any instalment gives the other party good grounds to conclude that a fundamental breach of contract will occur with respect to future instalments, he may declare the contract avoided for the future, provided that he does so within a reasonable time.

(3) A buyer who declares the contract avoided in respect of any delivery may, at the same time, declare it avoided in respect of deliveries already made or of future deliveries if, by reason of their interdependence, those deliveries could not be used for the purpose contemplated by the parties at the time of the conclusion of the contract.

Art. 73

1) Dans les contrats à livraisons successives, si l'inexécution par l'une des parties d'une obligation relative à une livraison constitue une contravention essentielle au contrat en ce qui concerne cette livraison, l'autre partie peut déclarer le contrat résolu pour ladite livraison.

2) Si l'inexécution par l'une des parties d'une obligation relative à une livraison donne à l'autre partie de sérieuses raisons de penser qu'il y aura contravention essentielle au contrat en ce qui concerne des obligations futures, elle peut déclarer le contrat résolu pour l'avenir, à condition de le faire dans un délai raisonnable.

3) L'acheteur qui déclare le contrat résolu pour une livraison peut, en même temps, le déclarer résolu pour les livraisons déjà reçues ou pour les livraisons futures si, en raison de leur connexité, ces livraisons ne peuvent être utilisées aux fins envisagées par les parties au moment de la conclusion du contrat.

Übersicht

	Rn.
I. Vorgeschichte	1
1. EKG	1
2. CISG	2
II. Aufgaben und Anwendungsbereich	3
1. Überblick	3
2. Rechtsvergleich	5
III. Gestörte Einzellieferung, Art. 73 I	7
1. Tatbestandsvoraussetzungen	7
2. Sukzessivlieferungsvertrag	8
3. Wesentliche Vertragsverletzung	11

4. Vertragsaufhebung – Form und Frist	13
5. Rechtsfolgen	15
IV. Vertragsaufhebung für die Zukunft, Art. 73 II	17
1. Tatbestandsvoraussetzungen	17
2. Gegenwärtige Pflichtverletzung	18
3. Kausalzusammenhang zwischen jetziger und künftiger Vertragsverletzung	19
4. Prognose der künftigen wesentlichen Vertragsverletzung	20
5. Vertragsaufhebung	23
a) Aufhebung ex nunc	23
b) Vorzeitige Anzeigepflicht	24
c) Form und Frist für die Aufhebungserklärung	25
d) Rechtsfolgen	27
6. Verhältnis zu Artt. 71, 72	28
V. Erweiterung des Aufhebungsrechts bei Zweckzusammenhang, Art. 73 III	29
1. Tatbestandsvoraussetzungen	29
2. Aufhebung nach Art. 73 I	30
3. Zweckzusammenhang	31
a) Interpendenz einzelner Teillieferungen	31
b) Massstäbe	32
4. Aufhebung nur für Vergangenheit oder Zukunft	34
5. Wirkungen	36
6. Form und Frist der Aufhebung	37
VI. Abgrenzung von Art. 73 und Art. 51	39
VII. Beweislast	40

Vorläufer und **Entwürfe:** Art. 75 EKG; Genfer E 1976 Art. 48; Wiener E 1977 Art. 50; New Yorker E 1977 Art. 64.

I. Vorgeschichte

1. EKG

1 Der Sukzessivlieferungsvertrag gehörte zu den Problemen, die bei den Vorarbeiten zum EKG von Anfang an behandelt wurden.[1] Die mit Art. 75 EKG gefundene **einheitliche Lösung** konnte sich auf eine in den nationalen Rechten weitgehend übereinstimmende Grundlage stützen,[2] sodass sich in der Entwicklungsgeschichte der Vorschrift keine wesentlichen Veränderungen ergaben.[3]

2. CISG

2 Das Übereinkommen hat in Art. 73 I[4] die Pflichtverletzung aus der aktuellen Einzellieferung als Ausgangspunkt für die ergänzenden Behelfe in den Abs. 2 und 3 genommen. Art. 73 II[5] und III[6] wurden gegenüber Art. 75 EKG geringfügig umformuliert.

---

[1] *Rabel* im „Blauen Bericht" von 1929, Ges. Aufs. Bd. 3, S. 381 ff., 442–444.
[2] *Rabel,* Recht des Warenkaufs, Bd. 1, § 66, S. 528 ff.
[3] Näher dazu *Dölle/Leser,* Art. 75 EKG, Rn. 1–3. Der in Art. 73 I geregelte Fall der Aufhebung bzgl. einer Teilleistung wurde im EKG den allgemeinen Regeln überlassen, da sich insoweit keine Besonderheiten ergaben.
[4] Im Wiener E 1977 als Art. 50 I enthalten; damit sollte auch der Verkäufer das Recht zur bloss teilweisen Vertragsaufhebung erhalten; dem Käufer war die Möglichkeit zur Teilaufhebung aufgrund Art. 51 CISG (Art. 32 Genfer E, Art. 33 Wiener E) bereits bekannt, vgl. YB VIII (1977), S. 55, Nr. 422 f.
[5] „Good reasons to fear" in Art. 75 EKG wurde in „good grounds to conclude" in Art. 73 II geändert (auch wegen der Einheitlichkeit mit Kap. V Abschnitt I), YB VIII (1977), S. 55, Nr. 427.
[6] Bereits in der Arbeitsgruppe wurde das bisherige „deliveries worthless to him" zu „could not be used" geändert, auch um einen möglichst einheitlichen Sprachgebrauch innerhalb des CISG zu erreichen, YB V (1974), S. 40 f., Nr. 118, 126.

II. Aufgaben und Anwendungsbereich

1. Überblick

Art. 73 enthält Sonderregelungen für die Vertragsaufhebung bei Störungen in der Abwicklung von Sukzessivlieferungsverträgen. Er erfasst dabei **drei verschiedene Situationen**. Abs. 1 sieht als Grundsatz die allgemeine Leistungsstörungsregel vor, dass sich das Vertragsaufhebungsrecht betreffend eine Teilleistung auf diese beschränkt. Die Vorschrift entspricht Art. 51 und will drastische Konsequenzen, wie sie sich aus der Verletzung blosser Teile des Vertrags ergeben, auf das Nötigste beschränken.[7] In Art. 73 II werden die für den Sukzessivlieferungsvertrag spezifischen künftigen Störungen erfasst, die sich aus einer Pflichtverletzung bei der aktuellen Einzellieferung ergeben. Hier wird dem Gläubiger ein Aufhebungsrecht für die Zukunft gewährt. Art. 73 II ist also, als vorgezogener Rechtsbehelf, mit Art. 72 verwandt.[8] Noch weitergehend zieht Art. 73 III die Konsequenz aus der gestörten Einzellieferung für den ganzen Vertrag: Der Käufer darf die für eine Einzellieferung erklärte Aufhebung auf den bereits erfüllten und/oder den noch ausstehenden Teil erstrecken, wenn der Zweckzusammenhang die wesentliche Störung der Einzellieferung auf andere Lieferungen oder auf den ganzen Vertrag ausstrahlen lässt.

Die Behelfe in Art. 73 I und II gelten für beide Vertragsteile in gleicher Weise.[9] Anderes gilt für Art. 73 III, der ausdrücklich ein Behelf lediglich des Käufers ist.

2. Rechtsvergleich[10]

Beim Sukzessivlieferungsvertrag entstehen durch seine zeitliche Erstreckung und die Mehrzahl der Lieferungen vermehrt **Störanfälligkeiten,** die zur Entwicklung spezifischer Behelfe geführt haben. Diese sind auch unter dem Gesichtspunkt der Verhältnismässigkeit und der Anpassung an die besonderen Bedürfnisse zu sehen. Der UCC knüpft an die wesentliche Störung der Einzellieferung an („non-conformity substantially impairing the value of that installment") und erlaubt, vereinfacht ausgedrückt, dem Käufer die Aufhebung des Vertrags nicht nur in Bezug auf diese Teillieferung, sondern auch betreffend den gesamten Vertrag, sofern dieser in seiner Gesamtheit wesentlich verletzt wird.[11] Im französischen Recht führt die „inexécution grave" bezüglich einer Teillieferung je nachdem, ob der Sukzessivlieferungsvertrag teilbar ist oder nicht, und je nach den weiteren Umständen zur Teilauflösung oder zur Vertragsauflösung für die Zukunft (résiliation gem. Art. 1184 Cc analog) oder zur rückwirkenden Auflösung des Gesamtvertrages (résolution gem. Art. 1184 Cc).[12] Im deutschen Recht findet sich in § 323 V 1 BGB die mit Art. 73 III vergleichbare Regelung, dass der Rücktritt vom gesamten Vertrag möglich ist, wenn die Teillieferung allein für den Gläubiger kein Interesse hat.[13] Für Österreich sieht § 918 II ABGB eine Art. 73 III ähnliche Regelung vor, lässt die Aufhebung für die Zukunft aber weitergehend bereits „wegen Verzögerung einer Teilleistung" zu.

Die **Einheitsrechtsprojekte** PECL und PICC treffen für Sukzessivlieferungsverträge Regelungen, die sich **im Ergebnis** kaum von den Lösungen des Art. 73 unterscheiden dürften: Art. 9:302 S. 1 PECL erlaubt bei Verträgen, die in mehreren Teilleistungen

---

[7] *Honnold/Flechtner,* Art. 73, Rn. 400.
[8] Zur Abgrenzung der beiden Behelfe vgl. unten Rn. 28.
[9] *Bianca/Bonell/Bennett,* Art. 73, Anm. 1.4.; *Schlechtriem,* Gemeinsame Bestimmungen, S. 159.
[10] Vgl. den rechtsvergleichenden Überblick bei *Schwenzer/Hachem/Kee,* Rn. 47.164 ff.
[11] Vgl. § 2–612 (3) UCC, dazu *White/Summers,* § 8-3.
[12] Vgl. zur Teilauflösung *Malaurie/Aynès,* Les obligations, Anm. 881., m. w. N.; vgl. auch Civ. 3e, 30.4.2003, Bull. Civ. III, no 87 = JCP 2004.II.10 031, Anm. *Jamin.*
[13] Zur fehlenden Regelung des Sukzessivlieferungsvertrags im früheren Leistungsstörungsrecht des BGB und zu den daraufhin durch die Rechtsprechung entwickelten Instrumenten unter Heranziehung der Figur der positiven Vertragsverletzung bzw. analoger Anwendung des § 326 BGB a. F. bei Aufspaltung des Vertrages in erbrachte und künftige Leistungen vgl. *Dölle/Leser,* Art. 75 EKG, Rn. 7.

erbracht werden, die Aufhebung des Vertrags betreffend eine Teilleistung, wenn diesbezüglich eine wesentliche Nichterfüllung („fundamental non-performance") vorliegt. Die Aufhebung des Gesamtvertrages (im Regelfall für die Zukunft) ist nur zulässig, wenn „the non-performance is fundamental to the contract as a whole".[14] Die Aufhebung des Sukzessivlieferungsvertrages auch für die Vergangenheit ermöglicht Art. 9:306 PECL; demgemäss darf der Empfänger einer Sache diese nachträglich zurückweisen, wenn sie auf Grund einer wesentlichen Nichterfüllung durch den anderen Teil für ihn ohne Wert ist.[15] Art. 9 II–IV CESL-Entwurf, Art. III. – 3:506 DCFR sehen eine ähnliche Regelung vor, die allerdings sowohl für die Sukzessivlieferung wie auch für das Einmalschuldverhältnis gilt,[16] behalten also die Unterscheidung, die im CISG zu Art. 51 einerseits und Art. 73 geführt hat, nicht bei. Den Materialien zur Entstehungsgeschichte der PICC schliesslich ist zu entnehmen, dass auch nach den UNIDROIT Principles – trotz eher verunglückter Kompromissformel in Art. 7.3.6 II – die Vertragsaufhebung bezüglich einer Teilleistung zulässig sein soll.[17] Das in Art. 7.3.6 II PICC aufgestellte Kriterium der Teilbarkeit soll nach dem Redaktorenkommentar bei einem Sukzessivlieferungsvertrag dann zur rückwirkenden Aufhebung des Gesamtvertrages für die Vergangenheit führen, wenn einzelne Teillieferungen ohne vollständige Gesamterfüllung für den Käufer nutzlos sind.[18]

III. Gestörte Einzellieferung, Art. 73 I

1. Tatbestandsvoraussetzungen

7   Art. 73 I gewährt dem Gläubiger in einem Sukzessivlieferungsvertrag das Recht, den Vertrag in Bezug auf eine Teillieferung aufzuheben, wenn diesbezüglich eine wesentliche Vertragsverletzung seitens des Schuldners vorliegt.

2. Sukzessivlieferungsvertrag

8   Art. 73 I erfasst den Sukzessivlieferungsvertrag durch die Formulierung „ein Vertrag mit aufeinander folgenden Lieferungen von Ware".[19] Ein Sukzessivlieferungsvertrag erfordert also **mindestens zwei aufeinander folgende Lieferungen.**[20] Entscheidend ist die **zeitliche Distanz,** die gegenwärtige und zukünftige Lieferungen unterscheidbar macht, da darauf die besonderen Behelfe des Sukzessivlieferungsvertrages beruhen.[21] Die einzelnen Lieferungen müssen voneinander trennbar und in der Art so selbstständig gegenüber dem

---

[14] Aus dem im Redaktorenkommentar Art. 9:302 PECL, Comment 1, gegebenen Beispielsfall 1 wird deutlich, dass die Aufhebung des Gesamtvertrages nur zulässig ist, wenn es auf Grund der Umstände sehr wahrscheinlich ist, dass sich die wesentliche Nichterfüllung bzgl. der Teilleistung zukünftig wiederholen wird. Es wird ausdrücklich auf Art. 9:304 PECL zum antizipierten Vertragsbruch Bezug genommen.
[15] Vgl. Art. 9:306 PECL, Comment, wo hervorgehoben wird, dass die Vorschrift insbesondere auch dann zur Anwendung kommen kann, wenn bei einem Sukzessivlieferungsvertrag die Nichterfüllung bzgl. einer Teilleistung die bereits erfolgten Teilleistungen nutzlos macht. Vgl. zur Gegenüberstellung von Art. 73 CISG und Art. 9:302 PECL *Kee,* 6 VJ (2002), 281 ff.
[16] Art. 9 II CESL-Entwurf: „in selbständigen Teilleistungen zu erfüllen oder auf andere Weise teilbar"; Art. III. – 3:506 II DCFR: „to be performed in separate parts or otherwise divisible".
[17] Nachweis hierzu bei *Hornung,* S. 177 ff. und 182.
[18] Vgl. Art. 7.3.6 PICC, Comment 3, Beispielsfall 6: Sukzessivkauf eines Bilderzyklus, der für den Käufer nur interessant ist, wenn er sämtliche Werke erhält.
[19] Vgl. die englische und frz. Originalfassung „contract for delivery of goods by instalments" bzw. „contrats à livraisons successives".
[20] Schiedsgericht der Hamburger freundschaftlichen Arbitrage, 29.12.1998, CISG-online 638 = IHR 2001, 35; HGer Zürich, 30.11.1998, CISG-online 415 = SZIER 1999, 185; Schiedsgericht der Börse für Landwirtschaftliche Produkte Wien, 10.12.1997, CISG-online 351 = östZRVgl 1998, 211: zwei Lieferungen von Braugerste als „vertragliche Einheit" i. S. d. Art. 73; *Staudinger/Magnus,* Art. 73, Rn. 6; *Piltz,* Internationales Kaufrecht, Rn. 5–296; MünchKommHGB/*Mankowski,* Art. 73, Rn. 3; MünchKomm/*P. Huber,* Art. 73, Rn. 2; *Witz/Salger/Lorenz/Lorenz,* Art. 73, Rn. 6; *Bamberger/Roth/Saenger,* Art. 73, Rn. 3.
[21] *Schlechtriem,* Internationales UN-Kaufrecht, Rn. 192.

Gesamtvertrag sein, dass man von einer Teillieferung sprechen kann, für die sich die darauf bezüglichen Pflichten beider Seiten nach den allgemeinen Regeln des Übereinkommens beurteilen lassen.[22] Dies ist – wie sich insbesondere aus Art. 73 III ergibt – nicht nur bei gleichartiger Ware der Fall, sondern auch dann, wenn unterschiedliche Teile einer Sachgesamtheit in Raten geliefert werden,[23] etwa eine Anlage in mehreren Komponenten oder diverse Materialien in Teilen. Auch ein kombinierter Vertrag, zum Beispiel die Lieferung von Soft- und Hardware, kann als Sukzessivlieferungsvertrag ausgestaltet sein, sofern die Lieferung in mehreren Schritten vorgesehen ist.[24] Die Teillieferungen müssen nicht jeweils gleich viel wert sein. Ebenso wenig ist erforderlich, dass die Spezifikation der Einzellieferungen oder die Preise und Modalitäten der Leistung, insbesondere auch hinsichtlich der Zeit, im vornherein festgelegt werden; sie können nachgeschoben werden.[25] Folglich fällt auch der bloss auf Abruf basierende Dauerliefervertrag unter Art. 73.[26]

Zahlung und Zahlungsmodalitäten sind zwar oft nach Einzellieferungen aufgetrennt;[27] es **9** sind aber auch andere Formen wie Gesamtzahlung, Zahlung in festen Raten ohne genaue Entsprechung zu den Lieferungen mit dem Vorbehalt einer Endabrechnung u. ä. anzutreffen, was ohne Einfluss auf den Charakter als Sukzessivlieferungsvertrag ist. Die **Ratenzahlung allein genügt jedenfalls nicht** für die Annahme eines Sukzessivlieferungsvertrages.[28]

Massgeblich für die Qualifizierung als Sukzessivlieferungsvertrag ist das Vorliegen eines **10** **einheitlichen Vertrags,** das heisst einer Vereinbarung, die in der Summe ihrer untergliederten Lieferungseinheiten ein Ganzes darstellt.[29] Als Sukzessivlieferungsvertrag im Sinne von Art. 73 kann demnach auch die Gesamtheit einzelner Lieferungen gelten, die von den Parteien als jeweils **selbständige Verträge** bezeichnet werden. Massgeblich ist, ob die Lieferungen in der Gesamtbetrachtung als zusammengehörige Teilleistungen aufzufassen sind. Indizien dafür sind insbesondere die Lieferung gleichartiger Ware,[30] die Tatsache, dass der Käufer pauschal für sämtliche Lieferungen bezahlt, dass die Zahlungsmodalitäten und/

---

[22] Sekretariatskommentar, Art. 64, Nr. 1, und *Bianca/Bonell/Bennett*, Art. 73, Anm. 2.1., stellen auf „separate lots" ab. Vgl. auch § 2–612 (1) UCC: „delivery of goods in separate lots to be separately accepted".

[23] HGer Zürich, 30.11.1998, CISG-online 415 = SZIER 1999, 185; Sekretariatskommentar, Art. 64, Nr. 4; *Achilles,* Art. 73, Rn. 2; *Honsell/Brunner/Hurni,* Art. 73, Rn. 2; *Staudinger/Magnus,* Art. 73, Rn. 6; *Bianca/Bonell/Bennett,* Art. 73, Anm. 2.5.; *Enderlein/Maskow/Strohbach,* Art. 73, Anm. 1.; *Bamberger/Roth/Saenger,* Art. 73, Rn. 3; MünchKomm/*P. Huber,* Art. 73, Rn. 2.

[24] Vgl. *Witz/Salger/Lorenz/Lorenz,* Art. 73, Rn. 6.

[25] OLG Innsbruck, 1.2.2005, CISG-online 1130 (zur Faktenlage ausführlicher OGH, 17.12.2003, CISG-online 828, sowie LG Innsbruck, 9.7.2004, CISG-online 1129); vgl. auch Int. Ct. Ukrainian CCI, 15.4.2004, CISG-online 1270; *Staudinger/Magnus,* Art. 73, Rn. 6.

[26] Vgl. ICC, 20.12.1999, CISG-online 1646 = IHR 2004, 21.

[27] Vgl. aus der jüngeren Rsp. etwa Shanghai First Intermediate People's Court (District Court), 25.12.2008, CISG-online 2059.

[28] Vgl. nur Gerechtshof Leeuwarden, 31.8.2005, CISG-online 1100, Erw. 2.7.2.; vgl. auch *Honsell/Brunner/Hurni,* Art. 73, Rn. 2; *Staudinger/Magnus,* Art. 73, Rn. 8; MünchKommHGB/*Mankowski,* Art. 73, Rn. 5; so auch die explizite Regelung in Art. 9 II CESL-Entwurf. A. A. *Bianca/Bonell/Knapp,* Art. 61, Anm. 2.12.: Art. 73 sei bei Ratenzahlung analog anzuwenden.

[29] Die Frage, ob es sich um einen Sukzessivlieferungsvertrag handelt oder nicht, wurde offen gelassen in LG Saarbrücken, 23.3.1992, CISG-online 60: Die Vertragsbeziehung gestaltet sich so, dass die Käuferin einzelne Bestellungen aufgab und der Verkäuferin diese mit ihren Auftragsbestätigungen bestätigte. In der Entscheidung, ob sie ein Vertragsangebot annahm oder ablehnte, war sie grundsätzlich frei.

[30] Vgl. Schiedsgericht der Börse für Landwirtschaftliche Produkte Wien, 10.12.1997, Erw. VII.1.2., CISG-online 351 = östZRVgl 1998, 211: „Die beiden Kontrakte der Parteien bilden nach Ansicht des Schiedsgerichtes wirtschaftlich insofern eine Einheit, als sie die sukzessive Lieferung qualitativ völlig gleichartiger Ware in Teilmengen im Zeitraum vom Jänner bis Juni 1997 unter gleichen rechtlichen Bedingungen – bei geringfügig abweichenden Zahlungskonditionen – vorsehen und am selben Tag vereinbart wurden. Es ist daher angezeigt, diese beiden Kontrakte als vertragliche Einheit anzusehen, die in Wahrheit eine Gesamtmenge an Braugerste als Kaufobjekt erfaßt, und sie deshalb in bezug auf die noch nicht zur Lieferung gelangten Teilmengen der für Sukzessivlieferungsverträge im Sinne des Art. 73 UN-Kaufrecht getroffenen Regelung zu unterstellen."; vgl. auch Schiedsgericht der Handelskammer Zürich, 31.5.1996, CISG-online 1291 = YB Comm. Arb. 1998, 128 ff.: „the various yearly Contracts 60-1, 60-2, 60-47 and those that would have followed must be considered, for the purposes of the Vienna Convention, to be one large installment contract in the sense of Art. 73"; LG Dresden, 29.5.2009, Erw. II.1., CISG-online 2174.

oder sonstigen Rahmenbedingungen für alle Einzelverträge dieselben sind,[31] oder die Tatsache, dass die Ware mittels einer einzigen Bestellung erfolgt, selbst wenn diese in ihrem Wortlaut die Lieferung in mehreren, eigenständigen Verträgen vorsieht; in diesem letzteren Fall kann ein zusätzlicher Hinweis auf die Zusammengehörigkeit der Einzelverträge deren fortlaufende Nummerierung sein (z. B. Vertrag Nr. 9604, Vertrag Nr. 9605, etc.).[32] Zur Abgrenzung von Art. 73 und Art. 51 vgl. unten Rn. 39 ff.

3. Wesentliche Vertragsverletzung

11   Bei der in Abs. 1 vorausgesetzten wesentlichen Vertragsverletzung kann es sich um die Verletzung sowohl von Verkäufer- wie von Käuferpflichten handeln. Unerheblich ist ihre Reihung im Gesamtvertrag.[33] Ob aufgehoben werden darf, bemisst sich an Artt. 49, 64. Es muss also entweder eine wesentliche Vertragsverletzung nach **Art. 25** vorliegen (Artt. 49 I lit. a), 64 I lit. a)),[34] oder aber es handelt sich um **Nichterfüllung** und nutzlos verstrichene Nachfrist (Artt. 49 I lit. b), 64 I lit. b)).[35]

12   Betrifft die Einzellieferung Teile eines zusammengehörenden Ganzen, dann hängt eine wesentliche Vertragsverletzung davon ab, **wie die Störung der Einzellieferung auf den Gesamtvertrag wirkt.** Soweit die Aufhebung des Gesamtvertrags nach Art. 73 III zulässig wäre, kann jedenfalls auch die veranlassende Einzellieferung allein aufgehoben werden.[36]

4. Vertragsaufhebung – Form und Frist

13   Für die Vertragsaufhebung gilt Art. 26. Die Teilaufhebungserklärung muss nicht notwendigerweise ausdrücklich erfolgen, solange sich aus den Erklärungen und dem Verhalten der vertragstreuen Partei ein entsprechender Wille **eindeutig ergibt.**[37] Eine Frist, innerhalb welcher die Aufhebung zu erklären ist, wird in Art. 73 nicht ausdrücklich geregelt. Aus der hier vertretenen allgemeinen Notwendigkeit einer Frist für das Aufhebungsrecht,[38] insbesondere aber daraus, dass Art. 73 I letztlich nur ein deklaratorischer Hinweis auf die Anwendbarkeit der allgemeinen Vorschriften – also auch der Artt. 49 II und 64 II – auf die Einzellieferung ist, folgt jedoch, dass die Teilaufhebung des Art. 73 I nicht fristlos möglich sein soll.[39] Vielmehr hat der Gläubiger seine Aufhebung innerhalb einer **angemessenen Frist** ab Erkennbarkeit des Aufhebungsrechts zu erklären.

---

[31] Schiedsgericht der Handelskammer Zürich, 31.5.1996, CISG-online 1291 = YB Comm. Arb. 1998, 128 ff.

[32] Id.

[33] Davon wird allgemein ausgegangen, ohne dass dies besonders hervorgehoben wird; vgl. etwa *Bianca/Bonell/Bennett*, Art. 73, Anm. 2.1.; *Enderlein/Maskow/Strohbach*, Art. 73, Anm. 1.; *Herber/Czerwenka*, Art. 73, Rn. 2; *von Scheven*, S. 240 f.

[34] Soweit es sich um selbstständige Einzellieferungen handelt, sind die unter Art. 25 entwickelten Fallgruppen (vgl. oben *Schroeter*, Art. 25 Rn. 17 ff.) auch hier entscheidend. Vgl. aus der Rechtsprechung etwa Shanghai First Intermediate People's Court (District Court), 25.12.2008, CISG-online 2059 (Qualitätsmangel); OLG Innsbruck, 1.2.2005, CISG-online 1130 (Qualitätsmängel); ICC, 20.12.1999, CISG-online 1646 = IHR 2004, 21 (einseitige Rabattänderung); Trib. Padova, 11.1.2005, CISG-online 967 = Riv. dr. int.priv. 2005, 791 (Nichtlieferung); LG Saarbrücken, 23.2.1992, CISG-online 60 (Nichtbezahlung).

[35] MünchKommHGB/*Mankowski*, Art. 73, Rn. 6; MünchKomm/*P. Huber*, Art. 73, Rn. 7; *Piltz*, Internationales Kaufrecht, Rn. 5–297; *Brunner*, Art. 73, Rn. 8; *Witz/Salger/Lorenz/Lorenz*, Art. 73, Rn. 10; a. A. *Vanwijk-Alexandre*, R. D. A. I. 2001, 353, 371 f.; *Honnold/Flechtner*, Art. 73, Rn. 400 a. E.; *Herber/Czerwenka*, Art. 73, Rn. 2.

[36] Vgl. Sekretariatskommentar, Art. 64, Nr. 4; *Staudinger/Magnus*, Art. 73, Rn. 13; *Bianca/Bonell/Bennett*, Art. 73, Anm. 2.5.; *Enderlein/Maskow/Strohbach*, Art. 73, Anm. 1.

[37] So zutreffend ICC, 8128/1995, CISG-online 526.

[38] Siehe dazu Art. 26 Rn. 16.

[39] *Schlechtriem*, Gemeinsame Bestimmungen, S. 161; ähnlich *Staudinger/Magnus*, Art. 73, Rn. 15; *Witz/Salger/Lorenz/Lorenz*, Art. 73, Rn. 10; MünchKommHGB/*Mankowski*, Art. 73, Rn. 8; *Honsell/Brunner/Hurni*, Art. 73, Rn. 12; *P. Huber/Mullis/P. Huber*, S. 350. A. A. *Ferrari u. a./Saenger*, Internationales Vertragsrecht, Art. 73, Rn. 5; *Bamberger/Roth/Saenger*, Art. 73, Rn. 5.

Weitere Voraussetzungen des Aufhebungsrechts wie die ordnungsgemässe **Untersuchung** 14
und Rüge nach Artt. 38, 39, 43 sind hinsichtlich der aufzuhebenden Teillieferung zu
beachten.[40] Des Weiteren ist die Aufhebung für den Käufer an die **Rückgabemöglichkeit
der Ware** nach Art. 82 I gebunden.

5. Rechtsfolgen

Wird die Einzellieferung aufgehoben, treten für diese die **Wirkungen der Vertrags-** 15
aufhebung ein, die in Artt. 81 ff. geregelt sind. Für den Gesamtvertrag bleibt es – unter
Vorbehalt der Möglichkeiten nach Art. 73 II und III – beim ursprünglichen Programm. Das
ist die Folge der durch Art. 73 I erfassten Verselbstständigung der Einzellieferung. Das Vertragsprogramm muss aber ggf. wegen der ausgefallenen Teilleistung neu angepasst werden.

Zusätzlich zur Teilaufhebung nach Art. 73 I kann der Gläubiger gegebenenfalls auch 16
Schadensersatz verlangen. Anstelle der Aufhebung bezüglich der Teillieferung kann er
auch die übrigen Rechtsbehelfe wie Erfüllung, Nachlieferung, Nachbesserung, Minderung
oder ein Aussetzungsrecht geltend machen.[41]

IV. Vertragsaufhebung für die Zukunft, Art. 73 II

1. Tatbestandsvoraussetzungen

Art. 73 II erlaubt dem Gläubiger, den Sukzessivlieferungsvertrag ex nunc aufzuheben. 17
Vorausgesetzt ist, dass 1) eine Teillieferung nicht richtig erfüllt wird, dass 2) deswegen 3)
triftige Gründe für die Annahme bestehen, dass 4) eine künftige wesentliche Vertragsverletzung zu erwarten ist, und dass 5) die Vertragsaufhebung innerhalb angemessener Frist ab
Erkennbarkeit der wahrscheinlichen künftigen wesentlichen Vertragsverletzung erklärt wird.

2. Gegenwärtige Pflichtverletzung

Für die Vertragsaufhebung nach Abs. 2 genügt, anders als bei Abs. 1, die **einfache** 18
„**Nichterfüllung**" einer Pflicht bezüglich einer Teillieferung", ohne dass es sich bereits um
eine wesentliche Vertragsverletzung handelt.[42] Die Vorschrift greift gerade auch dann ein,
wenn Störungen vorkommen, die noch unter der Wesentlichkeitsschwelle liegen.[43] **Beispielfälle** sind Verzögerungen der Lieferung oder der Zahlung, der Spezifikation oder
notwendiger Pläne, mangelnde Vertragsmässigkeit der Ware,[44] unzulässige Teillieferung etc.
Im Einzelfall kann es angezeigt sein, die schleppende Lieferung bzgl. einiger Teillieferungen
durch das Setzen einer angemessenen Nachfrist zur in Zukunft zu erwartenden wesentlichen Vertragsverletzung zu erheben.[45] Nicht erforderlich ist, dass aus der gegenwärtigen
Nichterfüllung noch Rechte hergeleitet werden können. Wenn etwa der Käufer die Mängelrüge unterlässt, so hindert ihn das nicht, die Schlechterfüllung zum Anlass für eine ex-
nunc-Aufhebung zu nehmen, sofern sich darauf seine Prognose zu einer künftigen wesentlichen Vertragsverletzung stützen lässt.[46]

---

[40] Staudinger/Magnus, Art. 73, Rn. 14; MünchKommHGB/Mankowski, Art. 73, Rn. 7.
[41] Vgl. auch Staudinger/Magnus, Art. 73, Rn. 16; MünchKommHGB/Mankowski, Art. 73, Rn. 9.
[42] Sekretariatskommentar, Art. 64, Nr. 6; Bianca/Bonell/Bennett, Art. 73, Anm. 2.7.; Enderlein/Maskow/Strohbach, Art. 73, Anm. 3.; Bamberger/Roth/Saenger, Art. 73, Rn. 8; Piltz, Internationales Kaufrecht, Rn. 5–298.
[43] Staudinger/Magnus, Art. 73, Rn. 18; MünchKommHGB/Mankowski, Art. 73, Rn. 11.
[44] Vgl. OLG Düsseldorf, 9.7.2010, CISG-online 2171, Rn. 89 ff. (wiederholte Lieferung von Konzentrat-statt Direktsaft); Shanghai First Intermediate People's Court (District Court), 25.12.2008, CISG-online 2059 (falsche Beschriftung von Champagnerflaschen in der Erstlieferung).
[45] Ausführlich hierzu Kimbel, 18 J. L. & Com. (1999), 301, 321–325, der sich unter Auswertung der ergangenen Rechtsprechung auch zur Frage äussert, wie eine angemessene Nachfrist im Rahmen eines Sukzessivlieferungsvertrags bemessen sein muss.
[46] Schiedsgericht der Börse für Landwirtschaftliche Produkte Wien, 10.12.1997, CISG-online 351 = östZRVgl 1998, 211: Die Tatsache, dass mangelhafte Teilleistungen wegen verspäteter Rügen nicht rückgege-

3. Kausalzusammenhang zwischen jetziger und künftiger Vertragsverletzung

19 Da der gegenwärtige Vertragsbruch die Basis für die Prognose bildet, dass eine künftige wesentliche Vertragsverletzung zu erwarten ist, muss diese Befürchtung aus der vorliegenden Vertragsverletzung herzuleiten sein. Das wird in der Regel bedeuten, dass **eine einzelne unerhebliche gegenwärtige Vertragsverletzung als Prognosebasis nicht genügt,** muss sich doch gerade aus ihr die Schlussfolgerung ergeben, dass eine künftige wesentliche Vertragsverletzung wahrscheinlich ist. Allerdings können mehrere solche unerhebliche Vertragsverletzungen in ihrer Gesamtheit den Schluss zulassen, dass eine künftige wesentliche Vertragsverletzung ansteht.[47] Der dabei anzulegende Massstab ist derjenige einer vernünftigen Person in den Schuhen des Gläubigers (Art. 8 II).

4. Prognose der künftigen wesentlichen Vertragsverletzung

20 Aus der Verletzung einer Pflicht hinsichtlich der Einzellieferung muss sich ein **„triftiger Grund"** (good grounds, sérieuses raisons) für die Annahme einer wesentlichen Vertragsverletzung bei einer künftigen Teillieferung ergeben. Die Wesentlichkeit der prognostizierten Vertragsverletzung beurteilt sich nach Art. 25, wobei deren Gewicht in Beziehung zum gesamten Volumen des verbliebenen Vertrags zu setzen ist.[48]

21 Die **Prognose** für die künftig zu erwartende Vertragsverletzung weist in der Frage des **Grades der Wahrscheinlichkeit** eine deutliche Verwandtschaft zum vorzeitigen Vertragsbruch in Art. 72 und zum Zurückhaltungsrecht in Art. 71 auf. In der Formulierung weichen sie aber voneinander ab: In Art. 71 I muss sich die drohende Vertragsverletzung „herausstellen" (it becomes apparent, il apparaît),[49] in Art. 72 muss die künftige wesentliche Vertragsverletzung „offensichtlich sein" (it is clear; il est manifeste),[50] während beim Sukzessivlieferungsvertrag der „triftige Grund zur Annahme der Erwartung einer wesentlichen Vertragsverletzung" erforderlich ist. Konkrete Massstäbe für die Differenzierung lassen sich aus den Formulierungen allein nicht entnehmen.[51] Sie müssen daher aus der **Funktion und der Schwere des jeweiligen Eingriffs** in den Vertrag gewonnen werden. Nach den Wirkungen lassen sich der Behelf in Art. 71 als schwächerer und vorläufiger, die Behelfe in Art. 72 und Art. 73 II als stärkere Behelfe einordnen. Die Vertragsaufhebung nach Art. 73 II nur für die Zukunft liegt als Reaktion auf eine bereits erfolgte, wenn auch nicht unbedingt wesentliche Vertragsverletzung auf einfacherer Ebene als die Aufhebung des ganzen Vertrages wegen vorzeitigen Vertragsbruchs. Damit ergibt sich bei einer **Stufung der Behelfe** eine Steigerung von Art. 71 I zu Art. 73 II und zu Art. 72 als dem stärksten. Dies ist in den Formulierungen des Übereinkommens nur rudimentär angelegt, ergibt sich aber aus dem vorstehenden funktionsadäquaten Vergleich der Behelfe.[52]

---

wickelt werden können, beeinträchtigt das Recht des Käufers nicht, aus der prognostischen Annahme, auch zukünftige Teilleistungen würden gleiche Mängel aufweisen, den Vertrag gem. Art. 73 II für die Zukunft aufzuheben.

[47] *Enderlein/Maskow/Strohbach*, Art. 25, Anm. 2.1. und 3.2.; *von Scheven*, S. 183 ff., 191 ff., 244 ff.; MünchKommHGB/*Mankowski*, Art. 73, Rn. 12; *Staudinger/Magnus*, Art. 73, Rn. 18; vgl. auch *Kimbel*, 18 J. L. & Com. (1999), 301, 320 ff.

[48] Vgl. Appellationsgericht Helsinki, 30.6.1998, CISG-online 1304: Ein bei mehreren Teillieferungen deutlich unter dem vereinbarten Minimum bleibender Vitamin-A-Anteil in Körperpflegeprodukten stellt einen triftigen Grund zur Annahme einer künftigen wesentlichen Vertragsverletzung dar; vgl. ferner MünchKommHGB/*Mankowski*, Art. 73, Rn. 14; MünchKomm/*P. Huber*, Art. 73, Rn. 14.

[49] Zur Entstehungsgeschichte vgl. Art. 71 Rn. 1.

[50] Zur Entstehungsgeschichte vgl. Art. 72 Rn. 1 f.

[51] Vgl. zu den Diskussionen um die Formulierung O. R., S. 431 ff.

[52] Für die hier vertretene Ansicht der Steigerung von Art. 71 I über Art. 73 II zu Art. 72 I auch *Bamberger/Roth/Saenger*, Art. 73, Rn. 9; *Witz/Salger/Lorenz/Lorenz*, Art. 73, Rn. 13; *Ferrari u. a./Saenger*, Internationales Vertragsrecht, Art. 73, Rn. 9; MünchKomm/*P. Huber*, Art. 73, Rn. 12; *Kröll u. a./Saidov*, Art. 73, Rn. 18; etwas anders *Honnold/Flechtner*, Art. 71, 73, Rn. 388, 401: Stufung von Art. 73 II über Art. 71 I zu Art. 72 I als höchster Anforderung an Prognose; ebenso *Neumayer/Ming*, Art. 72, Anm. 2., und Art. 73, Anm. 3.; *Karollus*, S. 87 und 163; vgl. auch *Nicholas*, L. Q. R. (1989), 201, 233; *Strub*, 38 Int'l & Comp. L. Q. (1989),

Sukzessivlieferungsvertrag; Aufhebung   22 **Art. 73**

In der bisher zu Art. 73 II ergangenen **Rechtsprechung** wurde ein triftiger Grund zur 22
Annahme der Erwartung einer wesentlichen Vertragsverletzung darin gesehen, dass der
Verkäufer trotz erfolgter Bezahlung bereits die erste Teillieferung nicht erbringen konnte.[53]
Auch die Tatsache, dass ein in laufender Geschäftsbeziehung mit seinem Käufer stehender
Verkäufer endgültig nicht in der Lage ist, die vereinbarte Ersatzlieferung für verdorbene
Ware vorzunehmen, berechtigt den Käufer dazu, den Sukzessivlieferungsvertrag gem.
Art. 73 II für die Zukunft aufzuheben.[54] Dem Nichterbringenkönnen von Teilleistungen
steht das Nicht(mehr)erbringenwollen von Teilleistungen gleich.[55] Weitere Fälle betreffen
die Weigerung des Schuldners, seinen Bezugsweg zu ändern, obwohl keine Gewähr dafür
besteht, dass dieser in Zukunft zuverlässiger sein wird,[56] die Tatsache, dass sämtliche bisher
erfolgten Teillieferungen mangelhaft waren und der Verkäufer den Verdacht, den künftigen
Teillieferungen würden gleichartige Qualitätsmängel anhaften, nicht entkräften konnte,[57]
oder die beharrliche Weigerung des Käufers, eine Zusicherung abzugeben, dass ein wirksames Re-Importverbot in Zukunft eingehalten werde.[58] Nicht erforderlich ist, dass alle
künftigen Teillieferungen in wesentlicher Weise vertragswidrig erscheinen. Entscheidend ist,
dass die **künftige ordnungsgemässe Erfüllung des Vertrags in gravierendem Ausmass in Frage gestellt** ist, sei es, dass etwa für einen auf die Gesamtvertragsdauer bezogen
beachtlichen Zeitraum gar nicht geliefert werden kann, sei es, dass wichtige Teile einer
Gesamtlieferung nicht oder nicht mangelfrei geliefert werden können.[59] Gleiches gilt für

---

475, 494. Nur zwischen Artt. 72 und 71 differenzierend und höhere Anforderungen an ersteren stellend *Enderlein/Maskow/Strohbach*, Art. 71, Anm. 2., und Art. 72, Anm. 1.; *Lookofsky*, Understanding the CISG, § 6.11, S. 124; nochmals anders bei *Bianca/Bonell/Bennett*, Art. 72, Anm. 2.2. und Art. 73, Anm. 2.7.; *Soergel/Lüderitz/Dettmeier*, Art. 73, Rn. 10; *Audit*, Vente Internationale, Anm. 169.; *Staudinger/Magnus*, Art. 73, Rn. 22, Art. 72, Rn. 9; *Honsell/Brunner/Hurni*, Art. 73, Rn. 15, die sowohl zwischen Art. 72 und 73 als auch zwischen Art. 71 und 72 abstufen und jedenfalls bei Art. 72 das strengste Prognoseerfordernis stellen. Nur zwischen Artt. 72 und 73 differenzierend und bei Art. 73 geringere Anforderungen stellend Schiedsgericht der Börse für Landwirtschaftliche Produkte Wien, 10.12.1997, CISG-online 351 = östZRVgl 1998, 211; *Schlechtriem*, GS Hellner, S. 229, 234 f.; *Bridge*, 25 J. L. & Com. (2005-06), 405, 414; *Azeredo da Silveira*, 2 Nordic J. Comm. L. (2005), 43 f.; *Jan*, S. 211 f.; *Piltz*, Internationales Kaufrecht, Rn. 5–299; *Achilles*, Art. 73, Rn. 4. Selbe Anforderungen an Artt. 71 und 72 stellend, an Art. 73 jedoch geringere *Herber/Czerwenka*, Art. 72, Rn. 2 und Art. 73, Rn. 4.
[53] HGer Zürich, 5.2.1997, CISG-online 327 = CLOUT Nr. 214.
[54] LG Ellwangen, 21.8.1995, CISG-online 279.
[55] Der Arb. Ct. Hungarian CCI, 25.5.1999, CISG-online 438 = CLOUT Nr. 265, urteilte, dass der Käufer einen Sukzessivlieferungsvertrag über Sauerkirschen gem. Art. 73 II für die Zukunft beenden dürfe, wenn der Verkäufer sich in Anbetracht deutlich gestiegener Marktpreise weigere, weitere Teillieferungen zu den im Rahmenvertrag vereinbarten Konditionen zu erbringen; ähnlich das Schiedsgericht der Hamburger freundschaftlichen Arbitrage, 29.12.1998, CISG-online 638 = CLOUT Nr. 299 = RIW 1999, 394: Der Verkäufer habe nicht nur die zweite Teillieferung, sondern jede zukünftige Lieferung zu den im Rahmenvertrag vereinbarten Konditionen abgelehnt, der Käufer könne daher die Rechte aus Art. 73 II geltend machen; vgl. auch HGer Zürich, 22.11.2010, Erw. IV. C.3., CISG-online 2160.
[56] MünchKommHGB/*Mankowski*, Art. 73, Rn. 13.
[57] OLG Düsseldorf, 9.7.2010, CISG-online 2171, Rn. 89 ff.; Schiedsgericht der Börse für Landwirtschaftliche Produkte Wien, 10.12.1997, CISG-online 351 = östZRVgl 1998, 211; Shanghai First Intermediate People's Court (District Court), 25.12.2008, CISG-online 2059; *Dingxi Longhai Dairy Ltd v. Becwood Technology Group L. L. C.*, U. S. C. App. (8th Cir.), 14.2.2011, CISG-online 2256 (Teillieferung in verschimmelter Verpackung).
[58] Vgl. CA Grenoble, 22.2.1995, CISG-online 151: Eine französische Jeanslieferantin (Berufungsklägerin) stand in Geschäftskontakt mit einer US-amerikanischen Abnehmerin (Berufungsbeklagte), die ihrerseits die Ware an Kunden in Afrika und Südamerika weiterveräusserte. Anlässlich der anstehenden zweiten Lieferung verlangte die Lieferantin von ihrer Geschäftspartnerin eine Erklärung über den Zielort und den endgültigen Abnehmer der Jeans, weil sie sich zum einen vertraglich gegenüber anderen ausländischen Jeanslieferanten zur Vermeidung der Bildung von Parallelmärkten verpflichtet habe und weil sie zum anderen auf dem US-amerikanischen Markt selbst nicht Lizenzinhaberin der vertriebenen Marke sei. Die beharrliche Weigerung der Berufungsbeklagten, die geforderte Erklärung abzugeben, wurde von der CA Grenoble als wesentliche Vertragsverletzung i. S. d. Art. 25 eingestuft, für deren Wiederholung in der Zukunft triftige Gründe sprächen, weshalb die Berufungsklägerin den Sukzessivlieferungsvertrag gem. Art. 73 II für die Zukunft habe aufheben dürfen.
[59] Vgl. Shanghai First Intermediate People's Court (Dist. Ct.), 25.12.2008, CISG-online 2059: („the trust between the parties was broken […] The mistrust between the parties arose mainly from the breach of the contract by the seller in delivering the first installment.").

Verletzungen der Zahlungspflicht, wenn das Gewicht der zu erwartenden Vertragsverletzung im Verhältnis zum noch ausstehenden Gesamtvertrag erheblich ist.[60]

5. Vertragsaufhebung

23 a) **Aufhebung ex nunc.** Das Aufhebungsrecht beschränkt sich gegenüber der normalen Vertragsaufhebung auf die zukünftigen Lieferungen, wobei **allfällige Leistungsvorbereitungen,** die eine der Parteien bereits vorgenommen hat, die Vertragsaufhebung für die Zukunft nicht hindern. Dies ist die Konsequenz der Teilbarkeit und relativen Selbstständigkeit der Einzellieferung.

24 b) **Vorzeitige Anzeigepflicht.** Eine **Informationspflicht** hinsichtlich der geplanten Vertragsaufhebung, um der anderen Seite eine Sicherheitsleistung zu ermöglichen,[61] ist nicht vorgesehen. Unter Berücksichtigung der im Sukzessivlieferungsvertrag bestehenden engen und unter Umständen länger dauernden Verbindungen der Parteien wäre eine solche Informationspflicht zwar durchaus angemessen gewesen, sie dürfte aber **nach jetziger Fassung nicht** in Art. 73 II hineinzulesen sein.[62] Jedoch kann der vertragstreue Teil gegebenenfalls gegen seine Schadensminderungspflicht aus Art. 77 verstossen, wenn er unvermittelt die Aufhebung des Rahmenvertrages gemäss Art. 73 II für die Zukunft erklärt, ohne zuvor Kontakt zu seinem Vertragspartner aufgenommen zu haben.[63]

25 c) **Form und Frist für die Aufhebungserklärung.** Für die Vertragsaufhebung gilt Art. 26. Die Aufhebungserklärung hat innerhalb angemessener Frist zu erfolgen, wobei die Frist mit der **Kenntnis** von der auslösenden Vertragsverletzung beginnt.[64] Dies ist wesentlich klarer, als die Frist mit Eintritt der Vertragsverletzung beginnen lassen zu wollen,[65] denn der Eintritt lässt sich in den Fällen, in denen nicht eine einzelne Vertragsverletzung, sondern die Summe mehrerer nicht vertragsgemässer Teillieferungen Anlass zur Befürchtung einer wesentlichen Vertragsverletzung gibt,[66] nicht genau bestimmen.

26 Die Angemessenheit der Frist ergibt sich aus den Umständen des Vertrages und richtet sich nach dem objektiven **Massstab des Art. 8 II.** So ist die Frist etwa auch dann gewahrt, wenn die Aufhebung zwar nicht sofort erfolgt, sondern erst, nachdem der Schuldner einen Ersatzlieferanten gefunden hat („sans être brutale").[67] Zu berücksichtigen ist unter anderem der zeitliche Abstand zur nächsten Teillieferung. Stellt die Pflichtverletzung hinsichtlich der aktuellen Teillieferung zugleich eine wesentliche Vertragsverletzung im Sinne des Art. 73 I dar und will der Gläubiger die Aufhebung sowohl für den gegenwärtigen Teil wie für die

---

[60] *Staudinger/Magnus,* Art. 73, Rn. 23.
[61] Zu den jeweiligen Informationspflichten in Art. 71 III und Art. 72 II vgl. oben *Fountoulakis,* Art. 71 Rn. 27 f. sowie Art. 72 Rn. 17 ff.
[62] So aber *Bridge,* 25 J.L. & Com. (2005-06), 405, 420, der über Art. 7 II das Abwendungsrecht des Schuldners durch Sicherheitenstellung (Artt. 71 III, 72 II) auf Art. 73 II übertragen will; wie hier *Kröll u. a./Saidov,* Art. 73, Rn. 26.
[63] A. a. offenbar *Vanwijk-Alexandre,* R. D. A. I. 2001, 353, 374; *Soergel/Lüderitz/Dettmeier,* Art. 73, Rn. 10.
[64] OLG Brandenburg, 18.11.2008, B. II.1.b)bb), CISG-online 1734; *Azeredo da Silveira,* 2 Nordic Journal of Commercial Law (2005), 44; *Staudinger/Magnus,* Art. 73, Rn. 24; *Herber/Czerwenka,* Art. 73, Rn. 5; *Bamberger/Roth/Saenger,* Art. 73, Rn. 11; *Ferrari u. a./Saenger,* Internationales Vertragsrecht, Art. 73, Rn. 11; MünchKommHGB/*Mankowski,* Art. 73, Rn. 16; *Brunner,* Art. 73, Rn. 13; *Honsell/Brunner/Hurni,* Art. 73, Rn. 23; m. E. auch *Kröll u. a./Saidov,* Art. 73, Rn. 27, der die Frist mit Kenntnis des triftigen Grundes für künftige Vertragsverletzungen beginnen lassen will. Dies ist aber in casu derselbe Zeitpunkt wie derjenige der Kenntnis von der Vertragsverletzung, denn Letztere muss gemäss Art. 73 II derart sein, dass sie die Prognose künftiger Vertragsverletzungen erlaubt. Da es nach hier vertretener Ansicht nicht auf die Kenntnis einer beliebigen, sondern vielmehr einer qualifizierten Vertragsverletzung ankommt – qualifiziert in dem Sinne, dass sie die Grundlage für die (objektivierte) Prognose weiterer Verletzungen bilden muss -, besteht m. E. kein Unterschied zwischen dem Zeitpunkt der Kenntnis einer Vertragsverletzung nach Art. 73 II und dem Zeitpunkt des Feststehens der Prognose.
[65] So aber *Bianca/Bonell/Bennett,* Art. 73, Anm. 2.7.
[66] Dazu vorne Rn. 18.
[67] CA Grenoble, 22.2.1995, CISG-online 151 = J. D. I. Nr. 3 1995, 632 ff.; zust. *Bridge,* 25 J. L. & Com. (2005-06), 405, 419 („commercially flexible and sensible").

künftigen Teillieferungen erklären, ist, wie bereits dargelegt, auch für Art. 73 I davon auszugehen, dass die Aufhebungserklärung innerhalb angemessener Frist erfolgen muss.[68]

d) Rechtsfolgen. Die Vertragsaufhebung für die Zukunft führt zu einer **Spaltung des** 27 **Gesamtvertrages.** Der bisher durchgeführte Teil des Sukzessivlieferungsvertrages einschliesslich der Teillieferung, die den triftigen Grund für die Annahme einer künftigen Störung gegeben hat – wenn sie nicht gem. Art. 73 I auch aufgehoben wurde – bleiben unberührt.[69] Auch Zahlungsverpflichtungen, Schadensersatzansprüche etc. für diesen Bereich bleiben bestehen. Für den in die Zukunft reichenden Teil des Vertrages entfallen die Pflichten für beide Seiten gem. Art. 81 I 1. Eine Rückabwicklung findet nur ausnahmsweise statt, etwa hinsichtlich einer erfolgten Vorauszahlung oder Überlassung von Geräten oder Lizenzen, die für den Gesamtvertrag bestimmt waren. Solche Elemente des Gesamtvertrages, die für die Gesamtdurchführung gedacht waren, stehen der Teilbarkeit des Vertrages nicht im Wege, bedürfen aber der Abwicklung in ähnlicher Weise wie nach einer vollen Aufhebung des Vertrages.[70]

6. Verhältnis zu Artt. 71, 72

In der Rechtsprechung werden Artt. 72 und 73 II in der Regel nebeneinander ange- 28 wandt.[71] Art. 73 II ist vom vorzeitigen Vertragsbruch des Art. 72 allerdings dadurch abzugrenzen, dass der Schuldner hier bereits eine wesentliche Vertragsverletzung in Bezug auf eine Teillieferung begangen hat, die die Prognose der künftigen Störung trägt. Wohl deshalb braucht es **bei Art. 73 II, anders als bei Art. 72 II, keine Anzeige** an den Schuldner, dass er die Vertragsaufhebung durch das Stellen ausreichender Sicherheiten abwenden könne. Dies mag bedauerlich sein,[72] macht aber die Differenzierung zwischen Artt. 73 II und 72 praktisch bedeutsam. Als weitere Unterschiede können hervorgehoben werden, dass Art. 73 II die Aufhebungserklärung ausdrücklich befristet („innerhalb angemessener Frist"), dass er geringere Anforderungen an die Prognose stellt[73] sowie dass er die Aufhebung auf künftige Teillieferungen beschränkt („Aufhebung ... für die Zukunft"). Art. 73 II sieht somit für die antizipierte Vertragsverletzung bei Sukzessivlieferungsverträgen spezifische Regeln vor, die von der allgemeinen Vorschrift in Art. 72 abweichen. Daraus ergibt sich ein **Vorrang** für den Behelf nach **Art. 73 II.**[74] Dagegen hindert das Vorliegen

---

[68] Vgl. allgemein oben Art. 26 Rn. 15f. und konkret oben Art. 73 Rn. 13. Netherlands Arbitration Institute, 15.10.2002, CISG-online 780, hat einen Verstoss gegen Art. 73 II darin gesehen, dass der Käufer bereits mehrere Monate lang (berechtigte) Mängelrügen erhoben, die Vertragsaufhebung für die Zukunft dann jedoch erst wenige Tage vor der vereinbarten nächsten Teillieferung erklärt hatte. Die Entscheidung spricht für einen Gleichlauf der Fristen in Art. 73 I und II; vgl. auch OLG Brandenburg, 18.11.2008, CISG-online 1734, B. II.1.b)bb): Keine Aufhebung innerhalb angemessener Frist bei Zuwarten von fast drei Monaten. Zur Notwendigkeit einer allgemeinen Frist für die Aufhebung und ihrer Herleitung aus der Entscheidungsreife *Schlechtriem,* Gemeinsame Bestimmungen, S. 161.
[69] *Herber/Czerwenka,* Art. 73, Rn. 3; *Bamberger/Roth/Saenger,* Art. 73, Rn. 10; *Witz/Salger/Lorenz/Lorenz,* Art. 73, Rn. 15.
[70] *Von Scheven,* S. 274 f.
[71] Vgl. nur AppGer Helsinki, 30.6.1998, CISG-online 1304; Schiedsgericht der Handelskammer Zürich, 31.5.1996, CISG-online 1291 = YB Comm. Arb. 1998, 128 ff.
[72] Dazu vorne Rn. 24.
[73] Vgl. Rn. 21.
[74] Zustimmend MünchKommHGB/*Mankowski,* Art. 73, Rn. 19; *Achilles,* Art. 73, Rn. 6; *Kröll u. a./Saidov,* Art. 73, Rn. 25; ähnlich *Brunner,* Art. 73, Rn. 11 (konkurrierende Anwendung, aber Art. 73 III geht bzgl. Rechtsfolgen als speziellere Regel vor). Nach anderer Meinung ist vom vorranglosen Überschneiden der Regelungsbereiche der Artt. 72 und 73 II auszugehen: *Herber/Czerwenka,* Art. 73, Rn. 10; *Bianca/Bonell/ Bennett,* Art. 73, Anm. 3.3.; *Soergel/Lüderitz/Dettmeier,* Art. 72, Rn. 2. Eine dritte Auffassung verneint das Vorliegen eines Konkurrenzverhältnisses, da sich die Anwendungsbereiche beider Normen nicht überschnitten: *Staudinger/Magnus,* Art. 73, Rn. 28; MünchKomm/*P. Huber,* Art. 73, Rn. 18. *Bamberger/Roth/Saenger,* Art. 73 Rn. 12, sowie *Ferrari u. a./Saenger,* Internationales Vertragsrecht, Art. 73, Rn. 12, weisen zu Recht darauf hin, dass die letztgenannte Auffassung – keine Überschneidung der Anwendungsbereiche – der hier vertretenen Auffassung des Vorrangs des Art. 73 II vor Art. 72 im praktischen Ergebnis gleicht.

der Voraussetzungen des Art. 73 II die Ausübung des Zurückbehaltungsrechts nach Art. 71 I nicht.[75]

V. Erweiterung des Aufhebungsrechts bei Zweckzusammenhang, Art. 73 III

1. Tatbestandsvoraussetzungen

29   Art. 73 III gilt nur für den Käufer und erlaubt ihm, unter gewissen Voraussetzungen den ganzen oder Teile des Gesamtvertrags aufzuheben. Er setzt voraus, dass der Verkäufer eine wesentliche Vertragsverletzung bezüglich einer Einzellieferung begangen hat (Art. 73 I), sowie, dass durch die wesentliche Vertragsverletzung hinsichtlich einer Teillieferung der Gesamtvertrag oder ein grösserer Teil davon wegen des inneren Zusammenhangs der Einzellieferungen direkt gestört wird. Gleichzeitig mit der Aufhebung betreffend die Einzellieferung muss auch diejenige betreffend die weiteren Vertragsteile erklärt werden.[76] Der Behelf in **Art. 73 III ist demnach nicht selbstständig, sondern erweitert die Reaktion** auf die Störung einer Einzellieferung auf den ganzen Vertrag oder Teile desselben.

2. Aufhebung nach Art. 73 I

30   Art. 73 III verlangt zunächst, dass der Käufer wegen einer wesentlichen Pflichtverletzung bezüglich einer Teillieferung zur Aufhebung berechtigt ist (Art. 73 I)[77] und sein Aufhebungsrecht auch ausübt.

3. Zweckzusammenhang

31   a) **Interpendenz einzelner Teillieferungen.** Im Gegensatz zum allgemeinen Vertrag mit aufeinander folgenden Lieferungen, bei dem die Einzellieferungen selbstständig und teilbar im Gesamtvertrag verbunden sind, ist hier zusätzlich ein **einheitlicher Erfolg** aller oder wenigstens mehrerer Einzellieferungen vorausgesetzt.[78] Der Zweckzusammenhang steht nicht in Widerspruch zum Erfordernis der Teilbarkeit des Gesamtvertrages, da teilbare Einzellieferungen im Rahmen des Gesamtvertrages auch beim einheitlichen Vertragsziel durchaus anzutreffen sind. Entscheidend ist, dass **die einzelnen Teillieferungen aufeinander aufbauen** und erst ihre Summe eine funktionsfähige Einheit ergibt. Beispiele sind etwa die einheitliche Materialversorgung bei der Herstellung eines Bauwerks (Fassadenverkleidung, Dach, Fenster), Lieferung der notwendigen Stoffe für eine Spezialfertigung, die einen bestimmten (Mindest-)Umfang erfordert, etwa im Chemie- oder Textilbereich, oder die Versorgung mit einem Produkt für einen bestimmten Käuferkreis nach entsprechender Vorbereitung durch Werbemassnahmen. Es sind regelmässig Fälle, in denen die versprochenen Lieferungen nicht ohne weiteres durch Lieferungen von dritter Seite ersetzt werden können.[79] Dabei müssen die bereits erbrachten bzw. die künftigen Lieferungen weder in

---

[75] Vgl. *Shuttle Packaging Systems, L. L. C. v. Jacob Tsonakis, INA S. A. and INA Plastics Corporation*, U. S. Dist. Ct. (W. D. Mich.), 17.12.2001, CISG-online 773 = 2001 U. S. Dist. LEXIS 21 630; ICC, 9448/1999, CISG-online 707 = 11:2 ICC Int. Ct. Arb. Bull. (2000), 103; OGH, 12.2.1998, CISG-online 349; *Staudinger/Magnus*, Art. 73, Rn. 28a; *Gabriel*, Contracts, S. 219; *Brunner*, Art. 73, Rn. 5.
[76] Sekretariatskommentar, Art. 64, Nr. 7; *Bamberger/Roth/Saenger*, Art. 73, Rn. 14; *Soergel/Lüderitz/Dettmeier*, Art. 73, Rn. 12.
[77] Wie hier MünchKomm/*P. Huber*, Art. 73, Rn. 21; a. A. *Staudinger/Magnus*, Art. 73, Rn. 30: Aushebungsrecht könne aus Art. 73 I oder II folgen; unklar MünchKommHGB/*Mankowski*, Art. 73, Rn. 22 (Art. 73 I oder II als Basis) gegenüber Rn. 27 (nur Art. 73 I).
[78] Vgl. Sekretariatskommentar, Art. 64, Nr. 7 f.; *Honnold/Flechtner*, Art. 73, Rn. 402 a. E.; *Herber/Czerwenka*, Art. 73, Rn. 7; *Piltz*, Internationales Kaufrecht, Rn. 5–301; *Staudinger/Magnus*, Art. 73, Rn. 32; vgl. auch *Achilles*, Art. 73, Rn. 7.
[79] Zur Beurteilung der Nichtverwendbarkeit von erfolgter Teillieferung und künftiger Lieferungen vgl. Sekretariatskommentar, Art. 64, Nr. 7 f.; *Schlechtriem*, Gemeinsame Bestimmungen, S. 161 f.

wesentlicher Weise vertragswidrig sein, noch müssen sie überhaupt zu beanstanden sein; es genügt, wenn ihr Nutzen für den Käufer wegen einer wesentlichen vertragswidrigen Teillieferung wegfällt.[80] Das Ausbleiben oder die Vertragswidrigkeit einer Lieferung machen die Erreichung des Vertragszieles unmöglich.

b) Massstäbe. Der Zweckzusammenhang enthält **objektive und subjektive Elemente.** 32
Die Zusammengehörigkeit einzelner Lieferungen zu einem einheitlichen Erfolg lässt sich zunächst objektiv bestimmen (Art. 8 II), wie es der Tendenz des Übereinkommens zur Objektivierung der Massstäbe allgemein entspricht.

Die Festlegung des Zwecks, also des Vertragsziels, enthält dagegen stets zumindest auch 33
subjektive Elemente.[81] Das Übereinkommen hat versucht, auch dieses Element zu objektivieren, indem es fordert, dass beide Parteien den Zweck beim Vertragsschluss „in Betracht gezogen haben" müssen (contemplated by the parties, envisagées par les parties).[82] Die eine Partei muss den Zweck daher zumindest als möglichen Vertragszweck der anderen Seite **erkannt haben,** wobei das Erkannthabenmüssen des Verwendungszwecks, wie bereits die Zusammengehörigkeit einzelner Lieferungen,[83] danach beurteilt wird, ob sich eine vernünftige Person in den Schuhen des Verkäufers (Art. 8 II) aufgrund der im Vertrag und der ihn begleitenden Umstände der Verwendungsvorstellungen des Käufers gewahr werden musste.[84]

4. Aufhebung nur für Vergangenheit oder Zukunft

Die Vertragsaufhebung ist in Art. 73 III nur hinsichtlich erbrachter **oder** künftiger Leis- 34
tungen vorgesehen. Sehr oft wird es aber so sein, dass der Zweck des gesamten Vertrages nicht mehr erreichbar ist. In Art. 75 EKG war die Möglichkeit zur **Aufhebung des Gesamtvertrages** ausdrücklich vorgesehen.[85] Aus der Vorgeschichte wie aus dem Sachzusammenhang ist zu schliessen, dass eine Verengung im Übereinkommen nicht beabsichtigt war.[86] Wenn das Vertragsziel insgesamt nicht mehr erreichbar ist, liegt eine wesentliche Verletzung des gesamten Vertrages vor, die auch zur Aufhebung des Ganzen berechtigt.[87]

Art. 73 III gibt dem Käufer ein **„Maximalrecht",**[88] wobei die äussere Grenze durch den 35
Zweckzusammenhang gesetzt wird. Der Käufer darf den Vertrag soweit aufheben, wie der Zweckzusammenhang reicht; er muss den Maximalrahmen aber nicht ausschöpfen.[89] Soweit für Lieferungen aus der Vergangenheit die Vertragsaufhebung erklärt wird, treten entsprechende Rückabwicklungspflichten ein.

5. Wirkungen

Die Aufhebung von Teilen des Vertrages oder des ganzen Vertrages kann zur Verschiebung 36
von Terminen, Anpassung von Rahmenbedingungen (z. B. Sicherheiten), aber auch zu

---

[80] *Staudinger/Magnus,* Art. 73, Rn. 33; MünchKommHGB/*Mankowski,* Art. 73, Rn. 24.
[81] Deshalb dürften die Begriffe des „Zweckzusammenhangs" und des von Art. 75 II EKG und § 323 V 1 BGB gewählten „Interessewegfalls" auch zu vergleichbaren Ergebnissen führen.
[82] Dazu Sekretariatskommentar, Art. 64, Nr. 7 f.
[83] Vgl. oben Rn. 8 ff.
[84] MünchKomm/*P. Huber,* Art. 73, Rn. 22; *Staudinger/Magnus,* Art. 73, Rn. 34; MünchKommHGB/*Mankowski,* Art. 73, Rn. 25; *Ferrari u. a./Saenger,* Internationales Vertragsrecht, Art. 73, Rn. 15.
[85] [...] Aufhebung des Vertrages für die künftigen Lieferungen oder für die bereits erhaltenen Lieferungen **oder für beide** [...] (Art. 75 II EKG).
[86] YB VII (1976), S. 128, Nr. 5; YB V (1974), S. 40, Nr. 117–126.
[87] CIETAC, 7.4.2005, CISG-online 1453; *Piltz,* Internationales Kaufrecht, Rn. 5–300, 5–302; *Kröll u. a./Saidov,* Art. 73, Rn. 31; *Bianca/Bonell/Bennett,* Art. 73, Anm. 2.8. f. (die die Wirkungen von Art. 73 III ohne weitere Begründung auf den Gesamtvertrag erstrecken).
[88] MünchKommHGB/*Mankowski,* Art. 73, Rn. 28.
[89] A. A. *Bridge,* 25 J. L. & Com. (2005-06), 405, 420: Die Option, lediglich eine beschränkte Anzahl an Teillieferungen aufzuheben, bestehe nicht.

besonderen Rückabwicklungspflichten führen.⁹⁰ Zu **Schadensersatzansprüchen,** die neben der Vertragsaufhebung bestehen können, vgl. Artt. 74 ff.

6. Form und Frist der Aufhebung

37 Die Voraussetzungen für die Aufhebungserklärung richten sich nach Art. 26. Die Erklärung muss **gleichzeitig** mit der Aufhebung der auslösenden Teillieferung nach Art. 73 I erfolgen. Eine spätere Erstreckung der Aufhebung, d. h. in zeitlichem Abstand zur Aufhebung der auslösenden Teillieferung, ist nicht zugelassen.⁹¹ Diese zeitliche Bindung stellt erhebliche Anforderungen an den Käufer, der sich entscheiden muss. Die Aufhebungserklärung nach Art. 73 III muss nicht separat zu der nach Art. 73 I erklärt werden, sondern es reicht eine **einheitliche** Erklärung.

38 Für die Aufhebungserklärung sowohl hinsichtlich der auslösenden Teillieferung wie auch hinsichtlich der übrigen Lieferungen ist im Übereinkommen eine **ausdrückliche Frist nicht vorgesehen.** Es gelten hierfür jedoch die gleichen Erwägungen zur Erforderlichkeit von Fristen wie für die Aufhebungsrechte in Art. 73 I und II.⁹²

VI. Abgrenzung von Art. 73 und Art. 51

39 Artt. 73 und 51 betreffen beide den Fall einer wesentlichen Störung einer Teilverpflichtung. Allerdings regelt Art. 73 die Situation, dass die Leistungen zeitlich nacheinander erfolgen sollen, wohingegen Art. 51 Leistungen betrifft, die grundsätzlich gleichzeitig erfolgen sollten, aber teilbar sind und aus technischen Gründen in Teilen erbracht werden.⁹³ Ein weiterer Unterschied besteht darin, dass Art. 73 I, II sowohl für den **Käufer als auch für den Verkäufer** gilt, wohingegen Art. 51 einen Rechtsbehelf einzig des Käufers darstellt. Bezüglich der wesentlichen Störung einer **Einzellieferung** bestehen im Ergebnis keine Unterschiede in den Rechtsfolgen, wenn man wie hier davon ausgeht, dass dem Käufer nicht nur bei Art. 51 I, sondern auch bei Art. 73 I sämtliche Rechtsbehelfe zur Verfügung stehen (d. h. nicht nur ein Aufhebungsrecht, sondern auch die Behelfe in Artt. 45, 71, 72).⁹⁴ Eine eigenständige Bedeutung kommt Art. 51 I im Rahmen von Art. 73 I dann zu, wenn innerhalb der Teillieferung nur ein Teil von der wesentlichen Vertragsverletzung betroffen ist; in diesem Falle kann der Vertrag, vorbehaltlich Art. 51 II, nur hinsichtlich dieses Teils aufgehoben werden.⁹⁵ Art. 73 III und 51 II weichen zwar im Wortlaut, wohl kaum aber in der zugrundeliegenden Wertung voneinander ab.⁹⁶ Die Frage, ob ein Vertrag als Sukzessivlieferungsvertrag anzusehen ist, wird aber im Hinblick auf **Art. 73 II** relevant,⁹⁷ indem dieser, da **zukunftsgerichtet,** von der Konzeption her nur auf Sukzessivlieferungsverträge passt. Ein Vorgehen über Art. 51 II hat hier den Vorteil, dass über Artt. 49 I b), 47 der gesamte Vertrag aufgehoben werden kann, ohne dass der Nachweis des „triftigen Grundes" in Art. 73 II erbracht werden muss.⁹⁸

---

⁹⁰ Auch bei der Vertragsaufhebung hinsichtlich künftiger Lieferungen kann ausnahmsweise eine ergänzende Rückabwicklung notwendig werden, vgl. *von Scheven,* S. 276 f.; *Bamberger/Roth/Saenger,* Art. 73, Rn. 14; *Achilles,* Art. 73, Rn. 8.
⁹¹ *Staudinger/Magnus,* Art. 73, Rn. 35; *Kröll u. a./Saidov,* Art. 73, Rn. 35.
⁹² S. dazu Art. 73 Rn. 13, 25 f.
⁹³ *Schlechtriem,* Internationales UN-Kaufrecht, Rn. 192; *Piltz,* Internationales Kaufrecht, Rn. 5–296.
⁹⁴ Vgl. oben Rn. 16.
⁹⁵ Vgl. oben *Müller-Chen,* Art. 51 Rn. 3; *Bianca/Bonell/Bennett,* Art. 73, Anm. 2.1.; *Staudinger/Magnus,* Art. 73, Rn. 7; *Ferrari u. a./Saenger,* Internationales Vertragsrecht, Art. 51, Rn. 2; *Huber/Mullis,* S. 295; *Honsell/Brunner/Hurni,* Art. 73, Rn. 7; a. A. *Kröll u. a./Saidov,* Art. 73, Rn. 14 (keine Anwendung von Art. 51 I im Rahmen von Art. 73 I).
⁹⁶ Vgl. zum Ganzen *Schlechtriem,* Internationales UN-Kaufrecht, Rn. 193 ff.
⁹⁷ Die Abgrenzung zwischen Artt. 73 und 51 wird in der Literatur jeweils unterschiedlich vorgenommen, vgl. etwa die a. A. bei MünchKomm/*P. Huber,* Art. 73, Rn. 3; *Staudinger/Magnus,* Art. 73, Rn. 7; *Bianca/Bonell/Bennett,* Art. 73, Anm. 3.2.
⁹⁸ *Ferrari u. a./Saenger,* Internationales Vertragsrecht, Art. 73, Rn. 16; *Kee,* 6 VJ (2002), 281, 282.

VII. Beweislast

Der Gläubiger, der sich auf einen oder mehrere der in Art. 73 enthaltenen Rechtsbehelfe **40**
beruft, muss beweisen, dass die jeweiligen Voraussetzungen vorliegen.[99]

---

[99] Vgl. Schiedsgericht der Börse für landwirtschaftliche Produkte Wien, 10.12.1997, CISG-online 351 = östZRVgl 1998, 211; ausführlich auch *Plate,* Beweislastverteilung, S. 148 ff.

Abschnitt II. Schadenersatz

Section II
Damages

Section II
Dommages-intérêts

Art. 74 [Umfang des Schadenersatzes]

Als Schadenersatz für die durch eine Partei begangene Vertragsverletzung ist der der anderen Partei infolge der Vertragsverletzung entstandene Verlust, einschließlich des entgangenen Gewinns, zu ersetzen. Dieser Schadenersatz darf jedoch den Verlust nicht übersteigen, den die vertragsbrüchige Partei bei Vertragsabschluß als mögliche Folge der Vertragsverletzung vorausgesehen hat oder unter Berücksichtigung der Umstände, die sie kannte oder kennen mußte, hätte voraussehen müssen.

Art. 74

Damages for breach of contract by one party consist of a sum equal to the loss, including loss of profit, suffered by the other party as a consequence of the breach. Such damages may not exceed the loss which the party in breach foresaw or ought to have foreseen at the time of the conclusion of the contract, in the light of the facts and matters of which he then knew or ought to have known, as a possible consequence of the breach of contract.

Art. 74

Les dommages-intérêts pour une contravention au contrat commise par une partie sont égaux à la perte subie et au gain manqué par l'autre partie par suite de la contravention. Ces dommages-intérêts ne peuvent être supérieurs à la perte subie et au gain manqué que la partie en défaut avait prévus ou aurait dû prévoir au moment de la conclusion du contrat, en considérant les faits dont elle avait connaissance ou aurait dû avoir connaissance, comme étant des conséquences possibles de la contravention au contrat.

Übersicht

	Rn.
I. Vorgeschichte	1
II. Grundgedanken und Systematik	3
1. Grundsätze	5
2. Verhältnis zu anderen Bestimmungen des CISG	9
3. Verhältnis zu anderen Rechtsbehelfen	10
III. Anwendungsbereich	11
1. Verletzung vertraglicher Pflichten	11
2. Verletzung von Obliegenheiten	13
3. Personenschäden	14
4. Ersatzberechtigte Personen und Drittschäden	15
IV. Form des Ersatzes	17
V. Umfang des Ersatzanspruchs	18
1. Allgemeines	18
2. Entstandener Verlust	20
a) Nichterfüllungsschaden	21
b) Begleitschäden	27
c) Folgeschäden	32
3. Entgangener Gewinn	36
4. Immaterielle Schäden	39
5. Zurechnung des Schadens	40
VI. Berechnung des Schadens	41
1. Konkrete und abstrakte Schadensberechnung	41
2. Vorteilsanrechnung	42
3. Gewinnabschöpfung	43
4. Zeitpunkt der Schadensberechnung	44

VII. Voraussehbarkeitsregel (S. 2) 45
   1. Allgemeines 45
   2. Relevante Personen und massgeblicher Zeitpunkt 47
   3. Massstab der Voraussehbarkeit 48
   4. Gegenstand der Voraussehbarkeit 50
   5. Beispiele 51
      a) Nichterfüllungsschäden 52
      b) Begleitschäden 53
      c) Folgeschäden 54
VIII. Vertragliche Haftungsregelungen 58
   1. Allgemeines 58
   2. Fixe Summen 59
   3. Haftungsbeschränkungen 60
IX. Einzelfragen 61
   1. Erfüllungsort für die Schadenersatzpflicht 61
   2. Verjährung 62
   3. Währung der Ersatzleistung 63
X. Beweisfragen 64
   1. Beweislast 64
   2. Beweismass 65
   3. Beweisführung 66

I. Vorgeschichte

Art. 74 regelt den Umfang von Schadenersatzansprüchen des Käufers oder des Verkäufers 1
bei Verletzung der jeweiligen vertraglichen Pflichten. Die Bestimmung wurde fast wörtlich
aus Art. 82 EKG übernommen. Sie gilt jedoch im Unterschied zu diesem auch im Falle der
Vertragsaufhebung, so dass Vorschriften, wie sie Artt. 86 und 87 EKG vorsahen, entfallen
konnten.[1]

Art. 74 enthält zwei wesentliche Grundgedanken: Den Grundsatz der **Totalreparation** 2
beziehungsweise des vollständigen Schadensausgleichs (principle of full compensation; principe de la réparation intégrale) und die Beschränkung der Haftung durch die **Voraussehbarkeitsregel**. Der Grundsatz des vollständigen Schadensausgleichs ist in vielen nationalen Rechtsordnungen ausdrücklich festgeschrieben.[2] Die Voraussehbarkeitsregel geht auf das französiche Recht (Art. 1150 Cc) und den englischen leading case *Hadley v. Baxendale*,[3] der seinerseits in die angloamerikanischen Kaufrechtskodifikationen[4] Eingang gefunden hat, zurück. Auch die PICC (vgl. Artt. 7.4.2 und 7.4.4), die PECL (Artt. 9:502 und 9:503) und der CESL-Entwurf (Artt. 160 f.)[5] sowie internationale Transportrechtskonventionen normieren den Grundsatz des vollständigen Schadensausgleichs und seine Beschränkung durch die Voraussehbarkeitsregel.[6]

---

[1] Eingehend zur Entstehungsgeschichte *Stoll*, 3. Aufl., Art. 74 Rn. 1.
[2] Vgl. Art. 9:502 PECL, Comment 2; Art. 7.4.2 PICC; Deutschland: §§ 249 ff. BGB; Frankreich: Art. 1149 Cc; Italien: Art. 1223 Cc; Niederlande: Art. 6:96 BW; Österreich: §§ 1323 ff. ABGB; Portugal: Art. 564 I Cc; Spanien: Art. 1106 Cc. Rechtsvergleichender Überblick bei *Stoll*, Haftungsfolgen, S. 179–181, 323–341.
[3] [1854] 9 Ex. 341; zur Entstehung der Vorhersehbarkeitsregel und zum Vergleich zwischen der Vorhersehbarkeit nach CISG und nach nationalen Rechten s. *Ferrari*, Foreseeability, S. 305 ff. ; anders jetzt *Ferrari*, 13 VJ (2009), 15, 28 ff. („not a derivative of the rule in *Hadley v. Baxendale*"), unter Hervorhebung der Unterschiede der Vorhersehbarkeit nach CISG und *Hadley v. Baxendale*.
[4] Ausführlich zum internen U.S.-amerikanischen Recht *Perillo*, Damages, S. 83 ff.
[5] Der Grundsatz der Totalreparation ergibt sich aus Art. 160 CESL-Entwurf, vgl. *Schmidt-Kessel/Remien*, Europäisches Kaufrecht, S. 511.
[6] Vgl. *Vékás*, Foreseeability, S. 170–172; *Magnus*, FS Herber, S. 30 ff. zum CMR und Warschauer Abkommen.

II. Grundgedanken und Systematik

3 Der in Art. 74 niedergelegte Grundsatz ist kurz aber aussagekräftig.[7] Der Gläubiger hat Anspruch auf **vollen Ausgleich** aller Nachteile, die ihm durch die Vertragsverletzung entstanden sind.[8] Entsprechend angloamerikanischem Vorbild (strict liability) hat der Schuldner ohne Rücksicht auf ein Verschulden für alle dem Gläubiger entstandenen Nachteile einzustehen, es sei denn, es liegt ein Entlastungsgrund nach Artt. 79, 80 CISG vor.[9] Die Bestimmung des Art. 74 ist grosszügig auszulegen. Der Schadenersatz hat sowohl das Interesse des Gläubigers an den mit der Erfüllung verbundenen Vorteilen (**Erfüllungsinteresse,** expectation interest) zu befriedigen als auch sein Interesse daran, nicht in Folge der Vertragsverletzung an anderen Rechtsgütern Schaden zu erleiden (**Integritätsinteresse,** indemnity interest).[10] Darüber hinaus ist auch das negative oder **Vertrauensinteresse** (reliance interest), d. h. die im Vertrauen auf den Bestand des Vertrages getätigten Aufwendungen, durch Art. 74 geschützt.[11] Die spezielle Erwähnung der Erstattungsfähigkeit auch des entgangenen Gewinns (loss of profit) hat lediglich klarstellende Funktion.[12]

4 Die in Art. 74 S. 2 niedergelegte **Voraussehbarkeitsregel** bildet nach h. M das Korrelat zur verschuldensunabhängigen Haftung der Parteien.[13] Die Haftungsbegrenzung ermöglicht es beiden Parteien, das mit der Eingehung des Vertrages verbundene finanzielle Risiko abzuschätzen und mögliche **Haftungsrisiken** entsprechend zu **versichern.**[14] Darüber hinaus hat die Voraussehbarkeitsregel den ökonomisch sicher sinnvollen (Neben-)Effekt, den **Informationsfluss** unter den Parteien zu fördern, indem sie angehalten werden, ungewöhnliche Schadensrisiken der anderen Partei im Zeitpunkt des Vertragsschlusses mitzuteilen.[15]

1. Grundsätze

5 Während der Grundsatz des vollen Schadensausgleichs unbestritten ist, ist seine Bedeutung im Einzelnen jedoch recht unklar.[16] Vor allem im deutschsprachigen Rechtskreis wird

---

[7] Vgl. *Honnold/Flechtner,* Art. 74, Rn. 403.

[8] OGH, 14.1.2002, CISG-online 643 = IHR 2002, 76, 80; OGH, 9.3.2000, CISG-online 573 = IHR 2001, 39, 40; Int. Schiedsgericht der Bundeskammer der gewerblichen Wirtschaft in Österreich, 15.6.1994, CISG-online 120 = 691 = RIW 1995, 590, 591; Sekretariatskommentar, Art. 70, Rn. 3; CISG-AC, Op. 6 *(Gotanda),* Comment 1.1; *P. Huber/Mullis/P. Huber,* S. 269; *Staudinger/Magnus,* Art. 74, Rn. 19; *Bianca/Bonell/ Knapp,* Art. 74, Anm. 3.2.; *Treitel,* Remedies for Breach, S. 82; *Schlechtriem,* Gemeinsame Bestimmungen, S. 163; *Audit,* Vente internationale, Anm. 172.; *Saidov,* Limiting Damages, I. 1.; ähnlich *Honnold/Flechtner,* Art. 74, Rn. 403. Kritisch *Honsell,* SJZ 1992, 361, 362, der jedoch zu Unrecht jenen Grundsatz mit der Differenzhypothese als „Produkt pandektistischer Begriffsjurisprudenz" gleichsetzt.

[9] *Neumayer/Ming,* Vor Art. 74, Anm. 2.; *Weber,* Vertragsverletzungsfolgen, S. 166, 191; *Audit,* Vente internationale, Anm. 171.; *Witz/Salger/Lorenz/Witz,* Art. 74, Rn. 1; *Herber/Czerwenka,* Art. 74, Rn. 3; *Roßmeier,* RIW 2000, 407, 408; *Karollus,* S. 206; *Ryffel,* S. 4–7, 37–41.

[10] OGH, 14.1.2002, CISG-online 643 = IHR 2002, 76, 80; *Karollus,* S. 214; *Staudinger/Magnus,* Art. 74, Rn. 20; *Witz/Salger/Lorenz/Witz,* Art. 74, Rn. 12; *Weber,* Vertragsverletzungsfolgen, S. 192; *Roßmeier,* RIW 2000, 407, 408.

[11] OGH, 14.1.2002, CISG-online 643 = IHR 2002, 76, 80; CISG-AC, Op. 6 *(Gotanda),* Comment 1.1; *Saidov,* Limiting Damages, I. 1; *Brölsch,* Schadensersatz; *Neumayer/Ming,* Art. 74, Anm. 1.; *Schneider,* 9 Pace Int'l L. Rev. (1997), 223, 228; zweifelnd *Karollus,* S. 215 f.; einschränkend *Witz/Salger/Lorenz/Witz,* Art. 74, Rn. 12 (frustrierte Aufwendungen nur im Rahmen des Erfüllungsinteresses ersatzfähig). Zum Ersatz frustrierter Aufwendungen im Falle der Rückabwicklung vgl. *Schmidt-Ahrendts,* IHR 2006, 67 ff.

[12] Vgl. Sekretariatskommentar, Art. 70, Rn. 3; *Witz/Salger/Lorenz/Witz,* Art. 74, Rn. 15; *Farnsworth,* 27 Am. J. Comp. L. (1979), 247, 249.

[13] *Witz/Salger/Lorenz/Witz,* Art. 74, Rn. 2; *U. Huber,* Leistungsstörungen, S. 729 („dogmatisch und praktisch untrennbar miteinander verbunden"); *Vékás,* Foreseeability, S. 159.

[14] *Schlechtriem,* Internationales UN-Kaufrecht, Rn. 302; *ders.,* Gemeinsame Bestimmungen, S. 166 f.; *Staudinger/Magnus,* Art. 74, Rn. 31; *Witz/Salger/Lorenz/Witz,* Art. 74, Rn. 27; *Karollus,* S. 217 f.; *Weber,* Vertragsverletzungsfolgen, S. 198; anderer, von der ökonomischen Analyse des Rechts beeinflusster Ansatz bei *Faust,* S. 216 ff.

[15] Vgl. *Faust,* S. 225 ff.

[16] S. *Schwenzer/Hachem,* Scope of Damages, S. 93.

insoweit vielfach unbesehen auf die unter deutschem Recht vertretene **Differenzhypothese** rekurriert und diese auf das CISG übertragen.[17] Die sämtlichen anderen Rechtskreisen fremde Differenzhypothese kann indes im Bereich des CISG nicht zur Anwendung gelangen, will man nicht die einheitliche Auslegung der Konvention gefährden.

Wie in den nationalen Rechtsordnungen ist der Schadenersatzanspruch primär auf **Kompensation** gerichtet. In zunehmendem Masse wird daneben jedoch heute die **Präventionsfunktion** des Schadenersatzes betont. Dies geht Hand in Hand damit, dass sich beim vertraglichen Schadenersatz das Hauptaugenmerk von der Betonung des rein rechnerischen ökonomischen Nutzens hin zum **Interesse** des Gläubigers **an vertragskonformer Erfüllung** verlagert.[18] 6

Diese in den nationalen Rechtsordnungen zu verzeichnende veränderte Sichtweise muss sich auch bei der Auslegung des CISG niederschlagen. Werden derartige Gedanken nicht berücksichtigt, besteht die Gefahr, dass nationale Gerichte dazu tendieren, nationales Recht konkurrierend zum CISG anzuwenden und damit die Vereinheitlichung in einem Kernbereich zu unterminieren. 7

Hieraus ergeben sich namentlich im Vergleich zu den Rechtsordnungen des deutschen Rechtskreises wichtige Unterschiede. Zunächst kann die im nationalen Recht vorgenommene **Grenzziehung zwischen materiellen und immateriellen Schäden** nicht unbesehen auf das CISG übertragen werden, zumal dieses keinen Ausschluss der Haftung für sogenannte immaterielle Schäden kennt. Zum anderen findet auch das rigide **Bereicherungsverbot** im CISG keine Anwendung. Wenngleich auch ein reiner Gewinnabschöpfungsanspruch aus Art. 74 nicht zu begründen sein mag, so kann der vom Schuldner durch die Vertragsverletzung erzielte Gewinn doch im Bereich der Schadensberechnung und -bemessung herangezogen werden. In diesem Zusammenhang können schliesslich auch **pönale Elemente** eine Rolle spielen,[19] selbst wenn ein eigentlicher **Strafschadenersatz** (punitive damages) vom CISG nicht vorgesehen ist. 8

2. Verhältnis zu anderen Bestimmungen des CISG

Art. 74 setzt das **Bestehen eines Schadenersatzanspruchs** des Käufers nach Art. 45 I lit. b oder des Verkäufers nach Art. 61 I lit. b voraus, die wiederum die Verletzung einer vertraglichen Pflicht zur Voraussetzung haben. Art. 74 als Grundnorm wird ergänzt durch Artt. 75 und 76, die **im Falle der Vertragsaufhebung** eine Berechnung des Mangelschadens anhand eines konkreten oder abstrakten Deckungsgeschäftes vorsehen. Begrenzt wird die Ersatzpflicht des Schuldners durch die in Art. 77 niedergelegte Schadensminderungspflicht des Gläubigers. Zu beachten ist auch Art. 44, wonach der Käufer, der für das Unterbleiben der Rüge nach Art. 39 I eine vernünftige Entschuldigung hat, entgangenen Gewinn jedenfalls nicht verlangen kann. 9

3. Verhältnis zu anderen Rechtsbehelfen

Schadenersatzansprüche nach Artt. 74 ff. können neben anderen Rechtsbehelfen wie dem **Erfüllungsanspruch** (Artt. 46 I, 62),[20] dem Recht auf **Minderung** des Kaufpreises (Art. 50) sowie der **Aufhebung** des Vertrages (Artt. 49 I, 64 I) geltend gemacht werden.[21] 10

---

[17] Vgl. OLG Koblenz, 24.2.2011, CISG-online 2301; HGer Zürich, 22.11.2010, CISG-online 2160; *Staudinger/Magnus*, Art. 74, Rn. 26 f.; MünchKomm/*P. Huber*, Art. 74, Rn. 22; *Honsell/Schönle/Th. Koller*, Art. 74, Rn. 13; kritisch dazu *Honsell*, SJZ 1992, 361, 362; vgl. auch *Brölsch*, Schadensersatz, S. 47 f.

[18] Grundlegend *Hachem*, FS Schwenzer, S. 647, 661 ff.; vgl. auch *Bock*, FS Schwenzer, S. 176, 185 ff.; *Coote*, 56 CLJ (1997), 541, 542 ff.; *Pearce/Halson*, 28 Oxford J. Legal Stud. (2008), 79, 80; *Schmidt-Ahrendts*, Disgorgement of Profits, S. 89, 83.

[19] A. A. CA Poitiers, 26.2.2009, CISG-online 2208, zustimmend *Piltz*, NJW 2011, 2261, 2266; MünchKomm/*P. Huber*, Art. 74, Rn. 16; *Staudinger/Magnus*, Art. 74, Rn. 17. Wohl auch *Kröll u. a./Gotanda*, Art. 74, Rn. 41.

[20] Der Erfüllungsanspruch unterliegt selbstverständlich Art. 28.

[21] Vgl. OGH, 22.4.2010, CISG-online 2296; vgl. auch *Berger/Scholl*, FS Schwenzer, S. 159, 169 ff.

Allein der Umfang des ersatzfähigen Schadens hängt davon ab, ob und welche anderen Rechtsbehelfe ausgeübt werden. Hat der Gläubiger einen anderen Rechtsbehelf ausgeübt und wurde dadurch der Schaden ganz oder teilweise beseitigt, so entfällt insoweit der Schadenersatzanspruch. Bei Kumulation von Schadenersatz und Vertragsaufhebung hat der Gläubiger einen einheitlichen Rechtsbehelf des **Schadenersatzes wegen Nichterfüllung.**[22] Wahlweise kann der Gläubiger Ersatz nach Massgabe des **Vertrauensinteresses** (reliance interest) verlangen, d. h. Ersatz der Aufwendungen, die er im Vertrauen auf die ordnungsgemässe Durchführung des Vertrages gemacht hat.[23]

III. Anwendungsbereich

1. Verletzung vertraglicher Pflichten

11   Schadenersatz ist geschuldet, wenn der Schuldner „eine seiner Pflichten nach dem Vertrag oder diesem Übereinkommen" nicht erfüllt (Artt. 45 I, 61 I). Die Vertragsverletzung braucht **nicht „wesentlich"** im Sinne des Art. 25 zu sein.[24] Auch die Verletzung der durch Aufhebung des Vertrages begründeten **Rückgewährpflichten** (Art. 81 II) zieht eine Haftung des Schuldners gem. Art. 74 nach sich,[25] beispielsweise wenn der Verkäufer nach Vertragsaufhebung die Rücknahme der Ware verweigert.[26]

12   Ausreichend ist die **objektive Verletzung** einer Vertragspflicht.[27] Es genügt, dass eine Verbindlichkeit bei Fälligkeit nicht oder schlecht erfüllt wird; ein Verschulden oder in Verzug setzen, etwa durch Mahnung oder Nachfristsetzung, ist nicht erforderlich.[28] Auch die ernsthafte und endgültige **Weigerung des Schuldners,** eine noch nicht fällige Verbindlichkeit zu erfüllen (vgl. Art. 72),[29] oder die Verweigerung einer Sicherheitsleistung, obwohl die geforderte Sicherheit Handelsbrauch oder Gepflogenheiten zwischen den Parteien entspricht, stellt eine zum Schadenersatz verpflichtende Vertragsverletzung dar.[30]

2. Verletzung von Obliegenheiten

13   Die Verletzung sogenannter Obliegenheiten zieht grundsätzlich **keine Schadenersatzpflicht** nach sich; die mit der Obliegenheit belastete Partei erleidet jedoch auf Grund der

---

[22] So auch *U. Huber*, Rechtsbehelfe der Parteien, S. 216. Im Zuge der Schuldrechtsreform wurde dieser Ansatz aufgegriffen: „§ 281 BGB n. F. spricht nun von Schadenersatz statt der Leistung"; vgl. dazu *Lorenz/Riehm*, Rn. 207; *Schlechtriem/Schmidt-Kessel*, SchuldR AT, Rn. 618 ff.
[23] Hierzu im Einzelnen unten Rn. 38.
[24] *Bamberger/Roth/Saenger*, Art. 74, Rn. 3; *Witz/Salger/Lorenz/Witz*, Art. 74, Rn. 5; *Weber*, Vertragsverletzungsfolgen, S. 193.
[25] *Roder Zelt- und Hallenkonstruktionen v. Rosedown Park Pty. Ltd. and Reginald R. Eustace,* 1995 Federal Court Reports (Australia), 216–240; *Honsell/Schönle/Th. Koller*, Art. 74, Rn. 21; *Achilles*, Art. 74, Rn. 2; *Staudinger/Magnus*, Art. 74, Rn. 9.
[26] Vgl. OLG München, 17.11.2006, CISG-online 1395.
[27] Vgl. dazu *Farnsworth*, Farnsworth on Contracts II, S. 448 f.; *Treitel*, Law of Contract, S. 746–757; *Witz/Salger/Lorenz/Witz*, Art. 74, Rn. 4; *Audit*, Vente internationale, Anm. 171.; *Weber*, Vertragsverletzungsfolgen, S. 193.
[28] KG Berlin, 24.1.1994, CISG-online 130 = RIW 1994, 683; *Asam/Kindler*, RIW 1989, 841; *Weber*, Vertragsverletzungsfolgen, S. 193; s. auch *Lando/Beale*, Part I and II, PECL Art. 9:501, Comment 3 (a). Das LG Flensburg, 19.1.2001, CISG-online 619 = IHR 2001, 202, 203 hat für die Verzugsvoraussetzungen hingegen fälschlicherweise auf das nationale Recht zurückgegriffen.
[29] *Fountoulakis*, Art. 72 Rn. 34; *Witz/Salger/Lorenz/Witz*, Art. 74, Rn. 5; *Karollus*, S. 163; *Stoll*, RabelsZ 52 (1988), 617, 627; *Weber*, Vertragsverletzungsfolgen, S. 194.
[30] *Staudinger/Magnus*, Art. 74, Rn. 10; *Herber/Czerwenka*, Art. 74, Rn. 2; *Enderlein/Maskow/Strohbach*, Art. 74, Anm. 1.; zu Einzelheiten *Stoll*, RabelsZ 52 (1988), 617, 627 unter Verweis auf § 2–609 UCC; a. A. *Schlechtriem*, Gemeinsame Bestimmungen, S. 159: Nach Art. 72 II habe zwar der Schuldner ein Recht zur Sicherheitsleistung, die Konvention verpflichte ihn aber nicht hierzu; abweichend auch *Neumayer/Ming*, Vor Art. 74, Anm. 2., die bei einer Verletzung von Art. 72 nur die Aufhebung des Vertrages zulassen wollen.

Versäumung **Rechtsnachteile**, wie insbes. den Verlust von Rechtsbehelfen.[31] Zu den Obliegenheiten zählen insbes. die **Schadensminderungspflicht** nach Art. 77 sowie die **Untersuchungs- und Rügepflicht** des Käufers nach Artt. 38, 39. Bezüglich letzterer steht es allerdings den Parteien frei, statt Verlust sämtlicher Rechtsbehelfe bei Rügepflichtverletzung eine Schadenersatzpflicht zu vereinbaren.[32] Die **Anzeigepflicht** des Verkäufers nach Art. 32 I oder die **Auskunftspflicht** nach Art. 32 III stellen echte Vertragspflichten dar.[33]

3. Personenschäden

Nicht in den Anwendungsbereich der Artt. 74 ff. fallen Personenschäden, die durch Produktfehler verursacht worden sind; die Haftung für solche Schäden richtet sich gem. Art. 5 nach dem jeweils anwendbaren nationalen Recht.[34] Dies gilt jedoch nicht für **Regressansprüche** des Käufers, der einem Abnehmer wegen Tod oder Körperverletzung Ersatz schuldet; diese sind als Vermögensschäden nach CISG zu beurteilen.[35] Auch für **Sachschäden** ist Art. 74 anwendbar. Soweit solche aus der Verletzung spezifischer Vertragspflichten resultieren ist die konkurrierende Anwendung nationalen Deliktsrechts ausgeschlossen.[36] Werden jedoch allgemeine, gegenüber jedermann bestehende Verkehrspflichten verletzt, ist der Rückgriff auf nationales Recht möglich.[37]

4. Ersatzberechtigte Personen und Drittschäden

Zum Schadenersatz berechtigt ist nur die durch die Vertragsverletzung betroffene **Vertragspartei**. Die **Erstreckung** der Vertragswirkungen **auf Dritte** bedarf entsprechender Vereinbarung, die allerdings auch stillschweigend oder beispielsweise über die „undisclosed agency" erfolgen kann. Rechtsfiguren wie der im deutschen Rechtskreis anerkannte **Vertrag mit Schutzwirkung für Dritte** oder die Einbeziehung Dritter nach § 2–318 UCC oder die französische action directe[38] sind dem CISG fremd.[39] Auch

---

[31] Wortlaut von Art. 39 I: „Der Käufer verliert das Recht, sich auf eine Vertragswidrigkeit der Ware zu berufen, wenn er sie dem Verkäufer nicht […]anzeigt […]".

[32] Vgl. oben Art. 39 Rn. 33b.

[33] Vgl. oben *Widmer Lüchinger*, Art. 32 Rn. 11 und 31; *Enderlein/Maskow/Strohbach*, Art. 74, Anm. 1.; zweifelnd noch *Stoll*, Schadensersatzpflicht, S. 260.

[34] Vgl. oben *Ferrari*, Art. 5 Rn. 3; *Schlechtriem/Schwenzer/Schwenzer/Hachem*, CISG Commentary, Art. 5, Rn. 4; *Schlechtriem*, Internationales UN-Kaufrecht, Rn. 39; *Honsell/Schönle/Th. Koller*, Art. 74, Rn. 2.

[35] Vgl. nunmehr auch *Schlechtriem*, Internationales UN-Kaufrecht, Rn. 39; *Schlechtriem/Schwenzer/Schwenzer/Hachem*, CISG Commentary, Art. 5, Rn. 10; *Th. Koller*, FS Wiegand, S. 422, 425; a. A. *Ernst*, Produkthaftung, S. 34 ff.

[36] Vgl. insbesondere *Herber*, FS Schlechtriem, S. 207 ff.; ders., IHR 2001, 187–190; *Köhler*, Spannungsverhältnis, S. 151; *D. Schneider*, UN-Kaufrecht und Produkthaftpflicht, S. 228 (deliktsrechtliche Ansprüche werden durch CISG verdrängt); OLG Jena, 26.5.1998, CISG-online 513; *Bianca/Bonell/Khoo*, Art. 5, Anm. 3.2.; *Honnold/Flechtner*, Art. 74, Rn. 73; *Herber/Czerwenka*, Art. 5, Rn. 5; *Enderlein/Maskow/Strohbach*, Art. 5, Anm. 1.2.; *Kuhlen*, Produkthaftung, S. 114; *Schmid*, Lückenfüllung und Normenkonkurrenz, S. 55; *Mather*, 20 J. L. & Com. (2001), 155, 161. A. A. Oberster Gerichtshof Israel, 17.3.2003, CISG-online 1980, Rn. 73 (auf die besonderen Umstände des Falls gestützt); *Miami Valley Paper, LLC v. Lebbing Eng'g GmbH*, U. S. Dist. Ct. (S. D. Ohio), 10.10.2006, CISG-online 1362; *Stoll/Gruber*, 4. Aufl., Art. 74 Rn. 7; dens., *Ferrari*, Art. 5 Rn. 12; ders., RabelsZ 71 (2007), 52, 74; *Schlechtriem/Schwenzer/Schlechtriem*, CISG Commentary, 2. Aufl., Art. 4, Rn. 23a; ders., Internationales UN-Kaufrecht, Rn. 40; *Lookofsky*, Understanding the CISG, S. 25 f., 76 ff.; ders., 13 Duke J. Comp. & Int'l L. (2003), 263, 285. Für Einzelfallentscheidungen *Hachem*, Property Damages, S. 17, 27 („no hard and fast rule"). Vgl. insgesamt dazu auch oben *Ferrari*, Art. 5 Rn. 11 ff.; ders., Art. 90 Rn. 3.

[37] Vgl. zu dieser Frage auch unten Rn. 35; *Schlechtriem/Schwenzer/Schwenzer/Hachem*, CISG Commentary, Art. 5, Rn. 6.

[38] Vgl. Civ. 1, 5.1.1999, CISG-online 431 = D. 1999, 383 ff., mit Anm. *C. Witz*, = Rev. crit. dr. int. privé 1999, 519 ff., m. Anm. *Heuzé*.

[39] Vgl. auch *P. Huber/Mullis/P. Huber*, S. 280; *Kröll u. a./Gotanda*, Art. 74, Rn. 50. Dies schliesst jedoch die Anwendbarkeit des CISG auf Ansprüche, die im Rahmen solcher nationalen Rechtsinstitute geltend gemacht werden, nicht aus, *Schlechtriem/Schwenzer/Schwenzer/Hachem*, CISG Commentary, Art. 4, Rn. 23; für eine

im nationalen Recht dienen sie primär dazu, Schwächen des Deliktsrechts auszugleichen.[40]

16   Nicht ausgeschlossen ist es jedoch, dass eine Vertragspartei die bei einem Dritten eingetretenen Schäden als eigene geltend macht, soweit es sich um eine zufällige **Schadensverlagerung** handelt.[41] Keine Probleme entstehen, wenn der Schaden in selbem Umfang auch hätte direkt beim Vertragsgläubiger eintreten können, wie insbes. der anhand objektiver Kriterien zu berechnende Mangelschaden. Hängt die Höhe des Schadens von der besonderen Situation des Geschädigten ab, kommt es entscheidend darauf an, ob es für den Schuldner erkennbar war, dass der Vertragsgläubiger die Interessen des (später geschädigten) Dritten verfolgt. Besondere Bedeutung erlangt diese Fragestellung im Zusammenhang mit **internationalen Konzernen,** wo häufig zwar eine Konzerntochter Vertragspartnerin ist, der Schaden jedoch bei der Konzernmutter oder einer –schwester eintritt.[42]

IV. Form des Ersatzes

17   Der Schadenersatz ist in **Geld** zu leisten; ein Recht auf **Naturalrestitution** kennt das CISG nicht.[43] Dies ergibt sich eindeutig aus der englischen Fassung des Art. 74 („damages [...] consist of a sum equal to the loss [...]"). Wegen des Ausschlusses der Naturalrestitution kann grundsätzlich auch nicht die **Befreiung von einer Verbindlichkeit** als Schadenersatz verlangt werden.[44] Insoweit ist jedoch Geldersatz möglich, da Ansprüche Dritter einen Haftpflichtschaden darstellen.[45]

V. Umfang des Ersatzanspruchs

1. Allgemeines

18   Das CISG schreibt zwar den Ersatz des durch die Vertragsverletzung entstandenen Verlustes einschliesslich des entgangenen Gewinns vor, definiert aber den ersatzfähigen Schaden nicht näher. Die Ersatzfähigkeit ist deshalb aus dem allgemeinen Ziel des **vollständigen Schadensausgleichs** im Rahmen des **konkreten Vertragszwecks** abzuleiten. Dabei ist stärker als im internen Recht des deutschen Rechtskreises, aber in Übereinstimmung mit neuen Entwicklungen im englischen Rechtskreis, das Erfüllungsprinzip in den Vordergrund zu stellen – das heisst der Zweck des Schadenersatzes, den Erfüllungsanspruch des Gläubigers zu schützen (dazu oben Rn. 6 ff.). Grenzüberschreitende Warenkaufverträge dienen regelmässig kommerziellen Zwecken. Marktgängige Ware hat regelmässig einen **Marktwert,** dasselbe gilt für **Nutzungsmöglichkeiten.** Auch dem Ruf und dem Ansehen eines Unternehmens und seiner Produkte (**goodwill,** reputation) ist heute regelmässig ein ökonomi-

---

detaillierte Argumentation *Schwenzer/M. Schmidt,* 13 VJ (2009), 109, 115 ff.; vgl. auch *Schlechtriem/C. Witz,* Convention de Vienne, Rn. 66.

[40] Vgl. die rechtsvergleichende Untersuchung zu den direkten Ansprüchen des Endabnehmers gegen den Hersteller in Europa bei *Ebers/Janssen/Meyer,* S. 3–73.

[41] *Honsell/Schönle/Th. Koller,* Art. 74, Rn. 11; *Achilles,* Art. 74, Rn. 3; *Soergel/Lüderitz/Dettmeier,* Vor Art. 74, Rn. 7; *Bamberger/Roth/Saenger,* Art. 74, Rn. 2; *Witz/Salger/Lorenz/Witz,* Art. 74, Rn. 10; *Staudinger/Magnus,* Art. 74, Rn. 14; *Weber,* Vertragsverletzungsfolgen, S. 195.

[42] Dazu ausführlich *Witz,* FS Schwenzer, S. 1795 ff., der über die Geltendmachung von Drittschäden hinaus die Einführung einer „schadensrechtlichen Organschaft" vorschlägt, die es dem kontrahierenden Unternehmen gestattet, den gesamten im Konzern aufgelaufenen Schaden zu liquidieren.

[43] *Bianca/Bonell/Knapp,* Art. 74, Anm. 2.3. und 3.1.; *Enderlein/Maskow/Strohbach,* Art. 74, Anm. 4.; *Honsell/Schönle/Th. Koller,* Art. 74, Rn. 41; *Neumayer/Ming,* Art. 74, Anm. 1.; *Staudinger/Magnus,* Art. 74, Rn. 24; *Karollus,* S. 213; *Schlechtriem,* Internationales UN-Kaufrecht, Rn. 286; *Soergel/Lüderitz/Dettmeier,* Vor Art. 74, Rn. 9.

[44] Vgl. *P. Huber/Mullis/P. Huber,* S. 270.

[45] Vgl. unten Rn. 32.

scher Wert beizumessen. Dasselbe gilt für **Erwerbschancen,** die oft mit hohen Aufwendungen „erkauft" werden.

Die namentlich aus dem deutschen Rechtskreis bekannte herkömmliche Differenzierung 19 zwischen **materiellen** und **immateriellen** Schäden kann unter dem CISG jedenfalls so nicht aufrecht erhalten werden. Vielmehr gilt es die Grenze gerade im Hinblick auf den Schutzzweck internationaler Kaufverträge neu zu ziehen. Von der so bestimmten Ersatzfähigkeit ist dann freilich die Frage der Vorhersehbarkeit (vgl. unten Rn. 45 ff.) sowie die Frage des Beweises (vgl. unten Rn. 64 ff.) zu unterscheiden.

2. Entstandener Verlust

Zum enstandenen Verlust gehören der **Nichterfüllungsschaden,** mögliche **Begleit-** 20 **schäden** (incidental damages) sowie **Folgeschäden** (consequential loss) der Vertragsverletzung. Zum Erfüllungsinteresse gehört auch die Nutzung einer Sache. Bei Verzug bzw. bis zur Vornahme eines Deckungsgeschäfts können deshalb Mietkosten konkret oder abstrakt als Schaden berechnet werden.[46]

a) **Nichterfüllungsschaden.** Der Nichterfüllungsschaden stellt das aufgrund der Leis- 21 tungsstörung primär oder unmittelbar entstehende Defizit dar.

Der eigentliche **Mangelschaden** besteht darin, dass bei Nichtlieferung der Käufer keinen 22 Gegenwert für die Kaufpreiszahlung erhält. Wird der Vertrag aufgehoben, berechnet sich der Mangelschaden anhand von Artt. 75, 76, d. h. nach den Kosten eines Deckungskaufes oder abstrakt nach dem Marktpreis. Aber auch wenn der Vertrag (noch) nicht aufgehoben ist, ist eine Berechnung des Mangelschadens über Art. 74 anhand eines Deckungsgeschäftes möglich soweit die entsprechenden weiteren Voraussetzungen vorliegen.[47] Solange der Vertrag nicht aufgehoben ist und der Käufer die nichtvertragsgemässe Ware behält, ist deren Wert von den Kosten des Deckungsgeschäfts in Abzug zu bringen; massgeblich ist dabei der Einkaufspreis zum Zeitpunkt der Lieferung der nichtkonformen Ware.[48]

Bei **vertragswidriger Beschaffenheit** der gelieferten Ware besteht der Mangelschaden 23 zunächst in der **Differenz** des objektiven Werts der mangelhaften Sache und demjenigen Wert, den die Sache im Zeitpunkt der Schadensberechnung bei vertragsgemässer Beschaffenheit hätte.[49] Diesen Minderwert kann der Käufer immer verlangen, unabhängig davon, ob er sich im Rahmen eines Weiterverkaufs realisiert (hat) oder nicht.[50] Kauft beispielsweise der Käufer Textilien mit der Massgabe, dass diese nicht durch Kinderarbeit hergestellt werden dürfen, so kann er bei vertragswidriger Herstellung auf jeden Fall die Differenz verlangen zwischen dem Preis, der für Ware bezahlt wird, die unter menschenwürdigen Umständen hergestellt wird, und jenem, der für unter menschenrechtswidrigen Bedingungen hergestellte Ware bezahlt wird. Wo die entsprechenden Marktpreise schwierig zu

---

[46] Vgl. das Fallbeispiel einer NGO, die nicht rechtzeitig mit Lastwagen beliefert wird, bei *Schwenzer/Hachem,* Scope of Damages, S. 94.

[47] Vgl. grundlegend *Schlechtriem,* FS Georgiades, S. 383, 387 ff.; CISG-AC, Op. 6 *(Gotanda),* Comment 8.1; *Honnold/Flechtner,* Artt. 75, 76, Rn. 410.2; *Saidov,* Law of Damages, p. 176; *Berger/Scholl,* FS Schwenzer, S. 159, 170; OLG Graz, 29.7.2004, CISG-online 1627, m. krit. Anm. *Bach,* IPRax 2009, 299, 301, 304; Audiencia Provincial de Palencia, 26.9.2005, CISG-online 1673; vgl. auch Chamber of National and International Arbitration of Milan, 28.9.2001, CISG-online 1582: Zuspruch von Schadensersatz basierend auf vor Vertragsaufhebung vorgenommenen Deckungsgeschäften, obwohl der Käufer dabei die Vorgaben der Konvention nicht beachtete; a. A. *P. Huber/Mullis/P. Huber,* S. 282; *P. Huber/Bach,* FS Bergsten, S. 585, 590 ff. (ohne Vertragsaufhebung können die Kosten des Deckungsgeschäfts nur als Aufwendungen zur Schadensminderung geltend gemacht werden); ebenso *P. Huber,* 3 Belgr. L. Rev. 2011, 150, 158 ff.

[48] *P. Huber/Bach,* FS Bergsten, S. 585, 594.

[49] *Audit,* Vente internationale, Anm. 172.; *Heuzé,* Anm. 449.; *Bianca/Bonell/Knapp,* Art. 74, Anm. 3.12.; *Honnold/Flechtner,* Art. 74, Rn. 405; *Karollus,* S. 156, 223; *Schlechtriem,* Gemeinsame Bestimmungen, S. 167; *Witz/Salger/Lorenz/Witz,* Art. 74, Rn. 18. Zum amerikanischen Recht § 2-714 (2) UCC; ähnlich auch sec. 53 (3) SGA (c. 54); vgl. auch *Rabel,* Recht des Warenkaufs, Bd. 1, S. 513.

[50] Ausführlich hierzu *Schwenzer/Hachem,* Scope of Damages, S. 94 ff.; a. A. *Schlechtriem,* 19 Pace Int'l L. Rev. (2007), 89, 98 ff.

bestimmen sind, kann auf die auf Grund des vertragswidrigen Verhaltens bei der Herstellung ersparten **Kosten** als **Minimalschaden** abgestellt werden.[51]

24 Kann die vertragswidrige Beschaffenheit durch **Nachbesserung** behoben werden, so kann der Mangelschaden anhand der hierfür erforderlichen **Aufwendungen** berechnet werden.[52] Hierzu zählen auch Kosten für den Austausch von Sachen, die der Käufer bereits eingebaut hatte.[53] Unterlässt der Käufer die konkrete Mängelbeseitigung, muss man ihm gestatten, den Mangelschaden **abstrakt auf Reparaturkostenbasis** zu berechnen. In beiden Fällen gilt es, das Nachbesserungsrecht des Verkäufers nach Art. 48 zu beachten, sofern der Verkäufer zur Mangelbeseitigung bereit ist und sie dem Käufer nach den Kriterien des Art. 48 auch zugemutet werden kann.[54] Konkrete oder abstrakte Nachbesserungskosten können freilich nur verlangt werden, soweit sie **angemessen** sind. Dies folgt aus der allgemeinen Schadensminderungspflicht nach Art. 77.[55]

25 Bei **Leistungsverzögerung** ist der Gläubiger ebenfalls berechtigt, Ersatz für den hieraus entstandenen Schaden zu verlangen. Bei **Lieferverzug des Verkäufers** kann der Käufer Ersatz für angemessene Massnahmen verlangen, die ihm die Zeit bis zum Eintreffen der Ware überbrücken helfen und Folgeschäden vermeiden.[56] Insbesondere können **Mietkosten** für eine Ersatzsache verlangt werden, und zwar unabhängig davon, ob diese tatsächlich angemietet wird oder nicht.[57] Ersatzfähig sind bei Lieferverzug auch die Mehrkosten eines Deckungskaufs (dazu oben Rn. 22). Bei **Zahlungsverzug des Käufers** kann der Verkäufer grundsätzlich Ersatz für die Kosten eines Überbrückungskredits[58] oder den Verlust einer gewinnbringenden Anlagemöglichkeit[59] verlangen. Die h. M. verlangt den konkreten Nachweis eines solchen Verlustes oder Gewinnausfalls.[60] Beim Nachweis des Verzugsschadens legt die Rechtsprechung allerdings einen recht grosszügigen Massstab an.[61] In der

---

[51] Vgl. *Schwenzer/Hachem*, Scope of Damages, S. 99 f.; *Schmidt-Ahrendts*, Disgorgement of Profits, S. 89, 101.
[52] BGH, 25.6.1997, CISG-online 277; *Delchi Carrier SpA v. Rotorex Corp.*, U. S. Ct. App. (2nd Cir.), 6.12.1995, CISG-online 140; OLG Hamm, 9.6.1995, CISG-online 146; AG München, 23.6.1995, CISG-online 368; MünchKomm/*P. Huber*, Art. 74, Rn. 35; *Bianca/Bonell/Knapp*, Art. 74, Anm. 3.12.; *Honnold/Flechtner*, Art. 74, Rn. 405; *Witz/Salger/Lorenz/Witz*, Art. 74, Rn. 18; *Audit*, Vente internationale, Anm. 172.; *Heuzé*, Anm. 449.; *Bianca/Bonelli*, Artt. 74–77, Anm. 6.; *Karollus*, S. 223.
[53] OLG Hamm, 9.6.1995, CISG-online 146; MünchKomm/*P. Huber*, Art. 74, Rn. 35; *Schlechtriem*, IPRax 1996, 256 f.
[54] *Karollus*, S. 144; *ders.*, ZIP 1993, 490 f.; *Bamberger/Roth/Saenger*, Art. 74, Rn. 5. Unberührt bleibt jedoch der Anspruch auf Ersatz von Verzögerungs- und Begleitschäden, vgl. oben *Müller-Chen*, Art. 48 Rn. 21; *Staudinger/Magnus*, Art. 48, Rn. 31, 33.
[55] *Bianca/Bonell/Will*, Art. 46, Anm. 2.2.2.2.
[56] Vgl. OLG Köln, 8.1.1997, CISG-online 217 (Einschalten einer Drittfirma für das Millen von Lederhäuten erforderlich, da die Verkäuferin mit der Lieferung von Millfässern in Verzug gekommen war).
[57] Vgl. hierzu *Schwenzer/Hachem*, Scope of Damages, S. 96.
[58] MünchKommHGB/*Mankowski*, Art. 74, Rn. 29; *Herber/Czerwenka*, Art. 74, Rn. 12; *Neumayer*, RIW 1994, 99, 106; Berufungsgericht für Ostfinnland, 27.3.1997, CISG-online 782.
[59] LG Stuttgart, 31.8.1989, CISG-online 11 = RIW 1989, 984, 985; AG Oldenburg, 24.4.1990, CISG-online 20 = IPRax 1991, 336, 338; *Asam*, RIW 1989, 942, 946.
[60] Vgl. LG Frankfurt a. M., 16.9.1991, CISG-online 26 = RIW 1991, 952, 954; OLG Frankfurt a. M., 18.1.1994, CISG-online 123 = NJW 1994, 1013, 1014; LG München I, 6.4.2000, CISG-online 665; LG Oldenburg, 9.11.1994, CISG Online 114 = RIW 1996, 65, 66; OLG Düsseldorf, 24.4.1997, CISG-online 385; LG Kassel, 15.2.1996, CISG-online 191; vgl. auch *Herber/Czerwenka*, Art. 74, Rn. 6, 9; *Karollus*, S. 224; *Staudinger/Magnus*, Art. 74, Rn. 25; *Witz/Salger/Lorenz/Witz*, Art. 74, Rn. 20; *Bamberger/Roth/Saenger*, Art. 74, Rn. 6; *Piltz*, NJW 2000, 553, 560 m. w. N.
[61] LG Hamburg, 26.9.1990, CISG-online 21 = RIW 1990, 1015, 1019 = IPRax 1991, 400, 403, mit zust. Anm. *Reinhart*, IPRax 1991, 376, 377 (Zinsverlust der italienischen Verkäuferin wird gem. § 287 ZPO in Höhe des behaupteten italienischen Diskontsatzes geschätzt); ICC, 7197/1992, J. D. I. 1993, 1028, 1034 = CLOUT Nr. 104 (Schreiben der Bank der Klägerin, dass diese für Bankkredit mindestens 12% Zinsen beansprache, als ausreichender Beweis); Int. Schiedsgericht der Bundeskammer der gewerblichen Wirtschaft in Österreich, 15.6.1994, CISG-online 120 = 691 = RIW 1995, 590, 591 (im Land des Verkäufers übliche Bankzinsen); ähnlich OLG Düsseldorf, 14.1.1994, CISG-online 119 (16,5% in Italien üblicher Zinssatz) unter Bestätigung von LG Krefeld, 28.4.1993, CISG-online 101; LG Berlin, 6.10.1992, CISG-online 173; LG Aachen, 3.4.1990, CISG-online 12 = RIW 1990, 491, 492; HGer Zürich, 10.7.1996, CISG-online 227 = SZIER 1997, 131, 132. Derselben Linie folgen grundsätzlich auch *Asam/Kindler*, RIW 1989, 841, 843–845, die die von der deutschen Rechtsprechung entwickelten Beweiserleichterungen als Fall der Schadensschätzung

Sache sollte auch hier eine **abstrakte Schadensberechnung** anhand marktgemässer Refinanzierungskosten zugelassen werden. Denn es kann nicht dem Schuldner zum Vorteil gereichen, dass der Gläubiger auf Grund besonders günstiger Umstände nicht mit Bankkredit arbeitet. In jedem Fall berechnet sich der Schaden nach CISG und nicht auf Basis der Zahlungsverzugs-Richtlinie.[62]

Als Folge des Zahlungsverzugs kann der Verkäufer auch einen **Kursverlust** oder einen **Geldentwertungsschaden** erleiden.[63] Auch hier ist streitig, ob eine Ersatzforderung des Gläubigers nur insoweit in Betracht kommt, als er nachweist, dass er bei rechtzeitiger Zahlung einen höheren Geldwert hätte realisieren können als es in Folge der verspäteten Zahlung möglich ist.[64] Richtiger Ansicht nach ist auch hier die Möglichkeit **abstrakter Berechnung** anzuerkennen. Dies gilt vor allem, wenn die Vertragswährung für den Gläubiger eine **Fremdwährung** ist. Hier kann unterstellt werden, dass der Gläubiger bei rechtzeitiger Zahlung den Betrag alsbald in die heimische Währung umgetauscht hätte.[65] Ist die Vertragswährung die Heimatwährung des Gläubigers, so können Schäden, die aus Geldentwertung durch Inflation resultieren, im Regelfall nicht ersetzt werden.[66] 26

b) Begleitschäden. Begleitschäden sind die durch die Vertragsverletzung veranlassten **Aufwendungen** des Gläubigers, die nicht der Befriedigung des Erfüllungsinteresses dienen, sondern zusätzliche Nachteile abwenden sollen.[67] Die Ersatzfähigkeit von Begleitschäden wird in Art. 74 zwar nicht ausdrücklich erwähnt; wegen des Grundsatzes der Totalreparation steht diese aber ausser Frage.[68] Zu ersetzen sind beispielsweise die infolge unberechtigter **Erfüllungsverweigerung** einer Partei entstandenen zusätzlichen Kosten der anderen Partei,[69] Aufwendungen des Verkäufers für **vergebliche Andienung** der 27

---

nach § 287 ZPO oder als Fall des Anscheinsbeweis ansehen und damit aus dem Anwendungsbereich des CISG herausnehmen.

[62] Richtlinie 2000/35/EG des Europäischen Parlaments und des Rates vom 29.6.2000 zur Bekämpfung von Zahlungsverzug im Geschäftsverkehr. Nach der h. M. hat das CISG grundsätzlich Vorrang gegenüber EU-Richtlinien, vgl. *Schlechtriem/Schwenzer/Schwenzer/Hachem*, CISG Commentary, Art. 90, Rn. 4 ff. Bezüglich der Zahlungsverzugs-Richtlinie im Speziellen *Perales Viscasillas*, 19 Pace Int'l L. Rev. 125, 127 ff.

[63] KG Wallis, 28.1.2009, CISG-online 2025. Gegen eine Qualifizierung als Schaden im Sinne von Art. 74 CISG aber nunmehr *McMahon*, FS Kritzer, S. 347, 353 ff., dessen Ablehnung freilich auf den Wertungen des internen U. S.-amerikanischen Rechts beruht.

[64] OLG Düsseldorf, 14.1.1994, CISG-online 119 unter Aufhebung von LG Krefeld, 28.4.1993, CISG-online 101; Hof Arnhem (NL), 15.4.1997, NIPR 1998, Nr. 101 = UNILEX; *Asam/Kindler*, RIW 1989, 841, 846 f.; *Honsell/Schönle/Th. Koller*, Art. 74, Rn. 38; *Piltz*, Internationales Kaufrecht, Rn. 5–549; *Staudinger/Magnus*, Art. 74, Rn. 48, 49; *Witz/Salger/Lorenz/Witz*, Art. 74, Rn. 21, 22 (Verzinsung von berücksichtigen). Nachweise zum deutschen und französischen Recht bei *Gruber*, Geldwertschwankungen, S. 118–122. Es fehlt aber auch nicht an Entscheidungen, die einen Wechselkursverlust der Zahlungswährung in der Verzugszeit ohne weitere Nachweise als ersatzfähigen Folgeschaden anerkennen, s. OLG München, 18.10.1978, *Schlechtriem/Magnus*, Art. 82 EKG, Nr. 11 = NJW 1979, 2480; RB Roermond, 6.5.1993, CISG-online 454; grosszügig auch *Soergel/Lüderitz/Dettmeier*, Art. 74, Rn. 7 und 19.

[65] HGer Zürich, 5.2.1997, CISG-online 327 = SZIER 1998, 75, 76 f. (wo allerdings Ersatz für den Kursverlust einer Fremdwährung abgelehnt wurde, weil die Zahlung noch nicht erfolgt war und der künftige Kurs ungewiss sei); OLG München, 9.12.1987, RIW 1988, 297, 299; *Asam*, RIW 1989, 841, 846 f.; *Witz/Salger/Lorenz/Witz*, Art. 74, Rn. 15; *Magnus*, RabelsZ 53 (1989), 116, 138; *Piltz*, Internationales Kaufrecht, Rn. 5–549; *ders.*, NJW 1994, 1101, 1106 Fn. 89; *Staudinger/Magnus*, Art. 74, Rn. 49; *Stoll*, Schadensersatzpflicht, S. 266 f.; *Weber*, Vertragsverletzungsfolgen, S. 201; kritisch *Soergel/Lüderitz/Dettmeier*, Art. 74, Rn. 7. *Saidov*, 13 VJ (2009), 197, 199 f. schlägt vor, den Schaden in der konkreten Verringerung des Werts des geschuldeten Betrags in der Heimatwährung des Gläubigers mit Blick auf die von diesem beabsichtigte Verwendung zu sehen.

[66] OLG Düsseldorf, 14.1.1994, CISG-online 916; MünchKomm/*P. Huber*, Art. 74, Rn. 52; *Witz/Salger/Lorenz/Witz*, Art. 74, Rn. 22; für die Ersatzfähigkeit hingegen *Saidov*, 13 VJ (2009), 197, 198 f.

[67] Vgl. § 2–710 und § 2–715 (1) UCC.

[68] *Schneider*, 9 Pace Int'l L. Rev. (1997), 223, 226; *Murphey*, 23 Geo. Wash. J. Int'l L. & Econ. (1989), 415, 459.

[69] OLG Hamm, 23.3.1978, in: *Schlechtriem/Magnus*, Art. 82 EKG, Nr. 8 = Art. 83, Nr. 4 (Wertverlust der zur Herstellung der Kaufsache gekauften Waren und Aufwendungen für Spezialwerkzeug). Hierher gehört auch der Fall, dass der Käufer bei einem Sukzessivlieferungsvertrag vertragswidrig die Lieferungen nicht abruft, BGH, 10.12.1986, NJW-RR 1987, 602, 603 = MDR 1987, 491.

Art. 74 28   Teil III. Kapitel V. Pflichten des Verkäufers und des Käufers. Abschnitt II

Ware[70] oder für deren Erhaltung und Lagerung, wenn der Käufer sie unberechtigt zurückweist,[71] die Zahlung des Zug um Zug zu leistenden Kaufpreises verweigert[72] oder vom Käufer bereitzustellender Laderaum auf dem Schiff verschmutzt ist.[73] Verzögert sich die Lieferung, weil der Käufer die vereinbarte **Bankgarantie** nicht stellt, so ist der Käufer grundsätzlich auch dafür verantwortlich, dass die Ware wegen der langen Lagerung Schaden nimmt.[74] Bei **Nichteinlösung** eines zahlungshalber gegebenen **Wechsels** oder Checks haftet der Käufer für die dadurch entstehenden Kosten.[75] Umgekehrt kann der Käufer **zusätzliche Transportkosten** verlangen, wenn der Verkäufer verspätet oder gänzlich unbrauchbare Ware liefert.[76] Erstattungsfähig sind auch Aufwendungen für die **Lagerung** verspätet eingetroffener oder mangelhafter Ware, wenn diese nach Aufhebung des Vertrages zurückgesendet wird,[77] ebenso **Mehraufwendungen bei Nachlieferung**[78] sowie Ersatz für zusätzliche Sortierkosten bei mangelhafter Ware.[79] Zu erstatten sind ferner angemessene Aufwendungen zur **Feststellung** sowie zur **Abwendung** oder **Minderung des Schadens**.[80] Kosten für die **Untersuchung** der Ware auf ihre Vertragsmässigkeit sind nur dann zu ersetzen, wenn der Vertrag aufgehoben wird oder wenn sie infolge Ersatzlieferung ein zweites Mal anfallen.[81] Bei sämtlichen Begleitschäden ist Art. 77 zu berücksichtigen; nur Aufwendungen, die angemessen und vernünftig sind, sind als Begleitschäden zu ersetzen.

28   Ein Sonderproblem stellt die Erstattung von **Rechtsverfolgungskosten** dar.[82] Dabei geht es einerseits um **Prozesskosten** (Gerichts- und Anwaltskosten), zum anderen auch um **vorprozessuale Rechtsverfolgungskosten**. Primär ist es den Parteien überlassen, eine ausdrückliche Regelung über die Verteilung der Rechtsverfolgungskosten im Vertrag[83] vorzusehen oder implizit im Wege einer Gerichtsstands- oder Schiedsklausel eine ihnen genehme Kostentragungsregelung zur Anwendung zu bringen. Ob bei fehlender ausdrücklicher Vereinbarung derartige Kosten als Schadenersatz im Rahmen von Art. 74 ersatzfähig

---

[70] *Heuzé*, Anm. 449.; *Witz/Salger/Lorenz/Witz*, Art. 74, Rn. 23; so auch schon OLG Hamm, 6.4.1978, in: *Schlechtriem/Magnus*, Art. 6 EAG, Nr. 4 = Art. 82 EKG, Nr. 9.
[71] OLG Braunschweig, 28.10.1999, CISG-online 510 = TranspR-IHR 2000, 4, 6 (Kosten für Einlagerung von Hirschfleisch im Kühlhaus und Mehrkosten bei Deckungsverkauf wie Provision, Telefonkosten, Transportkosten).
[72] Vgl. oben *Mohs*, Art. 63 Rn. 13; ICC, 7197/1992, J. D. I. 1993, 1029, 1033 f. = CLOUT Nr. 104; Int. Ct. Russian CCI, 9.9.1994, UNILEX; Int. Schiedsgericht der Bundeskammer der gewerblichen Wirtschaft in Österreich, 15.6.1994, CISG-online 120 = 691 = RIW 1995, 590, 591 = UNILEX; ICC, 7585/1992, J. D. I. 1995, 1015, 1019 = UNILEX. In dem im Text zuletzt genannten Fall ergibt sich die Haftung des Verkäufers auch schon aus Art. 85.
[73] Vgl. OLG Karlsruhe, 8.2.2006, CISG-online 1328.
[74] A. A. ICC, 7197/1992, J. D. I. 1993, 1028, 1035 f. = CLOUT Nr. 104, weil die Gefahr noch nicht übergegangen sei.
[75] Vgl. schon LG Konstanz, in: *Schlechtriem/Magnus*, Art. 82 EKG, Nr. 3 = Art. 90 EKG, Nr. 1; OLG Hamm, 14.11.1983, in: *Schlechtriem/Magnus*, Art. 82 EKG, Nr. 27 = Art. 8 EKG Nr. 8.
[76] Vgl. CIETAC, 9.11.2005, CISG-online 1444; OLG Köln, 14.8.2006, CISG-online 1405.
[77] *Delchi Carrier SpA v. Rotorex Corp.*, U. S. Ct. App. (2nd Cir.), 6.12.1995, CISG-online 140 = 10 F.3d. 1024; LG Landshut, 5.4.1995, CISG-online 193; *Kröll u. a./Gotanda*, Art. 74, Rn. 22.
[78] LG Oldenburg, 9.11.1994, CISG-online 114 = RIW 1996, 65, 66 (Reisekosten, Mautgebühren und Frachtkosten, selbst wenn Mängelbeseitigungskosten wegen unterlassener Mängelrüge nicht verlangt werden können).
[79] OLG Köln, 14. 8 2006, CISG-online 1405.
[80] BGH, 25.6.1997, CISG-online 277 = NJW 1997, 3311, 3313; *Bianca/Bonell/Knapp*, Art. 77, Anm. 2.6.; *Witz/Salger/Lorenz/Witz*, Art. 74, Rn. 13; *Staudinger/Magnus*, Art. 74, Rn. 54 und Art. 77, Rn. 20; rechtsvergleichend *Stoll*, Haftungsfolgen, S. 429 ff.; vgl. auch Niederlande: Art. 6:96 II BW.
[81] Weiter noch *Stoll/Gruber*, 4. Aufl., Art. 74 Rn. 19, die Ersatz für Untersuchungskosten schon bei mangelhafter Lieferung befürworten. Ebenso MünchKomm/*P. Huber*, Art. 74, Rn. 35; *Staudinger/Magnus*, Art. 38, Rn. 27 *Audit*, Vente internationale, Anm. 172.; *Herber/Czerwenka*, Art. 74, Rn. 12; vgl. ferner § 2–513 (2) UCC: „Expenses of inspection must be borne by the buyer but may be recovered from the seller if the goods do not conform and are rejected." Wie hier MünchKomm/*Gruber*, Art. 38, Rn. 66; *Brunner*, Art. 38, Rn. 14.
[82] Ausführlich *Jäger*, Attorney's Fees, *passim*.
[83] *Schlechtriem*, IHR 2006, 51 empfiehlt die Vereinbarung von Vertragsstrafen zur Vermeidung von Problemen beim Ersatz der Rechtsverfolgungskosten.

sind, kann nicht davon abhängig gemacht werden, ob die anwendbare lex fori Ersatz dieser Kosten als **materiell- oder prozessrechtlich** bewertet,[84] denn die Qualifikation divergiert zwischen den nationalen Rechtsordnungen; eine Anknüpfung an diese Qualifikation würde im Kernbereich des CISG zu uneinheitlicher Auslegung führen.

Weitgehend Einigkeit besteht heute, dass jedenfalls **prozessuale Rechtsverfolgungs-** 29
kosten nicht nach Art. 74 ersetzt werden;[85] über ihren Ersatz entscheiden die anwendbaren nationalen Kostentragungsregeln bzw. die anwendbare Schiedsordnung.[86] Hauptgrund für diese Lösung ist, dass die schadenersatzrechtliche Lösung einseitig den obsiegenden Kläger bevorzugen würde, während der obsiegende Beklagte mangels schadenersatzrechtlicher Anspruchsgrundlagen leer ausgehen würde.[87] Dies würde das dem CISG zugrundeliegende Prinzip der Gleichbehandlung der Parteien verletzten.[88] Auch Kosten, die über die prozessuale Kostenerstattung hinausgehen, können nicht im Wege des Schadenersatzes nach Art. 74 liquidiert werden.

Umstritten ist, ob **aussergerichtliche Rechtsverfolgungskosten** als Schaden im Sinne 30
des Art. 74 geltend gemacht werden können. Entsprechend der Lösung im nationalen Recht befürworten vorwiegend deutsche Gerichte und Autoren die Ersatzfähigkeit von Kosten für das aussergerichtliche Tätigwerden von Anwälten, soweit erforderlich.[89] Ein U. S.-amerikanisches Gericht[90] hielt vorprozessuale Rechtsverfolgungskosten in einem dictum dann als

---

[84] Vgl. vor allem CISG-AC, Op. 6 (*Gotanda*), Comment 5.2; *Gotanda*, 37 Geo. Wash. J. Int'l. L. & Econ. (2005), 95, 120 ff.; *Schlechtriem*, IHR 2006, 49, 51; vgl. auch *Orlandi*, 5 Uniform L. Rev. (2000), 23 ff.; zustimmend *Jäger*, Attorney's Fees, S. 160. Die Untauglichkeit dieser Unterscheidung betont etwa *Piltz*, FS Schwenzer, 1387, 1391 f. mit dem Hinweis, dass der Geltungsvorrang des CISG nicht auf materielles Recht beschränkt sei. A. A. *Zapata Hermanos Sucesores, S. A. v. Hearthside Baking Company, Inc. d/b/a Maurice Lenell Cooky Company*, U. S. Ct. App. (7th Cir.), 19.11.2002, CISG-online 684; *Flechtner/Lookofsky*, 7 VJ (2003), 93, 96; MünchKomm/*P. Huber*, Art. 74, Rn. 43; *Zeller*, Damages, S. 156 ff.

[85] So ausdrücklich *San Lucio et al. v. Import & Storage Services et al.*, U. S. Dist. Ct. (D. N. J.), 15.4.2009, CISG-online 1836 ('the CISG is silent with respect to the payment of attorneys' fees'); *Norfolk Southern Railway Company v. Power Source Supply, Inc.*, U. S. Dist. Ct. (W. D. Pa.), 25.7.2008, CISG-online 1776 („Plaintiff is not [...] allowed attorney's fees under Article 74 or any other part of the CISG."); vgl. auch CISG-AC, Op. 6 (*Gotanda*), Comment 5.1ff; *Honnold/Flechtner*, Art. 74, Rn. 408; *P. Huber/Mullis/P. Huber*, S. 278; a. A. *Piltz*, FS Schwenzer, S. 1387 ff.

[86] *Mullis*, RabelsZ 71 (2007), 35, 44 f.; MünchKomm/*P. Huber*, Art. 74, Rn. 43; *Brunner*, Art. 74, Rn. 31 *Brölsch*, Schadensersatz, S. 69; *Staudinger/Magnus*, Art. 74, Rn. 52; anders aber wohl CIETAC, 11.2.2000, CISG-online 1529; unklar Schiedsgericht der Handelskammer Hamburg, 21.3.1996, CISG-online 187; ICC, 7585/1992, CISG-online 105 („costs and expenses (legal costs, arbitration)"); CIETAC, 10.6.2002, CISG-online 1528.

[87] Vgl. *Zapata Hermanos Sucesores S. A. v. Hearthside Baking Company, Inc. d/b/a Maurice Lenell Cooky Company*, U. S. Ct. App. (7th Cir.), 19.11.2002, CISG-online 684, wo J. Posner ausdrücklich fragte: „Was, wenn der Beklagte gewinnen würde?"; vgl. auch *Schwenzer*, FS Tercier, S. 423. Dagegen *Piltz*, FS Schwenzer, S. 1387, 1395 f.: Benachteiligt sei immer die den Vertrag verletzende Partei, was der Wertung des CISG gerecht werde.

[88] Vgl. *Schlechtriem/Schwenzer/Schwenzer/Hachem*, CISG Commentary, Preamble, Rn. 8 und Art. 7, Rn. 34; vgl. auch *Schwenzer*, FS Tercier, S. 423; a. A. *Piltz*, FS Schwenzer, S. 1387, 1396 f., der nicht pauschal den Beklagten, sondern die den Vertrag verletzende Partei benachteiligt sieht.

[89] OLG München, 5.3.2008, CISG-online 1686; AG Landsberg, 21.6.2006, CISG-online 1460 bestätigt von OLG München, 17.11.2006, CISG-online 1395; OLG Köln, 3.4.2006, CISG-online 1218; OLG Düsseldorf, 22.7.2004, CISG-online 916; OLG Düsseldorf, 11.7.1996, CISG-online 201; OLG Düsseldorf, 14.1.1994, CISG-online 119; OLG Hamm, 2.4.2009, CISG-online 1978; LG Potsdam, 7.4.2009, CISG-online 1979 = 2164; LG Hamburg, 17.2.2009, CISG-online 1999; LG Lübeck, 30.12.2010, CISG-online 2292; LG München I, 18.5.2009, CISG-online 1998; KG Zug, 27.11.2008, CISG-online 2024; RB Rotterdam, 15.10.2008, CISG-online 1899; LG Coburg, 12.12.2006, CISG-online 1447; LG Bayreuth, 10.12.2004, CISG-online 1131; LG Frankfurt a. M., 16.9.1991, CISG-online 26; AG Alsfeld, 12.5.1995, CISG-online 170; AG Augsburg, 29.1.1996, CISG-online 172; AG Geldern, 17.8.2011, CISG-online 2302; HGer Aargau, 19.12.1997, CISG-online 418; Hof Arnhem, 15.4.1997, NIPR 1998, Nr. 101 = UNILEX; RB Zutphen, 27.2.2008, CISG-online 1692; RB Rotterdam, 15.10.2008, CISG-online 1899; RB Breda, 16.1.2009, CISG-online 1789; RB Rotterdam, 21.1.2009, CISG-online 1815; *P. Huber/Mullis/P. Huber*, S. 279; *Staudinger/Magnus*, Art. 74, Rn. 52; *Witz/Salger/Lorenz/Witz*, Art. 74, Rn. 13; *Herber/Czerwenka*, Art. 74, Rn. 7; anders noch *Stoll*, Schadensersatzpflicht, S. 267 f.; anders auch HGer Zürich, 22.11.2010, CISG-online 2160 für vorprozessuale Kosten, die sich direkt auf das Verfahren beziehen.

[90] *Zapata Hermanos Sucesores, S. A. v. Hearthside Baking Company, Inc. d/b/a Maurice Lenell Cooky Company*, U. S. Ct. App. (7th Cir.), 19.11.2002, CISG-online 684; zust. *Flechtner/Lookofsky*, 7 VJ (2003), 93 ff.

incidental damages für ersatzfähig, wenn sie der Schadensminderung dienten. Zur Begründung der generellen Ersatzfähigkeit wird geltend gemacht, dass sich ausserprozessuale Rechtsverfolgungskosten nur schwer von Aufwendungen zur Schadensabwehr trennen lassen und in nationalen Rechtsordnungen oft auch nicht von diesen getrennt werden.[91] Damit wird auch hier letztlich das **Prozess-/Sachrechtsargument** bemüht, das m. E. die Lösung nicht zu tragen vermag. Entscheidend ist auch hier, dass ein Ersatz nach Art. 74 zu einer nicht zu rechtfertigenden Besserstellung des obsiegenden Klägers im Vergleich zum obsiegenden Beklagten führen würde. Deshalb muss es auch hier dem **anwendbaren Prozessrecht** überlassen bleiben, ob und inwieweit vorprozessuale Kosten ersetzt werden.[92] Hingegen bleibt nationales Schadenersatzrecht ausgeschlossen, soweit es nicht um sittenwidriges Prozessieren (frivolous claims) geht; letzteres untersteht nationalem Deliktsrecht.

31 Die Kosten für die Einschaltung eines **Inkassobüros** werden nach h. M. nicht nach Art. 74 ersetzt.[93] Hierin wird eine sachlich nicht gerechtfertigte Massnahme zur Durchsetzung fälliger Forderungen gesehen, die gegen Art. 77 verstösst. Nach hier vertretener Auffassung handelt es sich auch insoweit um generell nicht als Schadenersatz erstattungsfähige ausserprozessuale Rechtsverfolgungskosten.

32 **c) Folgeschäden.** Als Folgeschäden kommen zusätzliche, über die Nichterfüllung als solche hinausgehende Verluste in Betracht. Hierzu zählen vor allem **Haftungsschäden,** d. h. Ansprüche Dritter gegen den Gläubiger wegen Nicht- oder nicht vertragsgemässer Erfüllung. So mag der Käufer die Ware weiter verkauft haben und nun vom Abnehmer wegen Nicht- oder nicht vertragsgemässer Erfüllung in Anspruch genommen werden, weil er selbst von seinem Verkäufer nicht beliefert oder ihm mangelhafte Ware geliefert wurde.[94] Hat sich der Käufer im Folgevertrag zu einer **Vertragsstrafe** verpflichtet, so kann auch diese grundsätzlich nach Art. 74 im Verhältnis zum Verkäufer liquidiert werden (vgl. zur Vorraussehbarkeit unten Rn. 56). Kosten einer fehlerbedingten **Rückrufaktion** sind ebenfalls ersatzpflichtige Folgeschäden. Umstritten ist, ob auch ein Haftungsschaden, der daraus resultiert, dass der Gläubiger aufgrund der Mangelhaftigkeit der vom Schuldner gelieferten Ware Dritten gegenüber für Personenschäden einstehen muss, nach CISG im Regressweg geltend gemacht werden kann oder ob ein solcher Anspruch vom Anwendungsbereich des CISG nach Art. 5 ausgeschlossen ist. Die früher überwiegende Meinung verneinte die Anwendung des CISG auf aus einer Körperverletzung resultierende Haftungsschäden.[95] In jüngerer Zeit mehren sich indes die Stimmen, die **Regressansprüche** nach CISG als Vermögensschaden des Käufers zulassen wollen.[96] Diese Auffassung überzeugt vor allem deshalb, weil so der Regress einheitlich behandelt werden kann und nicht zwischen einzelnen Posten der Haftpflichtbelastung des Käufers unterschieden werden muss. Auch der Verkäufer mag bei **Nichtabnahme** der Ware Haftungsschäden erleiden, etwa dann, wenn er von Verträgen mit Zulieferern Abstand nehmen muss und diesen gegenüber haftbar wird.[97]

---

[91] *Stoll/Gruber,* 4. Aufl., Art. 74 Rn. 20; LG Frankfurt a. M., 16.9.1991, CISG-online 26; *Staudinger/Magnus,* Art. 74, Rn. 52; *Witz/Salger/Lorenz/Witz,* Art. 74, Rn. 13; *Herber/Czerwenka,* Art. 74, Rn. 7.
[92] Ebenso *Magnus,* ZEuP 2010, 881, 900. Ausführlich zum Problemkreis *Schwenzer,* FS Tercier, S. 424 f.
[93] OLG Köln, 3.4.2006, CISG-online 1218; LG Frankfurt a. M., 16.9.1991, CISG-online 26; LG Berlin, 6.10.1992, CISG-online 173; LG Düsseldorf, 25.8.1994, CISG-online 451; AG Geldern, 17.8.2011, CISG-online 2302 (für ausländisches Inkassobüro); AG Tiergarten, 13.3.1997, CISG-online 412, mit zust. Anm. *Peter,* IPRax 1999, 159–161; a. A. *Soergel/Lüderitz/Dettmeier,* Art. 74, Rn. 6; *Staudinger/Magnus,* Art. 74, Rn. 52; *Witz/Salger/Lorenz/Witz,* Art. 74, Rn. 39; *Brunner,* Art. 74, Rn. 31; *Brölsch,* Schadensersatz, S. 72.
[94] BGH, 25.11.1998, CISG-online 353 = NJW 1999, 1259, 1261 wie LG Heidelberg, 2.10.1996, CISG-online 264 als erste Instanz; OLG Köln, 21.5.1996, CISG-online 254; *Staudinger/Magnus,* Art. 74, Rn. 45.
[95] *Stoll/Gruber,* 4. Aufl., Art. 74 Rn. 25; oben *Ferrari,* Art. 5 Rn. 8; *Brunner,* Art. 5, Rn. 1; *Witz/Salger/Lorenz/Lorenz,* Art. 5, Rn. 5; *Staudinger/Magnus,* Art. 5, Rn. 8; MünchKomm/*H. P. Westermann,* Art. 5, Rn. 3.
[96] *Schlechtriem/Schwenzer/Schwenzer/Hachem,* CISG Commentary, Art. 5, Rn. 10; *Schlechtriem,* Internationales UN-Kaufrecht, Rn. 39; *Honsell/Schönle/Th. Koller,* Art. 74, Rn. 35; *Th. Koller,* FS Wiegand, S. 421, 441 ff.; OLG Düsseldorf, 2.7.1993, CISG-online 74. Vgl. auch *Bridge,* Int'l Sale of Goods, Rn. 11.21
[97] LG Aachen, 14.5.1993, CISG-online 86.

Entsprechend den Grundsätzen zum Haftungsschaden sind **Rechtsverfolgungskosten,** 33
die dem Gläubiger vorprozessual oder im Verfahren mit Dritten entstanden sind, nach
Art. 74 grundsätzlich ersatzfähig.[98] Die Gründe, die zu einer Ablehnung der Ersatzfähigkeit
von Rechtsverfolgungskosten als Schaden im Verhältnis zwischen Gläubiger und Schuldner
führen,[99] liegen hier nicht vor.

Liefert der Verkäufer nicht oder nicht vertragsgemässe Ware, so kann dem Käufer ein 34
Folgeschaden insoweit entstehen, als sein geschäftliches Ansehen bei seiner Kundschaft
geschmälert wird, weil er seinerseits nicht oder nur mangelhafte Ware liefert (loss of
reputation, goodwill-Schaden). Weitgehend Einigkeit besteht, dass ein solcher **Reputationsschaden** nach Art. 74 grundsätzlich ersatzfähig ist.[100] Uneinigkeit besteht allenfalls, ob
es sich insoweit um einen **materiellen Schaden** handelt oder allenfalls um einen **immateriellen Schaden,** der jedoch ausnahmsweise ersetzt werden soll.[101] Im Hinblick auf die
ökonomische Bedeutung des goodwill dürfte kaum zweifelhaft sein, dass hier ein materieller
Schaden vorliegt, wenngleich Berechnung und das anzuwendende Beweismass unsicher und
umstritten sind.[102] Nicht verwechselt werden darf der Ersatz für Reputationsverlust mit dem
Verlangen nach **entgangenem Gewinn.** Der Reputationsverlust ist ein zusätzlicher Schadensposten. Entgangene Geschäftsabschlüsse und damit entgangene Gewinne belegen nur,
dass ein Reputationsverlust eingetreten ist. Seine Berechnung sollte sich an der Grösse des
Unternehmens, des Marktes, dem Wert einer Marke und den für die Wiederherstellung des
Rufes notwendigen Kosten orientieren.

Zu den Folgeschäden rechnen auch Schäden, die der Käufer aufgrund nicht vertrags- 35
gemässer Ware an seinem eigenen Sachbestand erleidet (sog. **Mangelfolgeschäden**), wie
z. B. der Verderb von Halbzeug durch Mängel einer gelieferten Maschine, der Verlust von
Rohstoffen, die mit untauglichem Material zusammen verarbeitet werden oder auch die
Zerstörung der Fabrikhalle des Käufers durch einen Brand, der durch einen Mangel der
gelieferten Maschine ausgelöst wurde.[103] Ist die grundsätzliche Ersatzfähigkeit dieser Mangelfolgeschäden nach Art. 74 unbestritten, so besteht doch in Rechtsprechung und Literatur
Uneinigkeit darüber, ob insoweit neben CISG **konkurrierend nationales Deliktsrecht**
zur Anwendung gelangen kann. Während teilweise vertreten wird, dass das anwendbare
nationale Recht diese Frage entscheiden müsse,[104] wollen Andere nationales Deliktsrecht im
Bereich der Anwendbarkeit des CISG bei Mangelfolgeschäden ausgeschlossen wissen.[105]

---

[98] Vgl. MünchKomm/*P. Huber,* Art. 74, Rn. 44; *Staudinger/Magnus,* Art. 74, Rn. 52.
[99] Vgl. oben Rn. 29 f.
[100] Vgl. CISG-AC, Op. 6 *(Gotanda),* Comment 7.1; *Schlechtriem,* Internationales UN-Kaufrecht, Rn. 299; ders., 19 Pace Int'l L. Rev. (2007), 89, 95; *P. Huber/Mullis/P. Huber,* S. 270; *Staudinger/Magnus,* Art. 74, Rn. 27; *Witz/Salger/Lorenz/Witz,* Art. 74, Rn. 14; MünchKomm/*P. Huber,* Art. 74, Rn. 39; *Brunner,* Art. 74, Rn. 20; *Honsell/Schönle/Th. Koller,* Art. 74, Rn. 7; *Saidov,* Limiting Damages, I. 2. d.; *ders.,* 25 J.L. & Com. (2006), 393 ff.; ausführlich *Leumann Liebster,* FS Schwenzer, S. 1031 ff.; a. A. noch LG München I, 30.8.2001, CISG-online 668; *Honsell,* SJZ 1992, 361, 364.
[101] Für Ersteres CISG-AC, Op. 6 *(Gotanda),* Comment 7.1; *Schlechtriem,* Internationales UN-Kaufrecht, Rn. 299; *Witz/Salger/Lorenz/Witz,* Art. 74, Rn. 14; *Leumann Liebster,* FS Schwenzer, S. 1031, 1035; *Saidov,* 13 VJ (2009), 197, 201; wohl auch *Honsell/Schönle/Th. Koller,* Art. 74, Rn. 7; für Letzteres *Staudinger/Magnus,* Art. 74, Rn. 50; MünchKomm/*P. Huber,* Art. 74, Rn. 39; *Brunner,* Art. 74, Rn. 20.
[102] Vgl. dazu unten Rn. 64 ff.
[103] Vgl. die Beispiele bei *Schlechtriem,* Internationales UN-Kaufrecht, Rn. 40.
[104] *Miami Valley Paper, LLC v. Lebbing Eng'g GmbH,* U. S. Dist. Ct. (S. D. Ohio), 10.10.2006, CISG-online 1362; Oberster Gerichtshof Israel, 17.3.2003, CISG-online 1980, Rn. 73 (auf die besonderen Umstände des Falls gestützt); *Stoll/Gruber,* 4. Aufl., Art. 74 Rn. 7; *Ferrari,* Art. 5 Rn. 12; *ders.,* RabelsZ 71 (2007), 52, 74; *Schlechtriem/Schwenzer/Schlechtriem,* CISG Commentary, 2. Aufl., Art. 4 Rn. 23a; *Soergel/Lüderitz/Dettmeier,* vor Art. 74, Rn. 14; *Soergel/Lüderitz/Fenge,* Art. 5, Rn. 4; *Staudinger/Magnus,* Art. 5, Rn. 14; *Bamberger/Roth/Saenger,* Art. 5, Rn. 3; *Brunner,* Art. 5, Rn. 2; *Honsell/Siehr,* Art. 5, Rn. 4; *Witz/Salger/Lorenz/Lorenz,* Art. 4, Rn. 28; *Lookofsky,* Understanding the CISG, S. 25 f., 76 ff.; *ders.,* 13 Duke J. Comp. & Int'l L. (2003), 263, 285.
[105] OLG Jena, 26.5.1998, CISG-online 513; *Bianca/Bonell/Khoo,* Art. 5, Anm. 3.2.; *Honnold/Flechtner,* Art. 5, Rn. 73; *Herber/Czerwenka,* Art. 5, Rn. 5; *Enderlein/Maskow/Strohbach,* Art. 5, Anm. 1.2.; *Kuhlen,* Produkthaftung, S. 114; *Schmid,* Lückenfüllung und Normenkonkurrenz, S. 55; *Mather,* 20 J. L. & Com. (2001), 155, 161.

Zutreffend erscheint eine **vermittelnde Auffassung:**[106] Mangelfolgeschäden an Sachen, die typischerweise von der Vertragswidrigkeit beeinträchtigt werden, wie z. B. das zu verarbeitende Material, müssen kaufrechtlicher Regelung vorbehalten bleiben. Wo es hingegen um allgemeine Sicherheitserwartungen geht und es auf Zufall beruht, dass der Käufer und nicht ein Dritter in seinem Sacheigentum geschädigt ist, wie z. B. Schäden an Einrichtungsgegenständen durch eine explodierende Maschine, kann auch der Käufer konkurrierend auf nationales Deliktsrecht zurückgreifen.[107]

3. Entgangener Gewinn

36 Während Verlust im Sinne des Art. 74 die Verminderung des schon bei Vertragsschluss vorhandenen Vermögens bedeutet, ist entgangener Gewinn jede durch die Vertragsverletzung **verhinderte Vermögensmehrung.** Beide Formen des Schadens stehen grundsätzlich einander gleich, jedoch kann bei unterlassener Mängelanzeige – selbst wenn diese entschuldbar ist – nach Art. 44 entgangener Gewinn nicht beansprucht werden.[108] Unter entgangenen Gewinn fällt zunächst der **Weiterverkaufsgewinn,** der dem Käufer in Folge Nichtbelieferung oder nicht vertragsmässiger Lieferung entgeht. Des Weiteren rechnen hierzu **Betriebsausfallschäden.** Aus dem Grundsatz der Totalreparation folgt, dass nicht nur der bis zum Zeitpunkt der Urteilsfindung entgangene, sondern auch der **in Zukunft** in voraussehbarer Weise erzielbare und berechenbare Gewinn zu vergüten ist.[109] Zu ersetzen ist nicht nur der sogenannte Reingewinn, sondern auch anteilsmässig fixe Kosten des Betriebs (sog. Generalunkosten).[110] In Abzug zu bringen sind jeweils ersparte Aufwendungen, die der Gläubiger bei Realisierung des entgangenen Gewinns getätigt hätte.[111]

37 Mit der neueren Auffassung ist auch die Vereitelung einer **Gewinnchance** (loss of chance) als grundsätzlich ersatzfähiger Schaden nach Art. 74 anzuerkennen.[112] Dass Gewinnchancen ein ökonomischer Wert zukommt, kann nicht bezweifelt werden.[113] Auch Art. 7.4.3 II PICC sieht den Ersatz einer verlorenen Gewinnchance vor.[114] Eine andere Frage ist es, wie diese Chancen berechnet werden und welche Anforderungen man an deren Beweis stellt.[115]

38 Anstelle des entgangenen Gewinns kann der Gläubiger auch vergeblich aufgewandte Kosten **(frustrierte Aufwendungen)** als Schaden nach Art. 74 ersetzen verlangen.[116] Hat

---

[106] So bereits *Schwenzer,* 9 Tel Aviv University Studies in Law (1989), 127 ff.; vgl. auch *Schlechtriem,* Internationales UN-Kaufrecht, Rn. 40; *Hachem,* Property Damage, S. 17, 27.

[107] Vgl. *Schlechtriem/Schwenzer/Schwenzer/Hachem,* CISG Commentary, Art. 5, Rn. 14; *Hachem,* Property Damage, S. 17, 27.

[108] Vgl. ICC, 9187/1999, CISG-online 705; *Weber,* Vertragsverletzungsfolgen, S. 196; *Witz/Salger/Lorenz/ Witz,* Art. 74, Rn. 15; *Heuzé,* Anm. 449.

[109] *Bianca/Bonell/Knapp,* Art. 74, Anm. 3.5.; *Kröll u. a./Gotanda,* Art. 74, Rn. 28; *Saidov,* Damages in Int'l Sales, S. 76; *Ziegler,* S. 209; so ausdrücklich Art. 9:501 PECL; Art. 7.4.3 PICC und Art. 159 II CESL-Entwurf; a. A. *Witz/Salger/Lorenz/Witz,* Art. 74, Rn. 15 (Frage des anwendbaren Verfahrensrechts).

[110] OLG Hamburg, 26.11.1999, CISG-online 515 = IHR 2001, 19, 21 f., mit zust. Anm. *Piltz; Delchi Carrier SpA v. Rotorex Corp.,* U. S. Ct. App. (2nd Cir.), 6.12.1995, CISG-online 140; *Bianca/Bonell/Knapp,* Art. 74, Anm. 3.10.–3.11.

[111] Vgl. HGer Zürich, 22.11.2010, CISG-online 2160.

[112] CISG-AC, Op. 6 *(Gotanda),* Comment 3.15; *Saidov,* 22 J. Cont. L. (2006), 1, 39 ff.; *ders.,* 25 J. L. & Com. (2006), 393, 400 ff.; *Schwenzer/Hachem,* Scope of Damages, S. 98; *Saidov,* Damages in Int'l Sales, S. 70 ff.; *ders.,* 13 VJ (2009), 197, 201; wohl auch *Brölsch,* Schadensersatz, S. 61; A. A. *Delchi Carrier SpA v. Rotorex Corp.,* U. S. Ct. App. (2nd Cir.), 6.12.1995, CISG-online 140; KG Zug, 14.12.2009, CISG-online 2026, unter 13.5; *Neumayer/Ming,* Art. 74, Anm. 1. Rechtsvergleichend dazu *Stoll,* Haftungsfolgen, S. 41 f.

[113] Vgl. *Schwenzer/Hachem,* Scope of Damages, S. 98.

[114] Dazu *Vogenauer/Kleinheisterkamp/McKendrick,* Art. 7.4.3 PICC, Rn. 3 f.

[115] Für eine Herabsetzung des Beweismasses in derartigen Fällen *Hachem,* FS Schwenzer, S. 647, 666. Vgl. auch *Saidov,* Damages in Int'l Sales, S. 169 f.

[116] Vgl. *Schlechtriem,* Internationales UN-Kaufrecht, Rn. 308; *Schmidt-Ahrendts,* IHR 2006, 63 ff., 68; *Bamberger/Roth/Saenger,* Art. 74, Rn 16; LG Berlin, 30.9.1992, CISG-online 70; CIETAC, 4.4.1997, CISG-online 1660: Normale Aufwendungen zur Erzielung des vorhersehbaren Gewinns seien im vor-

z. B. der Käufer im Hinblick auf das Eintreffen der bestellten Ware eine wegen Nichtlieferung des Verkäufers nutzlos gewordene Lagerhalle gebaut, so kann er ihre Kosten als Schadenersatz verlangen. Entsprechend der **Rentabilitätsvermutung** kann man davon ausgehen, dass solche Aufwendungen durch den Ertrag aus dem Vertrag abgedeckt worden wären. Frustrierte Aufwendungen stellen deshalb den **Mindestschaden** dar, dessen Ersatz für den Gläubiger insbes. dann Bedeutung erlangt, wenn ein weiter gehender entgangener Gewinn nicht nachgewiesen werden kann.[117]

4. Immaterielle Schäden

Das CISG enthält keinen ausdrücklichen Ausschluss der Haftung für immaterielle Schäden. Deshalb können an sich auch rein immaterielle Schäden ersatzfähig sein, wenn der **immaterielle Leistungszweck** Eingang in den Vertrag gefunden hat und der Schaden damit eine typische Folge der Leistungsstörung ist.[118] Begreift man freilich zutreffenderweise Schäden z. B. infolge Reputationsverlusts oder Verlusts einer Chance als materielle Schäden, sind kaum immaterielle Schäden denkbar, die vom Schutzzweck eines Kaufvertrages erfasst sein könnten. Namentlich **Schmerzensgeld** und **Genugtuungsansprüche** wegen „pain and suffering", „mental distress" und „loss of amenities" können nach Art. 74 nicht ersetzt verlangt werden.[119] Die Parteien eines internationalen Kaufvertrages versprechen und bezahlen nicht für ungestörten Lebensgenuss.[120]

5. Zurechnung des Schadens

Zu ersetzen ist nur der **durch die Vertragsverletzung** verursachte Schaden. Es ist erforderlich, grundsätzlich aber auch genügend, dass die Vertragsverletzung eine Bedingung für den Eintritt des schädlichen Erfolges darstellt (**conditio sine qua non**, „but-for rule").[121] Irrelevant ist, ob der Schaden durch die Vertragsverletzung unmittelbar oder nur mittelbar herbeigeführt wurde. Auch ist im CISG kein Raum für juristische **Kausalitätstheorien,** welche die schadensrechtliche Zurechnung auf wahrscheinliche oder nicht ganz fern liegende Kausalabläufe beschränken. Die Ausgrenzung entfernter Schäden, die ausserhalb des Verantwortungsbereichs des Schuldners liegen, hat allein über die Voraussehbarkeitsregel des Art. 74 S. 2 zu erfolgen.[122]

---

hersehbaren Gewinn enthalten und seien deshalb nicht als entgangener Gewinn ersatzfähig, wohingegen diejenigen Aufwendungen, die zur Erzielung des vorhersehbaren Gewinns nicht nötig waren, zusätzlich zum entgangenen Gewinn ersatzfähig seien. Vgl. auch Serbian Chamber of Commerce, 1.10.2007, CISG-online 1793: Fälschlicherweise Zuspruch des entgangenen Gewinns und zusätzlich der gesamten Zinsen, die der Käufer für einen Bankkredit zahlen musste, den er für die Sofortzahlung eines später aufgehobenen Vertrags aufgenommen hatte. Rechtsvergleichend Stoll, FS Neumayer, S. 313 ff.; Schackel, ZEuP 2001, 248 ff.

[117] Vgl. CIETAC, 31.10.2005, CISG-online 1715: Schadenersatz für frustrierte Aufwendungen wie Devisenhandels-, Überweisungs-, Importagentur- und Akkreditivgebühren. Vgl. auch CIETAC, 26.12.2005, CISG-online 1744.

[118] Stoll, FS Neumayer, S. 313, 327; grundsätzlich zustimmend Magnus, FS Herber, S. 28; Weber, Vertragsverletzungsfolgen, S. 195; Staudinger/Magnus, Art. 74, Rn. 27; ablehnend Honsell/Schönle/Th. Koller, Art. 74, Rn. 7; Schlechtriem, Internationales UN-Kaufrecht, Rn. 299; Ryffel, S. 50 f.; P. Huber/Mullis/P. Huber, S. 279 (immaterielle Schäden im Regelfall nicht ersatzfähig).

[119] Vgl. Kröll u. a./Gotanda, Art. 74, Rn. 39; Leumann Liebster, FS Schwenzer, S. 1031, 1041.

[120] Vgl. Schwenzer/Hachem, Scope of Damages, S. 100.

[121] KG Zug, 14.12.2009, CISG-online 2026, unter 11.2 (auch zur hypothetischen Kausalität bei einer Vertragsverletzung durch Unterlassen); Honsell/Schönle/Th. Koller, Art. 74, Rn. 22 f.; Staudinger/Magnus, Art. 74, Rn. 28, 29; Soergel/Lüderitz/Dettmeier, Vor Art. 74, Rn. 6; Witz/Salger/Lorenz/Witz, Art. 74, Rn. 26.

[122] Bianca/Bonell/Knapp, Art. 74, Anm. 2.6.; Honsell/Schönle/Th. Koller, Art. 74, Rn. 23; Heuzé, Anm. 451.; Bianca/Bonelli, Artt. 74–77, Anm. 2.; Soergel/Lüderitz/Dettmeier, Vor Art. 74, Rn. 6; Witz/Salger/Lorenz/Witz, Art. 74, Rn. 26; Achilles, Art. 74, Rn. 5; Weber, Vertragsverletzungsfolgen, S. 197.

VI. Berechnung des Schadens

1. Konkrete und abstrakte Schadensberechnung

41 Der dem Gläubiger durch eine Vertragsverletzung entstandene Schaden ist zunächst konkret zu berechnen.[123] Im Bereich des eigentlichen **Mangelschadens** sieht jedoch Art. 76 vor, dass bei Aufhebung des Vertrages die abstrakte Berechnung des Erfüllungsinteresses nach der Differenz zwischen Vertragspreis und Marktpreis gestattet ist, ohne dass der Schuldner einwenden kann, der Gläubiger habe tatsächlich kein Deckungsgeschäft geschlossen. Namentlich deutschsprachige Autoren halten Art. 76 für eine Ausnahmevorschrift und wollen eine abstrakte Schadensberechnung im Rahmen von Art. 74 nicht zulassen.[124] Diese Sichtweise kann zumindest im Bereich des Mangelschadens nicht aufrecht erhalten werden. Bei rechtsvergleichender Betrachtung zeigt sich, dass sich in den meisten Rechtskreisen starke Tendenzen zu einem Ersatz von **abstrakt berechneten Nutzungsausfallschäden** abzeichnen.[125] Allein das Prinzip des vollständigen Ausgleichs (vgl. hierzu oben Rn. 6 ff.) gebietet auch unter dem CISG die Zulässigkeit der abstrakten Schadensberechnung.[126] Es ist nicht zu rechtfertigen, warum ein Verkäufer von Lastwagen bei Verzögerung zwar dem Transporteur als Käufer Mietwagenkosten erstatten muss, derselbe Vertragsbruch jedoch ohne Konsequenzen bleibt, wenn der Käufer eine NGO ist, die mit diesen Lastwagen Lebensmittel in Krisengebiete liefern will.[127] Der abstrakte Nutzungsausfall kann dabei ohne weiteres berechnet werden, da Mietmärkte heute für praktisch alle Waren zur Verfügung stehen.[128]

2. Vorteilsanrechnung[129]

42 Erlangt der Gläubiger infolge des Vertragsbruchs oder der Schadenersatzleistung **Vorteile,** so ist fraglich, ob er sich diese anrechnen lassen muss. Ein **Verbot der Überkompensation** wird besonders von deutschsprachigen Autoren durch die strenge Anwendung der Differenztheorie betont.[130] In anderen Rechtskreisen wird demgegenüber eine mögliche Überkompensation als Begleiterscheinung des **Prinzips des Erfüllungsinteresses** und des **vollen Schadensausgleichs** hingenommen.[131] So ist beispielsweise die Figur des „Abzugs

---

[123] OLG Hamburg, 26.11.1999, CISG-online 515; *P. Huber/Mullis/P. Huber*, S. 271; *Herber/Czerwenka*, Art. 74, Rn. 9; *Neumayer/Ming*, Art. 74, Anm. 2.; *Staudinger/Magnus*, Art. 74, Rn. 25; *Schneider*, 9 Pace Int'l L. Rev. (1997), 223, 229 f.; vgl. auch Art. 7.4.3 PICC; a. A. *Honsell/Schönle*, 1. Aufl., Art. 74, Rn. 35–36; wohl auch *Honsell/Schönle/Th. Koller*, Art. 74, Rn. 19.

[124] *Stoll/Gruber*, 4. Aufl., Art. 74 Rn. 29; *Staudinger/Magnus*, Art. 74, Rn. 25; MünchKomm/*P. Huber*, Art. 74, Rn. 21; MünchKommHGB/*Mankowski*, Art. 74, Rn. 10; *Brunner*, Art. 74, Rn. 8; *Herber/Czerwenka*, Art. 74, Rn. 9; *Soergel/Lüderitz/Dettmeier*, Art. 74, Rn. 1; *Reinhart*, Art. 74, Rn. 3; *Brölsch*, Schadensersatz, S. 47.

[125] Rechtsvergleichend *Schwenzer/Hachem/Kee*, Rn. 44.240 ff. Zum internen deutschen Recht *Wagner*, Gutachten, A 25 ff., A 32; zur bisherigen Rechtslage GrS BGH, 9.7.1986, NJW 1987, 50; MünchKomm/*Oetker*, § 249 BGB, Rn. 58 ff. Zum internen schweizerischen Recht BaslerKomm/*Wiegand*, Art. 97 OR, Rn. 38; *Schwenzer*, OR AT, Rn. 14.06. Zum englischen Recht *McGregor*, Rn. 20–022; *Vanda Compania Limitada v Costa Rica v. Societe Maritime Nationale of Paris, (The ‚Ile aux Moines')* [1974] 2 Lloyd's Rep. 502.

[126] Vgl. *Semi-Materials Co., Ltd. v. MEMC Material Electronics, Inc.*, U.S. Dist. Lt. (E. D. Mo.), 10.1.2011, CISG-online 2168.

[127] Vgl. dazu ausführlich *Schwenzer/Hachem*, Scope of Damages, S. 95 ff.

[128] Vgl. *Schwenzer/Hachem*, Scope of Damages, S. 96.

[129] Grundlegend *M. Schmidt*, FS Schwenzer, S. 1499 ff. Vgl. auch *Spoorenberg/Fellrath*, IPRax 2009, 357 ff.; Art. 7.4.2 PICC, dazu *Vogenauer/Kleinheisterkamp/McKendrick*, Art. 7.4.2 PICC, Rn. 12.

[130] Vgl. *Stoll/Gruber*, 4. Aufl., Art. 74 Rn. 31; *Staudinger/Magnus*, Art. 74, Rn. 18, 22; *Witz/Salger/Lorenz/Witz*, Art. 74, Rn. 14; *Brölsch*, Schadensersatz, S. 43; ebenso OLG Koblenz, 24.2.2011, CISG-online 2301; anders *M. Schmidt*, FS Schwenzer, S. 1499, 1501 ff. unter Hinweis auf durch Schadensberechnung nach Artt. 75, 76 mögliche Überkompensationen und unter Ablehnung der Anwendung von Art. 84 II im Schadensrecht. In diese Richtung auch *Bock*, FS Schwenzer, S. 176, 187.

[131] Vgl. *McGregor*, Rn. 1–027; rechtsvergleichend *Schwenzer/Hachem/Kee*, Rn. 44.19 ff.; *Stoll*, Haftungsfolgen, S. 184; *Bock*, FS Schwenzer, S. 176, 187 (zum englischen Recht).

neu für alt" nur noch im deutschen Rechtskreis anerkannt.[132] Eine Anrechnung von Vorteilen kann deshalb nach Art. 74 CISG grundsätzlich nur befürwortet werden, soweit das Prinzip des Erfüllungsinteresses nicht entgegensteht.

3. Gewinnabschöpfung[133]

Nach herrschender Ansicht der deutschsprachigen Literatur zum CISG kann nach 43
Art. 74 keine Herausgabe des Verletzergewinns verlangt werden.[134] Auch in diesem Bereich hat es allerdings in den nationalen Rechtsordnungen in jüngerer Zeit Entwicklungen hin zu einer Abschöpfung des Verletzergewinns gegeben.[135] Entsprechend dem **Vorrang des Erfüllungsprinzips** muss auch im CISG der Grundsatz gelten, dass sich ein Vertragsbruch für den Schuldner nicht lohnen darf (**"breach of contract must not pay"**). Zwar werden bei internationalen Warenkäufen die Fälle eher selten sein, in denen der Gläubiger unter keinem Gesichtspunkt einen Schaden erlitten hat, der Schuldner hingegen Gewinn erzielen konnte.[136] Denkbar und notwendig ist indes ein Abstellen auf den Gewinn des Schuldners in folgenden **Fallkonstellationen:** Der Verkäufer verkauft die Waren ein zweites Mal und realisiert dabei einen höheren Preis als im Vertrag mit dem Käufer vereinbart.[137] Der Verkäufer, der sich verpflichtet hat, Ware unter menschenwürdigen und ökologisch vertretbaren Bedingungen herzustellen, senkt durch eine Vertragsverletzung seine Herstellungskosten und erhöht damit seinen Gewinn.[138] Entgegen einer entsprechenden Vertragsklausel beliefert der Käufer den europäischen Markt und realisiert dementsprechende Gewinne.[139] In all diesen Fällen gebietet das **Erfüllungsprinzip,** den vom Schuldner auf Grund der Vertragsverletzung erzielten Gewinn abzuschöpfen. Man mag hierin auch lediglich einen Modus der Berechnung des beim Gläubiger entstandenen Schadens sehen, wo dieser anders nur schwer oder gar nicht bewiesen werden kann.[140]

---

[132] *Stoll*, Haftungsfolgen, S. 181.
[133] Grundlegend *Bock*, FS Schwenzer, S. 176 ff.; rechtsvergleichend *dies.*, Gewinnherausgabe, *passim;* vgl. auch *Schmidt-Ahrendts*, Disgorgement of Profits, S. 89 ff.
[134] MünchKommHGB/*Mankowski*, Art. 74, Rn. 9; MünchKomm/*P. Huber*, Art. 74, Rn. 16; *Staudinger/Magnus*, Art. 74, Rn. 18; *Brölsch*, Schadensersatz, S. 44; *Honsell*, SJZ 1992, 361; *Hartmann*, IHR 2009, 189, 197 f.; *Schmidt-Ahrendts*, Disgorgement of Profits, S. 89, 98 ff.
[135] Vgl. rechtsvergleichend *Schwenzer/Hachem/Kee*, Rn. 44.250 ff.; Niederlande: Artt. 6.1.78, 6.1.104 BW; zum englischen Recht *Attorney General v. Blake* [2001] 1 A. C. 268 (H. L.); zum internen kanadischen Recht *Fridman*, Contracts, S. 765; zum internen deutschen Recht *Wagner*, Gutachten, A 83.
[136] Vgl. etwa den berühmten Fall *Attorney General v. Blake* [2001] 1 A. C. 268 (H. L.): Der Spion Blake war zur Sowjetunion übergelaufen und hatte 1989 eine Autobiographie verfasst, in der er Informationen preisgab, die zwar nicht mehr „confidential" waren, aber gleichwohl unter seine vertragliche Schweigepflicht fielen. Die britische Krone verlangte den von Blake mit dem Verlag vereinbarte Honorar, das House of Lords entschied zu ihren Gunsten. Vgl. dazu *Jones*, FS Schlechtriem, S. 763 und den Parallelfall in den USA *Snepp v. United States*, U. S. Supr. Ct., 19.2.1980, 444 U. S. 507.
[137] A. A. *Schmidt-Ahrendts*, Disgorgement of Profits, S. 89, 98 f. (aber für Beweiserleichterungen). Diese Konstellation wird oft auch als ökonomischer Vertragsbruch („efficient breach of contract") bezeichnet, d. h. der Einnahmen des Verkäufers aus dem zweiten Verkauf übersteigen den zu ersetzenden Schaden des ersten Käufers. Gegen dieses Konzept mit überzeugenden Argumenten bereits *Friedmann*, 18 J. Leg. Stud. (1989), 1 ff.
[138] Wohl anders *Schlechtriem*, 19 Pace Int'l L. Rev. (2007), 100 ff., der die Vereinbarung einer Schadenspauschalisierung under einer Vertragsstrafe als die einzigen Möglichkeiten des Käufers sieht, in Situationen Schadensersatz zu erhalten, in denen er keinen finanziellen Schaden erlitten hat, dagegen *Schwenzer/Hachem*, Scope of Damages, S. 95. A. A. auch *Schmidt-Ahrendts*, Disgorgement of Profits, S. 89, 101 f.
[139] A. A. *Schmidt-Ahrendts*, Disgorgement of Profits, S. 89, 99.
[140] Vgl. *Hachem*, FS Schwenzer, S. 647, 663 f.; *Schmidt-Ahrendts*, Disgorgement of Profits, S. 89, 98 ff.; dagegen *Hartmann*, IHR 2009, 189, 197 f., der eine funktionell bereicherungsrechtliche Gewinnherausgabe analog Art. 84 II bevorzugt. Noch weitergehend *Bock*, FS Schwenzer, S. 176 ff., die für die Schaffung eines originären Gewinnhaftungsanspruchs im Wege der inhaltlichen Weiterentwicklung der Konvention qua Rechtsvergleichung eintritt.

4. Zeitpunkt der Schadensberechnung

44 Bei **konkreter Schadensberechnung** kann sich der Schaden mit Zeitablauf verändern. Hier muss zwischen dem Zeitpunkt des Eintritts eines Schadens und dem Zeitpunkt seiner Bewertung unterschieden werden. Grundsätzlich ist für letzteres der Zeitpunkt der Urteilsfindung massgeblich,[141] so dass bis zu diesem Zeitpunkt Ereignisse nach Schadenseintritt berücksichtigt werden.[142] Dadurch wird auch vermieden, dass Preissteigerungen zwischen dem Eintritt des Schadens und dem rechtskräftigen Abschluss des Schadenersatzprozesses die Ersatzleistung entwerten.[143] Bei **abstrakter Schadensberechnung** des sog. Mangelschadens legt zunächst Art. 76 Abs. 1 den Zeitpunkt für die Schadensberechnung nach der Marktpreisregel fest. Ereignisse nach Schadenseintritt finden demnach nur Berücksichtigung, wenn ihr Eintritt in diesem Zeitpunkt als sicher vorhergesehen werden kann.[144] Bei abstrakter Berechnung eines Nutzungsausfalls ist auf den Zeitpunkt abzustellen, zu dem der Käufer die Ware in vertragsgemässem Zustand nach dem Vertrag hätte erhalten sollen.

VII. Voraussehbarkeitsregel (S. 2)[145]

1. Allgemeines

45 Die streng objektive Haftung des Schuldners für das gegebene Leistungsversprechen wird im CISG gemildert durch die **Begrenzung des Ersatzes** auf den voraussehbaren Schaden. Nach der Voraussehbarkeitsregel sind die Schadenszurechnung und der Umfang des Ersatzes unter Berücksichtigung des Vertragszwecks und der Umstände bei Vertragsschluss auf das für den Schuldner bei Vertragsschluss überschaubare Haftungsrisiko zu begrenzen. Die Voraussehbarkeitsregel betrifft allein die **Zurechnung der Haftungsfolgen,** und zwar unabhängig davon, ob den Schuldner ein **Verschulden** an der Vertragsverletzung trifft und wie schwer dieses Verschulden wiegt.[146] Sie gilt selbst dann, wenn der Schuldner **vorsätzlich** gegen vertragliche Pflichten verstossen hat.[147] Insoweit unterscheidet sie sich von Art. 9:503 PECL, wohingegen Art. 7.4.4 PICC und Art. 161 CESL-Entwurf dem Modell des CISG folgen.[148]

---

[141] Staudinger/*Magnus*, Art. 74, Rn. 55; Bamberger/Roth/Saenger, Art. 74, Rn. 2; *Roßmeier*, RIW 2000, 407, 412; Soergel/*Lüderitz*/Dettmeier, Vor Art. 74, Rn. 12; *Weber*, Vertragsverletzungsfolgen, S. 203 f.; *Ziegler*, S. 209. Dagegen ist nach *Neumayer/Ming*, Art. 74, Anm. 2. das Prozessrecht der lex fori massgebend für den Zeitpunkt, auf welchen die Schadensberechnung vorzunehmen ist. A. A. auch *Bianca/Bonell/Knapp*, Art. 74, Anm. 3.16., der einen nach den Umständen angemessenen Zeitpunkt („at an appropriate time") für massgebend hält, dabei aber wohl den Zeitpunkt des Schadenseintritts und dessen Feststellung im Auge hat; ähnlich *Sutton*, 50 Ohio St. L. J. (1989), 743.

[142] Vgl. *Hager*, FS Schwenzer, S. 681, 694.

[143] Zur Qualifizierung von Schadenersatzansprüchen als Geldwertschulden vgl. *Gruber*, Geldwertschwankungen, S. 105 ff. m. w. N.

[144] Vgl. *Hager*, FS Schwenzer, S. 681, 694 f.

[145] Rechtsvergleichend *Schwenzer/Hachem/Kee*, Rn. 44.85 ff.

[146] Darauf weist schon *Rabel*, Recht des Warenkaufs, Bd. 1, S. 509 nachdrücklich hin. S. ferner *Karollus*, S. 217; *Piltz*, Internationales Kaufrecht, Rn. 5–545; Witz/Salger/Lorenz/*Witz*, Art. 74, Rn. 2; Staudinger/*Magnus*, Art. 74, Rn. 32; *Bianca/Bonell/Knapp*, Art. 74, Anm. 2.15.; Herber/*Czerwenka*, Art. 74, Rn. 11; eingehend *Faust*, S. 26 f., 49 f., 314 ff. Dies entspricht auch der Rechtslage in England und den U. S. A.: *Treitel*, Remedies for Breach, S. 89; *Faust*, S. 117 f., auch mit Nachweisen zu Gegenstimmen in der U. S.-amerikanischen Literatur und Rechtsprechung.

[147] *Audit*, Vente internationale, Anm. 172.; *Bianca/Bonell/Knapp*, Art. 74, Anm. 2.15.; *Bianca/Bonelli*, Artt. 74–77, Anm. 2.; *Vékás*, Foreseeability, S. 160; einschränkend *Enderlein/Maskow/Strohbach*, Art. 74, Anm. 9., der die Herleitung einer solchen Beschränkung aus den allgemeinen Grundsätzen, die der Konvention zugrunde liegen, für möglich hält; zweifelnd *Heuzé*, Anm. 450. Anders entscheiden romanische Rechte, vgl. Frankreich: Art. 1150 Cc; Italien: Art. 1225 Cc und Spanien: Art. 1107 II Cc. In derartigen Fällen kommt allerdings eine Reduktion des Beweismasses in Bezug auf die Voraussehbarkeit in Betracht, vgl. unten Rn. 65.

[148] Ausführlich zur Vorhersehbarkeitsregel in CISG, PICC und PECL: *Saidov*, Damages in Int'l Sales, S. 101 ff.

Obwohl die Voraussehbarkeitsregel stark von der angloamerikanischen **contemplation** 46
rule[149] beeinflusst wurde, weicht sie doch von dieser in entscheidenden Punkten signifikant
ab.[150] Deshalb kann zur Auslegung des Art. 74 S. 2 nicht auf Rechtsprechung zum internen
Recht angloamerikanischer Staaten zurückgegriffen werden.[151]

2. Relevante Personen und massgeblicher Zeitpunkt

Anders als im angloamerikanischen Recht, das auf die „contemplation" beider Parteien 47
abstellt,[152] ist die Voraussehbarkeit des Schadens nach Art. 74 S. 2 allein aus der **Sicht der
vertragsbrüchigen Partei** zu beurteilen. Für die Beurteilung der Voraussehbarkeit ist der
Zeitpunkt des Vertragsschlusses massgebend. Irrelevant ist, ob der Schuldner nach diesem
Zeitpunkt Kenntnis von weiteren Schadensrisiken erlangt hat oder hätte erlangen müssen.[153]

3. Massstab der Voraussehbarkeit

Anders als im angloamerikanischen Rechtskreis, wo daran angeknüpft wird, ob der 48
Schadenseintritt als wahrscheinliche Folge (probable consequence) vorausgesehen wurde,
genügt es im Rahmen von Art. 74 S. 2, dass die vertragsbrüchige Partei den Schaden bei
Vertragsschluss als **„mögliche Folge"** (possible consequence) der Vertragsverletzung vorausgesehen hat oder hätte voraussehen müssen. Ein gewisses Mass an Wahrscheinlichkeit, wie es
von einer Reihe von Autoren gefordert wird,[154] ist nach dem Wortlaut des Art. 74 S. 2 nicht
erforderlich. Hervorzuheben ist jedoch, dass als „mögliche Folge" ohnehin nur das in
Betracht kommt, was unter **Berücksichtigung der konkreten Umstände** des Einzelfalls
vorausgesehen werden konnte, womit eine normative Begrenzung bewirkt wird.[155]

Die Voraussehbarkeit ist grundsätzlich nach einem **objektiven Massstab** zu beurteilen.[156] 49
Entscheidend ist, was eine **verständige Person** in den Schuhen des Schuldners in Kenntnis
der Umstände bei Vertragsschluss vorausgesehen hätte. Dabei sind **normative Elemente**
wie die vertragliche Risikoverteilung, der Vertragszweck und der Schutzzweck einzelner
Vertragspflichten zu berücksichtigen.[157] Die Voraussehbarkeitsregel wird durch ein **sub-**

---

[149] Vgl. *Hadley v. Baxendale* [1854] L.J.Ex. 179; § 2–715 (2) (a) UCC; *Faust*, S. 73 ff.; *Brölsch*, Schadensersatz, S. 50 ff.; *Saidov*, Limiting Damages, II. 2. Grundlegend noch immer *Rabel*, Recht des Warenkaufs,
Bd. 1, S. 483 ff.
[150] Vgl. sogleich Rn. 47 f.
[151] Unzutreffend deshalb *TeeVee Toons, Inc. (d/b/a TVT Records) & Steve Gottlieb, Inc. (d/b/a Biobox) v. Gerhard
Schubert GmbH*, U. S. Dist. Ct. (S. D. N. Y.), 23.8.2006, CISG-online 1272, wo das Gericht die Rechtsprechung zum internen U. S.-amerikanischen Recht heranzieht.
[152] *Treitel*, Remedies for Breach, S. 88 m. w. N.; *Ferrari*, 53 La. L. Rev. (1993), 1257, 1267–1269; *Vékás*,
Foreseeability, S. 159 f.; ebenso *Murphey*, 23 Geo. Wash. J. Int'l L. & Econ. (1989), 415–474.
[153] MünchKomm/*P. Huber*, Art. 74, Rn. 29, 33; *Honsell/Schönle/Th. Koller*, Art. 74, Rn. 28; *Neumayer/
Ming*, Art. 74, Anm. 3.; *Staudinger/Magnus*, Art. 74, Rn. 38; *Bianca/Bonell/Knapp*, Art. 74, Anm. 2.13.; *Heuzé*,
Anm. 450.; *Faust*, S. 10 ff.; *Brölsch*, Schadensersatz, S. 52 f.; *Saidov*, Limiting Damages, II. 2. (a) (iii) (b); vgl.
aber *ders.*, Damages in Int'l Sales, S. 119 f.: Der Zweck der Vorhersehbarkeitsregel, Parteien nur für diejenigen
Risiken haften zu lassen, die sie (in der Regel bei Vertragsschluss) übernommen haben, könne in gewissen
Fällen dazu führen, dass wegen einer nachträglichen Änderung der Risikoübernahme ein späterer Zeitpunkt
für die Beurteilung der Vorhersehbarkeit angemessen erscheine, z. B. bei Vertragsänderungen oder langfristigen Verträgen, die gewisse Bestimmungen zur späteren Bestimmung offenlassen.
[154] *Stoll/Gruber*, 4. Aufl., Art. 74 Rn. 35; *Soergel/Lüderitz/Dettmeier*, Art. 74, Rn. 15; *Witz/Salger/Lorenz/
Witz*, Art. 74, Rn. 28. Den Massstab „probable" des internen U. S.-amerikanischen Rechts auf das CISG
übertragen hat *Delchi Carrier SpA v. Rotorex Corp.*, U. S. Ct. App. (2nd Cir.), 6.12.1995, CISG-online 140.
[155] So zutr. *Farnsworth*, 27 Am. J. Comp. L. (1979), 247, 253.
[156] OGH, 14.1.2002, CISG-online 643; *Staudinger/Magnus*, Art. 74, Rn. 35; MünchKomm/*P. Huber*,
Art. 74, Rn. 30 ff.; *Enderlein/Maskow/Strohbach*, Art. 74, Anm. 10.; *Witz/Salger/Lorenz/Witz*, Art. 74,
Rn. 32; *Brunner*, Art. 74, Rn. 12; *Weber*, Vertragsverletzungsfolgen, S. 198; *Heuzé*, Anm. 450.; *Brölsch*, Schadensersatz, S. 53 f.; *Saidov*, Limiting Damages, II. 2. (a) (iii) (d); *Piltz*, Internationales Kaufrecht, Rn. 5–545.
[157] In diesem Sinne auch *U. Huber*, RabelsZ 43 (1979), 413, 469 f.; *Schlechtriem*, Internationales UN-Kaufrecht, Rn. 302; *Ziegler*, S. 210; *Staudinger/Magnus*, Art. 74, Rn. 35, 37; *Soergel/Lüderitz/Dettmeier*, Art. 74,
Rn. 16; *Witz/Salger/Lorenz/Witz*, Art. 74, Rn. 29, 30; auch schon *von Caemmerer*, 178 AcP (1978), 121,
142 f.; gegen die Berücksichtigung normativer Elemente *Faust*, 34 ff., 273 ff., 331 f.

jektives Element ergänzt.[158] Die Vorhersehbarkeit kann damit insbes. dadurch erweitert werden, dass der Gläubiger den Schuldner auf besondere, aus objektiver Sicht nicht voraussehbare Umstände hinweist.[159]

4. Gegenstand der Voraussehbarkeit

50 Gegenstand der Voraussehbarkeit sind allein die eingetretenen Schäden, nicht aber die Vertragsverletzung, die den Schadenersatzanspruch begründet.[160] Entscheidend ist daher, ob für den Schuldner – eine entsprechende Vertragsverletzung unterstellt – bei Vertragsschluss die **Möglichkeit des Schadenseintritts** und die **Natur des Schadens** voraussehbar waren. Der **Umfang des Schadens** muss zwar nicht genau ziffernmässig, jedoch im Wesentlichen voraussehbar gewesen sein.[161] Ist der Schadensumfang wesentlich höher als voraussehbar, dann hat sich ein anderes Schadensrisiko verwirklicht als das Voraussehbare.[162]

5. Beispiele

51 Um die Voraussehbarkeitsregel im Einzelfall praktikabel zu machen, wird in der deutschsprachigen Literatur eine Typisierung anhand von Fallgruppen vorgenommen.[163] Dies erscheint legitim, soweit die Voraussehbarkeit anhand eines objektiven Massstabs zu beurteilen ist. Die Fallgruppenbildung darf aber nicht dazu verleiten, die jeweiligen Umstände des Einzelfalles aus dem Blick zu verlieren.[164]

52 a) **Nichterfüllungsschäden.** Der sog. Nichterfüllungsschaden ist regelmässig voraussehbar.[165] Dazu gehört der **Mangelschaden** die Ware betreffend, aber auch Kosten für angemessene Massnahmen, um ersatzweise einen der Erfüllung entsprechenden Zustand herbeizuführen, wie z. B. **Reparatur-** oder **Mietkosten.**[166] Bei Zahlungsverzug sind regelmässig **Kreditkosten** voraussehbar.[167] Dasselbe gilt für **Wechselkursverluste.**[168]

---

[158] OGH, 14.1.2002, CISG-online 643; Polimeles Protodikio Athinon, 2009, CISG-online 2228, unter 2.2.11; *Staudinger/Magnus,* Art. 74, Rn. 36; *Enderlein/Maskow/Strohbach,* Art. 74, Anm. 8. Laut *Sutton,* 50 Ohio St. L. J. (1989), 743 f. weicht Art. 74 S. 2 insofern geringfügig von § 2–715 (2) (a) UCC ab.

[159] Vgl. *Faust,* S. 13; *Staudinger/Magnus,* Art. 74, Rn. 36.

[160] OGH, 14.1.2002, CISG-online 643 = IHR 2002, 76, 80; Polimeles Protodikio Athinon, 2009, CISG-online 2228, unter 2.2.11; *Herber/Czerwenka,* Art. 74, Rn. 10; *Honsell/Schönle/Th. Koller,* Art. 74, Rn. 24; *Witz/Salger/Lorenz/Witz,* Art. 74, Rn. 33; *Roßmeier,* RIW 2000, 407, 411; *U. Huber,* Haftung des Verkäufers, S. 28 f.; *Karollus,* S. 217; *Piltz,* Internationales Kaufrecht, Rn. 5–544; *Stoll,* Schadensersatzpflicht, S. 260 f.; *Weber,* Vertragsverletzungsfolgen, S. 198; *Vékás,* Foreseeability, S. 161.

[161] OGH, 14.1.2002, CISG-online 643; *Honnold/Flechtner,* Art. 74, Rn. 406; *Staudinger/Magnus,* Art. 74, Rn. 34; MünchKommHGB/*Mankowski,* Art. 74, Rn. 23; *Brunner,* Art. 74, Rn. 12; *Brölsch,* Schadensersatz, S. 53; *Saidov,* Limiting Damages, II. 2. (a) (iii) (e); *Enderlein/Maskow/Strohbach,* Art. 74, Anm. 8.; *Audit,* Vente internationale, Anm. 172.; *Vékás,* Foreseeability, S. 163 f.; *Murphey,* 23 Geo. Wash. J. Int'l L. & Econ. (1989), 415, 469 ff.; anders *Faust,* S. 28 f., 238 ff.

[162] Vgl. *Mullis,* RabelsZ 71 (2007), 35, 48. Vgl. auch Art. 7.4.4 PICC, dazu *Vogenauer/Kleinheisterkamp/McKendrick,* Art. 7.4.4 PICC, Rn. 4 f.

[163] Vgl. etwa *Schlechtriem,* Internationales UN-Kaufrecht, Rn. 303 ff.; *Staudinger/Magnus,* Art. 74, Rn. 31 ff.; MünchKomm/*P. Huber,* Art. 74, Rn. 25 ff.

[164] Für Zurückhaltung bei der Fallgruppenbildung auch: *Saidov,* Damages in Int'l Sales, S. 106 ff.

[165] OGH, 14.1.2002, CISG-online 643; *Honsell/Schönle/Th. Koller,* Art. 74, Rn. 30; *Schlechtriem,* Internationales UN-Kaufrecht, Rn. 303; *Neumayer/Ming,* Art. 74, Anm. 4. (die insoweit von „dommage direct" sprechen); *Roßmeier,* RIW 2000, 407, 411; *Staudinger/Magnus,* Art. 74, Rn. 40; *Stoll,* Schadensersatzpflicht, S. 262; *Weber,* Vertragsverletzungsfolgen, S. 199.

[166] OLG Köln, 8.1.1997, CISG-online 217; AG München, 23.6.1995, CISG-online 368; *Honsell/Schönle/Th. Koller,* Art. 74, Rn. 30; *Staudinger/Magnus,* Art. 74, Rn. 41; vgl. auch *P. Huber/Mullis/P. Huber,* S. 274 f., der richtigerweise betont, dass das Nachbesserungsrecht des Verkäufers gem. Art. 48 in diesem Kontext berücksichtigt werden muss.

[167] S. oben Rn. 16; *Roßmeier,* RIW 2000, 407, 411; *Staudinger/Magnus,* Art. 74, Rn. 44 m. w. N.; kritisch jedoch *Neumayer/Ming,* Art. 74, Anm. 6. Zinsen für einen Bankkredit, den der Käufer zur Finanzierung der Anzahlung aufgenommen hat, sind grundsätzlich vorhersehbar: Serbian Chamber of Commerce, 1.10.2007, CISG-online 1793. Bei ungewöhnlich hohen Zinsen kann es jedoch an der Vorhersehbarkeit fehlen, vgl. Berufungsgericht für Ostfinnland, 27.3.1997, CISG-online 782 (7% im Monat und 0,5% auf Rückstände); *Witz/Salger/Lorenz/Witz,* Art. 74, Rn. 31.

[168] Deshalb unzutr. Legfelsóbb Biróság (Oberster Gerichtshof von Ungarn), 2000, CISG-online 1687.

b) **Begleitschäden.** Auch Begleitschäden sind **regelmässig voraussehbar.** Bei Auf- 53
wendungen des Gläubigers, die nicht voraussehbar sind, dürfte bereits ein Verstoss gegen die
Schadensminderungspflicht nach Art. 77 vorliegen.[169] Für die vertragsbrüchige Partei nachteilige Marktentwicklungen sind vorhersehbar; dieses Risiko darf nicht aufgrund mangelnder Vorhersehbarkeit auf die andere Partei verlagert werden.

c) **Folgeschäden.** Die Voraussehbarkeitsregel kommt vor allem bei Folgeschäden zum 54
Tragen, da diese regelmässig durch die **besonderen Verhältnisse des Gläubigers,** die von
ihm getroffenen Dispositionen oder die wirtschaftlichen Rahmenbedingungen beeinflusst
werden.

Weitere **Verkaufsgewinne** sind beim Verkauf handelbarer Ware an einen Kaufmann 55
regelmässig vorhersehbar.[170] Bei **Betriebsausfallschäden** kommt es hingegen ganz auf die
Umstände des Einzelfalls an.[171] Bei Nichtabnahme der Ware durch den Käufer ist die
übliche **Handelsspanne** als Gewinn des Verkäufers voraussehbar.[172] **Frustrierte Aufwendungen** sind jedenfalls bis zur Höhe des zu erwartenden Gewinns voraussehbar.[173]

Bei Verkauf handelbarer Ware an eine Handelsfirma muss der Verkäufer damit rechnen, dass 56
die Lieferung vertragswidriger Ware den Käufer seinen Abnehmern gegenüber haftbar machen
kann[174] oder ihm mindestens Kosten aus der Rücknahme der Ware entstehen **(Haftungsschaden).**[175] In bestimmten Märkten (z. B. Automobilbranche) sind **Rückrufaktionen** voraussehbar. Auch **Vertragsstrafen** sind – soweit es den Gepflogenheiten der Parteien oder den
Gebräuchen der Branche entspricht (Art. 9) – im angemessenen Umfang grundsätzlich voraussehbar.[176] Der Verlust von **goodwill** ist jedenfalls voraussehbar, wenn der Zweck des Vertrags
zumindest auch auf die Förderung oder den Erhalt der Reputation des Käufers gerichtet ist,[177]
so z. B., wenn der Käufer erkennbar Wiederverkäufer in einem empfindlichen Markt ist.[178]

Mangelfolgeschäden, d. h. Schäden die durch Beeinträchtigung an anderen Sachen[179] 57
des Gläubigers entstehen, sind nach h. M.[180] immer voraussehbar, es sei denn, wenn bei-

---

[169] Zum Verhältnis zwischen Vorhersehbarkeit und Schadensminderung vgl. *Saidov,* Damages in Int'l Sales, S. 110.

[170] *Delchi Carrier SpA v. Rotorex Corp.,* U. S. Ct. App. (2nd Cir.), 6.12.1995; CISG-online 140; OGH, 6.2.1996, CISG-online 224; *Witz/Salger/Lorenz/Witz,* Art. 74, Rn. 34; *Bamberger/Roth/Saenger,* Art. 74, Rn. 9; *Herber/Czerwenka,* Art. 74, Rn. 12; *Neumayer/Ming,* Art. 74, Anm. 5.; *Stoll,* Schadensersatzpflicht, S. 263; *Vékás,* Foreseeability, S. 166.

[171] OGH, 28.4.2000, CISG-online 581; HGer Zürich, 10.2.1999, CISG-online 488; *Herber/Czerwenka,* Art. 74, Rn. 12; *Vékás,* Foreseeability, S. 166; *Schlechtriem,* Internationales UN-Kaufrecht, Rn. 305; gänzlich ablehnend *von Caemmerer,* 178 AcP (1978), 121, 147.

[172] OGH, 28.4.2000, CISG-online 581; *Kranz,* S. 220; *Staudinger/Magnus,* Art. 74, Rn. 43.

[173] *Schlechtriem,* Internationales UN-Kaufrecht, Rn. 308; *Schmidt-Ahrendts,* IHR 2006, 63, 68.

[174] OGH, 22.4.2010, CISG-online 2296 = IHR 2011, 38 f.; zustimmend für langjährige Geschäftsbeziehungen; *Saidov,* Damages in Int'l Sales, S. 108 f.

[175] OGH, 6.2.1996, CISG-online 224; BGer, 28.10.1998, CISG-online 413; OLG Köln, 21.5.1996, CISG-online 254; LG Landshut, 5.4.1995, CISG-online 193; *Witz/Salger/Lorenz/Witz,* Art. 74, Rn. 34; *Herber/Czerwenka,* Art. 74, Rn. 12; *Neumayer/Ming,* Art. 74, Anm. 5.; *Vékás,* Foreseeability, S. 167; *Karollus,* S. 215, 217; *Staudinger/Magnus,* Art. 74, Rn. 45.

[176] Int. Ct. Russian CCI, 23.12.2004, CISG-online 1188; vgl. aber CIETAC, 29.9.2004, CISG-online 1600: Vertragsstrafe unvorhersehbar, da sie bei der Gesellschaft anfiel, die den Käufer mit dem Abschluss eines Kaufvertrags mit einem Verkäufer beauftragt hatte, und aus Verträgen herrührte, die diese Gesellschaft mit Dritten nach Abschluss des Vertrags zwischen Käufer und Verkäufer abgeschlossen hatte, krit. dazu *Honsell/Schönle/Th. Koller,* Art. 74, Rn. 35. Vgl. LG Hamburg, 21.12.2001, CISG-online 1092 für einen Fall, in dem die Vertragsstrafe, obwohl grundsätzlich als vorhersehbar erachtet, unvorhersehbar war, da ihre konkrete Ausgestaltung über Gebühr nachteilig für den Käufer war.

[177] Vgl. *Leumann Liebster,* FS Schwenzer, S. 1031, 1047.

[178] Vgl. BGH WM 1980, 36 zum EKG; *Schlechtriem,* Internationales UN-Kaufrecht, Rn. 306; *Leumann Liebster,* FS Schwenzer, S. 1031, 1047 meint Indiz hierfür sei häufig ein gegenüber dem üblichen Marktpreis erhöhter Vertragspreis, den der Käufer als „reputationsfördernden Mehrpreis" zu zahlen bereit ist oder das Wissen des Verkäufers um Anforderungen gewisser Zertifikate, mit denen der Käufer die Ware ausstatten möchte. Grundsätzlich gegen die Vorhersehbarkeit von Reputationsschäden: Polimeles Protodikio Athinon, 2009, CISG-online 2228, unter 2.2.11.

[179] Vgl. oben Rn. 35.

[180] MünchKomm/*P. Huber,* Art. 74, Rn. 41; *Staudinger/Magnus,* Art. 74, Rn. 45 f.

spielsweise der Käufer die Ware bestimmungswidrig gebraucht und dabei ein Schaden entsteht.[181]

VIII. Vertragliche Haftungsregelungen

1. Allgemeines

58 Da die Artt. 74 ff. dispositiv sind, können die Parteien den Umfang ihrer Haftung ohne Weiteres vertraglich regeln. Denkbar sind einerseits die Festlegung **fixer Summen,** andererseits Haftungsbeschränkungen. Sind derartige Vereinbarungen in **Allgemeinen Geschäftsbedingungen** enthalten, so richtet sich deren Einbeziehung in den Vertrag nicht nach nationalem Recht, sondern nach den für den Vertragsschluss massgebenden Artt. 14, 18 und ist durch Auslegung nach Art. 8 zu ermitteln.[182] Die **Wirksamkeit** derartiger Vereinbarungen richtet sich nach dem subsidiär anwendbaren Vertragsstatut (lex causae).[183] Dabei sind allerdings die Massstäbe des CISG zu berücksichtigen.[184]

2. Fixe Summen[185]

59 Nach herkömmlichem Verständnis wird zwischen **Schadenspauschalierungen** (liquidated damages) und **Vertragsstrafen** (penalties) unterschieden.[186] Diese Unterscheidung hat in nationalen Rechtsordnungen insoweit Konsequenzen, als Vertragsstrafen insgesamt unzulässig sind[187] oder jedenfalls auf Antrag der belasteten Partei vom Gericht herabgesetzt werden können.[188] Die moderne Auffassung tendiert indes dahin, die begriffliche Unterscheidung zwischen Schadenspauschalen und Vertragsstrafen aufzugeben.[189] Die **Vereinbarung fixer Summen** wird danach für **grundsätzlich zulässig** gehalten;[190] im Falle eines groben Missverhältnisses zwischen vereinbarter Summe und eingetretenem Schaden ist jedoch häufig eine gerichtliche Herabsetzung möglich.[191] Diese Massstäbe sollten auch an eine Art. 74 im Sinne einer fixen Summe modifizierende Vertragsklausel angelegt wer-

---

[181] BGH, 24.3.1999, CISG-online 396; MünchKomm/*P. Huber,* Art. 74, Rn. 41; *Neumayer/Ming,* Art. 74, Anm. 5.; *Karollus,* S. 218; *Schlechtriem,* Internationales UN-Kaufrecht, Rn. 306; *Staudinger/Magnus,* Art. 74, Rn. 47; *Weber,* Vertragsverletzungsfolgen, S. 200; *Vékás,* Foreseeability, S. 162.

[182] BGH, 31.10.2001, CISG-online 617; OLG Zweibrücken, 31.3.1998, CISG-online 481; oben *Schroeter,* Art. 14 Rn. 33 f.; *Staudinger/Magnus,* Art. 14, Rn. 40; *Soergel/Lüderitz/Fenge,* Art. 14, Rn. 10; *Frense,* S. 44, 88–90; a. A. *Teklote,* S. 81 ff.

[183] ICC, 7197/1992, J.D.I. 1993, 1028, 1032 f.; OLG München, 8.2.1995, CISG-online 143; OLG Zweibrücken, 31.3.1998, CISG-online 481; insofern bestätigt von BGH, 24.3.1999, CISG-online 396; Gerechtshof Arnhem, 22.8.1995, CISG-online 317; RB Hasselt, 21.1.1997, CISG-online 360; *Berger,* RIW 1999, 401, 402; *Heuzé,* Anm. 450.; zu Schadenspauschalisierungen und Vertragsstrafen vgl. auch *Honnold/Flechtner,* Art. 74, Rn. 408.1. A. A. *Stoll/Gruber,* 4. Aufl., Art. 74 Rn. 49 f. Vgl. ausführlicher zu diesem Thema *Hachem,* 13 VJ (2009), 217, 222 ff.; *Mohs/Zeller,* 21 Mealey's Int'l Arb. Rep. (2006), 1 ff.

[184] Vgl. *Schlechtriem/Schwenzer/Hachem,* CISG Commentary, Art. 4, Rn. 38 ff.; *Ferrari,* Art. 4 Rn. 20 mit zahlreichen Nachweisen.

[185] Ausführlich *Hachem,* Agreed Sums, passim; CISG-AC, Op. 10 *(Hachem),* Rechtsvergleichend *Schwenzer/Hachem/Kee,* Rn. 44.266 ff.

[186] Vgl. zur Terminologie in nationalen Rechtsordnungen *Steltmann,* Vertragsstrafe, S. 22 ff.

[187] Dies gilt vor allem für die Länder des anglo-amerikanischen Rechtskreises. Vgl. für England die grundlegende Entscheidung *Dunlop Pneumatic Tyre Co, Ltd. v. New Garage and Motor Co., Ltd.* [1915] A. C. 79 sowie die Darstellung bei *McGregor,* Rn. 13–019; für die USA *Perillo,* S. 395 ff. Vgl. aber auch Deutschland: § 309 Nr. 5, 6 BGB für die Unterschiede bei der Behandlung von AGB.

[188] Vgl. z. B. Deutschland: § 343 I BGB; Frankreich: Art. 1150 Cc; Schweiz: Art. 160 III OR; für eine rechtsvergleichende Übersicht *Hachem,* Agreed Sums, S. 126 ff.; ders.,13 VJ (2009), 217 ff.

[189] Vgl. Art. 7.4.13 I PICC, dazu *Vogenauer/Kleinheisterkamp/McKendrick,* Art. 7.4.13 PICC, Rn. 2; Art. 9:509 I PECL. Vgl. dazu auch *Hachem,* Agreed Sums, S. 27.

[190] Vgl. CISG-AC, Op. 10 *(Hachem),* Comment 2.2; Art. 7.4.13 PICC, Comment 2.; *Lando/Beale,* Part I and II, Anm. A; *Berger,* RIW 1999, 401, 403 f. Aus der Rechtsprechung vgl. CIETAC, 9.11.2005, CISG-online 1444.

[191] Vgl. Art. 7.4.14 II PICC, dazu *Vogenauer/Kleinheisterkamp/McKendrick,* Art. 7.4.13 PICC, Rn. 16 ff.; Art. 9:509 II PECL. Vgl. hierzu und zu anderen Formen des Schulderschutzes CISG-AC, Op. 10 *(Hachem),* Comment 3.1–3.6.

den.¹⁹² Ob einer Vereinbarung einer fixen Summe **abschliessender Charakter** zukommt, d. h. ob sie nach dem Parteiwillen weitergehende Ersatzansprüche ausschliesst, ist durch Auslegung der jeweiligen Vereinbarung zu ermitteln.¹⁹³

3. Haftungsbeschränkungen¹⁹⁴

Die Parteien können durch entsprechende Vereinbarungen die Haftung **summenmäs-** 60 **sig** oder auf bestimmte **Schadensarten** oder **Handlungsformen beschränken** oder den Schadenersatz ganz **ausschliessen**. Bei der Beurteilung der **Gültigkeit** derartiger Klauseln sind auch im Rahmen des anwendbaren Vertragsstatuts die Wertungen des CISG, insbesondere das Prinzip des vollen Schadensausgleichs zu berücksichtigen.¹⁹⁵ Darüber hinaus können rechtsvergleichend übereinstimmend bestimmte Eckdaten festgestellt werden. So darf der Gläubiger nicht völlig rechtlos gestellt werden; es muss ihm zumindest ein **Minimalrechtsschutz** verbleiben.¹⁹⁶ Zum anderen wird übereinstimmend eine Wegbedingung der Haftung für **Vorsatz** und **grobe Fahrlässigkeit** nicht für zulässig erachtet.¹⁹⁷ Dies kann auch als allgemeines Prinzip im Sinne des Art. 7 II aus dem CISG abgeleitet werden.¹⁹⁸

IX. Einzelfragen

1. Erfüllungsort für die Schadenersatzpflicht

Die Schadenersatzpflicht ist an dem Ort zu erfüllen, an dem auch die verletzte **Primär-** 61 **pflicht** zu erfüllen ist.¹⁹⁹ Eine Anknüpfung an den Sitz des Gläubigers entsprechend Art. 57²⁰⁰ würde eine weitere Ausdehnung eines Klägergerichtsstands bedeuten.²⁰¹

2. Verjährung

Im Anwendungsbereich des **Verjährungsübereinkommens** verjähren auch Schaden- 62 ersatzansprüche nach Art. 8 in vier Jahren. Im Übrigen ist die Frage des auf die Verjährung anwendbaren Rechts in internationalen Verhältnissen höchst unsicher.²⁰² In den kontinentalen Rechtsordnungen wird die Verjährung regelmässig als Frage des materiellen Rechts angesehen und dementsprechend dem **Vertragsstatut** unterworfen.²⁰³ In vielen Rechts-

---

¹⁹² Vgl. CISG-AC, Op. 10 *(Hachem)*; Hachem, Agreed Sums, S. 167 ff.; *ders.*, 13 VJ (2009), 217, 227.
¹⁹³ ICC, 7585/1992, CISG-online 105 = J.D.I. 1995, 1015, 1019; CISG-AC, Op. 10 *(Hachem)*, Rule 8; Hachem, Agreed Sums, S. 177; *Staudinger/Magnus*, Art. 74, Rn. 60; *Berger*, RIW 1999, 401, 409; *Soergel/Lüderitz/Dettmeier*, Vor Art. 74, Rn. 13; *Mohs/Zeller*, 21 Mealey's Int'l Arb. Rep. (2006), 1, 2.
¹⁹⁴ Rechtsvergleichend *Schwenzer/Hachem/Kee*, Art. 44.295 ff.
¹⁹⁵ Vgl. *Schlechtriem/Schwenzer/Schwenzer/Hachem*, CISG Commentary, Art. 4, Rn. 38.
¹⁹⁶ Vgl. *Schwenzer/Hachem/Kee*, Rn. 44.310; *Schwenzer/Hachem*, 57 Am.J. Comp. L. (2009), 457, 474.
¹⁹⁷ OLG Zweibrücken, 31.3.1998, CISG-online 481, insofern bestätigt von BGH, 24.3.1999, CISG-online 396 = BGHZ 141, 129, 135; *Soergel/Lüderitz/Dettmeier*, Vor Art. 74, Rn. 13; *Staudinger/Magnus*, Art. 74, Rn. 59; *Witz/Salger/Lorenz/Witz*, Art. 74, Rn. 42; zu Einzelheiten *Frense*, S. 121–135; *Teklote*, S. 242–244; rechtsvergleichend *Schwenzer/Hachem/Kee*, Rn. 44.311 ff.; *Schwenzer/Hachem*, 57 Am.J. Comp. L. (2009), 457, 473 f. mit Verweisen auf nationale Bestimmungen. Zweifelnd MünchKomm/*P. Huber*, Art. 74, Rn. 56.
¹⁹⁸ Vgl. nur Artt. 35 III, 40, 42 II lit. a).
¹⁹⁹ *Soergel/Lüderitz/Dettmeier*, Vor Art. 74, Rn. 11; *Staudinger/Magnus*, Art. 74, Rn. 57; *Roßmeier*, RIW 2000, 407, 409; *Achilles*, Art. 74, Rn. 9; für Schadenersatz als Rechtsbehelf des Käufers vgl. oben *Müller-Chen*, Art. 45 Rn. 35.
²⁰⁰ So OLG Düsseldorf, 2.7.1993, CISG-online 74; *Herber/Czerwenka*, Art. 57, Rn. 14; *Piltz*, Internationales Kaufrecht, Rn. 5–565; *Hackenberg*, S. 151 f.; *Kröll u.a./Gotanda*, Art. 74, Rn. 30; *Witz/Salger/Lorenz/Witz*, Art. 74, Rn. 41.
²⁰¹ Vgl. auch *Staudinger/Magnus*, Art. 74, Rn. 57.
²⁰² Vgl. ausführlich hierzu *Schwenzer/Manner*, 23 Arb. Int'l (2007), 293 ff.
²⁰³ OLG Braunschweig, 28.10.1999, CISG-online 510; LG München I, 6.4.2000, CISG-online 665; LG Heidelberg, 2.10.1996, CISG-online 264; *Achilles*, Art. 74, Rn. 9; *Piltz*, Internationales Kaufrecht, Rn. 5–567; *Staudinger/Magnus*, Art. 74, Rn. 58; *Schwenzer/Manner*, 23 Arb. Int'l (2007), 293, 296 f.

ordnungen des Common Law hingegen, wird Verjährung auch heute noch als Frage des Prozessrechtes begriffen und dementsprechend der **lex fori** unterstellt.[204] In internationalen **Schiedsverfahren** spricht viel dafür, die Verjährungsregeln der PICC (Art. 10.1 ff.) anzuwenden,[205] die eine relative Verjährungsfrist von drei Jahren (Art. 10.2 I) bzw. eine absolute Verjährungsfrist von zehn Jahren (Art. 10.2 II) aufstellen.

3. Währung der Ersatzleistung

63 Nur selten werden die Parteien vereinbart haben, in welcher Währung der Schadenersatz zu leisten ist. Die für den **Kaufpreis** vereinbarte Währung ist nicht schlechthin auch für geschuldete Ersatzleistungen der einen oder anderen Partei massgebend.[206] Vielmehr ist für die Währung der Ersatzleistung die Zielsetzung der Artt. 74 ff. zu beachten, den Schaden des Gläubigers in vollem Umfang auszugleichen. Der Schaden ist deshalb grundsätzlich in derjenigen Währung zu bemessen, in welcher der Verlust des Gläubigers entstanden ist oder der entgangene Gewinn erzielt worden wäre.[207] Dies wird zumeist die **Währung am Sitz des Gläubigers** sein,[208] im Einzelfall kann der Schaden jedoch auch in einer anderen Währung eingetreten sein und ist dann in dieser zu ersetzen, z. B. ist bei Tätigung eines Deckungsgeschäfts die dabei verwendete Währung[209] und bei abstrakter Berechnung die Währung, in der die Ware üblicher Weise gehandelt wird, massgeblich.[210] Eine Ersetzungsbefugnis des Schuldners, wonach dieser auch in der Landeswährung des Zahlungsortes zu zahlen berechtigt ist, widerspricht grundsätzlich dem Prinzip des vollen Schadensausgleichs.[211]

X. Beweisfragen

1. Beweislast

64 Dass die Beweislast im CISG zwar nicht explizit aber doch mitgeregelt ist, ist heute nahezu unumstritten.[212] Nach h. M. trifft den **Gläubiger** die Beweislast jedenfalls für den **Umfang des Schadens** sowie den **Kausalzusammenhang** mit der haftungsbegründen-

---

[204] Vgl. *Schwenzer/Manner*, 23 Arb. Int'l (2007), 293, 296 f.
[205] Vgl. *Schwenzer/Manner*, 23 Arb. Int'l (2007), 293, 301 ff.
[206] *Remien*, RabelsZ 53 (1989), 245, 280; *Zmij*, ZfRVgl 1998, 21, 28; anders jedoch LG Berlin, 30.9.1992, CISG-online 70 (stets Vertragswährung).
[207] OLG Hamburg, 28.2.1997, CISG-online 261; MünchKomm/*P. Huber*, Art. 74, Rn. 53; *Kröll u. a./Gotanda*, Art. 74, Rn. 31; *Staudinger/Magnus*, Art. 74, Rn. 56; *ders.*, RabelsZ 53 (1989), 116, 134 f.; *Remien*, RabelsZ 53 (1989), 245, 264 ff.; *Achilles*, Art. 74, Rn. 6; *Saidov*, Damages in Int'l Sales, S. 265; *Zmij*, ZfRVgl 1998, 21, 27 ff.; *Wittinghofer/Becker*, IHR 2010, 225, 227 f. Dagegen für grundsätzliche Anwendung der Währung am Sitz des Gläubigers *Piltz*, Internationales Kaufrecht, Rn. 5–564; *Soergel/Lüderitz/Dettmeier*, Vor Art. 74, Rn. 9; *Roßmeier*, RIW 2000, 407, 412; *Bamberger/Roth/Saenger*, Art. 74, Rn. 2 Fn. 2 mit dem Argument, dass die Gegenansicht zu praktischen Schwierigkeiten bei der Umrechnung führe. Da der Gläubiger den Schaden i. d. R. im Sitzstaat ausgleichen wird, dürften diese Ansichten nur selten zu unterschiedlichen Ergebnissen führen. Für wahlweise Bemessung des Ersatzes in der Währung des Kaufpreises oder der Währung, in der der Schaden entstanden ist, Art. 7.4.12 PICC: („whichever is more appropriate"); die Wahl steht dabei dem Gläubiger zu, vgl. *Vogenauer/Kleinheisterkamp/McKendrick*, Art. 7.4.12 PICC, Rn. 4. Art. 9:510 PECL lässt dem Richter nach richterlichem Vorbild (vgl. dazu The Despina R. & the Folias, [1979] A. C. 685 (H. L.)) hingegen mehr Spielraum („currency which most appropriately reflects the aggrieved party's loss").
[208] MünchKomm/*P. Huber*, Art. 74, Rn. 53; *Staudinger/Magnus*, Art. 74, Rn. 56; *P. Huber/Mullis/P. Huber*, S. 280.
[209] Vgl. OLG Frankfurt a. M., 24.3.2009, CISG-online 2165 mit zustimmender Anmerkung von *Wittinghofer/Becker*, IHR 2010, 225, 227 f.
[210] Vgl. *Wittinghofer/Becker*, IHR 2010, 225, 229.
[211] Vgl. *Mohs*, Art. 53 Rn. 8. A. A. *Stoll/Gruber*, 4. Aufl., Art. 74 Rn. 30.
[212] BGH, 9.1.2002, CISG-online 651 (Frage der Folgen eines beweisrechtlichen Anerkenntnisses aber nicht im CISG geregelt); KG Wallis, 28.1.2009, CISG-online 2025; KG Zug, 14.12.2009, CISG-online 2026 unter 10.1; CISG-AC, Op. 6 *(Gotanda)*, Comment 2.1; oben *Ferrari*, Art. 4 Rn. 49; *ders.*, IPRax 2001, 354, 357; *Staudinger/Magnus*, Art. 4, Rn. 63–70; MünchKomm/*P. Huber*, Art. 74, Rn. 58; *Brunner*, Art. 74, Rn. 58; *Reimers-Zocher*, S. 128 ff.; eingehend *Antweiler*, S. 44 ff., 71–74; *T. M. Müller*, Beweislast, 26 ff. Unzutreffend OLG Koblenz, 22.4.2010, CISG-online 2163 (Beweislastregeln richten sich nach lex fori).

den Vertragsverletzung.²¹³ Umstritten ist die Beweislast für die **Vertragsverletzung**.²¹⁴ Grundsätzlich wird man auch diese dem Gläubiger auferlegen müssen; eine Differenzierung erscheint im Hinblick auf die Lieferung nicht vertragsgemässer Ware angebracht (vgl. oben Art. 35 Rn. 49). Ebenfalls umstritten ist die Beweislast für die **Vorhersehbarkeit** des Schadens. Richtiger Ansicht nach muss der Nachweis der Voraussehbarkeit des Schadens dem Gläubiger obliegen,²¹⁵ was freilich Beweiserleichterungen im Rahmen einer Typisierung von Fallgruppen²¹⁶ insbesondere beim sog. Mangelschaden nicht ausschliesst (s. oben Rn. 21).

2. Beweismass

Von einer Reihe von Gerichten und Autoren wird die Frage des Beweismasses als eine 65 solche des **Prozessrechtes** begriffen und deshalb der lex fori unterworfen.²¹⁷ Indessen kann die blosse Qualifikation von Beweisregeln als prozess- oder materiellrechtlich nicht entscheidend sein.²¹⁸ Die Zulassung unterschiedlicher nationaler Regeln zum Beweismass würde die einheitliche Auslegung und Anwendung des CISG und das Grundprinzip des vollen Schadensausgleichs selbst unterlaufen. Darüber hinaus ist zu Recht darauf hingewiesen worden, dass auch nach der oben geschilderten Auffassung richtigerweise das CISG selbst als Teil der lex fori zum Tragen kommen müsste.²¹⁹ Wie die Beweislast muss deshalb auch das Beweismass aus dem CISG selbst heraus entwickelt werden. Als Standard dafür bietet sich das Prinzip der „**reasonableness**" an.²²⁰ Nicht nur das CISG rekurriert an verschiedenen Stellen auf den Massstab einer „vernünftigen Person";²²¹ auch PICC, PECL und UNIDROIT Principles of Transnational Civil Procedure favorisieren einen derartigen Standard.²²² Der Gläubiger hat deshalb mit einem **vernünftigen Grad an Sicherheit** (reasonable degree of certainty) den ihm entstandenen Verlust und entgangenen Gewinn zu beweisen. Aus Gründen der Prävention mag man das Beweismass bei **vorsätzlichem Ver-**

---

²¹³ OLG Koblenz, 24.2.2011, CISG-online 2301; OLG Zweibrücken, 31.3.1998, CISG-online 481; KG Zug, 14.12.2009, CISG-online 2026, unter 11.; Trib. civ. e pen. Vigevano, 12.2.2000, CISG-online 493 = IHR 2001, 72, 77, mit zust. Anm. *Ferrari*, IPRax 2001, 354, 357; MünchKomm/*P. Huber*, Art. 74, Rn. 58; *Baumgärtel/Laumen-Hepting*, Art. 74 WKR, Rn. 2; *Honsell/Schönle/Th. Koller*, Art. 74, Rn. 46; *Staudinger/ Magnus*, Art. 74, Rn. 62; *Witz/Salger/Lorenz/Witz*, Art. 74, Rn. 40; *Jung*, S. 237 f.

²¹⁴ Für Beweispflichtigkeit des Gläubigers CISG-AC, Op. 6 *(Gotanda)*, Comment 2.2; HGer Zürich, 22.11.2005, CISG-online 1195, E. III 4c (aa); *Staudinger/Magnus*, Art. 74, Rn. 62; MünchKomm/*P. Huber*, Art. 74, Rn. 58; *Honsell/Schönle/Th. Koller*, Art. 74, Rn. 46; *Brunner*, Art. 74, Rn. 58; für Beweispflichtigkeit des Schuldners *Stoll/Gruber*, 4. Aufl., Art. 74 Rn. 51.

²¹⁵ OLG Bamberg, 13.1.1999, CISG-online 516; KG Zug, 14.12.2009, CISG-online 2026, unter 11.; Audiencia Provincial de Barcelona, 20.6.1997, CISG-online 338; *Brunner*, Art. 74, Rn. 58; MünchKomm/ *P. Huber*, Art. 74, Rn. 58; *Kröll u. a./Gotanda*, Art. 74, Rn. 48; *Witz/Salger/Lorenz/Witz*, Art. 74, Rn. 40; *Faust*, S. 324 f.; *Schlechtriem*, Internationales UN-Kaufrecht, Rn. 302; *Brölsch*, Schadensersatz, S. 50; a. A. *Staudinger/Magnus*, Art. 74, Rn. 62; MünchKommHGB/*Mankowski*, Art. 74, Rn. 46; *Enderlein/Maskow/Strohbach*, Art. 74, Anm. 10; *Herber/Czerwenka*, Art. 74, Rn. 13.

²¹⁶ Vgl. *Honsell/Schönle/Th. Koller*, Art. 74, Rn. 46: Tatsächliche Vermutung, Ausnahme bei aussergewöhnlichen Schäden.

²¹⁷ *Delchi Carrier SpA. v. Rotorex Corp.*, U. S. Ct. App. (2ⁿᵈ Cir.), 6.12.1995, CISG-online 140; HGer Zürich, 22.11.2010, CISG-online 2160 unter 3.4.; KG Zug, 14.12.2009, CISG-online 2026, unter 10.1; OLG Koblenz, 22.4.2010, CISG-online 2163; BezG Saane, 20.2.1997, CISG-online 426, E. 6.4.; *Stoll/Gruber*, 4. Aufl., Art 74 Rn. 53; *Staudinger/Magnus*, Art. 74, Rn. 61; MünchKomm/*P. Huber*, Art. 74, Rn. 57; *Herber/ Czerwenka*, Art. 74, Rn. 13.

²¹⁸ Vgl. v. a. CISG-AC, Op. 6 *(Gotanda)*, Comment 2.3; *Schwenzer/Hachem*, Scope of Damages S. 99; *Kröll u. a./Gotanda*, Art. 74, Rn. 13; *ders.*, 37 Geo. Wash. J. Int'l. L. & Econ. (2005), 95, 120 ff.; *Orlandi*, 5 Uniform L. Rev. (2000), 23.

²¹⁹ Vgl. *Th. Koller/Mauerhofer*, FS Schwenzer, S. 963, 971 f.

²²⁰ CISG-AC, Op. 6 *(Gotanda)*, Comment 2.1 ff.; *Saidov*, 22 J. Cont. L. (2006), 1, 5 ff.; *Mullis*, RabelsZ 71 (2007), 35, 49 ff.; *Schwenzer/Hachem*, Scope of Damages S. 99; *P. Huber/Mullis/P. Huber*, S. 281 f.; *Mohs*, AJP 2011, 425, 427; *Leumann Liebster*, FS Schwenzer, S. 1031, 1042; *Th. Koller/Mauerhofer*, FS Schwenzer, S. 963, 977 f. (unter ausdrücklicher Aufgabe der noch in *Honsell/Schönle/Th. Koller*, Art. 74, Rn. 49 vertretenen Gegenauffassung); a. A. *Schlechtriem*, 19 Pace Int'l L. Rev. (2007), 89, 97.

²²¹ Artt. 8 II, III; 25; 35 I lit. b); 60; 72 II; 75; 77; 79 I; 85; 86; 88 II.

²²² Vgl. Art. 7.4.3 PICC; Art. 9:501 II PECL; Art. 21.2 UNIDROIT Principles of Transnational Civil Procedure.

tragsbruch herabsetzen,²²³ was insbesondere in Bezug auf entgangenen Gewinn und Reputationsschäden von wichtiger Bedeutung ist. Aus dem Standard der „reasonableness" ergibt sich, dass bei nicht quantifizierbaren Schäden die Höhe des zugesprochenen Schadensersatzes auf eine vernünftige Schätzung des Gerichts zu stützen ist.²²⁴ Ein Rückgriff auf nationales Recht²²⁵ ist deshalb weder notwendig noch zulässig.²²⁶

3. Beweisführung

66 Die Art und Weise der Beweisführung, insbes. die zulässigen **Beweismittel,** bestimmen sich hingegen nach dem **Prozessrecht** der lex fori.²²⁷ Ob man aus Art. 8 III und Art. 11 S. 2, nach denen Erklärungen sowie insbesondere der Vertragsschluss auf jede Weise bewiesen werden können, auch durch Zeugen, einen allgemeinen dem CISG zu Grunde liegenden Grundsatz ableiten kann, erscheint fraglich.

---

²²³ Vgl. *Schwenzer/Hachem,* Scope of Damages, S. 93; *Hachem,* FS Schwenzer, S. 647, 666; vgl. auch *Th. Koller/Mauerhofer,* FS Schwenzer, S. 963, 979.

²²⁴ Vgl. CISG-AC, Op. 6 *(Gotanda),* Comment 2.9; *Leumann Liebster,* FS Schwenzer, S. 1031, 1045. Vgl. auch die entsprechende Lösung in Art. 7.4.3 III PICC.

²²⁵ So OLG Koblenz, 22.4.2010, CISG-online 2163; OLG München, 5.3.2008, CISG-online 1686; KG Zug, 14.12.2009, CISG-online 2026, unter 11.3; BezG Saane, 20.2.1997, CISG-online 426, E. 6.4.; AppGer Helsinki, 26.10.2000, CISG-online 1078; OLG Celle, 2.9.1998, CISG-online 506; offengelassen in BGer, 17.12.2009, CISG-online 2022 = BGE 136 III 56, 58

²²⁶ Vgl. *Mohs,* AJP 2011, 425, 427; in diese Richung auch *Th. Koller/Mauerhofer,* FS Schwenzer, S. 963, 973 f. (mit der Nähe zum materiellen Recht eine Anknüpfung an die lex causae begründend); a. A. *Brunner,* Art. 74, Rn. 57 (der allerdings eine einheitsrechtliche Lösung für vertretbar hält); *Staudinger/Magnus,* Art. 74, Rn. 61. *Th. Koller/Mauerhofer,* FS Schwenzer, S. 963, 979 konstatieren, dass bei nicht ziffernmässig nachweisbarem Schaden ein vernünftiger Grad eher erreicht ist als bei anderen Beweisthemen und kommen so zu einem ähnlichen Ergebnis.

²²⁷ *Staudinger/Magnus,* Art. 74, Rn. 61; MünchKomm/*P. Huber,* Art. 74, Rn. 57.

Art. 75 [Schadensberechnung bei Vertragsaufhebung und Deckungsgeschäft]

Ist der Vertrag aufgehoben und hat der Käufer einen Deckungskauf oder der Verkäufer einen Deckungsverkauf in angemessener Weise und innerhalb eines angemessenen Zeitraumes nach der Aufhebung vorgenommen, so kann die Partei, die Schadenersatz verlangt, den Unterschied zwischen dem im Vertrag vereinbarten Preis und dem Preis des Deckungskaufs oder des Deckungsverkaufs sowie jeden weiteren Schadenersatz nach Art. 74 verlangen.

Art. 75

If the contract is avoided and if, in a reasonable manner and within a reasonable time after avoidance, the buyer has bought goods in replacement or the seller has resold the goods, the party claiming damages may recover the difference between the contract price and the price in the substitute transaction as well as any further damages recoverable under article 74.

Art. 75

Lorsque le contrat est résolu et que, d'une manière raisonnable et dans un délai raisonnable après la résolution, l'acheteur a procédé à un achat de remplacement ou le vendeur à une vente compensatoire, la partie qui demande des dommages-intérêts peut obtenir la différence entre le prix du contrat et le prix de l'achat de remplacement ou de la vente compensatoire ainsi que tous autres dommages-intérêts qui peuvent être dus en vertu de l'article 74.

Übersicht

	Rn.
I. Grundgedanken	1
II. Voraussetzungen	2
1. Vornahme eines Deckungsgeschäfts	2
2. Nach Vertragsaufhebung	5
3. Angemessenheit des Deckungsgeschäfts	6
4. Anwendung der Vorhersehbarkeitsregel	8
III. Rechtsfolgen	9
1. Ersatz des Nichterfüllungsschadens	9
2. Ersatz weiterer Schäden	11
3. Verhältnis zu Artt. 74 und 76	13
IV. Beweisfragen	14

I. Grundgedanken

Art. 75 regelt wie schon Art. 85 EKG sowie vergleichbare Bestimmungen in nationalen Kaufrechten[1] und auf internationaler Ebene[2] die **konkrete Berechnung des Nichterfüllungsschadens** bei Vertragsaufhebung. Der Gläubiger kann sein Vertragsinteresse konkret nach Massgabe eines **Deckungsgeschäftes** berechnen, das er nach Aufhebung des Vertrages vorgenommen hat. Der ersatzberechtigte Käufer ist dann befugt, die Differenz zwischen dem Vertragspreis und dem höheren Preis eines Deckungskaufs, der ersatzberechtigte Verkäufer die Differenz zwischen dem Vertragspreis und dem bei einem Deckungsverkauf erzielten niedrigeren Preis als Nichterfüllungsschaden im engeren Sinne geltend zu machen. Art. 75 erleichtert damit dem Gläubiger die Berechnung und den Nachweis des

1

---

[1] Vgl. rechtsvergleichend *Schwenzer/Hachem/Kee*, Rn. 44.229 ff. Vgl. weiter Deutschland: § 376 III HGB; Italien: Art. 1516 Cc; Niederlande: Art. 7:37 BW; Österreich: § 376 II UGB; Schweiz: Artt. 191 II, 215 I OR; USA: § 2–706 (2) und § 2–712 UCC. Im französischen und belgischen Recht bedarf es einer richterlichen Ermächtigung (Art. 1144 Cc).

[2] Art. 7.4.5 PICC; Art. 9:506 PECL; Art. 164 CESL-Entwurf.

Nichterfüllungsschadens. Die Geltendmachung weiter gehender Schäden nach Art. 74 bleibt dem Gläubiger unbenommen.

II. Voraussetzungen

1. Vornahme eines Deckungsgeschäfts

2   Art. 75 setzt voraus, dass der Gläubiger ein Deckungsgeschäft vorgenommen hat; die blosse Möglichkeit, ein solches abzuschliessen, genügt nicht.[3] Nicht erforderlich ist hingegen, dass das Deckungsgeschäft bereits durchgeführt ist.[4] Das Deckungsgeschäft muss **auf den Kaufvertrag bezogen** sein, d. h. es muss dazu geeignet und bestimmt sein, das Erfüllungsinteresse des Gläubigers zu befriedigen.[5] Die Abgabe verdorbener Ware zur Entsorgung ist kein Deckungsverkauf.[6] Dasselbe gilt für die Anmietung von Ersatzware; diese Kosten können nicht nach Art. 75 wohl aber nach Art. 74 verlangt werden.[7] Hingegen kann der nicht belieferte Käufer zur Erfüllung der von ihm geschlossenen Lieferverträge auch andere von ihm bereits angeschaffte Ware verwenden und dem Verkäufer deren Anschaffungskosten in Rechnung stellen.[8] Ebenso kann der Verkäufer, der die gelieferte Ware nach Vertragsaufhebung noch nicht zurück erhalten hat, andere verfügbare Ware gleicher Art veräussern, um sein Erfüllungsinteresse bestmöglich zu befriedigen.[9] Art. 75 ist jedenfalls entsprechend anzuwenden, wenn der nicht belieferte Käufer sein Erfüllungsinteresse dadurch befriedigt, dass er die Ware im eigenen Betrieb herstellt. Die Herstellungskosten treten dann an die Stelle des Preises eines Deckungskaufs.[10]

3   Schwierigkeiten bei der Bestimmung eines Deckungsgeschäftes treten auf, wenn der Gläubiger ständig mit Ware der gekauften oder verkauften Art handelt.[11] Es besteht dann das Problem, dass der Gläubiger **wirtschaftlich ungünstige** Vertragsabschlüsse als angebliches Deckungsgeschäft auf den Schuldner abwälzt. Deshalb will eine Mindermeinung bei Fehlen einer auf ein bestimmtes Geschäft bezogenen Anzeige immer das erste nach Vertragsaufhebung getätigte Geschäft als Deckungsgeschäft ansehen.[12] Diese Auffassung erscheint indes als zu schematisch. Man wird dem Gläubiger nicht verwehren können, dass er nachweist, dass nicht gerade das erste Geschäft das Deckungsgeschäft darstellte. Gegebenenfalls

---

[3] *Herber/Czerwenka*, Art. 75, Rn. 5; *Bianca/Bonell/Knapp*, Art. 75, Anm. 3.1.; *Honsell/Schönle/Th. Koller*, Art. 75, Rn. 10.

[4] OLG Frankfurt a. M., 24.3.2009, CISG-online 2165; MünchKomm/*P. Huber*, Art. 75, Rn. 9; *Staudinger/Magnus*, Art. 75, Rn. 13; *Ferrari u. a./Saenger*, Internationales Vertragsrecht, Art. 76, Rn. 4.

[5] *Achilles*, Art. 75, Rn. 3; *Schmidt-Ahrendts*, Rechtsbehelfe, S. 79; *Hager*, FS Schwenzer, S. 681, 691 (unter besonderer Betonung des Lieferzeitpunkts). *Herber/Czerwenka*, Art. 75, Rn. 4 lehnen die Notwendigkeit ähnlicher Bestimmungen in Bezug auf Umfangs-, Lieferungs- und Bezahlungsregelungen ausdrücklich ab.

[6] OLG Hamm, 22.9.1992, CISG-online 57; zust. *Piltz*, NJW 1994, 1101, 1106; *Bamberger/Roth/Saenger*, Art. 75, Rn. 4; *Staudinger/Magnus*, Art. 75, Rn. 10; *Honsell/Schönle/Th. Koller*, Art. 75, Rn. 13.

[7] Vgl. zum UCC *Perillo*, Damages, S. 704.

[8] *Ferrari u. a./Saenger*, Internationales Vertragsrecht, Art. 76, Rn. 3. Enger *Staudinger/Magnus*, Art. 75, Rn. 14 (zeitlicher Zusammenhang erforderlich). A. A. *Honsell/Schönle/Th. Koller*, Art. 75, Rn. 7. Deckt sich der Käufer jedoch aus eigenen Beständen ein, ohne deren Anschaffungskosten in Rechnung zu stellen, so fehlt es an einem Deckungsgeschäft und die abstrakte Berechnung nach Art. 76 kommt zum Zuge, vgl. OLG Frankfurt a. M., 24.3.2009, CISG-online 2165.

[9] *Honsell/Schönle*, 1. Aufl., Art. 75, Rn. 21.

[10] *Bamberger/Roth/Saenger*, Art. 75, Rn. 4; im Ergebnis ebenso *Staudinger/Magnus*, Art. 75, Rn. 11; a. A. *P. Huber/Mullis/P. Huber*, S. 285; *Achilles*, Art. 75, Rn. 3; *Soergel/Lüderitz/Dettmeier*, Art. 75, Rn. 4; *Kröll u. a./Gotanda*, Art. 76, Rn. 13.

[11] Gemäss *Herber/Czerwenka*, Art. 75, Rn. 4 und *Honsell/Schönle*, 1. Aufl., Art. 75, Rn. 21 ist es nicht erforderlich, dem ursprünglichen Vertrag einen bestimmten Vertrag, den der Gläubiger im Zuge des normalen Geschäftsverkehrs abschliesst, zuzuordnen. Anders jetzt *Honsell/Schönle/Th. Koller*, Art. 75, Rn. 11.

[12] *Honnold/Flechtner*, Artt. 75, 76, Rn. 410.1; *P. Huber/Mullis/P. Huber*, S. 285; MünchKomm/*P. Huber*, Art. 75, Rn. 10; *Schmidt-Ahrendts*, Rechtsbehelfe, S. 80. CISG-AC, Op. 8 *(Gotanda)*, Comment 2.3.4 sieht darin vielmehr eine Möglichkeit für den Gläubiger als eine Vorschrift.

mag man mit Art. 77 korrigieren. Mögliche Beweislastprobleme kann der Gläubiger auf jeden Fall mit einer **Anzeige des Deckungsgeschäfts** vermeiden.[13]

Nicht zu verwechseln ist das Deckungsgeschäft mit dem **Selbsthilfeverkauf** nach Art. 88. Beim Deckungsgeschäft handelt der Gläubiger im eigenen Interesse und auf eigene Rechnung, auch wenn er die dadurch entstehenden Kosten als Schaden geltend machen kann.[14] Während beim Selbsthilfeverkauf der erzielte Erlös in vollem Umfang der anderen Partei gebührt, geht der bei einem Deckungsverkauf erzielte, den Vertragspreis übersteigende Mehrerlös den ersatzpflichtigen Käufer nichts an; ein solcher Gewinn des Verkäufers kann nicht zum Ausgleich eines weiteren, vom Verkäufer geltend gemachten Schadens herangezogen werden.[15] Entsprechendes gilt auch für einen Gewinn des Käufers bei Weiterveräusserung deckungshalber angeschaffter Ware.

2. Nach Vertragsaufhebung

Nach Art. 75 kann ein Deckungsgeschäft – anders als ein Selbsthilfeverkauf – erst nach Aufhebung des Kaufvertrages vorgenommen werden.[16] Welche Anforderungen an die **Aufhebungserklärung** zu stellen sind, ist im Rahmen von Art. 26 zu beantworten. So mag im Einzelfall das Verlangen des Differenzschadens[17] oder die vorherige Anzeige des Deckungsgeschäfts[18] ausreichen.[19] Vom Erfordernis vorgängiger Vertragsaufhebung macht die h. M. dann eine Ausnahme, wenn bei Vornahme des Deckungsgeschäftes feststeht, dass der Schuldner keinesfalls erfüllen wird, also insbesondere bei einer ernstlichen und endgültigen **Erfüllungsverweigerung**.[20] Es wäre mit dem Grundsatz von Treu und Glauben (Art. 7 I) nicht vereinbar, wenn die die Vertragserfüllung endgültig verweigernde Partei sich darauf berufen könnte, dass die andere Partei zuvor noch die Vertragsaufhebung hätte mitteilen müssen. Vertritt man indes die zu befürwortende Auffassung, dass eine Berechnung des Nichterfüllungsschadens anhand eines **konkreten Deckungsgeschäftes auch ohne Vertragsaufhebung** gemäss Art. 74 möglich ist (vgl. oben Art. 74 Rn. 22), so bedarf es einer derartigen teleologischen Reduktion des Art. 75 nicht. Die Unterschiede zwischen beiden Auffassungen in der Praxis sind allerdings zu vernachlässigen. Denn die nach Art. 74 erforderliche Vorhersehbarkeit, die in Art. 75 nicht verlangt wird (vgl. unten Rn. 8), dürfte im Hinblick auf die Vornahme eines konkreten Deckungsgeschäftes regelmässig gegeben sein.

---

[13] CISG-AC, Op. 8 *(Gotanda)*, Comment 2.3.4; *Honnold/Flechtner*, Artt. 75, 76, Rn. 410.1; *Saidov*, Damages in Int'l Sales, p. 178; *P. Huber/Mullis/P. Huber*, S. 285; *Brölsch*, Schadensersatz, S. 84. Eine Pflicht zur Anzeige besteht jedoch im Grundsatz nicht, vgl. *Saidov*, Damages in Int'l Sales, S. 185; *Ferrari u. a./Saenger*, Internationales Vertragsrecht, Art. 76, Rn. 4; *Honsell/Schönle/Th. Koller*, Art. 75, Rn. 11. *Stoll/Gruber*, 4. Aufl., Art. 75 Rn. 3 halten die Entstehung einer solchen Pflicht aus Handelsbräuchen i. S. d. Art. 9 I für möglich, lassen die Rechtsfolge bei Verletzung der Pflicht aber offen.

[14] *Karollus*, S. 219; *Weber*, Vertragsverletzungsfolgen, S. 201; *Hager*, Rechtsbehelfe des Verkäufers, S. 156 f.; *Witz/Salger/Lorenz/Witz*, Art. 75, Rn. 5; *Honsell/Schönle/Th. Koller*, Art. 75, Rn. 12.

[15] *Staudinger/Magnus*, Art. 75, Rn. 15; anders wohl *Witz/Salger/Lorenz/Witz*, Art. 75, Rn. 10; vgl. auch § 2–706 (6) (1) UCC: „The seller is not accountable to the buyer for any profit made on any resale.".

[16] Vgl. OLG Düsseldorf, 9.7.2010, CISG-online 2171 = IHR 2011, 116; vgl. auch ausdrücklich CISG-AC, Op. 8 *(Gotanda)*, Comment 2.3.3.

[17] Vgl. Schiedsgericht der Handelskammer Zürich, 31.5.1996, CISG-online 1291.

[18] Vgl. OLG Hamburg, 28.2.1997, CISG-online 261.

[19] Vgl. OLG Düsseldorf, 22.7.2004, CISG-online 916; ausführlich *Schmidt-Ahrendts*, Rechtsbehelfe, S. 73.

[20] Vgl. Oberster Gerichtshof Polen, 27.1.2006, CISG-online 1399; OLG Hamburg, 28.2.1997, CISG-online 261; OLG München, 15.9.2004, CISG-online 1013; OLG Bamberg, 13.1.1999, CISG-online 516; OLG Frankfurt a. M., 24.3.2009, CISG-online 2165; wohl auch Audiencia Provincial de Valencia, 31.3.2005, CISG-online 1369; wie hier *Staudinger/Magnus*, Art. 75, Rn. 8; *Achilles*, Art. 75, Rn. 2; *Witz/Salger/Lorenz/Witz*, Art. 75, Rn. 6; *Honsell/Schönle/Th. Koller*, Art. 75, Rn. 7; *Stoll*, RabelsZ 52 (1988), 617, 635; *Brölsch*, Schadensersatz, S. 83; *Weber*, Vertragsverletzungsfolgen, S. 201; wohl auch *P. Huber/Mullis/P. Huber*, S. 284; dagegen *Schmidt-Ahrendts*, Rechtsbehelfe, S. 76 ff.; *Ferrari u. a./Saenger*, Internationales Vertragsrecht, Art. 76, Rn. 3; wohl auch CISG-AC, Op. 8 *(Gotanda)*, Comment 2.3.3; *Berger/Scholl*, FS Schwenzer, S. 159, 170.

3. Angemessenheit des Deckungsgeschäfts

6   Die Schadensberechnung nach Art. 75 setzt voraus, dass das Deckungsgeschäft **in angemessener Weise** vorgenommen worden ist. Der Gläubiger muss beim Abschluss des Deckungsgeschäfts im Rahmen der einschlägigen kaufmännischen Übung wie ein vorsichtiger und umsichtiger Geschäftsmann der betreffenden Branche gehandelt haben.[21] Die Angemessenheit bezieht sich zunächst auf den **Preis** des Deckungsgeschäftes. Bei einem Deckungsverkauf muss der Verkäufer den höchsten erzielbaren Preis, bei einem Deckungskauf der Käufer den niedrigsten geforderten Preis anstreben;[22] beide Preise müssen nicht zwingend dem jeweiligen durchschnittlichen Marktpreis entsprechen.[23] Allerdings braucht der Gläubiger nur nahe liegende Geschäftschancen wahrzunehmen.[24] Es darf dem Käufer, der sich anderweitig eindecken muss, z. B. nicht zugemutet werden, eingehende Untersuchungen darüber anzustellen, wie er Ersatzware am vorteilhaftesten beschaffen kann.[25] Auch durch das konkrete Deckungsgeschäft entstehende Transaktionskosten müssen berücksichtigt werden.[26] Das Deckungsgeschäft muss auch bezüglich seines **Inhalts** angemessen sein. Dies bedeutet, dass z. B. bei einem Deckungskauf Ersatzware möglichst an dem Ort zu beschaffen ist, an dem der Verkäufer die Ware hätte liefern müssen.[27] Überhaupt muss der Deckungskauf grundsätzlich zu den **gleichen Bedingungen**[28] geschlossen werden wie der Kauf, für den er Ersatz bieten soll, und sich auf **Ware gleicher Art und Güte** beziehen.[29] Abweichungen können aber nach den Umständen gerechtfertigt sein.[30] Wenn sich der Käufer mit qualitativ schlechterer Ware zufrieden gibt, darf dies nicht dem Verkäufer zum Nachteil gereichen und kann als verhältnismässiges Deckungsgeschäft angesehen werden.

7   Das Deckungsgeschäft muss innerhalb eines **angemessenen Zeitraums** nach der Aufhebung des Vertrages vorgenommen werden.[31] Die Frist beginnt mit der **Aufhebungs-**

---

[21] ICC, 8128/1995, CISG-online 526; CISG-AC, Op. 8 *(Gotanda)*, Comment 2.3.1; *Herber/Czerwenka*, Art. 75, Rn. 4; *Staudinger/Magnus*, Art. 75, Rn. 16; *Soergel/Lüderitz/Dettmeier*, Art. 75, Rn. 5; *Achilles*, Art. 75, Rn. 4; *Witz/Salger/Lorenz/Witz*, Art. 75, Rn. 7; *Schmidt-Ahrendts*, Rechtsbehelfe, S. 84; *Weber*, Vertragsverletzungsfolgen, S. 202.

[22] Dies kann auch die Annahme eines neuen Angebots des Verkäufers beinhalten, wenn dessen Preis niedriger als derjenige ist, der für den Deckungskauf bezahlt werden müsste, vgl. CA Rennes, 27.5.2008, CISG-online 1746, zu dieser Thematik vgl. auch *Schwenzer/Manner*, FS Kritzer, S. 470, 486; Sekretariatskommentar, Art. 71, Nr. 4; *Bianca/Bonell/Knapp*, Art. 75, Anm. 2.4.; *Enderlein/Maskow/Strohbach*, Art. 75, Anm. 2.; *Neumayer/Ming*, Art. 75, Anm. 2.; *Roßmeier*, RIW 2000, 407, 409; grosszügiger *Soergel/Lüderitz/Dettmeier*, Art. 75, Rn. 5 unter Verweis auf § 2–712 UCC: „die Angemessenheit ist eingehalten, solange der Gläubiger nicht seine Schadensminderungspflicht verletzt".

[23] CIETAC, 4.6.1999, CISG-online 1806; *Saidov*, Damages in Int'l Sales, S. 179; CISG-AC, Op. 8 *(Gotanda)*, Comment 2.3.1; *Kröll u. a./Gotanda*, Art. 76, Rn. 16. Ein wesentlicher Preisunterschied deutet jedoch darauf hin, dass das Deckungsgeschäft nicht angemessen ist, vgl. *Honnold/Flechtner*, Artt. 75, 76, Rn. 410.2.

[24] Vgl. CISG-AC, Op. 8 *(Gotanda)*, Comment 2.3.1; *Witz/Salger/Lorenz/Witz*, Art. 75, Rn. 7. Vgl. auch *Schwenzer/Hachem/Kee*, Rn. 44.233.

[25] ICC, 8128/1995, CISG-online 526; *P. Huber/Mullis/P. Huber*, S. 286; *Heuzé*, Anm. 453.; *Staudinger/Magnus*, Art. 75, Rn. 4; MünchKomm/*P. Huber*, Art. 75, Rn. 13; *Soergel/Lüderitz/Dettmeier*, Art. 75, Rn. 7; *Witz/Salger/Lorenz/Witz*, Art. 75, Rn. 7.

[26] In diese Richung auch *M. Schmidt*, FS Schwenzer, S. 1499, 1511.

[27] *Honsell/Schönle/Th. Koller*, Art. 75, Rn. 17.

[28] Vgl. *Saidov*, Damages in Int'l Sales, S. 180. Möglich ist im Einzelfall auch eine Kompensation von abweichenden Bedingungen; so für die nachträgliche Berücksichtigung der Frachtkosten im Falle eines FOB-Deckungsgeschäfts für einen CFR-Vertrag, *Saidov*, 13 VJ (2009), 197, 215 unter Bezug auf CIETAC Award, 15.11.1996, CISG-online 1148; vgl. auch *Saidov*, Damages in Int'l Sales, S. 186 (Abzug der Mehrwertsteuer, Vergleich Einzelzahlung zu Ratenzahlung).

[29] *Honnold/Flechtner*, Artt. 75, 76, Rn. 410.2; *Staudinger/Magnus*, Art. 75, Rn. 17; *Witz/Salger/Lorenz/Witz*, Art. 75, Rn. 8; *Saidov*, Damages in Int'l Sales, S. 180 f. Ist die Herkunft der Ware im Vertrag ausdrücklich bestimmt, ist der Käufer im Rahmen eines Ersatzgeschäfts nicht verpflichtet, Güter anderer Herkunft zu beschaffen, vgl. CIETAC, 29.9.2004, CISG-online 1600 (Indisches Rapssamenmehl).

[30] CISG-AC, Op. 8 *(Gotanda)*, Comment 2.3.4 betont, dass die Vertragsbedingungen des Deckungsgeschäftes nicht identisch mit denen des aufgehobenen Vertrags sein müssen. Vgl. auch *Saidov*, Damages in Int'l Sales, S. 180 f.

[31] Vgl. *Ferrari u. a./Saenger*, Internationales Vertragsrecht, Art. 76, Rn. 6; *Saidov*, Damages in Int'l Sales, S. 184 f.; *Schmidt-Ahrendts*, Rechtsbehelfe, S. 80 f.

erklärung zu laufen.³² Im Falle der Vertragsaufhebung bei antizipiertem Vertragsbruch (Artt. 72, 73 II) ist für die Beurteilung der Angemessenheit abweichend auf den **ursprünglichen Lieferzeitpunkt** abzustellen,³³ soweit Art. 77 CISG nicht die Anknüpfung an einen früheren Zeitpunkt gebietet.³⁴ Welche Frist zur Vornahme des Deckungsgeschäftes angemessen ist, hängt von den Umständen des Einzelfalles ab.³⁵ Erweist sich der Abschluss eines angemessenen Deckungsgeschäftes als schwierig, müssen dem Gläubiger unter Umständen mehrere Monate zugestanden werden.³⁶ Hat die Ware einen Börsen- oder Marktpreis, wird der Zeitraum regelmässig kürzer zu bemessen sein.³⁷ Umstritten ist, ob auch ein **vorzeitiges Deckungsgeschäft,** also vor Aufhebung angeschaffte Ware, Grundlage für die Schadensberechnung nach Art. 75 sein kann.³⁸ Der Wortlaut des Art. 75 spricht gegen eine Anwendung auf ein vorzeitiges Deckungsgeschäft. Da der Käufer seinen Nichterfüllungsschaden jedoch auch bei Aufhebung des Vertrages unter Bezugnahme auf ein vor der Aufhebung getätigtes Deckungsgeschäft nach Art. 74 geltend machen kann,³⁹ spielt der Meinungsstreit für die Praxis kaum eine Rolle.

4. Anwendung der Vorhersehbarkeitsregel

Teilweise wird vertreten, dass die Vorhersehbarkeitsregel als allgemeines, dem CISG innewohnendes Prinzip nicht nur im Rahmen des Art. 74, sondern auch im Rahmen des Art. 75 bei **ungewöhnlichen Veränderungen des Preisgefüges,** mit denen der Schuldner nicht zu rechnen braucht, zur Anwendung komme.⁴⁰ Diese Auffassung ist indes abzulehnen.⁴¹ Hierfür spricht zunächst der Widerspruch zum ausdrücklichen Wortlaut der Bestimmung. Art. 75 will den Gläubiger in Bezug auf den Nichterfüllungsschaden besser stellen; nur für den Ersatz der übrigen Schäden wird er auf Art. 74 und damit die Vorhersehbarkeitsregel verwiesen. Gerade bei stark fluktuierenden Märkten muss – solange es sich um ein angemessenes Deckungsgeschäft handelt – das Risiko einer aussergewöhnlichen Veränderung des Preisgefüges dem vertragsbrüchigen Schuldner und nicht dem vertragstreuen Gläubiger auferlegt werden. Im Übrigen ist der aus einem Deckungsgeschäft entstehende Schaden ohnehin **regelmässig voraussehbar.**

---

³² Vgl. CISG-AC, Op. 8 *(Gotanda)*, Comment 2.3.2; *Ferrari u. a./Saenger,* Internationales Vertragsrecht, Art. 76, Rn. 6; *Roßmeier,* RIW 2000, 407, 409.
³³ Vgl. *Hager,* FS Schwenzer, S. 681, 691.
³⁴ Vgl. *Schlechtriem,* GS Hellner, S. 234, 235; so auch *Schlechtriem* in *Schlechtriem/P. Butler,* UN-Law, Rn. 311a (*P. Butler* schlägt jedoch einen differenzierteren Ansatz vor).
³⁵ Vgl. CISG-AC, Op. 8 *(Gotanda)*, Comment 2.3.2; *Achilles,* Art. 75, Rn. 3; *Honsell/Schönle/Th. Koller,* Art. 75, Rn. 21; *Heuzé,* Anm. 453.; *Staudinger/Magnus,* Art. 75, Rn. 18; *Bamberger/Roth/Saenger,* Art. 75, Rn. 6.
³⁶ OLG Düsseldorf, 14.1.1994, CISG-online 119 (drei Monate angemessen, da Absatz von Saisonware schwierig); OLG Hamburg, 28.2.1997, CISG-online 261 (Überlegungs- und Orientierungsfrist von zwei Wochen zugebilligt); vgl. auch die Entscheidung des Supreme Court von Queensland in *Downs Investments Pty Ltd. v. Perwaja Steel Sdn. Bhd.,* Sup. Ct. Queensland, 17.11.2000, CISG-online 587 (zwei Monate noch angemessen); *Schmidt-Ahrendts,* Rechtsbehelfe, S. 81.
³⁷ *Bamberger/Roth/Saenger,* Art. 75, Rn. 6; *Kröll u. a./Gotanda,* Art. 76, Rn. 19.
³⁸ Bejahend: *Staudinger/Magnus,* Art. 75, Rn. 14; enger MünchKomm/*P. Huber,* Art. 75, Rn. 12 (bei ernsthafter und endgültiger Erfüllungsverweigerung); verneinend: *Soergel/Lüderitz/Dettmeier,* Art. 75, Rn. 4; *Schmidt-Ahrendts,* Rechtsbehelfe, S. 83 f.; *Saidov,* Damages in Int'l Sales, S. 176 (aber für Ersatzfähigkeit nach Art. 74); *Kröll u. a./Gotanda,* Art. 76, Rn. 14 (für Ersatzfähigkeit nach Art. 74 oder 76); unklar in Bezug auf die Anwendung von Art. 75, aber ebenfalls für Ersatzfähigkeit nach Art. 74: *Honnold/Flechtner,* Artt. 75, 76, Rn. 410.2; offengelassen von OLG Düsseldorf, 9.7.2010, CISG-online 2171 = IHR 2011, 116, 121.
³⁹ Vgl. oben Art. 74 Rn. 22.
⁴⁰ *Honsell/Schönle/Th. Koller,* Art. 75, Rn. 26; *Staudinger/Magnus,* Art. 75, Rn. 3; *Saidov,* Damages in Int'l Sales, S. 118, 119; *Vékás,* Foreseeability, S. 165.
⁴¹ Vgl. *Schmidt-Ahrendts,* Rechtsbehelfe, S. 87 f.; MünchKomm/*P. Huber,* Art. 75, Rn. 16; *Faust,* S. 25 f.; *Witz/Salger/Lorenz/Witz,* Art. 75, Rn. 1, 12; *P. Huber/Mullis/P. Huber,* S. 283; *Reimers-Zocher,* S. 346.

III. Rechtsfolgen

1. Ersatz des Nichterfüllungsschadens

9 Nach Art. 75 kann der Gläubiger die **Differenz zwischen** dem **Vertragspreis und** dem Preis des **Deckungsgeschäftes** verlangen.[42] Ist das Deckungsgeschäft für den Gläubiger günstiger, so kommt Art. 75 nicht zur Anwendung.[43] Einen „Gewinn" braucht der Gläubiger nicht herauszugeben.[44]

10 Umstritten sind die Rechtsfolgen im Falle eines **nicht angemessenen Deckungsgeschäftes**. Nach überwiegender Auffassung gilt insoweit Art. 76, d. h. für die Schadensberechnung ist auf den **Marktpreis** abzustellen.[45] Nach anderer Auffassung ist der Schaden des Gläubigers auch in diesem Falle konkret zu berechnen, wobei der Schaden durch den **hypothetischen Schaden** bei Durchführung eines angemessenen Deckungsgeschäftes begrenzt ist.[46] Der Wortlaut des Art. 76, der davon ausgeht, dass überhaupt kein Deckungsgeschäft vorgenommen wurde, spricht für letztere Auffassung. Indessen sind die praktischen Unterschiede gering. Hat die Ware einen Marktpreis, so wird regelmässig als unter Berücksichtigung der Schadensminderungspflicht von Art. 77 anzunehmender angemessener Preis der Marktpreis zu verstehen sein.[47] Zu den Auswirkungen von besonders günstigen Deckungsgeschäften auf weitere geltendgemachte Schäden siehe unten Rn. 12a.

2. Ersatz weiterer Schäden

11 Der Ausgleich des mit dem Deckungsgeschäft verbundenen Preisnachteils reicht meist nicht aus, um den Gläubiger wirtschaftlich so zu stellen, wie er bei ordnungsgemässer Erfüllung des Vertrages stehen würde.[48] Deshalb bestimmt Art. 75, dass auch ein „weiterer Schaden" nach den allgemeinen Regeln des Art. 74, d. h. insbesondere im Rahmen der Voraussehbarkeit, zu ersetzen ist.[49] Als typischerweise ersatzfähige weitere Schäden kommen in Betracht: **Nebenkosten** des Deckungsgeschäftes, **Verzögerungs- oder Begleitschäden,** die durch die ersatzweise Befriedigung des allgemeinen Erfüllungsinteresses nicht gedeckt werden, z. B. Schaden wegen verspäteter Befriedigung des Kaufpreisanspruchs durch den Deckungsverkauf (Zinsschaden und Wechselkursverlust),[50] Mietkosten bis zum Zeitpunkt der Vornahme des Deckungskaufes, Kosten einer **vergeblichen Andienung** der Ware oder einer notwendig gewordenen **Zwischenlagerung** durch den Verkäufer[51] oder

---

[42] CISG-AC, Op. 8 *(Gotanda),* Comment 2.1.
[43] *Staudinger/Magnus,* Art. 75, Rn. 19; *Achilles,* Art. 75, Rn. 3; *Schmidt-Ahrendts,* Rechtsbehelfe, S. 92.
[44] MünchKomm/*P. Huber,* Art. 75, Rn. 17; *Schmidt-Ahrendts,* Rechtsbehelfe, S. 92.
[45] Sekretariatskommentar, Art. 71, Nr. 6; MünchKomm/*P. Huber,* Art. 76, Rn. 3; *Bianca/Bonell/Knapp,* Art. 75, Anm. 2.6.; *Kranz,* S. 221 f.; *Neumayer/Ming,* Art. 75, Anm. 2.; CISG-AC, Op. 8 *(Gotanda),* Comment 2.4.4; *Kröll u. a./Gotanda,* Art. 76, Rn. 20, 32; *Wittinghofer/Becker,* IHR 2010, 225, 226; *Ferrari u. a./ Saenger,* Internationales Vertragsrecht, Art. 76, Rn. 5 f.; *Soergel/Lüderitz/Dettmeier,* Art. 75, Rn. 10; *Witz/ Salger/Lorenz/Witz,* Art. 75, Rn. 3; *Staudinger/Magnus,* Art. 75, Rn. 20; *Schmidt-Ahrendts,* Rechtsbehelfe, S. 98 f.; *Sutton,* 50 Ohio St. L. J. (1989), 737, 745 f.; *P. Huber/Mullis/P. Huber,* S. 286 und *Piltz,* Internationales Kaufrecht, Rn. 5–524 wollen alternativ auch eine Berechnung nach Art. 74 zulassen.
[46] ICC, 6281/1989, J. D. I. 1989, 1114, 1119 = CLOUT Nr. 102; *Honnold/Flechtner,* Artt. 75, 76, Rn. 414 sieht dies als eine Möglichkeit; *Honsell/Schönle/Th. Koller,* Art. 75, Rn. 15; *Brölsch,* Schadensersatz, S. 86; *Roßmeier,* RIW 2000, 407, 409; zum EKG schon *Hager,* Rechtsbehelfe des Verkäufers, S. 215.
[47] *Schmidt-Ahrendts,* Rechtsbehelfe, S. 84 f. Vgl. auch *Honsell/Schönle/Th. Koller,* Art. 75, Rn. 15.
[48] *Staudinger/Magnus,* Art. 75, Rn. 4; *Witz/Salger/Lorenz/Witz,* Art. 75, Rn. 12; *Schmidt-Ahrendts,* Rechtsbehelfe, S. 89; *Brölsch,* Schadensersatz, S. 86.
[49] Vgl. auch § 2–706 (1) und § 2–713 (1) UCC 2003, wo klargestellt wird, dass neben der Differenz zwischen dem Vertragspreis und dem beim Deckungsgeschäft erzielten Preis nicht nur incidental damages, sondern auch consequential damages zu ersetzen sind.
[50] LG Krefeld, 28.4.1993, CISG-online 101; CISG-AC, Op. 8 *(Gotanda),* Comment 3.1; *Piltz,* NJW 1994, 1101, 1106.
[51] *Downs Investments Pty Ltd. v. Perwaja Steel Sdn. Bhd.,* Sup. Ct. Queensland, 17.11.2000, CISG-online 587; CISG-AC, Op. 8 *(Gotanda),* Comment 3.1; *Herber/Czerwenka,* Art. 75, Rn. 5; *Karollus,* S. 220; *Neumayer/*

Aufwendungen des Käufers zur **Entgegennahme der Ware,** die für das Deckungsgeschäft nutzlos sind.[52] Auch **frustrierte Aufwendungen** können neben dem nach Art. 75 geltend gemachten Differenzschaden ersatzfähig sein.[53]

Im Regelfall kommt **entgangener Gewinn** als weiterer Schaden nicht in Betracht;[54] denn das Deckungsgeschäft dient gerade auch dazu, dem Gläubiger die mit der Erfüllung des ursprünglichen Vertrages verbundenen Gewinnchancen zu erhalten. Nutzt er sie trotz ersatzweiser Herbeiführung der Erfüllung nicht, so ist es seine Sache. Eine derartige Doppelkompensation hat auszuscheiden.[55] Dies kann allerdings nicht gelten, wenn der Gläubiger geltend macht, ihm sei wegen der Notwendigkeit, ein Deckungsgeschäft zu schliessen, der Gewinn aus einem weiteren Geschäft entgangen, das er bei realer Erfüllung des aufgehobenen Kaufvertrages zusätzlich hätte tätigen können (Problem des „**lost volume**").[56] Dabei geht es darum, dass ein Verkäufer marktgängiger Waren auf Grund unbeschränkter Lieferkapazitäten eine beliebige Anzahl von Kaufinteressenten beliefern kann. In diesen Konstellationen ist allerdings bereits fraglich, ob man überhaupt von einem Deckungsgeschäft sprechen kann.[57] Im Ergebnis kann jedenfalls kein Zweifel daran bestehen, dass der Gläubiger berechtigt sein muss, anstelle der Schadensberechnung nach Art. 75 Ersatz des entgangenen Gewinns nach Art. 74 zu verlangen. Die in Art. 75 vorgesehene Möglichkeit der Schadensberechnung nach Massgabe eines Deckungsgeschäfts soll die Rechtsstellung des Gläubigers verstärken, nicht aber ein sonst gegebenes Recht auf Entschädigung einschränken. Demnach bleibt es dem Verkäufer unbenommen, anstelle der Schadensberechnung nach Art. 75, gemäss Art. 74 Ersatz für entgangenen Gewinn aus dem urpsrünglichen Geschäft, d. h. die Differenz zwischen dem Vertragspreis und den Selbstkosten zu fordern.[58] Umgekehrt kann der nicht belieferte Käufer Ersatz für den entgangenen Gewinn verlangen, den er in vorhersehbarer Weise bei Weiterveräusserung der Ware hätte erzielen können, einschliesslich Erstattung der Kosten für die vorübergehende Einlagerung der später zurückgesandten Ware.[59] Ein solcher Gewinnverlust ist jedenfalls dann voraussehbar, wenn der Schuldner wusste oder wissen musste, dass der Gläubiger ständig mit Waren der verkauften Art handelt. Bei dem Problem des „lost volume" geht es damit in Wahrheit nicht um entgangenen Gewinn aus einem Zweitgeschäft, sondern um den **Gewinn aus dem gescheiterten Erstgeschäft** und die Widerlegung des Einwandes der vertragsbrüchigen Partei, der Verlust dieses Gewinns habe durch ein Ersatzgeschäft wett gemacht werden können.

Ming, Art. 75, Anm. 3.; *Schlechtriem*, Gemeinsame Bestimmungen, S. 165; *Soergel/Lüderitz/Dettmeier*, Art. 75, Rn. 8; *Saidov*, Damages in Int'l Sales, S. 187.

[52] ICC, 8128/1995, CISG-online 526; CISG-AC, Op. 8 *(Gotanda)*, Comment 3.1.

[53] Vgl. *Schmidt-Ahrendts*, Rechtsbehelfe, S. 90 ff. mit Fallbeispiel zum deutschen Recht: BGH, 20.7.2005, NJW 2005, 2848 ff.

[54] LG München I, 6.4.2000, CISG-online 665; CISG-AC, Op. 8 *(Gotanda)*, Comment 1.3.1, 3.2; *P. Huber/Mullis/P. Huber*, S. 287; *Soergel/Lüderitz/Dettmeier*, Art. 75, Rn. 9; *Achilles*, Art. 75, Rn. 5; *Honsell/Schönle/Th. Koller*, Art. 75, Rn. 31; a. A. *Herber/Czerwenka*, Art. 75, Rn. 5; *Kranz*, S. 221; *Ryffel*, S. 74 Fn. 159; *Bamberger/Roth/Saenger*, Art. 75, Rn. 7.

[55] Vgl. *Kröll u. a./Gotanda*, Art. 76, Rn. 33; *Schmidt-Ahrendts*, Rechtsbehelfe, S. 94; *Saidov*, Damages in Int'l Sales, S. 187.

[56] Vgl. den Fall OGH, 28.4.2000, CISG-online 581, dazu und insgesamt *Schmidt-Ahrendts*, Rechtsbehelfe, S. 94 f.; *Saidov*, Limiting Damages, I. 2. (c); *Ferrari u. a./Saenger*, Internationales Vertragsrecht, Art. 76, Rn. 7; *Brölsch*, Schadensersatz, S. 87 ff.; *Bianca/Bonelli*, Artt. 74–77, Anm. 6.; *Honnold/Flechtner*, Artt. 75, 76, Rn. 415; *P. Huber/Mullis/P. Huber*, S. 287; *Sutton*, 50 Ohio St. L. J. (1989), 747, 748 unter Berufung auf die U. S.-amerikanische Rechtsprechung zu § 2–708 (2) UCC; *Karollus*, S. 220; *Witz/Salger/Lorenz/Witz*, Art. 75, Rn. 13; *Weber*, Vertragsverletzungsfolgen, S. 202; *Ziegel*, Remedial Provisions, S. 9–41; zweifelnd *Hellner*, UN Convention, S. 100. Vgl. auch *Kröll u. a./Gotanda*, Art. 76, Rn. 36 (kein Deckungsgeschäft, Berechnung nach Artt. 74, 76).

[57] Vgl. CISG-AC, Op. 8 *(Gotanda)*, Comment 3.4; *Schmidt-Ahrendts*, Rechtsbehelfe, S. 94 f.

[58] OLG Hamburg, 26.11.1999, CISG-online 515; CISG-AC, Op. 8 *(Gotanda)*, Comment 3.4; *Karollus*, S. 222, 223; *Schlechtriem*, Gemeinsame Bestimmungen, S. 165; *Lookofsky*, Understanding the CISG, S. 135, 153; *Bianca/Bonelli*, Artt. 74–77, Anm. 6.; einschränkend *Staudinger/Magnus*, Art. 75, Rn. 23.

[59] *Delchi Carrier S. p. A. v. Rotorex Corp.*, U. S. Ct. App. (2nd Cir.), 6.12.1995, CISG-online 140, dazu *Papandréou-Deterville*, D. 1997, Somm. 226; *Soergel/Lüderitz/Dettmeier*, Art. 75, Rn. 9.

12a Problematisch ist die Behandlung weiterer Schäden im Fall eines **besonders günstigen Deckungsgeschäfts**. Auf den ersten Blick erscheint es angemessen, die weiteren Schäden mit der für den Gläubiger positiven Differenz zwischen Marktpreis[60] und tatsächlich getätigtem Deckungskauf zu verrechnen.[61] Ist diese Differenz jedoch auf überobligatorischen Einsatz des Gläubigers zurückzuführen, so ist eine solche Verrechnung unangemessen; vielmehr steht die Differenz dem Gläubiger zu, so dass er seine weiteren Schäden vollumfänglich einfordern kann.[62] Geht die Differenz nicht auf besonderes Verhalten des Gläubigers sondern allein auf glückliche Zufälle zurück („windfall profits"), so gibt der Vertragsbruch des Schuldners den Ausschlag dafür, diese zufällige Differenz dem Gläubiger zugutekommen zu lassen und ihm wiederrum die weiteren Schäden vollumfänglich zuzusprechen.[63]

3. Verhältnis zu Artt. 74 und 76

13 Nach h. M. ist die **abstrakte Schadensberechnung** nach der Marktpreisregel gemäss Art. 76 **subsidiär** zur Geltendmachung des konkreten Differenzschadens nach Art. 75.[64] Dem Gläubiger steht also **kein Wahlrecht** zwischen den beiden Berechnungsmethoden zu. Hat der Gläubiger ein angemessenes Deckungsgeschäft im Sinne von Art. 75 vorgenommen, scheidet eine abstrakte Schadensberechnung nach Art. 76 aus.[65] Eine **Pflicht zur Vornahme eines Deckungsgeschäftes** kann sich aus der allgemeinen Schadensminderungspflicht des Art. 77 ergeben. Diese Obliegenheit nimmt dem Gläubiger die Möglichkeit der abstrakten Schadensberechnung nach Art. 76; er ist auf den Ersatz der Differenz zwischen Vertragspreis und abzuschliessendem Deckungsgeschäft beschränkt.[66] Zum Verhältnis zu Art. 74 vgl. oben Art. 74 Rn. 9, 20, 41, zu Art. 77 vgl. unten Art. 77 Rn. 10.

IV. Beweisfragen

14 Der Gläubiger muss beweisen, dass er **zur Vertragsaufhebung berechtigt** war und dies dem Schuldner ordnungsgemäss mitgeteilt hat.[67] Ferner obliegt ihm die Beweislast dafür, dass er ein **Deckungsgeschäft** in angemessener Weise und innerhalb eines angemessenen Zeitraums nach Vertragsaufhebung vorgenommen hat.[68] Beruft sich der Schuldner darauf, dass das Deckungsgeschäft auch früher hätte vorgenommen werden können, so macht er damit inzident eine Verletzung der **Schadensminderungspflicht** nach Art. 77 geltend und trägt dafür die Beweislast.[69]

---

[60] Zur Bedeutung des Marktpreises bei der Festlegung des angemessenen Preises, siehe oben Rn. 6.
[61] Vgl. *Kröll u. a./Gotanda*, Art. 76, Rn. 11.
[62] Vgl. *M. Schmidt*, FS Schwenzer, S. 1499, 1505 ff. Vgl. auch *Honsell/Schönle/Th. Koller*, Art. 75, Rn. 12.
[63] Vgl. *M. Schmidt*, FS Schwenzer, S. 1499, 1510.
[64] *Stoll/Gruber*, 4. Aufl., Art. 75 Rn. 2; *Schmidt-Ahrendts*, Rechtsbehelfe, S. 67.
[65] OLG Düsseldorf, 14.1.1994, CISG-online 119; OLG Hamm, 22.9.1992, CISG-online 57; Münch-Komm/*P. Huber*, Art. 75, Rn. 21; *Witz/Salger/Lorenz/Witz*, Art. 75, Rn. 11; *Staudinger/Magnus*, Art. 75, Rn. 22; *Herber/Czerwenka*, Art. 75, Rn. 4; *Schmidt-Ahrendts*, Rechtsbehelfe, S. 98; *Hager*, FS Schwenzer, S. 681, 692.
[66] BGer, 17.12.2009, CISG-online 2022 = BGE 136 III 56; *Mohs*, AJP 2011, 425, 428.
[67] *Baumgärtel/Laumen/Hepting*, Art. 75 WKR, Rn. 1; *Witz/Salger/Lorenz/Witz*, Art. 75, Rn. 14; *Heuzé*, Anm. 454. Zur Beweislast unter Art. 26 siehe oben *Fountoulakis*, Art. 26 Rn. 17.
[68] *Staudinger/Magnus*, Art. 75, Rn. 24; *Baumgärtel/Laumen/Hepting*, Art. 75 WKR, Rn. 2; a. A. *Soergel/Lüderitz/Dettmeier*, Art. 75, Rn. 11; *Honsell/Schönle/Th. Koller*, Art. 75, Rn. 35: Unangemessenheit des Deckungsgeschäfts vom Schuldner zu beweisen.
[69] Vgl. Hof van Beroep Gent, 20.10.2004, CISG-online 983: Es sei jedenfalls unklar, ob eine Partei sich explizit auf Art. 77 berufen muss oder ob staatliche Gerichte und Schiedsgerichte ex officio untersuchen müssen, ob der Gläubiger seine Schadensminderungspflicht verletzt hat, siehe auch unten Art. 77 Rn. 12.

Art. 76 [Schadensberechnung bei Vertragsaufhebung ohne Deckungsgeschäft]

(1) Ist der Vertrag aufgehoben und hat die Ware einen Marktpreis, so kann die Schadenersatz verlangende Partei, wenn sie keinen Deckungskauf oder Deckungsverkauf nach Art. 75 vorgenommen hat, den Unterschied zwischen dem im Vertrag vereinbarten Preis und dem Marktpreis zur Zeit der Aufhebung sowie jeden weiteren Schadenersatz nach Art. 74 verlangen. Hat jedoch die Partei, die Schadenersatz verlangt, den Vertrag aufgehoben, nachdem sie die Ware übernommen hat, so gilt der Marktpreis zur Zeit der Übernahme und nicht der Marktpreis zur Zeit der Aufhebung.

(2) Als Marktpreis im Sinne von Absatz 1 ist maßgebend der Marktpreis, der an dem Ort gilt, an dem die Lieferung der Ware hätte erfolgen sollen, oder, wenn dort ein Marktpreis nicht besteht, der an einem angemessenen Ersatzort geltende Marktpreis; dabei sind Unterschiede in den Kosten der Beförderung der Ware zu berücksichtigen.

Art. 76

(1) If the contract is avoided and there is a current price for the goods, the party claiming damages may, if he has not made a purchase or resale under article 75, recover the difference between the price fixed by the contract and the current price at the time of avoidance as well as any further damages recoverable under article 74. If, however, the party claiming damages has avoided the contract after taking over the goods, the current price at the time of such taking over shall be applied instead of the current price at the time of avoidance.

(2) For the purposes of the preceding paragraph, the current price is the price prevailing at the place where delivery of the goods should have been made or, if there is no current price at that place, the price at such other place as serves as a reasonable substitute, making due allowance for differences in the cost of transporting the goods.

Art. 76

1) Lorsque le contrat est résolu et que les marchandises ont un prix courant, la partie qui demande des dommages-intérêts peut, si elle n'a pas procédé à un achat de remplacement ou à une vente compensatoire au titre de l'article 75, obtenir la différence entre le prix fixé dans le contrat et le prix courant au moment de la résolution ainsi que tous autres dommages-intérêts qui peuvent être dus au titre de l'article 74. Néanmoins, si la partie qui demande des dommages-intérêts a déclaré le contrat résolu après avoir pris possession des marchandises, c'est le prix courant au moment de la prise de possession qui est applicable et non pas le prix courant au moment de la résolution.

2) Aux fins du paragraphe précédent, le prix courant est celui du lieu où la livraison des marchandises aurait dû être effectuée ou, à défaut de prix courant en ce lieu, le prix courant pratiqué en un autre lieu qu'il apparaît raisonnable de prendre comme lieu de référence, en tenant compte des différences dans les frais de transport des marchandises.

Übersicht

	Rn.
I. Grundgedanken	1
II. Voraussetzungen	2
1. Kein Deckungsgeschäft	2
2. Aufhebung des Vertrages	3
3. Vorhandensein eines Marktpreises	4
4. Vereinbarter Vertragspreis	5
5. Anwendung der Vorhersehbarkeitsregel	6
III. Rechtsfolgen	7
1. Ersatz des Nichterfüllungsschadens	7
a) Der für die Marktpreisberechnung massgebende Ort (Abs. 2)	8
b) Zeitpunkt der Schadensberechnung	10

2. Ersatz weiterer Schäden 13
3. Verhältnis zu Artt. 74 und 75 14
IV. Beweisfragen 15

I. Grundgedanken

1   Art. 76 entspricht im Grundsatz Art. 84 EKG[1] und stellt wie Art. 75 eine **Spezialvorschrift zu Art. 74** dar, deren Anwendbarkeit grundsätzlich eine Vertragsaufhebung voraussetzt. In nationalen Kaufrechten[2] sowie in internationalen Rechtsvereinheitlichungsprojekten[3] gibt es vergleichbare Bestimmungen. Nach Art. 76 kann die Partei, die den Vertrag aufgehoben hat, den Nichterfüllungsschaden, d. h. den durch das Scheitern des Vertrages unmittelbar verursachten Schaden, nach der **abstrakten Differenz** zwischen dem **Vertragspreis** und dem Marktpreis berechnen; ein konkreter Nachweis des Nichterfüllungsschadens ist deshalb entbehrlich.[4] Die Vorschrift beruht auf dem Gedanken, dass der Gläubiger das Recht hat, ein Deckungsgeschäft zum Marktpreis vorzunehmen.[5] Es soll dem Schuldner, der die Kosten eines Deckungsgeschäftes zu tragen hätte, nicht zum Vorteil gereichen, dass der ersatzberechtigte Gläubiger von einem solchen Geschäft tatsächlich abgesehen und sich anderweitig beholfen hat.[6] Die Schadensberechnung nach Art. 76 ist insoweit abstrakt, als dem wegen Nichterfüllung ersatzpflichtigen Verkäufer z. B. der Einwand abgeschnitten ist, der Käufer benötige in Wahrheit die Ware nicht, er habe sie nicht weiterveräussert oder werde von seinen Abnehmern trotz deren Nichtbelieferung nicht in Anspruch genommen. Ebensowenig wird der Verkäufer mit der Behauptung gehört, der nichtbelieferte Käufer habe die Ware unter dem Marktpreis weiterverkauft und deshalb sei dem Käufer nur der Gewinn aus diesem Geschäft entgangen, aber kein darüber hinaus gehender Schaden bis zur Differenz zwischen Vertragspreis und Marktpreis. Damit sichert Art. 76 dem Gläubiger im Ergebnis einen **Mindestschadenersatz**.[7] Soweit Art. 76 nicht anwendbar ist, kann der Gläubiger seinen Schaden nach der Marktpreisregel auch im Rahmen des Art. 74 berechnen.[8]

---

[1] Zur Entstehungsgeschichte und den Unterschieden zwischen beiden Bestimmungen s. *Stoll*, 3. Aufl., Art. 76 Rn. 1–3.
[2] Rechtsvergleichend *Schwenzer/Hachem/Kee*, Rn. 44.225; vgl. auch Deutschland: § 376 II HGB und die deutsche Entscheidungspraxis, die bei Kaufleuten die abstrakte Schadensberechnung nach dem Marktpreis generell zulässt (BGH, 19.6.1951, BGHZ 2, 310, 313; BGH, 2.3.1988, NJW 1988, 2234, 2236; BGH, 19.11.1997, WM 1998, 931 f.); Grossbritannien: sec. 50 (3), 51 (3) SGA; Italien: Art. 1518 Cc; Niederlande: Art. 7:36 BW; Österreich: § 376 II UGB; Schweiz: Art. 191 III und Art. 215 II OR; USA: §§ 2–708 (1) und 2–713 UCC.
[3] 7.4.6 PICC; Art. 9:507 PECL; Art. 165 CESL-Entwurf; rechtsvergleichender Überblick bei *Rabel*, Recht des Warenkaufs, Bd. 1, S. 170–173, 454–468.
[4] *Neumayer/Ming*, Art. 76, Anm. 1.; *Staudinger/Magnus*, Art. 76, Rn. 1, 6; einschränkend *Witz/Salger/Lorenz/Witz*, Art. 76, Rn. 1: Nicht abgeschnitten ist der Einwand, dass der Käufer wegen der Insolvenz seines Abnehmers ohnehin auf der Ware sitzengeblieben wäre.
[5] OLG Hamm, 22.9.1992, CISG-online 57; *Rabel*, Recht des Warenkaufs, Bd. 1, S. 170; *Staudinger/Magnus*, Art. 76, Rn. 6; *Farnsworth*, 27 Am. J. Comp. L. (1979), 247, 251 f.
[6] *Piltz*, Internationales Kaufrecht, Rn. 5–525; vgl. zur Grundkonzeption auch *Schmidt-Ahrendts*, Rechtsbehelfe, S. 97.
[7] So für die abstrakte Schadensberechnung schon *Rabel*, Recht des Warenkaufs, Bd. 1, S. 512. Für das CISG vgl. MünchKomm/*P. Huber*, Art. 76, Rn. 1; *Staudinger/Magnus*, Art. 76, Rn. 7; *Herber/Czerwenka*, Art. 76, Rn. 10; a. A. *Schmidt-Ahrendts*, Rechtsbehelfe, S. 98.
[8] Vgl. oben Art. 74 Rn. 41; vgl. auch CISG-AC, Op. 8 *(Gotanda)*, Comment 5; nach h. M. können Schäden nach Art. 74 demgegenüber dann nur konkret berechnet werden, vgl. OLG Celle, 2.9.1998, CISG-online 506; *Stoll/Gruber*, 4. Aufl., Art. 76 Rn. 2; *Herber/Czerwenka*, Art. 76, Rn. 11; *Roßmeier*, RIW 2000, 407, 410; *Stoll*, Schadensersatzpflicht, S. 266 f.

II. Voraussetzungen

1. Kein Deckungsgeschäft

Art. 76 ist entsprechend seinem Wortlaut und der Entstehungsgeschichte nur anwendbar, 2 sofern kein Deckungsgeschäft vorgenommen worden ist.[9] Kein Deckungsgeschäft liegt im allgemeinen vor, wenn sich ein Käufer aus eigenen Beständen eindeckt.[10] Bei **Vornahme eines Deckungsgeschäftes** hat die konkrete Schadensberechnung nach Art. 75 den Vorrang. Eine Schadensberechnung nach Art. 76 ist aber nach überwiegender Ansicht auch statthaft, wenn der Gläubiger ständig „im Markt" kauft und verkauft und deshalb nicht nachweisen kann, welches der getätigten Geschäfte als Deckungsgeschäft zu qualifizieren ist.[11] In diesen Fällen kann der Schuldner zwar einwenden, der Gläubiger habe ein Deckungsgeschäft vorgenommen, das zu einem geringeren Schaden geführt habe, er wird dies aber kaum nachweisen können.[12] In Ausnahmefällen kann der Schuldner jedoch gemäss Art. 77 eine **Herabsetzung** des abstrakt berechneten Schadens verlangen, wenn er nachweist, dass der Gläubiger – gerade weil er ständig „im Markt" kauft und verkauft – ein günstigeres Deckungsgeschäft hätte schliessen können und ihm der Abschluss des Deckungsgeschäfts nach den Umständen auch zumutbar war.[13] Eine ähnliche Situation ergibt sich, wenn der Käufer dem Verkäufer anbietet, die Ware zwar unter dem Vertragspreis, aber über dem Marktpreis abzunehmen; auch hier ist dem Verkäufer das Deckungsgeschäft in der Regel zuzumuten.[14] Es ist dann der Schadenersatz nach dem Preis des möglichen und zumutbaren Deckungsgeschäfts zu berechnen. Dies gilt freilich nicht in den Fällen eines „lost volume" (vgl. oben Art. 75 Rn 12).[15] Die überwiegende Auffassung[16] wendet die Marktpreisregel nach Art. 76 auch an, wenn das vom Gläubiger vorgenommene **Deckungsgeschäft nicht angemessen** im Sinne des Art. 75 ist (vgl. hierzu oben Art. 75 Rn. 10).

---

[9] OLG Graz, 29.7.2004, CISG-online 1627; OLG Hamm, 22.9.1992, CISG-online 57; KG Zug, 21.10.1999, CISG-online 491; *Honnold/Flechtner*, Artt. 75, 76, Rn. 414; *Stoll/Gruber*, 4. Aufl., Art. 76 Rn. 2; *Honsell/Schönle/Th. Koller*, Art. 76, Rn. 7; *Roßmeier*, RIW 2000, 407, 410; *Karollus*, S. 221 f.; *Schlechtriem*, Internationales UN-Kaufrecht, Rn. 312; *Soergel/Lüderitz/Dettmeier*, Art. 76, Rn. 3; *Staudinger/Magnus*, Art. 75, Rn. 3, 22 und Art. 76, Rn. 11; *Achilles*, Art. 76, Rn. 2; *Witz/Salger/Lorenz/Witz*, Art. 76, Rn. 5; a. A. *Herber*, Einführung, S. 45 f.; *U. Huber*, RabelsZ 43 (1979), 413, 470 f.; *Berger/Scholl*, FS Schwenzer, S. 160, 170.
[10] Vgl. OLG Frankfurt a. M., 24.3.2009, CISG-online 2165. Zur ausnahmsweisen Annahme eines Deckungsgeschäfts, wenn der Käufer die Anschaffungskosten für die verwendeten eigenen Bestände konkret geltend macht, vgl. oben Art. 75 Rn. 2.
[11] CISG-AC, Op. 8 *(Gotanda)*, Comment 4.1.5; *Kröll u. a./Gotanda*, Art. 76, Rn. 15; *Neumayer/Ming*, Art. 76, Anm. 1.; *Staudinger/Magnus*, Art. 76, Rn. 12: *Soergel/Lüderitz/Dettmeier*, Art. 76, Rn. 3; *Audit*, Vente internationale, Anm. 178.; *Heuzé*, Anm. 455.; *Witz/Salger/Lorenz/Witz*, Art. 76, Rn. 5; *P. Huber/Mullis/ P. Huber*, S. 288; *Ferrari u. a./Saenger*, Internationales Vertragsrecht, Art. 76, Rn. 3; *Piltz*, Internationales Kaufrecht, Rn. 5–526; *Bianca/Bonell/Knapp*, Art. 76, Anm. 2.4.; *Schlechtriem*, Einheitliches UN-Kaufrecht, S. 91. Insofern missverständlich OLG Hamm, 22.9.1992, CISG-online 57, wonach auf die abstrakte Schadensberechnung nach Art. 76 nur dann zurückgegriffen werden könne, wenn die Vornahme eines Deckungsgeschäfts unmöglich oder unzumutbar ist.
[12] Vgl. Sekretariatskommentar, Art. 72, Nr. 3; *Schlechtriem*, Gemeinsame Bestimmungen, S. 164 Fn. 32; *Heuzé*, Anm. 454.; LG Bielefeld, 18.1.1991, CISG-online 174 bestätigt von OLG Hamm, 22.9.1992, CISG-online 57; zustimmend *Hager*, FS Schwenzer, S. 681, 693; kritisch *Witz/Salger/Lorenz/Witz*, Art. 76, Rn. 7.
[13] *Reimers-Zocher*, S. 351–353; *Honsell/Schönle/Th. Koller*, Art. 76, Rn. 9. Ausführlich *Saidov*, Damages in Int'l Sales, S. 192 ff.
[14] *Saidov*, 13 VJ (2009), 197, 208 f. kritisiert zu Recht, dass dies von CIETAC Award, 1.3.1999, CISG-online 1136 übersehen wurde.
[15] *Stoll/Gruber*, 4. Aufl., Art. 76 Rn. 2. Zur Pflicht ein Deckungsgeschäft zur Schadensminderung vorzunehmen vgl. auch oben bei Art. 77 Rn. 10.
[16] Sekretariatskommentar, Art. 71, Nr. 6; CISG-AC, Op. 8 *(Gotanda)*, Comment 4.1.4; *Kröll u. a./Gotanda*, Art. 76, Rn. 14; *MünchKomm/P. Huber*, Art. 76, Rn. 3; *Bianca/Bonell/Knapp*, Art. 75, Anm. 2.6.; *Kranz*, S. 221 f.; *Neumayer/Ming*, Art. 75, Anm. 2.; *P. Huber/Mullis/P. Huber*, S. 288; *Piltz*, Internationales Kaufrecht, Rn. 5–524; *Soergel/Lüderitz/Dettmeier*, Art. 75, Rn. 10; *Witz/Salger/Lorenz/Witz*, Art. 75, Rn. 3; *Staudinger/ Magnus*, Art. 75, Rn. 20; *Schmidt-Ahrendts*, Rechtsbehelfe, S. 98 f.; *Sutton*, 50 Ohio St. L. J. (1989), 737, 745 f.; *Wittinghofer/Becker*, IHR 2010, 225, 226 f.

2. Aufhebung des Vertrages

3   Wie Art. 75 kommt auch Art. 76 nur zur Anwendung, wenn der Vertrag aufgehoben worden ist.[17] Die überwiegende Auffassung wendet indes auch Art. 76 wie bereits Art. 75 im Falle einer ernsthaften und endgültigen **Erfüllungsverweigerung** seitens des Schuldners an (vgl. oben Art. 75 Rn. 5). Nach hier vertretener Auffassung (vgl. oben Art. 74 Rn. 22, Art. 75 Rn. 5) ist auch **bei fehlender Vertragsaufhebung** eine Schadensberechnung anhand des jeweiligen Marktpreises im Rahmen von Art. 74 möglich.

3. Vorhandensein eines Marktpreises

4   Eine abstrakte Schadensberechnung nach Art. 76 ist nur möglich, wenn die Ware, die Gegenstand des Vertrages ist, einen Marktpreis hat. Dabei kann auf Art. 55 zurückgegriffen werden.[18] Unter Marktpreis ist danach der **Durchschnittspreis** zu verstehen, der allgemein für Waren gleicher Art berechnet wird, die in gleichartigen Geschäften unter vergleichbaren Bedingungen an einem bestimmten Ort mit einer gewissen Regelmässigkeit[19] durchgeführt werden.[20] Der Marktpreis hängt insbesondere auch von dem vorgesehenen Lieferzeitpunkt ab.[21] Soweit bei den Vertragsbedingungen Abweichungen bestehen, müssen sie rechnungsmässig angeglichen werden.[22] Der massgebende Marktpreis ist jeweils der **Grosshandelspreis,** nicht aber der um die Handelsspanne erhöhte Preis, der bei Weiterveräusserung im Einzelhandel erzielt werden kann.[23] Eine **amtliche oder nichtamtliche Notierung** ist nicht erforderlich;[24] sie ist jedoch gegebenenfalls zu berücksichtigen.[25] Fehlt es an einem Marktpreis, ist nach Art. 74 vorzugehen.

4. Vereinbarter Vertragspreis

5   Anders als nach Art. 75 genügt die **Bestimmbarkeit** des Kaufpreises nach Art. 55 nach dem Wortlaut des Art. 76 nicht. Die Schadensberechnung nach Art. 76 verlangt vielmehr, dass die Parteien einen **festen Vertragspreis** vereinbart haben („price fixed by the contract", „prix fixé dans le contrat").[26] Fehlt es an einem ausdrücklich oder stillschweigend vereinbarten Vertragspreis, kann der Gläubiger immer noch nach Art. 74 vorgehen.[27]

---

[17] MünchKomm/*P. Huber*, Art. 76, Rn. 2; *Witz/Salger/Lorenz/Witz*, Art. 76, Rn. 4; s. schon *Harlow & Jones v. Adras*, Oberster Gerichtshof Israels, 10.10.1982, in: *Schlechtriem/Magnus*, Art. 84 EKG, Nr. 1 zu Art. 84 EKG.

[18] Vgl. MünchKomm/*P. Huber*, Art. 76, Rn. 4; *Kröll u. a./Gotanda*, Art. 76, Rn. 11 („similar"); zweifelnd *Schmidt-Ahrendts*, Rechtsbehelfe, S. 101 ff.

[19] Vgl. *Saidov*, Damages in Int'l Sales, S. 201; *ders.,* 13 VJ (2009), 197, 209.

[20] Vgl. OLG Celle, 2.9.1998, CISG-online 506; CISG-AC, Op. 8 *(Gotanda)*, Comment 4.3.1; MünchKomm/*P. Huber*, Art. 76, Rn. 3; *Staudinger/Magnus*, Art. 76, Rn. 13; *Witz/Salger/Lorenz/Witz*, Art. 76, Rn. 3, 9; *Achilles*, Art. 76, Rn. 3. Vgl. aber *Honsell/Schönle/Th. Koller*, Art. 76, Rn. 13: rein objektive Feststellung der Verkäuflichkeit, kein tatsächlicher Handel in kritischer Zeit erforderlich.

[21] Vgl. OLG Düsseldorf, 15.8.2010, CISG-online 2171 = IHR 2011, 116, 122; *Hager*, FS Schwenzer, S. 681, 691; *Saidov*, 13 VJ (2009), 197, 214.

[22] CISG-AC, Op. 8 *(Gotanda)*, Comment 4.3.1; *Saidov*, Damages in Int'l Sales, S. 206 ff. Eine mittelbare Errechnung des Marktpreises durch Heranziehung des Marktpreises der Ware auf einer anderen Veredelungsstufe und Addition des fiktiven Veredelungsaufwands ist unzulässig, vgl. *Piltz*, NJW 1994, 1101, 1106; *Witz/Salger/Lorenz/Witz*, Art. 76, Rn. 9. Vgl. auch schon *Rabel*, Recht des Warenkaufs, Bd. 1, S. 461 f.

[23] *Stoll/Gruber*, 4 Aufl., Art. 76 Rn. 4; *Rabel*, Recht des Warenkaufs, Bd. 1, S. 462; a. A. bei Fehlen eines Grosshandelsmarktes: *Saidov*, Damages in Int'l Sales, S. 209.

[24] CISG-AC, Op. 8 *(Gotanda)*, Comment 4.3.1; MünchKomm/*P. Huber*, Art. 76, Rn. 4; *Enderlein/Maskow/Strohbach*, Art. 76, Anm. 2.; *Kröll u. a./Gotanda*, Art. 76, Rn. 11; *Honsell/Schönle/Th. Koller*, Art. 76, Rn. 12; *Neumayer/Ming*, Art. 76, Anm. 3.; *Staudinger/Magnus*, Art. 76, Rn. 13; *P. Huber/Mullis/P. Huber*, S. 288; *Weber*, Vertragsverletzungsfolgen, S. 203; *Witz/Salger/Lorenz/Witz*, Art. 76, Rn. 3.

[25] Nachweise bei MünchKomm/*P. Huber*, Art. 76, Rn. 4; *Staudinger/Magnus*, Art. 76, Rn. 13; *Enderlein/Maskow/Strohbach*, Art. 76, Anm. 2. Zurückhaltung bei der Annahme eines Marktpreises bei fehlender Preisnotierung empfehlen *Herber/Czerwenka*, Art. 76, Rn. 6.

[26] CISG-AC, Op. 8 *(Gotanda)*, Comment 4.2.1; *Kröll u. a./Gotanda*, Art. 76, Rn. 16 f.; MünchKomm/*P. Huber*, Art. 76, Rn. 10; *Honsell/Schönle/Th. Koller*, Art. 76, Rn. 10; *Staudinger/Magnus*, Art. 76, Rn. 25; *Roßmeier*, RIW 2000, 407, 410; *Weber*, Vertragsverletzungsfolgen, S. 203; *Witz/Salger/Lorenz/Witz*, Art. 76, Rn. 8.

[27] CISG-AC, Op. 8 *(Gotanda)*, Comment 4.2.2.

5. Anwendung der Vorhersehbarkeitsregel

Ähnlich wie im Rahmen von Art. 75 (vgl. oben Art. 75 Rn. 8) ist auch bei Art. 76 **6** umstritten, ob die Vorhersehbarkeitsregel des Art. 74 S. 2 im Rahmen des Art. 76 zur Anwendung gelangt.[28] Wie bei Art. 75 spricht jedoch bereits der Wortlaut gegen die Anwendung der Vorhersehbarkeitsregel, soweit es sich um Ersatz des Nichterfüllungsschadens handelt.[29] Mit dem **Prinzip des vollen Schadensausgleichs** wäre es nicht vereinbar, wenn der Schuldner sich darauf berufen könnte, dass sich nach Vertragsschluss die Preisverhältnisse in ganz aussergewöhnlicher Weise geändert haben, so dass er nicht damit rechnen musste.[30]

III. Rechtsfolgen

1. Ersatz des Nichterfüllungsschadens

Liegen die Voraussetzungen des Art. 76 vor, kann die ersatzberechtigte Partei als Nicht- **7** erfüllungsschaden i. e. S. die **Differenz zwischen dem Marktpreis und dem Vertragspreis** verlangen; dabei ist der Marktpreis zur Zeit der Vertragsaufhebung am Lieferort massgebend. Ersatz für darüber hinaus gehende Schäden kann nach Massgabe von Art. 74 verlangt werden.

a) **Der für die Marktpreisberechnung massgebende Ort (Abs. 2).** Nach Art. 76 II **8** ist der Marktpreis des Ortes massgebend, an dem die Lieferung der Ware hätte erfolgen sollen. Damit wird auf den **Lieferort i. S. d. Art. 31** verwiesen.[31] Teilweise wird geltend gemacht, die Bezugnahme auf den Lieferort im Sinne des Art. 31 passe nicht für den **Versendungskauf** nach Art. 31 lit. a), weil der Käufer einen Deckungskauf regelmässig nicht am Ort der Übergabe an den ersten Beförderer sondern erst am Bestimmungsort vornehme.[32] Dem ist freilich entgegen zu halten, dass es der Käufer in der Hand hat, am Bestimmungsort der Ware einen Deckungskauf vorzunehmen und seinen Schaden nach Art. 75 zu berechnen. Im Ergebnis sollte deshalb auch beim Versendungskauf der Marktpreis am Lieferort entscheiden.[33] Insbesondere im Rohstoffhandel kann als Lieferung im Sinne des Art. 76 II die Übergabe der die Ware repräsentierenden Dokumente gelten.[34]

Existiert am Lieferort kein Marktpreis, so ist nach Art. 76 II auf den Marktpreis eines **9** **angemessenen Ersatzortes** zurückzugreifen. Angemessen ist ein Ersatzort, wenn er unter Berücksichtigung der Transportkosten (Art. 76 II a. E.) **vergleichbare Bedingungen** bietet und für den schadenersatzpflichtigen Käufer oder Verkäufer am Wenigsten nachteilig ist.[35] Bei mehreren möglichen Ersatzorten ist grundsätzlich auf den räumlich nächsten abzustellen.[36]

---

[28] Befürwortend *Stoll/Gruber*, 4. Aufl., Art. 76 Rn. 6; *Staudinger/Magnus*, Art. 76, Rn. 6; *Honsell/Schönle/Th. Koller*, Art. 76, Rn. 26; *Saidov*, Damages in Int'l Sales, S. 118 f.

[29] Wie hier MünchKomm/*P. Huber*, Art. 76, Rn. 11; *Witz/Salger/Lorenz/Witz*, Art. 76, Rn. 12; Bamberger/Roth/*Saenger*, Art. 76, Rn. 3; *P. Huber/Mullis/P. Huber*, S. 283, 288; *Faust*, S. 25 f.

[30] A. A. *Stoll/Gruber*, 4. Aufl., Art. 76 Rn. 6.

[31] OLG Hamm, 22.9.1992, CISG-online 57; CIETAC Award, 9.1.2008, CISG-online 2056 (bei FOB-Vertrag: Preis im Bestimmungshafen); CISG-AC, Op. 8 *(Gotanda)*, Comment 4.5.1; *Honnold/Flechtner*, Artt. 75, 76, Rn. 413; *Staudinger/Magnus*, Art. 76, Rn. 18; MünchKomm/*P. Huber*, Art. 76, Rn. 7; MünchKommHGB/*Mankowski*, Art. 76, Rn. 7; *Brunner*, Art. 76, Rn. 3; *Baumgärtel/Laumen-Hepting*, Art. 76 WKR, Rn. 1; *Honsell/Schönle/Th. Koller*, Art. 76, Rn. 22; *Reimers-Zocher*, S. 351 f.; *Soergel/Lüderitz/Dettmeier*, Art. 76, Rn. 7; *Witz/Salger/Lorenz/Witz*, Art. 76, Rn. 12.

[32] So *Stoll/Gruber*, 4. Aufl., Art. 76 Rn. 9. Kritisch zur Verweisung auf den Lieferort *Audit*, Vente internationale, Anm. 178.; *Honnold/Flechtner*, Artt. 75, 76, Rn. 413; *Enderlein/Maskow/Strohbach*, Art. 76, Anm. 10.

[33] MünchKomm/*P. Huber*, Art. 76, Rn. 7; *Schmidt-Ahrendts*, Rechtsbehelfe, S. 108; *Sutton*, 50 Ohio St. L. J. (1989), 737, 746 f.

[34] Vgl. *Saidov*, 13 VJ (2009), 197, 211 f. (in Bezug auf CIF-Verträge).

[35] CISG-AC, Op. 8 *(Gotanda)*, Comment 4.5.2; *Kröll u. a./Gotanda*, Art. 76, Rn. 22; MünchKomm/*P. Huber*, Art. 76, Rn. 8; *Honsell/Schönle/Th. Koller*, Art. 76, Rn. 23; *Staudinger/Magnus*, Art. 76, Rn. 19; *Witz/Salger/Lorenz/Witz*, Art. 76, Rn. 11; *Brunner*, Art. 76, Rn. 3; *Schmidt-Ahrendts*, Rechtsbehelfe, S. 107.

[36] MünchKomm/*P. Huber*, Art. 76, Rn. 8; *Staudinger/Magnus*, Art. 76, Rn. 19; CISG-AC, Op. 8 *(Gotanda)*, Comment 4.5.2 erachtet den nächsten Ort sogar typischerweise als angemessenen Ersatzort.

Soweit feststellbar kann auch auf einen internationalen Marktpreis abgestellt werden, wobei jedoch die Umstände des Einzelfalls zu Modifikationen führen können.[37]

10 **b) Zeitpunkt der Schadensberechnung.** Nach Art. 76 I ist grundsätzlich der Marktpreis im **Zeitpunkt der Vertragsaufhebung** massgeblich.[38] Entsprechend Art. 27 ist dabei auf den Zeitpunkt der **Absendung der Aufhebungserklärung** abzustellen.[39] Der Gefahr, dass der Gläubiger mit seiner Aufhebungserklärung zuwartet und auf Kosten des vertragsbrüchigen Schuldners spekuliert, muss mit Anwendung der **Schadensminderungspflicht** nach Art. 77 begegnet werden,[40] so dass unter Umständen auf den Zeitpunkt der möglichen Vertragsaufhebung abzustellen ist.[41]

11 Hat der Gläubiger den Vertrag aufgehoben, nachdem er die Ware übernommen hat, so gilt der Marktpreis im **Zeitpunkt der Übernahme** (Art. 76 I 2). Diese Vorschrift betrifft allein den Käufer.[42] Sie findet selbst dann Anwendung, wenn der Käufer den Aufhebungsgrund, etwa die vertragswidrige Beschaffenheit der Ware, im Zeitpunkt der Übernahme der Ware noch gar nicht kannte.[43] Das Abstellen auf den Zeitpunkt der Übernahme verhindert zwar eine mögliche Spekulation durch den Käufer;[44] unangemessen erscheint diese Lösung jedoch dann, wenn der Marktpreis bis zum Zeitpunkt der Aufhebungserklärung erheblich gestiegen ist.[45] Hier bleibt dem Käufer nur, den weitergehenden Schaden nach Art. 74 zu berechnen.[46]

12 Besondere Probleme bereitet die Anwendung des Art. 76 beim **antizipierten Vertragsbruch**.[47] Hier kann weder auf den Marktpreis zum Zeitpunkt der Vertragsaufhebung, noch auf jenen zum Zeitpunkt der Erfüllung abgestellt werden, vielmehr sind hier die im Aufhebungszeitpunkt zu ermittelnden Preise für Ware, die erst im Erfüllungszeitpunkt zu liefern ist, zu Grunde zu legen.[48] Diese Preise sind gegebenenfalls anhand der Notierungen im Terminmarkt zu ermitteln.[49]

---

[37] Vgl. *Saidov*, Damages in Int'l Sales, S. 205; *ders.*, 13 VJ (2009), 197, 212 unter Verweis auf Schiedsgericht der Handelskammer Zürich, 31.5.1996, CISG-online 1291.
[38] Vgl. *Ferrari u. a./Saenger*, Internationales Vertragsrecht, Art. 76, Rn. 4; *Kröll u. a./Gotanda*, Art. 76, Rn. 19. Ebenso Art. 7.4.6 PICC; Art. 9:507 PECL und Art. 165 CESL-Entwurf, dazu *Schmidt-Kessel/Remien*, Europäisches Kaufrecht, S. 517; vgl. auch rechtsvergleichend *Schwenzer/Hachem/Kee*, Rn. 44.247; auf den Zeitpunkt der Fälligkeit der nicht erbrachten Leistung stellen hingegen ab: Deutschland: § 376 II HGB; Grossbritannien: sec. 51 (3) SGA; Italien: Art. 1518 Cc und Österreich: § 376 I UGB.
[39] CISG-AC, Op. 8 *(Gotanda)*, Comment 4.4.1; MünchKomm/*P. Huber*, Art. 76, Rn. 5; *Honsell/Schönle/Th. Koller*, Art. 76, Rn. 21; *Soergel/Lüderitz/Dettmeier*, Art. 76, Rn. 3; *Kranz*, S. 223 Fn. 5; *Staudinger/Magnus*, Art. 76, Rn. 15; *Witz/Salger/Lorenz/Witz*, Art. 76, Rn. 10; a. A. *Welser*, Vertragsverletzung des Verkäufers, S. 127; *Piltz*, Internationales Kaufrecht, Rn. 5–528; eingehend zu dieser Frage *Fountoulakis*, Art. 26 Rn. 11; *Schmidt-Ahrendts*, Rechtsbehelfe, S. 106. Für eine flexible Handhabung: *Saidov*, Damages in Int'l Sales, S. 205 f.
[40] *Kröll u. a./Gotanda*, Art. 76, Rn. 19; *Hellner*, UN Convention, S. 98 f.; *Kranz*, S. 224; *Neumayer/Ming*, Art. 76, Anm. 2; *Ryffel*, S. 77; *Witz/Salger/Lorenz/Witz*, Art. 76, Rn. 10; *Schlechtriem*, Internationales UN-Kaufrecht, Rn. 313; *ders.*, Gemeinsame Bestimmungen, S. 164; *Schmidt-Kessel*, RIW 1996, 60, 62. Vgl. auch *Saidov*, Damages in Int'l Sales, S. 197.
[41] *Schlechtriem*, Internationales UN-Kaufrecht, Rn. 313; vgl. dazu auch *Schwenzer/Manner*, FS Kritzer, S. 470, 481 ff.
[42] *Karollus*, S. 221; *Enderlein/Maskow/Strohbach*, Art. 78, Anm. 8.; *Witz/Salger/Lorenz/Witz*, Art. 76, Rn. 10; gemäss *Honnold/Flechtner*, Artt. 75, 76, Rn. 412 wird die Vorschrift selten auf Fälle anwendbar sein, in denen der Verkäufer den Vertrag aufhebt; eingehend zur Entstehungsgeschichte *Stoll*, 3. Aufl., Art. 76 Rn. 2; a. A. *Honsell/Schönle/Th. Koller*, Art. 76, Rn. 19; *Bamberger/Roth/Saenger*, Art. 76, Rn. 4.
[43] Vgl. CISG-AC, Op. 8 *(Gotanda)*, Comment 4.4.2.
[44] Vgl. CISG-AC, Op. 8 *(Gotanda)*, Comment 4.4.2; *Honsell/Schönle/Th. Koller*, Art. 76, Rn. 17.
[45] Vgl. die berechtigte Kritik bei *Enderlein/Maskow/Strohbach*, Art. 76, Anm. 9.; *Heuzé*, Anm. 455.; *Schmidt-Ahrendts*, Rechtsbehelfe, S. 106 f.; *Ryffel*, S. 78; *Schlechtriem*, Internationales UN-Kaufrecht, Rn. 314; *Witz/Salger/Lorenz/Witz*, Art. 76, Rn. 10; *Weber*, Vertragsverletzungsfolgen, S. 204; *Piltz*, Internationales Kaufrecht, Rn. 5–529.
[46] *A. A. Staudinger/Magnus*, Art. 76, Rn. 23; *Honsell/Schönle/Th. Koller*, Art. 76, Rn. 20.
[47] Hierzu ausführlich *Schlechtriem*, Internationales UN-Kaufrecht, Rn. 313a; *ders.*, GS Hellner, S. 240 ff.
[48] A. A. CISG-AC, Op. 8 *(Gotanda)*, Comment 4.4.3; *Kröll u. a./Gotanda*, Art. 76, Rn. 30: jeweiliger Preis zum Zeitpunkt der Vertragsaufhebung, falls kein Terminmarkt existiert; *Honsell/Schönle/Th. Koller*, Art. 76, Rn. 21: Vertragsaufhebung.
[49] Vgl. CISG-AC, Op. 8 *(Gotanda)*, Comment 4.4.2; *Hornung*, 4. Aufl., Art. 72 Rn. 25.

2. Ersatz weiterer Schäden

Als weitere Schäden, die neben der Preisdifferenz nach Art. 76 im Rahmen des Voraus- 13
sehbaren zu ersetzen sind, kommen dieselben Schadensposten in Betracht wie bei konkreter Berechnung des Nichterfüllungsschadens nach Art. 75.[50] Streitig ist, ob der Gläubiger neben der abstrakten Schadensberechnung nach Art. 76 **entgangenen Gewinn** geltend machen kann.[51] Nach zutreffender Ansicht kann die abstrakte Schadensberechnung nach Art. 76 den Anspruch auf entgangenen Gewinn nicht ausschliessen. Alles andere würde dem Grundsatz der vollen Schadloshaltung widersprechen. Es ist freilich stets zu prüfen, ob der Gläubiger den Schaden nicht durch ein rechtzeitiges Deckungsgeschäft hätte vermeiden können und müssen (Art. 77).[52] Auch **„lost volume"**, z. B. der Schaden durch erhöhte Produktionskosten wegen verminderter Auslastung, kann zusätzlich verlangt werden.[53] **Frustrierte Aufwendungen,** soweit sie nicht bereits durch die abstrakt berechnete Differenz miterfasst werden, können im Einzelfall ersatzfähig sein.[54]

3. Verhältnis zu Artt. 74 und 75

Bei Vorliegen eines angemessenen Deckungsgeschäfts im Sinne des Art. 75 CISG kommt 14
Art. 76 CISG nicht zur Anwendung (vgl. oben Rn. 2), insofern besteht **kein Wahlrecht** zwischen konkreter und abstrakter Schadensberechnung.[55] Freilich steht es dem Gläubiger frei, den weitergehenden Schaden im Rahmen von Art. 74 konkret oder abstrakt (vgl. oben Art. 74 Rn. 41) zu berechnen.[56]

IV. Beweisfragen

Der Gläubiger trägt die Beweislast dafür, dass er zur Schadensberechnung nach Art. 76 15
berechtigt ist, sowie für die **Höhe des Marktpreises**.[57] Hingegen hat der Schuldner nach dem Grundgedanken des **Art. 77** zu beweisen, dass der Gläubiger ein günstigeres Deckungsgeschäft vorgenommen hat oder hätte vornehmen müssen.[58]

---

[50] Vgl. oben Art. 75 Rn. 9 f.
[51] Befürwortend *Stoll/Gruber*, 4. Aufl., Art. 76 Rn. 13; MünchKomm/*P. Huber*, Art. 76, Rn. 14; *Bamberger/Roth/Saenger*, Art. 76, Rn. 3; *Enderlein/Maskow/Strohbach*, Art. 76, Anm. 3.; *Herber/Czerwenka*, Art. 76, Rn. 10; *Schmidt-Ahrendts*, Rechtsbehelfe, S. 110. Ablehnend CISG-AC, Op. 8 *(Gotanda)*, Comment 6.3; MünchKommHGB/*Mankowski*, Art. 76, Rn. 15; *Soergel/Lüderitz/Dettmeier*, Art. 76, Rn. 6; *Honsell/Schönle/Th. Koller*, Art. 76, Rn. 27.
[52] *Stoll/Gruber*, 4. Aufl., Art. 76 Rn. 13; *Roßmeier*, RIW 2000, 407, 410.
[53] Vgl. oben Art. 75 Rn. 12; CISG-AC, Op. 8 *(Gotanda)*, Comments 4.1.4, 6.4; *Schlechtriem*, Internationales UN-Kaufrecht, Rn. 314.
[54] Vgl. oben Art. 75 Rn. 11.
[55] CISG-AC, Op. 8 *(Gotanda)*, Comment 4.12; *Kröll u. a./Gotanda*, Art. 76, Rn. 13; *Staudinger/Magnus*, Art. 76, Rn. 24. Vgl. rechtsvergleichend *Saidov*, Damages in Int'l Sales, S. 191.
[56] Vgl. *Semi-Materials Co., Ltd. v. MEMC Electronic Materials, Inc.*, U.S. Dist. Lt. (E. D. Mo.), 10.1.2011, CISG-online 2168.
[57] OLG Celle, 2.9.1998, CISG-online 506; *Staudinger/Magnus*, Art. 76, Rn. 27; MünchKomm/*P. Huber*, Art. 76, Rn. 16; *Soergel/Lüderitz/Dettmeier*, Art. 76, Rn. 7; *Baumgärtel/Laumen-Hepting*, Art. 76 WKR, Rn. 1 f.; *Witz/Salger/Lorenz/Witz*, Art. 76, Rn. 12.
[58] OLG Hamm, 22.9.1992, CISG-online 57; MünchKomm/*P. Huber*, Art. 76, Rn. 16; *Baumgärtel/Laumen-Hepting*, Art. 76 WKR, Rn. 1; *Honsell/Schönle/Th. Koller*, Art. 76, Rn. 30; *Reimers-Zocher*, S. 351 f.; *Soergel/Lüderitz/Dettmeier*, Art. 76, Rn. 7; *Witz/Salger/Lorenz/Witz*, Art. 76, Rn. 12; *Ferrari u. a./Saenger*, Internationales Vertragsrecht, Art. 76, Rn. 5; *Staudinger/Magnus*, Art. 76, Rn. 27; a. A. *Achilles*, Art. 74, Rn. 5.

Art. 77 [Schadensminderungspflicht des Ersatzberechtigten]

Die Partei, die sich auf eine Vertragsverletzung beruft, hat alle den Umständen nach angemessenen Maßnahmen zur Verringerung des aus der Vertragsverletzung folgenden Verlusts, einschließlich des entgangenen Gewinns, zu treffen. Versäumt sie dies, so kann die vertragsbrüchige Partei Herabsetzung des Schadenersatzes in Höhe des Betrages verlangen, um den der Verlust hätte verringert werden sollen.

Art. 77

A party who relies on a breach of contract must take such measures as are reasonable in the circumstances to mitigate the loss, including loss of profit, resulting from the breach. If he fails to take such measures, the party in breach may claim a reduction in the damages in the amount by which the loss should have been mitigated.

Art. 77

La partie qui invoque la contravention au contrat doit prendre les mesures raisonnables, eu égard aux circonstances, pour limiter la perte, y compris le gain manqué, résultant de la contravention. Si elle néglige de le faire, la partie en défaut peut demander une réduction des dommages-intérêts égale au montant de la perte qui aurait dû être évitée.

Übersicht

	Rn.
I. Grundgedanken	1
II. Anwendungsbereich	3
1. Schadenersatzpflicht wegen Vertragsverletzung	3
2. Andere Rechtsbehelfe	4
3. Abgrenzung zu Art. 80	6
III. Umfang der Schadensminderungspflicht	7
1. Allgemeines	7
2. Einzelfälle	8
3. Deckungsgeschäfte im Besonderen	10
4. Aufwendungsersatz	11
IV. Rechtsfolgen (S. 2)	12
V. Beweislast	13

I. Grundgedanken

1   Art. 77 normiert wie schon Art. 88 EKG[1] eine Pflicht der ersatzberechtigten Partei, den Schaden zu mindern (**mitigation of damages**). Die Pflicht des Gläubigers, alles ihm Mögliche und Zumutbare zu tun, um den Eintritt des Schadens zu verhindern bzw. das Ausmass des Schadens zu mindern, ist Ausfluss des allgemeinen Grundsatzes von **Treu und Glauben** im internationalen Handelsverkehr,[2] und findet sich in den meisten nationalen Rechtsordnungen[3] und Projekten zur Rechtsvereinheitlichung[4] und wird bereits als **allgemeines Prinzip** insbesondere auch der internationalen Schiedsgerichtsbarkeit[5] betrachtet. Die Vorschrift des

---

[1] Zur Entstehungsgeschichte von Art. 77 und den geringfügigen Unterschieden zu Art. 88 EKG vgl. *Stoll*, 3. Aufl., Art. 77 Rn. 1, 2.

[2] *Herber/Czerwenka*, Art. 77, Rn. 4; *Neumayer/Ming*, Art. 77, Anm. 1.; *Staudinger/Magnus*, Art. 77, Rn. 2; *Witz/Salger/Lorenz/Witz*, Art. 77, Rn. 1; *Soergel/Lüderitz/Dettmeier*, Art. 77, Rn. 1; *P. Huber/Mullis/P. Huber*, S. 289; *Saidov*, Damages in Int'l Sales, S. 128.

[3] Vgl. Rechtsvergleichend *Schwenzer/Hachem/Kee*, Rn. 44.252 ff.; vgl. auch Deutschland: § 254 BGB; Italien: Art. 1227 Cc; Niederlande: Art. 6:101 BW; Österreich: § 1304 ABGB; Schweiz: Art. 44 I OR i. V. m. Art. 99 III OR; USA: Restatement of Contracts 2d, sec. 350; § 2–715 (2) UCC.

[4] Vgl. Art. 7.4.8 PICC; Art. 9:505 PECL und Art. 163 CESL-Entwurf.

[5] Vgl. ICC, 4761/1987, J. D. I. 1987, 1012, 1017 und ICC, 3344/1981, J. D. I. 1982, 978, 983 sowie *Watkins-Johnson v. Islamic Republic of Iran*, Iran-U. S. Claims Tribunal, 28.7.1989, CISG-online 9; *Audit*, Vente internationale, Anm. 173. Fn. 3.

Art. 77 beruht auf dem Grundgedanken, dass vermeidbarer Schaden (avoidable loss) nicht entschädigungswürdig ist.[6] Soweit der durch die Vertragsverletzung verursachte Schaden, einschliesslich des entgangenen Gewinns, durch angemessene Massnahmen hätte verringert werden können, ist er nicht ersatzfähig. Vollends sind Schäden vom Ersatz ausgeschlossen, die durch solche Massnahmen gänzlich behoben werden oder hätten verhütet werden können.[7]

Nach der im deutschen Rechtskreis üblichen Terminologie stellt die Schadensminderungspflicht keine Vertragspflicht, sondern lediglich eine **Obliegenheit** dar.[8] Ein Verstoss gegen die Schadensminderungspflicht zieht seinerseits keine Schadenersatzpflicht nach sich, sondern schliesst den Schadenersatz aus, soweit der Schaden hätte verhindert werden können. Nicht erforderlich ist, dass die Schadensminderungspflicht schuldhaft verletzt wurde. Auch eine Entlastung des Gläubigers nach Art. 79 ist grundsätzlich nicht vorgesehen. Wenn freilich der Schadensabwehr **Hindernisse** im Sinne des Art. 79 entgegenstehen, ist es kaum vorstellbar, dass angemessene Massnahmen zur Schadensabwehr überhaupt möglich sind.[9] Ob und inwieweit sich der Gläubiger im Rahmen des Art. 77 das **Verhalten dritter Personen** zurechnen lassen muss, ist in Art. 77 nicht geregelt. Insoweit kann jedoch ohne weiteres auf Art. 79 I und II zurückgegriffen werden.[10]

II. Anwendungsbereich

1. Schadenersatzpflicht wegen Vertragsverletzung

Die Vorschrift des Art. 77 bezieht sich auf alle Fälle einer Schadenersatzpflicht wegen Vertragsverletzung. Die Pflicht zur Schadensminderung greift dabei nicht erst ein, wenn der Schaden eingetreten ist, sondern auch schon **vor Eintritt des Schadens**.[11] So kann der Gläubiger gehalten sein, auf die Gefahr eines besonders hohen Schadens hinzuweisen.[12] Eine allgemeine Schadensminderungspflicht wird von der überwiegenden Auffassung auch bereits **vor der Begehung der Vertragsverletzung** bejaht, wenn diese – wie etwa im Falle eines vorweggenommenen Vertragsbruchs nach Art. 72 I – ernsthaft droht.[13] (Einzelheiten unten bei Rn. 5, 10).

2. Andere Rechtsbehelfe

Die Schadensminderungspflicht nach Art. 77 gilt nach Wortlaut, systematischer Stellung und Entstehungsgeschichte[14] nur für Schadenersatzansprüche.[15] Eine unmittelbare Anwen-

---

[6] BGH, 26.9.2012, CISG-online 2348; *Stoll/Gruber*, 4. Aufl., Art. 77 Rn. 1.
[7] *Enderlein/Maskow/Strohbach*, Art. 77, Anm. 5.; *Kranz*, S. 228; *Neumayer/Ming*, Art. 77, Anm. 1.; *Schlechtriem*, Gemeinsame Bestimmungen, S. 169.
[8] *Audit*, Vente internationale, Anm. 173.; *Bianca/Bonelli*, Artt. 74–77, Anm. 3.; *Witz/Salger/Lorenz/Witz*, Art. 77, Rn. 1; *Staudinger/Magnus*, Art. 77, Rn. 5; MünchKomm/*P. Huber*, Art. 74, Rn. 1; *P. Huber/Mullis/P. Huber*, S. 289; *Brunner*, Art. 77, Rn. 1; *Schlechtriem*, Internationales UN-Kaufrecht, Rn. 315; *Brölsch*, Schadensersatz, S. 95; a. A. *Hellner*, UN Convention, S. 99; *Saidov*, Limiting Damages, II. 4. (a). Zu den terminologischen Problemen mit dem Begriff „duty" vgl. *Treitel*, Law of Contract, S. 393.
[9] *Stoll/Gruber*, 4. Aufl., Art. 77, Rn. 2. Vgl. aber MünchKomm/*P. Huber*, Art. 77, Rn. 14; MünchKommHGB/*Mankowski*, Art. 77, Rn. 7; *Staudinger/Magnus*, Art. 77, Rn. 9; *Soergel/Lüderitz/Dettmeier*, Art. 77, Rn. 7, die Art. 79 für analog anwendbar halten.
[10] *Staudinger/Magnus*, Art. 77, Rn. 9; MünchKommHGB/*Mankowski*, Art. 77, Rn. 7; *Achilles*, Art. 77, Rn. 3.
[11] *Staudinger/Magnus*, Art. 77, Rn. 8; MünchKomm/*P. Huber*, Art. 77, Rn. 2; MünchKommHGB/*Mankowski*, Art. 77, Rn. 6; *Soergel/Lüderitz/Dettmeier*, Art. 77, Rn. 2; *Schwenzer/Manner*, FS Kritzer, S. 470, 481.
[12] *Bianca/Bonell/Knapp*, Art. 77, Anm. 3.11.; *Roßmeier*, RIW 2000, 407, 412; *Herber/Czerwenka*, Art. 77, Rn. 4; *Neumayer/Ming*, Art. 77, Anm. 4.; *Ryffel*, S. 81; *Staudinger/Magnus*, Art. 77, Rn. 8.
[13] Sekretariatskommentar, Art. 73, Nr. 4; MünchKommHGB/*Mankowski*, Art. 77, Rn. 6; MünchKomm/ *P. Huber*, Art. 74, Rn. 2; *Staudinger/Magnus*, Art. 74, Rn. 8; *Bianca/Bonell/Knapp*, Art. 77, Anm. 3.12.; *Brölsch*, Schadensersatz, S. 97; *Schwenzer/Manner*, FS Kritzer, S. 470, 481 ff.
[14] Vgl. *Honnold/Flechtner*, Art. 77, Rn. 419.3.
[15] Vgl. Sekretariatskommentar, Art. 73, Rn. 3; *Staudinger/Magnus*, Art. 77, Rn. 6; *Witz/Salger/Lorenz/ Witz*, Art. 77, Rn. 3; MünchKommHGB/*Mankowski*, Art. 77, Rn. 4.

dung auf andere Rechtsbehelfe kommt deshalb nach h. M. nicht in Betracht.[16] Dies bedeutet, dass der **Erfüllungsanspruch** oder das **Recht zur Vertragsaufhebung** als solche nicht unter Berufung auf Art. 77 abgewehrt werden können.[17] Allerdings ist mittlerweile allgemein anerkannt, dass das in Art. 77 niedergelegte und im internationalen Handel allgemein anerkannte Prinzip der Pflicht zur Schadensminderung auch auf andere Rechtsbehelfe ausstrahlen muss.[18] So mag eine spekulative Verzögerung der Vertragsaufhebung zwar nicht die Möglichkeit zur Vertragsaufhebung auszuschliessen, aus Art. 77 folgt jedoch eine Kürzung des dann möglichen Schadenersatzanspruchs.

5 Die Frage, ob der Verkäufer auf Erfüllung des Vertrages beharren darf, wenn der Schaden bei Vertragsaufhebung geringer ausfallen würde, stellt sich vor allem bei Verträgen über die Lieferung von herzustellenden Waren **(Werklieferungsvertrag)**. Verweigert der Käufer die Abnahme der Ware, noch ehe der Verkäufer die Ware fertig gestellt oder mit der Produktion begonnen hat, so stellt sich die Frage, ob der Verkäufer mit der Produktion fortfahren und die Durchführung des Vertrages dem Käufer aufzwingen kann, indem er den Kaufpreis fordert. Nationale Rechtsordnungen[19] gelangen nicht zu diesem Ergebnis, sei es, dass dem Käufer ein **Kündigungs- oder Rücktrittsrecht** zusteht, sei es, dass der Erfüllungsanspruch in diesem Fall ausgeschlossen wird. Auch unter dem CISG kann das Ergebnis nicht anders ausfallen, wobei sich zwei Wege anbieten. Entweder man wendet Art. 77 trotz anderslautender Entstehungsgeschichte direkt auf den Erfüllungsanspruch an und erachtet das Beharren auf dem Erfüllungsanspruch als Verletzung der Schadensminderungspflicht[20] oder man anerkennt den fortbestehenden Erfüllungsanspruch des Verkäufers, den dieser sich jedoch um die unnötigen Herstellungskosten kürzen lassen muss.[21]

3. Abgrenzung zu Art. 80

6 Das CISG folgt der namentlich im anglo-amerikanischen Recht vorgenommenen Unterscheidung zwischen „contributory/comparative negligence" und „mitigation of damages".[22] Art. 80 betrifft die **(Mit-)Verursachung der Nichterfüllung** durch den Gläubiger und schliesst sämtliche Rechtsbehelfe aus; Art. 77 regelt demgegenüber nur den Fall, dass der Gläubiger den allein vom Schuldner verursachten Schaden nicht vermieden oder gemindert hat.

---

[16] *Stoll/Gruber*, 4. Aufl., Art. 77 Rn. 4; MünchKomm/*P. Huber*, Art. 77, Rn. 3; *Brunner*, Art. 77, Rn. 2; *Heuzé*, Anm. 451.; *Bianca/Bonell/Knapp*, Art. 77, Anm. 3.1. ff.; *Witz/Salger/Lorenz/Witz*, Art. 77, Rn. 3; *Soergel/Lüderitz/Dettmeier*, Art. 77, Rn. 12; *Staudinger/Magnus*, Art. 77, Rn. 6; *Herber/Czerwenka*, Art. 77, Rn. 3; *Neumayer/Ming*, Art. 77, Anm. 5.; *P. Huber/Mullis/P. Huber*, S. 290; *Kröll u. a./Gotanda*, Art. 77, Rn. 6; *Kranz*, S. 227; *Piltz*, Internationales Kaufrecht, Rn. 5–553; *Brölsch*, Schadensersatz, S. 96; *Saidov*, Limiting Damages, II. 4. (a). A. A. *Honnold/Flechtner*, Art. 77, Rn. 419.3.
[17] Vgl. *Achilles*, Art. 77, Rn. 2 (Beschränkung von Erfüllungsansprüchen allenfalls durch das Verbot des venire contra factum proprium).
[18] MünchKomm/*P. Huber*, Art. 77, Rn. 3; *Staudinger/Magnus*, Art. 77, Rn. 6; *Brunner*, Art. 77, Rn. 2; MünchKommHGB/*Mankowski*, Art. 77, Rn. 4 f.; *Schlechtriem*, Internationales UN-Kaufrecht, Rn. 92; *Witz/Salger/Lorenz/Witz*, Art. 77, Rn. 3.
[19] Vgl. Deutschland: §§ 651 I 3, 649 BGB; Frankreich: Art. 1794 Cc; Grossbritannien: sec. 49 (1), (2) SGA; Italien: Art. 1671 Cc; Österreich: § 1168 I ABGB; Schweiz: Art. 377 OR sowie USA: § 2–709 (1) UCC; zum englischen und U. S.-amerikanischen Recht *Stoll*, RabelsZ 52 (1988), 617,638 f.; zu den PICC vgl. *Schwenzer*, 1 EJLR (1998/1999), 289, 293 ff. Art. 9:101 II PECL und Art. 132 II CESL-Entwurf gestehen grundsätzlich das Recht, Erfüllung zu verlangen, zu, es sei denn, ein angemessenes Deckungsgeschäft ist möglich oder die Erfüllung wäre unangemessen (letzteres nur PECL).
[20] MünchKomm/*P. Huber*, Art. 77, Rn. 3; *Staudinger/Magnus*, Art. 77, Rn. 6; MünchKommHGB/*Mankowski*, Art. 77, Rn. 5; wohl auch *Saidov*, Damages in Int'l Sales, S. 237 f.
[21] Vgl. *Stoll/Gruber*, 4. Aufl., Art. 77 Rn. 5; *Schwenzer/Manner*, FS Kritzer, S. 470, 483 ff.; wohl auch *Schlechtriem*, Internationales UN-Kaufrecht, Rn. 26.
[22] *Stoll/Gruber*, 4. Aufl., Art. 77, Rn. 6; *Th. Neumann*, Duty to Cooperate, S. 81; zum englischen Recht vgl. *Treitel*, Law of Contract, S. 910–915; ferner Deutschland: § 254 I und II BGB; Italien: Art. 1227 I und II Cc; Artt. 7.4.7 und 7.4.8 PICC; Artt. 9:504 und 9:505 PECL; Artt. 162 und 163 CESL-Entwurf; weitere Nachweise bei *Schwenzer/Hachem/Kee*, Rn. 44.254; *Lando/Beale*, Part I and II, Art. 9:505 Anm. 1.

III. Umfang der Schadensminderungspflicht

1. Allgemeines

Art. 77 verpflichtet die ersatzberechtigte Partei zur Vornahme **angemessener Massnahmen** der Schadensminderung, die unter den gegebenen Umständen nach Treu und Glauben erwartet werden dürfen.[23] Bei der Frage, welche Massnahmen angemessen sind, sind vorrangig Gepflogenheiten zwischen den Parteien und internationale Gebräuche zu berücksichtigen (Art. 9). Im Übrigen kommt es auf das Verhalten einer **verständigen Person** in gleicher Lage und unter denselben Umständen an (Art. 8 II).[24] Zu ausserordentlichen, unverhältnismässige Kosten erfordernden Anstrengungen ist der Gläubiger nicht verpflichtet.[25]

2. Einzelfälle

Massnahmen zur **Erhaltung der Ware** und die **Veräusserung** verderblicher Ware können nach Art. 77 geboten sein, auch wenn eine Verpflichtung zu solchen Massnahmen nach Artt. 85 bis 88 nicht besteht.[26] Ebenso kann eine Partei gehalten sein, **Rechtsmittel** gegen Hoheitsakte wie z. B. eine Beschlagnahme einzulegen, die der anderen Partei die Durchführung des Vertrages erschweren oder unmöglich machen.[27] Bei Lieferung vertragswidriger Ware kann der Käufer verpflichtet sein, den **Mangel selbst zu beheben,** um eine Ausbreitung des Mangels zu verhindern oder Folgeschäden entgegen zu wirken.[28] Dasselbe gilt, wenn der Käufer die Mangelbeseitigung wesentlich kostengünstiger vornehmen kann als der Verkäufer. Hat der Käufer die Mangelhaftigkeit der Ware erkannt, so ist er unter Umständen gehalten, die **Verwendung der Ware**[29] **oder die Produktion mit derselben**[30] **einzustellen,** es sei denn, der Verkäufer hat durch sein eigenes Verhalten Anlass dazu gegeben, die Ware weiter zu verwenden.[31] Vom Käufer vertragswidriger Ware kann auch verlangt werden, dass er seinen Abnehmern einen **Preisnachlass** gewährt, um eine mit einer Vertragsaufhebung verbundene Erhöhung des Schadens abzuwenden.[32] Unzumutbar ist es hingegen, vom Gläubiger eine **Vertragsverletzung** im Verhältnis zu seinen eigenen Vertragspartnern zu verlangen. Hingegen kann nach Art. 77 verlangt werden, dass sich der Gläubiger auf **Verhandlungen** mit dem Schuldner einlässt. So muss etwa der Verkäufer auch ein Angebot des vertragsbrüchigen Käufers annehmen, einen Teil der Ware zu einem niedrigeren Preis zu übernehmen, wenn dieser Preis noch über dem bei einem Deckungsverkauf zu erzielenden Preis liegt.[33] Nimmt der Verkäufer diese Gelegenheit nicht wahr,

---

[23] *Stoll/Gruber*, 4. Aufl., Art. 77 Rn. 7; *Ryffel*, S. 81; *Achilles*, Art. 77, Rn. 4; *Witz/Salger/Lorenz/Witz*, Art. 77, Rn. 9.
[24] OGH, 6.2.1996, CISG-online 224; OLG Koblenz, 24.2.2011, CISG-online 2301; *Roßmeier*, RIW 2000, 407, 411; *Bamberger/Roth/Saenger*, Art. 77, Rn. 3; *MünchKommHGB/Mankowski*, Art. 77, Rn. 10; *Schlechtriem*, Internationales UN-Kaufrecht, Rn. 315; *Soergel/Lüderitz/Dettmeier*, Art. 77, Rn. 4; *Herber/Czerwenka*, Art. 77, Rn. 5; *Kranz*, S. 229 Fn. 2; *Staudinger/Magnus*, Art. 77, Rn. 10; *P. Huber/Mullis/P. Huber*, S. 290.
[25] MünchKomm/*P. Huber*, Art. 77, Rn. 4; *Audit*, Vente internationale, Anm. 174.; Neumayer/Ming, Art. 77, Anm. 3.; *Witz/Salger/Lorenz/Witz*, Art. 77, Rn. 9; *Brunner*, Art. 77, Rn. 7; *Enderlein/Maskow/Strohbach*, Art. 77, Anm. 2.; *Bianca/Bonell/Knapp*, Art. 77, Anm. 2.3.; *P. Huber/Mullis/P. Huber*, S. 290.
[26] ICC, 7197/1992, CISG-online 36; *Herber/Czerwenka*, Art. 77, Rn. 6; *Kranz*, S. 231; *Weber*, Vertragsverletzungsfolgen, S. 205; *Bamberger/Roth/Saenger*, Art. 77, Rn. 3; *Staudinger/Magnus*, Art. 77, Rn. 13.
[27] *Staudinger/Magnus*, Art. 77, Rn. 18; *Herber/Czerwenka*, Art. 77, Rn. 6.
[28] District Court Komarno, 24.2.2009, CISG-online 1992 (Waschen von Kartoffeln); *Audit*, Vente internationale, Anm. 173.; *Bianca/Bonell/Knapp*, Art. 77, Anm. 2.2.; *Herber/Czerwenka*, Art. 77, Rn. 6; *Neumayer/Ming*, Art. 77, Anm. 4.; *Witz/Salger/Lorenz/Witz*, Art. 77, Rn. 9; *Roßmeier*, RIW 2000, 407, 412; *Enderlein/Maskow/Strohbach*, Art. 77, Anm. 2.; *Kranz*, S. 230 f.; *Staudinger/Magnus*, Art. 77, Rn. 14.
[29] Vgl. BGH, 24.3.1999, CISG-online 396 (Rebwachs); *P. Huber/Mullis/P. Huber*, S. 290.
[30] CA Rennes, 27.5.2008, CISG-online 1746.
[31] MünchKomm/*P. Huber*, Art. 77, Rn. 5; *Staudinger/Magnus*, Art. 77, Rn. 11.
[32] Vgl. OLG Koblenz, 19.10.2006, CISG-online 1407.
[33] CA Rennes, 27.5.2008, CISG-online 1746: Deckungskauf, obwohl Ware vom Verkäufer billiger hätte beschafft werden können, als unvernünftig erachtet; vgl. auch *Schwenzer/Manner*, FS Kritzer, S. 470, 486.

kann er nach Art. 74 nur die Differenz zwischen dem ursprünglichen Vertragspreis und dem vom Käufer angebotenen Preis verlangen.[34]

9   Es ist dem Gläubiger nach Art. 77 auch zuzumuten, den Schuldner auf die Gefahr eines besonders hohen Schadens **hinzuweisen,** der bei Nichterfüllung droht.[35] Allgemeine Massnahmen der Schadensvorsorge für den Fall einer möglichen Vertragsverletzung können jedoch nicht verlangt werden, soweit kein konkreter Anlass dafür besteht. Deshalb braucht der Gläubiger nicht durch Abschluss einer Betriebsausfallversicherung einer möglichen Nichterfüllung des Vertrages und ihren Folgen vorzubeugen.[36]

3. Deckungsgeschäfte im Besonderen

10 Grundsätzlich kann sich aus Art. 77 auch die Pflicht der von einer Vertragsverletzung betroffenen oder bedrohten Partei ergeben, zur Schadensminderung oder Schadensverhütung ein Deckungsgeschäft abzuschliessen.[37] Dabei müssen verschiedene Situationen unterschieden werden. Unzweifelhaft besteht eine Verpflichtung zum Abschluss eines Deckungsgeschäftes, wenn dies mit der **weiteren Durchführung des Kaufvertrages** vereinbar ist, d. h. wenn durch das Deckungsgeschäft Folgeschäden der Nicht- oder Schlechterfüllung des Vertrages abgewendet werden können (z. B. ein Haftungsschaden oder ein Gewinnverlust) und der Gläubiger nicht beabsichtigt, vom Vertrag Abstand zu nehmen.[38] Nach **Aufhebung des Vertrages** kann der Gläubiger gemäss Art. 77 verpflichtet sein, ein Deckungsgeschäft abzuschliessen, wenn danach der ersatzfähige Schaden geringer wäre als bei abstrakter Schadensberechnung nach der Marktpreisregel des Art. 76.[39] Der Gläubiger kann im Einzelfall sogar gehalten sein, mit dem vertragsbrüchigen Schuldner ein Deckungsgeschäft vorzunehmen.[40] Umstritten ist hingegen, ob dem Gläubiger vor allem im Falle des **antizipierten Vertragsbruchs** nach Art. 72 I auf Grund seiner Schadensminderungspflicht eine Pflicht zur Aufhebung des Vertrages obliegt oder ob er zuwarten und auf Erfüllung beharren darf, ohne seine Schadensminderungspflicht nach Art. 77 zu verletzen.[41] Praktisch

---

[34] Tribunal Supremo, 28.1.2000, CISG-online 503, dazu *Rosch, D.* 2002 Somm., 322–323.

[35] *Herber/Czerwenka,* Art. 77, Rn. 6; MünchKomm/*P. Huber,* Art. 77, Rn. 6; *Kranz,* S. 230; *Piltz,* Internationales Kaufrecht, Rn. 5–558; *Staudinger/Magnus,* Art. 77, Rn. 17; *Witz/Salger/Lorenz/Witz,* Art. 77, Rn. 11; *Ferrari u. a./Saenger,* Internationales Vertragsrecht, Art. 77, Rn. 4.

[36] *Honsell/Magnus,* Art. 77, Rn. 12; *Witz/Salger/Lorenz/Witz,* Art. 77, Rn. 10; *Neumayer/Ming,* Art. 77, Anm. 4.; *Bamberger/Roth/Saenger,* Art. 77, Rn. 4; *P. Huber/Mullis/P. Huber,* S. 290; a. A. *U. Huber,* RabelsZ 43 (1979), 413, 471; *Karollus,* S. 225; einschränkend *Herber/Czerwenka,* Art. 77, Rn. 6; *Roßmeier,* RIW 2000, 407, 412; *Ryffel,* S. 82 und *Staudinger/Magnus,* Art. 77, Rn. 14 (nur wenn üblich oder wegen besonderer Risiken angezeigt).

[37] Internationales Schiedsgericht der Bundeskammer der gewerblichen Wirtschaft in Österreich, 15.6.1994, CISG-online 120 = 691; OLG Hamburg, 28.2.1997, CISG-online 261; OLG Düsseldorf, 13.9.1996, CISG-online 407 (insbesondere wenn Kosten der Nachbesserung unangemessen hoch); OLG Celle, 2.9.1998, CISG-online 506, wie die Vorinstanz LG Göttingen, 31.7.1997, CISG-online 564; Hof van Beroep Antwerpen, 22.1.2007, CISG-online 1585; BGer, 17.12.2009, CISG-online 2022 = BGE 136 III 56, 59; *Mohs,* AJP 2011, 425, 428; *ders.,* FS Schwenzer, S. 1285, 1301; *Audit,* Vente internationale, Anm. 173.; *Bianca/Bonell/Knapp,* Art. 77, Anm. 2.2.; *Bianca/Bonell,* Artt. 74–77, Anm. 4.; *Herber/Czerwenka,* Art. 75, Rn. 7 und Art. 77, Rn. 6; *Enderlein/Maskow/Strohbach,* Art. 77, Anm. 2.; *Neumayer/Ming,* Art. 77, Anm. 3.; *Piltz,* Internationales Kaufrecht, Rn. 5–518, 5–559; *Roßmeier,* RIW 2000, 407, 412; *Soergel/Lüderitz/Dettmeier,* Art. 77, Rn. 4; *Staudinger/Magnus,* Art. 77, Rn. 11; enger *Witz/Salger/Lorenz/Witz,* Art. 77, Rn. 7, 8.

[38] Vgl. MünchKomm/*P. Huber,* Art. 77, Rn. 8; *P. Huber/Mullis/P. Huber,* S. 291. Vgl. schon RB Amsterdam, 17.12.1984, in: *Schlechtriem/Magnus,* Art. 88, Nr. 6; LG Heidelberg, 30.1.1979, in: *Schlechtriem/Magnus,* Art. 88 EKG, Nr. 2 = Art. 22 EKG, Nr. 2 (Deckungskauf bei Verzug).

[39] OLG Hamm, 22.9.1992, CISG-online 57; BGer, 17.12.2009, CISG-online 2022 = BGE 136 III 56, 59, m. krit. Anm. *Mohs,* AJP 2011, 425, 428 f., der Deckungsgeschäft auf gleicher Handelsstufe für unzumutbar hält; MünchKomm/*P. Huber,* Art. 77, Rn. 10. Vgl. auch *C. Witz,* D. H. 2012, 1144, 1153.

[40] Vgl. *Schwenzer/Manner,* FS Kritzer, S. 470, 486 f.; *Saidov,* 13 VJ (2009), 197, 208 f.; wohl auch *ders.,* Damages in Int'l Sales, S. 139.

[41] Die h. M. geht grundsätzlich von Letzterem aus, macht aber eine Ausnahme, wenn die Vertragsaufhebung aus spekulativen Gründen hinausgezögert wird und nur Schadensersatz als Rechtsbehelf zur Verfügung steht, vgl. OLG Braunschweig, 28.10.1999, CISG-online 510; OLG Düsseldorf, 14.1.1994, CISG-online 119; *Witz/Salger/Lorenz/Witz,* Art. 77, Rn. 7; *Neumayer/Ming,* Art. 77, Anm. 3.; *Heuzé,* Anm. 451.; *Saidov,* Limiting Damages, II. 4. (c); vgl. auch *Hager,* FS Schwenzer, S. 681, 691; enger aber wohl *Honnold/Flechtner,*

wird die Frage bei Waren, die starken **Preisschwankungen** unterliegen. Jedenfalls wenn sich Marktentwicklungen, die eindeutig zu Lasten der vertragsbrüchigen Partei gehen, klar abzeichnen, ist das Interesse des Gläubigers, bis zum Erfüllungszeitpunkt zuzuwarten, grundsätzlich nicht schützenswert.[42] Auf Grund der Schadensminderungspflicht des Art. 77 muss der Gläubiger als verpflichtet angesehen werden, rechtzeitig ein Deckungsgeschäft vorzunehmen.[43] Wo dies nicht der Fall ist, kann er Schadenersatz nur anhand eines fiktiven Deckungsgeschäfts in dem Zeitpunkt verlangen, in dem ein vernünftiger Gläubiger den Vertrag aufgehoben hätte.[44] In der Praxis wird dies meist auf eine Anwendung der Marktpreisregel des Art. 76 hinauslaufen. Schadensminderung kommt hingegen in den Fällen des „lost volume" nicht in Betracht, da hier gerade kein Deckungsgeschäft möglich ist.[45]

4. Aufwendungsersatz

Für Aufwendungen, die nach Art. 77 zur Abwendung oder Verminderung des Schadens geboten sind, kann die von der Vertragsverletzung betroffene Partei nach Art. 74 Ersatz fordern (vgl. oben Art. 74 Rn. 27).[46] Die Beschränkung auf **sachlich gebotene Aufwendungen** kann einerseits mit Art. 77 begründet[47] oder direkt auf Art. 74 gestützt werden. Für gänzlich ungeeignete Massnahmen kann kein Ersatz verlangt werden.[48]

IV. Rechtsfolgen (S. 2)

Die Verletzung der Schadensminderungspflicht führt nach Art. 77 S. 2 zu einer **Herabsetzung** des Schadenersatzanspruchs in dem Umfang, in dem der Schaden hätte vermieden werden können.[49] Entsprechend den Umständen des Einzelfalles kann auch jeglicher Ersatz **ausgeschlossen** sein.[50] Umstritten ist, ob es sich bei der Berufung auf eine Verletzung der Schadensminderungspflicht nach den Vorstellungen des deutschen Rechtskreises um eine anspruchsausschliessende **Einwendung,** die von Amtes wegen zu berücksichtigen ist, handelt oder lediglich um eine anspruchshemmende **Einrede**.[51] Vor anglo-amerikanischen

---

Art. 77, Rn. 419.2. Für eine generelle Pflicht zur Vertragsaufhebung aber *Bianca/Bonell/Knapp*, Art. 77, Anm. 3.
[42] Vgl. *Schlechtriem*, GS Hellner, S. 236 f.; *Schwenzer/Manner*, FS Kritzer, S. 470, 482 f.; *P. Huber/Mullis/P. Huber*, S. 290.
[43] Vgl. auch oben Fountoulakis, Art. 72 Rn. 20.
[44] Vgl. *Schlechtriem*, Internationales UN-Kaufrecht, Rn. 313.
[45] Vgl. MünchKomm/*P. Huber*, Art. 77, Rn. 10; *Kröll u. a./Gotanda*, Art. 77, Rn. 9; *Saidov*, Limiting Damages, II. 4. (d).
[46] So ausdrücklich Art. 7.4.9 II PICC; Art. 9:505 II PECL und Art. 163 II CESL-Entwurf.
[47] So die h. M., vgl. LG Düsseldorf, 25.8.1994, CISG-online 451; AG Alsfeld, 12.5.1995, CISG-online 170; *Herber/Czerwenka*, Art. 77, Rn. 6; *Piltz*, Internationales Kaufrecht, Rn. 5–561; *Staudinger/Magnus*, Art. 77, Rn. 16; *Witz/Salger/Lorenz/Witz*, Art. 77, Rn. 12; *Bianca/Bonelli*, Artt. 74–77, Anm. 3.
[48] Vgl. BGH, 25.6.1997, CISG-online 277; MünchKomm/*P. Huber*, Art. 77, Rn. 12.
[49] BGH, 24.3.1999, CISG-online 396; *Enderlein/Maskow/Strohbach*, Art. 77, Anm. 5.; *Soergel/Lüderitz/Dettmeier*, Art. 77, Rn. 9; *Karollus*, S. 225; *Reinhart*, Art. 77, Rn. 6; *Staudinger/Magnus*, Art. 77, Rn. 19; *Stoll*, Schadensersatzpflicht, S. 268; *U. Huber*, RabelsZ 43 (1979), 413, 471; *Bianca/Bonell/Knapp*, Art. 77, Anm. 2.5. und 2.11.; *Audit*, Vente internationale, Anm. 174.; *Bamberger/Roth/Saenger*, Art. 77, Rn. 6; *Witz/Salger/Lorenz/Witz*, Art. 77, Rn. 12; dagegen halten *Herber/Czerwenka*, Art. 77, Rn. 2, *Schlechtriem*, Internationales UN-Kaufrecht, Rn. 315 und *Trachsel*, Haftungsbefreiung, S. 393 Art. 77 für inhaltsgleich mit § 254 II 1 BGB; kritisch *Koziol*, ZEuP 1998, 593, 594 f., der darin eine bedauerliche Wiedererweckung der überwunden geglaubten Culpakompensationsregel sieht.
[50] BGH, 24.3.1999, CISG-online 396; OLG Koblenz, 24.2.2011, CISG-online 2301; MünchKomm/*P. Huber*, Art. 77, Rn. 13; *Staudinger/Magnus*, Art. 77, Rn. 19; *Witz/Salger/Lorenz/Witz*, Art. 77, Rn. 12; *P. Huber/Mullis/P. Huber*, S. 292.
[51] Einwendung: BGH, 24.3.1999, CISG-online 396; OGH, 6.2.1996, CISG-online 224; *Stoll/Gruber*, 4. Aufl., Art. 77 Rn. 12; *Achilles*, Art. 77, Rn. 1; *Soergel/Lüderitz/Dettmeier*, Art. 77, Rn. 11; *Witz/Salger/Lorenz/Witz*, Art. 77, Rn. 13; *Brunner*, Art. 77, Rn. 16; *Herber/Czerwenka*, Art. 77, Rn. 8; *Piltz*, NJW 2000, 553, 560; *Hutter*, S. 197; *Staudinger/Magnus*, Art. 77, Rn. 21; *P. Huber/Mullis/P. Huber*, S. 292; *Weber*, Vertragsverletzungsfolgen, S. 206. Einrede: *Karollus*, S. 225; *Schlechtriem*, Internationales UN-Kaufrecht, Rn. 316.

Gerichten und vor den meisten Schiedsgerichten dürfte jedenfalls eine Verletzung der Schadensminderungspflicht auf jeden Fall nur berücksichtigt werden, wenn der Schuldner sich darauf beruft.[52]

V. Beweislast

13 Beruft sich der **Schuldner** darauf, dass der Gläubiger die Schadensminderungspflicht nach Art. 77 verletzt hat, so trägt er insoweit die Beweislast.[53] Macht der **Gläubiger** im Rahmen von Art. 74 Aufwendungen zur Abwendung oder Verminderung des Schadens geltend, so ist er seinerseits hierfür beweispflichtig.[54]

---

[52] Vgl. *Treibacher Industrie, A. G. v. Allegheny Technologies, Inc.*, U. S. Ct. App. (11th Cir.), 12.9.2006, CISG-online 1278.

[53] OLG Koblenz, 24.2.2011, CISG-online 2301; AG München, 23.6.1995, CISG-online 368; *Castel Electronics Pty. Ltd. v. Toshiba Singapore Pte. Ltd.* Federal Court of Australia, 20.4.2011, CISG-online 2219, Rn. 327; *Baumgärtel/Laumen-Hepting*, Art. 77 WKR, Rn. 1; *Herber/Czerwenka*, Art. 77, Rn. 8; *Witz/Salger/Lorenz/Witz*, Art. 77, Rn. 13; *Hutter*, S. 198; *Staudinger/Magnus*, Art. 77, Rn. 22; *P. Huber/Mullis/P. Huber*, S. 289, 292; *Kröll u. a./Gotanda*, Art. 77, Rn. 11 ff.; differenzierend *Achilles*, Art. 77, Rn. 4, der dem Schuldner die Beweislast für das Vorliegen einer entsprechenden Minderungspflicht und den Umfang der Minderung auferlegt, während der Nachweis, dass die Obliegenheit erfüllt worden sei, dem Gläubiger obliege; ebenso OLG Celle, 2.9.1998, CISG-online 506; vgl. auch *Saidov*, Damages in Int'l Sales, S. 147 ff.

[54] MünchKomm/*P. Huber*, Art. 77, Rn. 16.

Abschnitt III. Zinsen

Section III.
Interest

Section III.
Intérêts

Art. 78 [Zinsen]

Versäumt eine Partei, den Kaufpreis oder einen anderen fälligen Betrag zu zahlen, so hat die andere Partei für diese Beträge Anspruch auf Zinsen, unbeschadet eines Schadenersatzanspruchs nach Artikel 74.

Art. 78

If a party fails to pay the price or any other sum that is in arrears, the other party is entitled to interest on it, without prejudice to any claim for damages recoverable under article 74.

Art. 78

Si une partie ne paie pas le prix ou toute autre somme due, l'autre partie a droit à des intérêts sur cette somme, sans préjudice des dommages-intérêts qu'elle serait fondée à demander en vertu de l'article 74.

Übersicht

	Rn.
I. Allgemeines	1
II. Vorgeschichte	4
III. Anwendungsbereich	4a
IV. Voraussetzungen der Zinszahlungspflicht	7
1. Fälligkeit	7
a) Kaufpreisanspruch	8
b) Andere Ansprüche	9
c) Festgelegte Höhe?	10
d) Minderung	13
e) Schadenersatz	14
2. Keine weiteren Voraussetzungen	17
3. Gegenrechte des Schuldners	19
a) Zahlungsansprüche	20
b) Andere Gegenansprüche	21
4. Wegfall des Anspruchs	22
a) Aufhebung des Vertrages	23
b) Minderung	24
V. Modalitäten der Zahlungspflicht	25
VI. Zinshöhe	26
1. Rückgriff auf nationales Recht oder Einheitslösung	27
a) Probleme einer Einheitslösung	28
b) Schwierigkeiten beim Rückgriff auf nationales Recht	32
c) Ergebnis	36
2. Einzelne nationale Zinssätze	37
3. Handelsbräuche	38
4. Vertragliche Regelung der Zinshöhe	39
5. Zinseszinsen	40
VII. Verhältnis zu anderen Ansprüchen	41
1. Schadenersatzansprüche	41
2. Zinsanspruch aus Art. 84 I	43
3. Prozesszinsen	45

Vorläufer und **Entwürfe:** Art. 83 EKG; Genfer E 1976 Art. 58; Wiener E 1977 Art. 55 I; New Yorker E 1978 Art. 69 I.

I. Allgemeines

1   Art. 78 normiert eine generelle Pflicht zur Zahlung von Zinsen auf fällige Geldbeträge. Er ergänzt Art. 84 I, der eine Verzinsung (nur) für den Anspruch auf Rückzahlung des Kaufpreises im Falle der Vertragsaufhebung vorsieht.

2   Beide Vorschriften legen einen Anspruch jedoch nur dem Grunde nach fest. Über die Höhe finden sich im CISG keine ausdrücklichen Regelungen. Versuche, auch die Zinshöhe zu regeln, scheiterten sowohl im Vorfeld als auch auf der Konferenz selbst. Die letztendlich erzielte Regelung stellt einen Kompromiss dar, der die „unüberbrückbaren Meinungsgegensätze zudecken sollte, um ein Scheitern der Konferenz zu verhindern".[1] Neben dem stark unterschiedlichen Zinsniveau in den einzelnen Vertragsstaaten spielten dabei auch grundlegende Vorbehalte gegen jegliche Zinspflicht eine Rolle, z. B. das grundsätzliche Zinsverbot in den arabischen Staaten.[2] Um zu verhindern, dass die wichtige Frage im CISG überhaupt keine Regelung findet, verständigte man sich auf eine Regelung dem Grunde nach und klammerte die Frage der Zinshöhe aus. Dass es über die offengebliebene Frage in Literatur und Rechtsprechung zu unterschiedlichen Auffassungen gekommen ist, kann angesichts der Vorgeschichte kaum verwundern.

3   Die dogmatische Einordnung des Zinsanspruchs ist umstritten und wird vor allem im Zusammenhang mit der Bestimmung der Zinshöhe diskutiert (dazu Rn. 29 f.). Unabhängig von diesem Streit sprechen die systematische Stellung des Art. 78 (innerhalb eines eigenen Abschnitts der Konvention) und der letzte Halbsatz der Vorschrift, wonach Ansprüche auf Schadenersatz unberührt bleiben, dafür, dass die für Schadenersatzansprüche geltenden Bestimmungen des CISG auf den Zinsanspruch aus Art. 78 nicht anwendbar sind. Dies gilt insbesondere für Art. 79 (hierzu Rn. 17).

II. Vorgeschichte

4   Art. 58 des Genfer E 1976 sah eine – aus Art. 83 EKG übernommene – Regelung über den Grund und die Höhe des Zinsanspruchs vor (1% über dem amtlichen Diskontsatz des Niederlassungslandes des Gläubigers). Die geschilderten Meinungsverschiedenheiten führten jedoch dazu, dass der Wiener E 1977 (Art. 55 I) und der New Yorker E 1978 (Art. 69 I) eine ausdrückliche Zinsregelung nur noch für den (jetzt von Art. 84 I erfassten) Fall der Rückzahlung des Kaufpreises nach Aufhebung des Vertrages enthielten. Erst auf der Wiener Konferenz wurde – gewissermaßen in letzter Minute – Art. 78 in seiner jetzigen Fassung eingefügt.[3]

III. Anwendungsbereich

4a   Art. 78 ist anwendbar für alle Zahlungsansprüche, die aus dem **Kaufvertrag** resultieren – unabhängig davon, ob es sich um Primäransprüche oder Sekundäransprüche handelt, und unabhängig davon, ob der Anspruch im Vertrag ausdrücklich vorgesehen ist oder sich aus den Bestimmungen des CISG oder des ergänzend anwendbaren nationalen Rechts ergibt. **Nicht** anwendbar dürfte die Vorschrift für Ansprüche sein, die zwar mit dem Kaufvertrag in Zusammenhang stehen, aber auf einer anderen Rechtsgrundlage beruhen. So wurde die Anwendung von Art. 78 auf einen auf das nationale Prozessrecht gestützten Anspruch auf Erstattung von **Prozesskosten** abgelehnt.[4] Zu Prozesszinsen vgl. unten Rn. 45 f.

---

[1] *Schlechtriem*, JZ 1988, 1037, 1047. Weitere Einzelheiten bei *Schlechtriem*, Internationales UN-Kaufrecht, Rn. 317 und *Bianca/Bonell/Nicholas*, Art. 78, Anm. 1.3.
[2] S. u. a. *Otto*, RIW 1992, 854 f.; *Cohen*, 26 U. Pa. L. Rev. (2005), 601, 614.
[3] Ausführlich zur Entstehungsgeschichte *Zoccolillo*, 1 VJ (1997), 3 ff.
[4] Gerechtshof Arnhem, 21.3.2006, CISG-online 1695.

Art. 78 erfasst neben dem Anspruch auf Zahlung des **Kaufpreises** auch alle anderen 5
Zahlungsansprüche. Zu letzteren gehören Ansprüche auf Erstattung von **Aufwendungen**, die eine Partei für die andere getätigt hat (z. B. vom Verkäufer verauslagte Transportkosten, die vereinbarungsgemäß dem Käufer zur Last fallen sollen), der Anspruch auf Rückzahlung eines Teils des bereits geleisteten Kaufpreises im Falle der **Minderung** nach Art. 50[5] sowie der Anspruch auf Erstattung von Lagerkosten gemäß Art. 87[6]. Wegen des Rückzahlungsanspruchs im Falle der Vertragsaufhebung s. Art. 84 I sowie unten Rn. 43 f.

Ob auch **Schadenersatzansprüche** zu verzinsen sind, wird z. T. angezweifelt. Gegen 6 eine Verzinsung nach Art. 78 ist vor allem vorgebracht worden, dass Schadenersatzansprüche nicht auf Zahlung eines festen Geldbetrages, sondern auf Ersatz eines bestimmten Wertes gerichtet seien.[7] Dies führt hin zu der allgemeineren Frage, ob die Anwendung des Art. 78 voraussetzt, dass der Anspruch seiner Höhe nach bereits fixiert, d. h. auf Zahlung einer „**liquidated sum**" gerichtet ist; dazu unten Rn. 10 ff. Zu Zinseszinsen s. Rn. 40.

IV. Voraussetzungen der Zinszahlungspflicht

1. Fälligkeit

Fälligkeit wird nur bei den sonstigen Zahlungsansprüchen ausdrücklich als Entstehungs- 7 voraussetzung genannt. Es besteht aber kein Zweifel daran, dass auch die Kaufpreisschuld erst vom Moment ihrer Fälligkeit an zu verzinsen ist.

a) Kaufpreisanspruch. Beim **Kaufpreisanspruch** bereitet die Frage nach dem **Zeit-** 8 **punkt** der Fälligkeit keine Probleme: Er richtet sich in erster Linie nach der Parteivereinbarung, mangels einer solchen nach Artt. 58 f.[8] Die Fälligkeit kann auch durch nachträgliche (Stundungs-)Vereinbarung auf einen späteren Zeitpunkt verlegt werden. Nimmt der Gläubiger erfüllungshalber einen Wechsel entgegen, liegt darin regelmäßig eine stillschweigende Stundungsabrede.[9]

b) Andere Ansprüche. Für **andere Ansprüche** hat das CISG den Fälligkeitszeitpunkt 9 nicht ausdrücklich geregelt. Mangels anderer Anhaltspunkte wird man davon auszugehen haben, dass solche Ansprüche sofort mit ihrem **Entstehen** fällig werden.[10]

c) Festgelegte Höhe? Verschiedentlich ist die Frage aufgeworfen worden, ob Art. 78 erst 10 dann greifen kann, wenn der betreffende Anspruch der Höhe nach festgelegt (**liquidated**) ist.[11] Aus dem Wortlaut der Vorschrift („fälliger Betrag", „sum that is in arrears", „somme due") lässt sich ein solches Erfordernis aber kaum entnehmen. Sachlich zwingende Gründe für eine vom Wortlaut abweichende Einschränkung der Zinszahlungspflicht sind nicht ersichtlich. Zinsen werden also auch für Zeiträume geschuldet, in denen der Anspruch bereits bestanden hat, seine genaue Höhe aber noch nicht festgelegt war.[12] Hiervon zu

---

[5] S. dazu auch *Müller-Chen*, Art. 50 Rn. 16.
[6] S. dazu Art. 87 Rn. 9.
[7] So *Heuzé*, Anm. 447., der im Ergebnis jedoch keine eindeutige Entscheidung treffen will. Für die Anwendung des Art. 78 auf Schadenersatzansprüche *Karollus*, S. 227; *Herber/Czerwenka*, Art. 78, Rn. 2; *Ferrari u. a./Ferrari*, Internationales Vertragsrecht, Art. 78, Rn. 4; *Soergel/Lüderitz/Dettmeier*, Art. 78, Rn. 3; seit 2005 auch *Staudinger/Magnus*, Art. 78, Rn. 8.
[8] Vgl. als Beispielsfälle OLG Koblenz, 19.10.2006, CISG-online 1407; Kantonsgericht Nidwalden, 23.5.2005, CISG-online 1086.
[9] LG Hamburg, 26.9.1990, CISG-online 21 = RIW 1990, 1015, 1018.
[10] S. dazu *Ferrari*, Art. 7 Rn. 52; ebenso *Ferrari u. a./Ferrari*, Internationales Vertragsrecht, Art. 78, Rn. 10; *Kröll u. a./Gotanda*, Art. 78, Rn. 18 f.; MünchKomm/*P. Huber*, Art. 78, Rn. 8; für Schadenersatz- und Aufwendungsersatzansprüche auch *Herber/Czerwenka*, Art. 78, Rn. 3; *Staudinger/Magnus*, Art. 78, Rn. 10.
[11] S. dazu beispielsweise *Honnold/Flechtner*, Art. 78, Rn. 422; *Bianca/Bonell/Nicholas*, Art. 78, Anm. 3.1.; *Achilles*, Art. 78, Rn. 3; Audiencia Provincial de Cuenca, 31.1.2005, CISG-online 1241; s. ferner bereits oben Rn. 6.
[12] Ebenso *Witz/Salger/Lorenz/Witz*, Art. 78, Rn. 5; *Brunner*, Art. 78, Rn. 3; *Ferrari u. a./Ferrari*, Internationales Vertragsrecht, Art. 78, Rn. 4; *Kröll u. a./Gotanda*, Art. 78, Rn. 9 f.; MünchKomm/*P. Huber*, Art. 78, Rn. 4; MünchKommHGB/*Ferrari*, Art. 78, Rn. 4; *Thiele*, 2 VJ (1998), 3 ff. sub II B.

unterscheiden sind Fälle, in denen die Anspruchshöhe zeitlichen Veränderungen unterliegt; s. dazu unten Rn. 15.

11 Im Einzelfall kann sich allerdings das praktische Problem stellen, dass der Schuldner schon deshalb nicht zahlen kann, weil er die **Höhe** des Anspruchs **nicht kennt** und ohne Mitwirkung des Gläubigers auch nicht in Erfahrung bringen kann. Sofern der Anspruch auf einer Vertragsverletzung des Schuldners beruht, sollten daraus keine Konsequenzen gezogen werden, denn auch die Unsicherheit über die Höhe der Forderung ist ja letztlich eine Folge des vertragswidrigen Verhaltens des Schuldners.

12 Entsprechende Unsicherheiten können aber auch ohne Vertragsverletzung des Schuldners entstehen, z. B. bei Ansprüchen auf Aufwendungsersatz oder auch beim Kaufpreisanspruch, wenn dessen Höhe von der – zunächst nicht genau festgelegten – Liefermenge abhängt. Wegen der fehlenden Entlastungsmöglichkeit nach Art. 79 mag es zwar auch hier vertretbar erscheinen, die Zinspflicht allein an die Entstehung des Anspruchs anzuknüpfen.[13] Dies könnte den Gläubiger aber zu einer Verzögerungstaktik verleiten, insbesondere wenn die nach Art. 78 zu zahlenden Zinsen eine für ihn lukrative Höhe erreichen. Man wird deshalb annehmen müssen, dass die Ansprüche stillschweigend so lange gestundet sind, bis der Gläubiger sie – beispielsweise in einer **Rechnung** – beziffert hat.[14] Macht der Gläubiger einen zu hohen Betrag geltend, sollte dies dem Beginn des Zinslaufs nicht entgegenstehen, denn der Schuldner hat die Möglichkeit, den aus seiner Sicht geschuldeten Betrag vorab zu zahlen; zahlt er zu wenig, fällt dies in seinen Risikobereich.[15]

13 d) **Minderung.** Im Falle der **Minderung** soll der Rückzahlungsanspruch des Käufers entsprechend dem Gedanken des Art. 84 I schon von dem Zeitpunkt an zu verzinsen sein, zu dem der Kaufpreis gezahlt worden ist.[16] Das leuchtet ein, erschiene es doch wenig sinnvoll, den Fall der vollständigen Rückzahlung des Kaufpreises anders zu behandeln als denjenigen der teilweisen Rückzahlung.

14 e) **Schadenersatz.** Bei Ansprüchen auf **Schadenersatz** ist nach dem hier vertretenen Ansatz grundsätzlich der Zeitpunkt maßgeblich, zu dem der zu ersetzende Schaden eingetreten ist, unabhängig davon, ob die genaue Höhe des Anspruchs schon feststeht oder nicht.

15 Etwas anderes gilt hingegen, wenn sich die Bewertung einzelner Schadensfolgen im Laufe der Zeit ändert, beispielsweise durch **Wertschwankungen.** Zinsen können dann nur von dem Zeitpunkt an verlangt werden, der der Wertberechnung zu Grunde liegt. Besteht der Schaden beispielsweise darin, dass die am 1. Februar gelieferte Kaufsache nicht den vertraglichen Anforderungen entspricht und deshalb statt 1000 nur noch 800 wert ist, und sinkt der Wert der gelieferten Sache am 1. März infolge von Marktschwankungen auf 700, kann der Gläubiger auf den Schadenersatzbetrag von 300 Zinsen erst ab März verlangen. Ihm darüber hinaus auch Zinsen (aus einem Betrag von 200) für Februar zuzusprechen, erschiene hingegen überzogen.[17]

Der Bewertungsstichtag im hier verstandenen Sinne darf allerdings nicht verwechselt werden mit dem Zeitpunkt, der für die Bestimmung des Schadensumfangs maßgeblich ist. Der Umfang der zu ersetzenden Schäden bestimmt sich grundsätzlich nach dem Tag, der allgemein für die Urteilsfällung maßgeblich ist.[18] Für die Bewertung dieser Schäden kann ein anderer Tag maßgeblich sein.

---

[13] So *Witz/Salger/Lorenz/Witz*, Art. 78, Rn. 5.
[14] Wie hier MünchKomm/*P. Huber*, Art. 78, Rn. 10; ähnlich *Soergel/Lüderitz/Dettmeier*, Art. 78, Rn. 3: „Sicherlich muss die Forderung mindestens beziffert geltend gemacht werden."
[15] Ebenso MünchKomm/*P. Huber*, Art. 78, Rn. 11; zur anderweitigen Rechtsprechung zum (internen) spanischen Recht s. *Grube*, RIW 1992, 634 f.
[16] So *Müller-Chen*, Art. 50 Rn. 16; *Heuzé*, Anm. 448.; *Enderlein/Maskow/Strohbach*, Art. 78, Anm. 4.3.; *Bamberger/Roth/Saenger*, Art. 78, Rn. 3; *Ferrari u. a./Ferrari*, Internationales Vertragsrecht, Art. 78, Rn. 9; MünchKomm/*P. Huber*, Art. 78, Rn. 9; MünchKommHGB/*Ferrari*, Art. 78, Rn. 9.
[17] Ebenso *Heuzé*, Anm. 448. a. E. Ähnliche Regelungen enthalten im deutschen Recht § 290 BGB (für Ansprüche aus Verzug) und § 849 BGB (für Ansprüche aus Delikt). In der 3. Aufl. dieses Kommentars war eine ergänzende Zinspflicht für den Zwischenzeitraum noch als denkbar angesehen worden.
[18] *Schwenzer*, Art. 74 Rn. 44.

Bei der Schadensberechnung nach Art. 75 sollte der Zinsanspruch aus Art. 78 konsequenterweise zu dem Zeitpunkt entstehen, in welchem das Deckungsgeschäft vorgenommen wird.[19] Bei der abstrakten Schadensberechnung nach Art. 76 sollten die dafür maßgeblichen Zeitpunkte – entweder derjenige der Vertragsaufhebung oder derjenige der Übernahme – auch für den Beginn der Zinspflicht maßgeblich sein.

2. Keine weiteren Voraussetzungen

Weitere Voraussetzungen nennt Art. 78 nicht. Aus diesem Schweigen des Gesetzes darf nicht etwa der Schluss gezogen werden, das Entstehen des Zinsanspruchs richte sich im Übrigen nach nationalem Recht. Vielmehr kommt darin zum Ausdruck, dass es grundsätzlich keiner weiteren Voraussetzungen als Fälligkeit und Nichtleistung bedarf.[20] Insbesondere ist nicht erforderlich, dass dem Gläubiger ein Schaden entsteht. Auch eine Entlastung nach Art. 79 ist dem Schuldner verwehrt.[21] Der Schuldner muss also z. B. auch dann nach Art. 78 Zinsen bezahlen, wenn er seine Leistung wegen einer Devisensperre nicht rechtzeitig erbringen konnte.[22] Schließlich bedarf es auch keiner vorherigen Mahnung durch den Gläubiger.[23] Für den Kaufpreisanspruch ergibt sich dies unmittelbar aus Art. 59, für andere Ansprüche muss der Gedanke dieser Vorschrift entsprechend herangezogen werden. Entsprechend dem Gedanken des Art. 80 besteht hingegen keine Zinspflicht, wenn die Nichterfüllung durch den Gläubiger verursacht wurde;[24] wegen der Voraussetzungen im Einzelnen vgl. die Kommentierung zu Art. 80.

Nach einer abweichenden Ansicht soll die Zinspflicht bei anderen Ansprüchen als demjenigen auf Zahlung des Kaufpreises erst dann einsetzen, wenn der Gläubiger seinen Anspruch gegenüber dem Schuldner **quantifiziert geltend gemacht** hat.[25] Ein derartiger Grundsatz lässt sich dem CISG indes nicht entnehmen. Der Wortlaut des Art. 78 und auch Art. 59 legen vielmehr nahe, dass es einer besonderen Geltendmachung des Anspruchs grundsätzlich **nicht** bedarf. Die Zinspflicht beginnt deshalb regelmäßig mit der Entstehung des Anspruchs. Für Ansprüche, deren Höhe dem Schuldner nicht bekannt ist, s. aber Rn. 11 f.

3. Gegenrechte des Schuldners

Unangemessen erscheint die Zinspflicht, soweit der Schuldner seinerseits gegen den Gläubiger einen fälligen Gegenanspruch hat.

---

[19] Ebenso *Witz/Salger/Lorenz/Witz*, Art. 78, Rn. 4.
[20] S. dazu nur *Bianca/Bonell/Nicholas*, Art. 78, Anm. 2.1. Ebenso zu Art. 83 EKG: HR, NJ 1992 Nr. 110; der Generalanwalt hat in diesem Verfahren ausdrücklich die Ansicht vertreten, dass auch zu CISG nichts anderes gelten könne.
[21] S. hierzu *Schlechtriem*, Internationales UN-Kaufrecht, Rn. 319; *Stoll*, Internationalprivatrechtliche Fragen, S. 509 f.; *ders.*, Schadensersatzpflicht, S. 279; *Achilles*, Art. 78, Rn. 3; *Brunner*, Art. 78, Rn. 2; *Enderlein/Maskow/Strohbach*, Art. 78, Anm. 2.1.; *Ferrari u. a./Ferrari*, Internationales Vertragsrecht, Art. 78, Rn. 12; *Kröll u. a./Gotanda*, Art. 78, Rn. 4; MünchKomm/*P. Huber*, Art. 78, Rn. 7; *Neumayer/Ming*, Art. 78, Anm. 1. f.; *Heuzé*, Anm. 448.; *Soergel/Lüderitz/Dettmeier*, Art. 78, Rn. 5; *Staudinger/Magnus*, Art. 78, Rn. 11; *Witz/Salger/Lorenz/Witz*, Art. 78, Rn. 4; AG Willisau, 12.3.2004, CISG-online 961.
[22] *Schlechtriem*, Einheitliches UN-Kaufrecht, S. 94.
[23] Beispiele aus der Rechtsprechung: OLG Köln, 3.4.2006, CISG-online 1218; Kantonsgericht Wallis, 27.5.2005, CISG-online 1137; KG Appenzell Ausserrhoden, 9.3.2006, CISG-online 1375; Tribunale di Padova, 31.3.2004, CISG-online 823; Rechtbank van Koophandel Hasselt, 20.9.2005, CISG-online 1496. Anders (ohne nähere Begründung) Turku Court of Appeal, 12.4.2002, CISG-online 660 und Audiencia Provincial de Valencia, 8.4.2008, CISG-online 2083: Der Beginn der Zinszahlungspflicht soll sich nach dem Vertragsstatut richten (nach finnischem Recht einen Monat nach Zahlungsaufforderung, nach spanischem Recht einen Tag nach dem vertraglich festgelegten Fälligkeitsdatum).
[24] MünchKomm/*P. Huber*, Art. 78, Rn. 7; *Enderlein/Maskow/Strohbach*, Art. 78, Anm. 2.1.; *Soergel/Lüderitz/Dettmeier*, Art. 78, Rn. 5.
[25] So *Enderlein/Maskow/Strohbach*, Art. 78, Anm. 4.2.; vgl. auch *Achilles*, Art. 78, Rn. 3; wie hier *Bamberger/Roth/Saenger*, Art. 78, Rn. 3; MünchKomm/*P. Huber*, Art. 78, Rn. 7; CIETAC, 31.12.1999, CISG-online 1805.

20 **a) Zahlungsansprüche.** Ist der **Gegenanspruch** ebenfalls auf **Zahlung** gerichtet, wird der Schuldner meist die Möglichkeit zur Aufrechnung haben. Folgt man der Ansicht, wonach sich Zulässigkeit und Wirkung einer Aufrechnung grundsätzlich nicht nach dem CISG, sondern nach dem ergänzend anwendbaren nationalen Recht richten,[26] so wäre der oben aufgestellte Grundsatz, dass sich die Zinspflicht dem Grunde ausschließlich nach den Regeln des CISG selbst bestimmt, an entscheidender Stelle durchbrochen. Zumindest soweit es um Ansprüche aus demselben Vertrag geht, sollte die Zinspflicht unabhängig von der Frage einer Aufrechnungsbefugnis oder eines Zurückbehaltungsrechts schon dann wegfallen, wenn (und soweit) sich zwei fällige Zahlungsansprüche gegenüberstehen.[27]

21 **b) Andere Gegenansprüche.** Hat der Schuldner einen andersartigen Gegenanspruch, wird sich mitunter schon aus dem CISG selbst ein **Zurückbehaltungsrecht** ergeben, etwa aus Art. 71 I oder aus Art. 81 II 2 oder auch in vorsichtiger Anlehnung an diese Vorschriften. Sofern dem Schuldner ein Zurückbehaltungsrecht zusteht, fehlt es an der Fälligkeit des Zahlungsanspruchs,[28] so dass Zinsen schon aus diesem Grund nicht geschuldet sind. Es stellt sich allenfalls die Frage, ob schon das bloße Bestehen des Zurückbehaltungsrechts ausreicht oder ob die Zinszahlungspflicht erst wegfällt, wenn es vom Schuldner geltend gemacht wird. Auch hier sollte grundsätzlich schon das Bestehen des Gegenanspruchs ausreichen. Anders ist es freilich, wenn der Gläubiger das Zurückbehaltungsrecht durch die Stellung von Sicherheiten abwenden kann; hier wird man die Ausübung des Zurückbehaltungsrechts durch den Schuldner verlangen müssen, damit der Gläubiger Gelegenheit hat, die Sicherheiten zu erbringen.[29]

4. Wegfall des Anspruchs

22 Erlischt der Hauptanspruch durch **Erfüllung** oder aus anderen Gründen, fällt auch die Pflicht zur Zahlung von Zinsen für die Zukunft weg.[30] In bestimmten Fällen kann darüber hinaus auch ein bereits entstandener Zinsanspruch wegfallen.

23 **a) Aufhebung des Vertrages.** Erlischt der bereits fällig gewesene Kaufpreisanspruch wegen **Vertragsaufhebung** (Art. 49), kann der Verkäufer auch für den Zeitraum zwischen Fälligkeit und Wirksamwerden der Aufhebungserklärung keine Zinsen mehr verlangen.[31] Hätte der Käufer den Kaufpreis rechtzeitig bezahlt, müsste nämlich der Verkäufer diesen seinerseits nach Art. 84 I vom Zeitpunkt der Zahlung an verzinsen.

24 **b) Minderung.** Im Falle der **Minderung** kann nichts anderes gelten, denn auch hier müsste der Verkäufer einen nicht geschuldeten Teil des Kaufpreises ggf. vom Zeitpunkt der Zahlung an verzinsen.

V. Modalitäten der Zahlungspflicht

25 Die näheren Einzelheiten der Zinszahlungspflicht, insbesondere **Zahlungsort** und geschuldete **Währung,** sind in Art. 78 **nicht** ausdrücklich geregelt. Auch insoweit erscheint ein Rückgriff auf nationales Recht indes unzulässig. Da der Zinsanspruch lediglich ein Anhängsel zur zu verzinsenden Hauptforderung darstellt, muss hinsichtlich Zahlungsort und

---

[26] So *Piltz,* Internationales Kaufrecht, Rn. 2–164; OLG Koblenz, 17.9.1993, CISG-online 91. Für eine im Wege der Lückenfüllung aus dem CISG selbst abgeleitete Aufrechnungsbefugnis im Falle der Rückabwicklung *Fountoulakis,* Art. 81 Rn. 21.
[27] Ebenso *Honnold/Flechtner,* Art. 78, Rn. 422 für den Beispielsfall, dass die noch nicht bezahlte Kaufsache einen Schaden verursacht hat.
[28] S. zum Zurückbehaltungsrecht nach Art. 71 I *Fountoulakis,* Art. 71 Rn. 10.
[29] Ebenso MünchKomm/*P. Huber,* Art. 78, Rn. 11; zur entsprechenden Unterscheidung im deutschen Recht BGH, 16.3.1973, BGHZ 60, 319, 323.
[30] Ebenso MünchKomm/*P. Huber,* Art. 78, Rn. 6.
[31] Ebenso *Piltz,* Internationales Kaufrecht, 1. Aufl., § 5, Rn. 410; CIETAC, 22.8.2005, CISG-online 1711.

Währung sowie sonstiger Zahlungsmodalitäten dasselbe gelten wie für die **Hauptforderung**.³²

VI. Zinshöhe

Die Zinshöhe ist in Art. 78 nicht festgelegt worden. Zu den Gründen hierfür s. bereits 26
Rn. 2. Die Art und Weise, wie diese Lücke geschlossen werden soll, ist umstritten.³³

1. Rückgriff auf nationales Recht oder Einheitslösung

Eine verbreitete Ansicht will die Lücke durch Rückgriff auf allgemeine Grundsätze des 27
CISG schließen und auf diese Weise doch eine international einheitliche Regelung erreichen.³⁴ Nach der – wohl überwiegenden – Gegenauffassung soll die Zinshöhe dagegen dem ergänzend anwendbaren nationalen Recht zu entnehmen sein, das wiederum nach Maßgabe der Kollisionsregeln des Forumstaats zu ermitteln ist.³⁵

---

³² Ebenso *Piltz*, Internationales Kaufrecht, Rn. 5–494; MünchKomm/*P. Huber*, Art. 78, Rn. 17.
³³ Umfassend zum Meinungsstand in Rechtsprechung und Literatur z. B. *Behr*, J. L. & Com. 17 (1998), 264 ff. und *Ferrari*, Int'l Bus. L. J. 1999, 86 ff.; *de Lukowicz, S.* 129 ff.; *Chengwei*, Nordic J. Comm. L. 2003, S. 22 ff. Eine umfassende Rechtsprechungsübersicht (Stand: Juli 2004) mit Auszügen aus allen zitierten Entscheidungen findet sich bei *Mazzotta*, http://www.cisg.law.pace.edu/cisg/biblio/mazzotta78.html (zuletzt besucht im Oktober 2012).
³⁴ *Honnold/Flechtner*, Art. 78, Rn. 420 mit Fn. 5; *Kröll u. a./Gotanda*, Art. 78, Rn. 27; *Neumayer/Ming*, Art. 78, Anm. 2.; *Neumayer*, RIW 1994, 99, 106; *Heuzé*, Anm. 449.; *Audit*, Vente internationale, S. 171; *Piltz*, Internationales Kaufrecht, Rn. 2–160; *Colligan*, 6 VJ (2002), 40, 55; *Zoccolillo*, 1 VJ (1997), 3, 43; *Thiele*, 2 VJ (1998), 3 ff. sub IV C 2. Auch die schiedsgerichtliche Praxis sieht bei der Festlegung der Zinsen häufig von einer Heranziehung kollisionsrechtlicher Vorschriften ab, vgl. dazu ICC, 1.1.1993, 6653/1993, CISG-online 71 = J. D. I. 1993, 1040, 1046 und dazu die Anmerkung von *J.-J. A.*, aaO., 1047, 1052.
³⁵ So *Behr*, J. L. & Com. 17 (1998), 264, 296 f.; *Achilles*, Art. 78, Rn. 5; *Bianca/Bonell/Nicholas*, Art. 78, Anm. 2.1.; *Enderlein/Maskow/Strohbach*, Art. 78, Anm. 2.2.; *Ferrari u. a./Ferrari*, Internationales Vertragsrecht, Art. 78, Rn. 18; *Herber/Czerwenka*, Art. 78, Rn. 6; *Karollus*, S. 227; *Kindler*, RIW 1991, 304, 305; *Magnus*, RabelsZ 53 (1989), 116, 140; MünchKomm/*P. Huber*, Art. 78, Rn. 15; MünchKommHGB/*Ferrari*, Art. 78, Rn. 18; *Piltz*, Internationales Kaufrecht, 1. Aufl., § 5, Rn. 412; *Reinhart*, IPRax 1991, 376, 377 f.; *Roßmeier*, RIW 2000, 407, 414; *Schlechtriem*, Internationales UN-Kaufrecht, Rn. 318; *ders.*, Uniform Sales Law, S. 100; *Soergel/Lüderitz/Dettmeier*, Art. 78, Rn. 8; *Staudinger/Magnus*, Art. 78, Rn. 12; *Stoll*, Internationalprivatrechtliche Fragen, S. 510; *Weber*, Vertragsverletzungsfolgen, S. 208. Aus der Rechtsprechung: OLG Düsseldorf, 10.2.1994, CISG-online 115; 22.7.2004, CISG-online 916; OLG Dresden, 23.10.2000, CISG-online 1935; OLG Frankfurt a. M., 24.3.2009, CISG-online 2165; OLG Karlsruhe, 20.7.2004, CISG-online 858; OLG Koblenz, 31.1.1997, CISG-online 256; 19.10.2006, CISG-online 1407; OLG Köln, 13.11.2000, CISG-online 657 = OLG-Rp. Köln 2001, 155; 3.4.2006, CISG-online 1218; OLG München, 11.3.1998, CISG-online 310; OLG Rostock, 27.7.1995, CISG-online 209; OLG Saarbrücken, 12.5.2010, CISG-online 2155; OLG Schleswig, 22.8.2002, CISG-online 710; OLG Stuttgart, 20.12.2004, CISG-online 997; BGer, 28.10.1998, CISG-online 413; CA Grenoble, 28.11.2002, CISG-online 787; CA Milano, 12.10.1998, CISG-online 430; Tribunale di Padova, 31.3.2004, CISG-online 823; *Chicago Prime Packers, Inc. v. Northam Food Trading Co.*, U. S. Dist. Ct. (N. D. Ill.), 21.5.2004, CISG-online 851 (anders noch *Zapata Hermanos Sucesores, S. a. v. Hearthside Baking Company, Inc. d/b/a Maurice Lenell Cooky Company*, U. S. Dist. Ct. (N. D. Ill.), 18.7.2001, CISG-online 599); *Treibacher Industrie, A. G. v. TDY Industries, Inc.*, U. S. Dist. Ct. (N. D. of Alabama), 27.4.2005, CISG-online 1178; *Guang Dong Light Headgear Factory Co., Ltd. v. ACI Intern., Inc.*, U. S. Dist. Ct. (Kansas), 28.4.2008, CISG-online 1682; *Norfolk Southern Railway Company v. Power Source Supply, Inc.*, U. S. Dist. Ct. (W. D. of Pennsylvania), 25.7.2008, CISG-online 1776; *San Lucio, S. r.l et al v. Import & Storage Services, LLC et al*, U. S. Dist. Ct. (New Jersey), 15.4.2009, CISG-online 1836; Hof van Beroep Antwerpen, 24.4.2006, CISG-online 1258; Hof van Beroep Gent, 11.10.2004, CISG-online 984; Gerechtshof 's-Hertogenbosch, 2.1.2007, CISG-online 1434; RB Rotterdam, 17.3.2010, CISG-online 2098; RB Breda, 16.1.2009, CISG-online 1789; Turku Court of Appeal, 12.4.2002, CISG-online 660; First Intermediate People's Court of Shanghai, 23.3.2004, CISG-online 1497; Krajský súd Zilina (Slowakische Republik), 29.3.2004, CISG-online 1857; Krajský súd Nitra (Slowakische Republik), 27.6.2006, CISG-online 1861; Szegedi Ítélőtábla (OLG Szegedin), 22.11.2007, CISG-online 1937. Aus der schiedsrichterlichen Praxis: ICC, 7153/1992, CISG-online 35 = J. D. I. 1992, 1005, 1007; ICC, 20.12.1999, CISG-online 1646; ICAC, 30.12.2003, CISG-online 1284; Tribunal of International Commercial Arbitration at the Russian Federation Chamber of Commerce and Industry, 9.6.2004, CISG-online 1239; Schiedsgericht der Hamburger freundlichen Arbitrage, 29.12.1998, CISG-online 638; Jugoslawische Handelskammer, 9.12.2002, CISG-online 2123; Russische Industrie- und Handelskammer, 29.12.2006, CISG-online 1945; Serbische Handelskammer, 5.1.2007, CISG-online 2233.

28 a) Probleme einer Einheitslösung. Unter dem Aspekt der Rechtsvereinheitlichung erscheint eine Lösung im erstgenannten Sinne durchaus wünschenswert. Dass auf der Wiener Konferenz über die Zinshöhe keine Einigung erzielt werden konnte, steht diesem Ansatz nicht zwingend im Wege, denn der schließlich verabschiedeten Fassung des Art. 78 lässt sich auch nicht entnehmen, dass die Bestimmung der Zinshöhe unter allen Umständen dem nationalen Recht überlassen bleiben sollte. Zudem befürworten auch einige Vertreter der zuletzt genannten Auffassung im Zusammenhang mit Art. 84 I eine einheitliche **Lückenfüllung** auf Grundlage des Übereinkommens, obwohl die Konferenz auch dort keine Einigung erzielen konnte.[36] Die entscheidende Schwierigkeit besteht jedoch darin, ein einheitliches Kriterium zu finden, das für alle Vertragsstaaten akzeptabel ist. Wenn die Konferenz diese Aufgabe nicht lösen konnte, ist gegenüber Lösungsvorschlägen aus Wissenschaft und Praxis besondere Vorsicht angebracht.

29 In der Sache besteht denn auch unter den Befürwortern einer einheitlichen Lösung Streit darüber, welcher Zinssatz maßgeblich sein soll. Zum Teil wird vorgeschlagen, den Zinssatz nach dem **Schaden** zu bemessen, der dem Gläubiger infolge der Nichtzahlung entstanden ist.[37] Andere sehen den Sinn des Art. 78 dagegen im **Ausgleich** zu Unrecht erlangter **Vorteile** und wollen die Zinsen deshalb nach der üblichen Höhe am Ort der Niederlassung des Schuldners bemessen.[38] Eine vermittelnde Auffassung will danach differenzieren, ob der Gläubiger infolge der Zahlungsverzögerung Kredit aufnehmen musste oder nicht.[39] Daneben ist auch der Vorschlag gemacht worden, die üblichen Zinsen am **Erfüllungsort**[40] oder einen internationalen Zinssatz wie den **Libor**[41] oder den **Euribor**[42] als Maßstab zu nehmen.[43] Schiedsgerichte umgehen das Problem mitunter, indem sie den Zinssatz nach billigem Ermessen festlegen.[44] Dieser Streit ist letztlich die Fortsetzung der Auseinandersetzungen auf der Wiener Konferenz, wo ja die unterschiedliche Zinshöhe in verschiedenen Ländern eine zentrale Rolle spielte. Wenn häufig mit dem auf pauschalierten Mindest-

---

[36] Für einen einheitlichen Zinssatz bei Art. 84 I: *Enderlein/Maskow/Strohbach*, Art. 84, Anm. 3. Für einen Rückgriff auf nationales Recht auch in diesem Zusammenhang *Bianca/Bonell/Tallon*, Art. 84, Anm. 2.1.; *Karollus*, S. 153; *Reinhart*, Art. 78, Rn. 3.

[37] *Honnold/Flechtner*, Art. 78, Rn. 421. Im Falle des Art. 84 I soll dagegen zu unterscheiden sein: Beruhe die Rückzahlungspflicht auf einer Vertragsverletzung des Verkäufers, so solle es bei der zu Art. 78 gefundenen Lösung sein Bewenden haben; anderenfalls seien die Vorteile maßgeblich, die dem Schuldner infolge der Nichtleistung entstanden sind (aaO. Rn. 451.2).

[38] *Bamberger/Roth/Saenger*, Art. 78, Rn. 5; *Neumayer/Ming*, Art. 78, Anm. 2.; *Neumayer*, RIW 1994, 99, 106; *Heuzé*, Anm. 449.; *Witz/Salger/Lorenz/Witz*, Art. 78, Rn. 9 a. E.; LG Berlin, 21.3.2003, CISG-online 785; Krajsky Súd Bratislava, 1.2.2007, CISG-online 1758; zu Art. 84 I auch *Fountoulakis*, Art. 84 Rn. 17.

[39] So *Thiele*, 2 VJ (1998), 3 ff. sub IV C 3c.

[40] So *Corterier*, 5 Int'l Trade & Bus. L. Ann. (2000), 33, 40 f.; *ders.*, ccisg.org, Art. 78 Rn. 26 ff. in Analogie zu Art. 76; ferner Wuhan Intermediate People's Court of Hubei Province, 11.5.2004, CISG-online 1499; Krajský súd Bratislava, 15.12.2005, CISG-online 1754; Jugoslawische Handelskammer, 28.1.2009, CISG-online 1856.

[41] London Interbank Offered Rate: Ein Referenzzinssatz, zu dem internationale Großbanken Geldmarktgeschäfte in London abschließen. Er wird täglich neu festgesetzt (http://www.bbalibor.com, zuletzt besucht im Oktober 2012).

[42] Euro Interbank Offered Rate: Ein Referenzzinssatz, der täglich auf der Basis der Zinssätze von Geschäftsbanken aus Ländern der Eurozone festgesetzt wird (http://www.euribor-ebf.eu, zuletzt besucht im Oktober 2012).

[43] *Audit*, Vente internationale, S. 171, der sich freilich für keine der hier aufgezeigten Möglichkeiten endgültig entschieden hat. Libor und Euribor werden mitunter auch von Gerichten und Schiedsgerichten herangezogen: Shanghai No. 1 Intermediate People's Court China, 19.3.2009, CISG-online 2060 (Libor); ICC, 1.1.1993, 6653/1993, CISG-online 71 = J.D.I. 1993, 1040, 1046 (Libor); Russische Industrie- und Handelskammer, 15.11.2006, CISG-online 2008 (Libor, auf der Grundlage des russischen Rechts, das für Fremdwährungsschulden den Rückgriff auf Marktzinssätze vorsieht); Serbische Handelskammer, 1.10.2007, CISG-online 1793 (Euribor); Serbische Handelskammer, 23.1.2008, CISG-online 1946 (Euribor).

[44] Jugoslawische Handelskammer, 24.9.2001, CISG-online 1854; CIETAC, 29.9.2004, CISG-online 1600; CIETAC, 12.8.2005, CISG-online 1709; CIETAC, 1.11.2006, CISG-online 1925; Schiedsgericht der Handelskammer Stockholm, 5.4.2007, CISG-online 1521; kritisch dazu und für die Anwendung von Marktzinssätzen wie dem Libor *Secomb*, FS Bergsten, S. 431, 439 ff. Umfassend und kritisch zur schiedsgerichtlichen Praxis *Gotanda*, 90 Am. J. Int'l L. (1996), S. 40 ff.

Schadenersatz oder aber auf Vorteilsausgleichung gerichteten Zweck des Art. 78 argumentiert wird, führt dies wenig weiter, da sich dem auch insoweit wenig aufschlussreichen Wortlaut des Art. 78 sowohl die eine als auch die andere Zielsetzung entnehmen lässt.[45] Deshalb vermag auch der Vorschlag, für die Zinshöhe in analoger Anwendung von Art. 76 an den Erfüllungsort anzuknüpfen[46], nicht zu überzeugen; er impliziert, dass Art. 78 auf Schadensausgleich abzielt, und unterliegt deshalb denselben Vorbehalten wie jede andere auf dieser Prämisse beruhende Argumentation. Auch das zuweilen für den Gedanken des Vorteilsausgleichs und für eine daraus abgeleitete Anknüpfung an den Niederlassungsort des Schuldners vorgebrachte Argument, Art. 78 solle eine Verzögerungstaktik des Schuldners verhindern, spricht nicht entscheidend für eine Lösung, denn dieser Zweck lässt sich durchaus auch mit einem Schadenersatzanspruch erreichen.[47]

Im Übrigen erscheint es sowohl bei einer Deutung als Mindest-Schadenersatz als auch bei einer Deutung als Vorteilsausgleich bzw. abzuschöpfende Bereicherung wenig sachgerecht, einfach an den Niederlassungsort des Gläubigers bzw. Schuldners oder an den Erfüllungsort anzuknüpfen, solange die Möglichkeit besteht, auch anderenorts Kapital anzulegen bzw. einen Kredit aufzunehmen. Zwar bedarf es im Rahmen des Art. 78 notwendigerweise einer gewissen Pauschalierung. Als am besten geeigneter Maßstab erscheinen dabei aber weder der Ort, an dem die Parteien ihre Niederlassung haben, noch der Ort, an dem die Verpflichtung zu erfüllen ist. Entscheidend erscheint vielmehr, dass die Höhe der üblichen Zinsen in aller Regel von der Währung, insbesondere von der jeweiligen **Inflationsrate** abhängt. Auch die Höhe des oben erwähnten Libor hängt von der Währung ab. Wenn man eine einheitliche Lösung sucht, sollte deshalb nicht an örtliche Gegebenheiten angeknüpft werden, sondern an die **Währung,** in welcher die zu verzinsende Hauptforderung zu erfüllen ist.[48] Wenn die Hauptforderung in einer Währung mit hoher Inflationsrate zu erbringen ist, gebührt dem Gläubiger bei verzögerter Zahlung sowohl unter dem Gesichtspunkt des Schadenersatzes als auch unter demjenigen des Vorteilsausgleichs ein eher hoher Zinssatz. Ist die Zahlung dagegen in einer „harten" Währung zu erbringen, wäre es unangebracht, dem Gläubiger daneben noch exorbitant hohe Zinsen zuzugestehen. Die ausschließliche Anknüpfung der Zinshöhe an einen bestimmten Ort kann diesem Zusammenhang nicht gerecht werden.[49] Die Anknüpfung an die Währung ist dafür weit besser geeignet.

Bei der danach verbleibenden Frage, welcher der im Währungsstaat geltenden Zinssätze maßgeblich sein soll, dürfen die näheren Umstände des Einzelfalles kaum Berücksichtigung finden, da es in Art. 78 ja darum geht, unabhängig von einem konkreten Schaden des Gläubigers (oder einer konkreten Bereicherung des Schuldners!) einen pauschalierten Ausgleich zu gewähren. Für diese Zwecke erscheint ein von der Notenbank festgesetzter **„Leitzins",** in den USA beispielsweise die „prime rate", am besten geeignet.[50] Dass auch

---

[45] Ebenso MünchKomm/*P. Huber,* Art. 78, Rn. 2.
[46] So *Corterier,* 5 Int'l Trade & Bus. L. Ann. (2000), 33, 40 f.; *ders.,* ccisg.org, Art. 78, Rn. 26 ff.
[47] Vgl. dazu auch *Honnold/Flechtner,* Art. 78, Rn. 420, nach dessen Ansicht Art. 78 sowohl den Gläubiger entschädigen als auch den Schuldner zur rechtzeitigen Zahlung anhalten soll.
[48] So auch *Piltz,* Internationales Kaufrecht, Rn. 2–160 und Rn. 5–495, sowie – im Zusammenhang mit kollisionsrechtlichen Erwägungen – *Basedow,* in: *Schlechtriem,* Einheitliches Kaufrecht und nationales Obligationenrecht, S. 288 f.; *Enderlein/Maskow/Strohbach,* Art. 78, Anm. 2.2.; *Schlechtriem,* RIW 1995, 592, 593 f.; Arb. Ct. Hungarian CCI, 5.12.1995, CISG-online 163, Umdruck S. 18 (insoweit nicht in NJW-RR 1996, 1145 f.); Rechtbank van Koophandel Ieper, 18.2.2002, CISG-online 747; Jugoslawische Handelskammer, 12.4.2002, CISG-online 1855; zweifelnd im Zusammenhang mit Art. 84 *Fountoulakis,* Art. 84 Rn. 18.
[49] Schon zu Art. 83 EKG, der die Zinsen ausdrücklich an den Diskontsatz am Niederlassungsort des Gläubigers band, haben verschiedene Gerichte entschieden, dass dies zu unbilligen Ergebnissen führe, wenn der Kaufpreis in einer anderen, „härteren" Währung zu zahlen sei. Zur Berechnung der Zinsen wurde der Kaufpreis deshalb zunächst in die Landeswährung des Verkäufers umgerechnet (OLG Düsseldorf, 27.11.1980, WM 1981, 1237 f. = *Schlechtriem/Magnus,* Nr. 11 zu Art. 83; dort auch weitere Nachweise, unter Nr. 7 und 20 auch zur Gegenauffassung); entsprechendes schlagen *Soergel/Lüderitz/Dettmeier,* Art. 78, Rn. 9 auch bei Anwendbarkeit von Art. 78 vor.
[50] Ebenso *Piltz,* Internationales Kaufrecht, Rn. 5–498.

dieser Zins nicht unbedingt den tatsächlichen Verhältnissen am Kredit- oder Anlagemarkt entspricht, stellt angesichts der angestrebten Pauschalierung keinen entscheidenden Nachteil dar. Wollte man dagegen auf irgendwelche Marktzinsen abstellen, stellten sich kaum lösbare Anschlussprobleme. So ließe sich kaum entscheiden, ob die Anlage- oder die Kreditzinsen maßgeblich sein sollen, ob auf kurz- oder langfristige Geschäfte abzustellen ist usw.[51] Zu überlegen wäre allenfalls, ob auf den Leitzins noch eine gewisse Marge – etwa 1 oder 2 Prozentpunkte – aufzuschlagen ist, weil die Parteien eines Kaufvertrages typischerweise mehr Zinsen bezahlen müssen als Banken.[52]

Für eine in **Euro** zu erbringende Zahlung erscheint am ehesten der **Hauptrefinanzierungszinssatz** (ggf. ebenfalls mit einem gewissen Aufschlag) geeignet.[53]

31a Die hier favorisierte Lösung kann sich ergänzend auch auf internationale Entwürfe zur Vereinheitlichung des Schuldrechts stützen. Sowohl die **UNIDROIT Principles** (Art. 7.4.9) als auch die **Principles of European Contract Law** (Art. 4:507 I bzw. Art. 9:508 I) erklären den Zinssatz für kurzfristige Kredite an erstklassige Kunden für die vereinbarte Währung am Zahlungsort für maßgeblich. In einigen Entscheidungen sind diese Regelungen als Ausdruck allgemeiner Prinzipien im Sinne von Art. 7 II CISG angesehen[54] oder zumindest dann als Richtschnur für die Ausübung des schiedsrichterlichen Ermessens herangezogen worden, wenn die Vertragsparteien aus Mitgliedstaaten von UNIDROIT stammen[55]. Die Heranziehung dieser Grundsätze als allgemeine Prinzipien im Sinne von Art. 7 II dürfte zwar nicht in Betracht kommen (vgl. *Ferrari*, Art. 7 Rn. 62). Die Konvergenz der verschiedenen Regelungen spricht aber durchaus dafür, auch für den Anwendungsbereich von Art. 78 zu demselben Ergebnis zu gelangen. Ob dies auch gilt, soweit die genannten Regelungen neben der Währung auch an den Zahlungsort anknüpfen, erscheint allerdings zweifelhaft.

31b Selbst wenn die hier vorgeschlagene Lösung abgelehnt wird, kann die Währung, in der die Hauptforderung zu erfüllen ist, von Bedeutung sein. Wenn beispielsweise der Zinssatz am Ort der Niederlassung des Gläubigers oder des Schuldners für maßgeblich erachtet wird und dieser Zinssatz seinerseits von der Währung abhängt, ist selbstverständlich der Zinssatz für diejenige Währung heranzuziehen, in der die Hauptforderung zu erfüllen ist.[56]

32 **b) Schwierigkeiten beim Rückgriff auf nationales Recht.** Greift man angesichts der gegen eine Einheitslösung bestehenden Bedenken auf das nach den Kollisionsregeln maßgebliche nationale Recht zurück, stellen sich in der Sache dieselben Probleme.[57] Zwar wird häufig ein Rückgriff auf das Vertragsstatut vorgeschlagen.[58] Nach europäischem IPR wäre

---

[51] Vgl. dazu *Gotanda*, 37 Georgetown Journal of International Law (2005), 95, 136 f., der den Marktzinssatz für Anlagegeschäfte heranziehen und eine vierteljährliche Zinseszinsberechnung vornehmen will.
[52] Vgl. dazu auch *Zapata Hermanos Sucesores, S. a. v. Hearthside Baking Company, Inc. d/b/a Maurice Lenell Cooky Company*, U. S. Dist. Ct (N. D. Ill.), 18.7.2001, CISG-online 599: Es sei absurd, dem Schuldner Kapital zu den Konditionen eines erstklassigen Kredits zu überlassen.
[53] Ebenso *Piltz*, Internationales Kaufrecht, Rn. 5–498; Serbische Handelskammer, 17.11.2008, CISG-online 2227; RB Hasselt, 10.5.2006, CISG-online 1259; anders (Maßgeblichkeit des Vertragsstatuts) das unmittelbar übergeordnete Gericht: Hof van Beroep Antwerpen, 24.4.2006, CISG-online 1258.
[54] ICC, 8128/1995, CISG-online 526; ICC, 8769/1996, UNILEX; Oberster Gerichtshof für Handelssachen der Republik Weißrussland, 20.5.2003, CISG-online 1352; Internationales Schiedsgericht der Bundeskammer der gewerblichen Wirtschaft in Österreich, 15.6.1994, CISG-online 691; näher dazu *Burkart*, S. 229 ff.; für eine Anlehnung an die genannten Entwürfe auch *Brunner*, Art. 78, Rn. 12; kritisch (de lege lata) *Eiselen*, PICC-Art. 78 CISG, sub g; allgemein zur Bedeutung der UNIDROIT-Principles vgl. *Ferrari*, Art. 7 Rn. 62.
[55] CIETAC, 2.9.2005, CISG-online 1712.
[56] Vgl. Shanghai High People's Court, 30.8.2005, CISG-online 1615: Zinssatz der Bank of China für Dollarforderungen; s. auch ICDR, 12.12.2007, CISG-online 1647: US-Geldmarktsatz (Treasury Bill Rate) wenn das US-Recht anwendbar *und* die Hauptforderung in US-Dollar zu zahlen ist.
[57] Einen detaillierten Überblick über den Meinungsstand gibt *Königer*, S. 57–65.
[58] So *Behr*, J. L. & Com. 17 (1998), 264, 298; *Enderlein/Maskow/Strohbach*, Art. 78, Anm. 2.2.; *Ferrari u. a./ Ferrari*, Internationales Vertragsrecht, Art. 78, Rn. 19; *Herber/Czerwenka*, Art. 78, Rn. 6; *Karollus*, S. 227; *Kindler*, RIW 1991, 304, 305; *Staudinger/Magnus*, Art. 78, Rn. 15. Vgl. auch ICC, 8611/1997, CISG-online 236: Anwendbar sei das Sachstatut, in besonderen Fällen das Währungsstatut.

dies das von den Parteien gewählte Recht (Art. 3 I VO 593/2008 – Rom I), mangels einer Vereinbarung regelmäßig das Recht des Staates, in welchem der Verkäufer seine Niederlassung hat (Art. 4 I Lit. a und Art. 19 I Rom I). In der **Rechtsprechung** der deutschen Instanzgerichte hat sich diese Auffassung inzwischen weitgehend durchgesetzt.[59] In der deutschen Literatur wird stattdessen aber auch eine Sonderanknüpfung an den Niederlassungsort des Schuldners,[60] den Niederlassungsort des Gläubigers[61] oder aber an die Währung, in der die Hauptforderung zu erfüllen ist,[62] vertreten. Daneben findet sich der Vorschlag, bei Verträgen, die dem CISG oder anderem internationalem Einheitsrecht unterliegen, anders anzuknüpfen als bei Verträgen, für die es kein solches Einheitsrecht gibt.[63] In einem Schiedsspruch der ICC ist das Recht des Erfüllungsorts[64] als maßgeblich angesehen worden. In den USA wurde das maßgebliche Recht in einer Entscheidung nach Maßgabe der einzelstaatlichen Kollisionsregeln bestimmt.[65] Die wohl überwiegende Auffassung wendet Bundesrecht an, das die Zinshöhe in das Ermessen des Gerichts stellt.[66]

Unter den zahlreichen Vorschlägen erscheint derjenige, an die für die Hauptforderung maßgebliche **Währung** anzuknüpfen, vorzugswürdig. Die oben Rn. 30 im Zusammenhang mit einer Einheitslösung angestellten Erwägungen treffen auch hier zu, denn für die Höhe des gesetzlichen Zinssatzes wird die Inflationsrate ebenfalls häufig eine nicht unbedeutende Rolle spielen. Auch im Falle einer kollisionsrechtlichen Lösung sollte deshalb der Staat maßgeblich sein, in dessen Währung die zu verzinsende Hauptforderung zu bezahlen ist. Wollte man dem nicht folgen, müsste es bei dem für den Vertrag im Allgemeinen maßgeblichen Recht verbleiben.

Schwierigkeiten bereitet die Bestimmung des Währungsstatuts, wenn die Hauptforderung in **Euro** zu erfüllen ist. Hier wird man vorrangig zu prüfen haben, ob der Vertrag sonstige Bezugspunkte zu einem bestimmten Staat der Euro-Zone aufweist. Ist dies nicht der Fall, sollte auf die Mindestsätze der Zahlungsverzug-Richtlinie zurückgegriffen werden.[67]

Eine entscheidende Abweichung gegenüber einer Einheitslösung ergibt sich hinsichtlich der Auswahl zwischen mehreren für ein bestimmtes Land geltenden Zinsen. Beschreitet man den Weg einer kollisionsrechtlichen Anknüpfung, darf nicht auf die im betreffenden Staat „üblichen" Zinsen zurückgegriffen werden. Maßgeblich ist vielmehr die von diesem Staat getroffene **gesetzliche** Regelung der Höhe von Verzugszinsen. Lässt sich eine derartige Vorschrift nicht ermitteln, ist nach funktionell vergleichbaren Regelungen zu suchen. Insbesondere in Ländern mit gesetzlichem **Zinsverbot** ist zu prüfen, ob das Gesetz vergleichbare Vergütungen vorsieht.[68] Erst wenn sich auch danach keine gesetzliche Zinshöhe

---

[59] S. dazu die Nachweise bei Rn. 27 a. E.
[60] *Stoll*, Internationalprivatrechtliche Fragen, S. 510; LG Heidelberg, 2.11.2005, CISG-online 1416.
[61] *Magnus*, RabelsZ 53 (1989), 116, 140 f.
[62] *Grunsky*, FS Merz, S. 147 ff., 151 f.; *Schlechtriem*, RIW 1995, 592, 593 f.; *Himmen*, Lückenfüllung, S. 174 ff.; bis zur 61. Aufl. auch *Palandt/Heldrich*, Art. 32 EGBGB, Rn. 5, der jetzt darauf verweist, dass das Währungsstatut für die Euro-Länder keine Unterscheidungskraft mehr habe. Für einen Rückgriff auf das Währungsstatut (nur) in dem Fall, dass die Heranziehung des Vertragsstatuts zu unbefriedigenden Ergebnissen führt: *Roßmeier*, RIW 2000, 407, 415.
[63] So *Königer*, S. 110–119, 131–136: Im ersten Fall soll das Währungsstatut maßgeblich sein, im anderen Fall das Vertragsstatut.
[64] ICC, 7153/1992, CISG-online 35 = J. D. I. 1992, 1005, 1007; s. dazu auch die Anmerkung von *Hascher*, aaO., S. 1009: Üblicherweise werde das Vertragsstatut, das Recht des Gläubigerlandes oder des Landes, in dessen Währung zu zahlen ist, herangezogen.
[65] *Chicago Prime Packers, Inc. v. Northam Food Trading Co.*, U. S. Dist. Ct. (N. D. Ill.), 21.5.2004, CISG-online 851.
[66] *Norfolk Southern Railway Company v. Power Source Supply, Inc.*, U. S. Dist. Ct (W. D. of Pennsylvania), 25.7.2008, CISG-online 1776 mit weiteren Nachweisen aus der US-Rechtsprechung.
[67] Näher zu dieser Richtlinie s. Rn. 37.
[68] Ebenso *Herber/Czerwenka*, Art. 78, Rn. 7; *Loewe*, Art. 78, S. 95; MünchKommHGB/*Ferrari*, Art. 78, Rn. 20; *Soergel/Lüderitz/Dettmeier*, Art. 78, Rn. 8; *Witz/Salger/Lorenz/Witz*, Art. 78, Rn. 10. Skeptisch *Schlechtriem*, Einheitliches UN-Kaufrecht, S. 94, Fn. 414; *ders.*, Uniform Sales Law, S. 100, Fn. 414: Im Falle eines nationalen Zinsverbots laufe Art. 78 leer. Anders *ders.*, Gemeinsame Bestimmungen, S. 171: Ein Leerlaufen lasse sich wohl nur mit sehr großzügiger Angleichung vermeiden.

ermitteln lässt, kann und sollte ergänzend auf den „üblichen" Zinssatz zurückgegriffen werden, wobei auch hier ein von der Notenbank festgesetzter „Leitzins" für die Zwecke des Art. 78 am besten geeignet erscheint.

35 In jedem Fall lassen sich nur solche nationalen Vorschriften heranziehen, die den Zinssatz unabhängig von den näheren Umständen des Einzelfalles festlegen. Vorschriften, die dem Gläubiger im Falle des Verzugs den Ersatz der von ihm konkret aufgewendeten Kreditkosten zusprechen, werden demgegenüber von den Regeln des CISG über Leistungsstörungen und Schadenersatz verdrängt.[69]

36 **c) Ergebnis.** Betrachtet man alles zusammen, erscheint es vorzugswürdig, eine Antwort auf die aufgeworfenen Sachfragen – die sich nach beiden Lösungsansätzen in gleicher Weise stellen – zunächst auf der Basis des **Einheitsrechts** zu suchen. Auf diese Weise lassen sich zum einen die in Rn. 34 geschilderten Probleme umgehen. Vor allem aber besteht zumindest die Hoffnung, doch noch eine allseits akzeptable Lösung zu finden und die ansonsten drohende Rechtszersplitterung zu vermeiden. Zwar mag die Gefahr bestehen, dass in Staaten, die sich auf der Wiener Konferenz aus grundlegenden Erwägungen heraus gegen eine Festlegung des Zinssatzes gewandt haben, auch der hier vorgeschlagene Weg der Lückenfüllung auf Ablehnung stößt. Dies sollte aber kein Grund sein, nicht zumindest den Versuch zu machen, in Wissenschaft und Praxis nach einer einheitlichen Lösung zu suchen.

2. Einzelne nationale Zinssätze[70]

37 Die Regelung des gesetzlichen Zinssatzes war früher sehr unterschiedlich.[71] In der EU ist für Geschäfte zwischen Unternehmern durch die Richtlinie zur Bekämpfung von Zahlungsverzug im Geschäftsverkehr[72] ein Mindestzinssatz vorgeschrieben, der mindestens acht Prozentpunkte über einem Bezugszinssatz liegen muss.[73] In Umsetzung der Richtlinie wird der Zinssatz bei Geschäften zwischen Unternehmern[74] und zum Teil auch zwischen Verbrauchern[75] an den Basiszinssatz angelehnt. Als Basiszinssatz wird teilweise der Hauptrefinanzierungs-Zinssatz der Europäischen Zentralbank verwendet, zum Teil ein davon abgeleiteter Zinssatz, der von der nationalen Zentralbank bekannt gemacht wird.[76] Auch außerhalb der EU verweist das Gesetz wegen der Zinshöhe zum Teil auf den jeweiligen Diskontsatz, so z. B. in der Schweiz.[77]

---

[69] Anders *Loewe*, Art. 78, S. 95, der solche Vorschriften ggf. als Regeln über den Zinsfuß auffassen will. Dagegen wiederum *Karollus*, S. 227, Fn. 110.

[70] Wegen weiterer Länder vgl. *Schwenzer/Hachem/Kee*, Rn. 46.79 ff.

[71] Einen Überblick über die Zinssätze in verschiedenen Vertragsstaaten geben *Piltz*, Internationales Kaufrecht, Rn. 5–496 und *Bonsau/Feuerriegel*, IPRax 2003, 421, 425.

[72] Richtlinie 2011/7/EU des Europäischen Parlaments und des Rates vom 16. Februar 2011 zur Bekämpfung von Zahlungsverzug im Geschäftsverkehr, AblEU Nr. L 48, S. 1. Diese Richtlinie ist vor dem 13. März 2013 umzusetzen. Zuvor lag der Mindestzinssatz bei sieben Prozentpunkten über dem Bezugszinssatz, vgl. Richtlinie 2000/35/EG des Europäischen Parlaments und des Rates vom 29. Juni 2000 zur Bekämpfung von Zahlungsverzug im Geschäftsverkehr, AblEG Nr. L 200, S. 35.

[73] Die Umsetzung der Richtlinien in den einzelnen Mitgliedsstaaten ist auf folgenden Seiten dokumentiert: RL 2011/7: http://eur-lex.europa.eu/LexUriServ/LexUriServ.do?uri=celex:72011L0007:de:not; RL 2000/35: http://eur-lex.europa.eu/LexUriServ/LexUriServ.do?uri=celex:72000L0035:de:not (zuletzt besucht im Oktober 2012).

[74] Deutschland: 8 Punkte über dem Basiszinssatz für Geschäfte, an denen kein Verbraucher beteiligt ist, § 288 II BGB. Österreich: 8 Punkte über dem Basiszinssatz für Geschäfte zwischen Unternehmern, § 1333 II ABGB. Italien: 7 Punkte über dem Zinssatz der EZB, Art. 4 des Decreto Legislativo n. 231 vom 9.10.2002 (G. U. n. 249).

[75] Deutschland: 5 Punkte über dem Basiszinssatz, § 288 I BGB. Feste Zinssätze bei Verbraucherbeteiligung gibt es dagegen in Österreich: 4%, § 1333 I i. V. m. § 1000 I ABGB.

[76] Letzteres gilt z. B. für Deutschland und Österreich.

[77] Nach Art. 104 I OR beträgt der gesetzliche Zinssatz 5%. Nach Art. 104 III OR kann unter Kaufleuten aber stattdessen der übliche Bankdiskont am Zahlungsort verlangt werden.

3. Handelsbräuche

Nach dem allgemeinen Grundsatz des Art. 9 kann sich die Höhe der geschuldeten Zinsen 38 auch aus einem Handelsbrauch ergeben. Nach Auffassung eines argentinischen Gerichts entspricht es internationalem Handelsbrauch, eine in US-Dollar zu erfüllende Verpflichtung mit dem jeweiligen Satz der „prime rate" zu erfüllen.[78] Dieser Handelsbrauch entspräche dem, was nach der hier vertretenen Auffassung im Wege der Lückenfüllung aus dem Übereinkommen selbst zu entnehmen ist.

4. Vertragliche Regelung der Zinshöhe

Den Parteien steht es selbstverständlich frei, die in den von Art. 78 erfassten Fällen 39 geschuldete Zinshöhe selbst vertraglich zu bestimmen.[79] Scheitern kann eine derartige Vereinbarung allenfalls an nationalen Nichtigkeitsvorschriften. Sieht etwa eine einzelstaatliche Bestimmung aus Gründen des Schuldnerschutzes eine Höchstgrenze für den Zinssatz vor, ist diese Vorschrift nach der auch hier anwendbaren Regel des Art. 4 S. 2 Lit. a) zu beachten.[80] Auch Schiedsgerichte sehen mitunter von der Anwendung einer vertraglichen Vereinbarung über die Zinshöhe ab, wenn diese unangemessen hoch ist.[81] Anderes gilt, wenn für die Vereinbarung eines höheren als des gesetzlichen Zinssatzes eine besondere Form vorgeschrieben wird, wie etwa in Art. 1284 III des italienischen Cc; derartige Formvorschriften sind im Bereich des CISG nach Art. 11 unbeachtlich.[82]

5. Zinseszinsen

Die Frage, ob der Schuldner auch Zinseszinsen zu leisten hat, ist in Art. 78 nicht 40 ausdrücklich geregelt. Dem Schweigen des Übereinkommens wird überwiegend entnommen, dass ein solcher Anspruch **nicht** besteht.[83] Ergänzend ist darauf hingewiesen worden, dass Zinseszinsen im internationalen Kaufrecht nicht üblich seien.[84] Letzteres wird in der neueren Literatur zwar zunehmend in Zweifel gezogen.[85] Dennoch erscheint es mit Wortlaut und Sinn von Art. 78 nur schwer vereinbar, Zinsansprüche ihrerseits einer Verzinsung zu unterwerfen, zumal sich die Anschlussfrage, nach welchem Zeitraum jeweils eine erneute Verzinsung stattfinden soll, auf der Grundlage des Übereinkommens wohl nicht beantworten lässt.

Aus wirtschaftlicher Sicht besteht allerdings ein enger Zusammenhang mit der **Zinshöhe**. 40a Eine Zinseszinsberechnung mit niedrigem Zinssatz kann zu demselben Zinsbetrag führen wie eine einfache Zinsberechnung mit höherem Zinssatz. Sofern die Zinshöhe entsprechend der überwiegenden Auffassung unter Rückgriff auf nationales Recht bestimmt wird, erscheint es deshalb konsequent, dem Gläubiger auch Zinseszinsen zu gewähren, wenn die

---

[78] Juzgado Nacional de 1ª Instancia en lo Comercial Nº 10, Buenos Aires, 23.10.1991, CISG-online 460; gegen die Annahme eines solchen Handelsbrauchs *Behr*, J. L. & Com. 17 (1998), 264, 299.
[79] Vgl. Russische Industrie- und Handelskammer, 7.4.2006, CISG-online 1943.
[80] Ebenso *Lookofsky*, The 1980 United Nations Convention, Rn. 297. Anders dagegen *Enderlein/Maskow/Strohbach*, Art. 78, Anm. 2.2., die Art. 78 gegenüber Art. 4 S. 2 Lit. a) als Sondervorschrift ansehen wollen.
[81] CIETAC, 1.7.2006, CISG-online 1970: Verdoppelung des Ausgangszinssatzes von 5% mit jedem Monat des Verzugs; Jugoslawische Handelskammer, 12.2.2002, CISG-online 2036: 0,1% pro Tag (also 36,5% pro Jahr).
[82] Anders beiläufig das LG Frankfurt a. M., 16.9.1991, CISG-online 26 = RIW 1991, 952, 954.
[83] So *Neumayer/Ming*, Art. 78, Rn. 3; *Achilles*, Art. 78, Rn. 4; *Brunner*, Art. 78, Rn. 1; *Ferrari u. a./Ferrari*, Internationales Vertragsrecht, Art. 78, Rn. 6; MünchKomm/*P. Huber*, Art. 78, Rn. 3; MünchKommHGB/*Ferrari*, Art. 78, Rn. 6; *Staudinger/Magnus*, Art. 78, Rn. 5; *Weber*, Vertragsverletzungsfolgen, S. 208; *Witz/Salger/Lorenz/Witz*, Art. 78, Rn. 11.
[84] So *Enderlein/Maskow/Strohbach*, Art. 78, Anm. 4.5.; ein Überblick über unterschiedliche nationale Regelungen findet sich bei *Schwenzer/Hachem/Kee*, Rn. 46.111 ff.
[85] Vgl. *Gotanda*, 37 Georgetown Journal of International Law (2005), 95, 137 f., der eine Summierung der Zinsen in vierteljährlichem Abstand für international üblich hält und deshalb auch auf der Grundlage von Art. 78 vornehmen will. Ähnlich *Kröll u. a./Gotanda*, Art. 78, Rn. 28.

einschlägige Rechtsordnung dies vorsieht.[86] Wenn die Zinshöhe entsprechend der hier favorisierten Auffassung auf der Grundlage des Übereinkommens einheitlich bestimmt wird, sollte hingegen aus den oben genannten Gründen von einer Zinseszinsberechnung Abstand genommen werden. Den berechtigten Interessen des Gläubigers kann durch einen Zuschlag auf den maßgeblichen Leitzins (vgl. oben Rn. 31) ausreichend Rechnung getragen werden.

40b Für möglich gehalten wurde ein Anspruch auf Zinseszinsen, wenn der Gläubiger für den ausstehenden Betrag einen **Kredit** aufgenommen hat und dafür seinerseits Zinseszinsen zu entrichten hat.[87] Diese Rechtsfolge kann indes allenfalls aus Art. 74 hergeleitet werden, nicht aber aus Art. 78.

VII. Verhältnis zu anderen Ansprüchen

1. Schadenersatzansprüche

41 **Schadenersatzansprüche** können nach dem ausdrücklichen Wortlaut der Vorschrift unabhängig von Art. 78 geltend gemacht werden. Dem Gläubiger steht also der Nachweis offen, dass er wegen der nicht rechtzeitigen Zahlung einen höheren (Zins-)Schaden erlitten hat. Welche Anforderungen dabei an den Nachweis der Kausalität zwischen Nichtzahlung und der Aufnahme eines Krediten zu stellen sind, ob es beispielsweise (wie nach deutschem Recht) ausreicht, wenn der Gläubiger laufend Bankkredit (mindestens) in Höhe der offenen Forderung in Anspruch nimmt, ist im Zusammenhang mit Artt. 74 ff. zu klären.[88] Steht dem Gläubiger danach ein Anspruch auf Ersatz des Zinsschadens zu, konkurriert dieser Anspruch ggf. mit demjenigen aus Art. 78.

42 Nicht zulässig wäre es dagegen, für einen auf Art. 74 gestützten Anspruch auf Ersatz von Zinsschäden wiederum gesetzliche Zinsen nach Art. 78 zu verlangen. Unabhängig davon, ob man die nach Art. 78 geschuldeten Zinsen als pauschalierten Mindest-Schadenersatz oder als Ausgleich für zu Unrecht erlangte Vorteile ansieht, kann es doch stets nur um Schäden oder Vorteile wegen nicht rechtzeitiger Erfüllung der Hauptforderung gehen. Wollte man dagegen auch Zinsansprüche einer erneuten Verzinsung nach Art. 78 unterwerfen, müssten konsequenterweise auch Ansprüche aus Art. 78 selbst wiederum Zinsen tragen usw. Dies dürfte kaum der Sinn der Vorschrift sein.

2. Zinsanspruch aus Art. 84 I

43 Das Verhältnis zu **Art. 84 I** wird nur selten ausdrücklich erörtert. Von einigen wird Art. 84 I als Sonderregelung gegenüber Art. 78 angesehen.[89] Danach bestimmt sich die gesetzliche Verzinsung des Anspruchs auf Rückzahlung des Kaufpreises im Falle der Aufhebung des Kaufvertrages allein nach Art. 84 I. Nach einer Gegenauffassung sollen beide Regelungen nebeneinander anwendbar sein.[90] Letzterem kann jedenfalls dann nicht gefolgt werden, wenn dies dazu führte, dass der Schuldner für ein und dieselbe Forderung zweimal Zinsen zahlen muss.[91] Naheliegend erscheint die Annahme von Anspruchskonkurrenz, mit der Folge, dass dem Gläubiger für dieselbe Forderung und denselben Zeitraum nur einmal Zinsen zustehen – sei es auf Grund von Art. 84 oder auf Grund von Art. 78.[92] In der Regel dürften beide Lösungen – Vorrang des Art. 84 I oder freie Anspruchskonkurrenz – zu denselben Ergebnissen führen.

---

[86] Im Ergebnis ebenso *Schlechtriem*, Internationales UN-Kaufrecht, Rn. 318.
[87] Hof van Beroep Antwerpen, 24.4.2006, CISG-online 1258.
[88] Allgemein zur Frage einer abstrakten Berechnung von Verzugsschäden *Schwenzer*, Art. 74 Rn. 20, 41.
[89] *Herber/Czerwenka*, Art. 78, Rn. 2; *Heuzé*, Anm. 447.; *Ferrari u. a./Ferrari*, Internationales Vertragsrecht, Art. 78, Rn. 3; MünchKommHGB/*Ferrari*, Art. 78, Rn. 3; *Kröll u. a./Gotanda*, Art. 78, Rn. 5.
[90] *Karollus*, S. 226 f.
[91] Wie hier *Witz/Salger/Lorenz/Witz*, Art. 78, Rn. 3.
[92] Dafür MünchKomm/*P. Huber*, Art. 78, Rn. 5.

Selbst wenn man die Artt. 78 und 84 I nebeneinander anwenden wollte, wäre es **44** jedenfalls nicht zulässig, den Zinsanspruch aus Art. 84 I nochmals einer Verzinsung nach Art. 78 zu unterwerfen.[93] Aus den in Rn. 42 genannten Gründen sollten Zinsansprüche auch in diesem Zusammenhang aus dem Anwendungsbereich des Art. 78 ausgeschlossen bleiben.

3. Prozesszinsen

Häufig wird die Ansicht vertreten, dass nationale Vorschriften über **Prozesszinsen** oder **45** „post-judgment interest" neben Art. 78 anwendbar seien.[94] Gerichte in den USA sprechen dem Gläubiger für den Zeitraum nach der Verurteilung sogar ausschließlich Zinsen nach der einschlägigen nationalen Bestimmung (28 U. S. C. § 1961(a)) zu, auch wenn sich daraus ein niedrigerer Zinssatz ergibt als aus Art. 78.[95] Beiden Ansätzen kann in dieser Allgemeinheit nicht zugestimmt werden. Sofern der Zinssatz unter Rückgriff auf nationales Recht bestimmt wird, erscheint es allerdings konsequent, insoweit auch diejenigen Vorschriften der maßgeblichen Rechtsordnung heranzuziehen, die dem Gläubiger nach Prozessbeginn oder nach Verurteilung einen höheren oder niedrigeren Zinssatz zusprechen.[96] Der Zinssatz für die Zeit vor und für die Zeit nach der Verurteilung sollte sich hinsichtlich ein und desselben Anspruchs aber nach derselben Rechtsordnung richten. Dies mag in Rechtssystemen, die vorprozessuale Zinsen dem materiellen Recht und Prozesszinsen dem Verfahrensrecht zuordnen, ungewohnt sein. Art. 78 unterscheidet aber nicht zwischen diesen beiden Zinskategorien. Deshalb ist kaum anzunehmen, dass die in Art. 78 vorgesehene Zinspflicht mit der Verurteilung zur Zahlung endet oder dass Prozesszinsen vom Regelungsbereich des CISG nicht erfasst werden[97]. Der Unterscheidung zwischen materiellem Recht und Prozessrecht sollte deshalb keine entscheidende Bedeutung zukommen.[98] Im Ergebnis ist die ergänzende Anwendung von Regelungen der *lex fori* über Prozesszinsen oder post-judgment interest ausgeschlossen, wenn die Zinshöhe durch eine ausländische Rechtsordnung – oder, entsprechend der hier favorisierten Auffassung – nach einheitlichen Grundsätzen bestimmt wird.

Unabhängig von dem dargestellten Meinungsstreit dürfte Einigkeit darüber bestehen, dass **46** die Zinsen aus Art. 78 und die im nationalen Recht vorgesehenen Prozesszinsen jedenfalls nicht kumuliert werden dürfen.

---

[93] So aber *Karollus*, S. 226 f.; wie hier *Achilles*, Art. 78, Rn. 2; MünchKomm/*P. Huber*, Art. 78, Rn. 5.
[94] *Honnold/Flechtner*, Art. 78, Rn. 420; *Bamberger/Roth/Saenger*, Art. 78, Rn. 6; MünchKommHGB/*Ferrari*, Art. 78, Rn. 7; *Staudinger/Magnus*, Art. 78, Rn. 6.
[95] *Norfolk Southern Railway Company v. Power Source Supply, Inc.*, U. S. Dist. Ct. (W. D. of Pennsylvania), 25.7.2008, CISG-online 1776.
[96] Ebenso *Schwenzer/Hachem/Kee*, Rn. 46.78.
[97] So aber *Gotanda*, FS Schwenzer, S. 597, 604 f.
[98] Ebenso *Schwenzer/Hachem/Kee*, Rn. 46.78. Zur unterschiedlichen Zuordnung von Prozesszinsen in einzelnen Ländern und US-Bundesstaaten vgl. ebenda Rn. 46.17 ff.

Abschnitt IV. Befreiungen
Section IV. Exemptions
Section IV. Exonération

Art. 79 [Hinderungsgrund außerhalb des Einflußbereiches des Schuldners]

(1) Eine Partei hat für die Nichterfüllung einer ihrer Pflichten nicht einzustehen, wenn sie beweist, daß die Nichterfüllung auf einem außerhalb ihres Einflußbereichs liegenden Hinderungsgrund beruht und daß von ihr vernünftigerweise nicht erwartet werden konnte, den Hinderungsgrund bei Vertragsabschluß in Betracht zu ziehen oder den Hinderungsgrund oder seine Folgen zu vermeiden oder zu überwinden.

(2) Beruht die Nichterfüllung einer Partei auf der Nichterfüllung durch einen Dritten, dessen sie sich zur völligen oder teilweisen Vertragserfüllung bedient, so ist diese Partei von der Haftung nur befreit,

a) wenn sie nach Abs. 1 befreit ist und
b) wenn der Dritte selbst ebenfalls nach Abs. 1 befreit wäre, sofern Abs. 1 auf ihn Anwendung fände.

(3) Die in diesem Artikel vorgesehene Befreiung gilt für die Zeit, während der der Hinderungsgrund besteht.

(4) Die Partei, die nicht erfüllt, hat den Hinderungsgrund und seine Auswirkung auf ihre Fähigkeit zu erfüllen der anderen Partei mitzuteilen. Erhält die andere Partei die Mitteilung nicht innerhalb einer angemessenen Frist, nachdem die nicht erfüllende Partei den Hinderungsgrund kannte oder kennen mußte, so haftet diese für den aus dem Nichterhalt entstehenden Schaden.

(5) Dieser Artikel hindert die Parteien nicht, ein anderes als das Recht auszuüben, Schadenersatz nach diesem Übereinkommen zu verlangen.

Art. 79

(1) A party is not liable for a failure to perform any of his obligations if he proves that the failure was due to an impediment beyond his control and that he could not reasonably be expected to have taken the impediment into account at the time of the conclusion of the contract or to have avoided or overcome it or its consequences.

(2) If the party's failure is due to the failure by a third person whom he has engaged to perform the whole or a part of the contract, that party is exempt from liability only if:

(a) he is exempt under the preceding paragraph; and
(b) the person whom he has so engaged would be so exempt if the provisions of that paragraph were applied to him.

(3) The exemption provided by this article has effect for the period during which the impediment exists.

Art. 79

1) Une partie n'est pas responsable de l'inexécution de l'une quelconque de ses obligations si elle prouve que cette inexécution est due à une empêchement indépendant de sa volonté et que l'on ne pouvait raisonnablement attendre d'elle qu'elle le prenne en considération au moment de la conclusion du contrat, qu'elle le prévienne ou le surmonte ou qu'elle en prévienne ou surmonte les conséquences.

2) Si l'inexécution par une partie est due à l'inexécution par un tiers qu'elle a chargé d'exécuter tout ou partie du contrat, cette partie n'est exonéré de sa responsabilité que dans le cas:

a) où elle l'est en vertu des dispositions du paragraphe précédent; et
b) où le tiers serait lui aussi exonéré si les dispositions de ce paragraphe lui étaient appliquées.

3) L'exonération prévue par le présent article produit effet pendant la durée de l'empêchement.

(4) The party who fails to perform must give notice to the other party of the impediment and its effect on his ability to perform. If the notice is not received by the other party within a reasonable time after the party who fails to perform knew or ought to have known of the impediment, he is liable for damages resulting from such non-receipt.

(5) Nothing in this article prevents either party from exercising any right other than to claim damages under this Convention.

4) La partie qui n'a pas exécuté doit avertir l'autre partie de l'empêchement et de ses effets sur sa capacité d'exécuter. Si l'avertissement n'arrive pas à destination dans un délai raisonnable à partir du moment où la partie qui n'a pas exécuté a connu ou aurait dû connaître l'empêchement, celle-ci est tenue à des dommages-intérêts du fait de ce défaut de réception.

5) Les dispositions du présent article n'interdisent pas à une partie d'exercer tous ses droits autres que celui d'obtenir des dommages-intérêts en vertu de la présente Convention.

Übersicht

	Rn.
I. Grundgedanken	1
1. Regelungsgehalt	1
2. Verhältnis zu anderen Vorschriften des CISG	3
3. Parallelen im (inter-)nationalen Handelsrecht	4
II. Anwendungsbereich von Art. 79	5
1. Nichterfüllung von Vertragspflichten	5
2. Lieferung vertragswidriger Ware	6
3. Obliegenheiten	7
4. Garantien, Vertragsstrafen, Schadenspauschalen	8
5. Wissenszurechnung	9
III. Voraussetzungen der Entlastung (Art. 79 I)	10
1. Allgemeine Voraussetzungen	10
a) Nicht beherrschbarer Hinderungsgrund	11
b) Unvorhersehbarkeit des Hinderungsgrundes	13
c) Unabwendbarkeit des Hindernisses und seiner Konsequenzen	14
d) Ursächlichkeit für die Nichterfüllung	15
2. Einzelfälle	16
a) Naturereignisse und -katastrophen	16
b) Staatliche Eingriffe	17
c) Organisationsrisiko	18
d) Personalrisiko	20
e) Arbeitskämpfe	21
f) Finanzielle Leistungsfähigkeit	25
g) Beschaffungsrisiko	26
h) Vertragsgemässheit der Ware	28
i) Wirtschaftliche Unmöglichkeit	30
j) (Ethische) Unzumutbarkeit	32
k) Verwendungsrisiko	33
IV. Haftung für Dritte (Art. 79 II)	34
1. Kreis der Dritten	34
2. Entlastung	39
3. Wissenszurechnung	40
V. Vorübergehende Leistungshindernisse (Art. 79 III)	41
VI. Benachrichtigungspflicht (Art. 79 IV)	43
1. Allgemeines	43
2. Mitteilung	44
3. Schadenersatzpflicht	47
VII. Wirkungen der Entlastung (Art. 79 V)	49
1. Befreiung von der Schadenersatzpflicht	49
2. Erfüllungsanspruch	52
3. Sonstige Rechtsbehelfe und Ansprüche	55

VIII. Vertragliche Abweichung 57
  1. Ausgestaltung der Haftungsbefreiung 57
  2. Garantien 58
IX. Beweislast 59

I. Grundgedanken

1. Regelungsgehalt

1   Art. 79 I regelt wie schon Art. 74 EKG[1] die Befreiung des Schuldners von der Schadenersatzpflicht, wenn er seine Verpflichtungen auf Grund eines unvorhersehbaren und unvermeidbaren Hinderungsgrundes nicht vertragsgemäss erfüllen kann. Art. 79 bildet die notwendige **Beschränkung** des dem CISG zu Grunde liegenden Grundsatzes der verschuldensunabhängigen **Garantiehaftung** („strict liability") bei Nichterfüllung des Vertrages.[2] Entstehungsgeschichte, Systematik und Wortlaut der Vorschrift machen deutlich, dass eine Befreiung nur unter ganz **engen Voraussetzungen** in Betracht kommen kann. Entsprechend diesem Ausgangsprinzip hat Art. 79 in der Praxis bislang noch keine grosse Bedeutung gespielt. Zwar haben Parteien wiederholt versucht, sich zur Entlastung auf Art. 79 zu berufen, sie sind damit in der Praxis jedoch nur höchst selten durchgedrungen.[3]

2   Art. 79 I wird ergänzt durch Art. 79 II, der klar stellt, dass sich der Schuldner nicht durch die **Übertragung von Leistungspflichten auf Dritte** entlasten kann. Er hat für deren Verhalten grundsätzlich gleich einzustehen, wie für das Verhalten eigener Leute. Die Abgrenzung der beiden Absätze[4] birgt gewisse Herausforderungen. Massgebliches Kriterium ist dabei das Beschaffungsrisiko:[5] Trägt es der Verkäufer, richtet sich seine Befreiung regelmäßig nach Art. 79 I, sonst nach Art. 79 II. Für den wichtigen Fall der Absatzkette bedeutet dies, dass Art. 79 I einschlägig ist, da der Verkäufer das Beschaffungsrisiko für die gesamte Kette trägt. Nur ausnahmsweise kommt in dieser Situation eine Entlastung nach Art. 79 II in Betracht.

2a Art. 79 III beschränkt die Befreiung auf die **Dauer des Hinderungsgrundes**; fällt der Hinderungsgrund weg, kann sich der Schuldner nicht mehr auf eine Befreiung von der Schadenersatzpflicht berufen. Art. 79 IV statuiert eine **Benachrichtigungspflicht** für die vom Hinderungsgrund betroffene Partei. Art. 79 V beschränkt die Wirkung der Befreiung auf den Bereich des **Schadenersatzes**.

2. Verhältnis zu anderen Vorschriften des CISG

3   Art. 79 bildet zusammen mit Art. 80, der die Folgen einer vom Gläubiger (mit-)verursachten Nichterfüllung regelt, einen gesonderten Abschnitt IV mit der Überschrift „**Befreiungen**". Während allerdings Art. 80 jegliche Berufung auf eine Vertragsverletzung und damit **sämtliche Rechtsbehelfe** ausschliesst, beschränkt sich die Wirkung des

---

[1] Zu den Unterschieden und zur Entstehungsgeschichte vgl. *Stoll*, 3. Aufl., Art. 79 Rn. 1–5; *Brunner*, Force majeure, S. 101 ff.
[2] Vgl. *Staudinger/Magnus*, Art. 79, Rn. 1; *Rathjen*, RIW 1999, 561; *Vischer*, Gemeinsame Bestimmungen, S. 174 f.; *Achilles*, Art. 79, Rn. 1; *Salger*, S. 15–18; *Mazzoni*, Riv. dir. com. 1991, I, 539, 553; *Brand*, Draft Digest, S. 395 f.; *Brunner*, Art. 79, Rn. 1; MünchKomm/*P. Huber*, Art. 79, Rn. 1; MünchKommHGB/*Mankowski*, Art. 79, Rn. 1; differenzierend *Schmidt-Kessel*, FS Schwenzer, S. 1513, 1520.
[3] Vgl. CISG-AC, Op. 7 (*Garro*), Comment 2; *Staudinger/Magnus*, Art. 79, Rn. 4; MünchKomm/*P. Huber*, Art. 79, Rn. 1. Für Fälle, in denen Art. 79 erfolgreich geltend gemacht wurde, vgl. *Raw Materials Inc. v. Manfred Forberich GmbH & Co. KG*, U. S. Dist. Ct. (N. D. Ill.), 6.7.2004, CISG-online 925; AG Willisau, 12.3.2004, CISG-online 961; Hof van Cassatie, 19.6.2009, CISG-online 1963; ICC, 8790/2000, CISG-online 1172; Trib. com. Besançon, 19.1.1998, CISG-online 557; Int. Ct. Russian CCI, 22.1.1997, CISG-online 1296; Int. Ct. Hungarian CCI, 10.12.1996, CISG-online 774; AG Charlottenburg, 4.5.1994, CISG-online 386.
[4] Vgl. dazu im Detail unten Rn. 34 ff.
[5] Vgl. dazu unten Rn. 26 f.

Art. 79 auf eine Befreiung von der Schadenersatzhaftung (dazu im Einzelnen unten Rn. 49 ff.).

3. Parallelen im (inter-)nationalen Handelsrecht[6]

Während die Haftung für Dritte, wie sie sich aus Art. 79 I und II ergibt, einem wohl in allen Rechtsordnungen anerkannten Grundsatz entspricht,[7] weicht der Befreiungstatbestand des Art. 79 I nicht unerheblich von ähnlichen Regelungen im nationalen Recht[8] und in Einheitsrechtsprojekten[9] ab. Im Unterschied zum CISG setzen die meisten Befreiungstatbestände nämlich nicht beim Schadensersatzanspruch als Sekundäranspruch, sondern beim **Erfüllungsanspruch** an.[10] Die Befreiung von der Schadenersatzhaftung wird in den Rechtsordnungen, die dem Verschuldensprinzip folgen, dann über das Vertretenmüssen geregelt. Ferner kennen viele Rechtsordnungen[11] und auch die Einheitsrechtsprojekte[12] anders als das CISG einen gesonderten **„hardship"-Tatbestand,** der die Fälle der blossen Leistungserschwerung oder der Leistungsentwertung, aber auch Fälle des Zweckfortfalls und der Zweckverfehlung erfasst. Auf der Rechtsfolgenseite sehen diese Regelungen eine **Anpassung des Vertrages** oder zumindest eine Pflicht zur Aufnahme von **Neuverhandlungen** vor.[13] In diesen Rechtsordnungen stellt sich freilich im besonderen Masse das Problem der Abgrenzung der beiden Befreiungstatbestände.[14] Die anglo-amerikanischen Rechtsordnungen kennen zwar verschiedene Befreiungstatbestände (impossibility, commercial impracticability und frustration of purpose), sehen jedoch die Möglichkeit einer Ver-

---

[6] Vgl. *Schwenzer*, 39 Vict. U. Well. L. Rev. (2009), 709, 710 ff.; *dies.*, FS Bucher, S. 723, 725, 726. Rechtsvergleichend *Schwenzer/Hachem/Kee*, Rn. 45.01 ff.; *Nottage*, 14 Ind. J. Global Legal Stud. (2007), 385.

[7] Deutschland: § 278 BGB; Italien: Art. 1228 Cc; Niederlande: Art. 6:76 BW; Österreich: § 1313a ABGB; Schweiz: Art. 101 OR; Türkei: Art. 116 I OR; rechtsvergleichend *Schwenzer/Hachem/Kee*, Rn. 44.74; *Herbot/Pauwels*, FS Neumayer, S. 335 f. mit Nachw. zum französischen und englischen Recht.

[8] Vgl. Deutschland: §§ 275 I, 283, 280 I BGB; Frankreich: Artt. 1147, 1148 Cc; Italien: Artt. 1218, 1256 Cc; Österreich: §§ 920, 1447 ABGB; Schweiz: Artt. 97, 119 OR; zu den ibero-amerikanischen Rechtsordnungen vgl. *E. Muñoz*, 14 VJ (2010), 175 ff.; zum chinesischen Recht vgl. *S.J. Yang*, FS Schwenzer, S. 1809 ff. Vgl. weiter rechtsvergleichend *Schwenzer/Hachem/Kee*, Rn. 45.24 ff.

[9] Vgl. die Art. 79 I nachgebildeten Art. 7.1.7 I PICC; Art. 8:108 I PECL; Art. 88 CESL-Entwurf.

[10] Vgl. *Schlechtriem*, Internationales UN-Kaufrecht, Rn. 288; *ders.*, Neues Schuldrecht, S. 77.

[11] Vgl. Deutschland: § 313 BGB (Störung der Geschäftsgrundlage); Italien: Artt. 1467–1469 Cc (sopravvenuta eccessiva onerosità); Niederlande: Art. 6:258 BW; Portugal: Art. 437 Cc. In Spanien, Österreich und der Schweiz ist die Möglichkeit der Vertragsanpassung wegen veränderter Umstände richterrechtlich anerkannt. Rechtsvergleichender Überblick bei *Jones/Schlechtriem*, Breach of Contract, Sec. 216–234; *Zweigert/Kötz*, S. 516 ff.; *Ommeslaghe*, Rev. dr. int. 1980, 7, 16–40; *Gruber*, Geldwertschwankungen, S. 516 ff.; *Rösler*, ERPL 2007, 483; vgl. darüber hinaus rechtsvergleichend *Schwenzer/Hachem/Kee*, Rn. 45.78; zu den ibero-amerikanischen Rechtsordnungen vgl. *E. Muñoz*, 14 VJ (2010), 175, 185. Das neue chinesische Vertragsrecht enthielt im Entwurfsstadium eine separate Vorschrift, die jedoch wieder gestrichen wurde, vgl. *S.J. Yang*, FS Schwenzer, S. 1809, 1810 f. In Frankreich und Belgien wird hingegen die théorie de l'imprévision weiter abgelehnt; dazu im Überblick *Gruber*, Geldwertschwankungen, S. 396 ff., 434 ff.

[12] Vgl. Art. 6.2.2 PICC (hardship) bzw. Art. 6:111 PECL (change of circumstances); Art. 89 CESL-Entwurf; vgl. im Überblick *Gruber*, Geldwertschwankungen, S. 553 ff.; *Bernardini*, Hardship e Force Majeure, S. 193–214; *Brunner*, Force majeure, S. 391 ff.; *Maskow*, Am. J. Comp. L. 40 (1992), 657, 661–663; *Fontaine*, Les dispositions relatives au hardship, S. 185–191; *Kessedjian*, Int'l Rev. L. & E. 25 (2005), 415, 420 ff.; *Lindström*, 1 Nordic J. Com. L. (2006), 1, 11 ff.

[13] Teilweise wird vertreten, dass diese Regelungen deshalb flexibler als das CISG seien, vgl. *Schlechtriem*, Internationales UN-Kaufrecht, Rn. 291; *ders.*, Neues Schuldrecht, S. 76; *Gruber*, Geldwertschwankungen, S. 545 f., 571. S. dazu jedoch unten Rn. 54.

[14] Vgl. zu den PICC *Bernardini*, Hardship e Force Majeure, S. 196–207; *Maskow*, Am. J. Comp. L. 40 (1992), 657, 663–665; *Fontaine*, Les dispositions relatives au hardship, S. 190 f.; *Draetta*, R. D. A. I. 2002, 347, 348–351; *Kessedjian*, Int'l Rev. L. & E. 25 (2005), 415, 420 ff.; *Lookofsky*, Int'l Rev. L. & E. 25 (2005), 434, 439 f. Im internen deutschen Recht ist das Verhältnis von § 313 BGB zu § 275 II BGB umstritten. Abweichend von der bisherigen Rechtslage (vgl. *Gruber*, Geldwertschwankungen, S. 439 f.) soll nach einer Auffassung auch die wirtschaftliche Unmöglichkeit von § 275 II BGB erfasst sein, der damit neben § 313 BGB zur Anwendung kommen soll, vgl. *Stoll*, JZ 2001, 589, 591 Fn. 15 unter Berufung auf den Wortlaut; nach a. A. soll nur die sog. praktische Unmöglichkeit erfasst sein, vgl. *Canaris*, JZ 2001, 499, 501 unter Berufung auf die Vorstellungen des Gesetzgebers; nach *Schlechtriem/Schmidt-Kessel*, SchuldR AT, Rn. 485 ist § 313 BGB Ergänzung zu § 275 II BGB.

Art. 79 5, 6   Teil III. Kapitel V. Pflichten des Verkäufers und des Käufers. Abschnitt IV

tragsanpassung nicht vor.[15] Dem CISG am nächsten kommen die skandinavischen Kaufgesetze, die die Entlastung des Schuldners in Anlehnung an Art. 79 über einen weiten, nicht auf Unmöglichkeit beschränkten Tatbestand regeln.[16]

II. Anwendungsbereich von Art. 79

1. Nichterfüllung von Vertragspflichten

5   Eine Entlastung nach Art. 79 ist in allen Fällen möglich, in denen eine Vertragspartei eine ihr obliegende Vertragspflicht nicht oder nicht gehörig erfüllt; dabei wird nicht nach dem Grund für die Nichterfüllung (Unmöglichkeit, Verzug oder Schlechtleistung) unterschieden. Dem einheitlichen Begriff der Nichterfüllung entspricht daher der **einheitliche Entlastungstatbestand** des Art. 79.[17] Primär erfasst werden Pflichtverletzungen, die eine Haftung nach Art. 45 oder Art. 61 auslösen; des Weiteren kommen aber auch die Verletzungen von **Nebenpflichten** oder von **Rückabwicklungspflichten** (Artt. 81 ff.) in Betracht.[18] Auch die Verletzung nur eines Teils des Vertrages fällt unter Art. 79.[19]

2. Lieferung vertragswidriger Ware

6   Entsprechend anglo-amerikanischer Auffassung wird von verschiedenen englischsprachigen Autoren vertreten, dass die Lieferung nicht vertragsgemässer Ware nicht unter Art. 79 falle, eine Befreiung deshalb nicht möglich sei.[20] Die inzwischen h. M. will indes Art. 79 auch auf diese Fallgruppe anwenden.[21] Dogmatische Gesichtspunkte – die Einheitlichkeit des Vertragsbruchstatbestandes nach CISG – sprechen für letztere Auffassung. Auch die

---

[15] Zum englischen Recht vgl. sec. 7 SGA; *Bridge*, Int'l Sale of Goods, Rn. 8.06–8.34; *Treitel*, Law of Contract, S. 805–863; zum amerikanischen Recht vgl. § 2–615 UCC und Restatement of Contracts 2d, sec. 261 (discharge by supervening impracticability); dazu *Bund*, 17 J. L. & Com. (1998), 381, 395–405; vgl. auch *Brunner*, Force majeure, S. 407 ff.; *Brand*, Draft Digest, S. 393 f.; eingehend *Treitel*, Unmöglichkeit, S. 20 ff., 86 ff.

[16] Vgl. §§ 27 und 40 des finnischen, norwegischen und schwedischen Kaufgesetzes.

[17] S. o. Art. 74 Rn. 12; *Witz/Salger/Lorenz/Salger*, Art. 79, Rn. 2; *Soergel/Lüderitz/Dettmeier*, Vor Art. 79, Rn. 3; *U. Huber*, östJBl. 1989, 273, 274; *Achilles*, Art. 79, Rn. 2; *Ziegler*, S. 218; *Bianca/Bonell/Tallon*, Art. 79, Anm. 2.4.1.; *Heuzé*, Anm. 468.; *Brunner*, Art. 79, Rn. 3; *ders.*, Force majeure, Ch. 4, § 7(I); MünchKommHGB/*Mankowski*, Art. 79, Rn. 19; differenzierend *Schmidt-Kessel*, FS Schwenzer, S. 1513, 1522 ff.

[18] So auch *Staudinger/Magnus*, Art. 79, Rn. 11; *Witz/Salger/Lorenz/Salger*, Art. 79, Rn. 2; *Soergel/Lüderitz/ Dettmeier*, Vor Art. 79, Rn. 3; *Achilles*, Art. 79, Rn. 3; MünchKomm/*P. Huber*, Art. 79, Rn. 3; *Kröll u. a./ Atamer*, Art. 79, Rn. 8; zweifelnd *Leser*, Vertragsaufhebung und Rückabwicklung, S. 245.

[19] Vgl. *Honnold/Flechtner*, Art. 79, Rn. 435.2; *Bianca/Bonell/Tallon*, Art. 79, Anm. 2.9.

[20] Vgl. *Honnold/Flechtner*, Art. 79, Rn. 427; *Nicholas*, Impracticability, S. 5–14; *ders.*, Prerequisites, S. 287 f.; *P. Huber/Mullis/P. Huber*, S. 258; *Lautenbach*, S. 18 f.; *Bianca/Bonell/Tallon*, Art. 79, Anm. 2.6.1. und 2.6.2.; *Bianca/Ponzanelli*, Art. 79, Anm. 4.; zweifelnd *Hudson*, S. 182–184, 193. Hinter der eingenenden Auslegung von Art. 79 I vor allem durch die amerikanische Literatur steht wohl die Sorge, dass über Art. 79 wieder Elemente einer Verschuldenshaftung ins CISG Eingang finden könnten; vgl. *Schlechtriem*, JZ 1999, 794, 795.

[21] Vgl. CISG-AC, Op. 7 (*Garro*), Comments 7, 10; *Staudinger/Magnus*, Art. 79, Rn. 12; *Rathjen*, RIW 1999, 561, 562; *Enderlein/Maskow/Strohbach*, Art. 79, Anm. 2.; *Herber/Czerwenka*, Art. 79, Rn. 8; *Piltz*, Internationales Kaufrecht, Rn. 4–227; *Heuzé*, Anm. 468.; *Audit*, Vente internationale, Anm. 181.; *Bamberger/Roth/ Saenger*, Art. 79, Rn. 2; *U. Huber*, RabelsZ 43 (1979), 413, 466; *Keil*, S. 36 f.; *Kranz*, S. 194; *Bund*, 17 J. L. & Com. (1998), 381, 403; *Brunner*, Art. 79, Rn. 21; *ders.*, Force majeure, Ch. 4, § 7(III)(4); MünchKomm/ *P. Huber*, Art. 79, Rn. 3; MünchKommHGB/*Mankowski*, Art. 79, Rn. 19; *Kruisinga*, Non-conformity, S. 127 f.; *Fischer*, Vor-und Nachteile, S. 58, 317; *Brölsch*, S. 116 f.; *Krüger*, S. 97 f., 166 ff.; *Bianca/Bonell/Tallon*, Art. 79, Anm. 2.4.1. ff.; *Soergel/Lüderitz/Dettmeier*, Art. 79, Rn. 15 ff.; *Schmidt-Kessel*, FS Schwenzer, S. 1513, 1520; *Stoll*, Schadensersatzpflicht, S. 275 f.; *Lookofsky*, Consequential Damages, S. 282 (jedoch mit der Einschränkung, die Anwendung des Art. 79 scheitere an der Vorhersehbarkeit jeden Mangels); *ders.*, Int'l Rev. L. & E. 25 (2005), 434, 437; so auch *Weber*, Vertragsverletzungsfolgen, S. 173; *Neumayer/Ming*, Art. 79, Anm. 2.; *Pichonnaz*, Anm. 1671.–1674.; *Salger*, S. 127; *Vischer*, Gemeinsame Bestimmungen, S. 177 f.; *Ziegler*, S. 218; *Flambouras*, 13 Pace Int'l L. Rev. (2001), 261, 276 f.; so auch LG Köln, 16.11.1995, CISG-online 265, bestätigt durch OLG Köln, 21.5.1996, CISG-online 254; OLG Zweibrücken, 31.3.1998, CISG-online 481; offengelassen von BGH, 24.3.1999, CISG-online 396 = BGHZ 141, 129, 132 f. (Rebwachs); vgl. auch *Flechtner*, Draft Digest, Art. 79, Rn. 8 f.

Entstehungsgeschichte[22] scheint diese Sichtweise zu unterstützen. In der Sache wird es freilich kaum Fälle geben, in denen sich der Verkäufer bei Vertragswidrigkeit der Ware auf Art. 79 berufen kann.[23] In der Regel haftet der Verkäufer **ohne Entlastungsmöglichkeit** für die Vertragsgemässheit. Ob der Verkäufer Fehler seiner Lieferanten erkennen konnte, spielt insoweit keine Rolle.[24]

3. Obliegenheiten

Bei Versäumung einer blossen Obliegenheit (vgl. oben Art. 74 Rn. 13) muss nach dem 7 Sinn der jeweiligen Regelung entschieden werden, inwiefern ein für die Säumnis ursächlicher Hinderungsgrund, der dem Einfluss der belasteten Partei entzogen ist, sie von den Folgen der Säumnis befreit. Da es hierbei nicht um Befreiung von einer Schadenersatzpflicht geht, sondern um die Vermeidung sonstiger Nachteile, kommt nur eine **analoge Anwendung** von Art. 79 in Betracht.[25] Für die Versäumung der **Rügepflicht** nach Artt. 39, 43 enthält Art. 44 jedoch eine Sonderregelung.[26]

4. Garantien, Vertragsstrafen, Schadenspauschalen

Nach Art. 79 V betrifft die Befreiung lediglich den aus den Regeln des CISG folgenden 8 Schadenersatzanspruch, nicht jedoch besondere, daneben bestehende **vertragliche Ansprüche** (s. dazu unten Rn. 51). Zur vertraglichen Änderung mittels Garantien s. unten Rn. 58.

5. Wissenszurechnung

Art. 79 I und II liegt das Prinzip zu Grunde, dass der Schuldner grundsätzlich für alle 9 Personen einzustehen hat, derer er sich bei der Erfüllung seiner Verbindlichkeit bedient. Als **allgemeiner Grundsatz** im Sinne des Art. 7 II kann hieraus abgeleitet werden, dass er sich auch das Wissen dieser Personen anrechnen lassen muss, wo es um **Kenntnis bzw. Kennenmüssen** bestimmter Umstände geht.[27]

III. Voraussetzungen der Entlastung (Art. 79 I)

1. Allgemeine Voraussetzungen

Der Schuldner ist nach Art. 79 entlastet, wenn die Nichterfüllung (a) auf **einem nicht** 10 **beherrschbaren Hinderungsgrund** beruht, der (b) **nicht vorhersehbar** und ferner (c) **unabwendbar** ist in dem Sinne, dass von dem Schuldner vernünftigerweise nicht erwartet werden konnte, den Hinderungsgrund und seine Folgen zu vermeiden oder zu überwinden. Des Weiteren ist Voraussetzung, dass (d) der Hinderungsgrund **ursächlich** ist für die Nichterfüllung. Richtungweisend für die Auslegung der Entlastungsklausel des Art. 79 ist dabei der Grundgedanke, dass die Erfüllung des Vertrages durch einen Grund verhindert wird, der sich der Beherrschung durch den Schuldner entzieht.

---

[22] Vgl. Sekretariatskommentar, Art. 65, Nr. 9, Beispiel 65 D.
[23] Vgl. CISG-AC, Op. 7 *(Garro)*, Comments 8, 11: „extremely heavy burden of proof" und 13; *Staudinger/ Magnus*, Art. 79, Rn. 12; MünchKomm/*P. Huber*, Art. 79, Rn. 19; *Brunner*, Art. 79, Rn. 21; *Stoll*, Schadensersatzpflicht, S. 275 f.
[24] Vgl. BGH, 24.3.1999, CISG-online 396 = BGHZ 141, 129, 134 (Rebwachs).
[25] So *Soergel/Lüderitz/Dettmeier*, Vor Art. 79, Rn. 3; *Staudinger/Magnus*, Art. 79, Rn. 14; *Ziegler*, S. 218; *Brunner*, Art. 79, Rn. 3; MünchKommHGB/*Mankowski*, Art. 79, Rn. 20; zurückhaltend MünchKomm/ *P. Huber*, Art. 79, Rn. 4.
[26] Vgl. MünchKomm/*P. Huber*, Art. 79, Rn. 4; *Bamberger/Roth/Saenger*, Art. 79, Rn. 2.
[27] Vgl. *Staudinger/Magnus*, Art. 79, Rn. 43; MünchKomm/*P. Huber*, Art. 79, Rn. 5; vgl. auch Art. 40, Rn. 6.

11 **a) Nicht beherrschbarer Hinderungsgrund.** Nur ein Hinderungsgrund, der ausserhalb des Einflussbereichs des Schuldners liegt, kann zu einer Entlastung nach Art. 79 führen. Die Einführung des Begriffes „impediment" sollte ein enges, objektives Verständnis der Befreiungsgründe gewährleisten.[28] Es kommen deshalb nur **objektive,** d. h. **ausserhalb der Person des Schuldners vorhandene Umstände** in Betracht, die der Erfüllung entgegenstehen.[29] Insofern kann man auch von „externen" Umständen sprechen oder von Zuständen der Aussenwelt, die jedoch auch den Leistungsgegenstand selbst umfasst.[30] Den Gegensatz bilden **persönliche Umstände,** die das Leistungsvermögen des Schuldners beeinträchtigen.[31] Die Abgrenzung zwischen der Risikosphäre des Schuldners und externen Leistungshindernissen ist primär anhand der **vertraglichen Risikoverteilung** vorzunehmen.[32] Darüber hinaus sind auch Gepflogenheiten und Handelsbräuche zu berücksichtigen.[33] Im Übrigen kann auf den **typischen Verantwortungsbereich** des Schuldners abgestellt werden, der insbesondere die Verantwortung für den persönlichen Bereich, wie die finanzielle Leistungsfähigkeit und die eigene Kontrollsphäre, das Beschaffungs-, Verwendungs- und Personalrisiko umfasst. Insoweit mag mangels anderer Anhaltspunkte auf Fallgruppen zurückgegriffen werden (vgl. Rn. 16 ff.).

12 Im Hinblick auf die generelle Befreiungsmöglichkeit nach Art. 79 spielt es keine Rolle, ob das Leistungshindernis anfänglich oder nachträglich, objektiv oder subjektiv, verschuldet oder unverschuldet, zeitweise oder dauernd besteht.[34] Für den Fall der **anfänglichen Unmöglichkeit** bedeutet dies, dass die Rechtsfolgen stets dem CISG zu entnehmen sind, und zwar selbst dann, wenn als subsidiäres Vertragsstatut ein Landesrecht in Betracht kommt,[35] nach welchem der auf eine anfänglich objektiv unmögliche Leistung gerichtete Vertrag nichtig ist.[36] Allerdings ist im Einzelfall zu prüfen, ob der Schuldner nicht im

---

[28] Dazu eingehend *Stoll*, 3. Aufl., Art. 79 Rn. 2.
[29] OLG München, 5.3.2008, CISG-online 1686.
[30] Vgl. *Herber/Czerwenka*, Art. 79, Rn. 8; *Piltz*, Internationales Kaufrecht, Rn. 4–234; *Kröll u. a./Atamer*, Art. 79, Rn. 44; *Staudinger/Magnus*, Art. 79, Rn. 16; *Heuzé*, Anm. 469.; *Liu*, Force Majeure, Nr. 4.3. Der Begriff darf nicht etwa mit dem ebenfalls engeren Begriff der „höheren Gewalt" im Sinne des deutschen Rechts oder dem Begriff der „force majeure" des französischen Rechts gleichgesetzt werden; treffend *Audit*, Vente internationale, Anm. 180.: „La convention adopte une notion autonome d'empêchement, laquelle doit être interpretée comme telle et non par référence à un système quelconque"; ebenso *Osman*, S. 160. Bedenklich daher die vor dem Hintergrund des anglo-amerikanischen Rechts vorgeschlagenen Definitionen von *Honnold/Flechtner*, Art. 79, Rn. 427 („a barrier to performance, such as delivery of the goods or transmission of the price rather than an aspect personal to the seller's performance") oder *Nicholas*, Impracticability, S. 5–14 („barrier to perform which is external to the party and the thing concerned"); zu eng auch *Bund*, 17 J. L. & Com. (1998), 381, 387 und *Heuzé*, Anm. 471.
[31] OLG München, 5.3.2008, CISG-online 1686 (Unvermögen des Verkäufers Eigentum an Auto zu verschaffen, da es gestohlen wurde).
[32] Vgl. *P. Huber/Mullis/P. Huber*, S. 259; *Staudinger/Magnus*, Art. 79, Rn. 16; MünchKomm/*P. Huber*, Art. 79, Rn. 7; *Brunner*, Art. 79, Rn. 6; *ders.*, Force majeure, S. 147 f.; *Schwenzer*, 39 Vict. U. Well. L. Rev. (2009), 709, 715; *dies.*, FS Bucher, S. 723, 729 f.
[33] Vgl. BGH, 24.3.1999, CISG-online 396 = BGHZ 141, 129, 133 (Rebwachs); OLG Hamburg, 28.2.1997, CISG-online 261; *Staudinger/Magnus*, Art. 79, Rn. 16; *P. Huber/Mullis/P. Huber*, S. 259; MünchKomm/*P. Huber*, Art. 79, Rn. 7.
[34] Vgl. *Staudinger/Magnus*, Art. 79, Rn. 17; *Bamberger/Roth/Saenger*, Art. 79, Rn. 3; MünchKomm/*P. Huber*, Art. 79, Rn. 7; MünchKommHGB/*Mankowski*, Art. 79, Rn. 18; *Piltz*, Internationales Kaufrecht, Rn. 4–235.
[35] Vgl. Österreich: § 878 ABGB; Schweiz: Art. 20 I OR; Frankreich: Artt. 1108, 1599 Cc; Italien: Art. 1346 Cc; Spanien: Artt. 1184, 1272, 1460 Cc. Im englischen Recht ist der Stückkauf gemäss sec. 6 SGA „void", wenn der Kaufgegenstand schon vor Vertragsschluss untergegangen ist und der Verkäufer dies nicht wusste. Nach common law Grundsätzen kommt bei Nichtexistenz des Vertragsgegenstandes Nichtigkeit wegen common mistake in Betracht; Einzelheiten sind aber ungewiss, s. *Chitty*, Chitty on Contracts, § 5–005– 5–019, 5–064–5–069. In dem bekannten, vom High Court of Australia entschiedenen Fall *McRae v. The Commonwealth Disposals Commission*, 84 C. L. R. 377 = *Smith/Thomas*, A Casebook on Contract, London: Sweet & Maxwell (1992), S. 485–489, der den Verkauf eines nicht existierenden Tankerwracks durch eine Regierungsbehörde zum Gegenstand hatte, ging das Gericht von der Wirksamkeit des Vertrages aus. Da die Regierungsbehörde sich nicht ausreichend vergewissert hatte, ob das Wrack tatsächlich existiert, kam auch keine Haftungsbefreiung in Betracht.
[36] Vgl. *Enderlein/Maskow/Strohbach*, Art. 79, Anm. 5.2.; *Herber/Czerwenka*, Art. 79, Rn. 24; *Honnold/Flechtner*, Art. 79, Rn. 432.3 Fn. 46; *U. Huber*, Haftung des Verkäufers, S. 16 Fn. 24; *Karollus*, S. 210; *Keil*, S. 120–122;

Hinblick auf seine anfängliche Leistungsfähigkeit eine **unbegrenzte Einstandspflicht** übernehmen wollte, die die Anwendung des Art. 79 ausschliesst.[37]

b) Unvorhersehbarkeit des Hinderungsgrundes. Selbst für einen Hinderungsgrund, **13** der ausserhalb des Einflussbereichs des Schuldners liegt, hat dieser einzustehen, wenn von ihm vernünftigerweise erwartet werden konnte, den Hinderungsgrund bei Vertragsschluss in Betracht zu ziehen. Entscheidend ist dabei, ob eine **vernünftige Person** in den Schuhen des Schuldners bei Vertragsschluss und unter Berücksichtigung der konkreten Umtände und von Handelsbräuchen mit der Existenz oder dem Eintritt bestimmter Leistungshindernisse rechnen musste.[38] War das Leistungshindernis bei Vertragsschluss vorhersehbar und hat der Schuldner keinen Vorbehalt geäussert, so übernimmt er das Risiko, dass die geschuldete Leistung wegen des vorhersehbaren Hindernisses verzögert oder vereitelt wird.[39]

c) Unabwendbarkeit des Hindernisses und seiner Konsequenzen. Auch ein Hin- **14** dernis, mit dem der Schuldner bei Vertragsschluss nicht zu rechnen brauchte, entlastet den Schuldner nicht, wenn ihm die Vermeidung oder Überwindung des Hindernisses oder seiner Konsequenzen möglich und zumutbar ist. Dabei sind gerade im internationalen Handelsverkehr sehr strenge Massstäbe anzulegen. Dem Schuldner ist die **Überwindung eines Hindernisses** zur Einhaltung des Vertrages regelmässig selbst dann zuzumuten, wenn der Schuldner hierdurch zu **erheblichen Mehraufwendungen** und zur Hinnahme eines Geschäftsverlustes genötigt wird.[40] So hat der Schuldner z. B. **alternative Beförderungsmöglichkeiten** in Betracht zu ziehen, selbst wenn dies mit erheblichen Mehrkosten verbunden ist.[41] Einem Verkäufer ist die Zahlung eines den Vertragspreis erheblich übersteigenden, neu eingeführten Mindestpreises an den Zulieferer zuzumuten, wenn der Staat des Zulieferers hiervon die Erteilung der Exportlizenz abhängig macht.[42] Der Schuldner kann auch gehalten sein, anstelle der nicht ausführbaren Leistung eine andere, nach der Handelsauffassung vernünftige **Ersatzleistung** („a commercially reasonable substitute") anzubieten, die den Vertragszweck ebenso gut erfüllt.[43] Der Schuldner muss in diesem Fall den Gläubi-

---

Schwenzer, 39 Vict. U. Well. L. Rev. (2009), 709, 717 f.; *dies.*, FS Bucher, S. 723, 731 ff.; *Kröll u. a./Atamer*, Art. 79, Rn. 48; *Staudinger/Magnus*, Art. 79, Rn. 33; vgl. auch den Sekretariatsbericht zu Art. 4 New Yorker E 1978, O. R., S. 17, Nr. 2. A. A. *Heuzé*, Anm. 470.; *Bianca/Bonell/Tallon*, Art. 79, Anm. 2.4.3.; *Lee*, 8 Dick J. Int'l L. (1990), 375, 386 f.; *Flambouras*, 13 Pace Int'l L. Rev. (2001), 261, 269 f.; im Sinne dieser Gegenmeinung auch die UNCITRAL-Arbeitsgruppe in ihrem Bericht zu Art. 50 Genfer E 1976, YB VII (1976), S. 130, Nr. 3.

[37] Vgl. *Staudinger/Magnus*, Art. 79, Rn. 17.
[38] Vgl. *Bianca/Bonell/Tallon*, Art. 79, Anm. 2.6.3.; *Pichonnaz*, Anm. 1734.–1739.; *Witz/Salger/Lorenz/Salger*, Art. 79, Rn. 5; *Salger*, S. 60 ff.; *Staudinger/Magnus*, Art. 79, Rn. 32; *Enderlein/Maskow/Strohbach*, Art. 79, Anm. 5.3.; *Heuzé*, Anm. 470.; *Piltz*, Internationales Kaufrecht, Rn. 4–241; *Soergel/Lüderitz/Dettmeier*, Art. 79, Rn. 3, 4; *MünchKomm/P. Huber*, Art. 79, Rn. 8; *MünchKommHGB/Mankowski*, Art. 79, Rn. 39; *Ryffel*, S. 92 f.; *Flambouras*, 13 Pace Int'l L. Rev. (2001), 261, 271; *Liu*, Force Majeure, Nr. 4.4; *Lindström*, 1 Nordic J. Com. L. (2006), 1, 8; *Brunner*, Force majeure, S. 156 ff.
[39] Vgl. *Bianca/Bonell/Tallon*, Art. 79, Anm. 2.6.3.; *Audit*, Vente internationale, Anm. 182.; *Kröll u. a./Atamer*, Art. 79, Rn. 50; *Neumayer/Ming*, Art. 79, Anm. 4.
[40] Vgl. *Heuzé*, Anm. 471.; *Karollus*, S. 209; *Piltz*, Internationales Kaufrecht, Rn. 4–244; *Staudinger/Magnus*, Art. 79, Rn. 34; anders *Achilles*, Art. 79, Rn. 8 (erheblicher Verlust bildet Grenze); *Brunner*, Force majeure, S. 322; *Liu*, Force Majeure, Nr. 4.5.
[41] Vgl. *Herber/Czerwenka*, Art. 79, Rn. 13; *Reinhart*, Art. 79, Rn. 6; *Ryffel*, S. 93. In den Suez-Kanalfällen hat die englische Rechtsprechung (vgl. *Tsakiroglou & Co. Ltd. v. Noblee & Thörl GmbH*, [1962] A. C. 93 (H. L.); dazu *Berman*, 63 Colum. L. Rev. (1963), 1413–1439) deshalb zu Recht den Schiffstransport um das Kap der guten Hoffnung wegen Sperrung des Suez-Kanals als „not commercially or fundamentally different" von einem Transport durch den Suez-Kanal angesehen und deshalb für zumutbar erachtet.
[42] Vgl. *Brauer & Co. (Great Britain) Ltd. v. James Clark (Brush) Materials Ltd.*, [1952] 2 All E. R. 497 (C. A.).
[43] Vgl. OLG Hamburg, 28.2.1997, CISG-online 261; AAA Interim Award, 23.10.2007, CISG-online 1645; *Audit*, Vente internationale, Anm. 182.; *Achilles*, Art. 79, Rn. 8; *Kröll u. a./Atamer*, Art. 79, Rn. 57; *Soergel/Lüderitz/Dettmeier*, Art. 79, Rn. 15; *Staudinger/Magnus*, Art. 79, Rn. 34; *Weber*, Vertragsverletzungsfolgen, S. 174; *Karollus*, S. 209; vgl. auch § 2–614 UCC; zurückhaltend *Enderlein/Maskow/Strohbach*, Art. 79, Anm. 13.6.; kritisch indes *Bianca/Bonell/Tallon*, Art. 79, Anm. 2.6.5. und 2.8. (es könne aber die Weigerung des Käufers, ein geringfügig verschiedenes „substitute" anzunehmen, gegen Treu und Glauben verstossen und ihn schadensersatzpflichtig machen).

ger nach Art. 79 IV benachrichtigen[44] und einen etwaigen Widerspruch des Gläubigers respektieren.[45] Welche Anstrengungen im Einzelfall dem Schuldner zumutbar sind, um das Leistungshindernis oder dessen Folgen zu überwinden, ist wiederum primär anhand der **vertraglichen Risikoverteilung** zu bestimmen.[46] Im Übrigen kommt eine Befreiung erst jenseits der **äussersten Opfergrenze** in Betracht.[47]

15 **d) Ursächlichkeit für die Nichterfüllung.** Die Entlastung des Schuldners nach Art. 79 setzt voraus, dass ein nicht vorhersehbarer und unabwendbarer Hinderungsgrund die **ausschliessliche Ursache** der Nichterfüllung ist.[48] Hingegen bleibt die Verantwortung des Schuldners bestehen, wenn die Nichterfüllung durch eine **Vertragsverletzung mitverursacht** ist, also etwa die Ware wegen schlechter Verpackung bei einem nicht vorhersehbaren Naturereignis verloren geht.[49] Gleiches muss gelten, wenn die Nichterfüllung auf dem **Zusammenwirken mehrerer Ereignisse** beruht, von denen jedenfalls eines vom Schuldner vorhersehbar war oder vermieden werden konnte.[50] An der Ursächlichkeit fehlt es auch, wenn sich der Schuldner bereits in Verzug befindet und der Hinderungsgrund bei rechtzeitiger Lieferung keine Auswirkungen gehabt hätte.[51]

2. Einzelfälle

16 **a) Naturereignisse und -katastrophen.** Eine Entlastung nach Art. 79 wird häufig in den klassischen Fällen sog. **höherer Gewalt**, z. B. bei Erdbeben, Überschwemmungen, Sturm, Dürre, Feuer, Frost etc., in Betracht kommen, wenn hieraus ein Leistungshindernis für den Schuldner resultiert.[52] Allerdings gilt es hier jeweils sorgfältig zu prüfen, ob das Naturereignis **nicht vorhersehbar** war, weil z. B. in einer bestimmten Region regelmässig mit Ernteausfällen wegen Dürre zu rechnen ist, oder seine Folgen nicht hätten überwunden werden müssen.[53] Einen Hinderungsgrund können auch Epidemien,[54]

---

[44] Vgl. *Staudinger/Magnus*, Art. 79, Rn. 47; *Karollus*, S. 209.
[45] Der Gläubiger ist dann zur Vertragsaufhebung berechtigt, wenn die Abweichung von der geschuldeten Leistung eine wesentliche Vertragsverletzung (Art. 25) bedeutet, *Bianca/Bonell/Tallon*, Art. 79, Anm. 2.8.; *Pichonnaz*, Anm. 1762. f.; *Staudinger/Magnus*, Art. 79, Rn. 47 (unwesentliche Änderungen habe der Gläubiger hinzunehmen).
[46] *P. Huber/Mullis/P. Huber*, S. 262.
[47] Vgl. MünchKomm/*P. Huber*, Art. 79, Rn. 9.
[48] Vgl. *Bianca/Bonell/Tallon*, Art. 79, Anm. 2.6.6.; *Heuzé*, Anm. 472.; *Bamberger/Roth/Saenger*, Art. 79, Rn. 3; *Lee*, 8 Dick. J. Int'l L. (1990), 375, 390 f.; *Flambouras*, 13 Pace Int'l L. Rev. (2001), 261, 273; *Staudinger/Magnus*, Art. 79, Rn. 31; a. A. *Enderlein/Maskow/Strohbach*, Art. 79, Anm. 3.4.; *Brunner*, Force majeure, S. 340 ff.
[49] Vgl. *Gustin*, R. D. A. I. 2001, 379, 396; a. A. *Trachsel*, Haftungsbefreiung, S. 376, 415 ff. (Schadensteilung entsprechend Art. 80 vorzunehmen). Wenn freilich der Verlust der Ware auch bei ordnungsgemässer Verpackung eingetreten wäre, fehlt es an der Mitursächlichkeit der vom Schuldner begangenen Vertragsverletzung. Der Anwendung des Art. 79 steht dann nichts im Wege; insoweit ist *Enderlein/Maskow/Strohbach*, Art. 79, Anm. 3.4. und *Heuzé*, Anm. 472. zuzustimmen; ebenso *Kröll u. a./Atamer*, Art. 79, Rn. 59.
[50] *Heuzé*, Anm. 472.
[51] Int. Ct. Bulgarian CCI, 24.4.1996, CISG-online 435 (Streik ukrainischer Bergleute); Int. Ct. Russian CCI, 16.6.2003, CISG-online 977; ebenso *Gustin*, R. D. A. I. 2001, 379, 396 (Lagerbrand nach Verzugseintritt); offengelassen: AAA Interim Award, 23.10.2007, CISG-online 1645.
[52] Vgl. *Keil*, S. 110 f.; *Bamberger/Roth/Saenger*, Art. 79, Rn. 4; *Soergel/Lüderitz/Dettmeier*, Art. 79, Rn. 8; *Enderlein/Maskow/Strohbach*, Art. 79, Anm. 3.6.; *Rathjen*, RIW 1999, 561; *Piltz*, Internationales Kaufrecht, Rn. 4–239; *Bianca/Bonell/Tallon*, Art. 79, Anm. 2.6.7.; *P. Huber/Mullis/P. Huber*, S. 259; MünchKomm/ *P. Huber*, Art. 79, Rn. 10 f.; MünchKommHGB/*Mankowski*, Art. 79, Rn. 34, 37; *Kröll u. a./Atamer*, Art. 79, Rn. 46; *Staudinger/Magnus*, Art. 79, Rn. 27; *Achilles*, Art. 79, Rn. 6; *Brunner*, Art. 79, Rn. 17; *Herber/Czerwenka*, Art. 79, Rn. 8; *Magnus*, CISG and Force Majeure, S. 1, 17; *Reinhart*, Art. 79, Rn. 4.
[53] Vgl. CIETAC, 30.11.1997, CISG-online 1412 (sofern Überflutungen in einem Gebiet nicht ungewöhnlich sind, gelten sie als vorhersehbar); CIETAC, 25.1.1996, CISG-online 1067 (Schneefall in einem schneereichen Gebiet im Dezember ist vorhersehbar); CIETAC, 14.3.1996, CISG-online 1523 (Lieferprobleme bei bereits vor Vertragsschluss erfolgter Überflutung sind vorhersehbar); *Raw Materials Inc. v. Manfred Forberich GmbH & Co., KG*, U. S. Dist. Ct. (N. D. Ill.), 6.7.2004, CISG-online 925 (dass der Hafen in St. Petersburg im Januar zufriert, ist grundsätzlich vorhersehbar; im entschiedenen Fall aber früheres Zufrieren und deshalb keine Vorhersehbarkeit).
[54] Vgl. *Keil*, S. 110 f.; *Bamberger/Roth/Saenger*, Art. 79, Rn. 4; *Soergel/Lüderitz/Dettmeier*, Art. 79, Rn. 8; *Enderlein/Maskow/Strohbach*, Art. 79, Anm. 3.6.; *Rathjen*, RIW 1999, 561; *Piltz*, Internationales Kaufrecht, Rn. 4–239; *Bianca/Bonell/Tallon*, Art. 79, Anm. 2.6.7.; MünchKomm/*P. Huber*, Art. 79, Rn. 10 f.; Münch-

kriegerische Handlungen[55] und terroristische Anschläge[56] sowie Sabotageakte darstellen.

b) Staatliche Eingriffe. Hoheitliche Eingriffe („fait du prince"), die die Erfüllung **17**
verhindern, liegen im Allgemeinen **ausserhalb des Einflussbereiches** der Parteien. Vor allem die deutschsprachige Literatur[57] vertritt deshalb die Auffassung, dass in Fällen der Kontingentierung oder von Export- oder Importverboten, Vorschriften über die Bewirtschaftung von Waren oder Devisen oder eines Handelsverbotes eine Befreiung nach Art. 79 in Betracht kommen könne. Vereinzelt sind auch Schiedsgerichte von einer Befreiung des Schuldners ausgegangen; so wurde z. B. das UN-Embargo gegen Jugoslawien als Hinderungsgrund für die Bezahlung des Kaufpreises an den jugoslawischen Verkäufer für die Dauer des Embargos anerkannt.[58] Wesentlich strenger zeigen sich indessen vor allem **russische** und **chinesische Schiedsgerichte:** Eine Vielzahl von Entscheidungen verneint hier die Befreiung bei Nichterteilung von Import- oder Exportlizenzen, bzw. bei Erlass entsprechender Verbote.[59] Zusätzlich wird insoweit häufig auf Vorhersehbarkeit im Zeitpunkt des Vertragsschlusses zurückgegriffen.[60] Im Einzelfall ist es deshalb den Parteien dringend anzuraten, **vertragliche Regelungen** über die Risikozuordnung für staatliche Eingriffe namentlich im Bereich der Import- und Exportlizenzen zu treffen. Soweit staatliche Eingriffe als befreiender Hinderungsgrund im Sinne des Art. 79 anerkannt werden, ist es zweifelhaft, ob sich ein **Staatsunternehmen** oder ein in staatlicher Hand befindliches Unternehmen hierauf zu seiner Entlastung berufen kann.[61] Auch insoweit will die überwiegende deutschsprachige Literatur eine Entlastung nicht generell ausschliessen, es sei denn, dass der Staatseingriff unmittelbar oder mittelbar dazu dient, das unternehmerische Risiko des Staatsunternehmens aufzuheben oder zu verhindern.[62]

c) Organisationsrisiko. Typischerweise hat der Schuldner für den **persönlichen Be- 18 reich** einzustehen. Umstände, die in seiner Person ihren Ursprung haben, führen nicht zu

---

KommHGB/*Mankowski*, Art. 79, Rn. 34, 37; *Staudinger/Magnus*, Art. 79, Rn. 27; *Achilles*, Art. 79, Rn. 6; *Brunner*, Art. 79, Rn. 17; *Herber/Czerwenka*, Art. 79, Rn. 8; *Magnus*, CISG and Force Majeure, S. 1, 17; *Reinhart*, Art. 79, Rn. 4.

[55] *Hilaturas Miel, SL v. Republic of Iraq*, U. S. Dist. Ct. (S. D. N. Y.), 20.8.2008, CISG-online 1777 = 573 F. Supp. 2d 781; *Kröll u. a./Atamer*, Art. 79, Rn. 46.

[56] Vgl. *Staudinger/Magnus*, Art. 79, Rn. 28; Sekretariatskommentar, Art. 65, Nr. 5; *Keil*, S. 110 f.; *Bamberger/Roth/Saenger*, Art. 79, Rn. 4; *Soergel/Lüderitz/Dettmeier*, Art. 79, Rn. 8; *Enderlein/Maskow/Strohbach*, Art. 79, Anm. 3.4.; *Rathjen*, RIW 1999, 561; *Piltz*, Internationales Kaufrecht, Rn 4–239; *Bianca/Bonell/Tallon*, Art. 79, Anm. 2.6.7.; MünchKomm/*P. Huber*, Art. 79, Rn. 10 f.; MünchKommHGB/*Mankowski*, Art. 79, Rn. 34, 37; *Achilles*, Art. 79, Rn. 6; *Brunner*, Art. 79, Rn. 17; *Enderlein/Maskow/Strohbach*, Art. 79, Anm. 3.6.; *Herber/Czerwenka*, Art. 79, Rn. 8; *Magnus*, CISG and Force Majeure, S. 1, 17; *Reinhart*, Art. 79, Rn. 4.

[57] Vgl. Sekretariatskommentar, Art. 65, Nr. 5; *Keil*, S. 111 f.; *Morscher*, S. 135 f.; *Staudinger/Magnus*, Art. 79, Rn. 28; *Achilles*, Art. 79, Rn. 5; *Brunner*, Art. 79, Rn. 19; *P. Huber/Mullis/P. Huber*, S. 259; MünchKommHGB/*Mankowski*, Art. 79, Rn. 35; *Magnus*, CISG and Force Majeure, S. 1, 17; *Kranz*, S. 199; *Piltz*, Internationales Kaufrecht, Rn. 4–239; *Reinhart*, Art. 79, Rn. 4.

[58] Int. Ct. Hungarian CCI, 10.12.1996, CISG-online 774.

[59] Vgl. CIETAC, 15.12.1998, CISG-online 1167; Int. Ct. Russian CCI, 24.11.1998, CISG-online 1525; CIETAC, 7.5.1997, CISG-online 1152; CIETAC, 31.12.1996, CISG-online 1524; Int. Ct. Russian CCI, 16.3.1995, CISG-online 526; CIETAC, 7.8.1993, CISG-online 1060; vgl. auch *Fisanich*, 10 Am. Rev. Int'l Arb. (1999), 101, 114.

[60] Vgl. CIETAC, 15.12.1998, CISG-online 1167; Int. Ct. Russian CCI, 24.11.1998, CISG-online 1525; Int. Ct. Russian CCI, 16.3.1995, CISG-online 526; CIETAC, 7.8.1993, CISG-online 1060.

[61] S. dazu *von Hoffmann*, S. 35–74, m. w. N.; *Khadjavi-Gontard/Hausmann*, RIW 1980, 533–544 und RIW 1983, 1–15; *Keil*, S. 112 ff.

[62] Vgl. *von Hoffmann*, S. 60–65; *Keil*, S. 116; *Staudinger/Magnus*, Art. 79, Rn. 29; MünchKomm/*P. Huber*, Art. 79, Rn. 11; MünchKommHGB/*Mankowski*, Art. 79, Rn. 36; *Keil*, S. 112 ff.; *Enderlein*, RIW 1988, 336. Deshalb überzeugt die englische Entscheidung *C. Czarnikow Ltd. v. Centrala Handlu Zagranicznego Rolimpex*, [1979] A. C. 351 nicht, dass ein von der polnischen Regierung nachträglich verhängtes Exportverbot für Zucker die polnische staatliche Aussenhandelsorganisation, die Zucker verkauft hatte, zu entlasten vermag, obwohl das Exportverbot dazu diente, die Folgen einer schlechten Zuckerrohrernte und eine Fehlkalkulation bei dem polnischen Monopolunternehmen abzumildern; s. *Gesang*, S. 103 f.; *von Hoffmann*, S. 62–65.

einer Entlastung nach Art. 79.⁶³ Selbst unvorhergesehene Erkrankung, Tod oder Verhaftung des Schuldners oder eines wichtigen Mitarbeiters entlasten den Schuldner nicht, weil solche in der Person liegende Leistungshindernisse nach dem üblichen Verständnis des Handels Teil des Risikobereichs des Schuldners sind. Der Schuldner hat ferner für seine **Kontrollsphäre** einzustehen, d. h. für Hindernisse, die auf der Beschaffenheit und Organisation seines gegenständlichen Herrschaftsbereichs beruhen, etwa auf dem Versagen von Produktions- oder Buchungsmaschinen oder Datenverarbeitungsanlagen.⁶⁴ Der Schuldner ist ausserdem für die richtige **Organisation** und den störungsfreien **Ablauf** der für die Vorbereitung und Durchführung des Vertrages nötigen Vorgänge verantwortlich; er hat insbesondere auch für geeignete Lagermöglichkeiten zu sorgen.⁶⁵ Eine Befreiung nach Art. 79 kann in diesen Fällen allenfalls in Betracht kommen, wenn die betriebliche Störung ihrerseits auf einen von aussen kommenden Hinderungsgrund (Naturkatastrophe, Seuche etc.) zurückzuführen ist.⁶⁶

19   Ein **Rechtsirrtum,** mag er auch entschuldbar sein, ist kein Hinderungsgrund im Sinne des Art. 79. Die richtige rechtliche Beurteilung der Vertragspflichten gehört zum typischen Risikobereich des Schuldners.⁶⁷

20   d) **Personalrisiko.** Der Schuldner hat für seine **eigenen Leute** einzustehen. Ihr Verhalten fällt in den typischen Verantwortungsbereich des Schuldners, weshalb sie keine „Dritte" im Sinne des Art. 79 II sind.⁶⁸ Auf ein Verschulden des Schuldners bei der **Auswahl oder Überwachung** seiner Leute oder des Personals selbst kommt es nicht an. Der Schuldner kann sich auch nicht durch den Nachweis entlasten, dass die Leistungsstörung durch Leute verursacht wurde, die gegen seine Weisung handelten, straffällig wurden oder überhaupt nicht bei der Erfüllung des Vertrages eingesetzt waren.⁶⁹ Dies muss selbst bei **Sabotageakten** durch das eigene Personal gelten.⁷⁰

21   e) **Arbeitskämpfe.** Zweifelhaft ist, inwieweit der Schuldner von der Haftung für Nichterfüllung befreit ist, wenn die Erfüllung durch Massnahmen des Arbeitskampfes (Streik oder Aussperrung) verhindert wird. Eine generelle Entscheidung verbietet sich.⁷¹ Vielmehr ist nach dem für Art. 79 massgebenden **Grundgedanken der mangelnden Beherrschbarkeit** eines Hinderungsgrundes nach den konkreten Umständen und unter Berücksichtigung des Vertragsinhaltes zu beurteilen, ob der Arbeitskampf den Verantwortungsbereich des Schuldners überschreitet.

---

⁶³ Vgl. *Karollus,* S. 208; *Rummel,* Schadenersatz, S. 186; *Pichonnaz,* Anm. 1688.; *Piltz,* Internationales Kaufrecht, Rn. 4–234; *Ryffel,* S. 90; *Staudinger/Magnus,* Art. 79, Rn. 18; *Achilles,* Art. 79, Rn. 5; *Flambouras,* 13 Pace Int'l L. Rev. (2001), 261, 267 f.; *Brunner,* Art. 79, Rn. 7.

⁶⁴ Vgl. *P. Huber/Mullis/P. Huber,* S. 260; *Soergel/Lüderitz/Dettmeier,* Art. 79, Rn. 5; *Enderlein/Maskow/Strohbach,* Art. 79, Anm. 4.1.; *Schlechtriem,* JZ 1999, 794, 795; *Herber/Czerwenka,* Art. 79, Rn. 8; *Neumayer/Ming,* Art. 79, Anm. 2.; *Piltz,* Internationales Kaufrecht, Rn. 4–238; *Staudinger/Magnus,* Art. 79, Rn. 18; *Bamberger/Roth/Saenger,* Art. 79, Rn. 4a; MünchKomm/*P. Huber,* Art. 79, Rn. 12; MünchKommHGB/*Mankowski,* Art. 79, Rn. 25; *Brunner,* Art. 79, Rn. 167 ff.; *Flambouras,* 13 Pace Int'l L. Rev. (2001), 261, 267 f.

⁶⁵ Int. Ct. Bulgarian CCI, 12.2.1998, CISG-online 436.

⁶⁶ Vgl. *Staudinger/Magnus,* Art. 79, Rn. 18; MünchKomm/*P. Huber,* Art. 79, Rn. 12.

⁶⁷ Vgl. *Staudinger/Magnus,* Art. 79, Rn. 18.

⁶⁸ Vgl. CISG-AC, Op. 7 *(Garro),* Comment 17; *P. Huber/Mullis/P. Huber,* S. 260; *Herber/Czerwenka,* Art. 79, Rn. 6, 15; *Herbots/Pauwels,* FS Neumayer, S. 343; *Achilles,* Art. 79, Rn. 9; *Rathjen,* RIW 1999, 561, 563; *Soergel/Lüderitz/Dettmeier,* Art. 79, Rn. 22; *Kröll u. a./Atamer,* Art. 79, Rn. 63; *Enderlein/Maskow/Strohbach,* Art. 79, Anm. 7.2.; *Karollus,* S. 213; *Keil,* S. 146 f.; *Neumayer/Ming,* Art. 79, Anm. 8.; *Pichonnaz,* Anm. 1692.; *Reinhart,* Art. 79, Rn. 5; *Schlechtriem,* Internationales UN-Kaufrecht, Rn. 294; *Staudinger/Magnus,* Art. 79, Rn. 37; *Vischer,* Gemeinsame Bestimmungen, S. 179; MünchKomm/*P. Huber,* Art. 79, Rn. 13; MünchKommHGB/*P. Mankowski,* Art. 79, Rn. 28; a. A. *Heuzé,* Anm. 474.

⁶⁹ Vgl. *Herber/Czerwenka,* Art. 79, Rn. 15; *U. Huber,* RabelsZ 43 (1979), 413, 466 f.; *Karollus,* S. 213; *Stoll,* Schadensersatzpflicht, S. 276; *Neumayer/Ming,* Art. 79, Anm. 8. Fn. 33; *Staudinger/Magnus,* Art. 79, Rn. 20; a. A. *Heuzé,* Anm. 474.; *Enderlein/Maskow/Strohbach,* Art. 79, Anm. 7.2.; *Rathjen,* RIW 1999, 561, 563.

⁷⁰ Vgl. *Soergel/Lüderitz/Dettmayer,* Art. 79, Rn. 5; a. A. *Staudinger/Magnus,* Art. 79, Rn. 20; *P. Huber/Mullis/P. Huber,* S. 260; MünchKomm/*P. Huber,* Art. 79, Rn. 15; MünchKommHGB/*Mankowski,* Art. 79, Rn. 28.

⁷¹ Vgl. *Schlechtriem,* Internationales UN-Kaufrecht, Rn. 293; *Ziegler,* S. 222 f.; a. A. *Staudinger/Magnus,* Art. 79, Rn. 21 und *U. Huber,* RabelsZ 43 (1979), 413, 476 f., die annehmen, jeder Streik sei unter den allgemeinen Voraussetzungen des Art. 79 I ein Entlastungsgrund.

Streik und Aussperrung im Rahmen einer **innerbetrieblichen Auseinandersetzung**, 22
die allein um die Arbeitsbedingungen im Unternehmen des Schuldners geführt wird,
gehören zum Personal- und Betriebsrisiko, das der Schuldner regelmässig zu tragen hat.[72]

Allgemeine, insbesondere **politische Streiks,** können dagegen geeignet sein, den 23
Schuldner zu entlasten.[73] Es bedarf freilich stets der Prüfung, ob die Möglichkeit eines
solchen Streiks nicht bei Vertragsschluss in Rechnung zu stellen war, ob seine Folgen nicht
durch geeignete Vorsorgemassnahmen, etwa Lagerhaltung, abgewendet werden konnten
und ob sie nicht durch zumutbare Massnahmen zu überwinden sind.[74]

Lieferschwierigkeiten wegen Verwicklung eines **Zulieferanten** in einen Arbeitskampf 24
gehören im Allgemeinen zum Beschaffungsrisiko, das der Schuldner zu tragen hat.[75] Eine
Entlastung kommt hier nur in Betracht, wenn der Schuldner gerade auf diesen Zulieferanten angewiesen ist, sei es aufgrund vertraglicher Verpflichtung oder weil eine andere
Lieferquelle nicht zur Verfügung steht. Entsprechendes gilt für den streikbedingten **Ausfall
allgemeiner Verkehrs- oder Versorgungsleistungen,** auf die der Schuldner angewiesen
ist, etwa bei Streik von Fluglotsen oder des Post-, Eisenbahn- und Zollpersonals.[76] Auch
hier muss sich der Schuldner gegebenenfalls um alternative Transportmittel und -wege
bemühen. Bei unvorhersehbarem Streik bei der eingeschalteten **Bank** hat der Zahlungsschuldner die Zahlung grundsätzlich über eine andere Bank zu organisieren.[77]

f) **Finanzielle Leistungsfähigkeit.** Die eigene finanzielle Leistungsfähigkeit gehört zum 25
typischen Verantwortungsbereich des Schuldners.[78] Dies umfasst auch die Beschaffung
von Devisen.[79] Der Geldschuldner trägt das Risiko, dass Zahlungen fristgerecht am Zahlungsort eintreffen.[80] Der Geldschuldner wird nicht dadurch entlastet, dass unzuverlässige
Mittelspersonen die Zahlung nicht an den Gläubiger weiterleiten.[81] In Betracht kommt
allenfalls eine Entlastung des Schuldners in Fällen, in denen ihm die Leistung an den
Gläubiger von staatlicher Seite untersagt wird, jedenfalls soweit es sich nicht um gegen den
Schuldner gerichtete Sanktionen sondern um Massnahmen zur Prävention von rechtswidrigem Verhalten des Gläubigers handelt.[82]

---

[72] Vgl. *Schlechtriem,* Internationales UN-Kaufrecht, Rn. 293; *Soergel/Lüderitz/Dettmeier,* Art. 79, Rn. 5; *Enderlein/Maskow/Strohbach,* Art. 79, Anm. 4.2.; *Brunner,* Force majeure, S. 169; *Keil,* S. 168; *Lautenbach,* S. 63; *Neumayer/Ming,* Art. 74, Anm. 3.; *Herbots/Pauwels,* FS Neumayer, S. 345; *Pichonnaz,* Anm. 1692.; *Rummel,* Schadensersatz, S. 190; *Ryffel,* S. 100; *Vischer,* Gemeinsame Bestimmungen, S. 179; *Brunner,* Art. 79, Rn. 9; differenzierend *Herber/Czerwenka,* Art. 79, Rn. 13, die darauf abstellen wollen, ob es dem Schuldner zuzumuten war, im Interesse der Erfüllung eines einzelnen Auftrages weitgehende Konzessionen an die Arbeitnehmer zu machen. Es geht indes nicht um Verschulden des Unternehmers, sondern um die Abgrenzung der Risikosphäre; anders *Schoop,* S. 136–142: das Personalrisiko sei durch das Direktionsrecht begrenzt.
[73] Vgl. *Keil,* S. 169; *Lautenbach,* S. 63; *Neumayer/Ming,* Art. 74, Anm. 3.; *Ryffel,* S. 100; *Herbots/Pauwels,* FS Neumayer, S. 345; *Vischer,* Gemeinsame Bestimmungen, S. 179; *Bianca/Ponzanelli,* Art. 79, Anm. 4.; *Piltz,* Internationales Kaufrecht, Rn. 4–239; *Achilles,* Art. 79, Rn. 6; *Brunner,* Art. 79, Rn. 9; *ders.,* Force majeure, S. 169; *MünchKomm/P. Huber,* Art. 79, Rn. 15; *MünchKommHGB/Mankowski,* Art. 79, Rn. 30; enger *Bamberger/Roth/Saenger,* Art. 79, Rn. 6 (nur politische Streiks entlasten).
[74] Vgl. *Schlechtriem,* Internationales UN-Kaufrecht, Rn. 293.
[75] Vgl. *Neumayer/Ming,* Art. 79, Anm. 3.; *Ryffel,* S. 100; *Schoop,* S. 197–200.
[76] Vgl. *Keil,* S. 169 f.; *Lautenbach,* S. 64.
[77] Vgl. MünchKommHGB/*Mankowski,* Art. 79, Rn. 31; a. A. *Staudinger/Magnus,* Art. 79, Rn. 21.
[78] Vgl. Sekretariatskommentar, Art. 65, Nr. 10 (bezüglich der Zahlungspflicht des Käufers); Schiedsgericht der Handelskammer Hamburg, 21.3.1996, CISG-online 187 = RIW 1996, 766, 769; *Soergel/Lüderitz/Dettmeier,* Art. 79, Rn. 6, 7; *Schlechtriem,* Internationales UN-Kaufrecht, Rn. 289a; *Audit,* Vente internationale, Anm. 182.; *Heuzé,* Anm. 469.; *Bianca/Bonell/Tallon,* Art. 79, Anm. 2.6.5.; *Enderlein/Maskow/Strohbach,* Art. 79, Anm. 4.1.; *Bamberger/Roth/Saenger,* Art. 79, Rn. 4a; *Ryffel,* S. 105; *Piltz,* Internationales Kaufrecht, Rn. 4238; *Staudinger/Magnus,* Art. 79, Rn. 18; *Welser,* Die Vertragsverletzung des Verkäufers, S. 129; *Karollus,* S. 208; *Kröll u. a./Atamer,* Art. 79, Rn. 47; *Brunner,* Art. 79, Rn. 10; *MünchKomm/P. Huber,* Art. 79, Rn. 16; MünchKommHGB/*Mankowski,* Art. 79, Rn. 27.
[79] Int. Ct. Russian CCI, 17.10.1995, CISG-online 207 = CLOUT Nr. 142; *Schmidt-Kessel,* FS Schwenzer, S. 1513, 1521.
[80] Vgl. *Staudinger/Magnus,* Art. 79, Rn. 18; MünchKommHGB/*Mankowski,* Art. 79, Rn. 27.
[81] AG Alsfeld, 12.5.1995, CISG-online 170 = NJW-RR 1996, 120 f.
[82] Vgl. *Schmidt-Kessel,* FS Schwenzer, S. 1513, 1521 f.; vgl. auch oben Rn. 17.

26 **g) Beschaffungsrisiko.** Beim **marktbezogenen Gattungskauf,** der im internationalen Handel die Regel darstellt, trägt der Verkäufer das Risiko, dass ihm die Beschaffung der Ware gelingt.[83] Er wird grundsätzlich nicht dadurch entlastet, dass ihn sein Lieferant im Stich lässt, die Preise gestiegen sind und deshalb die Beschaffung der Ware mit erheblichen zusätzlichen Aufwendungen verbunden ist oder dass die zur Lieferung ausersehene Ware durch Zufall untergeht. Solange noch Ersatzware auf dem Markt erhältlich ist, muss der Verkäufer bis zu einer „äussersten Opfergrenze" (vgl. dazu Rn. 30) alle Möglichkeiten einer **Ersatzbeschaffung** ausschöpfen.[84] Gelingt eine Ersatzbeschaffung nur mit Verspätung, kann sich der Verkäufer hinsichtlich der Verspätung entlasten, sofern er nachweist, dass er durch ein nicht beherrschbares und nicht vorhersehbares Ereignis an der rechtzeitigen Erfüllung gehindert wurde.[85] Durch entsprechende **Klauseln,**[86] namentlich solche wie „richtige und rechtzeitige Selbstbelieferung vorbehalten" kann der Verkäufer das Beschaffungsrisiko auf den Käufer abwälzen.

27 Bei einem **Gattungskauf ohne Marktbezug,** insbesondere einem Verkauf aus einer **bestimmten Produktion** oder einem **Vorrat,** trägt der Verkäufer nach dem Sinn des Vertrages nur das Risiko, Ware aus dieser Produktion oder dem Vorrat beschaffen zu können.[87] Vereitelung der Produktion oder Untergang des Vorrats auf Grund eines unvorhersehbaren und unabwendbaren Ereignisses entlasten den Schuldner. Geht ein Teil des Vorrats durch ein solches Ereignis verloren, sind vom Schuldner **verhältnismässige Teilleistungen** an alle Gläubiger, denen er Ware aus dem Vorrat verkauft hat, zu erwarten.[88] Ausnahmsweise können gravierende wirtschaftliche Gesichtspunkte eine andere Verteilung ökonomisch sinnvoll erscheinen lassen.[89] Demnach ist der Schuldner jeweils in Höhe des durch diese Verteilung auf einen Gläubiger entfallenden Anteils des untergegangenen Vorrats befreit. Ob er den dadurch auf jeden Gläubiger entfallenden Teil des verbleibenden Vorrats tatsächlich liefert, ist für die Befreiung in Bezug auf den untergegangenen Teil des Vorrats unerheblich. Es läge dann eine einfache Nichtlieferung vor, die die entsprechenden Rechtsfolgen (ohne Befreiung) nach sich zieht. Beim **Stückkauf** trifft den Verkäufer nur dann ein Beschaffungsrisiko, wenn er nach dem Inhalt oder dem Sinn des Vertrages die **Beschaffung** der verkauften Sache übernommen hat. Den Gegensatz zu einer solchen Beschaffungsschuld bildet die **Abgabeschuld,**[90] bei welcher der Verkäufer ein in seinem Vermögen befindliches Stück zu liefern übernimmt. Hier wird der Verkäufer dann befreit, wenn die Lieferung dieses Stücks durch ein unvorhersehbares und unabwendbares Ereignis untergeht.

---

[83] Vgl. CISG-AC, Op. 7 *(Garro),* Comment 13; *Soergel/Lüderitz/Dettmeier,* Art. 79, Rn. 6; *Staudinger/Magnus,* Art. 79, Rn. 22; *Brunner,* Art. 79, Rn. 11; *ders.,* Force majeure, S. 171 ff.; *P. Huber/Mullis/P. Huber,* S. 261; MünchKomm/*P. Huber,* Art. 79, Rn. 17; MünchKommHGB/*Mankowski,* Art. 79, Rn. 32; *Rathjen,* RIW 1999, 561 f.; *Gustin,* R. D. A. I. 2001, 379, 396; *Herber/Czerwenka,* Art. 79, Rn. 8; *U. Huber,* östJBl. 1989, 273, 277; *Karollus,* S. 208; *Vischer,* Gemeinsame Bestimmungen, S. 178; s. schon *von Caemmerer,* AcP 178 (1978), 121, 144 f.; BGH, 24.3.1999, CISG-online 396 = BGHZ 141, 129, 133 f. (Rebwachs); OLG Hamburg, 28.2.1997, CISG-online 261 (Eisen-Molybdän); ICC, 8128/1995, CISG-online 526; Schiedsgericht der Handelskammer Hamburg, 21.3.1996, CISG-online 187; RB 's-Hertogenbosch, 2.10.1998, CISG-online 1309.
[84] Vgl. MünchKomm/*P. Huber,* Art. 79, Rn. 17; *P. Huber/Mullis/P. Huber,* S. 262.
[85] Vgl. Sekretariatskommentar, Art. 65, Nr. 9, Beispiel 65 C.
[86] Vgl. OLG Hamburg, 28.2.1997, CISG-online 261, wo der Vorbehalt der deutschen Verkäuferin „richtige und rechtzeitige Selbstbelieferung vorbehalten" i. S. d. deutschen Rspr. (vgl. BGH, 14.11.1984, BGHZ 92, 396, 401) ausgelegt wird. S. hierzu auch die rechtsvergleichenden Hinweise bei *Rabel,* Recht des Warenkaufs, Bd. 1, S. 362; vgl. auch *Brunner,* Force majeure, S. 175 ff.; *P. Huber/Mullis/P. Huber,* S. 261; *Staudinger/Magnus,* Art. 79, Rn. 22; MünchKomm/*P. Huber,* Art. 79, Rn. 18; MünchKommHGB/*Mankowski,* Art. 79, Rn. 32.
[87] Vgl. *U. Huber,* östJBl. 1989, 273, 277; *ders.,* Haftung des Verkäufers, S. 18 f.; *Salger,* S. 56; *Staudinger/Magnus,* Art. 79, Rn. 23; *P. Huber/Mullis/P. Huber,* S. 261; *Piltz,* Internationales Kaufrecht, Rn. 4–238; vgl. auch *Brunner,* Force majeure, S. 180 ff. Ebenso ist das Risiko eines Bauern, der ein Termingeschäft über seine Ernte abschliesst, auf ebendiese begrenzt, er muss sich im Falle einer Missernte nicht anderweitig eindecken, vgl. Maastricht, 9.7.2008, CISG-online 1748, Anm. 3.8.
[88] Vgl. *Keil,* S. 126.
[89] Vgl. zum amerikanischen Recht § 2–615 (b) UCC.
[90] Vgl. hierzu *Heck,* S. 86 f.; vgl. auch *Piltz,* Internationales Kaufrecht, Rn. 4–230.

h) **Vertragsgemässheit der Ware.** Eine Entlastung nach Art. 79 ist grundsätzlich auch bei 28 Lieferung vertragswidriger oder mit Rechten Dritter belasteter Ware denkbar,[91] falls der Sach- oder Rechtsmangel durch unvorhersehbare und unbeherrschbare Ereignisse hervorgerufen worden ist. Allerdings dürften die Fälle, in denen eine derartige Entlastung in Betracht zu ziehen ist, in der Praxis äusserst selten sein.[92] Ist der Verkäufer **Hersteller,** so muss er für **Konstruktions-, Fabrikations-** und **Instruktionsfehler** ohne Entlastungsmöglichkeit einstehen.[93] Ebenso haftet der Verkäufer für **Entwicklungsfehler** der von ihm hergestellten Sache, die zwar den anerkannten Regeln der Technik und dem wissenschaftlichen Stand zur Zeit des Vertragsabschlusses und der Herstellung entspricht, jedoch nach späterer Erkenntnis als mangelhaft anzusehen ist.[94] Zur Entlastung im Zusammenhang mit der Geltendmachung unbegründeter Ansprüche Dritter vgl. oben Art. 41 Rn. 10, Art. 42 Rn. 6.

Dieselben Grundsätze sind auch dann anzuwenden, wenn der Verkäufer lediglich **Zwi-** 29 **schenhändler** ist.[95] Die abweichende Auffassung, wonach der Zwischenhändler nicht für verdeckte Mängel haftet, mit denen er angesichts der Zuverlässigkeit seines Lieferanten nicht zu rechnen brauchte und die er bei ordnungsgemässer Untersuchung nicht erkennen konnte,[96] widerspricht dem Grundgedanken des Art. 79.[97] Allein dies entspricht auch dem Grundsatz, dass der Verkäufer das Beschaffungsrisiko tragen muss.[98] Der Verkäufer hat hier zudem regelmässig einen Rückgriffsanspruch gegen seinen Lieferanten. So wird auch der Verkäufer, der gutgläubig ein gestohlenes Kraftfahrzeug weiter verkauft, nicht von seiner Schadenersatzpflicht nach Art. 79 befreit, wenn das Fahrzeug später beim Käufer beschlagnahmt wird.[99]

i) **Wirtschaftliche Unmöglichkeit.** Nach heute h. M.[100] kann auch die sog. wirtschaft- 30 liche Unmöglichkeit, d. h. eine Änderung der Marktbedingungen dergestalt, dass die

---

[91] Vgl. die Zitate zur h. L. oben in Rn. 6.
[92] Ebenso *Schmidt-Kessel,* FS Schwenzer, S. 1513, 1521.
[93] Vgl. *Staudinger/Magnus,* Art. 79, Rn. 25; *Rathjen,* RIW 1999, 561, 562; *Soergel/Lüderitz/Dettmeier,* Art. 79, Rn. 16; *Schlechtriem,* Internationales UN-Kaufrecht, Rn. 289a; *ders., JZ* 1999, 794, 795 (Teil der Kontrollsphäre); *ders.,* FS Welser, S. 979; *Stoll,* Schadensersatzpflicht, S. 272; *Kröll u. a./Atamer,* Art. 79, Rn. 75; *U. Huber,* Haftung des Verkäufers, S. 23; *ders.,* RabelsZ 43 (1979), 413, 496; MünchKomm/*P. Huber,* Art. 79, Rn. 19 f.; MünchKommHGB/*Mankowski,* Art. 79, Rn. 26; *Ryffel,* S. 107; *Heuzé,* Anm. 469.; *Brunner,* Art. 79, Rn. 21.
[94] Vgl. *Staudinger/Magnus,* Art. 79, Rn. 25; *Neumayer/Ming,* Art. 79, Rn. 2; *Schlechtriem,* Internationales UN-Kaufrecht, Rn. 292 Fn 327; *Heuzé,* Anm. 469.; *Rummel,* Schadensersatz, S. 186; *Brunner,* Art. 79, Rn. 21; MünchKomm/*P. Huber,* Art. 79, Rn. 20; MünchKommHGB/*Mankowski,* Art. 79, Rn. 26; vgl. auch BGH, 9.1.2002, CISG-online 651 = IHR 2002, 15; BGH, 24.3.1999, CISG-online 396 = BGHZ 141, 129, 134 (Rebwachs); wahrscheinlich auch *Schlechtriem/P. Butler,* UN Law, Rn. 292 Fn. 564; a. A. noch *Stoll/Gruber,* 4. Aufl., Art. 79 Rn. 39.
[95] Vgl. BGH, 24.3.1999, CISG-online 396 = BGHZ 141, 129, 133 f. (das mangelhafte, da pflanzenunverträgliche Rebwachs war direkt vom Hersteller an die Klägerin geliefert worden, ohne dass die Beklagte als Zwischenhändlerin Qualitätskontrollen vorgenommen hatte), mit zust. Anm. von *Schlechtriem,* JZ 1999, 794–797 und *Hohloch,* JuS 1999, 1235–1236 sowie krit. Anm. *Stoll,* LM CISG Nr. 6/7, 1749 ff.; ICC, 8128/1995, CISG-online 526; so auch *Staudinger/Magnus,* Art. 79, Rn. 26; *Brunner,* Art. 79, Rn. 22; *Achilles,* Art. 79, Rn. 5; *Bamberger/Roth/Saenger,* Art. 79, Rn. 4a; *Soergel/Lüderitz/Dettmeier,* Art. 79, Rn. 16; *U. Huber,* östJBl. 1989, 273, 284; *ders.,* Haftung des Verkäufers, S. 23; *Schlechtriem,* Internationales UN-Kaufrecht, Rn. 292; *Neumayer/Ming,* Art. 79, Anm. 10. (der Verkäufer „assume en effet le risque général de fournir une marchandise conforme au contrat"); *Heuzé,* Anm. 469.; *Ryffel,* S. 108; *Salger,* S. 128, 146 f.; im Ergebnis auch *Honnold/Flechtner,* Art. 79, Rn. 434; s. schon *von Caemmerer,* AcP 178 (1978), 121, 148 (der Verkäufer stehe dafür, dass seine Bezugsquelle mangelfreie Ware liefert, bis zur Grenze des gemeinen Werts der Ware schlechthin ein; kritisch sei aber die Frage der darüber hinausgehenden Schäden).
[96] Vgl. *Stoll/Gruber,* 4. Aufl., Art. 79 Rn. 40.
[97] Vgl. *Staudinger/Magnus,* Art. 79, Rn. 26; MünchKomm/*P. Huber,* Art. 79, Rn. 20; *Brunner,* Art. 79, Rn. 15; *Kröll u. a./Atamer,* Art. 79, Rn. 76; BGH, 24.3.1999, CISG-online 396 = BGHZ 141, 129, 134 (Rebwachs); LG Freiburg, 22.8.2002, CISG-online 711 = IHR 2003, 22.
[98] Vgl. BGH, 24.3.1999, CISG-online 396 = BGHZ 141, 129, 134 (Rebwachs).
[99] Vgl. OLG München, 5.3.2008, CISG-online 1686 = IHR 2008, 253, 256: Dies gilt selbst, wenn der Verkäufer seiner Nachforschungspflicht Herkunft des Fahrzeuges nachkam; vgl. auch LG Freiburg, 22.8.2002, CISG-online 711 = IHR 2003, 22.
[100] Vgl. Hof van Cassatie, 19.6.2009, CISG-online 1963; *Schlechtriem,* Internationales UN-Kaufrecht, Rn. 291; *Jones/Schlechtriem,* Breach of Contract, S. 136; *Staudinger/Magnus,* Art. 79, Rn. 22, 24; *Honnold/Flechtner,* Art. 79, Rn. 432.2,; *Brunner,* Art. 79, Rn. 23 f.; *ders.,* Force majeure, S. 213 ff.; MünchKomm/

Beschaffung oder Herstellung der Ware für den Verkäufer mit gemessen am Vertragspreis **unzumutbar hohen Kosten** verbunden ist, eine Entlastung nach Art. 79 rechtfertigen.[101] Dasselbe gilt bei einem extremen **Verfall der Kaufpreiswährung**.[102] Eine Entlastung nach Art. 79 kommt allerdings in diesen Fällen nur in Betracht, wenn die **äusserste Opfergrenze** überschritten ist.[103] Wann dies der Fall ist, muss auf Grund der Umstände des Einzelfalls entschieden werden. So stellen Preisänderungen von über 100% in der Regel noch keinen Entlastungsgrund dar.[104] Bei einem spekulativen Geschäft kann sogar eine Verdreifachung des Marktpreises hinzunehmen sein.[105] Derartige **Preisschwankungen** müssen als **vorhersehbar** gelten.[106]

31 Bei wirtschaftlicher Unmöglichkeit stellt sich insbesondere die Frage, ob eine **Pflicht zur Neuverhandlung** angenommen werden kann. Vergleiche dazu unten Rn. 54.

32 **j) (Ethische) Unzumutbarkeit.** Eine Entlastung nach Art. 79 ist grundsätzlich auch denkbar, wenn einer Partei aus ethischen Gründen die Durchführung des Vertrages nicht zugemutet werden kann.[107] Dies ist insbesondere denkbar beim Verkauf von sog. „**dual use goods**" d. h. Produkten, die dazu missbraucht werden können, chemische, biologische oder nukleare Waffen herzustellen. Erkennt der Verkäufer, dass der Käufer die Ware dergestalt (miss-)brauchen will oder dass sie bei Grenzübertritt vom Käuferstaat zu diesem Ziel beschlagnahmt werden soll, muss er bei Nichtlieferung jedenfalls nach Art. 79 entlastet sein, sofern man ihm nicht in diesen Fällen sogar ein Recht zur Vertragsaufhebung gewähren will.

33 **k) Verwendungsrisiko.** Dem Beschaffungsrisiko des Verkäufers entspricht das Verwendungsrisiko des Käufers.[108] Dieser kann die Abnahme der Ware nicht mit der Begründung verweigern, er könne die Ware wegen der schlechten Konjunktur nicht mehr[109] oder nicht mehr zu dem kalkulierten Preis **weiterverkaufen**.[110] Auch kann sich der Käufer nicht

---

[P.] *Huber*, Art. 79, Rn. 21; MünchKommHGB/*Mankowski*, Art. 79, Rn. 38; *Schwenzer*, 39 Vict. U. Well. L. Rev. (2009), 709, 713; *dies.*, FS Bucher, S. 723, 727; *Lookofsky*, Int'l Rev. L. & E. 25 (2005), 434, 438; *ders.*, The 1980 United Nations Convention, Rn. 302; *Mazzacano*, 2 Nordic J. Com. L. (2011), 1, 48; U. *Huber*, RabelsZ 43 (1979), 413, 477 f.; *Welser*, Die Vertragsverletzung des Verkäufers, S. 128; *Kröll u. a./Atamer*, Art. 79, Rn. 79; *Herber/Czerwenka*, Art. 79, Rn. 8; *Kranz*, S. 200; *Ryffel*, S. 105 f.; *Osman*, S. 160 f.; *Loewe*, Art. 79, S. 96: *Ziegler*, S. 221; *Keil*, S. 188–192; *Achilles*, Art. 79, Rn. 6; *Enderlein/Maskow/Strohbach*, Art. 79, Anm. 6.3.; zurückhaltender *Rathjen*, RIW 1999, 561, 562; *Neumayer/Ming*, Art. 79, Anm. 14.; *Vischer*, Gemeinsame Bestimmungen, S. 178 f.; *Caytas*, S. 438; *Pichonnaz*, Anm. 1771.–1779.; *Bernardini*, Hardship e Force Majeure, S. 206 f.; *Bamberger/Roth/Saenger*, Art. 79, Rn. 6 (wegen hoher Zumutbarkeitsschwelle kaum praktische Bedeutung); aber gemäss *Lookofsky*, Understanding the CISG, S. 141, dürfte die Voraussetzung der Vorhersehbarkeit in solchen Fällen kaum gegeben sein.

[101] Vgl. ausführlich *Schwenzer*, 39 Vict. U. Well. L. Rev. (2009), 709, 713 ff.; *dies.*, FS Bucher, S. 723, 728 ff.

[102] Vgl. *Staudinger/Magnus*, Art. 79, Rn. 24; *Brunner*, Force majeure, S. 222.

[103] So ausdrücklich CISG-AC, Op. 7 *(Garro)*, Comment 38; vgl. auch die Nachweise für die h. M. in Fn. 100.

[104] Vgl. CIETAC, 2.5.1996, CISG-online 1067; Int. Ct. Bulgarian CCI, 12.2.1998, CISG-online 436; RB Hasselt, 2.5.1995, CISG-online 371; CA Colmar, 12.6.2001, CISG-online 694; Civ. 1, 30.6.2004, CISG-online 870; vgl. auch *Brunner*, Force majeure, S. 431 ff.; *Schwenzer*, 39 Vict. U. Well. L. Rev. (2009), 709, 716 f.; *dies.*, FS Bucher, S. 723, 730 f.; anders aber belg. Hof van Cassatie, 19.6.2009, CISG-online 1963: Preisanstieg von 70% bereits ausreichend.

[105] Vgl. OLG Hamburg, 28.2.1997, CISG-online 261; ICC, 6281/1989, CISG-online 8; Trib. Monza, 14.1.1993, CISG-online 540.

[106] Vgl. RB Tongeren, 25.1.2005, CISG-online 1106; Civ. 1, 30.6.2004, CISG-online 870; CA Colmar, 12.6.2001, CISG-online 694; Int. Ct. Bulgarian CCI, 12.2.1998, CISG-online 436; RB Hasselt, 2.5.1995, CISG-online 371; Int. Ct. Russian CCI, 16.3.1995, CISG-online 526; ICC, 6281/1989, CISG-online 8.

[107] Vgl. hierzu grundlegend *Schwenzer/Leisinger*, GS Hellner, S. 249, 272 ff.

[108] Vgl. *Brauer & Co. (Great Britain) Ltd. v. James Clark (Brush) Materials Ltd.*, [1952] 2 All E. R. 497 (C. A.); *Kröll u. a./Atamer*, Art. 79, Rn. 72.

[109] Int. Ct. Bulgarian CCI, 12.2.1998, CISG-online 436.

[110] Civ. 1, 30.6.2004, CISG-online 870; CA Colmar, 12.6.2001, CISG-online 694; vgl. aber *Honnold/Flechtner*, Art. 79, Rn. 427.1, die eine Regelungslücke sehen, deren Beseitigung unter Rückgriff auf die Art. 79 zugrunde liegenden in Fällen von äusserst extremem Wertverlust zur Befreiung führen kann.

darauf berufen, sein **Verwendungszweck sei entfallen** oder es befänden sich mittlerweile modernere und bessere Produkte auf dem Markt.

IV. Haftung für Dritte (Art. 79 II)

1. Kreis der Dritten

Nach Massgabe des Art. 79 II haftet der Schuldner auch für sog. **Erfüllungsüberneh- 34 mer,** d. h. für Dritte, denen er die Erfüllung des Vertrages oder eines Teils des Vertrages übertragen hat.[111] Die Entstehungsgeschichte der Vorschrift zeigt, dass damit nur **eigenverantwortlich handelnde Personen** gemeint sind, die **nicht im Organisationsbereich** des Schuldners unter dessen Verantwortung tätig werden.[112] Nach h. M. sind daher die eigenen Leute des Schuldners nicht unter Art. 79 II zu subsumieren; für sie gilt vielmehr Art. 79 I (vgl. oben Rn. 20). Auch selbstständige Unternehmer, die in die betriebliche Organisation des Schuldners eingeordnet sind (z. B. Bereitstellung eines Krans mit Bedienung zum Verladen der Ware) unterfallen Art. 79 I. Hingegen dürfte in der Beauftragung eines **Spediteurs** mit der Versendung der Ware oder der Ausführung des Transports in Fällen, in denen die Versendung oder der Transport Teil der geschuldeten Leistung ist (sog. Bringschuld), regelmäßig eine partielle Erfüllungsübernahme durch einen Dritten im Sinne des Art. 79 II zu erblicken sein.[113] Die **genaue Unterscheidung** zwischen Erfüllungsgehilfen, für deren Verhalten der Schuldner schon nach Art. 79 I im Rahmen des Personalrisikos einstehen muss, und selbstständigen Dritten im Sinne des Art. 79 II ist nicht immer leicht;[114] im Ergebnis ist sie aber jedenfalls im Hinblick auf die praktischen Ergebnisse zumeist unerheblich.[115]

Im Einzelnen setzt eine Erfüllungsübernahme im Sinne von Art. 79 II voraus, dass der 35 Dritte nach Abschluss des Kaufvertrages zwecks dessen Erfüllung durch den Schuldner eingeschaltet wird.[116] Unzweifelhaft erfasst sind damit **Subunternehmer,** die Teile der vom Verkäufer zu erbringenden Leistung ausführen, und **Banken** und **Frachtführer,** soweit der Verkäufer zu Bank- oder Frachtleistungen verpflichtet ist.[117] Auch **eigene Leute des Gläubigers** können Dritte im Sinne des Art. 79 II sein.[118]

---

[111] Vgl. *Enderlein/Maskow/Strohbach,* Art. 79, Anm. 7.2.–7.4. sprechen von „Unterauftragnehmer". Die ursprünglich für solche Personen verwendete Bezeichnung „Subunternehmer" (subcontractor) wurde nur deshalb aufgegeben, weil sie in manchen Sprachen – so insbesondere im Deutschen – bei der eigenverantwortlichen Übertragung von Pflichten aus einem Kaufvertrag nicht gebräuchlich ist; dazu *Stoll,* 3. Aufl., Art. 79 Rn. 3; *Herbots/Pauwels,* FS Neumayer, S. 341.
[112] Vgl. *Bamberger/Roth/Saenger,* Art. 79, Rn. 7; *Herbots/Pauwels,* FS Neumayer, S. 343; *Rathjen,* RIW 1999, 561, 564; *Karollus,* S. 211 f.; *Keil,* S. 148; *Staudinger/Magnus,* Art. 79, Rn. 39; *Flambouras,* 13 Pace Int'l L. Rev. (2001), 261, 274; *Brunner,* Art. 79, Rn. 14; MünchKomm/*P. Huber,* Art. 79, Rn. 23; weiter *Soergel/Lüderitz/ Dettmeier,* Art. 79, Rn. 22; *Herber/Czerwenka,* Art. 79, Rn. 14; *Piltz,* Internationales Kaufrecht, Rn. 4–240; *Achilles,* Art. 79, Rn. 9; *Bianca/Bonell/Tallon,* Art. 79, Anm. 2.7.1.; *Neumayer/Ming,* Art. 79, Anm. 8., die die Anwendung des Art. 79 II auf alle bei der Vertragserfüllung eingeschalteten selbstständigen Dritten befürworten.
[113] Vgl. *Karollus,* S. 129, 212; *Stoll,* Schadensersatzpflicht, S. 277; *Schlechtriem,* FS Welser, S. 978 f.
[114] Vgl. AG Alsfeld, 12.5.1995, CISG-online 170 = NJW-RR 1996, 120, 121: Die Zahlung des Käufers an eine nichtbevollmächtigte „Marketing-Managerin" führt wegen des Bringschuldcharakters nicht zum Erlöschen des Kaufpreisanspruches. Nach Art. 79 trägt der Käufer das Risiko, dass ein Bote die Zahlung nicht weiterleitet; vgl. CISG-AC, Op. 7 *(Garro),* Comment 19.
[115] Vgl. auch *Schmidt-Kessel,* FS Schwenzer, S. 1513, 1525 f.
[116] Vgl. *Neumayer/Ming,* Art. 79, Anm. 9.; *Bridge,* Int'l Sale of Goods, Rn. 3.61 spricht treffend von „delegation"; *Bianca/Bonell/Tallon,* Art. 79, Anm. 2.7.1. („organic link" erforderlich); AppGer Tessin, 29.10.2003, CISG-online 912; vgl. auch *Brunner,* Art. 79, Force majeure, S. 185 ff.
[117] Vgl. *Staudinger/Magnus,* Art. 79, Rn. 40; MünchKommHGB/*Mankowski,* Art. 79, Rn. 49.
[118] Vgl. AG Alsfeld, 12.5.1995, CISG-online 170 = NJW-RR 1996, 120 f.; *Schmidt-Kessel,* FS Schwenzer, S. 1513, 1525 f.; vgl. aber *P. Huber/Mullis/P. Huber,* S. 263 f.

36 Für die Anwendung des Art. 79 II kommt es nicht darauf an, ob die Inanspruchnahme des Dritten für den Schuldner unausweichlich ist, etwa weil der Dritte über ein **Monopol** verfügt.[119] Eine entsprechende Einschränkung des Abs. 2 wurde bei den Vorbereitungen zum Wiener E 1977 abgelehnt.[120] Art. 79 II beruht nicht auf dem Gedanken der vom Schuldner zu verantwortenden Auswahl des Dritten, sondern soll verhindern, dass die Aufteilung der Vertragserfüllung dem Schuldner zum Vorteil gereicht. Art. 79 II ist selbst anwendbar, wenn die Einschaltung des Dritten dem Schuldner **vom Gläubiger aufgegeben** wurde oder auf einem Wunsch des Gläubigers beruht.[121] In diesem Fall kann jedoch u. U. die auf den Dritten zurückzuführende Vertragsverletzung dem Gläubiger über Art. 80 zuzurechnen sein (vgl. unten Art. 80 Rn. 5).

37 Nach heute h. M.[122] fallen **Zulieferanten** des Schuldners nicht unter Art. 79 II. Sie schaffen nur Vorbedingungen für die Leistung des Schuldners oder wirken an der Vorbereitung der Leistung mit, ohne mit der Erfüllung des Vertrages – sei es auch nur teilweise – betraut zu werden. Sie liefern etwa zur Herstellung der Ware benötigte Rohstoffe oder Halbfertigfabrikate an den Verkäufer oder auch die Ware selbst, sofern der Verkäufer nur Zwischenhändler oder Kommissionär ist. Leistungshindernisse, die durch Zulieferanten verursacht worden sind, sind nach der allgemeinen Regel des Art. 79 I zu behandeln. Die **Haftung für Zulieferanten** ist Teil des allgemeinen **Beschaffungsrisikos** (dazu oben Rn. 26). Der Verkäufer ist deshalb grundsätzlich nicht entlastet, wenn der Zulieferant nicht oder nicht vertragsgemässe Ware liefert, selbst wenn dies unvorhersehbar war.[123] Eine andere Beurteilung kann sich allenfalls dann rechtfertigen, wenn etwa ein Zulieferant die **einzige in Betracht kommende Lieferquelle** ist, er vielleicht ein Rohstoffmonopol hat, und die Zulieferung wegen unvorhersehbarer Ereignisse (Krieg, Ausfuhrsperre, Zerstörung des Betriebs) unterbleibt.[124]

38 Für selbstständige Dritte, die zwar bei der Vertragsdurchführung tätig werden, aber **keine Vertragspflicht des Schuldners** erfüllen (z. B. Transportperson beim Versendungs-

---

[119] *Keil*, S. 152; *Pichonnaz*, Anm. 1703. (hier sei aber der Entlastungsbeweis erleichtert); a. A. CISG-AC, Op. 7 *(Garro)*, Comment 20; *Loewe*, Art. 79, S. 97; *Neumayer/Ming*, Art. 79, Anm. 10. a. E.; *Schlechtriem*, JZ 1999, 794, 796.

[120] Dazu *Stoll*, 3. Aufl., Art. 79 Rn. 3.

[121] *Witz/Salger/Lorenz/Salger*, Art. 79, Rn. 9; *Soergel/Lüderitz/Dettmeier*, Art. 79, Rn. 22; *Bianca/Bonell/Tallon*, Art. 79, Anm. 2.7.1.; *Heuzé*, Anm. 474.; *Pichonnaz*, Anm. 1703.; *Trachsel*, Haftungsbefreiung, S. 387; grundsätzlich auch *Enderlein/Maskow/Strohbach*, Art. 79, Anm. 7.4.; a. A. CISG-AC, Op. 7 *(Garro)*, Comment 20; *Herber/Czerwenka*, Art. 79, Rn. 17, und ferner – unter Anwendung des Art. 80 – *Keil*, S. 152 f.; *Neumayer/Ming*, Art. 79, Anm. 8.; *Vischer*, Gemeinsame Bestimmungen, S. 180.

[122] Vgl. CISG-AC, Op. 7 *(Garro)*, Comment 18; *Staudinger/Magnus*, Art. 79, Rn. 40; MünchKommHGB/ *Mankowski*, Art. 79, Rn. 50; *Rathjen*, RIW 1999, 561, 564; *Achilles*, Art. 79, Rn. 9; *Herber/Czerwenka*, Art. 79, Rn. 17; *Schlechtriem*, Internationales UN-Kaufrecht, Rn. 294, ders., JZ 1999, 794, 796 f. (trotz erheblicher Bedenken); *Keil*, S. 153; *Ziegler*, S. 224; *Stoll*, Schadensersatzpflicht, S. 277; *Soergel/Lüderitz/Dettmeier*, Art. 79, Rn. 22; *Piltz*, Internationales Kaufrecht, Rn. 4–240; *Kröll u. a./Atamer*, Art. 79, Rn. 65; *Enderlein/Maskow/Strohbach*, Art. 79, Anm. 7.2.; *Audit*, Vente internationale, Anm. 183.; *Bianca/Ponzanelli*, Art. 79, Anm. 6.; *Rummel*, Schadenersatz, S. 191; *Karollus*, S. 212; *Honnold/Flechtner*, Art. 79, Rn. 434; *Flambouras*, 13 Pace Int'l L. Rev. (2001), 261, 274; *P. Huber/Mullis/P. Huber*, S. 260; *Lookofsky*, Understanding the CISG, S. 142 f.; *Herbots/Pauwels*, FS Neumayer, S. 346; *Neumayer/Ming*, Art. 79, Anm. 9.; *Vischer*, Gemeinsame Bestimmungen, S. 179; *Pichonnaz*, Anm. 1704.; *Weber*, Vertragsverletzungsfolgen, S. 175; *Welser*, Die Vertragsverletzung des Verkäufers, S. 131; in diesem Sinne auch OLG Hamburg, 28.2.1997, CISG-online 261; Schiedsgericht der Handelskammer Hamburg, 21.3.1996, CISG-online 187 = RIW 1996, 766, 769; offen gelassen vom Int. Ct. Russian CCI, 16.3.1995, CISG-online 205 = CLOUT Nr. 140.

[123] Vgl. BGer, 12.6.2006, CISG-online 1516 (sogar bei Restposten trägt der Verkäufer das Risiko, von seinem Lieferanten im Stich gelassen zu werden); Int. Ct. Russian CCI, 16.3.1995, CISG-online 205 = CLOUT Nr. 140 (keine Entlastung des Verkäufers, wenn der Produzent gezwungen ist, die Produktion zu unterbrechen); OLG Hamburg, 28.2.1997, CISG-online 261; Schiedsgericht der Handelskammer Hamburg, 21.3.1996, CISG-online 187 = RIW 1996, 766, 769 (chinesischer Hersteller verweigert Lieferung wegen Liquiditätsengpasses); CISG-AC, Op. 7 *(Garro)*, Comment 18; *Neumayer/Ming*, Art. 79, Anm. 10.

[124] CISG-AC, Op. 7 *(Garro)*, Comment 18; *Lautenbach*, S. 64; *Rathjen*, RIW 1999, 561, 562; es genügt aber nicht, dass der Zulieferant von der Regierung wegen der fälligen Rückführung eines staatlichen Kredits unter Druck gesetzt wird und deshalb nicht liefern kann.

kauf), haftet der Schuldner nicht und braucht sich dementsprechend auch nicht zu entlasten.[125]

2. Entlastung

Nach Art. 79 II hat der Schuldner einen **doppelten Entlastungsnachweis** zu erbringen: Er kann sich nur entlasten, wenn er nachweist, dass ein Erfüllungshindernis für ihn selbst nicht beherrschbar ist und ausserdem auch der Dritte, wäre er Schuldner, sich für seine Person nach Art. 79 I entlasten könnte. Da die Voraussetzungen des Art. 79 II **kumulativ** vorliegen müssen, führt die Vorschrift im Ergebnis zu einer **Haftungsverschärfung**.[126]

3. Wissenszurechnung

Das Zusammenspiel der Art. 79 I und Art. 79 II ergibt im Ergebnis eine umfassende Haftung des Schuldners für Dritte, die er in die Vertragsabwicklung eingeschaltet hat. Sie ist Ausdruck eines **allgemeinen Prinzips,** dass sich der Schuldner das Verhalten von Dritten zurechnen lassen muss, derer er sich zur Durchführung des Vertrages bedient. Der Schuldner muss sich daher nach Art. 79 I, II auch das Wissen von eigenen Leuten, sonstigen Erfüllungsgehilfen, Erfüllungsübernehmern und Zulieferanten zurechnen lassen, was insbesondere im Rahmen von Art. 40 Bedeutung erlangt.

V. Vorübergehende Leistungshindernisse (Art. 79 III)

Nicht beherrschbare Hindernisse, die der Leistung nur vorübergehend entgegenstehen, befreien den Schuldner nach Art. 79 III von der Schadenersatzpflicht nur während der **Dauer ihres Vorliegens.** Fällt das Leistungshindernis weg, so muss der Schuldner nunmehr wieder erfüllen.[127] Dies schliesst freilich nicht aus, dass der Gläubiger auf Grund der Verzögerung der Leistung – sofern sich diese als wesentliche Vertragsverletzung im Sinne des Art. 25 darstellt – ein Recht zur **Vertragsaufhebung** (Art. 49 I) erlangt hat. Hat er von diesem Recht Gebrauch gemacht, so bleibt die Vertragsaufhebung auch dann wirksam, wenn der Hinderungsgrund später wegfällt.[128]

Nicht geregelt ist die Frage, ob und unter welchen Voraussetzungen der Schuldner ohne Rücksicht auf eine Vertragsaufhebung durch den Gläubiger **endgültig befreit** wird, falls sich während des durch den Hinderungsgrund bedingten Verzuges die Verhältnisse grundlegend ändern und deshalb die Leistung einen wesentlich anderen Charakter erhält.[129] Ein

---

[125] Vgl. HGer Zürich, 10.2.1999, CISG-online 488; *Staudinger/Magnus,* Art. 79, Rn. 41; *Brunner,* Art. 79, Rn. 16; *Achilles,* Art. 79, Rn. 9; *Herbots/Pauwels,* FS Neumayer, S. 347 f.; *Piltz,* Internationales Kaufrecht, Rn. 4–240; *Karollus,* S. 212; MünchKommHGB/*Mankowski,* Art. 79, Rn. 45.

[126] CISG-AC, Op. 7 (*Garro*), Comment 20; *Staudinger/Magnus,* Art. 79, Rn. 39; *Schlechtriem,* JZ 1999, 794, 796; *ders.,* Internationales UN-Kaufrecht, Rn. 294; *ders.,* FS Welser, S. 981 f.; *Rathjen,* RIW 1999, 561, 563; *Keil,* S. 144; *Bamberger/Roth/Saenger,* Art. 79, Rn. 7; *Achilles,* Art. 79, Rn. 10; *Lautenbach,* S. 65; *Neumayer/ Ming,* Art. 79, Anm. 8.; *Ryffel,* S. 103; *Herbots/Pauwels,* FS Neumayer, S. 340; *Vischer,* Gemeinsame Bestimmungen, S. 180; *Rummel,* Schadensersatz, S. 190; anders *Enderlein/Maskow/Strohbach,* Art. 79, Anm. 7.3. (generelle Aussage verbietet sich); a. A. *U. Huber,* Haftung des Verkäufers, S. 21 (Erweiterung der Haftungsbefreiung); *Soergel/Lüderitz/Dettmeier,* Art. 79, Rn. 23. Von einer Haftungserleichterung ging auch noch die UNCITRAL-Arbeitsgruppe aus, vgl. *Keil,* S. 144. Wieder anders *Schmidt-Kessel,* FS Schwenzer, S. 1513, 1525 („schlichte Klarstellung").

[127] Vgl. *Soergel/Lüderitz/Dettmeier,* Art. 79, Rn. 27; *Staudinger/Magnus,* Art. 79, Rn. 44; *Achilles,* Art. 79, Rn. 11; *Stoll,* Schadensersatzpflicht, S. 279; *Neumayer/Ming,* Art. 79, Anm. 11.; *Bund,* 17 J. L. & Com. (1998), 381, 387; *Bartels/Motomura,* RabelsZ 43 (1979), 649, 667; *Liu,* Force Majeure, Nr. 9; MünchKommHGB/ *Mankowski,* Art. 79, Rn. 55; *Atamer,* FS Schwenzer, S. 83, 90.

[128] Vgl. MünchKomm/*P. Huber,* Art. 79, Rn. 25.

[129] Dieser Ansatz ist vom RG während des Ersten Weltkrieges entwickelt worden, um in Fällen Abhilfe zu schaffen, in denen der Verkäufer meist unter Berufung auf sog. Kriegsklauseln die Lieferung auf Grund der Kriegsereignisse zunächst nur ausgesetzt hatte, später aber wegen der Dauer des Krieges und der zwischen-

norwegischer Antrag, Abs. 3 in dieser Hinsicht zu ergänzen, fand auf der Wiener Konferenz keine Mehrheit.[130] Dies schliesst jedoch nicht aus, dem Schuldner in Ausnahmefällen die Berufung auf die **Unzumutbarkeit der Leistungserbringung** zu erlauben, wenn das Risiko unvermeidbar und unvorhersehbar war und die „Opfergrenze" überschritten wurde.[131]

VI. Benachrichtigungspflicht (Art. 79 IV)

1. Allgemeines

43   Die Partei, die sich auf Art. 79 beruft, ist verpflichtet, den Hinderungsgrund und dessen Auswirkungen auf die Vertragsdurchführung der anderen Partei mitzuteilen. Dies ist eine Ausprägung der allgemeinen dem CISG zu Grunde liegenden **Kooperationspflicht**. Die Mitteilung soll die andere Partei in die Lage versetzen abzuklären, ob sie gegebenenfalls selbst Abhilfemassnahmen treffen oder – bei Vorliegen einer wesentlichen Vertragsverletzung – vom Vertrag Abstand nehmen will. Führt der Hinderungsgrund dazu, dass der Schuldner seine Pflichten nur in annähernder Weise erfüllen kann, so schafft die Mitteilung auch die Basis für eine mögliche Vertragsanpassung.[132]

2. Mitteilung

44   In der Mitteilung müssen **Art, Schwere und Dauer des Leistungshindernisses** detailliert beschrieben werden. Die Mitteilung hat innerhalb einer **vernünftigen Frist**, nachdem die Befreiung suchende Vertragspartei den Hinderungsgrund kannte oder kennen musste, zu erfolgen. Unter Umständen ist eine **mehrstufige Mitteilung** erforderlich, wenn die Vertragspartei sich noch um Alternativlösungen bemüht bzw. diese fehlgeschlagen sind.[133]

45   Die Mitteilung ist grundsätzlich **formfrei**. Entgegen der Regel des Art. 27 trägt der Schuldner jedoch nach Art. 79 IV 2 das Risiko, dass die Mitteilung dem Gläubiger überhaupt zugeht und innerhalb der angemessenen Frist übermittelt wird.[134]

46   Bei **Kenntnis des Gläubigers** vom Vorliegen des Hinderungsgrundes besteht grundsätzlich keine Mitteilungspflicht.[135] Dasselbe gilt, wenn der **Hinderungsgrund** lediglich **droht**, aber noch nicht eingetreten ist. In beiden Fällen empfiehlt sich gleichwohl für den Schuldner eine klarstellende bzw. vorsorgliche Mitteilung.[136]

---

zeitlichen Preissteigerungen ganz vom Vertrag loskommen wollte (Nachweise bei *Gruber*, Geldwertschwankungen, S. 368 f.). Auch in der englischen doctrine of frustration of contract findet sich der Gedanke, dass sich im Falle einer Leistungserschwerung der Inhalt der Leistung wesentlich ändert und die Lieferung eines solchen aliuds nicht verlangt werden kann; vgl. *F. A. Tamplin Steamship Co. v. Anglo-Mexican Petroleum Products Co.*, [1916] 2 A. C. 397; *Davis Contractors Ltd. v. Fareham U. D. C.*, [1956] A. C. 696, 727.

[130] Vgl. O. R., S. 381, Nr. 52–70, und S. 383–385, Nr. 18–44.

[131] Vgl. *Honnold/Flechtner*, Art. 79, Rn. 435.1; *Keil*, S. 128 f., 190 f.; *Nicholas*, Impracticability, S. 5–16 ff.; *Schlechtriem*, Internationales UN-Kaufrecht, Rn. 291; *Karollus*, S. 210; *Gruber*, Geldwertschwankungen, S. 539; *Caytas*, S. 442.

[132] Vgl. *Staudinger/Magnus*, Art. 79, Rn. 47; MünchKommHGB/*Mankowski*, Art. 79, Rn. 59; *Benedick*, Informationspflichten, Rn. 499: die Mitteilung kann auch mit einem Angebot zur Vertragsänderung verbunden werden.

[133] Vgl. *Witz/Salger/Lorenz/Salger*, Art. 79, Rn. 11.

[134] Vgl. *Stern*, Erklärungen, S. 116 f.; *Soergel/Lüderitz/Dettmeier*, Art. 79, Rn. 28; *Enderlein/Maskow/Strohbach*, Art. 79, Anm. 11.; *Achilles*, Art. 79, Rn. 12; *Audit*, Vente internationale, Anm. 184.; *Karollus*, S. 211; MünchKomm/*P. Huber*, Art. 79, Rn. 30.

[135] Vgl. MünchKommHGB/*Mankowski*, Art. 79, Rn. 60.

[136] Vgl. MünchKommHGB/*Mankowski*, Art. 79, Rn. 60.

3. Schadenersatzpflicht

Unterlässt der Schuldner die nach Art. 79 IV 1 erforderliche Mitteilung oder ist diese 47 ungenau oder verspätet, so beeinflusst dies zwar nicht die nach Art. 79 I vorgesehene Entlastung,[137] der Schuldner ist jedoch zum Ersatz des Schadens verpflichtet, der spezifisch aus der Verletzung der Mitteilungspflicht resultiert. Regelmässig ist damit Ersatz des **Vertrauensschadens** des Gläubigers geschuldet; ein Anspruch auf das Erfüllungsinteresse besteht nicht.[138] Als Vertrauensschaden kommt etwa ein Haftpflichtschaden gegenüber Abnehmern oder entgangener Gewinn in Betracht, wenn der Käufer bei rechtzeitiger Benachrichtigung keine Folgegeschäfte abgeschlossen oder rechtzeitig Deckungsgeschäfte getätigt hätte.[139]

Auch die in Art. 79 IV 2 normierte Schadenersatzpflicht steht unter dem Vorbehalt, dass 48 der Schuldner sich durch den Nachweis entlastet, an der Benachrichtigung des Gläubigers oder an der rechtzeitigen Mitteilung durch einen **Hinderungsgrund** im Sinne des Art. 79 gehindert worden zu sein.[140] Dabei mag es sich um den gleichen Hinderungsgrund handeln, der bereits die Erfüllung verhindert hat, etwa um eine Naturkatastrophe oder einen Generalstreik im Lande des Schuldners. Für Verzögerung oder Vereitelung des Zugangs der Mitteilung durch ein Verhalten der mit der Übermittlung betrauten Anstalt oder Person hat jedoch der Schuldner nach Art. 79 II einzustehen.[141]

VII. Wirkungen der Entlastung (Art. 79 V)

1. Befreiung von der Schadenersatzpflicht

Die entlastende Wirkung eines Hinderungsgrundes im Sinne des Art. 79 I beschränkt sich 49 darauf, dass die Schadenersatzpflicht des Schuldners „nach diesem Übereinkommen" entfällt, soweit die Verhinderung reicht (Art. 79 V). Die Entlastung betrifft allein die vom Hinderungsgrund **betroffene Vertragspflicht,** der Bestand des Vertrages und die übrigen Pflichten werden nicht berührt.[142] Auch ändert die Entlastung nichts daran, dass die durch den Hinderungsgrund verursachte Nichterfüllung eine **Vertragsverletzung** darstellt.[143] Bei nur **teilweiser Verhinderung der Erfüllung** ist der Schuldner auch nur seiner Verantwortung für den nicht erfüllten Teil der Leistung enthoben.[144] Dem Gläubiger bleibt es unbenommen, seine Rechte hinsichtlich der von dem Hinderungsgrund nicht betroffenen Restleistung auszuüben; so kann er insbesondere auch den ganzen Vertrag nach Massgabe

---

[137] Vgl. *Benedick,* Informationspflichten, Rn. 497.
[138] Vgl. aber *Audit,* Vente internationale, Anm. 184.; *Achilles,* Art. 79, Rn. 13; *Karollus,* S. 210; *Flambouras,* 13 Pace Int'l L. Rev. (2001), 261, 273; anders *Staudinger/Magnus,* Art. 79, Rn. 49; *Herber/Czerwenka,* Art. 79, Rn. 21, die dem Käufer einen Anspruch auf Ersatz für entgangenen Gewinn zusprechen wollen, wenn er in Unkenntnis des Lieferhindernisses die Ware weiterverkauft hat. Dagegen spricht freilich, dass der Käufer auch bei rechtzeitiger Benachrichtigung keinen Gewinn erzielt hätte; anders auch *Soergel/Lüderitz/Dettmeier,* Art. 79, Rn. 28: ersatzfähig sind Mehrkosten eines Deckungsgeschäftes, wenn der Gläubiger bei rechtzeitiger Benachrichtigung ein günstigeres Deckungsgeschäft hätte abschliessen können.
[139] Vgl. *Staudinger/Magnus,* Art. 79, Rn. 49; *Bamberger/Roth/Saenger,* Art. 79, Rn. 9; *Herber/Czerwenka,* Art. 79, Rn. 21; MünchKommHGB/*Mankowski,* Art. 79, Rn. 62; *Soergel/Lüderitz/Dettmeier,* Art. 79, Rn. 28.
[140] Vgl. *Staudinger/Magnus,* Art. 79, Rn. 50; *Bianca/Bonell/Tallon,* Art. 79, Anm. 2.8.; *Pichonnaz,* Anm. 1790–1804.; *Stern,* Erklärungen, S. 116; *Achilles,* Art. 79, Rn. 13; *Piltz,* Internationales Kaufrecht, Rn. 4–248; MünchKomm/*P. Huber,* Art. 79, Rn. 31; MünchKommHGB/*Mankowski,* Art. 79, Rn. 63; zweifelnd *Karollus,* S. 211.
[141] *Stern,* Erklärungen, S. 116.
[142] Vgl. *Bridge,* Int'l Sale of Goods, Rn. 3.58; *Enderlein/Maskow/Strohbach,* Vorbem. 4. vor Abschnitt IV: Befreiungen; *Heuzé,* Anm. 475.; *Pichonnaz,* Anm. 1806.–1809.; *Gustin,* R. D. A. I. 2001, 379, 398 f.; *Brunner,* Art. 79, Rn. 38; *ders.,* Force majeure, S. 345.
[143] Vgl. *Piltz,* Internationales Kaufrecht, Rn. 4–253; *Staudinger/Magnus,* Art. 79, Rn. 51; *Karollus,* S. 211; *Enderlein/Maskow/Strohbach,* Art. 79, Anm. 13.2.; *Hudson,* S. 175; MünchKommHGB/*Mankowski,* Art. 79, Rn. 5.
[144] Vgl. *Honnold/Flechtner,* Art. 79, Rn. 435.2; *Bund,* 17 J. L. & Com. (1998), 381, 388; *Bianca/Bonell/Tallon,* Art. 79, Anm. 2.10.3.; *Liu,* Force Majeure, Nr. 10; *Magnus,* CISG and Force Majeure, S. 1, 21.

der allgemeinen Bestimmungen aufheben, wenn eine wesentliche Vertragsverletzung vorliegt, d. h. wenn er objektiv kein Interesse an der Teillieferung hat.[145]

50 Nicht geregelt ist die Frage, ob der Schuldner, der wegen des Leistungshindernisses zugleich einen Ersatzvorteil, etwa eine Versicherungs- oder Entschädigungssumme für verlorene oder beschlagnahmte Ware, erhält, zur Herausgabe eines solchen **stellvertretenden commodum** an den Gläubiger verpflichtet ist. Die inzwischen h. M.[146] bejaht einen derartigen Herausgabeanspruch in Analogie zu dem Gedanken des Art. 84 II lit. b. Voraussetzung ist freilich, dass es sich um ein eigentliches stellvertretendes commodum für die betroffene Ware handelt; die Herausgabe anderer Ersatzansprüche, wie z. B. Feuer- oder Betriebsausfallversicherungsansprüche, kommt nicht in Betracht.[147]

51 Nach Art. 79 V sind nur Schadenersatzansprüche nach dem CISG selbst ausgeschlossen. Ob von einer Befreiung auch vertragliche Vereinbarungen, d. h. **Vertragsstrafen** und **Schadenspauschalierungen,** betroffen sind, ist offen. Ein Antrag der damaligen DDR auf der Wiener Konferenz, Art. 79 V auch auf „penalties or liquidated damages" zu erstrecken, wurde ausdrücklich abgelehnt.[148] Welche Auswirkungen ein Hinderungsgrund im Sinne des Art. 79 I auf eine derartige vertragliche Vereinbarung hat, ist zunächst durch **Auslegung** der Vereinbarung zu ermitteln.[149] Die **Gültigkeit** derartiger Vereinbarungen bestimmt sich allerdings gemäss Art. 4 S. 2 lit. a nach dem anwendbaren nationalen Recht. Bei der insoweit vorzunehmenden **Inhaltskontrolle** derartiger Klauseln kann indes die Art. 79 zugrunde liegende Wertung als wichtige Auslegungshilfe herangezogen werden.[150] Im Zweifelsfall sollte die Befreiung dementsprechend auch auf Schadenersatzpauschalen und Strafen angewendet werden.[151]

2. Erfüllungsanspruch

52 Im Gegensatz zu Art. 74 EKG, der bei Vorliegen eines Hinderungsgrundes nicht nur den Anspruch auf Schadenersatz sondern auch den Anspruch auf Erfüllung ausschloss, lässt das CISG das Recht des Gläubigers auf **Erfüllung** gemäss Art. 79 V **grundsätzlich unberührt.** Auf der Wiener Konferenz war ein Antrag von deutscher Seite, bei einem dauernden Leistungshindernis den Erfüllungsanspruch auszuschliessen, mit der Begründung abgelehnt worden, dass sich bei tatsächlicher Unmöglichkeit in der Praxis keine Probleme ergeben, der kategorische Ausschluss des Erfüllungsanspruchs aber Nebenrechte des Gläubigers beeinträchtigen könne.[152] Die Aufrechterhaltung des Erfüllungsanspruchs in Fällen der Schuldnerentlastung nach Art. 79 ist durchaus sinnvoll, sofern die Erfüllung zu einem späteren Zeitpunkt, durch Reparatur oder Ersatzlieferung etc. möglich bleibt.[153]

---

[145] Vgl. *Honnold/Flechtner,* Art. 79, Rn. 435.2; *Bianca/Bonell/Tallon,* Art. 79, Anm. 2.10.3.; *Brunner,* Force majeure, S. 347 ff.

[146] Vgl. *Staudinger/Magnus,* Art. 79, Rn. 54; *Brunner,* Art. 79, Rn. 40; *ders.,* Force majeure, S. 349 ff.; *Achilles,* Art. 79, Rn. 14; MünchKommHGB/*Mankowski,* Art. 79, Rn. 11; *Piltz,* Internationales Kaufrecht, Rn. 4–251; *Kröll u. a./Atamer,* Art. 79, Rn. 26; *dies.,* FS Schwenzer, S. 83, 87 f.; *Bock,* FS Schwenzer, S. 175, 188.

[147] Vgl. *Staudinger/Magnus,* Art. 79, Rn. 54.

[148] Vgl. O. R., S. 135, 385 f.

[149] Vgl. CISG-AC, Op. 10 *(Hachem),* Rule 5; *Staudinger/Magnus,* Art. 79, Rn. 53; MünchKomm/*P. Huber,* Art. 79, Rn. 27; MünchKommHGB/*Mankowski,* Art. 79, Rn. 15; *Brunner,* Art. 79, Rn. 39; *ders.,* Force majeure, S. 347; *P. Huber/Mullis/P. Huber,* S. 265; *Rathjen,* RIW 1999, 561, 565.

[150] Vgl. *Staudinger/Magnus,* Art. 79, Rn. 53; MünchKommHGB/*Mankowski,* Art. 79, Rn. 15; *Rathjen,* RIW 1999, 561, 565; *Keil,* S. 45–48; *Piltz,* Internationales Kaufrecht, Rn. 4–246; *Berger,* RIW 1999, 401, 403; *Reinhart,* Art. 79, Rn. 12.

[151] CISG-AC, Op. 10 *(Hachem),* Rule 5; *Schwenzer,* 39 Vict. U. Well. L. Rev. (2009), 709, 719 f.; *dies.,* FS Bucher, S. 723, 734; *Hachem,* Agreed Sums, S. 173; *Kröll u. a./Atamer,* Art. 79, Rn. 15; offen gelassen von OLG Hamburg, 25.1.2008, CISG-online 1681, IHR 2008, 98, 101; a. A. MünchKommHGB/*Mankowski,* Art. 79, Rn 15.

[152] Vgl. O. R., S. 383 f. und die Ausführungen von *Hjerner* (Schweden), O. R., S. 384, Nr. 25; O. R., S. 381, Nr. 52–70, und S. 383–385, Nr. 18–44.

[153] Vgl. *Staudinger/Magnus,* Art. 79, Rn. 57; MünchKommHGB/*Mankowski,* Art. 79, Rn. 7; *Enderlein/Maskow/Strohbach,* Art. 79, Anm. 13.6.; *Piltz,* Internationales Kaufrecht, Rn. 4–252.

Bei **objektiver Unmöglichkeit** der Leistung, etwa bei Zerstörung des geschuldeten 53 Einzelgegenstandes, besteht indes Einigkeit, dass auch der Erfüllungsanspruch entfallen muss.[154] Dogmatisch kann dieses Ergebnis auf die Wertungen der Regeln über den Gefahrübergang sowie des Art. 79 selbst gestützt werden.[155] Ein Rückgriff auf Art. 28[156] erscheint wegen seiner Anbindung an subsidiär anwendbares nationales Recht und damit der Gefahr divergierender Lösungen nicht sachgerecht.

Andere Leistungshindernisse, insbesondere eine Leistungserschwerung wie sie auch im 54 Falle sog. **subjektiver Unmöglichkeit** vorliegt, führen nicht zum Erlöschen des Erfüllungsanspruchs.[157] Eine uneingeschränkte Zulassung der Erfüllungsklage oder gar die Verhängung von Zwangsstrafen würde freilich die von Art. 79 bezweckte Entlastung des Schuldners unterlaufen. Selbst wenn man in diesen Fällen ein Fortbestehen des Erfüllungsanspruchs annehmen will, so ist dieser jedenfalls für die Dauer der Leistungsbehinderung **nicht durchsetzbar** (enforceable).[158] Für die Fälle von „hardship" wird vorgeschlagen, die Anpassung des Vertrages über Art. 6.2.3 II PICC vorzunehmen,[159] indem diese als Handelsbrauch im Sinne des Art. 9 II CISG[160] oder als Teil der Grundprinzipien der Konvention im Sinne des Art. 7 II CISG[161] verstanden werden und soweit dessen Voraussetzungen vorliegen.[162] Freilich ist dieser Rückgriff nicht erforderlich. Abgesehen von den praktischen Schwierigkeiten, eine unwillige Partei zu konstruktiven und kooperativen Verhandlungen zu zwingen, erscheint es schwierig, sich überhaupt eine Situation vorzustellen, in der eine derartige Pflicht nötig sein könnte. Wenn der Schuldner wirtschaftliche Unmöglichkeit geltend macht und anbietet, unter anderen Vertragsbedingungen zu erfüllen, so ist der Gläubiger nicht berechtigt, den Vertrag aufzuheben, wenn von ihm vernünftiger-

---

[154] Vgl. oben *Müller-Chen*, Art. 28 Rn. 15 und Art. 46 Rn. 12; *Staudinger/Magnus*, Art. 79, Rn. 58; MünchKomm/*P. Huber*, Art. 79, Rn. 29; MünchKommHGB/*Mankowski*, Art. 79, Rn. 8 f.; *U. Huber*, Rechtsbehelfe der Parteien, S. 206; *Achilles*, Art. 79, Rn. 14; *Enderlein/Maskow/Strohbach*, Art. 79, Anm. 13.6.; *Witz/Salger/Lorenz/Salger*, Art. 79, Rn. 12; *Caytas*, S. 444; *Schmid*, Lückenfüllung und Normenkonkurrenz, S. 179; *Audit*, Vente internationale, Anm. 186.; *Plantard*, J. D. I. 1988, 311, 360 f.; *Bianca/Ponzanelli*, Art. 79, Anm. 8.; *Bianca/Bonell/Tallon*, Art. 79, Anm. 2.10.2. („specific performance does not make sense any more"); *Neumayer/Ming*, Art. 79, Anm. 13.; *Honnold/Flechtner*, Art. 79, Rn. 435.5; *Karollus*, S. 141; *Brunner*, Art. 79, Rn. 42 (Anwendung von Art. 7.2.2 PICC); *Kröll u. a./Atamer*, Art. 79, Rn. 32; unklar *Piltz*, Internationales Kaufrecht, Rn. 4–251, 5–169.

[155] So die heute überwiegende Meinung, vgl. *Staudinger/Magnus*, Art. 79, Rn. 58; MünchKommHGB/*Mankowski*, Art. 79, Rn. 8; MünchKomm/*P. Huber*, Art. 79, Rn. 29; *Enderlein/Maskow/Strohbach*, Art. 79, Anm. 13.6.; *U. Huber*, Rechtsbehelfe der Parteien, S. 206; *Witz/Salger/Lorenz/Salger*, Art. 79, Rn. 12; unklar *Piltz*, Internationales Kaufrecht, Rn. 4–251, 5–169. *Atamer*, FS Schwenzer, S. 83, 86 f., 92 f. spricht sich gegen die Anknüpfung an Art. 79 und für eine Orientierung an Art. 46 sowie eine Analogie zu Artt. 82, 84 aus.

[156] Vgl. *Staudinger/Magnus*, Art. 79, Rn. 59; MünchKommHGB/*Mankowski*, Art. 79, Rn. 9.

[157] Vgl. BGH, 27.11.2007, CISG-online 1617 = IHR 2008, 49, 53, m. Anm. *Schroeter*, EWiR 2008, 303; oben *Müller-Chen*, Art. 46 Rn. 12; *Soergel/Lüderitz/Dettmeier*, Art. 79, Rn. 25; *Karollus*, S. 141; *Staudinger/Magnus*, Art. 79, Rn. 60; *Achilles*, Art. 79, Rn. 14; *Flambouras*, 13 Pace Int'l L. Rev. (2001), 261, 275 f.; *Bamberger/Roth/Saenger*, Art. 79, Rn. 10; *Piltz*, Internationales Kaufrecht, Rn. 2–252. Vgl. auch Art. 6.2.1 PICC.

[158] Vgl. BGH, 27.11.2007, CISG-online 1617 = IHR 2008, 49, 53, m. Anm. *Schroeter*, EWiR 2008, 303; oben *Müller-Chen*, Art. 46 Rn. 12; *Soergel/Lüderitz/Dettmeier*, Art. 79, Rn. 25; *Karollus*, S. 141; *Staudinger/Magnus*, Art. 79, Rn. 60; *Achilles*, Art. 79, Rn. 14; *Schwenzer*, 39 Vict. U. Well. L. Rev. (2009), 709, 720; dies., FS Bucher, S. 723, 735; *Flambouras*, 13 Pace Int'l L. Rev. (2001), 261, 275 f.; *Bamberger/Roth/Saenger*, Art. 79, Rn. 10; *Piltz*, Internationales Kaufrecht, Rn. 2–252; *Atamer*, FS Schwenzer, S. 83, 94. Vgl. auch Art. 6.2.1 PICC.

[159] Belg. Hof van Cassatie, 19.6.2009, CISG-online 1963; vgl. auch *Brunner*, Art. 79, Rn. 27; *Kröll u. a./Atamer*, Art. 79, Rn. 86. Dagegen *Zeller*, Hardship, S. 113, 124 ff. Zu Art. 6.2.3 II PICC vgl. *Vogenauer/Kleinheisterkamp/McKendrick*, Art. 6.2.3 PICC, Rn. 1 ff.

[160] Für die Einordnung der PICC als internationale Handelsbräuche i. S. v. Art. 9, vgl. oben *Schmidt-Kessel*, Art. 9 Rn. 26.

[161] Belg. Hof van Cassatie, 19.6.2009, CISG-online 1963.

[162] So auch *Schlechtriem*, Internationales UN-Kaufrecht, Rn. 291; CISG-AC, Op. 7 (*Garro*), Comment 40; *Staudinger/Magnus*, Art. 79, Rn. 24; MünchKomm/*P. Huber*, Art. 79, Rn. 21; *Soergel/Lüderitz/Dettmeier*, Art. 79, Rn. 14; *Stoll*, Schadenersatzpflicht, S. 274; *Gruber*, Geldwertschwankungen, S. 545 f.; *Enderlein/Maskow/Strohbach*, Art. 79, Anm. 6.3.; *Keil*, S. 186; a. A. *Honnold/Flechtner*, Art. 79, Rn. 432.2.

weise erwartet werden kann, den Vertrag zu den angebotenen Bedingungen durchzuführen.[163]

3. Sonstige Rechtsbehelfe und Ansprüche

55 Bei Entlastung des Schuldners nach Art. 79 verbleiben dem Gläubiger, mit Ausnahme des Schadenersatzes, grundsätzlich alle sonstigen Rechtsbehelfe, die ihm nach der Konvention bei Nichterfüllung oder nicht gehöriger Erfüllung zustehen; Art. 79 V stellt dies ausdrücklich klar. Als sonstige Rechtsbehelfe des Gläubigers kommen in erster Linie die **Aufhebung des Vertrages** und die **Minderung** in Betracht.[164]

56 Ein sonstiges Recht des Gläubigers im Sinne des Art. 79 V, das von der Befreiung nicht betroffen wird, ist auch der auf Art. 78 gestützte Anspruch auf **Verzinsung** des Kaufpreises oder eines anderen fälligen Betrages. Die Zinspflicht nach Art. 78 ist nämlich keine Schadenersatzpflicht.[165] Die Pflicht zur Zahlung von Zinsen besteht daher auch dann fort, wenn der Geldschuldner etwa wegen eines Devisentransferverbots entlastet ist.[166] Auch **Aufwendungsersatzansprüche** nach Artt. 85, 86 werden nicht von einer möglichen Entlastung nach Art. 79 erfasst.[167]

VIII. Vertragliche Abweichung

1. Ausgestaltung der Haftungsbefreiung

57 Die Parteien können durch ausdrückliche oder stillschweigende Vereinbarung von Art. 79 abweichen und die Voraussetzungen oder Wirkungen der Entlastung ganz oder teilweise selbst regeln (Art. 6). Weit verbreitet im internationalen Handelsverkehr sind sog. **Höhere-Gewalt-Klauseln** („force majeure clauses").[168] Meist enthalten diese Klauseln einen langen Katalog von Ereignissen, die den Schuldner entlasten. Daneben oder anstelle dieses Katalogs

---

[163] Vgl. dazu ausführlich *Schwenzer*, 39 Vict. U. Well. L. Rev. (2009), 709, 721 ff., 724; *dies.*, FS Bucher, S. 723, 736 ff.; *dies./Hachem*, 57 Am. J. Comp. L. (2009), 457, 474 f. Ein derartiger Sachverhalt lag auch belg. Hof van Cassatie, 19.6.2009, CISG-online 1963 zugrunde.

[164] Vgl. Sekretariatskommentar, Art. 65, Anm. 8.; *Staudinger/Magnus*, Art. 79, Rn. 55 f.; *Bamberger/Roth/Saenger*, Art. 79, Rn. 10; *Bianca/Bonell/Tallon*, Art. 79, Anm. 2.10.; *Honnold/Flechtner*, Art. 79, Rn. 435.2, 435.6; *Piltz*, Internationales Kaufrecht, Rn. 4–253; *Soergel/Lüderitz/Dettmeier*, Art. 79, Rn. 25; *Herber/Czerwenka*, Art. 79, Rn. 22; *Heuzé*, Anm. 476.; *Enderlein/Maskow/Strohbach*, Art. 79, Anm. 13.2.–13.4.; *Achilles*, Art. 79, Rn. 14; MünchKomm/*P. Huber*, Art. 79, Rn. 28; MünchKommHGB/*Mankowski*, Art. 79, Rn. 12; *Liu*, Force Majeure, Nr. 8.1 ff.; *Atamer*, FS Schwenzer, S. 83, 96 f.; *Brunner*, Force majeure, S. 366 ff. Kritikwürdig ist insoweit die Lösung des CESL-Entwurfs, der seine entsprechenden Vorschriften Artt. 87–90 systematisch in Kapitel 9 „Allgemeine Bestimmungen" verortet und so zumindest den Eindruck erweckt, nicht nur Schadenersatzansprüche sondern alle Rechtsbehelfe auszuschliessen.

[165] Vgl. *Staudinger/Magnus*, Art. 79, Rn. 61; *Achilles*, Art. 79, Rn. 14; *Bamberger/Roth/Saenger*, Art. 79, Rn. 10; *Enderlein/Maskow/Strohbach*, Art. 79, Anm. 13.1. und Art. 78, Anm. 2.1.; *Soergel/Lüderitz/Dettmeier*, Art. 79, Rn. 25; *Herber/Czerwenka*, Art. 79, Rn. 22; *Honnold/Flechtner*, Art. 79, Rn. 435.6; *Piltz*, Internationales Kaufrecht, Rn. 4–253; *Schlechtriem*, Internationales UN-Kaufrecht, Rn. 317; *Stoll*, Schadensersatzpflicht, S. 279; MünchKomm/*P. Huber*, Art. 79, Rn. 28; MünchKommHGB/*Mankowski*, Art. 79, Rn. 13; *Flambouras*, 13 Pace Int'l L. Rev. (2001) 261, 282; AG Willisau, 12.3.2004, CISG-online 961; *Kröll u. a./Atamer*, Art. 79, Rn. 42; *dies.*, FS Schwenzer, S. 83, 96 f.; vgl. auch Int. Ct. Russian CCI, 13.5.2008, CISG-online 2103; a. A. *Audit*, Vente internationale, Anm. 185.

[166] Vgl. *Staudinger/Magnus*, Art. 79, Rn. 61.

[167] Vgl. *Staudinger/Magnus*, Art. 79, Rn. 62; MünchKommHGB/*Mankowski*, Art. 79, Rn. 13.

[168] Vgl. rechtsvergleichend *Schwenzer/Hachem/Kee*, Rn. 45.17 ff.; vgl. auch *Gesang*, S. 19 ff., 84 f.; *Rimke*, S. 228 f.; *Rösler*, ERPL 2007, 483, 484; *Böckstiegel*, RIW 1984, 1–7; *Salger*, S. 90–106. Internationale Verbände haben sich um eine Standardisierung solcher Klauseln bemüht: vgl. die von der ICC erarbeiteten Force Majeure Klauseln (ICC Force Majeure Clause 2003, ICC Publication Nr. 650; und dazu *Ramberg*, International Transactions, S. 50 ff.; vgl. auch ICC Force Majeure Clause 1985, ICC Publication Nr. 421 und dazu *Klotz/Barrett*, S. 241–255 sowie die leicht abgeänderte Force Majeure Clause im ICC Model International Sale Contract, ICC Publication Nr. 556) sowie die ECE-Lieferbedingungen, dazu *Gesang*, S. 137 ff.; *Bartels/Motomura*, RabelsZ 43 (1979), 649, 667–677. *Bund*, 17 J. L. & Com. (1998), 381, 405–412 empfiehlt dringend die Vereinbarung solcher Klauseln, um Streit um die Auslegung von Art. 79 zu vermeiden, und zeigt Gestaltungsmöglichkeiten auf; so auch *Honnold/Flechtner*, Art. 79, Rn. 432.1.

können die Parteien eine Generalklausel vereinbaren, die in der Regel Unvorhersehbarkeit und Nicht-Beherrschbarkeit sowie die Unabwendbarkeit des Leistungshindernisses, ggf. unter Festlegung einer Opfergrenze verlangen und damit Art. 79 I oder den nationalen Entlastungstatbeständen ähneln.[169] Auf der **Rechtsfolgenseite** bieten derartige Klauseln regelmässig mehr Flexibilität als Art. 79: Bei vorübergehenden Hindernissen sehen sie meist die Aussetzung der vertraglichen Pflichten, bei dauerhaften Hindernissen die Aufhebung des Vertrages oder eine Pflicht zur Neuverhandlung des Vertrages vor.[170] Häufig regeln die Parteien auch noch bestimmte Verfahrensfragen, deren Sanktionierung und die Verpflichtungen im Falle einer Rückabwicklung.[171] Neben solchen Höhere-Gewalt-Klauseln sind auch sog. **Hardship-Klauseln** (allgemeine Anpassungs-, Neuverhandlungs-, Härte-, Wirtschaftlichkeits- oder Revisionsklauseln) üblich.[172] Derartige Klauseln erfassen im Unterschied zu Art. 79 nicht nur die Fälle der Leistungserschwerung, sondern auch die Fälle der Leistungsentwertung, d. h. z. B. Veränderungen des Wechselkurses oder des Binnenwertes einer Währung. Auf der **Rechtsfolgenseite** sehen diese Klauseln in der Regel eine Pflicht zu Neuverhandlungen mit dem Ziel der Vertragsanpassung vor. Für den Fall des Scheiterns dieser Verhandlungen wird häufig die Einschaltung eines Dritten vorgesehen, der – je nach Vertragsgestaltung – Empfehlungen geben oder die Vertragsanpassung selbst vornehmen darf; andere Klauseln sehen im Fall des Scheiterns die Möglichkeit der Vertragsaufhebung vor. Hervorzuheben ist, dass derartige Klauseln zwar üblich sind, ihre Verwendung aber **keinem internationalen Handelsbrauch** im Sinne des Art. 9 II entspricht.[173] Sie erlangen deshalb nur Geltung, wenn die Parteien sich ausdrücklich oder stillschweigend beim Vertragsschluss auf sie bezogen haben.[174]

2. Garantien

Abweichend von Art. 79 kann der Schuldner auch eine absolute Garantie für sein Leistungsversprechen abgeben, so dass er ohne Rücksicht auf den Grund für die Nichterfüllung immer auch auf Schadenersatz haftet bzw. das Risiko für bestimmte Leistungshindernisse übernimmt. Eine solche Garantie liegt vor allem im Hinblick auf **anfängliche Leistungshindernisse** nahe, die den Parteien bekannt sind und deren Überwindung der Schuldner verspricht.[175] Im Übrigen dürfte bei der Auslegung von Garantien Zurückhaltung geboten sein. Da Art. 79 der Regelung in vielen Rechtsordnungen entspricht, gegenüber manchen die Haftung noch verschärft und auch von der Vertragspraxis allgemein akzeptiert wird, wird man eine ausdrückliche und eindeutige Erklärung verlangen müssen, dass der Schuldner auch das Risiko nicht beherrschbarer, unvorhersehbarer oder unüberwindbarer Leistungshindernisse übernehmen will.

---

[169] Vgl. *Horn*, Anpassung langfristiger Verträge, S. 27 ff.; *Fontaine*, Dr. prat. com. int. 1979, 469, 473 ff. mit zahlreichen Formulierungsbeispielen; *van Ommeslaghe*, Rev. dr. int. 1980, 7, 41 ff., 53 ff.; *Kahn*, J. D. I. 1975, 467, 469 ff. mit Beispielen aus der internationalen Vertragspraxis; *Gesang*, S. 29 ff.; *Draetta*, R. D. A. I. 2002, 347, 351–358 zu neueren Entwicklungen in der Vertragspraxis; vgl. auch OLG Hamburg, 28.2.1997, CISG-online 261.
[170] Vgl. *Fontaine*, Dr. prat. com. int. 1979, 469, 489 ff.; *Horn*, Anpassung langfristiger Verträge, S. 33 f.; *van Ommeslaghe*, Rev. dr. int. 1980, 7, 50; *Kahn*, J. D. I. 1975, S. 467, 478 ff.
[171] Vgl. *Fontaine*, Dr. prat. com. int. 1979, 469, 482 ff.; *Kahn*, J. D. I. 1975, S. 467, 477 f.
[172] Dazu im Überblick *Schwenzer/Hachem/Kee*, Rn. 45.79 ff.; *Fontaine*, Dr. prat. com. int. 1976, 7–49; *ders.*, Les clauses de hardship, S. 249–285 mit vielen Klauselbeispielen; *Martinek*, AcP 198 (1998), 329, 344 ff.; *Horn*, Anpassung langfristiger Verträge, S. 27 ff.; *Oppetit*, J. D. I. 1974, 794–814; *Rimke*, S. 229 ff.; weitere Nachweise bei *Gruber*, Geldwertschwankungen, S. 144–148. Beispiel: ICC Hardship Clause 2003, ICC Publication Nr. 650.
[173] Vgl. *van Ommeslaghe*, Rev. dr. int. 1980, 7, 15; *Osman*, S. 152 ff., 157; *Gruber*, Geldwertschwankungen, S. 550–553 m. w. N. auch zur Gegenansicht.
[174] *Bartels/Motomura*, RabelsZ 43 (1979), 649, 669.
[175] Vgl. *Achilles*, Art. 79, Rn. 5; *Herber/Czerwenka*, Art. 79, Rn. 10; *Neumayer/Ming*, Art. 79, Anm. 6.; *Staudinger/Magnus*, Art. 79, Rn. 17.

IX. Beweislast

59 Nach dem Wortlaut und Sinn des Art. 79 ist klar, dass der Schuldner die **Beweislast für entlastende Hinderungsgründe** im Sinne dieser Vorschrift trägt.[176] Dies gilt auch, wenn die Leistungsstörung auf dem Verhalten eines Erfüllungsübernehmers im Sinne von Art. 79 II beruht.[177] Macht der Gläubiger einen **Schadenersatzanspruch** nach Art. 79 IV 2 geltend, so muss er dessen Voraussetzungen beweisen.[178] Da der Nachweis des fehlenden Zugangs vom Gläubiger jedoch nicht zu erbringen ist, hat der Schuldner im Streitfall den **fristgerechten Zugang** der nach Art. 79 IV 1 erforderlichen Mitteilung zu beweisen.[179]

---

[176] Vgl. *Bianca/Bonell/Tallon*, Art. 79, Anm. 2.7.3.; *Heuzé*, Anm. 472.; *Neumayer/Ming*, Art. 79, Anm. 7.; *Soergel/Lüderitz/Dettmeier*, Art. 79, Rn. 21; *Achilles*, Art. 79, Rn. 15; *Herber/Czerwenka*, Art. 79, Rn. 26; *U. Huber*, RabelsZ 43 (1979), 413, 465; *Vischer*, Gemeinsame Bestimmungen, S. 175; *Brunner*, Force majeure, S. 382 f.

[177] Vgl. *Baumgärtel/Laumen-Hepting*, Art. 79 WKR, Rn. 8 und 9; *Bianca/Bonell/Tallon*, Art. 79, Anm. 2.7.3.

[178] Vgl. *Baumgärtel/Laumen-Hepting*, Art. 79 WKR, Rn. 10; *Witz/Salger/Lorenz/Salger*, Art. 79, Rn. 14; MünchKomm/*P. Huber*, Art. 79, Rn. 32.

[179] So mit Recht *Baumgärtel/Laumen-Hepting*, Art. 79 WKR, Rn. 10; *Achilles*, Art. 79, Rn. 15; dagegen *Staudinger/Magnus*, Art. 79, Rn. 66; *Witz/Salger/Lorenz/Salger*, Art. 79, Rn. 14; differenzierend *Bamberger/Roth/Saenger*, Art. 79, Rn. 11: Schuldner habe zumindest das Absenden der Mitteilung nachzuweisen.

Art. 80 [Verursachung der Nichterfüllung durch die andere Partei]

Eine Partei kann sich auf die Nichterfüllung von Pflichten durch die andere Partei nicht berufen, soweit diese Nichterfüllung durch ihre Handlung oder Unterlassung verursacht wurde.

Art. 80

A party may not rely on a failure of the other party to perform, to the extent that such failure was caused by the first party's act or omission.

Art. 80

Une partie ne peut pas se prévaloir d'une inexécution par l'autre partie dans la mesure où cette inexécution est due à un acte ou à une omission de sa part.

Übersicht

	Rn.
I. Grundgedanken der Regelung	1
II. Voraussetzungen der Befreiung	3
1. Handlung oder Unterlassung des Gläubigers	3
2. Ursächlichkeit für die Nichterfüllung	4
3. Beiderseitige Verursachung	7
III. Rechtsfolgen	8
1. Befreiung des Schuldners	8
2. Haftung des Gläubigers	10
IV. Beweislast	11

I. Grundgedanken der Regelung

Art. 80, der kein unmittelbares Vorbild im EKG hat und erst recht spät auf einen Antrag 1 der DDR[1] ins CISG aufgenommen wurde, sieht die **umfassende Befreiung** des Schuldners von seinen vertraglichen Pflichten vor, wenn der Gläubiger die Nichterfüllung verursacht hat. Die Vorschrift ist Ausdruck des allgemeinen Grundsatzes von Treu und Glauben (Art. 7 I):[2] Der Gläubiger soll keine Rechte wegen Nichterfüllung geltend machen können, wenn er diese selbst verursacht hat.[3] Viele Rechtsordnungen kennen vergleichbare Vorschriften;[4] im Unterschied zu diesen Bestimmungen regelt Art. 80 aber **nicht** die Folgen eines **Mitverschuldens des Gläubigers,** sondern die Befreiung des Schuldners von seiner Verantwortung für Leistungsstörungen, deren Ursache in der Gläubigersphäre liegt.[5]

Art. 80 bildet zusammen mit Art. 79 einen gesonderten Abschnitt „Befreiungen", der 2 Ausnahmen von der strengen, da verschuldensunabhängigen Garantiehaftung („strict liabili-

---

[1] Zur Entstehungsgeschichte eingehend *Stoll*, 3. Aufl., Art. 80 Rn. 1, 2; *Th. Neumann*, Duty to Cooperate, S. 59 ff. Vorbild war offenbar § 294 GIW; der Rechtsgedanke des Art. 80 war auch schon in Art. 74 III EKG enthalten. Vgl. auch O. R., S. 134–136.
[2] Zu weit jedoch *Th. Neumann*, Duty to Cooperate, S. 133 ff., der Art. 80 als umfassende Alternative zum allgemeinen Grundsatz von Treu und Glauben vorschlägt.
[3] BGH, 26.9.2012, CISG-online 2348; *Honsell/Magnus*, Art. 80, Rn. 1, 2; *Enderlein/Maskow/Strohbach*, Art. 80, Anm. 1.1.; *Rathjen*, RIW 1999, 561, 565; *Audit*, Vente internationale, Anm. 187.; *Heuzé*, Anm. 478.; *Herber/Czerwenka*, Art. 80, Rn. 2; *P. Huber/Mullis/P. Huber*, S. 265; *Reinhart*, Art. 80, Rn. 2; *Trachsel*, Haftungsbefreiung, S. 382; MünchKomm/*P. Huber*, Art. 80, Rn. 1; *Brunner*, Art. 80, Rn. 1; *Schmidt-Kessel*, Gläubigerfehlverhalten, § 11 (IX)(3).
[4] Vgl. Deutschland: § 254 I BGB; Italien: Art. 1227 I Cc; Portugal: Art. 570 Cc; Österreich: § 1304 ABGB; Schweiz: Artt. 44 I und 99 III OR; rechtsvergleichender Überblick bei *Lando/Beale*, Part. I and II, Anm. zu Art. 9:505; vgl. auch *Schwenzer/Hachem/Kee*, Rn. 45.120 ff.
[5] Ebenso Artt. 7.1.2, 7.4.7 PICC, dazu *Schäfer*, Failure of performance caused by other party, S. 246 ff.; Artt. 8:101 III, 9:504 PECL; Artt. 106 V, 131 III, 162 CESL-Entwurf, dazu *Schmidt-Kessel/Remien*, Europäisches Kaufrecht, S. 514.

ty") normiert. Im Unterschied zu Art. 79 sieht Art. 80 aber nicht nur eine Befreiung von der Schadenersatzhaftung vor, sondern der Gläubiger ist auch an der **Geltendmachung anderer Rechte** gehindert. Beide Vorschriften können nebeneinander zur Anwendung kommen;[6] wegen der umfassenden Befreiungswirkung von Art. 80 wird Art. 79 freilich bedeutungslos, wenn die Voraussetzungen beider Entlastungstatbestände vorliegen.[7] Art. 80 ist auch im Zusammenhang mit Art. 77 zu sehen, der den Fall betrifft, dass der Gläubiger den allein vom Schuldner verursachten Schaden nicht vermeidet oder eindämmt. Art. 80 erfasst hingegen den Fall, dass der Gläubiger selbst Ursache der Nichterfüllung ist. Beide Bestimmungen haben daher einen eigenständigen und klar voneinander abgegrenzten Anwendungsbereich (s. schon oben Art. 77 Rn. 6).

II. Voraussetzungen der Befreiung

1. Handlung oder Unterlassung des Gläubigers

3   Die Befreiung des Schuldners nach Art. 80 setzt voraus, dass der Gläubiger die Nichterfüllung durch Handeln oder Unterlassen verursacht hat. Unerheblich ist dabei, ob dem Gläubiger ein **Verschulden** zur Last fällt.[8] Auch auf Art. 79 kann er sich nicht berufen; insofern hat Art. 80 Vorrang vor Art. 79.[9] Als **Gläubigerhandlungen i. S. d. Art. 80** kommen fehlerhafte Anweisungen des Käufers oder die Bereitstellung mangelhafter Pläne in Betracht.[10] Dasselbe gilt, wenn der Käufer die Bedienungsanleitung nicht beachtet.[11] Unter Art. 80 fallen auch fehlerhafte Anweisungen des Käufers betreffend den Transport der Ware oder der Versuch des Käufers, sich die Ware absprachewidrig direkt vom Hersteller auf eigene Rechnung und unter Umgehung des Verkäufers liefern zu lassen.[12] Der Verursachung durch **aktives Handeln** steht ein **Unterlassen** gleich, wenn ein Handeln im Interesse des Gläubigers geboten und objektiv geeignet war, den Leistungserfolg zu ermöglichen.[13] Hierbei ist hauptsächlich an Fälle zu denken, in welchen der Gläubiger eine für den Erfolg erforderliche Mitwirkungshandlung verweigert, der Käufer es etwa unterlässt, die erforderliche Importgenehmigung zu besorgen oder die Anschrift mitzuteilen, an welche die Ware zu liefern ist.[14] Weitere Beispiele sind der unterbliebene Abruf oder die unter-

---

[6] Zum Teil wird Art. 80 als ein Sonderfall des Art. 79 gesehen: *Soergel/Lüderitz/Dettmeier*, Vor Art. 79, Rn. 2 und Art. 80, Rn. 1; zum Teil als eine eigenständige Vorschrift: *Herber/Czerwenka*, Art. 80, Rn. 2; *Trachsel*, Haftungsbefreiung, S. 383; *Th. Neumann*, Duty to Cooperate, S. 80.

[7] *Achilles*, Art. 80, Rn. 1; *Staudinger/Magnus*, Art. 80, Rn. 7, *Rathjen*, RIW 1999, 561, 565 und *Trachsel*, Haftungsbefreiung, S. 383 wollen sogar von einem Vorrang von Art. 80 ausgehen.

[8] OLG Koblenz, 31.1.1997, CISG-online 256; *Audit*, Vente internationale, Anm. 187.; *Heuzé*, Anm. 478.; *Achilles*, Art. 80, Rn. 2; *Stoll*, Schadensersatzpflicht, S. 280; *Herber/Czerwenka*, Art. 80, Rn. 4; *Neumayer/Ming*, Art. 80, Anm. 2.; *Piltz*, Internationales Kaufrecht, Rn. 4–224; *Reinhart*, Art. 80, Rn. 2; *Staudinger/Magnus*, Art. 80, Rn. 9, 11; *Schwenzer/Manner*, FS Kritzer, S. 470, 475; MünchKomm/*P. Huber*, Art. 80, Rn. 3; *Brunner*, Art. 80, Rn. 3; *Schmidt-Kessel*, Gläubigerfehlverhalten, § 11(IX)(3)(a).

[9] *Herber/Czerwenka*, Art. 80, Rn. 4; *Neumayer/Ming*, Art. 80, Anm. 2.; *Schlechtriem*, Internationales UN-Kaufrecht, Rn. 298; *Staudinger/Magnus*, Art. 80, Rn. 7; *P. Huber/Mullis/P. Huber*, S. 266; *Trachsel*, Haftungsbefreiung, S. 383; *Schwenzer/Manner*, FS Kritzer, S. 470, 475; MünchKomm/*P. Huber*, Art. 80, Rn. 3; *Brunner*, Art. 80, Rn. 3; *Kröll u. a./Atamer*, Art. 80, Rn. 2; a. A. *Soergel/Lüderitz/Dettmeier*, Art. 80, Rn. 3.

[10] Beispiel von *Maskow*, O. R., S. 393, Nr. 7. Vgl. ferner die oben von *Müller-Chen*, Art. 45 Rn. 3, gebildeten Beispiele für Verkäuferpflichten.

[11] Int. Ct. Russian CCI, 29.12.2004, CISG-online 1212.

[12] Vgl. den Sachverhalt in BGH, 15.2.1995, CISG-online 149 = NJW 1995, 2101 = IPRax 1996, 195 (Vorinstanzen LG Düsseldorf, 9.7.1992, CISG-online 42 und OLG Düsseldorf, 18.11.1993, CISG-online 92). In diesen Entscheidungen wird freilich zu Unrecht davon ausgegangen, der Verkäufer habe die Ware „geliefert". Hiergegen mit Recht *Schlechtriem*, EWiR 1995, 451 f. Zutreffender Hinweis auf Art. 80 bei *Schmidt-Kessel*, RIW 1996, 60, 64.

[13] *Trachsel*, Haftungsbefreiung, S. 384; *Honsell/Magnus*, Art. 80, Rn. 10. Vgl. auch *Kröll u. a./Atamer*, Art. 80, Rn. 6 („duty to act or cooperate"). Vgl. auch OLG Koblenz, 24.2.2011, CISG-online 2301: Verpflichtung oder Obliegenheit zum Handeln.

[14] Vgl. OGH, 6.2.1996, CISG-online 224 = ZfRVgl 1996, 248, 253 (Nichteröffnung eines Akkreditivs, weil Verkäufer abredewidrig Ladestelle nicht mitteilt), krit. dazu *Saidov*, Damages in Int'l Sales, S. 98 f.; OLG

bliebene Spezifikation der Ware seitens des Käufers sowie die unberechtigte Ablehnung der Nacherfüllung durch den Käufer.[15] Wiederholt wurde auch die Nichtzahlung vorangegangener Lieferungen unter Art. 80 subsumiert, wenn der Verkäufer deshalb weitere Lieferung unterliess,[16] bzw. die Nichtlieferung seitens des Verkäufers, auf Grund derer der Käufer zurückliegende Lieferungen nicht bezahlte.[17] In der Sache handelt es sich aber insoweit nicht um einen Fall des Art. 80, sondern um Ausübung eines Zurückbehaltungsrechts (vgl. unten Rn. 6). Das Handeln oder Unterlassen **einer Person, für die der Gläubiger** auf Grund seines Personalrisikos oder nach Art. 79 II **einstehen muss**, steht eigenem Handeln oder Unterlassen des Gläubigers gleich.[18] Das Fehlverhalten eines Spediteurs, der vom Käufer im eigenen Namen, aber für Rechnung der Verkäufers und in Erfüllung von dessen Nachbesserungspflicht beauftragt wurde, die vertragswidrige Ware zurückzubefördern, kann dem Käufer aber nicht zugerechnet werden.[19]

2. Ursächlichkeit für die Nichterfüllung

Das Handeln oder Unterlassen des Gläubigers muss die Nichterfüllung nicht nur im logischen Sinne verursacht haben, sondern auch objektiv geeignet gewesen sein, die Erfüllung des Vertrages ganz oder teilweise zu verhindern.[20] **Mittelbare Verursachung** genügt, sofern sich ein Risiko verwirklicht hat, das der Gläubiger durch sein Verhalten geschaffen hat und seinem Verantwortungsbereich zuzurechnen ist.[21] Lässt es etwa der Käufer an den erforderlichen Anweisungen oder Informationen fehlen, die der Verkäufer zur Fertigstellung der in Auftrag gegebenen Maschinen braucht, und wird infolge der dadurch bedingten Verzögerung der Fertigstellung das begonnene Werk beim Verkäufer durch Zufall zerstört, muss eine Befreiung des Verkäufers nach Art. 80 angenommen werden.

Die Befreiung nach Art. 80 setzt nicht voraus, dass sich das Gläubigerverhalten für den Schuldner als ein unvermeidliches Leistungshindernis i. S. d. Art. 79 darstellt. Dem Schuldner kann im Allgemeinen nicht zugemutet werden, Hindernisse zu überwinden, die der Gläubiger selbst der Erfüllung bereitet hat.[22] Ausnahmen sind jedoch nach dem Grundsatz von Treu und Glauben im Handelsverkehr denkbar; so kann der Schuldner bei **leicht überwindbaren**

München, 8.2.1995, CISG-online 143 (Käufer holt bestellte Fahrzeuge nicht ab); vgl. auch *Kyprianou v. Cyprus Textiles, Ltd.*, [1958] 2 Lloyd's Rep. 60 (Käufer verweigert zu Unrecht Auskunft, die Verkäufer für die Beantragung einer Exportlizenz braucht); vgl. auch *Stoll*, Schadensersatzpflicht, S. 280.

[15] OGH, 22.11.2011, CISG-online 2239; OLG Koblenz, 31.1.1997, CISG-online 256; *Achilles*, Art. 80, Rn. 2; *Piltz*, Internationales Kaufrecht, Rn. 4–223; *Saidov*, Damages in Int'l Sales, S. 100; *Rathjen*, RIW 1999, 561, 565.

[16] Int. Ct. Belarusian CCI, 5.10.1995, CISG-online 861; OLG München, 9.7.1997, CISG-online 282; OLG München, 1.7.2002, CISG-online 656.

[17] Handelskammer Zürich, 31.5.1996, CISG-online 1291.

[18] *Audit*, Vente internationale, Anm. 187.; *P. Huber/Mullis/P. Huber*, S. 266; *Soergel/Lüderitz/Dettmeier*, Art. 80, Rn. 2; *Herber/Czerwenka*, Art. 80, Rn. 5; *Herbots/Pauwels*, FS Neumayer, S. 351; *Neumayer/Ming*, Art. 80, Anm. 2.; *Staudinger/Magnus*, Art. 80, Rn. 11; *Kröll u. a./Atamer*, Art. 80, Rn. 4; MünchKomm/ *P. Huber*, Art. 80, Rn. 3; *Th. Neumann*, Duty to Cooperate, S. 169 ff. Auf der Wiener Konferenz sah man von einer Klarstellung in Art. 80 nur deshalb ab, weil eine solche Auslegung allgemein gebilligt wurde; vgl. O. R., S. 430, Nr. 88.

[19] Vgl. AG München, 23.6.1995, CISG-online 368.

[20] *Staudinger/Magnus*, Art. 80, Rn. 12; *Piltz*, Internationales Kaufrecht, Rn. 4–224; *Trachsel*, Haftungsbefreiung, S. 384 f.; MünchKomm/*P. Huber*, Art. 80, Rn. 5; MünchKommHGB/*Mankowski*, Art. 80, Rn. 6; zur Kausalität i. S. d. CISG vgl. auch oben Art. 74 Rn. 40. Die Heranziehung bestimmter Kausalitätstheorien ist hier gewiss nicht zu empfehlen. Die Anschauung des Verkehrs und des Handels über die Zurechnung dürften ausreichen, so auch *Bianca/Bonell/Tallon*, Art. 80, Anm. 2.1., der verlangt, dass die Nichterfüllung „imputable" sei. Zwischen „imputation" und „cause" unterscheidet *Th. Neumann*, Duty to Cooperate, S. 146, 152, der jede kausale Verbindung ausreichen lässt, S. 158. Zu eng wohl *Enderlein/Maskow/Strohbach*, Art. 80, Anm. 5.1., wonach die Nichterfüllung „eine charakteristische und im internationalen Handelsverkehr zu erwartende Folge" der Handlung des Gläubigers sein müsse.

[21] *Staudinger/Magnus*, Art. 80, Rn. 16; *Achilles*, Art. 80, Rn. 3; *Kröll u. a./Atamer*, Art. 80, Rn. 8; *Trachsel*, Haftungsbefreiung, S. 384; *Th. Neumann*, Duty to Cooperate, S. 158; *Brunner*, Art. 80, Rn. 5.

[22] *Stoll*, Schadensersatzpflicht, S. 280; *Kröll u. a./Atamer*, Art. 80, Rn. 9; grundsätzlich zustimmend *Enderlein/Maskow/Strohbach*, Art. 80, Anm. 3.3.

Art. 80 6, 7   Teil III. Kapitel V. Pflichten des Verkäufers und des Käufers. Abschnitt IV

Störungen durch den Gläubiger verpflichtet sein, sich um die Behebung der Störung zu bemühen.[23] Wenn z. B. der Käufer unklare oder widersprüchliche Angaben über die Spezifizierung der Ware macht, ist es dem Verkäufer im Allgemeinen zuzumuten, durch Nachfrage beim Käufer Klarheit zu schaffen.[24] Auch Anweisungen, einen bestimmten Werkstoff zu verwenden oder ein bestimmtes Unternehmen einzuschalten, bedeuten nicht zwingend, dass der Käufer damit alle mit der Anweisung verbundenen Risiken, etwa die mangelnde Eignung des Werkstoffs oder die unzulängliche Leistung des Dritten, konkludent auf sich genommen hat.[25] Man wird dabei stets prüfen müssen, ob der Schuldner nicht auf Grund des Vertrages oder allgemeiner Gepflogenheiten verpflichtet war, die **Anweisungen** des Gläubigers zu **prüfen**.[26] In vielen Fällen wird der Verkäufer nämlich über eine grössere Sachkunde verfügen als der Käufer; häufig werden beide Parteien einen Verursachungsbeitrag gesetzt haben.

6 An der Ursächlichkeit des Gläubigerverhaltens fehlt es auch, wenn dieses Verhalten die **Möglichkeit der Erfüllung** durch den Schuldner **nicht beeinträchtigt**. Verweigert der Käufer z. B. grundlos die Zahlung des fälligen Kaufpreises oder von Verbindlichkeiten aus früheren Geschäften, kann der Verkäufer die Lieferung der Ware nicht unter Berufung auf Art. 80 verweigern.[27] Die Vertragsverletzung seitens des Gläubigers ist zwar Anlass, aber nicht Ursache für die Nichterfüllung.[28] Auf ein **Leistungsverweigerungsrecht** kann sich der Schuldner in diesen Fällen nur nach Massgabe der Artt. 71–73, im Übrigen aber nach den Geboten von Treu und Glauben im internationalen Handel (Art. 7 I) berufen.[29]

3. Beiderseitige Verursachung

7 Höchst umstritten und noch nicht abschliessend geklärt ist die Frage, ob der Anwendungsbereich von Art. 80 nur eröffnet ist, wenn der Gläubiger die Nichterfüllung **allein verursacht** hat oder ob die Vorschrift auch Fälle erfasst, bei denen **beide Parteien** einen Verursachungsbeitrag zur konkreten Vertragsverletzung geleistet haben. Zum Teil wird der Anwendungsbereich von Art. 80 auf den Fall der alleinigen Verursachung durch den Gläubiger beschränkt; das Alles-oder-Nichts Prinzip des Art. 80 passe nicht in Fällen der beiderseitigen Verursachung.[30] Eine Aufteilung des Schadens habe in diesen Fällen nach Massgabe von Art. 77[31] oder den allgemeinen dem CISG zugrunde liegenden Grundsätzen[32] zu erfolgen. Die wohl h. M. vertritt hingegen unter Berufung auf den klaren

---

[23] *Enderlein/Maskow/Strohbach*, Art. 80, Anm. 3.3.; *Honsell/Magnus*, Art. 80, Rn. 5, 13; *Kröll u. a./Atamer*, Art. 80, Rn. 9; *P. Huber/Mullis/P. Huber*, S. 266 f.; *Th. Neumann*, Duty to Cooperate, S. 90, 161.
[24] Vgl. die Beispiele bei *Heuzé*, Anm. 478. Vgl. auch oben Art. 42 Rn. 17.
[25] So auch *Achilles*, Art. 80, Rn. 2; vgl. schon *Dölle/Stoll*, Art. 74 EKG, Rn. 127; anders *Trachsel*, Haftungsbefreiung, S. 387 f. (grundsätzlich Entlastung gegeben, es sei denn, der Schuldner hätte den vorgegebenen Werkstoff ohnehin verwendet oder den vorgegebenen Dritten ohnehin eingeschaltet).
[26] So richtig *Trachsel*, Haftungsbefreiung, S. 385, 406 f.; zustimmend *Kröll u. a./Atamer*, Art. 80, Rn. 9; vgl. auch *Saidov*, Damages in Int'l Sales, S. 97.
[27] *Honnold/Flechtner*, Art. 80, Rn. 436.5; wohl auch *Saidov*, Damages in Int'l Sales, S. 97 f.; a. A. Int. Ct. Belarusian CCI, 5.10.1995, CISG-online 861; OLG München, 9.7.1997, CISG-online 282; OLG München, 1.7.2002, CISG-online 656; Handelskammer Zürich, 31.5.1996, CISG-online 1291; wohl auch *Th. Neumann*, Duty to Cooperate, S. 178 f.
[28] *Achilles*, Art. 80, Rn. 3; *Honnold/Flechtner*, Art. 80, Rn. 436.5; anders wohl *Enderlein/Maskow/Strohbach*, Art. 80, Anm. 5.2.
[29] So richtig OLG Köln, 8.1.1997, CISG-online 217, während die Vorinstanz, das LG Aachen, 19.4.1996, CISG-online 165, fälschlicherweise Art. 80 anwandte; ebenso OLG München, 9.7.1997, CISG-online 282; für die Begründung eines allgemeinen Zurückbehaltungsrechts unter dem CISG vgl. CISG-AC, Op. 5 (*Schwenzer*), Comment 4.19.
[30] *Piltz*, Internationales Kaufrecht, Rn. 4–224; *P. Huber/Mullis/P. Huber*, S. 267; *Schmid*, Lückenfüllung und Normenkonkurrenz, S. 113–115; *Koziol*, ZEuP 1998, 593, 594, Fn. 7; *Soergel/Lüderitz/Dettmeier*, Art. 80, Rn. 2, 3; *Weber*, Vertragsverletzungsfolgen, S. 172; so auch *Stoll/Gruber*, 4. Aufl., Art. 80 Rn. 6; einschränkend *Achilles*, Art. 80, Rn. 4 (Art. 80 dann anwendbar, wenn Verursachungsbeitrag des Gläubigers überwiegt); ähnlich OLG Koblenz, 24.2.2011, CISG-online 2301 (Art. 80 bei deutlichem Überwiegen des Gläubigerbeitrags anwendbar).
[31] *Soergel/Lüderitz/Dettmeier*, Art. 80, Rn. 3.
[32] *Stoll/Gruber*, 4. Aufl., Art. 80 Rn. 6; *P. Huber/Mullis/P. Huber*, S. 267 f.

Wortlaut von Art. 80 („soweit") und die Entstehungsgeschichte[33] die Ansicht, dass Art. 80 auch und gerade bei beiderseitiger Verursachung anwendbar ist.[34] Da bei alleiniger Verursachung durch den Gläubiger der Schuldner ohnehin bereits nach Art. 79 entlastet sei, liefe Art. 80 ansonsten weitgehend leer. Die Rechtsfolgen seien unter Berücksichtigung des **Gewichts des jeweiligen Verursachungsbeitrages** zu bestimmen, wobei die gemachten Lösungsvorschläge stark voneinander abweichen. Letztlich ist die Frage nach der richtigen dogmatischen Grundlage zweitrangig. Wichtiger ist, wie und nach welchen Massstäben die Rechtsfolgen in einem solchen Fall zu bestimmen sind (s. unten Rn. 9). Art. 80 ist jedenfalls der Gedanke zu entnehmen, dass bei beiderseitiger Verursachung der Nichterfüllung der Beitrag des Gläubigers bei der Schadensverteilung zu berücksichtigen ist.[35]

III. Rechtsfolgen

1. Befreiung des Schuldners

Art. 80, der insoweit ungenau formuliert ist,[36] versagt dem Gläubiger das Recht, sich auf die Nichterfüllung „zu berufen". Gemeint ist offensichtlich, dass der Gläubiger – anders als in den Fällen des Art. 79 – keinerlei Rechte wegen Nichterfüllung geltend machen kann. Dementsprechend verliert der Gläubiger nicht nur das Recht auf Schadenersatz, sondern auch alle **sonstigen Rechtsbehelfe** wegen Nichterfüllung, insbesondere auch den Anspruch auf Erfüllung, das Recht zur Vertragsaufhebung[37] und das Recht zur Minderung des Kaufpreises.[38] Auch das Recht, nach Massgabe von Art. 78 **Fälligkeitszinsen** zu verlangen, entfällt.[39] Die Befreiung reicht indes nur so weit, als das Gläubigerverhalten kausal ist für die Nichterfüllung.[40] Wenn etwa der Verkäufer die Ware verspätet an die vom Gläubiger angegebene falsche Adresse versendet, kann der Gläubiger zwar wegen der Verspätung bis zur Versendung, nicht aber wegen der durch die Fehlleitung verursachten Verzögerung Verzugsfolgen geltend machen.[41] Zweifelhaft ist, ob Art. 80 dem Gläubiger nur ein rechtliches Vorgehen gegen den Schuldner verwehrt oder ihm auch versagt ist, bei einem

---

[33] Bei der Wiener Konferenz wurde der ursprüngliche Antrag der D.D.R. (A/CONF.97/C.1/L.217) dahin geändert, dass die Worte „if he has caused" durch „insofar as caused" ersetzt wurden (A/CONF.97/C.1/L.234), dies ausdrücklich mit Blick auf beiderseitige Verursachung (30th meeting); vgl. auch *Th. Neumann*, Duty to Cooperate, S. 196. Der Delegierte der B.R.D. beantragte darauf mündlich die Änderung der Worte „insofar as" in „to the extent that".

[34] *Audit*, Vente internationale, Anm. 188.; *Heuzé*, Anm. 478.; *Bianca/Bonell/Tallon*, Art. 80, Anm. 2.4.; *Enderlein/Maskow/Strohbach*, Art. 80, Anm. 6.; *Herber/Czerwenka*, Art. 80, Rn. 7, 8; *Neumayer/Ming*, Art. 80, Anm. 3.; *Rathjen*, RIW 1999, 561, 565; *Ziegler*, S. 239; *Staudinger/Magnus*, Art. 80, Rn. 14, 15; *Bamberger/Roth/Saenger*, Art. 80, Rn. 3; *Kröll u. a./Atamer*, Art. 80, Rn. 10; *Schlechtriem*, Internationales UN-Kaufrecht, Rn. 298; *Schwenzer/Manner*, FS Kritzer, S. 470, 477 f.; *Brunner*, Art. 80, Rn. 6; *ders.*, Force majeure, S. 114; *Th. Neumann*, Duty to Cooperate, S. 152 ff.; *Trachsel*, Haftungsbefreiung, S. 396 ff. sieht diese Fälle teilweise von Art. 80 erfasst und geht für die übrigen Fälle von einer Lücke aus, die nach den allgemeinen dem CISG zugrundeliegenden Grundsätzen, insbes. dem Grundsatz der Kooperation und Art. 85 S. 2, zu schliessen sei.

[35] In diesem Sinne auch *Schlechtriem*, Internationales UN-Kaufrecht, Rn. 298; *Trachsel*, Haftungsbefreiung, S. 399.

[36] Vgl. insoweit schon den kritischen Diskussionsbeitrag des norwegischen Delegierten *Rognlien* auf der Wiener Konferenz, O.R., S. 393, Nr. 6; ferner *Bianca/Bonell/Tallon*, Art. 80, Anm. 2.5.: „The text lacks precision."

[37] OGH, 22.11.2011, CISG-online 2239; *Honnold/Flechtner*, Art. 80, Rn. 436.1.

[38] *Enderlein/Maskow/Strohbach*, Art. 80, Anm. 3.1.; *Honsell/Magnus*, Art. 80, Rn. 14; *P. Huber/Mullis/P. Huber*, S. 265; *Soergel/Lüderitz/Dettmeier*, Art. 80, Rn. 6; *Piltz*, Internationales Kaufrecht, Rn. 4–225; *Heuzé*, Anm. 479.; *Trachsel*, Haftungsbefreiung, S. 389; MünchKomm/*P. Huber*, Art. 80, Rn. 7; *Brunner*, Art. 80, Rn. 7; *Schmidt-Kessel*, Gläubigerfehlverhalten, § 11(IX)(3)(b); vgl. auch ICC, 11 849/2003, CISG-online 1421 (bei fehlenden Angaben zur Eröffnung eines Akkreditivs durch den Käufer darf der Verkäufer nicht den Vertrag aufheben; die Nachfrist beginnt erst mit Kenntnis der Angaben zu laufen).

[39] *Staudinger/Magnus*, Art. 80, Rn. 17; *Bamberger/Roth/Saenger*, Art. 80, Rn. 4; *Neumayer/Ming*, Art. 80, Anm. 4.; *Heuzé*, Anm. 479.; MünchKomm/*P. Huber*, Art. 80, Rn. 7; *Brunner*, Art. 80, Rn. 7; *Schmidt-Kessel*, Gläubigerfehlverhalten, § 11(IX)(3)(b).

[40] *Kröll u. a./Atamer*, Art. 80, Rn. 13 f.

[41] *Achilles*, Art. 80, Rn. 5; *Trachsel*, Haftungsbefreiung, S. 389.

Vorgehen des Schuldners gegen ihn die **Einwendung** vorzubringen, der Schuldner habe nicht vertragsgemäss geleistet. Die Einordnung des Art. 80 in den Abschnitt „Befreiungen" spricht eher gegen eine solche Auslegung, der Wortlaut des Art. 80 aber dafür. Man wird wohl annehmen dürfen, dass Befreiung nach Art. 80 den Anspruch des Schuldners auf die Gegenleistung unberührt lässt, eben weil die Ursache der Nichterfüllung in den Verantwortungsbereich des Gläubigers fällt.[42] Doch wird sich der Schuldner dasjenige anrechnen lassen müssen, was er durch Wegfall seiner Leistungspflicht erspart hat oder ersparen könnte.[43] Der Schuldner soll durch den Wegfall seiner Leistungspflicht nicht besser gestellt werden, als er bei realer Durchführung des Vertrages stehen würde.

9   Bei **beidseitiger Verursachung** der Nichterfüllung sind die Rechtsfolgen differenziert zu beurteilen: Unstreitig sind auf **Geld** gerichtete Ansprüche des Gläubigers wie Schadenersatzansprüche, das Recht auf Minderung und auch der Zinsanspruch nach **Massgabe der Verursachungsbeiträge** zu mindern.[44] Bei der Gewichtung der Verursachungsbeiträge wird zum einen der Grad der Wahrscheinlichkeit zu berücksichtigen sein, mit der das Verhalten einer Partei den Schaden verursacht hat; aber auch die Berücksichtigung von Verschulden und der Schwere der Vertragsverletzung ist nicht ausgeschlossen.[45] Jedenfalls steht den Gerichten hier ein grosser Ermessensspielraum zu.[46] Andere Rechte wie die **Vertragsaufhebung** oder das Recht auf **Erfüllung** oder **Nacherfüllung** können hingegen nicht quotenmässig aufgeteilt sondern nur einheitlich ausgeübt werden. Verschiedene Autoren vertreten deshalb die Auffassung, dass diese Rechte nur ausgeübt werden können, wenn der Verursachungsbeitrag des Schuldners überwiegt.[47] Im Falle der Rückabwicklung sollen dann die jeweiligen Verursachungsbeiträge ggf. im Wege der Vorteilsausgleichung berücksichtigt werden.[48] Diese Lösung erscheint indessen zu mehr oder weniger zufälligen Ergebnissen zu führen, zumal die Bestimmung der jeweiligen Verursachungsbeiträge mehr oder minder im Ermessen des Gerichtes liegt und nicht mathematisch genau berechnet werden kann. Das Gewicht der jeweiligen Verursachungsbeiträge kann deshalb nicht entscheidend sein bei der Frage, ob der Gläubiger Vertragsaufhebung, Erfüllung oder ggf. Nacherfüllung verlangen kann.[49] Vielmehr sollte dies seiner eigenen Entscheidung überlassen bleiben, sofern er bereit ist, dem Schuldner einen **finanziellen Betrag** zu zahlen, der seinem Verursachungsbeitrag an der Vertragsverletzung entspricht.[50] Hat beispielsweise der Käufer dem Verkäufer fehlerhaftes Material zur Herstellung der Ware geliefert, was der Verkäufer jedoch erkennen konnte, und betrugen die jeweiligen Verursachungsbeiträge zwei Drittel (Käufer) und ein Drittel (Verkäufer), so sollte dem Käufer sein Anspruch auf Erfüllung

---

[42] *Achilles*, Art. 80, Rn. 6; *Staudinger/Magnus*, Art. 80, Rn. 18; *Soergel/Lüderitz/Dettmeier*, Art. 80, Rn. 6; *P. Huber/Mullis/P. Huber*, S. 265; MünchKomm/*P. Huber*, Art. 80, Rn. 8; *Kröll u. a./Atamer*, Art. 80, Rn. 15; vgl. auch Deutschland: § 326 II 1 BGB.

[43] *Achilles*, Art. 80, Rn. 6; *Staudinger/Magnus*, Art. 80, Rn. 18; MünchKomm/*P. Huber*, Art. 80, Rn. 8; *Brunner*, Art. 80, Rn. 9; *Kröll u. a./Atamer*, Art. 80, Rn. 15; vgl. auch Deutschland: § 326 II 2 BGB.

[44] BGH, 26.9.2012, CISG-online 2348 („jedenfalls bei teilbaren Rechtsbehelfen"); *Schlechtriem*, Internationales UN-Kaufrecht, Rn. 298; *Honsell/Magnus*, Art. 80, Rn. 12; *Achilles*, Art. 80, Rn. 4; *Enderlein/Maskow/Strohbach*, Art. 80, Anm. 6.; *Herber/Czerwenka*, Art. 80, Rn. 8; *Trachsel*, Haftungsbefreiung, S. 399; *Neumayer/Ming*, Art. 80, Anm. 3.; *Bianca/Bonell/Tallon*, Art. 80, Anm. 2.5.; *Audit*, Vente internationale, Anm. 188.; *Heuzé*, Anm. 479.; *Kröll u. a./Atamer*, Art. 80, Rn. 16 f.; *Schwenzer/Manner*, FS Kritzer, S. 470, 478 f.; MünchKomm/*P. Huber*, Art. 80, Rn. 6; *Brunner*, Art. 80, Rn. 6; *Th. Neumann*, Duty to Cooperate, S. 198.

[45] *Herber/Czerwenka*, Art. 80, Rn. 8; *Trachsel*, Haftungsbefreiung, S. 414 f.; anders *Bianca/Bonell/Tallon*, Art. 80, Anm. 2.5.

[46] *Audit*, Vente internationale, Anm. 188.; *Heuzé*, Anm. 479.; *Bianca/Bonell/Tallon*, Art. 80, Anm. 3.1.

[47] *Trachsel*, Haftungsbefreiung, S. 412; *Schäfer*, Nr. 4a; *Stoll/Gruber*, 4. Aufl., Art. 80 Rn. 10; *Kröll u. a./Atamer*, Art. 80, Rn. 19; einige Autoren verlangen sogar ein wesentliches Überwiegen, so MünchKomm/*P. Huber*, Art. 80, Rn. 6; *Staudinger/Magnus*, Art. 80, Rn. 14; *Brunner*, Art. 80, Rn. 6. Vgl. auch *Th. Neumann*, Duty to Cooperate, S. 199 f., der die Verursachungsbeiträge im Rahmen der Wesentlichkeit der Vertragsverletzung berücksichtigt.

[48] *Trachsel*, Haftungsbefreiung, S. 405 f.

[49] A. A. noch *Stoll/Gruber*, 4. Aufl., Art. 80 Rn. 10, denen zufolge Vertragsaufhebung nur möglich sein soll, wenn der Verursachungsbeitrag des Schuldners überwiegt und für sich betrachtet noch eine wesentliche Vertragsverletzung darstellt.

[50] Grundlegend hierzu *Schwenzer/Manner*, FS Kritzer, S. 470, 479 f.

erhalten bleiben, wenn er bereit ist, dem Verkäufer zwei Drittel der zusätzlichen Herstellungskosten zu ersetzen. In gleicher Weise müsste eine Vertragsaufhebung seitens des Käufers zulässig sein, wenn er bereit ist, zwei Drittel des beim Verkäufer eingetretenen Schadens zu ersetzen. Dieses Ergebnis erscheint nicht allein ökonomisch sinnvoll, sondern entspricht auch den Art. 77 zu Grunde liegenden Wertungen. Lediglich in Fällen, in denen der Verursachungsbeitrag des Schuldners praktisch vernachlässigbar ist, kann ein Ausschluss nicht finanzieller Rechtsbehelfe auf Grund von Art. 80 geboten sein.[51]

2. Haftung des Gläubigers

Stellt das Verhalten des Gläubigers, das den Ausschluss seiner Ansprüche begründet, eine Vertragsverletzung dar (z.B. Verletzung der Abnahmepflicht nach Art. 60), so kann der Schuldner Schadenersatz nach Massgabe der Artt. 61 I b, 74–77 verlangen. Unberührt bleiben auch sonstige Rechtsbehelfe des Schuldners wegen der vom Gläubiger begangenen Vertragsverletzung.[52]

IV. Beweislast

Wegen des Ausnahmecharakters von Art. 80 hat der Schuldner zu beweisen, dass die Handlung oder die Unterlassung des Gläubigers, auf die er sich beruft, zumindest mitursächlich für die Nichterfüllung ist.[53]

---

[51] Grundlegend hierzu *Schwenzer/Manner*, FS Kritzer, S. 470, 479 f.
[52] *Piltz*, Internationales Kaufrecht, Rn. 4–226; *Honsell/Magnus*, Art. 80, Rn. 6; *Heuzé*, Anm. 479.
[53] *Heuzé*, Anm. 479.; *Staudinger/Magnus*, Art. 80, Rn. 19; *Kröll u. a./Atamer*, Art. 80, Rn. 20; *Th. Neumann*, Duty to Cooperate, S. 91, 175 f.

Abschnitt V. Wirkungen der Aufhebung

Section V.
Effects of avoidance

Section V.
Effets de la résolution

Vorbemerkungen zu Artt. 81–84*

Übersicht

	Rn.
I. Anwendungsbereich	1
1. Aufhebung und Rückabwicklung	1
2. Aufhebungsrechte	2
3. Rechtsvergleich	3
4. Eigentumslage	4
5. Anwendung der Artt. 81 ff.	5
a) Nacherfüllung	5
b) Endgültige Leistungsbefreiung	6
c) Vertragliche Aufhebungsrechte und einvernehmliche Vertragsaufhebung	7
d) Teilrückabwicklung	8
II. Grundlinien der Regelung	9
1. Vertragsaufhebung und Schadensersatz	9
2. Wirkungen der Aufhebung	10

I. Anwendungsbereich

1. Aufhebung und Rückabwicklung

1   Die **Durchführung** und die **Wirkungen der Vertragsaufhebung** werden in Artt. 81–84 einheitlich geregelt (zur Anwendbarkeit im Rahmen des Nacherfüllungsanspruchs, Art. 46, sowie bei einvernehmlicher Vertragsaufhebung vgl. Rn. 5ff). Dabei sind die Vorschriften praktisch unverändert aus dem EKG übernommen worden. Das Rückabwicklungsregime des CISG ist eines der wenigen Gebiete, in welchem dem CISG kein moderner Wurf geglückt ist; vielmehr sind „Lücken geblieben und überkommene Lösungen, die sich kaum bewährt haben, beibehalten worden."[1] Artt. 81–84 werden ergänzt durch Artt. 26, 27, die Form und Modalitäten der Aufhebungserklärung regeln.

2. Aufhebungsrechte

2   Artt. 81–84 regeln grundsätzlich lediglich die **Folgen** der Vertragsaufhebung – mit Ausnahme von Art. 82, der in bestimmten Fällen eine „Sperre" des Aufhebungsrechts vorsieht und somit eine Voraussetzung für die Aufhebung betrifft. Ob ein Recht zur Aufhebung des Vertrags entstanden ist, ergibt sich jeweils aus den **Einzelvorschriften** im Rahmen der Verletzung der Pflichten durch Verkäufer oder Käufer. Aufhebungsrechte ergeben sich für den

---

*Anm. d.Verf.: Die Wirkungen der Vertragsaufhebung sind in der vorliegenden 6. Auflage von Prof. Dr. Christiana Fountoulakis bearbeitet worden. Dabei sind die Grundstruktur und Gliederung meines Vorgängers Dr. Rainer Hornung im Wesentlichen übernommen worden. Beibehalten worden sind auch manche der Problemanalysen und Wertentscheidungen, deren Neuformulierung ein Verlust gewesen wäre. Dr. Rainer Hornung sei an dieser Stelle herzlich gedankt.

[1] *Schlechtriem*, Internationales UN-Kaufrecht, Rn. 320; vgl. auch *Saidov*, 25 J. L. & Com. (2005), 443, 447 f.: Das CISG lasse zu viele Fragen in Zusammenhang mit der Rückabwicklung offen, um für internationale Handelsverträge der UNO eine praktikable Rechtswahl darzustellen.

Käufer aus Artt. 49 I lit. a), lit. b) sowie 51. Aufhebungsrechte des Verkäufers bestehen nach Artt. 64 I lit. a) und lit. b). Für beide Teile bestehen Aufhebungsrechte nach Artt. 72 und 73.

3. Rechtsvergleich

Dass die Aufhebung des Vertrages zur Rückgewähr der vertraglichen Leistungen führt, ist zwar den kontinental-europäischen Rechtsordnungen vertraut,[2] dem Common Law jedoch in dieser Grundsätzlichkeit und in diesem Ausmass fremd.[3] Der UCC etwa sieht kein allgemeines Rückerstattungsrecht des Verkäufers vor. Letzterem steht ein solches praktisch nur bei Insolvenz des Käufers zu, und auch dann nur unter engen Voraussetzungen.[4]

4. Eigentumslage

Die Eigentumslage an den gelieferten Waren nach erfolgter Aufhebung wird durch das CISG entsprechend der Selbstbeschränkung in Art. 4 lit. b) nicht geklärt. Dies kann insbesondere zur Folge haben, dass die Rückgewähr der Leistungen, wie sie im CISG vorgesehen ist (Art. 81 II), mit nationalem Insolvenzrecht kollidiert, wenn dieses den Gläubigern des Käufers dingliche Rechte an der erhaltenen Sache einräumt. Bei der Ausarbeitung von Art. 81 wurde es bewusst den einzelnen Rechtsordnungen überlassen, wie sie die Rangfolge verschiedener Gläubigerrechte entscheiden wollen.[5] Die Rückabwicklungsregeln des CISG nehmen auf die dingliche Wirkung der Vertragsaufhebung allerdings insofern Einfluss, als sie nationales Rückabwicklungsrecht – das dingliche Vindikationsansprüche vorsehen mag – ausschliessen. Insoweit sieht das CISG nämlich vor, dass der Vertrag für die Zeit der Vertragsliquidation gleichsam als Dach weiterbesteht.[6] Die **causa** für den Eigentumserwerb fällt demnach mit Aufhebung des Vertrages nicht fort, sondern **besteht** noch so lange, **bis die Rückabwicklung abgeschlossen** ist.[7] Erst danach werden nationale Rechte für die Frage relevant, ob mit Wegfall der causa gleichzeitig die Eigentumslage beeinflusst wird.

5. Anwendung der Artt. 81 ff.

a) Nacherfüllung. Artt. 81 ff. finden nicht nur bei Aufhebung des Vertrages Anwendung. Bei nicht vertragsgemässer Ware kann der Käufer **Ersatzlieferung** verlangen, Art. 46 II. Dieser Rechtsbehelf macht die Rückgabe der ersten, mangelhaften Lieferung erforderlich, ohne dass der Vertrag im Übrigen abgewickelt wird. Auf diese Rückgabe finden die Artt. 81 II, 82–84 zumindest entsprechende Anwendung,[8] zumal Artt. 82, 83 und 84 II lit. b) die Ersatzlieferung ausdrücklich mit erfassen. Die Ausübung des Ersatzlieferungsrechts ist von der „**unversehrten Rückgabe**" der ersten Leistung mit allen Einschränkungen des Grundsatzes in Art. 82 II abhängig.[9] Anwendung finden Artt. 81 II, 82–84 auch, wenn der

---

[2] Für eine internationale Übersicht vgl. *Schwenzer/Hachem/Kee,* Rn. 50.15 ff.; *Schlechtriem,* Restitution, Kapitel 3, VII; *Treitel,* Remedies, S. 382 ff.; *Laimer,* S. 122 ff.
[3] Sowohl das englische Recht (SGA, sec. 11; dazu *Benjamin's* Sale of Goods, Rn. 10–026 ff., 15–109, *Treitel,* Law of Contract, S. 806 ff., 908 ff. und *Chitty* On Contracts, Vol. II, Rn. 43–379 ff.) als auch der amerikanische UCC (vgl. §§ 2–702 und 2–703 UCC) gehen im Grundsatz nicht vom Anspruch auf Rückgewähr der Ware aus; siehe dazu *Honnold/Flechtner,* Art. 81, Rn. 444; *Ziegel,* Remedial Provisions, 9-1, 9–31: „British and American sales and restitutionary doctrines have long set their faces against allowing the seller to recover the goods involuntarily from the defaulting buyer." Vgl. auch unten *Fountoulakis,* Art. 81, Rn. 6 Fn. 14
[4] Vgl. § 2–702 (2), (3) UCC: Die Rechte des Käufers bei Weiterverkauf im normalen Geschäftsverkehr („ordinary course") und die Rechte gutgläubiger Dritterwerber gehen dem Rückerstattungsanspruch des Verkäufers vor.
[5] Legislative History, 33rd meeting, Rn. 77 f.
[6] Dazu unten *Fountoulakis,* Art. 81 Rn. 6–10.
[7] Vgl. *Schlechtriem,* Internationales UN-Kaufrecht, Rn. 330; vgl. auch *Honnold/Flechtner,* Art. 81, Rn. 444.1.
[8] UNCITRAL Digest, Vor Art. 81, Rn. 1; MünchKomm/*P. Huber,* Art. 81, Rn. 17; *Ferrari u. a./Ferrari,* Internationales Vertragsrecht, Art. 81, Rn. 2; *Staudinger/Magnus,* Art. 81, Rn. 20.
[9] Vgl. unten *Fountoulakis,* Art. 82 Rn. 2 ff.

Käufer **Nacherfüllung** im Sinne des Art. 46 III verlangt.[10] Dasselbe muss gelten, wenn der **Verkäufer** das Recht zur Nacherfüllung ausübt und infolgedessen die mangelhafte Erstlieferung zurückgegeben wird (Art. 48). Die Ware muss demnach grundsätzlich unversehrt zurückgegeben werden, allerdings angepasst an den mangelhaften Zustand bei Lieferung, der zur Nachlieferung führt.[11] Der Vertrag besteht im Übrigen weiter, für die Nacherfüllung (Artt. 46 II, III, 48) gelten die Vertragsregeln erneut in vollem Umfang. Lediglich hinsichtlich der zeitlichen Durchführung bedarf es der Anpassung.[12]

6 **b) Endgültige Leistungsbefreiung.** Artt. 81–84 können bei endgültiger Leistungsbefreiung nach Art. 79 analog angewandt werden.[13]

7 **c) Vertragliche Aufhebungsrechte und einvernehmliche Vertragsaufhebung.** Für vertraglich vereinbarte Aufhebungsrechte, wie sie die Gestaltungsfreiheit des Vertrages im Übereinkommen zulässt (Art. 6), sowie für die nachträgliche einvernehmliche Vertragsaufhebung **gelten Artt. 81, 84 sinngemäss**.[14] Anderes gilt bei Art. 82, der ausdrücklich auf den Fall zugeschnitten ist, dass der Verkäufer die vertragsbrüchige Partei ist; die einseitige Risikoverteilung zulasten des Verkäufers in Art. 82 II sollte nicht auf Fälle ausgedehnt werden, in denen der Vertrag durch den Verkäufer oder einvernehmlich aufgehoben wird.[15] Für die inhaltliche Kontrolle von Vertragsvereinbarungen, die einzelne Regeln der Rückabwicklung oder das Aufhebungsrecht insgesamt abändern oder ausschliessen, sieht das CISG keine Regeln vor; sie erfolgt nach den subsidiär anwendbaren Rechtsregeln, Art. 4 lit. a) i. V. m. Art. 7 II.

8 **d) Teilrückabwicklung.** Zur Vermeidung wirtschaftlicher Verluste berücksichtigt das Übereinkommen allgemein die Möglichkeit einer **teilweisen Verletzung** des Vertrages. Die Rückabwicklungsansprüche nach **Art. 81 II** orientieren sich, wenn der Vertrag oder der bereits nach Art. 51 abgespaltene Vertragsteil bis zur Aufhebung nur teilweise erfüllt worden sind, an den bereits erbrachten Leistungen in ihrem **tatsächlichen Umfang:**[16] Bei vollständig erfülltem Vertrag ist die ganze, bei teilweise erfülltem Vertrag die Teilleistung zurückzugewähren. Die Aufspaltung in Art. 51 ist der Rückabwicklung folglich sinnlogisch vorgelagert.[17] Eventuelle Wirkungen des Gesamtvertrages oder des bestehen bleibenden Vertragsteiles auf die Rückabwicklung sind allerdings möglich und analog den für die Abwicklung getroffenen Vereinbarungen in Art. 81 I zu behandeln.[18]

II. Grundlinien der Regelung

1. Vertragsaufhebung und Schadensersatz

9 Vertragsaufhebung und Schadensersatz sind, wie bereits im EKG,[19] als **selbstständige, aber kombinierte Behelfe** geregelt (vgl. auch Art. 83). Damit wird im Einheitskaufrecht

---

[10] OLG Karlsruhe, 19.12.2002, CISG-online 817 = IHR 2003, 125, m. Anm. *Hennecke,* IHR 2003, 268, 271 ff.
[11] OLG Karlsruhe, 19.12.2002, CISG-online 817 = IHR 2003, 125.
[12] Dazu oben *Müller-Chen,* Art. 46 Rn. 36 ff., Art. 48 Rn. 22 f.
[13] So auch *Staudinger/Magnus,* Art. 81, Rn. 4; *Bianca/Bonell/Tallon,* Art. 81, Anm. 2.1.
[14] Vgl. *Schlechtriem,* Internationales UN-Kaufrecht, Rn. 323; *Enderlein/Maskow/Strohbach,* vor Art. 81, Anm. 5.; *Ferrari u. a./Ferrari,* Internationales Vertragsrecht, Art. 81, Rn. 3; in der Rechtsprechung OGH, 29.6.1999, CISG-online 483 = östZRVgl 2000, 33: Soweit die Parteien die Rechtsfolgen ihrer einvernehmlichen Vertragsaufhebung nicht selbst regeln würden, kämen über Art. 7 II die Regeln der Artt. 81 ff. zur Anwendung – allerdings mit der hier abgelehnten (vgl. oben im Text sowie unten Art. 82 Rn. 29 f.) Konsequenz, dass dann auch Art. 82 zu berücksichtigen sei.
[15] Vgl. dazu unten *Fountoulakis,* Art. 82 Rn. 28–30.
[16] *Honnold/Flechtner,* Art. 81, Rn. 444; *Enderlein/Maskow/Strohbach,* Art. 81, Anm. 2; *Honsell/Weber,* Vorbem. Artt. 81–84, Rn. 13.
[17] Dies ergibt sich aus dem Aufbau des Übereinkommens, welches in Abschnitt III die Rechtsbehelfe und dann in Abschnitt V die Wirkungen regelt.
[18] Vgl. auch *Enderlein/Maskow/Strohbach,* vor Art. 81, Anm. 4.
[19] *Leser,* Vertragsaufhebung und Rückabwicklung, S. 227 f.

der Erkenntnis Rechnung getragen, dass Leistungsstörungen als Abweichungen vom Vertragsprogramm durch verschiedene Behelfe korrigiert und angepasst werden können.[20] Rechtsvergleichend ist die Kombination von Vertragsaufhebung und Schadensersatz denn auch praktisch durchwegs akzeptiert.[21]

2. Wirkungen der Aufhebung

Art. 81 I unterscheidet zwischen dem **Erlöschen der Primärleistungspflichten** und den weiter geltenden Rechten und Pflichten, insbesondere betreffend Schadensersatz und das Verfahren der Rückabwicklung.[22] Nach Aufhebung können beide Parteien die erbrachten Leistungen zurückfordern, Art. 81 II, soweit dem nicht ein Vorbehalt gegen die Erfüllung in Natur nach Art. 28 entgegensteht.[23] Es sind die Folgen des bereits (teilweise) erfüllten Vertrages zu beseitigen. Art. 82 enthält dabei als Kern eine **gefahrverteilende Regelung,** die den allgemeinen Regeln der Gefahrtragung in den Artt. 66 ff. im Rahmen der Rückabwicklung als speziellere Norm vorgeht.

Leitbild der Rückabwicklung ist die vollständige Rückgewähr der erhaltenen Leistungen auf beiden Seiten.[24] Dieses Leitbild ist auch der Grund dafür, dass die **Möglichkeit unversehrter Rückgabe** in Art. 82 I grundsätzlich zur Voraussetzung der Vertragsaufhebung gemacht wird. Die in Art. 82 II vom Grundsatz der unversehrten Rückgabe erlaubten **Ausnahmen überwiegen** die Regel allerdings bei Weitem.[25] Die Rückgewähr in natura wird ergänzt durch die Regel des Art. 84, wonach alle Vorteile zu erstatten sind, die den Parteien durch den vorübergehenden Leistungsaustausch zugefallen sind. Abs. 1 auferlegt dem Verkäufer die Pflicht, den empfangenen Kaufpreis vom Tag der Zahlung an zu **verzinsen.** Abs. 2 betrifft die Pflicht des Käufers, die **Vorteile zu vergüten,** die er aus der Ware gezogen hat. Zu beachten ist, dass Grenzen zwischen Rückabwicklung und Schadensersatz insbesondere im Bereich der Artt. 82 II und 84 und erst recht im Bereich dort nicht direkt geregelter, aber verwandter Fälle fliessend sind.[26] Gerade im Bereich der Vorteilsausgleichung mag das Schadensersatzrecht mit seinem festen **Orientierungspunkt am Interesse,** das sich aus der ordnungsgemässen Erfüllung des Vertrages ergibt, nicht selten das überlegenere Instrument sein.[27]

---

[20] Vgl. *Hellner,* UN Convention, S. 71, 81.
[21] Die Kombination von Rückabwicklung und Schadensersatz findet sich in praktisch sämtlichen Rechtsordnungen, vgl. *Schlechtriem,* Restitution, Kapitel 3, VII: *Treitel,* Remedies, S. 392 ff.; seit der Schuldrechtsmodernisierung auch im deutschen Recht, vgl. § 325 BGB. Vgl. auch Art. 8:102 PECL, Art. 7.3.5 II PICC, Artt. 106 VI, 131 IV CESL-Entwurf; Art. III.–3:509 III DCFR.
[22] Dazu näher unten *Fountoulakis,* Art. 81 Rn. 12 f. Zur Frage des Erfüllungsortes der gegenseitigen Rückgewähransprüche vgl. Art. 81 Rn. 23 ff.
[23] Zu diesem Vorbehalt näher unten Art. 81 Rn. 17.
[24] HGer St. Gallen, 3.12.2002, CISG-online 727, spricht davon, „den Status quo ante wieder herzustellen".
[25] *Enderlein/Maskow/Strohbach,* Art. 82, Anm. 1.2.; *Leser,* Rücktritt und Schadensersatz, S. 585 f.; *Ziegel,* Remedial Provisions, S. 9–26 ff.; *Coen,* S. 217; *Freiburg,* S. 256; vgl. auch OGH, 29.6.1999, CISG-online 483 = östZRVgl 2000, 33.
[26] Vgl. unten Art. 84 Rn. 32.
[27] Dazu unten Art. 84 Rn. 32.

Art. 81 [Erlöschen der Leistungspflichten; Rückgabe des Geleisteten]

(1) Die Aufhebung des Vertrages befreit beide Parteien von ihren Vertragspflichten, mit Ausnahme etwaiger Schadenersatzpflichten. Die Aufhebung berührt nicht Bestimmungen des Vertrages über die Beilegung von Streitigkeiten oder sonstige Bestimmungen des Vertrages, welche die Rechte und Pflichten der Parteien nach Vertragsaufhebung regeln.

(2) Hat eine Partei den Vertrag ganz oder teilweise erfüllt, so kann sie Rückgabe des von ihr Geleisteten von der anderen Partei verlangen.* Sind beide Parteien zur Rückgabe verpflichtet, so sind die Leistungen Zug um Zug zurückzugeben.

Art. 81

(1) Avoidance of the contract releases both parties from their obligations under it, subject to any damages which may be due. Avoidance does not affect any provision of the contract for the settlement of disputes or any other provision of the contract governing the rights and obligations of the parties consequent upon the avoidance of the contract.

(2) A party who has performed the contract either wholly or in part may claim restitution from the other party of whatever the first party has supplied or paid under the contract. If both parties are bound to make restitution, they must do so concurrently.

Art. 81

1) La résolution du contrat libère les deux parties de leurs obligations, sous réserve des dommages-intérêts qui peuvent être dus. Elle n'a pas d'effet sur les stipulations du contrat relatives au règlement des différends ou aux droits et obligations des parties en cas de résolution.

2) La partie qui a exécuté le contrat totalement ou partiellement peut réclamer restitution à l'autre partie de ce qu'elle a fourni ou payé en exécution du contrat. Si les deux parties sont tenues d'effectuer des restitutions, elles doivent y procéder simultanément.

Übersicht

	Rn.
I. Vorgeschichte	1
1. Vergleich gegenüber dem EKG	1
2. Unberücksichtigte Vorschläge	2
II. Voraussetzungen der Vertragsaufhebung	3
1. Entstehung des Anspruchs	3
2. Aufhebungserklärung	4
III. Wirkungen der Vertragsaufhebung	5
1. Befreiung von Primärpflichten	5
2. Ausschluss nationaler Rückabwicklungsregeln	6
3. Rechte Dritter	11
4. Fortbestehende Pflichten	12
a) Allgemeines	12
b) Insbesondere: Schadensersatz	13
5. Teilaufhebung	14
6. Anwendung bei übereinstimmender Vertragsaufhebungsvereinbarung	15
IV. Rückforderung des Geleisteten	16
1. Rückforderungsrecht	16
2. Form und Umfang der Rückgabe	17
3. Einschränkung durch Art. 82 I	19
4. Zug-um-Zug-Abwicklung	20
a) Grundsatz	20
b) Aufrechnung bzw. Verrechnung	21
5. Leistungsort der Rückgabe	23
a) Allgemeines	23

---

* Österreich, Schweiz: ihre Leistung von der anderen Partei zurückfordern.

b) Leistungsort für die Rückzahlung 24
c) Leistungsort für die Rückgabe der Ware 25
d) Kein allgemeines Prinzip des Rückleistungsorts am Sitz der
   vertragstreuen Partei 26
e) Bestimmung des Gerichtsstandes 27
6. Kosten der Rückgabe 28
7. Fristen für die Rückgabe; Annahmeverzug des Verkäufers in der
   Rückabwicklung 29
V. Beweislast 30

Vorläufer und **Entwürfe:** Art. 78 EKG; Genfer E 1976 Art. 51; Wiener E 1977 Art. 52; New Yorker E 1978 Art. 66.

I. Vorgeschichte

1. Vergleich gegenüber dem EKG

Art. 81 wurde in fast unveränderter Form von Art. 78 EKG übernommen. Zur Klarstellung wurde eingefügt, dass Klauseln zur Beilegung von Streitigkeiten durch die Aufhebung des Vertrages nicht ausgeschlossen werden.[1] Die heutige erweiterte Fassung mit Einbeziehung auch der „sonstigen Bestimmungen des Vertrages, welche die Rechte und Pflichten der Parteien nach Vertragsaufhebung regeln" fand bereits im Wiener E als Art. 52 Eingang.[2] Mit geringfügigen Änderungen wurde die Regelung auf der Wiener Konferenz, mit Art. 66 New Yorker E übereinstimmend, in das CISG übernommen.[3]   **1**

2. Unberücksichtigte Vorschläge

Nicht berücksichtigt in der endgültigen Fassung wurden Änderungsvorschläge zu einer nur eingeschränkten Rückabwicklung und zur Regelung sachenrechtlicher Fragen (Insolvenz und Eigentumsübergang);[4] ebenso wenig aufgenommen wurde die Teilbarkeitsvermutung bei komplexen Verträgen im Sinne des amerikanischen UCC,[5] Regeln zur Abgrenzung von Rückabwicklung und Schadensersatz[6] sowie ein Vorschlag zur gänzlichen Neuformulierung.[7] Auch die Tatsache, dass die beidseitige Rückabwicklung gerade im anglo-amerikanischen Rechtsraum ungewöhnlich ist, blieb schliesslich unberücksichtigt.[8]   **2**

II. Voraussetzungen der Vertragsaufhebung

1. Entstehung des Anspruchs

Das Recht zur Vertragsaufhebung ergibt sich aus den jeweiligen Störungstatbeständen, d. h. aus **Artt. 49, 51, 64, 72, 73**. Das Aufhebungsrecht steht jeder vertragstreuen Partei zu.[9]   **3**

---

[1] YB VII (1976), S. 132, Art. 51, Nr. 5.
[2] YB VIII (1977), S. 57 f., Art. 51, Nr. 462.
[3] *Bianca/Bonell/Tallon*, Art. 81, Anm. 1.1. Der an der Wiener Konferenz geäusserte Vorschlag, sich von dem aus dem EKG übernommenen Begriff der „avoidance" zu trennen, der Assoziationen mit den die Vertragswirksamkeit betreffenden englischen Fachtermini „void" und „voidable" weckt, und statt dessen den Begriff „discharge by breach" einzuführen, wurde aus Zeitgründen abgelehnt, vgl. Legislative History, 33rd Meeting, 2.4.1980, Nr. 83 f. Der von Artt. 9:301 ff. PECL, 7.3.1 PICC und Artt. III.–3:501 ff. DCFR gewählte Begriff „termination" wäre wohl auch im CISG glücklicher gewesen, ebenso der von §§ 2–703 (2) (f), 2–711 (2) (c) UCC 2003 verwandte Begriff der „cancellation". Beschwichtigend zum Begriff der „avoidance" *Ziegel*, Report, Art. 26, Anm. 1. („quite acceptable and not likely to cause confusion even among common law lawyers").
[4] Sämtl. YB V (1974), S. 42, Art. 78, Nr. 139 f.
[5] YB V (1974), S. 42, Art. 78, Nr. 141. Zum Problem der Teilrückabwicklung vgl. im Übrigen Vor Artt. 81–84 Rn. 8.
[6] YB V (1974), S. 42, Art. 78, Nr. 143. Vgl. dazu Art. 79 V und Art. 83.
[7] YB V (1974), S. 42, Art. 78, Nr. 143.
[8] YB VII (1976), S. 132, Art. 51, Nr. 9; Commentary, O. R., S. 57, Art. 66 E, Nr. 9.
[9] Vgl. auch Vor Artt. 81–84 Rn. 2 und Art. 26 Rn. 6.

Art. 81 4–7   Teil III. Kapitel V. Pflichten des Verkäufers und Käufers. Abschnitt V

2. Aufhebungserklärung

4   Form und Modalität der Erklärung der Vertragsaufhebung regeln **Artt. 26, 27.** Vgl. dort auch zur Frage des Zeitpunkts des Wirksamwerdens bzw. der Bindungswirkung der Aufhebungserklärung und zur Frage einer eventuellen Frist für die Ausübung.[10]

III. Wirkungen der Vertragsaufhebung

1. Befreiung von Primärpflichten

5   Durch die erklärte Vertragsaufhebung werden die **unerfüllten Primärpflichten** des Vertrages sowie die sie direkt unterstützenden Zusatzpflichten **aufgehoben**.[11] Beide Parteien werden durch eine wirksame Aufhebungserklärung unmittelbar befreit.[12] Sie gibt den Parteien die Dispositionsfreiheit zurück.

2. Ausschluss nationaler Rückabwicklungsregeln

6   International umstritten ist die Frage, welche Wirkung die Vertragsaufhebung auf den Bestand des Vertrages hat. Insofern stehen sich insbesondere zwei Positionen gegenüber. Nach der ersten Auffassung wird der Vertrag mit dessen Aufhebung nicht beseitigt, sondern in ein Abwicklungsverhältnis umgesteuert.[13] Nach der zweiten Auffassung hingegen wirkt die Aufhebung vertragsvernichtend, d. h. der Vertrag wird so behandelt, als ob er nie bestanden hat.[14]

7   Bedeutsam geworden ist der **Meinungsstreit** für die Frage, ob im Rahmen der Rückabwicklung auf nationale Rückabwicklungsregeln zurückgegriffen werden kann. Insbesondere interessiert, ob der Verkäufer dingliche Rechte an der Ware geltend machen kann oder aber auf obligatorische Rechte verwiesen ist. Geht man davon aus, dass die Vertragsaufhebung ex tunc wirkt, also vertragsvernichtende Wirkung hat, so fällt nach den weitaus

---

[10] Oben *Fountoulakis*, Art. 26 Rn. 7 ff., 11 f.

[11] *Bianca/Bonell/Tallon*, Art. 81, Anm. 2.2.; *Honnold/Flechtner*, Art. 81, Rn. 438; *Herber/Czerwenka*, Art. 81, Rn. 2; *Gabriel*, Contracts, S. 245; *Ferrari u. a./Ferrari*, Internationales Vertragsrecht, Art. 81, Rn. 11; Int. Ct. Ukrainian CCI, 5.7.2005, CISG-online 1361; BGH, 25.6.1997, CISG-online 277 = NJW 1997, 3311; KG Wallis, 21.2.2005, CISG-online 1193, Erw. 4.b) = IHR 2006, 155; vgl. auch Art. 9:305 I PECL; Art. 7.3.5 I PICC; Art. III.–3:509 I DCFR; Art. 8 I CESL-Entwurf.

[12] Vgl. oben *Fountoulakis*, Art. 26 Rn. 4.

[13] *Schlechtriem*, Internationales UN-Kaufrecht, Rn. 330; *Honsell/Weber*, Vorbem. 81–84, Rn. 10; Art. 81, Rn. 4 f.; *Staudinger/Magnus*, Vorbem. zu Artt. 81 ff., Rn. 2; oben Rn. 2; *Honnold/Flechtner*, Art. 81, Rn. 444.1; *Piltz*, Internationales Kaufrecht, Rn. 5–318; *Ferrari u. a./Ferrari*, Internationales Vertragsrecht, Art. 81, Rn. 9; *Herber/Czerwenka*, Art. 81, Rn. 7; *Reinhart*, Art. 81, Rn. 2; UNCITRAL Digest, Art. 81, Rn. 2; *Enderlein/Maskow/Strohbach*, Art. 81, Anm. 1.; *Jan*, S. 217 f.; *Bamberger/Roth/Saenger*, Art. 81, Rn. 3 f.; *Witz/Salger/Lorenz/Salger*, Art. 81, Rn. 2; MünchKommHGB/*Benicke*, Art. 81, Rn. 10; *Kazimierska*, Rn. 79, 147; *Soergel/Lüderitz/Dettmeier*, Art. 81, Rn. 1; *Vischer*, Gemeinsame Bestimmungen, S. 181; aus der Rspr. vgl. OGH, 29.6.1999, CISG-online 483 = östZRVgl 2000, 33: „Umsteuerung" in ein Abwicklungsverhältnis; ferner etwa HGer St. Gallen, 3.12.2002, CISG-online 727; LG Düsseldorf, 11.10.1995, CISG-online 180.

[14] *Wu*, 7 VJ (2003), 233, 239; *Heuzé*, Anm. 426.; *Goode*, Goode On Commercial Law, S. 1027 Fn. 66: „‚Avoid' appears to denote rescission **ab initio** (Hervorhebung im Original), followed by restitution on both sides but without prejudice to a right to damages"; *Bianca/Bonell/Tallon*, Art. 81, Anm. 2.5.; *Honnold/Flechtner*, Art. 81, Rn. 444. Im engl. und amerikanischen Recht kann der Verkäufer im Falle der Vertragsverletzung grundsätzlich nicht vom Käufer die Herausgabe der Kaufsache verlangen; insoweit stellt sich die Frage einer eventuellen dinglichen Wirkung der termination/cancellation nicht, vgl. dazu Vor. Artt. 81–84 Rn. 3. Wenn hingegen der vertragstreue Käufer die nicht vertragsgemässe Ware berechtigterweise zurückweist, soll das Eigentum auf den Verkäufer zurückfallen, so es denn überhaupt übergegangen ist. Hier geht es also weniger um die Konkursfestigkeit des Herausgabeanspruchs des Verkäufers als vielmehr um dessen Risiko für (weitere) Verschlechterungen der Sache. Ausserdem ermöglicht es die Annahme der lediglich auflösend bedingt erfolgten Eigentumsübertragung, die Weiterveräusserung oder Verpfändung von Dokumenten, die für eine bestimmte Ware stehen, nicht als „act inconsistent with the ownership of the seller" i. S. d. sec. 35 SGA anzusehen und deshalb das Zurückweisungsrecht des Käufers nicht auszuschliessen; vgl. insgesamt *Benjamin's Sale of Goods*, Rn. 12–065 i. V. m. Rn. 12–052, m. w. N. aus der Rspr.; *Chitty*, Chitty On Contracts, vol. I, Rn. 24–050 ff., mit Rechtsprechungsnachweisen; zu §§ 2–601, 2–602 UCC vgl. *White/Summers*, § 8-3.

meisten Rechtsordnungen[15] entweder das Eigentum automatisch an den ursprünglichen Eigentümer zurück (Konsensualprinzip) oder aber es entfällt die causa, so dass die Eigentumsübertragung von Anfang unwirksam war (Kausalitätsprinzip). Dem Sachgläubiger stehen damit dingliche, somit regelmässig stärkere – weil absolute und unverjährbare – Rechte zur Durchführung der Rückabwicklung zur Verfügung, wohingegen der Geldgläubiger blosse **in-personam**-Rechtsbehelfe in Händen hat.[16]

Versucht man, dem Wortlaut des Art. 81 I 1 („[d]ie Aufhebung des Vertrages befreit beide **8** Parteien von ihren Vertragspflichten") etwas zu der Frage von **ex-nunc- oder ex-tunc-Wirkung der Aufhebung** zu entnehmen, so erhält man wenig Anhaltspunkte, was sich auch darin widerspiegelt, dass sich sowohl die Vertreter der Rückabwicklungs- wie der ex-tunc-Theorie zur Untermauerung ihrer Position auf den Wortlaut stützen.[17] Bedeutsamer ist Art. 81 I 2, wonach bestimmte Pflichten und Vertragsbestimmungen trotz Aufhebung aufrecht erhalten bleiben. Dies könnte nun zwar als Grundsatz-Ausnahme-Regel verstanden werden, wonach – aus Praktikabilitätsgründen – gewisse Vertragsbestimmungen vorbehalten blieben, der Vertrag ansonsten aber als dahingefallen zu betrachten sei. Die Aufrechterhaltung einer ganzen Reihe von Zusatzpflichten steht aber im Widerspruch zur ex-tunc-Theorie, also dazu, dass die einstige Existenz eines Vertragsverhältnisses negiert wird. So können beispielsweise keine Geheimhaltungspflichten „fortwirken", wenn der Vertrag, der sie begründet hat, nie bestanden haben soll.

Dass nach h. L. Verletzungen der **nach** Vertragsaufhebung weiter bestehenden Pflichten **9** ebenfalls nach Art. 74 zu entschädigen sind, also zu vertraglichen Schadensersatzansprüchen führen,[18] könnte ebenfalls für die Rückabwicklungstheorie sprechen. Folgte man der ex-tunc-Theorie, müsste man konsequenterweise die Verletzung von nach Vertragsaufhebung entstandenen bzw. „weiter bestehenden" Pflichten (hier zeigt sich nochmals der rein sprachliche Widerspruch zur Vertragsvernichtungstheorie) nach nationalem (Delikts-)Recht beurteilen.

Scheint demnach Vieles für die Annahme eines ex nunc wirkenden Abwicklungsverhält- **10** nisses zu sprechen, ist dennoch Vorsicht angebracht, den Theorienstreit, der ja letztlich vor dem Hintergrund der nationalen Rechtsordnungen ausgetragen wird, nicht mit dem eigenen Vorverständnis zu betrachten. So sollte man sich hüten, der Theorie vom Abwicklungsverhältnis den deutschen dogmatischen Ansatz zugrunde legen zu wollen; vielmehr ist **autonom** auszulegen, welche Konsequenzen es hat, die Wirkungen der Aufhebung im CISG als „Umsteuerung in ein Abwicklungsverhältnis" zu begreifen.[19] Die hier entscheidende Frage ist, ob die Rückabwicklungsregeln des CISG von nationalem Rückabwicklungsrecht konkurrenziert bzw. abgelöst werden können. Dies ist klar zu verneinen.[20] Den

---

[15] Das Abstraktionsprinzip, wonach die dingliche Übereignung von dem zugrundeliegenden Schuldgeschäft unabhängig ist, bildet die grosse Ausnahme und gilt neben Deutschland z. B. noch in Griechenland (nur für bewegliche Sachen). Die Mehrheit der Rechtsordnungen sieht hingegen entweder vor, dass das Eigentum an der Ware automatisch mit Vertragsschluss übergeht (Konsensualprinzip), oder aber es bedarf zwar noch eines Übertragungsaktes, dem aber ein wirksamer Rechtsgrund, die causa, zugrunde liegt (Kausalitätsprinzip); vgl. zum Ganzen die Übersicht in *Schlechtriem*, Restitution, S. 283 ff.

[16] Vgl. die rechtsvergleichende Übersicht in *Schwenzer/Hachem/Kee*, Rn. 50.06 ff.

[17] *Krebs*, Rückabwicklung, S. 52, weist unter Angabe von Fundstellen darauf hin, dass sich „kuriorserweise" sowohl die Anhänger der Umsteuerungstheorie als auch die Verfechter des rückwirkenden Vertragswegfalls auf den Wortlaut des Art. 81 I 2 bezögen.

[18] Vgl. nur *Rolland*, FS Schlechtriem, S. 629, 651; *Schlechtriem*, Internationales UN-Kaufrecht, Rn. 331.

[19] So ausdrücklich auch *Coen*, S. 216; ähnlich *Krebs*, Rückabwicklung, S. 52: Die Entwicklungsgeschichte des CISG zeige, dass rechtstheoretische Grundfragen gerade nicht gelöst werden sollten. Da voraussichtlich ohnehin das Grundverständnis für den jeweils anderen dogmatischen Ansatz fehle, sei es angebracht, sich auf die von Artt. 81 ff. angebotenen praktischen Lösungen zu konzentrieren. Auch *Berg*, S. 73, warnt davor, aus der deutschen Theorie der Umsteuerung in ein Abwicklungsverhältnis zu weitgehende Rechtsfolgen zu ziehen. Einen guten, von dogmatischen Fragen abstrahierenden zusammenfassenden Überblick über die einzelnen Bestandteile des Rückabwicklungsprogramms bietet LG Krefeld, 19.12.1995, CISG-online 397, unter V. 3. der Entscheidungsgründe; mit dem Gesetzeswortlaut operierend ebenfalls LG Freiburg, 21.8.2002, CISG-online 711 = IHR 2003, 22.

[20] A. A. etwa *López Rodríguez*, 9 VJ (2005), 291, 298 („a cautious approach would refer this matter to the applicable domestic law.").

wohl wichtigsten Grund hierfür liefert Art. 7 I, also die Vorgabe, bei der Auslegung des CISG dessen einheitliche Anwendung zu fördern: Wie gezeigt worden ist, entstehen nach der ex-tunc-Theorie je nach nationalem Eigentumsübertragungskonzept unterschiedliche Eigentumslagen. Kann der Sachgläubiger nach nationalen, absolut wirkenden Rechtsbehelfen vorgehen, um die Ware zu erhalten, so wird er damit gegenüber dem Geldgläubiger besser gestellt, der immer nur einen obligatorischen Anspruch auf Rückzahlung hat. Das CISG will freilich die Differenzierung zwischen Rechtsbehelfen des Sachgläubigers und solchen des Geldgläubigers nicht vornehmen; vielmehr unterwirft es die **gesamte Rückabwicklung einem einheitlichen, autonom geregelten Regime, das (einzig) vertragliche Rückabwicklungsansprüche gewährt**. Dem Erfordernis der einheitlichen Anwendung des Übereinkommens wird deshalb einzig dann Genüge getan, wenn die Aufhebung ein einheitliches Abwicklungsverhältnis zur Folge hat und entsprechend nationale Rechte jeglicher Natur, seien sie vertraglich, bereicherungsrechtlich oder dinglich,[21] ausschliesst.[22] Es muss Gewähr dafür bestehen, dass, wer dem Übereinkommen untersteht, mit einem CISG-autonomen, abschliessenden Rückabwicklungsmechanismus konfrontiert wird und von nationalen Regeln nicht überrascht werden kann. Einzig dadurch wird dem Bedürfnis nach Rechtssicherheit Rechnung getragen.

3. Rechte Dritter

11   Das Rückabwicklungsregime des CISG **tangiert die Rechte Vertragsfremder nicht**. Beispielsweise kann der Dritterwerber durch nationale Mechanismen des gutgläubigen Erwerbs geschützt werden,[23] oder andere Gläubiger können in der Verteilung der Insolvenzmasse Priorität haben.[24]

4. Fortbestehende Pflichten

12   **a) Allgemeines.** Die in Art. 81 I genannten Pflichten, welche trotz der Aufhebung des Vertrages weiterbestehen, sollen nach den Materialien **keine erschöpfende Aufzählung** sein, sondern bloss als Beispiele dienen.[25] Ausdrücklich genannt ist zunächst der Schadensersatz als wichtigste fortbestehende Einzelpflicht, was freilich wegen des mehrfach erfolgenden Hinweises auf die Parallelität von Aufhebung und Schadensersatz im Übereinkommen[26] überflüssig ist. Aufgezählt in Art. 81 I werden ferner die Bestimmungen zur Beilegung von Streitigkeiten wie Schiedsklauseln,[27] Schadenspauschalierungen und Vertragsstrafen,[28] die damit auch den ganzen oder teilweisen Ausschluss von Schadensersatz-

---

[21] Vgl. die Übersicht bei *Schlechtriem*, Restitution, S. 695 ff.; *Schwenzer/Hachem/Kee*, Rn. 50.06 ff.; vgl. ferner *Schlechtriem/Coen/Hornung*, 2/3 European Review of Private Law (2001), 377, 391, die auch hervorheben, dass die Vielfalt und das Verhältnis der einzelnen nationalen Rückabwicklungsregeln untereinander insgesamt „a rather confusing picture" abgeben.
[22] So ausdrücklich auch ICC, 9978/1999, CISG-online 708 = 11 (2) ICC Int. Ct. Arb. Bull. (2000), 117; CISG-AC, Op. 9 *(Bridge)*, Opinion 1.5, Comment 3.8 ff.; *Magnus*, 25 J. L. & Com. (2005), 423, 431; *Mohs*, Effects of Avoidance, S. 252, 256.
[23] Sekretariatskommentar, Art. 66 E, Nr. 10; *Honnold/Flechtner*, Art. 81, Rn. 444.1; *Ziegel*, Report, Art. 81, Anm. 2. b); *Lookofsky*, The 1980 United Nations Convention, Rn. 312; *Kröll u. a./Bridge*, Art. 81, Rn. 16.
[24] *Usinor Industeel v. Leeco Steel Products, Inc.*, U. S. Dist. Ct. (N. D. Ill.), 28.3.2002, CISG-online 696 = 1326; vgl. auch *Audit*, Vente internationale, Anm. 189., 191.; *Lookofsky*, Understanding the CISG, S. 148.
[25] Sekretariatskommentar, Art. 66 E, Nr. 6; auch schon YB VII (1976), S. 132, Art. 51, Nr. 6.
[26] Vgl. Artt. 45 II, 61 II, ferner Artt. 75, 76, die ausdrücklich die Schadensberechnung **nach** Vertragsaufhebung regeln; zur Überflüssigkeit des Vorbehalts betr. Schadensersatzansprüche auch *Audit*, Vente internationale, Anm. 190.
[27] Vgl. etwa Int. Ct. Russian CCI, 13.6.2000, CISG-online 1083, Erw. 3.1.
[28] Vgl. Int. Ct. Ukrainian CCI, 18.11.2004, CISG-online 1271, Erw. 7; Economic Court of the Grodno Region (Weissrussland), 23.7.2008, CISG-online 2115; die Tatsache, dass Vertragsstrafen neben der Vertragsaufhebung bestehen bleiben, wurde ignoriert in Int. Ct. Russian CCI, 28.5.2004, CISG-online 1513, Erw. 3.6 („The Tribunal holds that the claim of the [Buyer] for recovery of the sanctions for delay in delivery is not compatible with [Buyer]'s claim for refund of the price of the goods, which follows from the fact of avoidance of the contract in respect of the first installment of the goods established by the Tribunal").

ansprüchen und von Aufhebungsrechten umfassen.²⁹ Die Gültigkeit solcher Ausschlussklauseln beurteilt sich je nach Art der Klausel nach dem anwendbaren (Schieds-)Prozessrecht und/oder nach den mittels Kollisionsrecht eruierten anwendbaren Rechtsregeln, vgl. Art. 4 lit. a).³⁰ Ferner bleiben bestehen die Bestimmungen des Vertrages, welche die Rechte und Pflichten der Parteien nach der Vertragsaufhebung regeln sollen.³¹ Soweit diese nicht bereits erwähnt sind, zählen hierher Pflichten zur Aufbewahrung oder Fürsorge für eine zurückzugebende Leistung der anderen Seite (Art. 86), Pflichten zur Rücksendung, Verwertung oder Weitergabe gelieferter Waren, ferner Geheimhaltungspflichten, die Rückgabe oder Rückgewähr von Sicherheiten, soweit sie nicht auch eventuelle Schadensersatzansprüche sichern sollen, sowie die Rückgabe von Plänen, Unterlagen, Mustern, mitübertragenen Rechten (Lizenzen) und Ähnliches. Diesen Vertragsbestimmungen ist gemein, dass sie regelmässig den zur Abwicklung fortgeltenden Teil des Vertrages bilden und deshalb auch und gerade im Falle der Vertragsaufhebung weiterbestehen sollen.³² Im Zweifel ist entscheidend, ob die Parteien das Fortbestehen einer Vertragsklausel nach Aufhebung bezweckten (Art. 8).³³ Ebenso darunter fallen Mitwirkungspflichten etwa für den Geldtransfer aus devisenbewirtschafteten Ländern und ggf. Zinssatz- und Wechselkursvereinbarungen.³⁴ Bestehen bleiben schliesslich auch Rechtswahlklauseln sowie force-majeure-Klauseln.³⁵ Es entfallen hingegen Nachbesserungs-, Minderungsrechte und Ersatzlieferungsansprüche, ungeachtet dessen, von welcher Seite sie geltend gemacht wurden.³⁶

b) Insbesondere: Schadensersatz. Schadenersatzansprüche, die **vor** der Vertragsaufhebung entstanden sind, bleiben von der Aufhebung unberührt, Art. 81 I 1, und zwar unabhängig davon, ob sie mit der die Vertragsaufhebung auslösenden Verletzung unmittelbar zusammenhängen oder nicht. **Nach** der Vertragsaufhebung können sich Schadensersatzansprüche aus der Verletzung von Pflichten, die trotz Aufhebung weiterhin existieren, ergeben, etwa aus der Verletzung von Geheimhaltungspflichten. Ebenso kann die Verletzung von Aufbewahrungspflichten, die zu Verschlechterung oder Verlust der Ware führt, sowie die Verletzung sonstiger Rückgabepflichten Schadensersatzansprüche auslösen.³⁷ Schliesslich ist auch entschädigungspflichtig, wer die Rückgabe der erhaltenen Leistung ungebührlich verzögert, ohne dass sich die andere Partei auf das Zug-um-Zug-Prinzip berufen kann, weil sie ihrerseits unter dem Vertrag keine zurückzuerstattende Leistung erbracht hatte.³⁸ Sämtliche dieser Schadensersatzansprüche beurteilen sich nach Artt. 74, 79.³⁹ Zur Rückerstattung der Kosten der Rückabwicklung gestützt auf Artt. 46 I lit. b), 61 I lit. b) i. V. m. 74 siehe Rn. 28.

---

²⁹ Vgl. auch Art. 9:305 I, II PECL; Art. 7.3.5 II PICC; Art. III.–3:509 II DCFR.
³⁰ Dazu *Schlechtriem*, Internationales UN-Kaufrecht, Rn. 41, 58; ICC, 9978/1999, CISG-online 708 = 11 (2) ICC Int. Ct. Arb. Bull. (2000), 117.
³¹ Vgl. Int. Ct. Russian CCI, 25.6.2004, CISG-online 1437, Erw. 3.5; *Bianca/Bonell/Tallon*, Art. 81, Anm. 2.3. f.; *Honnold/Flechtner*, Art. 81, Rn. 443; *Herber/Czerwenka*, Art. 81, Rn. 5; *Reinhart*, Art. 81, Rn. 2 f.
³² *Bianca/Bonell/Tallon*, Art. 81, Anm. 2.4.; *Enderlein/Maskow/Strohbach*, Art. 81, Anm. 1. und 5.; *Staudinger/Magnus*, Art. 81, Rn. 10; *Leser*, Rücktritt und Schadensersatz, S. 585.
³³ CISG-AC, Op. 9 *(Bridge)*, Opinion 1.2, Comment 3.3.
³⁴ *Witz/Salger/Lorenz/Salger*, Art. 81, Rn. 3.
³⁵ Vgl. CISG-AC, Op. 9 Bridge, Opinion 1.2, Comment 3.3, m. w. N.; *Kröll u. a./Bridge*, Art. 81, Rn. 8.
³⁶ *Witz/Salger/Lorenz/Salger*, Art. 81, Rn. 2.
³⁷ *Rolland*, FS Schlechtriem, S. 629, 651; MünchKomm/*P. Huber*, Art. 81, Rn. 16; *Witz/Salger/Lorenz/Salger*, Art. 81, Rn. 4; *Dimsey*, Consequences of Avoidance, S. 532; unrichtig daher ICC, 9978/1999, CISG-online 708 = 11 (2) ICC Int. Ct. Arb. Bull. (2000), 117: „[Art. 81 I] does not refer to a new claim for damages arising due to the seller's failure to refund the purchase price [but] rather provides for the continuation of any claims which may exist due to the seller's violation of his primary obligation".
³⁸ *Staudinger/Magnus*, Art. 81, Rn. 14, 16.
³⁹ CISG-AC, Op. 9 *(Bridge)*, Opinion 2.5, Comment 3.16; *Schlechtriem*, FS U. Huber, S. 563, 574; *Kröll u. a./Bridge*, Art. 81, Rn. 5 a. E.

5. Teilaufhebung

14 Kann der Käufer gemäss Art. 51 oder Art. 73 den Vertrag teilweise aufheben, erfolgt die Rückerstattung des Geleisteten gemäss Art. 81 II als Teil.[40]

6. Anwendung bei übereinstimmender Vertragsaufhebungsvereinbarung

15 Art. 81 findet auch bei einvernehmlicher Vertragsaufhebung sinngemäss Anwendung.[41] Häufiger als in den Fällen einseitiger Vertragsauflösung kann es hier allerdings sein, dass die Parteien spezielle Vereinbarungen betreffend die Rechtsfolgen nach Vertragsaufhebung treffen, die dann gemäss Art. 6 vor den Rückabwicklungsregeln des Art. 81 Vorrang haben.[42]

IV. Rückforderung des Geleisteten

1. Rückforderungsrecht

16 Als wichtigste Grundlage der Rückabwicklung gibt Art. 81 II jeder der beiden Parteien ein Rückforderungsrecht für das von ihr Geleistete. Die erbrachte(n) Leistung(en) werden **wechselseitig oder – bei Vorleistungen – einseitig rückerstattet;**[43] allerdings erfolgt die Rückerstattung nicht automatisch, sondern nur, sofern das Rückforderungsrecht geltend gemacht worden ist.[44] Auch der vertragstreue Verkäufer kann aufheben und die von ihm gelieferte Ware zurückverlangen, eine Variante, die dem anglo-amerikanischen Recht ferner liegt.[45]

2. Form und Umfang der Rückgabe

17 Das Rückforderungsrecht orientiert sich an der **Sache.**[46] Die konkret erbrachte Leistung ist **in natura** zurückzugeben, soweit nicht ein Vorbehalt nach Art. 28 besteht;[47] der Schutz-

---

[40] YB VII (1976), S. 131, Art. 51, Nr. 3; Sekretariatskommentar, Art. 66 E, Nr. 3; Int. Ct. Russian CCI, 28.5.2004, CISG-online 1513, Erw. 3.4.

[41] *Bamberger/Roth/Saenger,* Art. 81, Rn. 1; *Kröll u. a./Bridge,* Art. 81, Rn. 14; MünchKomm/*P. Huber,* Art. 81, Rn. 2; *Brunner,* Art. 81, Rn. 1; OLG Düsseldorf, 28.5.2004, CISG-online 850, Erw. C. II.1. = IHR 2004, 203: „einvernehmliche Rückabwicklung des Vertrages in entsprechender Anwendung der Art. 81 Abs. 2 S. 1 CISG"; vgl. auch OGH, 29.6.1999, CISG-online 483 = östZRVgl 2000, 33: „[D]ie Folgen einer einvernehmlichen Vertragsaufhebung regelt das UN-K nicht". Soweit die Parteien daher die Rechtsfolgen der einvernehmlichen Vertragsaufhebung, im speziellen die Gefahrtragung, den Leistungsort oder die Kostentragung, in ihrer Aufhebungsvereinbarung keiner privatautonomen Regelung unterziehen, muss die insoweit gebliebene Lücke in Auslegung nach Art 7 Abs 2 UN-K durch den Rückgriff auf die Art 81ff UN-K geschlossen werden."

[42] Insofern kann z. B. Int. Ct. Russian CCI, 3.3.1997, CISG-online 1298, nicht als Nachweis für die Nichtanwendbarkeit von Art. 81 auf einvernehmliche Vertragsaufhebungen herangezogen werden (so aber etwa *Gabriel,* Contracts, S. 246), da die Entscheidung lediglich davon spricht, dass „[t]he agreement of the parties prevails over the provisions of the Convention."

[43] Vgl. Schiedsgericht der Hamburger freundlichen Arbitrage, 29.12.1998, CISG-online 638 = RIW 1999, 394: Der Verkäufer konnte die Vorauszahlung für die nicht erbrachte Teilleistung gem. Art. 81 II zurückfordern; vgl. auch Int. Ct. Russian CCI, 15.4.1994, CISG-online 449. Nicht zur Anwendung kommt Art. 81 II hingegen, wenn sich im Rahmen eines nach CISG zu beurteilenden Kaufvertrages anderweitige Herausgabeansprüche ergeben: Wenn etwa zu Unrecht eine Rückerstattung erfolgt ist, so kann die Rückgabe des Rückerstattungsbetrages nicht nach Art. 81 II, sondern nur nach nationalem Bereicherungsrecht verlangt werden, vgl. OLG München, 28.1.1998, CISG-online 339 = RIW 1998, 559, 560.

[44] Foreign Trade Court of Arbitration attached to the Serbian Chamber of Commerce, 15.7.2008, CISG-online 1795.

[45] Vgl. *Honnold/Flechtner,* Art. 81, Rn. 444, mit dem Hinweis auf die praktischen Grenzen durch die Eigentumsverhältnisse und Rechte Dritter; *Schwenzer/Hachem/Kee,* Rn. 50.23 f.; vgl. auch *Whittington,* 37 Vict. U. Well. L. Rev. (2006), 421, 434 f. sowie vorne Fn. 14. Allerdings gilt im Falle der Aufhebung durch den Verkäufer Art. 82 nicht, vgl. dort Rn. 28 f.

[46] *Bianca/Bonell/Tallon,* Art. 81, Anm. 2.5.; *Honnold/Flechtner,* Art. 81, Rn. 444; *Nicholas,* 105 L. Q. R. (1989), 201, 227.

[47] So auch *Honnold/Flechtner,* Art. 81, Rn. 440.2 a. E.; *Herber/Czerwenka,* Art. 81, Rn. 8; *Bianca/Bonell/Tallon,* Art. 81, Anm. 2.6.; *Staudinger/Magnus,* Art. 28, Rn. 11; *Osuna,* Dealing with Avoidance, S. 492 f.;

zweck dieser Vorschrift greift, da das Vertragsgefüge gleichsam als Dach bis zur vollendeten Rückabwicklung weiterbesteht,[48] auch im Rückabwicklungsverhältnis.[49] Die Rückgabe einer Ersatzsache kommt nicht in Betracht.[50] Bei **Geld** bestimmt sich die Rückgabe nach der geleisteten Summe; diese ist in der von den Parteien für den Kaufpreis festgelegten Währung zurückzuerstatten;[51] ist die Währung ausnahmsweise nicht vertraglich festgelegt worden (vgl. Art. 55), so spricht der Restitutionscharakter von Artt. 81 ff. für die Rückzahlung in derjenigen Währung, auf die das Konto des Käufers, von dem er den Kaufpreisbetrag abhob, lautet.[52] Mögliche zwischenzeitliche Veränderungen des Wechselkurses bleiben vorbehaltlich anderslautender Vertragsvereinbarung unberücksichtigt.[53] Vielmehr spricht Art. 84 I dafür, den am Tag der Zahlung des Kaufpreises geltenden Wechselkurs anzuwenden.[54]

Art. 81 II regelt – neben der Funktion, als Grundlage für die Rückabwicklung insgesamt zu dienen – nur den Fall, dass die erbrachte Leistung noch **unverändert** beim Vertragspartner vorhanden ist. An diesem „einfachen" Fall orientiert sich die gesetzliche Lösung. In allen Fällen der Veränderung bestimmt sich der Umfang der Rückforderung nach den Artt. 82–84 einschliesslich der Zinspflicht für einen bereits bezahlten Kaufpreis. **18**

3. Einschränkung durch Art. 82 I

Für den Käufer ist die Einschränkung seines Aufhebungsrechts durch den **Grundsatz der unversehrten Rückgabe** in Art. 82 I zu beachten.[55] Bei Unmöglichkeit der unversehrten Rückgabe ist das Aufhebungsrecht blockiert. Diese Regel wird aber durch die Ausnahme in Art. 82 II zusammen mit den Regeln über die Vorteilsausgleichung in Art. 84 weitgehend abgewandelt, ja denaturiert; die Durchführung der Aufhebung ist trotz der Fassung des Übereinkommens danach die Regel.[56] **19**

4. Zug-um-Zug-Abwicklung

a) **Grundsatz.** Soweit auf beiden Seiten Rückforderungsrechte bestehen, sind sie Zug um Zug abzuwickeln.[57] Dies führt praktisch zu einem beiden Parteien zustehenden **Zurückbehaltungsrecht** solange, bis sich die andere Partei zur Rückgabe bereit er- **20**

Soergel/Lüderitz/Dettmeier, Art. 81, Rn. 7; *Bamberger/Roth/Saenger*, Art. 81, Rn. 4; MünchKommHGB/*Benicke*, Art. 81, Rn. 3; *Krebs*, L'article 28 CVIM, S. 159; *Coen*, S. 217; *Hornung*, S. 275 und 362 f.: Es wird darauf hingewiesen, dass eine Verurteilung zur Herausgabe der empfangenen Ware in Natur in den Ländern des Common Law ohnehin nur in Ausnahmefällen gerichtlich durchzusetzen ist, dazu oben *Müller-Chen*, Art. 28 Rn. 2.

[48] Vgl. oben Rn. 10.
[49] *Piltz*, Internationales Kaufrecht, Rn. 5–319; a. A. oben *Müller-Chen*, Art. 28 Rn. 6; *Neumayer/Ming*, Art. 81, Anm. 3.; *Honsell/Weber*, Art. 81, Rn. 16; *Heilmann*, S. 515; *Ferrari u. a./Ferrari*, Internationales Vertragsrecht, Art. 81, Rn. 18; MünchKomm/*P. Huber*, Art. 81, Rn. 8; offengelassen *bei Witz/Salger/Lorenz/Salger*, Art. 81, Rn. 4.
[50] Dazu unten *Fountoulakis*, Art. 82 Rn. 5.
[51] CISG-AC, Op. 9 *(Bridge)*, Opinion 2.4.
[52] Anders Art. 6.1.10 PICC, wonach bei fehlender Währungsangabe im Vertrag die Währung des Zahlungsortes gelte; diese Lösung wird auch von *Kröll u. a./Bridge*, Art. 81, Rn. 19 abgelehnt.
[53] ICC, 7660/1994, CISG-online 129 = ICC Ct. Bull. 1995, 69, 70; *Soergel/Lüderitz/Dettmeier*, Art. 81, Rn. 6; *Staudinger/Magnus*, Art. 81, Rn. 12.
[54] MünchKomm/*P. Huber*, Art. 28, Rn. 9; MünchKommHGB/*Benicke*, Art. 81, Rn. 6; *Staudinger/Magnus*, Art. 81, Rn. 12; *Soergel/Lüderitz/Dettmeier*, Art. 81, Rn. 6.
[55] Dazu unten Art. 82 Rn. 2 ff.
[56] Dazu *Fountoulakis*, Vor Artt. 81–84 Rn. 11 und im Einzelnen unten Art. 82 Rn. 10 ff. Die Regelung des Art. 82 II betrifft jedoch nur den Fall der Beeinträchtigung der Ware **vor** Erklärung der Aufhebung. Vgl. Art. 82 Rn. 27 zur Frage, ob darüber hinaus aus der Vorschrift allgemeine Haftungsgrundsätze auch für andere Fälle abzuleiten sind.
[57] CIETAC, 30.10.1991, CISG-online 842 = *Compilation of Selected Awards of the China International Economic and Trade Arbitration Commission, 1989–1995*, S. 429 (1997) (im chines. Original); Cour d'Appel Aix-en-Provence, 21.11.1996, CISG-online 1505; OLG Köln, 14.10.2002, CISG-online 709 = IHR 2003, 15 = RIW 2003, 300. Vgl. auch Art. 7.3.6 I PICC; Art. III.–3:511 I 2 i. V. m. Art. III.–1:101 IV DCFR.

Art. 81 21

klärt.⁵⁸ Nicht nur die zur Aufhebung berechtigte, sondern auch die andere Partei kann sich auf die Zug-um-Zug-Regel berufen, sie ist also nicht etwa vorleistungspflichtig.⁵⁹ Wo nur die eine Partei unter bestehendem Vertragsverhältnis geleistet hatte, greift die Zug-um-Zug-Regel allerdings ins Leere. Hier soll, bei unangemessener Verzögerung der Rückleistung, die rückleistungsberechtigte Partei **Schadensersatzansprüche**⁶⁰ und, bei Verzug in der Rückerstattung des Kaufpreises, Zinsansprüche nach Art. 78 geltend machen können.⁶¹ Zusätzlich zur Zug-um-Zug-Abwicklung steht das Zurückbehaltungsrecht in **Art. 71** zur Verfügung.⁶² Aus dogmatischer Sicht spricht nichts dagegen, da das Vertragsgefüge, wie gezeigt,⁶³ gewissermassen als Dach bis zur vollendeten Rückabwicklung weiterbesteht. Allerdings dürfte Art. 71 selten von Bedeutung sein, da seine Anwendungsvoraussetzungen gegenüber Art. 81 II strenger sind.⁶⁴ Relevant kann Art. 71 allenfalls dann werden, wenn die Parteien Art. 81 II vertraglich ausgeschlossen haben; hier wird die rückleistungsberechtigte Partei das, was sie zurückzugeben hat, (nur) unter den Voraussetzungen des Art. 71 zurückbehalten können, insbesondere sofortige Anzeige machen und bei Sicherheitenstellung durch den anderen ihrerseits mit der Rückabwicklung fortfahren müssen.⁶⁵

21 **b) Aufrechnung bzw. Verrechnung.** Eine Verrechnung oder Aufrechnung sieht das Übereinkommen nicht ausdrücklich vor. Dem in Artt. 81 II, 58 I verankerten Zug-um-Zug-Grundsatz kann insoweit nach zutreffender Ansicht der allgemeine Rechtsgrundsatz entnommen werden, dass **Forderungen, die aus ein und demselben, dem CISG unterstehenden Vertrag resultieren, gegeneinander aufgerechnet werden dürfen**.⁶⁶ Dies kann natürlich nur insoweit gelten, als es sich bei den gegeneinander aufgerechneten Forderungen um solche handelt, die Rechte und Pflichten der Parteien betreffen und damit Regelungsmaterie des CISG bilden (vgl. insbes. Art. 4). Die teilweise geäusserten Bedenken, wonach sich dem CISG keine Antwort zu den Fragen entnehmen lasse, ob und unter welchen Voraussetzungen die Aufrechnung erfolge (ipso iure, per gerichtliche Feststellung oder durch Erklärung?), und ab wann die aufgerechneten Forderungen erloschen seien,⁶⁷ sind nicht zu teilen: Die Artt. 84 II, 88 III, die ebenfalls eine Verrechnung gegenseitiger Ansprüche zulassen (indem sie die Auskehr lediglich des Überschusses anordnen), setzen

---

⁵⁸ *Staudinger/Magnus*, Art. 81, Rn. 14; *Honnold/Flechtner*, Art. 81, Rn. 444A; MünchKomm/*P. Huber*, Art. 81, Rn. 12; *Ferrari u. a./Ferrari*, Internationales Vertragsrecht, Art. 81, Rn. 19.
⁵⁹ Sekretariatskommentar, Art. 66 E, Nr. 9.
⁶⁰ Vgl. oben Rn. 13 sowie *Staudinger/Magnus*, Art. 81, Rn. 14.
⁶¹ *Kröll u. a./Bridge*, Art. 81, Rn. 22.
⁶² *Staudinger/Magnus*, Art. 81, Rn. 14; *Bianca/Bonell/Tallon*, Art. 81, Anm. 2.6.; *López Rodríguez*, 9 VJ (2005), 291, 298.
⁶³ Vgl. vorne Rn. 10.
⁶⁴ Zu seinen Tatbestandsvoraussetzungen vgl. Art. 71 Rn. 12 ff.
⁶⁵ Vgl. im Einzelnen oben Art. 71 Rn. 27 ff.
⁶⁶ So auch CISG-AC, Op. 9 (Bridge), Opinion 2.7, Comment 3.23; *Magnus*, Aufrechnung, S. 209, 221 ff.; *Staudinger/Magnus*, Art. 81, Rn. 15; *Kröll*, 25 J. L. & Com. (2005), 39, 52 f.; *Honsell/Weber*, Art. 81, Rn. 19; *Brunner*, Art. 81, Rn. 6; ausschliesslich betr. die Aufrechnung im Rückabwicklungsverhältnis *Bamberger/Roth/Saenger*, Art. 4, Rn. 19; *Saenger/Sauthoff*, IHR 2005, 189, 190; grunds. auch *Kröll u. a./Bridge*, Art. 84, Rn. 8 f.; BGer, 20.12.2006, CISG-online 1426, E. 2.2.1 = IHR 2007, 127; OLG München, 19.10.2006, CISG-online 1; 394, Erw. 3 = IHR 2007, 30, 32 ff.; OLG Düsseldorf, 21.4.2004, CISG-online II.2. = IHR 2005, 24 (impliciter); OLG Hamburg, 26.11.1999, CISG-online 515, Erw. I.b) = IHR 2001, 19; KG Zug, 14.12.2009, CISG-online 2026, Erw. 12; a. A. die Kommentierung von *Ferrari*, Art. 7 Rn. 55; *ders.*, 7 VJ (2003), 63, 88; *Bianca/Bonell/Tallon*, Art. 81, Anm. 2.6.; *Honnold/Flechtner*, Art. 81, Rn. 444A; MünchKomm/*P. Huber*, Art. 81, Rn. 13; *Ferrari u. a./Ferrari*, Internationales Vertragsrecht, Art. 81, Rn. 20; Multi-Member Court of First Instance of Athens (Griechenland), 4505/2009 (ohne Datum), CISG-online 2228, Erw. 2.2.6.; Juzgado de Primera Instancia de Badalona, 22.5.2006, CISG-online 1391; HGer St. Gallen, 3.12.2002, CISG-online 727 = IHR 2003, 181; Tribunale di Padova, 25.2.2004, CISG-online 819 = IHR 2005, 31; LG Mönchengladbach, 15.7.2003, CISG-online 813, Erw. II.2 = IHR 2003, 229, 230.
⁶⁷ *Schlechtriem*, Internationales UN-Kaufrecht, Rn. 42e: Aufrechnung auch konventionsinterner Ansprüche nur nach dem massgeblichen nationalen Recht zu beurteilen, da das CISG weder die Voraussetzungen der Verrechnung noch die Wirkungen bzw. deren Eintritt regelte; vgl. auch *Honnold/Flechtner*, Art. 81, Rn. 444A a. E.

implizit voraus, dass die verrechnende Seite ihren Gegenanspruch artikuliert und somit geltend macht. Dies lässt sich dahingehend verallgemeinern, dass die unter Art. 81 II erlaubte Verrechnung **erklärt** werden muss (Art. 7 II).[68] Auf eine Verrechnungserklärung abzustellen bietet sich auch angesichts dessen an, dass das CISG das Eintretenlassen von Rechtswirkungen ganz grundsätzlich jeweils von Erklärungen gegenüber der anderen Partei abhängig macht[69] und damit sowohl das Konzept der gerichtlichen Klage wie auch dasjenige des ipso-facto-Eintretens von Rechtswirkungen verwirft. Da eine Verrechnungserklärung nach der allgemeinen Regel des Art. 27 mit Absenden wirksam wird,[70] bietet es sich ferner an, als Zeitpunkt des Erlöschens der Forderungen denjenigen anzusehen, in dem die Verrechnung abgesandt wird. Die Bedenken gegen eine Aufrechnung unter dem CISG dürften sich heutzutage schliesslich insofern relativiert haben, als sowohl die PICC[71] als auch die europäischen Vereinheitlichungsprojekte[72] – trotz beträchtlicher Unterschiede in den einzelnen Rechtsordnungen –[73] international konsensfähige Regeln zur Aufrechnung erstellt haben.[74] Da die CISG-Praxis mit der – meist inzidenten – Aufrechnung konventionsinterner Ansprüche bisher keine Schwierigkeiten hatte,[75] ist es angesichts der vom Übereinkommen angestrebten Einheitlichkeit angebracht, für die Aufrechnung nicht auf die Eigenheiten des jeweiligen nationalen Rechts zu verweisen, sondern die Frage homogen, unter Verallgemeinerung der in Artt. 81 II, 84 II, 88 III bestehenden Regeln zu lösen.

Diese Lückenergänzung innerhalb des Übereinkommens gilt allerdings **nicht für vertragsfremde Forderungen**. Wenn nur eine der Forderungen dem CISG untersteht und auf die andere ein anderes Recht Anwendung findet, besteht für die Annahme allgemeiner Grundsätze (Art. 7 II) für die Zulässigkeit und die Modalitäten einer Aufrechnung im CISG kein Raum. Auch wenn Forderung und Gegenforderung aus zwei verschiedenen Verträgen stammen, die beide dem CISG unterliegen, ist eine Aufrechnung unter dem CISG, sofern die Parteien nichts anderes vereinbart haben, aus prozessualen Gründen ausgeschlossen. Die Frage, ob eine nicht aus demselben Vertragsverhältnis stammende Forderung gegen eine sich aus dem CISG-Vertrag ergebende Forderung aufgerechnet werden kann, unterliegt demnach dem anwendbaren **nationalen Recht.**[76]

5. Leistungsort der Rückgabe

a) Allgemeines. Bezüglich des Leistungsorts der Rückgabe fehlt eine Regelung im Übereinkommen. Es handelt sich hierbei um eine Lücke, die im Rahmen von Art. 7 II ohne Rückgriff auf nationales Kollisionsrecht ausgefüllt werden kann,[77] auch wenn die

---

[68] *Magnus*, Aufrechnung, S. 209, 221 ff.
[69] Vgl. nur Artt. 14 ff., 26 (im Unterschied zur früheren Vertragsaufhebung ipso facto); 39, 48 II–IV, 65, 71, 72, 73, 75, 76, 85–88.
[70] Vgl. oben *Schroeter*, Art. 27 Rn. 13; Art. 26 Rn. 11.
[71] Artt. 8.1–8.5 PICC.
[72] Artt. 13:101–13:107 PECL, Artt. III.-6:101–108 DCFR.
[73] Vgl. für einen Überblick *Fountoulakis*, Set-off Defences, S. 23 ff., 123 ff.; vgl. zudem für weitere europäische Rechtsordnungen die jeweiligen Anmerkungen im Redaktorenkommentar zu Artt. 13:101–13:107 PECL.
[74] Die wenigen verbleibenden Unterschiede betreffen Fragen ausserhalb der Regelungsmaterie des CISG, etwa die Möglichkeit der Aufrechnung mit zedierten Forderungen und den Ausschluss der Aufrechnung bei unverpfändbaren oder auf Delikt beruhenden Forderungen (vgl. *Fountoulakis*, Set-off Defences, S. 201 ff.); in diesen Fällen findet das CISG auf die Aufrechnung keine Anwendung, da die Forderungen nicht in den Geltungsbereich des CISG fallen (vgl. oben im Text).
[75] *Magnus*, Aufrechnung, S. 209, 223 f.
[76] OGH, 22.10.2001, CISG-online 614; OLG Karlsruhe, 20.7.2004, CISG-online 858; KG Zug, 14.12.2009, CISG-online 2026, Erw. 12; wohl auch BGer, 20.12.2006, CISG-online 1426, Erw. 2.2.1 = IHR 2007, 127; *Schwenzer/Fountoulakis/Fountoulakis*, S. 585; *Brunner*, Art. 4, Rn. 52 f.
[77] *Leser*, Vertragsaufhebung und Rückabwicklung, S. 242; *Schlechtriem*, Internationales UN-Kaufrecht, Rn. 331; *Kröll u. a./Bridge*, Art. 81, Rn. 23; *Audit*, Vente internationale, Anm. 55.; *ders.*, D. 1998, Somm. 288, 289; *Bamberger/Roth/Saenger*, Art. 81, Rn. 5; a. A. CA Paris, 14.1.1998, CISG-online 347; *Ferrari u. a./Ferrari*, Internationales Vertragsrecht, Art. 81, Rn. 22: Der Leistungsort sei über das nach IPR berufene nationale Recht zu eruieren.

differenzierte Regelung des Leistungsortes im Übereinkommen eine klare Entscheidung erschwert. Auszugehen ist von der Regelung des Leistungs- und Lieferungsortes für die **Primärleistungen des Vertrages** in den Artt. 31, 57. Sie gelten jeweils als **spiegelbildliche Regelung** für die Rückabwicklungspflicht.[78] Dabei wird man jeweils daran anzuknüpfen haben, was die Parteien für die Lieferung oder Zahlung konkret als jeweiligen Leistungsort vereinbart hatten.

24 **b) Leistungsort für die Rückzahlung.** Sofern die Parteien unter dem Vertrag für den Ort der Zahlung des Kaufpreises nichts anderes vereinbart hatten, war dieser nach Art. 57 am Ort der Niederlassung des Verkäufers zu zahlen. Bei der Rückabwicklung ist demzufolge **Leistungsort** der **Rückzahlung des Kaufpreises** der Ort der **Niederlassung des Käufers**.[79] Diese Auffassung wird auch von der Regelung des Art. 6.1.6 PICC getragen, wonach Geldschulden generell am Niederlassungsort des Gläubigers zu begleichen sind.[80] Das Argument, dass der Zahlungsort im Rahmen der Rückabwicklung nach dem über das IPR berufenen nationalen Recht zu bestimmen sei, weil sich der Festlegung der Niederlassung des Verkäufers als Zahlungsort in Art. 57 nicht zweifelsfrei entnehmen lasse, ob man das Prinzip der Leistung am **Verkäufer**sitz oder aber das allgemeine Prinzip der Leistung am **Gläubiger**sitz habe verankern wollen, und deshalb eine interne Lückenfüllung nicht möglich sei,[81] mag angesichts dessen, dass die Frage des Leistungsortes für die Rückabwicklung als Bestandteil der Rechtsfolgen bei Vertragsaufhebung durchaus ein „in diesem Übereinkommen geregelte[r] ... aber nicht ausdrücklich entschieden[er]" Gegenstand im Sinne von Art. 7 II ist,[82] nicht zu überzeugen.

25 **c) Leistungsort für die Rückgabe der Ware.** Erforderte die Lieferung der Ware nach Art. 31 lit. c die Abholung durch den Käufer bei der Niederlassung des Verkäufers bzw. beim Versendungskauf, die Übergabe durch den Verkäufer an den Beförderer (Art. 31 lit. a), so hat der Verkäufer die Ware beim Käufer abzuholen bzw. der Käufer die Ware zu versenden und hierzu einem Beförderer zur Übermittlung an den Verkäufer zu übergeben. Erfüllungsort bezüglich der Pflicht zur **Rückgabe der Ware** ist in diesen Fällen, vorbehältlich anderer Vereinbarung, ebenfalls der Ort der **Niederlassung des Käufers**.[83] Teilweise ist, vornehmlich aus Gründen der Effizienz, vorgeschlagen worden, als Leistungsort für die

---

[78] So auch *Soergel/Lüderitz/Dettmeier*, Art. 81, Rn. 10; *Staudinger/Magnus*, Art. 81, Rn. 19; *Schlechtriem*, Internationales UN-Kaufrecht, Rn. 331; *Piltz*, Internationales Kaufrecht, Rn. 5–320; *Leser*, Vertragsaufhebung und Rückabwicklung, S. 242, 252; MünchKomm/*P. Huber*, Art. 81, Rn. 15; *Osuna*, Dealing with Avoidance, S. 492. In der Rechtsprechung OGH, 29.6.1999, CISG-online 483 = östZRVgl 2000, 33: „Das UN-K [aufrecht] enthält keine Regelung über den Leistungsort der Rückgewähr; dennoch kann diese Lücke in Fehlen entsprechender Vereinbarungen im Rahmen von Art. 7 Abs. 2 UN-K[aufrecht] ohne Rückgriff auf die nationalen Regelungen ausgefüllt werden. [...] Der Leistungsort für die vertraglichen Primärleistungen ist spiegelbildlich auf die Rückabwicklungspflichten zu übertragen.": AG Sursee, 12.9.2008, CISG-online 1728, Erw. 6.1 f. = IHR 2009, 63; ähnlich LG Gießen, 17.12.2002, CISG-online 766.

[79] OLG Karlsruhe, 19.12.2002, CISG-online 817 = IHR 2003, 125; OLG Düsseldorf, 2.7.1993, CISG-online 74 = RIW 1993, 845 f.; LG Gießen, 17.12.2002, CISG-online 766 = IHR 2003, 276, 277; *Staudinger/Magnus*, Art. 81, Rn. 19; *Honsell/Weber*, Art. 81, Rn. 21; *Neumayer/Ming*, Art. 81, Anm. 4. m. w. N.; *Heilmann*, S. 526 f.; *Piltz*, Internationales Kaufrecht, Rn. 5–320; *Bamberger/Roth/Saenger*, Art. 81, Rn. 5; grundsätzlich auch CISG-AC, Op. 9 *(Bridge)*, Opinion 2.3: Sitz des Verkäufers von Käufer bestimmten Bankkonto; *Kröll u. a./Bridge*, Art. 81, Rn. 26. Dagegen halten *Herber/Czerwenka*, Art. 81, Rn. 12 und *Jan*, S. 218 f., unter Bezugnahme auf die Rspr. zum EKG den Ort der Niederlassung des Verkäufers für massgeblich; ebenso OLG Wien, 1.6.2004, CISG-online 954.

[80] CA Grenoble, 23.10.1993, CISG-online 1527 = Rev. crit. dr. int. pr. (1997), 756; kritisch hierzu mit dem – allerdings kaum überzeugenden – Argument, Art. 6.1.6 PICC dürfe als Auslegungshilfe nicht herangezogen werden, da die Vorschrift nach dem Zustandekommen des CISG entstanden sei, *Thiele*, RIW 2000, 892, 894.

[81] So z.B. CA Paris, 14.1.1998, CISG-online 347 = D. 1998, Somm. 288, mit krit. Anm. von *Audit*, der sich – wie oben (Fn. 77) erwähnt – im hier vertretenen Sinne für die Lückenfüllung nach Art. 7 II ausspricht.

[82] Vgl. die in Fn. 77 angeführte Literatur.

[83] Vgl. *Neumayer/Ming*, Art. 81, Anm. 4.; *Herber/Czerwenka*, Art. 81, Rn. 12; *Heilmann*, S. 523; *Piltz*, Internationales Kaufrecht, Rn. 5–324. Ebenso in der Rspr. OGH, 29.6.1999, CISG-online 483 = östZRVgl 2000, 33; KG Wallis, 21.2.2005, CISG-online 1193, Erw. 4.b) = IHR 2006, 155; LG Krefeld, 24.11.1992, CISG-online 62; a. A. *Ferrari u. a./Ferrari*, Internationales Vertragsrecht, Art. 81, Rn. 22.

Rückgabe der Ware grundsätzlich stets die Niederlassung des Käufers anzusehen.[84] Nach der hier vertretenen spiegelbildlichen Regelung hingegen ist in den Fällen, in denen Bringschuld vereinbart worden war, die Ware am **Sitz des Verkäufers** zurückzuerstatten.

d) Kein allgemeines Prinzip des Rückleistungsorts am Sitz der vertragstreuen 26
Partei. Nicht überzeugen kann die Auffassung, dass **alle Rückabwicklungspflichten** stets am Ort der **Niederlassung der vertragstreuen Partei** zu erfüllen seien, was sich gem. Art. 7 II über das allgemeine Prinzip von Treu und Glauben in die Rückabwicklungsregeln hineinlesen lasse.[85] Bereits auf technischer Ebene ist zweifelhaft, ob eine Regel mit so erheblichen praktischen Auswirkungen sich tatsächlich auf das allgemeine Prinzip von Treu und Glauben stützen lässt. Aber auch inhaltlich ist diesem moralisierenden Ansatz entgegenzusetzen, dass es einer dem CISG fremden Privatstrafe gleichkäme, allein aus der – gegebenenfalls unverschuldeten – wesentlichen Vertragsverletzung einer Partei auf einen allgemeinen Erfüllungsort beim vertragstreuen Teil zu schliessen. Eine Differenzierung nach im Sinne des Übereinkommens verschuldeter oder unverschuldeter wesentlicher Vertragsverletzung kommt für die rein finanzielle Fragen berührenden Kosten der Rückgabe direkt über Art. 79 in Betracht,[86] ist aber schon aus Gründen der Rechtssicherheit für die Frage des Erfüllungsorts in der Rückabwicklung ungeeignet.[87]

e) Bestimmung des Gerichtsstandes. Je nach Prozessrecht eröffnet der Erfüllungsort 27 gleichzeitig einen Gerichtsstand für Klagen aus dem Vertragsverhältnis.[88] In diesem Zusammenhang besteht reichhaltige Rechtsprechung zu Artt. 31, 57.[89] Der Leistungsort für die Rückgabe bzw. Rückzahlung im Rahmen der Rückabwicklung begründet einen entsprechenden Gerichtsstand.[90] Dies ist etwa in der Literatur zum EuGVÜ und zu dessen Parallelübereinkommen LugÜ oftmals kritisiert worden, weil gemäss Rechtsprechung des EuGH zum EuGVÜ auf den Erfüllungsort der jeweils streitigen Verpflichtung abzustellen war, was gerade in Verbindung mit Art. 57 (ggf. i. V. m. Art. 81(2)) zu einem reinen Klägergerichtsstand führte.[91] Die Diskussion hat mit Inkrafttreten der **EuGVVO**[92] für die Fälle, in denen der vertragliche Erfüllungsort in einem Migliedstaat liegt, ihre Bedeutung weitgehend verloren, denn die EuGVVO wie auch das entsprechend revidierte Luganer Parallelübereinkommen[93] stellen in Art. 5 I lit. b) 1. Spiegelstrich für den Gerichtsstand bei Kaufvertragsklagen auf einen **autonom bestimmten, einheitlichen Erfüllungsort** ab.[94] Die Problematik des reinen Klägergerichtsstands kann aber unter EuGVVO und revidiertem

---

[84] Vgl. CISG-AC, Op. 9 *(Bridge)*, Opinion 2.2, Comment 3.12; *Kröll u. a./Bridge*, Art. 81, Rn. 24 f.
[85] So aber *Thiele*, RIW 2000, 892, 894 f., der die Auffassung vertritt, dass die spiegelbildliche Anwendung der Erfüllungsortregeln des CISG durch die h. M. den vertragsbrüchigen Teil zu Unrecht privilegiere. Für die Niederlassung der vertragstreuen Partei als generellen Erfüllungsort der Rückabwicklung auch *Hackenberg*, S. 170 f.; ähnlich *Heuzé*, Anm. 444. f.; MünchKommHGB/*Benicke*, Art. 81, Rn. 8; *Brunner*, Art. 81, Rn. 8.
[86] Dazu hinten Rn. 28.
[87] I. E. ebenso *López Rodríguez*, 9 VJ (2005), 291, 297 f.; *Kröll u. a./Bridge*, Art. 81, Rn. 24 f. Weniger skeptisch *Schlechtriem*, Internationales UN-Kaufrecht, Rn. 331 („Denkbar und mit guten Gründen vertretbar wäre aber auch"), allerdings ohne nähere Begründung.
[88] Vgl. Art. 5 I EuGVVO, LugÜ; Art. 5, Ziff. 1 EuGVÜ.
[89] Vgl. insbes. die Nachweise bei *Mohs*, Art. 57 Rn. 23, sowie die entsprechende Rechtsprechungsübersicht im UNCITRAL Digest, Art. 31, Rn. 2 und insbes. Art. 57, Rn. 4 f.
[90] Vgl. *Schlechtriem*, Internationales UN-Kaufrecht, Rn. 331; OLG Hamm, 5.11.1997, CISG-online 381; OLG Düsseldorf, 12.7.1993, CISG-online 74 = RIW 1993, 845; CA Paris, 14.1.1998, CISG-online 347 = D. 1998, Somm. 288 (impliciter); a. A. LG Landshut, 5.4.1995, CISG-online 193.
[91] Vgl. statt vieler *Rauscher*, Verpflichtung und Erfüllungsort, S. 180 ff.; *Kropholler/von Hein*, Art. 5 EuGVO, Rn. 3, 23, m. w. N.; *Rauscher/Leible*, Art. 5 Brüssel I-VO, Rn. 40 ff.; *Siehr*, IPR, S. 242 f.
[92] EG-VO Nr. 44/2001 des Rates vom 22. Dezember 2000 über die gerichtliche Zuständigkeit und die Anerkennung und Vollstreckung von Entscheidungen in Zivil- und Handelssachen.
[93] Das an die Brüssel I-VO angeglichene Übereinkommen über die gerichtliche Zuständigkeit und die Vollstreckung gerichtlicher Entscheidungen in Zivil- und Handelssachen vom 21.2.1990 (SR 0.275.12) trat für die EU-Mitgliedstaaten, Norwegen und Dänemark am 1.1.2010, für die Schweiz am 1.1.2011 und für Island am 1.5.2011 in Kraft.
[94] Dazu statt vieler *Magnus*, IHR 2002, 45 ff.; *Mankowski*, IHR 2009, 46 ff.; *Ferrari*, Choice of Forum, S. 142 f., m. zahlr. Nachw.; vgl. auch oben *Widmer Lüchinger*, Art. 31 Rn. 87 ff.; *Mohs*, Art. 57 Rn. 25.

Art. 81 28, 29 Teil III. Kapitel V. Pflichten des Verkäufers und Käufers. Abschnitt V

Luganer Übereinkommen weiterhin bestehen, und zwar, über die Regel der spiegelbildlichen Anwendung von Artt. 31, 57, auch im Rahmen der Rückabwicklung, wenn nicht in einen Mitglied- bzw. Vertragsstaat geliefert wird (vgl. Art. 5 I lit. a), b) EuGVVO, LugÜ).[95]

6. Kosten der Rückgabe

28   Auch die Kosten der Rückgabe sind im Übereinkommen nicht ausdrücklich geregelt. Es liegt hier nahe, für den vertragstreuen Teil die Kosten der Rückgewähr (Rücktransport, Demontage) in die Berechnung des begleitenden **Schadensersatzes** mitaufzunehmen, während der vertragsverletzende Teil diese Kosten selbst tragen muss.[96] Soweit in einem Fall der Rückabwicklung der Schadensersatz über Art. 79 ausfällt, bleibt es bei der Belastung auch des vertragstreuen Teils mit den Rückgabekosten.[97] Hinsichtlich der Berechtigung zu Schadensersatz bei Verletzung der Rückgewährspflichten durch die eine Partei vgl. oben Rn. 13.

7. Fristen für die Rückgabe; Annahmeverzug des Verkäufers in der Rückabwicklung

29   Das CISG gibt keinen Zeitrahmen an, innerhalb dessen die Rückabwicklung stattzufinden hat. In spiegelbildlicher Anwendung der diesbezüglichen Vertragsbestimmungen für die Leistungserbringung unter bestehendem Vertrag (Art. 33) sollte für die Rückerstattung in erster Linie der vertraglich vereinbarte Termin oder die vereinbarte Frist massgeblich sein; mangels vertraglicher Abmachung hat die Rückerstattung innerhalb einer angemessenen Frist zu erfolgen, wobei sich die Angemessenheit an der Natur und Beschaffenheit der Ware und den sonstigen Umständen bemisst.[98] So dürften für verderbliche Ware oder solche mit volatilen Marktpreisen wesentlich kürzere Fristen gelten als für langlebige Güter. Verweigert der Verkäufer die Rücknahme der Ware, so verletzt er seine Abnahmepflicht aus dem Rückgewährschuldverhältnis und macht sich gemäss Art. 45 I lit. b) schadensersatzpflichtig. Zudem kann der Käufer gestützt auf das Zug-um-Zug-Prinzip (Art. 81 II) oder ggf. gestützt auf Art. 71[99] die eigene Leistung zurückhalten. Ein Rückgriff auf die nach dem Kollisionsrecht berufenen Rechtsregeln ist weder erforderlich noch zulässig.[100]

---

[95] Vgl. zum Ganzen *Rauscher/Leible*, Art. 5 Brüssel I-VO, Rn. 42.
[96] Sekretariatskommentar, Art. 66, Nr. 11; *Schlechtriem*, FS U. Huber, S. 563, 573; *Bianca/Bonell/Tallon*, Art. 81, Anm. 2.6.; *Bamberger/Roth/Saenger*, Art. 81, Rn. 7; MünchKommHGB/*Benicke*, Art. 81, Rn. 7; *Herber/Czerwenka*, Art. 81, Rn. 14; *Audit*, Vente internationale, Anm. 191.; *Neumayer/Ming*, Art. 81, Anm. 6.; *Honsell/Weber*, Art. 81, Rn. 22; *Soergel/Lüderitz/Dettmeier*, Art. 81, Rn. 2; *Lookofsky*, The 1980 United Nations Convention, Rn. 312; Int. Ct. Russian CCI, 21.12.2004, CISG-online 1187, Erw. 3.4; offengelassen in OGH, 29.6.1999, CISG-online 483 = östZRVgl 2000, 33. Für die Rückabwicklung unter PECL wird dieselbe Kostentragung vorgeschlagen, vgl. *Mazzotta*, Comparison, S. 509, 513 Fn. 23.
[97] Vgl. CISG-AC, Op. 9 *(Bridge)*, Opinion 2.8, Comment 3.17; *Bianca/Bonell/Tallon*, Art. 81, Anm. 2.6.; *Schlechtriem*, Internationales UN-Kaufrecht, Rn. 331; *Kröll u. a./Bridge*, Art. 81, Rn. 27.
[98] Für eine angemessene Frist, innerhalb welcher die Rückabwicklung zu erfolgen hat, auch CISG-AC, Op. 9 *(Bridge)*, Opinion 2.6, Comment 3.17; gemäss *Kröll u. a./Bridge*, Art. 81, Rn. 29 solle aber die Rückerstattung innerhalb des Zeitraums stattfinden, der dem Käufer für die Untersuchung der Ware unter Art. 38 zur Verfügung stand.
[99] So auch *Kröll u. a./Bridge*, Art. 81, Rn. 28. Zu dessen Anwendung im Rahmen der Rückabwicklung vgl. vorne Rn. 20.
[100] Vgl. auch HGer Zürich, 24.10.2003, CISG-online 857, Erw. 4.b)bb), das die Annahmeverzugsregeln konventionsimmanent entwickelte und insbes. dem Käufer ein Zurückhaltungsrecht bzgl. der eigenen Leistung einräumte. Der Fall betraf einen Ersatzlieferungsanspruch des Käufers, dem teilweise mangelhafte Matratzen geliefert worden waren, wobei der Verkäufer seiner Pflicht, die defekten Matratzen zurückzunehmen, nicht nachkam. Daraufhin hielt der Käufer zwei Ratenzahlungen zurück, was das HGer für zulässig hielt. Anders noch die 4. Aufl. in Rn. 19a, die auf den Annahmeverzug im Rahmen der Rückabwicklung das kollisionsrechtlich bestimmte nationale Recht angewandt wissen wollte (Art. 81 Rn. 19a); ebenso LG Landshut, 5.4.1995, CISG-online 193; wie hier *Staudinger/Magnus*, Art. 81, Rn. 17a.

V. Beweislast

Wer sich auf die Befreiung von ihren Vertragspflichten beruft (Art. 81 I) oder Rückgewähr erbrachter Leistungen verlangt (Art. 81 II), muss beweisen, dass die Voraussetzungen hierfür gegeben sind.[101] **30**

---

[101] *Bamberger/Roth/Saenger,* Art. 81, Rn. 8; *Staudinger/Magnus,* Art. 81, Rn. 22; MünchKomm/*P. Huber,* Art. 81, Rn. 18.

Art. 82 [Verlust der Rechte auf Vertragsaufhebung oder Ersatzlieferung wegen Unmöglichkeit der Rückgabe im ursprünglichen Zustand]

(1) Der Käufer verliert das Recht, die Aufhebung des Vertrages zu erklären oder vom Verkäufer Ersatzlieferung zu verlangen, wenn es ihm unmöglich ist, die Ware im wesentlichen in dem Zustand zurückzugeben, in dem er sie erhalten hat.

(2) Absatz 1 findet keine Anwendung,

a) wenn die Unmöglichkeit, die Ware zurückzugeben oder sie im wesentlichen in dem Zustand zurückzugeben, in dem der Käufer sie erhalten hat, nicht auf einer Handlung oder Unterlassung des Käufers beruht,

b) wenn die Ware ganz oder teilweise infolge der in Artikel 38 vorgesehenen Untersuchung untergegangen oder verschlechtert worden ist oder

c) wenn der Käufer die Ware ganz oder teilweise im normalen Geschäftsverkehr verkauft oder der normalen Verwendung entsprechend verbraucht oder verändert hat, bevor er die Vertragswidrigkeit entdeckt hat oder hätte entdecken müssen.

Art. 82

(1) The buyer loses the right to declare the contract avoided or to require the seller to deliver substitute goods if it is impossible for him to make restitution of the goods substantially in the condition in which he received them.

(2) The preceding paragraph does not apply:

(a) if the impossibility of making restitution of the goods or of making restitution of the goods substantially in the condition in which the buyer received them is not due to his act or omission;

(b) if the goods or part of the goods have perished or deteriorated as a result of the examination provided for in article 38; or

(c) if the goods or part of the goods have been sold in the normal course of business or have been consumed or transformed by the buyer in the course of normal use before he discovered or ought to have discovered the lack of conformity.

Art. 82

1) L'acheteur perd le droit de déclarer le contrat résolu ou d'exiger du vendeur la livraison de marchandises de remplacement s'il lui est impossible de restituer les marchandises dans un état sensiblement identique à celui dans lequel il les a reçues.

2) Le paragraphe précédent ne s'applique pas:

a) si l'impossibilité de restituer les marchandises ou de les restituer dans un état sensiblement identique à celui dans lequel l'acheteur les a reçues n'est pas due à un acte ou une omission de sa part;

b) si les marchandises ont péri ou sont détériorées, en totalité ou en partie, en conséquence de l'examen prescrit à l'article 38; ou

c) si l'acheteur, avant le moment où il a constaté ou aurait dû constater le défaut de conformité, a vendu tout ou partie des marchandises dans le cadre d'une opération commerciale normale ou a consommé ou transformé tout ou partie des marchandises conformément à l'usage normal.

Übersicht

	Rn.
I. Vorgeschichte	1
II. Verlust des Aufhebungsrechts, Abs. 1	2
1. Grundsatz der unversehrten Rückgabe	2
2. Rechtsvergleich	3
3. Unmöglichkeit der Rückgewähr	5
4. Bagatellregelung	6
5. Zeitpunkt	7
6. Rechtsfolgen	8
III. Ausnahmen von der unversehrten Rückgabe, Abs. 2	10
1. Grundgedanken der Regelung	10
2. Nicht auf „Handlung oder Unterlassung des Käufers beruhend", Abs. 2 lit. a)	13
a) Vertragsverletzung des Verkäufers	13
b) Höhere Gewalt	14
c) Weitere Fälle	15

      3. Untersuchung der Ware, Abs. 2 lit. b) 18
      4. Weiterverkauf, Verarbeitung und Gebrauch der Ware, Abs. 2 lit. c) 19
         a) Verwendungsrisiko des Verkäufers 19
         b) Verbrauch, Veränderung 20
         c) Gebrauch 21
         d) Weiterveräusserung 22
         e) Entsorgung wertloser Ware 24
         f) Zeitliche Sperrwirkung 25
         g) Normaler Geschäftsverkehr 26
  IV. Nachträglicher Untergang der Ware 27
  V. Anwendung von Art. 82 bei Aufhebung durch den Verkäufer bzw. bei
     einvernehmlicher Vertragsaufhebung? 28
  VI. Beweislast 31

Vorläufer und **Entwürfe:** Art. 79 EKG; Genfer E 1976 Art. 52; Wiener E 1977 Art. 53; New Yorker E 1978 Art. 67.

I. Vorgeschichte

Art. 82 stellt den einerseits gestrafften[1] und andererseits um den Zusatz in Art. 82 II lit. c) **1** ergänzten Nachfolger von Art. 79 EKG dar. Nunmehr bleibt, als wichtige Ausnahme vom Grundsatz der unversehrten Rückgabe, das Aufhebungsrecht auch bei Verkauf und nicht nur bei Verbrauch oder Veränderung der Ware erhalten. Durch diese Änderung erfolgte eine entscheidende Ausdehnung der Ausnahmen.[2]

II. Verlust des Aufhebungsrechts, Abs. 1

1. Grundsatz der unversehrten Rückgabe

Art. 82 I statuiert das aus dem römischen Recht stammende Prinzip der unversehrten **2** Rückgabe der Leistung. Der Käufer soll nur dann sein Recht zur Aufhebung des Vertrages ausüben dürfen, wenn er die empfangene Ware in intaktem Zustand zurückgeben kann; eine Rückabwicklung mit Ersatzansprüchen soll grundsätzlich nicht stattfinden. Gleiches gilt explizit für den **Ersatzlieferungsanspruch,** Art. 46 II, der ebenfalls eine Rückabwicklung hinsichtlich der fehlgeschlagenen Leistung erfordert. Die Einschränkung betrifft nur die Rückgabefähigkeit der Sache selbst, nicht auch anderer, vom Käufer zu retournierender Leistungen, etwa Kautionen u. Ä.[3]

2. Rechtsvergleich

Der Grundsatz der unversehrten Rückgabe fand sich auch in § 350 ff. BGB a. F., wurde **3** aber mit der Schuldrechtsreform durch die moderne Wertersatzlösung in § 346 II BGB abgelöst: Danach schliesst die Unmöglichkeit, den empfangenen Gegenstand heil herausgeben zu können, das Vertragsaufhebungsrecht nicht aus, sondern anstelle des untergegangenen, beschädigten etc. Gegenstandes ist Wertersatz zu leisten.[4] Ähnlichkeit zu Art. 82 weisen aber heute noch Art. 207 schweiz. OR,[5] Artt. 391–394 griech. ZGB, Art. 1647 I

---

[1] Sah Art. 79 II EKG noch die fünf Ausnahmefälle lit. a)–e) vor, wurde in Art. 82 II eine straffere Bündelung vorgenommen, die jedoch alle Varianten des Art. 79 II EKG inhaltlich erfasst, mit Ausnahme von lit. e), der in der Neuformulierung des Art. 82 I aufgegangen ist, YB V (1974), S. 70, Artt. 78–81, Nr. 9 und 10.
[2] YB V (1974), S. 43, Art. 79, Nr. 146.
[3] A. A. *Bamberger/Roth/Saenger,* Art. 82, Rn. 2; *Staudinger/Magnus,* Art. 82, Rn. 9; MünchKomm/*P. Huber,* Art. 82, Rn. 2; wie hier *Witz/Salger/Lorenz/Salger,* Art. 82, Rn. 1.
[4] Für einen Rechtsvergleich der Rückabwicklungsregeln im BGB, in anderen europäischen Kaufrechten sowie im CISG vgl. *Laimer,* S. 150 ff.; für einen Vergleich zwischen BGB, CISG, PICC und PECL s. *Boels,* S. 39 ff. Für einen internationalen Vergleich s. *Schwenzer/Hachem/Kee,* Rn. 50.27 ff.
[5] Dazu *Hartmann,* Rn. 491 ff.

frz. Cc, die skandinavischen Kaufgesetze[6] sowie manche der iberoamerikanischen Rechte[7] auf. Aber auch das amerikanische Recht kennt in § 2–608 (2) UCC die Bestimmung, wonach der Käufer, der die Abnahme der Ware verweigern will („revocation"), dies tun muss, bevor sich der Zustand der Ware – aus nicht mangelbehaftetem Grunde – wesentlich verändert hat („substantial change in condition of the goods").

4   Ähnlich dem revidierten deutschen Recht haben sich auch die Einheitsrechtsprojekte PICC und PECL für eine andere Lösung entschieden als sie das CISG vorsieht.[8] Nach Artt. 7.3.6 I 2 PICC bzw. 9:309 PECL führt die Unmöglichkeit, den empfangenen Gegenstand im Wesentlichen in unverändertem Zustand herausgeben zu können, in keinem Fall zum Ausschluss des Vertragsaufhebungsrechts; vielmehr muss anstelle des untergegangenen oder wesentlich verschlechterten, verarbeiteten oder weiterveräusserten Gegenstandes **Wertersatz** geleistet werden, soweit die Leistung tatsächlich einen messbaren Wert hatte.[9] Die Wertersatzlösung dürfte – was freilich bei Art. 84 noch näher zu prüfen sein wird[10] – den Vorzug haben, die Unsicherheiten der Auskehr des Surrogates nach Art. 84 II lit. b) zu vermeiden (das **commodum** muss nicht notwendigerweise dem tatsächlichen Wert der untergegangenen Ware entsprechen). Auch macht die generelle Aufrechterhaltung des Rechts zur Vertragsaufhebung die im Rahmen des CISG notwendige Definition und Auslegung der einzelnen Ausnahmetatbestände, bei denen die Vertragsaufhebung trotz Unmöglichkeit der Herausgabe zulässig bleibt, unnötig, wodurch die Regelung der Rückabwicklung insgesamt an Transparenz und Übersichtlichkeit gewinnt.[11] Freilich darf nicht verkannt werden, dass die Wertersatzlösung sich weit vom ursprünglichen Gedanken einer möglichst umfassenden Rückabwicklung in Natur entfernt und stattdessen die wechselseitige **Vorteilsausgleichung** in den Mittelpunkt stellt. Sie verdient aber als die „modernere" Lösung wegweisende Anerkennung.[12]

3. Unmöglichkeit der Rückgewähr

5   Unmöglich im Sinne von Art. 82 I wird die Rückgabe der Ware, wenn ihr **tatsächliche Hindernisse**[13] entgegenstehen; wirtschaftliche Hindernisse, etwa wesentliche Veränderungen im Marktwert der Ware, hindern die Aufhebung nicht.[14] Ein allfälliges Verschulden ist irrelevant. Unmöglich wird die Rückgewähr bei Untergang, Zerstörung, Beschädigung oder Verlust der Ware, ebenso bei Weiterveräusserung und Verarbeitung, sofern keine der in Abs. 2 enthaltenen Ausnahmen greift. Da das Übereinkommen von der Rückgabe der „empfangenen" Ware spricht, ist eine Rückabwicklung mit anderen Stücken aus derselben **Gattung**

---

[6] Vgl. §§ 57, 58 dänischer Sale of Goods Act; § 66 finnischer und schwedischer Sale of Goods Act.
[7] Vgl. dazu *Schwenzer/E. Muñoz/E. Muñoz*, Sec. Comp. Arts. 81–84, Rn. 4 f.
[8] Dies teilweise in ausdrücklicher Abgrenzung, vgl. Artt. 9:305–9:309 PECL, Note 6.
[9] Art. 9:309 PECL spricht von der Erstattung eines „reasonable amount for the value of the performance". Art. 7.3.6 I 2 PICC sieht vor, dass „allowance should be made in money whenever reasonable." Im Autorenkommentar wird herausgestrichen, dass der Zusatz „whenever reasonable" verdeutlichen soll, dass der Restitutionsschuldner zum Wertersatz nur dann verpflichtet ist, wenn die an ihn erbrachte Leistung auch tatsächlich einen Wert hat; vgl. Art. 7.3.6 PICC, Comment 2.
[10] S. unten Art. 82 Rn. 4.
[11] Vgl. zu allem *Hornung*, S. 150 ff.; *Laimer*, S. 143 ff.; *Kröll u. a./Bridge*, Art. 82, Rn. 25.
[12] Interessanterweise ist bereits im Rahmen der Vorarbeiten zum EKG von der israelischen Delegation der Vorschlag gemacht worden, die Ausschlusslösung durch die auch heute von den Einheitsrechtsprojekten bevorzugte Lösung zu ersetzen, s. Doc., 354, Art. 91. Dieser ist auch, in leicht veränderter Fassung, zunächst gebilligt, dann aber letztlich zugunsten der in Art. 79 EKG verkörperten Lösung aufgegeben worden, s. Doc., 391. Offensichtlich ist der zunächst positiv aufgenommene Vorschlag nur deshalb gescheitert, weil man es für problematisch hielt, kurz vor der Veröffentlichung des EKG ein System durch ein grundlegend anderes zu ersetzen (*Riese*, ein Vertreter der deutschen Delegation, betrachtete es als riskant, ein lange durchdachtes System durch ein „système bâclé en dernière minute" zu ersetzen, s. Actes, 181. Ähnliche Bedenken äusserte auch der Franzose *Tunc*, vgl. Actes, 172).
[13] *Bianca/Bonell/Tallon*, Art. 82, Anm. 1.1.; *Audit*, Vente internationale, Anm. 192. („altération physique"); vgl. auch der Rechtsprechung RB Rotterdam, 21.11.1996, CISG-online 541; vgl. auch *Hellner*, UN Convention, S. 82.
[14] *Hellwege*, Rückabwicklung, S. 578 f.; vgl. auch § 2-608 UCC, Official Comment 6.

ausgeschlossen. Letzteres würde Spekulationsmöglichkeiten für den Käufer eröffnen,[15] verbietet sich aber auch wegen der damit verbundenen Unklarheiten etwa hinsichtlich Qualität, Rechtsmängeln und insbesondere der Anwendung der Gefahrverteilungsregeln in Art. 82 II.[16] Den Parteien bleibt es indes unbenommen, eine andere Vereinbarung zu treffen.

4. Bagatellregelung

Die Sperre der unversehrten Rückgewähr ist dadurch eingeschränkt, dass die Ware vom **6** Käufer nur „**im Wesentlichen**" in dem Zustand zurückzugeben ist, in dem er sie erhalten hat". Damit sind **unwesentliche Veränderungen** für das Aufhebungsrecht **unschädlich**.[17] Ausschlaggebend ist, ob es dem Verkäufer vernünftigerweise zuzumuten ist, die Ware als Entsprechung dessen, was er geliefert hatte („*as the equivalent of that which he had delivered*"),[18] zurückzunehmen. Dies wird dann oft zu bejahen sein, wenn die Ware seit Erhalt an Wert gewonnen hat, etwa durch Lackierung oder Abschliff. Allerdings fällt **nicht jede Wertsteigerung** unter die Bagatellklausel:[19] Brennt z. B. der Käufer eigenwillige (wenn auch objektiv wertsteigernde) Verzierungen auf die vom Verkäufer gelieferten Trinkgläser, so ist nach dem Massstab des Art. 8 II zu beurteilen, ob dem Verkäufer die Rücknahme zumutbar ist.[20] Der Marktwert allein ist nicht entscheidend; vielmehr sind jeweils die Auffassung der am Verkehr beteiligten Kreise, der Verwendungszweck der Ware und die Einzelumstände, soweit sie für beide Parteien erkennbar waren, zu berücksichtigen.[21] Es wird darauf ankommen, ob der Verkäufer die zurückgewiesene Ware objektiv betrachtet als das von ihm Gelieferte anerkennen muss oder aber ob ihm – in seiner konkreten geschäftlichen Position – die durch den Käufer zwischenzeitlich vorgenommene Veränderung zugute kommt. **Abweichungen zum Schlechteren hin** hindern die Vertragsaufhebung nicht, wenn sie eindeutig belanglos sind; so schaden beispielsweise das Fehlen von – unbedeutenden – Schrauben oder die kurzfristige Benutzung einer Ledermöbelgarnitur nicht.[22] Aber auch geringfügige Verschlechterungen, die zu einer geldwerten Einbusse führen, lassen das Aufhebungsrecht nicht dahinfallen und sind lediglich in der Berechnung des begleitenden Schadensersatzes bzw. in der Vorteilsausgleichung zu berücksichtigen.[23]

5. Zeitpunkt

Massgeblicher Zeitpunkt für die Beurteilung der Unversehrtheit der Ware ist die **Abgabe** **7** **der Aufhebungserklärung**.[24] Beschädigung oder sonstige Beeinträchtigungen der Ware

---

[15] Vgl. *Staudinger/Magnus*, Art. 82, Rn. 5; *Ferrari u. a./Ferrari*, Internationales Vertragsrecht, Art. 82, Rn. 5; vgl. auch *Kröll u. a. /Bridge*, Art. 82, Rn. 15; *Honnold/Flechtner*, Art. 82, Rn. 445; *Brunner*, Art. 82, Rn. 4.
[16] Wie hier *Honsell/Weber*, Art. 82, Rn. 6; *Bamberger/Roth/Saenger*, Art. 82, Rn. 2; MünchKomm/*P. Huber*, Art. 82, Rn. 3; MünchKommHGB/*Benicke*, Art. 82, Rn. 4; a. A. *Bianca/Bonell/Tallon*, Art. 82, Anm. 2.1.
[17] *Enderlein/Maskow/Strohbach*, Art. 82, Anm. 2.1.; *Schlechtriem*, Internationales UN-Kaufrecht, Rn. 324; *Ferrari u. a./Ferrari*, Internationales Vertragsrecht, Art. 82, Rn. 7.
[18] Vgl. Sekretariatskommentar, Art. 67, Nr. 2 f.: „the change in condition of the goods must be of sufficient importance [so] that it would no longer be proper to require the seller to retake the goods *as the equivalent of that which he had delivered*" (Hervorhebung hinzugefügt).
[19] A. A. wohl *Magnus*, 25 J. L. & Com. (2005), 423, 430; *Staudinger/Magnus*, Art. 82, Rn. 8; *Brunner*, Art. 82, Rn. 5; *Ferrari u. a./Ferrari*, Internationales Vertragsrecht, Art. 82, Rn. 6: Verbesserungen der Ware seien stets als unwesentliche, nicht zum Verlust des Aufhebungsrechts führende Veränderungen aufzufassen.
[20] Ob der Fall allenfalls unter Art. 82 II lit. c) fällt, ist anhand dessen zu beurteilen, ob der Käufer die Verzierung vor Kenntnis bzw. Kennenmüssen der Vertragswidrigkeit anbrachte, vgl. unten Rn. 25.
[21] YB VII (1976), S. 133, Art. 52, Nr. 2 f.
[22] Vgl. OLG Oldenburg, 1.2.1995, CISG-online 253; für ein Gegenbsp. vgl. OLG Linz, 23.1.2006, CISG-online 1377: (normale) Abnutzung eines PKW sprengt die Bagatellgrenze des Abs. 1.
[23] *Bamberger/Roth/Saenger*, Art. 82, Rn. 3; *Staudinger/Magnus*, Art. 82, Rn. 6; *Honsell/Weber*, Art. 82, Rn. 8; a. A. *Schlechtriem*, Internationales UN-Kaufrecht, Rn. 324: Der Grundsatz der weitgehenden Vermeidung von Rückabwicklungen solle im Rahmen des Art. 82 dazu führen, dass auch geringfügige Verschlechterungen zum Dahinfallen des Aufhebungsrechts führen.
[24] So auch *Ferrari u. a./Ferrari*, Internationales Vertragsrecht, Art. 82, Rn. 7; MünchKomm/*P. Huber*, Art. 82, Rn. 6.

vor diesem Zeitpunkt sind unschädlich, solange nur der Käufer im Zeitpunkt des Absendens der Aufhebungserklärung die Ware im Wesentlichen unversehrt zurückgeben kann. Auf den Empfang der Aufhebungserklärung durch die andere Partei kommt es nicht an.[25] Wird die Rückgabe nach diesem Zeitpunkt unmöglich, hindert dies die Vertragsaufhebung nicht.[26] Da selbst in den nicht ausdrücklich so vorgesehenen Fällen von einer angemessenen Frist auszugehen ist, nach deren Ablauf die Aufhebung des Vertrags ausgeschlossen ist,[27] wird es auch zulässig sein, dass der Verkäufer dem Käufer eine Frist setzt, innerhalb welcher der Käufer die Aufhebung erklären kann.[28]

6. Rechtsfolgen

8   Kann die Ware – vorbehaltlich der Bagatellregelung – nicht unversehrt zurückgewährt werden, ist die Vertragsaufhebung **ausgeschlossen, sofern nicht eine der Ausnahmen des Art. 82 II vorliegt.** Eine Prüfung der Aufhebungssperre muss also in jedem Fall Art. 82 II mit umfassen.[29] Darf der Vertrag nicht mehr aufgehoben werden, bleiben dem Käufer die übrigen Rechtsbehelfe.[30]

9   Zu streng erscheint die Auffassung, dass es beim Ausschluss des Aufhebungsrechts bleiben soll, wenn zwar zum Zeitpunkt der Abgabe der Aufhebungserklärung die Ware nicht unversehrt zurückgewährt werden konnte, kurz darauf die unversehrte Rückgabe jedoch möglich wird, z.B. weil der Käufer die Ware inzwischen reparieren liess.[31] Aus Artt. 16 II lit. b), 29 II 2 lässt sich herauslesen, dass Erklärungen noch widerrufen bzw. modifiziert werden können, solange die andere Partei noch nicht im Vertrauen darauf gehandelt hat.[32] Entsprechend ist es hier angemessen, die Aufhebung noch so lange zuzulassen, wie der Verkäufer nicht darauf **vertraut** hat, dass der Käufer andere Rechtsbehelfe ergreift. Dies ergibt sich auch aus dem Grundgedanken des Art. 82, dem Verkäufer, der ja die Ursache zur Vertragsaufhebung gesetzt hat, die Gefahr möglichst weitgehend aufzuerlegen.[33]

III. Ausnahmen von der unversehrten Rückgabe, Abs. 2

1. Grundgedanken der Regelung

10   Der Grundsatz der unversehrten Rückgabe der Ware als Voraussetzung für die Ausübung des Aufhebungsrechts erfährt in Abs. 2 erhebliche Einschränkungen, die den **Grundsatz zur Ausnahme** machen.[34] Art. 82 II lit. a) und lit. b) auferlegen dem Verkäufer die Gefahr für Beeinträchtigungen der Ware, die auf seiner Vertragsverletzung basieren. Das ist am deutlichsten bei der Beeinträchtigung der Ware durch die erforderliche Untersuchung (lit. b)), liegt aber auch klar dem Fall der Verschlechterung der Ware durch den schon bei Lieferung vorhandenen Mangel[35] zu Grunde. Das Übereinkommen auferlegt dem vertrags-

---

[25] *Staudinger/Magnus*, Art. 82, Rn. 10; *Soergel/Lüderitz/Dettmeier*, Art. 82, Rn. 3; zur Absendetheorie vgl. Art. 26 Rn. 11.
[26] Dazu näher hinten Rn. 27.
[27] Zu den Ausschlussfristen für die Abgabe der Aufhebungserklärung vgl. oben *Fountoulakis*, Art. 26 Rn. 15 f.
[28] Vgl. dazu auch oben Art. 26 Rn. 16; *Honsell/Weber*, Art. 82, Rn. 10.
[29] *Leser*, Vertragsaufhebung und Rückabwicklung, S. 248 ff.; *Schlechtriem*, Internationales UN-Kaufrecht, Rn. 326 ff., 333.
[30] Dazu näher unten Art. 83 Rn. 3 ff.
[31] So noch die Vorauflage, Art. 82, Rn. 12; ebenso *Bamberger/Roth/Saenger*, Art. 82, Rn. 3a; *Ensthaler/Achilles*, GK-HGB, Art. 82, Rn. 5; *Honsell/Weber*, Art. 82, Rn. 12.
[32] Vgl. dazu auch oben *Fountoulakis*, Art. 26 Rn. 12.
[33] Dazu hinten Rn. 12.
[34] Vgl. oben Rn. 1 und Vor Artt. 81–84 Rn. 11; OGH, 29.6.1999, CISG-online 483 = östZRVgl 2000, 33.
[35] Im EKG, Art. 79 II lit. a), noch als „Vertragsverletzung, welche die Aufhebung rechtfertigt" getrennt erfasst und jetzt in Art. 82 II lit. a) aufgegangen, vgl. die Vorgeschichte oben Rn. 1.

brüchigen Verkäufer weiter das Risiko für alle Verschlechterungen oder Umstände, die zum Untergang der Ware führen, soweit sie nicht auf einer Handlung oder Unterlassung des Käufers beruhen (lit. a)).[36] Damit liegen die Risiken des Zufalls und der höheren Gewalt allein beim Verkäufer.

Art. 82 II lit. c) erfasst die Fälle, bei denen die gelieferte Ware im normalen Geschäftsgang weiter veräussert, verarbeitet oder verbraucht wurde, bevor der Mangel erkannt wurde. Hier geht es um das **Risiko der geschäftsüblichen Verwendung** der Sache, das ebenfalls der Verkäufer zu tragen hat, allerdings in abgeschwächter Form: Zum einen trifft den Käufer mit Erkennen des Mangels eine Einstandspflicht für die Ware;[37] zum anderen erhält der Verkäufer durch die Vorteilsausgleichung in Art. 84 II lit. b) die aus der Sache gezogenen Vorteile.[38]

Die einseitige oder doch vorwiegende **Belastung des Verkäufers** mit den Risiken der Rückabwicklung ist in diesem Ausmass durchaus fragwürdig,[39] und die Verursachung der Rückabwicklung durch die Vertragsverletzung des Verkäufers vermag die besonderen Gefahrverteilungsregeln des Art. 82 letztlich auch nicht befriedigend zu erklären.[40] Daher erscheint es auch sachgerecht, Art. 82 II lediglich bei Vertragsverletzung durch den Verkäufer anzuwenden. Ist hingegen der Käufer der vertragsbrüchige Teil oder heben die Parteien den Vertrag einvernehmlich auf, sollte eine andere Gefahrentragungsregel gefunden werden.[41]

2. Nicht auf „Handlung oder Unterlassung des Käufers beruhend",[42] Abs. 2 lit. a)

Die Frage, ob der Untergang oder die wesentliche Verschlechterung der Ware auf einem Handeln oder Unterlassen des Käufers beruht, ist **autonom** aus dem CISG heraus zu beantworten. Bei der Beurteilung der Vorraussetzungen von Art. 82 II a) sind Sorgfaltsmassstäbe und Haftungstatbestände nationalen Rechts folglich irrelevant.[43]

a) Vertragsverletzung des Verkäufers. Art. 82 II lit. a) belastet zunächst den Verkäufer mit allen **Risiken, die aus der mangelhaften Beschaffenheit oder Lieferung der Ware folgen**.[44] Hierzu gehören allgemein die weitere Verschlechterung der Ware infolge eines ihr bereits anhaftenden Mangels[45] (sogenannter „weiterfressender Mangel"), wie zum Beispiel der Verderb bereits mangelhafter Lebensmittel,[46] die Zerstörung eines gelieferten Kraftwagens durch fehlerhafte Bremsen,[47] die auf ihren Mangel zurückzuführende Explosion der gelieferten Maschine[48] etc. Hierher zu zählen ist auch die Unmöglichkeit der Herausgabe, weil die Ware wegen Sach-[49] oder Rechtsmangels[50] beschlagnahmt worden ist. Aber auch

---

[36] Vgl. hinten Rn. 13 ff.
[37] Vgl. hinten Rn. 25.
[38] Dazu unten Art. 84 Rn. 22 ff.
[39] Vgl. ausführlich aus rechtsvergleichender Sicht *Hornung*, S. 156 ff.
[40] Diese Erwägung lag aber wohl der Schaffung der Artt. 79 EKG und 82 zu Grunde.
[41] Vgl. hinten Rn. 28 ff.
[42] Es handelt sich hierbei um eine allgemeine Regel, die *Ernst Rabel* dem französischen Recht entnommen (vgl. *Rabel*, RheinZ 1 (1909), 187–226 (= Ges. Aufs. I, S. 103–140) und später in das Einheitskaufrecht eingeführt hat (*Rabel*, Recht des Warenkaufs, Bd. 1, S. 444; dann auch enthalten in Art. 99 E 1935 zum EKG, vgl. *Rabel*, Recht des Warenkaufs, Bd. 2, S. 392); umfassend zur Verteilung der Untergangsgefahr im Rahmen der Rückabwicklung gescheiterter Verträge nach französischem Recht *Hornung*, S. 122–132.
[43] Vgl. *Honnold/Flechtner*, Art. 82, Rn. 448.1; MünchKomm/*P. Huber*, Art. 82, Rn. 12; *Ferrari u. a./Ferrari*, Internationales Vertragsrecht, Art. 82, Rn. 9 Fn. 39.
[44] *Staudinger/Magnus*, Art. 82, Rn. 22; *Honsell/Weber*, Art. 82, Rn. 17 f.; *Neumayer/Ming*, Art. 82, Anm. 2.; *Reinhart*, Art. 82, Rn. 4; *Heuzé*, Anm. 428.; *Audit*, Vente internationale, Anm. 192.
[45] *Schlechtriem*, Internationales UN-Kaufrecht, Rn. 326.
[46] MünchKomm/*P. Huber*, Art. 82, Rn. 14.
[47] *Leser*, Vertragsaufhebung und Rückabwicklung, S. 246; *Schlechtriem*, Internationales UN-Kaufrecht, Rn. 326.
[48] *Audit*, Vente internationale, Anm. 192.
[49] Vgl. Hof's-Gravenhage, 23.4.2003, CISG-online 903 = IHR 2004, 119; *Medical Marketing International, Inc. v. Internazionale Medico Scientifica, S. R. L.*, U. S. Dist. Ct. (E. D. La.), 17.5.1999, CISG-online 387: Medizi-

Vertragsverletzungen anderer Art, wie Lieferung am falschen Ort oder zur falschen Zeit[51] oder mangelnde oder fehlerhafte Gebrauchsanweisungen, führen zur Belastung des Verkäufers mit dem Sachschicksal, soweit nicht der Käufer zur Abwendung der Gefahr[52] oder eventuellen Schadensminderung verpflichtet war.

14 **b) Höhere Gewalt.** Ebenfalls ausserhalb der Einflusssphäre des Käufers befinden sich **zufällige Einwirkungen,**[53] also Naturkatastrophen, staatliche Hoheitsakte etc. Hierher gehören auch **Einwirkungen Dritter,** die unvorhersehbar oder unvermeidbar sind, aber auch allenfalls vermeidbare Einwirkungen, sofern der Dritte nicht zur Einflusssphäre des Käufers gehört. Verliert etwa geliefertes Mehl, das im Käuferland wegen krebserregender Zusätze längere Zeit beschlagnahmt war, durch die Lagerung weiter an Qualität, ist der Käufer dafür nicht verantwortlich und kann den Vertrag nach wie vor aufheben, auch wenn er die Ware nicht im Wesentlichen im erhaltenen Zustand zurückgeben kann.[54] Dieser Massstab entspricht Art. 79 I, II.[55]

15 **c) Weitere Fälle.** Am schwierigsten sind die Fälle zu beurteilen, in denen sich die Ware im Besitz des Käufers befindet und dieser sie bereits in Betrieb genommen hat. Es geht hier darum, den **Risikobereich,** in dem der Käufer für den Untergang bzw. die Verschlechterung verantwortlich ist, festzulegen. Auf ein Verschulden kommt es nach der Struktur des Übereinkommens auch hier nicht an, doch sind dem Käufer selbstredend schuldhafte Verschlechterungen oder Einwirkungen auf die Sache durch ihn selbst sowie durch Personen, für die er einzustehen hat, klar zuzurechnen.[56]

16 Beruht die Unmöglichkeit auf einer **Unterlassung** des Käufers, so ist darauf abzustellen, ob sich das Risiko innerhalb der Herrschafts- und Einflusssphäre des Käufers befindet.[57] So greift etwa die Ausnahme von Art. 82 II a), wenn der Käufer die Sache lediglich an seiner Niederlassung zur Verfügung zu stellen hat (analog Art. 31 lit. c)), die Verladung also gerade nicht mehr zum Verantwortungsbereich des Käufers gehört, und die Sache später auf dem Rücktransport mangels hinreichender Sicherung beschädigt wird.[58] Allerdings vermag erst

---

nische Geräte waren beschlagnahmt worden, weil sie den Sicherheitsbestimmungen der USA nicht entsprachen. Das Gericht stufte die Vertragsverletzung der Verkäuferin als „fundamental" i. S. d. Art. 49 I lit. a) ein und liess die Vertragsaufhebung zu, ohne auf die Problematik der Unmöglichkeit der Herausgabe der Geräte ausdrücklich einzugehen; Einzelheiten bei *Schlechtriem*, IPRax 1999, 388.

[50] Vgl. LG Freiburg, 22.8.2002, CISG-online 711 = IHR 2003, 22: auf Verkauf eines fremden Pkw beruhende Beschlagnahme begründete eine Ausnahme nach Art. 82 II lit. a).

[51] Von *Soergel/Lüderitz/Dettmeier*, Art. 82, Rn. 6, wird etwa das Beispiel angeführt, dass die verspätet gelieferte Ware wegen zwischenzeitlichen Frosteinbruchs verdirbt.

[52] Zur Abwendung der Gefahren von der Sache vgl. Artt. 85 ff.

[53] *Leser*, FS Kitagawa, S. 445, 467 f.; *Enderlein/Maskow/Strohbach*, Art. 82, Anm. 7.; *Schlechtriem*, Internationales UN-Kaufrecht, Rn. 326; *Staudinger/Magnus*, Art. 82, Rn. 21; *Honsell/Weber*, Art. 82, Rn. 18; *Herber/Czerwenka*, Art. 82, Rn. 7; *Heuzé*, Art. 428.; *Audit*, Vente internationale, Anm. 192.

[54] Hof's-Gravenhage, 23.4.2003, CISG-online 903 = IHR 2004, 119. Vgl. auch Int. Ct. Russian CCI, 18.10.2005, CISG-online 1457: Wird die gelieferte Lackierungsmaschine bis zum Entdecken des Mangels von einem Dritten verwendet und kann sie später nicht im Wesentlichen im erhaltenen Zustand zurückgegeben werden, so stellt dies kein „Handeln des Käufers" (Abs. 2 lit. a)) dar.

[55] *Bianca/Bonell/Tallon*, Art. 82, Anm. 2.2.; MünchKommHGB/*Benicke*, Art. 82, Rn. 8; *Audit*, Vente internationale, Anm. 192.; *Soergel/Lüderitz/Dettmeier*, Art. 82, Rn. 5.

[56] *Bianca/Bonell/Tallon*, Art. 82, Anm. 2.2.; *Soergel/Lüderitz/Dettmeier*, Art. 82, Rn. 4; *Honsell/Weber*, Rn. 82, Rn. 16; *Karollus*, S. 150; MünchKommHGB/*Benicke*, Art. 82, Rn. 8; *Schlechtriem*, Internationales UN-Kaufrecht, Rn. 327. Art. 79 II lit. d) EKG enthielt noch ausdrücklich die Formulierung „Person […], für die er einzustehen hat". Die Änderung der Textfassung bedeutet aber keine sachliche Einschränkung des Risikobereichs. Während der Vorarbeiten für das EKG konnte sich der Vorschlag der Delegation Norwegens, das Wort „Handlung" („fait") durch „Verschulden" („faute") zu ersetzen, nicht durchsetzen; vgl. Doc., 354. A. A. wohl *Honnold/Flechtner*, Art. 82, Rn. 448.1[A]: unter „Handlung oder Unterlassung" i. S. v. Art. 82 II lit. a) sei nur verschuldetes Verhalten des Käufers zu verstehen.

[57] *Leser*, Vertragsaufhebung und Rückabwicklung, S. 246 f.; ähnlich auch *Soergel/Lüderitz/Dettmeier*, Art. 82, Rn. 5; *Hornung*, S. 158 f.; *Herber/Czerwenka*, Art. 82, Rn. 6.

[58] Vgl. OLG Karlsruhe, 19.12.2002, CISG-online 817 = IHR 2003, 125, m. Anm. *Hennecke*, IHR 2003, 268, 272 ff.

ein **risikoerhöhendes Verhalten** des Käufers zum Ausschluss des Aufhebungsrechts zu führen.[59]

Gründet die Unmöglichkeit auf einer **Handlung** des Käufers, so kommt es darauf an, ob **17** er zu diesem Umgang mit der Ware berechtigt war. Nicht jede Handlung, die die Unmöglichkeit herbeigeführt hat, schliesst das Aufhebungsrecht aus. In praktischer Hinsicht lautet die Frage, welchen **Gebrauch**[60] der Käufer von der Ware machen darf. Es ist, in Anlehnung an lit. c, zwischen der Phase zu unterscheiden, ab der der Käufer die Rückabwicklung als Möglichkeit erkennen konnte, und zwischen der Phase zuvor. Vor Kenntnis bzw. Kennenmüssen ist der normale Gebrauch der Ware zulässig.[61] Wird die Ware dabei beschädigt oder geht sie unter, schliesst dies das Aufhebungsrecht nicht aus. Mit der Kenntnis bzw. dem Kennenmüssen des Mangels jedoch wird über den Käufer, in Anlehnung an lit. c), die Sperre für eine unbeschränkte Weiterverwendung oder Veräusserung der Sache verhängt.[62] In der Sache trifft den Käufer ab diesem Zeitpunkt eine Einstandspflicht für die gelieferte Ware, die mit derjenigen nach Erklärung der Aufhebung zu vergleichen ist.[63]

3. Untersuchung der Ware, Abs. 2 lit. b)

Der Käufer darf den Vertrag auch dann aufheben, wenn die Sache als Folge der in Art. 38 **18** vorgesehenen und damit **berechtigten Untersuchung**[64] ganz oder teilweise verschlechtert oder zerstört wird. Die Untersuchung kann auf Mängel, aber auch auf Ursachen oder Möglichkeiten zur Behebung des Mangels hin erfolgt sein.[65] Art. 82 II lit. b) erfasst in erster Linie Fälle, in denen die Untersuchung ohne Eingriff in die Substanz nicht erfolgen kann, beispielsweise bei bestimmten chemischen Substanzen,[66] Nahrungsmitteln[67] etc., sowie Fälle, in denen die Untersuchung die Inbetriebnahme oder die Verarbeitung[68] der Ware erfordert. Die Risiken und Folgen der Untersuchung fallen bei Aufhebung damit allein dem Verkäufer zu.[69] Hat der Käufer die Untersuchung nicht mit angemessenen Mitteln bzw. auf andere Weise nicht ordnungsgemäss ausgeführt, so greift Art. 82 I lit. b) nicht, und es bleibt beim Wegfall des Aufhebungsrechts.[70]

4. Weiterverkauf, Verarbeitung und Gebrauch der Ware, Abs. 2 lit. c)

a) **Verwendungsrisiko des Verkäufers.** Wenn der Käufer die Ware im gewöhnlichen **19** Geschäftsverkehr verkauft oder sie ihrer normalen Verwendung gemäss verbraucht oder

---

[59] *Schlechtriem*, Internationales UN-Kaufrecht, Rn. 327; *Enderlein/Maskow/Strohbach*, Art. 82, Rn. 7; *Kappus*, RIW 1992, 528, 531; wohl auch *Herber/Czerwenka*, Art. 82, Rn. 6; *Achilles*, Art. 82, Rn. 7; zum Ganzen grundsätzlich *von Caemmerer*, FS Lorenz, S. 621 ff. = GS Bd. 2, S. 167 ff.
[60] „Gebrauch der Ware", der nirgends ausdrücklich erfasst wird (vgl. hinten Rn. 21), aber doch die Mehrheit aller Fälle ausmacht, tangiert sowohl Art. 82 II lit. a) oder lit. c) als auch die Bagatellregel des Abs. 1. Unabhängig davon, wo man den Gebrauch einstuft, sind die Rechtsfolgen jeweils dieselben.
[61] MünchKommHGB/*Benicke*, Art. 82, Rn. 9.
[62] Vgl. auch vorne Rn. 11 sowie hinten Rn. 25.
[63] Dazu hinten Rn. 25.
[64] *Bianca/Bonell/Tallon*, Art. 82, Anm. 2.3.; *Enderlein/Maskow/Strohbach*, Art. 82, Rn. 5; *Freiburg*, S. 262; BGH, 25.6.1997, CISG-online 277 = NJW 1997, 3311; LG Ellwangen, 21.8.1995, CISG-online 279.
[65] *Audit*, Vente internationale, Anm. 192.
[66] Vgl. BP International, Ltd. and BP Exploration & Oil, Inc. v. Empresa Estatal Petroleos de Ecuador, et al., U. S. Ct. App. (5th Cir.), 11.6.2003, CISG-online 730 = 332 F.3d 333 (Prüfung von Benzin auf Gummigehalt hin verlangte Entnahme von Proben).
[67] Vgl. AppGer Basel-Stadt, 22.8.2003, CISG-online 943 = IHR 2005, 117 (Prüfung vegetarischer Schnitzel auf gentechnisch veränderten Soja hin).
[68] Vgl. BGH, 25.6.1997, CISG-online 277 = NJW 1997, 3311: Art. 82 I schliesse die Rückabwicklung nicht aus, wenn für die Untersuchung des gelieferten Rohstahls auf Mängel hin dessen Verarbeitung notwendigerweise erforderlich sei. In diesem Fall basiere die Veränderung der Ware – bei der ohnehin von einer Verschlechterung nicht gesprochen werden könne – auf einer berechtigten Untersuchung i. S. d. Art. 82 II lit. b); ähnlich die erste Instanz, LG Krefeld, 19.12.1995, CISG-online 397.
[69] Für eine umfassende Gefahrtragung durch den Verkäufer ab Vertragsaufhebung *Honnold/Flechtner*, Art. 82, Rn. 448.1 [B].
[70] MünchKomm/*P. Huber*, Art. 82, Rn. 17.

verändert hat, bleibt sein Aufhebungsrecht bestehen. Art. 82 II lit. c) weist damit das **Verwendungsrisiko** dem Verkäufer zu, der durch seine wesentliche Vertragsverletzung das Aufhebungsrecht begründet hat.[71] War die Verwendung für den Käufer vorteilhaft, weil der Wert der gezogenen Vorteile den Kaufpreis unter Berücksichtigung einer allfälligen Minderung übersteigt, wird der Käufer am Vertrag festhalten. Ist der Vorteilswert hingegen geringer, wird er den Vertrag aufheben und vom Verkäufer den Betrag verlangen, um den der Kaufpreis den Wert der durch den Weiterverkauf gezogenen Nutzungen übersteigt. Die Interessen des Verkäufers werden (nur) dadurch geschützt, dass die Vertragsaufhebung fristgebunden ist[72] und es sich um eine „normale" Transaktion bzw. Verwendung gehandelt haben muss.[73]

20   **b) Verbrauch, Veränderung.** Die Fälle des Verbrauchs und der Veränderung der Sache sollen alle Vorgänge erfassen, die mit oder ohne Rest die Sachsubstanz in ihrem Wesen so verändern oder vernichten, dass ihre Rückgabe, soweit überhaupt physisch möglich, nicht mehr als Sache gleicher Art anzusehen wäre.[74] Die **Bagatellgrenze**[75] aus Art. 82 I ist auch hier anwendbar. Verbrauch als Vernichtung im wirtschaftlichen Sinne tritt etwa ein bei Brennstoffen, aber auch bei ausgebrachtem Dünger oder verarbeiteten Farben. Veränderung der Ware erfasst die Verarbeitung mit oder ohne Wertschöpfung,[76] beispielsweise die Einfärbung von Stoffen, das Zurechtschneiden von Holzbrettern, das Brennen von Ton. Die Übergänge sind freilich fliessend; eine scharfe Abgrenzung ist nicht möglich und wegen der gleichen Rechtsfolgen auch nicht nötig.[77] Die Vorteilsausgleichung gemäss Art. 84 bleibt getrennt zu prüfen.

21   **c) Gebrauch.** Der Gebrauch einer Sache ist zwischen „Veränderung" in lit. c), „Handeln" in lit. a) und „Rückgabe der Ware im Wesentlichen in dem Zustand, in dem er sie erhalten hat" in Abs. 1 anzusiedeln.[78] Der bestimmungsgemässe Gebrauch dürfte unter lit. c) fallen (und ggf. eine Ausgleichspflicht nach Art. 84 nach sich ziehen). Ob die Bagatellgrenze des Abs. 1 überschritten wird, ist beim **bestimmungsgemässen** Gebrauch nicht erheblich.[79] Werden z. B. gekaufte Lastwagen im normalen Geschäftsverkehr eingesetzt und führt dies zu einem erheblichen Werteverlust, bleibt der Käufer trotzdem nach lit. c) zur Aufhebung berechtigt, wenn er gutgläubig ist. Beim **nicht bestimmungsgemässen** Gebrauch ist ein Aufhebungsrecht nur dann gegeben, wenn die Bagatellgrenze des Abs. 1 nicht überschritten wird; von Abs. 2 wird der nicht bestimmungsgemässe Gebrauch nämlich nicht mehr gedeckt, ungeachtet dessen, ob der „Gebrauch" als solcher unter lit. a) oder lit. c) subsumiert wird.[80]

22   **d) Weiterveräusserung.** Der in lit. c) geregelte Ausnahmetatbestand erfasst neben den Fällen der Verarbeitung auch die Fälle der Weiterveräusserung.[81] Mit deren Einbeziehung, die in Art. 79 EKG noch nicht enthalten war, hat sich das CISG von der Grundidee einer möglichst vollständigen Rückabwicklung in Gestalt der gelieferten Sache entfernt. Die gelieferte Sache braucht nun nicht mehr zurückgegeben zu werden, sondern an ihre Stelle

---

[71] MünchKommHGB/*Benicke,* Art. 82, Rn. 13.
[72] Vgl. vorne *Fountoulakis,* Art. 26 Rn. 15 f.
[73] MünchKommHGB/*Benicke,* Art. 82, Rn. 13.
[74] Zum EKG *Dölle/Weitnauer,* Art. 79 EKG, Rn. 17–19.
[75] Vgl. oben Rn. 6 und Sekretariatskommentar, Art. 67, Nr. 3.
[76] *Bianca/Bonell/Tallon,* Art. 82, Anm. 2.4.
[77] So auch MünchKommHGB/*Benicke,* Art. 82, Rn. 14.
[78] Vgl. auch OLG Linz, 23.1.2006, CISG-online 1377, Erw. 6.1.
[79] MünchKommHGB/*Benicke,* Art. 82, Rn. 14.
[80] Beispiel: Hat der Käufer die gekauften Stoffballen entgegen der Anweisung heiss gewaschen, wird es für die Möglichkeit der Aufhebung darauf ankommen, ob er sie (dennoch) im Wesentlichen in dem Zustand zurückgeben kann, in dem er sie erhalten hat.
[81] Zur Entstehungsgeschichte vgl. oben Rn. 1. Für ein Beispiel des Weiterverkaufs im normalen Geschäftsbetrieb s. LG Ellwangen, 21.8.1995, CISG-online 279: Zwischen Lieferung und Feststellung der Vertragswidrigkeit packte der Käufer das Paprikapulver ab und lieferte es an diverse Lager aus.

tritt über Art. 84 der Ausgleich des Vorteils, das commodum ex negotiatione, das regelmässig, aber nicht notwendigerweise dem Wert der Sache entspricht.[82]

Unter **„normalem Geschäftsverkehr"** ist das Verhalten einer vernünftigen Person unter den entsprechenden Umständen zu verstehen.[83] Die Ware braucht nicht gemäss ihres ursprünglichen Erwerbszwecks weiterverarbeitet und als Bestandteil des vom Käufer vertriebenen Produkts veräussert worden zu sein; Weiterveräusserung im normalen Geschäftsverkehr gemäss Art. 82 II lit. c) ist auch jeder blosse Weiterverkauf der erworbenen Ware ohne vorherige Weiterverarbeitung, sofern dies **in den gegebenen Umständen ein ökonomisch sinnvolles Vorgehen** war.[84] Entsprechend hat selbst die Weiterveräusserung der Ware zu einem äusserst niedrigen Preis („Schrottpreis") als normales Geschäftsverhalten zu gelten, wenn für die Ware aufgrund ihrer Mangelhaftigkeit kein höherer Preis zu erzielen war. 22a

Neben der Weiterveräusserung werden nach der **ratio** der Vorschrift auch sonstige Formen des Eigentumsverlustes gemeint sein, so etwa das Einbringen der gekauften Ware in eine (Handels-)Gesellschaft mit eigener Rechtspersönlichkeit.[85] 22b

Für den (Weiter-)Verkauf ist **zeitlich** der nach dem massgeblichen Vertragsstatut zu bestimmende Vertragsschluss zwischen Käufer und Drittem massgeblich. Eine Übereignung oder Lieferung ist nicht erforderlich. Wie weit der Käufer sich gegenüber seinem Abkäufer bei Entdeckung eines Mangels der Ware noch vom Vertrag lösen kann, ist eine Frage, die der hierfür anwendbaren Rechtsordnung folgt. Der Weiterverkauf hindert jedenfalls die Vertragsaufhebung nicht. 23

e) Entsorgung wertloser Ware. Vom Wortlaut des Art. 82 nicht erfasst ist der Fall, dass die Ware wertlos war und der Käufer sie zwischenzeitlich entsorgt hat. Dieser Fall steht den in Art. 82 II enthaltenen Ausnahmen **wertungsmässig gleich:** Der Verkäufer kann nicht auf dem Weiterbestand des Vertrages beharren, wenn er selbst seine Pflicht nicht erfüllt hat.[86] 24

f) Zeitliche Sperrwirkung. Gemeinsam bleibt allen Fällen des lit. c), dass sie nur bis zur **Entdeckung bzw. Entdeckbarkeit der Vertragswidrigkeit** und damit der Möglichkeit der Vertragsaufhebung greifen. Von der Kenntnis der Rückgabemöglichkeit an entsteht für den Käufer eine potentielle Rückgabepflicht gemäss Art. 81 II, mit der sich eine weitere unbeschränkte Verfügung über die Sache oder ihre Verwendung nicht vereinbaren lässt.[87] Art. 82 I mit seinem Grundsatz der unversehrten Rückgabe entfaltet ab dann seine **Sperrwirkung.** Der Käufer kann den Vertrag nicht mehr aufheben, wenn er die Ware nicht mehr im Wesentlichen unversehrt zurückgeben kann, weil er sie verändert, verbraucht, gebraucht oder weiterverkauft hat, nachdem er Kenntnis hatte oder hätte haben müssen von seinem Aufhebungsrecht.[88] Dabei ist wiederum die Bagatellklausel in Art. 82 I zu beachten. Hat 25

---

[82] (Die früheren Fn. 77 und 78 bezogen sich auf den folgenden Text) Damit wandelt sich der ursprüngliche Rücktausch zu einer **Abrechnung der Vorteile,** wie ihn die PICC und die PECL vorsehen, und ist nicht mehr weit von einer Abrechnung eines Schadensersatzanspruch entfernt. Dazu *Leser,* Vertragsaufhebung und Rückabwicklung, S. 247 f., und Vor Artt. 81–84 Rn. 11. Allerdings bleibt als wesentlicher Unterschied die Orientierung an der (hypothetischen) Vermögenslage beim positiven Interesse, während die Rückabwicklung von der Sache und ihrem Schicksal ausgehend zur möglichst vollständigen Rückführung der Leistungen tendiert. Vgl. auch CIETAC, 31.12.2003, CISG-online 1465, Erw. IV.: Die Käuferin veräusserte einen Teil der Ware (in casu Kleidung) weiter, nachdem die Verkäuferin Schiedsklage erhoben hatte; da bezüglich des weiterveräusserten Teils Vertragsaufhebung unmöglich war (Abs. 2 lit. c)), gewährte das Schiedsgericht der Verkäuferin Schadensersatz anstelle der Rückleistung in Höhe des durch den Weiterverkauf erzielten Gewinns.
[83] Vgl. MünchKomm/*Benicke,* Art. 82, Rn. 17; *Ferrari u. a./Ferrari,* Internationales Vertragsrecht, Art. 82, Rn. 12; MünchKomm/Huber, Art. 82, Rn. 18.
[84] Vgl. *Kröll u. a./Bridge,* Art. 82, Rn. 23.
[85] Vgl. Int. Ct. Russian CCI, 18.10.2005, CISG-online 1457, Erw. 3.6: „the machine was deposited as a holding in the statutory fund of a Russian joint-stock company[,] which implies transfer of the title and forfeiture of the [Buyer]'s right to the machine."
[86] *Staudinger/Magnus,* Art. 82, Rn. 27; vgl. auch *Brunner,* Art. 82, Rn. 3.
[87] Vgl. auch *Mazzotta,* Restitution, S. 516; *Ferrari u. a./Ferrari,* Internationales Vertragsrecht, Art. 82, Rn. 13.
[88] Vgl. Cass., 3.11.2009, CISG-online 2004; OLG Linz, 23.1.2006, CISG-online 1377; OLG Koblenz, 27.9.1991, CISG-online 30. Vgl. auch die ähnliche Rechtslage bei Art. 82 II lit. a) Rn. 17.

der Gebrauch der Ware nach dem Zeitpunkt, indem die Vertragswidrigkeit entdeckt wurde oder hätte entdeckt werden müssen, nicht zu einer wesentlichen Veränderung geführt, so bleibt dem Käufer die Vertragsaufhebung gemäss Art. 82 I unbenommen.[89] Bei der Beurteilung der Frage, ob die Nutzung nach Entdecken oder Entdeckenmüssen des Mangels die Ware **wesentlich verändert,** sind insbesondere die Beschaffenheit der Ware, die Dauer und Intensität der Nutzung sowie der Aspekt, ob es sich um fabrikneue oder gebrauchte Ware handelt, zu berücksichtigen.[90] Dabei trägt der Käufer das Beweisrisiko: Ist die Ware nicht mehr im Wesentlichen im ursprünglichen Zustand, und kann nicht festgestellt werden, inwiefern die über den Zeitpunkt der Entdeckung des Mangels hinaus dauernde Nutzung den Zustand der Ware verschlechtert hat, so ist die Vertragsaufhebung ausgeschlossen.[91] Der Zeitpunkt, in dem die Vertragswidrigkeit zu entdecken ist, richtet sich nach der Untersuchungsfrist des Art. 38, was sich auch aus der Gleichstellung von „entdecken" und „hätte entdecken müssen" ergibt.[92]

26 g) **Normaler Geschäftsverkehr.** Alle Ausnahmen in Art. 82 II lit. c) stehen unter der weiteren Einschränkung, dass Verbrauch, Gebrauch, Veränderung oder Verkauf der Ware im **normalen Geschäftsverkehr** erfolgen. Vom geschäftsüblichen Ablauf nicht gedeckte Verhaltensweisen des Käufers, die zu Lasten des Risikos des Verkäufers gehen, werden von lit. c) nicht gedeckt, also etwa unwirtschaftliche Massnahmen wie die Verschleuderung der Ware (sofern dies nicht im Rahmen der Schadensminderung angesagt ist), aber auch die Verpfändungen derselben, um damit finanzielle Engpässe zu überbrücken.[93] Der Massstab für die Beurteilung, was zum normalen Geschäftsverkehr gehört („normal course of business", „dans le cadre d'une opération commerciale normale"), ist wiederum nach der vernünftigen Person des Art. 8 II zu bestimmen.

IV. Nachträglicher Untergang der Ware

27 Nach Erklärung der Aufhebung eintretende Unmöglichkeit ändert nichts am einmal ausgeübten Aufhebungsrecht. Das Aufhebungsrecht fällt nicht etwa nachträglich weg.[94] Allerdings wird der Verkäufer dem Anspruch des Käufers auf Rückzahlung des Kaufpreises oftmals einen Schadensersatzanspruch entgegenhalten können: Den Käufer, der den Vertrag aufgehoben hat und rückabwickeln möchte, trifft eine **Einstandspflicht** für die Ware. Bei Untergang, Verlust, Beschädigung etc. wird er dem Verkäufer in entsprechender Anwendung von Art. 74 schadensersatzpflichtig.[95] Kann sich der Käufer allerdings nach Art. 79 (analog) für Untergang, Verlust, Beschädigung etc. entlasten, so entfällt seine Haftung.

---

[89] BGer, 18.5.2009, CISG-online 1900, Erw. D.9.1. = IHR 2010, 27 sowie die Vorinstanz, AppGer Basel-Stadt, 26.9.2008, CISG-online 1732, Erw. 9 = IHR 2009, 164.

[90] Vgl. OLG Linz, 23.1.2006, CISG-online 1377: Weiterbenützung fabrikneuen Citroëns trotz Kenntnis der Mängel führt zu Ausschluss des Aufhebungsrechts; BGer, 18.5.2009, CISG-online 1900, Erw. D.9.1. = IHR 2010, 27: bei langlebigen Gütern bringt der Gebrauch in der Regel nur eine unwesentliche Veränderung mit sich; OLG Koblenz, 27.9.1991, CISG-online 30: Zuschneiden und Verarbeiten von Marmorplatten nach Entdeckung der Mängel schneidet Berufungsmöglichkeit auf erklärte Vertragsaufhebung ab.

[91] Vgl. Cass., 3.11.2009, CISG-online 2004: Ausschluss des Vertragsaufhebungsrechts wegen Weiterbenützung einer Maschine während fünf Jahren trotz Kenntnis der Mängel, wobei die Weiterbenützung den Zustand der Maschine verschlechtert hat, ohne dass der Sachverständige das Ausmass der Verschlimmerung durch die Weiterbenutzung quantifizieren konnte.

[92] So auch *Mohs*, IHR 2002, 59, 63; *Song*, S. 237.

[93] *Bianca/Bonell/Tallon*, Art. 82, Anm. 2.4.; *Schlechtriem*, Internationales UN-Kaufrecht, Rn. 329; vgl. aus der Rechtsprechung OLG Düsseldorf, 10.2.1994, CISG-online 115, das von „unter Preis verschleuderte[r] Restmenge" spricht.

[94] So aber *Enderlein/Maskow/Strohbach*, Art. 84, Anm. 1.3.; wie hier *Ferrari u. a./Ferrari*, Internationales Vertragsrecht, Art. 82, Rn. 3.

[95] Artt. 74, 79 sind auch nach Vertragsaufhebung via konventionsimmanente Lückenfüllung (Art. 7 II) anwendbar, vgl. bereits oben Art. 81 Rn. 13 sowie *Staudinger/Magnus*, Art. 74, Rn. 9; *Bamberger/Roth/Saenger*, Art. 82, Rn. 3a; *Freiburg*, S. 259; *Ziegler*, S. 196; *Ferrari u. a./Ferrari*, Internationales Vertragsrecht, Art. 82, Rn. 2; LG Krefeld, 19.12.1995, CISG-online 397.

V. Anwendung von Art. 82 bei Aufhebung durch den Verkäufer bzw. bei einvernehmlicher Vertragsaufhebung?

Art. 82 I spricht ausdrücklich von der Vertragsaufhebung bzw. Forderung nach Ersatz- **28** lieferung durch den Käufer.[96] Entsprechend einseitig fällt die Risikoverteilung in Art. 82 II aus, die ausschliesslich den Verkäufer belastet.[97] Hebt nun der **Verkäufer** den Vertrag auf und verlangt er die gelieferte Ware zurück – was insbesondere bei Zahlungsschwierigkeiten und -verzug des Käufers praktisch wird –[98], stellt sich die Frage, ob auch das Vertragsaufhebungsrecht des Verkäufers durch analoge Anwendung von Art. 82 gesperrt wird. Die Frage wird von der h. L. richtigerweise **verneint**.[99] Art. 82 ist nicht dahingehend entsprechend anwendbar, dass der vom Verkäufer zurückzugewährende Gegenstand unversehrt sein müsse, da es sich dabei um **Geld-** und damit Wertverschaffungsschulden handelt.[100] Art. 82 sperrt aber auch nicht das Vertragsaufhebungsrecht des Verkäufers bei Verlust oder Beschädigung der **Ware**: Art. 82 regelt den Interessenausgleich bei Unmöglichkeit der Rückgewähr der vertragstreuen Partei und baut folglich auf der Vertragsverletzung des Verkäufers auf.[101] Nicht sachgerecht ist deshalb die Beibehaltung dieser einseitigen Risikoverteilung bei Vertragsaufhebung durch den Verkäufer, die auf der Vertragsverletzung des Käufers beruht.[102] Vielmehr muss in diesem letzteren Fall der Verkäufer stets aufheben können, ungeachtet dessen, ob die Ware untergegangen ist oder nicht bzw. ob der Untergang auf einem der in Art. 82 II geregelten Gründe beruht. Ein allgemeines Prinzip dahingehend, dass der Käufer in den Fällen des Art. 82 II stets privilegiert werden soll, unabhängig davon, von welcher Partei die Vertragsaufhebung geltend gemacht wird, ist dem CISG nicht zu entnehmen.[103] Insbesondere besteht kein Art. 82 II lit. c) zugrundeliegender, verallgemeinerungsfähiger Grundsatz der „Privilegierung des gutgläubigen Weiterverkäufers".[104]

Kann die Ware bei Vertragsaufhebung durch den Verkäufer nicht zurückgegeben **29** **werden, so treten** anstelle des Rückleistungsanspruchs Schadenersatzansprüche, die auf eine analoge Anwendung der in Artt. 85, 86 verankerten Einstandspflicht in Verbindung mit Art. 74 zu stützen sind, von der sich der Käufer gegebenenfalls in entsprechender Anwendung von Art. 79 entlasten kann.[105]

Dasselbe muss auch für den Fall gelten, dass die Parteien den Vertrag **einvernehmlich** **30** **aufheben**.[106] Art. 82 auf ein vertraglich vereinbartes Rücktrittsrecht anzuwenden erscheint

---

[96] Zur Funktion von Art. 82 II als Gefahrverteilungsnorm vgl. Vor Artt. 81–84 Rn. 10 und oben Rn. 10 ff.
[97] Dazu vorne Rn. 12.
[98] *Leser*, Vertragsaufhebung und Rückabwicklung, S. 253 f.; *Honnold/Flechtner*, Art. 81, Rn. 444; vgl. auch *Osuna*, Dealing with Avoidance, S. 494.
[99] *Staudinger/Magnus*, Art. 82, Rn. 29; *Honsell/Weber*, Art. 82, Rn. 4; MünchKomm/*P. Huber*, Art. 82, Rn. 2; MünchKomm/*Benicke*, Art. 82, Rn. 21; *Verweyen/Foerster/Toufar*, S. 217.
[100] Vgl. *Honsell/Weber*, Art. 82, Rn. 4; OLG Karlsruhe, 14.2.2008, CISG-online 1649, Erw. II.1. = IHR 2008, 53.
[101] Vgl. *Schlechtriem*, Internationales UN-Kaufrecht, Rn. 323; vgl. dazu auch Vor Artt. 81–84 Rn. 7 sowie oben Rn. 12.
[102] Vgl. *Honsell/Weber*, Art. 82, Rn. 4.
[103] OLG Karlsruhe, 14.2.2008, CISG-online 1649, Erw. II.1. = IHR 2008, 53.
[104] OLG Karlsruhe, 14.2.2008, CISG-online 1649, Erw. II.1. = IHR 2008, 53: Die Käuferin stellte sich auf den Standpunkt, der Verkäufer dürfe den Vertrag nicht aufheben, da die Käuferin das fragliche Fahrzeug im normalen Geschäftsverkehr trotz Sachmängeln weiteräussert habe, bevor der Verkäufer wegen Nichtzahlung des Restkaufpreises den Vertrag aufhob. Sie stützte ihre Ansicht auf eine „im CISG zum Ausdruck kommend[e] Privilegierung des gutgläubigen Weiterverkäufers". Die Vorinstanz schützte die Auffassung der Käuferin, wohingegen das OLG sie verneinte, da der „Normzweck des Art 82 [nicht] gebiete, das Recht des Verkäufers zur Vertragsaufhebung an die ‚Gutgläubigkeit' des zur unversehrten Rückgabe der Ware nicht fähigen Käufers zu binden." (aaO)
[105] *Honsell/Weber*, Art. 82, Rn. 4; *Herber/Czerwenka*, Art. 82, Rn. 4.
[106] Vgl. OGH, 29.6.1999, CISG-online 483 = östZRVgl 2000, 33; *Soergel/Lüderitz/Dettmeier*, Art. 82, Rn. 1; *Boels*, S. 176.

(einzig) dort sachgerecht, wo dieses ähnliche Aufgaben wie das gesetzliche Aufhebungsrecht erfüllt, d. h. von Tatbeständen abhängig ist, die mit Artt. 49, 64, 72, 73 vergleichbar sind;[107] eine weitergehende Anwendung auf vereinbarte Aufhebungsrechte ist aus den oben Rn. 28 erwähnten Gründen nicht angebracht.

VI. Beweislast

31 Der Verkäufer, der sich auf den Verlust des Rechts des Käufers zur Vertragsaufhebung nach 82 I beruft, muss nachweisen, dass sich die Ware nicht mehr im Wesentlichen in dem Zustand befindet, in dem der Käufer sie erhalten hat. Die Beweislast für das Vorliegen eines Ausnahmefalles nach Art. 82 II liegt hingegen beim Käufer.[108]

---

[107] Vgl. OGH, 29.6.1999, CISG-online 483 = östZRVgl 2000, 33: entsprechende Anwendung von Art. 82 II lit. a) im Rahmen einvernehmlicher Vertragsaufhebung einzig deshalb, weil der Verkäufer die Vertragsverletzung zu vertreten hat; vgl. auch *Soergel/Lüderitz/Dettmeier*, Art. 82, Rn. 1.

[108] *Staudinger/Magnus*, Art. 82, Rn. 31 f.; *Bamberger/Roth/Saenger*, Art. 82, Rn. 9; MünchKomm/*P. Huber*, Art. 82, Rn. 21; differenzierend *Soergel/Lüderitz/Dettmeier*, Art. 82, Rn. 13.

Art. 83 [Fortbestand anderer Rechte des Käufers]

Der Käufer, der nach Artikel 82 das Recht verloren hat, die Aufhebung des Vertrages zu erklären oder vom Verkäufer Ersatzlieferung zu verlangen, behält alle anderen Rechtsbehelfe,* die ihm nach dem Vertrag und diesem Übereinkommen zustehen.

Art. 83	Art. 83
A buyer who has lost the right to declare the contract avoided or to require the seller to deliver substitute goods in accordance with article 82 retains all other remedies under the contract and this Convention.	L'acheteur qui a perdu le droit de déclarer le contrat résolu ou d'exiger du vendeur la livraison de marchandises de remplacement en vertu de l'article 82 conserve le droit de se prévaloir de tous les autres moyens qu'il tient du contrat et de la présente Convention.

Übersicht

	Rn.
I. Vorgeschichte	1
II. Anwendungsbereich	2
1. Grundsatz der Selbstständigkeit der Behelfe	2
2. Weiter bestehende Rechtsbehelfe	3
a) Minderung	3
b) Erfüllungs- und Nachbesserungsanspruch	4
c) Schadenersatz	5
d) Sonstige Rechte	6
3. Abgrenzungsfragen	7

Vorläufer und **Entwürfe:** Art. 80 EKG; Genfer E 1976 Art. 53; Wiener E 1977 Art. 54; New Yorker E 1978 Art. 68.

I. Vorgeschichte

Die Vorläufer des Art. 83 wurden jeweils im Zusammenhang mit den Änderungen der 1 Vorläufer der Artt. 81, 82 geringfügig verändert und erweitert, denn Art. 83 stellt eine **Ergänzung zu Art. 82** dar.[1] Entsprechend der Einfügung in Art. 82 I wurde auch in Art. 83 der Fall der Ersatzlieferung aufgenommen.[2] Im Übrigen ergaben sich nur leichte terminologische Entwicklungen, die schliesslich in die von der Endfassung des CISG übernommene Formulierung des Art. 53 Genfer E 1976 „retains all other remedies" mündeten.[3] Gedacht war bei „other remedies" insbesondere an den später in Art. 45 I b) verankerten Schadenersatz und die Minderung des Art. 50.[4] Art. 53 Genfer E 1976 fand dann praktisch unverändert Eingang[5] in das Übereinkommen.

---

* Schweiz: Rechte.
[1] *Bianca/Bonell/Tallon*, Art. 83, Anm. 1.; *Herber/Czerwenka*, Art. 83, Rn. 2; *Honnold/Flechtner*, Art. 83, Rn. 449. *Witz/Salger/Lorenz/Salger*, Kommentar zu Art. 83, sprechen zu Recht vom „lediglich klarstellenden Charakter" der Vorschrift. Die PICC verzichten denn auch ganz auf eine entsprechende Bestimmung.
[2] YB V (1974), S. 43, Art. 80, Nr. 154.
[3] YB VII (1976), S. 133, Art. 53 im Vergleich zu YB V (1974), S. 43, Art. 80, Nr. 154.
[4] YB VII (1976), S. 133, Art. 53; selbe Begründung in Sekretariatskommentar, Artt. 68 (bzgl. Art. 41 I lit. b)), 42 und 46 New Yorker E.
[5] Einzig der Zusatz „under the contract and this convention" wurde auf der Wiener Konferenz eingefügt, vgl. O. R., S. 164, Art. 68.

II. Anwendungsbereich

1. Grundsatz der Selbstständigkeit der Behelfe

2 Art. 83 soll (Schieds-)Richtern, denen die Aufhebungssperre des Art. 82 aufgrund ihrer eigenen Rechtstradition als Konzept widerstrebt, die Anwendung der Bestimmung erleichtern, indem er nochmals[6] den Grundsatz betont, dass bei Vertragsbruch **diverse Rechtsbehelfe unabhängig nebeneinander** bestehen (und der Käufer nicht etwa ohne Rechtsbehelfe bleibt).[7] Die Sperre der Vertragsaufhebung oder der Ersatzlieferung durch den Grundsatz der unversehrten Rückgabe der Sache in Art. 82 I blockiert also nicht die übrigen Behelfe, die aus der Vertragsverletzung erwachsen, wie Schadenersatz und Minderung.

2. Weiter bestehende Rechtsbehelfe

3 a) **Minderung.** Bei Verlust des Aufhebungsrechts nach Art. 82 kann der Käufer **stattdessen** Minderung (Art. 50) verlangen.[8] Einer Minderung auf Null, wie sie mehrheitlich bejaht wird,[9] steht Art. 83 nicht im Wege: Selbst wenn die Minderung **auf Null** faktisch zum selben Resultat führt wie die Vertragsaufhebung, wird sie aufgrund der ausdrücklichen Betonung der Eigenständigkeit der verschiedenen Rechtsbehelfe in Art. 83 nicht ausgeschlossen.

4 b) **Erfüllungs- und Nachbesserungsanspruch.** Der Nachbesserungsanspruch aus Art. 46 III kommt in den von Art. 82 II umfassten Fallgestaltungen meistens schon sinnlogisch nicht in Frage. War der Käufer bereits soweit, dass er die Vertragsaufhebung verlangen konnte, und verliert er dieses Recht einzig nach Art. 82, so wird die Nachbesserung in der Regel unzumutbar i. S. v. Art. 46 III sein. Ist die **Nachbesserung** dem Verkäufer aber ausnahmsweise zumutbar, so lässt Art. 83 die Geltendmachung des Anspruchs zu.[10] In Betracht kommt etwa ein Nachbesserungsrecht bei bereits weiterverkaufter Ware, beispielsweise das Auswechseln von Teilen an weiterverkauften Geräten.[11] Auch der **Erfüllungsanspruch** gem. Art. 46 I kann im Einzelfall fortbestehen, soweit dies mit Art. 82 II kompatibel ist: So kann der Käufer nach wie vor die Übertragung rechtsmangelfreier Ware verlangen.[12]

5 c) **Schadenersatz.** Die wohl grösste praktische Bedeutung von Art. 83 besteht in der Möglichkeit, trotz Verlust des Aufhebungsrechts vertraglichen Schadenersatz zu verlangen (Artt. 74–77).[13]

---

[6] Vgl. bereits Artt. 45, 61; vgl. auch *Honnold/Flechtner*, Art. 83, Rn. 449 („perhaps unnecessarily"); *Bianca/Bonell/Tallon*, Art. 83, Anm. 2.1. („probably useless").

[7] *Bianca/Bonell/Tallon*, Art. 83, Anm. 2.1.

[8] *Neumayer/Ming*, Art. 83, Anm. 1.; vgl. auch *Staudinger/Magnus*, Art. 83, Rn. 4; MünchKommHGB/*Benicke*, Art. 83, Rn. 3; *Honnold/Flechtner*, Art. 83, Rn. 449.1; *Bamberger/Roth/Saenger*, Art. 83, Rn. 1; *Achilles*, Art. 83, Rn. 1; *Soergel/Lüderitz/Dettmeier*, Art. 83, Rn. 1; *Witz/Salger/Lorenz/Salger*, Art. 83.

[9] Vgl. *Müller-Chen*, Art. 50 Rn. 13; *Schlechtriem*, Internationales UN-Kaufrecht, Rn. 202; *Staudinger/Magnus*, Art. 50, Rn. 23; OGH, 23.5.2005, CISG-online 1041 = IHR 2005, 165; BGH, 2.3.2005, CISG-online 999, Erw. II.3.a) = IHR 2005, 158.

[10] So die ganz h.A. in der Literatur: *Kröll u. a./Bridge*, Art. 83, Rn. 2; *Bamberger/Roth/Saenger*, Art. 83, Rn. 2; *Achilles*, Art. 83, Rn. 1; *Witz/Salger/Lorenz/Salger*, Art. 83; *Soergel/Lüderitz/Dettmeier*, Art. 83, Rn. 1; *Audit*, Vente internationale, Anm. 192.; *Ferrari u. a./Ferrari*, Internationales Vertragsrecht, Art. 83, Rn. 2; wohl auch *Bianca/Bonell/Tallon*, Art. 83, Anm. 1. Betont wird, dass die Nachbesserung nur hinsichtlich derjenigen Sachmängel verlangt werden könne, für die der Verkäufer hafte.

[11] *Witz/Salger/Lorenz/Salger*, Art. 83.

[12] *Honnold/Flechtner*, Art. 83, Rn. 449; vgl. auch *Staudinger/Magnus*, Art. 83, Rn. 4; *Honsell/Weber*, Art. 83, Rn. 2.

[13] *Staudinger/Magnus*, Art. 83, Rn. 4; MünchKommHGB/*Benicke*, Art. 83, Rn. 3; MünchKomm/*P. Huber*, Art. 83, Rn. 2; *Honsell/Weber*, Art. 83, Rn. 2; *Herber/Czerwenka*, Art. 83, Rn. 2; *Reinhart*, Art. 83, Rn. 4;

d) Sonstige Rechte. Offen gehalten wird ferner der Weg für **vertraglich vereinbarte** 6
Rechte aus dem Vertragsbruch, die nicht in Zusammenhang mit der Rückabwicklung stehen oder die die gesetzlichen Regelungen zur Rückabwicklung – insbesondere die Ausschlusswirkung von Art. 82 I – ausdrücklich abändern. Beispiele hierfür sind Konventionalstrafen[14] oder die Vereinbarung einer Schadenspauschale.[15]

3. Abgrenzungsfragen

Die Selbstständigkeit von Schadenersatz und Vertragsaufhebung – für die Minderung gilt 7
in beschränkterem Umfang dasselbe – schliesst Abgrenzungsprobleme nicht aus.[16] Das wird besonders deutlich, wenn der Schadenersatz durch Entlastung nach Art. 79 oder die Rückabwicklung nach Art. 82 I blockiert ist.

Wenn die Rückabwicklung ganz **entbehrlich** ist, weil noch keine Leistungen aus- 8
getauscht sind, oder wenn die Rückabwicklung mit unversehrten Leistungen durchgeführt ist, tauchen die Probleme nur am Rande auf, etwa bei der Vorteilsausgleichung für gezogene Nutzungen nach Art. 84 II lit. a) oder bei dem Ersatz für Kosten der Rückabwicklung beim Käufer. Ist aber die Rückabwicklung wegen weiterer vom Käufer verursachter Verschlechterungen der mangelhaften Ware **blockiert,** bleibt für den im Übrigen vertragstreuen Käufer die Frage nach der Berücksichtigung des Minderwerts der Ware im Schadenersatz, wenn er nicht Minderung wählt. Die beiden letzteren Wege stehen nur alternativ zur Verfügung.[17] Die Einbeziehung des Minderwerts der gelieferten Ware (vor der weiteren Verschlechterung) in den Schadenersatzanspruch ist nach der Struktur des Übereinkommens möglich. Sie muss dann die in Art. 82 enthaltenen Gefahrverteilungsregeln berücksichtigen,[18] d. h. innerhalb des Schadenersatzanspruches kann nur der durch Mangel verursachte Minderwert der Ware, nicht aber deren weiteres Schicksal, das zu Lasten des Risikos des Käufers geht (z. B. Art. 82 II lit. a)), berücksichtigt werden.[19] Der Käufer kann daher einem Kaufpreisanspruch des Verkäufers, der weiter besteht, nur diesen Schadenersatzanspruch entgegenstellen, ihn aber nicht durch die Aufhebung zu Fall bringen.

Honnold/Flechtner, Art. 83, Rn. 449; *Neumayer/Ming,* Art. 83, Anm. 1.; *Bamberger/Roth/Saenger,* Art. 83, Rn. 1; *Achilles,* Art. 83, Rn. 1; *Soergel/Lüderitz/Dettmeier,* Art. 83, Rn. 1; *Witz/Salger/Lorenz/Salger,* Art. 83.
[14] ICC, 9978/1999, CISG-online 708 = UNILEX = 11(2) ICC Int. Ct. Arb. Bull. (2000), 117.
[15] *Witz/Salger/Lorenz/Salger,* Art. 83; *Reinhart,* Art. 83, Rn. 3.
[16] Vgl. *Kröll u. a./Bridge,* Art. 83, Rn. 3; so bereits für das EKG *Dölle/Weitnauer,* vor Artt. 84–87 EKG, Rn. 5 ff. Vgl. zu Einzelfragen oben *Fountoulakis,* Art. 82 Rn. 27 und unten Art. 84 Rn. 10, 13 f., 23, 32.
[17] Dazu oben *Müller-Chen,* Art. 50 Rn. 18.
[18] Dazu oben Art. 82 Rn. 10–12.
[19] So auch *Kröll u. a./Bridge,* Art. 83, Rn. 5.

Art. 84 [Ausgleich von Vorteilen im Falle der Rückabwicklung]

(1) Hat der Verkäufer den Kaufpreis zurückzuzahlen, so hat er außerdem vom Tag der Zahlung an auf den Betrag Zinsen zu zahlen.

(2) Der Käufer schuldet dem Verkäufer den Gegenwert aller Vorteile, die er aus der Ware oder einem Teil der Ware gezogen hat,
a) wenn er die Ware ganz oder teilweise zurückgeben muß oder
b) wenn es ihm unmöglich ist, die Ware ganz oder teilweise zurückzugeben oder sie ganz oder teilweise im wesentlichen in dem Zustand zurückzugeben, in dem er sie erhalten hat, er aber dennoch die Aufhebung des Vertrages erklärt oder vom Verkäufer Ersatzlieferung verlangt hat.

Art. 84

(1) If the seller is bound to refund the price, he must also pay interest on it, from the date on which the price was paid.

(2) The buyer must account to the seller for all benefits which he has derived from the goods or part of them:
(a) if he must make restitution of the goods or part of them; or
(b) if it is impossible for him to make restitution of all or part of the goods or to make restitution of all or part of the goods substantially in the condition in which he received them, but he has nevertheless declared the contract avoided or required the seller to deliver substitute goods.

Art. 84

1) Si le vendeur est tenu de restituer le prix, il doit aussi payer des intérêts sur le montant de ce prix à compter du jour du paiement.

2) L'acheteur doit au vendeur l'équivalent de tout profit qu'il a retiré des marchandises ou d'une partie de celles-ci:
a) lorsqu'il doit les restituer en tout ou en partie; ou
b) lorsqu'il est dans l'impossibilité de restituer tout ou partie des marchandises ou de les restituer en tout ou en partie dans un état sensiblement identique à celui dans lequel il les a reçues et que néanmoins il a déclaré le contrat résolu ou a exigé du vendeur la livraison de marchandises de remplacement.

Übersicht

	Rn.
I. Vorgeschichte	1
1. Zinsregel, Abs. 1	1
2. Vorteilsausgleichung, Abs. 2	4
II. Normzweck und Anwendungsbereich	5
1. Ergänzung der Rückabwicklung	5
2. Anwendungsbereich	7
3. Geldansprüche/Verrechnung	9
4. Ausschluss nationalen Rückabwicklungsrechts	10
III. Verzinsung des Kaufpreises, Abs. 1	11
1. Pflicht des Verkäufers	11
a) Allgemeines	11
b) Verzinsung „vom Tag der Zahlung an"	12
c) Ende der Verzinsungspflicht	12a
2. Verhältnis zum Schadenersatz	13
a) Grundsatz	13
b) Berührungspunkte	14
3. Berechnung der Zinsen	15
a) Zinssatz am Ort der Niederlassung des Verkäufers	15
b) Abstrakte Zinsberechnung	20
4. Währung	20a
5. Über die Verzinsung hinausgehender Ausgleich für Geldentwertung	21
IV. Begleitende Vorteilsausgleichung, Abs. 2 Lit. a)	22
1. Vorteile	22
2. Früchte der Sache als Vorteil	25

     3. Gebrauchsvorteile 26
     4. Nutzungskosten, Aufwendungen 27
        a) Grundsatz 27
        b) Abzugsfähige Kosten 28
           aa) Allgemeines 28
           bb) Notwendige Aufwendungen 29
           cc) Luxuriöse Aufwendungen 30
           dd) Nützliche Aufwendungen 31
     5. Komplementärwirkung von Rückabwicklungs- und Schadensersatzregeln
        im CISG 32
     6. Nicht gezogene Nutzungen 33
  V. Vorteilsausgleichung durch Surrogat für die Sache, Abs. 2 lit. b) 34
     1. Vorteil als Surrogat 34
     2. Vorteilsausgleichung durch commodum ex re 35
     3. Vorteilsausgleichung durch commodum ex negotiatione 36
        a) Wertersatz 36
        b) Nettoerlös 38
        c) Bei fehlendem Surrogat 39
 VI. Beweislast 40

Vorläufer und **Entwürfe:** Art. 81 EKG; Genfer E 1976 Art. 54; Wiener E 1977 Art. 55; New Yorker E 1978 Art. 69.

I. Vorgeschichte

1. Zinsregel, Abs. 1

Die Entstehungsgeschichte von Art. 84 I steht in unmittelbarem Zusammenhang mit der **1** allgemeinen Zinsvorschrift des **Art. 78**.[1] Während die **Artt. 81, 83 EKG** und die ersten Entwürfe zum CISG noch allgemeine und feste Regeln für die Zinsberechnung vorsahen,[2] fanden sich entsprechende Vorschriften im Wiener E 1977 nicht mehr,[3] sodass nur noch die allgemeine Zinspflicht im Rahmen der Rückabwicklung vorgesehen war.[4] Seitdem fanden die Diskussionen um eine allgemeine Verzugszinspflicht einerseits[5] und die Verzinsung des Kaufpreises bei Rückabwicklung andererseits[6] getrennt statt. Die in die Kompromisslösung[7] des Art. 78 mündenden Diskussionen[8] basierten zum Einen auf grundsätzlichen Vorbehalten gegen Zinspflichten in islamisch geprägten Staaten,[9] zum Anderen auf Vorbehalten gegen den Basiszinssatz des Gläubigersitzes als Bemessungsgrundlage, wobei der Streit darüber, ob die Kreditkosten im Land des Schuldners oder des Gläubigers massgebend sein sollten,[10] von

---

[1] Vgl. oben *Bacher,* Art. 78 Rn. 1 ff.
[2] Allerdings gab es bereits hier erste Vorbehalte, vgl. YB VII (1976), S. 136 f., Art. 58.
[3] Vgl. Artt. 55 Wiener E, 69 New Yorker E; zur Diskussion, die zur Streichung von Art. 58 Genfer E führte, YB VIII (1977), S. 58, Art. 54, Nr. 468 f.; S. 60, Art. 58, Nr. 492 ff.
[4] *Schlechtriem,* Einheitliches UN-Kaufrecht, S. 93.
[5] Vgl. O. R., S. 223, Art. 73, Nr. 51 ff.; S. 415 ff.
[6] Vgl. O. R., S. 137 f., Art. 69, Nr. 1 ff.; S. 388 ff.
[7] Vgl. oben *Bacher,* Art. 78 Rn. 2; *Schlechtriem,* Einheitliches UN-Kaufrecht, S. 94; *Enderlein/Maskow/Strohbach,* Art. 78, Anm. 1.
[8] Vgl. im Einzelnen *Bacher,* Art. 78 Rn. 2 und O.R., S. 137 f., Art. 69, Nr. 1 ff. mit verschiedenen Vorschlägen zu einer Regelung; vgl. auch S. 223 ff., Art. 73, Nr. 51 ff.; S. 388 ff.; S. 415 ff.; S. 429 f., Art. 73, Nr. 70 ff. und schon zuvor YB VIII (1977), S. 60, Art. 58, Nr. 492 ff.
[9] So von Ägypten und Irak, vgl. O.R., S. 416, Art. 73, Nr. 10 und S. 418, Art. 73, Nr. 20.
[10] *Enderlein/Maskow/Strohbach,* Art. 78, Anm. 1.; *Schlechtriem,* Einheitliches UN-Kaufrecht, S. 93; *ders.,* Gemeinsame Bestimmungen, S. 171; in dieser Hinsicht bestand schon Streit wegen der Verweisung auf Art. 83 EKG in Art. 81 EKG. *Dölle/Weitnauer,* Art. 81 EKG, Rn. 3 sahen für die Zinsberechnung den Ort der Niederlassung des Käufers als des Gläubigers als massgeblich an, während *Mertens/Rehbinder,* Art. 81 EKG, Rn. 3 den Ort der Niederlassung des Verkäufers gelten lassen wollten; vgl. dazu auch *U. Huber,* RabelsZ 43 (1979), 413, 494.

handfesten Interessen einiger sozialistischer Länder an effektiver Devisenbeschaffung geprägt war.[11]

2   **Art. 83 EKG,** der die Verzugszinspflicht **schadensersatzrechtlich** begründete,[12] schien für die Rückabwicklung nicht zu passen,[13] gerade hinsichtlich der Entlastungsmöglichkeit des Art. 79.[14] Andere wiederum stellten darauf ab, dass entgangene Kapitalnutzung gerade als Schadensersatz geltend gemacht werden könne.[15]

3   Es verwundert angesichts der höchst unterschiedlichen Ausgangspositionen nicht, dass eine Einigung über eine **Berechnungsgrundlage** für Zinsen **nicht erzielt** werden konnte,[16] und die Kompromissformeln der Artt. 78 und 84 I stellen gegenüber dem englischen Vorschlag, die Zinsfrage ganz dem nationalen Recht zu überlassen,[17] bereits einen beachtlichen Fortschritt dar.

2. Vorteilsausgleichung, Abs. 2

4   Die Regelung der Vorteilsausgleichung folgt weitgehend **Art. 81 II EKG,** nur dass in Abs. 2 lit. b) die **Ersatzlieferung** einbezogen wurde.[18] Auch glich man die späteren Artt. 82 und 84 II lit. b) einander sprachlich an.[19]

II. Normzweck und Anwendungsbereich

1. Ergänzung der Rückabwicklung

5   Art. 84 ist (notwendiger) Bestandteil der Rückabwicklungsregeln.[20] Er regelt die Pflicht der Parteien, sich gegenseitig die Vorteile zu erstatten, die ihnen durch den vorübergehenden Leistungsaustausch zufielen. Die Parteien sollen wirtschaftlich in den Zustand ohne Austausch der Leistungen zurückversetzt werden.[21] Abs. 1 auferlegt deshalb dem Verkäufer die Pflicht, den empfangenen Kaufpreis vom Tag der Zahlung an zu **verzinsen.** Abs. 2 betrifft die Pflicht des Käufers, die **Vorteile zu vergüten,** die er aus der Ware gezogen hat. Abs. 2 lit. a) nimmt dabei auf den Fall der tatsächlichen (ganzen oder teilweisen)[22] Rückgewähr der Sache Bezug. Abs. 2 lit. b) betrifft die Fälle, in denen es dem Käufer unmöglich ist, die Sache unversehrt zurückzugeben, aber die Rückabwicklung dennoch statthaft ist.[23]

6   Den Regeln der Vorteilsausgleichung kann entnommen werden, dass das Ziel der Rückabwicklung grundsätzlich nicht nur durch Sachleistung, sondern auch durch Surrogat und Ausgleichsleistungen in Geld zu erreichen ist, sodass der Abstand zur Abwicklung mit einem Wertersatz- oder Schadensersatzanspruch verringert wird. Art. 84 ist **gegenüber** den **Scha-**

---

[11] *Schlechtriem*, Einheitliches UN-Kaufrecht, S. 94; *ders.*, Gemeinsame Bestimmungen, S. 171; vgl. auch *Enderlein/Maskow/Strohbach*, Art. 78, Anm. 1.
[12] Nicht unbestritten: vgl. dazu näher *Dölle/Weitnauer*, Art. 81 EKG, Rn. 3.
[13] *Bianca/Bonell/Nicholas*, Art. 78, Anm. 1.4.
[14] *Schlechtriem*, Einheitliches UN-Kaufrecht, S. 93; *ders.*, Gemeinsame Bestimmungen, S. 170 ff.; *Enderlein/Maskow/Strohbach*, Art. 78, Anm. 2.1.; *Neumayer/Ming*, Art. 84, Anm. 2.
[15] Vgl. O. R., S. 137 f., Art. 69, Nr. 4 a. E.; S. 223, Art. 73, Nr. 51 und die nachfolgende Diskussion; dazu *Schlechtriem*, Einheitliches UN-Kaufrecht, S. 93; *Honnold/Flechtner*, Art. 78, Rn. 420 ff.; *Bianca/Bonell/Nicholas*, Art. 78, Anm. 1.4.
[16] *Enderlein/Maskow/Strohbach*, Art. 78, Anm. 1.; *Bianca/Bonell/Nicholas*, Art. 78, Anm. 1.3.; *Schlechtriem*, Einheitliches UN-Kaufrecht, S. 93 f.
[17] Vgl. *Honnold/Flechtner*, Art. 78, Rn. 420 f.; *Bianca/Bonell/Nicholas*, Art. 78, Anm. 1.4.; O. R., S. 137 f., Art. 69, Nr. 4 a. E.
[18] YB V (1974), S. 44, Art. 81, Nr. 156.
[19] YB VII (1976), S. 133, Art. 54, Nr. 3.
[20] *Honnold/Flechtner*, Art. 84, Rn. 451.1; *Leser*, Vertragsaufhebung und Rückabwicklung, S. 248.
[21] MünchKommHGB/*Benicke*, Art. 84, Rn. 1; MünchKomm/*P. Huber*, Art. 84, Rn. 1.
[22] Zur Teilrückabwicklung vgl. oben *Fountoulakis*, Vor Artt. 81–84 Rn. 8; Art. 81 Rn. 14.
[23] Die Frage wird einzig relevant bei Aufhebung durch den Käufer. Bei Aufhebung durch den Verkäufer bzw. einvernehmlicher Vertragsaufhebung stellt sich die Frage, ob der Käufer die Ware in natura zurückgeben kann, nicht, vgl. oben *Fountoulakis*, Art. 82 Rn. 28 ff.

densersatzregeln selbstständig, weist aber freilich Schnitt- und Berührungspunkte dazu auf.[24] Diese werden bedeutsam, wenn, wie regelmässig, Rückabwicklung und Schadensersatz kumuliert werden, aber auch wenn der Schadensersatzanspruch gemäss Art. 79 blockiert ist.[25]

2. Anwendungsbereich

Art. 84 findet ausdrückliche Anwendung bei Vertragsaufhebung durch den **Käufer**[26] sowie bei blosser Teilaufhebung.[27] Für die Ersatzlieferung gilt Art. 84 II lit. b) ausdrücklich;[28] abgesehen von lit. b) wird Art. 84 bei Ausüben des Ersatzlieferungsanspruchs kaum relevant: Der Käufer zahlt den Kaufpreis bei Ersatzlieferung nicht zurück, so dass Abs. 1 gar nicht zum Zuge kommt. Im Falle des Abs. 2 lit. a) dürfte es nur selten zu Gebrauchsvorteilen der (mangelhaften) Ware kommen, die der Käufer herausgeben müsste.[29] Allerdings sollte der Käufer doch Ausgleich leisten müssen, wenn und soweit die Nacherfüllung zu einer Wertverbesserung führt.[30] Für die Vertragsaufhebung durch den **Verkäufer** ist die Anwendbarkeit von Art. 84 nicht explizit geregelt, doch rechtfertigt sie sich hier erst recht:[31] Muss der Käufer ausdrücklich (auch) dann Vorteile ausgleichen, wenn die Vertragsverletzung durch den Verkäufer verursacht worden ist (vgl. Art. 84 II lit. b)), so muss die Anordnung des Vorteilsausgleichs umso mehr gelten, wenn es der Käufer ist, der den Grund für die Aufhebung gesetzt hat.

Fraglich ist schliesslich, ob Art. 84 bei **einvernehmlicher Vertragsaufhebung** anzuwenden ist. Dies ist grundsätzlich zu bejahen,[32] wenn Art. 84 auch oft parteiautonom abgewandelt oder ausgeschlossen werden dürfte. Insbesondere wenn die Parteien mit der einvernehmlichen Aufhebung eine Per-Saldo-Lösung herbeiführen wollten, wird von einem stillschweigenden Ausschluss des Art. 84 auszugehen sein.

3. Geldansprüche/Verrechnung

Art. 84 gewährt sowohl hinsichtlich der Zinsen in Abs. 1 wie auch hinsichtlich der Vorteilsausgleichung in Abs. 2 jeweils **nur Geldansprüche**.[33] Stehen sich Ansprüche des Käufers, etwa auf Rückzahlung von Kaufpreis und Zinsen, und Geldansprüche des Verkäufers auf begleitende Vorteilsausgleichung oder als Surrogat gegenüber, so können diese

---

[24] Dazu bereits *Leser,* Vertragsaufhebung und Rückabwicklung, S. 251 f.
[25] Vgl. unten Rn. 32.
[26] Vgl. den Wortlaut in Art. 84 II: „Der Käufer schuldet [...] den Gegenwert aller Vorteile b) wenn [...] er [...] die Aufhebung des Vertrages erklärt [...] hat"; vgl. auch YB VII (1976), S. 133, Art. 54, Nr. 1; Sekretariatskommentar, Art. 69, Nr. 1; *Enderlein/Maskow/Strohbach,* Art. 84, Anm. 1.; *Jan,* S. 222; *Honnold/Flechtner,* Art. 84, Rn. 451 und 451.1.
[27] Vgl. den Wortlaut in Art. 84 II: „[...] a) wenn er die Ware ganz oder teilweise zurückgeben muss oder b) wenn es ihm unmöglich ist, die Ware ganz oder teilweise zurückzugeben oder sie ganz oder teilweise im Wesentlichen in dem Zustand zurückzugeben [...]". Vgl. auch *Schlechtriem,* Einheitliches UN-Kaufrecht, S. 102; *Enderlein/Maskow/Strohbach,* Art. 81, Anm. 8.
[28] Art. 84 II: „[...] lit. b) wenn [...] er [...] vom Verkäufer Ersatzlieferung verlangt hat".
[29] Vgl. auch *Enderlein/Maskow/Strohbach,* Art. 84, Anm. 5.2. („kaum praktische Bedeutung"); ähnl. *Honsell/Weber,* Art. 84, Rn. 5, 12; unklar *Staudinger/Magnus* (vgl. Art. 84, Rn. 14 einerseits und Rn. 20 andererseits).
[30] Siehe das von *Schlechtriem,* Internationales UN-Kaufrecht, Rn. 322, angeführte Beispiel eines als Ersatz gelieferten LKWs, dessen Wert von Bau- und Modelljahr abhängt und erheblich höher liegen kann als der des zurückzugebenden Fahrzeugs. A. A. MünchKomm/*P. Huber,* Art. 84, Rn. 11; *Soergel/Lüderitz/Dettmeier,* Art. 84, Rn. 3: keine Anwendung von Art. 84 II lit. a) auf die Ersatzlieferung.
[31] Vgl. OLG Karlsruhe, 14.2.2008, CISG-online 1649, E. II.3. = IHR 2008, 53; so auch *Staudinger/Magnus,* Art. 84, Rn. 25; *Honsell/Weber,* Art. 84, Rn. 6; MünchKomm/*P. Huber,* Art. 84, Rn. 20; MünchKomm/*Benicke,* Art. 82, Rn. 21; *Enderlein/Maskow/Strohbach,* Art. 84, Anm. 1., vgl. auch *Ferrari u. a./Ferrari,* Internationales Vertragsrecht, Art. 84, Rn. 4; *Brunner,* Art. 84, Rn. 2, 10.
[32] Anders die 4. Aufl. in Rn. 8: Anwendung von Art. 84 auf vertragliche Aufhebungsrechte und die einvernehmliche Vertragsaufhebung nur, soweit Art. 82 II anwendbar sei; ebenso *Enderlein/Maskow/Strohbach,* Vorbem. zu Art. 81, Anm. 4. und Art. 84, Anm. 6.; *Bianca/Bonell/Tallon,* Art. 84, Anm. 2.2.; wie hier *Schlechtriem,* Internationales UN-Kaufrecht, Rn. 323; *Staudinger/Magnus,* Art. 84, Rn. 25; *Brunner,* Art. 84, Rn. 2, 10; MünchKomm/*P. Huber,* Art. 84, Rn. 2.
[33] *Enderlein/Maskow/Strohbach,* Art. 84, Anm. 4.2.; *Leser,* Vertragsaufhebung und Rückabwicklung, S. 250; *Soergel/Lüderitz/Dettmeier,* Art. 84, Rn. 5.

verrechnet werden.³⁴ Entsprechend den Grundsätzen der Rückabwicklung hat die Zahlung der Zinsen ebenso wie die Rückgewähr des Kaufpreises am **Ort der Niederlassung des Käufers** zu erfolgen.³⁵

4. Ausschluss nationalen Rückabwicklungsrechts

10 Neben Art. 84 ist das Heranziehen nationaler Regeln über den Vorteilsausgleich ausgeschlossen.³⁶ Art. 84, gerade auch in Kombination mit den Schadensersatzvorschriften in Artt. 74, 77, 79, regelt die Frage des Vorteilsausgleichs bei der Rückabwicklung abschliessend.

III. Verzinsung des Kaufpreises, Abs. 1

1. Pflicht des Verkäufers

11 a) **Allgemeines.** Bei Aufhebung des Vertrages und der daraus gemäss Art. 81 II folgenden Pflicht des Verkäufers, den bereits empfangenen (Teil-)Kaufpreis zurückzuzahlen, muss der Verkäufer diesen vom Tag der Zahlung an zudem verzinsen.

12 b) **Verzinsung „vom Tag der Zahlung an".** Unter „Zahlung" ist der **Zeitpunkt des Empfangs** des Bar- oder Buchgeldes zu verstehen.³⁷ Nach anderer Ansicht solle es auf den Zeitpunkt ankommen, an dem die Zahlung im Sinne des Art. 58 erfolgte, unabhängig davon, ob der Verkäufer schon ab diesem Zeitpunkt tatsächlich über das Geld verfügen konnte oder nicht, da es nicht auf die konkrete, sondern die typisierte Möglichkeit der Zinserzielung durch den Verkäufer ankomme.³⁸ Diese Meinung verkennt freilich, dass Art. 84 I die Möglichkeit der Zinserlangung bereits dadurch typisiert, dass unabhängig davon, ob und wie der Verkäufer den erhaltenen Kaufpreis nutzte, eine Verzinsungspflicht besteht. Eine weitergehende Typisierung ist nicht gerechtfertigt. Der Zeitpunkt der effektiv empfangenen Zahlung lässt sich, nicht zuletzt, auch leichter beweisen (vgl. die u. U. schwer nachzuweisenden Konstellationen in Art. 58 II, III).

12a c) **Ende der Verzinsungspflicht.** Zinsen nach Art. 84 I sind geschuldet bis zum Zeitpunkt, in dem der Verkäufer den Kaufpreis **zurückerstattet**.³⁹ Dies folgt aus dem Art. 84 I zugrundeliegenden Gedanken der Vorteilsausgleichung.⁴⁰

---

³⁴ CISG-AC, Op. 9 Bridge, Opinion 3.3; *Kröll u. a./Bridge,* Art. 84, Rn. 3; LG Mönchengladbach, 15.7.2003, CISG-online 813, E. II.2 = IHR 2003, 229.

³⁵ Oben *Fountoulakis,* Art. 81 Rn. 24.

³⁶ So auch *Schlechtriem,* Internationales UN-Kaufrecht, Rn. 332; *Herber/Czerwenka,* Art. 84, Rn. 8; *Schmidt-Ahrendts,* IHR 2006, 67, 69; vgl. dazu bereits oben Art. 81 Rn. 10 sowie unten Rn. 32; a. A. *Neumayer/Ming,* Art. 84, Anm. 1., 3., die lediglich, wenn das nationale Rückabwicklungsrecht keinen Anspruch auf Herausgabe der Sache in natura gibt, über Art. 84 II vorgehen wollen.

³⁷ Vgl. Com., 11.5.2010, CISG-online 2184; CA Lyon, 18.9.2008, CISG-online 2209; Int. Ct. Russian CCI, 28.5.2004, CISG-online 1513, E. 3.5; Int. Ct. Russian CCI, 19.5.2004, CISG-online 1358, E. 3.6; RB Kortrijk, 4.6.2004, CISG-online 945; OLG Düsseldorf, 28.5.2004, CISG-online 850 = IHR 2004, 203; RB Zwolle, 22.1.2003, CISG-online 1023, E. 3.18; LG Dresden, 29.5.2009, CISG-online 2174, E. II.4.; CISG-AC, Op. 9 Bridge, Opinion 3.5, Comment 3.24; *Kröll u. a./Bridge,* Art. 84, Rn 10; MünchKomm/*P. Huber,* Art. 84, Rn. 5; *Piltz,* Internationales Kaufrecht, Rn. 5–320; *Bamberger/Roth/Saenger,* Art. 84, Rn. 2; *Herber/ Czerwenka,* Art. 84, Rn. 3; *Krebs,* S. 61; *Achilles,* Art. 84, Rn. 2; *Staudinger/Magnus,* Art. 84, Rn. 8; *Brunner,* Art. 84, Rn. 3.

³⁸ *Enderlein/Maskow/Strohbach,* Art. 84, Anm. 2.; *Witz/Salger/Lorenz/Salger,* Art. 84, Rn. 2; *Honsell/Weber,* Art. 84, Rn. 7; MünchKommHGB/*Benicke,* Art. 84, Rn. 6; *Ferrari u. a./Ferrari,* Internationales Vertragsrecht, Art. 84, Rn. 6. Vereinzelt geblieben ist die Auffassung, dass erst der Tag der Vertragsaufhebung als entscheidend für die Verzinsung anzusehen ist: (ital.) Pretura di Parma-Fidenza, 24.11.1989, CISG-online 316 = SZIER 1996, 49.

³⁹ Vgl. Tribunal of International Commercial Arbitration at the Russian Federation Chamber of Commerce and Industry, 1/1993, 15.4.1994, CISG-online 449; Pretura di Parma-Fidenza, 24.11.1989, CISG-online 316; a. A. Tribunal of International Commercial Arbitration at the Russian Federation Chamber of Commerce and Industry, 100/2002, 19.5.2004, CISG-online 1358 (Zinsen bis zu Einreichen der Klage geschuldet).

⁴⁰ Oben Rn. 5 sowie unten 16.

2. Verhältnis zum Schadenersatz

a) Grundsatz. Die Einbeziehung von Zinsen in die Rückabwicklung betont die Selbstständigkeit der Rückabwicklung gegenüber dem Schadenersatz.[41] Die Zinsen nach Art. 84 I sind nicht als Schadenersatz anzusehen, sondern als Vorteilsausgleichung.[42] Der Verkäufer konnte den empfangenen Betrag nutzen und mit ihm arbeiten, ohne dass ihm nach Aufhebung des Vertrages dieser Vorteil noch zusteht.[43] Aus der **Selbstständigkeit des Zinsanspruchs** in Art. 84 I folgt, dass eine Entlastung gem. Art. 79 hierfür nicht in Betracht kommt.[44] Dies lässt sich bereits aus Art. 79 V und dem Vorbehalt des Schadenersatzes in Art. 78 beim allgemeinen Zinsanspruch[45] ableiten. 13

b) Berührungspunkte. Überschneidungen zum Schadenersatzrecht können sich freilich dennoch ergeben: Art. 81 I sieht bei Vertragsaufhebung den Fortbestand bereits entstandener Schadenersatzansprüche ausdrücklich vor. Art. 74 als allgemeine Schadensersatzformel ist dabei so weit gefasst, dass er auch Zinsansprüche umfassen kann.[46] Ob nun ein Zinsanspruch unter Artt. 84, 78 oder 74 fällt, ist eine Frage der **Abgrenzung, die im Sinne der Spezialität vorzunehmen ist.** Zinsen auf den Kaufpreis werden primär nach vertraglicher Abmachung, ansonsten nach Art. 84 I berechnet. War der Käufer aber gezwungen, einen höher verzinslichen Kredit in Anspruch zu nehmen, so ist diese Position im Rahmen des Schadenersatzes für den über Art. 84 I hinausgehenden Teil zu berücksichtigen.[47] In diesen Fällen liegt dann ein weitergehender, ergänzender Schadenersatzanspruch vor. 14

3. Berechnung der Zinsen

a) Zinssatz am Ort der Niederlassung des Verkäufers. Höhe und Modalität der Berechnung der Zinsen sind im Übereinkommen offengelassen worden.[48] Rechtsprechung und Literatur bieten insbesondere zu Art. 78 höchst unterschiedliche Lösungsansätze an, welche entweder an den nationalen Rechten anknüpfen oder aber auf allgemeinen Grundsätzen des CISG beruhen („Einheitslösung").[49] Dieselben Lösungsansätze, die zu Art. 78 angeboten werden, finden sich auch im Rahmen der Diskussion zur Zinshöhe in Art. 84 I.[50] Klarheit und Kontinuität kann jedenfalls einzig eine **einheitliche Kollisionsnorm** 15

---

[41] Vgl. dazu oben *Fountoulakis*, Vor Artt. 81–84 Rn. 9 f.
[42] Vgl. oben Rn. 5 f.
[43] So auch *Bianca/Bonell/Tallon*, Art. 84, Anm. 2.1.; *Staudinger/Magnus*, Art. 78, Rn. 11.
[44] *Piltz*, Internationales Kaufrecht, Rn. 5–320; MünchKomm/*P. Huber*, Art. 84, Rn. 2.
[45] *Enderlein/Maskow/Strohbach*, Art. 78, Anm. 2.1.; *Schlechtriem*, Internationales UN-Kaufrecht, Rn. 319; *Stoll*, Internationalprivatrechtliche Fragen, S. 510.
[46] Art. 74 verlangt nur einen durch die Vertragsverletzung entstandenen Verlust, worunter auch Kreditkosten etc. fallen können. Art. 78 gewährt einen Zinsanspruch, soweit fällige Beträge nicht bezahlt werden, und Art. 84 I gibt dem Käufer nach Aufhebung den Zinsanspruch für den vom Verkäufer zurückzuzahlenden Kaufpreis. Damit können Zinsen auf drei Stufen erfasst werden.
[47] In diesem Sinne *Enderlein/Maskow/Strohbach*, Art. 78, Anm. 1. und 2.1.; *Vilus*, Provisions, S. 252; *Schlechtriem*, Einheitliches UN-Kaufrecht, S. 102, Fn. 449; MünchKomm/*P. Huber*, Art. 84, Rn. 6; *Brunner*, Art. 84, Rn. 4; *Ferrari u. a./Ferrari*, Internationales Vertragsrecht, Art. 84, Rn. 8. Für einen umfassenden Schadenersatzanspruch (der sich allein auf Art. 74 stützt) *Herber*, Einführung, S. 46; *Vischer*, Gemeinsame Bestimmungen, S. 182, der im Verzugsfall den Zins insgesamt als Schadenersatz ansehen will, dessen Höhe sich im Zweifel nach den Kreditkosten des Gläubigers richten soll. Demgegenüber findet nach der hier vertretenen Auffassung eine Einordnung der Zinsen in zwei Stufen statt, üblicher Zins und darüber hinausgehender Schaden. Dabei ist in Kauf zu nehmen, dass zwei verschiedene Bezugspunkte zu benutzen sind. Ein Argument für die Spaltung ergibt sich aus der Entlastungsmöglichkeit des Art. 79, der nur für den Schadenersatz gilt, vgl. Rn. 13.
[48] Vgl. zur Entstehungsgeschichte oben Rn. 1–3.
[49] Vgl. hierzu den Überblick oben bei *Bacher*, Art. 78 Rn. 26–39.
[50] Insbesondere bestimmen nach wie vor etliche (Schieds-)Gerichte die Zinshöhe im Rahmen des Art. 84 I nach dem Vertragsstatut: OLG Celle, 24.5.1995, CISG-online 152; Int. Ct. Russian CCI, 28.5.2004, CISG-online 1513, E. 3.5; Int. Ct. Russian CCI, 16.4.2003, CISG-online 1682, E. 3.3.2; Schiedsgericht der Hamburger freundlichen Arbitrage, 29.12.1998, CISG-online 638 = CLOUT Nr. 299 = RIW 1999, 394; KG Schaffhausen, 27.1.2004, CISG-online 960, E. 4. b) = SZIER 2005, 120; LG Freiburg, 22.8.2002, CISG-

herbeiführen,[51] wie sie sich aus dem Grundgedanken des Art. 84 I durchaus entwickeln lässt.

16   Für die Verzinsungspflicht im Rahmen von Art. 84 müssen die Besonderheiten beim Rückabwicklungsverhältnis im Auge behalten werden. Dazu ist zunächst erforderlich, die Diskussion um den anwendbaren Zinssatz in Art. 78 und denjenigen in Art. 84 I auseinander zu halten: Art. 78 befasst sich mit der Verzinsungspflicht fälliger Beträge. Die englische Fassung macht mit „sum that is in arrears" die Bezugnahme auf „verspätete" Beträge deutlich. Art. 78 findet also Anwendung bei Spätzahlung und damit bei Vertragsverletzung des Geldschuldners. Art. 84 I hingegen liegt der **Gedanke der Vorteilsausgleichung** zugrunde: Der Verkäufer soll einen – ggf. fingierten – Vorteil, den er durch den Erhalt und die Nutzung des Kaufpreises erhalten hat, auskehren, und zwar unabhängig davon, von welcher Partei die Vertragsverletzung, die zur Aufhebung geführt hat, herbeigeführt worden ist. Die Verzinsungspflicht des Art. 84 I hat demnach „bereicherungsrechtlichen" Charakter, der von der Frage, ob die Rückzahlung verspätet erfolgte, klar abzugrenzen ist. Deshalb ist die Frage des Zinssatzes bei Artt. 78 und 84 I getrennt zu behandeln.[52]

17   Entscheidend ist bei Art. 84 I, dass der Verkäufer den Kaufpreis erhielt und diesen für weitere Geschäfte nutzen konnte. Er hatte einen Geldbetrag zur Verfügung, den er sonst nicht gehabt hätte und für den er gegebenenfalls einen Kredit hätte aufnehmen müssen. Die Nutzungsmöglichkeit besteht im Verkäuferstaat, deshalb ist für die Zinsberechnung am Sitz des verpflichteten Verkäufers anzuknüpfen. Haben die Parteien keinen Zinssatz vereinbart,[53] ist folglich der **übliche Zinssatz am Ort der Niederlassung des Verkäufers** massgeblich.[54] Hier bestand die – wenn auch abstrakte – Möglichkeit zur Nutzung, die auszugleichen ist.

18   **Andere Anknüpfungen,** die in diesem Zusammenhang vorgeschlagen werden, werden dem Grundgedanken des Art. 84 I nicht gerecht. Der Gedanke etwa, dass dem Käufer der Zins am Ort seiner Niederlassung gebührt, weil er ihn während der entsprechenden Zeit hätte selbst erzielen können,[55] knüpft nicht an die Vorteilsausgleichung an, sondern hat

---

online 711 = IHR 2003, 22; Tribunale di Forlì, 11.12.2008, CISG-online 1729 = 1788 E. 4.. Auch ein wesentlicher Teil der Lehre spricht sich für die Heranziehung des über das IPR berufenen nationalen Rechts (Vertragsstatut bzw. Währungsstatut) aus, da das Abstellen auf eine materielle Sonderanknüpfung ein Mindestmass an Einigkeit zwischen den Verfassern des CISG voraussetze, das es niemals gegeben habe: *Bianca/Bonell/Tallon,* Art. 84, Anm. 2.1.; *Staudinger/Magnus,* Art. 84, Rn. 9; *Soergel/Lüderitz/Dettmeier,* Art. 84, Rn. 2; *Ferrari u. a./Ferrari,* Internationales Vertragsrecht, Art. 84, Rn. 7; *Herber/Czerwenka,* Art. 84, Rn. 3; *Enderlein/Maskow/Strohbach,* Art. 84, Anm. 3.; *Reinhart,* Art. 84, Rn. 3; *Schlechtriem,* Internationales UN-Kaufrecht, Rn. 318; *ders.,* RIW, 1995, 592, 593; *Ferrari u. a./Ferrari,* Internationales Vertragsrecht, Art. 84, Rn. 7; *Achilles,* Art. 84, Rn. 2; *Witz/Salger/Lorenz/Salger,* Art. 84, Rn. 2; MünchKomm/*P. Huber,* Art. 84, Rn. 6.
[51] Dazu auch *Lando,* Private International Law, S. 118; *Kröll u. a./Bridge,* Art. 84, Rn. 12; vgl. auch *Gabriel,* Contracts, S. 252.
[52] Vgl. zum Ganzen *Corterier,* Pace Int'l L. Rev. 2004, 1, 6 f.; *López Rodríguez,* 2 Nordic J. Com. L. 2005, Text bei Fn. 22; vgl. auch *Honnold/Flechtner,* Art. 84, Rn. 451.2, 452 a. E.
[53] Vgl. Int. Ct. Russian CCI, 16.6.2003, CISG-online 977, E. 3.4: Vereinbarung eines Zinssatzes von 3.25%.
[54] Sekretariatskommentar, Art. 69, Nr. 2; CISG-AC, Op. 9 Bridge, Opinion 3.4, Comment 3.27; *Bamberger/Roth/Saenger,* Art. 84, Rn. 3; *Honsell/Weber,* Art. 84, Rn. 10; *Hornung,* S. 330; *Vischer,* Gemeinsame Bestimmungen, S. 173, 182; *Neumayer/Ming,* Art. 84, Anm. 2.; *Kröll u. a./Bridge,* Art. 84, Rn. 11; *Piltz,* Internationales Kaufrecht, Rn. 5–321; *Audit,* Anm. 194.; *Brunner,* Art. 84, Rn. 3; *Corterier,* Pace Int'l L. Rev. 2004, 1, 16 f.; *López Rodríguez,* 2 Nordic J. Com. L. (2005), bei Fn. 22; *Tacheva,* Vertragsaufgebung, S. 217; vorsichtiger *Reinhart,* Art. 84, Rn. 3 und Art. 78, Rn. 5 („praktikabel"); *Enderlein/Maskow/Strohbach,* Art. 84, Anm. 2. („akzeptabel"); s. auch *Magnus,* ZEuP 1993, 79, 90, mit Nachweisen aus der Rechtsprechung in Fn. 66. Aus der Rspr. etwa OLG München, 8.2.1995, CISG-online 143; HGer Zürich, 5.2.1997, CISG-online 327 = CLOUT Nr. 214 = SZIER 1998, 75 = TranspR-IHR 1999, 12; Int. Ct. Russian CCI, 15.4.1994, CISG-online 449; LG Dresden, 29.5.2009, CISG-online 2174, E. II.4.; AG Sursee, 12.9.2008, E. 7., CISG-online 1728 = IHR 2009, 63. Die Massgeblichkeit der üblichen Zinsen am Ort der Niederlassung des Verkäufers befürworten im Übrigen auch für Art. 78 u. a. *Neumayer/Ming,* Art. 78, Anm. 2.; *Neumayer,* RIW 1994, 99, 106; *Heuzé,* Anm. 464.
[55] Vgl. Tribunal of International Commercial Arbitration at the Russian Federation Chamber of Commerce and Industry, 99/2002, 16.4.2003, CISG-online 1683; CIETAC, 30.11.1998, CISG-online 1281; *Bianca/Bonell/Tallon,* Art. 84, Anm. 2.1.

kompensatorischen Charakter, was allenfalls für den im Rahmen des Schadensersatzes berücksichtigten Zinsanspruch passen mag, nicht jedoch bei Art. 84 I.[56] Einiges für sich hat hingegen der Vorschlag, für die Bestimmung der Zinshöhe an das Währungsstatut anzuknüpfen.[57] Dies wird freilich dann nicht zu einer Lösung führen, wenn eine supranationale Währung wie der Euro vereinbart ist.[58] Ansonsten gelangt man auch bei Anknüpfung an das Währungsstatut zumindest theoretisch[59] meist zu der hier vertretenen Lösung, nämlich zur Anwendung des Zinssatzes am Ort der Niederlassung des Verkäufers.[60] Letztlich jedoch erscheint die **direkte Anknüpfung am Sitz des Verkäufers** für die Zinsberechnung deshalb **vorzugswürdig,** weil der später zurückzugewährende Kaufpreis unabhängig davon, ob er nun in einer harten oder inflationär geprägten Währung geleistet wurde, regelmässig dem Verkäufer in der am Ort seiner Niederlassung geltenden Währung von seinem Kreditinstitut gutgeschrieben wird. Daher vermag (nur) die Zugrundelegung des dortigen Zinsniveaus eine angemessene Vorteilsausgleichung zu erzielen.

Die Verzinsung richtet sich demnach in der Höhe nach den üblichen Zinsen am Ort der Niederlassung des Verkäufers.[61] Sie ist durch Anwendung der einschlägigen **Gesetze** und gegebenenfalls unter Zuhilfenahme des **Handelsbrauchs** zu bestimmen.[62] Im Übrigen ist für die Berechnung der Zinsen auf die Erläuterung zu Art. 78 zu verweisen. 19

b) Abstrakte Zinsberechnung. Der Zinssatz ist mit Rücksicht auf die Praktikabilität 20 der Lösung unabhängig von den Umständen der tatsächlichen Nutzung der empfangenen Geldsumme zu sehen und **abstrakt zu berechnen**.[63] Abzulehnen ist die Auffassung, dass nur die effektiv gezogenen Zinsen zu vergüten seien, mit der Begründung, dass es sich bei dem Ausgleichsanspruch des Art. 84 I dogmatisch um einen Bereicherungsanspruch handle.[64] Das Übereinkommen hat die Verzinsungspflicht an keine weiteren Voraussetzungen geknüpft ausser an die Rückzahlungspflicht des Verkäufers und sich insofern für einen typisierten Vorteilsausgleich entschieden.

---

[56] So aber *Honnold/Flechtner,* Art. 84, Rn. 451.2, für den Fall, dass die Vertragsaufhebung auf einer Vertragsverletzung durch den Verkäufer beruht: Hier solle im Sinne einer Sonderanknüpfung der Zinssatz am Sitz des Käufers herangezogen werden, da schadensersatzrechtlich gedacht und daher auf den Verlust des Käufers abgestellt werden müsse.

[57] Vgl. MünchKommHGB/*Benicke,* Art. 84, Rn. 5, mit der Begründung, da in der Zinshöhe für eine bestimmte Währung oft auch der zu erwartende inflationsbedingte Wertverlust enthalten sei, sei für die Zinshöhe primär die Währung entscheidend. Vgl. auch Art. 7.4.9 PICC, die primär auf den Zinssatz am Leistungsort für die Zahlung, sekundär aber auf denjenigen des Währungsstatuts abstellen.

[58] So auch *Corterier,* Pace Int'l L. Rev. (2004), 1, 8. Daran ändert auch die Zahlungsverzugsrichtlinie (2011/7/EU) nichts, da sie lediglich die Pflicht zur Zahlung von Verzugszinsen und nicht die Zinspflicht im Rahmen der Vorteilsausgleichung regelt. Zudem bestehen trotz der in der Zahlungsverzugsrichtlinie vorgegebenen Mindestsätze weiterhin nationale Abweichungen, so dass erst eine Prüfung sonstiger Bezugspunkte zu einem bestimmten Staat der Euro-Zone für die für die Bestimmung des Zinssatzes relevanten Rechtsordnung führt.

[59] D. h. wenn die Parteien ausnahmsweise keine Vereinbarung über die Währung getroffen haben und diesbezüglich keine Gebräuche oder Gepflogenheiten bestehen.

[60] Vgl. dazu oben *Mohs,* Art. 53 Rn. 5: Anknüpfung an die Währung führt in der Regel zur Währung am Sitz des Verkäufers.

[61] Vgl. die Nachweise in Fn. 54.

[62] In zahlreichen Staaten orientiert sich der gesetzliche Zinssatz am jeweiligen Basiszinssatz, wobei teilweise ein Aufschlag vorgenommen wird. Da die Zinspflicht im Rahmen der Rückabwicklung der Vorteilsausgleichung dient, wird man die Anwendung des Verzugszinssatzes des jeweiligen Staates (vgl. für die Euro-Zone dazu die Mindestzinssätze der Zahlungsverzugsrichtlinie) kaum über Art. 7 II in Art. 84 I hineinlesen können. Allerdings dürfte in Normalfall beim beiderseitigen Handelsgeschäft die „praktische Übung" für die Zinsorientierung am Basiszinssatz sprechen, zumal die Artt. 81, 83 EKG noch ausdrücklich auf diesen abgestellt hatten. Für den Fall, dass am Sitz des Verkäufers ein üblicher Zinssatz ganz fehlt, muss die Bestimmung dem Richter überlassen bleiben, vgl. *Honnold/Flechtner,* Art. 78, Rn. 421. Im Ergebnis übereinstimmend *Schlechtriem,* Gemeinsame Bestimmungen, S. 171, der die Heranziehung von Gebühren und Aufschlägen als funktional einer Verzinsung vergleichbar ansieht; dem folgend *Magnus,* RabelsZ 53 (1989), 116, 141, Fn. 118.

[63] CISG-AC, Op. 9 Bridge, Opinion 3.6; *Kröll u. a./Bridge,* Art. 84, Rn. 11; MünchKomm/*P. Huber,* Art. 84, Rn. 3; *Bamberger/Roth/Saenger,* Art. 84, Rn. 3.

[64] So aber *Honsell/Weber,* Art. 84, Rn. 11; *Honnold/Flechtner,* Art. 84, Rn. 452; *Neumayer/Ming,* Art. 84, Anm. 2.

4. Währung

20a Das Übereinkommen schweigt sich über die Frage, in welcher Währung die Zinsen auf den rückzuerstattenden Kaufpreis zu zahlen sind, aus. Hierbei ist wiederum auf den auf Vorteilsausgleichung bedachten Zweck von Art. 84 I abzustellen. Entsprechend ist die Zinszahlung in der Währung zu verrichten, in der der Verkäufer **die als Kaufpreis erhaltene Summe angelegt** hat. Dies entspricht der Währung, die der Verkäufer seinen geschäftlichen Beziehungen regelmässig zugrunde legt.[65] Im Zweifel ist auf die Währung am Ort der Niederlassung des Verkäufers abzustellen.

5. Über die Verzinsung hinausgehender Ausgleich für Geldentwertung

21 Die Verzinsung des zu restituierenden Kaufpreises wird regelmässig, aber nicht immer die zwischen Vertragsschluss und Vertragsaufhebung eingetretenen Binnen- oder Aussenwertverluste (Inflation bzw. Wechselkursschwankungen) auffangen. Reicht die Verzinsung ausnahmsweise zur gänzlichen Schadloshaltung des vertragstreuen Käufers nicht aus, so kann er nach Rechtsprechung[66] und Schrifttum[67] den Ausgleich des durch die Geldentwertung entstandenen Schadens über die **Artt. 45 I lit. b), 74** verlangen.

IV. Begleitende Vorteilsausgleichung, Abs. 2 Lit. a)

1. Vorteile

22 Der Käufer schuldet dem Verkäufer, wenn er die Sache gemäss Art. 81 zurückgibt oder wenn er gemäss Art. 84 II lit. b) das Surrogat des Wertersatzes als Vorteilsausgleichung schuldet, gleichzeitig den Gegenwert für alle Vorteile, die er aus der Ware oder einem Teil der Ware gezogen hat. Es entsteht damit ein **reiner Geldanspruch,**[68] der alle Vorteile der Sache dem Verkäufer zufliessen lässt. Es soll unabhängig davon, wer die Vertragsaufhebung verursacht oder erklärt hat, beim Käufer wie beim Verkäufer kein Vorteil zurückbleiben.[69]

---

[65] Vgl. *Kröll u. a./Bridge*, Art. 84, Rn. 14. Nicht überzeugend daher CIETAC, 10.3.1995, CISG-online 1065, wo auf die Währung abgestellt wurde, in der der Kaufpreis gezahlt wurde; denn damit wird übersehen, dass es unter Art. 84 I um das Ausgleichen von Vorteilen auf Seiten des Verkäufers geht.

[66] OLG Düsseldorf, 14.1.1994, CISG-online 119 = CLOUT Nr. 130; HGer Zürich, 5.2.1997, CISG-online 327 = CLOUT Nr. 214 = SZIER 1998, 75 = TranspR-IHR 1999, 12.

[67] *Staudinger/Magnus*, Art. 84, Rn. 11; *Piltz*, Internationales Kaufrecht, Rn. 5–321; *Asam/Kindler*, RIW 1989, 841, 846 ff.; *Burkart*, S. 244; im Ergebnis auch *Hornung*, S. 303.

[68] So auch *Witz/Salger/Lorenz/Salger*, Art. 84, Rn. 3; *Piltz*, Internationales Kaufrecht, Rn. 5–323. Nicht überzeugen kann dagegen die von *Neumayer/Ming*, Art. 84, Anm. 1., und ähnlich auch von *Krebs*, Rückabwicklung, S. 69 f., vertretene Ansicht, dass auch die Herausgabe der Früchte in Natur verlangt werden könne, wenn das subsidiär zur Anwendung kommende nationale Vindikationsrecht eine solche Naturalrestitution vorsehe. Auch *Coen*, S. 216, Fn. 534, wirft die Frage auf, ob die einheitliche Behandlung des Anspruchs auf Vorteilsausgleichung nicht ohnehin daran scheitere, dass die Sachfrüchte über die lex rei sitae je nach nationalem Sachenrecht wieder dem Käufer als Eigentümer zugeordnet würden. Die Rückerstattung in natura ist freilich bereits mit dem Wortlaut der Vorschrift („Gegenwert") nicht zu vereinbaren. Auf dogmatischer Ebene ist dieser Ansicht entgegenzuhalten, dass keine Regelungslücke besteht, vgl. dazu auch oben *Fountoulakis*, Art. 81 Rn. 10 sowie auch unten Rn. 31. Würde man dennoch die Naturalrestitution der Früchte zulassen, wäre das Ziel der Rechtsvereinheitlichung gefährdet. Tatsächlich wohnt der einheitsrechtlichen Regelung des Art. 84 II lit. a) eine Zuordnungsfunktion inne – der Käufer darf die Früchte behalten, muss aber den Gegenwert ersetzen –, das nationalen sachenrechtlichen Regeln vorgeht. Dogmatisch lässt sich dieses einheitsrechtlich wünschenswerte Ergebnis damit begründen, dass zwar nach der lex rei sitae möglicherweise das Eigentum an Sachfrüchten auf den Verkäufer zurückfällt, dass jedoch der Käufer dem Vindikationsanspruch ein perpetuiertes Recht zum Besitz aus Art. 84 II lit. a) entgegenhalten kann. Für einen einzig auf Geld gerichteten Vergütungsanspruch der gezogenen Sachnutzungen spricht darüber hinaus die grössere Praktikabilität im internationalen Geschäftsverkehr; vgl. zu allem *Hornung*, S. 330 f.

[69] Der Ansatz hat Parallelen zum Bereicherungsrecht. Die Anwendung nationaler bereicherungsrechtlicher Regelungen verbietet sich jedoch, da Art. 84 II den Vorteilsausgleich bei Rückabwicklung abschliessend regelt; vgl. hierzu *Leser*, Vertragsaufhebung und Rückabwicklung, S. 251; s. auch *Herber/Czerwenka*, Art. 84, Rn. 5; vgl. ferner Rn. 10, 31 f.

Daraus ergibt sich auch, dass Art. 84, anders als Art. 82, nicht nur bei Aufhebung durch den Käufer, sondern auch bei Aufhebung durch den Verkäufer oder bei einvernehmlicher Aufhebung Anwendung findet, wobei es den Parteien jeweils unbenommen ist, abweichende Regelungen zu treffen. Zur Anwendung auf die Ersatzlieferung vgl. vorne Rn. 7.

Dogmatisch ist die Vorteilsausgleichung gegenüber den Schadensersatzregeln **selbstständig**, so dass insbesondere die Entlastungsmöglichkeit des Art. 79 nicht greift. Art. 84 hat „bereicherungsähnlichen" Charakter, will also nicht Schaden kompensieren, sondern Vorteile abschöpfen. 23

Umfasst werden alle **Nutzungen**. Hierzu zählen die zivilen und natürlichen Früchte der Sache ebenso wie sämtliche Gebrauchsvorteile, die der Käufer durch Nutzung der Sache gezogen hat, und zwar unabhängig davon, ob sie im Zeitpunkt der Vertragsaufhebung noch vorhanden sind.[70] 24

2. Früchte der Sache als Vorteil

Für die natürlichen Früchte dienen als klassische Beispiele Junge von Muttertieren, Milch von der Kuh oder Wolle vom Schaf. Die zivilen Früchte sind für das Übereinkommen von grösserer Bedeutung. Zu ihnen zählen vor allem Vorteile – mit Ausnahme der eigenen Gebrauchsvorteile –, die sich aus Vermietung von Gegenständen, Überlassung von Lizenzen an Dritte gegen Entgelt, Zulassung der Vervielfältigung oder Kopie bei geschützten Werken etc. ergeben.[71] Die **Bewertung** der natürlichen Vorteile ist **objektiv** vorzunehmen, d. h. nach dem jeweiligen Markt- oder Börsenpreis. Für die zivilen Früchte sind die erlangten Entgelte massgeblich, solange sie den geschäftsüblichen Rahmen nicht verlassen. Auch hier muss eine objektive Bewertung vorgenommen werden. 25

3. Gebrauchsvorteile

Zu den Nutzungen zählen auch die Gebrauchsvorteile, d. h. die eigene Benutzung der Sache. Beispiele sind die Benutzung eines Kraftfahrzeugs, einer Maschine, aber auch die Benutzung von Software, Patenten und Lizenzen. Sie führen zum Wertersatz für die genossenen Vorteile, und zwar bestimmt nach dem Gebrauchswert, den die Ware **am Ort und zur Zeit der effektiven Nutzung objektiv** hat. Dies lässt sich meist aufgrund des Marktpreises für den Mietwert, den Lizenzpreis etc. der Ware bestimmen.[72] 26

4. Nutzungskosten, Aufwendungen

a) **Grundsatz.** Das Übereinkommen schweigt zu der Berücksichtigung von Kosten der Nutzung wie auch zum Ersatz von Aufwendungen[73] hinsichtlich der Sache. Aus dem Begriff der „Vorteile" in Art. 84 II sowie aus Sinn und Zweck der Norm lässt sich aber schliessen, dass nur die **Nettovorteile** der empfangenen Ware geschuldet sein sollen. Bezweckt ist ein möglichst vollständiger Rückaustausch,[74] wohingegen eine zusätzliche Belastung des Käufers mit Erhaltungskosten oder auch mit Kosten der Erlangung von Vorteilen nicht der Intention des Art. 84 II entspricht. Der Käufer darf Nutzungs- sowie 27

---

[70] *Staudinger/Magnus*, Art. 84, Rn. 18; *Bamberger/Roth/Saenger*, Art. 84, Rn. 4; MünchKomm/*P. Huber*, Art. 84, Rn. 9.
[71] *Ferrari u. a./Ferrari*, Internationales Vertragsrecht, Art. 84, Rn. 12; *Honsell/Weber*, Art. 84, Rn. 14; *Witz/Salger/Lorenz/Salger*, Art. 84, Rn. 3; *Staudinger/Magnus*, Art. 84, Rn. 17.
[72] *Schlechtriem*, Internationales UN-Kaufrecht, Rn. 332; *Bamberger/Roth/Saenger*, Art. 84, Rn. 4; *Honsell/Weber*, Art. 84, Rn. 14; *Ferrari u. a./Ferrari*, Internationales Vertragsrecht, Art. 84, Rn. 12; a. A. MünchKommHGB/*Benicke*, Art. 84, Rn. 10: zu ersetzen sei der Teil des Verkehrswertes, der dem Verhältnis von tatsächlicher zu möglicher Benutzungsdauer entspreche.
[73] Der Begriff der „Aufwendungen" (expenses; dépenses) ist den Artt. 85 I 2, 86 I 2 entnommen.
[74] *Leser*, Vertragsaufhebung und Rückabwicklung, S. 250; *Herber/Czerwenka*, Art. 84, Rn. 8; *Reinhart*, Art. 84, Rn. 7; *Hornung*, S. 351; in der Rechtsprechung LG Krefeld, 19.12.1995, CISG-online 397.

Aufwendungskosten – für die er die Beweislast trägt –[75] von den empfangenen Vorteilen direkt abziehen.[76]

28 **b) Abzugsfähige Kosten. aa) Allgemeines.** Art. 84 II lit. a) gibt keine Anhaltspunkte zum Umfang der Nutzungs- und Aufwendungskosten. Ein erster Orientierungspunkt ist insofern der Begriff der **„angemessenen Aufwendungen"** (reasonable expenses; dépenses raisonnables), den das CISG in Artt. 85, 86 I verwendet. Allerdings werden die angemessenen Aufwendungen dort nicht näher konkretisiert. Insbesondere wird nicht weiterführend zwischen „notwendigen – nützlichen – luxuriösen" Aufwendungen unterschieden, wie es klassischerweise den meisten kontinental-europäischen Rechten entspricht.[77] Für die systematische Erfassung der abzugsfähigen Kosten in Art. 84 II scheint es hilfreich zu sein, auf diese Kategorien abzustellen, ohne dass damit ein dogmatisches nationales Vorverständnis übernommen wird.[78]

29 **bb) Notwendige Aufwendungen.** Aus dem Normzweck der Artt. 85, 86 ist zu folgern, dass „angemessene" Aufwendungen diejenigen sind, die im Rahmen der Erhaltungspflicht erforderlich sind.[79] Für die Frage der Abzugsfähigkeit von Aufwendungen bei der Rückabwicklung ist in Artt. 85 S. 2 und 86 I 2 ein allgemeiner Grundsatz zu erblicken (Art. 7 II), der dem Käufer einen Anspruch auf **umfassenden Ersatz** der notwendigen Aufwendungen[80] gibt. Für die Anspruchsdurchsetzung bieten die Artt. 85 S. 2 und 86 I 2 ein Zurückbehaltungsrecht, das ebenfalls analog auf die Vertragsaufhebung angewandt werden kann.[81] Die Pflicht zur umfassenden Auskehr der Erhaltungsaufwendungen ist auch notwendiges Korrelat zur vollständigen Vergütung der gezogenen Nutzungen gemäss Art. 84 II lit. a).[82]

30 **cc) Luxuriöse Aufwendungen.** Fraglich ist, inwiefern Kosten, die über die „zur Erhaltung angemessenen Aufwendungen" hinaus gehen, zu erstatten sind. Es besteht zunächst weitgehende Einigkeit darin, dass reine „Luxusaufwendungen", die aus Gründen des Geschmacks oder der Liebhaberei gemacht werden, den Wert der Ware aber nicht steigern, **nicht ersatzfähig** sind: In Übereinstimmung mit den weitaus meisten nationalen Rechtsordnungen[83] kommt ein Ersatz generell nicht in Betracht, da diese Aufwendungen mit keinerlei greifbaren Vorteilen für den Rückgewährgläubiger verbunden sind.[84]

31 **dd) Nützliche Aufwendungen.** Uneinheitlich wird dagegen die Frage beantwortet, ob und inwieweit der Käufer Aufwendungen absetzen darf, die zwar nicht „angemessene Erhaltungskosten" darstellen, aber den Wert der Ware steigern. Hier bestehen in und

---

[75] OLG Karlsruhe, 14.2.2008, CISG-online 1649, E. II.4. = IHR 2008, 53.
[76] So auch *Staudinger/Magnus*, Art. 82, Rn. 17; *Bamberger/Roth/Saenger*, Art. 84, Rn. 4; *Piltz*, Internationales Kaufrecht, Rn. 5–323; *Ferrari u. a./Ferrari*, Internationales Vertragsrecht, Art. 84, Rn. 13; *Kröll u. a./Bridge*, Art. 84, Rn. 15.
[77] Vgl. nur Artt. 453–455 spanischer Cc; §§ 331, 332 ABGB; für die Schweiz Art. 65 OR sowie Artt. 939 I, II und 940 II ZGB, u. v. m. Die Unterscheidung geht bereits auf das römische Recht zurück, vgl. *Kaser/Knütel*, § 27.21. Einen ausführlichen rechtsvergleichenden Überblick über die verschiedenen Aufwendungsersatzregeln zahlreicher europäischer Rechtsordnungen bietet *Schlechtriem*, Restitution II, Kap. 5.
[78] Zur Möglichkeit, die klassische Unterscheidung als Anhaltspunkt bei Art. 84 II zu nehmen, vgl. auch *Schlechtriem*, Internationales UN-Kaufrecht, Rn. 332.
[79] Dazu unten *Bacher*, Art. 85 Rn. 12.
[80] In diesem Sinne *Neumayer/Ming*, Art. 84, Anm. 4.; *Herber/Czerwenka*, Art. 84, Rn. 8; *Staudinger/Magnus*, Art. 84, Rn. 26; *Hornung*, S. 355; *Berg*, S. 202; MünchKomm/*P. Huber*, Art. 84, Rn. 14.
[81] So *Hornung*, S. 351.
[82] Diese Argumentation vertraten bereits im Rahmen des EKG *Kropholler*, Internationales Einheitsrecht, S. 300; *Dölle/Wahl*, Art. 17 EKG, Rn. 114 (Ersatz der notwendigen Verwendungen auf Grund des Gebotes der *iustitia commutativa*).
[83] Vgl. auch hierzu den Überblick in *Schlechtriem*, Restitution II, Kap. 5.
[84] Vgl. *Bamberger/Roth/Saenger*, Art. 84, Rn. 4; *Berg*, S. 202; MünchKomm/*P. Huber*, Art. 84, Rn. 14; *Staudinger/Magnus*, Art. 84, Rn. 26 (implizit); *Herber/Czerwenka*, Art. 84, Rn. 8 (implizit); *Hornung*, S. 352. A. A. *Krebs*, Rückabwicklung, S. 79: Luxusverwendungen seien nach dem über das IPR berufenen nationalen Recht zu behandeln.

zwischen den nationalen Rechtsordnungen erhebliche rechtspolitisch motivierte Divergenzen: Dem bereicherungsrechtlichen Erfordernis des Ausgleichs ungerechtfertigt erlangter Vermögensvorteile steht der Gedanke der Vornahme der Aufwendungen auf eigenes Risiko gegenüber.[85] Vertreten wird sowohl die Ansicht, dass der Ersatz nützlicher Aufwendungen grundsätzlich nicht in Betracht komme,[86] wie auch, dass der Rückgewährschuldner zur vollen Vergütung der nützlichen Aufwendungen berechtigt sei.[87] Jedenfalls sollte eine einheitliche Lösung gefunden und die Frage nicht dem nationalen Recht überlassen werden,[88] da über den Grundsatz der Abzugsfähigkeit von Aufwendungen als solchen Einigkeit besteht, die zu klärende Frage demnach lediglich den Punkt betrifft, wie weit der Kreis abzugsfähiger Kosten zu ziehen ist. Der Blick auf Artt. 85, 86 hilft hier nicht weiter, da Art. 84 II davon ausgeht, der Käufer nutze die Ware, solange er noch keine Kenntnis vom Aufhebungsgrund erlangt hat, als seine eigene, statt, wie bei Artt. 85, 86, einer Erhaltungspflicht für den Verkäufer nachzukommen. Die Entscheidung wird vielmehr aus dem Normzweck des Art. 84 selbst zu entwickeln sein. Und zwar dürfte es sich anbieten, einen **Abzug für wertsteigernde Aufwendungen grundsätzlich zuzulassen**: Art. 84 soll verhindern, dass bei den Parteien ein wirtschaftlicher Vorteil zurückbleibt.[89] Ein solcher verbliebe dem Verkäufer jedoch, wenn der Käufer werterhöhende Aufwendungen nicht abziehen könnte. Akzeptabel erschiene es auch, wertsteigernde Kosten (einzig) als schadensrechtlichen Anspruch zuzulassen.[90] Ein Ausgleich über Art. 84 hat aber den wesentlichen Vorteil, dass weder ein Schaden nachzuweisen ist noch eine Entlastung nach Art. 79 möglich ist.[91]

5. Komplementärwirkung von Rückabwicklungs- und Schadensersatzregeln im CISG

Insgesamt ist für nationale Regeln zum Verwendungsersatz kein Raum.[92] Das CISG bietet abschliessende Regeln für die Vertragsrückabwicklung. Hierbei ist die Komplementärwirkung von Rückabwicklungs- und Schadensersatzregeln im CISG im Auge zu behalten. Die Schadensersatzregeln der Artt. 74 ff. sind insbesondere dann heranzuziehen, wenn dem vertragstreuen Verkäufer aus der (teilweisen) Vertragsdurchführung **nichtsachbezogene frustrierte Aufwendungen** entstanden sind.[93] Diese können rein kaufvertragsbezogen sein (etwa Notarskosten u. ä.), können sich aber insbesondere dann ergeben, wenn der Kaufvertrag ein zusätzliches arbeits- bzw. dienstvertragliches Element im Sinne des Art. 3 II

---

[85] So hat z. B. nach der richterrechtlichen französischen *théorie des impenses* auch der bösgläubige Restitutionsschuldner einen Anspruch auf den Ersatz seiner nützlichen Verwendungen im Rahmen der bestehenden Bereicherung (Nachweis bei *Hornung*, S. 336 ff.), während etwa im deutschen Eigentümer-Besitzer-Verhältnis der Ersatz nützlicher Verwendungen des bösgläubigen Besitzers generell ausgeschlossen ist (vgl. § 996 BGB). In der Schweiz kann der bösgläubige Schuldner nach Art. 940 I ZGB nur Ersatz für notwendige, nicht auch für nützliche Verwendungen verlangen; ebenso grundsätzlich in Spanien, Art. 453 span. Cc (mit Ausnahme der nützlichen Verwendungen, die eine erhöhte Fruchtziehung bewirkt haben, Art. 455 Cc); weitere Bsp. bei *Schlechtriem*, Restitution II, Kap. 5.
[86] *Honsell/Weber*, Art. 84, Rn. 22; *Herber/Czerwenka*, Art. 84, Rn. 8; *MünchKomm/P. Huber*, Art. 84, Rn. 14; *Soergel/Lüderitz/Dettmeier*, Art. 84, Rn. 6; *Brunner*, Art. 84, Rn. 6; *Ferrari u. a./Ferrari*, Internationales Vertragsrecht, Art. 84, Rn. 13.
[87] *Neumayer/Ming*, Art. 84, Anm. 4. m. w. N. in Fn. 24; *Heuzé*, Anm. 442.
[88] Anders die 4. Aufl., Rn. 20c: mit Blick auf die erheblichen Meinungsunterschiede und das vollständige Schweigen der Konvention zu nützlichen Verwendungen sei davon auszugehen, dass dieses Problem bis auf weiteres dem über das IPR berufenen nationalen Recht vorbehalten bleibe; ähnl. *Krebs*, Rückabwicklung, S. 78 f.: Die Ersatzfrage sei „zu kompliziert, als dass sie sich mit Hilfe allgemeiner Grundsätze zufriedenstellend beantworten liesse"; in diesem Sinne auch *Berg*, S. 202.
[89] Vgl. oben Rn. 5, 22.
[90] So etwa *Herber/Czerwenka*, Art. 84, Rn. 8; ähnlich *Bamberger/Roth/Saenger*, Art. 84, Rn. 4: Ausgleich der notwendigen Verwendungen über das Schadensersatzrecht des CISG; vgl. zum Meinungsstand *Schmidt-Ahrendts*, IHR 2006, 67, 70 ff.
[91] Vgl. vorne Rn. 23.
[92] Ebenso *Schlechtriem*, Internationales UN-Kaufrecht, Rn. 332; a. A. *Bianca/Bonell/Tallon*, Art. 84, Anm. 2.2.; *Neumayer/Ming*, Art. 84, Anm. 4.
[93] Vgl. *Schmidt-Ahrendts*, IHR 2006, 67, 70 ff. Vgl. zum Aufwendungsersatz *Schwenzer*, Art. 74 Rn. 27.

enthält, etwa die Montage der gelieferten Sache durch Mitarbeiter des Verkäufers oder eine Schulung der Mitarbeiter des Käufers. Die rein sachbezogenen Vorteilsausgleichungsregeln des Art. 84 II versagen hier grundsätzlich.[94] Umgekehrt wird man dem vertragstreuen Käufer einen begleitenden Schadensersatzanspruch aus Art. 74 zubilligen müssen, wenn er seine Mitarbeiter zur Schulung durch den Verkäufer abgestellt hat und die gelieferte Ware aus vom Verkäufer zu vertretenden Gründen für den vertraglich vereinbarten Gebrauch untauglich ist. Der Verkäufer hat hier selbstverständlich seinerseits keinen Ersatzanspruch für den Schulungsaufwand.

6. Nicht gezogene Nutzungen

33   Für Nutzungen, die nicht gezogen wurden, obwohl deren Ziehung allgemein verkehrsüblich ist und dem Käufer zuzumuten war, enthält das Übereinkommen ebenfalls keine ausdrückliche Regelung. Die Frage dürfte **in der Praxis weitgehend belanglos** sein: Man wird dem Käufer, der mangelhafte Ware erhalten hat, kaum vorhalten können, dass er die Ware theoretisch gewinnbringend hätte einsetzen können. Aber auch für den Fall der einvernehmlichen oder durch den Verkäufer ausgesprochenen Vertragsaufhebung wird die praktische Bedeutung gering sein: Der Verkäufer steht vor beträchtlichen Beweisschwierigkeiten, muss er doch nachweisen, dass und in welcher Höhe eine theoretische Nutzung geboten gewesen wäre. Zudem müsste auch im Rahmen des fiktiven Nutzungsausgleichs ein Abzug der fiktiven Abnutzung zugelassen werden[95] (genauso wie beim tatsächlichen Nutzungsausgleich lediglich der Nettovorteil geschuldet wird), was wiederum beweisbedürftig wäre. Für die wenigen Fälle jedoch, in denen die Frage praktisch wird, sollte ein **Ausgleich fiktiver Nutzungen nicht stattfinden.**[96] Solange der Käufer von seinem Aufhebungsrecht nicht wusste und auch nicht wissen musste, betrachtete er die Ware als seine eigene und nutzte sie entsprechend seinen konkreten Bedürfnissen.[97] Dazu gehört auch, dass er sie ggf. einstweilen gar nicht nutzte. Ihm nun vorzuwerfen, dass er sie hätte nutzen können, indem man ihn zu einem Ausgleich fiktiver Nutzungen verpflichtet, hat mit dem Zurückversetzen in den ursprünglichen wirtschaftlichen Zustand, dessen Zweck Art. 84 verfolgt, nichts mehr zu tun. Der Verkäufer kann aber ggf. nicht gezogene Nutzungen und Gebrauchsvorteile im Rahmen eines Schadensersatzanspruchs herausverlangen, wenn ihm dadurch ein Schaden entsteht.[98] Die Beweislast hinsichtlich der Zumutbarkeit liegt beim Verkäufer. Jedenfalls ist auch hier die Regelung des CISG abschliessend, so dass für nationale (Bereicherungs-)Regeln kein Raum ist.[99]

V. Vorteilsausgleichung durch Surrogat für die Sache, Abs. 2 lit. b)

1. Vorteil als Surrogat

34   Die Rückabwicklung kann auch dann möglich bleiben, wenn die Sache nicht im Wesentlichen unversehrt zurückgegeben werden kann. Dies gilt in den Fällen des Art. 82 II lit. c), wenn der Vertrag durch den **Käufer** aufgehoben wird, gilt aber auch im Falle der

---

[94] Zu denken wäre hier aber auch an eine Ausdehnung der Wertersatzlösung auf andere, ihrer Natur nach nicht rückgabefähige Leistungen und die daraus gezogenen Vorteile, vgl. *Schlechtriem*, Internationales UN-Kaufrecht, Rn. 333.
[95] *Witz/Salger/Lorenz/Salger*, Art. 84, Rn. 4.
[96] Vgl. OLG Oldenburg, 1.2.1995, CISG-online 253 = CLOUT Nr. 165; *Schlechtriem*, Internationales UN-Kaufrecht, Rn. 332; *Enderlein/Maskow/Strohbach*, Art. 84, Anm. 4.1.; *Staudinger/Magnus*, Art. 84, Rn. 19; *Herber/Czerwenka*, Art. 84, Rn. 5; *Achilles*, Art. 84, Rn. 3; *Piltz*, Internationales Kaufrecht, Rn. 5–323; *Ferrari u. a./Ferrari*, Internationales Vertragsrecht, Art. 84, Rn. 11.
[97] Vgl. auch vorne Rn. 31.
[98] *Witz/Salger/Lorenz/Salger*, Art. 84, Rn. 3; *Hornung*, S. 331.
[99] A. A. MünchKommHGB/*Benicke*, Art. 84, Rn. 11, der vorschlägt, nicht gezogene Nutzungen ggf. über nationales Bereicherungsrecht herauszuverlangen; vgl. auch *Neumayer/Ming*, Art. 84, Anm. 3.: Art. 84 II komme nur zur Anwendung, wenn kein entsprechender nationaler Behelf bestehe.

einvernehmlichen **Aufhebung** – sofern die Parteien nicht von Art. 84 abweichen – und erst recht bei Aufhebung durch den **Verkäufer**.[100] Anstelle der Sache hat der Käufer dem Verkäufer den **Gegenwert aller Vorteile** in Form einer Geldleistung zu gewähren, die er aus der Sache bei Veränderung oder Weiterverkauf gezogen hat. Damit tritt der **Wertersatzanspruch als Surrogat an die Stelle der Sache.** Die Rückabwicklung entfernt sich hier wesentlich vom ursprünglichen Rücktausch der Leistungen und nähert sich einer Gesamtabrechnung, wie sie sonst dem Schadensersatzanspruch entspricht.[101] Das Surrogat ist bei der Verwertung oder dem Verbrauch der Sache das commodum ex re (unten 2.), bei der Weiterveräusserung das commodum ex negotiatione (unten 3.).[102] In beiden Fällen wird der Sachwert als dem Vermögen des Käufers zugeflossen betrachtet und führt daher zum Ausgleichsanspruch.

2. Vorteilsausgleichung durch commodum ex re

Kann der Käufer die Ware nicht oder nicht im Wesentlichen in dem ursprünglichen Zustand zurückgeben, so muss er gemäss Abs. 2 lit. b) zumindest das herausgeben, was er für die Zerstörung oder Verschlechterung der Sache erlangt hat. Hierzu zählen insbesondere **Schadensersatz- oder Versicherungsansprüche** des Käufers, wenn die Sache ohne Zutun des Käufers verschlechtert oder untergegangen ist.[103] Wenn der Käufer die Ansprüche gegen den Dritten noch nicht geltend gemacht hat, ist er zur Abtretung dieser Ansprüche an den Verkäufer verpflichtet. Der Anspruch aus Art. 84 II lit. b) wandelt sich hier ausnahmsweise von einem Geldanspruch in einen Anspruch auf Abtretung.[104] 35

3. Vorteilsausgleichung durch commodum ex negotiatione

a) Wertersatz. Der Fall der Weiterveräusserung der Ware vor Kenntnis der Vertragsverletzung entfernt sich am weitesten vom ursprünglichen Rücktausch.[105] Hier stellt sich insbesondere die Frage, in welcher Höhe ein Gewinn des Käufers beim Weiterverkauf der Ware zu berücksichtigen ist. Art. 84 II lit. b) selbst konkretisiert den Wert der erlangten Vorteile, der herauszugeben ist, nicht.[106] Der Wortlaut von Art. 84 II, der von dem „Gegenwert **aller** Vorteile" (all benefits; l'équivalent de tout profit) spricht, könnte für sich genommen vermuten lassen, dass auch ein über den Marktverhältnissen liegender Verkaufserlös des Käufers an den Verkäufer herauszugeben wäre. Dies liesse sich insbesondere angesichts der Lektüre von Art. 7.3.6 I S. 2 PICC, Art. 9:309 PECL annehmen, die beide eine weichere Formulierung verwenden. So sprechen die PICC von einer „appropriate allowance in money" und die PECL von einem „reasonable amount for the value of the performance to the [party receiving the benefit]". Indes war durch die Formulierung keine Abweichung von Art. 84 II bezweckt; so nimmt der Autorenkommentar der PECL ausdrücklich Bezug auf CISG und PICC und streicht – in Abgrenzung zu nationalen Rechtsordnungen, die starrere Vorteilsausgleichsregeln kennen – heraus, dass „the Principles follow ULIS, CISG and Unidroit art. 7.3.6(1) in taking a broad flexible approach".[107] (Auch) Art. 84 II gewährt folglich einen **Ermessensspielraum** für die Frage, welche Vorteile der Käufer auszukehren hat. 36

Anhaltspunkte für die Berechnung des auszukehrenden commodum ex negotiatione lassen sich Art. 82 II lit. c) entnehmen. Danach ist auf den „Verkauf im normalen Geschäfts- 37

---

[100] S. dazu vorne Rn. 7.
[101] Zur Grenzziehung oben *Fountoulakis*, Vor Artt. 81–84 Rn. 11 sowie vorne Rn. 23.
[102] Zu dieser Unterscheidung vgl. bereits *Dölle/Weitnauer*, Art. 81 EKG, Rn. 9.
[103] *Herber/Czerwenka*, Art. 84, Rn. 7; *Staudinger/Magnus*, Art. 84, Rn. 23.
[104] MünchKomm/*P. Huber*, Art. 82, Rn. 17; *Staudinger/Magnus*, Art. 82, Rn. 23.
[105] Dazu vorne Rn. 6.
[106] Anders z. B. § 346 II S. 1 BGB, der ausdrücklich festhält, bei der Berechnung des Wertsatzes sei die vertraglich vereinbarte Gegenleistung massgeblich.
[107] Artt. 9:305-9:309 PECL, Note 8 (c).

verkehr" abzustellen. Daraus kann gefolgert werden, dass der Käufer nur zur Herausgabe des Erlöses verpflichtet ist, der bei einem **der allgemeinen Marktlage entsprechenden Weiterverkauf** zu erzielen war.[108] Er kann, wenn er z. B. durch sein Verhandlungsgeschick ein besonders hohes commodum ex negotiatione erzielt hat, den Mehrerlös aufgrund eines besonders günstigen Weiterverkaufs behalten. Auf den Verkauf entsprechend der allgemeinen Marktlage abzustellen rechtfertigt sich nicht nur in den Fällen des Art. 82 II, d. h. wenn der Käufer den Vertrag aufhebt bzw. der Verkäufer nacherfüllt, sondern auch bei einvernehmlicher Aufhebung und bei Aufhebung durch den Verkäufer. Die Gefahr der Spekulation durch den Verkäufer wäre ansonsten zu hoch.

38 b) **Nettoerlös.** Auch hier verlangt der Grundgedanke der Vorteilsausgleichung, dass als Vorteil aus der Veräusserung nur der Nettoerlös verstanden werden kann. Der Käufer kann Kosten, die nachweislich[109] aus der Verarbeitung, dem Verbrauch und im Zusammenhang mit dem Verkauf auftreten, **von seinem Erlös abziehen.** Dies betrifft insbesondere Kosten der Veräusserung, der Werbung, des Transports, ferner Personalkosten sowie Aufwendungen und Nachteile aus der Veräusserung und Verarbeitung.[110] Auch darf der Käufer Ersatzansprüche, die sein Abnehmer gegen ihn geltend macht, abziehen.[111]

39 c) **Bei fehlendem Surrogat.** In den seltenen Fällen, in denen der Käufer trotz Unmöglichkeit der Rückgewähr der Kaufsache in natura das Recht zur Vertragsaufhebung behält, ohne für die Sache ein Surrogat erhalten zu haben,[112] wird hinzunehmen sein, dass der Käufer den Anspruch auf Rückzahlung des vollen Kaufpreises hat und selbst nur die gezogenen Nutzungen vergüten muss.

VI. Beweislast

40 Der Käufer hat die Voraussetzungen des Zinsanspruchs nach Abs. 1 zu beweisen. Beruft sich der Verkäufer auf einen Anspruch auf Vorteilsausgleichung nach Abs. 2, so muss er grundsätzlich den Nachweis erbringen, dass die Tatbestandsvoraussetzungen erfüllt sind.[113] Da er aber über die „geschäftsüblichen" Vorteile hinaus nicht zu belegen vermag, welche konkreten Vorteile der Käufer tatsächlich gezogen hat, hat er lediglich die normalerweise zu erwartenden Vorteile zu beweisen; der Käufer kann dann seinerseits nachweisen, dass er tatsächlich weniger erwirtschaftet hat.[114]

---

[108] MünchKommHGB/*Benicke,* Art. 84, Rn. 16; *Krebs,* Rückabwicklung, S. 116: „nur solche Vorteile [sind] auszugleichen, die in der Substanz der Sache selbst gründen"; für Herausgabe des vollen Erlöses aber MünchKomm/*P. Huber,* Art. 84, Rn. 19; *Audit,* Vente internationale, Anm. 192. (der richtigerweise darauf hinweist, dass der Käufer i. d. R. Ersatzansprüchen des Zweitkäufers ausgesetzt sein wird, die er dem Ausgleichsanspruch des Verkäufers wiederum entgegensetzen kann); *Staudinger/Magnus,* Art. 84, Rn. 24; *Herber/ Czerwenka,* Art. 84, Rn. 6; differenzierend *Honsell/Weber,* Art. 84, Rn. 21: volle Gewinnabschöpfung nur dann, wenn der Vertrag vom Verkäufer aufgehoben wird, d. h. der Käufer vertragsbrüchig ist.

[109] Der Käufer trägt die Beweislast dafür, dass die abzugsfähigen Kosten auch tatsächlich angefallen sind, vgl. OLG Karlsruhe, 14.2.2008, CISG-online 1649, E. II.4. = IHR 2008, 53.

[110] CISG-AC, Op. 9 Bridge, Comment 3.29; MünchKomm/*P. Huber,* Art. 84, Rn. 18; *Ferrari u. a./Ferrari,* Internationales Vertragsrecht, Art. 84, Rn. 16.

[111] *Leser,* Vertragsaufhebung und Rückabwicklung, S. 250.

[112] *Hornung,* S. 152, bringt das Beispiel, dass ein lediglich haftpflichtversicherter PKW durch Blitzschlag vollkommen zerstört wird und sich bei der Untersuchung des Wracks schwerwiegende Mängel zeigen.

[113] CISG-AC, Op. 9 Bridge, Opinion 3.7; *Bamberger/Roth/Saenger,* Art. 84, Rn. 8; *Staudinger/Magnus,* Art. 84, Rn. 27.

[114] Vgl. OLG Karlsruhe, 14.2.2008, CISG-online 1649, E. II.4. = IHR 2008, 53; *Bamberger/Roth/Saenger,* Art. 84, Rn. 8; *Staudinger/Magnus,* Art. 84, Rn. 27; *Achilles,* Art. 84, Rn. 5; *Ferrari u. a./Ferrari,* Internationales Vertragsrecht, Art. 84, Rn. 18; diesbezüglich wertvolle Hinweise für die Vertragsgestaltung bei *Osuna,* Dealing with Avoidance, S. 498 f.

Abschnitt VI. Erhaltung der Ware
Section VI. Section VI.
Preservation of the goods Conservation des marchandises

Vorbemerkungen zu Artt. 85–88

Übersicht
	Rn.
I. Allgemeines	1
II. Folgen einer Pflichtverletzung	4
III. Analoge Anwendung	6

I. Allgemeines

Die Artt. 85 bis 88 verpflichten die Parteien unter gewissen Voraussetzungen, die Ware zu **verwahren** und für ihre **Erhaltung** zu sorgen, wenn sie vom Käufer zurückgewiesen bzw. nicht abgenommen wird. Häufig wird in solchen Situationen zunächst **unklar** sein, ob die Beanstandungen des Käufers berechtigt sind. Hinge die Verantwortlichkeit für das Schicksal der Ware in dieser Situation davon ab, wer in der Auseinandersetzung um die Vertragsmäßigkeit der Ware letztendlich Recht behält, könnten beide Seiten versucht sein, die Ware ihrem Schicksal zu überlassen – in der Hoffnung, dass die andere Partei die Konsequenzen zu tragen hat.[1] Artt. 85 ff. verhindern dies, indem sie je nach Situation den Käufer bzw. den Verkäufer auch dann zur Erhaltung der Ware verpflichten, wenn die andere Seite im Unrecht ist. 1

In der Literatur ist vorgeschlagen worden, die in Artt. 85 ff. normierten Verhaltensanforderungen dogmatisch jedenfalls zum Teil nicht als Pflichten, sondern als bloße **Obliegenheiten** anzusehen. Dies sei insbesondere bei Art. 86 geboten, da der Käufer in den dort geregelten Fällen regelmäßig schon Eigentum an der Ware habe, zumindest aber die Gefahr trage.[2] Der Hinweis auf die Eigentümerstellung ist im Zusammenhang mit CISG aber schon deshalb wenig hilfreich, weil sich die dinglichen Rechtsverhältnisse in jedem Fall nach unvereinheitlichtem nationalem Recht beurteilen. Die dogmatische Einordnung der Artt. 85 ff. hinge folglich vom jeweils anwendbaren nationalen Recht ab. Auch das Argument, dass der Käufer regelmäßig die Gefahr trage, kann kaum überzeugen: Ist der Käufer – wie dies Art. 86 voraussetzt – zur Zurückweisung der Ware berechtigt, so liegt die Gefahr eines zufälligen Untergangs oder einer zufälligen Verschlechterung der Ware wegen Art. 82 I nämlich regelmäßig beim Verkäufer. 2

Die **Systematik** der Vorschriften ist leicht zu verstehen: Art. 85 definiert die Situationen, in denen der **Verkäufer** zur Erhaltung der Ware verpflichtet ist. Art. 86 wendet sich demgegenüber an den **Käufer** und sieht zusätzlich zur Erhaltungspflicht unter bestimmten Voraussetzungen auch eine Pflicht zur Inbesitznahme vor. Artt. 87 und 88 wenden sich an **beide Parteien** und regeln wichtige Einzelheiten der Art und Weise, in der die Erhaltungspflicht zu erfüllen ist. 3

II. Folgen einer Pflichtverletzung

Eine Verletzung der Pflichten aus Artt. 85 ff. führt im Allgemeinen zu einem **Schadenersatzanspruch** des Berechtigten nach Maßgabe der Artt. 45, 61 und 74 ff.[3] Da in den 4

---
[1] Plastisch hierzu *Honnold/Flechtner*, Vor Artt. 85, Rn. 453; vgl. auch *Kröll u. a./Sono*, Vor Art. 85, Rn. 2.
[2] So *Neumayer/Ming*, Art. 86, Anm. 2.; hiergegen ausführlich *Jentsch*, S. 38 ff.
[3] *Achilles*, Art. 85, Rn. 5, Art. 86, Rn. 7, Art. 88, Rn. 4; *Enderlein/Maskow/Strohbach*, Vorbemerkung vor Art. 85, Anm. 3.; *Ferrari u. a./Ferrari*, Internationales Vertragsrecht, Art. 85, Rn. 9 und Art. 86, Rn. 14; *Kröll*

einschlägigen Situationen regelmäßig auch die Gegenseite vertragsbrüchig ist, kommt der Prüfung des Mitverursachungseinwands (Art. 77) besondere Bedeutung zu.

5   Eine Verletzung der **Erhaltungspflicht** aus Art. 85 oder Art. 86 hat darüber hinaus zur Folge, dass die zur Erhaltung verpflichtete Vertragspartei den aus einer Verschlechterung resultierenden Schaden nicht von der anderen Partei ersetzt verlangen kann, auch wenn auf diese bereits die Gefahr übergegangen ist.[4]

III. Analoge Anwendung

6   Die Artt. 85 und 86 CISG werden in verschiedenem Zusammenhang als Ausdruck eines dem CISG zu Grunde liegenden allgemeinen Grundsatzes bezeichnet.[5] So hat der österreichische Oberste Gerichtshof die Vorschriften zusammen mit anderen CISG-Artikeln als Beleg für ein allgemeines „Prinzip der Zug-um-Zug-Verpflichtung" angeführt.[6] In der Literatur wird der Vorschrift darüber hinaus der allgemeine Gedanke entnommen, dass diejenige Vertragspartei, in deren tatsächlichem Verantwortungsbereich sich die Ware befindet, eine Obhutspflicht für die Ware und eventuell auch für andere Gegenstände wie z. B. Verpackungsmaterial trifft.[7] Dies erscheint im Ansatz zutreffend. Dabei darf aber nicht übersehen werden, dass die Artt. 85 und 86 in Tatbestand und Rechtsfolge stark auf den Einzelfall abstellen und deshalb jede Verallgemeinerung und Schematisierung mit größter Vorsicht zu behandeln ist. Gerade weil die Artt. 85 ff. ihrerseits eine Ausprägung des allgemeinen Grundsatzes von Treu und Glauben darstellen, kann und muss sich die Beurteilung stets an den konkreten Umständen des jeweiligen Einzelfalles orientieren.

---

  u.a./Sono, Art. 85, Rn. 22, Art. 86, Rn. 15; *MünchKomm/P. Huber*, Art. 85, Rn. 11, Art. 86, Rn. 6; *Piltz*, Internationales Kaufrecht, Rn. 4–254; *Herber/Czerwenka*, Vor Art. 85, Rn. 4; *Soergel/Lüderitz/Dettmeier*, Art. 85, Rn. 9, Art. 86, Rn. 8, Art. 88, Rn. 10; *Staudinger/Magnus*, Art. 85, Rn. 13, Art. 86, Rn. 12; *Witz/Salger/Lorenz/Lorenz*, Art. 85, Rn. 12, Art. 88, Rn. 12. Zu den Einzelheiten eines Schadenersatzanspruchs ausführlich *Jentsch*, S. 131 ff.
  [4] CIETAC, 6.9.1996, CISG-online 1146.
  [5] Ausführlich dazu *Jentsch*, S. 70 ff.
  [6] OGH, 8.11.2005, CISG-online 1156.
  [7] So z. B. *MünchKomm/P. Huber*, Art. 85, Rn. 3; *MünchKommHGB/Mankowski*, Vor Art. 85, Rn. 5; *Staudinger/Magnus*, Art. 85, Rn. 19; speziell zur Obhutspflicht für Verpackungsmaterial siehe unten Art. 86 Rn. 21.

Art. 85 [Pflicht des Verkäufers zur Erhaltung der Ware]

Nimmt der Käufer die Ware nicht rechtzeitig ab* oder versäumt er, falls Zahlung des Kaufpreises und Lieferung der Ware Zug um Zug erfolgen sollen, den Kaufpreis zu zahlen, und hat der Verkäufer die Ware noch in Besitz oder ist er sonst in der Lage, über sie zu verfügen, so hat der Verkäufer die den Umständen angemessenen Maßnahmen zu ihrer Erhaltung zu treffen. Er ist berechtigt, die Ware zurückzubehalten, bis ihm der Käufer seine angemessenen Aufwendungen erstattet hat.

Art. 85

If the buyer is in delay in taking delivery of the goods or, where payment of the price and delivery of the goods are to be made concurrently, if he fails to pay the price, and the seller is either in possession of the goods or otherwise able to control their disposition, the seller must take such steps as are reasonable in the circumstances to preserve them. He is entitled to retain them until he has been reimbursed his reasonable expenses by the buyer.

Art. 85

Lorsque l'acheteur tarde à prendre livraison des marchandises ou qu'il n'en paie pas le prix, alors que le paiement du prix et la livraison doivent se faire simultanément, le vendeur, s'il a les marchandises en sa possession ou sous son contrôle, doit prendre les mesures raisonnables, eu égard aux circonstances, pour en assurer la conservation. Il est fondé à les retenir jusqu'à ce qu'il ait obtenu de l'acheteur le remboursement de ses dépenses raisonnables.

Übersicht

	Rn.
I. Allgemeines	1
II. Vorgeschichte	2
III. Voraussetzungen	3
1. Weigerung des Käufers	3
a) Abnahmeverweigerung	4
b) Zahlungsverweigerung	6
2. Besitz oder Verfügungsmöglichkeit des Verkäufers	8
a) Besitz	9
b) Verfügungsmöglichkeit	10
3. Keine sonstigen Voraussetzungen	11
IV. Rechtsfolgen	12
1. Erhaltungspflicht	12
2. Kostentragung	15
3. Zurückbehaltungsrecht	17
4. Verletzung der Erhaltungspflicht	18

Vorläufer und **Entwürfe**: Art. 91 EKG; Genfer E 1976 Art. 60; Wiener E 1977 Art. 60; New Yorker E 1978 Art. 74.

I. Allgemeines

Art. 85 verpflichtet den **Verkäufer** zur Erhaltung der Ware, falls der Käufer sie nicht abnimmt. Der Vorschrift kommt vor allem deshalb Bedeutung zu, weil der Verkäufer bei (unberechtigter) Nichtabnahme der Ware nach Art. 62 grundsätzlich berechtigt bleibt, den Kaufpreis zu fordern, und diesem Anspruch nicht das allgemeine Gebot zur Schadensminderung entgegengesetzt werden kann.[1] Nimmt man hinzu, dass in den von Art. 85 erfassten Fällen die Gefahr in der Regel auf den Käufer übergegangen ist, könnte es vorkommen, dass der Verkäufer die Ware verkommen lässt und dennoch den vollen Kaufpreis fordern

1

---

* Schweiz, Österreich: nimmt an.
[1] Dazu *Mohs*, Art. 62 Rn. 14.

Art. 85 2–5 Teil III. Kapitel V. Pflichten des Verkäufers und Käufers. Abschnitt VI

kann. Art. 85 schließt dies aus, indem er dem Verkäufer auferlegt, die Ware im Interesse des Käufers zu erhalten. Die Vorschrift übernimmt damit partiell dieselbe Funktion wie das allgemeine Schadensminderungsgebot.[2]

II. Vorgeschichte

2 Sowohl Art. 91 EKG als auch die Vorentwürfe zum CISG (Genfer E 1976, Art. 60; Wiener E 1977 Art. 60 und New Yorker E 1978 Art. 74) enthielten im Wesentlichen übereinstimmende Regelungen. In Art. 91 EKG waren die Voraussetzungen auf Verkäuferseite (Besitz oder Möglichkeit zur Verfügung über die Ware) noch nicht ausdrücklich normiert. In den Vorentwürfen zum CISG war der Fall, dass der Käufer sich bei Zug-um-Zug-Lieferung weigert, den Kaufpreis zu zahlen, noch nicht ausdrücklich einbezogen.

III. Voraussetzungen

1. Weigerung des Käufers

3 Erste Voraussetzung ist, dass der Käufer die Ware nicht rechzeitig abnimmt oder bei Zug-um-Zug-Lieferung die Zahlung des Kaufpreises versäumt.

4 **a) Abnahmeverweigerung.** Nach der ersten Alternative der Vorschrift genügt es, wenn der Käufer die Ware **nicht rechtzeitig abnimmt**. Nach der Rechtsprechung zum insoweit gleich lautenden Art. 91 EKG fällt darunter nicht nur der Fall einer verzögerten Abnahme, sondern auch der Fall einer endgültigen Abnahmeverweigerung.[3] Art. 85 ist auch dann anwendbar, wenn die Ware im Rahmen einer Ersatzlieferung nach bereits erfolgten Beanstandungen geliefert worden ist[4] und wenn der Käufer die bereits abgenommene Ware wieder zurückgegeben hat[5].

5 Ob die Weigerung zu Recht (etwa wegen nicht vertragsgemäßer Beschaffenheit der Ware) oder zu Unrecht erfolgt, ist nach dem Wortlaut unerheblich. Seiner Funktion nach erfasst Art. 85 allerdings nur den Fall der **unberechtigten** Weigerung.[6] Nur wenn der Käufer gegen seine Abnahmepflicht aus Artt. 53 und 60 verstößt und damit jedenfalls gemäß Art. 69 I die **Gefahr** auf ihn übergeht, bedarf es einer besonderen Verpflichtung des Verkäufers, im Interesse der Gegenseite tätig zu werden. Verweigert der Käufer die Abnahme hingegen zu Recht, liegt die Gefahr nach wie vor beim Verkäufer. Dieser ist dann schon im eigenen Interesse gehalten, für den Erhalt der Ware zu sorgen.[7] Praktische Auswirkungen hat diese dogmatische Unterscheidung freilich nur für die Frage, wer die **Erhaltungskosten** trägt. Ein Anspruch auf Aufwendungsersatz, wie ihn Art. 85 S. 2 zugrunde legt, ist nur dann angebracht, wenn sich der Käufer durch seine Weigerung vertragswidrig verhält. Für die in der Praxis vorrangige, weil ad hoc zu entscheidende Frage, was mit der zurückgewiesenen Ware geschehen soll, kommt es auf die Berechtigung der Zurückweisung hingegen nicht an. Der Verkäufer ist in jedem Fall gehalten, sich um die Ware zu kümmern, sei es, weil er noch selbst die Gefahr trägt, sei es, weil die Gefahr zwar

---

[2] Vgl. dazu *Honnold/Flechtner*, Art. 85, Rn. 454; *Kröll u. a./Sono*, Art. 85, Rn. 2.
[3] OLG Düsseldorf, 20.1.1983, in: *Schlechtriem/Magnus*, Art. 94 EKG, Nr. 1; ebenso *Kröll u. a./Sono*, Art. 85, Rn. 11; MünchKomm/*P. Huber*, Art. 85, Rn. 4; MünchKommHGB/*Mankowski*, Art. 85, Rn. 3.
[4] Im Ergebnis ebenso, aber für eine analoge Anwendung in diesem Fall MünchKomm/*P. Huber*, Art. 85, Rn. 4; *Soergel/Luederitz/Dettmeier*, Art. 85, Rn. 4.
[5] *Kröll u. a./Sono*, Art. 85, Rn. 10.
[6] Ebenso *Bianca/Bonell/Barrera Graf*, Art. 85, Anm. 2.2.; *Piltz*, Internationales Kaufrecht, Rn. 4–256.
[7] Ebenso *Kröll u. a./Sono*, Art. 85, Rn. 10 und *Soergel/Lüderitz/Dettmeier*, Art. 85, Rn. 2, der nach Gefahrübergang sogar eine generelle Erhaltungspflicht des Verkäufers unabhängig von Art. 85 annehmen will. Zum EKG s. LG Marburg, 1.11.1984, in: *Schlechtriem/Magnus*, Art. 48 EKG, Nr. 1. Anders MünchKomm/*P. Huber*, Art. 85, Rn. 13, der die herrschende Meinung für sich in Anspruch nimmt. Vermittelnd *Jentsch*, S. 52: Bis zur Lieferung komme Art. 85 nur deklaratorische Bedeutung zu.

übergegangen ist, er aber aus Art. 85 verpflichtet ist. Die Option, nichts zu unternehmen in der Hoffnung, dass die finanziellen Folgen einer Verschlechterung der Ware letztendlich den Käufer treffen, ist dem Verkäufer also genommen. Gerade darin liegt die entscheidende Bedeutung des Art. 85 S. 1.

b) Zahlungsverweigerung. Falls die Ware **Zug um Zug** gegen Zahlung des Kauf- 6 preises zu liefern ist, steht es der Abnahmeverweigerung gleich, wenn der Käufer sich **weigert zu zahlen.** Eine Zahlungsverweigerung liegt auch dann vor, wenn der Käufer vorbereitende Maßnahmen verweigert, zu denen er nach Art. 54 verpflichtet ist.[8] Nicht ausdrücklich von Art. 85 erfasst ist der Fall, dass der Kaufpreis **im Voraus** zu zahlen ist. In dieser Konstellation ist Art. 85 zumindest **entsprechend** anwendbar:[9] Hat der vorleistungspflichtige Käufer auch zum Zeitpunkt, zu dem die Lieferung erfolgen soll, noch nicht gezahlt, muss der Verkäufer die Ware nach Art. 58 I 2 ebenfalls nur Zug um Zug gegen Kaufpreiszahlung übergeben.

Auch im Falle der Zahlungsverweigerung wird man die Anwendung von Art. 85 auf den 7 Fall der **unberechtigten** Weigerung beschränken müssen. Die Ausführungen zu Rn. 5 gelten hier entsprechend.

2. Besitz oder Verfügungsmöglichkeit des Verkäufers

Den Verkäufer treffen nach Art. 85 nur dann Pflichten, wenn er in den unter 1 geschil- 8 derten Situationen noch im Besitz der Ware ist oder in der Lage ist, über sie zu verfügen.

a) Besitz. Im **Besitz** der Ware wird der Verkäufer vor allem dann bleiben, wenn der 9 Käufer sie bei ihm abholen muss oder wenn er sie durch eigene Leute zum Käufer bringen lässt.[10]

b) Verfügungsmöglichkeit. Die Frage, ob der Verkäufer noch **in der Lage** ist, über die 10 Ware zu **verfügen,** stellt sich, sobald die Ware in den Händen eines Dritten, etwa eines Frachtunternehmers ist. Eine ausreichende Verfügungsmöglichkeit im Sinne des Art. 85 setzt voraus, dass der Verkäufer das **Weisungsrecht** über die Beförderung innehat. Dies ist beispielsweise der Fall, wenn ein auf Order des Verkäufers lautender Frachtbrief ausgestellt ist.[11]

3. Keine sonstigen Voraussetzungen

Sonstige Voraussetzungen sind **nicht** erforderlich. Insbesondere ist unerheblich, ob das 11 **Eigentum** an der Ware bereits auf den Käufer übergegangen ist.[12] Maßgeblich für die Erhaltungspflicht ist allein der Umstand des **Gefahrübergangs.** Der Diskussion, ob Art. 85 schon vor Gefahrübergang anwendbar ist,[13] kommt andererseits allenfalls theoretische Bedeutung zu. In den von Art. 85 erfassten Fällen ist die Gefahr nämlich zumindest nach Art. 69 I auf den Käufer übergegangen. Scheitert der Gefahrübergang an fehlender Individualisierung der Ware (Art. 69 III), muss auch Art. 85 leer laufen, da sich die Erhaltungspflicht des Verkäufers ebenso wie die Kostenerstattungspflicht des Käufers nur auf näher individualisierte Waren beziehen kann. Unterbleibt der Gefahrübergang, weil der Käufer

---

[8] *Kröll u. a./Sono,* Art. 85, Rn. 13.
[9] Ebenso *Bamberger/Roth/Saenger,* Art. 85, Rn. 4; *Ferrari u. a./Ferrari,* Internationales Vertragsrecht, Art. 85, Rn. 4; *Herber/Czerwenka,* Art. 85, Rn. 2; *Kröll u. a./Sono,* Art. 85, Rn. 12; MünchKomm/*P. Huber,* Art. 85, Rn. 4; *Piltz,* Internationales Kaufrecht, Rn. 4–256; *Soergel/Lüderitz/Dettmeier,* Art. 85, Rn. 4; *Staudinger/ Magnus,* Art. 85, Rn. 6. Anders wohl *Enderlein/Maskow/Strohbach,* Art. 85, Anm. 2.
[10] Ebenso *Kröll u. a./Sono,* Art. 85, Rn. 16.
[11] Ebenso *Honnold/Flechtner,* Art. 85, Rn. 454; *Ferrari u. a./Ferrari,* Internationales Vertragsrecht, Art. 85, Rn. 5; *Kröll u. a./Sono,* Art. 85, Rn. 17. Weitere Beispiele bei *Bianca/Bonell/Barrera Graf,* Art. 85, Anm. 2.4. und bei *Jentsch,* S. 53 ff.
[12] Ebenso *Kröll u. a./Sono,* Art. 85, Rn. 15.
[13] Bejahend *Herber/Czerwenka,* Art. 85, Rn. 3

(noch) nicht zur Abnahme verpflichtet ist, scheidet die Anwendung von Art. 85 schon aus den in Rn. 5 genannten Gründen aus.

IV. Rechtsfolgen

1. Erhaltungspflicht

12   Sind die Voraussetzungen des Art. 85 erfüllt, muss der Verkäufer **angemessene Maßnahmen** zur Erhaltung der Ware treffen. Welche Maßnahmen danach geschuldet sind, lässt sich nur anhand der Umstände des Einzelfalles konkret bestimmen. Allgemein hat der Verkäufer die Ware zu lagern und vor schädlichen Einflüssen zu schützen. Dies kann im Einzelfall auch durch Hinterlegung bei einem Gericht erfolgen.[14] Je nach der Beschaffenheit der Ware können eine regelmäßige Überprüfung oder besondere Sicherungsmaßnahmen erforderlich sein. Bei verderblicher Ware statuiert Art. 88 II besondere Pflichten. Als angemessene Maßnahme ist auch die Verbringung der bereits ausgelieferten, aber noch nicht am Erfüllungsort eingetroffenen Waren an einen anderen Ort zum Zwecke der dortigen Einlagerung angesehen worden.[15]

Begrenzt wird der Pflichtenumfang durch den Maßstab der **Angemessenheit**. Gegenüber dem allgemeinen Haftungsmaßstab des Art. 79 bedeutet dies eine Erleichterung, weil der Verkäufer auch innerhalb seines Einflussbereichs von Maßnahmen absehen kann, die wegen der anfallenden Kosten oder aus sonstigen Gründen außer Verhältnis zum Wert der Ware und zu sonstigen drohenden Schäden stehen. Dabei sind auch die wohlverstandenen Interessen des Käufers zu berücksichtigen, denn dieser muss für alle angemessenen Maßnahmen die Kosten tragen (dazu unten Rn. 15 f.). Ob der Rahmen des Angemessenen überschritten ist, muss nach objektiven Maßstäben beurteilt werden.[16] Eine Beschränkung auf die Sorgfalt „in eigenen Angelegenheiten" dürfte der Vorschrift dagegen nicht zu entnehmen sein.[17]

12a   Wenn der Käufer finanziell nicht in der Lage ist, die Kosten zu erstatten, muss der Verkäufer nach überwiegender Auffassung in der Literatur dennoch Erhaltungsmaßnahmen durchführen, sofern er die Kosten durch einen möglichen Selbsthilfeverkauf decken kann.[18] Zumindest hinsichtlich des Umfangs der geschuldeten Erhaltungsmaßnahmen wird man hier aber zwischen dem Fall des Art. 85 und demjenigen des Art. 86 unterscheiden müssen: Dem Käufer, der den Kaufpreis noch nicht bezahlt hat, steht im Falle des Art. 86 theoretisch der gesamte Erlös des Selbsthilfeverkaufs zur Finanzierung der Erhaltungskosten zur Verfügung. Der Verkäufer muss durch den Selbsthilfeverkauf hingegen nicht nur die Erhaltungskosten, sondern auch den nicht gezahlten Kaufpreis abdecken.

13   Für Handlungen von **Gehilfen** hat der Verkäufer nach Maßgabe des Art. 79 einzustehen. Auch die Gehilfen brauchen freilich nur angemessene Erhaltungsmaßnahmen zu ergreifen. Das Verschulden **Dritter** sollte dem Verkäufer hingegen nicht angelastet werden. Wie bereits dargelegt (oben Rn. 5), liegt den von Art. 85 erfassten Fällen ein Vertragsbruch des Käufers zugrunde; zudem ist auch die Gefahr auf den Käufer übergegangen. In dieser Situation wäre es ungereimt, das Handeln eines – sorgfältig ausgewählten – Dritten dem Verkäufer zur Last zu legen.[19]

---

[14] Audiencia Provincial de Barcelona, 11.3.2002, CISG-online 1325; anders wohl MünchKommHGB/*Mankowski*, Art. 85, Rn. 6 unter Berufung auf KG Waadt, 17.5.1994, CISG-online 122.

[15] CIETAC, 27.2.1996, CISG-online 1033.

[16] Ebenso *Soergel/Lüderitz/Dettmeier*, Art. 85, Rn. 7; *Staudinger/Magnus*, Art. 85, Rn. 9.

[17] *Bamberger/Roth/Saenger*, Art. 85, Rn. 7; *Staudinger/Magnus*, Art. 85, Rn. 9; MünchKommHGB/*Mankowski*, Art. 85, Rn. 5; *Witz/Salger/Lorenz/Lorenz*, Art. 85, Rn. 9; Anders noch *Eberstein*, 2. Aufl., Art. 85 Rn. 11.

[18] *Schlechtriem*, Internationales UN-Kaufrecht, Rn. 338; MünchKomm/*P. Huber*, Art. 85, Rn. 4; MünchKommHGB/*Mankowski*, Art. 85, Rn. 3; *Staudinger/Magnus*, Art. 85, Rn. 12.

[19] Ebenso *Achilles*, Art. 85, Rn. 5; MünchKomm/*P. Huber*, Art. 85, Rn. 12; für den Sonderfall der Einlagerung bei Dritten auch *Soergel/Lüderitz/Dettmeier*, Art. 87, Rn. 4.

In **zeitlicher** Hinsicht unterliegt die Erhaltungspflicht ebenfalls keiner fest bestimmten **14** Grenze. Selbstverständlich endet die Pflicht dann, wenn der Käufer die Ware doch noch in Besitz nimmt. Entsprechendes gilt, wenn der Verkäufer nach Art. 64 die Aufhebung des Vertrages erklärt.[20] Der Verkäufer hat darüber hinaus unter bestimmten Voraussetzungen gemäß Art. 88 I die Möglichkeit und nach Maßgabe von Art. 88 II die Pflicht, die Aufbewahrung durch Verkauf der Ware zu beenden.[21] Wenn dem Käufer durch behördliche Verfügung aufgegeben wird, die Ware zu vernichten, endet auch die Erhaltungspflicht aus Art. 85.[22]

2. Kostentragung

Soweit sich die Aufwendungen zur Erhaltung der Ware im Rahmen des Angemessenen **15** halten, ist der Käufer zur Kostenerstattung verpflichtet. Ein solcher Erstattungsanspruch wird sich in der Regel schon aus Art. 61 I b) ergeben, weil sich der Käufer durch die unberechtigte Weigerung schadenersatzpflichtig gemacht hat.[23] Sofern ein solcher Ersatzanspruch aus besonderen Gründen – etwa wegen Art. 79 – ausgeschlossen ist, steht dem Verkäufer aus Art. 85 S. 2 dennoch ein Ersatzanspruch zu.[24]

Zu den zu erstattenden Kosten gehören insbesondere diejenigen einer **Einlagerung**.[25] **16** Für den Fall der Fremdlagerung ergibt sich dies schon aus Art. 87, für den Fall der Eigenlagerung gilt nach den in Rn. 15 zitierten Vorschriften nichts anderes. Je nach Lage des Falles kann auch eine **Vergütung** des Verkäufers für eigene Tätigkeiten angemessen sein.[26] Als Kosten der Erhaltung sind auch die Kosten für den **Rücktransport** der Ware angesehen worden, nachdem der Käufer sie am Erfüllungsort nicht abgenommen hatte.[27] Für Maßnahmen, die zur Erhaltung der Ware **ungeeignet** sind, besteht kein Anspruch auf Kostenerstattung.[28]

Nach Art. 78 ist der Ersatzanspruch zu **verzinsen**.[29] Ein Anspruch auf **Vorschuss** dürfte **16a** Art. 85 S. 2 nicht zu entnehmen sein.[30]

Die Kosten sind nach verbreiteter Auffassung in derjenigen **Währung** zu erstatten, in der **16b** sie angefallen sind.[31] Maßgeblich dürfte hierbei nicht die Währung sein, mit der die Kosten dem Verkäufer in Rechnung gestellt wurden, sondern die Währung, mit der sie bei ihm selbst angefallen sind. Sind die Kosten zum Beispiel in US-Dollar berechnet und nutzt der Verkäufer zur Zahlung ein in Euro geführtes Konto, so dürfte die maßgebliche Währung in der Regel der Euro sein, weil auch der Aufwand für die Konvertierung von Dollar in Euro

---

[20] *Kröll u. a./Sono*, Art. 85, Rn. 24; *Reinhart*, Art. 85, Rn. 6; MünchKomm/*P. Huber*, Art. 85, Rn. 9; MünchKommHGB/*Mankowski*, Vor Art. 85, Rn. 2 und Art. 85, Rn. 8; *Staudinger/Magnus*, Art. 85, Rn. 16; Hof van Beroep Gent, 3.10.2003, CISG-online 949.

[21] Vgl. Hof van Beroep Antwerpen, 24.4.2006, CISG-online 1258: Einlagerung von Holz für mehr als drei Monate war im Einzelfall unangemessen; CIETAC, 6.6.1991, CISG-online 854: Einlagerung von verderblichen Chemikalien für über zwei Jahre unangemessen; vgl. auch Art. 88 Rn. 12.

[22] CIETAC, 18.12.2002, CISG-online 1543.

[23] *Achilles*, Art. 85, Rn. 6; *Honnold/Flechtner*, Art. 85, Rn. 453; *Kröll u. a./Sono*, Art. 85, Rn. 28; CISG-AC Op 6 (Gotanda) Comment 4.2.

[24] So *Enderlein/Maskow/Strohbach*, Art. 85, Anm. 7.; *Ferrari u. a./Ferrari*, Internationales Vertragsrecht, Art. 85, Rn. 11; MünchKomm/*P. Huber*, Art. 85, Rn. 13; *Kröll u. a./Sono*, Art. 85, Rn. 29; *Staudinger/Magnus*, Art. 85, Rn. 17.

[25] ICAC, 25.4.1995, CISG-online 367; *Soergel/Lüderitz/Dettmeier*, Art. 85, Rn. 8.

[26] Ebenso *Achilles*, Art. 85, Rn. 6; *Brunner*, Art. 85, Rn. 9; *Kröll u. a./Sono*, Art. 85, Rn. 25; MünchKomm/ *P. Huber*, Art. 85, Rn. 14; MünchKommHGB/*Mankowski*, Art. 85, Rn. 11; *Soergel/Lüderitz/Dettmeier*, Art. 85, Rn. 8; *Staudinger/Magnus*, Art. 85, Rn. 17.

[27] Rechtbank van Koophandel Kortrijk, 3.10.2001, CISG-online 757.

[28] *Kröll u. a./Sono*, Art. 85, Rn. 26.

[29] Višje sodišče (Obergericht) Ljubljana, 14.12.2005, CISG-online 1959.

[30] Ebenso MünchKommHGB/*Mankowski*, Art. 85, Rn. 13; *Ferrari u. a./Ferrari*, Internationales Vertragsrecht, Art. 85, Rn. 13; *Jentsch*, S. 122 f.

[31] So MünchKommHGB/*Mankowski*, Art. 85, Rn. 12; *Soergel/Lüderitz/Dettmeier*, Art. 85, Rn. 8; *Staudinger/Magnus*, Art. 85, Rn. 17; *Ferrari u. a./Ferrari*, Internationales Vertragsrecht, Art. 85, Rn. 13.

zu den nach Art. 85 zu erstattenden Aufwendungen gehört, soweit er sich im Rahmen des Angemessenen hält.

3. Zurückbehaltungsrecht

17 Wegen des Anspruchs auf Ersatz der Erhaltungskosten steht dem Verkäufer gemäß Art. 85 S. 2 an der verkauften Ware ein Zurückbehaltungsrecht zu. Der Verkäufer braucht die Ware also nur Zug um Zug gegen Erstattung der Aufwendungen (und ggf. gegen Zahlung des Kaufpreises) zu liefern. Voraussetzung ist natürlich, dass dem Verkäufer ein solcher Erstattungsanspruch zusteht. Die Partei, die sich auf ein Zurückbehaltungsrecht beruft, muss also (spätestens) im Prozess vortragen, dass und welche Erhaltungskosten ihr entstanden sind.[32] Sofern ein Zurückbehaltungsrecht besteht, wird man dem anderen Teil die Befugnis einräumen müssen, dieses durch Stellung einer angemessenen Sicherheit abzuwenden.[33] So lässt sich verhindern, dass die Erhaltungskosten allein wegen des Streits um ihre Angemessenheit noch weiter ansteigen. Dadurch kann der Verkäufer zwar in die Situation kommen, die Freigabe der Sicherheit vor Gericht erstreiten zu müssen;[34] ein Streit um die Freigabe wird in der Regel aber mit weniger Risiken verbunden sein als ein Streit um das Zurückbehaltungsrecht.

4. Verletzung der Erhaltungspflicht

18 Siehe dazu Vor Art. 85 Rn. 4 f.

---

[32] Dies dürfte die eigentliche Aussage der (zu Art. 86 I 2 ergangenen) eher kryptisch gehaltenen Entscheidung Civ. 1, 4.1.1995, CISG-online 138 darstellen. Vgl. dazu auch MünchKomm/*P. Huber*, Art. 86, Rn. 8; MünchKommHGB/*Mankowski*, Art. 86, Rn. 10; *Kröll u. a./Sono*, Art. 85, Rn. 20.

[33] Ebenso *Achilles*, Art. 85, Rn. 7; *Brunner*, Art. 85, Rn. 10; *Bamberger/Roth/Saenger*, Art. 85, Rn. 10; *Enderlein/Maskow/Strohbach*, Art. 85, Anm. 6.; *Bianca/Bonell/Barrera Graf*, Art. 85, Anm. 3.1.; *Ferrari u. a./Ferrari*, Internationales Vertragsrecht, Art. 85, Rn. 14; *Herber/Czerwenka*, Art. 85, Rn. 6; MünchKomm/*P. Huber*, Art. 85, Rn. 15; MünchKommHGB/*Mankowski*, Art. 85, Rn. 16; *Staudinger/Magnus*, Art. 85, Rn. 18.

[34] Mit dieser Begründung wendet sich *Witz/Salger/Lorenz/Lorenz*, Art. 85, Rn. 11 gegen ein Abwendungsrecht.

Art. 86 [Pflicht des Käufers zur Inbesitznahme und Erhaltung der Ware]

(1) Hat der Käufer die Ware empfangen und beabsichtigt er, ein nach dem Vertrag oder diesem Übereinkommen bestehendes Zurückweisungsrecht auszuüben, so hat er die den Umständen angemessenen Maßnahmen zu ihrer Erhaltung zu treffen. Er ist berechtigt, die Ware zurückzubehalten, bis ihm der Verkäufer seine angemessenen Aufwendungen erstattet hat.

(2) Ist die dem Käufer zugesandte Ware ihm am Bestimmungsort zur Verfügung gestellt worden und übt er das Recht aus, sie zurückzuweisen, so hat er sie für Rechnung des Verkäufers in Besitz zu nehmen, sofern dies ohne Zahlung des Kaufpreises und ohne unzumutbare Unannehmlichkeiten oder unverhältnismäßige Kosten möglich ist. Dies gilt nicht,* wenn der Verkäufer oder eine Person, die befugt ist, die Ware für Rechnung des Verkäufers in Obhut zu nehmen, am Bestimmungsort anwesend ist. Nimmt der Käufer die Ware nach diesem Absatz in Besitz, so werden seine Rechte und Pflichten durch Absatz 1 geregelt.

Art. 86

(1) If the buyer has received the goods and intends to exercise any right under the contract or this Convention to reject them, he must take such steps to preserve them as are reasonable in the circumstances. He is entitled to retain them until he has been reimbursed his reasonable expenses by the seller.

(2) If goods dispatched to the buyer have been placed at his disposal at their destination and he exercises the right to reject them, he must take possession of them on behalf of the seller, provided that this can be done without payment of the price and without unreasonable inconvenience or unreasonable expense. This provision does not apply if the seller or a person authorized to take charge of the goods on his behalf is present at the destination. If the buyer takes possession of the goods under this paragraph, his rights and obligations are governed by the preceding paragraph.

Art. 86

1) If the buyer has received the goods and intends to exercise any right under the contract or this Convention to reject them, he must take such steps to preserve them as are reasonable in the circumstances. He is entitled to retain them until he has been reimbursed his reasonable expenses by the seller.

2) If goods dispatched to the buyer have been placed at his disposal at their destination and he exercises the right to reject them, he must take possession of them on behalf of the seller, provided that this can be done without payment of the price and without unreasonable inconvenience or unreasonable expense. This provision does not apply if the seller or a person authorized to take charge of the goods on his behalf is present at the destination. If the buyer takes possession of the goods under this paragraph, his rights and obligations are governed by the preceding paragraph.

Übersicht

	Rn.
I. Allgemeines	1
II. Vorgeschichte	2
III. Voraussetzungen der Erhaltungspflicht	3
1. Empfang der Ware	3
2. Absicht der Zurückweisung	4
a) Zurückweisungsrecht	5
b) Erkennbarkeit	7
IV. Voraussetzungen der Pflicht zur Inbesitznahme	8
1. Zusendung	9
2. Zurückweisung	11
3. Zumutbare Möglichkeit zur Inbesitznahme	13
a) Zahlung des Kaufpreises	14

---

* Schweiz: Dieser Absatz ist nicht anzuwenden.

b) Sonstige Nachteile 15
c) Verantwortlichkeit für Dritte 16a
4. Keine Anwesenheit des Verkäufers 17
5. Aufhebung des Vertrags 17a
V. Erhaltungspflicht, Kostentragung, Zurückbehaltung 18
VI. Sonstiges 21

Vorläufer und **Entwürfe:** Art. 92 EKG; Genfer E 1976 Art. 61; Wiener E 1977 Art. 61; New Yorker E 1978 Art. 75.

I. Allgemeines

1   Art. 86 legt als Gegenstück zu Art. 85 dem **Käufer** Erhaltungspflichten auf, wenn er die Ware zwar zurückweisen will (und darf), aber zunächst Besitz von ihr ergriffen hat. Ähnlich wie bei Art. 85 greift die Pflicht auch dann, wenn der Käufer die Ware noch nicht in Besitz hat, aber in der Lage ist, sie in Besitz zu nehmen.

II. Vorgeschichte

2   Bereits Art. 92 EKG enthielt eine im Wesentlichen gleich lautende Vorschrift. Die Vorentwürfe (Art. 61 Genfer E 1976 und Wiener E 1977 sowie Art. 75 New Yorker E 1978) unterscheiden sich davon nur in einzelnen sprachlichen Details. Der dritte Satz des zweiten Absatzes wurde erst in die Endfassung des Art. 86 aufgenommen.

III. Voraussetzungen der Erhaltungspflicht

1. Empfang der Ware

3   **Empfangen** hat der Verkäufer die Ware, wenn sie in seinen Besitz gelangt ist.[1]

2. Absicht der Zurückweisung

4   Weitere Voraussetzung ist, dass der Verkäufer beabsichtigt, ein ihm zustehendes Zurückweisungsrecht auszuüben.

5   a) **Zurückweisungsrecht.** Als **Grundlage** für ein solches Zurückweisungsrecht kommen alle Rechtsbehelfe in Betracht, die es mit sich bringen, dass der Käufer die gelieferte Ware zurückgeben kann. Dies ist vor allem bei Aufhebung des Vertrages (Artt. 49, 51 II, 72, 73) oder bei einem Anspruch auf Ersatzlieferung (Art. 46 II) der Fall. Ein Zurückweisungsrecht kann sich daneben auch aus Art. 52 (vorzeitige Lieferung oder Zuviellieferung) ergeben.[2] Denkbar ist ferner, dass der Käufer gemäß Art. 71 eine Teillieferung zurückweisen darf, weil die Erfüllung der übrigen Lieferverpflichtung infolge Vermögensverfalls des Verkäufers unsicher geworden ist.[3]

6   Die Erhaltungspflicht nach Art. 86 greift nur, wenn die Zurückweisung der Ware **zu Recht** erfolgt ist.[4] Steht dem Käufer in Wahrheit kein Zurückweisungsrecht zu, ist er schon

---

[1] *Bamberger/Roth/Saenger*, Art. 86, Rn. 2; *Ferrari u. a./Ferrari*, Internationales Vertragsrecht, Art. 86, Rn. 2; *Kröll u. a./Sono*, Art. 86, Rn. 6; *Soergel/Lüderitz/Dettmeier*, Art. 86, Rn. 2; *Witz/Salger/Lorenz/Lorenz*, Art. 86, Rn. 4.
[2] Ebenso *Enderlein/Maskow/Strohbach*, Art. 86, Anm. 3.1.; *Ferrari u. a./Ferrari*, Internationales Vertragsrecht, Art. 86, Rn. 3; *Herber/Czerwenka*, Art. 86, Rn. 2; *Kröll u. a./Sono*, Art. 86, Rn. 8; *Reinhart*, Art. 86, Rn. 2; *Soergel/Lüderitz/Dettmeier*, Art. 86, Rn. 2; *Staudinger/Magnus*, Art. 86, Rn. 10; vgl. auch Civ. 1, 4.1.1995, CISG-online 138 und dazu oben Art. 85 Rn. 17.
[3] So *Enderlein/Maskow/Strohbach*, Art. 86, Anm. 3.1.; *Ferrari u. a./Ferrari*, Internationales Vertragsrecht, Art. 86, Rn. 3; *Kröll u. a./Sono*, Art. 86, Rn. 8.
[4] Ebenso *Brunner*, Art. 86, Rn. 2.

im eigenen Interesse zur Erhaltung der Ware gehalten, da er zumindest nach Art. 69 I die Gefahr des Untergangs oder von Verschlechterungen trägt. Ein Anspruch auf Erstattung von Erhaltungskosten steht ihm in diesem Fall aber nicht zu.[5]

b) Erkennbarkeit. Entgegen einer gelegentlich vertretenen Ansicht ist nicht erforderlich, 7 dass der Käufer seine Zurückweisungsabsicht **sofort** bei Abnahme **manifestiert**.[6] Entdeckt er beispielsweise erst später, dass die Ware nicht vertragsgemäß ist, so ist er in gleicher Weise zur Erhaltung verpflichtet, sobald er die Absicht fasst, die Ware zurückzuweisen. Um Manipulationen hinsichtlich des Anspruchs auf Kostenerstattung auszuschließen, wird man allerdings verlangen müssen, dass sich diese Absicht nach außen erkennbar manifestiert.[7] Hat sich die Ware bereits zuvor verschlechtert, ist das Recht zur Vertragsaufhebung ohnehin nach Art. 82 I verlorengegangen.[8] Andererseits kann es nicht darauf ankommen, dass sich der Käufer schon endgültig für die Zurückweisung entschieden hat. Ein Schutzbedürfnis besteht vielmehr schon dann, wenn er die Zurückweisung als eine von mehreren Alternativen in Erwägung zieht.[9]

IV. Voraussetzungen der Pflicht zur Inbesitznahme

Ist der Käufer noch nicht im Besitz der Ware, zwingt ihn Art. 86 II unter gewissen 8 Voraussetzungen, sie in Besitz zu nehmen. Auch für diese Vorschrift ist der Gedanke maßgeblich, dass diejenige Partei, die die besseren Möglichkeiten zum Zugriff auf die Ware hat, im Konfliktfall zunächst für die Erhaltung der Ware zu sorgen hat, bis deren weiterer Verbleib geklärt ist.

1. Zusendung

Zunächst ist erforderlich, dass die Ware dem Käufer zugesandt worden ist. Ob darunter 9 nur ein Transport der Ware durch Dritte fällt,[10] ist letztlich unerheblich: Wird die Ware durch den Verkäufer selbst oder durch dessen eigene Leute zum Käufer transportiert, ist dieser schon nach Satz 2 von der Pflicht zur Inbesitznahme befreit.

Nach dem Sinn und Zweck der Vorschrift kann es auch keine Rolle spielen, ob die 10 Zusendung der Ware in vertragsgemäßer Art und Weise erfolgt ist. Einzige Voraussetzung ist in diesem Zusammenhang, dass die Ware am **Bestimmungsort** angeboten wird. Ist dies der Fall, muss der Käufer – bei Vorliegen der übrigen Voraussetzungen – die Ware auch dann in Besitz nehmen, wenn der Verkäufer sie vertragswidrig durch einen Dritten hat befördern lassen, statt sie selbst abzuliefern. Wird die Ware an einen **anderen Ort** geliefert, besteht für den Käufer grundsätzlich keine Verpflichtung.[11] Im Einzelfall kann allerdings eine analoge Anwendung der Vorschrift in Betracht kommen, wenn die Inbesitznahme für den Käufer ohne weiteres möglich ist;[12] dies gilt auch dann, wenn der

---

[5] Vgl. *Herber/Czerwenka*, Art. 86, Rn. 3; *Ferrari u. a./Ferrari*, Internationales Vertragsrecht, Art. 86, Rn. 2. Vgl. zum Ganzen Art. 85 Rn. 5.
[6] So aber *Bianca/Bonell/Barrera Graf*, Art. 86, Anm. 2.3. Wie hier *Bamberger/Roth/Saenger*, Art. 86, Rn. 2; *Enderlein/Maskow/Strohbach*, Art. 86, Anm. 3.2.; *Ferrari u. a./Ferrari*, Internationales Vertragsrecht, Art. 86, Rn. 2; MünchKomm/*P. Huber*, Art. 86, Rn. 4; MünchKommHGB/*Mankowski*, Art. 86, Rn. 5; *Soergel/Lüderitz/Dettmeier*, Art. 85, Rn. 2; *Staudinger/Magnus*, Art. 86, Rn. 10.
[7] Ebenso *Achilles*, Art. 86, Rn. 2; *Bamberger/Roth/Saenger*, Art. 86, Rn. 3; *Jentsch*, S. 59 f.
[8] Ebenso *Honnold/Flechtner*, Art. 86, Rn. 455.
[9] Ebenso *Honnold/Flechtner*, Art. 86, Rn. 455; *Krebs*, S. 112; *Kröll u. a./Sono*, Art. 86, Rn. 9; MünchKommHGB/*Mankowski*, Art. 86, Rn. 5.
[10] So *Soergel/Lüderitz/Dettmeier*, Art. 86, Rn. 3; *Kröll u. a./Sono*, Art. 86, Rn. 17; wie hier MünchKomm/*P. Huber*, Art. 86, Rn. 10.
[11] So ausdrücklich *Enderlein/Maskow/Strohbach*, Art. 86, Anm. 7.; *Bianca/Bonell/Barrera Graf*, Art. 86, Anm. 2.4.2.; *Kröll u. a./Sono*, Art. 86, Rn. 21.
[12] Ebenso MünchKomm/*P. Huber*, Art. 86, Rn. 10; *Ferrari u. a./Ferrari*, Internationales Vertragsrecht, Art. 86, Rn. 7 und wohl auch *Kröll u. a./Sono*, Art. 86, Rn. 21.

Verkäufer die Ware vertragswidrig zum Käufer sendet, obwohl Abholung beim Verkäufer vereinbart war.[13]

2. Zurückweisung

11 Weitere Voraussetzung ist, dass der Käufer **vor Annahme** von einem ihm zustehenden Zurückweisungsrecht Gebrauch macht. Wegen der möglichen Grundlagen eines Zurückweisungsrechts s. oben Rn. 5. Nimmt der Käufer die Ware zunächst entgegen und entschließt er sich erst danach zur Zurückweisung, kommt Absatz 1 zur Anwendung.

12 Nach einer verbreiteten Ansicht soll der Käufer auch dann von der Pflicht zur Inbesitznahme befreit sein, wenn er die Ware schon zu **einem früheren Zeitpunkt** zurückgewiesen hat, etwa weil er schon aus den ihm ausgehändigten Dokumenten entnehmen konnte, dass sie nicht vertragsgemäß ist.[14] Mit dem Zweck des Art. 86 II lässt sich dies allenfalls dann vereinbaren, wenn der Verkäufer infolge der frühzeitigen Zurückweisung die Möglichkeit erhalten hat, die Ware wieder in seine Obhut zu bringen. Bestand diese Möglichkeit nicht, so muss es bei der Pflicht des Käufers zur Inbesitznahme bleiben.[15] Und selbst wenn der Verkäufer die Ware nur aus Nachlässigkeit weiterhin ihrem Schicksal überlassen hat, wird man aus den in Rn. 8 angestellten Erwägungen heraus kaum anders entscheiden können.

3. Zumutbare Möglichkeit zur Inbesitznahme

13 Der Käufer ist nur dann zur Inbesitznahme verpflichtet, wenn ihm dies ohne unzumutbare Schwierigkeiten möglich ist.

14 a) **Zahlung des Kaufpreises. Keine** Pflicht zur Inbesitznahme trifft den Käufer insbesondere dann, wenn er die Ware nur gegen **Zahlung des Kaufpreises** übernehmen kann. Auch eine anstelle des Kaufpreises vorgesehene **Sicherheitsleistung** braucht der Käufer **nicht** zu erbringen.[16] Gibt der Transporteur hingegen zu erkennen, dass er trotz anderweitiger Vereinbarung bereit ist, die Ware auch ohne Zahlung zu übergeben, ist der Käufer aus den in Rn. 8 angestellten Erwägungen zur Übernahme verpflichtet.[17] Dasselbe gilt, wenn der Käufer die Ware schon vor der Anlieferung bezahlt hat.[18]

15 b) **Sonstige Nachteile.** Auch im Übrigen darf die Inbesitznahme nicht mit unzumutbaren **Unannehmlichkeiten** oder unverhältnismäßigen **Kosten** verbunden sein. Welche Anstrengungen und Ausgaben der Käufer hierbei auf sich zu nehmen hat, lässt sich nur anhand der konkreten Umstände des Einzelfalls bestimmen. Ebenso wie bei der Erhaltungspflicht ist auch hier in erster Linie das Verhältnis zwischen den erforderlichen Aufwendungen und dem drohenden Schaden von Bedeutung.[19]

16 Umstritten ist, welche Pflichten den Käufer treffen, wenn eine **rasche Verschlechterung** der Ware droht. Kontrovers diskutiert wird in diesem Zusammenhang vor allem die Bedeutung von Art. 88 II: Nach der einen Auffassung soll der Käufer trotz Art. 88 II nicht zur Inbesitznahme verpflichtet sein, wenn diese mit unverhältnismäßigen Kosten verbunden wäre.[20] Nach

---

[13] *Kröll u. a./Sono*, Art. 86, Rn. 19.
[14] So bereits Sekretariatskommentar, Art. 75, Nr. 4.; ebenso *Herber/Czerwenka*, Art. 86, Rn. 6; *Neumayer/Ming*, Art. 86, Anm. 3. a. E.
[15] Ebenso *Reinhart*, Art. 86, Rn. 6; *Kröll u. a./Sono*, Art. 86, Rn. 22; MünchKomm/*P. Huber*, Art. 86, Rn. 12; MünchKommHGB/*Mankowski*, Art. 86, Rn. 13; *Piltz*, Internationales Kaufrecht, Rn. 4–260; im Ergebnis wohl auch *Achilles*, Art. 86, Rn. 6, *Soergel/Lüderitz/Dettmeier*, Art. 86, Rn. 5 und *Staudinger/Magnus*, Art. 86, Rn. 19; gegen die Ansicht des Sekretariatskommentars auch *Enderlein/Maskow/Strohbach*, Art. 86, Anm. 7.
[16] *Enderlein/Maskow/Strohbach*, Art. 86, Anm. 10.1.; MünchKomm/*P. Huber*, Art. 86, Rn. 14.
[17] Ebenso *Kröll u. a./Sono*, Art. 86, Rn. 24.
[18] Ebenso *Kröll u. a./Sono*, Art. 86, Rn. 25.
[19] Vgl. zum Ganzen Art. 85 Rn. 12.
[20] So *Bianca/Bonell/Barrera Graf*, Art. 86, Anm. 2.9.; *Kröll u. a./Sono*, Art. 86, Rn. 27.

der Gegenansicht ist der Käufer wegen Art. 88 II verpflichtet, auch größere Kosten in Kauf zu nehmen und diese im Wege des sofortigen Selbsthilfeverkaufs wieder hereinzuholen.[21] Nach einer dritten Auffassung soll der Käufer wegen der mit einem Selbsthilfeverkauf verbundenen Risiken generell nicht verpflichtet sein, die Ware in Besitz zu nehmen, wenn absehbar ist, dass sofort ein Selbsthilfeverkauf vorzunehmen wäre.[22] Im Ergebnis dürfte keiner Ansicht uneingeschränkt zu folgen sein. Allerdings sollte die Möglichkeit eines Selbsthilfeverkaufs nach Art. 88 schon bei der Frage, ob eine Inbesitznahme zumutbar ist, Berücksichtigung finden. Die Übernahme von ansonsten nicht zumutbaren Kosten kann dem Käufer jedoch nur dann angesonnen werden, wenn ein Selbsthilfeverkauf im Einzelfall problemlos möglich ist und auch mit der Zwischenfinanzierung der Aufwendungen keine unzumutbaren Risiken verbunden sind.[23]

c) **Verantwortlichkeit für Dritte.** Die Pflicht zur Inbesitznahme trifft nur den **Käufer**. Dieser ist nach allgemeinen Regeln auch für das Verhalten der von ihm bei der Empfangnahme eingesetzten Hilfspersonen verantwortlich. Beim Streckengeschäft wird eine Verantwortlichkeit des Zwischenhändlers für den Endabnehmer verneint.[24]

4. Keine Anwesenheit des Verkäufers

Entsprechend dem in Rn. 8 dargestellten Grundgedanken ist der Käufer von der Pflicht zur Inbesitznahme befreit, wenn der Verkäufer am Bestimmungsort anwesend ist. In diesem Fall hat der Verkäufer selbst die Möglichkeit, sich um die zurückgewiesene Ware zu kümmern. Dasselbe gilt, wenn eine **andere Person** zugegen ist, die befugt ist, die Ware für Rechnung des Verkäufers in Obhut zu nehmen. Dies kann etwa ein vom Verkäufer eingeschalteter **Handelsvertreter** oder **-makler** sein. Ob eine Befugnis besteht, richtet sich nach dem Recht, das für die Beziehung zwischen dem Verkäufer und der anderen Person maßgeblich ist.[25] Ob eine mit der finanziellen Abwicklung betraute **Bank** die Voraussetzungen erfüllt, hängt vom Einzelfall ab; in der Regel wird sie nicht zu dem betreffenden Personenkreis zählen.[26]

5. Aufhebung des Vertrags

Die Pflicht des Käufers zum Erhalt der gelieferten Ware besteht – anders als die Erhaltungspflicht des Verkäufers (dazu Art. 85 Rn. 14) – auch im Falle einer Vertragsaufhebung fort.[27] Sie endet erst mit der Rückgabe oder mit einer Verwertung der Ware.

V. Erhaltungspflicht, Kostentragung, Zurückbehaltung

Hat der Käufer die Ware in den von Abs. 1 und 2 erfassten Fällen in Besitz genommen, treffen ihn dieselben Pflichten wie den Verkäufer im Fall des Art. 85. Wegen Einzelheiten kann auf Art. 85 Rn. 12–18 verwiesen werden. Im Falle des Abs. 2 gehören zu den vom Verkäufer zu ersetzenden Kosten auch diejenigen der Inbesitznahme.

Im Falle eines **Rechtsmangels** soll der Käufer nach verbreiteter Auffassung auch verpflichtet sein, rechtliche Vorkehrungen gegen Zugriffsversuche Dritter zu ergreifen.[28] Dies

---

[21] So *Enderlein/Maskow/Strohbach*, Art. 86, Anm. 3. und Art. 88, Anm. 5.; MünchKomm/*P. Huber*, Art. 86, Rn. 15.
[22] *Bamberger/Roth/Saenger*, Art. 86, Rn. 7; *Ferrari u. a./Ferrari*, Internationales Vertragsrecht, Art. 86, Rn. 9; MünchKommHGB/*Mankowski*, Art. 86, Rn. 14.
[23] Ähnlich *Jentsch*, S. 69.
[24] MünchKommHGB/*Mankowski*, Art. 86, Rn. 12; vgl. auch *Jentsch*, S. 69 f.
[25] So wohl auch *Kröll u. a./Sono*, Art. 86, Rn. 29.
[26] Wie hier *Kröll u. a./Sono*, Art. 86, Rn. 29; MünchKomm/*P. Huber*, Art. 86, Rn. 16. Generell ablehnend *Enderlein/Maskow/Strohbach*, Art. 86, Anm. 11.; *Ferrari u. a./Ferrari*, Internationales Vertragsrecht, Art. 86, Rn. 11.
[27] Vgl. *Fountoulakis*, Art. 81 Rn. 12; ebenso *Kröll u. a./Sono*, Art. 86, Rn. 14; für eine analoge Anwendung des Art. 86 in diesem Fall *Staudinger/Magnus*, Art. 85, Rn. 19.
[28] So *Bamberger/Roth/Saenger*, Art. 86, Rn. 2a; *Staudinger/Magnus*, Art. 86, Rn. 11; MünchKomm/*P. Huber*, Art. 86, Rn. 5; MünchKommHGB/*Mankowski*, Art. 86, Rn. 7.

dürfte nur dann in Betracht kommen, wenn der Verkäufer aufgrund fehlenden Besitzes, wegen der räumlichen Entfernung, wegen Eilbedürftigkeit oder aus sonstigen Gründen nicht in der Lage ist, solche Schritte selbst zu ergreifen.

20 Wenn der Käufer die ihm nach Art. 86 obliegende **Erhaltungspflicht verletzt** hat, können dem Verkäufer Ansprüche auf Schadenersatz zustehen.[29] Hat die Pflichtverletzung zu einer Verschlechterung der Ware geführt, verliert der Käufer darüber hinaus nach Art. 82 I das Recht, die Aufhebung des Vertrages zu erklären oder Ersatzlieferung zu verlangen.[30]

VI. Sonstiges

21 Eine analoge Anwendung von Art. 86 wird befürwortet, sofern der Käufer **Verpackungsmaterial** oder dergleichen erhält, das er dem Verkäufer zurückzusenden hat.[31] Dies erscheint zu weitgehend, zumal die Erhaltungspflicht in solchen Fällen nicht davon abhängen dürfte, ob das Verpackungsmaterial mangelhaft ist oder nicht. Allerdings sollten die dem Käufer insoweit obliegenden Nebenpflichten nicht nach nationalem Recht, sondern nach allgemeinen Grundsätzen des CISG beurteilt werden.[32] In diesem Zusammenhang mag Art. 86 als Ausprägung des allgemeinen Grundsatzes von Treu und Glauben heranzuziehen sein, soweit es um den Umfang der dem Käufer obliegenden Pflichten geht.[33]

---

[29] Vgl. dazu Vor Art. 85 Rn. 4 f.
[30] *Schlechtriem* Internationales UN-Kaufrecht, Rn. 336; *Brunner*, Art. 86, Rn. 11; MünchKomm/*P. Huber*, Art. 86, Rn. 6; MünchKommHGB/*Mankowski*, Art 86, Rn 8; *Staudinger/Magnus*, Art. 86, Rn. 12.
[31] So *Ferrari u. a./Ferrari*, Internationales Vertragsrecht, Art. 86, Rn. 5; *Staudinger/Magnus*, Art. 86, Rn. 23; *Jentsch*, S. 78 f.
[32] Anders MünchKommHGB/*Mankowski*, Art. 86, Rn. 6; beiläufig auch BGH, 5.2.1997, NJW 1997, 1578, 1579 zum EKG.
[33] Allgemein zur Bedeutung der Artt. 85 und 86 als Quelle für allgemeine Rechtsgrundsätze s. Vor Art. 85 Rn. 6.

Art. 87 [Einlagerung bei Dritten]

Eine Partei, die Maßnahmen zur Erhaltung der Ware zu treffen hat, kann die Ware auf Kosten der anderen Partei in den Lagerräumen eines Dritten einlagern, sofern daraus keine unverhältnismäßigen Kosten entstehen.

Art. 87	Art. 87
A party who is bound to take steps to preserve the goods may deposit them in a warehouse of a third person at the expense of the other party provided that the expense incurred is not unreasonable.	La partie qui est tenue de prendre des mesures pour assurer la conservation des marchandises peut les déposer dans les magasins d'un tiers aux frais de l'autre partie, à condition que les frais qui en résultent ne soient pas déraisonnables.

Übersicht

	Rn.
I. Allgemeines	1
II. Vorgeschichte	2
III. Voraussetzungen	3
IV. Rechtsfolgen	5
1. Sorgfältige Auswahl des Verwahrers	5
2. Versicherung	6
3. Erfüllungswirkung	7
4. Rechtsverhältnis zum Verwahrer	8
5. Kostentragung	9

Vorläufer und **Entwürfe:** Art. 93 EKG, Genfer E 1976 Art. 62; Wiener E 1977 Art. 62; New Yorker E 1978 Art. 76.

I. Allgemeines

Art. 87 stellt der nach Art. 85 bzw. 86 erhaltungspflichtigen Partei ein besonderes Mittel zur Verfügung, um dieser Pflicht nachzukommen. Die Vorschrift hat im Wesentlichen klarstellenden Charakter. **1**

II. Vorgeschichte

Dieselbe Regelung findet sich bereits in Art. 93 EKG sowie den Vorentwürfen zum CISG. **2**

III. Voraussetzungen

Art. 87 knüpft an das Bestehen einer **Erhaltungspflicht** nach Art. 85 oder Art. 86 an. Ist eine Partei danach zur Erhaltung der Ware verpflichtet, steht es in ihrem Ermessen, sie bei einem Dritten einzulagern. Zusätzliche Voraussetzungen, beispielsweise eine vorherige **Anzeige** an die andere Vertragspartei, sind **nicht** erforderlich.[1] **3**

Die einzige Beschränkung bilden die **Kosten**. Ebenso wie alle anderen Maßnahmen im Zusammenhang mit Artt. 85 ff. ist die Einlagerung nur zulässig, sofern daraus keine unverhältnismäßigen Kosten entstehen. Ist diese Grenze überschritten, hat dies freilich nur Auswirkungen auf den Erstattungsanspruch der einlagernden Partei (dazu Rn. 9). Ein Übergang der Einlagerungsgefahr findet hingegen nicht statt.[2] **4**

---
[1] MünchKomm/*P. Huber*, Art. 87, Rn. 2.
[2] *Karollus*, S. 97; *Kröll u. a./Sono*, Art. 87, Rn. 6; *Staudinger/Magnus*, Art. 87, Rn. 3.

IV. Rechtsfolgen

1. Sorgfältige Auswahl des Verwahrers

5   Entscheidet sich die erhaltungspflichtige Partei für eine Fremdeinlagerung, hat sie einen geeigneten Verwahrer auszuwählen. Verstößt sie gegen diese Pflicht, so ist sie dem anderen Teil zum Schadensersatz verpflichtet.[3] Für ein Verschulden des Dritten während der Verwahrung hat sie hingegen nicht einzustehen.[4]

2. Versicherung

6   Vereinzelt wird gefordert, die erhaltungspflichtige Partei müsse die eingelagerte Ware zusätzlich versichern.[5] In dieser Allgemeinheit geht dies sicherlich zu weit. Zwar kann nach den Umständen des Einzelfalles eine Versicherung geboten sein.[6] Ob dies der Fall ist, bestimmt sich jedoch nach dem allgemeinen Kriterium der Angemessenheit. Der Abschluss einer Versicherung kommt danach nur dann in Betracht, wenn dies ohne unverhältnismäßigen Aufwand möglich ist und den üblichen Gepflogenheiten in der betreffenden Branche entspricht.[7] Letzteres dürfte regelmäßig der Fall sein, wenn der Lagerhalter seine Haftung vertraglich ausgeschlossen hat.[8]

3. Erfüllungswirkung

7   Nicht ausdrücklich geregelt ist die Frage, ob die erhaltungspflichtige Partei durch die Einlagerung von ihrer Pflicht zur Lieferung bzw. Rückgabe der Ware frei wird. Einzelne nationale Rechte messen der **Hinterlegung** unter bestimmten Voraussetzungen mitunter Erfüllungswirkung bei. Dem **CISG** lässt sich eine solche Regelung dagegen auch **nicht** sinngemäß entnehmen. Da die Frage, auf welche Weise der Schuldner seine Verpflichtungen erfüllen kann, im CISG ansonsten umfassend geregelt ist, dürfte sich insoweit ein Rückgriff auf nationale Rechtsordnungen verbieten.[9] Selbst wenn der Schuldner bei der Einlagerung die besonderen Förmlichkeiten einhält, bei deren Beachtung nach den Regeln eines nationalen Rechts Erfüllungswirkung eintritt, tritt bei Anwendbarkeit des CISG folglich **keine Befreiung** von der Leistungspflicht ein.[10]

4. Rechtsverhältnis zum Verwahrer

8   Ebenfalls nicht geregelt sind die Rechtsbeziehungen zum einlagernden Dritten. Aus dem Schweigen der Konvention ist zu folgern, dass hierfür grundsätzlich die Vereinbarungen

---

[3] *Ferrari u. a./Ferrari*, Internationales Vertragsrecht, Art. 87, Rn. 3; *Kröll u. a./Sono*, Art. 87, Rn. 11.
[4] S. dazu bereits Art. 85 Rn. 13; ferner *Brunner*, Art. 87, Rn. 3; MünchKomm/*P. Huber*, Art. 87, Rn. 3 f.; MünchKommHGB/*Mankowski*, Art. 87, Rn. 4; *Soergel/Lüderitz/Dettmeier*, Art. 87, Rn. 4; *Staudinger/Magnus*, Art. 87, Rn. 5.
[5] So *Herber/Czerwenka*, Art. 87, Rn. 2; vermittelnd *Kröll u. a./Sono*, Art. 85, Rn. 25 und Art. 87, Rn. 12: Die einlagernde Partei sei nicht ohne weiteres verpflichtet, eine Versicherung abzuschließen, die andere Partei sei aber stets verpflichtet, eine angemessene Prämie für eine tatsächlich abgeschlossene Versicherung zu ersetzen.
[6] Bejaht wurde die Angemessenheit z. B. vom Hof van Beroep Antwerpen, 24.4.2006, CISG-online 1258.
[7] Ebenso *Bamberger/Roth/Saenger*, Art. 87, Rn. 3; *Kröll u. a./Sono*, Art. 87, Rn. 12.
[8] Dafür *Achilles*, Art. 87, Rn. 1; *Ferrari u. a./Ferrari*, Internationales Vertragsrecht, Art. 87, Rn. 5; *Witz/Salger/Lorenz/Lorenz*, Art. 87, Rn. 4; MünchKommHGB/*Mankowski*, Art. 87, Rn. 6; *Staudinger/Magnus*, Art. 87, Rn. 6.
[9] Ebenso *Bamberger/Roth/Saenger*, Art. 87, Rn. 4; *Witz/Salger/Lorenz/Lorenz*, Art. 87, Rn. 6.
[10] Ebenso *Schlechtriem*, Internationales UN-Kaufrecht, Rn. 339; *Achilles*, Art. 87, Rn. 2; *Brunner*, Art. 87, Rn. 3; *Herber/Czerwenka*, Art. 87, Rn. 5; *Kröll u. a./Sono*, Art. 87, Rn. 8; MünchKomm/*P. Huber*, Art. 87, Rn. 3; MünchKommHGB/*Mankowski*, Art. 87, Rn. 1 und 7; *Soergel/Lüderitz/Dettmeier*, Art. 87, Rn. 3; *Staudinger/Magnus*, Art. 87, Rn. 7. Für eine Befreiung *Enderlein/Maskow/Strohbach*, Art. 87, Anm. 1.2. (vgl. auch Art. 88, Anm. 2.3. zur Erfüllungswirkung eines Selbsthilfeverkaufs); *Neumayer/Ming*, Art. 87, Anm. 2.

zwischen dem Einlagernden und dem Verwahrer maßgeblich sind und keine unmittelbaren Rechte und Pflichten gegenüber der anderen Partei des Kaufvertrages entstehen. Mangels besonderer Vereinbarung hat also nur die einlagernde Partei einen Herausgabeanspruch gegen den Verwahrer; nur sie ist im Verhältnis zu ihm zur Zahlung einer Vergütung verpflichtet.[11]

5. Kostentragung

Die Kosten der Lagerung kann die einlagernde Partei von der Gegenseite ersetzt verlangen, soweit die Grenze des Unverhältnismäßigen nicht überschritten ist. Die in Artt. 85 und 86 vorgesehenen Zurückbehaltungsrechte erstrecken sich auch auf diesen Anspruch. Ein direkter Anspruch des Verwahrers gegen die andere Partei des Kaufvertrages ist im CISG nicht vorgesehen (dazu bereits oben Rn. 8). Gemäß Art. 78 sind die zu erstattenden Kosten zu verzinsen.[12]

---

[11] Ebenso *Honnold/Flechtner,* Art. 87, Rn. 456; *Kröll u. a./Sono,* Art. 87, Rn. 9.
[12] Višje sodišče (Obergericht) Ljubljana, 14.12.2005, CISG-online 1959.

Art. 88 [Selbsthilfeverkauf]

(1) Eine Partei, die nach Artikel 85 oder 86 zur Erhaltung der Ware verpflichtet ist, kann sie auf jede geeignete Weise verkaufen, wenn die andere Partei die Inbesitznahme oder die Rücknahme der Ware oder die Zahlung des Kaufpreises oder der Erhaltungskosten ungebührlich hinauszögert, vorausgesetzt, daß sie der anderen Partei ihre Verkaufsabsicht in vernünftiger Weise* angezeigt hat.

(2) Ist die Ware einer raschen Verschlechterung ausgesetzt oder würde ihre Erhaltung unverhältnismäßige Kosten verursachen, so hat die Partei, der nach Artikel 85 oder 86 die Erhaltung der Ware obliegt, sich in angemessener Weise um ihren Verkauf zu bemühen. Soweit möglich hat sie der anderen Partei ihre Verkaufsabsicht anzuzeigen.

(3) Hat eine Partei die Ware verkauft, so kann sie aus dem Erlös des Verkaufs den Betrag behalten, der den angemessenen Kosten der Erhaltung und des Verkaufs der Ware entspricht. Den Überschuß schuldet sie der anderen Partei.

Art. 88

(1) A party who is bound to preserve the goods in accordance with article 85 or 86 may sell them by any appropriate means if there has been an unreasonable delay by the other party in taking possession of the goods or in taking them back or in paying the price or the cost of preservation, provided that reasonable notice of the intention to sell has been given to the other party.

(2) If the goods are subject to rapid deterioration or their preservation would involve unreasonable expense, a party who is bound to preserve the goods in accordance with article 85 or 86 must take reasonable measures to sell them. To the extent possible he must give notice to the other party of his intention to sell.

(3) A party selling the goods has the right to retain out of the proceeds of sale an amount equal to the reasonable expenses of preserving the goods and of selling them. He must account to the other party for the balance.

Art. 88

1) La partie qui doit assurer la conservation des marchandises conformément aux articles 85 ou 86 peut les vendre par tous moyens appropriés si l'autre partie a apporté un retard déraisonnable à prendre possession des marchandises ou à les reprendre ou à payer le prix ou les frais de leur conservation, sous réserve de notifier à cette autre partie, dans des conditions raisonnables, son intention de vendre.

2) Lorsque les marchandises sont sujettes à une détérioration rapide ou lorsque leur conservation entraînerait des Frais déraisonnable, la partie qui est tenue d'assurer la conservation des marchandises conformément aux articles 85 ou 86 doit raisonnablement s'employer à les vendre. Dans la mesure du possible, elle doit notifier à l'autre partie son intention de vendre.

3) La partie qui vend le marchandises a le droit de retenir sur le produit de la vente un montant égal aux frais raisonnables de conservation et de vente des marchandises. Elle doit le surplus à l'autre partie.

Übersicht

	Rn.
I. Allgemeines	1
II. Vorgeschichte	2
III. Recht zum Selbsthilfeverkauf (Abs. 1)	3
1. Verzögerte Erfüllung	4
2. Ungebührliche Verzögerung	5
3. Hinderungsgründe	5a
4. Anzeige der Verkaufsabsicht	6
5. Modalitäten des Selbsthilfeverkaufs	9
IV. Pflicht zum Notverkauf (Abs. 2)	10
1. Gefahr der raschen Verschlechterung	11

---

* Schweiz: rechtzeitig.

2. Unverhältnismäßige Erhaltungskosten 12
3. Anzeige 13
4. Modalitäten des Notverkaufs 14
5. Keine erfolgsbezogene Pflicht 14a
V. Wirkungen gegenüber Dritten 15
IV. Verwendung des Verkaufserlöses 17

Vorläufer und **Entwürfe:** Artt. 94 und 95 EKG; Genfer E 1976 Art. 63; Wiener E 1977 Art. 63; New Yorker E 1978 Art. 77.

I. Allgemeines

Art. 88 normiert zum einen das allgemeine Recht der erhaltungspflichtigen Partei, die 1 Ware jederzeit im Wege des Selbsthilfeverkaufs zu veräußern. Unter bestimmten, in Absatz 2 genannten Voraussetzungen besteht sogar die Pflicht zum Verkauf (sog. Notverkauf). In beiden Fällen geht es darum, unnötige Beeinträchtigungen durch das Auflaufen hoher Lagerkosten oder durch den drohenden Verderb der Ware zu vermeiden. Art. 88 setzt stets voraus, dass die Partei, die den Notverkauf durchführt, gemäß Art. 85 oder Art. 86 zur Erhaltung der Ware verpflichtet ist. Fehlt es hieran, z. B. weil der Käufer die Abnahme zu Recht verweigert oder die bereits abgenommene Ware zu Unrecht zurückweisen will (vgl. dazu Art. 85 Rn. 5 und Art. 86 Rn. 6), ist für die Anwendung von Art. 88 kein Raum.[1]

II. Vorgeschichte

Das EKG hatte den Selbsthilfe- und den Notverkauf je in einem gesonderten Artikel geregelt 2 (Artt. 94 und 95). Inhaltlich entsprachen diese Vorschriften weitgehend der jetzigen Regelung. Die Vorentwürfe zum CISG fassten die beiden Fälle bereits in einer Vorschrift zusammen.

III. Recht zum Selbsthilfeverkauf (Abs. 1)

Absatz 1 knüpft an Art. 85 bzw. Art. 86 an und gibt der danach erhaltungspflichtigen Partei 3 unter bestimmten Voraussetzungen das **Recht,** die Ware zu verkaufen und damit den durch die Abnahmeverweigerung bzw. Zurückweisung entstandenen Schwebezustand zu beenden.

1. Verzögerte Erfüllung

Der Weg des Art. 88 I darf nur beschritten werden, wenn eine der folgenden Pflichten 4 nicht rechtzeitig erfüllt wird:
– die **Inbesitznahme** der Ware in den Fällen des Art. 85;
– die **Rücknahme** der Ware in den Fällen des Art. 86;
– die **Zahlung des Kaufpreises** im Falle des Art. 85;
– die **Zahlung der Erhaltungskosten** im Falle der Artt. 85, 86 oder 87.

Sinngemäß ist die Vorschrift auch dann anwendbar, wenn der Verkäufer im Fall des Art. 86 zwar zur Rücknahme der Sache bereit ist, aber eine von ihm Zug um Zug zu erbringende Leistung, insbesondere die **Rückzahlung des Kaufpreises** verweigert.[2] Entsprechendes muss gelten, wenn man dem Käufer im Falle der **Ersatzlieferung** ein Zurückbehaltungsrecht an der vertragswidrigen Ware einräumt:[3] Art. 88 I greift in diesem Fall auch

---
[1] Vgl. KG Zug, 30.11.1995, CISG-online 856, sub 4.4.
[2] Ebenso *Enderlein/Maskow/Strohbach,* Art. 88, Anm. 2.1.; *Ferrari u. a./Ferrari,* Internationales Vertragsrecht, Art. 88, Rn. 2; *Kröll u. a./Sono,* Art. 88, Rn. 13; MünchKommHGB/*Mankowski,* Art. 88, Rn. 3.
[3] Zur Frage, ob ein solches Zurückbehaltungsrecht besteht, s. *Müller-Chen,* Art. 46 Rn. 34 (verneinend), mit Nachweisen auch zur Gegenauffassung. Für ein Zurückbehaltungsrecht auch *Enderlein/Maskow/Strohbach,* Art. 88, Anm. 2.1.

dann, wenn der Verkäufer zwar zur Rücknahme bereit ist, die Ersatzlieferung aber verweigert.[4]

2. Ungebührliche Verzögerung

5   Ob eine Verzögerung „ungebührlich" ist, lässt sich – wie vieles im Zusammenhang mit den Artt. 85 ff. – nur anhand der Umstände des konkreten Einzelfalles sagen. Im Rahmen der dabei vorzunehmenden **Abwägung** ist vor allem die Höhe der bereits angefallenen **Kosten** zu beachten. Insbesondere wenn die berechtigte Befürchtung besteht, dass die Erhaltungskosten von der Gegenseite nicht oder nur unter Schwierigkeiten zu erlangen sein werden, kann ein Selbsthilfeverkauf schon nach relativ kurzer Zeit zulässig sein.[5] Der ungebührlichen Verzögerung steht die endgültige Verweigerung der geschuldeten Leistung gleich.[6] Hat der Verkäufer gemäß Art. 63 eine Nachfrist gesetzt, muss er sich selbst daran festhalten lassen und darf nicht vor Ablauf dieser Frist einen Selbsthilfeverkauf durchführen.[7]

3. Hinderungsgründe

5a   Wenn die Parteien ein **vertragliches Alleinvertriebsrecht** des Käufers vereinbart haben, dürfte es eine Frage der Vertragsauslegung im Einzelfall sein, ob der Verkäufer unter den Voraussetzungen des Art. 88 I dennoch zum Verkauf der Ware an Dritte berechtigt ist.[8] Auch wenn der Vertrag insoweit keine ausdrücklichen Vereinbarungen enthält, wird das berechtigte Interesse des Käufers an einem Erhalt seines Alleinvertriebsrechts besonders zu berücksichtigen sein. **Gewerbliche Schutzrechte** des Käufers – z. B. ein Patent oder eine Marke – bleiben durch Art. 88 I unberührt. Eine auf Treu und Glauben gestützte Befugnis des Verkäufers, die Ware trotz des Schutzrechts zu veräußern, kommt jedenfalls dann nicht in Betracht, wenn die Nichtabnahme auf einer Vertragsverletzung des Verkäufers beruht, z. B. auf einem Mangel der Kaufsache.[9] Auch in anderen Fällen dürfte eine verzögerte Pflichterfüllung des Käufers nicht ausreichen, um einen schutzrechtswidrigen Selbsthilfeverkauf durch den Verkäufer zu rechtfertigen.[10] Eine abweichende Beurteilung ist denkbar, wenn der Verkäufer keine andere zumutbare Möglichkeit hat, die ihm gegen den Käufer zustehenden Ansprüche aus dem Kaufvertrag zu realisieren.

4. Anzeige der Verkaufsabsicht

6   Der Weg des Selbsthilfeverkaufs darf erst beschritten werden, wenn dies der Gegenseite **zuvor** angezeigt wurde. Für die Anzeige ist **keine besondere Form** vorgeschrieben. Sie kann auch auf elektronischem Weg erfolgen.[11] Die Anzeige soll der Gegenseite nochmals die Möglichkeit geben, den Verkauf durch Erfüllung ihrer Pflichten abzuwenden.[12] Ein

---

[4] Ebenso *Ferrari u. a./Ferrari*, Internationales Vertragsrecht, Art. 88, Rn. 2; *Kröll u. a./Sono*, Art. 88, Rn. 13.
[5] So auch *Herber/Czerwenka*, Art. 88, Rn. 2; *Kröll u. a./Sono*, Art. 88, Rn. 14; MünchKomm/*P. Huber*, Art. 88, Rn. 3; MünchKommHGB/*Mankowski*, Art. 88, Rn. 4.
[6] So zu Art. 94 EKG: OLG Düsseldorf, 20.1.1983, in: *Schlechtriem/Magnus*, Art. 94, Nr. 1; s. ferner *Piltz*, Internationales Kaufrecht, Rn. 4–264; *Kröll u. a./Sono*, Art. 88, Rn. 14; MünchKomm/*P. Huber*, Art. 88, Rn. 3; *Staudinger/Magnus*, Art. 88, Rn. 7.
[7] *Mohs*, Art. 63 Rn. 12; ebenso *Schlechtriem*, Internationales UN-Kaufrecht, Rn. 342; *Brunner*, Art. 88, Rn. 5; *Ferrari u. a./Ferrari*, Internationales Vertragsrecht, Art. 88, Rn. 2; *Kröll u. a./Sono*, Art. 88, Rn. 15; MünchKomm/*P. Huber*, Art. 88, Rn. 5; MünchKommHGB/*Mankowski*, Art. 88, Rn. 6; *Staudinger/Magnus*, Art. 88, Rn. 12.
[8] Weitergehend (für ein Recht zum Selbsthilfeverkauf) MünchKomm/*P. Huber*, Art. 88, Rn. 6; MünchKommHGB/*Mankowski*, Art. 88, Rn. 6; *Staudinger/Magnus*, Art. 88, Rn. 11; anders *Piltz*, Internationales Kaufrecht, Rn. 4–263.
[9] Ebenso *Baier* RIW 2009, 845, 848.
[10] Großzügiger *Baier* RIW 2009, 845, 847.
[11] CISG-AC Op. 1 *(Ramberg)*, Comment 88.1; *Kröll u. a./Sono*, Art. 88, Rn. 18.
[12] *Bianca/Bonell/Barrera Graf*, Art. 88, Anm. 2.7.; *Enderlein/Maskow/Strohbach*, Art. 88, Anm. 3.1.; *Ferrari u. a./Ferrari*, Internationales Vertragsrecht, Art. 88, Rn. 2; *Soergel/Lüderitz/Dettmeier*, Art. 88, Rn. 2; s. ferner die Begründung zum Gesetzentwurf, BT-Drs. 11/3076, S. 61.

bloßer Widerspruch gegen die Verkaufsabsicht ist hingegen wirkungslos.[13] Die Anzeige ist nach Art. 27 **nicht zugangsbedürftig.**[14]

Nach einer bereits auf der Wiener Konferenz überwiegend vertretenen[15] Ansicht soll die Anzeige schon erfolgen können, **bevor** es zu einer „ungebührlichen" **Verzögerung** gekommen ist.[16] Dem wird man zustimmen müssen, da es der erhaltungspflichtigen Partei kaum zugemutet werden kann, zweimal eine Reaktion der Gegenseite abzuwarten. Soll die Anzeige ihre Warnfunktion behalten, darf sie freilich nicht zu jedem beliebigen Zeitpunkt erfolgen. Zu fordern ist vielmehr, dass zumindest die Voraussetzungen der **Artt. 85 bzw. 86** bereits erfüllt sind, d. h. dass die dort normierte Pflicht zur Erhaltung der Ware bereits entstanden ist.[17] 7

Wird die Pflicht zur vorherigen Anzeige **nicht erfüllt,** macht sich die Partei, die dennoch einen Selbsthilfeverkauf durchführt, schadenersatzpflichtig.[18] Zu ersetzen sind (nur) Schäden, die bei ordnungsgemäßer Anzeige nicht eingetreten wären.[19] Auf die Wirksamkeit des Verkaufs hat die Pflichtverletzung hingegen keinen Einfluss.[20] 8

5. Modalitäten des Selbsthilfeverkaufs

Für die Durchführung des Selbsthilfeverkaufs enthält Art. 88 keine konkreten Vorgaben: Der Verkauf ist „auf jede geeignete Weise" zulässig. Insbesondere muss also **keine bestimmte Form** (etwa öffentliche Versteigerung) eingehalten werden. Einzelstaatliche Regelungen, die besondere Erfordernisse vorsehen, sind nicht anwendbar.[21] Die Umstände und Bedingungen des Verkaufs, insbesondere der Kaufpreis, müssen freilich den Umständen des Falles angemessen sein. Wenn es für die Ware einen Börsen- oder Marktpreis gibt, darf sie allenfalls in Ausnahmefällen unter diesem Wert veräußert werden.[22] Ein solcher Ausnahmefall kann vorliegen, wenn ein Verkauf zum Marktpreis nur unter Inkaufnahme hoher Transportkosten möglich wäre.[23] Ein **Selbsteintritt** des Erhaltungspflichtigen ist grundsätzlich zulässig,[24] doch wird in diesen Fällen besonders sorgfältig zu prüfen sein, ob der Verkauf zu angemessenen Bedingungen erfolgt ist.[25] 9

---

[13] *Schlechtriem,* Internationales UN-Kaufrecht, Rn. 342; *Ferrari u. a./Ferrari,* Internationales Vertragsrecht, Art. 88, Rn. 4; *Kröll u. a./Sono,* Art. 88, Rn. 15; *Staudinger/Magnus,* Art. 88, Rn. 10.
[14] Ebenso *Bamberger/Roth/Saenger,* Art. 88, Rn. 4; *Ferrari u. a./Ferrari,* Internationales Vertragsrecht, Art. 88, Rn. 3; *Soergel/Lüderitz/Dettmeier,* Art. 88, Rn. 2; *Staudinger/Magnus,* Art. 88, Rn. 8; *Witz/Salger/Lorenz/Lorenz,* Art. 88, Rn. 8; OLG Graz, 16.9.2002, CISG-online 1198.
[15] O. R., S. 400 f.
[16] *Brunner,* Art. 88, Rn. 3; *Enderlein/Maskow/Strohbach,* Art. 88, Anm. 3.1.; *Herber/Czerwenka,* Art. 88, Rn. 6; *Piltz,* Internationales Kaufrecht, Rn. 4–264; *Kröll u. a./Sono,* Art. 88, Rn. 17; *Reinhart,* Art. 88, Rn. 3; *Staudinger/Magnus,* Art. 88, Rn. 8; *Witz/Salger/Lorenz/Lorenz,* Art. 88, Rn. 7.
[17] Ebenso MünchKomm/*P. Huber,* Art. 88, Rn. 4.
[18] *Enderlein/Maskow/Strohbach,* Art. 88, Anm. 3.2.; *Ferrari u. a./Ferrari,* Internationales Vertragsrecht, Art. 88, Rn. 6; *Herber/Czerwenka,* Art. 88, Rn. 7; *Kröll u. a./Sono,* Art. 88, Rn. 19; MünchKomm/*P. Huber,* Art. 88, Rn. 4; MünchKommHGB/*Mankowski,* Art. 88, Rn. 8; *Piltz,* Internationales Kaufrecht, Rn. 4–264; *Schlechtriem,* Internationales UN-Kaufrecht, Rn. 342.
[19] LG Köln, 5.12.2006, CISG-online 1440.
[20] Ebenso *Kröll u. a./Sono,* Art. 88, Rn. 19; MünchKomm/*P. Huber,* Art. 88, Rn. 4; *Witz/Salger/Lorenz/Lorenz,* Art. 88, Rn. 8. S. dazu allgemein unten Rn. 15 f.
[21] *Ferrari u. a./Ferrari,* Internationales Vertragsrecht, Art. 88, Rn. 5; *Kröll u. a./Sono,* Art. 88, Rn. 20; *Neumayer/Ming,* Art. 88, Anm. 2.; OLG Graz, 16.9.2002, CISG-online 1198; zu sachenrechtlichen Wirkungen s. aber unten Rn. 15.
[22] Ebenso *Kröll u. a./Sono,* Art. 88, Rn. 20; MünchKomm/*P. Huber,* Art. 88, Rn. 7; vgl. auch ICAC, 25.4.1995, CISG-online 367: Verkauf von Lkws zum Marktpreis ist zulässig.
[23] Vgl. CIETAC, 8.3.1996, CISG-online 1034: Lieferung von 500t Altpapier in eine Bergregion in China.
[24] *Schlechtriem,* Internationales UN-Kaufrecht, Rn. 341; *Herber/Czerwenka,* Art. 88, Rn. 5; MünchKommHGB/*Mankowski,* Art. 88, Rn. 7; *Piltz,* Internationales Kaufrecht, Rn. 4–263; *Staudinger/Magnus,* Art. 88, Rn. 13.
[25] Ebenso *Kröll u. a./Sono,* Art. 88, Rn. 23; MünchKomm/*P. Huber,* Art. 88, Rn. 7.

IV. Pflicht zum Notverkauf (Abs. 2)

10 Für zwei besondere Konstellationen sieht Abs. 2 nicht nur das Recht, sondern die Pflicht des Erhaltungspflichtigen zum Verkauf der Ware vor.

1. Gefahr der raschen Verschlechterung

11 Eine Pflicht zum Verkauf entsteht zum einen dann, wenn die Ware einer raschen Verschlechterung ausgesetzt ist. Dies wird vor allem bei leicht **verderblichen** Waren wie z. B. Lebensmitteln der Fall sein. Auch bei Lebensmitteln besteht aber keine Gefahr der Verschlechterung, wenn sie durch Tiefkühlen über längere Zeit ohne nennenswerte Qualitätsverluste lagerfähig gemacht werden können und die Kosten hierfür nicht ins Gewicht fallen.[26] Eine bloße **wirtschaftliche Verschlechterung** der Ware, z. B. ein Wertverlust durch rasch sinkende Marktpreise, reicht hingegen **nicht** aus.[27] Die gegenteilige Auffassung lässt sich mit dem Wortlaut des Übereinkommens kaum in Einklang bringen.[28] Sie steht in jedem Fall im Widerspruch zur Entstehungsgeschichte.[29] Drohender Wertverfall kann aber immerhin dazu führen, dass schon nach kurzer Zeit eine „ungebührliche" Verzögerung zu bejahen ist und damit ein Recht zum Selbsthilfeverkauf nach Art. 88 I entsteht.[30] Darüber hinaus wird es in der Regel nicht angemessen sein, für derartige Ware hohe Lagerkosten anfallen zu lassen, so dass die Pflicht zum Notverkauf aus der zweiten Alternative des Art. 88 II folgt. Wenn die Marktpreise typischerweise stark schwanken, die weitere Preisentwicklung also nicht absehbar ist, ist der Erhaltungspflichtige aber nicht dafür verantwortlich, spekulativ einen günstigen Verkaufstermin zu ermitteln.[31]

2. Unverhältnismäßige Erhaltungskosten

12 Alternativ ist ein Verkauf der Ware auch dann geboten, wenn die Erhaltungskosten die Grenze des Verhältnismäßigen zu überschreiten drohen. Ob diese Grenze überschritten ist, richtet sich auch in diesem Zusammenhang nach den Umständen des Einzelfalles.[32] Die Grenze ist jedenfalls dann überschritten, wenn die Erhaltungskosten den Wert der Ware zu übersteigen drohen. Dasselbe dürfte schon dann gelten, wenn die Kosten den Verlust, der bei einem Selbsthilfeverkauf droht, übersteigen würden.[33] Dies kann z. B. der Fall sein, wenn die Ware völlig unbrauchbar ist und nur noch als Abfall entsorgt werden kann.[34] Unverhältnismäßig können Erhaltungskosten auch dann sein, wenn sie geringer sind als der

---

[26] OLG Braunschweig, 28.10.1999, CISG-online 510 = TranspR-IHR 2000, 4 ff., sub 3 a: Lieferung von Wildfleisch.
[27] Ebenso OLG Braunschweig, 28.10.1999, CISG-online 510 = TranspR-IHR 2000, 4 ff., sub 3a; *Achilles*, Art. 88, Rn. 6; *Bamberger/Roth/Saenger*, Art. 88, Rn. 6; *Brunner*, Art. 88, Rn. 8; *Enderlein/Maskow/Strohbach*, Art. 88, Anm. 4.; *Ferrari u. a./Ferrari*, Internationales Vertragsrecht, Art. 88, Rn. 9; *Herber/Czerwenka*, Art. 88, Rn. 4; *Kröll u. a./Sono*, Art. 88, Rn. 27; *MünchKomm/P. Huber*, Art. 88, Rn. 10; *MünchKommHGB/Mankowski*, Art. 88, Rn. 9; *Neumayer/Ming*, Art. 88, Anm. 3.; *Piltz*, Internationales Kaufrecht, Rn. 4–262; *Reinhart*, Art. 88, Rn 6; *Schlechtriem*, Internationales UN-Kaufrecht, Rn. 340; *Soergel/Lüderitz/Dettmeier*, Art. 88, Rn. 5; *Staudinger/Magnus*, Art. 88, Rn. 15; *Witz/Salger/Lorenz/Lorenz*, Art. 88, Rn. 10.
[28] Für eine weite Auslegung des Ausdrucks „deterioration" dagegen *Bianca/Bonell/Barrera Graf*, Art. 88, Anm. 2.8.
[29] S. dazu O. R., S. 227: Durch Streichung des Wortes „loss" aus der Entwurfsfassung („subject to loss or rapid deterioration") sollte der Fall des rein wirtschaftlichen Wertverfalls aus dem Anwendungsbereich des Art. 88 II gerade ausgenommen werden. Es ist deshalb kaum haltbar, wenn die Entstehungsgeschichte als Argument *für* die Einbeziehung dieses Falls verwendet wird (so aber *Loewe*, Art. 88, S. 102 f.).
[30] Ebenso *Kröll u. a./Sono*, Art. 88, Rn. 27.
[31] So zutreffend *Jentsch*, S. 104 f.
[32] Aus der Rechtsprechung vgl. Hof van Beroep Antwerpen, 24.4.2006, CISG-online 1258: Einlagerung von Holz für mehr als drei Monate war im Einzelfall unangemessen; vgl. auch CIETAC, 6.6.1991, CISG-online 845: Einlagerung von Chemikalien für annähernd drei Jahre war unangemessen.
[33] So *Soergel/Lüderitz/Dettmeier*, Art. 88, Rn. 5.; *MünchKomm/P. Huber*, Art. 88, Rn. 11; *Staudinger/Magnus*, Art. 88, Rn. 16.
[34] Vgl. CIETAC, 7.4.2005, CISG-online 1453.

Wert der Ware, ihre Finanzierung aber für den Erhaltungspflichtigen mit unangemessen hohen Aufwendungen verbunden ist.[35]

3. Anzeige

Eine vorherige Anzeige der Verkaufsabsicht ist nur im Rahmen des **Möglichen** erforderlich. Entscheidend ist, ob der Verkauf trotz der Anzeige noch rechtzeitig vorgenommen werden kann, um die drohende Gefahr des Verderbs bzw. des unverhältnismäßigen Ansteigens der Erhaltungskosten auszuschalten.[36] Ebenso wie bei Absatz 1 ist die Anzeige nicht zugangsbedürftig (Art. 27).[37] 13

4. Modalitäten des Notverkaufs

Zur Durchführung des Notverkaufs kann auf die Ausführungen in Rn. 9 verwiesen werden. Auch hier muss sich der Erhaltungspflichtige um angemessene Verkaufsbedingungen bemühen. Wegen der besonderen Zwangslage kann freilich auch ein Verkauf zu relativ ungünstigen Bedingungen zulässig sein, sofern keine andere Möglichkeit besteht und im Fall des Nichtverkaufs noch größere Verluste drohen.[38] 14

5. Keine erfolgsbezogene Pflicht

Die Pflicht zum Notverkauf ist nicht erfolgsbezogen. Der Erhaltungspflichtige muss nicht unter allen Umständen einen Verkauf herbeiführen, sondern sich nur in angemessener Weise um einen Verkauf zu bemühen. Führen diese Bemühungen nicht zum Erfolg, ist er für den Untergang der Ware nicht ersatzpflichtig. Bemüht sich der Erhaltungspflichtige nicht in angemessener Weise oder nutzt er eine sich ihm bietende angemessene Verkaufsmöglichkeit nicht, so hat er hingegen den daraus entstehenden Schaden zu ersetzen.[39] 14a

V. Wirkungen gegenüber Dritten

Die Wirkungen des Selbsthilfe- oder Notverkaufs im Verhältnis zu Dritten sind im CISG nicht unmittelbar geregelt. In **schuldrechtlicher** Hinsicht unterliegt das Geschäft entweder den jeweiligen nationalen Vorschriften oder – sofern auch der Selbsthilfe- oder Notverkauf die Voraussetzungen der Artt. 1 ff. erfüllt – wiederum den Regeln des CISG. 15

Sachenrechtliche Wirkungen lassen sich dagegen weder Art. 88 noch sonstigen Bestimmungen des CISG entnehmen. Ob der Erhaltungspflichtige in der Lage ist, dritten Personen Eigentum an der Ware zu verschaffen, richtet sich allein nach dem auf Grund des Internationalen Privatrechts maßgeblichen nationalen Recht. In diesem Zusammenhang sind auch nationale Vorschriften von Bedeutung, die an eine besondere Form des Verkaufs (z. B. öffentliche Versteigerung) besondere sachenrechtliche Wirkungen wie z. B. einen erweiterten Gutglaubensschutz knüpfen. Soweit solche Vorschriften voraussetzen, dass der Erhaltungspflichtige gegenüber seinem Partner aus dem Kaufvertrag zum Selbsthilfe- oder Notverkauf berechtigt ist, ist freilich auch in diesem Zusammenhang allein Art. 88 maßgeblich. 16

IV. Verwendung des Verkaufserlöses

Sowohl beim Selbsthilfe- als auch beim Notverkauf ist der Erhaltungspflichtige gemäß Absatz 3 berechtigt, aus dem Verkaufserlös vorab die **Kosten** der **Erhaltung** und des **Verkaufs** 17

---

[35] *Ferrari u. a./Ferrari,* Internationales Vertragsrecht, Art. 88, Rn. 10.
[36] Ebenso *Kröll u. a./Sono,* Art. 88, Rn. 30.
[37] *Soergel/Lüderitz/Dettmeier,* Art. 88, Rn. 6.
[38] Ebenso *Kröll u. a./Sono,* Art. 88, Rn. 33; MünchKomm/*P. Huber,* Art. 88, Rn. 14.
[39] *Achilles,* Art. 88, Rn. 8; *Bamberger/Roth/Saenger,* Art. 88, Rn. 8; *Ferrari u. a./Ferrari,* Internationales Vertragsrecht, Art. 88, Rn. 12; *Kröll u. a./Sono,* Art. 88, Rn. 33; MünchKomm/*P. Huber,* Art. 88, Rn. 13; MünchKommHGB/*Mankowski,* Art. 88, Rn. 11; *Staudinger/Magnus,* Art. 88, Rn. 17.

der Ware abzudecken. Auch in diesem Zusammenhang gilt dies nur, soweit sich die Kosten im Rahmen des Angemessenen halten. Zu den Kosten des Verkaufs können auch Aufwendungen gehören, um die Ware (wieder) in einen verkaufsfähigen Zustand zu versetzen.[40]

18 Umstritten ist die Frage, ob der Erhaltungspflichtige vom Verkaufserlös **weitere Gegenansprüche** absetzen kann, beispielsweise einen Anspruch auf Zahlung oder Rückzahlung des Kaufpreises oder auf Schadenersatz.[41] Ein Recht zum unmittelbaren „Abzug" solcher Beträge lässt sich den Bestimmungen des CISG nicht entnehmen.[42] Andererseits tritt der Verkaufserlös an die Stelle der verkauften Ware, so dass anstelle einer Aufrechnungsmöglichkeit immerhin Zurückbehaltungsrechte nach Art. 58 I 2 oder Art. 81 I 2 greifen können.[43] Darüber hinaus bleibt in jedem Fall die Möglichkeit der Aufrechnung nach Maßgabe des jeweils anwendbaren nationalen Rechts.[44]

19 Um eine ordnungsgemäße Überprüfung zu ermöglichen, wird man dem Gegner einen Anspruch auf Rechnungslegung einräumen müssen.[45] Dies legt schon der englische Wortlaut des Art. 88 III 2 nahe, wonach der Verkaufende wegen des Überschusses mit der Gegenseite abzurechnen hat („must account").

20 Als **Erfüllungsort** für die Rückzahlungspflicht kommt in erster Linie derjenige Ort in Betracht, an dem die ursprüngliche Verpflichtung zu erfüllen war.[46] Bei einem Selbsthilfeverkauf durch den Verkäufer ist dies der Lieferort,[47] bei einem Selbsthilfeverkauf durch den Käufer der Ort, an dem die zurückgewiesene Sache zurückzugeben war. Die Auffassung, wonach die Rückzahlungspflicht an dem Ort zu erfüllen ist, an dem die Erhaltungspflicht zu erfüllen war,[48] dürfte in den meisten Fällen zu demselben Ergebnis führen.[49] Sofern dies nicht der Fall ist, erscheint es konsequenter, am Ort anzuknüpfen, an dem die Kaufsache zu liefern bzw. zurückzugeben war, weil der Verkaufserlös an die Stelle der Kaufsache tritt. Haben die Parteien einen Ort für die Lieferung der Kaufsache vereinbart und ergibt sich aus den Umständen des Einzelfalles, dass die Zahlung des Verkaufserlöses an diesem Ort keinen Sinn ergibt (z. B. wenn die Ware an einen Dritten geliefert werden sollte), erscheint es konsequent, entsprechend Art. 31 Lit. c an den Sitz des Schuldners der Zahlungsverpflichtung anzuknüpfen.[50]

---

[40] Vgl. ICAC, 25.9.1995, CISG-online 367: Serviceleistungen für eingelagerte Lkw.
[41] Für ein „Recht zum Einbehalt": *Staudinger/Magnus*, Art. 88, Rn. 25; *Brunner*, Art. 88, Rn. 13.
[42] Ebenso *Bianca/Bonell/Barrera Graf*, Art. 88, Anm. 2.10., Abs. 4. Anders für das EKG *Mertens/Rehbinder*, Artt. 94/95, Anm. 8.
[43] Ebenso *Herber/Czerwenka*, Art. 88, Rn. 8.
[44] So auch *Bamberger/Roth/Saenger*, Art. 88, Rn. 9; *Ferrari u. a./Ferrari*, Internationales Vertragsrecht, Art. 88, Rn. 15; *Herber/Czerwenka*, Art. 88, Rn. 8; *Kröll u. a./Sono*, Art. 88, Rn. 37; MünchKomm/*P. Huber*, Art. 88, Rn. 16; MünchKommHGB/*Mankowski*, Art. 88, Rn. 16; *Neumayer/Ming*, Art. 88, Anm. 5.; *Schlechtriem*, Internationales UN-Kaufrecht, Rn. 344; ähnlich *Enderlein/Maskow/Strohbach*, Art. 88, Anm. 9. Das OLG Hamburg hat es in seinem Urteil vom 26.11.1999, CISG-online 515 = IHR 2001, 19, 22, offen gelassen, ob sich die (bejahte) Aufrechnungsmöglichkeit unmittelbar aus CISG oder aus nationalem (deutschem) Recht ergibt. Ausführlich zu allen Aspekten der Aufrechnung *Saenger/Sauthoff*, IHR 2005, 189 ff.
[45] Dafür auch *Schlechtriem*, Internationales UN-Kaufrecht, Rn. 344; *Ferrari u. a./Ferrari*, Internationales Vertragsrecht, Art. 88, Rn. 14; *Herber/Czerwenka*, Art. 88, Rn. 8; *Kröll u. a./Sono*, Art. 88, Rn. 36; MünchKomm/*P. Huber*, Art. 88, Rn. 18; MünchKommHGB/*Mankowski*, Art. 88, Rn. 15; *Soergel/Lüderitz/Dettmeier*, Art. 88, Rn. 7; *Staudinger/Magnus*, Art. 88, Rn. 26.
[46] Ebenso *Bamberger/Roth/Saenger*, Art. 88, Rn. 9. Anders *Eberstein*, 2. Aufl., Art. 88, Rn. 31: grundsätzlich Bringschuld; für Bringschuld auch MünchKomm/*P. Huber*, Art. 88, Rn. 17; für Holschuld *Kröll u. a./Sono*, Art. 88, Rn. 39. Grundlegend anders *Ferrari u. a./Ferrari*, Internationales Vertragsrecht, Art. 88, Rn. 14: Der Erfüllungsort sei im CISG nicht geregelt und deshalb nach Maßgabe des nationalen Rechts zu bestimmen.
[47] Ebenso *Soergel/Lüderitz/Dettmeier*, Art. 88, Rn. 7.
[48] So MünchKommHGB/*Mankowski*, Art. 88, Rn. 15; *Staudinger/Magnus*, Art. 88, Rn. 24; differenzierend *Jentsch*, S. 109 ff.
[49] Allgemein zur Frage des Erfüllungsorts für Rückgabepflichten *Fountoulakis*, Art. 81 Rn. 23 ff. und CISG-AC Op. 9 *(Bridge)*, Comment 3.12 ff.
[50] So *Kröll u. a./Sono*, Art. 88, Rn. 39.

Teil IV. Schlußbestimmungen

Part IV. Quatrième partie.
Final provisions Dispositions finales

Vorbemerkungen zu Artt. 89–101

Übersicht
	Rn.
I. Allgemeines	1
II. Wesentlicher Inhalt der Schlussklauseln	6
1. Diplomatische Schlussklauseln	6
2. Vorrangklausel	8
3. Vorbehalte und ihre Wirkungen	9
4. Zeitlicher Anwendungsbereich	10
5. Inkrafttreten	11
6. Kündigung des Haager Kaufrechts	12

I. Allgemeines

Ein erster Entwurf der Schlussklauseln wurde vom Sekretariat, welches durch Entschließung Nr. 31/93 der Generalversammlung vom 16.12.1978 hierum ersucht worden war, bereits UNCITRAL vorgelegt und in revidierter Form auf der Konferenz eingebracht.[1] Dort wurden die Schlussklauseln im Zweiten Gesamtausschuss behandelt;[2] der daraus hervorgehende Entwurf[3] wurde alsdann vom Plenum erörtert und verabschiedet.[4] **1**

Die Schlussklauseln gehen auf denen anderer UNCITRAL-Übereinkommen zurück, nämlich des Verjährungsübereinkommens von 1974[5] und des Übereinkommens über die Beförderung von Gütern auf See (Hamburg-Regeln) von 1978.[6] Die die Schlussklauseln des CISG charakterisierenden Besonderheiten sind darauf zurückzuführen, dass kurz vor Fertigstellung des Übereinkommens die Wiener Vertragsrechtskonvention[7] in Kraft getreten war.[8] **2**

Wie bei allen mehrseitigen Verträgen enthalten die Schlussklauseln sowohl sogenannte **diplomatische Klauseln,**[9] die die Art und Weise der Annahme durch die Vertragsstaaten, das Inkrafttreten und die Kündigung regeln, als auch Bestimmungen über das **Verhältnis zu anderen Übereinkommen** und den **zeitlichen und räumlichen Geltungsbereich.**[10] Einen Doppelcharakter haben die Bestimmungen über **Vorbehalte,** die einer- **3**

---
[1] O. R., S. 66; vgl. auch *Schlechtriem/Schwenzer/Schlechtriem/Schwenzer/Hachem,* CISG Commentary, Intro to Arts 89–101, Rn. 1.
[2] Vgl. Report of the Second Committee O. R., S. 141 ff.
[3] O. R., S. 165.
[4] O. R., S. 229 ff.
[5] *Schroeter,* UN-Kaufrecht, S. 296.
[6] Vgl. auch *Schlechtriem/Schwenzer/Schlechtriem/Schwenzer/Hachem,* CISG Commentary, Intro to Arts 89–101, Rn. 2; *Staudinger/Magnus,* Vorbem. zu Artt. 89 ff., Rn. 1.
[7] BGBl. 1985 II, S. 926.
[8] *Herber/Czerwenka,* Vor Art. 89, Rn. 2; *Schlechtriem/Schwenzer/Schlechtriem/Schwenzer/Hachem,* CISG Commentary, Intro to Arts 89–101, Rn. 2.
[9] *Schlechtriem/Schwenzer/Schlechtriem/Schwenzer/Hachem,* CISG Commentary, Intro to Arts 89–101, Rn. 3 und 4.
[10] *Niemann,* S. 27; *Schlechtriem/Schwenzer/Schlechtriem/Schwenzer/Hachem,* CISG Commentary, Intro to Arts 89–101, Rn. 4.

seits die von den Vertragsstaaten zu erklärenden Vorbehalte abschließend aufführen,[11] andererseits aber auch die Wirkungen des jeweiligen Vorbehalts auf die Rechtsanwendung näher umschreiben.

4 Gemeinsam ist diesen Vorschriften, die wie alle anderen Vorschriften des CISG im Lichte von Art. 7 ausgelegt werden müssen,[12] dass sie von den Parteien nach h. L. in ihrer Gesamtheit **nicht abbedungen werden können,**[13] da sie sich nur an die Mitgliedstaaten richten, nicht auch an die Parteien der dem CISG unterliegenden Verträge.[14] Diese Ansicht ist neuerdings auch in der Rechtsprechung vertreten worden.[15]

5 Die verschiedenen Gruppen von Bestimmungen werden im Folgenden kurz charakterisiert. Die danach abgedruckten einzelnen Artikel sind insoweit erläutert, als dies für die praktische Anwendung des CISG erforderlich erscheint.

II. Wesentlicher Inhalt der Schlussklauseln

1. Diplomatische Schlussklauseln

6 Diplomatische Schlussklauseln finden sich in Artt. 89, 91, 98 und 101. Sie bestimmen den Generalsekretär der Vereinten Nationen zum Depositar, legen die Unterzeichnungsfrist fest, bestimmen, dass das Übereinkommen der Ratifikation (oder Annahme oder Genehmigung) bedarf und dass der Beitritt möglich ist. Vorbehalte sind nur zulässig, soweit sie ausdrücklich vorgesehen sind. Schließlich finden sich Regeln über die Kündigung des Übereinkommens.[16]

7 Diese Bestimmungen richten sich zunächst an die Staaten,[17] haben für den Rechtsanwender aber insofern Bedeutung, als sich daraus ergibt, ob das Übereinkommen für einen bestimmten Staat in Kraft ist, ggf. mit welchen Vorbehalten. In der BR Deutschland wird der Kreis der anderen Vertragsstaaten einschließlich des Zeitpunkts des Inkrafttretens sowie der von diesen Staaten notifizierten Vorbehalte im Bundesgesetzblatt (Teil II) bekannt gemacht.[18]

2. Vorrangklausel

8 Eine Vorrangklausel für andere internationale Übereinkommen findet sich in Art. 90. Diese hat rein materiellen Charakter[19] und legt fest, dass das CISG hinter bestimmten anderen Übereinkünften (materiell-rechtlichen Inhalts)[20] zurücktritt.[21]

---

[11] Siehe Art. 98 CISG.
[12] *Schlechtriem/Schwenzer/Schlechtriem/Schwenzer/Hachem* CISG Commentary, Intro to Arts 89–101, Rn. 2 aE; *Schroeter,* FS Kritzer, 2008, S. 425, 428.
[13] Vgl. *Czerwenka,* Rechtsanwendungsprobleme, S. 172; *Ferrari,* Rev. dr. aff. int. 2001, 401, 402; *Schlechtriem/Schwenzer/Schlechtriem/Schwenzer/Hachem* CISG Commentary, Intro to Arts 89–101, Rn. 2; *Staudinger/Magnus,* Art. 6, Rn. 53.
[14] *Ferrari u. a./Mankowski,* Internationales Vertragsrecht, Vor Art. 89, Rn. 4.
[15] Trib. Padova, Urt. v. 11.1.2005, CISG-online 967; Tribunale di Vigevano, 12.7.2000, CISG-online 493 = IHR 2001, 72, 74.
[16] *Schlechtriem/Schwenzer/Schlechtriem/Schwenzer/Hachem,* CISG Commentary, Intro to Arts 89–101, Rn. 4.
[17] *Brunner,* Vorbem. zu 89–101, Rn. 1
[18] Eine immer auf dem neuesten Stand gehaltene Liste der Vertragsstaaten mit Hinweis auf den Zeitpunkt des Inkrafttretens und der ggf. erklärten Vorbehalte findet sich auch unter der folgenden Internet-Adresse: http://www.uncitral.org.
[19] *Schlechtriem/Schwenzer/Schlechtriem/Schwenzer/Hachem* CISG Commentary, Intro to Arts 89–101, Rn. 5.
[20] Vgl. hierzu näher Art. 90 Rn. 4.
[21] *Achilles,* Art. 90, Rn. 1; *Schlechtriem/Schwenzer/Schlechtriem/Schwenzer/Hachem,* CISG Commentary, 2. Aufl., Intro to Arts 89–101, Rn. 5.

3. Vorbehalte und ihre Wirkungen

Die von den Staaten zu erklärenden Vorbehalte,[22] die der Vereinheitlichung des internationalen Kaufrechts sicher nicht zugute kommen,[23] sind in Artt. 92–96 **abschließend** aufgezählt.[24] Ihre Wirkungen sind dort näher geregelt. Einige der Vorbehalte können nur dann erklärt werden, wenn bestimmte Voraussetzungen vorliegen. Dies gilt in Bezug auf die Vorbehalte, die kraft Artikel 93, 94 und 96 erklärt werden können.[25] Wird ein Vorbehalt trotz Fehlens der erforderlichen Voraussetzungen erklärt,[26] müssen die Gerichte den Vorbehalt dennoch berücksichtigen. Gleiches gilt, wenn die Voraussetzungen bei Erklärung eine Vorbehalts zwar vorlagen, später aber weggefallen sind; nur dann, wenn der Vorbehaltsstaat eine an den Verwahrer gerichtete Rücknahmeerklärung ex Art. 97 Abs. 4 abgegeben hat, und diese auch wirksam geworden ist, können die Gerichte von der Berücksichtigung des Vorbehalts absehen.[27]

4. Zeitlicher Anwendungsbereich

Der zeitliche Anwendungsbereich des Übereinkommens bestimmt sich nach Art. 100, der in der Rechtsprechung auch oft herangezogen worden ist, um die Anwendbarkeit des Übereinkommens zu verneinen.[28] Danach gilt das Übereinkommen per se[29] nicht für Verträge, die vor seinem Inkrafttreten am 1.1.1988 abgeschlossen worden sind; damit Teil II des CISG gilt, darf das Angebot nicht vor seinem Inkrafttreten gemacht worden sein.

5. Inkrafttreten

Das Übereinkommen ist nach seinem Art. 99 I am 1.1.1988 in 11 Ländern in Kraft getreten. Für Deutschland ist es am 1.1.1991 in Kraft getreten.

6. Kündigung des Haager Kaufrechts

Den Vertragsstaaten wird durch Art. 99 III–IV eine Verpflichtung zur Kündigung der Haager Kaufrechtsübereinkommen auferlegt, weil diese mit dem CISG, das sachlich eine Fortentwicklung darstellt, inhaltlich nicht gänzlich vereinbar sind. Die BR Deutschland ist dieser Verpflichtung nachgekommen. EKG und EAG sind dementsprechend – nach Kündigung der Haager Kaufübereinkommen – mit Wirkung vom 31.12.1990 aufgehoben worden.[30] Sie bleiben jedoch für Verträge maßgebend, die vor dem 1.1.1991 abgeschlossen worden sind oder – hinsichtlich des EAG – bei denen das Angebot zum Vertragsabschluss vor dem 1.1.1991 zugegangen ist.[31]

---

[22] Damit die Vorbehalte ihre Wirkung entfalten können, müssen sie in der in Art. 97 vorgeschriebenen Art und Weise erklärt werden; es gibt keine anderen Mittel, im CISG vorgesehenen Vorbehalte Wirkungen entfalten zu lassen; vgl. auch *Schroeter*, 16 Pace Int'l L. Rev. (2004), 323; aA Civ. 1, 2.4.2008, CISG-online 1651.

[23] Vgl. diesbezüglich *Bailey*, 32 Cornell Int'l L. J. (1999), 273, 311 ff.

[24] Vgl. Art. 98 CISG; siehe in der Lehre *Brunner*, Vorbem. zu Art. 89–101, Rn. 3; *Flechtner*, 17 J. L. & Com. (1998), 187, 193; *Schlechtriem/Schwenzer/Schlechtriem/Schwenzer/Hachem*, CISG Commentary, Intro to Arts 89–101, Rn. 6.

[25] Vgl. *Schlechtriem/Schwenzer/Schlechtriem/Schwenzer/Hachem*, CISG Commentary, Intro to Arts 89–101, Rn. 7.

[26] Ein Beispielfall findet sich bei *Ferrari*, Art. 96 Rn. 2.

[27] Vgl. auch *Schroeter*, FS Kritzer, 2008, S. 425, 435 ff.

[28] Vgl. zuletzt etwa RB Dordrecht, 19.3.2008; CISG-online 1698; OLG Stuttgart, 1.3.2004, CISG-online 1044 (das Gericht hat jedoch übersehen, dass das CISG kraft Art. 1 Abs. 1 lit. b anwendbar war); RB Hasselt, 4.4.2000, CISG Belgium; BGH, 17.12.1997, CISG-online 296 = NJW-RR 1998, 680 ff.; OLG München, 9.8.1995, IPRax 1997, 38 ff.; Hof Amsterdam, 19.9.1996, NIPR 1998, Nr. 94; RB Arnhem, 27.5.1993, CISG-online 9; KG Waadt, 14.3.1993, CISG-online 84.

[29] Die Parteien können das CISG jedoch auch bei Fehlen der zeitlichen Anwendungsvoraussetzungen zur Anwendung bringen; vgl. hierzu statt aller *Ferrari*, Art. 6 Rn. 39 ff.

[30] Vgl. Art. 5 I VertragsG.

[31] Vgl. Art. 5 II VertragsG.

Art. 89 [Depositar]

Der Generalsekretär der Vereinten Nationen wird hiermit zum Verwahrer dieses Übereinkommens bestimmt.

Art. 89

The Secretary-General of the United Nations is hereby designated as the depositary for this Convention.

Art. 89

Le Secrétaire général de l'Organisation des Nations Unies est désigné comme dépositaire de la présente Convention.

1 Wie regelmäßig bei Übereinkommen, die im Rahmen der Vereinten Nationen ausgearbeitet und abgeschlossen werden,[1] nimmt der Generalsekretär die Aufgaben des Verwahrers (Depositars) wahr.[2]

2 Die **Aufgaben** des Verwahrers ergeben sich zum einen aus Art. 77 I der **Wiener Vertragsrechtskonvention,**[3] weshalb im CISG nicht – wie dies auch sonst häufig in internationalen Übereinkommen geschehen ist – nochmals gesagt zu werden brauchte, dass der Verwahrer insbesondere die von den Staaten erhaltenen Notifikationen an die anderen Vertragsstaaten zu übermitteln hat.[4] Zum anderen ergeben sich die Aufgaben des Verwahrers auch aus dem **CISG** selbst.[5] So zum Beispiel muss der Verwahrer ex Art. 99 IV sich mit der niederländischen Regierung als Verwahrer der Haager Kaufrechtsübereinkommen in Verbindung setzen, um die aus der Kündigung derselben durch die Vertragsstaaten des CISG notwendig gemachte Koordinierung sicherzustellen. Ferner muss der Depositar alle Erklärungen der Vertragsstaaten in bezug auf das CISG entgegennehmen,[6] wie etwa die Kündigung des CISG, die Vorbehaltserklärungen, etc.[7]

---

[1] Vgl. Art. 42 des Übereinkommens über die Verjährung beim internationalen Warenkauf von 1974; Art. 27 des Übereinkommens über die Beförderung von Gütern auf See (Hamburg-Regeln) von 1978; Art. 85 des Übereinkommens über internationale Wechsel von 1988; Art. 23 des Übereinkommens über unabhängige Garantien und Stand-by Letters of Credit von 1995; Art. 33 des Übereinkommens über die Abtretung von Forderungen im internationalen Handel; Art. 15 des Übereinkommens über die Nutzung elektronischer Kommunikation beim Abschluss grenzüberschreitender Verträge von 2005; Art. 87 des Übereinkommens über Verträge über die internationale Beförderung von Gütern ganz oder teilweise auf See von 2008.

[2] So auch *Bamberger/Roth/Saenger*, Art. 89, Rn. 1; *Ferrari u. a./Mankowski*, Internationales Vertragsrecht, Art. 89, Rn. 1; *Kröll u. a./Herre*, Art. 89, Rn. 1; *Schlechtriem/Schwenzer/Schlechtriem/Schwenzer/Hachem*, CISG Commentary, Art. 89, Rn. 1.

[3] Vgl. auch *Bianca/Bonell/Evans*, Art. 89, Anm. 2.2.

[4] In diesem Sinne auch *Schlechtriem/Schwenzer/Schlechtriem/Schwenzer/Hachem*, CISG Commentary, Art. 89, Rn. 2; *Witz/Salger/Lorenz/Witz*, Art. 89, Rn. 2.

[5] *Kröll u. a./Herre*, Art. 89, Rn. 2; *Staudinger/Magnus*, Art. 89, Rn. 2 m. w. Beispielen für sich aus dem CISG ergebende Aufgaben des Verwahrers; vgl. auch *Ferrari u. a./Mankowski*, Internationales Vertragsrecht, Art. 89, Rn. 2.

[6] *Kröll u. a./Herre*, Art. 89, Rn. 2.

[7] Vgl. *Witz/Salger/Lorenz/Witz*, Art. 89, Rn. 1.

Art. 90 [Konventionskonflikte]

Dieses Übereinkommen geht bereits geschlossenen oder in Zukunft zu schließenden völkerrechtlichen Übereinkünften, die Bestimmungen über in diesem Übereinkommen geregelte Gegenstände enthalten, nicht vor, sofern die Parteien ihre Niederlassung in Vertragsstaaten einer solchen Übereinkunft haben.

Art. 90

This Convention does not prevail over any international agreement which has already been or may be entered into and which contains provisions concerning the matters governed by this Convention, provided that the parties have their places of business in States parties to such agreement.

Art. 90

La présente Convention ne prévaut pas sur un accord international déjà conclu ou à conclure qui contient des dispositions concernant les matières régies par la présente Convention, à condition que les parties au contrat aient leur établissement dans des Etats parties à cet accord.

Mit der Zunahme der auf Vereinheitlichungsbestrebungen beruhenden Konventionen[1] werden **Konventionskonflikte**[2] immer wahrscheinlicher.[3] Dies haben auch die Konventionsgeber des CISG erkannt, weshalb sie eine Vorschrift eingeführt haben, die die Lösung ebensolcher Konflikte zum Gegenstand hat.[4] Dieser „toleranten"[5] Vorschrift nach, die ihr Vorbild in Art. 37 des Verjährungsübereinkommen hat,[6] tritt das CISG grundsätzlich hinter anderen – bereits geschlossenen oder auch noch zu schließenden –[7] internationalen Vereinbarungen zurück, die (auch nur teilweise)[8] die gleichen Rechtsmaterien betreffen.[9] Dieser **Nachrang**[10] setzt jedoch voraus, dass beide Vertragsparteien ihre Niederlassung in Vertragsstaaten der internationalen Vereinbarung haben,[11] selbst wenn diese das nicht als Anwendungsvoraussetzung verlangt.[12] Hat nur eine Vertragspartei ihre Niederlassung in einem Vertragstaat der Vereinbarung, dann geht das CISG vor.[13] **1**

---

[1] Vgl. diesbezüglich etwa *Ferrari*, IHR 2006, 1, 2; *ders.*, Factoring internazionale, S. 368; *Torsello*, Common Features, S. 259 ff.

[2] Vgl. allgemein zu Konventionskonflikten *Brière*, Les conflits de conventions internationales en droit privé, Paris: L. G. D. J. (2001); *Majoros*, RabelsZ 46 (1982), 84 ff.; *ders.*, Les Conventions internationales en matière de droit privé, Paris: Pèdone, Bd. 1 (1976), Bd. 2 (1980); *Volken*, Konventionskonflikte im internationalen Privatrecht, Zürich Schulthess (1977); *Wilting*, Vertragskonkurrenz im Völkerrecht, Köln: Heymanns (1994).

[3] Vgl. *Ferrari*, Uniform. L. Rev. 2000, 69, 73 ff.

[4] Siehe auch *Diez-Picazo/Calvo Caravaca*, Art. 90, S. 702 f.; *Schlechtriem/Schwenzer/Schlechtriem/Schwenzer/Hachem* CISG Commentary, Art. 90, Rn. 1.

[5] *Schroeter*, UN-Kaufrecht, § 9, Rn. 1.

[6] Vgl. *Bianca/Bonell/Evans*, Art 90, Anm. 1.1.; *Ferrari u. a./Mankowski*, Internationales Vertragsrecht, Art. 90, Rn. 1; *Herber/Czerwenka*, Art. 90, Rn. 1; *Schlechtriem/Schwenzer/Schlechtriem/Schwenzer/Hachem*, CISG Commentary, Art. 90, Rn. 1; *Schroeter*, UN-Kaufrecht, § 9, Rn. 5; *Winship*, 21 Cornell Int'l L. J. (1988), 487, 515 f.

[7] Vgl. *Ferrari u. a./Mankowski*, Internationales Vertragsrecht, Art. 90, Rn. 4; *Honsell/Siehr*, Art. 90, Rn. 2; *Piltz*, Internationales Kaufrecht, Rn. 2–171; *Schroeter*, UN-Kaufrecht, § 9, Rn. 68.

[8] Vgl. auch *Piltz*, Internationales Kaufrecht, Rn. 2–174.

[9] So auch *Achilles*, Art. 90, Rn. 1; *Ernst*, S. 96; *Kröll u. a./Herre*, Art. 90, Rn. 1; *Schroeter*, UN-Kaufrecht, § 9, Rn. 62; *Staudinger/Magnus*, Art. 90, Rn. 6.

[10] *Achilles*, Art. 90, Rn. 1; *Bianca/Bonell/Evans*, Art. 90, Anm. 2.1.; *Schroeter*, UN-Kaufrecht, § 9, Rn. 73; *Staudinger/Magnus*, Art. 90 Rn. 1; krit. *Piltz*, Internationales Kaufrecht, Rn. 2–171: Art. 90 schreibe nicht den Vorrang völkerrechtlicher Übereinkommen und daher auch nicht den Nachrang des CISG vor.

[11] *Herber/Czerwenka*, Art. 90, Rn. 5; *Honsell/Siehr*, Art. 90, Rn. 2; *Kröll u. a./Herre*, Art. 90, Rn. 1; *Schlechtriem/Schwenzer/Schlechtriem/Schwenzer/Hachem* CISG Commentary, Art. 90, Rn. 2; *Witz/Salger/Lorenz/Witz*, Art. 90, Rn. 1; a. A. *Piltz*, Internationales Kaufrecht, Rn. 2–171.

[12] So auch *Brunner*, Art. 90, Rn. 2; *Czerwenka*, Rechtsanwendungsprobleme, S. 163 f.; *Ferrari u. a./Mankowski*, Internationales Vertragsrecht, Art. 90, Rn. 3; *Schroeter*, UN-Kaufrecht, § 9, Rn. 106.

[13] Ebenso *Brunner*, Art. 90, Rn. 2; *Ferrari u. a./Mankowski*, Internationales Vertragsrecht, Art. 90, Rn. 3; *Honsell/Siehr*, Art. 90, Rn. 3; *Staudinger/Magnus*, Art. 90, Rn. 7; a. A. *Piltz*, Internationales Kaufrecht, Rn. 2–171, der die Ansicht vertritt, dass die Niederlassung nur einer Vertragspartei in einem Vertragstaat ausreiche, um diese vorgehen zu lassen.

2 Internationale Vereinbarung im Sinne der Vorschrift sind sowohl **multi-** als auch **bilaterale** Vereinbarungen.[14] Dafür spricht auch, dass für die vorgehende Vereinbarung eine andere Bezeichnung („agreement", „accord") gewählt worden ist als für das Übereinkommen selbst („convention"), man also den Kreis der vorgehenden Vereinbarungen auf alle internationalen Vereinbarungen ausdehnen wollte.

3 Ein Teil der Lehre vertritt – zum Teil sehr aggressiv[15] – die Ansicht, auch **EU-Richtlinien** seien von Art. 90 erfasst[16] und gingen dem CISG vor.[17] M. E. trifft dies jedoch nicht zu.[18] Die Richtlinien sind, genauso wie Verordnungen,[19] keine „international agreements";[20] daran ändert auch die Tatsache nichts, dass die Mitgliedsstaaten völkerrechtlich, durch den EG-Vertrag, „der im Hinblick auf seine Rechtsnatur grundsätzlich unter Art. 90 CISG [fällt]", aber „selbst anscheinend keine Bestimmungen über auch vom UN-Kaufrecht geregelte Gegenstände [enthält]",[21] zur Umsetzung der Richtlinien in nationales Recht verpflichtet sind.[22] Zwar ist das CISG bekanntlich erst nach dem EG-Vertrag vereinbart worden, was dazu verleiten könnte, allgemein vom Vorrang des EG-Vertrags auszugehen. Dies trifft aber nicht zu; die Vorrangklausel setzt m. E. voraus, dass vor Abschluss des CISG bereits kollidierende Rechte und Pflichten existieren. Selbst wenn man also die hier verworfene Ansicht vertreten würde, könnte dies lediglich zum Vorrang der zum Zeitpunkt des Abschlusses des CISG bereits existierenden, sich aus dem EG-Vertrag ergebenden Rechte und Pflichten führen. Hinsichtlich der nach Abschluss des CISG entstandenen kollidierenden Rechte und Pflichten muss aber immer vom Vorrang des CISG ausgegangen werden: Die mit dem EG-Vertrag entstandene abstrakte Verpflichtung zur Umsetzung von EG-Richtlinienrecht in nationales Recht allein kann nicht ausschlaggebend sein. Neben dieser eher theoretischen Begründung können auch **praktischere Gründe zugunsten des Vorranges des CISG** angeführt werden: Während das CISG nach fast fünfzigjährigen Vorarbeiten durchaus als ausgereiftes Regelungswerk angesehen werden kann und muss, kann Gleiches für die Richtlinien nicht gesagt werden, zumindest nicht immer.[23]

---

[14] Ebenso *Achilles,* Art. 90, Rn. 1; *Bamberger/Roth/Saenger,* Art. 90, Rn. 1; *Brunner,* Art. 90, Rn. 1; *Diez-Picazo/Calvo Caravaca,* Art. 90, S. 703; *Ferrari u. a./Mankowski,* Internationales Vertragsrecht, Art. 90, Rn. 4; *Herber,* IHR 2004, 89, 90; *Karollus,* S. 34; MünchKomm/*P. Huber,* Art. 90, Rn. 2; *Piltz,* Internationales Kaufrecht, Rn. 2–171; *Schlechtriem/Schwenzer/Schlechtriem/Schwenzer/Hachem* CISG Commentary, Art. 90, Rn. 2; *Schroeter,* UN-Kaufrecht, § 9, Rn. 10, Fn. 19; *Witz/Salger/Lorenz/Witz,* Art. 90, Rn. 2; so wohl auch *Loewe,* S. 104; a. A. *Enderlein/Maskow/Strohbach,* Art. 90, Anm. 5., die die Ansicht vertreten, nur multilaterale Vereinbarungen gingen dem Übereinkommen vor.

[15] *Herber,* IHR 2001, 187 ff.

[16] Vgl. etwa *Corvaglia,* S. 17; *Daun,* JuS 1997, 811, 813; *Ernst,* S. 114; *Herber,* in: FS Schlechtriem, S. 207, 220.

[17] So etwa *Herber,* MDR 1993, 106 f.; *Herber/Czerwenka,* Art. 90, Rn. 4; *Honsell/Siehr,* Art. 90, Rn. 7; *Witz/Salger/Lorenz/Witz,* Art. 90, Rn. 3; a. A. *Brunner,* Einl., Rn. 16.

[18] So bereits *Ferrari,* Unif. L. Rev. 2003, 177, 182; *Müller,* IHR 2005, 133, 134; *Piltz,* Rn. 2–69; ders., IHR 2002, 2, 4; vgl. auch Art. 5 Rn. 15.

[19] Ebenso *H.-F. Müller,* GPR 2006, 168, 173; *Piltz,* Internationales Kaufrecht, Rn. 2–177; *Schlechtriem/Schwenzer/Schlechtriem/Schwenzer/Hachem,* CISG Commentary, 2Art. 90, Rn. 5; vgl. aber *Ferrari u. a./Mankowski,* Internationales Vertragsrecht, Art. 90, Rn. 10: Für EG-Verordnungen besteht kein Umsetzungsspielraum der EU-Staaten, so dass jedenfalls „sie dieselbe unmittelbare Verbindlichkeit wie Staatsverträge haben", vgl. auch MünchKomm/*P. Huber,* Art. 90, Rn. 2.

[20] So ausdrücklich etwa *Kröll u. a./Mistelis,* Art. 2, Rn. 23.
Die ursprüngliche Version des Art. 90 ließ noch „conventions" dem CISG vorgehen; erst anlässlich der Wiener Diplomatischen Konferenz wurde dieser Begriff durch „any international agreement" ersetzt; zu den Gründen und Folgen dieser Wortlautänderung vgl. ausführlich *Schroeter,* UN-Kaufrecht, § 9, Rn. 7 ff.

[21] *Schroeter,* UN-Kaufrecht, § 9, Rn. 21; vgl. auch *Schlechtriem/Schwenzer/Schlechtriem/Schwenzer/Hachem* CISG Commentary, Art. 90, Rn. 5; *Schwenzer/Hachem/Kee,* Rn. 3.34.

[22] Ebenso *Achilles,* Art. 90, Rn. 2; *Bamberger/Roth/Saenger,* Art. 90, Rn. 1; *Brunner,* Art. 90, Rn. 3; *P. Huber,* IHR 2006, 228, 233; *Janssen,* EuLF 2003, 181, 183; *Köhler,* Die Haftung nach UN-Kaufrecht, S. 151 f.; *H.-F. Müller,* GPR 2006, 168, 173; ders., IHR 2005, 133, 134; MünchKomm/*Westermann,* Vor Art. 1, Rn. 17; *Schlechtriem/Schwenzer/Schlechtriem,* CISG Commentary, 2. Aufl., Art. 90, Rn. 13; *Staudinger/Magnus,* Art. 90, Rn. 4; *Wartenberg,* S. 44 f. und 47.

[23] Vgl. auch *Schlechtriem/Schwenzer/Schlechtriem,* CISG Commentary, 2. Aufl., Art. 90, Rn. 12b.

Der Vorrang des CISG muss m. E. auch aus „qualitativen" Gründen befürwortet werden.[24]

Fraglich ist, ob sich Art. 90 sowohl auf **materiellrechtliche** als auch **kollisionsrecht-** 4 **liche** Vereinbarungen bezieht. Unzweifelhaft statuiert Art. 90 den Vorrang von Vereinbarungen ersterer Art.[25] Vielfach wird auch vom Vorrang **kollisionsrechtlicher** Vereinbarungen ausgegangen.[26] Dies trifft m. E.[27] aber **nicht** zu.[28] Dies hängt damit zusammen, dass die materiellrechtlichen Abkommen andere Frage beantworten, als die kollisionsrechtlichen,[29] es sich also nicht um mit den gleichen Fragen beschäftigende Vereinbarungen handelt.[30] In Bezug auf das Verhältnis zischen dem **EVÜ**,[31] das trotz des Inkrafttretens der Rom I-VO noch Anwendung finden kann, und dem CISG führen die verschiedenen Ansichten zu keinem unterschiedlichen Ergebnis, da auch die Vertreter der hier abgelehnten Ansicht das CISG dem EVÜ vorgehen lassen,[32] mit der Begründung, dass das EVÜ seinerseits eine dem Art. 90 entsprechende Vorschrift enthalte und angesichts dieses negativen Konventionskonfliktes[33] das internationalprivatrechtliche Abkommen dem materiellrechtlichem weichen müsse.[34] Bisweilen wird der Vorrang des CISG damit begründet,[35] dass das CISG sich nur mit dem Kaufvertrag, das EVÜ aber mit den verschiedensten Vertragstypen beschäftige, das CISG demnach als *lex specialis* anzusehen sei und daher dem EVÜ vorgehen müsse. Diese Rechtfertigung mag im Verhältnis zum EVÜ gelten, bezüglich anderer IPR-Übereinkommen kann sie jedoch keine Geltung beanspruchen; so läßt sich der Vorrang des CISG gegenüber der doch in verschieden Vertragsstaaten des CISG geltenden, von dem Teil der Lehre, die sich auf das Prinzip, wonach „lex specialis derogat legi generali", beruft, aber übersehene Haager Konvention vom 15.6.1955 über das auf internationale Warenkaufverträge anzuwendende Recht nicht einfach damit rechtfertigen, dass das CISG bloß internationale Warenkaufverträge behandele, gilt dies doch auch hinsichtlich der Haager Konvention. Die „Spezialität" des CISG muß demnach anderweitig gerechtfertigt werden. Dies könnte etwa auf der Grundlage des Umstandes geschehen, dass das CISG die Internationalität genauer definiert, und so den eigenen Anwendungsbereich näher umschreibt – und so einschränkt –, während die Haager Konvention von einer Definition der Interna-

---

[24] IE ebenso *Kröll u. a./Herre,* Art. 90, Rn. 8, jedoch mit anderer Begründung: „there is a strong need of ignoring the EU law in oder to avoid very different results on the same matters due to this very complex body of law provided by the EU."
[25] Vgl. auch *Schlechtriem/Schwenzer/Schlechtriem/Schwenzer/Hachem,* CISG Commentary, Art. 90, Rn. 7.
[26] Vgl. *Achilles,* Art. 90, Rn. 2; *Czerwenka,* Rechtsanwendungsprobleme, S. 163; *Enderlein/Maskow/Strohbach,* Art. 90, Anm. 4.; *Ferrari u. a./Mankowski,* Internationales Vertragsrecht, Art. 90, Rn. 2; *Herber/Czerwenka,* Art. 90, Rn. 3; MünchKomm/*P. Huber,* Art. 90, Rn. 3; *Neumayer/Ming,* Art. 90, Anm. 1.; *Schlechtriem/ Schwenzer/Schlechtriem/Schwenzer/Hachem,* CISG Commentary, Art. 90, Rn. 8; *Schwenzer/Hachem/Kee,* Rn. 3.33; *Soergel/Lüderitz/Fenge,* Art. 90, Rn. 2; *Staudinger/Magnus,* Art. 90, Rn. 5; *Vékas,* IPRax 1987, 342, 343; *Winship,* Scope, S. 1–1, 1–41; *Witz/Salger/Lorenz/Witz,* Art. 90, Rn. 2.
[27] *Ferrari* IHR 2006, 1, 4.
[28] Ebenso *Bonell/Liguori,* Uniform L. Rev. 1997, 385, 392; *Brunner,* Einl., Rn. 12 und Art. 90, Rn. 3; *Honsell/Siehr,* Art. 90, Rn. 1 aE und 5 f.; *Kindler,* RIW 1988, 776, 780; *Lohmann,* Parteiautonomie, S. 41; *Winship,* 21 Cornell Int'l L. J. (1988), 487, 532.
[29] Vgl. hierzu auch *Ferrari,* Einheitsrecht, in: Basedow/Hopt/Zimmermann, Handwörterbuch des Europäischen Privatrechts, Bd. 1, 2009, S. 376, 376 f.
[30] Ebenso *Kampf,* RIW 2009, 297, 299; krit. gegen das im Text angesprochene Verständnis *Schroeter,* UN-Kaufrecht, § 9, Rn. 65.
[31] BGBl. 1986 II, S. 809.
[32] Vgl. statt aller *Staudinger/Magnus,* Art. 90, Rn. 17.
[33] Vgl. zu diesen negativen Konflikten, die sich nur dann ergeben können, wenn man die im Text vertretene Auffassung, Art. 90 beziehe sich lediglich auf materiellrechtliche Vereinbarungen, verwirft, da es keine materiellrechtliche Vereinbarung gibt, die sich mit im CISG geregelten Gegenständen beschäftigt und eine dem Art. 90 entsprechende Relationsnorm enthält, *Ferrari u. a./Mankowski,* Internationales Vertragsrecht, Art. 90, Rn. 12 ff.; *Schroeter,* UN-Kaufrecht, § 9, Rn. 74 ff.
[34] *Herber/Czerwenka,* Art. 90, Rn. 3; vgl. zum Verhältnis zwischen IPR und CISG, *Ferrari,* J. D. I. 2006, 27 ff.; *ders.,* CISG and PIL, S. 19; *ders.,* IHR 2012, 89; *Kampf* RIW 2009, 297.
[35] Vgl. *Schlechtriem/Schwenzer/ Schlechtriem/Schwenzer/Hachem,* CISG Commentary, Art. 90, Rn. 12.

tionalität der ihr unterliegenden Warenkaufverträge absieht und daher notwendigeweise einen weiteren Anwendungsbereich hat.[36]

5 Da Art. 90 eine normative **Vorrangregelung** ist, bedarf die Inanspruchnahme keiner ausdrücklichen Erklärung eines Vorbehaltes.[37] Die Rechtsfolgen der Vorschrift treten also ipso iure ein.[38] Dennoch hatte Ungarn bei der Ratifikation erklärt, dass es die Allgemeinen Bedingungen für Warenlieferungen zwischen Organisationen der Mitgliedsländer des RGW als dem Art. 90 unterworfen betrachte.[39] Der auch seitens der Lehre vertretene Vorrang der ALB wurde als „erheblicher Einbruch in den Anwendungsbereich des CISG" angesehen;[40] diese Aussage muss aber relativiert werden, da „die ALB/RGW nur noch Bedeutung [haben], soweit ihre Geltung erneuert worden ist".[41]

---

[36] So auch Trib. Vigevano, Urt. v. 12.7.2000, CISG-online 493.
[37] *Herber/Czerwenka*, Art. 90, Rn. 1; *Witz/Salger/Lorenz/Witz*, Art. 90, Rn. 1.
[38] *Diez-Picazo/Calvo Caravaca*, Art. 94, S. 704; *Ferrari u. a./Mankowski*, Internationales Vertragsrecht, Art. 90, Rn. 7; *Schlechtriem/Schwenzer/Schlechtriem/Schwenzer/Hachem*, CISG Commentary, Art. 90, Rn. 10; *Schroeter*, UN-Kaufrecht, § 9, Rn. 70.
[39] Vgl. auch Denkschrift, S. 62; *Witz/Salger/Lorenz/Witz*, Art. 90, Rn. 2 Fn. 4.
[40] *Herber*, 2. Aufl., Art. 90 Rn. 13.
[41] *Staudinger/Magnus*, Art. 90, Rn. 9; ebenso *Ferrari u. a./Mankowski*, Internationales Vertragsrecht, Art. 90, Rn. 7.

Art. 91 [Unterzeichnung, Ratifikation, Annahme, Genehmigung, Beitritt]

(1) Dieses Übereinkommen liegt in der Schlusssitzung der Konferenz der Vereinten Nationen über Verträge über den internationalen Warenkauf zur Unterzeichnung auf und liegt dann bis 30. September 1981 am Sitz der Vereinten Nationen in New York für alle Staaten zur Unterzeichnung auf.

(2) Dieses Übereinkommen bedarf der Ratifikation, Annahme oder Genehmigung durch die Unterzeichnerstaaten.

(3) Dieses Übereinkommen steht allen Staaten, die nicht Unterzeichnerstaaten sind, von dem Tag an zum Beitritt offen, an dem es zur Unterzeichnung aufgelegt wird.

(4) Die Ratifikations-, Annahme-, Genehmigungs- und Beitrittsurkunden werden beim Generalsekretär der Vereinten Nationen hinterlegt.

Art. 91

(1) This Convention is open for signature at the concluding meeting of the United Nations Conference on Contracts for the International Sale of Goods and will remain open for signature by all States at the Headquarters of the United Nations, New York until 30 September 1981.

(2) This Convention is subject to ratification, acceptance or approval by the signatory States.

(3) This Convention is open for accession by all States which are not signatory States as from the date it is open for signature.

(4) Instruments of ratification, acceptance, approval and accession are to be deposited with the Secretary-General of the United Nations.

Art. 91

1) La présente Convention sera ouverte à la signature à la séance de clôture de la Conférence des Nations Unies sur les contrats de vente internationale de marchandises et restera ouverte à la signature de tous les Etats au Siège de l'Organisation des Nations Unies, à New York, jusqu'au 30 septembre 1981.

2) La présente Convention est sujette à ratification, acceptation ou approbation par les Etats signataires.

3) La présente Convention sera ouverte à l'adhésion de tous les Etats qui ne sont pas signataires, à partir de la date à laquelle elle sera ouverte à la signature.

4) Les instruments de ratification, d'acceptation, d'pprobation ou d'adhésion seront déposés auprès du Secrétaire général de l'Organisation des Nations Unies.

Die Vorschrift ist Art. 28 des Übereinkommens über die Beförderung von Gütern auf See (Hamburg-Regeln) von 1978 nachgebildet,[1] der bereits im Hinblick auf die Wiener Vertragsrechtskonvention von den Vorschriften etwa des Verjährungsübereinkommens von 1974 abweicht.[2] **1**

Sachlich handelt es sich um eine Vorschrift, die sowohl die Unterzeichnung des Übereinkommens als auch die verschiedenen Möglichkeiten der Übernahme desselben behandelt.[3] Hinsichtlich der Unterzeichnung ist zu erwähnen, dass das Übereinkommen bis zum 30. September 1981 am Sitz der Vereinten Nationen in New York zur Unterzeichung (durch **alle völkerrechtlich anerkannten Staaten**,[4] also nicht nur UN-Mitglieder[5]) auflag.[6] Die bloße Unterzeichnung hat allerdings keine völkerrechtliche Wirkung.[7] Viel- **2**

---

[1] *Schlechtriem/Schwenzer/Schlechtriem/Schwenzer/Hachem*, CISG Commentary, Art. 91, Rn. 1.
[2] *Schlechtriem/Schwenzer/Schlechtriem/Schwenzer/Hachem*, CISG Commentary, Art. 91, Rn. 1.
[3] *Staudinger/Magnus*, Art. 91, Rn. 1.
[4] *Rudolph*, Art. 91, Rn. 4.
[5] Vgl. *Ferrari u. a./Mankowski*, Internationales Vertragsrecht, Art. 91, Rn. 1; *Reinhart*, Art. 91, Rn. 1.
[6] Das Übereinkommen ist innerhalb der vorgesehenen Frist gezeichnet worden von Chile, China, Dänemark, der DDR, der BR Deutschland, Finnland, Frankreich, Ghana, Italien, Jugoslawien, Lesotho, den Niederlanden, Norwegen, Österreich, Polen, Schweden, Singapur, Tschechoslowakei, Ungarn, Venezuela und den Vereinigten Staaten.
[7] *Bianca/Bonell/Evans*, Art. 91, Anm. 2.1.; *Reinhart*, Art. 91, Rn. 3; *Rudolph*, Art. 91, Rn. 2.

Art. 91 2   Teil IV. Schlussbestimmungen

mehr bedarf es auch – je nach internem Verfassungsrecht[8] – der Ratifikation, Annahme oder Genehmigung des Übereinkommens. Die Staaten, die das Übereinkommen nicht unterzeichnet haben,[9] können dem Übereinkommen beitreten.[10] Der **Beitritt** und die **Ratifikation,** Annahme und Genehmigung haben nach dem CISG **dieselben Wirkungen.**[11]

---

[8] *Brunner,* Art. 91, Rn. 1; *Staudinger/Magnus,* Art. 91, Rn. 2.
[9] Diese sog. Allstaaten-Klausel entspricht Art. 6 des Wiener Vertragsrechtsübereinkommens; in früheren Übereinkommen findet sich oft die Klausel, dass nur Mitgliedstaaten der UN oder einer ihrer Sonderorganisationen Vertragsstaat werden können.
[10] *Herber/Czerwenka,* Art. 91, Rn. 2; *Ferrari u. a./Mankowski,* Internationales Vertragsrecht, Art. 91, Rn. 3; *Rudolph,* Art. 91, Rn. 3, mit einer Liste von Beitrittsstaaten.
[11] Vgl. auch *Enderlein/Maskow/Strohbach,* Art. 91, Anm. 5.; *Ferrari u. a./Mankowski,* Internationales Vertragsrecht, Art. 91, Rn. 3; *Schlechtriem/Schwenzer/Schlechtriem/Schwenzer/Hachem,* CISG Commmentary, Art. 91, Rn. 3; *Witz/Salger/Lorenz/Witz,* Art. 91, Rn. 1.

Art. 92 [Teilweise Ratifikation, Annahme, Genehmigung oder Beitritt]

(1) Ein Vertragsstaat kann bei der Unterzeichnung, der Ratifikation, der Annahme, der Genehmigung oder dem Beitritt erklären, dass Teil II dieses Übereinkommens für ihn nicht verbindlich ist oder dass Teil III dieses Übereinkommens für ihn nicht verbindlich ist.

(2) Ein Vertragsstaat, der eine Erklärung nach Absatz 1 zu Teil II oder Teil III dieses Übereinkommens abgegeben hat, ist hinsichtlich solcher Gegenstände, die durch den Teil geregelt werden, auf den sich die Erklärung bezieht, nicht als Vertragsstaat im Sinne des Artikels 1 Absatz 1 zu betrachten.

Art. 92

(1) A Contracting State may declare at the time of signature, ratification, acceptance, approval or accession that it will not be bound by Part II of this Convention or that it will not be bound by Part III of this Convention.

(2) A Contracting State which makes a declaration in accordance with the preceding paragraph in respect of Part II or Part III of this Convention is not to be considered a Contracting State within paragraph (1) of article 1 of this Convention in respect of matters governed by the Part to which the declaration applies.

Art. 92

1) Tout Etat contractant pourra, au moment de la signature, de la ratification, de l'acceptation, de l'approbation ou de l'adhésion, déclarer qu'il ne sera pas lié par la deuxième partie de la présente Convention ou qu'il ne sera pas lié par la troisième partie de la présente Convention.

2) Un Etat contractant qui fait, en vertu du paragraphe précédent, une déclaration à l'égard de la dexième partie ou de la troisième partie de la présente Convention ne sera pas considéré comme étant un Etat contractant, au sens du paragraphe 1 de l'article premier de la Convention, pour les matières régies par la partie de la Convention à laquelle cette déclaration s'applique.

Als UNCITRAL 1978 im New Yorker E die Entwürfe für die beiden in Teil II und Teil III geregelten Materien vereinigte, wurde auf Wunsch der skandinavischen Länder[1] zugleich beschlossen,[2] dass es den Mitgliedsstaaten freistehen müsse, trotz Zusammenfassung der – in den Haager Kaufrechtsübereinkommen noch in EAG und EKG getrennten[3] – Regeln über den Abschluss von Kaufverträgen einerseits und über die Rechte und Pflichten der Vertragsparteien aus Verträgen andererseits diese Teile gesondert anzunehmen. 1

Die Erklärung ist ein echter **Vorbehalt**.[4] Sie muss bei der Ratifikation, Annahme, Genehmigung oder dem Beitritt abgegeben werden;[5] eine anlässlich der Unterzeichnung abgegebene Erklärung hat lediglich die Funktion einer Ankündigung, da der Vorbehalt in diesem Fall nur wirksam ist, wenn er später, d. h., bei der Ratifikation, Annahme oder Genehmigung, bestätigt wird.[6] Nach vorbehaltlosem Inkrafttreten des Übereinkommens kann die Vorbehaltswirkung nur durch teilweise Kündigung des Übereinkommens herbeigeführt werden.[7] Der Vorbehalt kann jederzeit zurückgenommen werden.[8] 2

---

[1] Vgl. *Brunner*, Art. 92, Rn. 1; *Ferrari*, IHR 2006, 1, 5; *Ferrari u. a./Mankowski*, Internationales Vertragsrecht, Art. 92, Rn. 1; *Herber/Czerwenka*, Art. 92, Rn. 1; MünchKomm/*P. Huber*, Art. 92, Rn. 1; *Schlechtriem/Schwenzer/Schlechtriem/Schwenzer/Hachem*, CISG Commentary, Art. 92, Rn. 1; *Witz/Salger/Lorenz/Witz*, Art. 92, Rn. 1.

[2] UNCITRAL YB IX (1978), S. 13.

[3] Vgl. *Dölle/Dölle*, Einl. XXXVI.

[4] *Herber/Czerwenka*, Art. 92, Rn. 1; *Schlechtriem/Schwenzer/ Schlechtriem/Schwenzer/Hachem*, CISG Commentary, Art. 92, Rn. 1.

[5] *Ferrari u. a./Mankowski*, Internationales Vertragsrecht, Art. 92, Rn. 3.

[6] Siehe Art. 97 I.

[7] *Achilles*, Art. 92, Rn. 1; *Ferrari u. a./Mankowski*, Internationales Vertragsrecht, Art. 92, Rn. 3; *Staudinger/Magnus*, Art. 92, Rn. 4.

[8] Vgl. Art. 97 IV.

Art. 92 3   Teil IV. Schlussbestimmungen

3   Bei dem **Vorbehalt** handelt es sich, im Gegensatz zu anderen im CISG vorgesehenen Vorbehalten,[9] um einen sich auf die **Vertragsstaateneigenschaft auswirkenden** Vorbehalt.[10] Dies ergibt sich unschwer aus dem Wortlaut des Abs. 2, der die Wirkungen des Vorbehaltes klarstellt. Demzufolge ist ein Staat hinsichtlich des von ihm durch den Vorbehalt ausgeschlossenen Teils nicht als Vertragsstaat anzusehen.[11] In der praktischen Konsequenz bedeutet dies, dass wenn auch nur eine der Parteien ihre Niederlassung in einem Vorbehaltsstaat hat, das CISG nie ex Art. 1 I lit. a) in toto Anwendung finden kann.[12] Kraft Art. 1 I lit. a) können nur die Teile des CISG Anwendung finden, die in beiden Staaten, in denen die Parteien ihre Niederlassung haben, in Kraft sind.[13] Dies schließt eine Anwendung der Vorschriften des vom Vorbehaltsstaat ausgeschlossenen Teils aber nicht unbedingt aus.[14] Vielmehr hängt dies davon ab, ob das IPR des Forumsstaates auf das Recht eines Vertragsstaates verweist, der den Vorbehalt nicht erklärt hat.[15] In diesem Fall kann der ausgeschlossene Teil des CISG über Art. 1 I lit. b) Anwendung finden,[16] sofern alle Voraussetzungen vorliegen.[17] Dies gilt auch dann, wenn die angerufenen Gerichte die eines Vertragsstaates sind, der den Vorbehalt gemäß Art. 92 eingelegt hat;[18] dies ist auch von der Rechtsprechung bestätigt worden.[19]

---

[9] Siehe etwa Art. 95 und Art. 96.

[10] So auch *Ferrari*, Applicabilità ed applicazioni, S. 79; *Ferrari u. a./Mankowski*, Internationales Vertragsrecht, Art. 92, Rn. 5; MünchKommHGB/*Benicke*, Art. 1, Rn. 30; *Torsello*, Uniform L. Rev. 2000, 85, 97.

[11] *Achilles*, Art. 92, Rn. 1; *Herber/Czerwenka*, Art. 92, Rn. 3; *Honsell/Siehr*, Art. 92, Rn. ;1; *Kröll u. a./Herre*, Art. 92, Rn. 1 und 3; *Lookofsky*, 80 Nordic J. Int'l L. (2011), 295, 299; MünchKomm/*P. Huber*, Art. 92, Rn. 2; *Piltz*, Internationales Kaufrecht, Rn. 2–89; *Sannini*, L'Applicazione, S. 69; *Schlechtriem/Schwenzer/Schlechtriem/Schwenzer/Hachem*, CISG Commentary, Art. 92, Rn. 3; *Staudinger/Magnus*, Art. 92, Rn. 5.

[12] So auch *Ferrari*, Applicabilità ed applicazioni, S. 80; *Ferrari u. a./Mankowski*, Internationales Vertragsrecht, Art. 92, Rn. 6; *Fogt*, ZEuP 2002, 580, 587; *Honsell/Siehr*, Art. 1 Rn. 22 f.; *Johannsen*, S. 340; *Lookofsky*, 18 J. L. & Com. (1999), 289, 292; MünchKomm/*P. Huber*, Art. 92, Rn. 2; *Schlechtriem/Schwenzer/Schlechtriem/Schwenzer/Hachem*, CISG Commentary, Art. 92, Rn. 3; *Torsello*, Uniform L. Rev. 2000, 85, 98.

[13] Falsch daher OLG Naumburg, 27.4.1999, CISG-online 512 = TranspR-IHR 2000, 22 f.: „Nach Art. 1 Abs. 1 lit a CISG ist das Übereinkommen bei Kaufverträgen über Waren anzuwenden, wenn die Parteien ihren Sitz in Vertragsstaaten haben. Sowohl Deutschland (Sitz der Beklagten), als auch Dänemark (Sitz jedenfalls der Verkaufsniederlassung der Klägerin – vgl. Art. 28 Abs. 2 S. 2 EGBGB -) sind Vertragsstaaten des Übereinkommens [...]. „Damit ist das Abkommen anzuwenden und geht den Vorschriften des BGB vor"; falsch auch OLG Frankfurt a. M., 4.3.1994, CISG-online 110 (schwedisch-deutscher Kaufvertrag, der dem Gericht nach ex Art. 1 I lit. a) dem CISG unterliegt; kritisch zu diesen Urteilen auch *Fogt*, ZEuP 2002, 580, 587 Fn. 22.

[14] So auch *Ferrari*, IHR 2006, 1, 5; *Herber/Czerwenka*, Art. 92, Rn. 3; *Lookofsky*, 80 Nordic J. Int'l L. (2011), 295, 299; *ders.*, 18 J. L. & Com. (1999), 289, 294 f.

[15] *Achilles*, Art. 92, Rn. 1; *Enderlein/Maskow/Strohbach*, Art. 92, Anm. 6.; *Ferrari*, Applicabilità ed applicazioni, S. 80 ff.; *Ferrari u. a./Mankowski*, Internationales Vertragsrecht, Art. 92, Rn. 6; *Flechtner*, 17 J. L. & Com. (1998), 187, 193 f.; *Lookofsky*, Understanding the CISG in Scandinavia, S. 19; *ders.*, 18 J. L. & Com. (1999), 289, 294 f.; *Magnus*, ZEuP 1997, 823, 827 f.

[16] Vgl. *Brunner*, Art. 92, Rn. 3; *Ferrari*, J. D. I. 2006, 27, 44; *Honnold/Flechtner*, Art. 92, Rn. 467; *Honsell/Siehr*, Art. 92, Rn. 1; *Lookofsky*, 80 Nordic J. Int'l L. (2011), 295, 300; MünchKomm/*P. Huber*, Art. 92, Rn. 2; MünchKommHGB/*Benicke*, Art. 1, Rn. 30; *Rudolph*, Art. 92, Rn. 2; *Schlechtriem/Schwenzer/Schlechtriem/Schwenzer/Hachem*, CISG Commentary, Art. 92, Rn. 3; *Witz/Salger/Lorenz/Witz*, Art. 92, Rn. 2; a. A. – ohne Begründung – LG Bielefeld, 12.12.2003, CISG-online 905: Anwendung der BGB-Vorschriften zum Vertragsschluss, obwohl der deutsch-dänische Vertrag aufgrund einer Rechtswahl deutschem Recht, also dem Recht eines Vertragsstaates, unterstellt worden war.

[17] Siehe in der Rechtsprechung *Mitchell Aircraft Spares Inc. v. European Aircraft Service AB*, U. S. Dist. Ct. (N. D. Ill.), 27.10.1998, CISG-online 444 = U. S. Dist. Lexis 17 030 (Teil II des CISG kam nicht zur Anwendung, da der Forumsstaat einen Vorbehalt nach Art. 95 eingelegt hatte und die Vorschriften des IPR auf das Recht des Forumsstaates verwiesen); Stadtgericht Budapest, 21.5.1996, CISG-online 252 (die IPR-Vorschriften des Forumsstaates verwiesen auf schwedisches Recht, d. h. das Recht eines Vorbehaltsstaates nach Art. 92, weshalb internes schwedisches Recht auf in Teil II geregelte Fragen Anwendung fand); OLG Rostock, 27.7.1995, CISG-online 209 (die IPR Vorschriften des Forumsstaates verwiesen auf dänisches Recht, d. h. das Recht eines Vorbehaltsstaates nach Art. 92, weshalb internes dänisches Recht auf in Teil II geregelte Fragen Anwendung fand); ICC, 7585/1992, CISG-online 105; unklar hingegen OLG München, 8.3.1995, CISG-online 145 (deutsch-finnischer Kaufvertrag).

[18] Ebenso *Achilles*, Art. 92, Rn. 1; *Ferrari u. a./Mankowski*, Internationales Vertragsrecht, Art. 92, Rn. 6; *Herber/Czerwenka*, Art. 92, Rn. 3; *Lookofsky*, 39 Am. J. Comp. L. (1991), 403 ff.; *Schlechtriem/Schwenzer/Schlechtriem/Schwenzer/Hachem*, CISG Commentary, Art. 92, Rn. 3; *Schroeter*, FS Kritzer, S. 425, 439; *Witz/Salger/Lorenz/Witz*, Art. 92, Rn. 2.

[19] Østre Landsret, 23.4.1998, CISG-online 486; vgl. hierzu *Lookofsky*, 80 Nordic J. Int'l L. (2011), 295, 300.

Hat einer der beteiligten Staaten die Erklärung hinsichtlich Teil II, der andere hinsichtlich 4
Teil III abgegeben[20], so ist die Anwendung dieser Teile ex Art. 1 I lit. a) ausgeschlossen. Die
Anwendung der ausgeschlossenen Teile ist zwar über Art. 1 I lit. b) möglich, jedoch nach
anwendbarem IPR gesondert zu prüfen.[21]

---

[20] Es sei angemerkt, dass bislang noch kein Staat einen Vorbehalt hinsichtlich Teil III des CISG abgegeben hat.
[21] So auch *Bianca/Bonell/Evans,* Art. 92, Anm. 2.3. und 2.4.; *Schlechtriem/Schwenzer/Schlechtriem/Schwenzer/ Hachem,* CISG Commentary, Art. 92, Rn. 4; vgl auch *Kröll u. a./Herre* , Art. 92, Rn. 7.

Art. 93 [Föderative Staaten]

(1) **Ein Vertragsstaat, der zwei oder mehr Gebietseinheiten umfasst, in denen nach seiner Verfassung auf die in diesem Übereinkommen geregelten Gegenstände unterschiedliche Rechtsordnungen angewendet werden, kann bei der Unterzeichnung, der Ratifikation, der Annahme, der Genehmigung oder dem Beitritt erklären, dass dieses Übereinkommen sich auf alle seine Gebietseinheiten oder nur auf eine oder mehrere derselben erstreckt; er kann seine Erklärung jederzeit durch eine neue Erklärung ändern.**

(2) **Die Erklärungen sind dem Verwahrer zu notifizieren und haben ausdrücklich anzugeben, auf welche Gebietseinheiten das Übereinkommen sich erstreckt**

(3) **Erstreckt sich das Übereinkommen aufgrund einer Erklärung nach diesem Artikel auf eine oder mehrere, jedoch nicht auf alle Gebietseinheiten eines Vertragsstaats und liegt die Niederlassung einer Partei in diesem Staat, so wird diese Niederlassung im Sinne dieses Übereinkommens nur dann als in einem Vertragsstaat gelegen betrachtet, wenn sie in einer Gebietseinheit liegt, auf die sich das Übereinkommen erstreckt.**

(4) **Gibt ein Vertragsstaat keine Erklärung nach Absatz 1 ab, so erstreckt sich das Übereinkommen auf alle Gebietseinheiten dieses Staates.**

Art. 93

(1) If a Contracting State has two or more territorial units in which, according to its constitution, different systems of law are applicable in relation to the matters dealt with in this Convention, it may, at the time of signature, ratification, acceptance, approval or accession, declare that this Convention is to extend to all its territorial units or only to one or more of them, and may amend its declaration by submitting another declaration at any time.

(2) These declarations are to be notified to the depositary and are to state expressly the territorial units to which the Convention extends.

(3) If, by virtue of a declaration under this article, this Convention extends to one or more but not all of the territorial units of a Contracting State, and if the place of business of a party is located in that State, this place of business, for the purposes of this Convention, is considered not to be in a Contracting State, unless it is in a territorial unit to which the Convention extends.

(4) If a Contracting State makes no declaration under paragraph (1) of this article, the Convention is to extend to all territorial units of that State.

Art. 93

1) Tout Etat contractant qui comprend deux ou plusieurs unités territoriales dans lesquelles, selon sa constitution, des systèmes de droit différents s'appliquent dans les matières régies par la présente Convention pourra, au moment de la signature, de la ratification, de l'acceptation, de l'approbation ou de l'adhésion, déclarer que la présente Convention s'appliquera à toutes ses unités territoriales ou seulement à l'une ou plusieurs d'entre elles et pourra à tout moment modifier cette déclaration en faisant une nouvelle déclaration.

2) Ces déclarations seront notifiées au dépositaire et désigneront expressément les unités territoriales auxquelles la Convention s'applique.

3) Si, en vertu d'une déclaration faite conformément au présent article, la présente Convention s'applique à l'une ou plusieurs des unités territoriales d'un Etat contractant, mais non pas à toutes, et si l'établissement d'une partie au contrat est situé dans cet Etat, cet établissement sera considéré, aux fins de la présente Convention, comme n'étant pas situé dans un Etat contractant, à moins qu'il ne soit situé dans une unite territoriale à laquelle la Convention s'applique.

4) Si un Etat contractant ne fait pas de déclaration en vertu du paragraphe 1 du présent article, la Convention s'appliquera à l'ensemble du territoire de cet Etat.

Föderative Staaten   1–3 **Art. 93**

Die Vorschrift enthält die sogenannte **Bundesstaaten-Klausel**,[1] die auch in anderen 1
Einheitssachrechtskonventionen enthalten ist.[2] Sie soll es einem Bundesstaat ermöglichen, auch dann dem CISG wenigstens für einzelne seiner Gebietseinheiten beizutreten, wenn dies ihm mangels eigener Gesetzgebungszuständigkeit für das in dem CISG geregelte Rechtsgebiet nicht mit Wirkung für alle seine Gliederungen gestattet ist.[3] Die Bestimmung wurde insbesondere von Australien und Kanada verlangt.[4]

Das Sekretariat hatte mit dem Entwurf der Schlussklauseln noch zwei Alternativen für die 2
Regelung vorgeschlagen;[5] während die Alternative I davon ausging, dass ein Bundesstaat die Anwendung einzelner Artikel, für die er keine Gesetzgebungszuständigkeit hat, aussetzen kann, enthielt Alternative II die – letztlich beschlossene – Regelung, welche einzelne Gebietsteile von der Anwendung auszunehmen gestattet. In der Diskussion im Zweiten Gesamtausschuss[6] wurde mit Recht hervorgehoben, dass die Nichtanwendung einzelner Artikel bei einem komplexen Übereinkommen wie dem CISG praktisch nicht durchführbar sei. Deshalb entschied sich die Diplomatische Konferenz für die Alternative II, die allerdings noch verbessert wurde.[7]

Die Vorschrift ermöglicht es, durch eine Erklärung bei der Unterzeichnung – die aber der 3
späteren Bestätigung in den in Art. 97 I vorgesehenen Formen bedarf –, der Ratifikation, Annahme, Genehmigung oder dem Beitritt[8] die Geltung des Übereinkommens auf bestimmte Gebietseinheiten eines Vertragsstaates, wie etwa Bundesstaaten, Kantone, Regionen, Provinzen, etc.,[9] die jedoch eine gewisse staatsrechtliche Eigenständigkeit haben müssen, zu beschränken.[10] Diese Erklärung, die kraft Abs. 1 Hs. 2 jederzeit durch eine neue Erklärung geändert werden kann,[11] wirkt sich – genauso wie eine gemäß Art. 92 abgegebene Erklärung – auf die **Vertragsstaateneigenschaft** des die Erklärung abgebenden Staates dahingehend aus, dass nur jene Gebietseinheiten als Teil eines Vertragsstaates des Übereinkommens anzusehen sind, auf die sich die Geltung des Übereinkommens erstreckt.[12] Hat demnach eine Vertragspartei ihre Niederlassung in einem Gebietsteil, auf den sich die Geltung des CISG nicht erstreckt, so gilt diese als in einem Nichtvertragsstaat gelegen,[13] mit der Folge, dass das Übereinkommen nicht über Art. 1 I lit. a) Anwendung finden kann.[14] Das CISG kann

---

[1] Vgl. *Brunner*, Art. 93, Rn. 1; *Date-Bah*, 11 Ghana L. Rev. (1979), 50, 52; *Flechtner*, 17 J. L. & Com. (1998), 187, 194; *Kröll u. a./Herre*, Art. 93, Rn. 1; *Schlechtriem/Schwenzer/Schlechtriem/Schwenzer/Hachem*, CISG Commentary, Art. 93, Rn. 1; *Schroeter*, IHR 2004, 7, 11; *Torsello*, Uniform L. Rev. 2000, 85, 93; *Volken*, Anwendungsvoraussetzungen, S. 89; *Witz/Salger/Lorenz/Witz*, Art. 93, Rn. 1.
[2] Vgl. etwa Art. 87 des Übereinkommens über internationale Wechsel von 1988; Art. 25 des Übereinkommens über unabhängige Garantien und Stand-by Letters of Credit von 1995; Art. 35 des Übereinkommens über die Abtretung von Forderungen im internationalen Handel von 2001; Art. 18 des Übereinkommens über die Nutzung elektronischer Kommunikation beim Abschluss grenzüberschreitender Verträge von 2005; Art. 92 des Übereinkommens über Verträge über die internationale Beförderung von Gütern ganz oder teilweise auf See von 2008.
[3] *Achilles*, Art. 93, Rn. 1; *Herber/Czerwenka*, Art. 93, Rn. 1; *MünchKomm/P. Huber*, Art. 93, Rn. 1; vgl. auch IHR 2004, 7, 12.
[4] *Brunner*, Art. 93, Rn. 1; *Reinhart*, Art. 93, Rn. 1; *Rudolph*, Art. 93, Rn. 1; *Schlechtriem*, Einheitliches UN-Kaufrecht, S. 107; *Schlechtriem/Schwenzer/Schlechtriem/Schwenzer/Hachem*, CISG Commentary, Art. 93, Rn. 1.
[5] Vgl. O. R. S. 67; hierzu eingehend *Bianca/Bonell/Evans*, Art. 93, Anm. 1.1. ff.; *Ferrari u. a./Mankowski*, Internationales Vertragsrecht, Art. 94, Rn. 4; *Schlechtriem/Schwenzer/Schlechtriem/Schwenzer/Hachem*, CISG Commentary, Art. 93, Rn. 2.
[6] O. R. S. 434 ff.
[7] O. R. S. 434 ff., 445 ff.
[8] *Rudolph*, Art. 93, Rn. 2.
[9] Art. 93 sieht eine Vorbehaltsmöglichkeit „nur für territorial gespaltene, nicht aber für personell oder religiös gespaltene Staaten [vor]", *Ferrari u. a./Mankowski*, Internationales Vertragsrecht, Art. 94, Rn. 3.
[10] Vgl. *Schlechtriem/Schwenzer/Schlechtriem/Schwenzer/Hachem*, CISG Commentary, Art. 93, Rn. 3; *Staudinger/Magnus*, Art. 93, Rn. 4.
[11] Diese Möglichkeit geht anscheinend davon aus, dass die Zahl der Gebietsteile, in denen das Übereinkommen keine Anwendung finden soll, eher zurückgeht als zunimmt; so *Herber*, 2. Aufl., Art. 93 Rn. 3.
[12] *Staudinger/Magnus*, Art. 93, Rn. 7; *Torsello*, Uniform L. Rev. 2000, 85, 93.
[13] *Flechtner*, 17 J. L. & Com. (1998), 187, 194; *Schlechtriem/Schwenzer/Schlechtriem/Schwenzer/Hachem*, CISG Commentary, Art. 93, Rn. 5.
[14] *Bianca/Bonell/Evans*, Anm. 2.4.; *Diez-Picazo/Calvo Caravaca*, Art. 93, S. 715; *Ferrari*, Applicabilità ed applicazioni, S. 82; *MünchKommHGB/Benicke*, Art. 1, Rn. 31; *Herber/Czerwenka*, Art. 93, Rn. 4.

dennoch zur Anwendung kommen, sofern das Recht, auf das die Kollisionsnormen des Forumsstaates verweisen, nicht das des Gebietsteils ist, auf das sich die Geltung des CISG nicht erstreckt und sofern alle anderen Anwendungsvoraussetzungen vorliegen.[15]

4 **Ohne eine ausdrückliche Erklärung** nach Art. 93 erstreckt sich die Geltung des Übereinkommens auf das gesamte Gebiet des Vertragsstaates.[16] Daher muß davon ausgegagen werden, dass das CISG auch für Makau gilt, obwohl anläßlich der Rückführung Makaus das CISG nicht auf die Liste der Übereinkommen gesetzt hat, die auch für Makau gelten sollten.[17] Dieser Umstand ist nämlich nicht ausreichend, um die Wirkungen einer Erklärung nach Art. 93 entfalten zu lassen. Gleiches gilt auch in Bezug auf Hong Kong.[18]

5 Gibt ein Vertragsstaat ursprünglich keine Erklärung ab, wonach sich das CISG nicht auf alle Gebietseinheiten erstreckt, kann ein nachträglicher Vorbehalt nicht erklärt werden.[19] Der Vertragsstaat müsste, um den gewünschten Effekt zu erreichen, das CISG kündigen und abermals – mit Nichtanwendungsvorbehalt – dem CISG beitreten.[20]

---

[15] Ebenso *Ferrari*, IHR 2006, 1, 6; *Honsell/Siehr*, Art. 1, Rn. 24; *Staudinger/Magnus*, Art. 93, Rn. 7.

[16] *Brunner*, Art. 93, Rn. 3; *Diez-Picazo/Calvo Caravaca*, Art. 93, S. 715; *Herber/Czerwenka*, Art. 93, Rn. 3; MünchKomm/*P. Huber*, Art. 93, Rn. 1; *Reinhart*, Art. 93, Rn. 4; *Rudolph*, Art. 93, Rn. 1; *Schlechtriem/Schwenzer/Schlechtriem/Schwenzer/Hachem*, CISG Commentary, Art. 93, Rn. 4.

[17] *Schlechtriem/Schwenzer/Schlechtriem/Schwenzer/Hachem*, CISG Commentary, Art. 93, Rn. 4; *Schroeter*, IHR 2004, 7, 13 f.; a. a. Cour Cass., 2.4.2008, CISG-online 1651.

[18] *Electrocraft Arkansas, Inc. v. Super Electric Motors, Ltd and Raymond O'Gara*, U. S. District Court, ED of Arkansas, Western Division, 19.8.2010, CISG-online 2149; *Electrocraft Arkansas, Inc. v. Super Electric Motors, Ltd et al.*; U. S. District Court, ED of Arkansas, Western Division, 23.12.2009, CISG-online 2045; *CNA Int'l Inc. v. Guangdong Kelon Electronical Holdings et al.*, U. S. District Court, N. D. of Illinois, 3.9.2008, CISG-online 2043; OGH, 31.8.2005, CISG-online 1093; OLG Innsbruck, 1.2.2005, CISG-online 1130; Hof van Beroep Antwerpen, 14.2.2002, CISG-online 995; OLG Hamm, 12.11.2001, CISG-online 1430; RB Turnhout, 18.1.2001, CISG-online 994; a. a. *Innotex Precision Limited v. Horei Image Products, Inc., et al.*, U. S. District Court, ND of Georgia, Atlanta Division, 17.12.2009, CISG-online 2044; *Hannaford (trading as Torrens Valley Orchards) v Australian Farmlink*, Federal Court of Australia (South Australia Registry), 24.10.2008, CISG-online 1743; Cour Cass., 2.4.2008, CISG-online 1651.

[19] *Schlechtriem/Schwenzer/Schlechtriem/Schwenzer/Hachem*, CISG Commentary, Art. 93, Rn. 3; vgl. auch *Schroeter*, IHR 2004, 7, 13; a. a. *Ferrari u. a./Mankowski*, Internationales Vertragsrecht, Art. 93, Rn. 2.

[20] *Achilles*, Art. 93, Rn. 1.

Art. 94 [Erklärung über Nichtanwendung des Übereinkommens]

(1) Zwei oder mehr Vertragsstaaten, welche gleiche oder einander sehr nahekommende Rechtsvorschriften für Gegenstände haben, die in diesem Übereinkommen geregelt werden, können jederzeit erklären, dass das Übereinkommen auf Kaufverträge und ihren Abschluss keine Anwendung findet, wenn die Parteien ihre Niederlassung in diesen Staaten haben. Solche Erklärungen können als gemeinsame oder als aufeinander bezogene einseitige Erklärungen abgegeben werden.

(2) Hat ein Vertragsstaat für Gegenstände, die in diesem Übereinkommen geregelt werden, Rechtsvorschriften, die denen eines oder mehrerer Nichtvertragsstaaten gleich sind oder sehr nahe kommen, so kann er jederzeit erklären, dass das Übereinkommen auf Kaufverträge oder ihren Abschluss keine Anwendung findet, wenn die Parteien ihre Niederlassung in diesen Staaten haben.

(3) Wird ein Staat, auf den sich eine Erklärung nach Absatz 2 bezieht, Vertragsstaat, so hat die Erklärung von dem Tag an, an dem das Übereinkommen für den neuen Vertragsstaat in Kraft tritt, die Wirkung einer nach Absatz 1 abgegebenen Erklärung, vorausgesetzt, dass der neue Vertragsstaat sich einer solchen Erklärung anschließt oder eine darauf bezogene einseitige Erklärung abgibt.

Art. 94

(1) Two or more Contracting States which have the same or closely related legal rules on matters governed by this Convention may at any time declare that the Convention is not to apply to contracts of sale or to their formation where the parties have their places of business in those States. Such declarations may be made jointly or by reciprocal unilateral declarations.

(2) A Contracting State which has the same or closely related legal rules on matters governed by this Convention as one or more non-Contracting States may at any time declare that the Convention is not to apply to contracts of sale or to their formation where the parties have their places of business in those States.

(3) If a State which is the object of a declaration under the preceding paragraph subsequently becomes a Contracting State, the declaration made will, as from the date on which the Convention enters into force in respect of the new Contracting State, have the effect of a declaration made under paragraph (1), provided that the new Contracting State joins in such declaration or makes a reciprocal unilateral declaration.

Art. 94

1) Deux ou plusieurs Etats contractants qui, dans des matières régies par la présente Convention, appliquent des règles juridiques identiques ou voisines peuvent, à tout moment, déclarer que la Convention ne s'appliquera pas aux contrats de vente ou à leur formation lorsque les parties ont leur établissement dans ces Etats. De telles déclarations peuvent être faites conjointement ou être unilatérales et reciproques.

2) Un Etat contractant qui, dans des matières régies par la présente Convention, applique des règles juridiques identiques ou voisines de celles d'un ou de plusieurs Etats non contractants peut, à tout moment, déclarer que la Convention ne s'appliquera pas aux contrats de vente ou à leur formation lorsque les parties ont leur établissement dans ces Etats.

3) Lorsqu'un Etat à l'égard duquel une déclaration a été faite en vertu du paragraphe précédent devient par la suite un Etat contractant, la déclaration mentionnée aura, à partir de la date à laquelle la présente Convention entrera en vigueur à l'égard de ce nouvel Etat contractant, les effets d'une déclaration faite en vertu du paragraphe 1, à condition que le nouvel Etat contractant s'y associe ou fasse une déclaration unilatérale à titre réciproque.

Die Vorschrift, die ein Vorbild in den Einführungskonventionen zum Haager Kaufrecht und in Art. 34 des Verjährungsübereinkommens hat[1] und auf Wunsch der skandinavischen Länder eingeführt wurde,[2] hat den Zweck, Staaten, die ihr Kaufrecht **weitgehend an-** **1**

---

[1] Siehe *Bianca/Bonell/Evans*, Art. 94, Anm. 1.2.; *Czerwenka*, S. 139; eingehend zur Entstehungsgeschichte vgl. *Schroeter*, UN-Kaufrecht, § 10, Rn. 5–9.

[2] Vgl. *Ferrari*, IHR 2006, 1, 6; O. R. S. 436; *Ferrari u. a./Mankowski*, Internationales Vertragsrecht, Art. 94, Rn. 4; *Schroeter*, UN-Kaufrecht, § 10, Rn. 2; *Volken*, Anwendungsvoraussetzungen, S. 89, spricht von der

einander angeglichen haben, wobei irrelevant ist, wie es zu dieser Angleichung gekommen ist,[3] ob durch Rechtsetzung oder Richterrecht, die Anwendung des CISG **in ihrem Verhältnis zueinander** zu erlassen.[4] Wann das Kaufrecht als ausreichend angeglichen gilt, um zur Nichtanwendung des CISG zu führen, entscheiden die Staaten selbst,[5] was durchaus nicht unproblematisch ist,[6] etwa im Fall einer nur in einem der Vorbehaltsstaaten nach der Erklärung erfolgten Rechtsänderung.[7] Mit dieser Vorschriften haben die Konventionsgeber (implizit) dem Ergebnis eventueller **regionaler Rechtsvereinheitlichungsbestrebungen** (unter bestimmten Bedingungen) **Vorrang** eingeräumt.[8]

2 Der **Erklärung** des Vorbehaltes, deren Erfordernis bewirkt, „dass im Rahmen der vorausgehenden internen Beschlussfassung eine Erörterung der Wünschbarkeit einer zukünftigen (teilweisen) Nichtanwendung des UN-Kaufrechts stattfindet",[9] und die im Gegensatz zu den Erklärungen einiger anderer Vorbehalte **jederzeit**[10] abgegeben werden und, was sich bereits aus dem Gesagten ergibt, auch nur Teilkomplexe des CISG betreffen kann,[11] bedarf es nicht,[12] soweit die Rechtsangleichung auf einer **internationalen Vereinbarung** beruht, da in einem solchen Fall die zwischen den Vertragsstaaten des CISG vereinbarten Regeln bereits kraft **Art. 90** denen des CISG vorgehen.[13]

3 Fraglich ist, ob die gemäß Art. 94 gemachten Erklärungen die Anwendung des CISG auch[14] in **Vertragsstaaten,** die eine solche **Erklärung nicht abgegeben** haben, ausschließen, wenn beide Vertragsparteien ihre Niederlassung in Vorbehaltsstaaten haben.[15] M. E. ist

---

„Skandinavienklausel", da bei der Ausarbeitung der Vorschrift vor allem an die Rechtsvereinheitlichung im skandinavischen Raum gedacht wurde.

[3] *Ferrari u. a./Mankowski,* Internationales Vertragsrecht, Art. 94, Rn. 3; *Herber,* IHR 2004, 89, 90; *Rudolph,* Art. 94, Rn. 5; *Schlechtriem/Schwenzer/Schlechtriem/Schwenzer/Hachem,* CISG Commentary, Art. 94, Rn. 5; *Schroeter,* UN-Kaufrecht, § 10, Rn. 4.

[4] Siehe auch *Lookofsky,* 18 J. L. & Com. (1999), 289, 290; *Rudolph,* Art. 94, Rn. 1; *Schlechtriem/ Schwenzer/Schlechtriem/Schwenzer/Hachem,* CISG Commentary, Art. 94, Rn. 1; *Schroeter,* UN-Kaufrecht, § 10, Rn. 43.

[5] *Achilles,* Art. 94, Rn. 2; *Brunner,* Art. 94, Rn. 2; *Enderlein/Maskow/Strohbach,* Art. 94, Anm. 1.; *Ferrari u. a./Mankowski,* Internationales Vertragsrecht, Art. 94, Rn. 10; *Flechtner,* 17 J. L. & Com. (1998), 187, 194; *Neumayer/Ming,* Art. 94, Anm. 1., Fn. 1; *Reinhart,* Art. 94, Rn. 4; *Schlechtriem/Schwenzer/Schlechtriem/Schwenzer/Hachem,* CISG Commentary, Art. 94, Rn. 5; *Schroeter,* UN-Kaufrecht, § 10, Rn. 20; *Staudinger/Magnus,* Art. 94, Rn. 5.

[6] *Torsello,* Uniform L. Rev. 2000, 85, 94 ff.

[7] Vgl. hierzu *Kröll u. a./Herre,* Art. 94, Rn. 7, der darauf hinweist, dass sich das Recht der skandinavischen Vorbehaltsstaaten nach denErklärungen der Vorbehalte geändert hat.

[8] *Schroeter,* UN-Kaufrecht, § 10, Rn. 5; vgl. auch *Ferrari u. a./Mankowski,* Internationales Vertragsrecht, Art. 94, Rn. 1 f.; *H.-F. Müller,* GPR 2006, 168, 173; allgemein zum Verhältnis von CISG und regionaler Rechtsvereinheitlichung auf dem Gebiet des Kaufrechts, vgl. *Ferrari,* Uniform L. Rev. 2003, 177 ff.; *ders.,* Rev. dr. aff. int. 2004, 445 ff.; *Šarčević,* Regional Unification, S. 3 ff.; *Schlechtriem,* Uniform L. Rev. 2003, 173 ff.

[9] *Schroeter,* UN-Kaufrecht, § 10, Rn. 27.

[10] *Ferrari u. a./Mankowski,* Internationales Vertragsrecht, Art. 94, Rn. 11; *Herber,* IHR 2004, 89, 90; *Rudolph,* Art. 94, Rn. 3; *Schlechtriem/Schwenzer/Schlechtriem/Schwenzer/Hachem,* CISG Commentary, Art. 94, Rn. 8; *Schroeter,* UN-Kaufrecht, § 10, Rn. 30.

[11] *Achilles,* Art. 94, Rn. 2; *Brunner,* Art. 94, Rn. 3; *Ferrari u. a./Mankowski,* Internationales Vertragsrecht, Art. 94, Rn. 13; *Janssen,* EuLF 2003, 181, 183; MünchKomm/*P. Huber,* Art. 94, Rn. 1; *Rudolph,* Art. 94, Rn. 2; *Schroeter,* UN-Kaufrecht, § 10, Rn. 33 ff.; *Witz/Salger/Lorenz/Witz,* Art. 94, Rn. 1; krit. hierzu *Kröll u. a./Herre,* Art. 94, Rn. 4; die im Text vertretene Ansicht missverstehend, *Schlechtriem/Schwenzer/Schlechtriem/ Schwenzer/Hachem,* CISG Commentary, Art. 94, Rn. 4.

[12] *Schlechtriem/Schwenzer/Schlechtriem/Schwenzer/Hachem,* CISG Commentary, Art. 94, Rn. 1; *Schroeter,* UN-Kaufrecht, § 10, Rn. 14.

[13] *Achilles,* Art. 94, Rn. 1; *Brunner,* Art. 94, Rn. 1 a. E.; *Ferrari u. a./Mankowski,* Internationales Vertragsrecht, Art. 94, Rn. 3; *Herber,* IHR 2004, 89, 90; *Herber/Czerwenka,* Art. 94, Rn. 6; MünchKomm/*P. Huber,* Art. 94, Rn. 1; *Rudolph,* Art. 94, Rn. 5; *Schlechtriem/Schwenzer/Schlechtriem/Schwenzer/Hachem,* CISG Commentary, Art. 94, Rn. 1; *Staudinger/Magnus,* Art. 94, Rn. 6; *Witz/Salger/Lorenz/Witz,* Art. 94, Rn. 2.

[14] Dass die Gerichte der Vorbehaltsstaaten das CISG nicht ex Art. 1 Abs. 1 lit. a zur Anwendung kommen lassen können, ist h. M.; vgl. statt aller *Schlechtriem/Schwenzer/Schlechtriem/Schwenzer/Hachem,* CISG Commentary, Art. 94, Rn. 6; *Staudinger/Magnus,* Art. 94, Rn. 7.

[15] Die Frage offen lassend MünchKomm/*P. Huber,* Art. 94, Rn. 1.

diesbezüglich die Ansicht der Lehre abzulehnen, die diese Frage bejaht;[16] vielmehr muss davon ausgegangen werden, dass das CISG anzuwenden ist.[17] Es handelt sich nicht um einen dem in Art. 92 und Art. 93 enthaltenen Vorbehalt ähnlichen Vorbehalt: Die **Vertragsstaateneigenschaft** des eine Erklärung gemäß Art. 94 abgebenden Staates bleibt **unberührt**,[18] weshalb die Gerichte eines Nichtvorbehaltsstaates den üblichen Weg zur Bestimmung der Anwendbarkeit des CISG anzuwenden haben,[19] also die Anwendbarkeit des CISG ex Art. 1 I lit. a) oder 1 I lit. b) untersuchen müssen.[20]

Keine Zweifel scheint die Frage aufzuwerfen, ob die **Wahl des Rechts** eines Nicht- 4 vorbehaltsstaates durch die in verschiedene Vorbehaltsstaaten niedergelassenen Vertragsparteien zur Anwendung des CISG führen kann: Das CISG kann in diesem Fall, soweit das IPR des Forumsstaates eine Rechtswahl zulässt und sofern alle anderen Anwendungsvoraussetzungen vorliegen, durchaus zur Anwendung kommen und zwar auch vor Gerichten eines Vorbehaltsstaates.[21]

An dieser Stelle muss man sich fragen, ob eine Erklärung gemäß Art. 94 zur Lösung des 5 bereits angesprochenen Problems des **Verhältnisses des CISG zu Richtlinien**[22] beitragen kann. Dies könnte etwa durch Erklärung der (auch nur **teilweisen**) **Nichtanwendung**[23] des CISG von EU-Staaten geschehen. Da es, wie bereits erwähnt,[24] irrelevant ist, auf welche Weise es zu der weitgehenden Angleichung der Rechtsvorschriften gekommen ist, muss davon ausgegangen werden, dass den EU Staaten die Möglichkeit einer mit der Absicht, den Verordnungen bzw. Richtlinien Vorrang zu gewähren, gemachten Erklärung der (auch nur teilweisen) Nichtanwendung durchaus zugestanden werden muss.[25]

---

[16] So etwa *Achilles*, Art. 94, Rn. 3; *Brunner*, Art. 94, Rn. 4; *Enderlein/Maskow/Strohbach*, Art. 94, Anm. 2.; *Flechtner*, 17 J. L. & Com. (1998), 187, 194; MünchKommHGB/*Benicke*, Art. 1, Rn. 31; *Schlechtriem/Schwenzer/Schlechtriem/Schwenzer/Hachem*, CISG Commentary, Art. 94, Rn. 7; *Schroeter*, UN-Kaufrecht, § 10, Rn. 61; *Staudinger/Magnus*, Art. 94, Rn. 7; *Torsello*, Uniform L. Rev. 2000, 85, 97; *Witz/Salger/Lorenz/Witz*, Art. 94, Rn. 4.

[17] Ebenso *Czerwenka*, S. 139 f.; *Diez-Picazo/Calvo Caravaca*, Art. 94, S. 718; *Ferrari*, Uniform L. Rev. 2003, 177, 184; *Ferrari u. a./Mankowski*, Internationales Vertragsrecht, Art. 94, Rn. 14; *Honsell/Siehr*, Art. 94, Rn. 2; *Reinhart*, Art. 94, Rn. 7.

[18] *Ferrari*, IHR 2006, 1, 6; *Ferrari u. a./Mankowski*, Internationales Vertragsrecht, Art. 94, Rn. 14; a. A. *Flechtner*, 17 J. L. & Com. (1998), 187, 194: „[this reservation] amounts to an alteration in the meaning of the term „Contracting State" for the purposes of the scope provision (Article 1) of the Convention." Ebenso MünchKommHGB/*Benicke*, Art. 1, Rn. 31; *Torsello*, Uniform L. Rev. 2000, 85, 94 ff.

[19] Ebenso *Czerwenka*, S. 139 f.; *Honsell/Siehr*, Art. 94, Rn. 2; a. A. *Achilles*, Art. 94, Rn. 3; *Ferrari u. a./Mankowski*, Internationales Vertragsrecht, Art. 94, Rn. 14; *Staudinger/Magnus*, Art. 94, Rn. 7; *Witz/Salger/Lorenz/Witz*, Art. 94, Rn. 4; a. A. *Kröll u. a./Herre*, Art. 94, Rn. 5.

[20] A. A. MünchKommHGB/*Benicke*, Art. 1, Rn. 31.

[21] Ebenso *Achilles*, Art. 94, Rn. 3; *Kröll u. a./Herre* , Art. 94, Rn. 6; MünchKomm/*P. Huber*, Art. 94, Rn. 1 a. E.; *Schlechtriem/Schwenzer/Schlechtriem/Schwenzer/Hachem*, CISG Commentary, Art. 94, Rn. 8; *Schroeter*, UN-Kaufrecht, § 10, Rn. 53, Fn. 95; *Staudinger/Magnus*, Art. 94, Rn. 7; *Witz/Salger/Lorenz/Witz*, Art. 94, Rn. 4; im Ergebnis wohl auch *Bianca/Bonell/Evans*, Anm. 3.1.

[22] Vgl. Art. 5 Rn. 15 und Art. 90 Rn. 3.

[23] Die Möglichkeit, auch nur Teilkomplexe auszunehmen, ist in der Lehre durchaus vertreten worden; vgl. *Herber*, 2. Aufl., Art. 94 Rn. 4: „Der Wortlaut deutet darauf hin, daß nicht nur – wie ausdrücklich im Text hervorgehoben – der gesamte Teil I oder II von der Anwendung ausgenommen werden kann, sondern auch kleinere Teilkomplexe. Es darf sich dabei aber nicht um einzelne Vorschriften handeln. die Regelung der Produkthaftung etwa dürfte ein hinreichend weites Gebiet sein."

[24] Vgl. Rn. 1.

[25] Überzeugend in diesem Sinne *Schroeter*, UN-Kaufrecht, § 10, Rn. 10 ff.; a. A. noch *Ferrari*, 4. Aufl., Art. 94, Rn. 5; MünchKommHGB/*Ferrari*, 2. Aufl., Art. 94, Rn. 5.

Art. 95 [Erklärung zum Ausschluss der Anwendung des Art. 1 Abs. 1 lit. b)]

Jeder Staat kann bei der Hinterlegung seiner Ratifikations-, Annahme-, Genehmigungs- oder Beitrittsurkunde erklären, dass Artikel 1 Absatz 1 Buchstabe b für ihn nicht verbindlich ist.

Art. 95

Any State may declare at the time of the deposit of its instrument of ratification, acceptance, approval or accession that it will not be bound by subpara-graph (1) (b) of article 1 of this Convention.

Art. 95

Tout Etat peut déclarer, au moment du dépôt de son instrument de ratification, d'acceptation, d'approbation ou d'adhésion, qu'il ne sera pas lié par l'alinéa b) du paragraphe 1 de l'article premier de la présente Convention.

1 Die Vorschrift geht zurück auf einen zunächst im Zweiten Gesamtausschuss abgelehnten[1] und im Plenum der Diplomatischen Konferenz wiederholten und letztlich angenommen Antrag der Tschechoslowakei[2] und ist Konsequenz der gegenüber der Einführung des Art. 1 I lit. b), der zur Anwendung des Übereinkommens über das IPR des Forumsstaates führt[3] und den Anwendungsbereich des Übereinkommens erweitert,[4] geäußerten Kritik.[5] Eine ähnliche Vorbehaltsmöglichkeit[6] sahen auch die Einführungskonventionen zu den Haager Kaufgesetzen vor,[7] doch kam dieser Vorbehaltsmöglichkeit eine andere Funktion zu, nämlich die, den bereits sehr weiten Anwendungsbereich des Haager Kaufrechts einzugrenzen.[8]

2 Welche **Wirkung** dieser als Kompromiss qualifizierter Vorbehalt[9] hat, ist zum Teil umstritten.[10] Unzweifelhaft ist jedoch, dass **Gerichte eines Vorbehaltsstaates** das Übereinkommen ohne weiteres ex Art. 1 I lit. a) anwenden können,[11] nicht aber kraft Art. 1 I lit. b).[12]

---

[1] O. R., S. 439.
[2] Vgl. O. R., S. 229 f.; vgl. auch *Ferrari u. a./Mankowski*, Internationales Vertragsrecht, Art. 95, Rn. 2.
[3] Vgl. Art. 1, Rn. 69 ff.
[4] *Schlechtriem/Schwenzer/Schlechtriem/Schwenzer/Hachem*, CISG Commentary, Art. 95, Rn. 1.
[5] Ausführlich zu den Gründen, die zur Einführung dieser Vorschrift geführt haben, vgl. neuerdings *G. Bell*, 9 Singapore YB. Int'l L. (2005), 55, 58 ff.; vgl. auch *Ragno*, Convenzione di Vienna e Diritto europeo, S. 112 f.
[6] Siehe Art. III der jeweiligen Einführungskonventionen.
[7] *Enderlein/Maskow/Strohbach*, Art. 95 Anm. 2. a. E., sprechen nicht von einer „ähnlichen", sondern von einer „gleichen Vorbehaltsmöglichkeit", was aber nicht zutrifft.
[8] *Herber*, 2. Aufl., Art. 95 Rn. 2.
[9] Vgl. *Schlechtriem*, 36 Vict. U. Well. L. Rev. (2005), 781, 783; *Ubertaite*, 7 Eur. J. L. Ref. (2005), 277, 278 und 281.
[10] Vgl. hierzu eingehend Art. 1, Rn. 77 ff.; siehe außerdem auch *Bernasconi*, Neth. Int'l L. Rev. 1999, 137 ff.; *Ferrari*, NIPR 1995, 317 ff.; *ders.*, Riv. dir. civ. 1995, 669 ff.; *ders.*, Int. Bus. L. J. 2002, 961 ff.; *ders.*, IHR 2006, 248 ff.; *Pünder*, RIW 1990, 869 ff.
[11] Vgl. auch *G. Bell*, 9 Singapore YB. Int'l L. (2005), 55, 56; *Ferrari*, IHR 2006, 248, 249; *Ferrari u. a./Mankowski*, Internationales Vertragsrecht, Art. 95, Rn. 4; *Sannini*, L'applicazione, S. 75; *Schlechtriem*, 36 Vict. U. Well. 783, L. Rev. (2005), 781, 783; *Schlechtriem/Schwenzer/Schlechtriem/Schwenzer/Hachem*, CISG Commentary, Art. 95, Rn. 2. Für Fälle, in denen staatliche Gericht und Schiedsgerichte das Übereinkommen ex Art. 1 I a) auf Kaufverträge angewendet haben, die zwischen Parteien mit Sitz in verschiedenen Vertragsstaaten hatten, von denen mindestens einer ein Vorbehaltsstaat im Sinne von Art. 95 war, vgl. *CSS Antenna, Inc. v. Amphenol-Tuchel Electronics, GmbH*, U. S. District Court of Maryland, 8.2.2011, CISG-online 2177 (deutsch-amerikanischer Vertrag); *Hanwha Corporation v. Cedar Petrochemicals, Inc.*, U. S. Dist. Ct. (S. D. N. Y.), 18 January 2011, CISG-online 2178 (amerikanisch-koreanischer Vertrag); *Golden Valley Grape Juice and Wine, LLC v. Centrisys Corporation et al.*, U. S. District Court (E. D. of California), 21.1.2010, CISG-online 2089 (amerikanisch-australischer Vertrag); *Electrocraft Arkansas, Inc. v. Electric Motors, Ltd et al.*, U. S. District Court (E. D. of Arkansas, Western Division), 23.12.2009, CISG-online 2045 (chinesisch-amerikanischer Vertrag); *Cedar Petrochemicals, Inc. v. Dongbu Hannong Chemical Co., Ltd.*, U. S. Dist. Ct. (S. D. N. Y.), 19.7.2007, CISG-online 1509

Erklärung zum Ausschluss der Anwendung des Art. 1 Abs. 1 lit. b) 3, 4 **Art. 95**

Unzweifelhaft ist ferner, dass Gerichte eines Vorbehaltsstaates das CISG dann nicht 3 anwenden werden, wenn die Kollisionsnormen des Forumsstaates auf die **lex fori** verweisen.[13]

Bezüglich der anderen möglichen (aber umstrittenen) Fallkonstellationen sei auf die 4 Ausführungen zu Art. 1 verwiesen.[14]

(amerikanisch-koreanischer Vertrag); *Tee Vee Toons, Inc. et al v. Gerhard Schubert GmbH,* U. S. Dist. Ct. (S. D. N. Y.), 23.8.2006, CISG-online 1272 = 2006 WL 2 463 537 (S. D. N. Y.) (deutsch-amerikanischer Vertrag); *Raw Materials Inc. v. Manfred Forberich GmbH & Co., KG,* U. S. District Court, Northern District of Illinois, Eastern Division, 6.7.2004, CISG-online 1665 (deutsch-amerikanischer Vertrag); *Chicago Prime Packers, Inc. v. Northam Food Trading Co., et al.,* U. S. District Court, Northern District of Illinois, Eastern Division, 21.5.2004, CISG-online 851 = IHR 2004, 156 ff. (amerikanisch-kanadischer Vertrag); *Chateau des Charmes Wines Ltd. v. Sabaté USA, Sabaté S. a.,* U. S. District Court, Northern District of California, 10.11.2003, CISG-online 809 (französisch-amerikanischer Vertrag); *Ajax Tool Works, Inc. v. Can-Eng Manufacturing Ltd.,* U. S. Dist. Ct. (N. D. Ill.), 29.1.2003, CISG-online 772 = 2003 U. S. Dist. LEXIS 1306 (kanadisch-amerikanischer Vertrag); *Schmitz-Werke GmbH & Co., Plaintiff-Appellee, v. Rockland Industries, Inc.,* U. S. Ct. App. (4th Cir.), 21.6.2002, CISG-online 625 = 37 Fed. Appx. 687 (deutsch-amerikanischer Vertrag); *Magellan International v. Salzgitter Handel,* U. S. Dist. Ct. (N. D. Ill.), CISG-online 439 = 76 Federal Supplement 2d 919 = 40 UCC Rep Serv 2d 321 (N. D. Ill. 1999) (deutsch-amerikanischer Vertrag); *KSTP-FM, LLC v. Specialized Communications, Inc. and Adtronics Signs, Ltd.,* U. S. Dist. Ct. (D. Minn.), 9.3.1999, CISG-online 471 (kanadisch-amerikanischer Vertrag); *Mitchell Aircraft Spares, Inc. v. European Aircraft Service AB,* U. S. Dist. Ct. (N. D. Ill.), 28.10.1998, CISG-online 342 = 1998 WL 754 801 (N. D. Ill., 1998) (amerikanisch-schwedischer Kaufvertrag); CA Grenoble, 22.2.1995, CISG-online 151 = J. D. I. 1995, 632 ff. (französisch-amerikanischer Kaufvertrag); *Delchi Carrier SpA v. Rotorex Corp.,* U. S. Ct. App. (2nd Cir.), 6.12.1995, CISG-online 140 = 10 F. 3d 1024 (2nd Cir. 1995) (amerikanisch-italienischer Kaufvertrag); *S. V. Braun Inc. v. Alitalia Linee Aeree Italiane SpA,* U. S. Dist. Ct. (S. D. N. Y.), 6.4.1994, CISG-online 112 = 1994 WL 495 787 (S. D. N. Y.) (amerikanisch-ungarischer Kaufvertrag); ICC, 7399/1993, CISG-online 748 = ICC Ct. Bull. 2/1995, 68 f. (amerikanisch-schweizerischer Vertrag); *José Luis Morales y/o Son Export, S. A., de C. V., de Hermosillo Sonora, México v. Nez Marketing de Los Angeles California, E. U. A.,* Comision para la Proteccion del Comercio Exterior de Mexico, 4.5.1993, CISG-online 75 = Diario Oficial de 27.5.1993, 17 ff. (mexikanisch-amerikanischer Vertrag); ICC, 7531/1994, CISG-online 565 = ICC Ct. Bull. 2/1995, 67 f. (chinesisch-österreichischer Kaufvertrag); LG Heidelberg, 3.7.1992, CISG-online 38 (amerikanisch-deutscher Kaufvertrag); *Filanto SpA v. Chilewich International Corp.,* U. S. Dist. Ct. (S. D. N. Y.), 14.4.1992, CISG-online 45 = 789 F. Supp. 1229 ff. (S. D. N. Y. 1992) (italienisch-amerikanischer Kaufvertrag).

[12] Vgl. Vor Artt. 1–6, Rn. 22.
[13] So auch G. *Bell,* 9 Singapore YB. Int'l L. (2005), 55, 63; *Ferrari u. a./Saenger,* Internationales Vertragsrecht, Art. 1, Rn. 19; *Karollus,* S. 32; *Kröll u. a./Herre,* Art. 95, Rn. 3; MünchKommHGB/*Benicke,* Art. 1, Rn. 38; *Pelichet,* Vente internationale, S. 43 f.; *Siehr,* RabelsZ 52 (1988), 587, 608 f.
[14] Art. 1, Rn. 77 ff.

Art. 96 [Erklärung über Schriftform]

Ein Vertragsstaat, nach dessen Rechtsvorschriften Kaufverträge schriftlich zu schließen oder nachzuweisen sind, kann jederzeit eine Erklärung nach Artikel 12 abgeben, dass die Bestimmungen der Artikel 11 und 29 oder des Teils II dieses Übereinkommens, die für den Abschluss eines Kaufvertrages, seine Änderung oder Aufhebung durch Vereinbarung oder für ein Angebot, eine Annahme oder eine sonstige Willenserklärung eine andere als die schriftliche Form gestatten, nicht gelten, wenn eine Partei ihre Niederlassung in diesem Staat hat.

Art. 96

A Contracting State whose legislation requires contracts of sale to be concluded in or evidenced by writing may at any time make a declaration in accordance with article 12 that any provision of article 11, article 29, or Part II of this Convention, that allows a contract of sale or its modification or termination by agreement or any offer, acceptance, or other indication of intention to be made in any form other than in writing, does not apply where any party has his place of business in that State.

Art. 96

Tour Etat contractant dont la législation exige que les contrats de vente soient conclus ou constatés par écrit peut à tout moment déclarer, conformément à l'article 12, que toute disposition de l'article 11, de l'article 29 ou de la deuxième partie de la présente Convention autorisant une forme autre que la forme écrite pour la conclusion, la modification ou la résiliation amiable d'un contrat de vente, ou pour toute offre, acceptation ou autre manifestation d'intention, ne s'applique pas dès lors que l'une des parties a son établissement dans cet Etat.

1   Der Vorbehalt wurde als ein **Kompromiss**[1] schon in den New Yorker E aufgenommen;[2] während die westlichen Industriestaaten für die – schon im Haager Kaufrecht niedergelegte – Garantie der Formfreiheit eintraten, wünschten die Staatshandelsländer das Formerfordernis der Schriftform. Als Kompromiss wurde in Art. 11 die Formfreiheit statuiert, jedoch der Vorbehalt des Art. 96 aufgenommen, dessen Wirkungen in Art. 12 umschrieben sind.

2   Der Vorbehalt kann, genauso wie der ex Art. 94, **jederzeit** erklärt werden,[3] also auch nach Inkrafttreten des CISG in einem bestimmten Staat, etwa weil dort Formerfordernisse eingeführt werden.[4] Er darf, so der Wortlaut des Art. 96, nur von einem Staat erklärt werden, der selbst in seinem **Heimatrecht die Schriftform** für Kaufverträge vorschreibt.[5] Das Erfordernis muss grundsätzlich für alle Kaufverträge gelten, nicht nur für einzelne Arten;[6] dies ergibt sich auch aus der Tatsache, dass ein niederländischer Antrag, auch ein eingeschränktes Formerfordernis genügen zu lassen, auf der Konferenz ausführlich erörtert,

---

[1] *Ferrari*, Vendita internazionale, S. 227; *Ferrari u. a./Mankowski*, Internationales Vertragsrecht, Art. 96, Rn. 1; *Garro/Zuppi* S. 69; *Herber/Czerwenka*, Art. 96, Rn. 1; MünchKomm/*Westermann*, Art. 12, Rn. 1; *Schlechtriem/Schwenzer/Schlechtriem/Schwenzer/Hachem*, CISG Commentary, Art. 96, Rn. 1; *Wang/Andersen*, Uniform L. Rev. 2003, 870; a. A. *Maskow*, Perspective of the Socialist Countries, S. 39, 52, wonach Art. 96 keinen Kompromiss darstelle, sondern eher den Beweis für die Unmöglichkeit, eine allgemein akzeptable Lösung zu finden.
[2] Artikel X, UNCITRAL YB IX (1978), S. 21.
[3] *Audit* S. 73; *Comoglio* Riv. trim. dir. proc. civ. 1990, 785, 793 f.; *Ferrari*, Vendita internazionale, S. 228; *Herber/Czerwenka*, Art. 96, Rn. 2; *Kröll u. a./Herre*, Art. 96, Rn. 2; *Wey* RdNr. 469; diese Erweiterung der Vorbehaltsmöglichkeit wurde auf der Konferenz auf deutschen Antrag beschlossen; vgl. O. R., S. 444; vgl. auch *Schlechtriem/Schwenzer/Schlechtriem/Schwenzer/Hachem*, CISG Commentary, Art. 96, Rn. 2, Fn. 3.
[4] *Kröll u. a./Herre*, Art. 96, Rn 2.
[5] Siehe auch *Bianca/Bonell/Evans*, Art. 96, Anm. 3.1.; *Ferrari*, IHR 2004, 1, 5; *Kröll u. a./Herre*, Art. 96, Rn 4; MünchKomm/*P. Huber*, Art. 96, Rn. 1; *Reinhart*, Art. 96, Rn. 2; *Rehbinder*, Vertragsschluß, S. 154; *Rudolph*, Art. 96, Rn. 2; *Schlechtriem/Schwenzer/Schlechtriem/Schwenzer/Hachem*, CISG Commentary, Art. 96, Rn. 2; *Walther/Morawietz*, IHR 2006, 252.
[6] *Ferrari u. a./Mankowski*, Internationales Vertragsrecht, Art. 96, Rn. 2; *Kröll u. a./Herre*, Art. 96, Rn 4; *Schlechtriem/Schwenzer/Schlechtriem/Schwenzer/Hachem*, CISG Commentary, Art. 96, Rn. 2; *Witz/Salger/Lorenz/Witz*, Art. 96, Rn. 1.

Erklärung über Schriftform 3 **Art. 96**

letztendlich aber abgelehnt wurde.⁷ Mit dieser Voraussetzung kollidieren aber die Erklärungen sowohl Argentiniens als auch Chiles, die einen Vorbehalt erklärt haben, obwohl deren nationales Recht ein Formerfordernis nicht zwingend vorschreibt.⁸ Welche Folgen dies auf Verträge zwischen Parteien hat, von denen mindestens eine ihre Niederlassungen in einen dieser beiden Staaten hat, ergibt sich nicht aus dem CISG, sondern muss auf der Grundlage des ungültige Vorbehalte regelnden Völkerrechts entschieden werden.⁹

Die **Wirkung** des oft kritisierten Vorbehalts¹⁰ ist dahin definiert, dass die Formfreiheit **3** des Art. 11 nicht notwendigerweise gilt, wenn eine der Kaufvertragsparteien ihren Sitz in einem Vorbehaltsstaat hat.¹¹ Der Grundsatz der Formfreiheit wird somit, unter bestimmten Voraussetzungen, beschränkt, was jedoch nicht unbedingt dazu führt, dass der nicht schriftlich geschlossene Kaufvertrag ungültig sei.¹² Diese **Beschränkung** wirkt sich jedoch nicht auf alle generell vom Grundsatz der Formfreiheit erfassten Erklärungen¹³ aus.¹⁴ Vielmehr unterliegen der Beschränkung lediglich der **Vertragsschluss** und die einvernehmliche **Vertragsänderung bzw. -aufhebung,**¹⁵ sowie die in Teil II des CISG geregelten Erklärungen, wie etwa Angebot, Widerruf,¹⁶ Rücknahme,¹⁷ Annahme. Im Rahmen der **Vertragsabwicklung** (Teil III) bedeutsame Erklärungen, wie etwa die Erklärung der Vertragsaufhebung und die Mängelrüge,¹⁸ die Minderungserklärung, die Nachfristsetzung und die Spezifikation,¹⁹ können selbst dann in **jeder Form** abgegeben werden, wenn eine der Parteien ihre maßgebliche Niederlassung in einem Vorbehaltsstaat hat.²⁰ Hat (mindestens) eine Vertragspartei ihre maßgebliche Niederlassung in einem Vorbehaltsstaat, dann sind die Gerichte eines Vertragsstaates nicht berechtigt, von dem Formerfordernis ohne weiteres abzusehen.²¹ Er ist andererseits auch nicht verpflichtet, das Formerfordernis des Vorbehaltsstaates ohne weiteres zur Anwendung kommen zu lassen²²

---

⁷ Vgl. die Erörterungen im Ersten Gesamtausschuss, O. R., S. 271 ff.
⁸ So auch *Ferrari,* IHR 2004, 1, 5; *Garro,* 17 J. L. & Com. (1998), 187, 228 f.; *Torsello,* Uniform L. Rev. 2000, 85, 111; a. A. *Kröll u. a./Perales Viscasillas,* Art. 12, Rn. 2, Fn. 6.
⁹ So nun auch *Schlechtriem/Schwenzer/Schlechtriem/Schwenzer/Hachem,* CISG Commentary, Art. 96, Rn. 2 a. E.; *Schroeter,* FS Kritzer, S. 425, 436; a. A. MünchKomm/*Westermann,* Art. 12, Rn. 3: „die Wirkungen des Vorbehaltes treten nur ein, wenn der Vorbehalt nach Art. 96 zulässig ist".
¹⁰ Vgl. hierzu statt aller *Walther/Morawietz,* IHR 2006, 252 ff.; *Wang/Andersen,* Uniform L. Rev. 2003, 870 ff.
¹¹ *Ferrari,* IHR 2004, 1, 5; *Flechtner,* 17 J. L. & Com. (1998), 187, 196; *Lohmann,* Privatautonomie, S. 345.
¹² A. A. *Forestal Guarani S. a. v. Daros International, Inc.,* U. S. Court of Appeals (3 rd. Cir.), 21.7.2010, CISG-online 2112; *Zhejiang Shaoxing Yongli Printing and Dyeing Co., Ltd v. Microflock Textile Group Corporation,* U. S. District Court (S. D. of Florida), 19.5.2008, CISG-online 1771.
¹³ Vgl. hierzu MünchKommHGB/*Ferrari,* Art. 11, Rn. 2 f.
¹⁴ So auch *Ferrari u. a./Saenger,* Internationales Vertragsrecht, Art. 12, Rn. 2; *Rudolph,* Art. 12, Rn. 1.
¹⁵ Ebenso *Bamberger/Roth/Saenger,* Art. 12, Rn. 1; *Patti,* Nuove leggi civ. comm. 1989, 44, 49; Staudinger/*Magnus,* Art. 12, Rn. 6.
¹⁶ A. A. *Enderlein/Maskow/Strohbach* Anm. 1.
¹⁷ A. A. *Schlechtriem/Schwenzer/Schlechtriem/Schmidt-Kessel,* CISG Commentary, Art. 12, Rn. 6, die die Meinung vertreten, die Vorschrift gelte nicht für die Rücknahme eines Angebots; ebenso MünchKomm/*Westermann,* Art. 12, Rn. 1.
¹⁸ Ausdrücklich diese Beispiele nennend etwa *Ferrari,* Vendita internazionale, S. 229, *Herber/Czerwenka,* Art. 12, Rn. 3; *Patti,* Nuove leggi civ. comm. 1989, 44, 49; *Rudolph,* Art. 12, Rn. 1.
¹⁹ Diese Beispiele finden sich bei Staudinger/*Magnus,* Art. 12, Rn. 7.
²⁰ So auch *Bamberger/Roth/Saenger,* Art. 12, Rn. 1; *Bianca/Bonell/Rajski,* Art. 12, Anm. 2.2; *Brunner,* Art. 12, Rn. 1; *Enderlein/Maskow/Strohbach,* Art. 12, Anm. 1; *Ferrari u. a./Saenger,* Internationales Vertragsrecht, Art. 12, Rn. 2; *Honsell/Melis,* Art. 12, Rn. 3; *Staudinger/Magnus,* Art. 12, Rn. 7; *Wey,* Rn. 404 und 481; *Witz/Salger/Lorenz/Witz,* Art. 11–12, Rn. 11.
²¹ MünchKommHGB/*Ferrari,* Art. 11, Rn. 11; *Schlechtriem/Schwenzer/Schlechtriem/Schwenzer/Hachem,* CISG Commentary, Art. 96, Rn. 3.
²² Ebenso *Achilles,* Art. 96, Rn. 1; *Audit,* S. 73; *Bamberger/Roth/Saenger,* Art. 12, Rn. 2; *Bernstein/Lookofsky,* § 2–14; *Bianca/Bonell/Rajski,* Art. 12, Anm. 2.3.; *Brunner,* Art. 12, Rn. 1; *Enderlein/Maskow/Strohbach,* Art. 12, Anm. 2.2.; *Eörsi,* General Provisions, S. 2–1, 2–33; *Ferrari,* Writing requirements, S. 206, 213; *ders.,* Vendita internazionale, S. 230 f.; *Ferrari u. a./Mankowski,* Internationales Vertragsrecht, Art. 12, Rn. 4; *Herber/Czerwenka,* Art. 12, Rn. 4; *Honnold/Flechtner,* Art. 12, Rn. 129; *Jametti Greiner,* Der Vertragsabschluss, S. 43, 47; MünchKommHGB/*Ferrari,* Art. 11, Rn. 11 und Art. 12, Rn. 4; MünchKommBGB/*P. Huber,* Art. 96, Rn. 1; MünchKomm/*Westermann,* Art. 12, Rn. 2; *Neumayer/Ming,* Art. 96, Anm. 1.; *Rudolph,* Art. 12,

– so auch die neuere Rechtsprechung.²³ Dies folgt unter anderem daraus, dass der Vorschlag, bei Vorbehalt ohne weiteres die Formvorschriften des Vorbehaltsstaates gelten zu lassen, abgelehnt wurde.²⁴ Daraus ergibt sich m. E.,²⁵ dass das **Internationale Privatrecht** des angerufenen Gerichts bestimmt, welches Recht über die Form entscheidet.²⁶ Verweist das Kollisionsrecht auf das Recht eines Vorbehaltsstaates, sind dessen Formvorschriften relevant.²⁷ Verlangt dieses Recht Schriftform, dann ist, da sich die auf der Grundlage einer Erklärung nach Art. 96 ergebende Beschränkung des Grundsatzes der Formfreiheit nicht auf Art. 13 auswirkt, dieses Erfordernis auch dann erfüllt, wenn die Erklärung mittels Telegramm oder Fernschreiben abgegeben worden ist.²⁸ Verweist das Kollisionsrecht hingegen auf das Recht eines Vertragsstaates, das keine Erklärung gemäß Art. 96 abgegeben hat, bleibt es bei der im CISG festgesetzten Formfreiheit ex Art. 11.²⁹ „Dem Vorbehaltsstaat wird damit nichts Unbilliges zugemutet, denn er müsste ja auch Formfreiheit

---

Rn. 3; *Schlechtriem/Schwenzer/Schlechtriem*, CISG Commentary, 2. Aufl., Art. 96, Rn. 3; *Staudinger/Magnus*, Art. 12, Rn. 8; *Wey*, Rn. 475; ebenso in der Rechtsprechung *Forestal Guarani S. a. v. Daros International, Inc.*, US. Court of Appeals (3rd Circ.), 21.7.2010, CISG-online 2112; a. A. *Rehbinder*, S. 143, 154 f.; *Stoffel*, Formation du contrat, S. 55, 60; *Vékás*, IPRax 1987, 342, 344; ebenso in der *Forestal Guarani, S. a. v. Daros International, Inc.*, U. S. District Court, New Jersey, 7.10.2008, CISG-online 1779; *Zhejiang Shaoxing Yongli Printing and Dyeing Co., Ltd v. Microflock Textile Group Corporation*, U. S. District Court, S. D. of Florida, 19.5.2008, CISG-online 1771; Tribunal of International Commercial Arbitration at the Russian Federation Chamber of Commerce and Industry, 16.2.2004, CISG-online1181; Tribunal of International Commercial Arbitration at the Russian Federation Chamber of Commerce and Industry, 16.2.1998, CISG-online 1303; RB Hasselt, 2.5.1995, CISG-online 371.
²³ RB Rotterdam, 12.7.2001, NIPR 2001, Nr. 278; HR, 7.11.1997, CISG-online 551 = NIPR 1998, Nr. 91.
²⁴ Vgl. UNCITRAL YB IX (1978), S. 45; vgl. auch *Bianca/Bonell/Evans*, Art. 96, Anm. 1.2; *Kröll u. a./Perales Viscasillas*, Art. 12, Rn. 7 und dort Fn. 18 a. E.
²⁵ Vgl. hierzu auch *Ferrari*, IHR 2004, 1 ff.; *ders.*, Writing requirements, S. 206 ff.
²⁶ Ebenso *Achilles*, Art. 96, Rn. 1; *Bamberger/Roth/Saenger*, Art. 96, Rn. 1; *Brunner*, Art. 12, Rn. 1; *Ferrari u. a./Mankowski*, Internationales Vertragsrecht, Art. 96, Rn. 4; *Herber/Czerwenka*, Art. 96, Rn. 3; *Honsell/Melis*, Art. 12, Rn. 4; MünchKomm/*P. Huber*, Art. 96, Rn. 1; MüKomm/*Westermann*, Art. 12 Rn. 2; *Piltz*, Internationales Kaufrecht, Rn. 3–128; *Rudolph*, Art. 96, Rn. 4; *Schlechtriem/Schwenzer/Schlechtriem/Schmidt-Kessel*, CISG Commentary, Art. 12, Rn. 2; *Schlechtriem/Schwenzer/Schlechtriem/Schwenzer/Hachem*, CISG Commentary, Art. 96, Rn. 3; *Staudinger/Magnus*, Art. 96, Rn. 7; *Wey*, Rn. 473; in der Rechtsprechung vgl. *Forestal Guarani S. a. v. Daros International, Inc.*, US. Court of Appeals (3rd Cir.), 21.7.2010, CISG-online 2112; a. A. *Sedgwick*, 34 Suffolk Transnat'l L. Rev. (2011), 273; *Stoffel*, Formation du contrat, S. 60; a. A. auch *Forestal Guarani, S. a. v. Daros International, Inc.*, U. S. District Court, New Jersey, 7.10.2008, CISG-online 1779; *Zhejiang Shaoxing Yongli Printing and Dyeing Co., Ltd v. Microflock Textile Group Corporation*, U. S. District Court, S. D. of Florida, 19.5.2008, CISG-online 1771; Tribunal of International Commercial Arbitration at the Russian Federation Chamber of Commerce and Industry, 16.2.2004, CISG-online1181; die Frage untersuchend, ohne jedoch eine Antwort zu geben *Walther/Morawietz*, IHR 2006, 252 ff.
²⁷ So ausdrücklich RB Hasselt, 2.5.1995, CISG-online 371 (Kaufvertrag zwischen einem belgischen Käufer und einem chilenischen Verkäufer); vgl. in der Lehre *Brunner*, Art. 96, Rn. 3; *Ferrari*, Writing requirements, S. 206, 214; *Honsell/Melis*, Art. 96, Rn. 4; *Kröll u. a./Perales Viscasillas*, Art. 12, Rn. 9; *Witz/Salger/Lorenz/Witz*, Art. 12, Rn. 12.
²⁸ So auch *Bamberger/Roth/Saenger*, Art. 13 CISG, Rn. 2; *Herber/Czerwenka*, Art. 12 Rn. 2; *Witz/Salger/Lorenz/Witz*, Art. 11–12, Rn. 13.
²⁹ So in der Rechtsprechung etwa *Forestal Guarani S. a. v. Daros International, Inc.*, U.S. Court of Appeals (3 rd. Cir.), 21.7.2010, CISG-online 2112; RB Rotterdam, 12.7.2001, CISG-online 968 = NIPR 2001, Nr. 278, HR, 7.11.1997, CISG-online 551 = NIPR 1998, Nr. 91; Stadtgericht Budapest, 24.3.1992, CISG-online 61; in der Lehre vgl. *Adame Goddard* S. 126; *Ferrari*, Writing requirements, S. 206. 214; *Hosell/Melis* RdNr. 4; *U. Huber* RabelsZ 43 (1979) 413, 434 f.; *Kröll u. a./Perales Viscasillas* RdNr. 10; *Schlechtriem/Schwenzer/Schlechtriem/Schmidt-Kessel*, CISG Commentary, Art. 12, Rn. 3; a. A. *Flechtner*, 17 J. L. & Com. (1998), 187, 196 f.; a. A. *Ferrari u. a./Mankowski*, Internationales Vertragsrecht, Art. 96, Rn. 4: „[Der Vorbehalt] macht nur die Regeln der CISG nicht anwendbar und überlasst die Regelung der Form dem anwendbaren Recht. Art. 11 wird also auch als Teil der lex causae nicht wieder anwendbar."; a. A. auch *Kröll u. a./Herre*, Art. 96, Rn. 6; a. A. auch *Forestal Guarani, S. a. v. Daros International, Inc.*, U. S. District Court, New Jersey, 7.10.2008, CISG-online 1779; *Zhejiang Shaoxing Yongli Printing and Dyeing Co., Ltd v. Microflock Textile Group Corporation*, U. S. District Court (S. D. of Florida,) 19.5.2008, CISG-online 1771; Tribunal of International Commercial Arbitration at the Russian Federation Chamber of Commerce and Industry, 16.2.2004, CISG-online 1181; auf die Frage hinweisend, ohne sie jedoch zu beantworten, *P. Huber/Mullis/P. Huber*, S. 38.

hinnehmen, wenn über das IPR des Forumsstaates nationale Regeln, die Formfreiheit vorsehen, zur Anwendung kämen."[30]

---

[30] Unten *Schmidt-Kessel*, Art. 12, Rn. 3.

Art. 97 [Wirksamkeitsvoraussetzungen einer Vorbehaltserklärung]

(1) Erklärungen, die nach diesem Übereinkommen bei der Unterzeichnung abgegeben werden, bedürfen der Bestätigung bei der Ratifikation, Annahme oder Genehmigung.

(2) Erklärungen und Bestätigungen von Erklärungen bedürfen der Schriftform und sind dem Verwahrer zu notifizieren.

(3) Eine Erklärung wird gleichzeitig mit dem Inkrafttreten dieses Übereinkommens für den betreffenden Staat wirksam. Eine Erklärung, die dem Verwahrer nach diesem Inkrafttreten notifiziert wird, tritt jedoch am ersten Tag des Monats in Kraft, der auf einen Zeitabschnitt von sechs Monaten nach ihrem Eingang beim Verwahrer folgt. Aufeinander bezogene einseitige Erklärungen nach Artikel 94 werden am ersten Tag des Monats wirksam, der auf einen Zeitabschnitt von sechs Monaten nach Eingang der letzten Erklärung beim Verwahrer folgt.

(4) Ein Staat, der eine Erklärung nach diesem Übereinkommen abgibt, kann sie jederzeit durch eine an den Verwahrer gerichtete schriftliche Notifikation zurücknehmen. Eine solche Rücknahme wird am ersten Tag des Monats wirksam, der auf einen Zeitabschnitt von sechs Monaten nach Eingang der Notifikation beim Verwahrer folgt.

(5) Die Rücknahme einer nach Artikel 94 abgegebenen Erklärung macht eine von einem anderen Staat nach Artikel 94 abgegebene, darauf bezogene Erklärung von dem Tag an unwirksam, an dem die Rücknahme wirksam wird.

Art. 97

(1) Declarations made under this Convention at the time of signature are subject to confirmation upon ratification, acceptance or approval.

(2) Declarations and confirmations of declarations are to be in writing and be formally notified to the depositary.

(3) A declaration takes effect simultaneously with the entry into force of this Convention in respect of the State concerned. However, a declaration of which the depositary receives formal notification alter such entry into force takes effect on the first day of the month following the expiration of six months after the date of its receipt by the depositary. Reciprocal unilateral declarations under article 94 take effect on the first day of the month following the expiration of six months after the receipt of the latest declaration by the depositary.

(4) Any State which makes a declaration under this Convention may withdraw it at any time by a formal notification in writing addressed to the depositary. Such withdrawal is to take effect on the first day of the month following the expiration of six months after the date of the receipt of the notification by the depositary.

(5) A withdrawal of a declaration made under article 94 renders inoperative, as from the date on which the withdrawal takes effect, any reciprocal declaration made by another State under that article.

Art. 97

1) Les déclarations faites en vertu de la présente Convention lors de la signature sont sujettes à confirmation lors de la ratification, de l'acceptation ou de l'approbation.

2) Les déclarations, et la confirmation des déclarations, seront faites par écrit et formellement notifiées au dépositaire.

3) Les déclarations prendront effet à la date de l'entrée en vigueur de la présente Convention à l'égard de l'Etat déclarant. Cependant, les déclarations dont le dépositaire aura reçu notification formelle après cette date prendront effet le premier jour du mois suivant l'expiration d'un délai de six mois à compter de la date de leur réception par le dépositaire. Les déclarations unilatérales et réciproques faites en vertu de l'article 94 prendront effet le premier jour du mois suivant l'expiration d'une période de six mois après la date de la réception de la dernière déclaration par le dépositaire.

4) Tout Etat qui fait une déclaration en vertu de la présente Convention peut à tout moment la retirer par une notification formelle adressée par écrit au dépositaire. Ce retrait prendra effet le premier jour du mois suivant l'expiration d'une période de six mois après la date de réception de la notification par le dépositaire.

5) Le retrait d'une déclaration faite en vertu de l'article 94 rendra caduque, à partir de la date de sa prise d'effet, toute déclaration réciproque faite par un autre Etat en vertu de ce même article.

Diese Vorschrift bedarf keiner Erläuterung.

Art. 98 [Zulässigkeit von Vorbehalten]

Vorbehalte sind nur zulässig, soweit sie in diesem Übereinkommen ausdrücklich für zulässig erklärt werden.

Art. 98
No reservations are permitted except those expressly authorized in this Convention.

Art. 98
Aucune réserve n'est autorisée autre que celles qui sont expressément autorisées par la présente Convention.

Art. 98 findet sich in gleicher Form in den meisten rechtsvereinheitlichenden Übereinkommen.[1] Sie bedürfen keiner näheren Erörterung. 1

Die Unzulässigkeit nicht aufgeführter Vorbehalte, die aber nach Art. 19 der Wiener Vertragsrechtskonvention möglich wären,[2] bedeutet nicht per se, dass Staaten nicht **andere Erklärungen** abgeben könnten.[3] Ihre **Wirkung** bemisst sich nach sowohl nach Art. 7 Abs. 1 als auch nach allgemeinem Völkerrecht.[4] 2

---

[1] *Schlechtriem/Schwenzer/Schlechtriem/Schwenzer/Hachem,* CISG Commentary, Art. 98, Rn. 1.
[2] Vgl. *Ferrari u. a./Mankowski,* Internationales Vertragsrecht, Art. 98, Rn. 1; MünchKomm/P. *Huber,* Art. 98, Rn. 1; *Staudinger/Magnus,* Art. 98, Rn. 1.
[3] Vgl. *Bianca/Bonell/Evans,* Art. 98, Anm. 2.3.; *Ferrari u. a./Mankowski,* Internationales VertragsrechtArt. 98, Rn. 2; *Kröll u. a./Herre,* Art. 98, Rn. 1; *Schlechtriem/Schwenzer/Schlechtriem/Schwenzer/Hachem,* CISG Commentary, Art. 98, Rn. 2.
[4] Ebenso *Herber/Czerwenka,* Art. 98, Rn. 2.

Art. 99 [Zeitpunkt des Inkrafttretens]

(1) Vorbehaltlich des Absatzes 6 tritt dieses Übereinkommen am ersten Tag des Monats in Kraft, der auf einen Zeitabschnitt von zwölf Monaten nach Hinterlegung der zehnten Ratifikations-, Annahme-, Genehmigungs- oder Beitrittsurkunde einschließlich einer Urkunde, die eine nach Artikel 92 abgegebene Erklärung enthält, folgt.

(2) Wenn ein Staat dieses Übereinkommen nach Hinterlegung der zehnten Ratifikations-, Annahme-, Genehmigungs- oder Beitrittsurkunde ratifiziert, annimmt, genehmigt oder ihm beitritt, tritt dieses Übereinkommen mit Ausnahme des ausgeschlossenen Teils für diesen Staat vorbehaltlich des Absatzes 6 am ersten Tag des Monats in Kraft, der auf einen Zeitabschnitt von zwölf Monaten nach Hinterlegung seiner Ratifikations-, Annahme-, Genehmigungs- oder Beitrittsurkunde folgt.

(3) Ein Staat, der dieses Übereinkommen ratifiziert, annimmt, genehmigt oder ihm beitritt und Vertragspartei des Haager Übereinkommens vom 1. Juli 1964 zur Einführung eines Einheitlichen Gesetzes über den Abschluss von internationalen Kaufverträgen über bewegliche Sachen (Haager Abschlussübereinkommen von 1964) oder des Haager Übereinkommens vom 1. Juli 1964 zur Einführung eines Einheitlichen Gesetzes über den internationalen Kauf beweglicher Sachen (Haager Kaufrechtsübereinkommen von 1964) ist, kündigt gleichzeitig das Haager Kaufrechtsübereinkommen von 1964 oder das Haager Abschlussübereinkommen von 1964 oder gegebenenfalls beide Übereinkommen, indem er der Regierung der Niederlande die Kündigung notifiziert.

(4) Eine Vertragspartei des Haager Kaufrechtsübereinkommens von 1964, die das vorliegende Übereinkommen ratifiziert, annimmt, genehmigt oder ihm beitritt und nach Artikel 92 erklärt oder erklärt hat, dass Teil II dieses Übereinkommens für sie nicht verbindlich ist, kündigt bei der Ratifikation, der Annahme, der Genehmigung oder dem Beitritt das Haager Kaufrechtsübereinkommen von 1964, indem sie der Regierung der Niederlande die Kündigung notifiziert.

(5) Eine Vertragspartei des Haager Abschlussübereinkommens von 1964, die das vorliegende Übereinkommen ratifiziert, annimmt, genehmigt oder ihm beitritt und nach Artikel 92 erklärt oder erklärt hat, dass Teil III dieses Übereinkommens für sie nicht verbindlich ist, kündigt bei der Ratifikation, der Annahme, der Genehmigung oder dem Beitritt das Haager Abschlussübereinkommen von 1964, indem sie der Regierung der Niederlande die Kündigung notifiziert.

(6) Für die Zwecke dieses Artikels werden Ratifikationen, Annahmen, Genehmigungen und Beitritte bezüglich dieses Übereinkommens, die von Vertragsparteien des Haager Abschlussübereinkommens von 1964 oder des Haager Kaufrechtsübereinkommens von 1964 vorgenommen werden, erst wirksam, nachdem die erforderlichen Kündigungen durch diese Staaten bezüglich der genannten Übereinkommen selbst wirksam geworden sind. Der Verwahrer dieses Übereinkommens setzt sich mit der Regierung der Niederlande als Verwahrer der Übereinkommen von 1964 in Verbindung, um die hierfür notwendige Koordinierung sicherzustellen.

Art. 99

(1) This Convention enters into force, subject to the provision of paragraph (6) of this article, on the first day of the month following the expiration of twelve months after the date of deposit of the tenth instrument of ratification, acceptance, approval or accession, including an instrument which contains a declaration made under article 92.

Art. 99

1) La présente Convention entrera en vigueur, sous réserve des dispositions du paragraphe 6 du présent article, le premier jour du mois suivant l'expiration d'une période de douze mois après la date du dépôt du dixième instrument de ratification, d'acceptation, d'approbation ou d'adhésion, y compris tout instrument contenant une déclaration faite en vertu de l'article 92.

Zeitpunkt des Inkrafttretens

(2) When a State ratifies, accepts, approves or accedes to this Convention after the deposit of the tenth instrument of ratification, acceptance, approval or accession, this Convention, with the exception of the Part excluded, enters into force in respect of that State, subject to the provisions of paragraph (6) of this article, on the first day of the month following the expiration of twelve months after the date of the deposit of its instrument of ratification, acceptance, approval or accession.

(3) A State which ratifies, accepts approves or accedes to this Convention and is a party to either or both the Convention relating to a Uniform Law on the Formation of Contracts for the International Sale of Goods done at The Hague an 1 July 1964 (1964 Hague Formation Convention) and the Convention relating to a Uniform Law on the International Sale of Goods done at The Hague on 1 July 1964 (1964 Hague Sales Convention) shall at the same time denounce, as the case may be, either or both the 1964 Hague Sales Convention and the 1964 Hague Formation Convention by notifying the Government of the Netherlands to that effect.

(4) A State party to the 1964 Hague Sales Convention which ratifies, accepts, approves or accedes to the present Convention and declares or has declared under article 92 that it will not be bound by Part II of this Convention shall at the time of ratification, acceptance, approval or accession denounce the 1964 Hague Sales Convention by notifying the Government of the Netherlands to that effect.

(5) A State party to the 1964 Hague Formation Convention which ratifies, accepts, approves or accedes to the present Convention and declares or has declared under article 92 that it will not be bound by Part III of this Convention shall at the time of ratification, acceptance, approval or accession denounce the 1964 Hague Formation Convention by notifying the Government of the Netherlands to that effect.

(6) For the purpose of this article, ratifications, acceptances, approvals and accessions in respect of this Convention by States parties to the 1964 Hague Formation Convention or to the 1964 Hague Sales Convention shall not be effective until such denunciations as may be required on the part of those States in respect of the latter two Conventions have themselves become effective. The depositary of this Convention shall consult with the Government of the Netherlands, as the depositary of the 1964 Conventions, so as to ensure necessary coordination in this respect.

2) Lorsqu'un Etat ratifiera, acceptera ou approuvera la présente Convention ou y adhérera après le dépôt du dixième instrument de ratification, d'acceptation, d'approbation ou d'adhésion, la Convention, à l'exception de la partie exclue, entrera en vigueur à l'égard de cet Etat, sous réserve des dispositions du paragraphe 6 du présent article, le premier jour du mois suivant l'expiration d'une période de douze mois après la date du dépôt de l'instrument de ratification, d'acceptation, d'approbation ou d'adhésion.

3) Tout Etat qui ratifiera, acceptera ou approuvera la présente Convention ou y adhérera et qui est partie à la Convention portant loi uniforme sur la formation des contrats de vente internationale des objets mobiliers corporels faite à La Haye le 1er juillet 1964 (Convention de La Haye de 1964 sur la formation) ou à la Convention portant loi uniforme sur la vente internationale des objets mobiliers corporels faite à La Haye le 1er juillet 1964 (Convention de La Haye de 1964 sur la vente), ou à ces deux conventions, dénoncera en mîme temps, selon le cas, la Convention de La Haye de 1964 sur la vente ou la Convention de La Haye sur la formation, ou ces deux conventions, en adressant une notification à cet effet au Gouvernement néerlandais.

4) Tout Etat partie à la Convention de La Haye de 1964 sur la vente qui ratifiera, acceptera ou approuvera la présente Convention ou y adhérera et qui déclarera ou aura déclaré en vertu de l'article 92 qu'il n'est pas lié par la deuxième partie de la Convention, dénoncera, au moment de la ratification, de l'acceptation, de l'approbation ou de l'adhésion, la Convention de La Haye de 1964 sur la vente en adressant une notification à cet effet au Gouvernement néerlandais.

5) Tour Etat partie à la Convention de La Haye de 1964 sur la vente [richtig: sur la formation] qui ratifiera, acceptera ou approuvera la présente Convention ou y adhérera et qui déclarera ou aura déclaré en vertu de l'article 92 qu'il n'est pas lié par la troisième partie de la Convention, dénoncera, au moment de la ratification, de l'acceptation, de l'approbation ou de l'adhésion, la Convention de La Haye de 1964 sur la formation en adressant une notification à cet effet au Gouvernement néerlandais.

6) Aux fins du présent article, les ratifications, acceptations, approbations et adhésions effectuées à l'égard de la présente Convention par des Etats parties à la Convention de La Haye de 1964 sur la formation ou à la Convention de La Haye de 1964 sur la vente ne prendront effet qu'à la date à laquelle les dénonciations éventuellement requises de la part desdits Etats à l'égard de ces deux conventions auront elles-mîmes pris effet. Le dépositaire de la présente Convention s'entendra avec le Gouvernements néerlandais, dépositaire des conventions de 1964, pour assurer la coordination nécessaire à cet égard.

Ferrari

Art. 99 1   Teil IV. Schlussbestimmungen

1   Diese Vorschrift bestimmt, wann das Übereinkommen international (Abs. 1) und einzelstaatlich (Abs. 2) in Kraft tritt,[1] und dass ein Vertragsstaat nicht zugleich Vertragsstaat des Übereinkommens und des Haager Kaufrechts sein kann.

---

[1] *Ferrari u. a./Mankowski,* Internationales Vertragsrecht, Art. 99, Rn. 1.

Art. 100 [Zeitlicher Anwendungsbereich]

(1) **Dieses Übereinkommen findet auf den Abschluss eines Vertrages nur Anwendung, wenn das Angebot zum Vertragsabschluß an oder nach dem Tag gemacht wird, an dem das Übereinkommen für die in Artikel 1 Absatz 1 Buchstabe a genannten Vertragsstaaten oder den in Artikel 1 Absatz 1 Buchstabe b genannten Vertragsstaat in Kraft tritt.**

(2) **Dieses Übereinkommen findet nur auf Verträge Anwendung, die an oder nach dem Tag geschlossen werden, an dem das Übereinkommen für die in Artikel 1 Absatz 1 Buchstabe a genannten Vertragsstaaten oder den in Artikel 1 Absatz 1 Buchstabe b genannten Vertragsstaat in Kraft tritt.**

Art. 100

(1) This Convention applies to the formation of a contract only when the proposal for concluding the contract is made on or after the date when the Convention enters into force in respect of the Contracting States referred to in subparagraph (1) (a) or the Contracting State referred to in subparagraph (1) (b) of article 1.

(2) This Convention applies only to contracts concluded on or after the date when the Convention enters into force in respect of the Contracting States referred to in subparagraph (1) (a) or the Contracting State referred to in Subparagraph (1) (b) of article 1.

Art. 100

1) La présente Convention s'applique à la formation des contrats conclus à la suite d'une proposition intervenue après l'entrée en vigueur de la Convention à l'égard des Etats contractants visés à l'alinéa a) du paragraphe 1 de l'article premier ou de l'Etat contractant visé à l'alinéa b) du paragraphe 1 de l'article premier.

2) La présente Convention s'applique uniquement aux contrats conclus après son entrée en vigueur à l'égard des Etats contractants visés à l'alinéa a) du paragraphe 1 de l'article premier ou de l'Etat contractant visé à l'alinéa b) du paragraphe 1 de l'article premier.

Die Vorschrift regelt den zeitlichen Anwendungsbereich des Übereinkommens,[1] wobei sie zwischen der Anwendbarkeit des Teil II und des Teil III unterscheidet. **1**

Hinsichtlich **Teil II** statuiert Art. 100, dass die Vorschriften zum Vertragsabschluss nur dann Anwendung finden, wenn das Angebot nach Inkrafttreten des CISG in den für Art. 1 I lit. a) relevanten Staaten oder im für Art. 1 I lit. b) maßgeblichen Staat gemacht worden ist. Es reicht nicht aus, dass der Vertrag nach dem Inkrafttreten des CISG in den erwähnten Staaten geschlossen worden ist.[2] Entscheidend ist diesbezüglich der Zeitpunkt der **Abgabe des Angebots**.[3] **2**

Damit **Teil III** Anwendung finden kann, ist es notwendig, dass der internationale Kaufvertrag nicht vor Inkrafttreten des Übereinkommens in den erwähnten Staaten abgeschlossen worden ist.[4] Dies bedeutet m. E. aber nicht, dass es immer ausreiche, dass die Annahmeerklärung dem Offerenten nach dem Zeitpunkt des Inkrafttretens in den erwähnten Staaten **3**

---

[1] Vgl. *Achilles*, Art. 100, Rn. 1; *Brunner*, Art. 100, Rn. 1; *Ferrari u. a./Mankowski*, Internationales VertragsrechtArt. 100, Rn. 1; *Schlechtriem/Schwenzer/Schlechtriem/Schwenzer/Hachem*, CISG Commentary, Art. 100, Rn. 1; vgl. in der Rechtsprechung etwa BGH, 17.12.1997, NJW-RR 1998, 680.

[2] Ebenso *Bianca/Bonell/Evans*, Art. 100, Anm. 2.2.; Schlechtriem/Schwenzer/*Schlechtriem/Schwenzer/Hachem*, CISG Commentary, Art. 100, Rn. 2; *Staudinger/Magnus*, Art. 100, Rn. 5.

[3] Vgl. *Brunner*, Art. 100, Rn. 2; *Czerwenka*, Rechtsanwendungsprobleme, S. 155; *Ferrari u. a./Mankowski*, Internationales VertragsrechtArt. 100, Rn. 4; *Karollus*, S. 36; *Niemann*, S. 69; *Schlechtriem/Schwenzer/Schlechtriem/Schwenzer/Hachem*, CISG Commentary, Art. 100, Rn. 2.

[4] Siehe auch *Achilles*, Art. 100, Rn. 2; vgl. in der Rechtsprechung BGH, 17.12.1997, CISG-online 296 = NJW-RR 1998, 680: mangelnde Anwendbarkeit des CISG, „weil Art. 100 Abs. 2 CISG dessen zeitlichen Geltungsbereich auf Verträge beschränkt, die an oder nach dem Tag geschlossen worden sind, an dem das CISG in dem betreffenden Vertragsstaat in Kraft getreten ist. „Das war in Deutschland erst am 1. Januar 1991 (BGBl. 1990 II, 1477) und damit nach dem Vertragsschluß der Parteien am 18. Januar 1990 der Fall".

zugegangen ist.[5] Es kann durchaus sein, dass eine Annahmeerklärung nach Inkrafttreten des Übereinkommens zugeht, der Vertrag aber bereits davor abgeschlossen worden ist und zwar dann, wenn der Zeitpunkt des Vertragsschlusses sich nach der sogenannten „mail-box rule" bestimmt, nach der die bloße Absendung an den richtigen Adressaten zum Vertragsabschluß führt.[6] In Bezug auf Art. 100 II führt dies dazu, dass der Hinweis auf den Vertragsschluss nicht unbedingt so verstanden werden muss, dass der Zugang nach Inkrafttreten des CISG in den genannten Staaten ausreiche.[7] Dies trifft nur dann zu, wenn auf den Vertragsabschluß die Vorschriften des Teil II oder die eines Rechts Anwendung finden, das von der Zugangstheorie (oder einer Theorie, die den Zeitpunkt des Vertragsabschlusses noch weiter hinausschiebt, wie die etwas in Italien der Fall ist) ausgeht.

---

[5] So nun auch *Schlechtriem/Schwenzer/Schlechtriem/Schwenzer/Hachem*, CISG Commentary, Art. 100, Rn. 3; a. A. *Bianca/Bonell/Evans*, Art. 100, Anm. 2.; *Brunner*, Art. 100, Rn. 3; *Ferrari u. a./Mankowski*, Internationales Vertragsrecht, Art. 100, Rn. 6; *Herber/Czerwenka*, Art. 100, Rn. 2, *Staudinger/Magnus*, Art. 100, Rn. 10.

[6] Beispielhaft sei der folgende Fall genannt: Absendung der Annahme am 30.12. des Jahres x, Zugang am 3.1. des darauffolgenden Jahres. Findet auf den Vertragsabschluß das Recht eine Staates Anwendung, das von der mail-box rule ausgeht, so kann das Übereinkommen keine Anwendung finden, selbst wenn das Übereinkommen in den maßgeblichen Staaten am 1.1. in Kraft getreten ist, also vor Zugang der Annameerklärung; a. A. *Ferrari u. a./Mankowski*, Internationales Vertragsrecht, Art. 100, Rn. 7.

[7] So aber *Herber/Czerwenka*, Art. 100, Rn. 2.

Art. 101 [Kündigung des Übereinkommens]

(1) Ein Vertragsstaat kann dieses Übereinkommen oder dessen Teil II oder Teil III durch eine an den Verwahrer gerichtete schriftliche Notifikation kündigen..

(2) Eine Kündigung wird am ersten Tag des Monats wirksam, der auf einen Zeitabschnitt von zwölf Monaten nach Eingang der Notifikation beim Verwahrer folgt. Ist in der Notifikation eine längere Kündigungsfrist angegeben, so wird die Kündigung nach Ablauf dieser längeren Frist nach Eingang der Notifikation beim Verwahrer wirksam.

Art. 101

(1) A Contracting State may denounce this Convention, or Part II or Part III of the Convention, by a formal notification in writing addressed to the depositary.

(2) The denunciation takes effect on the first day of the month following the expiration of twelve months after the notification is received by the depositary. Where a longer period for the denunciation to take effect is specified in the notification, the denunciation takes effect upon the expiration of such longer period after the notification is received by the depositary.

Art. 101

1) Tout Etat contractant pourra dénoncer la présente Convention, ou la deuxième ou la troisième partie de la Convention, par une notification formelle adressée par écrit au dépositaire.

2) La dénonciation prendra effet le premier jour du mois suivant l'expiration d'une période de douze mois après la date de réception de la notification par le dépositaire. Lorsqu'une période plus longue pour la prise d'effet de la dénonciation est spécifiée dans la notification, la dénonciation prendra effet à l'expiration de la période en question après la date de réception de la notification.

Diese Vorschrift bedarf keiner Erläuterung.

[Unterzeichnungsklausel]

Geschehen zu Wien am 11. April 1980 in einer Urschrift in arabischer, chinesischer, englischer, französischer, russischer und spanischer Sprache, wobei jeder Wortlaut gleichermaßen verbindlich ist.

Zu Urkund dessen haben die unterzeichneten, hierzu von ihren Regierungen gehörig befugten Bevollmächtigten dieses Übereinkommen unterschrieben.

Done at Vienna, this day of eleventh day of April, one thousand nine hundred and eighty, in a single original, of which the Arabic, Chinese, English, French, Russian and Spanish texts are equally authentic.

In witness whereof the undersigned plenipotentiaries, being duly authorized by their respective Governments, have signed this Convention.

Fait à Vienne, le onze avril mil neuf cent quatrevingt, en un seul original, dont les textes anglais, arabe, chinois, espagnol, français et russe sont également authentiques.

En foi de quoi les plénipotentiairies sous-signés, dûment autorisés par leurs gouvernements respectifs, ont signé la présente Convention.

1   Die Vorschrift legt fest, welche **Fassungen verbindlich** sind[1] (die arabische, chinesische, englische, französische, russische und spanische). Daraus folgt, dass die von den Vertretern der deutschsprachigen Ländern gemeinsam erarbeitete deutsche Übersetzung, genauso wie alle anderen Übersetzungen, lediglich als Anwendungshilfen anzusehen sind.[2]

2   Es kann durchaus vorkommen, dass die verschiedenen, gleichermaßen verbindlichen Fassungen Auslegungszweifel entstehen lassen; sind diese auch nicht durch einen Vergleich untereinander zu bereinigen, muss der **englischen** (und, bisweilen, auch der französischen) Fassung besonderes **Gewicht zukommen,**[3] da die Diskussionen und Formulierungsvorschläge auf der Diplomatischen Konferenz im wesentlichen in englischer Sprache gemacht worden sind.[4]

---

[1] Vgl. *Hager,* FS Huber, S. 319, 323; *Schlechtriem/Schwenzer/Schlechtriem/Schwenzer/Hachem,* CISG Commentary, Witness Cl., Rn. 1.

[2] Vgl. hierzu MünchKommHGB/*Ferrari,* Art. 7, Rn. 29 f.; *Schlechtriem/Schwenzer/Schlechtriem,* CISG Commentary, 2. Aufl., Witness Cl., Rn. 3; *Staudinger/Magnus,* Art. 7, Rn. 15.

[3] Vgl. auch *Achilles,* Unterzeichnungsklausel, Rn. 1; *Brunner,* Art. 7, Rn. 5; *Ferrari u. a./Saenger,* Internationales Vertragsrecht, Art. 7, Rn. 2; *Gruber,* Methoden, S. 142; *Hager,* FS Huber, S. 319, 324; *Honsell/Melis,* Art. 7, Rn. 10; *Honsell/Siehr,* Unterzeichnungsklausel, Rn. 1; *Kröll u. a./Herre,* Art. 101, Rn. 4; *J. Meyer,* RabelsZ 69 (2005), 457, 480; *Piltz,* Rn. 2–82; *Schlechtriem/Schwenzer/Schlechtriem/Schwenzer/Hachem,* CISG Commentary, Witness Cl., Rn. 3; *Schroeter,* UN-Kaufrecht, § 9, Rn. 2, Fn. 4; *Staudinger/Magnus,* Art. 7, Rn. 17 und 33; *Vogel,* S. 8; *Wulf,* UN3; -Kaufrecht und eCommerce, S. 38; a. A. *Flechtner,* 17 J. L. & Com. (1998), 187, 208, der sich gegen die Bevorzugung, auch im Falle eines Widerspruchs der verschiedenen verbindlichen Textfassungen, der englischen Originalfassung ausspricht.

[4] Vgl. BGer, 13.11.2003, CISG-online 840: „Bei Unklarheiten über den Wortlaut ist auf die Originaltexte abzustellen, wobei der englischen und sekundär der französischen Fassung eine erhöhte Bedeutung zukommt, da Englisch und Französisch die offiziellen Konferenzsprachen waren und die Verhandlungen hauptsächlich auf Englisch geführt wurden".

Gesetz zu dem Übereinkommen der Vereinten Nationen vom 11. April 1980 über Verträge über den internationalen Warenkauf sowie zur Änderung des Gesetzes zu dem Übereinkommen vom 19. Mai 1956 über den Beförderungsvertrag im internationalen Straßengüterverkehr (CMR) [VertragsG]

Vom 5. Juli 1989

(BGBl. 1989 II 586) in der Fassung des Schuldrechtsmodernisierungsgesetzes vom 26.11.2001 (BGBl. 2001 I 3138)

Der Bundestag hat das folgende Gesetz beschlossen:

Erster Teil. Zustimmung zu dem Übereinkommen vom 11. April 1980 über Verträge über den internationalen Warenkauf sowie Vorschriften zur Ausführung des Übereinkommens

Art. 1 [Zustimmung]

Dem in New York am 26. Mai 1981 von der Bundesrepublik Deutschland unterzeichneten Übereinkommen der Vereinten Nationen vom 11. April 1980 über Verträge über den internationalen Warenkauf wird zugestimmt. Das Übereinkommen wird nachstehend mit einer amtlichen deutschen Übersetzung veröffentlicht.

Die Zuständigkeit des Bundestages zur Zustimmung zu dem Übereinkommen ergibt sich aus Art. 59 II 1 GG. 1

Die deutsche Übersetzung wurde im Jahre 1983 von Vertretern der Bundesrepublik, der damaligen DDR, Österreichs und der Schweiz erarbeitet. Soweit Divergenzen im Sprachgebrauch geblieben sind, meint „amtliche deutsche Übersetzung" den in der Bundesrepublik geltenden Text.[1] 2

Obwohl das Gesetz im Wesentlichen die „Zustimmung" des zuständigen Gesetzgebungsorgans enthält, wird es nach den Richtlinien des Auswärtigen Amtes[2] zur Vermeidung von Missverständnissen nicht als „Zustimmungsgesetz", sondern als „Vertragsgesetz" bezeichnet. 3

Art. 2 [Anwendung aufgrund IPR-Verweisung]

Führen die Regeln des internationalen Privatrechts zur Anwendung des Rechts eines Staates, der eine Erklärung nach Artikel 95 des Übereinkommens von 1980 abgegeben hat, so bleibt Artikel 1 Abs. 1 Buchstabe b des Übereinkommens außer Betracht.

---

[1] Zur Frage, ob für die Auslegung der deutsche Text oder der Wortlaut der Originalfassungen des Übereinkommens maßgebend ist, s. *Schlechtriem/Schwenzer/Schwenzer/Hachem*, CISG Commentary, Intro to Arts 1–6, Rn. 15 f., Art. 7 Rn. 21.

[2] Richtlinien für die Behandlung völkerrechtlicher Verträge (RvV), § 21, S. 47, Stand 1.12.1987.

1. Normzweck

1 Da die Bundesrepublik Deutschland von dem Vorbehalt des Art. 95 keinen Gebrauch gemacht hat, kann das Übereinkommen vor deutschen Gerichten auch dann Anwendung finden, wenn die Voraussetzungen des Art. 1 I lit. a) – beide Parteien sind in unterschiedlichen Vertragsstaaten niedergelassen – im konkreten Fall nicht erfüllt sind, aber Art. 1 I lit. b) eingreift. Nach Art. 1 I lit. b) ist das CISG anzuwenden, wenn die Regeln des internationalen Privatrechts (bei einem deutschen Forum also Artt. 3 ff. Rom I-VO[1]) „zur Anwendung des Rechts eines Vertragsstaates führen."[2] Mit Art. 2 VertragsG hat der deutsche Gesetzgeber eine einfachgesetzliche Regelung zu der letztgenannten Konstellation geschaffen, deren Inhalt zudem in einer Erklärung niedergelegt wurde, welche die Bundesrepublik Deutschland bei Hinterlegung der Ratifikationsurkunde gegenüber dem Verwahrer des Übereinkommens (Art. 89) abgegeben hat.[3]

2 Art. 2 VertragsG verfolgt dabei das **Ziel,** im Anwendungsbereich des Art. 1 I lit. b) die Wirkung einer kollisionsrechtlichen Verweisung auf das Recht eines Vertragsstaates **einzuschränken,** falls dieser Vertragsstaat von dem Vorbehalt des Art. 95 Gebrauch gemacht und Art. 1 I lit. b) des Übereinkommens daher selbst nicht in Kraft gesetzt hat. Dieser Regelungsansatz beruht auf der Erwägung, dass Art. 1 I lit. b) für Vertragsstaaten (auch) die Funktion einer internen Verteilungsnorm hat, d. h. bei Zuständigkeit des Gerichtes eines Vertragsstaates darüber entscheidet, ob das Übereinkommen oder internes Kaufrecht anwendbar ist, wenn die Anwendungsvoraussetzungen des Art. 1 I lit. a) nicht gegeben sind, aber das IPR des angerufenen Gerichts auf die lex fori verweist.[4] Art. 2 VertragsG soll nun bewirken, dass das Gleiche bei Verweisung auf das Recht eines anderen Vertragsstaates gilt: Muss ein deutsches Gericht auf Grund einer Verweisung durch das deutsche IPR das Recht eines Vertragsstaates anwenden, so sollen dessen Normen über die Anwendbarkeit von Einheitskaufrecht oder internem Sachrecht ebenfalls zu beachten sein. Hat dieser Vertragsstaat Art. 1 I lit. b) nicht eingeführt und wendet er deshalb das CISG nur an, wenn die Voraussetzungen des Art. 1 I lit. a) gegeben sind, dann soll das deutsche Gericht ebenso entscheiden.[5]

3 Das Normverständnis des deutschen Gesetzgebers und der daraus abgeleitete Lösungsansatz des Art. 2 VertragsG hat im Schrifttum vielfach Zustimmung erfahren.[6] Er ist freilich **keineswegs zwingend,**[7] weil die Erklärung eines Vorbehalts nach Art. 95 eben nicht die Wirkung hat, dem erklärenden Staat die Eigenschaft eines „Vertragsstaates" i. S. d. Art. 1 I lit. b) zu nehmen – eine dahingehende Rechtsfolge ist in Art. 95 (im Gegensatz zu Art. 92 II) gerade nicht vorgesehen.[8] Zudem führt Art. 1 I lit. b) seinem klaren Wortlaut nach zur

---

[1] Die Rom I-VO findet nach ihrem Art. 28 auf Verträge Anwendung, die ab dem 17.12.2009 geschlossen wurden. Für ältere Verträge gelten einstweilen weiterhin Artt. 27 ff. EGBGB a. F.
[2] Zu den Einzelheiten s. *Ferrari*, Art. 1 Rn. 69 ff.
[3] Die Erklärung lautete: „Nach Auffassung der Regierung der Bundesrepublik Deutschland sind Vertragsparteien des Übereinkommens, die eine Erklärung nach Artikel 95 des Übereinkommens abgegeben haben, nicht als Vertragsstaaten im Sinne des Artikels 1 Absatz 1 Buchstabe b des Übereinkommens anzusehen. Deshalb besteht keine Verpflichtung und übernimmt die Bundesrepublik Deutschland keine Verpflichtung, diese Bestimmung anzuwenden, wenn die Regeln des internationalen Privatrechts zur Anwendung des Rechts einer Vertragspartei führen, die erklärt hat, daß Artikel 1 Absatz 1 Buchstabe b des Übereinkommens für sie nicht verbindlich ist. Vorbehaltlich dieser Bemerkung gibt die Regierung der Bundesrepublik Deutschland keine Erklärung nach Artikel 95 des Übereinkommens ab." (BGBl. 1990 II S. 1477).
[4] Vgl. hierzu *Czerwenka*, Rechtsanwendungsprobleme, S. 158 f.; *Piltz*, NJW 1989, 615, 620; *Drobnig*, FS von Overbeck, S. 29 („Rang- bzw. sachliche Kollisionsnormen"); ebenso (zur Factoring-Konvention) *Weller*, RIW 1999, 161, 162 f.; gründlich zu den verschiedenen Konstellationen auch *Pünder*, RIW 1990, 869; a. A. *Siehr*, RabelsZ 52 (1988), 587, 607.
[5] Vgl. Begründung zum VertragsG, BT-Drs. 11/3076, S. 6.
[6] *Heuzé*, Anm. 116.; *Honnold/Flechtner*, Art. 1, Rn. 47.5; MünchKommHGB/*Benicke*, Art. 1, Rn. 39; *Neumayer/Ming*, Art. 1, Anm. 8.; *Schlechtriem*, Internationales UN-Kaufrecht, Rn. 18; *Soergel/Lüderitz/Fenge*, Art. 1, Rn. 16.
[7] Anders noch *Schlechtriem*, 4. Auflage, Art. 2 VertragsG Rn. 1.
[8] *Ferrari*, Art. 1 Rn. 78; *Schroeter*, FS Kritzer, S. 446 f.

Anwendbarkeit des Übereinkommens[9] und nicht, wie vom deutschen Gesetzgeber zugrunde gelegt, zur Anwendbarkeit des in Bezug genommenen Rechts jenes Vertragsstaates. Die besseren Gründe sprechen daher für die Gegenansicht, nach welcher ein kollisionsrechtlicher Verweis auf das Recht eines Art. 95-Vorbehaltsstaates im Rahmen des Art. 1 I lit. b) zur Anwendbarkeit des Übereinkommens und nicht des unvereinheitlichten Kaufrechts des Vorbehaltsstaates führt.[10]

2. Normanwendung, praktische Bedeutung

Nach den Vorgaben des Art. 2 VertragsG hat ein deutsches Gericht bei Verweisung auf das Recht eines Vertragsstaates im Rahmen des Art. 1 I lit. b) zu **prüfen,** ob dieser Vertragsstaat von dem **Vorbehalt** nach Art. 95 Gebrauch gemacht hat.[11] Ob eine der Parteien in Deutschland niedergelassen ist, spielt keine Rolle: Auch wenn ein deutsches Gericht (ausnahmsweise) für Ansprüche aus einem Kaufvertrag zuständig ist, der zwischen einer Partei in einem Vorbehalts-Vertragsstaat (etwa den USA oder China) und einer Partei in einem Nichtvertragsstaat geschlossen wurde, greift bei einer Verweisung auf das Recht des Vorbehalts-Vertragsstaates Art. 2 VertragsG ein und führt zur Maßgeblichkeit des unvereinheitlichten Sachrechts des Vorbehalts-Vertragsstaates. Gelangt das Übereinkommen hingegen bereits aufgrund von **Art. 1 I lit. a)** zur Anwendung, ist Art. 2 VertragsG von vornherein **nicht einschlägig.**

Regelungsgegenstand des Art. 2 VertragsG ist damit eine Sonderkonstellation, die **praktisch außerordentlich selten** ist; sie hat vor deutschen Gerichten bislang keine Bedeutung erlangt.[12] Hintergrund ist zum einen die mittlerweile große Anzahl an Vertragsstaaten, aufgrund derer die Anwendung des Übereinkommens über Art. 1 I lit. a) der Regelfall und das Eingreifen des Art. 1 I lit. b) die (in ihrer Bedeutung ständig zurückgehende) Ausnahme geworden ist.[13] Zum anderen wirkt sich aus, dass faktisch nahezu ausschließlich solche international-kaufrechtlichen Streitfälle vor deutsche Gerichte gelangen, an denen eine deutsche Partei beteiligt ist – zur Anwendbarkeit des Art. 2 VertragsG kann es daher nur kommen, wenn ein Kaufvertrag zwischen einer deutschen Partei und einer Gegenpartei aus einem Nichtvertragsstaat vorliegt, das IPR aber ausnahmsweise das Recht eines dritten Staates (welcher den Vorbehalt nach Art. 95 erklärt hat) beruft; daneben kommen Rechtsstreitigkeiten aus bestimmten Kaufverträgen ohne jede deutsche Beteiligung in Frage, die vor deutschen Gerichten ebenfalls rar sind. Aus heutiger Perspektive spricht daher viel für die Einschätzung, dass Art. 2 VertragsG eine im Grunde überflüssige Spezialregelung enthält.

3. Völkerrechtskonformität der Regelung

a) Art. 2 VertragsG und die deutsche Interpretationserklärung. Indem Art. 2 VertragsG anordnet, dass Art. 1 I lit. b) des Übereinkommens in den tatbestandlich von Art. 2 VertragsG erfassten Fällen „außer Betracht" bleibt, ist diese Übereinkommensnorm mit dem so beschriebenen Inhalt in deutsches Recht transformiert worden. Die parallele völkerrechtliche Erklärung der Bundesrepublik Deutschland gegenüber dem Übereinkommensverwah-

---

[9] Vgl. den Wortlaut des Art. 1 I lit. b): „*Dieses Übereinkommen* ist auf Kaufverträge über Waren zwischen Parteien anzuwenden [...] wenn die Regeln des internationalen Privatrechts zur Anwendung des Rechts eines Vertragsstaats führen" (meine Hervorhebung).
[10] *Ferrari,* Art. 1 Rn. 78; *Honsell/Siehr,* Art. 1, Rn. 17; *Karollus,* S. 31; *Piltz,* Internationales Kaufrecht, Rn. 2–105; *Schroeter,* FS Kritzer, S. 447; *Siehr,* RabelsZ 52 (1988), 587, 601 ff. So im Ergebnis (aber ohne Begründung) auch OLG Düsseldorf, 2.7.1993, CISG-online 74 = RIW 1993, 845.
[11] Vorbehaltsstaaten s. Anh. I.
[12] OLG Düsseldorf, 2.7.1993, CISG-online 74 = RIW 1993, 845 hatte über einen entsprechenden Fall zu entscheiden, in dem der Kaufvertrag zwischen einer Verkäuferin aus dem U.S.-amerikanischen Gliedstaat Indiana und einer deutschen Käuferin noch vor Inkrafttreten des CISG für Deutschland abgeschlossen worden war: Das OLG gelangte über Art. 1 I lit. b) CISG i.V.m. Art. 28 II EGBGB zur Anwendbarkeit des CISG; krit. *Schlechtriem,* EWiR 1993, 1075.
[13] S. *Bridge,* Int'l Sale of Goods, Rn. 2.45: „The Article 95 problem is a dying one, the victim of the success of the CISG".

rer[14] stellt ihrem Wortlaut und Sinn nach keinen Teilvorbehalt,[15] sondern eine **Interpretationserklärung** dar.[16] Als solche verstößt sie zwar nicht gegen Art. 98, ist aber mit den Vorgaben des Art. 7 I **unvereinbar,** weil letztere Übereinkommensregel die Interpretation der Bestimmungen des CISG der Maßgabe der internationalen Einheitlichkeit unterwirft und die betreffende Aufgabe implizit den Gerichten zuweist. Es ist den einzelnen Vertragsstaaten daher völkervertraglich verwehrt, die von ihnen bevorzugte Auslegung einzelner Übereinkommensnormen rechtlich bindend festzuschreiben.[17]

7 **b) Folgen für die Rechtsanwendung.** Praktische Folgen könnte der vorstehende Befund freilich nur dann zeitigen, wenn sich eine i. S. des Art. 7 I international einheitliche Auslegung des Art. 1 I lit. b) (bzw. des Art. 95) gebildet hätte, die inhaltlich von Art. 2 VertragsG abweicht. Bislang ist dies weder eingetreten, noch steht eine dahingehende Entwicklung aufgrund der geringen praktischen Relevanz der betreffenden Fallkonstellation[18] für die Zukunft zu erwarten. Sollte eine entsprechende Auslegungsdivergenz eintreten, so wird man die deutschen Gerichte trotz der sich in diesem Fall materialisierenden Völkerrechtswidrigkeit des deutschen Rechts für an Art. 2 VertragsG gebunden halten müssen:[19] Obwohl sie grundsätzlich zur völkerrechtskonformen Auslegung deutschen Gesetzesrechts verpflichtet sind,[20] dürften der klare Wortlaut des Art. 2 VertragsG und der erkennbare Wille des historischen Gesetzgebers hier Versuchen entgegen stehen, die Gerichte der Bundesrepublik Deutschland zur – rechtspolitisch wünschenswerten – Übernahme einer gegenteiligen Übereinkommensinterpretation zu ermächtigen oder gar zu verpflichten.[21]

Art. 3 [Verjährung von Ansprüchen wegen vertragswidriger Beschaffenheit]

Auf die Verjährung der dem Käufer nach Art. 45 des Übereinkommens von 1980 zustehenden Ansprüche wegen Vertragswidrigkeit der Ware ist § 438 Abs. 3 des Bürgerlichen Gesetzbuchs auch anzuwenden, wenn die Vertragswidrigkeit auf Tatsachen beruht, die der Verkäufer kannte oder über die er nicht in Unkenntnis sein konnte und die er dem Käufer nicht offenbart hat.

1 **1.** Das CISG enthält keine Verjährungsvorschriften.[1] Das **UN-Übereinkommen über die Verjährung beim internationalen Warenkauf vom 14.6.1974**[2] dürfte in absehbarer Zeit von der Bundesrepublik nicht ratifiziert werden. In den neuen Bundesländern trat das von der ehemaligen DDR ratifizierte Verjährungsübereinkommen[3] mit Wirkung zum 3. Oktober 1990 außer Kraft.[4] Für die **Verjährung** gilt deshalb **unvereinheitlichtes Recht,** es sei denn, das IPR des Forums verweist auf das Recht eines Vertragsstaates des

---

[14] S. o. Rn. 1.
[15] So aber *Reinhart,* Art. 2 VertragsG, Rn. 1; *Soergel/Lüderitz/Fenge,* Art. 1, Rn. 16.
[16] *Ferrari,* Art. 1 Rn. 79; *Herber/Czerwenka,* Art. 1, Rn. 19; MünchKomm/*P. Huber,* Art. 2 VertragsG, Rn. 3; *Schroeter,* IHR 2004, 7, 15; *ders.,* FS Kritzer, S. 454; *Staudinger/Magnus,* Art. 1, Rn. 112.
[17] *Schroeter,* IHR 2004, 7, 15; *ders.,* FS Kritzer, S. 455; *Staudinger/Magnus,* Art. 2 VertragsG, Rn. 6.
[18] S. o. Rn. 5.
[19] *Ferrari,* Art. 1 Rn. 79.
[20] Vgl. BVerfG, 26.3.1987, BVerfGE 74, 358, 370; *Schroeter,* UN-Kaufrecht, § 5, Rn. 51 m. w. N.
[21] *Herber/Czerwenka,* Art. 2 VertragsG, Rn. 2; *Schroeter,* UN-Kaufrecht, § 5, Rn. 62; *ders.,* IHR 2004, 7, 15; a. A. *Staudinger/Magnus,* Art. 1, Rn. 112 und Art. 2 VertragsG, Rn. 6: die Interpretation des Übereinkommens durch Art. 2 VertragsG sei für den deutschen Rechtsanwender nur solange verbindlich, als sie der international vorherrschenden Auffassung entspricht.
[1] Missverständlich OLG Zweibrücken, 26.7.2002, CISG-online 688 = IHR 2002, 67, 69 („außer in Art. 39"); zutreffend OLG Brandenburg, 19.3.2009, CISG-online 2289.
[2] S. hier die Kommentierung von *Müller-Chen;* ferner *Landfermann,* RabelsZ 39 (1975), 253, 263 ff.
[3] Die DDR hatte sowohl das Übereinkommen von 1974 als auch das Protokoll zur Änderung des Verjährungsübereinkommens vom 11. April 1980 ratifiziert, in Geltung war das Übereinkommen seit 1. März 1990.
[4] S. Schreiben des Bundesministers der Justiz vom 10.6.1992, DtZ 1992, 241; *Piltz,* Internationales Kaufrecht, 1. Auflage, § 5, Rn. 84; *Herber,* MDR 1993, 105; *ders.,* BB 1991, Beilage 14, gegen *Enderlein/Graefrath,* Supplement Deutsche Einigung – Rechtsentwicklung, BB 1991, Beilage 6.

Verjährungsübereinkommens und dessen Anwendungsvoraussetzungen, insbesondere Art. 3, sind erfüllt.[5]

2. Die anwendbaren Verjährungsvorschriften sind, auch wenn sie in Prozessgesetze eingestellt sein sollten, grundsätzlich als materielles Recht zu qualifizieren und deshalb dem durch Artt. 3 ff., 12 I lit. d) Rom I-VO berufenen **Vertragsstatut** zu entnehmen.[6] Eine davon abweichende Sonderanknüpfung für solche „Rest"-fragen kann nicht befürwortet werden, da – und solange – es an allgemein akzeptierten Regeln dafür fehlt und die „dépeçage" des hilfsweise berufenen Schuldstatuts zu unsicheren und schwer berechenbaren Ergebnissen führt.[7]

3. Bei **Maßgeblichkeit deutschen Rechts** als Vertragsstatut[8] gelten die Verjährungsvorschriften der §§ 194 ff., 438, 479 BGB. Das gilt nach Art. 3 VertragsG auch für alle Ansprüche und Rechtsbehelfe wegen vertragswidriger Beschaffenheit (Rn. 4, 6). Ansonsten verjähren Ansprüche der Parteien in drei Jahren ab Schluss des Jahres ihrer Entstehung, §§ 195, 199 I BGB, soweit ihre Entstehung – wie regelmäßig – von einer Mitwirkung des Berechtigten abhängt, wie z. B. beim Vertragsschluss, bei der Vertragsaufhebung, bei Inbesitznahme oder Einlagerung der Ware (Aufwendungsersatzansprüche), sodass ihre Entstehung ihm bekannt oder für ihn ohne grobe Fahrlässigkeit erkennbar ist. Rechtsbehelfe wegen Nichtlieferung oder verzögerter Lieferung dürften hinsichtlich der Tatsachen, die sie entstehen lassen, ebenfalls stets erkennbar sein und deshalb in 3 Jahren ab Schluss des Entstehungsjahres verjähren. Anwendung der äußersten Fristen von 10 bzw. 30 Jahren nach § 199 III Nr. 1 oder 2 BGB, die unabhängig von Kenntnis oder Kenntnismöglichkeit ablaufen, dürfte deshalb wohl nur bei Verletzung von Nebenpflichten und in Ausnahmefällen beim Vorteilsausgleich nach Art. 84 II in Betracht kommen. Das Gestaltungsrecht „Vertragsaufhebung" ist wie der Rücktritt nach BGB durch § 218 BGB an diese Verjährungsfristen angekoppelt; Entsprechendes gilt nach § 438 V BGB (analog) für das Minderungsrecht.

4. Ansprüche des Käufers wegen Mängeln unterliegen der Sonderverjährung des § 438 BGB; Art. 3 VertragsG in der Fassung des SchuldModG setzt das als selbstverständlich voraus. Das Recht des Käufers, wegen Mängeln zu mindern oder den Vertrag aufzuheben, verfristet nach §§ 438 IV 1, V, 218 BGB. Der Vorteil, dass für die Verjährung von Mängelansprüchen und -rechten BGB- und CISG-Käufe gleichbehandelt werden, kann aber eine vor allem für ausländische Parteien bei Maßgeblichkeit deutschen Verjährungsrechts überraschende Verkürzung ihrer Ansprüche und Rechte auf Aufhebung oder Minderung bedeuten: Ihre Rechtsbehelfe sind auch bei ordnungsgemäßer Rüge, die die konventionsinterne zweijährige Ausschlussfrist des Art. 39 II außer Kraft setzt, zumeist zwei Jahre – § 438 I Nr. 3 BGB – nach Ablieferung verfristet.[9] Auch die bei entschuldbarer Rügeversäumnis nach Art. 44 fortbestehenden Ansprüche verfristen nach deutschem Verjährungsrecht. Diese für ausländische Vertragsparteien einschneidende Verkürzung ihrer Rechtsbehelfe muss sie zu schleuniger Rechtsverfolgung zwecks Hemmung der Verjährung nach § 204 I BGB, jedenfalls aber zur Aufnahme verjährungshemmender Verhandlungen – § 203 BGB – veranlassen.

Rechtsbehelfe des Käufers wegen Sachmängeln sind nach § 438 I Nr. 3 BGB regelmäßig in 2 Jahren verfristet.[10] Handelt es sich bei der Ware um Baumaterial i. S. d. § 438 I Nr. 2b)

---

[5] OGH, 25.6.1998, CISG-online 352 = EvBl 1998, 922, 923 f.

[6] OLG Brandenburg, 19.3.2009, CISG-online 2289; LG Heilbronn, 15.9.1997, CISG-online 562; vgl. zur Qualifikation statt aller *Palandt/Thorn*, Art. 12 Rom I (IPR), Rn. 8; speziell zum italienischen (häufig anzuwendenden) Verjährungsrecht bei CISG-Verträgen s. *Asam*, RIW 1992, 798–802 m. w. N.; für Österreich s. OGH, 25.6.1998, CISG-online 352 = EvBl 1998, 922, 923 f.: Schuldstatut. Übersicht ausländischer Verjährungsregeln s. *Lando/Clive/Prüm/Zimmermann*, Part III, PECL Art. 14:201, Comments 2, 3; PECL Art. 14:202, Comment 1.

[7] Für eine solche Sonderanknüpfung aber *Stoll*, Internationalprivatrechtliche Fragen, S. 507 f.; *ders.*, IPRax 1993, 75–79.

[8] Zu dieser Voraussetzung s. LG Heilbronn, 15.9.1997, CISG-online 562.

[9] Vgl. die zutreffende Kritik von *C. Witz*, D. 2002, 2860, 2862.

[10] Zum unglücklichen Festhalten des Gesetzgebers an dem deutschen dogmatischen Glaubenssatz, dass nur Ansprüche verjähren können – § 194 I BGB –, die Gestaltungsrechte Rücktritt (= Aufhebung im CISG) und

BGB, dessen vertragswidrige Beschaffenheit die Mangelhaftigkeit eines Bauwerks verursacht hat, dann beträgt die Verjährungsfrist 5 Jahre. Für arglistig verschwiegene Mängel, für die die Regelfristen gelten – § 438 III BGB – kann die Frist bis zu 10, evtl. sogar 30 Jahre betragen, § 199 III Nr. 1 oder Nr. 2 BGB. Art. 3 VertragsG modifiziert freilich verbal die Voraussetzungen für die Geltung der allgemeinen Verjährungsfristen dahin, dass *auch* unterbliebene Offenbarung bei Kenntnis oder grobfahrlässiger Unkenntnis des Verkäufers hinsichtlich der Vertragswidrigkeit – und nicht nur „Arglist" wie in § 438 III BGB – die Geltung der Regelfrist auslöst; in der Sache sind damit jedoch im Wesentlichen die Arglistfälle der Rspr. zu §§ 123, 477 I 1 BGB a. F. gemeint.[11] Art. 39 II CISG bleibt von *dieser* Fristverlängerung an sich unberührt, d. h. auf vertragliche Ansprüche des Käufers anwendbar (s. aber Rn. 7), doch schneiden die dem Art. 3 VertragsG gleich lautenden Artt. 40, 43 I dem Verkäufer die Berufung auf Art. 39 ohnehin ab.

Auch die Verjährungshemmung des § 479 II BGB gilt, wenn etwa der Importeur/Käufer an Verbraucher verkauft hat und von diesen in Anspruch genommen wird, sodass für seine Regressansprüche nach CISG eine Fristverlängerung von bis zu 5 Jahren eintreten kann.[12] Allerdings kann der Käufer mangels Rüge schon vorher, d. h. nach 2 Jahren, mit seinen Rechtsbehelfen durch Art. 39 II abgeschnitten sein.[13]

6   Art. 3 VertragsG unterstellt alle Ansprüche des Käufers wegen Vertragswidrigkeit der Ware bei Maßgeblichkeit deutschen Rechts als Vertragsstatut dem § 438 BGB.[14] Das gilt für (Ansprüche und Rechte wegen) Qualitätsmängel(n), Minderlieferung, Verpackungsfehler(n), Falschlieferungen und Aufwendungen des Käufers zur Mangelbeseitigung.[15] Ob „vertragswidrige Beschaffenheit" im CISG **Rechtsmängel** umfasst, ist streitig.[16] Art. 3 VertragsG ist jedoch unabhängig von der Bedeutung der Begriffe im CISG als Teil des deutschen Verjährungsrechts auszulegen und umfasst – wie auch der in Bezug genommene Art. 45 – Ansprüche und Rechte des Käufers wegen jeglicher Vertragswidrigkeit. Angesichts der weitgehenden Gleichbehandlung von Vertragswidrigkeiten auf Grund des SchuldModG gilt deshalb Art. 3 VertragsG auch für Rechtsmängel;[17] im Übrigen geht es um ein rein theoretisches Problem, da auch bei Beschränkung des Art. 3 VertragsG auf Sachmängel für Rechtsmängel die Sonderverjährungsfristen aus § 438 BGB gelten würden. Damit kann im Falle dinglicher Herausgabeansprüche eines Dritten eine 30-jährige Verjährungsfrist eingreifen, § 438 I Nr. 1a) BGB.[18] Das gilt allerdings nur für bestehende dingliche Herausgabe-

---

Minderung deshalb mit Erhebung der Verjährungseinrede gegen den Nacherfüllungsanspruch des Käufers nach Ausübung unwirksam werden müssen – §§ 218, 438 IV 1 BGB –, s. *Schlechtriem*, SchuldR BT, Rn. 68, 103.

[11] Vgl. zu Art. 3 VertragsG a. F. OLG Zweibrücken, 26.7.2002, CISG-online 688 = IHR 2002, 67, 69; *Palandt/Weidenkaff*, § 438, Rn. 12 unter Verweis auf Nachweise bei *Palandt/Ellenberger*, § 123, Rn. 2, 7, 8.
[12] S. *Magnus*, RIW 2002, 577, 583.
[13] A. A. *Magnus*, RIW 2002, 577, 583. Aber Art. 3 VertragsG will und kann nicht Art. 39 II derogieren.
[14] LG Mainz, 26.11.1998, CISG-online 563 = IHR 2001, 203, 205.
[15] LG Mainz, 26.11.1998, CISG-online 563 = IHR 2001, 203, 205: „Jede vertragswidrige Beschaffenheit der erworbenen Sache fällt unter Art. 3 Vertragsgesetz, und zwar unabhängig davon, ob es sich hierbei um einen Mangelfolgeschaden oder nur einen Minderwertschaden handelt oder ob eine auf die vertragsgemäße Beschaffenheit bezogene Nebenpflicht verletzt worden ist"; *Magnus*, RIW 2002, 577, 580.
[16] Umfassend (und differenzierend) hierzu *Mohs*, IHR 2002, 59–66.
[17] A. A. *Staudinger/Magnus*, Art. 3 VertragsG, Rn. 5. Die Frage, ob für das in Art. 3 VertragsG für die Anwendung des § 438 III BGB vorausgesetzte Wissen oder vorwerfbare Nichtwissen des Verkäufers auf Grund Art. 40 und 43 II zwischen Sach- und Rechtsmängeln zu differenzieren sei (so *Magnus*, RIW 2002, 577, 581 f.), ist wohl ein Scheinproblem: Art. 3 VertragsG ist als Teil des deutschen Verjährungsrechts autonom auszulegen und lässt die Regelfristen bei Kenntnis oder grobfahrlässiger Unkenntnis des Verkäufers ohne Differenzierung zwischen den Arten der vertragswidrigen Beschaffenheit anwendbar werden.
[18] Für eine teleologische Anpassung dieser Frist, falls die Herausgabeansprüche des Dritten anders als die deutsche rei vindicatio in kürzerer Frist verjähren, an diese kürzere Frist *Magnus*, RIW 2002, 577, 582. Das erscheint nicht nötig, weil der Dritte seine verjährten Herausgabeansprüche nicht durchsetzen und deshalb der Käufer nicht mehr evinciert werden kann (§ 438 I Nr. 1 Lit. a) BGB formuliert: „verlangt werden *kann*"); gibt er freiwillig heraus, sollte das nicht zu Lasten des Verkäufers gehen. Hat der Käufer dagegen kurz vor Ablauf der Verjährungsfrist für die Ansprüche des Dritten an diesen herausgegeben, dann könnte eine entsprechende zeitliche Verkürzung seiner Ansprüche gegen den Verkäufer zu einer im Vergleich zum internen Recht kaum vertretbaren Regressverkürzung führen.

ansprüche, nicht für bloß behauptete.[19] Art. 3 VertragsG erfasst selbstverständlich auch Rechtsbehelfe des Käufers wegen Belastung der Ware mit gewerblichen und anderen immateriellen Schutzrechten – Art. 42 –.

5. Art. 3 VertragsG gilt nur für vertragliche Ansprüche des Käufers nach CISG. **Außer- 7 vertragliche Ansprüche** verjähren nach dem Deliktsstatut, sodass die Probleme der Weiterfresserschäden auch in Fällen grenzüberschreitender Kaufvertrag vorstellbar sind.[20] Soweit fraudulöses Verschweigen von Mängeln nach dem maßgeblichen Deliktsstatut außervertragliche Schadenersatzansprüche auslöst, gilt die Verjährungsfrist des Deliktsstatuts; Art. 39 II bleibt, da das CISG Ansprüche wegen fraudulöser Schädigung nicht abschließend regeln wollte (s. Vor Artt. 14–24 Rn. 36), auf diese Ansprüche unanwendbar.

6. Trotz Verlust seines Aufhebungs- und Minderungsrechts auf Grund Verjährung seiner 8 Rechtsbehelfe wegen Mängeln – § 438 IV 1, V – kann der Käufer den noch nicht gezahlten Kaufpreis **zurückbehalten**. § 438 IV 2, V BGB ist als Teil der Vorschriften des Verjährungsstatuts zu sehen, denn er schränkt Verjährungswirkungen ein; eines Rückgriffs auf ein aus Prinzipien des CISG zu entwickelndes Zurückbehaltungsrecht des CISG bedarf es nicht.[21] Soweit der Käufer den Kaufpreis wegen eines durch Verjährung verlorenen Minderungsrechts einbehält, kann er nur in Höhe des Minderungsbetrages zurückhalten,[22] mindert also im Ergebnis trotz Ablaufs der Verjährungsfrist. Hat er voll oder jedenfalls zu viel gezahlt, kann er jedoch nicht zurückfordern, § 214 II 1 BGB. Im Falle der Zurückhaltung des Kaufpreises wegen eines – durch Verjährung verloren gegangenen – Aufhebungsrechts könnte der Käufer u. U. die mangelhafte Ware behalten, ohne etwas zu zahlen. Dieser Fall wird bei CISG-Käufen nicht häufig auftreten, da wegen Mängeln nur unter strengen Voraussetzungen aufgehoben werden kann (s. Art. 25 Rn. 43 ff.), ein Aufhebungsrecht also selten verloren geht. Falls der Käufer jedoch hätte aufheben können, muss auch bei einem CISG-Vertrag dem Verkäufer die Möglichkeit zur Lösung aus dem nicht mehr sachangemessen durchführbaren Vertrag gegeben werden. Eine Implantierung des Rücktrittsrechts aus § 438 IV 3 BGB in das CISG lässt sich mit dem Argument vertreten, dass es die Einschränkung der Verjährungswirkung durch das verbleibende Zurückbehaltungsrecht modifiziert und deshalb ebenfalls Teil des dem subsidiär eingreifenden Vertragsstatuts unterstehenden Verjährungsregimes ist. Zur Auflösung der Pattsituation kann jedoch auch in – vorzuziehender – konventionsinterner Lückenfüllung ein Aufhebungsrecht auf Art. 64 I lit. a) gestützt werden, da eine Geltendmachung des Zurückbehaltungsrechts, etwa Einbehaltung des vollen Kaufpreises trotz Verjährung der Mängelansprüche des Käufers, unangemessen ist und einer unberechtigten Erfüllungsweigerung gleichsteht.

7. Soweit Maßgeblichkeit deutschen Rechts gegeben ist, sind auch die für **Neubeginn 9 der Verjährungsfrist** und ihre **Hemmung** geltenden Vorschriften – §§ 203–213 BGB – anzuwenden.[23]

---

[19] A. A. *Magnus*, RIW 2002, 577, 582.
[20] S. zu Mangelfolgeschäden an Sachgütern des Käufers *Schlechtriem*, Internationales UN-Kaufrecht, Rn. 40.
[21] *Schlechtriem*, Internationales UN-Kaufrecht, Rn. 42d, 20b; *W. Witz*, FS Schlechtriem, S. 291 ff., 295 f.
[22] *Mansel/Budzikiewicz*, S. 125, Rn. 33.
[23] Vgl. OLG Brandenburg, 19.3.2009, CISG-online 2289; OLG Zweibrücken, 26.7.2002, CISG-online 688 = IHR 2002, 67, 69; OLG Düsseldorf, 28.2.2001, CISG-online 1448.

Zweiter Teil.
Änderung des Gesetzes zu dem Übereinkommen vom 19. Mai 1956 über den Beförderungsvertrag im internationalen Straßengüterverkehr (CMR)

Art. 4 (hier nicht abgedruckt)

Dritter Teil. Schlussbestimmungen

Art. 5 [Aufhebung von EAG und EKG]

(1) Das Einheitliche Gesetz über den internationalen Kauf beweglicher Sachen vom 17. Juli 1973 (BGBl. I S. 856) und das Einheitliche Gesetz über den Abschluß von internationalen Kaufverträgen über bewegliche Sachen vom 17. Juli 1973 (BGBl. I S. 868) werden aufgehoben.

(2) Für Verträge, die Gegenstand des Einheitlichen Gesetzes über den internationalen Kauf beweglicher Sachen sind, bleibt dieses Einheitliche Gesetz maßgebend, sofern der Vertrag vor dem Tage geschlossen wird, an dem das Übereinkommen von 1980 für die Bundesrepublik Deutschland in Kraft tritt. Für den Abschluß solcher Verträge bleibt das Einheitliche Gesetz über den Abschluß von internationalen Kaufverträgen über bewegliche Sachen maßgebend, sofern das Angebot zum Abschluß des Vertrages vor dem Tage gemacht wird, an dem das Übereinkommen von 1980 für die Bundesrepublik Deutschland in Kraft tritt.

Art. 5 ist eingefügt worden auf Grund einer Empfehlung des Rechtsausschusses. Die **1** förmliche Aufhebung der Haager Kaufgesetze war erforderlich, da die in Art. 99 III, VI vorgesehene Kündigung der Haager Kaufrechtsübereinkommen nicht zugleich das Außerkrafttreten von EKG und EAG bewirkte. Die Regelung stellt sicher, dass das CISG in vollem Umfang an die Stelle des bisherigen Einheitskaufrechts tritt.

Art. 5 II enthält eine Übergangsregelung (intertemporales Privatrecht), die gewährleisten **2** soll, dass Verträge und Vertragsangebote, die vom CISG noch nicht erfasst werden, nach EAG und EKG zu behandeln sind.

Art. 6 (gegenstandslos)

Art. 6 enthielt die übliche Berlinklausel. Durch Gesetz vom 14. September 1989[1] hatte das Berliner Abgeordnetenhaus beschlossen, dass CISG in Berlin Anwendung findet. Seit Inkrafttreten des Einigungsvertrages ist die Bestimmung gegenstandslos.

Art. 7 [Inkrafttreten des Gesetzes]

(1) Mit Ausnahme der Artikel 2, 3 und 5 tritt dieses Gesetz am Tage nach seiner Verkündung in Kraft. Die Artikel 2, 3 und 5 treten an dem Tage in Kraft, an dem das Übereinkommen von 1980 für die Bundesrepublik Deutschland in Kraft tritt.

---

[1] GVBl. 1989, S. 1699.

(2) **Der Tag, an dem das Übereinkommen von 1980 nach seinem Artikel 99 für die Bundesrepublik Deutschland in Kraft tritt, ist im Bundesgesetzblatt bekanntzugeben.**

Die Zustimmung zum CISG ist am 14.7.1989 in Kraft getreten.[1] Das Übereinkommen sowie die Artt. 2, 3 und 5 VertragsG sind nach Art. 99 III, VI i. V. m. Art. 12 des Übereinkommens zur Einführung eines Einheitlichen Gesetzes über den internationalen Kauf beweglicher Sachen vom 1. Juli 1964 und Art. X des Übereinkommens zur Einführung eines Einheitlichen Gesetzes über den Abschluss von internationalen Kaufverträgen über bewegliche Sachen vom 1. Juli 1964 erst zum 1. Januar 1991 in Kraft getreten.[2] Die Neufassung des Art. 3 VertragsG gilt ab 1.1.2002; Übergangsregelung s. Art. 229 § 6 EGBGB.

---

[1] Verkündung erfolgte in BGBl. 1989 II, 586 f.
[2] BGBl. 1990 II, 1477.

Übereinkommen über die Verjährung beim internationalen Warenkauf

Vom 14. Juni 1974

– in der Fassung des Protokolls vom 11. April 1980 –

Einleitung

I.

Am 14. Juni 1974 verabschiedete eine diplomatische Konferenz in New York das Übereinkommen der Vereinten Nationen über die Verjährung beim internationalen Warenkauf.[1] Die nach Art. 44 VerjÜbk erforderliche Hinterlegung von zehn Ratifikations- oder Beitrittsurkunden wurde erst am 21. Januar 1988 erreicht. Das Verjährungsübereinkommen ist daher am 1. August 1988 in Kraft getreten.[2] 1

Die Verabschiedung des CISG am 11. April 1980 in Wien machte eine Anpassung des Verjährungsübereinkommens notwendig, weil die definitive Fassung des CISG in manchen Punkten von den Vorarbeiten, auf deren Grundlage 1974 das Verjährungsübereinkommen abgeschlossen worden war, abwich.[3] Auf der Wiener Konferenz wurde deswegen am 11. April 1980 das Protokoll zur Änderung des Übereinkommens über die Verjährung beim internationalen Warenkauf beschlossen,[4] um den räumlichen und sachlichen Anwendungsbereich des Verjährungsübereinkommens dem CISG anzupassen.[5] Das Änderungsprotokoll ist am 1. August 1988 in Kraft getreten.[6] 2

Das Ergebnis dieser Angleichung ist das Übereinkommen der Vereinten Nationen über die Verjährung beim internationalen Warenkauf in der Fassung des Protokolls vom 11. April 1980. Obwohl das Verjährungsübereinkommen 1974 gemäss Art. 44a VerjÜbk 1980 in gewissen Fällen weiterhin angewendet werden muss, wird gestützt auf die Erwartung, dass die Zukunft dem ergänzten Verjährungsabkommen gehören wird, nachstehend nur das ergänzte Übereinkommen abgedruckt und kommentiert.[7] Die Bestimmungen der alten Fassung werden nur noch in den Fussnoten wiedergegeben. 3

Die ehemalige DDR hatte das Verjährungsübereinkommen ratifiziert und war auch dem Änderungsprotokoll beigetreten. Das Übereinkommen in der Fassung des Protokolls war vom 1. März 1990 bis zum Beitritt der ehemaligen DDR zum Geltungsbereich des Grund- 4

---

[1] *Loewe*, Einl VerjÜbk, S. 187; *Esslinger*, 13 Int'l Q. (2001), 472, 473 ff.; zur Ausarbeitung des Übereinkommens s. *Nestor*, FS Schmitthoff, S. 292 ff.; zur diplomatischen Konferenz s. *Landfermann*, RabelsZ 39 (1975), 253, 255 f.

[2] Gegenwärtig ist das Verjährungsübereinkommen 1974 in 27 Staaten in Kraft, s. Vertragsstaatenliste im Anhang II.

[3] *Enderlein/Maskow/Strohbach*, Vorbem. VerjÜbk; *Loewe*, Einl ÄndProt, 226; *Jaffé*, S. 19; *Staudinger/Magnus*, Anhang II zum CISG, Rn. 9.

[4] Das Änderungsprotokoll (UN-Doc. A/Conf. 97/18, annex II) ist in der englischen Originalfassung und in der deutschen Übersetzung abgedruckt in RabelsZ 51 (1987), 186 ff.

[5] *Loewe*, Einl VerjÜbk, S. 189; Das Änderungsprotokoll änderte Artt. 3, 4, 31, 34, 37 und 40 des Verjährungsübereinkommens 1974 und fügte neu Artt. 36a, 43a, 43b, 44a und 45a hinzu.

[6] Art. IX Abs. 1 ÄndProt; dem Änderungsprotokoll sind bislang 19 Staaten beigetreten, s. Vertragsstaatenliste im Anhang II.

[7] Der englische Originaltext ist in der RabelsZ 39 (1975), 342 ff. und bei *Loewe*, S. 231 ff. abgedruckt, der auch die französische Originalfassung (S. 246 ff.) wiedergibt. Weder beim Verjährungsübereinkommen 1974 noch beim Änderungsprotokoll ist Deutsch Abkommenssprache. Eine Übersetzungskonferenz der deutschsprachigen Länder erstellte eine amtliche Übersetzung; vgl. dazu *Schlechtriem*, Einl I.

gesetzes am 3. Oktober 1990 in Kraft. Die Bundesrepublik Deutschland ist dem Übereinkommen bislang nicht beigetreten.[8] Österreich und die Schweiz haben weder das Verjährungsübereinkommen 1974 ratifiziert, noch sind sie dem Änderungsprotokoll beigetreten.[9]

II.

5   Das Verjährungsübereinkommen enthält in vier Teilen Bestimmungen zur Dauer, dem Beginn, der Unterbrechung und der Verlängerung der Verjährung.[10] Die Verjährungsfrist beträgt vier Jahre (Art. 8). Sie kann unter gewissen Voraussetzungen bis zur Höchstfrist von zehn Jahren verlängert werden (Art. 23). Durch die einheitliche Regelung können Unsicherheiten bei der Ermittlung des anwendbaren Rechtes und dessen Inhalt abgebaut werden. Dies trägt auch dazu bei, das unerwünschte Forum Shopping einzudämmen.[11] Zudem vereinheitlicht das Verjährungsübereinkommen nicht nur die Verjährung, sondern auch gewisse Fragen im Zusammenhang mit der Wirkung der Einleitung eines Verfahrens in einem Staat (Art. 30).[12]

6   Wenn auch manche Lösungen des Verjährungsübereinkommens den Bedürfnissen des internationalen Handels nicht immer optimal gerecht werden und sich zum Teil deutlich von den nationalen Rechtsordnungen unterscheiden,[13] so muss das Übereinkommen insgesamt als gelungen bezeichnet werden.[14] Es ist ein wichtiger Schritt auf dem Weg zu einer umfassenden Kaufrechtsvereinheitlichung, und es ist darum zu bedauern, dass ausser Norwegen noch kein Mitgliedsstaat des Europäischen Wirtschaftsraums das Verjährungsübereinkommen ratifiziert hat. Eine Ratifikation sollte von den Vertragsstaaten des CISG daher in Betracht gezogen werden.[15]

Präambel
Die Vertragsstaaten dieses Übereinkommens –
in Anbetracht dessen, dass der internationale Handel einen wichtigen Beitrag zur Förderung freundschaftlicher Beziehungen zwischen den Staaten leistet,
in der Überzeugung, dass die Annahme einheitlicher Regeln über die Verjährung beim internationalen Warenkauf die Entwicklung des Welthandels erleichtern würde –
haben folgendes vereinbart:

Die Präambel stimmt inhaltlich mit der Präambel des CISG überein,[16] weshalb auf die diesbezügliche Kommentierung verwiesen wird.[17]

---

[8] Es war anfänglich kontrovers, ob das Verjährungsübereinkommen nach dem Beitritt der DDR zum Grundgesetz auch für die Bundesrepublik Deutschland gilt, s. z. B. dafür *Enderlein*, UN-Verjährungsübereinkommen, S. 65; *Thorn*, IPRax 1993, 215; dagegen *Herber*, BB 1990, Beil. 37, 1, 5. Die ablehnende Haltung setzte sich schließlich durch (*Staudinger/Magnus*, Art. 3 VertragsG, Rn. 4).
[9] Zum aktuellen Stand der Ratifikationen s. die Vertragsstaatenliste im Anhang II.
[10] Teil I enthält das materielle Verjährungsrecht (Artt. 8–30), Teil II die Anwendungsbestimmungen, Teil III die Erklärungen und Vorbehalte und Teil IV die Schlussbestimmungen; Sekretariatskommentar VerjÜbk, Präambel, Nr. 6; *Girsberger*, Verjährung und Verwirkung, S. 158 ff.; *Hill*, 25 Tex. Int'l L. J. (1990), 1, 5; *Sono*, 35 La. L. Rev. (1975), 1127, 1128.
[11] *Winship*, 28 Int'l Law. (1994), 1071, 1077; vgl. auch *Landfermann*, RabelsZ 39 (1975), 253, 274 f.; *Nelson*, 24 Int'l Law. (1990), 583, 584; *Sono*, La. L. Rev. (1975), 1127, 1128, 1130 f.
[12] *Sono*, La. L. Rev. (1975), 1127, 1133; *Smit*, 23 Am. J. Comp. L. (1975), 337, 350.
[13] Z. B. die einheitliche Vierjahresfrist, die auch für die Verjährung von Sachmängelansprüchen gilt, s. Art. 8 Rn. 2; oder die fehlende Möglichkeit, die Verjährungsfrist vertraglich verkürzen zu können, s. Art. 22 Rn. 4.
[14] *Smit*, 23 Am. J. Comp. L. (1975), 337, 355; *Enderlein*, UN-Verjährungsübereinkommen, S. 75, 80 f.; a. A. *Herber*, RIW 1974, 577, 579.
[15] So auch *Enderlein*, UN-Verjährungsübereinkommen, S. 80 f.; *Loewe*, Einl VerjÜbk, S. 188.
[16] Second Committee, Summary Records, O. R., S. 460.
[17] *Ferrari*, Präambel Rn. 3 ff.

Teil I. Allgemeine Bestimmungen

Anwendungsbereich

Art. 1 [Einführende Bestimmungen: Gegenstand und Definitionen]*

(1) Dieses Übereinkommen bestimmt die Voraussetzungen, unter denen die gegenseitigen Ansprüche zwischen einem Käufer und einem Verkäufer, die sich aus einem internationalen Kaufvertrag über bewegliche Sachen** (Waren) ergeben oder auf die Verletzung, Aufhebung oder Unwirksamkeit eines solchen Vertrages beziehen, wegen Ablaufs einer bestimmten Zeit nicht mehr ausgeübt werden können. Diese Zeitspanne wird im folgenden als „Verjährungsfrist" bezeichnet.

(2) Dieses Übereinkommen berührt nicht eine besondere Frist, innerhalb derer eine Partei als Voraussetzung für den Erwerb oder die Ausübung ihres Anspruchs der anderen Partei eine Mitteilung zu machen oder eine andere Handlung als die Einleitung eines Rechtsverfahrens vorzunehmen hat.

(3) In diesem Übereinkommen
a) bezeichnen die Ausdrücke „Käufer", „Verkäufer" und „Partei" Personen, die Waren kaufen oder verkaufen oder die vereinbaren, Waren zu kaufen oder zu verkaufen, sowie deren Nachfolger in die Rechte und Pflichten aus dem Kaufvertrag;
b) bezeichnet der Ausdruck „Gläubiger" eine Partei, die einen Anspruch geltend macht, unabhängig davon, ob der Anspruch auf die Zahlung einer Geldsumme gerichtet ist oder nicht;
c) bezeichnet der Ausdruck „Schuldner" eine Partei, gegen die ein Gläubiger einen Anspruch geltend macht;
d) bezeichnet der Ausdruck „Vertragsverletzung" die Nichterfüllung des Vertrages durch eine Partei oder jede nicht vertragsgemäße Erfüllung;
e) umfaßt der Ausdruck „Rechtsverfahren" jedes gerichtliche, schiedsrichterliche oder Verwaltungsverfahren;
f) umfaßt der Ausdruck „Person" auch Gesellschaften, Vereinigungen oder andere Rechtsträger, die klagen oder verklagt*** werden können, unabhängig davon, ob sie dem privaten oder dem öffentlichen Recht angehören;
g) umfaßt der Ausdruck „schriftlich" auch Mitteilungen durch Telegramm oder Fernschreiben;
h) bezeichnet der Ausdruck „Jahr" ein Jahr nach dem Gregorianischen Kalender.

Übersicht

	Rn.
I. Allgemeines	1
II. Sachlicher Anwendungsbereich	2
1. Grundsatz (Abs. 1)	2
a) Begriff der Verjährung	3
b) Ansprüche aus oder im Zusammenhang mit einem Kaufvertrag	4
2. Ausnahme (Abs. 2)	6
III. Definitionskatalog (Abs. 3)	8
1. Allgemeines	8
2. Ausgewählte Definitionen	9
a) Parteien des Kaufvertrages (lit. a))	9

---

* Die Überschriften gehören nicht zum offiziellen Text des Übereinkommens. Sie sind dem Sekretariatskommentar VerjÜbk entnommen.
** Für Österreich: bewegliche körperliche Sachen.
*** Für Österreich: geklagt.

b) Person (lit. f)) 10
c) Jahr (lit. h)) 11

I. Allgemeines

1 Art. 1 verfolgt ein doppeltes Ziel: In Abs. 1 und 2 wird zum einen der **sachliche Anwendungsbereich** des Verjährungsübereinkommens geregelt und in Abs. 3 werden zum anderen nach dem Vorbild anglo-amerikanischer Gesetze gewisse Begriffe definiert, um eine möglichst einheitliche Auslegung und Anwendung des Übereinkommens zu gewährleisten.[1]

II. Sachlicher Anwendungsbereich

1. Grundsatz (Abs. 1)

2 Das Verjährungsübereinkommen legt nach Art. 1 I die Voraussetzungen fest, unter denen kaufvertragliche Ansprüche verjähren. Die Bestimmung des sachlichen Anwendungsbereichs des Übereinkommens hängt damit vom Begriff der Verjährung und der kaufvertraglichen Ansprüche ab.

3 **a) Begriff der Verjährung.** Das Wesen der Verjährung wird in Abs. 1 dahingehend umschrieben, dass ein Anspruch wegen Ablaufs einer bestimmten Zeit **nicht mehr ausgeübt** werden kann.[2] Diese etwas vage Formulierung dient dem Ziel, sowohl die prozessrechtliche Konzeption der Verjährung des Common Law[3] als auch das materiellrechtliche Verständnis der meisten anderen Rechtsordnungen[4] zu erfassen.[5] Der Begriff der Verjährung darf somit nicht mit einem bestimmten nationalen System in Verbindung gebracht werden,[6] sondern muss nach den Grundsätzen von Art. 7 VerjÜbk autonom ausgelegt werden.

4 **b) Ansprüche aus oder im Zusammenhang mit einem Kaufvertrag.** Das Übereinkommen betrifft Ansprüche zwischen einem **Käufer und Verkäufer** sowie deren **Rechtsnachfolgern**.[7] **Dies stellt klar, dass Ansprüche Dritter sowie Ansprüche gegen Dritte ausgeschlossen sind.**[8] So fällt z. B. die Klage eines Einzelhändlers, der Ware von einem Grosshändler erworben hat, gegen den Hersteller nicht in den Anwendungsbereich des Übereinkommens.[9]

---

[1] *Enderlein/Maskow/Strohbach*, Art. 1 VerjÜbk, Anm. 6.
[2] *Enderlein/Maskow/Strohbach*, Art. 1 VerjÜbk, Anm. 7.
[3] *Cheshire/Fifoot/Furmston*, S. 713; *Hill*, 25 Tex. Int'l L.J. (1990), 1, 6; seit Inkrafttreten des Foreign Limitation Period Act 1984 am 1.10.1985 wird in England die Verjährung im internationalen Verhältnis als materiellrechtlich qualifiziert: Auf Ansprüche, die vor einem englischen Gericht nach ausländischem Recht beurteilt werden, wird grundsätzlich die Verjährungsfrist der lex causae angewandt (sec. 1 (1)), s. *Chitty* On Contracts, § 29–151; *Jaffé*, S. 34; zur uneinheitlichen Lage in den USA s. *Girsberger*, Verjährung und Verwirkung, S. 57 ff.; rechtsvergleichender Überblick zum prozessrechtlichen Verständnis der Verjährung in Common Law Countries, mit Hinweis darauf, dass die moderne Tendenz eher Richtug materiellrechtliches Verständnis geht: *Schwenzer/Hachem/Kee*, Rn. 51.8 ff.
[4] *Girsberger*, Verjährung und Verwirkung, S. 27 ff., 50 f.; *Zimmermann*, JZ 2000, 853, 856 f.; so auch Art. 10 I lit. d) EuIPRÜ; rechtsvergleichender Überblick zur Verjährung als materiellrechtliche Frage in Civil Law Countries: *Schwenzer/Hachem/Kee*, Rn. 51.6 ff.; so auch Art. III.-7:101 DCFR, Art. 10(1)(d) Rom I-VO, Kap. 14 PECL, Kap. 10 PICC.
[5] O. R. VerjÜbk, S. 137 ff., Nr. 19 ff.; Sekretariatskommentar VerjÜbk, Art. 1, Nr. 1; *Loewe*, Art. 1 VerjÜbk, S. 192; *Landfermann*, RabelsZ 39 (1975), 253, 257; *Hill*, 25 Tex. Int'l L.J. (1990), 1, 6; *Krapp*, 19 J. World Trade L. (1985), 343, 345; *Sumulong*, 50 Philippine L.J. (1975), 318, 326. Der Unterschied wirkt sich auf das auf die Verjährung anwendbare Recht aus: Die anglo-amerikanischen Rechtsordnungen wenden hauptsächlich die *lex fori* an, die kontinentalen Rechte hingegen die *lex causae*; *Burr*, S. 19 ff., 53 ff.
[6] *Smit*, 23 Am. J. Comp. L. (1975), 337, 339.
[7] Art. 1 III lit. a) VerjÜbk.
[8] Sekretariatskommentar VerjÜbk, Art. 1, Nr. 3, 7; *Enderlein/Maskow/Strohbach*, Art. 1 VerjÜbk, Anm. 3.; *Smit*, 23 Am. J. Comp. L. (1975), 337, 339.
[9] Sekretariatskommentar VerjÜbk, Art. 1, Nr. 7.

Sodann erfasst das Verjährungsübereinkommen nur **vertragliche Ansprüche**, die sich 5
aus einem **internationalen Kaufvertrag**[10] ergeben oder sich auf einen solchen beziehen.[11]
Mit dieser Umschreibung soll die Unsicherheit ausgeräumt werden, ob Ansprüche aus der
Verletzung, Aufhebung oder Unwirksamkeit des Vertrages „sich aus dem Vertrag ergeben".
Damit fallen z. B. die Ansprüche aus der Rückabwicklung eines Kaufvertrags in Folge eines
Willensmangels unter das Verjährungsübereinkommens; ausgeschlossen sind hingegen **deliktische Ansprüche**.[12]

2. Ausnahme (Abs. 2)

Das Verjährungsübereinkommen schliesst **Ausschlussfristen** aus, innerhalb derer eine 6
Partei der anderen als Voraussetzung für den Erwerb oder die Ausübung eines Anspruches
Anzeige zu erstatten hat.[13] Hierzu gehören etwa die Zweijahresfrist für die Mängelrüge in
Art. 39 II CISG, die kurze Mängelrügefrist in § 377 HGB („unverzüglich") oder in sec. 2–
607 (3)(a) UCC („reasonable time")[14] oder die Erklärung der Vertragsaufhebung innerhalb
angemessener Frist in Art. 49 II CISG.[15] Eine Ausschlussfrist kann weder gehemmt noch
unterbrochen werden und wird oft von Amtes wegen berücksichtigt.[16]

Ausschlussfristen werden von den Verjährungsfristen nach dem **formalrechtlichen Kri-** 7
terium abgegrenzt, ob zur Ausübung des Anspruches innerhalb der Frist ein Rechtsverfahren einzuleiten ist.[17] In diesem Fall handelt es sich um eine Verjährungsfrist, anderenfalls
um eine Ausschlussfrist.[18] Eine Unterscheidung der Fristen nach materiellen Kriterien war
nicht möglich, da oft eine Ausschlussfrist in einer Rechtsordnung funktionell einer Verjährungsfrist in einer anderen Rechtsordnung entspricht.[19]

III. Definitionskatalog (Abs. 3)

1. Allgemeines

Die meisten Definitionen in Abs. 3 werden – soweit sie nicht selbsterklärend sind – im 8
Kontext der Vorschrift betrachtet, welche auf den fraglichen Begriff abstellt. Aus diesem
Grund wird für die Definition der **„Vertragsverletzung"** in lit. d) auf Art. 10 verwiesen,
für den Begriff des **„Verfahrens"** in lit. e) auf Art. 15 und für die Definition der **„Schriftlichkeit"** auf den gleich lautenden Art. 13 CISG.

2. Ausgewählte Definitionen

a) **Parteien des Kaufvertrages (lit. a))**. In den Begriff der „Parteien" eines Kaufver- 9
trages werden in lit. a) auch ihre **Rechtsnachfolger** einbezogen. Primär sind dies Personen,

---

[10] Zum Begriff des internationalen Kaufvertrags vgl. Art. 2. *Staudinger/Magnus*, Anhang II zum CISG, Rn. 19.
[11] Die Formulierung geht zurück auf einen Antrag der tschechischen Delegation, O. R. VerjÜbk, S. 51, Nr. 10; S. 136 ff., Nr. 3 ff.
[12] *Staudinger/Magnus*, Anhang II zum CISG, Rn. 22; Sekretariatskommentar VerjÜbk, Art. 1, Nr. 6.
[13] Sekretariatskommentar VerjÜbk, Art. 1, Nr. 9; *Girsberger*, Verjährung und Verwirkung, S. 29 ff.
[14] Siehe dazu *Hill*, 25 Tex. Int'l L. J. (1990), 1, 7; *Nelson*, 24 Int'l Law. (1990), 583, 588 f.; *White/Summers*, Vol. 1, S. 611 ff.
[15] Vgl. dazu *Müller-Chen*, Art. 49 Rn. 30 ff.; weitere Beispiele bei *Girsberger*, Verjährung und Verwirkung, S. 167 f.
[16] So ausdrücklich Artt. 2964 und 2969 ital. Cc; *Girsberger*, Verjährung und Verwirkung, S. 41.
[17] *Landfermann*, RabelsZ 39 (1975), 253, 258; *Krapp*, 19 J. World Trade L. (1985), 343, 345 f.; *Loewe*, Art. 1 VerjÜbk, S. 193; *Girsberger*, Verjährung und Verwirkung, S. 165.
[18] *Enderlein/Maskow/Strohbach*, Art. 1 VerjÜbk, Anm. 8.; zum Einfluss der Ausschlussfristen auf die Verjährungsfrist s. Art. 8 Rn. 3.
[19] So ist z. B. die Ausschlussfrist des § 121 BGB oder des Art. 1109 frz. Cc i. V. m. Art. 1304 frz. Cc eine Verjährungsfrist (Nichtigkeitsklage wegen Irrtums), s. *Landfermann*, RabelsZ 39 (1975), 253, 258; *Girsberger*, Verjährung und Verwirkung, S. 167 f.

welche die Schuld übernommen haben oder denen die Forderung abgetreten wurde. Praktisch bedeutsam sind insoweit die Factoringinstitute oder die Konkursverwaltung einer Vertragspartei.[20]

10 **b) Person (lit. f)).** Das Verjährungsübereinkommen versteht gemäss lit. f) unter einer „Person" alle **Zusammenschlüsse,** die prozessuale **Aktiv- oder Passivlegitimation** besitzen. Dies soll verdeutlichen, dass das Verjährungsübereinkommen unabhängig von der rechtlichen oder organisatorischen Struktur der Partei des Kaufvertrages anzuwenden ist.[21] Unter das Übereinkommen fallen daher nicht nur juristische Personen, sondern auch Vereinigungen ohne eigene Rechtspersönlichkeit.[22] Für die Anwendbarkeit des Verjährungsübereinkommens ist es des Weiteren unerheblich, ob die Person nach dem Verständnis des nationalen Rechtes eine **privat- oder öffentlich-rechtliche Grundlage** hat.[23] Dadurch werden nicht nur staatliche Unternehmen in den Geltungsbereich des Übereinkommens einbezogen, sondern auch die Staaten selbst.[24]

11 **c) Jahr (lit. h)).** Auf Antrag Singapurs wurde in lit. h) klargestellt, dass unter einem „Jahr" ein Jahr nach dem **Gregorianischen Kalender** zu verstehen ist,[25] da auch andere Kalender gebräuchlich sind."[26]

Art. 2 [Definition eines internationalen Kaufvertrages]

Für die Zwecke dieses Übereinkommens

a) wird ein Kaufvertrag über Waren als international angesehen, wenn der Käufer und der Verkäufer zur Zeit des Vertragsabschlusses ihre Niederlassungen in verschiedenen Staaten haben;

b) wird die Tatsache, daß die Parteien ihre Niederlassungen in verschiedenen Staaten haben, nicht berücksichtigt, wenn sie sich nicht aus dem Vertrag oder aus Verhandlungen oder Auskünften ergibt, die vor oder bei Vertragsabschluß zwischen den Parteien geführt oder von ihnen erteilt worden sind;

c) gilt, wenn eine Partei eines Kaufvertrages über Waren Niederlassungen in mehr als einem Staat hat, als ihre Niederlassung diejenige, die unter Berücksichtigung der zur Zeit des Vertragsabschlusses den Parteien bekannten oder von ihnen in Betracht gezogenen Umstände die engste Beziehung zu dem Vertrag und zu seiner Erfüllung hat;

d) ist, wenn eine Partei keine Niederlassung hat, ihr gewöhnlicher Aufenthalt maßgebend;

e) wird weder berücksichtigt, welche Staatsangehörigkeit die Parteien haben, noch ob sie Kaufleute oder Nichtkaufleute sind oder ob der Vertrag bürgerlich-rechtlicher* Art ist.

Die Kriterien für die Festlegung der Internationalität des Kaufvertrages in Art. 2 stimmen inhaltlich mit Artt. 1 und 10 CISG überein. Es wird deshalb auf die diesbezüglichen Ausführungen verwiesen.[1] Die zum Teil von der entsprechenden Vorschrift des CISG abweichenden Formulierungen schaden dieser inhaltlichen Kongruenz nicht.

---

[20] *Enderlein/Maskow/Strohbach,* Art. 1 VerjÜbk, Anm. 11.
[21] Sekretariatskommentar VerjÜbk, Art. 1, Nr. 10.
[22] Z.B. die Bürgerlich-rechtliche Gesellschaft (§ 705 BGB) oder die Offene Handelsgesellschaft (§ 124 I HGB).
[23] Sekretariatskommentar VerjÜbk, Art. 1, Nr. 10; *Enderlein/Maskow/Strohbach,* Art. 1 VerjÜbk, Anm. 15.
[24] Das Verjährungsübereinkommen berührt nicht die Frage, ob die Staaten vor den Gerichten Immunität beanspruchen können, s. Sekretariatskommentar VerjÜbk, Art. 1, Nr. 10.
[25] O.R. VerjÜbk, S. 52, Nr. 10, 13, S. 137, Nr. 14.
[26] *Enderlein/Maskow/Strohbach,* Art. 1 VerjÜbk, Anm. 17.
* Für Österreich und die Schweiz: handels- oder zivilrechtlicher.
[1] Zu Art. 2 lit. a) s. *Ferrari,* Art. 1 Rn. 8 f., 40 ff.; zu Art. 2 lit. b)–2 lit. d) s. *Ferrari,* Art. 10 Rn. 5 ff.; zu Art. 2 lit. e) s. *Ferrari,* Art. 1 Rn. 59 f.

Art. 3 [Anwendungsbereich]

(1) Dieses Übereinkommen ist nur anzuwenden
a) wenn die Parteien des Vertrages über den internationalen Warenkauf zur Zeit des Vertragsabschlusses ihre Niederlassung in Vertragsstaaten haben; oder
b) wenn nach den Regeln des internationalen Privatrechts das Recht eines Vertragsstaates auf den Kaufvertrag anzuwenden ist.

(2) Dieses Übereinkommen ist nicht anzuwenden, wenn die Parteien seine Anwendung ausdrücklich ausgeschlossen haben.

Übersicht

	Rn.
I. Vorgeschichte	1
II. Die Vorschrift im Einzelnen	2
1. Abs. 1: Anwendungsvoraussetzungen	2
a) Allgemeines	2
b) Vorbehaltsmöglichkeit	3
2. Abs. 2: Anwendungsausschluss	4

I. Vorgeschichte

Art. 3 VerjÜbk 1974 sah die Anwendung des Übereinkommens grundsätzlich nur dann 1 vor, wenn die Parteien des Kaufvertrages ihre Niederlassung in Vertragsstaaten haben.[1] Demgegenüber bestimmte schon der Entwurf des CISG, dass das Kaufrechtsübereinkommen anzuwenden ist, wenn die Regeln des internationalen Privatrechts zur Anwendung des Rechtes eines Vertragsstaates führen. Auf der Wiener Konferenz wurde der **Geltungsbereich** des Verjährungsübereinkommens durch Art. I ÄndProt zumindest teilweise an die Vorschriften des CISG angeglichen.[2]

II. Die Vorschrift im Einzelnen

1. Abs. 1: Anwendungsvoraussetzungen

a) Allgemeines. Trotz teilweise abweichender Formulierungen entspricht die Bestimmung des **räumlichen Anwendungsbereiches** in Art. 3 I VerjÜbk inhaltlich Art. 1 I CISG. Es wird deshalb auf die diesbezüglichen Ausführungen verwiesen.[3]

b) Vorbehaltsmöglichkeit. Das harte Ringen auf der diplomatischen Konferenz um die 3 Angleichung des Anwendungsbereiches an das CISG hatte zur Folge, dass in Art. 36a den Vertragsstaaten die Möglichkeit gegeben wird, die Anwendung des Übereinkommens auf **Nichtvertragsstaaten** auszuschliessen.[4] Für diese Staaten gilt Art. 3 I in der alten Fassung. Da Art. 36a VerjÜbk Art. 95 CISG entspricht, wird für die Einzelheiten auf die diesbezüglichen Ausführungen verwiesen.[5]

---

[1] *Alte Fassung:* (1) Dieses Übereinkommen ist nur anzuwenden, wenn die Parteien des internationalen Kaufvertrages über Waren zurzeit des Vertragsabschlusses ihre Niederlassungen in Vertragsstaaten haben. (2) Soweit dieses Übereinkommen nichts anderes bestimmt, ist es unabhängig von dem Recht anzuwenden, das sonst auf Grund der Regeln des internationalen Privatrechts anzuwenden wäre. (3) Dieses Übereinkommen ist nicht anzuwenden, wenn die Parteien seine Anwendung ausdrücklich ausgeschlossen haben.

[2] Die Angleichung war umstritten: Second Committee, Summary Records, O.R., S. 465 ff.; zur Nichtanpassung von Art. 30, der funktionell mit Art. 3 zusammenhängt, s. Art. 30 Rn. 6; *Enderlein/Maskow/Strohbach*, Art. 3 VerjÜbk, Anm. 1.

[3] *Ferrari*, Art. 1 Rn. 12 ff.; s. auch *Girsberger*, Verjährung und Verwirkung, S. 159 ff.

[4] Bislang haben nur die USA sowie die Slowakische und Tschechische Republik von der Vorbehaltsmöglichkeit Gebrauch gemacht, s. Art. 36a Rn. 1 (Fn. 1) und Vertragsstaatenliste in Anhang II.

[5] *Ferrari*, Art. 95 Rn. 1 ff.

2. Abs. 2: Anwendungsausschluss

4 Im Unterschied zu Art. 6 CISG, der den Ausschluss des CISG auch stillschweigend zulässt,[6] muss der Ausschluss des Verjährungsübereinkommens **ausdrücklich**[7] erfolgen und sich auf das gesamte Übereinkommen beziehen.[8] Wird das Übereinkommen ausgeschlossen, kommt das von den Parteien gewählte oder ein nach den Regeln des internationalen Privatrechtes zu ermittelndes nationales Recht zur Anwendung.[9]

5 Über Art. 3 II hinaus kann das Verjährungsabkommen in zwei weiteren Fällen ausgeschlossen werden. Vereinbaren die Parteien in ihrem Vertrag, dass Ansprüche nur erworben oder ausgeübt werden können, wenn diese der anderen Partei innerhalb einer bestimmten Zeit **angezeigt** werden, wird das Übereinkommen ausgeschlossen, da das Übereinkommen auf diese Fristen gemäss Art. 1 II keine Anwendung findet.[10] Die gleiche Wirkung hat die Vereinbarung nach Art. 22 III, dass ein **schiedsrichterliches Verfahren** in einer kürzeren Frist als der im Abkommen vorgesehenen Verjährungsfrist eingeleitet werden muss.[11]

Art. 4 [Ausschluß bestimmter Käufe und Warenarten]

Dieses Übereinkommen findet keine Anwendung auf den Kauf
a) **von Waren für den persönlichen Gebrauch oder den Gebrauch in der Familie oder im Haushalt, es sei denn, daß der Verkäufer vor oder bei Vertragsabschluß weder wußte noch wissen mußte, daß die Ware für einen solchen Gebrauch gekauft wurde;**
b) **bei Versteigerungen;**
c) **auf Grund von Zwangsvollstreckungs- oder anderen gerichtlichen Maßnahmen;**
d) **von Wertpapieren oder Zahlungsmitteln;**
e) **von Seeschiffen, Binnenschiffen, Luftkissenfahrzeugen oder Luftfahrzeugen;**
f) **von elektrischer Energie.**

Art. 4 VerjÜbk 1974 wurde durch Art. II. ÄndProt abgeändert.[1] Art. 4 in der Fassung des Änderungsprotokolls entspricht nun Art. 2 CISG, weshalb auf die diesbezüglichen Ausführungen verwiesen wird.[2]

Art. 5 [Ausschluß bestimmter Ansprüche]

Dieses Übereinkommen gilt nicht für Ansprüche, die gegründet sind auf
a) **Tod oder Körperverletzung einer Person;**
b) **nukleare Schäden, die durch die verkaufte Ware verursacht wurden;**
c) **ein Recht auf vorzugsweise Befriedigung, ein Pfandrecht oder eine andere dingliche Sicherung;**
d) **eine in einem Rechtsverfahren ergangene richterliche oder schiedsrichterliche Entscheidung;**

---

[6] *Ferrari*, Art. 6 Rn. 18 ff.
[7] Sekretariatskommentar VerjÜbk, Art. 3, Nr. 7; *Landfermann*, RabelsZ 39 (1975), 253, 264 f.; *Staudinger/Magnus*, Anhang II zum CISG, Rn. 15.
[8] A. A. *Enderlein/Maskow/Strohbach*, Art. 3 VerjÜbk, Anm. 6.
[9] Sekretariatskommentar VerjÜbk, Art. 3, Nr. 8; *Enderlein/Maskow/Strohbach*, Art. 3 VerjÜbk, Anm. 6.
[10] *Smit*, 23 Am. J. Comp. L. (1975), 337, 339 f.
[11] Vgl. Art. 22 Rn. 4; *Smit*, 23 Am. J. Comp. L. (1975), 337, 341.
[1] *Alte Fassung:* Dieses Übereinkommen gilt nicht den Kauf a) von Waren für den persönlichen Gebrauch, den Gebrauch in der Familie oder im Haushalt; b) bei Versteigerungen; c) auf Grund einer Beschlagnahme oder einer anderen gerichtlichen Massnahme; d) von Wertpapieren und Zahlungsmitteln; e) von Seeschiffen, Binnenschiffen und Luftfahrzeugen; f) von elektrischer Energie.
[2] *Ferrari*, Art. 2 Rn. 4 ff.

e) einen nach dem Recht des Ortes, an dem die Vollstreckung begehrt wird, vollstreckbaren Titel;
f) einen Wechsel oder einen Scheck.

Übersicht

	Rn.
I. Allgemeines	1
II. Die Vorschrift im Einzelnen	2
1. Ansprüche aus Tod und Körperverletzung (lit. a)	2
2. Ansprüche aus Atomhaftpflicht (lit. b)	3
3. Ansprüche aus Sicherungsrechten des Verkäufers (lit. c)	4
4. Ansprüche aus richterlichen oder schiedsrichterlichen Entscheidungen (lit. d)	5
5. Ansprüche aus vollstreckbaren Titeln (lit. e)	6
6. Ansprüche aus einem Wechsel oder Scheck (lit. f)	7

I. Allgemeines

Art. 5 ergänzt Artt. 4 und 6, indem Ansprüche ausgeschlossen werden, die nicht in einem **1** unmittelbaren Zusammenhang mit der handelsrechtlichen Natur des Kaufvertrages stehen.[1]

II. Die Vorschrift im Einzelnen

1. Ansprüche aus Tod und Körperverletzung (lit. a)

Der Ausschluss von Ansprüchen aus Tod und Körperverletzung entspricht Art. 5 CISG, **2** weshalb auf die diesbezüglichen Ausführungen verwiesen wird.[2]

2. Ansprüche aus Atomhaftpflicht (lit. b)

Die auf kaufvertragliche Ansprüche im engeren Sinn zugeschnittenen Verjährungsregeln **3** sind für Ansprüche aus nuklearen Schäden unangemessen, weil solche Schäden oft erst sehr lange nach dem schädigenden Ereignis zu Tage treten.[3] Auf Grund ihrer häufig **deliktischen** Natur werden sie ohnehin nicht vom Verjährungsübereinkommen erfasst.

3. Ansprüche aus Sicherungsrechten des Verkäufers (lit. c)

Die Sicherungsrechte des Verkäufers bei Nichtzahlung des Kaufpreises oder im Konkurs **4** des Käufers sind in der Praxis eng mit Fragen des (nationalen) **Zwangsvollstreckungsrechtes** verknüpft. Dies führte zu einem **Verzicht,** die Auswirkungen der Verjährung des kaufrechtlichen Anspruches auf die Sicherungsrechte zu regeln.[4] Dieser Ausschluss betrifft z. B. den Anspruch des Verkäufers auf Rückgabe der unbezahlten Ware bei Vereinbarung eines Eigentumsvorbehaltes.[5]

4. Ansprüche aus richterlichen oder schiedsrichterlichen Entscheidungen (lit. d)

Ansprüche, die auf einer richterlichen oder schiedsrichterlichen Entscheidung beruhen, **5** werden in lit. d) ausgeschlossen, auch wenn die Entscheidung sachlich einen Anspruch aus

---

[1] *Enderlein/Maskow/Strohbach,* Art. 5 VerjÜbk, Anm. 1.
[2] *Ferrari,* Art. 5 Rn. 3 ff.; *Staudinger/Magnus,* Anhang II zum CISG, Rn. 20.
[3] Art. VI der Wiener Konvention über die zivilrechtliche Verantwortlichkeit für nukleare Schäden vom 21. Mai 1963 sieht Verjährungsfristen von 10 und 20 Jahren vor.
[4] Vgl. auch Art. 4 lit. b) CISG, welcher die Wirkungen, die der Kaufvertrag auf das Eigentum der Ware hat, ausschließt, s. *Ferrari,* Art. 4 Rn. 29 ff.
[5] Sekretariatskommentar VerjÜbk, Art. 5, Nr. 3; *Enderlein/Maskow/Strohbach,* Art. 5 VerjÜbk, Anm. 4.

oder im Zusammenhang mit einem internationalen Kaufvertrag betrifft.[6] Durch die **Ausklammerung** der **Urteilsverjährung**[7] wird zum Ausdruck gebracht, dass das Verjährungsübereinkommen ausschliesslich die Anspruchsverjährung regelt.[8]

5. Ansprüche aus vollstreckbaren Titeln (lit. e)

6 Der **Ausschluss** der Vollstreckungsverjährung nach lit. e) erfolgt aus den gleichen Gründen wie der Ausschluss der Urteilsverjährung. Unter einem vollstreckbaren Titel (titre exécutoire) sind Dokumente zu verstehen, welche die gleiche Wirkung wie eine richterliche oder schiedsrichterliche Entscheidung haben, aber nicht als solche qualifiziert werden.[9]

6. Ansprüche aus einem Wechsel oder Scheck (lit. f)

7 Hat der Käufer für die Ware einen Wechsel oder Scheck ausgestellt, fällt die Verjährung der Forderung aus dem Wertpapier nach lit. f) nicht unter das Übereinkommen, weil die Wechselverjährung in besonderen **internationalen Abkommen** geregelt ist[10] und Wechsel oder Schecks häufig in das Vermögen vertragsfremder Personen gelangen, die mit dem Kaufvertrag nichts zu tun haben.[11]

Art. 6 [Verträge über herzustellende Waren oder Dienstleistungen]

(1) Dieses Übereinkommen ist auf Verträge nicht anzuwenden, bei denen der überwiegende Teil der Pflichten des Verkäufers in der Ausführung von Arbeiten oder anderen Dienstleistungen besteht.

(2) Den Kaufverträgen stehen die Verträge über die Lieferung herzustellender oder zu erzeugender Waren gleich, es sei denn, daß der Besteller einen wesentlichen Teil der für die Herstellung oder Erzeugung notwendigen Stoffe selbst zur Verfügung zu stellen hat.

Art. 6 entspricht Art. 3 CISG, lediglich die Reihenfolge der Absätze ist vertauscht. Es wird daher auf die Ausführungen zu Art. 3 CISG verwiesen.[1]

Art. 7 [Auslegung zur Förderung der Einheitlichkeit]

Bei der Auslegung und Anwendung dieses Übereinkommens sind sein internationaler Charakter und die Notwendigkeit, die Einheitlichkeit des Rechtes zu fördern, zu berücksichtigen.

Art. 7 entspricht Art. 7 I CISG fast wörtlich,[1*] weshalb auf die diesbezüglichen Ausführungen verwiesen wird.[2*]

---

[6] Sekretariatskommentar VerjÜbk, Art. 5, Nr. 5.
[7] § 197 I Nr. 3 BGB (30 Jahre); in Frankreich beträgt die Frist grundsätzlich 30 Jahre: Soc. 7.10.1981, Bull. Civ. V, n° 762; Art. 3:324 BW (20 Jahre); Art. 137 II OR und Art. 2953 ital. Cc (10 Jahre); sec. 24 (1) Limitation Act 1980 (6 Jahre); *Loewe*, Art. 5 VerjÜbk, S. 198; *Enderlein/Maskow/Strohbach*, Art. 5 VerjÜbk, Anm. 5.; rechtsvergleichend *Spiro*, Begrenzung privater Rechte, S. 381 ff.; *Burr*, S. 102 ff.
[8] Sekretariatskommentar VerjÜbk, Art. 5, Nr. 5.
[9] Z. B. notariell beglaubigte Verträge, aussergerichtliche Vergleiche oder schriftliche Schuldanerkenntnisse: *Sumulong*, 50 Philippine L. J. (1975), 318, 337.
[10] Art. 70 Einheitliches Wechselgesetz vom 7.6.1930: Verjährungsfristen zwischen sechs Monaten und drei Jahren; Art. 52 Einheitliches Scheckgesetz vom 19.3.1931: Sechs Monate.
[11] Sekretariatskommentar VerjÜbk, Art. 5, Nr. 7; *Enderlein/Maskow/Strohbach*, Art. 5 VerjÜbk, Anm. 6.
[1] *Ferrari*, Art. 3 Rn. 4 ff.
[1*] Im Unterschied zum CISG fehlt die Bezugnahme auf den Grundsatz von Treu und Glauben und eine Regel zur Lückenfüllung. Die praktische Bedeutung dieser Diskrepanz darf jedoch nicht überschätzt werden, denn die von Art. 7 VerjÜbk bei der Auslegung geforderte Berücksichtigung des internationalen Charakters und der Notwendigkeit, die Einheitlichkeit des Rechtes zu fördern, trägt indirekt dem Grundgedanken von Art. 7 II CISG Rechnung.
[2*] *Ferrari*, Art. 7 Rn. 4 ff.

Dauer und Beginn der Verjährungsfrist

Art. 8 [Länge der Verjährungsfrist]
Die Verjährungsfrist beträgt vier Jahre.

Übersicht
	Rn.
I. Vorgeschichte	1
II. Einheitsfrist	2
1. Allgemeines	2
2. Verkürzung der Verjährungsfrist durch Ausschlussfrist	3

I. Vorgeschichte

Bei der Festlegung der **Dauer** der Verjährung musste ein Mittelweg zwischen den divergierenden nationalen Rechtsordnungen gefunden werden.[1] Auf der diplomatischen Konferenz setzten sich einige Entwicklungsländer – die im internationalen Handel häufig als Käufer auftreten – und Grossbritannien für eine fünfjährige, die Industriestaaten für eine dreijährige Frist ein.[2] Schliesslich einigte man sich im Sinne eines mathematischen Kompromisses auf **vier Jahre**.[3] Dabei wurde berücksichtigt, dass eine längere Frist bei einem internationalen Kauf wegen der räumlichen Distanz zwischen den Parteien, der unterschiedlichen Sprachen und Rechtssysteme eher gerechtfertigt ist als bei einem rein nationalen Vertrag. Andererseits durfte die Frist auch nicht zu lang bemessen sein, um nicht die Schutzfunktion der Verjährung zu gefährden.[4]

---

[1] Auf kaufrechtliche Ansprüche finden verschiedene Fristen Anwendung, wobei durch die Zweijahresfrist in Art. 5 I RL 1999/44/EG v. 25.5.1999 zu bestimmten Aspekten des Verbrauchsgüterkaufs und der Garantien für Verbrauchsgüter eine gewisse Annäherung an die Vierjahresfrist stattgefunden hat. Trotzdem bleiben Unterschiede bestehen: **Verjährung der Gewährleistungsrechte:** *Deutschland:* 2 Jahre ab Ablieferung (§ 438 I 3 BGB); *Schweiz:* 1 Jahr ab Ablieferung (Art. 210 I OR), ab 1.1.2013 gilt neu eine zweijährige Frist; bei Kulturgütern 1 Jahr nach Entdeckung des Mangels (Art. 210 Ibis OR; neu: Art. 210 III OR), dazu *Amstutz et al./Müller-Chen*, Art. 210, Rn. 6 ff.; *Österreich:* 3 Jahre für unbewegliche Sachen, 6 Monate für bewegliche Sachen ab Ablieferung (§ 933 ABGB); *Frankreich:* 2 Jahre ab Entdeckung des Mangels (Art. 1648 Cc); *Italien:* 1 Jahr ab Übergabe (Art. 1495 III Cc); *Spanien:* 6 Monate ab Übergabe (Art. 1490 Cc); *Niederlande:* Für Schadenersatz 5 Jahre ab Entdeckung des Schadens (Art. 3:310 BW); *Dänemark:* 3 Jahre (§ 3 I Neues dänisches Verjährungsgesetz (Gesetz Nr. 522 vom 6.6.2007, in der Fassung der letzten Änderung vom 19.12.2008, Gesetz Nr. 1336); die kurze Frist muss im „Zusammenhang mit der neuen allgemeinen Suspensionsregelung verstanden werden, wonach [...] die Frist erst bei Kenntnis (oder Kennen-Müssen) des Gläubigers [vom Anspruch bzw. der Person des Schuldners] zu laufen beginnt: *Fötschl*, RIW 2011, 696, 698). *England:* 6 Jahre ab Übergabe (sec. 5 Limitation Act 1980); *USA:* 4 Jahre ab Übergabe (§ 2–725 I UCC) (gemäss § 2–725 I UCC 2003 gilt folgendes: (1) Except as otherwise provided (...), an action for breach of any contract for sale must be commenced within the later of four years after the right of action has accrued under subsection (2) or (3) or one year after the breach was or should have been discovered, but no longer than five years after the right of action accrued.); **Verjährung weiterer kaufrechtlicher Ansprüche:** *Österreich, Dänemark:* 30 Jahre (§ 1478 ABGB, § 3 III 1 Neues dänisches Verjährungsgesetz für Personen- und Verunreinigungsschäden); *Niederlande:* 20 Jahre (Art. 3:306 BW); *Spanien:* 15 Jahre (Art. 1964 Cc); *Schweiz, Italien, Dänemark:* 10 Jahre (Art. 127 OR, Art. 2946 Cc, § 3 III 3 Neues dänisches Verjährungsgesetz für alle anderen Forderungen); *England:* 6 Jahre (sec. 5 Limitation Act 1980); *Frankreich:* 5 Jahre (Art. 2224 Cc); *USA:* 4 Jahre (§ 2–725 I UCC); *Deutschland:* 3 Jahre (§ 195 BGB); in einigen Staaten unterliegt der Kaufpreisanspruch beim Konsumentengeschäft einer besonderen Verjährungsfrist.

[2] O.R. VerjÜbk, S. 177 ff., Nr. 22 ff.; *Landfermann*, RabelsZ 39 (1975), 253, 266; *Sumulong*, 50 Philippine L. J. (1975), 318, 340 ff. Civil Law Staaten haben eher kurze Fristen (2 bis 5 Jahre), Common Law Staaten eher längere Fristen: *S. J. Yang*, S. 393; *Penda Matipé*, S. 477.

[3] *Loewe*, Einl VerjÜbk, S. 189; *Sumulong*, 50 Philippine L. J. (1975), 318, 338 f.

[4] O. R. VerjÜbk, S. 177, Nr. 26; Sekretariatskommentar VerjÜbk, Art. 8, Nr. 1.

II. Einheitsfrist

1. Allgemeines

2   Alle Ansprüche, die sich aus einem internationalen Kaufvertrag ergeben oder sich auf die Verletzung, Aufhebung oder Unwirksamkeit eines solchen Vertrages beziehen, unterliegen der vierjährigen Verjährungsfrist.[5] Art. 10 UNCITRAL-Entwurf sah zusätzlich eine zweijährige Frist für **Ansprüche aus** offenen und eine achtjährige Frist für Ansprüche aus verborgenen **Mängeln** vor.[6] Diese Fristen und ihre konkrete Ausgestaltung waren im ersten Ausschuss und im Plenum heftig umstritten.[7] Sie wurden schliesslich im Plenum zugunsten der Einheitsfrist wieder gestrichen.[8] Damit hängt die Länge der Verjährung nicht von der Unterscheidung zwischen einer Nicht- und Schlechtlieferung ab.

2. Verkürzung der Verjährungsfrist durch Ausschlussfrist

3   Im Zusammenhang mit der Verjährung von Ansprüchen aus der Vertragswidrigkeit der Ware ist an **Art. 39 II CISG** zu erinnern. Danach verliert der Käufer das Recht, sich auf die Vertragswidrigkeit zu berufen, wenn er sie nicht spätestens innerhalb von zwei Jahren nach tatsächlicher Übergabe der Ware dem Verkäufer anzeigt.[9] Diese zweijährige **Ausschlussfrist** beginnt im gleichen Zeitpunkt zu laufen wie die vierjährige Verjährungsfrist des Übereinkommens (Art. 10 II) und verkürzt die dem Käufer zur Verfügung stehende Zeit, seine Rechte aus der Vertragswidrigkeit der Ware geltend zu machen. Bei Anwendung des CISG verliert daher der Käufer bei verborgenen Sachmängeln die Vorteile, die ihm durch die vierjährige Frist des Übereinkommens erwachsen.[10]

Art. 9 [Allgemeine Regel zum Beginn der Verjährungsfrist]

(1) **Vorbehaltlich der Artikel 10, 11 und 12 beginnt die Verjährungsfrist an dem Tag zu laufen, an dem der Anspruch fällig wird.**

(2) **Der Beginn der Verjährungsfrist wird nicht hinausgeschoben**

a) **durch das Erfordernis einer Mitteilung an eine Partei im Sinn des Artikels 1 Absatz 2 oder**

b) **durch die Bestimmung in einer Schiedsvereinbarung, daß kein Recht entsteht, bevor ein Schiedsspruch ergangen ist.**

Übersicht

	Rn.
I. Abs. 1: Fälligkeit des Anspruches	1
II. Abs. 2: Keine Veränderung des Beginns der Verjährungsfrist	2

---

[5] Diese Frist bedeutet teils eine Verlängerung, teils eine Verkürzung nationaler Verjährungsfristen: *Zimmermann*, JZ 2000, 853, 863; *Enderlein/Maskow/Strohbach*, Art. 8 VerjÜbk, Anm. 1.; z.B. Mexiko 60 Tage, Portugal 1 Jahr bei Willensmängeln: *E. Muñoz*, S. 522; zur Kritik an der Vierjahresfrist s. *Herber*, BB 1991, Beil. 14, 7, 9; *Krapp*, 19 J. World Trade L. (1985), 343, 351; *Spiro*, in: *Hoyer/Posch*, 202 f.; gemäss Art. 14:201 PECL beträgt die regelmässige Verjährungsfrist 3 Jahre.

[6] O.R. VerjÜbk, S. 6; Kommentar UNCITRAL-Entwurf, O.R. VerjÜbk, S. 19 f., Art. 10, Nr. 1 f.; *Landfermann*, RabelsZ 39 (1975), 253, 266 ff.; *Enderlein/Maskow/Strohbach*, Art. 10 VerjÜbk, Anm. 3.; *Loewe*, Art. 10 VerjÜbk, S. 202; *ders.*, FS Zepos II, S. 415 f.; *Nestor*, FS Schmitthoff, S. 300; zur kritischen Haltung der Entwicklungsländer s. *Sumulong*, 50 Philippine L.J. (1975), 318, 343 ff.

[7] O.R. VerjÜbk, S. 59 ff., Nr. 67 ff.; *Landfermann*, RabelsZ 39 (1975), 253, 266 f.

[8] O.R. VerjÜbk, S. 119 ff., Nr. 17 ff.; S. 177 f., Nr. 28 ff.; S. 185 f., Nr. 1 ff.; S. 205 ff., Nr. 1 ff.; S. 209 ff., Nr. 1 ff.; *Nestor*, FS Schmitthoff, S. 300; *Krapp*, 19 J. World Trade L. (1985), 343, 353 f.; *Enderlein/Maskow/Strohbach*, Art. 8 VerjÜbk, Anm. 2.; *Loewe*, FS Zepos II, S. 415 f.; viele nationale Rechtsordnungen unterscheiden zwischen versteckten und offenen Mängeln: *E. Muñoz*, S. 523.

[9] Vgl. *Schwenzer*, Art. 39 Rn. 22 ff.

[10] *Krapp*, 19 J. World Trade L. (1985), 343, 352 f.; *Lookofsky*, Understanding the CISG in Scandinavia, S. 132.

I. Abs. 1: Fälligkeit des Anspruches

Die Verjährung der von der Konvention erfassten Ansprüche beginnt nach der international anerkannten Grundregel von Art. 9 I mit der **Fälligkeit** des Anspruches zu laufen.[1] Ob ein bestimmter Anspruch besteht, beurteilt sich nach dem anwendbaren Recht.[2] Das Gleiche gilt grundsätzlich für die Frage, wann ein Anspruch fällig wird. Von diesem Grundsatz weicht das Verjährungsübereinkommen jedoch in gewissen Fällen ab, um Schwierigkeiten bei der Bestimmung des Fälligkeitszeitpunktes zu beseitigen.[3]

1

II. Abs. 2: Keine Veränderung des Beginns der Verjährungsfrist

Art. 9 II hat die Aufgabe, Unterschiede im Beginn der Verjährungsfrist zu eliminieren. Es kommt häufig vor, dass das anwendbare Recht oder der internationale Kaufvertrag eine Partei verpflichtet, als Voraussetzung für den Erwerb oder die Ausübung eines Anspruches der anderen Partei eine **Mitteilung** zu machen. Damit wird zum Teil die Folge verbunden, dass die Verjährungsfrist erst mit Zugang der Mitteilung zu laufen beginnt.[4] Da diese **Ausschlussfristen** nach Art. 1 II vom Verjährungsübereinkommen nicht erfasst werden, würde der Beginn der Verjährungsfrist in diesen Fällen vom anwendbaren Recht abhängen. Um dies zu verhindern, bestimmt Art. 9 II lit. a), dass der Beginn der Verjährungsfrist durch eine solche Anzeige nicht hinausgeschoben wird.

2

In Schiedsvereinbarungen findet sich oft die Bestimmung, dass ein Anspruch erst entsteht und ein gerichtliches Verfahren erst eingeleitet werden kann, nachdem ein Schiedsverfahren durchgeführt wurde.[5] Diese sog. **Scott-Avery-Klausel** beeinflusst den Beginn der Verjährungsfrist gemäss Art. 9 II lit. b) nicht.[6]

3

Art. 10 [Spezielle Regeln: Vertragsverletzung, Vertragswidrigkeit, Täuschung]

(1) **Ein Anspruch aus einer Vertragsverletzung wird an dem Tag fällig, an dem die Vertragsverletzung begangen wird.**

(2) **Ein Anspruch aus einer Vertragswidrigkeit der Ware wird an dem Tag fällig, an dem die Ware dem Käufer tatsächlich übergeben oder ihre Annahme vom Käufer abgelehnt wird.**

(3) **Ein Anspruch auf Grund einer Täuschung, die vor oder bei Abschluß des Vertrages oder während seiner Erfüllung begangen wurde, wird an dem Tag fällig, an dem die Täuschung erkannt wurde oder vernünftigerweise hätte erkannt werden können.**

---

[1] Z. B. § 199 I BGB; Art. 130 I OR; § 1478 ABGB; Frankreich: Civ. 1, 27.10.1982, Bull. Civ. I, n°308 (*Mazeaud/Chabas*, 1209 f.); Art. 2935 ital. Cc; Art. 1969 span. Cc; Art. 3:313 BW; sec. 5 Limitation Act 1980; § 2–725 (1) UCC; rechtsvergleichend *Spiro*, Begrenzung privater Rechte, 36 ff.; *Lapiashvili*, S. 353, für das osteuropäische und zentralasiatische System; *Zimmermann*, JZ 2000, 853, 864 f.
[2] Sekretariatskommentar VerjÜbk, Art. 9, Nr. 2.
[3] Artt. 10–12 VerjÜbk; Sekretariatskommentar VerjÜbk, Art. 9, Nr. 1.
[4] Sekretariatskommentar VerjÜbk, Art. 9, Nr. 3; *Enderlein/Maskow/Strohbach*, Art. 9 VerjÜbk, Anm. 2.; a. A. *Staudinger/Magnus*, Anhang II zum CISG, Rn. 25.
[5] *Enderlein/Maskow/Strohbach*, Art. 9 VerjÜbk, Anm. 4.
[6] Die Klausel geht zurück auf den englischen Fall *Scott v. Avery* [1856] 5 H. L. C. 811; s. Chitty On Contracts, § 29–060; Sekretariatskommentar VerjÜbk, Art. 9, Nr. 4; *Enderlein/Maskow/Strohbach*, Art. 9 VerjÜbk, Anm. 4.

Übersicht

	Rn.
I. Allgemeines	1
II. Die Vorschrift im Einzelnen	2
1. Anspruch aus Vertragsverletzung	2
a) Begriff der Vertragsverletzung	2
b) Beginn der Verjährungsfrist	3
2. Anspruch aus Vertragswidrigkeit	4
a) Begriff der Vertragswidrigkeit	4
b) Beginn der Verjährungsfrist	5
aa) Tatsächliche Übergabe	5
bb) Ablehnung der Annahme der Ware	6
3. Anspruch auf Grund einer Täuschung	7
a) Tatbestand der Täuschung	7
b) Beginn der Verjährungsfrist	8

I. Allgemeines

1 Die Verjährungsfrist beginnt nach der Regel von Art. 9 mit der Fälligkeit des Anspruches zu laufen. Um Unsicherheiten auszuschalten, wann gewisse Anspruchsarten fällig werden, enthält Art. 10 besondere Bestimmungen für Ansprüche aus einer **Vertragsverletzung**, aus der **Vertragswidrigkeit der Ware** und auf Grund einer **Täuschung**.[1]

II. Die Vorschrift im Einzelnen

1. Anspruch aus Vertragsverletzung

2 **a) Begriff der Vertragsverletzung.** Das Übereinkommen definiert in Art. 1 III lit. d) den Begriff der Vertragsverletzung als *„Nichterfüllung des Vertrages durch eine Partei oder jede nicht vertragsgemässe Erfüllung".*[2] Dieses Verständnis lehnt sich an das anglo-amerikanische Konzept des *breach of contract* an,[3] das auch Eingang in das CISG gefunden hat.[4] Der **Tatbestand der Vertragsverletzung** ist demnach immer dann erfüllt, wenn die Leistung des Schuldners im Verhältnis zum vertraglichen Versprechen ein Defizit ausweist.[5] Ein Verschulden ist nicht erforderlich.[6] Der Einheitsbegriff der Vertragsverletzung erfährt allerdings eine Einschränkung, indem Abs. 2 die Vertragswidrigkeit der Ware ausklammert.

3 **b) Beginn der Verjährungsfrist.** Die Verjährung eines Anspruches aus einer **Vertragsverletzung** beginnt nach Abs. 1 im Zeitpunkt der Verletzungshandlung. Diese unter dem Vorbehalt von Abs. 2 für alle Vertragsverletzungen geltende Regel stammt aus dem Common Law,[7] den kontinentaleuropäischen Rechtsordnungen ist sie in dieser Allgemeinheit nicht geläufig.[8] Unterschiede ergeben sich insbesondere beim vertraglichen **Schadenersatzanspruch,** der nicht auf das Erfüllungsinteresse gerichtet ist. Dieser beginnt gemäß Art. 10 I am Tag zu laufen, an dem die Leistung hätte erbracht werden sollen, nach deutschem Recht hingegen erst, wenn der Anspruch entstanden ist, was neben der Erfül-

---

[1] Sekretariatskommentar VerjÜbk, Art. 10, Nr. 1.
[2] Zu den Ansprüchen aus Vertragsverletzung s. im einzelnen Artt. 45 ff. und 61 ff. CISG; weitere Beispiele finden sich im Sekretariatskommentar VerjÜbk, Art. 10, Nr. 2 (Bsp. 10A–10D).
[3] *Landfermann*, RabelsZ 39 (1975), 253, 266; *Krapp*, 19 J. World Trade L. (1985), 343, 350; *Sumulong*, 50 Philippine L. J. (1975), 318, 343.
[4] *Schwenzer*, Art. 79 Rn. 1; *Ziegler*, S. 204 f.; *Neumayer/Ming*, Art. 79, Anm. 1.
[5] Vgl. z. B. Art. 6: 74 Abs. 1 BW; Restatement (Second) of Contracts § 235 (2) (1981): „When performance of a duty under a contract is due, any nonperformance is a breach".
[6] *Loewe*, Art. 10 VerjÜbk, S. 201.
[7] Sec. 5 Limitation Act 1980; s. dazu *Cheshire/Fifoot/Furmston*, S. 707; *Chitty* On Contracts, § 29–028; § 2–725 II UCC, s. dazu *Chen*, 7 Int'l Q. (1995), 400, 415 ff.; *Hill*, 25 Tex. Int'l L. J. (1990), 1, 12 f.
[8] *Loewe*, Art. 10 VerjÜbk, S. 201; *Landfermann*, RabelsZ 39 (1975), 253, 266.

2. Anspruch aus Vertragswidrigkeit

a) Begriff der Vertragswidrigkeit. Art. 10 II geht wie Art. 35 CISG von einem **4** einheitlichen Begriff der Vertragswidrigkeit aus.[10] Er umfasst damit die Qualitätsabweichung, die Quantitätsabweichung, die Lieferung eines aliud und Verpackungsfehler.[11] Darunter fallen aber auch Rechtsmängel, die im CISG separat geregelt sind.[12]

b) Beginn der Verjährungsfrist. aa) Tatsächliche Übergabe. Die Verjährung eines **5** Anspruches aus einer Vertragswidrigkeit beginnt mit der tatsächlichen Übergabe der Ware an den Käufer oder mit der Ablehnung ihrer Annahme zu laufen.[13] Unter tatsächlicher Übergabe ist die **physische Aushändigung** der Ware an den Käufer zu verstehen.[14] Es spielt keine Rolle, ob die Gefahr oder das Eigentum an der Ware bereits auf den Käufer übergegangen ist oder ob die tatsächliche Übergabe vorzeitig, rechtzeitig oder verspätet erfolgt.[15] Vorausgesetzt wird für den Fristbeginn hingegen, dass der Käufer die Ware tatsächlich untersuchen kann.[16]

bb) Ablehnung der Annahme der Ware. Für den Fristbeginn wird die Ablehnung der **6** Annahme der Ware der tatsächlichen Übergabe an den Käufer in Abs. 2 gleichgestellt. Der Beginn der Verjährungsfrist wird nicht verändert, wenn der Käufer zu einem späteren Zeitpunkt die Ware doch noch annimmt.[17]

3. Anspruch auf Grund einer Täuschung

a) Tatbestand der Täuschung. Tatbestand und Rechtsfolgen von Ansprüchen auf **7** Grund einer Täuschung **vor** oder **bei Abschluss** eines Vertrages berühren die Gültigkeit des Vertrages und werden nicht vom CISG, sondern vom unvereinheitlichten nationalen Recht erfasst.[18] Auch die **während** der **Erfüllung** begangene Täuschung, z. B. hinsichtlich der Qualität der Ware, fällt unter Art. 10 III.[19] Eine Täuschung des Gläubigers während der Laufzeit der Verjährung kann unter Umständen eine Verlängerung der Verjährungsfrist nach Art. 21 zur Folge haben.[20]

b) Beginn der Verjährungsfrist. Ein Anspruch auf Grund einer Täuschung wird erst **8** bei **Kenntnis,** bzw. **Erkennbarkeit** der Täuschung durch den Vertragspartner fällig.[21] Ob

---

[9] § 199 I (1). BGB: *Palandt/Heinrichs*, § 199, Rn. 14 ff.
[10] Sekretariatskommentar VerjÜbk, Art. 10, Nr. 3; s. ausführlich zur Vertragswidrigkeit *Schwenzer*, Art. 35 Rn. 6 ff.
[11] Artt. 41 f. CISG.
[12] *Enderlein/Maskow/Strohbach*, Art. 10 VerjÜbk, Anm. 3.; *Loewe*, Art. 10 VerjÜbk, S. 202.
[13] Als Beginn der Frist bei defekter Ware gelten in nationalen Rechtsordnungen das Lieferdatum (z. B. Peru, Spanien), „the date of effective, real delivery" (z. B. Ecuador, El Salvador), das Datum, an dem der Mangel ersichtlich wurde (z. B. Argentinien) oder das Datum des Vertragsschlusses (z. B. Portugal): *E. Muñoz*, S. 524. Rechtsvergleichend *Krapp*, Verjährung, S. 96 ff.
[14] Sekretariatskommentar VerjÜbk, Art. 10, Nr. 4; *Hill*, 25 Tex. Int'l L.J. (1990), 1, 16; *Loewe*, Art. 10 VerjÜbk, S. 203; *Smit*, 23 Am. J. Comp. L. (1975), 337, 341; *E. Muñoz*, S. 526; so auch Art. 39 II CISG, s. dazu *Schwenzer*, Art. 39 Rn. 24.
[15] Sekretariatskommentar VerjÜbk, Art. 10, Nr. 4 (Bsp. 10E); *Enderlein/Maskow/Strohbach*, Art. 10 VerjÜbk, Anm. 4.; *Hill*, 25 Tex. Int'l L.J. (1990), 1, 16.
[16] Sekretariatskommentar VerjÜbk, Art. 10, Nr. 4; *Loewe*, Art. 10 VerjÜbk, S. 202; *Enderlein/Maskow/Strohbach*, Art. 10 VerjÜbk, Anm. 4.; *Smit*, 23 Am. J. Comp. L. (1975), 337, 341.
[17] Sekretariatskommentar VerjÜbk, Art. 10, Nr. 6.
[18] Art. 4 S. 2 lit. a) CISG (*Ferrari*, Art. 4 Rn. 25); z. B. §§ 123 f. BGB; § 870 ABGB; Artt. 28, 30 f. OR; Art. 1116 frz. Cc; Art. 1439 ital. Cc; sec. 32 (1) Limitation Act 1980; *Enderlein/Maskow/Strohbach*, Art. 10 VerjÜbk, Anm. 5.; *Loewe*, Art. 10 VerjÜbk, S. 203.
[19] *Enderlein/Maskow/Strohbach*, Art. 10 VerjÜbk, Anm. 6.
[20] S. Art. 21 Rn. 2 f.; *Smit*, 23 Am. J. Comp. L. (1975), 337, 342.
[21] So wie Art. 10 III VerjÜbk sec. 32 (1) Limitation Act 1980, s. auch *Peco Arts, Inc. v. Hazlitt Galley, Ltd.* [1983] 3 All E. R. 193; im deutschen sowie auch im argentinischen und venezolanischen (*E. Muñoz*, S. 522)

der Getäuschte auf Grund der konkreten Umstände des Einzelfalles eine Täuschung vernünftigerweise hätte erkennen können, soll nicht zu streng beurteilt werden, da dieser Zeitpunkt in der Regel umstritten und nicht einfach zu beweisen ist.[22]

Art. 11 [Ausdrückliche Garantie]

Hat der Verkäufer hinsichtlich der verkauften Ware eine ausdrückliche Garantie für einen gewissen Zeitraum gegeben, der kalendermäßig oder anderweitig bestimmt sein kann, so beginnt die Verjährungsfrist für einen Anspruch aus der Garantie an dem Tag zu laufen, an dem der Käufer dem Verkäufer den Umstand anzeigt, auf den er seinen Anspruch gründet, spätestens jedoch am Tag des Ablaufs der Garantiefrist.

Übersicht

	Rn.
I. Allgemeines	1
II. Die Vorschrift im Einzelnen	2
1. Garantiefrist	2
2. Beginn der Verjährungsfrist	3

I. Allgemeines

1 Art. 11 ist eine Ausnahme zur Regel von Art. 10 II, wonach bei einem Anspruch aus einer Vertragswidrigkeit die Frist mit der tatsächlichen Übergabe zu laufen beginnt. Im internationalen Handel übernimmt der Verkäufer vielfach eine ausdrückliche **Garantie** *(express undertaking/garantie expresse)* für die Ware.[1]

II. Die Vorschrift im Einzelnen

1. Garantiefrist

2 Die Garantie ist das Versprechen des Verkäufers, dass die Ware für eine bestimmte Zeit für den üblichen oder für einen bestimmten Zweck geeignet bleibt oder besondere Eigenschaften oder Merkmale behalten wird.[2] Sie muss **ausdrücklich** erfolgen und kalendermässig oder anderweitig bestimmt sein. Es genügt nach Art. 11, wenn die Garantie für einen **gewissen,** d. h. unbestimmten Zeitraum gegeben wird. Die Dauer ist in diesen Fällen nach den Umständen des Einzelfalls zu bemessen.[3]

2. Beginn der Verjährungsfrist

3 Die Verjährungsfrist beginnt beim Bestehen einer ausdrücklichen Garantie nicht mit der tatsächlichen Übergabe, sondern mit der Verständigung des Verkäufers über den Grund des Anspruches, d. h. mit der **Mängelrüge** des Käufers, zu laufen. Entscheidend ist der Tag der **Absendung** der Anzeige des Mangels, da diese nicht empfangsbedürftig ist.[4] Erfolgt innerhalb der Garantiefrist keine Anzeige des Mangels, z. B. weil er verborgen ist, beginnt die Verjährungsfrist mit dem Ablauf der Garantiezeit.[5]

Recht beginnt die Anfechtungsfrist wegen Täuschung erst bei positiver Kenntnis zu laufen (§ 124 II 1 BGB), s. *Palandt/Heinrichs*, § 124, Rn. 2 Einige nationale Regelungen (z. B. Brasilien und Chile) sehen aber einen Beginn der Frist ab Vertragsschluss vor, s. *E. Muñoz*, S. 522.

[22] *Krapp,* 19 J. World Trade L. (1985), 343, 350.
[1] *Enderlein/Maskow/Strohbach,* Art. 11 VerjÜbk, Anm. 1.
[2] Zur Garantie s. *Schwenzer,* Art. 36 Rn. 7 ff.
[3] *Schwenzer,* Art. 36 Rn. 9 f.
[4] *Enderlein/Maskow/Strohbach,* Art. 11 VerjÜbk, Anm. 2.; so auch § 377 IV HGB; Art. 27 CISG.
[5] Die nationalen Rechtsordnungen weichen von der Regel in Art. 11 zum Teil ab; maßgebend ist grundsätzlich der Zeitpunkt der Ablieferung der Ware: Deutschland: § 438 II BGB, dazu *Palandt/Weidenkaff,* § 438,

Art. 12 [Aufhebung des Vertrages vor Erfüllung; Sukzessivlieferungsverträge]

(1) Erklärt eine Partei in einem Fall, der in dem auf den Vertrag anzuwendenden Recht vorgesehen ist, vor dem für die Erfüllung festgesetzten Tag die Aufhebung des Vertrages, so beginnt die Verjährungsfrist an dem Tag zu laufen, an dem die Erklärung an die andere Partei gerichtet wird. Wird die Aufhebung des Vertrages nicht vor dem für die Erfüllung festgesetzten Tag erklärt, so beginnt die Verjährungsfrist erst an diesem Tag zu laufen.

(2) Die Verjährungsfrist für einen Anspruch aus der Verletzung eines Vertrages, der mehrere aufeinanderfolgende Lieferungen oder Ratenzahlungen vorsieht, beginnt für jede einzelne Lieferung oder Rate an dem Tag zu laufen, an dem die betreffende Vertragsverletzung eingetreten ist. Erklärt eine Partei nach dem auf den Vertrag anzuwendenden Recht wegen dieser Vertragsverletzung die Aufhebung des Vertrages, so beginnt die Verjährungsfrist für alle Lieferungen oder Raten an dem Tag zu laufen, an dem die Erklärung an die andere Partei gerichtet wird.

Übersicht

	Rn.
I. Vertragsaufhebung vor der Erfüllung (Abs. 1)	1
1. Voraussetzungen	1
a) Allgemeines	1
b) Aufhebungserklärung	2
2. Beginn der Verjährungsfrist	3
II. Ansprüche aus einem Sukzessivlieferungsvertrag (Abs. 2)	4
1. Vertragsverletzung hinsichtlich einer Einzelleistung	4
2. Aufhebung des Vertrages	5

I. Vertragsaufhebung vor der Erfüllung (Abs. 1)

1. Voraussetzungen

a) Allgemeines. Die Anwendung der Vorschrift von Art. 12 I setzt voraus, dass der 1 Gläubiger nach dem anwendbaren Recht berechtigt ist, bei einer Vertragsverletzung den Vertrag schon vor der Fälligkeit aufzuheben. Lehnt der Schuldner z. B. bereits vor Fälligkeit die Erfüllung seiner Leistung ab (**antizipierter Vertragsbruch**, Art. 72 CISG), steht dem Gläubiger in den meisten Rechtsordnungen unter bestimmten Voraussetzungen das Recht zu, sich vom Vertrag zu lösen.[1]

b) Aufhebungserklärung. Das Verjährungsübereinkommen knüpft die Anwendbarkeit 2 von Art. 12 I daran, dass die Vertragsaufhebung durch eine **unmissverständliche Erklärung** ausgeübt wird.[2] Sieht das massgebliche Recht eine Vertragsaufhebung ipso iure vor, richtet sich der Beginn der Verjährungsfrist nach Art. 10 I.[3]

2. Beginn der Verjährungsfrist

Wurde eine Aufhebungserklärung abgegeben, beginnt die Verjährungsfrist am Tag der 3 **Absendung** der Erklärung zu laufen.[4] Erklärt die betroffene Partei jedoch die Aufhebung

---

Rn. 13 ff.; *Magnus*, RIW 2002, 577, 580 ff.; Schweiz: Art. 210 I OR, dazu *Amstutz et al./Müller-Chen*, Art. 210 OR, Rn. 11; USA: § 2–725 (3) (c) UCC, dazu *Hill*, 25 Tex. Int'l L. J. (1990), 1, 17; *Chen*, 7 Int'l Q. (1995), 400, 416 ff.

[1] Zum deutschen Recht vgl. *Emmerich*, S. § 22 I 2; zum englischen Recht s. *Cheshire/Fifoot/Furmston*, S. 596; zum UCC s. *Hill*, 25 Tex. Int'l L. J. (1990), 1, 17 ff.; zum CISG s. *Fountoulakis*, Art. 72 Rn. 11 ff.

[2] So generell im UN-Kaufrechtsübereinkommen, s. *Müller-Chen*, Art. 49 Rn. 24; Sekretariatskommentar VerjÜbk, Art. 12, Nr. 5; *Enderlein/Maskow/Strohbach*, Art. 12 VerjÜbk, Anm. 4.; *Loewe*, Art. 12 VerjÜbk, S. 204.

[3] Sekretariatskommentar VerjÜbk, Art. 12, Nr. 5.

[4] S. auch Art. 27 CISG; *Enderlein/Maskow/Strohbach*, Art. 12 VerjÜbk, Anm. 3.

des Vertrages nicht vor dem Erfüllungszeitpunkt, beginnt die Verjährung in Übereinstimmung mit Art. 10 I erst mit dem Zeitpunkt der Vertragsverletzung zu laufen, der mit dem Zeitpunkt der Fälligkeit des Anspruches zusammenfällt.[5]

II. Ansprüche aus einem Sukzessivlieferungsvertrag (Abs. 2)

1. Vertragsverletzung hinsichtlich einer Einzelleistung

4   Die Verjährung von Ansprüchen, die sich aus der Verletzung einer Teilleistung ergeben, beginnt in Übereinstimmung mit Art. 10 I und II am Tag der jeweiligen Verletzung des **Sukzessivlieferungsvertrages**.[6]

2. Aufhebung des Vertrages

5   Ob und unter welchen Voraussetzungen eine Partei auf Grund der Verletzung einer **Teilleistung** den Vertrag aufheben kann und ob diese Aufhebung ex nunc oder ex tunc wirkt, wird vom Verjährungsübereinkommen nicht geregelt. Massgebend ist dafür das auf den Sukzessivlieferungsvertrag anwendbare Recht.[7]

6   Die Frist beginnt für alle Lieferungen oder Raten mit der Absendung der Erklärung der Vertragsaufhebung zu laufen. Dadurch wird ein einheitlicher Beginn der Verjährungsfrist für **alle** Teilleistungen des Vertrages bewirkt, was eine Verlängerung der Verjährungsfrist für schon erbrachte Teilleistungen zur Folge hat.[8] Ob Art. 12 allerdings schon verjährte Ansprüche aus der Verletzung einer früheren Teilleistung wiederaufleben lässt, erscheint zweifelhaft, da sonst bei längerfristigen Dauerschuldverträgen die zehnjährige Höchstfrist von Art. 23 unter Umständen erheblich überschritten werden könnte.[9]

7   In Art. 12 ist nicht geregelt, wann die Verjährungsfrist zu laufen beginnt, wenn eine Partei nur die Aufhebung des Vertrages in Bezug auf eine **Teillieferung** erklärt.[10] Analog zur Lösung von Art. 12 II ist für diesen Fall anzunehmen, dass die Verjährungsfrist mit der Absendung der Erklärung der Vertragsaufhebung zu laufen beginnt.[11]

Unterbrechung und Verlängerung der Verjährungsfrist

Art. 13 [Gerichtsverfahren]

Die Verjährungsfrist wird unterbrochen, wenn der Gläubiger eine Handlung vornimmt, die nach dem Recht des angerufenen Gerichtes als Einleitung eines gerichtlichen Verfahrens gegen den Schuldner oder als Geltendmachung des Anspruchs in einem bereits gegen den Schuldner eingeleiteten solchen Verfahren zu dem Zweck, Befriedigung oder Anerkennung des Anspruchs zu erlangen, angesehen wird.

---

[5] Sekretariatskommentar VerjÜbk, Art. 12, Nr. 2 (Bsp. 12A): Der am 1. Juni geschlossene Kaufvertrag setzt den Liefertermin auf den 1. Dezember fest. Am 1. Juli informiert der Verkäufer den Käufer, dass er ihm die vertraglich versprochene Ware nicht liefern wird. Wartet der Käufer mit seiner Aufhebungserklärung bis zum 1. Dezember zu, beginnt die Verjährung dann zu laufen, da der Verkäufer erst ab diesem Zeitpunkt in Verzug gerät, d. h. eine Vertragsverletzung begeht.
[6] Sekretariatskommentar VerjÜbk, Art. 12, Nr. 6 (Bsp. 12B); zum Common Law s. *Jaffé*, S. 119.
[7] Z. B. Art. 72 II und III CISG, s. *Fountoulakis*, Art. 72 Rn. 17 ff., Art. 73 Rn. 29 ff.; zu § 2–612 UCC s. *Hill*, 25 Tex. Int'l L. J. (1990), 1, 13 ff.
[8] Sekretariatskommentar VerjÜbk, Art. 12, Nr. 7 f.; *Loewe*, Art. 12 VerjÜbk, S. 205.
[9] Zweifelnd auch *Enderlein/Maskow/Strohbach*, Art. 12 VerjÜbk, Anm. 8.
[10] S. *Fountoulakis*, Art. 73 Rn. 7 ff.
[11] So auch *Babiak*, 6 Temp. Int'l & Comp. L. J. (1992), 113, 138.

Übersicht

	Rn.
I. Voraussetzungen der Unterbrechung der Verjährungsfrist	1
1. Allgemeines	1
2. Einleitung eines gerichtlichen Verfahrens	2
3. Geltendmachung eines Anspruches in einem laufenden Verfahren	3
II. Wirkung der Einleitung eines gerichtlichen Verfahrens	4

I. Voraussetzungen der Unterbrechung der Verjährungsfrist

1. Allgemeines

Das Verjährungsübereinkommen sieht vor, dass bei Eintritt bestimmter Ereignisse oder Zustände die Verjährungsfrist nicht weiterläuft *(„ceases to run")*. Obwohl Tatbestand und Wirkungen dieses Vorganges nicht exakt der in vielen Rechtsordnungen bekannten **Unterbrechung** oder **Hemmung** der Verjährung entsprechen,[1] wurde in der deutschen Übersetzung auf den Begriff des „Nichtweiterlaufens" wegen seiner sprachlichen Schwerfälligkeit verzichtet. Statt dessen findet sich der Begriff der „Unterbrechung", der aber nicht mit einem bestimmten nationalen System gleichgesetzt werden darf.

2. Einleitung eines gerichtlichen Verfahrens

In Übereinstimmung mit den meisten nationalen Rechtsordnungen bestimmt Art. 13, dass die Einleitung eines gerichtlichen Verfahrens die Verjährungsfrist unterbricht.[2] Es ist der anwendbaren lex fori zu entnehmen, wie und wann die entsprechenden prozessualen Handlungen vorgenommen werden müssen, um das Verfahren einzuleiten.[3] Die **gehörige Fortsetzung** der Klage wird im Verjährungsübereinkommen im Gegensatz etwa zum deutschen und österreichischen Recht nicht verlangt.[4] Es wird lediglich gefordert, dass die prozessuale Handlung zum Zweck der Geltendmachung oder Anerkennung eines Anspruchs vorgenommen wird und nicht nur zum Zweck der Unterbrechung der Verjährungsfrist.[5]

3. Geltendmachung eines Anspruches in einem laufenden Verfahren

Der Einleitung eines gerichtlichen Verfahrens steht die Geltendmachung eines Anspruches in einem bereits laufenden Verfahren gleich. Ob, unter welchen Voraussetzungen und in welchem Zeitpunkt der Gläubiger seine Klage erweitern darf, hängt von den Vorschriften des Rechtes des angerufenen Gerichtes ab.[6]

---

[1] *Landfermann*, RabelsZ 39 (1975), 253, 269; *Enderlein/Maskow/Strohbach*, Art. 13 VerjÜbk, Vorbem.; *Krapp*, 19 J. World Trade L. (1985), 343, 355; *Nestor*, FS Schmitthoff, S. 301; kritisch *Smit*, 23 Am.J. Comp. L. (1975), 337, 343; zur Unterbrechung s. rechtsvergleichend *Spiro*, Begrenzung privater Rechte, S. 286 ff. und *Schwenzer/Hachem/Kee*, Rn. 51.39 ff.

[2] Vgl. z. B. §§ 204 I 1 BGB; Art. 135 Ziff. 2 OR; § 1497 ABGB; Artt. 2241 ff. frz. Cc; Art. 2943 I ital. Cc; Art. 1973 span. Cc; Art. 3:316 Abs. 1 BW.

[3] Z. B. Klageerhebung, Zustellung einer gerichtlichen Anordnung oder der Klage, Beantragung einstweiligen Rechtsschutzes (§ 203 (b) (3) N. Y.-CPLR), Ladung zu einem amtlichen Sühneversuch oder Antrag auf Erlass eines Zahlungsbefehles; Sekretariatskommentar VerjÜbk, Art. 13, Nr. 2; *Jaffé*, S. 127 ff.; *Enderlein/Maskow/Strohbach*, Art. 13 VerjÜbk, Anm. 1.; *Nestor*, FS Schmitthoff, S. 301; *Loewe*, Art. 13 VerjÜbk, S. 205; zum deutschen Recht s. § 203 BGB (Verhandlungen zwischen dem Gläubiger und dem Schuldner führen bei allen Ansprüchen zur Hemmung der Verjährung).

[4] § 204 II BGB; § 1497 ABGB.

[5] *Loewe*, Art. 13 VerjÜbk, S. 205.

[6] Sekretariatskommentar VerjÜbk, Art. 13, Nr. 3; *Enderlein/Maskow/Strohbach*, Art. 13 VerjÜbk, Anm. 2.

II. Wirkung der Einleitung eines gerichtlichen Verfahrens

4   Die Einleitung eines gerichtlichen Verfahrens oder die Geltendmachung eines Anspruches in einem laufenden Verfahren bewirkt die **Unterbrechung** der Verjährungsfrist: Die Frist läuft nicht weiter.[7] Damit beginnt aber nicht eine neue Verjährungsfrist, so dass die Unterbrechung in ihrer Wirkung der Hemmung der Verjährungsfrist ähnelt.[8]

Art. 14 [Schiedsverfahren]

(1) **Haben die Parteien vereinbart, ihre Streitigkeit einem Schiedsgericht zu unterbreiten, so wird die Verjährungsfrist unterbrochen, sobald eine der Parteien das schiedsrichterliche Verfahren auf die in der Schiedsvereinbarung oder in dem auf das Verfahren anzuwendenden Recht vorgesehene Weise einleitet.**

(2) **Sind hierüber keinerlei Bestimmungen vorhanden, so gilt das schiedsrichterliche Verfahren als an dem Tag eingeleitet, an dem der Antrag, den strittigen Anspruch dem Schiedsgericht zu unterbreiten, am Ort des gewöhnlichen Aufenthalts oder der Niederlassung der anderen Partei oder bei Fehlen eines solchen Ortes am Ort ihres letzten bekannten Aufenthalts oder ihrer letzten bekannten Niederlassung zugestellt wird.**

Übersicht

	Rn.
I. Allgemeines	1
II. Zeitpunkt der Einleitung des Schiedsverfahrens	3

I. Allgemeines

1   Die Unterbrechung der Verjährung durch Einleitung eines **schiedsrichterlichen Verfahrens** setzt voraus, dass die Parteien in ihrem Kaufvertrag eine Schiedsklausel vereinbart haben oder dass der Schuldner sich auf das Verfahren einlässt.[1]

2   Art. 14 II entspricht Art. 3 II der UNCITRAL-Schiedsgerichtsregeln vom 15. Dezember 1976 bzw. Art. 21 des UNCITRAL-Musterschiedsverfahrensgesetzes 1985 in der Fassung 2006.[2]

---

[7] Die nationalen Rechtsordnungen unterscheiden sich hinsichtlich der Wirkung der Unterbrechung: Neubeginn der Frist nach Beendigung der Unterbrechung bzw. Hemmung: § 212 BGB; § 1497 ABGB (*Koziol/Welser/Kletečka*, Band I, S. 232); Civ. 1, 5.6.1973, Bull. Civ. I, n° 193; Art. 2945 II ital. Cc; die neue Verjährung beginnt neu unmittelbar mit Eintritt des Unterbrechungsgrundes: Artt. 137 f. OR (*Spiro*, Begrenzung privater Rechte, S. 377 ff.) und grundsätzlich Art. 3:319 Abs. 1 BW; die Frist läuft trotz Klageerhebung weiter: § 2–725 III UCC (*Hill*, 25 Tex. Int'l L.J. (1990), 1, 20 (Fn. 105)); *Nelson*, 24 Int'l Law. (1990), 583, 591; *Smit*, 23 Am.J. Comp. L. (1975), 337, 342); rechtsvergleichende Übersicht bei *Burr*, S. 86; *Sumulong*, 50 Philippine L.J. (1975), 318, 348; *Zimmermann*, JZ 2000, 853, 855 f.

[8] *Enderlein/Maskow/Strohbach*, Art. 13 VerjÜbk, Vorbem.

[1] Obligatorisch, d. h. ohne Parteivereinbarung durchzuführende Schiedsverfahren fallen nicht unter Art. 14, sondern unter Art. 13: Sekretariatskommentar VerjÜbk, Art. 14, Nr. 1 (Fn. 1); *Enderlein/Maskow/Strohbach*, Art. 14 VerjÜbk, Anm. 3.

[2] Art. 3 II: „Arbitral proceedings shall be deemed to commence on the date on which the notice of arbitration is received by the respondent"; Art. 21: „Unless otherwise agreed by the parties, the arbitral proceedings in respect of a particular dispute commence on the date on which a request for that dispute to be referred to arbitration is received by the respondent"; anders Art. 4 II ICC-Schiedsgerichtsordnung („Der Tag, an dem die Klage beim Sekretariat eingeht, gilt in jedem Fall als Beginn des Schiedsverfahrens").

II. Zeitpunkt der Einleitung des Schiedsverfahrens

Gemäß Art. 14 I entscheidet primär die **Schiedsvereinbarung** und subsidiär das auf das Schiedsverfahren anzuwendende Recht *(lex arbitri),* wie das schiedsrichterliche Verfahren einzuleiten ist.[3] 3

Enthält weder die Schiedsvereinbarung noch das anwendbare Recht eine Vorschrift darüber, wann das Schiedsverfahren als eingeleitet anzusehen ist, wird die **Zustellung des Antrages,** den strittigen Anspruch dem Schiedsgericht zu unterbreiten, für massgebend erklärt. Entscheidend ist somit weder die Kenntnisnahme noch das blosse Absenden, sondern die Zustellung des Antrags am Ort des gewöhnlichen Aufenthaltes oder der Niederlassung der anderen Partei. Der Antragsteller trägt damit das Risiko der Übermittlung.[4] 4

Art. 15 [Rechtsverfahren wegen Todes, Konkurses oder ähnlichem]

In allen anderen als den in den Artikeln 13 und 14 bezeichneten Rechtsverfahren einschließlich solcher, die eingeleitet werden wegen
a) des Todes oder der Geschäftsunfähigkeit des Schuldners,
b) des Konkurses oder einer Zahlungsunfähigkeit des Schuldners, die dessen gesamtes Vermögen betrifft, oder
c) der Auflösung oder der Liquidation einer Gesellschaft, einer Vereinigung oder eines anderen Rechtsträgers, wenn es sich dabei um den Schuldner handelt,
wird die Verjährungsfrist unterbrochen, wenn der Gläubiger seinen Anspruch in einem solchen Verfahren geltend macht, um Befriedigung oder Anerkennung des Anspruchs zu erlangen, es sei denn, daß das für das Verfahren geltende Recht etwas anderes bestimmt.

Übersicht

	Rn.
I. Einleitung eines Rechtsverfahrens zur Verjährungsunterbrechung	1
II. Vorrang des nationalen Rechtes	2

I. Einleitung eines Rechtsverfahrens zur Verjährungsunterbrechung

Neben den gerichtlichen oder schiedsrichterlichen Verfahren gibt es **weitere Rechtsverfahren,** welche die Verjährungsfrist unterbrechen.[1] Art. 15 zählt beispielhaft[2] einige solcher Verfahren auf, in denen der Gläubiger seine Ansprüche aus einem internationalen Kaufvertrag geltend machen kann. Es wird nicht vorausgesetzt, dass der Gläubiger das Rechtsverfahren einleitet, dieses kann auch von Amtes wegen oder vom Schuldner eingeleitet werden.[3*] Im letzteren Fall wird die Verjährung aber erst unterbrochen, wenn der Gläubiger seinen Anspruch zum Zweck der Befriedigung oder Anerkennung geltend macht. 1

---

[3] *Enderlein/Maskow/Strohbach,* Art. 14 VerjÜbk, Anm. 2.
[4] Sekretariatskommentar VerjÜbk, Art. 14, Nr. 2; *Enderlein/Maskow/Strohbach,* Art. 14 VerjÜbk, Anm. 5.
[1] Unter den Begriff des Rechtsverfahrens fallen nach der Legaldefinition von Art. 1 III lit. e) auch Verwaltungsverfahren, nicht jedoch Strafprozesse.
[2] Vgl. den französischen Originaltext: „(...) Il en est ainsi *notamment* des procédures introduites à l'occasion (...)"; Sekretariatskommentar VerjÜbk, Art. 15, Nr. 1; *Enderlein/Maskow/Strohbach,* Art. 15 VerjÜbk, Anm. 3.
[3*] Sekretariatskommentar VerjÜbk, Art. 15, Nr. 1; *Loewe,* Art. 15 VerjÜbk, S. 207.

II. Vorrang des nationalen Rechtes

2 Den aufgezählten Rechtsverfahren ist gemeinsam, dass sie nicht nur Ansprüche zwischen den Kaufvertragsparteien, sondern in erheblichem Ausmaß auch Rechte **Dritter** betreffen, die mit dem internationalen Kaufvertrag unter Umständen nur in einem entfernten Zusammenhang stehen. Diese Personen verlassen sich auf die Geltung der für sie gebräuchlichen nationalen Vorschriften, insbesondere auf die Bestimmungen zur Frage, in welcher Frist Ansprüche angemeldet werden müssen. Aus diesem Grund gewährt das Verjährungsübereinkommen dem auf diese Verfahren anwendbaren Recht den **Vorrang**.[3] Bestimmt z. B. das auf die Zwangsvollstreckung anwendbare Recht, dass ein Gläubiger seinen Anspruch verliert, wenn er ihn nicht innerhalb eines bestimmten Zeitraumes angemeldet hat, kann er sich nicht darauf berufen, dass die Geltendmachung des Anspruches nach Art. 15 die Verjährungsfrist unterbricht, wenn er den nach dem anwendbaren Recht massgeblichen Zeitpunkt verpasst hat.[4]

Art. 16 [Gegenansprüche]

Für die Zwecke der Artikel 13, 14 und 15 gilt eine Handlung, durch die ein Gegenanspruch geltend gemacht wird, als an demselben Tag vorgenommen wie die Handlung, durch die der Anspruch geltend gemacht wurde, gegen den der Gegenanspruch erhoben wird, sofern sich Anspruch und Gegenanspruch auf denselben Vertrag oder auf mehrere im Rahmen desselben Geschäftes abgeschlossene Verträge beziehen.

Übersicht

	Rn.
I. Geltendmachung eines Gegenanspruches	1
1. Allgemeines	1
2. Form	2
3. Konnexität	3
II. Zeitpunkt der Unterbrechung der Verjährungsfrist	4

I. Geltendmachung eines Gegenanspruches

1. Allgemeines

1 In Art. 16 werden Anspruch und Gegenanspruch verjährungsrechtlich gleichgeschaltet.[1]

2. Form

2 Das Verjährungsübereinkommen enthält keine Bestimmungen darüber, in welcher Form der **Gegenanspruch** in einem Rechtsverfahren nach Artt. 13–15 zu erheben ist. Massgebend ist insofern das auf das Verfahren anwendbare Recht.[2] In der Regel wird der Gegenanspruch durch eine Widerklage oder eine Aufrechnungserklärung geltend gemacht. Die Aufrechnung fällt jedoch nicht unter Art. 16, sondern ist in Art. 25 II speziell geregelt.

---

[3] Sekretariatskommentar VerjÜbk, Art. 15, Nr. 2; *Enderlein/Maskow/Strohbach*, Art. 15 VerjÜbk, Anm. 5.
[4] Weitere Beispiele in: Sekretariatskommentar VerjÜbk, Art. 15, Bsp. 15B-15C.
[1] *Loewe*, Art. 16 VerjÜbk, S. 207.
[2] Sekretariatskommentar VerjÜbk, Art. 16, Nr. 1 (Fn. 1).

3. Konnexität

Die verjährungsrechtliche Wirkung von Art. 16 tritt nur ein, wenn zwischen Anspruch und Gegenanspruch ein sachlicher Zusammenhang besteht. Konnexität ist gegeben, wenn die Forderungen aus demselben **Vertrag** oder zumindest aus mehreren im Rahmen desselben **Geschäftes** abgeschlossenen Verträgen stammen. Nicht gefordert ist hingegen, dass die Forderungen denselben Inhalt haben. Der englische Originaltext, der von *„transaction"* spricht, liefert einen Hinweis darauf, dass mit „Geschäft" nicht die gesamte geschäftliche Beziehung zwischen den Parteien gemeint ist, sondern ein sachlich und zeitlich begrenzter geschäftlicher Vorgang.[3]

II. Zeitpunkt der Unterbrechung der Verjährungsfrist

Besteht ein sachlicher Zusammenhang zwischen Anspruch und Gegenanspruch, tritt für den Gegenanspruch eine **rückwirkende** Unterbrechung der Verjährungsfrist ein.[4] Ist der Gegenanspruch im Zeitpunkt der Erhebung der Hauptklage nicht verjährt, kann die Widerklage demnach selbst dann erhoben werden, wenn die Forderung inzwischen verjährt ist. Diese Lösung hat den Vorteil, dass dem Erstbeklagten Zeit für Vergleichsverhandlungen verbleibt.[5]

Art. 17 [Verfahren ohne Sachentscheidung]

(1) **Ist innerhalb der Verjährungsfrist ein Anspruch in einem Rechtsverfahren nach Artikel 13, 14, 15 oder 16 geltend gemacht, dieses Verfahren jedoch ohne eine Entscheidung in der Sache selbst beendet worden, so gilt die Verjährungsfrist als nicht unterbrochen.**

(2) **Wenn bei Beendigung dieses Verfahrens die Verjährungsfrist abgelaufen ist oder nur noch weniger als ein Jahr zu laufen hat, steht dem Gläubiger eine Frist von einem Jahr, gerechnet vom Tag der Beendigung des Verfahrens, zu.**

Übersicht

	Rn.
I. Keine Unterbrechung der Verjährungsfrist (Abs. 1)	1
II. Nachfrist (Abs. 2)	2

I. Keine Unterbrechung der Verjährungsfrist (Abs. 1)

Die Einleitung eines gerichtlichen, schiedsrichterlichen oder sonstigen Rechtsverfahrens oder die Geltendmachung eines Gegenanspruches bewirkt gemäss Artt. 13 bis 16, dass die Verjährungsfrist nicht weiterläuft. Die rechtzeitige Einleitung eines Rechtsverfahrens würde daher verhindern, dass der Anspruch vor Ablauf der Höchstfrist von zehn Jahren (Art. 23) verjähren kann.[1] Um dies zu verhindern, bestimmt Art. 17 I, dass die Unterbrechung der Verjährungsfrist als **nicht eingetreten** gilt, wenn das Rechtsverfahren ohne Entscheidung

---

[3] Sekretariatskommentar VerjÜbk, Art. 16, Nr. 3; *Loewe*, Art. 16 VerjÜbk, S. 207.
[4] *Enderlein/Maskow/Strohbach*, Art. 16 VerjÜbk, Anm. 2.
[5] *Enderlein/Maskow/Strohbach*, Art. 16 VerjÜbk, Anm. 2.
[1] Sekretariatskommentar VerjÜbk, Art. 17, Nr. 1; *Smit*, 23 Am. J. Comp. L. (1975), 337, 343; *Sono*, 35 La. L. Rev. (1975), 1127, 1132; so wie hier das deutsche Recht (§ 204 I 1 BGB), anders aber (zumindest theoretisch) das schweizerische und US-amerikanische Recht, *Krapp*, ZSR 1984, 289, 312; *Spiro*, Begrenzung privater Rechte, S. 377 ff.

in der Hauptsache[2] endet.[3] Damit wird der Beklagte davor geschützt, dass der Kläger durch prozessuale Hinhaltetaktik die Verjährungsfrist nach Belieben verlängern kann.[4] Ein Verfahren kann aus verschiedenen Gründen **ohne Sachentscheidung** enden: Die Klage wird vom Gläubiger zurückgezogen oder nicht weiter betrieben, das Gericht tritt wegen mangelnder örtlicher oder sachlicher Zuständigkeit nicht auf die Klage ein, die Klage wird wegen prozessualer Mängel abgewiesen oder die Entscheidung eines Schiedsgerichtes wird vor einem ordentlichen Gericht angefochten und aufgehoben.[5] All diese Gründe werden von Art. 17 erfasst.[6]

II. Nachfrist (Abs. 2)

2   Endet das Rechtsverfahren ohne Entscheidung in der Hauptsache, gilt die Verjährungsfrist als weitergelaufen. Dies kann zur Folge haben, dass der geltend gemachte Anspruch im Verlaufe des Verfahrens verjährt. Ist dies geschehen oder läuft die Verjährungsfrist noch weniger als ein Jahr, gewährt Art. 17 II dem Gläubiger eine **Nachfrist** von einem Jahr,[7] um seinen Anspruch in einem neuen Verfahren zu verfolgen.[8] Diese Ausschlussfrist beginnt mit der Beendigung des Rechtsverfahrens zu laufen.[9] Dem Gläubiger wird so eine **Ablaufshemmung** gewährt: Die Verjährung geht nicht früher als ein Jahr nach dem erfolglosen Verfahren zu Ende.[10]

Art. 18 [Gesamtschuld; Regreß]

(1) **Ist ein Rechtsverfahren gegen einen Schuldner eingeleitet worden, so wird die in diesem Übereinkommen vorgesehene Verjährungsfrist gegenüber einer anderen Person, die mit dem Schuldner gesamtschuldnerisch haftet, unterbrochen, wenn der Gläubiger den Gesamtschuldner innerhalb dieser Frist schriftlich von der Einleitung des Verfahrens verständigt.**

(2) **Ist ein Rechtsverfahren gegen einen Käufer von dessen Abnehmer eingeleitet worden, so wird die in diesem Übereinkommen vorgesehene Verjährungsfrist in bezug auf den Anspruch des Käufers gegen den Verkäufer unterbrochen, wenn der Käufer den Verkäufer innerhalb dieser Frist schriftlich von der Einleitung des Verfahrens verständigt.**

---

[2] Ob bei Abweisung der Klage eine erneute Klageerhebung zulässig ist, richtet sich nicht nach dem Verjährungsübereinkommen, sondern nach dem anwendbaren Recht; Art. 16 UNCITRAL-Entwurf enthielt noch Bestimmungen zu dieser Problematik, s. Kommentar UNCITRAL-Entwurf, O. R. VerjÜbk, S. 24, Art. 16, Nr. 2 ff. und *Smit*, 23 Am. J. Comp. L. (1975), 337, 344; *Loewe*, FS Zepos II, S. 417; *Nelson*, 24 Int'l Law. (1990), 583, 592.

[3] Dies entspricht sachlich § 204 II BGB; *Enderlein/Maskow/Strohbach*, Art. 17 VerjÜbk, Anm. 2.; *Loewe*, Art. 17 VerjÜbk, S. 208; *Krapp*, 19 J. World Trade L. (1985), 343, 355.

[4] *Nelson*, 24 Int'l Law. (1990), 583, 591 f.; den gleichen Zweck erfüllen z. B. § 204 II BGB, § 1497 ABGB und Art. 3:316 Abs. 2 BW, die für die Unterbrechung der Verjährungsfrist eine gehörige Fortsetzung der Klage voraussetzen.

[5] Sekretariatskommentar VerjÜbk, Art. 17, Nr. 1; *Sono*, 35 La. L. Rev. (1975), 1127, 1132; *Enderlein/Maskow/Strohbach*, Art. 17 VerjÜbk, Anm. 1.

[6] Dies im Unterschied zu § 2–725 III UCC, der die Rücknahme oder die unterlassene Fortsetzung der Klage nicht erfasst: *Hill*, 25 Tex. Int'l L. J. (1990), 1, 20.

[7] Im deutschen und niederländischen Recht hat der Kläger sechs Monate Zeit, eine neue Klage zu erheben (§ 204 II BGB; Art. 3:316 Abs. 2 BW; § 2–725 (4) UCC 2003), im schweizerischen Recht nur 30 Tage (Art. 63 I ZPO).

[8] Ob eine erneute Erhebung der Klage zulässig ist, hängt von dem auf das Verfahren anwendbaren Recht ab, s. Sekretariatskommentar VerjÜbk, Art. 17, Nr. 2 (Fn. 1).

[9] Das anwendbare Recht bestimmt, in welchem Zeitpunkt das Rechtsverfahren als beendigt gilt.

[10] So auch zum schweizerischen Recht *Spiro*, Begrenzung privater Rechte, S. 335 ff. mit zahlreichen rechtsvergleichenden Hinweisen.

(3) Ist ein in den Absätzen 1 und 2 bezeichnetes Verfahren beendet, so gilt die Verjährungsfrist in bezug auf den Anspruch des Gläubigers oder des Käufers gegen den Gesamtschuldner oder den Verkäufer nicht als auf Grund der Absätze 1 und 2 unterbrochen; dem Gläubiger oder dem Käufer steht jedoch eine weitere Frist von einem Jahr, gerechnet vom Tag der Beendigung des Verfahrens, zu, wenn an diesem Tag die Verjährungsfrist bereits abgelaufen war oder nur noch weniger als ein Jahr zu laufen hatte.

Übersicht

	Rn.
I. Unterbrechung bei gesamtschuldnerischer Haftung (Abs. 1)	1
1. Fragestellung	1
2. Rechtsvergleichung	2
3. Lösung des Übereinkommens	3
a) Allgemeines	3
b) Verständigung des Schuldners	4
II. Unterbrechung beim Regress des Käufers (Abs. 2)	5
III. Nachfrist (Abs. 3)	7

I. Unterbrechung bei gesamtschuldnerischer Haftung (Abs. 1)

1. Fragestellung

Haften dem Gläubiger mehrere Schuldner als **Gesamtschuldner,** steht es in seinem 1 Belieben, von welchem Schuldner er die Leistung fordert. Damit stellt sich die Frage nach dem persönlichen Umfang der Unterbrechung, d. h. ob die Einleitung des Rechtsverfahrens gegen einen Schuldner die Verjährungsfrist auch gegenüber den anderen Mitverpflichteten unterbricht.[1]

2. Rechtsvergleichung

Die nationalen Rechtsordnungen beantworten diese Frage ganz unterschiedlich.[2] Nach 2 deutschem Recht (§ 425 BGB) hat die Unterbrechung rein persönliche Wirkung, soweit sich aus dem Schuldverhältnis nicht etwas anderes ergibt. Umgekehrt legen andere Rechtsordnungen der Unterbrechung generell[3] oder nur für bestimmte Fälle[4] Wirkung auch gegen die Mitverpflichteten bei.

3. Lösung des Übereinkommens

a) **Allgemeines.** Die **Unterbrechung der Verjährungsfrist** gegenüber einem Schuld- 3 ner wirkt nach Art. 18 I zunächst **nur** gegenüber diesem Schuldner.[5] Die Frist für die Gesamtschuld **läuft** damit trotz Einleitung des Rechtsverfahrens gegen die Mitschuldner **weiter.**[6] Dies bringt den Gläubiger unter Umständen in eine missliche Lage. Denn er kann nicht immer im Voraus sicher sein, dass der ausgewählte Schuldner zahlungskräftig ist oder dass sich das erstrittene Urteil vollstrecken lässt. Um sich die Option offenzuhalten, einen anderen gesamtschuldnerisch haftenden Schuldner ins Recht zu fassen, müsste er gegen

---

[1] Vgl. zur ganzen Problematik *Spiro,* Begrenzung privater Rechte, S. 430 ff.
[2] Sekretariatskommentar VerjÜbk, Art. 18, Nr. 2.
[3] Artt. 1206 und 2245 I frz. Cc; Art. 1974 I span. Cc; sowie Art. 136 OR.
[4] Nur im Falle der Geltendmachung des Anspruches durch den Gläubiger, nicht aber bei Anerkenntnis des Schuldners: Artt. 1309, 1310 I ital. Cc; sec. 29 (5) und 31 (6) Limitation Act 1980 (dazu *Cheshire/Fifoot/Furmston,* S. 713); *Spiro,* Begrenzung privater Rechte, S. 432.
[5] Die Vorschrift war angesichts der unterschiedlichen Lösungen der nationalen Rechtsordnungen umstritten, s. *Loewe,* FS Zepos II, S. 418; in der Sache gleich § 425 II BGB.
[6] *Girsberger,* Verjährung und Verwirkung, S. 177.

jeden Solidarschuldner ein Verfahren anstrengen. Wird der Gläubiger aber schon im ersten Verfahren befriedigt, sind durch das zweite Verfahren unnötige Kosten angefallen.

4   **b) Verständigung des Schuldners.** Um diese unerwünschten Folgen zu verhindern, kann der Gläubiger die Verjährungsfrist auch gegenüber dem oder den anderen Solidarschuldner(n) unterbrechen, indem er ihn oder sie innerhalb der Verjährungsfrist **schriftlich** über die Einleitung des Rechtsverfahrens **verständigt**.[7] Dies erlaubt der benachrichtigten Partei, Beweise zu sichern und abzuklären, ob sie sich in das laufende Verfahren einschalten will.[8] Die Mitteilung muss dem Gesamtschuldner zu einem Zeitpunkt zugehen, in dem die Verjährungsfrist ihm gegenüber noch nicht abgelaufen ist.[9]

II. Unterbrechung beim Regress des Käufers (Abs. 2)

5   Der Regelung des Abs. 2 liegt der Fall zu Grunde, dass der Käufer von einem Abnehmer z. B. wegen einer Vertragswidrigkeit der Ware in Anspruch genommen wird.[10] Da der Käufer diese Kosten in der Regel nicht alleine tragen will, wird er versuchen, diese auf dem **Regressweg** auf den Verkäufer abzuwälzen. Leitet der Abnehmer das Verfahren gegen den Käufer aber erst gegen Ende der Verjährungsfrist ein, läuft der Käufer Gefahr, dass sein Anspruch gegen den Verkäufer verjährt. Dies kann dazu führen, dass er gezwungen wird, in einem Zeitpunkt ein Rechtsverfahren gegen den Verkäufer einzuleiten, in dem noch nicht feststeht, ob der Abnehmer mit seiner Klage erfolgreich sein wird.[11]

6   Art. 18 II ermöglicht es dem Käufer, mit der **Regressklage** gegen den Verkäufer solange abzuwarten, bis er weiss, ob überhaupt Anlass dazu besteht.[12] Die Unterbrechung der Verjährung gegenüber dem Verkäufer setzt allerdings wie in Abs. 1 voraus, dass der Verkäufer von der Einleitung des Verfahrens gegen den Käufer schriftlich benachrichtigt wird.

III. Nachfrist (Abs. 3)[13]

7   Mit der Beendigung des Rechtsverfahrens des Gläubigers gegen den Solidarschuldner (Abs. 1) oder des Abnehmers gegen den Käufer (Abs. 2) gilt die Verjährungsfrist als **weitergelaufen**.[14] Ist der Gläubiger gegen den ins Recht gefassten Schuldner nicht oder bloss teilweise durchgedrungen, oder hat der Abnehmer erfolgreich gegen den Käufer geklagt, verbleibt dem Gläubiger oder dem Käufer noch **ein** Jahr, um seine Ansprüche gegen einen anderen Solidarschuldner, bzw. den Verkäufer durchzusetzen.

8   Art. 18 III setzt bei der Gewährung der Nachfrist bei Ablauf der Verjährungsfrist oder bei einem kürzeren Zeitraum als einem Jahr allerdings stillschweigend voraus, dass der Gläubiger oder Käufer im ersten Verfahren die Verjährungsfrist gegenüber dem Solidarschuldner oder Verkäufer durch eine Mitteilung wirksam **unterbrochen** hat.[15] Unterblieb diese Anzeige und ist der Anspruch gegen den Solidarschuldner oder den Verkäufer zwischenzeitlich

---

[7] Sekretariatskommentar VerjÜbk, Art. 18, Nr. 3.
[8] Die Form und Voraussetzungen der Teilnahme am Prozess wird durch das auf das Verfahren anwendbare Recht bestimmt: *Loewe*, Art. 10 VerjÜbk, S. 209; *Nelson*, 24 Int'l Law. (1990), 583, 592.
[9] *Loewe*, Art. 18 VerjÜbk, S. 209; *Nestor*, FS Schmitthoff, S. 303.
[10] Es ist unerheblich, ob Käufer und Abnehmer ihre Niederlassung in verschiedenen Vertragsstaaten haben: *Enderlein/Maskow/Strohbach*, Art. 18 VerjÜbk, Anm. 4.
[11] Sekretariatskommentar VerjÜbk, Art. 18, Nr. 5.
[12] *Loewe*, FS Zepos II, S. 418; in der Sache gleich § 204 I Nr. 6 BGB.
[13] Die Regelung in Abs. 3 entspricht funktionell Art. 17 II; Sekretariatskommentar VerjÜbk, Art. 18, Nr. 7; *Smit*, 23 Am. J. Comp. L. (1975), 337, 343.
[14] Missverständlich *Enderlein/Maskow/Strohbach*, Art. 18 VerjÜbk, Anm. 6.: Die Verjährungsfrist läuft nicht mit der Beendigung des zuerst eingeleiteten Verfahrens weiter, sondern es wird so gehalten, als ob sie gar nie unterbrochen worden wäre (s. Sekretariatskommentar VerjÜbk, Art. 18, Nr. 7).
[15] Ungenau *Enderlein/Maskow/Strohbach*, Art. 18 VerjÜbk, Anm. 7.

verjährt, kommt der Kläger nicht in den Genuss der Nachfrist. Hat die Verjährungsfrist noch mehr als ein Jahr zu laufen, steht dem Kläger die effektiv verbleibende Zeit zur Verfügung.

Art. 19 [Wiederbeginn der Verjährungsfrist]

Nimmt der Gläubiger in dem Staat, in dem der Schuldner seine Niederlassung hat, vor Ablauf der Verjährungsfrist eine andere Handlung als die in den Artikeln 13, 14, 15 und 16 bezeichneten Handlungen vor, die nach dem Recht dieses Staates den Wiederbeginn einer Verjährungsfrist bewirkt, so beginnt an dem von diesem Recht bestimmten Tag eine neue Frist von vier Jahren zu laufen.

Übersicht

	Rn.
I. Vorgeschichte	1
II. Unterbrechung der Verjährungsfrist ohne Einleitung eines Verfahrens	2
1. Voraussetzungen	2
2. Wirkung	3

I. Vorgeschichte

Die Vorschrift geht zurück auf eine Initiative Frankreichs und Belgiens, deren nationales Recht die Unterbrechung der Verjährungsfrist auch durch Handlungen **außerhalb** eines Rechtsverfahrens vorsieht.[1] Die Aufnahme dieser Bestimmung in das Verjährungsübereinkommen hat die nicht unproblematische Folge, dass nationales Recht in das System des internationalen Einheitsrechtes einbricht, weshalb Art. 19 auf der diplomatischen Konferenz umstritten war.[2] Schließlich setzte sich aber die Meinung durch, dass eine zusätzliche Möglichkeit, die Verjährungsfrist zu unterbrechen, im internationalen Handel wegen des erhöhten Zahlungsrisikos gerechtfertigt sei.[3]

II. Unterbrechung der Verjährungsfrist ohne Einleitung eines Verfahrens

1. Voraussetzungen

Der Gläubiger kann die Verjährungsfrist durch eine andere Handlung als die Einleitung eines Rechtsverfahrens nur dann unterbrechen, wenn das Recht des Staates, in dem der Schuldner seine Niederlassung hat, dies erstens zulässt und wenn die Handlung des Gläubigers zweitens einen **Wiederbeginn** des Fristenlaufes bewirkt.[4] Dadurch werden Schuldner, deren nationales Recht diese Möglichkeit nicht kennt, vor einer Unterbrechung der Verjährung geschützt, die ihnen nicht vertraut ist. Art. 19 wird daher nur praktisch für Gläubiger, deren Schuldner ihre Niederlassung in Frankreich, Belgien, Italien, Spanien oder einer anderen vom Code civil beeinflussten Rechtsordnung haben. Der Gläubiger kann dort die Verjährungsfrist durch eine **außergerichtliche Handlung**, z. B. durch eine förmliche Zahlungsaufforderung (Art. 2244 frz. Cc) oder eine schriftliche Mahnung (Art. 2943 IV ital. Cc; Art. 1973 span. Cc), unterbrechen.[5]

---

[1] *Loewe*, FS Zepos II, S. 419.
[2] O. R. VerjÜbk, S. 123 ff., Nr. 23 f.; S. 213 f., Nr. 1 ff.; *Landfermann*, RabelsZ 39 (1975), 253, 269; *Sumulong*, 50 Philippine L. J. (1975), 318, 353.
[3] *Enderlein/Maskow/Strohbach*, Art. 19 VerjÜbk, Anm. 4.
[4] Sekretariatskommentar VerjÜbk, Art. 19, Nr. 1; *Loewe*, Art. 19 VerjÜbk, S. 210; *Enderlein/Maskow/Strohbach*, Art. 19 VerjÜbk, Anm. 3.
[5] Art. 3:311 BW differenziert nach der Art des Anspruches: Nach Abs. 1 kann die Verjährung des Erfüllungsanspruches durch eine schriftliche Mitteilung, in der die Erfüllung unmissverständlich gefordert wird,

2. Wirkung

3 Wurde die Verjährungsfrist unterbrochen, beginnt in Abweichung der Regeln von Artt. 13 ff. eine **neue** Frist von **vier** Jahren gemäß Art. 8.[6] Der Beginn der Verjährungsfrist richtet sich nach dem anwendbaren nationalen Recht.

4 Der UNCITRAL-Entwurf sah in Art. 18 noch vor, dass durch die fortgesetzten Unterbrechungen und durch den Beginn neuer Verjährungsfristen ein Zeitraum von **acht** Jahren nicht überschritten werden darf.[7] Diese Begrenzung wurde jedoch fallen gelassen, so dass die allgemeine Höchstfrist von zehn Jahren zur Anwendung gelangt (Art. 23).

Art. 20 [Anerkenntnis]

(1) Erkennt der Schuldner vor Ablauf der Verjährungsfrist seine Schuld gegenüber dem Gläubiger schriftlich an, so beginnt an dem Tag dieses Anerkenntnisses eine neue Verjährungsfrist von vier Jahren zu laufen.

(2) Die Zahlung von Zinsen oder die teilweise Erfüllung einer Schuld durch den Schuldner hat dieselbe Wirkung wie ein Anerkenntnis nach Absatz 1, sofern aus der Zahlung oder Erfüllung vernünftigerweise geschlossen werden kann, daß der Schuldner seine Schuld anerkennt.

Übersicht

	Rn.
I. Voraussetzungen	1
1. Grundsatz: Schriftlichkeit	1
2. Ausnahme: Konkludentes Schuldanerkenntnis	2
3. Anerkenntnis vor Ablauf der Verjährungsfrist	3
II. Wirkung der Unterbrechung	4

I. Voraussetzungen

1. Grundsatz: Schriftlichkeit

1 Die Unterbrechung der Verjährung durch **Anerkenntnis der Schuld** ist den meisten nationalen Rechtsordnungen bekannt.[1] Während aber die kontinentaleuropäischen Rechtsordnungen ein stillschweigendes Anerkenntnis zulassen, verlangt das Common Law aus Gründen der Beweissicherung und der Rechtssicherheit Schriftlichkeit.[2] Trotz kritischer Stimmen setzten sich auf der diplomatischen Konferenz die Staaten des Common Law mit ihrer Position durch.[3] Die verjährungsunterbrechende Wirkung des Anerkenntnisses hängt damit nach Art. 20 I davon ab, dass es **schriftlich** erfolgt.[4]

---

unterbrochen werden; Abs. 2 verlangt für die verjährungsunterbrechende Wirkung der Mitteilung im Falle aller anderen Ansprüche zusätzlich, dass innerhalb von sechs Monaten nach der Mitteilung ein Rechtsverfahren eingeleitet wird.

[6] *Loewe*, Art. 19 VerjÜbk, S. 210; *Smit*, 23 Am. J. Comp. L. (1975), 337, 344.
[7] *Nestor*, FS Schmitthoff, S. 303; *Loewe*, FS Zepos II, S. 419.
[1] § 212 I 1 BGB; § 1497 ABGB; Art. 135 Ziff. 1 OR; Art. 2240 frz. Cc; Art. 2944 ital. Cc; Art. 1973 span. Cc; Art. 3:318 BW; sec. 29 (5) Limitation Act 1980 lässt eine Unterbrechung der Verjährung durch Anerkenntnis grundsätzlich nur bei *debt* zu, d. h. bei einer Forderung, die auf eine ziffernmäßig fest bestimmte Geldsumme gerichtet ist (*Cheshire/Fifoot/Furmston*, S. 711 ff.); *Spiro*, Begrenzung privater Rechte, S. 348 ff.
[2] Sec. 30 Limitation Act 1980.
[3] O. R. VerjÜbk, S. 68, Nr. 120; S. 214 f., Nr. 9 ff.; *Landfermann*, RabelsZ 39 (1975), 253, 270; *Enderlein/Maskow/Strohbach*, Art. 20 VerjÜbk, Anm. 1.; kritisch *Loewe*, FS Zepos II, S. 419 („wirklichkeitsfremder und störender Formalismus"); zustimmend *Krapp*, 19 J. World Trade L. (1985), 343, 355 f.
[4] Zur Legaldefinition der Schriftlichkeit s. Art. 1 III lit. g).

2. Ausnahme: Konkludentes Schuldanerkenntnis

Aus der **Zahlung von Zinsen** oder der **teilweisen Erfüllung einer Schuld** wird auf 2
ein Schuldanerkenntnis geschlossen, wenn diese Handlungen vernünftigerweise als Anerkenntnis gedeutet werden können. Hauptfall einer teilweisen Erfüllung ist die Teilzahlung; es sind aber auch andere Formen denkbar, wie z. B. die unvollständige Reparatur einer defekten Maschine. Ob aus einer dieser Handlungen vernünftigerweise auf ein Anerkenntnis geschlossen werden darf, hängt von den Umständen des Einzelfalles ab. Dabei müssen die Einzelheiten des Kaufvertrages und seiner Erfüllung sowie die gängige Praxis zwischen den Parteien genauso wie die Geschäftsusanzen des betreffenden Wirtschaftszweiges beachtet werden.[5] Es ist z. B. nicht als Anerkenntnis zu werten, wenn der Schuldner die Forderung zwar bestreitet, aber das leistet, was er schuldig zu sein meint.[6]

3. Anerkenntnis vor Ablauf der Verjährungsfrist

Der Schuldner muss seine Schuld vor Ablauf der Verjährungsfrist anerkennen, um die 3
Verjährungsfrist zu unterbrechen. Ein Anerkenntnis vermag daher die Verjährungsfrist **nicht**
wieder **aufleben** zu lassen, falls der Anspruch schon verjährt ist.[7] Obwohl nur Abs. 1 dieses
Erfordernis ausdrücklich nennt, muss es nach Sinn und Zweck der Regelung auch für die
Formen des konkludenten Schuldanerkenntnisses nach Abs. 2 gelten.[8]

II. Wirkung der Unterbrechung

Wie bei Art. 19 beginnt bei der Unterbrechung der Verjährungsfrist durch Anerkenntnis 4
der Schuld eine neue Frist von vier Jahren zu laufen.[9]

Art. 21 [Verlängerung der Verjährungsfrist bei höherer Gewalt]

Wurde der Gläubiger durch einen Umstand, auf den er keinen Einfluß hatte und den er weder vermeiden noch überwinden konnte, daran gehindert, die Verjährungsfrist zu unterbrechen, so wird die Verjährungsfrist so verlängert, daß sie nicht früher als ein Jahr nach dem Tag abläuft, an dem der Umstand zu bestehen aufgehört hat.

Übersicht

	Rn.
I. Voraussetzungen der Verlängerung der Verjährungsfrist	1
1. Hinderungsgrund	1
a) Voraussetzungen	1
b) Beispiele	2
2. Hinderung an der Unterbrechung der Verjährungsfrist	3
II. Mechanismus der Verlängerung der Verjährungsfrist	4

---

[5] Sekretariatskommentar VerjÜbk, Art. 20, Nr. 3.
[6] *Loewe*, Art. 20 VerjÜbk, S. 210.
[7] *Sumulong*, 50 Philippine L. J. (1975), 318, 353 f.; a. A. *Jaffé*, S. 108; anders noch ein Vorschlag der Arbeitsgruppe: YB I (1968–1970), S. 227, Nr. 78 ff.; YB III (1972), S. 112; *Nestor*, FS Schmitthoff, S. 304.
[8] So auch *Smit*, 23 Am. J. Comp. L. (1975), 337, 344.
[9] S. Art. 19 Rn. 3 f.; der Grundsatz, dass mit der Anerkenntnis die Verjährung im ganzen neu beginnt, gilt in vielen nationalen Rechtsordnungen: § 212 BGB; Art. 137 II OR; Art. 2945 I ital. Cc; Art. 3:319 Abs. 1 BW.

I. Voraussetzungen der Verlängerung der Verjährungsfrist

1. Hinderungsgrund

1   a) **Voraussetzungen.** Die Verlängerung der Verjährungsfrist setzt voraus, dass der Gläubiger durch Umstände ausserhalb des von ihm kontrollierten Einfluss- und Verantwortungsbereiches,[1] die **unvermeidbar** und **unüberwindbar** sind, an der Unterbrechung der Verjährungsfrist gehindert wird. Das Verjährungsübereinkommen umschreibt damit den Tatbestand der **force majeure**, ohne diesen systembelasteten Begriff zu gebrauchen, da er in den verschiedenen nationalen Rechtsordnungen unterschiedlich ausgelegt wird.[2] Angesichts der Vielfalt der möglichen Sachverhalte kann nicht generell gesagt werden, welche präventiven Massnahmen gegen Hindernisse zu ergreifen sind und welches Mass an Anstrengung dem Gläubiger zugemutet wird, das einmal eingetretene Hindernis zu überwinden. Um die Verjährungsfrist nicht allzu sehr auszudehnen, ist jedoch ein **strenger** Massstab an die Bemühungen des Gläubigers anzulegen.[3]

2   b) **Beispiele.** Als Hinderungsgrund nach Art. 21 in Frage kommen etwa ein Krieg und eine damit verbundene Unterbrechung der **Kommunikationsmöglichkeiten** zwischen den betreffenden Ländern, der **Stillstand** der **Rechtspflege** im Land des Schuldners oder die **Irreführung** des Gläubigers hinsichtlich der Person des Schuldners oder der Existenz der Forderung.[4]

2. Hinderung an der Unterbrechung der Verjährungsfrist

3   Der Hinderungsgrund muss den Gläubiger daran hindern, eine nach dem Verjährungsübereinkommen (Artt. 13–16) oder nach dem nationalen Recht (Art. 19) vorgesehene verjährungsunterbrechende Handlung vorzunehmen. Die **Verlängerung** der Verjährungsfrist setzt daher erst dann ein, wenn der Gläubiger alle ihm zur Verfügung stehenden Möglichkeiten zur Unterbrechung der Verjährungsfrist ausgeschöpft hat.[5]

II. Mechanismus der Verlängerung der Verjährungsfrist

4   Hindert ein Umstand den Gläubiger an der Unterbrechung der Verjährungsfrist, wird die Verjährungsfrist unter Umständen verlängert. Die dem Gläubiger nach Wegfall des Hindernisses zur Verfügung stehende Zeit entspricht dabei nicht starr der gehemmten Zeit.[6] Die **Verlängerung** der Verjährungsfrist wird vielmehr so bestimmt, dass dem Gläubiger vom Wegfall des Hinderungsgrundes an noch mindestens ein Jahr verbleibt, um seinen Anspruch gerichtlich geltend zu machen. Hat die Verjährungsfrist deshalb noch mindestens ein Jahr zu laufen, nachdem der Hinderungsgrund zu bestehen aufgehört hat, wird die vierjährige Frist nicht verlängert. Die Verjährungsfrist kann nie über die allgemeine Höchstfrist von zehn Jahren hinaus verlängert werden.[7]

---

[1] *Schwenzer*, Art. 79 Rn. 10 ff.
[2] Sekretariatskommentar VerjÜbk, Art. 21, Nr. 1; *Sumulong*, 50 Philippine L.J. (1975), 318, 354; *Loewe*, Art. 21 VerjÜbk, S. 211.
[3] Sekretariatskommentar VerjÜbk, Art. 21, Nr. 1.
[4] *Enderlein/Maskow/Strohbach*, Art. 21 VerjÜbk, Anm. 1.; *Smit*, 23 Am.J. Comp. L. (1975), 337, 345; s. auch Art. 1496 ABGB und Art. 3:321 Abs. 1 lit. f BW.
[5] Sekretariatskommentar VerjÜbk, Art. 21, Nr. 1 (Fn. 1); *Enderlein/Maskow/Strohbach*, Art. 21 VerjÜbk, Anm. 3.
[6] *Enderlein/Maskow/Strohbach*, Art. 21 VerjÜbk, Anm. 2.; *Loewe*, Art. 21 VerjÜbk, S. 211.
[7] Sekretariatskommentar VerjÜbk, Art. 21, Nr. 2 (Fn. 4); *Enderlein/Maskow/Strohbach*, Art. 21 VerjÜbk, Anm. 2.

Änderung der Verjährungsfrist durch die Parteien

Art. 22 [Änderung durch die Parteien]

(1) Außer in den Fällen des Absatzes 2 kann die Verjährungsfrist durch eine Erklärung oder Vereinbarung der Parteien nicht geändert werden.

(2) Während des Laufes der Verjährungsfrist kann der Schuldner diese jederzeit durch eine an den Gläubiger gerichtete schriftliche Erklärung verlängern. Diese Erklärung kann wiederholt werden.

(3) Dieser Artikel berührt nicht die Gültigkeit einer Bestimmung des Kaufvertrages, wonach ein schiedsrichterliches Verfahren innerhalb einer kürzeren als der in diesem Übereinkommen vorgesehenen Verjährungsfrist eingeleitet werden muß, vorausgesetzt, daß diese Bestimmung nach dem auf den Kaufvertrag anzuwendenden Recht gültig ist.

Übersicht

	Rn.
I. Grundsatz: Keine Änderung der Verjährungsfrist	1
II. Ausnahmen	2
1. Allgemeines	2
2. Verlängerung	3
3. Verkürzung	4

I. Grundsatz: Keine Änderung der Verjährungsfrist

Die Parteien können die Verjährungsfrist unter dem Vorbehalt von Abs. 2 und 3 weder durch einseitige Erklärung noch durch Vertrag verändern. Diese im Vergleich zu vielen nationalen Rechtsordnungen **schuldnerfreundliche** Bestimmung geht auf das Bestreben zurück, die schwächere Vertragspartei zu schützen und zu verhindern, dass die wirtschaftlich mächtigere Partei eine für sie günstige Fristlänge gegen den Willen des Vertragspartners durchsetzt.[1] **1**

II. Ausnahmen

1. Allgemeines

Der Grundsatz der **Unabänderlichkeit** der Verjährungsfrist gilt nicht uneingeschränkt. Neben den in Art. 22 II und III vorgesehenen Ausnahmen gibt es noch weitere Möglichkeiten, wie die Parteien die Länge der Verjährungsfrist beeinflussen können.[2] Zunächst können die Parteien nach Art. 3 II das Verjährungsübereinkommen als Ganzes **abbedingen**. Vereinbaren die Parteien sodann, dass der Erwerb oder die Ausübung eines Anspruches von einer weniger als vier Jahre betragenden **Ausschlussfrist** abhängt, ändern sie dadurch indirekt auch die Verjährungsfrist, da das Übereinkommen gemäß Art. 1 II auf derartige Ausschlussfristen nicht anwendbar ist. **2**

---

[1] Sekretariatskommentar VerjÜbk, Art. 22, Nr. 3; *Enderlein/Maskow/Strohbach*, Art. 22 VerjÜbk, Anm. 1.; *Loewe*, Art. 22 VerjÜbk, S. 212; *Sumulong*, 50 Philippine L.J. (1975), 318, 354; die Vorschrift war umstritten, YB I (1968–1970), S. 228 ff., Nr. 93 ff.

[2] *Krapp*, 19 J. World Trade L. (1985), 343, 356; *Smit*, 23 Am.J. Comp. L. (1975), 337, 346; *Landfermann*, RabelsZ 39 (1975), 253, 271; rechtsvergleichende Übersicht bei *Schwenzer/Hachem/Kee*, Rn. 51.16 ff.

2. Verlängerung

3   Der Schuldner (und *nur* er) kann die Verjährungsfrist durch einseitige, schriftliche Erklärung verlängern.³ Dies ist nur zulässig, solange die Verjährungsfrist **läuft**, d. h. weder vorher noch nachher.⁴ Eine Verlängerung der Frist über die Höchstgrenze von zehn Jahren hinaus ist nicht statthaft.⁵ Diese ausgewogene Regelung schützt einerseits den Schuldner, indem er vom Gläubiger nicht im Voraus zu einer unvorteilhaften Ausgestaltung der Verjährungsfrist gezwungen werden kann. Anderseits ermöglicht es Abs. 2 aber, eine überhastete Einleitung eines Rechtsverfahrens zu verhindern und Zeit für Verhandlungen zu schaffen.⁶

3. Verkürzung

4   Das Verjährungsübereinkommen lässt eine Verkürzung der Verjährungsfrist durch einseitige Erklärung oder durch Vertrag im Gegensatz zu vielen Rechtsordnungen prinzipiell nicht zu.⁷ Staaten mit kurzen Verjährungsfristen für die Sachmängelgewährleistung versuchten auf der diplomatischen Konferenz vergeblich durchzusetzen, dass die für sie lange Vierjahresfrist vertraglich verkürzt werden kann. Die Entwicklungsländer machten geltend, dass die wirtschaftlich starken Verkäufer aus den Industrienationen die vierjährige Frist des Übereinkommens in den Allgemeinen Geschäftsbedingungen regelmäßig verkürzen würden, womit die Käufer um den Schutz der längeren Frist gebracht würden.⁸ Wollen die Parteien die Verjährungsfrist verkürzen, müssen sie gemäß Art. 22 III im Kaufvertrag vereinbaren, dass ein **Schiedsgerichtsverfahren** in einer weniger als vier Jahre betragenden Frist eingeleitet werden muss. Das Übereinkommen anerkennt die Gültigkeit einer solchen Klausel, wenn das auf den Kaufvertrag anwendbare Recht sie zulässt.⁹

Allgemeine Begrenzung der Verjährungsfrist

Art. 23 [Höchstfrist]

Ungeachtet der Bestimmungen dieses Übereinkommens läuft jede Verjährungsfrist spätestens zehn Jahre nach dem Tag ab, an dem sie nach den Artikeln 9, 10, 11 und 12 zu laufen begonnen hat.

---

³ Nach deutschem Recht (§ 202 II BGB) ist die Verlängerung der Verjährungsfrist grundsätzlich auf höchstens 30 Jahre zulässig (*Palandt/Heinrichs*, § 202, Rn. 3 f.). Im schweizerischen Recht kann die gesetzliche Einjahresfrist für Ansprüche aus Gewährleistung verlängert werden, allerdings nicht über die allgemeine Zehnjahresfrist von Art. 127 OR hinaus (BGE 99 II 185). Im österreichischen (§ 1502 ABGB) und im französischen Recht (Art. 2250 Cc) ist die Verlängerung der Verjährungsfrist zulässig, solange sie nicht im Voraus vereinbart wurde. Art. 2936 ital. Cc und § 2–725 I UCC untersagen eine Verlängerung generell.
⁴ Sekretariatskommentar VerjÜbk, Art. 22, Nr. 3; ungenau *Krapp*, ZSR 1984 I, 289, 312 („Nach Art. 22 kann die Verjährungszeit *jederzeit* (…) verlängert werden").
⁵ Art. 21 II UNCITRAL-Entwurf sah für die Verlängerung der Verjährungsfrist ursprünglich eine Höchstgrenze von acht Jahren vor, s. *Nestor*, FS Schmitthoff, S. 304; *Loewe*, FS Zepos II, S. 419; Sekretariatskommentar VerjÜbk, Art. 22, Nr. 2; *Enderlein/Maskow/Strohbach*, Art. 22 VerjÜbk, Anm. 3.; *Sumulong*, 50 Philippine L. J. (1975), 318, 355.
⁶ Sekretariatskommentar VerjÜbk, Art. 22, Nr. 4; *Smit*, 23 Am. J. Comp. L. (1975), 337, 346.
⁷ Zulässigkeit der Verkürzung statuieren § 202 BGB (*Palandt/Heinrichs*, § 202, Rn. 2); § 1502 ABGB (s. *Koziol/Welser/Kletečka*, Band I, S. 234); Art. 129 OR e contrario für die kaufvertraglichen Verjährungsfristen (s. *Schwenzer*, OR AT, Rn. 84.11); Art. 2250 frz. Cc (*Mazeaud/Chabas*, S. 1226); § 2–725 I UCC (die Frist kann höchstens bis auf ein Jahr verkürzt werden); zum Verzicht auf die Geltendmachung der Verjährung s. Art. 24 Rn. 4 f.
⁸ *Landfermann*, RabelsZ 39 (1975), 253, 270 f.
⁹ Die Verknüpfung der Gültigkeit der Verkürzung der Verjährungsfrist mit der Gültigkeit der vertraglichen Vereinbarung weist darauf hin, dass das Verjährungsübereinkommen einer materiellrechtlichen Konzeption der Verjährung folgt, s. *Loewe*, Art. 22 VerjÜbk, S. 212; *Smit*, 23 Am. J. Comp. L. (1975), 337, 347.

Übersicht

	Rn.
I. Vorgeschichte	1
II. Höchstfrist	2

I. Vorgeschichte

Der UNCITRAL-Entwurf enthielt für verschiedene Tatbestände eine spezielle Höchstfrist.[1] Diese wurden aber zu Gunsten einer allgemeinen zehnjährigen Höchstfrist gestrichen.[2] Die **Begrenzung** der Verjährungsfrist durch Art. 23 war allerdings auf der diplomatischen Konferenz aus verschiedenen Gründen umstritten.[3] Letztlich setzte sich aber die Ansicht durch, dass es dem Zweck des Übereinkommens, die Verjährungsfrist klar und überschaubar zu begrenzen, zuwiderlaufen würde, wenn Rechtsverfahren noch nach zehn Jahren zugelassen würden.[4] 1

II. Höchstfrist

Zehn Jahre nach dem Beginn der Verjährungsfrist nach Artt. 9–12 verjährt jeder Anspruch, der in den Geltungsbereich des Verjährungsübereinkommens fällt.[5] Art. 23 ist eine **zwingende** Norm; die Parteien können auf ihre Anwendung nicht verzichten.[6] Die Höchstgrenze darf in keinem Fall überschritten werden. Sie gilt selbst dann, wenn der Gläubiger wegen höherer Gewalt während der ganzen zehn Jahre an der Geltendmachung des Anspruches gehindert wurde; sie ist schliesslich auch auf die der Unterbrechung nach Artt. 19 und 20 folgende Vierjahresfrist anwendbar.[7] 2

Wird die Zehnjahresfrist überschritten, kann ein Anspruch während eines laufenden Verfahrens verjähren. Dies ist jedoch nicht weiter problematisch, denn die **Wirkung** der Verjährung gemäss Art. 25 I besteht darin, dass kein Anspruch in einem **nach** Ablauf der Verjährungsfrist eingeleiteten Rechtsverfahren anerkannt wird.[8] Dem Schuldner steht damit die Einrede der Verjährung nicht zur Verfügung, wenn der Anspruch in einem laufenden Rechtsverfahren verjährt.[9] 3

---

[1] Art. 18 I (acht Jahre bei Wiederbeginn der Frist nach einer Unterbrechung der Verjährungsfrist durch andere Handlung als die Einleitung eines Rechtsverfahrens), Art. 20 (acht Jahre bei Hinderung des Gläubigers an der Unterbrechung wegen höherer Gewalt) und Art. 21 II UNCITRAL-Entwurf (acht Jahre bei Verlängerung der Verjährungsfrist durch den Schuldner), s. dazu *Smit*, 23 Am.J. Comp. L. (1975), 337, 347.

[2] Die Länge der Höchstfristen in den nationalen Rechtsordnungen variiert erheblich: Deutschland, Österreich, Schweiz (für Kulturgüter): 30 Jahre (§ 197 BGB, § 1478 ABGB, Art. 210 Ibis OR); Niederlande: 20 Jahre (Art. 3:306 BW); Spanien: 15 Jahre (Art. 1964 Cc); Schweiz, Italien: 10 Jahre (Art. 127 OR, Art. 2946 Cc); England: 6 Jahre (sec. 5 Limitation Act 1980); Frankreich: 5 Jahre (Art. 2224 Cc); USA: 4 Jahre (§ 2–725 (1) UCC; gemäss § 2–725 (1) UCC 2003 beträgt die Höchstfrist unter bestimmten Voraussetzungen 5 Jahre); rechtsvergleichender Überblick bei *Schwenzer/Hachem/Kee*, Rn. 51.23 ff. Die Civil Law Staaten haben grundsätzlich bedeutend längere Verjährungsfristen als die Common Law Staaten.

[3] O. R. VerjÜbk, S. 225 f., Nr. 34 ff.; S. 226 ff., Nr. 1 ff.; S. 230 ff., Nr. 1 ff.; *Enderlein/Maskow/Strohbach*, Art. 23 VerjÜbk, Anm. 2.; *Smit*, 23 Am.J. Comp. L. (1975), 337, 347 f.

[4] Sekretariatskommentar VerjÜbk, Art. 23, Nr. 1; *Loewe*, FS Zepos II, S. 419 f.

[5] S. dazu Art. 1 Rn. 4 f.

[6] *Loewe*, Art. 23 VerjÜbk, S. 213.

[7] Sekretariatskommentar VerjÜbk, Art. 23, Nr. 1 (Fn. 2); *Enderlein/Maskow/Strohbach*, Art. 23 VerjÜbk, Anm. 1.; *Loewe*, Art. 23 VerjÜbk, S. 212; *Krapp*, ZSR 1984, 289, 313.

[8] S. Art. 25 Rn. 1.

[9] *Smit*, 23 Am.J. Comp. L. (1975), 337, 347; s. auch O. R. VerjÜbk, S. 227, Nr. 13.

Wirkungen des Ablaufs der Verjährungsfrist

Art. 24 [Einrede der Verjährung]

Der Ablauf der Verjährungsfrist wird in einem Rechtsverfahren nur berücksichtigt, wenn eine am Verfahren beteiligte Partei ihn geltend macht.

Übersicht

	Rn.
I. Vorgeschichte	1
II. Einrede der Verjährung	2
1. Allgemeines	2
2. Verzicht auf die Verjährung	3
3. Vorbehalt gemäss Art. 36	5

I. Vorgeschichte

1 Die Frage, ob der Eintritt der Verjährung in einem Rechtsverfahren **von Amtes wegen** oder nur auf **Einrede** des Beklagten zu beachten ist, war auf der diplomatischen Konferenz umstritten. Es standen sich insofern die Interessen der Industriestaaten und der Entwicklungsländer gegenüber. Die nationalen Rechtsordnungen der ersten Gruppe sehen meist die einredeweise Geltendmachung der Verjährung vor,[1] während in manchen Staaten der zweiten Gruppe der Richter die Verjährung ex officio zu berücksichtigen hat,[2] da die Verjährung als Frage der öffentlichen Ordnung angesehen wird.[3] Schliesslich setzte sich die Position der Industriestaaten durch, wonach die Verjährung nur beachtet wird, wenn sie von einer Partei geltend gemacht wird.[4]

II. Einrede der Verjährung

1. Allgemeines

2 Die Verjährungskonvention bestimmt lediglich, dass der Eintritt der Verjährung nur berücksichtigt wird, wenn eine am Verfahren beteiligte Partei ihn **geltend** macht. In welchem Verfahrensstadium und in welcher Form dies zu geschehen hat, bleibt dem auf das Rechtsverfahren anwendbaren Recht überlassen.[5]

2. Verzicht auf die Verjährung

3 Art. 24 sagt nichts darüber aus, ob der Schuldner auf die Verjährung durch einseitige Erklärung oder vertraglich verzichten kann. Aus dem Grundsatz der einredeweisen Geltendmachung der Verjährung lässt sich nicht schon auf die Zulässigkeit des Verzichtes schliessen.

---

[1] Z.B. deutscher Rechtskreis (§ 214 I BGB, § 1501 ABGB; Art. 142 OR), romanische Rechte (z.B. Art. 2247 frz. Cc, Art. 2938 ital. Cc), Niederlande: Art. 3:322 Abs. 1 BW; zum Common Law s. z.B.: R.S.C., Ord. 18, r. 8; *Chitty On Contracts*, § 29–110; *Spiro*, Begrenzung privater Rechte, S. 553.

[2] Albanien, Indien, Pakistan, gewisse afrikanische Staaten, s. *Krapp*, 19 J. World Trade L. (1985), 343, 357; rechtsvergleichende Übersicht bei *Burr*, S. 14 ff.

[3] O.R. VerjÜbk, S. 72, Nr. 145 ff., S. 229, Nr. 34 ff.; *Enderlein/Maskow/Strohbach*, Art. 24 VerjÜbk, Anm. 2.

[4] Sekretariatskommentar VerjÜbk, Art. 24, Nr. 1 f.; *Enderlein/Maskow/Strohbach*, Art. 24 VerjÜbk, Anm. 2.; *Loewe*, Art. 24 VerjÜbk, S. 213; *Landfermann*, RabelsZ 39 (1975), 253, 271; *Spiro*, Begrenzung privater Rechte, S. 553 ff.; *Sumulong*, 50 Philippine L.J. (1975), 318, 356.

[5] Sekretariatskommentar VerjÜbk, Art. 24, Nr. 1 (Fn. 1); *Loewe*, Art. 24 VerjÜbk, S. 213; *Enderlein/Maskow/Strohbach*, Art. 24 VerjÜbk, Anm. 1.; *Girsberger*, Verjährung und Verwirkung, S. 179.

Denn die Geltendmachung kann oft noch nachgeholt werden, der Verzicht ist unwiderruflich, auch für spätere Rechtsverfahren.[6]

Der **Verzicht** auf die Verjährung ist in den meisten Rechtsordnungen dann zulässig, wenn **4** er nach Eintritt der Verjährung oder bei noch laufender Verjährung im Hinblick auf die bereits verstrichene Verjährungszeit erfolgt. Ausgeschlossen ist hingegen der Verzicht im Voraus, etwa bei Begründung der Forderung.[7] Den gleichen Grundsätzen folgt die Erschwerung der Verjährung, insbesondere die Verlängerung der Frist, selbst wenn sie keinem vollständigen Verzicht gleichkommt.[8] Im Verhältnis zu den nationalen Rechtsordnungen lässt das Übereinkommen eine Erschwerung der Verjährung nur in engen Grenzen zu: Solange die Verjährungsfrist läuft, kann der Schuldner sie bis zur Höchstfrist von zehn Jahren verlängern (Art. 22). Eine Anerkennung der Möglichkeit des gänzlichen Verzichtes auf die Verjährung würde m. E. dem in dieser Regelung zum Ausdruck gelangenden **Schuldnerschutz** widersprechen.[9] Ein Verzicht nach Eintritt der Verjährung ist zudem im Ergebnis mit Art. 22 I unvereinbar, da dieser eine Verlängerung der Frist in diesem Zeitpunkt nicht gestattet.[10]

3. Vorbehalt gemäss Art. 36

Um den Interessen der Entwicklungsländer entgegenzukommen, gibt Art. 36 den Vertragsstaaten die Möglichkeit, Art. 24 **auszuschliessen**.[11] Die Gerichte des Vorbehaltsstaates sind dann gehalten, die Verjährung von Amtes wegen zu beachten.

Art. 25 [Wirkung der Verjährung; Aufrechnung]

(1) **Vorbehaltlich des Absatzes 2 sowie des Artikels 24 wird kein Anspruch in einem nach Ablauf der Verjährungsfrist eingeleiteten Rechtsverfahren anerkannt oder durchgesetzt.**

(2) **Ungeachtet des Ablaufs der Verjährungsfrist kann sich eine Partei auf ihren Anspruch als Verteidigungsmittel oder zum Zweck der Aufrechnung gegen einen von der anderen Partei geltend gemachten Anspruch berufen, in dem zuletzt genannten Fall jedoch nur, wenn**

a) **die beiden Ansprüche sich auf denselben Vertrag oder auf mehrere im Rahmen desselben Geschäftes abgeschlossene Verträge beziehen oder**
b) **die Ansprüche zu irgendeinem Zeitpunkt vor Ablauf der Verjährungsfrist gegeneinander hätten aufgerechnet werden können.**

Übersicht

	Rn.
I. Wirkung der Verjährung (Abs. 1)	1
II. Aufrechnung oder Verteidigung mit verjährtem Anspruch (Abs. 2)	3
1. Allgemeines	3
2. Voraussetzungen der Aufrechnung	4

---

[6] *Spiro*, Begrenzung privater Rechte, S. 547 (Fn. 21).
[7] Art. 141 I OR (s. *Schwenzer*, OR AT, Rn. 83.07); § 1502 ABGB (s. *Koziol/Welser/Kletečka*, Band I, S. 234); Art. 2250 frz. Cc; Art. 2937 II ital. Cc; Art. 3:322 Abs. 2 und 3 BW; im englischen Recht ist der Verzicht auch vor Eintritt der Verjährung zulässig, wenn eine ausreichende consideration gegeben wurde: *Pearson v. Dublin Corp.* [1907] A. C. 351, 368; *Chitty* On Contracts, § 29–115; im deutschen Recht ist der rechtsgeschäftliche Verzicht außer bei Haftung wegen Vorsatzes im Voraus möglich, vgl. § 202 BGB (s. *Palandt/Heinrichs*, § 202, Rn. 3 f.; zum Ganzen rechtsvergleichend *Spiro*, Begrenzung privater Rechte, S. 544 ff. und S. 847 ff.
[8] Vgl. die Zusammenstellung der nationalen Vorschriften in Art. 22 Rn. 3 (Fn. 3) und bei *Spiro*, Begrenzung privater Rechte, S. 848.
[9] So wohl auch *Loewe*, Art. 25 VerjÜbk, S. 214.
[10] S. Art. 22 Rn. 3.
[11] Bislang hat noch kein Vertragsstaat den Vorbehalt nach Art. 36 erklärt.

I. Wirkung der Verjährung (Abs. 1)

1 In Art. 25 I kommt zum Ausdruck, dass die Verjährung den Bestand des Rechtes **unberührt** lässt.[1] Der Eintritt der Verjährung hindert vielmehr die gerichtliche oder schiedsrichterliche Durchsetzung des Anspruches, falls das Rechtsverfahren nach Ablauf der Verjährungsfrist eingeleitet wurde und der Schuldner gemäss Art. 24 die Verjährung geltend gemacht hat.[2]

2 Der Anwendungsbereich von Abs. 1 ist beschränkt auf die Wirkung der Verjährung auf die Anerkennung und Durchsetzung eines Anspruches in einem **Rechtsverfahren**. Welche Rechte dem Gläubiger aus einem Pfand oder einer anderen Kreditsicherung zustehen, wenn der gesicherte Anspruch verjährt ist, muss vom anwendbaren Recht beantwortet werden.[3]

II. Aufrechnung oder Verteidigung mit verjährtem Anspruch (Abs. 2)

1. Allgemeines

3 Trotz Eintritt der Verjährung lässt es das Verjährungsübereinkommen in Abweichung von Art. 25 I zu, dass sich eine Partei als **Verteidigungsmittel** oder zum Zweck der **Aufrechnung** auf ihren Anspruch beruft. Ein solches Verteidigungsmittel kann die Einrede der ungerechtfertigten Bereicherung oder die Erhebung einer Widerklage sein, wenn der geltend gemachte Anspruch im Zeitpunkt der Klageerhebung noch nicht verjährt war (Art. 16).[4] Durch Art. 25 II werden die Rechte der Parteien in Fällen, in denen der Beginn der Verjährungsfrist ihrer Ansprüche unterschiedlich ist, aneinander angeglichen.[5]

2. Voraussetzungen der Aufrechnung

4 Das Verjährungsübereinkommen regelt die Frage der Aufrechnung mit einem verjährten Anspruch. Ob eine Aufrechnung überhaupt zulässig ist, richtet sich nach dem anwendbaren nationalen Recht.[6] Eine Partei kann sich zum Zweck der Aufrechnung in zwei Fällen auf ihren verjährten Anspruch berufen.[7] Sie ist dazu erstens berechtigt, wenn eine **wirtschaftliche Konnexität** zwischen den beiden Ansprüchen besteht (Art. 25 II lit. a)). Die Aufrechnung ist in diesem Fall jederzeit möglich, d. h. selbst dann, wenn die Forderung des Aufrechnenden schon verjährt war, als die Hauptforderung entstand.[8] Beziehen sich die Ansprüche nicht auf den gleichen Vertrag oder stammen sie nicht aus dem gleichen Geschäft, kann zweitens immer

---

[1] So auch z. B. § 214 I BGB; zum englischen Recht s. *Cheshire/Fifoot/Furmston*, S. 713; *Enderlein/Maskow/Strohbach*, Präambel VerjÜbk, Anm. 2.; *Burr*, S. 9; in gewissen romanischen Rechtsordnungen geht der Anspruch als solcher durch den Zeitablauf unter: Art. 2934 I ital. Cc; Art. 1930 II span. Cc; anders aber in Frankreich (Artt. 1234 und 2219 Cc): *Mazeaud/Chabas*, S. 1200.

[2] Sekretariatskommentar VerjÜbk, Art. 25, Nr. 1; *Enderlein/Maskow/Strohbach*, Art. 25 VerjÜbk, Anm. 2.; *Sumulong*, 50 Philippine L.J. (1975), 318, 357; zur Klageverjährung im Allgemeinen s. *Girsberger*, Verjährung und Verwirkung, S. 27 ff.

[3] S. Art. 5 Rn. 4; Sekretariatskommentar VerjÜbk, Art. 25, Nr. 2; *Enderlein/Maskow/Strohbach*, Art. 25 VerjÜbk, Anm. 1.

[4] Zum Unterschied zwischen der Widerklage und der Aufrechnung s. Sekretariatskommentar VerjÜbk, Art. 25, Nr. 3; *Enderlein/Maskow/Strohbach*, Art. 25 VerjÜbk, Anm. 3.

[5] *Sumulong*, 50 Philippine L.J. (1975), 318, 357.

[6] Sekretariatskommentar VerjÜbk, Art. 25, Nr. 3 (Fn. 4); *Enderlein/Maskow/Strohbach*, Art. 25 VerjÜbk, Anm. 4.; *Loewe*, Art. 20 VerjÜbk, S. 214; *Krapp*, 19 J. World Trade L. (1985), 343, 357.

[7] Es findet sich in den nationalen Rechten keine entsprechende Vorschrift; zumeist kann mit einer verjährten Forderung nur dann aufgerechnet werden, wenn die Verjährung eingetreten ist, nachdem sich die beiden Forderungen bereits aufrechenbar gegenübergestanden haben, vgl. z. B. § 215 BGB; Art. 120 III OR; Art. 1242 II ital. Cc; Art. 6:130 Abs. 1 BW; *Henriksens Rederi A/S v. T.H.Z. Rolimpex* [1974] Q.B. 233; *Chitty On Contracts*, § 29–125; *Spiro*, Begrenzung privater Rechte, S. 510 f.

[8] Sekretariatskommentar VerjÜbk, Art. 25, Nr. 3 (Bsp. 25A); *Enderlein/Maskow/Strohbach*, Art. 25 VerjÜbk, Anm. 7.

dann aufgerechnet werden, wenn die beiden Ansprüche zu irgendeinem früheren Zeitpunkt, d. h. **vor Ablauf** der Verjährungsfrist, aufgerechnet werden konnten (Art. 25 II lit. b)).[9]

Art. 26 [Vertragserfüllung nach Eintritt der Verjährung]

Erfüllt der Schuldner seine Schuld nach Ablauf der Verjährungsfrist, so hat er kein Recht auf Rückforderung, selbst wenn er zum Zeitpunkt der Erfüllung nicht wußte, daß die Verjährungsfrist abgelaufen war.

Die Vorschrift entspricht dem international verbreiteten Grundsatz,[1] dass die freiwillige Erfüllung eines verjährten Anspruches den Schuldner nicht zur Rückforderung des Geleisteten berechtigt.[2] Es wird dadurch verdeutlicht, dass die Verjährung die Durchsetzbarkeit des Anspruches hindert, nicht aber das Recht an sich zum Erlöschen bringt.[3] Art. 26 betrifft nur Rückforderungsansprüche, die mit dem Eintritt der Verjährung begründet werden. Er lässt die Rückforderung aus anderen Rechtsgründen, z. B. wegen arglistiger Täuschung, unberührt.[4] Das Recht auf Rückforderung besteht selbst dann nicht, wenn der Schuldner in Unkenntnis der Verjährung geleistet hat.[5]

Art. 27 [Zinsen]

Der Ablauf der Verjährungsfrist hinsichtlich der Hauptschuld hat die gleiche Wirkung hinsichtlich der Pflicht, Zinsen für diese Schuld zu zahlen.

Die Vorschrift bringt zum Ausdruck, dass die **Zinsforderung** als Nebenforderung von der Kapitalforderung abhängt und innerhalb der gleichen Frist verjährt.[1*] Zur Regelung der Zinsen bei einem internationalen Kaufvertrag wird auf Art. 78 CISG verwiesen.[2*]

Berechnung der Verjährungsfrist

Art. 28 [Grundsatz]

(1) Die Verjährungsfrist wird so berechnet, daß sie am Ende des Tages abläuft, dessen Datum dem des Tages entspricht, an dem die Frist zu laufen begonnen hat. Bei Fehlen des entsprechenden Datums läuft die Verjährungsfrist am Ende des letzten Tages des letzten Monats der Frist ab.

---

[9] Sekretariatskommentar VerjÜbk, Art. 25, Nr. 3 (Bsp. 25B); *Enderlein/Maskow/Strohbach,* Art. 25 VerjÜbk, Anm. 6.; *Krapp,* 19 J. World Trade L. (1985), 343, 357; *Smit,* 23 Am. J. Comp. L. (1975), 337, 349.

[1] S. nur § 214 II BGB; Art. 63 II OR; § 1432 ABGB; Art. 1371 frz. Cc; Art. 2940 ital. Cc; zum englischen Recht *Cheshire/Fifoot/Furmston,* S. 713; *Girsberger,* Verjährung und Verwirkung, S. 41.

[2] *Loewe,* Art. 26 VerjÜbk, S. 214; *Krapp,* 19 J. World Trade L. (1985), 343, 357; *Sumulong,* 50 Philippine L.J. (1975), 318, 358.

[3] S. auch Art. 25 Rn. 1; *Enderlein/Maskow/Strohbach,* Art. 26 VerjÜbk, Anm. 1.; *Smit,* 23 Am. J. Comp. L. (1975), 337, 349; *Nelson,* 24 Int'l Law. (1990), 583, 594.

[4] Sekretariatskommentar VerjÜbk, Art. 26, Nr. 2; *Enderlein/Maskow/Strohbach,* Art. 26 VerjÜbk, Anm. 1.; *Nelson,* 24 Int'l Law. (1990), 583, 594.

[5] So auch das deutsche Recht (§ 214 II BGB).

[1*] Die Frage der Verjährungsfrist der Zinsforderung wird in den nationalen Rechtsordnungen unterschiedlich beantwortet, ohne dass eine Lösung als vorherrschend bezeichnet werden kann; vgl. z. B. § 217 BGB, der allerdings allgemeiner von Nebenleistungen spricht; Art. 133 OR; Art. 2254 III frz. Cc; anders jedoch § 1480 ABGB (die Zinsforderung verjährt unabhängig von der Hauptforderung in drei Jahren, s. *Koziol/Welser/Kletečka,* Band I, S. 226) und Art. 2948 IV ital. Cc (selbstständige Verjährung der Zinsforderung in fünf Jahren); im niederländischen Recht verjährt der Anspruch auf Zinsen aus einer Geldforderung selbstständig in fünf Jahren (Art. 3:308 BW), sonstige Nebenforderungen verjähren hingegen mit der Hauptforderung (Art. 3:312 BW); *Enderlein/Maskow/Strohbach,* Art. 27 VerjÜbk, Anm. 1.; *Loewe,* Art. 27 VerjÜbk, S. 215.

[2*] *Bacher,* Art. 78 Rn. 1 ff.

(2) Die Verjährungsfrist wird nach dem Datum des Ortes berechnet, an dem das Rechtsverfahren eingeleitet wird.

Übersicht

	Rn.
I. Allgemeines	1
II. Fristberechnung	2
1. Fristende (Abs. 1)	2
2. Maßgeblicher Ort (Abs. 2)	3

I. Allgemeines

1 Bei der **Berechnung** der Verjährungsfrist folgt das Übereinkommen dem Grundsatz der **Zivilkomputation**, d. h. es wird nur nach vollen Tagen gerechnet. Da das Verjährungsübereinkommen ausschliesslich Jahresfristen kennt, wirft die Fristberechnung keine grossen Schwierigkeiten auf.

II. Fristberechnung

1. Fristende (Abs. 1)

2 Die in Art. 28 I 1 aufgestellte Regel entspricht in ihrer Wirkung der international vorherrschenden Methode, den **ersten** Tag der Frist bei der Berechnung **auszuschließen** und den **letzten** Tag **mitzuzählen**.[1] In beiden Fällen endet die Jahresfrist – vorbehaltlich der Feiertagsregelung von Art. 29 – mit einem Wochen-, Monats- oder Jahrestag, der jenem Tag entspricht, auf den das die Frist auslösende Ereignis gefallen ist. Art. 28 I 2 trägt den Besonderheiten des **Schaltjahres** Rechnung.[2]

2. Maßgeblicher Ort (Abs. 2)

3 Abs. 2 nimmt Rücksicht auf das Bestehen verschiedener Kalendersysteme[3] und auf die Datumsgrenze. Maßgebend für die Fristberechnung ist der Ort, an dem das Rechtsverfahren **eingeleitet** wird.[4]

Art. 29 [Auswirkung von Feiertagen]

Fällt der letzte Tag der Verjährungsfrist auf einen gesetzlichen Feiertag oder auf einen anderen gerichtsfreien Tag, so daß die erforderliche Rechtshandlung an dem Ort, an dem der Gläubiger nach Artikel 13, 14 oder 15 ein Rechtsverfahren einleitet oder einen Anspruch geltend macht, nicht vorgenommen werden kann, so wird die Verjährungsfrist bis zum Ende des ersten Tages nach dem gesetzlichen Feiertag oder gerichtsfreien Tag verlängert, an dem an diesem Ort ein solches Verfahren eingeleitet oder ein solcher Anspruch geltend gemacht werden kann.

---

[1] Z. B. §§ 187 f. BGB; Art. 132 I OR; § 902 I ABGB; Art. 2229 frz. Cc; Art. 2963 II ital. Cc; Art. 3:101 BW; *Pritam Kaur v. S. Russel & Sons, Ltd.* [1973] Q. B. 336; *Chitty* On Contracts, § 29–063; Art. 3 I Europäisches Übereinkommen über die Berechnung von Fristen vom 16. Mai 1972 (Vertragsstaaten: Liechtenstein, Luxemburg, Österreich, Schweiz).

[2] Ist der erste Tag der Frist der 29. Februar und endet die Frist nicht in einem Schaltjahr, läuft sie am 28. Februar ab: Sekretariatskommentar VerjÜbk, Art. 28, Nr. 1.

[3] Nach der Legaldefinition von Art. 1 I lit. h) ist immer der Gregorianische Kalender maßgeblich, s. Art. 1 Rn. 1.

[4] Bsp.: Die Verjährungsfrist beginnt im Staat X am 1. März. Staat Y, in dem das Rechtsverfahren eingeleitet wird, liegt jenseits der Datumsgrenze, so dass die Frist dort am 2. März beginnt. Dieses Datum, d. h. der 2. März, bestimmt auch das Ende der Frist.

Fällt das Ende der Frist auf einen am Ort des Rechtsverfahrens staatlich anerkannten **Feiertag** oder **dies non juridicus,**[1] verlängert Art. 29 in Übereinstimmung mit der Regelung der meisten Rechtsordnungen die Verjährungsfrist bis zum nächstfolgenden Werktag.[2]

Internationale Wirkung

Art. 30 [Handlungen oder Umstände mit internationaler Wirkung]

Für die Zwecke dieses Übereinkommens sind die in den Artikeln 13 bis 19 bezeichneten Handlungen oder Umstände, die in einem Vertragsstaat vorgenommen worden oder eingetreten sind, in einem anderen Vertragsstaat wirksam, vorausgesetzt, daß der Gläubiger alle angemessenen Schritte unternommen hat, um sicherzustellen, daß der Schuldner so bald wie möglich von den betreffenden Handlungen oder Umständen verständigt wird.

Übersicht

	Rn.
I. Gegenstand und Vorgeschichte der Vorschrift	1
II. Voraussetzungen der internationalen Wirkung	2
1. Fristwahrende Handlungen oder Umstände	2
2. Verständigung des Schuldners	3
III. Internationale Wirkung	4
IV. Verhältnis zu Art. 3 VerjÜbk	6

I. Gegenstand und Vorgeschichte der Vorschrift

Die Beantwortung der Frage, welche Wirkung den Handlungen des Gläubigers, die dieser zur **Wahrung der Verjährungsfrist** in einem Staat vornimmt, in einem anderen Staat zukommen soll, war bei der Ausarbeitung des Übereinkommens bis zuletzt umstritten.[1*] Durchgesetzt hat sich schliesslich die Lösung, dass die Vornahme einer Handlung oder der Eintritt eines Ereignisses nach Artt. 13 bis 19 nur dann eine internationale Wirkung hat, wenn sie in einem **Vertragsstaat** erfolgt und der Schuldner über die entsprechenden Vorgänge informiert wird. Dies hat zur Konsequenz, dass es dem unvereinheitlichten Recht der Vertragsstaaten überlassen bleibt, ob Handlungen des Gläubigers in einem **Nichtvertragsstaat** Einfluss auf die Verjährung haben.[2*] 1

II. Voraussetzungen der internationalen Wirkung

1. Fristwahrende Handlungen oder Umstände

Das Übereinkommen zählt in Art. 30 die Gründe auf, die auch zu einer Unterbrechung der Verjährungsfrist in einem anderen Vertragsstaat führen, nämlich die Einleitung eines **gericht-** 2

---

[1] *Girsberger,* Verjährung und Verwirkung, S. 175.
[2] Vgl. z. B. § 193 BGB; Art. 132 II i. V. m. Art. 78 I OR; Art. 7 décret no 72–788 vom 28.8.1972 (D.1972 475); Art. 2963 III ital. Cc; *Pritam Kaur v. S. Russel & Sons, Ltd.* [1973] Q. B. 336; *Chitty On Contracts,* § 29–064; Art. 5 Europäisches Übereinkommen über die Berechnung von Fristen vom 16. Mai 1972; s. auch Sekretariatskommentar VerjÜbk, Art. 29, Nr. 1 ff.
[1*] O. R. VerjÜbk, S. 74 f., Nr. 174 ff.; S. 237 ff., Nr. 1 ff.; S. 240, Nr. 1 ff.; zur Entstehungsgeschichte s. *Landfermann,* RabelsZ 39 (1975), 253, 272; *Loewe,* Art. 30 VerjÜbk, S. 216; *ders.,* FS Zepos II, S. 417 f.; *Enderlein/Maskow/Strohbach,* Art. 30 VerjÜbk, Anm. 1.; *Sono,* 35 La. L. Rev. (1975), 1127, 1133; *Sumulong,* 50 Philippine L. J. (1975), 318, 360 f.
[2*] Kommentar UNCITRAL-Entwurf, O. R. VerjÜbk, S. 30, Art. 29, Nr. 4; Sekretariatskommentar VerjÜbk, Art. 30, Nr. 2 (Fn. 4); *Enderlein/Maskow/Strohbach,* Art. 30 VerjÜbk, Anm. 1.; *Loewe,* Art. 30 VerjÜbk, S. 217.

lichen, schiedsrichterlichen oder **sonstigen Verfahrens** (Artt. 13 bis 18) oder die **Vornahme** einer **Handlung,** die nach dem Recht des Forumstaates des Schuldners den Wiederbeginn einer Verjährungsfrist bewirkt (Art. 19). Die Unterbrechung der Verjährungsfrist wegen **Anerkenntnis** der Schuld (Art. 20) oder **höherer Gewalt** (Art. 21) wird in Art. 30 ebenso wenig erwähnt wie die **Änderung** der **Verjährungsfrist** durch die Parteien (Art. 22). Die Wirksamkeit dieser Handlungen und Ereignisse hängt nicht vom Ort ab, an dem sie vorgenommen worden oder eingetreten sind. Sie müssen daher von den Vertragsstaaten auch dann anerkannt werden, wenn sie sich in einem **Nichtvertragsstaat** abgespielt haben.[3]

2. Verständigung des Schuldners

3   Der Gläubiger muss alle angemessenen Maßnahmen treffen, um den Schuldner so bald wie möglich zu **verständigen.** Dieses Erfordernis soll unbillige Ergebnisse vermeiden, wenn das Recht am Ort der Einleitung der Klage eine Notifizierung des Schuldners nicht vorschreibt.[4]

III. Internationale Wirkung

4   Sind die Voraussetzungen von Art. 30 erfüllt, sind die **Handlungen** oder **Ereignisse,** die in einem **Vertragsstaat** vorgenommen worden oder eingetreten sind, auch in einem anderen **Vertragsstaat** wirksam. Hat z. B. der Gläubiger durch die Einleitung eines Gerichtsverfahrens die Verjährung im Vertragsstaat A gemäss Art. 13 unterbrochen und wird das Verfahren ohne Entscheidung in der Sache selbst beendet, weil das Gericht sich für unzuständig erklärt, kann der Gläubiger nach der Regel von Art. 17 i. V. m. Art. 30 eine neue Klage im Vertragsstaat B einleiten, selbst wenn die vierjährige Verjährungsfrist (Art. 8) mittlerweile abgelaufen ist.[5]

5   Die eng mit der Verjährung bei mehrfacher Klageerhebung zusammenhängenden Fragen, ob dem ausländischen Urteil **materielle Rechtskraft** zukommt und ob das ausländische Urteil eine inländische **Vollstreckung** wegen des Eintrittes der Verjährung verhindert, werden im Verjährungsübereinkommen nicht geregelt.[6]

IV. Verhältnis zu Art. 3 VerjÜbk

6   Nach der Regel von Art. 3 I lit. b) findet das Übereinkommen unter bestimmten Voraussetzungen auch dann Anwendung, wenn eine der Parteien ihre Niederlassung in einem Nichtvertragsstaat hat. Gemäß Art. 30 haben aber in diesem **Nichtvertragsstaat gemäss Artt. 13–19** vorgenommene Handlungen in einem anderen **Vertragsstaat keine Wirkung.** Der unauflösbare **Widerspruch** zwischen den beiden Vorschriften ist entstanden, weil auf der Wiener Konferenz bei der Erarbeitung des Änderungsprotokolls Art. 30 dem neuen Geltungsbereich des Übereinkommens nicht angepasst wurde.[7]

---

[3] Sekretariatskommentar VerjÜbk, Art. 30, Nr. 3; *Enderlein/Maskow/Strohbach,* Art. 30 VerjÜbk, Anm. 2.; *Loewe,* Art. 30 VerjÜbk, S. 217; *Landfermann,* RabelsZ 39 (1975), 253, 272; *Smit,* 23 Am. J. Comp. L. (1975), 337, 350.

[4] *Girsberger,* Verjährung und Verwirkung, S. 177; Sekretariatskommentar VerjÜbk, Art. 30, Nr. 5; *Sumulong,* 50 Philippine L. J. (1975), 318, 361; *Krapp,* 19 J. World Trade L. (1985), 343, 358; *Sono,* 35 La. L. Rev. (1975), 1127, 1137.

[5] *Sono,* 35 La. L. Rev. (1975), 1127, 1134; s. auch Sekretariatskommentar VerjÜbk, Art. 30, Nr. 1 (Bsp. 30B).

[6] Sekretariatskommentar VerjÜbk, Art. 30, Nr. 1 (Fn. 1); *Girsberger,* Verjährung und Verwirkung, S. 178, 209 f.; *Landfermann,* RabelsZ 39 (1975), 253, 272 f.; *Sono,* 35 La. L. Rev. (1975), 1127, 1135 f.; vgl. aber noch Art. 16 UNCITRAL-Entwurf, dazu Kommentar UNCITRAL-Entwurf, O. R. VerjÜbk, S. 24, Art. 16, Nr. 2 ff.

[7] Second Committee, Summary Records, O. R., S. 473 f.; *Enderlein/Maskow/Strohbach,* Art. 30 VerjÜbk, Anm. 4.

Teil II. Anwendungsbestimmungen

Art. 31 [Föderative Staaten]

(1) Ein Vertragsstaat, der zwei oder mehr Gebietseinheiten umfaßt, in denen nach seiner Verfassung auf die in diesem Übereinkommen geregelten Fragen unterschiedliche Rechtsordnungen angewendet werden, kann bei der Unterzeichnung, bei der Ratifikation oder beim Beitritt erklären, daß dieses Übereinkommen auf alle seine Gebietseinheiten oder nur auf eine oder mehrere derselben angewendet wird; er kann diese Erklärung jederzeit durch eine neue Erklärung ändern.

(2) Die Erklärungen sind dem Generalsekretär der Vereinten Nationen zu übermitteln und haben ausdrücklich die Gebietseinheiten anzuführen, in denen das Übereinkommen angewendet wird.

(3) Gibt ein in Absatz 1 bezeichneter Vertragsstaat bei der Unterzeichnung, bei der Ratifikation oder beim Beitritt keine Erklärung ab, so ist das Übereinkommen in allen Gebietseinheiten dieses Staates anzuwenden.

(4) Erstreckt sich das Übereinkommen auf Grund seiner Erklärung nach diesem Artikel auf eine oder mehrere, jedoch nicht auf alle Gebietseinheiten eines Vertragsstaates und liegt die Niederlassung einer Partei in diesem Staat, so wird diese Niederlassung im Sinne dieses Übereinkommens nur dann als in einem Vertragsstaat gelegen betrachtet, wenn sie in einer Gebietseinheit liegt, auf die sich das Übereinkommen erstreckt.

Art. 31 IV wurde durch Art. III ÄndProt hinzugefügt. Die Vorschrift betrifft **föderative Staaten** und entspricht Art. 93 CISG, weshalb auf die diesbezüglichen Ausführungen verwiesen wird.[1]

Art. 32 [Föderative Staaten, betroffene Rechtsordnung]

Wird in diesem Übereinkommen auf das Recht eines Staates verwiesen, in dem unterschiedliche Rechtsordnungen angewendet werden, so ist diese Verweisung dahin auszulegen, daß sie sich auf die Vorschriften derjenigen Rechtsordnung bezieht, die betroffen ist.

Verweist das Verjährungsübereinkommen zur Lösung einer Frage auf nationales Recht,[1*] bestimmt sich das anzuwendende Recht nach den Regeln des internationalen Privatrechts des Forums. Existieren in einem **föderativen Staat,** wie z. B. den USA, verschiedene Rechtsordnungen, muss entschieden werden, welche Rechtsordnung massgebend ist. Art. 32 stellt klar, dass das innerstaatlich anwendbare Recht nach den gleichen Grundsätzen ermittelt werden soll wie das nationale Recht.[2*]

Art. 33 [Zeitlicher Geltungsbereich]

Jeder Vertragsstaat wendet dieses Übereinkommen auf die Verträge an, die an oder nach dem Tag des Inkrafttretens des Übereinkommens abgeschlossen werden.

---

[1] *Ferrari,* Art. 93 Rn. 1 ff.
[1*] Z. B. Artt. 12, 13, 14 I, 15, 19, 22 III VerjÜbk.
[2*] Sekretariatskommentar VerjÜbk, Art. 32, Nr. 1.

Diese Bestimmung regelt den **zeitlichen Geltungsbereich**[1] des Verjährungsübereinkommens und entspricht Art. 100 II CISG.[2]

Teil III. Erklärungen und Vorbehalte

Art. 34 [Erklärung über die Nichtanwendung des Übereinkommens]

(1) Zwei oder mehr Vertragsstaaten, welche gleiche oder einander sehr nahekommende Rechtsvorschriften für Gegenstände haben, die in diesem Übereinkommen geregelt werden, können jederzeit erklären, daß das Übereinkommen auf Verträge über den internationalen Warenkauf keine Anwendung findet, wenn die Parteien ihre Niederlassung in diesen Staaten haben. Solche Erklärungen können als gemeinsame oder als aufeinander bezogene einseitige Erklärungen abgegeben werden.

(2) Hat ein Vertragsstaat, der für Gegenstände, die in diesem Übereinkommen geregelt werden, Rechtsvorschriften, die denen eines oder mehrerer Nichtvertragsstaaten gleich sind oder sehr nahekommen, so kann er jederzeit erklären, daß das Übereinkommen auf Verträge über den internationalen Warenkauf keine Anwendung findet, wenn die Parteien ihre Niederlassung in diesen Staaten haben.

(3) Wird ein Staat, auf den sich eine Erklärung nach Absatz 2 bezieht, Vertragsstaat, so hat die Erklärung von dem Tag an, an dem das Übereinkommen für den neuen Vertragsstaat in Kraft tritt, die Wirkung einer nach Absatz 1 abgegebenen Erklärung, vorausgesetzt, daß der neue Vertragsstaat sich einer solchen Erklärung anschließt oder eine darauf bezogene einseitige Erklärung abgibt.

1 Art. 34 wurde durch Art. IV ÄndProt neu gefasst.[1*] Die Vorschrift entspricht Art. 94 CISG, weshalb auf die diesbezüglichen Ausführungen verwiesen wird.[2*]

2 **Norwegen** erklärte als bislang einziger Vertragsstaat bei der Unterzeichnung und bestätigte bei der Ratifikation, dass das Verjährungsübereinkommen nicht auf Kaufverträge zwischen Parteien, die beide ihre Niederlassung im Gebiet der nordischen Staaten (d. h. Norwegen, Dänemark, Finnland, Island und Schweden) haben, anwendbar ist.[3*]

Art. 35 [Erklärung zur Anwendung des Übereinkommens auf Nichtigkeitsklagen]

Ein Vertragsstaat kann bei der Hinterlegung seiner Ratifikations- oder Beitrittsurkunde erklären, daß er dieses Übereinkommen auf Klagen, die die Nichtigkeit eines Vertrages zum Gegenstand haben, nicht anwenden wird.

1 Art. 35 ist eine Konzession an Rechtsordnungen, die verlangen, dass die Nichtigkeit des Vertrages mit einer **Nichtigkeitsklage** *(action for annulment/action en annulation)* geltend gemacht wird und dafür spezielle Verjährungsregeln vorsehen.[1**] Macht ein Staat von der

---

[1] Sekretariatskommentar VerjÜbk, Art. 33, Nr. 1; *Loewe*, Art. 33 VerjÜbk, S. 219; zum Inkrafttreten des Übereinkommens vgl. Art. 44.

[2] *Ferrari*, Art. 100 Rn. 2 f.

[1*] *Alte Fassung:* Zwei oder mehr Vertragsstaaten können jederzeit erklären, dass Kaufverträge zwischen einem Verkäufer mit Niederlassung in einem dieser Staaten und einem Käufer mit Niederlassung in einem anderen dieser Staaten diesem Übereinkommen nicht unterliegen, weil die betreffenden Staaten auf die in diesem Übereinkommen geregelten Fragen die gleichen oder einander sehr nahe kommende Rechtsvorschriften anwenden.

[2*] *Ferrari*, Art. 94 Rn. 1 f.

[3*] Da Norwegen nur Vertragsstaat der Verjährungskonvention in der Fassung vom 14. Juni 1974 ist, bezieht sich der Vorbehalt auf Art. 34 in der ursprünglichen Form (s. Fn. 259).

[1**] Z. B. Art. 1304 frz. Cc (action en nullité): Fünf Jahre; *Girsberger*, Verjährung und Verwirkung, S. 163 f., 170.

Vorbehaltsmöglichkeit Gebrauch, kommt das nationale Recht zur Anwendung.² Allerdings dürften solche Nichtigkeitsklagen nicht häufig sein, denn die Nichtigkeit wird im Allgemeinen einer Leistungsklage gegenüber eingewendet.³
Bislang hat noch kein Staat den Vorbehalt nach Art. 35 erklärt. 2

Art. 36 [Erklärung zur einredeweisen Geltendmachung der Verjährung]

Ein Staat kann bei der Hinterlegung seiner Ratifikations- oder Beitrittsurkunde erklären, daß er sich nicht verpflichtet, Artikel 24 anzuwenden.

Die Erklärung eines Vorbehaltes gemäss Art. 36 bedeutet, dass die Gerichte und Schiedsgerichte des betreffenden Staates die Verjährung in Abweichung von Art. 24 **von Amtes wegen** zu berücksichtigen haben.¹ Die Gründe, die zu dieser Vorbehaltsmöglichkeit geführt haben, sind bereits bei Art. 24 erläutert worden.²* 1

Bislang hat noch kein Staat den Vorbehalt nach Art. 36 erklärt. 2

Art. 36a [Vorbehalt zum Anwendungsbereich des Übereinkommens]

Jeder Staat kann bei Hinterlegung seiner Beitrittsurkunde oder seiner Notifikation nach Art. 43a erklären, daß Artikel 3 in der Fassung des Artikels I des Protokolls von 1980 für ihn nicht verbindlich ist. Eine Erklärung nach dem vorliegenden Artikel bedarf der Schriftform und ist dem Verwahrer zu notifizieren.

Art. 36a wurde durch Art. XII ÄndProt hinzugefügt und ermöglicht es jedem Vertragsstaat zu erklären, dass die Anwendung der Konvention auf Parteien in **Nichtvertragsstaaten ausgeschlossen** wird.¹** Für solche Staaten gilt Art. 3 in der nicht geänderten Fassung des Übereinkommens von 1974. Der Vorbehalt kann sowohl beim (direkten) Beitritt zum Änderungsprotokoll gemäss Art. 43b abgegeben werden als auch beim (indirekten) Beitritt durch Notifikation des Verwahrers anlässlich der Ratifikation oder des Beitrittes zum Übereinkommen von 1974 gemäß Art. 43a. 1

Art. 36a entspricht im Übrigen Art. 95 CISG, weshalb auf die diesbezüglichen Ausführungen verwiesen wird.²** 2

Art. 37 [Verhältnis zu anderen internationalen Vereinbarungen]

Dieses Übereinkommen geht bereits geschlossenen oder in Zukunft zu schließenden internationalen Vereinbarungen, die Bestimmungen über in diesem Übereinkommen geregelte Gegenstände enthalten, nicht vor, sofern Verkäufer und Käufer ihre Niederlassung in Vertragsstaaten einer solchen Vereinbarung haben.

---

² Sekretariatskommentar VerjÜbk, Art. 35, Nr. 1.
³ *Loewe,* FS Zepos II, S. 414.
¹ *Girsberger,* Verjährung und Verwirkung, S. 164.
²* Art. 24 Rn. 1.
¹** Bislang haben die Slowakische und Tschechische Republik sowie die USA in Übereinstimmung mit Art. XII ÄndProt einen Vorbehalt zur Anwendung des Übereinkommens abgegeben; die USA haben den Vorbehalt erklärt, „because the broader application of the Convention would come at the expense of the application of U.S law (...) and the uncertainties introduced by non-uniform rules of conflict of laws", *Nelson,* 24 Int'l Law. (1990), 583, 596; zu den Auswirkungen vgl. *Bernstein/Lookofsky,* S. 146 f.
²** *Ferrari,* Art. 95 Rn. 1 ff.

Art. 37 wurde durch Art. V ÄndProt neu gefasst.[1] Die Vorschrift regelt das Verhältnis der Verjährungskonvention zu anderen **internationalen Vereinbarungen** und entspricht Art. 90 CISG, weshalb auf die diesbezüglichen Ausführungen verwiesen wird.[2]

Art. 38 [Erklärung zur Definition des internationalen Kaufvertrages]

(1) **Ein Vertragsstaat, der einem bestehenden Übereinkommen über den internationalen Warenkauf angehört, kann bei der Hinterlegung seiner Ratifikations- oder Beitrittsurkunde erklären, daß er dieses Übereinkommen ausschließlich auf die in dem bestehenden Übereinkommen definierten internationalen Kaufverträge über Waren anwenden wird.**

(2) **Diese Erklärung verliert ihre Wirkung am ersten Tag des Monats, der auf den Ablauf einer Frist von zwölf Monaten nach Inkrafttreten eines im Rahmen der Vereinten Nationen geschlossenen neuen Übereinkommens über den internationalen Warenkauf folgt.**

Es war ursprünglich die Funktion von Art. 38, den Vertragsstaaten der **Haager Kaufrechtsübereinkommen** von 1964 die Möglichkeit zu verschaffen, den Anwendungsbereich des Verjährungsübereinkommens dem Anwendungsbereich der Haager Abkommen anzupassen.[1*] Die Vorschrift ist jedoch praktisch **bedeutungslos** geworden, da kein Vertragsstaat der Haager Kaufgesetze dem Verjährungsübereinkommen beigetreten ist. Es ist auch nicht zu erwarten, dass einer der Staaten, der noch Mitglied der Haager Kaufrechtsabkommen ist,[2*] dem Verjährungsabkommen beitritt, ohne vorher oder gleichzeitig das CISG zu ratifizieren,[3] was ohnehin die Kündigung der Haager Kaufgesetze zur Folge hat (Art. 99 CISG).

Art. 39 [Zulässigkeit von Vorbehalten]

Andere als die in den Artikeln 34, 35, 36 und 38 vorgesehenen Vorbehalte sind nicht zulässig.

1 Die Bestimmung findet ihre Entsprechung in Art. 98 CISG, weshalb auf die dortige Kommentierung verwiesen wird.[1**]

2 Eine Erklärung nach Art. 31 gilt nicht als **Vorbehalt,** so dass sie von Art. 39 nicht erfasst wird.[2**]

Art. 40 [Wirksamkeitsvoraussetzungen einer Vorbehaltserklärung]

(1) **Die auf Grund dieses Übereinkommens abgegebenen Erklärungen sind an den Generalsekretär der Vereinten Nationen zu richten und werden gleichzeitig mit dem Inkrafttreten dieses Übereinkommens für den die Erklärung abgebenden Staat wirksam. Nach diesem Inkrafttreten abgegebene Erklärungen werden am ersten Tag des Monats wirksam, der auf den Ablauf einer Frist von sechs Monaten nach dem Tag ihres Eingangs beim Generalsekretär der Vereinten Nationen folgt.**

---

[1] *Alte Fassung:* Dieses Übereinkommen geht bereits geschlossenen oder in Zukunft zu schliessenden Übereinkommen, die Bestimmungen über in diesem Übereinkommen geregelte Fragen enthalten, nicht vor, sofern Verkäufer und Käufer ihre Niederlassung in Vertragsstaaten eines dieser Übereinkommen haben.

[2] *Ferrari,* Art. 90 Rn. 1 ff.

[1*] Sekretariatskommentar VerjÜbk, Art. 38, Nr. 1; ausführlich *Landfermann,* RabelsZ 39 (1975), 253, 261 ff.; *Smit,* 23 Am. J. Comp. L. (1975), 337, 352 ff.; *Enderlein/Maskow/Strohbach,* VerjÜbk, Anm. 1. f.

[2*] Gambia, Grossbritannien, Israel, San Marino.

[3] Sekretariatskommentar VerjÜbk, Art. 38, Nr. 2.

[1**] *Ferrari,* Art. 98 Rn. 2.

[2**] *Enderlein/Maskow/Strohbach,* Art. 39 VerjÜbk, Anm. 1.; *Loewe,* Art. 39 VerjÜbk, S. 223.

Aufeinander bezogene einseitige Erklärungen nach Artikel 34 werden am ersten Tag des Monats wirksam, der auf einen Zeitabschnitt von sechs Monaten nach Eingang der letzten Erklärung beim Generalsekretär der Vereinten Nationen folgt.

(2) Ein Staat, der eine Erklärung auf Grund dieses Übereinkommens abgegeben hat, kann sie jederzeit durch eine an den Generalsekretär der Vereinten Nationen gerichtete Notifikation zurücknehmen. Diese Zurücknahme wird am ersten Tag des Monats wirksam, der auf den Ablauf einer Frist von sechs Monaten nach dem Tag ihres Eingangs beim Generalsekretär der Vereinten Nationen folgt. Im Fall einer Erklärung nach Artikel 34 macht die Zurücknahme vom Zeitpunkt ihres Wirksamwerdens an auch jede damit übereinstimmende Erklärung unwirksam, die ein anderer Staat nach dem Übereinkommen abgegeben hat.

Art. 40 I wurde durch Art. VI ÄndProt abgeändert.[1] Die Bestimmung entspricht Art. 97 III–V CISG, weshalb auf die diesbezüglichen Ausführungen verwiesen wird.[2]

Teil IV. Schlußbestimmungen

Art. 41 [Unterzeichnung]

Dieses Übereinkommen liegt bis zum 31. Dezember 1975 am Sitz der Vereinten Nationen für alle Staaten zur Unterzeichnung aus.

Art. 41 stimmt sachlich mit Art. 91 I CISG überein, weshalb auf die diesbezüglichen Ausführungen verwiesen wird.[1*] 1

Bis zum Ablauf der Frist **unterzeichneten** Brasilien, Bulgarien, Costa Rica, die ehemalige Deutsche Demokratische Republik, Ghana, die Mongolei, Nicaragua, Norwegen, Polen, die ehemalige Tschechoslowakei, die ehemalige UdSSR, die Ukraine, Ungarn und Weissrussland das Übereinkommen. 2

Art. 42 [Ratifikation]

Dieses Übereinkommen bedarf der Ratifikation. Die Ratifikationsurkunden sind beim Generalsekretär der Vereinten Nationen zu hinterlegen.

Im Unterschied zu Art. 91 II CISG spricht Art. 42 nur von der **Ratifikation** des Übereinkommens.[1**] Damit werden jedoch andere Formen der endgültigen Bindung an die Konvention, wie Annahme oder Genehmigung, nicht ausgeschlossen.[2**]

Art. 43 [Beitritt]

Dieses Übereinkommen steht allen Staaten zum Beitritt offen. Die Beitrittsurkunden sind beim Generalsekretär der Vereinten Nationen zu hinterlegen.

Die Vorschrift entspricht Artt. 89 und 91 III CISG, weshalb auf die diesbezüglichen Ausführungen verwiesen wird.[1***]

---

[1] In der alten Fassung fehlte in Abs. 1 der Satz: „Aufeinander bezogene einseitige Erklärungen nach Artikel 34 werden am ersten Tag des Monats wirksam, der auf einen Zeitabschnitt von sechs Monaten nach Eingang der letzten Erklärung beim Generalsekretär der Vereinten Nationen folgt".

[2] *Ferrari*, Art. 98 Rn. 1 f.

[1*] *Ferrari*, Art. 91 Rn. 1 f.

[1**] Zum gegenwärtigen Stand der Ratifikationen s. Vertragsstaatenliste, Anhang II.

[2**] Vgl. *Ferrari*, Art. 91 Rn. 2; Art. 11 Wiener Vertragsrechtskonvention.

[1***] *Ferrari*, Art. 89 Rn. 2; Art. 91 Rn. 1 f.; zum gegenwärtigen Stand der Beitritte siehe Vertragsstaatenliste, Anhang II.

Art. 43a [Beitritt zur ergänzten Fassung]

Ratifiziert ein Staat nach Inkrafttreten des Protokolls von 1980 das Verjährungsübereinkommen von 1974 oder tritt er ihm bei, so stellt die Ratifikation oder der Beitritt auch einen Beitritt zum Übereinkommen in der Fassung des Protokolls dar, sofern der Staat dies dem Verwahrer notifiziert.

Art. 43a entspricht Art. X ÄndProt und hat den Zweck, den **Beitritt** zum Verjährungsübereinkommen in der Fassung des Protokolls zu **erleichtern** und den administrativen Aufwand zu reduzieren.[1] Ratifiziert ein Staat das Verjährungsübereinkommen 1974 oder tritt er ihm bei, genügt eine Mitteilung an den Generalsekretär der Vereinten Nationen, um auch dem Verjährungsübereinkommen in der Fassung des Änderungsprotokolls beizutreten. Die Hinterlegung einer zweiten Beitrittsurkunde ist damit im Unterschied zum Beitritt nach Art. 43b nicht nötig. Die Wirkung des Beitrittsverfahrens gemäß Art. 43a ist, dass im betreffenden Staat beide Fassungen des Verjährungsübereinkommens in Kraft sind.[2]

Art. 43b [Beitritt zur ergänzten Fassung]

Der Beitritt eines Staates, der nicht Vertragsstaat des Verjährungsübereinkommens von 1974 ist, zum Protokoll von 1980 hat vorbehaltlich des Artikels 44a die Wirkung eines Beitritts zu jenem Übereinkommen in der durch dieses Protokoll geänderten Fassung.

Art. 43b geht auf Art. VIII Abs. 2 ÄndProt[1*] zurück und sieht ein **vereinfachtes Beitrittsverfahren** zum Verjährungsübereinkommen in der geänderten Fassung vor.[2*] Der Beitritt zum Änderungsprotokoll hat demgemäss nicht nur einen Beitritt zum Verjährungsübereinkommen 1980 zur Folge, sondern unter den Voraussetzungen von Art. 44a gleichzeitig auch einen Beitritt zum nicht ergänzten Übereinkommen von 1974.[3]

Art. 44 [Inkrafttreten]

(1) **Dieses Übereinkommen tritt am ersten Tag des Monats in Kraft, der auf den Ablauf einer Frist von sechs Monaten nach der Hinterlegung der zehnten Ratifikations- oder Beitrittsurkunde folgt.**

(2) **Für jeden Staat, der nach Hinterlegung der zehnten Ratifikations- oder Beitrittsurkunde dieses Übereinkommen ratifiziert oder ihm beitritt, tritt das Übereinkommen am ersten Tag des Monats in Kraft, der auf den Ablauf einer Frist von sechs Monaten nach der Hinterlegung seiner Ratifikations- oder Beitrittsurkunde folgt.**

Im Unterschied zu Art. 99 I und II CISG[1**] enthält Art. 44 für das **Inkrafttreten** des Verjährungsübereinkommens eine Frist von sechs Monaten.[2**]

---

[1] Die Vorschrift ist eine modifizierte Version von Art. 40 V lit. a) Wiener Vertragsrechtskonvention: „Jeder Staat, der nach dem Inkrafttreten der Ergänzungsvereinbarung Vertragspartei wird, ist, wenn er keine andere Absicht zum Ausdruck bringt: (a) als Partei des ergänzten Vertrages anzusehen (...)"; Second Committee, Summary Records, O. R., S. 461 f.
[2] *Enderlein/Maskow/Strohbach*, Art. 43a VerjÜbk, Anm. 1.; zur Geltung der beiden Fassungen s. Art. 44a Rn. 2.
[1*] Art. VIII Abs. 2 ÄndProt wurde auf der Wiener Konferenz von der österreichischen Delegation eingebracht, s. Second Committee, Summary Records, O. R., S. 462 f.
[2*] Eine Unterzeichnung des Übereinkommens mit nachfolgender Ratifikation ist nicht notwendig, s. *Enderlein/Maskow/Strohbach*, Art. 43b VerjÜbk, Anm. 2.
[3] Art. 44a Rn. 1.
[1**] Vgl. *Ferrari*, Art. 99 Rn. 1.
[2**] Zum Zeitpunkt des Inkrafttretens des Übereinkommens in den Vertragsstaaten siehe Vertragsstaatenliste, Anhang II.

Art. 44a [Gleichzeitiger Beitritt zu beiden Fassungen]

Jeder Staat, der Vertragsstaat des Verjährungsübereinkommens von 1974 in der durch das Protokoll von 1980 geänderten Fassung wird, ist, falls er dem Verwahrer nichts Gegenteiliges notifiziert, auch als Vertragsstaat des nicht geänderten Übereinkommens in bezug auf jeden Vertragsstaat der Konvention zu betrachten, der noch nicht Vertragsstaat des Protokolls von 1980 ist.

Art. 44a entspricht Art. XI ÄndProt und wäre systematisch korrekter als Art. 43c einzuordnen gewesen.[1] Die Vorschrift ist notwendig, weil das Verjährungsübereinkommen 1980 die alte Fassung ergänzt, nicht aber abgelöst hat. Es gibt weiterhin Staaten, die nur dem nicht ergänzten Übereinkommen von 1974 angehören.[2] Tritt ein Staat, ohne Vertragspartei des Verjährungsübereinkommens 1974 zu sein, nach Art. 43b der **ergänzten Fassung** bei, wird er gemäss Art. 44a als Vertragsstaat der nicht ergänzten Fassung des Übereinkommens in Bezug auf jeden Vertragsstaat betrachtet, der noch nicht dem Verjährungsübereinkommen 1980 beigetreten ist. Der Beitritt zum nicht ergänzten Übereinkommen findet **automatisch** statt, es sei denn, der beitretende Staat widerspreche dem Beitritt. Praktisch bedeutsam wird die Anwendung der nicht ergänzten Fassung vor allem beim räumlichen Anwendungsbereich von Art. 3 Verjährungsübereinkommen 1974, der keine Anwendung des Übereinkommens auf Nichtvertragsstaaten vorsieht.[3]

Das Verjährungsübereinkommen in der **Fassung des Protokolls** gilt somit einerseits im Verhältnis der Staaten, welche Vertragsparteien der neuen Fassung sind und anderseits zwischen Staaten, die Vertragsstaaten beider Fassungen sind. Das **nicht ergänzte** Übereinkommen gilt zum einen zwischen den Vertragsstaaten der alten Fassung und zum anderen zwischen den Staaten, die nur dem Verjährungsübereinkommen 1974 angehören und denjenigen, die nach Art. 43b dem ergänzten Abkommen beigetreten sind.

Art. 45 [Kündigung]

(1) **Jeder Vertragsstaat kann dieses Übereinkommen durch eine an den Generalsekretär der Vereinten Nationen gerichtete Notifikation kündigen.**

(2) **Die Kündigung wird am ersten Tag des Monats wirksam, der auf den Ablauf einer Frist von zwölf Monaten nach dem Eingang der Notifikation beim Generalsekretär der Vereinten Nationen folgt.**

Die Vorschrift bedarf keiner Erläuterung.

Art. 45a [Kündigung des Änderungsprotokolls]

Ein Vertragsstaat, für den das Protokoll von 1980 in Anwendung der Absätze 1 und 2 des Artikels XIII des Protokolls von 1980 außer Kraft tritt, bleibt Vertragsstaat des nicht geänderten Verjährungsübereinkommens von 1974, es sei denn, dass er das nicht geänderte Übereinkommen nach dessen Artikel 45 kündigt.

Art. 45a entspricht Art. XIII Abs. 3 ÄndProt. Eine **Kündigung** des **Änderungsprotokolls**[1*][4] hat nur eine Kündigung des Verjährungsübereinkommens in der ergänzten Fas-

---

[1] *Enderlein/Maskow/Strohbach*, Art. 44a VerjÜbk, Anm. 1.; Second Committee, Summary Records, O. R., S. 463 f.
[2] Bosnien-Herzegowina, Burundi, die Dominikanische Republik, Ghana, Jugoslawien, Norwegen und die Ukraine.
[3] Vgl. Art. 3 Rn. 1; Art. 30 Rn. 6; *Loewe*, Art. VIII ÄndProt, S. 227.
[4] Art. XIII Abs. 1 und 2 ÄndProt lauten: (1) Ein Vertragsstaat kann dieses Protokoll kündigen, indem er dies dem Verwahrer notifiziert. (2) Die Kündigung wird an dem ersten Tag des Monats wirksam, der auf einen Zeitabschnitt von zwölf Monaten nach Eingang der Notifikation beim Verwahrer folgt.

VerjÜbk Art. 46

sung zur Folge. Umgekehrt berührt eine Kündigung des Verjährungsübereinkommens 1974 nach Art. 45 den Bestand des Änderungsprotokolls und des ergänzten Verjährungsübereinkommens nicht.[1]

2   Die alte Fassung des Verjährungsübereinkommens wird **automatisch** außer Kraft treten, sobald alle Vertragsstaaten dem Übereinkommen in der Fassung des Protokolls beigetreten sind (Art. 59 Wiener Vertragsrechtskonvention)."

Art. 46 [Originalsprachen]

Die Urschrift dieses Übereinkommens, dessen chinesischer, englischer, französischer, russischer und spanischer Wortlaut gleichermaßen verbindlich ist, wird beim Generalsekretär der Vereinten Nationen hinterlegt.

Im Unterschied zum UN-Kaufrechtsübereinkommen[1*] wurde das Verjährungsübereinkommen 1974 nur in fünf Sprachen erstellt, weil arabisch damals noch keine offizielle Sprache der Vereinten Nationen war. Schon das Änderungsprotokoll von 1980 wurde aber auch auf arabisch abgefasst und mittlerweile hat der Generalsekretär der Vereinten Nationen eine **arabische** Übersetzung des Verjährungsübereinkommens angefertigt. Diese hat den gleichen Status wie die anderen **authentischen** Fassungen des Übereinkommens.[2]

---

[1] *Enderlein/Maskow/Strohbach*, Art. 45a VerjÜbk, Anm. 4.; *Loewe*, Art. XIII ÄndProt, S. 229.
[1*] Vgl. *Ferrari*, Unterzeichnung Rn. 1.
[2] Der arabische Text wurde am 2.4.1993 angenommen (A/CN.470 1992.Treaties-5); veraltet: *Enderlein/Maskow/Strohbach*, Art. 46 VerjÜbk, Anm. 1.; *Loewe*, Art. 46 VerjÜbk, S. 226.

Anhang

I. Vertragsstaaten des Übereinkommens der Vereinten Nationen über Verträge über den internationalen Warenkauf – CISG –

Staat	Unterzeichnung	Ratifikation/ Annahme/ Genehmigung Beitritt/ Nachfolge	Inkrafttreten	Vorbehalte/Erklärungen
Ägypten		6.12.1982	1.1.1988	
Albanien		13.5.2009	1.6.2010	
Argentinien		19.7.1983	1.1.1988	Art. 96[1]
Armenien		2.12.2008	1.1.2010	Artt. 95, 96[1a]
Australien		17.3.1988	1.4.1989	Art. 93[2]
Belgien		31.10.1996	1.11.1997	
Benin		29.7.2011	1.8.2012	
Bosnien-Herzegowina		12.1.1994	6.3.1992	
Brasilien		4.3.2013	1.4.2014	
Bulgarien		9.7.1990	1.8.1991	
Bundesrepublik Deutschland*	26.5.1981	21.12.1989	1.1.1991	Art. 95[3]
Burundi		4.9.1998	1.10.1999	
Chile	11.4.1980	7.2.1990	1.3.1991	Art. 96[4]
China	30.9.1981	11.12.1986	1.1.1988	Artt. 95, 96[5]
Dänemark	26.5.1981	14.2.1989	1.3.1990	Artt. 92, 93, 94 I, II[6]
Dominikanische Republik		7.6.2010	1.7.2011	
Ecuador		27.1.1992	1.2.1993	
Ehemalige Jugoslawische Republik Mazedonien		22.11.2006	17.11.1991	
El Salvador		27.11.2006	1.12.2007	
Estland		20.9.1993	1.10.1994	Art. 96[7]
Finnland	26.5.1981	15.12.1987	1.1.1989	Artt. 92, 94 I, II[8]
Frankreich	27.8.1981	6.8.1982	1.1.1988	
Gabrun		15.12.2004	1.1.2006	
Georgien		16.8.1994	1.9.1995	
Ghana	11.4.1980	–	–	
Griechenland		12.1.1998	1.2.1999	
Guinea		23.1.1991	1.2.1992	
Honduras		10.10.2002	1.11.2003	
Irak		5.3.1990	1.4.1991	
Island		10.5.2001	1.6.2002	Art. 94[8a]
Israel		22.1.2002	1.2.2003	
Italien	30.9.1981	11.12.1986	1.1.1988	
Japan		1.7.2008	1.8.2009	
Kanada		23.4.1991	1.5.1992	Artt. 93, (95)[9]

Anh. I

I. Vertragsstaaten

Staat	Unterzeich-nung	Ratifikation/ Annahme/ Genehmigung Beitritt/ Nachfolge	Inkrafttreten	Vorbehalte/Erklärungen
Kirgisistan		11.5.1999	1.6.2000	
Kolumbien		10.7.2001	1.8.2002	
Korea, Republik		17.2.2004	1.3.2005	
Kroatien**		8.6.1998	8.10.1991	
Kuba		2.11.1994	1.12.1995	
Lettland		31.7.1997	1.8.1998	Art. 96[10]
Lesotho	18.6.1981	18.6.1981	1.1.1988	
Libanon		21.11.2008	1.12.2009	
Liberia		16.9.2005	1.10.2006	
Litauen		18.1.1995	1.2.1996	Art. 96[11]
Luxemburg		30.1.1997	1.2.1998	
Mauretanien		20.8.1999	1.9.2000	
Mexiko		29.12.1987	1.1.1989	
Moldau, Republik		13.10.1994	1.11.1995	
Mongolei		31.12.1997	1.1.1999	
Montenegro		23.10.2006	3.6.2006	
Neuseeland		22.9.1994	1.10.1995	Art. 93[12]
Niederlande	29.5.1981	13.12.1990	1.1.1992	
Norwegen	26.5.1981	20.7.1988	1.8.1989	Artt. 92, 94 I, II[13]
Österreich	11.4.1980	29.12.1987	1.1.1989	
Paraguay		13.1.2006	1.2.2007	
Polen	28.9.1981	19.5.1995	1.6.1996	
Peru		25.3.1999	1.4.2000	
Rumänien		22.5.1991	1.6.1992	
Russische Föderation***		16.8.1990	1.9.1991	Art. 96[14]
Sambia		6.6.1986	1.1.1988	
San Marino		22.2.2012	1.3.2013	
Sankt Vincent und die Grenadinen[14a]		12.9.2000	1.10.2001	
Singapur	11.4.1980	16.2.1995	1.3.1996	Art. 95[15]
Schweden	26.5.1981	15.12.1987	1.1.1989	Artt. 92, 94 I, II[16]
Schweiz		21.2.1990	1.3.1991	
Serbien und Montenegro[16a]		12.3.2001	27.4.1992	
Slowakische Republik****		28.5.1993	1.1.1993	Art. 95[17]
Slowenien		7.1.1994	25.6.1991	
Spanien		24.7.1990	1.8.1991	
Syrien		19.10.1982	1.1.1988	
Tschechische Republik****		30.9.1993	1.1.1993	Art. 95[18]
Türkei		7.7.2012	1.8.2011	
Uganda		12.2.1992	1.3.1993	
Ukraine		3.1.1990	1.2.1991	Art. 96[19]
Ungarn	11.4.1980	16.6.1983	1.1.1988	Artt. 96, (90)[20]
Uruguay		25.1.1999	1.2.2000	

I. Vertragsstaaten **Anh. I**

Staat	Unterzeichnung	Ratifikation/ Annahme/ Genehmigung Beitritt/ Nachfolge	Inkrafttreten	Vorbehalte/Erklärungen
USA	31.8.1981	11.12.1986	1.1.1988	Art. 95[21]
Usbekistan		27.11.1996	1.12.1997	
Venezuela	28.9.1981	–	–	
Weißrußland		9.10.1989	1.11.1990	Art. 96[22]
Zypern		7.3.2005	1.4.2006	

*Unterzeichnungen: 18; Ratifikation, Annahme, Genehmigung, Beitritt, Nachfolge: 79
Stand 11.4.2013
Quelle: Office of Legal Affairs, Treaty Section, United Nations, New York, N. Y. 10017 (USA)
Internetdokument: www.uncitral.org/en-index.htm
(dort auch der jeweils aktuelle Status)*

* Das Übereinkommen wurde von der ehemaligen DDR am 13.8.1981 unterzeichnet, am 23.2.1989 ratifiziert und trat dort bereits am 1.3.1990 in Kraft.

** Die Republik Kroatien hat beschlossen, aufgrund des Verfassungsentschlusses der Souveränität und Unabhängigkeit der Republik Kroatien vom 25.6.1991 und des Beschlusses des kroatischen Parlaments vom 8.10.1991 sowie kraft der Nachfolge der ehemaligen Republik Jugoslawiens bezüglich des Territoriums Kroatiens, als Vertragsstaat der Konvention mit Wirkung vom 8.10.1991 zu gelten. Dies war der Tag, an welchem Kroatien alle konstitutionellen und rechtlichen Verbindungen zu Jugoslawien gelöst und dessen internationale Verpflichtungen übernommen hat.

*** Die Russische Föderation hat am 24.12.1991 die Nachfolge der ehemaligen Sowjetunion als Mitglied der Vereinten Nationen angetreten und damit die Rechte und Pflichten der Sowjetunion aus der Charta der Vereinten Nationen und den multilateralen Verträgen übernommen, die beim Generalsekretär hinterlegt waren.

**** Die ehemalige Tschechoslowakei hat das Übereinkommen am 1.9.1981 unterzeichnet und am 5.3.1990 die Ratifikationsurkunde hinterlegt. Das Übereinkommen trat daraufhin am 1.4.1991 in Kraft. Die Slowakische Republik hat am 28.5.1993 eine Urkunde hinterlegt, in der sie als Rechtsnachfolger der ehemaligen Tschechoslowakei ausgewiesen wurde. Die Tschechische Republik hat am 30.9.1993 für sich eine Urkunde entsprechenden Inhalts hinterlegt. Das Übereinkommen konnte deshalb in der Slowakischen Republik und in der Tschechischen Republik mit Wirkung vom 1.1.1993, dem Zeitpunkt der Staatennachfolge, in Kraft treten.

[1] Argentinien hat bei Hinterlegung der Beitrittsurkunde folgende Erklärung abgegeben:
„Nach den Artikeln 96 und 12 des Übereinkommens der Vereinten Nationen über Verträge über den internationalen Warenkauf gelten die Bestimmungen der Artikel 11 und 29 oder des Teils II des Übereinkommens, die für den Abschluß eines Kaufvertrages, seine Änderung oder Aufhebung durch Vereinbarung oder für ein Angebot, eine Annahme oder eine sonstige Willenserklärung eine andere als die schriftliche Form gestatten, nicht, wenn eine Partei ihre Niederlassung in der Argentinischen Republik hat."
(BGBl. 1990 II S. 1477).

[1a] Armenien hat bei Hinterlegung der Beitrittsurkunde folgende Erklärungen abgegeben:
„1. Nach Artikel 95 des Übereinkommens erklärt die Republik Armenien, dass sie Artikel 1 Absatz 1 Buchstabe b des Übereinkommens nicht auf Parteien anwenden wird, die erklären, dass Artikel 1 Absatz 1 Buchstabe b des Übereinkommens für sie nicht verbindlich ist.
2. Nach den Artikeln 12 und 96 des Übereinkommens erklärt die Republik Armenien, dass die Bestimmungen der Artikel 11 und 29 oder des Teils II des genannten Übereinkommens, die für den Abschluss eines Kaufvertrags, seine Änderung oder Aufhebung durch Vereinbarung oder für ein Angebot, eine Annahme oder eine sonstige Willenserklärung eine andere als die schriftliche Form gestatten, nicht gelten, wenn eine Partei ihre Niederlassung in der Republik Armenien hat."
(BGBl. 2010 II S. 826).

² Australien hat bei Hinterlegung der Beitrittsurkunde folgende Erklärung abgegeben:
„Das Übereinkommen gilt für alle australischen Staaten und Festlandterritorien sowie für alle Außengebiete mit Ausnahme der Weihnachtsinsel, der Kokosinseln (Keelinginseln) und der Ashmore- und Cartierinseln."
(BGBl. 1990 II S. 1478).
³ Die Bundesrepublik Deutschland hat bei Hinterlegung der Ratifikationsurkunde folgende Erklärung abgegeben:
„Nach Auffassung der Regierung der Bundesrepublik Deutschland sind Vertragsparteien des Übereinkommens, die eine Erklärung nach Artikel 95 des Übereinkommens abgegeben haben, nicht als Vertragsstaaten im Sinne des Artikels 1 Absatz 1 Buchstabe b des Übereinkommens anzusehen. Deshalb besteht keine Verpflichtung und übernimmt die Bundesrepublik Deutschland keine Verpflichtung, diese Bestimmung anzuwenden, wenn die Regeln des internationalen Privatrechts zur Anwendung des Rechts einer Vertagspartei führen, die erklärt hat, daß Artikel 1 Absatz 1 Buchstabe b des Übereinkommens für sie nicht verbindlich ist. Vorbehaltlich dieser Bemerkung gibt die Regierung der Bundesrepublik Deutschland keine Erklärung nach Artikel 95 des Übereinkommens ab."
(BGBl. 1990 II S. 1477).
⁴ Chile hat bei Hinterlegung der Ratifikationsurkunde folgende Erklärung abgegeben:
„Der Staat Chile erklärt nach den Artikeln 12 und 96 des Übereinkommens, daß die Bestimmungen der Artikel 11 und 29 oder des Teils II des Übereinkommens, die für den Abschluß eines Kaufvertrages, seine Änderung oder Aufhebung durch Vereinbarung oder für ein Angebot, eine Annahme oder eine sonstige Willenserklärung eine andere als die schriftliche Form gestatten, nicht gelten, wenn eine Partei ihre Niederlassung in Chile hat."
(BGBl. 1990 II S. 1480).
⁵ China hat bei Hinterlegung der Genehmigungsurkunde folgende Erklärung abgegeben:
„Die Volksrepublik China betrachtet sich durch Artikel 1 Absatz 1 Buchstabe b und Artikel 11 sowie die Bestimmungen des Übereinkommens, die sich auf den Inhalt des Artikels 11 beziehen, nicht als gebunden."
(BGBl. 1990 II S. 1478).
Am 16.1.2013 zog China diesen Vorbehalt mit Wirkung zum 1.8.2013 insoweit zurück, als er den Ausschluss von Artikel 11 und der sich auf dessen Inhalt beziehenden weiteren Artikel umfasst.
(http://www.unis.unvienna.org/unis/pressrels/2013/unisl180.html).
⁶ Dänemark hat bei Hinterlegung der Ratifikationsurkunde folgende Erklärung abgegeben:
„Bei der Ratifikation des Übereinkommens erklärt das Königreich Dänemark
1. nach Artikel 92 Absatz 1, daß Teil II des Übereinkommens für Dänemark nicht verbindlich ist,
2. nach Artikel 93 Absatz 1, daß das Übereinkommen nicht für die Färöer und Grönland gilt,
3. nach Artikel 94 Absatz 1 in Verbindung mit Absatz 3, daß das Übereinkommen auf Kaufverträge keine Anwendung findet, wenn eine der Parteien ihre Niederlassung in Dänemark, Finnland, Norwegen oder Schweden und die andere Partei ihre Niederlassung in einem anderen dieser Staaten hat,
4. nach Artikel 94 Absatz 2, daß das Übereinkommen auf Kaufverträge keine Anwendung findet, wenn eine der Parteien ihre Niederlassung in Dänemark, Finnland, Norwegen oder Schweden und die andere Partei ihre Niederlassung in Island hat."
(BGBl. 1990 II S. 1478).
Am 2.7.2012 zog Dänemark die unter 1. aufgeführte Erklärung mit Wirkung zum 1.2.2013 zurück (http://treaties.un.org/Pages/ViewDetails.aspx?src=TREATY&mtdsg_no=X-10&chapter=10&lang=en#1).
⁷ Estland hat bei Hinterlegung seiner Beitrittsurkunde nach den Artikeln 12 und 96 des Übereinkommens erklärt, dass die Bestimmungen der Artikel 11 und 29 oder des Teils II dieses Übereinkommens, die für den Abschluss eines Kaufvertrags, seine Änderung oder Aufhebung durch Vereinbarung oder für ein Angebot, eine Annahme oder eine sonstige Willenserklärung eine andere als die schriftliche Form gestatten, nicht gelten, wenn eine Partei ihre Niederlassung in Estland hat.
(BGBl. 1994 II S. 10).
⁸ Finnland hat bei Hinterlegung der Ratifikationsurkunde folgende Erklärung abgegeben:
„1. Nach Artikel 92 ist Teil II dieses Übereinkommens (Abschluß des Vertrages) für Finnland nicht verbindlich.
2. Nach Artikel 94 wird das Übereinkommen in bezug auf Schweden nach Absatz 1 und sonst nach Absatz 2 auf Kaufverträge keine Anwendung finden, wenn die Parteien ihre Niederlassung in Finnland, Schweden, Dänemark, Island oder Norwegen haben."
(BGBl. 1990 II S. 1478 f.).

I. Vertragsstaaten Anh. I

Am 28.11.2011 zog Finnland die unter 1. aufgeführte Erklärung mit Wirkung zum 1.6.2012 zurück (http://treaties.un.org/Pages/ViewDetails.aspx?src=TREATY&mtdsg_no=X-10&chapter=10&lang=en#12).

[8a] Island hat in einer Bekanntmachung vom 12.3.2003 erklärt, dass das Übereinkommen nach Art. 94 Absatz 1 nicht auf Kaufverträge oder deren Abschluss anwendbar sei, wenn die Parteien ihre Niederlassung in Dänemark, Finnland, Island oder Schweden haben (http://www.unicitral.org/en-index.htm)."

[9] Kanada hat bei Hinterlegung der Beitrittsurkunde zunächst folgende Erklärung abgegeben:
„Die Regierung von Kanada erklärt nach Artikel 93 des Übereinkommens, daß dieses sich auf Alberta, Britisch-Kolumbien, Manitoba, Neubraunschweig, Neufundland, Neuschottland, Ontario, Prince Edward Island und die Nordwest-Territorien erstreckt. Ferner erklärt die Regierung von Kanada nach Artikel 95 des Übereinkommens, daß dessen Artikel 1 Absatz 1 Buchstabe b in bezug auf Britisch-Kolumbien für sie nicht verbindlich ist.
Später hat Kanada den Generalsekretär der Vereinten Nationen notifiziert, dass es die Anwendung des Übereinkommens der Vereinten Nationen vom 11. April 1980 über den internationalen Warenkauf nach Artikel 93 dieses Übereinkommens mit Wirkung vom 1. Mai 1992 auf Québec und Saskatchewan und mit Wirkung vom 1. Januar 1993 auf Yukon erstreckt.
Ferner notifizierte Kanada am 31. Juli 1992 die Rücknahme seiner bei Hinterlegung der Beitrittsurkunde nach Artikel 95 abgegebene Erklärung zu Artikel 1 Absatz 1 Buchstabe b des Übereinkommens. Nach Artikel 97 Absatz 4 dieser Übereinkunft ist die Rücknahme am 1. Februar 1993 wirksam geworden.
(BGBl. 1992 II S. 449, 1993 II S. 738).

[10] Lettland hat bei Hinterlegung der Beitrittsurkunde folgende Erklärung abgegeben:
„Nach Artikel 96 des Übereinkommens erklärt die Republik Lettland, daß die Bestimmungen der Artikel 11 und 29 oder des Teils II des Übereinkommens, die für den Abschluß eines Kaufvertrags, seine Änderung oder Aufhebung durch Vereinbarung oder für ein Angebot, eine Annahme oder eine sonstige Willenserklärung eine andere als die schriftliche Form gestatten, nicht gelten, wenn eine Partei ihre Niederlassung in der Republik Lettland hat."
(BGBl. 1998 II S. 880).
Am 13.11.2012 zog Lettland die aufgeführte Erklärung zurück (http://treaties.un.org/Pages/ViewDetails.aspx?src=TREATY&mtdsg_no=X-10&chapter=10&lang=en#12).

[11] Die Republik Litauen hat bei Hinterlegung ihrer Beitrittsurkunde folgende Erklärung abgegeben:
„Nach den Artikeln 12 und 96 des Übereinkommens erklärt die Republik Litauen, daß die Bestimmungen der Artikel 11 und 29 oder des Teils II des Übereinkommens, die für den Abschluß eines Kaufvertrags, seine Änderung oder Aufhebung durch Vereinbarung oder für ein Angebot, eine Annahme oder eine sonstige Willenserklärung eine andere als die schriftliche Form gestatten, nicht gelten, wenn eine Partei ihre Niederlassung in der Republik Litauen hat."
(BGBl. 1995 II S. 814).

[12] Neuseeland hat anlässlich seines Beitritts erklärt, daß das Übereinkommen auf folgende Gebiete keine Anwendung findet: Cookinseln, Niue und Tokelau.
(BGBl. 1995 II S. 231).

[13] Norwegen hat bei Hinterlegung der Ratifikationsurkunde folgende Erklärung abgegeben:
„1. Nach Artikel 92 Absatz 1 erklärt die Regierung des Königreichs Norwegen, daß Teil II dieses Übereinkommens (Abschluß des Vertrages) für Norwegen nicht verbindlich ist.
2. Nach Artikel 94 erklärt die Regierung des Königreichs Norwegen in bezug auf Finnland und Schweden nach Absatz 1 und sonst nach Absatz 2, daß das Übereinkommen auf Kaufverträge keine Anwendung findet, wenn die Parteien ihre Niederlassung in Norwegen, Dänemark, Finnland, Island oder Schweden haben."
(BGBl. 1990 II S. 1479).

[14] Die Sowjetunion hat bei Hinterlegung der Beitrittsurkunde folgende Erklärung abgegeben:
„Nach den Artikeln 12 und 96 des Übereinkommens erklärt die Union der Sozialistischen Sowjetrepubliken, daß die Bestimmungen der Artikel 11 und 29 oder des Teils II des Übereinkommens, die für den Abschluß eines Kaufvertrages, seine Änderung oder Aufhebung durch Vereinbarung oder für ein Angebot, eine Annahme oder eine sonstige Willenserklärung eine andere als die schriftliche Form gestatten, nicht gelten, wenn eine Partei ihre Niederlassung in der Union der Sozialistischen Sowjetrepubliken hat."
(BGBl. 1991 II S. 675).

[14a] Art. 1 Absatz 1 Buchstabe b ist für diesen Staat unverbindlich (http://www.unicitral.org/en-index.htm).

[15] Die Republik Singapur hat bei Hinterlegung der Ratifikationsurkunde folgende Erklärung abgegeben:

„Nach Artikel 95 des Übereinkommens ist Artikel 1 Absatz 1 Buchstabe b für die Regierung der Republik Singapur nicht verbindlich; sie wendet das Übereinkommen nur auf Kaufverträge über Waren zwischen den Parteien an, die ihre Niederlassung in verschiedenen Staaten haben, wenn diese Staaten Vertragsstaaten sind."

(BGBl. 1995 II S. 814).

[16] Schweden hat bei Hinterlegung der Ratifikationsurkunde folgende Erklärung abgegeben:

„1. Nach Artikel 92 ist Teil II dieses Übereinkommens (Abschluß des Vertrages) für Schweden nicht verbindlich.

2. Nach Artikel 94 wird das Übereinkommen in bezug auf Finnland nach Absatz 1 und sonst nach Absatz 2 auf Kaufverträge keine Anwendung finden, wenn die Parteien ihre Niederlassung in Schweden, Finnland, Dänemark, Island oder Norwegen haben."

(BGBl. 1990 II S. 1479).

Am 25.5.2012 zog Schweden die unter 1. aufgeführte Erklärung mit Wirkung zum 1.12.2012 zurück (http://treaties.un.org/Pages/ViewDetails.aspx?src=TREATY&mtdsg_no=X-10&chapter=10&lang=en#12).

[16a] Das ehemalige Jugoslawien hatte das Übereinkommen am 11. April 1980 unterzeichnet und am 27. März 1985 ratifiziert. Das Übereinkommen war am 1.1.1988 für Jugoslawien in Kraft getreten. Mit Bekanntmachung vom 12. März 2001 gab Jugoslawien folgende Erklärung ab: Das Übereinkommen ist für Jugoslawien am 27. April 1992, zum Zeitpunkt der Staatennachfolge, in Kraft getreten (http://www.uncitral.org/en-index.htm).

[17] Die Tschechoslowakei hat bei Hinterlegung der Ratifikationsurkunde eine Erklärung abgegeben, wonach Artikel 1 Absatz 1 Buchstabe b des Übereinkommens für sie nicht verbindlich ist.

(BGBl. 1990 II S. 1480).

[18] Die Tschechoslowakei hat bei Hinterlegung der Ratifikationsurkunde eine Erklärung abgegeben, wonach Art. 1 Abs. 1 Buchstabe b des Übereinkommens für sie nicht verbindlich ist.

(BGBl. 1990 II S. 1480).

[19] Die Ukraine hat bei Hinterlegung der Beitrittsurkunde folgende Erklärung abgegeben:

„Nach den Artikeln 12 und 96 des Übereinkommens erklärt die Ukrainische Sozialistische Sowjetrepublik, daß die Bestimmungen der Artikel 11 und 29 oder des Teils II des Übereinkommens, die für den Abschluß eines Kaufvertrages, seine Änderung oder Aufhebung durch Vereinbarung oder für ein Angebot, eine Annahme oder eine sonstige Willenserklärung eine andere als die schriftliche Form gestatten, nicht gelten, wenn eine Partei ihre Niederlassung in der Ukrainischen Sozialistischen Sowjetrepublik hat."

(BGBl. 1990 II S. 1480).

[20] Ungarn hat bei Hinterlegung der Ratifikationsurkunde folgende Erklärung abgegeben:

„Es [Ungarn] ist der Auffassung, daß die Allgemeinen Bedingungen für Warenlieferungen zwischen Organisationen der Mitgliedländer des Rates für Gegenseitige Wirtschaftshilfe/GCD CMEA, 1968/1975, in der Fassung von 1979 den Bestimmungen des Artikels 90 des Übereinkommens unterliegen.

Es erklärt nach den Artikeln 12 und 96 des Übereinkommens, daß die Bestimmungen der Artikel 11 und 29 oder des Teils II des Übereinkommens, die für den Abschluß eines Kaufvertrages, seine Änderung oder Aufhebung durch Vereinbarung oder für ein Angebot, eine Annahme oder eine sonstige Willenserklärung eine andere als die schriftliche Form gestatten, nicht gelten, wenn eine Partei ihre Niederlassung in der Ungarischen Volksrepublik hat."

(BGBl. 1990 II S. 1479 f.).

[21] Die Vereinigten Staaten haben bei Hinterlegung der Ratifikationsurkunde folgende Erklärung abgegeben:

„Nach Artikel 95 ist Artikel 1 Absatz 1 Buchstabe b für die Vereinigten Staaten nicht verbindlich."

(BGBl. 1990 II S. 1480).

[22] Weißrußland hat bei Hinterlegung der Beitrittsurkunde folgende Erklärung abgegeben:

„Die Weißrussische Sozialistische Sowjetrepublik erklärt nach den Artikeln 12 und 96 des Übereinkommens, daß die Bestimmungen der Artikel 11 und 29 oder des Teils II dieses Übereinkommens, die für den Abschluß eines Kaufvertrages, seine Änderung oder Aufhebung durch Vereinbarung oder für ein Angebot, eine Annahme oder eine sonstige Willenserklärung eine andere als die schriftliche Form gestatten, nicht gelten, wenn eine Partei ihre Niederlassung in der Weißrussischen Sozialistischen Sowjetrepublik hat."

(BGBl. 1990 II S. 1481).

II. Vertragsstaaten des Übereinkommens über die Verjährung beim internationalen Warenkauf – VerjÜbk –*

Staat	Unterzeichnung	Ratifikation/ Annahme/ Genehmigung Beitritt/ Nachfolge	Inkrafttreten	Änderungsprotokoll Beitritt+
Ägypten		6.12.1982	1.8.1988	6.12.1982
Argentinien		9.10.1981	1.8.1988	19.7.1983
Belgien		1.8.2008	1.3.2009	1.8.2008
Benin		28.7.2011	1.2.2012	
Bosnien-Herzegowina**		12.1.1994	6.3.1992	
Brasilien	14.6.1974	–	–	
Bulgarien	24.2.1975	–	–	
Burundi		4.9.1998	1.4.1999	
Costa Rica	30.8.1974	–	–	
Dominikanische Republik		23.12.1977	1.8.1988	30.7.2010
Ghana	5.12.1974	7.10.1975	1.8.1988	
Guinea		23.1.1991	1.8.1991	23.1.1991
Kuba		2.11.1994	1.6.1995	2.11.1994
Liberia		16.9.2005	1.4.2006	16.9.2005
Mexiko		21.1.1988	1.8.1988	21.1.1988
Moldau, Republik		28.8.1997	1.3.1998	28.8.1997
Mongolei	14.6.1974	–	–	
Montenegro		23.10.2006	3.6.2006	6.8.2012
Nicaragua	13.5.1975	–	–	
Norwegen	11.12.1975	20.3.1980[1]	1.8.1988	
Paraguay		18.8.2003	1.3.2004	18.8.2003
Polen	14.6.1974	19.5.1995	1.12.1995	19.5.1995
Rumänien		23.4.1992	1.11.1992	23.4.1992
Russische Föderation***	14.6.1974			
Sambia		6.6.1986	1.8.1988	6.6.1986
Serbien****		12.3.2001	27.4.1992	
Slowakische Republik*****		28.5.1993	1.1.1993	28.5.1993[2]
Slowenien		2.8.1995	1.3.1996	2.8.1995
Tschechische Republik*****		30.9.1993	1.1.1993	30.9.1993[2]
Uganda		12.2.1992	1.9.1992	12.2.1992
Ukraine	14.6.1974	13.9.1993	1.4.1994	
Ungarn	14.6.1974	16.6.1983	1.8.1988	16.6.1983
Uruguay		1.4.1997	1.11.1997	1.4.1997
USA		5.5.1994[3]	1.12.1994	5.5.1994
Weißrußland	14.6.1974	23.1.1997	1.8.1997	23.1.1997

Anh. II

Übereinkommen: Unterzeichnungen: 12; Ratifikation, Annahme, Genehmigung, Beitritt, Nachfolge: 29
Änderungsprotokoll: Ratifikation, Annahme, Genehmigung, Beitritt, Nachfolge: 22
Stand 11.4.2013
Quelle: Office of Legal Affairs, Treaty Section, United Nations, New York, N. Y. 10017 (USA)
Internetdokument: www.uncitral.org/en-index.htm
(dort auch der jeweils aktuelle Status)

+ Soweit nicht anders vermerkt, ist das Änderungsprotokoll für die aufgeführten Staaten gleichzeitig mit dem Übereinkommen in Kraft getreten.
* Deutschland und die Schweiz sind dem Übereinkommen bislang noch nicht beigetreten.
** Bosnien-Herzegowina hat am 12.1.1994 eine Urkunde hinterlegt, in der es als Nachfolger des ehemaligen Jugoslawien ausgewiesen wird.
*** Die Russische Föderation hat am 24.12.1991 die Nachfolge der ehemaligen Sowjetunion als Mitglied der Vereinten Nationen angetreten und damit die Rechte und Pflichten der Sowjetunion aus der Charta der Vereinten Nationen und den multilateralen Verträgen übernommen, die beim Generalsekretär hinterlegt waren.
**** Das ehemalige Jugoslawien war dem Übereinkommen am 27.11.1978 beigetreten. Mit Bekanntmachung vom 12.3.2001 gab Jugoslawien folgende Erklärung ab: Das Übereinkommen ist für Jugoslawien am 27.4.1992, zum Zeitpunkt der Staatennachfolge, in Kraft getreten (http://www.uncitral.org/en-index-htm).
***** Die ehemalige Tschechoslowakei hat das Übereinkommen am 29.8.1975 unterzeichnet und am 26.5.1977 die Ratifikationsurkunde hinterlegt. Das Übereinkommen trat daraufhin am 1.8.1988 in Kraft. Dem Änderungsprotokoll ist die ehemalige Tschechoslowakei am 5.3.1990 beigetreten; es trat für sie am 10.10.1990 in Kraft.
Die Slowakische Rebulik hat am 28.5.1993 eine Urkunde hinterlegt, in der sie als Rechtsnachfolgerin der ehemaligen Tschechoslowakei ausgewiesen wurde. Die Tschechische Republik hat am 30.9.1993 für sich eine Urkunde entsprechenden Inhalts hinterlegt. Übereinkommen und Änderungsprotokoll konnten deshalb in der Slowakischen Republik und in der Tschechischen Republik mit Wirkung vom 1.1.1993, dem Zeitpunkt der Staatennachfolge, in Kraft treten.
[1] Bei der Unterzeichnung des Übereinkommens sowie bei Hinterlegung der Ratifikationsurkunde hat Norwegen in Übereinstimmung mit Art. 34 des Übereinkommens erklärt, dass das Übereinkommen nicht anwendbar sei auf Kaufverträge zwischen Parteien, die beide ihre Niederlassung im Gebiet der nordischen Staaten (d. h. Norwegen, Dänemark, Finnland, Island und Schweden) haben.
[2] Bei Hinterlegung der Beitrittsurkunde zum Änderungsprotokoll hat die Tschechoslowakei in Übereinstimmung mit Art. XII des Änderungsprotokolls erklärt, dass Art. I des Änderungsprotokolls für sie nicht verbindlich sei. Dies bedeutet, dass für sie bzw. ihre Nachfolgestaaten Art. 3 des Verjährungsübereinkommens in der alten Fassung gilt.
[3] Bei Hinterlegung der Beitrittsurkunde haben die USA in Übereinstimmung mit Art. XII des Änderungsprotokolls erklärt, dass Art. I des Änderungsprotokolls für sie nicht verbindlich sei.

III. Materialien zu CISG und VerjÜbk

1. Working Group

1. Report of the Secretary-General: Analysis of replies and comments by Governments on the Hague Conventions of 1964, (A/CN.9/31), YB I (1968-70), S. 159–176.
2. Report of the W. G., first session, New York 5–16 Jan.1970, (A/CN.9/35), (Organisation, Zielsetzung), YB I (1968-70), S. 176–202.
3. Note by the Secretary-General: Analysis of comments and proposals relating to articles 1–17 of ULIS 1964, (A/CN.9/WG.2/WP.6), YB II (1971), S. 37–49.
4. Report of the W. G., second session, Geneva, 7–18 Dec.1970, (A/CN.9/52), (Beratung über Artt. 1–17 ULIS), YB II (1971), S. 50–66.
5. Report of the Secretary-General: „Delivery" in ULIS, (A/CN.9/WG.2/WP.8), YB III (1972), S. 31 ff.; „Ipso facto avoidance" in ULIS, (A/CN.9/WG.2/WP.9), YB III (1972), S. 41–54.
6. Note by the Secretary-General: Analysis of comments and proposals relating to articles 18–55 of ULIS, (A/CN.9/WG.2/WP.10), YB III (1972), S. 54 ff.; Analysis of comments and proposals relating to articles 1–17 of ULIS, (A/CN.9/WG.2/WP.11), YB III (1972), S. 54–69.
7. Report of the W. G., third session, Geneva 17–28 Jan.1972, (A/CN.9/62, Add.1 and Add.2), (Beratung und Entscheidung über Artt. 1–55 ULIS), YB III (1972), S. 77–95.
8. Note by the Secretary-General: Analysis of comments and proposals by Governments relating to Artt. 56–70 of ULIS, (A/CN.9/WG.2/WP.15), YB IV (1973), S. 31–35.
9. Report of the Secretary-General: Obligations of the Seller in an International Sale of Goods, consolidation of work done by the W. G. and suggested solutions for unresolved problems, (A/CN.9/WG.2/WP.16), YB IV (1973), S. 36–61.
10. Report of the W. G., fourth session, New York, 22 Jan.–2 Feb.1973, (A/CN.9/75), (Fortführung der Beratung über Artt. 18–55 ULIS, Beratung über Artt. 56–70 ULIS), YB IV (1973), S. 61–79.
11. Report of the W. G., fifth session, Geneva, 21 Jan.–1 Feb.1974, (A/CN.9/87), (Fortführung der Beratungen über Artt. 58–70 ULIS, Beratung über Artt. 71–101 ULIS), YB V (1974), S. 29 ff. Revised text of the Uniform Law on the International Sale of Goods as approved or deferred for further consideration by the W. G. at its first five sessions, (A/CN.9/87, annex I), YB V (1974), S. 29–51. Texts of comments and proposals by representatives: Artt. 56–70 of ULIS, (A/CN.9/87, annex II), YB V (1974), S. 60–65. Artt. 71–101 of ULIS, (A/CN.9/87, annex III), YB V (1974), S. 65–79. Report of the Secretary-General: issues presented by chapters IV to VI of ULIS, (A/CN.9/87, annex IV), (Verpflichtungen des Käufers; gemeinsame Bestimmungen für die Verpflichtungen des Verkäufers und des Käufers; Gefahrübergang), YB V (1974), S. 80–94.
12. Report of the W. G., sixth session, New York, 27 Jan.–7 Feb.1975, (Fertigstellung des Entwurfs eines Übereinkommens über den internationalen Warenkauf), (A/CN.9/100), YB VI (1975), S. 49–62. Revised text of the Convention on the International Sale of Goods as approved or deferred for further consideration by the W. G. at its first six sessions, (A/CN.9/100, annex I), YB VI (1975), S. 63–69. Text of comments and proposals of representatives on the revised text of a Uniform Law on the International Sale of Goods as approved or deferred for further consideration by the W. G. at its first five sessions, (A/CN.9/100, annex II), YB VI (1975), S. 70–87. Report of the Secretary-General: pending questions with respect to the revised text of a Uniform Law on the International Sale of Goods, (A/CN.9/100, annex III and IV), YB VI (1975), S. 88–113.

13. Report of the Secretary-General: general conditions of sale and standard contracts, (A/CN.9/98), YB VI (1975), S. 114–118.

14. Report of the W. G., seventh session, Geneva, 5–16 Jan.1976, (Beratungen über den Entwurf eines Übereinkommens über den internationalen Warenkauf, Abschluß und Gültigkeit von Verträgen im internationalen Warenkauf), (A/CN.9/116), YB VII (1976), S. 87–89. Draft Convention on the International Sale of Goods, (A/CN.9/116, annex I), YB VII (1976), S. 89–96. Commentary on the draft Convention on the International Sale of Goods, (A/CN.9/116, annex II), YB VII (1976), S. 96–142.

15. Report of the W. G., eighth session, New York, 4–14 Jan.1977, (Abschluß von internationalen Warenkaufverträgen), (A/CN.9/128), YB VIII (1977), S. 73–88. Draft Convention on the Formation of Contracts for the International Sale of Goods as approved or deferred for further consideration by the W. G. at its eighth session, (A/CN.9/128, annex I), YB VIII (1977), S. 88–90. Report of the Secretary-General: Formation and Validity of Contracts for the International Sale of Goods, (A/CN.9/128, annex II), YB VIII (1977), S. 90–109.

16. Comments by Governments and international organizations on the draft Convention on the International Sale of Goods, (A/CN.9/125 and A/CN.9/125/Add.1 to 3), YB VIII (1977), S. 109–142. Report of the Secretary-General: analysis of comments by Governments and international organizations on the draft Convention on the International Sale of Goods as adopted by the W. G., (A/CN.9/126), YB VIII (1977), S. 142–163.

17. Report of the Secretary-General: draft Convention on the International Sale of Goods; draft articles concerning implementation and other final clauses, (A/CN.9/135), YB VIII (1977), S. 164–168.

18. Report of the W. G., ninth session, Geneva, 19–30 Sept.1977, (Auslegung, Gültigkeit, Fertigstellung des Entwurfs des Übereinkommens über den Abschluß von Verträgen über den internationalen Warenkauf), (A/CN.9/142), YB IX (1978), S. 61–63. (Text des „Formation Draft 1977" im Annex, S. 83 f.; Arbeitspapiere dazu S. 85–105).

19. Report of the Secretary-General: commentary on the draft Convention on the Formation of Contracts for the International Sale of Goods, (A/CN.9/144), YB IX (1978), S. 106–121.

20. Report of the Secretary-General: incorporation of the provisions of the draft Convention on the Formation of Contracts for the International Sale of Goods into the draft Convention on the International Sale of Goods, (A/CN.9/145), YB IX (1978), S. 121–126.

21. Report of the Secretary-General: analytical compilation of comments by Governments and international organizations on the draft Convention on the Formation of Contracts for the International Sale of Goods as adopted by the W. G. and on the draft of a uniform law for the unification of certain rules relating to validity of contracts for the international sale of goods prepared by UNIDROIT, (A/CN.9/146 and Add. 1–4), YB IX (1978), S. 127–146.

2. UNCITRAL

1. Report of UNCITRAL, tenth session, Vienna, 23 May–17 June 1977, (Ausarbeitung des Wiener E 1977), (A/32/17), YB VIII (1977), S. 11–21 (Text des Entwurfes S. 15–21).

2. Report of UNCITRAL, eleventh session, New York, 30 May–16 June 1978, (Fertigstellung des New Yorker E 1978), (A/33/17), YB IX (1978), S. 11–21 (Text des Entwurfes S. 14–21).

3. Diplomatic Conference

1. United Nations Conference on Contracts for the International Sale of Goods, Vienna, 10 March–11 April 1980, Official Records, Documents of the Conference and Summary

Records of the Plenary Meetings and of the Meetings of the Main Committees, United Nations, New York (1981) (A/CONF.97/19).

2. Text of the draft Convention on Contracts for the International Sale of Goods approved by UNCITRAL (New Yorker E 1978), (A/CONF.97/5), O. R., S. 5–14; auch abgedruckt bei *Honnold,* Uniform Law, S. 641–658.

3. Commentary on the draft Convention on Contracts for the International Sale of Goods, prepared by the Secretariat (Sekretariatskommentar), (A/CONF.97/5), O. R., S. 14–70; zum Text s. auch http://www.cisg-online.ch/cisg/materials-commentary.html.

4. Analysis of comments and proposals by Governments and international organizations on the draft Convention on Contracts for the International Sale of Goods . . ., prepared by the Secretary-General, (A/CONF.97/9), O. R., S. 71–82.

5. Report of the First Committee, (A/CONF.97/11), O. R., S. 82–141.

6. Report of the Second Committee, (A/CONF.97/12), O. R., S. 141–154.

7. Final Act of the United Nations Conference on Contracts for the International Sale of Goods, (A/CONF.97/18), O. R., S. 176 f.; YB XI (1980), S. 149–150; in englischer und französischer Sprache auch abgedruckt bei *Schlechtriem,* Einheitliches UN-Kaufrecht, S. 112–119.

8. United Nations Convention on Contracts for the International Sale of Goods, (A/CONF.97/18, annex I), O. R., S. 178–190; YB XI (1980), S. 151–162; deutsche Fassung (en) mit teilweise abweichenden Formulierungen s. RabelsZ 51 (1987), S. 134–187; Text auch abgedruckt bei Bianca/Bonell, S. 683–840 (in arabischer, chinesischer, französischer, englischer, russischer, spanischer, deutscher und italienischer Sprache); Text in verschiedenen Sprachen auch im Internet unter http://www.cisg-online.ch/cisg/materials-text.html.

4. Ratifikation und Vertragsgesetz

Deutschland

1. Gesetzesentwurf der Bundesregierung: Entwurf eines Gesetzes zu dem Übereinkommen der Vereinten Nationen vom 11. April 1980 über Verträge über den internationalen Warenkauf sowie zur Änderung des Gesetzes zu dem Übereinkommen vom 19. Mai 1956 über den Beförderungsvertrag im internationalen Straßengüterverkehr (CMR): BT-Drs. 11/3076 (7.10.1988).

2. Denkschrift der Bundesregierung zum Übereinkommen, BT-Drs. 11/3076 (7.10.1988), S. 38–64.

3. Gesetz zu dem Übereinkommen der Vereinten Nationen vom 11. April 1980 über Verträge über den internationalen Warenkauf sowie zur Änderung des Gesetzes zu dem Übereinkommen vom 19. Mai 1956 über den Beförderungsvertrag im internationalen Straßengüterverkehr (CMR): (VertragsG) vom 5.7.1989, BGBl. II S. 586–587, in der Fassung des Gesetzes zur Modernisierung des Schuldrechts vom 26.11.2001, BGBl. I S. 3138.

Österreich

1. Erläuterungen zur Regierungsvorlage zum Übereinkommen der Vereinten Nationen über Verträge über den internationalen Warenkauf vom 12.5.1987, 94 BlgNR, XVII.GP, S. 45.

2. Gesetz vom 29.12.1987, BGBl. 1988, S. 1530.

Schweiz

Botschaft betreffend das Wiener Übereinkommen über Verträge über den internationalen Warenkauf vom 11.1.1989, BBl. 1989 I, S. 745.

5. Übereinkommen über die Verjährung beim internationalen Warenkauf vom 14. Juni 1974

a. Working Group

Reports of Working Group, YB I (1968–1970), S. 218–232; YB II (1971), S. 74–112; YB III (1972), S. 109–110.

b. UNCITRAL

Report of UNCITRAL, fifth session, New York, 10 April–5 May 1972, YB III (1972), S. 11–16.

c. Diplomatic Conference

United Nations Conference on Prescription (Limitation) in the International Sale of Goods, Official Records: Documents of the Conference and Summary Records of the Plenary Meetings and of the Meetings of the Main Committees (New York, 20 May–14 June 1974), New York: United Nations (1975) (A/Conf. 63/16).

Text of the Draft Convention on Prescription (Limitation) in the International Sale of Goods, prepared by the United Nations Commission on International Trade Law, (A/Conf. 63/4), O. R., S. 4–10.

Commentary on the Draft Convention on Prescription (Limitation) in the International Sale of Goods, prepared by the Secretariat, (A/Conf. 63/5), O. R., S. 10–33; YB III (1972), S. 115–142.

Analytical Compilation of Comments and Proposals by Governments and International Organizations on the Draft Convention on Prescription (Limitation) in the International Sale of Goods, prepared by the Secretariat, (A/Conf. 63/6), O. R., S. 33–50.

Report of the First Committee, (A/Conf. 63/9), O. R., S. 50–81.

Report of the Second Committee, (A/Conf. 63/12), O. R., S. 81–87.

Final Act of the United Nations Conference on Prescription (Limitation) in the International Sale of Goods, (A/Conf. 63/14), O. R., S. 99–100; YB V (1974), S. 209–210.

United Nations Convention on Prescription (Limitation) in the International Sale of Goods, (A/Conf. 63/15), O. R., S. 101–105; YB V (1974), S. 210–215.

Commentary on the Convention on the Limitation Period in the International Sale of Goods, prepared by the United Nations Office of Legal Affairs, (A/Conf. 63/17), O. R., S. 1–62; YB X (1979), S. 145–173 (Sekretariatskommentar).

6. Protokoll zur Änderung des Übereinkommens über die Verjährung beim internationalen Warenkauf vom 11. April 1980

Protocol Amending the Convention on the Limitation Period in the International Sale of Goods, (A/Conf. 97/18, annex II), YB XI (1980), S. 162–164; deutsche Fassung s. RabelsZ 51 (1987), 187–195.

IV. Incoterms® 2010

Die Regeln der ICC zur Auslegung nationaler und internationaler Handelsklauseln

Gültig ab 1. Januar 2011
(ICC-Publikation Nr. 560 ED)[1]

Einführung

(nicht abgedruckt)

[I.] Klauseln für alle Transportarten

[1.] EXW

AB WERK
(... benannter Lieferort)

ANWENDUNGSHINWEIS

Diese Klausel kann unabhängig von der gewählten Transportart verwendet werden, auch dann, wenn mehr als eine Transportart zum Einsatz kommt. Sie eignet sich für den nationalen Warenhandel, für den internationalen Handel ist hingegen FCA üblicherweise besser geeignet.

„Ab Werk" bedeutet, dass der Verkäufer liefert, wenn er die Ware dem Käufer beim Verkäufer oder an einem anderen benannten Ort (z. B. Werk, Fabrik, Lager usw.) zur Verfügung stellt. Der Verkäufer muss die Ware weder auf ein abholendes Transportmittel verladen, noch muss er sie zur Ausfuhr freimachen, falls dies erforderlich sein sollte.

Die Parteien sind gut beraten, die Stelle innerhalb des benannten Lieferortes so präzise wie möglich zu bezeichnen, da der Verkäufer die Kosten und Gefahren bis zu dieser Stelle zu tragen hat. Der Käufer trägt alle Kosten und Gefahren, die bei der Übernahme der Ware an der gegebenenfalls vereinbarten Stelle am benannten Lieferort entstehen.

EXW stellt die Mindestverpflichtung für den Verkäufer dar. Die Klausel sollte mit Vorsicht angewendet werden, da:

a) der Verkäufer gegenüber dem Käufer keine Verpflichtung hat, die Ware zu verladen, selbst wenn der Verkäufer in der Praxis dazu besser in der Lage wäre. Falls der Verkäufer die Ware verlädt, tut er dieses auf Gefahr und Kosten des Käufers. In Fällen, in denen der Verkäufer besser in der Lage ist, die Ware zu verladen, ist es meist sinnvoller, die FCA-Klausel zu verwenden, da sie den Verkäufer verpflichtet, auf seine Gefahr und Kosten zu verladen.

b) ein Käufer, der von einem Verkäufer auf EXW-Basis zur Ausfuhr kauft, sich bewusst sein sollte, dass der Verkäufer gegenüber dem Käufer nicht verpflichtet ist, die Ware für die Ausfuhr freizumachen. Er ist lediglich verpflichtet, den Käufer so zu unterstützen, dass dieser die Ausfuhr durchführen kann. Käufer sind daher gut beraten, EXW nicht zu verwenden, wenn es ihnen nicht möglich ist, direkt oder indirekt die Ausfuhrabfertigung vorzunehmen.

---

[1] Abgedruckt mit freundlicher Genehmigung der Internationalen Handelskammer (ICC Deutschland).

c) der Käufer gegenüber dem Verkäufer nur eine eingeschränkte Verpflichtung hat, diesem Informationen hinsichtlich der Ausfuhr der Ware zur Verfügung zu stellen, obwohl es sein kann, dass der Verkäufer diese Informationen z. B. aus steuerlichen Gründen oder aufgrund von Meldepflichten benötigt.

A. Verpflichtungen des Verkäufers

A1. Allgemeine Verpflichtungen des Verkäufers

Der Verkäufer hat die Ware und die Handelsrechnung in Übereinstimmung mit dem Kaufvertrag bereitzustellen und jeden sonstigen vertraglich vereinbarten Konformitätsnachweis zu erbringen.

Jedes Dokument, auf das in A1–A10 Bezug genommen wird, kann auch ein entsprechender elektronischer Beleg oder ein entsprechendes elektronisches Verfahren sein, wenn dies zwischen den Parteien vereinbart oder üblich ist.

A2. Lizenzen, Genehmigungen, Sicherheitsfreigaben und andere Formalitäten

Falls zutreffend, hat der Verkäufer den Käufer auf dessen Verlangen, Gefahr und Kosten bei der Beschaffung der Ausfuhrgenehmigung oder anderer behördlicher Genehmigungen, die für die Ausfuhr der Ware erforderlich sind, zu unterstützen.

Falls zutreffend, hat der Verkäufer auf Verlangen, Gefahr und Kosten des Käufers diesem alle ihm vorliegenden Informationen, die für die Sicherheitsfreigabe der Ware erforderlich sind, zur Verfügung zu stellen.

A3. Beförderungs- und Versicherungsverträge

a. Beförderungsvertrag
Der Verkäufer hat gegenüber dem Käufer keine Verpflichtung, einen Beförderungsvertrag abzuschließen.
b. Versicherungsvertrag
Der Verkäufer hat gegenüber dem Käufer keine Verpflichtung, einen Versicherungsvertrag abzuschließen. Jedoch hat der Verkäufer dem Käufer auf dessen Verlangen, Gefahr und (gegebenenfalls entstehende) Kosten jene Informationen zur Verfügung zu stellen, die der Käufer für den Abschluss einer Versicherung benötigt.

A4. Lieferung

Der Verkäufer hat die Ware zu liefern, indem er sie dem Käufer am genannten Lieferort an der gegebenenfalls vereinbarten Stelle zur Verfügung stellt, jedoch ohne Verladung auf das abholende Beförderungsmittel. Wurde am benannten Lieferort keine bestimmte Stelle vereinbart und kommen mehrere Stellen in Betracht, kann der Verkäufer die Stelle auswählen, die für den Zweck am besten geeignet ist. Der Verkäufer hat die Ware zum vereinbarten Zeitpunkt oder innerhalb des vereinbarten Zeitraums zu liefern.

A5. Gefahrenübergang

Der Verkäufer trägt bis zur Lieferung gemäß A4 alle Gefahren des Verlustes oder der Beschädigung der Ware, mit Ausnahme von Verlust oder Beschädigung unter den in B5 beschriebenen Umständen.

A6. Kostenverteilung

Der Verkäufer hat alle die Ware betreffenden Kosten zu tragen bis diese gemäß A4 geliefert worden ist, ausgenommen solcher Kosten, die vom Käufer wie in B6 vorgesehen zu tragen sind.

A7. Benachrichtigungen an den Käufer

Der Verkäufer hat den Käufer über alles Nötige zu benachrichtigen, damit dieser die Ware übernehmen kann.

A8. Transportdokument

Der Verkäufer hat gegenüber dem Käufer keine Verpflichtung.

A9. Prüfung – Verpackung – Kennzeichnung

Der Verkäufer hat die Kosten jener Prüfvorgänge (wie Qualitätsprüfung, Messen, Wiegen und Zählen) zu tragen, die notwendig sind, um die Ware gemäß A4 zu liefern.

Der Verkäufer hat auf eigene Kosten die Ware zu verpacken, es sei denn, es ist handelsüblich, die jeweilige Art der verkauften Ware unverpackt zu transportieren. Der Verkäufer kann die Ware in der für ihren Transport geeigneten Weise verpacken, es sei denn, der Käufer hat den Verkäufer vor Vertragsschluss über spezifische Verpackungsanforderungen in Kenntnis gesetzt. Die Verpackung ist in geeigneter Weise zu kennzeichnen.

A10. Unterstützung bei Informationen und damit verbundene Kosten

Der Verkäufer hat, falls zutreffend, dem Käufer auf dessen Verlangen, Gefahr und Kosten rechtzeitig alle Dokumente und Informationen, einschließlich sicherheitsrelevanter Informationen, die der Käufer für die Aus- und/oder Einfuhr der Ware und/oder für ihren Transport bis zum endgültigen Bestimmungsort benötigt, zur Verfügung zu stellen oder ihn bei deren Beschaffung zu unterstützen.

B. Verpflichtungen des Käufers

B1. Allgemeine Verpflichtungen des Käufers

Der Käufer hat den im Kaufvertrag genannten Preis der Ware zu zahlen.

Jedes Dokument, auf das in B1–B10 Bezug genommen wird, kann auch ein entsprechender elektronischer Beleg oder ein entsprechendes elektronisches Verfahren sein, wenn dies zwischen den Parteien vereinbart oder üblich ist.

B2. Lizenzen, Genehmigungen, Sicherheitsfreigaben und andere Formalitäten

Falls zutreffend, obliegt es dem Käufer, auf eigene Gefahr und Kosten die Aus- und Einfuhrgenehmigung oder andere behördliche Genehmigungen zu beschaffen sowie alle Zollformalitäten für die Ausfuhr der Ware zu erledigen.

B3. Beförderungs- und Versicherungsverträge

a. Beförderungsvertrag
  Der Käufer hat gegenüber dem Verkäufer keine Verpflichtung, einen Beförderungsvertrag abzuschließen.

b. Versicherungsvertrag

Der Käufer hat gegenüber dem Verkäufer keine Verpflichtung, einen Versicherungsvertrag abzuschließen.

B4. Übernahme

Der Käufer muss die Ware übernehmen, wenn A4 und A7 entsprochen worden ist.

B5. Gefahrenübergang

Der Käufer trägt alle Gefahren des Verlustes oder der Beschädigung der Ware ab dem Zeitpunkt, an dem sie wie in A4 vorgesehen geliefert worden ist.

Falls der Käufer es unterlässt, gemäß B7 zu benachrichtigen, trägt der Käufer alle Gefahren des Verlustes oder der Beschädigung der Ware ab dem vereinbarten Lieferzeitpunkt oder ab Ablauf des vereinbarten Lieferzeitraums, vorausgesetzt, die Ware ist eindeutig als die vertragliche Ware kenntlich gemacht worden.

B6. Kostenverteilung

Der Käufer hat:
a. alle die Ware betreffenden Kosten ab dem Zeitpunkt der Lieferung wie in A4 vorgesehen zu tragen;
b. alle zusätzlichen Kosten zu tragen, die entweder dadurch entstanden sind, dass die ihm zur Verfügung gestellte Ware nicht übernommen worden oder keine Benachrichtigung gemäß B7 erfolgt ist, vorausgesetzt, die Ware ist eindeutig als die vertragliche Ware kenntlich gemacht worden;
c. falls zutreffend, alle Zölle, Steuern und andere Abgaben sowie die bei der Ausfuhr fälligen Kosten der Zollformalitäten zu tragen; und
d. alle dem Verkäufer durch die in A2 vorgesehene Unterstützung entstandenen Kosten und Abgaben zu erstatten.

B7. Benachrichtigungen an den Verkäufer

Wann immer der Käufer berechtigt ist, innerhalb eines vereinbarten Zeitraums den Zeitpunkt und/oder innerhalb des benannten Ortes die Stelle für die Warenübernahme zu bestimmen, hat er den Verkäufer in angemessener Weise darüber zu benachrichtigen.

B8. Liefernachweis

Der Käufer hat dem Verkäufer einen angemessenen Nachweis der Warenübernahme zu erbringen.

B9. Prüfung der Ware

Der Käufer hat die Kosten für jede vor der Verladung zwingend erforderliche Warenkontrolle (pre-shipment inspection) zu tragen, einschließlich behördlich angeordneter Kontrollen des Ausfuhrlandes.

B10. Unterstützung bei Informationen und damit verbundene Kosten

Der Käufer hat dem Verkäufer rechtzeitig alle sicherheitsrelevanten Informationsanforderungen mitzuteilen, so dass der Verkäufer die Verpflichtungen entsprechend A10 erfüllen kann.

Der Käufer hat dem Verkäufer alle Kosten und Abgaben zu erstatten, die dem Verkäufer durch das Zurverfügungstellen oder die Unterstützung bei der Beschaffung der Dokumente und Informationen wie in A10 vorgesehen entstanden sind.

[2.] FCA

FREI FRACHTFÜHRER
(... benannter Lieferort)

ANWENDUNGSHINWEIS

Diese Klausel kann unabhängig von der gewählten Transportart verwendet werden, auch dann, wenn mehr als eine Transportart zum Einsatz kommt.

„Frei Frachtführer" bedeutet, dass der Verkäufer die Ware dem Frachtführer oder einer anderen vom Käufer benannten Person beim Verkäufer oder an einem anderen benannten Ort liefert. Die Parteien sind gut beraten, die Stelle innerhalb des benannten Lieferortes so genau wie möglich zu bezeichnen, da an dieser Stelle die Gefahr auf den Käufer übergeht.

Beabsichtigen die Parteien, die Ware beim Verkäufer zu liefern, sind sie angehalten, dessen Adresse als benannten Lieferort anzugeben. Beabsichtigen die Parteien hingegen, dass die Ware an einem anderen Ort geliefert wird, so müssen sie diesen anderen Lieferort genau angeben.

FCA verpflichtet den Verkäufer, falls zutreffend, die Ware zur Ausfuhr freizumachen, Jedoch hat der Verkäufer keine Verpflichtung, die Ware zur Einfuhr freizumachen, Einfuhrzölle zu zahlen oder Einfuhrzollformalitäten zu erledigen.

A. Verpflichtungen des Verkäufers

A1. Allgemeine Verpflichtungen des Verkäufers

Der Verkäufer hat die Ware und die Handelsrechnung in Übereinstimmung mit dem Kaufvertrag bereitzustellen und jeden sonstigen vertraglich vereinbarten Konformitätsnachweis zu erbringen.

Jedes Dokument, auf das in A1–A10 Bezug genommen wird, kann auch ein entsprechender elektronischer Beleg oder ein entsprechendes elektronisches Verfahren sein, wenn dies zwischen den Parteien vereinbart oder üblich ist.

A2. Lizenzen, Genehmigungen, Sicherheitsfreigaben und andere Formalitäten

Falls zutreffend, hat der Verkäufer auf eigene Gefahr und Kosten die Ausfuhrgenehmigung oder andere behördliche Genehmigungen zu beschaffen sowie alle Zollformalitäten zu erledigen, die für die Ausfuhr der Ware erforderlich sind.

A3. Beförderungs- und Versicherungsverträge

a. Beförderungsvertrag
Der Verkäufer hat gegenüber dem Käufer keine Verpflichtung, einen Beförderungsvertrag abzuschließen. Wenn es der Käufer jedoch verlangt oder es Handelspraxis ist und der Käufer keine gegenteilige Anweisung rechtzeitig erteilt, kann der Verkäufer einen Beförderungsvertrag zu üblichen Bedingungen auf Gefahr und Kosten des Käufers abschließen. In beiden Fällen kann es der Verkäufer ablehnen, den Beförderungsvertrag abzuschließen, wovon er den Käufer umgehend in Kenntnis zu setzen hat.

b. Versicherungsvertrag
Der Verkäufer hat gegenüber dem Käufer keine Verpflichtung, einen Versicherungsvertrag abzuschließen. Jedoch hat der Verkäufer dem Käufer auf dessen Verlangen, Gefahr und (gegebenenfalls entstehende) Kosten jene Informationen zur Verfügung zu stellen, die der Käufer für den Abschluss einer Versicherung benötigt.

A4. Lieferung

Der Verkäufer hat die Ware an den Frachtführer oder eine andere vom Käufer benannte Person an der gegebenenfalls vereinbarten Stelle am benannten Ort zum vereinbarten Zeitpunkt oder innerhalb des vereinbarten Zeitraums zu liefern.

Die Lieferung ist abgeschlossen:
a. falls der benannte Ort beim Verkäufer liegt, wenn die Ware auf das vom Käufer bereitgestellte Beförderungsmittel verladen worden ist.
b. in allen anderen Fällen, wenn die Ware dem Frachtführer oder einer anderen vom Käufer benannten Person auf dem Beförderungsmittel des Verkäufers entladebereit zur Verfügung gestellt wird.

Wenn der Käufer am benannten Lieferort keine bestimmte Stelle gemäß B7 d mitgeteilt hat und mehrere Stellen in Betracht kommen, kann der Verkäufer jene Stelle auswählen, die für den Zweck am besten geeignet ist.

Sofern der Käufer den Verkäufer nicht anderweitig benachrichtigt, kann der Verkäufer die Ware zur Beförderung in der Weise übergeben, wie es Menge und/oder Art der Ware verlangen.

A5. Gefahrenübergang

Der Verkäufer trägt bis zur Lieferung gemäß A4 alle Gefahren des Verlustes oder der Beschädigung der Ware, mit Ausnahme von Verlust oder Beschädigung unter den in B5 beschriebenen Umständen.

A6. Kostenverteilung

Der Verkäufer hat zu tragen
a. alle die Ware betreffenden Kosten bis diese gemäß A4 geliefert worden ist, ausgenommen solcher Kosten, die wie in B6 vorgesehen vom Käufer zu tragen sind; und
b. falls zutreffend, die Kosten der für die Ausfuhr notwendigen Zollformalitäten sowie alle Zölle, Steuern und andere Abgaben, die bei der Ausfuhr fällig werden.

A7. Benachrichtigungen an den Käufer

Der Verkäufer hat den Käufer auf dessen Gefahr und Kosten in angemessener Weise darüber zu benachrichtigen, entweder, dass die Ware gemäß A4 geliefert worden ist, oder dass der Frachtführer oder eine andere vom Käufer benannte Person die Ware innerhalb der vereinbarten Frist nicht übernommen hat.

A8. Transportdokument

Der Verkäufer hat auf eigene Kosten dem Käufer den üblichen Nachweis zu erbringen, dass die Ware gemäß A4 geliefert worden ist.

Der Verkäufer hat den Käufer auf dessen Verlangen, Gefahr und Kosten bei der Beschaffung eines Transportdokuments zu unterstützen.

A9. Prüfung – Verpackung – Kennzeichnung

Der Verkäufer hat die Kosten jener Prüfvorgänge (wie Qualitätsprüfung, Messen, Wiegen und Zählen), die notwendig sind, um die Ware gemäß A4 zu liefern, sowie die Kosten für alle von den Behörden des Ausfuhrlandes angeordneten Warenkontrollen vor der Verladung (pre-shipment inspection) zu tragen.

Der Verkäufer hat auf eigene Kosten die Ware zu verpacken, es sei denn, es ist handelsüblich, die jeweilige Art der verkauften Ware unverpackt zu transportieren. Der Verkäufer kann die Ware in der für ihren Transport geeigneten Weise verpacken, es sei denn, der

Käufer hat den Verkäufer vor Vertragsschluss über spezifische Verpackungsanforderungen in Kenntnis gesetzt. Die Verpackung ist in geeigneter Weise zu kennzeichnen.

A10. Unterstützung bei Informationen und damit verbundene Kosten

Der Verkäufer hat, falls zutreffend, dem Käufer auf dessen Verlangen, Gefahr und Kosten rechtzeitig alle Dokumente und Informationen, einschließlich sicherheitsrelevanter Informationen, die der Käufer für die Einfuhr der Ware und/oder für ihren Transport bis zum endgültigen Bestimmungsort benötigt, zur Verfügung zu stellen oder ihn bei deren Beschaffung zu unterstützen.

Der Verkäufer hat dem Käufer alle Kosten und Abgaben zu erstatten, die dem Käufer durch das Zurverfügungstellen oder die Unterstützung bei der Beschaffung der in B10 vorgesehenen Dokumente und Informationen entstanden sind.

B. Verpflichtungen des Käufers

B1. Allgemeine Verpflichtungen des Käufers

Der Käufer hat den im Kaufvertrag genannten Preis der Ware zu zahlen.

Jedes Dokument, auf das in B1–B10 Bezug genommen wird, kann auch ein entsprechender elektronischer Beleg oder ein entsprechendes elektronisches Verfahren sein, wenn dies zwischen den Parteien vereinbart oder üblich ist.

B2. Lizenzen, Genehmigungen, Sicherheitsfreigaben und andere Formalitäten

Falls zutreffend, obliegt es dem Käufer, auf eigene Gefahr und Kosten die Einfuhrgenehmigung oder andere behördliche Genehmigungen zu beschaffen sowie alle Zollformalitäten für die Einfuhr der Ware und für ihre Durchfuhr durch jedes Land zu erledigen.

B3. Beförderungs- und Versicherungsverträge

a. Beförderungsvertrag
Der Käufer hat auf eigene Kosten den Vertrag über die Beförderung der Ware vom benannten Lieferort abzuschließen, es sei denn, der Beförderungsvertrag ist vom Verkäufer wie in A3 a vorgesehen abgeschlossen worden.
b. Versicherungsvertrag
Der Käufer hat gegenüber dem Verkäufer keine Verpflichtung, einen Versicherungsvertrag abzuschließen.

B4. Übernahme

Der Käufer muss die Ware übernehmen, wenn sie wie in A4 vorgesehen geliefert worden ist.

B5. Gefahrenübergang

Der Käufer trägt alle Gefahren des Verlustes oder der Beschädigung der Ware ab dem Zeitpunkt, an dem sie wie in A4 vorgesehen, geliefert worden ist.
Falls
a. der Käufer es unterlässt gemäß B7, über die Benennung eines Frachtführers oder einer anderen in A4 vorgesehenen Person zu benachrichtigen; oder
b. der Frachtführer oder die vom Käufer wie in A4 vorgesehen benannte Person es unterlässt, die Ware zu übernehmen,
trägt der Käufer alle Gefahren des Verlustes oder der Beschädigung der Ware:

i. ab dem vereinbarten Zeitpunkt oder, mangels eines vereinbarten Zeitpunkts,
ii. ab dem vom Verkäufer nach A7 mitgeteilten Zeitpunkt innerhalb des vereinbarten Zeitraums; oder, falls kein solcher Zeitpunkt mitgeteilt wurde,
iii. ab dem Ablaufdatum eines vereinbarten Lieferzeitraums,

vorausgesetzt, die Ware ist eindeutig als die vertragliche Ware kenntlich gemacht worden.

B6. Kostenverteilung

Der Käufer hat zu tragen
a. alle die Ware betreffenden Kosten ab dem Zeitpunkt, an dem sie wie in A4 vorgesehen geliefert worden ist, ausgenommen, falls zutreffend, die Kosten der für die Ausfuhr notwendigen Zollformalitäten sowie alle Zölle, Steuern und andere in A6 b genannte Abgaben, die bei der Ausfuhr fällig werden;
b. alle zusätzlichen Kosten, die entweder dadurch entstehen, dass:
  i. der Käufer es unterlässt, einen Frachtführer oder eine andere in A4 vorgesehene Person zu benennen, oder
  ii. der Frachtführer oder die vom Käufer benannte Person wie in A4 vorgesehen es unterlässt, die Ware zu übernehmen, oder
  iii. der Käufer es unterlässt, gemäß B7 angemessen zu benachrichtigen,
vorausgesetzt, die Ware ist eindeutig als die vertragliche Ware kenntlich gemacht worden; und
c. falls zutreffend, alle Zölle, Steuern und andere Abgaben sowie die Kosten der Zollformalitäten, die bei der Einfuhr der Ware fällig werden, und die Kosten für ihre Durchfuhr durch jedes Land.

B7. Benachrichtigungen an den Verkäufer

Der Käufer hat den Verkäufer zu benachrichtigen:
a. rechtzeitig über den Namen des Frachtführers oder einer anderen in A4 vorgesehenen Person, um dem Verkäufer die Lieferung der Ware gemäß A4 zu ermöglichen;
b. wenn erforderlich, über den innerhalb des vereinbarten Lieferzeitraums gewählten Zeitpunkt, an dem der Frachtführer oder die benannte Person die Ware übernehmen wird;
c. über die Transportart, die von der benannten Person eingesetzt wird; und
d. über die Stelle der Warenübernahme innerhalb des benannten Ortes.

B8. Liefernachweis

Der Käufer hat den wie in A8 vorgesehen zur Verfügung gestellten Liefernachweis anzunehmen.

B9. Prüfung der Ware

Der Käufer hat die Kosten für jede vor der Verladung zwingend erforderliche Warenkontrolle (pre-shipment inspection) zu tragen, mit Ausnahme behördlich angeordneter Kontrollen des Ausfuhrlandes.

B10. Unterstützung bei Informationen und damit verbundene Kosten

Der Käufer hat dem Verkäufer rechtzeitig alle sicherheitsrelevanten Informationsanforderungen mitzuteilen, so dass der Verkäufer die Verpflichtungen entsprechend A10 erfüllen kann.

Der Käufer hat dem Verkäufer alle Kosten und Abgaben zu erstatten, die dem Verkäufer durch das Zurverfügungstellen oder die Unterstützung bei der Beschaffung der Dokumente und Informationen wie in A10 vorgesehen entstanden sind.

Der Käufer hat, falls zutreffend, dem Verkäufer rechtzeitig auf dessen Verlangen, Gefahr und Kosten alle Dokumente und Informationen, einschließlich sicherheitsrelevanter Informationen, die der Verkäufer für den Transport und die Ausfuhr der Ware sowie für ihre Durchfuhr durch jedes Land benötigt, zur Verfügung zu stellen oder ihn bei deren Beschaffung zu unterstützen.

[3.] CPT

FRACHTFREI
(… benannter Bestimmungsort)

ANWENDUNGSHINWEIS

Diese Klausel kann unabhängig von der gewählten Transportart verwendet werden, auch dann, wenn mehr als eine Transportart zum Einsatz kommt.

„Frachtfrei" bedeutet, dass der Verkäufer die Ware dem Frachtführer oder einer anderen vom Verkäufer benannten Person an einem vereinbarten Ort (falls ein solcher Ort zwischen den Parteien vereinbart ist) liefert, und dass der Verkäufer den Beförderungsvertrag abzuschließen und die für die Beförderung der Ware bis zum benannten Bestimmungsort entstehenden Frachtkosten zu zahlen hat.

Werden die Klauseln CPT, CIP, CFR oder CIF verwendet, erfüllt der Verkäufer seine Lieferpflicht, sobald er die Ware dem Frachtführer übergibt und nicht, wenn die Ware den Bestimmungsort erreicht.

Diese Klausel beinhaltet zwei kritische Punkte, da Gefahren- und Kostenübergang an verschiedenen Orten stattfinden. Die Parteien sind gut beraten, im Vertrag sowohl den Lieferort, an dem die Gefahr auf den Käufer übergeht, als auch den benannten Bestimmungsort, bis zu welchem der Verkäufer den Beförderungsvertrag abzuschließen hat, so genau wie möglich anzugeben. Kommen mehrere Frachtführer für die Beförderung zum vereinbarten Bestimmungsort zum Einsatz und verständigen sich die Parteien hinsichtlich der Lieferung nicht auf eine bestimmte Stelle, so geht die Gefahr immer dann über, wenn die Ware dem ersten Frachtführer übergeben worden ist. Die Auswahl der Stelle, an der die Lieferung erfolgen soll, liegt in diesen Fällen gänzlich im Ermessen des Verkäufers, während der Käufer darauf keinen Einfluss hat. Wünschen die Parteien einen späteren Gefahrenübergang (zum Beispiel in einem See- oder Flughafen), dann müssen sie dies in ihrem Kaufvertrag festlegen.

Die Parteien sind außerdem gut beraten, innerhalb des vereinbarten Bestimmungsortes die Stelle so genau wie möglich anzugeben, da die Kosten bis zu dieser Stelle zu Lasten des Verkäufers gehen. Dem Verkäufer wird geraten, mit dieser Wahl genau übereinstimmende Beförderungsverträge zu verschaffen. Entstehen dem Verkäufer gemäß seinem Beförderungsvertrag Kosten im Zusammenhang mit der Entladung am benannten Bestimmungsort, dann ist der Verkäufer nicht berechtigt, diese Kosten vom Käufer zurückzufordern, sofern nichts anderes zwischen den Parteien vereinbart worden ist.

CPT verpflichtet den Verkäufer, falls zutreffend, die Ware zur Ausfuhr freizumachen. Jedoch hat der Verkäufer keine Verpflichtung, die Ware zur Einfuhr freizumachen, Einfuhrzölle zu zahlen oder Einfuhrzollformalitäten zu erledigen.

A. Verpflichtungen des Verkäufers

A1. Allgemeine Verpflichtungen des Verkäufers

Der Verkäufer hat die Ware und die Handelsrechnung in Übereinstimmung mit dem Kaufvertrag bereitzustellen und jeden sonstigen vertraglich vereinbarten Konformitätsnachweis zu erbringen.

Jedes Dokument, auf das in A1–A10 Bezug genommen wird, kann auch ein entsprechender elektronischer Beleg oder ein entsprechendes elektronisches Verfahren sein, wenn dies zwischen den Parteien vereinbart oder üblich ist.

A2. Lizenzen, Genehmigungen, Sicherheitsfreigaben und andere Formalitäten

Falls zutreffend, hat der Verkäufer auf eigene Gefahr und Kosten die Ausfuhrgenehmigung oder andere behördliche Genehmigungen zu beschaffen sowie alle Zollformalitäten zu erledigen, die für die Ausfuhr der Ware und für ihre Durchfuhr durch jedes Land vor Lieferung erforderlich sind.

A3. Beförderungs- und Versicherungsverträge

a. Beförderungsvertrag
Der Verkäufer hat für die Ware einen Beförderungsvertrag von der gegebenenfalls vereinbarten Lieferstelle am Lieferort bis zum benannten Bestimmungsort oder einer gegebenenfalls vereinbarten Stelle an diesem Ort abzuschließen oder zu verschaffen. Der Beförderungsvertrag ist zu den üblichen Bedingungen auf Kosten des Verkäufers abzuschließen und hat die Beförderung auf der üblichen Route und in der handelsüblichen Weise zu beinhalten. Ist keine bestimmte Stelle vereinbart und ergibt sie sich auch nicht aus der Handelspraxis, kann der Verkäufer die Stelle am Lieferort und am benannten Bestimmungsort auswählen, die für den Zweck am besten geeignet ist.

b. Versicherungsvertrag
Der Verkäufer hat gegenüber dem Käufer keine Verpflichtung, einen Versicherungsvertrag abzuschließen. Jedoch hat der Verkäufer dem Käufer auf dessen Verlangen, Gefahr und (gegebenenfalls entstehende) Kosten jene Informationen zur Verfügung zu stellen, die der Käufer für den Abschluss einer Versicherung benötigt.

A4. Lieferung

Der Verkäufer hat die Ware zu liefern, indem er sie an den gemäß A3 beauftragten Frachtführer zum vereinbarten Zeitpunkt oder innerhalb des vereinbarten Zeitraums übergibt.

A5. Gefahrenübergang

Der Verkäufer trägt bis zur Lieferung gemäß A4 alle Gefahren des Verlustes oder der Beschädigung der Ware, mit Ausnahme von Verlust oder Beschädigung unter den in B5 beschriebenen Umständen.

A6. Kostenverteilung

Der Verkäufer hat zu tragen
a. alle die Ware betreffenden Kosten bis diese gemäß A4 geliefert worden ist, ausgenommen solcher Kosten, die wie in B6 vorgesehen vom Käufer zu tragen sind;
b. die Fracht- und alle anderen aus A3 a entstehenden Kosten, einschließlich der Kosten für die Verladung der Ware und aller Abgaben für die Entladung am Bestimmungsort, die gemäß Beförderungsvertrag vom Verkäufer zu tragen sind; und
c. falls zutreffend, die Kosten der für die Ausfuhr notwendigen Zollformalitäten sowie alle Zölle, Steuern und andere Abgaben, die bei der Ausfuhr fällig werden, und die Kosten für die Durchfuhr der Ware durch jedes Land, die gemäß Beförderungsvertrag zu Lasten des Verkäufers gehen.

A7. Benachrichtigungen an den Käufer

Der Verkäufer hat den Käufer zu benachrichtigen, dass die Ware gemäß A4 geliefert worden ist.

Der Verkäufer hat den Käufer über alles Nötige zu benachrichtigen, damit dieser die üblicherweise notwendigen Maßnahmen zur Übernahme der Ware treffen kann.

A8. Transportdokument

Falls handelsüblich oder falls der Käufer es verlangt, hat der Verkäufer auf eigene Kosten dem Käufer das oder die übliche(n) Transportdokument(e) für den gemäß A3 vertraglich vereinbarten Transport zur Verfügung zu stellen.

Dieses Transportdokument muss die vertragliche Ware erfassen und innerhalb der zur Versendung vereinbarten Frist datiert sein. Falls vereinbart oder handelsüblich, muss das Dokument den Käufer auch in die Lage versetzen, die Herausgabe der Ware bei dem Frachtführer am benannten Bestimmungsort einfordern zu können, und es dem Käufer ermöglichen, die Ware während des Transports durch Übergabe des Dokuments an einen nachfolgenden Käufer oder durch Benachrichtigung an den Frachtführer zu verkaufen.

Wird ein solches Transportdokument als begebbares Dokument und in mehreren Originalen ausgestellt, muss ein vollständiger Satz von Originalen dem Käufer übergeben werden.

A9. Prüfung – Verpackung – Kennzeichnung

Der Verkäufer hat die Kosten jener Prüfvorgänge (wie Qualitätsprüfung, Messen, Wiegen und Zählen), die notwendig sind, um die Ware gemäß A4 zu liefern, sowie die Kosten für alle von den Behörden des Ausfuhrlandes angeordneten Warenkontrollen vor der Verladung (pre-shipment inspection) zu tragen.

Der Verkäufer hat auf eigene Kosten die Ware zu verpacken, es sei denn, es ist handelsüblich, die jeweilige Art der verkauften Ware unverpackt zu transportieren. Der Verkäufer kann die Ware in der für ihren Transport geeigneten Weise verpacken, es sei denn, der Käufer hat den Verkäufer vor Vertragsschluss über spezifische Verpackungsanforderungen in Kenntnis gesetzt. Die Verpackung ist in geeigneter Weise zu kennzeichnen.

A10. Unterstützung bei Informationen und damit verbundene Kosten

Der Verkäufer hat, falls zutreffend, dem Käufer auf dessen Verlangen, Gefahr und Kosten rechtzeitig alle Dokumente und Informationen, einschließlich sicherheitsrelevanter Informationen, die der Käufer für die Einfuhr der Ware und/oder für ihren Transport bis zum endgültigen Bestimmungsort benötigt, zur Verfügung zu stellen oder ihn bei deren Beschaffung zu unterstützen.

Der Verkäufer hat dem Käufer alle Kosten und Abgaben zu erstatten, die dem Käufer durch das Zurverfügungstellen oder die Unterstützung bei der Beschaffung der in B10 vorgesehenen Dokumente und Informationen entstanden sind.

B. Verpflichtungen des Käufers

B1. Allgemeine Verpflichtungen des Käufers

Der Käufer hat den im Kaufvertrag genannten Preis der Ware zu zahlen.

Jedes Dokument, auf das in B1–B10 Bezug genommen wird, kann auch ein entsprechender elektronischer Beleg oder ein entsprechendes elektronisches Verfahren sein, wenn dies zwischen den Parteien vereinbart oder üblich ist.

B2. Lizenzen, Genehmigungen, Sicherheitsfreigaben und andere Formalitäten

Falls zutreffend, obliegt es dem Käufer, auf eigene Gefahr und Kosten die Einfuhrgenehmigung oder andere behördliche Genehmigungen zu beschaffen sowie alle Zollformalitäten für die Einfuhr der Ware und für ihre Durchfuhr durch jedes Land zu erledigen.

B3. Beförderungs- und Versicherungsverträge

a. Beförderungsvertrag
Der Käufer hat gegenüber dem Verkäufer keine Verpflichtung, einen Beförderungsvertrag abzuschließen.
b. Versicherungsvertrag
Der Käufer hat gegenüber dem Verkäufer keine Verpflichtung, einen Versicherungsvertrag abzuschließen. Allerdings hat der Käufer dem Verkäufer auf dessen Verlangen die für den Abschluss einer Versicherung notwendigen Informationen zur Verfügung zu stellen.

B4. Übernahme

Der Käufer muss die Ware übernehmen, wenn sie wie in A4 vorgesehen geliefert worden ist, und hat sie vom Frachtführer am benannten Bestimmungsort entgegenzunehmen.

B5. Gefahrenübergang

Der Käufer trägt alle Gefahren des Verlustes oder der Beschädigung der Ware ab dem Zeitpunkt, an dem sie wie in A4 vorgesehen geliefert worden ist.

Falls der Käufer es unterlässt, gemäß B7 zu benachrichtigen, hat er alle Gefahren des Verlustes oder der Beschädigung der Ware ab dem vereinbarten Lieferzeitpunkt oder ab Ablauf des vereinbarten Lieferzeitraums zu tragen, vorausgesetzt, die Ware ist eindeutig als die vertragliche Ware kenntlich gemacht worden.

B6. Kostenverteilung

Der Käufer hat, vorbehaltlich der Bestimmungen in A3 a, zu tragen
a. alle die Ware betreffenden Kosten ab dem Zeitpunkt, an dem sie wie in A4 vorgesehen geliefert worden ist, ausgenommen, falls zutreffend, die Kosten der für die Ausfuhr notwendigen Zollformalitäten sowie alle Zölle, Steuern und andere in A6 c genannten Abgaben, die bei der Ausfuhr fällig werden;
b. alle die Ware betreffenden Kosten und Abgaben während des Transports bis zu ihrer Ankunft am vereinbarten Bestimmungsort, sofern solche Kosten und Abgaben gemäß Beförderungsvertrag nicht zu Lasten des Verkäufers gehen;
c. die Entladekosten, sofern solche Kosten gemäß Beförderungsvertrag nicht zu Lasten des Verkäufers gehen;
d. alle zusätzlichen Kosten, sollte der Käufer die Benachrichtigung gemäß B7 unterlassen, ab dem für die Versendung vereinbarten Zeitpunkt oder ab Ablauf des hierfür vereinbarten Zeitraums, vorausgesetzt, die Ware ist eindeutig als die vertragliche Ware kenntlich gemacht worden; und
e. falls zutreffend, alle Zölle, Steuern und andere Abgaben sowie die Kosten der Zollformalitäten, die bei der Einfuhr der Ware fällig werden, sowie die Kosten für ihre Durchfuhr durch jedes Land, sofern sie nicht in den Kosten des Beförderungsvertrags enthalten sind.

B7. Benachrichtigungen an den Verkäufer

Wann immer der Käufer berechtigt ist, den Zeitpunkt für die Versendung der Ware und/ oder den benannten Bestimmungsort oder die Stelle für die Entgegennahme der Ware innerhalb dieses Ortes zu bestimmen, hat er den Verkäufer in angemessener Weise darüber zu benachrichtigen.

B8. Liefernachweis

Der Käufer hat das wie in A8 vorgesehen zur Verfügung gestellte Transportdokument anzunehmen, wenn dieses mit dem Vertrag übereinstimmt.

B9. Prüfung der Ware

Der Käufer hat die Kosten für jede vor der Verladung zwingend erforderliche Warenkontrolle (pre-shipment inspection) zu tragen, mit Ausnahme behördlich angeordneter Kontrollen des Ausfuhrlandes.

B10. Unterstützung bei Informationen und damit verbundene Kosten

Der Käufer hat dem Verkäufer rechtzeitig alle sicherheitsrelevanten Informationsanforderungen mitzuteilen, so dass der Verkäufer die Verpflichtungen entsprechend A10 erfüllen kann.

Der Käufer hat dem Verkäufer alle Kosten und Abgaben zu erstatten, die dem Verkäufer durch das Zurverfügungstellen oder die Unterstützung bei der Beschaffung der Dokumente und Informationen wie in A10 vorgesehen entstanden sind.

Der Käufer hat, falls zutreffend, dem Verkäufer rechtzeitig auf dessen Verlangen, Gefahr und Kosten alle Dokumente und Informationen, einschließlich sicherheitsrelevanter Informationen, die der Verkäufer für den Transport und die Ausfuhr der Ware sowie für ihre Durchfuhr durch jedes Land benötigt, zur Verfügung zu stellen oder ihn bei deren Beschaffung zu unterstützen.

[4.] CIP

FRACHTFREI VERSICHERT
(… benannter Bestimmungsort)

ANWENDUNGSHINWEIS

Diese Klausel kann unabhängig von der gewählten Transportart verwendet werden, auch dann, wenn mehr als eine Transportart zum Einsatz kommt.

„Frachtfrei versichert" bedeutet, dass der Verkäufer die Ware dem Frachtführer oder einer anderen vom Verkäufer benannten Person an einem vereinbarten Ort (falls ein solcher Ort zwischen den Parteien vereinbart ist) liefert, und dass der Verkäufer den Beförderungsvertrag abzuschließen und die für die Beförderung der Ware bis zum benannten Bestimmungsort entstehenden Frachtkosten zu zahlen hat.

Der Verkäufer schließt auch einen Versicherungsvertrag gegen die vom Käufer getragene Gefahr des Verlustes oder der Beschädigung der Ware während des Transports ab. Der Käufer sollte beachten, dass der Verkäufer bei Verwendung von CIP lediglich verpflichtet ist, eine Versicherung mit einer Mindestdeckung abzuschließen. Wünscht der Käufer einen höheren Versicherungsschutz, wird er dies entweder ausdrücklich mit dem Verkäufer vereinbaren oder eigene zusätzliche Versicherungsvorkehrungen treffen müssen.

Werden die Klauseln CPT, CIP, CFR oder CIF verwendet, erfüllt der Verkäufer seine Lieferpflicht, sobald er die Ware dem Frachtführer übergibt und nicht, wenn die Ware am Bestimmungsort ankommt.

Diese Klausel beinhaltet zwei kritische Punkte, da Gefahren- und Kostenübergang an verschiedenen Orten stattfinden. Die Parteien sind gut beraten, im Vertrag sowohl den Lieferort, an dem die Gefahr auf den Käufer übergeht, als auch den benannten Bestimmungsort, bis zu welchem der Verkäufer den Beförderungsvertrag abzuschließen hat, so genau wie möglich anzugeben. Kommen mehrere Frachtführer für die Beförderung zum vereinbarten Bestimmungsort zum Einsatz und verständigen sich die Parteien hinsichtlich der Lieferung nicht auf eine bestimmte Stelle, geht die Gefahr immer dann über, wenn die Ware an den ersten Frachtführer übergeben worden ist. Die Auswahl der Stelle, an dem die Lieferung erfolgen soll, liegt in diesen Fällen gänzlich im Ermessen des Verkäufers, während der Käufer darauf keinen Einfluss hat. Wünschen die Parteien einen späteren Gefahrenübergang (zum Beispiel in einem See- oder Flughafen), dann müssen sie dies in ihrem Kaufvertrag festlegen.

Die Parteien sind außerdem gut beraten, innerhalb des vereinbarten Bestimmungsortes die Stelle so genau wie möglich anzugeben, da die Kosten bis zu dieser Stelle zu Lasten des Verkäufers gehen. Dem Verkäufer wird geraten, mit dieser Wahl genau übereinstimmende Beförderungsverträge zu verschaffen. Entstehen dem Verkäufer gemäß seinem Beförderungsvertrag Kosten im Zusammenhang mit der Entladung am benannten Bestimmungsort, dann ist der Verkäufer nicht berechtigt, diese Kosten vom Käufer zurückzufordern, sofern nichts anderes zwischen den Parteien vereinbart ist.

CIP verpflichtet den Verkäufer, falls zutreffend, die Ware zur Ausfuhr freizumachen. Jedoch hat der Verkäufer keine Verpflichtung, die Ware zur Einfuhr freizumachen, Einfuhrzölle zu zahlen oder Einfuhrzollformalitäten zu erledigen.

A. Verpflichtungen des Verkäufers

A1. Allgemeine Verpflichtungen des Verkäufers

Der Verkäufer hat die Ware und die Handelsrechnung in Übereinstimmung mit dem Kaufvertrag bereitzustellen und jeden sonstigen vertraglich vereinbarten Konformitätsnachweis zu erbringen.

Jedes Dokument, auf das in A1–A10 Bezug genommen wird, kann auch ein entsprechender elektronischer Beleg oder ein entsprechendes elektronisches Verfahren sein, wenn dies zwischen den Parteien vereinbart oder üblich ist.

A2. Lizenzen, Genehmigungen, Sicherheitsfreigaben und andere Formalitäten

Falls zutreffend, hat der Verkäufer auf eigene Gefahr und Kosten die Ausfuhrgenehmigung oder andere behördliche Genehmigungen zu beschaffen sowie alle Zollformalitäten zu erledigen, die für die Ausfuhr der Ware und für ihre Durchfuhr durch jedes Land vor Lieferung erforderlich sind.

A3. Beförderungs- und Versicherungsverträge

a. Beförderungsvertrag
   Der Verkäufer hat für die Ware einen Beförderungsvertrag von der gegebenenfalls vereinbarten Lieferstelle am Lieferort bis zum benannten Bestimmungsort oder einer gegebenenfalls vereinbarten Stelle an diesem Ort abzuschließen oder zu verschaffen. Der Beförderungsvertrag ist zu den üblichen Bedingungen auf Kosten des Verkäufers abzuschließen und hat die Beförderung auf der üblichen Route und in der handelsüblichen Weise zu beinhalten. Ist keine bestimmte Stelle vereinbart und ergibt sie sich auch nicht aus der Handelspraxis, kann der Verkäufer die Stelle am Lieferort und am benannten Bestimmungsort auswählen, die für den Zweck am besten geeignet ist.

b. Versicherungsvertrag
Der Verkäufer hat auf eigene Kosten eine Transportversicherung abzuschließen, die zumindest der Mindestdeckung gemäß den Klauseln (C) der Institute Cargo Clauses (LMA/IUA) oder ähnlichen Klauseln entspricht. Die Versicherung ist bei Einzelversicherern oder Versicherungsgesellschaften mit einwandfreiem Leumund abzuschließen und muss den Käufer oder jede andere Person mit einem versicherbaren Interesse an der Ware berechtigen, Ansprüche direkt bei dem Versicherer geltend zu machen.
Der Verkäufer muss auf Verlangen und Kosten des Käufers, vorbehaltlich der durch den Käufer zur Verfügung gestellten vom Verkäufer benötigten Informationen, zusätzliche Deckung, falls erhältlich, beschaffen, wie z. B. entsprechend den Klauseln (A) oder (B) der Institute Cargo Clauses (LMA/IUA) oder ähnlicher Klauseln, und/oder der Institute War Clauses und/oder der Institute Strikes Clauses (LMA/IUA) oder ähnlicher Klauseln.
Die Versicherung muss zumindest den im Vertrag genannten Preis zuzüglich zehn Prozent (d. h. 110 %) decken und in der Währung des Vertrags ausgestellt sein.
Der Versicherungsschutz muss die Ware ab dem Lieferort, wie in A4 und A5 festgelegt, bis mindestens zum benannten Bestimmungsort decken.
Der Verkäufer hat dem Käufer die Versicherungspolice oder einen sonstigen Nachweis über den Versicherungsschutz zu übermitteln.
Ferner hat der Verkäufer dem Käufer auf dessen Verlangen, Gefahr und (gegebenenfalls entstehende) Kosten jene Informationen zur Verfügung zu stellen, die der Käufer für den Abschluss einer zusätzlichen Versicherung benötigt.

A4. Lieferung

Der Verkäufer hat die Ware zu liefern, indem er sie an den gemäß A3 beauftragten Frachtführer zum vereinbarten Zeitpunkt oder innerhalb des vereinbarten Zeitraums übergibt.

A5. Gefahrenübergang

Der Verkäufer trägt bis zur Lieferung gemäß A4 alle Gefahren des Verlustes oder der Beschädigung der Ware, mit Ausnahme von Verlust oder Beschädigung unter den in B5 beschriebenen Umständen.

A6. Kostenverteilung

Der Verkäufer hat zu tragen
a. alle die Ware betreffenden Kosten bis diese gemäß A4 geliefert worden ist, ausgenommen solcher Kosten, die wie in B6 vorgesehen vom Käufer zu tragen sind;
b. die Fracht- und alle anderen aus A3 a entstehenden Kosten einschließlich der Kosten für die Verladung der Ware und aller Abgaben für die Entladung am Bestimmungsort, die gemäß Beförderungsvertrag vom Verkäufer zu tragen sind;
c. die aus A3b resultierenden Kosten für die Versicherung; und
d. falls zutreffend, die Kosten der für die Ausfuhr notwendigen Zollformalitäten sowie alle Zölle, Steuern und andere Abgaben, die bei der Ausfuhr fällig werden, und die Kosten für die Durchfuhr der Ware durch jedes Land, die gemäß Beförderungsvertrag zu Lasten des Verkäufers gehen.

A7. Benachrichtigungen an den Käufer

Der Verkäufer hat den Käufer zu benachrichtigen, dass die Ware gemäß A4 geliefert worden ist.
Der Verkäufer hat den Käufer über alles Nötige zu benachrichtigen, damit dieser die üblicherweise notwendigen Maßnahmen zur Übernahme der Ware treffen kann.

A8. Transportdokument

Falls handelsüblich oder falls der Käufer es verlangt, hat der Verkäufer auf eigene Kosten dem Käufer das oder die übliche(n) Transportdokument(e) für den gemäß A3 vertraglich vereinbarten Transport zur Verfügung zu stellen.

Dieses Transportdokument muss die vertragliche Ware erfassen und innerhalb der zur Versendung vereinbarten Frist datiert sein. Falls vereinbart oder handelsüblich, muss das Dokument den Käufer auch in die Lage versetzen, die Herausgabe der Ware bei dem Frachtführer am benannten Bestimmungsort einfordern zu können und es dem Käufer ermöglichen, die Ware während des Transports durch Übergabe des Dokuments an einen nachfolgenden Käufer oder durch Benachrichtigung an den Frachtführer zu verkaufen.

Wird ein solches Transportdokument als begebbares Dokument und in mehreren Originalen ausgestellt, muss ein vollständiger Satz von Originalen dem Käufer übergeben werden.

A9. Prüfung – Verpackung – Kennzeichnung

Der Verkäufer hat die Kosten jener Prüfvorgänge (wie Qualitätsprüfung, Messen, Wiegen und Zählen), die notwendig sind, um die Ware gemäß A4 zu liefern, sowie die Kosten für alle von den Behörden des Ausfuhrlandes angeordneten Warenkontrollen vor der Verladung (pre-shipment inspection) zu tragen.

Der Verkäufer hat auf eigene Kosten die Ware zu verpacken, es sei denn, es ist handelsüblich, die jeweilige Art der verkauften Ware unverpackt zu transportieren. Der Verkäufer kann die Ware in der für ihren Transport geeigneten Weise verpacken, es sei denn, der Käufer hat den Verkäufer vor Vertragsschluss über spezifische Verpackungsanforderungen in Kenntnis gesetzt. Die Verpackung ist in geeigneter Weise zu kennzeichnen.

A10. Unterstützung bei Informationen und damit verbundene Kosten

Der Verkäufer hat, falls zutreffend, dem Käufer auf dessen Verlangen, Gefahr und Kosten rechtzeitig alle Dokumente und Informationen, einschließlich sicherheitsrelevanter Informationen, die der Käufer für die Einfuhr der Ware und/oder für ihren Transport bis zum endgültigen Bestimmungsort benötigt, zur Verfügung zu stellen oder ihn bei deren Beschaffung zu unterstützen.

Der Verkäufer hat dem Käufer alle Kosten und Abgaben zu erstatten, die dem Käufer durch das Zurverfügungstellen oder die Unterstützung bei der Beschaffung der in B10 vorgesehenen Dokumente und Informationen entstanden sind.

B. Verpflichtungen des Käufers

B1. Allgemeine Verpflichtungen des Käufers

Der Käufer hat den im Kaufvertrag genannten Preis der Ware zu zahlen.

Jedes Dokument, auf das in B1–B10 Bezug genommen wird, kann auch ein entsprechender elektronischer Beleg oder ein entsprechendes elektronisches Verfahren sein, wenn dies zwischen den Parteien vereinbart oder üblich ist.

B2. Lizenzen, Genehmigungen, Sicherheitsfreigaben und andere Formalitäten

Falls zutreffend, obliegt es dem Käufer, auf eigene Gefahr und Kosten die Einfuhrgenehmigung oder andere behördliche Genehmigungen zu beschaffen sowie alle Zollformalitäten für die Einfuhr der Ware und für ihre Durchfuhr durch jedes Land zu erledigen.

B3. Beförderungs- und Versicherungsverträge

a. Beförderungsvertrag
Der Käufer hat gegenüber dem Verkäufer keine Verpflichtung, einen Beförderungsvertrag abzuschließen.
b. Versicherungsvertrag
Der Käufer hat gegenüber dem Verkäufer keine Verpflichtung, einen Versicherungsvertrag abzuschließen. Allerdings hat der Käufer dem Verkäufer auf dessen Verlangen die für den Abschluss einer vom Käufer verlangten in A3 b vorgesehenen zusätzlichen Versicherung notwendigen Informationen zur Verfügung zu stellen.

B4. Übernahme

Der Käufer muss die Ware übernehmen, wenn sie wie in A4 vorgesehen geliefert worden ist, und hat sie vom Frachtführer am benannten Bestimmungsort entgegenzunehmen.

B5. Gefahrenübergang

Der Käufer trägt alle Gefahren des Verlustes oder der Beschädigung der Ware ab dem Zeitpunkt, an dem sie wie in A4 vorgesehen geliefert worden ist.

Falls der Käufer es unterlässt, gemäß B7 zu benachrichtigen, hat er alle Gefahren des Verlustes oder der Beschädigung der Ware ab dem vereinbarten Lieferzeitpunkt oder ab Ablauf des vereinbarten Lieferzeitraums zu tragen, vorausgesetzt, die Ware ist eindeutig als die vertragliche Ware kenntlich gemacht worden.

B6. Kostenverteilung

Der Käufer hat, vorbehaltlich der Bestimmungen in A3 a, zu tragen
a. alle die Ware betreffenden Kosten ab dem Zeitpunkt, an dem sie wie in A4 vorgesehen geliefert worden ist, ausgenommen, falls zutreffend, die Kosten der für die Ausfuhr notwendigen Zollformalitäten sowie alle Zölle, Steuern und andere in A6 d genannte Abgaben, die bei der Ausfuhr fällig werden;
b. alle die Ware betreffenden Kosten und Abgaben während des Transports bis zu ihrer Ankunft am vereinbarten Bestimmungsort, sofern solche Kosten und Abgaben gemäß Beförderungsvertrag nicht zu Lasten des Verkäufers gehen;
c. die Entladekosten, sofern solche Kosten gemäß Beförderungsvertrag nicht zu Lasten des Verkäufers gehen;
d. alle zusätzlichen Kosten, sollte der Käufer die Benachrichtigung gemäß B7 unterlassen, ab dem für die Versendung vereinbarten Zeitpunkt oder ab Ablauf der hierfür vereinbarten Frist, vorausgesetzt, die Ware ist eindeutig als die vertragliche Ware kenntlich gemacht worden;
e. falls zutreffend, alle Zölle, Steuern und andere Abgaben sowie die Kosten der Zollformalitäten, die bei der Einfuhr der Ware fällig werden, sowie die Kosten für ihre Durchfuhr durch jedes Land, sofern sie nicht in den Kosten laut Beförderungsvertrag enthalten sind; und
f. die Kosten für jede zusätzlich auf Verlangen des Käufers nach A3 und B3 abgeschlossene Versicherung.

B7. Benachrichtigungen an den Verkäufer

Wann immer der Käufer berechtigt ist, den Zeitpunkt für die Versendung der Ware und/oder den benannten Bestimmungsort oder die Stelle für die Entgegennahme der Ware innerhalb dieses Ortes zu bestimmen, hat er den Verkäufer in angemessener Weise darüber zu benachrichtigen.

B8. Liefernachweis

Der Käufer hat das wie in A8 vorgesehen zur Verfügung gestellte Transportdokument anzunehmen, wenn dieses mit dem Vertrag übereinstimmt.

B9. Prüfung der Ware

Der Käufer hat die Kosten für jede vor der Verladung zwingend erforderliche Warenkontrolle (pre-shipment inspection) zu tragen, mit Ausnahme behördlich angeordneter Kontrollen des Ausfuhrlandes.

B10. Unterstützung bei Informationen und damit verbundene Kosten

Der Käufer hat dem Verkäufer rechtzeitig alle sicherheitsrelevanten Informationsanforderungen mitzuteilen, so dass der Verkäufer die Verpflichtungen entsprechend A10 erfüllen kann.

Der Käufer hat dem Verkäufer alle Kosten und Abgaben zu erstatten, die dem Verkäufer durch das Zurverfügungstellen oder die Unterstützung bei der Beschaffung der Dokumente und Informationen wie in A10 vorgesehen entstanden sind.

Der Käufer hat, falls zutreffend, dem Verkäufer rechtzeitig auf dessen Verlangen, Gefahr und Kosten alle Dokumente und Informationen, einschließlich sicherheitsrelevanter Informationen, die der Verkäufer für den Transport und die Ausfuhr der Ware sowie für ihre Durchfuhr durch jedes Land benötigt, zur Verfügung zu stellen oder ihn bei deren Beschaffung zu unterstützen.

[5.] DAT

GELIEFERT TERMINAL
(... benannter Terminal im Bestimmungshafen/-ort)

ANWENDUNGSHINWEIS

Diese Klausel kann unabhängig von der gewählten Transportart verwendet werden, auch dann, wenn mehr als eine Transportart zum Einsatz kommt.

„Geliefert Terminal" bedeutet, dass der Verkäufer die Ware liefert, sobald die Ware von dem ankommenden Beförderungsmittel entladen wurde und dem Käufer an einem benannten Terminal im benannten Bestimmungshafen oder -ort zur Verfügung gestellt wird. „Terminal" kann jeder Ort sein, unabhängig davon, ob überdacht oder nicht, wie z. B. ein Kai, eine Lagerhalle, ein Containerdepot oder ein Straßen-, Schienen- oder Luftfrachtterminal. Der Verkäufer trägt alle Gefahren, die im Zusammenhang mit der Beförderung der Ware zum und der Entladung im Terminal im benannten Bestimmungshafen oder -ort entstehen.

Die Parteien sind gut beraten, den Terminal und, wenn möglich, eine bestimmte Stelle innerhalb des Terminals im benannten Bestimmungshafen oder -ort so genau wie möglich zu bezeichnen, da die Gefahr bis zu dieser Stelle der Verkäufer trägt. Dem Verkäufer wird geraten, einen mit dieser Wahl genau übereinstimmenden Beförderungsvertrag zu verschaffen.

Falls die Parteien jedoch des Weiteren beabsichtigen, dass der Verkäufer die mit dem Umschlag und dem Weitertransport der Ware vom Terminal zu einem anderen Ort in Zusammenhang stehenden Gefahren und Kosten tragen soll, dann sollten die Klauseln DAP oder DDP verwendet werden.

DAT verpflichtet den Verkäufer, falls zutreffend, die Ware zur Ausfuhr freizumachen. Jedoch hat der Verkäufer keine Verpflichtung, die Ware zur Einfuhr freizumachen, Einfuhrzölle zu zahlen oder Einfuhrzollformalitäten zu erledigen.

A. Verpflichtungen des Verkäufers

A1. Allgemeine Verpflichtungen des Verkäufers

Der Verkäufer hat die Ware und die Handelsrechnung in Übereinstimmung mit dem Kaufvertrag bereitzustellen und jeden sonstigen vertraglich vereinbarten Konformitätsnachweis zu erbringen.

Jedes Dokument, auf das in A1–A10 Bezug genommen wird, kann auch ein entsprechender elektronischer Beleg oder ein entsprechendes elektronisches Verfahren sein, wenn dies zwischen den Parteien vereinbart oder üblich ist.

A2. Lizenzen, Genehmigungen, Sicherheitsfreigaben und andere Formalitäten

Falls zutreffend, hat der Verkäufer auf eigene Gefahr und Kosten die Ausfuhrgenehmigung und andere behördliche Genehmigungen zu beschaffen sowie alle Zollformalitäten zu erledigen, die für die Ausfuhr der Ware und für ihre Durchfuhr durch jedes Land vor Lieferung erforderlich sind.

A3. Beförderungs- und Versicherungsverträge

a. Beförderungsvertrag
Der Verkäufer hat für die Ware auf eigene Kosten einen Beförderungsvertrag bis zum benannten Terminal im vereinbarten Bestimmungshafen oder -ort abzuschließen. Ist kein bestimmter Terminal vereinbart oder ergibt er sich nicht aus der Handelspraxis, kann der Verkäufer den Terminal im vereinbarten Bestimmungshafen oder -ort wählen, der für den Zweck am besten geeignet ist.
b. Versicherungsvertrag
Der Verkäufer hat gegenüber dem Käufer keine Verpflichtung, einen Versicherungsvertrag abzuschließen. Jedoch hat der Verkäufer dem Käufer auf dessen Verlangen, Gefahr und (gegebenenfalls entstehende) Kosten jene Informationen zur Verfügung zu stellen, die der Käufer für den Abschluss einer Versicherung benötigt.

A4. Lieferung

Der Verkäufer hat die Ware von dem ankommenden Beförderungsmittel zu entladen und sie dann dem Käufer zu liefern, indem er sie an dem gemäß A3 a benannten Terminal im Bestimmungshafen oder -ort zum vereinbarten Zeitpunkt oder innerhalb des vereinbarten Zeitraums zur Verfügung stellt.

A5. Gefahrenübergang

Der Verkäufer trägt bis zur Lieferung gemäß A4 alle Gefahren des Verlustes oder der Beschädigung der Ware, mit Ausnahme von Verlust oder Beschädigung unter den in B5 beschriebenen Umständen.

A6. Kostenverteilung

Der Verkäufer hat zu tragen
a. zusätzlich zu den aus A3 a entstehenden Kosten alle die Ware betreffenden Kosten bis diese gemäß A4 geliefert worden ist, ausgenommen solcher Kosten, die wie in B6 vorgesehen vom Käufer zu tragen sind; und
b. falls zutreffend, die Kosten der für die Ausfuhr notwendigen Zollformalitäten sowie alle Zölle, Steuern und andere Abgaben, die bei der Ausfuhr fällig werden, und die Kosten für die Durchfuhr der Ware durch jedes Land vor Lieferung gemäß A4.

A7. Benachrichtigungen an den Käufer

Der Verkäufer hat den Käufer über alles Nötige zu benachrichtigen, damit dieser die üblicherweise notwendigen Maßnahmen zur Übernahme der Ware treffen kann.

A8. Transportdokument

Der Verkäufer hat auf eigene Kosten dem Käufer ein Dokument zur Verfügung zu stellen, das diesem die Übernahme der Ware wie in A4/B4 vorgesehen ermöglicht.

A9. Prüfung – Verpackung – Kennzeichnung

Der Verkäufer hat die Kosten jener Prüfvorgänge (wie Qualitätsprüfung, Messen, Wiegen und Zählen), die notwendig sind, um die Ware gemäß A4 zu liefern, sowie die Kosten für alle von den Behörden des Ausfuhrlandes angeordneten Warenkontrollen vor der Verladung (pre-shipment inspection) zu tragen.

Der Verkäufer hat auf eigene Kosten die Ware zu verpacken, es sei denn, es ist handelsüblich, die jeweilige Art der verkauften Ware unverpackt zu transportieren. Der Verkäufer kann die Ware in der für ihren Transport geeigneten Weise verpacken, es sei denn, der Käufer hat den Verkäufer vor Vertragsschluss über spezifische Verpackungsanforderungen in Kenntnis gesetzt. Die Verpackung ist in geeigneter Weise zu kennzeichnen.

A10. Unterstützung bei Informationen und damit verbundene Kosten

Der Verkäufer hat, falls zutreffend, dem Käufer auf dessen Verlangen, Gefahr und Kosten rechtzeitig alle Dokumente und Informationen, einschließlich sicherheitsrelevanter Informationen, die der Käufer für die Einfuhr der Ware und/oder für ihren Transport bis zum endgültigen Bestimmungsort benötigt, zur Verfügung zu stellen oder ihn bei deren Beschaffung zu unterstützen.

Der Verkäufer hat dem Käufer alle Kosten und Abgaben zu erstatten, die dem Käufer durch das Zurverfügungstellen oder die Unterstützung bei der Beschaffung der in B10 vorgesehenen Dokumente und Informationen entstanden sind.

B. Verpflichtungen des Käufers

B1. Allgemeine Verpflichtungen des Käufers

Der Käufer hat den im Kaufvertrag genannten Preis der Ware zu zahlen.

Jedes Dokument, auf das in B1–B10 Bezug genommen wird, kann auch ein entsprechender elektronischer Beleg oder ein entsprechendes elektronisches Verfahren sein, wenn dies zwischen den Parteien vereinbart oder üblich ist.

B2. Lizenzen, Genehmigungen, Sicherheitsfreigaben und andere Formalitäten

Falls zutreffend, muss der Käufer auf eigene Gefahr und Kosten die Einfuhrgenehmigung oder andere behördliche Genehmigungen beschaffen sowie alle Zollformalitäten für die Einfuhr der Ware erledigen.

B3. Beförderungs- und Versicherungsverträge

a. Beförderungsvertrag

Der Käufer hat gegenüber dem Verkäufer keine Verpflichtung, einen Beförderungsvertrag abzuschließen.

b. Versicherungsvertrag

Der Käufer hat gegenüber dem Verkäufer keine Verpflichtung, einen Versicherungsvertrag abzuschließen. Allerdings hat der Käufer dem Verkäufer auf dessen Verlangen die für den Abschluss einer Versicherung notwendigen Informationen zur Verfügung zu stellen.

B4. Übernahme

Der Käufer muss die Ware übernehmen, wenn sie wie in A4 vorgesehen geliefert worden ist.

B5. Gefahrenübergang

Der Käufer trägt alle Gefahren des Verlustes oder der Beschädigung der Ware ab dem Zeitpunkt, an dem sie wie in A4 vorgesehen geliefert worden ist.
Falls
a. der Käufer seine Verpflichtungen gemäß B2 nicht erfüllt, trägt er alle daraus resultierenden Gefahren des Verlustes oder der Beschädigung der Ware; oder
b. der Käufer es unterlässt, gemäß B7 zu benachrichtigen, trägt er alle Gefahren des Verlustes oder der Beschädigung der Ware ab dem vereinbarten Lieferzeitpunkt oder ab Ablauf des vereinbarten Lieferzeitraums,

vorausgesetzt, die Ware ist eindeutig als die vertragliche Ware kenntlich gemacht worden.

B6. Kostenverteilung

Der Käufer hat zu tragen
a. alle die Ware betreffenden Kosten ab dem Zeitpunkt, an dem sie wie in A4 vorgesehen geliefert worden ist;
b. alle zusätzlichen Kosten, die dem Verkäufer entstehen, falls der Käufer seine Verpflichtungen gemäß B2 nicht erfüllt oder es unterlässt, gemäß B7 zu benachrichtigen, vorausgesetzt, die Ware ist eindeutig als die vertragliche Ware kenntlich gemacht worden; und
c. falls zutreffend, die Kosten der Zollformalitäten sowie alle Zölle, Steuern und andere Abgaben, die bei der Einfuhr der Ware fällig werden.

B7. Benachrichtigungen an den Verkäufer

Wann immer der Käufer berechtigt ist, den Zeitpunkt der innerhalb einer vereinbarten Lieferfrist und/oder die Stelle für die Warenübernahme im benannten Terminal zu bestimmen, hat er den Verkäufer in angemessener Weise darüber zu benachrichtigen.

B8. Liefernachweis

Der Käufer hat das wie in A8 vorgesehen zur Verfügung gestellte Transportdokument anzunehmen.

B9. Prüfung der Ware

Der Käufer hat die Kosten für jede vor der Verladung zwingend erforderliche Warenkontrolle (pre-shipment inspection) zu tragen, mit Ausnahme behördlich angeordneter Kontrollen des Ausfuhrlandes.

B10. Unterstützung bei Informationen und damit verbundene Kosten

Der Käufer hat dem Verkäufer rechtzeitig alle sicherheitsrelevanten Informationsanforderungen mitzuteilen, so dass der Verkäufer die Verpflichtungen entsprechend A10 erfüllen kann.

Der Käufer hat dem Verkäufer alle Kosten und Abgaben zu erstatten, die dem Verkäufer durch das Zurverfügungstellen oder die Unterstützung bei der Beschaffung der Dokumente und Informationen wie in A10 vorgesehen entstanden sind.

Der Käufer hat, falls zutreffend, dem Verkäufer rechtzeitig auf dessen Verlangen, Gefahr und Kosten alle Dokumente und Informationen, einschließlich sicherheitsrelevanter Informationen, die der Verkäufer für den Transport und die Ausfuhr der Ware sowie für ihre Durchfuhr durch jedes Land benötigt, zur Verfügung zu stellen oder ihn bei deren Beschaffung zu unterstützen.

[6.] DAP

GELIEFERT BENANNTER ORT
(... benannter Bestimmungsort)

ANWENDUNGSHINWEIS

Diese Klausel kann unabhängig von der gewählten Transportart verwendet werden, auch dann, wenn mehr als eine Transportart zum Einsatz kommt.

„Geliefert benannter Ort" bedeutet, dass der Verkäufer liefert, wenn die Ware dem Käufer auf dem ankommenden Beförderungsmittel entladebereit am benannten Bestimmungsort zur Verfügung gestellt wird. Der Verkäufer trägt alle Gefahren, die im Zusammenhang mit der Beförderung zum benannten Ort stehen.

Die Parteien sind gut beraten, die Stelle innerhalb des benannten Bestimmungsortes so genau wie möglich zu bezeichnen, da die Gefahren bis zu dieser Stelle zu Lasten des Verkäufers gehen. Dem Verkäufer wird geraten, mit dieser Wahl genau übereinstimmende Beförderungsverträge zu verschaffen. Entstehen dem Verkäufer gemäß seinem Beförderungsvertrag Kosten im Zusammenhang mit der Entladung am Bestimmungsort, dann ist der Verkäufer nicht berechtigt, diese Kosten vom Käufer zurückzufordern, sofern nichts anderes zwischen den Parteien vereinbart ist.

DAP verpflichtet den Verkäufer, falls zutreffend, die Ware zur Ausfuhr freizumachen. Jedoch hat der Verkäufer keine Verpflichtung, die Ware zur Einfuhr freizumachen, Einfuhrzölle zu zahlen oder Einfuhrzollformalitäten zu erledigen. Falls die Parteien wünschen, dass der Verkäufer die Ware zur Einfuhr freimacht, Einfuhrzölle zahlt und die Einfuhrzollformalitäten erledigt, sollte die DDP-Klausel verwendet werden.

A. Verpflichtungen des Verkäufers

A1. Allgemeine Verpflichtungen des Verkäufers

Der Verkäufer hat die Ware und die Handelsrechnung in Übereinstimmung mit dem Kaufvertrag bereitzustellen und jeden sonstigen vertraglich vereinbarten Konformitätsnachweis zu erbringen.

Jedes Dokument, auf das in A1–A10 Bezug genommen wird, kann auch ein entsprechender elektronischer Beleg oder ein entsprechendes elektronisches Verfahren sein, wenn dies zwischen den Parteien vereinbart oder üblich ist.

A2. Lizenzen, Genehmigungen, Sicherheitsfreigaben und andere Formalitäten

Falls zutreffend, hat der Verkäufer auf eigene Gefahr und Kosten die Ausfuhrgenehmigung und andere behördliche Genehmigungen zu beschaffen sowie alle Zollformalitäten zu erledigen, die für die Ausfuhr der Ware und für ihre Durchfuhr durch jedes Land vor Lieferung erforderlich sind.

A3. Beförderungs- und Versicherungsverträge

a. Beförderungsvertrag
Der Verkäufer hat für die Ware auf eigene Kosten einen Beförderungsvertrag bis zum benannten Bestimmungsort oder zu der gegebenenfalls vereinbarten Stelle am benannten Bestimmungsort abzuschließen. Ist keine bestimmte Stelle vereinbart oder ergibt sie sich nicht aus der Handelspraxis, kann der Verkäufer jene Stelle am benannten Bestimmungsort auswählen, die für den Zweck am besten geeignet ist.

b. Versicherungsvertrag
Der Verkäufer hat gegenüber dem Käufer keine Verpflichtung, einen Versicherungsvertrag abzuschließen. Jedoch hat der Verkäufer dem Käufer auf dessen Verlangen, Gefahr und (gegebenenfalls entstehende) Kosten jene Informationen zur Verfügung zu stellen, die der Käufer für den Abschluss einer Versicherung benötigt.

A4. Lieferung

Der Verkäufer hat die Ware zu liefern, indem er sie dem Käufer auf dem ankommenden Beförderungsmittel entladebereit am benannten Bestimmungsort an der gegebenfalls vereinbarten Stelle zum vereinbarten Zeitpunkt oder innerhalb des vereinbarten Zeitraums zur Verfügung stellt.

A5. Gefahrenübergang

Der Verkäufer trägt bis zur Lieferung gemäß A4 alle Gefahren des Verlustes oder der Beschädigung der Ware, mit Ausnahme von Verlust oder Beschädigung unter den in B5 beschriebenen Umständen.

A6. Kostenverteilung

Der Verkäufer hat zu tragen
a. zusätzlich zu den aus A3 a entstehenden Kosten alle die Ware betreffenden Kosten bis diese gemäß A4 geliefert worden ist, ausgenommen solcher Kosten, die wie in B6 vorgesehen vom Käufer zu tragen sind;
b. alle Abgaben für die Entladung am Bestimmungsort, die gemäß Beförderungsvertrag vom Verkäufer zu tragen sind; und
c. falls zutreffend, die Kosten der für die Ausfuhr notwendigen Zollformalitäten sowie alle Zölle, Steuern und andere Abgaben, die bei der Ausfuhr fällig werden, und die Kosten für die Durchfuhr der Ware durch jedes Land vor Lieferung gemäß A4.

A7. Benachrichtigungen an den Käufer

Der Verkäufer hat den Käufer über alles Nötige zu benachrichtigen, damit dieser die üblicherweise notwendigen Maßnahmen zur Übernahme der Ware treffen kann.

A8. Transportdokument

Der Verkäufer hat auf eigene Kosten dem Käufer ein Dokument zur Verfügung zu stellen, das diesem die Übernahme der Ware wie in A4/B4 vorgesehen ermöglicht.

A9. Prüfung – Verpackung – Kennzeichnung

Der Verkäufer hat die Kosten jener Prüfvorgänge (wie Qualitätsprüfung, Messen, Wiegen und Zählen), die notwendig sind, um die Ware gemäß A4 zu liefern, sowie die Kosten für alle von den Behörden des Ausfuhrlandes angeordneten Warenkontrollen vor der Verladung (pre-shipment inspection) zu tragen.

Der Verkäufer hat auf eigene Kosten die Ware zu verpacken, es sei denn, es ist handelsüblich, die jeweilige Art der verkauften Ware unverpackt zu transportieren. Der Verkäufer kann die Ware in der für ihren Transport geeigneten Weise verpacken, es sei denn, der Käufer hat den Verkäufer vor Vertragsschluss über spezifische Verpackungsanforderungen in Kenntnis gesetzt. Die Verpackung ist in geeigneter Weise zu kennzeichnen.

A10. Unterstützung bei Informationen und damit verbundene Kosten

Der Verkäufer hat, falls zutreffend, dem Käufer auf dessen Verlangen, Gefahr und Kosten rechtzeitig alle Dokumente und Informationen, einschließlich sicherheitsrelevanter Informationen, die der Käufer für die Einfuhr der Ware und/oder für ihren Transport bis zum endgültigen Bestimmungsort benötigt, zur Verfügung zu stellen oder ihn bei deren Beschaffung zu unterstützen.

Der Verkäufer hat dem Käufer alle Kosten und Abgaben zu erstatten, die dem Käufer durch das Zurverfügungstellen oder die Unterstützung bei der Beschaffung der in B10 vorgesehenen Dokumente und Informationen entstanden sind.

B. Verpflichtungen des Käufers

B1. Allgemeine Verpflichtungen des Käufers

Der Käufer hat den im Kaufvertrag genannten Preis der Ware zu zahlen.

Jedes Dokument, auf das in B1–B10 Bezug genommen wird, kann auch ein entsprechender elektronischer Beleg oder ein entsprechendes elektronisches Verfahren sein, wenn dies zwischen den Parteien vereinbart oder üblich ist.

B2. Lizenzen, Genehmigungen, Sicherheitsfreigaben und andere Formalitäten

Falls zutreffend, muss der Käufer auf eigene Gefahr und Kosten die Einfuhrgenehmigung oder andere behördliche Genehmigungen beschaffen, sowie alle Zollformalitäten für die Einfuhr der Ware erledigen.

B3. Beförderungs- und Versicherungsverträge

a. Beförderungsvertrag
Der Käufer hat gegenüber dem Verkäufer keine Verpflichtung, einen Beförderungsvertrag abzuschließen.
b. Versicherungsvertrag
Der Käufer hat gegenüber dem Verkäufer keine Verpflichtung, einen Versicherungsvertrag abzuschließen. Allerdings hat der Käufer dem Verkäufer auf dessen Verlangen die für den Abschluss einer Versicherung notwendigen Informationen zur Verfügung zu stellen.

B4. Übernahme

Der Käufer muss die Ware übernehmen, wenn sie wie in A4 vorgesehen geliefert worden ist.

B5. Gefahrenübergang

Der Käufer trägt alle Gefahren des Verlustes oder der Beschädigung der Ware ab dem Zeitpunkt, an dem sie wie in A4 vorgesehen geliefert worden ist.
Falls
a. der Käufer seine Verpflichtungen gemäß B2 nicht erfüllt, trägt er alle daraus resultierenden Gefahren des Verlustes oder der Beschädigung der Ware; oder
b. der Käufer es unterlässt, gemäß B7 zu benachrichtigen, trägt er alle Gefahren des Verlustes oder der Beschädigung der Ware ab dem vereinbarten Lieferzeitpunkt oder ab Ablauf des vereinbarten Lieferzeitraums,
vorausgesetzt, die Ware ist eindeutig als die vertragliche Ware kenntlich gemacht worden.

B6. Kostenverteilung

Der Käufer hat zu tragen
a. alle die Ware betreffenden Kosten ab dem Zeitpunkt, an dem sie wie in A4 vorgesehen geliefert worden ist;
b. alle Entladekosten, die erforderlich sind, um die Ware vom ankommenden Beförderungsmittel am benannten Bestimmungsort zu übernehmen, sofern diese Kosten gemäß Beförderungsvertrag nicht zu Lasten des Verkäufers gehen;
c. alle zusätzlichen Kosten, die dem Verkäufer entstehen, falls der Käufer seine Verpflichtungen gemäß B2 nicht erfüllt oder es unterlässt, gemäß B7 zu benachrichtigen, vorausgesetzt, die Ware ist eindeutig als die vertragliche Ware kenntlich gemacht worden; und
d. falls zutreffend, die Kosten für die Zollformalitäten sowie alle Zölle, Steuern und andere Abgaben, die bei der Einfuhr der Ware fällig werden.

B7. Benachrichtigungen an den Verkäufer

Wann immer der Käufer berechtigt ist, den Zeitpunkt innerhalb einer vereinbarten Lieferfrist und/oder die Stelle für die Warenübernahme am benannten Bestimmungsort zu bestimmen, hat er den Verkäufer in angemessener Weise darüber zu benachrichtigen.

B8. Liefernachweis

Der Käufer hat das wie in A8 vorgesehen zur Verfügung gestellte Transportdokument anzunehmen.

B9. Prüfung der Ware

Der Käufer hat die Kosten für jede vor der Verladung zwingend erforderliche Warenkontrolle (pre-shipment inspection) zu tragen, mit Ausnahme behördlich angeordneter Kontrollen des Ausfuhrlandes.

B10. Unterstützung bei Informationen und damit verbundene Kosten

Der Käufer hat dem Verkäufer rechtzeitig alle sicherheitsrelevanten Informationsanforderungen mitzuteilen, so dass der Verkäufer die Verpflichtungen entsprechend A10 erfüllen kann.

Der Käufer hat dem Verkäufer alle Kosten und Abgaben zu erstatten, die dem Verkäufer durch das Zurverfügungstellen oder die Unterstützung bei der Beschaffung der Dokumente und Informationen wie in A10 vorgesehen entstanden sind.

Der Käufer hat, falls zutreffend, dem Verkäufer rechtzeitig auf dessen Verlangen, Gefahr und Kosten alle Dokumente und Informationen, einschließlich sicherheitsrelevanter Informationen, die der Verkäufer für den Transport und die Ausfuhr der Ware sowie für ihre Durchfuhr durch jedes Land benötigt, zur Verfügung zu stellen oder ihn bei deren Beschaffung zu unterstützen.

[7.] DDP

GELIEFERT VERZOLLT
(... benannter Bestimmungsort)

ANWENDUNGSHINWEIS

Diese Klausel kann unabhängig von der gewählten Transportart verwendet werden, auch dann, wenn mehr als eine Transportart zum Einsatz kommt.

„Geliefert verzollt" bedeutet, dass der Verkäufer liefert, wenn er die zur Einfuhr freigemachte Ware dem Käufer auf dem ankommenden Beförderungsmittel entladebereit am benannten Bestimmungsort zur Verfügung stellt. Der Verkäufer trägt alle Kosten und Gefahren, die im Zusammenhang mit der Beförderung der Ware bis zum Bestimmungsort stehen und hat die Verpflichtung, die Ware nicht nur für die Ausfuhr, sondern auch für die Einfuhr freizumachen, alle Abgaben sowohl für die Aus- als auch für die Einfuhr zu zahlen sowie alle Zollformalitäten zu erledigen.

DDP stellt die Maximalverpflichtung für den Verkäufer dar.

Die Parteien sind gut beraten, die Stelle innerhalb des benannten Bestimmungsortes so genau wie möglich zu bezeichnen, da die Kosten und Gefahren bis zu dieser Stelle vom Verkäufer zu tragen sind. Dem Verkäufer wird geraten, mit dieser Wahl genau übereinstimmende Beförderungsverträge zu verschaffen. Entstehen dem Verkäufer gemäß seinem Beförderungsvertrag Kosten im Zusammenhang mit der Entladung am Bestimmungsort, dann ist der Verkäufer nicht berechtigt, diese Kosten vom Käufer zurückzufordern, sofern nichts anderes zwischen den Parteien vereinbart ist.

Die Parteien sind gut beraten, DDP nicht zu verwenden, wenn der Verkäufer nicht in der Lage ist, direkt oder indirekt die Einfuhrabfertigung zu erledigen.

Wenn die Parteien wünschen, dass der Käufer alle Gefahren und Kosten der Einfuhrabfertigung trägt, sollte die DAP-Klausel verwendet werden.

Alle Mehrwertsteuern und andere im Zusammenhang mit der Einfuhr anfallende Steuern gehen zu Lasten des Verkäufers, sofern nicht ausdrücklich etwas anderes im Kaufvertrag vereinbart wurde.

A. Verpflichtungen des Verkäufers

A1. Allgemeine Verpflichtungen des Verkäufers

Der Verkäufer hat die Ware und die Handelsrechnung in Übereinstimmung mit dem Kaufvertrag bereitzustellen und jeden sonstigen vertraglich vereinbarten Konformitätsnachweis zu erbringen.

Jedes Dokument, auf das in A1–A10 Bezug genommen wird, kann auch ein entsprechender elektronischer Beleg oder ein entsprechendes elektronisches Verfahren sein, wenn dies zwischen den Parteien vereinbart oder üblich ist.

Anh. IV

A2. Lizenzen, Genehmigungen, Sicherheitsfreigaben und andere Formalitäten

Falls zutreffend, hat der Verkäufer auf eigene Gefahr und Kosten die Aus- und Einfuhrgenehmigung und andere behördliche Genehmigungen zu beschaffen sowie alle Zollformalitäten zu erledigen, die für die Ausfuhr der Ware, ihre Durchfuhr durch jedes Land und ihre Einfuhr erforderlich sind.

A3. Beförderungs- und Versicherungsverträge

a. Beförderungsvertrag
Der Verkäufer hat für die Ware auf eigene Kosten einen Beförderungsvertrag bis zum benannten Bestimmungsort oder zu der gegebenenfalls vereinbarten Stelle am benannten Bestimmungsort abzuschließen. Ist keine bestimmte Stelle vereinbart oder ergibt sie sich nicht aus der Handelspraxis, kann der Verkäufer jene Stelle am benannten Bestimmungsort auswählen, die für den Zweck am besten geeignet ist.
b. Versicherungsvertrag
Der Verkäufer hat gegenüber dem Käufer keine Verpflichtung, einen Versicherungsvertrag abzuschließen. Jedoch hat der Verkäufer dem Käufer auf dessen Verlangen, Gefahr und (gegebenenfalls entstehende) Kosten jene Informationen zur Verfügung zu stellen, die der Käufer für den Abschluss einer Versicherung benötigt.

A4. Lieferung

Der Verkäufer hat die Ware zu liefern, indem er sie dem Käufer auf dem ankommenden Beförderungsmittel entladebereit am benannten Bestimmungsort an der gegebenenfalls vereinbarten Stelle zum vereinbarten Zeitpunkt oder innerhalb des vereinbarten Zeitraums zur Verfügung stellt.

A5. Gefahrenübergang

Der Verkäufer trägt bis zur Lieferung gemäß A4 alle Gefahren des Verlustes oder der Beschädigung der Ware, mit Ausnahme von Verlust oder Beschädigung unter den in B5 beschriebenen Umständen.

A6. Kostenverteilung

Der Verkäufer hat zu tragen
a. zusätzlich zu den aus A3 a entstehenden Kosten alle die Ware betreffenden Kosten bis diese gemäß A4 geliefert worden ist, ausgenommen solcher Kosten, die wie in B6 vorgesehen vom Käufer zu tragen sind;
b. alle Abgaben für die Entladung am Bestimmungsort, die gemäß Beförderungsvertrag vom Verkäufer zu tragen sind; und
c. falls zutreffend, die Kosten der für die Aus- und Einfuhr notwendigen Zollformalitäten sowie alle Zölle, Steuern und andere Abgaben, die bei der Aus- und Einfuhr der Ware fällig werden, und die Kosten für ihre Durchfuhr durch jedes Land vor Lieferung gemäß A4.

A7. Benachrichtigungen an den Käufer

Der Verkäufer hat den Käufer über alles Nötige zu benachrichtigen, damit dieser die üblicherweise notwendigen Maßnahmen zur Übernahme der Ware treffen kann.

A8. Transportdokument

Der Verkäufer hat auf eigene Kosten dem Käufer ein Dokument zur Verfügung zu stellen, das diesem die Übernahme der Ware wie in A4/B4 vorgesehen ermöglicht.

A9. Prüfung – Verpackung – Kennzeichnung

Der Verkäufer hat die Kosten jener Prüfvorgänge (wie Qualitätsprüfung, Messen, Wiegen und Zählen), die notwendig sind, um die Ware gemäß A4 zu liefern, sowie die Kosten für alle von den Behörden des Aus- oder Einfuhrlandes angeordneten Warenkontrollen vor der Verladung (pre-shipment inspection) zu tragen.

Der Verkäufer hat auf eigene Kosten die Ware zu verpacken, es sei denn, es ist handelsüblich, die jeweilige Art der verkauften Ware unverpackt zu transportieren. Der Verkäufer kann die Ware in der für ihren Transport geeigneten Weise verpacken, es sei denn, der Käufer hat den Verkäufer vor Vertragsschluss über spezifische Verpackungsanforderungen in Kenntnis gesetzt. Die Verpackung ist in geeigneter Weise zu kennzeichnen.

A10. Unterstützung bei Information und damit verbundene Kosten

Der Verkäufer hat, falls zutreffend, dem Käufer auf dessen Verlangen, Gefahr und Kosten rechtzeitig alle Dokumente und Informationen, einschließlich sicherheitsrelevanter Informationen, die der Käufer für den Transport der Ware bis zum endgültigen Bestimmungsort, falls zutreffend, vom benannten Bestimmungsort benötigt, zur Verfügung zu stellen oder ihn bei deren Beschaffung zu unterstützen.

Der Verkäufer hat dem Käufer alle Kosten und Abgaben zu erstatten, die dem Käufer durch das Zurverfügungstellen oder die Unterstützung bei der Beschaffung der in B10 vorgesehenen Dokumente und Informationen entstanden sind.

B. Verpflichtungen des Käufers

B1. Allgemeine Verpflichtungen des Käufers

Der Käufer hat den im Kaufvertrag genannten Preis der Ware zu zahlen.

Jedes Dokument, auf das in B1–B10 Bezug genommen wird, kann auch ein entsprechender elektronischer Beleg oder ein entsprechendes elektronisches Verfahren sein, wenn dies zwischen den Parteien vereinbart oder üblich ist.

B2. Lizenzen, Genehmigungen, Sicherheitsfreigaben und andere Formalitäten

Falls zutreffend, muss der Käufer den Verkäufer auf dessen Verlangen, Gefahr und Kosten dabei unterstützen, die Einfuhrgenehmigung oder andere behördliche Genehmigungen für die Einfuhr der Ware zu beschaffen.

B3. Beförderungs- und Versicherungsverträge

a. Beförderungsvertrag

Der Käufer hat gegenüber dem Verkäufer keine Verpflichtung, einen Beförderungsvertrag abzuschließen.

b. Versicherungsvertrag

Der Käufer hat gegenüber dem Verkäufer keine Verpflichtung, einen Versicherungsvertrag abzuschließen. Allerdings hat der Käufer dem Verkäufer auf dessen Verlangen die für den Abschluss einer Versicherung notwendigen Informationen zur Verfügung zu stellen.

B4. Übernahme

Der Käufer muss die Ware übernehmen, wenn sie wie in A4 vorgesehen geliefert worden ist

B5. Gefahrenübergang

Der Käufer trägt alle Gefahren des Verlustes oder der Beschädigung der Ware ab dem Zeitpunkt, an dem sie wie in A4 vorgesehen geliefert worden ist.
Falls
a. der Käufer seine Verpflichtungen gemäß B2 nicht erfüllt, trägt er alle daraus resultierenden Gefahren des Verlustes oder der Beschädigung der Ware; oder
b. der Käufer es unterlässt, gemäß B7 zu benachrichtigen, trägt er alle Gefahren des Verlustes oder der Beschädigung der Ware ab dem vereinbarten Lieferzeitpunkt oder ab Ablauf des vereinbarten Lieferzeitraums,
vorausgesetzt, die Ware ist eindeutig als die vertragliche Ware kenntlich gemacht worden.

B6. Kostenverteilung

Der Käufer hat zu tragen
a. alle die Ware betreffenden Kosten ab dem Zeitpunkt, an dem sie wie in A4 vorgesehen geliefert worden ist;
b. alle Entladekosten, die erforderlich sind, um die Ware vom ankommenden Beförderungsmittel am benannten Bestimmungsort zu übernehmen, sofern diese Kosten gemäß Beförderungsvertrag nicht zu Lasten des Verkäufers gehen; und
c. alle zusätzlichen Kosten, die entstehen, falls der Käufer seine Verpflichtungen gemäß B2 nicht erfüllt, oder es unterlässt, gemäß B7 zu benachrichtigen, vorausgesetzt, die Ware ist eindeutig als die vertragliche Ware kenntlich gemacht worden.

B7. Benachrichtigungen an den Verkäufer

Wann immer der Käufer berechtigt ist, den Zeitpunkt innerhalb einer vereinbarten Lieferfrist und/oder die Stelle für die Warenübernahme am benannten Bestimmungsort zu bestimmen, hat er den Verkäufer in angemessener Weise darüber zu benachrichtigen.

B8. Liefernachweis

Der Käufer hat den wie in A8 vorgesehen zur Verfügung gestellten Liefernachweis anzunehmen.

B9. Prüfung der Ware

Der Käufer hat gegenüber dem Verkäufer keine Verpflichtung, die Kosten für die vor der Verladung zwingend erforderlichen, von den Behörden des Aus- oder Einfuhrlandes angeordneten Warenkontrollen (pre-shipment inspection) zu tragen.

B10. Unterstützung bei Informationen und damit verbundene Kosten

Der Käufer hat dem Verkäufer rechtzeitig alle sicherheitsrelevanten Informationsanforderungen mitzuteilen, so dass der Verkäufer die Verpflichtungen entsprechend A10 erfüllen kann.
Der Käufer hat dem Verkäufer alle Kosten und Abgaben zu erstatten, die dem Verkäufer durch das Zurverfügungstellen oder die Unterstützung bei der Beschaffung der Dokumente und Informationen wie in A10 vorgesehen entstanden sind.

Der Käufer hat, falls zutreffend, dem Verkäufer rechtzeitig auf dessen Verlangen, Gefahr und Kosten alle Dokumente und Informationen, einschließlich sicherheitsrelevanter Informationen, die der Verkäufer für Transport, Aus- und Einfuhr der Ware sowie für ihre Durchfuhr durch jedes Land benötigt, zur Verfügung zu stellen oder ihn bei deren Beschaffung zu unterstützen.

[II.] Klauseln für den See- und Binnenschiffstransport

[8.] FAS

FREI LÄNGSSEITE SCHIFF
(... benannter Verschiffungshafen)

ANWENDUNGSHINWEIS

Diese Klausel ist ausschließlich für den See- und Binnenschiffstransport geeignet.

„Frei Längsseite Schiff" bedeutet, dass der Verkäufer liefert, wenn die Ware längseits des vom Käufer benannten Schiffs (z.B. an einer Kaianlage oder auf einem Binnenschiff) im benannten Verschiffungshafen gebracht ist. Die Gefahr des Verlustes oder der Beschädigung der Ware geht über, wenn sich die Ware längseits des Schiffs befindet. Der Käufer trägt ab diesem Zeitpunkt alle Kosten.

Die Parteien sind gut beraten, die Ladestelle im benannten Verschiffungshafen so genau wie möglich zu bestimmen, da die Kosten und Gefahren bis zu dieser Stelle zu Lasten des Verkäufers gehen. Diese Kosten und damit verbundene Umschlagskosten (handling charges) können entsprechend der Hafenpraxis variieren.

Der Verkäufer ist verpflichtet, die Ware entweder längseits des Schiffs zu liefern oder bereits so für die Verschiffung gelieferte Ware zu verschaffen. Der Hinweis „zu verschaffen" bezieht sich hier auf mehrere hintereinander geschaltete Verkäufe in einer Verkaufskette („string sales"), die insbesondere im Rohstoffhandel vorkommen.

Bei containerisierter Ware ist es für den Verkäufer üblich, die Ware nicht längseits des Schiffs, sondern an den Frachtführer im Terminal zu übergeben. In derartigen Fällen wäre die FAS-Klausel ungeeignet und es sollte die FCA-Klausel verwendet werden.

FAS verpflichtet den Verkäufer, falls zutreffend, die Ware zur Ausfuhr freizumachen. Jedoch hat der Verkäufer keine Verpflichtung, die Ware zur Einfuhr freizumachen, Einfuhrzölle zu zahlen oder Einfuhrzollformalitäten zu erledigen.

A. Verpflichtungen des Verkäufers

A1. Allgemeine Verpflichtungen des Verkäufers

Der Verkäufer hat die Ware und die Handelsrechnung in Übereinstimmung mit dem Kaufvertrag bereitzustellen und jeden sonstigen vertraglich vereinbarten Konformitätsnachweis zu erbringen.

Jedes Dokument, auf das in A1–A10 Bezug genommen wird, kann auch ein entsprechender elektronischer Beleg oder ein entsprechendes elektronisches Verfahren sein, wenn dies zwischen den Parteien vereinbart oder üblich ist.

A2. Lizenzen, Genehmigungen, Sicherheitsfreigaben und andere Formalitäten

Falls zutreffend, hat der Verkäufer auf eigene Gefahr und Kosten die Ausfuhrgenehmigung oder andere behördliche Genehmigungen zu beschaffen sowie alle Zollformalitäten zu erledigen, die für die Ausfuhr der Ware erforderlich sind.

A3. Beförderungs- und Versicherungsverträge

a. Beförderungsvertrag
Der Verkäufer hat gegenüber dem Käufer keine Verpflichtung, einen Beförderungsvertrag abzuschließen. Wenn es der Käufer jedoch verlangt oder es in der Handelspraxis üblich ist und der Käufer keine gegenteilige Anweisung rechtzeitig erteilt, kann der Verkäufer zu üblichen Bedingungen den Beförderungsvertrag auf Gefahr und Kosten des Käufers abschließen. In beiden Fällen kann der Verkäufer es ablehnen, den Beförderungsvertrag abzuschließen, wovon er den Käufer umgehend in Kenntnis zu setzen hat.

b. Versicherungsvertrag
Der Verkäufer hat gegenüber dem Käufer keine Verpflichtung, einen Versicherungsvertrag abzuschließen. Jedoch hat der Verkäufer dem Käufer auf dessen Verlangen, Gefahr und (gegebenenfalls entstehende) Kosten, jene Informationen zur Verfügung zu stellen, die der Käufer für den Abschluss einer Versicherung benötigt.

A4. Lieferung

Der Verkäufer hat die Ware entweder durch Bereitstellung längsseits des vom Käufer benannten Schiffs an der gegebenenfalls vom Käufer benannten Ladestelle im benannten Verschiffungshafen zu liefern oder indem er die so gelieferte Ware verschafft. In beiden Fällen hat der Verkäufer die Ware zum vereinbarten Zeitpunkt oder innerhalb des vereinbarten Zeitraums und in der im Hafen üblichen Weise zu liefern.

Falls keine bestimmte Ladestelle durch den Käufer angegeben worden ist, kann der Verkäufer die für den Zweck am besten geeignete Stelle innerhalb des benannten Verschiffungshafens auswählen. Falls die Parteien vereinbart haben, dass die Lieferung innerhalb eines Zeitraums stattfinden soll, hat der Käufer die Möglichkeit, den Zeitpunkt innerhalb dieser Frist zu wählen.

A5. Gefahrenübergang

Der Verkäufer trägt bis zur Lieferung gemäß A4 alle Gefahren des Verlustes oder der Beschädigung der Ware, mit Ausnahme von Verlust oder Beschädigung unter den in B5 beschriebenen Umständen.

A6. Kostenverteilung

Der Verkäufer hat zu tragen
a. alle die Ware betreffenden Kosten bis diese gemäß A4 geliefert worden ist, ausgenommen solcher Kosten, die wie in B6 vorgesehen vom Käufer zu tragen sind; und
b. falls zutreffend, die Kosten der für die Ausfuhr notwendigen Zollformalitäten sowie alle Zölle, Steuern und andere Abgaben, die bei der Ausfuhr fällig werden.

A7. Benachrichtigungen an den Käufer

Der Verkäufer hat den Käufer, auf dessen Gefahr und Kosten, in angemessener Weise darüber zu benachrichtigen, entweder, dass die Ware gemäß A4 geliefert worden ist oder dass das Schiff die Ware nicht innerhalb der vereinbarten Frist geladen hat.

A8. Transportdokument

Der Verkäufer hat auf eigene Kosten dem Käufer den üblichen Nachweis zu erbringen, dass die Ware gemäß A4 geliefert worden ist.

Sofern es sich bei einem solchen Nachweis nicht um ein Transportdokument handelt, hat der Verkäufer den Käufer auf dessen Verlangen, Gefahr und Kosten bei der Beschaffung eines Transportdokuments zu unterstützen.

A9. Prüfung – Verpackung – Kennzeichnung

Der Verkäufer hat die Kosten jener Prüfvorgange (wie Qualitätsprüfung, Messen, Wiegen und Zählen), die notwendig sind, um die Ware gemäß A4 zu liefern, sowie die Kosten für alle von den Behörden des Ausfuhrlandes angeordneten Warenkontrollen vor der Verladung (pre-shipment inspection) zu tragen.

Der Verkäufer hat auf eigene Kosten die Ware zu verpacken, sofern es nicht handelsüblich ist, die jeweilige Art der verkauften Ware unverpackt zu transportieren. Der Verkäufer kann die Ware in der Weise verpacken, die für ihren Transport angemessen ist, es sei denn, der Käufer hat den Verkäufer über spezifische Verpackungsanforderungen vor Vertragsschluss in Kenntnis gesetzt. Die Verpackung ist in geeigneter Weise zu kennzeichnen.

A10. Unterstützung bei Informationen und damit verbundene Kosten

Der Verkäufer hat, falls zutreffend, dem Käufer auf dessen Verlangen, Gefahr und Kosten rechtzeitig alle Dokumente und Informationen, einschließlich sicherheitsrelevanter Informationen, die der Käufer für die Einfuhr der Ware und/oder für ihren Transport bis zum endgültigen Bestimmungsort benötigt, zur Verfügung zu stellen oder ihn bei deren Beschaffung zu unterstützen.

Der Verkäufer hat dem Käufer alle Kosten und Abgaben zu erstatten, die dem Käufer durch das Zurverfügungstellen oder die Unterstützung bei der Beschaffung der in B10 vorgesehenen Dokumente und Informationen entstanden sind.

B. Verpflichtungen des Käufers

B1. Allgemeine Verpflichtungen des Käufers

Der Käufer hat im Kaufvertrag genannten Preis der Ware zu zahlen.

Jedes Dokument, auf das in B1–B10 Bezug genommen wird, kann auch ein entsprechender elektronischer Beleg oder ein entsprechendes elektronisches Verfahren sein, wenn dies zwischen den Parteien vereinbart oder üblich ist.

B2. Lizenzen, Genehmigungen, Sicherheitsfreigaben und andere Formalitäten

Falls zutreffend, obliegt es dem Käufer, auf eigene Gefahr und Kosten die Einfuhrgenehmigung oder andere behördliche Genehmigungen zu beschaffen sowie alle Zollformalitäten für die Einfuhr der Ware und für ihre Durchfuhr durch jedes Land zu erledigen.

B3. Beförderungs- und Versicherungsverträge

a. Beförderungsvertrag
   Der Käufer hat auf eigene Kosten den Vertrag über die Beförderung der Ware vom benannten Verschiffungshafen abzuschließen, sofern der Beförderungsvertrag nicht vom Verkäufer wie in A3 a vorgesehen abgeschlossen wurde.
b. Versicherungsvertrag
   Der Käufer hat gegenüber dem Verkäufer keine Verpflichtung, einen Versicherungsvertrag abzuschließen.

B4. Übernahme

Der Käufer muss die Ware übernehmen, wenn sie wie in A4 vorgesehen geliefert worden ist.

B5. Gefahrenübergang

Der Käufer trägt alle Gefahren des Verlustes oder der Beschädigung der Ware ab dem Zeitpunkt, an dem sie wie in A4 vorgesehen geliefert worden ist.
Falls
a. der Käufer es unterlässt, gemäß B7 zu benachrichtigen; oder
b. das vom Käufer benannte Schiff nicht rechtzeitig eintrifft oder die Ware nicht übernimmt oder schon vor dem gemäß B7 festgesetzten Zeitpunkt keine Ladung mehr annimmt;
dann trägt der Käufer alle Gefahren des Verlustes oder der Beschädigung der Ware ab dem vereinbarten Lieferzeitpunkt oder ab Ablauf des für Lieferung vereinbarten Zeitraums, vorausgesetzt, die Ware ist eindeutig als die vertragliche Ware kenntlich gemacht worden.

B6. Kostenverteilung

Der Käufer hat zu tragen
a. alle die Ware betreffenden Kosten ab dem Zeitpunkt, an dem sie wie in A4 vorgesehen geliefert worden ist, ausgenommen, falls zutreffend, die Kosten der für die Ausfuhr notwendigen Zollformalitäten sowie alle Zölle, Steuern und andere in A6 b genannte Abgaben, die bei der Ausfuhr fällig werden;
b. alle zusätzlichen Kosten, die entweder dadurch entstehen, dass:
  i. der Käufer die angemessene Benachrichtigung gemäß B7 unterlässt, oder
  ii. das vom Käufer benannte Schiff nicht rechtzeitig eintrifft, die Ware nicht übernehmen kann oder schon vor der gemäß B7 mitgeteilten Lieferzeit keine Ladung mehr annimmt,
vorausgesetzt, die Ware ist eindeutig als die vertragliche Ware kenntlich gemacht worden; und
c. falls zutreffend, alle Zölle, Steuern und andere Abgaben sowie Kosten der Zollformalitäten, die bei der Einfuhr der Ware fällig werden, sowie die Kosten für ihre Durchfuhr durch jedes Land.

B7. Benachrichtigungen an den Verkäufer

Der Käufer hat dem Verkäufer in angemessener Weise den Namen des Schiffs, die Ladestelle und, falls erforderlich, die gewählte Lieferzeit innerhalb des vereinbarten Zeitraums anzugeben.

B8. Liefernachweis

Der Käufer hat den wie in A8 vorgesehen zur Verfügung gestellten Liefernachweis anzunehmen.

B9. Prüfung der Ware

Der Käufer hat die Kosten für jede vor der Verladung zwingend erforderliche Warenkontrolle (pre-shipment inspection) zu tragen, mit Ausnahme behördlich angeordneter Kontrollen des Ausfuhrlandes.

B10. Unterstützung bei Informationen und damit verbundene Kosten

Der Käufer hat dem Verkäufer rechtzeitig alle sicherheitsrelevanten Informationsanforderungen mitzuteilen, so dass der Verkäufer die Verpflichtungen entsprechend A10 erfüllen kann.

Der Käufer hat dem Verkäufer alle Kosten und Abgaben zu erstatten, die dem Verkäufer durch das Zurverfügungstellen oder die Unterstützung bei der Beschaffung der Dokumente und Informationen wie in A10 vorgesehen entstanden sind.

Der Käufer hat, falls zutreffend, dem Verkäufer rechtzeitig auf dessen Verlangen, Gefahr und Kosten alle Dokumente und Informationen, einschließlich sicherheitsrelevanter Informationen, die der Verkäufer für den Transport und die Ausfuhr der Ware sowie für ihre Durchfuhr durch jedes Land benötigt, zur Verfügung zu stellen oder ihn bei deren Beschaffung zu unterstützen.

[9.] FOB

FREI AN BORD
(... benannter Verschiffungshafen)

ANWENDUNGSHINWEIS

Diese Klausel ist ausschließlich für den See- und Binnenschiffstransport geeignet.

„Frei an Bord" bedeutet, dass der Verkäufer die Ware an Bord des vom Käufer benannten Schiffs im benannten Verschiffungshafen liefert oder die bereits so gelieferte Ware verschafft. Die Gefahr des Verlustes oder der Beschädigung der Ware geht über, wenn die Ware an Bord des Schiffs ist. Der Käufer trägt ab diesem Zeitpunkt alle Kosten.

Der Verkäufer ist verpflichtet, die Ware entweder an Bord des Schiffs zu liefern oder bereits so für die Verschiffung gelieferte Ware zu verschaffen. Der Hinweis „zu verschaffen" bezieht sich hier auf mehrere hintereinander geschaltete Verkäufe in einer Verkaufskette („string sales"), die insbesondere im Rohstoffhandel vorkommen.

FOB kann ungeeignet sein, wenn die Ware dem Frachtführer übergeben wird, bevor sie sich auf dem Schiff befindet, z. B. bei containerisierter Ware, welche üblicherweise am Terminal geliefert wird. In derartigen Fällen sollte die FCA-Klausel verwendet werden.

FOB verpflichtet den Verkäufer, falls zutreffend, die Ware zur Ausfuhr freizumachen. Jedoch hat der Verkäufer keine Verpflichtung, die Ware zur Einfuhr freizumachen, Einfuhrzölle zu zahlen oder Einfuhrzollformalitäten zu erledigen.

A. Verpflichtungen des Verkäufers

A1. Allgemeine Verpflichtungen des Verkäufers

Der Verkäufer hat die Ware und die Handelsrechnung in Übereinstimmung mit dem Kaufvertrag bereitzustellen und jeden sonstigen vertraglich vereinbarten Konformitätsnachweis zu erbringen.

Jedes Dokument, auf das in A1–A10 Bezug genommen wird, kann auch ein entsprechender elektronischer Beleg oder ein entsprechendes elektronisches Verfahren sein, wenn dies zwischen den Parteien vereinbart oder üblich ist.

A2. Lizenzen, Genehmigungen, Sicherheitsfreigaben und andere Formalitäten

Falls zutreffend, hat der Verkäufer auf eigene Gefahr und Kosten die Ausfuhrgenehmigung oder andere behördliche Genehmigungen zu beschaffen sowie alle Zollformalitäten zu erledigen, die für die Ausfuhr der Ware erforderlich sind.

A3. Beförderungs- und Versicherungsverträge

a. Beförderungsvertrag
Der Verkäufer hat gegenüber dem Käufer keine Verpflichtung, einen Beförderungsvertrag abzuschließen. Wenn es der Käufer jedoch verlangt oder es in der Handelspraxis üblich ist und der Käufer keine gegenteilige Anweisung rechtzeitig erteilt, kann der Verkäufer zu üblichen Bedingungen den Beförderungsvertrag auf Gefahr und Kosten des Käufers abschließen. In beiden Fällen kann der Verkäufer es ablehnen, den Beförderungsvertrag abzuschließen, wovon er den Käufer umgehend in Kenntnis zu setzen hat.

b. Versicherungsvertrag
Der Verkäufer hat gegenüber dem Käufer keine Verpflichtung, einen Versicherungsvertrag abzuschließen. Jedoch hat der Verkäufer dem Käufer auf dessen Verlangen, Gefahr und (gegebenenfalls entstehende) Kosten, jene Informationen zur Verfügung zu stellen, die der Käufer für den Abschluss einer Versicherung benötigt.

A4. Lieferung

Der Verkäufer hat die Ware zu liefern, entweder, indem er sie an Bord des vom Käufer benannten Schiffs an der gegebenenfalls vom Käufer bestimmten Ladestelle im benannten Verschiffungshafen verbringt oder indem er die so gelieferte Ware verschafft. In beiden Fällen hat der Verkäufer die Ware zum vereinbarten Zeitpunkt oder innerhalb des vereinbarten Zeitraums und in der im Hafen üblichen Weise zu liefern.

Falls keine bestimmte Ladestelle durch den Käufer angegeben worden ist, kann der Verkäufer die für den Zweck am besten geeignete Stelle innerhalb des benannten Verschiffungshafens auswählen.

A5. Gefahrenübergang

Der Verkäufer trägt bis zur Lieferung gemäß A4 alle Gefahren des Verlustes oder der Beschädigung der Ware, mit Ausnahme von Verlust oder Beschädigung unter den in B5 beschriebenen Umständen.

A6. Kostenverteilung

Der Verkäufer hat zu tragen
a. alle die Ware betreffenden Kosten bis diese gemäß A4 geliefert worden ist, ausgenommen solcher Kosten, die wie in B6 vorgesehen vom Käufer zu tragen sind; und
b. falls zutreffend, die Kosten der für die Ausfuhr notwendigen Zollformalitäten sowie alle Zölle, Steuern und andere Abgaben, die bei der Ausfuhr fällig werden.

A7. Benachrichtigungen an den Käufer

Der Verkäufer hat den Käufer, auf dessen Gefahr und Kosten, in angemessener Weise darüber zu benachrichtigen, entweder, dass die Ware gemäß A4 geliefert worden ist oder dass das Schiff die Ware nicht innerhalb der vereinbarten Frist geladen hat.

A8. Transportdokument

Der Verkäufer hat auf eigene Kosten dem Käufer den üblichen Nachweis zu erbringen, dass die Ware gemäß A4 geliefert worden ist.

Sofern es sich bei einem solchen Nachweis nicht um ein Transportdokument handelt, hat der Verkäufer den Käufer auf dessen Verlangen, Gefahr und Kosten bei der Beschaffung eines Transportdokuments zu unterstützen.

A9. Prüfung – Verpackung – Kennzeichnung

Der Verkäufer hat die Kosten jener Prüfvorgänge (wie Qualitätsprüfung, Messen, Wiegen und Zählen), die notwendig sind, um die Ware gemäß A4 zu liefern, sowie die Kosten für alle von den Behörden des Ausfuhrlandes angeordneten Warenkontrollen vor der Verladung (pre-shipment inspection) zu tragen.

Der Verkäufer hat auf eigene Kosten die Ware zu verpacken, sofern es nicht handelsüblich ist, die jeweilige Art der verkauften Ware unverpackt zu transportieren. Der Verkäufer kann die Ware in der Weise verpacken, die für ihren Transport angemessen ist, es sei denn, der Käufer hat den Verkäufer über spezifische Verpackungsanforderungen vor Vertragsschluss in Kenntnis gesetzt. Die Verpackung ist in geeigneter Weise zu kennzeichnen.

A10. Unterstützung bei Informationen und damit verbundene Kosten

Der Verkäufer hat, falls zutreffend, dem Käufer auf dessen Verlangen, Gefahr und Kosten rechtzeitig alle Dokumente und Informationen, einschließlich sicherheitsrelevanter Informationen, die der Käufer für die Einfuhr der Ware und/oder für ihren Transport bis zum endgültigen Bestimmungsort benötigt, zur Verfügung zu stellen oder ihn bei deren Beschaffung zu unterstützen.

Der Verkäufer hat dem Käufer alle Kosten und Abgaben zu erstatten, die dem Käufer durch das Zurverfügungstellen oder die Unterstützung bei der Beschaffung der in B10 vorgesehenen Dokumente und Informationen entstanden sind.

B. Verpflichtungen des Käufers

B1. Allgemeine Verpflichtungen des Käufers

Der Käufer hat den im Kaufvertrag genannten Preis der Ware zu zahlen.

Jedes Dokument, auf das in B1–B10 Bezug genommen wird, kann auch ein entsprechender elektronischer Beleg oder ein entsprechendes elektronisches Verfahren sein, wenn dies zwischen den Parteien vereinbart oder üblich ist.

B2. Lizenzen, Genehmigungen, Sicherheitsfreigaben und andere Formalitäten

Falls zutreffend, obliegt es dem Käufer, auf eigene Gefahr und Kosten die Einfuhrgenehmigung oder andere behördliche Genehmigungen zu beschaffen sowie alle Zollformalitäten für die Einfuhr der Ware und für ihre Durchfuhr durch jedes Land zu erledigen.

B3. Beförderungs- und Versicherungsverträge

a. Beförderungsvertrag

Der Käufer hat auf eigene Kosten den Vertrag über die Beförderung der Ware vom benannten Verschiffungshafen abzuschließen, sofern der Beförderungsvertrag nicht vom Verkäufer wie in A3 a vorgesehen abgeschlossen wurde.

b. Versicherungsvertrag

Der Käufer hat gegenüber dem Verkäufer keine Verpflichtung, einen Versicherungsvertrag abzuschließen.

B4. Übernahme

Der Käufer muss die Ware übernehmen, wenn sie wie in A4 vorgesehen geliefert worden ist.

B5. Gefahrenübergang

Der Käufer trägt alle Gefahren des Verlustes oder der Beschädigung der Ware ab dem Zeitpunkt, an dem sie wie in A4 vorgesehen geliefert worden ist.
Falls
a. der Käufer die Benachrichtigung gemäß B7 über die Benennung eines Schiffs unterlässt; oder
b. das vom Käufer benannte Schiff nicht rechtzeitig eintrifft, um es dem Verkäufer zu ermöglichen, seine Pflichten entsprechend A4 zu erfüllen, es die Ware nicht übernehmen kann oder schon vor dem gemäß B7 festgesetzten Zeitpunkt keine Ladung mehr annimmt;
dann trägt der Käufer alle Gefahren des Verlustes oder der Beschädigung der Ware:
  i. ab dem vereinbarten Zeitpunkt, oder mangels eines vereinbarten Zeitpunkts,
  ii. ab dem vom Verkäufer gemäß A7 mitgeteilten Zeitpunkt innerhalb des vereinbarten Zeitraums oder, falls kein solcher Zeitpunkt mitgeteilt wurde,
  iii. ab dem Ablaufdatum eines vereinbarten Lieferzeitraums,
vorausgesetzt, die Ware ist eindeutig als die vertragliche Ware kenntlich gemacht worden.

B6. Kostenverteilung

Der Käufer hat zu tragen
a. alle die Ware betreffenden Kosten ab dem Zeitpunkt, an dem sie wie in A4 vorgesehen geliefert worden ist, ausgenommen, falls zutreffend, die Kosten der für die Ausfuhr notwendigen Zollformalitäten sowie alle Zölle, Steuern und andere in A4 b genannte Abgaben, die bei der Ausfuhr fällig werden;
b. alle zusätzlichen Kosten, die entweder dadurch entstehen, dass:
  i. der Käufer die angemessene Benachrichtigung gemäß B7 unterlässt, oder
  ii. das vom Käufer benannte Schiff nicht rechtzeitig eintrifft, die Ware nicht übernehmen kann oder schon vor der gemäß B7 mitgeteilten Lieferzeit keine Ladung mehr annimmt,
vorausgesetzt, die Ware ist eindeutig als die vertragliche Ware kenntlich gemacht worden; und
c. falls zutreffend, alle Zölle, Steuern und andere Abgaben sowie die Kosten der Zollformalitäten, die bei der Einfuhr der Ware sowie ihrer Durchfuhr durch jedes Land fällig werden.

B7. Benachrichtigungen an den Verkäufer

Der Käufer hat dem Verkäufer in angemessener Weise den Namen des Schiffs, die Ladestelle und, falls erforderlich, die gewählte Lieferzeit innerhalb des vereinbarten Lieferzeitraums anzugeben.

B8. Liefernachweis

Der Käufer hat den wie in A8 vorgesehen zur Verfügung gestellten Liefernachweis anzunehmen.

B9. Prüfung der Ware

Der Käufer hat die Kosten für jede vor der Verladung zwingend erforderliche Warenkontrolle (pre-shipment inspection) zu tragen, mit Ausnahme behördlich angeordneter Kontrollen des Ausfuhrlandes.

B10. Unterstützung bei Informationen und damit verbundene Kosten

Der Käufer hat dem Verkäufer rechtzeitig alle sicherheitsrelevanten Informationsanforderungen mitzuteilen, so dass der Verkäufer die Verpflichtungen entsprechend A10 erfüllen kann.

Der Käufer hat dem Verkäufer alle Kosten und Abgaben zu erstatten, die dem Verkäufer durch das Zurverfügungstellen oder die Unterstützung bei der Beschaffung der Dokumente und Informationen wie in A10 vorgesehen entstanden sind.

Der Käufer hat, falls zutreffend, dem Verkäufer rechtzeitig auf dessen Verlangen, Gefahr und Kosten alle Dokumente und Informationen, einschließlich sicherheitsrelevanter Informationen, die der Verkäufer für den Transport und die Ausfuhr der Ware sowie für ihre Durchfuhr durch jedes Land benötigt, zur Verfügung zu stellen oder ihn bei deren Beschaffung zu unterstützen.

[10.] CFR

KOSTEN UND FRACHT
(… benannter Bestimmungshafen)

ANWENDUNGSHINWEIS

Diese Klausel ist ausschließlich für den See- und Binnenschiffstransport geeignet.

„Kosten und Fracht" bedeutet, dass der Verkäufer die Ware an Bord des Schiffs liefert oder die bereits so gelieferte Ware verschafft. Die Gefahr des Verlustes oder der Beschädigung der Ware geht über, wenn die Ware an Bord des Schiffs ist. Der Verkäufer hat den Beförderungsvertrag abzuschließen und die Kosten und Fracht zu tragen, die für die Beförderung der Ware zum benannten Bestimmungshafen erforderlich sind.

Werden die Klauseln CPT, CIP, CFR oder CIF verwendet, erfüllt der Verkäufer seine Lieferpflicht, wenn er die Ware dem Frachtführer in der gemäß der gewählten Klausel bestimmten Weise übergibt und nicht, wenn die Ware den Bestimmungsort erreicht.

Diese Klausel beinhaltet zwei kritische Punkte, da Gefahren- und Kostenübergang an verschiedenen Orten stattfinden. Während der Vertrag in jedem Fall einen Bestimmungshafen angibt, muss er nicht den Verschiffungshafen angeben. Dort allerdings geht die Gefahr auf den Käufer über. Falls der Verschiffungshafen für den Käufer von besonderer Bedeutung ist, sind die Parteien gut beraten, diesen im Vertrag so genau wie möglich zu bezeichnen.

Die Parteien sind gut beraten, die Stelle im vereinbarten Bestimmungshafen so genau wie möglich zu bezeichnen, da die Kosten bis zu dieser Stelle zu Lasten des Verkäufers gehen. Dem Verkäufer wird geraten, mit dieser Wahl genau übereinstimmende Beförderungsverträge zu verschaffen. Entstehen dem Verkäufer nach seinem Beförderungsvertrag Kosten im Zusammenhang mit der Entladung an der bestimmten Stelle im Bestimmungshafen, dann ist der Verkäufer nicht berechtigt, diese Kosten vom Käufer zurückzufordern, sofern nichts anderes zwischen den Parteien vereinbart ist.

Der Verkäufer ist verpflichtet, die Ware entweder an Bord des Schiffs zu liefern oder bereits so für die Verschiffung an den Bestimmungsort gelieferte Ware zu verschaffen. Zusätzlich ist der Verkäufer verpflichtet, entweder einen Beförderungsvertrag abzuschließen oder einen solchen Vertrag zu verschaffen. Der Hinweis „zu verschaffen" bezieht sich hier auf mehrere hintereinander geschaltete Verkäufe in einer Verkaufskette („string sales"), die insbesondere im Rohstoffhandel vorkommen.

CFR kann ungeeignet sein, wenn die Ware dem Frachtführer übergeben wird, bevor sie sich auf dem Schiff befindet, z. B. bei containerisierter Ware, welche üblicherweise am Terminal geliefert wird. In derartigen Fällen sollte die CPT-Klausel verwendet werden.

Anhang **Anh. IV**

CFR verpflichtet den Verkäufer, falls zutreffend, die Ware zur Ausfuhr freizumachen. Jedoch hat der Verkäufer keine Verpflichtung, die Ware zur Einfuhr freizumachen, Einfuhrzölle zu zahlen oder Einfuhrzollformalitäten zu erledigen.

A. Verpflichtungen des Verkäufers

A1. Allgemeine Verpflichtungen des Verkäufers

Der Verkäufer hat die Ware und die Handelsrechnung in Übereinstimmung mit dem Kaufvertrag bereitzustellen und jeden sonstigen vertraglich vereinbarten Konformitätsnachweis zu erbringen.

Jedes Dokument, auf das in A1–A10 Bezug genommen wird, kann auch ein entsprechender elektronischer Beleg oder ein entsprechendes elektronisches Verfahren sein, wenn dies zwischen den Parteien vereinbart oder üblich ist.

A2. Lizenzen, Genehmigungen, Sicherheitsfreigaben und andere Formalitäten

Falls zutreffend, hat der Verkäufer auf eigene Gefahr und Kosten die Ausfuhrgenehmigung oder andere behördliche Genehmigungen zu beschaffen sowie alle Zollformalitäten zu erledigen, die für die Ausfuhr der Ware erforderlich sind.

A3. Beförderungs- und Versicherungsverträge

a. Beförderungsvertrag
Der Verkäufer muss einen Vertrag über die Beförderung der Ware von der gegebenenfalls vereinbarten Lieferstelle am Lieferort bis zum benannten Bestimmungshafen oder einer gegebenenfalls vereinbarten Stelle in diesem Hafen abschließen oder verschaffen. Der Beförderungsvertrag muss zu den üblichen Bedingungen auf Kosten des Verkäufers abgeschlossen werden und die Beförderung auf der üblichen Route mit einem Schiff der Bauart gewährleisten, die normalerweise für den Transport der verkauften Warenart verwendet wird.

b. Versicherungsvertrag
Der Verkäufer hat gegenüber dem Käufer keine Verpflichtung, einen Versicherungsvertrag abzuschließen. Jedoch hat der Verkäufer dem Käufer auf dessen Verlangen, Gefahr und (gegebenenfalls entstehende) Kosten jene Informationen zur Verfügung zu stellen, die der Käufer für den Abschluss einer Versicherung benötigt.

A4. Lieferung

Der Verkäufer hat die Ware zu liefern, entweder, indem er sie an Bord des Schiffs verbringt oder indem er die so gelieferte Ware verschafft. In beiden Fällen hat der Verkäufer die Ware zum vereinbarten Zeitpunkt oder innerhalb des vereinbarten Zeitraums und in der im Hafen üblichen Weise zu liefern.

A5. Gefahrenübergang

Der Verkäufer trägt bis zur Lieferung gemäß A4 alle Gefahren des Verlustes oder der Beschädigung der Ware, mit Ausnahme von Verlust oder Beschädigung unter den in B5 beschriebenen Umständen.

A6. Kostenverteilung

Der Verkäufer hat zu tragen

a. alle die Ware betreffenden Kosten bis diese gemäß A4 geliefert worden ist, ausgenommen solcher Kosten, die wie in B6 vorgesehen vom Käufer zu tragen sind;
b. die Fracht und alle anderen aus A3 a entstehenden Kosten einschließlich der Kosten für die Verladung der Ware an Bord und aller Entladekosten im vereinbarten Entladehafen, die nach dem Beförderungsvertrag vom Verkäufer zu tragen sind; und
c. falls zutreffend, die Kosten der für die Ausfuhr notwendigen Zollformalitäten sowie alle Zölle, Steuern und andere Abgaben, die bei der Ausfuhr fällig werden, und die Kosten für die Durchfuhr der Ware durch jedes Land, soweit diese nach dem Beförderungsvertrag vom Verkäufer zu tragen sind.

A7. Benachrichtigungen an den Käufer

Der Verkäufer hat den Käufer über alles Nötige zu benachrichtigen, damit dieser die üblicherweise notwendigen Maßnahmen zur Übernahme der Ware treffen kann.

A8. Transportdokument

Der Verkäufer hat auf eigene Kosten dem Käufer unverzüglich das übliche Transportdokument für den vereinbarten Bestimmungshafen zur Verfügung zu stellen.

Dieses Transportdokument muss über die vertragliche Ware lauten, ein innerhalb der für die Verschiffung vereinbarten Frist liegendes Datum tragen, den Käufer berechtigen, die Herausgabe der Ware im Bestimmungshafen von dem Frachtführer zu verlangen und, sofern nichts anderes vereinbart wurde, es dem Käufer ermöglichen, die Ware während des Transports an einen nachfolgenden Käufer durch Übertragung des Dokuments oder durch Mitteilung an den Frachtführer zu verkaufen.

Wird ein solches Transportdokument als begebbares Dokument und in mehreren Originalen ausgestellt, muss ein vollständiger Satz von Originalen dem Käufer übergeben werden.

A9. Prüfung – Verpackung – Kennzeichnung

Der Verkäufer hat die Kosten jener Prüfvorgänge (wie Qualitätsprüfung, Messen, Wiegen und Zählen), die notwendig sind, um die Ware gemäß A4 zu liefern, sowie die Kosten für alle von den Behörden des Ausfuhrlandes angeordneten Warenkontrollen vor der Verladung (pre-shipment inspection) zu tragen.

Der Verkäufer hat auf eigene Kosten die Ware zu verpacken, sofern es nicht handelsüblich ist, die jeweilige Art der verkauften Ware unverpackt zu transportieren. Der Verkäufer kann die Ware in der Weise verpacken, die für ihren Transport angemessen ist, es sei denn, der Käufer hat den Verkäufer über spezifische Verpackungsanforderungen vor Vertragsschluss in Kenntnis gesetzt. Die Verpackung ist in geeigneter Weise zu kennzeichnen.

A10. Unterstützung bei Informationen und damit verbundene Kosten

Der Verkäufer hat, falls zutreffend, dem Käufer auf dessen Verlangen, Gefahr und Kosten rechtzeitig alle Dokumente und Informationen, einschließlich sicherheitsrelevanter Informationen, die der Käufer für die Einfuhr der Ware und/oder für ihren Transport bis zum endgültigen Bestimmungsort benötigt, zur Verfügung zu stellen oder ihn bei deren Beschaffung zu unterstützen.

Der Verkäufer hat dem Käufer alle Kosten und Abgaben zu erstatten, die dem Käufer durch das Zurverfügungstellen oder die Unterstützung bei der Beschaffung der in B10 vorgesehenen Dokumente und Informationen entstanden sind.

B. Verpflichtungen des Käufers

B1. Allgemeine Verpflichtungen des Käufers

Der Käufer hat den im Kaufvertrag genannten Preis der Ware zu zahlen.

Jedes Dokument, auf das in B1–B10 Bezug genommen wird, kann auch ein entsprechender elektronischer Beleg oder ein entsprechendes elektronisches Verfahren sein, wenn dies zwischen den Parteien vereinbart oder üblich ist.

B2. Lizenzen, Genehmigungen, Sicherheitsfreigaben und andere Formalitäten

Falls zutreffend, obliegt es dem Käufer, auf eigene Gefahr und Kosten die Einfuhrgenehmigung oder andere behördliche Genehmigungen zu beschaffen sowie alle Zollformalitäten für die Einfuhr der Ware und für ihre Durchfuhr durch jedes Land zu erledigen.

B3. Beförderungs- und Versicherungsverträge

a. Beförderungsvertrag
Der Käufer hat gegenüber dem Verkäufer keine Verpflichtung, einen Beförderungsvertrag abzuschließen.
b. Versicherungsvertrag
Der Käufer hat gegenüber dem Verkäufer keine Verpflichtung, einen Versicherungsvertrag abzuschließen. Allerdings hat der Käufer dem Verkäufer auf dessen Verlangen die notwendigen Informationen für den Abschluss einer Versicherung zur Verfügung zu stellen.

B4. Übernahme

Der Käufer muss die Ware übernehmen, wenn sie wie in A4 vorgesehen geliefert worden ist, und sie von dem Frachtführer im benannten Bestimmungshafen entgegennehmen.

B5. Gefahrenübergang

Der Käufer trägt alle Gefahren des Verlustes oder der Beschädigung der Ware ab dem Zeitpunkt, an dem sie wie in A4 vorgesehen geliefert worden ist.

Falls der Käufer es unterlässt, gemäß B7 zu benachrichtigen, trägt er alle Gefahren des Verlustes oder der Beschädigung der Ware ab dem für die Verschiffung vereinbarten Zeitpunkt oder ab Ablauf der hierfür vereinbarten Frist, vorausgesetzt, die Ware ist eindeutig als die vertragliche Ware kenntlich gemacht worden.

B6. Kostenverteilung

Der Käufer hat, vorbehaltlich der Bestimmungen in A3 a, zu tragen
a. alle die Ware betreffenden Kosten ab dem Zeitpunkt, an dem sie wie in A4 vorgesehen geliefert worden ist, ausgenommen, falls zutreffend, die Kosten der für die Ausfuhr notwendigen Zollformalitäten sowie alle Zölle, Steuern und andere in A6 c genannte Abgaben, die bei der Ausfuhr fällig werden;
b. alle die Ware betreffenden Kosten und Abgaben während des Transports bis zu ihrer Ankunft im Bestimmungshafen, es sei denn, solche Kosten und Abgaben gehen gemäß dem Beförderungsvertrag zu Lasten des Verkäufers;
c. die Entladekosten, einschließlich Kosten für Leichterung und Kaigebühren, es sei denn, diese Kosten und Abgaben sind nach dem Beförderungsvertrag vom Verkäufer zu tragen;

d. alle zusätzlichen Kosten, die entstehen, sollte er die Benachrichtigung gemäß B7 unterlassen, ab dem für die Verschiffung vereinbarten Zeitpunkt oder ab Ablauf der hierfür vereinbarten Frist, vorausgesetzt, die Ware ist eindeutig als die vertragliche Ware kenntlich gemacht worden; und
e. falls zutreffend, alle Zölle, Steuern und andere Abgaben sowie die Kosten der Zollformalitäten, die bei der Einfuhr der Ware und, soweit nicht im Beförderungsvertrag enthalten, bei ihrer Durchfuhr durch jedes Land anfallen.

B7. Benachrichtigungen an den Verkäufer

Wann immer der Käufer berechtigt ist, den Zeitpunkt für die Verschiffung der Ware und/oder die Stelle für die Entgegennahme der Ware innerhalb des benannten Bestimmungshafens zu bestimmen, hat er den Verkäufer in angemessener Weise darüber zu benachrichtigen.

B8. Liefernachweis

Der Käufer hat das wie in A8 vorgesehen zur Verfügung gestellte Transportdokument anzunehmen, wenn dieses mit dem Vertrag übereinstimmt.

B9. Prüfung der Ware

Der Käufer hat die Kosten für jede vor der Verladung zwingend erforderliche Warenkontrolle (pre-shipment inspection) zu tragen, mit Ausnahme behördlich angeordneter Kontrollen des Ausfuhrlandes.

B10. Unterstützung bei Informationen und damit verbundene Kosten

Der Käufer hat dem Verkäufer rechtzeitig alle sicherheitsrelevanten Informationsanforderungen mitzuteilen, so dass der Verkäufer die Verpflichtungen entsprechend A10 erfüllen kann.

Der Käufer hat dem Verkäufer alle Kosten und Abgaben zu erstatten, die dem Verkäufer durch das Zurverfügungstellen oder die Unterstützung bei der Beschaffung der Dokumente und Informationen wie in A10 vorgesehen entstanden sind.

Der Käufer hat, falls zutreffend, dem Verkäufer rechtzeitig auf dessen Verlangen, Gefahr und Kosten alle Dokumente und Informationen, einschließlich sicherheitsrelevanter Informationen, die der Verkäufer für den Transport und die Ausfuhr der Ware sowie für ihre Durchfuhr durch jedes Land benötigt, zur Verfügung zu stellen oder ihn bei deren Beschaffung zu unterstützen.

[11.] CIF

KOSTEN, VERSICHERUNG UND FRACHT
(... benannter Bestimmungshafen)

ANWENDUNGSHINWEIS

Diese Klausel ist ausschließlich für den See- und Binnenschiffstransport geeignet.

„Kosten, Versicherung und Fracht" bedeutet, dass der Verkäufer die Ware an Bord des Schiffs liefert oder die bereits so gelieferte Ware verschafft. Die Gefahr des Verlustes oder der Beschädigung der Ware geht über, wenn die Ware an Bord des Schiffs ist. Der Verkäufer hat den Beförderungsvertrag abzuschließen sowie die Kosten und Fracht zu tragen, die für die Beförderung der Ware zum benannten Bestimmungshafen erforderlich sind.

Der Verkäufer schließt auch einen Versicherungsvertrag gegen die vom Käufer getragene Gefahr des Verlustes oder der Beschädigung der Ware während des Transports ab. Der

Käufer sollte beachten, dass gemäß der CIF-Klausel der Verkäufer nur verpflichtet ist, eine Versicherung mit Mindestdeckung abzuschließen. Wünscht der Käufer einen höheren Versicherungsschutz, wird er dies entweder ausdrücklich mit dem Verkäufer vereinbaren oder eigene zusätzliche Versicherungsvorkehrungen treffen müssen.

Werden die Klauseln CPT, CIP, CFR oder CIF verwendet, erfüllt der Verkäufer seine Lieferpflicht, sobald er die Ware dem Frachtführer in der nach der gewählten Klausel bestimmten Weise übergibt und nicht, wenn die Ware den Bestimmungsort erreicht.

Diese Klausel beinhaltet zwei kritische Punkte, da Gefahren- und Kostenübergang an verschiedenen Orten stattfinden. Während der Vertrag in jedem Fall den Bestimmungshafen angibt, muss er nicht den Verschiffungshafen angeben. Dort allerdings geht die Gefahr auf den Käufer über. Falls der Verschiffungshafen für den Käufer von besonderer Bedeutung ist, sind die Parteien gut beraten, diesen im Vertrag so genau wie möglich zu bezeichnen.

Die Parteien sind gut beraten, die Stelle im vereinbarten Bestimmungshafen so genau wie möglich zu bezeichnen, da die Kosten bis zu dieser Stelle zu Lasten des Verkäufers gehen. Dem Verkäufer wird geraten, mit dieser Wahl genau übereinstimmende Beförderungsverträge zu verschaffen. Entstehen dem Verkäufer nach seinem Beförderungsvertrag Kosten im Zusammenhang mit der Entladung an der bestimmten Stelle im Bestimmungshafen, dann ist der Verkäufer nicht berechtigt, diese Kosten vom Käufer zurückzufordern, sofern nichts anderes zwischen den Parteien vereinbart ist.

Der Verkäufer ist verpflichtet, die Ware entweder an Bord des Schiffs zu liefern oder bereits so für die Verschiffung an den Bestimmungsort gelieferte Ware zu verschaffen. Zusätzlich ist der Verkäufer verpflichtet, entweder einen Beförderungsvertrag abzuschließen oder einen solchen Vertrag zu verschaffen. Der Hinweis „zu verschaffen" bezieht sich hier auf mehrere hintereinander geschaltete Verkäufe in einer Verkaufskette („string sales"), die insbesondere im Rohstoffhandel vorkommen.

CIF kann ungeeignet sein, wenn die Ware dem Frachtführer übergeben wird, bevor sie sich auf dem Schiff befindet, z. B. bei containerisierter Ware, welche üblicherweise am Terminal geliefert wird. In derartigen Fällen sollte die CIP-Klausel verwendet werden.

CIF verpflichtet den Verkäufer, falls zutreffend, die Ware zur Ausfuhr freizumachen. Jedoch hat der Verkäufer keine Verpflichtung, die Ware zur Einfuhr freizumachen, Einfuhrzölle zu zahlen oder Einfuhrzollformalitäten zu erledigen.

A. Verpflichtungen des Verkäufers

A1. Allgemeine Verpflichtungen des Verkäufers

Der Verkäufer hat die Ware und die Handelsrechnung in Übereinstimmung mit dem Kaufvertrag bereitzustellen und jeden sonstigen vertraglich vereinbarten Konformitätsnachweis zu erbringen.

Jedes Dokument, auf das in A1–A10 Bezug genommen wird, kann auch ein entsprechender elektronischer Beleg oder ein entsprechendes elektronisches Verfahren sein, wenn dies zwischen den Parteien vereinbart oder üblich ist.

A2. Lizenzen, Genehmigungen, Sicherheitsfreigaben und andere Formalitäten

Falls zutreffend, hat der Verkäufer auf eigene Gefahr und Kosten die Ausfuhrgenehmigung oder andere behördliche Genehmigungen zu beschaffen sowie alle Zollformalitäten zu erledigen, die für die Ausfuhr der Ware erforderlich sind.

A3. Beförderungs- und Versicherungsverträge

a. Beförderungsvertrag
Der Verkäufer muss einen Vertrag über die Beförderung der Ware von der gegebenenfalls vereinbarten Lieferstelle am Lieferort bis zum benannten Bestimmungshafen oder einer gegebenenfalls vereinbarten Stelle in diesem Hafen abschließen oder verschaffen. Der Beförderungsvertrag ist zu den üblichen Bedingungen auf Kosten des Verkäufers abzuschließen und hat die Beförderung auf der üblichen Route mit einem Schiff der Bauart zu gewährleisten, die normalerweise für den Transport der verkauften Warenart verwendet wird.

b. Versicherungsvertrag
Der Verkäufer hat auf eigene Kosten eine Transportversicherung abzuschließen, die zumindest der Mindestdeckung gemäß den Klauseln (C) der Institute Cargo Clauses (LMA/IUA) oder ähnlichen Klauseln entspricht. Die Versicherung ist bei Einzelversicherern oder Versicherungsgesellschaften mit einwandfreiem Leumund abzuschließen und muss den Käufer oder jede andere Person mit einem versicherbaren Interesse an der Ware berechtigen, Ansprüche direkt bei dem Versicherer geltend zu machen.

Der Verkäufer muss auf Verlangen und Kosten des Käufers, vorbehaltlich der durch den Käufer zur Verfügung gestellten vom Verkäufer benötigten Informationen, zusätzliche Deckung, falls erhältlich, beschaffen, wie z. B. Deckung entsprechend den Klauseln (A) oder (B) der Institute Cargo Clauses (LMA/IUA) oder ähnlichen Klauseln und/oder der Institute War Clauses und/oder der Institute Strikes Clauses (LMA/IUA) oder ähnlichen Klauseln.

Die Versicherung muss zumindest den im Vertrag genannten Preis zuzüglich zehn Prozent (d. h. 110 %) decken und in der Währung des Vertrags ausgestellt sein.

Der Versicherungsschutz muss die Ware ab der Lieferstelle, wie in A4 und A5 festgelegt, bis mindestens zum benannten Bestimmungshafen decken.

Der Verkäufer hat dem Käufer die Versicherungspolice oder einen sonstigen Nachweis über den Versicherungsschutz zu übermitteln.

Ferner hat der Verkäufer dem Käufer auf dessen Verlangen, Gefahr und (gegebenenfalls entstehende) Kosten jene Informationen zur Verfügung zu stellen, die der Käufer für den Abschluss einer zusätzlichen Versicherung benötigt.

A4. Lieferung

Der Verkäufer hat die Ware zu liefern, entweder, indem er sie an Bord des Schiffs verbringt oder indem er die so gelieferte Ware verschafft. In beiden Fällen hat der Verkäufer die Ware zum vereinbarten Zeitpunkt oder innerhalb des vereinbarten Zeitraums und in der im Hafen üblichen Weise zu liefern.

A5. Gefahrenübergang

Der Verkäufer trägt bis zur Lieferung gemäß A4 alle Gefahren des Verlustes oder der Beschädigung der Ware, mit Ausnahme von Verlust oder Beschädigung unter den in B5 beschriebenen Umständen.

A6. Kostenverteilung

Der Verkäufer hat zu tragen
a. alle die Ware betreffenden Kosten bis diese gemäß A4 geliefert worden ist, ausgenommen solcher Kosten, die wie in B6 vorgesehen vom Käufer zu tragen sind;
b. die Fracht und alle anderen aus A3 a entstehenden Kosten einschließlich der Kosten für die Verladung der Ware an Bord und alle Entladekosten im vereinbarten Entladehafen, die nach dem Beförderungsvertrag vom Verkäufer zu tragen sind;
c. die aus A3 b resultierenden Kosten für die Versicherung; und

d. falls zutreffend, die Kosten der für die Ausfuhr notwendigen Zollformalitäten sowie alle Zölle, Steuern und andere Abgaben, die bei der Ausfuhr fällig werden, und die Kosten für die Durchfuhr der Ware durch jedes Land, soweit diese nach dem Beförderungsvertrag vom Verkäufer zu tragen sind.

A7. Benachrichtigungen an den Käufer

Der Verkäufer hat den Käufer über alles Nötige zu benachrichtigen, damit dieser die üblicherweise notwendigen Maßnahmen zur Übernahme der Ware treffen kann.

A8. Transportdokument

Der Verkäufer hat auf eigene Kosten dem Käufer unverzüglich das übliche Transportdokument für den vereinbarten Bestimmungshafen zur Verfügung zu stellen.

Dieses Transportdokument muss über die vertragliche Ware lauten, ein innerhalb der für die Verschiffung vereinbarten Frist liegendes Datum tragen, den Käufer berechtigen, die Herausgabe der Ware im Bestimmungshafen von dem Frachtführer zu verlangen und, sofern nichts anderes vereinbart wurde, es dem Käufer ermöglichen, die Ware während des Transports an einen nachfolgenden Käufer durch Übertragung des Dokuments oder durch Mitteilung an den Frachtführer zu verkaufen.

Wird ein solches Transportdokument als begebbares Dokument und in mehreren Originalen ausgestellt, muss ein vollständiger Satz von Originalen dem Käufer übergeben werden.

A9. Prüfung – Verpackung – Kennzeichnung

Der Verkäufer hat die Kosten jener Prüfvorgänge (wie Qualitätsprüfung, Messen, Wiegen und Zählen), die notwendig sind, um die Ware gemäß A4 zu liefern, sowie die Kosten für alle von den Behörden des Ausfuhrlandes angeordneten Warenkontrollen vor der Verladung (pre-shipment inspection) zu tragen.

Der Verkäufer hat auf eigene Kosten die Ware zu verpacken, es sei denn, es ist handelsüblich, die jeweilige Art der verkauften Ware unverpackt zu transportieren. Der Verkäufer kann die Ware in der für ihren Transport geeigneten Weise verpacken, es sei denn, der Käufer hat den Verkäufer vor Vertragsschluss über spezifische Verpackungsanforderungen in Kenntnis gesetzt. Die Verpackung ist in geeigneter Weise zu kennzeichnen.

A10. Unterstützung bei Informationen und damit verbundene Kosten

Der Verkäufer hat, falls zutreffend, dem Käufer auf dessen Verlangen, Gefahr und Kosten rechtzeitig alle Dokumente und Informationen, einschließlich sicherheitsrelevanter Informationen, die der Käufer für die Einfuhr der Ware und/oder für ihren Transport bis zum endgültigen Bestimmungsort benötigt, zur Verfügung zu stellen oder ihn bei deren Beschaffung zu unterstützen.

Der Verkäufer hat dem Käufer alle Kosten und Abgaben zu erstatten, die dem Käufer durch das Zurverfügungstellen oder die Unterstützung bei der Beschaffung der in B10 vorgesehenen Dokumente und Informationen entstanden sind.

B. Verpflichtungen des Käufers

B1. Allgemeine Verpflichtungen des Käufers

Der Käufer hat den im Kaufvertrag genannten Preis der Ware zu zahlen.

Jedes Dokument, auf das in B1–B10 Bezug genommen wird, kann auch ein entsprechender elektronischer Beleg oder ein entsprechendes elektronisches Verfahren sein, wenn dies zwischen den Parteien vereinbart oder üblich ist.

B2. Lizenzen, Genehmigungen, Sicherheitsfreigaben und andere Formalitäten

Falls zutreffend, obliegt es dem Käufer, auf eigene Gefahr und Kosten die Einfuhrgenehmigung oder andere behördliche Genehmigungen zu beschaffen sowie alle Zollformalitäten für die Einfuhr der Ware und für ihre Durchfuhr durch jedes Land zu erledigen.

B3. Beförderungs- und Versicherungsverträge

a. Beförderungsvertrag
Der Käufer hat gegenüber dem Verkäufer keine Verpflichtung, einen Beförderungsvertrag abzuschließen.
b. Versicherungsvertrag
Der Käufer hat gegenüber dem Verkäufer keine Verpflichtung, einen Versicherungsvertrag abzuschließen. Allerdings hat der Käufer dem Verkäufer auf dessen Verlangen alle für den Abschluss einer vom Käufer verlangten in A3 b vorgesehenen zusätzlichen Versicherung notwendigen Informationen zur Verfügung zu stellen.

B4. Übernahme

Der Käufer muss die Ware übernehmen, wenn sie wie in A4 vorgesehen geliefert worden ist, und sie von dem Frachtführer im benannten Bestimmungshafen entgegennehmen.

B5. Gefahrenübergang

Der Käufer trägt alle Gefahren des Verlustes oder der Beschädigung der Ware ab dem Zeitpunkt, an dem sie wie in A4 vorgesehen geliefert worden ist.
Falls der Käufer es unterlässt, gemäß B7 zu benachrichtigen, trägt er alle Gefahren des Verlustes oder der Beschädigung der Ware ab dem für die Verschiffung vereinbarten Zeitpunkt oder ab Ablauf der hierfür vereinbarten Frist, vorausgesetzt, die Ware ist eindeutig als die vertragliche Ware kenntlich gemacht worden.

B6. Kostenverteilung

Der Käufer hat, vorbehaltlich der Bestimmungen in A3 a, zu tragen
a. alle die Ware betreffenden Kosten ab dem Zeitpunkt, an dem sie wie in A4 vorgesehen geliefert worden ist, ausgenommen, falls zutreffend, die Kosten der für die Ausfuhr notwendigen Zollformalitäten sowie alle Zölle, Steuern und andere in A6 d genannte Abgaben, die bei der Ausfuhr fällig werden;
b. alle die Ware betreffenden Kosten und Abgaben während des Transports bis zu ihrer Ankunft im Bestimmungshafen, es sei denn, solche Kosten und Abgaben gehen gemäß dem Beförderungsvertrag zu Lasten des Verkäufers;
c. die Entladekosten, einschließlich Kosten für Leichterung und Kaigebühren, es sei denn, diese Kosten und Abgaben sind nach dem Beförderungsvertrag vom Verkäufer zu tragen;
d. alle zusätzlichen Kosten, sollte er die Benachrichtigung gemäß B7 unterlassen, ab dem für die Verschiffung vereinbarten Zeitpunkt oder ab Ablauf der hierfür vereinbarten Frist, vorausgesetzt, die Ware ist eindeutig als die vertragliche Ware kenntlich gemacht worden;
e. falls zutreffend, alle Zölle, Steuern und andere Abgaben sowie die Kosten der Zollformalitäten, die bei der Einfuhr der Ware und, soweit nicht im Beförderungsvertrag enthalten, bei ihrer Durchfuhr durch jedes Land anfallen; und
f. die Kosten für jede zusätzlich auf Verlangen des Käufers gemäß A3 b und B3 b abgeschlossene Versicherung.

B7. Benachrichtigungen an den Verkäufer

Wann immer der Käufer berechtigt ist, den Zeitpunkt für die Verschiffung der Ware und/ oder die Stelle für die Entgegennahme der Ware innerhalb des benannten Bestimmungshafens zu bestimmen, hat er den Verkäufer in angemessener Weise darüber zu benachrichtigen.

B8. Liefernachweis

Der Käufer hat das wie in A8 vorgesehen zur Verfügung gestellte Transportdokument anzunehmen, wenn dieses mit dem Vertrag übereinstimmt.

B9. Prüfung der Ware

Der Käufer hat die Kosten für jede vor der Verladung zwingend erforderliche Warenkontrolle (pre-shipment inspection) zu tragen, mit Ausnahme behördlich angeordneter Kontrollen des Ausfuhrlandes.

B10. Unterstützung bei Informationen und damit verbundene Kosten

Der Käufer hat dem Verkäufer rechtzeitig alle sicherheitsrelevanten Informationsanforderungen mitzuteilen, so dass der Verkäufer die Verpflichtungen entsprechend A10 erfüllen kann.

Der Käufer hat dem Verkäufer alle Kosten und Abgaben zu erstatten, die dem Verkäufer durch das Zurverfügungstellen oder die Unterstützung bei der Beschaffung der Dokumente und Informationen wie in A10 vorgesehen entstanden sind.

Der Käufer hat, falls zutreffend, dem Verkäufer rechtzeitig auf dessen Verlangen, Gefahr und Kosten alle Dokumente und Informationen, einschließlich sicherheitsrelevanter Informationen, die der Verkäufer für den Transport und die Ausfuhr der Ware sowie für ihre Durchfuhr durch jedes Land benötigt, zur Verfügung zu stellen oder ihn bei deren Beschaffung zu unterstützen.

V. UNIDROIT PRINCIPLES OF INTERNATIONAL COMMERCIAL CONTRACTS 2010[1]

Preamble

(Purpose of the Principles)
These Principles set forth general rules for international commercial contracts.
They shall be applied when the parties have agreed that their contract be governed by them.[1(*)]
They may be applied when the parties have agreed that their contract be governed by general principles of law, the lex mercatoria or the like.
They may be applied when the parties have not chosen any law to govern their contract.
They may be used to interpret or supplement international uniform law instruments.
They may be used to interpret or supplement domestic law.
They may serve as a model for national and international legislators.

Chapter 1 – General Provisions

Article 1.1 *(Freedom of contract)*
The parties are free to enter into a contract and to determine its content.

Article 1.2 *(No form required)*
Nothing in these Principles requires a contract, statement or any other act to be made in or evidenced by a particular form. It may be proved by any means, including witnesses.

Article 1.3 *(Binding character of contract)*
A contract validly entered into is binding upon the parties. It can only be modified or terminated in accordance with its terms or by agreement or as otherwise provided in these Principles.

Article 1.4 *(Mandatory rules)*
Nothing in these Principles shall restrict the application of mandatory rules, whether of national, international or supranational origin, which are applicable in accordance with the relevant rules of private international law.

Article 1.5 *(Exclusion or modification by the parties)*
The parties may exclude the application of these Principles or derogate from or vary the effect of any of their provisions, except as otherwise provided in the Principles.

---

[1] Abgedruckt mit freundlicher Genehmigung der UNIDROIT.

[1] (*) Parties wishing to provide that their agreement be governed by the Principles might use the following words, adding any desired exceptions or modifications:
„This contract shall be governed by the UNIDROIT Principles (2010) [except as to Articles …]".
Parties wishing to provide in addition for the application of the law of a particular jurisdiction might use the following words:
„This contract shall be governed by the UNIDROIT Principles (2010) [except as to Articles…], supplemented when necessary by the law of [jurisdiction X]".

Article 1.6 *(Interpretation and supplementation of the Principles)*

(1) In the interpretation of these Principles, regard is to be had to their international character and to their purposes including the need to promote uniformity in their application.

(2) Issues within the scope of these Principles but not expressly settled by them are as far as possible to be settled in accordance with their underlying general principles.

Article 1.7 *(Good faith and fair dealing)*

(1) Each party must act in accordance with good faith and fair dealing in international trade.

(2) The parties may not exclude or limit this duty.

Article 1.8 *(Inconsistent behaviour)*

A party cannot act inconsistently with an understanding it has caused the other party to have and upon which that other party reasonably has acted in reliance to its detriment.

Article 1.9 *(Usages and practices)*

(1) The parties are bound by any usage to which they have agreed and by any practices which they have established between themselves.

(2) The parties are bound by a usage that is widely known to and regularly observed in international trade by parties in the particular trade concerned except where the application of such a usage would be unreasonable.

Article 1.10 *(Notice)*

(1) Where notice is required it may be given by any means appropriate to the circumstances.

(2) A notice is effective when it reaches the person to whom it is given.

(3) For the purpose of paragraph (2) a notice „reaches" a person when given to that person orally or delivered at that person's place of business or mailing address.

(4) For the purpose of this Article „notice" includes a declaration, demand, request or any other communication of intention.

Article 1.11 *(Definitions)*

In these Principles
- „court" includes an arbitral tribunal;
- where a party has more than one place of business the relevant „place of business" is that which has the closest relationship to the contract and its performance, having regard to the circumstances known to or contemplated by the parties at any time before or at the conclusion of the contract;
- „obligor" refers to the party who is to perform an obligation and „obligee" refers to the party who is entitled to performance of that obligation.
- „writing" means any mode of communication that preserves a record of the information contained therein and is capable of being reproduced in tangible form.

Article 1.12 *(Computation of time set by parties)*

(1) Official holidays or non-business days occurring during a period set by parties for an act to be performed are included in calculating the period.

(2) However, if the last day of the period is an official holiday or a non-business day at the place of business of the party to perform the act, the period is extended until the first business day which follows, unless the circumstances indicate otherwise.

(3) The relevant time zone is that of the place of business of the party setting the time, unless the circumstances indicate otherwise.

Chapter 2 – Formation and Authority of Agents

Section 1: Formation

Article 2.1.1 *(Manner of formation)*

A contract may be concluded either by the acceptance of an offer or by conduct of the parties that is sufficient to show agreement.

Article 2.1.2 *(Definition of offer)*

A proposal for concluding a contract constitutes an offer if it is sufficiently definite and indicates the intention of the offeror to be bound in case of acceptance.

Article 2.1.3 *(Withdrawal of offer)*

(1) An offer becomes effective when it reaches the offeree.

(2) An offer, even if it is irrevocable, may be withdrawn if the withdrawal reaches the offeree before or at the same time as the offer.

Article 2.1.4 *(Revocation of offer)*

(1) Until a contract is concluded an offer may be revoked if the revocation reaches the offeree before it has dispatched an acceptance.

(2) However, an offer cannot be revoked

  (a) if it indicates, whether by stating a fixed time for acceptance or otherwise, that it is irrevocable; or
  (b) if it was reasonable for the offeree to rely on the offer as being irrevocable and the offeree has acted in reliance on the offer.

Article 2.1.5 *(Rejection of offer)*

An offer is terminated when a rejection reaches the offeror.

Article 2.1.6 *(Mode of acceptance)*

(1) A statement made by or other conduct of the offeree indicating assent to an offer is an acceptance. Silence or inactivity does not in itself amount to acceptance.

(2) An acceptance of an offer becomes effective when the indication of assent reaches the offeror.

(3) However, if, by virtue of the offer or as a result of practices which the parties have established between themselves or of usage, the offeree may indicate assent by performing an act without notice to the offeror, the acceptance is effective when the act is performed.

Article 2.1.7 *(Time of acceptance)*

An offer must be accepted within the time the offeror has fixed or, if no time is fixed, within a reasonable time having regard to the circumstances, including the rapidity of the means of communication employed by the offeror. An oral offer must be accepted immediately unless the circumstances indicate otherwise.

Article 2.1.8 *(Acceptance within a fixed period of time)*

A period of acceptance fixed by the offeror begins to run from the time that the offer is dispatched. A time indicated in the offer is deemed to be the time of dispatch unless the circumstances indicate otherwise.

Article 2.1.9 *(Late acceptance. Delay in transmission)*

(1) A late acceptance is nevertheless effective as an acceptance if without undue delay the offeror so informs the offeree or gives notice to that effect.

(2) If a communication containing a late acceptance shows that it has been sent in such circumstances that if its transmission had been normal it would have reached the offeror in due time, the late acceptance is effective as an acceptance unless, without undue delay, the offeror informs the offeree that it considers the offer as having lapsed.

Article 2.1.10 *(Withdrawal of acceptance)*

An acceptance may be withdrawn if the withdrawal reaches the offeror before or at the same time as the acceptance would have become effective.

Article 2.1.11 *(Modified acceptance)*

(1) A reply to an offer which purports to be an acceptance but contains additions, limitations or other modifications is a rejection of the offer and constitutes a counter-offer.

(2) However, a reply to an offer which purports to be an acceptance but contains additional or different terms which do not materially alter the terms of the offer constitutes an acceptance, unless the offeror, without undue delay, objects to the discrepancy. If the offeror does not object, the terms of the contract are the terms of the offer with the modifications contained in the acceptance.

Article 2.1.12 *(Writings in confirmation)*

If a writing which is sent within a reasonable time after the conclusion of the contract and which purports to be a confirmation of the contract contains additional or different terms, such terms become part of the contract, unless they materially alter the contract or the recipient, without undue delay, objects to the discrepancy.

Article 2.1.13 *(Conclusion of contract dependent on agreement on specific matters or in a particular form)*

Where in the course of negotiations one of the parties insists that the contract is not concluded until there is agreement on specific matters or in a particular form, no contract is concluded before agreement is reached on those matters or in that form.

Article 2.1.14 *(Contract with terms deliberately left open)*

(1) If the parties intend to conclude a contract, the fact that they intentionally leave a term to be agreed upon in further negotiations or to be determined by a third person does not prevent a contract from coming into existence.

(2) The existence of the contract is not affected by the fact that subsequently

    (a) the parties reach no agreement on the term; or

    (b) the third person does not determine the term,

provided that there is an alternative means of rendering the term definite that is reasonable in the circumstances, having regard to the intention of the parties.

Article 2.1.15 *(Negotiations in bad faith)*

(1) A party is free to negotiate and is not liable for failure to reach an agreement.

(2) However, a party who negotiates or breaks off negotiations in bad faith is liable for the losses caused to the other party.

(3) It is bad faith, in particular, for a party to enter into or continue negotiations when intending not to reach an agreement with the other party.

Article 2.1.16 *(Duty of confidentiality)*

Where information is given as confidential by one party in the course of negotiations, the other party is under a duty not to disclose that information or to use it improperly for its own purposes, whether or not a contract is subsequently concluded. Where appropriate, the remedy for breach of that duty may include compensation based on the benefit received by the other party.

Article 2.1.17 *(Merger clauses)*

A contract in writing which contains a clause indicating that the writing completely embodies the terms on which the parties have agreed cannot be contradicted or supplemented by evidence of prior statements or agreements. However, such statements or agreements may be used to interpret the writing.

Article 2.1.18 *(Modification in a particular form)*

A contract in writing which contains a clause requiring any modification or termination by agreement to be in a particular form may not be otherwise modified or terminated. However, a party may be precluded by its conduct from asserting such a clause to the extent that the other party has reasonably acted in reliance on that conduct.

Article 2.1.19 *(Contracting under standard terms)*

(1) Where one party or both parties use standard terms in concluding a contract, the general rules on formation apply, subject to Articles 2.1.20 – 2.1.22.

(2) Standard terms are provisions which are prepared in advance for general and repeated use by one party and which are actually used without negotiation with the other party.

Article 2.1.20 *(Surprising terms)*

(1) No term contained in standard terms which is of such a character that the other party could not reasonably have expected it, is effective unless it has been expressly accepted by that party.

(2) In determining whether a term is of such a character regard shall be had to its content, language and presentation.

Article 2.1.21 *(Conflict between standard terms and non-standard terms)*

In case of conflict between a standard term and a term which is not a standard term the latter prevails.

Article 2.1.22 *(Battle of forms)*

Where both parties use standard terms and reach agreement except on those terms, a contract is concluded on the basis of the agreed terms and of any standard terms which are common in substance unless one party clearly indicates in advance, or later and without undue delay informs the other party, that it does not intend to be bound by such a contract.

Section 2: Authority of Agents

Article 2.2.1 *(Scope of the Section)*

(1) This Section governs the authority of a person („the agent") to affect the legal relations of another person („the principal") by or with respect to a contract with a third party, whether the agent acts in its own name or in that of the principal.

(2) It governs only the relations between the principal or the agent on the one hand, and the third party on the other.

(3) It does not govern an agent's authority conferred by law or the authority of an agent appointed by a public or judicial authority.

Article 2.2.2 *(Establishment and scope of the authority of the agent)*

(1) The principal's grant of authority to an agent may be express or implied.

(2) The agent has authority to perform all acts necessary in the circumstances to achieve the purposes for which the authority was granted.

Article 2.2.3 *(Agency disclosed)*

(1) Where an agent acts within the scope of its authority and the third party knew or ought to have known that the agent was acting as an agent, the acts of the agent shall directly affect the legal relations between the principal and the third party and no legal relation is created between the agent and the third party.

(2) However, the acts of the agent shall affect only the relations between the agent and the third party, where the agent with the consent of the principal undertakes to become the party to the contract.

Article 2.2.4 *(Agency undisclosed)*

(1) Where an agent acts within the scope of its authority and the third party neither knew nor ought to have known that the agent was acting as an agent, the acts of the agent shall affect only the relations between the agent and the third party.

(2) However, where such an agent, when contracting with the third party on behalf of a business, represents itself to be the owner of that business, the third party, upon discovery of the real owner of the business, may exercise also against the latter the rights it has against the agent.

Article 2.2.5 *(Agent acting without or exceeding its authority)*

(1) Where an agent acts without authority or exceeds its authority, its acts do not affect the legal relations between the principal and the third party.

(2) However, where the principal causes the third party reasonably to believe that the agent has authority to act on behalf of the principal and that the agent is acting within the scope of that authority, the principal may not invoke against the third party the lack of authority of the agent.

Article 2.2.6 *(Liability of agent acting without or exceeding its authority)*

(1) An agent that acts without authority or exceeds its authority is, failing ratification by the principal, liable for damages that will place the third party in the same position as if the agent had acted with authority and not exceeded its authority.

(2) However, the agent is not liable if the third party knew or ought to have known that the agent had no authority or was exceeding its authority.

Article 2.2.7 *(Conflict of interests)*

(1) If a contract concluded by an agent involves the agent in a conflict of interests with the principal of which the third party knew or ought to have known, the principal may avoid the contract. The right to avoid is subject to Articles 3.2.9 and 3.2.11 to 3.2.15.

(2) However, the principal may not avoid the contract

　(a) if the principal had consented to, or knew or ought to have known of, the agent's involvement in the conflict of interests; or

　(b) if the agent had disclosed the conflict of interests to the principal and the latter had not objected within a reasonable time.

Article 2.2.8 *(Sub-agency)*

An agent has implied authority to appoint a sub-agent to perform acts which it is not reasonable to expect the agent to perform itself. The rules of this Section apply to the sub-agency.

Article 2.2.9 *(Ratification)*

(1) An act by an agent that acts without authority or exceeds its authority may be ratified by the principal. On ratification the act produces the same effects as if it had initially been carried out with authority.

(2) The third party may by notice to the principal specify a reasonable period of time for ratification. If the principal does not ratify within that period of time it can no longer do so.

(3) If, at the time of the agent's act, the third party neither knew nor ought to have known of the lack of authority, it may, at any time before ratification, by notice to the principal indicate its refusal to become bound by a ratification.

Article 2.2.10 *(Termination of authority)*

(1) Termination of authority is not effective in relation to the third party unless the third party knew or ought to have known of it.

(2) Notwithstanding the termination of its authority, an agent remains authorised to perform the acts that are necessary to prevent harm to the principal's interests.

Chapter 3 – Validity

Section 1: General Provisions

Article 3.1.1 *(Matters not covered)*

This Chapter does not deal with lack of capacity.

Article 3.1.2 *(Validity of mere agreement)*

A contract is concluded, modified or terminated by the mere agreement of the parties, without any further requirement.

Article 3.1.3 *(Initial impossibility)*

(1) The mere fact that at the time of the conclusion of the contract the performance of the obligation assumed was impossible does not affect the validity of the contract.

(2) The mere fact that at the time of the conclusion of the contract a party was not entitled to dispose of the assets to which the contract relates does not affect the validity of the contract.

Article 3.1.4 *(Mandatory character of the provisions)*

The provisions on fraud, threat, gross disparity and illegality contained in this Chapter are mandatory.

Section 2: Grounds for Avoidance

Article 3.2.1 *(Definition of mistake)*

Mistake is an erroneous assumption relating to facts or to law existing when the contract was concluded.

Article 3.2.2 *(Relevant mistake)*

(1) A party may only avoid the contract for mistake if, when the contract was concluded, the mistake was of such importance that a reasonable person in the same situation as the party in error would only have concluded the contract on materially different terms or would not have concluded it at all if the true state of affairs had been known, and

    (a) the other party made the same mistake, or caused the mistake, or knew or ought to have known of the mistake and it was contrary to reasonable commercial standards of fair dealing to leave the mistaken party in error; or

    (b) the other party had not at the time of avoidance reasonably acted in reliance on the contract.

(2) However, a party may not avoid the contract if

    (a) it was grossly negligent in committing the mistake; or

    (b) the mistake relates to a matter in regard to which the risk of mistake was assumed or, having regard to the circumstances, should be borne by the mistaken party.

Article 3.2.3 *(Error in expression or transmission)*

An error occurring in the expression or transmission of a declaration is considered to be a mistake of the person from whom the declaration emanated.

Article 3.2.4 *(Remedies for non-performance)*

A party is not entitled to avoid the contract on the ground of mistake if the circumstances on which that party relies afford, or could have afforded, a remedy for non-performance.

Article 3.2.5 *(Fraud)*

A party may avoid the contract when it has been led to conclude the contract by the other party's fraudulent representation, including language or practices, or fraudulent non-disclosure of circumstances which, according to reasonable commercial standards of fair dealing, the latter party should have disclosed.

Article 3.2.6 *(Threat)*

A party may avoid the contract when it has been led to conclude the contract by the other party's unjustified threat which, having regard to the circumstances, is so imminent and serious as to leave the first party no reasonable alternative. In particular, a threat is unjustified if the act or omission with which a party has been threatened is wrongful in itself, or it is wrongful to use it as a means to obtain the conclusion of the contract.

Article 3.2.7 *(Gross disparity)*

(1) A party may avoid the contract or an individual term of it if, at the time of the conclusion of the contract, the contract or term unjustifiably gave the other party an excessive advantage. Regard is to be had, among other factors, to

(a) the fact that the other party has taken unfair advantage of the first party's dependence, economic distress or urgent needs, or of its improvidence, ignorance, inexperience or lack of bargaining skill, and
(b) the nature and purpose of the contract.

(2) Upon the request of the party entitled to avoidance, a court may adapt the contract or term in order to make it accord with reasonable commercial standards of fair dealing.

(3) A court may also adapt the contract or term upon the request of the party receiving notice of avoidance, provided that that party informs the other party of its request promptly after receiving such notice and before the other party has reasonably acted in reliance on it. Article 3.2.10(2) applies accordingly.

Article 3.2.8 *(Third persons)*

(1) Where fraud, threat, gross disparity or a party's mistake is imputable to, or is known or ought to be known by, a third person for whose acts the other party is responsible, the contract may be avoided under the same conditions as if the behaviour or knowledge had been that of the party itself.

(2) Where fraud, threat or gross disparity is imputable to a third person for whose acts the other party is not responsible, the contract may be avoided if that party knew or ought to have known of the fraud, threat or disparity, or has not at the time of avoidance reasonably acted in reliance on the contract.

Article 3.2.9 *(Confirmation)*

If the party entitled to avoid the contract expressly or impliedly confirms the contract after the period of time for giving notice of avoidance has begun to run, avoidance of the contract is excluded.

Article 3.2.10 *(Loss of right to avoid)*

(1) If a party is entitled to avoid the contract for mistake but the other party declares itself willing to perform or performs the contract as it was understood by the party entitled to avoidance, the contract is considered to have been concluded as the latter party understood it. The other party must make such a declaration or render such performance promptly after having been informed of the manner in which the party entitled to avoidance had understood the contract and before that party has reasonably acted in reliance on a notice of avoidance.

(2) After such a declaration or performance the right to avoidance is lost and any earlier notice of avoidance is ineffective.

Article 3.2.11 *(Notice of avoidance)*

The right of a party to avoid the contract is exercised by notice to the other party.

Article 3.2.12 *(Time limits)*

(1) Notice of avoidance shall be given within a reasonable time, having regard to the circumstances, after the avoiding party knew or could not have been unaware of the relevant facts or became capable of acting freely.

(2) Where an individual term of the contract may be avoided by a party under Article 3.2.7, the period of time for giving notice of avoidance begins to run when that term is asserted by the other party.

Article 3.2.13 (Partial avoidance)

Where a ground of avoidance affects only individual terms of the contract, the effect of avoidance is limited to those terms unless, having regard to the circumstances, it is unreasonable to uphold the remaining contract.

Article 3.2.14 (Retroactive effect of avoidance)

Avoidance takes effect retroactively.

Article 3.2.15 (Restitution)

(1) On avoidance either party may claim restitution of whatever it has supplied under the contract, or the part of it avoided, provided that the party concurrently makes restitution of whatever it has received under the contract, or the part of it avoided.

(2) If restitution in kind is not possible or appropriate, an allowance has to be made in money whenever reasonable.

(3) The recipient of the performance does not have to make an allowance in money if the impossibility to make restitution in kind is attributable to the other party.

(4) Compensation may be claimed for expenses reasonably required to preserve or maintain the performance received.

Article 3.2.16 (Damages)

Irrespective of whether or not the contract has been avoided, the party who knew or ought to have known of the ground for avoidance is liable for damages so as to put the other party in the same position in which it would have been if it had not concluded the contract.

Article 3.2.17 (Unilateral declarations)

The provisions of this Chapter apply with appropriate adaptations to any communication of intention addressed by one party to the other.

Section 3: Illegality

Article 3.3.1 (Contracts infringing mandatory rules)

(1) Where a contract infringes a mandatory rule, whether of national, international or supranational origin, applicable under Article 1.4 of these Principles, the effects of that infringement upon the contract are the effects, if any, expressly prescribed by that mandatory rule.

(2) Where the mandatory rule does not expressly prescribe the effects of an infringement upon a contract, the parties have the right to exercise such remedies under the contract as in the circumstances are reasonable.

(3) In determining what is reasonable regard is to be had in particular to:
    (a) the purpose of the rule which has been infringed;
    (b) the category of persons for whose protection the rule exists;
    (c) any sanction that may be imposed under the rule infringed;
    (d) the seriousness of the infringement;
    (e) whether one or both parties knew or ought to have known of the infringement;
    (f) whether the performance of the contract necessitates the infringement; and
    (g) the parties' reasonable expectations.

Article 3.3.2 (Restitution)

(1) Where there has been performance under a contract infringing a mandatory rule under Article 3.3.1, restitution may be granted where this would be reasonable in the circumstances.

(2) In determining what is reasonable, regard is to be had, with the appropriate adaptations, to the criteria referred to in Article 3.3.1(3).

(3) If restitution is granted, the rules set out in Article 3.2.15 apply with appropriate adaptations.

Chapter 4 – Interpretation

Article 4.1 (Intention of the parties)

(1) A contract shall be interpreted according to the common intention of the parties.

(2) If such an intention cannot be established, the contract shall be interpreted according to the meaning that reasonable persons of the same kind as the parties would give to it in the same circumstances.

Article 4.2 (Interpretation of statements and other conduct)

(1) The statements and other conduct of a party shall be interpreted according to that party's intention if the other party knew or could not have been unaware of that intention.

(2) If the preceding paragraph is not applicable, such statements and other conduct shall be interpreted according to the meaning that a reasonable person of the same kind as the other party would give to it in the same circumstances.

Article 4.3 (Relevant circumstances)

In applying Articles 4.1 and 4.2, regard shall be had to all the circumstances, including
(a) preliminary negotiations between the parties;
(b) practices which the parties have established between themselves;
(c) the conduct of the parties subsequent to the conclusion of the contract;
(d) the nature and purpose of the contract;
(e) the meaning commonly given to terms and expressions in the trade concerned;
(f) usages.

Article 4.4 (Reference to contract or statement as a whole)

Terms and expressions shall be interpreted in the light of the whole contract or statement in which they appear.

Article 4.5 (All terms to be given effect)

Contract terms shall be interpreted so as to give effect to all the terms rather than to deprive some of them of effect.

Article 4.6 (Contra proferentem rule)

If contract terms supplied by one party are unclear, an interpretation against that party is preferred.

Article 4.7 (Linguistic discrepancies)

Where a contract is drawn up in two or more language versions which are equally authoritative there is, in case of discrepancy between the versions, a preference for the interpretation according to a version in which the contract was originally drawn up.

Article 4.8 (Supplying an omitted term)

(1) Where the parties to a contract have not agreed with respect to a term which is important for a determination of their rights and duties, a term which is appropriate in the circumstances shall be supplied.

(2) In determining what is an appropriate term regard shall be had, among other factors, to

   (a) the intention of the parties;
   (b) the nature and purpose of the contract;
   (c) good faith and fair dealing;
   (d) reasonableness.

Chapter 5 – Content and Third Party Rights

Section 1: Content

Article 5.1.1 (Express and implied obligations)

The contractual obligations of the parties may be express or implied.

Article 5.1.2 (Implied obligations)

Implied obligations stem from

(a) the nature and purpose of the contract;
(b) practices established between the parties and usages;
(c) good faith and fair dealing;
(d) reasonableness.

Article 5.1.3 (Co-operation between the parties)

Each party shall cooperate with the other party when such co-operation may reasonably be expected for the performance of that party's obligations.

Article 5.1.4 (Duty to achieve a specific result. Duty of best efforts)

(1) To the extent that an obligation of a party involves a duty to achieve a specific result, that party is bound to achieve that result.

(2) To the extent that an obligation of a party involves a duty of best efforts in the performance of an activity, that party is bound to make such efforts as would be made by a reasonable person of the same kind in the same circumstances.

Article 5.1.5 (Determination of kind of duty involved)

In determining the extent to which an obligation of a party involves a duty of best efforts in the performance of an activity or a duty to achieve a specific result, regard shall be had, among other factors, to

(a) the way in which the obligation is expressed in the contract;
(b) the contractual price and other terms of the contract;
(c) the degree of risk normally involved in achieving the expected result;
(d) the ability of the other party to influence the performance of the obligation.

Article 5.1.6 *(Determination of quality of performance)*

Where the quality of performance is neither fixed by, nor determinable from, the contract a party is bound to render a performance of a quality that is reasonable and not less than average in the circumstances.

Article 5.1.7 *(Price determination)*

(1) Where a contract does not fix or make provision for determining the price, the parties are considered, in the absence of any indication to the contrary, to have made reference to the price generally charged at the time of the conclusion of the contract for such performance in comparable circumstances in the trade concerned or, if no such price is available, to a reasonable price.

(2) Where the price is to be determined by one party and that determination is manifestly unreasonable, a reasonable price shall be substituted notwithstanding any contract term to the contrary.

(3) Where the price is to be fixed by a third person, and that person cannot or will not do so, the price shall be a reasonable price.

(4) Where the price is to be fixed by reference to factors which do not exist or have ceased to exist or to be accessible, the nearest equivalent factor shall be treated as a substitute.

Article 5.1.8 *(Contract for an indefinite period)*

A contract for an indefinite period may be ended by either party by giving notice a reasonable time in advance.

Article 5.1.9 *(Release by agreement)*

(1) An obligee may release its right by agreement with the obligor.

(2) An offer to release a right gratuitously shall be deemed accepted if the obligor does not reject the offer without delay after having become aware of it.

Section 2: Third Party Rights

Article 5.2.1 *(Contracts in favour of third parties)*

(1) The parties (the „promisor" and the „promisee") may confer by express or implied agreement a right on a third party (the „beneficiary").

(2) The existence and content of the beneficiary's right against the promisor are determined by the agreement of the parties and are subject to any conditions or other limitations under the agreement.

Article 5.2.2 *(Third party identifiable)*

The beneficiary must be identifiable with adequate certainty by the contract but need not be in existence at the time the contract is made.

Article 5.2.3 *(Exclusion and limitation clauses)*

The conferment of rights in the beneficiary includes the right to invoke a clause in the contract which excludes or limits the liability of the beneficiary.

Article 5.2.4 *(Defences)*

The promisor may assert against the beneficiary all defences which the promisor could assert against the promisee.

Article 5.2.5 *(Revocation)*

The parties may modify or revoke the rights conferred by the contract on the beneficiary until the beneficiary has accepted them or reasonably acted in reliance on them.

Article 5.2.6 *(Renunciation)*

The beneficiary may renounce a right conferred on it.

Section 3: Conditions

Article 5.3.1 *(Types of condition)*

A contract or a contractual obligation may be made conditional upon the occurrence of a future uncertain event, so that the contract or the contractual obligation only takes effect if the event occurs (suspensive condition) or comes to an end if the event occurs (resolutive condition).

Article 5.3.2 *(Effect of conditions)*

Unless the parties otherwise agree :
(a) the relevant contract or contractual obligation takes effect upon fulfilment of a suspensive condition;
(b) the relevant contract or contractual obligation comes to an end upon fulfilment of a resolutive condition.

Article 5.3.3 *(Interference with conditions)*

(1) If fulfilment of a condition is prevented by a party, contrary to the duty of good faith and fair dealing or the duty of co-operation, that party may not rely on the non-fulfilment of the condition.

(2) If fulfilment of a condition is brought about by a party, contrary to the duty of good faith and fair dealing or the duty of co-operation, that party may not rely on the fulfilment of the condition.

Article 5.3.4 *(Duty to preserve rights)*

Pending fulfilment of a condition, a party may not, contrary to the duty to act in accordance with good faith and fair dealing, act so as to prejudice the other party's rights in case of fulfilment of the condition.

Article 5.3.5 *(Restitution in case of fulfilment of a resolutive condition)*

(1) On fulfilment of a resolutive condition, the rules on restitution set out in Articles 7.3.6 and 7.3.7 apply with appropriate adaptations.

(2) If the parties have agreed that the resolutive condition is to operate retroactively, the rules on restitution set out in Article 3.2.15 apply with appropriate adaptations.

Chapter 6 – Performance

Section 1: Performance in General

Article 6.1.1 *(Time of performance)*

A party must perform its obligations:
(a) if a time is fixed by or determinable from the contract, at that time;

(b) if a period of time is fixed by or determinable from the contract, at any time within that period unless circumstances indicate that the other party is to choose a time;
(c) in any other case, within a reasonable time after the conclusion of the contract.

Article 6.1.2 *(Performance at one time or in instalments)*

In cases under Article 6.1.1(b) or (c), a party must perform its obligations at one time if that performance can be rendered at one time and the circumstances do not indicate otherwise.

Article 6.1.3 *(Partial performance)*

(1) The obligee may reject an offer to perform in part at the time performance is due, whether or not such offer is coupled with an assurance as to the balance of the performance, unless the obligee has no legitimate interest in so doing.

(2) Additional expenses caused to the obligee by partial performance are to be borne by the obligor without prejudice to any other remedy.

Article 6.1.4 *(Order of performance)*

(1) To the extent that the performances of the parties can be rendered simultaneously, the parties are bound to render them simultaneously unless the circumstances indicate otherwise.

(2) To the extent that the performance of only one party requires a period of time, that party is bound to render its performance first, unless the circumstances indicate otherwise.

Article 6.1.5 *(Earlier performance)*

(1) The obligee may reject an earlier performance unless it has no legitimate interest in so doing.

(2) Acceptance by a party of an earlier performance does not affect the time for the performance of its own obligations if that time has been fixed irrespective of the performance of the other party's obligations.

(3) Additional expenses caused to the obligee by earlier performance are to be borne by the obligor, without prejudice to any other remedy.

Article 6.1.6 *(Place of performance)*

(1) If the place of performance is neither fixed by, nor determinable from, the contract, a party is to perform:

(a) a monetary obligation, at the obligee's place of business;

(b) any other obligation, at its own place of business.

(2) A party must bear any increase in the expenses incidental to performance which is caused by a change in its place of business subsequent to the conclusion of the contract.

Article 6.1.7 *(Payment by cheque or other instrument)*

(1) Payment may be made in any form used in the ordinary course of business at the place for payment.

(2) However, an obligee who accepts, either by virtue of paragraph (1) or voluntarily, a cheque, any other order to pay or a promise to pay, is presumed to do so only on condition that it will be honoured.

Article 6.1.8 *(Payment by funds transfer)*

(1) Unless the obligee has indicated a particular account, payment may be made by a transfer to any of the financial institutions in which the obligee has made it known that it has an account.

(2) In case of payment by a transfer the obligation of the obligor is discharged when the transfer to the obligee's financial institution becomes effective.

Article 6.1.9 *(Currency of payment)*

(1) If a monetary obligation is expressed in a currency other than that of the place for payment, it may be paid by the obligor in the currency of the place for payment unless

 (a) that currency is not freely convertible; or
 (b) the parties have agreed that payment should be made only in the currency in which the monetary obligation is expressed.

(2) If it is impossible for the obligor to make payment in the currency in which the monetary obligation is expressed, the obligee may require payment in the currency of the place for payment, even in the case referred to in paragraph (1)(b).

(3) Payment in the currency of the place for payment is to be made according to the applicable rate of exchange prevailing there when payment is due.

(4) However, if the obligor has not paid at the time when payment is due, the obligee may require payment according to the applicable rate of exchange prevailing either when payment is due or at the time of actual payment.

Article 6.1.10 *(Currency not expressed)*

Where a monetary obligation is not expressed in a particular currency, payment must be made in the currency of the place where payment is to be made.

Article 6.1.11 *(Costs of performance)*

Each party shall bear the costs of performance of its obligations.

Article 6.1.12 *(Imputation of payments)*

(1) An obligor owing several monetary obligations to the same obligee may specify at the time of payment the debt to which it intends the payment to be applied. However, the payment discharges first any expenses, then interest due and finally the principal.

(2) If the obligor makes no such specification, the obligee may, within a reasonable time after payment, declare to the obligor the obligation to which it imputes the payment, provided that the obligation is due and undisputed.

(3) In the absence of imputation under paragraphs (1) or (2), payment is imputed to that obligation which satisfies one of the following criteria in the order indicated:

 (a) an obligation which is due or which is the first to fall due;
 (b) the obligation for which the obligee has least security;
 (c) the obligation which is the most burdensome for the obligor;
 (d) the obligation which has arisen first.

If none of the preceding criteria applies, payment is imputed to all the obligations proportionally.

Article 6.1.13 *(Imputation of non-monetary obligations)*

Article 6.1.12 applies with appropriate adaptations to the imputation of performance of non-monetary obligations.

Article 6.1.14 *(Application for public permission)*

Where the law of a State requires a public permission affecting the validity of the contract or its performance and neither that law nor the circumstances indicate otherwise

(a) if only one party has its place of business in that State, that party shall take the measures necessary to obtain the permission;

(b) in any other case the party whose performance requires permission shall take the necessary measures.

Article 6.1.15 *(Procedure in applying for permission)*

(1) The party required to take the measures necessary to obtain the permission shall do so without undue delay and shall bear any expenses incurred.

(2) That party shall whenever appropriate give the other party notice of the grant or refusal of such permission without undue delay.

Article 6.1.16 *(Permission neither granted nor refused)*

(1) If, notwithstanding the fact that the party responsible has taken all measures required, permission is neither granted nor refused within an agreed period or, where no period has been agreed, within a reasonable time from the conclusion of the contract, either party is entitled to terminate the contract.

(2) Where the permission affects some terms only, paragraph (1) does not apply if, having regard to the circumstances, it is reasonable to uphold the remaining contract even if the permission is refused.

Article 6.1.17 *(Permission refused)*

(1) The refusal of a permission affecting the validity of the contract renders the contract void. If the refusal affects the validity of some terms only, only such terms are void if, having regard to the circumstances, it is reasonable to uphold the remaining contract.

(2) Where the refusal of a permission renders the performance of the contract impossible in whole or in part, the rules on non-performance apply.

Section 2: Hardship

Article 6.2.1 *(Contract to be observed)*

Where the performance of a contract becomes more onerous for one of the parties, that party is nevertheless bound to perform its obligations subject to the following provisions on hardship.

Article 6.2.2 *(Definition of hardship)*

There is hardship where the occurrence of events fundamentally alters the equilibrium of the contract either because the cost of a party's performance has increased or because the value of the performance a party receives has diminished, and

(a) the events occur or become known to the disadvantaged party after the conclusion of the contract;

(b) the events could not reasonably have been taken into account by the disadvantaged party at the time of the conclusion of the contract;

(c) the events are beyond the control of the disadvantaged party; and

(d) the risk of the events was not assumed by the disadvantaged party.

Article 6.2.3 *(Effects of hardship)*

(1) In case of hardship the disadvantaged party is entitled to request renegotiations. The request shall be made without undue delay and shall indicate the grounds on which it is based.

(2) The request for renegotiation does not in itself entitle the disadvantaged party to withhold performance.

(3) Upon failure to reach agreement within a reasonable time either party may resort to the court.

(4) If the court finds hardship it may, if reasonable,

> (a) terminate the contract at a date and on terms to be fixed, or
> (b) adapt the contract with a view to restoring its equilibrium.

Chapter 7 – Non-performance

Section 1: Non-performance in General

Article 7.1.1 *(Non-performance defined)*

Non-performance is failure by a party to perform any of its obligations under the contract, including defective performance or late performance.

Article 7.1.2 *(Interference by the other party)*

A party may not rely on the non-performance of the other party to the extent that such non-performance was caused by the first party's act or omission or by another event for which the first party bears the risk.

Article 7.1.3 *(Withholding performance)*

(1) Where the parties are to perform simultaneously, either party may withhold performance until the other party tenders its performance.

(2) Where the parties are to perform consecutively, the party that is to perform later may withhold its performance until the first party has performed.

Article 7.1.4 *(Cure by non-performing party)*

(1) The non-performing party may, at its own expense, cure any non-performance, provided that

> (a) without undue delay, it gives notice indicating the proposed manner and timing of the cure;
> (b) cure is appropriate in the circumstances;
> (c) the aggrieved party has no legitimate interest in refusing cure; and
> (d) cure is effected promptly.

(2) The right to cure is not precluded by notice of termination.

(3) Upon effective notice of cure, rights of the aggrieved party that are inconsistent with the non-performing party's performance are suspended until the time for cure has expired.

(4) The aggrieved party may withhold performance pending cure.

(5) Notwithstanding cure, the aggrieved party retains the right to claim damages for delay as well as for any harm caused or not prevented by the cure.

Article 7.1.5 *(Additional period for performance)*

(1) In a case of non-performance the aggrieved party may by notice to the other party allow an additional period of time for performance.

(2) During the additional period the aggrieved party may withhold performance of its own reciprocal obligations and may claim damages but may not resort to any other remedy. If it receives notice from the other party that the latter will not perform within that period, or if upon expiry of that period due performance has not been made, the aggrieved party may resort to any of the remedies that may be available under this Chapter.

(3) Where in a case of delay in performance which is not fundamental the aggrieved party has given notice allowing an additional period of time of reasonable length, it may terminate the contract at the end of that period. If the additional period allowed is not of reasonable length it shall be extended to a reasonable length. The aggrieved party may in its notice provide that if the other party fails to perform within the period allowed by the notice the contract shall automatically terminate.

(4) Paragraph (3) does not apply where the obligation which has not been performed is only a minor part of the contractual obligation of the non-performing party.

Article 7.1.6 *(Exemption clauses)*

A clause which limits or excludes one party's liability for non-performance or which permits one party to render performance substantially different from what the other party reasonably expected may not be invoked if it would be grossly unfair to do so, having regard to the purpose of the contract.

Article 7.1.7 *(Force majeure)*

(1) Non-performance by a party is excused if that party proves that the non-performance was due to an impediment beyond its control and that it could not reasonably be expected to have taken the impediment into account at the time of the conclusion of the contract or to have avoided or overcome it or its consequences.

(2) When the impediment is only temporary, the excuse shall have effect for such period as is reasonable having regard to the effect of the impediment on the performance of the contract.

(3) The party who fails to perform must give notice to the other party of the impediment and its effect on its ability to perform. If the notice is not received by the other party within a reasonable time after the party who fails to perform knew or ought to have known of the impediment, it is liable for damages resulting from such non-receipt.

(4) Nothing in this Article prevents a party from exercising a right to terminate the contract or to withhold performance or request interest on money due.

Section 2: Right to Performance

Article 7.2.1 *(Performance of monetary obligation)*

Where a party who is obliged to pay money does not do so, the other party may require payment.

Article 7.2.2 *(Performance of non-monetary obligation)*

Where a party who owes an obligation other than one to pay money does not perform, the other party may require performance, unless

(a) performance is impossible in law or in fact;
(b) performance or, where relevant, enforcement is unreasonably burdensome or expensive;
(c) the party entitled to performance may reasonably obtain performance from another source;
(d) performance is of an exclusively personal character; or
(e) the party entitled to performance does not require performance within a reasonable time after it has, or ought to have, become aware of the non-performance.

Article 7.2.3 *(Repair and replacement of defective performance)*

The right to performance includes in appropriate cases the right to require repair, replacement, or other cure of defective performance. The provisions of Articles 7.2.1 and 7.2.2 apply accordingly.

Article 7.2.4 *(Judicial penalty)*

(1) Where the court orders a party to perform, it may also direct that this party pay a penalty if it does not comply with the order.

(2) The penalty shall be paid to the aggrieved party unless mandatory provisions of the law of the forum provide otherwise. Payment of the penalty to the aggrieved party does not exclude any claim for damages.

Article 7.2.5 *(Change of remedy)*

(1) An aggrieved party who has required performance of a non-monetary obligation and who has not received performance within a period fixed or otherwise within a reasonable period of time may invoke any other remedy.

(2) Where the decision of a court for performance of a non-monetary obligation cannot be enforced, the aggrieved party may invoke any other remedy.

Section 3: Termination

Article 7.3.1 *(Right to terminate the contract)*

(1) A party may terminate the contract where the failure of the other party to perform an obligation under the contract amounts to a fundamental non-performance.

(2) In determining whether a failure to perform an obligation amounts to a fundamental non-performance regard shall be had, in particular, to whether

- (a) the non-performance substantially deprives the aggrieved party of what it was entitled to expect under the contract unless the other party did not foresee and could not reasonably have foreseen such result;
- (b) strict compliance with the obligation which has not been performed is of essence under the contract;
- (c) the non-performance is intentional or reckless;
- (d) the non-performance gives the aggrieved party reason to believe that it cannot rely on the other party's future performance;
- (e) the non-performing party will suffer disproportionate loss as a result of the preparation or performance if the contract is terminated.

(3) In the case of delay the aggrieved party may also terminate the contract if the other party fails to perform before the time allowed it under Article 7.1.5 has expired.

Article 7.3.2 *(Notice of termination)*

(1) The right of a party to terminate the contract is exercised by notice to the other party.

(2) If performance has been offered late or otherwise does not conform to the contract the aggrieved party will lose its right to terminate the contract unless it gives notice to the other party within a reasonable time after it has or ought to have become aware of the offer or of the non-conforming performance.

Article 7.3.3 *(Anticipatory non-performance)*

Where prior to the date for performance by one of the parties it is clear that there will be a fundamental non-performance by that party, the other party may terminate the contract.

Article 7.3.4 *(Adequate assurance of due performance)*

A party who reasonably believes that there will be a fundamental non-performance by the other party may demand adequate assurance of due performance and may meanwhile withhold its own performance. Where this assurance is not provided within a reasonable time the party demanding it may terminate the contract.

Article 7.3.5 *(Effects of termination in general)*

(1) Termination of the contract releases both parties from their obligation to effect and to receive future performance.

(2) Termination does not preclude a claim for damages for non-performance.

(3) Termination does not affect any provision in the contract for the settlement of disputes or any other term of the contract which is to operate even after termination.

Article 7.3.6 *(Restitution with respect to contracts to be performed at one time)*

(1) On termination of a contract to be performed at one time either party may claim restitution of whatever it has supplied under the contract, provided that such party concurrently makes restitution of whatever it has received under the contract.

(2) If restitution in kind is not possible or appropriate, an allowance has to be made in money whenever reasonable.

(3) The recipient of the performance does not have to make an allowance in money if the impossibility to make restitution in kind is attributable to the other party.

(4) Compensation may be claimed for expenses reasonably required to preserve or maintain the performance received.

Article 7.3.7 *(Restitution with respect to contracts to be performed over a period of time)*

(1) On termination of a contract to be performed over a period of time restitution can only be claimed for the period after termination has taken effect, provided the contract is divisible.

(2) As far as restitution has to be made, the provisions of Article 7.3.6 apply.

Section 4: Damages

Article 7.4.1 *(Right to damages)*

Any non-performance gives the aggrieved party a right to damages either exclusively or in conjunction with any other remedies except where the non-performance is excused under these Principles.

Article 7.4.2 *(Full compensation)*

(1) The aggrieved party is entitled to full compensation for harm sustained as a result of the non-performance. Such harm includes both any loss which it suffered and any gain of which it was deprived, taking into account any gain to the aggrieved party resulting from its avoidance of cost or harm.

(2) Such harm may be non-pecuniary and includes, for instance, physical suffering or emotional distress.

Article 7.4.3 *(Certainty of harm)*

(1) Compensation is due only for harm, including future harm, that is established with a reasonable degree of certainty.

(2) Compensation may be due for the loss of a chance in proportion to the probability of its occurrence.

(3) Where the amount of damages cannot be established with a sufficient degree of certainty, the assessment is at the discretion of the court.

Article 7.4.4 *(Foreseeability of harm)*

The non-performing party is liable only for harm which it foresaw or could reasonably have foreseen at the time of the conclusion of the contract as being likely to result from its non-performance.

Article 7.4.5 *(Proof of harm in case of replacement transaction)*

Where the aggrieved party has terminated the contract and has made a replacement transaction within a reasonable time and in a reasonable manner it may recover the difference between the contract price and the price of the replacement transaction as well as damages for any further harm.

Article 7.4.6 *(Proof of harm by current price)*

(1) Where the aggrieved party has terminated the contract and has not made a replacement transaction but there is a current price for the performance contracted for, it may recover the difference between the contract price and the price current at the time the contract is terminated as well as damages for any further harm.

(2) Current price is the price generally charged for goods delivered or services rendered in comparable circumstances at the place where the contract should have been performed or, if there is no current price at that place, the current price at such other place that appears reasonable to take as a reference.

Article 7.4.7 *(Harm due in part to aggrieved party)*

Where the harm is due in part to an act or omission of the aggrieved party or to another event for which that party bears the risk, the amount of damages shall be reduced to the extent that these factors have contributed to the harm, having regard to the conduct of each of the parties.

Article 7.4.8 *(Mitigation of harm)*

(1) The non-performing party is not liable for harm suffered by the aggrieved party to the extent that the harm could have been reduced by the latter party's taking reasonable steps.

(2) The aggrieved party is entitled to recover any expenses reasonably incurred in attempting to reduce the harm.

Article 7.4.9 *(Interest for failure to pay money)*

(1) If a party does not pay a sum of money when it falls due the aggrieved party is entitled to interest upon that sum from the time when payment is due to the time of payment whether or not the non-payment is excused.

(2) The rate of interest shall be the average bank short-term lending rate to prime borrowers prevailing for the currency of payment at the place for payment, or where no such rate exists at that place, then the same rate in the State of the currency of payment. In the absence of such a rate at either place the rate of interest shall be the appropriate rate fixed by the law of the State of the currency of payment.

(3) The aggrieved party is entitled to additional damages if the non-payment caused it a greater harm.

Article 7.4.10 *(Interest on damages)*

Unless otherwise agreed, interest on damages for non-performance of non-monetary obligations accrues as from the time of non-performance.

Article 7.4.11 *(Manner of monetary redress)*

(1) Damages are to be paid in a lump sum. However, they may be payable in instalments where the nature of the harm makes this appropriate.

(2) Damages to be paid in instalments may be indexed.

Article 7.4.12 *(Currency in which to assess damages)*

Damages are to be assessed either in the currency in which the monetary obligation was expressed or in the currency in which the harm was suffered, whichever is more appropriate.

Article 7.4.13 *(Agreed payment for non-performance)*

(1) Where the contract provides that a party who does not perform is to pay a specified sum to the aggrieved party for such non-performance, the aggrieved party is entitled to that sum irrespective of its actual harm.

(2) However, notwithstanding any agreement to the contrary the specified sum may be reduced to a reasonable amount where it is grossly excessive in relation to the harm resulting from the non-performance and to the other circumstances.

Chapter 8 – Set-off

Article 8.1 *(Conditions of set-off)*

(1) Where two parties owe each other money or other performances of the same kind, either of them („the first party") may set off its obligation against that of its obligee („the other party") if at the time of set-off,
- (a) the first party is entitled to perform its obligation;
- (b) the other party's obligation is ascertained as to its existence and amount and performance is due.

(2) If the obligations of both parties arise from the same contract, the first party may also set off its obligation against an obligation of the other party which is not ascertained as to its existence or to its amount.

Article 8.2 *(Foreign currency set-off)*

Where the obligations are to pay money in different currencies, the right of set-off may be exercised, provided that both currencies are freely convertible and the parties have not agreed that the first party shall pay only in a specified currency.

Article 8.3 *(Set-off by notice)*

The right of set-off is exercised by notice to the other party.

Article 8.4 *(Content of notice)*

(1) The notice must specify the obligations to which it relates.

(2) If the notice does not specify the obligation against which set-off is exercised, the other party may, within a reasonable time, declare to the first party the obligation to which set-off relates. If no such declaration is made, the set-off will relate to all the obligations proportionally.

Article 8.5 *(Effect of set-off)*

(1) Set-off discharges the obligations.

(2) If obligations differ in amount, set-off discharges the obligations up to the amount of the lesser obligation.

(3) Set-off takes effect as from the time of notice.

Chapter 9 – Assignment of Rights, Transfer of Obligations, Assignment of Contracts

Section 1: Assignment of Rights

Article 9.1.1 *(Definitions)*

„Assignment of a right" means the transfer by agreement from one person (the „assignor") to another person (the „assignee"), including transfer by way of security, of the assignor's right to payment of a monetary sum or other performance from a third person („the obligor").

Article 9.1.2 *(Exclusions)*

This Section does not apply to transfers made under the special rules governing the transfers:

(a) of instruments such as negotiable instruments, documents of title or financial instruments, or
(b) of rights in the course of transferring a business.

Article 9.1.3 *(Assignability of non-monetary rights)*

A right to non-monetary performance may be assigned only if the assignment does not render the obligation significantly more burdensome.

Article 9.1.4 *(Partial assignment)*

(1) A right to the payment of a monetary sum may be assigned partially.

(2) A right to other performance may be assigned partially only if it is divisible, and the assignment does not render the obligation significantly more burdensome.

Article 9.1.5 *(Future rights)*

A future right is deemed to be transferred at the time of the agreement, provided the right, when it comes into existence, can be identified as the right to which the assignment relates.

Article 9.1.6 *(Rights assigned without individual specification)*

A number of rights may be assigned without individual specification, provided such rights can be identified as rights to which the assignment relates at the time of the assignment or when they come into existence.

Article 9.1.7 *(Agreement between assignor and assignee sufficient)*

(1) A right is assigned by mere agreement between the assignor and the assignee, without notice to the obligor.

(2) The consent of the obligor is not required unless the obligation in the circumstances is of an essentially personal character.

Article 9.1.8 *(Obligor's additional costs)*

The obligor has a right to be compensated by the assignor or the assignee for any additional costs caused by the assignment.

Article 9.1.9 *(Non-assignment clauses)*

(1) The assignment of a right to the payment of a monetary sum is effective notwithstanding an agreement between the assignor and the obligor limiting or prohibiting such an assignment. However, the assignor may be liable to the obligor for breach of contract.

(2) The assignment of a right to other performance is ineffective if it is contrary to an agreement between the assignor and the obligor limiting or prohibiting the assignment. Nevertheless, the assignment is effective if the assignee, at the time of the assignment, neither knew nor ought to have known of the agreement. The assignor may then be liable to the obligor for breach of contract.

Article 9.1.10 *(Notice to the obligor)*

(1) Until the obligor receives a notice of the assignment from either the assignor or the assignee, it is discharged by paying the assignor.

(2) After the obligor receives such a notice, it is discharged only by paying the assignee.

Article 9.1.11 *(Successive assignments)*

If the same right has been assigned by the same assignor to two or more successive assignees, the obligor is discharged by paying according to the order in which the notices were received.

Article 9.1.12 *(Adequate proof of assignment)*

(1) If notice of the assignment is given by the assignee, the obligor may request the assignee to provide within a reasonable time adequate proof that the assignment has been made.

(2) Until adequate proof is provided, the obligor may withhold payment.

(3) Unless adequate proof is provided, notice is not effective.

(4) Adequate proof includes, but is not limited to, any writing emanating from the assignor and indicating that the assignment has taken place.

Article 9.1.13 *(Defences and rights of set-off)*

(1) The obligor may assert against the assignee all defences that the obligor could assert against the assignor.

(2) The obligor may exercise against the assignee any right of set-off available to the obligor against the assignor up to the time notice of assignment was received.

Article 9.1.14 *(Rights related to the right assigned)*

The assignment of a right transfers to the assignee:

(a) all the assignor's rights to payment or other performance under the contract in respect of the right assigned, and
(b) all rights securing performance of the right assigned.

Article 9.1.15 *(Undertakings of the assignor)*

The assignor undertakes towards the assignee, except as otherwise disclosed to the assignee, that:
(a) the assigned right exists at the time of the assignment, unless the right is a future right;
(b) the assignor is entitled to assign the right;
(c) the right has not been previously assigned to another assignee, and it is free from any right or claim from a third party;
(d) the obligor does not have any defences;
(e) neither the obligor nor the assignor has given notice of set-off concerning the assigned right and will not give any such notice;
(f) the assignor will reimburse the assignee for any payment received from the obligor before notice of the assignment was given.

Section 2: Transfer of Obligations

Article 9.2.1 *(Modes of transfer)*

An obligation to pay money or render other performance may be transferred from one person (the „original obligor") to another person (the „new obligor") either
(a) by an agreement between the original obligor and the new obligor subject to Article 9.2.3, or
(b) by an agreement between the obligee and the new obligor, by which the new obligor assumes the obligation.

Article 9.2.2 *(Exclusion)*

This Section does not apply to transfers of obligations made under the special rules governing transfers of obligations in the course of transferring a business.

Article 9.2.3 *(Requirement of obligee's consent to transfer)*

The transfer of an obligation by an agreement between the original obligor and the new obligor requires the consent of the obligee.

Article 9.2.4 *(Advance consent of obligee)*

(1) The obligee may give its consent in advance.

(2) If the obligee has given its consent in advance, the transfer of the obligation becomes effective when a notice of the transfer is given to the obligee or when the obligee acknowledges it.

Article 9.2.5 *(Discharge of original obligor)*

(1) The obligee may discharge the original obligor.

(2) The obligee may also retain the original obligor as an obligor in case the new obligor does not perform properly.

(3) Otherwise the original obligor and the new obligor are jointly and severally liable.

Article 9.2.6 *(Third party performance)*

(1) Without the obligee's consent, the obligor may contract with another person that this person will perform the obligation in place of the obligor, unless the obligation in the circumstances has an essentially personal character.

(2) The obligee retains its claim against the obligor.

Article 9.2.7 (Defences and rights of set-off)

(1) The new obligor may assert against the obligee all defences which the original obligor could assert against the obligee.

(2) The new obligor may not exercise against the obligee any right of set-off available to the original obligor against the obligee.

Article 9.2.8 (Rights related to the obligation transferred)

(1) The obligee may assert against the new obligor all its rights to payment or other performance under the contract in respect of the obligation transferred.

(2) If the original obligor is discharged under Article 9.2.5(1), a security granted by any person other than the new obligor for the performance of the obligation is discharged, unless that other person agrees that it should continue to be available to the obligee.

(3) Discharge of the original obligor also extends to any security of the original obligor given to the obligee for the performance of the obligation, unless the security is over an asset which is transferred as part of a transaction between the original obligor and the new obligor.

Section 3: Assignment of Contracts

Article 9.3.1 (Definitions)

„Assignment of a contract" means the transfer by agreement from one person (the „assignor") to another person (the „assignee") of the assignor's rights and obligations arising out of a contract with another person (the „other party").

Article 9.3.2 (Exclusion)

This Section does not apply to the assignment of contracts made under the special rules governing transfers of contracts in the course of transferring a business.

Article 9.3.3 (Requirement of consent of the other party)

The assignment of a contract requires the consent of the other party.

Article 9.3.4 (Advance consent of the other party)

(1) The other party may give its consent in advance.

(2) If the other party has given its consent in advance, the assignment of the contract becomes effective when a notice of the assignment is given to the other party or when the other party acknowledges it.

Article 9.3.5 (Discharge of the assignor)

(1) The other party may discharge the assignor.

(2) The other party may also retain the assignor as an obligor in case the assignee does not perform properly.

(3) Otherwise the assignor and the assignee are jointly and severally liable.

Article 9.3.6 (Defences and rights of set-off)

(1) To the extent that the assignment of a contract involves an assignment of rights, Article 9.1.13 applies accordingly.

(2) To the extent that the assignment of a contract involves a transfer of obligations, Article 9.2.7 applies accordingly.

Article 9.3.7 *(Rights transferred with the contract)*

(1) To the extent that the assignment of a contract involves an assignment of rights, Article 9.1.14 applies accordingly.

(2) To the extent that the assignment of a contract involves a transfer of obligations, Article 9.2.8 applies accordingly.

Chapter 10 – Limitation Periods

Article 10.1 *(Scope of the Chapter)*

(1) The exercise of rights governed by the Principles is barred by the expiration of a period of time, referred to as „limitation period", according to the rules of this Chapter.

(2) This Chapter does not govern the time within which one party is required under the Principles, as a condition for the acquisition or exercise of its right, to give notice to the other party or to perform any act other than the institution of legal proceedings.

Article 10.2 *(Limitation periods)*

(1) The general limitation period is three years beginning on the day after the day the obligee knows or ought to know the facts as a result of which the obligee's right can be exercised.

(2) In any event, the maximum limitation period is ten years beginning on the day after the day the right can be exercised.

Article 10.3 *(Modification of limitation periods by the parties)*

(1) The parties may modify the limitation periods.

(2) However they may not

    (a) shorten the general limitation period to less than one year;
    (b) shorten the maximum limitation period to less than four years;
    (c) extend the maximum limitation period to more than fifteen years.

Article 10.4 *(New limitation period by acknowledgement)*

(1) Where the obligor before the expiration of the general limitation period acknowledges the right of the obligee, a new general limitation period begins on the day after the day of the acknowledgement.

(2) The maximum limitation period does not begin to run again, but may be exceeded by the beginning of a new general limitation period under Article 10.2(1).

Article 10.5 *(Suspension by judicial proceedings)*

(1) The running of the limitation period is suspended

    (a) when the obligee performs any act, by commencing judicial proceedings or in judicial proceedings already instituted, that is recognised by the law of the court as asserting the obligee's right against the obligor;
    (b) in the case of the obligor's insolvency when the obligee has asserted its rights in the insolvency proceedings; or
    (c) in the case of proceedings for dissolution of the entity which is the obligor when the obligee has asserted its rights in the dissolution proceedings.

(2) Suspension lasts until a final decision has been issued or until the proceedings have been otherwise terminated.

Article 10.6 *(Suspension by arbitral proceedings)*

(1) The running of the limitation period is suspended when the obligee performs any act, by commencing arbitral proceedings or in arbitral proceedings already instituted, that is recognised by the law of the arbitral tribunal as asserting the obligee's right against the obligor. In the absence of regulations for arbitral proceedings or provisions determining the exact date of the commencement of arbitral proceedings, the proceedings are deemed to commence on the date on which a request that the right in dispute should be adjudicated reaches the obligor.

(2) Suspension lasts until a binding decision has been issued or until the proceedings have been otherwise terminated.

Article 10.7 *(Alternative dispute resolution)*

The provisions of Articles 10.5 and 10.6 apply with appropriate modifications to other proceedings whereby the parties request a third person to assist them in their attempt to reach an amicable settlement of their dispute.

Article 10.8 *(Suspension in case of force majeure, death or incapacity)*

(1) Where the obligee has been prevented by an impediment that is beyond its control and that it could neither avoid nor overcome, from causing a limitation period to cease to run under the preceding Articles, the general limitation period is suspended so as not to expire before one year after the relevant impediment has ceased to exist.

(2) Where the impediment consists of the incapacity or death of the obligee or obligor, suspension ceases when a representative for the incapacitated or deceased party or its estate has been appointed or a successor has inherited the respective party's position. The additional one-year period under paragraph (1) applies accordingly.

Article 10.9 *(Effects of expiration of limitation period)*

(1) The expiration of the limitation period does not extinguish the right.

(2) For the expiration of the limitation period to have effect, the obligor must assert it as a defence.

(3) A right may still be relied on as a defence even though the expiration of the limitation period for that right has been asserted.

Article 10.10 *(Right of set-off)*

The obligee may exercise the right of set-off until the obligor has asserted the expiration of the limitation period.

Article 10.11 *(Restitution)*

Where there has been performance in order to discharge an obligation, there is no right of restitution merely because the limitation period has expired.

Chapter 11 – Plurality of Obligors and of Obligees

Section 1: Plurality of Obligors

Article 11.1.1 *(Definitions)*

When several obligors are bound by the same obligation towards an obligee:

(a) the obligations are joint and several when each obligor is bound for the whole obligation;
(b) the obligations are separate when each obligor is bound only for its share.

Article 11.1.2 *(Presumption of joint and several obligations)*

When several obligors are bound by the same obligation towards an obligee, they are presumed to be jointly and severally bound, unless the circumstances indicate otherwise.

Article 11.1.3 *(Obligee's rights against joint and several obligors)*

When obligors are jointly and severally bound, the obligee may require performance from any one of them, until full performance has been received.

Article 11.1.4 *(Availability of defences and rights of set–off)*

A joint and several obligor against whom a claim is made by the obligee may assert all the defences and rights of set-off that are personal to it or that are common to all the co-obligors, but may not assert defences or rights of set-off that are personal to one or several of the other co-obligors.

Article 11.1.5 *(Effect of performance or set–off)*

Performance or set-off by a joint and several obligor or set-off by the obligee against one joint and several obligor discharges the other obligors in relation to the obligee to the extent of the performance or set-off.

Article 11.1.6 *(Effect of release or settlement)*

(1) Release of one joint and several obligor, or settlement with one joint and several obligor, discharges all the other obligors for the share of the released or settling obligor, unless the circumstances indicate otherwise.

(2) When the other obligors are discharged for the share of the released obligor, they no longer have a contributory claim against the released obligor under Article 11.1.10.

Article 11.1.7 *(Effect of expiration or suspension of limitation period)*

(1) Expiration of the limitation period of the obligee's rights against one joint and several obligor does not affect:

  (a) the obligations to the obligee of the other joint and several obligors; or
  (b) the rights of recourse between the joint and several obligors under Article 11.1.10.

(2) If the obligee initiates proceedings under Articles 10.5, 10.6 or 10.7 against one joint and several obligor, the running of the limitation period is also suspended against the other joint and several obligors.

Article 11.1.8 *(Effect of judgment)*

(1) A decision by a court as to the liability to the obligee of one joint and several obligor does not affect:

  (a) the obligations to the obligee of the other joint and several obligors; or
  (b) the rights of recourse between the joint and several obligors under Article 11.1.10.

(2) However, the other joint and several obligors may rely on such a decision, except if it was based on grounds personal to the obligor concerned. In such a case, the rights of recourse between the joint and several obligors under Article 11.1.10 are affected accordingly.

Article 11.1.9 *(Apportionment among joint and several obligors)*

As among themselves, joint and several obligors are bound in equal shares, unless the circumstances indicate otherwise.

Article 11.1.10 *(Extent of contributory claim)*

A joint and several obligor who has performed more than its share may claim the excess from any of the other obligors to the extent of each obligor's unperformed share.

Article 11.1.11 (Rights of the obligee)

(1) A joint and several obligor to whom Article 11.1.10 applies may also exercise the rights of the obligee, including all rights securing their performance, to recover the excess from all or any of the other obligors to the extent of each obligor's unperformed share.

(2) An obligee who has not received full performance retains its rights against the co-obligors to the extent of the unperformed part, with precedence over co-obligors exercising contributory claims.

Article 11.1.12 (Defences in contributory claims)

A joint and several obligor against whom a claim is made by the co-obligor who has performed the obligation :
(a) may raise any common defences and rights of set-off that were available to be asserted by the co-obligor against the obligee ;
(b) may assert defences which are personal to itself ;
(c) may not assert defences and rights of set-off which are personal to one or several of the other co-obligors.

Article 11.1.13 (Inability to recover)

If a joint and several obligor who has performed more than that obligor's share is unable, despite all reasonable efforts, to recover contribution from another joint and several obligor, the share of the others, including the one who has performed, is increased proportionally.

Section 2: Plurality of Obligees

Article 11.2.1 (Definitions)

When several obligees can claim performance of the same obligation from an obligor:
(a) the claims are separate when each obligee can only claim its share;
(b) the claims are joint and several when each obligee can claim the whole performance;
(c) the claims are joint when all obligees have to claim performance together.

Article 11.2.2 (Effects of joint and several claims)

Full performance of an obligation in favour of one of the joint and several obligees discharges the obligor towards the other obligees.

Article 11.2.3 (Availability of defences against joint and several obligees)

(1) The obligor may assert against any of the joint and several obligees all the defences and rights of set-off that are personal to its relationship to that obligee or that it can assert against all the co-obligees, but may not assert defences and rights of set-off that are personal to its relationship to one or several of the other co-obligees.

(2) The provisions of Articles 11.1.5, 11.1.6, 11.1.7 and 11.1.8 apply, with appropriate adaptations, to joint and several claims.

Article 11.2.4 (Allocation between joint and several obligees)

(1) As among themselves, joint and several obligees are entitled to equal shares, unless the circumstances indicate otherwise.

(2) An obligee who has received more than its share must transfer the excess to the other obligees to the extent of their respective shares.

Anh. VI

VI. Entscheidungsregister

Gericht, Datum	Fundstelle	Art. Rn.
Argentinien		
Cámara Nacional de Apelaciones en lo Comercial, 14.10.1993	CISG-online 87	**Vor 14–24** 10; **18** 7a; **78** 38
Cámara Nacional de Apelaciones en lo Comercial, 31.10.1995	CISG-online 299	**Vor 66–70** 16; **67** 10
Cámara Nacional de Apelaciones en lo Comercial, 24.4.2000	CISG-online 699	**1** 71; **35** 49
Cámara Nacional de Apelaciones en lo Comercial, 31.5.2007	CISG-online 1517	**53** 4
Cámara Nacional de Apelaciones en lo Comercial, 24.6.2010	CISG-online 2132	**26** 8
Cámara Nacional de Apelaciones en lo Comercial, 7.10.2010	CISG-online 2156; UNILEX	**1** 71; **53** 18
Juzgado Nacional de Primera Instancia en lo Comercial, 20.5.1991	CISG-online 461	**9** 14, 21, 26; **53** 38
Juzgado Nacional de Primera Instancia en lo Comercial No. 10, 23.10.1991	CISG-online 460	**9** 21; **78** 38
Juzgado Nacional de Primera Instancia en lo Comercial No. 10, 6.10.1994	CISG-online 378	**6** 5; **7** 48; **9** 21
Juzgado Nacional de Primera Instancia en lo Comercial No. 26, 2.7.2003	CISG Pace	**7** 41
Juzgado Nacional de Primera Instancia en lo Comercial No. 26, 17.3.2003	CISG-online 1844	**4** 41

Parteien	Gericht, Datum	Fundstelle	Art. Rn.
Australien			
McRae v. The Commonwealth Disposals Commission	High Court of Australia, 27.8.1951	[1951] HCA 79	**79** 12
Roder Zelt- und Hallenkonstruktionen GmbH v. Rosedown Park Pty. Ltd. and Reginald R. Eustace	Federal Court of Australia, 28.4.1995	CISG-online 218; 1995 FCR 216	**4** 30; **8** 5, 31; **18** 3; **23** 7; **25** 66; **26** 8, 14; **30** 8; **64** 7, 12; **72** 13; **74** 11
Hannaford (t/as Torrens Valley Orchards) v. Australian Farmlink Pty. Ltd.	Federal Court of Australia, 24.10.2008	CISG-online 1782	**1** 64; **7** 17; **50** 4; **93** 4
Olivaylle Pty Ltd. v. Flotweg GmbH & Co KGAA	Federal Court of Australia, 20.5.2009	CISG-online 1902	**6** 15
Cortem SpA v. Centrolmatic Pty. Ltd.	Federal Court of Australia, 13.8.2010	CISG-online 2128	**35** 12, 17a
Castel Electronics Pty. Ltd. v. Toshiba Singapore Pte. Ltd.	Federal Court of Australia, 20.4.2011	CISG-online 2219	**Vor 1–6** 22; **1** 77; **35** 34; **77** 13
Castel Electronics Pty. Ltd. v. Toshiba Singapore Pte. Ltd.	Federal Court of Australia, 28.9.2010	CISG-online 2158	**1** 76
Fryer Holdings v. Liaoning MEC Group	Supreme Court of New South Wales, 30.1.2012	CISG-online 2325	**35** 12, 15

VI. Entscheidungsregister   Anh. VI

Kingston Estate Wines Pty. Ltd.   **Supreme Court of**   CISG-online 1891   **8** 1, 43
v. Vetreria Etrusca S. r. l.   **South Australia,**
                                    14.3.2008

Downs Investment Pty Ltd. v. Per- **Supreme Court of** CISG-online 587;   **1** 71; **25** 66; **54** 7;
waja Stell Sdn. Bhd.   **Queensland,**   2000 QSC 421   **64** 9; **72** 12, 12a, 35,
                                    17.11.2000   37; **75** 7, 11

Gericht, Datum	Fundstelle	Art. Rn.
Belgien		
Hof van Cassatie, 19.6.2009	CISG-online 1963	**4** 9; **7** 5, 6, 9, 46, 55; **53** 3; **79** 1, 30, 54
Hof van Beroep Antwerpen, 18.6.1996	CISG-online 758	**4** 13, 40
Hof van Beroep Antwerpen, 4.11.1998	CISG-online 1310	**14** 37, 44; **50** 4
Hof van Beroep Antwerpen, 27.6.2001	CISG-online 2342	**40** 2
Hof van Beroep Antwerpen, 14.2.2002	CISG-online 995	**1** 64; **93** 4
Hof van Beroep Antwerpen, 3.1.2005	CISG-online 1001	**3** 12
Hof van Beroep Antwerpen, 24.4.2006	CISG-online 1258	**6** 22; **8** 17; **78** 27, 31, 40; **85** 14; **87** 6; **88** 12
Hof van Beroep Antwerpen, 22.1.2007	CISG-online 1585	**64** 7
Hof van Beroep Gent, 26.4.2000	CISG-online 1316	**71** 27
Hof van Beroep Gent, 15.5.2002	CISG-online 746	**1** 72, 73; **7** 48, 49; **Vor 14–24** 23; **14** 26; **29** 2, 8
Hof van Beroep Gent, 31.1.2002	CISG-online 1349	**53** 30
Hof van Beroep Gent, 15.5.2002	CISG-online 746	**3** 5; **7** 48; **57** 23
Hof van Beroep Gent, 3.10.2003	CISG-online 949	**85** 14
Hof van Beroep Gent, 29.10.2003	CISG-online 1654	**3** 12
Hof van Beroep Gent, 28.1.2004	CISG-online 830	**35** 49; **39** 37; **35** 51; **45** 10
Hof van Beroep Gent, 10.5.2004	CISG-online 991	**25** 57
Hof van Beroep Gent, 17.5.2004	CISG-online 990	**4** 35
Hof van Beroep Gent, 24.6.2004	CISG-online 987	**4** 10
Hof van Beroep Gent, 4.10.2004	CISG-online 985	**4** 35; **14** 33
Hof van Beroep Gent, 11.10.2004	CISG-online 984	**78** 27
Hof van Beroep Gent, 20.10.2004	CISG-online 983	**25** 67; **64** 13
Hof van Beroep Gent, 8.11.2004	CISG-online 982	**14** 6; **19** 8a 11, 17; **75** 14
Hof van Beroep Gent, 24.11.2004	CISG-online 966	**3** 12
Hof van Beroep Gent, 14.11.2008	CISG-online 1908	**3** 5, 13, 17; **6** 7; **38** 9
CA Liège, 28.4.2003	CISG-online 944	**4** 9, 15; **Vor 14–24** 12
Trib. com. Bruxelles, 11.9.1984	*Schlechtriem/Magnus*, Art. 10 EKG, Nr. 7	**25** 22
Trib. com. Bruxelles, 13.11.1992	CISG-online 458	**1** 75, 81
Trib. com. Bruxelles, 5.10.1994	CISG-online 447	**1** 75
Trib. com. Nivelles, 19.9.1995	CISG-online 366	**1** 81; **4** 6, 38; **8** 15, 53, 56; **14** 16, 37, 40, 54
Trib. com. Namur, 15.1.2002	CISG-online 759	**6** 18, 22; **45** 28
RB Hasselt, 23.2.1994	CISG-online 456	**1** 75, 81; **79** 30
RB Hasselt, 16.3.1994	CISG-online 455	**1** 81
RB Hasselt, 24.1.1995	CISG-online 375	**1** 75, 81; **Vor 14–24** 19
RB Hasselt, 1.3.1995	CISG-online 373	**1** 81; **71** 10
RB Hasselt, 2.5.1995	CISG-online 371	**1** 81; **12** 2; **29** 5; **74** 53; **79** 30; **96** 3
RB Hasselt, 18.10.1995	CISG-online 364	**1** 75, 81; **8** 22, 24
RB Hasselt, 8.11.1995	CISG-online 363	**1** 75, 81
RB Hasselt, 9.10.1996	CISG-online 361	**1** 75, 81
RB Hasselt, 21.1.1997	CISG-online 360	**1** 81; **39** 15; **74** 58
RB Hasselt, 17.6.1998	CISG-online 760	**4** 40
RB Hasselt, 2.12.1998	CISG-online 761	**7** 17; **14** 55

Anh. VI

Gericht, Datum	Fundstelle	Art. Rn.
RB Hasselt, 28.4.1999	CISG Belgium	7 17
RB Hasselt, 2.6.1999	CISG-online 762	10 5; 14 59, 63
RB Hasselt, 4.10.1999	CISG-online 763	6 18, 22
RB Hasselt, 4.4.2000	CISG Belgium	Vor 89–101 10
RB Hasselt, 19.9.2001	CISG-online 604	3 12
RB Hasselt, 6.3.2002	CISG-online 622	7 17; 39 17
RB Hasselt, 22.5.2002	CISG-online 703	11 13
RB Hasselt, 13.5.2003	CISG Belgium	1 59
RB Hasselt, 4.2.2004	CISG-online 863	3 13
RB Hasselt, 14.9.2004	CISG Pace	3 5
RB Hasselt, 14.9.2005	CISG Belgium	6 22
RB Hasselt, 20.9.2005	CISG-online 1496	1 8, 40; 78 17
RB Hasselt, 15.2.2006	CISG-online 1257	6 22
RB Hasselt, 19.4.2006	CISG-online 1389	4 24; Vor 14–24 12
RB Hasselt, 10.5.2006	CISG-online 1259	78 31
RB Hasselt, 28.6.2006	CISG Belgium	6 22
RB Ieper, 29.1.2001	CISG-online 606	4 35; 7 48, 52
RB Ieper, 18.2.2002	CISG-online 764	6 18; 7 48; 78 30; 79 37
RB Kortrijk, 3.10.2001	CISG-online 757	33 7, 17; 85 16
RB Kortrijk, 4.6.2004	CISG-online 945	25 48; 49 24
RB Kortrijk, 8.12.2004	CISG-online 1511	8 53a; 14 59, 60; 29 7
RB Mechelen, 18.1.2002	CISG-online 1432	14 51, 57, 64
RB Tongeren, 25.1.2005	CISG-online 1106	6 18; 7 48; 15 4, 6; 18 4, 7a; 79 30
RB Turnhout, 18.1.2001	CISG-online 994	1 64; 93 4
RB Utrecht, 15.4.2009	CISG Pace	6 15
RB Veurne, 25.4.2001	CISG-online 765	1 59; 14 37, 59
RB Veurne, 15.1.2003	CISG-online 1056	39 17

China

Gericht, Datum	Fundstelle	Art. Rn.
Supreme Court of People's Republic of China, 21.9.2005	CISG-online 1611	1 31
Shanghai Higher People's Court, 17.5.2007	CISG-online 1976	6 5, 18
Shanghai First Intermediate People's Court, 23.3.2004	CISG-online 1497	Vor 1–6 22; 4 34; 78 27
Shanghai First Intermediate People's Court, 30.8.2005	CISG-online 1615	78 31b
Shanghai First Intermediate People's Court, 25.12.2008	CISG-online 2059	25 45; 40 5; 73 9, 11, 18, 22
Shanghai First Intermediate People's Court, 19.3.2009	CISG-online 2060	Vor 1–6 22; 78 29
Wuhan Intermediate People's Court of Hubei Province, 11.5.2004	CISG-online 1499	78 29
Xiamen Intermediate People's Court, 9.5.1994	UNILEX	9 6

Dänemark

Gericht, Datum	Fundstelle	Art. Rn.
Højesteret, 15.2.2001	CISG-online 601	31 76, 92
Sø og Handelsretten, 1.7.1992	CISG-online 459; UfR 1992, A, 920	57 23
Sø og Handelsretten, 31.1.2002	CISG-online 679 = 868	35 10; 38 14; 39 17; 44 17
Østre Landsret Kobenhaven, 22.1.1996	CISG-online 362; UfR 1996, 616	57 23
Østre Landsret, 23.4.1998	CISG-online 486	1 65; 18 9; 92 3
Vestre Landsret, 10.11.1999	CISG-online 704	39 16; 49 32

VI. Entscheidungsregister

Gericht, Datum	Fundstelle	Art. Rn.
Dist. Ct. Copenhagen, 19.10.2007	CISG-online 2150	**1** 34; **2** 12
Deutschland		
RG, 8.2.1902	RGZ 50, 191	**18** 14
RG, 13.7.1904	RGZ 58, 406	**24** 42
RG, 17.6.1905	RGZ 61, 125	**24** 9
RG, 29.1.1906	RGZ 62, 331	**31** 40
RG, 22.5.1908	RGZ 68, 407	**15** 2
RG, 24.11.1916	RGZ 89, 123	**47** 6
RG, 20.2.1918	RGZ 92, 232	**19** 9
RG, 11.3.1918	LZ 1918, 1208	**31** 84
RG, 14.4.1920	RGZ 99, 20	**24** 35
RG, 4.5.1920	RGZ 99, 56	**31** 38
RG, 1.11.1921	RGZ 103, 129	**31** 18
RG, 20.12.1921	RGZ 103, 312	**18** 7a
RG, 17.2.1922	Recht 1922, Nr. 1391	**18** 5
RG, 5.1.1923	JW 1923, 457	**35** 51
RG, 5.1.1925	RGZ 110, 34	**24** 42
RG, 19.5.1925	RGZ 111, 23	**31** 92
RG, 21.10.1926	RGZ 115, 162	**31** 36
RG, 20.5.1930	RGZ 129, 109	**18** 18
BGH, 19.6.1951	BGHZ 2, 310	**76** 1
BGH, 9.7.1952	BGH LM § 854	**31** 57
BGH, 29.3.1978	NJW 1978, 2394	**39** 33
BGH, 29.10.1956	BGHZ 22, 19	**Vor 81–84** 6
BGH, 14.2.1958	WM 1958, 456	**25** 36
BGH, 2.10.1963	WM 1963, 1185	**32** 15
BGH, 3.12.1964	BGHZ 43, 21	**4** 34
BGH, 29.1.1968	BGHZ 49, 356	**46** 25
BGH, 27.3.1968	BGHZ 50, 32	**31** 79
BGH, 9.7.1970	BGHZ 54, 236	**29** 7
BGH, 10.12.1970	WM 1971, 158	**25** 63
BGH, 1.12.1971	NJW 1972, 246	**72** 27
BGH, 16.3.1973	BGHZ 60, 319	**78** 21
BGH, 21.12.1973	BGHZ 62, 71	**9** 16
BGH, 20.9.1974	NJW 1975, 778	**42** 5
BGH, 15.4.1975	BGHZ 64, 183	**4** 34
BGH, 30.4.1975	WM 1975, 562	**44** 10
BGH, 18.6.1975	WM 1975, 917	**9** 26; **30** 3
BGH, 2.6.1976	BGHZ 66, 378	**29** 16, 17
BGH, 30.6.1976	NJW 1976, 1886	**14** 41
BGH, 7.7.1976	NJW 1976, 2075	**14** 16
BGH, 3.11.1976	BGHZ 67, 271	**24** 42
BGH, 24.11.1976	BGHZ 67, 359	**25** 16
BGH, 1.12.1976	NJW 1977, 580	**72** 27
BGH, 11.2.1977	BGHZ 67, 395	**25** 7
BGH, 16.3.1977	NJW 1977, 1150	**38** 14
BGH, 20.4.1977	BB 1977, 1019	**38** 13
BGH, 29.3.1978	NJW 1978, 2394	**39** 33
BGH, 28.3.1979	WM 1979, 761	**49** 23; **73** 27
BGH, 28.3.1979	NJW 1979, 1779	**1** 15; **6** 18
BGH, 4.4.1979	BGHZ 74, 136	**57** 23
BGH, 24.10.1979	Schlechtriem/Magnus, Art. 82 EKG, Nr. 1; MDR 1980, 308	**25** 35; **74** 38
BGH, 13.2.1980	NJW 1980, 990	**24** 35

Anh. VI

Gericht, Datum	Fundstelle	Art. Rn.
BGH, 22.10.1980	BGHZ 78, 257	**31** 90; **81** 17
BGH, 24.10.1980	IPRax 1981, 96	**1** 18
BGH, 26.11.1980	NJW 1981, 1156	**1** 31; **6** 21, 23
BGH, 28.1.1981	BGHZ 79, 281	**29** 17
BGH, 26.6.1981	BGHZ 81, 75	**42** 5
BGH, 13.5.1982	NJW 1982, 2783	**4** 34
BGH, 2.6.1982	NJW 1982, 2730	**1** 46; **35** 10; **38** 5; **39** 16; **49** 26
BGH, 26.10.1983	RIW 1984, 151	**6** 21, 25
BGH, 8.3.1984	NJW 1984, 1885	**14** 14
BGH, 14.3.1984	RIW 1984, 559	**1** 7, 28; **71** 6; **72** 27
BGH, 22.5.1984	BGHZ 91, 243	**74** 53
BGH, 2.7.1984	NJW 1985, 550	**25** 63
BGH, 25.10.1984	NJW 1985, 555	**53** 16
BGH, 14.11.1984	BGHZ 92, 396	**79** 18, 26
BGH, 26.11.1984	BGHZ 93, 29	**29** 17
BGH, 30.1.1985	BGHZ 93, 338	**31** 55, 57
BGH, 20.3.1985	NJW 1985, 1838	**19** 23
BGH, 22.5.1985	ZIP 1985, 1204	**38** 29
BGH, 4.12.1985	BGHZ 96, 313	**6** 14, 18, 22
BGH, 18.12.1985	NJW-RR 1986, 415	**18** 3, 18
BGH, 23.4.1986	BB 1986, 1395	**9** 6
BGH, 24.9.1986	BGHZ 98, 263	**31** 73, 89, 90, 92
BGH, 9.7.1986	NJW 1987, 50	**74** 41
BGH, 10.12.1986	NJW-RR 1987, 602	**74** 27
BGH, 13.5.1987	BGHZ 101, 49	**27** 1, 10
BGH, 8.7.1987	BGH WM 1987, 1254	**49** 45
BGH, 16.9.1987	BGHZ 101, 337	**38** 14
BGH, 30.10.1987	WM 1988, 12; BGHZ 102, 152	**Vor 14–24** 5; **14** 16
BGH, 2.3.1988	NJW 1988, 2234	**76** 1
BGH, 16.9.1988	NJW-RR 1989, 396	**18** 14
BGH, 15.3.1989	NJW-RR 1989, 757	**24** 8, 19
BGH, 8.6.1989	NJW 1990, 1986	**42** 5
BGH, 5.7.1989	RIW 1989, 741	**40** 4, 12
BGH, 17.1.1990	BGHZ 110, 88	**25** 10; **49** 50
BGH, 31.1.1990	BGHZ 110, 197	**42** 1, 5
BGH, 28.3.1990	NJW 1990, 1655	**18** 7a
BGH, 27.6.1990	NJW 1990, 3077	**14** 22; **55** 13, 17
BGH, 5.7.1990	BB 1990, 1662	**49** 46
BGH, 28.11.1990	RIW 1991, 151	**1** 7, 28, 29; **74** 53
BGH, 5.12.1990	BGHZ 113, 106	**31** 18, 29, 30
BGH, 17.4.1991	WM 1991, 1398	**27** 5; **29** 16
BGH, 19.6.1991	BB 1991, 1732; NJW 1991, 2633	**19** 23; **39** 33
BGH, 25.9.1991	IPRax 1993, 242	**7** 3, 30; **39** 1
BGH, 10.10.1991	BGHZ 115, 324	**38** 29
BGH, 21.11.1991	NJW 1992, 1234	**Vor 14–24** 5
BGH, 12.2.1992	BGHZ 117, 190	**14** 41
BGH, 25.3.1992	NJW-RR 1992, 886	**39** 21
BGH, 26.3.1992	CISG-online 67; IPRax 1992, 373	**57** 23
BGH, 28.1.1993	NJW 1993, 1126	**11** 4
BGH, 3.12.1993	NJW 1993, 1789	**9** 25
BGH, 9.3.1994	EuZW 1994, 635	**9** 24
BGH, 19.4.1994	NJW 1994, 188	**24** 34

VI. Entscheidungsregister   Anh. VI

Gericht, Datum	Fundstelle	Art. Rn.
BGH, 20.10.1994	NJW-RR 1995, 179	**29** 16
BGH, 27.10.1994	NJW 1995, 190	**24** 40; **27** 8
BGH, 28.11.1994	IPRax 1996, 124	**14** 30; **16** 10; **74** 7
BGH, 7.12.1994	NJW 1995, 665	**24** 44
BGH, 14.2.1995	NJW 1995, 1281	**18** 9
BGH, 15.2.1995	CISG-online 149	**29** 10; **49** 27, 30; **72** 4; **80** 3
BGH, 8.3.1995	CISG-online 144; BGHZ 129, 75	**4** 52; **8** 44; **35** 17; **39** 15, 17; **45** 10; **49** 32; **60** 2
BGH, 22.3.1995	WM 1995, 339	**19** 20
BGH, 7.6.1995	NJW 1995, 2217	**24** 31
BGH, 2.11.1995	NJW 1996, 919	**14** 14
BGH, 3.4.1996	CISG-online 135; BGHZ 132, 290	**7** 10; **8** 29; **25** 2, 9, 19, 21, 35, 36, 44, 50, 51, 61, 64; **34** 5; **35** 9, 10, 17; **58** 16; **64** 2, 4, 5
BGH, 27.6.1996	WM 1996, 2209	**14** 8, 12
BGH, 4.12.1996	CISG-online 260; NJW-RR 1997, 690	**3** 5; **6** 17; **8** 2, 48; **35** 14; **39** 6; **57** 23
BGH, 11.12.1996	CISG-online 225; NJW 1997, 870	**1** 63; **8** 22, 40, 45, 47, 60; **57** 23; **67** 11
BGH, 22.1.1997	WM 1997, 1713	**12** 2
BGH, 5.3.1997	RIW 1997, 958; NJW 1997, 1775	**58** 5
BGH, 25.6.1997	CISG-online 277; NJW 1997, 3311; IPRax 1999, 375; EuZW 1998, 29	**26** 9; **39** 33; **49** 24, **51** 7; **74** 24, 27; **77** 11; **81** 8; **82** 22
BGH, 23.7.1997	CISG-online 276	**1** 32, 71; **6** 16; **7** 54; **11** 7; **Vor 14–24** 41
BGH, 23.7.1997	CISG-online 285	**1** 31, 32
BGH, 30.7.1997	ZIP 1997, 1694	**13** 2
BGH, 10.10.1997	NJW-RR 1998, 590	**29** 3
BGH, 19.11.1997	WM 1998, 931	**76** 1
BGH, 26.11.1997	NJW 1998, 976	**24** 20, 31, 42
BGH, 17.12.1997	CISG-online 296	**Vor 89–101** 10; **100** 3
BGH, 12.2.1998	CISG-online 343	**1** 18, 71; **4** 10, 38
BGH, 10.7.1998	NJW 1998, 3268	**Vor 81** 8
BGH, 8.9.1998	NJW 1998, 3636	**Vor 14–24** 38; **14** 29
BGH, 25.11.1998	CISG-online 353	**6** 22; **7** 49, 50; **8** 37; **39** 33; **74** 32
BGH, 26.2.1999	NJW-RR 1999, 927	**Vor 14–24** 6
BGH, 24.3.1999	CISG-online 396	**7** 9; **Vor 14–24** 5; **14** 35; **35** 18; **45** 1, 23, 26; **74** 57, 58, 60; **77** 8, 12; **79** 6, 26, 28, 40
BGH, 3.11.1999	CISG-online 475	**38** 17; **39** 6, 8, 15, 17, 20
BGH, 18.10.2000	NJW 2000, 221	**11** 16
BGH, 24.10.2000	NJW-RR 2001, 484	**19** 9
BGH, 10.5.2001	NJW 2001, 2626	**11** 15
BGH, 12.10.2001	WM 2002, 819	**24** 5
BGH, 31.10.2001	CISG-online 617; BGHZ 149, 113; NJW 2002, 370	**1** 59; **2** 8, 24; **4** 15, 21, 23; **7** 49, 54; **8** 38, 52, 53; **Vor 14–24** 7; **14** 33, 36, 40, 41, 42, 43, 47, 68; **45** 36; **53** 40; **74** 58
BGH, 7.11.2001	CISG-online 682; IHR 2002, 31	**14** 13; **57** 21, 24
BGH, 12.2.2001	NJW 2002, 1565	**24** 7, 8

Anh. VI

Gericht, Datum	Fundstelle	Art. Rn.
BGH, 9.1.2002	CISG-online 651; RIW 2002, 396	**4** 49, 50, 52; **6** 17, 35; **7** 35, 49, 56; **14** 76; **19** 6, 19, 21, 23, 30, 31, 35; **35** 52, 55; **45** 10; **74** 51; **79** 28, 40, 53
BGH, 6.2.2002	WM 2002, 2381	**Vor 14–24** 38
BGH, 16.4.2002	WM 2002, 2383	**Vor 14–24** 38
BGH, 5.7.2002	NJW 2002, 3164	**11** 13
BGH, 18.7.2002	NJW 2002, 3253	**8** 34
BGH, 2.10.2002	CISG-online 700	**2** 28
BGH, 19.11.2002	NJW 2003, 507	**14** 15
BGH, 4.12.2003	WM 2004, 182	**11** 15
BGH, 9.2.2004	BGHZ 158, 43	**Vor 14–24** 30
BGH, 25.2.2004	CISG-online 1051	**57** 23
BGH, 15.3.2004	ZIP 2004, 1047	**25** 63
BGH, 30.6.2004	CISG-online 847; NJW 2004, 3181	**4** 51, 52; **7** 17; **39** 17; **40** 4, 12
BGH, 2.3.2005	CISG-online 999; NJW-RR 2005, 1218	**7** 5, 9, 12, 15, 17; **35** 14, 17; **36** 4; **50** 13
BGH, 1.6.2005	NJW-RR 2005, 1518	**8** 52
BGH, 20.7.2005	NJW 2005, 2848	**75** 11
BGH, 11.1.2006	CISG-online 1200; IHR 2006, 82	**41** 7, 10; **43** 2; **44** 5
BGH, 14.6.2006	NJW 2006, 2976	**14** 49
BGH, 27.11.2007	CISG-online 1617; IHR 2008, 49; CLOUT No. 721	**4** 25; **8** 6, 17; **25** 18; **45** 22; **53** 3; **61** 14; **62** 16; **64** 34
BGH, 9.7.2008	CISG-online 1717	**3** 13; **57** 25
BGH, 22.4.2009	NJW 2009, 2606	**31** 99
BGH, 11.5.2010	CISG-online 2125	**1** 71, 72; **6** 22
BGH, 11.11.2010	NJW-RR 2011, 130	**29** 10
BGH, 13.4.2011	BGHZ 189, 196; NJW 2011, 2278	**46** 45
BGH, 26.9.2012	CISG-online 2348	**35** 13; **77** 1; **80** 1, 9
BGH, 7.11.2012	CISG-online 2374	**8** 40a, 45; **9** 26
OLG Bamberg, 23.2.1979	RIW 1979, 566	**6** 7; **39** 5, 9, 14
OLG Bamberg, 13.1.1999	CISG-online 516	**1** 71; **26** 2; **74** 43, 51; **75** 5
KG, 7.4.1919	Recht 1920, Nr. 1140	**18** 14
KG Berlin, 5.7.1983	Schlechtriem/Magnus, Art. 39 EKG, Nr. 37	**39** 8, 11; **75** 5
KG Berlin, 30.4.1984	MDR 1984, 760	**84** 11
KG Berlin, 24.1.1994	CISG-online 130; RIW 1994, 683	**53** 4, 5
OLG Brandenburg, 18.11.2008	CISG-online 1734; IHR 2009, 10569	**7** 27, 49; **25** 10, 15, 51; **60** 8; **63** 5; **64** 2, 4, 5, 7, 13, 18, 21; **73** 25, 26
OLG Brandenburg, 19.3.2009	CISG-online 2289	**3** 1, 2, 9
OLG Braunschweig, 28.10.1999	CISG-online 510; CLOUT No. 361; TranspR-IHR 2000, 4	**Vor 14–24** 10, 13; **57** 29; **58** 5, 8; **64** 37; **74** 27, 62; **77** 10; **88** 11
OLG Braunschweig, 4.2.2003	NJW 2003, 1053	**46** 40
OLG Bremen, 4.3.1994	CISG-online 110	**14** 8
OLG Celle, 2.3.1984	RIW 1985, 571	**6** 22; **31** 82; **32** 30
OLG Celle, 2.9.1986	IPRax 1987, 313	**35** 14; **39** 9

VI. Entscheidungsregister
Anh. VI

Gericht, Datum	Fundstelle	Art. Rn.
OLG Celle, 24.5.1995	CISG-online 152	**6** 18, 21, 22, 25; **7** 49; **8** 2, 47; **25** 37; **47** 6, 9; **49** 20, 24; **84** 13
OLG Celle, 9.5.1996	NJW-RR 1997, 662	**Vor 14–24** 38
OLG Celle, 2.9.1998	CISG-online 506	**8** 55; **14** 33; **49** 27; **55** 17; **74** 65; **76** 2, 4, 15; **77** 10, 13
OLG Celle, 11.11.1998	CISG-online 507; IPRax 1999, 456	**57** 21, 22, 24
OLG Celle, 10.3.2004	CISG-online 824	**6** 7; **39** 5, 10; **40** 4
OLG Celle, 24.7.2009	CISG-online 1906; NJW-RR 2010, 136	**7** 49, 54; **8** 53; **14** 33, 40, 50, 55
OLG Dresden, 9.7.1998	CISG-online 559; IHR 2001, 18	**Vor 1–6** 34; **9** 4, 20; **Vor 14–24** 20; **53** 16
OLG Dresden, 27.12.1999	CISG-online 511	**1** 8; **6** 18, 22, 25; **8** 20, 29; **71** 4
OLG Dresden, 23.10.2000	CISG-online 1935	**78** 27
OLG Dresden, 10.11.2006	CISG-online 1625	**15** 4; **16** 3; **18** 4, 7a; **24** 2, 23, 43, 44
OLG Dresden, 21.3.2007	CISG-online 1626	**30** 24
OLG Dresden, 11.6.2007	CISG-online 1720; IHR 2008, 162	**3** 14; **Vor 14–24** 14; **14** 37
OLG Dresden, 27.5.2010	CISG-online 2182	**Vor 1–6** 22; **1** 77; **35** 41, 42
OLG Dresden, 30.11.2010	CISG-online 2183; IHR 2011, 142	**1** 24, 40; **3** 5; **Vor 14–24** 18, 19, 21, 25, 45; **14** 3, 27; **18** 15; **21** 6, 7
OLG Düsseldorf, 27.11.1980	*Schlechtriem/Magnus,* Art. 83 EKG, Nr. 11	**78** 30
OLG Düsseldorf, 20.1.1983	*Schlechtriem/Magnus,* Art. 76 EKG, Nr. 4	**42** 1; **85** 4; **88** 5
OLG Düsseldorf, 17.11.1983	*Schlechtriem/Magnus,* Art. 62 EKG, Nr. 4	**25** 22; **75** 3
OLG Düsseldorf, 24.10.1984	RIW 1985, 404	**38** 16
OLG Düsseldorf, 9.7.1986	RIW 1987, 943	**31** 90
OLG Düsseldorf, 27.11.1986	RIW 1987, 221	**35** 49
OLG Düsseldorf, 6.7.1988	ZIP 1988, 1415	**19** 19
OLG Düsseldorf, 14.12.1988	IPRax 1990, 178	**38** 16
OLG Düsseldorf, 6.1.1989	NJW-RR 1989, 1330	**Vor 14–24** 12
OLG Düsseldorf, 8.1.1993	CISG-online 76	**1** 72; **6** 22; **7** 13; **38** 31; **39** 16, 17, 30, 36
OLG Düsseldorf, 12.3.1993	CISG-online 82	**8** 1; **29** 11; **39** 17
OLG Düsseldorf, 2.7.1993	CISG-online 74; RIW 1993, 845	**1** 81; **5** 8; **6** 20, 27; **7** 18, 55; **45** 35; **57** 29; **74** 32, 61; **81** 18
OLG Düsseldorf, 18.11.1993	CISG-online 92; CLOUT No. 130	**25** 40; **64** 6; **80** 3
OLG Düsseldorf, 14.1.1994	CISG-online 119	**14** 35; **25** 17; **51** 1; **72** 12; **74** 25, 26, 30; **75** 6, 7; **77** 10; **84** 15a
OLG Düsseldorf, 10.2.1994	CISG-online 115; NJW-RR 1994, 506	**4** 39; **25** 10, 37, 49; **35** 10; **39** 6, 17; **47** 14, 17, **49** 6, 8, 15, 16; **51** 1; **74** 20; **78** 27; **82** 28
OLG Düsseldorf, 10.2.1994	CISG-online 116	**1** 73; **4** 39; **6** 25; **38** 16; **39** 17
OLG Düsseldorf, 8.3.1996	WM 1996, 1489	**14** 35

Gericht, Datum	Fundstelle	Art. Rn.
OLG Düsseldorf, 11.7.1996	CISG-online 201; RIW 1996, 958	**61** 7, 13
OLG Düsseldorf, 13.9.1996	CISG-online 407	**77** 10
OLG Düsseldorf, 11.7.1996	CISG-online 201	**1** 31; **4** 39; **Vor 14–24** 41; **74** 30
OLG Düsseldorf, 24.4.1997	CISG-online 385	**25** 32, 37, 38, 39, 40; **71** 4; **72** 12; **74** 25
OLG Düsseldorf, 15.2.2001	CISG-online 658	**14** 16
OLG Düsseldorf, 25.7.2003	CISG-online 919	**14** 40, 41, 76; **19** 23
OLG Düsseldorf, 23.1.2004	CISG-online 918	**25** 51; **38** 10; **39** 7, 16; **40** 4, 7
OLG Düsseldorf, 30.1.2004	CISG-online 821	**8** 5, 55, 56; **9** 8; **Vor 14–24** 10; **14** 37, 40, 66
OLG Düsseldorf, 21.4.2004	CISG-online 914	**1** 59, 71, 73, 79; **7** 9
OLG Düsseldorf, 21.4.2004	CISG-online 915	**4** 20; **7** 9; **8** 54a, 57; **Vor 14–24** 3, 5; **14** 35, 40, 46, 64, 76; **18** 7a; **24** 34; **25** 25, 39
OLG Düsseldorf, 28.5.2004	CISG-online 850; IHR 2004, 203	**1** 43; **4** 39; **29** 13; **58** 11
OLG Düsseldorf, 22.7.2004	CISG-online 916; IHR 2005, 29	**4** 39; **25** 66, 67; **27** 14; **59** 2; **61** 19; **64** 7, 15, 34; **74** 30; **75** 5; **78** 27
OLG Düsseldorf, 20.12.2004	CISG-online 997	**4** 39
OLG Düsseldorf, 24.7.2007	CISG-online 1531	**57** 7
OLG Düsseldorf, 9.7.2010	CISG-online 2171; IHR 2011, 116	**1** 15; **25** 22, 50, 56; **26** 6a; **73** 18, 22; **75** 5, 7
OLG Düsseldorf, 23.3.2011	CISG-online 2218	**4** 21; **8** 53; **Vor 14–24** 10; **14** 37, 40, 51, 59, 60; **29** 7, 8
OLG Frankfurt a. M., 27.4.1976	NJW 1977, 1015	**72** 27
OLG Frankfurt a. M., 27.11.1979	Schlechtriem/Magnus, Art. 6 EAG, Nr. 8; Art. 4 EAG, Nr. 1	**Vor 14–24** 3; **18** 7
OLG Frankfurt a. M., 28.4.1981	IPRax 1982, 242	**19** 8
OLG Frankfurt a. M., 21.9.1982	Schlechtriem/Magnus, Art. 19 EKG, Nr. 8	**31** 22
OLG Frankfurt a. M., 13.6.1991	CISG-online 23	**1** 73, 81; **4** 52; **35** 49; **39** 6; **45** 10
OLG Frankfurt a. M., 17.9.1991	CISG-online 28	**1** 81; **3** 5, 10; **8** 39; **25** 15, 29, 31, 68; **49** 12, 24; **82** 13
OLG Frankfurt a. M., 18.1.1994	CISG-online 123; CLOUT No. 79; NJW 1994, 1013	**25** 46, 57; **39** 6; **46** 24, 31; **49** 13, 15; **53** 4; **60** 15; **74** 25; **78** 27
OLG Frankfurt a. M., 4.3.1994	CISG-online 110	**1** 65; **Vor 14–24** 38; **14** 16, 19, 26; **19** 8a; **92** 3
OLG Frankfurt a. M., 20.4.1994	CISG-online 125	**Vor 1–6** 34; **7** 15, 36, 55; **35** 17, 57
OLG Frankfurt a. M., 14.12.1994	CISG-online 216	**25** 7
OLG Frankfurt a. M., 31.3.1995	CISG-online 137	**8** 1, 47, 48, 51; **19** 8a
OLG Frankfurt a. M., 23.5.1995	CISG-online 185	**18** 7c, 8; **19** 8a; **39** 37
OLG Frankfurt a. M., 5.7.1995	CISG-online 258	**9** 22, 24; **Vor 14–24** 20, 21, 22
OLG Frankfurt a. M., 30.8.2000	CISG-online 594	**6** 21, 22; **8** 5, 51; **14** 4; **18** 7a
OLG Frankfurt a. M., 6.10.2004	CISG-online 996	**1** 15, 73; **7** 43; **29** 10
OLG Frankfurt a. M., 26.6.2006	CISG-online 1385	**Vor 14–24** 10; **19** 8a, 19, 23, 30

VI. Entscheidungsregister   Anh. VI

Gericht, Datum	Fundstelle	Art. Rn.
OLG Frankfurt a. M., 24.3.2009	CISG-online 2165; IHR 2010, 250	Vor 14–24 14b, 14c; 14 45; 18 14; 21 8, 9; 25 15, 41, 66; 74 63; 75 2, 5; 76 2
OLG Hamburg, 31.1.1910	SeuffArch. 65 Nr. 160	31 80
OLG Hamburg, 20.1.1925	OLGRspr. 44, 130	18 14
OLG Hamburg, 9.7.1980	Schlechtriem/Magnus, Art. 2 EAG, Nr. 2	Vor 14–24 3
OLG Hamburg, 30.12.1980	Schlechtriem/Magnus, Art. 39 EKG, Nr. 17	10 7
OLG Hamburg, 3.3.1982	RIW 1982, 435	38 14
OLG Hamburg, 15.2.1991	EWiR 1991, 547	Vor 14–24 41
OLG Hamburg, 14.12.1994	CISG-online 216	25 19
OLG Hamburg, 28.2.1997	CISG-online 261	7 49; 25 29, 41; 26 10; 47 5; 49 5; 74 30; 75 5, 7; 77 10; 79 11, 14, 18, 26, 29, 30, 35
OLG Hamburg, 4.7.1997	CISG-online 1299	14 10
OLG Hamburg, 5.10.1998	CISG-online 473; TranspR-IHR 1999, 37	1 19, 31; 6 22; 8 5, 6, 29, 44, 51; 29 3; 61 19
OLG Hamburg, 26.11.1999	CISG-online 515; IHR 2001, 19	1 71; 4 39, 55; 49 32; 61 19; 74 36, 41; 75 12; 88 18
OLG Hamburg, 26.1.2000	CISG-online 509	6 22
OLG Hamburg, 13.6.2002	WM 2003, 581	14 16
OLG Hamburg, 25.1.2008	CISG-online 1681; IHR 2008, 98	4 6, 38, 40; 16 2, 4; 25 32, 51, 53, 68; 26 12; 79 51; 59 8
OLG Hamm, 23.3.1978	Schlechtriem/Magnus, Art. 82 EKG, Nr. 8; Art. 83, Nr. 4	74 27
OLG Hamm, 6.4.1978	Schlechtriem/Magnus, Art. 6 EAG, Nr. 4; Art. 7 EAG, Nr. 2	18 8; 19 8; 74 18
OLG Hamm, 7.12.1978	Schlechtriem/Magnus, Art. 6 EAG, Nr. 5; Art. 7 EAG, Nr. 3	18 8; 19 8
OLG Hamm, 29.1.1979	Schlechtriem/Magnus, Art. 7 EAG, Nr. 4; Art. 55 EKG, Nr. 1	32 30; 74 34
OLG Hamm, 21.3.1979	Schlechtriem/Magnus, Art. 7 EAG, Nr. 4	19 8
OLG Hamm, 5.4.1979	Schlechtriem/Magnus, Art. 88 EKG, Nr. 3; Art. 60 EKG, Nr. 1	77 4,
OLG Hamm, 3.10.1979	RIW 1980, 662	6 18
OLG Hamm, 8.12.1980	Schlechtriem/Magnus, Art. 26 EKG, Nr. 3	25 35; 33 9, 13
OLG Hamm, 16.2.1981	Schlechtriem/Magnus, Art. 2 EKG, Nr. 4; Art. 39 EKG, Nr. 19	Vor 14–24 1; 39 10
OLG Hamm, 6.7.1981	Schlechtriem/Magnus, Art. 40 EKG, Nr. 3	40 4
OLG Hamm, 17.9.1981	Schlechtriem/Magnus, Art. 39 EKG, Nr. 22; Art. 40 EKG, Nr. 4	35 14; 39 7; 40 4
OLG Hamm, 17.12.1981	Schlechtriem/Magnus, Art. 6 EAG, Nr. 11; Art. 7 EAG, Nr. 8	18 4; 19 8
OLG Hamm, 29.4.1982	IPRax 1983, 231	6 22; 35 15; 81 2

1371

Anh. VI

Gericht, Datum	Fundstelle	Art. Rn.
OLG Hamm, 14.4.1983	Schlechtriem/Magnus, Art. 33 EKG, Nr. 13	**35** 14
OLG Hamm, 20.6.1983	RIW 1983, 952; NJW 1984, 1307	**4** 6; **6** 12, 22; **25** 8; **71** 11
OLG Hamm, 14.11.1983	Schlechtriem/Magnus, Art. 82 EKG, Nr. 27	**74** 27
OLG Hamm, 19.12.1983	Schlechtriem/Magnus, Art. 40 EKG, Nr. 7	**40** 4, 6
OLG Hamm, 25.6.1984	Schlechtriem/Magnus, Art. 3 EAG, Nr. 5	**11** 4
OLG Hamm, 10.10.1988	IPRax 1991, 324	**Vor 14–24** 13
OLG Hamm, 22.10.1990	CR 1991, 335	**38** 19
OLG Hamm, 7.2.1992	NJW-RR 1992, 1201	**42** 1
OLG Hamm, 22.9.1992	CISG-online 57	**8** 19, 34; **9** 21; **14** 31a, 31b, 31c, 31d; **18** 8; **19** 9, 13; **25** 18, 67; **49** 27; **64** 13; **75** 2; **76** 1, 2, 8, 15; **77** 10
OLG Hamm, 8.2.1995	CISG-online 141	**8** 38, 41, 42; **14** 66; **24** 36, 37, 38, 39; **29** 10
OLG Hamm, 9.6.1995	CISG-online 146	**4** 6, 35, 38, 39; **6** 22, 25; **45** 27; **46** 45, 46; **48** 8; **74** 24
OLG Hamm, 3.11.1997	CISG-online 381	**1** 31
OLG Hamm, 23.6.1998	CISG-online 434	**6** 7; **31** 50, 63; **33** 15; **71** 10, 20
OLG Hamm, 12.11.2001	CISG-online 1430	**1** 64; **2** 5; **25** 38, 39; **93** 4
OLG Hamm, 20.9.2005	IPRax 2007, 125	**Vor 14–24** 12, 13
OLG Hamm, 6.12.2005	CISG-online 1221; IHR 2006, 84	**8** 52; **57** 25
OLG Hamm, 2.4.2009	CISG-online 1978; IHR 2010, 59, 61	**1** 46; **2** 7, 20; **6** 7, 15, 17, 18, 22, 25, 26, 31; **Vor 14–24** 36; **39** 6, 8, 17; **40** 4, 5; **74** 30
OLG Hamm, 30.11.2010	CISG-online 2217; RdL 2011, 129	**6** 22; **8** 45, 46; **29** 14, 15, 24, 27; **35** 16
OLG Jena, 26.5.1998	CISG-online 513	**6** 42; **66** 21; **74** 14, 35
OLG Jena, 27.8.2008	CISG-online 1820; NJW 2009, 689	**14** 2; **18** 7a
OLG Jena, 10.11.2010	CISG-online 2216; IHR 2011, 79	**Vor 1–6** 22; **1** 77; **4** 20; **8** 36, 53, 53b; **Vor 14–24** 4; **14** 33, 37, 40, 43, 76; **29** 7, 8
OLG Karlsruhe, 12.2.1975	RIW 1975, 225	**25** 41
OLG Karlsruhe, 14.4.1978	Schlechtriem/Magnus, Art. 56 EKG, Nr. 2	**35** 14
OLG Karlsruhe, 29.12.1983	Schlechtriem/Magnus, Art. 39 EKG, Nr. 40	**39** 14
OLG Karlsruhe, 25.7.1986	RIW 1986, 818	**27** 11; **39** 14
OLG Karlsruhe, 25.3.1988	NJW-RR 1989, 19	**14** 2
OLG Karlsruhe, 20.11.1992	CISG-online 54; CLOUT No. 317; NJW-RR 1993, 1316	**Einl; 8** 40, 44, 45, 51; **31** 76; **58** 37; **67** 11; **69** 18
OLG Karlsruhe, 25.6.1997	CISG-online 263	**1** 71; **4** 42; **6** 7, 22; **7** 9, 51; **38** 14, 17; **44** 5a
OLG Karlsruhe, 19.12.2002	CISG-online 817	**25** 48; **31** 53, 54; **49** 6
OLG Karlsruhe, 10.12.2003	CISG-online 911	**1** 71; **4** 35, 45; **29** 6
OLG Karlsruhe, 20.7.2004	CISG-online 858; IHR 2004, 246	**4** 21, 35, 39; **6** 7; **7** 17, 21; **14** 37, 44, 64; **25** 39; **61** 19; **78** 27

VI. Entscheidungsregister   Anh. VI

Gericht, Datum	Fundstelle	Art. Rn.
OLG Karlsruhe, 8.2.2006	CISG-online 1328; IHR 2006, 106	60 2; 61 7, 13
OLG Karlsruhe, 14.2.2008	CISG-online 1649; IHR 2008, 53	7 17; 39 6; 45 10; 63 8, 9; 64 23, 35; 74 27; 82 28; 84 7, 27, 38, 40
OLG Karlsruhe, 12.6.2008	CISG-online 1716	3 14, 15
OLG Koblenz, 9.1.1981	IPRax 1982, 20	6 21, 25
OLG Koblenz, 21.1.1983	Schlechtriem/Magnus, Art. 56 EKG, Nr. 7	14 9
OLG Koblenz, 23.12.1983	Schlechtriem/Magnus, Art. 6 EAG, Nr. 14	18 4
OLG Koblenz, 16.3.1984	Schlechtriem/Magnus, Art. 1 EAG, Nr. 11	Vor 14–24 1; 11 5
OLG Koblenz, 18.5.1984	Schlechtriem/Magnus, Art. 44 EKG, Nr. 6	25 42; 35 15; 40 4, 6; 51 11
OLG Koblenz, 1.3.1985	Schlechtriem/Magnus, Art. 56 EKG, Nr. 10	14 9
OLG Koblenz, 10.5.1985	RIW 1985, 737	25 14
OLG Koblenz, 6.2.1987	RIW 1987, 313	Vor 14–24 1; 25 24
OLG Koblenz, 23.12.1988	RIW 1989, 384	18 15
OLG Koblenz, 3.3.1989	RIW 1989, 310	38 16; 39 9
OLG Koblenz, 23.2.1990	CISG-online 19	1 74, 81; 31 90
OLG Koblenz, 28.3.1991	RIW 1991, 592	39 9
OLG Koblenz, 27.9.1991	CISG-online 30	1 73, 74; 82 27
OLG Koblenz, 16.1.1992	CISG-online 47	4 30; 14 16; 30 8
OLG Koblenz, 17.9.1993	CISG-online 91; RIW 1993, 934	1 31, 38, 72; 4 39; 6 22; 53 8; 61 19; 78 20
OLG Koblenz, 31.1.1997	CISG-online 256	8 1, 48, 51, 61; 25 15, 47, 48; 39 8, 30; 48 14, 15; 49 7, 12, 32; 78 27; 80 3
OLG Koblenz, 11.9.1998	CISG-online 505	38 14; 44 7
OLG Koblenz, 18.11.1999	CISG-online 570	4 39; 38 10, 17; 39 15, 17, 37
OLG Koblenz, 4.10.2002	CISG-online 716	14 40; 19 13, 14, 22; 31 76; 67 11
OLG Koblenz, 10.10.2006	CISG-online 1438	25 69; 50 13; 53 21
OLG Koblenz, 19.10.2006	CISG-online 1407; CLOUT No. 723	27 4, 9, 10; 39 11; 78 8, 27
OLG Koblenz, 14.12.2006	CISG-online 1408	66 19, 21
OLG Koblenz, 21.11.2007	CISG-online 1733; OLGR Koblenz 2008, 493	25 10, 55
OLG Koblenz, 1.3.2010	CISG-online 2126; NJW-RR 2010, 1004	14 4; 19 5, 13
OLG Koblenz, 22.4.2010	CISG-online 2163	74 64, 65
OLG Koblenz, 22.4.2010	CISG-online 2290	35 51, 55
OLG Koblenz, 24.2.2011	CISG-online 2301	35 47; 74 5, 42, 64; 77 7, 12, 13; 80 3, 7
OLG Köln, 29.6.1978	MDR 1980, 1023	40 4
OLG Köln, 24.10.1984	RIW 1985, 404	38 16
OLG Köln, 14.7.1986	BB 1988, 20	38 14
OLG Köln, 16.3.1988	RIW 1988, 555; NJW 1988, 2182	Vor 14–24 19; 9 24
OLG Köln, 1.12.1989	CR 1990, 323	24 34
OLG Köln, 27.11.1991	CISG-online 31	1 40

Anh. VI

Gericht, Datum	Fundstelle	Art. Rn.
OLG Köln, 22.2.1994	CISG-online 127	6 22, 25; **Vor 14–24** 19, 22; **18** 9; **29** 2, 11; **49** 32
OLG Köln, 26.8.1994	CISG-online 132	1 34, 38, 40; **3** 5, 13
OLG Köln, 21.5.1996	CISG-online 254	1 8, 34, 40; **7** 52; **Vor 14–24** 3; **35** 37; **74** 32, 56; **79** 6, 39
OLG Köln, 8.1.1997	CISG-online 217	1 71; **8** 56; **31** 76, 92; **39** 7; **45** 23; **71** 25; **74** 25, 52; **80** 6
OLG Köln, 21.8.1997	CISG-online 290	**38** 16; **39** 17
OLG Köln, 13.11.2000	CISG-online 657	1 41, 46, 48; **78** 27
OLG Köln, 28.5.2001	CISG-online 681	1 31; **4** 39
OLG Köln, 16.7.2001	CISG-online 609	1 31; **31** 76, 90, 94; **67** 11
OLG Köln, 14.10.2002	CISG-online 709	25 47, 55; **81** 16
OLG Köln, 15.9.2004	CISG-online 1057	1 31
OLG Köln, 21.12.2005	CISG-online 1201; IHR 2006, 86	7 49, 54; **Vor 14–24** 13; **14** 40; **57** 25, 26
OLG Köln, 13.2.2006	CISG-online 1219	4 35, 39
OLG Köln, 3.4.2006	CISG-online 1218	6 7; **8** 5; **59** 5; **74** 30, 31; **78** 17, 27
OLG Köln, 24.5.2006	CISG-online 1232	6 7; **Vor 14–24** 10, 13; **19** 22, 35
OLG Köln, 14.8.2006	CISG-online 1405	**74** 27
OLG Köln, 12.1.2007	CISG-online 1581	**38** 13
OLG Köln, 30.4.2007	IHR 2007, 164	**57** 25; **61** 19
OLG Köln, 2.7.2007	CISG-online 1811	8 11, 26, 27
OLG Köln, 19.5.2008	CISG-online 1700; IHR 2008, 26	4 39; **26** 10a; **29** 13
OLG München, 19.12.1957	NJW 1958, 426	**30** 3
OLG München, 12.8.1977	NJW 1978, 499	**40** 4
OLG München, 16.10.1978	Schlechtriem/Magnus, Art. 82 EKG, Nr. 11	**74** 17, 26
OLG München, 17.10.1986	RIW 1986, 998	**31** 92
OLG München, 9.12.1987	RIW 1988, 297; CISG-online 1530	25 43; **74** 26
OLG München, 2.3.1994	CISG-online 108; CLOUT No. 83	4 39; **49** 32; **64** 34
OLG München, 8.2.1995	CISG-online 142	3 5; **44** 5, 7
OLG München, 8.2.1995	CISG-online 143	**Vor 1–6** 16; 1 65; **8** 44; **18** 8a; **19** 8a; **29** 9; **44** 5, 6; **74** 58; **77** 4; **80** 3; **84** 13; **92** 3
OLG München, 8.3.1995	CISG-online 145	**11** 7, 12; **Vor 14–24** 13, 17, 45; **79** 53
OLG München, 9.8.1995	IPRax 1997, 38	**74** 7, 21
OLG München, 22.9.1995	CISG-online 208	1 31; **Vor 14–24** 41
OLG München, 3.7.1996	WM 1996, 2335	25 63
OLG München, 9.7.1997	CISG-online 281	1 71; **3** 12; **6** 7
OLG München, 9.7.1997	CISG-online 282; BB 1997, 2295	1 31, 71; **6** 18; **39** 7; **53** 12, 22, 42; **57** 7, 23, 24; **59** 4; **61** 19; **80** 6
OLG München, 21.1.1998	CISG-online 536	4 35
OLG München, 28.1.1998	CISG-online 339; RIW 1998, 559; IHR 2001, 23	1 71; **8** 5; **58** 6; **61** 19; **81** 11

VI. Entscheidungsregister   **Anh. VI**

Gericht, Datum	Fundstelle	Art. Rn.
OLG München, 11.3.1998	CISG-online 310	1 71; 4 39; 18 8; 19 20, 22; 38 13, 14; 39 17, 35; 78 27
OLG München, 3.12.1999	CISG-online 585	3 17; 7 33; 31 82
OLG München, 1.7.2002	CISG-online 656	47 1
OLG München, 13.11.2002	CISG-online 786	35 9; 38 7
OLG München, 15.9.2004	CISG-online 1013; IHR 2005, 70, 71	7 9, 27, 50; 25 37; 49 6; 75 5
OLG München, 3.4.2006	CISG-online 1218	58 5
OLG München, 19.10.2006	CISG-online 1394; IHR 2007, 30	47 11; 58 5; 63 5, 7; 64 23
OLG München, 17.11.2006	CISG-online 1395	14 33; 27 1, 4, 10; 74 30
OLG München, 5.3.2008	CISG-online 1686; IHR 2008, 253	4 29, 30; 45 2; 74 30, 65; 79 11, 29
OLG München, 14.1.2009	CISG-online 2011; IHR 2009, 201	2 5; 7 49; 8 53; 14 40, 43, 51, 64, 69
OLG München, 18.5.2009	CISG-online 1998	61 13
OLG München, 11.7.2011,	unveröff.; AZ 34 Sch 15/10	4 9
OLG Naumburg, 28.6.1993	BB 1993, 1622	27 9
OLG Naumburg, 27.4.1999	CISG-online 512	1 65; 19 8a, 8b, 13; 27 4, 9; 33 8, 16; 39 11; 47 6, 8; 92 3
OLG Nürnberg, 20.9.1995	CISG-online 267	25 61; 47 5
OLG Oldenburg, 27.4.1982	Schlechtriem/Magnus, Art. 26 EKG, Nr. 5	25 13, 18; 49 5
OLG Oldenburg, 1.2.1995	CISG-online 253	84 16
OLG Oldenburg, 28.2.1996	CISG-online 189	14 4
OLG Oldenburg, 22.9.1998	CISG-online 508	25 37; 66 5
OLG Oldenburg, 28.4.2000	CISG-online 683	39 6, 7, 17; 40 5
OLG Oldenburg, 5.12.2000	CISG-online 618	7 27; 38 2, 14; 39 17, 33
OLG Oldenburg, 20.12.2007	CISG-online 1644; IHR 2008, 112	3 5; 4 21, 52; 6 17; Vor 14–24 10, 14b, 14c; 14 40, 59; 57 25
OLG Rostock, 27.7.1995	CISG-online 209	Vor 1–6 16; 1 65; 74 20; 78 27; 92 3
OLG Rostock, 24.9.1997	NJW-RR 1998, 526	24 14
OLG Rostock, 10.10.2001	CISG-online 671; IHR 2003, 17	1 8; 6 21, 22, 25; 14 12, 19; 55 15
OLG Rostock, 25.9.2002	CISG-online 672	35 8; 39 5, 30; 40 7; 52 7, 10
OLG Saarbrücken, 2.10.1991	NJW 1992, 987	Vor 14–24 12
OLG Saarbrücken, 13.1.1993	CISG-online 83	3 5; 8 48, 52, 54; 9 14; 14 37, 44; 18 4, 7a, 8; 38 14, 23, 25; 39 6, 17, 35
OLG Saarbrücken, 3.6.1998	CISG-online 354	39 6, 15, 16
OLG Saarbrücken, 14.2.2001	CISG-online 610	1 24; 3 4, 5
OLG Saarbrücken, 17.1.2007	CISG-online 1642; IHR 2008, 55	35 11, 29; 44 4, 5, 6, 8
OLG Saarbrücken, 12.5.2010	CISG-online 2155	1 24, 73; 3 5; 53 2; 57 16; 78 27
OLG Saarbrücken, 30.5.2011	CISG-online 2225	1 71
OLG Schleswig, 22.8.2002	CISG-online 710	1 65; 35 50; 38 17; 39 7, 16; 66 19; 78 17
OLG Schleswig, 29.10.2002	CISG-online 717; IHR 2003, 67	Vor 1–6 25, 34, 35; 1 15, 34, 76; 8 16; 14 31a, 31b; 18 7a; Vor 66–70 16
OLG Schleswig, 24.10.2008	CISG-online 2020	Vor 1–6 34; 4 34

Gericht, Datum	Fundstelle	Art. Rn.
OLG Stuttgart, 16.6.1987	IPRax 1988, 293	**8** 54; **14** 63
OLG Stuttgart, 28.6.1988	Schlechtriem/Magnus, Art. 26 EKG, Nr. 5	**25** 18
OLG Stuttgart, 21.8.1995	CISG-online 150	**4** 39; **39** 17
OLG Stuttgart, 28.2.2000	CISG-online 583	**1** 24, 46; **3** 5; **8** 5, 51; **10** 5; **14** 4
OLG Stuttgart, 12.3.2001	CISG-online 841	**25** 45, 52; **38** 10; **49** 15
OLG Stuttgart, 20.12.2004	CISG-online 997	**4** 45a; **7** 55; **78** 27
OLG Stuttgart, 1.3.2004	CISG-online 1044	**Vor 89–101** 10
OLG Stuttgart, 15.5.2006	CISG-online 1414	**8** 49, 60; **Vor 14–24** 10
OLG Stuttgart, 31.3.2008	CISG-online 1658	**1** 54; **2** 11, 15; **6** 21, 22, 26, 31; **7** 17; **8** 47; **45** 27; **49** 32
OLG Stuttgart, 18.4.2011	CISG-online 2226; IHR 2011, 236	**19** 8a
OLG Stuttgart, 30.5.2011	CISG-online 2225	**1** 73; **4** 4; **7** 17
OLG Zweibrücken, 31.3.1998	CISG-online 481	**8** 52, 53; **Vor 14–24** 4, 5; **14** 35, 37, 68; **74** 58, 60; **79** 6, 14, 29, 39,40
OLG Zweibrücken, 26.7.2002	CISG-online 688	**4** 35; **6** 22
OLG Zweibrücken, 2.2.2004	CISG-online 877	**35** 9; **40** 4; **42** 1
LG Aachen, 3.4.1990	CISG-online 12	**1** 74, 81; **7** 13; **35** 9; **39** 17; **74** 25
LG Aachen, 14.5.1993	CISG-online 86; RIW 1993, 760	**4** 9, 24, 45; **29** 6; **31** 18; **35** 45; **57** 29; **60** 3; **61**20; **74** 32; **79** 31
LG Aachen, 20.7.1995	CISG-online 169	**7** 36; **74** 20
LG Aachen, 19.4.1996	CISG-online 165	**65** 1, 14
LG Aachen, 22.6.2010	CISG-online 2162; IHR 2011, 82	**8** 41, 53a, 53b, 54a, 55; **Vor 14–24** 13, 14b, 14c; **29** 7
LG Augsburg, 12.7.1994	CISG-online 390	**8** 36, 41
LG Aurich, 8.5.1998	CISG-online 518	**18** 4
LG Baden-Baden, 14.8.1991	CISG-online 24	**1** 81; **19** 13; **39** 35
LG Bamberg, 13.4.2005	CISG-online 1402	**2** 9; **4** 35; **14** 7; **18** 7a
LG Bamberg, 23.10.2006	CISG-online 1400; IHR 2007, 113	**2** 7; **4** 39; **6** 18, 25; **39** 17; **57** 25; **67** 20
LG Bayreuth, 10.12.2004	CISG-online 1131	**74** 30
LG Berlin, 30.9.1992	CISG-online 70	**8** 39; **72** 12; **74** 38, 63
LG Berlin, 6.10.1992	CISG-online 173	**74** 25, 31
LG Berlin, 15.9.1994	CISG-online 399	**26** 6; **35** 15; **71** 8, 12, 22a
LG Berlin, 24.3.1998	CISG-online 742	**1** 73; **4** 34; **7** 55
LG Berlin, 25.5.1999	CISG-online 1311	**38** 14
LG Berlin, 21.3.2003	CISG-online 785	**38** 14; **78** 29
LG Bielefeld, 5.6.1987	IPRax 1988, 229	**18** 15
LG Bielefeld, 18.1.1991	CISG-online 174	**18** 15; **76** 2
LG Bielefeld, 24.11.1998	CISG-online 697; CLOUT No. 363; IHR 2001, 199	**57** 8
LG Bielefeld, 15.8.2003	CISG-online 906	**39** 14
LG Bielefeld, 12.12.2003	CISG-online 905	**1** 65; **92** 3
LG Bielefeld, 9.11.2010	CISG-online 2204; BeckRS 2011, 08294	**1** 73; **53** 30
LG Bochum, 24.1.1996	CISG-online 175	**27** 7
LG Braunschweig, 16.11.1982	RIW 1983, 372	**6** 12, 25
LG Braunschweig, 30.7.2001	CISG-online 689	**1** 71

VI. Entscheidungsregister   Anh. VI

Gericht, Datum	Fundstelle	Art. Rn.
LG Coburg, 12.12.2006,	CISG-online 1447	8 44, 53, 53a; 14 37, 40, 55, 59; 74 30
LG Darmstadt, 29.5.2001	CISG-online 686	38 17; 39 17, 37; 50 3; 71 4, 21
LG Dortmund, 23.9.1981	Schlechtriem/Magnus, Art. 3 EAG, Nr. 4	Vor 14–24 3; 18 7; 25 31; 74 44
LG Dresden, 29.5.2009	CISG-online 2174	71 9a, 52; 73 10; 84 12, 17
LG Duisburg, 16.7.1976	Schlechtriem/Magnus, Art. 43 EKG, Nr. 2	74 36
LG Duisburg, 17.4.1996	CISG-online 186; RIW 1996, 774	53 22
LG Düsseldorf, 17.11.1983	Schlechtriem/Magnus, Art. 26 EKG, Nr. 6; Art. 71 EKG, Nr. 2	25 30; 33 17
LG Düsseldorf, 9.7.1992	CISG-online 42	80 3
LG Düsseldorf, 23.6.1994	CISG-online 179	38 17
LG Düsseldorf, 25.8.1994	CISG-online 451	39 11; 74 31; 77 11
LG Düsseldorf, 11.10.1995	CISG-online 180	4 35; 6 28; 8 48; 26 6; 81 9
LG Ellwangen, 21.8.1995	CISG-online 279	1 15; 25 45; 29 11; 35 17; 47 9; 73 23a; 79 40; Vor 81 16; 82 22, 23
LG Ellwangen, 13.12.2002	NJW 2003, 517	46 18, 40
LG Essen, 10.6.1980	MDR 1981, 148	74 20
LG Flensburg, 24.3.1999	CISG-online 719; IHR 2001, 202	31 18; 50 15; 53 21
LG Flensburg, 19.1.2001	CISG-online 619	1 34; 40 12; 74 12
LG Frankenthal, 17.4.1997	CISG-online 479	9 8
LG Frankfurt a. M., 2.5.1990	CISG-online 183	8 42
LG Frankfurt a. M., 16.9.1991	CISG-online 26	26 10; 49 24; 74 25, 30, 31; 75 5; 78 39; 81 8; 82 6
LG Frankfurt a. M., 6.7.1994	CISG-online 257	4 52; 9 18
LG Frankfurt a. M., 13.7.1994	CISG-online 118	4 39
LG Frankfurt a. M., 11.4.2005	CISG-online 1014; IHR 2005, 161	25 55; 38 16, 24, 25
LG Freiburg, 26.4.2002	CISG-online 690; IHR 2002, 72	57 7, 14
LG Freiburg, 22.8.2002	CISG-online 711; IHR 2011, 22	4 29, 30; Vor 14–24 25; 14 28; 25 37; 49 32; 79 29; 81 9d; 82 19; 84 13
LG Gera, 29.6.2006	CISG-online 1852	2 5
LG Gießen, 5.7.1994	CISG-online 111	39 35
LG Gießen, 17.12.2002	CISG-online 766; IHR 2003, 276	Vor 14–24 10, 13; 14 40; 57 25, 31
LG Görlitz, 27.5.2010	CISG-online 2181	26 6
LG Göttingen, 31.7.1997	CISG-online 564	8 54; 14 55, 61, 62, 65, 66; 77 10
LG Hagen, 15.10.1997	CISG-online 311	1 71; 4 39
LG Halle, 27.3.1998	CISG-online 521	49 5
LG Hamburg, 14.11.1975	RIW 1977, 425	25 8
LG Hamburg, 18.8.1976	Schlechtriem/Magnus, Art. 86 EKG, Nr. 4	31 10
LG Hamburg, 14.5.1984	Schlechtriem/Magnus, Art. 8 EKG, Nr. 13	Vor 14–24 1
LG Hamburg, 26.9.1990	CISG-online 21; RIW 1990, 1015; EuZW 1991, 188	1 19, 40, 74, 81; 4 34, 45; 8 5, 16, 19; 9 21; 14 4; 29 2, 6, 10; 53 14, 21; 58 6; 74 25; 78 8

Gericht, Datum	Fundstelle	Art. Rn.
LG Hamburg, 23.10.1995	CISG-online 395	**25** 39
LG Hamburg, 19.6.1997	CISG-online 283	**8** 7; **Vor 14–24** 10
LG Hamburg, 21.12.2001	CISG-online 1092	**18** 5; **21** 8
LG Hamburg, 26.11.2003	CISG-online 875	**Vor 14–24** 27; **16** 9; **18** 4, 5, 14; **20** 1
LG Hamburg, 6.9.2004	CISG-online 1085	**38** 18; **39** 17
LG Hamburg, 17.2.2009	CISG-online 1999	**74** 30
LG Hamburg, 6.9.2011	unveröff.; AZ 312 O 316/11	**6** 15
LG Hannover, 1.12.1993	CISG-online 244	**39** 7, 35; **61** 13; **74** 20
LG Hannover, 21.4.2009	CISG-online 2298	**14** 37, 51
LG Heidelberg, 30.1.1979	*Schlechtriem/Magnus*, Art. 3 EAG, Nr. 2; Art. 22 EKG, Nr. 2; IHR 2012, 59	**11** 4; **Vor 14–24** 23; **14** 25, 27, 37, 51; **33** 14; **74** 50; **77** 10
LG Heidelberg, 21.4.1981	*Schlechtriem/Magnus*, Art. 39 EKG, Nr. 21; Art. 56 EKG, Nr. 4	**14** 9; **31** 83; **39** 7, 33
LG Heidelberg, 3.7.1992	CISG-online 38	**Vor 1–6** 22; **1** 38, 77; **25** 42; **51** 9; **95** 2
LG Heidelberg, 2.10.1996	CISG-online 264	**74** 32, 62
LG Heidelberg, 2.11.2005	CISG-online 1416	**78** 32
LG Heilbronn, 15.9.1997	CISG-online 562	**Vor 1–6** 34; **4** 35; **8** 53, 54; **Vor 14–24** 3; **14** 40, 63; **25** 46, 48
LG Kassel, 22.6.1995	CISG-online 370	**1** 73; **4** 34; **39** 37
LG Kassel, 21.9.1995	CISG-online 192	**25** 66; **54** 7; **63** 8, 9; **64** 9, 34
LG Kassel, 15.2.1996	CISG-online 190	**1** 72, 73; **6** 22; **8** 16, 36, 41, 42; **18** 7a, 8a, 18; **24** 37, 38; **29** 6, 9; **39** 14
LG Kassel, 15.2.1996	CISG-online 191; NJW-RR 1996, 1146	**6** 22; **39** 14; **27** 7; **53** 42; **74** 25
LG Kiel, 27.7.2004	CISG-online 1534	**9** 23; **Vor 14–24** 19, 20
LG Konstanz, 1976	*Schlechtriem/Magnus*, Art. 82 EKG, Nr. 3; Art. 90 EKG, Nr. 1	**31** 83; **74** 27
LG Konstanz, 3.6.1983	*Schlechtriem/Magnus*, Art 82 EKG, Nr. 26; Art. 83 EKG, Nr. 16	**74** 20
LG Konstanz, 6.12.1984	*Schlechtriem/Magnus*, Art. 39 EKG, Nr. 47	**35** 49
LG Köln, 11.7.1978	*Schlechtriem/Magnus*, Art. 39 EKG, Nr. 8	**27** 5
LG Köln, 16.11.1995	CISG-online 265	**1** 39; **79** 6, 39
LG Köln, 5.12.2006	CISG-online 1440	**18** 7a; **39** 9, 30; **88** 8
LG Krefeld, 24.11.1992	CISG-online 62	**81** 18
LG Krefeld, 28.4.1993	CISG-online 101	**8** 2; **72** 12; **74** 25, 26; **75** 11
LG Krefeld, 19.12.1995	CISG-online 397	**74** 18; **81** 9d; **82** 13, 22; **84** 20
LG Krefeld, 20.9.2006	CISG-online 1459; IHR 2007, 161	**Vor 1–6** 34; **57** 14, 16
LG Lahn-Gießen, 16.6.1978	*Schlechtriem/Magnus*, Art. 39 EKG, Nr. 6	**39** 7
LG Landshut, 14.7.1976	NJW 1977, 2033	**18** 8; **19** 9

VI. Entscheidungsregister   Anh. VI

Gericht, Datum	Fundstelle	Art. Rn.
LG Landshut, 5.4.1995	CISG-online 193	2 5; 6 1, 7, 18, 25; 25 57; 35 8, 9; 38 14, 17; 40 12; 74 27, 56; 81 19, 27, 29; 84 13
LG Landshut, 12.6.2008	CISG-online 1703; IHR 2008, 184	2 5; 4 20, 34; 7 43; 9 23; Vor 14–24 5, 19, 20
LG Lübeck, 30.12.2010	CISG-online 2292	38 16, 25; 40 12; 74 30
LG Mainz, 26.11.1998	CISG-online 563	3 12, 14
LG Mannheim, 16.2.2004	IHR 2006, 106	7 17
LG Marburg, 22.4.1982	Schlechtriem/Magnus, Art. 2 EAG, Nr. 4	Vor 14–24 3
LG Marburg, 1.11.1984	Schlechtriem/Magnus, Art. 48 EKG, Nr. 1	85 5
LG Marburg, 12.12.1995	CISG-online 148	39 6, 37
LG Memmingen, 1.12.1993	CISG-online 73	3 5; 11 12; 74 16
LG Memmingen, 13.9.2000	CISG-online 820	14 62, 64, 67, 76
LG Mönchengladbach, 22.5.1992	CISG-online 56	8 4, 36, 38
LG Mönchengladbach, 15.7.2003	CISG-online 813	1 73; 4 39
LG Mönchengladbach, 25.7.2003	CISG-online 919	7 54
LG München I, 3.7.1989	CISG-online 4	1 81; 39 7
LG München I, 8.2.1995	CISG-online 203	1 16, 38; 39 6
LG München I, 20.3.1995	CISG-online 164	39 9; 49 24, 32
LG München I, 29.5.1995	CISG-online 235	1 38; 6 18; 14 33
LG München I, 25.1.1996	CISG-online 278	4 41
LG München I, 6.5.1997	CISG-online 341	1 73
LG München I, 6.4.2000	CISG-online 665	26 13; 45 27; 71 11, 38; 74 25, 62; 75 12
LG München I, 16.11.2000	CISG-online 667	38 17
LG München I, 30.8.2001	CISG-online 668	74 34
LG München I, 27.2.2002	CISG-online 654	1 24; 3 5; 25 51; 35 14, 21, 24; 38 14; 39 10; 46 26; 49 7, 8
LG München I, 29.11.2005	CISG-online 1567	25 52
LG München I, 18.5.2009	CISG-online 1998; IHR 2010, 150	7 43; 35 52; 39 16, 37; 45 23; 74 30
LG München II, 20.2.2002	CISG-online 712	1 20; 2 11; 39 16
LG Münster, 24.5.1977	Schlechtriem/Magnus, Art. 82 EKG, Nr. 6	33 13
LG Münster, 29.8.2008	CISG-online 2167	39 17
LG Neubrandenburg, 3.8.2005	CISG-online 1190; IHR 2006, 26	4 20, 21; 6 7; 7 17, 49, 54; 8 53; 9 22; Vor 14–24 19, 21, 22; 14 20, 40, 51, 55, 59; 55 5, 10, 15; 57 25
LG Nürnberg-Fürth, 26.7.1994	CISG-online 266	47 5
LG Nürnberg-Fürth, 27.2.2003	CISG-online 818; IHR 2004, 20	31 93; 57 7, 10, 25
LG Oldenburg, 6.7.1994	CISG-online 274	25 55; 84 10, 41
LG Oldenburg, 9.11.1994	CISG-online 114	38 9; 45 26; 46 47; 49 32; 74 25, 27; 84 13
LG Oldenburg, 1.2.1995	CISG-online 253	84 16
LG Oldenburg, 25.2.1995	CISG-online 197	3 5; 6 7
LG Oldenburg, 28.2.1996	CISG-online 189	8 16; 14 10, 41
LG Oldenburg, 27.3.1996	CISG-online 188	25 40
LG Osnabrück, 19.2.1982	Schlechtriem/Magnus, Art. 59 EKG, Nr. 11	39 37
LG Paderborn, 25.6.1996	CISG-online 262	38 13

Anh. VI

Gericht, Datum	Fundstelle	Art. Rn.
LG Potsdam, 7.4.2009	CISG-online 1979 = 2164	**74** 30
LG Regensburg, 17.12.1998	CISG-online 514	**48** 17
LG Saarbrücken, 23.3.1992	CISG-online 60	**9** 23, 24; **Vor 14–24** 21; **73** 16
LG Saarbrücken, 2.7.2002	CISG-online 713	**6** 25; **39** 7, 17
LG Saarbrücken, 25.11.2002	CISG-online 718	**9** 14
LG Saarbrücken, 1.6.2004	CISG-online 1228	**25** 58
LG Siegen, 15.10.1976	Schlechtriem/Magnus, Art. 88 EKG, Nr. 1; Art. 74 EKG, Nr. 2	**79** 37
LG Siegen, 29.1.1986	Schlechtriem/Magnus, Art. 39 EKG, Nr. 50	**38** 16
LG Stendal, 12.10.2000	CISG-online 592; IHR 2001, 30	**6** 5; **7** 48; **25** 10; **40** 12; **49** 16; **50** 3; **58** 25, 32, 33; **59** 1
LG Stuttgart, 31.8.1989	CISG-online 11	**1** 81; **7** 18; **38** 13, 16; **39** 17; **74** 25
LG Stuttgart, 13.8.1991	CISG-online 33	**27** 6, 9
LG Stuttgart, 15.8.2009	CISG-online 2019	**39** 6, 17, 37
LG Stuttgart, 29.10.2009	CISG-online 2017	**1** 48; **50** 8
LG Stuttgart, 11.11.2009	CISG-online 2018	**71** 9, 28, 53
LG Tübingen, 18.6.2003	CISG-online 784	**35** 52; **39** 17
LG Trier, 12.10.1995	CISG-online 160	**6** 7; **38** 13; **40** 4; **45** 27; **74** 15
LG Trier, 7.12.2000	CISG-online 595; IHR 2001, 35	**57** 5, 8
LG Trier, 28.6.2001	CISG-online 673	**39** 11
LG Trier, 8.1.2004	CISG-online 910	**4** 40; **7** 17; **8** 53, 56; **14** 40, 59
LG Zwickau, 19.3.1999	CISG-online 519	**7** 52; **14** 70
AG Albstadt, 10.3.1989	IPRax 1989, 247	**31** 25
AG Alsfeld, 12.5.1995	CISG-online 170; NJW-RR 1996, 120	**4** 34; **57** 20; **74** 30; **77** 11; **79** 25
AG Augsburg, 29.1.1996	CISG-online 172	**39** 17; **74** 30
AG Cloppenburg, 14.4.1993	CISG-online 85	**2** 5; **46** 45; **50** 7
AG Duisburg, 13.4.2000	CISG-online 659; IHR 2001, 114	**1** 46; **2** 11; **4** 6, 39; **9** 8; **14** 70; **31** 70, 76; **61** 19; **67** 12, 30; **69** 4
AG Frankfurt a. M., 31.1.1991	CISG-online 34	**4** 39; **71** 21
AG Freiburg, 6.7.2007	CISG-online 1596	**27** 9
AG Geldern, 17.8.2011	CISG-online 2302	**1** 73; **8** 5, 46; **39** 5; **74** 30, 31
AG Hamburg Altona, 14.12.2000	CISG-online 692; IPRax 2001, 582	**64** 13
AG Kehl, 6.10.1995	CISG-online 162	**8** 53, 54, 54a; **14** 63, 76; **19** 9, 23, 28, 30; **24** 16; **38** 14, 16
AG Kempen, 28.8.2006	NJW 2007, 1215	**24** 44
AG Ludwigsburg, 21.12.1990	CISG-online 17	**25** 39, 40; **49** 2
AG Landsberg, 21.6.2006	CISG-online 1493	**74** 30
AG München, 23.6.1995	CISG-online 368	**4** 39; **48** 11, 23; **74** 24, 52, 41; **77** 13; **80** 3
AG Nordhorn, 14.6.1994	CISG-online 259	**4** 20, 21; **8** 46, 48, 51, 54; **14** 44, 64; **25** 25, 40; **74** 5
AG Oldenburg, 24.4.1990	CISG-online 20	**1** 20, 81; **49** 5, 24; **74** 25

VI. Entscheidungsregister   Anh. VI

Gericht, Datum	Fundstelle	Art. Rn.
AG Riedlingen, 21.10.1994	CISG-online 358	**38** 16; **39** 16
AG Tiergarten, 13.3.1997	CISG-online 412	**74** 31
AG Zweibrücken, 14.10.1992	CISG-online 46	**26** 10; **49** 24; **73** 5

Estland

Tallinna Ringkonnakohus, 19.2.2004	CISG-online 826	**14** 2

Europäischer Gerichtshof

EuGH, 6.10.1976 (de Bloos/Bouyer)	Rs. 14/76; NJW 1977, 490; ECR 1976, I-1479	**31** 89; **57** 23
EuGH, 6.10.1976 (Tessili/Dunlop)	Rs. 12/76; ECR 1976, I-1473	**31** 89; **57** 23
EuGH, 15.1.1987	Slg. 1987, I-239	**31** 89
EuGH, 29.6.1994	CISG-online 272; ECR 1994, I-2913; IPRax 1995, 31	**31** 89; **57** 23
EuGH, 20.2.1997	Slg. 1997, I-911	**9** 16, 20, 22, 24, 25; **Vor 14–24** 12
EuGH, 16.3.1999	Slg. 1999, I-1597, Nr. 25	**9** 16, 20
EuGH, 1.6.1999	Slg. 1999, I-3055	**9** 16
EuGH, 28.9.1999 (GIE Groupe Concorde/ Kapitän des Schiffes „Suhadiwarno Panjan")	RIW 1999, 951; ECR 1999, I-6307	**31** 89; **57** 23
EuGH, 5.10.1999 (Leathertex/Bodetex)	RIW 1999, 953	**31** 89
EuGH, 6.4.2000	Slg. 2000, I-02519	**42** 13a
EuGH, 19.2.2002 (Besix/Kretzschmar)	Slg. 2002, I-1699	**31** 89; **45** 35
EuGH, 17.9.2002	NJW 2002, 3195	**Vor 14–24** 38
EuGH, 7.1.2004	Rs. 60/02	**42** 13a
EuGH, 3.5.2007	ECR 2007, I-3699	**57** 25
EuGH, 9.7.2009	Rs. C-204/08	**31** 89
EuGH, 25.2.2010 (Car Trim/Keysafety Systems S. r. l.)	Rs. C-381/08	**31** 89
EuGH, 11.3.2010	Rs. C-19/09	**31** 89
EuGH, 9.6.2011 (Electorsteel Europe SA/ Edil Centro SpA)	Rs. C-87/10; NJW 2011, 3018	**57** 25

Europäischer Gerichtshof für Menschenrechte

EGMR, 22.10.1996	Sammlung 1996-IV Rn. 50	**39** 25

Finnland

Appellationsgericht Helsinki, 30.6.1998	CISG-online 1304	**25** 45
Appellationsgericht Helsinki, 29.1.1998	UNILEX	**9** 20, 21
Appellationsgericht Helsinki, 26.10.2000	CISG-online 1078	**74** 65
Appellationsgericht Ostfinnland, 27.3.1997	CISG-online 782	**74** 25, 52
Appellationsgericht Turku, 18.2.1997	CISG-online 1297	**25** 40
Appellationsgericht Turku, 12.4.2002	CISG-online 660	**49** 29; **78** 17, 27

Frankreich

Ass. plén., 1.12.1995	J. C. P. 1996, II, 22, 565; D. 1996, 13	**14** 15; **55** 12
Civ. 1, 29.11.1994	J. C. P. 1995, II, 22, 371	**14** 15
Civ. 1, 4.1.1995	CISG-online 138	**1** 46; **4** 4; **14** 15; **19** 8b, 13; **35** 8; **55** 1; **85** 17; **86** 5
Civ. 1, 23.1.1996	CISG-online 159	**25** 58; **35** 9

Anh. VI

Gericht, Datum	Fundstelle	Art. Rn.
Civ. 1, 14.5.1996	J. C. P. 1997, I, 4009	**35** 46
Civ. 1, 2.12.1997	CISG-online 294	**1** 71; **31** 90
Civ. 1, 27.1.1998	CISG-online 309	**1** 71; **8** 36; **18** 9
Civ. 1, 16.7.1998	CISG-online 344	**1** 71; **Vor 14–24** 10; **18** 8; **19** 8a, 9, 23; **31** 89, 90
Civ. 1, 5.1.1999	Rev. crit. dr. int. Priv. 1999, 519	**4** 8
Civ. 1, 26.5.1999	CISG-online 487	**25** 58; **39** 17
Civ. 1, 26.6.2001	CISG-online 598	**Vor 1–6** 24; **1** 75; **6** 7, 18, 25
Civ. 1, 26.6.2001	CISG-online 600	**1** 71; **31** 94
Civ. 1, 26.6.2001	CISG-online 695; D. 2001, 2593	**6** 7; **57** 23
Civ. 1, 19.3.2002	CISG-online 662	**8** 39; **42** 17
Civ. 1, 30.6.2004	CISG-online 870	**1** 22; **8** 30; **Vor 14–24** 41; **14** 9; **79** 30
Civ. 1, 4.10.2005	CISG-online 1097; J. C. P. 2005, IV, 3342	**39** 17; **40** 5
Civ. 1, 25.10.2005	CISG-online 1226	**6** 18, 25
Civ. 1, 2.4.2008	CISG-online 1651	**1** 64; **4** 34; **Vor 89–101** 9; **93** 4
Civ. 1, 11.5.2010	CISG-online 2184	**84** 12
Civ. 2, 18.1.2001	J. C. P. 2001, IV, 1413	**31** 94
Com., 28.11.1956	Bull. Civ. III, Nr. 317	**18** 18
Com., 3.11.1988	Bull. Civ. I, Nr. 291	**31** 94
Com., 1.3.1994	Rev. crit. dr. int. Privé 1994, 672	**31** 94
Com., 17.12.1996	CISG-online 220	**35** 14; **39** 29
Com., 7.4.1998	J. C. P. 1999, éd. E, 579	**Vor 14–24** 38
Com., 21.11.2000	D. 2001, 123	**53** 29
Com., 24.9.2003	CISG-online 791	**35** 51; **42** 1; **79** 53
Com., 13.2.2007	CISG-online 1561	**Vor 14–24** 3
Com., 20.2.2007	CISG-online 1492	**6** 22
Com., 16.9.2008	CISG-online 1821 = 1851	**39** 25; **40** 4, 5
Com., 3.2.2009	CISG-online 1843	**39** 28
Com., 3.11.2009	CISG-online 2004	**6** 18
Com., 8.11.2011	CISG-online 2310	**26** 15
Req., 27.2.1894	D. P. 1894, I, 216	**73** 5
Req., 31.10.1923	Gaz. Pal. 1924.1.18	**73** 5
CA Amiens, 27.9.2007	CISG-online 1934	**35** 14; **39** 28
CA Aix-en-Provence, 1.7.2005	CISG-online 1096	**39** 17
CA Chambéry, 25.5.1993	CISG-online 223	**3** 10
CA Colmar, 26.9.1995	CISG-online 226	**6** 22
CA Colmar, 24.10.2000	CISG-online 578	**14** 44, 57, 63, 64, 75, 76; **39** 17; **46** 43
CA Colmar, 12.6.2001	CISG-online 694	**1** 12, 13, 15; **2** 5; **61** 7; **79** 20, 30
CA Colmar, 13.11.2002	CISG-online 792	**42** 17
CA Colmar, 26.2.2008	CISG-online 1657	**3** 5, 15
CA Grenoble, 21.10.1989	CISG France	**74** 7, 12
CA Grenoble, 16.6.1993	CISG-online 90	**57** 23
CA Grenoble, 22.2.1995	CISG-online 151; J. D. I. 1995, 632	**Vor 1–6** 22; **1** 77; **7** 49, 50; **8** 5, 15; **25** 15, 67, 68; **64** 18, 21; **73** 23a; **95** 2
CA Grenoble, 29.3.1995	CISG-online 156	**29** 9

Gericht, Datum	Fundstelle	Art. Rn.
CA Grenoble, 26.4.1995	CISG-online 153	1 75; 3 12; 8 36
CA Grenoble, 26.4.1995	CISG-online 154	3 12; 25 47; 49 7
CA Grenoble, 13.9.1995	CISG-online 157	1 72; 4 6, 38; 6 22; 8 15; 9 8; 35 17, 29; 39 17
CA Grenoble, 15.5.1996	CISG-online 219	35 49; 45 10
CA Grenoble, 23.10.1996	CISG-online 305 = 1527	57 31
CA Grenoble, 4.2.1999	CISG-online 443; TranspR-IHR 1999, 43	25 67; 63 1; 64 15, 19
CA Grenoble, 21.10.1999	CISG-online 574	8 44; 18 9; 25 37
CA Grenoble, 28.11.2004	CISG-online 787	78 27
CA Lyon, 18.9.2008	CISG-online 2209	84 12
CA Mons, 8.3.2001	CISG-online 605	35 51; 45 10
CA Paris, 22.4.1992	CISG-online 222	1 46, 75; 4 8, 9; 23 1
CA Paris, 10.11.1993	CISG-online 80; J. C. P. 1994, II, 22314	57 23
CA Paris, 6.4.1995	CISG-online 139	84 13
CA Paris, 13.12.1995	CISG-online 312	Vor 14–24 10; 14 37, 59; 18 4, 8a, 13; 29 7, 8
CA Paris, 15.10.1997	CISG-online 293	6 7
CA Paris, 14.1.1998	CISG-online 347; D. Somm. 1998, 288	1 34, 71; 7 55; 57 31; 81 23, 24, 27
CA Paris, 4.3.1998	CISG-online 535	31 89
CA Paris, 18.3.1998	CISG-online 533	31 89; 46 45
CA Paris, 14.6.2001	CISG-online 693	3 15; 49 32
CA Paris, 6.11.2001	CISG-online 677	Vor 1–6 24; 6 7, 22, 38; 39 17; 40 5
CA Paris, 10.9.2003	CISG-online 788	4 9; 18 4; 24 38
CA Paris, 4.6.2004	CISG-online 872	25 55
CA Paris, 18.11.2009	CISG-online 2237	14 9
CA Paris, 7.10.2009	CISG-online 2034	39 26
CA Poitiers, 26.2.2009	CISG-online 2208	Vor 1–6 22; 1 77; 74 8
CA Rennes, 27.5.2008	CISG-online 1746	18 7a, 7c; 19 8a; 26 8; 49 7
CA Rouen, 2.5.1979	Gaz. Pal. 1980, I, Somm. 81	31 94, 96
CA Rouen, 19.12.2006	CISG-online 1933	4 10
CA Rouen, 19.12.2007	CISG-online 1933	35 14; 39 22, 23; 40 4, 5
CA Versailles, 11.7.1985	Juris Data 042231	35 42
CA Versailles, 29.1.1998	CISG-online 337	25 45, 46; 39 17; 47 6
CA Versailles, 13.10.2005	CISG-online 1433	4 34
Trib. com. Besançon, 19.2.1998	CISG-online 557	79 1, 40
Trib. com. Poitiers, 9.12.1996	CISG-online 221	25 37
Trib. de Grande Instance Versailles, 23.11.2004	CISG-online 953	42 17
Trib. de Grande Instance de Strasbourg, 22.12.2006	CISG-online 1629	63 8; 64 15

Griechenland

Court of Appeals of Piraeus, 520/2008	CISG Pace	2 12
Polimeles Protodikio Athinon, 2282/2009	CISG Pace	6 7
Polimeles Protodikio Athinon, 4505/2009	CISG-online 2228	Vor 1–6 34; 1 48; 2 7; 4 35; 6 7, 18, 22; 7 9, 43, 47; 26 6a; 35 7, 12, 47, 52; 39 29, 37; 74 49, 50

Anh. VI

Gericht, Datum	Fundstelle	Art. Rn.
Monomeles Protodikio Athinon, 8161/2009	CISG-online 2294	**39** 17
Monomeles Protodikio Thessalonikis, 16319/2007	CISG-online 2295	**23** 7
Monomeles Protodikio Thessalonikis, 43945/2007	CISG Pace	**4** 39

Parteien	Gericht, Datum	Fundstelle	Art. Rn.
Israel			
Harlow & Jones Ltd. v. Adras	**Oberster Gerichtshof Israels,** 10.10.1982	Schlechtriem/Magnus, Art. 84 EKG, Nr. 1	**49** 27; **76** 3
Pamesa Ceramica v. Yisrael Mendelson Ltd.	**Oberster Gerichtshof Israels,** 17.3.2009	CISG-online 1980	**39** 28; **40** 2, 5; **74** 14, 35

Gericht, Datum	Fundstelle	Art. Rn.
Italien		
Cass., 24.6.1968	Riv. dir. int priv. proc. 1969, 914	**7** 9
Cass., 13.1.1978	Schlechtriem/Magnus, Art. 19 EKG, Nr. 1	**31** 90
Cass., 9.6.1995	CISG-online 314	**57** 23
Cass., 7.8.1998	CISG-online 538	**8** 51
Cass., 14.12.1999	Giust. Civ. 2000, 2333; CISG-online 1317;	**1** 31
Cass., 19.6.2000	CLOUT No. 647	Vor **1–6** 3; **6** 5; **31** 82; **57** 23
Cass., 18.10.2002	Nr. 14837 (unveröffentlicht)	Vor **1–6** 34
Cass., 20.4.2004	CISG-online 927	Vor **1–6** 34
Cass., 27.9.2006	CISG-online 1393; ZEuP 2008, 165	**57** 25
Cass., 13.10.2006	CISG-online 1404	Vor **14–24** 4
Cass., 5.10.2009	CISG-online 2105	Vor **1–6** 34; **1** 75
Cass., 3.11.2009	CISG-online 2004	**82** 25
CA Genova, 24.3.1995	CISG-online 315	**9** 26; **53** 36
CA Milano, 20.3.1998	CISG-online 348	**8** 51; **25** 30, 39; **26** 10; **49** 5
CA Milano, 12.10.1998	CISG-online 413	**78** 27
CA Milano, 11.12.1998	CISG-online 430	**7** 49; **63** 8
Trib. Busto Arsizio, 13.12.2001	CISG-online 1323; Riv. dir. int. priv. proc. 2003, 150	**25** 23; **49** 32
Trib. Cuneo, 31.1.1996	CISG-online 268	**7** 17, 18; **39** 17; **25** 8, 13
Trib. Forlì, 11.12.2008	Case No n.2280/2007; CISG-online 1729 = 1788	Vor **1–6** 34; **1** 12, 13, 34, 39, 40, 45, 46, 61; **6** 7, 15, 18; **7** 12, 17, 18; **10** 2; **25** 15, 18, 29, 37, 47, 51, 68; **49** 2; **84** 15
Trib. Forlì, 16.2.2009	CISG-online 1780	Vor **1–6** 34; **1** 13, 34, 39, 48; **3** 17; **6** 7, 18; **7** 9, 12, 17, 18; **46** 7
Trib. Forlì, 26.9.2009	CISG-online 2336	**39** 11, 17
Trib. Modena, 9.12.2005	CISG-online 1398	Vor **1–6** 7; **1** 73, 75; **7** 9, 43
Trib. Monza, 29.3.1993	CISG-online 102	**1** 72; **79** 30, 31

Anh. VI

VI. Entscheidungsregister

Gericht, Datum	Fundstelle	Art. Rn.
Trib. Padova, 25.2.2004	CISG-online 819; IHR 2005, 31	**Vor 1–6** 34; **1** 13, 34, 40, 71; **4** 6, 34, 35, 38; **6** 26; **7** 9, 10, 12, 13, 14, 17, 18, 24, 48, 49, 50, 52, 56; **59** 3
Trib. Padova, 31.3.2004	CISG-online 823; IHR 2005, 33	**Vor 1–6** 34; **7** 18, 52; **58** 5; **59** 2; **63** 3, 5
Trib. Padova, 11.1.2005	CISG-online 967	**Vor 1–6** 34; **1** 12, 13, 34, 45; **6** 9, 20, 21, 42, 43; **7** 12, 13, 17, 18, 67; **10** 2; **Vor 89–101** 4
Trib. Padova, 10.1.2006	CISG-online 1157; CLOUT No. 652	**Vor 1–6** 34; **1** 13, 34; **3** 17; **7** 17, 18, 38, 59; **57** 25, 26
Trib. Pavia, 29.12.1999	CISG-online 678; Corr. giur. 2000, 932	**Vor 1–6** 34; **1** 34, 71, 75; **4** 49, 50; **7** 24
Trib. Reggio Emilia, 3.7.2000	CISG-online 771	**31** 90
Trib. Reggio Emilia, 12.4.2011	CISG-online 2229	**1** 71; **7** 17, 18
Trib. Rovereto, 24.8.2006	CISG-online 1374	**8** 53, 54; **14** 33, 37, 40, 74
Trib. Rovereto, 21.12.2007	CISG-online 1590	**Vor 1–6** 34; **7** 17, 18, 49, 54; **14** 40, 42, 43
Trib. Rimini, 26.11.2002	CISG-online 737	**Vor 1–6** 34; **1** 34, 61, 71; **4** 50; **7** 13, 17, 24, 48, 50, 52; **39** 17
Trib. Verona, 17.12.1997	Riv. vr. giur. ec. Impr. 1998, 22	**1** 75
Trib. Vigevano, 12.7.2000	CISG-online 493; IHR 2001, 72	**Vor 1–6** 34; **1** 40, 42, 48, 61, 63, 69, 71; **4** 34, 35, 39, 49, 50, 52; **6** 7, 9, 18, 25, 26; **7** 13; **38** 14; **74** 51; **90** 4
Pretura di Parma-Fidenza, 24.11.1989	CISG-online 316	**25** 18; **49** 17; **84** 12, 12a

Kanada

CA Québec, 12.4.2011	CISG-online 2278	**8** 44
Supreme Court of British Columbia, 21.8.2003	CISG-online 1017	**14** 40
Ontario Superior Court of Justice, 31.8.1999	CISG-online 433	**52** 10
Ontario Superior Court of Justice, 6.10.2003	CISG-online 1436	**Vor 14–24** 30; **25** 39
Ontario Superior Court of Justice, 28.10.2005	CISG-online 1139	**19** 8b; **29** 8
Quebec Superior Court of Justice, 29.7.2005	CISG Pace	**4** 25

Litauen

Lietuvos Apeliacinio teismo Civiliniv, 27.3.2000	CISG-online 1512	**Vor 14–24** 10

Mexiko

Primer Tribunal Colegiado en Materia Civil del Primer Circuito, 10.3.2005	CISG-online 1004	**7** 49; **14** 3; **19** 5
Tribunal de Apelación de Baja California, 24.3.2006	CISG-online 1392	**59** 1
Comisión para la Protección del Comercio Exterior de México, 4.5.1995	CISG-online 75	**Vor 1–6** 22; **1** 77; **11** 13; **95** 2
Comisión para la Protección del Comercio Exterior de México, 29.4.1996	CISG-online 350	**7** 52; **18** 13; **23** 1; **34** 8; **35** 11

Anh. VI

Gericht, Datum	Fundstelle	Art. Rn.
Comisión para la Protección del Comercio Exterior de México, 30.11.1998	CISG-online 504	**6** 10; **7** 26, 49
Juzgado Sexto de Primera Instancia del Partido de Tijuana, Baja California, 14.7.2000	CISG-online 571; IHR 2001, 38	**53** 42; **58** 37, 38
Juzgado Sexto de Primera Instancia del Partido de Tijuana, Baja California, 30.8.2005	CISG-online 1158	**59** 1

Parteien	Gericht, Datum	Fundstelle	Art. Rn.
Neuseeland			
RJ & AM Smallmon v. Transport Sale sand Grant Alan Miller Limited	**High Court New Zealand**, 30.7.2010	CISG-online 2113	**7** 9, 17, 21; **35** 12, 17, 23
RJ & AM Smallmon v. Transport Sales Limited and Grant Alan Miller	**CA New Zealand**, 22.7.2011	CISG-online 2215	**7** 9, 17; **35** 17, 23

Gericht, Datum	Fundstelle	Art. Rn.
Niederlande		
HR, 26.9.1997	CISG-online 286	**1** 71; **31** 90
HR, 7.11.1997	CISG-online 551	**8** 60; **14** 4; **96** 3
HR, 20.2.1998	CISG-online 313; NJB 1998, 566	**1** 71, 81; **39** 6
HR, 28.1.2005	CISG-online 1002	**4** 20, 21; **8** 1, 52, 59; **14** 33
HR, 4.2.2005	CISG-online 1003	**39** 14
HR, 21.5.2010	CISG-online 2096	**6** 22
Gerechtshof Amsterdam, 8.6.1977	Schlechtriem/Magnus, Art. 22 EKG, Nr. 1	**33** 14
Gerechtshof Amsterdam, 16.7.1992	CISG-online 48	**1** 31
Gerechtshof Amsterdam, 20.11.1997	CISG-online 553; NIPR 1998 No 220	**57** 23
Gerechtshof Arnhem, 22.8.1995	CISG-online 317	**1** 34; **4** 40; **8** 30; **74** 58
Gerechtshof Arnhem, 7.5.1996	NIPR 14 (1996), Nr. 397	**6** 22
Gerechtshof Arnhem, 15.4.1997	UNILEX	**74** 26, 30
Gerechtshof Arnhem, 9.2.1999	CISG-online 1338	**7** 49
Gerechtshof Arnhem, 27.4.1999	CISG-online 741	**3** 12, 13; **14** 55; **35** 17; **39** 17
Gerechtshof Arnhem, 21.10.2000	CISG-online 1533	**8** 53a
Gerechtshof Arnhem, 17.4.2004	CISG-online 946	**8** 52
Gerechtshof Arnhem, 21.3.2006	CISG-online 1695	**78** 4a
Gerechtshof Arnhem, 18.7.2006	CISG-online 1266	**39** 37
Gerechtshof Arnhem, 12.9.2006	CISG-online 1736	**2** 41
Gerechtshof Arnhem, 17.1.2007	CISG-online 1476	**8** 5
Gerechtshof Arnhem, 7.10.2008	CISG-online 1749	**8** 9; **47** 5
Gerechtshof Arnhem, 14.10.2008	CISG-online 1818; EJCL 2009, 40	**8** 3; **14** 4
Gerechtshof Arnhem, 9.3.2010	CISG-online 2095	**Einl**; **6** 7; **8** 3, 5
Gerechtshof 's-Gravenhage, 23.4.2003	CISG-online 903	**7** 49; **25** 45, 55; **49** 32
Gerechtshof 's-Gravenhage, 17.2.2009	unveröff.	**2** 7
Gerechtshof 's-Hertogenbosch, 26.2.1992	CISG-online 65	**1** 81; **4** 42; **7** 51
Gerechtshof 's-Hertogenbosch, 26.10.1994	CISG-online 318	**57** 23
Gerechtshof 's-Hertogenbosch, 24.4.1996	CISG-online 321	**9** 8, 18, 19; **14** 73

VI. Entscheidungsregister   Anh. VI

Gericht, Datum	Fundstelle	Art. Rn.
Gerechtshof 's-Hertogenbosch, 19.11.1996	CISG-online 323	1 38; **Vor 14–24** 10; **19** 20, 27
Gerechtshof 's-Hertogenbosch, 5.2.1997	CISG-online 542	**57** 23
Gerechtshof 's-Hertogenbosch, 2.10.1998	CISG-online 1309	**79** 26
Gerechtshof 's-Hertogenbosch, 16.10.2002	CISG-online 816	**14** 33, 40, 41, 42, 44, 59
Gerechtshof 's-Hertogenbosch, 25.2.2003	CISG-online 1834	**19** 8b, 13
Gerechtshof 's-Hertogenbosch, 2.1.2007	CISG-online 1434; CLOUT No. 828	**7** 43; **53** 24
Gerechtshof 's-Hertogenbosch, 29.5.2007	CISG-online 1550	**14** 33, 59
Gerechtshof 's-Hertogenbosch, 13.11.2007	CISG Pace	**6** 22
Gerechtshof 's-Hertogenbosch, 9.3.2010	CISG-online 2341	**8** 5; **38** 15, 22; **39** 16; **78** 27
Gerechtshof 's-Hertogenbosch, 18.1.2011	CISG-online 2179	**1** 12, 13; **4** 20
Gerechtshof Leeuwarden, 3.6.1996	NIPR 14 (1996), Nr. 404	**6** 22
Gerechtshof Leeuwarden, 31.8.2005	CISG-online 1100	**6** 22; **29** 10; **47** 1
RB Alkmaar, 22.7.1982	*Schlechtriem/Magnus*, Art. 19 EKG, Nr. 7	**31** 89
RB Alkmaar, 2.5.1985	*Schlechtriem/Magnus*, Art. 33 EKG, Nr. 19	**35** 28; **74** 25
RB Almelo, 28.1.1998	unveröffentlicht	**4** 4
RB Amsterdam, 17.12.1984	*Schlechtriem/Magnus*, Art. 88, Nr. 6	**77** 10
RB Amsterdam, 5.10.1994	CISG-online 446	**1** 81; **4** 42; **24** 3, 15
RB Amsterdam, 3.6.2009	CISG-online 2065	**Präambel** 7; **7** 17
RB Arnhem, 16.2.1984	*Schlechtriem/Magnus*, Art. 82 EKG, Nr. 29	**74** 20
RB Arnhem, 25.2.1993	CISG-online 98	**1** 81; **4** 39
RB Arnhem, 27.5.1993	CISG-online 99	**Vor 89–101** 10
RB Arnhem, 30.12.1993	CISG-online 104	**1** 81
RB Arnhem, 17.7.1997	CISG-online 548	**36** 3
RB Arnhem, 8.7.1999	CISG-online 1431	**14** 55
RB Arnhem, 17.3.2004	CISG-online 946	**4** 21; **14** 33
RB Arnhem, 1.3.2006	CISG-online 1475	**2** 7; **7** 43; **63** 1
RB Arnhem, 28.6.2006	CISG-online 1265	**1** 38; **3** 5; **6** 7, 22
RB Arnhem, 17.1.2007	CISG-online 1455	**1** 65; **7** 52; **Vor 14–24** 10; **14** 33, 70
RB Arnhem, 14.11.2007	unveröffentlicht	**4** 15
RB Arnhem, 5.11.2008	CISG-online 1751	**2** 7; **11** 11
RB Arnhem, 11.2.2009	CISG online 1813	**27** 4, 6
RB Arnhem, 29.7.2009	CISG-online 1939	**7** 17; **25** 15, 69; **27** 4, 9; **49** 28, 31; **58** 27, 31; **71** 9
RB Breda, 27.2.2008	CISG-online 2252	**7** 5, 9; **9** 25; **14** 33, 51
RB Breda, 16.1.2009	CISG-online 1789	**6** 7; **78** 27
RB Den Haag, 17.9.1982	*Schlechtriem/Magnus*, Art. 74 EKG, Nr. 6	**79** 23
RB Dordrecht, 21.11.1990	CISG-online 16	**1** 81
RB Dordrecht, 19.3.2008	CISG-online 1698	**Vor 89–101** 10
RB 's-Gravenhage, 7.6.1995	CISG-online 369	**1** 72; **6** 22
RB Harleem, 15.12.2005	CISG-online 1696	**2** 12
RB Harleem, 3.12.2008	CISG-online 1816	**1** 73
RB Middelburg, 25.1.1995	CISG-online 374	**4** 39
RB Middelburg, 1.12.1999	NIPR 18 (2000), Nr. 188	**4** 42

Anh. VI

Gericht, Datum	Fundstelle	Art. Rn.
RB Middelburg, 2.4.2008	CISG-online 1737	2 41; 6 22
RB Kortrijk, 27.6.1997	CISG-online 529	57 23
RB Roermond, 19.12.1991	CISG-online 29	1 81; 38 14; 40 12
RB Roermond, 6.5.1993	CISG-online 454	1 73; 4 39; 74 26
RB Rotterdam, 21.11.1996	CISG-online 541	82 5
RB Rotterdam, 14.10.1999	CISG-online 1312	8 53a; 14 44, 59
RB Rotterdam, 12.7.2001	CISG-online 968	18 9; 29 5
RB Rotterdam, 1.11.2001	NIPR 2001, Nr. 114	1 13
RB Rotterdam, 15.10.2008	CISG-online 1899	74 30
RB Rotterdam, 5.11.2008	CISG-online 1817	6 22
RB Rotterdam, 25.2.2009	CISG-online 1812; EJCL 2009, 105	7 17, 49; Vor 14–24 14b; 14 40, 61
RB Rotterdam, 3.2.2010	CISG-online 2097	6 22
RB Rotterdam, 17.3.2010	CISG-online 2098	7 43; 78 27
RB Rotterdam, 2.6.2010	CISG-online 2098	39 28
RB Rotterdam, 13.10.2010	CISG-online 2297	Vor 14–24 14b
RB Rotterdam, 29.12.2010	CISG-online 2180	6 7
RB Utrecht, 1.8.2001	CISG-online 2299; NJ 2002, 157	Vor 14–24 51
RB Utrecht, 21.1.2009	CISG-online 1814	7 17; 8 53; Vor 14–24 10; 14 37, 40, 55, 61
RB Utrecht, 15.4.2009	CISG Pace	6 15
RB Zutphen, 29.5.1997	CISG-online 546	4 20; Vor 14–24 3; 14 33
RB Zutphen, 27.2.2008	CISG-online 1692	39 16; 74 30
RB Zwolle, 1.3.1995	CISG-online 372	42 29; Vor 14–24 4; 14 33
RB Zwolle, 5.3.1997	CISG-online 545	7 49
RB Zwolle, 22.1.2003	CISG-online 1023	8 52
RB Zwolle, 21.5.2003	IHR 2005, 34	6 18; 14 33
RB Zwolle, 9.12.2009	CISG-online 2069	7 43; 8 52; 35 17

Österreich

Gericht, Datum	Fundstelle	Art. Rn.
OGH, 26.6.1974	östJBl. 1975, 89	9 24
OGH, 3.11.1981	SZ 54/152	42 1
OGH, 12.6.1986	ZfRV 1988, 126, 130	Vor 14–24 30c
OGH, 7.6.1990	CISG-online 13	19 23
OGH, 28.4.1993	CISG-online 100	9 24; Vor 14–24 21
OGH, 22.12.1993	Ecolex 1994, 316	9 24
OGH, 27.10.1994	CISG-online 133	3 8, 9, 12
OGH, 10.11.1994	CISG-online 117; IPRax 1996, 137	1 12, 34, 40, 46; 6 7; 8 47, 51; 14 9, 12; 53 9; 55 10; 57 15
OGH, 24.10.1995	CISG-online 166	1 18; 4 35
OGH, 6.2.1996	CISG-online 224; RdW 1996, 203	2 46; 4 9, 15; 8 44, 52, 53, 54; 9 8, 16; 11 15; 14 9, 33, 36, 37, 38, 48, 68, 70, 71, 73; 19 5; 26 2, 6, 8, 10, 14; 29 6; 41 4, 16a; 45 23, 26; 49 23, 24; 53 18; 54 5, 6, 8; 74 55, 56; 77 7, 12; 80 3
OGH, 15.1.1997	IPRax 1998, 294	14 38
OGH, 11.2.1997	CISG-online 298	2 8; 6 7
OGH, 20.3.1997	CISG-online 269	Vor 1–6 5; 1 63, 71; 4 34; 8 6, 22, 47; 19 8b; 26 9; 51 6
OGH, 24.4.1997	CISG-online 291	4 37; 8 5

VI. Entscheidungsregister   Anh. VI

Gericht, Datum	Fundstelle	Art. Rn.
OGH, 18.6.1997	CISG-online 292	**8** 14; **14** 4, **18** 4
OGH, 12.2.1998	CISG-online 349	**1** 72; **6** 22; **71** 11, 17, 25a; **73** 28
OGH, 10.3.1998	CISG-online 356; östZRVgl 1998, 161	**6** 28; **57** 31
OGH, 26.5.1998	ZfRVgl 2000, 77	**4** 35, 38
OGH, 25.6.1998	CISG-online 352	**3 VertragsG** 1, 2
OGH, 30.6.1998	CISG-online 410	**27** 4, 7, 9, 13; **39** 11, 16,34
OGH, 10.9.1998	CISG-online 409	**1** 63; **8** 40; **31** 76, 92
OGH, 10.9.1998	CISG-online 646	**31** 90, 92
OGH, 15.10.1998	CISG-online 380	**Vor 1–6** 3; **1** 3, 40; **4** 26; **6** 5; **8** 54; **9** 5, 6, 7, 10, 12, 14, 16, 19, 20; **27** 5; **38** 15; **39** 11, 15, 17, 33; **44** 6, 7
OGH, 11.3.1999	CISG-online 524	**35** 25
OGH, 19.5.1999	CISG-online 484	**39** 22
OGH, 29.6.1999	CISG-online 483	**4** 41; **7** 55; **25** 29; **29** 4, 13; **35** 10; **Vor 81–84** 5; **81** 9, 9c, 17; **82** 13, 18
OGH, 27.8.1999	CISG-online 485	**Vor 1–6** 3; **6** 5; **38** 13; **39** 17
OGH, 9.3.2000	CISG-online 573	**1** 63; **6** 7; **7** 52; **8** 60; **19** 8a; **74** 3
OGH, 21.3.2000	CISG-online 641	**Vor 1–6** 3; **4** 27; **6** 5; **9** 5, 6, 7, 10, 12, 14, 16, 19, 20; **14** 73; **39** 16
OGH, 13.4.2000	CISG-online 576	**4** 6; **35** 17, 46
OGH, 28.4.2000	CISG-online 581; IHR 2001, 206	**49** 23, 27; **64** 34; **74** 55; **75** 12
OGH, 7.9.2000	CISG-online 642	**4** 13, 20, 35, 38; **7** 54; **25** 25; **46** 48; **49** 7, 49
OGH, 5.7.2001	CISG-online 652; ZfRVgl 2002, 25	**25** 48; **39** 33
OGH, 7.9.2001	CISG-online 642	**4** 13, 20, 35, 38; **7** 54; **Vor 14–24** 3; **25** 10; **46** 48; **49** 7, 49
OGH, 13.9.2001	CISG-online 644	**19** 22
OGH, 22.10.2001	CISG-online 613	**4** 9, 15, 17, 34, 35, 39, 41
OGH, 22.10.2001	CISG-online 614	**4** 3; **6** 18, 22, 29; **53** 8; **61** 19
OGH, 14.1.2002	CISG-online 643	**3** 15; **4** 35; **7** 52; **38** 15,16, 18, 20; **39** 6, 7, 17; **74** 3, 49, 50, 52
OGH, 17.4.2002	CISG-online 1020	**44** 4, 5
OGH, 18.12.2002	CISG-online 1279	**Vor 1–6** 34; **7** 47; **Vor 14–24** 7; **57** 30
OGH, 27.2.2003	CISG-online 794; IHR 2004, 25	**9** 20, 21; **35** 16, 17, 25; **40** 5
OGH, 17.12.2003	CISG-online 828	**1** 64; **6** 1, 7, 18; **8** 41, 52, 53, 54a; **14** 33, 36, 38, 61, 63, 64, 65, 66, 68
OGH, 29.3.2004	CISG-online 926	**57** 29
OGH, 21.4.2004	CISG-online 1048	**3** 5; **6** 22
OGH, 14.12.2004	CISG-online 1018	**57** 25
OGH, 26.1.2005	CISG-online 1045	**6** 7, 22
OGH, 23.5.2005	CISG-online 1041	**Vor 1–6** 34; **7** 9, 30; **50** 6, 13

Anh. VI

Gericht, Datum	Fundstelle	Art. Rn.
OGH, 24.5.2005	CISG-online 1046	**6** 7; **27** 4, 9, 10; **39** 11, 37
OGH, 21.6.2005	CISG-online 1047; IHR 2005, 195	**1** 38; **6** 7; **25** 21, 23, 27, 29, 30; **51** 4
OGH, 31.8.2005	CISG-online 1093	**1** 64; **8** 52; **14** 33, 36, 37, 38, 44, 62, 68, 69, 70, 71; **18** 7a; **93** 4
OGH, 8.9.2005	CISG-online 1901	**57** 25
OGH, 8.11.2005	CISG-online 1156; IHR 2006, 87	**Vor 1–6** 24; **1** 73; **3** 5, 13, 15, 17, 18; **4** 45a; **6** 7; **7** 55; **45** 22; **58** 27; **Vor 85–88** 6
OGH, 29.11.2005	CISG-online 1227	**14** 39, 45, 62
OGH, 25.1.2006	CISG-online 1223	**35** 17
OGH, 12.9.2006	CISG-online 1364	**4** 50, 51, 52; **7** 56; **35** 51; **42** 4, 6, 11, 27, 29
OGH, 30.11.2006	CISG-online 1417	**4** 45a; **7** 55
OGH, 19.4.2007	CISG-online 1495	**35** 17
OGH, 4.7.2007	CISG-online 1560	**6** 17, 18, 21
OGH, 19.12.2007	CISG-online 1628	**39** 22, 23, 34
OGH, 3.4.2008	CISG-online 1680; IHR 2008, 188	**57** 25
OGH, 6.11.2008	CISG-online 1833	**8** 54a; **Vor 14–24** 14; **14** 61, 62, 63
OGH, 2.4.2009	CISG-online 1889	**6** 15, 18, 21, 22; **39** 17, 33
OGH, 22.4.2010	CISG-online 2296	**74** 10, 56
OGH, 31.8.2010	CISG-online 2236; 4 Ob 98/10f; IHR 2011, 85, 87	**39** 6, 8, 16, 17; **51** 2
OGH, 22.11.2011	CISG-online 2239; IHR 2012, 114	**25** 47, 47, 51; **49** 5; **80** 3, 8
OGH, 14.2.2012	CISG-online 2308	**40** 2, 12
OLG Graz, 9.11.1995	CISG-online 308	**9** 18; **50** 8, 9, 15
OLG Graz, 24.2.1999	CISG-online 797	**Vor 14–24** 2; **14** 10; **29** 13
OLG Graz, 28.9.2000	CISG-online 798	**1** 31; **6** 22; **49** 5, 24
OLG Graz, 24.1.2002	CISG-online 801	**64** 32
OLG Graz, 7.3.2002	CISG-online 669	**1** 15; **9** 24; **Vor 14–24** 21; **14** 70
OLG Graz, 16.9.2002	CISG-online 1198	**27** 4; **88** 9
OLG Graz, 29.7.2004	CISG-online 1627	**1** 46, 59; **Vor 14–24** 30a; **26** 7, 10; **64** 32
OLG Wien, 1.6.2004	CISG-online 954	**3** 13; **57** 31
OLG Innsbruck, 1.7.1994	CISG-online 107	**4** 52; **35** 51; **36** 13; **45** 22
OLG Innsbruck, 1.2.2005	CISG-online 1130	**8** 36, 52, 54a; **14** 65, 66, 68, 69; **93** 4
OLG Innsbruck, 18.12.2007	CISG-online 1735	**3** 5, 7, 14, 15; **6** 7; **29** 14, 19
OLG Linz, 23.3.2005	CISG-online 1376	**Vor 1–6** 5; **4** 20, 21, 39; **6** 22; **8** 52; **Vor 14–24** 3; **18** 7a; **19** 9, 10, 19, 21; **25** 25
OLG Linz, 1.6.2005	CISG-online 1088	**38** 15
OLG Linz, 8.8.2005	CISG-online 1087	**4** 35; **6** 7, 18, 22; **8** 53, 54a; **14** 45, 62, 65, 66, 68, 69, 71
OLG Linz, 23.1.2006	CISG-online 1377	**6** 8, 18, 19, 20, 21, 22, 26, 31, 38; **Vor 14–24** 14c
OLG Linz, 24.9.2007	CISG-online 1583	**3** 5; **6** 7; **39** 22, 23, 24

VI. Entscheidungsregister   Anh. VI

Gericht, Datum	Fundstelle	Art. Rn.
LG Salzburg, 2.2.2005	CISG-online 1189	**7** 17
BezG Wien, 20.2.1993	CISG-online 53	**7** 13
HGer Wien, 4.3.1997	CISG-online 743	**Vor 1–6** 3; **6** 5

Polen

Supreme Court of Poland, 19.12.2003	CISG-online 1222	**4** 6, 38
Supreme Court of Poland, 27.1.2006	CISG-online 1399	**1** 31; **26** 10; **75** 12
Supreme Court of Poland, 11.5.2007	CISG-online 1790	**7** 17, 47; **25** 21, 22

Russland

Supreme Arbitration Court, 16.12.2009	CISG-online 2339	**26** 17
Federal Arbitration Court for the Moscow Region, 26.5.2003	CISG-online 836	**1** 30
Federal Arbitration Court for the Western Siberia Circuit, 6.8.2002	CISG-online 2282	**71** 22a

Parteien	Gericht, Datum	Fundstelle	Art. Rn.
Schottland			
Philip & Co. v. Knoblauch	**Court of Sessions,** 1907	Session Cases, 994	**14** 30

Gericht, Datum	Fundstelle	Art. Rn.
Schweiz		
BGer, 28.1.1924	BGE 50 II 13	**18** 15
BGer, 2.2.1954	BGE 80 II 26	**14** 30
BGer, 14.2.1956	BGE 82 II 238	**42** 1
BGer, 18.4.1958	BGE 84 II 158	**Vor 66–70** 18, 19
BGer, 7.6.1988	BGE 114 II 131	**45** 32
BGer, 27.10.1988	BGE 114 II 250	**9** 24
BGer, 24.9.1990	BGE 116 II 436	**47** 9
BGer, 5.12.1995	BGE 121 III 453	**38** 7
BGer, 18.1.1996	CISG-online 214; BGE 122 III 43	**57** 9, 23; **58** 6
BGer, 15.1.1997	BGE 123 III 16	**45** 16
BGer, 28.10.1998	CISG-online 413	**7** 54; **25** 51, 52; **49** 7; **74** 56, 65; **78** 27
BGer, 11.7.2000	CISG-online 627	**1** 63; **4** 33
BGer, 15.9.2000	CISG-online 770	**Vor 1–6** 7, 31; **4** 3, 6, 8; **25** 15, 19, 22, 24, 29, 32, 39, 40, 47; **33** 9, 13; **47** 6; **49** 24, 27
BGer, 22.12.2000	CISG-online 628	**4** 4, 15; **8** 26; **35** 7
BGer, 19.8.2002	http://www.bger.ch	**45** 2, 16, 28
BezG, 28.5.2002	CISG-online 676	**39** 6; **49** 24
BGer, 4.8.2003	CISG-online 804	**8** 5, 24; **14** 4
BGer, 13.11.2003	CISG-online 840; BGE 130 III 258	**60** 2
BGer, 19.2.2004	CISG-online 839	**4** 3
BGer, 7.7.2004	CISG-online 848	**4** 39, 50, 51, 52; **7** 56; **35** 51; **45** 10
BGer, 13.11.2004	CISG-online 840	**45** 9
BGer, 5.4.2005	CISG-online 1012	**8** 12, 21, 23, 36, 60; **9** 22; **18** 7a; **19** 8a, 8b
BGer, 12.6.2006	CISG-online 1516	**79** 37

Anh. VI

Gericht, Datum	Fundstelle	Art. Rn.
BGer, 20.12.2006	CISG-online 1426; IHR 2007, 127; SZIER 2008, 173; ZEuP 2008, 318, 333	**4** 39; **6** 7; **49** 20; **61** 19; **71** 28
BGer, 17.7.2007	CISG-online 1515	**6** 22
BGer, 13.11.2007	CISG-online 1618	**25** 44; **49** 13
BGer, 16.12.2008	CISG-online 1800	**1** 75; **2** 7
BGer, 18.5.2009	CISG-online 1900; IHR 2010, 27	**4** 35; **25** 45, 48, 51, 54, 56; **49** 7, 31, 35; **82** 25
BGer, 16.12.2009	CISG-online 2047; IHR 2010, 258	**25** 12
BGer, 17.12.2009	CISG-online 2022	**45** 23; **75** 13; **77** 10
BGer, 16.9.2010	CISG-online 2220	**1** 71
BGer, 17.4.2012	CISG-online 2346	**42** 6, 29
BGer, 16.7.2012	CISG-online 2371; BGE 138 III 601	**35** 52
HGer Aargau, 26.9.1997	CISG-online 329	**25** 15, 68; **58** 5; **59** 1
HGer Aargau, 19.12.1997	CISG-online 418	**74** 30
HGer Aargau, 11.6.1999	CISG-online 494	**4** 34; **50** 16
HGer Aargau, 5.11.2002	CISG-online 715	**3** 5; **7** 17; **25** 47, 48; **48** 15, 26; **49** 8
HGer Aargau, 25.1.2005	CISG-online 1091; IHR 2006, 34	**1** 24; **3** 5; **53** 8
HGer Aargau, 19.6.2007	CISG-online 1741	**1** 63
HGer Aargau, 20.9.2007	CISG-online 1742	**1** 34; **6** 7, 12
HGer Aargau, 5.2.2008	CISG-online 1740	**8** 3, 6, 19, 46, 50
HGer Aargau, 5.2.2008	CISG-online 1739	**4** 6, 17, 38; **8** 3, 61
HGer Aargau, 10.3.2010	CISG-online 2176; SZIER 2011, 551	**1** 13, 15, 31, 34, 63; **3** 5; **4** 15; **6** 12, 18, 31; **7** 55; **47** 1; **71** 3
HGer Bern, 30.10.2001	CISG-online 734	**39** 29
HGer Bern, 17.1.2002	CISG-online 725	**39** 29
HGer St. Gallen, 24.8.1995	CISG-online 247	**4** 4, 9
HGer St. Gallen, 5.12.1995	CISG-online 245	**14** 4
HGer St. Gallen, 3.12.2002	CISG-online 727; SZIER 2003, 107; IHR 2003, 181	**3** 5; **6** 7, 22; **26** 6; **63** 8, 14; **64** 20, 34; **Vor 81–84** 11; **81** 9, 11, 16
HGer St. Gallen, 11.2.2003	CISG-online 960	**39** 17
HGer St. Gallen, 29.4.2004	CISG-online 962; SZIER 2005, 115	**1** 24; **3** 5; **58** 5
HGer St. Gallen, 15.6.2010	CISG-online 2159; IHR 2011, 149	**8** 2, 55; **Vor 14–24** 14b, 14c; **18** 7a; **19** 8a
HGer Zürich, 9.9.1993	CISG-online 79	**1** 81; **3** 5; **4** 49, 50; **7** 56
HGer Zürich, 26.4.1995	CISG-online 248	**1** 31; **3** 12, 17; **4** 33, 40, 50, 52; **5** 3, 9, 11, 12; **7** 56; **25** 47
HGer Zürich, 21.9.1995	CISG-online 246	**39** 17; **74** 16
HGer Zürich, 10.7.1996	CISG-online 227	**14** 13; **18** 7a; **19** 8a; **29** 7, 8, 10; **74** 25; **78** 27
HGer Zürich, 5.2.1997	CISG-online 327	**73** 23a; **74** 26; **84** 13, 15a
HGer Zürich, 21.9.1998	CISG-online 416	**39** 7
HGer Zürich, 30.11.1998	CISG-online 415	**Vor 1–6** 34; **1** 15, 71; **4** 34, 41; **8** 29; **35** 32, 49; **38** 14; **39** 17

VI. Entscheidungsregister   **Anh. VI**

Gericht, Datum	Fundstelle	Art. Rn.
HGer Zürich, 10.2.1999	CISG-online 488	**3** 10; **4** 45, 52; **8** 61; **31** 10, 32; **33** 13; **45** 28; **50** 8; **79** 7; **74** 55, 38, 44; **79** 38
HGer Zürich, 8.4.1999	CISG-online 489	**1** 31
HGer Zürich, 17.2.2000	CISG-online 637	**3** 13
HGer Zürich, 9.7.2002	CISG-online 727	**3** 5, 18; **6** 22
HGer Zürich, 24.10.2003	CISG-online 857	**4** 45; **6** 7; **7** 17; **8** 5, 40, 44; **9** 8, 10; **25** 68; **29** 6
HGer Zürich, 22.12.2005	CISG-online 1195	**4** 39, 52; **6** 7
HGer Zürich, 25.6.2007	CISG-online 1564; IHR 2008, 31	**3** 5; **25** 39
HGer Zürich, 25.10.2007	CISG-online 1564; SZIER 2008, 180	**45** 16; **48** 15; **49** 5, 24, 25
HGer Zürich, 25.6.2010	CISG-online 2161	**1** 24; **3** 5; **4** 50; **8** 3, 21, 53a, 61
HGer Zürich, 22.11.2010	CISG-online 2160; IHR 2011, 151	**1** 15; **25** 37; **73** 22; **74** 5, 30, 36, 65
AppGer Basel-Stadt, 22.8.2003	CISG-online 943; IHR 2005, 117	**1** 71; **25** 45; **35** 32
AppGer Basel-Stadt, 26.9.2008	CISG-online 1732; IHR 2009, 164	**4** 35, 39; **8** 19, 21, 36; **82** 25
AppGer Tessin, 10.2.1996	CISG-online 233	**4** 34; **78** 27
AppGer Tessin, 8.6.1999	CISG-online 497	**39** 34
AppGer Tessin, 15.12.1999	CISG-online 422	**1** 28
AppGer Tessin, 29.10.2003	CISG-online 912	**3** 17; **8** 19; **79** 35
Cour de Justice Genève, 10.10.1997	CISG-online 295	**1** 71; **39** 29
Cour de Justice Genève, 9.10.1998	CISG-online 424	**2** 35
Cour de Justice Genève, 13.9.2002	CISG-online 722	**Vor 14–24** 22; **18** 17
Cour de Justice Genève, 15.11.2002	CISG-online 853	**4** 3, 52; **50** 4, 6
Cour de Justice Genève, 19.9.2003	CISG-online 854	**59** 1
Cour de Justice Genève, 20.1.2006	CISG-online 1504	**3** 5; **4** 50, 51
OGer Aargau, 3.3.2009	CISG-online 2013	**Vor 1–6** 34; **1** 24, 34, 35, 63; **2** 7; **3** 5, 13, 14, 18; **6** 18, 21, 22; **41** 4
OGer Bern, 11.2.2004	CISG-online 1191	**4** 49, 50, 52; **7** 52; **27** 4; **38** 8
OGer Bern, 19.5.2008	CISG-online 1738	**6** 5, 18; **Vor 14–24** 10; **14** 33, 40, 60; **29** 8
OGer Luzern, 8.1.1997	CISG-online 228	**1** 31, 32; **3** 12; **39** 17
OGer Luzern, 12.5.2003	CISG-online 846; ZBJV 2004, 704	**35** 51; **39** 17; **79** 56
OGer Thurgau, 19.12.1995	CISG-online 496	**4** 38, 39; **8** 1, 5, 30; **14** 4, 24
OGer Thurgau, 11.9.2003	CISG-online 1810	**Vor 1–6** 34
OGer Thurgau, 12.12.2006	CISG-online 1566	**7** 41, 43
OGer Zug, 24.3.1998	CISG-online 897	**35** 49; **38** 14
OGer Zug, 5.7.2005	CISG-online 1155	**8** 30
OGer Zug, 21.6.2004	IHR 2006, 112	**1** 71
OGer Zug, 16.12.2006	CISG-online 1565	**Vor 1–6** 24; **3** 5
OGer Zug, 19.12.2006	CISG-online 1427	**3** 13, 15, 17; **49** 7
KG Aargau, 20.9.2007	CISG-online 1742	**3** 5; **6** 22
KG Appenzell Ausserrhoden, 10.3.2003	CISG-online 852; IHR 2004, 254	**58** 29
KG Appenzell Ausserrhoden, 9.3.2006	CISG-online 1375	**7** 17, 21; **39** 17; **78** 17
KG Basel-Land, 5.10.1999	CISG-online 492	**Vor 14–24** 22; **29** 6, 9
KG Bern-Laupen, 29.1.1999	CISG-online 701	**1** 72, 76; **3** 13, 14, 15

Anh. VI

Gericht, Datum	Fundstelle	Art. Rn.
KG Glarus, 6.11.2008	CISG-online 1996; IHR 2010, 152; SZIER 2011, 563	25 57; 35 13, 14; 39 17; 51 6
KG Freiburg, 11.10.2004	CISG-online 964	8 19; Vor 14–24 21; 14 19; 18 7, 13, 16; 19 11
KG Jura, 3.11.2004	CISG-online 965	Vor 1–6 34; 1 46, 75; 2 8, 17; 6 5, 17, 18, 19, 20, 22; Vor 14–24 2; 14 4, 42, 59
KG Jura, 26.7.2007	CISG-online 1723; SZIER 2008, 192	49 7
KG Nidwalden, 5.6.1996	CISG-online 332	2 7
KG Nidwalden, 3.12.1997	CISG-online 331	1 71; 6 25
KG Nidwalden, 23.5.2005	CISG-online 1086; IHR 2005, 253	Vor 1–6 7; 1 75; 4 3, 35, 50, 52, 53; 7 56; Vor 14–24 12; 35 52; 53 21, 42; 78 8
KG Obwalden, 16.8.2005	CISG-online 1727	1 75
KG Schaffhausen, 25.2.2002	CISG-online 723	1 12, 13; 3 17
KG Schaffhausen, 20.10.2003	CISG-online 957	Vor 1–6 7, 34; 4 3
KG Schaffhausen, 13.11.2003	CISG Pace	4 50, 52
KG Schaffhausen, 27.1.2004	CISG-online 960	1 24; 3 5; 25 58; 38 14; 60 2
KG St. Gallen, 12.8.1997	CISG-online 330; CLOUT No. 216	58 16
KG St. Gallen, 3.12.2002	CISG-online 727	1 71; 6 18
KG St. Gallen, 11.2.2003	CISG-online 900	38 17
KG St. Gallen, 13.5.2008	CISG-online 1768; IHR 2009, 161	4 25; Vor 14–24 36
KG St. Gallen, 15.6.2010	CISG-online 2159	1 24; 3 5; 6 7, 15
KG Waadt, 14.3.1993	CISG-online 84	Vor 89–100 10
KG Waadt, 6.12.1993	CISG-online 457	1 75
KG Waadt, 29.6.1994	CISG-online 134	Vor 1–6 5; 1 63; 6 5
KG Waadt, 17.5.1994	CISG-online 122	85 12
KG Waadt, 11.3.1996	CISG-online 333	1 12, 13
KG Waadt, 30.6.1998	CISG-online 419	4 41
KG Waadt, 26.5.2000	SZIER 2002, 146	31 32
KG Waadt, 11.4.2002	CISG-online 899	2 5; 6 5
KG Waadt, 24.11.2004	CISG-online 1842	6 5
KG Wallis, 29.6.1994	CISG-online 134	Vor 1–6 3
KG Wallis, 20.12.1994	CISG-online 302; CLOUT No. 197	59 1
KG Wallis, 28.10.1997	CISG-online 328	35 34, 35
KG Wallis, 29.6.1998	CISG-online 420	33 15
KG Wallis, 30.6.1998	CISG-online 419	53 6, 9
KG Wallis, 2.12.2002	CISG-online 733	64 6
KG Wallis, 3.8.2003	CISG-online 895	1 46; 4 41
KG Wallis, 19.8.2003	CISG-online 895	53 6
KG Wallis, 21.2.2005	CISG-online 1193	Vor 1–6 5; 1 63; 4 33; 6 7; 25 35, 45; 39 7; 49 7
KG Wallis, 27.5.2005	CISG-online 1137	4 16, 50; 53 6
KG Wallis, 23.5.2006	CISG-online 1532	1 44, 46; 10 2; 53 4, 6
KG Wallis, 27.10.2006	CISG-online 1563	1 13, 75; 4 41; 53 4, 6, 9
KG Wallis, 27.4.2007	CISG-online 1721; SZIER 2008, 184	4 17, 34, 41; 7 43; 49 7; 53 4, 6; 55 5, 14, 15; 58 1
KG Wallis, 28.1.2009	CISG-online 2025	4 9, 15, 50, 52; 9 26; 14 25, 73; 18 7a; 19 8a; 25 28; 29 2, 9, 14, 19, 20; 30 14; 45 10; 47 6; 49 20, 23; 51 6; 74 26, 64

VI. Entscheidungsregister   Anh. VI

Gericht, Datum	Fundstelle	Art. Rn.
KG Zug, 15.12.1994	SZIER 1997, 134	**74** 20
KG Zug, 16.3.1995	CISG-online 230	**6** 22
KG Zug, 30.11.1995	CISG-online 856	**88** 1
KG Zug, 16.10.1997	CISG-online 335	**1** 71; **53** 23
KG Zug, 25.2.1999	CISG-online 490	**3** 12, 13, 15
KG Zug, 21.10.1999	CISG-online 491	**1** 13, 34; **76** 2
KG Zug, 12.12.2002	CISG-online 720	**64** 6
KG Zug, 11.12.2003	CISG-online 958	**6** 18, 22; **Vor 14–24** 11, 13; **14** 33, 59, 60; **19** 9; **29** 7, 8
KG Zug, 21.6.2004	CISG-online 1213	**8** 61
KG Zug, 2.12.2004	CISG-online 1194; IHR 2006, 158	**8** 61; **58** 5, 35
KG Zug, 30.8.2007	CISG-online 1722; SZIER 2008, 187	**25** 50, 52; **49** 24
KG Zug, 13.5.2008	CISG-online 1768	**53** 32
KG Zug, 27.11.2008	CISG-online 2024	**6** 7; **74** 30
KG Zug, 14.12.2009	CISG-online 2026	**1** 24; **3** 5, 13, 14, 18; **Vor 14–24** 2, 12, 20, 21, 22; **25** 49; **26** 8; **29** 2, 9, 14, 19, 20; **45** 10; **47** 6; **49** 20, 23; **51** 6; **74** 37, 40, 64, 65; **81** 21, 22
ZGer Basel-Stadt, 21.12.1992	CISG-online 55	**1** 81; **4** 9, 15; **9** 19, 22, 23, 24; **11** 6; **Vor 14–24** 21
ZGer Basel-Stadt, 3.12.1997	CISG-online 346; CLOUT No. 221; TranspR-IHR 1999, 11; SZIER 1999, 190	**57** 6, 9
ZGer Basel-Stadt, 8.11.2006	CISG-online 1731; SZIER 2011, 450	**3** 17; **47** 6
AG Sursee, 12.9.2008	CISG-online 1728; IHR 2009, 63	**1** 19, 63, 71; **4** 3, 9, 34; **7** 43; **9** 4, 8, 20, 21; **14** 70; **29** 2, 11, 13, 33; **45** 17; **81** 23; **84** 17
AG Willisau, 12.3.2004	CISG-online 961	**78** 17; **79** 1, 56
BezG Arbon, 9.12.1994	CISG-online 376	**4** 6, 38
BezG Laufen, 7.5.1993	CISG-online 136	**Vor 1–6** 7, 16, 31; **1** 75, 76, 81; **3** 12; **4** 3, 8; **7** 9
BezG Saane, 20.2.1997	CISG-online 426	**54** 5; **64** 10, 21; **74** 65
BezG Sissach, 5.11.1998	CISG-online 1466	**Vor 1–6** 34; **7** 41
BezG St. Gallen, 3.7.1997	CISG-online 336; SZIER 1998, 84	**1** 71; **8** 51; **14** 19, 21; **53** 4, 8; **55** 5, 6, 14
BezG Weinfelden, 23.11.1998	CISG-online 428	**6** 22
KreisG St. Gallen, 16.10.2009	CISG-online 2023	**11** 11; **18** 4
Pretore della giurisdizione di Locarno-Campagna, 16.12.1991	CISG-online 27	**1** 81; **9** 2
Pretore della giurisdizione di Locarno-Campagna, 27.4.1992	CISG-online 68	**1** 71; **7** 18, 55
Pretore del Distretto di Lugano, 19.4.2007	CISG-online 1724; SZIER 2008, 193	**25** 46; **49** 31

Serbien

High Commercial Court, 19.12.2006	CLOUT 916	**1** 12, 13
High Commercial Court, 22.4.2008	CISG-online 1990	**1** 31, 48

Anh. VI

Parteien	Gericht, Datum	Fundstelle	Art. Rn.
Singapur			
Chwee Kin Keong and Others v. Digilandmall.com Pte. Ltd.	High Ct. Sing., 12.4.2004	CISG-online 1641	Vor 14–24 25

Gericht, Datum	Fundstelle	Art. Rn.
Slowakische Republik		
Supreme Court Slovak Republic, 30.4.2008	CISG-online 1873	4 35; 8 44
Supreme Court Slovak Republic, 19.6.2008	CISG-online 1875	Vor 1–6 22
Supreme Court Slovak Republic, 12.12.2008	CISG-online 1955	Vor 1–6 22
Najvyšší súd Slovenskej republiky, 19.6.2008	CISG-online 1875	18 8a, 9; 19 8b; 29 6, 8
Krajský súd Košiciach, 22.5.2007	CISG-online 1898	4 6, 38; 29 10
Krajský súd Košiciach, 28.5.2007	CISG-online 1950	25 12
Krajský súd Zilina, 29.3.2004	CISG-online 1857	78 27
Krajský súd Žiline, 25.10.2007	CISG-online 1761	25 58
Krajský súd Nitra, 27.6.2006	CISG-online 1861	78 27
Krajský súd Bratislava, 15.12.2005	CISG-online 1754	78 29
Krajský súd Bratislava, 1.2.2007	CISG-online 1758	78 29
Krajský súd Bratislava, 10.7.2007	CISG-online 1828	6 25
Okresný súd Nitra, 27.2.2006	CISG-online 1755	18 4
Regional Court Nitra, 15.10.2008	CISG-online 1877	Vor 1–6 22
Regional Court Nitra, 3.11.2008	CISG-online 1954	39 17
Dist. Ct. Brezno, 24.6.2008	CISG-online 2198	Vor 1–6 22
Dist. Ct. Brezno, 21.7.2009	CISG-online 2195	Vor 1–6 22
Dist. Ct. Nitra, 29.6.2006	CISG-online 1757	61 9
Dist. Ct. Nitra, 29.5.2008	CISG-online 1766	Vor 1–6 22; 4 9
Dist. Ct. Nitra, 29.10.2008	CISG-online 2213	Vor 1–6 22
Dist. Ct. Nitra, 15.1.2009	CISG-online 2212	Vor 1–6 22
Dist. Ct. Dolny Kubin, 21.1.2008	CISG-online 1762	58 21
Dist. Ct. Dolny Kubin, 17.6.2008	CISG-online 1874	Vor 1–6 22
Dist. Ct. Dolny Kubin, 24.11.2008	CISG-online 1879	Vor 1–6 22
Dist. Ct. Dolny Kubin, 1.4.2010	CISG-online 2192	Vor 1–6 22
Dist. Ct. Komarno, 24.2.2009	CISG-online 1992	Vor 1–6 22; 39 16, 77
Slowenien		
OGer Ljubljana, 14.12.2005	CISG-online 1959	85 16a; 87 9
BerufungsG Lujubljana, 9.4.2008	CISG-online 2238; EJCL 2010, 143	16 4
Spanien		
Tribunal Supremo, 17.2.1998	CISG-online 1333	Vor 14–24 10, 11
Tribunal Supremo, 28.1.2000	CISG-online 503	18 4; 29 6, 7; 77 8
Tribunal Supremo, 9.12.2008	CISG-online 2100	Vor 1–6 22; 1 77
Audiencia Provincial de Barcelona, 20.6.1997	CISG-online 338	74 46, 51
Audiencia Provincial de Barcelona, 12.2.2002	CISG-online 1324	25 60, 61; 49 11
Audiencia Provincial de Barcelona, 11.3.2002	CISG-online 1325	85 12
Audiencia Provincial de Barcelona, 27.11.2003	CISG-online 1102; CLOUT No. 556	55 1
Audiencia Provincial de Barcelona, 28.4.2004	CISG-online 931	25 45

VI. Entscheidungsregister   Anh. VI

Gericht, Datum	Fundstelle	Art. Rn.
Audiencia Provincial de Barcelona, 24.3.2009	CISG-online 2042	25 62; 35 15; 39 11, 14, 16, 37
Audiencia Provincial de Cáceres, 14.7.2010	CISG-online 2131	8 17
Audiencia Provincial de Cuenca, 31.1.2005	CISG-online 1241	78 10
Audiencia Provincial de Granada, 2.3.2000	CISG-online 756	1 77
Audiencia Provincial de La Coruña, 21.6.2002	CISG-online 1049	39 17
Audiencia Provincial de Córdoba, 31.10.1997	CISG-online 502	67 10
Audiencia Provincial de Madrid, 20.2.2007	CISG-online 1637	8 26; 25 21, 28, 45
Audiencia Provincial de Madrid, 10.3.2009	CISG-online 2084	8 1
Audiencia Provincial de Madrid, 14.7.2009	CISG-online 2087	Vor 1–6 22; 1 77
Audiencia Provincial de Murcia, 15.7.2010	CISG-online 2130	14 31a, 31b
Audiencia Provincial de Navarra, 23.7.1999	CISG-online 1342	57 23
Audiencia Provincial de Navarra, 27.3.2000	CISG-online 575; CLOUT No. 397	58 27
Audiencia Provincial de Navarra, 27.12.2007	CISG-online 1798	7 49; 8 1
Audiencia Provincial de Pontevedra, 19.12.2007	CISG-online 1688	7 43
Audiencia Provincial de Valencia, 7.6.2003	CISG-online 948	7 4, 17; 35 51
Audiencia Provincial de Valencia, 31.3.2005	CISG-online 1369	75 5
Audiencia Provincial de Valencia, 13.3.2007	CISG-online 1719	4 35; 6 7
Audiencia Provincial de Valencia, 8.4.2008	CISG-online 2083	78 17
Audiencia Provinciale de Zaragoza, 31.3.2009	CISG-online 2085	7 17
Juzgado de primera instancia e instrucción de Tudela, 29.3.2005	CISG-online 1016	49 15

Tschechien

Oberster Gerichtshof Tschechien, 29.3.2006	CISG-online 1747	35 12

Ungarn

Legfelsóbb Biróság, 25.9.1992	CISG-online 63; 1993 J. L. & Com., 31	55 17
Szegedi Ítéltábla, 22.11.2007	CISG-online 1937	3 5; 78 27
Appellationsgericht Szeged, 5.12.2008	CISG-online 1938	39 6, 17
Fovárosi Biróság Budapest, 10.1.1992	CISG-online 43	23 1, 4
Fovárosi Biróság Budapest, 24.3.1992	CISG-online 61; CLOUT No. 52; IPRax 1993, 263	9 8; 12 2, 3; 14 8, 9, 21; 53 5; 55 4; 96 3
Fovárosi Biróság Budapest, 19.3.1996	CISG-online 289	1 31
Fovárosi Biróság Budapest, 21.5.1996	CISG-online 252	Vor 1–6 16; 1 65; 92 3
Fovárosi Biróság Budapest, 1.7.1997	CISG-online 309	8 6

Anh. VI

Gericht, Datum	Fundstelle	Art. Rn.
Fovárosi Biróság Budapest, 17.6.1997	CISG-online 288	Vor 14–24 38, 41
Dist. Ct. Galanta, 15.12.2006	CISG-online 1863	7 43
Dist. Ct. Namestovo, 13.7.2010	CISG-online 2189	Vor 1–6 22; 1 77
Dist. Ct. Trnava, 17.9.2008	CISG-online 1991	Vor 1–6 22; 4 6, 38
Dist. Ct. Trnava, 17.11.2008	CISG-online 2136	Vor 1–6 22
Dist. Ct. Trnava, 17.12.2008	CISG-online 2203	Vor 1–6 22
Dist. Ct. Trnava, 20.10.2010	CISG-online 2188	Vor 1–6 22
Dist. Ct. Trnava, 9.3.2011	CISG-online 2210	Vor 1–6 22; 1 77
Dist. Ct. Trnava, 13.5.2011	CISG-online 2191	Vor 1–6 22; 1 77
Dist. Ct. Trnava, 19.5.2011	CISG-online 2190	Vor 1–6 22; 1 77
Dist. Ct. Zvolen, 5.11.2009	CISG-online 2194	Vor 1–6 22

Parteien	Gericht, Datum	Fundstelle	Art. Rn.
USA			
Snepp v. United States	U. S. Sup. Ct., 19.2.1980	444 U. S. 507	74 43
Delchi Carrier S. p. A. v. Rotorex Corp.	U. S. Ct. App. (2nd Cir.), 6.12.1995	CISG-online 140	Vor 1–6 22; 1 16, 77; 6 18; 7 9, 10; 25 45, 46, 58; 35 25; 74 27, 36, 37, 47; 75 11; 95 2; 75 12
Valero Marketing & Supply Company v. Greeni Trading Oy	U. S. Ct. App. (3rd Cir.), 19.7.2007	CISG-online 1510; IHR 2008, 35	7 19; 29 7, 9; 47 3, 14
Forestal Guarani S. A. v. Daros International, Inc.	U. S. Ct. App. (3rd Cir.), 21.7.2010	CISG-online 2112	Vor 1–6 33; 1 77; 7 5, 9, 19, 30; 12 2; 29 4; 96 3
T & S Brass & Bronze Works, Inc. v. Pic-Air, Inc.	U. S. Ct. App. (4th Cir.), 12.5.1986	1 UCC Rep. 2d 433	48 12
Schmitz-Werke GmbH & Co. v. Rockland Industries, Inc.	U. S. Ct. App. (4th Cir.), 21.6.2002	CISG-online 625	Vor 1–6 22; 1 77; 7 10, 30; 35 49; 95 2
Beijing Metals & Minerals Import/Export Corp. v. American Business Center, Inc.	U. S. Ct. App. (5th Cir.), 15.6.1993	CISG-online 89	Vor 1–6 22; 8 32; 11 13, 32; Vor 14–24 36
BP International Ltd. and BP Exploration & Oil Inc. v. Empresa Estatal Petroleos de Ecuador and Saybolt Inc.	U. S. Ct. App. (5th Cir.), 11.6.2003	CISG-online 730; US App. LEXIS 12013	6 18; 9 26; 14 73; 60 8, 9
Zapata Hermanos Sucesores, S. A. Hearthside v. Baking Co., Inc.	U. S. Ct. App. (7th Cir.), 19.11.2002	CISG-online 684	Einl; Präambel 6; 74 28
Chicago Prime Packers, Inc. v. Northam Food Trading Co.	U. S. Ct. App. (7th Cir.), 23.5.2005	CISG-online 1026	Vor 1–6 24; 7 10; 35 51; 45 10
Dingxi Longhai Dairy Ltd. v. Becwood Technology Group L. L. C.	U. S. Ct. App. (8th Cir.), 14.2.2011	CISG-online 2256	73 22
GPL Treatment Ltd. v. Louisiana-Pacific Corp.	U. S. Ct. App. (9th Cir.), 12.4.1995	CISG-online 147	11 13
Chateau de Charmes Wines Ltd. v. Sabate USA Inc.	U. S. Ct. App. (9th Cir.), 5.5.2003	CISG-online 767; IHR 2003, 295	8 5, 50; Vor 14–24 10, 11; 14 51, 59; 18 8a; 29 7, 8

VI. Entscheidungsregister   Anh. VI

Parteien	Gericht, Datum	Fundstelle	Art. Rn.
Chateau de Charmes Wines Ltd. v. Sabate USA Inc.	U. S. Ct. App. (9th Cir.), 10.11.2003	CISG-online 809	8 5, 50; **Vor 14–24** 10, 11; **14** 51, 59; **18** 8a; **29** 7, 8; **95** 2
MCC-Marble Ceramic Center, Inc. v. Ceramica Nuova D'Agostino S. p. A.	U. S. Ct. App. (11th Cir.), 29.6.1998	CISG-online 342	**1** 71; **7** 10; **8** 10, 12, 32, 33, 35, 40, 42, 44, 54; **11** 13; **14** 62, 63, 68
Treibacher Industrie, AG v. Allegheny Technologies, Inc.	U. S. Ct. App. (11th Cir.), 12.9.2006	CISG-online 1278	**8** 40, 40a, 44; **9** 3, 6, 14; **77** 12
American Biophysics v. Dubois Marine Specialties, a/k/a Dubois Motor Sports	U. S. Dist. Ct. (D. R. I.), 30.1.2006	CISG-online 1176	**6** 22
Allied Semi-Conductors international Ltd. v. Pulsar Components International, Inc.	U. S. Dist. Ct. (E. D. N. Y.), 17.12.1993	842 F. Supp. 653	**48** 4
Interag Company Ltd. v. Stafford Phase Corporation	U. S. Dist. Ct. (S. D. N. Y.), 22.5.1990	CISG-online 18	**50** 1
Filanto, S. p. A. v. Chilewich Internat. Corp.	U. S. Dist. Ct. (S. D. N. Y.), 14.4.1992	CISG-online 45	**Vor 1–6** 22; **1** 77; **4** 40; **8** 32, 36, 38, 51; **11** 13; **Vor 14–24** 10, 15; **18** 9; **19**
S. V. Braun Inc. v. Alitalia-Linee Aeree Italiana S. p. A.	U. S. Dist. Ct. (S. D. N. Y.), 6.4.1994	CISG-online 112	**Vor 1–6** 22; **1** 77; **50** 2; **95** 2
Graves Import Co. Ltd. et al. v. Chilewich Int'l Corp.	U. S. Dist. Ct. (S. D. N. Y.), 22.9.1994	CISG-online 128	**29** 19
Helen Kaminski Pty. Ltd. v. Marketing Austrialian Products Inc.	U. S. Dist. Ct. (S. D. N. Y.), 21.7.1997	CISG-online 297; CLOUT No. 187	**1** 31, 71; **6** 18; **7** 18; **Vor 14–24** 41; **54** 8; **61** 18; **64** 9
Calzaturificio Claudia S. N. C. v. Olivieri Footwear Ltd.	U. S. Dist. Ct. (S. D. N. Y.), 6.4.1998	CISG-online 440	**7** 10; **8** 32, 33, 44, 60; **11** 13; **Vor 14–24** 22; **19** 8a
Fercus S. r. l. v. Mario Palazzo and others	U. S. Dist. Ct. (S. D. N. Y.), 8.8.2000	CISG-online 588	**11** 13
St. Paul Guardian Insurance Company and Travelers Insurance Company, as subrogees of Shared Imaging, Inc. v. Neuromed Medical Systems & Support GmbH, et al.	U. S. Dist. Ct. (S. D. N. Y.), 26.3.2002	CISG-online 615; 2002 US Dist. LEXIS, 5096	**4** 29, 34; **6** 18; **7** 9, 11, 15, 17; **9** 26; **14** 73; **53** 36; **Vor 66–70** 16
Geneva Pharmaceuticals Technology Corp. v. Barr Laboratories, Inc.	U. S. Dist. Ct. (S. D. N. Y.), 10.5.2002	CISG-online 653; 201 F. Supp. 2d 236	**Präambel** 7; **4** 15; **5** 12; **Vor 14–24** 37; **14** 5, 9, 10; **16** 1, 11, 13, 14; **18** 18, 22; **60** 8, 9
Genpharm Inc. v. Pliva-Lachema A. S., Pliva d. d.	U. S. Dist. Ct. (N. D. N. Y.), 19.3.2005	CISG-online 1006	**Vor 1–6** 24; **7** 9, 10, 30; **Vor 14–24** 41
Multi-Juice, S. A. v. Snapple Beverage Corp.	U. S. Dist. Ct. (S. D. N. Y.), 1.6.2006	CISG-online 1229	**7** 19
TeeVee Toons, Inc. (d/b/a TVT Records) & Steve Gottlieb, Inc. (d/b/a Biobox) v. Gerhard Schubert GmbH	U. S. Dist. Ct. (S. D. N. Y.), 23.8.2006	CISG-online 1272	**Einl**; **1** 77; **2** 5; **3** 13, 15; **4** 25, 53; **6** 12, 18; **7** 19a, 24; **8** 32, 35; **Vor 14–24** 36; **14** 45; **29** 17, 20; **39** 17; **74** 46; **95** 2

Anh. VI

Parteien	Gericht, Datum	Fundstelle	Art. Rn.
Cedar Petrochemicals, Inc. v. Dongbu Hannong Chemical Co., Ltd.	U. S. Dist. Ct. (S. D. N. Y.), 19.7.2007	CISG-online 1509	**1** 77; **4** 10; **6** 18; **10** 5; **95** 2; **7** 9, 10
Macromex Srl. v. Globex International, Inc.	U. S. Dist. Ct. (S. D. N. Y.), 16.4.2008	CISG-online 1653	
Hilaturas Miel, S. L. v. Republic of Iraq	U. S. Dist. Ct. (S. D. N. Y.), 20.8.2008	CISG-online 1777; 573 F. Supp. 2d 781	**7** 9, 10; **Vor 14–24** 30; **25** 12
Doolim Corp. v. R Doll L. L. C. et al.	U. S. Dist. Ct. (S. D. N. Y.), 29.5.2009	CISG-online 1892	**2** 5; **6** 21; **25** 66; **71** 16, 46
Guangxi Nanning Baiyang Food Co. Ltd. v. Long River International, Inc.	U. S. Dist. Ct. (S. D. N. Y.), 30.3.2010	CISG-online 2091	**Vor 1–6** 22
Ho Myung Moolsan, Co. Ltd. v. Manitou Mineral Water, Inc.	U. S. Dist. Ct. (S. D. N. Y.), 2.12.2010	CISG-online 2170	**6** 18, 25
Hanwha Corporation v. Cedar Petrochemicals, Inc.	U. S. Dist. Ct. (S. D. N. Y.), 18.1.2011	CISG-online 2178	**Vor 1–6** 22; **1** 77; **6** 18; **14** 24; **18** 7a; **19** 8a, 9, 15, 23; **95** 2
Cedar Petrochemicals, Inc. v. Dongbu Hannong Chemical Co., Ltd.	U. S. Dist. Ct. (S. D. N. Y.), 28.9.2011	CISG-online 2338	Einl; **1** 77; **4** 10; **6** 18; **10** 5; **95** 2
Solae, L. L. C. v. Hershey Canada, Inc.	U. S. Dist. Ct. (D. Del.), 9.5.2008	CISG-online 1769; IHR 2007, 240	**11** 12; **19** 27
Forestal Guarani S. A. v. Daros International, Inc.	U. S. Dist. Ct. (D. N. J.), 7.12.2008	CISG-online 1779	**6** 7, 18; **96** 3
Valero Marketing & Supply Company v. Greeni Oy	U. S. Dist. Ct. (D. N. J.), 15.6.2005	CISG-online 1028	**6** 18; **Vor 14–24** 45
Valero Marketing & Supply Company v. Greeni; Oy & Greeni Trading Oy	U. S. Dist. Ct. (D. N. J.), 4.4.2006	CISG-online 1216	**25** 39, 40; **49** 5
Forestal Guarani S. A. v. Daros International, Inc.	U. S. Dist. Ct. (D. N. J.), 7.8.2008	CISG-online 1779	**12** 2
San Lucio, S. r. I et al. v. Import & Storage Services, L. L. C. et al.	U. S. Dist. Ct. (D. N. J.), 15.4.2009	CISG-online 1836	**7** 43, 52; **78** 27
Viva Vino Import v. Farnese Vini	U. S. Dist. Ct. (E. D. Pa.), 29.8.2000	CISG-online 675	**1** 31; **Vor 14–24** 41; **74** 7
Amco Ukrservice & Promriladamco v. American Meter Company	U. S. Dist. Ct. (E. D. Pa.), 29.3.2004	CISG-online 1409	**Vor 14–24** 41
Amco Ukrservice & Promriladamco v. American Meter Company	U. S. Dist. Ct. (E. D. Pa.), 29.3.2004	CISG-online 1664	**1** 28, 31
ECEM European Chemical Marketing B. V. v. The Purolite Company	U. S. Dist. Ct. (E. D. Pa.), 29.1.2010	CISG-online 2090	**1** 40; **8** 32
Traynor v. Walters	U. S. Dist. Ct. (M. D. Pa.), 15.5.1972	10 UCC Rep. 967	**48** 4

VI. Entscheidungsregister   Anh. VI

Parteien	Gericht, Datum	Fundstelle	Art. Rn.
American Mint L. L. C. v. GOSoftware, Inc.	U. S. Dist. Ct. (M. D. Pa.), 16.8.2005	CISG-online 1104	Vor 1–6 24; 1 48; 6 18; 4 10; 6 7, 22
American Mint LLC v. GO-Software, Inc.,	U. S. Dist. Ct. (M. D. Pa.), 6.1.2006	CISG-online 1175	1 38; 10 5
Norfolk Southern Railway Company v. Power Source Supply, Inc.	U. S. Dist. Ct. (W. D. Pa.), 25.7.2008	CISG-online 1776	8 3; 19 21, 22; 29 4, 7; 35 12; 78 27, 32, 45
MSS, Inc. v. Maser Corporation	U. S. Dist. Ct. (D. Md.), 18.7.2011	CISG-online 2222	4 9, 15
Gruppo Essenziero Italiano, S. p. A. v. Aromi D'Italia, Inc.	U. S. Dist. Ct. (D. Md.), 27.7.2011	CISG-online 2223	1 31; 5 12; Vor 14–24 41
CSS Antenna, Inc. v. Amphenol-Tuchel Electronics GmbH	U. S. Dist. Ct. (D. Md.), 8.2.2011	CISG-online 2177	Vor 1–6 22; 1 77; 8 52, 53, 53a; Vor 14–24 10; 14 37; 19 8a; 29 8; 95 2
Medical Marketing International Inc. v. Internazionale Medico Scientifica S. r. l.	U. S. Dist. Ct. (E. D. La.), 17.5.1999	CISG-online 387	7 5, 17; Vor 14–24 41; 25 55; 35 17; 82 19
China North Chemical Industries Corp. v. Beston Chemical Corp.	U. S. Dist. Ct. (S. D. Tex.), 7.2.2006	CISG-online 1177	Vor 1–6 22; 9 26; 14 73; Vor 66–70 23
Sky Cast, Inc. v. Global Direct Distribution, L. L. C.	U. S. Dist. Ct. (E. D. Ky.), 18.3.2008	CISG-online 1652; IHR 2009, 24	Einl; 1 63; Vor 14–24 37
Easom Automation Systems, Inc. v. Thyssenkrupp Fabco Corp.	U. S. Dist. Ct. (E. D. Mich.), 28.9.2007	CISG-online 1601; IHR 2008, 34	6 18, 22; 18 5
Key Safety Systems, Inc. v. Invista, S. A. R. L., L. L. C.	U. S. Dist. Ct. (E. D. Mich.), 16.9.2008	CISG-online 1778	17 2
Shuttle Packaging Systems, L. L. C. v. Jacob Tsonakis, INA S. A. and INA Plastics Corporation	U. S. Dist. Ct. (W. D. Mich.), 17.12.2001	CISG-online 773	25 66; 29 4, 6; 39 17; 58 28; 64 6
Victoria Alloys, Inc. V. Fortis Bank SA/NV,	U. S. Dist. Ct. (N. D. Ohio), 10.4.2004	CISG-online 589	4 30
Miami Valley Paper, L. L. C. v. Lebbing Eng'g GmbH	U. S. Dist. Ct. (S. D. Ohio), 26.3.2009	CISG-online 1880	4 25; 8 32; 11 12; 49 7
Miami Valley Paper, L. L. C. v. Lebbing Eng'g GmbH	U. S. Dist. Ct. (S. D. Ohio), 10.10.2006	CISG-online 1362	Einl; 4 25; Vor 14–24 36, 37; 35 47; 74 46
Mitchell Aircraft Spares Inc. v. European Aircraft Service AB	U. S. Dist. Ct. (N. D. Ill.), 28.10.1998	CISG-online 444	Vor 1–6 16; 1 71, 77; 8 32; 79 16; 92 3; 95 2
Magellan International Corp. v. Salzgitter Handel GmbH	U. S. Dist. Ct. (N. D. Ill.), 7.12.1999	CISG-online 439	Vor 1–6 22; 1 77; 8 47; 18 7a, 8; 19 8a, 28; 25 64; 28 2; 95 2

Anh. VI

Parteien	Gericht, Datum	Fundstelle	Art. Rn.
Zapata Hermanos Sucsores, S. A. v. Hearthside Baking Co., Inc.	U. S. Dist. Ct. (N. D. Ill.), 28.8.2001	CISG-online 599	**Einl**; **8** 32; **78** 27, 31
Zapata Hermanos Sucsores, S. A. v. Hearthside Banking Co., Inc.	U. S. Dist. Ct. (N. D. Ill.), 13.3.2002	CISG-online 663	**Einl**
Usinor Industeel v. Leeco Steel Products, Inc.	U. S. Dist. Ct. (N. D. Ill.), 28.3.2002	CISG-online 696 = 1326	**Vor 1–6** 24; **4** 10, 29, 30; **7** 17; **81** 11
Ajax Tool Works, Inc. v. Can-Eng Manufacturing Ltd.	U. S. Dist. Ct. (N. D. Ill.), 29.1.2003	CISG-online 772	**Vor 1–6** 22; **1** 77; **6** 18, 20, 22; **74** 20; **95** 2
Chicago Prime Packers, Inc. v. Northam Food Trading Co., et al.	U. S. Dist. Ct. (N. D. Ill.), 21.5.2004	CISG-online 851; IHR 2004, 156	**7** 17, 24; **38** 14; **78** 27, 32
Raw Materials Inc. v. Manfred Forberich GmbH & Co. KG	U. S. Dist. Ct. (N. D. Ill.), 6.7.2004	CISG-online 925	**7** 10; **29** 4, 6, 9; **7**; **95** 2
Caterpillar, Inc. and Caterpillar Mexico, S. A. v. Usinor Industeel, Usinor Industeel (U. S. A.), Inc. and Leeco Steel Products, Inc.	U. S. Dist. Ct. (N. D. Ill.), 30.3.2005	CISG-online 1007	**7** 51
CAN Int'l Inc. v. Guangdong Kelon Electronical Holdings et al.	U. S. Dist. Ct. (N. D. Ill.), 3.9.2008	CISG-online 2043	**1** 64; **7** 17; **93** 4
Electrocraft Arkansas, Inc. v. Super Electric Motors, Ltd. et al.	U. S. Dist. Ct. (E. D. Ark.), 23.12.2009	CISG-online 2045	**Einl**; **1** 64, 77; **4** 25; **5** 12; **35** 47; **93** 4; **95** 2
Electrocraft Arkansas, Inc. v. Super Electric Motors, Ltd. et al.	U. S. Dist. Ct. (E. D. Ark.), 2.4.2010	CISG-online 2093	**Vor 1–6** 22
Electrocraft Arkansas, Inc. v. Super Electric Motors, Ltd. et al.	U. S. Dist. Ct. (E. D. Ark.), 19.8.2010	CISG-online 2149	**1** 64; **93** 4
Klif et al. v. Grace Label, Inc.	U. S. Dist. Ct. (S. D. Iowa), 25.1.2005	CISG-online 1666	**1** 40
KSTP-FM, L. L. C. v. Specialized Communications, Inc. and Adtronics Signs, Ltd.	U. S. Dist. Ct. (D. Minn.), 9.3.1999	CISG-online 471	**Vor 1–6** 22; **1** 77; **95** 2
Travelers Property Casualty Company of America et al. v. Saint-Gobain Technical Fabrics Canada Ltd.	U. S. Dist. Ct. (D. Minn.), 31.1.2007	CISG-online 1435; IHR 2007, 240	**6** 7, 18, 22; **7** 10; **14** 33; **19** 27
BTC-USA Corp. v. Novacare et al.	U. S. Dist. Ct. (D. Minn.), 16.6.2008	CISG-online 1773	**Vor 14–24** 10; **29** 2, 8, 9
Dingxi Longhai Dairy, Ltd. v. Becwood Technology Group, L. L. C.	U. S. Dist. Ct. (D. Minn.), 1.7.2008	CISG-online 1774	**Vor 14–24** 36
Semi-Materials Co., Ltd. v. MEMC Electronic Materials, Inc.	U. S. Dist. Ct. (E. D. Mo.), 10.1.2010	CISG-online 2168	**74** 41; **76** 14

VI. Entscheidungsregister   Anh. VI

Parteien	Gericht, Datum	Fundstelle	Art. Rn.
Semi-Materials Co., Ltd. v. MEMC Electronic Materials, Inc.	U. S. Dist. Ct. (E. D. Mo.), 10.1.2010	CISG-online 2169	Vor 1–6 22; 1 77
Golden Valley Grape Juice and Wine, LLC v. Centrisys Corp. et al.	U. S. Dist. Ct. (E. D. Cal.), 21.1.2010	CISG-online 2089	1 77; 4 9, 40; 6 18; Vor 14–24 10; 14 44, 75; 18 2, 7a, 95 2
Supermicro Computer Inc. v. Digitechnic, S. A.	U. S. Dist. Ct. (N. D. Cal.), 30.1.2001	CISG-online 612	8 12
Asante Technologies, Inc. v. PMC-Sierra, Inc.	U. S. Dist. Ct. (N. D. Cal.), 27.7.2001	CISG-online 616	Präambel 7; Vor 1–6 24; 1 40; 4 13; 6 18, 21, 22; 10 8
McDowell Valley Vineyards, Inc. v. Sabaté USA Inc. et al.	U. S. Dist. Ct. (N. D. Cal.), 2.11.2005	CISG Pace	Vor 1–6 34; 10 7
Barbara Berry, S. A. de C. V. v. Ken M. Spooner Farms	U. S. Dist. Ct. (W. D. Wash.), 13.4.2006	CISG-online 1354	4 15, 16; 7 17; 8 52; 9 24; Vor 14–24 3, 21; 18 7a
Prime Start Ltd. v. Maher Forest Products Ltd. et al.	U. S. Dist. Ct. (W. D. Wash.), 17.7.2006	CISG-online 1242	1 80
Guang Dong Light Headgear Factory Co., Ltd. v. ACI International, Inc.	U. S. Dist. Ct. (D. Kan.), 28.9.2007	CISG-online 1602	14 4
Guang Dong Light Headgear Factory Co., Ltd. v. ACI Intern., Inc.	U. S. Dist. Ct. (D. Kan.), 28.4.2008	CISG-online 1682	78 27
Belcher-Robinson, L. L. C. v. Linamar Corporation, et al.	U. S. Dist. Ct. (M. D. Ala.), 31.3.2010	CISG-online 2092	Vor 1–6 22; 1 77; Vor 14–24 10; 19 8a, 9, 18
Treibacher Industrie, AG v. TDY Industries, Inc.	U. S. Dist. Ct. (N. D. Ala.), 27.4.2005	CISG-online 1178	4 25; 58 5; 78 27
Impuls I. D. Internacional, S. L., Impuls I. D. Systems, Inc., and PSIAR, S. A. v. Psion-Teklogix Inc.	U. S. Dist. Ct. (S. D. Fla.), 22.11.2002	CISG-online 783	1 51, 77
Zhejiang Shaoxing Yongli Printing and Dyeing Co. v. Microflock Textile Group Corp.	U. S. Dist. Ct. (S. D. Fla.), 19.5.2008	CISG-online 1771	Vor 1–6 22; 4 9; 6 7; 12 2; 18 7a; 96 3
Innotex Precision Limited v. Horei Image Products, Inc., et al.	U. S. Dist. Ct. (N. D. Ga.), 17.12.2009	CISG-online 2044	1 64; 7 17; 93 4
In re: Siskiyou Evergreen, Inc. Debtor	U. S. Bankr. D. Or., 29.3.2004	CISG-online 1174	7 17; 39 6
In re: East Coast Brokers & Packers, Inc.	U. S. Bankr. M. D. Fla., 12.10.1990	14 UCC 2d 461	49 32
A. C. Carpenter, Inc. v. Boyer Potato Chips	U. S. Dept. Agric., 2.12.1969	7 UCC Rep. Serv. 493	38 16
Orbisphere Corp. v. United States	Ct. Int'l Trade, 24.10.1989	CISG-online 7	6 1, 18; 7 10

Anh. VI

Parteien	Gericht, Datum	Fundstelle	Art. Rn.
Pasta Zara S. p. A. v. United States, American Italian Pasta Company, et al.	Ct. Int'l Trade, 7.4.2010	CISG-online 2094	Vor 1–6 22; 1 77
C9 Ventures v. SVC West L. P.	Cal. App. 4 Dist., 27.1.2012	CISG-online 2307	14 51; 29 8
Ricklefs v. Clemens	Supr. Ct. Kann., 25.1.1975	16 UCC Rep. Serv. 322	41 7
Vision Systems, Inc. v. EMC Corporation	Supr. Ct. Mass., 28.2.2005	CISG-online 1005	1 40; 10 11
American Container, Corp. v. Hanley Trucking Corp.	N. J. Super. Ct., 31.7.1970	7 UCC Rep. Serv. 1301	41 7
Dejesus v. Cat Auto Tech. Corp.	N. Y. Ct. Cl., 23.5.1994	23 UCC Rep. 2d 755	48 17

Parteien	Jahr	Fundstelle	Art. Rn.
Vereinigtes Königreich (ohne Schottland)			
Attorney-General v. Blake	2000	[2001] 1 A. C. 268 (H. L.)	74 43
A. V. Pound & Co. Ltd. v. M. W. Hardy & Co. Inc.	1956	[1956] A. C. 588	31 85
Brauer & Co. (Great Britain) Ltd. v. James Clark (Brush) Materials Ltd.	1952	[1952] 2 All E. R. 497	79 14
Cehave N. V. v. Bremer Handelsgesellschaft m. b. H. (The Hansa Nord)	1976	[1976] Q. B. 44	35 15
Czarnikow Ltd. v. Centrala Handlu Zagranicznego Rolimpex Czarnikow v. Koufos	1979	[1979] A. C. 351	79 17
	1969	[1969] 1 A. C. 350	74 35
Davis Contractors Ltd. v. Fareham U. D. C.	1956	[1956] A. C. 696	79 42
Dickinson v. Dodds Dunlop Pneumatic Tyre Co., Ltd. v. New Garage and Motor Co., Ltd.	1876	[1876] 2 Ch. D. 463 [1915] A. C. 79	16 3
Entores Ltd. v. Miles Far East Corp.	1955	[1955] 2 All E. R. 493	24 41
Equitable Trust Company of New York v. Dawson Partners Ltd.	1927	[1927] 27 Ll. L. R. 49	25 63
F. A. Tamplin Steamship Co. v. Anglo-Mexican Petroleum Products Co.	1916	[1916] 2 A. C. 397	79 42
Hadley v. Baxendale	1854	[1854] L. J. Ex. 179	73 35; 74 46
Kyprianou v. Cyprus Textiles, Ltd.	1958	[1958] 2 Lloyd's Rep. 60	80 3
Lombard North Central p. l. c. v. Butterworth	1987	[1987] 2 W. L. R. 7	25 39
Niblett, Ltd. v. Confectioners Butterworth	1921	[1921] 3 K. B. 387 (C. A.)	41 7
The Despina R. & The Folias	1977	[1979] A. C. 685 (H. L.)	74 63
Tito v. Waddell	1977	[1977] Ch. D. 106, 326	28 15
Tinn v. Hoffmann & Co.	1873	[1873] 29 L. T. 271	18 5

VI. Entscheidungsregister   Anh. VI

Parteien	Jahr	Fundstelle	Art. Rn.
Tsakiroglou & Co. Ltd. v. Noblee Thörl GmbH	1962	[1962] A. C. 93 (H. L.)	79 14.
Quenerduaine v. Cole	1883	[1883] 32 W. R. 185	18 5
Vanda Compania Limitada of Costa Rica v. Société Maritime Nationale of Paris, (The 'Ile aux Moines')	1974	[1974] 2 Lloyd's Rep. 502	74 41
Rugby Group Ltd. v. Pro Force Ltd., C. A. (England	2006	CISG-online 1424; EWCA Civ 69 (C. A.)	8 32, 35
Wahda Bank v. Arab Bank p. l. c.	1995	(1996) 1 Lloyd's Rep. 470	Vor 14–24 30c
The Square Mile Partnership Ltd. v. Fitzmaurice McCall Ltd. (C. A.)	2006	CISG-online 1423	8 32

Gericht, Datum	Fundstelle	Art. Rn.
Vietnam		
People's Supreme Court Appeal Division in Ho Chi Minh City, 5.4.1996	UNILEX	8 35, 50; **29** 17
Weissrussland		
Oberster Gerichtshof für Handelssachen der Republik Weißrussland, 20.5.2003	CISG-online 1352	78 31a
Economic Court of the Grodno Region, 23.7.2008	CISG-online 2115	81 12
Schiedsgerichte		
American Arbitration Association, 23.10.2007	CISG-online 1645	7 9, 10, 41, 49, 54; **25** 40; **29** 4, 6, 8; **49** 5; **79** 15
Arb. Ct. Bulgarian CCI, 24.4.1996	CISG-online 435	79 15
Arb. Ct. Bulgarian CCI, 30.11.1998	CISG-online 1832	14 20
Arb. Ct. Bulgarian CCI, 12.2.1998	CISG-online 436	79 30
Arb. Ct. Hungarian CCI, 17.1.1994	CISG-online 251	1 82
Arb. Ct. Hungarian CCI, 17.11.1995	CISG-online 250	54 5, 7, 8; **71** 22a
Arb. Ct. Hungarian CCI, 5.12.1995	CISG-online 163	1 63; **3** 5, 7, 8; **39** 16; **78** 30
Arb. Ct. Hungarian CCI, 10.12.1996	CISG-online 774	66 7, 35; **79** 17
Arb. Ct. Hungarian CCI, 8.5.1997	CISG-online 307	1 82
Arb. Ct. Hungarian CCI, 25.5.1999	CISG-online 438	73 23a
Arbitration Institute of the Stockholm Chamber of Commerce, 5.6.1998	CISG-online 379	7 52; **35** 15; **40** 4, 5, 11
Arbitration Institute of the Stockholm Chamber of Commerce, 5.4.2007	CISG-online 1521	1 85; **25** 35, 51; **35** 32, 50; **78** 29
Bulgarska turgosko-promishlena palata, 24.4.1996	CISG-online 435	1 59; **79** 24
Bulgarska turgosko-promishlena palata, 12.2.1998	CISG-online 436	7 55; **8** 54; **31** 83; **79** 18, 20, 30
Chamber of National and International Arbitration of Milan, 28.9.2001	CISG-online 1582	71 7, 9c
CIETAC, 1.1.1989	CISG-online 1230	71 22a
CIETAC, 6.6.1991	CISG-online 845	85 14; **88** 12
CIETAC, 30.10.1991	CISG-online 842	25 45
CIETAC, 1.4.1993	CISG-online 1428	19 13
CIETAC, 7.8.1993	CISG-online 1060	79 17
CIETAC, 10.3.1995	CISG-online 1065	84 20a
CIETAC, 23.4.1995	CISG-online 1031	58 5; **64** 9, 10
CIETAC, 30.1.1996	CISG-online 1120	72 35

Anh. VI

Gericht, Datum	Fundstelle	Art. Rn.
CIETAC, 27.2.1996	CISG-online 122	**85** 12
CIETAC, 8.3.1996	CISG-online 1034	**88** 9
CIETAC, 14.3.1996	CISG-online 1523	**79** 16
CIETAC, 29.3.1996	CISG-online 2279	**72** 35
CIETAC, 2.5.1996	CISG-online 1067	**79** 16
CIETAC, 10.5.1996	CISG-online 1067	**79** 30
CIETAC, 6.9.1996	CISG-online 1146	**Vor 85–88** 5
CIETAC, 15.11.1996	CISG-online 1148	**75** 6
CIETAC, 18.12.1996	CISG-online 2281	**71** 22a
CIETAC, 31.12.1996	CISG-online 1524	**79** 17
CIETAC, 15.4.1997	CISG-online 1162	**29** 6
CIETAC, 23.4.1997	CISG-online 1151	**65** 1, 4
CIETAC, 7.5.1997	CISG-online 1152	**79** 17
CIETAC, 30.11.1997	CISG-online 1412	**79** 16
CIETAC, 30.11.1998	CISG-online 1281	**84** 18
CIETAC, 15.12.1998	CISG-online 1167	**79** 17
CIETAC, 25.12.1998	CISG-online 1135	**14** 6, 13
CIETAC, 28.1.1999	CISG-online 1206	**53** 18
CIETAC, 1.3.1999	CISG-online 1136	**76** 2
CIETAC, 1.1.2000	CISG-online 1614	**25** 52
CIETAC, 11.2.2000	CISG-online 1529	**74** 29
CIETAC, 23.5.2000	CISG-online 1461	**29** 8
CIETAC, 29.9.2000	CISG-online 1592	**60** 8; **62** 16
CIETAC, 22.3.2001	CISG-online 1442	**60** 8
CIETAC, 24.2.2002	CISG-online 1825	**53** 30
CIETAC, 10.6.2002	CISG-online 1528	**19** 13, 16, 17; **74** 29
CIETAC, 15.7.2002	CISG-online 1553	**4** 17
CIETAC, 9.9.2002	CISG-online 1555	**53** 10
CIETAC, 8.12.2002	CISG-online 1543	**85** 14
CIETAC, 27.12.2002	CISG-online 2205	**71** 9a, 14
CIETAC, 3.6.2003	CISG-online 1451	**39** 17
CIETAC, 3.12.2003	CISG-online 1469	**4** 15
CIETAC, 12.3.2004	CISG-online 1599	**4** 34
CIETAC, 1.9.2004	CISG-online 1910	**4** 34, 40
CIETAC, 29.9.2004	CISG-online 1600	**78** 29
CIETAC, 21.2.2005	CISG-online 1706	**58** 5
CIETAC, 28.2.2005	CISG-online 1580	**4** 34; **64** 7
CIETAC, 7.4.2005	CISG-online 1453	**88** 12
CIETAC, 10.5.2005	CISG-online 1022	**25** 39
CIETAC, 25.5.2005	CISG-online 1685	**55** 15; **64** 7, 9
CIETAC, 1.6.2005	CISG-online 1909	**4** 15
CIETAC, 13.6.2005	CISG-online 1707	**3** 5
CIETAC, 12.8.2005	CISG-online 1709	**78** 29
CIETAC, 22.8.2005	CISG-online 1711	**78** 17
CIETAC, 2.9.2005	CISG-online 1712	**78** 31a
CIETAC, 15.9.2005	CISG-online 1714	**59** 1; **64** 9, 10
CIETAC, 1.10.2005	CISG-online 1914	**4** 34
CIETAC, 21.10.2005	CISG-online 1472	**4** 25
CIETAC, 9.11.2005	CISG-online 1444	**4** 40; **74** 27, 59
CIETAC, 7.12.2005	CISG-online 2124	**4** 40
CIETAC, 9.12.2005	CISG-online 1445	**8** 29
CIETAC, CISG/2005/22 (ohne Datum)	CISG-online 1912	**4** 34
CIETAC, 23.2.2006	CISG-online 2050	**1** 82
CIETAC, 1.3.2006	CISG-online 2051	**1** 82
CIETAC, 1.4.2006	CISG-online 1967	**1** 82

VI. Entscheidungsregister   Anh. VI

Gericht, Datum	Fundstelle	Art. Rn.
CIETAC, 1.5.2006	CISG-online 1917	**1** 82
CIETAC, 1.6.2006	CISG-online 1918	**1** 82
CIETAC, 1.7.2006	CISG-online 1970	**78** 39
CIETAC, 3.8.2006	CISG-online 1919	**1** 82
CIETAC, 1.9.2006	CISG-online 1924	**1** 82
CIETAC, 18.9.2006	CISG-online 2053	**1** 82
CIETAC, 20.9.2006	CISG-online 1473	**1** 82
CIETAC, 1.11.2006	CISG-online 1925	**1** 82; **78** 29
CIETAC, 1.11.2006	CISG-online 1926	**1** 82
CIETAC, 1.12.2006	CISG-online 1927	**1** 82
CIETAC, 14.2.2007	CISG-online 1929	**1** 82
CIETAC, 1.5.2007	CISG-online 1975	**1** 82; **25** 45
CIETAC, 30.6.2007	CISG-online 1930	**1** 82
CIETAC, 24.7.2007	CISG-online 2055	**1** 82; **25** 28, 45
CIETAC, 10.12.2007	CISG-online 1932	**4** 34
CIETAC, 9.1.2008	CISG-online 2056	**76** 8
CIETAC, 18.4.2008	CISG-online 2057	**1** 82; **4** 29, 30; **35** 12, 17
Corte Arbitrale ad hoc di Firenze, 19.4.1994	CISG-online 124	**6** 22
Dänisches Ad-hoc-Tribunal, 10.11.2000	CISG-online 2154	**35** 12
Foreign Trade Court of Arbitration attached to the Serbian Chamber of Commerce, 15.7.2008	CISG-online 1795	**8** 1; **26** 8; **30** 8; **63** 8; **81** 16
ICC, 2216/1974	J. D. I. 1975, 917	**79** 30
ICC, 2508/1976	J. D. I. 1977, 939	**79** 30
ICC, 2708/1976	J. D. I. 1977, 943	**79** 30
ICC, 3344/1981	J. D. I. 1982, 978	**77** 1
ICC, 4761/1987	J. D. I. 1987, 1012	**77** 1; **79** 30
ICC, 5713/1989	CISG-online 3	**1** 83, 84; **38** 16
ICC, 5953/1989	J. D. I. 1990, 1056	**79** 30
ICC, 6149/1990	YB Comm. Arb. 20 (1995), 41	**1** 84
ICC, 6281/1989	UNILEX	**75** 10; **79** 30
ICC, 6653/1993	CISG-online 71	**1** 82; **4** 48; **6** 22; **7** 56; **24** 43; **35** 49; **78** 27, 29; **84** 13
ICC, 7153/1992	CISG-online 35	**1** 82; **78** 27, 32
ICC, 7197/1992	CISG-online 36; J. D. I. 1993, 1028	**1** 82; **4** 40; **54** 5; **74** 25, 27, 58; **77** 8
ICC, 7585/1992	CISG-online 105; J. D. I. 1995, 1015	**1** 65; **25** 66; **54** 7; **61** 9; **63** 7; **64** 7, 20; **74** 27, 29, 59; **92** 3
ICC, 7331/1994	CISG-online 106	**1** 19, 84; **8** 5
ICC, 7399/1994	ICC Ct. Bull. 2/1995, 68	**Vor 1–6** 22; **1** 77; **95** 2
ICC, 7531/1994	CISG-online 565	**Vor 1–6** 22; **1** 46, 77; **48** 9; **95** 2
ICC, 7565/1994	CISG-online 566	**6** 22; **39** 26
ICC, 7660/1994	CISG-online 129	**3** 5, 17; **4** 35; **6** 22; **39** 26
ICC, 7731/1994	ICC Ct. Bull., Nov. 1995, 73	**39** 34
ICC, 7819/1999	ICC Ct. Bull., 2001, 56	**55** 11
ICC, 7844/1994	CISG-online 567	**1** 15; **3** 5; **6** 22; **14** 31a, 31b; **18** 14; **23** 3
ICC, 7645/1995	CISG-online 844	**25** 41
ICC, 7754/1995	CISG-online 834	**25** 47

Anh. VI

Gericht, Datum	Fundstelle	Art. Rn.
ICC, 8128/1995	CISG-online 526; J. D. I. 1996, 1024	**7** 55, 62; **25** 13, 15, 29; **73** 17; **25** 7; **75** 6, 11; **78** 31a; **79** 29
ICC, 8213/1995	UNILEX	**9** 11
ICC, 8324/1995	CISG-online 596; J. D. I. 1996, 1019	**1** 72, 73; **6** 22; **8** 17, 21, 46; **14** 19; **55** 15
ICC, 8486/1996	J. D. I. 1998, 1047	**79** 30
ICC, 8611/1997	CISG-online 236	**4** 7; **7** 26, 58; **8** 44; **14** 69, 71; **18** 7a, 8; **19** 9; **33** 5; **71** 4; **78** 32
ICC, 8769/1996		**78** 31a
ICC, 8786/1997	CISG-online 775	**7** 50; **25** 10, 39
ICC, 8817/1997	CISG-online 749	**9** 9; **7** 52, 63
ICC, 8873/1997	CISG-online 776	**9** 26; **79** 30
ICC, 8908/1998	J. D. I. 1998, 1017	**1** 75; **7** 52
ICC, 9029/1998	CISG-online 751	**9** 26
ICC, 9083/1999	UNILEX	**35** 8; **37** 7; **40** 7
ICC, 9117/1998	CISG-online 706	**7** 63; **29** 14; **33** 10, 13
ICC, 9187/1999	CISG-online 777	**6** 22; **25** 36; **38** 10; **40** 6; **44** 6; **74** 36
ICC, 9479/1999	CISG-online 705	**9** 26
ICC, 3.11.1999	UNILEX	**39** 29
ICC, 9875/1999	unveröffentlicht	**9** 26
ICC, 9978/1999	UNILEX	**25** 37; **45** 2
ICC, 10274/1999	CISG-online 708	**64** 9
ICC, 10274/1999	CISG-online 1159; YB. Comm. Arb. 89 2004, 102	
ICC, 20.12.1999	CISG-online 1646; IHR 2004, 21	**Vor 14–24** 30a, 30d, 30e; **25** 37; **78** 27
ICC, 8790/2000	CISG-online 1172	**79** 1
ICC, 9781/2000	CISG-online 1202	**3** 13
ICC, 10022/2000	UNILEX	**9** 26
ICC, 11333/2003	CISG-online 1420	**1** 82; **4** 35; **6** 18, 22
ICC, 11849/2003	CISG-online 1421; YB. Comm. Arb. 2006, 148	**1** 31; **4** 35; **6** 18, 39; **7** 49; **25** 10; **27** 8; **53** 10; **54** 6; **58** 5, 29; **63** 8; **64** 21, 22, 27, 32
ICC, 12713/2004	CISG-online 2066	**1** 31
ICC, 10303/2008	CISG-online 2137	**1** 82
ICDR, 12.12.2007	CISG-online 1647	**78** 31b
Int. Ct. Russian CCI, 13.1.1992	CISG-online 1622	**61** 9
Int. Ct. Russian CCI, 15.4.1994	CISG-online 449	**81** 11; **84** 12a, 13, 17
Int. Ct. Russian CCI, 9.9.1994	UNILEX	**74** 27
Int. Ct. Russian CCI, 3.3.1995	CISG-online 204; CLOUT No. 139; UNILEX	**1** 82; **14** 19; **55** 5
Int. Ct. Russian CCI, 16.3.1995	CISG-online 205	**1** 82; **75** 5; **79** 17, 30
Int. Ct. Russian CCI, 25.4.1995	CISG-online 206	**1** 82; **72** 12a
Int. Ct. Russian CCI, 25.4.1995	CISG-online 367	**85** 16; **88** 9
Int. Ct. Russian CCI, 17.10.1995	CISG-online 207; CLOUT No. 142	**54** 1; **57** 20
Int. Ct. Russian CCI, 22.1.1996	CISG-online 1830	**1** 82; **53** 30; **79** 25
Int. Ct. Russian CCI, 22.1.1997	CISG-online 1296	**79** 1
Int. Ct. Russian CCI, 21.2.1997	CISG-online 781	**8** 44
Int. Ct. Russian CCI, 5.6.1997	UNILEX	**9** 26
Int. Ct. Russian CCI, 2.9.1997	CISG Pace	**2** 42

VI. Entscheidungsregister
Anh. VI

Gericht, Datum	Fundstelle	Art. Rn.
Int. Ct. Russian CCI, 21.1.1998	CISG-online 1246	**41** 7
Int. Ct. Russian CCI, 22.1.1998	CISG-online 2283	**71** 22a
Int. Ct. Russian CCI, 16.2.1998	CISG-online 1303	**96** 3
Int. Ct. Russian CCI, 4.4.1998	CISG-online 1334	**25** 66
Int. Ct. Russian CCI, 6.4.1998	CISG-online 778	**2** 39
Int. Ct. Russian CCI, 5.10.1998	CISG-online 1831; CLOUT No. 468	**64** 6
Int. Ct. Russian CCI, 24.11.1998	CISG-online 1525	**79** 17
Int. Ct. Russian CCI, 27.7.1999	CISG-online 779	**9** 26
Int. Ct. Russian CCI, 24.1.2000	CISG-online 1042	**6** 22; **45** 23
Int. Ct. Russian CCI, 13.6.2000	CISG-online 1083	**81** 12
Int. Ct. Russian CCI, 24.1.2002	CISG-online 887	**60** 8
Int. Ct. Russian CCI, 6.9.2002	CISG-online 892	**6** 22
Int. Ct. Russian CCI, 11.10.2002	CISG-online 893	**6** 22
Int. Ct. Russian CCI, 9.12.2002	CISG Pace	**7** 54
Int. Ct. Russian CCI, 16.4.2003	CISG-online 1683	**84** 18
Int. Ct. Russian CCI, 16.6.2003	CISG-online 977	**6** 22; **79** 15
Int. Ct. Russian CCI, 25.6.2003	CISG-online 978	**6** 22; **49** 24
Int. Ct. Russian CCI, 17.9.2003	CISG-online 979	**6** 22
Int. Ct. Russian CCI, 30.12.2003	CISG-online 1284	**78** 27
Int. Ct. Russian CCI, 3.2.2004	CISG-online 1180	**4** 15
Int. Ct. Russian CCI, 16.2.2004	CISG-online 1181	**9** 16; **29** 6, 14; **96** 3
Int. Ct. Russian CCI, 9.3.2004	CISG-online 1184	**1** 30
Int. Ct. Russian CCI, 9.4.2004	CISG-online 1207	**14** 13, 19
Int. Ct. Russian CCI, 12.4.2004	CISG-online 1208	**6** 22
Int. Ct. Russian CCI, 19.5.2004	CISG-online 1358	**84** 12, 12a
Int. Ct. Russian CCI, 24.5.2004	CISG-online 1210	**4** 40
Int. Ct. Russian CCI, 28.5.2004	CISG-online 1513	**7** 41
Int. Ct. Russian CCI, 9.6.2004	CISG-online 1239	**4** 17, 35, 40; **12** 2; **78** 27
Int. Ct. Russian CCI, 25.6.2004	CISG-online 1437	**25** 48
Int. Ct. Russian CCI, 22.10.2004	CISG-online 1359	**6** 22
Int. Ct. Russian CCI, 2.11.2004	CISG-online 1285	**25** 26; **49** 5
Int. Ct. Russian CCI, 5.11.2004	CISG-online 1360	**6** 15
Int. Ct. Russian CCI, 21.12.2004	CISG-online 1187	**25** 45
Int. Ct. Russian CCI, 23.12.2004	CISG-online 1188	**74** 56
Int. Ct. Russian CCI, 19.9.2005	CISG-online 1287	**63** 8
Int. Ct. Russian CCI, 13.1.2006	CISG-online 1622	**4** 40; **7** 43; **61** 9
Int. Ct. Russian CCI, 13.2.2006	CISG-online 1623	**7** 43; **59** 4
Int. Ct. Russian CCI, 1.3.2006	CISG-online 1941	**4** 40
Int. Ct. Russian CCI, 7.3.2006	CISG-online 1942	**7** 43
Int. Ct. Russian CCI, 7.4.2006	CISG-online 1943	**1** 82; **78** 39
Int. Ct. Russian CCI, 13.4.2006	CISG-online 1944	**30** 14
Int. Ct. Russian CCI, 19.5.2006	CISG-online 2006	**1** 82
Int. Ct. Russian CCI, 15.11.2006	CISG-online 2008	**7** 43; **78** 29
Int. Ct. Russian CCI, 29.12.2006	CISG-online 1945	**78** 27
Int. Ct. Russian CCI, 30.1.2007	CISG-online 1886	**1** 82
Int. Ct. Russian CCI, 8.2.2008	CISG-online 2102	**7** 49
Int. Ct. Russian CCI, 13.5.2008	CISG-online 2103	**79** 56
Int. Ct. Ukrainian CCI, 25.11.2002	CISG-online 1267	**25** 68; **29** 19
Int. Ct. Ukrainian CCI, 10.10.2003	CISG-online 1268	**1** 30
Int. Ct. Ukrainian CCI, 14.4.2004	CISG-online 1270	**4** 35
Int. Ct. Ukrainian CCI, 18.11.2004	CISG-online 1371	**25** 40; **49** 5
Int. Ct. Ukrainian CCI, 27.5.2005	CISG-online 1456	**8** 29, 51a
Int. Ct. Ukrainian CCI, 5.7.2005	CISG-online 1361	**25** 61, 69; **49** 5
Int. Ct. Ukrainian, 15.2.2006	CISG-online 1961	**1** 82

Gericht, Datum	Fundstelle	Art. Rn.
Internationales Schiedsgericht der Bundeskammer der gewerblichen Wirtschaft (Wien), 15.6.1994	CISG-online 120 = 691	1 82; 4 42; 6 22; 7 51; 8 50; 16 1; 39 33a; 74 3, 16, 18, 53; 77 10; 78 31a
Internationales Schiedsgericht der Bundeskammer der gewerblichen Wirtschaft (Wien), 15.6.1994	CISG-online 121	1 82; 4 42; 6 22; 7 51; 8 50; 39 33a
Iran-US Claims Tribunal, 28.7.1989	YB. Comm. Arb. 15 (1990), 220	1 83, 84
Iran-US Claims Tribunal, 28.7.1989	CISG Pace	
Netherlands Arbitration Institute, (1990), 220	CISG-online 780	7 5; 35 15, 46, 51; 45 10; 71 21, 31, 38; 73 26
Netherlands Arbitration Institute, 15.10.2002	CISG-online 740	72 12a
Netherlands Arbitration Institute, 10.2.2005	CISG-online 1621	Vor 14–24 10; 14 44, 51, 69, 71
Netherlands Arbitration Institute, 17.5.2005	CISG-online 1422	6 22
Schiedsgericht der Börse für landwirtschaftliche Produkte in Wien, 10.12.1997	CISG-online 351; östZRVgl 1998, 211	6 22; 8 11, 24, 25, 26; 9 1, 6; 25 45, 67; 38 9; 39 30
Schiedsgericht der Hamburger freundschaftlichen Arbitrage, 4.1.1965	Straatmann/Ulmer, E 4d Nr. 3	79 32
Schiedsgericht der Hamburger freundschaftlichen Arbitrage, 6.3.1970	Straatmann/Ulmer, E 4d Nr. 4	79 32
Schiedsgericht der Hamburger freundschaftlichen Arbitrage, 21.6.1996	CISG-online 465	7 26
Schiedsgericht der Hamburger freundschaftlichen Arbitrage, 30.8.1996	YB. Comm. Arb. 1997, 57	1 72
Schiedsgericht der Hamburger freundschaftlichen Arbitrage, 29.12.1998	CISG-online 638	8 2, 46; 25 37; 64 34; 73 23a; 78 27; 81 11; 84 13
Schiedsgericht der Handelskammer Hamburg, 21.3.1996	CISG-online 187	1 72, 82; 6 22; 8 1, 2, 46; 25 66; 47 17; 49 6; 74 29, 53; 79 16, 26, 29, 37
Schiedsgericht der Handelskammer Hamburg, 21.6.1996	RIW 1996, 771	74 20
Schiedsgericht der Handelskammer Zürich, 31.5.1996	CISG-online 1291; YB. Comm. Arb. 1998, 128	1 63; 2 35; 4 25; Vor 14–24 30a, 36; 58 27; 71 9; 73 10
Schiedsgericht der Jugoslawischen Handelskammer, 15.4.1999	CISG-online 1587	2 39
Schiedsgericht der Jugoslawischen Handelskammer, 27.9.2001	CISG-online 1854	78 29
Schiedsgericht der Jugoslawischen Handelskammer, 12.2.2002	CISG-online 2036	78 39
Schiedsgericht der Jugoslawischen Handelskammer, 12.4.2002	CISG-online 1855	78 30
Schiedsgericht der Jugoslawischen Handelskammer, 9.12.2002	CISG-online 2123	7 48
Schiedsgericht der serbischen Handelskammer, 5.1.2007	CISG-online 2233	78 27
Schiedsgericht der serbischen Handelskammer, 1.10.2007	CISG-online 1793	1 82; 25 37; 78 29
Schiedsgericht des Waren-Vereins der Hamburger Börse e. V., 27.11.1979	HSG Bd. 3 E 6b, Nr. 78	46 25
Schiedsgericht des Vereins der am Kaffeehandel beteiligten Firmen, 9.11.1973	HSG, A5 No. 43	64 39

VI. Entscheidungsregister

Anh. VI

Gericht, Datum	Fundstelle	Art. Rn.
Serbian Chamber of Commerce, 21.2.2005	CISG-online 2038	**39** 17
Serbian Chamber of Commerce, 30.10.2006	CISG-online 2081	**1** 82
Serbian Chamber of Commerce, 13.11.2007	CISG-online 1794	**1** 31
Serbian Chamber of Commerce, 23.1.2008	CISG-online 1946	**1** 82; **35** 9; **41** 7
Serbian Chamber of Commerce, 15.7.2008	CISG-online 1795	**1** 15, 82; **4** 30; **7** 17
Serbian Chamber of Commerce, 28.1.2009	CISG-online 1856	**1** 31, 82; **6** 18, 22; **7** 17, 52
Serbian Chamber of Commerce, 17.8.2009	CISG-online 2039	**6** 15, 16; **77** 1

Sachregister

Die fett gedruckten Zahlen bezeichnen die Artikel, die mageren Zahlen die Randnummern; „Vor" bezeichnet die Vorbemerkung vor einem Artikel bzw. mehreren Artikeln.

ab Kai, Zeitpunkt der Lieferung **33** 10
ab Lager, Ort der Lieferung **31** 72
ab Pflanzung 31 72
ab Schiff (DAP), Bestimmung des Zeitpunkts der Lieferung innerhalb der Lieferfrist **33** 10, beim Verkauf schwimmender Ware **31** 79 ff., Zeitpunkt der Lieferung **33** 10
ab Terminal, Ort der Lieferung **31** 74
ab Werk (EXW), Ausfuhrabgaben und -zölle **31** 84, Exportgenehmigung **31** 85, Inhalt der Lieferpflicht **31** 72, Liefertermin **33** 10, Ort der Lieferung **31** 72
Abbedingung des CISG Vor 14–24 14a ff., in AGB **Vor 14–24** 14c, materielle Einigung **Vor 14–24** 14b ff.
Abdingbarkeit *s. Ausschluss der Konvention, Parteiautonomie,* bei der Minderung **50** 19, beim Recht des Käufers auf Erfüllung **46** 48, beim Recht des Verkäufers auf Nacherfüllung **48** 31, der Rechtsbehelfe **45** 36 f., bei der Vertragsaufhebung **49** 49 f.
Ablehnungsandrohung, Entbehrlichkeit bei Nachfristsetzung **47** 5, bei Nachfristsetzung als bedingte Erklärung der Vertragsaufhebung **49** 23, 39
Abnahme 60 1 ff., der Dokumente **60** 6, Mitwirkungspflichten bei Lieferung **60** 7, Ort der A. **60** 3, vertragswidriger Ware **60** 2, der Ware **60** 2, Zeit der A. **60** 4
Abnahme der Ware 28 6, **31** 30, 76, 79, **33** 3, 5, 12, **60** 2, im Fall der Bringschuld **31** 76, Frist **33** 5, Klage auf A. **28** 6, Pflicht zur A. und Pflicht zur Angabe der Bestimmungsorts **31** 30, unterlassener Abruf als Verletzung der Abnahmepflicht **33** 12, bei Vereinbarung der Klauseln „frei Frachtführer", FAS, FOB **31** 79, Zeitpunkt **33** 3, *(s. a. Empfangszeit)*
Abnahmepflicht bei Teillieferung **51** 4, Verletzung der A. und wesentliche Vertragsverletzung **25** 67
Abruf 33 11 f.
Absendetheorie 26 11, **27** 1 f.
Absendung 27 9, der Erklärung der Inanspruchnahme auf Ersatzlieferung **46** 33, der Erklärung der Vertragsaufhebung **49** 25, 28, 30
Absichtserklärung 14 26, *s. a. letter of intent*
absolute Berechnung der Minderung *s. Minderung*
abstrakte Schadensberechnung bei antizipiertem Vertragsbruch **76** 12, Aufhebung des Vertrags **76** 3, Begriff **76** 1, bei Erfüllungsverweigerung **76** 3, Ersatz entgangenen Gewinns **76** 13, Ersatz weiteren Schadens **76** 13, bei Geldentwertung **74** 26, Grundsatz der Totalreparation **76** 6, Hinauszögern der Vertragsaufhebung **76** 10, und konkrete Schadensberechnung **74** 41, bei Kursverlust **74** 26, lost volume **76** 13, maßgeblicher Ort **76** 8 f., maßgeblicher Zeitpunkt **76** 10 ff., bei nicht angemessenem Deckungsgeschäft **76** 2, Nichterfüllungsschaden **76** 7 ff., Nutzungsausfallschaden **74** 41, auf Reparaturkostenbasis **74** 24, und Schadensminderungspflicht **76** 2, Übernahmezeitpunkt **76** 11, Verhältnis zur konkreten S. **76** 2, 13, bei Verzögerungsschaden **74** 25, Vertragspreis **76** 5, Voraussehbarkeitsregel **76** 6, Voraussetzungen **76** 2 ff., Zeitpunkt der **74** 44
abstrakte Schadensberechung, Schadensminderungspflicht **77** 10
Abtretbarkeit 53 29
Abtretung 4 38, **53** 29, A. des Herausgabeanspruchs als Lieferung **31** 58
Abwahl *s. Ausschluss der Konvention, Parteiautonomie*
Abweichende Vereinbarungen *s. Abdingbarkeit*
Abweichung der Annahme von der Offerte *s. Annahme der Offerte, Gegenofferte*
Abwicklungsverhältnis *s. Vertragsaufhebung*
Abzahlungsgeschäft 1 26
actio quanti minoris 50 1
action directe 74 15
Adressierung 31 39 f., **32** 3
AGB *s. Allgemeine Geschäftsbedingungen,* Haftungsausschluss zugunsten des Käufers **61** 16 ff.
Agenturvertrag Vor 14–24 41
Akkreditiv 9 8, **28** 6, **34** 2, 3, **57** 22, **58** 9, Anspruch des Käufers auf Stellung des A. **28** 6, und Erfüllungsort für die Übergabe der Dokumente **34** 3, Zeitpunkt der Übergabe der Dokumente **34** 2
Aliud 35 10, wesentlicher Vertragsbruch *s. a. Falschlieferung*
Allgemeine Geschäftsbedingungen 4 20 f., **6** 14, 17, 30, **8** 8a, 11, 52 ff., **9** 8, **11** 16, **Vor 14–24** 1, 3, 9, **14** 32 ff., **19** 4 f., 19 f., **25** 10, **27** 6, **45** 36 f., 48, **48** 31, **49** 49 f., **50** 19, Änderung **14** 58, Auslegung **8** 8a, 59, Ausschluss der Konvention **6** 14, 17, Ausschluss der Minderung **50** 19, Ausschluss des Erfüllungsanspruchs **46** 48, Ausschluss des Nacherfüllungsrechts **48** 31, **49** 50, Ausschluss des Rechts zur Vertragsaufhebung **49** 49, battle of

Sachregister

Fette Zahlen = Artikel

forms **8** 11, **19** 4, 19 f., Bedeutung der Sprache für die Einbeziehung **14** 61 ff., Beweislast **14** 76, Einbeziehung **8** 52 ff., **Vor 14–24** 4, **14** 32 ff., E-Mail **14** 44, 49 ff., Erweiterung des Erfüllungsanspruchs **46** 48, als Gepflogenheit **14** 69, Gültigkeit **4** 20 f., als Handelsbrauch **14** 73, Hinterlegung bei Handelskammer **14** 55, Inhaltskontrolle **14** 34, international übliche **14** 53, Internet **14** 49, Kenntnisverschaffungsobliegenheit **14** 41, **18** 8, kollidierende Geschäftsbedingungen **8** 11, **19** 4, 19 f., Kontrolle **Vor 14–24** 3 ff., Kontrollmaßstab **45** 37, laufende Geschäftsbeziehung **14** 51, Musterverträge **9** 8, **14** 32, Offerte **14** 36, Regelung des Transportrisikos bei Erklärungen **27** 6, Schriftformklauseln **11** 16, stillschweigende Einbeziehung **14** 38, Tagespreisklauseln **14** 15, Transparenzgebot **Vor 14–24** 4, **14** 14, überraschende Klauseln **8** 57, **Vor 14–24** 5, **14** 35, Verhandlungssprache **14** 62, Vertragssprache **14** 63, Vertragsstatut **45** 36, Vorrang der Individualabrede **8** 58, Weltsprache **14** 65, wesentliche Vertragsverletzung **25** 25, Widersprüche zwischen AGB **8** 11, **19** 4 f., 19 f., Zeitpunkt der Kenntnisnahme **14** 59

allgemeine Grundsätze des Übereinkommens, Beweislastverteilung **7** 56, favor contractus **7** 54, Formfreiheit **7** 52, Lückenfüllung **7** 41, Pflicht zur Erfüllung von Leistungspflichten innerhalb angemessener Frist **32** 6, **34** 1, reasonableness **7** 53, Schadensminderung **7** 52, Treu und Glauben **7** 49 f., venire contra factum proprium **7** 50, Vertrauensschutz **7** 54, Vorhersehbarkeit des Schadens **7** 52, Vorrang der Parteiautonomie **7** 48, Zinsanspruch **7** 52

Änderung von Verträgen s. *Vertragsänderung*

Anfechtung s. *Willensmängel*

Angebot, Auslegung **8** 3, der Nachbesserung **46** 26, der nachträglichen Erfüllung durch den Verkäufer **48** 30, **49** 27, 41

Angebot eines Vertragsschlusses s. *Offerte*

Anlagenliefervertrag 3 18

Annahme, Folgen der A. der vorzeitigen Lieferung **52** 4, Folgen der A. der Zuvielleferung **52** 10

Annahme der Konvention s. *Ratifikation*

Annahme der Offerte, A. der Gegenofferte **19** 12, Abgrenzung wesentlicher von unwesentlicher Abweichung von der Offerte **19** 8, 13, mit Abweichung **21** 14, keine Annahme bei Äußerung von Erwartungen **19** 7, keine Abweichung bei Äußerung von Vorschlägen **19** 7, Abweichung der A. von der Offerte **19** 5, 10–18, angemessene Frist **18** 15, Auftragsbestätigung als A. **18** 4, Beginn der Annahmefrist **20** 1–4, Bindungswille **18** 4, EDI **18** 5, Endtermin für A. **20** 1, Ergänzungen in der Annahmeerklärung **19** 6, falsa demonstratio **19** 5, Frist **18** 14 f., durch Fristsetzung erloschene Offerte **21** 3, Gegenofferte **19** 10–12, Gerichtsstandsklausel als wesentliche Abweichung von der Offerte **19** 8a, Geschäftsfähigkeit **18** 3, Gewährleistungsbürgschaft als wesentliche Abweichung von der Offerte **19** 9, Gründe **21** 5, günstige Abweichungen als unwesentliche Abweichung von der Offerte **19** 8b, Kommunikationsmittel **18** 5, Kreuzofferten als A. **18** 10, Kündigungsvorbehalt als wesentliche Abweichung von der Offerte **19** 9, Mengenabweichungen als wesentliche Abweichung von der Offerte **19** 8a, mirror image rule **19** 1, nachträgliche Modifikation der A. **22** 5, nicht zugangsbedürftige A. **18** 18, Preisänderung als wesentliche Abweichung von der Offerte **19** 8a, Rechtsfolgen unwesentlicher Abweichung der A. von der Offerte **19** 14 ff., Rechtsfolgen von Ergänzungen in der Annahmeerklärung **19** 14, Rechtsfolgen wesentlicher Abweichung der A. von der Offerte **19** 10–12, Rechtswahlklauseln als wesentliche Abweichung von der Offerte **19** 9, Rücknahme **18** 12, **22** 1–7, Rücktrittsvorbehalt als wesentliche Abweichung von der Offerte **19** 9, Schweigen **18** 5, „sonstiges Verhalten" **18** 7, Spekulationsgefahr bei verspäteter Annahmeerklärung **21** 23, Überlegungsfrist **18** 15, Untätigkeit **18** 9, unwesentliche Abweichung von der Offerte **19** 13, unwesentliche Ergänzungen in der Annahmeerklärung **19** 14, Verpackungsart als wesentliche Abweichung von der Offerte **19** 9, Versendungsart als wesentliche Abweichung von der Offerte **19** 9, verspätete A. **21** 4, Vertragsschluss **21** 6, Vertragsstrafe als wesentliche Abweichung von der Offerte **19** 9, Vertretungsmacht für Annahme **18** 3, wesentliche Abweichung von der Offerte **19** 13, Widerruf der Annahme **18** 12, Widerrufsvorbehalt **18** 12, Willenserklärung **18** 3, Willensmängel **18** 3, Wirksamkeit der Annahmeerklärung **18** 11, zugangslose Zustimmungsäußerung **18** 20, Zugangsprinzip **18** 13, Zustimmungsäußerung aufgrund Offerte s. a. *annahmeäquivalente Handlungen; Billigung verspäteter Annahme; Widerspruch*

annahmeäquivalente Handlungen 18 19, aufgrund Gepflogenheit **18** 21, aufgrund Handelsbrauchs **18** 21, aufgrund Rahmenvertrags **18** 21, Rücknahme **18** 22, Zeitpunkt der Wirkung **18** 22

Annahmefrist, Zeitzone **18** 14

Annahmeverzug 31 62 ff., 75, **81** 29, und Gefahrübergang **31** 62, bei Rückabwicklung **81** 29

Anrufbeantworter, mündliche Erklärung **24** 13, Zugang **24** 13

Ansprüche Dritter 41 9–12, Form der Geltendmachung **41** 11, „frivole" A. **41** 10, aufgrund Schutzrechtes **42** 6, Sicherungsrechte **41** 4, unbegründete A. **41** 10, aufgrund Verhaltens des Käufers **41** 13, vertragswidrige Kostenbelas-

tung der Ware durch den Beförderer **31** 37, vertragswidrige Kostenbelastung der Ware durch den Lagerhalter **31** 60, *s. a. Rechtsmangel*
anticipatory breach 72 2, 6, 33, Beginn der Verjährungsfrist **12 VerjÜbk** 1, *s. a. Vertragsverletzung, künftige wesentliche*
antizipierte Vertragsverletzung bei Sukzessivlieferungsvertrag **73** 17 ff.
Antizipierter Vertragsbruch, Abdingbarkeit **72** 5, Abgrenzung zu anderen Rechtsbehelfen **72** 10, Beweislast **72** 42, Deckungsgeschäft bei **75** 7, Normzweck **72** 4, Rechtsvergleich **72** 6 ff., Schadenminderungspflicht **77** 3, 10, Vorgeschichte **72** 1 ff.
Anweisung an den Beförderer als Lieferung **31** 79
anwendbares Recht, deutsches Recht als Vertragsstatut bei Verjährung **3 VertragsG** 3, auf Eigentumslage **30** 7, Formstatut **12** 2 f., lex rei sitae **30** 7, **41** 2, Sachnormcharakter des Art. 1 I b) **2 VertragsG** 1, UNIDROIT-Principles als objektiv anwendbares Recht **7** 59–61, Verteilungsnorm **2 VertragsG** 1, Vertragsstatut bei allgemeinen Geschäftsbedingungen **45** 36, Vertragsstatut bei Verjährung **3 VertragsG** 3, Vorbehalt nach Art. 95 **2 VertragsG** 2, bei Vorbehalt nach Art. 96 **12** 2 f., Währung als Anknüpfungspunkt für den Zinssatz **78** 30, 33, *s. a. IPR*
Anwendung, kollisionsrechtliche 1 1, 4 ff., 69–76, Haager Übereinkommen von 1955 **1** 75, und lex mercatoria **1** 84, objektive Anknüpfung **1** 73, Rechtswahl **1** 72, Renvoi **1** 71, Sachnormcharakter des Art. 1 I b) **2 VertragsG** 1, Schiedsgerichte **1** 82–84, Verteilungsnorm **2 VertragsG** 1, Vertragsgesetz **1** 79, Vorbehalt nach Art. 95 **Vor 1–6** 21 f., **1** 77–81, **2 VertragsG** 2, Wahl des Übereinkommens **6** 39–43
Anwendungsbereich des Verjährungsübereinkommens, einzelne Gebietsteile **31 VerjÜbk**, **32 VerjÜbk**, räumlicher A. **2 VerjÜbk**, **3 VerjÜbk** 2 ff., sachlicher A. **1 VerjÜbk** 2 ff., zeitlicher A. **33 VerjÜbk,** *s. a. Ausschluss der Anwendung des Verjährungsübereinkomens; Vorbehalte*
Anwendungsbereich, persönlich-räumlicher Vor 1–6 3 f., **1** 40–60, Autonome Anwendung **1** 63–68, gewöhnlicher Aufenthalt **10** 9 f., Internationalität **1** 40–43, Kaufmannseigenschaft unerheblich **1** 59 f., lex mercatoria **1** 84, Niederlassung der Parteien **1** 44–47, Schiedsgerichte **1** 82–84, Staatsangehörigkeit unerheblich **1** 59 f., Vertragsstaaten **1** 64, Vorbehalt nach Art. 92 **Vor 1–6** 15 f., **1** 65, Vorbehalt nach Art. 93 **Vor 1–6** 17 f., **1** 66, Vorbehalt nach Art. 94 **Vor 1–6** 19 f., **1** 67, Vorbehalte **1** 65–68, Wahl des Übereinkommens **6** 39–43, *s. a. Niederlassung*
Anwendungsbereich, sachlicher Vor 1–6 3 f., **1** 12–39, **Vor 14–24** 41, Abzahlungsgeschäft **1** 26, Agenturvertrag **Vor 14–24** 41, Anlagenliefervertrag **3** 18, Aufhebungsvereinbarung **1** 19, ausgeschlossene Verträge **1** 25, Bedarfsdeckungsvertrag **Vor 14–24** 41, Dokumentenkauf **1** 37, **2** 34, Eigenhändlervertrag **Vor 14–24** 41, Fixkauf **1** 20, Franchisevertrag **1** 32, Gegengeschäfte **1** 30, Geltungsbereich der Vertragsschlussvorschriften **Vor 14–24** 1 ff., **14** 2, gemischter Vertrag **3** 19, Kauf an Warenbörse **2** 29, Kauf auf Probe **1** 23, Kauf nach Muster **1** 16, Kauf nach Probe **1** 16, Kauf von Elektrizität **2** 46, Kauf von Wasserfahrzeugen **2** 38–41, Kauf von Wertpapieren **2** 34–36, Kauf von Zahlungsmitteln **2** 37, Kaufoption **1** 21, **Vor 14–24** 41, Kaufvertrag **1** 12–15, Leasingvertrag **1** 28, 29, Liefervertrag mit arbeits- oder dienstvertraglichen Pflichten **3** 12–20, Liefervertrag mit Montageverpflichtung **3** 17, Mietkaufvertrag **1** 27, promesse de vente **Vor 14–24** 41, Rahmenvereinbarung **Vor 14–24** 41, Rückkaufvertrag **Vor 14–24** 41, Sale-and-lease-back Geschäft **1** 29, Schenkungsvertrag **1** 33, Spezifikationskauf **1** 17, Sukzessivlieferungsvertrag **1** 15, Tauschvertrag **1** 30, Verbrauchsgüterkauf **1** 7–26, Veredelungsvertrag **3** 9, Versendungskauf **1** 18, Versteigerungen **2** 2, 27–30, Vertriebsvertrag **1** 31, Vorkaufvertrag **Vor 14–24** 41, Vorvertrag **1** 21, **Vor 14–24** 41, Wahl des Übereinkommens **6** 39–43, Werklieferungsvertrag **1** 24, **3** 4–11, Wiederkaufvertrag **Vor 14–24** 41, Zwangsvollstreckung **2** 31–33
Anwendungsbereich, zeitlicher 100 1–3, **33 VerjÜbk**
Anzeige, Absendeprinzip **27** 1, der Bereitstellung der Ware **31** 51 f., der Erfüllungsbereitschaft durch den Verkäufer **48** 25 ff., 30, **49** 27, 41, bei künftiger wesentlicher Vertragsverletzung **72** 17 ff., Sukzessivlieferungsvertrag, vorzeitige A. der Vertragsaufhebung **73** 24, unangemessene A. **72** 27, Zurückbehaltungs- und Anhalterecht *s. a. Rüge*
arbeitsfreie Tage, Annahme **20** 6, Fristberechnung **20** 5, Zugang **20** 6
Arbeitskampf, Aussperrung **79** 21
Arbeitskämpfe, Ausfall allgemeiner Verkehrs- oder Versorgungsleistungen **79** 24, Haftungsbefreiung **79** 21 ff., beim Zulieferanten **79** 24
Arglist des Verkäufers 35 37, 48, **41** 24, **42** 28, bezüglich der Vertragswidrigkeit der Ware **35** 37, 48
arglistige Schädigung als Grenze der Bindung an die Offerte **16** 13
arglistige Täuschung 46 30
Atlanta Agreement 35 7
attachment, Zugang **24** 6, Zugangsbindung **24** 42
Aufenthalt *s. gewöhnlicher Aufenthalt*
Aufhebungserklärung *s. Erklärung der Vertragsaufhebung, s. Vertragsaufhebung,* bei antizipiertem Vertragsbruch **72** 37 ff., Fristen für bei antizi-

1415

Sachregister

piertem Vertragsbruch **72** 38 f., Wirkungen **72** 40
Aufhebungsgründe *s. Vertragsaufhebung, Voraussetzungen*
Aufhebungslage, Vorrang der Vertragsaufhebung bei A. **48** 17
Aufhebungsvereinbarung 1 19
Aufhebungsvertrag, Auslegung **8** 1
Aufklärungspflichten 45 3
Aufrechnung 4 39, **8** 5, **45** 27, **78** 20, **81** 21 f., **88** 18, **25 VerjÜbk** 3 f., Auslegung des Aufrechnungsverbots **8** 5, mit Erlös aus Selbsthilfe- und Notverkauf **88** 18, durch den Käufer **61** 19, in der Rückabwicklung **81** 21 f., mit dem Schadensersatzanspruch **45** 27, mit verjährtem Anspruch **25 VerjÜbk** 3 f., Zahlungsklauseln als Aufrechnungsverbot **61** 19, und Zinsanspruch **78** 20
Auftragsbestätigung 18 4, als Annahme **18** 4, als kaufmännisches Bestätigungsschreiben **18** 4
Auftragsvergabe durch öffentliche Hand *s. öffentliche Auftragsvergabe*
Aufwendungen bei Vorteilsausgleichung 84 28 ff., luxuriöse A. **84** 30, notwendige A. **84** 29, nützliche A. **84** 31
Aufwendungsersatz, Schadensminderungspflicht **77** 11
Auktion, Internet-Auktion **Vor 14–24** 28
Ausfallprobe 38 9
Ausgleich von Vorteilen **84** 5 ff.
Auslegung Präambel 4, **7** 5–40, **8, 7 VerjÜbk** 1, Allgemeine Geschäftsbedingungen **8** 52 ff., 59, Angebot **8** 3, Aufhebungserklärung **8** 1, Aufhebungsvertrag **8** 1, Berücksichtigung der Verhandlungen **8** 31 ff., contra proferentem **8** 47 f., Erklärungen **8** 1, Erklärungsbewusstsein **8** 7, favor negotii **8** 49, Formvorschriften **8** 13, Gegenstände, nicht geregelte **8** 5, Geschäftsgrundlage **8** 8, Gültigkeit **8** 6, Irrtumsrisiko **8** 6, Konsens **8** 3 f., merger clauses **8** 35, parol evidence rule **8** 31 ff., Privatautonomie **8** 9, Regeln, nationale **8** 1, Schweigen **8** 2, 36, Sorgfalt des Erklärungsempfängers **8** 14 ff., Sprachrisiken **8** 41 ff., Treu und Glauben **8** 30, Verhalten **8** 2, Verhalten nach Vertragsschluss **8** 50 f., Verkehrsschutz **8** 9, Vermutung der Richtigkeit und Vollständigkeit **8** 34, Vertrag **8** 3 ff., Vertrag als Ganzes **8** 5, 29, Vertragsergänzung **8** 11, 25 ff., Vertragsschluss **8** 1, 3, Willensmängel **8** 6
Auslegung der Konventionen 7 5–40, **7 VerjÜbk** 1, ausländische Rechtsprechung **7** 18–24, Auslegungsgrundsätze **7** 8–27, Auslegungsmethoden **7** 28–40, autonome Auslegung **7** 9–14, Bindung an ausländische Rechtsprechung **7** 23, CISG-online **7** 21, CLOUT **7** 19, Einheitlichkeit der Anwendung **7** 15–17, historische A. **7** 36, Internet und CISG **7** 21, Originalfassungen **7** 31, Präambel **Präambel** 4, Rechtsvergleichung **7** 40, Rückgriff auf die Lehre **7** 9,

systematische A. **7** 37–39, Textinterpretation **7** 30–35, Treu und Glauben **7** 25–27, UNILEX **7** 20, Wiener Vertragsrechtskonvention **7** 33
Auslegung des Kaufvertrags, objektive Auslegungskriterien **8** 7–9, Rahmenvereinbarung hinsichtlich Auslegung **14** 9, Reihenfolge der Auslegungskriterien **8** 2, subjektive Auslegungskriterien **8** 4–6
Ausscheiden der Ware und Lieferung **31** 50
Ausschließlichkeitsbindung 49 12, 30
Ausschluss der Anwendung des Verjährungsübereinkomens 3 VerjÜbk 4 f., **22 VerjÜbk** 2, A. von Ansprüchen aus Atomhaftpflicht **5 VerjÜbk** 3, A. von Ansprüchen aus Entscheidungen **5 VerjÜbk** 5, A. von Ansprüchen aus Sicherungsrechten des Verkäufers **5 VerjÜbk** 4, A. von Ansprüchen aus Tod oder Körperverletzung **5 VerjÜbk** 2, A. von Ansprüchen aus vollstreckbaren Titeln **5 VerjÜbk** 6, A. von Ansprüchen aus Wechsel oder Scheck **5 VerjÜbk** 7
Ausschluss der Konvention durch Vertrag, allgemeine Geschäftsbedingungen **6** 14, 17, 30, ausdrücklicher A. **6** 15–17, Ausschlussvereinbarung **6** 12–14, Beweislast **6** 38, dispositive Natur des Übereinkommens **6** 5–7, einseitiger A. **6** 13, Gerichtsstandsvereinbarung **6** 31, Haager Kaufrecht **6** 1–4, Hinweispflicht des Richters **6** 27, Incoterms **6** 29, Rechtswahl **6** 15 f., 20, Schiedsgerichtsvereinbarung **6** 32, stillschweigender A. **6** 1, 18–32, teilweiser A. **6** 33–35, Verhandeln auf Grundlage des nationalen Rechts **6** 25–27, *s. a. Parteiautonomie*
Ausschluss des CISG Vor 14–24 14a ff., in AGB **Vor 14–24** 14c, materielle Einigung **Vor 14–24** 14b ff.
Ausschlussfrist, Anwendungsbereich **39** 22, 40 9, Begriff **1 VerjÜbk** 6, Bösgläubigkeit des Verkäufers **39** 22, Einfluss der A. auf den Beginn der Verjährungsfrist **9 VerjÜbk** 2, Fristbeginn **39** 24, Fristende **39** 25, und Garantiefrist **39** 26, Hemmung und Unterbrechung **39** 23, und Verjährung **39** 28 f., **1 VerjÜbk** 6 f., **8 VerjÜbk** 3, Verkürzung oder Verlängerung **39** 26, 35, zweijährige A. für die Geltendmachung von Sachmängeln **44** 1
Ausschreibung, Vertragsschluss **Vor 14–24** 30
Außervertragliche Ansprüche, Verjährung **3 VertragsG** 7
Aussperrung 79 21
Autonome Anwendung 1 63–68

Banken als Erfüllungsgehilfen bei der Übergabe von Dokumenten **34** 3
Bankgarantien 9 8, **28** 12, **45** 3, **48** 4, **49** 12
battle of forms 8 11, **19** 4, 19 f., Gepflogenheiten **19** 29, Leistungsvorbereitungen **19** 31, Restgültigkeitstheorie **19** 23, 25 ff., Scheitern des Vertragsschlusses **19** 24, Theorie des letzten Wortes **19** 22, *s. a. Allgemeine Geschäftsbedingun-*

Magere Zahlen = Randnummern

Sachregister

gen, Vertragsdurchführung, einvernehmliche **19** 30, Vertragsinhalt **19** 34 ff., vorausgegangener mündlicher Vertragsschluss **19** 27
Bedarfsdeckungsvertrag Vor 14–24 41
Bedingung, bedingte Vertragsaufhebung **49** 23, Lieferung unter B. **31** 55 f., in Offerte **14** 31a ff., Zeitpunkt des Vertragsschlusses **23** 3
Beförderer 31 19–28, 32, 36, 38, 77, 79 f., **32** 16, 21 f., **67** 5, Auswahl **32** 17, Begriff **31** 19–28, erster B. **31** 20, Haftung des Verkäufers für den B. **31** 32, 36, 38, 77, Haftung des Verkäufers für den B. beim Verkauf rollender oder schwimmender Ware **31** 79 f., Mehrheit **31** 20, Selbständigkeit als Begriffsmerkmal **31** 19, 23, Spediteur als B. **31** 25–28, **32** 21 f.
Beförderung, Begriff **31** 13–16, bei Bringschuld **31** 76, Eingriffe des Verkäufers **31** 41–43, Erforderlichkeit nach dem Vertrag **31** 17 f., 70 ff., Pflicht des Verkäufers zum Abschluss des Beförderungsvertrags **32** 1, 15–30, bei Schickschuld **31** 2, 32, durch den Verkäufer **31** 21 f.
Beförderungsmittel 32 19
Beförderungsvertrag 32 1, 15–30, Abschluss durch Spediteur **32** 21 f., Abschluss mit Unterfrachtführer **32** 23, Abschluss zu üblichen Bedingungen **32** 20, Haftungsfreizeichnung des Beförderers **32** 20, Rechtsfolgen der Verletzung der Pflicht zum Abschluss eines angemessenen B. **32** 30, Tarif **32** 20
Beförderungsverzögerung (Annahme) 21 5, 16–21, Bedeutung **21** 19, Erkennbarkeit **21** 18, Gründe **21** 17, Verwahrung gegen transportverzögerte Annahme **21** 20
Befreiung des Schuldners bei Gläubigerfehlverhalten, Anspruch des S. auf die Gegenleistung **80** 8, beiderseitige Verursachung **80** 9, Fälligkeitszinsen **80** 9, Schadenersatz und sonstige Rechtsbehelfe **80** 8, Vertragsverletzung des Gläubigers **80** 10
Befreiung des Schuldners bei Gläubigerverursachung, Voraussetzungen **80** 3 ff.
Befreiung von der Haftung 31 76 f., **79,** bei Transportstörungen im Fall der Bringschuld gemäß Art. 79 **31** 76 f.
begebbares Dokument 31 58 f., **34** 4
Beginn der Verjährungsfrist 9 VerjÜbk 1 ff., bei Anspruch auf Grund einer Täuschung **10 VerjÜbk** 7 f., bei Anspruch aus einer Garantie **11 VerjÜbk** 2 f., bei Anspruch aus einer Vertragswidrigkeit der Ware **10 VerjÜbk** 4 ff., bei Anspruch aus Vertragsverletzung **10 VerjÜbk** 2 f., Einfluss der Ausschlussfrist auf B. **9 VerjÜbk** 2, und Schiedsvereinbarung **9 VerjÜbk** 3, und Scott-Avery-Klausel **9 VerjÜbk** 3, bei Sukzessivlieferungsvertrag **12 VerjÜbk** 4 ff., bei Vertragsaufhebung vor Erfüllung **12 VerjÜbk** 1
Begleitschaden bei Ausübung des Nacherfüllungsrechts **48** 21, und Erfüllungsanspruch **45** 26, bei Ersatzlieferung **46** 36, bei Lieferung vertragswidriger Ware **46** 36, bei Nachfristsetzung **47** 19, bei Vertragsaufhebung **45** 27
Begleitschaden (incidental damages), Aufwendungen **74** 27, Ersatzfähigkeit **74** 27, infolge unberechtigter Erfüllungsverweigerung **74** 27, Rechtsverfolgungskosten *s. dort*, Voraussehbarkeit **74** 53
Behelfe, Unabhängigkeit der **83** 2 ff.
Beitritt zum Änderungsprotokoll 1980 43a f. VerjÜbk
Beitritt zur Konvention *s. Ratifikation*
Beladen des Fahrzeugs des Beförderers bei Schickschuld **31** 29, 35, des Fahrzeugs des Käufers bei Holschuld **31** 54
Benachrichtigung des Käufers von der Bereitstellung der Ware **31** 51
Berechnung der Verjährungsfrist 28 VerjÜbk 1 ff., **29 VerjÜbk**
Beschädigung der für den Käufer bereitgestellten Ware beim Verkäufer **31** 62, der Ware nach Gefahrübergang **31** 62 f.
Beschaffungsrisiko 79 26 f., 30, 37, 40, Haftung für Zulieferanten **79** 37, Haftungsbefreiung **79** 26
Beschlagnahme wegen Eigenschaften der Ware **41** 6, gestohlener Ware **41** 7, wegen Rechten Dritter **41** 7
Besitzerwerb des Käufers und Lieferung **30** 2
Besitzkonstitut 31 50
Bestätigungsschreiben *s. kaufmännisches B.*
Bestellprobe 35 27
Bestimmtheit *s. Offerte*
Bestimmungsbefugnis *s. Offerte*
Bestimmungsort 32 18, **38** 21 f., Untersuchung der Ware **38** 21 f.
Beweisführung 35 49, Schadensersatzanspruch **74** 66
Beweisgegenstand, Vertragswidrigkeit der Ware **35** 50
Beweislast 1 42, 48, **2** 22 f., **3** 11, 20, **4** 48–53, **7** 56, **25** 16, **27** 9, **29** 14, **31** 63, 80, **32** 8, **33** 15, 20, **35** 51 f., **36** 13, **39** 37 f., **40** 12, **41** 25, **42** 29, **43** 12, **45** 9 f., **46** 16, 31, 33, 40, **47** 13, **48** 13, 26, 29, **49** 13, 20, 25, 28, 34, 39, **50** 15, **53** 42, **64** 38 ff., **65** 25 ff., **74** 64, **75** 14, **76** 15, **77** 13, **79** 59, **80** 11, Abnahmepflicht **60** 19, Absendung einer Erklärung **27** 9, Anwendbarkeit des CISG nach Art. 3 II **3** 20, Ausschluss des Übereinkommens **6** 38, Beweislastumkehr **35** 52, Eignung für bestimmten Gebrauchszweck **35** 53, Erkennbarkeit der Internationalität **1** 48, Erkennbarkeit des persönlichen Gebrauchs **2** 22 f., Gläubigerverursachung der Nichterfüllung **80** 11, Haftungsbefreiung **79** 59, Hinderungsgrund **79** 59, Internationalität **1** 42, Kauf nach Muster oder Probe **35** 53, Kaufpreis nach Nettogewicht **56** 5, Kaufpreiszahlungspflicht **53** 42, Kaufvertrag mit offenem Preis **55** 18, Kenntnis der Vertragswidrigkeit der Ware **35** 54, **40** 12, Marktpreisregel **76** 15, Miss-

1417

Sachregister

Fette Zahlen = Artikel

brauchseinwand bei Formmangel **29** 14, Nachfrist zur Erfüllung **63** 16 ff., Nichterfüllung **45** 9 f., Rechtsmangel **41** 25, Rechtsmängelanzeige **43** 12, Rüge **39** 37 f., Schadensersatzanspruch **74** 64, Schadensersatzanspruch wegen Verletzung der Benachrichtigungspflicht **79** 59, Schadensberechnung bei Deckungsgeschäft **75** 14, Schadensminderungspflicht **77** 13, Schutzrechtsbelastung **42** 29, Spezifizierung der Ware **65** 25 ff., Vernehmbarkeit der Erklärung **24** 43, Vertragsänderung **29** 14, Vertragsaufhebung durch den Verkäufer **64** 38 ff., Vertragsverletzungen **45** 9 f., Vertragswidrigkeit der Ware **35** 51 ff., Voraussehbarkeit bei wesentlicher Vertragsverletzung **25** 26 ff., Wechsel der Niederlassung des Verkäufers **57** 33, Werklieferungsvertrag **3** 11, mit der Zahlung verbundene Pflicht **54** 9, Zahlungsort **57** 33, Zahlungszeit **58** 37 ff., Zugang von Erklärungen **24** 43, Zurückbehaltungsrechte **58** 39

Beweislast des Käufers, Erklärung der Vertragsaufhebung **49** 13, 25, 28, 39, Lieferzeit **33** 15, 20, Nachfristsetzung im Fall der Vertragsaufhebung **47** 13, **49** 39, rechtzeitige Absendung des Ersatzlieferungsverlangens **46** 33, rechtzeitiger Widerspruch gegen ein nachträgliches Erfüllungsangebot des Verkäufers **48** 26, Unzumutbarkeit der Mängelbeseitigung durch den Verkäufer **48** 13, der Werte bei Minderung **50** 15, Wesentlichkeit der Vertragsverletzung des Verkäufers **46** 31, **49** 13

Beweislast des Verkäufers, Angebot der nachträglichen Erfüllung **48** 29, Einhaltung der Nachfrist **49** 20, 39, Fehlerfreiheit der Ware bei Übernahme einer Haltbarkeitsgarantie **36** 13, Kenntnis des Käufers von der Lieferung **49** 28, Kenntnis des Käufers von der Vertragsverletzung **49** 34, Lieferung **45** 10, **49** 20, Unmöglichkeit der Nachbesserung **46** 40, Unzumutbarkeit der Erfüllung **46** 16, Unzumutbarkeit der Nachbesserung **46** 40, Vereinbarung eines von Art. 33c) abweichenden Lieferzeitpunkts **33** 15, vertragsmäßiger Zustand der Ware bei Gefahrübergang **31** 80, **32** 8, **45** 10, für nicht zu vertretende Unmöglichkeit **46** 16, Vorhandensein auf dem Transport verkaufter Ware **31** 80, Vorhandensein der ab Lager gekauften Ware **31** 63

Beweismaß, Berücksichtigung präventiver Gesichtspunkte **74** 65, bei entgangenem Gewinn **74** 65, bei Goodwill-Schaden **74** 65, reasonable certainty **74** 65, Regelungsbereich **35** 49, Schadenersatzanspruch **74** 65, Vertragswidrigkeit der Ware **35** 55, bei Verzögerungsschaden **74** 25

Beweismittel s. Form

Beweiswürdigung 11 12

Bezugsverträge 60 8

Billigkeit 44 4 f.

Billigung verspäteter Annahme 21 6 ff., Erklärungsmittel **21** 9, modifizierende B. **21** 11, Rücknahme **21** 12, unverzüglich **21** 8, Verständigung des Akzeptanten **21** 7, als Willenserklärung **21** 7

Bindung an Offerte, arglistige Schädigung als Grenze **16** 13, Ausgestaltung als unwiderruflich **16** 8 f., Bindungswille des Offerenten **14** 1, 23, **16** 8 f., Rechtsfolge der Widerrufssperre bei der Offerte **16** 13, aufgrund Vertrauens **16** 11, Widerruflichkeit der Offerte **16** 7, Widerrufssperre **16** 4, 6

Bindungswille des Annehmenden **18** 4, des Offerenten **14** 1, 23, **16** 8 f.

Bindungswirkung, Erfüllungsanspruch **45** 14 f., Gebräuche **9** 7, Minderung **27** 14, **45** 17 ff., Nachfristsetzung **27** 14, **45** 14, **47** 3, 14–20, unbefristete Mahnung **47** 21, Versendungsanzeige **32** 9, Vertragsaufhebung **49** 45

Börse, Vertragsschluss **Vor 14–24** 29

Bösgläubigkeit des Verkäufers, hinsichtlich der Vertragswidrigkeit der Ware **40** 4 ff.

Bote, Absendeprinzip **27** 1, Erklärungsmittel **27** 7, laufender B. **27** 7, reitender B. **27** 7, s. a. Empfangsbote; Erklärungsbote

Bräuche, Berücksichtigung bei Schadensminderungspflicht **77** 7

breach of contract s. Vertragsverletzung

Bringschuld, Abschluss des Beförderungsvertrages **32** 16, Beförderung durch Dritte **31** 77, Einfuhrabgaben **31** 84, Exportgenehmigung **31** 85, Lieferschuld als B. **31** 76, Pflicht zur Verschaffung von Dokumenten als B. **34** 13

Brüssler Übereinkommen, Zahlungsort **57** 23

Brüssler Verordnung, Zahlungsort **57** 25 ff.

CAD s. „cash against documents"

„cash against documents" 53 16, Aufrechnungsverbot **61** 19, Untersuchungsrecht des Käufers vor Zahlung **58** 35, Zahlungsort **57** 10, Zahlungszeit **58** 5, 15

„cash against invoice", Aufrechnungsverbot **61** 19, Untersuchungsrecht des Käufers vor Zahlung **58** 35, Zahlungsort **57** 7, Zahlungszeit **58** 5

„cash before delivery", Aufrechnungsverbot **61** 19, Zahlungsort **57** 7, Zahlungszeit **58** 5

„cash on delivery", Aufrechnungsverbot **61** 19, Zahlungsort **57** 7

CBD s. „cash before delivery"

CE-Kennzeichnung 35 14

CESL 25 2, CISG als Vorbild **Vor 14–24** 47, CISG-konforme Auslegung **Vor 14–24** 51

CFR, Abschluss des Beförderungsvertrages **32** 15, Inhalt der Lieferpflicht **31** 73 f., Ort der Lieferung **31** 73, Verschiffungsanzeige **32** 4

chat program, Offerte, Fristbeginn **20** 3a

chat room 27 5

CIF, Abschluss des Beförderungsvertrages **32** 15, Gerichtsstand des Erfüllungsortes **31** 92, Inhalt der Lieferpflicht **31** 74, Kosten des Transports **31** 83, Ort der Lieferung **31** 73, Sammelladung **32** 4, Verschiffungsanzeige **32** 4

Magere Zahlen = Randnummern

Sachregister

CIP 31 72
CISG-AC Einl, 7 19a
CISG-online 7 21
CLOUT 7 19
COD *s. „cash on delivery"*
commercial impracticability 79 4
commodum ex negotiatione 84 36
commodum ex re 84 35
condition 25 2, 35 4
consideration 11 11, 16 2, 29 4
Container, Beladung 31 54
contemplation rule *s. Voraussehbarkeitsregel*
contra proferentem, Auslegung 8 47 f.
CPT, Inhalt der Lieferpflicht **31** 72, Ort der Lieferung 31 72
CTO-Dokument 32 3 f., 49 18
culpa in contrahendo 4 46, **Vor 14–24** 1, 32 ff., 38 ff., 16 14, 18 23, 29 13, **35** 47, **41** 23, **45** 30, Missbrauchseinwand bei Formverstoß 29 13, Schweigen 18 23, Verhandlungsstadium **Vor 14–24** 33

D/A *s. „documents against acceptance"*
DAP, Ort der Lieferung 31 74
DAT, Ort der Lieferung 31 74
Dauer der Verjährungsfrist *s. Verjährungsfrist*
DCFR 25 2
DDP 31 74, 85
Deckungsgeschäft 28 1 f., **46** 14, **49** 27, **75** 1 ff., **77** 10, Abgrenzung zum Selbsthilfeverkauf 75 4, Angemessenheit 75 6, bei antizipiertem Vertragsbruch 75 7, Anzeige 75 3, Begriff 75 3, Beweis 75 3, bei Erfüllungsverweigerung 75 5, Ersatz weiterer Schäden 75 11, Frist zur Vornahme 75 7, Gewinn aus dem Geschäft 75 4, marktgängige Ware 75 3, Nichterfüllung der Lieferpflicht **46** 14, **49** 27, Pflicht zur Vornahme 75 13, Rechtsfolgen bei Unangemessenheit 75 10, und Schadenminderungspflicht 75 13 f., 14, Schadensminderungspflicht 77 10, Verpflichtung zur Vornahme 28 1–2, Vertragsaufhebung als Voraussetzung 75 5, und Voraussehbarkeitsregel 75 8, vorzeitiges 75 7
Deliktshaftung 5 2–8, 35 47 f., **41** 23, **42** 27 f., **45** 31, **1 VerjÜbk** 5, Personenschäden 5 2–7, Rechtsmangel 41 23 f., Schmerzensgeld 5 5, Schutzrechtsbelastung **42** 27 f., Verjährung **1 VerjÜbk** 5, des Verkäufers 45 31, Vertragswidrigkeit der Ware 35 47 f.
Demontage 45 27
Depositar 89 1 f.
Destinationsvorbehalt 31 30
detriment *s. wesentliche Vertragsverletzung*
Devisen, Finanzielle Leistungsfähigkeit des Schuldners 79 25, staatlicher Eingriff **79** 17, Zinsen 79 56
Devisenkontrolle 53 26
Devisenrecht 28 7
Devisensperre 28 15, keine Befreiung von Zinspflicht **78** 17

Diskontsatz, Ablösung durch Bezugszinssatz **78** 31, als Maßstab für Zinshöhe **78** 31
Dispositionsfreiheit, Wiedergewinnung der D. **72** 4
Dispositivität *s. Ausschluss der Konvention, Parteiautonomie*
Dissens Vor 14–24 6
Distanzkauf 31 18
do ut des *s. Synallagma*
„**documents against acceptance**" 53 16
„**documents against payment**" **53** 16, Zahlungsort 57 7
Dokumente 1 37, **30** 6, **34** 1–13, **38** 7, **45** 3, 5, **46** 6, **48** 3 ff., **49** 11, 18 ff., **57** 9, 10, 11, **58** 16, **60** 6, Aufnahme von Dokumenten **60** 6, Erfüllungsanspruch **46** 6, fehlerhafte D. **34** 5, 12, **48** 3 f., **49** 11, 18 f., Form der Übergabe **34** 4, Gerichtsstand **34** 13, Nachfristsetzung für die Verschaffung der D. **49** 19, Nichterfüllung der Pflicht zur Übergabe von D. als Vertragsverletzung **34** 5, **45** 3, 5, **49** 19, Ort der Übergabe **34** 3, Pflicht des Verkäufers zur Übergabe **30** 6, **34** 1, Recht des Verkäufers zur Auswechslung fehlerhafter D. **34** 6–12, **48** 4 f., Rechtsfolgen der Nichterfüllung der Pflicht zur Übergabe der D. **34** 5, **49** 19, Untersuchungs- und Rügepflicht **38** 7, Zahlung gegen Dokumente **57** 9, 10, Zeitpunkt der Übergabe **34** 2
Dokumente, unreine als wesentliche Vertragsverletzung 25 63
Dokumentenakkreditiv 53 17 ff., **54** 5 ff., Aufforderung zur Stellung eines D. **59** 1, Rechtsbehelfe des Verkäufers **54** 8, Untersuchungsrecht vor Zahlung **58** 35 f., Vertragsaufhebung **64** 9 ff., Zahlungsort **57** 7, 10, Zahlungszeit **58** 5, 15, Zurückbehaltungsrecht **58** 29
Dokumentengeschäft und wesentliche Vertragsverletzung 25 62 ff.
Dokumenteninkasso 34 3
Dokumentenkauf 1 37, 2 34, **49** 19
Dokumentenstrenge und wesentliche Vertragsverletzung 25 62
D/P *s. „documents against payment"*
Dreiparteienvertrag Vor 14–24 30a ff.
Dritte, Banken **79** 35, doppelter Entlastungsnachweis **79** 39, Einschaltung D. vom Gläubiger aufgegeben **79** 36, Frachtführer **79** 35, Gläubigerverantwortung für Nichterfüllung durch D. **80** 3, Haftung des Schuldners **79** 34 ff., Haftungsverschärfung **79** 39, selbständige D. **79** 38, Spediteur **79** 34, Subunternehmer **79** 35, Untersuchung der Ware durch D. **38** 10, Zulieferanten **79** 37
Drittschäden, undisclosed agency **74** 15, zufällige Schadensverlagerung **74** 16
dual use goods 79 32

ECE-Lieferbedingungen 8 8
e-commerce *s. elektronische Kommunikation,* Vertragsschluss **Vor 14–24** 25 ff.

1419

Sachregister

Fette Zahlen = Artikel

EDI 18 5
EG-Recht 5 14 f., **90** 3, **94** 5, EG-Richtlinien **90** 3, **94** 5, Produkthaftungsrichtlinie **5** 14 f., Vorrang der Konvention **90** 3
Eigenes Recht s. *innerstaatliches Recht*
Eigenhändlervertrag Vor 14–24 41
Eigenschaften, spezielle E. der Ware **46** 24
Eigentum 4 4, 29–31, **41** 2, **42** 4, **45** 3, **46** 6, **Vor 81–84** 4, **81** 6 ff., anwendbares Recht **30** 7, Eigentumsvorbehalt **4** 30, geistiges E. **42** 4, (s. a. *Immaterialgüterrechte*), Pflicht zur Verschaffung **30** 7, Rechtsfolgen der Nichterfüllung der Pflicht zur Verschaffung **45** 3, **46** 6, bei Rückabwicklung **Vor 81–84** 4, **81** 6 ff., Übertragung **4** 4, **41** 2
Eigentumsvorbehalt 30 8
Eil- und Notfälle, Fälligkeit der Lieferpflicht bei Bestellung in E. **33** 17
Einheitliche Richtlinien für Inkassi (ERI 522) 53 16
Einheitlichkeit der Anwendung s. *Auslegung*
Einheitsfrist s. *Verjährungsfrist*
Einigung, bedingte **14** 31a ff.
Einigungsmangel, Kaufpreis **Vor 14–24** 6
Einigungsvorgang, ungeregelter s. *Vertragsschluss*
Einlagerung der Ware 87 1 ff., als Erfüllungssurrogat **87** 7
Einleitung eines Gerichtsverfahrens, internationale Wirkung **30 VerjÜbk** 2, s. a. *Unterbrechung der Verjährungsfrist*
Einleitung eines Schiedsverfahrens, internationale Wirkung **30 VerjÜbk** 2, s. a. *Unterbrechung der Verjährungsfrist*
Einrede der Verjährung 24 VerjÜbk 1 f.
Einrede des nichterfüllten Vertrags 33 4
Einstandspflicht für die Ware und Rückabwicklung **82** 27
„Einwurf-Einschreiben" 24 20
Einzelhändler, wesentliche Vertragsverletzung bei Lieferung mangelhafter Ware an den E. **46** 25
Einzellieferung, Abgrenzung zur Teillieferung **73** 8 ff., gestörte E. **73** 11 ff., Sukzessivlieferungsvertrag **73** 9
Eisenbahn 31 19
electronic commerce s. *elektronische Kommunikation*
Electronic Data Interchange (EDI), Zugang **24** 29
Elektrizität 2 46, keine Anwendung des VerjÜbk auf Kauf von E. **4 VerjÜbk**
elektronische Erklärung, Zugang **24** 6, 22–30
elektronische Kommunikation 11 4, 16, **13** 2, **Vor 14–24** 15, 25 ff., **18** 5, 5a, **21** 9, 16, 18, 20, **27** 7, als geeignetes Mittel **27** 7, Schriftform **13** 2, verspätete Annahme **21** 9, 16, 18, 20, s. a. *E-Mail; Internet; Kommunikation, elektronische; Signatur, elektronische*

Elektronische Kommunikationsmittel, Schriftform bei Vertragsänderung **29** 7
E-Mail 11 4, **13** 2, **18** 4, 5, 15, 17, **20** 3, 3a, **24** 12, 14, **27** 5, 9, **39** 11, **43** 5, Absendung **27** 9, angemessene Frist für Annahme der Offerte **18** 15, Mängelrüge **39** 11, **43** 5, keine mündliche Erklärung **18** 17, Offerte, Fristbeginn **20** 3a, Schriftform **13** 2, Übermittlungsrisiko **27** 5, unmittelbare Übermittlungsart **20** 3a, Zugang **24** 24
Embargo 28 15
Empfängerhorizont 8 4, 7, 19 ff.
Empfangsbote, Zugang von Erklärungen **24** 7, 8
Empfangszeit 33 5
Endtermin für Annahme der Offerte 20 1
entgangener Gewinn 44 1, 10
Entlastung s. *Haftungsbefreiung*
Entschuldigung der Nichtvornahme der Rüge **39** 22, der Versäumung der Rügefrist **39** 22, **44** 4–9a
Entsorgung der Ware, Grundsatz der unversehrten Rückgabe **82** 24
ERA/ERI 9 26
Erfüllung der Zahlungspflicht 57 20, Scheck **53** 14, Überweisung **53** 12, Wechsel **53** 14
Erfüllung in Natur s. *Erfüllungsanspruch*, Anspruch des Verkäufers s. a. *Erfüllungsanspruch; specific performance*
Erfüllungsanspruch 28 1 f., 4, 6, **35** 43, **45** 14 f., **46** 1 ff., 17, 29, 39, **48** 1, **62** 4 ff., **77** 4 ff., **79** 52, Abnahme der Ware oder Erfüllung einer sonstigen Pflicht **62** 15, Ausschluss des **46** 7 ff., Bindungswirkung der Geltendmachung **45** 14 f., Einschränkung der Durchsetzbarkeit des E. durch Art. 28 **46** 8, Einschränkung durch Leistungshindernisse **46** 9 ff., Ersatzlieferung **46** 4, 17 ff., als Grundprinzip des Einheitskaufrechts **28** 1 f., **46** 1, Haftungsbefreiung **79** 52, des Käufers **28** 6, **46** 6 ff., Kaufpreisklage **62** 14, Nachbesserung **28** 6, **46** 5, **39** ff., praktische Bedeutung **28** 4, als Rechtsbehelf **46** 29, Schadensminderungspflicht **77** 4 f., unvereinbare Rechtsbehelfe **46** 7, des Verkäufers **28** 6, **48** 1, **62** 13, bei Vertragswidrigkeit der Ware **35** 43, Vorrang des E. **46** 1 f., Zahlung des Kaufpreises s. a. *specific performance*
Erfüllungsgehilfe s. *Hilfspersonen*
Erfüllungsklage auf Abnahme s. *Abnahme der Ware,* Abweisung der E. **28** 5, 21, auf Nachbesserung **28** 6, Selbsthilfeverkauf s. a. *specific performance*
Erfüllungsort 28 9, **31** 87 ff., **45** 31 f., **47** 16, **74** 61, und anwendbares Recht **28** 9, Gerichtsstand für die Lieferung **31** 87 ff., Schadenersatzanspruch **74** 61, für Schadensersatzanspruch **45** 31 f., und Wahrung der Frist **47** 16
Erfüllungsortsvereinbarungen und Gerichtsstand **31** 92, 96
Erfüllungsübernehmer, Begriff **79** 34, Haftung des Schuldners **79** 34 ff.

Magere Zahlen = Randnummern **Sachregister**

Erfüllungsverweigerung 47 17, 49 6, 17, 27, 38, 46, 48, **72** 33, 37 ff., **12 VerjÜbk** 1, vor Ablauf der Nachfrist 47 17, 49 17, 38, Beginn der Verjährungsfrist **12 VerjÜbk** 1, bezüglich der Ersatzlieferung 49 38, bezüglich der Nachbesserung 49 6, 38, Form und Frist der Aufhebungserklärung **72** 37 ff., unbefristetes Recht des Käufers zur Erklärung der Vertragsaufhebung 49 38, unrechtmäßige Erklärung der Vertragsaufhebung als E. 49 46, 48, als wesentliche Vertragsverletzung 49 6
Erfüllungszwang 28 10–15, 18
Ergänzungen in der Annahmeerklärung s. *Annahme der Offerte*
Erhaltung der Ware Vor 85 1 ff., **85** 5, 11 ff., **86** 16, **87** 9, und Gefahrübergang **85** 5, 11, und Hilfspersonen **85** 13, Inhalt der Erhaltungspflicht **85** 12, Kosten **85** 15, **87** 9, Pflicht zur Inbesitznahme bei drohender Verschlechterung **86** 16, Zurückbehaltungsrecht wegen der Kosten **85** 17, **87** 9
Erhaltungspflicht des Käufers bei vorzeitiger Lieferung **52** 3, bei Zuviellieferung **52** 9
Erhaltungspflicht des Verkäufers, Haftung 45 3, bei Holschulden im Fall des Annahmeverzugs **31** 62
Erklärung auf anderem Weg als mündlich 24 6, Auslegung 8 1, Funk 18 17, 24 5, mündliche E. 18 17, 24 5, 27 5, durch schlüssiges Verhalten 26 7 f., Telephon 18 17, Vernehmbarkeit 27 5, zugangsbedürftige E. 24 3, Zugangsvoraussetzungen 24 31
Erklärung der Vertragsaufhebung 26 7 ff., 49 23 ff., Absendung als ausreichende E. 49 25, Adressat 26 14, Änderung der V. 26 11, trotz Angebots der Mängelbeseitigung 48 17 f., 49 41 f., bedingte E. 49 23, Beschränkung auf einen Teil des Vertrags 49 26, **51** 1, 6, Beweislast 49 13, 25, 28, 39, Bindung an die E. 45 16, Bindungswirkung 26 11 f., Form 26 7, 49 24, Frist für E. bei Nichteinhaltung des Liefertermins 49 27 ff., Frist für E. bei sonstigen Vertragsverletzungen 49 30 ff., Fristen 26 15 f., 49 27 ff., Inhalt 49 24, Inhaltliche Klarheit 26 8, durch den Käufer **81** 3, **82** 28, **84** 7, Kombination mit Mängelrüge oder Nachfristsetzung 26 9, konkludente E. 49 24, als massgeblicher Zeitpunkt für Beurteilung der Unversehrtheit **82** 7, Mittelbare 26 14, Sprache 49 24, Übermittlungsrisiko 26 11, unberechtigte E. 49 44, 48, bei Unmöglichkeit 49 23, Verbindung mit Nachfristsetzung 49 23, 40, durch den Verkäufer **81** 3, **82** 28 f., **84** 7, Wegfall der Verpflichtung zur 26 10, Widerruf der E. 26 12
Erklärungsbote, Zugang von Erklärungen 24 9
Erkundigungspflicht des Käufers in bezug auf Rechtsmängel 43 4, des Käufers in bezug auf Schutzrechte 42 14, 17, des Verkäufers bei Versendung an den falschen Ort **31** 39, des Verkäufers in bezug auf Schutzrechte 42 14

Erlöschen der Leistungspflichten 81 5 ff.
Ersatzfähigkeit von Aufwendungen 84 28 ff.
Ersatzlieferung 31 62, 35 43, 38 9, 39 13, 44 15, 45 14, 46 3 f., 17 ff., 23–36, 48 5 ff., 9–11, 14, 20, 49 8, 15, 20, 33, 35, 38, **70** 2–4, **Vor 81–84** 5, Anspruch des Käufers auf E. 46 3 f., 17 ff., 35, Begriff 46 19, Beschädigung der Ware beim Verkäufer nach Bereitstellen der Ware **31** 62, Bindung des Käufers an den Anspruch auf E. 45 14, bei Fehlschlagen der Nachbesserung 46 26, Frist für die Geltendmachung des Anspruchs auf E. 46 33, beim Gattungskauf 46 18, Geltendmachung mit Rüge 39 13, Grundsatz der unversehrten Rückgabe **Vor 81–84** 5, Kosten der E. 46 4, 48 8, Nachfrist bei der E. 45 14, 48 10, 49 8, 33, 38, Recht des Verkäufers zur E. 44 15, 46 32, 48 6, 20, Rechtsfolgen 46 36 ff., bei Rechtsmangel 46 22, Rückgabe der mangelhaften Sache 46 34, beim Spezieskauf 46 18, 48 5, Unmöglichkeit der E. infolge verspäteter Rüge 44 15, Unmöglichkeit der Mängelbeseitigung durch E. s. *Unmöglichkeit,* Untersuchung der Ware 38 9, Unzumutbarkeit bei den Käufer 49 9–11, Verlust der Ware beim Verkäufer und Pflicht zur E. **31** 62, bei verspäteter Rüge 44 15, Vertragsaufhebung bei Nichterfüllung des Anspruchs auf E. 49 15, 20, 35, bei Vertragswidrigkeit der Ware 35 43, wesentliche Vertragsverletzung als Voraussetzung des Anspruchs auf E. 46 23–32, wesentliche Vertragsverletzung und Recht des Verkäufers zur E. 48 14, 20
Ersatzteil, Liefertermin 33 17, bei Nachbesserung 46 44
Ersatzvornahme 46 46, der Nachbesserung durch den Käufer 46 46
Erwerbschancen, kommerzieller Wert 74 18
essentialia contractus s. *Offerte*
estoppel s. *venire contra factum proprium*
Ethische Prinzipien 35 9, 19
Ethische Unzumutbarkeit 79 32, dual use goods 79 32
EuGVO und Erfüllungsort für die Lieferung **31** 93 ff., Zahlungsort **57** 25 ff.
EuGVÜ und Erfüllungsort **31** 88, 99, Zahlungsort **57** 23
Euro, Hauptrefinanzierungssatz der EZB **78** 31, Zinssatz **78** 31
ex Tank 31 72
Export- und Importverbote, Haftungsbefreiung **79** 17
Exportabgaben 31 84
Exportgenehmigung 30 6
Exportgenehmigung (EXW) 31 85 f., wesentliche Vertragsverletzung **25** 29
Exportverbot 46 13 f., als Rechtsmangel 41 6
EXW, Ausfuhrabgaben und −zölle **31** 84, Inhalt der Lieferpflicht **31** 72, Ort der Lieferpflicht **31** 72

1421

Sachregister

Fette Zahlen = Artikel

Fairer Handel 35 19
Fälligkeit s. *Zahlungszeit*, des Anspruchs auf Lieferung **33** 4, 7 ff., des Anspruchs auf Lieferung bei Vorleistungspflicht des Käufers **33** 4, als Beginn der Verjährungsfrist 9 **VerjÜbk** 1
Fälligkeit des Kaufpreisanspruchs 31 56, 61, 78 7 ff., Lieferung **31** 56, 61, als Voraussetzung für Zinsanspruch **78** 7 ff.
Fälligkeitszinsen und Kreditkosten **78** 35, 41, und Schadenersatz **78** 41 f., und Verzugsschaden **78** 41
falsa demonstratio 19 5
Falschangaben, fahrlässige 35 47, **41** 23, **42** 27
Falschlieferung 31 34, **35** 4, 10, **38** 7, **39** 30, **40** 5, **45** 7, **46** 18, 20, 24, Bösgläubigkeit des Verkäufers **40** 5, Gutgläubigkeit des Verkäufers **35** 10, Kenntnis des Verkäufers **35** 10, **40** 5, Lieferung nicht vertragsgemäßer Ware **31** 34, **46** 20, Offensichtlichkeit **35** 10, beim Spezieskauf **46** 18, 24, unterlassene oder nicht gehörige Rüge **39** 30, Untersuchung der Ware **38** 7, als Vertragsverletzung **45** 7, wesentliche Vertragsverletzung **46** 20, 24
FAS, Abschluss des Beförderungsvertrages **31** 75, Exportgenehmigung **31** 85, Exportzoll **31** 84, Inhalt der Lieferpflicht **31** 74, Ort der Lieferung **31** 73, unterlassene Mitwirkung des Käufers **31** 75, Verschiffungsanzeige **32** 5, Zeitpunkt der Lieferung **33** 10
favor contractus 7 54
FCA, Abschluss des Beförderungsvertrages **32** 15, Beladen des Fahrzeugs durch den Verkäufer **31** 54, 72, Exportgenehmigung **31** 85, Exportzoll **31** 84, Inhalt der Lieferpflicht **31** 74, Ort der Lieferpflicht **31** 72, unterlassene Benennung des Transportmittels durch den Käufer **31** 75, Zeitpunkt der Lieferung **33** 10
Fehlerbegriff 35 6
Fehlerbegriff, subjektiver 35 6
Fernkauf, Anzeige des Lieferzeitpunkts **33** 10
Fiktion, Anzeige der Erfüllungsbereitschaft **48** 28
Fixgeschäft 1 20, **25** 39, 41, **48** 15, **49** 5, 9, 28, Incoterms-Klausel **25** 41, Lieferung nach dem Liefertermin **49** 28, Lieferung nicht vertragsmäßiger Ware **48** 15, **49** 9, Überschreitung des Liefertermins als wesentliche Vertragsverletzung **48** 15, **49** 5, Vertragsaufhebung **49** 9, 28
Flugzeuge s. *Luftfahrzeuge*
FOB, Abschluss des Beförderungsvertrags **32** 15, Exportzoll **31** 84
FOB Flughafen 31 74
„FOB verschifft" 32 15 (Fn. 41), erweitertes FOB-Geschäft **32** 15 (Fn. 41), Gerichtsstand des Erfüllungsortes **31** 92, Inhalt der Lieferpflicht **31** 74, **32** 15 (Fn. 41), Ort der Lieferung **31** 73, uneigentliches FOB-Geschäft **32** 15 (Fn. 41), Unterlassung der Benennung des Schiffs durch den Käufer **31** 75, Verschiffungsanzeige **32** 5, Zeitpunkt der Lieferung **33** 10

FOB-Transport 31 74, 83
Folgeschaden bei Nachfristsetzung **47** 19
Folgeschäden (consequential damages), Goodwill-Schaden **74** 33, Haftungsschäden **74** 32, Mangelfolgeschaden **74** 35, Personenschäden **74** 32, Rechtsverfolgungskosten **74** 33, Vertragsstrafe **74** 32, Voraussehbarkeit **74** 54
force majeure clauses 79 57
Form 4 13, anwendbares Recht bei Vorbehalt nach Art. 96 **12** 2 f., Aufhebung des Sukzessivlieferungsvertrages bei Zweckzusammenhang **73** 37, Aufhebung des Sukzessivlieferungsvertrages für die Zukunft **73** 25, Aufhebungserklärung **26** 7, **49** 24, Aufhebungserklärung bei gestörter Einzellieferung des Sukzessivlieferungsvertrages **73** 13, der Aufhebungserklärung wegen künftiger wesentlicher Vertragsverletzung **72** 21, 37, Auslegungsregeln **8** 13, Beweismittelbeschränkung als Formvorschriften **11** 12, beweisrechtliche Formvorschriften **11** 12, consideration **11** 11, der Erklärung über die Sicherheitsleistung bei künftiger wesentlicher Vertragsverletzung **72** 32, Formfreiheit **7** 52, **11** 1–16, Formvorschriften eines Vorbehaltsstaats **13** 4, Handelsbrauch **11** 6, 16, parol evidence rule **11** 13, Qualifikation von Formvorschriften **11** 15, Sprache als F. **11** 14, verbraucherschützende Formvorschriften **11** 14, vereinbarte F. **11** 16, Vereinbarung in Allgemeinen Geschäftsbedingungen **11** 16, Vorbehalt nach Art. 96 **Vor 1–6** 23, **11** 2, **12** 2 f., **13** 4, s. a. *Schriftform*
Formbedürftigkeit, Gerichtsstandsklausel **11** 7, Grundstücksgeschäfte **11** 7, Schiedsklausel **11** 7, vereinbarte Formvorschriften **29** 5–9, Wettbewerbsabrede **11** 7
Formfreiheit 7 52, **11** 1–16, Vertragsänderungen **11** 4, 8, Vertragsaufhebung **11** 8, Vertragsergänzung **11** 8, Vertragsschluss **11** 5, Vorkorrespondenz **11** 4
Formvereinbarung, Auslegung **11** 16
Formverstoß, Heilung **29** 11, 13, Missbrauchseinwand **29** 10–13, Sanktionen **11** 11
Frachtbrief 32 3
Frachtbriefdoppel, Nachfrist für Übergabe **49** 18, Pflicht zur Übergabe **30** 6, **34** 1
frachtfrei (CPT), Inhalt der Lieferpflicht **31** 72, Ort der Lieferung **31** 72, Transportkosten **31** 83, Zollkosten **31** 84
frachtfrei versichert (CIP) 31 72
Frachtführer 31 19
Franchisevertrag 1 32
frei Bahnstation 31 74
frei Frachtführer (FCA), Abschluss des Beförderungsvertrages **32** 15, Beladen des Fahrzeugs durch den Verkäufer **31** 54, 72, Exportgenehmigung **31** 85, Exportzoll **31** 84, Inhalt der Lieferpflicht **31** 72, Ort der Lieferung **31** 72, unterlassene Benennung des Transportmittels durch den Käufer **31** 75, Versendungsanzeige **32** 1 ff., Zeitpunkt der Lieferung **33** 10

Magere Zahlen = Randnummern **Sachregister**

frei Haus 31 76, Beförderungsvertrag **32** 16, Bringschuld **31** 76, **32** 16, Ort der Lieferung **31** 76
frei Waggon 31 74
freibleibend 14 25, **33** 14
Freizeichnung 32 20, **35** 41 f., **36** 11, **41** 19a, **42** 24a, **45** 36 f., des Beförderers **32** 20, *s. a. Abdingbarkeit,* bei Belastung mit gewerblichen Schutzrechten **42** 24a, bei Haltbarkeitsgarantie **36** 11, bei Rechtsmangel **41** 19a, bei Vertragswidrigkeit der Ware **35** 41 f.
fremde Sache, Verkauf **41** 3, 22
Frist, Abgrenzung der Rüge- und Untersuchungsfrist **39** 15, Absendeprinzip bei Fristsetzung **27** 4, Annahmeerklärung **18** 14 f., Aufhebung des Sukzessivlieferungsvertrages bei Zweckzusammenhang **73** 37 f., Aufhebung des Sukzessivlieferungsvertrages für die Zukunft **73** 25 f., Aufhebungserklärung **26** 15 f., Aufhebungserklärung bei gestörter Einzellieferung im Rahmen eines Sukzessivlieferungsvertrags **73** 13, Aufhebungserklärung bei vorzeitiger Erfüllungsverweigerung **72** 38 f., Ausschlussfrist für Rüge **39** 22–29, Beginn der Annahmefrist **20** 1, Beginn der F. zur Erklärung der Vertragsaufhebung **49** 34 ff., Berechnung **20** 5, keine Gewährung einer zusätzlichen F. durch das Gericht **45** 29, Rüge **39** 15–21, Untersuchung der Ware **38** 15–26, Zeitzone **18** 14
Frist, angemessene 47 6, Annahme **18** 15, Annahme per Telefax **18** 15, Annahme per Telex **18** 15, beim Anspruch auf Nachlieferung **46** 29, 33, 43, bei der Erklärung der Vertragsaufhebung **49** 28, 31 f., 42, Erklärung der Vertragsaufhebung nach Lieferung **49** 28, Erklärung der Vertragsaufhebung nach Nachfristsetzung **49** 42, Erklärung der Vertragsaufhebung nach nachträglichem Erfüllungsangebot des Verkäufers **49** 42, Lieferung **33** 16 f., bei Nachfrist *s. dort,* Nichterfüllung des Anspruchs auf Nachbesserung innerhalb F. und wesentliche Vertragsverletzung **46** 29, Rüge **39** 1 ff., 15 ff., Übergabe der Dokumente **34** 2, Überlegungsfrist bei Annahme der Offerte **18** 15, bei Widerspruch gegen die Anzeige der Erfüllungsbereitschaft **48** 26
Fristversäumnis und Rechtsbehelfe **45** 21, **49** 33
Fristwahrung im Ausland *s. internationale Wirkung*
Früchte 84 25
frustration of purpose 79 4
Funk, mündliche Erklärung **18** 17, **24** 5, sofortige Übermittlungsart **20** 3, Übermittlungsrisiko **27** 5

Garantie 36 1 f., 1 ff., 7 ff., **79** 8, 58, **11 VerjÜbk** 3, absolute G. **79** 58, anfängliche Leistungshindernisse **79** 58, Anwendungsbereich **36** 7, Befreiung von der Haftung **79** 58, Beginn der Verjährung **11 VerjÜbk** 3, Beweislast **36** 12 f., Dauer **36** 9 f., Haftungsbefreiung **79** 8, Haftungsbegrenzung **36** 11, Handelsbrauch **36** 8
Garantiefrist 11 VerjÜbk 2, Anzeige der Vertragswidrigkeit der Ware **39** 27, und Ausschlussfrist für Rüge **39** 26
Garantiehaftung des Verkäufers **45** 23
Gattungskauf 46 18, **48** 5, **79** 26 f., Anspruch auf Ersatzlieferung **46** 18, Beschaffungsrisiko **79** 26 f., marktbezogener G. **79** 26, nicht marktbezogener G. **79** 27, Recht zur zweiten Andienung **48** 5
Gattungsschuld 35 15, durchschnittliche Qualität **35** 15
Gebrauch, Bestimmung der Ware zum eigenen G. des Käufers und wesentliche Vertragsverletzung **46** 25
Gebrauch der Ware, Grundsatz der unversehrten Rückgabe **82** 17, 21
Gebräuche, Auslegung **8** 12, 26, 45 f., Beachtlichkeit **9** 12 ff., Begriff **9** 6, 11, Bekanntheit und Beachtung **9** 16 f., Einigung **9** 6 f., Gerichtsstandsvereinbarungen **9** 25, Gültigkeit **4** 26 f., **9** 2, 5, Internationaler Handel **9** 11, Internationalität **9** 18, kaufmännisches Bestätigungsschreiben **9** 22 ff., Prozessuale Behandlung **9** 20, Schiedsklausel **9** 25, *s. a. Gepflogenheiten, Handelsbrauch*
Gebrauchsanweisung 35 14
Gebrauchsmuster 42 4
Gebrauchsvorteile 84 26
Gebrauchszweck *s. Verwendungszweck*
Gefahrbegriff 66 4 f., Hoheitliche Eingriffe **66** 6 ff.
Gefahrtragung 31 11, 61 ff., 75 ff., **32** 8, 14, **66** 12 ff., 16 ff., 27 ff., **67** 19 ff., **68** 4 ff., **69** 17 ff., **70** 5 ff., **82** 10, **85** 5, 11, anfängliche Unmöglichkeit **68** 4 ff., Annahmeverzug **31** 11, 62, 75, zwischen Bereitstellung der Ware und Übernahme durch den Käufer **31** 61 ff., bei Bringschulden **31** 76, und Erhaltungspflicht **85** 5, 11, Gefahrbegriff *s. dort,* Gefahrrückfall **70** 10 ff., und Haftung **66** 16 ff., Vergleich mit ICC Incoterms® **67** 19 ff., **68** 4 ff., Verhältnis zu ICC Incoterms® **Vor 66–70** 23 f., Individualisierung *s. dort,* und Kaufpreisklage **66** 27 ff., Konkretisierung *s. Individualisierung,* und Lieferung **31** 11, Lieferung an sonstigem Ort **69** 17 ff., periculum est emptoris **Vor 66–70** 5 ff., Pflichtverletzung des Käufers **69** 15 f., Pflichtverletzung des Verkäufers **66** 16 ff., Platzkauf **69** 5 ff., Preisgefahr **31** 62, 77, reisende Ware **68** 4 ff., res perit domino **Vor 66–70** 8 ff., Rückabwicklung **82** 10, Sammelladungen *s. dort,* Übergabe der Ware **Vor 66–70** 11 ff., **66** 17 ff., Untergang durch Handlung oder Unterlassung des Käufers **31** 75, Veränderung des Transports **66** 12 ff., bei Verkauf rollender oder schwimmender Ware **31** 80 f., nach Versen-

1423

Sachregister

dungsanzeige **32** 8, 14, Versendungskauf *s. dort,* Verzug **69** 9 ff., und wesentliche Vertragsverletzung **70** 5 ff., Zurverfügungstellen der Ware **31** 62 ff.

Gefahrtragungsregeln in der Rückabwicklung, Übertragung auf andere Fälle? **82** 28 ff.

Gefahrübergang 28 2, **45** 10, und Beweislast **45** 10, als maßgeblicher Zeitpunkt für die Vertragswidrigkeit der Ware **36** 3 f.

Gegenanspruch, Verjährung des G. **16 VerjÜbk** 1 ff.

Gegenfrist, Setzung durch den Verkäufer **47** 17

Gegengeschäfte 1 30

Gegenkauf (counterpurchase) 53 28

Gegenofferte 19 11–12, Mindestforfordernisse **19** 11

Gegenstände, geregelte 4 8–11, Beweislast **4** 48–53, Form **4** 13, Lückenfüllung bei G. **7** 42 f., positive Vertragsverletzung **4** 46, Rechte und Pflichten der Parteien **4** 10 f., Vergleich **4** 45, Vertragsschluss **4** 9, Verwirkung **4** 42, Wegfall der Geschäftsgrundlage **4** 44

Gegenstände, nicht geregelte 4 4–7, 12–41, 48–53, Abtretung **4** 38, Aufrechnung **4** 39, culpa in contrahendo **4** 46, Eigentumsübertragung **4** 4, 29–31, Eigentumsvorbehalt **4** 30, Gebräuche und Gepflogenheiten **9** 4, Gültigkeit des Vertrages **4** 4, 15–28, Gültigkeit von Vertragsstrafevereinbarungen **4** 40, Kartellabreden **4** 14, Personenschäden **5** 3–7, Schuldübernahme **4** 37, Sittenverstoß **4** 18, Stellvertretung **4** 34, Verfahrensrecht **4** 33, Verjährung **4** 35 f., Verstoß gegen die guten Sitten **4** 18, Vertragsauslegung **8** 5, *s. a. Gültigkeit des Vertrages*

Gehilfen *s. Hilfspersonen*

geistiges Eigentum *s. Immaterialgüterrechte*

Geldwertverlust, Entschädigung im Rahmen der Rückabwicklung **84** 21

geliefert Grenze, Gerichtsstand des Erfüllungsortes **31** 92

geliefert verzollt (DDP) 31 85

„Geliefert"-Klauseln, Ort der Lieferung **31** 74

Geltungsbereich *s. Anwendungsbereich, persönlicher; Anwendungsbereich, sachlicher; Anwendungsbereich, zeitlicher*

Gemeinschaftsrecht *s. EG-Recht*

Genehmigung der Ware bei Unterlassen der Rüge **39** 30

Genehmigung der Konvention *s. Ratifikation*

Genehmigung des Vertragsschlusses durch Dritte, Rückwirkung **18** 14, Zeitpunkt des Vertragsschlusses **23** 4

Genfer Konventionen über gezogene Wechsel und Eigenwechsel 53 13

Gepflogenheiten, Auslegung **8** 12, 26, 44, **14** 9, Beendigung **9** 9, Begriff **9** 8, Berücksichtigung bei Schadensminderungspflicht **77** 7, beim Distanzkauf **31** 18, Untersuchung der Ware **38** 11, beim Verkauf eingelagerter Ware **31** 59, Vorrang und Nachrang **9** 10, Zugangsbedürftigkeit

von Erklärungen **27** 6, *s. a. Gebräuche, Handelsbrauch*

gerichtliches Verfahren, internationale Wirkung **30 VerjÜbk** 2, ohne Sachentscheidung **17 VerjÜbk** 1 f., *s. a. Unterbrechung der Verjährungsfrist*

Gerichtsstand und Bestimmungsort **31** 90, 92, 94 ff., bei Erfüllungsvereinbarungen **31** 92, 96, und Incoterms **31** 92, 96, bei Lieferortvereinbarungen **31** 92, 96

Gerichtsstand des Erfüllungsorts 31 88 ff., **34** 13, **45** 34 f., **57** 10 ff., **81** 27, für Ansprüche auf Schadenersatz und aus Vertragsaufhebung **45** 34 f., und Dokumentenübergabe **31** 94, **34** 13, nach EuGVO **31** 93 ff., **34** 13, nach EuGVÜ **31** 88, 99, für die Lieferung nach Lugano Übereinkommen **31** 89 ff., bei Rückabwicklung **81** 27, am Sitz der Zahlstelle **34** 13, für die Übergabe von Dokumenten **34** 13, beim Versendungskauf **31** 90, 92

Gerichtsstandsklausel 57 28, Fortbestehen der bei Vertragsrückabwicklung **81** 12

Gerichtsstandsvereinbarungen 8 5, 10, **9** 25, **11** 7, **Vor 14–24** 9 ff., 11, 29 2, Auslegung **8** 5, äußerer Konsens **Vor 14–24** 10, Formbedürftigkeit **11** 7, Gebräuche **9** 25, Schriftform **Vor 14–24** 11, Vereinbarung im Rahmen einer Vertragsänderung **29** 2

Gesamtschuldner *s. Unterbrechung der Verjährungsfrist*

gesamtschuldnerische Haftung *s. Unterbrechung der Verjährungsfrist*

Gesamtvertrag, Sukzessivlieferungsvertrag **73** 8 ff.

Geschäftsbesorgung 32 15

Geschäftsfähigkeit 4 17, **Vor 14–24** 1, **15** 7 f., **17** 6, **18** 3, Annahme der Offerte **18** 3, beschränkte G. **Vor 14–24** 2, Einfluss fehlender G. auf Offerte **15** 6, **17** 6, fehlende G. **Vor 14–24** 2

Geschäftsgrundlage, Auslegung **8** 8

Geschäftsverkehr, normaler und Grundsatz der unversehrten Rückgabe **82** 26

Geschmacksmuster 42 4

Gestaltung des Vertrages *s. Gestaltungsrecht*

Gestaltungsrecht 26 2, 7 ff., 10a, Recht zur Minderung *s. ius variandi,* Recht zur Vertragsaufhebung *s. ius variandi*

Gewährleistungsansprüche, Verjährung **3 VertragsG** 4–6

Gewährleistungsbürgschaft als wesentliche Abweichung von der Offerte **19** 9

gewerbliche Schutzrechte *s. Immaterialgüterrechte*

Gewicht der Ware, Kaufpreis **53** 2, **56** 1 ff.

Gewinn, entgangener 44 1, 10, **74** 3, 36 ff., Abgrenzung zu Goodwill-Schaden **74** 34, neben abstrakter Schadensberechnung **76** 13, Betriebsausfallschaden **74** 36, Beweismaß **74** 65, frustrierte Aufwendungen anstelle von **74** 38,

lost volume **75** 12, Vereitelung einer Gewinnchance (loss of chance) **74** 37, Weiterverkaufsgewinn **74** 36
Gewinnabschöpfung 74 42
gewöhnlicher Aufenthalt 10 9 f.
Gläubigerfehlverhalten, Handeln Dritter **80** 3, Handlung oder Unterlassung **80** 3, leicht überwindbare Störungen **80** 5, Ursächlichkeit **80** 4 ff., verschuldensunabhängig **80** 3
Gläubigerverantwortung für Nichterfüllung
s. *Gläubigerfehlverhalten,* Beweislast **80** 11, Entlastung des G. **80** 5, Rechtsfolgen **80** 8 ff.
Gnadenfrist 45 29
Good manufacturing practices 35 9, 14
Goodwill-Schaden, Abgrenzung zu entgangenem Gewinn **74** 34, Berechnung **74** 34, Beweismaß **74** 65, Ersatzfähigkeit **74** 34, kommerzieller Wert **74** 18, Voraussehbarkeit **74** 56
Gültigkeitsfragen 4 4, 15–28, **9** 5, **Vor 14–24** 1, 2, **35** 45 f., **41** 22 f., **42** 27, **1 VerjÜbk** 5, **35 VerjÜbk** 1, Allgemeine Geschäftsbedingungen **4** 20 f., Anfechtung **4** 24 f., Gebräuche **4** 26 f., **9** 2, 5, Geschäftsfähigkeit **4** 17, Identitätsirrtum **4** 25, Inhaltsirrtum **4** 25, Irrtum über Eigenschaften **4** 24 f., Irrtum über Leistungsfähigkeit **4** 24, Irrtumsanfechtung bei Rechtsmangel **41** 23, Irrtumsanfechtung bei Schutzrechtsbelastung **42** 27, Irrtumsanfechtung bei Vertragswidrigkeit der Ware **35** 45 f., Kartellabreden **4** 14, Nichtigkeit des Vertrages **1 VerjÜbk** 5, Nichtigkeit wegen Verkauf einer fremden Sache **41** 22, Rechtsfähigkeit **4** 17, **Vor 14–24** 2, Sittenverstoß **4** 18, Täuschung **4** 25, Verbotsgesetz **Vor 14–24** 2, Verbraucherschutzrecht **4** 19, Verstoß gegen die guten Sitten **4** 18, Vorbehalt zur Anwendung des Verjährungsübereinkommens auf die Nichtigkeit des Vertrags **35 VerjÜbk** 1, Willensmängel **4** 22–25, *s. a. Willensmängel*
gute Sitten s. *Sittenverstoß*
guter Glaube s. *Treu und Glauben*
gutgläubiger Erwerb 41 2 f.

Haager Kaufrecht Vor 1–6 1 f., **1** 1 ff.
Haftung des Gläubigers wegen Verletzung von Mitwirkungspflichten 80 11
Haftung für Dritte 79 34 ff.
Haftungsausschluss 35 5, 34 ff., **38** 29, **40** 11, arglistiges Handeln bei Vertragswidrigkeit der Ware **40** 11, grobe Fahrlässigkeit bei Vertragswidrigkeit der Ware **40** 11, Kenntnis des Käufers von Vertragswidrigkeit der Ware **35** 5, 34, Qualitätssicherungsvereinbarungen **38** 29, vertragliche Leistungsbeschreibung **35** 38
Haftungsbefreiung, anfängliche Unmöglichkeit **79** 12, Arbeitskämpfe **79** 21 ff., Aufwendungsersatzansprüche **79** 56, Befreiungswirkung **79** 49 ff., Beschaffungsrisiko **79** 26, Beweislast **79** 59, eigene Leute **79** 20, Entwicklungsfehler **79** 28, Erfüllungsanspruch **79** 52, Erkrankung des Schuldners **79** 18, ethische Unzumutbarkeit **79** 32, finanzielle Leistungsfähigkeit des Schuldners **79** 25, Garantie **79** 8, 58, Gläubigerverursachung **80** 1 ff., Hersteller **79** 28, höhere Gewalt **79** 16, innerbetriebliche Auseinandersetzung **79** 22, des Käufers **61** 14 ff., Kaufpreisklage **62** 17, Konstruktions-, Fabrikations- und Instruktionsfehler **79** 28, Kontrollsphäre des Schuldners **79** 18, kriegerische oder terroristische Handlungen **79** 16, Leistungshindernis **79** 12, Minderung **79** 55, Monopol Dritter **79** 36, Naturereignisse und -katastrophen **79** 16, Nebenpflichten **79** 5, objektive Unmöglichkeit **79** 53, Obliegenheiten **79** 7, Organisationsrisiko **79** 18, Personalrisiko **79** 20, Rechtsirrtum **79** 19, Regelungsgehalt des Art. 79 **79** 1 f., Rückabwicklungspflichten **79** 5, Sabotageakt **79** 16, Schadenspauschale **79** 8, 51, sonstige Rechtsbehelfe **79** 55, Staatliche Eingriffe **79** 17, Staatsunternehmen **79** 17, stellvertretendes commodum **79** 50, subjektive Unmöglichkeit **79** 54, teilweise Verhinderung **79** 49, Unmöglichkeit **79** 5, Unzumutbarkeit bei vorübergehenden Leistungshindernissen **79** 42, Verhältnis von Art. 79 zu Art. 80 **79** 3, **80** 1, Verschuldensprinzip **79** 4, vertragliche Abreden **79** 57 f., Vertragsaufhebung **79** 55, Vertragsstrafe **79** 8, 51, Vertragswidrige Ware **79** 6, vertragswidrige Ware **79** 28 f., Verwendungsrisiko **79** 33, Verzinsung geschuldeter Beträge **79** 56, Verzug **79** 5, Voraussetzungen **79** 10 ff., Vorübergehende Leistungshindernisse **79** 41 ff., Zwischenhändler **79** 29
Haftungsbeschränkungen, Wirksamkeit **74** 60
Haftungsregelungen 74 58 ff.
Haltbarkeitsgarantie 36 2, 7 ff., 13
Handelsbrauch, angemessene Frist für Annahme **18** 15, annahmeäquivalente Handlungen **18** 19 f., beim Distanzkauf **31** 18, Empfangszeit **33** 5, Exportabgaben **31** 84, Feststellung des gewöhnlichen Gebrauchszwecks **35** 16, Formen für Rechtsgeschäfte **11** 6, 16, Garantie **36** 8, Hauptrefinanzierungssatz der EZB, als Maßstab für Zinshöhe bei Euro-Forderungen **78** 31, Incoterms **30** 3, Pflicht zur Anzeige der Vertragswidrigkeit **44** 18, Pflicht zur Übergabe von Dokumenten **30** 6, **34** 1, Pflicht zur Verschaffung eines negotiablen Dokuments **31** 59, **34** 4, Pflicht zur Versendungsanzeige **32** 13 f., Preisbestimmung **14** 15, Untersuchung der Ware **38** 11 ff., zweite Andienung **34** 7, *s. a. Gebräuche, Gepflogenheiten*
Handelsware, mangelhafte H. und wesentliche Vertragsverletzung **46** 25
hardship 79 4
Hardship-Klauseln 79 57
Hemmung, Verjährung **3 VertragsG** 9
Hemmung der Verjährung 79 16, **82** 14, **3 VertragsG** 9, **13 VerjÜbk** 1, **17 VerjÜbk** 2, **21 VerjÜbk** 1 ff., **30 VerjÜbk** 2

Sachregister

Fette Zahlen = Artikel

Hersteller Vor 14–24 30c
Herstellungspraktiken 35 7
Hilfspersonen s. *Erfüllungsübernehmer*, Bank **34** 3, Beförderer **31** 32, 36, 38, 77, **32** 16, 23, Einstandspflicht des Verkäufers **36** 1, 6, **40** 5, Erfüllungsgehilfen **79** 21, Organe juristischer Personen **Vor 14–24** 2, Spediteur **31** 79, **32** 21 f., Stellvertretung **1** 41, **4** 34, Stellvertretung durch Agenten **Vor 14–24** 2, Stellvertretung durch Organe juristischer Personen **Vor 14–24** 2, Verstoß gegen Erhaltungspflicht **85** 13, Vorlieferant **31** 24, 35, **32** 24, Wissenszurechnung **40** 6, Zugang von Erklärungen bei Stellvertretung **24** 7, s. a. *Empfangsbote, Erklärungsbote*
Hinderungsgrund, alternative Beförderung **79** 14, äußerste Opfergrenze **79** 14, Begriff **79** 11, Benachrichtigungspflicht **79** 43 ff., Beweislast **79** 59, Export- und Importverbote **79** 17, externe Umstände **79** 11, formfreie Mitteilung **79** 45, Inhalt der Mitteilung **79** 44, Kenntnis des Gläubigers **79** 46, Kontingentierung **79** 17, persönliche Umstände **79** 11, Schadenersatz bei Verletzung der Benachrichtigungspflicht **79** 47 f., typischer Verantwortungsbereich **79** 11, Unabwendbarkeit **79** 14, Unvorhersehbarkeit **79** 13, Ursächlichkeit **79** 15, vernünftige Ersatzleistung **79** 14, vertragliche Risikoverteilung **79** 11, 14
Hinterlegung s. *Einlagerung der Ware*
Hinterlegungsschein, Übergabe des H. und Lieferung **31** 58
Höchstfrist s. *allgemeine Begrenzung der Verjährungsfrist*
Hoheitliche Eingriffe, Aus- und Einfuhrverbote **66** 11, und Gefahrübergang **66** 6 ff.
höhere Gewalt 79 20, 30, 51, **21 VerjÜbk** 1 ff., Einfluss auf die Unterbrechung der Verjährungsfrist **21 VerjÜbk** 1 ff.
Höhere Gewalt, Grundsatz der unversehrten Rückgabe **82** 14
höhere Gewalt, Haftungsbefreiung **79** 16, internationale Wirkung der h. G. **30 VerjÜbk** 2
Höhere-Gewalt-Klauseln 79 57
höherwertige Ware 52 11
Holschuld 31 3, 45, Anzeige der Lieferbereitschaft **31** 51, **33** 13, Beladen des Käuferfahrzeuges **31** 54, Empfangszeit **33** 5, Gefahrübergang **31** 62, hinsichtlich des letzten Teilstücks des Transports **31** 74

Immaterialgüterrechte 1 36, **37** 6, **42** 3–29, 4, **43** 2 ff., Abgrenzung zum Rechtsmangel **42** 4 f., Ansprüche Dritter **42** 6, Anzeigepflicht **43** 2 ff., Arglist des Verkäufers **42** 28, Ausschluss der Haftung wegen I. **42** 16–24a, Bestehen von I. **42** 3, Beweislast **42** 29, Erkundigungspflicht des Käufers **42** 14, 17, Erkundigungspflicht des Verkäufers **42** 14, Gebrauchsmuster **42** 4, geistiges Eigentum **42** 4, Geschmacksmuster **42** 4, gewerbliches Eigentum **42** 4,

Internationale Abkommen **42** 3, Irrtumsanfechtung **42** 27, im Käuferstaat **42** 12, Kenntnis des Käufers **42** 16–18, 20, Kenntnis des Verkäufers **42** 14 f., maßgeblicher Zeitpunkt **42** 8, Nachbesserungsanspruch **42** 23, 25, Nachlieferungsanspruch **42** 25, Namensrecht **42** 5, Patent **42** 4, Persönlichkeitsrecht **42** 5, Recht zur Mängelbeseitigung **37** 6, Rechte des Verkäufers als I. **42** 7, Rechtsbehelfe des Käufers **42** 25–28, Rechtsbehelfe des Verkäufers **42** 22 f., technische Anweisungen **42** 19 ff., aufgrund technischer Anweisungen des Käufers **42** 19, territoriale Begrenzung **42** 3, 9 ff., im Transitstaat **42** 13a, Urheberrecht **42** 4, Verbietungsrecht aus Eigentum **42** 5, Verfahrenspatent **42** 4, Verjährung der Ansprüche **43** 7, im Verkäuferstaat **42** 13, 22 f., im Verwendungsstaat **42** 10 ff., als Ware **1** 36, Warenzeichen **42** 4
immaterieller Schaden, Abgrenzung zu materiellem Schaden **74** 8, 19, Arten **74** 39, Goodwill-Schaden **74** 34
Immobilien 1 35
implied terms s. *Vertragsergänzung*
Importabgaben 31 84
Importgenehmigung 31 85 f.
Importverbot als Rechtsmangel **41** 6
Incoterms 9 26, **30** 3 f., **31** 71 ff., 83 ff., **32** 13, 27, **33** 10, **34** 2
INCOTERMS 53 36, Abnahme der Ware **60** 5
Incoterms, Bestimmung des Liefertermins **33** 10
INCOTERMS, Dokumente **58** 16
Incoterms und Gerichtsstand **31** 92, 96
INCOTERMS als Handelsbrauch **14** 73, Mitwirkungspflichten des Käufers bei der Lieferung **60** 8 ff.
Incoterms, Pflicht zur Beschaffung von Dokumenten **34** 2, Pflicht zur Versendungsanzeige **32** 13
INCOTERMS, Rechnung **59** 5
Incoterms, Versicherungspflicht **32** 27
INCOTERMS, Warendokumente **58** 16, Zahlungsort **57** 7, 12, Zahlungszeit **58** 5, 8, 11, 12
Incoterms-Klausel, Fixgeschäft **25** 41
Individualisierung und Gefahrtragung **67** 29 ff., **69** 24, Sammelladungen **67** 31 ff.
Indossament 34 4
Informationspflicht, besondere Umstände im Land des Käufers **60** 9, Sukzessivlieferungsvertrag, I. bezüglich Vertragsaufhebung **73** 24, Wechsel der Niederlassung durch den Verkäufer **57** 17
Informationspflichten 11 14, **Vor 14–24** 6b, 39 f., **31** 82, **32** 31, **35** 13, 23, Auskunftspflicht des Verkäufers **32** 31, Erfüllungsort **31** 82, des Verkäufers bei fehlender Zweckeignung **35** 23, des Verkäufers bei unbrauchbarer Ware **35** 13
Inkrafttreten des Verjährungsübereinkommens 44 VerjÜbk

1426

Magere Zahlen = Randnummern **Sachregister**

innerstaatliches Recht Vor 1–6 29–33, bei Art. 28 **28** 9 ff., 16, konkurrierende Rechtsbehelfe des i. R. **35** 45 f., 47, **45** 30–32, Lückenfüllung durch i. R. **7** 57 f., Revisibilität des CISG nach i. R. **1** 76, und specific performance **28** 10–11
internationale Wirkung fristwahrender Handlungen im Ausland 30 VerjÜbk 1 ff., Verhältnis zu Art. 3 VerjÜbk **30 VerjÜbk** 6, Voraussetzungen **30 VerjÜbk** 2 ff.
Internationale Zuständigkeit, Abtretung des Kaufpreiszahlungsanspruchs **57** 22, 24, Gerichtsstandsklausel **57** 28, Schiedsklausel **57** 28, Wechsel der Niederlassung durch den Verkäufer **57** 24, Zahlungsort **57** 23 ff.
Internationaler Handelsbrauch s. *Gebräuche*
Internationalität 1 4, 40–43, **2 VerjÜbk,** Beweislast **1** 42, 48, Erkennbarkeit **1** 48, Stellvertretung **1** 41
Internet 7 21, **11** 4, **13** 2, **14** 13, 15, 28, **18** 5, 15, 17, Offerte **14** 28
Internet-Auktion, Vertragsschluss **Vor 14–24** 28
invitatio ad offerendum 14 29, culpa in contrahendo **14** 29
IPR, Anwendungsbereich **1** 69–76, Verhältnis zum Anwendungsbereich **Vor 1–6** 6 f., Verhältnis zum CISG **Vor 1–6** 34 f., s. a. *anwendbares Recht; Anwendung, kollisionsrechtliche*
ipso facto avoidance 26 1 f., **49** 23
Irrtumsanfechtung s. *Willensmängel*
ius variandi 45 14–20, **46** 7, nach Erklärung der Minderung **27** 14, kein i. v. nach Erklärung der Vertragsaufhebung **46** 7

just in time-Vertrag 33 7, Untersuchung der Ware **38** 29

Kaiteilschein, Pflicht zur Übergabe **30** 6, **34** 1, bei Sammelsendung **32** 4
Kasse gegen Dokumente, Erfüllungsort für die Übergabe der Dokumente **34** 13, bei Zuviellieferung **49** 11, **52** 8
Kauf an Warenbörse 2 29
Kauf auf Probe 1 23
Kauf für persönlichen Gebrauch s. *Verbrauchsgüterkauf*
Kauf nach Muster 1 16, **35** 3, 24–27, Beweislast **35** 53, Untersuchung der Ware **38** 9, wesentliche Vertragsverletzung beim **46** 24
Kauf nach Muster oder Probe 1 16, **35** 24 ff., 53, **38** 9
Kauf nach Probe 1 16, **35** 3, 24–27, Beweislast **35** 53, Untersuchung der Ware **38** 9, wesentliche Vertragsverletzung beim **46** 24
Käuferpflichten, Verletzung als wesentlicher Vertragsbruch **25** 66 ff.
kaufmännisches Bestätigungsschreiben 9 22, **11** 6, **Vor 14–24** 2, 4, 15, 18 ff., **18** 4, 29 2, Auftragsbestätigung als k. B. **18** 4, Handelsbrauch **Vor 14–24** 18 ff.

Kaufmannseigenschaft 1 59 f.
Kaufoption 1 21, **Vor 14–24** 41
Kaufpreis, Bestimmung **53** 2, Bestimmung des Nettogewichts **56** 4, „brutto für netto" **56** 3, nach dem Gewicht der Ware **53** 2, **56** 1 ff., iustum pretium (angemessener Preis) **53** 3, Kaufpreisklage s. *Kaufpreisklage,* Leistungsverweigerungsrecht **45** 22, Marktpreis **53** 2, **55** 1 ff., Pflicht zur Zahlung bei Vertragsaufhebung **45** 27, Pflicht zur Zahlung bei vorzeitiger Lieferung **52** 4, Preis pro Einheit **56** 2, pretium certum **55** 1 ff.
Kaufpreisklage 53 25, **62** 1 ff., Konkurrierende Rechtsbehelfe **62** 19, Widersprüchliche Rechtsbehelfe **62** 12
Kaufvertrag 1 12–15, **3** 5 f., bedingter **14** 31a ff., Gleichstellung mit Werklieferungsvertrag **3** 5 f.
Kausalität, Schadenszurechnung **74** 40
Kenntnis, Beweislast für K. der Vertragswidrigkeit der Ware seitens des Verkäufers **40** 12, des Käufers von der Vertragswidrigkeit der Ware **35** 4 f., 34 ff., 54, Rechtsfolgen der K. des Verkäufers **40** 9, des Verkäufers von der Vertragswidrigkeit der Ware **35** 10, **38** 24, **39** 32, **40** 2–8, von der Vertragsverletzung **49** 34, Zeitpunkt **40** 8, als Zugangsvoraussetzung **24** 18
Kenntnisnahme, Möglichkeit der K. als Zugangsvoraussetzung **24** 18
Klauselkontrolle s. *allgemeine Geschäftsbedingungen*
Know-how 1 38, **42** 14
kollidierende Standardbedingungen s. *Battle of forms*
Kollisionsnorm des Art. 28 28 22
Kommissionsgeschäfte, Einkaufskommission **1** 43, Verkaufskommission **1** 43
Kommunikation, elektronische 11 4, 16, **18** 5
Kommunikationsmittel 27 7, Annahme **18** 5, „Einwurf-Einschreiben" **24** 44, Erklärungsmittel unmittelbarer Kommunikation **20** 3, interaktives K. **18** 17, nach den Umständen geeignete K., s. a. *E-Mail, Funk, Telefax, Telegramm, Telephon, Telex*
Konkretisierung 31 32, **61** ff., s. *Individualisierung,* durch Bereitstellung **31** 61 ff., durch Versendung **31** 32
konkurrierende Rechtsbehelfe des nationalen Rechts, culpa in contrahendo bei Vertragswidrigkeit der Ware **35** 47, Deliktshaftung bei Vertragswidrigkeit der Ware **35** 47, Irrtumsanfechtung und Vertragswidrigkeit der Ware **35** 45 f., Produkthaftung für Sachschäden **5** 9–13, Rechtsbehelfe des Käufers **45** 30, s. a. *innerstaatliches Recht*
Konkurs, Einfluss des K. des Erklärenden auf Offerte **15** 6, **17** 6
Konnossement, Nachfrist **49** 18 f., Pflicht zur Übergabe **30** 6, **34** 1 f., „unreines" K. **34** 8, vertragswidriges K. **34** 8, Zeitpunkt der Über-

Sachregister

Fette Zahlen = Artikel

gabe **34** 2, Zuordnung der Ware zum Kaufvertrag **32** 3 f., über Zuviellieferung **52** 8
Konsens, Auslegung **8** 4
Konsens, äußerer Vor **14–24** 1
Konsensprinzip Vor **14–24** 24
Konsumentenkauf *s. Verbrauchsgüterkauf*
Konventionalstrafe, Fortbestehen der bei Vertragsrückabwicklung **81** 12
Kosten 34 3, 11, Abnahme **31** 83, der Aufbewahrung der Zuviellieferung **52** 9, der Behebung des Mangels in der Vertragserfüllung **48** 8, Belastung des Käufers infolge fehlerhafter Beschaffenheit der Dokumente **34** 11 f., Erhaltung und Einlagerung der Ware **85** 15, **87** 9, Lieferung **31** 83, Messen, Zählen, Wiegen **31** 83, der Nachbesserung **37** 14, 16, *s. Nachbesserung*, Qualitätsprüfung **31** 83, Rückgewähr **81** 28, des Transports der Ware **31** 83, **32** 25, Transportversicherung **32** 26 f., Untersuchung der Ware **38** 27, unverhältnismäßige K. der Nachbesserung **34** 11, **46** 40, Verpackung **31** 53, 83, Vorteilsausgleichung **84** 27 ff., der vorzeitigen Lieferung **52** 3 f.
Kreditkosten und Fälligkeitszinsen **78** 35, 41
Kündigung des Änderungsprotokolls 1980 **45a VerjÜbk** 1 f., des Verjährungsübereinkommens **45 VerjÜbk,** des Vertrages **73** 23, des Werklieferungsvertrages **28** 16
Kündigungsvorbehalt als wesentliche Abweichung von Offerte **19** 9

Ladeschein, Individualisierung der Ware durch L. **32** 3, Nachfrist **49** 18, Übergabe als Lieferung **31** 79, Zeitpunkt der Übergabe **34** 2
Lagerhalter, Haftung des Verkäufers für den L. **31** 63
Lagerschein, Lieferung durch Übergabe des L. **31** 58, Nachfrist **49** 18, Nachfrist für Verschaffung **49** 18, Orderlagerschein und Lieferung **31** 58, Pflicht zur Übergabe **34** 1 f.
lastenfreier Erwerb 41 2, **42** 3
L/C *s. Dokumentenakkreditiv*
Leasing 1 28, 29
Leistungsbestimmung, Zeitpunkt des Vertragsschlusses **23** 5
Leistungsentwertung 79 4, vertragliche Regelung **79** 57
Leistungserfolg 31 4
Leistungserschwerung 79 4, vertragliche Regelung **79** 57
Leistungsfähigkeit, finanzielle, Einstandspflicht des Schuldners **79** 25
Leistungsgefahr 31 62 ff., 77
Leistungsort bei Rückabwicklung **81** 23 ff.
Leistungsverweigerungsrecht 45 22, **80** 6
Leitzins, Bezugszinssatz **78** 31, Diskontsatz **78** 31, Hauptrefinanzierungssatz der EZB **78** 31, Maßstab für Zinshöhe **78** 31, 34, prime rate **78** 31
letter of intent 14 12, 26

Leutehaftung *s. Hilfspersonen*
lex mercatoria 1 84
lex rei sitae *s. anwendbares Recht*
LIBOR 78 29 f.
Lieferort 31 39 f., 46, 68, 70 ff., 78, **47** 16, „anderer bestimmter Ort" **31** 70–82, Fabrik **31** 46, Grube **31** 46, Rechtsfolgen der Lieferung am falschen Ort **31** 39 f., 68, 78, beim Spezieskauf **31** 46, und Stelle **31** 46, und Wahrung der Frist **47** 16
Lieferortvereinbarungen und Gerichtsstand **31** 92, 96
Lieferschein, Lieferung durch L. **31** 58 f., Pflicht zur Übergabe **30** 6, **34** 1
Liefertermin 25 38, **33** 7, 14, 17, 19, **45** 6, **47** 11, **49** 5, 17, **52** 2, und Nachfristsetzung **47** 11, „schnellstmöglich" **33** 7, „sofort" **33** 17, Überschreitung des L. **49** 5, 17, Überschreitung des L. als wesentliche Vertragsverletzung **45** 6, ungewisses Ereignis als L. **33** 19, unverbindlicher L. **33** 14, und vorzeitige Lieferung **52** 2, wesentliche Vertragsverletzung **25** 38
Lieferung, Anspruch des Käufers auf L. **28** 6, **45** 12, 14, **46** 6–16, Dokumentenübergabe **31** 58 f., 83, **49** 18, Eigentumsverschaffung **30** 7, einseitiger Akt **31** 4, 75 f., Erfüllung bei Artabweichung **35** 10, am falschen Ort **31** 39 f., 68, 78, bei Festlegung eines „anderen bestimmten Orts" **31** 70–82, frei ... **31** 74, 76, Gefahrübergang **31** 11, Hauptpflicht des Verkäufers **30** 2, Leistungshandlung **31** 4, nicht vertragsgemäßer Ware **31** 33, 65 f., **49** 7, 15, 30, *s. a. Vertragswidrigkeit der Ware,* „schnellstmöglich" **33** 7, „sofort" **33** 17, Teilbarkeit der L. **51** 2, durch Übergabe an den Beförderer **31** 13–44, 74, durch Übergabe an den Käufer **31** 76, durch Versendung der Ware **31** 13–44, 74, verspätete L. *s. Lieferung, verspätete,* vorzeitige L. **33** 6, **52** 1–5, *s. a. Lieferung, vorzeitige,* zukünftige L. **73** 17 ff., durch Zur-Verfügung-Stellen der Ware **31** 45–69, 74
Lieferung, vorzeitige 52 1–5, Beginn der Rügefrist **39** 21, Beginn der Untersuchungsfrist **38** 20, Begriff **37** 4 f., Recht zur Mängelbeseitigung **37** 36 ff.
Lieferungseinheit 73 10
Lieferverträge mit arbeits- oder dienstvertraglichen Pflichten 3 12–20, Anlagenliefervertrag **3** 18, Einheitlichkeit des Vertrages **3** 12, Montageverpflichtung **3** 17, Rechtsfolgen der Anwendbarkeit des CISG **3** 16, sonstiger gemischter Vertrag **3** 19, Wertrelation **3** 13–15, *s. a. Montagepflicht*
Lieferzeitpunkt *s. Liefertermin*
lineare Berechnung der Minderung 50 8
lost volume 75 12, Schadensminderungspflicht **77** 10
Lückenfüllung 7 41–69, Analogie **7** 47, Frist für Erklärung der Vertragsaufhebung **26** 15 f., durch innerstaatliches Recht **7** 57 f., kaufmän-

Magere Zahlen = Randnummern **Sachregister**

nisches Bestätigungsschreiben **Vor 14–24** 18 f., UNIDROIT-Principles **7** 59–69, Vorrang der Parteiautonomie **7** 48, s. *Allgemeine Grundsätze des Übereinkommens*
Luftfahrzeuge 2 42, 45, **4 VerjÜbk,** keine Anwendung des Verjährungsübereinkommens auf Kauf von L. **4 VerjÜbk**
Luftkissenfahrzeuge 2 43 ff., keine Anwendung des Verjährungsübereinkommens auf Kauf von L. **4 VerjÜbk**
Lugano Übereinkommen, Zahlungsort **57** 23 ff., 25, 27 ff.
Lugano-Übereinkommen und Erfüllungsort für die Lieferung **31** 89 ff.

Mahnung 33 2, **47** 4 f., 21, **78** 17, Bindungswirkung **47** 21, mit Nachfristsetzung **47** 4 f., Verzug ohne Mahnung **33** 2, keine Voraussetzung für Zinsanspruch **78** 17
Mangel, Recht zur selbstständigen Beseitigung durch den Käufer bei Nachfristsetzung **47** 14
Mangel in der Erfüllung 48 3 f., Art und Weise der Behebung **48** 5 ff.
Mangelfolgeschaden 44 10, **74** 35, Eintritt nach Versäumung der Rügefrist **44** 10, Verhältnis zu nationalem Deliktsrecht **74** 35
Mangelhaftigkeit s. *Vertragswidrigkeit*
Manifestation 11 14, Pflicht zur M. **11** 14a
Manifestationsmöglichkeit 11 14
Marke 42 4
Markierung 32 5
Marktpreis, Vorhandensein **76** 4, und Vorteilsausgleichung **84** 36 f.
Marktpreisregel 76 1 ff., bei antizipiertem Vertragsbruch **76** 12, Aufhebung des Vertrages **76** 3, Begriff **76** 1, Beweis eines Deckungsgeschäfts **76** 15, bei Erfüllungsverweigerung **76** 3, Hinauszögern der Vertragsaufhebung **76** 10, maßgeblicher Ort **76** 8 f., maßgeblicher Zeitpunkt **76** 10 ff., Nichterfüllungsschaden **76** 7 ff., Übernahmezeitpunkt **76** 11, Vertragspreis **76** 5, Voraussetzungen **76** 3, Vorrang eines Deckungsgeschäfts **76** 2, Vorrang eines realen Deckungsgeschäfts s. *Schadensberechnung*
Maßstab des Vernünftigen s. *reasonableness*
Material-Adverse-Change-Klausel 64 12
Mehrparteienvertrag Vor 14–24 30a ff.
merger clauses 8 35
Mietkaufvertrag 1 27
Minderung 50, 78 13, 24, Abweichende Vereinbarung **50** 19, Berechnungsmethode **50** 8, 9, Beweislast für den Wert der Ware **50** 16, keine Bindung an **45** 17 ff., Erklärung der Minderung **50** 4 ff., maßgeblicher Ort für die Berechnung **50** 12, maßgeblicher Zeitpunkt für die Berechnung **50** 9 ff., Rechtsfolgen **50** 16 ff., bei Rechtsmangel **41** 20, Unabhängigkeit vom Schaden des Käufers **50** 14, trotz Versäumnis der Rügefrist **44** 14, bei Vertragswidrigkeit der Ware **35** 32, 43, Verzinsung des Rückzahlungsanspruchs **78** 13, Voraussetzungen **50** 2–7, Wegfall des Zinsanspruchs **78** 24, bei wertloser Ware **50** 13, Zinsen auf Rückzahlungsanspruch **50** 15
Minderung des Kaufpreises, Rückzahlungsort **57** 31
Mindestinhalt der Offerte 14 3, Abweichung durch Parteivereinbarung **14** 3
mirror image rule 19 1
Mitteilung, Hinderungsgrund **79** 43 ff.
Mitteilungen 27 1 ff., Verlust **27** 10, Verspätung **27** 11, Zugang **24** 1 ff.
Mitverschulden des Käufers bei Verwendung der mangelhaften Ware **44** 13
Mitverschulden des Gläubigers 80 1
Mitwirkungshandlung des Gläubigers 80 3
Mitwirkungspflichten des Käufers 31 75, 33 12
Mitwirkungspflichtendes Käufers 31 75, 33 12
Montageanleitung 35 14
Montagefehler, Recht des Verkäufers zur Beseitigung **48** 4, wesentliche Vertragsverletzung **49** 12
Montagepflicht 3 17, **28** 6, **45** 3, **48** 4, **49** 12, Anspruch auf Erfüllung **28** 6, keine Anwendung des Verjährungsübereinkommens auf Liefervertrag mit M. **6 VerjÜbk,** Erfüllungsort **31** 82, Nichterfüllung **45** 3, Nichterfüllung als wesentliche Vertragsverletzung **49** 12

Nachbesserung 25 47, **28** 6, **35** 43, **37** 10, **38** 9, **41** 20 f., **42** 16 ff., 23, **44** 1, **46** 5, 26 ff., **39** ff., **47** 14, 16, **48** 8, 15, 20, **49** 7 f., 38, **70** 7, Angebot **46** 26, Anspruch auf **46** 5, 39 ff., Anspruch bei Rechtsmangel **41** 20 f., Anspruch bei Schutzrechtsbelastungen **42** 16 ff., Anspruch bei technischen Anweisungen **42** 23, kein Anspruch bei Versäumung der Rügefrist trotz vernünftiger Entschuldigung **44** 1, und Erfüllungsklage **28** 6, Ersatzteillieferung **46** 44, Fehlschlagen der N. **46** 46, Kosten der N. **46** 45, **48** 8, Möglichkeit der N. und wesentliche Vertragsverletzung **25** 47, Nachfrist für **46** 27, 45, **47** 1, 14, 16, **49** 8, 38, Nichterfüllung des Anspruchs als wesentliche Vertragsverletzung **46** 26, **49** 8, Ort **46** 45, Untersuchung der Ware **38** 9, Unzumutbarkeit für den Verkäufer **46** 40, 42, bei Vertragswidrigkeit der Ware **35** 43, bei vorzeitiger Lieferung **37** 10, und wesentliche Vertragsverletzung **25** 47, **46** 26, 28, 30, **48** 15, 20, **49** 7 f., Zeitverlust durch N. als wesentliche Vertragsverletzung **46** 30, **48** 15, Zwischenhändler **46** 40
Nachbesserungsanspruch, Rechtsfolgen der Nichterfüllung des N. **46** 46 f.
Nacherfüllung 45 19, 26, **48** 6, 14, 18, 21 ff., **50** 17, Rechtsfolgen **48** 22 f.
Nacherfüllungsrecht, mehrfaches N. **48** 6, und Minderung **45** 19, **48** 19, **50** 17, und Schaden-

1429

Sachregister

Fette Zahlen = Artikel

ersatz **45** 26, **48** 21, und Vertragsaufhebung durch den Käufer **48** 14, 18, 23, Wahlrecht des Verkäufers **48** 6
Nachfrist 25 6, 21, **34** 5, **39** 13, **47** 1, 3, 6 ff., **48** 10, 30, **49** 11 f., 20 f., 28, 39, 60, **63** 1 ff., **64** 2, 19 ff., angemessene Frist **47** 6, 10, Beweislast **47** 13, **49** 20, 39, 60, Bindungswirkung **47** 3, 14–20, Erfüllung vor Ablauf der **47** 16, **49** 20, Ersatz des Verzögerungsschadens **47** 18, vor Fälligkeit **47** 11, Form **47** 12, Gegenfristsetzung durch den Verkäufer **48** 30, **49** 21, Geltendmachung mit Rüge **39** 13, Lieferung nach Ablauf der **49** 28, zu kurze N. **47** 7–9, zu lange N. **47** 10, bei der Nachbesserung *s. dort,* bei Nichterfüllung **25** 10 f., 49, für sonstige Pflichten des Verkäufers (außer der Lieferpflicht) **47** 1, **49** 12, für die Übergabe der Dokumente **34** 5, **49** 11, Übermittlungsrisiko **47** 12, und unzumutbare Verzögerung **48** 10, bei der Vertragsaufhebung *s. dort,* und Vertragsstrafe **47** 20, bei vertragswidriger Beschaffenheit der Ware **25** 11, 49
Nachfrist zur Erfüllung durch den Käufer 63 1 ff., Angemessenheit **63** 8 ff., bestimmte Nachfrist **63** 7, bezüglich jedweder Pflicht **63** 1, 4, nutzloser Ablauf **63** 14, Vertragsaufhebung durch den Verkäufer **64** 2, 19 ff., Vorläufige Präklusion der anderen Rechtsbehelfe des Verkäufers **63** 2, 11 ff., zeitliche Anforderung an Nachfristsetzung **63** 5
Namensrecht 42 5
nationales Recht *s. innerstaatliches Recht*
Natur des Übereinkommens Vor 1–6 24 f.
Naturalrestitution 74 17
Nebenpflichten 45 3, **47** 5, des Käufers **42** 23, Nebenleistungspflichten und wesentliche Vertragsverletzung **25** 68 f.

negligent misrepresentation **Vor 14–24** 37

Negligent misrepresentation 35 47
negotiables Dokument 34 4
„net cash", Aufrechnungsverbot **61** 19, Zahlungsort **57** 7, 15
Nettovorteil in der Rückabwicklung 84 27 ff.
Neubeginn, Verjährung **3 VertragsG** 9
Neuverhandlungspflicht 79 4, 30, 57
Nichterfüllung 45 2, 5, 8, 11, **51** 1 f., 5–8, **73** 11, **79** 5, **80** 1 ff., beiderseitige Verursachung **80** 7, 9, Gläubigerhandeln **80** 1 ff., Haftungsbefreiung **79** 5, Handlung oder Unterlassen des Gläubigers **80** 3, Rechtsbehelfe bei N. **45** 5, 11, Rechtsbehelfe bei teilweiser N. **51** 5–8, vom Schuldner nicht zu vertretende N. **45** 8, bei Sukzessivlieferungsverträgen **73** 11, Tatbestand der N. **45** 2, 5, 8, teilweise N. **51** 1 f., Verursachung durch beide Parteien *s. Vertragsverletzung*
Nichterfüllungsschaden, abstrakte Schadensberechnung **74** 24 ff., *s. a.* abstrakte Schadensberechnung, Ersatz des **75** 9, Mangelschaden **74** 20, 22 ff., anhand von Mietkosten **74** 25, Nutzungsmöglichkeiten **74** 20, Voraussehbarkeit **74** 52
Nichtigkeit *s. Gültigkeitsfragen*
Nichtlieferung 45 6, Falschlieferung **31** 34, **46** 20, 24, Nichtverschaffung der Dokumente als N. **49** 18, wegen Unmöglichkeit **49** 6, verspätete Lieferung **49** 5, als Vertragsverletzung **45** 6, Vertragswidrigkeit der Ware **31** 33, 65 f., als wesentliche Vertragsverletzung **25** 37, **49** 5
Niederlassung 1 44–47, **10** 4–8, **31** 49, 76, 90 f., Haager Kaufrecht **10** 4, Hauptniederlassung **10** 4–8, des Käufers als Ort der Lieferung **31** 76, Liaison-office **1** 46, Mehrheit von Niederlassungen und Erfüllungsort **31** 49, 90, Tochtergesellschaft **1** 47, des Verkäufers als Ort der Lieferung **31** 49, 90 f., Zweigniederlassung **10** 4–8
Notverkauf 88 10 ff., Aufrechnung mit Erlös **88** 18, Pflicht zum N. bei Gefahr der Verschlechterung **88** 11
Novation, Auslegung **8** 5
Nutzungen bei Vorteilsausgleichung 84 24 ff., Gebrauchsvorteile **84** 26, natürliche Früchte **84** 24 f., nicht gezogene N. **84** 33, zivile Früchte **84** 24 f.
Nutzungsmöglichkeiten, kommerzieller Wert **74** 18

Objektivierung der Maßstäbe 72 15, **73** 32 f.
Obliegenheiten 38 3 ff., **44** 16, **45** 4, **74** 9, **79** 7, **Vor 85–88** 2, Haftungsbefreiung **79** 7, Rüge **38** 3 f., Untersuchung **38** 5, Verhaltensanforderungen aus Artt. 85 ff. **Vor 85–88** 2
Offenbarungspflicht des Verkäufers hinsichtlich der Vertragswidrigkeit der Ware **40** 7
Offener Preis 55 1 ff., angemessener Preis **55** 17, Bestimmungsrecht **55** 8, 12, 13, Beweislast **55** 18, Irrtum **55** 11, Marktpreis **55** 15, Marktpreis im Zeitpunkt des Vertragsschlusses **55** 16, Preisfestsetzung **55** 14 ff., pretium certum **55** 1, Vertragserfüllung **55** 6, Vorvertrag (agreement to agree) **55** 5
Offensichtlichkeit der künftigen wesentlichen Vertragsverletzung **72** 14 ff.
öffentliches Recht und Qualitätsstandards und Vertragsmäßigkeit der Ware **35** 17
öffentlich-rechtliche Belastungen als Rechtsmangel **41** 5 ff.
Offerte Vor 14–24 2, 5, **14 ff.,** Ablehnung **17** 1–3, allgemeine Geschäftsbedingungen **14** 36, bedingte **14** 31a ff., Bestimmbarkeit des Inhalts der Offerte **14** 3, Bestimmtheit von Ware, Menge, Preis in Offerte **14** 3, Bestimmungsbefugnis **14** 5, Bindung **16** 8 ff., 11, Einfluss des Konkurses des Erklärenden **15** 6, **17** 6, Einfluss des Todes des Erklärenden **15** 6, **17** 6, Einfluss fehlender Geschäftsfähigkeit **15** 6, **17** 6, Endtermin für Annahme **20** 1, Erlöschen **17** 1, 4 ff.,

Magere Zahlen = Randnummern **Sachregister**

6, essentialia contractus **14** 3, freibleibend **14** 25, Fristablauf **17** 4 f., Fristbeginn **20** 3a, Gegenofferte **19** 11–12, Kreuzofferten **Vor 14–24** 15, **18** 10, Mindestinhalt **14** 3 ff., mündliche O. **18** 16, als Pro-Forma-Rechnung **14** 26, Rücknahme **15** 3, sans engagement **14** 25, Tagespreisklauseln **14** 15, Transparenzgebot **14** 6, Verpflichtungswille bei O. **14** 1, Widerruflichkeit **16** 1–13, Widerrufssperre **16** 4, 6, Willenserklärung **14** 1 ff., Wirksamwerden **15** 1, without obligation **14** 25, *s. a. Mindestinhalt der O., Publikumsofferte, Vertragsschluss*
Opfergrenze 79 14, 26, 30, 42, 57
opting in Vor 14–24 14d
Opting-in *s. Rechtswahl*
Orderlagerschein, Übergabe und Lieferung der Ware **31** 58
Orderpapiere 34 4
Organe, juristischer Personen **Vor 14–24** 2, *s. a. Hilfspersonen*
Ort, maßgeblicher O. für die Berechnung der Minderung **50** 12, der Nachbesserung **46** 45, **48** 7, der Übergabe von Dokumenten **34** 3, der Versendung **31** 31, Versendung zum unrichtigen O. **32** 30

pacta sunt servanda 28 1
Pacta sunt servanda 62 1
Paketdienste 31 19
parol evidence rule 8 31 ff., **11** 13, *s. a. Form*
Parteiautonomie 1 85, **6** 5–11, 33 ff., **7** 48, 62–69, **Vor 14–24** 17, **28** 24, Art. 28 nicht dispositiv **28** 24, Ausnahmen von der Dispositivität **6** 8–11, **28** 24, dispositive Natur der Konvention **6** 5–7, teilweiser Ausschluss der Konvention **6** 33–35, und UNIDROIT-Principles **7** 62–69, Vertragsschlussverfahren **Vor 14–24** 17, Vorrang vor Lückenfüllung **7** 48, *s. a. Ausschluss der Konvention*
Parteien des Kaufvertrages 1 VerjÜbk 9, Definition **1 VerjÜbk** 9
Parteiwille, Vorrang vor Lückenfüllung **7** 48
Patent 42 4
PECL *s. Principles of European Contract Law*
peius 35 4, *s. a. Vertragswidrigkeit der Ware*
periculum est emptoris Vor 66–70 5 ff.
Personalrisiko des Schuldners 79 20
Personenschäden 5, 3–7, **74** 14, 32, als Folgeschaden **74** 32, Regressansprüche **74** 14, 32, Rückgriffsansprüche **5** 8, Schmerzensgeld **5** 5
Persönlichkeitsrecht 42 5
Pfandrecht des Frachtführers **41** 4, des Lagerhalters **41** 4
Pfandrecht des Frachtführers/Lagerhalters 41 4
Pflicht zu Neuverhandlungen 79 31
Pflichten des Käufers 53–60, Abnahme der Ware **53** 31, **60** 1 ff., andere Pflichten (als Kaufpreiszahlung und Abnahme) **53** 40, **60** 18, Haupt- und Nebenpflichten **53** 1, Kaufpreiszahlung **53** 1 ff., Kooperations- und Informationspflichten **53** 39, Lieferung von Teilen der für die Herstellung oder Erzeugung der Ware notwendigen Stoffe **53** 35 f., Obliegenheiten **53** 1, Rechtsbehelfe des Verkäufers *s. Rechtsbehelfe des Verkäufers,* Spezifikation der Ware *s. Spezifikation,* Stellung von Sicherheiten **53** 31 ff., Währung **53** 8
Pflichtverletzung *s. Vertragsverletzung*
PICC 9 26, *s. a. UNIDROIT-Principles,* Verjährung **53** 27
positive Vertragsverletzung 4 46, und Vertragsmäßigkeit der Ware **35** 11
Post 31 19
Postfach, Zugang **24** 19
Präambel, Auslegung **Präambel** 4, Bedeutung **Präambel** 3, 4
Preis 14 3, 8–11, **55,** Bestimmung durch Handelsbrauch **14** 15, Festsetzung **14** 8, pretium certum **14** 18, unbestimmter P. **14** 13, *s. a. Fälligkeit des Kaufpreisanspruchs, Zahlung des Kaufpreises*
pretium certum *s. Preis*
Primärpflichten, Befreiung von **81** 5
Principles of European Contract Law 25 2
Produktabnahmevertrag (buy-back transaction) 53 28
Produkthaftung 5 1, 3–15, **25** 16, Fehler als wesentliche Vertragsverletzung **25** 16, Haager Kaufrecht **5** 1, Personenschäden **5** 3–7, Produkthaftungsrichtlinie **5** 14 f., Sachschäden **5** 9–13
Prognose, künftige Vertragsverletzung beim Sukzessivlieferungsvertrag **73** 20 ff., künftige wesentliche Vertragsverletzung **72** 14 ff., Stufung der P. der Vertragsverletzung **73** 21, vernünftige Person *s. a. künftige Vertragsstörung, Verschlechterungseinrede, Vertragsverletzung, künftige wesentliche*
promesse de vente Vor 14–24 41
proportionale Berechnung der Minderung 50 8
Prozessrecht *s. Verfahrensrecht*
Prozesszinsen 78 45
Publikumsofferte, grundsätzlich nur invitatio ad offerendum **14** 30, Rücknahme **15** 4, Widerruf **16** 3, Widerrufssperre **16** 4, Wirksamwerden **15** 2, *s. a. Offerte*
pVV *s. positive Vertragsverletzung*

Qualitätssicherungsvereinbarungen 38 29
Quantitätsabweichung 25 42, **31** 44, 69, **35** 4, 8, **39** 10, 30, 51, **40** 5, 51, **51** 5 f., 9, **52** 6–10, 6–11, **70** 10, Lieferung höherwertiger Ware **52** 11, Recht des Käufers zur Aufhebung des Kaufvertrags im ganzen **51** 9, Recht des Verkäufers zur Teillieferung **51** 5, Rüge **39** 10, wesentliche Vertragsverletzung **25** 42, Zulässigkeit **31** 44, 69, Zuviellieferung **35** 8, **39** 30, **52** 6–10, Zuweniglieferung **35** 8, **39** 30, 51, **51** 5 f.

1431

Sachregister

Fette Zahlen = Artikel

Rahmenvereinbarung Vor 14–24 41, hinsichtlich Auslegung **14** 9, über Schriftform **29** 6
Ratenzahlung 73 9 f., 9
Ratifikation 91 1 f., **42 VerjÜbk, 43 VerjÜbk,** durch föderative Staaten **93** 1–4, Teilratifikation **92** 1–4, des VerjÜbk 1974 **43a VerjÜbk,** des VerjÜbk 1980 **44a VerjÜbk** 1 f., Vorbehalt für regionale Rechtsvereinheitlichung **94** 1–5
reasonableness 7 53
Rechnung 59 4 ff., Pflicht zur Übergabe **30** 6, **34** 1
Recht zur Mängelbeseitigung 37 2 ff., Anwendungsbereich **37** 6, erfolglose Ausübung **37** 11, durch Ersatzlieferung **37** 9, Erscheinungsformen **37** 7 f., Grenzen **37** 12 ff., durch Nachbesserung **37** 10, durch Nachlieferung **37** 8, Rechtsfolgen **37** 15 ff., bei Rechtsmangel **37** 6, Schadenersatzanspruch des Käufers **37** 14, 16, bei Schutzrechtsbelastung **37** 6, unvollständige Mängelbeseitigung **37** 11, Unzumutbarkeit **37** 12 f., vorzeitige Lieferung **37** 4 f., Weigerung des Käufers **37** 17
Recht zur zweiten Andienung 48 1
Rechte Dritter s. *Ansprüche Dritter*
Rechtsbehelfe s. *konkurrierende R. des nationalen Rechts,* Selbstständigkeit der **83** 2 ff., Wechsel des R. **45** 14
Rechtsbehelfe des Verkäufers 53 41, **61–65,** antizipierter Vertragsbruch **61** 10, Aufrechnung durch den Käufer **61** 19, einheitliches Vertragsbruchskonzept **61** 4, Erfüllungsanspruch **61** 6, **62** 1 ff., s. *Erfüllungsanspruch,* Gnadenfrist **61** 3, 18, konkurrierende Ansprüche nach nationalem Recht **61** 20, konkurrierende Rechtsbehelfe **61** 2, 12 ff., Nichterfüllung einer mit der Zahlung verbundenen Pflicht **54** 8, Schadenersatz **61** 7, Schadenminderungspflicht **62** 16, **64** 35 ff., Selbsthilfeverkauf **62** 18, Sukzessivlieferungsvertrag **61** 10, Verjährungsfristen **61** 21, verspäteter Zahlung **58** 18, Vertragsaufhebung s. *Vertragsaufhebung durch den Verkäufer,* Vertragsstrafe **61** 9, vorzeitiger Zahlung **58** 19 ff.
Rechtsfähigkeit 4 17, **Vor 14–24** 2, mangelnde R. **Vor 14–24** 2
Rechtsmangel 35 5, **37** 6, **41** 3 ff., 14, 17 ff., **42** 4 f., **43** 7, **45** 10, **46** 6, 22, **48** 3, **49** 10, 3 **VertragsG** 6, Abgrenzung zu Sachmangel **35** 5, **41** 6, Abgrenzung zur Schutzrechtsbelastung **42** 4 f., Anspruch auf Beseitigung **46** 6, 22, Anspruchsverjährung 3 **VertragsG** 6, Arglist des Verkäufers **41** 24, Ausschluss der Haftung **41** 17 ff., Belastung mit Steuern und Zöllen **41** 7, Beschlagnahme gestohlener Ware **41** 7, Beweislast **41** 25, **45** 10, dingliche Rechte Dritter **41** 4, Einwilligung des Käufers in R. **41** 17 f., Erfüllungsanspruch **41** 21, Export- und Importverbote **41** 6, Irrtumsanfechtung **41** 23, Kenntnis des Käufers **41** 17, maßgeblicher Zeitpunkt **41** 15, Minderung **41** 20 f., Nachbesserungsanspruch **41** 20 f., Nachlieferungsanspruch **41** 20 f., obligatorische Rechte Dritter **41** 4, öffentlich-rechtliche Belastungen **41** 5 f., Recht des Verkäufers zur Beseitigung **37** 6, **48** 3, Rechte des Verkäufers als R. **41** 14, Rechtsbehelfe des Käufers **41** 20 ff., Schadensersatz **41** 21, schuldrechtliche Bindung als R. **41** 4, Sicherungsrechte Dritter **41** 4, Verjährung der Ansprüche **43** 7, Verkauf einer fremden Sache **41** 3, Vertragsaufhebung **41** 21, als wesentliche Vertragsverletzung **41** 21, **49** 10
Rechtsmängelanzeige, Anzeigepflicht **43** 2 ff., Beweislast **43** 12, Entbehrlichkeit bei Kenntnis des Verkäufers **43** 9 f., Frist zur Ausübung **43** 3 f., Übermittlungsrisiko **43** 5
Rechtsmissbrauch, Berücksichtigung von Amts wegen **29** 12, Formverstoß **29** 10 f., Wechsel von Erfüllungsanspruch zu anderen Rechtsbehelfen **45** 15, Wechsel von Erfüllungsanspruch zu Vertragsaufhebung **45** 15, Zugangsverhinderung **24** 41
Rechtsverfahren s. *gerichtliches Verfahren*
Rechtsverfolgungskosten, außergerichtliche Kosten **74** 28, 30, als Folgeschaden **74** 33, Inkassokosten **74** 31, Prozesskosten **74** 28 f., Qualifikation **74** 28
Rechtsvergleichung 7 40
Rechtswahl 1 72 f., **6** 15–32, Rechtswahlklauseln als wesentliche Abweichung von der Offerte **19** 9, Wahl des Übereinkommens **6** 39–43
Regelungsbereich s. *Gegenstände, nicht geregelte*
Regress, Unterbrechung der Verjährungsfrist beim R. des Käufers **18 VerjÜbk** 5 f.
Reparaturaufwand und Minderung **50** 8
repentir s. *Widerruf von Erklärungen*
Reputationsschaden 74 18
res perit domino Vor 66–70 8 ff.
Restgültigkeitstheorie s. *battle of forms*
Revisibilität 1 76
Risikobereiche, Grundsatz der unversehrten Rückgabe **82** 15 ff.
Rollfuhrspediteur 31 20, 27
Rückabwicklung, Annahmeverzug **81** 29, Aufrechnung **81** 21 f., autonome Regelung im CISG **81** 10, Beweislast **81** 30, Eigentumslage **Vor 81–84** 4, einvernehmliche Vertragsaufhebung **81** 15, s. a. *Vertragsaufhebungsrecht,* Entdeckung des Mangels **82** 25, Entstehungsgeschichte **81** 1 f., fortbestehende Pflichten **81** 12 f., frustrierte Aufwendungen **84** 32, und Gebrauch der Ware **82** 21, Gefahrtragung **82** 10, Gerichtsstand **81** 27, Kombination mit Schadensersatz **Vor 81–84** 9, Kosten **81** 28, Leistungsort **81** 23 ff., und nationales Recht **81** 6 ff., Nettovorteil **84** 27 ff., 38, und Rechte Dritter **81** 11, trotz Rückgabeunmöglichkeit im Rahmen der PICC und der PECL **82** 4, Rückzahlungsort **57** 31, und Schadensersatz **Vor 81–84** 9, **81** 13, **82** 6, 27, **84** 6, 23, 31 f., 32, Surrogat **84** 34 ff., Teilrückabwicklung **Vor**

Magere Zahlen = Randnummern

Sachregister

81–84 10 f., Umsteuerung in sverhältnis **81** 6 ff., 12, 20, Unmöglichkeit der Rückgabe **82** 5, und Verarbeitung der Ware **82** 19 ff., und Verbrauch der Ware **82** 20, und Weiterverkauf der Ware **82** 22 f., Zug-um Zug-Abwicklung **81** 20
Rückgabe, Bagatellregelung **82** 6, der gelieferten Ware bei Geltendmachung des Anspruchs auf Ersatzlieferung **46** 34, Gerichtsstand **81** 27, Grundsatz der unversehrten Rückgabe und Aufhebung durch Verkäufer **82** 28 f., Grundsatz der unversehrten Rückgabe und einvernehmliche Vertragsaufhebung **82** 30, Leistungsort **81** 25, in natura **81** 17 ff., Unmöglichkeit unversehrter R. **82** 5 ff., 5, unversehrte R. **Vor 81–84** 11, unversehrte R.: Ausnahmen **Vor 81–84** 10 f., unversehrte R. bei der Ersatzlieferung **Vor 81–84** 5, unversehrte R. und Rücktritt des Verkäufers **81** 17 ff., **82** 2
Rückkaufvertrag Vor 14–24 41
Rücknahme, Annahme **18** 12, **22** 1–7, annahmeäquivalenter Handlungen **18** 22, Gegenofferte **19** 11, nachträgliche Modifikation der R. **22** 6, Offerte **15** 3, Publikumsofferte **15** 4, Rechtsfolge der R. für Offerte **15** 5, Unterscheidung von Widerruf **22** 1
Rücksendung der vertragswidrigen Ware **46** 34
Rücktritt 26 4, 10, **49** 1 ff., **Vor 81–84** 5, Verhältnis zum Schadenersatz **26** 4, 10
Rücktrittsvorbehalt als wesentliche Abweichung von Offerte **19** 9
Rückzahlung, Zahlungsort **81** 24
Rüge 34 5, **38** 3, 7, **39**, **50** 3, **52** 4, Abdingbarkeit **39** 34 ff., Adressat **39** 14, angemessene Frist **39** 15 ff., Anwendungsbereich **39** 5, Ausschlussfrist **39** 22 ff., Bedeutung für Minderung **50** 3, Bedeutung für Nachbesserungsverlangen **46** 33, 43, Bedeutung für Nacherfüllungsverlangen **46** 33, Beweislast **39** 37 f., bei dauerhafter Ware **39** 9, 16 f., Form **39** 11 ff., Inhalt der Anzeige **39** 6 ff., Kenntnis des Verkäufers von der Vertragswidrigkeit der Ware **39** 31, **40** 2 ff., Offenbarungspflicht des Verkäufers **40** 7, Parteivereinbarungen **39** 12, 34 ff., keine Pflicht zur vorzeitigen R. bei vorzeitiger Lieferung **52** 4, Rechtsfolgen bei unterlassener oder nicht gehöriger Anzeige **39** 30 ff., **40** 9 f., Rechtsnatur **38** 3, Rügepflicht als Obliegenheit **44** 16, Substantiierung der R. **39** 6–10, Teillieferung **39** 10, bei verderblicher Ware **39** 9, 16 f., bei vertraglicher Garantiefrist **39** 27, bei vertragswidrigen Dokumenten **34** 5, **38** 7, Verwirkung **39** 33a, Verzicht des Verkäufers **39** 33, vorsätzliche Vertragsverletzung **39** 16, bei vorzeitiger Lieferung **39** 21, Wahl der Rechtsbehelfe **39** 13, Zweck **38** 3
Rügefrist 39 15 ff., Beginn **39** 19 ff., Fristwahrung **39** 18, Rechtsmängelanzeige **43** 3 f., Weihnachten **44** 8
Rügepflicht, Verletzung der **74** 13

Sache, Verkauf einer fremden Sache **41** 3, 22, s. a. vertretbare Sachen
Sachgesamtheit 73 8
Sachgesamtheiten 1 34
Sachmangel 41 5 ff., Abgrenzung zum Rechtsmangel **41** 5 ff.
Sachmängelgewährleistung 46 3 ff., 17 ff.
Sachnormcharakter des Art. 1 I b) 2 VertragsG 1
Sachschäden, Schutzzweck des Vertrags **74** 14
Saisonware 49 5, 29, 32
sale and lease back 1 29, **31** 50
Sammelladungen, Gefahrtragung **67** 29 ff., Individualisierung **67** 31 ff., pro-rata-Verteilung **67** 34, reisende Ware **68** 22 ff.
Sammelsendung 32 4
sans engagement 14 25
Schaden, Aufwendungen **74** 10, Begleitschaden (incidental damages) s. dort, Betriebsausfallschaden **74** 36, Drittschäden **74** 15 f., entgangener Gewinn **74** 3, s. Gewinn, entgangener, Ersatzfähigkeit **74** 18, Erwerbschancen **74** 18, Folgeschäden (consequential damages) s. dort, frustrierte Aufwendungen **74** 38, Geldentwertung **74** 26, Goodwill-Schaden s. dort, immaterieller s. dort, Integritätsinteresse (indemnity interest) **74** 3, Kosten der Rechtsverteidigung **41** 21, Kursverlust **74** 26, Mangelfolgeschaden **74** 35, negatives oder Vertrauensinteresse (reliance interest) **74** 3, Nichterfüllungsschaden **75** 1, s. dort, Nutzungsmöglichkeiten **74** 18, Personenschäden **5** 3–8, **74** 14, positives oder Erfüllungsinteresse (expectation interest) **74** 3, Rechtsverfolgungskosten s. dort, Sachschäden **74** 14, Verzögerungsschaden **74** 25, voraussehbarer s. dort, Vorhersehbarkeit **7** 52, zufällige Schadensverlagerung **74** 16, Zurechnung **74** 40
Schadenersatz, Bereicherungsverbot **74** 8, Form des **74** 17, in Geld **74** 17, Gewinnabschöpfung **74** 8, Kompensationsfunktion **74** 6, Naturalrestitution **74** 17, wegen Nichterfüllung **74** 10, Präventionsfunktion **74** 6, Punitive Damages **74** 8, Rechtsbehelf des Verkäufers **61** 7, bei Sukzessivlieferungsvertrag **73** 16, 36, Zahlungsort **57** 29
Schadenersatzanspruch, berechtigte Personen **74** 15 f., Beweisführung **74** 66, Beweislast **74** 64, Beweismaß **74** 65, Erfüllungsort **74** 61, Erfüllungsprinzip **74** 6 ff., 18, Gewinnabschöpfung **74** 42, Grundsatz der Totalreparation **74** 2, 5, Haftungsbeschränkungen **74** 60, künftige wesentliche Vertragsverletzung **72** 41, Nachbesserungsrecht des Verkäufers **74** 24, Umfang **74** 18 ff., undisclosed agency **74** 15, Verhältnis zu anderen Rechtsbehelfen **74** 10, Verhältnis zu fixer Summe **74** 59, Verhältnis zum Deliktsrecht **74** 14, Verjährung **74** 62, verschuldensunabhängig **74** 3, Voraussehbarkeitsregel s. dort, Währung der Ersatzleistung **74** 63

1433

Sachregister

Fette Zahlen = Artikel

Schadenersatzpflicht, Entlastung/Befreiung **79** 1 ff., Garantiehaftung **79** 1

Schadenminderungspflicht, Kaufpreisklage **62** 16, Selbstspezifikation des Verkäufers **65** 19, Verletzung der **74** 13, Vertragsaufhebung durch Verkäufer **64** 35 ff.

Schadensberechnung 26 10, **74, 75** 1, 2, **76** 1 ff., **10** ff., abstrakte *s. abstrakte Schadensberechnung,* abstrakte und konkrete **74** 41, Art. 74 als Grundnorm **74** 9, Aufwendungen für Nachbesserung **74** 24, ersparte Kosten **74** 23, Gewinnabschöpfung **74** 42, Goodwill-Schaden **74** 34, konkrete S. **75** 1, konkrete und abstrakte **76** 13, bei Mangelschaden **74** 41, anhand des Marktwerts **74** 18, 23, maßgeblicher Zeitpunkt **26** 10, Nichterfüllungsschaden **75** 2, pönale Elemente **74** 8, Rentabilitätsvermutung **74** 38, Schadensschätzung *s. Deckungsgeschäft; Marktpreisregel,* Verletzergewinn **74** 8, Vorteilsausgleichung **74** 42, Zeitpunkt der **74** 44

Schadensberechnung, abstrakte *s. abstrakte Schadensberechnung*

Schadensersatz bei Rückabwicklung **81** 13, bei Vertragsrückabwicklung **81** 13

Schadensersatzanspruch als ergänzender Anspruch **84** 13 f., 21, 32, und Fälligkeitszinsen **78** 41 f., des Käufers bei Schutzrechtsbelastung **42** 25, **44** 10, 13, des Käufers bei Vertragswidrigkeit der Ware **35** 43, des Käufers wegen Untersuchungskosten **38** 27, des Käufers wegen Vertragsverletzung des Verkäufers **31** 10, **45** 23–28, Konkurrenz zum Missbrauchseinwand bei Formverstoß **29** 13, Kumulation von Schaden und Rücktritt **74** 10, Mängelbeseitigung **37** 16, Minderung **50** 18, und Nacherfüllungsrecht **45** 26, **48** 21, wegen Nichterfüllung **45** 27, Rechtsmangel **41** 21, Rückgriffsansprüche wegen Personenschäden **5** 8, Schadensminderungspflicht **77** 4, Verbindung mit anderen Rechtsbehelfen **45** 25 ff., des Verkäufers bei Schutzrechtsbelastung aufgrund technischer Anweisungen des Käufers **42** 23, des Verkäufers wegen unterlassener Anzeige der Vertragswidrigkeit **44** 16, des Verkäufers wegen unterlassener Versendungsanzeige **32** 11, Verletzung von Artt. 85 ff. **Vor 85–88** 4, Verletzung von Informationspflichten durch den Verkäufer **42** 15, 21, und Vertragsaufhebung **34** 5, 12, **45** 27, **49** 2, 7, 46, und Vorteilsausgleichung **84** 6, 23, 31 f., 32, vorzeitige Lieferung **52** 4, und Zins **84** 13 f., Zuviellieferung **52** 9 f.

Schadensminderungspflicht 7 52, **28** 2, **44** 11 f., **46** 14 f., **49** 27, **62** 14, **64** 27, **71** 26, **73** 24, **77** 1–12

Schadensminderungspflicht (mitigation of damages) 7 52, **77** 1–12, Abbestellung einer Werklieferung **77** 5, Abgrenzung zu contributory negligence **77** 6, angemessene Maßnahmen **77** 7 ff., Antizipierter Vertragsbruch **77** 3, 10, Aufwendungsersatz **77** 11, Berücksichtigung von Bräuchen und Gepflogenheiten **77** 7, Beweislast **77** 13, Deckungsgeschäft **77** 10, drohender Schaden **77** 3, als Einwendung oder Einrede **77** 12, Erfüllungsanspruch **77** 4 f., Erhaltung der Ware **77** 8, Herstellung trotz Widerspruchs des Käufers **77** 5, Hinweispflicht bei drohendem Schaden **77** 9, des Käufers und Versäumung der Rügefrist **44** 11 ff., 16, lost volume **77** 10, Marktpreisregel **77** 10, Obliegenheit **77** 2, Pflicht zur Vornahme eines Deckungsgeschäftes **28** 2, **46** 14 f., **49** 27, Preisschwankungen **77** 10, Rechtsfolgen **77** 12, Schadensvermeidung **77** 3, Sukzessivlieferungsvertrag **73** 24, Treu und Glauben **77** 1, Umfang **77** 7 ff., Veräußerung verderblicher Ware **77** 8, Verhalten Dritter **77** 2, Verhandlungen mit dem Schuldner **77** 8, Vertragsaufhebung **77** 4, 10, vor Vertragsverletzung **77** 3

Schadenspauschale, Haftungsbefreiung **79** 8, 51, Verhältnis zum Schadenersatzanspruch **74** 59

Schadensschätzung nach § 287 ZPO und Minderung **50** 15

Scheck, Zahlungsort **57** 7

Scheingeschäft 8 7

Schenkungsvertrag 1 33

Schickschuld 31 2

Schiedsgerichte 1 82 ff., Anspruch auf Erfüllung in Natur vor Sch. **28** 9, Erfüllungsklage **28** 9, Gnadenfrist **45** 29

Schiedsklausel 8 5, **9** 25, **11** 7, **18** 9, **29** 2, **57** 28, **81** 12, Auslegung **8** 5, Formbedürftigkeit **11** 7, Fortbestehen der bei Vertragsrückabwicklung **81** 12, Gebräuche **9** 25, Vereinbarung im Rahmen einer Vertragsänderung **29** 2

Schiffe *s. Wasserfahrzeuge*

Schiffsangabe 32 5

schlüssiges Verhalten als Erklärung der Vertragsaufhebung **26** 7 f.

„schnellstmögliche" Lieferung 33 7

Schönheitsfehler 46 40

Schriftform 11 2, **12** 5, **13** 1–4, **18** 5, **29** 5–9, E-Mail **13** 2, Formerfordernis **29** 9, Formvorschriften eines Vorbehaltsstaates **13** 4, Konsens **29** 8, Schriftformklauseln **29** 5–9, Telefax **13** 2, **18** 5, **29** 7, Telegramm **13** 2, **29** 7, Telex **13** 2, **29** 7, Vorbehalt nach Art. 96 **11** 2, Vorbehaltsstaaten **12** 5, **13** 4, *s. a. Form*

Schuldbeitritt als Vertragsänderung **29** 10

Schuldübernahme 4 37

Schutzland, Maßgeblichkeit des Rechts **42** 3

Schutzpflichten 45 3, Verletzung **25** 17

Schutzrechtsbelastung *s. Immaterialgüterrechte*

Schwebezustand bei künftigen Störungen 72 38 f.

Schweigen 14 16, als Annahme **18** 9, **48** 2, 27, Auslegung **8** 2, 36

Schweigen als Annahme 18 9, **48** 2, 27

Scott-Avery-Klausel und Beginn der Verjährungsfrist **9 VerjÜbk** 3

Magere Zahlen = Randnummern **Sachregister**

Selbsteintritt des Spediteurs 31 27
Selbsthilfeverkauf 31 62, **62** 18, **75** 4, **88** 3 ff., 18, Aufrechnung mit Erlös **88** 18, Kaufpreisklage **62** 18, Rechtsbehelfe des Verkäufers **62** 18
Selbsttransport, Lieferung **31** 21–23
Sicherheitsleistung, angemessene Frist für S. **72** 26 f., ausreichende S. **72** 29 ff., Nichtstellen von Sicherheiten **72** 31, 35a, Wirkungen **72** 30 ff.
Sicherungsrechte Dritter 41 4
Signatur, digitale s. Signatur, elektronische
Signatur, elektronische 13 2, s. a. E-Mail, elektronische Kommunikation
Sittenverstoß 4 18
SMS, Zugang **24** 30
„sofortige" Lieferung 33 17
Software 1 38, Bestimmtheit des Angebots **14** 5
„sonstige" Pflichten" des Verkäufers 30 9, 45 3, Erfüllungsanspruch des Käufers **46** 6
Sorgfaltspflichten, Verstoß und „vernünftige Entschuldigung" bei Versäumung der Rügefrist **44** 4
Sortierung teilweise mangelhafter Ware 51 11
specific performance 28 2 f., 10, 22, Haftungsbefreiung s. a. Erfüllung in Natur, Erfüllungsanspruch, Erfüllungsklage
Spediteur 31 25–28, 77, **32** 21 ff., Abschluss des Beförderungsvertrags **32** 21 f., als Beförderer i. S. d. Art. 31 **31** 25–28, Haftung des Verkäufers für den S. **31** 77, **32** 21 f., Übergabe an den S. **31** 25–28
Spekulationsgefahr, verspätete Annahmeerklärung **21** 23, Vertragsaufhebung **26** 16, Vertragsaufhebung wegen antizipierten Vertragsbruchs **72** 38
Sperrwirkung, zeitliche und Grundsatz der unversehrten Rückgabe **82** 25
Spezielle Eigenschaften der Ware 46 24
Spezieskauf 46 18, **48** 5, Anspruch auf Ersatzlieferung **46** 18, Beseitigung eines Sachmangels durch Ersatzlieferung **48** 5, Falschlieferung **46** 18
Spezifikation 1 17, **65** 1 ff., **80** 5, unterbliebene S. **80** 5
Spezifikation der Ware 53 35, **65** 1 ff., abweichende Spezifizierung des Käufers **65** 15, allgemeines Prinzip hinter Art. 65 **65** 24, Angemessene Frist für abweichende Spezifizierung druch Käufer **65** 12 f., Aufforderung zur Spezifikation durch den Verkäufer **65** 7 ff., Beweislast **65** 25 ff., Nichtvornahme durch den Käufer **65** 5 ff., Schadenminderungspflicht **65** 19, dem Verkäufer bekannte Bedürfnisse des Käufers **65** 10, als vertragliche Pflicht **65** 4
Sprache, Anfechtung wegen Sprachirrtums **24** 40, **27** 8, Auslegung von Erklärungen **8** 4a, deutsche Übersetzung des CISG Vor 1–6 26–28, Eignung als Erklärungsmittel **27** 8, **49** 24, Einbeziehung von AGB **14** 61 ff., als Form **11** 14, Mitteilungen **27** 8, Originalfassungen **7** 31,

Sprachirrtum **24** 38, **27** 8, Vertragssprache **27** 8, Zugang von Erklärungen **24** 36
Sprachrisiken 8 41 ff.
Sprachrisiko, Zugang von Erklärungen **24** 36
Staatsangehörigkeit 1 59 f.
Standby letter of credit 53 39
statutes of frauds 11 12
stellvertretendes commodum 79 50
Stellvertretung s. Hilfspersonen
Steuern, Belastung mit S. als Rechtsmangel **41** 7
Stichprobe 38 14
Streckengeschäft 31 24, 35, **32** 24
Streik s. Arbeitskampf, Haftungsbefreiung **79** 21 ff., politischer S. **79** 23
strict liability 74 3
Strom s. Elektrizität
Stückkauf, Abgabeschuld **79** 27, Beschaffungsschuld **79** 27
Stundung, Nachfristsetzung keine S. **47** 18, 20
substantial detriment s. wesentliche Vertragsverletzung
Subunternehmer 79 35
Sukzessivlieferungsvertrag 1 15, **38** 9, **51** 3, **73**, **12 VerjÜbk** 4 ff., Beginn der Verjährung **12 VerjÜbk** 4 ff., Begriff **73** 8 ff., Beweislast **73** 40, Einzellieferung **73** 9, gegenwärtige Pflichtverletzung **73** 18, Gesamtvertrag **73** 8 ff., gestörte Einzellieferung **73** 7 ff., konkludente Aufhebungserklärung bei gestörter Einzellieferung **73** 13, Nichterfüllung **73** 11, Prognose der künftigen wesentlichen Pflichtverletzung **73** 20 ff., Rechtsvergleich **73** 5 f., Regelungsüberblick **73** 3 f., Umfang der Aufhebung **73** 34 f., Untersuchung der Ware **38** 9, Vergleich mit PICC und PECL **73** 6, Verhältnis von mangelhafter Einzellieferungen der S. und teilweiser Nichterfüllung **73** 39, Verhältnis zu Zurückbehaltungsrecht und Vertragsaufhebung bei antizipiertem Vertragsbruch **73** 28, Vertragsaufhebung bei gestörter Einzellieferung **73** 7 ff., Vertragsaufhebung bei Zweckzusammenhang **73** 29 ff., Vertragsaufhebung für die Zukunft **73** 17 ff., Vorgeschichte **73** 1 f., wesentliche Vertragsverletzung **73** 11 f., Zweckzusammenhang **73** 31 ff.
Surrogat in der Rückabwicklung **84** 34 ff.

Tagespreisklauseln 14 15
Tank, Lieferung aus dem T. **31** 72
Tauschhandel 53 28
Täuschung, Beginn der Verjährung **10 VerjÜbk** 7 f.
Tauschvertrag 1 30
Teilaufhebung 81 14, bei Sukzessivlieferungsverträgen **73** 15 f., 27, 34 f.
Teilbarkeit des Vertrages 73 31 ff.
Teillieferung 26 6, **31** 44, 69, **39** 10, **51** 4, 9, **73** 39, Recht des Käufers zur Aufhebung des Kaufvertrags im ganzen **51** 9, Recht des Verkäufers zur T. **51** 4, Rüge **39** 10, Sukzessivliefe-

1435

Sachregister

Fette Zahlen = Artikel

rungsvertrag **73** 39, Vertragsaufhebung **51** 9, Zulässigkeit **31** 44, 69
Teilrückabwicklung Vor 81–84 8
Telefax, Absendung **27** 9, angemessene Frist für Annahme der Offerte **18** 15, Schriftform **13** 2, **18** 5, Übermittlungsrisiko **27** 5, „umgehende" Antwort **18** 15, unmittelbare Übermittlungsart **20** 3, vereinbarte Schriftform **29** 7, Zugang **24** 23
Telegramm, Schriftform **13** 2, Übermittlungsrisiko **27** 5, vereinbarte Schriftform **29** 7
Telephon, mündliche Erklärung **18** 17, **24** 5, Übermittlungsrisiko **27** 5, unmittelbare Übermittlungsart **20** 3, Zugang **24** 5
Telex, angemessene Frist für Annahme der Offerte **18** 15, Schriftform **13** 2, Übermittlungsrisiko **27** 5, unmittelbare Übermittlungsart **20** 3, vereinbarte Schriftform **29** 7, Zugang **24** 23
Theorie des letzten Wortes s. *battle of forms*
Tod des Erklärenden, Einfluss auf Offerte **15** 6, **17** 6
Totalreparation, Grundsatz **74** 2
Transitstaat, Schutzrechtsbelastung im T. **42** 13a
Transparenzgebot Vor 14–24 4, **14** 6
Transport, Weisungen des Käufers hinsichtlich des T. **32** 28 f.
Transportgefahr, Bringschuld **32** 16, und fehlerhaftes Verhalten des Beförderers **31** 32, 36, 38, vertragliche Lieferklauseln **31** 77
Transportkosten 31 83, **32** 25
Transportroute 32 19
Transportschaden infolge mangelhafter Verpackung **31** 35 f., infolge unsachgemäßer Versendung **32** 30
Transportversicherung 32 26 ff., 31, Incoterms **32** 27, Kosten **32** 26 f., Pflicht zur T. **32** 26 f., Rechtsfolgen der Verletzung der Pflicht zur T. **32** 30
Transportversicherungspolice, fehlende T. **32** 30, fehlerhafte T. **34** 8, 10, Pflicht zur Übergabe **30** 6, **34** 1
Treu und Glauben 7 5, 25–27, 49 ff., **8** 30, **30** 6, **31** 32, 39 f., 49, 68, 78, **32** 18, 28 f., **33** 13, **34** 5, **45** 16, **46** 10, **47** 3, **49** 27, 42, **51** 4, **52** 3, 7, **80** 1, 7 VerjÜbk, Abtretung des Ersatzanspruchs gegen den Beförderer **31** 40, Auslegung **8** 30, Befreiung des Schuldners bei Gläubigerverursachung **80** 1, Bestimmungsort der Lieferung **32** 18, Bindung an die Vertragsaufhebung **45** 16, Bindung des Käufers an den geltend gemachten Erfüllungsanspruch **47** 3, Bindung des Käufers an die Ablehnung des nachträglichen Erfüllungsangebots des Verkäufers **49** 42, langdauernde Leistungshindernisse **46** 10, Pflicht des Käufers zur Übernahme der Ware zu einem anderen als dem vertraglich oder gesetzlich bestimmten Lieferort **31** 49, 68, 78, Pflicht des Verkäufers zum Widerspruch gegen unzweckmäßige Versandanweisungen des Käufers **32** 29, Pflicht des Verkäufers zur Anzeige der Lieferbereitschaft vor Ablauf der Lieferfrist **33** 13, Schranken des Anspruchs auf Erfüllung **46** 10, venire contra factum proprium **45** 16, Versendungsort **31** 32, verspätete Rüge der Vertragswidrigkeit von Dokumenten **34** 5, Verwirkung des Schadensersatzanspruchs des Käufers **49** 27, Weisungsrecht des Käufers hinsichtlich der Versendung der Ware **32** 28, Zurückweisung der Ware bei Versendung an den falschen Ort **31** 39 f., Zurückweisung von Teillieferungen **51** 4, Zurückweisung von Zuviellieferung **52** 7, Zurückweisung vorzeitig gelieferter Ware **52** 3
triftiger Grund, Sukzessivlieferungsvertrag **73** 20 ff.

Übergabe an den Beförderer **31** 29 ff., an den Beförderer „zur Übermittlung an den Käufer" **31** 30, Beginn der Verjährungsfrist bei Ü. **10** VerjÜbk **5**, von Dokumenten **30** 6, **34** 1 ff., und Eigentumsverschaffung **30** 7, Lieferung durch Ü. an den Käufer **31** 76
Übermittlungsfehler 27 12
Übermittlungsrisiko 27 3, 12, Ablehnung des Nacherfüllungsangebots **48** 26, Erklärung der Vertragsaufhebung **26** 11, **49** 25, Geltendmachung des Anspruchs auf Ersatzlieferung **46** 33, Nachfristsetzung **47** 12, nachträgliches Angebot der Erfüllung durch den Verkäufer **48** 29, Rechtsfolgen des Verlustes einer Mitteilung **27** 10, Rechtsmängelanzeige **43** 5
überraschende Klauseln Vor 14–24 5, **14** 35
Umladung 31 36, **32** 19
Umleitung der Ware, Beginn der Untersuchungsfrist **38** 23 ff., Kenntnis des Verkäufers **38** 24
Umsteuerung s. *Abwicklungsverhältnis, Vertragsaufhebung,* in Vertragsrückabwicklungsverhältnis **81** 6 ff., 12, 20
Umverpackung 31 36
UN Global Compact 35 7
UN Übereinkommen über die Verjährung beim internationalen Warenkauf 53 27
UN Übereinkommen über internationale gezogene Wechsel und internationale Eigenwechsel 53 13
UNCITRAL Modellgesetz über internationale Überweisungen 53 11
ungerechtfertigte Bereicherung bei Lieferung höherwertiger Ware **52** 11
Ungewissheit der Erstattung von Auslagen **48** 9
UNIDROIT-Principles 25 2, Lückenfüllung durch U. **7** 59–69, materiellrechtliche Verweisung **7** 66, als objektiv anwendbares Recht **7** 59–61, Parteiautonomie **7** 62–69, Schiedsgerichte **7** 69, vor staatlichen Gerichten **7** 61, s. a. PICC
UNILEX 7 20
Universalitätsprinzip Vor 1–6 10, **1** 5
Unmöglichkeit 28 15, **31** 62, **45** 17, **46** 9 ff., 34, **49** 6, **79** 5, 12 ff., 53 f., **82** 5, 8 f., anfäng-

Magere Zahlen = Randnummern

liche U. **49** 6, anfängliche und Gefahrübergang **68** 4 ff., und Annahmeverzug **31** 62 ff., der Beseitigung des Mangels **45** 17 (Fn. 33), Bösgläubigkeit des Verkäufers **68** 14 ff., kein Erfüllungsanspruch bei feststehender U. **28** 15, **46** 12, Haftungsbefreiung **79** 5, 12, der Nachbesserung **45** 17 (Fn. 33), nicht zu vertretende U. **46** 12, der Rückgabe der gelieferten Ware **46** 9, 34, der Rückgewähr **82** 5, der Rückgewähr, Rechtsfolgen **82** 8 f., Rückwirkung des Gefahrübergangs **68**. 5 f., 7 ff., subjektive s. *Unvermögen*, vorübergehende U. **28** 41 ff., **46** 10, 12, als wesentliche Vertragsverletzung **49** 6
Unmöglichkeit, objektive, Haftungsbefreiung **79** 53
Unmöglichkeit, subjektive, Haftungsbefreiung **79** 54
Unterbrechung der Verjährungsfrist durch Anerkenntnis **20 VerjÜbk** 1 ff., Beendigung des Rechtsverfahrens ohne Sachentscheidung **17 VerjÜbk** 1 f., Begriff **13 VerjÜbk** 1, Einfluss höherer Gewalt auf die U. **21 VerjÜbk** 1 f., Einleitung eines Rechtsverfahrens **13 VerjÜbk** 1 ff., **15 VerjÜbk** 1 f., Einleitung eines Schiedsverfahrens **14 VerjÜbk** 1 ff., Geltendmachung eines Anspruches in einem laufenden Verfahren **13 VerjÜbk** 3, Geltendmachung eines Gegenanspruches **16 VerjÜbk** 4, bei gesamtschuldnerischer Haftung **18 VerjÜbk** 1 ff., Hinderung an der U. **21 VerjÜbk** 3, internationale Wirkung der U. **30 VerjÜbk** 1 ff., Nachfrist **17 VerjÜbk** 2, **18 VerjÜbk** 7 f., Regress des Käufers **18 VerjÜbk** 5 f., Vornahme einer außergerichtlichen Handlung **19 VerjÜbk** 2 ff., Wirkung der U. **13 VerjÜbk** 4, **19 VerjÜbk** 3 f., **20 VerjÜbk** 4
Unterfrachtführer 32 23
Untergang, nachträglicher der Ware und Grundsatz der unversehrten Rückgabe **82** 27
Unterlassungspflicht 45 3, **49** 12
Untersuchung der Dokumente 34 5
Untersuchung der Ware 38, Abdingbarkeit **38** 28, Anwendungsbereich **38** 7–9, Art und Weise **38** 10 ff., Ausfallprobe **38** 9 bei Bestimmungsort **38** 21 f., „cash against documents" **58** 35, Dokumente **34** 5, **38** 7, durch Dritte **38** 10, bei Ersatzlieferung **38** 9, fortlaufende U. **39** 20, Frist **38** 15 ff., Fristausschluss oder -verlängerung **38** 28 ff., Fristbeginn **38** 19 ff., Gebräuche **38** 11, Grundstoffe **38** 17, just in time-Verträge **38** 29, bei Kauf nach Muster oder Probe **38** 9, Kosten **38** 19, und Mängelrüge **38** 3 ff., Maschinen **38** 14, 16 f., Modalitäten **38** 10 ff., bei Nachbesserung **38** 9, durch neutrale Prüfstelle **38** 10, als Obliegenheit **38** 5, bei originalverpackter Ware **38** 14, Ort der Untersuchung der Ware vor Zahlung **58** 34, Parteivereinbarungen **38** 11, 29 ff., Pflicht des Käufers bei „vernünftiger Entschuldigung" **44** 10, 12, Pflicht des Verkäufers **40** 5, Rechtsnatur **38** 3 ff., und Rück-

abwicklung **82** 18, keine Schadensersatzpflicht des Käufers bei unterlassener U. **44** 16, Stellung des Käufers **38** 18, Stichproben **38** 14, Sukzessivlieferungsvertrag **38** 9, bei Umleitung oder Weiterversendung **38** 23 ff., Untersuchungsort **38** 12, 31, bei verderblicher Ware **38** 14, 16, beim Verkauf reisender Ware **38** 21, beim Versendungskauf **38** 21, vor Vertragsschluss **35** 35, bei vorzeitiger Lieferung **38** 20, bei Weiterverkauf **38** 23, vor Zahlung **58** 2, 33 ff., Zeitpunkt **38** 15 ff., Zweck **38** 3 f.
Untersuchungspflicht, Verletzung der **74** 13
Unterzeichnung 91 1 f., **41 VerjÜbk** 1 f.
Unterzeichnungsklausel 46 VerjÜbk
Unverhältnismäßigkeit 34 11
Unvermögen 28 15, **46** 12, **79** 54
unverzüglich, Billigungserklärung bei verspäteter Annahme **21** 8, Widerspruch **19** 15 ff.
Unzumutbarkeit der Anzeige bei künftiger wesentlicher Vertragsverletzung **72** 23 f., Behebung des Mangels durch den Verkäufer **48** 6, 9–13, Beweislast **46** 40, **48** 13, Erfüllung **46** 12, als Kriterium der wesentlichen Vertragsverletzung **46** 24 f., Mängelbeseitigung für den Käufer **37** 12 f., Nachbesserung für den Verkäufer **46** 40, 42, Nachbesserung und wesentliche Vertragsverletzung **46** 30, Unannehmlichkeiten bei Behebung des Mangels in der Erfüllung **34** 11, **48** 11, Untersuchung der Ware **34** 11, **38** 25, Verzögerung bei der Beseitigung des Mangels **48** 10
Urheberrecht 42 4
Ursprungszeugnis 30 6, **34** 1

venire contra factum proprium 7 50, **9** 8, Zahlungszeit **57** 7, **63** 5
Veränderung der Ware und Rückabwicklung **82** 5 ff.
Veränderung der Ware, Grundsatz der unversehrten Rückgabe **82** 20
Veränderungsrisiko 27 3, 12
Verarbeitung, Bestimmung der Ware zur V. und wesentliche Vertragsverletzung **46** 25
Veräußerung der Ware, Grundsatz der unversehrten Rückgabe **82** 22 f.
Verbrauch der Ware, Grundsatz der unversehrten Rückgabe **82** 20
Verbraucherschutzrecht 2 24–26, **4** 19, keine Anwendung des Verjährungsübereinkommens auf Verbrauchergeschäfte **4 VerjÜbk,** Formvorschriften **11** 14, missbräuchliche Klauseln s. *Verbrauchsgüterkauf*
Verbrauchsgüterkauf 2 7–26, Erkennbarkeit des persönlichen Gebrauchs **2** 15–21, Familie **2** 13, Haushalt **2** 13, s. a. *Verbraucherschutzrecht*
Veredelungsvertrag 3 9
Verfahrenspatent 42 4
Verfahrensrecht 4 33
Verfrachter 31 19
Vergaberecht s. *öffentliche Auftragsvergabe*

Sachregister

Fette Zahlen = Artikel

Vergleich 4 45
Verhältnis zu anderen Übereinkommen 37 VerjÜbk
Verjährung 4 35 f., **39** 16 ff., **28** f., **43** 7, **45** 33, **74** 62, **3 VertragsG** 1–9, **VerjÜbk,** Ansprüche aus der Nichtigkeit des Vertrages **1 VerjÜbk** 5, Ansprüche des Käufers **45** 33, Begriff **1 VerjÜbk** 3, deliktische Ansprüche **1 VerjÜbk** 5, Einrede der V. **24 VerjÜbk** 2 ff., Kaufpreiszahlungsanspruch **53** 27, kaufrechtliche Ansprüche **1 VerjÜbk** 5, **8 VerjÜbk** 2, Neubeginn und Hemmung **3 VertragsG** 9, Rechtsbehelfe des Verkäufers **61** 21, Rechtsmangel **43** 7, Schadenersatzanspruch **74** 62, in Schiedsverfahren **74** 62, Schutzrechtsbelastung **43** 7, Sonderfristen für Gewährleistungsansprüche **3 VertragsG** 4–6, Verhältnis zur Ausschlussfrist für Rüge **39** 28 f., Verzicht auf die V. **24 VerjÜbk** 3 f., Wirkung der V. **23 VerjÜbk** 3, **24 VerjÜbk** 1 f., **25 VerjÜbk** 1 f., **26 VerjÜbk,** *s. a. Verjährungsfrist, Unterbrechung der Verjährungsfrist*
Verjährungsfrist, allgemeine Begrenzung der V. **23 VerjÜbk** 2 f., Beginn bei Ansprüchen aus einer Vertragswidrigkeit der Ware **9 VerjÜbk** 2, **10 VerjÜbk** 4 ff., Berechnung der V. **28 VerjÜbk** 1 ff., Dauer **8 VerjÜbk** 1 ff., Einheitsfrist **8 VerjÜbk** 2, Wirkung des Ablaufs der V. **23 VerjÜbk** 3, **24 VerjÜbk** 2, **25 VerjÜbk** 1 ff., **26 VerjÜbk,** Zinsen **27 VerjÜbk**
Verjährungsübereinkommen 3 VertragsG 1, Anwendungsausschluss durch die Parteien **3 VerjÜbk** 4 f., Verhältnis zu anderen Übereinkommen **37 VerjÜbk,** Vertragsstaaten **Anhang II**
Verkäuferhaftung, Nichterfüllung einer Vertragspflicht **45** 2
Verkäuferpflichten bei Rückabwicklung **84** 11 ff.
Verkürzung der Verjährungsfrist *s. Änderung der Verjährungsfrist*
Verlängerung der Verjährungsfrist *s. Änderung der Verjährungsfrist*
Verletzung von Nebenpflichten als wesentliche Vertragsverletzung **25** 68
Vermutung der Richtigkeit und Vollständigkeit 8 34
Vernehmbarkeit, Erklärung **27** 5
vernünftige Person 72 15, **73** 32 f., **82** 25 f.
Verordnung 97/5/EC über grenzüberschreitende Überweisungen 53 11
Verpackung 19 9, 13, **31** 35, 53, 83, **35** 11, **28** ff., Angemessenheit **35** 31, Beginn der Untersuchungsfrist **38** 25, Bestandteil der Ware **35** 31, bei Holschuld **31** 53, Kennzeichnung **35** 29, Kosten **31** 83, mangelhafte V. **31** 35 f., Parteivereinbarung **35** 11, Pflicht zur V. **35** 30, Üblichkeit **35** 29, Verpackungsart als wesentliche Abweichung von Offerte **19** 9, 13, bei Versendungskauf **31** 83, Vertragsmäßigkeit der Ware **35** 11

Verrechnung *s. Aufrechnung,* in der Rückabwicklung **81** 21 f.
Verschlechterungseinrede, Objektivierung der Maßstäbe **71** 14, 20, 45, *s. a. Prognose*
Verschulden 45 8, 10, Nichterfüllung und V. **45** 8, bei Vertragsbruch **61** 5, Vertragsverletzung und V. **45** 10
Versendungsanzeige 32 1, 11, 14, Bindung des Verkäufers **32** 9, Inhalt **32** 5, Rechtsfolgen der Verletzung der Pflicht zur V. **32** 8 ff., 14, vertragliche Pflicht zur V. **32** 13 f., Zeitpunkt **32** 6, 12 ff.
Versendungskauf 1 18, **19** 9, **31** 2, 11, 17 f., 17., 73 f., **32** 1, 17, 30, **38** 21, **50** 9, **57** 3, 15 ff., **58** 7, 11, 13, **67** 2 ff., **71** 32, 35, Anhalterecht **71** 32, 35, Beförderer **67** 12 ff., Beginn der Untersuchungsfrist **38** 21, mit Bestimmung eines besonderen Versendungsortes **31** 73 f., Erforderlichkeit der Beförderung **67** 9 ff., Gefahrtragung **67** 17 ff., 22 ff., Gefahrübergang **31** 11, Minderung **50** 9, Pflicht zum Abschluss des Beförderungsvertrags **32** 1, 17, 30, Versendungsart als wesentliche Abweichung von Offerte **19** 9, Zurückbehaltung von Dokumenten **67** 27 f.
Versendungsort 31 31, 74
Versicherungsansprüche als commodum ex re **84** 35
Verspätung, Mitteilung **27** 11
Versteigerung, Internet-Auktion **Vor 14–24** 28
Versteigerungen 2 2, 27–30, 32, keine Anwendung des Verjährungsübereinkommens auf V. **4 VerjÜbk**
Verteilungsnorm 2 VertragsG 1
Vertrag, Auslegung **8** 3 ff.
Vertrag, der die Beförderung der Ware vorsieht, Zahlungsort **57** 12, 16, Zahlungszeit **58** 12
Vertrag mit Schutzwirkung zugunsten Dritter 74 16
Vertragsänderung 29, 1 ff., durch Abnahme der Zuviellieferung **52** 10, Annahme **29** 8, durch Annahme vorzeitiger Lieferung **52** 5, Formfreiheit **11** 4, 8, konkludente Annahme **29** 8, Schuldbeitritt **29** 10, Vertragsübernahme **29** 10
Vertragsanpassung 79 4, 43, 57
Vertragsaufhebung 11 8, **26** 1 ff., **29** 1 ff., **75** 5, **Vor 81–84** 1 ff., 1 f., **81** 3 ff., 12, 14, **82** 5, **83** 2, **84** 1 ff., 22 ff., 32 ff., Abgrenzung zur Aufhebungsvereinbarung **26** 10a, Anwendungsfälle **26** 6, Aufhebung der Primärpflichten **26** 4 ff., Aufwendungen, frustrierte **84** 32, Auslöser für V. **26** 6, Befreiungswirkung **81** 5, Behelfe **83** 2 ff., Beweislast **26** 17, **75** 14, Bindung des Käufers an unrechtmäßige Erklärung der V. *s. Vertragsaufhebung durch den Käufer,* dogmatische Einordnung der Rückerstattungspflichten **Vor 81–84** 4, **81** 6 ff., Durchführung **Vor 81–84** 1 f., Entstehungsgeschichte **26** 1 ff., Erklärung

1438

Magere Zahlen = Randnummern

Sachregister

der **75** 5, ex nunc **73** 23, 27, ex-nunc- bzw. ex-tunc-Wirkung **81** 6 ff., Formfreiheit **11** 8, fortbestehende Pflichten **81** 12, Mitteilung **26** 11 f., Normzweck **26** 4 ff., Rechtsvergleich **26** 5, **Vor 81–84** 3, Rechtzeitigkeit der Aufhebungserklärung **26** 15 f., rückwirkende Vertragsvernichtung nach romanischer Dogmatik **81** 6, und Schadensersatz **Vor 81–84** 9, Schadensminderungspflicht **77** 4, 10, durch schlüssiges Verhalten **26** 7 f., als Surrogat der Rückgabe **84** 34 ff., teilweise V. **Vor 81–84** 8, **81** 14, Unmöglichkeit der Rückgabe **82** 5, Vereinbarung, einvernehmliche **84** 7, Verhältnis zum Schadensersatz **26** 15, Voraussetzungen **26** 6, **81** 3 f., und Vorteilsausgleichung **84** 5 ff., 22 ff., Wirkungen **26** 4, **81** 5 ff., und Zins **84** 1 ff., 11 ff., für die Zukunft **73** 23 ff., *s. a. Abwicklungsverhältnis*

Vertragsaufhebung durch den Käufer, Ablauf einer vom Käufer gesetzten Nachfrist **49** 15, 20 ff., Angebot der Erfüllung durch den Verkäufer nach Erklärung der V. durch den Käufer **48** 30, bedingte V. **49** 23, 39, Bindung an die Erklärung der V. **45** 16, Bindung des Käufers **45** 16, Bindung des Käufers an unrechtmäßige Erklärung der V. **46** 7, **49** 44 f., wegen Erfüllungsverweigerung des Verkäufers **49** 6, Frist **49** 27, 42, Geltendmachung mit Rüge **39** 13, Gestaltungswirkung **45** 16, **49** 43, nach Nachfristsetzung **49** 15, 22, 32, 42, wegen Nichterfüllung des Anspruchs auf Ersatzlieferung **46** 38, wegen Nichterfüllung des Anspruchs auf Nachbesserung **46** 47, wegen Nichterfüllung des Anspruchs auf Verschaffung von Dokumenten **49** 11, 18, wegen Nichterfüllung von Nebenpflichten **49** 12, 20, Rechtsfolgen bei berechtigter V. **49** 43, Rechtsfolgen bei unberechtigter V. **49** 44 ff., wegen Rechtsmangels **49** 10, teilweise V. **49** 26, **Vor 51** 4, 84, **51** 1, wegen Unmöglichkeit **49** 6, unrechtmäßige Erklärung der V. **49** 44 ff., Unwiderruflichkeit mit Zugang der Erklärung **45** 16, **49** 43, wegen verspäteter Lieferung **49** 5, 15 ff., Vertragswidrigkeit der Ware **35** 43, **49** 7 ff., Vorbehalt der V. **48** 14, Wegfall des Zinsanspruchs **78** 23, wesentliche Vertragsverletzung **49** 4–14

Vertragsaufhebung durch den Verkäufer 64 1 ff., andauernde Vertragsverletzung **64** 29 ff., Beweislast **64** 38 ff., Insolvenz des Käufers **64** 12, Mitteilung der Vertragsaufhebungserklärung **64** 32, Nichtabnahme der Ware **64** 13 ff., Nichtaufnahme konformer Dokumente **64** 15, Nichterfüllung einer anderen Pflicht **64** 17 ff., Nichterfüllung einer mit der Zahlung verbundenen Pflicht **64** 10, Nichtzahlung **64** 6 ff., Nichtzahlung oder Nichtabnahme innerhalb Nachfrist **64** 2, 19 ff., Präklusion **64** 31, Schadensersatz **64** 34, ultima ratio Rechtsbehelf **64** 4, Verhältnis zum Erfüllungsanspruch **64** 35 ff., „verspätete Erfüllung" **64** 23 ff., verspätete Zahlung **64** 7 ff., vertraglich geschaffenes zusätzliches Aufhebungsrecht **64** 21, wesentlicher Vertragsbruch durch den Käufer **64** 2, 5 ff., Wirkungen der Vertragsaufhebung **64** 33, zeitliche Begrenzungen **64** 3, 22 ff.

Vertragsaufhebungsrecht Vor 81–84 2, **81** 3, einvernehmliche Vertragsaufhebung **Vor 81–84** 7, des Käufers **Vor 81–84** 5, Rechtsmangel **41** 21, Schutzrechtsbelastung **42** 25, Schutzrechtsbelastung aufgrund technischer Anweisungen des Käufers **42** 23, des Verkäufers **Vor 81–84** 5, Verlust **26** 15 f., vertragliches V. **Vor 81–84** 7, **84** 7

Vertragsaufsage 72 35, Widerrufbarkeit der **72** 36

Vertragsauslegung, ergänzende *s. Auslegung; Vetragsergänzung*

Vertragsbruch *s. Vertragsverletzung*

Vertragsergänzung 8 11, 25 ff., **9** 1 f., **29** 1 ff., Formfreiheit **11** 8

Vertragsfreiheit *s. Parteiautonomie*

Vertragsgesetz 1 79, **1 VertragsG** 3

Vertragsinhalt, Bestimmung **8** 21 ff., Gestaltung **Vor 14–24** 42

Vertragsmäßigkeit der Ware 31 33, **35, 36,** Abgrenzung zum Rechtsmangel **35** 5, Bestellprobe **35** 27, bestimmter Verwendungszweck **35** 18 ff., durchschnittliche Qualität **35** 15, Gattungsschuld **35** 15, Gebrauchsanweisung **35** 14, bei Gefahrübergang **36** 3 f., gewöhnlicher Verwendungszweck **35** 13 ff., Haltbarkeit **35** 14, Handelbarkeit **35** 14 f., Handelsbräuche **35** 16, Hilfspersonen **36** 1, 6, bei Kauf nach Muster oder Probe **35** 24 ff., objektive Kriterien zur Bestimmung **35** 12 ff., Pflicht zur Lieferung von vertragsmäßiger Ware **31** 33, Qualität der Ware **35** 9, subsidiäre Bestimmung **35** 12, Verpackung **35** 11, 28 ff., vertragliche Leistungsbeschreibung **35** 6 f., Wiederverkäuflichkeit **35** 14 f., Zeitpunkt **36** 1 ff.

Vertragsprogramm, Anpassung des V.s **73** 15, 36

Vertragsschluss 4 9, Ausschreibung **Vor 14–24** 30, äußerer Konsens **Vor 14–24** 1, bedingter **14** 13a ff., Börse **Vor 14–24** 29, Einigung ohne Offerte und Annahme **Vor 14–24** 23 f., Einigungsvorgang **Vor 14–24** 1, 15 ff., Formfreiheit **11** 5, Gebräuche und Gepflogenheiten **9** 3, 7, Geltungsbereich der Vertragsschlussvorschriften **Vor 14–24** 1 ff., Internet-Auktion **Vor 14–24** 28, Konsensprinzip **Vor 14–24** 24, Kreuzofferten **Vor 14–24** 15 f., Mehrparteienvertrag **Vor 14–24** 30a ff., Parteiautonomie und Vertragsschlussverfahren **Vor 14–24** 17, Scheitern des V. bei battle of forms **19** 24, ungeregelter Einigungsvorgang **Vor 14–24** 17, trotz verspäteter Annahme möglich **21** 6, Warenbörse **Vor 14–24** 29, Zeitpunkt **23** 1–6, Zeitpunkt des V. bei Leistungsbestimmung **23** 5, Zeitpunkt des V. bei verspäteter Annahmeerklärung **21** 10, *s. a.*

1439

Sachregister

Fette Zahlen = Artikel

Annahme der Offerte, kaufmännisches Bestätigungsschreiben, Offerte
Vertragssprache, allgemeine Geschäftsbedingungen **14** 63
Vertragsstaat, Definition **1** 64, Liste der Vertragsstaaten **Anhang I,** Liste der Vertragsstaaten des Verjährungsübereinkommens **Anhang II,** Vorbehalte **1** 65–68
Vertragsstatut *s. anwendbares Recht*
Vertragsstrafe 4 40, **19** 9, **47** 20, **74** 32, 56, 59, **79** 8, 51, **81** 12, Fortbestehen der bei Vertragsrückabwicklung **81** 12, Gültigkeit **4** 40, Haftungsbefreiung **79** 8, 51, bei Nachfristsetzung **47** 20, Verfall als Folgeschaden **74** 32, Verhältnis zum Schadenersatzanspruch **74** 59, Voraussehbarkeit **74** 56, wesentliche Abweichung von Offerte **19** 9
Vertragsübernahme als Vertragsänderung **29** 10
Vertragsverletzung 25 1 ff., **45** 5, **46** 23–32, **48** 15, 23, **49** 4–14, 20 ff., **51** 1, 6, 9–11, **52** 4, 8, **64** 1 ff., **5** ff., **71** 3, 13 ff., **72** 13 ff., 21, 30, 33 ff., 41, **73** 11 f., 17 ff., **74** 11 f., **80** 3, 6, 9, **82** 13, **10 VerjÜbk** 2 f., **12 VerjÜbk** 1, Beginn der Verjährung **10 VerjÜbk** 2 f., Begriff **45** 5, beiderseitige V. **80** 7, 9, Einzellieferung beim Sukzessivlieferungsvertrag **73** 12, Gegenreaktion des Gläubigers **80** 6, Gläubigerverursachung **80** 3 ff., Nachfristsetzung beim Sukzessivlieferungsvertrag **73** 11, Obliegenheiten **74** 13, Rückgewährpflichten **74** 11, unerhebliche V. bei Sukzessivlieferungsvertrag **73** 19, des Verkäufers und Grundsatz der unversehrten Rückgabe **82** 13, vorzeitige Erfüllungsverweigerung **72** 33 ff., vorzeitige Lieferung als V. **52** 4, Wegfall bei Gläubigerverursachung *s. Nichterfüllung,* Weigerung des Schuldners **74** 12, Wesentlichkeit der **74** 11
Vertragsverletzung durch den Käufer, Rechtsbehelfe des Verkäufers **61** 1 ff., wesentlicher Vertragsbruch **64** 1 ff., 5 ff.
Vertragsverletzung, künftige 71 3 ff., 13 ff., Beurteilungskriterien **71** 13 f., *s. a. Prognose*
Vertragsverletzung, künftige wesentliche 72 14 ff., Abwendung der Vertragsaufhebung durch Sicherheitsleistung **72** 17 ff., 30, Beginn der Verjährungsfrist **12 VerjÜbk** 1, Begriff **72** 13, Form und Frist der Anzeige **72** 21, Form und Frist der Sicherheitsleistung **72** 32, Prognose **72** 14 ff., Schadenersatz **72** 41, vorherige Anzeige der Vertragsaufhebung **72** 17 ff., *s. a. Prognose*
Vertragsverletzung, wesentliche 25 1 ff., **46** 23–32, **48** 15, **49** 4–14, **51** 6, 9–11, Nichterstattung einer Versendungsanzeige **32** 12, Recht zur Vertragsaufhebung **49** 4 ff., Rechtsmängel **41** 19a, 21, Sachmangel **49** 7–9, Schutzrechtsbelastung **42** 25, Schutzrechtsbelastung aufgrund technischer Anweisungen des Käufers **42** 23, teilweise Nichterfüllung **51** 1 ff., Transportversicherung **32** 31, Versendung an den falschen Bestimmungsort **32** 30, Vertragswidrigkeit der Ware **35** 43, zugesicherte Eigenschaften **46** 24, Zuviellieferung **52** 8
Vertragswidrige Beschaffenheit, Anspruchsverjährung **3 VertragsG** 4–6
Vertragswidrigkeit der Dokumente 34 5, 12, **48** 3, 5, **49** 11, 18
Vertragswidrigkeit der Ware, Abgrenzung zum Rechtsmangel **35** 5, Anerkennung durch den Verkäufer **39** 33, Anspruch auf Ersatzlieferung **46** 17 ff., 35, Anspruch auf Nachbesserung **46** 39 ff., Anzeige **35** 40, **39** 1 ff., *s. a. Rüge,* Anzeige der Garantiefrist **39** 27, Arglist des Verkäufers **35** 37, Artabweichung **35** 10, ins Auge springende V. **35** 34, **40** 4, Beginn der Verjährung des Anspruches aus der V. **10 VerjÜbk** 4 ff., Begriff **35** 4, **46** 20, Beweisfragen **35** 49 ff., Beweislast **31** 80, **32** 8, **35** 51 ff., **45** 9 f., Beweismaß **35** 55, Bösgläubigkeit des Verkäufers **40** 2 ff., dogmatische Einordnung **35** 2, Eintritt nach Gefahrübergang **36** 5 ff., Entdeckung und Rückabwicklung **82** 25, Entlastung **79** 6, Erfüllungsanspruch **35** 43, Ersatzlieferung **35** 43, Falschlieferung **31** 34, **35** 4, 10, **46** 20, Fehlerbegriff **35** 6, Freizeichnungsklauseln **35** 41 f., Garantie **36** 7 ff., bei Gefahrübergang **36** 3 f., Haftungsausschluss **35** 34 ff., Haftungsbefreiung **79** 28 ff., höherwertige Ware **52** 11, Irrtumsanfechtung **35** 45 f., auf den Käufer zurückzuführende V. **35** 33, Kenntnis der Käufers **35** 34 ff., Kenntnis des Verkäufers **40** 4 ff., Lieferung **31** 33, Mängelbeseitigungsanspruch **35** 36, Minderung **35** 43, Nachbesserung **35** 43, Nichterfüllung **45** 5, Offenbarung durch Verkäufer **40** 7, peius **35** 4, wegen Pflichtverletzung des Verkäufers **35** 6, Qualitätsabweichung **35** 4, 8, **40** 5, Quantitätsabweichung **35** 4, 8, **40** 5, 51, Recht des Käufers zur Vertragsaufhebung **35** 43, **49** 7 ff., 37, Rechtsbehelfe **35** 43 ff., **39** 13, Rüge **39** 1 ff., Sachmangel **46** 23–32, Schadenersatz **35** 43, unerhebliche Abweichungen **35** 2, 32, unerheblicher Fehler **35** 32, **46** 4, Untersuchung der Ware **38** 3 ff., verborgener Mangel **36** 4, **39** 34, Verjährung der Ansprüche **39** 28 f., Verjährungsfrist **8 VerjÜbk** 2, Verpackungsfehler **35** 11, **36** 4, Voraussetzung der Minderung **50** 2, vorzeitige Lieferung **37** 2 ff., und wesentliche Vertragsverletzung **25** 43 ff., **35** 43, **46** 23–32, **48** 15, **49** 7 ff., zugesicherte Eigenschaft **35** 37
Vertrauensschutz 7 54
vertretbare Sachen, kein Ersatzlieferungsanspruch bei Spezieskauf **46** 18, Recht des Verkäufers zur Ersatzlieferung bei Spezieskauf **48** 5
Vertriebshändlervertrag Vor 14–24 41
Vertriebsvertrag 1 31, **Vor 14–24** 41
Verwahrung gegen transportverzögerte Annahme 21 20
Verwendungsrisiko, Grundsatz der unversehrten Rückgabe **82** 19

Sachregister

Magere Zahlen = Randnummern

Verwendungsrisiko des Gläubigers 79 33
Verwendungszweck, bestimmter 35 18 ff., Informationspflicht des Verkäufers **35** 23, Kauf nach Muster oder Probe **35** 24 ff., Kenntnis des Verkäufers **35** 20 ff., Sachkunde des Käufers **35** 23, vertragliche Vereinbarung **35** 20, Vertrauen auf Sachkenntnis des Verkäufers **35** 23, Zeitpunkt der Bekanntgabe **35** 22
Verwendungszweck, gewöhnlicher 35 13 ff., Feststellung **35** 14 ff., Haftung für unüblichen Verwendungszweck **35** 13, Handelbarkeit **35** 15, Informationspflicht des Verkäufers bei Abweichung **35** 13, kaufmännische Verwendung **35** 14, öffentlich-rechtliche Schutzvorschriften **35** 17, Wiederverkäuflichkeit **35** 14
Verwertbarkeit der Ware 25 52 ff.
Verwirkung 4 42, **7** 51, des Schadenersatzanspruchs des Käufers **49** 27
Verzicht auf Einwand nicht gehöriger Rüge **39** 33, stillschweigender V. **8** 2, auf die Verjährung **24 VerjÜbk** 3 f.
Verzögerungsrisiko 27 3
Verzögerungsschaden s. Verzugsschaden
Verzug, Haftungsbefreiung **79** 5, des Verkäufers als wesentliche Vertragsverletzung **25** 38, Vertragsaufhebung wegen V. des Verkäufers **49** 5, 15, Zahlungsverzug **25** 66, Zinsen **78** 7 ff.
Verzugsschaden 45 26, **46** 36, **47** 18, **48** 21, **78** 41, bei Ersatzlieferung **46** 36, und Fälligkeitszinsen **78** 41, bei Nachbesserung **48** 21, bei Nachfristsetzung **47** 18
Videokonferenz, Erklärungsabgabe **18** 17
völkerrechtliche Vereinbarungen 90 1–5
Vollständigkeitsklauseln 29 6
Voraussehbarer Schaden 74 47 ff.
voraussehbarer Schaden, Begleitschäden **74** 53, Betriebsausfallschäden **74** 55, Folgeschäden **74** 54, frustrierte Aufwendungen **74** 55, Gegenstand **74** 50, Goodwill-Schaden **74** 56, Haftungsschaden **74** 56, Mangelfolgeschäden **74** 57, Maßstab **74** 48, Nichterfüllungsschaden **74** 52, objektives Element **74** 49, relevante Personen **74** 47, relevanter Zeitpunkt **74** 47, subjektives Element **74** 49
Voraussehbarkeitsregel 74 2, 45 ff., s. a. voraussehbarer Schaden, Begrenzung des Ersatzes **74** 45, contemplation rule **74** 4, und contemplation rule **74** 46, bei Deckungsgeschäft **75** 8, Verschuldensunabhängigkeit **74** 45, voraussehbarer Schaden s. dort, Zurechnung der Haftungsfolgen **74** 45
Vorbehalt, geheimer 8 7
Vorbehalte Vor 1–6 8–23, **1** 65–68, Anwendung des VerjÜbk auf Nichtigkeitsklagen **35 VerjÜbk** 1 f., zur Anwendung von Art. 24 VerjÜbk **24 VerjÜbk** 5, **36 VerjÜbk** 1 f., nach Art. 34 VerjÜbk **34 VerjÜbk** 1 f., nach Art. 38 VerjÜbk **38 VerjÜbk,** nach Art. 92 **Vor 1–6** 15 f., **1** 65, **Vor 14–24** 44 f., nach Art. 93 **Vor 1–6** 17 f., **1** 66, nach Art. 94 **Vor 1–6** 19 f., **1** 67, nach Art. 95 **Vor 1–6** 21 f., **1** 77–81, **2 VertragsG** 2, nach Art. 96 **Vor 1–6** 23, **11** 2, **12** 2 f., zum Geltungsbereich des VerjÜbk **36a VerjÜbk** 1 f., Unzulässigkeit nicht aufgeführter Vorbehalte **39 VerjÜbk** 1 f., Vertragsgesetz **1** 79
Vorbehalte nach Art. 95 2 VertragsG 2
Vorbehaltsklausel, Art. 28 als V. **28** 11
Vorbildfunktion des CISG Vor 14–24 46 ff.
Vorgaben, öffentlich-rechtliche **35** 17
Vorkaufvertrag Vor 14–24 41
vorläufiger Rechtsschutz 71 39
Vorleistungspflicht 57 14, des Käufers und Fälligkeit des Anspruchs auf Lieferung **33** 4, Verkäufer **33** 4, Wegfall **71** 5
Vorlieferant als Erfüllungsgehilfe hinsichtlich der Versendung **31** 24, 35, **32** 24
Vorratsschuld 31 46, **79** 27, Haftungsbefreiung **79** 27, Ort der Lieferung **31** 46
Vorteile bei Vorteilsausgleichung, Begriff **84** 22, Gegenwert **84** 22, 34, Geldanspruch **84** 22, Nutzungen **84** 24 ff., als Surrogat **84** 34 ff.
Vorteilsausgleichung, Aufwendungen **84** 28 ff., begleitende V. **84** 5 ff., bereicherungsähnlicher Charakter **84** 16, 23, und Beweislast **84** 40, commodum ex negotiatione **84** 36, commodum ex re **84** 35, bei Ersatzlieferung **84** 7, Geldanspruch **84** 9, 22, Grundgedanke **84** 5, und Grundsatz der Totalreparation **74** 42, Kosten **84** 27 ff., keine Naturalerstattung der Sachfrüchte **84** 22, im Rahmen der PICC und der PECL **84** 36, und Schadensersatz **84** 6, 21, 23, 31 f., 32, als Surrogat der Rückgabe **84** 34 ff., Verhältnis zu nationalem Recht **84** 10, 31, 33, Zinsen **84** 11 ff., 15 ff.
Vorvertrag 1 21, **Vor 14–24** 41, Anwendbarkeit der Artt. 14 ff. **Vor 14–24** 41
Vorzeitige Erfüllungsverweigerung, Begriff **72** 33, ernsthafte und endgültige **72** 35, Erscheinungsformen **72** 35
Vorzeitige Lieferung, Zurückbehaltungsrecht des Käufers **60** 12

Wahl des CISG Vor 14–24 14d
Wahlrecht des Käufers zwischen Rechtsbehelfen **45** 12 f., des Verkäufers zwischen Ersatzlieferung und Nachbesserung **46** 35, **48** 6
Währung 53 4, 4 ff., **74** 63, **78** 30, 33, als Anknüpfungspunkt für den Zinssatz **78** 30, 33, im CISG geregelter, nicht entschiedener Gegenstand **53** 5, Effektivklausel **53** 9, kollisionsrechtliche Lösung **53** 6, Recht des Käufers zur Zahlung in Währung des Zahlungsorts **53** 8, Recht des Verkäufers, Zahlung in Währung des Zahlungsorts zu verlangen **53** 9, der Schadensersatzleistung **74** 63, Unmöglichkeit der Zahlung in vertraglichen Währung **53** 9, vertragliche Währung **53** 4, Währungsschaden **53** 9, am Zahlungsort **53** 5
Währungsrecht 28 7

Sachregister

Fette Zahlen = Artikel

Währungsstatut *s. anwendbares Recht*
Wandelung 49 1 ff.
Ware, Begriff **1** 34–39, bewegliche körperliche Sachen **1** 34, Dokumentenkauf **1** 37, Immobilien **1** 35, Know-how **1** 38, Sachgesamtheiten **1** 34, Software **1** 38, Verkehrsfähigkeit **1** 39
Ware, eingelagerte, Lieferung **31** 58, 60, nicht vorhandene Ware **31** 60, Ort der Lieferung **31** 46, 58, Verlust **31** 63
Ware, frei zugängliche, Gefahrübergang **31** 64, Inhalt der Lieferpflicht **31** 57
Ware, höherwertige 52 11
Ware, reisende, Haftung des Verkäufers **31** 80 f., Inhalt der Lieferpflicht **31** 79
Warenbörse, Vertragsschluss **Vor 14–24** 29
Warnhinweise 35 14
Warnpflichten des Verkäufers **45** 3
Warnungen, Absendeprinzip **27** 4
warranty 35 4
Wasserfahrzeuge 2 38–41, 44 f., keine Anwendung des Verjährungsübereinkommens auf Kauf von Schiffen **4 VerjÜbk**
Website, Annahme **18** 15, EDI **24** 29, Offerte, Fristbeginn **20** 3a
Wechsel, Zahlungsort **57** 7
Wegfall der Geschäftsgrundlage 4 44, **79** 4, *s. Geschäftsgrundlage*
Weihnachten und Versäumung der Rügefrist **44** 8
Weisungen des Käufers hinsichtlich des Transports **32** 28 f.
Weiterveräußerung, Bestimmung der Ware zur W. und wesentliche Vertragsverletzung **46** 25
Weiterversendung der Ware, Beginn der Untersuchungsfrist **38** 23, Kenntnis des Verkäufers **38** 24
Weltsprache, Zugang von Erklärungen **24** 38
Werbeaussagen 35 7, **36** 8
Werklieferungsvertrag 1 24 f., **3** 4–11, **28** 16, **77** 5, **6 VerjÜbk,** keine Anwendung des Verjährungsübereinkommens auf W. **6 VerjÜbk,** Arbeitsanweisungen **3** 10, Gleichstellung mit Kaufvertrag **3** 5 f., und Schadensminderungspflicht **77** 5, Veredelungsvertrag **3** 9
Wertangabe, Pflicht zur W. bei Versendung der Ware **32** 26
Wertersatz in der Rückabwicklung **82** 3 f.
Wertersatzanspruch für Früchte **84** 24 f., für Gebrauchsvorteile **84** 26, für Nutzungen **84** 24 ff., als Surrogat **84** 23 ff.
Wertpapiere 2 34–37, keine Anwendung des Verjährungsübereinkommens auf den Kauf von W. **4 VerjÜbk**
Wertschwankungen, Einfluss auf Zinsanspruch **78** 15
wesentliche Vertragsverletzung, Dokumente **49** 11, Erfüllungsverweigerung **49** 9, Fixgeschäft **49** 5, Liefertermin **49** 5, Lieferung nicht vertragsmäßiger Ware **48** 15, 23, **49** 7 f., und Nacherfüllungsrecht des Verkäufers **48** 15,

und Nachfrist **49** 20 ff., Rechtsmängel **49** 10, Sachmangel **48** 15
Wesentliche Vertragsverletzung bei Sukzessivlieferungsverträgen **73** 11 f.
wesentliche Vertragsverletzung, Unmöglichkeit der Lieferung **49** 6, Unterlassungspflichten **49** 12, Unvermögen zur Leistung **49** 6
wesentlicher Teil der Pflichten 71 9 ff., 13 f.
Wesentlicher Vertragsbruch durch den Käufer **64** 1 ff., 5 ff., Nichtabnahme **64** 13 ff., Nichterfüllung einer anderen Pflicht **64** 17 ff., Nichtzahlung **64** 6 ff.
Wettbewerbsabrede, Auslegung **8** 5, Formbedürftigkeit **11** 7
Widerruf der Aufhebungserklärung **26** 12
Widerruf von Erklärungen, Gegenofferte **19** 11, Unterscheidung von Rücknahme **22** 1, Widerruf der Annahme **18** 12, **21** 15, des Widerrufs **16** 3, Widerrufsvorbehalt als wesentliche Abweichung der Annahme von Offerte **19** 9, *s. a. Bindung an die Offerte, Widerruflichkeit der Offerte*
Widerruflichkeit der Offerte 16 1–13, Ende durch Abschluss des Vertrages **16** 4, Ende durch Absenden der Annahmeerklärung **16** 4, Gegenofferte **19** 11, Rechtsfolge der Widerrufssperre der Offerte **16** 13, des Widerrufs **16** 3, Widerrufssperre **16** 4, 6, *s. a. Bindung an die Offerte, Offerte, Widerruf von Erklärungen*
Widerrufsrechte Vor 14–24 7 f.
Widerrufssperre *s. Bindung an die Offerte, Offerte, Widerruflichkeit der Offerte*
Widerspruch, absendebedürftig **19** 16, gegen Annahme mit unwesentlichen Abweichungen **19** 15, gegen die Anzeige der Erfüllungsbereitschaft **48** 26, unverzüglich **19** 16 f., Wirkung **19** 18
Wiederkaufvertrag Vor 14–24 41
Wiederkehrschuldverhältnis 73 8
Wiener Vertragsrechtsübereinkommen Präambel 4, **7** 33, **89** 2
Willensmängel 4 22–25, **8** 6, **Vor 14–24** 2, **14** 3, **24** 36, **27** 8, **35** 45 f., **41** 23, **42** 27, **71** 21, bei Annahme der Offerte **18** 3, Auslegung **8** 6, Ausschluss der Irrtumsanfechtung **71** 21, Identitätsirrtum **4** 25, Inhaltsirrtum **4** 25, Irrtum über Eigenschaften **4** 24 f., Irrtum über Leistungsfähigkeit **4** 24, Irrtumsanfechtung bei Rechtsmangel **41** 23, Irrtumsanfechtung bei Schutzrechtsbelastung **42** 27, Irrtumsanfechtung bei Vertragswidrigkeit der Ware **35** 45 f., Sprachirrtum **24** 36, **27** 8, Täuschung **4** 25
Wirksamkeit des Vertrages *s. Gültigkeitsfragen*
Wissenszurechnung 79 9, 40
without obligation 14 25

Zahlung, Anrechnung von Zahlungen **53** 24, Bankformalitäten **54** 5 ff., Devisenkontrolle **54** 2 ff., Direktabbuchung **57** 8, Erfüllungswirkung *s. Erfüllung der Zahlungspflicht,* Stundung **57** 7,

Magere Zahlen = Randnummern

58 6, **63** 13, Teilzahlung **53** 23, vorzeitige Zahlung **58** 19 ff., Z. durch Dritte **53** 30, Zahlungskosten **53** 22, **57** 8, 19, Zahlungsmittel *s. Zahlungsmittel*, Zahlungsort *s. Zahlungsort*, Zahlungszeit *s. Zahlungszeit*
Zahlung des Kaufpreises, Anspruch auf Erfüllung **28** 6 f.
Zahlungsaufforderung 59 1 ff., Rückzahlung des Kaufpreises **59** 8, Vertragsstrafe **59** 8, Zinsen **59** 8
Zahlungsgarantie 53 38, **54** 5 ff., Vertragsaufhebung **64** 10
Zahlungsklauseln, Aufrechnungsverbot **61** 19, Untersuchung der Ware vor Zahlung **58** 35, Zahlungsort **57** 7, Zahlungszeit **58** 5
Zahlungsmittel 2 37, Bargeld **53** 10 ff., Dokumentenakkreditiv **53** 17 ff., **54** 5, Dokumenteninkasso **53** 15, **57** 10, Kauf von Z. **2** 37, Offene Rechnung **53** 10 ff., Überweisung **53** 10 ff., Wechsel **53** 13, **54** 5
Zahlungsort 57 1 ff., Abtretung **57** 21, Anspruch auf Rückzahlung des Kaufpreises **57** 31, Bankkonto **57** 6, „cash against documents" **57** 10, Internationale Zuständigkeit **57** 4, 22 ff., Niederlassung des Verkäufers **57** 2, Offene Rechnung **57** 15, Schadenersatzanspruch **57** 29, Verträge, die die Beförderung der Ware vorsehen **57** 12, 16, Verträge über Ware, die bei Dritten lagert **57** 13, 16, Verträge über Ware, die sich auf dem Transport befindet **57** 16, vertraglicher Z. **57** 5, Vertragsstrafe **57** 30, Wechsel der Niederlassung durch den Verkäufer **57** 17, Zahlung gegen Ware oder Dokumente **57** 9 ff.
Zahlungsverzug, EG-Richtlinie **78** 33a, 37
Zahlungszeit, Anzeige der Lieferbereitschaft (notice of readiness) **58** 5, „cash against documents" **58** 5, 15, Rechnung **58** 5, Verträge, die die Beförderung der Ware erfordern **58** 12, 17, Verträge über Ware, die bei Dritten lagert **58** 14, Verträge über Ware, die sich auf dem Transport befindet **58** 13, vertragliche Z. **58** 5 ff., vorzeitige Zahlung **58** 19 f., Z. gegen Ware und Dokumente **58** 7 ff., Zahlung gegen Dokumente **58** 15 ff., Zur-Verfügung-Stellen am Ort der Niederlassung des Käufers oder einem anderen vereinbarten Ort **58** 11, Zur-Verfügung-Stellen am Ort der Niederlassung des Verkäufers, der Produktion oder der Lagerung **58** 8
Zeit der Nachbesserung **46** 45
Zeitpunkt, just in time-Vertrag **33** 5, für Kenntnis des Käufers von Vertragswidrigkeit der Ware **40** 8, maßgeblicher Z. für die Berechnung der Minderung **50** 9 ff., der Übergabe von Dokumenten **34** 2, für Vertragsmäßigkeit der Ware **36** 3 ff., vorzeitige Lieferung **37** 4 ff., **38** 20
Zinsanspruch 7 52, keine Befreiung durch Devisensperre **78** 17, Einfluss von Wertschwankungen **78** 15, Entfallen bei Aufrechnungslage **78** 20, Entfallen durch Minderung **78** 24, Entfallen durch Vertragsaufhebung **78** 23, Entfallen durch Zurückbehaltungsrecht **78** 20 f., Fälligkeit als Voraussetzung **78** 7 ff., Mahnung keine Voraussetzung **78** 17
Zinsen 50 16, **53** 21, **78** 1 ff., 13, 26–40, 45, **84**, 1 ff., 11 ff., **20 VerjÜbk** 2, **27 VerjÜbk**, Höhe **78** 26–40, Prozesszinsen **78** 45, Richtlinie zur Bekämpfung von Zahlungsverzug im Geschäftsverkehr **58** 22, auf Rückzahlungsanspruch bei Minderung **78** 13, Verjährung **27 VerjÜbk**, bei verspäteter Zahlung und Minderung **50** 16, Zahlung von Z. und Anerkenntnis **20 VerjÜbk** 2, Zahlungsaufforderung **59** 2, Zahlungsort **57** 32, Zahlungszeit **58** 21, Zinseszinsen **78** 40
Zinsen in der Vorteilsausgleichung 84 11 ff., Beginn der Verzinsungspflicht **84** 11 f., Berechnungsgrundlagen **84** 15, 17, Pflicht des Verkäufers **84** 11, und Schadensersatz **84** 13 f., 21, üblicher Zinssatz am Verkäufersitz **84** 11 ff.
Zinseszinsen 78 40
Zinshöhe, Anknüpfung an die Vertragswährung **78** 30, 33, Bezugszinssatz als Maßstab **78** 31, Diskontsatz als Maßstab **78** 31, Euro **78** 31, Handelsbrauch zur Z. **78** 38, Hauptrefinanzierungssatz der EZB als Maßstab **78** 31, Leitzins als Maßstab **78** 31, 34, LIBOR **78** 29 f., prime rate als Maßstab **78** 31
zollamtliche Abfertigung 31 32
Zölle 31 84, Belastung mit Z. als Rechtsmangel **41** 7
Zugang 18 13, **24** 1–15, 23 f., **26** 11 f., **27** 1 f., 1 ff., Annahme der Offerte **18** 13, Anrufbeantworter **24** 13, der Aufhebungserklärung **26** 11 ff., Beweislast **24** 43, Einschreiben **24** 20, E-Mail **24** 24, Empfangsbote **24** 7, 8, Erklärungsbote **24** 7, Postfach **24** 19, SMS **24** 30, Spam-Filter **24** 25, Stellvertretung **24** 7, Telefax **24** 23, Telex **24** 23, Vernehmung **24** 5, Website **24** 28, Weltsprache **24** 38, World Wide Web **24** 28, Zustellung als Z. **24** 15
Zugangsbedürftigkeit, Annahme der Offerte **18** 7, Anzeige der Bereitschaft zur Nacherfüllung **48** 29
zugesicherte Eigenschaften 35 37
Zug-um-Zug-Abwicklung 71 5, 9 ff., und Ersatzlieferung **46** 34, Rückabwicklung **81** 20
Zug-um-Zug-Erfüllung 57 9, **58** 1
Zulieferanten, Haftung des Schuldners **79** 37
Zumutbarkeit *s. Unzumutbarkeit*
Zurückbehaltung des Kaufpreises trotz Verjährung von Justizleistungsansprüchen 3 VertragsG 8
Zurückbehaltungsrecht 45 22, **58** 2, 23 ff., **60** 11 ff., **61** 8, **71** 3, 3 ff., 10, 25 ff., 37, 41 ff., 52, **80** 3, **85** 17, **87** 9, Abdingbarkeit **71** 11, Abnahmepflicht **60** 11 ff., allgemeines Z. **58** 26 ff., **71** 9, Auflösung des Schwebezustandes **71** 41 ff., Ausübung **71** 25 ff., Ausübung des Z. **58** 32, Beweislast **71** 53, wegen Erhaltungskosten **85**

1443

Sachregister

Fette Zahlen = Artikel

17, **87** 9, nach Fälligkeit **71** 9, Informationspflicht **71** 27 ff., des Käufers **58** 25, des Käufers bei Verletzung einer anderen Pflicht als der Lieferpflicht **58** 29, des Käufers bei vertragswidriger Ware **58** 28, **60** 15 ff., Konkurrenzverhältnis zu nationalen Z. **71** 31, nach nationalem Recht **58** 31, bei nicht-synallagmatischen Leistungen **71** 9a, Normzweck **71** 3, Schadenersatzansprüche **71** 30, 51 f., Schwebezustand bei künftigen Störungen **71** 10, 29, 37, 42 f., 47, bei Sekundärpflichten **71** 8, Selbsthilfeverkauf des Verkäufers **58** 30, Störungsgründe **71** 6, 15 ff., bei Sukzessivlieferungsverträgen **71** 7, Umfang der zurückgehaltenen Leistung **71** 9b, unberechtigte Ausübung **71** 30, 52, Vergleich mit PECL, PICC **71** 5, Verhältnis zu Artt. 72, 73 **71** 2, 49, des Verkäufers **58** 23 ff., des Verkäufers bei wesentlicher Verletzung einer anderen Pflicht als der Zahlungs- bzw. Abnahmepflicht durch den Käufer **58** 30, verspätete Lieferung **60** 14, vertragswidrige Ware oder Dokumente **60** 15 ff., Voraussetzungen **71** 12 ff., Vorgeschichte **71** 1, und Vorleistungspflicht **71** 5, vorzeitige Lieferung **60** 12, Wegfall **71** 41 ff., Wirkung **71** 25 ff., zeitliche Grenzen **71** 26, und Zinsanspruch **78** 20 f., *s. a. Schwebezustand bei künftigen Störungen,* und Zug-um-Zug-Leistung **71** 5, Zuviel-Lieferung **60** 13

Zurückweisung, nicht vertragskonformer Ware **31** 66, **46** 19, **49** 17, der Teillieferung **51** 4, der vorzeitigen Lieferung **52** 3, der Zuviellieferung **52** 7 ff.

Zurückweisung nicht vertragskonformer Ware 31 66, **46** 19, **49** 17, **60** 3

Zurverfügungstellen der Ware 31 45, 69, 74, 76, 79

Zur-Verfügung-Stellen der Ware an den Käufer, Ort der Niederlassung des Käufers oder ein anderer vereinbarter Ort **57** 11, Ort der Niederlassung des Verkäufers, der Produktion oder der Lagerung **57** 8

Zustellung als Zugang 24 15

Zustimmungsäußerung *s. Annahme, annahmeäquivalente Handlungen*

Zuviellieferung 35 8, **39** 30, **52** 6–11

Zuviel-Lieferung, Zurückbehaltungsrecht des Käufers **60** 13

Zuweniglieferung 35 8, **39** 30, **51** 5 f.

Zwangsvollstreckung 2 31–33, keine Anwendung des Verjährungsübereinkommens auf Z. **4 VerjÜbk**

Zweckfortfall 79 4

Zweckverfehlung 79 4

Zweckzusammenhang, Sukzessivlieferungsvertrag **73** 31 ff.

zweite Andienung 34 6, 12